AN MMY MONOGRAPH

Publications of
THE INSTITUTE OF MENTAL MEASUREMENTS
Edited by Oscar Krisen Buros

EDUCATIONAL, PSYCHOLOGICAL, AND PERSONALITY TESTS OF 1933 AND 1934

EDUCATIONAL, PSYCHOLOGICAL, AND PERSONALITY TESTS OF 1933, 1934, AND 1935

EDUCATIONAL, PSYCHOLOGICAL, AND PERSONALITY TESTS OF 1936

THE NINETEEN THIRTY-EIGHT MENTAL MEASUREMENTS YEARBOOK

THE NINETEEN FORTY MENTAL MEASUREMENTS YEARBOOK

THE THIRD MENTAL MEASUREMENTS YEARBOOK

THE FOURTH MENTAL MEASUREMENTS YEARBOOK

THE FIFTH MENTAL MEASUREMENTS YEARBOOK

TESTS IN PRINT

THE SIXTH MENTAL MEASUREMENTS YEARBOOK

READING TESTS AND REVIEWS

PERSONALITY TESTS AND REVIEWS

THE SEVENTH MENTAL MEASUREMENTS YEARBOOK

TESTS IN PRINT II

ENGLISH TESTS AND REVIEWS

FOREIGN LANGUAGE TESTS AND REVIEWS

INTELLIGENCE TESTS AND REVIEWS

MATHEMATICS TESTS AND REVIEWS

PERSONALITY TESTS AND REVIEWS II

READING TESTS AND REVIEWS II

SCIENCE TESTS AND REVIEWS

SOCIAL STUDIES TESTS AND REVIEWS

VOCATIONAL TESTS AND REVIEWS

INTELLIGENCE
TESTS AND REVIEWS

EDITORIAL ASSOCIATE
Joan Stein Paszamant

EDITORIAL ASSISTANT
Sandra Boxer Discenza

PRODUCTION AND SECRETARIAL
Mary Anne Miller Becker
Doris Greene McCan
Barbara Ruis Martko
Mary T. Mooney
Natalie J. Rosenthal Turton

INTELLIGENCE
TESTS AND REVIEWS

A Monograph
Consisting of the Intelligence Sections of the
SEVEN MENTAL MEASUREMENTS YEARBOOKS (1938–72)
and
TESTS IN PRINT II (1974)

Edited by
OSCAR KRISEN BUROS
Director, The Institute of Mental Measurements

THE GRYPHON PRESS
HIGHLAND PARK · NEW JERSEY
1975

DESIGNED BY LUELLA BUROS

COPYRIGHT 1975 BY OSCAR KRISEN BUROS, PUBLISHED BY THE GRYPHON PRESS, 220 MONTGOMERY STREET, HIGHLAND PARK, NEW JERSEY 08904. No part of this publication may be reproduced in any form, nor may any of the contents be used in an informational storage, retrieval, or transmission system without the prior written permission of the publisher.

LC 75-8112, ISBN 910674-17-5

MANUFACTURED BY QUINN & BODEN COMPANY, INC., RAHWAY, NEW JERSEY
PRINTED IN THE UNITED STATES OF AMERICA

To
Pat and Allan

TABLE OF CONTENTS

	PAGE
MMY TEST REVIEWERS	xi
PREFACE	xv
INTRODUCTION	xvii
INTELLIGENCE TESTS	
TESTS IN PRINT II	1
INTELLIGENCE TEST REVIEWS	
FIRST MENTAL MEASUREMENTS YEARBOOK	147
SECOND MENTAL MEASUREMENTS YEARBOOK	174
THIRD MENTAL MEASUREMENTS YEARBOOK	244
FOURTH MENTAL MEASUREMENTS YEARBOOK	351
FIFTH MENTAL MEASUREMENTS YEARBOOK	464
SIXTH MENTAL MEASUREMENTS YEARBOOK	611
SEVENTH MENTAL MEASUREMENTS YEARBOOK	793
TIP II SCANNING INDEX	1030
PUBLISHERS DIRECTORY AND INDEX	1065
INDEX OF TITLES	1069
INDEX OF NAMES	1076
INTELLIGENCE SCANNING INDEX	1126

MMY TEST REVIEWERS

Murray Aborn	4:361
C. J. Adcock	5:383
J. Stanley Ahmann	6:495, 7:358
Lewis E. Albright	6:512
William D. Altus	4:340, 4:361
Anne Anastasi	1:1037, 1:1058, 2:1398
	2:1424, 3:216, 3:222, 3:265, 7:352
James M. Anderson	3:295, 4:363, 6:553
Gwen F. Arnold	4:336, 4:349
Mary C. Austin	6:553
J. Douglas Ayers	7:437
Andrew R. Baggaley	6:468
Leonard L. Baird	7:445, 7:448
Benjamin Balinsky	4:359
Rachel S. Ball	2:1407
Charlotte E. K. Banks	4:314
	4:337, 5:327, 5:367
Robert H. Bauernfeind	7:369
Brent Baxter	3:221, 3:252
Nancy Bayley	2:1406, 2:1407, 3:276
	3:285, 5:404, 5:411, 5:414
George K. Bennett	4:355, 7:445
Ralph F. Berdie	6:450
Robert G. Bernreuter	2:1387, 4:320
Marion A. Bills	3:215
	3:216, 3:221, 3:246
L. B. Birch	6:520
Harold H. Bixler	3:268
Donald B. Black	6:445, 6:493
J. M. Blackburn	2:1376
Morton Bortner	6:471, 6:490, 6:518
John E. Bowers	6:449
E. J. G. Bradford	3:266, 4:291
Hubert E. Brogden	3:269
Andrew W. Brown	2:1379, 2:1399
Emily T. Burr	3:222, 3:265
Alvin G. Burstein	6:540, 7:429
Cyril Burt	3:225, 5:313, 5:326
H. J. Butcher	7:347
Joel T. Campbell	7:332, 7:372
John B. Carroll	7:442
Burton M. Castner	2:1383, 2:1406
Psyche Cattell	1:1044, 1:1049
	1:1053, 3:256, 3:274
Raymond B. Cattell	2:1384, 2:1389
Clinton I. Chase	7:442
W. V. Clemans	6:456
Charles N. Cofer	3:266, 3:284
John Cohen	3:270
Roberta R. Collard	7:402, 7:420
W. D. Commins	1:1039, 1:1040
	1:1042, 2:1202, 2:1664
	3:217, 3:224, 4:318, 4:319
Stuart A. Courtis	1:1049
Lee J. Cronbach	5:379, 7:334, 7:384
William M. Cruickshank	4:340
Edward E. Cureton	4:317, 4:320
John T. Dailey	4:280, 4:281
	5:318, 5:336, 5:352
Reginald R. Dale	5:374
John C. Daniels	5:387, 5:392
Frederick B. Davis	4:285, 5:322
Paul C. Davis	6:454, 6:525
Harold A. Delp	4:350, 4:363
Robert G. Demaree	4:279
Richard F. Docter	7:419

Jerome E. Doppelt	4:342, 6:464
N. M. Downie	6:448, 6:485, 6:513
Raleigh M. Drake	3:259, 4:287, 4:300, 4:325, 5:316, 5:326
James Drever	2:1414
Robert C. Droege	7:401
Philip H. DuBois	7:344
Jack W. Dunlap	2:1377
James A. Dunn	7:352
S. S. Dunn	6:454
Marvin D. Dunnette	6:513
Walter N. Durost	4:325, 5:349, 5:380, 6:488
August Dvorak	2:1398
Norman Eagle	5:358
Howard Easley	2:1398, 2:1418, 2:1424
Dorothy H. Eichorn	6:516, 7:428, 7:434
W. G. Emmett	3:236, 4:289, 4:294
Henry Feinberg	1:1058
George A. Ferguson	3:237, 4:308, 4:327, 5:390, 6:445, 6:493
Warren G. Findley	6:450
Joshua A. Fishman	5:377, 5:391
John C. Flanagan	1:1054, 3:252, 4:331
Charles D. Flory	3:245, 3:251, 3:269
John P. Foley, Jr.	5:395, 7:401
Hanford M. Fowler	4:299, 5:308, 5:322
Charles Fox	2:1381
Elizabeth D. Fraser	5:360, 5:405, 5:416, 6:447, 6:536
Frank S. Freeman	5:314, 5:350
David Freides	7:425, 7:431
Joseph L. French	7:404
Robert L. French	6:461
Gustav J. Froehlich	5:319, 5:320, 6:440
Eugene L. Gaier	5:371
Eric F. Gardner	7:346, 7:359
Henry E. Garrett	2:1404, 2:1427, 3:223, 4:302, 5:349, 5:381
James R. Glennon	6:484
Goldine C. Gleser	6:547
Bert A. Goldman	6:441, 6:494, 7:338
Marcel L. Goldschmid	7:343, 7:428
Florence L. Goodenough	2:1382, 2:1383, 2:1406, 3:264
Russel F. Green	6:452, 6:468, 7:382, 7:391
William R. Grove	4:335
Wilson H. Guertin	5:414
J. P. Guilford	2:1398, 3:217, 3:238, 3:244, 4:293, 4:304, 5:70, 5:326
Nelson G. Hanawalt	5:401
Albert J. Harris	7:351
Louis D. Hartson	1:1051
Mary R. Haworth	5:413, 6:537
Alfred B. Heilbrun, Jr.	5:371
Alice W. Heim	4:312, 5:324, 5:325, 5:347, 6:457, 6:470
V. A. C. Henmon	1:1038
Edwin R. Henry	4:316, 4:317
John R. Hills	6:442
Philip Himelstein	7:418, 7:424
C. B. Hindley	6:523
Marshall S. Hiskey	6:517, 7:409
James R. Hobson	3:225
Raymond H. Holden	7:402
Marjorie P. Honzik	6:527, 6:528, 7:411
Kenneth D. Hopkins	7:389
John L. Horn	7:419
John E. Horrocks	6:495, 6:496
Carl I. Hovland	3:218, 3:263, 4:293, 4:304
Duncan Howie	5:295, 5:694
Cyril J. Hoyt	5:359
Lloyd G. Humphreys	6:472
John D. Hundleby	6:491
E. Patricia Hunt	2:1400, 2:1410
Jane V. Hunt	7:423, 7:424
Arthur R. Jensen	7:334, 7:399
Frank B. Jex	6:525
H. Gwynne Jones	6:514, 6:519
A. M. Jordan	2:1392
Raymond A. Katzell	7:381
T. J. Keating	2:1385, 2:1414, 2:1417
J. A. Keats	5:321, 5:390, 6:544
Gertrude Keir	4:306, 4:323
Truman L. Kelley	2:1427
James E. Kennedy	6:478, 6:509, 6:562, 7:399
Grace H. Kent	2:1390, 2:1391, 2:1394, 2:1414, 2:1426, 3:273
Kate L. Kogan	3:302, 4:339
William S. Kogan	4:339
Frederic Kuder	3:248, 3:249, 3:250
F. Kuhlmann	2:1384, 2:1413
Theos A. Langlie	1:1051
Charles R. Langmuir	3:232
J. S. Lawes	6:510, 6:529
Richard Ledgerwood	1:1048

D. Welty Lefever	5:342, 5:362, 6:480	Myrtle L. Pignatelli	2:1387, 2:1426
Roger T. Lennon	5:379	A. E. G. Pilliner	5:307, 5:320, 5:531, 6:469
Philip M. Levy	6:501, 6:520	Rudolf Pintner	1:1042, 1:1051, 1:1053
John Liggett	5:340, 5:357, 6:506	Stanley D. Porteus	2:1387, 2:1419
W. Line	2:1393, 2:1411	M. L. Kellmer Pringle	4:306, 5:327, 5:367, 5:387
Jane Loevinger	4:333	Albert I. Rabin	5:416
Irving Lorge	3:245, 3:269	S. Rachman	6:447
C. M. Louttit	4:356	James H. Ricks, Jr.	5:311
Kenneth Lovell	7:408	Cyril A. Rogers	5:356
James Lumsden	5:298	John H. Rosenbach	7:338, 7:359
Howard B. Lyman	6:441, 6:530, 7:351, 7:429	Benjamin Rosner	6:491
Boyd R. McCandless	4:358, 4:363, 6:533, 6:534, 7:335	John W. M. Rothney	1:1062
Arthur C. MacKinney	7:400	Arthur B. Royse	5:386, 6:470, 6:511
Louis L. McQuitty	4:279	David G. Ryans	6:448, 6:478, 6:509
James Mainwaring	5:385, 5:388	C. Sanders	5:296, 5:297, 5:307
Herschel T. Manuel	2:1428, 4:350	H. J. Sants	6:465
Melvin R. Marks	6:484	I. David Satlow	5:389
Stanley S. Marzolf	3:236, 3:255	Willis C. Schaefer	4:281, 4:319
Francis N. Maxfield	1:1061, 1:1062, 2:1388, 2:1426	William Schofield	4:360
James Maxwell	4:291	Fred J. Schonell	4:272
Ivan N. Mensh	4:342, 4:346, 4:360, 4:364	William B. Schrader	4:274, 4:275, 4:329, 5:382, 6:472, 6:500
William B. Michael	5:308, 5:309, 5:377, 6:466, 7:346, 7:359	Richard E. Schutz	6:496, 7:391
T. R. Miles	5:337, 5:393, 6:469, 6:479	Gladys C. Schwesinger	4:300, 4:356
John E. Milholland	5:314, 5:350, 6:453, 7:370, 7:381	Harold G. Seashore	4:338
		David Segel	1:1037, 4:302
		Melvin I. Semmel	7:446
G. A. V. Morgan	5:405	Walter C. Shipley	3:228, 3:258, 3:259
Alice E. Moriarty	7:405	A. B. Silverstein	7:432, 7:434
Louis C. Nanassy	5:311	Patrick Slater	3:241
Charles O. Neidt	5:349	William Sloan	5:409
T. Ernest Newland	6:516, 6:517, 6:541, 7:410, 7:418	C. Ebblewhite Smith	2:1409, 2:1422
		I. Macfarlane Smith	5:315, 5:343
Joseph Newman	4:360, 4:364	Percival Smith	2:1381, 2:1389
John Nisbet	5:369, 5:398, 6:479, 6:510, 7:331	Charles D. Smock	7:335
		C. Spearman	2:1427
Stanley D. Nisbet	4:289, 6:499, 7:342	Julian C. Stanley	5:322, 6:443, 6:766
Raymond C. Norris	5:354	Naomi Stewart	4:292, 5:332, 6:503, 6:560
Robert D. North	7:392	Charles A. Stickland	4:334
Jum C. Nunnally	7:378	Norman D. Sundberg	5:413
R. T. Osborne	7:431	Abraham J. Tannenbaum	6:453
Gerald R. Patterson	5:416	Calvin W. Taylor	5:321
David A. Payne	6:439, 7:358	Erwin K. Taylor	4:276, 4:331, 5:366, 6:512, 6:379, 7:380, 7:394
E. A. Peel	4:307, 5:357, 5:377	Hugh Taylor	7:403
L. S. Penrose	3:228	Florence M. Teagarden	2:1406, 2:1407, 3:276, 3:281, 5:332
Douglas A. Pidgeon	5:301, 5:350, 6:466		
Ellen V. Piers	6:530, 6:534, 6:537		

Lorene Teegarden	2:1401
Mildred C. Templin	4:353, 4:354
W. Wesley Tennyson	5:359
Albert S. Thompson	6:544
Godfrey H. Thomson	2:1386, 2:1427
Robert L. Thorndike	2:1377, 3:224, 3:263, 7:448
David V. Tiedeman	4:301, 5:319, 5:320
Carol K. Tittle	7:343, 7:360
Arthur E. Traxler	1:1042
Robert C. Tryon	2:1427
William W. Turnbull	3:245
Austin H. Turney	1:1049, 2:1378
F. T. Tyler	3:231, 3:237, 3:268
Leona E. Tyler	5:342, 6:545, 6:546
Philip E. Vernon	7:445
David A. Walker	7:398
W. D. Wall	4:314, 4:337
Wimburn L. Wallace	6:440, 6:442, 7:330, 7:344
Norman E. Wallen	6:462
F. W. Warburton	4:290, 5:325, 5:369
Ruth W. Washburn	3:226, 3:274, 3:296
Robert I. Watson	3:298
David Wechsler	2:1419, 3:228, 3:239, 3:258
Henry Weitz	7:382
Beth L. Wellman	3:281, 3:286
F. L. Wells	1:1062, 2:1426, 2:1429, 3:225, 3:275
Emmy E. Werner	6:522, 6:526, 7:405, 7:423
Alexander G. Wesman	5:380
George Westby	4:297, 4:313, 4:314
Carroll A. Whitmer	2:1379, 2:1388, 3:243, 3:254, 3:256
Warren W. Willingham	6:461, 6:472
John M. Willits	5:305, 5:389
R. Winterbourn	5:299, 5:300, 5:333
Dael L. Wolfle	4:305, 4:315, 4:316
Leroy Wolins	6:556
Frank B. Womer	6:439
D. A. Worcester	2:1418, 3:242, 3:255
Ll. Wynn Jones	2:1430
Alfred Yates	5:362
Wayne S. Zimmerman	6:449, 6:487

PREFACE

IT IS my considered belief that most standardized tests are poorly constructed, of questionable or unknown validity, pretentious in their claims, and likely to be misused more often than not. This conviction began to form 48 to 50 years ago when I was taking courses in testing at the University of Minnesota. I vividly recall presenting a paper entitled "Common Fallacies in the Use of Standardized Tests" in an advanced educational psychology class taught by Professor W. S. Miller, a paper in which I criticized some of the views of my instructors. Shortly thereafter, I had the good fortune to read a book which was a landmark in the consumer movement—*Your Money's Worth* by Stuart Chase and F. J. Schlink. It was this book which led to the founding of Consumers' Research, Inc., an organization which tests and evaluates commonly used commercial products. This book and the establishment of Consumers' Research stimulated me to begin thinking about a test users' research organization to evaluate tests.

After failing to secure financial support for the initiation of a test users' research organization, I scaled down my objectives to the establishment of a cooperative test reviewing service which would report on and evaluate standardized tests used in education, industry, and psychology. One hundred thirty-three specialists in a wide variety of disciplines cooperated by contributing "frankly critical reviews" for *The 1938 Mental Measurements Yearbook* (also called *The First Yearbook*). Later yearbooks (each volume supplementing earlier volumes) were published in 1941, 1949, 1953, 1959, 1965, and 1972.

The objectives of the *Mental Measurements Yearbooks* (MMY's) have remained essentially the same since they were first presented in detail in *The 1940 Mental Measurements Yearbook* (also called *The Second Yearbook*): (*a*) to provide information about tests published as separates throughout the English-speaking world; (*b*) to present frankly critical test reviews written by testing and subject specialists representing various viewpoints; (*c*) to provide extensive bibliographies of verified references on the construction, use, and validity of specific tests; (*d*) to make readily available the critical portions of test reviews appearing in professional journals; and (*e*) to present fairly exhaustive listings of new and revised books on testing along with evaluative excerpts from representative reviews in professional journals.

As important as the above objectives are, I place even greater importance on these less tangible objectives: (*f*) to impel test authors and publishers to publish better tests and to provide test users with detailed information on the validity and limitations of these tests; (*g*) to inculcate in test users a keener awareness of the values and limitations of standardized tests; (*h*) to stimulate contributing reviewers to think through more carefully their own beliefs and values relevant to testing; (*i*) to suggest to test users better methods of appraising tests in light of their own particular needs; and (*j*) to impress upon test users the need to suspect all tests unaccompanied by detailed data on their construction, validity, uses, and limitations—

even when products of distinguished authors and reputable publishers.

As the number of published tests and, especially, the related literature increased tremendously over the years, the MMY's became increasingly more encyclopedic in scope. Many test users, however, are interested in only one or two areas of testing. To meet their needs, we announced in 1941 plans for publishing monographs in English, foreign languages, intelligence, mathematics, personality, reading, science, social studies, and vocations. Unfortunately, we were too optimistic; it was over a quarter of a century before we were able to finance the publication of the first monograph, *Reading Tests and Reviews* (RTR I), published in 1968.

The next monograph, *Personality Tests and Reviews* (PTR I), was published in 1970. The core of these two monographs, RTR I and PTR I, consists of a reprinting of the reading and personality sections, respectively, of the first six MMY's and a new section listing both in print and out of print tests in the area represented by the monograph.

Despite the use of a large amount of reprinted material, the preparation and publication of these two monographs turned out to be very costly. Since sales later proved insufficient to finance similar monographs in other areas, we temporarily abandoned our plans for additional monographs.

Following the publication of *The Seventh Yearbook* in early 1972, we began devoting all of our time to the completion of *Tests in Print II: An Index to Tests, Test Reviews, and the Literature on Specific Tests* (TIP II). In mid-1974, while TIP II was in press, it suddenly occurred to me that up-to-date monographs could be prepared at a manageable cost by reprinting a given section of TIP II along with the corresponding sections of the seven MMY's. As a consequence, we are now publishing monographs in nine areas: second monographs in personality and reading, and first monographs in English, foreign languages, intelligence, mathematics, science, social studies, and vocations. Hopefully, the publication of these monographs will make our material available to many test users who might otherwise not consult the MMY's and TIP II. Broadening the readership of our test reviews will bring us closer to achieving our objectives.

We believe that this volume contains the most carefully prepared bibliographies available for specific intelligence tests. More than 13,000 references on specific tests have been presented, all of which (except unpublished theses) I have personally examined to make sure that they meet our criteria for relevancy. We never rely on secondary sources in listing articles, books, chapters, and monographs. If we are unable to locate a reference for firsthand examination, we do not include it in our bibliographies.

Although these bibliographies are probably unequaled in their accuracy, comprehensiveness, and relevancy, we know of no instance where any of them has been cited in a test manual, article, or book dealing with a specific test. What disturbs us even more, however, is that some authors present parts of our material as their own. We feel strongly that proper credit should be given when our bibliographies are used. We suggest that authors and publishers of tests generating a substantial number of references consider referring readers to our bibliographies in their test manuals and then supplementing them with their own list of references.

It has been particularly hectic preparing nine MMY monographs simultaneously. Fortunately, I have been assisted by a dedicated staff. Although other people worked for shorter periods of time, there are seven whom I would like to name for special recognition: Mary Anne Miller Becker, Sandra Boxer Discenza, Doris Greene McCan, Barbara Ruis Martko, Mary T. Mooney, Joan Stein Paszamant, and Natalie J. Rosenthal Turton. I am greatly indebted to my staff colleagues for their assistance in producing these nine derivative monographs.

We plan to publish *The Eighth Mental Measurements Yearbook* in 1977, followed by *Tests in Print III* in 1978. The intelligence sections of these volumes will supplement and update the material in this monograph.

OSCAR KRISEN BUROS

Highland Park, New Jersey
February 24, 1975

INTRODUCTION

FOR THE past 40 years we have been providing test users in education, industry, and psychology with a series of publications designed to assist them in the selection and use of tests which best meet their needs. We maintained an annual production schedule for our first four volumes (1935–38); since then, however, the intervals between books have been quite irregular with publication dates 1941, 1949, 1953, 1959, 1961, 1965, 1968, 1970, 1972, and 1974. Our publications through 1974 include three test bibliographies, seven *Mental Measurements Yearbooks,* two monographs, and two *Tests in Print*.[1] Nine derivative mono-

---

[1] The first fourteen publications (1935–1974), edited by Oscar K. Buros and now published by The Gryphon Press, are listed from the most recent to the oldest:
  a) *Tests in Print II: An Index to Tests, Test Reviews, and the Literature on Specific Tests,* December 1974. Pp. xxxix, 1107. $70.
  b) *The Seventh Mental Measurements Yearbook,* Vols. I and II, 1972. Pp. xl, 935; vi, 937–1986. $70 per set.
  c) *Personality Tests and Reviews: Including an Index to The Mental Measurements Yearbooks,* 1970. Pp. xxxi, 1659. $45. For reviews, see 7:B120.
  d) *Reading Tests and Reviews: Including a Classified Index to The Mental Measurements Yearbooks,* 1968. Pp. xxii, 520. $20. For reviews, see 7:B121.
  e) *The Sixth Mental Measurements Yearbook,* 1965. Pp. xxxvii, 1714. $45. (Reprinted 1971) For reviews, see 7:B122.
  f) *Tests in Print: A Comprehensive Bibliography of Tests for Use in Education, Psychology, and Industry,* 1961. Pp. xxix, 479. $15. (Reprinted 1974) For reviews, see 6:B105.
  g) *The Fifth Mental Measurements Yearbook,* 1959. Pp. xxix, 1292. $35. (Reprinted 1961) For reviews, see 6:B104.
  h) *The Fourth Mental Measurements Yearbook,* 1953. Pp. xxv, 1163. $30. (Reprinted 1974) For reviews, see 5:B84.
  i) *The Third Mental Measurements Yearbook,* 1949. Pp. xv, 1047. $25. (Reprinted 1974) For reviews, see 4:B71.
  j) *The Nineteen Forty Mental Measurements Yearbook,* 1941. Pp. xxv, 674. $20. (Reissued 1972) For reviews, see 3:788 and 4:B70.
  k) *The Nineteen Thirty Eight Mental Measurements Yearbook,* 1938. Pp. xv, 415. $17.50. (Reissued 1972) For reviews, see 2:B858.
  l) *Educational, Psychological, and Personality Tests of 1936: Including a Bibliography and Book Review Digest of Measurement Books and Monographs of 1933–36,* 1937. Pp. 141. Out of print. For reviews, see 1:B326.
  m) *Educational, Psychological, and Personality Tests of 1933, 1934, and 1935,* 1936. Pp. 83. *Out of print.* For reviews, see 36:B46.
  n) *Educational, Psychological, and Personality Tests of 1933 and 1934,* 1935. Pp. 44. *Out of print.* For a review, see 36:B45.

graphs—this volume and eight others—are being published in 1975. A brief description of our first fourteen publications follows.

FIRST THREE PUBLICATIONS

Although the earliest three publications are noncritical bibliographies, the original intent had been to prepare an annual critical review of new tests for journal publication. It soon became apparent, however, that this was far beyond the capacity of a single individual. A more modest goal was substituted, the publication of an annual bibliography of tests, as described in the Introduction to the first one:

> To locate the standard tests recently published in specific areas is a laborious task. The usual bibliographic aids for locating periodical, monograph, and book publications are of little value in locating standard tests. New tests are being published so rapidly that the test technicians themselves find it difficult to locate the test titles of the past year without an inordinate amount of searching. For these reasons, the writer has undertaken the task of preparing a bibliography of psychological, achievement, character, and personality tests published in 1933 and 1934. This bibliography will be the first of a series to be published annually by the School of Education, Rutgers University.[2]

This 44-page bibliography lists 257 tests that were new, revised, or supplemented in 1933 and 1934. Many of these tests, usually revised editions, are still in print today.

Similar test bibliographies [3] were published in 1936 and 1937. During this time, attempts were being made to obtain a grant to initiate a

---

[2] *Educational, Psychological, and Personality Tests of 1933 and 1934,* p. 5.
[3] *Educational, Psychological, and Personality Tests of 1933, 1934, and 1935.*
Educational, Psychological, and Personality Tests of 1936.

research organization which would serve as a bureau of standards for the evaluation of educational and psychological tests. It was only after we despaired of raising such funds that we decided to set up a test reviewing service.

THE SEVEN MMY'S

Since tests, unlike books, were rarely reviewed in professional journals, it was a revolutionary step forward when we published *The 1938 Mental Measurements Yearbook* 37 years ago. In his Foreword, Clarence E. Partch's comments reflect our excitement and mood in those early days:

> The publication of *The 1938 Mental Measurements Yearbook of the School of Education, Rutgers University* is likely to prove a landmark of considerable importance in the history of tests and measurements. Heretofore, despite the obvious need of test users for frank evaluations of tests by competent reviewers, few standardized tests have been critically appraised in the professional journals and textbooks for students of education and psychology. Now, for the first time, a large number of frankly evaluative reviews by able test technicians, subject-matter specialists, and psychologists are available to assist test users in making more discriminating selections from among the hundreds of tests on the market.[4]

Except for a few test authors and publishers who objected to unfavorable reviews, *The 1938 Yearbook* (also referred to as *The First Yearbook*) was enthusiastically acclaimed in this country and abroad. It took some time, however, before most of the protesting publishers were able to accept unfavorable test reviews with equanimity.

Before *The 1938 Yearbook* was off the press, we began sending out invitations to review tests for a 1939 yearbook. Unfortunately, because of financing and production problems, we were unable to maintain our annual production schedule. It took us over two years to publish the next volume, *The 1940 Mental Measurements Yearbook*.

Much enlarged and greatly improved over its predecessor, *The 1940 Yearbook* (also referred to as *The Second Yearbook*) has been the prototype for all later yearbooks. In addition to the increased number of tests, reviews, and references, there were many qualitative changes: (*a*) The objectives which have characterized all MMY's were presented in detail for the first time. (*b*) The format was standardized. (*c*) The classification of tests was changed from 40 specific categories to 12 broad categories. (*d*) The practice of including very short reviews of 100 words or less was discontinued. (*e*) The review coverage was extended to old tests and to tests previously reviewed as well as new tests. (*f*) The instructions given to reviewers concerning the preparation of their test reviews were presented. (*g*) The reactions of test authors and publishers—most of them objecting strenuously to unfavorable reviews—were reprinted for the first and last time.

In the Preface of *The 1940 Yearbook* we announced that the yearbooks would be published every two years. Because of World War II, however, *The Third Mental Measurements Yearbook* was not published until 1949. Except for its larger size and more thorough preparation, *The Third Yearbook*—like all later yearbooks—is very similar in its coverage, format, indexing, and organization to *The 1940 Yearbook*. There were, however, several improvements: (*a*) The "Classified Index of Tests," an expanded table of contents, was introduced. (*b*) Stars and asterisks were used preceding test titles to indicate, respectively, tests listed in a yearbook for the first time and tests revised or supplemented since last listed. (*c*) Asterisks were used at the end of a reference to indicate that the reference had been examined personally for accuracy and relevance. (*d*) Whenever possible, the abstract in *Psychological Abstracts* was cited for each reference. (*e*) Two improvements were made in the name index. Previously authors of references for specific tests had been indexed merely by citing the test for which the reference appears. After locating the test, one then had to search through the references to find those by that author. The new index eliminated this searching by citing each reference both to the test number and the reference number. Secondly, the index was converted into an "analytic index" in which *"test," "rev," "exc," "bk,"* and *"ref"* were used to indicate whether a citation referred to authorship of a test, review, excerpted review, book, or reference. These five features have been included in all later yearbooks.

In *The Fourth Mental Measurements Yearbook,* published in 1953, our review coverage was extended for the first time to many tests restricted to testing programs administered by organizations such as the College Entrance Ex-

---

[4] *The 1938 Mental Measurements Yearbook*, p. xi.

amination Board. Six years later, in 1959, *The Fifth Yearbook* was published. Upon the completion of that volume, we were concerned that some cutbacks would be necessary to stem the phenomenal growth of production costs, as well as the ever increasing length of each MMY. As a result, we decided to discontinue specific test bibliographies and almost all reviews of foreign tests. The appreciative reviews *The Fifth Yearbook* received, however, especially those mentioning the value of the specific bibliographies to students of testing, caused us to reconsider. Consequently, despite the expanding literature on specific tests, we decided to continue all features of the earlier volumes. As a result, it took us six years to publish in 1965 *The Sixth Mental Measurements Yearbook*, a 1,751-page volume, approximately one-third larger than the previous yearbook. In addition to its more extensive coverage, *The Sixth Yearbook* presents a comprehensive listing of all tests in print as of mid-1964. The latest yearbook to date, *The Seventh Yearbook*, was published in 1972. This massive two-volume work of 2,032 pages may well be considered the zenith of the MMY's.

Like all other volumes published since 1938, *The Seventh Yearbook* supplements rather than supplants earlier yearbooks. For complete coverage, therefore, a reader must have access to all seven MMY's. A person using only the latest, *The Seventh Yearbook*, will miss a tremendous amount of valuable information in the six earlier volumes. Although the more recent yearbooks—especially the last three—are of greatest value, the third and fourth yearbooks also contain much useful information on many in print tests. Even though the first two yearbooks are mainly of historical interest, they also include some critical information on currently used tests. Our faith in the value of the first four MMY's, published between 1938 and 1953, is attested to by our reissuing of the first and second yearbooks in 1972 and reprinting of the third and fourth in 1974. Consequently, all seven yearbooks are now in print.

EARLIER MMY MONOGRAPHS

It is with amusement and wonder that we look back at some of the dreams of our youth. *The 1940 Mental Measurements Yearbook* was the first yearbook published by my wife and myself. In those depression days, money was scarce but printing was cheap and penny postcards could be used for advertising. Borrowed capital of $3,500 was sufficient to launch us into book publishing. Even before our first book was off the press we were planning to publish not only a new MMY every two years, but also a series of derivative monographs. Our plans were confidently announced in the Preface of *The 1940 Yearbook* thus:

In order to make the material in the yearbooks more easily accessible to individuals who are interested in only a small part of each volume, a new series of monographs is being planned. If the first two or three monographs prove successful, others will eventually be prepared to cover tests in each of the following fields: business education, English and reading, fine arts, foreign languages, health and physical education, home economics, industrial arts, intelligence, mathematics, sciences, social studies, and vocational aptitudes. The first publication in each field will include: a comprehensive bibliography of all standard tests in print in that area; a reprinting, in part or in full, of all reviews of these tests which have appeared in previous yearbooks or in the journal literature; new reviews written especially for the monograph (to be, in turn, reprinted, in part or in full, in the following yearbook); and an extensive list of references on the construction, validation, use, and limitations of the tests. Separates in each field will be issued every four, six, or eight years depending upon the frequency of test publication. These monographs will range in size from fifty to two hundred pages. This new series will make it possible for an individual to purchase, at a nominal cost, every four, six, or eight years a monograph devoted solely to the tests and reviews of most interest to him.[5]

However, the publishing of the MMY's alone, even at intervals of 4 to 8 years, proved to be so time consuming and difficult that initiating the monograph series had to be continually postponed. But the dreams were never abandoned.

In 1968, 27 years after the monograph series was initially announced, the first monograph, *Reading Tests and Reviews* (RTR I), was published. This 542-page volume consists of a comprehensive bibliography of reading tests as of May 1968 and a reprinting of the reading sections of the first six MMY's. A second monograph, *Personality Tests and Reviews* (PTR I), was published two years later. This 1,695-page volume lists all personality tests as of June 1969 and provides a reprinting of the personality sections of the first six MMY's. The preparation of these two monographs turned out to be too costly and time consuming to justify working on monographs in other areas.

[5] *The 1940 Mental Measurements Yearbook*, p. xx.

TIP I AND TIP II

In 1961, we published the ninth volume in the MMY series: *Tests in Print: A Comprehensive Bibliography of Tests for Use in Education, Psychology, and Industry*. The objectives and nature of *Tests in Print* (hereafter called *Tests in Print I* or TIP I) are described in its Introduction as follows:

> The objectives of *Tests in Print* are threefold: first, to present a comprehensive bibliography of tests—achievement, aptitude, intelligence, personality, and certain sensory-motor skills—published as separates and currently available in English-speaking countries; second, to serve as a classified index and supplement to the volumes of the *Mental Measurements Yearbook* series published to date; third, to give a wider distribution to the excellent recommendations for improving test manuals made by committees of the American Psychological Association, the American Educational Research Association, and the National Council on Measurements Used in Education.[6]

TIP I lists 2,967 tests—2,126 in print and 841 out of print as of early 1961, and also serves as a master index to the contents of the first five MMY's. Originally, we had planned to publish a new edition of TIP shortly after the publication of each new MMY, but poor sales of TIP I caused these plans to be abandoned. *The Sixth Yearbook*, in effect, served as a new edition of *Tests in Print* by referring to the tests in TIP I which were still in print as of mid-1964. Surprisingly, however, sales of the 1961 *Tests in Print* began to pick up after publication of *The Sixth Yearbook* in 1965. This unexpected upturn encouraged us to begin devoting all of our time to the preparation of a new edition of TIP immediately after approving the last proofs for *The Seventh Yearbook*.

Tests in Print II: An Index to Tests, Test Reviews, and the Literature on Specific Tests (TIP II) was published in December 1974. Like the 1961 volume, *Tests in Print II* presents: (a) a comprehensive bibliography of all known tests published as separates for use with English-speaking subjects; (b) a classified index to the contents of the test sections of the seven *Mental Measurements Yearbooks* published to date; and (c) a reprinting of the 1974 APA-AERA-NCME *Standards for Educational and Psychological Tests*.

In addition, TIP II introduces the following new features: (d) comprehensive bibliographies through 1971 on the construction, use, and validity of specific tests; (e) a classified list of tests which have gone out of print since TIP I; (f) a cumulative name index for each test with references; (g) a title index covering in print and out of print tests, as well as inverted, series, and superseded titles in the MMY's and monographs; (h) an analytic name index covering all authors of tests, reviews, excerpts, and references in the MMY's and monographs; (i) a publishers directory with a complete listing of each publisher's test titles; (j) a classified scanning index which describes the population for which each test is intended; (k) identification of foreign tests and journals by presenting the country of origin in brackets immediately after a test entry or journal title; (l) inclusions of factual statements implying criticism such as "1971 tests identical with tests copyrighted 1961 except for format," and "no manual"; (m) listing of test titles at the foot of each page to permit immediate identification of pages consisting only of references or names; and (n) directions on how to use the book and an expanded table of contents printed on the endpages to greatly facilitate its use.

TIP II contains 2,467 in print test entries, 16.0 percent more than in TIP I. Table 1 presents a breakdown of the number of tests and new references in TIP II by classification. Personality—the area in which we know the least about testing—has, as it did in 1961, the greatest number of tests. Although the percentage of personality tests is 17.9, 44.9 percent of the TIP II references are for personality tests. Three categories—intelligence, personality, and

TABLE 1
TESTS AND NEW REFERENCES
IN TESTS IN PRINT II

Classification	Tests		References	
	Number	Percent	Number	Percent
Achievement Batteries	50	2.0	438	2.6
English	131	5.3	220	1.3
Fine Arts	35	1.4	229	1.4
Foreign Languages	105	4.3	81	.5
Intelligence	274	11.1	4,039	24.4
Mathematics	168	6.8	166	1.0
Miscellaneous	291	11.8	866	5.2
Multi-Aptitude	26	1.1	235	1.4
Personality	441	17.9	7,443	44.9
Reading	248	10.1	837	5.1
Science	97	3.9	72	.4
Sensory-Motor	62	2.5	382	2.3
Social Studies	85	3.4	49	.3
Speech and Hearing	79	3.2	216	1.3
Vocations	375	15.2	1,301	7.8
Total	2,467	100.0	16,574	99.9

---
[6] *Tests in Print*, p. xv.

vocations—make up 44.2 percent of tests and 77.1 percent of the references in TIP II.

INTELLIGENCE TESTS AND REVIEWS

This volume's subtitle, *A Monograph Consisting of the Intelligence Sections of the Seven Mental Measurements Yearbooks (1938–72) and Tests in Print II (1974)*, succinctly describes its contents. In addition to the 146-page reprint from TIP II and the 883-page section of reprints from the seven MMY's, *Intelligence Tests and Reviews* (ITR) includes a publishers directory, title index, name index, and an intelligence scanning index. The TIP II scanning index is reprinted in full also.

TIP II TESTS REPRINT

The section of this volume reprinted from *Tests in Print II*, TIP II Tests, contains a bibliography of in print intelligence tests, references for specific tests, cumulative name indexes for specific tests with references, and lists of tests which have gone out of print since appearing in TIP I. (The out of print tests are listed alphabetically at the ends of the subsections "Group," "Individual," and "Specific.") The first three of these categories will be described in more detail.

INTELLIGENCE TESTS

The TIP II reprint section lists 274 intelligence tests in print as of early 1974—15.1 percent more tests than were listed 14 years ago in TIP I (Table 2). While the number of group tests decreased 5.8 percent, individual tests increased 45.0 percent, and specific tests increased 103.7 percent. The marked increase in the specific tests category is largely due to the inclusion of creativity tests.

Table 3 presents statistics on the number of tests new or revised (or supplemented) since

TABLE 2
In Print Intelligence Tests
in TIP II and TIP I

	TIP II		TIP I	
	Number	Percent	Number	Percent
Group	161	58.8	171	71.8
Individual	58	21.2	40	16.8
Specific	55	20.1	27	11.3
Total	274	100.1	238	99.9

TABLE 3
In Print Intelligence Tests
New, Revised (or Supplemented)
Since the 7th MMY

Classification	Tests	Percent		
		New	Revised	Total
Group	161	6.8	22.4	29.2
Individual	58	15.5	6.9	22.4
Specific	55	32.7	14.5	47.2
Total	274	13.9	17.5	31.4

the 7th MMY. Of the 274 intelligence tests listed, 13.9 percent (38 tests) are new since the 7th MMY; 17.5 percent (48 tests) revised or supplemented.

Unlike the long test entries in the *Mental Measurements Yearbooks*, the TIP II entries in this volume are short entries supplying the following information:

a) TITLE. Test titles are printed in boldface type. Secondary or series titles are set off from main titles by a colon. Titles are always presented exactly as reported in the test materials. Stars precede titles of tests listed for the first time in TIP II; asterisks precede titles of tests which have been revised or supplemented since last listed.

b) TEST POPULATION. The grade, chronological age, or semester range, or the employment category is usually given. Commas are used to indicate separate grade levels. "Grades 1.5–2.5, 2–3, 4–12, 13–17" means that there are four test booklets: a booklet for the middle of the first grade through the middle of the second grade, a booklet for the beginning of the second grade through the end of the third grade, a booklet for grades 4 through 12 inclusive, and a booklet for undergraduate and graduate students in colleges and universities. "First, second semester" means that there are two test booklets: one covering the work of the first semester, the other covering the work of the second semester. "1, 2 semesters" indicates that the second booklet covers the work of the two semesters. "Ages 10-2 to 11-11" means ages 10 years 2 months to 11 years 11 months and "Grades 4-6 to 5-9" means the sixth month in the fourth grade through the ninth month in the fifth grade. "High school and college" denotes a single test booklet for both levels; "High school, college" denotes two test booklets, one for high school and one for college.

c) COPYRIGHT DATE. The range of copyright dates (or publication dates if not copyrighted) includes the various forms, accessories, and editions of a test. When the publication date differs from the copyright date, both dates are given; e.g., "1971, c1965–68" means that the test materials were copyrighted between 1965 and 1968 but were not published until 1971. Publication or copyright dates enclosed in brackets do not appear on the test materials but were obtained from other sources.

d) ACRONYM. An acronym is given for many tests.

e) SPECIAL COMMENTS. Some entries contain special notations, such as: "for research use only"; "revision of the *ABC Test*"; "tests administered monthly at centers throughout the United States"; "subtests available as separates"; and "verbal creativity." "For research use only" should be interpreted to mean that the *only* use of the test should be in research designed to assess its usefulness; contrary to what the implications seem to be, "for research use only" does not mean that a test has any use, whatsoever, as a research instrument. Tests used in research studies should have demonstrated validity before being selected as research tools. A statement such as "verbal creativity" is intended to further describe what the test claims to measure.

f) PART SCORES. The number and description of part scores is presented.

g) FACTUAL STATEMENTS IMPLYING CRITICISM. Some of the test entries include factual statements which imply criticism of the test, such as "1970 test identical with test copyrighted 1960" and "no manual."

h) AUTHOR. For most tests, all authors are reported. In the case of tests which appear in a new form each year, only authors of the most recent forms are listed. Names are reported exactly as printed on test materials. Names of editors are generally not reported.

i) PUBLISHER. The name of the publisher or distributor is reported for each test. Foreign publishers are identified by listing the country in brackets immediately following the name of the publisher. The Publishers Directory and Index must be consulted for a publisher's address.

j) FOREIGN ADAPTATIONS. Revisions and adaptations of tests for foreign use are listed in parentheses following the description of the original edition.

k) CLOSING ASTERISK. An asterisk following the publisher's name indicates that the entry was prepared from a first-hand examination of the test materials.

l) SUBLISTINGS. Levels, editions, subtests, or parts of a test which are available in separate booklets are sometimes presented as sublistings with titles set in small capitals. Sub-sublistings are indented with titles set in italic type.

m) CROSS REFERENCES. Except for tests being listed for the first time, a test entry includes a second paragraph with cross references to relevant material which may be found in the MMY reprint sections in this volume, or, in rare instances, to material in other sections of the MMY's. These cross references may be to "additional information" reported in longer entries, or to reviews, excerpts, and references for specific tests.

REFERENCES

The specific test biblographies in this monograph contain 13,468 references on the construction, use, and validity of specific tests—11,798 of these references for tests currently in print. Forty percent of the references for in print tests are for the last two trienniums reported on, 1966–71.

Table 4 presents reference counts for the 59 tests with 25 or more references through 1971. The *Stanford-Binet Intelligence Scale*, first published in 1916, leads with 1,408 references —36.0 percent more than its nearest competitor, the *Wechsler Intelligence Scale for Children*. One hundred seventy (12.1 percent) of the references for the S-B were published at least 50 years ago. Six tests are responsible for 46.2 percent of the references: *Stanford-Binet*

TABLE 4
INTELLIGENCE TESTS WITH 25 OR MORE REFERENCES THROUGH 1971

Test (Rank)	References
Stanford-Binet Intelligence Scale (1)	1,408
Wechsler Intelligence Scale for Children (2)	1,035
Wechsler-Bellevue Intelligence Scale (3)	990
Wechsler Adult Intelligence Scale (4)	938
College Board Scholastic Aptitude Test (5)	567
Progressive Matrices (6)	509
Goodenough-Harris Drawing Test (7)	388
Torrance Tests of Creative Thinking (8)	331
Cooperative School and College Ability Tests (9)	319
Peabody Picture Vocabulary Test (10)	299
California Test of Mental Maturity (11)	277
Otis Self-Administering Tests of Mental Ability (12)	262
Porteus Maze Test (13)	241
Otis Quick-Scoring Mental Ability Tests (14)	202
Ohio State University Psychological Test (15)	169
Lorge-Thorndike Intelligence Tests (16)	150
Miller Analogies Test (17)	142
Kuhlmann-Anderson Test (18.5)	129
Remote Associates Test (18.5)	129
Wonderlic Personnel Test (20)	123
Gesell Developmental Schedules (21)	108
Henmon-Nelson Tests of Mental Ability (22)	102
Alternate Uses (23.5)	101
Benton Visual Retention Test (23.5)	101
California Short-Form Test of Mental Maturity (25)	95
Culture Fair Intelligence Test (26)	89
Wechsler Memory Scale (27)	88
Wechsler Preschool and Primary Scale of Intelligence (28)	86
Graduate Record Examinations Aptitude Test (29.5)	84
Consequences (29.5)	84
Army General Classification Test (31)	78
Columbia Mental Maturity Scale (32)	77
Block-Design Test (33)	74
Full-Range Picture Vocabulary Test (34)	73
Arthur Point Scale of Performance Tests (35.5)	70
Leiter International Performance Scale (35.5)	70
Revised Beta Examination (37)	65
Kent Series of Emergency Scales (38)	61
Mill Hill Vocabulary Scale (39)	58
Christensen-Guilford Fluency Tests (40)	52
College Qualification Tests (41)	50
Cattell Infant Intelligence Scale (42.5)	49
Hidden Figures Test (42.5)	49
Quick Test (44)	48
Merrill-Palmer Scale of Mental Tests (45)	46
AH4, AH5, and AH6 Tests (46.5)	43
Slosson Intelligence Test (46.5)	43
Pintner-Cunningham Primary Test (48)	41
Concept Mastery Test (49)	40
Moray House Verbal Reasoning Tests (50)	38
Healy Pictorial Completion Tests (51.5)	37
Proverbs Test (51.5)	37
Bayley Scales of Infant Development (54)	31
Leiter Adult Intelligence Scale (54)	31
Minnesota Scholastic Aptitude Test (54)	31
Hiskey-Nebraska Test of Learning Aptitude (56)	27
Pressey Classification and Verifying Tests (57)	26
Adaptability Test (58.5)	25
Seguin-Goddard Formboard (58.5)	25
Total for 59 in print tests	10,941
Total for remaining 215 tests	857
Grand total for in print tests	11,798

Intelligence Scale (1,408 references), *Wechsler Intelligence Scale for Children* (1,035 references), *Wechsler-Bellevue Intelligence Scale* (990 references), *Wechsler Adult Intelligence Scale* (938 references), *College Board Scholastic Aptitude Test* (567 references), and *Progressive Matrices* (509 references). The 59 tests with 25 or more references account for

92.7 percent of all references for in print intelligence tests.

Current trends on the literature output for specific tests are shown in Table 5. Six tests generated 47.0 percent of the references in 1969–71: *Wechsler Intelligence Scale for Children* (322 references), *Wechsler Adult Intelligence Scale* (262 references), *College Board Scholastic Aptitude Test* (176 references), *Torrance Tests of Creative Thinking* (148 references), *Stanford-Binet Intelligence Scale* (147 references), and *Peabody Picture Vocabulary Test* (135 references). In the last three trienniums for which references are reported, the average number of references per year has increased from 506 in the years 1963–65 to 844 in 1969–71. The current rate is probably 1,000 or more references per year.

These specific test bibliographies cover not only the literature of the English-speaking world, but also the literature in English published in non-English-speaking countries. Our goal has been to include all published material—articles, books, chapters, and research monographs—as well as unpublished theses. We do not list as references research reports prepared for internal organizational use, prepublication reports, ERIC material, or abstracts of documents which are reproduced only on receipt of a purchase order (e.g., JSAS manuscripts). Secondary sources (e.g., *Psychological Abstracts*) may provide leads, but if the original publication cannot be located and examined, the reference is not used. We do, however, rely on secondary sources (primarily *Dissertation Abstracts International*) for unpublished theses. Except for doctoral dissertations abstracted in DAI, in recent years all thesis entries have been checked for accuracy by the degree-granting institutions.

References for a given test immediately follow the test entry. They are numbered consecutively for each test as they appear in the first through the seventh MMY and TIP II. References which appeared in earlier volumes are referred to but not repeated; e.g., "23–133. *See* 5:416" means references 23–133 can be found following test 416 in the section "Fifth MMY Reviews" in this volume.

References are arranged in chronological order by year of publication and alphabetically by authors within years. No references later than 1971 have been included. Supplementary bibliographies will be provided in the forthcoming 8th MMY for those tests which are listed again in that volume; the bibliographies for other tests will be brought up to date in *Tests in Print III*, scheduled for publication after the 8th MMY.

CUMULATIVE NAME INDEXES

A cumulative name index has been provided for every in print test having references to facilitate the search for an author's writings relevant to that test. To simplify indexing, forenames were reduced to initials. Authors not consistent in reporting their names will find their publications listed under two or more citations. On the other hand, a given

TABLE 5
INTELLIGENCE TESTS
WITH 15 OR MORE REFERENCES
IN THE TRIENNIUM 1969–71

Test (Rank)	'69–71	'66–68	'63–65
Wechsler Intelligence Scale for Children (1)	322	245	168
Wechsler Adult Intelligence Scale (2)	262	265	190
College Board Scholastic Aptitude Test (3)	176	139	113
Torrance Tests of Creative Thinking (4)	148	115	60
Stanford-Binet Intelligence Scale (5)	147	117	84
Peabody Picture Vocabulary Test (6)	135	108	38
Progressive Matrices (7)	105	104	61
Cooperative School and College Ability Tests (8)	89	76	86
Goodenough-Harris Drawing Test (9)	82	84	41
Wechsler Preschool and Primary Scale of Intelligence (10)	67	19	
California Test of Mental Maturity (11)	56	48	45
Remote Associates Test (12)	53	48	25
Lorge-Thorndike Intelligence Tests (13)	51	39	33
Hidden Figures Test (14)	35	13	1
Otis Quick-Scoring Mental Ability Tests (16)	34	40	37
Wechsler-Bellevue Intelligence Scale (16)	34	37	70
Alternate Uses (16)	34	37	17
Slosson Intelligence Test (18)	30	13	
Graduate Record Examinations Aptitude Test (19.5)	29	17	14
Consequences (19.5)	29	22	20
Benton Visual Retention Test (21)	28	23	18
Miller Analogies Test (22)	25	25	15
Porteus Maze Test (23)	24	31	27
Culture Fair Intelligence Test (24)	22	24	16
Wechsler Memory Scale (25)	21	13	11
California Short-Form Test of Mental Maturity (26)	20	22	21
Columbia Mental Maturity Scale (27)	19	13	8
AH4, AH5, and AH6 Tests (28.5)	18	6	5
Quick Test (28.5)	18	17	10
Otis-Lennon Mental Ability Test (30.5)	16		
Christensen-Guilford Fluency Tests (30.5)	16	20	11
College Qualification Tests (33.5)	15	9	11
Bayley Scales of Infant Development (33.5)	15	13	3
Gesell Developmental Schedules (33.5)	15	12	12
Thinking Creatively With Sounds and Words (33.5)	15	1	1
Total for the 35 in print tests	2,205	1,815	1,272
Total for the remaining 239 tests	328	373	246
Grand total for in print tests	2,533	2,188	1,518

name may represent two or more persons. In all cases, however, the references present names exactly as they appear in the publication referenced.

MMY REVIEWS REPRINT

This 883-page chapter is a reprinting of the intelligence test sections of the seven *Mental Measurements Yearbooks* presented in their order of publication: 1st MMY (1938, 27 pages), 2nd MMY (1941, 70 pages), 3rd MMY (1949, 107 pages), 4th MMY (1953, 113 pages), 5th MMY (1959, 147 pages), 6th MMY (1965, 182 pages), and 7th MMY (1972, 237 pages). This chapter brings together in a single well-indexed volume a tremendous amount of information on intelligence testing covering the past 50 years and more. The yearbooks must still be consulted, however, for information about books on intelligence testing. With a few exceptions (e.g., Terman and Merrill's *Measuring Intelligence*, 1937), the book review sections of the *Mental Measurements Yearbooks* contain all excerpted reviews of books on intelligence testing.

This chapter presents 574 original test reviews written by 271 specialists, 145 excerpted test reviews, and 9,429 references on the construction, use, and validity of specific tests (Table 6). Over three-quarters of the reviews and excerpts are for tests currently in print, although not always the most recent editions. Of the 13,468 references in this chapter and the preceding chapter, from the yearbooks and TIP II, 92.4 percent are for tests in print.

The contributing reviewers represent a wide range of interests and viewpoints. Every effort was made to select reviewers who would be considered highly competent by a sizable group of test users. Our practice of publishing multiple reviews of given tests makes it possible to give representation to differing viewpoints among reviewers. The test reviews in a given yearbook are not limited to new and revised tests; old tests, especially those generating considerable research and writing, are frequently reviewed in successive yearbooks.

In order to make sure that persons invited to review would know what was expected of them, a sheet entitled "Suggestions to MMY Reviewers" was enclosed with each letter of invitation. The suggestions follow:

1. Reviews should be written with the following major objectives in mind:
 a) To provide test users with carefully prepared appraisals of tests for their guidance in selecting and using tests.
 b) To stimulate progress toward higher professional standards in the construction of tests by commending good work, by censuring poor work, and by suggesting improvements.
 c) To impel test authors and publishers to present more detailed information on the construction, validity, reliability, uses, and possible misuses of their tests.
2. Reviews should be concise, the average review running from 600 to 1,200 words in length. The average length of the reviews written by one person generally should not exceed 1,000 words. Except for reviews of achievement batteries, multi-factor batteries, and tests for which a literature review is made, longer reviews should be prepared only with the approval of the Editor.
3. Reviews should be frankly critical, with both strengths and weaknesses pointed out in a judicious manner. Descriptive comments should be kept to the minimum necessary to support the critical portions of the review. Criticism should be as specific as possible; implied criticisms meaningful only to testing specialists should be avoided. Reviews should be written primarily for the rank and file of test users. An indication of the relative importance and value of a test with respect to competing tests should be presented whenever possible. If a reviewer considers a competing test better than the one being reviewed, the competing test should be specifically named.
4. If a test manual gives insufficient, contradictory, or ambiguous information regarding the construction, validity, and use of a test, reviewers are urged to write directly to authors and publishers for further information. Test authors and publishers should, however, be held responsible for presenting adequate data in test manuals—failure to do so should be pointed out. For comments made by reviewers based upon unpublished information received personally from test authors or publishers, the source of the unpublished information should be clearly indicated.
5. Reviewers will be furnished with the test entries which will precede their reviews. Information presented in the entry should not be repeated in reviews unless needed for evaluative purposes.
6. The use of sideheads is optional with reviewers.
7. Each review should conclude with a paragraph presenting a concise summary of the reviewer's overall evaluation of the test. The summary should be as explicit as possible. Is the test the best of its kind? Is it recommended for use? If other tests are better, which of the competing tests is best?

TABLE 6
REVIEWS, EXCERPTS, AND REFERENCES FOR THE 394 INTELLIGENCE TESTS IN THIS VOLUME

Reprint	Tests	Rev's	Exc's	Ref's
TIP II	274			4,039
7th MMY	121	87	42	4,058
6th MMY	131	114	13	1,623
5th MMY	122	111	1	1,393
4th MMY	94	89	25	1,036
3rd MMY	77	79	15	939
2nd MMY	57	69	19	380
1st MMY	26	25	30	
Total	394[1]	574	145	13,468

[1] The total number of different tests in all publications is 394—274 in print and 120 out of print.

INTRODUCTION

8. A separate review should be prepared for each test. Each review should begin on a new sheet. The test and forms reviewed should be clearly indicated. Your name, title, position, and address should precede each review, e.g.: John Doe, Professor of Education and Psychology, University of Maryland, College Park, Maryland. The review should begin a new paragraph immediately after the address.

9. All reviews should be typed double spaced and in triplicate. Two copies of each review should be submitted to the Editor; one copy should be retained by the reviewer.

10. If for any reason a reviewer thinks he is not in a position to write a frankly critical review in a scholarly and unbiased manner, he should request the Editor to substitute other tests for review.

11. Reviewers may not invite others to collaborate with them in writing reviews unless permission is secured from the Editor.

12. Most tests will be reviewed by two or more persons in order to secure better representation of various viewpoints. Noncritical content which excessively overlaps similar materials presented by another reviewer may be deleted. Reviews will be carefully edited, but no important changes will be made without the consent of the reviewer. Galley proofs (unaccompanied by copy) will be submitted to reviewers for checking.

13. The Editor reserves the right to reject any review which does not meet the minimum standards of the MMY series.

14. Each reviewer will receive a complimentary copy of *The Seventh Mental Measurements Yearbook*.

The long test entries in the section Seventh MMY Reviews contain all the information in the short TIP II entries plus the following:

a) INDIVIDUAL OR GROUP TEST. All tests are group tests unless otherwise indicated.

b) FORMS, PARTS, AND LEVELS. All available forms, parts, and levels are listed with copyright dates.

c) PAGES. The number of pages on which print occurs is reported for test booklets, manuals, technical reports, profiles, and other nonapparatus accessories.

d) FACTUAL STATEMENTS IMPLYING CRITICISM. Much more so than short entries, the long entries include factual statements implying criticism of the following type: "no data on reliability," "no data on validity," "no norms," "norms for grade 5 only," "no description of the normative population," "no norms for difference scores," "test copyrighted in 1970 identical with test copyrighted in 1960," and "statistical data based on earlier forms."

e) MACHINE SCORABLE ANSWER SHEETS. All types of machine scorable answer sheets available for use with a specific test are reported: Digitek (OpScan Test Scoring and Document Scanning System), IBM 805 (IBM Test Scoring Machine), IBM 1230 (IBM Optical Mark Reader), MRC (MRC Scoring and Reporting Service), NCS (NCS Scoring and Reporting Service), and NCS Sentry/70, and a few other answer sheets less widely used.

f) COST. Price information is reported for test packages (usually 20 to 35 tests), answer sheets, all other accessories, and specimen sets. The statement "$5.20 per 35 tests" means that all accessories are included unless separate prices are given for accessories. The statement also means 35 tests of one level, one edition, or one part unless stated otherwise. Quantity discounts and special discounts are not reported. Specimen set prices include copies of each level and part—but not all forms—unless otherwise indicated. Since 1970 prices are reported, the latest catalog of a test publisher should be consulted for current prices.

g) SCORING AND REPORTING SERVICES. Scoring and reporting services provided by publishers are reported along with information on costs. Special computerized scoring and interpretation services are sometimes given in separate entries immediately following the test entry.

h) TIME. The number of minutes of actual working time allowed examinees and the approximate length of time needed for administering a test are provided whenever obtainable. The latter figure is always enclosed in parentheses. Thus, "50(60) minutes" indicates that the examinees are allowed 50 minutes of working time and that a total of 60 minutes is needed to administer the test. When the time necessary to administer a test has been obtained through correspondence with the test publisher or author, the time is enclosed in brackets.

RUNNING HEADS AND FEET

To use this volume most efficiently, it is important to take advantage of the information given at the top and bottom of each page in the test and review sections. Both test entry and page numbers are given in the running heads. However, since all citations in the indexes and cross references are to entry numbers, these numbers, found next to the outside margins on facing pages, can be used as guide numbers in locating a particular test. The entry number on the left-hand page corresponds to the test embodying the first line of type on that page; the entry number on the right-hand page refers to the test containing the last line of type on that page. The test titles corresponding to these guide numbers are given in the running feet at the bottom of the page. Thus, the reader can quickly identify the first and last test discussed on each pair of facing pages.

The first reprint section, from *Tests in Print II*, has guide numbers in the range 323 to 594; the second reprint section, from the seven MMY's, has the successive ranges: 1:1037 to 1:1062, 2:1376 to 2:1430.1, 3:214 to 3:302, 4:267 to 4:364, 5:295 to 5:416, 6:432 to 6:562, and 7:328 to 7:448. The digit preceding the colon in the guide number corresponds to the number of the yearbook being reprinted. The numbers following the colon are the test entry numbers within that yearbook.

TIP II SCANNING INDEX

The complete TIP II Scanning Index, a classified listing of all tests in TIP II, has been reprinted to provide readers with an overview of tests available in areas other than intelligence. The 2,467 tests are divided into the categories delineated in Table 1 of this Introduction. Since the intelligence section of the TIP II Scanning Index will be of most interest to readers of this monograph, we have reprinted that section (entitled Intelligence Scanning Index) at the end of this volume for convenient reference. This end-of-the-book index is especially useful for locating tests suitable for a given population, since descriptions of these populations are reported immediately following the test titles.

PUBLISHERS DIRECTORY AND INDEX

Instead of giving only the entry numbers of the tests of a given publisher, as in our earlier publications, this Publishers Directory and Index gives both test titles and entry numbers. Stars denote the 33 publishers with test catalogs listing 10 or more tests (not necessarily intelligence tests). Tests not originating in the country of publication are identified by listing in brackets the country in which the test was originally prepared and published.

All addresses have been checked by the publishers (except for one publisher who did not reply to our four requests for verification), and are accurate through 1973. However, with such a large number of publishers (including many author-publishers), some address changes must be expected.

The directory lists 84 publishers of intelligence tests, 54.8 percent of which publish only one intelligence test. Their geographical distribution covers 8 foreign countries: Great Britain, 10 publishers; Canada, 5; India, 2; South Africa, 2; Australia, 1; The Netherlands, 1; New Zealand, 1; and Papua New Guinea, 1.

The seven publishers with 10 or more intelligence tests are: Psychological Corporation, 27 tests; Sheridan Psychological Services, Inc., 22; Australian Council for Educational Research, 17; NFER Publishing Co. Ltd., 14; Stoelting Co., 13; George G. Harrap & Co. Ltd., 12; and National Institute for Personnel Research, 11.

INDEX OF TITLES

This cumulative title index includes (*a*) intelligence tests in print as separates as of February 1, 1974; (*b*) out of print or status unknown intelligence tests; and (*c*) tests reclassified since last listed in the intelligence sections of the seven *Mental Measurements Yearbooks*.

Citations are to test entry numbers, not to pages. Numbers without colons refer to in print tests listed in the first reprint section (TIP II Tests) in this volume; numbers with colons refer to tests out of print, status unknown, or reclassified since last listed with intelligence tests. Unless preceded by the word "consult," all numbers containing colons refer to tests in this volume. To obtain the latest information on a test no longer classified with intelligence tests, the reader is directed to consult TIP II. For example, "Chicago Tests of Primary Mental Abilities, 3:225, reclassified, *consult* SRA Primary Mental Abilities, T2:1087" indicates that the test was last listed as an intelligence test in the *Third Yearbook* but has been reclassified and the title changed to *SRA Primary Mental Abilities;* for the latest information, test 1087 in TIP II must be consulted. Superseded titles are listed with cross references to the current title. Tests which are part of a series are listed under their individual titles and also their series titles. Acronyms for tests having 10 or more references are presented at the end of the Index of Titles.

INDEX OF NAMES

This cumulative index is an analytical index distinguishing between authorship of a test, test review, excerpted review, or reference dealing with a specific test. Furthermore, the index indicates whether the relevant test is in print or out of print. Numbers with colons refer to out of print or status unknown tests. Unless preceded by the word "consult," all numbers containing colons refer to tests in this volume.

Forenames have been reduced to initials to lower the cost of indexing. Since authors are not always consistent in how they list their names, two or more listings may refer to the same person. On the other hand, the use of initials sometimes results in one name representing two or more persons. Reference to the cited material in the text will resolve these difficulties in almost all cases.

Except for test authors, the use of the Index of Names is a two-step process. For example, if the name index reports *"rev,* 348" for C. Burt, the reader must look at the cross reference for test 348 in TIP II Tests to learn where Burt's review may be found in the yearbooks. Similarly, if the name index reports *"ref,* 518" for C. Burt, the reader must look at the Cumulative Name Index for test 518 to learn where, in this volume, Burt's reference or references on that test may be found. For example, in the main Index of Names, a reference listed for S. D. Porteus is *"ref, 518."* Looking in the Cumulative Name Index for test 518, the reader will find that Porteus is the author of 50 references for this test, each cited by number, so the reader can quickly locate them in the list of references under the test entry.

INTELLIGENCE
TESTS AND REVIEWS

Reprinted from *Tests in Print II*

INTELLIGENCE – TIP II

GROUP

[323]

A.C.E.R. Advanced Test B40. Ages 13 and over; 1940–66; formerly called *Adult Test (B40)*; 1965 test identical with test copyrighted 1940 except for 2 revised items; 1966 manual identical with manual published 1964 except for key to 2 items; Australian Council for Educational Research [Australia]. *

For additional information, see 7:328 (4 references); for a review by C. Sanders, see 5:296 (3 references).

REFERENCES THROUGH 1971

1-3. See 5:296.
4-7. See 7:328.
8. ANDERSON, A. W. "School of Entry and First-Year Aca-

demic Performance in the University of Western Australia." *Austral J Higher Ed* 1:20–3 N '61. *
9. HOGBEN, D. "The Academic Progress of Science Students in the University of Western Australia." *Austral J Higher Ed* 1:24–8 N '61. *
10. SMALL, J. J. "A Case Study Approach to Success and Failure Among First Year Students in New Zealand." *Austral J Higher Ed* 1:80–90 N '63.*
11. POND, L. "A Study of High-Achieving and Low-Achieving University Freshmen." *Austral J Higher Ed* 2:73–8 N '64. *
12. START, K. B. "Intelligence and the Improvement in a Gross Motor Skill After Mental Practice." *Brit J Ed Psychol* 34:85–90 F '64. * (*PA* 38:7246)
13. ADCOCK, C. J., AND WEBBERLEY, M. "Primary Mental Abilities." *J General Psychol* 84(2):229–43 Ap '71. * (*PA* 46:4979)

CUMULATIVE NAME INDEX

Adcock, C. J.: 13
Anderson, A. W.: 4, 6, 8
Cook, P. H.: 1
Hogben, D.: 5, 7, 9
Hohne, H. H.: 2–3
Pond, L.: 11
Sanders, C.: *rev*, 5:296
Small, J. J.: 10
Start, K. B.: 12
Webberley, M.: 13

[324]

*A.C.E.R. Advanced Tests AL and AQ.** College and superior adults; 1953–73; 2 tests; D. Spearritt (manual); Australian Council for Educational Research [Australia]. *
a) TEST AL. 1953–55; linguistic.
b) TEST AQ. 1953–73; quantitative; 1973 metric edition identical with test published 1954 except for 2 new and 4 revised items.

For additional information and a review by Duncan Howie, see 5:295.

REFERENCES THROUGH 1971

1. POND, L. "A Study of High-Achieving and Low-Achieving University Freshmen." *Austral J Higher Ed* 2:73–8 N '64. *
2. CHEONG, GEORGE S. C. "Relations Among Age, Schooling, Differential Aptitude Test, and the ACER Test." *Ed & Psychol Meas* 30(2):479–82 su '70. *
3. GAUDRY, ERIC, AND SPIELBERGER, CHARLES D. "Anxiety and Intelligence in Paired-Associate Learning." *J Ed Psychol* 61(5):386–91 O '70. * (*PA* 45:1705)

CUMULATIVE NAME INDEX

Cheong, G. S. C.: 2
Gaudry, E.: 3
Howie, D.: *rev*, 5:295
Pond, L.: 1
Spielberger, C. D.: 3

[325]

*A.C.E.R. Higher Tests.** Ages 13 and over; 1944–73; formerly called *A.C.E.R. General Ability Test: Advanced M;* 3 scores: linguistic, quantitative, total; 2 parts; D. Spearritt (original manual), M. L. Clark (revised manual), and B. Christeson (form W); Australian Council for Educational Research [Australia]. *
a) FORMS ML AND WL [LINGUISTIC]. 1973 metric edition of form WL identical with form published 1959 except for 2 revised items.
b) FORMS MQ AND WQ [QUANTITATIVE]. 1973 metric edition identical with forms published 1948 (MQ) and 1959 (WQ) except for 6 new and 5 revised items for MQ and 4 new and 2 revised items for WQ.

For additional information, see 6:432 (1 reference); for a review by C. Sanders, see 5:297.

REFERENCES THROUGH 1971

1. See 6:432.
2. PHILLIPS, G. R. "A Study of Psychological Tests for the Selection of Trainee Nurses: 1, General Approach." *Personnel Prac B* 20:28–32 D '64. * (*PA* 39:10886)

CUMULATIVE NAME INDEX

Casey, D. L.: 1
Mason, P. L.: 1
Phillips, G. R.: 2
Sanders, C.: *rev*, 5:297

[326]

A.C.E.R. Intermediate Test A. Ages 10-0 to 14-0; 1938–61; 1961 test essentially the same as *A.C.E.R. General Test A* ['38]; Australian Council for Educational Research [Australia]. *

For additional information, see 6:433. For excerpts from related book reviews, see 3:1110 (1 excerpt) and 2:B1005 (1 excerpt).

[327]

*A.C.E.R. Intermediate Tests C and D.** Ages 10-0 to 14-0; 1939–72; 2 tests; Australian Council for Educational Research [Australia]. *
a) TEST C. 1939–53; formerly called *A.C.E.R. General Test C. Out of print.*
b) TEST D. 1947–72; 1972 metric edition of test identical with test published 1947 except for 3 new and 5 revised items; not available to government schools; D. Spearritt (original manual) and M. L. Clark (revised manual).

For additional information and a review by James Lumsden, see 5:298 (2 references).

REFERENCES THROUGH 1971

1–2. See 5:298.
3. DEWING, K. "Some Correlates of Creativity Test Performance in Seventh Grade Children." *Austral J Psychol* 22(3):269–76 D '70. * (*PA* 46:889)

CUMULATIVE NAME INDEX

Brownless, V. T.: 2
Dewing, K.: 3
Dunn, S.: 1
Dunn, S. S.: 2
Lumsden, J.: *rev*, 5:298
Spearritt, D.: 1

[328]

A.C.E.R. Junior Non-Verbal Test. Ages 8.5–12.0; 1949–53; manual by D. Spearritt; Australian Council for Educational Research [Australia]. *

For additional information and a review by D. A. Pidgeon, see 5:301 (1 reference).

REFERENCES THROUGH 1971

1. See 5:301.
2. HOWIE, DUNCAN. "Scholastic Aptitude, Reasoning, Fluency and Concentration." *Austral J Psychol* 2:100–13 D '50. * (*PA* 26:737)
3. COCHRANE, R. G.; ELKINS, J.; AND RICHMOND, DAWN M. "Analysis of Fourth Grade Testing." *Slow Learning Child* (Australia) 16(3):131–42 N '69. * (*PA* 44:18351)
4. ELKINS, J. "Some Recent Queensland Norms for Widely Used Standardized Tests." *Slow Learning Child* (Australia) 18(3):142–7 N '71. *

CUMULATIVE NAME INDEX

Cochrane, R. G.: 3
Dunn, S.: 1
Elkins, J.: 3–4
Howie, D.: 2
Pidgeon, D. A.: *rev*, 5:301
Richmond, D. M.: 3
Spearritt, D.: 1

[329]

A.C.E.R. Junior Test A. Ages 8.5–12.0; 1946–58; formerly called *General Test T;* Australian Council for Educational Research [Australia]. *

For additional information, see 6:434; for a review by R. Winterbourn, see 5:299.

[330]

A.C.E.R. Lower Grades General Ability Scale, Second Edition. Ages 6-6 to 9-1; 1962–66; 5 scores: picture vocabulary, picture arrangement, picture analogies, picture series, total; 1964 test identical with test copyrighted 1962 except for minor revisions in format; manual by M. L. Clark; Australian Council for Educational Research [Australia]. *

For additional information, see 7:329.

REFERENCES THROUGH 1971

1. ELKINS, J. "Some Recent Queensland Norms for Widely Used Standardized Tests." *Slow Learning Child* (Australia) 18(3):142–7 N '71. *

CUMULATIVE NAME INDEX

Elkins, J.: 1

[331]

*AH4, AH5, and AH6 Tests.** Ages 10 and over, 13 and over, 16 and over; 1955–73; 4 tests; A. W. Heim,

K. P. Watts (c), and V. Simmonds (c); NFER Publishing Co. Ltd. [England]. *

a) AH4: GROUP TEST OF GENERAL INTELLIGENCE (1968 REVISION). Ages 10 and over; 1955–73; 2 editions.
  1) *Hand Scored Edition.* 1955–70.
  2) *Machine Scorable Edition.* 1973; manual by Peter Saville and Janice Hare.

b) AH5: GROUP TEST OF HIGH-GRADE INTELLIGENCE. Ages 13 and over; 1956–68.

c) AH6: GROUP TESTS OF HIGH-LEVEL INTELLIGENCE. Ages 16 and over; 1970; 2 tests: SEM for Scientists, Engineers and Mathematicians (potential or qualified), AG for Arts and General.

For additional information and a review by John Nisbet, see 7:331 (12 references); for a review by John Liggett of AH5 and the original edition of AH4, see 6:506; for reviews by George A. Ferguson of AH4 and J. A. Keats of AH5, see 5:390 (11 references).

REFERENCES THROUGH 1971

1–11. See 5:390.
12–23. See 7:331.
24. HEIM, ALICE W., AND WALLACE, JEAN G. "The Effects of Repeatedly Retesting the Same Group on the Same Intelligence Test: Part 1, Normal Adults." *Q J Exp Psychol* (England) 1:151–9 O '49. * (*PA* 25:6022)
25. DAVIDSON, M. A.; LEE, D.; PARNELL, R. W.; AND SPENCER, S. J. G. "The Detection of Psychological Vulnerability in Students." *J Mental Sci* (England) 101:810–25 O '55. * (*PA* 30:7161)
26. HUDSON, L. "A Differential Test of Art/Science Aptitude." *Nature* (England) 186:413–4 Ap 30 '60. *
27. EVANS, E. G. S. "Reasoning Ability and Personality Differences Among Student-Teachers." *Brit J Ed Psychol* 34:305–14 N '64. * (*PA* 39:8718)
28. GIBBONS, K. C., AND SAVAGE, R. D. "Intelligence Study Habits and Personality Factors in Academic Success—A Preliminary Report." *Durham Res R* (England) 5:8–12 S '65. *
29. OJHA, A. B.; KELVIN, R. P.; AND LUCAS, C. J. "A Note on Season of Birth and Intelligence." *Brit J Ed Psychol* 36:94–5 F '66. * (*PA* 40:6630)
30. POPPLETON, PAMELA K. "Puberty, Family Size and the Educational Progress of Girls." *Brit J Ed Psychol* 38:286–92 N '68. * (*PA* 43:6777)
31. STRINGER, PETER, AND TYSON, MOYA. "University Selection Interviewers' Ratings Related to Interviewee Self-Image." *Occup Psychol* (England) 42:49–60 Ja '68. * (*PA* 43:4563)
32. LI, ANITA KING-FUN. "Student Attitudes and Teacher Training Performance." *Ed Res* (England) 12(1):60–3 N '69. *
33. BRIERLEY, HARRY. "A Fully Automated Intellectual Test." *Brit J Social & Clin Psychol* 10(3):286–8 S '71. * (*PA* 48:3255)
34. BYRNE, P. S., AND FREEMAN, JAMES. "Postgraduate Training for General Practice: An Assessment of Aptitudes and Abilities of Trainee Entrants." *Brit J Med Ed* 5(4):293–304 D '71. *
35. CHILD, DENNIS, AND SMITHERS, ALAN. "Some Cognitive and Affective Factors in Subjective Choice." *Res Ed* (England) 5:1–9 My '71. *
36. CRAWSHAW, JOYCE E. "Investigation Into Correlation Between Scores on Tests of Creativity and Ability in Modern Educational Dance." *Brit J Phys Ed* 2(6):xliii–xlv N '71. *
37. DACEY, JOHN S., AND MADAUS, GEORGE F. "An Analysis of Two Hypotheses Concerning the Relationship Between Creativity and Intelligence." *J Ed Res* 64(5):213–6 Ja '71. * (*PA* 46:4712)
38. FRANSELLA, FAY. "A Personal Construct Theory and Treatment of Stuttering." *J Psychosom Res* (England) 15(4):433–8 D '71. *
39. HAMILTON, V., AND FREEMAN, P. "Academic Achievement and Student Personality Characteristics: Multivariate Study." *Brit J Sociol* 22(1):31–52 Mr '71. * (*PA* 47:3755)
40. HARTLEY, JAMES, AND HOLT, JANET. "The Validity of a Simplified Version of Baddeley's Three-Minute Reasoning Test." *Ed Res* (England) 14(1):70–3 N '71. * (*PA* 49:10254)
41. MEHRYAR, A. H., AND SHAPURIAN, R. "The Reliability and Validity of the Persian Form of AH5." *Brit J Ed Psychol* 41(2):209–13 Je '71. * (*PA* 47:9657)
42. SINGH, AMARJIT. "Norms for First-Year Student Nurses: General Intelligence and Personality." *Nursing Times* (England) 67(30, sup):117–9 Jl 29 '71. *
43. WATERS, W. E. "Migraine: Intelligence, Social Class, and Familial Prevalence." *Brit Med J* 2(5753):77–81 Ap 10 '71. * (*PA* 47:3566)

CUMULATIVE NAME INDEX

Allen, A.: 18
Banks, C.: 19
Batts, V.: 2
Beard, R. M.: 12
Brierley, H.: 33
Byrne, P. S.: 34
Cane, V. R.: 4
Child, D.: 35
Cortis, G. A.: 17
Crawshaw, J. E.: 36
Dacey, J.: 18
Dacey, J. S.: 37
Davidson, M. A.: 25
Evans, E. G. S.: 27
Ferguson, G. A.: *rev,* 5:390
Fransella, F.: 38
Freeman, J.: 34
Freeman, P.: 39
Gallop, R.: 20
Gibbons, K. C.: 28
Hamilton, V.: 21, 39
Harrison, G. J.: 16
Hartley, J.: 40
Heim, A. W.: 1–5, 10, 24
Holt, J.: 40
Hudson, L.: 26
Jones, E. M.: 19
Kardak, V. S.: 19
Keats, J. A.: *rev,* 5:390
Kelvin, R. P.: 13, 15, 29
Lee, D.: 25
Li, A. K. F.: 32
Liggett, J.: *rev,* 6:506
Lucas, C. J.: 13, 15, 19, 29
Madaus, G.: 18
Madaus, G. F.: 37
Mehryar, A. H.: 22, 41
Nisbet, J.: *rev,* 7:331
Ojha, A. B.: 13, 15, 29
Parnell, R. W.: 25
Pilkington, G. W.: 16
Poppleton, P. K.: 30
Povey, R. M.: 23
Savage, R. D.: 28
Shapurian, R.: 22, 41
Singh, A.: 42
Smithers, A.: 35
Spencer, S. J. G.: 25
Stringer, P.: 31
Tarpey, M. S.: 14
Tyson, M.: 31
Wallace, J. G.: 5–7, 24
Waters, W. E.: 43
Watts, K. P.: 8–9, 11

[332]

APT Performance Test. Adults; 1954–57; 2 tests: verbal, quantitative; distribution restricted to clients; Bentley Barnabas; Associated Personnel Technicians, Inc. *

For additional information, see 5:302.

REFERENCES THROUGH 1971

1. SANCHEZ, JOHN TRIJILLO. *A Statistical Appraisal of the APT Form of the Wonderlic Personnel Test.* Master's thesis, Kansas State College (Manhattan, Kan.), 1954.

CUMULATIVE NAME INDEX

Sanchez, J. T.: 1

[333]

Abstract Reasoning: Differential Aptitude Tests. Grades 8–12 and adults; 1947–73; 2 editions; George K. Bennett, Harold G. Seashore, and Alexander G. Wesman; Psychological Corporation. * For the complete battery entry, see 1069.

a) FORM A. 1947–59. *Out of print.*
b) FORM T. 1947–73; 1972 test identical with tests copyrighted 1947 and 1961 except for item sequence.

For reviews of the complete battery, see 7:673 (1 review, 1 excerpt), 6:767 (2 reviews), 5:605 (2 reviews), 4:711 (3 reviews), and 3:620 (1 excerpt).

REFERENCES THROUGH 1971

1. WILLIAMS, NANCY. "A Study of the Validity of the Verbal Reasoning Subtests and the Abstract Reasoning Subtest of the Differential Aptitude Tests." *Ed & Psychol Meas* 12:129–31 sp '52. * (*PA* 27:5914)
2. PASRICHA, P. "A Try-out of Abstract Reasoning Test With Children of Baroda." *J Voc & Ed Guid* (India) 9:118–21 Ag '63. * (*PA* 38:6571)
3. GILES, GEORGE C., JR. "Predictive Validity of Progressive Matrices and Two Other Nonlanguage Tests of Mental Ability." *J Ed Meas* 1:65–7 Je '64. * (*PA* 39:7757)
4. SCHRECK, THOMAS C. "Selected Factors Related to Academic Success in College." *Ed & Psychol R* (India) 4:71–6 Ap '64. *
5. MARTIN, WILLIAM T. "Analysis of the Abstracting Function in Reasoning Using an Experimental Test." *Psychol Rep* 21:593–8 O '67. * (*PA* 42:4815)
6. KIRKPATRICK, JAMES J.; EWEN, ROBERT B.; BARRETT, RICHARD S.; AND KATZELL, RAYMOND A. *Testing and Fair Employment: Fairness and Validity of Personnel Tests for Different Ethnic Groups,* pp. 17–9, 25–7, 51–69. New York: New York University Press, 1968. Pp. x, 145. *
7. GRANT, DONALD L., AND BRAY, DOUGLAS W. "Validation of Employment Tests for Telephone Company Installation and Repair Occupations." *J Appl Psychol* 54(1):7–14 F '70. * (*PA* 44:5738)

CUMULATIVE NAME INDEX

Barrett, R. S.: 6
Bray, D. W.: 7
Ewen, R. B.: 6
Giles, G. C.: 3
Grant, D. L.: 7
Katzell, R. A.: 6
Kirkpatrick, J. J.: 6
Martin, W. T.: 5
Pasricha, P.: 2
Schreck, T. C.: 4
Williams, N.: 1

[334]
Academic Alertness "AA": Individual Placement Series. Adults; 1957–66; 7 scores: general knowledge, arithmetic, vocabulary, reasoning ability, logical sequence, accuracy, total; J. H. Norman; Personnel Research Associates, Inc. *

For additional information and a review by Joel T. Campbell, see 7:332.

[335]
Academic Aptitude Test: Non-Verbal Intelligence: Acorn National Aptitude Tests. Grades 7–16 and adults; 1943–57; 4 scores: spatial relations, physical relations, graphic relations, total; 1957 test identical with test copyrighted 1944; Andrew Kobal, J. Wayne Wrightstone, and Karl R. Kunze; Psychometric Affiliates. *

For additional information, see 5:303; for a review by William B. Schrader, see 4:274.

[336]
Academic Aptitude Test: Verbal Intelligence: Acorn National Aptitude Tests. Grades 7–16 and adults; 1943–52; 4 scores: general information, mental alertness, comprehension of relations, total; 1952 test identical with test copyrighted 1943 except for minor changes; Andrew Kobal, J. Wayne Wrightstone, and Karl R. Kunze; Psychometric Affiliates. *

For additional information, see 5:304; for a review by William B. Schrader, see 4:275; for a review by Marion A. Bills, see 3:215.

[337]
Adaptability Test. Job applicants; 1942–67; Joseph Tiffin and C. H. Lawshe; Science Research Associates, Inc. *

For additional information, see 7:333 (6 references); for a review by John M. Willits, see 5:305 (13 references); for reviews by Anne Anastasi and Marion A. Bills, see 3:216 (3 references).

REFERENCES THROUGH 1971
1–3. See 3:216.
4–16. See 5:305.
17–22. See 7:333.
23. LAWSHE, C. H., AND PATINKA, PAUL J. "An Empirical Comparison of Two Methods of Test Selection and Weighting." *J Appl Psychol* 42:210–2 Je '58. * (*PA* 33:9093)
24. WRIGHTSMAN, LAWRENCE S., JR. "The Effects of the Purported Validity of a Test Upon Level of Motivation and Performance." *J Ed Res* 54:153–6 D '60. *
25. GRUENFELD, LEOPOLD W. "Selection of Executives for a Training Program." *Personnel Psychol* 14:421–31 w '61. * (*PA* 37:3922)

CUMULATIVE NAME INDEX

Albright, L. E.: 15–6	Page, H. E.: 17
Anastasi, A.: *rev*, 3:216	Patinka, P. J.: 23
Baehner, V. M.: 21	Patton, W. M.: 14
Berg, I. A.: 12	Poe, W. A.: 12
Bills, M. A.: *rev*, 3:216	Pred, G. D.: 5
Buel, W. D.: 21	Rosensteel, R. K.: 13
Chandler, R. E.: 18	Sartain, A. Q.: 3
Giese, W. J.: 7	Stromberg, E. L.: 6
Gruenfeld, L. W.: 20, 25	Thornton, G. R.: 1
Guion, R. M.: 22	Tiffin, J.: 2
Hadley, J. M.: 8–9	Wallace, S. R.: 11
Kahn, D. F.: 4, 8–9	Willits, J. M.: *rev*, 5:305
Kazmier, L. J.: 19	Wrightsman, L. S.: 24
Lawshe, C. H.: 1–2, 10, 23	

[338]
Advanced Test N. Ages 15 and over; 1951–52; not available to government schools; Australian Council for Educational Research [Australia]. *

For additional information and reviews by A. E. G. Pilliner and C. Sanders, see 5:307.

[339]
American School Intelligence Test. Grades kgn–3, 4–6, 7–9, 10–12; 1961–63; ASIT; tests for grades 4–12 "developed from the *Illinois General Intelligence Scale*" ('20–26) for grades 3–8; Willis E. Pratt, M. R. Trabue, Rutherford B. Porter, and George A. W. Stouffer, Jr.; Bobbs-Merrill Co., Inc. *

For additional information and reviews by David A. Payne and Frank B. Womer, see 6:439 (1 reference).

REFERENCES THROUGH 1971
1. See 6:439.

CUMULATIVE NAME INDEX

Hofforth, R. A.: 1	Womer, F. B.: *rev*, 6:439
Payne, D. A.: *rev*, 6:439	

[340]
*****Analysis of Learning Potential.** Grades 1, 2–3, 4–6, 7–9, 10–12; 1970–71; ALP; *complete test option:* 2 scores derived from the same total raw score: learning potential ("estimate of the pupil's general learning ability" compared to the same age group), general composite ("estimate of the pupil's general learning ability" compared to the same grade group); in grades 4–12 a reading-mathematics difference score (called "reading-mathematics composite prognostic differential") is also reported; *reading prognostic subtests option:* reading composite prognostic score ("an estimate of the pupil's capacity for school learning" in reading compared to the same grade group); *mathematics prognostic subtests option:* mathematics composite prognostic score ("an estimate of the pupil's capacity for school learning" in mathematics compared to the same grade group); Walter N. Durost, Eric F. Gardner, Richard Madden, and George A. Prescott; Harcourt Brace Jovanovich, Inc. *

For additional information and reviews by Lee J. Cronbach and Arthur R. Jensen, see 7:334.

REFERENCES THROUGH 1971
1. GIRARD, JUDITH ANDERSON FUNK. *A Study of the Correlations Between the Gates-MacGinitie Reading Comprehension Test and Various Subtests From the Analysis of Learning Potential.* Doctor's thesis, University of Northern Colorado (Greeley, Colo.), 1971. (*DAI* 32:5468A)
2. HEYDENBERK, WARREN ROBERT. *A Comparison of Four Methods of Estimating Reading Potential.* Doctor's thesis, University of Northern Colorado (Greeley, Colo.), 1971. (*DAI* 32:3558A)

CUMULATIVE NAME INDEX

Cronbach, L. J.: *rev*, 7:334	Heydenberk, W. R.: 2
Girard, J. A. F.: 1	Jensen, A. R.: *rev*, 7:334

[341]
Analysis of Relationships. Grades 12–16 and industry; 1960; manual subtitle is *A Test of Mental Ability*; Edwin E. Ghiselli; Consulting Psychologists Press, Inc. *

For additional information and reviews by Gustav J. Froehlich and Wimburn L. Wallace, see 6:440 (2 references).

REFERENCES THROUGH 1971
1–2. See 6:440.
3. ROSS, PAUL F., AND DUNFIELD, NEIL M. "Selecting Salesmen for an Oil Company." *Personnel Psychol* 17:75–84 sp '64. *

CUMULATIVE NAME INDEX

Dunfield, N. M.: 3	Ross, P. F.: 3
Froehlich, G. J.: *rev*, 6:440	Wallace, W. L.: *rev*, 6:440
Ghiselli, E. E.: 1–2	

[341A]
The Army Alpha Examination: First Nebraska Revision. Grades 6–16 and adults; 1937–40; a revision of *Army Group Examination Alpha*; 4 scores: verbal, numerical computation, relationships, total; 1940 test

identical with test copyrighted 1937; J. P. Guilford; Sheridan Psychological Services, Inc. *

For additional information and a review by Robert G. Demaree (with Louis L. McQuitty), see 4:279 (5 references); for a review by W. D. Commins, see 1:1039; see also 3:220 (77 references for *Army Group Examination Alpha* and revisions).

REFERENCES THROUGH 1971
1–4. See 3:220 (61, 66, 69, 73).
5. See 4:279.

CUMULATIVE NAME INDEX
Blakemore, A. M.: 2
Commins, W. D.: *rev,* 1:1039
Demaree, R. G.: *rev,* 4:279
Guilford, J. P.: 1, 5
Hay, E. N.: 2–3
McQuitty, L. L.: *rev,* 4:279
Rabin, A. I.: 4
Weinik, H. M.: 4

[342]
Army General Classification Test, First Civilian Edition. Grades 9–16 and adults; 1940–60; AGCT; 1947 test identical with the 1940 form 1a of the Army edition; test by Personnel Research Section, the Adjutant General's Office, War Department; Science Research Associates, Inc. *

For additional information and reviews by Bert A. Goldman and Howard B. Lyman, see 6:441 (5 references); see also 5:310 (17 references); for a review by John T. Dailey, see 4:280 (15 references); for an excerpted review, see 3:219 (14 references).

REFERENCES THROUGH 1971
1–14. See 3:219.
15–29. See 4:280.
30–46. See 5:310.
47–51. See 6:441.
52. LAYMAN, JAMES W., AND BOGUSLAVSKY, GEORGE W. "The Relationship Between Ability and Achievement in the Army Specialized Training Program." *J Psychol* 18:45–54 Jl '44. * (*PA* 19:254)
53. BINGHAM, WALTER V. "Inequalities in Adult Capacity—From Military Data." *Sci* 104:147–52 Ag 16 '46. * (*PA* 20:3967)
54. FOX, VERNON. "A Study of the Promotion of Enlisted Men in the Army." *J Appl Psychol* 31:298–305 Je '47. * (*PA* 21:4101)
55. WILLIAMS, S. B., AND LEAVITT, H. J. "Prediction of Success in Learning Japanese." *J Appl Psychol* 31:164–8 Ap '47. * (*PA* 21:2796)
56. ALTUS, W. D. "Some Correlates of Enlisted Grades in a Specialized Type of Army Installation." *J Social Psychol* 31:303–4 My '50. * (*PA* 25:3446)
57. FUCHS, EDMUND F., AND CHYATTE, CONRAD. "On the Intelligence of Soldier Criminals." *J Crim Law Criminol & Police Sci* 40:753–5 Mr–Ap '50. * (*PA* 25:1927)
58. CANTER, AARON HERMAN. "Direct and Indirect Measures of Psychological Deficit in Multiple Sclerosis: Part 1." *J General Psychol* 44:3–25 Ja '51. * (*PA* 25:7027)
59. CANTER, AARON HERMAN. "Direct and Indirect Measures of Psychological Deficit in Multiple Sclerosis: Part 2." *J General Psychol* 44:27–50 Ja '51. * (*PA* 25:7028)
60. MASON, CHARLES F. "Pre-Illness Intelligence of Mental Hospital Patients." *J Consult Psychol* 20:297–300 Ag '56. * (*PA* 31:7418)
61. FIRESTONE, RICHARD W. "Education, Intelligence, and Military Recruit Performance." *J Clin Psychol* 13:93–5 Ja '57. * (*PA* 32:6039)
62. WEINSTEIN, SIDNEY, AND TEUBER, HANS-LUKAS. "Effects of Penetrating Brain Injury on Intelligence Test Scores." *Sci* 125:1036–7 My 24 '57. * (*PA* 32:5817)
63. WEINSTEIN, SIDNEY, AND TEUBER, HANS-LUKAS. "The Role of Preinjury Education and Intelligence Level in Intellectual Loss After Brain Injury." *J Comp & Physiol Psychol* 50:535–9 O '57. * (*PA* 33:4493)
64. BRADLEY, ARTHUR DICKINSON. *Estimating Success in Technical and Skilled Trade Courses Using a Multivariate Statistical Analysis.* Doctor's thesis, University of Minnesota (Minneapolis, Minn.), 1958. (*DA* 21:313)
65. ROSS, ALAN O. "Brain Injury and Intellectual Performance." *J Consult Psychol* 22:151–2 Ap '58. * (*PA* 35:3415)
66. CROUCH, HENRIETTA H. "An Inquiry Into the Relationship of Achievement Scores and Certain Variables in an Adult High School." *J Ed Res* 55:323–6 Ap '62. * (*PA* 38:6558)
67. CURRIE, JOHN S.; ANDERSON, RICHARD J.; AND PRICE, A. COOPER. "Timed Block Counting as a Test for Organic Brain Impairment." *J Gerontol* 20:372–3 Jl '65. *
68. SILVER, MIRIAM ROST. *Characteristics and Functions of Teacher-Aides in Classes for Trainable Mentally Retarded Children.* Doctor's thesis, University of Pittsburgh (Pittsburgh, Pa.), 1965. (*DA* 27:988A)
69. WOLINS, LEROY, AND PERLOFF, ROBERT. "The Factorial Composition of AGCT 'Subtests' Along With College Aptitude Items and High School Grades." *Ed & Psychol Meas* 25:73–8 sp '65. * (*PA* 39:13028)
70. BINGHAM, WILLIAM C.; BURKE, HENRY R.; AND MURRAY, STEWART. "Raven's Progressive Matrices: Construct Validity." *J Psychol* 62:205–9 Mr '66. * (*PA* 40:7203)
71. KINGSLEY, LEONARD, AND STRUENING, ELMER L. "Changes in Intellectual Performance of Acute and Chronic Schizophrenics." *Psychol Rep* 18:791–800 Je '66. * (*PA* 40:10283)
72. BLUMENKRANTZ, JACK; WILKIN, WENDELL R.; AND TUDDENHAM, READ D. "Relationships Between the Progressive Matrices and AGCT-3a Among Older Military Personnel." *Ed & Psychol Meas* 28:931–5 au '68. * (*PA* 43:3317)
73. PERLMAN, LEONARD G. *A Predictive Model for the Identification of Potential Dropouts From Vocational Training in a Comprehensive Rehabilitation Center.* Doctor's thesis, Pennsylvania State University (University Park, Pa.), 1968. (*DA* 29:3424A)
74. TUDDENHAM, R. D.; BLUMENKRANTZ, J.; AND WILKIN, W. R. "Age Changes on AGCT: A Longitudinal Study of Average Adults." *J Consult & Clin Psychol* 32:659–63 D '68. * (*PA* 43:4017)
75. WATSON, CHARLES G., AND KLETT, WILLIAM G. "Prediction of WAIS IQ's From the Shipley-Hartford, the Army General Classification Test and the Revised Beta Examination." *J Clin Psychol* 24:338–41 Jl '68. * (*PA* 42:16437)
76. BURKE, HENRY R., AND BINGHAM, WILLIAM C. "Raven's Progressive Matrices: More on Construct Validity." *J Psychol* 72(2):247–51 Jl '69. * (*PA* 44:71)
77. HOLLENDER, JOHN W., AND BROMAN, HARVEY J. "Intellectual Assessment in a Disadvantaged Population." *Meas & Eval Guid* 2(1):19–24 sp '69. *
78. PERLMAN, LEONARD G., AND HYLBERT, KENNETH W. "Identifying Potential Dropouts at a Rehabilitation Center." *Rehabil Counsel B* 13(2):217–25 D '69. *

CUMULATIVE NAME INDEX
Adjutant General's Office, Classification and Replacement Branch, Personnel Research Section: 5
Altus, W. D.: 19, 21, 56
Anderson, R. J.: 51, 67
Aylesworth, H. C.: 22
Bailey, H. W.: 16
Barnette, W. L.: 39
Barrett, R. S.: 46
Bernard, J.: 35
Billeter, P. E.: 4
Bingham, W. C.: 70, 76
Bingham, W. V.: 53
Bittner, R. H.: 18
Blumenkrantz, J.: 72, 74
Boguslavsky, G. W.: 52
Bond, G. L.: 30
Bradley, A. D.: 64
Bradley, G. H.: 23
Broman, H. J.: 77
Burke, H. R.: 70, 76
Callis, R.: 36
Canter, A. H.: 58–9
Chappell, T. L.: 36, 40
Christensen, T. E.: 8
Chyatte, C.: 57
Conover, D. M.: 6
Crites, J. O.: 50
Crouch, H. H.: 66
Cureton, E. E.: 24
Currie, J. S.: 67
Dailey, J. T.: *rev,* 4:280
Dallenbach, K. M.: 16
Darley, J. G.: 48
DuBois, P. H.: 26, 37
Duncan, A. J.: 0
Estes, B. W.: 49
Ferson, R. F.: 32
Firestone, R. W.: 61
Fox, V.: 54
Fruchter, B.: 33
Fuchs, E. F.: 57
Fulk, B. E.: 34
Glaser, R.: 27–8, 38
Goldman, A.: *rev,* 6:441
Griffith, R. M.: 49
Harrell, M. S.: 7
Harrell, T. W.: 7, 9, 17, 34
Hollender, J. W.: 77
Hylbert, K. W.: 78
Jacobs, O.: 38
Jensen, M. B.: 11
Johnson, R. H.: 30, 43
Kent, E. G.: 51
Kingsley, L.: 71
Kirkpatrick, J. J.: 24
Klett, W. G.: 75
Layman, J. W.: 52
Leavitt, H. J.: 55
LeShan, L.: 47
Lyerly, O.: 47
Lyman, H. B.: *rev,* 6:441
Marvin, S.: 47
Mason, C. F.: 31, 60
Mullineaux, J. E.: 41
Murray, S.: 70
Otterness, W. B.: 43
Patterson, C. H.: 42–4
Perlman, L. G.: 73, 78
Perloff, R.: 45, 69
Peterson, L. R.: 43
Price, A. C.: 51, 67
Renzaglia, G. A.: 36
Ross, A. O.: 65
Rotter, J. B.: 11
Silver, M. R.: 68
Spohrer, M. A.: 36
Stewart, N.: 12–3
Struening, E. L.: 71
Super, D. E.: 25, 50
Tamminen, A. W.: 29
Teuber, H. L.: 62–3
Thompson, R. B.: 15
Tuddenham, R. D.: 20, 72, 74
War Department, Adjutant General's Office, Personnel Research Section: 14
Watson, C. G.: 75
Watson, R. I.: 26, 37
Weinstein, S.: 62–3
Wilkin, W. R.: 72, 74
Williams, S. B.: 55
Wolins, L.: 45, 69
Zerof, S. A.: 49

[343]
★**The BITCH Test (Black Intelligence Test of Cultural Homogeneity).** Adolescents and adults; 1972; BITCH; a vocabulary test of Afro-American

expressions used as an intelligence test for blacks and as "a measure of sensitivity and responsivity" to black experience when administered to whites; manual also uses the other titles: *The Bitch-100: A Culture-Specific Test* and *Black Intelligence Test of Cultural Homogeneity;* Robert L. Williams; Williams and Associates. *

[344]

*Boehm Test of Basic Concepts. Grades kgn–2; 1969–71, c1967–71; BTBC; Ann E. Boehm; Psychological Corporation. *

For additional information, reviews by Boyd R. McCandless and Charles D. Smock, and excerpted reviews by Frank S. Freeman, George Lawlor, Victor H. Noll, and Barton B. Proger, see 7:335 (1 reference).

REFERENCES THROUGH 1971

1. See 7:335.
2. VANE, JULIA R. "Importance of Considering Background Factors When Evaluating the Effects of Compensatory Education Programs Designed for Young Children." *J Sch Psychol* 9(4):393–8 w '71. * (PA 47:11817)

CUMULATIVE NAME INDEX

Boehm, A. E.: 1
Freeman, F. S.: *exc*, 7:335
Lawlor, G.: *exc*, 7:335
McCandless, B. R.: *rev*, 7:335
Noll, V. H.: *exc*, 7:335
Proger, B. B.: *exc*, 7:335
Smock, C. D.: *rev*, 7:335
Vane, J. R.: 2

[345]

*Business Test. Clerical workers; 1952–71; intelligence; 1971 test identical with test copyrighted in 1952; Edward N. Hay; Aptitude Test Service, Inc. *

For additional information and reviews by Louis C. Nanassy and James H. Ricks, Jr., see 5:311.

[346]

CGA Mental Ability Tests. Grades 6–9, 9–12; 1957–68; items identical with *The Henmon-Nelson Tests of Mental Ability;* for use in Canada only; Canadian Guidance Associates; distributed by Guidance Centre [Canada]. *

For additional information, see 7:336.

[347]

★C.P.66 Test. Ages 13 and over; 1966; CP66 is acronym for Comparability Project 1966; title on test booklet is *Aptitude Test C.P. 66;* 3 scores: verbal, quantitative, total; Ian M. Connaughton; NFER Publishing Co. Ltd. [England]. *

REFERENCES THROUGH 1971

1. CONNAUGHTON, I. M., AND SKURNIK, L. S. "The Comparative Effectiveness of Several Short-Cut Item Analysis Procedures." *Brit J Ed Psychol* 39(3):225–32 N '69. * (PA 44:9257)

CUMULATIVE NAME INDEX

Connaughton, I. M.: 1   Skurnik, L. S.: 1

[348]

California Short-Form Test of Mental Maturity, 1963 Revision. Grades kgn–1.5, 1.5–3.5, 3–4, 4–6, 6–7, 7–8, 9–12, 12–16 and adults; 1938–65; CTMM-SF; all items drawn from the long form, *California Test of Mental Maturity;* 7 scores: logical reasoning, numerical reasoning, verbal concepts, memory, language total, nonlanguage total, total; Elizabeth T. Sullivan, Willis W. Clark, and Ernest W. Tiegs; CTB/McGraw-Hill. *

For the regular edition entry, see 349.

For additional information, see 7:337 (41 references); for a review by Julian C. Stanley, see 6:443 (11 references); for a review by Cyril Burt of an earlier edition, see 5:313 (15 references); for an excerpted review by Laurance F. Shaffer, see 4:282. For reference to reviews of the regular edition, see 349.

REFERENCES THROUGH 1971

1–15. See 5:313.
16–26. See 6:443.
27–67. See 7:337.
68. WOODY, CLIFFORD. *Aptitudes, Achievements and Interests of High School Pupils.* University of Michigan, Bureau of Educational Reference and Research Bulletin No. 157. Ann Arbor, Mich.: School of Education, the University, 1945. Pp. vi, 159. *
69. EELLS, KENNETH; DAVIS, ALLISON; HAVIGHURST, ROBERT J.; HERRICK, VERGIL E.; AND TYLER, RALPH W. *Intelligence and Cultural Differences: A Study of Cultural Learning and Problem-Solving.* Chicago, Ill.: University of Chicago Press, 1951. Pp. xii, 388. * (PA 27:5738)
70. KITTELL, JACK E. "Bilingualism and Language: Non-Language Intelligence Scores of Third-Grade Children." *J Ed Res* 52:263–8 Mr '59. * (PA 34:4038)
71. MORRISON, IDA E., AND PERRY, IDA F. "Spelling and Reading Relationships With Incidence of Retardation and Acceleration." *J Ed Res* 52:222–7 F '59. * (PA 34:2012)
72. LLOYD, DAVID O. "Comparison of Standardized Test Results of Indian and Non-Indian in an Integrated School System." *J Am Indian Ed* 1:8–16 Je '61. *
73. KITTELL, JACK E. "Intelligence-Test Performance of Children from Bilingual Environments." *El Sch J* 64:76–83 N '63. *
74. POLLARD, ALICE G. *A Comparison of the Performance of a Group of Intellectually Retarded Children on Three Group Tests of Intelligence.* Master's thesis, Catholic University of America (Washington, D.C.), 1963.
75. BACKE, EDWARD B. *Predicting the Outcome in Second Year Algebra.* Master's thesis, Northern Illinois University (DeKalb, Ill.), 1964.
76. DIZNEY, HENRY F., AND YAMAMOTO, KAORU. "Note on Effects of Practice and Fatigue in Group Testing of Intelligence and Achievement." *Psychol Rep* 16:537–8 Ap '65. * (PA 39:10193)
77. FOSTER, MARION E. "A Comparison of Reading Achievement of Christchurch, New Zealand and Edmonton Alberta Public School Students of the Same Age and Number of Years of Schooling." *Alberta J Ed Res* (Canada) 11:21–31 Mr '65. * (PA 39:16455)
78. SINKS, NAOMI B., AND POWELL, MARVIN. "Sex and Intelligence as Factors in Achievement in Reading in Grades 4 Through 8." *J Genetic Psychol* 106:67–79 Mr '65. * (PA 39:12952)
79. GRAY, JAMES A. *A Study to Determine the Effectiveness of Certain Lehi Junior High School Variables in Predicting Senior High School Success.* Master's thesis, Brigham Young University (Provo, Utah), 1966.
80. WHITTEMORE, ROBERT G.; ECHEVERRIA, BEN P.; AND GRIFFIN, JOHN V. "Can We Use Existing Tests for Adult Basic Education?" *Adult Ed* 17:19–29 au '66. *
81. CICIRELLI, VICTOR G. "Sibling Constellation, Creativity, IQ, and Academic Achievement." *Child Develop* 38:481–90 Je '67. * (PA 41:10210)
82. SCHORR, MORTIMER. *A Study to Determine the Relationships Between Non-Language Mental Maturity and Achievement in the California Physical Performance Test.* Master's thesis, Humboldt State College (Arcata, Calif.), 1967.
83. DATTA, LOIS-ELLIN, AND SCHAEFER, EARL. "Sex and Scholastic Aptitude as Variables in Teachers' Ratings of the Adjustment and Classroom Behavior of Negro and Other Seventh-Grade Students." *J Ed Psychol* 59:94–101 Ap '68. * (PA 42:9407)
84. KELSEY, ANN E. *A Study of the Relationship Between Ability and Achievement.* Master's thesis, Texas Tech College (Lubbock, Tex.), 1968.
85. PAGE, BEN H. *Predicting Performance in Seventh Grade Advanced Mathematics at Kearns Junior High School.* Master's thesis, University of Utah (Salt Lake City, Utah), 1969.
86. ELEFAÑO, INOCENCIA PATIÑO. *Predicting the Educability of Children From Low Socioeconomic Status Homes.* Doctor's thesis, Rutgers—The State University (New Brunswick, N.J.), 1970. (*DAI* 32:667A)
87. MOULIN, EUGENE K. "The Effects of Client-Centered Group Counseling Using Play Media on the Intelligence, Achievement, and Psycholinguistic Abilities of Underachieving Primary School Children." *El Sch Guid & Counsel* 5(2):85–98 D '70. *
88. SMALL, JAMES FRANKLIN, II. *Auditory-Vocal and Visual-Motor Language Orientations in Elementary School Children.* Doctor's thesis, Duke University (Durham, N.C.), 1970. (*DAI* 31:6268B)
89. SMITH, PHILIP D., JR. *A Comparison of the Cognitive and Audiolingual Approaches to Foreign Language Instruction: The Pennsylvania Foreign Language Project.* Philadelphia, Pa.: Center for Curriculum Development, Inc., 1970. Pp. xxv, 380. *
90. DOUGHTY, EARL. "Test Rankings and Selection Procedures for Identifying Gifted Intermediate Elementary Students." *Ill Sch Res* 8(1):29–32 f '71. *
91. FRIEDRICHS, THOMAS DONNELLY. *Prediction of First Grade Teachers' Ratings and Objective Achievement From*

92. HALL, LUCIEN T., JR. "The Prediction of Success in Each of Six Four-Year Selections of Secondary Mathematics Courses." *Sch Sci & Math* 71(8):693–6 N '71. *
93. LIEDTKE, WERNER. "Mathematics Learning and Pupil Characteristics." *Alberta J Ed Res* (Canada) 17(3):143–53 S '71. * (*PA* 48:1864)
94. O'PIELA, JOAN MARIE. *Identification of Predictor Variables of Success in First Grade Reading in Culturally Disadvantaged Inner-City Children Who Have Had a Preschool Experience.* Doctor's thesis, Wayne State University (Detroit, Mich.), 1971. (*DAI* 32:6109A)
95. STACY, BOBBY FANT. *A Comparison of Academic Achievement and Mental Maturity Test Scores of Negro High School Seniors in Predominantly White Schools With Academic Achievement and Mental Maturity Test Scores of Negro Seniors in Predominantly Negro Schools.* Doctor's thesis, Mississippi State University (State College, Miss.), 1971. (*DAI* 32:1815A)

CUMULATIVE NAME INDEX

Allen, J. C. Y.: 43
Altenhaus, C. B.: 33
Backe, E. B.: 75
Barnett, T. M.: 51
Bashaw, J. A.: 29
Berg, I. A.: 3
Bliesmer, E. P.: 9
Bregoli, E. J.: 6
Bristol, J. L.: 44
Burke, B. P.: 55
Burt, C.: *rev*, 5:313
Bushey, J. T.: 59
Carbonari, J. P.: 56
Carron, T. J.: 60
Cashen, V. M.: 61
Cauble, B. L.: 34
Cicirelli, V. G.: 81
Clegg, H. D.: 22
Cognata, A.: 45
Cowne, L.: 8
Datta, L. E.: 83
Davis, A.: 69
Decker, R. L.: 22
Denum, D. C.: 30
Dizney, H. F.: 76
Doughty, E.: 90
Drew, A. S.: 23, 35
Echeverria, B. P.: 80
Edelstein, G.: 26
Edgar, M.: 15
Eells, K.: 69
Elefano, O.: 86
Elley, W. B.: 25
Feldt, L. S.: 17
Finley, C. J.: 45
Foster, M. E.: 77
Fowler, W. L.: 11, 13
Friedrichs, T. D.: 91
Frost, B. P.: 38
Furr, K. D.: 62
Gray, J. A.: 79
Griffin, J. V.: 86
Gundersen, R. O.: 17
Hall, L. T.: 63, 92
Hanna, G. S.: 52
Havighurst, R. J.: 69
Herrick, V. E.: 69
Hopkins, K. D.: 42
Jenkins, A. C.: 46
Johnson, H. S.: 39
Kelsey, A. E.: 84
Kittell, J. E.: 70, 73
Klugman, S. F.: 14
Koo, G. Y.: 18
Kopff, R. G.: 47
Leach, K. W.: 2
Liedtke, W.: 93
Lloyd, D. O.: 72
MacArthur, R. S.: 19, 25, 37, 57
McCullough, J. L.: 64
McDonnell, M. W.: 24
McHugh, A. F.: 27
MacKinney, A. C.: 21
MacNeil, R. L.: 53
Mars, D.: 66
Mattick, W. E.: 31
Mayhon, W. G.: 48
Mickler, J. E.: 32
Miller, B. B.: 67
Mitchell, J. V.: 12
Morrison, I. E.: 71
Moulin, E. K.: 87
Mouly, G. J.: 15
Nelson, M. O.: 26
North, R. D.: 10
Oas, R. T.: 65
Olson, A. V.: 49–50
Olson, N. H.: 54
O'Neil, W. J.: 7
O'Piela, J. M.: 94
Page, B. H.: 85
Perry, I. F.: 71
Poe, W. A.: 3
Pollard, A. G.: 74
Powell, M.: 78
Rainey, R. G.: 40
Raleigh, W. H.: 4
Ramirez, W. G.: 58
Ramseyer, G. C.: 61
Rooks, I.: 28
Schaefer, E.: 83
Schorr, M.: 82
Shaffer, L. F.: *exc*, 4:282
Shaffer, R. G.: 36
Silver, C. E.: 1
Sinks, N. B.: 78
Slayton, W. G.: 41
Small, J. F.: 88
Smith, P. D.: 89
Stack, S. E.: 16
Stacy, B. F.: 95
Stanley, J. C.: *rev*, 6:443
Stephans, P.: 21
Swan, R. J.: 42
Taylor, E. A.: 5
Thompson, J. M.: 45
Tyler, R. W.: 69
Warren, P. A.: 20
West, L. W.: 37
Whittemore, R. G.: 80
Wilson, F. R.: 62
Wolins, L.: 21
Woody, C.: 68
Yamamoto, K.: 76

[349]

California Test of Mental Maturity, 1963 Revision. Grades kgn–1.5, 1.5–3.5, 4–6, 7–9, 9–12, 12–16 and adults; 1936–65; CTMM; 8 scores: logical reasoning, spatial relationships, numerical reasoning, verbal concepts, memory, language total, nonlanguage total, total; Elizabeth T. Sullivan, Willis W. Clark, and Ernest W. Tiegs; CTB/McGraw-Hill. * For the short form entry, see 348.

For additional information and reviews by Bert A. Goldman and John H. Rosenbach, see 7:338 (102 references); see also 6:444 (30 references); for reviews by Frank S. Freeman and John E. Milholland of an earlier edition, see 5:314 (34 references); see also 4:282 (24 references); for a review by Henry E. Garrett and excerpted reviews by W. Line and one other, see 3:223 (10 references); for reviews by Raymond B. Cattell and F. Kuhlmann and an excerpted review by David Kopel, see 2:1384 (5 references); for reviews by W. D. Commins, Rudolf Pintner, and Arthur E. Traxler, and an excerpted review, see 1:1042. For reference to reviews of the short form, see 348.

REFERENCES THROUGH 1971

1–5. See 2:1384.
6–15. See 3:223.
16–39. See 4:282.
40–73. See 5:314.
74–103. See 6:444.
104–205. See 7:338.
206. BONNEY, MERL E. "The Relative Stability of Social, Intellectual, and Academic Status in Grades II to IV, and the Inter-Relationships Between These Various Forms of Growth." *J Ed Psychol* 34:88–102 F '43. * (*PA* 17:3943)
207. HANSEN, CARL W. "Factors Associated With Successful Achievement in Problem Solving in Sixth Grade Arithmetic." *J Ed Res* 38:111–8 O '44. * (*PA* 19:1039)
208. WAGGONER, R. W., AND ZEIGLER, THORNTON WOODWARD. "Psychiatric Factors in Medical School Students Who Fail." *Am J Psychiatry* 103:369–76 N '46. * (*PA* 21:1671)
209. SMITH, HERBERT A. "The Relationship Between Intelligence and the Learning Which Results From the Use of Educational Sound Motion Pictures." *J Ed Res* 43:241–9 D '49. * (*PA* 24:3879)
210. STRAUS, MURRAY A. "Mental Ability and Cultural Needs: A Psychocultural Interpretation of the Intelligence Performance of Ceylon University Entrants." *Indian J Psychol* 25:21–32 pts 1–4 '50. * (*PA* 27:7158)
211. CURTIN, JAMES T. *A Factor Analysis of Verbal and Non-Verbal Tests of Intelligence.* Washington, D.C.: Catholic University of America, 1951. Pp. vii, 63. * (*PA* 27:981)
212. HOPKA, ERICH. "Correlation of College Freshmen Chemistry Marks With Some California Mental Maturity Test Scores." *Trans Kans Acad Sci* 55:465–7 D '52. * (*PA* 27:7409)
213. STRAUS, MURRAY A. "Subcultural Variation in Ceylonese Mental Ability: A Study in National Character." *J Social Psychol* 39:129–41 F '54. * (*PA* 28:8662)
214. KRANTZ, L. L. "The Relationship of Reading Abilities and Basic Skills of the Elementary School to Success in the Interpretation of the Content Materials in the High School." *J Exp Ed* 26:97–114 D '57. * (*PA* 33:4579)
215. COLEMAN, J. M.; ISCOE, IRA; AND BRODSKY, MARVIN. "The 'Draw-A-Man' Test as a Predictor of School Readiness and as an Index of Emotional and Physical Maturity." *Pediatrics* 24:275–81 Ag '59. *
216. HIRSCH, MONROE J. "The Relationship Between Refractive State of the Eye and Intelligence Test Scores." *Am J Optom* 36:12–21 Ja '59. * (*PA* 34:1099)
217. MCBEE, GEORGE, AND DUKE, RALPH L. "Relationship Between Intelligence, Scholastic Motivation, and Academic Achievement." *Psychol Rep* 6:3–8 F '60. * (*PA* 34:8404)
218. SNIDER, JAMES G., AND COLADARCI, ARTHUR P. "Intelligence Test Performance of Acculturated Indian Children." *Calif J Ed Res* 11:34–6+ Ja '60. * (*PA* 34:7662)
219. MCGUIRE, CARSON. "Sex Role and Community Variability in Test Performances." *J Ed Psychol* 52:61–73 Ap '61. * (*PA* 38:3207)
220. TOBIAS, MILTON, AND MICHAEL, WILLIAM B. "An Exploration Into Child Ecology: Physiological and Maturational Indices as Predictors of Measures of Achievement, Aptitude, and Adjustment." *Ed & Psychol Meas* 21:967–74 w '61. *
221. CURRY, ROBERT L. "The Effect of Socio-Economic Status on the Scholastic Achievement of Sixth-Grade Children: Part I," *Brit J Ed Psychol* 32:46–9 F '62. * (*PA* 37:2007)
222. WILLIAMS, J. R., AND KNECHT, WALTER W. "Teachers' Ratings of High-School Students on 'Likability' and Their Relation to Measures of Ability and Achievement." *J Ed Res* 56:152–5 N '62. *
223. ANDERSON, HARRY E., JR., AND SLIVINSKE, ALEC J. "A Study of Intelligence and Achievement at the Fourth-, Fifth-, and Sixth-Grade Levels." *J Exp Ed* 31:425–32 su '63. *
224. BAYLOR, CONSTANCE C. *The Predictive Efficiency of the California Test of Mental Maturity.* Master's thesis, Glassboro State College (Glassboro, N.J.), 1963.
225. BLACK, DONALD B., AND FOSTER, MARION E. "A Comparative Study of the Performance in Arithmetic of Edmonton, Alberta, and Christchurch, New Zealand, Public School Pupils of Comparable Age and Grade Level." *Alberta J Ed Res* (Canada) 9:49–59 Mr '63. *
226. KAMII, CONSTANCE K., AND WEIKART, DAVID P. "Marks, Achievement, and Intelligence of Seventh Graders Who Were

Retained (Nonpromoted) Once in Elementary School." *J Ed Res* 56:452–9 My–Je '63. *

227. PETERS, HERBERT D. "Performance of Hopi Children on Four Intelligence Tests." *J Am Indian Ed* 2:27–31 Ja '63. *

228. RUSH, ALLEN C. "Better Police Personnel Selection." *Police Chief* 30:18+ S '63. *

229. TOBIAS, MILTON, AND MICHAEL, WILLIAM B. "Dimensions of Biological and Psychological Function in Two Samples of Children in the Third Grade." *Psychol Rep* 12:759–62 Je '63. * (*PA* 38:5756)

230. YOUNG, FRANCIS A. "Reading, Measures of Intelligence and Refractive Errors." *Am J Optom* 40:257–64 My '63. *

231. BARBEE, EUNICE W. *A Comparison of the Validity of Individual and Group Administration of Intelligence Tests With First Grade Pupils.* Master's thesis, Furman University (Greenville, S.C.), 1964.

232. NADEAU, CORINNE. *A Comparison of the Performance of a Group of Intellectually Normal Children on Three Group Tests of Intelligence.* Master's thesis, Catholic University of America (Washington, D.C.), 1964.

233. ROBERTS, HERBERT CLIVE. *Predicting Performance in Shorthand at Skyline High School.* Master's thesis, University of Utah (Salt Lake City, Utah), 1964.

234. TRITES, DAVID K., AND COBB, BART B. "Problems in Air Traffic Management: 4, Comparison of Pre-Employment, Job Related Experience With Aptitude Tests as Predictors of Training and Job Performance of Air Traffic Control Specialists." *Aerospace Med* 35:428–36 My '64. *

235. PETERSON, DONALD FREDERICK. *A Predictive Study of Success in First Year Bookkeeping.* Master's thesis, San Diego State College (San Diego, Calif.), 1965.

236. ROZYNKO, VITALLI, AND WENK, ERNEST. "Intellectual Performance of Three Delinquent Groups of Different Ethnic Origin." Abstract. *J Consult Psychol* 29:282 Je '65. * (*PA* 39:12810, title only)

237. CENTER, CLARE CALL. *A Correlational Study of the Relationship Between Eighth Grade Test Scores and First Semester Grades at Del Oro High School.* Master's thesis, Sacramento State College (Sacramento, Calif.), 1966.

238. GOOD, RONALD K. *Factors Used to Predict Achievement in Algebra I.* Master's thesis, Millersville State College (Millersville, Pa.), 1966.

239. LANE, BETTY RUBINO. *A Study of the Predictive Values of the Tests Being Used to Determine Success in Algebra I in the Lockport Township High Schools.* Master's thesis, Northern Illinois University (DeKalb, Ill.), 1966.

240. TAGG, HOWARD R. *Correlation Between Intelligence Test Scores and Modern Mathematics Test Scores of Fifty Seventh-Grade Hillcrest Junior High School Students.* Master's thesis, Brigham Young University (Provo, Utah), 1966.

241. WILSON, GERALD E. *An Investigation of the Relationship of Mental Ability to Manual Dexterity and Coordination in Adolescents.* Master's thesis, California State College (Long Beach, Calif.), 1966.

242. AMUNRUD, KATHERINE D. *A Study of Intelligence and Personality Factors Influencing Teacher Effectiveness.* Master's thesis, Northwestern University (Evanston, Ill.), 1967.

243. HUFF, BETTY. *The Predictive Value of Standardized Testing in Relation to Mathematical Achievement at Virginia High School.* Master's thesis, East Tennessee State University (Johnson City, Tenn.), 1967.

244. HURLEY, JOHN R. "Parental Malevolence and Children's Intelligence." *J Consult Psychol* 31:199–204 Ap '67. * (*PA* 41:7151)

245. PARK, GAIL RODNEY. *The Predictive Efficiency of Selected Data for Eighth Grade Algebra Students at Bonneville Junior High.* Master's thesis, University of Utah (Salt Lake City, Utah), 1967.

246. CHANCELLOR, GEORGE A., JR. *Standardized Tests as Predictors of Academic Success in Either One or Two Forms of High School Biology.* Master's thesis, Stetson University (DeLand, Fla.), 1968.

247. CRUMLEY, FRANCES S. *The Relationship of Personal-Social Adjustment and Intellectual Capacity to the Academic Achievement of Ninety-Three Junior High School Students.* Master's thesis, East Tennessee State University (Johnson City, Tenn.), 1968.

248. DE LUCA, JOSEPH N. "Motivation and Performance in Chronic Schizophrenia." *Psychol Rep* 22:1261–9 Je '68. * (*PA* 42:19082)

249. OBERSTEIN, RITA M. *Reading Achievement: Its Relationship to Visual Motor Perception and Mental Age in First and Third Grade Students.* Master's thesis, Adelphi University (Garden City, N.Y.), 1968.

250. COFFEY, FRANK HOLMES. *The Relationship of Intelligence to Creativity.* Master's thesis, Wisconsin State University (Oshkosh, Wis.), 1969.

251. KING, F. J.; ROBERTS, DENNIS; AND KROPP, RUSSELL P. "Relationship Between Ability Measures and Achievement Under Four Methods of Teaching Elementary Set Concepts." *J Ed Psychol* 60(3):244–7 Je '69. * (*PA* 43:13392)

252. LOWE, WALTER EDWARD, SR. *A Study of the Relationship Between the Socioeconomic Status and the Reading Performance of Negro Students Enrolled in the Public Schools of Caroline County, Virginia.* Doctor's thesis, George Washington University (Washington, D.C.), 1969. (*DAI* 31:1141A)

253. MORE, ARTHUR. "The Relation of High School Grades, Achievement and Intelligence Test Scores to Success in Dental School." *Can Counsellor* 3(1):56–8 Ja '69. *

254. SHIELDS, RUTH VIRGINIA. *Relationship of Schematic Concept Formation to Mental Ability in Adolescents.* Master's thesis, Southern Methodist University (Dallas, Tex.), 1969.

255. ELLISON, ROBERT L.; JAMES, LAWRENCE R.; FOX, DAVID G.; AND TAYLOR, CALVIN W. *The Identification of Talent Among Negro and White Students From Biographical Data.* An unpublished report to the U.S. Office of Education, Research Project No. 9-H-033, Institute for Behavioral Research in Creativity, 1970. Pp. iv, 71. *

256. HOOPES, JANET L.; SHERMAN, EDMUND A.; LAWDER, ELIZABETH; ANDREWS, ROBERTA G.; AND LOWER, KATHERINE D. *A Follow-Up Study of Adoptions (Vol. II): Post-Placement Functioning of Adopted Children.* New York: Child Welfare League of America, Inc., 1970. Pp. v, 126. *

257. PLUMLEIGH, GEORGE ELWOOD, JR. *The Relationship of Selected Variables to the Ability of First-Grade Children to Read and Interpret Maps.* Doctor's thesis, University of Southern California (Los Angeles, Calif.), 1970. (*DAI* 31:5946A)

258. POMERANTZ, NORMAN ELIOT. *An Investigation of the Relationship Between Intelligence and Reading Achievement for Various Samples of Bilingual Spanish-Speaking Children.* Doctor's thesis, New Mexico State University (University Park, N.M.), 1970. (*DAI* 31:4558A)

259. WONZER, ANN CUSHMAN. *A Study of the Relationships Among Creativity, Intelligence, and Achievement Measures Based on Longitudinal Data.* Doctor's thesis, University of Michigan (Ann Arbor, Mich.), 1970. (*DAI* 32:1205A)

260. BROUSSEAU, PAULA JOAN. *A Study of the Interrelationships of Reading Ability, Listening Ability and Intelligence of Ninth and Tenth Grade Students.* Doctor's thesis, Southern Illinois University (Carbondale, Ill.), 1971. (*DAI* 32:4828A)

261. CHOATE, HUBERT HUGH. *Selected Factors Contributing to Learning Potential of Children of Spanish Heritage.* Doctor's thesis, University of Southern California (Los Angeles, Calif.), 1971. (*DAI* 32:3778A)

262. DEBERARDINIS, ACHILLE. *The Relationship Between Group IQ Sub-Scale Discrepancy and Specific Reading Comprehension Abilities.* Doctor's thesis, University of Rochester (Rochester, N.Y.), 1971. (*DAI* 32:1393A)

263. ENDE, RUSSELL S. "Reading for Understanding in Grades 7, 8, and 9." *Ill Sch Res* 7(2):32–7 w '71. *

264. HAFNER, LAWRENCE E.; GWALTNEY, WAYNE; AND ROBINSON, RICHARD. "Reading in Bookkeeping: Predictions and Performance." *J Read* 14(8):537–46 My '71. *

265. HAYNES, ELIZABETH FINGER. *An Analysis of the Relationships Between Pupil Performance in the Learning of Transformational Grammar and Intelligence Test Scores.* Doctor's thesis, University of Virginia (Charlottesville, Va.), 1971. (*DAI* 32:4591A)

266. HOLLY, KEITH ALLEN. *Structure-of-Intellect Factor Abilities and a Self-Concept Measure in Mathematics Relative to Performance in High School Modern Algebra.* Doctor's thesis, University of Southern California (Los Angeles, Calif.), 1971. (*DAI* 32:2484A)

267. HOPKINS, KENNETH D., AND BIBELHEIMER, MILO. "Five-Year Stability of Intelligence Quotients From Language and Nonlanguage Group Tests." *Child Develop* 42(2):645–9 Je '71. * (*PA* 47:652)

268. RAMSEYER, GARY C., AND CASHEN, VALJEAN M. "The Effect of Practice Sessions on the Use of Separate Answer Sheets by First and Second Graders." *J Ed Meas* 8(3):177–81 f '71. *

269. ROTTER, DORIS M.; LANGLAND, LOIS; AND BERGER, DALE. "The Validity of Tests of Creative Thinking in Seven-Year-Old Children." *Gifted Child Q* 15(4):273–8 w '71. * (*PA* 48:5633)

270. SEITHER, FRANCES GARDNER. *An Investigation of the Predictive Validity of Selected Admission Screening Measures Relative to Success in Practical Nursing.* Doctor's thesis, University of Maryland (College Park, Md.), 1971. (*DAI* 32:5890B)

271. SHAVER, JAMES P., AND NUHN, DEE. "The Effectiveness of Tutoring Underachievers in Reading and Writing." *J Ed Res* 65(3):107–12 N '71. * (*PA* 48:1878)

272. STEVENS, FRANCES ANN BENNETT. *Predicting Third Grade Reading Achievement for Mexican-American Students From Lower Socioeconomic Levels.* Doctor's thesis, New Mexico State University (University Park, N.M.), 1971. (*DAI* 32:5480A)

273. TAYLOR, ALTON L. "Regression Analysis of Antecedent Measures of Slow Sections in High School Biology." *Sci Ed* 55(3):395–402 Jl–S '71. *

274. WETHERELL, RICHARD H. *A Study of the Relationship Between Visual Perception and School Achievement.* Doctor's thesis, University of Southern Mississippi (Hattiesburg, Miss.), 1971. (*DAI* 32:2324A)

275. WICKWIRE, PATRICIA JOANNE NELLOR. *The Academic Achievement and Language Development of American Children of Latin Heritage: Factors of Intellect, Home Educational*

Environment, and Personality. Doctor's thesis, University of Texas (Austin, Tex.), 1971. (*DAI* 32:6232A)

276. WILLIAMS, J. R.; DEWITT, WILLARD R.; AND HURT, ROBERT W. "Ability, Likability, and Motivation of Students as They Relate to Prediction of Achievement." *J Ed Res* 65(4):155-8 D '71. * (*PA* 48:1873)

277. WILLIAMS, PATSY RUTH. *Comparison of the Cattell Culture Fair Test With the California Mental Maturity Test.* Master's thesis, Southern Methodist University (Dallas, Tex.), 1971.

CUMULATIVE NAME INDEX

Altus, G. T.: 53, 59
American Gas Association, Personnel Committee: 43
Amunrud, K. D.: 242
Anderson, H. E.: 86-7, 123, 178, 223
Anderson, M.: 204
Andrews, R. G.: 256
Arena, T.: 192
Arnold, E. R.: 40
Arth, A. A.: 167
Bailey, A. E.: 8
Bailey, H. K.: 26
Baldauf, R. J.: 99
Baldwin, J. W.: 94
Barbee, E. W.: 231
Barnowe, T. J.: 18
Barry, C. A.: 75
Barz, A. I.: 179
Baylor, C. C.: 224
Benoit, E. P.: 62
Berger, D.: 269
Bessemer, D. W.: 98
Bibelheimer, M.: 267
Bibelheimer, M. H.: 119
Bish, G. G.: 124
Black, B.: 225
Bliesmer, E. P.: 60
Bobbe, C.: 100
Boger, J. H.: 44
Bolton, F. B.: 14
Boney, J. D.: 125, 143
Bonney, M. E.: 206
Bosworth, D. L.: 158
Boyce, R. W.: 136
Boyd, H. F.: 62
Bradshaw, D. H.: 126
Brady, W. J.: 137
Breen, J. M.: 138
Brendemuehl, F. L.: 80, 157
Brodsky, M.: 215
Brousseau, P. J.: 260
Buck, J. R.: 127
Burnette, R.: 92
Caffrey, J.: 58
Caldwell, J. R.: 193
California Test Bureau, Division of Professional Services: 61
Callaway, W. R.: 180
Campbell, W.: 100
Canabal, J. V.: 194
Carl, P. M.: 41
Carlson, H. B.: 31
Carney, R. E.: 95
Carroll, I. V.: 195
Cashen, V. M.: 268
Cassel, R. N.: 79, 88
Cattell, R. B.: *rev,* 2:1384
Center, C. C.: 237
Centi, P.: 89
Chambers, J. A.: 76
Chancellor, G. A.: 246
Choate, H. H.: 261
Church, A. M.: 19
Clark, B. P.: 98
Clark, J. H.: 27, 104
Clark, W. W.: 28-9, 45, 48, 96
Cleveland, G. A.: 158
Cline, V. B.: 101
Clymer, T.: 80, 90, 102
Cobb, B. B.: 97, 128, 164, 234
Coffey, F. H.: 250
Coffey, H. S.: 16
Coladarci, A. P.: 218
Coleman, J. C.: 61
Coleman, J. M.: 215
Colgan, R. L.: 168
Commins, W. D.: *rev,* 1:1042
Comrey, A. L.: 54
Cooke, B. E. M.: 169
Cooper, J. G.: 72

Coppedge, F. L.: 144, 181
Coppedge, L. L.: 145
Corrigan, F. V.: 196
Cox, O.: 182
Crumley, F. S.: 247
Cunningham, W.: 146
Curry, R. L.: 109, 221
Curtin, J. T.: 211
Damm, V. J.: 197
Davis, W. A.: 20
DeBerardinis, A.: 262
De Boer, D. L.: 129
Deich, R. F.: 170
Dejmek, F. W.: 21
De Luca, J. N.: 248
DeWitt, W. R.: 276
Dirr, P. M.: 147
Dizney, H.: 130-1
Driscoll, J. A.: 46
Duke, R. L.: 217
Elias, J. Z.: 36
Elley, W. B.: 103
Ellison, R. L.: 255
Ende, R.: 159
Ende, R. S.: 263
Erlandson, F. L.: 77
Evans, M. C.: 22
Failor, L. M.: 7
Fleming, E.: 131
Foster, M. E.: 225
Fox, D. G.: 255
Freeman, F. S.: *rev,* 5:314
French, J. L.: 91
Fuller, G. B.: 159
Fuqua, N. V.: 148
Gallagher, J. J.: 62
Gardner, S. F.: 118
Garrett, H. E.: *rev,* 3:223
Gates, J. A.: 198
Gilman, R. H.: 160
Goldman, B. A.: *rev,* 7:338
Good, R. K.: 238
Gordon, M. A.: 188
Griess, J. A.: 149
Gundersen, R. O.: 107
Gwaltney, W.: 264
Hackman, R. B.: 23
Hafner, L. E.: 264
Hammer, E. F.: 49
Hansen, C. W.: 207
Harootunian, B.: 151-2
Harootunian, B. A.: 108
Hatfield, R. C.: 171
Havighurst, R. J.: 20
Haynes, E. F.: 265
Henderson, N.: 31
Herrmann, M.: 23
Hieronymus, A. N.: 183
High, W. S.: 54
Hindsman, E.: 113
Hirsch, M. J.: 216
Hoepfner, R.: 139, 150
Hoffman, C. B.: 110
Holly, K. A.: 266
Hoopes, J. L.: 256
Hopka, E.: 212
Hopkins, K. D.: 119, 184, 267
Huff, B.: 243
Hurley, J. R.: 244
Hurt, R. W.: 276
Iscoe, I.: 215
Jackson, B. J.: 42
Jacobs, R. E.: 81
James, H. B.: 255
Jennings, E.: 113
Johnson, J. K.: 199
Johnson, W. E.: 111
Jones, A. L.: 75
Jones, K. J.: 200
Jones, P. P.: 200
Jogeward, P. A.: 132
Kamii, C. K.: 226

Kandel, A.: 153
Keach, C. C.: 154
King, F. J.: 113, 251
King, P.: 77
Knecht, W. W.: 222
Knezevich, S. J.: 12
Kopel, D.: *exc,* 2:1384
Kortmeyer, H. A.: 78
Krantz, L. L.: 214
Krebs, S. O.: 74
Krop, H.: 185
Kropp, R. P.: 251
Kuhlmann, F.: *rev,* 2:1384
Kurek, A.: 164
Lamberti, E.: 100
Lane, B. R.: 239
Langland, L.: 269
Lauten, D. A. H.: 172
Lawder, E.: 256
Leton, D. A.: 123
Line, W.: *exc,* 3:223
Lloyd, B. A.: 161
Lloyd, R.: 161
Lovett, C. J.: 186
Lowe, W. E.: 252
Lower, K. D.: 256
Lucier, O.: 92
MacArthur, R. S.: 103, 115, 175
McBee, G.: 217
McCall, J. R.: 55
McCall, R. A.: 140
McCall, R. B.: 140
McCauley, J. H.: 141
McCracken, R. A.: 201
McDonald, D.: 6
McGuire, C.: 93, 113, 219
McHugh, A. F.: 68
McLeod, J. D.: 173
Mandel, R.: 162
Manolakes, G.: 51, 56
Manson, M. P.: 32
Maples, V. S.: 187
Marshall, J.: 174
Marshall, T. A.: 57
Maxfield, F. N.: 2
Mehrens, W. A.: 84
Meyers, C. E.: 193
Michael, W. B.: 193, 220, 229
Milholland, J. E.: *rev,* 5:314
Moe, L.: 106
More, A.: 253
Moulin, E. K.: 202
Mullen, N. D.: 201
Mumaw, M. J.: 120
Nadeau, C.: 232
Nair, R. K.: 33
Needham, W. E.: 101
Nelson, A. G.: 9
Nicholson, A.: 69, 73
Nolan, E. G.: 17
Norman, R. D.: 98
Norrell, G.: 77
Nuhn, D.: 271
Oberstein, R. M.: 249
Olson, D. R.: 115
Onarheim, J.: 15
Ordahl, V. E.: 13
Osborne, R. T.: 82
Owen, J. C.: 70
Parish, R. L.: 155
Park, G. R.: 245
Parker, A. D.: 156
Paxson, R. C.: 136
Peters, H. D.: 227
Petersen, H.: 139
Peterson, D. F.: 235
Pintner, R.: *rev,* 1:1042
Plessas, G. P.: 121
Plumb, G. R.: 37
Plumleigh, G. E.: 257
Pomerantz, N. E.: 258
Ramsey, W.: 83
Ramseyer, G. C.: 268

Rattan, M. S.: 175
Rawlings, T. D.: 105
Ray, M. R.: 176
Richards, J. M.: 101
Ringness, T. A.: 203
Rinsland, H. D.: 30
Roberts, D.: 251
Roberts, H. C.: 233
Robinson, R.: 264
Rosenbach, J. H.: *rev,* 7:338
Rosilda, M.: 38
Rotter, D. M.: 269
Rozynko, V.: 236
Rubin, S. S.: 116
Rush, A. C.: 228
Schell, R. E.: 163
Schellenberg, E. D.: 24
Schrader, D. R.: 193
Schwellenbach, J. A.: 50
Seither, F. G.: 270
Shanner, W. M.: 64
Shaver, J. P.: 271
Sheldon, W. D.: 51, 56
Sheppard, C.: 100
Sherman, E. A.: 256
Shields, R. V.: 188, 254
Sitkei, E. G.: 184
Skubic, V.: 204
Slivinske, A. J.: 223
Smith, H. A.: 209
Smith, P. D.: 189
Smith, R. H.: 133
Smith, T. W.: 58, 65-6
Snider, J. G.: 218
Spiers, D. E.: 142
Stake, R. E.: 84
Stancik, E. J.: 79, 88
Stein, H. L.: 25
Stevens, F. A. B.: 272
Stevens, J. C.: 178
Strang, R.: 10
Straus, M. A.: 39, 210, 213
Stroud, J. B.: 183
Sutherland, K.: 190
Sweeney, F. J.: 52
Tagg, H. R.: 240
Tate, M. W.: 67
Taylor, A. L.: 273
Taylor, C. W.: 255
Thomas, H.: 177
Tiegs, E. W.: 1
Tilker, H. A.: 163
Tobias, M.: 220, 229
Topetzes, N. J.: 71
Traxler, A. E.: 3-5; *rev,* 1:1042
Trites, D. K.: 134, 164, 234
Trowbridge, N.: 95
Tully, G. E.: 165
Vertein, L. D.: 112
Voss, C. E.: 67
Waggoner, R. W.: 208
Wagner, H. E.: 166
Waldron, C.: 135
Walsh, N. E.: 122
Weikart, D. P.: 226
Welch, W. B.: 47
Welna, C. T.: 85
Welter, M. B.: 114
Wenk, E.: 236
Wetherell, R. H.: 274
White, W. F.: 178
Wickwire, P. J. N.: 275
Wiley, L. N.: 34
Williams, J. R.: 222, 276
Williams, P. R.: 277
Willmarth, J. G.: 191
Wilson, G. E.: 241
Winans, J. M.: 35
Wonzer, A. C.: 259
Woody, C.: 11
Young, F. A.: 230
Younge, J. W.: 205
Zeigler, T. W.: 208

[350]

Canadian Academic Aptitude Test. Grades 8.5–9.0; 1959–68; CAAT; a test in the *Canadian Test Battery, Grades 8–9;* 3 parts; Ontario Institute for Studies in Education; distributed by Guidance Centre [Canada]. * For the complete battery entry, see 1047.

a) PART I, VERBAL REASONING.

b) PART 2, MATHEMATICAL REASONING.
c) PART 3, NON-VERBAL REASONING. 1962 test identical with test copyrighted 1959.
For additional information, see 7:339 (1 reference); for reviews by Donald B. Black and George A. Ferguson, see 6:445 (2 references).

REFERENCES THROUGH 1971
1–2. See 6:445.
3. See 7:339.

CUMULATIVE NAME INDEX

Black, D. B.: rev, 6:445
D'Oyley, V. R.: 1–2
Ferguson, G. A.: rev, 6:445
Khan, S. B.: 3
Roberts, D. M.: 3

[351]

Canadian Cognitive Abilities Test. Grades kgn–1, 2–3; 1954–70; CCAT; adaptation of *Cognitive Abilities Test*; original test by Robert L. Thorndike, Elizabeth Hagen, and Irving Lorge; adaptation by Edgar N. Wright; Thomas Nelson & Sons (Canada) Ltd. [Canada]. *
For additional information, see 7:340.

[352]

Canadian Lorge-Thorndike Intelligence Tests, Multi-Level Edition. Grades 3–9; 1954–67; CLTIT; adaptation of *Lorge-Thorndike Intelligence Tests, Multi-Level Edition*; 3 scores: verbal, non-verbal, composite; original test by Irving Lorge, Robert L. Thorndike, and Elizabeth Hagen; adaptation by Edgar N. Wright; Thomas Nelson & Sons (Canada) Ltd. [Canada]. *
For additional information, see 7:341.

[353]

★**Canadian Scholastic Aptitude Test.** Candidates for college entrance; 1968–73; CSAT; test administered annually in April and December at centers established by the publisher; 2 scores: verbal, mathematical; French edition available; Service for Admission to College and University [Canada]. * For the testing program entry, see 1060.

REFERENCES THROUGH 1971
1. D'OYLEY, VINCENT R. "Development of the SACU Tests." *Sch Guid Worker* (Canada) 26(4):12–6 Mr-Ap '71. *
2. ELLEY, W. B. "SACU English Language Achievement and Verbal Aptitude Tests." *Interchange* (Canada) 2(3):83–6 '71. * (PA 48:5618)
3. ELLIOTT, H. A. "SACU and the SACU Tests: Past, Present, and Future." *Sch Guid Worker* (Canada) 26(4):6–11 Mr-Ap '71. *
4. EVANS, G. T. "The Canadian Scholastic Aptitude Test: Mathematical Sections." *Interchange* (Canada) 2(3):86–90 '71. * (PA 48:5620)
5. HOLMES, MARK. "The Relationship Between SACU Test Scores and Other Criteria of High School Academic Performance." *Sch Guid Worker* (Canada) 26(4):25–30 Mr-Ap '71. *
6. ROSEVEAR, DAVID. "Reflections on the Mathematics Section of CSAT." *Sch Guid Worker* (Canada) 26(4):31–3 Mr-Ap '71. *

CUMULATIVE NAME INDEX

D'Oyley, V. R.: 1
Elley, W. B.: 2
Elliott, H. A.: 3
Evans, G. T.: 4
Holmes, M.: 5
Rosevear, D.: 6

[354]

Cattell Intelligence Tests. Mental ages 4–8, 8–11, 11–15, 15 and over; 1930–52; 4 levels; R. B. Cattell; George G. Harrap & Co. Ltd. [England]. *
a) SCALE 0 (DARTINGTON SCALE). Mental ages 4–8; 1933. *Out of print.* Identical with Scale 1 of *IPAT Culture Fair Intelligence Test* (see 364a1).
b) SCALE 1 (NON-VERBAL), NEW EDITION, REVISED. Mental ages 8–11; 1930–52.
c) SCALE 2, NEW EDITION, REVISED. Mental ages 11–15; 1930–52.
d) SCALE 3, NEW EDITION, REVISED. Mental ages 15 and over; 1930–52.
For additional information and a review by I. Macfarlane Smith, see 5:315 (9 references); for a review by Godfrey H. Thomson, see 2:1386 (3 references).

REFERENCES THROUGH 1971
1–3. See 2:1386 (There is no reference 4.)
5–13. See 5:315.
14. CATTELL, RAYMOND B. "Intelligence Levels in Schools of the South-West." *Forum Ed* (England) 8:201–5 N '30. * (PA 5:2058)
15. PEEL, E. A., AND GRAHAM, D. "Differentiation of Ability in Primary School Children." *Durham Res R* (England) 1(2):40–8 S '51. *
16. PEEL, E. A., AND GRAHAM, D. "Differentiation of Ability in Primary School Children—II." *Durham Res R* (England) 1(3):31–4 S '52. * (PA 27:5157)

CUMULATIVE NAME INDEX

Bristol, H.: 1
Cattell, R. B.: 1–3, 10, 14
Chase, V. E.: 6
Crawford, J. M.: 12
Fitt, A. B.: 11
Graham, D.: 15–6
Halstead, H.: 6
Moore, B. G. R.: 13
O'Connor, N.: 12
Peel, E. A.: 13, 15–6
Rogers, C. A.: 11
Rohan, J. C.: 5
Slater, P.: 7
Smith, C. A.: 8
Smith, I. M.: rev, 5:315
Thomson, G. H.: rev, 2:1386
Tizard, J.: 12
Uhrbrock, R. S.: 9

[355]

Chicago Non-Verbal Examination. Ages 6 and over; 1936–54; Andrew W. Brown, Seymour P. Stein, and Perry L. Rohrer; Psychological Corporation. *
For additional information and a review by Raleigh M. Drake, see 5:316 (10 references); for reviews by Robert G. Bernreuter, Myrtle Luneau Pignatelli, and S. D. Porteus, see 2:1387.

REFERENCES THROUGH 1971
1–10. See 5:316.
11. CARY, LEE ALLAN. *A Comparative Analysis of the Sub-Test Scores of Two Groups of Deaf Children for the Chicago Non-Verbal Examination and the Reading and Arithmetic Reasoning Sections of the Stanford Achievement Test.* Doctor's thesis, University of Denver (Denver, Colo.), 1964. (DA 25:7023)
12. FARRANT, ROLAND H. "The Intellective Abilities of Deaf and Hearing Children Compared by Factor Analyses." *Am Ann Deaf* 109:306–25 My '64. * (PA 39:2442)
13. GOETZINGER, CORNELIUS P.; WILLS, ROBERT C.; AND DEKKER, LYNN CROUTER. "Non-Language IQ Tests Used With Deaf Pupils." *Volta R* 69:500–6 O '67. *
14. LARSON, STANFORD S. *A Comparison of Two Non-Verbal Intelligence Tests as Predictors of Academic Success of Navajo Students.* Master's thesis, Utah State University (Logan, Utah), 1967.
15. SEIDEL, H. E., JR.; BARKLEY, MARY JO; AND STITH, DORIS. "Evaluation of a Program for Project Head Start." *J Genetic Psychol* 110:185–97 Je '67. * (PA 41:11718)
16. MCLELLAND, PAUL EUGENE. *A Comparative Study of the Reasoning Ability of Two Groups of Hearing Impaired Children in a Residential School.* Doctor's thesis, University of Virginia (Charlottesville, Va.), 1968. (DA 29:3005A)

CUMULATIVE NAME INDEX

Allen, R. M.: 4
Barkley, M. J.: 15
Bernreuter, R. G.: rev, 2:1387
Bessell, H.: 4
Brown, A. W.: 1–2
Cary, L. A.: 11
Cotton, C. B.: 2
Dekker, L. C.: 13
Drake, R. M.: rev, 5:316
Ewing, R. M.: 5
Farrant, R. H.: 12
Goetzinger, C. P.: 13
Iscoe, I.: 10
Johnson, E. H.: 3
Larson, S. S.: 14
Lavos, G.: 6, 9
Lawrence, W. C.: 8
Levine, B.: 10
McLelland, P. E.: 16
Newland, T. E.: 8
Pignatelli, M. L.: rev, 2:1387
Porteus, S. D.: rev, 2:1387
Roper, G. E.: 7
Seidel, H. E.: 15
Stith, D.: 15
Wills, R. C.: 13

[356]

★**Cognitive Abilities Test.** Grades kgn–1, 2–3, 3–12; 1954–72; CAT; Robert L. Thorndike, Elizabeth Hagen, and Irving Lorge (a); Houghton Mifflin Co. *

a) PRIMARY BATTERIES. Grades kgn–1, 2–3; 1954–68; revision of Levels 1 and 2 of still-in-print *Lorge-Thorndike Intelligence Tests;* 2 levels.
1) *Primary 1.* Grades kgn–1.
2) *Primary 2.* Grades 2–3.
b) MULTI-LEVEL EDITION. Grades 3–12; 1971–72; 3 scores: verbal, quantitative, nonverbal.

For additional information, reviews by Marcel L. Goldschmid and Carol K. Tittle, and an excerpted review by Richard C. Cox, see 7:343.

[357]
*College Board Scholastic Aptitude Test. Candidates for college entrance; 1926–73; SAT; test administered on specified dates at centers established by the publisher; 2 scores: verbal, mathematical; special editions available for the visually handicapped; program administered for the College Entrance Examination Board by Educational Testing Service. * For the testing program entry, see 1048.

For additional information and reviews by Philip H. DuBois and Wimburn L. Wallace of an earlier form, see 7:344 (298 references); for reviews by John E. Bowers and Wayne S. Zimmerman, see 6:449 (79 references); for a review by John T. Dailey, see 5:318 (20 references); for a review by Frederick B. Davis, see 4:285 (22 references). For reviews of the testing program, see 6:760 (2 reviews).

REFERENCES THROUGH 1971
1–22. See 4:285.
23–42. See 5:318.
43–121. See 6:449.
122–419. See 7:344.
420. BRIGHAM, CARL C.; ANGIER, ROSWELL P.; MACPHAIL, ANDREW H.; ROGERS, DAVID C.; AND STONE, CHARLES L. "General Report [First] on the Scholastic Aptitude Test." *Col Entr Exam Board Ann Rep* 26:159–98 S '26. * (PA 1:1627)
421. BRIGHAM, CARL C.; ANGIER, ROSWELL P.; MACPHAIL, ANDREW H.; ROGERS, DAVID C.; AND STONE, CHARLES L. "General Report [Second] on the Scholastic Aptitude Test, June 25, 1927." *Col Entr Exam Board Ann Rep* 27:173–211 S '27. * (PA 2:1390)
422. BRIGHAM, CARL C. "General Report [Third] on the Scholastic Aptitude Test, June 23, 1928." *Col Entr Exam Board Ann Rep* 28:147–99 S '28. * (PA 3:965)
423. BRIGHAM, CARL C. "General Report [Fourth] on the Scholastic Aptitude Test, June 19, 1929." *Col Entr Exam Board Ann Rep* 29:161–200 S '29. * (PA 4:913)
424. BROLYER, CECIL R. "General Report [Fifth] on the Scholastic Aptitude Test, June 21, 1930." *Col Entr Exam Board Ann Rep* 30:203–32 S '30. * (PA 5:1681)
425. CRAWFORD, ALBERT BEECHER. "Forecasting Freshman Achievement." *Sch & Soc* 31:125–32 Ja 25 '30. *
426. BROLYER, CECIL R. "General Report [Sixth] on the Scholastic Aptitude Test, June 20, 1931." *Col Entr Exam Board Ann Rep* 31:173–205 S '31. * (PA 6:1652)
427. BRIGHAM, CARL C. *A Study of Error: A Study and Evaluation of Methods Used in Six Years of Study of the Scholastic Aptitude Test of the College Entrance Examination Board.* New York: College Entrance Examination Board, 1932. Pp. xiii, 384. * (PA 6:4597)
428. BROLYER, CECIL R. "General Report [Seventh] on the Scholastic Aptitude Test, June 25, 1932." *Col Entr Exam Board Ann Rep* 32:173–95 S '32. * (PA 7:1170)
429. CRAWFORD, ALBERT B. AND BURNHAM, PAUL S. "Entrance Examinations and College Achievement." *Sch & Soc* 36:344–52, 378–84 S 10, 17 '32. * (PA 7:349)
430. BROLYER, CECIL R. "General Report [Eighth] on the Scholastic Aptitude Test, June 24, 1933." *Col Entr Exam Board Ann Rep* 33:171–96 S '33. * (PA 8:1362)
431. BROLYER, CECIL R. "General Report [Ninth] on the Scholastic Aptitude Test, June 23, 1934." *Col Entr Exam Board Ann Rep* 34:157–82 S '34. * (PA 9:924)
432. BRIGHAM, CARL C. *Examining Fellowship Applicants: A Report Made to the Social Science Research Council on the Method of Selecting Fellows for First-Year Graduate Study.* Social Science Research Council Bulletin No. 23. Princeton, N.J.: Princeton University Press, 1935. Pp. vii, 58. * (PA 10:1724)
433. BROLYER, CECIL R. "General Report [Tenth] on the Scholastic Aptitude Test, June 22, 1935." *Col Entr Exam Board Ann Rep* 35:151–74 S '35. * (PA 10:1725)
434. BROLYER, CECIL R. "General Report [Eleventh] on the Scholastic Aptitude Test, June 13, 1936." *Col Entr Exam Board Ann Rep* 36:145–53 S '36. *
435. BROLYER, CECIL R. "General Report [Twelfth] on the Scholastic Aptitude Test." *Col Entr Exam Board Ann Rep* 37:135–43 S '37. *
436. LANDRY, HERBERT A. "The Relative Predictive Value of Certain College Entrance Criteria." *J Exp Ed* 5:256–60 Mr '37. * (PA 11:3887)
437. STALNAKER, JOHN M. "Thirteenth Annual Report on the Scholastic Aptitude Test." *Col Entr Exam Board Ann Rep* 38:79–95 S '38. * (PA 13:2733)
438. STALNAKER, JOHN M., AND STALNAKER, RUTH C. "Fourteenth Annual Report on the Scholastic Aptitude Test." *Col Entr Exam Board Ann Rep* 39:97–114 S '39. *
439. WOLF, RALPH ROBINSON, JR. "Differential Forecasts of Achievement and Their Use in Educational Counseling." *Psychol Monogr* 51(1):1–53 '39. * (PA 13:6506)
440. CHILD, IRVIN L., AND SHELDON, WILLIAM H. "The Correlation Between Components of Physique and Scores on Certain Psychological Tests." *Char & Pers* 10:23–34 S '41. * (PA 16:1040)
441. STALNAKER, JOHN M. "Identification of the Best Southern Negro High-School Seniors." *Sci Mo* 67:237–9 S '48. * (PA 23:1269)
442. DAVIS, JUNIUS A., AND FREDERIKSEN, NORMAN. "Public and Private School Graduates in College." *J Teach Ed* 6:18–22 Mr '55. * (PA 30:3359)
443. SARASON, IRWIN G. "Test Anxiety, General Anxiety, and Intellectual Performance." *J Consult Psychol* 21:485–90 D '57. * (PA 33:3867)
444. SEVIER, FRANCIS A. C. "Testing the Assumptions Underlying Multiple Regression." *J Exp Ed* 25:323–30 Je '57. * (PA 33:5133)
445. BIERI, JAMES; BRADBURN, WENDY M.; AND GALINSKY, M. DAVID. "Sex Differences in Perceptual Behavior." *J Personality* 26:1–12 Mr '58. * (PA 33:5426)
446. FRENCH, JOHN W. "The Relationship of Home and School Experiences to Scores on Achievement Tests." *J Ed Psychol* 50:75–82 Ap '59. * (PA 35:2795)
447. WORELL, LEONARD. "Level of Aspiration and Academic Success." *J Ed Psychol* 50:47–54 Ap '59. * (PA 35:2783)
448. FREDERIKSEN, NORMAN, AND GILBERT, ARTHUR C. F. "Replication of a Study of Differential Predictability." *Ed & Psychol Meas* 20:759–67 w '60. * (PA 35:7953)
449. ALTUS, WILLIAM D. "Questionnaire Items and Types of Intelligence." *J Genetic Psychol* 98:265–71 Je '61. * (PA 36:2KK65A)
450. GETTYS, RICHARD H. *An Analysis of Variables at Spartanburg High School in Predicting College Success.* Master's thesis, Furman University (Greenville, S.C.), 1963.
451. HEARD, WILLIAM G.; FINLEY, JUDSON R.; AND STAATS, ARTHUR W. "The Relationship of Intelligence-Test Scores to the Ease of Language Conditioning." *J Genetic Psychol* 103:227–31 D '63. * (PA 38:7786)
452. SCHNEYER, J. WESLEY. "Factors Associated With the Progress of Students Enrolled in a College Reading Program." *J Ed Res* 56:340–5 Mr '63. *
453. WESTCOTT, MALCOLM R., AND RANZONI, JANE H. "Correlates of Intuitive Thinking." *Psychol Rep* 12:595–613 Ap '63. * (PA 38:4257)
454. AIKEN, LEWIS R., JR. "Rank in High School Graduating Classes of Various Sizes as a Predictor of College Grades." *J Ed Res* 58:56–60 O '64. *
455. AIKEN, LEWIS R., JR. "Some Nomographs for Academic Prediction Work." *Ed & Psychol Meas* 24:913–20 w '64. * (PA 39:8678)
456. BEHRING, DANIEL W. *The Prediction of Academic Success From an Inventory of Student Preferences for Activities.* Master's thesis, Ohio University (Athens, Ohio), 1964.
457. BROD, DIANE; KERNOFF, PHYLLIS; AND TERWILLIGER, ROBERT F. "Anxiety and Semantic Differential Responses." *J Abn & Social Psychol* 68:570–4 N '64. * (PA 39:4647)
458. FOREE, SHERRELL S. *Selection of Factors for Prediction of Scholastic Success in Introductory Food and Nutrition Courses.* Master's thesis, Texas Technological College (Lubbock, Tex.), 1964.
459. SPIELBERGER, CHARLES D., AND WEITZ, HENRY. "Improving the Academic Performance of Anxious College Freshmen: A Group-Counseling Approach to the Prevention of Underachievement." *Psychol Monogr* 78(13):1–20 '64. * (PA 39:5919)
460. BOVINETTE, ROBERT L. *Establishing a Prediction Equation for Determining Academic Success at MacMurray College.* Master's thesis, Northern Illinois University (DeKalb, Ill.), 1965.
461. BURKE, RONALD J., AND MAIER, NORMAN R. F. "Attempts to Predict Success on an Insight Problem." *Psychol Rep* 17:303–10 Ag '65. * (PA 40:1115)
462. CAUTELA, JOSEPH R., AND BARLOW, DAVID H. "The Relation Between Intelligence and Critical Flicker Fusion." *Psychon Sci* 3:559–60 D 15 '65. * (PA 40:2219)
463. HOWELL, WALLACE J. "Influence of Curriculum Enrichment in a High School Honors Group on College Board

Examination Scores." *J Ed Res* 59:113-4 N '65. * (*PA* 40:3332)

464. LARIMORE, DAVID LEE. *A Study of the Relationship Between the Scholastic Aptitude Test Scores and Converted High School Rank Scores and Success in a School of Education.* Master's thesis, North Carolina State University (Raleigh, N.C.), 1965.

465. MATHIS, CLAUDE, AND PARK, YOUNG HORN. "Some Factors Relating to Success in Student Teaching." *J Ed Res* 58:420-2 My-Je '65. * (*PA* 39:16472)

466. BURKE, RONALD J. "The Relationship of Some Interest, Intellectual Ability, and Nonintellectual Ability Tests to Problem-Solving Success and Effective Use of Hints in Individual Problem-Solving." *Mich Acad Sci Arts & Letters* 51:353-60 '66. * (*PA* 41:14722)

467. DENNY, J. PETER. "Effects of Anxiety and Intelligence on Concept Formation." *J Exp Psychol* 72:596-602 O '66. *

468. HILLS, JOHN R. "Diversity and the Effect of Selective Admissions." *J Ed Meas* 3:235-42 f '66. *

469. HILLS, JOHN R.; BUSH, MARILYN L.; AND KLOCK, JOSEPH A. "Keeping College Prediction Equations Current." *J Ed Meas* 3:33-4 sp '66. *

470. PHILLIPS, LYNDA N. *A Statistical Analysis of Selected Factors Influencing Performance of Students Enrolled in Physics 218 at Texas A & M University.* Master's thesis, Texas A & M University (College Station, Tex.), 1966.

471. BAGGALEY, ANDREW R., AND CAMPBELL, JAMES P. "Multiple-Discriminant Analysis of Academic Curricula by Interest and Aptitude Variables." *J Ed Meas* 4:143-9 f '67. * (*PA* 42:4434)

472. CROW, JOHNNY LEE. *Factors Associated With Improvement in Ability to Visualize Shapes Described by Orthographic Projection Drawings.* Master's thesis, North Carolina State University (Raleigh, N.C.), 1967.

473. MARKS, EDMOND. "Student Perceptions of College Persistence, and Their Intellective, Personality and Performance Correlates." *J Ed Psychol* 58:210-21 Ag '67. * (*PA* 41:15798)

474. NEIDT, CHARLES O., AND HEDLUND, DALVA E. "The Relationship Between Changes in Attitudes Toward a Course and Final Achievement." *J Ed Res* 61:56-8 O '67. *

475. NICHOLI, ARMAND M., JR. "Harvard Dropouts: Some Psychiatric Findings." *Am J Psychiatry* 124:651-8 N '67. * (*PA* 42:5637)

476. WALKER, C. EUGENE, AND TAHMISIAN, JAMES. "Birth Order and Student Characteristics: A Replication." Abstract. *J Consult Psychol* 31:219 Ap '67. * (*PA* 41:7349, title only)

477. CARRUTH, BETTY RUTH ROBERTS. *Development of Criteria for Student Placement in an Introductory Food and Nutrition Course.* Master's thesis, Texas Tech University (Lubbock, Tex.), 1968.

478. COY, MICHAEL. *Factorial Study of Variables Related to College Grade Point Average.* Master's thesis, Humboldt State College (Arcata, Calif.), 1968.

479. DIMALTA, VINCENT F. *Statistical Differences Between Science and Non-Science Freshmen Entering Indiana University of Pennsylvania During the Fall Term, 1967.* Master's thesis, Indiana University of Pennsylvania (Indiana, Pa.), 1968.

480. GENTRY, JOANNE. "Abstract of a Study of the Relationship Between High School Grades and Test Scores and the Achievement of Students Enrolled in BEOA 326 (Shorthand) at Ball State University in the Autumn Quarter of 1966." *Ball State J Bus Educators* 40:12-6 N '68. *

481. OPPENHEIM, DON B. "The Relation Between Intelligence and Different Patterns of Feedback in a Linear Teaching Program." *J Exp Ed* 36:82-5 sp '68. *

482. PETERSON, RICHARD E. "Predictive Validity of a Brief Test of Academic Aptitude." *Ed & Psychol Meas* 28:441-4 su '68. * (*PA* 42:19279)

483. TILLINGHAST, B. S., AND NORRIS, BETTY N. "The Relation of Selected Admission Variables to Student Achievement." *Nursing Outl* 16:58 Jl '68. *

484. BROUSSEAU, MARY ALINE. *Comparison of Disciplined and Non-Disciplined Women Residents Marquette University 1967-68.* Doctor's thesis, Marquette University (Milwaukee, Wis.), 1969. (*DAI* 31:4451A)

485. KLEIN, STEPHEN P.; FREDERIKSEN, NORMAN; AND EVANS, FRANKLIN R. "Anxiety and Learning to Formulate Hypotheses." *J Ed Psychol* 60(6):465-75 D '69. * (*PA* 44:3087)

486. LAPP, C. J. "Evaluation and Selection of Graduate Students." *Eng Ed* 60(2):112-6 O '69. *

487. LINDEMAN, RICHARD H.; GORDON, RICHARD E.; AND GORDON, KATHERINE K. "Further Relationships Between Blood Chemical Values and College Student Performance and Attitudes." *J Am Col Health Assn* 18(2):156-61 D '69. *

488. ROGGENKAMP, RONALD R. *A Study to Determine the Validity of Using College Entrance Exams and I.Q. as Predictors of College Performance for Falls City Senior High Graduates.* Master's thesis, Kearney State College (Kearney, Neb.), 1969.

489. WILLIAMS, HELEN B. *Interests and Prediction of Academic Performance of Associate Degree Nursing Students.* Master's thesis, Alfred University (Alfred, N.Y.), 1969.

490. *Normative Data for the 1969-70 Freshman Class, University System of Georgia.* Atlanta, Ga.: Regents of the University System of Georgia, November 1970. Pp. xi, 94. *

491. ASTIN, ALEXANDER W. "How Colleges Are Rated." *Change H* 2(6):11+ N-D '70. *

492. BARRETT, S BARRE. *A Study of the Interrelationship and Influences of Scholastic Aptitude and Perception Upon Aesthetic Sensitivity in College Students.* Doctor's thesis, University of Kansas (Lawrence, Kan.), 1970. (*DAI* 31:5835A)

493. BEAN, ANDREW GEORGE. *Personality Measures as Multiple Moderators in the Prediction of College Student Attrition.* Doctor's thesis, University of Pennsylvania (Philadelphia, Pa.), 1970. (*DAI* 32:229A)

494. BELLICO, RUSSELL PAUL. *The Relationship of Selected Factors to Academic Achievement in Economics.* Doctor's thesis, University of Massachusetts (Amherst, Mass.), 1970. (*DAI* 31:5022A)

495. BROWN, JOAN LOBIS. *A Descriptive Analysis of Some Common Predictors of Academic Achievement Applied in a Predominantly Black State University in North Carolina.* Master's thesis, Wake Forest University (Winston-Salem, N.C.), 1970.

496. CHERDACK, ARTHUR NORMAN. *The Predictive Validity of the Scholastic Aptitude Test for Disadvantaged College Students Enrolled in a Special Education Program.* Doctor's thesis, University of California (Los Angeles, Calif.), 1970. (*DAI* 31:5193A)

497. CHRISTOFF, PATRICK LEO. *The Relationship Between Attendance at a Summer Orientation Program, Expectation-Press Congruence, and Selected Behavioral Correlates.* Doctor's thesis, University of Maryland (College Park, Md.), 1970. (*DAI* 31:4454A)

498. D'ANGELO, ROCCO DOMENICK. *Variations in Instructional and General Expenditures Associated With Seven Administrative Factors in Private Liberal Arts Colleges for the Academic Year, 1966-67.* Doctor's thesis, Ohio University (Athens, Ohio), 1970. (*DAI* 31:4484A)

499. DANIERE, ANDRE, AND MECHLING, JERRY. "Direct Marginal Productivity of College Education in Relation to College Aptitude of Students and Production Costs of Institutions." *J Hum Resources* 5(1):51-70 w '70. *

500. ELLISON, ROBERT L.; JAMES, LAWRENCE R.; FOX, DAVID G.; AND TAYLOR, CALVIN W. *The Identification of Talent Among Negro and White Students From Biographical Data.* An unpublished report to the U.S. Office of Education, Research Project No. 9-H-033, Institute for Behavioral Research in Creativity, 1970. Pp. iv, 71. *

501. GARMS, JOE D. "A Nonintellectual Scale for Predicting Achievement in Introductory Psychology." *Psychol* 7(1):40-3 F '70. * (*PA* 44:13377)

502. GRUNEBERG, MICHAEL M. "Scholastic Aptitude and Attainment Related to Employment Choice: A Study of Senior Secondary School Leavers in Scotland." *Voc Aspect Ed* (England) 22(53):159-68 N '70. *

503. HARTNETT, RODNEY T. "Differences in Selected Attitudes and College Orientations Between Black Students Attending Traditionally Negro and Traditionally White Institutions." *Sociol Ed* 43(4):419-36 f '70. * (*PA* 47:9611)

504. KALOGER, JAMES HERACLES. *Characteristics of Grosse Pointe High School Students in Advanced Placement Programs.* Doctor's thesis, University of Michigan (Ann Arbor, Mich.), 1970. (*DAI* 31:6440A)

505. KIRKENDALL, DON R., AND GRUBER, JOSEPH J. "Canonical Relationships Between the Motor and Intellectual Achievement Domains in Culturally Deprived High School Pupils." *Res Q* 41(4):496-502 D '70. * (*PA* 46:5712)

506. MOORE, LELAND B. *Predicting Levels of Success in Baccalaureate Technology Curriculums.* Doctor's thesis, Southern Illinois University (Carbondale, Ill.), 1970. (*DAI* 31:5151A)

507. MORRISON, JOHN W. "The Vocational Response of High School Students to Science Courses." *Sch Sci & Math* 70(8):720-34 N '70. *

508. NOWKA, HARRY EDWARD. *The Relationship Between Student Characteristics and Collegiate Termination of Vocational Business Certificate Holders.* Doctor's thesis, Oklahoma State University (Stillwater, Okla.), 1970. (*DAI* 31:5151A)

509. OATES, WALLACE E., AND QUANDT, RICHARD E. "The Effectiveness of Graduate Students as Teachers of the Principles of Economics." *J Econ Ed* 1(2):131-8 sp '70. *

510. PINTEL, GERALD. *The Effectiveness of Admissions Criteria in Relation to the Timely Completion of a Business Administration Curriculum by Students Enrolled in a Community College.* Doctor's thesis, New York University (New York, N.Y.), 1970. (*DAI* 32:1303A)

511. ROBERTS, JOSEPH PORTER. *Intellectually Gifted Adolescents: A Multivariate Analysis of Certain Educationally Relevant Attributes.* Doctor's thesis, University of Virginia (Charlottesville, Va.), 1970. (*DAI* 31:4588A)

512. SHINN, STEVEN MARKHAM. *A Comparative Investigation of Three Predictors of Academic Success at Springfield College.* Master's thesis, Springfield College (Springfield, Mass.), 1970.

513. WALL, K. WAYNE. "The Continuing Problem of Predicting Success in the Basic College Speech Course." *Speech Teach* 19(4):310–2 N '70. *
514. WILSON, KENNETH M. "Increasing Selectivity and Institutional Grading Standards." *Col & Univ* 46(1):46–53 f '70. *
515. YOUNG, RICHARD O. "A Study of Sophomores Who Used Career Counseling Services." *J Col Stud Personnel* 11(6):457 N '70. * (*PA* 45:8960)
516. *Normative Data for the 1970–71 Freshman Class, University System of Georgia.* Atlanta, Ga.: Regents of the University System of Georgia, November 1971. Pp. xi, 95. *
517. ALKER, HENRY A., AND CLOSSON, MICHAEL B. "Admission Standards, Institutional Racism, and Black Student Political Participation." Abstract. *Proc 79th Ann Conv Am Psychol Assn* 6(1):397–8 '71. * (*PA* 46:3703)
518. ASTIN, ALEXANDER W. *Predicting Academic Performance in College: Selectivity Data for 2300 American Colleges.* New York: Free Press, 1971. Pp. ix, 299. * (*PA* 48:3832, title only)
519. BACKMAN, MARGARET E., AND STEINDLER, FRANCES M. "Cognitive Abilities Related to Attrition in a Collegiate Nursing Program." *Nursing Outl* 19(12):807–8 D '71. *
520. BACKMAN, MARGARET E., AND STEINDLER, FRANCES M. "Prediction of Achievement in a Collegiate Nursing Program and Performance on State Board Examinations." *Nursing Outl* 19(7):487 Jl '71. *
521. BADGETT, JOHN L.; HOPE, LANNES H.; AND KERLEY, S. AUSTON. "The Relationship Between Self-Concept and Academic Aptitude of Entering Male College Freshmen." *Psychol* 8(2):43–7 My '71. * (*PA* 47:5736)
522. BELZ, HELENE FULTON. *The Relation of Convergent and Divergent Thinking Processes to Complex Problem-Solving.* Doctor's thesis, Stanford University (Stanford, Calif.), 1971. (*DAI* 32:5604A)
523. BLANCHFIELD, W. C. "College Dropout Identification: A Case Study." *J Exp Ed* 40(2):1–4 w '71. * (*PA* 48:1856)
524. BOHRNSTEDT, GEORGE W.; LAMBERT, PHILIP; AND BORGATTA, EDGAR F. "The Reliability and Validity of Quick Tests with High School Seniors." *J Exp Ed* 39(4):22–3 su '71. * (*PA* 47:1573)
525. BRADY, WILLIAM JOHN. *A Comparison of the Academic Performances of Native Students and Junior College Transfer Students in the Colleges of Agriculture, Business, and Education at the University of Georgia.* Doctor's thesis, University of Georgia (Athens, Ga.), 1971. (*DAI* 32:5561A)
526. BRANDENBURG, JUDITH BERMAN. *The Relationship Between Future Time Perspective and Academic Achievement: The Relationship of Three Dimensions of Future Time Perspective to Academic Achievement With Respect to Scholastic Aptitude, Sex and Socioeconomic Status Among College Freshmen.* Doctor's thesis. New York University (New York, N.Y.), 1971. (*DAI* 32:2982B)
527. BURKE, RONALD J. "Correlates of the Ability to Fragment and Reorganize Stored Information." *J General Psychol* 84(2):183–9 Ap '71. * (*PA* 46:4255)
528. BURNHAM, PAUL S., AND HEWITT, BENJAMIN A. "Advanced Placement Scores: Their Predictive Validity." *Ed & Psychol Meas* 31(4):939–45 w '71. * (*PA* 48:1631)
529. CARRUTH, BETTY RUTH, AND LAMB, MINA W. "Prediction of Student Performance Through Pretesting in Food and Nutrition: Home Economics Majors and Nonmajors." *J Home Econ* 63(1):41–4 Ja '71. *
530. CHAMBERS, JEAN FORBES. *Predicting the Academic Achievement Level of Deaf Students.* Doctor's thesis, University of Arizona (Tucson, Ariz.), 1971. (*DAI* 31:6396A)
531. CHAUNCEY, HENRY. "Educational Testing and Human Diversity." *Ed Rec* 52(2):117–24 sp '71. *
532. CLARK, KENNETH, AND PLOTKIN, LAWRENCE. "Aptitude Test Bias." Letter. *Sci* 174(4016):1278–9 D 12 '71. *
533. CREIGHTON, SAMUEL LESLEY. *The Quest for New Methods for Predicting the Academic Achievement of Economically Disadvantaged College Students.* Doctor's thesis, University of Toledo (Toledo, Ohio), 1971. (*DAI* 32:3717A)
534. DAVIS, JUNIUS A., AND TEMP, GEORGE. "Is the SAT Biased Against Black Students?" *Col Board R* 81:4–9 f '71. *
535. DENNEHY, ROBERT F. *The Relationship Between "Satisfaction" and "Satisfactoriness" in a Sample of College Freshmen: An Exploration of the Applicability of the Minnesota Theory of Work Adjustment to Scholastic Performance.* Doctor's thesis, New York University (New York, N.Y.), 1971. (*DAI* 32:5543A)
536. DINNAN, JAMES A.; BICKLEY, RACHEL T.; AND WILLIAMS, JOHN C. "Syntagmatic Oral Responses and SAT Scores of College Freshmen." *Yearb Nat Read Conf* 20:17–9 '71. *
537. DI SCIPIO, WILLIAM J. "Divergent Thinking: A Complex Function of Interacting Dimensions of Extraversion-Introversion and Neuroticism-Stability." *Brit J Psychol* 62(4):545–50 N '71. * (*PA* 47:8899)
538. FEDELL, JOHN C. *A Study of the Relationship Between the Need for Academic Achievement Motive and Student Grade Point Average at the Community College Level.* Doctor's thesis, American University (Washington, D.C.), 1971. (*DAI* 32:1332A)
539. GOOLSBY, THOMAS M., JR., AND WILLIAMSON, DONALD A. "Use of the ROTC Qualifying Examination for Selection of Students to Enroll in Advanced Courses in ROTC as Juniors." *Ed & Psychol Meas* 31(2):513–6 su '71. *
540. HENDRICKSON, GERRY F. "The Effect of Differential Option Weighting on Multiple-Choice Objective Tests." *J Ed Meas* 8(4):291–6 w '71. * (*PA* 47:9651)
541. IRVINE, DONALD W. "Predicting the Persistence of Summer Trial Freshmen." *Cont Ed* 42(4):184–6 F '71. *
542. JAMES, REUBEN J. *Traits Associated With the Initial and Persistent Interest in the Study of College Science.* Doctor's thesis, State University of New York (Buffalo, N.Y.), 1971. (*DAI* 32:1296A)
543. KEPKA, EDWARD J., AND BRICKMAN, PHILIP. "Consistency Versus Discrepancy as Clues in the Attribution of Intelligence and Motivation." *J Pers & Social Psychol* 20(2):223–9 N '71. * (*PA* 47:6717)
544. KINCANNON, SUE GUNTER. *The Relationship of Selected Variables and Length of College Attendance at the University of Arkansas.* Doctor's thesis, University of Arkansas (Fayetteville, Ark.), 1971. (*DAI* 32:740A)
545. KIPNIS, DAVID, AND RESNICK, JEROME H. "Experimental Prevention of Underachievement Among Intelligent Impulsive College Students." *J Consult & Clin Psychol* 36(1):53–60 F '71. * (*PA* 45:10969)
546. LINN, MOTT ROBERTSON. *Achievement, Aptitude, Interest, and Personality Variables as Predictors of Curriculum, Graduation, and Placement.* Doctor's thesis, University of Pennsylvania (Philadelphia, Pa.), 1971. (*DAI* 32:1857A)
547. MACCHIA, WALTER. *Prediction of Senior Year SAT Scores From Freshman Year SCAT Scores and Final Grade Averages in English and Algebra.* Master's thesis, Jersey City State College (Jersey City, N.J.), 1971.
548. McCONNELL, DARLENE S. "A Study to Determine the Difference Between Selected Factors and Success in Shorthand I (BEOA 321) at Ball State University." *Ball State J Bus Educators* 43(1):9–14 N '71. *
549. MICHALSKI, STANLEY F., JR. "Development and Evaluation of a Visual-Aural Program in Conceptual Understanding of the Basic Elements of Music." *J Res Music Ed* 19(1):92–7 sp '71. * (*PA* 47:1824)
550. MOLNAR, GEORGE E.; DELAURETIS, ROBERT J.; AND LEBOLD, WILLIAM K. "Discriminant and Regression Models of College Persistence and Vocational Decisions." Abstract. *Proc 79th Ann Conv Am Psychol Assn* 6(2):519–20 '71. * (*PA* 46:5707)
551. MORGAN, ROBERT EARLE. *A Study of the Choices of Majors of Gardner-Webb College's Senior Class 1970–1971.* Doctor's thesis, University of North Carolina (Chapel Hill, N.C.), 1971. (*DAI* 32:4991A)
552. MUHLENKAMP, ANN F. "Prediction of State Board Scores in a Baccalaureate Prgoram." *Nursing Outl* 19(1):57 Ja '71. *
553. PFEIFER, C. MICHAEL, JR., AND SEDLACEK, WILLIAM E. "The Validity of Academic Predictors for Black and White Students at a Predominantly White University." *J Ed Meas* 8(4):253–61 w '71. * (*PA* 47:11785)
554. POWERS, RICHARD J. *Selected Noncognitive Variables as Predictors of Academic Achievement.* Doctor's thesis, St. John's University (Jamaica, N.Y.), 1971. (*DAI* 32:4194B)
555. SCHELLHAMMER, JAMES ROBERT. *A Longitudinal Analysis of the Academic Performance of Probationary Matriculants at Indiana University.* Doctor's thesis, Indiana University (Bloomington, Ind.), 1971. (*DAI* 32:1885A)
556. SHERRILL, DAVID, AND DRUGER, MARVIN. "Relationships Among Student Variables in an Audio-Tutorial Biology Course." *J Res Sci Teach* 8(2):191–4 '71. *
557. SIEGELMAN, MARVIN. "SAT and High School Average Predictions of Four Year College Achievement." *Ed & Psychol Meas* 31(4):947–50 w '71. * (*PA* 48:1871)
558. SMITH, JOHN STEPHEN. *A Multivariate Combination of Academic and Non-Academic Factors Related to Student Attrition.* Doctor's thesis, University of Pittsburgh (Pittsburgh, Pa.), 1971. (*DAI* 32:6786A)
559. SNYDER, C. R., AND RAY, WILLIAM J. "Observed Body Movement in the College Test-Taking Situation and Scores on the Scholastic Aptitude Test." *Percept & Motor Skills* 32(1):265–6 F '71. * (*PA* 46:3733)
560. STANLEY, JULIAN C. "Predicting College Success of the Educationally Disadvantaged: Admission to Selective Colleges Should Be Based Substantially on Test Scores and High School Grades." *Sci* 171(3972):640–7 F 19 '71. * (*PA* 46:9771)
561. SZABO, MICHAEL, AND FELDHUSEN, JOHN F. "Success in an Independent Study Science Course at the College Level as Related to Intellective, Personality, and Biographical Variables." *J Res Sci Teach* 8(3):225–9 '71. *
562. TEMP, GEORGE. "Validity of the SAT for Blacks and Whites in Thirteen Integrated Institutions." *J Ed Meas* 8(4):245–51 w '71. * (*PA* 47:11635)
563. THOMAS, CHARLES LEO. *The Relative Effectiveness of High School Grades and Standardized Test Scores for Predicting College Grades of Black Students.* Doctor's thesis, Johns

Hopkins University (Baltimore, Md.), 1971. (*DAI* 32:2495A)

564. ULIN, RICHARD O., AND BELSKY, THEODORE B. "Screening Prospective English Teachers: Criteria for Admission to Teacher Education Programs." *Res Teach Engl* 5(2):165–78 f '71. *

565. WHEELER, ROBERT G. "Computer Predicts Student Success as They Register." *Col Mgmt* 6(4):36–8 Ap '71. *

566. WILHELM, HOWARD MCDONALD. *Predicting Academic Achievement at a Multipurpose College.* Doctor's thesis, University of Virginia (Charlottesville, Va.), 1971. (*DAI* 32:4261A)

567. WING, CLIFF W., AND WALLACH, MICHAEL A. *College Admissions and the Psychology of Talent.* New York: Holt, Rinehart & Winston, Inc., 1971. Pp. ix, 165. * (*PA* 46:3701)

CUMULATIVE NAME INDEX

Abell, A. P.: 224
Adinolfi, A. A.: 376
Aiken, L. R.: 105–6, 138, 207, 278, 454–5
Alker, H. A.: 330–1, 517
Allen, R. J.: 74
Allison, R. B.: 26
Altus, W. D.: 51, 75, 171, 449
Anderson, C. E.: 332
Anderson, S. B.: 86
Andrews, F. M.: 259
Angers, W. P.: 76, 98
Angier, R. P.: 420–1
Angoff, W. H.: 37–8, 107–8, 172, 212, 279, 415–6
Asher, J. W.: 313
Asher, W.: 158
Astin, A. W.: 491, 518
Bachman, J. G.: 139
Bachrach, P. B.: 173
Backman, M. E.: 519–20
Badgett, J. L.: 521
Baer, D. J.: 208
Baggaley, A. R.: 471
Baker, D.: 160
Ballantyne, R. H.: 124
Barlow, D. H.: 462
Barrett, S. B.: 492
Barritt, L. S.: 128–9, 212
Beals, E. W.: 280
Bean, A. G.: 493
Bechtold, D. W.: 333
Behling, M. A.: 334
Behring, D. W.: 174, 209, 335, 456
Bell, E. L.: 210
Bellico, R. P.: 494
Belsky, T. B.: 564
Belz, H. F.: 522
Benson, P. H.: 239
Berdie, R. F.: 84
Berkey, R.: 140
Biaggio, A. M. B.: 175
Bickley, R. T.: 536
Bieri, J.: 445
Black, D. B.: 52, 61
Blanchfield, W. C.: 523
Bobbitt, J. M.: 24
Bohrnstedt, G. W.: 524
Borgatta, E. F.: 291, 524
Botel, M.: 25
Botwin, D. E.: 229
Bovinette, R. L.: 460
Bowers, J. E.: rev, 6:449
Boyd, J. D.: 33
Boyden, B. W.: 141
Bradburn, W. M.: 445
Brady, W. J.: 176, 525
Brandenburg, J. B.: 526
Braun, J. R.: 336
Brickman, P.: 543
Brigham, C. C.: 420–3, 427, 432
Brod, D.: 457
Brody, E. B.: 337, 377
Brolyer, C. R.: 424, 426, 428, 430–1, 433–5
Brooks, W. N.: 281
Brothers, C. T.: 378
Brousseau, M. A.: 484
Brown, J. L.: 379, 495
Buckeye, D. A.: 282
Buescher, R. M.: 338
Burgess, T. C.: 339
Burke, R. J.: 461, 466, 527
Burnham, P. S.: 429, 528
Burns, R. L.: 109

Bush, M. L.: 152–4, 189–91, 469
Buszek, B. R.: 283
Butler, J. H.: 284
Butzow, J. W.: 240
Campanile, S. C.: 380
Campbell, D. P.: 381
Campbell, J. P.: 211, 471
Canning, H.: 241
Caputo, D. V.: 197
Carlsmith, L.: 142
Carlson, J. A.: 331
Carruth, B. R.: 529
Carruth, B. R. R.: 477
Cassel, R. N.: 340
Casselman, G. G.: 402
Cautela, J. R.: 462
Centra, J. A.: 382–3, 406
Chambers, J. F.: 530
Chandler, M. O.: 417
Chansky, N. M.: 177
Chase, C. I.: 128–9, 178, 212, 285, 384
Chastain, K.: 341
Chauncey, H.: 87, 143, 531
Cherdack, A. N.: 496
Cherry, A. L.: 342
Child, I. L.: 440
Christoff, P. L.: 497
Clark, E. W.: 130
Clark, K.: 532
Clawar, H. J.: 286
Cleary, T. A.: 287–8
Closson, M. B.: 517
Coffman, W. E.: 110, 242, 298
Cole, C. W.: 243
Colgan, R. T.: 289
College Entrance Examination Board: 36, 111, 144–5, 179, 385–6
Combs, H. T.: 387
Conley, H. W.: 343
Conrad, H. S.: 11
Cook, R. L.: 290
Cooper, C. J.: 146
Corsini, R. J.: 291
Costello, J. J.: 180
Cox, A.: 96
Coy, M.: 478
Craddick, R. A.: 213
Crawford, A. B.: 425, 429
Creighton, S. L.: 533
Crouch, J. G.: 292
Crow, J. L.: 472
Crowder, D. G.: 78
Dailey, J. T.: rev, 5:318
D'Angelo, R. D.: 498
Daniere, A.: 499
Darley, J. G.: 88
Davis, F. B.: rev, 4:285
Davis, J. A.: 48, 442, 534
Dear, R. E.: 55
Delauretis, R. J.: 388, 550
Dempster, D.: 156
Dennehy, R. F.: 535
Denny, J. P.: 467
Dickason, D. G.: 344
Dickey, O. W.: 214
Dickter, M. R.: 2–4
Dieppa, J. J.: 147
Dimalta, V. F.: 479
Dinnan, J. A.: 536
Di Scipio, W. J.: 537
Doermann, H.: 293
Dole, A. A.: 235
Domino, G.: 389
Donlon, T. F.: 416
Donnan, H.: 294
Dowd, R. J.: 244

Druger, M.: 556
DuBois, P. H.: rev, 7:344
Duggan, J. M.: 53
Dunn, D. C.: 390
Dye, J. M.: 181
Dyer, H. S.: 22, 27, 43–4
Eichsteadt, A. C.: 340
Ellison, R. L.: 500
Emory, L. B.: 58, 65, 77–9, 93
Entwisle, F. N.: 98
Eriksen, C. W.: 161
Esser, B. F.: 89, 345
Evans, F. R.: 485
Evans, J. D.: 346
Even, A.: 295
Evenson, A. B.: 39
Fedell, J. C.: 538
Feeney, M. M.: 40
Feldhusen, J. F.: 313, 561
Finger, J. A.: 131, 182
Finley, P. J.: 451
Fishman, J. A.: 45
Fitzpatrick, M. R.: 215
Flaugher, R. L.: 296–7, 347
Fleming, W. G.: 46–7, 54, 90, 183
Flora, L. D.: 216
Floyd, W. A.: 245
Foree, S. S.: 458
Foulkes, D.: 91
Fox, D. G.: 500
Frankel, E.: 62–3
Franz, G.: 48, 58, 65, 78
Frederiksen, N.: 14, 442, 448, 485
Fremer, J.: 298, 417
French, J. W.: 24, 34, 41, 55, 92, 148, 446
Fricke, B. G.: 391
Frields, S. I.: 246
Fujita, G. Y.: 392
Funkenstein, D. H.: 112
Galinsky, M. D.: 445
Gallant, T. F.: 184
Gallessich, J. M.: 247
Gamble, K. R.: 299
Garcia, M.: 48
Gardner, F. E.: 49
Garms, J. D.: 248, 501
Gentry, J.: 480
Gerry, R.: 249
Gershon, A.: 96
Gettys, R. H.: 450
Giessow, F. J.: 122
Gilbert, A. C. F.: 56–7, 64, 448
Gladney, M. B.: 302
Goolsby, T. M.: 539
Gordon, K. K.: 487
Gordon, R. E.: 487
Graff, R. W.: 300
Grieneeks, L.: 397
Gruber, E. C.: 113
Gruber, J. J.: 505
Gruneberg, M. M.: 502
Gummere, R. F.: 42
Halladay, R. E.: 217
Hamm, B. H.: 301
Harris, J.: 250
Hart, M. E.: 149
Hartnett, R. T.: 393, 503
Harville, D. L.: 348
Haun, K. W.: 185
Heard, W. G.: 451
Heaxt, S.: 91
Hedlund, D. E.: 474
Heil, L. M.: 186
Hemmeter, J. T.: 384
Hendrickson, G. F.: 540
Herbstritt, R. L.: 187
Hermann, M. G.: 331
Hewitt, B. A.: 528
Highley, F. S.: 394
Hills, J. R.: 58, 65, 77–9, 93, 114, 150–4, 188–91, 302–3, 395, 468–9
Hilton, T. L.: 251, 288
Hindle, P. G.: 141
Holland, J. L.: 50, 59, 66, 80, 134
Hoover, M.: 96
Hope, L. H.: 521
Hornaday, J. A.: 100
Horton, C. P.: 362

Howell, J. J.: 304
Howell, W. J.: 463
Howlett, J. L.: 349
Hoyt, D. P.: 121, 305
Hurwitz, H. L.: 67
Hutchcraft, G.: 360
Hutchins, H. C.: 224
Ihlanfeldt, W. I.: 396
Irvine, D. W.: 192, 218, 541
Ivanoff, J. M.: 155
Ivey, A. E.: 219
Jacobs, P. I.: 115, 220
James, L. R.: 500
James, R. J.: 542
Jansen, D. G.: 252
Jeffreys, L. C.: 94
Jex, F. B.: 221
Johnson, A. P.: 17, 98
Johnson, R. W.: 306
Jones, J. G.: 397
Jones, R. A.: 96, 118, 160
Jordan, M. L.: 398
Judd, L. R.: 350
Judge, E. M.: 222
Juola, A. E.: 68, 116
Kaloger, J. H.: 504
Kantrowitz, J. L.: 223
Kaplan, M.: 352
Karas, S. F.: 351
Karlins, M.: 352
Katz, M.: 96
Kaufmann, J. D.: 156
Keenen, C. B.: 253
Keesee, C. G.: 254
Kellner, H.: 299
Kendrick, S. A.: 255–6
Keochakian, S. V.: 306
Kepka, E. J.: 543
Kerley, S. A.: 521
Kernoff, P.: 457
Ketcham, H. E. (Mrs.): 69
Kincannon, S. G.: 544
King, R. G.: 44
Kipnis, D.: 545
Kirk, C. R.: 307
Kirkendall, D. R.: 505
Klein, S. P.: 201, 485
Klock, J. A.: 114, 152–4, 188–91, 469
Kovacs, A. R.: 308
Kuder, G. F.: 6
Lamb, M. W.: 529
Lambert, P.: 524
Landry, H. A.: 436
Lapp, C. J.: 486
Lare, J. H.: 132
Larimore, D. L.: 464
Leach, A. R.: 133
Leathers, R. K.: 257
Leaver, E.: 193
LeBold, W. K.: 326, 388, 550
Lee, E. E.: 353
LeMay, M.: 399
Lemons, C. D.: 194
Levine, H. G.: 117
Levine, R. L.: 37
Lewis, S. C.: 114
Lightsey, R.: 379
Lin, Y. G.: 400
Lindeman, R. H.: 487
Lindquist, E. F.: 157
Linn, M. R.: 546
Linn, R. L.: 382–3, 406
Lins, L. J.: 224
Lord, F. M.: 309
Loret, P. G.: 70
Ludlow, H. G.: 128–9, 285, 360
Lyden, B. A.: 401
Lyons, W. A.: 117
McCall, J. N.: 28
Macchia, M.: 547
Maccoby, E. E.: 227
McConnell, D. S.: 548
McCormick, J. H.: 158
McEntire, E. M.: 310
McIntosh, W. A.: 274
McKeachie, W. J.: 400
McKelpin, J. P.: 195
MacPhail, A. H.: 420–1
Magoon, R. A.: 258
Magrab, R.: 354
Maier, N. R. F.: 402, 461
Malcolm, R. W.: 225
Malecki, G. S.: 29

College Board Scholastic Aptitude Test

Malloy, J. P.: 155
Mann, M. J.: 81
Manning, W. H.: 311
Marks, E.: 159, 473
Marquette, A. J.: 312
Marsh, F. E.: 123
Martin, H. T.: 101
Masten, S. H.: 95
Masters, P. B.: 77, 79, 93
Mathis, C.: 465
Mayer, J.: 241
Meadows, M. E.: 226
Mechling, J.: 499
Mednick, M. T.: 259
Melton, R. S.: 297
Merwin, J. C.: 169
Michael, W. B.: 96, 118, 160, 276, 398
Michalski, S. F.: 549
Miller, C. D.: 243
Miller, C. L.: 313
Miller, D. M.: 355
Miller, J. M.: 11
Mock, W. L.: 82
Mollenkopf, W. G.: 18
Molnar, G. E.: 388, 550
Moore, H.: 1
Moore, L. B.: 506
Morgan, J. M.: 404
Morgan, L. B.: 314
Morgan, R. E.: 551
Morningstar, M.: 306
Morrison, J. W: 507
Mueller, K. A.: 119
Muhlenkamp, A. F.: 552
Munday, L.: 196, 315
Myers, A. E.: 251
Myers, C. T.: 297
Myers, R. C.: 19, 23
Neidt, C. O.: 474
Nelsen, E. A.: 227
Nelson, B. E.: 356
Newman, S. H.: 24
Nicholi, A. M.: 475
Nichols, R. C.: 134
Nicholson, E.: 403
Nicholson, J.: 414
Norris, B. N.: 483
Notestine, E. B.: 357
Nowka, H. E.: 508
Oates, W. E.: 509
O'Connor, P.: 355
Oliver, R. A. C.: 97
Olsen, M. A.: 30
Oppenheim, D. B.: 481
O'Reilly, J. P.: 392
O'Zee, W. F.: 228
Pallone, N. J.: 83
Park, Y. H.: 465
Parres, J. G.: 35
Parry, M. E.: 242, 383
Passons, W. R.: 260
Paul, G. L.: 161
Payne, D. A.: 261
Pearson, R.: 15, 31
Peixotto, H. E.: 8
Pertusio, C. B.: 316
Peterson, F. E.: 219
Peterson, R. E.: 482
Pfeifer, C. M.: 553
Pfeiffer, M. G.: 364
Phillips, L. N.: 470
Pintel, G.: 510
Pipher, J. A.: 71
Plapp, J. M.: 197
Plotkin, L.: 532
Pomeroy, M. C.: 128–9
Porter, A. C.: 266
Powers, R. J.: 554
Preas, N. B.: 358
Preston, R. C.: 25
Price, R. L.: 359
Prien, E. P.: 229
Psathas, G.: 197
Pugh, R.: 200, 231
Pugh, R. C.: 285, 317, 360, 404
Quandt, R. E.: 509
Quiller, G. F.: 125
Quinlan, C. A.: 162
Range, L. H.: 262
Ranzoni, J. H.: 453
Ray, W. J.: 559
Reck, M.: 318
Reeling, P. A.: 361

Reid, J. W.: 98
Reiner, J. R.: 405
Reitzel, J.: 250
Resnick, J. H.: 545
Richman, E.: 135
Roberts, B. B.: 319
Roberts, B. T.: 362
Roberts, J. P.: 511
Roberts, S. O.: 362
Robinson, B. V.: 198
Robinson, F. K.: 199
Rock, D. A.: 296, 347, 406
Rogers, D. C.: 420–1
Roggenkamp, R. R.: 488
Rose, J. R.: 155
Rosen, N. A.: 72
Rowe, L. M.: 230
Russell, J. W.: 136
Sachtleben, C. C.: 263
Sarason, I. G.: 443
Sassenrath, J. M.: 200, 231, 264, 317
Saunders, H. R.: 232
Savitsky, J. C.: 365
Schellhammer, J. R.: 555
Scherer, G. A. C.: 163
Schlesser, G. E.: 131, 182
Schneyer, J. W.: 452
Schoemer, J. R.: 320
Schrader, W. B.: 30, 418–9
Schuerhoff, C.: 352
Schultz, C. B.: 201
Schultz, D. G.: 19–20
Seashore, H.: 32
Sedlacek, W. E.: 553
Seltzer, C. C.: 12
Sevier, F. A. C.: 444
Sgan, M. R.: 164
Shanner, W. M.: 6
Shaw, H. S.: 99
Shay, C. T.: 149
Sheldon, W. H.: 440
Sherrill, D.: 556
Sherron, R. H.: 363, 407
Shinn, S. M.: 512
Siegel, A. I.: 364
Siegelman, M.: 557
Sieveking, N. A.: 365
Skager, R. W.: 201
Skinner, S. B.: 408
Smith, C.: 350
Smith, D.: 96
Smith, D. E.: 39
Smith, J. S.: 558
Smith, P. M.: 165
Snyder, C. R.: 559
Sockloff, A. L.: 366
Southworth, J. A.: 306
Spaulding, G.: 120
Spaulding, H.: 60
Spiegel, J. A.: 367
Spielberger, C. D.: 459
Staats, A. W.: 451
Stalnaker, J. M.: 9, 13, 437–8, 441
Stalnaker, R. C.: 9, 438
Stanley, J. C.: 265–6, 303, 370, 395, 560
Staples, J. D.: 202
Starkman, S. S.: 203
Steige, R.: 126
Steindler, F. M.: 519–20
Steininger, M.: 409
Stewart, C. J.: 267
Stewart, E. E.: 419
Stimson, R. C.: 321
Stix, D. L.: 268
Stone, C. L.: 420–1
Stone, M. H.: 368
Stovall, E. M.: 233
Strahan, R.: 410
Stricker, G.: 204
Strickland, J. A.: 103
Stroup, A. L.: 411
Sullivan, G. V.: 234
Sutter, E. M. G.: 269
Swanson, E. O.: 84
Szabo, M.: 369, 561
Tahmisian, J.: 476
Tatham, C. B.: 235
Taylor, C. W.: 500
Taylor, P. H.: 298
Temp, G.: 534, 562
Terwilliger, R. F.: 457
Thomas, C. L.: 370, 563

Thorndike, R. L.: 10
Threatt, R.: 137
Tiedeman, D. V.: 32
Tillinghast, B. S.: 483
Tobias, S.: 371
Trafton, H.: 1
Traxler, A. E.: 16, 21
Trebbe, E. S.: 219
Turrentine, E. M.: 127
Ulin, R. O.: 564
Utgard, R. O.: 372
Vaughan, R. P.: 322
Vaughn, H. A.: 261
Veal, L. R.: 166
Veldman, D. J.: 323
Vick, M. C.: 100
Virene, E. P.: 5
Vroman, C.: 412
Walberg, H. J.: 270
Walker, C. E.: 476
Walker, P.: 167
Wall, K. W.: 513
Wallace, W. L.: rev, 7:344
Wallach, M. A.: 567
Walters, N. R.: 271
Watley, D. J.: 85, 101, 168–9, 205, 373
Watson, L. W.: 374
Webb, S. C.: 28, 170, 236, 272
Weber, C. O.: 7
Weiss, K. P.: 413

Weitz, H.: 459
Weitzner, M.: 173
Wertheimer, M.: 163
Westcott, M. R.: 453
Wexler, A. H.: 73
Wheeler, R. G.: 565
Whetstone, R. D.: 206
Whitla, D. K.: 102, 324
Wiersma, W.: 119
Wilcox, L.: 412
Wilhelm, H. M.: 566
Williams, C. M.: 240
Williams, H. B.: 489
Williams, J. C.: 536
Williams, R. H.: 273
Williamson, D. A.: 539
Willingham, W. W.: 103, 121, 325
Willis, C. G.: 414
Wilson, K. M.: 514
Windholz, G.: 274
Wing, C. W.: 567
Wolf, R. R.: 439
Wood, D. A.: 326
Worell, L.: 447
Yeremian, T. S.: 275
Young, R. O.: 515
Zarfoss, N. J.: 327
Zimmerman, J. J.: 375
Zimmerman, W. S.: 276; rev, 6:449

[358]

College Qualification Tests. Candidates for college entrance; 1955–61; CQT; 2 editions; distribution of Forms B and C restricted to colleges and universities; George K. Bennett, Marjorie G. Bennett, Wimburn L. Wallace, and Alexander G. Wesman; Psychological Corporation. *

a) COMBINED BOOKLET EDITION. 6 scores: verbal, numerical, information (science, social studies, total), total.

b) SEPARATE BOOKLET EDITION.

1) *Test V* [*Verbal*].
2) *Test N* [*Numerical*].
3) *Test I* [*Information*]. 3 scores: science, social studies, total.

For additional information, see 7:345 (24 references); for reviews by Ralph F. Berdie and Warren G. Findley, see 6:450 (11 references); for reviews by Gustav J. Froehlich, A. E. G. Pilliner, and David V. Tiedeman, see 5:320.

REFERENCES THROUGH 1971

1–11. See 6:450.
12–35. See 7:345.
36. ROBERTSON, MALCOLM H. "Test Scores and Self-Estimates of Two Curricula Groups." *Personnel & Guid J* 38:746–50 My '60. * (*PA* 35:2767)
37. CUMMINGS, ROGER W., AND KIRK, BARBARA A. ["Norms of the College Qualification Test."] Letter. *J Counsel Psychol* 9:282 f '62. *
38. SEASHORE, HAROLD G. "Women Are More Predictable Than Men." *J Counsel Psychol* 9:261–70 f '62. * (*PA* 38:3194)
39. OBST, FRANCES. "A Study of Abilities of Women Students Entering the Colleges of Letters and Science and Applied Arts at the University of California, Los Angeles." *J Ed Res* 57:84–6 O '63. *
40. TROY, ELIZABETH MCGOLDRICK. *A Study of the Predictive Value of Eleven Variables Used at King's College to Determine General Scholastic Achievement of Two Hundred Forty-Three Entering Students.* Master's thesis, Marywood College (Scranton, Pa.), 1965.
41. CUMMINS, EMERY J. "A Study of Differences Among Four Types of Disciplinary Offenders on Selected Cognitive and Affective Measures." *J Ed Res* 60:444–7 Jl–Ag '67. *
42. DELONG, JOAN J. *The College Qualification Tests and Predictability of First Semester Grade Point Average at Chadron State College.* Master's thesis, Chadron State College (Chadron, Neb.), 1969.
43. ARNDT, JOHN RICHARD. *A Study of Selected Factors Characterizing Freshmen Who Entered Michigan State University in Fall 1968 Identified as Under-, Over- or Normal Achievers After One Term of College.* Doctor's thesis, Michigan State University (East Lansing, Mich.), 1970. (*DAI* 32:191A)
44. DUTHLER, BERNARD THOMAS. *A Study of the Prediction of Transfer Students' Academic Success in a College of Educa-*

tion. Doctor's thesis, University of Toledo (Toledo, Ohio), 1970. (*DAI* 31:4457A)
45. JOHNS, DANIEL JAY. *Correlates of Academic Success in a Predominantly Black, Open-Door, Public, Urban Community College*. Doctor's thesis, University of Virginia (Charlottesville, Va.), 1970. (*DAI* 31:4464A)
46. KALLINGAL, ANTHONY K. *Differential Validities of Selected Variables in the Prediction of College Success for Blacks and Whites*. Doctor's thesis, Michigan State University (East Lansing, Mich.), 1970. (*DAI* 31:5848A
47. KALLINGAL, ANTHONY. "The Prediction of Grades for Black and White Students at Michigan State University." *J Ed Meas* 8(4):263–5 w '71. *
48. SMITH, DONALD MICHAEL. *The Validity of Factor Score Estimates of Speed and Accuracy as Predictors of First Term Grade Point Average*. Doctor's thesis, Florida State University (Tallahassee, Fla.), 1971. (*DAI* 32:6228A)
49. SMITH, LELAND. "A 5-Year Follow-Up Study of High Ability Achieving and Nonachieving College Freshmen." *J Ed Res* 64(5):220–2 Ja '71. * (*PA* 46:5716)
50. WILLETT, ELIZABETH A.; RIFFEL, P. A.; BREEN, LAWRENCE J.; AND DICKSON, ELINOR J. "Selection and Success of Students in a Hospital School of Nursing." *Can Nurse* 67(1):41–5 Ja '71. *

CUMULATIVE NAME INDEX

Abell, A. P.: 24
Arndt, J. R.: 43
Bauer, R.: 25
Bennett, G. K.: 4
Berdie, R. F.: *rev*, 6:450
Borgatta, E. F.: 27
Boyce, R. W.: 17
Breen, L. J.: 50
Bunger, F. A.: 13
Buszek, B. R.: 26
Cassel, R. N.: 30
Cooper, C. J.: 15
Corsini, R. J.: 27
Cummings, R. W.: 10, 37
Cummins, E. J.: 41
Darley, J. G.: 8
DeLong, J. J.: 42
Dickson, E. J.: 50
Dreyer, D. E.: 31
Duthler, B. T.: 44
Eichsteadt, A. C.: 30
Elton, C. F.: 18, 32
Findley, W. G.: *rev*, 6:450
Froehlich, G. J.: *rev*, 5:320
Goodstein, L. D.: 10
Greenland, T. C.: 28
Hartford, D. L.: 12
Hutchins, H. C.: 24
Ikenberry, S. O.: 14
Jenkins, N. L.: 33
Johns, D. J.: 45
Johnson, R. J.: 34
Juola, A. E.: 5–7, 16, 22
Kafer, L. G.: 23
Kallingal, A.: 47
Kallingal, A. K.: 46
Kirk, B. A.: 1, 10, 37
Lehmann, I. J.: 19
Leonard, L. C.: 34
Lins, L. J.: 24
Lueptow, L. B.: 29
McKay, W. R.: 20
Mehrens, W. A.: 25
Mills, D. H.: 21
Obst, F.: 39
Paxson, R. C.: 17
Pilliner, A. E. G.: *rev*, 5:320
Rao, S. N.: 9, 11
Riffel, P. A.: 50
Robertson, M. H.: 36
Seashore, H.: 2
Seashore, H. G.: 38
Smith, D. M.: 48
Smith, L.: 49
Spaulding, H.: 3
Tiedeman, D. V.: *rev*, 5:320
Troy, E. M.: 40
Vinsonhaler, J. F.: 25
Vohs, A. P.: 35
Wesman, A. G.: 4
Willett, E. A.: 50

[359]

Concept Mastery Test. Grades 15–16 and graduate students and applicants for executive and research positions; 1956, c1950; CMT; Lewis M. Terman; Psychological Corporation. *

For additional information, see 6:451 (8 references); for reviews by J. A. Keats and Calvin W. Taylor, see 5:321 (4 references).

REFERENCES THROUGH 1971

1–4. See 5:321.
5–12. See 6:451.
13. CAMPBELL, MARY LOU. *Verbal Analogies Tests: A Comparison of Vocabulary and Reasoning Components Using the Miller Analogies Test and the Concept Mastery Test*. Master's thesis, University of Utah (Salt Lake City, Utah), 1964.
14. CHASE, CLINTON I.; LUDLOW, H. GLENN; AND PUGH, RICHARD C. *Predicting Success for Master's Degree Students in Education*. Indiana Studies in Prediction No. 5. Bloomington, Ind.: Bureau of Educational Studies and Testing, Indiana University, 1964. Pp. v, 25. *
15. CHASE, CLINTON I.; LUDLOW, H. GLENN; PUGH, RICHARD C.; AND POMEROY, MARTHA C. *Predicting Success for Advanced Graduate Students in Education*. Indiana Studies in Prediction No. 4. Bloomington, Ind.: Bureau of Educational Studies and Testing, Indiana University, 1964. Pp. v, 18. *
16. KNAPP, ROBERT H. "An Experimental Study of a Triadic Hypothesis Concerning the Sources of Aesthetic Imagery." *J Proj Tech & Pers Assess* 28:49–54 Mr '64. * (*PA* 39:1641)
17. FLEISCHER, GERALD, AND COHEN, IRA S. "The Relationship Between Test Anxiety and Tests of Creativity." Abstract. *Proc Ann Conv Am Psychol Assn* 73:311–2 '65. * (*PA* 39:15458)
18. GLAD, JOAN ROGERS BOURNE. *Evaluation of the Remedial Reading Program in Utah Public Schools*. Doctor's thesis, University of Utah (Salt Lake City, Utah), 1965. (*DA* 26:5864)
19. MCDERMID, CHARLES D. "Some Correlates of Creativity in Engineering Personnel." *J Appl Psychol* 49:14–9 F '65. * (*PA* 39:7782)
20. ALEXAKOS, C. E. "Predictive Efficiency of Two Multivariate Statistical Techniques in Comparison With Clinical Predictions." *J Ed Psychol* 57:297–306 O '66. * (*PA* 40:12756)
21. BYERS, JOE L. "A Set of Norms for the Concept Mastery Test Based Upon a Sample of Students in Teacher Education." *Calif J Ed Res* 17:133–43 My '66. * (*PA* 40:9429)
22. WELSH, GEORGE S. "Comparison of D-48, Terman CMT, and Art Scale Scores of Gifted Adolescents." Abstract. *J Consult Psychol* 30:88 F '66. * (*PA* 40:4105)
23. GAMEWELL, JOYCE. *An Investigation of the Use of Two Instruments for Assessing Intellective and Nonintellective Aspects of Intelligence as Predictors of Post Degree Success of Psychology Graduate Students*. Doctor's thesis, Colorado State College (Greeley, Colo.), 1967. (*DA* 28:3022A)
24. LAUGHLIN, PATRICK R. "Incidental Concept Formation as a Function of Creativity and Intelligence." *J Pers & Social Psychol* 5:115–9 Ja '67. * (*PA* 41:3958)
25. NEIDT, CHARLES O., AND HEDLUND, DALVA E. "The Relationship Between Changes in Attitudes Toward a Course and Final Achievement." *J Ed Res* 61:56–8 O '67. *
26. SLAKTER, MALCOLM J. "Risk Taking On Objective Examinations." *Am Ed Res J* 4:31–43 Ja '67. * (*PA* 41:7850)
27. WALLEN, NORMAN E., AND CAMPBELL, MARY LOU A. "Vocabulary and Non-verbal Reasoning Components of Verbal Analogies Tests (Miller Analogies Test and Concept Mastery Test)." *J Ed Res* 61:87–9 O '67. *
28. WELSH, GEORGE S. "Verbal Interests and Intelligence: Comparison of Strong VIB, Terman CMT, and D-48 Scores of Gifted Adolescents." *Ed & Psychol Meas* 27:349–52 su '67. * (*PA* 41:13633)
29. ZAHN, JANE C. "Some Characteristics of Successful and Less Successful Overseas Community Development Advisers." *Adult Ed* 18:15–23 f '67. *
30. GRIMSRUD, RICHARD ARLO. *A Method for Predicting Success in a Counselor Education Training Program*. Doctor's thesis, University of Minnesota (Minneapolis, Minn.), 1968. (*DA* 29:2115A)
31. MCCLOUD, THOMAS E. "Persistency as a Motivational Factor of Vocational Interest in the Prediction of Academic Success of Twelfth-Grade Superior Students." *Psychol* 5:34–46 N '68. * (*PA* 43:5984)
32. ROHLF, RICHARD JOHN. *A Higher-Order Alpha Factor Analysis of Interest, Personality, and Ability Variables, Including an Evaluation of the Effect of Scale Interdependency*. Doctor's thesis. University of Kansas (Lawrence, Kan.), 1968. (*DA* 29:1758A)
33. SLAKTER, MALCOLM J. "The Penalty for Not Guessing." *J Ed Meas* 5:141–4 su '68. *
34. SLAKTER, MALCOLM J., AND RODEN, AUBREY H. "Comparison of a Disguised and Reported Measure of Risk Taking on Objective Examinations." *Alberta J Ed Res* (Canada) 14:123–8 Je '68. * (*PA* 44:4173)
35. HINRICHS, J. R. "Comparison of 'Real Life' Assessments of Management Potential With Situational Exercises, Paper-and-Pencil Ability Tests, and Personality Inventories." *J Appl Psychol* 53(5):425–32 O '69. * (*PA* 44:1442)
36. KRAUT, ALLEN I. "Intellectual Ability and Promotional Success Among High Level Managers." *Personnel Psychol* 22(3):281–90 au '69. * (*PA* 44:9440)
37. LAUGHLIN, PATRICK R.; BRANCH, LAURENCE G.; AND JOHNSON, HOMER H. "Individual Versus Triadic Performance on a Unidimensional Complementary Task as a Function of Initial Ability Level." *J Pers & Social Psychol* 12(2):144–50 Je '69. * (*PA* 43:12897)
38. WELSH, GEORGE S. *Gifted Adolescents: A Handbook of Test Results*. Greensboro, N.C.: Prediction Press, June 1969. Pp. viii, 89. *
39. ROHLF, RICHARD J. "A Higher-Order Alpha Factor Analysis of Interest, Personality, and Ability Variables, Including an Evaluation of the Effect of Scale Interdependency." *Ed & Psychol Meas* 31(2):381–96 su '71. * (*PA* 46:11516)
40. WELSH, GEORGE S. "Vocational Interests and Intelligence in Gifted Adolescents." *Ed & Psychol Meas* 31(1):155–64 sp '71. * (*PA* 46:10645)

CUMULATIVE NAME INDEX

Alexakos, C. E.: 20
Barthol, R. P.: 3
Bayley, N.: 2, 6
Branch, L. G.: 37
Byers, J. L.: 21
Camp, W. L.: 9
Campbell, M. L.: 13
Campbell, M. L. A.: 27
Chase, C. I.: 14–5
Cohen, I. S.: 17
Curtis, H. A.: 10
Fleischer, G.: 17
Gamewell, J.: 23
Glad, J. R. B.: 18
Grimsrud, R. A.: 30
Hedlund, D. E.: 25
Hinrichs, J. R.: 35
Johnson, H. H.: 37
Keats, J. A.: *rev*, 5:321
Kennedy, W. A.: 11
Kirk, B. A.: 3
Knapp, R. H.: 16
Kraut, A. I.: 36
Kropp, R. P.: 10
Laughlin, P. R.: 24, 37
Ludlow, H. G.: 14–5
McCloud, T. E.: 31
McDermid, C. D.: 19

MacKinnon, D. W.: 8
McNemar, Q.: 5-6
Marshall, H.: 6
Neidt, C. O.: 25
Oden, M. H.: 2, 6-7
Pomeroy, M. C.: 15
Pugh, R. C.: 14-5
Roden, A. H.: 34
Rohlf, R. J.: 32, 39
Rothney, J. W. M.: 9
Slakter, M. J.: 26, 33-4
Smith, A. H.: 11
Sullivan, E. B.: 6
Taylor, C. W.: *rev*, 5:321
Taylor, D. W.: 4, 12
Terman, L. M.: 6-7
Thorndike, R. L.: 1
Wallen, N. E.: 27
Welsh, G. S.: 22, 28, 38, 40
Zahn, J. C.: 29

[360]
Cooperative Academic Ability Test. Superior grade 12 students; 1963-64; AAT; also published in 1966 as Level 1 of *Cooperative School and College Ability Tests: Series 2*, Forms A and B; 3 scores: verbal, mathematical, total; Cooperative Tests and Services. *

For additional information, reviews by Eric F. Gardner and William B. Michael, and an excerpted review by Kenneth D. Hopkins (with Darrell L. Sander), see 7:346 (3 references).

REFERENCES THROUGH 1971
1-3. See 7:346.

CUMULATIVE NAME INDEX
Clawar, H. J.: 2
Conklin, R. C.: 3
Gardner, E. F.: *rev*, 7:346
Hopkins, K. D.: *exc*, 7:346
Michael, W. B.: *rev*, 7:346
Ogston, D. G.: 3
Sander, D. L.: *exc*, 7:346
Traxler, A. E.: 1

[361]
*****Cooperative School and College Ability Tests.**
1955-73; SCAT; 3 scores: verbal, quantitative, total; 2 editions; Cooperative Tests and Services. *
a) ORIGINAL SERIES [70 MINUTE TESTS]. Grades 4-6, 6-8, 8-10, 10-12, 12-14, 15-16; 1955-63; 6 levels.
1) *School Ability Test.* Grades 4-6, 6-8, 8-10, 10-12; Braille and large type editions are available from American Printing House for the Blind, Inc.
2) *College Ability Test.* Grades 12-14, 15-16.
b) SERIES 2 [40 MINUTE TESTS]. Grades 4-6, 7-9, 10-12, 12-14; 1955-73.

For additional information, a review by H. J. Butcher, and excerpted reviews by S. David Farr, Esin Kaya, and Douglas McKie (with Peggy Rae Koopman) of Series 2, see 7:347 (186 references); for a review by Russel F. Green of the original series, see 6:452 (64 references); for reviews by Frederick B. Davis, Hanford M. Fowler, and Julian C. Stanley, see 5:322 (7 references).

REFERENCES THROUGH 1971
1-7. See 5:322.
8-71. See 6:452.
72-257. See 7:347.

258. CLIFF, ROSEMARY. "The Predictive Value of Chance-Level Scores." *Ed & Psychol Meas* 18:607-16 au '58. * (*PA* 33:9269)
259. FOREHAND, G. A., JR., AND McQUITTY, LOUIS C. "Configurations of Factor Standings as Predictors of Educational Achievement." *Ed & Psychol Meas* 19:31-43 sp '59. * (*PA* 34:119)
260. DAHLKE, ARNOLD E., AND DANA, RICHARD H. "Intraindividual Verbal-Numerical Discrepancies and Personality." Abstract. *J Consult Psychol* 27:182 Ap '63. *
261. CHABASSOL, DAVID J., AND MANSON, GORDON G. "An Investigation to Identify Creativity in Teaching." *Alberta J Ed Res* (Canada) 10:201-8 D '64. *
262. EDMONDS, WILLIAM S. "Sex Differences in the Verbal Ability of Socio-Economically Depressed Groups." *J Ed Res* 58:61-4 O '64. *
263. GAZDA, GEORGE M., AND FOLDS, JANELL H. "The Effects of Three Methods of Test Interpretation on the Recall of Test Scores and Change in Self Concept." *J Stud Pers Assn Teach Ed* 4:10-21 D '64. *
264. HUGHES, DONALD L. *A Study to Predict the Academic Success of Low Achieving High School Students at Brigham Young University With Selected Tests.* Master's thesis, Brigham Young University (Provo, Utah), 1964.
265. KATZ, STANLEY S. "Selection and Evaluation of Students in Medical Technology Degree Programs." *Am J Med Technol* 30:51-63 Ja '64. *
266. ALTUS, WILLIAM D. "Birth Order and Mean Score on a Ten-Item Aptitude Test." *Psychol Rep* 16:956 Je '65. * (*PA* 39:14628)
267. BARGER, BEN, AND HALL, EVERETTE. "The Interaction of Ability Levels and Socioeconomic Variables in the Prediction of College Dropouts and Grade Achievement." *Ed & Psychol Meas* 25:501-8 su '65. * (*PA* 39:14896)
268. ELLIOTT, MERLE H., AND BADAL, ALDEN W. "Achievement and Racial Composition of Schools." *Calif J Ed Res* 16:158-66 S '65. * (*PA* 40:1478)
269. KIMBALL, WEBSTER H. *Persistence and Success Prediction in Accounting.* Master's thesis, California State College (Long Beach, Calif.), 1965.
270. LUNDQUIST, RUSSELL M. *Prognosis of Success in Ninth Grade Algebra.* Master's thesis, Mankato State College (Mankato, Minn.), 1965.
271. PEDERSEN, DARHL M. "The Measurement of Individual Differences in Perceived Personality-Trait Relationships and Their Relation to Certain Determinants." *J Social Psychol* 65:233-58 Ap '65. * (*PA* 39:14976)
272. AMAREL, MARIANNE; CHEEK, FRANCES E.; AND STIERHEM, ROBERT J. "Studies in the Sources of Variation in Cloze Scores: 1, The Raters." *J Abn Psychol* 71:444-8 D '66. * (*PA* 41:1574)
273. HARDING, WILLIAM THOMAS. *Differential Verbal and Quantitative Scores and Interests.* Master's thesis, Illinois State University (Normal, Ill.), 1966.
274. PHELPS, ARTHUR M. *Predicting First Semester Grades in the Junior College Two-Year Terminal Vocational-Technical Programs.* Master's thesis, Stetson University (DeLand, Fla.), 1966.
275. BIDINIAN, ROSE JOHNSON. *Predicting Probability of Success in Selected First Semester Curriculum Areas of Sacramento State College.* Master's thesis, Sacramento State College (Sacramento, Calif.), 1967.
276. HUFF, BETTY. *The Predictive Value of Standardized Testing in Relation to Mathematical Achievement at Virginia High School.* Master's thesis, East Tennessee State University (Johnson City, Tenn.), 1967.
277. STEWART, LAWRENCE H.; DOLE, ARTHUR A.; AND HARRIS, YEUELL Y. "Cultural Differences in Abilities During High School." *Am Ed Res J* 4:19-29 Ja '67. * (*PA* 41:7189)
278. WILLIAMSON, MALCOLM L., AND HOPKINS, KENNETH D. "The Use of 'None-of-These' Versus Homogeneous Alternatives on Multiple-Choice Tests: Experimental Reliability and Validity Comparisons." *J Ed Meas* 4:53-8 su '67. *
279. ZOOK, HOWARD A. *A Comparative Study of the Validity of Three Variables as Predictors of GPI at Kearney State College.* Master's thesis, Kearney State College (Kearney, Neb.), 1967.
280. BLAI, BORIS, JR. "Measuring Educational Progress Through 'Before' and 'After' Testing." *Psychol* 5:39-41 My '68. * (*PA* 42:14567)
281. GENTRY, JOANNE. "Abstract of a Study of the Relationship Between High School Grades and Test Scores and the Achievement of Students Enrolled in BEOA 326 (Shorthand) at Ball State University in the Autumn Quarter of 1966." *Ball State J Bus Educators* 40:12-6 N '68. *
282. GOEDICKE, RITA. *The Relation Between Academic Success and Personality Variables.* Master's thesis, University of Alberta (Edmonton, Alta., Canada), 1968.
283. MILLER, RICHARD H. "Students Show a Preparation Increase but No Increase in Grades Was Shown." *Col & Univ* 45(1):28-30 f '69. *
284. MORE, ARTHUR. "The Relation of High School Grades, Achievement and Intelligence Test Scores to Success in Dental School." *Can Counsellor* 3(1):56-8 Ja '69. *
285. BACHMAN, ALFRED MORRY. "The Relationship Between a Seventh-Grade Pupil's Academic Self-Concept and Achievement in Mathematics." *J Res Math Ed* 1(3):173-9 My '70. *
286. CARPENTER, CORINNE TAYLOR. *Study of the Relationship of Selected Factors to the Performance of Business Education Graduates at Grambling College on the Commons Section of the National Teacher Examinations.* Doctor's thesis, Indiana University (Bloomington, Ind.), 1970. (*DAI* 31:5900A)
287. DURHAM, JAMES ALFRED, JR. *An Analysis of Academic Success Predictors for Selected Students at a Florida Junior College.* Doctor's thesis, University of Southern Mississippi (Hattiesburg, Miss.), 1970. (*DAI* 31:5790A)
288. EDDY, BERDYNE BUTCHER. *A Study of the Relationship of Selected Student Characteristics to Persistence and Withdrawal of a Sample of Full-Time Freshmen at a Community College.* Doctor's thesis, American University (Washington, D.C.), 1970. (*DAI* 32:89A)
289. ELBERFELD, STEPHAN, AND LOVE, BETHOLENE. "Identification of Aptitude Criteria for Medical Technology." *Am J Med Technol* 36(8):388-99 Ag '70. *
290. FOXWORTH, CHARLES LEONARD. *Factors Related to Academic Performance of Students Admitted to the Roswell Community College 1958-1967.* Doctor's thesis, Louisiana State University (Baton Rouge, La.), 1970. (*DAI* 31:4487A)
291. HALCROW, JOHN HAROLD. *The Relationship of Selected Variables to the Academic Performance of Transfer Students at the University of North Dakota.* Doctor's thesis, University of North Dakota (Grand Forks, N.D.), 1970. (*DAI* 32:6759A)
292. KALOGER, JAMES HERACLES. *Characteristics of Grosse*

Pointe High School Students in Advanced Placement Programs. Doctor's thesis, University of Michigan (Ann Arbor, Mich.), 1970. (DAI 31:6440A)

293. KIMBLES, SAMUEL LEWIS. *A Measure of Cultural Deprivation.* Doctor's thesis, University of Southern California (Los Angeles, Calif.), 1970. (DAI 31:4552A)

294. PARSLEY, JAMES FRANCIS, JR. *A Comparison of the Ability of Ninth Grade Students to Apply Several Critical Thinking Skills to Problematic Content Presented Through Two Different Media.* Doctor's thesis, Ohio University (Athens, Ohio), 1970. (DAI 31:4629A)

295. POINDEXTER, CHARLES CRAWFORD, JR. *Degrees and Dropouts: A Profile of Student Characteristics in North Carolina Community Colleges.* Doctor's thesis, University of North Carolina (Chapel Hill, N.C.), 1970. (DAI 31:5776A)

296. ROBERTS, JOSEPH PORTER. *Intellectually Gifted Adolescents: A Multivariate Analysis of Certain Educationally Relevant Attributes.* Doctor's thesis, University of Virginia (Charlottesville, Va.), 1970. (DAI 31:4588A)

297. RUSSELL, WENDELL PHILLIPS. *Intellectual and Non-Intellectual Factors Affecting the Attrition Rate of Students Entering Virginia Union University in 1965.* Doctor's thesis, University of Virginia (Charlottesville, Va.), 1970. (DAI 31:4474A)

298. SCHRECK, JOHN FREDERICK. *An Experimental Study of the Influence of Human Color Sensitivity Upon the Reliability of Student Responses on the School and College Ability Test Series II, Forms 1A and 1B.* Doctor's thesis, American University (Washington, D.C.), 1970. (DAI 32:1347A)

299. SODHI, SURINDER. "Personality Factors in Second Language Acquisition." *Ed & Psychol R* (India) 10(2):70–6 Ap '70. *

300. AUSTIN, GILBERT R., AND RYAN, BRUCE. "Computer Assisted Guidance in Predicting Probable Admission to Institutions of Higher Education." *J Ed Data Processing* 8(2–3):18–23 '71. *

301. BAUER, DAVID H. "The Effect of Test Instructions, Test Anxiety, Defensiveness, and Confidence in Judgment on Guessing Behavior in Multiple-Choice Test Situations." *Psychol Sch* 8(3):208–15 Jl '71. * (PA 47:9634)

302. BRADLEY, RICHARD W., AND SANBORN, MARSHALL S. "Using Tests to Predict Four-Year Patterns of College Grade Point." *J Col Stud Personnel* 12(2):138–42 Mr '71. * (PA 46:5699)

303. CLARK, NEWTON CECIL, JR. *Test Anxiety, Locus of Control, and Feedback in Self-Instruction.* Doctor's thesis, George Peabody College for Teachers (Nashville, Tenn.), 1971. (DAI 32:1912A)

304. DAMPEL, DAVID D., AND SEYMOUR, WARREN R. "The Academic Success of Black Students: A Dilemma." *J Col Stud Personnel* 12(4):243–7 Jl '71. *

305. DIXON, PAUL W.; FUKUDA, NOBUKO K.; AND BERENS, ANNE E. "A Factor Analysis of EPPS Scales, Ability, and Achievement Measures." *J Exp Ed* 39(4):31–41 su '71. * (PA 47:1723)

306. FRANK, AUSTIN C. "Men's Strong Vocational Interest Blank Academic Achievement Scale: An Attempted Validation." *J Counsel Psychol* 18(4):324–7 Jl '71. * (PA 46:11572)

307. HALL, LUCIEN T., JR. "The Prediction of Success in Each of Six Four-Year Selections of Secondary Mathematics Courses." *Sch Sci & Math* 71(8):693–6 N '71. *

308. HEATON, JEAN MOSSMAN. *Adolescent Orientation, Achievement and Family Interaction.* Doctor's thesis, Florida State University (Tallahassee, Fla.), 1971. (DAI 32:6486B)

309. KIRBY, BARBARA JANE. *An Analysis of the Relationships Between Academic Performance and Scores on Licensure Examinations of Mortuary Science Students at Miami-Dade Junior College 1966–1969.* Doctor's thesis, University of Miami (Coral Gables, Fla.), 1971. (DAI 32:3122A)

310. LESCARBEAU, WILFRED J. *A Study of the Relationship Between Selected Fine Manipulative Motor Abilities and Achievement in the Introductory Physical Science Course.* Doctor's thesis, University of Houston (Houston, Tex.), 1971. (DAI 33:900A)

311. MACCHIA, WALTER. *Prediction of Senior Year SAT Scores From Freshman Year SCAT Scores and Final Grade Averages in English and Algebra.* Master's thesis, Jersey City State College (Jersey City, N.J.), 1971. *

312. PANDEY, R. E. "The SCAT and Race." *Psychol Rep* 28(2):459–62 Ap '71. * (PA 46:7456)

313. ROSENFELD, MICHAEL, AND HILTON, THOMAS L. "Negro-White Differences in Adolescent Educational Growth." *Am Ed Res J* 8(2):267–83 Mr '71. *

314. SISSON, ELEANOR RUTH. *A Longitudinal Study of Recent Counselor Information as a Broader Base for Academic Prediction.* Doctor's thesis, Purdue University (Lafayette, Ind.), 1971. (DAI 32:3045A)

315. STEPHENSON, ROBERT S., AND BEARD, JACOB G. "Common Dimensions of the School, Social, and Economic Environment in Florida: An Empirical Study." *Fla J Ed Res* 13:49–57 '71. *

316. TAYLOR, ALTON L. "Regression Analysis of Antecedent Measures of Slow Sections in High School Biology." *Sci Ed* 55(3):395–402 Jl–S '71. *

317. TISDALE, JOSEPH CHRISTOPHER, III. *Prediction of Success in First-Year Community College Mathematics.* Doctor's thesis, University of Virginia (Charlottesville, Va.), 1971. (DAI 32:4385A)

318. WAGMAN, MORTON. "Clinical and Research Use of the Strong Vocational Interest Blank Academic Achievement Scale." *J Counsel Psychol* 18(4):337–430 Jl '71. * (PA 46:11599)

319. WEBB, HAROLD QUENTIN. *The Prognostic Potential of Selected Factors for Predicting Achievement in the Study of High School Bookkeeping and Accounting.* Doctor's thesis, Ohio State University (Columbus, Ohio), 1971. (DAI 32:3645A)

CUMULATIVE NAME INDEX

Ackerman, T. J.: 112
Aichele, D. B.: 206
Aleamoni, L. M.: 202
Allgood, E. V.: 91
Alspaugh, C. A.: 232
Altus, W. D.: 266
Amarel, M.: 272
Ames, R.: 72
Anderson, H. E.: 113
Anderson, R. E.: 81
Anderson, S. B.: 48
Angers, W. P.: 55
Asher, W.: 106
Atkinson, B. H.: 92
Austin, G. R.: 300
Bachman, A. M.: 285
Badal, A. W.: 268
Barger, B.: 114, 117, 267
Barry, J. R.: 113
Bartlett, C. J.: 23
Bates, C. O.: 82
Bauer, D. H.: 301
Baumeister, A. A.: 23
Beard, J. G.: 315
Belk, F. E.: 141
Bellamy, R. Q.: 225
Berens, A. E.: 186, 210, 236–7, 305
Berry, C. A.: 24
Bidinian, R. J.: 275
Bierley, R.: 18
Black, D. B.: 9, 14, 25
Black, H. P.: 115
Blai, B.: 280
Bohrnstedt, G. W.: 214
Boney, J. D.: 93, 142
Borgatta, E. F.: 214
Bowers, J.: 233
Boyce, R. W.: 94, 116
Bradley, R. C.: 162
Bradley, R. W.: 302
Bray, D. W.: 143, 241
Broad, E. J.: 15
Brodsky, S. L.: 95
Brodsky, S. M.: 96
Broe, J. R.: 77
Brown, W. T.: 182
Buegel, H. F.: 26
Butcher, H. J.: *rev,* 7:347
Byler, J. T.: 144
Cameron, H. K.: 183
Carleton, F. O.: 234
Carpenter, C. T.: 286
Carver, R. P.: 207
Cassel, R. N.: 27
Chabassol, D. J.: 163, 184, 261
Chambers, J. L.: 117
Cheek, F. E.: 272
Cheers, A. L.: 58
Clark, N. C.: 303
Clarke, R. B.: 164
Cliff, R.: 258
Clyde, R. B.: 39
Condon, C. F.: 121
Cooper, L. R.: 97
Crawford, W. R.: 83
Crowell, O.: 235
Cummings, R. W.: 51
Cunningham, R.: 208
Curtis, H. A.: 40
Dahlke, A. E.: 260
Dampel, D. D.: 304
Dana, R. H.: 260
Daniel, K. B.: 165
Daniel, K. laV. B.: 84
Darley, J. G.: 49
Davis, F. B.: *rev,* 5:322
Davis, L. E.: 118
Davis, S. E.: 185
De Beruff, E.: 209
DeHart, A. L.: 78
Denham, E. C.: 145
Denny, T.: 121

De Sena, P. A.: 119
DeWees, J. P.: 28
Dick, W.: 85
Distefano, M. K.: 146
Dixon, P. W.: 186, 210, 236–7, 305
Dole, A. A.: 277
Doleys, E. J.: 59
Drum, D. J.: 211
Durham, J. A.: 287
Eddy, J. B.: 288
Edmonds, W. S.: 262
Edwards, M. P.: 120
Eells, K.: 41
Elberfeld, S.: 289
Elias, R. M.: 239
Elliott, M. H.: 268
Endler, N. S.: 60, 98
Engelhart, M. D.: 16
Engen, H. B.: 99
Entwisle, F. N.: 55
Evans, R. W.: 100
Evenson, A. B.: 5
Faragher, J. P.: 238
Farley, J.: 44
Farr, S. D.: *exc,* 7:347
Farrar, R. D.: 187
Fee, F.: 188
Feldhusen, J. F.: 121, 239
Ferris, M. J.: 166
Fleming, W. G.: 10–11, 17
Folds, J. H.: 122, 147, 263
Follman, J.: 212–3
Fontes, P. J.: 189
Ford, R. N.: 214
Ford, Z. B.: 148
Fordham, S. L.: 86
Forehand, G. A.: 259
Forrest, D. V.: 149
Fortna, R. O.: 61
Foster, G. R.: 215
Fowler, H. M.: *rev,* 5:322
Fox, L. J.: 167
Foxworth, C. L.: 290
Francis, R. L.: 123
Frank, A. C.: 240, 306
Frary, R. B.: 217
Friedman, S. M.: 150
Fukuda, N. K.: 186, 210, 236–7, 305
Gagni, A. O.: 190
Gazda, G. M.: 147, 263
Gelatt, H. B.: 164
Gentry, J.: 281
George, W. E.: 216
Ginther, M. L.: 191
Goedicke, R.: 282
Goldman, B. A.: 62
Goodstein, L. D.: 51
Goolsby, T. M.: 168, 217
Graham, W. R.: 201
Grant, D. L.: 143, 241
Greco, G. F.: 169
Green, J. L.: 242
Green, R. F.: *rev,* 6:452
Gremillion, B. J.: 6
Griffin, W. M.: 101
Grimsley, G.: 124
Gross, A. T.: 102
Gross, N.: 151
Guilliams, C. I.: 152
Gulutsan, M.: 255
Gustafson, M. C.: 42
Haakonsen, H. O.: 218
Halcrow, J. H.: 291
Hall, B. W.: 139
Hall, E.: 114, 267
Hall, L. T.: 219, 307
Hardesty, D. L.: 192
Harding, W. T.: 273
Hare, R. D.: 103
Harris, Y. Y.: 277
Harvey, E. D.: 220
Haugen, E. S.: 104

Hayes, E. M.: 221
Heaton, J. M.: 308
Hedley, C. N.: 193-4
Hernandez, D.: 212-3
Hicks, J. M.: 243
Hilliard, A. G.: 87
Hills, J. R.: 195, 244
Hilton, T. L.: 170, 313
Hinrichs, J. R.: 222
Holtby, V. J.: 125
Hood, A. B.: 88
Hopkins, K. D.: 138, 278
Hornaday, J. A.: 57
Huff, B.: 276
Hughes, D. L.: 264
Husemoller, K. E.: 223
Hutchins, B. E.: 196
Ingram, J. A.: 171
Irvine, S. H.: 224
Ivanoff, J. M.: 36
Johnson, A. P.: 55
Johnson, E. L.: 50
Jones, A. L.: 24, 29
Jones, W. S.: 192
Juola, A. E.: 30
Kaloger, J. H.: 292
Katz, S. S.: 265
Kaya, E.: *exc*, 7:347
Kennedy, P. E.: 12, 43
Khan, S. B.: 197, 245
Kilpatrick, A. R.: 126
Kimball, W. H.: 269
Kimbell, F. T.: 31
Kimbles, S. L.: 293
Kirby, B. J.: 309
Kirk, B. A.: 51, 240, 253-4
Klugh, H. E.: 18
Kogan, N.: 140
Kooker, E. W.: 225
Koopman, P. R.: *exc*, 7:347
Kranzler, G. D.: 246
Kropp, R. P.: 40, 74
Lasco, R. A.: 217
Leard, J. L.: 153
Lease, G. C.: 19
Leep, A. G.: 127
Lescarbeau, W. J.: 310
Leutenegger, R. R.: 128
Lewis, J. W.: 52-3
Libby, W. L.: 247
Lieberman, L. R.: 117
Liggitt, W. A.: 63
Lohnes, P. R.: 172
Long, J. M.: 32, 105
Love, B.: 289
Lucier, O.: 44
Lundquist, R. M.: 270
Lundsteen, S. W.: 154
Lunn, M. S.: 75
Lyon, J. T.: 155
Lyons, R. A.: 226
Macchia, W.: 311
McCormick, J. H.: 106
McGee, J. E.: 198
McGuire, D.: 173
McIntire, P. H.: 172
McKie, D.: *exc*, 7:347
MacNeil, R. L.: 174
McQuitty, L. L.: 259
Madaus, G. F.: 175
Malnig, L. R.: 73
Mann, M. J.: 45
Manson, G. G.: 261
Manuel, H. T.: 3
Martin, B. E.: 162
Massad, C. E.: 176
Mayer, R. W.: 13
Means, H. R.: 156
Michael, W. B.: 154
Milam, O. H.: 33
Miller, B. B.: 248
Miller, R. H.: 199, 283
Miller, W.: 212-3
Miller, W. E.: 157
Moan, C. E.: 251
More, A.: 284
Morper, J.: 158
Morris, R. O.: 129
Motley, H. C.: 227
Mott, D. D.: 20
Moyel, I. S.: 83
Mueller, T. H.: 128
Munday, L.: 130, 200
Myers, A. E.: 170
Nash, J. M.: 249

Nicholson, J.: 257
North, R. D.: 1, 4
Orr, D. B.: 201
Osborn, L. R.: 64
O'Shaughnessy, M. M.: 34
Otte, H. W.: 131
Owen, C.: 79
Pace, J. L.: 250
Pandey, R. E.: 312
Parsley, J. F.: 294
Patterson, B.: 177
Paxson, R. C.: 116
Pearson, M. A.: 54, 65
Pedersen, D. M.: 271
Pemberton, W. A.: 66
Perry, J. O.: 80
Phelps, A. M.: 274
Phillips, R. M.: 228
Pipher, J. A.: 35
Pohlmann, V. C.: 132
Poindexter, C. C.: 295
Poland, H. V.: 76
Pratt, M.: 202
Prediger, D. J.: 133
Rardin, D. R.: 251
Reams, J. W.: 89
Reid, J. W.: 55
Reilly, H. E.: 134
Renzaglia, G. A.: 59
Rice, M. L.: 146
Riechard, D. E.: 252
Ritchie, R. W.: 107
Roberts, J. P.: 296
Ronan, R. J.: 229
Rosenfeld, M.: 313
Rossmann, J. E.: 253-4
Rudd, J. P.: 56
Russell, W. P.: 297
Ryan, B.: 300
Sanborn, M. P.: 302
Sarason, I. G.: 67
Saruk, A.: 255
Schreck, J. F.: 298
Schusler, M. M.: 159
Seymour, W. R.: 304
Sherman, D. M.: 58
Sherman, V. M. S. R.: 108
Sisson, E. R.: 314
Slayton, W. G.: 135
Smith, D. E.: 5
Smith, R. G.: 136
Smith, W. N.: 68
Sober, K. A.: 110
Sodhi, S.: 299
Sommerfeld, R. E.: 69
Sours, C. F. R.: 230
Stanley, J. C.: 195, 244; *rev*, 5:322
Steinberg, D.: 60
Stephenson, R. S.: 315
Stewart, L. H.: 109, 277
Stierhem, R. J.: 272
Stivers, R. E.: 160
Stoker, H. W.: 74
Stone, D. B.: 137
Summers, G. W.: 124
Swan, R. J.: 138
Swanson, J. R.: 161
Taylor, A. L.: 316
Tempero, H. E.: 36
Tenopyr, M. L.: 178-9
Terwilliger, J. S.: 70
Thacker, J. H.: 180
Thomas, D. C.: 163, 184
Tisdale, J. C.: 317
Tracy, N. H.: 69
Traxler, A. E.: 2, 37
Treffinger, D. J.: 239
Tseng, M.: 203
Tully, G. E.: 139, 161
Tyler, L. E.: 120
Van Derslice, J. F.: 204
Vick, M. C.: 57
Vincent, J.: 7
Wagman, M.: 318
Wagner, E. E.: 110
Waiches, V. C.: 46
Wallach, M. A.: 140
Ward, G.: 33
Ward, R.: 181, 188
Webb, H. Q.: 319
Webb, J. B.: 256
Weber, L. A.: 111, 119
Weeks, J. S.: 21
Weisgerber, C. A.: 231

Wellck, A. A.: 71
Wershow, I. R.: 128
White, A. J.: 22
Williams, C. L.: 8
Williams, R. A.: 90
Williamson, M. L.: 278

Willis, C. G.: 257
Wilson, A. V.: 205
Wright, J. H.: 243
Zabel, R. L.: 38
Zook, H. A.: 279
Zuckowsky, L. M.: 47

[362]
*Cotswold Junior Ability Tests. Ages 8.5-9.5, 9.5-10.5; 1949-69; 2 levels; tests A, B, C, and E are out of print; C. M. Fleming; Robert Gibson & Sons, Glasgow, Ltd. [Scotland]. *

a) JUNIOR MENTAL ABILITY D. Ages 8.5-9.5; 1967-69, c1957.

b) JUNIOR MENTAL ABILITY F. Ages 9.5-10.5; 1967-69, c1961.

For additional information concerning earlier forms, see 5:323.

[363]
*Cotswold Measurement of Ability. Ages 10-12; 1947-70; earlier forms entitled *Cotswold Measurement of Mental Ability* and *Cotswold Mental Ability Test*; C. M. Fleming; Robert Gibson & Sons, Glasgow, Ltd. [Scotland]. *

For additional information and a review by A. W. Heim of earlier forms, see 5:324.

REFERENCES THROUGH 1971
1. JONES, W. R., AND STEWART, W. A. C. "Bilingualism and Verbal Intelligence." *Brit J Psychol* (Stat Sect) 4:3-8 Mr '51. * (*PA* 25:7930)

CUMULATIVE NAME INDEX
Heim, A. W.: *rev*, 5:324   Stewart, W. A. C.: 1
Jones, W. R.: 1

[364]
*Culture Fair Intelligence Test. Ages 4-8 and mentally retarded adults, 8-14 and average adults, 13-16 and superior adults or grades 9-16 and superior adults; 1933-73; CFIT; formerly called *Culture Free Intelligence Test*; 2 editions; Raymond B. Cattell and A. K. S. Cattell (Scales 2 and 3).

a) IPAT CULTURE FAIR INTELLIGENCE TEST. 1933-73; formerly called *IPAT Culture Free Intelligence Test*; test booklet titles are *Test of g: Culture Fair* or *Test of g: Culture Free*; 3 levels; Institute for Personality and Ability Testing. *

1) *Scale 1*. Ages 4-8 and mentally retarded adults; 1933-69; test copyrighted 1950 identical with *Cattell Intelligence Tests, Scale 0: Dartington Scale* (see 354*a*) copyrighted 1933.

2) *Scale 2*. Ages 8-14 and average adults; 1949-73.

3) *Scale 3*. Ages 13-16 and superior adults; 1950-73; Form A copyrighted 1963 identical with Form A copyrighted 1959 except for slight change in scale of some drawings.

b) CATTELL CULTURE FAIR INTELLIGENCE TEST. 1960-61; 2 levels; Bobbs-Merrill Co., Inc. *

1) *Scale 2*. Ages 8-14 and average adults; 1960; test copyrighted 1960 identical with Forms A (1957) and B (1960) of Scale 2 of *IPAT Culture Fair Intelligence Test* presented in a single test booklet.

2) *Scale 3*. Grades 9-16 and superior adults; 1961; test copyrighted 1961 identical with Forms A (1959) and B (1961) of Scale 3 of *IPAT Culture Fair Intelligence Test* presented in a single test booklet.

For additional information and reviews by John E. Milholland and Abraham J. Tannenbaum, see 6:453 (15 references); for a review by I. Macfarlane Smith of *a*, see 5:343 (11 references); for reviews by Raleigh M. Drake and Gladys C. Schwesinger, see 4:300 (2 references).

REFERENCES THROUGH 1971
1-2. See 4:300.
3-13. See 5:343.

14-28. See 6:453.
29. ELLIS, EARNEST. *A Comparison of the Wechsler Intelligence Scale for Children and the I.P.A.T. Culture Free Intelligence Test.* Master's thesis, San Francisco State College (San Francisco, Calif.), 1953.
30. ROGERS, LORENE L., AND PELTON, RICHARD B. "Effect of Glutamine on IQ Scores of Mentally Deficient Children." *Tex Rep Biol & Med* 15:84-90 sp '57. * (PA 31:8272)
31. RODD, WILLIAM G. "The Role of a 'Culture Free' Intelligence Test." *J Ed* (Hong Kong) 20:10-7 '62. *
32. MOORE, RICHARD V. *Comparative Influences of Material Incentives on Cattell Culture-Free Intelligence Scores for Children From Different Socio-economic Groups.* Master's thesis, Kent State University (Kent, Ohio), 1963.
33. POLLARD, ALICE G. *A Comparison of the Performance of a Group of Intellectually Retarded Children on Three Group Tests of Intelligence.* Master's thesis, Catholic University of America (Washington, D.C.), 1963.
34. DOMINO, GEORGE. "Comparison of the D48, Cattell Culture Fair, and Army Beta Tests in a Sample of College Males." *J Consult Psychol* 28:468-9 O '64. * (PA 39:5052)
35. FARRANT, ROLAND H. "The Intellective Abilities of Deaf and Hearing Children Compared by Factor Analyses." *Am Ann Deaf* 109:306-25 My '64. * (PA 39:2442)
36. KEARNEY, GEORGE E. "Comment on 'The Use of a Non-Verbal Test of Intelligence in the Trust Territory of the Pacific' by Jordheim and Olsen." *Am Anthrop* 66:1395-6 D '64. *
37. KING, A. RICHARD. "Comments on Jordheim and Olsen's Use of a Non-Verbal Test of Intelligence in the Pacific Islands Trust Territory." Letter. *Am Anthrop* 66:640-4 Je '64. *
38. NADEAU, CORINNE. *A Comparison of the Performance of a Group of Intellectually Normal Children on Three Group Tests of Intelligence.* Master's thesis, Catholic University of America (Washington, D.C.), 1964.
39. GERSTEIN, ALVIN I. "Development of a Selection Program for Nursing Candidates." *Nursing Res* 14:254-7 su '65. *
40. KIDD, ALINE H., AND RIVOIRE, JEANNE L. "The Culture-Fair Aspects of the Development of Spatial Perception." *J Genetic Psychol* 106:101-11 Mr '65. * (PA 39:12291)
41. RAO, SHARADAMBA. "Use of Culture Free Intelligence Tests in India." *Indian J Psychol* 40:61-5 Je '65. * (PA 40:9359)
42. RAO, SHARADAMBA. "A Useful Intelligence Test for Senior High School and College Students in India." *Indian J Psychol* 40:19-26 Mr '65. * (PA 40:5453)
43. STEWART, HORACE F., JR., AND KEELER, CLYDE E. "A Comparison of the Intelligence and Personality of Moon-Child Albino and Control Cuna Indians." *J Genetic Psychol* 106:319-24 Je '65. * (PA 39:14888)
44. CATTELL, R. B.; SEALY, A. P.; AND SWENEY, A. B. "What Can Personality and Motivation Source Trait Measurements Add to the Prediction of School Achievement?" *Brit J Ed Psychol* 36:280-95 N '66. * (PA 41:804)
45. HORN, JOHN L., AND CATTELL, RAYMOND B. "Age Differences in Primary Mental Ability Factors." *J Gerontol* 21:210-20 Ap '66. *
46. MACARTHUR, R. S., AND MOSYCHUK, H. "Lower and Upper Socio-economic Group Contrasts in Long-Term Predictability of Grade Nine Achievement." *J Ed Meas* 3:167-8 su '66. *
47. TATHAM, CLIFFORD B., AND DOLE, ARTHUR A. "Academic Success of Foreign Undergraduates." *J Col Stud Personnel* 7:167-71 My '66. *
48. AINSWORTH, MARJORIE E. "The Relationship Between Motivation, Personality, Intelligence and School Attainment in a Secondary Modern School." *Brit J Ed Psychol* 37:135-7 F '67. * Abstract of master's thesis, University of Manchester (Manchester, England), 1966.
49. CATE, CLARENCE C. "Test Behavior of ESL Students." *Calif J Ed Res* 18:184-7 S '67. * (PA 42:4480)
50. HORN, JOHN L., AND CATTELL, RAYMOND B. "Age Differences in Fluid and Crystallized Intelligence." *Acta Psychologica* (Netherlands) 26(2):107-29 '67. * (PA 41:10446)
51. HUMPHREYS, LLOYD G. "Critique of Cattell's 'Theory of Fluid and Crystallized Intelligence: A Critical Experiment.'" *J Ed Psychol* 58:129-36 Je '67. * (PA 41:10447)
52. LARSON, STANFORD S. *A Comparison of Two Non-Verbal Intelligence Tests as Predictors of Academic Success of Navajo Students.* Master's thesis, Utah State University (Logan, Utah), 1967.
52a. MOGOR, ALBERT GARY. *The Concurrent Validity of Scale 2, Cattell Culture Fair Test of Intelligence for Three Levels of Socioeconomic Status.* Master's thesis, New Mexico State University (University Park, N.M.), 1967.
53. ALZOBAIE, ABDUL JALIL; METFESSEL, NEWTON S.; AND MICHAEL, WILLIAM B. "Alternative Approaches to Assessing the Intellectual Abilities of Youth From a Culture of Poverty." *Ed & Psychol Meas* 28:449-55 su '68. * (PA 42:19264)
54. ARNOLD, RICHARD D. "Reliability Coefficients of Certain Tests Used in the San Antonio Language Research Project." Abstract. *AERA Paper Abstr* 1968:92 '68. *
55. AX, ALBERT F., AND BAMFORD, JACQUELINE L. "Validation of a Psychophysiological Test of Aptitude for Learning Social Motives." *Psychophysiol* 5:16-32 S '68. * (PA 43:3943)
56. BECICA, BOZA. *A Comparison of Selected Characteristics of Students With Higher Grades in Their Foreign Language Courses Than in Their Nonlanguage Courses.* Doctor's thesis, University of Texas (Austin, Tex.), 1968. (DA 29:4315A)
57. CATTELL, RAYMOND B., AND BUTCHER, H. J. *The Prediction of Achievement and Creativity,* pp. 161-79, passim. Indianapolis, Ind.: Bobbs-Merrill Co., Inc., 1968. Pp. xiv, 386. *
58. CATTELL, RAYMOND BERNARD. "Are I.Q. Tests Intelligent?" *Psychol Today* 1:56-62 Mr '68. *
59. DOMINO, GEORGE. "Culture-Free Tests and the Academic Achievement of Foreign Students." Abstract. *J Consult & Clin Psychol* 32:102 F '68. * (PA 42:7843)
60. GADDES, W. H.; MCKENZIE, AUDREY; AND BARNSLEY, ROGER. "Psychometric Intelligence and Spatial Imagery in Two Northwest Indian and Two White Groups of Children." *J Social Psychol* 75:35-42 Je '68. * (PA 42:13575)
61. HARRIS, A. J., AND LOVINGER, R. J. "Longitudinal Measures of the Intelligence of Disadvantaged Negro Adolescents." *Sch R* 76:60-6 Mr '68. * (PA 43:3138)
62. MACARTHUR, R. S. "Assessing Intellectual Potential of Native Canadian Pupils: A Summary." *Alberta J Ed Res* (Canada) 14:115-22 Je '68. * (PA 44:4170)
63. MACARTHUR, RUSSELL. "Some Differential Abilities of Northern Canadian Native Youth." *Int J Psychol* (France) 3(1):43-50 '68. * (PA 42:15325)
64. PELOSI, JOHN WILLIAM. *A Study of the Effects of Examiner Race, Sex, and Style on Test Responses of Negro Examinees.* Doctor's thesis, Syracuse University (Syracuse, N.Y.), 1968. (DA 29:4105A)
65. SCHLICHT, WILLIAM J., JR.; ANDERSON, DERWYN L.; HELIN, WILLIAM C.; HIPPE, DOUGLAS L.; LISTIAK, RICHARD L.; MOSER, RICHARD J.; AND WALKER, JAMES L. "Creativity and Intelligence: Further Findings." *J Clin Psychol* 24:458 O '68. * (PA 43:4025)
66. WILLARD, LOUISA A. "A Comparison of Culture Fair Test Scores With Group and Individual Intelligence Test Scores of Disadvantaged Negro Children." *J Learn Dis* 1:584-9 O '68. * (PA 45:3968)
67. ARNOLD, RICHARD D. "Reliability of Test Scores for the Young 'Bilingual' Disadvantaged." *Read Teach* 22(4):341-5 Ja '69. *
68. KANDERIAN, SUAD SIROP. *Study of the Relationship Between School Achievement and Measures of Intelligence and Creativity for Students in Iraq.* Doctor's thesis, University of Southern California (Los Angeles, Calif.), 1969. (DAI 31:644A)
69. MACARTHUR, RUSSELL S. "Some Cognitive Abilities of Eskimo, White, and Indian-Métis Pupils Aged 9 to 12 Years." *Can J Behav Sci* 1(1):50-9 Ja '69. * (PA 44:12319)
70. WIGGINS, NANCY; HOFFMAN, PAUL J.; AND TABER, THOMAS. "Types of Judges and Cue Utilization in Judgments of Intelligence." *J Pers & Social Psychol* 12(1):52-9 My '69. * (PA 43:11266)
71. ISMAIL, A. H., AND KIRKENDALL, D. R. "Relationship Among Three Domains of Development," pp. 451-60. In *Contemporary Psychology of Sport.* Proceedings of the Second International Congress of Sport Psychology, Washington, D.C., 1968. Chicago, Ill.: Athletic Institute, 1970. Pp. xix, 878. *
72. KAKKAR, S. B. "Popularity, Intelligence, Economic Status and Academic Achievement." *Indian J Psychol* 45(3):233-7 S '70. *
73. KALEHOFF, DOROTHY W. *Selected Personal Characteristics of the Adult Basic Education Student in Mississippi.* Doctor's thesis, Mississippi State University (State College, Miss.), 1970. (DAI 31:5109A)
74. KNIGHT, DAVID, AND ALCORN, JOHN D. "Comparisons of the Performance of Educationally Disadvantaged Adults and Elementary Children on Selected Measures of Reading Performance." *South J Ed Res* 4(4):262-72 O '70. *
75. SINGH, R. N. "A Study of the Scores on Cattell's Culture Fair Test of Intelligence (Scale 2) in an Indian Background: A Special Reference to Socio-Economic Variable." Doctor's thesis abstract. *Indian Psychol R* 7(1):74-6 Jl '70. *
76. VROMAN, CLYDE, AND WILCOX, LEE. "Research on A.I.D. Sponsored Foreign Students." *Col & Univ* 45(4):717-23 su '70. *
77. ADCOCK, C. J., AND WEBBERLEY, M. "Primary Mental Abilities." *J General Psychol* 84(2):229-43 Ap '71. * (PA 46:4979)
78. BARTON, K.; DIELMAN, T. E.; AND CATTELL, R. B. "The Prediction of School Grades From Personality and IQ Measures." *Personality* 2(4):325-33 w '71. * (PA 48:7878)
79. COWDEN, JAMES E.; PETERSON, WILLIAM M.; AND PACHT, ASHER R. "The Validation of a Brief Screening Test for Verbal Intelligence at Several Correctional Institutions in Wisconsin." *J Clin Psychol* 27(2):216-8 Ap '71. * (PA 46:7125)
80. DIELMAN, T. E.; BARTON, K.; AND CATTELL, R. B. "The Prediction of Junior High School Achievement From Objective Motivation Tests." *Personality* 2(4):279-87 w '71. * (PA 48:7881)
81. GOODWIN, NANCY-LEE. *The Prediction of Artistic Performance From Cognitive and Non-Cognitive Measures.* Doctor's thesis, University of Illinois (Urbana, Ill.), 1971. (DAI 32:4419A)

82. GREENBERG, BERNARD L., AND GREENBERG, SALLY H. "The Measurement of College Potential in the Hearing Handicapped." *Am Ann Deaf* 116(3):372-81 Je '71. * (*PA* 47:1410)
83. KNIGHT, DAVID, AND ALCORN, JOHN D. "Comparisons of the Performance of Educationally Disadvantaged Adults and Elementary Children on Selected Measures of Reading Performance." *Yearb Nat Read Conf* 19(2):113-7 '71. *
84. LANDRY, RICHARD G. "The Factorial Orthogonality of the Torrance Tests of Creative Thinking and the Culture-Fair Intelligence Tests." *Col Ed Rec Univ N Dak* 57(2):20-6 N '71. *
85. POWELL, RICHARD R., AND POHNDORF, RICHARD H. "Comparison of Adult Exercisers and Nonexercisers on Fluid Intelligence and Selected Physiological Variables." *Res Q* 42(1):70-7 Mr '71. * (*PA* 46:6635)
86. SINGH, AMIR, AND HUNDAL, P. S. "Age Differences in Fluid and Crystallized Intelligence." *Indian J Psychol* 46(1):85-94 Mr '71. *
87. WILLIAMS, PATSY RUTH. *Comparison of the Cattell Culture Fair Test With the California Mental Maturity Test.* Master's thesis, Southern Methodist University (Dallas, Tex.), 1971.
88. ZEDECK, SHELDON. "Identification of Moderator Variables by Discriminant Analysis in a Multipredictable Group Validation Model." *J Appl Psychol* 55(4):364-71 Ag '71. * (*PA* 47:1947)

CUMULATIVE NAME INDEX

Adcock, C. J.: 77
Ainsworth, M. E.: 48
Alcorn, J. D.: 74, 83
Alvi, S. A.: 25
Alzobaie, A. J.: 53
Anastasi, A.: 6
Anderson, D. L.: 65
Arnold, R. D.: 54, 67
Attwell, A. A.: 24
Ax, A. F.: 55
Bailey, L. L.: 10
Bamford, J. L.: 55
Barnsley, R.: 60
Barratt, E. S.: 21
Barton, K.: 78, 80
Becica, B.: 56
Bensberg, G. J.: 7
Buss, F. H.: 15
Butcher, H. J.: 57
Cate, C. C.: 49
Cattell, R. B.: 2, 8, 26, 44-5, 50, 57-8, 78, 80
Chambers, J. A.: 16
Clark, M.: 21
Cooper, J. G.: 13, 22
Cordova, F. A.: 4, 6
Cowden, J. E.: 79
Dielman, T. E.: 78, 80
Dingman, H. F.: 24
Dole, A. A.: 47
Domino, G.: 34, 59
Drake, R. M.: *rev,* 4:300
Elley, W. B.: 28
Ellis, E.: 29
Farrant, R. H.: 20, 35
Fowler, W. L.: 11-2
Gaddes, W. H.: 60
Gerstein, A. I.: 39
Gibson, Q. H.: 3
Goodwin, N. L.: 81
Greenberg, B. L.: 82
Greenberg, S. H.: 82
Harris, A. J.: 61
Helin, W. C.: 65
Hippe, D. L.: 65
Hoffman, P. J.: 70
Horn, J. L.: 45, 50
Humphreys, L. G.: 51
Hundal, P. S.: 86
Ismail, A. H.: 71
Jordheim, G. D.: 27
Kakkar, S. B.: 72
Kalehoff, D. W.: 73
Kanderian, S. S.: 68
Kearney, G. E.: 36
Keehn, J. D.: 9
Keeler, C. E.: 43
Kidd, A. H.: 18, 23, 40
King, A. R.: 37
Kirkendall, D. R.: 71
Knapp, R. R.: 19
Knight, D.: 74, 83
Landry, R. G.: 84
Larson, S. S.: 52
Lipton, J.: 21
Listiak, R. L.: 65
Lovinger, R. J.: 61
MacArthur, R.: 63
MacArthur, R. S.: 28, 46, 62, 69
McKenzie, A.: 60
Marquart, D. I.: 10
Metfessel, N. S.: 53
Meyers, E.: 24
Michael, W. B.: 53
Milholland, J. E.: *rev,* 6:453
Mogor, A. G.: 52a
Moore, R. V.: 32
Moser, R. J.: 65
Mosychuk, H.: 46
Nadeau, C.: 38
Olsen, I. A.: 27
Orpet, R. E.: 24
Pacht, A. R.: 79
Pelosi, J. W.: 64
Pelton, R. B.: 30
Peterson, W. M.: 79
Pierce-Jones, J.: 1
Pohndorf, R. H.: 85
Pollard, A. G.: 33
Powell, R. R.: 85
Prothro, E. T.: 9
Rao, S.: 41-2
Rivoire, J. L.: 40
Rodd, W. G.: 17, 31
Rogers, L. L.: 30
Schlicht, W. J.: 65
Schwartz, I. H.: 5
Schwesinger, G. C.: *rev,* 4:300
Sealy, A. P.: 44
Singh, A.: 86
Singh, R. N.: 75
Sloan, W.: 7
Smith, I. M.: *rev,* 5:343
Stewart, H. F.: 43
Sweney, A. B.: 44
Taber, T.: 70
Tannenbaum, A. J.: *rev,* 6:453
Tatham, C. B.: 47
Tyler, F. T.: 1
Vroman, C.: 76
Walker, J. L.: 65
Webberley, M.: 77
Wiggins, N.: 70
Wilcox, L.: 76
Willard, L. A.: 66
Williams, P. R.: 87
Xydias, N.: 14
Zedeck, S.: 88

[365-6]

The D48 Test. Grades 5 and over; 1963, c1961; intelligence; translation of the French edition published in 1948; for research use only; translation and American manual by John D. Black; Consulting Psychologists Press, Inc. *

For additional information and reviews by Paul C. Davis and S. S. Dunn, see 6:454 (3 references).

REFERENCES THROUGH 1971

1-3. See 6:454.
4. DOMINO, GEORGE. "Comparison of the D48, Cattell Culture Fair, and Army Beta Tests in a Sample of College Males." *J Consult Psychol* 28:468-9 O '64. * (*PA* 39:5052)
5. BOYD, MAYNARD E. *Characteristics of the D48 Test When Used at the College Level.* Master's thesis, Marshall University (Huntington, W.Va.), 1966.
6. CANTWELL, ZITA M. "Relationships Between Scores on the Standard Progressive Matrices (1938) and on the D.48 Test of Non-Verbal Intelligence and 3 Measures of Academic Achievement." *J Exp Ed* 34:28-31 su '66. * (*PA* 40:11152)
7. WELSH, GEORGE S. "Comparison of D-48, Terman CMT, and Art Scale Scores of Gifted Adolescents." Abstract. *J Consult Psychol* 30:88 F '66. * (*PA* 40:4105)
8. BOYD, MAYNARD E., AND WARD, GEORGE, II. "Validities of the D-48 Test for Use With College Students." *Ed & Psychol Meas* 27:1137-8 w '67. * (*PA* 42:8933)
9. RAFI, A. ABI. "The Progressive Matrices (1938) and the Dominoes (D48) Tests: A Cross-Cultural Study." *Brit J Ed Psychol* 37:117-9 F '67. *
10. WELSH, GEORGE S. "Verbal Interests and Intelligence: Comparison of Strong VIB, Terman CMT, and D-48 Scores of Gifted Adolescents." *Ed & Psychol Meas* 27:349-52 su '67. * (*PA* 41:13633)
11. DOMINO, GEORGE. "Culture-Free Tests and the Academic Achievement of Foreign Students." Abstract. *J Consult & Clin Psychol* 32:102 F '68. * (*PA* 42:7843)
12. DOMINO, GEORGE. "A Non-Verbal Measure of Intelligence for Totally Blind Adults." *New Outl Blind* 62:247-52 O '68. *
13. KARNES, LUCIA ROONEY. *The Comparison of Eighth-Grade Reading and Nonreading Boys on the Lorge-Thorndike Tests, Wechsler Intelligence Scale for Children, the D48 Test, and the Welsh Figure Preference Test, GW Scale.* Doctor's thesis, University of North Carolina (Chapel Hill, N.C.), 1968. (*DAI* 30:585A)
14. WELSH, GEORGE S. *Gifted Adolescents: A Handbook of Test Results.* Greensboro, N.C.: Prediction Press, June 1969. Pp. viii, 89. *
15. CHISSOM, BRAD S., AND LIGHTSEY, RALPH. "A Comparison of the D-48 Test and the Otis Quick Score for High School Dropouts." *Ed & Psychol Meas* 31(2):525-7 su '71. *
16. WELSH, GEORGE S. "Vocational Interests and Intelligence in Gifted Adolescents." *Ed & Psychol Meas* 31(1):155-64 sp '71. * (*PA* 46:10645)

CUMULATIVE NAME INDEX

Boyd, M. E.: 5, 8
Cantwell, Z. M.: 6
Chissom, B. S.: 15
Cronholm, B.: 2
Davis, P. C.: *rev,* 6:454
Domino, G.: 3-4, 11-2
Dunn, S. S.: *rev,* 6:454
Gough, H. G.: 3
Karnes, L. R.: 13
Keehn, J. D.: 1
Lightsey, R.: 15
Prothro, E. T.: 1
Rafi, A. A.: 9
Schalling, D.: 2
Ward, G.: 8
Welsh, G. S.: 7, 10, 14, 16

[367]

Deeside Non-Verbal Reasoning Test: English-Welsh Bilingual Version. Ages 10-12; 1961-63; distribution restricted to directors of education; W. G. Emmett; George G. Harrap & Co. Ltd. [England]. *

For additional information, see 6:455.

[368]

Deeside Picture Puzzles. Ages 6.5-8.5; 1956-58; W. G. Emmett; George G. Harrap & Co. Ltd. [England]. *

For additional information and reviews by Charlotte E. K. Banks and M. L. Kellmer Pringle, see 5:327.

[369]

Dennis Test of Scholastic Aptitude. Grades 4-8, 5-8; DTSA; 1961-63; William H. Dennis; the Author. *

For additional information, see 7:348.

[370]

Detroit General Intelligence Examination. Grades 7-12; 1938-54; consists of 8 of the 10 subtests used to get an intelligence score in the *Detroit General Apti-*

tudes Examination; 1954 test identical with subtests copyrighted 1938; Harry J. Baker and Paul H. Voelker; Bobbs-Merrill Co., Inc. *

For additional information, see 5:328.

[371]

Doppelt Mathematical Reasoning Test. Grades 16–17 and employees; 1954–68; DMRT; distribution restricted and test administered at specified licensed university centers; Jerome E. Doppelt; Psychological Corporation. *

For additional information, see 7:349 (2 references); for a review by W. V. Clemans, see 6:456 (2 references).

REFERENCES THROUGH 1971

1–2. See 6:456.
3–4. See 7:349.

CUMULATIVE NAME INDEX

Carleton, F. O.: 4
Clark, F. E.: 1
Clemans, W. V.: *rev,* 6:456
Hardesty, D. L.: 3
Jones, W. S.: 3
Roemmich, H.: 2
Schwartz, M. M.: 1

[372]

Draw-A-Man Test for Indian Children. Ages 6–10; 1956–66; adaptation of *Goodenough Intelligence Test;* Pramila Phatak; distributed by Anand Agencies [India]. *

For additional information and an excerpted review by M. A. Faroqi, see 7:350 (4 references).

REFERENCES THROUGH 1971

1–4. See 7:350.
5. MAJUMDAR, S. K. "Relationship Between Old (1956) and New (1966) Norms for Goodenough's Draw-a-Man Test (Pramila Phatak's Indian Adaptation) on Normal and Retarded Children." *Indian Ed R* 4(2):97–102 Jl '69. *

CUMULATIVE NAME INDEX

Faroqi, M. A.: *exc,* 7:350
Majumdar, S. K.: 5
Misra, A. N.: 4
Phatak, P.: 1–3

[373]

The Essential Intelligence Test. Ages 8–12; 1940–52; manual title is *Essential Junior Intelligence Test;* Fred J. Schonell and R. H. Adams; Oliver & Boyd [Scotland]. *

For additional information and a review by R. Winterbourn, see 5:333; for a review by F. W. Warburton, see 4:290.

REFERENCES THROUGH 1971

1. PEEL, E. A., AND GRAHAM, D. "Differentiation of Ability in Primary School Children." *Durham Res R* (England) 1(2):40–8 S '51. *
2. PEEL, E. A., AND GRAHAM, D. "Differentiation of Ability in Primary School Children—II." *Durham Res R* (England) 1(3):31–4 S '52. * (*PA* 27:5157)
3. MADDOX, H. "Mental Age Scales." *Brit J Ed Psychol* 29:72–3 F '59. * (*PA* 34:2731)
4. NISBET, J. D., AND ILLESLEY, R. "The Influence of Early Puberty on Test Performance at Age Eleven." *Brit J Ed Psychol* 33:169–76 Je '63. * (*PA* 38:4096)
5. RILEY, CONAL STUART. "The Relationship Between Reading Ability and Verbal Intelligence Test Performance." Abstract. *Brit J Ed Psychol* 36:117 F '66. * (*PA* 40:7056, title only)
6. HOROBIN, GORDON; OLDMAN, DAVID; AND BYTHEWAY, BILL. "The Social Differentiation of Ability." *Sociology* 1:113–29 My '67. *
7. NISBET, J. D., AND ENTWISTLE, N. J. "Intelligence and Family Size, 1949–1965." *Brit J Ed Psychol* 37:188–93 Je '67. * (*PA* 41:15274)

CUMULATIVE NAME INDEX

Bytheway, B.: 6
Entwistle, N. J.: 7
Graham, D.: 1–2
Horobin, G.: 6
Illesley, R.: 4
Maddox, H.: 3
Nisbet, J. D.: 4, 7
Oldman, D.: 6
Peel, E. A.: 1–2
Riley, C. S.: 5
Warburton, F. W.: *rev,* 4:290
Winterbourn, R.: *rev,* 5:333

Detroit General Intelligence Examination

[374]

Executive Employment Review. Applicants for executive level positions; 1964–70; revision of *General Interest Review;* formerly called *General Employment Review;* 4 scores: vocabulary, mathematics, perception-general knowledge, total; no manual; L & L Associates. *

For additional information, see 7:992c.

[375]

Figure Reasoning Test: A Non-Verbal Intelligence Test, Second Edition. Ages 10 and over; 1949–62; 1962 test identical with test copyrighted 1949 except for format; John C. Daniels; Crosby Lockwood Staples [England]. *

For additional information and a review by A. W. Heim, see 6:457; for reviews by E. J. G. Bradford and James Maxwell and an excerpted review, see 4:291 (1 reference).

REFERENCES THROUGH 1971

1. See 4:291.
2. MESSER, MICHAEL E., AND ALLEN, ROBERT M. "Verbal Recognition and Non-Verbal Reasoning of Retardates." *Percept & Motor Skills* 28(1):334 F '69. * (*PA* 43:11764)

CUMULATIVE NAME INDEX

Allen, R. M.: 2
Bradford, E. J. G.: *rev,* 4:291
Daniels, J. C.: 1
Heim, A. W.: *rev,* 6:457
Maxwell, J.: *rev,* 4:291
Messer, M. E.: 2

[376-7]

*****Fundamental Achievement Series.** Semiliterate job applicants and employees; 1968–70, c1965–70; FAS; 3 scores: numerical, verbal, total; 2 tests; distribution of Form A restricted to personnel departments; George K. Bennett and Jerome E. Doppelt; Psychological Corporation. *

a) NUMERICAL.
b) VERBAL.

For additional information, a review by Norman Frederiksen, and an excerpted review by Lewis R. Aiken, Jr., see 7:978.

[378]

*****General Mental Ability Test: ETSA Test 1A.** Job applicants; 1960–72, c1957–66; manual and technical handbook by S. Trevor Hadley and George A. W. Stouffer, Jr.; test by Psychological Services Bureau; Educators'-Employers' Tests & Services Associates. *

For the complete battery entry, see 2106.

For reviews of the complete battery, see 6:1025 (2 reviews).

[379]

General Verbal Practice Tests G1–G3. Ages 10–11; 1954–61; to be given at least 3 weeks before administering a verbal intelligence test in order to equalize coaching effects; distribution restricted to directors of education; published for the National Foundation for Educational Research in England and Wales; Ginn & Co. Ltd. [England]. *

For additional information, see 6:458.

[380]

*****Gilliland Learning Potential Examination.** Ages 6 and over; 1966–71; GLPE; an intelligence test "for use with remedial readers and the culturally disadvantaged"; 1 to 4 scores: total score for all subjects, nonreading-noncultural, predicted comprehension, and visual memory for subjects with reading problems; some subtests may be omitted in grades 3 and over to obtain a quick score and in grades 3 and under to obtain a primary score; Hap Gilliland; Montana Reading Publications. *

For additional information and reviews by Albert J. Harris and Howard B. Lyman, see 7:351.

[381]
Goodenough-Harris Drawing Test. Ages 3–15; 1926–63; revision and extension of the *Goodenough Intelligence Test;* Florence L. Goodenough and Dale B. Harris; Harcourt Brace Jovanovich, Inc. *
For additional information, reviews by Anne Anastasi and James A. Dunn, and excerpted reviews by M. L. Kellmer Pringle, Marjorie P. Honzik, Carol Hunter, Adolph G. Woltmann, Marvin S. Kaplan, and Mary J. Rouse, see 7:352 (158 references); see also 6:460 (43 references) and 5:335 (34 references); for a review by Naomi Stewart of the original edition, see 4:292 (60 references).

REFERENCES THROUGH 1971
1–60. See 4:292.
61–94. See 5:335.
95–137. See 6:460.
138–295. See 7:352.
296. HECKMAN, SAMUEL B. Chap. 3, "A Comparative Study of Group Intelligence Tests Applicable to Children of Kindergarten Age," pp. 17–44. In *Contributions to Education, Vol 1.* Edited by J. Carleton Bell. Yonkers, N.Y.: World Book Co., 1924. Pp. ix, 364. *
297. CUNNINGHAM, BESS V. "Measurement of Intelligence by Drawings: A Review." *J Ed Psychol* 18:66–7 Ja '27. *
298. WAGONER, LOVISA C., AND ARMSTONG, EDNA M. "The Motor Control of Children as Involved in the Dressing Process." *J Genetic Psychol* 35:84–97 Mr '28. * (*PA* 2:3692)
299. PORTEUS, STANLEY D. Chap. 23, "Aboriginal Children's Intelligence," pp. 408–20. In his *The Psychology of a Primitive People: A Study of the Australian Aborigine.* New York: Longmans, Green & Co., 1931. Pp. xvi, 438. * (*PA* 6:1168, title only)
300. DAVENPORT, E. LEE. "The Intelligence Quotients of Mexican and Non-Mexican Siblings." *Sch & Soc* 36:304–6 S 3 '32. * (*PA* 7:232)
301. EELLS, WALTER CROSBY. "Mental Ability of the Native Races of Alaska." *J Appl Psychol* 17:417–38 Ag '33. * (*PA* 8:478)
302. SCHILLER, BELLE. "Verbal, Numerical and Spatial Abilities of Young Children." *Arch Psychol* 161:1–69 Mr '34. * (*PA* 8:3874)
303. ANDERSON, H. DEWEY, AND EELLS, WALTER CROSBY. *Alaska Natives: A Survey of Their Sociological and Educational Status,* pp. 298–370. Stanford, Calif.: Stanford University Press, 1935. Pp. xvi, 472. * (*PA* 9:2346)
304. TIEBOUT, CAROLYN. "The Measurement of Quality in Children's Painting by the Scale Method." *Psychol Monogr* 48(1):85–94 '36. * (*PA* 11:391)
305. TIEBOUT, CAROLYN, AND MEIER, NORMAN C. "Artistic Ability and General Intelligence." *Psychol Monogr* 48(1):95–125 '36. * (*PA* 11:392)
306. WEISENBURG, THEODORE; ROE, ANNE; AND MCBRIDE, KATHARINE E. *Adult Intelligence: A Psychological Study of Test Performances.* New York: Commonwealth Fund, 1936. Pp. xiii, 155. * (*PA* 10:3771)
307. SPRINGER, N. NORTON. "A Comparative Study of the Intelligence of a Group of Deaf and Hearing Children." *Am Ann Deaf* 83:138–52 Mr '38. * (*PA* 13:750)
308. SPRINGER, N. NORTON. "The Influence of General Social Status on the Emotional Stability of Children." *J Genetic Psychol* 53:321–8 D '38. * (*PA* 13:3348)
309. ABEL, THEODORA M. "Subnormal Girls With Discrepant Test Patterns." *J Appl Psychol* 23:398–404 Je '39. * (*PA* 13:5668)
310. MOTT, SINA M. "The Growth of an Abstract Concept." *Child Develop* 10:21–5 Mr '39. * (*PA* 13:4408)
311. ROHRER, JOHN H. "The Test Intelligence of Osage Indians." *J Social Psychol* 16:99–105 Ag '42. * (*PA* 16:4724)
312. SEASHORE, HAROLD G., AND BAVELAS, ALEX. "A Study of Frustration in Children." *J Genetic Psychol* 61:279–314 D '42. * (*PA* 17:1002)
313. GREENE, CHARLOTTE L. "A Study of Personal Adjustment in Mentally Retarded Girls." *Am J Mental Def* 49:472–6 Ap '45. * (*PA* 20:145)
314. NOTCUTT, B. "The Measurement of Zulu Intelligence." *J Social Res* (South Africa) 1:195–206 D '50. * (*PA* 27:4186)
315. BENNETT, EDWARD M., AND JOHANNSEN, DOROTHEE E. "Psychodynamics of the Diabetic Child." *Psychol Monogr* 68(11):1–23 '54. * (*PA* 29:6072)
316. GUREVITZ, SAUL, AND HELME, WILLIAM H. "Effects of Electroconvulsive Therapy on Personality and Intellectual Functioning of the Schizophrenic Child." *J Nerv & Mental Dis* 120:213–26 S–O '54. * (*PA* 29:7650)
317. KARLSEN, BJÖRN. *A Comparison of Some Educational and Psychological Characteristics of Successful and Unsuccessful Readers at the Elementary School Level.* Doctor's thesis, University of Minnesota (Minneapolis, Minn.), 1954. (*DA* 15:456)
318. GÜNZBURG, H. C. "Projection in Drawings: A Case Study." *Brit J Med Psychol* 28:72–81 pt 1 '55. * (*PA* 30:1028)
319. WHEELER, JOHN I., JR., AND CALDWELL, BETTYE MCDONALD. "Psychological Evaluation of Women With Cancer of the Breast and of the Cervix." *Psychosom Med* 17:256–68 Jl–Ag '55. * (*PA* 30:5074)
320. DENNIS, WAYNE, AND NAJARIAN, PERGROUHI. "Infant Development Under Environmental Handicap." *Psychol Monogr* 71(7):1–13 '57. * (*PA* 33:5830)
321. HELLER, ARTHUR D. "The Draw-a-Person Test in Mental Defectives." *Mental Health* (England) 16:90–5 S '57. * (*PA* 33:1636)
322. MELIKIAN, LEVON. "Preference for Delayed Reinforcement: An Experimental Study Among Palestinian Arab Refugee Children." *J Social Psychol* 50:81–6 Ag '59. * (*PA* 35:3240)
323. SAMPSON, OLIVE C. "The Speech and Language Development of 5-Year-Old Children." *Brit J Ed Psychol* 29:217–22 N '59. *
324. CURTI, MARGARET WOOSTER. "Intelligence Tests of White and Colored Children in Grand Cayman." *J Psychol* 49:13–27 Ja '60. * (*PA* 34:7628)
325. CARKHUFF, ROBERT R. "The Face Supplement: A Quick Index of Intelligence for Adult Subnormals." *J Clin Psychol* 18:346–7 Jl '62. * (*PA* 39:1721)
326. CARKHUFF, ROBERT R. "Perseveration of Habit in Drawing Tasks as a Characteristic Distinguishing Mental Defectives From Normals." *J Clin Psychol* 18:413–5 O '62. * (*PA* 39:5658)
327. MACKAY, G. W. S., AND VERNON, P. E. "The Measurement of Learning Ability." *Brit J Ed Psychol* 33:177–86 Je '63. * (*PA* 38:4067)
328. PETERS, HERBERT D. "Performance of Hopi Children on Four Intelligence Tests." *J Am Indian Ed* 2:27–31 Ja '63. *
329. TAYLOR, JAMES BENTLEY. "The Structure of Ability in the Lower Intellectual Range." *Am J Mental Def* 68:766–74 My '64. * (*PA* 39:1793)
330. KING, AUDREY J., AND WAKE, F. R. "The Effect of Motivation on 'Draw-a-Man' Scores." *Ont Psychol Assn Q* (Canada) 19(4):97–101 '66. *
331. MCPHERSON, MARION WHITE; POPPLESTONE, JOHN A.; AND EVANS, KATHERINE A. "Perceptual Carelessness, Drawing Precision, and Oral Activity Among Six-Year-Olds." *Percept & Motor Skills* 22:327–30 F '66. * (*PA* 40:5241)
332. SPOCK, ALEXANDER, AND STEDMAN, DONALD J. "Psychologic Characteristics of Children With Cystic Fibrosis." *N C Med J* 27:426–8 S '66. *
333. MOLEMA, SEODI Y. *A Comparison of Associative and Conceptual Thinking as Indicated by Two Non-Language Tests Among 'Lower and Higher Socioeconomic Negro Children in Elementary School.* Master's thesis, Catholic University of America (Washington, D.C.), 1967.
334. VERNON, PHILIP E. "A Cross-Cultural Study of 'Creativity Tests' With 11-Year Boys." *New Res Ed* (England) 1:135–46 Je '67. *
335. BELLER, E. KUNO. "Intellectual Development in Educationally Disadvantaged Pre-School Children." *Proc 1966 Ann Read Inst Temple Univ* 5:73–83 '68. *
336. DE-NOUR, ATARA K.; SHALTIEL, JUDITH; AND CZACZKES, J. W. "Emotional Reactions of Patients on Chronic Hemodialysis." *Psychosom Med* 30:521–33 S–O '68. * (*PA* 43:8624)
337. DOMRATH, RICHARD P. "Constructional Praxis and Visual Perception in School Children." *J Consult & Clin Psychol* 32:186–92 Ap '68. * (*PA* 42:8174)
338. GLUCKSMAN, MYRON L.; HIRSCH, JULES; MCCULLY, ROBERT S; BARRON, BRUCE A.; AND KNITTLE, JEROME L. "The Response of Obese Patients to Weight Reduction: 2, A Quantitative Evaluation of Behavior." *Psychosom Med* 30:359–73 Jl–Ag '68. * (*PA* 43:2314)
339. MONEY, JOHN; COHEN, STEPHEN M.; LEWIS, VIOLA; AND DRASH, PHILIP W. Chap. 40, "Human Figure Drawings as Index of Body Image in Dwarfism," pp. 582–91. In *Human Growth, Body Composition, Cell Growth, Energy, and Intelligence.* Edited by Donald B. Cheek. Philadelphia, Pa.: Lea & Febiger, 1968. Pp. xxx, 781. *
340. PRENTICE, NORMAN M., AND BIERI, JAMES. "Intellectual Development of Culturally Deprived Children in a Day Care Program." Abstract. *Proc 76th Ann Conv Am Psychol Assn* 3:599–600 '68. * (*PA* 43:1328, title only)
341. GRANDOVIC, MARGARET CLARK. *A Study of the Usefulness of the Bender Gestalt Test With Young Educable Retarded Children Using the Koppitz Procedures.* Doctor's thesis, Temple University (Philadelphia, Pa.), 1969. (*DAI* 32:1335A)
342. HARRIS, DALE B. *Comparison of Timed and Untimed Presentation of the Goodenough-Harris Test of Intellectual Maturity.* Public Health Service Publication No. 1000, Series 2, No. 35. Washington, D.C.: United States Government Printing Office, June 1969. Pp. vi, 16. *
343. MAJUMDAR, S. K. "Relationship Between Old (1956) and New (1966) Norms for Goodenough's Draw-a-Man Test (Pramila Phatak's Indian Adaptation) on Normal and Retarded Children." *Indian Ed R* 4(2):97–102 Jl '69. *

344. SINHA, MAYA. *A Study of the Harris Revision of the Goodenough Draw-A-Man Test.* Doctor's thesis, University of London (London, England), 1969.
345. CICERO, JANE. *An Analysis of the Effectiveness of the Goodenough Draw-A-Person Test in Predicting Achievement Among Selected Third Graders.* Master's thesis, John Carroll University (Cleveland, Ohio), 1970.
346. EAVES, LINDA C.; NUTTALL, J. C.; KLONOFF, H.; AND DUNN, H. G. "Developmental and Psychological Test Scores in Children of Low Birth Weight." *Pediatrics* 45(1):9-20 Ja '70. * Correction: 45(5):886-7 My '70. *
347. HARRIS, DALE B.; ROBERTS, JEAN; AND PINDNER, GLENN D. "Intellectual Maturity of Children as Measured by the Goodenough-Harris Drawing Test." *Vital & Health Stat Series* 11(105):1-40 D '70. * (*PA* 50:2691)
348. HARTMAN, ROBERT KINTZ. *An Investigation of the Incremental Validity of Human Figure Drawings in the Diagnosis of Learning Disabilities.* Doctor's thesis, University of Connecticut (Storrs, Conn.), 1970. (*DAI* 31:6403A)
349. KEOGH, BARBARA K., AND VORMELAND, ODDVAR. "Performance of Norwegian Children on the Bender Gestalt and Draw-A-Person Tests." *Scand J Ed Res* (Norway) 14(3):105-11 '70. * (*PA* 47:10628)
350. LECRONE, EDDIE M. *A Comparison of the Goodenough-Harris "Self" and "Adult" Drawings of Children Having Corrected Cleft-Palates With Similar Drawings of Children Having No Speech Impediments.* Master's thesis, Northern Illinois University (DeKalb, Ill.), 1970.
351. MUSGROVE, WALTER J. "Comparisons of Low Socioeconomic Black and White Kindergarten Children." *Acad Ther* 6(2):163-7 w '70. *
352. NATHAN, SUSAN, AND PISULA, DOROTHY. "Psychological Observations of Obese Adolescents During Starvation Treatment." *J Am Acad Child Psychiatry* 9(4):722-40 O '70. * (*PA* 45:8849)
353. NORDÉN, K. "The Structure of Abilities in a Group of Deaf Adolescents." *Ed & Psychol Interactions* (Sweden) 32:1-22 '70. * (*PA* 44:15094)
354. WHITE, GENEVIEVE. *Procedures for Predicting Children's Success in First Grade Achievement.* Master's thesis, Arkansas State University (State University, Ark.), 1970.
355. ABLES, BILLIE S. "The Use of the Draw-A-Man Test With Borderline Retarded Children Without Pronounced Pathology." *J Clin Psychol* 27(2):262-3 Ap '71. * (*PA* 46:7068)
356. ACUFF, NANCY HAMBLEN. *Paternal Effectiveness in a Selected Cognitive Task.* Doctor's thesis, Ohio State University (Columbus, Ohio), 1971. (*DAI* 32:3771A)
357. ARMENTROUT, JAMES A. "Effects of Perceptual Training on Children's Human Figure Drawings." *J Genetic Psychol* 119(2):281-7 D '71. * (*PA* 47:11789)
358. BRAUN, JEAN S., AND BRANE, MARIA. "Comparison of the Performance of Children With Dysrhythmia Grade 1 and Normal EEG on Psychological Tests." Abstract. *Proc 79th Ann Conv Am Psychol Assn* 6(1):457-8 '71. * (*PA* 46:5135)
359. CONNERS, C. KEITH. "The Effect of Stimulant Drugs on Human Figure Drawings in Children With Minimal Brain Dysfunction." *Psychopharmacologia* (West Germany) 19(4):329-33 '71. * (*PA* 46:3568)
360. GAYTON, WILLIAM F.; EVANS, H. EUGENE; AND WILSON, WINSTON S. "Comparative Validity of Harris Point and Quality Scales." *Percept & Motor Skills* 33(3):1111-3 D '71. * (*PA* 48:687)
361. GOLDSTEIN, HARRIS S., AND PECK, ROSALIND. "Cognitive Functions in Negro and White Children in a Child Guidance Clinic." *Psychol Rep* 28(2):379-84 Ap '71. * (*PA* 46:7556)
362. HALL, JOSEPH C., AND CHANSKY, NORMAN M. "Relationships Between Selected Ability and Achievement Tests in an Economically Disadvantaged Negro Sample." *Psychol Rep* 28(3):741-2 Je '71. * (*PA* 46:11501)
363. IRETON, HAROLD; QUAST, WENTWORTH; AND GANTCHER, PHYLLIS. "The Draw-A-Man Test as an Index of Developmental Disorders in a Pediatric Outpatient Population." *Child Psychiatry & Hum Develop* 2(1):42-9 f '71. * (*PA* 49:4143)
364. JENSEN, DIANA E.; PRANDONI, JOGUES R.; AND ABUDABBEH, NUHA N. "Figure Drawings by Sex Offenders and a Random Sample of Offenders." *Percept & Motor Skills* 32(1):295-300 F '71. * (*PA* 46:3356)
365. JENSEN, OLIVE MARIE JACOBSON. *Differences in Perception Through Teaching Drawing in Contrasting Groups of Fifth Grade Students.* Doctor's thesis, University of Minnesota (Minneapolis, Minn.), 1971. (*DAI* 32:3156A)
366. JOHNSON, DALE L., AND JOHNSON, CARMEN A. "Comparison of Four Intelligence Tests Used With Culturally Disadvantaged Children." *Psychol Rep* 28(1):209-10 F '71. * (*PA* 46:5736)
367. L'ABATE, LUCIANO. "Receptive-Expressive Functions in Kindergarten Children and Adolescents." *Psychol Sch* 8(3):253-9 Jl '71. * (*PA* 47:9699)
368. LAOSA, LUIS M.; SWARTZ, JON D.; AND HOLTZMAN, WAYNE H. "Human Figure Drawings by Normal Children Over Four Years of Repeated Testing." Abstract. *Proc 79th Ann Conv Am Psychol Assn* 6(1):167-8 '71. * (*PA* 46:2607)
369. LEHMAN, ELYSE BRAUCH, AND LEVY, BERNARD I. "Discrepancies in Estimates of Children's Intelligence: WISC and Human Figure Drawings." *J Clin Psychol* 27(1):74-6 Ja '71. * (*PA* 46:1427)
370. LEVI, HELENE S., AND WELCHER, DORIS W. "Social Class and Race as Determinants of the Sex of Human Figures Drawn by Seven-Year-Olds." *Johns Hopkins Med J* 129(1):10-8 Jl '71. *
371. LEVY, IRWIN S. "The Harris-Goodenough Drawing Test and Educable Mentally Retarded Adolescents." *Am J Mental Def* 75(6):760-1 My '71. *
372. MCCORMICK, CLARENCE C., AND SCHNOBRICH, JANICE N. "Perceptual-Motor Training and Improvement in Concentration in a Montessori Preschool." *Percept & Motor Skills* 32(1):71-7 F '71. * (*PA* 46:3865)
373. MCGILLIGAN, ROBERT P.; YATER, ALLAN C.; AND HUESING, RALPH. "Goodenough-Harris Drawing Test Reliabilities." *Psychol Sch* 8(4):359-62 O '71. * (*PA* 47:11621)
374. MOORE, MARY, AND WELCHER, DORIS W. "A Descriptive Analysis of the Seven-Year Psychological Data." *Johns Hopkins Med J* 128(6):332-46 Je '71. *
375. MUSGROVE, WALTER J., AND LAWSON, JOHN R. "A Comparison of Lower Class Negro and White Children on Three Standardized Tests." *J Negro Ed* 40(1):53-5 w '71. *
376. MYKLEBUST, HELMER R.; BANNOCHIE, MARGARET N.; AND KILLEN, JAMES R. Chap. 9, "Learning Disabilities and Cognitive Processes," pp. 213-51. In *Progress in Learning Disabilities, Vol. 2.* Edited by Helmer R. Myklebust. New York: Grune & Stratton, Inc., 1971. Pp. ix, 404. *
377. O'KEEFE, RIP; LESKOSKY, RICHARD J.; O'BRIEN, THOMAS G.; YATER, ALLAN C.; AND BARCLAY, ALLAN. "Influences of Age, Sex, and Ethnic Origin on Goodenough-Harris Drawing Test Performances by Disadvantaged Preschool Children." *Percept & Motor Skills* 33(3):708-10 D '71. * (*PA* 48:691)
378. OWEN, FREYA WEAVER; ADAMS, PAULINE AUSTIN; FORREST, THOMAS; STOLZ, LOIS MEEK; AND FISHER, SARA. "Learning Disorders in Children: Sibling Studies." *Monogr Soc Res Child Develop* 36(4):1-77 N '71. * (*PA* 48:12196)
379. PARKER, HARRY J.; STERNLOF, RICHARD E.; AND MCCOY, JOHN F. "Objective Versus Individual Mental Ability Tests With Former Head Start Children in the First Grade." *Percept & Motor Skills* 32(1):287-92 F '71. * (*PA* 46:3868)
380. PELC, ROBERT E. "Advancement Along a Complexity Gradient in Perceptual Level and Brain Damage." *Percept & Motor Skills* 32(1):251-4 F '71. * (*PA* 46:3322)
381. SAPIR, SELMA G. "Learning Disability and Deficit Centered Classroom Training." *Cognitive Studies* 2:324-38 '71. * (*PA* 49:1359, title only)
382. SCHAEFER, CHARLES E., AND STERNFIELD, MELVIN. "Comparative Validity of the Harris Quality and Point Scales." *Percept & Motor Skills* 33(3):997-8 D '71. * (*PA* 48:1325)
383. SINHA, MAYA. "Draw-A-Man Test Scores of British and Non-British Children." *Indian Ed R* 6(2):79-87 Jl '71. *
384. STRUEMPFER, D. J. W. "Validation of Two Quality Scales for Children's Figure Drawings." *Percept & Motor Skills* 32(3):887-93 Je '71. * (*PA* 47:2675)
385. WELCHER, DORIS W.; MELLITS, E. DAVID; AND HARDY, JANET B. "A Multivariate Analysis of Factors Affecting Psychological Performance." *Johns Hopkins Med J* 129(1):19-35 Jl '71. *
386. WELLS, DONALD G., AND PEDRINI, DUILIO T. "Relationships Among Wechsler Adult Intelligence Scale, Goodenough-Harris, and Peabody Picture Vocabulary Tests With Institutionalized Retarded Adults." *Percept & Motor Skills* 33(1):227-32 Ag '71. * (*PA* 47:3549)
387. WICKWIRE, PATRICIA JOANNE NELLOR. *The Academic Achievement and Language Development of American Children of Latin Heritage: Factors of Intellect, Home Educational Environment, and Personality.* Doctor's thesis, University of Texas (Austin, Tex.), 1971. (*DAI* 32:6232A)
388. YATER, ALLAN C.; BARCLAY, ALLAN; AND LESKOSKY, RICHARD. "Goodenough-Harris Drawing Test and WPPSI Performance of Disadvantaged Preschool Children." *Percept & Motor Skills* 33(3):967-70 D '71. * (*PA* 48:698)

CUMULATIVE NAME INDEX

Abel, T. M.: 309
Abercrombie, M. L.: 189
Ables, B. S.: 355
Abudabbeh, N. N.: 364
Acuff, N. H.: 356
Adams, P. A.: 378
Alexander, D.: 190
Alexander, T.: 132
Alzobaie, A. J.: 175
Anastasi, A.: 72, 141; rev, 7:352
Anderson, H. D.: 303
Ansbacher, H. L.: 66, 186
Armentrout, J. A.: 357
Armon, V.: 108
Armstrong, E. M.: 298
Armstrong, J. G.: 232
Arth, A. A.: 233
Auricchio, E. W.: 191
Aymat, F.: 253

Bach, L. C.: 234
Badri, M. B.: 176-7
Bailey, R. B.: 88
Balinky, J. L.: 160
Ballinger, T.: 260
Bannochie, M. N.: 376
Barclay, A.: 223, 377, 388
Barclay, N. A.: 277
Barnsley, R.: 239
Barron, B. A.: 338
Bassett, J. E.: 283
Battin, R.: 235
Bavelas, A.: 312
Beller, E. K.: 335
Bender, L.: 28, 65
Bennett, E. M.: 315
Benton, J. G.: 197
Berdie, R. F.: 40
Berger, A.: 79
Berkowitz, M. C.: 262

Berrien, F. K.: 16
Bevan, W. E.: 263
Beyer, F. N.: 64
Bieri, J.: 340
Birch, J. W.: 52
Bishop, J. S.: 283
Blackburn, I.: 286
Bliss, M.: 79
Bobitt, D.: 200
Boehncke, F. C.: 26
Brane, M.: 358
Braun, J. S.: 358
Brenner, A.: 89
Brenner, M. W.: 192, 209
Briggs, P. F.: 161
Brill, M.: 17, 23
Britton, J. H.: 67, 80
Brodsky, M.: 100
Bromwich, R. M.: 210
Broverman, D. M.: 162
Buchanan, B. A.: 236
Butler, B. V.: 269
Byrd, C.: 264
Caldwell, B. M.: 319
Campbell, H. E.: 265
Carkhuff, R. R.: 125, 193, 325–6
Carlson, J. S.: 279
Carney, R. E.: 126
Chansky, N. M.: 362
Chase, J. M.: 31
Chodorkoff, J.: 133
Cicero, J.: 345
Clawson, A.: 127
Cobb, K.: 68
Cohen, D. N.: 13
Cohen, H.: 156
Cohen, S. M.: 339
Coleman, J. M.: 100, 117
Collier, H. L.: 114
Conners, C. K.: 359
Corah, N. L.: 157
Corah, P. L.: 157
Cundick, B. P.: 280
Cunningham, B. V.: 297
Curti, M. W.: 167, 324
Curtin, M. E.: 17
Czaczkes, J. W.: 336
Danford, B. H.: 163
D'Angelo, R. Y.: 56, 141
Darke, R. A.: 49
Datta, A.: 18
Datta, L.: 211
Davenport, E. L.: 300
Davies, J.: 225
DeBurger, R. A.: 116
deJesús, C.: 69, 72
de Moreau, M.: 237
Dennis, W.: 33–4, 91, 109, 147, 194, 320
Denny, C.: 116
De-Nour, A. K.: 336
Dodd, J. M.: 195
Dokecki, P. R.: 266
Domrath, R. P.: 337
Donnelly, F.: 242
Doris, R. E.: 83
Dörken, H.: 140
Dowlen, C. L.: 144
Drash, P. W.: 339
Drexler, H. G.: 112
Dudek, S. Z.: 267
Dunn, H. G.: 346
Dunn, J. A.: 212–4; rev, 7:352
Dunn, M. B.: 143
Dyett, E. G.: 6
Earl, C. J. C.: 138
Easley, G. T.: 164
Eaves, L. C.: 346
Eells, W. C.: 301, 303
Egan, R. A.: 253
Eggers, M. M.: 7
Ehrhardt, A. A.: 190
Eisen, V. W.: 97, 131
Eklund, S.: 178
Ellerd, A. A.: 58
Estes, B. W.: 116
Etuk, E. E. S.: 215
Evans, H. E.: 360
Evans, K. A.: 331
Eysenck, H. J.: 281
Eysenck, S. B. G.: 281
Fahmy, M.: 165
Farrant, R. H.: 166

Farrell, M.: 209
Fiedler, F. E.: 53
Fine, M. J.: 238
Fingert, H. H.: 27
Finley, C. J.: 137
Fisher, J.: 81
Fisher, S.: 378
Forrest, T.: 378
Frede, M. C.: 266
Fukada, N.: 179
Fuller, C. W.: 149
Gaddes, W. H.: 239
Gantcher, P.: 363
Gautney, D. B.: 266
Gayton, W. F.: 282–3, 360
Geil, G. A.: 36, 49–50
Gellert, E.: 240
Georgas, J. G.: 241
Gilbert, J. G.: 128
Gillman, S.: 192, 209
Gitlitz, H. B.: 14
Glowatsky, E.: 73
Glucksman, M. L.: 338
Goffeney, B.: 269
Goldberg, J. S.: 267
Goldenberg, S.: 142
Goldstein, H. S.: 361
Goodenough, F. L.: 1–2, 57
Gorelick, J.: 113
Gowan, J. C.: 217
Grandovic, M. C.: 341
Granick, S.: 134
Gray, J. E.: 263
Greene, C. L.: 313
Grinder, R. E.: 167
Gross, D. G.: 99
Gross, M.: 248
Gunther, M. K.: 45
Gunzburg, H. C.: 84, 318
Gurevitz, S.: 316
Hagin, R. A.: 171
Hall, J. C.: 268, 362
Hall, M. R.: 128
Handrich, M.: 275
Hanna, R.: 117
Hanson, E.: 256
Hanvik, L. J.: 74
Harckham, L. D.: 284
Hardy, J. B.: 385
Harman, M. E.: 285
Harris, B. R.: 267
Harris, D. B.: 57, 101, 135, 288, 342, 347
Harris, R. E.: 81
Hartman, R. K.: 348
Havighurst, R. J.: 37, 45
Haward, L. R. C.: 82, 85–6
Haworth, M. R.: 130
Heckman, S. B.: 296
Heller, A. D.: 321
Helme, W. H.: 316
Henderson, K.: 102
Henderson, N. B.: 269
Hepburn, A. W.: 242
Herron, W. G.: 92
Hildreth, G.: 9
Hiler, E. W.: 196
Hinrichs, W. E.: 19
Hirsch, J.: 338
Hirschenfang, S.: 118, 197
Holden, R. H.: 153
Holowinsky, I. Z.: 179
Holtzman, W. H.: 368
Honzik, M. P.: exc, 7:352
Hozier, A.: 150
Huesing, R.: 373
Hughes, L. S.: 11
Hullett, J.: 200
Hunkin, V.: 139
Hunt, B.: 93
Hunter, C.: exc, 7:352
Huysamen, G. K.: 258
Ingram, T. T. S.: 286
Ireton, H.: 202, 363
Isard, E. S.: 119
Iscoe, I.: 100, 117
Israelite, J.: 22
Janke, L. L.: 37
Jaramillo, S.: 197
Jeeves, M. A.: 183
Jensen, D. E.: 364
Jensen, O. M. J.: 365
Johannsen, D. E.: 315
Johnson, A. P.: 58
Johnson, C. A.: 216, 366

Johnson, D. L.: 216, 366
Johnson, G. B.: 75
Jones, A. W.: 94
Kagan, J. R.: 27
Kaplan, M. S.: exc, 7:352
Karlsen, B.: 317
Kaspar, J. C.: 185, 188
Kelton, W. W.: 117
Kennedy, W. A.: 168
Keogh, B. K.: 243–4, 349
Keogh, J. F.: 244
Kernan, J. S.: 198
Kessler, R. T.: 173
Khatena, J.: 180, 217
Killen, J. R.: 376
King, A. J.: 330
Kirschner, F. E.: 245
Klonoff, H.: 346
Knittle, J. L.: 338
Kogan, K. L.: 54
Koppitz, E. M.: 110, 181, 237
Kraft, I. A.: 235
Kraft, R. B.: 246
Krop, H. D.: 247
L'Abate, L.: 367
Lahey, H. L.: 58
Laosa, L. M.: 368
Larsen, R. V.: 253
Lasky, D. I.: 119
Lawson, J. R.: 375
Lecrone, E. M.: 350
Lehman, E. B.: 369
Leppke, R. D.: 218
Leskosky, R.: 388
Leskosky, R. J.: 377
Lessing, E. E.: 120
Lester, E. P.: 267
Levi, H. S.: 370
Levine, H. A.: 248
Levinson, B. M.: 103, 154
Levy, B. I.: 369
Levy, I. S.: 249, 371
Levy, L. R.: 8
Lewis, V.: 339
Lindner, R. S.: 129, 168
Lockyer, L.: 231
Loudon, M. L.: 170
Luong, C. K. M.: 250
McAninch, M.: 199
McBride, K. F.: 306
McCarthy, D.: 24, 38
McClellan, D. A.: 251
McCormick, C. C.: 372
McCoy, J. F.: 257, 379
McCully, R. S.: 338
McCurdy, H. G.: 48
McElwee, E. W.: 10, 15
McGilligan, R.: 277
McGilligan, R. P.: 373
McHugh, A. F.: 70
McHugh, G.: 41–2
Mackay, G. W. S.: 327
McKenzie, A.: 239
McPherson, M. W.: 331
Magnusson, D.: 111
Majumdar, S. K.: 343
Maloney, M. P.: 270
Manuel, H. T.: 11
Marquis, D. P.: 71
Marshall, A.: 219
Mason, A. W.: 220, 286
Maurer, K. M.: 53
Medinnus, G. R.: 200
Meier, J. H.: 182
Meier, N. C.: 305
Melikian, L.: 322
Mellits, E. D.: 385
Menzel, E. W.: 20
Merz, W. R.: 287
Midkiff, K. L.: 87
Mienie, C. J. P.: 259
Miezitis, S. A.: 252
Millichap, J. G.: 253
Minsky, R.: 271
Mitchell, A. C.: 104
Molema, S. Y.: 333
Money, J.: 190, 221, 339
Moore, M.: 374
Morse, N. C.: 89
Mott, S. M.: 43, 310
Muralidharan, R.: 294
Murphy, M. M.: 90
Musgrove, W. J.: 351, 375
Muzekari, L. H.: 222
Myklebust, H. R.: 376

Najarian, P.: 320
Nase, R. R.: 272
Nash, H.: 288
Nathan, S.: 352
Needham, N. R.: 39
Nelson, S.: 161
Nielsen, H. H.: 121, 273
Noone, A.: 231
Norden, K.: 353
Norman, R. D.: 87
Notcutt, B.: 314
Nuttall, J. C.: 346
Oakley, C. A.: 29
O'Brien, T. G.: 377
Ochs, E.: 59
Ogilvie, D. S.: 151
Ohtsuki, K.: 96
O'Keefe, R.: 377
Olivier, K.: 223
Ouellette, F. E.: 169
Owen, F. W.: 378
Painter, G.: 201
Panther, E. E.: 224
Papadopoulou, E.: 241
Papavassiliou, I. T.: 76
Parker, H. J.: 257, 379
Patterson, R. M.: 93
Payne, L. E.: 270
Peck, R.: 361
Pedrini, D. T.: 229–30, 386
Pelc, R. E.: 380
Peters, H. D.: 328
Peterson, F.: 61
Petrie, R. G.: 289
Phatak, P.: 98, 105, 122, 155
Pickup, K. T.: 136
Pindner, G. D.: 347
Pisula, D.: 352
Popplestone, J. A.: 106, 331
Porteus, S. D.: 299
Prandoni, J. R.: 364
Pratt, I. E.: 45
Prentice, N. M.: 340
Price, P. C.: 117
Price-Williams, D.: 216
Pringle, M. L. K.: 136; exc, 7:352
Quast, W.: 202, 363
Rajalakshmi, R.: 183
Randall, R. R.: 195
Rawl, M. F.: 254
Raymond, C. S.: 285
Redbird, H. M.: 158
Reichenberg-Hackett, W.: 77
Rich, T. A.: 94
Richey, M. H.: 107, 184
Ringe, K.: 273
Roberton, M. A.: 255
Roberts, J.: 347
Robinault, I. P.: 148
Robinson, H. A.: 203, 256
Roche, D.: 274, 290
Roche, P. J. D.: 274
Roe, A.: 306
Rohrer, J. H.: 311
Rohrs, F. W.: 130
Roland, W. A.: 82, 85–6
Rosen, E. K.: 77
Rosenzweig, S.: 46, 54
Rottersman, L.: 60
Rouse, M. J.: exc, 7:352
Russell, R. W.: 35
Russell, T.: 281
Sak, H. G.: 225
Sampson, O. C.: 323
Santos, B.: 152
Sapir, S. G.: 381
Saunders, M. H.: 291
Schaefer, C. E.: 382
Schilder, P.: 27
Schiller, B.: 302
Schnobrich, J. N.: 372
Schulman, J. L.: 185, 188
Scott, M.: 178
Sears, R.: 51
Seashore, H. G.: 312
Sedberry, M. E.: 117
Sells, S. B.: 204
Shaltiel, J.: 336
Shipp, D. E.: 170
Shrimali, P. L.: 47
Siegel, S.: 53
Silver, A. A.: 95, 171
Silverstein, A. B.: 205
Singer, M. T.: 159

Goodenough-Harris Drawing Test

Singh, B.: 123
Sinha, M.: 292, 344, 383
Sinnett, E. R.: 71
Sjah, A.: 124
Smith, A. A.: 225
Smith, F. O.: 25
Spadafore, G. J.: 293
Spock, A.: 332
Spoerl, D. T.: 30
Spotts, J. V.: 107
Spotts, W. S.: 167
Springer, N. N.: 32, 307-8
Springfield, L.: 264
Stedman, D. J.: 332
Steer, M. D.: 112
Steinman, W. M.: 226
Sternfield, M.: 382
Sternlof, R. E.: 257, 379
Stewart, N.: rev, 4:292
Stolz, L. M.: 378
Stone, P. A.: 186
Stonesifer, F. A.: 55
Struempfer, D. J. W.: 384
Strümpfer, D. J. W.: 258-9
Sturgis, L. H.: 253
Sundberg, N.: 260
Swartz, J. D.: 368
Sweeney, N. R.: 172
Tauber, R.: 206
Taylor, J. B.: 207, 329
Telford, C. W.: 12, 61
Teska, P. T.: 291
Thomas, R. M.: 124
Thompson, C. W.: 261
Thompson, J. M.: 137
Thorpe, J. S.: 187
Throne, F. M.: 185, 188
Tiebout, C.: 304-5
Tobias, J.: 113
Tracy, D. B.: 238
Trowbridge, N.: 126
Tsao, D. F.: 62

Tuska, S. A.: 78
Tyson, M. C.: 189
Utsugi, E.: 96
Vahar, M.: 179
Vane, J. R.: 131, 173, 227
Varva, F. I.: 145
Vernon, P. E.: 327, 334
Vogel, F. X.: 228
Vormeland, O.: 349
Vroegh, K.: 275
Wagoner, L. C.: 298
Wake, F. R.: 330
Wang, C.: 221
Warren, A. S.: 114
Watkins, D. G.: 208
Watson, B. L.: 276
Weir, M. W.: 117
Weisenburg, T.: 306
Welcher, D. W.: 370, 374, 385
Wells, D. G.: 229-30, 386
Werner, E. E.: 294
West, J. H.: 115
West, P. C.: 174
Wheeler, J. I.: 319
White, G.: 354
White, M. F. R.: 44
Whitten, C. F.: 133
Wickwire, P. J. N.: 387
Williams, B. K.: 295
Williams, J. H.: 21
Williams, M. L.: 5
Wilson, J. L.: 146
Wilson, W. S.: 360
Winter, W. D.: 71
Woltmann, A. G.: exc, 7:352
Yater, A. C.: 277, 373, 377, 388
Yen, S. M. Y.: 278
Yepsen, L. N.: 3-4
Yule, W.: 231
Zangwill, O. L.: 209

[382]

*The Graduate Record Examinations Aptitude Test. Graduate school candidates; 1949-73; GREAT; 2 scores: verbal, quantitative; Educational Testing Service. * For the testing program entry, see 1053.

For additional information concerning earlier forms, see 7:353 (43 references); for reviews by Robert L. French and Warren W. Willingham, see 6:461 (17 references); for a review by John T. Dailey, see 5:336 (7 references); for reviews by J. P. Guilford and Carl I. Hovland, see 4:293 (2 references). For an excerpt from a related book review, see 7:B113. For reviews of the testing program, see 7:667 (1 review) and 5:601 (1 review).

REFERENCES THROUGH 1971

1-2. See 4:293.
3-9. See 5:336.
10-26. See 6:461.
27-69. See 7:353.
70. WYETH, EZRA R. "Evaluation of the Effectiveness of the Leadership Training Program in the Area of the Deaf at San Fernando Valley State College." *Am Ann Deaf* 110:479-82 S '65. * (*PA* 40:5848)
71. HOUSTON, SAMUEL R. "Generating a Projected Criterion of Graduate School Success via Normative Judgment Analysis." *J Exp Ed* 37:53-8 w '68. *
72. JARDIN, ROBERT PATRICK. *An Analysis of Peer Ratings and Subordinate Ratings as a Potential Feedback and Self-Selection Device for School Counselor Candidates.* Doctor's thesis, American University (Washington, D.C.), 1970. (*DAI* 32:178A)
73. ROBERTS, PAMELA T. *An Analysis of the Relationship Between Graduate Record Examination Scores and Success in the Graduate School of Wake Forest University.* Master's thesis, Wake Forest University (Winston-Salem, N.C.), 1970.
74. CRAWFORD, FRANCES W. *An Investigation of the Graduate Record Examination and Other Variables Used as Predictors of Success in the Graduate Program of the Department of Psychology of East Tennessee State University.* Master's thesis, East Tennessee State University (Johnson City, Tenn.), 1971.
75. ELSTER, RICHARD S.; GITHENS, WILLIAM H.; AND WISKOFF, MARTIN. "Predicting the Graduate School Performance of Military Officers," pp. 91-8. In *Second Annual Symposium: Psychology in the Air Force, 20-22 April 1971.* Edited by Hal W. Hendrick. Colorado Springs, Colo.: United States Air Force Academy, [1971]. Pp. x, 409. *

76. HANSEN, W. LEE. "Prediction of Graduate Performance in Economics." *J Econ Ed* 3(1):49-53 f '71. *
77. HARRIS, JOHN A. *A Study of Selected Graduate Students' Performances on Graduate Record Examination, Iowa Silent Reading Test, and Grade-Point Average.* Master's thesis, Fort Valley State College (Ft. Valley, Ga.), 1971.
78. LEDFORD, KENNETH B. *An Analysis of the Predictive Value of the Graduate Record Examination in Relation to Success in Four Disciplines at East Tennessee State University.* Master's thesis, East Tennessee State University (Johnson City, Tenn.), 1971.
79. MARSTON, ALBERT R. "It Is Time to Reconsider the Graduate Record Examination." *Am Psychologist* 26(7):653-5 Jl '71. * (*PA* 47:11620)
80. MERENDA, PETER F., AND REILLY, RAYMOND. "Validity of Selection Criteria in Determining Success of Graduate Students in Psychology." *Psychol Rep* 28(1):259-66 F '71. * (*PA* 46:5705)
81. MICHAEL, WILLIAM B.; JONES, ROBERT A.; AL-AMIR, HUDHAIL; PULLIAS, CALVIN M.; JACKSON, MICHEL; AND GOO, VALERIE. "Correlates of a Pass-Fail Decision for Admission to Candidacy in a Doctoral Program in Education." *Ed & Psychol Meas* 31(4):965-7 w '71. * (*PA* 48:1832)
82. PAYNE, DAVID A.; WELLS, ROBERT A.; AND CLARKE, ROBERT R. "Another Contribution to Estimating Success in Graduate School: A Search for Sex Differences and Comparison Between Three Degree Types." *Ed & Psychol Meas* 31(2):497-503 su '71. *
83. WITTMER, JOE, AND LISTER, JAMES L. "The Graduate Record Examination, 16 PF Questionnaire, and Counseling Effectiveness." *Counselor Ed & Sup* 10(3):293 sp '71. *
84. WRIGHT, MATTHEW THOMAS. *An Analysis of Selected Factors of Education Doctoral Programs at Washington State University.* Doctor's thesis, Washington State University (Pullman, Wash.), 1971. (*DAI* 32:4388A)

CUMULATIVE NAME INDEX

Al-Amir, H.: 81
Alexakos, C. E.: 47
Angoff, W. H.: 5, 7
Baillie, G. S.: 27
Bass, A. R.: 66
Besco, R. O.: 13-4
Blackburn, M.: 53, 63
Borg, W. R.: 24
Breimeier, K. H.: 42
Burdick, L. A.: 31
Capps, M. P.: 8
Carbonari, J. P.: 48
Chimonides, S. G.: 54
Cieboter, F. J.: 55
Clarke, R. R.: 82
Colvin, G. F.: 49
Conway, M. T.: 10
Crawford, F. W.: 74
Creager, J. A.: 35
Crosby, D. W.: 4
Cureton, E. E.: 43
Dailey, J. T.: rev, 5:336
DeCosta, F. A.: 8
Donaghy, R. T.: 46
Duperre, M. R.: exc, 7:B113
Elster, R. S.: 75
Elton, C. F.: 36
Ewen, R. B.: 56
Frank, A. C.: 57
French, R. L.: rev, 6:461
Gab, D.: 58, 64, 69
Gibbons, B. D.: 16
Githens, W. H.: 75
Goo, V.: 81
Green, E. J.: 68
Guilford, J. P.: rev, 4:293
Hackman, J. R.: 53, 63, 66
Hall, E.: 34
Hansen, W. L.: 76
Harlow, S. D.: 69
Harris, J. A.: 77
Harrison, C. W.: 60
Horton, C. P.: 61
Houston, S. R.: 62, 71
Hovland, C. I.: rev, 4:293
Howard, J. S.: 20
Huber, J. T.: 44
Jackson, M.: 81
Jardin, R. P.: 72
Johnson, B. G.: 28
Johnson, J. W.: 21
Jones, R. A.: 16, 81
King, D. C.: 14
King, F. J.: 29
Kirk, B. A.: 57
Law, A.: 15
Ledford, K. B.: 78

Lister, J. L.: 83
Maberly, N. C.: 22, 25
Madaus, G. F.: 37
Manuel, H. T.: 6
Marston, A. R.: 79
Mehrabian, A.: 59, 67
Merenda, P. F.: 80
Michael, W. B.: 16, 81
Moghrabi, K. M.: 38
Mosher, R. L.: 46
Newman, R. I.: 50
Nichols, R. C.: 32
Nielsen, W.: 17
Palmer, R. H.: 39
Payne, D. A.: 82
Poniatowski, R. A.: 33
Pullias, C. M.: 81
Rawls, D. J.: 60
Rawls, J. R.: 60
Reilly, R.: 80
Richter, W. R.: 51
Rindone, R.: 40
Roberts, B. T.: 61
Roberts, P. T.: 73
Roberts, S. O.: 61
Robertson, M.: 17, 34
Robinson, D. W.: 9
Roscoe, J. T.: 62
Rudman, J.: 26
Rupiper, O. J.: 11
Saum, J. A.: 1, 3
Schultz, M. K.: 5, 7
Scott, T. B.: 43
Sleeper, M. L.: 18
Sprinthall, N. A.: 46
Stafford, J. W.: 2
Stein, R. F.: 68
Stricker, G.: 44
Thomsen, S. J.: 19
Tookey, M. D.: 52
Tucker, H.: 41
Tully, G. E.: 23, 29
Walsh, J. J.: 37
Wells, R. A.: 82
White, G. W.: 45
Whiteley, J. M.: 46
Wiggins, N.: 53, 63, 66
Williams, J. D.: 64, 69
Williams, O. H.: 12
Willingham, W. W.: rev, 6:461
Wiskoff, M.: 75
Wittmer, J.: 83
Woodard, D. B.: 65
Wright, M. T.: 84
Wyeth, E. R.: 70
Zimmerman, W. G.: 30

[383]

★**Group Test for Indian South Africans.** Standards 4–6, 7–8, 9–10; 1967–71; GTISA; adaptation for Indian pupils of the *New South African Group Test*; 3 scores: verbal, nonverbal, total; 3 levels; Human Sciences Research Council [South Africa]. *
a) JUNIOR. Standards 4–6; 1968–71; Indian standardization by F. W. O. Heinichen, R. J. Prinsloo, and S. Oosthuizen.
b) INTERMEDIATE. Standards 7–8; 1967–69.
c) SENIOR. Standards 9–10; 1968–69.

[384]

Group Test 36. Ages 10–14; 1937–45; verbal intelligence; National Institute of Industrial Psychology; NFER Publishing Co. Ltd. [England]. *
For additional information, see 4:296.

REFERENCES THROUGH 1971

1. HOLLIDAY, FRANK. "An Investigation Into the Selection of Apprentices for the Engineering Industry." *Occup Psychol* (England) 14:69–81 Ap '40. * (*PA* 14:3710)
2. SHUTTLEWORTH, CLIFFORD W. "Tests of Technical Aptitude." *Occup Psychol* (England) 16:175–82 O '42. *
3. FRISBY, C. B.; VINCENT, D. F.; AND LANCASHIRE, RUTH. *Tests for Engineering Apprentices: A Validation Study*. National Institute of Industrial Psychology, Report 14. London: the Institute, 1959. Pp. iii, 24. *
4. JAMIESON, G. H. "Psychological Aspects of Craftsmanship in Pottery-Making at a Secondary School." *Brit J Ed Psychol* 35:179–82 Je '65. * (*PA* 39:16457)

CUMULATIVE NAME INDEX

Frisby, C. B.: 3
Holliday, F.: 1
Jamieson, G. H.: 4
Lancashire, R.: 3
Shuttleworth, C. W.: 2
Vincent, D. F.: 3

[385]

Group Test 75. Ages 12–13; 1957; nonverbal intelligence; National Institute of Industrial Psychology; NFER Publishing Co. Ltd. [England]. *
For additional information, see 5:338.

REFERENCES THROUGH 1971

1. JAMIESON, G. H. "Psychological Aspects of Craftsmanship in Pottery-Making at a Secondary School." *Brit J Ed Psychol* 35:179–82 Je '65. * (*PA* 39:16457)

CUMULATIVE NAME INDEX

Jamieson, G. H.: 1

[386]

Group Test 91. Industrial applicants; 1949–68; verbal intelligence; National Institute of Industrial Psychology; NFER Publishing Co. Ltd. [England]. *
For additional information, see 7:354.

REFERENCES THROUGH 1971

1. CASTLE, P. F. C., AND GARFORTH, F. I. DE LA P. "Selection, Training and Status of Supervisors: 1, Selection." *Occup Psychol* (England) 25:109–23 Ap '51. * (*PA* 26:5858)

CUMULATIVE NAME INDEX

Castle, P. F. C.: 1
Garforth, F. I. de la P.: 1

[386A]

★**Group Test 95.** Ages 14 and over; [1972]; verbal intelligence; no manual; National Institute of Industrial Psychology; NFER Publishing Co. Ltd. [England]. *

[387]

*****Group Test of Learning Capacity: Dominion Tests.** Grades kgn–1, 4–6, 7–9, 10–12 and adults; 1934–70; formerly called *Group Test of Intelligence*; various titles used by publisher: *Dominion Group Test of Learning Capacity, Dominion Tests of Learning Capacity*; 4 levels; Ontario Institute for Studies in Education; distributed by Guidance Centre [Canada]. *
a) PRIMARY. Grades kgn–1; 1934–56. Out of print. (Replaced by *OISE Picture Reasoning Test: Primary*.)
b) JUNIOR. Grades 4–6; 1940–56.
c) MACHINE-SCORING GROUP TEST OF LEARNING CAPACITY, MACHINE- AND HAND-SCORING EDITION. Grades 7–9, 10–12 and adults; 1934–70; revision of *Quick-Scoring Group Test of Learning Capacity: Dominion Tests* (test items identical except for deletion of 5 items); 2 levels; technical report by Mohindra P. Gill, Ross E. Traub, and R. Schweiker.
  1) *Intermediate*. Grades 7–9; 1934–70.
  2) *Advanced*. Grades 10–12 and adults; 1939–70.
For additional information and reviews by Donald B. Black and George A. Ferguson of the intermediate and advanced levels, see 6:493; for additional information concerning the primary and junior levels, see 5:341; for a review by W. G. Emmett, see 4:294 (3 references); for a review by F. T. Tyler, see 3:231.

REFERENCES THROUGH 1971

1–3. See 4:294.
4. PIPHER, J. A. "An Appraisal of the Use of the Dominion Group Test of Learning Capacity (Advanced) in the Atkinson Study of Utilization of Student Resources." *Ont J Ed Res* (Canada) 3:17–23 O '60. *
5. RUSSELL, H. H., AND DILLING, H. J. "Comparison of General Intelligence Test Results and Student Achievement in Grade 8 and Grade 9 of Scarborough Schools." *Ont J Ed Res* (Canada) 8:267–77 sp '66. *
6. GORDON, JAMES ROSCOE. *Listening, Attitude, and Intelligence Tests to Predict Academic Achievement*. Doctor's thesis, Colorado State College (Greeley, Colo.), 1968. (*DA* 29:2522A)

CUMULATIVE NAME INDEX

Black, D. B.: *rev*, 6:493
Department of Educational Research, Ontario College of Education, University of Toronto: 2
Dilling, H. J.: 5
Emmett, W. G.: *rev*, 4:294
Ferguson, G. A.: *rev*, 6:493
Gordon, J. R.: 6
Ontario Commercial Teachers' Association: 2
Phillips, A. J.: 1
Pipher, J. A.: 4
Russell, H. H.: 5
Tyler, F. T.: *rev*, 3:231
Yule, D. L. G.: 3

[388]

Group Tests 70 and 70B. Ages 15 and over; 1939–70; subtest of *N.I.I.P. Engineering Apprentice Selection Test Battery*; nonverbal intelligence; National Institute of Industrial Psychology; NFER Publishing Co. Ltd. [England]. * For the complete battery entry, see 2345.
For additional information, see 7:355 (5 references); for a review by George Westby of form 70, see 4:297 (5 references).

REFERENCES THROUGH 1971

1–5. See 4:297.
6–10. See 7:355.
11. SLATER, PATRICK, AND BENNETT, ELIZABETH. "The Development of Spatial Judgment and Its Relation to Some Educational Problems." *Occup Psychol* (England) 17:139–55 Jl '43. *
12. ADCOCK, CYRIL. "A Re-Analysis of Slater's Spatial Judgment Research." *Occup Psychol* (England) 22:213–6 O '48. * (*PA* 23:1691)
13. HIMMELWEIT, HILDE T., AND SUMMERFIELD, ARTHUR. "Student Selection—An Experimental Investigation: II." *Brit J Sociol* 2:59–75 Mr '51. * (*PA* 26:542)
14. GASKILL, P. Chap. 9, "Tests of Ability and Attainments: Pilot Experiments in Selection and Guidance," pp. 188–212. In *Educational Guidance and the Deaf Child*. Edited by A. W. G. Ewing. Manchester, England: Manchester University Press, 1957. Pp. xiii, 345. *
15. MURPHY, K. P. Chap. 11, "Tests of Abilities and Attainments: Pupils in Schools for the Deaf Aged Twelve," pp. 252–77. In *Educational Guidance and the Deaf Child*. Edited by A. W. G. Ewing. Manchester, England: Manchester University Press, 1957. Pp. xiii, 345. *
16. CATTELL, RAYMOND B., AND SCHEIER, IVAN H. "The Objective Test Measurement of Neuroticism, U.I. 23 (—)." *Indian J Psychol* 33:217–36 pt 4 '58. * (*PA* 35:3427, title only)
17. MEHROTRA, S. N. "An Educational-Vocational Guidance Project for Intermediate Students: A Follow-Up Study." *Indian J Psychol* 34:148–62 pt 3 '59. * (*PA* 36:4KJ48M)
18. MOSHIN, S. M. "Plea for a Scientific Aptitude Test and

a Preliminary Report of the Development of Such Test." *Indian J Psychol* 34:36-42 pt 1 '59. *
19. DAS, RHEA S. "Validity Information Exchange, No. 14-05: D.O.T. Code 2-66.01, Police Lieutenant." *Personnel Psychol* 14:459-61 w '61. *

CUMULATIVE NAME INDEX

Adcock, C.: 12
Aga, H.: 10
Bennett, E.: 11
Cattell, R. B.: 16
Das, R. S.: 19
Dhar, C.: 7
Frisby, C. B.: 8
Gaskill, P.: 14
Himmelweit, H. T.: 13
Jog, R. N.: 9-10
Lancashire, R.: 8
Marr, E.: 7
Mehrotra, S. N.: 6, 17
Mills, L. F.: 2
Moshin, S. M.: 18
Murphy, K. P.: 15
Parry, J. B.: 4
Scheier, I. H.: 16
Slater, P.: 1, 11
Summerfield, A.: 13
Vernon, P. E.: 3-4
Vincent, D. F.: 8
Westby, G.: *rev,* 4:297

[389]

Group Tests 72 and 73. Industrial applicants; 1949-68; nonverbal intelligence; National Institute of Industrial Psychology; NFER Publishing Co. Ltd. [England]. *

For additional information, see 7:356 (1 reference).

REFERENCES THROUGH 1971

1. See 7:356.

CUMULATIVE NAME INDEX

Castle, P. F. C.: 1   Garforth, F. I. de la P.: 1

[390]

Group Tests 90A and 90B. Ages 15 and over; 1950-70; subtest of *N.I.I.P. Engineering Apprentice Selection Test Battery;* verbal intelligence; National Institute of Industrial Psychology; NFER Publishing Co. Ltd. [England]. * For the complete battery entry, see 2345.

For additional information, see 7:357 (1 reference); for a review by John Liggett of form 90A, see 5:340.

REFERENCES THROUGH 1971

1. See 7:357.
2. VINCENT, D. F. "The Linear Relationship Between Age and Score of Adults in Intelligence Tests." *Occup Psychol* (England) 26:243-9 O '52. * (*PA* 27:7044)
3. GARSIDE, R. F. "The Prediction of Examination Marks of Mechanical Engineering Students at King's College, Newcastle." *Brit J Psychol* 48:219-20 Ag '57. * (*PA* 33:2157)

CUMULATIVE NAME INDEX

Garside, R. F.: 3
Liggett, J.: *rev,* 5:340
Vincent, D. F.: 2
Williams, A. P.: 1

[391]

The Henmon-Nelson Tests of Mental Ability.
Grades kgn-2, 3-6, 6-9, 9-12, 13-17; 1931-73; 2 editions; Tom A. Lamke (except *b*1) and Martin J. Nelson; Houghton Mifflin Co. *

a) REVISED EDITION. Grades 3-6, 6-9, 9-12, 13-17; 1931-61; 4 levels.
 1) *Grades 3-6.* 1931-58.
 2) *Grades 6-9.* 1931-57.
 3) *Grades 9-12.* 1931-58.
 4) *Grades 13-17.* 1931-61; 3 scores: quantitative, verbal, total; Paul C. Kelso.

b) 1973 REVISION. Grades kgn-2, 3-6, 6-9, 9-12; 1931-73; 4 levels; no manual; Joseph L. French.
 1) *Primary Battery.* Grades kgn-2; 1973.
 2) *Grades 3-6.* 1931-73.
 3) *Grades 6-9.* 1931-73.
 4) *Grades 9-12.* 1931-73.

For additional information, a review by Norman E. Wallen, and an excerpted review by John O. Crites of the college level, see 6:462 (11 references); for reviews by D. Welty Lefever and Leona E. Tyler and an excerpted review by Laurance F. Shaffer of the other levels in the Revised Edition, see 5:342 (14 references); for a review by H. M. Fowler of an earlier edition, see

4:299 (25 references); for reviews by Anne Anastasi, August Dvorak, Howard Easley, and J. P. Guilford and an excerpted review by Francis N. Maxfield, see 2:1398.

REFERENCES THROUGH 1971

1-25. See 4:299.
26-39. See 5:342.
40-50. See 6:462.
51. BYRNS, RUTH. "The Mental Ability of Twins." *Sch & Soc* 40:671-2 N 17 '34. * (*PA* 9:1187)
52. LYON, VERGIL E. "The Variation of High School Senior and College Freshman Classes." *J Exp Ed* 3:25-35 S '34. * (*PA* 9:1418)
53. OMWAKE, KATHARINE T.; DEXTER, EMILY S.; AND LEWIS, L. WAYVE. "The Inter-Relations of Certain Physiological Measurements and Aspects of Personality." *Char & Pers* 3:64-71 S '34. * (*PA* 9:291)
54. BYRNS, RUTH. "Intelligence and Nationality of Wisconsin School Children." *J Social Psychol* 7:455-70 N '36. * (*PA* 11:4220)
55. OLANDER, HERBERT T., AND WALKER, BERT S. "Can Teachers Estimate I.Q.'s?" *Sch & Soc* 44:744-6 D 5 '36. * (*PA* 11:1490)
56. DENNIS, FLAVIUS ELIAS. *An Investigation of the Mental Ability, Educational Achievement, and Neurotic Tendencies of a Group of Partially Seeing Pupils.* Master's thesis, University of Colorado (Boulder, Colo.), 1939. (Abstract: *Univ Colo Studies* 26:48)
57. MACKENZIE, D. M. "Placement Tests and Freshman Week." *Sch & Soc* 50:351-2 S 9 '39. * (*PA* 14:547)
58. MORRIS, CHARLES M. "A Critical Analysis of Certain Performance Tests." *J Genetic Psychol* 54:85-105 Mr '39. * (*PA* 13:5387)
59. FROEHLICH, GUSTAV J. *The Prediction of Academic Success at the University of Wisconsin, 1909-1941.* Bulletin of the University of Wisconsin, Serial No. 2574, General Series No. 2358. Madison, Wis.: Bureau of Guidance and Records, the University, 1941. Pp. 44. * (*PA* 16:3775)
60. JOHNSON, DONALD M., AND REYNOLDS, FLOYD. "A Factor Analysis of Verbal Ability." *Psychol Rec* 4:183-95 Ja '41. * (*PA* 15:3315)
61. DEXTER, EMILY S. "Relation of Imagination to Certain Other Factors." *J General Psychol* 28:139-41 Ja '43. * (*PA* 17:1106)
62. SPOERL, DOROTHY TILDEN. "The Academic and Verbal Adjustment of College Age Bilingual Students." *J Genetic Psychol* 64:139-57 Mr '44. * (*PA* 18:2275)
63. BERRY, GEORGE S. "An Experiment in Self-Analysis." *J Ed Psychol* 37:111-24 F '46. * (*PA* 20:2061)
64. MOSER, W. E. "Vocational Preference as Related to Mental Ability." *Occupations* 27:460-1 Ap '49. * (*PA* 23:4870)
65. BARRETT, HARRY O. "Differences in Intelligence Between Two- and Four-Year Course Pupils in a Commercial High School." *J Ed Res* 44:143-7 O '50. * (*PA* 25:5681)
66. EELLS, KENNETH; DAVIS, ALLISON; HAVIGHURST, ROBERT J.; HERRICK, VERGIL E.; AND TYLER, RALPH W. *Intelligence and Cultural Differences: A Study of Cultural Learning and Problem-Solving.* Chicago, Ill.: University of Chicago Press, 1951. Pp. xii, 388. * (*PA* 27:5738)
67. WILLIAMS, HENRIETTA V., AND MCQUARY, JOHN P. "The High-School Performance of College Freshmen." *Ed Adm & Sup* 39:303-8 My '53. * (*PA* 28:4955)
68. PROTHRO, E. TERRY. "An Alternative Approach in Cross-Cultural Intelligence Testing." *J Psychol* 39:247-51 Ap '55. * (*PA* 29:8553)
69. HOFSTAETTER, PETER R.; O'CONNOR, JAMES P.; AND SUZIEDELIS, ANTANAS. "Sequences of Restricted Associative Responses and Their Personality Correlates." *J General Psychol* 57:219-27 O '57. * (*PA* 33:9818)
70. LITTLE, J. KENNETH. "The Persistence of Academically Talented Youth in University Studies." *Ed Rec* 40:237-41 Jl '59. * (*PA* 34:4815)
71. PIPPERT, RALPH REINHARD. *The Prediction of the Correctness of Post-High School Written Language Performance.* Doctor's thesis, University of Wisconsin (Madison, Wis.), 1959. (*DA* 20:2104)
72. MARTIN, JACK R. "The Correlation Between Preadmission Tests and Graduation From Nursing School." *J Nursing Ed* 1:3-4+ D '62. *
73. KIENLEN, JOSEPH S. *A Study to Predict the Success of Students in Plane Geometry in Worland High School, Worland, Wyoming.* Master's thesis, Fort Hays Kansas State College (Hays, Kan.), 1963.
74. MUMAW, MYRON JAY. *Test Predictability for Culturally Deprived Students.* Master's thesis, Ohio State University (Columbus, Ohio), 1963.
75. GLIDDEN, GEORGE WAYNE. *Factors That Influence Achievement in Senior High School American History.* Doctor's thesis, University of Nebraska (Lincoln, Neb.), 1964. (*DA* 25:3429)
76. ZAHN, JANE. "Dropout and Academic Ability in University Extension Courses." *Adult Ed* 15:35-46 au '64. *
77. RIGHTHAND, HERBERT. "Identifying Technical Institute Dropouts." *Personnel & Guid J* 44:68-72 S '65. *

78. SWAN, ROBERT J., AND HOPKINS, KENNETH D. "An Investigation of Theoretical and Empirical Chance Scores on Selected Standardized Group Tests." *Calif J Ed Res* 16:34–41 Ja '65. * (*PA* 39:10156)

79. PEARSON, RICHARD E., AND OHLSEN, MERLE M. "Factors Associated With Teacher Over- Or Under-Estimation of Student Intellectual Ability." *J Stud Pers Assn Teach Ed* 5:1–13 Ap '66. *

80. RENFER, MARY EMMA FEWELL. *Predicting Success in the Study of Descriptive Linguistics.* Doctor's thesis, University of Southern California (Los Angeles, Calif.), 1966. (*DA* 27:1268A)

81. CONKLIN, BERNICE B. *The Correlation of High School Students' Intelligence and Aptitude in Relation to the Understanding of Automated Data Processes.* Master's thesis, San Diego State College (San Diego, Calif.), 1967.

82. SCHURDAK, JOHN J. "An Approach to the Use of Computers in the Instructional Process and an Evaluation." *Am Ed Res J* 4:59–73 Ja '67. * (*PA* 41:7907)

83. WESTBROOK, BERT W., AND SELLERS, JAMES R. "Critical Thinking, Intelligence, and Vocabulary." *Ed & Psychol Meas* 27:443–6 su '67. * (*PA* 41:13634)

84. GORDON, EDWIN. "A Study of the Efficacy of General Intelligence and Musical Aptitude Tests in Predicting Achievement in Music." *Council Res Music Ed B* 13:40–5 sp '68. * (*PA* 42:15436)

85. HANSEN, EDA A. *The Relationship Between Grade Point Averages of the Henmon-Nelson Test of Mental Ability and the American College Test.* Master's thesis, Utah State University (Logan, Utah), 1968.

86. MANN, LESTER; HAUGHEY, CHARLES; TREFSGAR, THEODORE F.; AND KEFFER, CHARLES E. "Achievement and Personality Measurements Associated With Progress in a Programmed Course in Decimals and Fractions at a Fifth Grade Level." *Scientia Paedagogica Experimentalis* (Belgium) 5(1):76–83 '68. * (*PA* 45:3108)

87. MUNDAY, LEO. "Correlations Between ACT and Other Predictors of Academic Success in College." *Col & Univ* 44:67–76 f '68. *

88. SEWELL, WILLIAM H., AND SHAH, VIMAL P. "Social Class, Parental Encouragement, and Educational Aspirations." *Am J Sociol* 73:559–72 Mr '68. * (*PA* 42:11147)

89. WELCH, WAYNE W., AND ROTHMAN, ARTHUR I. "The Success of Recruited Students in a New Physics Course." *Sci Ed* 52:270–3 Ap '68. *

90. BERGER, VINCENT F.; MUNZ, DAVID C.; SMOUSE, ALBERT D.; AND ANGELINO, HENRY. "The Effects of Item Difficulty Sequencing and Anxiety Reaction Type on Aptitude Test Performance." *J Psychol* 71(2):253–8 Mr '69. * (*PA* 43:8674)

91. HAMILTON, DOROTHY DEE HOWE. *A Comparison of School Achievement, Teachers' Ratings, Self-Ratings, and a Personality Score as Predictors of Creative Thinking Potential.* Doctor's thesis, University of Nebraska (Lincoln, Neb.), 1969. (*DAI* 30:2905A)

92. HIERONYMUS, A. N., AND STROUD, JAMES B. "Comparability of IQ Scores on Five Widely Used Intelligence Tests." *Meas & Eval Guid* 2(3):135–40 f '69. * (*PA* 44:13285)

93. WALBERG, HERBERT J. "Predicting Class Learning: An Approach to the Class as a Social System." *Am Ed Res J* 6(4):529–42 N '69. * (*PA* 45:7078)

94. WESTPHAL, M. ELIZABETH; LEUTENEGGER, RALPH R.; AND WAGNER, DOROTHEA L. "Some Psycho-Acoustic and Intellectual Correlates of Achievement in German Language Learning of Junior High School Students." *Mod Lang J* 53(4):258–66 Ap '69. * (*PA* 44:21623)

95. CASSEL, RUSSELL N., AND KNOX, PATRICIA. "Improving High School Learning Predictions With Multiple Junior High Test Scores." *Calif J Ed Res* 21(1):14–20 Ja '70. *

96. JOHNSON, MARIE LOUISE. *Black Adolescents' Nonstandard English and Its Relation to Intellectual Skills.* Doctor's thesis, Illinois Institute of Technology (Chicago, Ill.), 1970. (*DAI* 31:7573B)

97. WALBERG, HERBERT J., AND AHLGREN, ANDREW. "Predictors of the Social Environment of Learning." *Am Ed Res J* 7(2):153–67 Mr '70. * (*PA* 46:11680)

98. WALKER, LARRY DALE. *The Effect of Reactive Inhibition and Extroversion on the Standardized Test Scores of Selected Groups of Students.* Doctor's thesis, Mississippi State University (State College, Miss.), 1970. (*DAI* 31:6249B)

99. BERMAN, GRAHAM, AND EISENBERG, MILDRED. "Psycho-Social Aspects of Academic Achievement." *Am J Orthopsychiatry* 41(3):406–15 Ap '71. * (*PA* 46:7673)

100. BUTLER, RALPH BACKSTROM. *Aptitude Test Performance of Negro College Students as Affected by Item Difficulty Sequence, Anxiety Reaction Type, and Sex Differences.* Doctor's thesis, University of Oklahoma (Norman, Okla.), 1971. (*DAI* 32:3776A)

101. DAVIS, GARY A., AND BELCHER, TERENCE L. "How Shall Creativity Be Measured? Torrance Tests, RAT, Alpha Biographical, and IQ." *J Creative Behav* 5(3):153–61 '71. *

102. VAUGHAN, MARGERY, AND MYERS, R. E. "Examination of Musical Process as Related to Creative Thinking." *J Res Music Ed* 19(3):337–41 f '71. * (*PA* 48:5879)

CUMULATIVE NAME INDEX

Ahlgren, A.: 97
Allen, R. M.: 24
Alteneder, L. E.: 5, 9
Anastasi, A.: *rev*, 2:1398
Angelino, H.: 90
Bailey, A. E.: 14
Barbe, W.: 28
Barrett, H. O.: 43, 65
Beckham, A. S.: 8
Belcher, T. L.: 101
Berger, V. F.: 90
Berman, G.: 99
Berry, G. S.: 63
Bessell, H.: 24
Blosser, G. H.: 47
Bond, E. A.: 1
Bond, G. L.: 27
Bushong, G. E.: 20
Butler, R. B.: 100
Byrns, R.: 51, 54
Carlile, A. B.: 33
Carr, A.: 46
Cassel, R. N.: 95
Christ, A. F.: 6
Condell, J. F.: 44
Conklin, B. B.: 81
Crites, J. O.: *exc*, 6:462
Cummings, R. W.: 45
Davis, A.: 66
Davis, G. A.: 101
Davis, W. A.: 21
Demand, J. W.: 15
Dennis, F. E.: 56
Dexter, E. S.: 53, 61
Dodson, M. H.: 26
Drake, L. E.: 2
Dvorak, A.: *rev*, 2:1398
Easley, H.: *rev*, 2:1398
Eells, K.: 66
Eisenberg, M.: 99
Embree, R. B.: 25
Emerick, L. M.: 7
Failor, L. M.: 10-1
Fowler, H. M.: *rev*, 4:299
Fowler, W. L.: 36, 39
Froehlich, G. J.: 12, 59
Frook, W. F.: 23
Glidden, G. W.: 75
Goodstein, L. D.: 45
Gordon, E.: 84
Grilk, W.: 28
Guilford, J. P.: *rev*, 2:1398
Haas, L.: 22
Hamilton, D. D. H.: 91
Hansen, E. A.: 85
Hartson, L. D.: 13, 16
Haughey, C.: 86
Havighurst, R. J.: 21, 66
Henmon, V. A. C.: 2–3
Herrick, V. E.: 66
Hieronymus, A. N.: 92
Hofstaetter, P. R.: 69
Hopkins, K. D.: 78
Hult, E.: 17
Johnson, D. M.: 60
Johnson, M. L.: 96
Johnson, R. H.: 27
Jurjevich, R.: 48
Justman, J.: 31
Kaczkowski, H. R.: 40
Keffer, C. E.: 86
Kienlen, J. S.: 73
Kirk, B. A.: 45
Knezevich, S. J.: 18
Knight, R.: 41
Knox, P.: 95
Lamke, T. A.: 35, 37
Laver, A. B.: 42
Lefever, D. W.: *rev*, 5:342
Leutenegger, R. R.: 94
Lewis, L. W.: 53
Lien, A. J.: 29
Lins, L. J.: 19
Little, J. K.: 70
Lyon, V. E.: 52
Mackenzie, D. M.: 57
McQuary, J. P.: 67
Mann, L.: 86
Martin, J. R.: 72
Maxfield, F. N.: *exc*, 2:1398
Mitchell, J. V.: 38
Morris, C. M.: 4, 58
Moser, W. E.: 64
Mumaw, M. J.: 74
Munday, L.: 87
Munz, D. C.: 90
Myers, R. E.: 102
Nelson, M. J.: 3
O'Connor, J. P.: 69
Ohlsen, M. M.: 79
Olander, H. T.: 55
Omwake, K. T.: 53
Pearson, R. E.: 79
Penfold, D. J.: 30
Pippert, R. R.: 71
Prothro, E. T.: 68
Randall, R. S.: 34
Renfer, M. E. F.: 80
Reynolds, F.: 60
Righthand, H.: 77
Rothman, A. I.: 89
Sax, G.: 46
Schroeder, W. L.: 49
Schurdak, J. J.: 82
Sellers, J. R.: 83
Sewell, W. H.: 88
Shaffer, L. F.: *exc*, 5:342
Shah, V. P.: 88
Smith, V. E.: 32
Smouse, A. D.: 90
Spoerl, D. T.: 62
Sprow, A. J.: 13
Stennett, R. G.: 41
Stroud, J. B.: 92
Suziedelis, A.: 69
Swan, R. J.: 78
Tobias, S.: 50
Trefsgar, T. F.: 86
Turner, G. H.: 30
Tyler, L. E.: *rev*, 5:342
Tyler, R. W.: 66
Vaughan, M.: 102
Wagner, D. L.: 94
Walberg, H. J.: 93, 97
Walker, B. S.: 55
Walker, L. D.: 98
Wallen, N. E.: *rev*, 6:462
Weiner, M.: 50
Welch, W. W.: 89
Westbrook, B. W.: 83
Westphal, M. E.: 94
Williams, H. V.: 67
Wrightstone, J. W.: 31
Zahn, J.: 76

[392]

Illinois Index of Scholastic Aptitude. Grades 9–12; 1966; IISA; B. Everard Blanchard; Western Psychological Services. *

For additional information and reviews by J. Stanley Ahmann and David A. Payne, see 7:358.

[393]

Inventory No. 2. Ages 16 and over; 1956; "a mental ability test"; Stevens, Thurow and Associates, Inc. *

For additional information, see 6:463.

[394]

Junior Scholastic Aptitude Test, Revised Edition. Grades 7–9; 1935–60; for independent schools; 2 scores:

verbal, numerical; 1959–60 tests identical with tests copyrighted 1957 except for cover page directions; Secondary Education Board (original edition); Geraldine Spaulding (revised edition); distributed for the National Association of Independent Schools by Educational Records Bureau. *

For additional information and a review by Jerome E. Doppelt, see 6:464 (5 references); see also 5:345 (7 references) and 3:233 (3 references).

REFERENCES THROUGH 1971

1-3. See 3:233.
4-10. See 5:345.
11-15. See 6:464.
16. TRAXLER, ARTHUR E. "A Note on the Correlation of the Secondary Education Board Junior Scholastic Aptitude Test With the College Entrance Examination Board Scholastic Aptitude Test." *Ed Rec B* 51:63–5 Ja '49. * (*PA* 23:3453)
17. TRAXLER, ARTHUR E. "A Further Study of Relationship Between the SEB Junior Scholastic Aptitude Test and the CEEB Scholastic Aptitude Test." *Ed Rec B* 53:48–51 Ja '50. * (*PA* 24:3898)
18. TOWNSEND, AGATHA. "The Junior Scholastic Aptitude Test in the Independent-School Program." *Ed Rec B* 57:58–65 Jl '51. * (*PA* 26:1107)
19. CLAWAR, HARRY J. "Some Examples of Best-Weighted Combinations of Junior Scholastic Aptitude Test Verbal and Numerical Scores When Predicting Standardized Achievement Test Performance." *Ed Rec B* 93:34–40 F '68. *

CUMULATIVE NAME INDEX

Clawar, H. J.: 19
Doppelt, J. E.: *rev*, 6:464
Jungeblut, A.: 14
Spaulding, G.: 8–12, 15
Townsend, A.: 3, 5, 18
Traxler, A. E.: 1–2, 4–7, 16–7
Vecchione, N.: 13

[395]

Kelvin Measurement of Ability in Infant Classes. Ages 5–8; 1935; C. M. Fleming; Robert Gibson & Sons, Glasgow, Ltd. [Scotland]. *

For additional information, see 5:346.

REFERENCES THROUGH 1971

1. THACKRAY, D. V. *The Relationship Between Reading Readiness and Reading Progress.* Master's thesis, University of London (London, England), 1964. (Abstract: *Brit J Ed Psychol* 35:252–4)

CUMULATIVE NAME INDEX

Thackray, D. V.: 1

[396]

Kelvin Measurement of Mental Ability. Ages 8–12; 1933; C. M. Fleming; Robert Gibson & Sons, Glasgow, Ltd. [Scotland]. *

For additional information, see 1:1047.

[397]

The Kingston Test of Intelligence. Ages 10–12; 1953–63; M. E. Hebron; George G. Harrap & Co. Ltd. [England]. *

For additional information and a review by H. J. Sants, see 6:465; for a review by A. W. Heim, see 5:347.

[398]

***Kuhlmann-Anderson Test, Seventh Edition.** Grades kgn, 1, 2, 3–4, 4–5, 5–7, 7–9, 9–12; 1927–67; KAT, also MAP; publisher uses title *Kuhlmann-Anderson Measure of Academic Potential* in promotional literature; 8 levels; F. Kuhlmann (fourth and earlier editions) and Rose G. Anderson; Personnel Press. *

a) BOOKLETS K, A, B, AND CD. Grades kgn, 1, 2, 3–4; 1927–65.

b) SEPARATE ANSWER SHEET EDITION. Grades 4–5, 5–7, 7–9, 9–12; 1927–67.

1) *Booklets D and EF.* Grades 4–5, 5–7; 1927–67.
2) *Booklets G and H.* Grades 7–9, 9–12; 1927–65; 3 scores: verbal, quantitative, total.

For additional information, reviews by William B. Michael and Douglas A. Pidgeon, and an excerpted review by Frederick B. Davis, see 6:466 (11 references); see also 5:348 (15 references); for reviews by Henry E. Garrett and David Segel of an earlier edition, see 4:302 (10 references); for reviews by W. G. Emmett and Stanley S. Marzolf, see 3:236 (25 references); for a review by Henry E. Garrett, see 2:1404 (15 references); for reviews by Psyche Cattell, S. A. Courtis, and Austin H. Turney, see 1:1049.

REFERENCES THROUGH 1971

1–15. See 2:1404.
16–40. See 3:236.
41–50. See 4:302.
51–65. See 5:348.
66–76. See 6:466.
77. HENRY, MARY BESS. "The Kuhlmann-Anderson Test of Intelligence—IX to Maturity." *Ed Res B* (Los Angeles City Schools) 8:15 D '28. *
78. MCALPIN, ALICE S. "Changes in the Intelligence Quotients of Negro Children." *J Negro Ed* 1:44–8 Ap '32. * (*PA* 8:3826)
79. COERS, WALTER CLARENCE. *Comparative Achievement of White and Mexican Junior High School Pupils.* Master's thesis, George Peabody College for Teachers (Nashville, Tenn.), 1933.
80. NILSON, KENNETH. "Certain Intelligence Aspects of a Group of Physically Disabled Pupils in Minnesota Public Schools." *J Ed Res* 26:513–6 Mr '33. * (*PA* 7:3061)
81. PRICE, ORVILLE K. *Comparative Validity and Reliability of Four Intelligence Tests in the Ninth Grade.* Master's thesis, University of Kentucky (Lexington, Ky.), 1933.
82. JAGGERS, CRADDOCK H. "The Relation of Intelligence to Behavior in School Children." *Peabody J Ed* 11:254–9 My '34. * (*PA* 9:997)
83. LEE, J. MURRAY, AND HUGHES, W. HARDIN. "Predicting Success in Algebra and Geometry." *Sch R* 42:188–96 Mr '34. *
84. LONG, HOWARD H. "The Intelligence of Colored Elementary Pupils in Washington, D.C." *J Negro Ed* 3:205–22 Ap '34. * (*PA* 8:3699)
85. LONG, HOWARD HALE. "Test Results of Third-Grade Negro Children Selected on the Basis of Socio-Economic Status." *J Negro Ed* 4:192–212, 523–52 Ap, O '35. * (*PA* 10:1089)
86. CHARLES, C. M. "A Comparison of the Intelligence Quotients of Incarcerated Delinquent White and American Negro Boys and of Groups of St. Louis Public School Boys." *J Appl Psychol* 20:499–510 Ag '36. * (*PA* 11:400)
87. OLANDER, HERBERT T., AND WALKER, BERT S. "Can Teachers Estimate I.Q.'s?" *Sch & Soc* 44:744–6 D 5 '36. * (*PA* 11:1490)
88. RYANS, DAVID G. "An Experimental Study of the Transfer of Training With Special Attention to the Relation of Intelligence Test Performance." *J Ed Psychol* 27:492–500 O '36. * (*PA* 11:1523)
89. TIEBOUT, CAROLYN. "The Measurement of Quality in Children's Painting by the Scale Method." *Psychol Monogr* 48(1):85–94 '36. * (*PA* 11:391)
90. TIEBOUT, CAROLYN, AND MEIER, NORMAN C. "Artistic Ability and General Intelligence." *Psychol Monogr* 48(1):95–125 '36. * (*PA* 11:392)
91. CRISSEY, ORLO L. *Mental Development as Related to Institutional Residence and Educational Achievement.* University of Iowa Studies in Child Welfare Vol. 13, No. 1. Iowa City, Iowa: the University, 1937. Pp. 81. * (*PA* 11:3477)
92. DESING, MINERVA F. *The Relation of Pupil Achievement Gain to Certain Personal and Environmental Elements.* Philadelphia, Pa.: University of Pennsylvania, 1940. Pp. xii, 169. *
93. BOYNTON, PAUL L. "The Relationship Between Children's Tested Intelligence and Their Hobby Participations." *J Genetic Psychol* 58:353–62 Je '41. * (*PA* 16:374)
94. BONNEY, MERL E. "The Relative Stability of Social, Intellectual, and Academic Status in Grades II to IV, and the Inter-Relationships Between These Various Forms of Growth." *J Ed Psychol* 34:88–102 F '43. * (*PA* 17:3943)
95. KOBLER, FRANK J. "Cultural Differences in Intelligence." *J Social Psychol* 18:279–303 S '43. * (*PA* 18:1145)
96. GILL, LESTER N., AND GILL, MYRTLE PAINE. "The Correlation of Reading Rate With Intelligence Scores of Grade School Children After Training in Phonics." *Proc Iowa Acad Sci* 51:377–81 '44. * (*PA* 20:3306)
97. LEWIS, W. DRAYTON. "Sex Distribution of Intelligence Among Inferior and Superior Children." *J Genetic Psychol* 67:67–75 S '45. * (*PA* 20:592)
98. ROBINSON, MARY LOUISE, AND MEENES, MAX. "The Relationship Between Test Intelligence of Third Grade Negro Children and the Occupations of Their Parents." *J Negro Ed* 16:136–41 w '47. * (*PA* 21:2933)
99. TOWNSEND, AGATHA. "An Investigation of Certain Relationships of Spelling With Reading and Academic Aptitude." *J Ed Res* 40:465–71 F '47. * (*PA* 21:3763)
100. JOHNSON, J. T. "On the Nature of Problem-Solving in Arithmetic." *J Ed Res* 43:110–5 O '49. * (*PA* 24:2791)
101. EELLS, KENNETH; DAVIS, ALLISON; HAVIGHURST, ROBERT J.; HERRICK, VERGIL E.; AND TYLER, RALPH W. *Intelligence and Cultural Differences: A Study of Cultural Learning*

and *Problem-Solving*. Chicago, Ill.: University of Chicago Press, 1951. Pp. xii, 388. * (*PA* 27:5738)
102. WALLIHAN, ROBERT SYLVANUS. *A Comparative Study of Retardation in the Primary Grades of the San Diego, California, City Schools*. Doctor's thesis, University of Colorado (Boulder, Colo.), 1955. (*DA* 16:1418)
103. HEBER, RICK F. "The Relation of Intelligence and Physical Maturity to Social Status of Children." *J Ed Psychol* 47:158-62 Mr '56. * (*PA* 31:7514)
104. EDWARDS, ROBERTA MILLER. *Factorial Comparison of Arithmetic Performance of Girls and Boys in the Sixth Grade*. Washington: D.C.: Catholic University of America, 1957. Pp. viii, 45. * (*PA* 32:842)
105. LARSON, ROBERT E., AND SELLAND, CYNTHIA T. "A Comparison of Reading Ages With Mental Ages." *J Ed Res* 52:55-9 O '58. * (*PA* 34:2105)
106. SMITH, GARY RICHARD. *An Examination of Selected Measures of Achievement and Aptitude for Use in Normative Grade Placement of Science Concepts on Light*. Doctor's thesis, Northwestern University (Evanston, Ill.), 1960. (*DA* 21:2952)
107. WOZENCRAFT, MARIAN. "Sex Comparisons of Certain Abilities." *J Ed Res* 57:21-7 S '63. *
108. BRYAN, QUENTIN R. "Relative Importance of Intelligence and Visual Perception in Predicting Reading Achievement." *Calif J Ed Res* 15:44-8 Ja '64. * (*PA* 38:9228)
109. MOORE, EARL JAMES. *A Study of the Relationship Between High School and College Scholarship and Selected Test Results for Grades K-12*. Doctor's thesis, University of South Dakota (Vermillion, S.D.), 1964. (*DA* 27:679A)
110. NORTH, ROBERT D. "An Appraisal of the Kuhlmann-Anderson Seventh Edition Test for Grades K-3 in Independent Schools." *Ed Rec B* 85:48-54 F '64. *
111. SHAFFER, RAYMOND GEORGE. *A Study of Four Group Intelligence Tests to Identify Ambiguous Pictures as a Factor Which Causes Some Children to Select Incorrect Answers*. Doctor's research study No. 1, Colorado State College (Greeley, Colo.), 1964. (*DA* 25:1014)
112. JOHNSON, MARILYN C. *Relationship Between Kuhlmann-Anderson Intelligence Tests and Reading Ability in Grade 3*. Master's thesis, University of Tulsa (Tulsa, Okla.), 1965.
113. NORTH, ROBERT D. "Kuhlmann-Anderson and Stanford Achievement Test Results of Sixth-Grade Students in Suburban Public Schools." *Ed Rec B* 88:67-70 Jl '65. *
114. NORTH, ROBERT D. "Kuhlmann-Anderson Seventh Edition IQs of Pupils in Independent Elementary Schools." *Ed Rec B* 87:50-6 F '65. *
115. RAINEY, ROBERT G. "A Study of Four School-Ability Tests." *J Exp Ed* 33:305-19 su '65. * (*PA* 39:12306)
116. WIMBY, EUGENE B. *A Comparative Study of the Kuhlmann-Anderson and the Otis Quick Scoring Intelligence Tests as Predictors of High School Performance*. Master's thesis, Atlanta University (Atlanta, Ga.), 1965.
117. YAMAMOTO, KAORU, AND DIZNEY, HENRY F. "Effects of Three Sets of Test Instructions on Scores on an Intelligence Scale." *Ed & Psychol Meas* 25:87-94 sp '65. * (*PA* 39:13029)
118. CUNNINGHAM, WILLIAM. *A Thirteen-Year Retrospective Study of Standardized Test Data*. Doctor's thesis, Western Reserve University (Cleveland, Ohio), 1966. (*DA* 27:3305A)
119. DAVIS, BARBARA H. *Comparison of the Row Peterson First Year Readiness Test Scores and the Kuhlmann-Anderson IQ as Predictors of Reading Achievement in Second Grade Boys*. Master's thesis, Kent State University (Kent, Ohio), 1966.
120. ZWIER, MARCIA D. "Interrelations Among Measured and Perceived Psychosocial Variables." *Percept & Motor Skills* 22:910 Je '66. * (*PA* 40:10998)
121. PATTERSON, BARBARA. *Comparison of Students From High and Low Socio-Economic Backgrounds Using Kuhlmann-Anderson and SCAT Total Test Scores*. Master's thesis, California State College (Hayward, Calif.), 1967.
122. GORDON, JAMES ROSCOE. *Listening, Attitude, and Intelligence Tests to Predict Academic Achievement*. Doctor's thesis, Colorado State College (Greeley, Colo.), 1968. (*DA* 29:2522A)
123. MAZUR, JOSEPH LAWRENCE. *Validity of Scholastic Aptitude Scores as Predictors of Achievement*. Doctor's thesis, Case Western Reserve University (Cleveland, Ohio), 1968. (*DAI* 30:171A)
124. GOFF, CHARLES EDWARD. *A Study of the Relationship Between Noncognitive Factors and General Intelligence to Academic Achievement at the Junior High School Level*. Doctor's thesis, Boston University (Boston, Mass.), 1969. (*DAI* 31:220A)
125. HIERONYMUS, A. N., AND STROUD, JAMES B. Comparability of IQ Scores on Five Widely Used Intelligence Tests." *Meas & Eval Guid* 2(3):135-40 f '69. * (*PA* 44:13285)
126. ANNESLEY, FRED; ODHNER, FRED; MADOFF, ELLEN; AND CHANSKY, NORMAN. "Identifying the First Grade Underachiever." *J Ed Res* 63(10):459-62 Jl-Ag '70. *
127. JOSE, TERESITA A. "Convergent-Divergent Thinking Abilities and Risk-Taking in Children." *Philippine J Psychol* 3(1):22-35 Je '70. * (*PA* 49:11231)
128. BRESKIN, STEPHEN, AND RICH, KENNETH D. "Correlation of Non-Verbal Rigidity and Intelligence in Elementary School Children." *Percept & Motor Skills* 32(1):194 F '71. * (*PA* 46:2729)
129. GWALTNEY, WAYNE KEITH. *Reading in Upward Bound: An Evaluation of a Reading Improvement Course and an Analysis of Some Correlates of Reading Achievement*. Doctor's thesis, University of Georgia (Athens, Ga.), 1971. (*DAI* 32:3557A)

CUMULATIVE NAME INDEX

Adkins, D. C.: 18-9
Allen, M. M.: 22, 33-4, 37
Anderson, R. G.: 15, 40
Annesley, F.: 126
Bailey, A. E.: 29
Bailey, H. K.: 50
Barnowe, T. J.: 47
Beach, S.: 62
Berson, P. M.: 20
Bliesmer, E. P.: 54, 60
Bond, G. L.: 51
Bonney, M. E.: 94
Boynton, R. L.: 9, 93
Bradway, K. P.: 12
Breskin, S.: 128
Bruce, M.: 23
Bryan, Q. R.: 108
Cabanski, C. L.: 38
Cantoni, L. J.: 55
Carlton, T.: 30
Cattell, P.: 6; *rev*, 1:1049
Cavell, A. C.: 21
Chambers, J. A.: 69
Chansky, N.: 126
Chapanis, A.: 38
Charles, C. M.: 7, 86
Coers, W. C.: 79
Courtis, S. A.: *rev*, 1:1049
Crissey, O. L.: 91
Cunningham, W.: 118
Davis, A.: 101
Davis, B. H.: 119
Davis, F. B.: *exc*, 6:466
Davis, W. A.: 49
Desing, M. F.: 92
Dizney, H. F.: 117
Edwards, R. M.: 104
Eells, K.: 101
Emmett, W. G.: *rev*, 3:236
Garrett, H. E.: *rev*, 2:1404, 4:302
Gentry, D. E.: 45
Gibbons, C. C.: 43
Gill, L. N.: 96
Gill, M. P.: 96
Goff, C. E.: 124
Gordon, J. R.: 122
Gwaltney, W. K.: 129
Hales, W. M.: 13
Hartson, L. D.: 25, 46
Havighurst, R. J.: 49, 101
Heber, R. F.: 103
Henry, M. B.: 77
Herrick, V. E.: 101
Hieronymus, A. N.: 125
Hilden, A. H.: 10
Hinkelman, E. A.: 56
Hoffeditz, E. L.: 12
Holland, P. E.: 35
Holsopple, I. G.: 66
Hughes, W. H.: 83
Jaggers, C. H.: 82
Johnson, J. T.: 100
Johnson, M. C.: 112
Johnson, R. H.: 51
Jose, T. A.: 127
Kelly, P. O.: 16
Knight, R.: 70
Kobler, F. J.: 95
Kuhlmann, F.: 1-4, 8, 31
Larson, R. E.: 105
Lee, J. M.: 83
Leon, J. F.: 57
Lewis, W. D.: 97
Lloyd, C. J.: 67
Long, H. H.: 84-5
Love, M. I. 62
McAlpin, A. S.: 78
Madoff, E.: 126
Marzolf, S. S.: *rev*, 3:236
Mazur, J. L.: 123
Meenes, M.: 98
Meier, N. C.: 90
Michael, W. B.: *rev*, 6:466
Moore, E. J.: 109
Mullen, F. A.: 32
Murphy, L. W.: 42
Nash, P. G.: 63
Nemzek, C. L.: 11, 17
Nilson, K.: 80
North, R. D.: 61, 65, 73-4, 110, 113-4
Odhner, F.: 126
Odoroff, M. E.: 31
Olander, H. T.: 87
Patterson, B.: 121
Pidgeon, D. A.: *rev*, 6:466
Price, W. C.: 81
Racky, D. J.: 71
Rainey, R. G.: 115
Rich, K. D.: 128
Richie, A.: 53
Robinson, M. L.: 98
Roslow, S.: 24
Ryans, D. G.: 88
Sawyer, C. R.: 41
Schena, R. A.: 75
Seagoe, M. V.: 44
Segel, D.: *rev*, 4:302
Selland, C. T.: 105
Shaffer, R. G.: 111
Skeels, H. M.: 10
Smith, G. R.: 106
Sniffen, A. M.: 76
Spache, G.: 14, 26
Spaulding, G.: 52
Sprow, A. J.: 25
Steckel, M. L.: 5
Stroud, J. B.: 125
Tiebout, C.: 89-90
Tilton, J. W.: 48
Townsend, A.: 36, 99
Traxler, A. E.: 27-8, 58-9, 64
Turney, A. H.: *rev*, 1:1049
Tyler, R. W.: 101
Vecchione, N.: 72
Walker, B. S.: 87
Wallihan, R. S.: 102
Williams, W. C.: 38
Wimberly, S. E.: 39
Wimby, E. G.: 116
Wozencraft, M.: 107
Yamamoto, K.: 117
Zwier, M. D.: 120

[399]

Kuhlmann-Finch Tests. Grades 1, 2, 3, 4, 5, 6, 7-9, 10-12; 1951-60; catalog uses the title *Kuhlmann-Finch Scholastic Aptitude Tests;* 1957 test identical with tests copyrighted 1951-52; Frank H. Finch; American Guidance Service, Inc. *

For additional information and reviews by Walter N. Durost, Henry E. Garrett, and Charles O. Neidt, see 5:349 (3 references).

REFERENCES THROUGH 1971

1-3. See 5:349.
4. SCHMUCK, RICHARD A., AND SCHMUCK, ROBERT W. "Upward Mobility and I.Q. Performance." *J Ed Res* 55:123-7 N '61. * (*PA* 36:5GC23S)
5. CLYMER, THEODORE. "A Study of the Influence of Reading

Ability on the Validity of Group Intelligence Tests." *Slow Learning Child* (England) 10:76–84 N '63. *
6. SNIFFEN, ALLAN MEAD. *A Correlation Study of Group Intelligence Tests With Achievement in Reading and Arithmetic in Grade Four: An Investigation of the Effectiveness of Using Group Intelligence Test Scores for Evaluating Academic Achievement in the Tool Subject Areas of Reading and Arithmetic in Public Elementary Schools.* Doctor's thesis, New York University (New York, N.Y.), 1963. (*DA* 24:826)
7. LARSON, ANNE A. *A Study to Determine the Correlation Between a Set of Scores Received on the SRA Primary Mental Abilities Test Given in Kindergarten and a Set of Scores Received on the Kuhlmann-Finch Group Intelligence Test in Third Grade.* Master's thesis, Moorehead State College (Moorehead, Minn.), 1966.
8. DOMRATH, RICHARD P. "Constructional Praxis and Visual Perception in School Children." *J Consult & Clin Psychol* 32:186–92 Ap '68. * (*PA* 42:8174)
9. MENDENHALL, DIANA R. *The Influences of Various Methods of Test Interpretation of the Kuhlmann-Finch Tests.* Master's thesis, Wisconsin State University (Platteville, Wis.), 1970.

CUMULATIVE NAME INDEX

Clymer, T.: 5
Coleman, W.: 1
Domrath, R. P.: 8
Durost, W. N.: *rev*, 5:349
Edgar, M.: 3
Frandsen, A. N.: 2
Garrett, H. E.: *rev*, 5:349
Grimes, J. W.: 2
Larson, A. A.: 7
Mendenhall, D. R.: 9
Mouly, G. J.: 3
Neidt, C. O.: *rev*, 5:349
Schmuck, R. A.: 4
Schmuck, R.: 4
Sniffen, A. M.: 6
Ward, A. W.: 1

[400]

Lorge-Thorndike Intelligence Tests. Grades kgn–13; 1954–66; LTIT; 2 editions; Irving Lorge, Robert L. Thorndike, and Elizabeth Hagen (*b*); Houghton Mifflin Co. *

a) SEPARATE LEVEL EDITION. Grades kgn–1, 2–3, 4–6, 7–9, 10 12; 1954 62; 5 levels; 2 tests (verbal, nonverbal) for levels 3–5.
 1) *Level 1, Nonverbal Battery.* Grades kgn–1.
 2) *Level 2, Nonverbal Battery.* Grades 2–3.
 3) *Level 3.* Grades 4–6.
 4) *Level 4.* Grades 7–9.
 5) *Level 5.* Grades 10–12.

b) MULTI-LEVEL EDITION. Grades 3–13; 1954–66; revision of levels 3–5 of the separate level edition; 3 scores: verbal, nonverbal, composite; 8 levels (grades 3, 4, 5, 6, 7, 8–9, 10–11, 12–13) in a single booklet; test for grades 12–13 also available as a separate (see 401).

For additional information and a review by Carol K. Tittle of the multi-level edition, see 7:360 (95 references); see also 6:467 (11 references); for reviews by Frank S. Freeman, John E. Milholland, and D. A. Pidgeon of the separate level edition, see 5:350 (6 references).

REFERENCES THROUGH 1971

1–6. See 5:350.
7–17. See 6:467.
18–112. See 7:360.
113. NEWTON, BERTHA M. "A Study of Certain Factors Related to Achievement in Spelling." *Alberta J Ed Res* (Canada) 7:202–8 D '61. * (*PA* 36:5KL02N)
114. CONVERSE, HAROLD D., AND COURTNEY, JOHN MICHAEL. "A Comparative Study of the Lorge-Thorndike Group Intelligence Tests With an Individual Intelligence Test." *J Res Services* 1:1–5 My '62. *
115. POLLARD, ALICE G. *A Comparison of the Performance of a Group of Intellectually Retarded Children on Three Group Tests of Intelligence.* Master's thesis, Catholic University of America (Washington, D.C.), 1963.
116. NADEAU, CORINNE. *A Comparison of the Performance of a Group of Intellectually Normal Children on Three Group Tests of Intelligence.* Master's thesis, Catholic University of America (Washington, D.C.), 1964.
117. RAPHAEL, SHARON. *The Relationship of Intelligence and Personality on the Reading Achievement of Culturally Deprived Second-Grade Students.* Master's thesis, Central Connecticut State College (New Britain, Conn.), 1965.
118. ROFF, MERRILL, AND SELLS, S. B. "Relations Between Intelligence and Sociometric Status in Groups Differing in Sex and Socio-Economic Background." *Psychol Rep* 16:511–6 Ap '65. * (*PA* 39:9929)
119. TRAD, MICHAEL, JR. *Intelligence: Relationship With Achievement of Junior High School Students.* Master's thesis, Illinois State University (Normal, Ill.), 1965.
120. MACARTHUR, R. S., AND MOSYCHUK, H. "Lower and Upper Socioeconomic Group Contrasts in Long-Term Predictability of Grade Nine Achievement." *J Ed Meas* 3:167–8 su '66. *
121. BATH, JOHN A. "Mental Ability of Residents in a State School for Dependent and Neglected Youth." *Psychol Rep* 20:469–70 Ap '67. * (*PA* 41:8716)
122. GUSTAFSON, RAYMOND G. *Predicting Student Success in Ninth Grade Algebra in the Public Schools of Watertown, Minnesota.* Master's thesis, St. Cloud State College (St. Cloud, Minn.), 1967.
123. HOHENSHIL, THOMAS H. *The Effects of Discouragement on the Verbal Section of a Group Intelligence Test.* Master's thesis, Kent State University (Kent, Ohio), 1967.
124. RUDNICK, MARK; STERRITT, GRAHAM M.; AND FLAX, MORTON. "Auditory and Visual Rhythm Perception and Reading Ability." *Child Develop* 38:581–7 Je '67. * (*PA* 41:10263)
125. YAMAMOTO, KAORU. "Creativity and Unpredictability in School Achievement." *J Ed Res* 60:321–5 Mr '67. *
126. OHNMACHT, FRED W. "Correlates of Change in Academic Achievement." *J Ed Meas* 5:41–4 sp '68. *
127. AMES, WILBUR S. "Reading Programs: Use of Test Data as a Vital Factor." *Clearing House* 43(9):515–8 My '69. *
128. HAMMOND, LONNIE L. *A Non-Linear Relationship Study of Personality and Intelligence.* Master's thesis, East Tennessee State University (Johnson City, Tenn.), 1969.
129. EHRHART, PATRICIA MAULDIN. *A Study of Selected Mental Ability Tests as Predictors of Achievement for Chamorro Pupils.* Master's thesis, University of Guam (Agana, Guam), 1970.
130. MANCOTT, ANATOL. "Prediction of Performance in Chemistry II." *Nursing Outl* 18(11):57 N '70. *
131. MIRON, MORDECHAI. *Principles for Equivalent Cross-Cultural Utilization of Group Intelligence Tests.* Doctor's thesis, University of Pittsburgh (Pittsburgh, Pa.), 1970. (*DAI* 31:6474A)
132. MITCHELL, KATHARINE E. *An Early Predictive Test and Its Relationship to Junior High School Achievement.* Doctor's thesis, Syracuse University (Syracuse, N.Y.), 1970. (*DAI* 32:97A)
133. BUSCH, JOHN CHRISTIAN, AND DE RIDDER, LAWRENCE M. "Note on Control for Intelligence in Studies of Field Dependence With Young Children." *Percept & Motor Skills* 32(1):337–8 F '71. * (*PA* 46:2634)
134. COUNTS, PERRY DALMOND. *A Study of the Relationship Between Academic Achievement and Creativity.* Doctor's thesis, University of Tennessee (Knoxville, Tenn.), 1971. (*DAI* 32:4342A)
135. DACEY, JOHN S., AND MADAUS, GEORGE F. "An Analysis of Two Hypotheses Concerning the Relationship Between Creativity and Intelligence." *J Ed Res* 64(5):213–6 Ja '71. * (*PA* 46:4712)
136. FOLLMAN, JOHN; LOWE, A. J.; AND WILEY, RUSSELL. "Correlational and Factor Analysis of Critical Reading and Thinking Test Scores—Twelfth Grade." *Yearb Nat Read Conf* 20:128–36 '71. *
137. GREEN, RICHARD B., AND ROHWER, WILLIAM D., JR. "SES Differences on Learning and Ability Tests in Black Children." *Am Ed Res J* 8(4):601–9 N '71. * (*PA* 47:11611)
138. JENSEN, ARTHUR R. "Do Schools Cheat Minority Children?" *Ed Res* (England) 14(1):3–28 N '71. * (*PA* 49:11953)
139. JOHNSON, ROGER; FOLLMAN, JOHN; WILEY, RUSSELL; LOWE, A. J.; AND MILLER, WILLIAM. "Canonical and Partial Correlation of Critical Reading and Critical Thinking Test Scores—Twelfth Grade." *Yearb Nat Read Conf* 20:137–41 '71. *
140. KAUFFMAN, JAMES M.; WEAVER, S. JOSEPH; AND WEAVER, ANN. "Age and Intelligence as Correlates of Perceived Family Relationships of Underachievers." *Psychol Rep* 28(2):522 Ap '71. * (*PA* 46:7758)
141. KAUFMAN, ALAN S. "Piaget and Gesell: A Psychometric Analysis of Tests Built From Their Tasks." *Child Develop* 42(5):1341–60 N '71. * (*PA* 48:4592)
142. LOWE, A. J.; FOLLMAN, JOHN; BURLEY, WADE; AND FOLLMAN, JOHNNY. "Psychometric Analysis of Critical Reading and Critical Thinking Test Scores—Twelfth Grade." *Yearb Nat Read Conf* 20:142–7 '71. *
143. PROGER, BARTON B.; MCGOWAN, JOHN R.; BAYUK, ROBERT J., JR.; MANN, LESTER; TREVORROW, RUTH L.; AND MASSA, EDWARD. "The Relative Predictive and Construct Validities of the Otis-Lennon Mental Ability Test, the Lorge-Thorndike Intelligence Test, and the Metropolitan Readiness Test in Grades Two and Four: A Series of Multivariate Analyses." *Ed & Psychol Meas* 31(2):529–38 su '71. *
144. RICHMOND, BERT O. "Creative and Cognitive Abilities of White and Negro Children." *J Negro Ed* 40(2):111–6 sp '71. * (*PA* 47:7566)
145. ROSENOFF, CHARLES B., AND WILLIAMS, JOHN D. "A Comparison of the Lorge-Thorndike Intelligence Test Total IQ and the General Aptitude Test Battery Aptitude G." *Col Ed Rec Univ N Dak* 56(9):167–70 Je '71. *
146. SMITH, I. LEON. "IQ, Creativity, and Achievement: Interaction and Threshold." *Multiv Behav Res* 6(1):51–62 Ja '71. * (*PA* 46:9753)
147. TAYLOR, ALTON L. "Regression Analysis of Antecedent

Measures of Slow Sections in High School Biology." *Sci Ed* 55(3):395–402 Jl–S '71. *

148. WILLIAMSON, HELEN THORWORTH. *Tolerance of Ambiguity and Creativity Thinking in Elementary School Children: A Study of the Relationships Among Tolerance of Ambiguity, Intelligence, Training in Creative Thinking, and Flexibility of Concept Formation.* Doctor's thesis, New York University (New York, N.Y.), 1971. (*DAI* 32:6821A)

149. YOLOYE, EMMANUEL AYOTUNDE. "The Effect of Schooling on the Performance of Bilingual Students in Tests of Intelligence." *Res Ed* (England) 5:25–34 My '71. * (*PA* 47:3646)

150. YOUNG, WILLIAM T. "The Role of Musical Aptitude, Intelligence, and Academic Achievement in Predicting the Musical Attainment of Elementary Instrumental Music Students." *J Res Music Ed* 19(4):385–98 w '71. * (*PA* 48:7918)

CUMULATIVE NAME INDEX

Abdel-Ghaffar, A. S. A. K.: 28
Allison, D. E.: 105
Alzobaie, A. J.: 71
Ames, W. S.: 127
Anderson, W. F.: 11
Bailey, R. J.: 45
Balow, I. H.: 19
Barrett, T. C.: 24
Bath, J. A.: 121
Bayuk, R. J.: 143
Bland, R. B.: 86
Boersma, F. J.: 72
Brendemuehl, F. L.: 61
Bromer, J. A.: 12
Brown, B.: 33
Burley, W.: 142
Busch, P. C.: 133
Caldwell, J. R.: 106
Canabal, J. V.: 107
Caplan, S. W.: 16
Cave, R. L.: 62, 108
Cicchetti, D. V.: 73
Constantinides, P. D.: 46
Converse, H. D.: 114
Counts, P. D.: 134
Courtney, J. M.: 114
Cropley, A. J.: 63
Dacey, J. S.: 135
Demopoulos, C. G.: 32
De Ridder, L. M.: 133
Deutsch, M.: 33
Doherty, V. W.: 13
Dudek, S. Z.: 87–8, 109
Dyer, G. B.: 88
Dykstra, R.: 54
Eagle, N.: 55
Edwards, A. J.: 34
Ehrhart, P. M.: 129
Elley, W. B.: 17
Felton, T. A.: 89
Fischer, R. F.: 22
Fitzgerald, L. A.: 21
Flax, M.: 124
Follman, J.: 136, 139, 142
Freeman, F. S.: *rev*, 5:350
Glad, J. R. B.: 47
Gnauck, J.: 10
Goldberg, J. S.: 87–8
Green, R. B.: 137
Gundersen, R. O.: 20
Gustafson, R. G.: 122
Hage, D. S.: 7–8
Hammond, L. L.: 128
Harms, C. R.: 23
Harris, B. R.: 87
Hayes, R. E. M.: 90
Hieronymus, A. N.: 91
Hill, K. T.: 38
Hohenshil, T. H.: 123
Hopkins, K. D.: 52
Huck, C. S.: 85
Ingebo, G. S.: 13
Jensen, A. R.: 138
Johnson, J. M.: 12
Johnson, R.: 139
Jungeblut, A.: 35
Kaczkowski, H.: 10
Kakkar, S. B.: 74
Kandel, A.: 56
Kangas, R. D.: 48
Karnes, F. R.: 75
Karzen, J. M.: 49
Katzenmeyer, W. G.: 25
Kauffman, J. M.: 140
Kaufman, A. S.: 141
Keach, C. C.: 57
Kerfoot, J. F.: 36
Kilgore, L. L.: 14
King, M. L.: 85
Kirby, M. E.: 34
Klein, R. A.: 37
Knief, L. M.: 2, 9
Lanier, P. E.: 64
Lehmann, I. J.: 96
Lehrer, B. E.: 76
Lerner, E.: 73
Lessing, E. E.: 92
Lester, E. P.: 87–8, 109
Leutenegger, R. R.: 103
Lowe, A. J.: 136, 139, 142
MacArthur, R.: 78
MacArthur, R. S.: 17, 27, 42, 77, 80, 93, 120
McComas, W.: 65
McComas, W. C.: 66
McCutcheon, N. S.: 94
McGowan, J. R.: 143
Madaus, G. F.: 135
Mancott, A.: 79, 95, 130
Mann, L.: 143
Massa, E.: 143
Mattick, W. E.: 29
Mehrens, W. A.: 96
Metfessel, N. S.: 71
Meyers, C. E.: 106
Michael, W. B.: 71, 106
Milholland, J. E.: *rev*, 5:350
Miller, W.: 139
Miron, M.: 131
Mitchell, K. E.: 132
Morper, J.: 58
Mortensen, J. B.: 26
Mosychuk, H.: 120
Motley, H. C.: 97
Muir, R.: 109
Nadeau, C.: 116
Newton, B. M.: 113
Nikas, G. B.: 98
North, R. D.: 3
Nye, M. R.: 110
Oas, R. T.: 99
O'Bryan, K.: 72
Ohnmacht, F.: 81
Ohnmacht, F. W.: 59, 126
Olson, D. R.: 27
Owen, J. C.: 4
Panther, E. E.: 67
Pidgeon, D. A.: *rev*, 5:350
Pollard, A. G.: 115
Proger, B. B.: 143
Rainey, R. G.: 50
Raphael, S.: 117
Rattan, M. S.: 80
Ray, J. R.: 51
Rice, V.: 68
Richmond, B. O.: 144
Roberts, D. E.: 18
Robertson, J. W.: 69
Rodgers, D. C.: 100
Roff, M.: 118
Rohwer, W. D.: 137
Rosen, C. L.: 81
Rosenau, C. B.: 145
Rosner, B.: 1
Ruble, R. A.: 16
Rudnick, M.: 124
Sarason, S. B.: 38
Sattabanasuk, T.: 82
Schlueter, M. P.: 30
Schrader, D. R.: 106
Segel, D.: 16
Sells, S. B.: 118
Sevransky, P.: 12
Shaffer, R. G.: 39
Shea, C. A.: 40, 83
Shigaki, I. S.: 101
Smith, I. L.: 111, 146
Sonneman, L. J.: 31
Sterritt, G. M.: 124
Stroud, J. B.: 8–9, 91
Suvetor, H.: 49
Swan, R. J.: 52
Taylor, A. L.: 41, 147
Thompson, G.: 49
Tittle, C. K.: *rev*, 7:360
Torrance, E. P.: 102
Trad, M.: 119
Traxler, A. E.: 5–6
Trevornow, R. L.: 143
Wagner, D. L.: 103
Ward, G.: 60, 65
Wartenberg, H.: 70
Weaver, A.: 140
Weaver, S. J.: 140
West, L. W.: 42
Weston, L. D.: 84
Westphal, M. E.: 103
Wiley, R.: 136, 139
Williams, B. L.: 43
Williams, J. D.: 145
Williamson, H. T.: 148
Willis, J.: 112
Wolf, W.: 85
Womer, F. B.: 15
Yamamoto, K.: 44, 125
Yoloye, E. A.: 53, 149
Young, W. T.: 104, 150
Zagorin, S. W.: 92
Zimbardo, P. G.: 38

[401]

Lorge-Thorndike Intelligence Tests, College Edition. Grades 12–13; 1954–66; LTIT-H; Level H of the Multi-Level Edition (see 400); 3 scores: verbal, nonverbal, composite; Irving Lorge, Robert L. Thorndike, and Elizabeth Hagen; Houghton Mifflin Co. *

For additional information and reviews by Eric F. Gardner, William B. Michael, and John H. Rosenbach, see 7:359.

[402]

***Mental Alertness: Tests A/1 and A/2.** Job applicants with 9–11, 12 or more years of education; 1945–68; 2 levels; no manual; National Institute for Personnel Research [South Africa]. *

a) TEST A/2. Job applicants with 9–11 years of education; 1945–68; revision of Test A(G) of the South African Air Force.

b) TEST A/1. Job applicants with 12 or more years of education; 1945–62; revision of Test A(F) of the South African Air Force.

For additional information, see 7:362.

[403]

Mill Hill Vocabulary Scale. Ages 4 and over, 11–14, 14 and over; 1943–58; intelligence; 2 editions; John C. Raven; H. K. Lewis & Co. Ltd. [England]. *

a) ORAL DEFINITIONS FORM. Ages 4 and over; consists of all words from both forms of the junior and senior levels below.

b) WRITTEN TEST. Ages 11–14, 14 and over. (Australian edition of senior level: Australian Council for Educational Research [Australia].)

For additional information and a review by Morton Bortner, see 6:471 (16 references); see also 4:303 (7 references); for a review by David Wechsler, see 3:239 (3 references).

REFERENCES THROUGH 1971

1–3. See 3:239.
4–10. See 4:303.
11–26. See 6:471.
27. CROWN, SIDNEY. "An Experimental Study of Psychological Changes Following Prefrontal Lobotomy." *J General Psychol* 47:3–41 Jl '52. * (*PA* 27:6024)
28. DAVIES-EYSENCK, MARGARET. "Cognitive Factors in Epilepsy." *J Neurol Neurosurg & Psychiatry* (England) 15:39–44 F '52. * (*PA* 27:2918)
29. FOULDS, G. A. "The Reliability of Psychiatric, and the Validity of Psychological, Diagnoses." *J Mental Sci* (England) 101:851–62 O '55. * (*PA* 30:7165)
30. HOPKINS, BARBARA, AND POST, FELIX. "The Significance of Abstract and Concrete Behaviour in Elderly Psychiatric Patients and Control Subjects." *J Mental Sci* (England) 101:841–50 O '55. * (*PA* 30:7000)
31. MEYER, VICTOR, AND YATES, AUBREY J. "Intellectual Changes Following Temporal Lobectomy for Psychomotor Epilepsy: Preliminary Communication." *J Neurol Neurosurg & Psychiatry* (England) 18:44–52 F '55. * (*PA* 29:7775)
32. MONTGOMERY, G. W. G. "Predicting Success in Engineering." *Occup Psychol* (England) 36:59–68 Ja–Ap '62. *
33. ROSS, JEAN. "Predicting Practical Skill in Engineering Apprentices." *Occup Psychol* (England) 36:69–74 Ja–Ap '62. *
34. SAMPSON, OLIVE C. "Reading Skill at Eight Years in

Relation to Speech and Other Factors." *Brit J Ed Psychol* 32:12–7 F '62. *

35. FOULDS, G. A., AND OWEN, ANNA. "Speed and Accuracy on Mazes in Relation to Diagnosis and Personality." *Brit J Social & Clin Psychol* 3:34–5 F '64. * (*PA* 38:8870)

36. GIBSON, H. B. "A Slang Vocabulary Test as an Indicator of Delinquent Association." *Brit J Social & Clin Psychol* 3:50–5 F '64. * (*PA* 38:8999)

37. KENDRICK, D. C. "Assessment of Pre-Morbid Intelligence of Elderly Patients With Diffuse Brain Pathology." *Psychol Rep* 15:188 Ag '64. * (*PA* 39:1389)

38. VINODA, K. S. "A Comparative Study of the Personality Characteristics of Attempted Suicides, Psychiatric Patients and Normals." *Trans All-India Inst Mental Health* 5:67–74 D '65. * (*PA* 40:7860)

39. GIBSON, H. B. "The Validation of a Technique for Measuring Delinquent Association by Means of Vocabulary." *Brit J Social & Clin Psychol* 5:190–5 S '66. * (*PA* 40:13338)

40. LEY, P.; SPELMAN, M. S.; DAVIES, ANN D. M.; AND RILEY, S. "The Relationships Between Intelligence, Anxiety, Neuroticism and Extraversion." *Brit J Ed Psychol* 36:185–91 Je '66. * (*PA* 40:10100)

41. HERON, ALASTAIR, AND CHOWN, SHEILA. *Age and Function.* London: J. & A. Churchill Ltd., 1967. Pp. x, 182. *

42. PAYNE, R. W.; NETLEY, C. T.; AND SLOANE, R. B. "Rigidity, Drive and Conditioning in Neurotics." *Brit J Psychol* 58:111–26 My '67. * (*PA* 42:10857)

43. MONTGOMERY, G. W. G. "A Factorial Study of Communication and Ability in Deaf School Leavers." *Brit J Ed Psychol* 38:27–37 F '68. * (*PA* 42:12755)

44. MUNRO, HELLE. "Verbal Fluency in Test and Group Situations." *Brit J Proj Psychol & Pers Study* 13:25–9 Je '68. * (*PA* 45:946)

45. FARLEY, FRANK H. "Further Data on Multiple-Choice Versus Open-Ended Estimates of Vocabulary." *Brit J Social & Clin Psychol* 8(1):67–8 F '69. * (*PA* 43:7551)

46. JAMIESON, G. HARRY. "Prior Learning and Response Flexibility in Two Age Groups." *J Gerontol* 24(2):179–83 Ap '69. *

47. ROMNEY, DAVID. "The Validity of Certain Tests of Overinclusion." *Brit J Psychiatry* 115(522):591–2 My '69. * (*PA* 44:3689)

48. FOULDS, G. A. "Progressive Matrices and the Mill Hill Vocabulary Scale as a Diagnostic Aid Among Psychiatric Patients." *Brit J Social & Clin Psychol* 9(1):80–2 F '70. *

49. GIBSON, H. B., AND WEST, D. J. "Social and Intellectual Handicaps as Precursors of Early Delinquency." *Brit J Criminol* 10(1):21–32 Ja '70. * (*PA* 44:16949)

50. IRVING, G.; ROBINSON, R. A.; AND MCADAM, W. "The Validity of Some Cognitive Tests in the Diagnosis of Dementia." *Brit J Psychiatry* 117(537):149–56 Ag '70. * (*PA* 45:4539)

51. KEAR-COLWELL, J. J. "The B Factor Scale of the 16 PF as a Measure of Intelligence in Psychiatric Patients." *J Clin Psychol* 26(4):477–9 O '70. * (*PA* 45:4540)

52. MCKERRACHER, D. W.; ZWIRNER, W.; AND HARSHMAN, R. C. "Personality and Attainment: A Pilot Study." *West Psychologist* (Canada) 1(2):62–70 Ja '70. *

53. ORME, J. E. "A Practical Guide to Estimating Intelligence, Attainments and Intellectual Deficit." *Acta Psychologica* (Netherlands) 32(2):145–61 Ap '70. * (*PA* 44:16684)

54. PECK, DAVID F. "The Conversion of Progressive Matrices and Mill Hill Vocabulary Raw Scores Into Deviation IQ's." *J Clin Psychol* 26(1):67–70 Ja '70. * (*PA* 44:10420)

55. WARDER, JOHN; PRESLY, ALLAN S.; AND KIRK, JOAN. "Intelligence and Literacy in Prison and Hospital Populations." *Brit J Criminol* 10(3):286–7 Jl '70. * (*PA* 46:1469)

56. EYSENCK, HANS J. "Relation Between Intelligence and Personality." *Percept & Motor Skills* 32(2):637–8 Ap '71. * (*PA* 46:10929)

57. LOVIUS, B. B. J. "Speech and Intelligence in Adult Cleft-Palate Patients." *Dental Prac & Dental Rec* 21(8):290–3 Ap '71. *

58. SPELMAN, MICHAEL S.; HARRISON, ARTHUR W.; AND MELLSOP, GRAHAM W. "Grid Test for Schizophrenic Thought Disorder in Acute and Chronic Schizophrenia." *Psychol Med* (England) 1(3):234–8 My '71. * (*PA* 47:11296)

CUMULATIVE NAME INDEX

Bortner, M.: *rev,* 6:471
Chown, S.: 41
Costa, L. D.: 21
Crown, S.: 27
Davies, A. D. M.: 40
Davies-Eysenck, M.: 28
Desai, M.: 3
Desai, M. M.: 17
Dixon, P.: 22–4
Dunsdon, M. I.: 12–4, 18
Eysenck, H. J.: 3, 56
Farley, F. H.: 45
Foulds, G. A.: 4–5, 8–9, 16, 22–4, 29, 35, 48
Furneaux, W. D.: 3
Gibson, H. B.: 36, 39, 49
Gordon, I. E.: 19
Graham, C.: 25
Halstead, H.: 3
Hamilton, V.: 26
Harrison, A. W.: 58
Harshman, R. C.: 52
Heron, A.: 41
Himmelweit, H. T.: 2–3
Hopkins, B.: 30
Irving, G.: 50
Jamieson, G. H.: 46
Kear-Colwell, J. J.: 51
Kelley, J.: 11
Kendrick, D. C.: 37
Kirk, J.: 55
Ley, P.: 40
Lovius, B. B. J.: 57
Lynn, R.: 19
McAdam, W.: 50
McClelland, M.: 24
McClelland, W. J.: 24
McKerracher, D. W.: 52
McKinlay, M.: 3
Marum, O.: 3
Mellsop, G. W.: 58
Meyer, V.: 31
Montgomery, G. W. G.: 32, 43
Munro, H.: 44
Netley, C. T.: 42
Orme, J. E.: 15, 53
Owen, A.: 35
Payne, R. W.: 42
Peck, D. F.: 54
Petrie, A.: 3, 10
Pinkerton, P.: 11
Post, F.: 30
Powell, M. B.: 10
Presly, A. S.: 55
Raven, J. C.: 1, 4–6
Rees, W. L.: 3
Riley, S.: 40
Roberts, J. A. F.: 13–4, 18
Robinson, R. A.: 50
Romney, D.: 47
Ross, J.: 33
Sampson, O. C.: 34
Slater, P.: 7
Sloane, R. B.: 42
Spelman, M. S.: 40, 58
Vaughan, H. G.: 21
Venables, E. C.: 20
Vinoda, K. S.: 38
Walshaw, J. B.: 1
Warder, J.: 55
Wechsler, D.: *rev,* 3:239
West, D. J.: 49
Yap, P. M.: 3
Yates, A. J.: 31
Zwirner, W.: 52

[404]

Miller Analogies Test. Candidates for graduate school; 1926–70; MAT; Forms J and R also published under the title *Advanced Personnel Test* for use in business; distribution restricted and test administered at specified licensed university centers; W. S. Miller (test); Psychological Corporation. *

For additional information, see 7:363 (57 references); for reviews by Lloyd G. Humphreys, William B. Schrader, and Warren W. Willingham, see 6:472 (26 references); for a review by John T. Dailey, see 5:352 (28 references); for reviews by J. P. Guilford and Carl I. Hovland, see 4:304 (16 references).

REFERENCES THROUGH 1971

1–16. See 4:304.
17–44. See 5:352.
45–70. See 6:472.
71–127. See 7:363.

128. SORENSON, HERBERT. "Adult Ages as a Factor in Learning." *J Ed Psychol* 21:451–9 S '30. * (*PA* 5:108)

129. BLAKE, ROBERT R. "The Relation Between Childhood Environment and the Scholastic Aptitude and Intelligence of Adults." *J Social Psychol* 29:37–41 F '49. * (*PA* 23:4132)

130. DUMLER, MARVIN J. "A Study of Factors Related to Gains in the Reading Rate of College Students Trained With the Tachistoscope and Accelerator." *J Ed Res* 52:27–30 S '58. * (*PA* 33:10956)

131. WIDENER, SUE ELLEN. *A Statistical Analysis for Predicting Success in Graduate School.* Master's thesis, East Tennessee State University (Johnson City, Tenn.), 1964.

132. "Science and Nursing Knowledge of Graduate Students." *Nursing Outl* 15:53 D '67. *

133. HARTSOCK, WOODROW WILSON. *The Prediction of Academic Performance in a Seminary.* Master's thesis, Southern Methodist University (Dallas, Tex.), 1967.

134. FELKER, SALLY ANNA. *The Relationship Between Communication and Discrimination Skills and Selected Factors of Personality, Intellect, and Experience in Counselor Trainees.* Doctor's thesis, Kent State University (Kent, Ohio), 1970. (*DAI* 31:5122A)

135. JARDIN, ROBERT PATRICK. *An Analysis of Peer Ratings and Subordinate Ratings as a Potential Feedback and Self-Selection Device for School Counselor Candidates.* Doctor's thesis, American University (Washington, D.C.), 1970. (*DAI* 32:178A)

136. POROZNY, GEORGE HAROLD JOHN. *Relationship of Selected Intellectual and Personal Factors to Completion of the Business Education Doctoral Program at Selected American Universities.* Doctor's thesis, University of North Dakota (Grand Forks, N.D.), 1970. (*DAI* 31:6488A)

137. AYERS, JERRY B. "Predicting Quality Point Averages in Master's Degree Programs in Education." *Ed & Psychol Meas* 31(2):491–5 su '71. *

138. BURRELL, LEON FREDERICK. *Non-Academic Variables as They Relate to Academic Achievement of Male Black Doctoral Candidates.* Doctor's thesis, Michigan State University (East Lansing, Mich.), 1971. (*DAI* 32:4863A)

139. DOPPELT, JEROME E. "Differences Between the Miller Analogies Test Scores of People Tested Twice." *Ed & Psychol Meas* 31(3):735–44 au '71. * (*PA* 47:7556)

140. KOOKER, EARL W. "The Relationship Between Performance in a Graduate Course in Statistics and the Miller Analogies Test and the Watson-Glaser Critical Thinking Appraisal." *J Psychol* 77(2):165–9 Mr '71. * (*PA* 46:1772)

141. PAYNE, DAVID A.; WELLS, ROBERT A.; AND CLARKE, ROBERT R. "Another Contribution to Estimating Success in Graduate School: A Search for Sex Differences and Comparison

Between Three Degree Types." *Ed & Psychol Meas* 31(2):497–503 su '71. *

142. WRIGHT, MATTHEW THOMAS. *An Analysis of Selected Factors of Education Doctoral Programs at Washington State University.* Doctor's thesis, Washington State University (Pullman, Wash.), 1971. (*DAI* 32:4388A)

CUMULATIVE NAME INDEX

Abrahams, N.: 81
Ainsworth, L. L.: 89
Armstrong, H. C.: 34
Ashbrook, J. B.: 75
Ayers, J. B.: 137
Badal, A. W.: 48
Bentley, J. C.: 90
Berdie, R. F.: 20
Bessent, E. W.: 61
Binford, M. L.: 73
Bishop, R.: 17
Blake, R. R.: 129
Blatt, S. J.: 74
Boernke, C.: 96
Boone, S. W.: 77
Boyce, R. D.: 55
Bradfield, A. F.: 9
Brams, J. M.: 36
Buckton, L.: 29
Burdock, E. I.: 56
Burrell, L. F.: 138
Butler, M. J.: 86
Callis, R.: 79
Campbell, M. L.: 80
Campbell, M. L. A.: 106
Carleton, F. O.: 122
Carlson, R.: 112
Cash, W. L.: 85
Cheek, F.: 56
Clark, F. E.: 52
Clarke, R. R.: 141
Cockrum, L. V.: 21
Coladarci, A. P.: 57
Colver, R. M.: 62
Cook, W. W.: 3
Cureton, E. E.: 17, 99
Cureton, L. W.: 17
Dailey, J. T.: *rev*, 5:352
De Beruff, E.: 113
DiGiorgio, A. J.: 114
Donaghy, R. T.: 107
Doppelt, J. E.: 12, 29, 139
Dugan, W. E.: 2
Dumler, M. J.: 130
Dunnette, M. D.: 39, 81
Durnall, E. J.: 27
Ebert, F. J.: 58
Eckhoff, C. M.: 91
England, G. W.: 60
Ewen, R. B.: 115
Fahey, G. L.: 23
Feinberg, A.: 82
Feldman, M. J.: 40
Felker, S. A.: 134
Fernandes, L. M.: 123
Fischer, R. F.: 92
Fiske, D. W.: 10, 15
Fox, A. M.: 89
Fuller, E. M.: 4
Gab, D.: 121, 127
Gab, D. D.: 116
Gade, E. M.: 85
Geertsma, R.: 32
Gill, G.: 102
Glading, J. C.: 71
Glaser, R.: 13–4, 28
Goldberg, L. R.: 49
Greenberg, B. S.: 63
Grimsrud, R. A.: 108
Guilford, J. P.: *rev*, 4:304
Hahn, M. E.: 5
Hall, E.: 84
Hardesty, D. L.: 109
Harlow, S. D.: 127
Harrison, C. W.: 119
Hartsock, W. W.: 133
Hountras, P. T.: 30, 35
Hovland, C. I.: *rev*, 4:304
Humphreys, L. G.: *rev*, 6:472
Hyman, S. R.: 37, 72
Jacobs, O.: 28
James, K. R.: 59
Jansen, D. G.: 100
Jardin, R. P.: 135
Jenson, R. E.: 6, 24
Johnston, F. N.: 100
Jones, W. S.: 109

Katz, D.: 51
Kelly, E. L.: 10, 15, 49
Kendall, W. E.: 5
King, P.: 67
Kirchner, W. K.: 39
Koltveit, T. H.: 83
Kooker, E. W.: 140
Lane, R. G.: 92
Laurent, H.: 110
Layton, W. L.: 20
Leafgren, F.: 67
Lehmkuhl, C. B.: 78
Lief, H. I.: 87
Lief, V. F.: 87
Locke, L. F.: 65
Lovegren, L. A.: 1
Luton, J. N.: 46
McClintock, C.: 51
McGreevy, C. P.: 101
Marascuilo, L. A.: 102
Mednick, M. T.: 70
Meer, B.: 31–2
Mehrabian, A.: 117, 124
Merle, S.: 111
Merwin, J. C.: 95
Moffett, C. R.: 45
Monahan, R. D.: 88
Moore, J. C.: 93
Moore, R. B.: 64
Mosher, R. L.: 107
Nelson, R. J.: 60
Nunnery, M. Y.: 47, 50
Oliver, J. A.: 16
Paterson, D. G.: 26
Payne, D. A.: 94, 141
Penn, N. E.: 92
Pepinsky, H. N.: 42
Peterson, T. T.: 41
Platz, A.: 51
Porozny, G. H. J.: 136
Poston, W. K.: 118
Prediger, D. J.: 79
Prien, E. P.: 125
Rawls, D. J.: 119
Rawls, J. R.: 119
Robertson, M.: 84
Robinson, D. W.: 43
Ross, J. A.: 76
Schmitt, J. A.: 103
Schofield, W.: 95
Schrader, W. B.: *rev*, 6:472
Schwartz, M. M.: 52
Scott, C. W.: 66
Scott, T. B.: 99
Seibel, D. W.: 104
Smith, I. L.: 126
Smith, L. M.: 38
Smolinsky, M. P.: 120
Sorenson, H.: 128
Spielberger, C. D.: 53, 62
Sprinthall, N. A.: 107
Stafford, J. W.: 18
Steffire, B.: 67
Stein, M. I.: 31–2, 74
Sternal, W.: 85
Stordahl, K. E.: 105
Streit, L. R.: 19
Strowig, R. W.: 22
Thumin, F. J.: 96
Travers, R. M. W.: 11
Tronca, W. F.: 25
Tully, G. E.: 68
Tuttle, C. E.: 94
Votaw, D. F.: 44
Waggoner, G. H.: 54
Wallace, W. L.: 11
Wallen, N. E.: 106
Ward, D. V.: 97
Ward, J. H.: 33
Watley, D. J.: 98
Watters, G. V.: 26
Webster, E. C.: 16
Wells, R. A.: 141
Wernimont, P.: 81
Wexler, N.: 66
Whiteley, J. M.: 107
Widener, S. E.: 131

Williams, J. D.: 121, 127
Willingham, W. W.: *rev*, 6:472
Winn, A.: 16
Wrenn, C. G.: 7

Wright, M. T.: 142
Young, K. M.: 87
Zagorski, H. J.: 8
Zubin, J.: 56

[405]

★**Minnesota Scholastic Aptitude Test.** High school and college; 1969–70, c1940–70; MSAT; short form of *Ohio State University Psychological Test,* Form 23; originally prepared for use in Minnesota secondary schools; Wilbur L. Layton; original test by Herbert A. Toops; Wilbur L. Layton. *

REFERENCES THROUGH 1971

1. LAYTON, WILBUR L. "Construction of a Short Form of the Ohio State University Psychological Examination." *Yearb Nat Council Meas Used Ed* 12(pt 1):81–5 '55. *
2. SWANSON, EDWARD O., AND BERDIE, RALPH F. "Predictive Validities in an Institute of Technology." *Ed & Psychol Meas* 21:1001–8 w '61. * Errata: 22:258 su '62.
3. BERDIE, RALPH F.; LAYTON, WILBUR L.; HAGENAH, THEDA; AND SWANSON, EDWARD O. *Who Goes to College? Comparison of Minnesota College Freshmen, 1930–1960.* Minneapolis, Minn.: University of Minnesota Press, 1962. Pp. vii, 56. *
4. RAY, PHILIP BOND. *A Descriptive Study of Certain Characteristics of "High Creative" Freshman Arts College Students as Compared With "High Academic Potential" Students.* Doctor's thesis, University of Minnesota (Minneapolis, Minn.), 1962. (*DA* 24:1924)
5. LESTER, ROBERT ANDREW. *The Relationship of SVIB and ACT Scores to Differential Academic Achievement.* Doctor's thesis, University of Minnesota (Minneapolis, Minn.), 1963. (*DA* 24:1076)
6. HAAK, LOUIS ANDREW. *An Investigation of the Validation Characteristics of Four Statistical Techniques in the Prediction of Certain Educational Achievement Variables.* Doctor's thesis, University of Minnesota (Minneapolis, Minn.), 1964. (*DA* 26:867)
7. HOOD, ALBERT B., AND BERDIE, RALPH F. "The Relationship of Ability to College Attendance." *Col & Univ* 39:309–18 sp '64. *
8. SPACE, MARGARET NIVEN. *A Study of Individual Predictability Based on Intra-Individual Variability on Certain Achievement Measures.* Doctor's thesis, University of Minnesota (Minneapolis, Minn.), 1964. (*DA* 26:879)
9. WATLEY, DONIVAN J. "Type, Location, and Size of High School and Prediction of Achievement in an Institute of Technology." *Ed & Psychol Meas* 24:331–8 su '64. * (*PA* 39:5987)
10. CAMPBELL, DAVID P. "A Cross-Sectional and Longitudinal Study of Scholastic Abilities Over Twenty-Five Years." *J Counsel Psychol* 12:55–61 sp '65. * (*PA* 39:10814)
11. HEWER, VIVIAN H. "Are Tests Fair to College Students From Homes With Low Socio-Economic Status?" *Personnel & Guid J* 43:764–9 Ap '65. * (*PA* 39:16441)
12. BERDIE, RALPH F., AND HOOD, ALBERT B. "How Effectively Do We Predict Plans for College Attendance?" *Personnel & Guid J* 44:487–93 Ja '66. * (*PA* 40:5899)
13. BERDIE, RALPH F., AND STEIN, JUNE. "A Comparison of New University Students Who Do and Do Not Seek Counseling." *J Counsel Psychol* 13:310–7 f '66. * (*PA* 40:12631)
14. CAMPBELL, JOHN P. "Comparison of Criterion Clusters Obtained by Analyzing the Homogeneity of a Set of Regression Equations and the Matrix of Intercorrelations." *Ed & Psychol Meas* 26:405–17 su '66. * (*PA* 40:12757)
15. HAKEL, MILTON D. "Prediction of College Achievement From the Edwards Personal Preference Schedule Using Intellectual Ability as a Moderator." *J Appl Psychol* 50:336–40 Ag '66. * (*PA* 40:11489)
16. BROWN, F. G., AND SCOTT, D. A. "Differential Predictability in College Admissions Testing." *J Ed Meas* 4:163–6 f '67. *
17. HOOD, ALBERT B. "A Method of Comparing Student Achievement Levels at Different Colleges." *Personnel & Guid J* 45:799–803 Ap '67. *
18. HOOD, ALBERT B. "Predicting College Achievement of Students From Farm Backgrounds." *Personnel & Guid J* 45:996–1000 Je '67. *
19. PETRIK, NORMAN D. "Socio-Economic Status, Vocational Interests, and Persistence in Selected College Curricula." *Voc Guid Q* 16:39–44 S '67. *
20. WATLEY, DONIVAN J., AND MERWIN, JACK C. "An Attempt to Improve Prediction of College Success by Adjusting for High School Characteristics." *Am Ed Res J* 4:229–40 My '67. * (*PA* 41:14173)
21. LUNDGREN, ELIZABETH J. "Predicting Student Success in Medical Technology and Clinical Laboratory Assistant Programs." *Am J Med Technol* 34:349–61 Je '68. *
22. MUNDAY, LEO. "Correlations Between ACT and Other Predictors of Academic Success in College." *Col & Univ* 44:67–76 f '68. *
23. BERDIE, RALPH F. "Intra-Individual Temporal Variability

and Predictability." *Ed & Psychol Meas* 29(2):235–57 su '69. * (*PA* 44:17502)
24. TAYLOR, RONALD G., AND HANSON, GARY R. "Pre-College Math-Workshop and Freshman Achievement." *J Ed Res* 63(4):157–60 D '69. *
25. BIGGS, DONALD A.; ROTH, JOHN D.; AND STRONG, STANLEY R. "Self-Made Academic Predictions and Academic Performance." *Meas & Eval Guid* 3(2):81–5 su '70. * (*PA* 45:1357)
26. BYERLY, RICHARD LEE. *The Use of Multiple Regression and Path Analysis in Analyzing Success in Journalism at Iowa State University.* Doctor's thesis, Iowa State University (Ames, Iowa), 1970. (*DAI* 31:4617A)
27. ERNEST, DAVID J. "The Predication of Academic Success of College Music Majors." *J Res Music Ed* 18(3):273–6 f '70. * (*PA* 45:8994)
28. HANSON, GARY R., AND TAYLOR, RONALD G. "Interaction of Ability and Personality: Another Look at the Drop-Out Problem in an Institute of Technology." *J Counsel Psychol* 17(6):540–5 N '70. * (*PA* 45:3036)
29. IM, IN JAE. *A Multivariate Analysis of the Relationship of Academic, Personality, and Family Background Variables to the Different Patterns of Collegiate Attendance.* Doctor's thesis, University of Minnesota (Minneapolis, Minn.), 1970. (*DAI* 32:240A)
30. SHERMAN, RICHARD C., AND POE, CHARLES A. "Factor-Analytic Scales of a Normative Form of the EPPS." *Meas & Eval Guid* 2(4):243–8 w '70. *
31. FRYETT, HOWARD LESLIE. *An Interpretation of Student Self Concept and Analysis of Relationships Between the Self and Selected Characteristics of Business Education Students Enrolled in Minnesota Area Vocational-Technical Schools.* Doctor's thesis, University of North Dakota (Grand Forks, N.D.), 1971. (*DAI* 33:76A)

CUMULATIVE NAME INDEX

Berdie, R. F.: 2–3, 7, 12–3, 23
Biggs, D. A.: 25
Brown, F. G.: 16
Byerly, R. L.: 26
Campbell, D. P.: 10
Campbell, J. P.: 14
Ernest, D. J.: 27
Fryett, H. L.: 31
Haak, L. A.: 6
Hagenah, T.: 3
Hakel, M. D.: 15
Hanson, G. R.: 24, 28
Hewer, V. H.: 11
Hood, A. B.: 7, 12, 17–8
Im, I. J.: 29
Layton, W. L.: 1, 3
Lester, R. A.: 5
Lundgren, E. J.: 21
Merwin, J. C.: 20
Munday, L.: 22
Petrik, N. D.: 19
Poe, C. A.: 30
Ray, P. B.: 4
Roth, J. D.: 25
Scott, D. A.: 16
Sherman, R. C.: 30
Space, M. N.: 8
Stein, J.: 13
Strong, S. R.: 25
Swanson, E. O.: 2–3
Taylor, R. G.: 24, 28
Watley, D. J.: 9, 20

[406]
Mitchell Vocabulary Test. Adults; 1958; intelligence; [A. Mitchell]; distributed by NFER Publishing Co. Ltd. [England]. *

For additional information, see 6:473 (1 reference).

REFERENCES THROUGH 1971
1. See 6:473.

CUMULATIVE NAME INDEX

Semeonoff, B.: 1   Trist, E.: 1

[407]
Modified Alpha Examination Form 9. Grades 7–12 and adults; 1941–51; a revision of *Army Group Examination Alpha*; 3 scores: numerical, verbal, total; F. L. Wells; Psychological Corporation. *

For additional information and a review by Dael Wolfle, see 4:305 (8 references); see also 3:220 (77 references for *Army Group Examination Alpha* and revisions).

REFERENCES THROUGH 1971

1–3. See 3:220(68, 70, 72).
4–8. See 4:305.
9. RUBIN, EDMUND JOSEPH. *Performance of Totally-Blind and Sighted Subjects on Tests of Abstraction.* Doctor's thesis, Fordham University (New York, N.Y.), 1963. (*DA* 24:2989)
10. MATHAE, DAVID E. "Norms and Correlations of Scores From the Modified Alpha Examination Form 9 and the Shipley Institute of Living Scale for Hospitalized Female Neuropsychiatric Patients." *Newsl Res Psychol* 10:22–6 My '68. *

CUMULATIVE NAME INDEX

Allen, R. M.: 7
Bennett, G. K.: 1
Bessell, H.: 7
Demand, J. W.: 3
Eimicke, V. W.: 4, 8
Fish, H. L.: 4
Mathae, D. E.: 10
Murray, J. E.: 6
Rubin, E. J.: 9
Savage, B. M.: 2
Seltzer, C. C.: 5
Wells, F. L.: 2
Wolfle, D.: *rev*, 4:305

[408]
Moray House Picture Tests. Ages 6.5–8.5; 1944–61; 2 tests; Department of Education, University of Edinburgh; University of London Press Ltd. [England]. *
a) MORAY HOUSE PICTURE INTELLIGENCE TEST 1. Ages 6.5–8.5; 1944–48; test booklet title is *Picture Intelligence Test 1*; Margaret A. Mellone.
b) MORAY HOUSE PICTURE TEST 2. Ages 6.5–8.0; 1961.

For additional information concerning *b*, see 6:475; for reviews by Gertrude Keir and M. L. Kellmer Pringle of *a*, see 4:306 (5 references).

REFERENCES THROUGH 1971

1–5. See 4:306.
6. PEEL, E. A., AND GRAHAM, D. "Differentiation of Ability in Primary School Children." *Durham Res R* (England) 1(2):40–8 S '51. *
7. PEEL, E. A., AND GRAHAM, D. "Differentiation of Ability in Primary School Children—II." *Durham Res R* (England) 1(3):31–4 S '52. * (*PA* 27:5157)
8. POTTS, ERIC. "A Factorial Study of the Relationship Between the Child's Vocabulary and His Reading Progress at the Infants' Stage." Abstract. *Brit J Ed Psychol* 30:84–6 F '60. *
9. NISBET, J. D., AND ILLESLEY, R. "The Influence of Early Puberty on Test Performance at Age Eleven." *Brit J Ed Psychol* 33:169–76 Je '63. * (*PA* 38:4096)
10. HOROBIN, GORDON; OLDMAN, DAVID; AND BYTHEWAY, BILL. "The Social Differentiation of Ability." *Sociology* 1:113–29 My '67. *
11. NISBET, J. D., AND ENTWISTLE, N. J. "Intelligence and Family Size, 1949–1965." *Brit J Ed Psychol* 37:188–93 Je '67. * (*PA* 41:15274)
12. PUMFREY, P. D. "Effect of Selection Procedure on the Placement of Children in Special Schools." *Res Ed* (England) 5:10–24 My '71. *

CUMULATIVE NAME INDEX

Bytheway, B.: 10
Emmett, W. C.: 4
Entwistle, N. J.: 11
Graham, D.: 6–7
Horobin, G.: 10
Hughes, H. O.: 5
Illesley, R.: 9
Keir, G.: *rev*, 4:306
Mellone, M. A.: 1–3
Nisbet, J. D.: 9, 11
Oldman, D.: 10
Peel, E. A.: 6–7
Potts, E.: 8
Pringle, M. L. K.: *rev*, 4:306
Pumfrey, P. D.: 12

[409]
Moray House Verbal Reasoning Tests. Ages 8.5–10.5, 10–12, 12–14.5, 13.5 and over; 1930–72; formerly listed as *Moray House Intelligence Tests*; 5 levels; Godfrey Thomson Unit, University of Edinburgh; University of London Press Ltd. [England]. *
a) MORAY HOUSE JUNIOR REASONING TEST FOR NINE YEAR OLDS. Ages 8.5–10.5; 1947–70; formerly called *Moray House Junior Intelligence Test*.
b) MORAY HOUSE VERBAL REASONING TEST. Ages 10–12; 1930–72; formerly called *Moray House Intelligence Tests*; 1–3 new forms issued annually; distribution of forms 75–89 restricted to education authorities.
c) MORAY HOUSE VERBAL REASONING TEST: VERNIER TEST 2. Ages 10–12 of above average ability; 1954–57. *Out of print.*
d) MORAY HOUSE VERBAL REASONING TEST (ADV.). Ages 12–14.5; 1940–68.
e) MORAY HOUSE VERBAL REASONING TEST (ADULT) 1. Ages 13.5 and over; 1952–70; formerly called *Moray House Adult Intelligence Test 1*.

For additional information, see 7:364 (3 references); see also 6:474 (13 references) and 5:353 (2 references); for a review by Patrick Slater of earlier forms, see 3:241 (2 references); for a review by C. Ebblewhite Smith, see 2:1409.

REFERENCES THROUGH 1971

1–2. See 3:241.
3–4. See 5:353.
5–17. See 6:474.

Minnesota Scholastic Aptitude Test

18-20. See 7:364.
21. SUTHERLAND, H. E. G. "The Relationship Between IQ and Size of Family." *J Ed Psychol* 20:81-90 F '29. * (*PA* 3:2242)
22. MCRAE, HUGH. "The Inconstancy of Group Test IQ's." *Brit J Ed Psychol* 12:59-70 F '42. * (*PA* 16:2905)
23. RUTTER, D. "An Inquiry Into the Predictive Value of the Grammar School Entrance Examination." *Durham Res R* (England) 1(1):3-11 Jl '50. *
24. JONES, W. R. "The Influence of Reading Ability in English on the Intelligence Test Scores of Welsh-Speaking Children." *Brit J Ed Psychol* 23:114-20 F '53. * (*PA* 28:4835)
25. PEEL, E. A. "Footnote on 'Practice Effects Between Three Consecutive Tests of Intelligence.'" *Brit J Ed Psychol* 23:126 F '53. * (*PA* 28:4382)
26. SMITH, I. MACFARLANE. "The Development of a Spatial Test." *Durham Ed R* (England) 1(5):19-33 S '54. * (*PA* 29:7298)
27. DOCKRELL, W. B. "The Relationship Between Socio-Economic Status, Intelligence and Attainment in Some Scottish Primary Schools." *Indian Psychol B* 4:1-6 Ja '59. * (*PA* 37:4715)
28. KING, NORMAN W. "Sources of Fluctuation in Scores From Successive Group Intelligence Tests." Abstract of bachelor's thesis. *Brit J Ed Psychol* 30:83 F '60. *
29. PILLINER, A. E. G.; SUTHERLAND, J.; AND TAYLOR, E. G. "Zero Error in Moray House Verbal Reasoning Tests." *Brit J Ed Psychol* 30:53-62 F '60. *
30. MANLEY, D. R. "Mental Ability in Jamaica: (An Examination of the Performance of Children in the Jamaican Common Entrance Examination, 1959)." *Social & Econ Studies* (Jamaica) 12:51-71 Mr '63. * (*PA* 38:767)
31. NISBET, J. D., AND ILLESLEY, R. "The Influence of Early Puberty on Test Performance at Age Eleven." *Brit J Ed Psychol* 33:169-76 Je '63. * (*PA* 38:4096)
32. HALLWORTH, H. J. "Personality Ratings of Adolescents: A Study in a Comprehensive School." *Brit J Ed Psychol* 34:171-7 Je '64. * (*PA* 39:3180)
33. HOROBIN, GORDON; OLDMAN, DAVID; AND BYTHEWAY, BILL. "The Social Differentiation of Ability." *Sociology* 1:113-29 My '67. *
34. NISBET, J. D., AND ENTWISTLE, N. J. "Intelligence and Family Size, 1949-1965." *Brit J Ed Psychol* 37:188-93 Je '67. * (*PA* 41:15274)
35. HADDON, F. A., AND LYTTON, HUGH. "Teaching Approach and the Development of Divergent Thinking Abilities in Primary Schools." *Brit J Ed Psychol* 38:171-80 Je '68. * (*PA* 42:17790)
36. HOCKEY, S. W. "Intelligence, Common Entrance and the General Certificate of Education." *Brit J Ed Psychol* 38:140-7 Je '68. * (*PA* 43:17796)
37. RICHARDS, P. N., AND BOLTON, N. "Type of Mathematics Teaching, Mathematical Ability and Divergent Thinking in Junior School Children." *Brit J Ed Psychol* 41(1):32-7 F '71. * (*PA* 46:9822)
38. WILSON, J. D. "Predicting Levels of First Year University Performance." *Brit J Ed Psychol* 41(2):163-70 Je '71. * (*PA* 47:9821)

CUMULATIVE NAME INDEX

Armstrong, H. G.: 15
Bolton, N.: 37
Boyne, A. W.: 18
Buchan, J.: 16
Bytheway, B.: 33
Clark, J. R.: 18
Dempster, J. J. B.: 4
Dockrell, W. B.: 27
Emmett, W. G.: 10, 14
Entwistle, N. J.: 19, 34
Haddon, F. A.: 35
Hallworth, H. J.: 32
Herbert, N.: 17
Hockey, S. W.: 36
Horobin, G.: 33
Illesley, R.: 31
Jones, W. R.: 11, 24
King, N. W.: 28
Lambert, C. M.: 7
Lytton, H.: 35
McIntosh, D. M.: 20
McRae, H.: 22
Manley, D. R.: 30

Nisbet, J.: 16
Nisbet, J. D.: 31, 34
Oldman, D.: 33
Peel, E. A.: 8-9, 12, 15, 25
Pilliner, A. E. G.: 29
Richards, P. N.: 37
Rodger, A. G.: 1
Rutter, D.: 23
Slater, P.: *rev*, 3:241
Smith, C. E.: *rev*, 2:1409
Smith, I. M.: 26
Sutherland, H. E. G.: 21
Sutherland, J.: 29
Taylor, E. G.: 29
Thomson, G. H.: 2-3, 5-6
Turnbull, G. H.: 17
Walker, D. A.: 20
Welsh, J.: 19
Wilmut, F. S.: 10
Wilson, J. D.: 38
Wiseman, S.: 13
Wrigley, J.: 13

[410]

[N.B. Group Tests.] Ages 5-6, 7-8; 1958; 2 levels; Human Sciences Research Council [South Africa]. *
a) N.B. GROUP TEST FOR FIVE AND SIX YEAR OLDS.
b) N.B. GROUP TEST FOR SEVEN AND EIGHT YEAR OLDS.
For additional information, see 6:477.

[411]

New South African Group Test. Ages 8-11, 10-14, 13-17; 1931-65; NSAGT; 3 scores: verbal, nonverbal, total; 3 levels; Human Sciences Research Council [South Africa]. *
a) JUNIOR. Ages 8-11; 1931-65.
b) INTERMEDIATE. Ages 10-14; 1931-63.
c) SENIOR. Ages 13-17; 1931-65.
For additional information, see 7:365 (3 references).

REFERENCES THROUGH 1971

1-3. See 7:365.
4. STRÜMPFER, D. J. W. "The Relation of Draw-A-Person Test Variables to Psychometric and Inventory Measures." *J Social Res* (South Africa) 15(1):1-9 '66. * (*PA* 42:2613)

CUMULATIVE NAME INDEX

Elder, C. M.: 1
Mienie, C. J. P.: 3
Strümpfer, D. J. W.: 3-4
Sugarman, L.: 2

[412]

★**Non-Language Test of Verbal Intelligence—Form 768.** Class 8 (ages 11-13); 1968; 4 scores: analogy, classification, opposites, picture arrangement; S. Chatterji and Manjula Mukerjee; Statistical Publishing Society [India]. *

REFERENCES THROUGH 1971

1. CHATTERJI, S., AND MUKERJEE, MANJULA. "The Development of Non-Language Test of Verbal Intelligence." *J Psychol Res* (India) 11:58-68 My '67. * (*PA* 42:6379)
2. CHATTERJI, S., AND MUKERJEE, M. "Verbal Intelligence as Measured by the NLTVI and Its Relation With Different Subjects Taught in School." *Psychol Studies* (India) 15(2):71-83 Jl '70. *

CUMULATIVE NAME INDEX

Chatterji, S.: 1-2
Mukerjee, M.: 1-2

[413]

Non-Readers Intelligence Test. Ages 6-9 to 8-11; 1964; D. Young; University of London Press Ltd. [England]. *
For additional information, see 7:366.

[414]

Non-Verbal Reasoning Test. Job applicants and industrial employees; 1961; Raymond J. Corsini (test) and Measurement Research Division, Industrial Relations Center, University of Chicago (manual); the Center. * [The publisher has not replied to our four requests to check the accuracy of this entry.]
For additional information and reviews by James E. Kennedy and David G. Ryans, see 6:478.

REFERENCES THROUGH 1971

1. LAURENT, HARRY. Chap. 1, "Research on the Identification of Management Potential," pp. 1-34. In *Predicting Managerial Success.* Edited by John A. Myers, Jr. Ann Arbor, Mich.: Foundation for Research on Human Behavior, April 1968. Pp. v, 173. *
2. BAEHR, MELANY E.; FURCON, JOHN E.; AND FROEMEL, ERNEST C. *Psychological Assessment of Patrolman Qualifications in Relation to Field Performance.* Washington, D.C.: United States Government Printing Office, 1969. Pp. vii, 246. *

CUMULATIVE NAME INDEX

Baehr, M. E.: 2
Froemel, E. C.: 2
Furcon, J. E.: 2
Kennedy, J. E.: *rev* 6:478
Laurent, H.: 1
Ryans, D. G.: *rev* 6:478

[415]

Non-Verbal Tests. Ages 8 to 11-0, 10 to 12, 10 to 15; 1947-65; 3 levels; published for the National Foundation for Educational Research in England and Wales; Ginn & Co. Ltd. [England]. *
a) NON-VERBAL TESTS 1-2. Ages 10 to 12; 1947-59; 2 forms.
1) *Non-Verbal Test 1.* 1947-59; test booklet title is *A Scale of Non-Verbal Mental Ability;* J. W. Jenkins. (An Australian adaptation, *Jenkins Non-Verbal*

Test, is available from Australian Council for Educational Research [Australia].)
2) *Non-Verbal Test 2.* 1948–51; D. M. Lee and J. W. Jenkins.
b) NON-VERBAL TEST DH. Ages 10 to 15; 1953–58; formerly called *Non-Verbal Test 3;* B. Calvert (test) and I. Macfarlane Smith (original manual).
c) NON-VERBAL TEST BD. Ages 8 to 11-0; 1953–65; formerly called *Non-Verbal Test 5;* D. A. Pidgeon.

For additional information, see 7:367 (1 reference); for reviews by T. R. Miles and John Nisbet, see 6:479 (1 reference); for a review by Cyril A. Rogers, see 5:356 (1 reference); for a review by E. A. Peel of the original edition, see 4:307 (3 references).

REFERENCES THROUGH 1971

1-3. See 4:307.
4. See 5:356.
5. See 6:479.
6. See 7:367.
7. JONES, W. R., AND STEWART, W. A. C. "Bilingualism and Verbal Intelligence." *Brit J Psychol* (Stat Sect) 4:3–8 Mr '51. * (PA 25:7930)
8. JONES, W. R. "The Influence of Reading Ability in English on the Intelligence Test Scores of Welsh-Speaking Children." *Brit J Ed Psychol* 23:114–20 F '53. * (PA 28:4835)
9. MCINTYRE, W. "Difficulty of Understanding Instructions as a Factor in Coaching and Practice Effects in Intelligence Testing." Abstract. *Brit J Ed Psychol* 24:122–3 Je '54. * (PA 29:2456)
10. SMITH, I. MACFARLANE. "The Development of a Spatial Test." *Durham Ed R* (England) 1(5):19–33 S '54. * (PA 29:7298)
11. DUNN, S., AND SPEARRITT, D. "A Comparative Study of the Reliability of Some Verbal and Non-Verbal Intelligence Tests." *Austral J Psychol* 7:169–74 D '55. * (PA 31:1030)
12. DUNN, S. S., AND BROWNLESS, V. T. "Differences in Test and Retest Responses of a Group of Children to a Verbal and a Non-Verbal Test." *Austral J Psychol* 8:84–7 Je '56. * (PA 31:7910)
13. MORGAN, G. A. V. "Verbal Abilities of Primary School Children." *Durham Ed R* (England) 2(7):97–107 S '56. *
14. LEWIS, D. G. "Differences in Attainment Between Primary-Schools in Mixed-Language Areas: Their Dependence on Intelligence and Linguistic Background." *Brit J Ed Psychol* 30:63–70 F '60. *
15. LLOYD, F., AND PIDGEON, D. A. "An Investigation Into the Effects of Coaching on Non-Verbal Test Material With European, Indian and African Children." *Brit J Ed Psychol* 31:145–51 Je '61. * (PA 36:3KJ45L)
16. LOVELL, K.; SHAPTON, D.; AND WARREN, N. S. "A Study of Some Cognitive and Other Disabilities in Backward Readers of Average Intelligence as Assessed by a Non-Verbal Test." *Brit J Ed Psychol* 34:58–64 F '64. * (PA 38:9233)
17. NISBET, J. D., AND ENTWISTLE, N. J. "Intelligence and Family Size, 1949–1965." *Brit J Ed Psychol* 37:188–93 Je '67. * (PA 41:15274)
18. PARKER, D. H. H. "Musical Perception and Backwardness in Reading." *Ed Res* (England) 12(3):244–6 Je '70. * (PA 47:1754)

CUMULATIVE NAME INDEX

Brownless, V. T.: 12
Dunn, S.: 11
Dunn, S. S.: 12
Entwistle, N. J.: 6, 17
Jones, W. R.: 4, 7–8
Lewis, D. G.: 5, 14
Lloyd, F.: 15
Lovell, K.: 16
McIntyre, W.: 9
Miles, T. R.: *rev,* 6:479
Mills, L. F.: 1
Morgan, G. A. V.: 13
Nisbet, J.: *rev,* 6:479
Nisbet, J. D.: 17
Parker, D. H. H.: 18
Peel, E. A.: 2; *rev,* 4:307
Pidgeon, D. A.: 15
Rogers, C. A.: *rev,* 5:356
Scott, G. C.: 3
Shapton, D.: 16
Smith, I. M.: 10
Spearritt, D.: 11
Stewart, W. A. C.: 7
Warren, N. S.: 16
Welsh, J.: 6

[416]

The Northumberland Mental Tests. Ages 10–12.5; 1922; manual and higher level test (for ages 11–16) are out of print; Godfrey H. Thomson; George G. Harrap & Co. Ltd. [England]. *

REFERENCES THROUGH 1971

1. THOMSON, GODFREY H. "The Northumberland Mental Tests." *Brit J Psychol* 12:201–22 D '21. *
2. BALLARD, PHILIP BOSWOOD. Chap. 11, "The Northumberland Mental Tests," pp. 76–89. In his *Group Tests of Intelligence.* London: University of London Press, Ltd., 1922. Pp. x, 252. *

Non-Verbal Tests

3. WILSON, J. H. "Comparison of Certain Intelligence Scales." *Brit J Psychol* 15:44–63 Jl '24. *
4. BOWIE, S., AND LAWS, A. R. "A School Intelligence Test." *Forum Ed* (England) 3:134–40 Je '25. *
5. STAINER, W. J. "Intelligence Tests in Scholarship Examinations." *Forum Ed* (England) 3:32–9 F '25. *
6. RUSSELL, J. B. "The Measurement of Intelligence in a Rural Area." *Brit J Psychol* 20:274–95 Ja '30. * (PA 4:2940)
7. GHOSH, S. "Investigation Into the Validity of an Intelligence-Test-Element Such as the Hindustani Test (A6, B6) in the Northumberland Mental Test (No. 1)." *Indian J Psychol* 6:61–70 Ja '31. * (PA 6:909)
8. WILSON, J. H. "The Exactness of '*g*' as Determined by Certain Intelligence Tests." *Brit J Psychol* 26:93–8 Jl '35. *
9. NIJHAWAN, HARBANS KAUR. *The Reliability and Validity of the Northumberland Intelligence Test.* Doctor's thesis, University College, University of London (London, England), 1956.
10. NIJHAWAN, H. K. "The Reliability and Validity of the Northumberland Test of Intelligence." *Psychol Studies* (India) 10:115–20 Jl '65. * (PA 39:15255)

CUMULATIVE NAME INDEX

Ballard, P. B.: 2
Bowie, S.: 4
Ghosh, S.: 7
Laws, A. R.: 4
Nijhawan, H. K.: 9–10
Russell, J. B.: 6
Stainer, W. J.: 5
Thomson, G. H.: 1
Wilson, J. H.: 3, 8

[417]

OISE Picture Reasoning Test: Primary. Grades 1–2; 1969–70; replaces *Group Test of Learning Capacity: Dominion Tests: Primary;* Ontario Institute for Studies in Education; distributed by Guidance Centre [Canada]. *

For additional information, see 7:368.

[418]

The Ohio Penal Classification Test. Penal institutions; 1952–54; also available for industrial use under the title *Ohio Classification Test* ('57); 5 scores: block counting, digit-symbol, number series, memory span, total; DeWitt E. Sell; manual for industrial edition by the author and Robert W. Scollay and Leroy N. Vernon; Psychometric Affiliates. *

For additional information and a review by Norman Eagle, see 5:358.

REFERENCES THROUGH 1971

1. KERR, WILLARD A., AND MCGEHEE, EDWARD M. "Creative Temperament as Related to Aspects of Strategy and Intelligence." *J Social Psychol* 62:211–6 Ap '64. * (PA 39:5126)
2. KELLEHER, EDWARD J.; KERR, WILLARD A.; AND MELVILLE, NORBERT T. "The Prediction of Subprofessional Nursing Success." *Personnel Psychol* 21:379–88 au '68. * (PA 47:4063)

CUMULATIVE NAME INDEX

Eagle, N.: *rev,* 5:358
Kelleher, E. J.: 2
Kerr, W. A.: 1–2
McGehee, E. M.: 1
Melville, N. T.: 2

[419]

***Ohio State University Psychological Test.** Grades 9–16 and adults; 1919–68; OSUPT; 4 scores: same-opposites, analogies, reading comprehension, total; Herbert A. Toops; originally published by the Ohio College Association; now distributed by Wilbur L. Layton. *

For additional information and a review by Cyril J. Hoyt (with W. Wesley Tennyson), see 5:359 (29 references); for a review by George A. Ferguson, see 4:308 (23 references); for a review by J. P. Guilford, see 3:244 (28 references); for reviews by Louis D. Hartson, Theos A. Langlie, and Rudolf Pintner, see 1:1051.

REFERENCES THROUGH 1971

1–28. See 3:244.
29–51. See 4:308.
52–80. See 5:359.
81. ERFFMEYER, C. E. "Intelligence Tests as an Aid in the Diagnosis of Academic Maladies." *Sch & Soc* 20:317–20 S 6 '24. *
82. WHINERY, S. M. "Psychological Test Ratings and College Entrance Age." *Sch & Soc* 24:370–2 S 18 '26. * (PA 1:506)

83. FARNSWORTH, P. R.; SEASHORE, R. H.; AND TINKER, M. A. "Speed in Simple and Serial Action as Related to Performance in Certain 'Intelligence' Tests." *J Genetic Psychol* 34:537–51 D '27. * (*PA* 2:1700)
84. EDGERTON, HAROLD A., AND TOOPS, HERBERT A. *Academic Progress: A Follow-Up Study of the Freshmen Entering the University in 1923.* Ohio State University Studies, Contributions in Administration, No. 1. Columbus, Ohio: Ohio State University Press, 1929. Pp. x, 150. *
85. NEEL, MARY O., AND MEAD, A. R. "Correlations Between Certain Group Factors in Preparation of Secondary School Teachers." *Ed Adm & Sup* 17:675–6 D '31. *
86. FREEMAN, FRANK S. "The Factor of Speed." *J General Psychol* 6:462–8 Ap '32. * (*PA* 7:773)
87. HARTSON, L. D. "The Validation of the Rating Scales Used With Candidates for Admission to Oberlin College." *Sch & Soc* 36:413–6 S 24 '32. * (*PA* 7:354)
88. PATRICK, JAMES R., AND ROWLES, EMMETT. "Intercorrelations Among Metabolic Rate, Vital Capacity, Blood Pressure, Intelligence, Scholarship, Personality and Other Measures on University Women." *J Appl Psychol* 17:507–21 O '33. * (*PA* 8:2498)
89. LYON, VERGIL E. "The Variation of High School Senior and College Freshman Classes." *J Exp Ed* 3:25–35 S '34. * (*PA* 9:1418)
90. CLARK, GENEVIEVE Y., AND SOUTH, EARL B. "Some Suggestions for Measuring Nursing Aptitude." *Am J Nursing* 35:865–71 S '35. * (*PA* 10:550)
91. LORENZ, ALICE B., AND MCCLURE, WILLIAM E. "The Influence of Color Blindness on Intelligence and Achievement of College Men." *J Appl Psychol* 19:320–30 Je '35. * (*PA* 10:85)
92. SMITH, HARRY P. "Psychological Examinations Administered by Syracuse University." *Sch & Soc* 41:134–6 Ja 26 '35. * (*PA* 9:2986)
93. STRABEL, EUNICE. "How Academically Apt Are Collegiate College Students?" *Sch & Soc* 41:814–6 Je 15 '35. * (*PA* 9:4822)
94. WELLER, DALE C. *Predictive Value of the Ohio State University Psychological Test Toward College Success.* Master's thesis, University of Wyoming (Laramie, Wyo.), 1936.
95. HARTSON, L. D. "Intellectual Output of Sixty-One Secondary Schools." *J Higher Ed* 9:42–4 Ja '38. * (*PA* 12:2632)
96. READ, CECIL B. "The Prediction of Scholastic Success in a Municipal University." *Sch & Soc* 48:187–8 Ag 6 '38. * (*PA* 12:6645)
97. STUIT, DEWEY B. "A Follow-Up Study of Freshmen in the Teachers College of the University of Nebraska." *Sch & Soc* 48:282–4 Ag 27 '38. * (*PA* 13:558)
98. HARTSON, L. D. "Relative Value of School Marks and Intelligence Tests as Bases for Rating Secondary Schools." *Sch & Soc* 49:354–6 Mr 18 '39. * (*PA* 13:3849)
99. ODGERS, JOHN GARNET, JR. *An Attempt to Broaden the Bases of Prognosis for Marginal Students in the College of Education.* Master's thesis, Ohio State University (Columbus, Ohio), 1939.
100. SHEDDAN, BOYD R., AND WITMER, LOUISE R. "Employment Tests for Relief Visitors." *J Appl Psychol* 23:270–9 Ap '39. * (*PA* 13:4837)
101. OSBORN, RICHARDS C. "How Is Intellectual Performance Related to Social and Economic Background." *J Ed Psychol* 34:215–28 Ap '43. * (*PA* 17:4276)
102. LANE, G. GORHAM. "Studies in Pilot Selection: I, The Prediction of Success in Learning to Fly Light Aircraft." *Psychol Monogr* 61(5):1–17 '47. * (*PA* 22:5166)
103. PORTENIER, LILLIAN G. "Abilities and Interests of Japanese-American High School Seniors." *J Social Psychol* 25:53–61 F '47. * (*PA* 21:3177)
104. ROACH, JAMES H. L. "Autosuggestion in Extroverts and Introverts." *J Personality* 15:215–21 Mr '47. * (*PA* 22:2536)
105. BUMGARNER, FAYNE. "Social Factors and OSPE Scores for 46 Women Enrolled in the University of Oklahoma Fall Semester 1951." *Proc Okla Acad Sci* 32:110–3 '52. * (*PA* 27:3781)
106. SMITH, ALLAN B. *The Prediction of Scholastic Success for Freshman Entrants to the University of Connecticut 1933–1951.* Doctor's thesis, University of Connecticut (Storrs, Conn.), 1953. (*DA* 13:1121)
107. MALLINSON, GEORGE GREISEN, AND SAMS, CONWAY C. "The Relationship Among Scientific Knowledge, Intelligence, and Achievement in General Psychology." *J Ed Res* 48:29–36 S '54. * (*PA* 29:3341)
108. MERRILL, REED M. "An Evaluative Study of Probation Students' Academic Performance in a University." *J Ed Res* 48:37–45 S '54. * (*PA* 29:4639)
109. MARTIN, JUDSON PHILLIPS. *Prediction of Scholastic Success as One Phase of Counseling Service for Entering Freshmen in a State Teachers College.* Doctor's thesis, University of Wisconsin (Madison, Wis.), 1955. (*DA* 16:267)
110. CHAHBAZI, PARVIZ. "Use of Projective Tests in Predicting College Achievement." *Ed & Psychol Meas* 16:538–42 w '56. * (*PA* 32:939)
111. MUNGER, PAUL. "Student Persistence in College." *Personnel & Guid J* 35:241–3 D '56. * (*PA* 31:8836)
112. PIHLBLAD, C. T., AND GREGORY, C. L. "The Role of Test Intelligence and Occupational Background as Factors in Occupational Choice." *Sociometry* 19:192–9 S '56. * (*PA* 31:8191)
113. HILL, SUZANNE D. "The Relationship Between Grades and a Predictive Test Battery in the School of Pharmacy of the George Washington University." *J Appl Psychol* 41:61–2 F '57. * (*PA* 32:946)
114. SHERWOOD, EMILY J. *An Investigation of the Relationship Between the Academic Achievement and Goal-Orientations of College Students.* Doctor's thesis, Temple University (Philadelphia, Pa.), 1957. (*DA* 17:2924)
115. CHAMPION, JOHN MILLS. *A Method For Predicting Success of Commerce Students.* Doctor's thesis, Purdue University (Lafayette, Ind.), 1958. (*DA* 19:2134)
116. NEBERGALL, ROGER E. "An Experimental Investigation of Rhetorical Clarity." *Speech Monogr* 25:243–54 N '58. *
117. PIERSON, LEROY R. "High School Teacher Prediction of College Success." *Personnel & Guid J* 37:142–5 O '58. * (*PA* 36:2KJ42P)
118. WEBB, SAM C., AND GOODLING, RICHARD A. "Test Validity in a Methodist Theology School." *Ed & Psychol Meas* 18:859–66 w '58. * (*PA* 34:2123)
119. PAERATAKUL, CHAWAL. "Differences in Performance on the Doctoral Admission Examinations at Indiana University by Thai Students, Foreign Non-Thai Students, and American Students." *B Sch Ed Ind Univ* 35(3):41–64 My '59. * (*PA* 34:6571)
120. SPAULDING, HELEN. "The Prediction of First-Year Grade Averages in a Private Junior College." *Ed & Psychol Meas* 19:627–8 w '59. * (*PA* 34:6574)
121. BARTLETT, CLAUDE J.; RONNING, ROYCE R.; AND HURST, JOHN G. "A Study of Classroom Evaluation Techniques With Special Reference to Application of Knowledge." *J Ed Psychol* 51:152–8 Je '60. * (*PA* 35:3871)
122. BROWN, DONALD JAMES. *An Investigation of the Relationships Between Certain Personal Characteristics of Guidance Counselors and Performance in Supervised Counseling Interviews.* Doctor's thesis, Ohio State University (Columbus, Ohio), 1960. (*DA* 21:810)
123. GARRETT, WILEY S. "Prediction of Academic Success in a School of Nursing." *Personnel & Guid J* 38:500–3 F '60. * (*PA* 35:3954)
124. JUOLA, ARVO E. "Predictive Validity of Five College-Level Academic Aptitude Tests at One Institution." *Personnel & Guid J* 38:637–41 Ap '60. * (*PA* 35:2791)
125. KETCHAM, HERBERT E., (MRS.) "Reading Tests and College Performance," pp. 63–6. In *Research and Evaluation in College Reading.* Ninth Yearbook of the National Reading Conference for College and Adults. Ft. Worth, Tex.: Texas Christian University Press, 1960. Pp. 137. *
126. McFARLAND, JOHN ANTHONY. *A Study to Determine the Correlation Between the Ohio State University Psychological Test Scores and Academic Success Among Students at North Idaho Junior College.* Master's thesis, Gonzaga University (Spokane, Wash.), 1960.
127. PEDERSEN, FRANK, AND MARLOWE, DAVID. "Capacity and Motivational Differences in Verbal Recall." *J Clin Psychol* 16:219–22 Ap '60. * (*PA* 36:2HJ19P)
128. TOOPS, HERBERT A. "A Comparison, by Work-Limit and Time-Limit, of Item Analysis Indices for Practical Test Construction." *Ed & Psychol Meas* 20:251–66 su '60. * (*PA* 35:6395)
129. ISARD, ELEANORE S., AND LASKY, DAVID I. "A Discrepancy Score Method in Predicting Scholastic Achievement of College Freshmen Counseled During Probation." *Personnel & Guid J* 39:725–8 My '61. * (*PA* 36:1KL25I)
130. LUNN, MERVEL SAMUEL, JR. *The Prediction of Success of Students Enrolled in Professional Education Courses at the University of Oklahoma.* Doctor's thesis, University of Oklahoma (Norman, Okla.), 1961. (*DA* 22:1490)
131. PETERS, FRANK R., AND PLOG, EUGENIA L. "The Effectiveness of the ACT for Selection and Placement at the Ohio State University." *Ed Res B* 40:232–41+ D '61. *
132. RISHEL, DARRELL FRED. *The Development and Validation of Instruments and Techniques for the Selective Admission of Applicants for Graduate Studies in Counselor Education.* Doctor's thesis, Pennsylvania State University (University Park, Pa.), 1961. (*DA* 22:2271)
133. CASH, W. L., JR. "Relationship of Personality Traits and Scholastic Aptitude to Academic Achievement in Theological Studies." *J Psychol Studies* 13:105–10 Je '62 [issued F '64]. *
134. DARLEY, JOHN G. "The Basis for Equivalent Scores on the Annual Editions of the American Council on Education Psychological Examination (ACE), 1941 to 1954," pp. 170–83. In his *Promise and Performance: A Study of Ability and Achievement in Higher Education.* Berkeley, Calif.: Center for Study of Higher Education, University of California, 1962. Pp. vii, 191. *
135. TURRENTINE, EDGAR MAYER. *Predicting Success in Practice Teaching in Music.* Doctor's thesis, State University of Iowa (Iowa City, Iowa), 1962. (*DA* 23:2814)
136. BROWN, ELIZABETH A., AND CRITES, JOHN O. "The Ohio State Psychological Test Today: A Current Evaluation for Counseling." *Personnel & Guid J* 41:677–9 Ap '63. * (*PA* 39:1718)

Ohio State University Psychological Test

137. HUGHES, BILLIE EDWARD. *Predicting Achievement in a Graduate School of Education.* Doctor's thesis, North Texas State University (Denton, Tex.), 1963. *(DA 24:1448)*
138. JARMIN, MARTIN VALENCIA. *Prediction of Success in the Student Teaching Program for Prospective Teachers of Vocational Agriculture at the New York State College of Agriculture at Cornell University.* Doctor's thesis, Cornell University (Ithaca, N.Y.), 1963. *(DA 24:3219)*
139. LAND, MELVIN. "Psychological Tests as Predictors for Scholastic Achievement of Dental Students." *J Dental Ed* 27:25–30 Mr '63. *
140. PORTER, ALBERT. "Intelligence-Test Score as a Predictor of Executive Success." *J Bus* 36:65–8 Ja '63. * [The *Ohio State University Psychological Examination*—not the "Otis intelligence test"—was used in this study according to the author.]
141. VORREYER, WARREN J. "Relationship of Selected Adjustment Factors, College Ability, and Achievement to Drop-Outs and Nondrop-Outs of College Freshmen." *J Ed Res* 56:362–5 Mr '63. *
142. WEAVER, WENDELL W., AND KINGSTON, ALBERT J. "A Factor Analysis of the Cloze Procedure and Other Measures of Reading and Language Ability." *J Commun* 13:252–61 D '63. * *(PA 39:188)*
143. ZIMMERMAN, WILLIAM GEORGE, JR. *An Analysis of Selected Aspects of the Master of Education Program at the University of Miami.* Doctor's thesis, University of Miami (Coral Gables, Fla.), 1963. *(DA 28:95A)*
144. BROWN, FREDERICK G., AND DUBOIS, THOMAS E. "Correlates of Academic Success for High-Ability Freshman Men." *Personnel & Guid J* 42:603–7 F '64. * *(PA 39:5820)*
145. CALLIS, ROBERT, AND PREDIGER, DALE J. "Predictors of Achievement in Counseling and Guidance Graduate Study." *Counselor Ed & Sup* 3:63–9 w '64. *
146. DE SANTE, DAVID A. *The Effectiveness of the Ohio State University Psychological Examination in Predicting First Year Scholastic Averages of the Class of 1966 College of Liberal Arts, and Local Application at Niagara University.* Master's thesis, Niagara University (Niagara University, N.Y.), 1964.
147. FEINBERG, ABRAHAM. *The Relative Efficiency of Several Variables Used in the Selection Process for Candidates in a Graduate Certification Program.* Doctor's thesis, Rutgers—The State University (New Brunswick, N.J.), 1964. *(DA 25:2871)*
148. CHAIKA, JOHN J. *Norms and Validity of the Total Scores of the Ohio State Psychological Examination, Form 26, in Predicting First Year Averages in the College of Business Administration of Niagara University.* Master's thesis, Niagara University (Niagara University, N.Y.), 1965.
149. HEWER, VIVIAN H. "Are Tests Fair to College Students From Homes With Low Socio-Economic Status?" *Personnel & Guid J* 43:764–9 Ap '65. * *(PA 39:16441)*
150. LYNCH, PETER L. *A Study of the Effectiveness of the Ohio State University Psychological Examination in Predicting First Year Averages in the College of Liberal Arts in the Class of 1967 at Niagara University.* Master's thesis, Niagara University (Niagara University, N.Y.), 1965.
151. SCIORTINO, RIO. "Relationships Among Originality, Intelligence, Scholastic Achievement, and Scholastic Ability Measures." *Psychol Rep* 17:943–54 D '65. * *(PA 40:4218)*
152. TOLLEFSON, BRUCE E. *The Conditioning and Extinction of Verbal Responses as a Function of Scores on the Ohio State Psychological Examination.* Master's thesis, University of Wyoming (Laramie, Wyo.), 1965.
153. BELK, FLOYD EDMOND. *The Construction of a Simple Instrument to Predict Junior College Freshmen Attrition.* Doctor's thesis, Oklahoma State University (Stillwater, Okla.), 1966. *(DA 27:4061A)*
154. HAVENS, ROBERT INNIS. *An Exploratory Search for Characteristic Patterns of High Performance Rated and Low Performance Rated Counselor-Candidates in a Counselling Practicum.* Doctor's thesis, University of Michigan (Ann Arbor, Mich.), 1966. *(DA 28:104A)*
155. OWENS, THOMAS R., AND ROADEN, ARLISS L. "Predicting Academic Success in Master's Degree Programs in Education." *J Ed Res* 60:124–6 N '66. *
156. PRIEN, ERICH P., AND BOTWIN, DAVID E. "The Reliability and Correlates of an Achievement Index." *Ed & Psychol Meas* 26:1047–52 w '66. * *(PA 41:4998)*
157. BREIMEIER, KENNETH H. *Relationship Between Various Psychological Measures in Use at Theological Seminaries.* Comments by James E. Dittes. Occasional Papers No. 1. Washington, D.C.: Ministry Studies Board, 1967. Pp. iii, 59. *
158. LANE, JAMES ALBERT. *Assessment of Physically Handicapped Adult Students in College.* Doctor's thesis, Ohio State University (Columbus, Ohio), 1967. *(DA 28:3511A)*
159. NELSON, ARVID KAYE. *Differential Predictability of Academic Success.* Doctor's thesis, University of Missouri (Columbia, Mo.), 1967. *(DA 28:3975A)*
160. DENNEY, LOREN L. *The Relationships Between Teaching Method, Critical Thinking and Other Selected Teacher Traits.* Doctor's thesis, University of Missouri (Columbia, Mo.), 1968. *(DA 29:2586A)*
161. GRIMSRUD, RICHARD ARLO. *A Method for Predicting Success in a Counselor Education Training Program.* Doctor's thesis, University of Minnesota (Minneapolis, Minn.), 1968. *(DA 29:2115A)*
162. KEOUGH, MARY JOAN. *The Validity of the Ohio State Psychological Examination in Predicting First Year Averages of the College of Nursing at Niagara University.* Master's thesis, Niagara University (Niagara University, N.Y.), 1968.
163. LEVINE, LOUIS GERALD. *The Relationship of Selected Intellective Factors in the High School Record to First Semester Community College Grade Point Average.* Doctor's thesis, Case Western Reserve University (Cleveland, Ohio), 1968. *(DA 29:4286A)*
164. MUNDAY, LEO. "Correlations Between ACT and Other Predictors of Academic Success in College." *Col & Univ* 44:67–76 f '68. *
165. PENDERGAST, MARY CARITA. *Assessment of a Psychological Screening Program for Candidates to a Religious Congregation of Women.* Doctor's thesis, Fordham University (New York, N.Y.), 1968. *(DA 29:2572A)*
166. DIGIORGIO, ANTHONY JOSEPH. *Discriminant Function Analysis of Measured Characteristics Among Committed Career Groups With Requisite Graduate Training.* Doctor's thesis, Purdue University (Lafayette, Ind.), 1969. *(DAI 30:4769A)*
167. DIELMAN, T. E., AND WILSON, WARNER R. "Convergent and Discriminant Validity of Three Measures of Ability, Aspiration-Level, Achievement, Adjustment and Dominance." *J Ed Meas* 7(3):185–90 f '70. * *(PA 45:4915)*
168. HUGHES, LOIS JUNE. *Selected Factors as Related to Success in Student Teaching of Home Economics.* Doctor's thesis, University of Missouri (Columbia, Mo.), 1970. *(DAI 31:5249A)*
169. JANSEN, DAVID G.; ROBB, GEORGE P.; AND BONK, EDWARD C. "Characteristics of High-Rated and Low-Rated Master's Degree Candidates in Counseling and Guidance." *Counselor Ed & Sup* 9(3):162–70 sp '70. * *(PA 46:5559)*

CUMULATIVE NAME INDEX

Alluisi, E. A.: 73
Anneser, R.: 74
Bartlett, C. J.: 121
Beck, R. L.: 16
Belk, F. E.: 153
Bell, G. B.: 58
Bernard, H. W.: 17
Bond, G. L.: 54
Bonk, E. C.: 169
Botwin, D. E.: 156
Boyd, J. D.: 69
Boyer, L. E.: 75
Bradt, K. H.: 58
Breimeier, K. H.: 157
Brinegar, V.: 4
Brown, D. J.: 122
Brown, E. A.: 136
Brown, F. G.: 144
Bumgarner, F.: 105
Byrns, R. K.: 3
Cahow, A. C.: 18
Callis, R.: 145
Carlile, A. B.: 63
Carter, W. R.: 28, 51
Cash, W. L.: 64, 133
Chahbazi, P.: 70, 76, 110
Chaika, J. J.: 148
Champion, J. M.: 115
Clark, G. Y.: 2, 90
Conner, H. T.: 65
Cooprider, H. A.: 37
Crites, J. O.: 136
Darley, J. G.: 134
Denney, L. L.: 160
De Sante, D. A.: 146
Dielman, T. E.: 167
DiGiorgio, A. J.: 166
Dittes, J. E.: 157
Di Vesta, F. J.: 38, 42
Dubois, T. E.: 144
Duncan, C. P.: 58
Edberg, G.: 53
Edgerton, H. A.: 84
Erffmeyer, C. E.: 81
Farnsworth, P. R.: 83
Feinberg, A.: 147
Ferguson, G. A.: *rev,* 4:308
Frank, G.: 4
Freeman, F. S.: 86
Garrett, W. S.: 26, 123
Gentry, D. E.: 32
Goeckerman, R. W.: 72
Goodling, R. A.: 118
Greene, J. E.: 14
Gregory, C. L.: 112
Grimsrud, R. A.: 161
Guiler, W. S.: 1
Guilford, J. P.: *rev,* 3:244
Gunning, I. C.: 5
Hanna, J. V.: 57
Hardin, R. A.: 29
Hartson, L. D.: 6, 21, 25, 34, 87, 95, 98
Hartson, L. S.: *rev,* 1:1051
Havens, R. I.: 154
Hendrix, O. R.: 59
Hertel, J. P.: 38, 42
Heston, J. C.: 23
Hewer, V. H.: 78, 149
Hill, S. D.: 113
Holmes, J. L.: 68
Houk, C. C.: 77
Hoyt, C. J.: *rev,* 5:359
Hoyt, D. P.: 66
Hughes, B. E.: 137
Hughes, L. J.: 168
Hurst, J. G.: 121
Ingram, L. M.: 39
Isard, E. S.: 129
James, R. W.: 47
Jansen, D. G.: 169
Jarmin, M. V.: 138
Jenkins, J. J.: 60
Johnson, R. H.: 54
Juola, A. E.: 124
Keough, M. J.: 162
Ketcham, H. E. (Mrs.): 125
Kingston, A. J.: 142
Kinzer, J. R.: 61, 67
Kinzer, L. G.: 61, 67
Kirk, H. A.: 52
Kirkpatrick, F. H.: 19
Kohn, H. A.: 10
Koken, J. E.: 75
Krueger, A. F.: 27
Ladieu, G. B.: 20
Land, M.: 139
Lane, G. G.: 102
Lane, J. A.: 158
Langlie, T. A.: *rev,* 1:1051
Lasky, D. I.: 129
Laslett, H. R.: 37
Laughlin, W. P.: 31
Layton, W. L.: 55, 71
Levine, L. G.: 163
Lorenz, A. B.: 91
Lowrie, K. H.: 24
Lunn, M. S.: 130
Lynch, P. L.: 150
Lyon, V. E.: 89
McClure, W. E.: 91
MacDonald, G. L.: 43
McFarland, J. A.: 126
Major, C. L.: 30
Mallinson, G. G.: 107
Marlowe, D.: 127
Martin, J. P.: 109
Mead, A. R.: 85

Merrill, R. M.: 108
Munday, L.: 164
Munger, P.: 111
Munger, P. F.: 72
Nebergall, R. E.: 116
Neel, M. O.: 85
Nelson, A. K.: 159
Newman, S. E.: 58
Norman, W. T.: 66
Odgers, J. G.: 99
Osborn, R. C.: 101
Owens, T. R.: 155
Paeratakul, C.: 119
Patrick, J. R.: 88
Paulsen, G. B.: 36
Pedersen, F.: 127
Pendergast, M. C.: 165
Peters, F. R.: 131
Pierson, L. R.: 117
Pihlblad, C. T.: 112
Pintner, R.: rev, 1:1051
Plog, E. L.: 131
Portenier, L. G.: 40–1, 48, 103
Porter, A.: 140
Porter, J. P.: 8
Prediger, D. J.: 145
Prien, E. P.: 156
Quaid, T. D. D.: 7, 11
Read, C. B.: 96
Reusser, W. C.: 4
Richards, J. M.: 79
Rinsland, H. D.: 44
Rishel, D. F.: 132
Roach, J. H. L.: 104
Roaden, A. L.: 155
Robb, G. P.: 169
Ronning, R. R.: 121
Rowles, E.: 88
Ryan, S. E.: 49
Sabeh, R.: 50
Samenfeld, H. W.: 62
Sams, C. C.: 107
Saum, A. L.: 12
Schmitz, R. M.: 68
Sciortino, R.: 151
Seashore, R. H.: 83
Selover, R. B.: 8
Sharp, H. C.: 35
Sheddan, B. R.: 100
Sherwood, E. J.: 114
Smith, A. B.: 106
Smith, H. P.: 92
South, E. B.: 2, 90
Spaulding, H.: 120
Sprow, A. J.: 21
Stackhouse, H. A.: 80
Staton, T. F.: 14
Stopher, E. C.: 22
Strabel, E.: 93
Stuit, D. B.: 9, 13, 97
Tennyson, W. W.: rev, 5:359
Thompson, R. B.: 33
Tinker, M. A.: 83
Tollefson, B. E.: 152
Toops, H. A.: 15, 84, 128
Turrentine, E. M.: 135
Uhrbrock, R. S.: 45
Vorreyer, W. J.: 141
Weaver, W. W.: 142
Webb, S. C.: 118
Weller, D. C.: 94
Welsh, M. L.: 56
Whinery, S. M.: 82
Wilson, W. R.: 167
Witmer, L. R.: 100
Woodruff, A. D.: 42
Wrenn, C. G.: 46
Zimmerman, W. G.: 143

[419A]

★Oral Verbal Intelligence Test. Ages 7.5–14; 1973; OVIT; D. Young; University of London Press Ltd. [England]. *

[420]

The Oregon Academic Ranking Test. Gifted children grades 3–7; 1965; OART; for rapid identification of the top 3 percent; 9 scores: making sentences, making comparisons, numbers, secret words, working problems, reasoning, completing sentences, sayings, total; Charles H. Derthick; Western Psychological Services. *

For additional information and a review by Robert H. Bauernfeind, see 7:369.

[421]

O'Rourke General Classification Test, Senior Grade. Grades 12–13 and adults; 1927–42; L. J. O'Rourke; O'Rourke Publications. *

For additional information and a review by Marion A. Bills, see 3:246 (3 references).

REFERENCES THROUGH 1971

1–3. See 3:246.
4. CUMMINGS, D. E. "Iron Men for Iron Ships." *Personnel J* 6:87–92 Ag '27. * (*PA* 2:736)
5. "Validity Information Exchange, No. 7-095: D.O.T. Code 7-94.112 and 7-94.100, Tool and Die and Machinist Apprentice." *Personnel Psychol* 7:573 w '54. *

CUMULATIVE NAME INDEX

Bills, M. A.: rev, 3:246
Cummings, D. E.: 4
Davidson, C. M.: 1–2
Lawshe, C. H.: 3
Thornton, G. R.: 3

[422]

The "Orton" Intelligence Test, No. 4. Ages 10–14; 1931; Robert Gibson & Sons, Glasgow, Ltd. [Scotland]. *

For additional information, see 1:1052.

[423]

Otis Employment Tests. Applicants for employment; 1943, c1922; tests identical with Forms A and B of *Otis Self-Administering Tests of Mental Ability;* Arthur S. Otis; Harcourt Brace Jovanovich, Inc. *

For additional information, see 4:310. For reference to a review of the *Otis Self-Administering Tests of Mental Ability,* see 426.

REFERENCES THROUGH 1971

1. HILL, G. H.; STOUTENBOROUGH, ANN; AND SAUNDERS, WILLIAM J., JR. "Normative Data Information Exchange, No. 29." *Personnel Psychol* 9:539–40 w '56. *
2. COOK, JOHN M., AND FARBRO, PATRICK C. "Normative Data Information Exchange, No. 10-3." *Personnel Psychol* 10:97 sp '57. *
3. SHORE, RICHARD P. "Normative Data Information Exchange, Nos. 11-27, 11-28." *Personnel Psychol* 11:593–4 w '58. *
4. SHORE, RICHARD P. "Validity Information Exchange, No. 11-22: D.O.T. Code 1-02.01, Bookkeeping-Machine Operator (Banking)." *Personnel Psychol* 11:435–6 au '58. *
5. SHORE, RICHARD P. "Validity Information Exchange, No. 11-23: D.O.T. Code 1-06.02, Teller." *Personnel Psychol* 11:437 au '58. *
6. SHORE, RICHARD P. "Validity Information Exchange, No. 11-24: D.O.T. Code 1-25.68, Proof-Machine Operator." *Personnel Psychol* 11:438–9 au '58. *
7. ARON, JOEL E., AND HECHT, ROBERT M. "Normative Data Information Exchange, No. 12-26." *Personnel Psychol* 12:645 w '59. *
8. KAZMIER, LEONARD J. "Normative Data Information Exchange, No. 12-20." *Personnel Psychol* 12:502 au '59. *
9. HARRELL, THOMAS W. "The Relation of Test Scores to Sales Criteria." *Personnel Psychol* 13:65–9 sp '60. * (*PA* 35:7192)
10. MACKINNEY, ARTHUR C., AND WOLINS, LEROY. "Validity Information Exchange, No. 13-01, Foreman II, Home Appliance Manufacturing." *Personnel Psychol* 13:443–7 w '60. *
11. RHODE, JACK FERDINAND. *A Pilot Study of the Prediction of Salesmen's Success in an Electronics Organization.* Doctor's thesis, University of Minnesota (Minneapolis, Minn.), 1963. (*DA* 25:2283)

CUMULATIVE NAME INDEX

Aron, J. E.: 7
Cook, J. M.: 2
Farbro, P. C.: 2
Harrell, T. W.: 9
Hecht, R. M.: 7
Hill, G. H.: 1
Kazmier, L. J.: 8
MacKinney, A. C.: 10
Rhode, J. F.: 11
Saunders, W. J.: 1
Shore, R. P.: 3–6
Stoutenborough, A.: 1
Wolins, L.: 10

[424]

Otis-Lennon Mental Ability Test. Grades kgn, 1.0–1.5, 1.6–3, 4–6, 7–9, 10–12; 1936–70; revision of still-in-print *Otis Quick-Scoring Mental Ability Tests;* Arthur S. Otis and Roger T. Lennon; Harcourt Brace Jovanovich, Inc. *

For additional information, a review by John E. Milholland, and excerpted reviews by Arden Grotelueschen and Arthur E. Smith, see 7:370 (6 references). For reference to reviews of the *Otis Quick-Scoring Mental Ability Tests,* see 425.

REFERENCES THROUGH 1971

1–6. See 7:370.
7. ADKISSON, JACK. *A Study of the Value of Selected Curiosity Tests for Predicting Academic Achievement in First and Second-Grades.* Doctor's thesis, North Texas State University (Denton, Tex.), 1970. (*DAI* 31:5833A)
8. BUDDE, ELAINE HELEN. *The Relationship Between Performance of Kindergarten Children on Selected Motor Tests and the Metropolitan Readiness Tests—Otis-Lennon Mental Ability Test,* Doctor's thesis, University of Wisconsin (Madison, Wis.), 1970. (*DAI* 31:5820A)
9. EHRHART, PATRICIA MAULDIN. *A Study of Selected Mental Ability Tests as Predictors of Achievement for Chamorro Pupils.* Master's thesis, University of Guam (Agana, Guam), 1970.
10. EICHELBERGER, R. TONY. *Practice Effects of Repeated IQ Testing and the Relationship Between IQ Change Scores and Selected Individual Characteristics.* Doctor's thesis, Southern Illinois University (Carbondale, Ill.), 1970. (*DAI* 31:5196A)
11. CHISSOM, BRAD S., AND THOMAS, JERRY R. "Multivariate Validity of the Otis-Lennon Mental Ability Tests Primary I Level." *Ed & Psychol Meas* 31(4):991–3 w '71. * (*PA* 48:1635)
12. GRUEN, RONALD STEVEN. *Prediction of End-of-Year Reading Achievement for First and Third Grade Pupils.* Doctor's thesis, Pennsylvania State University (University Park, Pa.), 1971. (*DAI* 32:6198A)
13. HASSON, DAVID JOSEPH. *An Evaluation of Two Methods*

of Test Item Selection. Doctor's thesis, University of Maine (Orono, Me.), 1971. (*DAI* 32:6200A)

14. PROGER, BARTON B.; MCGOWAN, JOHN R.; BAYUK, ROBERT J., JR.; MANN, LESTER; TREVORROW, RUTH L.; AND MASSA, EDWARD. "The Relative Predictive and Construct Validities of the Otis-Lennon Mental Ability Test, the Lorge-Thorndike Intelligence Test, and the Metropolitan Readiness Test in Grades Two and Four: A Series of Multivariate Analyses." *Ed & Psychol Meas* 31(2):529–38 su '71. *

15. RICE, JAMES A. "Head Start Screening: Effectiveness of a Teacher-Administered Battery." *Percept & Motor Skills* 32(2): 675–8 Ap '71. * (*PA* 46:11733)

16. TRIDER, MARY S. "The Right to Read and Standardized Testing: A Necessary Dimension." *Read Teach* 24(4):320–30 Ja '71. * (*PA* 46:11521)

CUMULATIVE NAME INDEX

Adkisson, J.: 7
Bayuk, R. J.: 14
Bligh, H. F.: 3
Breuer, C. E.: 4
Budde, E. H.: 8
Burkhalter, W. D.: 1
Chissom, B. S.: 11
Cotler, S.: 5
Cox, O.: 2
Ehrhart, P. M.: 9
Eichelberger, R. T.: 10
Grotelueschen, A.: *exc,* 7:370
Gruen, R. S.: 12
Hanna, G. S.: 3
Hasson, D. J.: 13
Lenke, J. M.: 3
McGowan, J. R.: 14
Mann, L.: 14
Massa, E.: 14
Milholland, J. E.: *rev,* 7:370
Orleans, J. B.: 3
Palmer, R. J.: 5
Proger, B. B.: 14
Rice, J. A.: 15
Skripol, J. N.: 6
Smith, A. E.: *exc,* 7:370
Thomas, J. R.: 11
Trevorrow, R. L.: 14
Trider, M. S.: 16

[425]

Otis Quick-Scoring Mental Ability Tests. Grades 1–4, 4–9, 9–16; 1936–54; 3 levels; Beta and Gamma levels are revisions of still-in-print *Otis Self-Administering Tests of Mental Ability;* for revised edition, see 424; Arthur S. Otis; Harcourt Brace Jovanovich, Inc. *

a) ALPHA TEST. Grades 1–4; 1936–54; 2 editions.

1) *Alpha Test [Long Form].* 3 scores: nonverbal, verbal, total. *Out of print.*

2) *Alpha Short Form.*

b) BETA TEST. Grades 4–9; 1937–54.

c) GAMMA TEST. Grades 9–16; 1937–54.

For additional information, see 6:481 (24 references); for reviews by D. Welty Lefever and Alfred Yates, see 5:362 (33 references); for a review by Frederic Kuder, see 3:249 (9 references); for a review by F. Kuhlmann, see 2:1413; for a review by C. Spearman of this and the *SRA Primary Mental Abilities,* see 2:1427; for reviews by Psyche Cattell and R. Pintner and excerpted reviews by J. A. Long and one other, see 1:1053. For reference to reviews of the earlier edition, see 426.

REFERENCES THROUGH 1971

1–9. See 3:249.
10–42. See 5:362.
43–66. See 6:481.

67. WILLMOTT, JOHN N. "High School Boys Electing Industrial Arts: A Study of Certain Factors Differentiating the Industrial Arts Group From the Group Not Electing Industrial Arts." *Teach Col Contrib Ed* 836:1–71 '41. * (*PA* 16:2490)

68. SHEPARD, EUGENE L. "Measurements of Certain Nonverbal Abilities of Urban and Rural Children." *J Ed Psychol* 33:458–62 S '42. * (*PA* 17:809)

69. THOMPSON, GEORGE G., AND WITRYOL, SAM L. "The Relationship Between Intelligence and Motor Learning Ability, as Measured by a High Relief Finger Maze." *J Psychol* 22:237–46 O '46. * (*PA* 21:713)

70. SUPER, DONALD E.; BRAASCH, WILLIAM F., JR.; AND SHAY, JOSEPH B. "The Effect of Distractions on Test Results." *J Ed Psychol* 38:373–7 O '47. * (*PA* 22:2159)

71. POTTER, MURIEL CATHERINE. "Perception of Symbol Orientation and Early Reading Success." *Teach Col Contrib Ed* 939:1–69 '49. * (*PA* 24:6511)

72. BARRETT, HARRY O. "Differences in Intelligence Between Two- and Four-Year Course Pupils in a Commercial High School." *J Ed Res* 44:143–7 O '50. * (*PA* 25:5681)

73. EELLS, KENNETH; DAVIS, ALLISON; HAVIGHURST, ROBERT J.; HERRICK, VERGIL E.; AND TYLER, RALPH W. *Intelligence and Cultural Differences: A Study of Cultural Learning and Problem-Solving.* Chicago, Ill.: University of Chicago Press, 1951. Pp. xii, 388. * (*PA* 27:5738)

74. PEEL, E. A., AND GRAHAM, D. "Differentiation of Ability in Primary School Children." *Durham Res R* (England) 1(2): 40–8 S '51. *

75. PEEL, E. A., AND GRAHAM, D. "Differentiation of Ability in Primary School Children—II." *Durham Res R* (England) 1(3):31–4 S '52. * (*PA* 27:5157)

76. CARTER, ROBERT SCRIVEN. "Non-Intellectual Variables Involved in Teachers' Marks." *J Ed Res* 47:81–95 O '53. * (*PA* 28:6587)

77. COLEMAN, JAMES C. "Perceptual Retardation in Reading Disability Cases." *J Ed Psychol* 44:497–503 D '53. * (*PA* 28:7966)

78. GRAHAM, D. "The Differentiation of Ability in Primary School-Children: A Comment." *Durham Res R* (England) 1(4):27–30 S '53. * (*PA* 28:8077)

79. GREEN, CLINTON WALLACE. "The Relationship Between Intelligence as Determined by Intelligence Tests and the Ability to Learn as Determined by Performance on Learning Tests." *J Ed Res* 47:191–200 N '53. * (*PA* 28:6494)

80. GARDINER, CHARLES S.; HALL, HENRY E.; AND PARKER, LEE L., JR. "Identification and Measurement of Case Worker Characteristics: Part II." *Pub Personnel R* 16:153–9 Jl '55. * (*PA* 30:3654)

81. HARRINGTON, MARY JAMES, AND DURRELL, DONALD D. "Mental Maturity Versus Perception Abilities in Primary Reading." *J Ed Psychol* 46:375–80 O '55. * (*PA* 30:7676)

82. WEBB, WILSE B. "Self-Evaluations, Group Evaluations, and Objective Measures." *J Consult Psychol* 19:210–2 Je '55. * (*PA* 30:2935)

83. BRICE, MARSHALL MOORE. *A Comparison of Subjective Predictions With Objective Predictions of College Achievement.* Doctor's thesis, University of Virginia (Charlottesville, Va.), 1956. (*DA* 16:1622)

84. BEAMER, GEORGE C., AND BONK, EDWARD C. "Reliability of Mental Ability Tests." *J Counsel Psychol* 4:322 w '57. * (*PA* 33:5720)

85. CURRIE, CAROLINE. *The Relationship of Certain Selected Factors to Achievement in Freshman Composition.* Doctor's thesis, Northwestern University (Evanston, Ill.), 1957. (*DA* 18:884)

86. HUTSON, BILLY T., AND VINCENT, NICHOLAS M. "Motivation and Prognosis in Shorthand." *J Bus Ed* 33:29–31 O '57. *

87. OLSON, GARETH RAYMOND. *A Study of Predictive Efficiency of Selected Mental and Motor Measures and Success in Athletics.* Doctor's thesis, University of Minnesota (Minneapolis, Minn.), 1958. (*DA* 19:2530)

88. PEGNATO, CARL V. *An Evaluation of Various Initial Methods of Selecting Intellectually Gifted Children at the Junior High School Level.* Doctor's thesis, Pennsylvania State University (University Park, Pa.), 1958. (*DA* 19:1254)

89. BURCHINAL, LEE G. "Social Status, Measured Intelligence, Achievement, and Personality Adjustment of Rural Iowa Girls." *Sociometry* 22:75–80 Mr '59. * (*PA* 34:1254)

90. HAROOTUNIAN, BERJ AVEDIS. *The Relationships Among Tests of Intelligence, Learning, and Reasoning.* Doctor's thesis, University of Pennsylvania (Philadelphia, Pa.), 1959. (*DA* 20:203)

91. KELLY, JOHN PATRICK. *The Influence of Reading Ability on Group Intelligence Test Scores.* Doctor's thesis, State University of Iowa (Iowa City, Iowa), 1959. (*DA* 20:3629)

92. LIGHTHALL, FREDERICK; RUEBUSH, BRITTON; SARASON, SEYMOUR; AND ZWEIBELSON, IRVING. "Change in Mental Ability as a Function of Test Anxiety and Type of Mental Test." *J Consult Psychol* 23:34–8 F '59. * (*PA* 34:981)

93. OLANDER, HERBERT T., AND KLEYLE, HELEN M. "Differences in Personal and Professional Characteristics of a Selected Group of Elementary Teachers With Contrasting Success Records." *Ed Adm & Sup* 45:191–8 Jl '59. * (*PA* 34:6582)

94. FITZGERALD, LOUIS ALLEN. *Some Effects of Reading Ability on Group Intelligence Test Scores in the Intermediate Grades.* Doctor's thesis, State University of Iowa (Iowa City, Iowa), 1960. (*DA* 21:1844)

95. HOLOWINSKY, IVAN ZENOVI. *The Relationship Between Intelligence (80–110 I.Q.) and Achievement in Basic Educational Skills for a Selected Sample in Camden, New Jersey.* Doctor's thesis, Temple University (Philadelphia, Pa.), 1961. (*DA* 22:1509)

96. MORRISON, HUGH E., AND COLLISTER, E. GORDON. "The Use of Difference Scores in the Interpretation of Test Results in Elementary Schools." *Univ Kan B Ed* 16:19–25 N '61. *

97. TURRENTINE, EDGAR MAYER. *Predicting Success in Practice Teaching in Music.* Doctor's thesis, State University of Iowa (Iowa City, Iowa), 1962. (*DA* 23:2814)

98. BABBOTT, EDWARD FRENCH. *The Differential Effectiveness of Eight 9th Grade Variables in Predicting Success in Three 10th Grade Academic Subjects at Summit High School: A Study in Differential Prediction.* Doctor's thesis, New York University (New York, N.Y.), 1963. (*DA* 25:993)

99. BOND, CONSTANCE MCCURRY. *A Study of the Predictive Value of Two Measures of Scholastic Aptitude in the Middle Elementary Grades.* Master's thesis, Northern Illinois University (DeKalb, Ill.), 1963.

100. GUSTAFSON, EDWIN A. *A Study of the Relationship of IQ Scores to the Grades and Curriculum Choices Among the Students of Little Falls High School.* Master's thesis, St. Cloud State College (St. Cloud, Minn.), 1963.

101. HAAS, MARY GERALDINE. *A Comparative Study of Critical*

Thinking, Flexibility of Thinking, and Reading Ability Involving Religious and Lay College Seniors. Doctor's thesis, Fordham University (New York, N.Y.), 1963. (*DA* 24:622)

102. PETERS, HERBERT D. "Performance of Hopi Children on Four Intelligence Tests." *J Am Indian Ed* 2:27–31 Ja '63. *

103. SILVAROLI, NICHOLAS JOSEPH. *Intellectual and Emotional Factors as Predictors of Children's Success in First Grade Reading.* Doctor's thesis, Syracuse University (Syracuse, N.Y.), 1963. (*DA* 24:5098)

104. URAY, RICHARD MARTIN. *An Analysis of Scores Made by a Group of Radio Announcers in Texas on Selected Psychological Tests.* Doctor's thesis, University of Houston (Houston, Tex.), 1963. (*DA* 25:950)

105. WEBER, LYLE E. *An Experimental Study on the Effect of Age, Reading Score, I.Q., and Sex on High School Students' Ability to Learn to Typewrite.* Master's thesis, Northwestern University (Evanston, Ill.), 1963.

106. CHARLES, C. M. "Bicultural Children and Science Achievement." *Sci Ed* 48:93–6 F '64. *

107. JOHNSON, EDWARD E. "Time Concepts as Related to Sex, Intelligence and Academic Performance." *J Ed Res* 57:377–9 Mr '64. *

108. LYSAUGHT, JEROME P. "Further Analysis of Success Among Auto-Instructional Programmers." *Teaching Aid News* 4:6–11 O 15 '64. *

109. LYSAUGHT, JEROME P. "Selecting Instructional Programmers: New Research Into Characteristics of Successful Programmers." *Training Directors J* 18:8–14 Je '64. *

110. LYSAUGHT, JEROME P., AND PIERLEONI, ROBERT G. "A Comparison of Predicted and Actual Success in Auto-Instructional Programing." *J Programed Instr* 3(4):14–23 '64. * (*PA* 40:13506)

111. MCCORMICK, JAMES H., AND ASHER, WILLIAM. "Aspects of the High School Record Related to the First Semester College Grade Point Average." *Personnel & Guid J* 42:699–703 Mr '64. *

112. SHAFFER, RAYMOND GEORGE. *A Study of Four Group Intelligence Tests to Identify Ambiguous Pictures as a Factor Which Causes Some Children to Select Incorrect Answers.* Doctor's research study No. 1, Colorado State College (Greeley, Colo.), 1964. (*DA* 25:1014)

113. SLATER, RICHARD D. "The Equivalency of IBM Mark-Sense Answer Cards and IBM Answer Sheets When Used as Answer Formats for a Precisely-Timed Test of Mental Ability." *J Ed Res* 57:545–7 Jl–Ag '64. *

114. BRADY, WILLIAM JOSEPH. *Twenty Quantitative Predictors of Academic Success in College as Measured by Grade Point Averages.* Doctor's thesis, University of Connecticut (Storrs, Conn.), 1965. (*DA* 26:5121)

115. CASTIGLIONE, LAWRENCE VIRGIL. *The Relation of Intelligence to Selected Measures of Creativity.* Doctor's thesis, New York University (New York, N.Y.), 1965. (*DA* 27:1278E)

116. CAUTELA, JOSEPH R., AND BARLOW, DAVID H. "The Relation Between Intelligence and Critical Flicker Fusion." *Psychon Sci* 3:559–60 D 15 '65. * (*PA* 40:2219)

117. DICKEN, CHARLES F., AND BLACK, JOHN D. "Predictive Validity of Psychometric Evaluations of Supervisors." *J Appl Psychol* 49:34–47 F '65. * (*PA* 39:8793)

118. ESTES, BETSY WORTH. "Relationships Between the Otis, 1960 Stanford-Binet and WISC." *J Clin Psychol* 21:296–7 Jl '65. * (*PA* 39:15230)

119. FOSTER, MARION E. "A Comparison of Reading Achievement of Christchurch, New Zealand and Edmonton Alberta Public School Students of the Same Age and Number of Years of Schooling." *Alberta J Ed Res* (Canada) 11:21–31 Mr '65. * (*PA* 39:16455)

120. GOSHAL, AVTAR H. SINGH. "Indian Adaptation of Otis Mental Ability Test Gamma C—A Normative Study." *J Indian Acad Appl Psychol* 2:24–9 Ja '65. * (*PA* 39:12284)

121. JAMAL, SHABNAM. "The Validity of Raven's Coloured Progressive Matrices and Otis Quick Scoring Mental Ability Test for Pakistani Children." *B Ed & Res* (Pakistan) 4(1):25–41 '65. *

122. JUSTMAN, JOSEPH. "Academic Aptitude and Reading Test Scores of Disadvantaged Children Showing Varying Degrees of Mobility." *J Ed Meas* 2:151–5 D '65. * (*PA* 40:5943)

123. PETIT, JEAN L. *Selecting Variables Found in the Cumulative Folder of Belvidere High School Students Predicting Academic Success.* Master's thesis, Northern Illinois University (DeKalb, Ill.), 1965.

124. PLAPP, JON M.; PSATHAS, GEORGE; AND CAPUTO, DANIEL V. "Intellective Predictors and Success in Nursing School." Abstract. *Proc Ann Conv Am Psychol Assn* 73:307–8 '65. * (*PA* 39:16458)

125. PLAPP, JON M.; PSATHAS, GEORGE; AND CAPUTO, DANIEL V. "Intellective Predictors of Success in Nursing School." *Ed & Psychol Meas* 25:565–77 su '65. * (*PA* 39:15259)

126. SCOTT, RUSSELL H.; PHIPPS, GRANT T.; AND MORGART, HELEN S. "Prediction of Success in a Dental Assisting Course." *J Dental Ed* 29:348–57 D '65. *

127. STAPLES, JOHN DIXON. *An Experimental Study to Identify the Basic Abilities Needed to Detect Typescript Errors With Implications for the Improvement of Instruction in Typewriting.* Doctor's thesis, University of North Dakota (Grand Forks, N.D.), 1965. (*DA* 27:1693A)

128. WIMBY, EUGENE B. *A Comparative Study of the Kuhlmann-Anderson and the Otis Quick Scoring Intelligence Tests as Predictors of High School Performance.* Master's thesis, Atlanta University (Atlanta, Ga.), 1965.

129. BRENNAN, JOSEPH T., JR. *Estimating Expected Reading Achievement in the Junior High School.* Doctor's thesis, University of Pittsburgh (Pittsburgh, Pa.), 1966. (*DA* 27:4033A)

130. CASHMAN, JEROME PATRICK. *A Study of the Relationship Between Organic Factors, Certain Selected Variables and Progress in a Reading Improvement Program.* Doctor's thesis, Fordham University (New York, N.Y.), 1966. (*DA* 27:1648A)

131. CONAWAY, BARON DARVIS. *A Modification of Group Intelligence Test Administration and Its Relation to the Reading Abilities of Sixth-Grade Pupils.* Doctor's thesis, Auburn University (Auburn, Ala.), 1966. (*DA* 27:945A)

132. DARBES, ALEX. "Some Test Characteristics of Female Student Beauticians." *Proc W Va Acad Sci* 37:286–8 F '66. * (*PA* 40:8250)

133. DIRR, PIERRE MARIE. *Intellectual Variables in Achievement in Modern Algebra.* Doctor's thesis, Catholic University of America (Washington, D.C.), 1966. (*DA* 27:2873A)

134. FOX, A. M., AND AINSWORTH, L. L. "Otis Prediction of Graduate Education Course Grades." *Ed & Psychol Meas* 26:1055–6 w '66. * (*PA* 41:4990)

135. GAY, CLEVELAND JOHNSON. *Academic Achievement and Intelligence Among Negro Eighth Grade Students as a Function of the Self Concept.* Doctor's thesis, North Texas State University (Denton, Tex.), 1966. (*DA* 27:112A)

136. HAROOTUNIAN, BERJ. "Intelligence and the Ability to Learn." *J Ed Res* 59:211–4 Ja '66. * (*PA* 40:6627)

137. JEX, FRANK B. *Predicting Academic Success Beyond High School.* Salt Lake City, Utah: University of Utah Bookstore, 1966. Pp. vi, 41. *

138. KANDEL, ARTHUR. *Discrepancies Between the Stanford-Binet and Three Group Tests of Intelligence in the Identification of Low I.Q. Children.* Doctor's thesis, Catholic University of America (Washington, D.C.), 1966. (*DA* 27:1659A)

139. KEACH, CHARLES CAMPBELL. *Discrepancies Between the Stanford-Binet and Three Group Tests of Intelligence in the Identification of High I.Q. Children.* Doctor's thesis, Catholic University of America (Washington, D.C.), 1966. (*DA* 27:1660A)

140. MCCORMICK, ALBERT GRANT. *An Investigation of Reading Skills, General Mental Ability and Personality Variables Used in the Selection of Practical Nursing Students.* Doctor's thesis, Oklahoma State University (Stillwater, Okla.), 1966. (*DA* 27:4136A)

141. MCCRORY, MARGARET ANNE. *An Analysis of Mental Emotional and Social Factors Related to Success in Student Teaching.* Doctor's thesis, Boston University (Boston, Mass.), 1966. (*DA* 27:3318A)

142. RUSSELL, H. H., AND DILLING, H. J. "Comparison of General Intelligence Test Results and Student Achievement in Grade 8 and Grade 9 of Scarborough Schools." *Ont J Ed Res* (Canada) 8:267–77 sp '66. *

143. SAVAGE, R. D., AND O'CONNOR, D. J. "The Assessment of Reading and Arithmetic Retardation in the School." *Brit J Ed Psychol* 36:317–8 N '66. *

144. SCHUSLER, MARIAN M. "Prediction of Grades by Computer for High School Students: A Cross-Validation and Experimental Placement Study." *J Ed Data Processing* 3:97–110 su '66. *

145. STAFFORD, RICHARD LINDSAY. *The Effects of Creativity and Intelligence on Information Seeking Strategies Used in a Problem Solving Task by Sixth Grade Boys.* Doctor's thesis, University of Houston (Houston, Tex.), 1966. (*DA* 27:973B)

146. WEBER, DORIS S. *The Relationship Between Verbal and Non-Verbal Ability and Achievement in Elementary Mathematics.* Master's thesis, Adelphi University (Garden City, N.Y.), 1966.

147. WHITTEMORE, ROBERT G.; ECHEVERRIA, BEN P.; AND GRIFFIN, JOHN V. "Can We Use Existing Tests for Adult Basic Education?" *Adult Ed* 17:19–29 au '66. *

148. AINSWORTH, L. L., AND FOX, A. M. "Otis IQ: Forecasting Efficiency for Undergraduate Education Courses." *Ed & Psychol Meas* 27:431 su '67. *

149. BHUSHAN, VIDYA. "The Translation of the Otis Quick-Scoring Mental Ability Tests Into Hindi Language." *J Ed & Psychol* (India) 24:192–5 Ja '67. *

150. HUSTON, BEATRICE MOORE. *A Normative Survey of the Personal and Academic Characteristics of the Freshmen Women Students Enrolled in Mary Hardin-Baylor College, 1966–1967.* Doctor's thesis, Baylor University (Waco, Tex.), 1967. (*DA* 28:1209A)

151. SANTORO, ROSEANN MARIE. *The Relationship of Reading Achievement to Specific Measures of Visual Perception, Visual-Motor Perception and Intelligence.* Doctor's thesis, Fordham University (New York, N.Y.), 1967. (*DA* 28:4010A)

152. SERVIS, MARGERY, AND FROST, REUBEN B. "Qualities Related to Success in Women's Physical Education Professional Preparation Program." *Res Q* 38:283–90 My '67. *

153. TUCKER, WILLIAM FRANCIS. *The Prediction of Achievement in Selected High School Subjects From Junior High School*

Data. Doctor's thesis, New York University (New York, N.Y.), 1967. *(DA* 28:1317A)

154. WILLIAMS, JACK, AND FOX, A. M. "Prediction of Performance in Student Teaching." *Ed & Psychol Meas* 27:1169-70 w '67. * *(PA* 42:9491)

155. WINSTON, WILMA ESSEX. *A Correlation Between Language Achievement and Musical Aptitude of Thirty Sixth Grade Pupils at Booker T. Washington School, East Gadsden, Alabama.* Master's thesis, Alabama A & M College (Normal, Ala.), 1967.

156. AHMAD, FARRUKH Z. "Is the Otis Quick Scoring Mental Ability Test a Good Predictor of Academic Success in West Pakistan?" *Ed & Psychol Meas* 28:947-9 au '68. * *(PA* 43:4513)

157. ARTH, ALFRED ARTHUR. *A Study of the Relationship Between Non-Completion and Intelligence Exhibited by Sixth Grade Elementary School Students.* Doctor's thesis, University of Oklahoma (Norman, Okla.), 1968. *(DA* 29:1666A)

158. BAILEY, LARRY J. "Factors Related to Success in Practical Nursing Programs." *Nursing Outl* 16:59 N '68. *

159. BUSZEK, BEATRICE R. "Differential Treatment of Test Scores." *Col & Univ* 43:294-307 sp '68. *

160. GREEN, JOHNNIE HENDERSON. *An Analysis of Academic Proficiency of the 1965-66 Beginning Freshman Class, School of Business, Texas Southern University, Houston, Texas.* Doctor's thesis, University of Houston (Houston, Tex.), 1968. *(DA* 29:3323A)

161. HARRIS, A. J., AND LOVINGER, R. J. "Longitudinal Measures of the Intelligence of Disadvantaged Negro Adolescents." *Sch R* 76:60-6 Mr '68. * *(PA* 43:3138)

162. HAYDEN, DAVID LEE. *Factors of Intelligence of College Students in the Philippines as Determined by the Otis Quick-Scoring Mental Ability Test, Gamma, FM, and the Measure of Intellectual Maturation.* Doctor's thesis, Catholic University of America (Washington, D.C.), 1968. *(DA* 29:3874A)

163. MACARTHUR, R. S. "Assessing Intellectual Potential of Native Canadian Pupils: A Summary." *Alberta J Ed Res* (Canada) 14:115-22 Je '68. * *(PA* 44:4170)

164. MACARTHUR, RUSSELL. "Some Differential Abilities of Northern Canadian Native Youth." *Int J Psychol* (France) 3(1):43-50 '68. * *(PA* 42:15325)

165. PUGH, RICHARD C. "Tests for Creative Thinking—Potential for School Testing Programs." *B Sch Ed Ind Univ* 44(6):1-30 N '68. * *(PA* 46:5483)

166. RUTHERFORD, BRENT M., AND KOPLYAY, JANOS B. "Program COGITO: Computerized General IQ Testing—Otis, in the FORTRAN IV Language." *Ed & Psychol Meas* 28:177-9 sp '68. * *(PA* 42:11395)

167. SOLKOFF, NORMAN. "The Use of Personality and Attitude Tests in Predicting the Academic Success of Medical and Law Students." *J Med Ed* 43:1250-3 D '68. * *(PA* 44:7336)

168. STOCK, WILLIAM H., JR. *Some Psychological and Physiological Factors Affecting Excellence in Acting.* Doctor's thesis, Michigan State University (East Lansing, Mich.), 1968. *(DA* 29:3716A)

169. ARMBRUST, ROBERT. *An Investigation of the Role of Selected Non-Verbal Intelligence Factors in Beginning Drafting Success.* Doctor's thesis, Southern Illinois University (Carbondale, Ill.), 1969. *(DAI* 30:2895A)

170. BOWERS, JOHN. "Interactive Effects of Creativity and IQ on Ninth-Grade Achievement." *J Ed Meas* 6(3):173-7 f '69. * *(PA* 44:15469)

171. DE BOTTARI, LINDA. "Primary School Correlates of Secondary School Achievement." *Personnel & Guid J* 47(7):675-8 Mr '69. * *(PA* 43:13362)

172. ERTL, JOHN P., AND SCHAFER, EDWARD W. P. "Brain Response Correlates of Psychometric Intelligence." *Nature* 223(5204):421-2 Jl 26 '69. *

173. FAIRCHILD, PATRICIA CARLETTE. *Grade Point Average and Variance as Criteria of College Academic Performance.* Doctor's thesis, University of Oklahoma (Norman, Okla.), 1969. *(DAI* 30:3318A)

174. GROPPER, ROBERT L. *Comprehension of Narrative Passages by Fourth-Grade Children as a Function of Listening Rate and Eleven Predictor Variables.* Doctor's thesis, George Peabody College for Teachers (Nashville, Tenn.), 1969. *(DAI* 30:4827A)

175. HIERONYMUS, A. N., AND STROUD, JAMES B. "Comparability of IQ Scores on Five Widely Used Intelligence Tests." *Meas & Eval Guid* 2(3):135-40 f '69. * *(PA* 44:13285)

176. MEEHAN, KATHRYN S. *Predicting Future Achievement From the Detroit Beginning First Grade Intelligence Test and the Otis Quick Scoring Test of Mental Ability.* Master's thesis, Jersey City State College (Jersey City, N.J.), 1969.

177. MORE, ARTHUR. "The Relation of High School Grades, Achievement and Intelligence Test Scores to Success in Dental School." *Can Counsellor* 3(1):56-8 Ja '69. *

178. NELSON, C. MICHAEL, AND HUDSON, FLOYD G. "Predicting the Reading Achievement of Junior High School EMR Children." *Am J Mental Def* 74(3):415-20 N '69. * *(PA* 44:5559)

179. ROGGENKAMP, RONALD R. *A Study to Determine the Validity of Using College Entrance Exams and I.Q. as Predictors of College Performance for Falls City Senior High Graduates.* Master's thesis, Kearney State College (Kearney, Neb.), 1969.

180. TOLOR, ALEXANDER. "Incidence of Underachievement at the High School Level." *J Ed Res* 63(2):63-5 O '69. *

181. URLOCKER, WILFRID THOMAS. *A Pilot Study to Determine the Validity of the Otis Quick-Scoring Mental Ability Beta Test and the Dominion Achievement Test in Silent Reading Type II: Diagnostic Test in Paragraph Reading in Predicting Grade VII Averages at St. Anthony Senior Elementary School.* Master's thesis, Niagara University (Niagara University, N.Y.), 1969.

182. BEINKE, JAMES L. *A Study to Determine the Correlation of a System of Teacher Evaluation to Otis IQ Scores and the Gordon Musical Aptitude Profile Test.* Master's thesis, Wisconsin State University (Whitewater, Wis.), 1970.

183. BICKLEY, A. C.; DINNAN, JAMES A.; AND BICKLEY, RACHEL. "Language Responses as a Predictor of Performance on Intelligence Tests." *J Read Behav* 2(4):291-4 f '70. * *(PA* 46:4980)

184. CHASE, CLINTON I. "Comparable Intelligence Test Performance by Extreme Social Classes." Abstract. *Proc 78th Ann Conv Am Psychol Assn* 5(2):645-6 '70. * *(PA* 44:18350)

185. ISMAIL, A. H., AND KIRKENDALL, D. R. "Relationship Among Three Domains of Development," pp. 451-60. In *Contemporary Psychology of Sport.* Proceedings of the Second International Congress of Sport Psychology, Washington, D.C., 1968. Chicago, Ill.: Athletic Institute, 1970. Pp. xix, 878. *

186. KENNETT, K. F., AND CROPLEY, A. J. "Intelligence, Family Size and Socio-Economic Status." *J Biosocial Sci* (England) 2(3):227-36 Jl '70. * *(PA* 46:4670)

187. LEUNES, ARNOLD, AND CHRISTENSEN, LARRY. "Reliability and Inmate Test Results." *Correct Psychologist* 4(3):85-93 N-D '70. * *(PA* 49:2670)

188. LYSAUGHT, JEROME P., AND PIERLEONI, ROBERT G. "Predicting Individual Success in Programing Self-Instructional Materials." *AV Commun R* 18(1):5-24 sp '70. * *(PA* 44:13334)

189. PARTIN, RONALD L. *The Value of Four Selected Test Scores in Predicting Advanced Placement American History Test Scores.* Master's thesis, Bowling Green State University (Bowling Green, Ohio), 1970.

190. PIERLEONI, ROBERT G., AND LYSAUGHT, JEROME P. "A Decision Ladder for Predicting Programmer Success." *NSPI J* 9(5):6-7 + Je '70. *

191. SMITH, I. MACFARLANE. "The Use of Diagnostic Tests for Assessing the Abilities of Overseas Students Attending Institutions of Further Education, Part I." *Voc Aspect Ed* (England) 22(51):1-8 Mr '70. *

192. BAILEY, KENT G., AND GIBBY, ROBERT G., SR. "Developmental Differences in Self-Ratings on Intelligence." *J Clin Psychol* 27(1):51-4 Ja '71. * *(PA* 46:791)

193. CHASE, CLINTON I., AND PUGH, RICHARD C. "Social Class and Performance on an Intelligence Test." *J Ed Meas* 8(3):197-202 f '71. * *(PA* 47:11604)

194. CHISSOM, BRAD S., AND LIGHTSEY, RALPH. "A Comparison of the D-48 Test and the Otis Quick Score for High School Dropouts." *Ed & Psychol Meas* 31(2):525-7 su '71. *

195. FARR, JAMES L.; O'LEARY, BRIAN S.; AND BARTLETT, C. J. "Ethnic Group Membership as a Moderator of the Prediction of Job Performance." *Personnel Psychol* 24(4):609-36 w '71. *

196. LANGEVIN, R. "Is Curiosity a Unitary Construct?" *Can J Psychol* 25(4):360-74 au '71. * *(PA* 47:5607)

197. LEMKE, ELMER A., AND KIRCHNER, JOHN H. "A Multivariate Study of Handwriting, Intelligence, and Personality Correlates." *J Pers Assess* 35(6):584-92 D '71. * *(PA* 47:10876)

198. SHANLEY, LUKE A.; WALKER, RONALD E.; AND FOLEY, JEANNE M. "Social Intelligence: A Concept in Search of Data." *Psychol Rep* 29(3):1123-32 D '71. * *(PA* 48:1661)

199. SMITH, I. MACFARLANE. "The Use of Diagnostic Tests for Assessing the Abilities of Overseas Students Attending Institutions of Further Education, Part II." *Voc Aspect Ed* (England) 23(54):39-48 Ap '71. *

200. SMITH, RICHARD LEE. *A Factor-Analytic Study of Critical Reading/Thinking, Influenceability, and Related Factors.* Doctor's thesis, University of Maine (Orono, Me.), 1971. *(DAI* 32:6229A)

201. VARNER, DONALD GILES. *The Relationship of Selected Cumulative Grade Point Averages to Intelligence Quotient.* Master's thesis, Eastern Illinois University (Charleston, Ill.), 1971.

202. WILSON, GLENN D.; TUNSTALL, OLIVE A.; AND EYSENCK, H. J. "Individual Differences in Tapping Performance as a Function of Time on the Task." *Percept & Motor Skills* 33(2):375-8 O '71. * *(PA* 47:6073)

CUMULATIVE NAME INDEX

Ahmad, F. Z.: 156	Bailey, A. E.: 1
Ainsworth, L. L.: 134, 148	Bailey, K. G.: 192
Allen, R. M.: 14	Bailey, L. J.: 158
Alvi, S. A.: 61	Barlow, D. H.: 116
Anderson, S. B.: 23	Barnes, P. J.: 28
Armbrust, R.: 169	Barnette, W. L.: 16
Arth, A. A.: 157	Barrett, H. O.: 72
Asher, W.: 111	Barron, E. M.: 17
Babbott, E. F.: 98	Bartlett, C. J.: 195

Otis Quick-Scoring Mental Ability Tests

Beamer, G. C.: 84
Beinke, J. L.: 182
Bessell, H.: 14
Bhushan, V.: 149
Bickley, A. C.: 183
Bickley, R.: 183
Bininger, M. L.: 4
Black, J. D.: 117
Blosser, G. H.: 62
Boger, J. H.: 20
Bolin, B. J.: 29
Bolton, F. B.: 9
Bond, C. M.: 99
Bonk, E. C.: 84
Bowers, J.: 170
Braasch, W. F.: 70
Brady, W. J.: 114
Brennan, J. T.: 129
Brice, M. M.: 83
Burchinal, L. G.: 89
Buszek, B. R.: 159
Campbell, R. J.: 46
Caputo, D. V.: 124-5
Carter, R. S.: 76
Cashman, J. P.: 130
Cass, J. C.: 52
Castiglione, L. V.: 115
Cattell, P.: *rev*, 1:1053
Cautela, J. R.: 116
Charles, C. M.: 106
Chase, C. I.: 184, 193
Chissom, B. S.: 194
Christensen, L.: 187
Clark, G. E.: 33
Clymer, T.: 63
Coleman, J. C.: 77
Collister, E. G.: 96
Conaway, B. D.: 131
Croft, E. J.: 48
Cropley, A. J.: 186
Crouch, M. S.: 24
Currie, C.: 85
Darbes, A.: 53, 132
Davis, A.: 73
Davis, W. A.: 12
de Bottari, L.: 171
Delancy, E. O.: 26
Di Bona, L. J.: 54
Dicken, C. F.: 117
Dilling, H. J.: 142
Dinnan, J. A.: 183
Dirr, P. M.: 133
Donohue, H. H.: 17
Dufficy, E. C.: 45
Durrell, D. D.: 81
Echeverria, B. P.: 147
Edgar, M.: 40
Eells, K.: 73
Engelhart, M. D.: 49
Ertl, J. P.: 172
Estes, B. W.: 118
Eysenck, H. J.: 202
Fairchild, P. C.: 173
Farr, J. L.: 195
Fitzgerald, L. A.: 94
Foley, J. M.: 198
Foster, M. E.: 119
Fox, A. M.: 134, 148, 154
Frost, R. B.: 152
Fruchter, B.: 21
Gardiner, C. S.: 80
Gay, C. J.: 135
Gibby, R. G.: 192
Goshal, A. H. S.: 120
Graham, D.: 74-5, 78
Green, C. W.: 79
Green, J. H.: 160
Griffin, J. V.: 147
Gropper, R. L.: 174
Gustafson, E. A.: 100
Haas, M. G.: 101
Hall, H. E.: 80
Harootunian, B.: 136
Harootunian, B. A.: 90
Harrington, M. J.: 81
Harris, A. J.: 161
Havighurst, R. J.: 12, 73
Hayden, D. L.: 162
Herrick, V. E.: 73
Hieronymus, A. N.: 175
Higgins, C.: 64
Holmes, J. A.: 43
Holowinsky, I. Z.: 95
Hudson, F. G.: 178
Hurd, A. W.: 15

Huston, B. M.: 150
Hutson, B. T.: 86
Ismail, A. H.: 185
Jamal, S.: 121
Jex, F. B.: 137
Johnson, E. E.: 107
Justman, J.: 22, 122
Kandel, A.: 138
Keach, C. C.: 139
Kelly, J. P.: 91
Kennett, K. F.: 186
Kerr, J.: 10
Kirchner, J. H.: 197
Kirkendall, D. R.: 185
Kleyle, H. M.: 93
Koplyay, J. B.: 166
Kuder, F.: *rev*, 3:249
Kuhlmann, F.: *rev*, 2:1413
Langevin, R.: 196
Larsen, R. P.: 11
Laver, A. B.: 50
Lefever, D. W.: *rev*, 5:362
Lemke, E. A.: 197
Lennon, R. T.: 18, 34
LeUnes, A.: 187
Lighthall, F.: 92
Lightsey, R.: 194
Long, J. A.: *exc*, 1:1053
Long, J. R.: 35
Lovinger, R. J.: 161
Lysaught, J. P.: 108-10, 188, 190
MacArthur, R.: 164
MacArthur, R. S.: 163
McCormick, A. G.: 140
McCormick, J. H.: 111
McCrory, M. A.: 141
McQueen, R.: 47
Marinaccio, L. V.: 56
Meehan, K. S.: 176
Mitchell, J. V.: 30
More, A.: 177
Morgart, H. S.: 126
Morrison, H. E.: 96
Mouly, G. J.: 40
Nelson, C. M.: 178
Nicholson, A.: 36, 41
North, R. D.: 37, 42
Norton, D. P.: 51
O'Connor, D. J.: 143
Olander, H. T.: 93
O'Leary, B. S.: 195
Olson, G. R.: 87
Parker, L. L.: 80
Partin, R. L.: 189
Peel, E. A.: 13, 74-5
Pegnato, C. V.: 88
Peters, H. D.: 102
Petit, J. L.: 123
Phipps, G. T.: 126
Pierleoni, R. G.: 110, 188, 190
Pintner, R.: *rev*, 1:1053
Plapp, J. M.: 124-5
Potter, M. C.: 71
Preische, W. A.: 2
Psathas, G.: 124-5
Pugh, G. S.: 8
Pugh, R. C.: 165, 193
Purdy, B. F.: 19
Ridley, W. N.: 25
Roberts, H. E.: 57
Roggenkamp, R. R.: 179
Rosinski, E. F.: 55
Ruebush, B.: 92
Russell, H. H.: 142
Rutherford, B. M.: 166
Santoro, R. M.: 151
Sarason, S.: 92
Savage, R. D.: 143
Schafer, E. W. P.: 172
Schusler, M. M.: 144
Schutz, R. E.: 34
Scott, R. H.: 126
Servis, M.: 152
Shaffer, R. G.: 112
Shanley, L. A.: 198
Shaw, G. S.: 44
Shay, J. B.: 70
Shepard, E. L.: 68
Shuman, J. T.: 3, 5-6
Siebert, L. A.: 58, 65
Silvaroli, N. J.: 103
Slater, R. D.: 113
Slutzky, J. E.: 22
Smith, I. M.: 191, 199

Smith, R. L.: 200
Solkoff, N.: 167
Spearman, C.: *rev*, 2:1427
Speer, G. S.: 38
Stafford, R. L.: 145
Staples, J. D.: 127
Stock, W. H.: 168
Strickland, J. A.: 60
Stroud, J. B.: 175
Super, D. E.: 70
Thompson, G. G.: 69
Tiedeman, D. V.: 52
Tobias, S.: 66
Tolor, A.: 180
Tucker, W. F.: 153
Tunstall, O. A.: 202
Turrentine, E. M.: 97
Tyler, R. W.: 73
Uray, R. M.: 104
Urlocker, W. T.: 181
Varner, D. G.: 201
Vincent, N. M.: 86

von Wittich, B.: 59
Walker, R. E.: 198
Webb, W. B.: 82
Weber, D. S.: 146
Weber, E. G.: 7
Weber, L. E.: 105
Weiner, M.: 66
Wellman, F. E.: 39
Whittemore, R. G.: 147
Williams, J.: 154
Williams, K. C.: 47
Willingham, W. W.: 60
Willmott, J. N.: 67
Wilson, G. D.: 202
Wimby, E. B.: 128
Winston, W. E.: 155
Wityrol, S. L.: 69
Wittenborn, J. R.: 11
Wrightstone, J. W.: 22
Yates, A.: *rev*, 5:362
Zweibelson, I.: 31, 92

[426]
Otis Self-Administering Tests of Mental Ability. Grades 4–9, 9–16; 1922–29; Arthur S. Otis and Thomas N. Barrows (Forms D, intermediate C); Harcourt Brace Jovanovich, Inc. (Australian adaptation: Ages 9–14, 12.5 and over; 1936–73; 1972–73 metric editions identical with tests published 1936–51 except for 2–9 revised items; manuals by D. Spearritt; Australian Council for Educational Research [Australia]. New Zealand adaptation: Ages 9–14, 12–17; 1937–69; New Zealand Council for Educational Research [New Zealand].) * For later edition entries, see 424 and 425.

For additional information, see 5:363 (52 references); for a review by Frederic Kuder, see 3:250 (71 references). For additional information concerning the original Australian edition, see 2:1412.

REFERENCES THROUGH 1971

1–71. See 3:250.
72–123. See 5:363.
124. BINNEWIES, W. G. "Freshmen Grades and Mental Tests: A Correlation Made at South Dakota State College, Brookings." *Ed Adm & Sup* 9:161–2 Mr '23. *
125. HUGHES, J. M. "The Use of Tests in the Evaluation of Factors Which Condition the Achievement of Pupils in High School Physics." *J Ed Psychol* 16:217–31 Ap '25. *
126. KEENER, E. E. "Mental Ability of Freshman High-School Pupils." *J Ed Res* 11:113–22 F '25. *
127. ODELL, C. W. "Some Data as to the Effect of Previous Testing Upon Intelligence Test Scores." *J Ed Psychol* 16:482–6 O '25. *
128. SCHREIBER, EDWIN W. "A Study of the Factors of Success in First-Year Algebra." *Math Teach* 18:65–78, 141–63 F, Mr '25. *
129. BEAR, ROBT. B. "Factors in the Achievement of College Freshmen." *Sch & Soc* 24:802–4 D 25 '26. * (*PA* 1:689)
130. BRIGHAM, CARL C.; ANGIER, ROSWELL P.; MACPHAIL, ANDREW H.; ROGERS, DAVID C.; AND STONE, CHARLES L. "The Otis Self-Administering Test." *Col Entr Exam Board Ann Rep* 26:185–7 S '26. *
131. ELDER, HARRY E. "Percentile Rank in Intelligence as a Prognosis in Algebra." *Sch R* 34:542–6 S '26. *
132. GROVES, J. W. "Some Correlations in a Teacher-Training Class." *J Ed Res* 13:305–6 Ap '26. *
133. HURD, A. W. "The Intelligence Quotient as a Prognosis of Success in Physics." *Sch R* 34:123–8 F '26. *
134. LACY, L. D. "Relative Intelligence of White and Colored Children." *El Sch J* 26:542–6 Mr '26. *
135. PEAK, HELEN, AND BORING, EDWIN G. "The Factor of Speed in Intelligence." *J Exp Psychol* 9:71–94 Ap '26. * (*PA* 1:64)
136. JANUS, MORRIS. *I.Q. as Indicative of Achievement in Townsend Harris Hall High School.* Master's thesis, College of the City of New York (New York, N.Y.), 1927.
137. KORNHAUSER, ARTHUR W. "Test and High-School Records as Indicators of Success in an Undergraduate School of Business." *J Ed Res* 16:342–56 D '27. * (*PA* 2:1072)
138. LANIER, LYLE H. "Prediction of the Reliability of Mental Tests and Tests of Special Abilities." *J Exp Psychol* 10:69–113 Ap '27. * (*PA* 2:1692)
139. ANDERSON, ERNEST MITCHELL. *Individual Differences in the Reading Ability of College Students.* The University of Missouri Bulletin, Vol. 29, No. 39: Education Series, No. 25. Columbia, Mo.: the University, 1928. Pp. 79. *
140. BEAR, ROBERT M. "Factors Affecting the Success of College Freshmen." *J Appl Psychol* 12:517–23 O '28. * (*PA* 3:460)

141. BROWN, WILLIAM M. *Validity of Certain Group Intelligence Tests.* Master's thesis, State College of Washington (Pullman, Wash.), 1928.
142. BURGER, BERTRAND. *Correlations of Standardized English Tests, School Marks in English and Intelligence Tests.* Master's thesis, College of the City of New York (New York, N.Y.), 1928.
143. FOWLER, O. F. "The Civic Attitudes of High School Sophomores." *Sch R* 36:25-37 Ja '28. *
144. GARRISON, K. C. "Correlation Between Intelligence Test Scores and Success in Certain Rational Organization Problems." *J Appl Psychol* 12:621-30 D '28. * (*PA* 3:1747)
145. GARRISON, K. C. "Intelligence Test Scores and Choice of Major Field." *Sch & Soc* 28:630-2 N 17 '28. * (*PA* 3:923)
146. GARRISON, KARL C. *An Analytic Study of Rational Learning.* George Peabody College for Teachers Contributions to Education, No. 44. Nashville, Tenn.: the College, 1928. Pp. 52. * (*PA* 2:2701)
147. MAIN, H. V. "A Simplified Table for Otis I.Q." *Sch Sci & Math* 28:730 O '28. *
148. SPENCE, RALPH B. "Factors Related to College Achievement." *Teach Col Rec* 29:504-14 Mr '28. * (*PA* 2:2326)
149. TRAVIS, LEE EDWARD, AND HUNTER, THEODORE A. "The Relation Between 'Intelligence' and Reflex Conduction Rate." *J Exp Psychol* 11:342-54 O '28. * (*PA* 3:987)
150. BALYEAT, RAY M. "The General Health and Mental Activity of Allergic Children." *Am J Dis Children* 37:1193-7 Je '29. * (*PA* 4:3885)
151. GARRISON, KARL C. "An Investigation of Some Simple Speed Activities." *J Appl Psychol* 13:167-72 Ap '29. * (*PA* 3:3428)
152. KEFAUVER, GRAYSON N. "Need of Equating Intelligence Quotients Obtained From Group Tests." *J Ed Res* 19:92-101 F '29. * (*PA* 3:2105)
153. PETERSON, JOSEPH, AND LANIER, LYLE H. Part 2, "Comparisons of Certain Mental Abilities in White and Negro Adults," pp. 103-56. In their *Studies in the Comparative Abilities of Whites and Negroes.* Mental Measurements Monographs, Serial No. 5. Baltimore, Md.: Williams & Wilkins Co., 1929. Pp. vi, 156. * (*PA* 3:2316)
154. PRICE, J. ST. CLAIR. "The Intelligence of Negro College Freshmen." *Sch & Soc* 30:749-54 N 30 '29. * (*PA* 4:739)
155. SCHUTTE, T. H. "Students' Estimates of Their Ability and Achievement." *J Ed Res* 20:394-6 D '29. * (*PA* 4:883)
156. WOOD, MARGARET M. "Mental Test Findings With Armenian, Turkish, Greek and Bulgarian Subjects." *J Appl Psychol* 13:266-73 Je '29. * (*PA* 3:3737)
157. COMMINS, W. D. "A Factor in Language Ability." *J Ed Res* 21:77-8 Ja '30. *
158. DAVIS, THOMAS ROYAL. *The Prognostic Value of Certain Tests for Predicting the Success of High School Freshmen.* Master's thesis, University of Chicago (Chicago, Ill.), 1930.
159. GRAHAM, JAMES L. "A Quantitative Comparison of Certain Mental Traits of Negro and White College Students." *J Social Psychol* 1:97-121, 267-85 F, My '30. * (*PA* 5:503)
160. MORLEY, CLYDE A. "The Reliability of the Achievement Quotient." *J Ed Psychol* 21:351-60 My '30. * (*PA* 4:4052)
161. ODELL, CHARLES W. *Predicting the Scholastic Success of College Students.* University of Illinois Bulletin, Vol. 28, No. 5; Bureau of Educational Research Bulletin No. 37. Urbana, Ill.: the Bureau, 1930. Pp. 43. *
162. BRAY, WILLIS JOSEPH. "Achievement in General Chemistry as It Is Related to Certain Learning Abilities." *Sci Ed* 16:149-60 D '31. *
163. BROOKS, FOWLER D. "Predicting Scholarship in the Junior High School." *Ann Conf Ed Meas* 18:73-80 '31. *
164. SIMS, VERNER MARTIN. "The Influence of Blood Relationship and Common Environment on Measured Intelligence." *J Ed Psychol* 22:56-65 Ja '31. * (*PA* 5:2290)
165. SYMONDS, P. M. "Shall the I.Q. Be Used for Sectioning in the High School?" *J Ed Res* 24:138-40 S '31. * (*PA* 6:505)
166. BOUSFIELD, MAUDELLE B. "The Intelligence and School Achievement of Negro Children." *J Negro Ed* 1:388-95 O '32. * (*PA* 8:3671)
167. BOWMAN, HERBERT LLOYD. "Reported Preference and Performance in Problem Solving According to Intelligence Groups." *J Ed Res* 25:295-9 Ap-My '32. * (*PA* 6:3381)
168. ENGELHART, MAX D. "The Relative Contribution of Certain Factors to Individual Differences in Arithmetical Problem Solving Ability." *J Exp Ed* 1:19-27 S 15 '32. * (*PA* 7:1126)
169. GRACE, ALONZO G. "The Relationship of Mental Ability to Occupational Choices of Adults." *Voc Guid Mag* 10:354-8 My '32. * (*PA* 7:2543)
170. HENDRICKSON, GORDON, AND HUSKEY, JOHN F. "Extroversion as a Factor Conditioning Achievement in the Fifth and Sixth Grades of an Elementary School." *J Ed Res* 25:6-13 Ja '32. * (*PA* 6:2005)
171. MCMURRY, ROBERT N. "Efficiency, Work-Satisfaction and Neurotic Tendency: A Study of Bank Employees." *Personnel J* 11:201-10 D '32. * (*PA* 7:1086)
172. MALLER, J. B. "Age Versus Intelligence as Basis for Prediction of Success in High School." *Teach Col Rec* 33:402-15 F '32. * (*PA* 6:2015)

173. MILLER, ANDREW J., AND MANWILLER, C. E. "A Study of Trade School Pupils." *Pittsburgh Sch* 6:219-69 My-Je '32. *
174. DURRELL, DONALD D. "The Influence of Reading Ability on Intelligence Measures." *J Ed Psychol* 24:412-6 S '33. * (*PA* 8:654)
175. BOYNTON, PAUL L., AND LOWE, PAUL E. "The Developmental Age of Industrial School Boys." *Child Develop* 5:59-62 Mr '34. * (*PA* 8:4803)
176. BROWN, ANDREW W.; LYON, VERNE W.; AND STEIN, SEYMOUR. "The Influence of Distraction Upon Mental-Test Performance." *Psychol Clinic* 22(4):213-9 '34. * (*PA* 9:1086)
177. JAGGERS, CRADDOCK H. "The Relation of Intelligence to Behavior in School Children." *Peabody J Ed* 11:254-9 My '34. * (*PA* 9:997)
178. LASLETT, H. R., AND MANNING, JUANITA. "A Delinquency Survey of a Medium-Size High School." *J Juvenile Res* 18:71-8 Ap '34. * (*PA* 8:5147)
179. PATTERSON, HERBERT. "The Chronological Age of Highly Intelligent Freshmen." *Peabody J Ed* 12:19-20 Jl '34. * (*PA* 9:953)
180. TRIPLETT, RICHARD J. "Intelligence of Commercial College Students." *Personnel J* 13:92-3 Ag '34. * (*PA* 8:5668)
181. FINCH, F. H., AND NEMZEK, C. L. "Attendance and Achievement in the High School." *Sch & Soc* 41:207-8 F 9 '35. * (*PA* 9:2967)
182. LEAHY, A. M. "Nature-Nurture and Intelligence." *Genetic Psychol Monogr* 17:236-308 Ag '35. * (*PA* 9:5664)
183. MITCHELL, CLAUDE. "Prognostic Value of Intelligence Tests." *J Ed Res* 28:577-81 Ap '35. * (*PA* 9:3904)
184. ODOROFF, M. E. "A Correlational Method Applicable to the Study of the Time Factor in Intelligence Tests." *J Ed Psychol* 26:307-11 Ap '35. * (*PA* 9:4843)
185. QUAYLE, MARGARET SIDNEY. "A Study of Some Aspects of Satisfaction in the Vocation of Stenography." *Teach Col Contrib Ed* 659:1-121 '35. * (*PA* 10:2644)
186. WELLS, F. L., AND HYLAN, N. W. "Psychometric Practice in Adults of Superior Intelligence." *Am J Orthopsychiatry* 5:286-301 Jl '35. * (*PA* 10:1224)
187. BENTON, ARTHUR L. "Influence of Incentives Upon Intelligence Test Scores of School Children." *J Genetic Psychol* 49:494-7 D '36. * (*PA* 11:2971)
188. FENDRICK, PAUL, AND BOND, GUY. "Delinquency and Reading." *J Genetic Psychol* 48:236-43 Mr '36. * (*PA* 10:3619)
189. HILL, HARRY SEGNER. "Correlation Between I.Q.'s of Bilinguals at Different Ages on Different Intelligence Tests." *Sch & Soc* 44:89-90 Jl 18 '36. * (*PA* 10:5164)
190. LORGE, IRVING. "The Influence of the Test Upon the Nature of Mental Decline as a Function of Age." *J Ed Psychol* 27:100-10 F '36. * (*PA* 10:3760)
191. MOORE, JOSEPH E. "A Comparative Study of the Educational Achievement of Delinquent and Dependent Boys." *Peabody J Ed* 14:1-6 Jl '36. * (*PA* 11:969)
192. OLANDER, HERBERT T., AND WALKER, BERT S. "Can Teachers Estimate I.Q.'s?" *Sch & Soc* 44:744-6 D 5 '36. * (*PA* 11:1490)
193. STEER, MAX D. "The General Intelligence of College Stutterers." *Sch & Soc* 44:862-4 D 26 '36. * (*PA* 11:1427)
194. TIEBOUT, CAROLYN, AND MEIER, NORMAN C. "Artistic Ability and General Intelligence." *Psychol Monogr* 48(1):95-125 '36. * (*PA* 11:1392)
195. FERGUSON, HENRY H. "Incentives and an Intelligence Test." *Austral J Psychol & Philos* 15:39-53 Mr '37. * (*PA* 11:3924)
196. MOORE, JOSEPH E. "A Comparative Study of the Intelligence of Delinquent and Dependent Boys." *J Ed Psychol* 28:355-66 My '37. * (*PA* 12:478)
197. SCHMITZ, SYLVESTER B. "Predicting Success in College: A Study of Various Criteria." *J Ed Psychol* 28:465-73 S '37. * (*PA* 12:538)
198. SEASHORE, R. H.; STOCKFORD, L. B. O.; AND SWARTZ, B. K. "A Correlational Analysis of Factors in Speed of Reading Tests." *Sch & Soc* 46:187-92 Ag 7 '37. * (*PA* 11:5346)
199. STONE, C. P., AND BARKER, R. G. "Aspects of Personality and Intelligence in Post Menarcheal and Premenarcheal Girls of the Same Chronological Age." *J Comp Psychol* 23:439-45 Je '37. * (*PA* 11:4871)
200. GOLDBERG, WOOLF. *The Carnegie Examinations at Temple University: A Study of the Examinations of the Carnegie Foundation in the Teachers College of Temple University.* Philadelphia, Pa.: Temple University, 1938. Pp. 105. *
201. MANNING, FRANK LEROY. "How Accurately Can We Predict Success in College?" *J Am Assn Col Reg* 14:35-8 O '38. * (*PA* 13:4365)
202. OTIS, JAY L. "The Prediction of Success in Power Sewing Machine Operating." *J Appl Psychol* 22:350-66 Ag '38. * (*PA* 13:1688)
203. KRUEGER, RAYMOND LESLIE. "Grades and Intelligence Quotients. (A Study of the Figures for Three Years in One Private School.)" *Sch & Soc* 50:60-4 Jl 8 '39. * (*PA* 13:5920)
204. POND, FREDERICK L. "Influence of Reading Abilities on School Success in Grade IX." *Sch R* 48:437-44 Je '40. *
205. RIES, ARTHUR J. *A Survey of the Intelligence and Achievement Scores of White and Negro Children Entering the*

Otis Self-Administering Tests of Mental Ability

Junior High Schools of Louisville in September, 1938. Master's thesis, University of Louisville (Louisville, Ky.), 1940.

206. BEAN, KENNETH L. "Negro Responses to Verbal and Non-Verbal Test Materials." *J Psychol* 13:343-53 Ap '42. * (PA 16:3487)

207. ROHRER, JOHN H. "The Test Intelligence of Osage Indians." *J Social Psychol* 16:99-105 Ag '42. * (PA 16:4724)

208. WILSON, M. T. "Detection of Reading Difficulties in a Rural Public School." *Training Sch B* 39:41-6 My '42. * (PA 16:3818)

209. EBERT, ELIZABETH, AND SIMMONS, KATHERINE. *The Brush Foundation Study of Child Growth and Development: I, Psychometric Tests.* Monographs of the Society for Research in Child Development, Vol. 8, No. 2, Serial No. 35. Washington, D.C.: the Society, National Research Council, 1943. Pp. xiv, 113. * (PA 18:3322)

210. OSBORNE, AGNES ELIZABETH. "The Relationship Between Certain Psychological Tests and Shorthand Achievement." *Teach Col Contrib Ed* 873:1-58 '43. *

211. LORGE, IRVING. "Schooling Makes a Difference." *Teach Col Rec* 46:483-92 My '45. * (PA 19:2773)

212. CLARK, WALTER H. "Perseverance and Repetition as Factors in Gain in IQ." *J Ed Psychol* 37:557-62 D '46. * (PA 21:1420)

213. BROWER, DANIEL. "The Experimental Study of Imagery: I, The Relation of Imagery to Intelligence." *J General Psychol* 36:229-31 Ja '47. * (PA 22:2927)

214. LANE, G. GORHAM. "Studies in Pilot Selection: I, The Prediction of Success in Learning to Fly Light Aircraft." *Psychol Monogr* 61(5):1-17 '47. * (PA 22:5166)

215. STAUDT, VIRGINIA M. "The Relationship of Testing Conditions and Intellectual Level to Errors and Correct Responses in Several Types of Tasks Among College Women." *J Psychol* 26:125-40 Jl '48. * (PA 23:1163)

216. KNEHR, CHARLES A., AND SOBOL, ALBERT. "Mental Ability of Prematurely Born Children at Early School Age." *J Psychol* 27:355-61 Ap '49. * (PA 23:4160)

217. BRUCE, MARTIN MARC. *The Importance of Certain Personality Characteristics, Skills and Abilities in Effectiveness as a Factory Foreman.* Doctor's thesis, New York University (New York, N.Y.), 1952. (DA 13:116)

218. HANES, BERNARD. *A Factor Analysis of the MMPI, Aptitude Test Data and Personal Information Using a Population of Criminals.* Doctor's thesis, Ohio State University (Columbus, Ohio), 1952. (DA 18:1483)

219. LAWRENCE, P. J. "Some Characteristics of Incorrect Responses to Intelligence Test Items." *Austral J Psychol* 9:1-11 Je '57. *

220. KRATTIGER, JOHN TRUBERT. *An Evaluation of the Freshman Testing Program of Southeastern State College of Oklahoma.* Doctor's thesis, University of Oklahoma (Norman, Okla.), 1958. (DA 19:718)

221. LAVER, A. B. "Testing in Canada: Report No. 1." *Can Psychologist* 8:102-3 O '59. *

222. BROWN, THELMA E. "Factors Relating to Turnover Among Veterans Administration Nursing Assistants." *J Clin & Exp Psychopathol* 22:226-34 D '61. *

223. HASCALL, EDWARD O. "Predicting Success in High School Foreign Language Study." *Personnel & Guid J* 40:361-7 D '61. * (PA 36:4KL61H)

224. ROTH, ROBERT M., AND GILBERT, JEAN. "AF: A New Approach to the Concept of Achievement." *J Ed Res* 55:90-2 O '61. *

225. BLAZSANYIK, J. "Clinical Diagnostic Use of P.M. 38 and Verbal Tests." *Austral J Psychol Res* 3:5-8 au '62. *

226. CRANE, WILLIAM J. "Screening Devices for Occupational Therapy Majors." *Am J Occup Ther* 16:131-2 My-Je '62. * (PA 37:4078)

227. DARLEY, JOHN G. "The Basis for Equivalent Scores on the Annual Editions of the American Council on Education Psychological Examination (ACE), 1941 to 1954," pp. 170-83. In his *Promise and Performance: A Study of Ability and Achievement in Higher Education.* Berkeley, Calif.: Center for Study of Higher Education, University of California, 1962. Pp. vii, 191. *

228. ROOS, PHILIP, AND LEWIS, JERRY M. "Differential Abstraction Deficits in a Normal Population." *J Nerv & Mental Dis* 134:535-8 Je '62. * (PA 37:3708)

229. SUPER, DONALD E., AND CRITES, JOHN O. *Appraising Vocational Fitness by Means of Psychological Tests, Revised Edition*, pp. 102-9. New York: Harper & Brothers, 1962. Pp. xv, 688. * (PA 37:2038)

230. ADKINS, ARLIE ANDREW. *Prediction of College Success at Middle Tennessee State College.* Doctor's thesis, University of Florida (Gainesville, Fla.), 1963. (DA 25:211)

231. BECKER, JAMES A. "An Exploratory Factor Analytic Study of Interests, Intelligence, and Personality." *Psychol Rep* 13:847-51 D '63. * (PA 38:8399)

232. BLAKENEY, ADOLPH L. *An Analysis of the Relationships Between Certain Ability and Personality Variables and Clinical Performance During Psychiatric-Mental Health Nursing Education.* Doctor's thesis, University of Alabama (University, Ala.), 1963. (DA 25:1732)

233. HACKETT, JOHN R., AND FARNUM, HOLLIS B. "A New Look at the Evening College Student." *Adult Ed* 13:148-52 sp '63. *

234. JONES, KENNETH J. "Predicting Achievement in Chemistry: A Model." *J Res Sci Teach* 1:226-31 S '63. *

235. TWAIN, DAVID C., AND BROOKS, EDWARD M. "A Comparison of Wechsler, Revised Beta and Otis Scores of Delinquents." *Brit J Criminol* 3:288-90 Ja '63. *

236. WOEHLKE, ARNOLD B., AND WILDER, DAVID H. "Differences in Difficulty of Forms A and B of the Otis Self-Administering Test of Mental Ability." *Personnel Psychol* 16:395-8 w '63. * (PA 38:8440)

237. CREELMAN, ARTHUR G. *The Prediction of Physics Grades at the University Level From Previously Recorded Data.* Master's thesis, University of British Columbia (Vancouver, B.C., Canada), 1964.

238. SPITZER, MORTON EDWARD, AND MCNAMARA, WALTER J. "A Managerial Selection Study." *Personnel Psychol* 17:19-40 sp '64. * (PA 39:2945)

239. DOUGLAS, MARCELINE J. *A Study of Test-Retest Scores of the Otis Test of Mental Ability for Seabreeze High School Students.* Master's thesis, Stetson University (DeLand, Fla.), 1965.

240. HARRISON, BARBARA. *The Development of Local Norms for the Otis Mental Ability Test and the Iowa Tests of Basic Skills With Selected Relationships to Teacher Marks in Orange, Connecticut.* Master's thesis, Southern Connecticut State College (New Haven, Conn.), 1965.

241. JOG, R. N., AND AGA, H. "A Comparative Study of the Prediction of Academic Achievement of Engineering." *J Voc & Ed Guid* (India) 12:45-50 My '66. *

242. LEVY, RUSSELL H. "The Gauging of Academic Achievement Among 'Court-Labelled' Delinquent Boys (Second of a Series)." *J Correct Ed* 18:14-7 O '66. *

243. LEVY, RUSSELL H., AND HENNING, JOHN A. "The Gauging of Achievement Among 'Court-Labelled' Delinquent Boys." *J Correct Ed* 18:16-8+ Ap '66. *

244. LEVY, RUSSELL H., AND MOORE, WINSTON E. "Cross-Sectional Psychometric Evaluation of Court-Labelled Delinquent Boys." *J Correct Ed* 18:7-9 Jl '66. *

245. MCCREARY, J. R. "Reading Tests With Maori Children." *N Zeal J Ed Studies* 1(1-2):40-50 '66. *

246. DONELSON, KENNETH L. "Variables Distinguishing Between Effective and Ineffective Writers in the Tenth Grade." *J Exp Ed* 35:37-41 su '67. *

247. HAWKES, NORMA JEANNE. *Analysis of Channel Selection by Junior Secondary School Students on the Reorganized Curriculum in British Columbia Schools.* Doctor's thesis, University of Oregon (Eugene, Ore.), 1967. (DA 28:3463A)

248. HINMAN, SUSAN LEE. *A Predictive Validity Study of Creative Managerial Performance.* Greensboro, N.C.: Creativity Research Institute of the Richardson Foundation, Inc., November 1967. Pp. vi, 124. *

249. MOFFIE, D. J., AND GOODNER, SUSAN. *A Predictive Validity Study of Creative and Effective Managerial Performance.* Greensboro, N.C.: Creativity Research Institute of the Richardson Foundation, Inc., December 1967. Pp. 80. *

250. WELSCH, LAWRENCE A. *The Supervisor's Employee Appraisal Heuristic: The Contribution of Selected Measures of Employee Aptitude, Intelligence and Personality.* Doctor's thesis, University of Pittsburgh (Pittsburgh, Pa.), 1967. (DA 28:4321A)

251. BILES, DAVID. "Test Performance and Imprisonment." *Austral & N Zeal J Criminol* (Australia) 1:46-58 Mr '68. *

252. LEVY, RUSSELL H. "Group Administered Intelligence Tests Which Appropriately Reflect the Magnitude of Mental Retardation Among Wards of the Illinois Youth Commission." *J Correct Ed* 20:7-10 su '68. *

253. SOLKOFF, NORMAN. "The Use of Personality and Attitude Tests in Predicting the Academic Success of Medical and Law Students." *J Med Ed* 43:1250-3 D '68. * (PA 44:7336)

254. THUMIN, FRED J. "Ability Scores as Related to Age Among Male Job Applicants." *J Gerontol* 23:390-2 Jl '68. *

255. ELLEY, W. B. "Changes in Mental Ability in New Zealand School Children." *N Zeal J Ed Studies* 4(2):140-55 N '69. * (PA 47:4547)

256. WITT, NORMAN ERNEST. *A Study of Significant Factors Which Tend to Predict Selection as a Candidate for the Position of Commercial Airline Pilot.* Doctor's thesis, University of California (Los Angeles, Calif.), 1969. (DAI 30:3291A)

257. BRADLEY, M. "Statistical Comparison of the Otis Self-Administering Tests of Mental Ability and PSC Examinations 302A and 5A (GIT Series)." *Studies Pers Psychol* (Canada) 2(1):74-80 Ap '70. * (PA 46:4042)

258. DODD, W. E.; WOLLOWICK, H. B.; AND MCNAMARA, W. J. "Task Difficulty as a Moderator of Long-Range Prediction." *J Appl Psychol* 54(3):265-70 Je '70. * (PA 44:13452)

259. GROSVENOR, THEODORE. "Refractive State, Intelligence Test Scores, and Academic Ability." *Am J Optom* 47(5):355-61 My '70. * (PA 46:4624)

260. THUMIN, FRED J. "Comparative Study of Three Mental Ability Tests." *J Indus Psychol* 5(1):1-7 Mr '70. * (PA 45:7117)

261. COWDEN, JAMES E.; PETERSON, WILLIAM M.; AND PACHT, ASHER R. "The Validation of a Brief Screening Test

for Verbal Intelligence at Several Correctional Institutions in Wisconsin." *J Clin Psychol* 27(2):216–8 Ap '71. * (*PA* 46:7125)
262. ELKINS, J. "Some Recent Queensland Norms for Widely Used Standardized Tests." *Slow Learning Child* (Australia) 18(3):142–7 N '71. *

CUMULATIVE NAME INDEX

Aamodt, G. P.: 22
Abt, L. E.: 88
Achard, F. H.: 79
Adkins, A. A.: 230
Aga, H.: 241
Ames, V.: 57
Anderson, E. M.: 139
Angier, R. P.: 130
Bailey, A. E.: 50
Bair, J. T.: 98
Balinsky, B.: 35
Balyeat, R. M.: 150
Barbe, W. B.: 111
Barker, R. G.: 199
Barnabas, B.: 63
Bass, H.: 8
Baxter, B.: 45, 51
Beamer, G. C.: 113
Bean, K. L.: 206
Bear, R. B.: 129
Bear, R. M.: 140
Becker, J. A.: 231
Benton, A. L.: 187
Biles, D.: 251
Binnewies, W. G.: 124
Blair, G. M.: 52
Blakemore, A. M.: 53-4
Blakeney, A. L.: 232
Blazsanyik, J.: 225
Blum, M. L.: 46
Bond, G.: 188
Bond, G. L.: 96
Bonk, E. C.: 113
Boring, E. G.: 135
Bousfield, M. B.: 166
Bowman, H. L.: 167
Boynton, P. L.: 175
Bradley, M.: 257
Bray, W. J.: 162
Brice, M. M.: 114
Brigham, C. C.: 130
Brooks, E. M.: 235
Brooks, F. D.: 3, 163
Broom, M. E.: 12
Brower, D.: 213
Brown, A. W.: 176
Brown, T. E.: 222
Brown, W. M.: 141
Bruce, M. M.: 104, 107-8, 112, 115, 118, 217
Burger, B.: 142
Candee, B.: 46
Case, H. W.: 70, 101
Cattell, P.: 13-4, 17
Chapanis, A.: 31
Clark, G. Y.: 11
Clark, W. H.: 212
Clarke, F. H.: 79
Cohen, E. R.: 36
Cole, R. D.: 10
Commins, W. D.: 157
Cook, P. H.: 81
Copeland, H. A.: 28, 32
Cowden, J. E.: 261
Crane, W. J.: 226
Creelman, A. G.: 237
Crider, B.: 58
Crites, J. O.: 229
Crooks, W. R.: 47
Cushman, C. L.: 4
Darley, J. G.: 227
Davies, F. R. J.: 44
Davis, T. R.: 158
Dessotnekoff, N.: 74
Dodd, W. E.: 258
Donelson, K. L.: 246
Douglas, M. J.: 239
du Mas, F. M.: 116, 123
Durrell, D. D.: 174
Ebert, E.: 209
Edmonson, L. D.: 93
Elder, H. E.: 131
Elkins, J.: 262
Elley, W. B.: 255
Engelhart, M. D.: 168
Failor, L. M.: 41
Farnum, H. B.: 233
Fee, M.: 23

Fendrick, P.: 188
Ferguson, H. H.: 195
Ferguson, L. W.: 47
Finch, F. H.: 181
Flemming, C. W.: 65
Flemming, E. G.: 65
Flottman, E. A.: 34
Forlano, G.: 60
Fowler, O. F.: 143
Freeman, K. H.: 86
Garrison, K. C.: 78, 144-6, 151
Gaudet, F. J.: 49
Gilbert, J.: 224
Goldberg, W.: 200
Goldfarb, W.: 48
Goodner, S.: 249
Gordon, H. C.: 18
Grace, A. G.: 169
Graham, J. L.: 159
Greenly, R. J.: 39
Grosvenor, T.: 259
Groves, J. W.: 132
Guiler, W. S.: 5
Gunnell, D. C.: 117
Hackett, J. R.: 233
Halliday, R. W.: 109
Hanes, B.: 109, 218
Harrell, W.: 42
Harris, A. J.: 33
Harrison, B.: 240
Hartson, L. D.: 80
Hascall, E. O.: 223
Hawkes, N. J.: 247
Hay, E. N.: 53-4, 59
Hecht, R.: 118
Hendrickson, G.: 170
Henning, J. A.: 243
Hill, H. S.: 189
Hinman, S. L.: 248
Holmes, F. J.: 95
Hovland, C. I.: 37, 40
Hughes, J. M.: 125
Hunter, T. A.: 149
Hurd, A. W.: 133
Huskey, J. F.: 170
Hylan, N. W.: 186
Isaacs, A.: 72
Jaggers, C. H.: 177
Janus, M.: 136
Jog, R. N.: 241
Johnson, A. P.: 43
Johnson, G.: 102
Johnson, G. B.: 105
Johnson, R. H.: 96
Jones, K. J.: 234
Kamman, J. F.: 52
Keener, E. E.: 126
Kefauver, G. N.: 152
Kirkpatrick, F. H.: 60
Knehr, C. A.: 216
Kogan, K. L.: 89
Kornhauser, A. W.: 137
Krattiger, J. T.: 220
Krueger, R. L.: 203
Krueger, W. C. F.: 29
Kuder, F.: *rev,* 3:250
Kuhlmann, F.: 10
Kushner, R. E.: 84
Lacy, L. D.: 134
Lane, G. G.: 214
Lange, I. D.: 6
Lanier, L. H.: 138, 153
Lanigan, M. A.: 85
Laslett, H. R.: 178
Laver, A. B.: 221
Lawrence, P. J.: 119, 219
Leahy, A. M.: 182
Levy, R. H.: 242-4, 252
Lewis, J. M.: 228
Lorge, I.: 30, 190, 211
Lowe, P. E.: 175
Lyon, V. W.: 176
MacBride, K.: 123
McCreary, J. R.: 245
McGehee, W.: 55
McGeoch, J. A.: 1
McMurry, R. N.: 171

McNamara, W. J.: 238, 258
MacPhail, A. H.: 130
Main, H. V.: 147
Maller, J. B.: 172
Manning, F. L.: 201
Manning, J.: 178
Manwiller, C. E.: 173
Meier, N. C.: 194
Miles, C. C.: 19-20, 24
Miles, W. R.: 20
Miller, A. J.: 173
Miller, W. S.: 2
Milton, C. R.: 103
Mitchell, C.: 183
Moffie, D. J.: 55, 103, 249
Moore, H.: 25
Moore, J. E.: 191, 196
Moore, W. E.: 244
Morley, C. A.: 160
Nemzek, C. L.: 21, 181
Niemi, G. M.: 61
Nutting, R. E.: 117
Odell, C. W.: 7, 127, 161
Odoroff, M. E.: 184
Olander, H. T.: 192
Older, H. J.: 56
Ordahl, V. E.: 66
Osborne, A. E.: 210
Otis, J. L.: 202
Oxlade, M.: 82
Oxlade, M. N.: 83, 87, 99
Pacht, A. R.: 261
Patterson, H.: 179
Peak, H.: 135
Peterson, J.: 153
Peterson, W. M.: 261
Pond, F. L.: 204
Poruben, A.: 97
Price, J. St. C.: 154
Quayle, M. S.: 185
Redmond, M.: 44
Ries, A. J.: 205
Riess, B.: 75
Riker, B. L.: 49
Rogers, D. C.: 130
Rohrer, J. H.: 207
Roos, P.: 228
Rosenzweig, S.: 89
Roth, R. M.: 224
Sartain, A. Q.: 62, 67-9
Saunders, W. J.: 120-1
Schmitz, B. S.: 197
Schreiber, E. W.: 128
Schutte, T. H.: 155
Seagoe, M. V.: 76

Seashore, H.: 110
Seashore, H. G.: 106
Seashore, R. H.: 198
Seidenfeld, M. A.: 38
Shah, S. A.: 122
Shultz, I. T.: 63
Simmons, K.: 209
Sims, V. M.: 164
Sobol, A.: 216
Solkoff, N.: 253
South, E. B.: 11
Spence, R. B.: 148
Spitzer, M. E.: 238
Staudt, V. M.: 215
Steckel, M. L.: 15
Steer, M. D.: 193
Stein, S.: 176
Stevens, S. N.: 26
Stockford, L. B. O.: 198
Stone, C. L.: 130
Stone, C. P.: 199
Stone, I. R.: 35
Super, D. E.: 94, 229
Swartz, B. K.: 198
Symonds, P. M.: 165
Taylor, D. H.: 16
Teepe, E. A.: 77
Thorndike, R. L.: 71
Thumin, F. J.: 254, 260
Tiebout, C.: 194
Tiedeman, D. V.: 110
Tiffin, J.: 39
Toll, C. H.: 73
Torgerson, T. L.: 22
Trafton, H.: 25
Travis, L. E.: 149
Traxler, A. E.: 27, 64
Triplett, R. J.: 180
Turney, A. H.: 23
Twain, D. C.: 235
Vaccaro, J. J.: 100
Walker, B. S.: 192
Walker, K. F.: 83
Wells, F. L.: 186
Welsch, L. A.: 250
Wightwick, B.: 90
Wilder, D. H.: 236
Wilson, M. T.: 208
Witt, N. E.: 256
Woehlke, A. B.: 236
Wollowick, H. B.: 258
Wonderlic, E. F.: 26, 37, 40
Wood, M. M.: 156
Yela, M.: 91
Zakolski, F. C.: 92

[427]
Pacific Reasoning Series Tests: Pacific Test Series. Job applicants in Papua New Guinea; 1962–68; PRST; I. G. Ord; Australian Council for Educational Research [Australia]. *

For additional information, see 7:371 (1 reference).

REFERENCES THROUGH 1971
1. See 7:371.

CUMULATIVE NAME INDEX
Bennett, M. J.: 1

[428]
Pattern Perception Test. Ages 6 and over; 1943; no manual; L. S. Penrose; Kennedy-Galton Centre [England]. *

For additional information and a review by Alice W. Heim, see 4:312 (3 references).

REFERENCES THROUGH 1971
1-3. See 4:312.
4. LEE, TERENCE. "The Selection of Student Nurses: A Revised Procedure." *Occup Psychol* (England) 33:209–16 O '59. *

CUMULATIVE NAME INDEX
Heim, A. W.: *rev,* 4:312
Lee, T.: 4
Penrose, L. S.: 1-2
Petrie, A.: 3
Powell, M. B.: 3

[429]
Performance Alertness "PA" (With Pictures): Individual Placement Series. Adults; 1961–66; J. H. Norman; Personnel Research Associates, Inc. *

For additional information and a review by Joel T. Campbell, see 7:372.

[430]

Personal Classification Test. Business and industry; 1953–59; no manual for Form H; W. E. Brown, W. H. E. Geiger, R. W. Henderson, and L. C. Steckle; William, Lynde & Williams. *

For additional information, see 6:483.

[431]

Personnel Research Institute Classification Test. Adults; 1943–54; formerly called *Classification Test for Industrial and Office Personnel;* Jay L. Otis, Evelyn Katz (Form A), Robert W. Henderson (A), Mary Aiken (A), David J. Chesler (Form B), and Gardner E. Lindzey (B); Personnel Research Institute. *

For additional information and reviews by James R. Glennon and Melvin R. Marks, see 6:484 (2 references). For reviews by Louise Witmer Cureton and Albert K. Kurtz of this and other tests in the *Personnel Research Institute Clerical Battery,* see 4:729.

REFERENCES THROUGH 1971

1–2. See 6:484.
3. HILTON, ANDREW C.; BOLIN, STANLEY F.; PARKER, JAMES W., JR.; TAYLOR, ERWIN K.; AND WALKER, WILLIAM B. "The Validity of Personnel Assessments by Professional Psychologists." *J Appl Psychol* 39:287–93 Ag '55. * (*PA* 30:5294)

CUMULATIVE NAME INDEX

Bolin, S. F.: 3　　　　Marks, M. R.: *rev,* 6:484
Campbell, J. T.: 2　　Otis, J. L.: 1
Chesler, D. J.: 1　　　Parker, J. W.: 3
Glennon, J. R.: *rev,* 6:484　Taylor, E. K.: 3
Hilton, A. C.: 3　　　　Walker, W. B.: 3

[432]

Personnel Research Institute Factory Series Test. Applicants for routine industrial positions; 1950–56; Jay L. Otis and Alfred H. Exton; Personnel Research Institute. *

For additional information and a review by N. M. Downie, see 6:485.

[433]

Personnel Tests for Industry. Trade school and adults; 1945–69; PTI; 3 tests; Psychological Corporation. *

a) PTI-VERBAL TEST. 1952–69; PTI-V; Alexander G. Wesman.

b) PTI-NUMERICAL TEST. 1952–69; PTI-N; Jerome E. Doppelt.

c) PTI-ORAL DIRECTIONS TEST. 1945–54; ODT; Charles R. Langmuir.

For additional information, see 7:373 (3 references); for a review by Erwin K. Taylor, see 5:366; see also 4:309 (1 reference); for reviews by Charles D. Flory, Irving Lorge, and William W. Turnbull of the *Oral Directions Test,* see 3:245.

REFERENCES THROUGH 1971

1. See 4:309.
2–4. See 7:373.
5. VACCARO, JOSEPH JOHN. *A Study of Psychological Factors That Contrast the Most and Least Efficient Psychiatric Aides in Mental Hospitals.* Doctor's thesis, Fordham University (New York, N.Y.), 1951.
6. SANUA, VICTOR D. "A Note on the Spanish Language Form of the Oral Directions Test of Intelligence." *J Appl Psychol* 40:350–2 O '56. * (*PA* 31:7968)
7. DOPPELT, JEROME E., AND SEASHORE, HAROLD G. "Psychological Testing in Correctional Institutions." *J Counsel Psychol* 6:81–92 sp '59. * (*PA* 34:6012)
8. STERN, FERDINAND, AND GORDON, LEONARD V. "Ability to Follow Instructions as a Predictor of Success in Recruit Training." *J Appl Psychol* 45:22–4 F '61. * (*PA* 36:2LD22S)
9. RAFFEL, SHERMAN C.; SWINK, RICHARD; AND LAMPTON, T. D. "The Influence of Chlorphenesin Carbamate and Carisoprodol on Psychological Test Scores." *Curr Ther Res* 11(9):553–60 S '69. *

CUMULATIVE NAME INDEX

Campbell, S. C.: 2　　Sanua, V. D.: 6
Davis, J. A.: 4　　　　Seashore, H. G.: 1, 7
Doppelt, J. E.: 7　　　Stern, F.: 8
Flory, C. D.: *rev,* 3:245　Swink, R.: 9
Gordon, L. V.: 8　　　Taylor, E. K.: *rev,* 5:366
Haber, W.: 3　　　　　Turnbull, W. W.: *rev,* 3:245
Lampton, T. D.: 9　　Vaccaro, J. J.: 5
Lorge, I.: *rev,* 3:245　Wolfe, R. N.: 4
Raffel, S. C.: 9

[434]

Picture Test A. Ages 7-0 to 8-1; 1955–70; formerly called *Picture Test 1* and, earlier, *Picture Intelligence Test 1;* 1970 test identical with test published 1955 except for title; 1961 manual identical with 1955 manual; Joan E. Stuart; published for the National Foundation for Educational Research in England and Wales; Ginn & Co. Ltd. [England]. *

For additional information, see 7:374; for reviews by Charlotte E. K. Banks and M. L. Kellmer Pringle, see 5:367.

[435]

*Pintner-Cunningham Primary Test. Grades kgn–2; 1923–66; revision of *Pintner-Cunningham Primary Mental Test;* a test in the *Pintner General Ability Tests: Verbal Series;* tests for grades 2–12 are out of print; Rudolf Pintner, Bess V. Cunningham, and Walter N. Durost; Harcourt Brace Jovanovich, Inc. *

For additional information, see 5:368a; for an excerpted review by J. Wayne Wrightstone, see 2:1416. For reviews of the *Pintner General Ability Tests: Verbal Series,* see 3:255 (2 reviews) and 2:1416 (2 excerpts).

REFERENCES THROUGH 1971

1. PINTNER, R., AND CUNNINGHAM, BESS V. "The Problem of Group Intelligence Tests for Very Young Children." *J Ed Psychol* 13:465–72 N '22. *
2. CUNNINGHAM, BESS V. "The Prognostic Value of a Primary Group Test: A Study of Intelligence and Relative Achievement in the First Grade." *Teach Col Contrib Ed* 139:1–54 '23. *
3. FORAN, THOMAS GEORGE. "A Study of Some Group Intelligence Tests in the First Grade." *Cath Ed R* 22:81–9 F '24. *
4. HECKMAN, SAMUEL B. Chap. 3, "A Comparative Study of Group Intelligence Tests Applicable to Children of Kindergarten Age," pp. 17–44. In *Contributions to Education, Vol. 1.* Edited by J. Carleton Bell. Yonkers, N.Y.: World Book Co., 1924. Pp. ix, 364. *
5. PRESSEY, LUELLA C. "The Prognostic Value of a Primary Group Test: A Review." *J Ed Res* 11:223–4 Mr '25. *
6. RAYBOLD, EMMA. "An Experiment With Primary Intelligence Tests." *Ed Res B* (Los Angeles City Schools) 4:8 Je 15 '25. *
7. VIELE, ADA B. "A Study of Four Primary Mental Tests." *El Sch J* 25:675–81 My '25. *
8. HIRSCH, NATHANIEL D. MTTRON. "A Study of Natio-Racial Mental Differences." *Genetic Psychol Monogr* 1:231–406 My–Jl '26. * (*PA* 2:179)
9. KOCH, HELEN LOIS, AND SIMMONS, RIETTA. "A Study of the Test-Performance of American, Mexican, and Negro Children." *Psychol Monogr* 35(5):1–116 '26. *
10. BERG, B. C., AND PARKS, ETTA. "Comparison of the Scores on Pintner-Cunningham Test at the Beginning of the Kindergarten Course in the Second Grade." *J Ed Res* 15:293–4 Ap '27. *
11. FOX, EDNA J. "The Diagnostic Value of Group Tests as Determined by the Qualitative Differences Between Normal and Feeble-Minded Children." *J Appl Psychol* 11:127–34 Ap '27. * (*PA* 2:2945)
12. PINTNER, RUDOLF. "The Pintner-Cunningham Primary Test." *J Ed Psychol* 18:52–8 Ja '27. * (*PA* 1:977)
13. JAMIESON, ELMER, AND SANDIFORD, PETER. "The Mental Capacity of Southern Ontario Indians." *J Ed Psychol* 19:313–28, 536–51 My, N '28. * (*PA* 2:2841, 3:817)
14. KUHLMANN, F. "The Kuhlmann-Anderson Intelligence Tests Compared With Seven Others." *J Appl Psychol* 12:545–94 D '28. * (*PA* 3:1751)
15. MCGRAW, MARY LOUISE, AND MANGOLD, MARIE CECILIA. "Group Intelligence Tests in the Primary Grades." *Cath Univ Am Ed Res B* 4(2):1–41 F '29. * (*PA* 3:3902)
16. SANGREN, PAUL V. "Comparative Validity of Primary Intelligence Tests." *J Appl Psychol* 13:394–412 Ag '29. * (*PA* 3:4324)

17. DEPUTY, ERBY CHESTER. "Predicting First-Grade Reading Achievement: A Study in Reading Readiness." *Teach Col Contrib Ed* 426:1–61 '30. * (*PA* 7:2114)
18. JONES, CHARLES H. *Reliability of Group Intelligence Tests Administered to Children From Foreign Language Homes.* Master's thesis, New York State College for Teachers (Albany, N.Y.), 1930.
19. PORTER, M. POWELL, AND LAUDERBACH, J. CALVIN. "On the Constancy of the IQ." *Sch & Soc* 33:675–6 My 16 '31. * (*PA* 5:3570)
20. SEAGOE, M. V. "An Evaluation of Certain Intelligence Tests." *J Appl Psychol* 18:432–6 Je '34. * (*PA* 8:6140)
21. WALKER, ELLIS WOODS. *The Predictive Value of the Pintner-Cunningham Primary Mental Test: A Follow-up Study.* Master's thesis, Birmingham-Southern College (Birmingham, Ala.), 1935.
22. GRANT, ALBERT. "A Comparison of the Metropolitan Readiness Tests and the Pintner-Cunningham Primary Mental Test." *El Sch J* 38:118–26 O '37. * (*PA* 15:3195)
23. GRANT, ALBERT. "The Comparative Validity of the Metropolitan Readiness Tests and the Pintner-Cunningham Primary Mental Tests." *El Sch J* 38:599–605 Ap '38. * (*PA* 12:4990)
24. GATES, ARTHUR I. "A Further Evaluation of Reading Readiness Tests." *El Sch J* 40:577–91 Ap '40. * (*PA* 15:3581)
25. BAILEY, ALBERT ERNEST. *The Relative Validity of Ten Different Intelligence Tests.* Doctor's thesis, University of Washington (Seattle, Wash.), 1942.
26. HERR, SELMA E. "The Effect of Pre-First-Grade Training Upon Reading Readiness and Reading Achievement Among Spanish-American Children." *J Ed Psychol* 37:87–102 F '46. * (*PA* 20:2076)
27. MOREAU, MARGARET. "Long Term Prediction of Reading Success." *Calif J Ed Res* 1:173–6 S '50. *
28. SAWREY, JAMES M. "The Predictive Effectiveness of Two Non-Verbal Tests of Intelligence Used in the First Grade in the Santa Clara County Schools." Abstract. *Calif J Ed Res* 6:133 My '55. *
29. WALLIHAN, ROBERT SYLVANUS. *A Comparative Study of Retardation in the Primary Grades of the San Diego, California, City Schools.* Doctor's thesis, University of Colorado (Boulder, Colo.), 1955. (*DA* 16:1418)
30. BRENNER, ANTON, AND MORSE, NANCY C. "The Measurement of Children's Readiness for School." *Papers Mich Acad Sci Arts & Letters* 41:333–40 '56. * (*PA* 37:6453)
31. MORGAN, ELMER F., JR. "Efficacy of Two Tests in Differentiating Potentially Low From Average and High First Grade Achievers." *J Ed Res* 53:300–4 Ap '60. *
32. AVAKIAN, SONIA ASTRID. "An Investigation of Trait Relationships Among Six-Year-Old Children." *Genetic Psychol Monogr* 63:339–94 My '61. * (*PA* 36:1FF39A)
33. GNAUCK, JOHANNA, AND KACZKOWSKI, HENRY. "Prediction of Junior High School Performance." *Ed & Psychol Meas* 21:485–8 su '61. * (*PA* 36:2KL85G)
34. GASKILL, A. R., AND FOX, W. C. "How Useful Are Psychological Tests for Screening Underage School Beginners?" *J Ed Res* 57:333–6 F '64. * (*PA* 39:5832)
35. WIDEEN, MARVIN FRANK. *The Predictive Validity of the Pintner-Cunningham Primary Test, Form A.* Master's thesis, University of Saskatchewan (Saskatoon, Sask., Canada), 1964.
36. LOHNES, PAUL R., AND MARSHALL, THOMAS O. "Redundancy in Student Records." *Am Ed Res J* 2:19–23 Ja '65. *
37. BEAUCHAMP, JOAN M. *The Relationship Between Selected Factors Associated With Reading Readiness and the First Grade Reading Achievement of Students Instructed in the Initial Teaching Alphabet.* Doctor's thesis, Syracuse University (Syracuse, N.Y.), 1967. (*DA* 28:1200A)
38. BOND, GUY L., AND DYKSTRA, ROBERT. "The Cooperative Research Program in First-Grade Reading Instruction." *Read Res Q* 2:5–142 su '67. * (*PA* 42:4557)
39. WILSON, ROBERT M., AND ANDERSON, CATHIE A. "Prediction of Success in Reading." *Acad Ther* 4(3):199–200 sp '69. * (*PA* 43:17992)
40. BILKA, LOISANNE PFEIFER. *An Evaluation of the Predictive Value of Certain Reading Readiness Measures as Related to Method of Instruction, Sex, and Mental Age.* Doctor's thesis, University of Pittsburgh (Pittsburgh, Pa.), 1970. (*DAI* 31:5922A)
41. SANDY, CLAUDE ASHBURN. *The Effects of Material Reward, Sex, Race, and Socioeconomic Strata on the Pintner-Cunningham Primary Test Scores of Kindergarten Students.* Doctor's thesis, University of Virginia (Charlottesville, Va.), 1970. (*DAI* 31:5213A)

CUMULATIVE NAME INDEX

Anderson, C. A.: 39
Avakian, S. A.: 32
Bailey, A. E.: 25
Beauchamp, J. M.: 37
Berg, B. C.: 10
Bilka, L. P.: 40
Bond, G. L.: 38
Brenner, A.: 30
Cunningham, B. V.: 1–2
Deputy, E. C.: 17
Dykstra, R.: 38
Foran, T. G.: 3
Fox, E. J.: 11
Fox, W. C.: 34
Gaskill, A. R.: 34
Gates, A. I.: 24
Gnauck, J.: 33
Grant, A.: 22–3
Heckman, S. B.: 4
Herr, S. E.: 26
Hirsch, N. D. M.: 8
Jamieson, E.: 13
Jones, C. H.: 18
Kaczkowski, H.: 33
Koch, H. L.: 9
Kuhlmann, F.: 14
Lauderbach, J. C.: 19
Lohnes, P. R.: 36
McGraw, M. L.: 15
Mangold, M. C.: 15
Marshall, T. O.: 36
Moreau, M.: 27
Morgan, E. F.: 31
Morse, N. C.: 30
Parks, E.: 10
Pintner, R.: 1, 12
Porter, M. P.: 19
Pressey, L. C.: 5
Raybold, E.: 6
Sandiford, P.: 13
Sandy, C. A.: 41
Sangren, P. V.: 16
Sawrey, J. M.: 28
Seagoe, M. V.: 20
Simmons, R.: 9
Viele, A. B.: 7
Walker, E. W.: 21
Wallihan, R. S.: 29
Wideen, M. F.: 35
Wilson, R. M.: 39
Wrightstone, J. W.: exc, 2: 1416

[436]
★**Preliminary Scholastic Aptitude Test/National Merit Scholarship Qualifying Test.** Grades 10–12; 1959–73; PSAT/NMSQT; formerly called *Preliminary Scholastic Aptitude Test;* "a two-hour version of the [College Board] *Scholastic Aptitude Test*"; for guidance in grades 10–12 and scholarship testing in grade 11; administered in October at participating secondary schools; 3 scores: verbal, mathematical, selection index (for scholarship consideration by NMSC); program administered for College Entrance Examination Board and National Merit Scholarship Corporation by Educational Testing Service. *

For additional information concerning earlier forms, see 7:375 (10 references); for a review by Wayne S. Zimmerman, see 6:487 (2 references).

REFERENCES THROUGH 1971

1-2. See 6:487.
3-12. See 7:375.
13. SKAGER, RODNEY W.; BUSSIS, ANNE M.; AND SCHULTZ, CHARLES B. "Comparison of Information Scales and Like-Indifferent-Dislike Scales as Measures of Interest." *Psychol Rep* 16:251–61 F '65. * (*PA* 39:8691)
14. PARTIN, RONALD L. *The Value of Four Selected Test Scores in Predicting Advanced Placement American History Test Scores.* Master's thesis, Bowling Green State University (Bowling Green, Ohio), 1970.
15. DISPENZIERI, ANGELO; GINIGER, SEYMOUR; REICHMAN, WALTER; AND LEVY, MARGUERITE. "College Performance of Disadvantaged Students as a Function of Ability and Personality." *J Counsel Psychol* 18(4):298–305 Jl '71. * (*PA* 46:11687)
16. RUTLAND, EUGENE. *A Study to Determine the Influence of the Preliminary Scholastic Aptitude Test on the Results on the Scholastic Aptitude Test Scores of a Group of Students Enrolled in the Senior Class at the Wilcox County High School, Rochelle, Georgia.* Master's thesis, Fort Valley State College (Ft. Valley, Ga.), 1971.

CUMULATIVE NAME INDEX

Brady, W. J.: 4
Bussis, A. M.: 13
Clawar, H. J.: 8
Cleary, T. A.: 9
Coffman, W. E.: 1
College Entrance Examination Board: 12
Dempster, D.: 3
Dispenzieri, A.: 15
Frields, S. I.: 6
Giniger, S.: 15
Harasymiw, S. J.: 10
Helm, C. E.: 10
Hilton, T. L.: 7, 9
Kaufmann, J. D.: 3
Levy, M.: 15
Manning, W. H.: 11
Myers, A. E.: 7
Partin, R. L.: 14
Reichman, W.: 15
Rutland, E.: 16
Schultz, C. B.: 13
Seibel, D. W.: 2, 5
Skager, R. W.: 13
Zimmerman, W. S.: rev, 6:487

[437]
★**Preschool and Early Primary Skill Survey, Preliminary Edition.** Ages 3-3 to 7-2; 1971; PEPSS; 4 or 5 scores: picture recognition, picture relationship, picture sequence, total, form completion (optional); John A. Long, Jr., Morton Morris, and George A. W. Stouffer, Jr.; distributed by Mafex Associates, Inc. *

[438]
[**Pressey Classification and Verifying Tests.**] Grades 1–2, 3–6, 7–12 and adults; 1922–58; 3 levels; S. L. Pressey (except a) and L. C. Pressey; Bobbs-Merrill Co., Inc. *

a) PRIMARY CLASSIFICATION TEST. Grades 1–2; 1922.
b) PRESSEY INTERMEDIATE CLASSIFICATION-VERIFYING TESTS. Grades 3–6; 1922–58; 1958 test identical with tests copyrighted 1922 and 1923 except for format, directions, and minor changes in a few items; 2 tests.
 1) *Pressey Intermediate Classification Test.*
 2) *Pressey Intermediate Verifying Test.*
c) PRESSEY SENIOR CLASSIFICATION-VERIFYING TESTS. Grades 7–12 and adults; 1922–58; 2 tests.
 1) *Pressey Senior Classification Test.*
 2) *Pressey Senior Verifying Test.* 1958 test identical with test copyrighted 1922 except for format, directions, and minor changes in a few items.
For additional information and a review by Walter N. Durost, see 6:488 (11 references).

REFERENCES THROUGH 1971

1–11. See 6:488.
12. FORAN, THOMAS GEORGE. "A Study of Some Group Intelligence Tests in the First Grade." *Cath Ed R* 22:81–9 F '24. *
13. HECKMAN, SAMUEL B. Chap. 3, "A Comparative Study of Group Intelligence Tests Applicable to Children of Kindergarten Age," pp. 17–44. In *Contributions to Education, Vol. 1.* Edited by J. Carleton Bell. Yonkers, N.Y.: World Book Co., 1924. Pp. ix, 364. *
14. MILLER, W. S. "The Variation and Significance of Intelligence Quotients Obtained From Group Tests." *J Ed Psychol* 15:359–66 S '24. *
15. PRESSEY, L. W. "The Primary Classification Test." *J Ed Res* 9:305–14 Ap '24. *
16. PRESSEY, S. L., AND LONG, GLENN S. "A New Idea in Intelligence Testing." *Ed Res B* 3:365–8 D 10 '24. *
17. STROUD, J. B. "A Study of the Relation of Intelligence Test Scores on Public School Children to the Economic Status of Their Parents." *J Genetic Psychol* 35:105–10 Mr '28. * (*PA* 2:3758)
18. MCGRAW, MARY LOUISE, AND MANGOLD, MARIE CECILIA. "Group Intelligence Tests in the Primary Grades." *Cath Univ Am Ed Res B* 4(2):1–41 F '29. * (*PA* 3:3902)
19. SOUTH, EARL B., AND CLARK, GENEVIEVE Y. "Some Uses of Psychological Tests in Schools of Nursing." *Am J Nursing* 29:1495–501 D '29. * (*PA* 4:1740)
20. NEMZEK, CLAUDE L.; CRONIN, MARION; AND BRANNOM, EDNA. "Motor Ability of High-School Girls." *J Ed Res* 26:593–4 Ap '33. * (*PA* 7:4070)
21. DODGE, ARTHUR F. "Occupational Ability Patterns." *Teach Col Contrib Ed* 658:1–97 '35. * (*PA* 9:5877)
22. BRENTLINGER, W. H. "The Abilities and Occupational History of Transients: A Preliminary Study." *J Appl Psychol* 20:105–13 F '36. * (*PA* 10:3673)
23. FIALKIN, H. N., AND BECKMAN, R. O. "The Influence of Month of Birth on the Intelligence Test Scores of Adults." *J Genetic Psychol* 52:203–9 Mr '38. * (*PA* 13:172)
24. PATERSON, DONALD G.; SCHNEIDLER, GWENDOLEN G.; AND WILLIAMSON, EDMUND G. *Student Guidance Techniques*, pp. 63–6. New York: McGraw-Hill Book Co., Inc., 1938. Pp. xviii, 316. * (*PA* 12:2131)
25. NEMZEK, CLAUDE L. "A Note Concerning Direct and Differential Prediction of Academic Success." *J Social Psychol* 15:325–30 My '42. * (*PA* 16:4543)
26. SHULTZ, IRVIN T., AND RUSH, HARVEY. "Comparison of the Occupational Ranking and Interests, Education and Intelligence of Patients at Sunnyside Sanatorium." *J Appl Psychol* 26:218–26 Ap '42. * (*PA* 16:4184)

CUMULATIVE NAME INDEX

Beckman, R. O.: 23
Bender, W. R. G.: 11
Berman, I. R.: 7
Brannom, E.: 20
Brentlinger, W. H.: 22
Clark, G. Y.: 19
Cronin, M.: 20
Dodge, A. F.: 21
Durost, W. N.: rev, 6:488
Fialkin, H. N.: 23
Finch, F. H.: 6
Foran, T. G.: 12
Ghiselli, E. E.: 10
Green, H. J.: 7
Hackman, R. C.: 9
Heckman, S. B.: 13
Henmon, V. A. C.: 1
Long, G. S.: 16
Lorge, I.: 8
Loveless, H. E.: 11
McGraw, M. L.: 18
Mangold, M. C.: 18
Miller, W. S.: 3, 5, 14
Nemzek, C. L.: 20, 25
Paterson, D. G.: 7, 24
Pressey, L. C.: 2
Pressey, L. W.: 15
Pressey, S. L.: 2, 16
Rush, H.: 26
Sangren, P. V.: 4
Schneidler, G. G.: 24
Shultz, I. T.: 26
South, E. B.: 19
Streitz, R.: 1
Stroud, J. B.: 17
Trabue, M. R.: 7
Williamson, E. G.: 24

Progressive Matrices. Ages 5 and over; 1938–65; PM; 3 levels; J. C. Raven; H. K. Lewis & Co. Ltd.

[England]. * (United States distributor: Psychological Corporation.)
a) STANDARD PROGRESSIVE MATRICES. Ages 6 and over; 1938–60; manual also uses the title *Progressive Matrices (1938), 1956 Revision;* 1956 test identical with test copyrighted 1938 except for 1 revised item and item sequence; 1960 manual identical with 1956 manual except for bibliography.
b) COLOURED PROGRESSIVE MATRICES. Ages 5–11 and mental patients and senescents; 1947–63.
c) ADVANCED PROGRESSIVE MATRICES. Ages 11 and over; 1943–65; 2 editions.
 1) *Progressive Matrices (1947): Set 1.* For use either as a practice test for Set 2 or as a rough screening test.
 2) *Advanced Progressive Matrices, Set 2: 1962 Revision.*

For additional information, see 7:376 (194 references); for a review by Morton Bortner, see 6:490 (78 references); see also 5:370 (62 references); for reviews by Charlotte Banks, W. D. Wall, and George Westby, see 4:314 (32 references); for reviews by Walter C. Shipley and David Wechsler of the 1938 edition, see 3:258 (13 references); for a review by T. J. Keating, see 2:1417 (8 references).

REFERENCES THROUGH 1971

1–8. See 2:1417.
9–21. See 3:258.
22–53. See 4:314.
54–115. See 5:370.
116–193. See 6:490.
194–387. See 7:376.
388. ADCOCK, CYRIL. "A Re-Analysis of Slater's Spatial Judgment Research." *Occup Psychol* (England) 22:213–6 O '48. * (*PA* 23:1691)
389. BIESHEUVEL, S. Chap. 4, "Psychological Tests and Their Applications to Non-European Peoples," pp. 87–126. In *The Yearbook of Education, 1949.* London: Evans Brothers Ltd., 1949. Pp. xv, 660. *
390. WICKHAM, MARY. "Follow-Up of Personnel Selection in the A.T.S." *Occup Psychol* (England) 23:153–69 Jl '49. * (*PA* 24:1504)
391. NOTCUTT, B. "The Measurement of Zulu Intelligence." *J Social Res* (South Africa) 1:195–206 D '50. * (*PA* 27:4186)
392. SUTTON, R. V., AND MITCHELL, L. "Preliminary Report on the Validation of Aptitude Tests for the Selection of Articled Clerks." *B Nat Inst Pers Res* (South Africa) 3:4–13 F '51. * (*PA* 27:1488)
393. DAVIES-EYSENCK, MARGARET. "Cognitive Factors in Epilepsy." *J Neurol Neurosurg & Psychiatry* (England) 15:39–44 F '52. * (*PA* 27:2918)
394. KALDEGG, A. "Migraine Patients: A Discussion of Some Test Results." *J Mental Sci* (England) 98:672–82 O '52. * (*PA* 27:6067)
395. PINKERTON, PHILIP, AND KELLEY, JOSEPH. "An Attempted Correlation Between Clinical and Psychometric Findings in Senile-Arteriosclerotic Dementia." *J Mental Sci* (England) 98:244–55 Ap '52. * (*PA* 27:585)
396. STRUCKETT, PAULINE B. A. "Effect of Prefrontal Lobotomy on Intellectual Functioning in Chronic Schizophrenia." *Arch Neurol & Psychiatry* 69:293–304 Mr '53. * (*PA* 28:1346)
397. PITTS, R., AND SIMON, A. "A Psychological and Educational Study of a Group of Male Prisoners." *Brit J Ed Psychol* 24:106–21 Je '54. * (*PA* 29:2748)
398. SMITH, I. MACFARLANE. "The Development of a Spatial Test." *Durham Ed R* (England) 1(5):19–33 S '54. * (*PA* 29:7298)
399. FOULDS, G. A. "The Reliability of Psychiatric, and the Validity of Psychological, Diagnoses." *J Mental Sci* (England) 101:851–62 O '55. * (*PA* 30:7165)
400. HOPKINS, BARBARA, AND POST, FELIX. "The Significance of Abstract and Concrete Behaviour in Elderly Psychiatric Patients and Control Subjects." *J Mental Sci* (England) 101:841–50 O '55. * (*PA* 30:7000)
401. MARCUS, B. "Intelligence, Criminality and the Expectation of Recidivism." *Brit J Deling* 6:147–51 S '55. * (*PA* 30:4914)
402. MEYER, VICTOR, AND YATES, AUBREY J. "Intellectual Changes Following Temporal Lobectomy for Psychomotor Epilepsy: Preliminary Communication." *J Neurol Neurosurg & Psychiatry* (England) 18:44–52 F '55. * (*PA* 29:7775)
403. PICHOT, PIERRE. "Language Disturbances in Cerebral Disease; Concept of Latent Aphasia." *Arch Neurol & Psychiatry* 74:92–6 Jl '55. * (*PA* 30:3225)
404. JAHODA, GUSTAV. "Assessment of Abstract Behavior in a

Non-Western Culture." *J Abn & Social Psychol* 53:237-43 S '56. * (*PA* 32:2798)

405. JORDAN, THOMAS E. "Psychological Findings in a Case of Von Recklinghausen's Disease and Hyperpituitarism." *J Clin Psychol* 12:389-91 O '56. * (*PA* 32:4470)

406. WARBURTON, F. W., AND VENABLES, E. C. "Relationship Between the Intelligence of Technical College Students and Size of Family." *Eug R* (England) 47:245 Ja '56. * (*PA* 31:2530)

407. BAUER, ROBERT W., AND JOHNSON, DERWOOD E. "The Question of Deterioration in Alcoholism." Abstract. *J Consult Psychol* 21:296 Ag '57. * (*PA* 33:1669)

408. HANDEL, AMOS. "The Suitability of Certain Non-Verbal Tests for Testing Immigrants in Israel." *J Ed Res* 51:55-8 S '57. * (*PA* 33:2164)

409. MUNDY, LYDIA. "Environmental Influence on Intellectual Function as Measured by Intelligence Tests." *Brit J Med Psychol* 30:194-201 pt 3 '57. * (*PA* 33:791)

410. YOUNG, CECIL, AND MCCONNELL, FREEMAN. "Retardation of Vocabulary Development in Hard of Hearing Children." *Excep Children* 23:368-70 My '57. * (*PA* 33:4509)

411. CALLAWAY, ENOCH, III, AND BAND, RAYMOND I. "Some Psychopharmacological Effects of Atropine: Preliminary Investigation of Broadened Attention." *Arch Neurol & Psychiatry* 79:91-102 Ja '58. * (*PA* 33:5502)

412. HILDEBRAND, H. P. "A Factorial Study of Introversion-Extraversion." *Brit J Psychol* 49:1-11 F '58. * (*PA* 33:8632)

413. VIEL, BENJAMIN, AND REQUENA, MARIANO. "Analysis of the Results Obtained With the Entrance Examination in the School of Medicine of the University of Chile." *J Med Ed* 33:352-62 Ap '58. * (*PA* 34:2291)

414. JAHODA, GUSTAV. "Development of the Perception of Social Differences in Children From 6 to 10." *Brit J Psychol* 50:159-75 My '59. * (*PA* 34:2826)

415. JARVIE, HUGH. "Problem-Solving Deficits Following Wounds of the Brain." *J Mental Sci* (England) 106:1377-82 O '60. * (*PA* 35:5145)

416. MORAN, R. E. "Levels of Attainment of Educable Subnormal Adolescents." *Brit J Ed Psychol* 30:201-10 N '60. * (*PA* 37:3584)

417. RAO, C. K. VASUDEVA. "Intelligence in a Group of Convicts: An Analysis of 35 Cases." *Trans All-India Inst Mental Health* 1:44-53 D '60. * (*PA* 37:3649)

418. WILLIAMS, MOYRA. "The Effect of Past Experience on Mental Test Performance in the Elderly." *Brit J Med Psychol* 33:215-9 pt 2 '60. * (*PA* 36:4FI15W)

419. DOWIS, JAMES L., AND BUCHANAN, CHARLES E. "Some Relationships Between Intellectual Efficiency and the Severity of Psychiatric Illness." *J Psychol* 51:371-81 Ap '61. * (*PA* 35:6905)

420. BIGGS, J. B. "The Relation of Neuroticism and Extraversion to Intelligence and Educational Attainment." *Brit J Ed Psychol* 32:188-99 Je '62. * (*PA* 37:3123)

421. BRENGELMANN, JOHANNES C., AND LINDAHL, LESLIE E. H. "Personality, Task Difficulty, and Level of Memory Performance." *Archiv für die Gesamte Psychologie* (West Germany) 114:242-59 D '62. * (*PA* 38:1179)

422. DAS, J. P., AND MITRA, A. K. "Relative Effectiveness of Electric Shock and Praise and Reproof in Verbal Conditioning." *J General Psychol* 67:141-6 Jl '62. * (*PA* 37:2442)

423. KNEHR, CHARLES A. "Psychological Assessment of Differential Impairment in Cerebral Organic Conditions and Schizophrenics." *J Psychol* 54:165-89 Jl '62. * (*PA* 37:3695)

424. ORME, J. E. "Intelligence and Season of Birth." *Brit J Med Psychol* 35:233-4 pt 3 '62. * (*PA* 37:4963)

425. PIERCY, MALCOLM M., AND SMYTH, V. O. G. "Right Hemisphere Dominance for Certain Non-Verbal Intellectual Skills." *Brain* (England) 85:775-90 D '62. *

426. SAMPSON, OLIVE C. "Reading Skill at Eight Years in Relation to Speech and Other Factors." *Brit J Ed Psychol* 32:12-7 F '62. *

427. SHAFFER, JOHN W.; FREINEK, WILFRIED R.; WOLF, SIDNEY; FOXWELL, NANCY H.; AND KURLAND, ALBERT A. "A Controlled Evaluation of Chlordiazepoxide (Librium) in the Treatment of Convalescing Alcoholics." *J Nerv & Mental Dis* 137:494-507 N '63. * (*PA* 39:5332)

428. HALLWORTH, H. J. "Personality Ratings of Adolescents: A Study in a Comprehensive School." *Brit J Ed Psychol* 34:171-7 Je '64. * (*PA* 39:3180)

429. JUEL-NIELSEN, NIELS. "Individual and Environment: A Psychiatric-Psychological Investigation of Monozygotic Twins Reared Apart." *Acta Psychiatrica Scandinavica Supplementum* (Denmark) 183:1-292 '64. *

430. LEVITA, ERIC; RIKLAN, MANUEL; AND COOPER, IRVING S. "Cognitive and Perceptual Performance in Parkinsonism as a Function of Age and Neurological Impairment." *J Nerv & Mental Dis* 139:516-20 D '64. * (*PA* 39:10554)

431. DAS, RHEA S. "An Application of Factor and Canonical Analysis to Multivariate Data." *Brit J Math & Stat Psychol* 18:57-67 My '65. * (*PA* 39:13270)

432. DIXON, JAMES C. "Cognitive Structure in Senile Conditions With Some Suggestions for Developing a Brief Screening Test of Mental Status." *J Gerontol* 20:41-9 Ja '65. *

433. JAMAL, SHABNAM. "The Validity of Raven's Coloured Progressive Matrices and Otis Quick Scoring Mental Ability Test for Pakistani Children." *B Ed & Res* (Pakistan) 4(1):25-41 '65. *

434. KNEHR, CHARLES A. "Revised Approach to Detection of Cerebral Damage: Progressive Matrices Revisited." *Psychol Rep* 17:71-7 Ag '65. * (*PA* 40:1891)

435. BARRY, ALAN J.; STEINMETZ, JOHN R.; PAGE, HENRY F.; AND RODAHL, KAARE. "The Effects of Physical Conditioning on Older Individuals: 2, Motor Performance and Cognitive Function." *J Gerontol* 21:192-9 Ap '66. *

436. BEVANS, H. G. "Confidence (Probability) Scoring for the Standard Progressive Matrices (1956) and the Advanced Matrices." Abstract. *B Brit Psychol Soc* 19:A15 Ap '66. *

437. EVANS, LIONEL. "A Comparative Study of the Wechsler Intelligence Scale for Children (Performance) and Raven's Progressive Matrices With Deaf Children." *Teach Deaf* (England) 64:76-82 Mr '66. *

438. MACARTHUR, R. S., AND MOSYCHUK, H. "Lower and Upper Socioeconomic Group Contrasts in Long-Term Predictability of Grade Nine Achievement." *J Ed Meas* 3:167-8 su '66. *

439. ARNOLD, ELIZABETH M. "Is Temporal Integration a Distinct Mental Ability?" *Austral J Psychol* 19:41-7 Ap '67. * (*PA* 41:11914)

440. KINSBOURNE, MARCEL. "Effect of Focal Cerebral Lesions on Perspective and Movement Reversals." *J Nerv & Mental Dis* 144:139-44 F '67. * (*PA* 41:12356)

441. LEVITA, ERIC, AND RIKLAN, MANUEL. "Patterns of Psychological Function Before, After Unilateral, and After Bilateral Thalamic Surgery." *Percept & Motor Skills* 24:619-26 Ap '67. * (*PA* 41:9973)

442. MOLEMA, SEODI Y. *A Comparison of Associative and Conceptual Thinking as Indicated by Two Non-Language Tests Among Lower and Higher Socioeconomic Negro Children in Elementary School.* Master's thesis, Catholic University of America (Washington, D.C.), 1967.

443. CHOPRA, SUKHENDRA L. "Measured Intelligence and Academic Achievement as Related to Urban-Rural Residence." Letter. *Rural Sociol* 33:214-7 Je '68. * (*PA* 43:730)

444. DAVIES, ANN D. M. "Measurement of Mental Deterioration in Aging and Brain Damage." Discussion by Walter W. Surwillo. *Interdiscipl Topics Gerontol* 1:78-92 '68. *

445. DE-NOUR, ATARA K.; SHALTIEL, JUDITH; AND CZACZKES, J. W. "Emotional Reactions of Patients on Chronic Hemodialysis." *Psychosom Med* 30:521-33 S-O '68. * (*PA* 43:8624)

446. FREYBERG, P. S. "Fluctuations in Children's Cognitive Test Scores Over a Two-Year Period." *Brit J Ed Psychol* 38:82-6 F '68. * (*PA* 42:12731)

447. HALSTEAD, HERBERT, AND NEAL, C. DAVID. "Intelligence and Personality in Drug Addicts: A Pilot Study." *Brit J Addict* 63:237-40 D '68. *

448. HICHENS, JOHN H. "Speed, Level, Power and Progressive Matrices." Abstract. *Papers Psychol* (Northern Ireland) 2:72-3 O '68. *

449. JACOBS, PAUL I. "The Development, Use and Evaluation of Self-Instructional Programs in Israel." *J Exp Ed* 36:59-69 sp '68. *

450. JENSEN, ARTHUR R. "Patterns of Mental Ability and Socioeconomic Status." *Proc Nat Acad Sci* 60:1330-7 Ag 15 '68. *

451. MONTGOMERY, G. W. G. "A Factorial Study of Communication and Ability in Deaf School Leavers." *Brit J Ed Psychol* 38:27-37 F '68. * (*PA* 42:12755)

452. BROADHURST, ANNE. "Time Estimation Related to Personality, Cognitive Speed and Schizophrenia." *Life Sci* (England) 8(pt 2, 2):69-78 Ja 15 '69. * (*PA* 45:2722)

453. FREEMAN, JAMES; M'COMISKY, JAMES G.; AND BUTTLE, DEREK. "Student Selection: A Comparative Study of Student Entrants to Architecture and Economics." *Ed Sci* (England) 3(3):189-97 D '69. *

454. HASETH, KJELL; SHAGASS, CHARLES; AND STRAUMANIS, JOHN J. "Perceptual and Personality Correlates of EEG and Evoked Response Measures." *Biol Psychiatry* 1(1):49-60 Ja '69. * (*PA* 46:4440)

455. IRVINE, S. H. "How Fair Is Culture? Factorial Studies of Raven's Progressive Matrices Across Cultures in Africa," pp. 372-87. In *Developments in Educational Testing: The Proceedings of an International Conference Held Under the Aegis of the Pädagogisches Zentrum, Berlin, Vols. 1 and 2.* Edited by Karlheinz Ingenkamp. London: University of London Press Ltd., 1969. Pp. 446, 502. *

456. JAMIESON, G. HARRY. "Prior Learning and Response Flexibility in Two Age Groups." *J Gerontol* 24(2):179-83 Ap '69. *

457. WETHERICK, N. E.; FITZSIMMONS, ELIZABETH K.; AND HILLS, D. A. "Inductive Thinking in Subnormals." *J Mental Subnorm* (England) 15(2):79-84 D '69. * (*PA* 44:16917)

458. BEACH, JOE EDWARD. *A Study of the Relationship of Intelligence and Academic Achievement of a Selected Group of Deaf Pupils.* Master's thesis, Mississippi State University (State College, Miss.), 1970.

459. BLANTON, WILLIAM ELGIT. *The Interactive Effects of Perceptual Centration and Decentration on Reading Readiness and Reading Achievement at the First Grade Level.* Doctor's thesis, University of Georgia (Athens, Ga.), 1970. (*DAI* 31:5837A)

460. BOLLINGER, RICK LEONARD. *Communication Abilities of*

"Chronic Brain Syndrome" Patients. Doctor's thesis, University of Washington (Seattle, Wash.), 1970. (DAI 32:610B)

461. COMSTOCK, JOHN ALLAN. *The Relationship Between Clinically Derived Scores of Employability and Employability Scores Predicted by an Employability Model for Mentally Retarded Adolescents.* Doctor's thesis, University of Minnesota (Minneapolis, Minn.), 1970. (DAI 32:271A)

462. DAS, J. P.; JACHUCK, KASTURI; AND PANDA, T. P. Chap. 23, "Cultural Deprivation and Cognitive Growth," pp. 587–604. In *Social-Cultural Aspects of Mental Retardation: Proceedings of the Peabody-NIMH Conference.* Edited by H. Carl Haywood. New York: Appleton-Century-Crofts, 1970. Pp. xvii, 798. *

463. DAVAGE, P. P. E., AND WILKINSON, V. J. "The Intelligence of Voluntary Mental Hospital Admissions: A Pilot Study." *N Zeal Med J* 72(459):96–8 Ag '70. *

464. DICKER, LEO. *Retardation of 9–14 Year Old Deaf Students on the 1938 Raven's Progressive Matrices.* Doctor's thesis, University of Kansas (Lawrence, Kan.), 1970. (DAI 31:5884A)

465. DURR, LEWIS. "Personality Profile of the Successful Pilot." *Airline Mgmt & Marketing* 2(10):79–80+ O '70. *

466. ELEFAÑO, INOCENCIA PATIÑO. *Predicting the Educability of Children From Low Socioeconomic Status Homes.* Doctor's thesis, Rutgers—The State University (New Brunswick, N.J.), 1970. (DAI 32:667A)

467. FAROQI, M. A. "A Study of Errors Made by Children on Progressive Matrices Test." *J Ed Res & Exten* (India) 7(2):65–73 O '70. *

468. FEIN, SOPHIA RICHMAN. *Conceptual Tempo and Abstract Reasoning in College Students: A Study of the Effects of Individual Differences in Speed and Confidence of Judgment on Abstract Reasoning Performance of College Females.* Doctor's thesis, New York University (New York, N.Y.), 1970. (DAI 31:5840A)

469. NORDÉN, K. "The Structure of Abilities in a Group of Deaf Adolescents." *Ed & Psychol Interactions* (Sweden) 32:1–22 '70. * (PA 44:15094)

470. PAITICH, DANIEL. "The Clarke Automated Psychological Examination and Report (CAPER)." *Ont Psychologist* (Canada) 2(5):304–14 '70. *

471. SHANAN, JOEL; KEDAR, HANNAH; ELIAKIM, MARCEL; OSTER, ZVI H.; AND PRYWES, MOSHE. "Evolution of Selection Methods for Admission to Medical School: 3, Psychological Tests in the Selection of Medical Students." *Israel J Med Sci* 6(1):132–44 Ja–F '70. *

472. WOOSTER, ARTHUR D. "Social and Ethnic Differences in Understanding the Spoken Word." *Brit J Dis Commun* 5(2):118–25 O '70. *

473. BART, LEONARD EUGENE. *A Comparison of the Effectiveness of Televised and Conventional Administrations of Objective Scales.* Doctor's thesis, St. John's University (Jamaica, N.Y.), 1971. (DAI 32:2980B)

474. BERRY, J. W. "Ecological and Cultural Factors in Spatial Perceptual Development." *Can J Behav Sci* 3(4):324–36 O '71. * (PA 47:8577)

475. BEYEL, VIRGINIA; FRACCHIA, JOHN; SHEPPARD, CHARLES; AND MERLIS, SIDNEY. "Relationships Among Raven Progressive Matrices Avoidable and Atypical Errors and Bender Gestalt Errors." *Percept & Motor Skills* 33(3):1269–70 D '71. * (PA 48:3366)

476. BIGGS, J. B.; FITZGERALD, D.; AND ATKINSON, SONIA M. "Convergent and Divergent Abilities in Children and Teachers' Ratings of Competence and Certain Classroom Behaviours." *Brit J Ed Psychol* 41(3):277–86 N '71. * (PA 47:11600)

477. BOLTON, BRIAN. "A Factor Analytic Study of Communication Skills and Nonverbal Abilities of Deaf Rehabilitation Clients." *Multiv Behav Res* 6(4):485–501 O '71. * (PA 47:11373)

478. CANTWELL, ZITA M. "Teachers' Perceptions of Levels of Performances of Students From an Economically Disadvantaged Urban Area." *Percept & Motor Skills* 32(2):593–4 Ap '71. * (PA 46:11646)

479. CARLSON, J. S. "Some Relationships Between Class Inclusion, Perceptual Capabilities, Verbal Capabilities and Race." *Hum Develop* (Switzerland) 14(1):30–8 '71. * (PA 47:2617)

480. CARLSON, JERRY S. "Some Relationships Between Verbal and Perceptual Capabilities and the Development of Relative Thinking." *J Genetic Psychol* 118(1):115–9 Mr '71. * (PA 46:8724)

481. CHEYNE, WILLIAM M., AND JAHODA, GUSTAV. "Emotional Sensitivity and Intelligence in Children From Orphanages and Normal Homes." *J Child Psychol & Psychiatry* (England) 12(2):77–90 Je '71. * (PA 47:4505)

482. DESHPANDE, M. V. "Sex Differences on Raven's Matrices Test—(Coloured Form)." *J Psychol Res* (India) 15(3):101–3 S '71. *

483. EISENTHAL, SHERMAN, AND HARFORD, THOMAS. "Correlation Between the Raven Progressive Matrices Scale and the Shipley Institute of Living Scale." *J Clin Psychol* 27(2):213–5 Ap '71. * (PA 46:7158)

484. EYSENCK, HANS J. "Relation Between Intelligence and Personality." *Percept & Motor Skills* 32(2):637–8 Ap '71. * (PA 46:10929)

485. FITZ-GIBBON, CAROL T. *An Investigation of Advanced Progressive Matrices (1962) as a Selection Instrument for Mentally Gifted Students in Inner-City Schools.* Master's thesis, University of California (Los Angeles, Calif.), 1971.

486. FURR, KARL D., AND LANDRUS, GARY. "Raven Progressive Matrices Norms for Toronto, Canada." *Ont Psychologist* (Canada) 3(3):160–2 '71. *

487. GRANICK, SAMUEL. "Brief Tests and Their Interrelations as Intelligence Measures of Aged Subjects." Abstract. *Proc 79th Ann Conv Am Psychol Assn* 6(2):599–600 '71. * (PA 46:4727)

488. GREEN, RICHARD B., AND ROHWER, WILLIAM D., JR. "SES Differences on Learning and Ability Tests in Black Children." *Am Ed Res J* 8(4):601–9 N '71. * (PA 47:11611)

489. GUINAGH, BARRY J. "An Experimental Study of Basic Learning Ability and Intelligence in Low-Socioeconomic-Status Children." *Child Develop* 42(1):27–36 Mr '71. * (PA 46:4669)

490. HUNDAL, P. S., AND SINGH, MOHINDER. "A Factor Analytical Study of Intellectual and Non-Intellectual Characteristics." *Multiv Behav Res* 6(4):503–14 O '71. * (PA 47:11735)

491. JACOBS, PAUL I., AND VANDEVENTER, MARY. "The Learning and Transfer of Double-Classification Skills by First Graders." *Child Develop* 42(1):149–59 Mr '71. * (PA 46:4642)

492. JENSEN, ARTHUR R. "Do Schools Cheat Minority Children?" *Ed Res* (England) 14(1):3–28 N '71. * (PA 49:11953)

493. JONES, BEN MORGAN. "Verbal and Spatial Intelligence in Short and Long Term Alcoholics." *J Nerv & Mental Dis* 153(4):292–7 O '71. * (PA 47:11157)

494. KLINGELHOFER, E. L. "A Note on Language, School, and Examiner Effects on the Performance of Tanzanian Schoolchildren on Raven's Standard Progressive Matrices Test." *J Social Psychol* 83(1):145–6 F '71. * (PA 45:8230)

495. LANGEVIN, R. "Is Curiosity a Unitary Construct?" *Can J Psychol* 25(4):360–74 au '71. * (PA 45:5607)

496. LEMKE, ELMER A., AND KIRCHNER, JOHN H. "A Multivariate Study of Handwriting, Intelligence, and Personality Correlates." *J Pers Assess* 35(6):584–92 D '71. * (PA 47:10876)

497. LOVIUS, B. B. J. "Speech and Intelligence in Adult Cleft-Palate Patients." *Dental Prac & Dental Rec* 21(8):290–3 Ap '71. *

498. MATHER, LEONARD JOSEPH. *A Causal Comparative Study of Intellectual Functioning in Good and Poor Readers.* Doctor's thesis, Catholic University of America (Washington, D.C.), 1971. (DAI 32:1920A)

499. MOHAN, VIDHU, AND MOHAN, JITENDRA. "Scores on Two Intelligence Tests and Seasons of Birth." *Psychologia* (Japan) 14(3–4):170–4 D '71. * (PA 49:863)

500. MOYLES, E. WILLIAM, AND WOLINS, MARTIN. "Group Care and Intellectual Development." *Develop Psychol* 4(3):370–80 My '71. * (PA 46:6543)

501. PRICE, JAMES DAVID. *Analysis of Changes in Intelligence Test Scores of Mexican-American Youth Assigned to Special Classes in Relation to Jensen's Two-Level Theory of Mental Abilities.* Doctor's thesis, University of Arizona (Tucson, Ariz.), 1971. (DAI 32:3125A)

502. PRINGLE, ROGER K., AND HAANSTAD, MARTIN. "Estimating WAIS IQs From Progressive Matrices and Shipley-Hartford Scores." *J Clin Psychol* 27(4):479–81 O '71. * (PA 47:8929)

503. RAMIREZ, JUDITH VALLA. "Effects of Tutorial Experiences on the Problem-Solving Behavior of Sixth-Graders." *Calif J Ed Res* 22(2):80–90 Mr '71. *

504. RAO, S. NARAYANA. "A Prognostic Study of Achievement in Relation to Academic Adjustment." *Indian Ed R* 6(2):196–213 Jl '71. *

505. ROHWER, WILLIAM D., JR.; AMMON, MARY SUE; SUZUKI, NANCY; AND LEVIN, JOEL R. "Population Differences and Learning Proficiency." *J Ed Psychol* 62(1):1–14 F '71. * (PA 46:3844)

506. ROHWER, WILLIAM D., JR., AND LEVIN, JOEL R. "Elaboration Preferences and Differences in Learning Proficiency." *Cognitive Studies* 2:127–48 '71. * (PA 49:1354, title only)

507. THORSEN, ERIC EDWARD. *The Heritability of "G" and Figural Divergent Thinking.* Doctor's thesis, Boston College (Chestnut Hill, Mass.), 1971. (DAI 32:1351A)

508. WEINER, PAUL S. "The Cognitive Functioning of Language Deficient Children." *Cognitive Studies* 2:338–63 '71. *

509. WILSON, GLENN D.; TUNSTALL, OLIVE A.; AND EYSENCK, H. J. "Individual Differences in Tapping Performance as a Function of Time on the Task." *Percept & Motor Skills* 33(2):375–8 O '71. * (PA 47:6073)

CUMULATIVE NAME INDEX

Adcock, C.: 388
Aftanas, M. S.: 341
Air, D. H.: 370
Alexander, J. F.: 387
Allebach, N. L.: 77
Allen, R. M.: 118
Almgren, P. E.: 342
Ammon, M. S.: 505
Anderson, H. E.: 278, 308
Anderson, R. A.: 217
Anderson, R. P.: 250
Andersson, A. L.: 342
Archibald, Y. M.: 279–80, 309
Arnold, E. M.: 439

Atkinson, S. M.: 476
Attwell, A. A.: 177
Baer, C. J.: 204
Band, R. I.: 411
Banks, C.: 50; rev, 4:314
Bannister, D.: 207, 281
Bannon, W. J.: 330
Barkley, M. J.: 304
Barratt, E. S.: 97
Barry, A. J.: 435
Bart, L. E.: 473
Basu, K.: 297
Bauer, R. W.: 407
Beach, H. D.: 182

Beach, J. E.: 458
Beck, E. J.: 218
Bennett, C. M.: 106
Bennett, E.: 56
Berry, J. W.: 474
Besijn, J. W.: 384
Bevan, W. E.: 343
Bevans, H. G.: 436
Beyel, V.: 475
Biesheuvel, S.: 116, 389
Biggs, J. B.: 420, 476
Bingham, W. C.: 254, 345
Birkemeyer, F.: 219, 236
Birren, J. E.: 213
Blanton, W. E.: 459
Blazsanyik, J.: 167
Blue, A. W.: 344
Blumenkrantz, J.: 310
Boeke, P. E.: 384
Bolin, B. J.: 83
Bollinger, R. L.: 460
Bolton, B.: 477
Bolton, F. B.: 84
Bortner, M.: *rev*, 6:490
Botwinick, J.: 213
Bradford, E. J. G.: 11
Bradley, B. H.: 220
Brengelmann, J. C.: 421
Brimble, A. R.: 230
Broadhurst, A.: 452
Bromley, D. B.: 69
Brown, R.: 149
Buchanan, C. E.: 419
Bucklow, M.: 103
Budoff, M.: 282
Burke, H. R.: 112, 254, 345
Burnett, A.: 182
Buttle, D.: 453
Caine, T. A.: 121
Callaway, E.: 411
Canabal, J. V.: 368
Cankardas, A.: 119
Cantwell, Z. M.: 255, 283, 478
Carleton, F. O.: 93
Carlson, J. S.: 369, 479-80
Casey, D. L.: 150
Cashdan, A.: 237
Cassel, R. H.: 34
Castetter, J. S.: 98
Cate, C. C.: 284
Cattell, R. B.: 120
Cheyne, W. M.: 481
Chopra, S. L.: 443
Chown, S.: 289
Chun, R. W. M.: 323
Clark, P. J.: 154
Collins, L.: 334-5, 366
Collins, M. G.: 118
Colonna, A.: 256
Comstock, J. A.: 461
Cook, C.: 278, 308
Cooper, I. S.: 430
Costa, L. D.: 346
Costello, C. G.: 126
Cowley, J. J.: 116
Crawford, A.: 85
Crawford, J. M.: 48
Crickmore, L.: 311
Crookes, T. G.: 155
Curr, W.: 99
Curtin, M. E.: 156
Czaczkes, J. W.: 445
Das, J. P.: 312, 422, 462
Das, R. S.: 431
Dasgupta, P.: 297
Dash, S. C.: 127
Davage, P. P. E.: 463
Davidson, M.: 3
Davies, A. D. M.: 265, 444
Davies-Eysenck, M.: 393
Davis, L.: 115
Davis, W. E.: 370
Davison, L.: 115
DeBurger, R. A.: 156
DeCharms, R.: 132
Dekker, L. C.: 287
Denny, C.: 156
De-Nour, A. K.: 445
De Renzi, E.: 238
Desai, M.: 19, 62
Desai, M. M.: 86, 142
Deshpande, M. V.: 482
DeWolfe, A. S.: 370
Dhar, C.: 198

Dicker, L.: 464
Dils, C. W.: 143
Dingman, H. F.: 177
Dirks, D. D.: 204
Dixon, J. C.: 432
Dixon, P.: 169-71
Dizzonne, M. F.: 370
Domino, G.: 313
Doughty, P.: 103
Dowis, J. L.: 419
Durr, J.: 465
Dutta, D.: 297
Dutta, T.: 312
Dwarshuis, L.: 303
Edelstein, G.: 189
Edholm, O. G.: 15
Edwards, A. E.: 183
Eisenthal, S.: 347, 351, 483
Elefaño, I. P.: 466
Eliakim, M.: 471
Elkin, L.: 314
Elley, W. B.: 168, 188
Elonen, A. S.: 71
Esbenshade, A. A.: 203
Esher, F. J. S.: 54
Estes, B. W.: 156
Evans, L.: 437
Evans, R. B.: 184, 221
Ewert, J. C.: 87
Eysenck, H. J.: 12, 16, 19, 484, 509
Eysenck, M. D.: 17
Faglioni, P.: 238, 256
Faroqi, M. A.: 467
Fein, S. R.: 468
Feinberg, I.: 157
Fiedler, E. R.: 349
Finney, B. J.: 315
Finnie, F. R.: 316
Fiorentino, D.: 334-5, 348, 366, 372
Fitch, M. J.: 257
Fitzgerald, D.: 476
Fitz-Gibbon, C. T.: 485
Fitzsimmons, E. K.: 457
Fleming, J. M.: 285
Forbes, A. R.: 222
Foulds, G. A.: 26-7, 35, 42-3, 121, 128, 169-71, 223, 371, 399
Foxwell, N. H.: 427
Fracchia, J.: 372-3, 475
Fracchia, J. F.: 348
Frank, H.: 349
Freeman, J.: 453
Freinek, W. R.: 427
French, J. G.: 155
Freyberg, P. S.: 258, 446
Frisby, C. B.: 208
Fuller, C. W.: 199
Furneaux, W. D.: 19
Furr, K. D.: 486
Gabriel, K. R.: 78
Ganguly, A. K.: 286
Garman, E. M.: 157
Gaskill, P.: 104
Gibbens, T. C. N.: 214
Gibson, H. B.: 374
Gibson, Q. H.: 15, 57
Giles, G. C.: 224
Gill, M. R.: 94
Goetzinger, C. P.: 204, 287
Goetzinger, M. R.: 350
Gordon, I. E.: 160
Gourlay, N.: 99
Gowan, J. C.: 226, 294
Grabow, J. D.: 323
Granick, S.: 487
Gray, J. E.: 343
Green, M. W.: 87
Green, R. B.: 488
Grosvenor, T.: 375
Guinagh, B. J.: 489
Gupta, G. C.: 259
Gupta, K. P.: 239
Gupta, S.: 259
Gwynne Jones, H.: 100
Haanstad, M.: 502
Hake, D.: 149
Hall, J. C.: 105
Hallworth, H. J.: 428
Halstead, H.: 13, 18-9, 44, 447
Hamilton, V.: 185
Handel, A.: 408

Harding, D. W.: 14
Harford, T.: 288, 317, 347, 351, 483
Harris, D. B.: 129
Häseth, K.: 454
Hazari, A.: 144, 376
Hegge, T. G.: 71
Heim, A. W.: 45, 59
Heron, A.: 289
Hichens, J. H.: 448
Higashimachi, W. H.: 186
Higdon, B. P.: 158
Higgins, C.: 122
Hildebrand, H. P.: 412
Hills, D. A.: 457
Himmelweit, H. T.: 19
Holden, R. H.: 51
Hopkins, B.: 70, 75, 400
Horwitz, M.: 346
Houchins, R. R.: 350
Hundal, P. S.: 490
Hutchins, B. E.: 318
Hwang, C. H.: 352
Irvine, S. H.: 230, 260, 353-4, 455
Irving, G.: 377
Iscoe, I.: 79, 90, 269
Jachuck, K.: 462
Jacobs, G. F.: 116
Jacobs, P. I.: 261, 319, 378, 449, 491
Jahoda, G.: 404, 414, 481
Jain, K. S. P.: 225
Jamal, S.: 433
Jamieson, G. H.: 456
Jamuar, K. K.: 159
Jarvie, H.: 415
Jastak, J.: 36
Jensen, A. R.: 130, 450, 492
Johnson, C. A.: 290
Johnson, D. E.: 407
Johnson, D. L.: 290
Johnson, E. Z.: 63-4, 71-3
Johnson, J. E.: 379
Johnson, S. A. H.: 262
Jones, B. M.: 493
Jones, L. V.: 279-80
Jordan, T. E.: 88, 106, 131-2, 172, 405
Juel-Nielsen, N.: 429
Jurjevich, R. M.: 291-2
Kakkar, A.: 240
Kaldegg, A.: 394
Kanungo, R.: 127
Kasper, S.: 113
Kear-Colwell, J. J.: 380
Keating, T. J.: *rev*, 2:1417
Kebbon, L.: 241
Kedar, H.: 471
Keehn, J. D.: 89
Keir, G.: 37
Kelley, J.: 395
Kenchaveeraiah, B.: 320
Kern, F. E.: 278, 308
Khatena, J.: 226, 242-3, 293-4
Kiang, C. G.: 226
Kilburn, K. L.: 263-4
King, W. H.: 187
Kingsley, L.: 355
Kinsbourne, M.: 440
Kirchner, J. H.: 496
Kirk, J.: 386
Klein, J.: 244
Klingelhofer, E. L.: 295, 494
Klonoff, H.: 60
Knehr, C. A.: 101, 173, 423, 434
Knief, L. M.: 133
Kobler, F. J.: 81
Kothari, S.: 362, 381
Kullberg, G.: 342
Kumar, P.: 296
Kundu, R.: 227
Kurland, A. A.: 427
Kuroda, Y.: 134
Landrus, G.: 486
Lange, U. A.: 356
Langevin, R.: 495
Larson, K. H.: 228
Lemke, E. A.: 496
Levin, J. R.: 505-6
Levine, B.: 79, 90
Levine, B. D.: 74

Levinson, B. M.: 135-6, 174, 205
Levita, E.: 430, 441
Ley, P.: 265
Li, A. K.: 229
Lindall, L. E. H.: 421
Lingwood, J.: 65
Loranger, A. W.: 137, 145
Lovius, B. B. J.: 497
Lunzer, E. A.: 146
Lynn, R.: 160
McAdam, W.: 377
MacArthur, R.: 322
MacArthur, R. S.: 147, 168, 188, 210, 230, 234, 321, 333, 357, 438
McClelland, M.: 171
McClelland, W. J.: 171
M'Comisky, J. G.: 453
McConnell, F.: 410
Macdonald, H. A.: 358
McDonald, R. P.: 245
McDonnell, M. W.: 175
McGee, E.: 82
McKinlay, M.: 19
McLeod, H. N.: 161, 176
McNamara, J. R.: 359
Maher, B. A.: 148
Maitra, A. K.: 246
Majumdar, P. K.: 297
Malpass, L. F.: 149
Mandel, R.: 298
Marcus, B.: 401
Marmorston, J.: 184, 221
Marr, E.: 198
Marriage, A.: 214
Martin, A. W.: 80
Martin, D. R.: 58
Martin, F.: 202
Marum, O.: 19
Marzolf, S. S.: 96
Mason, P. L.: 150
Mather, L. J.: 498
Matthews, C. G.: 323
Maxwell, A. E.: 123
Mears, F. G.: 299
Mehrotra, K. K.: 324-5
Mehrotra, S. N.: 138, 197
Meier, J. H.: 247
Melton, K.: 264
Menon, A. S.: 320
Merlis, M.: 373
Merlis, S.: 334-5, 348, 366, 372-3, 475
Meyer, V.: 402
Meyers, E.: 177
Michael, W. B.: 271
Midkiff, K. L.: 91
Miller, F. M.: 4
Miller, L. E.: 359
Mills, L. F.: 25
Misiak, H.: 137, 145
Mitchell, L.: 392
Mitra, A. K.: 422
Mogensen, A.: 231
Mohan, J.: 499
Mohan, V.: 499
Molema, S. Y.: 442
Montemagni, G.: 181
Montgomery, G. W. G.: 209, 266, 451
Moore, B. G. R.: 52
Morán, R. E.: 416
Morris, A. B.: 152
Morrison, M.: 215
Moshin, S. M.: 139
Mosychuk, H.: 438
Moyles, E. W.: 500
Mueller, M. W.: 248-9, 326
Mundy, L.: 123, 409
Munro, H.: 327
Murray, S.: 254
Neal, C. D.: 447
Nelson, M. O.: 189
Netherton, A. H.: 358
Newbrough, J. R.: 338
Newcomb, W. B.: 300
Nicholson, C. L.: 360, 382
Nickols, J.: 301
Nickols, J. E.: 178
Nordén, K.: 469
Norman, R. D.: 91
Notcutt, B.: 38, 391
Nyman, G. E.: 151
O'Connor, N.: 48, 53, 66

Progressive Matrices

Oléron, P.: 46
Olson, D. R.: 210
Orme, J. E.: 107, 162, 267, 328, 383, 424
Orpet, R. E.: 177
Orton, R.: 58
Oster, Z. H.: 471
Owens, R. T.: 361
Oxlade, M.: 23
Oziel, L. J.: 379
Page, H. F.: 435
Paitich, D.: 470
Panda, T. P.: 462
Pande, C. G.: 362
Parry, J. B.: 41
Payne, J. F.: 363
Peel, E. A.: 52
Penfold, D. J.: 67
Penrose, L. S.: 1
Periaswamy, T. M.: 329
Petrie, A.: 19
Phelps, H. B.: 206
Phillips, C. J.: 330
Phillips, G. R.: 232
Pichot, P.: 403
Piercy, M. M.: 425
Pinkerton, P.: 395
Pitts, R.: 397
Porterfield, C. L.: 359
Post, F.: 400
Pottash, M. E.: 331
Presly, A. S.: 281, 386
Price, J. D.: 501
Price-Williams, D.: 290
Pringle, R. K.: 502
Proctor, C. H.: 154
Prothro, E. T.: 89
Prywes, M.: 471
Qualtere, T. J.: 108
Raaheim, K.: 200
Radford, J.: 268
Radzan, M.: 207
Rafi, A. A.: 302
Ramirez, J. V.: 503
Rao, C. K. V.: 417
Rao, S. N.: 179, 190, 332, 504
Rath, R.: 117, 201
Rattan, M. S.: 333
Raven, J. C.: 1, 4-6, 8-10, 24, 26-8, 43, 59, 109
Reddy, I. K. S.: 332
Rees, W. L.: 19
Requena, M.: 413
Rich, C. C.: 191, 250
Richardson, E. J.: 81
Riklan, M.: 430, 441
Riley, S.: 265
Rimoldi, H. J. A.: 29-30
Ritter, W.: 346
Robinson, R. A.: 377
Rodahl, K.: 435
Rohwer, W. D.: 488, 505-6
Romney, D.: 364
Rosenberg, C. M.: 365
Ross, J.: 211
Roth, M.: 70, 75
Royce, J. R.: 341
Royo, D.: 202
Rubin, J.: 161, 176
Rudolf, C. de M.: 31
Rustin, S. L.: 235
Sampson, O. C.: 426
Sanderson, R. E.: 263-4
Satter, G.: 82, 92
Scheier, I. H.: 120
Schepers, J. M.: 180
Schindler, K.: 115
Schnell, R. R.: 303
Schut, D.: 384
Seidel, H. E.: 304
Seim, S.: 385
Semler, I. J.: 269
Sen (Chakraborty), A.: 227
Shaffer, J. W.: 427
Shagass, C.: 454
Shaltiel, J.: 445
Shanan, J.: 251, 471
Shantz, C. U.: 270
Sharon, M.: 251
Shaw, C. N.: 252
Sheppard, C.: 334-5, 348, 366, 372-3, 475
Shipley, W. C.: rev, 3:258
Sigel, I. E.: 192

Simon, A.: 397
Singh, M.: 490
Sinha, U.: 47, 50, 336
Sitkei, E. G.: 271
Sivers, C. H.: 122
Slater, P.: 18, 20, 22, 32, 55-6, 207
Smith, G. J. W.: 151
Smith, I. M.: 398
Smyth, V. O. G.: 425
Spearman, C.: 7
Spearman, C. E.: 2
Spelman, M. S.: 265
Sperrazzo, G.: 114, 140
Stacey, C. L.: 93-4
Steinmetz, J. R.: 435
Stephenson, G. R.: 196
Stith, D.: 304
Straumanis, J. J.: 454
Stroud, J. B.: 133, 165
Struckett, P. B. A.: 396
Struhs, I.: 102
Sullivan, A.: 110
Sullivan, A. M.: 182
Surwillo, W. W.: 444
Sutton, R. V.: 392
Suzuki, N.: 505
Sydiaha, D.: 305
Sydow, D. W.: 76
Tagiuri, R.: 181
Taibl, R. M.: 61
Tamhankar, V. S.: 337
Taylor, A. J. W.: 306
Tesi, G.: 181, 212
Thakur, G. P.: 376
Thompson, W. H.: 323
Thorsen, E. E.: 507
Tizard, J.: 48, 53
Tonn, M. H.: 233
Tracht, V. S.: 33, 124
Tuddenham, R. D.: 115, 310
Tulkin, S. R.: 338
Tully, G. E.: 307
Tunstall, O. A.: 509
Turner, G. H.: 67
Uleman, A. L.: 384
Urmer, A. H.: 152
Valentine, M.: 141
Vandenberg, S. G.: 154
Vandeventer, M.: 319, 378, 491
Varadachar, D.: 194
Varva, F. I.: 195
Vaughan, H. G.: 346
Vejleskov, H.: 339
Venables, E. C.: 163-4, 193, 406
Vernon, P. E.: 21, 39-41, 49
Viel, B.: 413
Voggenthaler, A. L.: 125
Waite, A.: 6
Walker, A.: 214
Wall, W. D.: rev, 4:314
Wallace, J. G.: 45
Walton, D.: 95
Wamba, D. E.: 96
Wang, F. Y.: 272
Warburton, F. W.: 406
Warder, A.: 386
Wattimena, D. M.: 340
Wechsler, D.: rev, 3:258
Weiner, P. S.: 508
Weingarten, G.: 387
Wendland, L. V.: 152
Wepman, J. M.: 279-80, 309
West, D. J.: 374
West, L. W.: 234
Westby, G.: rev, 4:314
Wetherick, N. E.: 273, 457
Wickham, M.: 390
Wiechers, J. E.: 80
Wilcock, J. C.: 274
Wilkin, W. R.: 310
Wilkins, W. L.: 114, 140
Wilkinson, V. J.: 463
Williams, J. R.: 274
Williams, M.: 418
Wills, R. C.: 287
Wilson, G. D.: 509
Wilson, L.: 68
Wine, D. B.: 183
Wirt, R.: 253
Wober, M.: 367
Wolf, S.: 427
Wolf, W.: 165

Wolf, W. S.: 153
Wolins, M.: 500
Wolk, R. L.: 235
Wooster, A. D.: 472
Wysocki, B. A.: 111, 119

Yap, P. M.: 19
Yates, A. J.: 166, 216, 275-7, 402
Young, C.: 410
Young, H. B.: 181, 212

[440]

Proverbs Test. Grades 5-16 and adults; 1954-56; 2 scores: abstract, concrete; Donald R. Gorham; Psychological Test Specialists. *

For additional information and reviews by Eugene L. Gaier and Alfred B. Heilbrun, Jr., see 5:371 (4 references).

REFERENCES THROUGH 1971

1-4. See 5:371.
5. O'REILLY, P. O., AND HARRISON, K. "Experimentation With an Objective Test Battery." *Can Psychiatric Assn J* 5:108-23 Ap '60. *
6. O'REILLY, P. O., AND HARRISON, K. "The Gorham Proverbs Test." *Dis Nerv System* 21:382-5 Je '60. *
7. GORHAM, DONALD R. "Verbal Abstraction in Psychiatric Illness: Assay of Impairment Utilizing Proverbs." *J Mental Sci* 107:52-9 Ja '61. * (*PA* 36:1JP52G)
8. HERRON, WILLIAM G. "Abstract Ability in the Process-Reactive Classification of Schizophrenia." *J General Psychol* 67:147-54 Jl '62. * (*PA* 37:3691)
9. SATZ, PAUL AND CARROLL, L. T. "Utilization of the Proverbs Test as a Projective Instrument: An Objective Approach Through Language Behavior." *J General Psychol* 67:205-13 O '62. * (*PA* 37:8020)
10. GORHAM, DONALD R. "Additional Norms and Scoring Suggestions for the Proverbs Test." *Psychol Rep* 13:487-92 O '63. * (*PA* 38:8415)
11. HARKEY, SHARON M., AND HOWELL, ROBERT J. "The Effect of Anxiety as Measured by the Taylor MAS Scale on Performance on the Gorham Proverb Tests." *J Clin Psychol* 19:106-8 Ja '63. * (*PA* 39:1667)
12. RUBIN, EDMUND JOSEPH. *Performance of Totally-Blind and Sighted Subjects on Tests of Abstraction.* Doctor's thesis, Fordham University (New York, N.Y.), 1963. (*DA* 24:2989)
13. HOLTZMAN, WAYNE H.; GORHAM, DONALD R.; AND MORAN, LOUIS J. "A Factor-Analytic Study of Schizophrenic Thought Processes." *J Abn & Social Psychol* 69:355-64 O '64. * (*PA* 39:8491)
14. LEWINSOHN, PETER M., AND NICHOLS, ROBERT C. "The Evaluation of Changes in Psychiatric Patients During and After Hospitalization." *J Clin Psychol* 20:272-9 Ap '64. * (*PA* 39:8200)
15. PETTINATO, GAETANO CARL. *The Effect of Stress and the Sex of the Examiner of the Conceptual Performance of Male Schizophrenics.* Doctor's thesis, Temple University (Philadelphia, Pa.), 1964. (*DA* 25:1343)
16. SUEHS, JAMES ERNEST. *A Comparative Study of Brain-Damaged and Schizophrenic Subjects on Several Psychological Tests.* Doctor's thesis, University of Houston (Houston, Tex.), 1964. (*DA* 25:1347)
17. FOGEL, MAX L. "The Proverbs Test in the Appraisal of Cerebral Disease." *J General Psychol* 72:269-75 Ap '65. * (*PA* 39:12281)
18. GOLDSTEIN, ROBERT H., AND SALZMAN, LEONARD F. "Proverb Word Counts as a Measure of Overinclusiveness in Delusional Schizophrenics." *J Abn Psychol* 70:244-5 Ag '65. * (*PA* 39:16197)
19. SMITH, LAURENCE C., JR. "The Effects of Heat Stroke on Cognitive Functioning." *Proc Ann Conf Air Force Behav Sci* 11:130-42 Jl '65. *
20. WEISSMAN, HERBERT, AND KOSTLAN, ALBERT. "Use of the Proverbs Test in Differential Diagnosis in the Intensive Treatment Setting." *Newsl Res Psychol* 7:33-4 My '65. *
21. MAY, A. E. "Anxiety and Overinclusion." *Brit J Psychiatry* 112:41-2 Ja '66. * (*PA* 40:5745)
22. SALZMAN, LEONARD F.; GOLDSTEIN, ROBERT H.; ATKINS, ROBERT; AND BABIGIAN, HAROUTUN. "Conceptual Thinking in Psychiatric Patients." *Arch Gen Psychiatry* 14:55-9 Ja '66. * (*PA* 40:4443)
23. SHIMKUNAS, ALGIMANTAS M.; GYNTHER, MALCOLM D.; AND SMITH, KATHLEEN. "Abstracting Ability of Schizophrenics Before and During Phenothiazine Therapy." *Arch Gen Psychiatry* 14:79-83 Ja '66. * (*PA* 40:4468)
24. GOLDSTEIN, ROBERT H., AND SALZMAN, LEONARD F. "Cognitive Functioning in Acute and Remitted Psychiatric Patients." *Psychol Rep* 21:24-6 Ag '67. * (*PA* 42:2738)
25. JURJEVICH, R. M. "Intellectual Assessment With Gorham's Proverbs Test, Raven's Progressive Matrices, and WAIS." *Psychol Rep* 20:1285-6 Je '67. * (*PA* 41:15271)
26. LASKY, LAWRENCE. "Alternate Forms of the Multiple Choice Version of the Proverbs Test." *J Psychol* 65:59-60 Ja '67. * (*PA* 41:4746)
27. LEWINSOHN, PETER M., AND NICHOLS, ROBERT C. "Dimensions of Change in Mental Hospital Patients." *J Clin Psychol* 23:498-503 O '67. * (*PA* 42:2624)

28. MARTIN, WILLIAM T. "Analysis of the Abstracting Function in Reasoning Using an Experimental Test." *Psychol Rep* 21:593–8 O '67. * (*PA* 42:4815)
29. SHIMKUNAS, ALGIMANTAS M.; GYNTHER, MALCOLM D.; AND SMITH, KATHLEEN. "Schizophrenic Responses to the Proverbs Test: Abstract, Concrete, or Autistic?" *J Abn Psychol* 72:128–33 Ap '67. * (*PA* 41:7605)
30. TURNER, WILLIAM J. "The Usefulness of Diphenylhydantoin in Treatment of Nonepileptic Emotional Disorders." *Int J Neuropsychiatry* 3(sup 2):S8–20 D '67. * (*PA* 42:14005)
31. POWELL, J. C. "The Interpretation of Wrong Answers From a Multiple Choice Test." *Ed & Psychol Meas* 28:403–12 su '68. * (*PA* 42:18104)
32. AFTANAS, M. S., AND ROYCE, J. R. "A Factor Analysis of Brain Damage Tests Administered to Normal Subjects With Factor Score Comparisons Across Ages." *Multiv Behav Res* 4(4):459–81 O '69. * (*PA* 44:11030)
33. KINGSLEY, LEONARD. "Functioning of Acute and Chronic Schizophrenics on Measures of Abstract Reasoning." *J Clin Psychol* 25(2):144–7 Ap '69. * (*PA* 43:14470)
34. L'ABATE, LUCIANO, AND GALE, ELLIOT N. "Neurological Status and Psychological Functioning." *Percept & Motor Skills* 29(3):999–1007 D '69. * (*PA* 46:5330)
35. SHIMKUNAS, ALGIMANTAS M. "Reciprocal Shifts in Schizophrenic Thought Processes." *J Abn Psychol* 76(3):423–6 D '70. * (*PA* 45:6724)
36. REED, J. L. "The Relationship Between Results on Some Psychological Tests and Outcome in Schizophrenia." *Acta Psychiatrica Scandinavica* (Denmark) 47(3):223–9 '71. * (*PA* 44:11030)
37. SMITH, ROGER C. "Use of the Proverbs Test for the Identification of Psychotic Disorder." *J Clin Psychol* 27(2):227 Ap '71. * (*PA* 46:7083)

CUMULATIVE NAME INDEX

Aftanas, M. S.: 32
Atkins, R.: 22
Babigian, H.: 22
Carroll, L. T.: 9
Elmore, C. M.: 4
Fogel, M. L.: 17
Gaier, E. L.: *rev*, 5:371
Gale, E. N.: 34
Goldstein, R. H.: 18, 22, 24
Gorham, D. R.: 1–2, 4, 7, 10, 13
Gynther, M. D.: 23, 29
Harkey, S. M.: 11
Harrison, K.: 5–6
Heilbrun, A. B.: *rev*, 5:371
Herron, W. G.: 8
Holtzman, W. H.: 13
Howell, R. J.: 11
Jurjevich, R. M.: 25
Kingsley, L.: 33
Kostlan, A.: 20
L'Abate, L.: 34
Lasky, L.: 26
Lewinsohn, P. M.: 14, 27
Martin, W. T.: 28
May, A. E.: 21
Moran, L. J.: 13
Nichols, R. C.: 14, 27
O'Reilly, P. O.: 5–6
Pettinato, G. C.: 15
Pounders, C. J.: 3
Powell, J. C.: 31
Reed, J. L.: 36
Royce, J. R.: 32
Rubin, E. J.: 12
Salzman, L. F.: 18, 22, 24
Satz, P.: 9
Shimkunas, A. M.: 23, 29, 35
Smith, K.: 23, 29
Smith, L. C.: 19
Smith, R. C.: 37
Suehs, J. E.: 16
Turner, W. J.: 30
Weissman, H.: 20

[441]
Public School Primary Intelligence Test. Grades 2–4; 1924–56; revision of *Detroit Primary Intelligence Test;* 1954 test identical with test copyrighted 1924 except for minor changes; Harry J. Baker; Bobbs-Merrill Co., Inc. *

For additional information, see 5:329*a;* for a review by W. Line of this and two other Detroit intelligence tests, see 2:1393.

REFERENCES THROUGH 1971

1. KUHLMANN, F. "The Kuhlmann-Anderson Intelligence Tests Compared With Seven Others." *J Appl Psychol* 12:545–94 D '28. * (*PA* 3:1751)
2. KUHLMANN, F. "Effect of Degree of Difficulty on Operation of Intelligence Tests." *J Juvenile Res* 14:8–21 Ja '30. * (*PA* 4:2866)
3. SEAGOE, M. V. "An Evaluation of Certain Intelligence Tests." *J Appl Psychol* 18:432–6 Je '34. * (*PA* 8:6140)
4. TILTON, J. W. "The Relation Between IQ and Trait Difference as Measured by Group Intelligence Tests." *J Ed Psychol* 38:343–52 O '47. * (*PA* 22:2066)

CUMULATIVE NAME INDEX

Kuhlmann, F.: 1–2
Seagoe, M. V.: 3
Tilton, J. W.: 4

[442]
Purdue Non-Language Personnel Test. Business and industry; 1957–69; abbreviated revision of *Purdue Non-Language Test;* Joseph Tiffin; University Book Store. *

Proverbs Test

For additional information, see 7:377; for reviews by John D. Hundleby and Benjamin Rosner of the earlier test, see 6:491.

REFERENCES THROUGH 1971

1. GRUENFELD, LEOPOLD W. "Selection of Executives for a Training Program." *Personnel Psychol* 14:421–31 w '61. * (*PA* 37:3922)

CUMULATIVE NAME INDEX

Gruenfeld, L. W.: 1
Hundleby, J. D.: *rev*, 6:491
Rosner, B.: *rev*, 6:491

[443]
Quantitative Evaluative Device. Entering graduate students; 1959–62; also called QED; tests administered at college centers established by the author; "potential for quantitative sophistication"; R. E. Stake; Lincoln Test Service. *

For additional information, see 6:492 (1 reference).

REFERENCES THROUGH 1971

1. See 6:492.
2. STAKE, ROBERT EARL. *Predicting Success in Quantification at the Graduate Level.* Master's thesis, University of Nebraska (Lincoln, Neb.), 1955.

CUMULATIVE NAME INDEX

Stake, R. E.: 1–2

[444]
RBH Test of Learning Ability. Business and industry; 1947–63; TLA; 3 editions; Richardson, Bellows, Henry & Co., Inc. *

a) FORMS S AND T.
b) FORMS DS-12 AND DT-12. Identical with Forms S and T except for removal of directions from testing time; formerly titled *Test for Office Personnel;* 1961 test identical with tests copyrighted 1947.
c) FORM ST. Consists of Forms S and T combined.

For additional information and a review by Erwin K. Taylor, see 7:379 (2 references); see also 6:504 (2 references).

REFERENCES THROUGH 1971

1–2. See 6:504.
3–4. See 7:379.
5. SPARKS, CHARLES P. "Validity of Psychological Tests." *Personnel Psychol* 23(1):39–46 sp '70. * (*PA* 44:17556)

CUMULATIVE NAME INDEX

Dunfield, N. M.: 3
MacNaughton, J. F.: 4
Moore, C. L.: 4
Osborn, H. G.: 4
Perrine, M. W.: 1
Ross, P. F.: 3
Sparks, C. P.: 2, 5
Taylor, E. K.: *rev*, 7:379
Waite, W. D.: 2

[445]
RBH Test of Non-Verbal Reasoning. Business and industry; 1948–63; catalog uses title *The RBH Non-Verbal Reasoning Test;* Richardson, Bellows, Henry & Co., Inc. *

For additional information and a review by Erwin K. Taylor, see 7:380 (1 reference); see also 6:505 (3 references).

REFERENCES THROUGH 1971

1–3. See 6:505.
4. See 7:380.

CUMULATIVE NAME INDEX

Benson, D.: 3
Cuomo, S.: 1–2
Hanson, R.: 3
Kirchner, W.: 3
MacNaughton, J. F.: 4
Meyer, H. H.: 2
Moore, C. L.: 4
Osburn, H. G.: 4
Taylor, E. K.: *rev*, 7:380

[446]
Reasoning Tests for Higher Levels of Intelligence. College entrants; 1954; C. W. Valentine; Oliver & Boyd [Scotland]. *

For additional information and a review by Reginald R. Dale, see 5:374.

REFERENCES THROUGH 1971

1. VALENTINE, C. W. "The Use of a New Reasoning Test for Selection of University and Training College Students." *Brit J Ed Psychol* 31:227–31 N '61. * (PA 36:5KK27V)
2. HALLWORTH, H. J. "An Analysis of C. W. Valentine's Reasoning Test for Higher Levels of Intelligence." *Brit J Ed Psychol* 33:41–6 F '63. * (PA 38:954)
3. EVANS, E. G. S. "Reasoning Ability and Personality Differences Among Student-Teachers." *Brit J Ed Psychol* 34:305–14 N '64. * (PA 39:8718)
4. ELTON, CHARLES F. "The Effect of Logic Instruction on the Valentine Reasoning Test." *Brit J Ed Psychol* 35:339–41 N '65. * (PA 40:3374)
5. BACKHOUSE, J. K. "The Use of Valentine's Reasoning Tests in an Investigation Into Transfer From Mathematics to Reasoning." *Brit J Ed Psychol* 37:121–3 F '67. *
6. PILKINGTON, G. W., AND HARRISON, G. J. "The Relative Value of Two High Level Intelligence Tests, Advanced Level, and First Year University Examination Marks for Predicting Degree Classification." *Brit J Ed Psychol* 37:382–9 N '67. * (PA 42:6148)
7. BANKS, C.; KARDAK, V. S.; JONES, E. M.; AND LUCAS, C. J. "The Relation Between Mental Health, Academic Performance and Cognitive Test Scores Among Chemistry Students." *Brit J Ed Psychol* 40(1):74–9 F '70. * (PA 44:11366)

CUMULATIVE NAME INDEX

Backhouse, J. K.: 5
Banks, C.: 7
Dale, R. R.: *rev*, 5:374
Elton, C. F.: 4
Evans, E. G. S.: 3
Hallworth, H. J.: 2
Harrison, G. J.: 6
Jones, E. M.: 7
Kardak, V. S.: 7
Lucas, C. J.: 7
Pilkington, G. W.: 6
Valentine, C. W.: 1

[447]

Revised Beta Examination. Ages 16–59; 1931–57; revision of *Army Group Examination Beta* ('20); nonlanguage; 1946 revision by Robert M. Lindner and Milton Gurvitz; basic revision by C. E. Kellogg and N. W. Morton; Psychological Corporation. *

For additional information and a review by Bert A. Goldman, see 6:494 (13 references); see also 5:375 (14 references); for reviews by Raleigh M. Drake and Walter C. Shipley, see 3:259 (5 references); for reviews by S. D. Porteus and David Wechsler, see 2:1419 (4 references).

REFERENCES THROUGH 1971

1–4. See 2:1419.
5–9. See 3:259.
10–23. See 5:375.
24–36. See 6:494.
37. BERAN, MARIANNE; PERKINS, JOHN C.; AND SCOLLON, ROBERT W. "Psychological Studies on Patients Undergoing Nonconvulsive Electric-Stimulation Treatment." *Am J Psychiatry* 109:367–74 N '52. * (PA 27:5168)
38. HANES, BERNARD. *A Factor Analysis of the MMPI, Aptitude Test Data and Personal Information Using a Population of Criminals.* Doctor's thesis, Ohio State University (Columbus, Ohio), 1952. (DA 18:1483)
39. DUNHAM, RALPH E. "Factors Related to Recidivism in Adults." *J Social Psychol* 39:77–91 F '54. * (PA 28:8866)
40. MARTIN, RICHARD PANTALL. *The Adjustment of Latin-American Male Students in Selected Private Secondary Schools in the United States.* Doctor's thesis, Northwestern University (Evanston, Ill.), 1954. (DA 14:1605)
41. PANTON, JAMES H. "The Relationship Between Education and Measures of Intelligence and Educational Achievement Within a State Prison Population." *J Correct Ed* 12:18–20 Ja '60. *
42. WOODS, JAMES E., AND MYERS, ROGER A. "A Comparison of IQ Scores on the Revised Beta Examination and the Wechsler Adult Intelligence Scale." *Rehabil Counsel B* 7:54–8 S '63. *
43. DOMINO, GEORGE. "Comparison of the D48, Cattell Culture Fair, and Army Beta Tests in a Sample of College Males." *J Consult Psychol* 28:468–9 O '64. * (PA 39:5052)
44. LEVINE, BERNARD L. *A Sub-Test Comparison of Negro and White Delinquents on the Revised Beta Examination.* Master's thesis, De Paul University (Chicago, Ill.), 1964.
45. WATSON, CHARLES G., AND CAHOON, D. D. "A Note on the Relationship Between the Revised Beta Examination and the Wechsler Adult Intelligence Scale." *Rehabil Counsel B* 8:47–9 D '64. *
46. BORTNER, RAYMAN W. "The IES Test and a Performance Measure of Intelligence." *Percept & Motor Skills* 22:171–5 F '66. * (PA 40:5449)
47. LEVY, RUSSELL H., AND MOORE, WINSTON E. "Cross-Sectional Psychometric Evaluation of Court-Labelled Delinquent Boys." *J Correct Ed* 18:7–9 Jl '66. *
48. WATSON, CHARLES G., AND BAUGH, VERNER S. "Patterns of Psychiatric Patients on the Revised Beta Examination." *J Clin Psychol* 22:188–90 Ap '66. * (PA 40:7861)
49. WHITTEMORE, ROBERT G.; ECHEVERRIA, BEN P.; AND GRIFFIN, JOHN V. "Can We Use Existing Tests for Adult Basic Education?" *Adult Ed* 17:19–29 au '66. *
50. BARTZ, WAYNE R. "Relationship of WAIS, BETA and Shipley-Hartford Scores." *Psychol Rep* 22:676 Ap '68. * (PA 42:12089)
51. DOMINO, GEORGE. "Culture-Free Tests and the Academic Achievement of Foreign Students." Abstract. *J Consult & Clin Psychol* 32:102 F '68. * (PA 42:7843)
52. FUNKHOUSER, THOMAS R. "Correlational Study of the 'Revised Beta Examination' in a Female Retarded Population." *Am J Mental Def* 72:875–8 My '68. * (PA 42:13754)
53. LEVY, RUSSELL H. "Group Administered Intelligence Tests Which Appropriately Reflect the Magnitude of Mental Retardation Among Wards of the Illinois Youth Commission." *J Correct Ed* 20:7–10 su '68. *
54. PATRICK, JERRY H., AND OVERALL, JOHN E. "Validity of Beta IQ's for White Female Patients in a State Psychiatric Hospital." *J Clin Psychol* 24:343–5 Jl '68. * (PA 42:16422)
55. WATSON, CHARLES G., AND KLETT, WILLIAM G. "Prediction of WAIS IQ's From the Shipley-Hartford, the Army General Classification Test and the Revised Beta Examination." *J Clin Psychol* 24:338–41 Jl '68. * (PA 42:16437)
56. FOSTER, ASHLEY. "The Use of Psychological Testing in Rehabilitation Planning for Alaskan Native People." *Austral Psychologist* 4(2–3):146–52 N '69. * (PA 46:5260)
57. OSBORNE, R. T. "Psychometric Correlates of the Visual Evoked Potential." *Acta Psychologica* (Netherlands) 29(3):303 My '69. * (PA 44:1912)
58. PHILLIPS, RICHARD MARTIN. *A Multiple Regression Study of Academic Prediction at Gallaudet College.* Doctor's thesis, University of Maryland (College Park, Md.), 1969. (DAI 30:5257A)
59. RAFFEL, SHERMAN C.; SWINK, RICHARD; AND LAMPTON, T. D. "The Influence of Chlorphenesin Carbamate and Carisoprodol on Psychological Test Scores." *Curr Ther Res* 11(9):553–60 S '69. *
60. ROCHESTER, DEAN E., AND BODWELL, AARON. "Beta-WAIS Comparisons for Illiterate and Indigent Male and Female Negroes." *Meas & Eval Guid* 3(3):164–8 f '70. * (PA 45:9974)
61. SMITH, HARRY ELMER. *The Beta-WAIS Relationship and the Intercorrelations Among Beta Subtests for a Youthful Offender Population.* Master's thesis, Millersville State College (Millersville, Pa.), 1970.
62. BOLTON, BRIAN. "A Factor Analytic Study of Communication Skills and Nonverbal Abilities of Deaf Rehabilitation Clients." *Multiv Behav Res* 6(4):485–501 O '71. * (PA 47:11373)
63. DUDLEY, HAROLD K., JR.; WILLIAMS, JACK D.; AND OVERALL, JOHN E. "Relationships of Beta IQ Scores to Socio-Cultural Factors in a Psychiatric Population." *J Clin Psychol* 27(1):68–74 Ja '71. * (PA 46:1421)
64. LIBB, J. WESLEY, AND COLEMAN, JOHN M. "Correlation Between the WAIS and Revised Beta, Wechsler Memory Scale and Quick Test in a Vocational Rehabilitation Center." *Psychol Rep* 29(3):863–5 D '71. * (PA 47:9410)
65. MILLER, BRIAN P. "IQ Tests and Minority Groups." *Training & Develop J* 25(10):26–7 O '71. * (PA 48:2801)

CUMULATIVE NAME INDEX

Alessi, S. L.: 16
Alper, T. G.: 24
Bartz, W. R.: 50
Baugh, V. S.: 48
Bennett, G. K.: 5, 9
Beran, M.: 37
Bitterman, M. E.: 27
Bluett, C. G.: 17
Bodwell, A.: 60
Bolton, B.: 62
Boring, E. G.: 24
Bortner, R. W.: 35, 46
Brooks, E. M.: 36
Cahoon, D. D.: 45
Cohen, L. M.: 31
Coleman, J. M.: 64
Coppinger, N. W.: 35
Cuomo, S.: 29
Domino, G.: 43, 51
Doppelt, J. E.: 32
Drake, R. M.: *rev*, 3:259
Dudley, H. K.: 63
Dunham, R. E.: 39
Durrett, H. L.: 34
Echeverria, B. P.: 49
Elias, J. Z.: 15
Fear, R. A.: 5
Foster, A.: 56
Funkhouser, T. R.: 52
Garrett, H. E.: 25
Goldman, B. A.: *rev*, 6:494
Griffin, J. V.: 49
Gurvitz, M.: 8
Hafemeister, N.: 13
Hanes, B.: 38
Holzberg, J. D.: 16
Horton, S. P.: 4
Hsiao, S. L.: 30
Johnson, D. L.: 7
Kellogg, C. E.: 3
Klett, W. G.: 55
Klugman, S. F.: 6
Knapp, W.: 18
Lampton, T. D.: 59
Lavos, G.: 20–1
Levine, B. L.: 44
Levy, R. H.: 47, 53
Libb, J. W.: 64
Lindner, R. M.: 8
McMurry, R. N.: 7
Marcuse, F. L.: 27
Martin, R. P.: 40
Meyer, H. H.: 29
Miller, B. P.: 65
Montagu, M. F. A.: 26
Moore, W. E.: 19
Moore, W. E.: 47
Morton, N. W.: 3, 11
Murphy, L. W.: 10
Myers, R. A.: 42
Ni, L.: 30
Osborne, R. T.: 57

Overall, J. E.: 54, 63
Panton, J. H.: 33, 41
Pastore, N.: 28
Patrick, J. H.: 54
Perkins, J. C.: 37
Phillips, R. M.: 58
Porteus, S. D.: *rev*, 2:1419
Raffel, S. C.: 59
Rochester, D. E.: 60
Ross, L. W.: 12, 19
Saucer, R. T.: 35
Scollon, R. W.: 37
Seashore, H. G.: 32
Shipley, W. C.: *rev*, 3:259
Smith, H. E.: 61
Stotsky, B. A.: 22
Swink, R.: 59
Toal, R.: 23
Twain, D. C.: 36
Watson, C. G.: 45, 48, 55
Wechsler, D.: *rev*, 2:1419
Wegman, M.: 13
Wesman, A. G.: 9
Whittemore, R. G.: 49
Williams, H. M.: 13
Williams, J. D.: 63
Woods, J. E.: 42
Woods, W. A.: 23
Yerbury, E. C.: 16
Yerkes, R. M.: 1-2
Yoakum, C. S.: 1
Zakolski, F. C.: 14

[448]

The Ryburn Group Intelligence Tests. Ages 6.5–12.5, 9.5–15.5; [1936–40]; H. V. Clark; Robert Gibson & Sons, Glasgow, Ltd. [Scotland]. *

For additional information, see 2:1421.

[449]

***SRA Nonverbal Form.** Ages 12 and over; 1946–73; formerly called *SRA Non-Verbal Classification Form*; Robert N. McMurry and Joseph E. King; Science Research Associates, Inc. *

For additional information and a review by W. D. Commins, see 4:318; for an excerpted review, see 3:261 (incorrectly listed under 3:260 in the first printing of *The Third Mental Measurements Yearbook*).

REFERENCES THROUGH 1971

1. BUSWELL, G. T. "The Relationship Between Rate of Thinking and Rate of Reading." *Sch R* 59:339-46 S '51. *
2. EBER, HERBERT W.; COCHRANE, CARL M.; AND BRANCA, ALBERT A. "Brief Intellectual Assessment of Patients With Behavior Disorders." Abstract. *J Consult Psychol* 18:396 D '54. * (*PA* 29:7271, title only)
3. FOOTE, RICHARD PAUL. *The Prediction of Success in Automotive Mechanics in a Vocational-Industrial Curriculum on the Secondary School Level.* Doctor's thesis, New York University (New York, N.Y.), 1960. (*DA* 21:3014)
4. HOLDEN, RAYMOND H.; MENDELSON, MARTIN A.; AND DEVAULT, SPENCER. "Relationship of the WAIS to the SRA Non-Verbal Test Scores." *Psychol Rep* 19:987-90 D '66. * (*PA* 41:3721)
5. LEVY, RUSSELL H. "The Gauging of Academic Achievement Among 'Court-Labelled' Delinquent Boys (Second of a Series)." *J Correct Ed* 18:14-7 O '66. *
6. LEVY, RUSSELL H., AND MOORE, WINSTON E. "Cross-Sectional Psychometric Evaluation of Court-Labelled Delinquent Boys." *J Correct Ed* 18:7-9 Jl '66. *
7. PHILLIPS, ROBERT, AND BERG, THOMAS. "Use of the SRA Verbal and Non-Verbal Forms at Gallaudet College." *J Rehabil Deaf* 1:59-62 O '67. *
8. KIRKPATRICK, JAMES J.; EWEN, ROBERT B.; BARRETT, RICHARD S.; AND KATZELL, RAYMOND A. *Testing and Fair Employment: Fairness and Validity of Personnel Tests for Different Ethnic Groups*, pp. 17-9, 25-7, 51-69. New York: New York University Press, 1968. Pp. x, 145. *
9. LEVY, RUSSELL H. "Group Administered Intelligence Tests Which Appropriately Reflect the Magnitude of Mental Retardation Among Wards of the Illinois Youth Commission." *J Correct Ed* 20:7-10 su '68. *
10. STRATTON, ALBERT J. "Validity of the SRA Non-Verbal Form for Adults." *Psychol Rep* 22:163-7 F '68. * (*PA* 42:10577)
11. PHILLIPS, RICHARD MARTIN. *A Multiple Regression Study of Academic Prediction at Gallaudet College.* Doctor's thesis, University of Maryland (College Park, Md.), 1969. (*DAI* 30:5257A)
12. ODELL, LOUISE M. "Maternal Intellectual Functioning." *Johns Hopkins Med J* 128(6):362-8 Je '71. *

CUMULATIVE NAME INDEX

Barrett, R. S.: 8
Berg, T.: 7
Branca, A. A.: 2
Buswell, G. T.: 1
Cochrane, C. M.: 2
Commins, W. D.: *rev*, 4:318
DeVault, S.: 4
Eber, H. W.: 2
Ewen, R. B.: 8
Foote, R. P.: 3
Holden, R. H.: 4
Katzell, R. A.: 8
Kirkpatrick, J. J.: 8
Levy, R. H.: 5–6, 9
Mendelson, M. A.: 4
Moore, W. E.: 6
Odell, L. M.: 12
Phillips, R.: 7
Phillips, R. M.: 11
Stratton, A. J.: 10

[450]

***SRA Pictorial Reasoning Test.** Ages 14 and over; 1966–73; PRT; "to measure the learning potential of individuals from diverse backgrounds with reading difficulties"; test by Robert N. McMurry and Phyllis D. Arnold; manual by Bruce A. Campbell with the editorial assistance of Marita Schofield; Science Research Associates, Inc. *

For additional information, reviews by Raymond A. Katzell and John E. Milholland, and an excerpted review by John L. Horn, see 7:381.

[451]

***SRA Short Test of Educational Ability.** Grades kgn–1, 2–3, 3–6, 6–9, 9–12; 1966–72; STEA; approximately 80 percent of the items were taken from *SRA Primary Mental Abilities* and *SRA Tests of Educational Ability*; Science Research Associates, Inc. *

For additional information, reviews by Russel F. Green and Henry Weitz, and an excerpted review by Raynard J. Dooley (rejoinder by W. Paul Jones), see 7:382 (2 references).

REFERENCES THROUGH 1971

1–2. See 7:382.
3. JONES, W. PAUL, AND DEBLASSIE, RICHARD R. "Social Class Contrasts in Short Term Predictability of Grade 7 Achievement." *J Ed Res* 65(1):11-4 S '71. *

CUMULATIVE NAME INDEX

DeBlassie, R. R.: 3
Dooley, R. J.: *exc*, 7:382
Green, R. F.: *rev*, 7:382
Jones, W. P.: 1–3; *exc*, 7:382
Weitz, H.: *rev*, 7:382

[452]

***SRA Verbal Form.** Grades 7–16 and adults; 1946–73; formerly called *SRA Verbal Classification Form*; abbreviated adaptation of *Thurstone Test of Mental Alertness* which is an abbreviated adaptation of *American Council on Education Psychological Examination for High School Students*, 1940 Edition; 3 scores: quantitative, linguistic, total; test by Thelma Gwinn Thurstone and L. L. Thurstone; manual by Bruce A. Campbell with the editorial assistance of LaVonne Macaitis and Marita Schofield; Science Research Associates, Inc. *

For additional information, see 7:383 (2 references); for reviews by W. D. Commins and Willis C. Schaefer, see 4:319.

REFERENCES THROUGH 1971

1–2. See 7:383.
3. PHILLIPS, ROBERT, AND BERG, THOMAS. "Use of the SRA Verbal and Non-Verbal Forms at Gallaudet College." *J Rehabil Deaf* 1:59-62 O '67. *

CUMULATIVE NAME INDEX

Berg, T.: 3
Commins, W. D.: *rev*, 4:319
Filer, R. J.: 1
Grigg, A. E.: 1
Phillips, R.: 3
Phillips, R. M.: 2
Schaefer, W. C.: *rev*, 4:319

[453]

Safran Culture Reduced Intelligence Test. Grades 1–6, 4 and over; 1960–69; SCRIT; C. Safran; the Author [Canada]. *

For additional information and a review by Lee J. Cronbach, see 7:384 (6 references); see also 6:497 (1 reference).

REFERENCES THROUGH 1971

1. See 6:497.
2–7. See 7:384.
8. NEVILLE, MARY H., AND FROST, BARRY P. "Differential Achievement in Reading and Arithmetic." *Alberta J Ed Res* (Canada) 10:192-200 D '64. *

CUMULATIVE NAME INDEX

Cronbach, L. J.: *rev*, 7:384
Frost, B. P.: 3, 8
MacArthur, R.: 5
MacArthur, R. S.: 2, 4, 6

Revised Beta Examination

Neville, M. H.: 8
Rattan, M. S.: 6
Safran, C.: 1
Solis, M. M.: 7
West, L. W.: 2

[454]

Scholastic Mental Ability Tests. Grades kgn–1, 2–3, 4–5, 6–8; 1953–67; SMAT; various titles used by publisher; Oliver F. Anderhalter; Scholastic Testing Service, Inc. *

For additional information, see 7:385; for reviews by Walter N. Durost and Alexander G. Wesman of earlier editions, see 5:380.

[455]

Schubert General Ability Battery. Grades 12–16 and adults; 1946–65; 5 scores: vocabulary, analogies, arithmetic problems, syllogisms, total; 1965 test identical with test copyrighted 1946 except for 4 revised items and 3 omitted items; 1965 manual identical with manual published 1953 except for revised analogies norms for grade 12 boys; Herman J. P. Schubert and Daniel S. P. Schubert (test); Herman J. P. Schubert. *

For additional information, see 7:386 (1 reference); for a review by William B. Schrader, see 5:382.

REFERENCES THROUGH 1971
1. See 7:386.

CUMULATIVE NAME INDEX
Drebus, R. W.: 1
Neidt, C. O.: 1
Schrader, W. B.: rev, 5:382

[456]

Scott Company Mental Alertness Test. Applicants for office positions; 1923; Scott Co.; Stoelting Co. *

REFERENCES THROUGH 1971
1. FRYER, DOUGLAS, AND SPARLING, E. J. "Intelligence and Occupational Adjustment." *Occupations* 12:55–63 Je '34. *

CUMULATIVE NAME INDEX
Fryer, D.: 1
Sparling, E. J.: 1

[457]

Ship Destination Test. Grades 9 and over; 1955–56; general reasoning; Paul R. Christensen and J. P. Guilford; Sheridan Psychological Services, Inc. *

For additional information and a review by William B. Schrader, see 6:500 (8 references); for a review by C. J. Adcock, see 5:383.

REFERENCES THROUGH 1971
1–8. See 6:500.
9. MARKS, ALVIN; MICHAEL, WILLIAM B.; AND KAISER, HENRY F. "Comparison of Manual and Analytic Techniques of Rotation in a Factor Analysis of Aptitude Test Variables." *Psychol Rep* 7:519–22 D '60. * (*PA* 35:2792)
10. MERRIFIELD, P. R.; GUILFORD, J. P.; CHRISTENSEN, P. R.; AND FRICK, J. W. "Interrelationships Between Certain Abilities and Certain Traits of Motivation and Temperament." *J General Psychol* 65:57–74 Jl '61. * (*PA* 36:2HD57M)
11. DE MILLE, RICHARD. "Intellect After Lobotomy in Schizophrenia: A Factor Analytic Study." *Psychol Monogr* 76(16):1–18 '62. * (*PA* 38:2784)
12. LOCKE, EDWIN A. "Some Correlates of Classroom and Out-of-Class Achievement in Gifted Science Students." *J Ed Psychol* 54:238–48 O '63. * (*PA* 38:4649)
13. PIMSLEUR, PAUL. "A Study of Foreign Language Learning Ability: Parts 1 and 2," pp. 57–72. In *Report of the Twelfth Annual Round Table Meeting on Linguistics and Language Studies.* Edited by Michael Zarechnak. Washington, D.C.: Georgetown University Press, 1963. Pp. 132. *
14. LEMKE, ELMER A.; KLAUSMEIER, HERBERT J.; AND HARRIS, CHESTER W. "Relationship of Selected Cognitive Abilities to Concept Attainment and Information Processing." *J Ed Psychol* 58:27–35 F '67. * (*PA* 41:3959)
15. VERY, PHILIP S. "Differential Factor Structures in Mathematical Ability." *Genetic Psychol Monogr* 75:169–207 My '67. * (*PA* 41:10451)
16. BERGER, RAYMOND M. "Selection of Systems Analysts and Programmer Trainees." *Proc Ann Computer Personnel Res Conf* 6:44–63 '68. *
17. BROWN, STEPHEN W.; GUILFORD, J. P.; AND HOEPFNER, RALPH. "Six Semantic-Memory Abilities." *Ed & Psychol Meas* 28:691–717 au '68. * (*PA* 43:4427)
18. GUILFORD, J. P., AND HOEPFNER, RALPH. "Comparisons of Varimax Rotations With Rotations to Theoretical Targets." *Ed & Psychol Meas* 29(1):3–22 sp '69. * (*PA* 44:15668)
19. KRAUT, ALLEN I. "Intellectual Ability and Promotional Success Among High Level Managers." *Personnel Psychol* 22(3):281–90 au '69. * (*PA* 44:9440)
20. VANDENBERG, STEVEN G. "A Twin Study of Spatial Ability." *Multiv Behav Res* 4(3):273–94 Jl '69. * (*PA* 44:356)
21. BALDWIN, THOMAS S. "Relationships Among Student Achievement and 'Pure Factors' of Intellect." *J Indus Teach Ed* 9(1):15–25 f '71. *

CUMULATIVE NAME INDEX
Adcock, C. J.: rev, 5:383
Baldwin, T. S.: 21
Berger, R. M.: 1, 16
Brown, S. W.: 17
Christensen, P. R.: 1, 4, 8, 10
de Mille, R.: 11
Frick, J. W.: 8, 10
Guilford, J. P.: 1, 4, 8, 10, 17–8
Haney, R.: 3, 5
Harris, C. W.: 14
Hills, J. R.: 2
Hoepfner, R.: 17–8
Jones, R. A.: 3, 5
Kaiser, H. F.: 6–7, 9
Kettner, N. W.: 4
Klausmeier, H. J.: 14
Kraut, A. I.: 19
Lemke, E. A.: 14
Locke, E. A.: 12
Marks, A.: 6–7, 9
Merrifield, P. R.: 8, 10
Michael, W. B.: 3, 5–7, 9
Pimsleur, P.: 13
Schrader, W. B.: rev, 6:500
Vandenberg, S. G.: 20
Very, P. S.: 15

[458]

Short Form Test of Academic Aptitude. Grades 1.5–3.4, 3.5–4, 5–6, 7–9, 9–12; 1936–70; SFTAA; revision of still-in-print *California Test of Mental Maturity;* 3 scores: language, nonlanguage, total; Elizabeth T. Sullivan, Willis W. Clark, and Ernest W. Tiegs; CTB/McGraw-Hill. *

For additional information, see 7:387.

[459]

The Simplex GNV Intelligence Tests. Ages 11–13.0; 1952–57; titles on tests are, for example for form 1, *The Simplex Intelligence Test GNV 1;* C. A. Richardson; George G. Harrap & Co. Ltd. [England]. *

For additional information and a review by Philip M. Levy, see 6:501 (2 references).

REFERENCES THROUGH 1971
1–2. See 6:501.

CUMULATIVE NAME INDEX
Levy, P. M.: rev, 6:501
Nisbet, J. D.: 2
Shuttleworth, C. W.: 1

[460]

The Simplex Group Intelligence Scale. Ages 10 and over; 1922–39; C. A. Richardson; George G. Harrap & Co. Ltd. [England]. *

For additional information and a review by James Mainwaring, see 5:385.

REFERENCES THROUGH 1971
1. WILSON, J. H. "Comparison of Certain Intelligence Scales." *Brit J Psychol* 15:44–63 Jl '24. *
2. JONES, D. CARADOG, AND CARR-SAUNDERS, A. M. "The Relation Between Intelligence and Social Status Among Orphan Children." *Brit J Psychol* 17:343–64 Ap '27. * (*PA* 1:2271)
3. DALE, A. BARBARA. "The Use of Mental Tests With University Women Students." *Brit J Ed Psychol* 5:59–75 F '35. * (*PA* 9:3448)

CUMULATIVE NAME INDEX
Carr-Saunders, A. M.: 2
Dale, A. B.: 3
Jones, D. C.: 2
Mainwaring, J.: rev, 5:385
Wilson, J. H.: 1

[461]

[The Simplex Junior Intelligence Tests.] Ages 7–14; 1932–51; 2 forms; C. A. Richardson; George G. Harrap & Co. Ltd. [England]. *

a) THE SIMPLEX JUNIOR INTELLIGENCE SCALE. 1932.
b) THE SIMPLEX JUNIOR 'A' INTELLIGENCE TEST. 1950–51; test booklet title is *The Simplex Junior 'A' Test.*

For additional information and a review by Arthur B. Royse, see 5:386 (1 reference); see also 4:322 (2 references).

REFERENCES THROUGH 1971
1-2. See 4:322.
3. See 5:386.
4. LAWRENCE, EVELYN M. "An Investigation Into the Relation Between Intelligence and Inheritance." *Brit J Psychol Monogr Sup* 16:1–80 '31. *
5. RICHARDSON, C. A., AND STOKES, C. W. "The Growth and Variability of Intelligence." *Brit J Psychol Monogr Sup* 18:1–83 '33. * (*PA* 9:4390)
6. McRAE, HUGH. "The Inconstancy of Group Test IQ's." *Brit J Ed Psychol* 12:59–70 F '42. * (*PA* 16:2905)
7. MADDOX, H. "Mental Age Scales." *Brit J Ed Psychol* 29:72–3 F '59. * (*PA* 34:2731)
8. KING, W. H. "The Development of Scientific Concepts in Children." *Brit J Ed Psychol* 33:240–52 N '63. * (*PA* 38:8062)

CUMULATIVE NAME INDEX

Curr, W.: 3 Maddox, H.: 7
Gourlay, N.: 3 Richardson, C. A.: 5
Keir, G.: 1 Royse, A. B.: *rev,* 5:386
King, W. H.: 8 Stokes, C. W.: 5
Lawrence, E. M.: 4 Wilson, J. T.: 2
McRae, H.: 6

[462]
Sleight Non-Verbal Intelligence Test. Ages 8–9, 6–10; 1931–63; 2 tests; George F. Sleight and Preston Education Committee (revision of *a*); George G. Harrap & Co. Ltd. [England]. *
a) SLEIGHT NON-VERBAL INTELLIGENCE TEST: PRESTON REVISION. Ages 8–9; 1931–63; distribution restricted to directors of education.
b) SLEIGHT NON-VERBAL INTELLIGENCE TEST. Ages 6–10; 1931.
For additional information, see 6:502 (1 reference); for reviews by John C. Daniels and M. L. Kellmer Pringle of *b*, see 5:387.

REFERENCES THROUGH 1971
1. See 6:502.
2. PEEL, E. A., AND GRAHAM, D. "Differentiation of Ability in Primary School Children." *Durham Res R* (England) 1(2):40–8 S '51. *
3. PEEL, E. A., AND GRAHAM, D. "Differentiation of Ability in Primary School Children—II." *Durham Res R* (England) 1(3):31–4 S '52. * (*PA* 27:5157)
4. GRAHAM, D. "The Differentiation of Ability in Primary School-Children: A Comment." *Durham Res R* (England) 1(4):27–30 S '53. * (*PA* 28:8077)

CUMULATIVE NAME INDEX

Daniels, J. C.: *rev,* 5:387 Peel, E. A.: 2–3
Graham, D.: 2–4 Pringle, M. L. K.: *rev,* 5:387
Lytton, H.: 1

[463]
The Southend Test of Intelligence. Ages 10–12; 1939–53; revision of *Southend Group Test of Intelligence;* M. E. Hebron and W. Stephenson; George G. Harrap & Co. Ltd. [England]. *
For additional information and a review by James Mainwaring, see 5:388; for a review by Gertrude Keir of the original edition, see 4:323 (1 reference); for an excerpted review, see 2:1423.

REFERENCES THROUGH 1971
1. See 4:323.

CUMULATIVE NAME INDEX

Keir, G.: *rev,* 4:323 Peel, E. A.: 1
Mainwaring, J.: *rev,* 5:388

[464]
Spiral Nines, Sixth Edition. Job applicants with 7–8 years of education; 1960–65; also called *Nines;* intelligence; no manual; National Institute for Personnel Research [South Africa]. *
For additional information, see 7:388 (2 references).

REFERENCES THROUGH 1971
1-2. See 7:388.

CUMULATIVE NAME INDEX

Brimble, A. R.: 1 MacArthur, R. S.: 1
Irvine, S. H.: 1–2

[465]
Test of Adult College Aptitude. Evening college entrants; 1966; TACA; King M. Wientge and Philip H. DuBois; TACA Development Fund. *
For additional information and a review by Kenneth D. Hopkins, see 7:389.

[466]
***Test of Perceptual Organization.** Ages 12 and over; 1967–70; formerly called *Test of Abstract Reasoning;* William T. Martin; Psychologists and Educators, Inc. *
For additional information, see 7:390 (1 reference).

REFERENCES THROUGH 1971
1. See 7:390.

CUMULATIVE NAME INDEX

Martin, W. T.: 1

[467]
Tests of General Ability. Grades kgn–2, 2–4, 4–6, 6–9, 9–12; 1959–60, c1957–60; TOGA; test booklets for grades 4–12 have the title *SRA Tests of General Ability;* 3 scores: verbal (cultural), reasoning (noncultural), total; John C. Flanagan; Science Research Associates, Inc. *
For additional information, reviews by John E. Horrocks and Richard E. Schutz, and an excerpted review by Laurence Siegel, see 6:496.

REFERENCES THROUGH 1971
1. BERNARDONI, LOUIS C. "Results of the TOGA With First Grade Children." *J Am Indian Ed* 1:24 8 Jc '61. *
2. CATE, CLARENCE C. "Test Behavior of ESL Students." *Calif J Ed Res* 18:184–7 S '67. * (*PA* 42:4480)
3. CONN, LANE K.; EDWARDS, CARL N.; ROSENTHAL, ROBERT; AND CROWNE, DOUGLAS. "Perception of Emotion and Response to Teachers' Expectancy by Elementary School Children." *Psychol Rep* 22:27–34 F '68. * (*PA* 42:11118)
4. STOUGH, KENNETH FRANCIS. *An Analysis of Selected Factors as Predictors of Success in Vocational Industrial Certification Courses.* Doctor's thesis, University of Maryland (College Park, Md.), 1968. (*DA* 29:2595A)
5. BRAGG, JANE K. *Six Predictive Reading Capacity Formulas With Actual Reading Achievement for Children in Grades 3–6.* Master's thesis, Rutgers—The State University (New Brunswick, N.J.), 1971.
6. DAVISON, DONALD G., AND KILGORE, JOHN H. "A Model for Evaluating the Effectiveness of Economic Education in Primary Grades." *J Econ Ed* 3(1):17–25 f '71. *
7. FIELDER, WILLIAM R.; COHEN, RONALD D.; AND FEENEY, STEPHANIE. "An Attempt to Replicate the Teacher Expectancy Effect." *Psychol Rep* 29(3):1223–8 D '71. * (*PA* 48:1638)
8. LOWELL, ROBERT E. "Reading Readiness Factors as Predictors of Success in First Grade Reading." *J Learn Dis* 4(10):563–7 D '71. * (*PA* 47:11782)

CUMULATIVE NAME INDEX

Bernardoni, L. C.: 1 Fielder, W. R.: 7
Bragg, J. K.: 5 Horrocks, J. E.: *rev,* 6:496
Cate, C. C.: 2 Kilgore, J. H.: 6
Cohen, R. D.: 7 Lowell, R. E.: 8
Conn, L. K.: 3 Rosenthal, R.: 3
Crowne, D.: 3 Schutz, R. E.: *rev,* 6:496
Davison, D. G.: 6 Siegel, L.: *exc,* 6:496
Edwards, C. N.: 3 Stough, K. F.: 4
Feeney, S.: 7

[468]
***Tests of General Ability: Inter-American Series.** Preschool, grades kgn–1.5, 2–3, 4–6, 7–9, 10–13.5; 1961–73; TGA; revision of *Tests of General Ability: Cooperative Inter-American Tests;* 6 levels; parallel editions in English and Spanish; Herschel T. Manuel; Guidance Testing Associates. *
a) PRESCHOOL LEVEL. Ages 4–5; 1966–73; 3 scores: verbal-numerical, nonverbal, total.
b) LEVEL 1—PRIMARY. Grades kgn–1.5; 1962–73; 3 scores: same as in *a*.
c) LEVEL 2—PRIMARY. Grades 2–3; 1964–73; 3 scores: same as in *a*.

d) LEVEL 3—ELEMENTARY. Grades 4–6; 1961–73; 4 scores: verbal, nonverbal, numerical, total.
e) LEVEL 4—INTERMEDIATE. Grades 7–9; 1962–73; 4 scores: same as in *d*.
f) LEVEL 5—ADVANCED. Grades 10–13.5; 1962–67; 4 scores: same as in *d*.

For additional information and reviews by Russel F. Green and Richard E. Schutz, see 7:391 (2 references); for reviews by Raleigh M. Drake and Walter N. Durost of the earlier edition, see 4:325 (8 references).

REFERENCES THROUGH 1971
1–8. See 4:325.
9–10. See 7:391.
11. CHENAULT, VIVIAN MARGARET. *A Study of the Cooperative Inter-American Tests of General Ability and Reading at the Primary Level.* Master's thesis, University of Texas (Austin, Tex.), 1951.

CUMULATIVE NAME INDEX

Chenault, V. M.: 11
Drake, R. M.: *rev,* 4:325
Dunham, C. V.: 6
Durost, W. N.: *rev,* 4:325
Fife, R. H.: 8
Green, R. F.: *rev,* 7:391
Kelley, F.: 3
McCranie, J.: 2
Manuel, H. T.: 8–10
Schutz, R. E.: *rev,* 7:391
Stovall, F. L.: 1, 7
Willhauk, R. C.: 4
Zaccaria, M. A.: 5

[469]
Thurstone Test of Mental Alertness. Grades 9–12 and adults; 1943–68; TTMA; abbreviated adaptation of *American Council on Education Psychological Examination for High School Students,* 1940 Edition; for a shorter adaptation of this test, see *SRA Verbal Form;* 3 scores: quantitative, linguistic, total; Thelma Gwinn Thurstone and L. L. Thurstone; Science Research Associates, Inc. *

For additional information and a review by Robert D. North, see 7:392 (4 references); for a review by Joshua A. Fishman, see 5:391; see also 4:326 (3 references); for reviews by Anne Anastasi and Emily T. Burr of an earlier edition, see 3:265.

REFERENCES THROUGH 1971
1–3. See 4:326.
4–7. See 7:392.
8. BASS, BERNARD M. "Further Evidence on the Dynamic Character of Criteria." *Personnel Psychol* 15:93–7 sp '62. * (PA 37:3906)
9. MAHER, HOWARD. "Validity Information Exchange, No. 16-01: D.O.T. Code 0-06.71, Feature Writer; 0-06.73, Columnist; 0-06.92, Copyreader (Rewrite Man)." *Personnel Psychol* 16:71–3 sp '63. *
10. MAHER, HOWARD. "Validity Information Exchange, No. 16-02: D.O.T. Code 1-87.26, Advertising Space Salesman." *Personnel Psychol* 16:74–7 sp '63. *
11. BENTZ, V. JON. Chap. 7, "The Sears Experience in the Investigation, Description, and Prediction of Executive Behavior," pp. 147–205; critique by Ross Stagner, pp. 206–27. In *Measuring Executive Effectiveness.* Edited by Frederic R. Wickert and Dalton E. McFarland. New York: Appleton-Century-Crofts, 1967. Pp. viii, 242. *
12. FARR, JAMES L.; O'LEARY, BRIAN S.; AND BARTLETT, C. J. "Ethnic Group Membership as a Moderator of the Prediction of Job Performance." *Personnel Psychol* 24(4):609–36 w '71. *

CUMULATIVE NAME INDEX

Anastasi, A.: *rev,* 3:265
Bartlett, C. J.: 12
Bass, B. M.: 8
Bentz, V. J.: 6, 11
Borg, W. R.: 3
Burr, E. T.: *rev,* 3:265
Farr, J. L.: 12
Fife, I. E.: 2
Fishman, J. A.: *rev,* 5:391
Hackney, K. U.: 1
Maher, H.: 2, 9–10
North, R. D.: *rev,* 7:392
O'Leary, B. S.: 12
Peterson, F. E.: 4
Stagner, R.: 11
Vivers, B. B.: 5
Wheeler, R. W.: 7

[470]
The Undergraduate Program Aptitude Test. Grades 15–16; 1969–73; formerly called *The Undergraduate Record Examinations: Aptitude Test;* test available to colleges for local administration; 2 scores: verbal, quantitative; Educational Testing Service. * For the testing program entry, see 1062.

For additional information, see 7:393. For reviews of the testing program, see 7:671 (2 reviews).

[471]
The Verbal Power Test of Concept Equivalence. Ages 14 and over; 1959–63; VPT; E. Francesco; Western Psychological Services. *

For additional information and a review by Erwin K. Taylor, see 7:394; see also 6:508 (3 references).

REFERENCES THROUGH 1971
1–3. See 6:508.
4. FRANCESCO, E. "Performance of the VPT With Low-Variance Samples." *J Social Psychol* 62:343–9 Ap '64. * (PA 39:5057)
5. BORGATTA, EDGAR F. "Intelligent Word Associations." *Multiv Behav Res* 6(3):301–11 Jl '71. * (PA 47:4828)
6. LAMBERT, PHILIP; HANSEN, LEE H.; AND BORGATTA, EDGAR F. "Intelligent Word Associations in High School Students." *J Ed Res* 64(6):269–70 F '71. * (PA 46:11510)

CUMULATIVE NAME INDEX

Borgatta, E. F.: 5–6
Francesco, E.: 1–4
Hansen, L. H.: 6
Lambert, P.: 6
Taylor, E. K.: *rev,* 7:394

[472]
Verbal Reasoning. Job applicants and industrial employees; 1958–61; Raymond J. Corsini, Richard Renck, and Measurement Research Division, Industrial Relations Center, University of Chicago (manual); the Center. *

For additional information and reviews by James E. Kennedy and David G. Ryans, see 6:509.

[473]
Verbal Reasoning: Differential Aptitude Tests. Grades 8–12 and adults; 1947–73; 2 editions; George K. Bennett, Harold G. Seashore, and Alexander G. Wesman; Psychological Corporation. * For the complete battery entry, see 1069.
a) FORM A. 1947–59. *Out of print.*
b) FORM T. 1947–73; revision of Forms L and M ('61).

For reviews of the complete battery, see 7:673 (1 review, 1 excerpt), 6:767 (2 reviews), 5:605 (2 reviews), 4:711 (3 reviews), and 3:620 (1 excerpt).

REFERENCES THROUGH 1971
1. WILLIAMS, NANCY. "A Study of the Validity of the Verbal Reasoning Subtest and the Abstract Reasoning Subtest of the Differential Aptitude Tests." *Ed & Psychol Meas* 12:129–31 sp '52. * (PA 27:5914)
2. CATTELL, RAYMOND B., AND SCHEIER, IVAN H. "The Objective Test Measurement of Neuroticism, U.I. 23 (—)." *Indian J Psychol* 33:217–36 pt 4 '58. * (PA 35:3427, title only)
3. MOSHIN, S. M. "Plea for a Scientific Aptitude Test and a Preliminary Report of the Development of Such Test." *Indian J Psychol* 34:36–42 pt 1 '59. *
4. MILTON, OHMER. "Primitive Thinking and Reasoning Among College Students." *J Higher Ed* 31:218–20 Ap '60. *
5. AIJAZ, SAIYID MOHAMMAD. *Predictive Validity of the Three Versions of the "Verbal Reasoning" and the "Numerical Ability" Subtests of the Differential Aptitude Tests for East Pakistan.* Doctor's research study No. 1, Colorado State College (Greeley, Colo.), 1963. (DA 24:1068)
6. DAYAL, P. "Study of the Relationship Between a Verbal Intelligence Test (B.P.T. 15) and Verbal Reasoning Plus Numerical Ability Test Scores of the D.A.T." *J Voc & Ed Guid* (India) 10:83–9 Ag '64. * (PA 39:5114)
7. BUSBY, WALTER ALVIN. *A Multivariate Analysis of the Relationship of Academic Motivation, Aptitude, Socio-Economic Status, and Age to Persistence in Adult Evening School.* Doctor's thesis, Michigan State University (East Lansing, Mich.), 1965. (DA 26:4414)
8. CHAUDHRY, GHULAM MOHAMMED, AND KAYANI, MOHAMMED RASHID. "A Comparative Study of the DAT Verbal Reasoning, ACE Psychological Examination and Cooperative English Comprehension Tests as Predictors of Academic Success in the Institute of Education and Research, University of the Panjab." *B Ed & Res* (Pakistan) 4(2):1–21 '65. *
9. BAROYA, GEORGE MANORANJAN. *Reliability, Validity, and Comparability of Forms L and M of the "Verbal Reasoning" and the "Numerical Ability" Subtests of the Differential Aptitude Tests for Use in East Pakistan.* Doctor's research study No. 1, Colorado State College (Greeley, Colo.), 1966. (DA 27:2865A)

10. CAIN, RALPH W. "Relationships of Verbal Reasoning and Numerical Ability to Achievement in First-Year Algebra." *Sch Sci & Math* 66:131–4 F '66. *
11. HASHMI, SHAMIM AHMAD. *Effect of Previous Academic Achievement on the Performance of First-Year College Students of East Pakistan on the "Verbal Reasoning" and the "Numerical Ability" Subtests of the Differential Aptitude Tests.* Doctor's research study No. 1, Colorado State College (Greeley, Colo.), 1966. (*DA* 27:2391A)
12. NELSON, LEONARD THEODORE, JR. *The Relationship Between Verbal, Visual-Spatial, and Numerical Abilities and the Learning of the Mathematical Concept of Function.* Doctor's thesis, University of Michigan (Ann Arbor, Mich.), 1968. (*DAI* 30:218A)

CUMULATIVE NAME INDEX

Aijaz, S. M.: 5   Hashmi, S. A.: 11
Baroya, G. M.: 9   Kayani, M. R.: 8
Busby, W. A.: 7   Milton, O.: 4
Cain, R. W.: 10   Moshin, S. M.: 3
Cattell, R. B.: 2   Nelson, L. T.: 12
Chaudhry, G. M.: 8   Scheier, I. H.: 2
Dayal, P.: 6   Williams, N.: 1

[474]

Verbal Tests (Adv.). Ages 12–13; 1954–67; 5 tests; distribution restricted to directors of education; published for National Foundation for Educational Research in England and Wales; Ginn & Co. Ltd. [England]. *
a) VERBAL TEST (ADV.) 1. 1954–55; D. A. Pidgeon.
b) VERBAL TEST (ADV.) 2. 1957. *Out of print.*
c) VERBAL TEST (ADV.) 3. 1958.
d) VERBAL TEST (ADV.) 4. 1960.
e) VERBAL TEST (ADV.) 5. 1962–67.

For additional information, see 7:395; for reviews by J. S. Lawes and John Nisbet of Tests 1–4, see 6:510.

[475]

Verbal Tests BC, CD, C, and D. Ages 8-0 to 10-6, 9-0 to 11-6, 9-6 to 12-0; 1953–66; 3 levels; published for the National Foundation for Educational Research in England and Wales; Ginn & Co. Ltd. [England]. *
a) VERBAL TEST BC. Ages 8-0 to 10-6; 1953–62; formerly called *Primary Verbal Test 1;* adaptation of *A.C.E.R. Junior A Test* and *A.C.E.R. Junior B Test;* D. A. Pidgeon.
b) VERBAL TESTS CD AND C. Ages 9-0 to 11-6; 1959–66; 2 tests.
   1) *Verbal Test CD.* Ages 9-0 to 11-6; formerly called *Primary Verbal Test 2;* Valerie Land.
   2) *Verbal Test C.* Ages 9-4 to 11-0; formerly called *Primary Verbal Test 2G.*
c) VERBAL TEST D. Ages 9-6 to 12-0; 1962; formerly called *Primary Verbal Test 3;* T. Neville Postlethwaite.

For additional information, see 7:396; for reviews by John Nisbet and F. W. Warburton of *a*, see 5:369.

[476]

Verbal Tests EF and GH. Ages 11.0–13.5, 13.5–15.0; 1960–66; 2 levels; Valerie Land and Olive Wood (*a*); published for the National Foundation for Educational Research in England and Wales; Ginn & Co. Ltd. [England]. *
a) VERBAL TEST EF. Ages 11.0–13.5; 1960; formerly called *Secondary Verbal Test 1.*
b) VERBAL TEST GH. Ages 13.5–15.0; 1962–66; formerly called *Secondary Verbal Test 2.*

For additional information, see 7:397; for a review by Stanley Nisbet of *a*, see 6:499.

[477]

*****Verbal Tests 15–23 and 69.** Ages 10–12; 1951–72; 10 tests; new test published annually; tests 1–2 and 4–14 are out of print; distribution restricted to directors of education; published for the National Foundation for Educational Research in England and Wales; Ginn & Co. Ltd. [England]. *
a) VERBAL TEST 15. 1964–65.
b) VERBAL TEST 16. 1965–66.
c) VERBAL TEST 17. 1966–67.
d) VERBAL TEST 18. 1967–68.
e) VERBAL TEST 19. 1968–69.
f) VERBAL TESTS 20 AND 69. 1969–70; 2 editions.
   1) *Verbal Test 20.* 1969–70.
   2) *Verbal Test 69.* 1969; multiple choice version of form 20A.
g) VERBAL TEST 21. 1970–71.
h) VERBAL TEST 22. 1971.
i) VERBAL TEST 23. 1972.

For additional information and a review by David A. Walker of tests 13–20, see 7:398; for a review by Arthur B. Royse of earlier tests, see 6:511 (1 reference).

REFERENCES THROUGH 1971

1. See 6:511.

CUMULATIVE NAME INDEX

Butcher, H. J.: 1   Royse, A. B.: *rev*, 6:511
Moreton, C. A.: 1   Walker, D. A.: *rev*, 7:398

[478]

★**WLW Employment Inventory III.** Job applicants; 1954–72; approximately 65 percent of the items are from *WLW Culture Fair Inventory, WLW Mental Alertness Inventory,* and *WLW Employment Inventory, Short Form;* 4 scores: verbal, numerical, nonverbal, total; L. D. Edmonson, W. E. Brown, T. L. Chappell, W. H. E. Geiger, R. W. Henderson, T. E. Sutherland, W. S. Jones, and L. C. Steckle; William, Lynde & Williams. *

[479]

★**WLW Mental Alertness Inventory.** Job applicants; 1955; 3 scores: verbal, nonverbal, total; R. W. Henderson, W. E. Brown, T. L. Chappell, L. D. Edmonson, W. H. E. Geiger, R. L. Kaiser, L. E. Saddler, and L. C. Steckle; William, Lynde & Williams. *

[480]

Wesman Personnel Classification Test. Grades 8–16 and adults; 1946–65; WPCT; title on Forms A and B is *Personnel Classification Test;* 3 scores: verbal, numerical, total; Alexander G. Wesman; Psychological Corporation. *

For additional information, a review by Arthur C. MacKinney, and an excerpted review by Jack C. Merwin, see 7:400 (7 references); see also 5:399 (8 references); for reviews by John C. Flanagan and Erwin K. Taylor, see 4:331 (3 references); for an excerpted review, see 3:253.

REFERENCES THROUGH 1971

1–3. See 4:331.
4–11. See 5:399.
12–18. See 7:400.
19. GARBER, W. F. "Evaluation of Psychometric Tests for Optometry." *Optom Weekly* 40:1927-32+, 1953–7 D 22, 29 '49. * (*PA* 24:3477)
20. FRANKLE, A. H. "Indirect Measurement of Personal Adjustment by Use of a Conventional Industrial Aptitude Test." *Proc Inter Congr Appl Psychol* 16:284–90 '68. *

CUMULATIVE NAME INDEX

Abrahams, N.: 16   Gerken, C. d'A.: 5
Abt, L. E.: 1   Gilbert, H. B.: 3–4
Ash, P.: 12–3   Haner, C. F.: 6
Baier, D. E.: 9–10   Holt, W. G.: 7, 11
Cottle, W. C.: 11   Kirchner, W. K.: 14
Dugan, R. D.: 9–10, 15 MacKinney, A. C.: *rev*, 7:400
Dunnette, M. D.: 14, 16 Merwin, J. C.: *exc*, 7:400
Flanagan, J. C.: *rev*, 4:331 Ottman, D. K.: 11
Frankle, A. H.: 20   Parry, M. E.: 18
Garber, W. F.: 19   Perrine, M. W.: 8

Poruben, A.: 2
Taylor, E. K.: *rev,* 4:331
Vincent, N. L.: 15
Welsch, L. A.: 17
Wernimont, P.: 16
Williams, J. E.: 5

[481]

The Western Personnel Tests. College and adults; 1962; WPT; Robert L. Gunn and Morse P. Manson; Western Psychological Services. *

For additional information and reviews by Lewis E. Albright and Erwin K. Taylor, see 6:512.

REFERENCES THROUGH 1971

1. MONROE, KENTON L. "Note on the Estimation of the WAIS Full Scale IQ." *J Clin Psychol* 22:79–81 Ja '66. * (*PA* 40:4217)

CUMULATIVE NAME INDEX

Albright, L. E.: *rev,* 6:512
Monroe, K. L.: 1
Taylor, E. K.: *rev,* 6:512

[482]

*__Wonderlic Personnel Test.__ Adults; 1938–72; WPT; Forms D and F are adaptations of *Otis Self-Administering Tests of Mental Ability,* Higher Form; E. F. Wonderlic; E. F. Wonderlic & Associates, Inc.*

For additional information and reviews by Robert C. Droege and John P. Foley, Jr., see 7:401 (28 references); for reviews by N. M. Downie and Marvin D. Dunnette, see 6:513 (17 references); see also 5:400 (59 references); for reviews by H. E. Brogden, Charles D. Flory, and Irving Lorge, see 3:269 (7 references); see also 2:1415 (2 references).

REFERENCES THROUGH 1971

1–2. See 2:1415.
3–9. See 3:269.
10–68. See 5:400.
69–85. See 6:513.
86–113. See 7:401.
114. GUEST, LESTER, AND NUCKOLS, ROBERT. "A Laboratory Experiment in Recording in Public Opinion Interviewing." *Int J Opin & Attitude Res* (Mexico) 4:336–52 f '50. * (*PA* 25:7387)
115. WEIDER, ARTHUR. "Some Aspects of an Industrial Mental Hygiene Program." *J Appl Psychol* 35:383–5 D '51. * (*PA* 26:6560)
116. BASS, BERNARD M. "Validity Information Exchange, No. 10-25: D.O.T. Code 1-85.22, Salesman, Foodstuffs." *Personnel Psychol* 10:343–4 au '57. *
117. BIAMONTE, A. J. "A Study of the Effect of Attitudes on the Learning of Computer Programming." *Proc Ann Computer Personnel Res Conf* 3:68–74 '65. *
118. GETZELS, J. W., AND CSIKSZENTMIHALYI, M. Chap. 15, "The Study of Creativity in Future Artists: The Criterion Problem," pp. 349–68. In *Experience, Structure and Adaptability.* Edited by O. J. Harvey. New York: Springer Publishing Co., Inc., 1966. Pp. ix, 406. *
119. GORDON, BRUCE F., AND DENNIS, RICHARD A. "Characteristics and Performance Predictors of 7094 Computer Service Operators." *Proc Ann Computer Personnel Res Conf* 4:96–106 '66. *
120. BLANK, STANLEY S. "An Examination of the Usefulness of Various Psychological Instruments for Predicting Department Managers' Ratings of Clerical Sales Personnel." *Can Counsellor* 2:46–50 Ja '68. *
121. BOTTEGAL, J. DAVID, AND DECKER, ROBERT L. "An Industrial Test-Validation to Meet the Requirements of Title VII of the Civil Rights Act of 1964." *Proc W Va Acad Sci* 41(1969): 204–9 '70. *
122. Cox, WRAY KENT. *Personality, Intelligence, and Work Performance of Disadvantaged Adolescents.* Doctor's thesis, University of Missouri (Columbia, Mo.), 1971. (*DAI* 32:4939A)
123. GLUSKINOS, URY, AND BRENNAN, THOMAS F. "Selection and Evaluation Procedure for Operating Room Personnel." *J Appl Psychol* 55(2):165–9 Ap '71. * (*PA* 46:3909)

CUMULATIVE NAME INDEX

Albright, L. E.: 64, 67, 72, 85, 100, 102
American Gas Association, Personnel Committee: 30
Aursand, I. M.: 43
Barnabas, B.: 48–9
Barrett, R. S.: 65
Barton, G.: 69
Bass, B. M.: 35, 116
Benson, D.: 80
Biamonte, A. J.: 117
Blakemore, A.: 26
Blank, S. S.: 120
Bolanovich, D. J.: 5
Boneau, C. A.: 54, 59
Bottegal, J. D.: 121
Braaten, L. J.: 43
Brailey, L. G.: 78
Brennan, T. F.: 123
Bridgman, C. S.: 66
Brogden, H. E.: *rev,* 3:269
Browne, C.: 76
Busch, A. C.: 73–4
Butler, P. C.: 104
Campbell, J. T.: 78
Canfield, A. A.: 56
Capwell, D. F.: 15
Carlson, W. A.: 3
Chesler, D. J.: 14
Coats, J. E.: 82
Cox, W. K.: 122
Csikszentmihalyi, M.: 118
Cuomo, S.: 50
Decker, R. L.: 121
Dennis, R. A.: 119
Dignan, F.: 66
Doub, B. A.: 19
Downie, N. M.: *rev,* 6:513
Droege, R. C.: *rev,* 7:401
Dulsky, S. G.: 20
Dunn, R. E.: 81
Dunnette, M. D.: *rev,* 6:513
Fiske, D. W.: 13
Fitzpatrick, E. D.: 41, 44–6, 51, 57
Flory, C. D.: *rev,* 3:269
Foley, J. P.: *rev,* 7:401
Garner, R. G.: 82
Getzels, J. W.: 118
Glaser, R.: 16
Glennon, J. R.: 64, 67, 72, 85
Gluskinos, U.: 123
Goldhor, H.: 55
Goldman, S.: 103
Gordon, B. F.: 119
Grohsmeyer, F. A.: 36
Guest, L.: 114
Haner, C. F.: 37
Hanson, R.: 80
Harding, F. D.: 52
Harrison, R.: 53
Hawkins, W. A.: 79
Hay, E. N.: 21, 27, 31, 38
Hodgson, R. W.: 89
Holmes, F. J.: 22–3
Hoskins, J. E.: 90
Hovland, C. I.: 1–2
Hunt, W.: 53
Huttner, L.: 70
Irish, T. E.: 99
Jackson, T. A.: 53
Jacobson, C. F.: 10
Jennings, E. E.: 32
Jensen, M. B.: 8
Jerdee, T. H.: 87
Jex, F. B.: 92
Johnson, D. L.: 7
Kaplan, M.: 105
Karlins, M.: 105
Karstendiek, B.: 35
Kazmier, L. J.: 75–6
Keillor, J. S.: 109
Keim, L.: 93
King, D. C.: 83
Kirchner, W.: 80
Knauft, E. B.: 17, 39
Kopff, R. G.: 94
Krout, M. H.: 20
Kushmar, H. S.: 56
Laing, D. M.: 4
Laney, A. R.: 28
Lindzey, G.: 18
Lindzey, G. E.: 11
Lord, R. M.: 106
Lorge, I.: *rev,* 3:269
McCarty, J. J.: 40–1, 44–6, 51, 57, 60–3
McCullough, G.: 35
MacKinney, A. C.: 77
McMurry, F. D.: 100
McMurry, R. N.: 7
McNamara, W. J.: 84
Mahoney, T. A.: 87
Martin, F.: 42
Meyer, H. H.: 29, 50
Miller, R. B.: 24
Mitchell, M. D.: 100
Morrison, W. E.: 88
Nash, A. N.: 87
Neel, R. G.: 81
Nuckols, R.: 114
Parry, M. E.: 101
Penfield, R. V.: 95
Phillips, J. C.: 68
Prien, E. P.: 78, 110
Pruitt, R. C.: 35
Richardson, B. K.: 107
Robbins, J. E.: 83
Roberts, W. H.: 12
Ronan, W. W.: 111
Rotter, J. B.: 8
Rowe, F. B.: 86
Ruda, E.: 102
Rusmore, J.: 42
Rusmore, J. T.: 104
Schuerhoff, C.: 105
Schuh, A. J.: 98
Seashore, H. G.: 33
Shott, G. L.: 85
Skard, Ø.: 43
Skolnicki, J.: 71
Smith, W. J.: 64, 67, 72
Spaethe, M.: 66
Stene, D. M.: 70
Thompson, C. E.: 9
Thumin, F.: 103
Thumin, F. J.: 91, 112
Walker, F. C.: 58
Weaver, H. B.: 54, 59
Wechsler, I. R.: 25
Weider, A.: 115
Westberg, W. C.: 41, 44–6
Wevrick, L.: 113
Wille, G. R.: 108
Wittenberg, A.: 91
Wolins, L.: 77
Wonderlic, E. F.: 1–2, 6, 96–7
Woodward, R. H.: 73–4
Wright, J. H.: 4
Young, M. B.: 47

[Out of Print Since TIP I]

A.C.E.R. Junior B Test, 6:435 (1 review, 1 reference)
A.C.E.R. Test W.N.V., 6:436
American Council on Education Psychological Examination for College Freshmen, 6:438 (8 reviews, 535 references)
American Council on Education Psychological Examination for High School Students, 5:309 (4 reviews, 12 references)
Army Group Examination Alpha, 4:281 (2 reviews, 87 references)
Army Group Examination Alpha: Schrammel-Brannan Revision, 1:1040 (1 review); see also *Army Group Examination Alpha* and revisions, 3:220 (77 references)
Benge Employment Tests (status unknown), 3:221 (2 reviews)
California Analogies and Reasoning Test, 6:442 (2 reviews, 2 excerpts)
California Capacity Questionnaire, 3:222 (2 reviews)
Cardall-Miles Test of Mental Alertness (status unknown), 6:446
Carlton Intelligence Tests, 7:342 (1 review)

Carlton Picture Intelligence Test, 6:447 (2 reviews)
Classification Test 40-A, 6:448 (2 reviews)
Cole-Vincent Group Intelligence Test for School Entrants, 3:226 (1 review)
College Placement Test, 5:319 (2 reviews)
Comprehension Tests: Supplementary Mentality Tests for Superior Adults, T:741
Daneshill Intelligence Test, 5:325 (2 reviews)
Davis-Eells Test of General Intelligence or Problem-Solving Ability, 5:326 (3 reviews, 36 references)
Dawson Mental Test, 2:1389 (2 reviews, 2 excerpts)
Detroit Advanced First-Grade Intelligence Test, 2:1392 (1 review)
Detroit Advanced Intelligence Test, 5:329c (1 review, 6 references—3, 4, 6, 7, 8, 9)
Detroit Alpha Intelligence Test, 5:329b (1 review, 7 references—1, 3, 5, 6, 8, 10, 11)
Detroit Beginning First-Grade Intelligence Test, 1:1044 (1 review, 1 excerpt)
Dominion Group Test of Intelligence, 5:330
Duplex Series of Ability Tests, 4:289 (2 reviews, 1 excerpt, 2 references)
Easel Age Scale, 5:332 (2 reviews)
FR-CR Test, 4:339 (1 review, 1 reference); now available only as a subtest of *Leiter Adult Intelligence Scale,* 504
General Intelligence: Northumberland Standardised Tests (1925 Series), T:760
Gestalt Continuation Test (status unknown), 6:459 (3 references)
Group Tests 33 and 33B, 5:339 (11 references)
Group Test 90A, 5:340 (1 review)
Inductive Reasoning Test, 3:232 (1 review)
Job Alertness Tests, T:776
Junior School Grading Test, 2:1400 (1 review)
Kentucky General Ability Test, 3:234 (1 review, 3 references); revised edition was available only as a part of *Kentucky Classification Battery,* 4:301 (1 review, 4 references)
Kingsway Intelligence Tests, 3:235 (2 excerpts)
Laycock Mental Ability Test, 3:237 (2 reviews)
Leiter Adaptation of Arthur's Stencil Design Test, 4:347 (1 excerpt, 1 reference); now available only as a subtest of *Leiter Adult Intelligence Scale,* 504
Leiter Adaptation of the Painted Cube Test, 4:348 (1 excerpt, 1 reference); now available only as a subtest of *Leiter Adult Intelligence Scale,* 504
Lowry-Lucier Reasoning Test Combination, 7:361 (2 reviews, 7 references)
Maddox Verbal Reasoning Test, 6:469 (2 reviews, 1 excerpt)
Manchester General Ability Test (Senior), 6:470 (3 reviews, 1 reference)
Multi-Racial Picture Intelligence Tests Suitable for Use in African and Asian Schools, 6:476
New Rhode Island Intelligence Test, 5:354 (1 review, 6 references)
Non-Language Multi-Mental Test, 3:243 (1 review, 1 reference)
"Northern" Test of Educability, T:805
Orally Presented Group Test of Intelligence for Juniors, 5:360 (1 review, 2 references)
Otis Classification Test, 3:247 (1 excerpt, 3 references)
Otis General Intelligence Examination, 3:248 (1 review)
Otis Group Intelligence Scale, 6:480 (1 review, 44 references)
Partington's Pathways Test, 4:355 (1 review, 1 excerpt, 1 reference); now available only as a subtest of *Leiter Adult Intelligence Scale,* 504

Pintner General Ability Tests: Non-Language Series, 3:254 (1 review)
Pintner General Ability Tests: Verbal Series, 5:368 (2 reviews, 2 excerpts, 23 references); the lowest level, *Pintner-Cunningham Primary Test,* 435, is still in print
Purdue Non-Language Test, 6:491 (2 reviews)
Quick Word Test, 7:378 (1 review, 2 excerpts, 8 references)
Roback Mentality Tests for Superior Adults, T:837
SRA College Classification Tests, 5:376
SRA Tests of Educational Ability, 6:495 (5 reviews, 1 excerpt, 1 reference)
School Aptitude Test: Thanet Mental Tests, 2:1422 (1 review)
Schrammel General Ability Test, 6:498 (1 review)
Scientific Ingenuity and Juristic Aptitude Test, T:848
Selective Service System College Qualification Test, T:851
Survey of Mental Maturity: California Survey Series, 6:503 (1 review)
Terman-McNemar Test of Mental Ability, 4:324 (4 reviews, 62 references)
Test of General Knowledge, 2:1425 (1 reference)
Test of Word-Number Ability, 5:389 (3 reviews, 1 reference)
Tomlinson Junior School Test, 5:392 (1 review)
Verbal and Non-Verbal Test 1, 5:393 (1 review)
Verbal Capacity Sampler, 5:394
Vocabulary Tests, 5:398 (1 review)
WLW Culture Fair Inventory, 7:399 (2 reviews)
"West Riding" Tests of Mental Ability, 2:1430 (1 review)
"West Yorkshire" Group Test of Intelligence, 4:332

INDIVIDUAL

[483]
Arthur Point Scale of Performance Tests. Ages 4.5 or 5.5 to superior adults; 1925–47; 2 editions; Grace Arthur. *

a) FORM I. Ages 5.5 to superior adults; 1925–43; 10 tests: *Knox Cube Test (Arthur Revision), Seguin Form Board (Arthur Revision), Two-Figure Form Board, Casuist Form Board, Manikin Test, Feature Profile Test, Mare and Foal Formboard, Healy Pictorial Completion Test I, Porteus Maze Test (1924 Series), The Block-Design Test (Arthur Modification)*; Stoelting Co.

b) REVISED FORM II. Ages 4.5 to superior adults; 1933–47; 5 tests: *Knox Cube Test (Arthur Revision), Seguin Form Board (Arthur Revision), Arthur Stencil Design Test I, Porteus Maze Test (Arthur Revision), Healy Pictorial Completion Test II*; Psychological Corporation.

For additional information and a review by William R. Grove, see 4:335 (12 references); for an excerpted review, see 3:271 (20 references); for reviews by Andrew W. Brown and Carroll A. Whitmer and an excerpted review by Donald Snedden, see 2:1379 (17 references). For excerpts from related book reviews, see 2:B830 (1 excerpt), 1:B304 (7 excerpts), and 36:B19 (1 excerpt).

REFERENCES THROUGH 1971
1–16. See 2:1379.
17–35. See 3:271.
36–47. See 4:335.
48. BALKEN, EVA RUTH; MAURER, SIEGFRIED; AND FALSTEIN, EUGENE K. "Variations in Psychological Measurements Associated With Increased Feeding of Vitamins A, D, B_1, and B_2 and

Iron in Dementia Praecox." *J Comp Psychol* 21:387-403 Je '36. * (*PA* 10:5019)

49. HINTON, RALPH T., JR. "The Role of the Basal Metabolic Rate in the Intelligence of Ninety Grade-School Students." *J Ed Psychol* 27:546-50 O '36. * (*PA* 11:1247)

50. NAROSNY, ELEANOR HELEN. *A Comparative Study of the Performanie of Juvenile Delinquents and Educational Problem Children on the Stanford-Binet and Grace Arthur Scales.* Master's thesis, Ohio State University (Columbus, Ohio), 1937.

51. HASLAM, PHYLLIS. *The Prediction of Ability on the Arthur Point Performance Scale From the Merrill-Palmer Scale.* Master's thesis, State University of Iowa (Iowa City, Iowa), 1938.

52. HINTON, RALPH T., JR. "A Further Study of the Role of the Basal Metabolic Rate in the Intelligence of Children." *J Ed Psychol* 30:309-14 Ap '39. * (*PA* 13:5602)

53. BIJOU, S. W., AND MCCANDLESS, B. R. "An Approach to a More Comprehensive Analysis of Mentally Retarded Pre-Delinquent Boys." *J Genetic Psychol* 65:147-60 S '44. * (*PA* 19:440)

54. ZIMMERMAN, FREDERIC T.; BURGEMEISTER, BESSIE B.; AND PUTNAM, TRACY J. "A Group Study of the Effect of Glutamic Acid Upon Mental Functioning in Children and Adolescents." *Psychosom Med* 9:175-83 My-Je '47. * (*PA* 21:3474)

55. JOSEPH, ALICE, AND MURRAY, VERONICA F. *Chamorros and Carolinians of Saipan: Personality Studies,* pp. 119-35, 329-36, passim. Cambridge, Mass.: Harvard University Press, 1951. Pp. xviii, 381. * (*PA* 26:3359)

56. COHEN, BERTRAM D., AND COLLIER, MARY J. "A Note on the WISC and Other Tests of Children Six to Eight Years Old." *J Consult Psychol* 16:226-7 Je '52. * (*PA* 27:5145)

57. GELLERMAN, SAUL W. "Forms I and II of the Arthur Performance Scales With Mental Defectives." *J Consult Psychol* 16:127-31 Ap '52. * (*PA* 27:2719)

58. JOHNSON, ELIZABETH Z. "Sex Differences and Variability in the Performance of Retarded Children on Raven, Binet and Arthur Tests." *J Clin Psychol* 8:298-301 Jl '52. * (*PA* 27:5981)

59. MANOLAKES, GEORGE, AND SHELDON, WILLIAM D. "A Comparison of the Grace Arthur, Revised Form II, and the Stanford-Binet, Revised Form L." *Ed & Psychol Meas* 12:105-8 sp '52. * (*PA* 27:5886)

60. GLOWATSKY, EDWARD. "The Verbal Element in the Intelligence Scores of Congenitally Deaf and Hard of Hearing Children." *Am Ann Deaf* 98:328-35 My '53. * (*PA* 28:7921)

61. VARVA, FRANK IRVIN. *An Investigation of the Effect of Auditory Deficiency Upon Performance With Special Reference to Concrete and Abstract Tasks.* Doctor's thesis, University of Pittsburgh (Pittsburgh, Pa.), 1956. (*DA* 16:2532)

62. SHONTZ, FRANKLIN C. "Evaluation of Intellectual Potential in Hemiplegic Individuals." *J Clin Psychol* 13:267-9 Jl '57. * (*PA* 32:5816)

63. LEVINSON, BORIS M. "A Research Note on the Knox Cubes as an Intelligence Test for Aged Males." *J Gerontol* 15:85-6 Ja '60. * (*PA* 35:6234)

64. SHECHTMAN, AUDREY M. *The Relationship of Variability in Children's Verbal and Non-Language Test Performance to Current and Later Behavioral Functions.* Doctor's thesis, University of Minnesota (Minneapolis, Minn.), 1961. (*DA* 22:2065)

65. BERGÈS, JEAN, AND LÉZINE, IRÈNE. *The Imitation of Gestures: A Technique for Studying the Body Schema and Praxis of Children Three to Six Years of Age,* pp. 83-7. Clinics in Developmental Medicine No. 18. Translated from the 1963 French edition by Arthur H. Parmelee, Jr. Published for the Spastics Society Medical Education and Information Unit, 1965. Pp. x, 116. *

66. KOWITZ, GERALD T., AND LEVY, LOIS E. "Underachievement in Deaf Children." *Am Ann Deaf* 110:414-9 My '65. * (*PA* 39:15990)

67. SANTORO, ROSEANN MARIE. *The Relationship of Reading Achievement to Specific Measures of Visual Perception, Visual-Motor Perception and Intelligence.* Doctor's thesis, Fordham University (New York, N.Y.), 1967. (*DA* 28:4010A)

68. SILBERBERG, NORMAN E., AND BOURESTOM, NORMAN C. "The Knox Cubes as a Screening Measure of Intelligence for Hemiparetic Patients." *J Clin Psychol* 24:348-9 Jl '68. * (*PA* 42:16431)

CUMULATIVE NAME INDEX

Abel, T. M.: 28
Arthur, G.: 1-6, 8, 10, 16, 22, 24a, 25, 42-3, 45
Balken, E. R.: 48
Bensberg, G. J.: 44
Bergès, J.: 65
Bijou, S. W.: 23, 38, 53
Bishop, H. M.: 15
Bourestom, N. C.: 68
Boynton, P. L.: *exc,* 1:B304
Brown, A. W.: 9; *rev,* 2:1379
Bruce, M.: 20
Burchard, E. M. L.: 24
Burgemeister, B. B.: 54
Capwell, D. F.: 29
Cohen, B. D.: 56
Collier, M. J.: 56
Cook, J. M.: 45
Deahl, K.: 17
DiTolla, E. E.: 19
Emerson, M. R.: *exc,* 1:B304
Falstein, E. K.: 48
Frazeur, H. A.: 34
Gellerman, S. W.: 57
Glowatsky, E.: 60
Grove, W. R.: *rev,* 4:335
Hamilton, M. E.: 40
Haslam, P.: 51
Havighurst, R. J.: 26
Hilden, A. H.: 13
Hilkevitch, R. R.: 26
Hinton, R. T.: 49, 52
Hoakley, Z. P.: 34
Hultsch, C. L.: 27
Humm, K. A.: 14, 18
Hunt, E. P.: *exc,* 36:B19
Johnson, E. Z.: 58
Joseph, A.: 55
Knight, M. W.: 11
Kogan, K. L.: 41
Kowitz, G. T.: 66
Levinson, B. M.: 63
Levy, L. E.: 66
Lézine, I.: 65
Line, W.: *exc,* 1:B304
McBrearty, J. F.: 46
McCandless, B. R.: 53
MacKane, K.: 10.1
Mahan, H. C.: 12
Manolakes, G.: 59
Maurer, S.: 48
Maxfield, F. N.: *exc,* 1:B304
Murray, V. F.: 55
Myklebust, H. R.: 24
Narosny, E. H.: 50
Patterson, R. M.: 32, 39
Putnam, T. J.: 54
Riley, G.: 7
Roberts, A. D.: 30
Rosenzweig, S.: 41
Santoro, R. M.: 67
Sarason, E. K.: 33, 35
Sarason, S. B.: 21, 33, 35
Seidl, J. C.: 37
Shechtman, A. M.: 64
Sheldon, W. D.: 59
Shontz, F. C.: 62
Shotwell, A. M.: 31
Shrubsall, F. C.: *exc,* 1:B304
Shuttleworth, F. K.: *exc,* 1:B304
Silberberg, N. E.: 68
Skeels, H. M.: 13
Sloan, W.: 44
Snedden, D.: *exc,* 2:1379
Varva, F. I.: 61
Wallin, J. E. W.: 27
Watson, R. I.: 47
Whitmer, C. A.: *rev,* 2:1379
Wisler, M. L.: 36
Woodrow, H.: 1
Zimmerman, F. T.: 54

[484]

Bayley Scales of Infant Development. Ages 2-30 months; 1969; BSID; 2 scores: mental, motor, plus 30 behavior ratings; Nancy Bayley; Psychological Corporation. *

For additional information and reviews by Roberta R. Collard and Raymond H. Holden, see 7:402 (20 references).

REFERENCES THROUGH 1971

1-20. See 7:402.

21. ROSENBLITH, JUDY F. "Prognostic Value of Behavioral Assessments of Neonates." *Biologia Neonatorum* (Switzerland) 6(1-2):76-103 '64. *

22. VANDENBERG, STEVEN G.; STAFFORD, RICHARD E.; AND BROWN, ANNE E. Chap. 10, "The Louisville Twin Study," pp. 153-204. In *Progress in Human Behavior Genetics.* Edited by Steven G. Vandenberg. Baltimore, Md.: Johns Hopkins Press, 1968. Pp. xi, 356. *

23. HERMAN, SUSAN JANE. *The Relationship Between Maternal Variable Scores and Infant Performance in a Negro Experimental Stimulation Training Population.* Doctor's thesis, University of Florida (Gainesville, Fla.), 1970. (*DAI* 32:239A)

24. KILBRIDE, JANET E.; ROBBINS, MICHAEL C.; AND KILBRIDE, PHILIP L. "The Comparative Motor Development of Baganda, American White, and American Black Infants." *Am Anthrop* 72(6):1422-8 D '70. * (*PA* 46:8847)

25. BAYLEY, NANCY, AND HUNT, JANE V. "Explorations Into Patterns of Mental Development and Prediction From Bayley Scales of Infant Development," pp. 52-71. In *Minnesota Symposia on Child Psychology, Vol. 5.* Edited by John P. Hill. Minneapolis, Minn.: University of Minnesota Press, 1971. Pp. xiii, 216. *

26. BLAINE, HENRY MYRATE, II. *The Relationship of Attention Span in a Selected Group of Infants to Performance on a Test of Mental Abilities.* Doctor's thesis, University of Alabama (University, Ala.), 1971. (*DAI* 32:2511A)

27. GOFFENEY, BARBARA; HENDERSON, NORMAN B.; AND BUTLER, BRUCE V. "Negro-White, Male-Female Eight-Month Developmental Scores Compared With Seven-Year WISC and Bender Test Scores." *Child Develop* 42(2):595-604 Je '71. * (*PA* 47:651)

28. HIGUCHI, JUDITH L. *Applications of the Bayley Scales of Infant Development to Multiply Handicapped Children.* Master's thesis, George Peabody College (Nashville, Tenn.), 1971.

29. HUNT, JANE V., AND BAYLEY, NANCY. "Explorations Into Patterns of Mental Development From the Bayley Scales of Infant Development." *Minn Symposia Child Psychol* 5:52-71 '71. *

30. ROBINSON, HALBERT B., AND ROBINSON, NANCY M. "Longitudinal Development of Very Young Children in a Comprehensive Day Care Program: The First Two Years." *Child Develop* 42(6):1673-83 D '71. * (*PA* 48:8827)

31. WELCHER, DORIS W.; MELLITS, E. DAVID; AND HARDY, JANET B. "A Multivariate Analysis of Factors Affecting Psychological Performance." *Johns Hopkins Med J* 129(1):19-35 Jl '71. *

CUMULATIVE NAME INDEX

Adelman, M.: 19
Barot, J.: 2
Bayley, N.: 1, 7, 11, 25, 29
Blaine, H. M.: 26
Broman, S. H.: 20
Brown, A. E.: 22
Butler, B. V.: 27
Campbell, F. A.: 17
Carr, J.: 16
Cohen, A. I.: 3
Collard, R. R.: *rev,* 7:402
Combs, A.: 4
Erickson, M. T.: 17
Estes, B.: 4
Fiedler, M.: 20
Francis-Williams, J.: 8
Gannon, D. R.: 12
Gerson, E. F.: 13, 15

Goffeney, B.: 27
Gravem, H.: 18
Hardy, J. B.: 31
Henderson, N. B.: 27
Herman, S. J.: 23
Higuchi, J. L.: 28
Holden, R. H.: *rev*, 7:402
Hunt, J. V.: 25, 29
Ireton, H.: 18
Johnson, N. M.: 17
Jones, W. S.: 19
Kilbride, J. E.: 24
Kilbride, P. L.: 24
Klatskin, E. H.: 5
Kohen-Raz, R.: 6, 9, 14
Lord, R. M.: 19
McGarry, M. E.: 5
Man, E. B.: 19
Mellits, E. D.: 31

Mendelson, M. A.: 10
Patel, A.: 2
Phatak, P.: 2
Poffenberger, T.: 2
Robbins, M. C.: 24
Robinson, H. B.: 30
Robinson, J. S.: 11
Robinson, N. M.: 30
Rosenblith, J. F.: 21
Schaefer, E. S.: 1
Stafford, R. E.: 22
Steward, M. S.: 5
Thwing, E.: 18
Vanderberg, S. G.: 22
Welcher, D. W.: 31
Werner, E. E.: 7
Willerman, L.: 20
Yule, W.: 8

[485]

★**Bingham Button Test.** Disadvantaged children ages 3–6; 1967; BBT; "knowledge and understanding of simple terms and relationships"; William J. Bingham; Bingham Button Test. *

[486]

Canadian Intelligence Test, 1966 Revision. Ages 3–16; 1940–66; formerly called *Canadian Intelligence Examination;* modification of the 1916 *Stanford Revision of the Binet-Simon Intelligence Scale;* Carman E. Stothers, Beverly R. Collier, James W. Covert, and James C. Williams; McGraw-Hill Ryerson Ltd. [Canada]. *

For additional information and a review by Hugh Taylor, see 7:403; for a review by Gwen F. Arnold of the 1947 edition, see 4:336; for excerpted reviews by Clara Blacklock and one other, see 3:272 (1 reference).

REFERENCES THROUGH 1971

1. See 3:272.

CUMULATIVE NAME INDEX

Arnold, G. F.: *rev*, 4:336
Blacklock, C.: *exc*, 3:272
Stothers, C. E.: 1
Taylor, H.: *rev*, 7:403

[487]

Cattell Infant Intelligence Scale. Ages 3–30 months; 1940–60; downward extension of *Stanford-Binet Intelligence Scale, Second Revision;* Psyche Cattell; Psychological Corporation. *

For additional information, see 6:515 (22 references); for reviews by Florence M. Teagarden and Beth L. Wellman and excerpted reviews by Rachel Stutsman Ball, C. M. Louttit, T. L. McCulloch, Norma V. Scheidemann, and Helen Speyer, see 3:281–2.

REFERENCES THROUGH 1971

1–22. See 6:515.
23. SIMON, ABRAHAM J., AND BASS, LIBBY G. "Toward a Validation of Infant Testing." *Am J Orthopsychiatry* 26:340–50 Ap '56. * (PA 31:4713)
24. DENNIS, WAYNE, AND NAJARIAN, PERGROUHI. "Infant Development Under Environmental Handicap." *Psychol Monogr* 71(7):1–13 '57. * (PA 33:5830)
25. HOHMAN, LESLIE B., AND FREEDHEIM, DONALD K. "A Study of IQ Retest Evaluations on 370 Cerebral Palsied Children." *Am J Phys Med* 38:180–7 O '59. *
26. WIEMERS, IRENE HOLLINGSWORTH. *Evaluating Adequacy of Adjustment in Normal Infants.* Doctor's thesis, University of Utah (Salt Lake City, Utah), 1960. (DA 21:2791)
27. DUNPHY, DONAL, AND PESSIN, VIVIAN. "Correlation Between Cord Blood Oxygen Values and Psychological Test Scores." *J Iowa Med Soc* 52:212–6 Ap '62. *
28. BIERMAN, JESSIE M.; CONNOR, ANGIE; VAAGE, MARILYN; AND HONZIK, MARJORIE P. "Pediatricians' Assessments of the Intelligence of Two-Year-Olds and Their Mental Test Scores." *Pediatrics* 34:680–90 N '64. *
29. KARELITZ, SAMUEL; FISICHELLI, VINCENT R.; COSTA, JOAN; KARELITZ, RUTH; AND ROSENFIELD, LAURA. "Relation of Crying Activity in Early Infancy to Speech and Intellectual Development at Age Three Years." *Child Develop* 35:769–77 S '64. * (PA 39:4513)
30. GERSON, ELAINE F., AND SCOTT, ROLAND B. "Growth and Development of Negro Infants: 7, The Relationship of Parental Attitudes and Socioeconomic Pressures to Intelligence and Gross Motor Quotients During the Second Year of Life." *Med Ann DC* 35:5–8 Ja '66. *
31. LUSZKI, WALTER A. "Intellectual Functioning of Spastic Cerebral Palsied." *Cereb Palsy J* 27:7–9 Mr–Ap '66. * (PA 40:8010)
32. MATHENY, ADAM P., JR. "Improving Diagnostic Forecasts Made on a Developmental Scale." *Am J Mental Def* 71:371–5 N '66. * (PA 41:1706)
33. SIDERITS, MARY ANNE TERESA. *Indices of Change in the Cattell-Binet Ratings of Intellectually Sub-Average Children.* Doctor's thesis, University of Michigan (Ann Arbor, Mich.), 1966. (DA 27:2519B)
34. STOTT, LELAND H., AND BALL, RACHEL STUTSMAN. *Infant and Preschool Mental Tests: Review and Evaluation.* Monographs of the Society for Research in Child Development, Vol. 30, No. 3, Serial No. 101. Chicago, Ill.: University of Chicago Press, 1966. Pp. iv, 151. * (PA 40:7220)
35. ALPERN, GERALD D. "Measurement of 'Untestable' Autistic Children." *J Abn Psychol* 72:478–86 D '67. * (PA 42:4183)
36. LINDE, LEONARD M.; RASOF, BEATRICE; AND DUNN, OLIVE JEAN. "Mental Development in Congenital Heart Disease." *J Pediatrics* 71:198–203 Ag '67. *
37. RASOF, BEATRICE; LINDE, LEONARD M.; AND DUNN, OLIVE JEAN. "Intellectual Development in Children With Congenital Heart Disease." *Child Develop* 38:1043–53 D '67. * (PA 42:7687)
38. WERNER, EMMY; SIMONIAN, KENNETH; BIERMAN, JESSIE M.; AND FRENCH, FERN E. "Cumulative Effect of Perinatal Complications and Deprived Environment on Physical, Intellectual, and Social Development of Preschool Children." *Pediatrics* 39:490–505 Ap '67. *
39. BONACCORSI, MARIE-THÉRÈSE; GAGNON, JACQUES; DESTROOPER, JOHAN; AND TOUSIGNANT, FRANCINE. "The Relationship Between Mongoloid Phenotype and Genotype: A Comparative Study of the Psychological and Social Developments of Diplo 21/Triplo 21 Mosaic and Standard Trisomy 21." *Proc 4th World Congr Psychiatry* 1966(pt 3):1584–6 '68. *
40. ERICKSON, MARILYN T. "The Predictive Validity of the Cattell Infant Intelligence Scale for Young Mentally Retarded Children." *Am J Mental Def* 72:728–33 Mr '68. * (PA 42:11047)
41. GOLDEN, MARK, AND BIRNS, BEVERLY. "Social Class and Cognitive Development in Infancy." *Merrill-Palmer Q* 14:139–49 Ap '68. * (PA 43:2423)
42. WERNER, EMMY E.; HONZIK, MARJORIE P.; AND SMITH, RUTH S. "Prediction of Intelligence and Achievement at Ten Years From Twenty Months Pediatric and Psychologic Examinations." *Child Develop* 39:1063–75 D '68. * (PA 43:8145)
43. WERNER, EMMY E.; SIMONIAN, KENNETH; AND SMITH, RUTH S. "Ethnic and Socioeconomic Status Differences in Abilities and Achievement Among Preschool and School-Age Children in Hawaii." *J Social Psychol* 75:43–59 Je '68. * (PA 42:13553)
44. ALPERN, GERALD D., AND KIMBERLIN, CAROLYN C. "Short Intelligence Test Ranging From Infancy Levels Through Childhood Levels for Use With the Retarded." *Am J Mental Def* 75(1):65–71 Jl '70. * (PA 45:1185)
45. BAYLEY, NANCY. Chap. 16, "Development of Mental Abilities," pp. 1163–209. In *Carmichael's Manual of Child Psychology, Third Edition, Vol. 1.* Edited by Paul H. Mussen. New York: John Wiley & Sons, Inc. 1970. Pp. xiii, 1519. *
46. ERICKSON, MARILYN T.; JOHNSON, NANCY M.; AND CAMPBELL, FRANCES A. "Relationships Among Scores on Infant Tests for Children With Developmental Problems." *Am J Mental Def* 75(1):102–4 Jl '70. * (PA 45:926)
47. BECKWITH, LEILA. "Relationships Between Attributes of Mothers and Their Infants' IQ Scores." *Child Develop* 42(4):1083–97 O '71. * (PA 48:2692)
48. GOLDEN, MARK; BIRNS, BEVERLY; BRIDGER, WAGNER; AND MOSS, ABIGAIL. "Social-Class Differentiation in Cognitive Development Among Black Preschool Children." *Child Develop* 42(1):37–45 Mr '71. * (PA 46:4621)
49. HUSTED, J.; WALLIN, K.; AND WOODEN, H. "The Psychological Evaluation of Profoundly Retarded Children With the Use of Concrete Reinforcers." *J Psychol* 77(2):173–9 Mr '71. * (PA 46:1701)

CUMULATIVE NAME INDEX

Allen, R. M.: 15
Alpern, G. D.: 35, 44
Ball, R. S.: 34; *exc*, 3:282
Bass, L. G.: 23
Bayley, N.: 45
Beckwith, L.: 47
Bierman, J. M.: 28, 38
Birns, B.: 41, 48
Bonaccorsi, M. T.: 39
Bridger, W.: 48
Brodie, F. H.: 14
Campbell, F. A.: 46
Cattell, P.: 1–2, 10, 18
Cavanaugh, M. C.: 12
Cohen, I.: 12
Connor, A.: 28

Costa, J.: 29
Dennis, W.: 24
Destrooper, J.: 39
Dunn, O. J.: 36–7
Dunphy, D.: 12, 27
Erickson, M. T.: 40, 46
Escalona, S.: 4–5, 20
Fisichelli, V. R.: 29
Freedheim, D. K.: 25
French, F. E.: 38
Fromm, E.: 13
Gagnon, J.: 39
Gallagher, J. J.: 11
Gerson, E. F.: 30
Gerstein, R. A.: 3
Goldberg, I. D.: 12

Golden, M.: 41, 48
Harms, I. E.: 6, 16
Hartman, L. D.: 13
Hohman, L. B.: 25
Honzik, M. P.: 28, 42
Husted, J.: 49
Johnson, N. M.: 46
Karelitz, R.: 29
Karelitz, S.: 29
Kimberlin, C. C.: 44
Kiatskin, E. H.: 8
Kralovich, A. M.: 17
Linde, L. M.: 36-7
London, S. K.: 22
Louttit, C. M.: *exc*, 3:282
Luszki, W. A.: 31
McCulloch, T. L.: *exc*, 3:282
Marschak, M.: 13
Matheny, A. P.: 32
Miller, E.: 9
Moriarty, A.: 20
Moss, A.: 48
Najarian, P.: 24
Norris, M.: 14
Pease, D.: 21
Pessin, V.: 27
Rasof, B.: 36-7
Ringwall, E. A.: 12
Rosauer, J. K.: 21
Rosenfeld, G. B.: 9
Rosenfeld, L.: 29
Scheidemann, N. V.: *exc*, 3:281
Scott, R. B.: 30
Siderits, M. A. T.: 33
Simon, A. J.: 23
Simonian, K.: 38, 43
Smith, R. S.: 42-3
Spaulding, P. J.: 14
Speyer, H.: *exc*, 3:282
Spiker, C. C.: 16
Stott, L. H.: 34
Teagarden, F. M.: *rev*, 3:281
Tousignant, F.: 39
Vaage, M.: 28
Wallin, K.: 49
Watson, R. I.: 7
Wellman, B. L.: *rev*, 3:281
Werner, E.: 38
Werner, E. E.: 42-3
Wieners, I. H.: 26
Wiggin, M. K.: 19
Wolins, L.: 21
Wooden, H.: 49

[488]

★**Classification Tasks, Experimental Edition.** Ages 5-9; 1971; for research use only; 2 scores (response, response plus explanation) for each of 2 tasks (cross-classification, equivalence); Mary Nixon; Australian Council for Educational Research [Australia]. *

REFERENCES THROUGH 1971

1. NIXON, MARY. *Children's Classification Skills.* Hawthorn, Vic., Australia: Australian Council for Educational Research, 1971. Pp. 107. *

CUMULATIVE NAME INDEX

Nixon, M.: 1

[489]

*__Columbia Mental Maturity Scale, Third Edition.__ Ages 3.5-9; 1954-72; CMMS; Bessie B. Burgemeister, Lucille Hollander Blum, and Irving Lorge; Harcourt Brace Jovanovich, Inc. *

For additional information and reviews by Marshall S. Hiskey and T. Ernest Newland of an earlier edition, see 6:517 (22 references); see also 5:402 (12 references).

REFERENCES THROUGH 1971

1-13. See 5:402.
14-35. See 6:517.
36. STEPHENSON, GEORGE ROTHWELL. *Form Perception, Abstract Thinking and Intelligence Test Validity in Cerebral Palsy.* Doctor's thesis, Columbia University (New York, N.Y.), 1957. (*DA* 17:1600)
37. BOONE, DANIEL R. "Communication Skills and Intelligence in Right and Left Hemiplegics." *J Speech & Hearing Disorders* 24:241-8 Ag '59. * (*PA* 34:8233)
38. LEREA, LOUIS, AND KOHUT, SUZANNE. "A Comparative Study of Monolinguals and Bilinguals in a Verbal Task Performance." *J Clin Psychol* 17:49-52 Ja '61. * (*PA* 37:2480)
39. BRENGELMANN, JOHANNES C., AND STANDEN, JOHN L. "Task Difficulty and Response Time in the Retardate." *Training Sch B* 60:89-93 Ag '63. * (*PA* 38:4557)
40. SONNEMAN, LAWRENCE J. *A Study of the Relationships Between Four Tests of Intelligence and One Test of Scholastic Achievement.* Doctor's thesis, State University of South Dakota (Vermillion, S.D.), 1963. (*DA* 24:4555)
41. BIBB, JOHN JAMES, JR. *A Study of the Quick Test as a Screening Instrument for Educable Mentally Retarded Children.* Doctor's thesis, University of Virginia (Charlottesville, Va.), 1964. (*DA* 25:3386) (Abstract: *Ed R* 2:69-71)
42. MARLEY, ALBERT D. *A Validity Study of the Columbia Mental Maturity Scale and the Peabody Picture Vocabulary Test, Using the Wechsler Intelligence Scale for Children as the Validating Criterion, With a Selected Sample of Educable Mentally Retarded Children.* Doctor's research study No. 1, Colorado State College (Greeley, Colo.), 1964. (*DA* 25:5386)
43. TUTTLE, LESTER EUGENE, JR. *The Comparative Effect on Intelligence Test Scores of Negro and White Children When Certain Verbal and Time Factors Are Varied.* Doctor's thesis, University of Florida (Gainesville, Fla.), 1964. (*DA* 25:7093)
44. BRENGELMANN, JOHANNES C., AND HILLMAN, WILLIAM A., JR. "Determinants of Learning in the Retardate: A Pilot Study." *Training Sch B* 61:156-62 F '65. * (*PA* 39:10570)
45. BRENGELMANN, JOHANNES C., AND HILLMAN, WILLIAM A., JR. "Perceptual and Conceptual Response Time Effects in the Retardate." *Training Sch B* 62:57-65 Ag '65. * (*PA* 40:713)
46. CORWIN, BETTY JANE. "The Influence of Culture and Language on Performance of Individual Ability Tests." *J Sch Psychol* 3:41-7 sp '65. * (*PA* 39:15217)
47. BRENGELMANN, JOHANNES C., AND HILLMAN, WILLIAM A., JR. "Response Time to Passed and Failed Problems in the Retardate." *Training Sch B* 63:128-35 N '66. * (*PA* 41:3230)
48. BRUNJE, JOHN. *Suitability of the Revised Columbia Mental Maturity Scale for Use With Educable Mentally Retarded Children.* Master's thesis, Fresno State College (Fresno, Calif.), 1966.
49. HIRSCHENFANG, SAMUEL; JARAMILLO, SELENE; AND BENTON, JOSEPH G. "Comparison of Scores on the Revised Stanford-Binet (L), Columbia Mental Maturity Scale (CMMS) and Goodenough Draw-A-Man Test of Children With Neurological Disorders." *Psychol Rep* 19:15-6 Ag '66. * (*PA* 40:12564)
50. ROBINSON, H. ALAN. "Reliability of Measures Related to Reading Success of Average, Disadvantaged, and Advantaged Kindergarten Children." Comments by Samuel Weintraub. *Read Teach* 20:203-9 D '66. * (*PA* 41:3344)
51. ROSENBERG, LEON A., AND STROUD, MICHAEL. "Limitations of Brief Intelligence Testing With Young Children." *Psychol Rep* 19:721-2 D '66. * (*PA* 41:4999)
52. TUTTLE, LESTER EUGENE, JR. "The Comparative Effect on Intelligence Test Scores of Negro and Caucasian Children When Certain Verbal and Time Factors Are Varied by Use of the WISC, PPVT and CMMS." *Fla J Ed Res* 8:49-61 Ja '66. *
53. BUFFMIRE, JUDY A. *A Comparative Study of the Performance of Retarded Children on the Columbia Mental Maturity Scale.* Master's thesis, University of Utah (Salt Lake City, Utah), 1967.
54. MILLER, BILLY. *A Comparison of the Columbia Mental Maturity Scale, the Leiter International Performance Scale, and the Wright Short Form of the Stanford Binet, Form L-M, With the Full Scale Stanford Binet, Form L-M, on a Group of Trainable Retardates.* Master's thesis, Central Missouri State College (Warrensburg, Mo.), 1967.
55. BERMAN, ALLAN. *An Investigation of the Relationship Between Cerebral Dominance and Intelligence.* Doctor's thesis, Louisiana State University (Baton Rouge, La.), 1968. (*DA* 29:3476B)
56. HYMAN, JOANNE R. *A Study of Concept Identification in Elementary School Children Using the Columbia Mental Maturity Scale.* Master's thesis, Kent State University (Kent, Ohio), 1968.
57. LEREA, LOUIS, AND SINCLAIR, JANET K. "A Preliminary Study of Verbal Style Among Normal and Speech Defective Children." *Psychol Rec* 18:75-80 Ja '68. * (*PA* 42:9318)
58. SEKYRA, FRANCIS, III, AND ARNOULT, JOSEPH FRANCIS, III. "Negro Intellectual Assessment With Three Instruments Contrasting Caucasian and Negro Norms." *J Learn Dis* 1:564-9 O '68. * (*PA* 45:2174)
59. STERNLOF, R. E.; PARKER, H. J.; AND MCCOY, J. F. "Relationships Between the Goodenough DAM Test and the Columbia Mental Maturity Test for Negro and White Headstart Children." *Percept & Motor Skills* 27:424-6 O '68. * (*PA* 43:5328)
60. DUNDORE, JAMES M., JR. *A Study of the Relationship Between Scores Earned on the Columbia Mental Maturity Scale and Peabody Picture Vocabulary Test and School Achievement of Culturally Disadvantaged Negro Children.* Master's thesis, Mississippi State University (State College, Miss.), 1969.
61. FREY, JOAN H. *A Study of the Feasibility of Using the Columbia Mental Maturity Scale to Predict School Achievement of Young Deaf Children.* Master's thesis, University of Tennessee (Knoxville, Tenn.), 1969.
62. GIOIOSO, JOSEPH V., AND ADERMAN, MORRIS. "The Combination Test as a Quick Screening Device to Differentiate Levels of Retardation." *Psychol Rep* 25(3):843-8 D '69. * (*PA* 44:18906)
63. GROSS, MORRIS. "Learning Readiness in Two Groups: A Study in 'Cultural Deprivation.'" *Jewish Ed* 39(1):36-48 Ja '69. *
64. NICHOLSON, CHARLES L. "The Use of Four Screening Instruments." *Ann Inter Conf Assn Children Learn Dis* 6:101-7 '69. *
65. VINGOE, FRANK J.; BIRNEY, S. DARYL; AND KORDINAK, S. THOMAS. "Note on Psychological Screening of Preschool Children." *Percept & Motor Skills* 29(2):661-2 O '69. * (*PA* 44:4182)
66. GOLDSTEIN, LEO S.; COLLER, ALAN R.; DILL, JOHN; AND TILIS, HOWARD S. "The Effect of a Special Curriculum for Disadvantaged Children on Test-Retest Reliabilities of Three Standardized Instruments." *J Ed Meas* 7(3):171-4 f '70. * (*PA* 45:4917)
67. NICHOLSON, CHARLES L. "Correlations Among CMMS, PPVT, and RCPM for Cerebral Palsied Children." *Percept & Motor Skills* 30(3):715-8 Je '70. * (*PA* 44:17151)
68. REUTER, JEANETTE, AND MINTZ, JOANNE. "Columbia

Mental Maturity Scale as a Test of Concept Formation."
J Consult & Clin Psychol 34(3):387–93 Je '70. * (*PA* 44:13635)
69. BART, LEONARD EUGENE. *A Comparison of the Effectiveness of Televised and Conventional Administrations of Objective Scales.* Doctor's thesis, St. John's University (Jamaica, N.Y.), 1971. (*DAI* 32:2980B)
70. BERMAN, ALLAN. "The Problem of Assessing Cerebral Dominance and Its Relationship to Intelligence." *Cortex* (Italy) 7(4):372–86 D '71. * (*PA* 49:11336)
71. HOLLINGSWORTH, JACK DAREL. *A Comparison of Motor Ability of Mentally Retarded Children of Specific Mental and Chronological Ages and Normal Children.* Doctor's thesis, University of Georgia (Athens, Ga.), 1971. (*DAI* 32:3760A)
72. JEFFREE, D. M., AND CASHDAN, A. "Severely Subnormal Children and Their Parents: An Experiment in Language Improvement." *Brit J Ed Psychol* 41(2):184–94 Je '71. * (*PA* 47:9728)
73. KANFER, FREDERICK H.; DUERFELDT, PRYSE H.; MARTIN, BARBARA; AND DORSEY, THOMAS E. "Effects of Model Reinforcement, Expectation to Perform, and Task Performance on Model Observation." *J Pers & Social Psychol* 20(2):214–7 N '71. * (*PA* 47:6449)
74. L'ABATE, LUCIANO. "Receptive-Expressive Functions in Kindergarten Children and Adolescents." *Psychol Sch* 8(3):253–9 Jl '71. * (*PA* 47:9699)
75. PARKER, HARRY J.; STERNLOF, RICHARD E.; AND MCCOY, JOHN F. "Objective Versus Individual Mental Ability Tests With Former Head Start Children in the First Grade." *Percept & Motor Skills* 32(1):287–92 F '71. * (*PA* 46:3868)
76. SWIZE, LYDIA MARIE. *The Relationship Between Performance on Piagetian Conservation Tasks and Intelligence and Achievement in Educable Mentally Retarded Children.* Doctor's thesis, University of Northern Colorado (Greeley, Colo.), 1971. (*DAI* 32:3806A)
77. SWIZE, MYRON THEODORE. *Prediction of Piagetian Conservation for Second Grade Mexican-American and Anglo-American Children.* Doctor's thesis, University of Northern Colorado (Greeley, Colo.), 1971. (*DAI* 32:5624A)
78. VANCE, SANDRA B. *A Comparison of the Wechsler Intelligence Scale for Children and the Columbia Mental Maturity Scale With Mental Retardates.* Master's thesis, East Tennessee State University (Johnson City, Tenn.), 1971.

CUMULATIVE NAME INDEX

Aderman, M.: 62
Akel, M.: 26
Allen, R. M.: 16, 19
Alling, R. L.: 8
Arnoult, J. F.: 58
Barratt, E. S.: 5
Bart, L. E.: 69
Benoit, E. P.: 21
Benton, J. G.: 49
Berko, M. J.: 17
Berman, A.: 55, 70
Bibb, J. J.: 41
Birney, S. D.: 65
Bligh, H. F.: 24
Block, Z.: 28
Blum, L. H.: 14–5
Boone, D. R.: 37
Boyd, H. F.: 21
Brengelmann, J. C.: 39, 44–5, 47
Brunje, J.: 48
Buffmire, J. A.: 53
Burgemeister, B. B.: 14–5
Canter, A.: 6
Cashdan, A.: 72
Coller, A. R.: 66
Collier, H. L.: 29
Collins, M. G.: 16
Cooper, J. G.: 13
Corwin, B. J.: 46
Dill, J.: 66
Dorsey, T. E.: 73
Duerfeldt, P. H.: 73
Dundore, J. M.: 60
Dunn, L. M.: 25
Estes, B. W.: 26
Fleming, K.: 33
French, J.: 20
Frey, J. H.: 61
Gallagher, J. J.: 21–2
Gioioso, J. V.: 62
Goldstein, L. S.: 66
Gross, D. G.: 23
Gross, M.: 63
Gusloff, R. F.: 18
Harley, R. K.: 25
Hillman, W. A.: 44–5, 47
Hirschenfang, S.: 30–1, 49
Hiskey, M. S.: *rev*, 6:517
Hollingsworth, J. D.: 71
Hyman, J. R.: 56
Jaramillo, S.: 49
Jeffree, D. M.: 72
Johnson, G. O.: 8
Jones, R. L.: 27
Kanfer, F. H.: 73
Kodman, F.: 26, 34
Kohut, S.: 38
Kordinak, S. T.: 65
L'Abate, L.: 74
Lantz, B.: 9
Lerea, L.: 38, 57
Levinson, B. M.: 28
Lorge, I.: 15
Lorge, I. D.: 14
McCoy, J. F.: 59, 75
Marley, A. D.: 42
Martin, B.: 73
Mascia, G. V.: 35
May, W. T.: 11
Mill, C. R.: 3
Miller, B.: 54
Miller, E.: 2
Mintz, J.: 68
Neely, J. H.: 8
Newland, T. E.: *rev*, 6:517
Nicholson, C. L.: 64, 67
Parker, H. J.: 59, 75
Perry, H. W.: 11
Reuter, J.: 68
Robinson, H. A.: 50
Rosenberg, L. A.: 51
Rosenblum, J.: 4
Rosenfeld, G. B.: 2
Sandler, J.: 19
Sekyra, F.: 58
Shontz, F. C.: 12
Sinclair, J. K.: 57
Smith, B. S.: 32
Sonneman, J. J.: 40
Standen, J. L.: 39
Stephenson, G. R.: 36
Sternlof, R. E.: 59, 75
Strother, C. R.: 1
Stroud, M.: 51
Swize, L. M.: 76
Swize, M. T.: 77
Taylor, E. A.: 10
Tilis, H. S.: 66
Turner, C. J.: 3
Tuttle, L. E.: 43, 52
Vance, S. B.: 78
Vingoe, F. J.: 65
Warren, S. A.: 29
Waters, J. E.: 34
Weintraub, S.: 50
Whipple, C. I.: 34
Witsaman, L. R.: 27
Wolf, R.: 9
Worcester, D. A.: 20

[490]
Cooperative Preschool Inventory, Revised Edition. Ages 3–6; 1965–70; CPI; achievement in areas necessary for success in school; test booklet title is *Preschool Inventory;* standardized on disadvantaged children; Bettye M. Caldwell; Cooperative Tests and Services. *

For additional information, a review by Joseph L. French, and an excerpted review by Dale Carlson, see 7:404 (5 references).

REFERENCES THROUGH 1971

1–5. See 7:404.
6. SONTAG, MARVIN; SELLA, ADINA P.; AND THORNDIKE, ROBERT L. "The Effect of Head Start Training on the Cognitive Growth of Disadvantaged Children." *J Ed Res* 62(9):387–9 My–Je '69. * (*PA* 46:1899)
7. SLAUGHTER, DIANA T. "Parental Potency and the Achievements of Inner-City Black Children." *Am J Orthopsychiatry* 40(3):433–40 Ap '70. * (*PA* 45:8989)
8. FORMANEK, RUTH, AND WOOG, PIERRE. "Attitudes of Preschool and Elementary School Children to Authority Figures." *Child Study J* 1(2):100–10 w '71. * (*PA* 47:7523)
9. ROBINSON, HALBERT B., AND ROBINSON, NANCY M. "Longitudinal Development of Very Young Children in a Comprehensive Day Care Program: The First Two Years." *Child Develop* 42(6):1673–83 D '71. * (*PA* 48:8827)

CUMULATIVE NAME INDEX

Allerhand, M. E.: 1
Asbury, C. A.: 4
Caldwell, B. M.: 2
Carlson, D.: *exc*, 7:404
Datta, L.: 3
Formanek, R.: 8
French, J. L.: *rev*, 7:404
Hoops, H. R.: 5
Howard, M. J.: 5
McKinnon, A. J.: 5
Robinson, H. B.: 9
Robinson, N. M.: 9
Sella, A. P.: 6
Slaughter, D. T.: 7
Sontag, M.: 6
Thorndike, R. L.: 6
Woog, P.: 8

[491]
Crichton Vocabulary Scale. Ages 4–11; 1950; John C. Raven; H. K. Lewis & Co. Ltd. [England]. *

For additional information and a review by Morton Bortner, see 6:518 (1 reference); for reviews by Charlotte Banks and W. D. Wall, see 4:337.

REFERENCES THROUGH 1971

1. See 6:518.
2. JAHODA, GUSTAV. "Development of the Perception of Social Differences in Children From 6 to 10." *Brit J Psychol* 50:159–75 My '59. * (*PA* 34:2826)
3. PAYNE, J. F. "A Comparative Study of the Mental Ability of Seven- and Eight-Year-Old British and West Indian Children in a West Midland Town." *Brit J Ed Psychol* 39(3):326–7 N '69. *
4. WOOSTER, ARTHUR D. "Social and Ethnic Differences in Understanding the Spoken Word." *Brit J Dis Commun* 5(2):118–25 O '70. *

CUMULATIVE NAME INDEX

Banks, C.: *rev*, 4:337
Bortner, M.: *rev*, 6:518
Jahoda, G.: 2
Payne, J. F.: 3
Ravenette, A. T.: 1
Wall, W. D.: *rev*, 4:337
Wooster, A. D.: 4

[492]
Denver Developmental Screening Test. Ages 2 weeks to 6 years; 1968–70; DDST; 4 scores: gross motor, fine motor-adaptive, language, personal-social; William K. Frankenburg, Josiah B. Dodds, and Alma W. Fandal (manual); Ladoca Project and Publishing Foundation, Inc. *

For additional information and reviews by Alice E. Moriarty and Emmy E. Werner, see 7:405 (6 references).

REFERENCES THROUGH 1971

1–6. See 7:405.
7. "Development Screening Test." *Nursing Mirror & Midwives J* (England) 130(5):27–9 Ja 30 '70. *

Columbia Mental Maturity Scale

8. HILL, BEVERLY E. *Developmental Screening of the Pre-School Child.* Master's thesis, Dominican College (San Rafael, Calif.), 1970.
9. BLACK, ROBERT BEN. *An Investigation of Early Childhood Development as Related to Age and Social Class.* Doctor's thesis, Ohio University (Athens, Ohio), 1971. (*DAI* 32:4934A)
10. FRANKENBURG, WILLIAM K.; CAMP, BONNIE W.; AND VAN NATTA, PEARL A. "Validity of the Denver Developmental Screening Test." *Child Develop* 42(2):475-85 Je '71. * (*PA* 47:596)
11. FRANKENBURG, WILLIAM K.; CAMP, BONNIE W.; VAN NATTA, PEARL A.; DEMERSSEMAN, JOHN A.; AND VOORHEES, SUSAN F. "Reliability and Stability of the Denver Developmental Screening Test." *Child Develop* 42(5):1315-25 N '71. * (*PA* 48:4065)
12. FRANKENBURG, WILLIAM K.; GOLDSTEIN, ARNOLD D.; AND CAMP, BONNIE W. "The Revised Denver Developmental Screening Test: Its Accuracy as a Screening Instrument." *J Pediatrics* 79(6):988-95 D '71. *

CUMULATIVE NAME INDEX

Black, R. B.: 9
Camp, B. W.: 10-2
Desmersseman, J. A.: 11
Dodds, J. B.: 1
Frankenburg, W. K.: 1, 3, 10-2
Goldstein, A. D.: 12
Hill, B. E.: 8
Koupernik, C.: 2
Moriarty, A. E.: *rev,* 7:405
Ratner, G.: 5
Robischon, P.: 4
Sandler, L.: 5
Smith, J. H.: 6
Stafford, C.: 5
VanCampen, J.: 5
Van Natta, P. A.: 10-1
Voorhees, S. F.: 11
Weismar, R.: 5
Werner, E. E.: *rev,* 7:405

[493]

Detroit Tests of Learning Aptitude. Ages 3 and over; 1935-68; DTLA; 20 scores: pictorial absurdities, verbal absurdities, pictorial opposites, verbal opposites, motor speed and precision, auditory attention span (for unrelated words, for related syllables), oral commissions, social adjustment A, visual attention span (for objects, for letters), orientation, free association, memory for designs, number ability, social adjustment B, broken pictures, oral directions, likenesses and differences, total; Harry J. Baker and Bernice Leland; Bobbs-Merrill Co., Inc. *

For additional information, see 7:406 (10 references); for a review by F. L. Wells, see 3:275 (1 reference); for reviews by Anne Anastasi and Henry Feinberg and an excerpted review by D. A. Worcester (with S. M. Corey) of an earlier edition, see 1:1058.

REFERENCES THROUGH 1971

1. See 3:275.
2-11. See 7:406.
12. ENGELHARDT, GEORGE MICHAEL. *Predicting Rehabilitation of Socially Maladjusted Boys From the Detroit Tests of Learning Aptitude.* Doctor's thesis, Wayne State University (Detroit, Mich.), 1969. (*DAI* 32:6191A)
13. FALK, LIBBY JANET. *A Profile of Learning Abilities and Behavioral Characteristics of Elementary School-Age Children With Phenylketonuria.* Doctor's thesis, Temple University (Philadelphia, Pa.), 1971. (*DAI* 32:1913A)
14. MYKLEBUST, HELMER R.; BANNOCHIE, MARGARET N.; AND KILLEN, JAMES R. Chap. 9, "Learning Disabilities and Cognitive Processes," pp. 213-51. In *Progress in Learning Disabilities, Vol. 2.* Edited by Helmer R. Myklebust. New York: Grune & Stratton, Inc., 1971. Pp. ix, 404. *

CUMULATIVE NAME INDEX

Anastasi, A.: *rev,* 1:1058
Ashlock, P.: 4
Ashlock, P. R.: 2
Banas, N.: 8
Bannochie, M. N.: 14
Bruininks, R. H.: 9
Charry, L. B.: 5
Chiappone, A. D.: 7
Corey, S. M.: 1; *exc,* 1:1058
Engelhardt, G. M.: 11-2
Falk, L. J.: 13
Feinberg, H.: *rev,* 1:1058
Hudson, F. G.: 10
Killen, J. R.: 14
Myklebust, H. R.: 14
Nelson, C. M.: 10
Sandstedt, B.: 3
Wartenberg, H.: 6
Wells, F. L.: *rev,* 3:275
Wills, I. H.: 8
Worcester, D. A.: 1; *exc,* 1:1058

[494]

A Developmental Screening Inventory. Ages 1-18 months; 1966; DSI; test consists of selected items from *Gesell Developmental Schedules;* abnormal development; history and observation ratings in 5 areas: adaptive, gross motor, fine motor, language, personal-social; Hilda Knobloch, Benjamin Pasamanick, and Earl S. Sherard, Jr.; Hilda Knobloch. *

For additional information, see 7:407 (1 reference).

REFERENCES THROUGH 1971

1. See 7:407.
2. KNOBLOCH, HILDA, AND PASAMANICK, BENJAMIN. "A Developmental Questionnaire for Infants Forty Weeks of Age: An Evaluation." *Monogr Soc Res Child Develop* 20(2):1-112 '55. * (*PA* 31:673)
3. KNOBLOCH, HILDA; RIDER, ROWLAND; PASAMANICK, BENJAMIN; AND HARPER, PAUL. "An Evaluation of a Questionnaire on Infant Development." *Am J Pub Health* 45:1309-20 O '55. * (*PA* 30:8137)

CUMULATIVE NAME INDEX

Harper, P.: 3
Knobloch, H.: 1-3
Pasamanick, B.: 1-3
Rider, R.: 3
Sherard, E. S.: 1

[495]

***English Picture Vocabulary Test.** Ages 5-8, 7-11, 11 and over; 1962-68; EPVT; derived from *Peabody Picture Vocabulary Test;* 3 levels; M. A. Brimer and Lloyd M. Dunn; Educational Evaluation Enterprises [England]. *

a) TEST 1. Ages 5-8; 1962-66.
b) TEST 2. Ages 7-11; 1962-66.
c) TEST 3. Ages 11 and over; 1968.

For additional information and a review by Kenneth Lovell of Tests 1-2, see 7:408 (5 references); for reviews by L. B. Birch and Philip M. Levy, see 6:520.

REFERENCES THROUGH 1971

1-5. See 7:408.
6. WOOSTER, ARTHUR D. "Social and Ethnic Differences in Understanding the Spoken Word." *Brit J Dis Commun* 5(2):118-25 O '70. *
7. CHEYNE, WILLIAM M., AND JAHODA, GUSTAV. "Emotional Sensitivity and Intelligence in Children From Orphanages and Normal Homes." *J Child Psychol & Psychiatry* (England) 12(2):77-90 Je '71. * (*PA* 47:4505)
8. CONRAD, R. "The Chronology of the Development of Covert Speech in Children." *Develop Psychol* 5(3):398-405 N '71. * (*PA* 47:4506)
9. CREED, C. D., AND ROBINSON, W. P. "Intelligence Test Scores in the Evaluation of a 'Use of Language' Programme for Infant School Children." *Res Ed* (England) 6:1-11 N '71. * (*PA* 48:12239)

CUMULATIVE NAME INDEX

Bannon, W. J.: 2
Birch, L. B.: *rev,* 6:520
Brimer, M. A.: 3
Cheyne, W. M.: 7
Conrad, R.: 8
Creed, C. D.: 9
Horne, I. E.: 4
Jahoda, G.: 7
Levy, P. M.: *rev,* 6:520
Lovell, K.: *rev,* 7:408
Marshall, A.: 1
O'Kelly, E.: 5
Phillips, C. J.: 2
Robinson, W. P.: 9
Wedell, K.: 4
Wooster, A. D.: 6

[496]

Full-Range Picture Vocabulary Test. Ages 2 and over; 1948; Robert B. Ammons and Helen S. Ammons; Psychological Test Specialists. *

For additional information, see 6:521 (30 references); for reviews by William D. Altus and William M. Cruickshank, see 4:340 (10 references).

REFERENCES THROUGH 1971

1-10. See 4:340.
11-40. See 6:521.
41. JENSEN, MILTON B., AND SCHMID, JOHN. "An Analysis of Some Clinical Judgments on Male Basic Airmen Who Failed the Group Psychological Tests." *J Clin Psychol* 10:325-32 O '54. * (*PA* 29:4753)
42. STEPHENSON, GEORGE ROTHWELL. *Form Perception, Abstract Thinking and Intelligence Test Validity in Cerebral Palsy.* Doctor's thesis, Columbia University (New York, N.Y.), 1957. (*DA* 17:1600)
43. TIKOFSKY, RONALD SHERWOOD. *An Investigation of Some Possible Relationships Between Neurologic and Psychologic Techniques in the Study of Aphasia.* Doctor's thesis, University of Utah (Salt Lake City, Utah), 1957. (*DA* 18:1903)
44. WINTHROP, HENRY. "Scoring, Validation, and Construction Problems in the Picture Recognition Type of Vocabulary Test." *J General Psychol* 56:269-79 Ap '57. * (*PA* 33:11039)
45. YOUNG, CECIL, AND MCCONNELL, FREEMAN. "Retardation

of Vocabulary Development in Hard of Hearing Children." *Excep Children* 23:368–70 My '57. * (*PA* 33:4509)

46. INGLIS, JAMES. "Learning, Retention, and Conceptual Usage in Elderly Patients With Memory Disorder." *J Abn & Social Psychol* 59:210–5 S '59. * (*PA* 34:3317)

47. WINITZ, HARRIS. "Language Skills of Male and Female Kindergarten Children." *J Speech & Hearing Res* 2:377–86 D '59. * (*PA* 34:5895)

48. WINTHROP, HENRY. "Relative Variability With Visually Mediated Vocabulary Among the Retarded." *Psychol Rep* 5:318 Je '59. * (*PA* 34:3186)

49. DOEHRING, DONALD G., AND ROSENSTEIN, JOSEPH. "Visual Word Recognition by Deaf and Hearing Children." *J Speech & Hearing Res* 3:320–6 D '60. * (*PA* 35:2488)

50. SCHUELL, HILDRED; JENKINS, JAMES; AND LANDIS, LYDIA. "Relationship Between Auditory Comprehension and Word Frequency in Aphasia." *J Speech & Hearing Res* 4:30–6 Mr '61. * (*PA* 35:6801)

51. SPRAGUE, ANN LEE. *The Relationship Between Selected Measures of Expressive Language and Motor Skill in Eight-Year-Old Boys.* Doctor's thesis, State University of Iowa (Iowa City, Iowa), 1961. (*DA* 21:3696)

52. OHLSEN, ROBERT L., JR. *The Effects of Concretion and Abstraction on Vocabulary Performance of Mentally Retarded, Average and Bright Children.* Doctor's thesis, University of Kansas (Lawrence, Kan.), 1963. (*DA* 25:1664)

53. GROSSBERG, JOHN M. "A Comparison of the Full-Range Picture Vocabulary Test and WISC in Clinical Use." Abstract. *J Consult Psychol* 28:188 Ap '64. * (*PA* 39:1732, title only)

54. JACKSON, CECIL LEE. *Factor Structure of the Wechsler Intelligence Scale for Children and Selected Reference Tests at Pre-School Level and After First Grade: A Longitudinal Study.* Doctor's thesis, University of Georgia (Athens, Ga.), 1964. (*DA* 25:6052)

55. RUGG, ROGER H. *A Comparison of the Relative Effectiveness of the Peabody Picture Vocabulary Test and the Ammons Full Range Picture Vocabulary Test With Educable Mentally Retarded Children.* Master's thesis, Sacramento State College (Sacramento, Calif.), 1964.

56. STERNE, DAVID M. "Use of a Picture Vocabulary in Evaluating Comprehension in Residual Aphasia After CVA." *J Clin Psychol* 20:357–9 Jl '64. * (*PA* 39:10543)

57. HEDGER, MABLE F. Chap. 3, "An Analysis of Three Picture Vocabulary Tests for Use With the Deaf," pp. 12–9. In *Research Studies on the Psycholinguistic Behavior of Deaf Children.* Edited by Joseph Rosenstein and Walter H. MacGinitie. CEC Research Monograph, Series B, No. B-2. Washington, D.C.: Council for Exceptional Children, 1965. Pp. v, 40. *

58. KIMBRELL, DON L. "Comparison of PPVT, FRPVT, RS-B, and Academic Achievement Scores Among Institutionalized Educable Mental Retardates." *Percept & Motor Skills* 23:1178 D '66. * (*PA* 41:6185)

59. LINDSEY, JAMES MORRISON. *The Factorial Organization of Intelligence in Children as Related to the Variables of Age, Sex and Subculture.* Doctor's thesis, University of Georgia (Athens, Ga.), 1966. (*DA* 27:3664B)

60. VELLUTINO, FRANK R., AND HOGAN, TERRENCE P. "The Relationship Between the Ammons and WAIS Test Performances of Unselected Psychiatric Subjects." *J Clin Psychol* 22:69–71 Ja '66. * (*PA* 40:4221)

61. COOPER, G. DAVID; YORK, MICHAEL W.; DASTON, PAUL G.; AND ADAMS, HENRY B. "The Porteus Test and Various Measures of Intelligence With Southern Negro Adolescents." *Am J Mental Def* 71:787–92 Mr '67. * (*PA* 41:8879)

62. OSBORNE, R. T.; ANDERSON, HARRY E., JR.; AND BASHAW, W. L. "The Stability of the WISC Factor Structure at Three Age Levels." *Multiv Behav Res* 2:443–51 O '67. * (*PA* 42:6388)

63. SILVERSTEIN, A. B., AND HILL, THOMAS VERNON. "Comparability of Three Picture Vocabulary Tests With Retarded School Children." *Training Sch B* 64:58–61 Ag '67. * (*PA* 42:1057)

64. SYDIAHA, DANIEL. "Prediction of WAIS IQ for Psychiatric Patients Using the Ammons' FRPV and Raven's Progressive Matrices." *Psychol Rep* 20:823–6 Je '67. * (*PA* 41:13602)

65. DICKINSON, THOMAS C.; NEUBERT, JOAN; AND MCDERMOTT, DOROTHY. "Relationship of Scores on the Full-Range Picture Vocabulary Test and the Wechsler Adult Intelligence Scale in a Vocational Rehabilitation Setting." *Psychol Rep* 23:1263–6 D '68. * (*PA* 43:8448)

66. FINE, MARVIN J., AND TRACY, D. B. "Performance of Normal and EMR Boys on the FRPV and GHDT." *Am J Mental Def* 72:648–52 Mr '68. * (*PA* 42:11049)

67. CARDONE, SAMUEL S., AND OLSON, RONALD E. "Chlorpromazine and Body Image: Effects on Chronic Schizophrenics." *Arch Gen Psychiatry* 20(5):576–82 My '69. * (*PA* 43:16118)

68. FRANK, HARRY, AND FIEDLER, EDNA R. "A Multifactor Behavioral Approach to the Genetic-Etiological Diagnosis of Mental Retardation." *Multiv Behav Res* 4(2):131–45 Ap '69. * (*PA* 43:16258)

69. GIOIOSO, JOSEPH V., AND ADERMAN, MORRIS. "The Combination Test as a Quick Screening Device to Differentiate Levels of Retardation." *Psychol Rep* 25(3):843–8 D '69. * (*PA* 44:18906)

70. HOGAN, TERRENCE P. "Relationship Between the Ammons IQ Norms and WAIS Test Performances of Psychiatric Subjects." *J Clin Psychol* 25(3):275–6 Jl '69. * (*PA* 44:3679)

71. MARKIDES, M. "The Speech of Deaf and Partially-Hearing Children With Special Reference to Factors Affecting Intelligibility." *Brit J Dis Commun* 5(2):126–40 O '70. * (*PA* 46:7484)

72. GRANICK, SAMUEL. "Brief Tests and Their Interrelations as Intelligence Measures of Aged Subjects." Abstract. *Proc 79th Ann Conv Am Psychol Assn* 6(2):599–600 '71. * (*PA* 46:4727)

73. MOORE, N. I. "Cognitive Styles and the Schizophrenias and Character Disorders." *Percept & Motor Skills* 33(2):475–82 O '71. * (*PA* 47:7200)

CUMULATIVE NAME INDEX

Adams, H. B.: 61
Aderman, M.: 69
Aguero, A.: 5
Allen, R. M.: 14, 18–9, 22
Altus, W. D.: rev, 4:340
Ammons, H. S.: 1
Ammons, R. B.: 1–3, 5–9, 13
Anderson, H. E.: 62
Arnold, P. R.: 6
Attwell, A. A.: 36
Bashaw, W. L.: 62
Bensberg, G. J.: 16
Black, A. D.: 24
Blatt, S. J.: 25
Burgin, J.: 40
Cardone, S. S.: 67
Carroll, J. B.: 37
Carson, A. S.: 29
Collins, M. G.: 18
Condell, J. F.: 26
Cooper, G. D.: 61
Coppinger, N. W.: 4, 13
Cruickshank, W. M.: rev, 4:340
Daston, P. G.: 61
Dickinson, T. C.: 65
Dingman, H. F.: 36
Doehring, D. G.: 49
Dunn, L. M.: 27
Ehrmann, L. C.: 20
Fiedler, E. R.: 68
Fillmore, A. R.: 17
Fine, M. J.: 66
Fisher, G. M.: 30
Frank, H.: 68
Gioioso, J. V.: 69
Granick, S.: 72
Grinder, R. E.: 24
Grossberg, J. M.: 53
Harley, R. K.: 27
Hedger, M. F.: 57
Hermann, R. S.: 6
Hill, T. V.: 63
Ho, D.: 38
Hogan, T. P.: 60, 70
Holden, R. H.: 10
Holmes, J. C.: 2
Huth, R. W.: 3
Inglis, J.: 46
Jackson, C. L.: 54
James, P.: 39
Jenkins, J.: 50
Jenkins, J. J.: 37
Jensen, M. B.: 41
Katz, I. S.: 11
Kimbrell, D. L.: 58
King, G. F.: 20
Kobler, F. J.: 15
Landis, L.: 50
Larson, W. L.: 7
Lindsey, J. M.: 59
McConnell, F.: 45
McDermott, D.: 65
Manahan, N.: 8
Markides, M.: 71
Mead, D. F.: 32
Meyers, E.: 36
Moed, G.: 39
Moore, N. I.: 73
Morgan, E. F.: 31
Neubert, J.: 65
Norman, R. D.: 32
Ohlsen, R. L.: 52
Olson, R. E.: 67
Orpet, R. E.: 36
Osborne, R. T.: 62
Rabin, A. I.: 20, 29
Rachiele, L. D.: 9
Richardson, E. J.: 15
Rosenstein, J.: 49
Rugg, R. H.: 55
Sanders, C. C.: 21
Schmid, J.: 41
Schuell, H.: 37, 50
Scoggins, B. J.: 33
Shearn, C. R.: 7
Shotwell, A. M.: 30
Silverstein, A. B.: 63
Simkins, L.: 40
Sloan, W.: 16
Smith, B. S.: 35
Smith, L. M.: 17
Sprague, A. L.: 51
Stenger, C. A.: 14, 19, 22
Stephenson, G. R.: 42
Sterne, D. M.: 34, 56
Sydiaha, D.: 64
Templin, M. C.: 23
Thornton, T. E.: 14, 19, 22
Tikofsky, R. S.: 43
Tracy, D. B.: 66
Tucker, D. A.: 12
Vellutino, F. R.: 60
White, D. T.: 38
Wight, B. W.: 39
Winitz, H.: 28, 47
Winthrop, H.: 44, 48
York, D. H.: 30
York, M. W.: 61
Young, C.: 45

[497]

Gesell Developmental Schedules, 1940 Series. Ages 4 weeks to 6 years; 1925–49; GDS; Arnold Gesell and others; Psychological Corporation. *

For additional information and a review by Emmy E. Werner, see 6:522 (27 references); see also 4:341 (5 references); for reviews by Nancy Bayley and Florence M. Teagarden, see 3:276 (28 references). For excerpts from related book reviews, see 3:277 (11 excerpts), 3:278 (4 excerpts), 3:279 (8 excerpts), 3:280 (1 excerpt), 2:B912 (3 excerpts), 2:B913 (13 excerpts), 2:B914 (6 excerpts), 2:B915 (8 excerpts), and 2:B916 (15 excerpts).

REFERENCES THROUGH 1971

1–28. See 3:276.
29–33. See 4:341.
34–60. See 6:522.

61. GESELL, ARNOLD, AND LORD, ELIZABETH EVANS. "A Psychological Comparison of Nursery School Children From Homes

of Low and High Economic Status." *J Genetic Psychol* 34:339–56 S '27. * (*PA* 2:751)
62. GESELL, ARNOLD L. "Developmental Diagnosis of Infant and Child: Its Role in Clinical Medicine." *Post Grad Med J* (England) 1:29–35 Ja '47. * (*PA* 21:4408)
63. BERKO, MARTIN J. "Measurement of Behavioral Development in Cerebral Palsy." *Cereb Palsy R* 15:16–7 Je–Jl '54. * (*PA* 29:6688)
64. APGAR, VIRGINIA; GIRDANY, B. R.; MCINTOSH, R.; AND TAYLOR, H. C., JR. "Neonatal Anoxia: 1, A Study of the Relation of Oxygenation at Birth to Intellectual Development." *Pediatrics* 15:653–62 Je '55. *
65. DU PAN, R. MARTIN, AND ROTH, S. "The Psychologic Development of a Group of Children Brought Up in a Hospital Type Residential Nursery." *J Pediatrics* 47:124–9 Jl '55. * (*PA* 30:4251)
66. KNOBLOCH, HILDA, AND PASAMANICK, BENJAMIN. "A Developmental Questionnaire for Infants Forty Weeks of Age: An Evaluation." *Monogr Soc Res Child Develop* 20(2):1–112 '55. * (*PA* 31:673)
67. KNOBLOCH, HILDA; RIDER, ROWLAND; PASAMANICK, BENJAMIN; AND HARPER, PAUL. "An Evaluation of a Questionnaire on Infant Development." *Am J Pub Health* 45:1309–20 O '55. * (*PA* 30:8137)
68. FISH, BARBARA. "The Detection of Schizophrenia in Infancy: A Preliminary Report." *J Nerv & Mental Dis* 125:1–24 Ja–Mr '57. * (*PA* 33:4353)
69. GEBER, MARCELLE, AND DEAN, R. F. A. "Gesell Tests on African Children." *Pediatrics* 20:1055–65 D '57. *
70. KNOBLOCH, HILDA, AND PASAMANICK, BENJAMIN. "The Relationship of Race and Socioeconomic Status to the Development of Motor Behavior Patterns in Infants." *Psychiatric Res Rep* 10:123–33 D '58. * (*PA* 35:1971)
71. KNOBLOCH, HILDA, AND PASAMANICK, BENJAMIN. "Environmental Factors Affecting Human Development, Before and After Birth." *Pediatrics* 26:210–8 Ag '60. *
72. WIEMERS, IRENE HOLLINGSWORTH. *Evaluating Adequacy of Adjustment in Normal Infants.* Doctor's thesis, University of Utah (Salt Lake City, Utah), 1960. (*DA* 21:2791)
73. PELZ, KURT; PIKE, FRANCES; AND AMES, LOUISE B. "A Proposed Battery of Childhood Tests for Discriminating Between Different Levels of Intactness of Function in Elderly Subjects." *J Genetic Psychol* 100:23–40 Mr '62. * (*PA* 37:975)
74. WOODWARD, MARY, AND STERN, DIANA J. "Developmental Patterns of Severely Subnormal Children." *Brit J Ed Psychol* 33:10–21 F '63. * (*PA* 38:673)
75. AMES, LOUISE B., AND ILG, FRANCES L. "Sex Differences in Test Performance of Matched Girl-Boy Pairs in the Five-to-Nine-Year-Old Age Range." *J Genetic Psychol* 104:25–34 Mr '64. * (*PA* 39:4582)
76. FISHLER, KAROL; SHARE, JACK; AND KOCH, RICHARD. "Adaptation of the Gesell Developmental Scales for Evaluation of Development in Children With Down's Syndrome (Mongolism)." *Am J Mental Def* 68:642–6 Mr '64. *
77. SHARE, JACK; KOCH, RICHARD; WEBB, ALLEN; AND GRALIKER, BETTY. "The Longitudinal Development of Infants and Young Children With Downs Syndrome (Mongolism)." *Am J Mental Def* 68:689–92 My '64. * (*PA* 39:2533)
78. STECHLER, GERALD. "A Longitudinal Follow-Up of Neonatal Apnea." *Child Develop* 35:333–48 Je '64. * (*PA* 39:4520)
79. DONOFRIO, A. F. "Clinical Value of Infant Testing." *Percept & Motor Skills* 21:571–4 O '65. * (*PA* 40:2973)
80. FISHLER, KAROL; GRALIKER, BETTY V.; AND KOCH, RICHARD. "The Predictability of Intelligence with Gesell Developmental Scales in Mentally Retarded Infants and Young Children." *Am J Mental Def* 69:515–25 Ja '65. * (*PA* 39:9821)
81. WALTERS, C. ETTA. "Prediction of Postnatal Development From Fetal Activity." *Child Develop* 36:801–8 Je '65. * (*PA* 39:14616)
82. DICKS-MIREAUX, MARIE-JOSÉ. "Development of Intelligence of Children With Down's Syndrome: Preliminary Report." *J Mental Def Res* (England) 10:89–93 Je '66. * (*PA* 41:1827)
83. FISHLER, KAROL; KOCH, RICHARD; DONNELL, GEORGE; AND GRALIKER, BETTY V. "Psychological Correlates in Galactosemia." *Am J Mental Def* 71:116–25 Jl '66. * (*PA* 40:11430)
84. GERSON, ELAINE F., AND SCOTT, ROLAND B. "Growth and Development of Negro Infants: 7, The Relationship of Parental Attitudes and Socioeconomic Pressures to Intelligence and Gross Motor Quotients During the Second Year of Life." *Med Ann DC* 35:5–8 Ja '66. *
85. KNOBLOCH, HILDA; PASAMANICK, BENJAMIN; AND SHERARD, EARL S., JR. "A Developmental Screening Inventory for Infants." *Pediatrics* 38(sup):1095–108 D '66. *
86. STOTT, LELAND H., AND BALL, RACHEL STUTSMAN. *Infant and Preschool Mental Tests: Review and Evaluation.* Monographs of the Society for Research in Child Development, Vol. 30, No. 3, Serial No. 101. Chicago, Ill.: University of Chicago Press, 1966. Pp. iv, 151. * (*PA* 40:7220)
87. AMES, LOUISE B. "Predictive Value of Infant Behavior Examinations," pp. 207–39. In *Exceptional Infant: The Normal Infant*, Vol. 1. Edited by Jerome Hellmuth. Seattle, Wash.: Special Child Publications, 1967. Pp. 568. *
88. FULLER, RENEE. "Psychological Results in Treated Phenylketonuria: 1, Gesell Findings." *Proc Am Psychopath Assn* 56:153–80, 190–2 '67. *
89. KNOBLOCH, HILDA, AND PASAMANICK, BENJAMIN. "Prediction From the Assessment of Neuromotor and Intellectual Status in Infancy." *Proc Am Psychopath Assn* 56:387–400 '67. *
90. LINDE, LEONARD M.; RASOF, BEATRICE; AND DUNN, OLIVE JEAN. "Mental Development in Congenital Heart Disease." *J Pediatrics* 71:198–203 Ag '67. *
91. RASOF, BEATRICE; LINDE, LEONARD M.; AND DUNN, OLIVE JEAN. "Intellectual Development in Children With Congenital Heart Disease." *Child Develop* 38:1043–53 D '67. * (*PA* 42:7687)
92. WALTERS, C. ETTA. "Comparative Development of Negro and White Infants." *J Genetic Psychol* 110:243–51 Je '67. * (*PA* 41:11696)
93. ROE, KIKI VLACHOULI. *A Longitudinal Study of Infant Vocalizations.* Doctor's thesis, University of California (Los Angeles, Calif.), 1968. (*DA* 29:3472B)
94. AYRES, A. JEAN. "Relation Between Gesell Developmental Quotients and Later Perceptual-Motor Performance." *Am J Occup Ther* 23(1):11–7 Ja–F '69. * (*PA* 44:439)
95. DALES, RUTH J. "Motor and Language Development of Twins During the First Three Years." *J Genetic Psychol* 114(2):263–71 Je '69. * (*PA* 43:17029)
96. LEVESQUE, CLAIRE E. *The Correlation Between the Gesell Developmental Examination and Four Common Ability Tests.* Master's thesis, Southern Connecticut State College (New Haven, Conn.), 1969.
97. MURALIDHARAN, RAJALAKSHMI. "Developmental Norms of Children Aged 2½–5 Years: A Pilot Study." *Indian Ed R* 4(1):67–91 Ja '69. * (*PA* 46:840)
98. BAYLEY, NANCY. Chap. 16, "Development of Mental Abilities," pp. 1163–209. In *Carmichael's Manual of Child Psychology*, Third Edition, Vol. 1. Edited by Paul H. Mussen. New York: John Wiley & Sons, Inc., 1970. Pp. xiii, 1519. *
99. CRANDALL, VIRGINIA C., AND BATTLE, ESTHER S. "The Antecedents and Adult Correlates of Academic and Intellectual Achievement." *Minn Symposia Child Psychol* 4:36–93 '70. *
100. DEMPSEY, MARIA PETRA. *A Comparative Study of the Developmental Quotients of the 30–36-Months-Old Negro and Indian Child as Measured by the Gesell Schedules.* Doctor's thesis, Florida State University (Tallahassee, Fla.), 1970. (*DAI* 31:5660A)
101. HELSETH, BETTY J. *A Comparative Study of Intelligence and Maturity as Measured by the Gesell Developmental Placement Test and Other Selected Tests.* Master's thesis, Pacific Lutheran University (Tacoma, Wash.), 1970.
102. PARMELEE, ARTHUR H., JR., AND SCHULTE, FRANZ J. "Developmental Testing of Pre-Term and Small-for-Date Infants." *Pediatrics* 45(1):21–8 Ja '70. *
103. BARBER, LUCIE W. "Effect of an Infancy Curriculum on Motor and Personal-Social Behaviors." *Char Potential* 5(3):128–47 F '71. * (*PA* 45:7837)
104. BARBER, LUCIE W. "Language Development in Infants Enrolled in the Infancy Design." *Char Potential* 5(3):118–28 F '71. * (*PA* 45:7838)
105. BECKWITH, LEILA. "Relationships Between Attributes of Mothers and Their Infants' IQ Scores." *Child Develop* 42(4):1083–97 O '71. * (*PA* 48:2692)
106. COLLARD, ROBERTA R. "Exploratory and Play Behaviors of Infants Reared Apart in an Institution and in Foster and Middle-Class Homes." *Child Develop* 42(4):1003–15 O '71. * (*PA* 48:2709)
107. GRANTHAM-MCGREGOR, SALLY M., AND HAWKE, W. A. "Development Assessment of Jamaican Infants." *Develop Med & Child Neurol* (England) 13(5):582–9 O '71. *
108. POPOVICS, ALEXANDER J. *A Comparison of the Effectiveness of Actuarial and Clinical Scoring of the Gesell Incomplete Man Test as a Predictor of School Success.* Master's thesis, Southern Connecticut State College (New Haven, Conn.), 1971.

CUMULATIVE NAME INDEX

Adams, D. K.: *exc*, 2:B913, 2:B916
Aldrich, C. G.: 6
Allen, R. M.: 42
Amatruda, C. S.: 11, 13, 17, 20, 22, 31
Ames, L. B.: 20, 23–7, 34, 54, 57, 73, 75, 87
Anderson, J. E.: *exc*, 2:B912
Anderson, L. D.: 16
Apgar, V.: 64
Astrachan, M. A.: 40
Ayres, A. J.: 94
Ball, R. S.: 86
Barber, L. W.: 103–4
Bartelme, P.: 8
Bass, L. G.: 39
Battle, E. S.: 99
Bayley, N.: 98; *rev*, 3:276; *exc*, 2:B913, 2:B916
Beckwith, L.: 105
Berko, M. J.: 63
Bolt, R. A.: *exc*, 3:B279

Brown, C. W.: 8
Castner, B. M.: 17, 20
Coghill, G. E.: *exc*, 2:B912
Collard, R. R.: 106
Cox, G. M.: 8
Crandall, V. C.: 99
Curti, M.: *exc*, 2:B915
Curti, M. W.: 12
Dales, R. J.: 95
Dean, R. F. A.: 69
DeGooyer, M. W.: 40
Dempsey, M. P.: 100
Dicks-Mireaux, M. J.: 82
Doll, E. A.: 6; *exc*, 3:277
Dolly, A.: 47
Donnell, G.: 83
Donofrio, A. F.: 79
Drillien, C. M.: 45, 50
Dunn, O. J.: 90–1
Du Pan, R. M.: 65
Edwards, A. S.: *exc*, 2:B916
Escalona, S.: 32–3, 51
Firestone, M. H.: *exc*, 3:277

Gesell Developmental Schedules

Fish, B.: 68
Fishler, K.: 76, 80, 83
Foxe, A. N.: exc, 3:277
Fuller, R.: 88
Gardner, D. B.: 43
Gardner, W. H.: exc, 3:277
Geber, M.: 69
Gerson, E. F.: 84
Gerstein, R. A.: 30
Gesell, A.: 1-5, 10-1, 13, 17, 20, 22, 26-7, 31, 34, 36, 61
Gesell, A. L.: 62
Girdany, B. R.: 64
Good, C. V.: exc, 3:277
Goodenough, F. L.: exc, 2:B915
Graliker, B.: 77
Graliker, B. V.: 58, 80, 83
Grant, W. W.: 40
Grantham-McGregor, S. M.: 107
Halverson, H. M.: 20
Harper, P.: 67
Hawke, W. A.: 107
Helseth, B. I.: 101
Henderson, E. M.: 12
Hendrick, I.: exc, 3:B279
Hildreth, G.: exc, 2:B916
Howard, W. H. R.: 44
Hrdlicka, A.: exc, 3:B279
Ilg, F. L.: 20, 24, 34, 57, 75
Illingworth, R. S.: 48, 52
Irwin, O. C.: exc, 2:B914
Janoff, I. Z.: 40
Jenkins, J. W.: exc, 3:B279
Jensen, K.: exc, 2:B916
Kasambi, K.: 29
Knobloch, H.: 44, 49, 56, 66-7, 70-1, 85, 89
Koch, H. L.: exc, 3:277
Koch, R.: 55, 58, 76-7, 80, 83
Koshuk, R. P.: exc, 2:B916
Koza, C.: 59
Kugel, R. B.: 40, 46
Lamm, S. S.: exc, 2:B916
Learned, J.: 34
Leiter, R. G.: exc, 2:B916
Levesque, C. E.: 96
Liddicoat, R.: 59
Linde, L. M.: 90-1
Line, W.: exc, 3:278
Lis, E. F.: 47
Lord, E. E.: 61; exc, 3:278
McIntosh, R.: 64
MacRae, J. M.: 38
Malcove, L.: exc, 2:B916
Marshall, F. B.: 12
Mead, M.: 28
Moriarty, A.: 51
Munn, N. L.: exc, 2:B915
Muralidharan, R.: 97
Myers, B. J.: 40
Nelson, A. K.: exc, 2:B916

Nelson, V.: 21
Nelson, V. L.: 14-5, 18-9
Norman, R. D.: 37
Parmelee, A. H.: 102
Pasamanick, B.: 49, 56, 66-7, 70-1, 85, 89
Pease, D.: 53
Peatman, J. G.: exc, 2:B916
Pelz, K.: 73
Pelz, K. S.: 54
Pike, F.: 54, 73
Popovics, A. J.: 108
Rasof, B.: 90-1
Ribble, M. A.: exc, 2:B916
Rich, G. J.: exc, 2:B916
Richards, T. W.: 14-5, 18-9, 21
Rider, R.: 67
Riess, A.: 40
Roe, K. V.: 93
Rosauer, J. K.: 53
Roth, S.: 65
Ruess, A. L.: 47
Russell, E. C.: 40
Ryan, M. S.: exc, 2:B913
Ryans, D. G.: exc, 2:B914
Sayers, M. P.: 44
Schmidt, A. G.: exc, 2:B914
Schulte, F. J.: 102
Scott, R. B.: 84
Share, J.: 55, 58, 76-7
Sherard, E. S.: 85
Shirley, M.: exc, 2:B913
Sievers, D. J.: 37
Silver, A. A.: 35
Simon, A. J.: 39
Stechler, G.: 78
Steckel, M. L.: 7
Steggerda, M.: 12
Stern, D. J.: 74
Stoddard, G. D.: exc, 2:B915
Stott, L. H.: 86
Swiger, M. K.: 43
Symmes, E. F.: 9
Taylor, H. C.: 64
Teagarden, F. M.: rev, 3:276
Thompson, H.: 11, 13, 17, 20
Valentine, C. W.: exc, 2:B913, 2:B915, 3:B279
Veeder, B. S.: exc, 2:B912
Walters, C. E.: 81, 92
Washburn, A. A.: exc, 3:277
Webb, A.: 55, 58, 77
Welch, L.: exc, 3:278
Werner, E. E.: rev, 6:522
Wiemers, I. H.: 72
Wile, I. S.: exc, 2:B914
Wilson, M. G.: 60
Wilson, M. T.: exc, 3:277
Wittenborn, J. R.: 40
Wolins, L.: 53
Wolk, S. M.: 41
Woodward, M.: 74

[498]
Haptic Intelligence Scale for Adult Blind. Blind and partially sighted adults; 1964; HIS; 7 scores: digit symbol, block design, object assembly, object completion, pattern board, bead arithmetic, total; Harriett C. Shurrager and Phil S. Shurrager; Harriett C. Shurrager. *

For additional information and a review by Marshall S. Hiskey, see 7:409 (9 references).

REFERENCES THROUGH 1971
1-9. See 7:409.
10. MILLER, LAURENCE RICHARD. *A Factor Analytic Study of Cognitive Variables in Congenitally Blind Individuals.* Doctor's thesis, Case Western Reserve University (Cleveland, Ohio), 1970. (DAI 32:248A)

CUMULATIVE NAME INDEX

Alston, P. P.: 9
Avery, C. D.: 7-8
Curtis, W. S.: 6
Dauterman, W. L.: 3
Eber, H. W.: 4
Gallagher, P.: 5
Hiskey, M. S.: rev, 7:409
Kamin, H. S.: 2
Miller, L. R.: 10
Naddeo, C. L.: 6
Porter, T. L.: 9
Saxon, J. P.: 9
Shapiro, B.: 5
Streitfeld, J. W.: 7-8
Suinn, R. M.: 3
Watson, S. B.: 1

[499]
Hiskey-Nebraska Test of Learning Aptitude. Ages 3-17 (deaf and hearing); 1941-66; HNTLA; revision of *Nebraska Test of Learning Aptitude;* Marshall S. Hiskey; the Author. *

For additional information and a review by T. Ernest Newland, see 7:410 (14 references); for a review by William Sloan of an earlier edition, see 5:409 (8 references); for a review by Mildred C. Templin, see 4:353 (1 reference); see also 3:289 (3 references).

REFERENCES THROUGH 1971
1-3. See 3:289.
4. See 4:353.
5-12. See 5:409.
13-26. See 7:410.
27. VASA, STANLEY FRANK. *A Comparison of Selected Intelligence Scales With Bilingual Children.* Doctor's thesis, University of Nebraska (Lincoln, Neb.), 1971. (DAI 32:802A)

CUMULATIVE NAME INDEX

Bach, L. C.: 21
Casjens, C. C.: 17
Davis, K. A.: 8
Gentile, J. R.: 19
Giangreco, C. J.: 18, 20
Hiskey, M. S.: 1-3, 11-2
Howard, J. O.: 25
Kirk, S. A.: 13
Lane, H. S.: 14
Lewis, J. F.: 26
Ludlow, M. E.: 5
MacPherson, J. G.: 6, 14
Mira, M. P.: 16
Morris, B. E. J. VanC.: 22
Morris, G. L.: 23
Newland, T. E.: rev, 7:410
Paul, G. T.: 24
Perry, J.: 13
Perry, J. A.: 7
Ross, G.: 9
Sloan, W.: rev, 5:409
Templin, M. C.: rev, 4:353
Thomure, E.: 4
Varva, F. I.: 15
Vasa, S. F.: 27
Walsh, R.: 10

[500]
The Immediate Test: A Quick Verbal Intelligence Test. Adults; 1951; Raymond J. Corsini; Sheridan Psychological Services, Inc. *

For additional information and reviews by Jerome E. Doppelt and Ivan Norman Mensh, see 4:342 (1 reference).

REFERENCES THROUGH 1971
1. See 4:342.
2. NEWTON, G. MACKIE. "A Comparison of the Immediate Test and WAIS Verbal Scale in Vocational Rehabilitation Use." *J Clin Psychol* 21:300 Jl '65. * (PA 39:15368)
3. CULL, JOHN G., AND HARDY, RICHARD E. "Correlation Between the Immediate Test and the Wechsler Adult Intelligence Scale Verbal Scale in the Rehabilitation Setting." *J Psychol* 77(2):203-5 Mr '71. * (PA 46:1627)

CUMULATIVE NAME INDEX

Corsini, R.: 1
Cull, J. G.: 3
Doppelt, J. E.: rev, 4:342
Hardy, R. E.: 3
Mensh, I. N.: rev, 4:342
Newton, G. M.: 2

[501]
★**Individual Scale for Indian South Africans.** Ages 8-17; 1971; ISISA; adaptation for Indian pupils of the *New South African Individual Scale;* 13 scores: verbal (vocabulary, comprehension, similarities, problems, memory, total), nonverbal (pattern completion, blocks, absurdities, form board, mazes, total), total; R. J. Prinsloo and F. W. O. Heinichen in collaboration with D. J. Swart; Human Sciences Research Council [South Africa]. *

[502]
Kahn Intelligence Tests: Experimental Form. Ages 1 month and over (particularly the verbally or culturally handicapped); 1960; KIT; uses same test objects as *Kahn Test of Symbol Arrangement;* main scale plus 6 optional scales: brief scale, concept formation, recall, motor coordination, scale for use with the deaf, scale for use with the blind; Theodore C. Kahn; Psychological Test Specialists. *

For additional information and a review by Marjorie P. Honzik, see 7:411 (6 references); see also 6:524 (2 references).

Gesell Developmental Schedules

REFERENCES THROUGH 1971

1–2. See 6:524.
3–8. See 7:411.
9. CHAWLA, TILAK R. "Cultural Factors and Kahn Intelligence Test." *Indian Psychol R* 6(2):77–9 Ja '70. * (*PA* 46:9569)

CUMULATIVE NAME INDEX

Carse, W. T.: 4–5
Chawla, T. R.: 9
Chovan, W. L.: 8
Cupp, M. E.: 3
Eppley, E. B.: 6
Fretwell, L. N.: 3
Hathaway, M. L.: 8
Honzik, M. P.: *rev,* 7:411
Kahn, T. C.: 1–2
Kroske, W. H.: 3
McDaniel, E. D.: 4
Roffman, P. O.: 7

[503]

Kent Series of Emergency Scales. Ages 5–7, 6–8, 6.5–10, 9–14; 1932–46; 4 scales; Grace H. Kent; Psychological Corporation. *

a) SCALE A. Ages 5–7; 1944–46; formerly called *Andover School-Entrance Test.*

b) SCALES B AND C. Ages 6–8, 6.5–10; 1946.

c) SCALE D. Ages 9–14; 1932–46; revision of *Emergency Test* (also called *Kent E-G-Y Test*).

For additional information and a review by Ivan Norman Mensh, see 4:346 (8 references); for a review by Charles N. Cofer, see 3:284 (26 references).

REFERENCES THROUGH 1971

1–26. See 3:284.
27–34. See 4:346.
35. TROWBRIDGE, LOWELL; MOORE, MERRILL; AND GRAY, M. GENEVA. "An Estimate of the Intelligence of Alcoholic Patients at the Haymarket Square Relief Station as Related to Chronological Age, Marital Status, and Occupation." *New Engl J Med* 221:59–62 Jl 13 '39. * (*PA* 14:1437)
36. WILSON, M. T. "Detection of Reading Difficulties in a Rural Public School." *Training Sch B* 39:41–6 My '42. * (*PA* 16:3818)
37. ORR, DAVID HAMILTON. *A Field Study of a Psychiatric Aide Applicant Group at a State Mental Hospital.* Doctor's thesis, University of Kentucky (Lexington, Ky.), 1950. (*DA* 18:666)
38. CROWLEY, MIRIAM E. "The Use of the Kent EGY for the Detection of Malingering." *J Clin Psychol* 8:332–7 O '52. * (*PA* 27:5864)
39. DELP, HAROLD A. "Correlations Between the Kent EGY and the Wechsler Batteries." *J Clin Psychol* 9:73–5 Ja '53. * (*PA* 27:7764)
40. MASON, EVELYN P. "Some Correlates of Self-Judgments of the Aged." *J Gerontol* 9:324–37 Jl '54. * (*PA* 29:5429)
41. ROBINOWITZ, RALPH. "Performances of Hospitalized Psychiatric Patients on the Kent Emergency Test and the Wechsler-Bellevue Intelligence Scale." *J Clin Psychol* 12:199–200 Ap '56. * (*PA* 31:4711)
42. GOERTZEN, STAN M. "A Study of Some Aspects of the Kent E.G.Y. Scales." *Calif J Ed Res* 8:140 My '57. *
43. WEST, DORAL N. "Reducing Chance in Test Selection." *Personnel & Guid J* 36:420–1 F '58. * (*PA* 33:6935)
44. GYNTHER, MALCOLM D., AND MAYER, ANNE D. "The Prediction of Mental Deficiency by Means of the Kent-EGY." *Am J Mental Def* 64:988–90 My '60. * (*PA* 35:6834)
45. GUERRANT, JOHN; ANDERSON, WILLIAM W.; FISCHER, AMES; WEINSTEIN, MORTON R.; JAROS, R. MARY; AND DESKINS, ANDREW. Chap. 5, "Psychological Considerations," pp. 66–92. In their *Personality in Epilepsy.* Springfield, Ill.: Charles C Thomas, Publisher, 1962. Pp. xii, 112. *
46. KATZ, LAWRENCE, AND CROOK, HAMILTON. "Use of the Kent E-G-Y With an Aged Population." *J Gerontol* 17:186–9 Ap '62. * (*PA* 37:2953)
47. CLORE, GERALD L., JR. "Kent E-G-Y: Differential Scoring and Correlation With the WAIS." Abstract. *J Consult Psychol* 27:372 Ag '63. * (*PA* 38:2665)
48. CLORE, GERALD L., JR. "The Kent E-G-Y: Differential Scoring and Correlation With the WAIS." *Newsl Res Psychol* 5:9 F '63. *
49. McDONALD, ROBERT L.; GYNTHER, MALCOLM D.; AND CHRISTAKOS, ARTHUR C. "Relations Between Maternal Anxiety and Obstetric Complications." *Psychosom Med* 25:357–63 Jl–Ag '63. * (*PA* 38:9104)
50. NELSON, DON A. "Group vs. Individual Administration of the Kent E-G-Y." *Newsl Res Psychol* 5:12–3 F '63. *
51. GENDEL, HOWARD, AND RICE, WARREN. "Correlation of the Kent EGY With WAIS IQ's and Scaled Scores." *Newsl Res Psychol* 6:43–4 Ag '64. *
52. MEER, BERNARD, AND BAKER, JANET A. "Reliability of Measurements of Intellectual Functioning of Geriatric Patients." *J Gerontol* 20:410–4 Jl '65. *
53. SCHWARTZ, MARK S. "Relationships Between the Kent EGY and WAIS Scores, Functioning Levels and Subtests in a Veterans Neuropsychiatric Population." *Newsl Res Psychol* 7:8–9 My '65. *
54. PIERCE, ROBERT C. Chap. 4, "Intellectual Functioning and Mental Health," pp. 82–100. In *Aging and Mental Disorder in San Francisco: A Social Psychiatric Study.* By Marjorie Fiske Lowenthal, Paul L. Berkman, and Associates. San Francisco, Calif.: Jossey-Bass Inc., Publishers, 1967. Pp. xix, 341. *
55. PIERCE, ROBERT C. Chap. 6, "Intellectual Status Compared," pp. 112–9. In *Aging and Mental Disorder in San Francisco: A Social Psychiatric Study.* By Marjorie Fiske Lowenthal, Paul L. Berkman, and Associates. San Francisco, Calif.: Jossey-Bass Inc., Publishers, 1967. Pp. xix, 341. *
56. PIERCE, ROBERT C., AND BERKMAN, PAUL L. Chap. 11, "Change in Intellectual Functioning," pp. 176–89. In *Aging and Mental Disorder in San Francisco: A Social Psychiatric Study.* By Marjorie Fiske Lowenthal, Paul L. Berkman, and Associates. San Francisco, Calif.: Jossey-Bass Inc., Publishers, 1967. Pp. xix, 341. *
57. DE CASTRO, FERNANDO J.; VAUGHN, KENNETH L.; AND GIBSON, RALPH M. "A Rapid Screening Psychometric Test: Evaluation of the Kent Emergency Scale." *Clin Pediatrics* 8(5):258–62 My '69. *
58. O'CONNOR, PATRICIA A.; SCHWARTZ, EDWARD M.; AND ROKICKI, ROBERT R. "Use of the Kent Scales to Evaluate Development in Children." *Univ Mich Med Center J* 35(4):217–9 O–D '69. *
59. TEMPLER, DONALD I., AND HARTLAGE, LAWRENCE C. "Physicians' I.Q. Estimates and Kent I.Q. Compared With WAIS I.Q." *J Clin Psychol* 25(1):74–5 Ja '69. * (*PA* 43:10025)
60. DE CASTRO, F. J., AND GIBSON, R. M. "Psychometric Screening by Allied Medical Personnel." *Clin Pediatrics* 9(4):192 Ap '70. *
61. MYKLEBUST, HELMER R.; BANNOCHIE, MARGARET N.; AND KILLEN, JAMES R. Chap. 9, "Learning Disabilities and Cognitive Processes," pp. 213–51. In *Progress in Learning Disabilities,* Vol. 2. Edited by Helmer R. Myklebust. New York: Grune & Stratton, Inc., 1971. Pp. ix, 404. *

CUMULATIVE NAME INDEX

Anderson, W. W.: 45
Baker, J. A.: 52
Bannochie, M. N.: 61
Benton, A. L.: 6
Berkman, P. L.: 56
Biegel, M. M.: 29
Bilodeau, I. M.: 34
Bongiovanni, A. M.: 26
Burchard, E. M. L.: 4
Cannicott, R. G.: 31, 34
Christakos, A. C.: 49
Clore, G. L.: 47–8
Cofer, C. N.: 29; *rev,* 3:284
Crook, H.: 46
Crowley, M. E.: 38
Cummings, S. B.: 33
de Castro, F. J.: 57, 60
Delp, H. A.: 39
Demarest, R.: 28
Deskins, A.: 45
Drummond, W. A.: 23
Elwood, M. I.: 4
Fischer, A. M.: 45
Gendel, H.: 51
Gibson, R. M.: 57, 60
Goertzen, S. M.: 42
Gray, M. G.: 35
Greenwood, E. D.: 18
Guerrant, J.: 45
Gynther, M. D.: 44, 49
Harris, H. I.: 27
Harris, J. D.: 23
Hartlage, L. C.: 59
Hoffeditz, E. L.: 3
Hogan, H. P.: 7
Hunt, W. A.: 19, 27, 30
Hutchens, W. H.: 5
Jackson, M. M.: 27
Jaros, R. M.: 45
Katz, L.: 46
Kent, G. H.: 1–2, 11, 15, 20, 24
Killen, J. R.: 61
Klebanoff, S. G.: 30
Knott, J. R.: 31, 34
Koenig, F. J.: 12
Lester, D. W.: 25
Lewinski, R. J.: 13, 16, 21
McDonald, R. L.: 49
McIntire, J. T.: 3
MacPhee, H. M.: 33
Mason, E. P.: 40
Mayer, A. D.: 44
Meer, B.: 52
Mensh, I. N.: 30; *rev,* 4:346
Miles, D. W.: 25
Moore, M.: 35
Mullen, F. A.: 14, 17
Myklebust, H. R.: 61
Nelson, D. A.: 50
O'Connor, P. A.: 58
Older, H. J.: 19
Orr, D. H.: 37
Pierce, R. C.: 54–6
Rautman, A. L.: 22
Rice, W.: 51
Robinowitz, R.: 41
Rokicki, R. R.: 58
Rudolf, G. de M.: 8, 32
Schwartz, E. M.: 58
Schwartz, M. S.: 53
Senti, M. M.: 18
Sharp, A. A.: 9
Sloan, W.: 9
Smith, J.: 12
Snider, H. L.: 18
Solomon, P.: 27
Springer, N. N.: 10
Teagarden, F. M.: 4–5
Templer, D. I.: 59
Trowbridge, L.: 35
Umberger, J. P.: 34
Vaughn, K. L.: 57
Weinstein, M. R.: 45
West, D. N.: 43
Wheeler, J. A.: 23
Wilkins, W. L.: 25
Williams, M.: 30
Williams, S. B.: 23
Wilson, M. T.: 36
Wittson, C. L.: 27
Wright, H. F.: 33

[504]

***The Leiter Adult Intelligence Scale.** Adults; 1949–72; LAIS; revision of *Leiter-Partington Adult Performance Scale;* includes *The FR-CR Test, Partington's Pathways Test, The Leiter Adaptation of Arthur's Stencil Design Test,* and *The Leiter Adapta-*

tion of the Painted Cube Test; 3 scores: verbal, performance, total; Russell Graydon Leiter; Stoelting Co. *

For additional information, reviews by Paul C. Davis and Frank B. Jex, and an excerpted review by Laurance F. Shaffer, see 6:525 (15 references); for reviews by Harold A. Delp and Herschel Manuel and an excerpted review by Laurance F. Shaffer of the original edition, see 4:350 (4 references). For a review of *The FR-CR Test,* see 4:339; for an excerpted review of *The Leiter Adaptation of Arthur's Stencil Design Test,* see 4:347; for an excerpted review of *The Leiter Adaptation of the Painted Cube Test,* see 4:348; and for reviews of *Partington's Pathways Test,* see 4:355 (1 review, 1 excerpt).

REFERENCES THROUGH 1971

1-4. See 4:350.
5-19. See 6:525.
20. PAYNE, R. W. "Some Aspects of Perception and Thought Disorder in Schizophrenic Subjects." *Schweizerische Zeitschrift für Psychologie und Ihre Anwendungen* (Switzerland) 17(4): 300-8 '58. * (PA 34:1791)
21. CRAWFORD, PAUL L. "The Relative Sensitivity of the LAIS, WAIS, and PM in Differentiating Between Psychopathic and Psychotic Patients in a Mental Hospital." *Psychol Service Center J* 11(2):93-7 '59. * (PA 34:4374)
22. CRAWFORD, PAUL L. "The Statistical Significance of Difference in Performance on the Leiter Adult Intelligence Scale, the Wechsler Adult Intelligence Scale, and the Porteus Maze by a Heterogeneous Mental Hospital Population." *Psychol Service Center J* 11(2):89-92 '59. * (PA 34:4510)
23. SCHERER, ISIDORE W., AND WINNE, JOHN F. "A Five Year Follow-Up Study of the Pathways Test With Lobotomized Patients." *Psychol Service Center J* 11(2):98-101 '59. * (PA 34:4408)
24. DOERRING, PAUL LUTHER. *Psychological Deficits in Children as Sequelae of Western and St. Louis Encephalitis.* Doctor's thesis, Stanford University (Stanford, Calif.), 1962. (DA 23:2006)
25. WASSENAAR, G. M. C. "The Effect of General Anxiety as an Index of Lability on the Performance of Various Psychomotor Tasks." *J General Psychol* 71:351-7 O '64. * (PA 39:3667)
26. CRAWFORD, PAUL L., AND SNYDER, WILLIAM U. "Differentiating the Psychopath and Psychoneurotic With the LAIS." Abstract. *J Consult Psychol* 30:178 Ap '66. * (PA 40:6637, title only)
27. BERKE, NORMAN DANIEL. *An Investigation of Adult Negro Illiteracy: Prediction of Reading Achievement and Description of Educational Characteristics of a Sample of City Core Adult Negro Illiterates.* Doctor's thesis, State University of New York (Buffalo, N.Y.), 1967. (DA 28:931A)
28. BLUNDELL, ELIZABETH. "A Psychological Study of the Effects of Surgery on Eighty-Six Elderly Patients." *Brit J Social & Clin Psychol* 6:297-303 D '67. * (PA 42:7707)
29. GOLDSAMT, MILTON R. "An Evaluation of the Leiter Adult Intelligence Scale (LAIS)." *Percept & Motor Skills* 28(3): 959-71 Je '69. * (PA 43:16633)
30. LUBER, SHULA A., AND WALKER, RONALD E. "Sex Difference on the Free Recall-Controlled Recall Test of the Leiter Adult Intelligence Scale." *J Clin Psychol* 25(4):412-3 O '69. * (PA 44:10417)
31. CLARK, JACK MANNING. *The Prediction of Gain in Reading Among Adult Illiterates From an Analysis of Items on the Wechsler, Leiter and Davis-Eells Scales.* Doctor's thesis, State University of New York (Buffalo, N.Y.), 1971. (DAI 32:2512A)

CUMULATIVE NAME INDEX

Adjutant General's Office, Classification and Replacement Branch, Personnel Research Section: 1
Armitage, S. G.: 2
Berke, N. D.: 27
Blundell, E.: 28
Brown, R. C.: 4
Clark, J. M.: 31
Cozan, L. W.: 12, 15
Crawford, P. L.: 21-2, 26
Davis, P. C.: *rev,* 6:525
Delp, H. A.: *rev,* 4:350
Doerman, L. H.: 4
Doerring, P. L.: 24
Gaitz, C. M.: 19
George, E. I.: 16
Goldsamt, M. R.: 29
Hewlett, J. H. G.: 17
International Psychological Service Center: 5
Jex, F. B.: *rev,* 6:525
Leiter, R. G.: 3, 6-7, 9, 13
Luber, S. A.: 30
Manuel, H.: *rev,* 4:350
Mattussek, P.: 16
Partington, J. E.: 3, 8-9
Payne, R. W.: 16-7, 20
Scherer, I. W.: 23
Shaffer, L. F.: *exc,* 4:350, 6:525
Snyder, W. U.: 26
Sydow, D. W.: 14
Vinson, D. B.: 18-9
Walker, R. E.: 30
Wassenaar, G. M. C.: 25
Watson, N.: 10-1
Weaver, H. B.: 4
Winne, J. F.: 23

Leiter Adult Intelligence Scale

---

[505]
Leiter International Performance Scale. Ages 2-18, 3-8; 1936-55; 2 editions; Russell Graydon Leiter and Grace Arthur (*b*); Stoelting Co. *
a) 1948 REVISION. Ages 2-18; 1936-52.
b) ARTHUR ADAPTATION. Ages 3-8; 1952-55; author recommends use with *Arthur Point Scale of Performance Tests.*

For additional information and a review by Emmy E. Werner, see 6:526 (10 references); see also 5:408 (17 references); for a review by Gwen F. Arnold and an excerpted review by Laurance F. Shaffer of *a,* see 4:349 (25 references). For an excerpt from a related book review, see 2:B989.

REFERENCES THROUGH 1971

1-25. See 4:349.
26-42. See 5:408.
43-52. See 6:526.
53. VARVA, FRANK IRVIN. *An Investigation of the Effect of Auditory Deficiency Upon Performance With Special Reference to Concrete and Abstract Tasks.* Doctor's thesis, University of Pittsburgh (Pittsburgh, Pa.), 1956. (DA 16:2532)
54. BRENGELMANN, JOHANNES C., AND HILLMAN, WILLIAM A., JR. "Determinants of Learning in the Retardate: A Pilot Study." *Training Sch B* 61:156-62 F '65. * (PA 39:10570)
55. KORST, JOSEPH W. *A Comparison of the Results Obtained for the Peabody Picture Vocabulary Test and the Leiter International Performance Scale With Children Having Functional Articulatory Disorders.* Master's thesis, Wichita State University (Wichita, Kan.), 1965.
56. STEWART, HORACE F., JR., AND KEELER, CLYDE E. "A Comparison of the Intelligence and Personality of Moon-Child Albino and Control Cuna Indians." *J Genetic Psychol* 106:319-24 Je '65. * (PA 39:14888)
57. CLEGG, STANLEY J., AND WHITE, WILLIAM F. "Assessment of General Intelligence of Negro Deaf Children in a Public Residential School for the Deaf." *J Clin Psychol* 22:93-4 Ja '66. * (PA 40:4523)
58. GENTILE, J. RONALD. "In Search of Research: Four Children's Tests." *J Sch Psychol* 5:1-13 au '66. * (PA 41:3335)
59. KORST, JOSEPH W. "A Comparison of Results From the Peabody Vocabulary Test and Leiter International Performance Scale With Children Having Functional Articulatory Disorders." *Cereb Palsy J* 27:3-5 Ja-F '66. * (PA 40:5851)
60. MCBRIDE, DON W. "Longitudinal Study of Performance of Childhood Aphasics on Mental Ability Tests," pp. 118-25. In *Special Education: Strategies for Educational Progress.* Selected Convention Papers, 44th Annual CEC Convention, 1966. Washington, D.C.: Council for Exceptional Children, [1966]. Pp. viii, 259. *
61. BEANS, DAVID T. *The Leiter International Performance Scale as a Measure of Intelligence in Navahos.* Master's thesis, Utah State University (Logan, Utah), 1967.
62. MIEZITIS, SOLVEIGA AUSMA. *An Exploratory Study of Divergent Production in Preschoolers.* Doctor's thesis, University of Toronto (Toronto, Ont., Canada), 1968. (DAI 30:589A)
63. COSTELLO, JOAN, AND DICKIE, JOYCE. "Leiter and Stanford-Binet IQ's of Preschool Disadvantaged Children." Abstract. *Develop Psychol* 2(2):314 Mr '70. * (PA 44:6523)
64. KING, SUSAN HOFMAN. *The Relationships Between Mental Age, Level of Language Functioning and Social Acceptability in the Trainable Mentally Retarded.* Doctor's thesis, Louisiana State University (Baton Rouge, La.), 1970. (DAI 31:5691B)
65. MATHER, LEONARD JOSEPH. *A Causal Comparative Study of Intellectual Functioning in Good and Poor Readers.* Doctor's thesis, Catholic University of America (Washington, D.C.), 1971. (DAI 32:1920A)
66. MYKLEBUST, HELMER R.; BANNOCHIE, MARGARET N.; AND KILLEN, JAMES R. Chap. 9, "Learning Disabilities and Cognitive Processes," pp. 213-51. In *Progress in Learning Disabilities,* Vol. 2. Edited by Helmer R. Myklebust. New York: Grune & Stratton, Inc., 1971. Pp. ix, 404. *
67. NEDLER, SHARI, AND SEBERA, PEGGY. "Intervention Strategies for Spanish-Speaking Preschool Children." *Child Develop* 42(1):259-67 Mr '71. * (PA 46:5743)
68. ROBINSON, HALBERT B., AND ROBINSON, NANCY M. "Longitudinal Development of Very Young Children in a Comprehensive Day Care Program: The First Two Years." *Child Develop* 42(6):1673-83 D '71. * (PA 48:8827)
69. RUBINO, C. A.; KROCCO, D.; AND SHEA, M. "An Analysis of Right Hemispheric Deficits in the Moderately Retarded Child as Measured by the WISC and Leiter." *Ont Psychologist* (Canada) 3(2):85-95 '71. * (PA 47:9488)
70. WEINER, PAUL S. "Stability and Validity of Two Measures of Intelligence Used With Children Whose Language Development Is Delayed." *J Speech & Hearing Res* 14(2):254-61 Je '71. * (PA 48:5419)

CUMULATIVE NAME INDEX

Allen, R. M.: 43, 50
Alper, A. E.: 40
Arnold, G. F.: 15, 28; rev, 4:349
Arthur, G.: 18, 30
Bannochie, M. N.: 66
Beans, D. T.: 61
Benefiel, R. C.: 5
Benoit, E. P.: 37
Bensberg, G. J.: 29, 31
Bessent, T. E.: 22
Beverly, L.: 31
Birch, J. R.: 24, 36, 52
Birch, J. W.: 21, 24, 36, 52
Boehncke, F. C.: 2
Boyd, H. F.: 37
Brengelmann, J. C.: 47, 54
Burns, P. P.: 34
Clegg, S. J.: 57
Collins, M. G.: 43
Cooper, J. G.: 41
Costello, J.: 63
Craig, A. L.: 3
Darby, H. E.: 6
Dean, C. C.: 10
Dickie, J.: 63
Dreger, R. M.: 35
Earle, E. S.: 14
Evans, M. L.: 33
Gallagher, J. J.: 37
Gentile, J. R.: 58
Glenn, R. T.: 25
Goulard, L. J.: 19
Goulard, S. E.: 7
Herrick, C. J.: 11
Hillman, W. A.: 54
Hunt, B. M.: 48
Hunter, M.: 11
Keeler, C. E.: 56
Kenny, J. T.: 47
Killen, J. R.: 66
King, S. H.: 64
Korst, J. W.: 55, 59
Krocco, D.: 69
Leiter, R. G.: 1, 4, 8, 20, 26–7, 45
McBride, D. W.: 60
Madeley, C. B.: 16
Maisel, R. N.: 50
Mather, L. J.: 65
Matthews, J.: 21
Michea, C. A.: 13
Miezitis, S. A.: 62
Mira, M. P.: 51
Molino, H. S.: 9
Myklebust, H. R.: 66
Nedler, S.: 67
Orgel, A. R.: 35
Peisner, E. F.: 38
Porteus, S. D.: 11
Rinsland, H. D.: exc, 2:B989
Robinson, H. B.: 68
Robinson, N. M.: 68
Rubino, C. A.: 69
Sebera, P.: 67
Shaffer, L. F.: exc, 4:349
Sharp, H. C.: 39, 42
Shea, M.: 69
Sloan, W.: 29
Stewart, H. F.: 56
Stroud, J. B.: 49
Stuckless, E. R.: 52
Tallarico, R. B.: 50
Tate, M. E.: 23, 32
Varva, F. I.: 53
Weiner, P. S.: 70
Werner, E. E.: rev, 6:526
White, W. F.: 57
Williams, R. M.: 12
Wilson, B. A.: 44
Wolf, W.: 49
Wolf, W. S.: 46

[506]

★**McCarthy Scales of Children's Abilities.** Ages 2.5–8.5; 1972, c1970–72; MSCA; 6 scores: verbal, perceptual-performance, quantitative, composite (general cognitive), memory, motor; Dorothea McCarthy; Psychological Corporation. *

[507]

Merrill-Palmer Scale of Mental Tests. Ages 24–63 months; 1926–31; Rachel Stutsman; Stoelting Co. *

For additional information and a review by Marjorie P. Honzik, see 6:527 (16 references); for reviews by Nancy Bayley, B. M. Castner, Florence L. Goodenough, and Florence M. Teagarden, see 2:1406 (13 references). For excerpts from related book reviews, see 2:B1123 (5 excerpts).

REFERENCES THROUGH 1971

1–13. See 2:1406.
14–29. See 6:527.
30. WOOLEY, HELEN T. "The Validity of Standards of Mental Measurement in Young Childhood." *Sch & Soc* 21:476–82 Ap 18 '25. *
31. GOODENOUGH, FLORENCE L. "The Reliability and Validity of the Wallin Peg Boards." *Psychol Clinic* 16:199–215 O '27. * (*PA* 2:1395)
32. BALDWIN, BIRD T., AND WELLMAN, BETH L. "The Peg Board as a Means of Analyzing Form Perception and Motor Control in Young Children." *J Genetic Psychol* 35:389–414 S '28. * (*PA* 3:1358)
33. WAGONER, LOVISA C., AND ARMSTRONG, EDNA M. "The Motor Control of Children as Involved in the Dressing Process." *J Genetic Psychol* 35:84–97 Mr '28. * (*PA* 2:3692)
34. HERTZBERG, OSCAR E. "The Relationship of Motor Ability to the Intelligence of Kindergarten Children." *J Ed Psychol* 20:507–19 O '29. * (*PA* 4:373)
35. GOODENOUGH, FLORENCE L. "Inter-Relationships in the Behavior of Young Children." *Child Develop* 1:29–48 Mr '30. * (*PA* 4:3637)
36. VANCE, THOMAS F. "The Effect of Size of Peg and Form Boards Upon the Performance Scores of Young Children." *Proc Iowa Acad Sci* 40:181–4 '33. * (*PA* 9:3048)
37. WELLMAN, BETH L. "Mental Measurement of Preschool Children: A Review." *J Ed Res* 26:536–7 Mr '33. *
38. HASLAM, PHYLLIS. *The Prediction of Ability on the Arthur Point Performance Scale From the Merrill-Palmer Scale.* Master's thesis, State University of Iowa (Iowa City, Iowa), 1938.
39. SKEELS, HAROLD M.; UPDEGRAFF, RUTH; WELLMAN, BETH L.; AND WILLIAMS, HAROLD M. *A Study of Environmental Stimulation: An Orphanage Preschool Project*, pp. 60–73. University of Iowa Studies in Child Welfare, Vol. 15, No. 4. Iowa City, Iowa: the University, 1938. Pp. 191. * (*PA* 13:1758)
40. GROVER, V. M. "The Coloured Nursery School Child and the Merrill Palmer Test." Abstract. *Proc South African Psychol Assn* 3:26–7 '52. * (*PA* 30:2881, title only)
41. MORIARTY, ALICE. "Coping Patterns of Preschool Children in Response to Intelligence Test Demands." *Genetic Psychol Monogr* 64:3–127 Ag '61. * (*PA* 36:2FF03M)
42. KLATSKIN, ETHELYN HENRY. "Relationships of Deficits in Intelligence Test Performance of Preschool Children to Perinatal Experience." *J Consult Psychol* 28:228–33 Je '64. * (*PA* 39:4590)
43. KEIR, GERTRUDE. "The Merrill-Palmer Test With the Children From the Island of Tristan da Cunha." *J Child Psychol & Psychiatry* (England) 7:133–42 O '66. * (*PA* 41:4399, title only)
44. STOTT, LELAND H., AND BALL, RACHEL STUTSMAN. *Infant and Preschool Mental Tests: Review and Evaluation.* Monographs of the Society for Research in Child Development, Vol. 30, No. 3, Serial No. 101. Chicago, Ill.: University of Chicago Press, 1966. Pp. iv, 151. * (*PA* 40:7220)
45. DUROJAIYE, M. O. A., AND SUCH, M. "Predicting Educational Suitability of Children in an Assessment Unit." *J Exp Ed* 40(2):27–36 w '71. * (*PA* 47:11608)
46. TAKACS, CAROL PAULA. *Comparison of Mental Abilities Between Lower Socioeconomic Status Five-Year-Old Negro and White Children on Individual Intelligence Measures.* Doctor's thesis, Kent State University (Kent, Ohio), 1971. (*DAI* 32:3806A)

CUMULATIVE NAME INDEX

Aldrich, C. G.: 15
Allan, M. E.: 20
Anderson, L. D.: 18
Armstrong, E. M.: 33
Baldwin, B. T.: 32
Ball, R. S.: 44
Barrett, H. E.: 14
Bayley, N.: rev, 2:1406
Beck, S. J.: exc, 2:B1123
Bristol, H.: 10
Burks, B. S.: exc, 2:B1123
Castner, B. M.: rev, 2:1406
Chesire, L. E.: 3
Coffey, H. S.: 17
Crump, E. P.: 28
DeForrest, R.: 13, 19
Doll, E. A.: 15
Driscoll, G. P.: 6
Durojaiye, M. O. A.: 45
Ebert, E.: 21
Goodenough, F. L.: 31, 35; rev, 2:1406
Gordon, R. G.: 7
Grover, V. M.: 40
Haines, M. S.: 24–5
Harris, D. B.: 22
Haslam, P.: 38
Hatt, E.: 3
Hertzberg, O. E.: 34
Hoefer, C.: 4
Honzik, M. P.: rev, 6:527
Horton, C. P.: 28
Hurst, J. G.: 27, 29
Kawin, E.: 4
Keir, G.: 43
Klatskin, E. H.: 42
Koch, H. L.: 14
Linder, M. G.: 4
Line, W.: exc, 2:B1123
Mohr, E.: 4
Moriarty, A.: 41
Mowrer, W. M. C.: 8
Oberlin, D. S.: 11
Schmidt, A. G.: exc, 2:B1123
Simmons, K.: 21
Skeels, H. M.: 39
Smitter, F. W.: 16
Stott, L. H.: 44
Stutsman, R.: 1–3, 5, 9, 23
Such, M.: 45
Sweeny, M. E.: 3
Takacs, C. P.: 46
Taylor, M. W.: 4
Teagarden, F. M.: rev, 2:1406
Updegraff, R.: 39
Vance, T. F.: 36
Wagoner, L. C.: 33
Walsh, R.: 26
Wellman, B. L.: 12, 32, 37, 39
Williams, H. M.: 39
Wilson, C. A.: 3
Wooley, H. T.: 30
Young, F. M.: 20

[508]

★**Minnesota Child Development Inventory.** Ages 1–6; 1968–72; MCDI; observations by mother; 8 scores: gross motor, fine motor, expressive language, comprehension-conceptual, situation comprehension, self help, personal-social, general development; Harold R. Ireton and Edward J. Thwing; NCS Interpretive Scoring Systems. *

[509]

Minnesota Preschool Scale. Ages 1.5–6.0; 1932–40; MPS; 3 scores: verbal, nonverbal, total; Florence L. Goodenough, Katherine M. Maurer, and M. J. Van Wagenen; American Guidance Service, Inc. *

For additional information and a review by Marjorie P. Honzik, see 6:528 (3 references); see also 4:351 (2 references); for a review by Beth L. Wellman, see 3:286 (2 references); for reviews by Rachel Stutsman Ball, Nancy Bayley, and Florence M. Teagarden of the original edition, see 2:1407 (3 references). For excerpts from related book reviews, see 4:352 (5 excerpts), 3:287 (5 excerpts), and 3:288 (2 excerpts).

REFERENCES THROUGH 1971

1-3. See 2:1407.
4-5. See 3:286.
6-7. See 4:351.
8-10. See 6:528.
11. GOODENOUGH, FLORENCE L. "Inter-Relationships in the Behavior of Young Children." *Child Develop* 1:29-48 Mr '30. * (*PA* 4:3637)
12. WELLMAN, BETH L. *The Intelligence of Preschool Children as Measured by the Merrill-Palmer Scale of Performance Tests.* University of Iowa Studies in Child Welfare, Vol. 15, No. 3. Iowa City, Iowa: the University, 1938. Pp. 150. * (*PA* 13:1730)

CUMULATIVE NAME INDEX

Ball, R. S.: *rev*, 2:1407
Bayley, N.: *rev*, 2:1407; *exc*, 3:287, 4:352
Coffey, H. S.: 6
Cronbach, L. J.: *exc*, 4:352
Curti, M. W.: 2
DeForrest, R.: 3, 7
Eysenck, H. J.: *exc*, 4:352
Fleming, C. M.: *exc*, 4:352
Froehlich, G. J.: *exc*, 3:287
Goodenough, F. L.: 4, 11
Honzik, M. P.: *rev*, 6:528
Lyle, J. G.: 8-10
McNemar, Q.: *exc*, 4:352
Maurer, K. M.: 4-5
Mowrer, W. M. C.: 1
Olson, W. C.: *exc*, 3:287
Steggerda, M.: 2
Teagarden, F. M.: *rev*, 2:1407
Valentine, C. W.: *exc*, 3:287
Wellman, B. L.: 12; *rev*, 3:286

[510]

New Guinea Performance Scales. Pre-literates ages 17 and over; 1961-71; NGPS; based (except *f*) on the unpublished *PIR Test* used for screening for the Pacific Island Regiment; test (except *e*) is essentially the same as the *Queensland Test* except for minor differences in some of the testing materials and differences in administration, scoring, and norms population; 6 tests; 7 scores: 6 scores listed below plus total; I. G. Ord; Society for New Guinea Psychological Research and Publications [Papua New Guinea]. *
a) CUBE IMITATION TEST. An adaptation of *Knox Cube Test: Pintner Modification.*
b) BEAD THREADING TEST.
c) PASSALONG TEST. Modification of a subtest of *Alexander Performance Scale*; test booklet title is *Passalong Test (New Guinea Version).*
d) FORM ASSEMBLY TEST.
e) OBSERVATION TEST.
f) DESIGN CONSTRUCTION TEST. Published separately as *Pacific Design Construction Test.*

For additional information, see 7:412 (4 references).

REFERENCES THROUGH 1971

1-4. See 7:412.

CUMULATIVE NAME INDEX

Ord, I. G.: 1-4

[511]

New South African Individual Scale. Ages 6-17; 1964; NSAIS; 12 scores: verbal (vocabulary, comprehension, reasoning, problems, memory, total), nonverbal (pattern completion, blocks, absurdities, form board, total), total; both power and power-time scores are obtained for 4 subtests (problems, pattern completion, blocks, absurdities), verbal total, nonverbal total, and overall total; Human Sciences Research Council [South Africa]. *

For additional information, see 7:413 (1 reference).

REFERENCES THROUGH 1971

1. See 7:413.

CUMULATIVE NAME INDEX

Mienie, C. J. P.: 1   Strümpfer, D. J. W.: 1

[512]

Non-Verbal Intelligence Tests for Deaf and Hearing Subjects. Ages 3-16; 1939-59; NVIT, also

SON; record booklet title is *S.O.N. Snijders-Oomen Non-Verbal Intelligence Scale*; 9 scores: mosaic, picture memory, arrangement, analogies, completion, Knox cubes, drawing, sorting, IQ; J. Th. Snijders and N. Snijders-Oomen; distributed by Swets and Zeitlinger B.V. [The Netherlands]. (South African standardization entitled *Snijders-Oomen Non-Verbal Intelligence Scale.* 1964; W. Backer; Human Sciences Research Council [South Africa].) *

For additional information and a review by J. S. Lawes, see 6:529 (2 references).

REFERENCES THROUGH 1971

1-2. See 6:529.
3. HART, N. W. M. "The Use of the S.O.N. Test With Deaf Children in Queensland as a Measure of Their Academic Potential." *Spec Sch B* 5:11-23 N '63. *
4. MONTGOMERY, G. W. G. "A Factorial Study of Communication and Ability in Deaf School Leavers." *Brit J Ed Psychol* 38:27-37 F '68. * (*PA* 42:12755)
5. KEARNEY, JACQUELINE E. "A New Performance Scale of Cognitive Capacity for Use With Deaf Subjects." *Am Ann Deaf* 114(1):2-14 Ja '69. * (*PA* 43:7197)
6. CANABAL, JUANA VILLANUEVA. *Comparison of Deaf and Normally Hearing Children on Analogy Items Under Different Methods of Instruction at Different Age Levels.* Doctor's thesis, St. John's University (Jamaica, N.Y.), 1970. (*DAI* 31:3700B)
7. GASKILL, P.; LONGWORTH, A.; AND NEILSON, J. R. "The Administration of Snijders-Oomen Non-Verbal Intelligence Tests to Deaf Children." *Teach Deaf* (England) 68(400):137-42 Mr '70. *

CUMULATIVE NAME INDEX

Canabal, J. V.: 6
Gaskill, P.: 7
Hart, N. W. M.: 3
Kearney, J. E.: 5
Lawes, J. S.: *rev*, 6:529
Longworth, A.: 7
Montgomery, G. W. G.: 4
Neilson, J. R.: 7
Neuhaus, M.: 2
Snijders, J. T.: 1
Snijders-Oomen, N.: 1

[513]

The Ohwaki-Kohs Tactile Block Design Intelligence Test for the Blind. Blind ages 6 and over; 1965; OKTBD; record booklet title is *The Ohwaki-Kohs Tactile Block-Design Intelligence Test*; adaptation of *Kohs' Block Design Test*; for American revision, see 527; Yoshikazu Ohwaki; Western Psychological Services. *

For additional information and an excerpted review by Richard J. Rankin, see 7:414 (4 references).

REFERENCES THROUGH 1971

1-4. See 7:414.
5. SUINN, RICHARD M. "The Theory of Cognitive Style: A Partial Replication." *J General Psychol* 77:11-5 Jl '67. * (*PA* 41:14063)

CUMULATIVE NAME INDEX

Bozzo, M. T.: 2
Dauterman, W.: 4
Hariu, T.: 1
Hayasaka, K.: 1
Miyake, K.: 1
Ohwaki, M.: 1
Ohwaki, Y.: 1
Rankin, R. J.: *exc*, 7:414
Shapiro, B.: 4
Suinn, R. M.: 3-5
Tanno, Y.: 1
Zecca, G.: 2

[514]

Pacific Design Construction Test. Illiterates and semiliterates in Papua New Guinea; 1962-68; PDCT; based upon *Kohs' Block-Design Test* and block design subtest of *Wechsler Adult Intelligence Scale*; subtest of *New Guinea Performance Scales*; subtest (with minor modifications) of *Queensland Test* in which it is called *Pattern Matching Test*; I. G. Ord; Australian Council for Educational Research [Australia]. *

For additional information, see 7:415 (3 references).

REFERENCES THROUGH 1971

1-3. See 7:415.
4. ORD, I. G. "The P.I.R. Test and Derivatives." *Austral Psychologist* 2:137-46 Mr '68. * (*PA* 42:18798)

CUMULATIVE NAME INDEX

Kearney, G. E.: 2   Ord, I. G.: 1, 3-4

Minnesota Preschool Scale

[515]

The Passalong Test: A Performance Test of Intelligence. Ages 8 and over; 1932–37; W. P. Alexander; Stoelting Co. *

For additional information and reviews by James Drever, T. J. Keating, and Grace H. Kent, see 2:1414 (5 references).

REFERENCES THROUGH 1971

1–5. See 2:1414.
6. PRICE, E. J. J. "The Nature of the Practical Factor (F)." *Brit J Psychol* 30:341–51 Ap '40. * (*PA* 14:3783)
7. BRADFORD, E. J. G. "Performance Tests in the Diagnosis of Mental Deficiency." *Brit J Med Psychol* 19:394–414 pts 3–4 '43. * (*PA* 17:3783)
8. AMIN, D. L. "Differences Among the Deaf and Hearing Children." *Indian J Psychol* 21:91–2 pts 1–4 '46. * (*PA* 22:4571)
9. BRADFORD, E. J. G. "Selection for Technical Education: Parts I and II." *Brit J Ed Psychol* 16:20–31, 69–81 F, Je '46. * (*PA* 20:2887, 4881)
10. KAPAT, G., AND BHATTACHARYYA, C. C. "Some Critical Observations on Pass-along Test." *Indian J Psychol* 23:51–4 pts 1–4 '48. * (*PA* 28:6032, title only)
11. BIESHEUVEL, S. Chap. 4, "Psychological Tests and Their Applications to Non-European Peoples," pp. 87–126. In *The Yearbook of Education, 1949.* London: Evans Brothers Ltd., 1949. Pp. xv, 660. *
12. YELA, MARIANO. "Application of the Concept of Simple Structure to Alexander's Data." *Psychometrika* 14:121–35 Je '49. * (*PA* 24:1066)
13. WOODWARD, JOHN C. *Relationship of the Passalong Intelligence Test and Eighth Grade Achievement.* Master's thesis, University of Nebraska (Lincoln, Neb.), 1953.
14. RAY-CHOWDHURY, K. "Imagery and Performance Tests of Intelligence." *Indian Psychol B* 2:25–30 S '57. * (*PA* 37:4964)
15. JAYALAKSHMI, G. "Correlation of Tests of Psychomotor Ability With Intelligence and Non-motor Tests." *J Psychol Res* (India) 3:78–84 S '59. *
16. RAO, C. K. VASUDEVA. "Intelligence in a Group of Convicts: An Analysis of 35 Cases." *Trans All-India Inst Mental Health* 1:44–53 D '60. * (*PA* 37:3649)
17. KUNDU, RAMANATH. "An Investigation Into the Relationship Between Intelligence and Memory." *J Psychol Res* (India) 7:32–6 Ja '63. * (*PA* 38:2685)
18. FAHMY, MOSTAFA. "Initial Exploring of the Intelligence of Shilluk Children: Studies in the Southern Sudan." *Vita Hum* (Switzerland) 7(3–4):164–77 '64. * (*PA* 39:7815)
19. CHATTERJEE, NEERA. "A Comparison of Performance of Tribal and Non-Tribal Boys of Tripura (India) on Five Performance Tests." *J Psychol Res* (India) 9:151–8 S '65. * (*PA* 40:6561)
20. DEB, SUBIMAL, AND RAY, TAPATI. "Nature of Consistency Between Scores of Two Different Performance Tests in Normal and Subnormals." *Psychol Studies* (India) 13:16–20 Ja '68. *

CUMULATIVE NAME INDEX

Alexander, W. P.: 1–2
Amin, D. L.: 8
Bhattacharyya, C. C.: 10
Biesheuvel, S.: 11
Bradford, E. J. G.: 7, 9
Chatterjee, N.: 19
Deb, S.: 20
Drever, J.: rev, 2:1414
Earl, C. J. C.: 3
Fahmy, M.: 18
Fowler, H. L.: 5
Jayalakshmi, G.: 15
Kapat, G.: 10
Keating, T. J.: rev, 2:1414
Kent, G. H.: rev, 2:1414
Kundu, R.: 17
Price, E. J. J.: 6
Rao, C. K. V.: 16
Ray, T.: 20
Ray-Chowdhury, K.: 14
Vernon, P. E.: 4
Woodward, J. C.: 13
Yela, M.: 12

[516]

Peabody Picture Vocabulary Test. Ages 2.5–18; 1959–70; PPVT; Lloyd M. Dunn; American Guidance Service, Inc. *

For additional information, see 7:417 (201 references); for reviews by Howard B. Lyman and Ellen V. Piers, see 6:530 (21 references).

REFERENCES THROUGH 1971

1–21. See 6:530.
22–223. See 7:417.
224. BRENGELMANN, JOHANNES C., AND HILLMAN, WILLIAM A., JR. "Determinants of Learning in the Retardate: A Pilot Study." *Training Sch B* 61:156–62 F '65. * (*PA* 39:10570)
225. LIEBERMAN, J. NINA. "Playfulness and Divergent Thinking: An Investigation of Their Relationship at the Kindergarten Level." *J Genetic Psychol* 107:219–24 D '65. * (*PA* 40:5252)
226. BENGER, KATHLYN. *A Study of the Relationships Between Perception, Personality, Intelligence and Grade One Reading Achievement.* Master's thesis, University of Alberta (Edmonton, Alta., Canada), 1966.
227. CORAH, NORMAN L.; JONES, SALLY ANN; AND MILLER, BARBARA B. "The Relation of Verbal Intelligence and Color-Form Discriminative Ability to Children's Color-Matching and Form-Matching Behavior." *J Psychol* 62:221–8 Mr '66. * (*PA* 40:7569)
228. SPOCK, ALEXANDER, AND STEDMAN, DONALD J. "Psychologic Characteristics of Children With Cystic Fibrosis." *N C Med J* 27:426–8 S '66. *
229. TILLMANS, SUSAN JEAN. *A Pilot Program on Language Development for Cerebral Palsied Children.* Master's thesis, St. Cloud State College (St. Cloud, Minn.), 1967.
230. BELLER, E. KUNO. "Intellectual Development in Educationally Disadvantaged Pre-School Children." *Proc 1966 Ann Read Inst Temple Univ* 5:73–83 '68. *
231. BURNS, GARY W. *A Comparison of the Peabody Picture Vocabulary Test With the Stanford-Binet Intelligence Scale and With the Wechsler Intelligence Scale for Children.* Master's thesis, Sacramento State College (Sacramento, Calif.), 1968.
232. GIEBINK, JOHN W., AND MARDEN, MARY L. "Verbal Expression, Verbal Fluency, and Grammar Related to Cultural Experience." *Psychol Sch* 5:365–8 O '68. * (*PA* 43:5912)
233. IRVINE, JAMES. *Correlates of Grade One Achievement.* Master's thesis, University of Alberta (Edmonton, Alta., Canada), 1968.
234. PAULUS, DIETER H., AND RENZULLI, JOSEPH S. "Improving the Validity of the Peabody Picture Vocabulary Test Through Item Analysis." *Univ Va Ed R* 6:67–71 '68. *
235. SMITH, MARSHALL P. "Intellectual Differences in Five-Year-Old Underprivileged Girls and Boys With and Without Pre-Kindergarten School Experience." *J Ed Res* 61:348–50 Ap '68. *
236. TEASDALE, G. R., AND KATZ, F. M. "Psycholinguistic Abilities of Children From Different Ethnic and Socio-Economic Backgrounds." *Austral J Psychol* 20:155–9 D '68. * (*PA* 45:3957)
237. FEDIO, PAUL, AND MIRSKY, ALLAN F. "Selective Intellectual Deficits in Children With Temporal Lobe or Centrencephalic Epilepsy." *Neuropsychologia* (England) 7(4):287–300 S '69. * (*PA* 44:4022)
238. GROSS, MORRIS. "Learning Readiness in Two Groups: A Study in 'Cultural Deprivation.'" *Jewish Ed* 39(1):36–48 Ja '69. *
239. BENNINGER, CLEO A. *A Study of the Interrelations Among Articulation, Chronological Age, Memory for Digits and Sentences, and Measures of the Peabody Picture Vocabulary Test for Kindergarten Children.* Master's thesis, Sacramento State College (Sacramento, Calif.), 1970.
240. COMSTOCK, JOHN ALLAN. *The Relationship Between Clinically Derived Scores of Employability and Employability Scores Predicted by an Employability Model for Mentally Retarded Adolescents.* Doctor's thesis, University of Minnesota (Minneapolis, Minn.), 1970. (*DAI* 32:271A)
241. KARNES, MEREL B.; TESKA, JAMES A.; AND HODGINS, AUDREY S. "The Effects of Four Programs of Classroom Intervention on the Intellectual and Language Development of 4-Year-Old Disadvantaged Children." *Am J Orthopsychiatry* 40(1):58–76 Ja '70. * (*PA* 45:1373)
242. KING, SUSAN HOFMAN. *The Relationships Between Mental Age, Level of Language Functioning and Social Acceptability in the Trainable Mentally Retarded.* Doctor's thesis, Louisiana State University (Baton Rouge, La.), 1970. (*DAI* 31:5691B)
243. LANEY, BILLIE JOHNSON. *A Comparative Study of Expressive and Comprehensive Vocabulary Development in Male and Female Kindergarten Children.* Doctor's thesis, East Texas State University (Commerce, Tex.), 1970. (*DAI* 31:4386A)
244. WHITMAN, MYRON A. "Discrimination Learning as a Function of MA, IQ and Institutionalization." *Training Sch B* 67(2):123–30 Ag '70. * (*PA* 44:21460)
245. ALI, FAIZUNISA, AND COSTELLO, JOAN. "Modification of the Peabody Picture Vocabulary Test." *Develop Psychol* 5(1):86–91 Jl '71. * (*PA* 46:8740)
246. AMDUR, JEANETTE LORRAINE READ. *Oral Language Abilities in a Low Socio-Economic Status Kindergarten Spanish-Surnamed Population Varying in Reading Achievement.* Doctor's thesis, University of Denver (Denver, Colo.), 1971. (*DAI* 32:779A)
247. BART, LEONARD EUGENE. *A Comparison of the Effectiveness of Televised and Conventional Administrations of Objective Scales.* Doctor's thesis, St. John's University (Jamaica, N.Y.), 1971. (*DAI* 32:2980B)
248. BERG, NORMAN L., AND BERG, SANDRA D. "Comparison of Verbal Intelligence of Young Children From Low and Middle Socioeconomic Status." *Psychol Rep* 28(2):559–62 Ap '71. * (*PA* 46:6531)
249. BIGELOW, GORDON S. "Field Dependence-Field Independence in 5- to 10-Year-Old Children." *J Ed Res* 64(9):397–400 My–Je '71. * (*PA* 47:6507)
250. BURLAND, R., AND CARROLL, V. M. "The Misuse of a Test of a Specific Ability as an Estimate of General Ability." *B Brit Psychol Soc* 24(85):317–8 O '71. * (*PA* 48:3515)
251. CARLSON, J. S. "Some Relationships Between Class Inclu-

sion, Perceptual Capabilities, Verbal Capabilities and Race." *Hum Develop* (Switzerland) 14(1):30-8 '71. * (*PA* 47:2617)

252. CARLSON, JERRY S. "Some Relationships Between Verbal and Perceptual Capabilities and the Development of Relative Thinking." *J Genetic Psychol* 118(1):115-9 Mr '71. * (*PA* 46:8724)

253. COSTELLO, JOAN, AND ALI, FAIZUNISA. "Reliability and Validity of Peabody Picture Vocabulary Test Scores of Disadvantaged Preschool Children." *Psychol Rep* 28(3):755-60 Je '71. * (*PA* 46:11495)

254. DE LACEY, P. R. "Classificatory Ability and Verbal Intelligence Among High-Content Aboriginal and Low Socioeconomic White Australian Children." *J Cross-Cultural Psychol* 2(4):393-6 D '71. * (*PA* 48:655)

255. DE LACEY, P. R. "Verbal Intelligence, Operational Thinking and Environment in Part-Aboriginal Children." *Austral J Psychol* 23(2):145-9 Ag '71. * (*PA* 47:10681)

256. DICK, ROBERT MARCUS, II. *Screening Identification of First Grade Problems in an American Indian Population.* Doctor's thesis, University of North Carolina (Chapel Hill, N.C.), 1971. (*DAI* 32:1209B)

257. DOLL, PADDY A.; FAGOT, HACKER J.; AND HIMBERT, JOANNA D. "Experimenter Effect on Sex-Role Preference Among Black and White Lower-Class Male Children." *Psychol Rep* 29(3):1295-301 D '71. * (*PA* 48:709)

258. ELLIOTT, R., AND MACKAY, D. N. "Social Competence of Subnormal and Normal Children Living Under Different Types of Residential Care." *Brit J Mental Subnormal* 17(32):48-53 Je '71. * (*PA* 47:11471)

259. FALK, LIBBY JANET. *A Profile of Learning Abilities and Behavioral Characteristics of Elementary School-Age Children With Phenylketonuria.* Doctor's thesis, Temple University (Philadelphia, Pa.), 1971. (*DAI* 32:1913A)

260. FAY, WARREN H., AND BUTLER, BRUCE V. "Echo-Reaction as an Approach to Semantic Resolution." *J Speech & Hearing Res* 14(3):645-51 S '71. * (*PA* 48:2699)

261. HALL, JOSEPH C., AND CHANSKY, NORMAN M. "Relationships Between Selected Ability and Achievement Tests in an Economically Disadvantaged Negro Sample." *Psychol Rep* 28(3):741-2 Je '71. * (*PA* 46:11501)

262. HARDY, MIRIAM P.; MELLITS, DAVID; AND WILLIG, SHARON N. "Reading: A Function of Language Usage." *Johns Hopkins Med J* 129(1):43-53 Jl '71. *

263. HEYDENBERK, WARREN ROBERT. *A Comparison of Four Methods of Estimating Reading Potential.* Doctor's thesis, University of Northern Colorado (Greeley, Colo.), 1971. (*DAI* 32:3558A)

264. HINTON, GEORGE G., AND KNIGHTS, ROBERT M. "Children With Learning Problems: Academic History, Academic Prediction, and Adjustment Three Years After Assessment." *Excep Children* 37(7):513-9 Mr '71. * (*PA* 47:3663)

265. JEFFREE, D. M., AND CASHDAN, A. "Severely Subnormal Children and Their Parents: An Experiment in Language Improvement." *Brit J Ed Psychol* 41(2):184-94 Je '71. * (*PA* 47:9728)

266. JERROLDS, BOB W.; CALLAWAY, BYRON; AND GWALTNEY, WAYNE. "A Comparative Study of Three Tests of Intellectual Potential, Three Tests of Reading Achievement, and the Discrepancy Scores Between Potential and Achievement." *J Ed Res* 65(4):168-72 D '71. * (*PA* 48:1647)

267. JERUCHIMOWICZ, RITA; COSTELLO, JOAN; AND BAGUR, J. SUSANA. "Knowledge of Action and Object Words: A Comparison of Lower- and Middle-Class Negro Preschoolers." *Child Develop* 42(2):455-64 Je '71. * (*PA* 47:637)

268. JOESTING, JOAN, AND JOESTING, ROBERT. "Correlation of Scores on the Picture Interpretation Test and Stanford-Binet Form L-M IQs." *Psychol Rep* 28(3):906 Je '71. * (*PA* 46:10576)

269. JOHNSON, DALE L., AND JOHNSON, CARMEN A. "Comparison of Four Intelligence Tests Used With Culturally Disadvantaged Children." *Psychol Rep* 28(1):209-10 F '71. * (*PA* 46:5736)

270. KASPAR, JOSEPH C.; MILLICHAP, J. GORDON; BACKUS, RENO; CHILD, DAVID; AND SCHULMAN, JEROME L. "A Study of the Relationship Between Neurological Evidence of Brain Damage in Children and Activity and Distractibility." *J Consult & Clin Psychol* 36(3):329-37 Je '71. * (*PA* 46:9475)

271. KOOLS, JOSEPH A.; WILLIAMS, AMANDA F.; VICKERS, MARJORIE JO; AND COELL, ANN. "Oral and Limb Apraxia in Mentally Retarded Children With Deviant Articulation." *Cortex* (Italy) 7(4):387-400 D '71. * (*PA* 49:11425)

272. L'ABATE, LUCIANO. "Receptive-Expressive Functions in Kindergarten Children and Adolescents." *Psychol Sch* 8(3):253-9 Jl '71. * (*PA* 47:9699)

273. MCCALL, CAROL IRENE. *An Investigation of Language Deficiency in a Female Prison Population.* Doctor's thesis, University of Florida (Gainesville, Fla.), 1971. (*DAI* 32:6101B)

274. MCCOOK, WILLIAM. *A Statistical Analysis of the Item Validity of the Peabody Picture Vocabulary Test.* Master's thesis, University of Connecticut (Storrs, Conn.), 1971.

275. MCCORMICK, CLARENCE C., AND SCHNOBRICH, JANICE N. "Perceptual-Motor Training and Improvement in Concentration in a Montessori Preschool." *Percept & Motor Skills* 32(1):71-7 F '71. * (*PA* 46:3865)

276. MALONEY, MICHAEL P.; WARD, MICHAEL P.; SCHENCK, HERBERT U.; AND BRAUCHT, GEORGE N. "Re-Evaluation of the Use of the Quick Test With a Sample of Institutionalized Mentally Retarded Subjects." *Psychol Rep* 29(3):1155-9 D '71. * (*PA* 48:1517)

277. MARSHALL, M. S., AND BENTLER, P. M. "IQ Increases of Disadvantaged Minority-Group Children Following Innovative Enrichment Program." *Psychol Rep* 29(3):805-6 D '71. * (*PA* 47:9836)

278. MATHENY, ADAM P., JR. "Comparability of WISC and PPVT Scores Among Young Children." *Excep Children* 38(2):147-50 O '71. * (*PA* 48:3673)

279. MILGRAM, NORMAN A. "IQ Constancy in Disadvantaged Negro Children." *Psychol Rep* 29(1):319-26 Ag '71. * (*PA* 47:2652)

280. NEDLER, SHARI, AND SEBERA, PEGGY. "Intervention Strategies for Spanish-Speaking Preschool Children." *Child Develop* 42(1):259-67 Mr '71. * (*PA* 46:5743)

281. ODELL, LOUISE M. "Maternal Intellectual Functioning." *Johns Hopkins Med J* 128(6):362-8 Je '71. *

282. O'PIELA, JOAN MARIE. *Identification of Predictor Variables of Success in First Grade Reading in Culturally Disadvantaged Inner-City Children Who Have Had a Preschool Experience.* Doctor's thesis, Wayne State University (Detroit, Mich.), 1971. (*DAI* 32:6109A)

283. PASEWARK, RICHARD A.; FITZGERALD, BERNARD J.; AND GLOECKLER, TED. "Relationship of Peabody Picture Vocabulary Test and Wechsler Intelligence Scale for Children in an Educable Retarded Group: A Cautionary Note." *Psychol Rep* 28(2):405-6 Ap '71. * (*PA* 46:7516)

284. RADIN, NORMA. "Maternal Warmth, Achievement Motivation, and Cognitive Functioning in Lower-Class Preschool Children." *Child Develop* 42(5):1560-6 N '71. * (*PA* 48:4724)

285. RASKIN, LARRY M.; OFFENBACH, STUART I.; AND SCOONOVER, DELMER L. "A Developmental Study of PPVT Temporal Stability Over Two 6-Mo. Intervals." *Psychol Rep* 28(2):501-2 Ap '71. * (*PA* 46:7458)

286. ROBINSON, HALBERT B., AND ROBINSON, NANCY M. "Longitudinal Development of Very Young Children in a Comprehensive Day Care Program: The First Two Years." *Child Develop* 42(6):1673-83 D '71. * (*PA* 48:8827)

287. ROHWER, WILLIAM D., JR.; AMMON, MARY SUE; SUZUKI, NANCY; AND LEVIN, JOEL R. "Population Differences and Learning Proficiency." *J Ed Psychol* 62(1):1-14 F '71. * (*PA* 46:3844)

288. ROHWER, WILLIAM D., JR., AND LEVIN, JOEL R. "Elaboration Preferences and Differences in Learning Proficiency." *Cognitive Studies* 2:127-48 '71. * (*PA* 49:1354, title only)

289. ROSENBERG, JOHN BENJAMIN. *The Relationship of Minor Congenital Anomalies to Behavioral and Intellectual Variables in Early School Age Children.* Doctor's thesis, Temple University (Philadelphia, Pa.), 1971. (*DAI* 32:2384B)

290. ROURKE, B. P.; YOUNG, G. C.; AND FLEWELLING, R. W. "The Relationships Between WISC Verbal-Performance Discrepancies and Selected Verbal, Auditory-Perceptual, Visual-Perceptual, and Problem-Solving Abilities in Children With Learning Disabilities." *J Clin Psychol* 27(4):475-9 O '71. * (*PA* 47:9738)

291. SEDA, MARIA S. A., AND MICHAEL, JOAN J. "The Concurrent Validity of the Sprigle School Screening Readiness Test for a Sample of Preschool and Kindergarten Children." *Ed & Psychol Meas* 31(4):995-7 w '71. * (*PA* 48:1660)

292. SELMAN, ROBERT L. "The Relation of Role Taking to the Development of Moral Judgment in Children." *Child Develop* 42(1):79-91 Mr '71. * (*PA* 46:4699)

293. SILOAC, KENNETH THOMAS. *An Investigation of Selected Perceptual Abilities in Educable Retarded and Normal Children.* Doctor's thesis, Wayne State University (Detroit, Mich.), 1971. (*DAI* 32:6719B)

294. STAFFIERI, J. ROBERT. "Performance of Preschool Children on the Quick Test (QT)." *Psychol Rep* 29(2):472 O '71. * (*PA* 47:9667)

295. SWIZE, LYDIA MARIE. *The Relationship Between Performance on Piagetian Conservation Tasks and Intelligence and Achievement in Educable Mentally Retarded Children.* Doctor's thesis, University of Northern Colorado (Greeley, Colo.), 1971. (*DAI* 32:3806A)

296. THOMAS, CLIFTON D.; ALCORN, JOHN D.; AND HOLMES, WILLIAM R. "Intellectual Performance of Headstart Children." *South J Ed Res* 5(1):51-6 Ja '71. *

297. TOLIVER, GLORIA DEAN. *The Measurement of Language Abilities of Black Children From Low Socioeconomic Environments.* Doctor's thesis, Ohio State University (Columbus, Ohio), 1971. (*DAI* 32:1903B)

298. WEINER, PAUL S. "Stability and Validity of Two Measures of Intelligence Used With Children Whose Language Development Is Delayed." *J Speech & Hearing Res* 14(2):254-61 Je '71. * (*PA* 48:5419)

299. WELLS, DONALD G., AND PEDRINI, DUILIO T. "Relationships Among Wechsler Adult Intelligence Scale, Goodenough-Harris, and Peabody Picture Vocabulary Tests With Institutionalized Retarded Adults." *Percept & Motor Skills* 33(1):227-32 Ag '71. * (*PA* 47:3549)

300. WILLIAMS, JOHN E., AND ROUSSEAU, CYNTHIA A. "Evaluation and Identification Responses of Negro Preschoolers to the Colors Black and White." *Percept & Motor Skills* 33(2):587-99 O '71. * (*PA* 47:6522)

301. WOLF, GERALD PHILLIP. *The Reliability and Validity of the Peabody Picture Vocabulary Test With Institutionalized Educable Retarded Children and Adolescents and Its Use as a Group Test With This Population.* Doctor's thesis, Catholic University of America (Washington, D.C.), 1971. (*DAI* 32:1871A)

CUMULATIVE NAME INDEX

Abramson, T.: 153
Alcorn, J. D.: 296
Ali, F.: 245, 253
Allen, R. M.: 28, 154-6, 175, 190
Allerhand, M. E.: 81
Amdur, J. L. R.: 246
Ammon, M. S.: 287
Anastasiow, N. J.: 191
Anderson, B. B.: 117, 192
Anderson, D. E.: 118
Anderson, H. E.: 109
Ando, K.: 119
Archer, L. S.: 193
Asbury, C. A.: 157
Ayers, J. B.: 82
Bach, L. C.: 120
Backus, R.: 270
Bagur, J. S.: 267
Bart, L. E.: 247
Bashaw, W. L.: 82, 109
Baumann, K. S.: 158
Beck, R.: 194
Becker, J. T.: 159, 182
Belden, B. R.: 195
Belden, E.: 139
Beller, E. K.: 230
Benger, K.: 121, 226
Benninger, C. A.: 239
Bentler, P. M.: 277
Berg, N. L.: 248
Berg, S. D.: 248
Bigelow, G. S.: 83, 249
Billy, H. T.: 222
Birch, H. G.: 172
Birnbrauer, J. S.: 131
Blue, C. M.: 160
Bonner, M. W.: 122, 195
Borich, G. D.: 191
Borosage, V.: 123
Brady, J. J.: 128, 164
Braucht, G. N.: 276
Brengelmann, J. C.: 224
Bridges, J. S.: 212
Bromwich, R. M.: 84
Brooks, S.: 6
Brooks, S. T.: 3
Brosseau, J. F.: 89
Brown, L. F.: 85-6, 111
Brown, R.: 218
Bruininks, R. H.: 196-7
Budoff, M.: 17
Burland, R.: 250
Burnett, A.: 38
Burns, G. W.: 231
Butler, B. V.: 260
Callaway, B.: 198, 266
Carlson, J. S.: 251-2
Carr, D. L.: 86
Carroll, V. M.: 250
Cartwright, G. P.: 124
Cashdan, A.: 265
Chansky, N. M.: 261
Child, D.: 270
Childers, P. R.: 55
Cochran, M. L.: 161, 199
Coell, A.: 271
Cohen, S.: 149
Coller, A. R.: 206
Comstock, J. A.: 240
Corah, N. L.: 227
Cork, E.: 125
Corwin, B. J.: 39, 87
Costello, J.: 200, 245, 253, 267
Coyle, F. A.: 125
Crawford, V. B.: 162
Cromwell, R. L.: 74
Crowell, D.: 57
Crowell, D. C.: 90
Cundick, B. P.: 201
Curry, D. R.: 163
Danford, B. H.: 29
Dans, C.: 125
Datta, L. E.: 88
Deich, R. F.: 126
de Lacey, P. R.: 254-5
Dick, R. M.: 256
Dill, J.: 206
DiLorenzo, L. T.: 127-8, 164
Dingman, H. F.: 184
Dockrell, W. B.: 89
Doll, P. A.: 257
Dundore, J. M.: 165
Dunn, L. M.: 1, 3, 8, 74
Dunn-Rankin, P.: 90
Edmonds, P.: 5
Eisenson, J.: 149
Eklund, S.: 40
Elkin, L.: 129
Elliott, E.: 258
Elliott, R. N.: 166
Emerick, L. L.: 56
English, R. A.: 167
Ernhart, C. B.: 130, 202
Fagot, H. J.: 257
Falk, L. J.: 259
Familant, R. P.: 92
Fargo, G.: 57
Fargo, G. A.: 90
Fay, W. H.: 260
Fedio, P.: 237
Feldman, D. H.: 196
Feldt, L. S.: 75
Fitzgerald, B. J.: 203, 283
Flax, M. L.: 118
Fleming, J. W.: 188
Flewelling, R. W.: 290
Floyd, W. A.: 30
Fong, L. J.: 219
Fuchigami, R. Y.: 90
Fulton, R. T.: 91
Gabet, Y.: 184
Gage, G. E.: 41
Galli, A. P.: 204
Garber, M.: 205
Gardner, A. M.: 131
Garrett, J.: 2
Giebink, J. W.: 232
Gilmore, S. I.: 92
Gleason, J. B.: 207
Gloeckler, T.: 203, 283
Goldstein, L. S.: 206
Goodglass, H.: 207
Gordon, J. M.: 90
Gorelick, J.: 9
Graubard, P. S.: 93
Graves, G. R.: 24
Greemore, R.: 94
Griffith, J.: 185
Gropper, R. L.: 168
Gross, M.: 238
Grossman, M.: 208
Gwaltney, W.: 266
Hale, J. R.: 95
Hall, J. C.: 169, 261
Hammill, D.: 42
Hammill, D. D.: 45-6, 58, 64, 96, 132
Hardy, M. P.: 262
Harley, R. K.: 1
Hartman, B. T.: 10
Haupt, T. D.: 28
Haywood, H. C.: 133
Heal, L. W.: 133
Hedger, M. F.: 43
Herndon, J. D.: 11
Heydenberk, W. R.: 263
Hill, T. V.: 112
Hillman, W. A.: 224
Himbert, J. D.: 257
Himelstein, P.: 11
Hinton, O. G.: 264
Hodgins, A. S.: 241
Holmes, W. R.: 299
Hottel, J. V.: 6, 8
Howard, J. L.: 97
Hubschman, E.: 209
Hudson, F. G.: 178
Hughes, R. B.: 44
Hyde, M. R.: 207
Irvine, J.: 233
Irwin, O. C.: 42, 45-6, 58-64, 96, 98-101, 132
Ivanoff, J. M.: 47, 136
Jackson, C. L.: 31
James, P.: 19
Jeffree, D. M.: 265
Jerrolds, B. W.: 266
Jeruchimowicz, R.: 267
Joesting, J.: 268
Joesting, R.: 268
Johnson, C. A.: 269
Johnson, C. M.: 134
Johnson, D. L.: 269
Jones, R. W.: 28
Jones, S. A.: 227
Joselson, M. L.: 210
Kahn, H.: 65
Kaliski, M. S.: 209
Kaplan, B. E.: 135, 211
Karnes, M. B.: 241
Kaspar, J. C.: 54, 270
Katz, F. M.: 236
Kaufman, H. J.: 136
Keim, R. P.: 170
Kicklighter, R. M.: 66
Kidder, J. W.: 167
Kilburn, K. L.: 67
Kimbrell, D. L.: 4
King, S. H.: 242
Kirk, G. E.: 171
Klapper, Z. S.: 172
Kløve, H.: 73
Knights, R. M.: 264
Koh, T. H.: 102
Kools, J. A.: 271
Korst, J. W.: 48, 68, 99-101
Krippner, S.: 25
L'Abate, L.: 272
Laney, B. J.: 243
Lavitt, J. A.: 103
Leonhardt, T. M.: 191
Leppke, R. D.: 104
Lessler, K.: 44, 212
Levin, J. R.: 287-8
Lieberman, J. N.: 225
Lindsey, J. M.: 69
Lloyd, L. L.: 105
Lockyer, L.: 213
Lucker, W. G.: 197
Lyman, H. B.: rev, 6:530
McArthur, C. R.: 137
McCall, C. I.: 273
McClary, G. O.: 173
McClellan, D. A.: 138
McCook, W.: 274
McCormick, C. C.: 275
MacKay, D. N.: 258
McLeod, C. M.: 214
McManis, D. L.: 105
Madow, A. A.: 102
Maier, L. J.: 80
Malerstein, A. J.: 139
Maloney, M. P.: 276
Mandel, R.: 214
Manning, G. C.: 33
Marden, M. L.: 232
Marley, A. D.: 32
Marshall, A. S.: 277
Matheny, A. P.: 278
Matthews, C. G.: 18, 33, 73
Mauser, A. J.: 140
Mayans, A. E.: 70
Mazer, M.: 174
Meier, J. H.: 49
Mein, R.: 12
Mellits, D.: 262
Melton, R. S.: 67
Messer, M. E.: 175
Michael, J. J.: 291
Miezitis, S.: 183
Miezitis, S. A.: 141
Milgram, N. A.: 106-7, 147, 279
Miller, B. B.: 227
Millichap, J. G.: 270
Miner, L.: 185
Minsky, R.: 176
Mirsky, A. F.: 237
Moed, G.: 19
Moffitt, P.: 216
Moss, J. W.: 5
Mueller, M. W.: 13, 50-1, 142, 177
Myers, P. I.: 132
Nation, J. E.: 34
Naumann, T. F.: 41
Nedler, S.: 280
Nelson, C. M.: 178
Nelson, P. C.: 108
Nesbitt, M. C.: 143
Nicholson, C. L.: 179, 215
Norris, R. C.: 6
Noyes, M.: 57
Noyes, M. H.: 90
Nurcombe, B.: 216
Nurss, J. R.: 221
O'Connor, G.: 184
Odell, L. M.: 281
Offenbach, S. I.: 285
Omer, J. L.: 180
O'Piela, J. M.: 282
Osborne, R. T.: 109
Ozer, M. N.: 107
Palmer, F. H.: 217
Panther, E. E.: 110
Pasewark, R. A.: 203, 283
Patterson, H. J.: 22
Paulus, D. H.: 146, 181, 234
Pedrini, D. T.: 116, 161, 299
Piers, E. V.: rev, 6:530
Plant, W. T.: 97, 144
Polizzotto, E. A.: 209
Pool, D. A.: 218
Purseglove, E. M.: 17
Radin, N.: 284
Raskin, L. M.: 219, 285
Rawl, M. F.: 145
Reger, R.: 14
Reitan, R. M.: 18
Renzulli, J. S.: 77, 146, 151, 181, 234
Rice, D.: 14
Rice, J. A.: 85-6, 111, 147
Rieber, M.: 148
Roberts, A. J.: 220
Robinson, H. B.: 286
Robinson, N. M.: 286
Rohwer, W. D.: 287-8
Rolland, J. C.: 105
Rood, T. M.: 26
Rosenberg, J. B.: 289
Rosenberg, L. A.: 72
Rourke, B. P.: 290
Rousseau, C. A.: 300
Rugg, R. H.: 35
Rutter, M.: 213
Sabatino, D. A.: 182
Sanderson, R. E.: 67
Scharf, M. P.: 36
Schenck, H. U.: 276
Schnobrich, J. N.: 275
Schoeninger, D. W.: 212
Schulman, J. L.: 54, 270
Scoggins, B. J.: 7
Scoonover, D. L.: 285
Scott, M.: 40
Sebera, P.: 280
Seda, M. S. A.: 291
Selman, R. L.: 292
Shane, J. F.: 52
Shaw, D. J.: 73
Shipe, D.: 74, 183
Shipe, D. M.: 15
Shotwell, A. M.: 184
Sibley, S. A.: 191
Silberberg, N. E.: 75
Siloac, K. T.: 293
Silverstein, A. B.: 112
Smith, M. P.: 235
Smith, P. B.: 113
Southern, M. L.: 144
Spock, A.: 228
Staffieri, J. R.: 294
Stark, J.: 149
Stedman, D. J.: 228
Sterne, D. M.: 150
Strandberg, T. E.: 185
Strong, R. T.: 53
Stroud, M.: 72
Suzuki, N.: 287
Swize, L. M.: 295
Talkington, L. W.: 194
Tauber, R.: 76

Peabody Picture Vocabulary Test

Taylor, J. R.: 20
Teasdale, G. R.: 186, 236
Tempero, H. E.: 47
Tenhoff, M. L.: 23
Teska, J. A.: 241
Thomas, C. D.: 296
Throne, F. M.: 54
Tilis, H. S.: 206
Tillinghast, B. S.: 77, 151
Tillmans, S. J.: 229
Tobias, J.: 9
Toliver, G. D.: 297
Tolley, J.: 152
Tuttle, L. E.: 37, 78
Uhl, N. P.: 221
Vickers, M. J.: 271
Wakefield, H. E.: 137
Walker, A. J. M.: 187
Wallach, E. S.: 156
Ward, M. P.: 276
Ward, W. C.: 79
Ware, W. B.: 205
Weaver, A. S.: 115
Weeks, R. W.: 21
Weiner, P. S.: 298
Wells, D. G.: 116, 299
Whipple, C. I.: 80
Whitman, M. A.: 244
Wight, B. W.: 19
Williams, A. F.: 271
Williams, J. E.: 300
Williams, T. M.: 188
Willig, S. N.: 262
Winschel, J. F.: 27
Wolf, G. P.: 301
Wolfensberger, W.: 16
Womack, M.: 148
Woody, R. H.: 222
Yen, S. M. Y.: 189
Young, G. C.: 290
Zaeske, A.: 223
Zunich, M.: 152

[517]

Pictorial Test of Intelligence. Ages 3–8; 1964; PTI; prepublication titles were *North Central Individual Test of Mental Ability* and *Pictorial Intelligence Test;* 7 scores: picture vocabulary, form discrimination, information and comprehension, similarities, size and number, immediate recall, total; Joseph L. French; Houghton Mifflin Co. *

For additional information and reviews by Philip Himelstein and T. Ernest Newland, see 7:418 (17 references); see also 6:531 (2 references).

REFERENCES THROUGH 1971

1–2. See 6:531.
3–19. See 7:418.
20. MANDELBAUM, DAVID. *The Feasibility of an Audio-Taped Administration of the Pictorial Test of Intelligence.* Master's thesis, Pennsylvania State University (University Park, Pa.), 1971.

CUMULATIVE NAME INDEX

Bonfield, J. R.: 11
Brito, H.: 10
Dell, D.: 10
Elliott, R. N.: 18
French, J. L.: 1–3
Gentile, J. R.: 7
Greer, D.: 3
Himelstein, P.: *rev*, 7:418
Honstead, C. A.: 8
Howard, J. L.: 9
Jenson, G.: 4
Lee, R.: 10
Mandelbaum, D.: 20
Mueller, M. W.: 5–6, 12, 18
Newland, T. E.: *rev*, 7:418
Ortiz, K. K.: 13
Pasewark, R. A.: 10
Patterson, N. J.: 14
Plant, W. T.: 9, 15
Sawyer, R. N.: 10, 16
Smith, E.: 10
Southern, M. L.: 15
Vogler, J. D.: 17
Wasserberger, M.: 10

[518]

The Porteus Maze Test. Ages 3 and over; 1914–65; PMT; 2 scores: quantitative, qualitative; 3 editions and 2 supplements; Stanley D. Porteus. *

a) VINELAND REVISION. Ages 3 and over; 1914–24; Stoelting Co.

b) VINELAND REVISION: NEW SERIES. Ages 3 and over; 1914–65; Psychological Corporation.

c) PORTEUS MAZE EXTENSION. Ages 7 and over; 1953–65; for use only as a supplement to the *Vineland Revision: New Series;* Psychological Corporation.

d) PORTEUS MAZE SUPPLEMENT. Ages 7 and over; 1959–65; a retesting series; Psychological Corporation.

e) BRITISH EDITION. Ages 3 and over; 1914–65; George G. Harrap & Co. Ltd. [England].

For additional information, reviews by Richard F. Docter and John L. Horn, and excerpted reviews by William D. Altus, H. B. Gibson, D. C. Kendrick, and Laurance F. Shaffer, see 7:419 (67 references); see also 6:532 (38 references) and 5:412 (28 references); for reviews by C. M. Louttit and Gladys C. Schwesinger, see 4:356 (56 references). For excerpts from related book reviews, see 6:B400 (3 excerpts), 4:357 (4 excerpts), 1:B453 (2 excerpts), and 36:B210 (3 excerpts).

Peabody Picture Vocabulary Test

REFERENCES THROUGH 1971

1–56. See 4:356.
57–84. See 5:412.
85–122. See 6:532.
123–189. See 7:419.
190. BASSETT, DOROTHY M., AND PORTEUS, STANLEY D. "Sex Differences in Porteus Maze Test Performance." *Training Sch B* 17:1–16 N '20. *
191. PORTEUS, S. D. Chap. 4, "Porteus Maze Tests," pp. 75–115. In his *Studies in Mental Deviations*. Publications of the Training School at Vineland, N.J., Department of Research, No. 24, October 1922. Vineland, N.J.: the School, 1923. Pp. xi, 276. *
192. FOX, J. TYLOR. "The Response of Epileptic Children to Mental and Educational Tests." *Brit J Med Psychol* 4:235–48 N '24. *
193. HERRING, JOHN P. "Diagnosis of Feeble-Mindedness by Subjective Means." *J Ed Psychol* 17:270–4 Ap '26. *
194. BABCOCK, MARJORIE E. *Applications of Clinical Psychology in Hawaii.* University of Hawaii Research Publications No. 1. Honolulu, Hawaii: Mercantile Press, 1927. Pp. 88. *
195. PETERSON, JOSEPH. "A Review of *Temperament and Race.*" *Am J Psychol* 40:640–1 O '28 *; PORTEUS, S. D. "A Protest." *Am J Psychol* 41:336–8 Ap '29 *; PETERSON, JOSEPH. "A Reply to Porteus' 'Protest.'" *Am J Psychol* 41:338–41 Ap '29. *
196. BROOM, EUSTACE. "The Validity of Four Individual Tests of Mental Ability." *Ed Res B* (Los Angeles City Schools) 8:9–10 Mr '29. *
197. TREAT, KATHARINE. "Tests for Garment Machine Operators." *Personnel J* 8:19–28 Je '29. * (*PA* 3:3767)
198. PORTEUS, STANLEY D. Chap. 21, "Tests of Temperament and Intelligence," pp. 351–77. In his *The Psychology of a Primitive People: A Study of the Australian Aborigine.* New York: Longmans, Green & Co., 1931. Pp. xvi, 438. * (*PA* 6:1168, title only)
199. PORTEUS, STANLEY D. Chap. 23, "Aboriginal Children's Intelligence," pp. 408–20. In his *The Psychology of a Primitive People: A Study of the Australian Aborigine.* New York: Longmans, Green & Co., 1931. Pp. xvi, 438. * (*PA* 6:1168, title only)
200. PORTEUS, STANLEY D. "Mentality of Australian Aborigines." *Oceania* (Australia) 4:30–6 S '33. *
201. REICHARD, J. D. "The Intelligence of the Prospective Immigrant: 1, A Study of the Mental Ability, Measured by Language and Non-Language Tests, of Applicants for Immigrant Visas at Warsaw, Poland." *Pub Health B* 206:1–35 Jl '33. * (*PA* 8:1774)
202. SHAKOW, DAVID, AND MILLARD, MARY S. "A Psychometric Study of One Hundred and Fifty Adult Delinquents." *J Social Psychol* 6:437–57 N '35. * (*PA* 10:3652)
203. WEISENBURG, THEODORE; ROE, ANNE; AND MCBRIDE, KATHARINE E. *Adult Intelligence: A Psychological Study of Test Performances.* New York: Commonwealth Fund, 1936. Pp. xiii, 155. * (*PA* 10:3771)
204. COWLES, KATHARINE. *The Correlation of Non-Language Mental Tests and Scholastic Achievement of Deaf Children.* Master's thesis, Temple University (Philadelphia, Pa.), 1937.
205. MARSH, CHARLES JUDD. *Performance Test Abilities of Adults.* Doctor's thesis, Stanford University (Stanford, Calif.), 1938.
206. MORRIS, CHARLES M. "A Critical Analysis of Certain Performance Tests." *J Genetic Psychol* 54:85–105 Mr '39. * (*PA* 13:5387)
207. PENROSE, L. S. "Intelligence Test Scores of Mentally Defective Patients and Their Relatives." *Brit J Psychol* 30:1–18 Jl '39. * (*PA* 13:5734)
208. PETERS, MARY FRIDIANA. *A Comparative Study of Some Measures of Emotional Instability in School Children.* Lafayette, Ind.: St. Francis Community Press, 1939. Pp. x, 71. *
209. MUENCH, GEORGE A. "A Follow-Up of Mental Defectives After Eighteen Years." *J Abn & Social Psychol* 39:407–18 O '44. * (*PA* 19:420)
210. BIESHEUVEL, S. Chap. 4, "Psychological Tests and Their Applications to Non-European Peoples," pp. 87–126. In *The Yearbook of Education,* 1949. London: Evans Brothers Ltd., 1949. Pp. xv, 660. *
211. PETRIE, ASENATH. "Personality Changes After Pre-Frontal Leucotomy." *Brit J Med Psychol* 22:200–1 pts 3–4 '49. * (*PA* 25:2002)
212. PETRIE, ASENATH. "Preliminary Report of Changes After Prefrontal Leucotomy." *J Mental Sci* (England) 95:449–55 Ap '49. * (*PA* 24:278)
213. JENSEN, MILTON B., AND SCHMID, JOHN. "An Analysis of Some Clinical Judgments on Male Basic Airmen Who Failed the Group Psychological Tests." *J Clin Psychol* 10:325–2 O '54. * (*PA* 29:4753)
214. FOULDS, G. A. "The Reliability of Psychiatric, and the Validity of Psychological, Diagnoses." *J Mental Sci* (England) 101:851–62 O '55. * (*PA* 30:7165)
215. GARDNER, M. J.; HAWKINS, H. M.; JUDAH, L. N.; AND MURPHREE, O. D. "Objective Measurement of Psychiatric Changes Produced by Chlorpromazine and Reserpine in Chronic Schizophrenia." *Psychiatric Res Rep* 1:77–83 Jl '55. * (*PA* 30:8411)
216. PORTEUS, STANLEY D. "Some Commonsense Implications

of Psychosurgery." *Brit J Med Psychol* 28:167-76 pts 2-3 '55. * (PA 30:2982)

217. Tow, P. Macdonald. Chap. 22, "Porteus Mazes," pp. 171-80. In his *Personality Changes Following Frontal Leucotomy.* London: Oxford University Press, 1955. Pp. xv, 262. * (PA 30:8319)

218. Durling, Dorothy, and Esen, Fatma Munire. "Irregular Test Profiles Correlated With Personality Traits." *Am J Mental Def* 61:409-12 O '56. * (PA 32:1772)

219. Dennis, Wayne, and Najarian, Pergrouhi. "Infant Development Under Environmental Handicap." *Psychol Monogr* 71(7):1-13 '57. * (PA 33:5830)

220. Garrison, Mortimer, Jr. "A Comparison of Psychological Measures in Mentally Retarded Boys Over a Three-Year Period as a Function of Etiology." *Training Sch B* 55:54-60 N '58. * (PA 34:1664)

221. Smith, Aaron, and Kinder, Elaine F. "Changes in Psychological Test Performances of Brain-Operated Schizophrenics After 8 Years." *Sci* 129:149-50 Ja 16 '59. * (PA 34:4700)

222. Rao, C. K. Vasudeva. "Intelligence in a Group of Convicts: An Analysis of 35 Cases." *Trans All-India Inst Mental Health* 1:44-53 D '60. * (PA 37:3649)

223. Shapiro, M. B.; Kessell, R.; and Maxwell, A. E. "Speed and Quality of Psychomotor Performance in Psychiatric Patients." *J Clin Psychol* 16:266-71 Jl '60. * (PA 36:2HI66S)

224. Porteus, Stanley D., and Diamond, A. L. "Measurement of Psychomotor Perseverative Tendencies." Letter. *Nature* (England) 189(4765):691-2 F 25 '61. *

225. Jenkins, C. David. "The Relation of EEG Slowing to Selected Indices of Intellective Impairment." *J Nerv & Mental Dis* 135:162-70 Ag '62. *

226. Agnew, Neil, and Agnew, Mary. "Drive Level Effects on Tasks of Narrow and Broad Attention." *Q J Exp Psychol* 15:58-62 F '63. * (PA 37:7549)

227. Conners, C. Keith, and Eisenberg, Leon. "The Effects of Methylphenidate on Symptomatology and Learning in Disturbed Children." *Am J Psychiatry* 120:458-63 N '63. * (PA 38:6177)

228. Helper, Malcolm M.; Wilcott, R. C.; and Garfield, Sol L. "Effects of Chlorpromazine on Learning and Related Processes in Emotionally Disturbed Children." *J Consult Psychol* 27:1-9 F '63. * (PA 37:7710)

229. Smith, Aaron. "Mental Deterioration in Chronic Schizophrenia." *J Nerv & Mental Dis* 139:479-87 N '64. *

230. Bromley, D. B. "Age Differences in the Porteus Maze Test." *Proc Int Congr Gerontol* 6:225-8 '65. *

231. Mussen, Paul H., and Parker, Ann L. "Mother Nurturance and Girls' Incidental Imitative Learning." *J Pers & Social Psychol* 2:94-7 Jl '65. * (PA 39:12022)

232. Meier, Manfred J., and French, Lyle A. "Longitudinal Assessment of Intellectual Functioning Following Unilateral Temporal Lobectomy." *J Clin Psychol* 22:22-7 Ja '66. * (PA 40:4283)

233. Porteus, Stanley D., and David, Kenneth. "Australid Mental Development and Geriatric Decline." *Percept & Motor Skills* 23:75-87 Ag '66. *

234. Porteus, Stanley D. *A Psychologist of Sorts: The Autobiography and Publications of the Inventor of the Porteus Maze Tests.* Palo Alto, Calif.: Pacific Books, Publishers, 1969. Pp. x, 325. *

235. Meier, Manfred J. "Effects of Focal Cerebral Lesions on Contralateral Visuomotor Adaptation to Reversal and Inversion of Visual Feedback." *Neuropsychologia* (England) 8(3): 269-79 Jl '70. * (PA 44:21410)

236. Erikson, Robert V., and Roberts, Alan H. "Some Ego Functions Associated With Delay of Gratification in Male Delinquents." *J Consult & Clin Psychol* 36(3):378-82 Je '71. * (PA 46:9318)

237. Falconer, A. D. "Measurement of Cognitive Function in Two Groups of Alcoholics." *J Alcoholism* (England) 6(4): 118-23 w '71. *

238. Freston, Cyrus Wheelock, II. *Verbal and Porteus Maze Performance of Learning Disabled Children: Effects of Methylphenidate and Input Organization.* Doctor's thesis, University of Texas (Austin, Tex.), 1971. (DAI 32:6246A)

239. Logothetis, John; Haritos-Fatouros, Mary; Constantoulakis, Mathios; Economidou, Joanna; Augoustaki, Olga; and Loewenson, Ruth B. "Intelligence and Behavioral Patterns in Patients With Cooley's Anemia (Homozygous Beta-thalassemia); A Study Based on 138 Consecutive Cases." *Pediatrics* 48(5):740-4 N '71. *

240. Meichenbaum, Donald H., and Goodman, Joseph. "Training Impulsive Children to Talk to Themselves." *J Abn Psychol* 77(2):115-26 Ap '71. * (PA 46:3785)

241. Shipe, Dorothy. "Impulsivity and Locus of Control as Predictors of Achievement and Adjustment in Mildly Retarded and Borderline Youth." *Am J Mental Def* 76(1):12-22 Jl '71. * (PA 47:5484)

CUMULATIVE NAME INDEX

Aaronson, B. S.: 80, 116
Adams, H. B.: 155
Aftanas, M. S.: 174
Agnew, M.: 226
Agnew, N.: 226
Altus, W. D.: *exc*, 7:419
Andrews, R. S.: 145
Anthony, A. A.: 117-8
Armlin, N. J.: 144
Arnold, G. F.: 38, 60
Aronson, H.: 96
Augoustaki, O.: 239
Babcock, M. E.: 194
Barclay, J. E.: 83, 103
Barnsley, R.: 165
Barry, J. R.: 106, 146
Bassett, D. M.: 190
Bennett, H. J.: 76
Bentley, M.: *exc*, 4:357
Berman, I. R.: 45
Bernreuter, R. G.: 15
Bernstein, L.: 114
Biesheuvel, S.: 210
Blumenkrantz, J.: 136
Bochner, S.: 157, 162
Borum, E.: 136
Bourestom, N. C.: 164
Briggs, P. F.: 119
Bromley, D. B.: 230
Broom, E.: 196
Broverman, D. M.: 132
Burdock, E. I.: 109
Burnand, G.: 110, 154
Burt, C.: 6, 44
Byrum, M.: 122
Caine, T. M.: 88, 92
Cannell, C. F.: 30
Carson, M. K.: 46
Chun, R. W. M.: 169
Clark, G. R.: 187
Cohen, S.: 175
Conners, C. K.: 183, 227
Constantoulakis, M.: 239
Cooper, G. D.: 155
Cotler, S.: 182
Cowles, K.: 204
Craft, M.: 110, 137
Crawford, J. M.: 51
Crawford, P. L.: 127-8
Cronbach, L. J.: *exc*, 4:357
Crown, S.: 124
Culver, H. S.: 103
Cunningham, K. S.: 3
Dahlgren, H.: 136
Daston, P. G.: 79, 155
David, K.: 162, 233
David, K. H.: 156-7
Davidson, K. S.: 104
Dennis, W.: 219
Dentler, R. A.: 111
Desai, M. M.: 73
Dewey, D. M.: 15
Diamond, A. L.: 113, 224
Docter, R. F.: 62, 68, 97-8; *rev*, 7:419
Drewery, J.: *exc*, 6:B400
Durling, D.: 218
Earl, C. J. C.: 24
Ebert, E.: 123
Economidou, J.: 239
Eisenberg, L.: 227
Erikson, R. V.: 147, 172, 236
Erlick, D.: 48
Esen, F. M.: 218
Everstine, L.: 106
Ewing, J. A.: 176
Fabisch, W.: 110
Fahmy, M.: 133
Falconer, A. D.: 237
Farnham, L. J.: 122
Feldman, R. C.: 138
Fish, C. C.: 158
Fisher, S.: 47
Floor, L.: 187
Fooks, G.: 81
Foulds, G. A.: 52, 61, 69, 88, 91-2, 130, 134, 214
Fox, J. T.: 192
French, L. A.: 232
Freston, C. W.: 238
Frost, B. P.: 139
Fry, H. R.: 16
Fulkerson, S. C.: 146
Fuller, C. W.: 129
Gaddes, W. H.: 165
Gambaro, S.: 148
Gardner, M. J.: 215
Garfield, S. L.: 228
Garrison, M.: 220
Gaw, F.: 9-10
Gibbens, T. C. N.: 84, 131
Gibson, H. B.: *exc*, 7:419
Gilberstadt, H.: 166
Goldenberg, S.: 125
Goodman, J.: 240
Gorelick, J.: 115
Grabow, J. D.: 169
Grajales, M. C.: 59
Gregor, A. J.: 120-1; *exc*, 6:B400
Hanson, H. B.: 45
Haritos-Fatouros, M.: 239
Havighurst, R. J.: 34
Hawkins, H. M.: 215
Helper, M. M.: 228
Henker, B. A.: 99
Herrick, C. J.: 31
Herring, J. P.: 193
Heston, L. C.: 30
Hicks, J. A.: 17
Hoggart, K.: 154
Horn, J. L.: *rev*, 7:419
Howard, M. T.: 164
Hunter, H.: 154
Hunter, M.: 31
Janke, L. L.: 34
Jarrahi-Zadeh, A.: 176
Jarrett, R. F.: 57
Jenkins, C. D.: 225
Jensen, M. B.: 107, 213
Jones, F. D.: 53
Joseph, A.: 86
Judah, L. N.: 215
Judson, A. J.: 100
Justiss, W. A.: 126
Kahana, B.: 170
Kainer, R. K.: 140
Kane, F. J.: 176
Karpeles, L. M.: 21
Kendrick, D. C.: *exc*, 7:419
Kepner, R. D.: 36
Kerridge, D.: 110
Kessell, R.: 223
Kinder, E. F.: 221
Kiresuk, T. J.: 159
Kivitz, M. S.: 187
Klee, G. D.: 96
Kleman, J. P.: 102-3, 106
LaBarba, R. C.: 141
Lachenbruch, P. A.: 176
Landis, C.: 48
Lefkowitz, M. M.: 167
Leibowitz, M.: 149
Lester, O. P.: 12
Lighthall, F. K.: 104
Loewenson, R. B.: 239
Logothetis, J.: 239
Looker, A.: 183
Loranger, A. W.: 93, 101
Louttit, C. M.: 18, 23; *rev*, 4:356
McAloon, F. W.: 168
McBride, K. E.: 203
McDonald, J. R.: 19
McFadden, J. H.: *exc*, 36: B210
McGee, E.: 71
McKenzie, A.: 165
Mackler, B.: 111
McPherson, D. A.: 120
Malmquist, C. P.: 159
Marriage, A.: 131
Marsh, J.: 205
Martin, W. E.: 184
Matthews, C. G.: 169
Maxwell, A. E.: 223
Meichenbaum, D. H.: 240
Meier, M. J.: 150, 160-1, 177, 184, 232, 235
Millard, M. S.: 202
Minski, L.: 73
Misiak, H.: 93, 101
Montgomery, R. P.: 13
Morgenthau, D. R.: 7
Morris, C. M.: 25, 206
Muench, G. A.: 209
Muralidharan, R.: 189
Murphree, O. D.: 215
Murray, V. F.: 86
Mussen, P. H.: 231
Myatt, M. F.: 63
Najarian, P.: 219
O'Connor, N.: 51, 64
Okayama, M.: 177

O'Keefe, E. J.: 185
Owen, A.: 134
Palkes, H.: 170
Palmer, R. J.: 182
Parker, A. L.: 231
Penrose, L. S.: 207
Peretz, D.: 109
Peters, H. N.: 42-3, 53; *exc*, 6:B400
Peters, M. F.: 208
Peterson, J.: 14, 195
Petrie, A.: 211-2
Phillips, E. L.: 45
Piddington, M.: 85
Piddington, R.: 85
Pierce, R. A.: 142
Pintner, R.: *exc*, 1:B453
Porteus, S. D.: 1-2, 4-5, 8, 15, 22, 26, 28, 31, 33, 35-6, 39-40, 42-3, 49-50, 54, 65-6, 70, 74, 77, 82-3, 89, 94-5, 102-3, 108, 112-3, 121, 143, 162, 171, 178, 190-1, 195, 198-200, 216, 224, 233-4
Poull, L. E.: 13
Prange, A. J.: 181
Pulleine, R. H.: 16
Purcell, K.: 78, 114
Query, W. T.: 186
Ralph, D. W.: 17
Rankin, R.: 152
Rankin, R. J.: 151
Rao, C. K. V.: 222
Reichard, J. D.: 201
Resch, J. A.: 150, 161
Riley, J. E.: 144
Roberts, A. H.: 147, 172, 236
Roe, A.: 203
Rosén, A. S.: 173
Rosen, M.: 187
Royce, J. R.: 174
Ruebush, B. K.: 104, 122
Russell, J.: 162
Sacks, J. M.: 79
Salzinger, K.: 109
Salzinger, S.: 109
Sanderson, M. H.: 41
Sarason, S. B.: 104
Satter, G.: 71, 75
Schalling, D.: 173
Schell, R. E.: 148, 163
Schmid, J.: 213
Schmidt, A. G.: *exc*, 36:B210
Schwesinger, G. C.: *rev*, 4:356

Shaffer, L. F.: *exc*, 4:357, 7:419
Shakow, D.: 202
Shapiro, M. B.: 223
Sharp, E. Y.: 188
Shimota, H. E.: 87
Shipe, D.: 241
Simmons, K.: 123
Small, K.: 72
Smith, A.: 105, 221, 229
Spano, R. M.: 159
Sparling, M. E.: 32
Stackman, H.: 23
Stephenson, G.: 110
Sterne, D. M.: 153, 179
Stewart, M.: 170
Stone, C. L.: *exc*, 36:B210
Story, J. L.: 160
Stotsky, B. A.: 79
Sunukjian, H.: 47
Sutton, S.: 109
Sydow, D. W.: 67
Telford, C. W.: 14, 20
Thomas, R. R.: 81
Thompson, K.: 151-2
Thompson, W. H.: 169
Tilker, H. A.: 163
Tilton, J. W.: *exc*, 1:B453
Tizard, J.: 51, 55
Tobias, J.: 115
Tow, P. M.: 217
Trail, B. M.: 180
Treadway, C. R.: 181
Treat, K.: 197
Turnbull, J. W.: 114
Van de Castle, R. L.: 176
van der Kolk, J. J.: 29
Vernon, P. E.: 27
Verrill, B. V.: 90
Waite, R. R.: 104
Walker, A.: 131
Wassenaar, G. M. C.: 135
Watson, R. I.: 56
Weisenburg, T.: 203
Werner, E. E.: 189
Whybrow, P. C.: 181
Wilcott, R. C.: 228
Winder, C. L.: 68
Worcester, D. A.: *exc*, 4:357
Worthington, M. R.: 11
Wright, C.: 37
York, M. W.: 155
Zeckel, A.: 29
Zubin, J.: 109

[519]

Preschool Attainment Record, Research Edition. Ages 6 months to 7 years; 1966-67; PAR; 9 scores: ambulation, manipulation, rapport, communication, responsibility, information, ideation, creativity, total; Edgar A. Doll; American Guidance Service, Inc. *

For additional information, a review by Roberta R. Collard, and an excerpted review by C. H. Ammons, see 7:420 (5 references).

REFERENCES THROUGH 1971

1-5. See 7:420.
6. JORDAN, THOMAS E. "Early Developmental Adversity and the First Two Years of Life." *Multiv Behav Res Monogr* 6(1): 1-80 '71. * (*PA* 49:2132)
7. PHILLIPS, DORIS CAMPBELL. *An Exploratory Study of the Relationship Between Mothers' Individualization of Their Children and the Children's Developmental Progress.* Doctor's thesis, Washington University (St. Louis, Mo.), 1971. (*DAI* 32:2201A)

CUMULATIVE NAME INDEX

Ammons, C. H.: *exc*, 7:420
Blair, J. R.: 4
Bowling, D. H.: 5
Clifford, M.: 3
Collard, R. R.: *rev*, 7:420
Doll, E. A.: 1-2
Jordan, T. E.: 6
McKnight, E. L.: 1
Owens, E. P.: 5
Phillips, D. C.: 7
Spitznagel, A.: 3
Stedman, D. J.: 3

[520]

Queensland Test. Ages 7 and over; 1968-70; QT; based (except for pattern matching subtest) on the unpublished *PIR Test* used for screening for the Pacific Island Regiment; essentially the same as 5 of the 6 subtests in *New Guinea Performance Scales* except for minor differences in some testing materials and differences in administration, scoring, and norms population; for the selection of subjects "likely to be able to learn rapidly the complex skills of westernized urbanized cultures from among groups who had had little contact with that culture"; 6 scores: *Knox Cube Test,* beads, modified *Passalong Test,* form assembly, pattern matching, total; D. W. McElwain, G. E. Kearney, and I. G. Ord (test and record form); Australian Council for Educational Research [Australia]. * (United States distributor: Educational and Industrial Testing Service.)

For additional information, see 7:421 (7 references).

REFERENCES THROUGH 1971

1-7. See 7:421.
8. BIANCHI, G. N.; MCELWAIN, D. W.; AND CAWTE, J. E. "The Dispensary Syndrome in Australian Aborigines: Origins of Their Bodily Preoccupation and Sick Role Behavior." *Brit J Med Psychol* 43(4):375-82 D '70. *

CUMULATIVE NAME INDEX

Bianchi, G. N.: 8
Cawte, J. E.: 8
Kearney, G. E.: 2, 4
Kearney, J. E.: 3, 6-7
McElwain, D. W.: 8
Ord, I. G.: 1, 5

[521]

Quick Screening Scale of Mental Development. Ages 6 months to 10 years; 1963; 6 mental age ratings: body coordination, manual performance, speech and language, listening attention and number, play interests, general mental level (mean of preceding 5 ratings); Katharine M. Banham; Psychometric Affiliates. *

For additional information and a review by Boyd R. McCandless, see 6:533.

[522]

The Quick Test. Ages 2 and over; 1958-62; QT; picture vocabulary; R. B. Ammons and C. H. Ammons; Psychological Test Specialists. *

For additional information and excerpted reviews by Peter F. Merenda and B. Semeonoff, see 7:422 (30 references); for reviews by Boyd R. McCandless and Ellen V. Piers, see 6:534 (3 references).

REFERENCES THROUGH 1971

1-3. See 6:534.
4-33. See 7:422.
34. DIXON, JAMES C. "Cognitive Structure in Senile Conditions With Some Suggestions for Developing a Brief Screening Test of Mental Status." *J Gerontol* 20:41-9 Ja '65. *
35. MERENDA, PETER F. "The Provisional Manual for the Quick Test: A Review." *Ed & Psychol Meas* 25:268-71 sp '65. *
36. FLOWER, RICHARD M.; VIEHWEG, RICHARD; AND RUZICKA, WILLIAM R. "The Communicative Disorders of Children With Kernicteric Athetosis: 2, Problems in Language Comprehension and Use." *J Speech & Hearing Disorders* 31:60-8 F '66. * (*PA* 40:9108)
37. PATON, RICHARD. "Use of the Quick Test With Retarded Children." *Ont Psychol Assn Q* (Canada) 19:60-3 su '66. *
38. BOHRNSTEDT, GEORGE W.; LAMBERT, PHILIP; AND BORGATTA, EDGAR F. "The Reliability and Validity of Quick Tests With High School Seniors." *J Exp Ed* 39(4):22-3 su '71. * (*PA* 47:1573)
39. ERNHART, CLAIRE B.; JORDAN, THOMAS E.; AND SPANER, STEVEN D. "Maternal Quick Test (QT) Scores in Child Development Research." *Psychol Rep* 28(2):669-70 Ap '71. * (*PA* 46:6594)
40. JERROLDS, BOB W.; CALLAWAY, BYRON; AND GWALTNEY, WAYNE. "A Comparative Study of Three Tests of Intellectual Potential, Three Tests of Reading Achievement, and the Discrepancy Scores Between Potential and Achievement." *J Ed Res* 65(4):168-72 D '71. * (*PA* 48:1647)
41. JOESTING, JOAN, AND JOESTING, ROBERT. "Comparison of Scores on Quick Test and Stanford-Binet, Form L-M." *Psychol Rep* 29(3):1178 D '71. * (*PA* 48:1648)
42. JOESTING, JOAN, AND JOESTING, ROBERT. "The Quick Test as a Screening Device in a Welfare Setting." *Psychol Rep* 29(3):1289-90 D '71. * (*PA* 48:992)
43. LAMBERT, PHILIP; HANSEN, LEE H.; AND BORGATTA, EDGAR F. "Intelligent Word Associations in High School Students." *J Ed Res* 64(6):269-70 F '71. * (*PA* 46:11510)
44. LEVINE, NIRA R. "Validation of the Quick Test for Intel-

ligence Screening of the Elderly." *Psychol Rep* 29(1):167-72 Ag '71. * (*PA* 47:2717)
45. LIBB, J. WESLEY, AND COLEMAN, JOHN M. "Correlation Between the WAIS and Revised Beta, Wechsler Memory Scale and Quick Test in a Vocational Rehabilitation Center." *Psychol Rep* 29(3):863-5 D '71. * (*PA* 47:9410)
46. MALONEY, MICHAEL P.; WARD, MICHAEL P.; SCHENCK, HERBERT U.; AND BRAUCHT, GEORGE N. "Re-Evaluation of the Use of the Quick Test With a Sample of Institutionalized Mentally Retarded Subjects." *Psychol Rep* 29(3):1155-9 D '71. * (*PA* 48:1517)
47. SEITZ, FRANK C., AND BRAUCHT, GEORGE N. "Ammons' Quick Test as a Measure of Adult Intelligence in a Psychiatric Sample." *Psychol Rep* 29(2):356-8 O '71. * (*PA* 47:9302)
48. STAFFIERI, J. ROBERT. "Performance of Preschool Children on the Quick Test (QT)." *Psychol Rep* 29(2):472 O '71. * (*PA* 47:9667)

CUMULATIVE NAME INDEX

Abidin, R. R.: 13
Ammons, C. H.: 2
Ammons, R. B.: 2
Anderson, J.: 12
Andrews, R. J.: 12
Barclay, A.: 16, 26
Bibb, J. J.: 4
Bohrnstedt, G. W.: 38
Bonfield, J. R.: 20
Borgatta, E. F.: 38, 43
Braucht, G. N.: 46-7
Burgess, T. C.: 1, 3
Byrne, A. V.: 13
Callaway, B.: 40
Carlisle, A. L.: 6
Cole, S.: 14, 18
Coleman, J. M.: 45
Colvin, C. R.: 32
Connolly, J. K.: 21
Coyle, F. A.: 22
Cull, J. G.: 32
Davis, W. E.: 33
Dixon, J. C.: 34
Dizzone, M. F.: 33
Doyle, E. D.: 7
Eaton, A. E.: 10
Erdberg, P.: 22
Ernhart, C. B.: 39
Feldman, S. E.: 23
Flower, R. M.: 36
Griffith, J.: 31
Gwaltney, W.: 40
Hansen, L. H.: 43
Houston, C.: 24-5
Jerrolds, B. W.: 40
Joesting, J.: 41-2
Joesting, R.: 41-2
Jordan, T. E.: 39

Kearsley, R. B.: 10
King, F. W.: 15
Lambert, P.: 38, 43
Lamp, R. E.: 16, 26
Levine, N. R.: 27, 44
Libb, J. W.: 45
McCandless, B. R.: *rev*, 6:534
McMenemy, R. A.: 9
Maloney, M. P.: 46
Mednick, M. T.: 17, 28
Merenda, P. F.: 35; *exc*, 7:422
Methvin, M.: 5
Metzger, R.: 11
Miner, L.: 31
Ogilvie, R. D.: 8
Otto, W.: 9, 24-5
Paton, R.: 37
Piers, E. V.: *rev*, 6:534
Pless, I. B.: 10
Plotkin, R. R.: 19
Quattlebaum, L. F.: 29-30
Ruzicka, W. R.: 36
Schenck, H. U.: 46
Seitz, F. C.: 47
Semeonoff, B.: *exc*, 7:422
Snider, M.: 10
Spaner, S. D.: 39
Staffieri, J. R.: 48
Stewart, H.: 18
Strandberg, T. E.: 31
Viehweg, R.: 36
Ward, M. P.: 46
White, W. F.: 29-30
Whitney, V.: 11
Williams, R.: 14, 18
Wirls, C. J.: 19
Wright, D. D.: 3

[523]
Ring and Peg Tests of Behavior Development. Birth to age 6; 1958-64; experimental; 6 scores: ambulative, manipulative, communicative, social adaptive, emotive, total; Katharine M. Banham; Psychometric Affiliates. *

For additional information and reviews by Jane V. Hunt and Emmy E. Werner, see 7:423.

[524]
Slosson Intelligence Test. Ages 2 weeks and over; 1961-63; SIT; based in part upon *Stanford-Binet Intelligence Scale, Third Revision* and *Gesell Developmental Schedules;* Richard L. Slosson; Slosson Educational Publications, Inc. *

For additional information and reviews by Philip Himelstein and Jane V. Hunt, see 7:424 (31 references).

REFERENCES THROUGH 1971

1-31. See 7:424.
32. MESINGER, JOHN F. "An Intelligence Test to Assess Compensatory Education Programs for Disadvantaged Youth?" *Univ Va Ed R* 7:52-8 '69. *
33. MILLER, CHARLES K. "Conservation in Blind Children." *Ed Visually Handicapped* 1(4):101-5 D '69. * (*PA* 44:9017)
34. CHARLTON, NORMAN WOOD, II. *An Investigation of Selected Visual-Perceptual and Motor Parameters of Young Trainable Mentally Retarded Children.* Doctor's thesis, University of Houston (Houston, Tex.), 1970. (*DAI* 32:271A)

35. KAPEL, MARILYN B., AND KAPEL, DAVID E. "Hebrew English Reading Achievement in a Jewish Day School: A Comparison Among Reading Achievements and Attitudes Towards the Two Languages." *Jewish Ed* 40(3):23-32 w '70. *
36. MAXWELL, MICHAEL T. *The Relationship Between the Wechsler Intelligence Scale for Children and the Slosson Intelligence Test.* Master's thesis, Eastern Montana College (Billings, Mont.), 1970.
37. RUDOLPH, LINDA. *Correlates of the Slosson Intelligence Test, Wechsler Adult Intelligence Scale, ACT Scores and Grade Point Averages.* Master's thesis, Austin Peay State University (Clarksville, Tenn.), 1970.
38. ARMSTRONG, ROBERT J., AND MOONEY, ROBERT F. "The Slosson Intelligence Test: Implications for Reading Specialists." *Read Teach* 24(4):336-40+ Ja '71. * (*PA* 46:11492)
39. ARMSTRONG, ROBERT J.; MOONEY, ROBERT F.; AND JENSEN, JOHN A. "A Short, Reliable, Easy to Administer Individual Intelligence Test for Special Class Placement." *Child Study J* 1(3):156-63 sp '71. * (*PA* 48:1701)
40. GARRISON, MORTIMER, JR., AND HAMMILL, DONALD D. "Who Are the Retarded?" *Excep Children* 38(1):13-20 S '71. * (*PA* 47:7598)
41. HEDL, JOHN J., JR.; O'NEIL, HAROLD F., JR.; AND HANSEN, DUNCAN N. "Affective Nature of Computer-Based Testing Procedures." Abstract. *Proc 79th Ann Conv Am Psychol Assn* 6(2):535-6 '71. * (*PA* 46:5468)
42. LESSLER, KEN, AND GALINSKY, M. DAVID. "Relationship Between Slosson Intelligence Test and WISC Scores in Special Education Candidates." *Psychol Sch* 8(4):341-4 O '71. * (*PA* 47:9677)
43. MAXWELL, MICHAEL T. "The Relationship Between the Wechsler Intelligence Scale for Children and the Slosson Intelligence Test." *Child Study J* 1(3):164-71 sp '71. * (*PA* 48:1709)

CUMULATIVE NAME INDEX

Ames, L. B.: 3
Armstrong, R. J.: 38-9
Bonfield, J. R.: 4
Burns, L. M.: 5
Carlisle, A. L.: 24
Charlton, N. W.: 34
Colarusso, R.: 26
Crandell, J. M.: 26
DeLapa, G.: 1, 6
Duggan, M. D.: 7
Fagert, C. M.: 8
Galinsky, M. D.: 42
Garrison, M.: 40
Gillespie, P. H.: 25
Hammill, D.: 14
Hammill, D.: 26, 40
Hansen, D. N.: 41
Hedl, J. J.: 41
Himelstein, P.: *rev*, 7:424
Houston, C.: 9-10
Hunt, J. V.: *rev*, 7:424
Hutton, J. B.: 15, 27
Ivanoff, J.: 18
Jacobson, A.: 31
Jensen, J. A.: 39
Jongeward, P. A.: 16-7

Kapel, D. E.: 35
Kapel, M. B.: 35
Kaufman, H.: 18
Keany, M.: 11
Kilduff, C. T.: 19
Lessler, K.: 42
McRae, J.: 12
Maxwell, M. T.: 36, 43
Meissler, G. R.: 28
Mesinger, J. F.: 32
Miller, C. K.: 33
Mooney, R. F.: 38-9
Nash, M. S.: 20
Nicholson, C. L.: 21, 29
O'Keefe, S. L.: 2
O'Neil, H. F.: 41
O'Neill, H. D.: 22
Otto, W.: 9-10
Rudolph, L.: 37
Shepherd, C. W.: 23
Shinedling, M. M.: 24
Stuhler, A. M.: 30
Swanson, M. S.: 31
Weaver, R.: 24
Whitacre, R. L.: 13

[525]
Stanford-Binet Intelligence Scale. Ages 2 and over; 1916-73; S-B; 2 editions; Lewis M. Terman and Maud A. Merrill; Houghton Mifflin Co. * (British edition: George G. Harrap & Co. Ltd. [England].)
a) SECOND REVISION. 1916-37; title on test material is *Revised Stanford-Binet Scales;* only printed materials available.
b) THIRD REVISION. 1916-73; a single form combination of items selected from Forms L and M ('37) of the second revision; test materials and directions in 1972 standardization identical with 1960 edition except for minor changes in two items; Samuel R. Pinneau (1960 norms) and Robert L. Thorndike (1972 norms).

For additional information and a review by David Freides of the third revision, see 7:425 (258 references); for a review by Elizabeth D. Fraser and excerpted reviews by Benjamin Balinsky, L. B. Birch, James Maxwell, Marie D. Neale, and Julian C. Stanley, see 6:536 (110 references); for reviews by Mary R. Haworth and Norman D. Sundberg of the second revision, see 5:413 (121 references); for a review by Boyd R. McCandless, see 4:358 (142 references); see also 3:292 (217 references); for excerpted reviews by Cyril Burt, Grace H. Kent, and M. Krugman, see 2:1420 (132 references); for reviews by Francis N. Maxfield, J. W. M. Rothney, and F. L. Wells, see 1:1062. For excerpts from related book reviews, see 6:B396 (2 excerpts), 3:293 (6 excerpts), 3:294 (2 excerpts), 2:B1093 (3 excerpts), and 1:B497 (23 excerpts).

REFERENCES THROUGH 1971

1–134. See 2:1420.
135–351. See 3:292.
352–493. See 4:358.
494–620. See 5:413.
621–728. See 6:536.
729–986. See 7:425.
987. PYLE, W. H. "A Suggestion for the Improvement and Extension of Mental Tests." *J Ed Psychol* 3:95–6 F '12. *
988. HICKS, VINNIE CRANDALL. "The Value of the Binet Mental Age Tests for First-Grade Entrants." *J Ed Psychol* 6:157–66 Mr '15. *
989. HOUSER, J. DAVID. "The Relation of Spelling Ability to General Intelligence and to Meaning Vocabulary." *El Sch J* 16:190–9 D '15. *
990. TERMAN, LEWIS M., AND KNOLLIN, H. E. "Some Problems Relating to the Detection of Borderline Cases of Mental Deficiency." *J Psycho-Asthenics* 20:1–15 S–D '15. *
991. WILLIAMS, J. HAROLD. "The Problem of the Delinquent Boy." *Child* 6:29–32 O '15. *
992. BRIGGER, GRETCHEN. "A Study of Twenty-Five Repeaters at the Associated Charities, Portland, Oregon." *J Delinq* 1:187–94 S '16. *
993. TERMAN, LEWIS M. "Mentality Tests: A Symposium." *J Ed Psychol* 7:348–51 Je '16. *
994. WELLS, F. L. "The Measurement of Intelligence: A Review." *Sch & Soc* 4:296–8 Ag 19 '16. *
995. DOLL, E. A. "The Measurement of Intelligence: A Review." *J Ed Psychol* 8:111–6 F '17. *
996. DOWNEY, J. E. "University Instructors Tested by the Stanford Scale." Abstract. *Psychol B* 14:70–1 F '17. *
997. DOWNEY, JUNE E. "The Stanford Adult Intelligence Tests." *J Delinq* 2:144–55 My '17. *
998. KOHS, SAMUEL C. "The Stanford (1915) and the Vineland (1911) Revisions of the Binet Scale." *Psychol R* 24:174–9 Mr '17. *
999. PRATT, CARROL C. "The Measurement of Intelligence: A Review." *J Appl Psychol* 1:191–2 Je '17. *
1000. WELLS, F. L. "Aphasic Performance in the Terman Vocabulary Test." *J Ed Psychol* 8:483–7 O '17. *
1001. COLE, LAWRENCE W. "Mental Age and School Entrance." *Sch & Soc* 8:418–9 O 5 '18. *
1002. DOWNEY, JUNE E. "The Constancy of the I.Q." *J Delinq* 3:122–31 My '18. *
1003. LACY, WILLIAM I. "A Study of 100 Retarded Fourth Grade Pupils Tested by the Binet Scale." *Psychol Clinic* 12:16–23 Mr 15 '18. *
1004. MATEER, FLORENCE. "The Diagnostic Fallability of Intelligence Ratios." *Pedagog Sem* 25:369–92 D '18. *
1005. MAXFIELD, FRANCIS N. "Some Mathematical Aspects of the Binet-Simon Tests." *J Ed Psychol* 9:1–12 Ja '18. *
1006. CALDWELL, HELEN HUBBERT. "Adult Tests of the Stanford Revision Applied to College Students." *J Ed Psychol* 10:477–88 D '19. *
1007. CHASE, H. W., AND CARPENTER, C. C. "The Response of a Composite Group to the Stanford Revision of the Binet-Simon Tests." *J Ed Psychol* 10:179–88 Ap '19. *
1008. GORDON, KATE. "Report of Psychological Tests of Orphan Children." *J Delinq* 4:46–55 Ja '19. *
1009. SAAM, THEODORE. "Intelligence Tests as an Aid in Supervision." *El Sch J* 20:26–32 S '19. *
1010. SUNNE, DAGNY. "The Relation of Scholarships to the Yerkes and Terman Adult Tests." *J Ed Psychol* 10:520–4 D '19. *
1011. TERMAN, LEWIS M. "Some Data on the Binet Test of Naming Words." *J Ed Psychol* 10:29–35 Ja '19. *
1012. WALLIN, J. E. WALLACE. "The Value of the Intelligence Quotient for Individual Diagnosis." *J Delinq* 4:109–24 My '19. *
1013. WASHBURN, M. F. "A Note on the Terman Superior Adult Tests, as Applied to Vassar Freshmen." *Am J Psychol* 30:310 Jl '19. *
1014. WASHBURNE, CARLETON W. "A Classified Scale for Measuring Intelligence." *J Ed Psychol* 10:309–22 S '19. *
1015. BUCKINGHAM, B. R. "The Intelligence of School Children: A Review." *J Ed Res* 1:144–7 F '20. *
1016. CLARK, WILLIS W. "Success Record of Delinquent Boys in Relation to Intelligence." *J Delinq* 5:174–82 S '20. *
1017. DERRICK, S. M. "A Comparative Study of the Intelligence of Seventy-Five White and Fifty-Five Colored College Students by the Stanford Revision of the Binet-Simon Scale." *J Appl Psychol* 4:316–29 D '20. *
1018. DICKSON, VIRGIL E. "What First-Grade Children Can Do in School as Related to What Is Shown by Mental Tests." *J Ed Res* 2:475–80 Je '20. *
1019. EDMONDSON, MARGARET B. "A Mental Survey of First-Grade School Children." *Pedagog Sem* 27:354–70 D '20. *
1020. FRASIER, GEORGE W. "The Measurement of Intelligence as an Aid to Administration." *Ed Adm & Sup* 6:361–6 O '20. *
1021. NORTON, JOHN K. "The Mental Ages of a Group of 127 Prostitutes." *J Delinq* 5:63–6 My '20. *
1022. PINTNER, RUDOLF, AND NOBLE, HELEN. "The Classification of School Children According to Mental Age." *J Ed Res* 2:713–28 N '20. *
1023. PROCTOR, W. M. "Psychological Tests as a Means of Measuring the Probable School Success of High School Pupils." *J Ed Res* 1:258–70 Ap '20. *
1024. PROCTOR, W. M. "The Use of Psychological Tests in the Educational Guidance of High School Pupils." *J Ed Res* 1:369–81 My '20. *
1025. ROSENOW, CURT. "The Stability of the Intelligence Quotient." *J Delinq* 5:160–73 S '20. *
1026. RUCH, G. M., AND STRACHAN, LEXIE. "Intelligence Ratings by Group Scales and by the Stanford Revision of the Binet Tests." *J Ed Psychol* 11:421–9 N '20. *
1027. SCHWEGLER, R. A., AND WINN, EDITH. "A Comparative Study of the Intelligence of White and Colored Children." *J Ed Res* 2:838–48 D '20. *
1028. TERMAN, LEWIS M. "The Use of Intelligence Tests in the Grading of School Children." *J Ed Res* 1:20–32 Ja '20. *
1029. WALCOTT, GREGORY D. "The Intelligence of Chinese Students." *Sch & Soc* 11:474–80 Ap 17 '20. *
1030. CHASSELL, CLARA F., AND CHASSELL, LAURA M. "A Survey of the Three First Grades of the Horace Mann School by Means of Psychological Tests and Teachers' Estimates, and a Statistical Evaluation of the Measures Employed." *J Ed Psychol* 12:72–81, 243–52 F, My '21. *
1031. DECAMP, J. E. "Studies in Mental Tests: Army Alpha, Thurstone IV, and Binet-Simon (SR)." *Sch & Soc* 14:353–8 O 1 '21. *
1032. GARRISON, S. C. "Fluctuation of Intelligence Quotient." *Sch & Soc* 13:647–9 Je 4 '21. *
1033. GATES, ARTHUR I. "An Experimental and Statistical Study of Reading and Reading Tests." *J Ed Psychol* 12:303–14, 378–91, 445–64 S, O, N '21. *
1034. MATHEWS, JULIA. "Irregularity in Intelligence Tests of Delinquents." *J Delinq* 6:355–61 Mr '21. *
1035. ODELL, C. W. "Correlation of Certain Intelligence Tests for the Lower Grades." *J Ed Res* 3:308–10 Ap '21. *
1036. OTIS, ARTHUR S., AND KNOLLIN, HERBERT E. "The Reliability of the Binet Scale and of Pedagogical Scales." *J Ed Res* 4:121–42 S '21. *
1037. POULL, LOUISE E. "Constancy of I.Q. in Mental Defectives, According to the Stanford-Revision of Binet Tests." *J Ed Psychol* 12:323–4 S '21. *
1038. PROCTOR, WILLIAM MARTIN. *The Use of Psychological Tests in the Educational and Vocational Guidance of High School Pupils, Revised Edition.* Journal of Educational Research Monographs No. 1. Bloomington, Ill.: Public School Publishing Co., 1921. Pp. 125. *
1039. ROOT, W. T. "Two Cases Showing Marked Change in I.Q." *J Appl Psychol* 5:156–8 Je '21. *
1040. TERMAN, L. M. "Mental Growth and the I.Q." *J Ed Psychol* 12:325–41, 401–7 S, O '21. *
1041. WALLIN, J. E. WALLACE. "A Comparison of Three Methods for Making the Initial Selection of Presumptive Mental Defectives." Abstract. *Psychol B* 18:85–6 F '21. *
1042. WALLIN, J. E. WALLACE. "A Comparison of Three Methods for Making the Initial Selection of Presumptive Mental Defectives." *Sch & Soc* 13:31–45 Ja 8 '21. *
1043. WALLIN, J. E. WALLACE. "The Results of Retests by Means of the Binet Scale." *J Ed Psychol* 12:392–400 O '21. *
1044. WEEKS, ANGELINA L. "Terman Vocabulary as a Group Test." *J Ed Psychol* 12:532–6 D '21. *
1045. WEISMAN, FRANCES. "The Use of Mental Tests in the Whitman School." *J Ed Res* 4:155–8 S '21. *
1046. BAKER, HARRY J. "Mental Tests as an Aid in the Analysis of Mental Constitution." *J Appl Psychol* 6:349–77 D '22. *
1047. BALDWIN, BIRD T. "The Relation Between Mental and Physical Growth." *J Ed Psychol* 13:193–203 Ap '22. *
1048. BROWN, GILBERT L. "Intelligence as Related to Nationality." *J Ed Res* 5:324–7 Ap '22. *
1049. CALDWELL, HELEN HUBBERT. "Adult Tests of the Stanford Revision Applied to University Faculty Members." *J Exp Psychol* 5:247–62 Ag '22. *
1050. CLARK, WILLIS W. "Home Conditions and Native Intelligence." *J Delinq* 7:17–23 Ja '22. *
1051. COBB, MARGARET V. "One Element in the Probable Error of a Mental Age Measurement." *J Ed Psychol* 13:236–40 Ap '22. *
1052. COBB, MARGARET V. "Tentative Order of Difficulty of the Terman Vocabulary With Very Young Children." *J Ed Psychol* 13:357–62 S '22. *
1053. COWDERY, KARL M. "Measures of General Intelligence as Indices of Success in Trade Learning." *J Appl Psychol* 6:311–30 D '22. *
1054. DAWSON, CHARLES D. "Classification of Kindergarten

Stanford-Binet Intelligence Scale

Children for First Grade by Means of the Binet Scale." *J Ed Res* 6:412–22 D '22. *

1055. FREEMAN, FRANK N. "The Mental Age of Adults." Editorial. *J Ed Res* 6:441–4 D '22. *

1056. GATES, ARTHUR I. "The Correlations of Achievement in School Subjects With Intelligence Tests and Other Variables." *J Ed Psychol* 13:129–39, 223–35, 277–85 Mr, Ap, My '22. *

1057. GLENN, IRENE. "A Report on the Correlation of Psychological Tests With Academic and Manual Subjects." *J Ed Psychol* 13:496–500 N '22. *

1058. GUILER, WALTER S. "How Different Mental Tests Agree in Rating Children." *El Sch J* 22:734–44 Je '22. *

1059. JOHNSON, BUFORD, AND SCHRIEFER, LOUISE. "A Comparison of Mental Age Scores Obtained by Performance Tests and the Stanford Revision of the Binet-Simon Scale." *J Ed Psychol* 13:408–17 O '22. *

1060. LINCOLN, EDWARD A. "The Constancy of Intelligence Quotients (A Case Study)." *J Ed Psychol* 13:484–95 N '22. *

1061. LINCOLN, EDWARD A. "Time-Saving in the Stanford-Binet Test." *J Ed Psychol* 13:94–7 F '22. *

1062. MITCHELL, DAVID. "Psychological Examination and Pre-School Age Children." *Sch & Soc* 15:561–8 My 20 '22. *

1063. ROOT, W. T. "The Intelligence Quotient From Two Viewpoints." *J Appl Psychol* 6:267–75 S '22. *

1064. TEAGARDEN, FLORENCE M. "'The Constancy of the IQ' Again." *J Ed Psychol* 13:366–72 S '22. *

1065. WALLIN, J. E. W. "Intelligence Irregularity as Measured by Scattering in the Binet Scale." *J Ed Psychol* 13:140–51 Mr '22. *

1066. AVERY, GEORGE T. "A Study of the Binet and Terman Intelligence Tests With Eleven-Year-Old Children." *J Ed Res* 7:429–33 My '23. *

1067. BALDWIN, B. T. "Additional Data From Consecutive Stanford-Binet Tests." *J Ed Res* 8:375 N '23. *

1068. COLVIN, STEPHEN S., AND ALLEN, RICHARD D. "Mental Tests and Linguistic Ability." *J Ed Psychol* 14:1–20 Ja '23. *

1069. DEBUSK, B. W. "The Economic Status and the Intelligence of Children." *J Ed Res* 8:370–2 N '23. *

1070. EATON, H. T. "The Intelligence of Pupils Who Repeat." *Sch & Soc* 17:139–40 F 3 '23. *

1071. GATES, ARTHUR I., AND LASALLE, JESSIE. "The Relative Predictive Values of Certain Intelligence and Educational Tests Together With a Study of the Effect of Educational Achievement Upon Intelligence Test Scores." *J Ed Psychol* 14:517–39 D '23. *

1072. GORDON, KATE. "Some Notes on the Mental Status of the Left-Handed." *J Delinq* 8:154–7 My–Jl '23. *

1073. GRAY, P. L., AND MARSDEN, R. E. "The Constancy of the Intelligence Quotient." *Brit J Psychol* 13:315–24 Ja '23. *

1074. GRAY, P. L., AND MARSDEN, R. E. "The Stanford-Binet Tests in Some English Schools." *J Ed Res* 8:150–5 S '23. *

1075. JORDAN, A. M. "The Validation of Intelligence Tests." *J Ed Psychol* 14:348–66, 414–28 S, O '23. *

1076. ORDAHL, GEORGE. "Diagnosis of the Unstable Moron." *J Delinq* 8:99–112 Mr '23. *

1077. PORTEUS, S. D. Chap. 7, "Binet-Simon Scale," pp. 187–208. In his *Studies in Mental Deviations*. Publications of the Training School at Vineland, N.J., Department of Research, No. 24, October 1922. Vineland, N.J.: the School, 1923. Pp. xi, 276. *

1078. ROOT, W. T. "Transmutation of Scores Between Binet Tests and Group Tests." *J Ed Res* 7:338–43 Ap '23. *

1079. SCRIPTURE, MAY KIRK, AND KITTREDGE, WINIFRED BOYD. "An Attempt to Determine Another Etiological Factor of Stuttering Through Objective Measurement." *J Ed Psychol* 14:162–73 Mr '23. *

1080. WALLIN, J. E. W. "The Diagnostic Findings From Seven Years of Experience in the Same School Clinic." *J Delinq* 8:169–95 My–Jl '23. *

1081. WILNER, CHARLES F. "Mental Age Equivalents for a Group of Non-Reading Tests of the Herring Revision of the Binet-Simon Tests." *J Ed Psychol* 14:296–9 My '23. *

1082. GATES, ARTHUR I., AND LASALLE, JESSIE. "A Study of Writing Ability and Its Relation to Other Abilities Based on Repeated Tests During a Period of 20 Months." *J Ed Psychol* 15:205–16 Ap '24. *

1083. GATES, ARTHUR I.; ASSISTED BY GRACE A. TAYLOR, ELOISE BOEKER, AND DOROTHY VAN ALSTYNE. "The Nature and Educational Significance of Physical Status and of Mental, Physiological, Social and Emotional Maturity." *J Ed Psychol* 15:329–58 S '24. *

1084. GRAVES, KATHARINE B. "The Influence of Specialized Training on Tests of General Intelligence." *Teach Col Contrib Ed* 143:1–78 '24. *

1085. GRAY, P. L., AND MARSDEN, R. E. "The Constancy of the Intelligence Quotient—Further Results." *Brit J Psychol* 15:169–73 O '24. *

1086. HART, HORNELL. "Correlations Between Intelligence Quotients of Siblings." *Sch & Soc* 20:382 S 20 '24. *

1087. HECKMAN, SAMUEL B. Chap. 3, "A Comparative Study of Group Intelligence Tests Applicable to Children of Kindergarten Age," pp. 17–44. In *Contributions to Education, Vol. I*. Edited by J. Carleton Bell. Yonkers, N.Y.: World Book Co., 1924. Pp. ix, 364. *

1088. HERRING, JOHN P. "Herring Revision of the Binet-Simon Tests." *J Ed Psychol* 15:172–9 Mr '24. *

1089. HEWES, AMY; HOLT, MILDRED; MERANSKI, SOPHIE; AND SNELL, JULIA. "Mental Age and School Attainment of 1007 Retarded Children in Massachusetts." *J Ed Psychol* 15:297–301 My '24. *

1090. MERRILL, MAUD A. "On the Relation of Intelligence to Achievement in the Case of Mentally Retarded Children." *Comp Psychol Monogr* 2(10):1–100 S '24. *

1091. MERRIMAN, CURTIS. "The Intellectual Resemblance of Twins." *Psychol Monogr* 33(5):1–58 '24. *

1092. MITCHELL, DAVID. "Psychological Examination of Pre-School Age Children: A Demonstration of the Classification of Children According to Ability." *Pedagog Sem* 31:108–46 Je '24. *

1093. SHELDON, WILLIAM H. "The Intelligence of Mexican Children." *Sch & Soc* 19:139–42 F 2 '24. *

1094. ABERNETHY, ETHEL M. "Correlations in Physical and Mental Growth." *J Ed Psychol* 16:458–66, 539–46 O, N '25. *

1095. CARMICHAEL, LEONARD. "Eidetic Imagery and the Binet Test." *J Ed Psychol* 16:251–2 Ap '25. *

1096. DASHIELL, J. F., AND GLENN, W. D. "A Re-examination of a Socially Composite Group With Binet and With Performance Tests." *J Ed Psychol* 16:335–40 My '25. *

1097. DAVIDSON, HELEN PYE. *Some Effects of Training on the Stanford Binet Scale*. Master's thesis, Stanford University (Stanford, Calif.), 1925.

1098. DEVOSS, JAMES C. Chap. 12, "Specialization of the Abilities of Gifted Children," pp. 307–62. In *Genetic Studies of Genius: Vol. I, Mental and Physical Traits of a Thousand Gifted Children*. By Lewis M. Terman. Palo Alto, Calif.: Stanford University Press, 1925. Pp. xv, 648. *

1099. FERNALD, MABLE R., AND ARLITT, ADA H. "A Psychological Study of a Group of Crippled Children of Various Types." *Sch & Soc* 21:449–52 Ap 11 '25. *

1100. FUKUDA, TONAN. "A Survey of the Intelligence and Environment of School Children." *Am J Psychol* 36:124–39 Ja '25. *

1101. GARRISON, S. C., AND ROBINSON, M. S. "A Study of Re-Tests." *J Ed Res* 11:190–6 Mr '25. *

1102. GATES, ARTHUR I., AND TAYLOR, GRACE A. "An Experimental Study of the Nature of Improvement Resulting From Practice in a Mental Function." *J Ed Psychol* 16:583–92 D '25. *

1103. GOODENOUGH, F. L. "The Reading Tests of the Stanford Achievement Scale and Other Variables." *J Ed Psychol* 16:523–31 N '25. *

1104. HARTER, DORIS IRENE. *Some Results of Coaching Some of the Tests of the Stanford Revision of the Binet-Simon Scale*. Master's thesis, Stanford University (Stanford, Calif.), 1925.

1105. HILDRETH, GERTRUDE HOWELL. "The Resemblance of Siblings in Intelligence and Achievement." *Teach Col Contrib Ed* 186:1–65 '25. *

1106. JOHNSON, BUFORD J. Chap. 4, "Mental Development as Measured by Graded Series of Tests," pp. 79–107. In his *Mental Growth of Children in Relation to the Rate of Growth in Bodily Development: A Report of the Bureau of Educational Experiments, New York City*. New York: E. P. Dutton & Co., 1925. Pp. 160. *

1107. JONES, A. M. "An Analytical Study of One Hundred Twenty Superior Children." *Psychol Clinic* 16:19–76 Ja–F '25. * (*PA* 3:1656)

1108. JONES, VERNON A. "A Study of Children's Ability to Note Similarities and Differences." *J Ed Psychol* 16:253–60 Ap '25. *

1109. KOLB, LAURENCE. "The Relation of Intelligence to the Etiology of Drug Addiction." *Am J Psychiatry* 82:163–7 Jl '25. * (*PA* 1:618)

1110. RAND, GERTRUDE. "A Discussion of the Quotient Method of Specifying Test Results." *J Ed Psychol* 16:599–618 D '25. *

1111. RAYBOLD, EMMA. "An Experiment With Primary Intelligence Tests." *Ed Res B* (Los Angeles City Schools) 4:8 Je 15 '25. *

1112. RUGG, L. S. "Retests and the Constancy of the IQ." *J Ed Psychol* 16:341–3 My '25. *

1113. SUNNE, DAGNY. "Comparison of White and Negro Children by the Terman and Yerkes-Bridges Revisions of the Binet Tests." *J Comp Psychol* 5:209–20 Je '25. * (*PA* 1:1409)

1114. WILSON, G. M. "Standard Deviations of Age Scores and Quotients in Typical Groups." *J Ed Psychol* 16:193–207 Mr '25. *

1115. WOODS, ELIZABETH L. "Intellectual and Emotional Improvement in Nutrition Classes." *Ed Res B* (Los Angeles City Schools) 5:6–11 O '25. *

1116. WOOLEY, HELEN T. "The Validity of Standards of Mental Measurement in Young Childhood." *Sch & Soc* 21:476–82 Ap 18 '25. *

1117. BROOKS, FOWLER D. "The Accuracy of Group Test Mental Ages and Intelligence Quotients of Junior High School Pupils." *Sch R* 34:333–42 My '26. *

1118. CASEY, MARY LOUISE. *Some Results of Training in Material Similar to the Stanford Revision of the Binet-Simon Scale*. Master's thesis, Stanford University (Stanford, Calif.), 1926.

1119. DARSIE, MARVIN L. "The Mental Capacity of American-Born Japanese Children." *Comp Psychol Monogr* 3(15):1–89 Ja '26. * (*PA* 1:133)

1120. GATES, ARTHUR I. "A Study of the Role of Visual Per-

Stanford-Binet Intelligence Scale

1120. ception, Intelligence, and Certain Associative Processes in Reading and Spelling." *J Ed Psychol* 17:433-45 O '26. * (*PA* 1:175)
1121. GRAHAM, VIRGINIA TAYLOR. "The Intelligence of Chinese Children in San Francisco." *J Comp Psychol* 6:43-71 F '26. * (*PA* 1:663)
1122. GRAY, P. L., AND MARSDEN, R. E. "The Constancy of the Intelligence Quotient—Final Results." *Brit J Psychol* 17: 20-6 Jl '26. *
1123. HOLLINGWORTH, LETA S. "Musical Sensitivity of Children Who Test Above 135 IQ (Stanford-Binet)." *J Ed Psychol* 17:95-109 F '26. *
1124. HOLLINGWORTH, LETA S., AND MONAHAN, JANE E. "Tapping-Rate of Children Who Test Above 135 IQ (Stanford-Binet)." *J Ed Psychol* 17:505-18 N '26. * (*PA* 1:285)
1125. LACY, L. D. "Relative Intelligence of White and Colored Children." *El Sch J* 26:542-6 Mr '26. *
1126. MERRILL, MAUD A. "Mental Differences Among Juvenile Delinquents." *J Delinq* 10:312-23 Mr '26. *
1127. MINOGUE, BLANCHE M. "The Constancy of the I.Q. of Mental Defectives." *Mental Hyg* 10:751-8 O '26. * (*PA* 1:870)
1128. STRACHAN, LEXIE. "Distribution of Intelligence Quotients of Twenty-Two Thousand Primary-School Children." *J Ed Res* 14:169-77 O '26. * (*PA* 1:209)
1129. SULLIVAN, ELIZABETH T. "The Use of a Psychographic Representation of Results of the Stanford Revision of the Binet-Simon Tests." *J Delinq* 10:284-5 plus 2 inserts Ja '26. *
1130. WECHSLER, DAVID. "On the Influence of Education on Intelligence as Measured by the Binet-Simon Tests." *J Ed Psychol* 17:248-57 Ap '26. *
1131. WORTHINGTON, MYRTLE RAYMAKER. "Performance Test Scores of Behavior and Non-Behavior Children." *Welfare Mag* 17:97-103 O '26. * (*PA* 1:439)
1132. WORTHINGTON, MYRTLE RAYMAKER. "A Study of Some Commonly Used Performance Tests." *J Appl Psychol* 10:216-27 Je '26. *
1133. ASHER, E. J. "Training Needs of Reform School Boys Experimentally Determined." *J Delinq* 11:151-8 S '27. * (*PA* 2:746)
1134. BROOM, M. EUSTACE. "A Study of the Constancy of the I.Q." *Ed Res B* (Los Angeles City Schools) 7:2-3 O-N '27. *
1135. MONAHAN, JANE E., AND HOLLINGWORTH, LETA S. "Neuro-Muscular Capacity of Children Who Test Above 135 IQ (Stanford-Binet)." *J Ed Psychol* 18:88-96 F '27. * (*PA* 1:1170)
1136. SEROTA, KATHRYN EWART. "A Comparative Study of One Hundred Italian Children at the Six-Year Level." *Psychol Clinic* 16:216-31 O '27. * (*PA* 2:1347)
1137. SLOCOMBE, C. S. "Why the IQ Is Not, and Cannot Be Constant." *J Ed Psychol* 18:421-3 S '27. * (*PA* 2:277)
1138. STALNAKER, ELIZABETH M., AND ROLLER, R. D., JR. "A Study of One Hundred Nonpromoted Children." *J Ed Res* 16: 265-70 N '27. * (*PA* 2:781)
1139. WALTERS, FRED C. "A Statistical Study of Certain Aspects of the Time Factor in Intelligence." *Teach Col Contrib Ed* 248:1-82 '27. *
1140. ABELSON, HAROLD H. Chap. 12, "What Hope for the Low I.Q.?" pp. 64-70. In *Contributions to Education, Vol. 2.* Edited by J. Carleton Bell and Ambrose L. Suhrie. Yonkers, N.Y.: World Book Co., 1928. Pp. xi, 425. * (*PA* 2:2313)
1141. BIDDLE, A. E. "An Analytical Study of One Class in High School." *Psychol Clinic* 17:97-118 S-O '28. * (*PA* 3: 1676)
1142. BURKS, BARBARA STODDARD. "The Relative Influence of Nature and Nurture Upon Mental Development: A Comparative Study of Foster Parent-Foster Child Resemblance and True Parent-True Child Resemblance." *Yearb Nat Soc Study Ed* 27(1):219-316 '28. * (*PA* 2:2464)
1143. CASEY, MARY L.; DAVIDSON, HELEN P.; AND HARTER, DORIS I. "Three Studies on the Effect of Training in Similar and Identical Material Upon Stanford-Binet Test Scores." *Yearb Nat Soc Study Ed* 27(1):431-9 '28. * (*PA* 2:2338)
1144. DENWORTH, KATHARINE M. "The Effect of Length of School Attendance Upon Mental and Educational Ages." *Yearb Nat Soc Study Ed* 27(2):67-91 '28. * (*PA* 2:2608)
1145. DIETSCH, MILDRED KATHRYN. *A Correlation of the Intelligence Quotients of the Drawing Test With the Stanford Binet.* Master's thesis, Ohio State University (Columbus, Ohio), 1928.
1146. ESTABROOKS, G. H. "The Relation Between Cranial Capacity, Relative Cranial Capacity and Intelligence in School Children." *J Appl Psychol* 12:524-9 O '28. * (*PA* 3:499)
1147. FREEMAN, FRANK N.; HOLZINGER, KARL J.; AND MITCHELL, BLYTHE CLAYTON. "The Influence of Environment on the Intelligence, School Achievement, and Conduct of Foster Children." *Yearb Nat Soc Study Ed* 27(1):102-217 '28. * (*PA* 2: 2469)
1148. FREEMAN, FRANK S. "Influence of Educational Attainment Upon Tests of Intelligence." *J Ed Psychol* 19:230-42 Ap '28. * (*PA* 2:2651)
1149. GREENE, KATHARINE B. "The Influence of Specialized Training on Tests of General Intelligence." *Yearb Nat Soc Study Ed* 27(1):421-8 '28. * (*PA* 2:2063)
1150. HALLOWELL, D. K. "Mental Tests for Pre-School Children." *Psychol Clinic* 16:235-76 N-D '28. * (*PA* 2:2948)
1151. HILDRETH, GERTRUDE. "The Effect of School Environment Upon Stanford Binet Tests of Young Children." *Yearb Nat Soc Study Ed* 27(1):355-9 '28. * (*PA* 2:1649)
1152. HOEFER, CAROLYN, AND HARDY, MATTIE CRUMPTON. "The Influence of Improvement in Physical Condition on Intelligence and Educational Achievement." *Yearb Nat Soc Study Ed* 27(1):371-87 '28. * (*PA* 2:2342)
1153. JONES, ALICE M. "A Vocabulary Study of Children in a Foreign Industrial Community." *Psychol Clinic* 17:13-21 Mr '28. * (*PA* 2:2950)
1154. LINCOLN, EDWARD A. "Studies of the Validity of the Dearborn General Intelligence Examinations." *J Ed Psychol* 19:346-9 My '28. * (*PA* 2:2952)
1155. MCANULTY, ELLEN ALICE. "A Comparison of the Terman, the National and the Stanford Binet Tests." *Ed Res B* (Los Angeles City Schools) 8:5-7 O '28. *
1156. MATTHEW, JANET, AND LUCKEY, BERTHA. "Notes on Factors That May Alter the Intelligence Quotient in Successive Examinations." *Yearb Nat Soc Study Ed* 27(1):411-9 '28. * (*PA* 2:2345)
1157. MURPHY, MILES. "The Ten Year Level of Competency." *Psychol Clinic* 17:33-60 My-Je '28. *
1158. ROGERS, AGNES L.; DURLING, DOROTHY; AND MCBRIDE, KATHARINE. "The Constancy of the IQ and the Training of Examiners." *J Ed Psychol* 19:257-62 Ap '28. * (*PA* 2:2657)
1159. ROGERS, AGNES L.; DURLING, DOROTHY; AND MCBRIDE, KATHARINE. "The Effect on the Intelligence Quotient of Change From a Poor to a Good Environment." *Yearb Nat Soc Study Ed* 27(1):323-31 '28. * (*PA* 2:1708)
1160. THORNDIKE, ROBERT L.; FLEMMING, CECILE WHITE; HILDRETH, GERTRUDE; AND STANGER, MARGARET. "Retest Changes in the IQ in Certain Superior Schools." *Yearb Nat Soc Study Ed* 27(2):351-61 '28. *
1161. WAGONER, LOVISA C., AND ARMSTRONG, EDNA M. "The Motor Control of Children as Involved in the Dressing Process." *J Genetic Psychol* 35:84-97 Mr '28. * (*PA* 2:3692)
1162. WITTY, PAUL A. "Some Results of a Pre-School Clinic." *J Genetic Psychol* 35:139-41 Mr '28. * (*PA* 2:3694)
1163. WOODWORTH, R. S. "Computing the Standard Deviation and Probable Error of a Binet Mental Age." Abstract. *Psychol R* 25:167 Mr '28. *
1164. ABT, ISAAC A.; ADLER, HERMAN M.; AND BARTELME, PHYLLIS. "The Relationship Between the Onset of Speech and Intelligence." *J Am Med Assn* 93:1351-5 N 2 '29. * (*PA* 4: 1285)
1165. BROOM, EUSTACE. "The Validity of Four Individual Tests of Mental Ability." *Ed Res B* (Los Angeles City Schools) 8:9-10 Mr '29. *
1166. CHIPMAN, CATHERINE E. "The Constancy of the Intelligence Quotient of Mental Defectives." *Psychol Clinic* 18:103-11 My-Je '29. * (*PA* 4:1110)
1167. FORD, CHARLES A. "The Variability of I.Q.'s for Psychopaths Retested Within Fifteen Days." *Psychol Clinic* 18:199-204 N-D '29. * (*PA* 4:4082)
1168. HERTZBERG, OSCAR E. "The Relationship of Motor Ability to the Intelligence of Kindergarten Children." *J Ed Psychol* 20:507-19 O '29. * (*PA* 4:373)
1169. MCCLURE, W. E., AND GOLDBERG, BRONETT. "Intelligence of Unmarried Mothers." *Psychol Clinic* 18:119-27 My-Je '29. * (*PA* 4:1202)
1170. MARSDEN, R. E. "The Intelligence of Children in Some Remote Country Schools." *Forum Ed* (England) 7:83-90 Je '29. * (*PA* 3:4320)
1171. RUCH, FLOYD L. "Defensibility of Certain Abridgments of the Stanford Achievement Examination." *J Ed Res* 20:66-9 Je '29. *
1172. THURSTONE, L. L., AND JENKINS, RICHARD L. "Birth Order and Intelligence." *J Ed Psychol* 20:641-51 D '29. * (*PA* 4:1057)
1173. CARROLL, HERBERT A., AND HOLLINGWORTH, LETA S. "The Systematic Error of Herring-Binet in Rating Gifted Children." *J Ed Psychol* 21:1-11 Ja '30. * (*PA* 4:1840)
1174. CATTELL, PSYCHE. "Comparability of I.Q.'s Obtained From Different Tests at Different I.Q. Levels." *Sch & Soc* 31: 437-42 Mr '30. * (*PA* 4:2561)
1175. CATTELL, PSYCHE. "IQ's and the Otis' Measure of Brightness." *J Ed Res* 22:31-5 Je '30. * (*PA* 4:3726)
1176. COX, JOHN FREMONT. *Differences Between Negro and Native White Convicts Tested With the Stanford-Binet Scale and Retested With a Reorganized Form of This Scale.* Master's thesis, University of Pittsburgh (Pittsburgh, Pa.), 1930.
1177. DAVENPORT, CHARLES B., AND MINOGUE, BLANCHE M. "The Intelligence Quotient and the Physical Quotient: Their Fluctuation and Intercorrelation." *Hum Biol* 2:473-507 D '30. * (*PA* 6:440)
1178. DEARBORN, WALTER F., AND CATTELL, PSYCHE. "The Intelligence and Achievement of Private School Pupils." *J Ed Psychol* 21:197-211 Mr '30. * (*PA* 4:2864)
1179. KEEN, ANGELINE M. "Growth Curves and IQ's as Determined by Testing Large Families." *Sch & Soc* 32:737-42 N 29 '30. * (*PA* 5:1740)
1180. ALTMAIER, CARL L. "The Performance Level of Children in the Sixth Grade in Two Philadelphia Public Schools." *Psychol Clinic* 19:233-57 Ja '31. * (*PA* 5:3986)
1181. BROOKS, FOWLER D. "Predicting Scholarship in the Junior High School." *Ann Conf Ed Meas* 18:73-80 '31. *

Stanford-Binet Intelligence Scale

1182. CATTELL, PSYCHE. "Why Otis' 'IQ' Cannot Be Equivalent to the Stanford-Binet IQ." *J Ed Psychol* 22:599–603 N '31. * (PA 6:906)
1183. HSIAO, HSIAO HUNG. "The Status of the First-Born With Special Reference to Intelligence." *Genetic Psychol Monogr* 9:1–118 Ja–F '31. * (PA 5:2689)
1184. LAWRENCE, EVELYN M. "An Investigation Into the Relation Between Intelligence and Inheritance." *Brit J Psychol Monogr Sup* 16:1–80 '31. *
1185. LEE, MARY V. "The Children's Orthopedic Hospital: A Survey of the Intelligence of Crippled Children." *J Ed Res* 23:164–6 F '31. * (PA 5:2503)
1186. DAWSON, SHEPHERD. "Intelligence and Fertility." *Brit J Psychol* 23:42–51 Jl '32. * (PA 7:2829)
1187. MCELWEE, EDNA WILLIS. "An Analysis of the Binet Test of Naming Words." *Psychol Clinic* 21:59–61 Mr–My '32. * (PA 7:379)
1188. OBELKEVICH, HENRY. *A Comparison of Detroit Boy Truants With Boy Non-Truants on Stanford-Binet Test Failures and on Certain Tangible Home Factors*. Master's thesis, University of Alabama (University, Ala.), 1932.
1189. RICHARDS, T. W. "Psychological Tests in the First Grade." *Psychol Clinic* 21:235–42 D–F '32–33. * (PA 8:665)
1190. RICHARDS, T. W. "The Relationship of Psychological Tests in the First Grade to School Progress: A Follow-Up Study." *Psychol Clinic* 21:137–71 S–N '32. *
1191. STEINER, MELVIN ARTHUR. "Yearly Variation in the Average Intelligence of Pupils Entering the First Grade." *J Ed Psychol* 23:161–72 Mr '32. * (PA 6:3003)
1192. UPDEGRAFF, RUTH. "The Determination of a Reliable Intelligence Quotient for the Young Child." *J Genetic Psychol* 41:152–66 S '32. * (PA 7:2164)
1193. WELLMAN, BETH L. "The Effect of Pre-School Attendance Upon IQ." *J Exp Ed* 1:48–69 D '32. * (PA 7:3106)
1194. BECKHAM, ALBERT SIDNEY. "A Study of the Intelligence of Colored Adolescents of Different Social-Economic Status in Typical Metropolitan Areas." *J Social Psychol* 4:70–91 F '33. * (PA 7:2459)
1195. CATTELL, PSYCHE. "The Heinis Personal Constant as a Substitute for the IQ." *J Ed Psychol* 24:221–8 Mr '33. * (PA 7:4176)
1196. DURRELL, DONALD D. "The Influence of Reading Ability on Intelligence Measures." *J Ed Psychol* 24:412–6 S '33. * (PA 8:654)
1197. EELLS, WALTER CROSBY. "Mental Ability of the Native Races of Alaska." *J Appl Psychol* 17:417–38 Ag '33. * (PA 8:478)
1198. FARSON, MABEL R. "A Comparison of Orthogenic Backward Children and Regular Grade Children at the Six Year Performance Level." *Psychol Clinic* 22:149–80 S–N '33. * (PA 8:5685)
1199. HARRIMAN, PHILIP L. "Ethical Discrimination as a Function of Intelligence." *Sch & Soc* 38:812 D 16 '33. * (PA 8:3175)
1200. HEILMAN, J. D. "Sex Differences in Intellectual Abilities." *J Ed Psychol* 24:47–62 Ja '33. * (PA 7:2121)
1201. LINE, W., AND KAPLAN, E. "Variation in I.Q. at the Preschool Level." *J Exp Ed* 2:95–100 D '33. * (PA 8:2316)
1202. MCCLURE, W. E. "Intelligence of Six Hundred Juvenile Delinquents." *J Juvenile Res* 17:35–43 Ja '33. * (PA 7:2509)
1203. MURPHY, MILES. "The Relation Between Intelligence and Age of Walking in Normal and Feeble-Minded Children." *Psychol Clinic* 22:187–97 S–N '33. * (PA 8:5712)
1204. OUTHIT, MARION CURRIE. "A Study of the Resemblance of Parents and Children in General Intelligence." *Arch Psychol* 149:1–60 Ap '33. * (PA 8:310)
1205. REICHARD, J. D. "The Intelligence of the Prospective Immigrant: 1, A Study of the Mental Ability, Measured by Language and Non-Language Tests, of Applicants for Immigrant Visas at Warsaw, Poland." *Pub Health B* 206:1–35 Jl '33. * (PA 8:1774)
1206. SCHELL, M. "Infection by Intestinal Protozoa in Relation to the Intelligence of Siblings." *Child Develop* 4:253–8 S '33. * (PA 8:721)
1207. SIMMONS, PERSIS WHITE. "Statistical Results of an Eight Year Testing Program of a Psychological Clinic in a Charity Hospital." *Psychol Clinic* 22:128–37 Je–Ag '33. * (PA 8:4681)
1208. BRYAN, ALICE I. "Organization of Memory in Young Children." *Arch Psychol* 162:1–56 Mr '34. * (PA 8:3836)
1209. CUNNINGHAM, BESS V. "Infant IQ Ratings Evaluated After an Interval of Seven Years." *J Exp Ed* 3:84–7 D '34. * (PA 9:2493)
1210. RAPPAPORT, MITCHELL E. "The Selection of the Intelligence Quotient Divisor for Clinical Cases Between Fourteen and Nineteen Years of Age." *J Ed Psychol* 25:101–14 F '34. * (PA 8:2812)
1211. STEINBACH, ALEXANDER ALAN. "Intelligence and Juvenile Delinquency." *El Sch J* 34:691–7 My '34. * (PA 8:4682)
1212. ANDERSON, H. DEWEY, AND EELLS, WALTER CROSBY. *Alaska Natives: A Survey of Their Sociological and Educational Status*, pp. 298–370. Stanford, Calif.: Stanford University Press, 1935. Pp. xvi, 472. * (PA 9:2346)
1213. ASHER, E. J. "The Inadequacy of Current Intelligence Tests for Testing Kentucky Mountain Children." *J Genetic Psychol* 46:480–6 Je '35. * (PA 9:6005)
1214. AXELBAUM, ETHEL M. *Differences Between the Kohs and Stanford-Binet in a Group of Artistically Gifted Children*. Master's thesis, Columbia University (New York, N.Y.), 1935.
1215. BRADWAY, KATHERINE PRESTON. "Paternal Occupational Intelligence and Mental Deficiency." *J Appl Psychol* 19:527–41 O '35. * (PA 10:2019)
1216. LANE, HOWARD A., AND WITTY, PAUL A. "The Mental Ability of Delinquent Boys." *J Juvenile Res* 19:1–12 Ja '35. * (PA 9:4718)
1217. LEAHY, A. M. "Nature-Nurture and Intelligence." *Genetic Psychol Monogr* 17:236–308 Ag '35. * (PA 9:5664)
1218. LINCOLN, EDWARD A. "A Study of Changes in the Intelligence Quotients of Superior Children." *J Ed Res* 29:272–5 D '35. * (PA 10:2764)
1219. LONG, HOWARD HALE. "Test Results of Third-Grade Negro Children Selected on the Basis of Socio-Economic Status." *J Negro Ed* 4:192–212, 523–52 Ap, O '35. * (PA 10:1089)
1220. MCELWEE, EDNA WILLIS. "Differences in Reading Attainment of Italian and Jewish Children." *J Appl Psychol* 19:730–2 D '35. * (PA 10:3637)
1221. ROTHBART, H. B., AND HAW, ARTHUR B. "Basal Metabolism in Children of Normal and Subnormal Intelligence With Blood Cholesterol and Creatinine Values." *Am J Dis Children* 49:672–88 Mr '35. *
1222. SHAKOW, DAVID, AND MILLARD, MARY S. "A Psychometric Study of One Hundred and Fifty Adult Delinquents." *J Social Psychol* 6:437–57 N '35. * (PA 10:3652)
1223. CANADY, HERMAN G. "The Effect of 'Rapport' on the I.Q.: A New Approach to the Problem of Racial Psychology." *J Negro Ed* 5:209–19 Ap '36. * (PA 10:4136)
1224. FENDRICK, PAUL, AND BOND, GUY. "Delinquency and Reading." *J Genetic Psychol* 48:236–43 Mr '36. * (PA 10:3619)
1225. HILL, HARRY SEGNER. "Correlation Between I.Q.'s of Bilinguals at Different Ages on Different Intelligence Tests." *Sch & Soc* 44:89–90 Jl 18 '36. * (PA 10:5164)
1226. HINTON, RALPH T., JR. "The Role of the Basal Metabolic Rate in the Intelligence of Ninety Grade-School Students." *J Ed Psychol* 27:546–50 O '36. * (PA 11:1247)
1227. JENKINS, MARTIN D. "A Socio-Psychological Study of Negro Children of Superior Intelligence." *J Negro Ed* 5:175–90 Ap '36. * (PA 10:4157)
1228. LORGE, IRVING, AND HOLLINGWORTH, LETA S. "Adult Status of Highly Intelligent Children." *J Genetic Psychol* 49:215–26 S '36. * (PA 11:3007)
1229. SKEELS, HAROLD M. "The Relation of the Foster Home Environment to the Mental Development of Children Placed in Infancy." *Child Develop* 7:1–5 Mr '36. * (PA 10:4443)
1230. SMITTER, FAITH WINTERS. *The Serviceability of the Merrill-Palmer and the Stanford-Binet Scales for Ages Three to Six*. Master's thesis, University of Southern California (Los Angeles, Calif.), 1936.
1231. WEISENBURG, THEODORE; ROE, ANNE; AND MCBRIDE, KATHARINE E. *Adult Intelligence: A Psychological Study of Test Performances*. New York: Commonwealth Fund, 1936. Pp. xiii, 155. * (PA 10:3771)
1232. BAYLEY, NANCY, AND JONES, HAROLD E. "Environmental Correlates of Mental and Motor Development: A Cumulative Study From Infancy to Six Years." *Child Develop* 8:329–41 D '37. * (PA 12:3201)
1233. CRISSEY, ORLO L. *Mental Development as Related to Institutional Residence and Educational Achievement*. University of Iowa Studies in Child Welfare Vol. 13, No. 1. Iowa City, Iowa: the University, 1937. Pp. 81. * (PA 11:3477)
1234. GLANVILLE, A. DOUGLAS. "Psychometric Patterns in Industrial School Boys." *Delaware State Med J* 11:91–4 Ap '37. * (PA 11:4270)
1235. HONZIK, MARJORIE P., AND JONES, HAROLD E. "Mental-Physical Relationships During the Preschool Period." *J Exp Ed* 6:139–46 D '37. * (PA 12:3216)
1236. JASTAK, JOSEPH. "Psychometric Patterns of State Hospital Patients." *Delaware State Med J* 11:87–91 Ap '37. * (PA 11:4152)
1237. KYTE, GEORGE C. "Causes of First-Grade Non-Promotion in the Light of Measured Intelligence." *El Sch J* 37:415–28 F '37. * (PA 11:3886)
1238. NAROSNY, ELEANOR HELEN. *A Comparative Study of the Performance of Juvenile Delinquents and Educational Problem Children on the Stanford-Binet and Grace Arthur Scales*. Master's thesis, Ohio State University (Columbus, Ohio), 1937.
1239. NOTTINGHAM, RUTH D. "A Psychological Study of Forty Unmarried Mothers." *Genetic Psychol Monogr* 19:157–228 My '37. * (PA 11:4670)
1240. PINESS, GEORGE; MILLER, HYMAN; AND SULLIVAN, ELLEN G. "The Intelligence Rating of the Allergic Child." *J Allergy* 8:168–74 Ja '37. * (PA 12:994)
1241. WELLMAN, BETH L. "Mental Growth From Preschool to College." *J Exp Ed* 6:127–38 D '37. * (PA 12:3244)
1242. WOLF, S. J. "A Comparative Study of Two Groups of Girls of Relatively Equal Intelligence but Differing Markedly in Achievement." *J Appl Psychol* 21:304–10 Je '37. * (PA 11:4815)
1243. LAMSON, EDNA E. "To What Extent Are Intelligence

Stanford-Binet Intelligence Scale

1243. Quotients Increased by Children Who Participate in a Rich, Vital School Curriculum?" *J Ed Psychol* 29:67-70 Ja '38. * (PA 12:3950)
1244. ROBERTS, CHARLES STEPHEN. "Ordinal Position and Its Relationship to Some Aspects of Personality." *J Genetic Psychol* 53:173-213 Je '38. * (PA 13:2034)
1245. SKEELS, HAROLD M.; UPDEGRAFF, RUTH; WELLMAN, BETH L.; AND WILLIAMS, HAROLD M. *A Study of Environmental Stimulation: An Orphanage Preschool Project*, pp. 37-60. University of Iowa Studies in Child Welfare, Vol. 15, No. 4. Iowa City, Iowa: the University, 1938. Pp. 191. * (PA 13:1758)
1246. WELLMAN, BETH L. *The Intelligence of Preschool Children as Measured by the Merrill-Palmer Scale of Performance Tests.* University of Iowa Studies in Child Welfare, Vol. 15, No. 3. Iowa City, Iowa: the University, 1938. Pp. 150. * (PA 13:1730)
1247. WILE, IRA S., AND DAVIS, ROSE M. "A Study of the Behavior of 250 Children With Mental Age Ten Years." *Am J Orthopsychiatry* 8:689-709 O '38. * (PA 13:1345)
1248. ABEL, THEODORA M. "Subnormal Girls With Discrepant Test Patterns." *J Appl Psychol* 23:398-404 Je '39. * (PA 13:5668)
1249. BIJOU, S. W. "Psychometric Similarities Between Habitual Criminals and Psychotics." *Delaware State Med J* 11:126-9 My '39. * (PA 14:3687)
1250. BRODY, LEON. "Adult Intelligence and Pre-Adult Schooling." *Sch & Soc* 49:746-8 Je 10 '39. * (PA 13:5063)
1251. HINTON, RALPH T., JR. "A Further Study of the Role of the Basal Metabolic Rate in the Intelligence of Children." *J Ed Psychol* 30:309-14 Ap '39. * (PA 13:5602)
1252. JASTAK, JOSEPH. "Psychometric Changes Following Insulin Therapy." *Delaware State Med J* 11:114-9 My '39. * (PA 14:3410)
1253. PENROSE, L. S. "Intelligence Test Scores of Mentally Defective Patients and Their Relatives." *Brit J Psychol* 30:1-18 Jl '39. * (PA 13:5734)
1254. TEAGARDEN, FLORENCE M. "The Intelligence of Diabetic Children With Some Case Reports." *J Appl Psychol* 23:337-46 Je '39. * (PA 13:5613)
1255. WELLS, F. L. "The Plan of Search at Various Levels of Abstraction." *J General Psychol* 21:163-85 Jl '39. * (PA 14:242)
1256. BAYLEY, NANCY. "Mental Growth in Young Children." *Yearb Nat Soc Study Ed* 39(2):11-47 '40. * (PA 14:3260)
1257. BRADLEY, CHARLES, AND GREEN, EMILY. "Psychometric Performance of Children Receiving Amphetamine (Benzedrine) Sulfate." *Am J Psychiatry* 97:388-94 S '40. * (PA 15:1997)
1258. CONRAD, HERBERT S., AND JONES, HAROLD E. "A Second Study of Familial Resemblance in Intelligence: Environmental and Genetic Implications of Parent-Child and Sibling Correlations in the Total Sample." *Yearb Nat Soc Study Ed* 39(2):97-141 '40. * (PA 14:2870)
1259. FRANDSEN, ARDEN, AND BARLOW, FRANCES P. "Influence of the Nursery School on Mental Growth." *Yearb Nat Soc Study Ed* 39(2):143-8 '40. * (PA 14:3202)
1260. GRAHAM, VIRGINIA TAYLOR. "Psychological Studies of Hypoglycemia Therapy." *J Psychol* 10:327-58 O '40. * (PA 15:1337)
1261. HONZIK, MARJORIE PYLES. "Age Changes in the Relationship Between Certain Environmental Variables and Children's Intelligence." *Yearb Nat Soc Study Ed* 39(2):185-205 '40. * (PA 14:2888)
1262. JENKINS, RICHARD L.; BROWN, ANDREW W.; AND CISLER, LILLIAN E. "Influence of Syphilis on Intelligence of Children." *Am J Dis Children* 60:341-51 Ag '40. * (PA 15:3627)
1263. KATZ, EVELYN. "The Relationship of IQ to Height and Weight From Three to Five Years." *J Genetic Psychol* 57:65-82 S '40. * (PA 15:1109)
1264. KVARACEUS, W. C. "Intelligence Quotients of Retarded Children in the Same Families." *El Sch J* 40:527-8 Mr '40. * (PA 15:4066)
1265. LAYMAN, JAMES W. "A Quantitative Study of Certain Changes in Schizophrenic Patients Under the Influence of Sodium Amytal." *J General Psychol* 22:67-86 Ja '40. * (PA 14:2439)
1266. SPEER, GEORGE S. "The Intelligence of Foster Children." *J Genetic Psychol* 57:49-55 S '40. * (PA 15:1128)
1267. PAGE, JAMES D. "Twin, Sibling and Chance IQ Differences." *J Ed Psychol* 32:73-6 Ja '41. * (PA 15:2947)
1268. ROFF, MERRILL. "A Statistical Study of the Development of Intelligence Test Performance." *J Psychol* 11:371-86 Ap '41. * (PA 15:3738)
1269. DULSKY, STANLEY G. "Affect and Intellect: An Experimental Study." *J General Psychol* 27:199-220 O '42. * (PA 17:77)
1270. MCRAE, HUGH. "The Inconstancy of Group Test IQ's." *Brit J Ed Psychol* 12:59-70 F '42. * (PA 16:2905)
1271. WILSON, M. T. "Detection of Reading Difficulties in a Rural Public School." *Training Sch B* 39:41-6 My '42. * (PA 16:3818)
1272. JENKINS, MARTIN D. "Case Studies of Negro Children of Binet IQ of 160 and Above." *J Negro Ed* 12:159-66 sp '43. * (PA 17:2410)
1273. BIJOU, S. W., AND MCCANDLESS, B. R. "An Approach to a More Comprehensive Analysis of Mentally Retarded Delinquent Boys." *J Genetic Psychol* 65:147-60 S '44. * (PA 19:440)
1274. BROWN, FRED. "A Comparative Study of the Intelligence of Jewish and Scandinavian Kindergarten Children." *J Genetic Psychol* 64:67-92 Mr '44. * (PA 18:2003)
1275. MUENCH, GEORGE A. "A Follow-Up of Mental Defectives After Eighteen Years." *J Abn & Social Psychol* 39:407-18 O '44. * (PA 19:420)
1276. SPOERL, DOROTHY TILDEN. "The Academic and Verbal Adjustment of College Age Bilingual Students." *J Genetic Psychol* 64:139-57 Mr '44. * (PA 18:2275)
1277. FALK, R.; PENROSE, L. S.; AND CLARK, E. A. "The Search for Intellectual Deterioration Among Epileptic Patients." *Am J Mental Def* 49:469-71 Ap '45. * (PA 20:139)
1278. KEIR, GERTRUDE. "An Experiment in Mental Testing Under Hypnosis." *J Mental Sci* (England) 91:346-52 Jl '45. * (PA 20:425)
1279. SPIEGEL, HERBERT; SHOR, JOEL; AND FISHMAN, SIDNEY. "An Hypnotic Ablation Technique for the Study of Personality Development: A Preliminary Report." *Psychosom Med* 7:273-8 S '45. * (PA 20:209)
1280. WAGGONER, R. W., AND ZEIGLER, THORNTON WOODWARD. "Psychiatric Factors in Medical School Students Who Fail." *Am J Psychiatry* 103:369-76 N '46. * (PA 21:1671)
1281. MARTIN, FLORENCE. "Comparative Study of Intelligence of Children From Private Homes and Those From an Institutional Home." *Peabody J Ed* 24:198-202 Ja '47. * (PA 21:3950)
1282. SLOAN, WILLIAM, AND HARMAN, HARRY H. "Constancy of IQ in Mental Defectives." *J Genetic Psychol* 71:177-85 D '47. * (PA 22:3525)
1283. ZIMMERMAN, FREDERIC T.; BURGEMEISTER, BESSIE B.; AND PUTNAM, TRACY J. "A Group Study of the Effect of Glutamic Acid Upon Mental Functioning in Children and Adolescents." *Psychosom Med* 9:175-83 My-Je '47. * (PA 21:3474)
1284. COLLINS, JEANNE. "The Correlation Between Perseveration Test Scores and the Intelligence Quotient: An Experimental Study." *J Genetic Psychol* 72:47-55 Mr '48. * (PA 22:4834)
1285. ZIMMERMAN, FREDERIC T.; BURGEMEISTER, BESSIE B.; AND PUTNAM, TRACY J. "The Ceiling Effect of Glutamic Acid Upon Intelligence in Children and in Adolescents." *Am J Psychiatry* 104:593-9 Mr '48. * (PA 23:634)
1286. SKODAK, MARIE, AND SKEELS, HAROLD M. "A Final Follow-Up Study of One Hundred Adopted Children." *J Genetic Psychol* 75:85-125 S '49. * (PA 24:3651)
1287. ASHER, PATRIA, AND SCHONELL, F. ELEANOR. "A Survey of 400 Cases of Cerebral Palsy in Childhood." *Arch Dis Childh* (England) 25:360-79 D '50. * (PA
1288. GERVER, JOHN M., AND DAY, RICHARD. "Intelligence Quotient of Children Who Have Recovered From Erythroblastosis Fetalis." *J Pediatrics* 36:342-8 Mr '50. * (PA 24:4490)
1289. KREEZER, GEORGE L., AND SMITH, FRANKLIN W. "The Relation of the Alpha Rhythm of the Electroencephalogram, and Intelligence Level in the Non-Differentiated Familial Type of Mental Deficiency." *J Psychol* 29:47-51 Ja '50. * (PA 24:4170)
1290. ALBERT, K.; HOCH, P.; AND WAELSCH, H. "Glutamic Acid and Mental Deficiency." *J Nerv & Mental Dis* 114:471-91 D '51. * (PA 26:4871)
1291. REED, HOMER R. "The Intelligence of Epileptics." *J Genetic Psychol* 78:145-52 Je '51. * (PA 26:2942)
1292. BENSBERG, GERARD J., JR. "The Relation of Academic Achievement of Mental Defectives to Mental Age, Sex, Institutionalization and Etiology." *Am J Mental Def* 58:327-30 O '53. * (PA 28:4530)
1293. GHOSH, S. P., AND SEN, ROMA. "An Attempt to Standardise the Bengali Adaptation of Terman 'M' Form." *Indian J Psychol* 28:111-5 pts 1-4 '53. * (PA 29:2446)
1294. REYNOLDS, MAYNARD CLINTON. "A Study of the Relationships Between Auditory Characteristics and Specific Silent Reading Abilities." *J Ed Res* 46:439-49 F '53. * (PA 28:1492)
1295. BAYLEY, NANCY. "Some Increasing Parent-Child Similarities During the Growth of Children." *J Ed Psychol* 45:1-21 Ja '54. * (PA 28:7257)
1296. GUREVITZ, SAUL, AND HELME, WILLIAM H. "Effects of Electroconvulsive Therapy on Personality and Intellectual Functioning of the Schizophrenic Child." *J Nerv & Mental Dis* 120:213-26 S-O '54. * (PA 29:7650)
1297. PAZEIAN, BESSIE. "Classification and Treatment Problems in a Case of Encephalopathy." *J Clin Psychol* 10:149-55 Ap '54. * (PA 29:1376)
1298. UECKER, ALBERT E.; FRENCH, LYLE A.; AND JOHNSON, DAVID R. "Psychological Studies of Seven Epileptic Hemiparetics Before and After Hemispherectomy." *Arch Neurol & Psychiatry* 72:555-64 N '54. * (PA 29:6114)
1299. BAYLEY, NANCY. "On the Growth of Intelligence." *Am Psychologist* 10:805-18 D '55. * (PA 30:6898)
1300. GRANICK, SAMUEL. "Intellectual Performance as Related to Emotional Instability in Children." *J Abn & Social Psychol* 51:653-6 N '55. * (PA 31:2632)
1301. SONTAG, L. W.; BAKER, CHARLES T.; AND NELSON, VIRGINIA. "Personality as a Determinant of Performance." *Am J Orthopsychiatry* 25:555-62 Jl '55. * (PA 30:4173)
1302. MONEY, JOHN. "Psychologic Studies in Hypothyroidism: Recommendations for Case Management." *Arch Neurol & Psychiatry* 76:296-309 S '56. * (PA 31:4827)

1303. Pearson, John S., and Amacher, Phyllis L. "Intelligence Test Results and Observations of Personality Disorder Among 3594 Unwed Mothers in Minnesota." *J Clin Psychol* 12: 16–21 Ja '56. * (*PA* 30:4476)

1304. Rebhun, Albert M. "The Level-Sharpening Dimension as Manifested in Other Perceptual or Non-Perceptual Tasks." *Psychol Newsl* 7:43–6 Ja–F '56. * (*PA* 31:1767)

1305. Schoonover, Sarah M. "A Longitudinal Study of Sibling Resemblances in Intelligence and Achievement." *J Ed Psychol* 47:436–42 N '56. * (*PA* 32:4617)

1306. Ellis, N. R., and Sloan, W. "Relationship Between Intelligence and Simple Reaction Time in Mental Defectives." *Percept & Motor Skills* 7:65–7 Je '57. * (*PA* 32:3041)

1307. Levinson, Boris M. "A Comparative Study of the Intelligence of Jewish Preschool Boys and Girls of Orthodox Parentage." *J Genetic Psychol* 90:17–22 Mr '57. * (*PA* 35:2198)

1308. Levinson, Boris M. "The Intelligence of Applicants for Admission to Jewish Day Schools." *Jewish Social Studies* 19:129–40 Jl–O '57. * (*PA* 34:2728, 35:781)

1309. Lewis, D. G. "The Normal Distribution of Intelligence: A Critique." *Brit J Psychol* 48:98–104 My '57. * (*PA* 32:5220)

1310. Mundy, Lydia. "Environmental Influence on Intellectual Function as Measured by Intelligence Tests." *Brit J Med Psychol* 30:194–201 pt 3 '57. * (*PA* 33:791)

1311. Baker, Charles T.; Sontag, Lester W.; and Nelson, Virginia L. "Individual and Group Differences in the Longitudinal Measurement of Change in Mental Ability." *Monogr Soc Res Child Develop* 23(2):11–85 '58. * (*PA* 33:5719)

1312. Garrison, Mortimer, Jr. "A Comparison of Psychological Measures in Mentally Retarded Boys Over a Three-Year Period as a Function of Etiology." *Training Sch B* 55:54–60 N '58. * (*PA* 34:1664)

1313. Sontag, Lester W., and Baker, Charles T. "Personality, Familial, and Physical Correlates of Change in Mental Ability." *Monogr Soc Res Child Develop* 23(2):87–143 '58. * (*PA* 33:5729)

1314. Braen, Bernard B., and Masling, Joseph M. "Intelligence Tests Used With Special Groups of Children." *Excep Children* 26:42–5 S '59. * (*PA* 35:2194)

1315. Hirsch, Monroe J. "The Relationship Between Refractive State of the Eye and Intelligence Test Scores." *Am J Optom* 36:12–21 Ja '59. * (*PA* 34:1099)

1316. Hohman, Leslie B., and Freedheim, Donald K. "A Study of IQ Retest Evaluations on 370 Cerebral Palsied Children." *Am J Phys Med* 38:180–7 O '59. *

1317. Hunt, Betty M. "Performance of Mentally Deficient Brain-Injured Children and Mentally Deficient Familial Children on Construction From Patterns." *Am J Mental Def* 63:679–87 Jl '59. * (*PA* 34:1669)

1318. Sampson, Olive C. "The Speech and Language Development of 5-Year-Old Children." *Brit J Ed Psychol* 29:217–22 N '59. *

1319. Moran, R. E. "Levels of Attainment of Educable Subnormal Adolescents." *Brit J Ed Psychol* 30:201–10 N '60. * (*PA* 37:3584)

1320. Dunphy, Donal, and Pessin, Vivian. "Correlation Between Cord Blood Oxygen Values and Psychological Test Scores." *J Iowa Med Soc* 52:212–6 Ap '62. *

1321. Jenkins, C. David. "The Relation of EEG Slowing to Selected Indices of Intellective Impairment." *J Nerv & Mental Dis* 135:162–70 Ag '62. *

1322. Worden, Don K., and Vignos, Paul J., Jr. "Intellectual Function in Childhood Progressive Muscular Dystrophy." *Pediatrics* 29:968–77 Je '62. *

1323. Chodorkoff, Joan, and Whitten, Charles F. "Intellectual Status of Children With Sickle Cell Anemia." *J Pediatrics* 63:29–35 Jl '63. *

1324. Francis, Gary Mills. *Mental Age as a Criterion of School Entrance.* Master's thesis, University of Utah (Salt Lake City, Utah), 1963.

1325. Haan, Norma. "Proposed Model of Ego Functioning: Coping and Defense Mechanisms in Relationship to IQ Change." *Psychol Monogr* 77(8):1–23 '63. * (*PA* 38:4234)

1326. Young, Francis A. "Reading Measures of Intelligence and Refractive Errors." *Am J Optom* 40:257–64 My '63. *

1327. Karelitz, Samuel; Fisichelli, Vincent R.; Costa, Joan; Karelitz, Ruth; and Rosenfield, Laura. "Relation of Crying Activity in Early Infancy to Speech and Intellectual Development at Age Three Years." *Child Develop* 35:769–77 S '64. * (*PA* 39:4513)

1328. Klatskin, Ethelyn Henry. "Relationships of Deficits in Intelligence Test Performance of Preschool Children to Perinatal Experience." *J Consult Psychol* 28:228–33 Je '64. * (*PA* 39:4590)

1329. Pollitt, Ernesto, and Money, John. "Studies in the Psychology of Dwarfism: 1, Intelligence Quotient and School Achievement." *J Pediatrics* 64:415–21 Mr '64. *

1330. Qureshi, Mohammed Y. "Performance on Individual Ability Tests as a Function of Various Scoring Cutoffs." *Ed & Psychol Meas* 24:481–512 f '64. * (*PA* 39:3173)

1331. Reinhart, Richard A. "Some Relationships Between Early Rheumatic Fever, Intelligence and Anxiety Scores." *J Child Psychol & Psychiatry* (England) 6:243–50 D '65. * (*PA* 40:8694)

1332. Silverstein, A. B. "'Validity' of Short-Form Intelligence Tests." *J Consult Psychol* 29:392–3 Ag '65. * (*PA* 39:15267)

1333. Spreen, Otfried, and Benton, Arthur L. "Comparative Studies of Some Psychological Tests for Cerebral Damage." *J Nerv & Mental Dis* 140:323–33 My '65. * (*PA* 40:700)

1334. Money, John, and Lewis, Viola. "IQ, Genetics and Accelerated Growth: Adrenogenital Syndrome." *Johns Hopkins Med J* 118:365–73 My '66. *

1335. Paton, Richard. "Use of the Quick Test With Retarded Children." *Ont Psychol Assn Q* (Canada) 19:60–3 su '66. *

1336. Ball, T. S., and Wilsoncroft, W. E. "Perceptual-Motor Deficits and the Phi Phenomenon." *Am J Mental Def* 71:797–800 My '67. * (*PA* 41:9259)

1337. Gittelman, Martin, and Birch, Herbert G. "Childhood Schizophrenia: Intellect, Neurologic Status, Perinatal Risk, Prognosis, and Family Pathology." *Arch Gen Psychiatry* 17:16–25 Jl '67. * (*PA* 41:15552)

1338. Harter, Susan. "Mental Age, IQ, and Motivational Factors in the Discrimination Learning Set Performance of Normal and Retarded Children." *J Exp Child Psychol* 5:123–41 Je '67. * (*PA* 41:12393)

1339. Linde, Leonard M.; Rasof, Beatrice; and Dunn, Olive Jean. "Mental Development in Congenital Heart Disease." *J Pediatrics* 71:198–203 Ag '67. *

1340. Money, John; Drash, Philip W.; and Lewis, Viola. "Dwarfism and Hypopituitarism: Statural Retardation Without Mental Retardation." *Am J Mental Def* 72:122–6 Jl '67. * (*PA* 41:15732)

1341. Qureshi, Mohammed Y. "The Invariance of Certain Ability Factors." *Ed & Psychol Meas* 27:803–10 w '67. * (*PA* 42:8734)

1342. Beller, E. Kuno. "Intellectual Development in Educationally Disadvantaged Pre-School Children." *Proc 1966 Ann Read Inst Temple Univ* 5:73–83 '68. *

1343. Drash, Philip W.; Greenberg, Nancy E.; and Money, John. Chap. 39, "Intelligence and Personality in Four Syndromes of Dwarfism," pp. 568–81. In *Human Growth, Body Composition, Cell Growth, Energy, and Intelligence.* Edited by Donald B. Cheek. Philadelphia, Pa.: Lea & Febiger, 1968. Pp. xxx, 781. *

1344. Prentice, Norman M., and Bieri, James. "Intellectual Development of Culturally Deprived Children in a Day Care Program." Abstract. *Proc 76th Ann Conv Am Psychol Assn* 3:599–600 '68. * (*PA* 43:1328, title only)

1345. Pringle, M. L. Kellmer, and Cox, T. "The Association Between Sarason's Test Anxiety and Intelligence Test Performance." *Ed Sci* (England) 2:227–36 S '68. *

1346. Smith, Marshall P. "Intellectual Differences in Five-Year-Old Underprivileged Girls and Boys With and Without Pre-Kindergarten School Experience." *J Ed Res* 61:348–50 Ap '68. *

1347. Babson, S. Gorham; Henderson, Norman; and Clark, William M., Jr. "The Preschool Intelligence of Oversized Newborns." *Pediatrics* 44(4):536–8 O '69. *

1348. Barclay, A. "Longitudinal Changes in Intellectual and Social Development of Non-Institutionalized Retardates." *Am J Mental Def* 73(5):831–7 Mr '69. * (*PA* 43:10216)

1349. Bozarth, Dorothy Craig. *The Relationship of Intelligence Test Scatter and Self-Concept.* Master's thesis, Millersville State College (Millersville, Pa.), 1969.

1350. Bruch, Catherine. "A Creative Score From the Stanford-Binet and Its Application." *CEC Selected Conv Papers* 1969:1–3 '69. *

1351. Fraser, Don. "Mental Abilities of British Columbia Indian Children." *Can Counsellor* 3(3):42–8 Je '69. *

1352. Fraser, William D. *Mental Abilities of British Columbia Indian Children.* Master's thesis, University of British Columbia (Vancouver, B.C., Canada), 1969.

1353. Gross, Morris. "Learning Readiness in Two Groups: A Study in 'Cultural Deprivation.'" *Jewish Ed* 39(1):36–48 Ja '69. *

1354. Honzik, Marjorie P.; Collart, Donna S.; Robinson, Saul J.; and Finley, Knox H. "Sex Differences in Verbal and Performance IQ's of Children Undergoing Open-heart Surgery." *Sci* 164(3878):445–7 Ap 25 '69. * (*PA* 45:6906)

1355. Sontag, Marvin; Sella, Adina P.; and Thorndike, Robert L. "The Effect of Head Start Training on the Cognitive Growth of Disadvantaged Children." *J Ed Res* 62(9):387–9 My–Je '69. * (*PA* 46:1899)

1356. Brown, Joe, and Zemanek, Don. "Variables Affecting the Gross Motor Performance of Trainable Retardates," pp. 489–98. In *Contemporary Psychology of Sport.* Proceedings of the Second International Congress of Sport Psychology, Washington, D.C., 1968. Chicago, Ill.: Athletic Institute, 1970. Pp. xix, 878. *

1357. Eaves, Linda C.; Nuttall, J. C.; Klonoff, H.; and Dunn, H. G. "Developmental and Psychological Test Scores in Children of Low Birth Weight." *Pediatrics* 45(1):9–20 Ja '70. * Correction: 45(5):886–7 My '70. *

1358. Gross, Morris B. "Pre-School Prediction of Academic Achievement." Abstract. *Psychol Rep* 26(1):278 F '70. * (*PA* 45:5056)

1359. Karnes, Merel B.; Teska, James A.; and Hodgins, Audrey S. "The Effects of Four Programs of Classroom Inter-

1359. vention on the Intellectual and Language Development of 4-Year-Old Disadvantaged Children." *Am J Orthopsychiatry* 40(1):58–76 Ja '70. * *(PA* 45:1373)
1360. O'KELLY, E. "A Method for Detecting Slow Learning Juniors." *Ed Res* (England) 12(2):135–9 F '70. *
1361. SHATUS, ERWIN L. "Validation of the Wechsler Preschool and Primary Scale of Intelligence With the Stanford-Binet, Form L-M, on Culturally Deprived Children." *South J Ed Res* 4(1):18–36 Ja '70 [My '71]. *
1362. SIMMERS, CATHERINE POWELL. *Cognitive Correlates of Attitudinal Rigidity.* Doctor's thesis, Case Western Reserve University (Cleveland, Ohio), 1970. *(DAI* 32:1348A)
1363. SLAUGHTER, DIANA T. "Parental Potency and the Achievements of Inner-City Black Children." *Am J Orthopsychiatry* 40(3):433–40 Ap '70. * *(PA* 45:8989)
1364. WHITE, GENEVIEVE. *Procedures for Predicting Children's Success in First Grade Achievement.* Master's thesis, Arkansas State University (State University, Ark.), 1970.
1365. WRIGHT, ELSIE LOUISE. *A Correlational Study of Selected Sociological Variables and Two Ranges of Stanford-Binet Intelligence Quotients Among Culturally Disadvantaged Preschool Children.* Doctor's thesis, University of Alabama (University, Ala.), 1970. *(DAI* 31:5219A)
1366. ABLES, BILLIE S. "The Use of the Draw-A-Man Test With Borderline Retarded Children Without Pronounced Pathology." *J Clin Psychol* 27(2):262–3 Ap '71. * *(PA* 46:7068)
1367. ACHENBACH, THOMAS M. "Stanford-Binet Short-Form Performance of Retarded and Nonretarded Persons Matched for MA." *Am J Mental Def* 76(1):30–2 Jl '71. * *(PA* 47:7069)
1368. ARMSTRONG, ROBERT J., AND MOONEY, ROBERT F. "The Slosson Intelligence Test: Implications for Reading Specialists." *Read Teach* 24(4):336–40+ Ja '71. * *(PA* 46:11492)
1369. ARMSTRONG, ROBERT J.; MOONEY, ROBERT F.; AND JENSEN, JOHN A. "A Short, Reliable, Easy to Administer Individual Intelligence Test for Special Class Placement." *Child Study J* 1(3):156–63 sp '71. * *(PA* 48:1701)
1370. BERSOFF, DONALD N. "Short Forms of Individual Intelligence Tests for Children: Review and Critique." *J Sch Psychol* 9(3):310–20 '71. * *(PA* 47:8924)
1371. BROWN, DARRELL LEE. *Variations in Test Response of Preschool Children by Sex and Socioeconomic Level Related to Guilford's Structure-of-Intellect.* Doctor's thesis, University of Pittsburgh (Pittsburgh, Pa.), 1971. *(DAI* 32:4412A)
1372. BRUCH, CATHERINE B. "Modification of Procedures for Identification of the Disadvantaged Gifted." *Gifted Child Q* 15(4):267–72 w '71. * *(PA* 48:5647)
1373. BUCK, CAROL; GREGG, ROSE; HARPER, MARY; AND SNIDER, SANDRA. "The Effect of Kindergarten Experiences Upon IQ Test Performance." *Psychol Sch* 8(1):62–4 Ja '71. * *(PA* 46:7677)
1374. BUDOFF, M.; MESKIN, J.; AND HARRISON, R. H. "Educational Test of the Learning-Potential Hypothesis." *Am J Mental Def* 76(2):159–69 S '71. * *(PA* 47:9717)
1375. DUROJAIYE, M. O. A., AND SUCH, M. "Predicting Educational Suitability of Children in an Assessment Unit." *J Exp Ed* 40(2):27–36 w '71. * *(PA* 47:11608)
1376. ELLIOTT, R., AND MACKAY, D. N. "Social Competence of Subnormal and Normal Children Living Under Different Types of Residential Care." *Brit J Mental Subnormal* 17(32):48–53 Je '71. * *(PA* 47:11471)
1377. FIELDS, DONALD L., AND GIBSON, DAVID. "Forecasting Mental Growth for At-Home Mongols (Down's Syndrome)." *J Mental Def Res* (England) 15(3):163–8 S '71. * *(PA* 49:11377)
1378. FOREHAND, REX, AND GORDON, DONALD A. "Application of Two Short Forms of the Stanford-Binet With Retardates." *Am J Mental Def* 75(6):763–4 My '71. *
1379. GAYTON, WILLIAM F. "An Evaluation of Two Short Forms of the Stanford-Binet, Form L-M, for Use With a Child Guidance Population." *Psychol Rep* 28(2):355–7 Ap '71. * *(PA* 46:7553)
1380. GOLDEN, MARK; BIRNS, BEVERLY; BRIDGER, WAGNER; AND MOSS, ABIGAIL. "Social-Class Differentiation in Cognitive Development Among Black Preschool Children." *Child Develop* 42(1):37–45 Mr '71. * *(PA* 46:4621)
1381. HERSH, JEFFREY B. "Effects of Referral Information on Testers." *J Consult & Clin Psychol* 37(1):116–22 Ag '71. * *(PA* 47:1578)
1382. HERTZIG, MARGARET E., AND BIRCH, HERBERT G. "Longitudinal Course of Measured Intelligence in Preschool Children of Different Social and Ethnic Backgrounds." *Am J Orthopsychiatry* 41(3):416–26 Ap '71. * *(PA* 46:6537)
1383. HUIZINGA, RALEIGH JAMES. *The Relationship of the Illinois Test of Psycholinguistic Abilities to the Stanford-Binet Form L-M and the Wechsler Intelligence Scale for Children.* Doctor's thesis, University of Arizona (Tucson, Ariz.), 1971. *(DAI* 32:3823A)
1384. JACOBSON, LEONARD I.; BERGER, STEPHEN E.; BERGMAN, RONALD L.; MILLHAM, JIM; AND GREESON, LARRY E. "Effects of Age, Sex, Systematic Conceptual Learning, Acquisition of Learning Sets, and Programmed Social Interaction on the Intellectual and Conceptual Development of Preschool Children From Poverty Backgrounds." *Child Develop* 42(5):1399–415 N '71. * *(PA* 48:5847)

1385. JOESTING, JOAN, AND JOESTING, ROBERT. "Comparison of Scores on Quick Test and Stanford-Binet, Form L-M." *Psychol Rep* 29(3):1178 D '71. * *(PA* 48:1648)
1386. JOHNSON, DALE L., AND JOHNSON, CARMEN A. "Comparison of Four Intelligence Tests Used With Culturally Disadvantaged Children." *Psychol Rep* 28(1):209–10 F '71. * *(PA* 46:5736)
1387. JORDAN, THOMAS E. "Early Developmental Adversity and the First Two Years of Life." *Multiv Behav Res Monogr* 6(1):1–80 '71. * *(PA* 49:2132)
1388. KANGAS, JON, AND BRADWAY, KATHERINE. "Intelligence at Middle Age: A Thirty-Eight-Year Follow-Up." *Develop Psychol* 5(2):333–7 S '71. * *(PA* 47:2985)
1389. KARADENES, MARK. *A Comparison of Differences in Achievement and Learning Abilities Between Anglo and Mexican-American Children When the Two Groups Are Equated by Intelligence.* Doctor's thesis, University of Virginia (Charlottesville, Va.), 1971. *(DAI* 32:4422A)
1390. KOLLER, JAMES RAYMOND. *Mental Age: A Test of Certain Underlying Assumptions.* Doctor's thesis, University of Missouri (Columbia, Mo.), 1971. *(DAI* 32:2485A)
1391. LEITHWOOD, KENNETH A. "Motor, Cognitive, and Affective Relationships Among Advantaged Preschool Children." *Res Q* 42(1):47–53 Mr '71. * *(PA* 46:6539)
1392. LEVINSON, ELIZABETH J. "The Modification of Intelligence by Training in the Verbalization of Word Definitions and Simple Concepts." *Child Develop* 42(5):1361–80 N '71. * *(PA* 48:4673)
1393. LEWIS, RUTH. "Survey of the Intelligence of Cleft-Lip and Cleft-Palate Children in Ontario." *Brit J Dis Commun* 6(1):17–25 Ap '71. * *(PA* 49:9395)
1394. LOBL, MICHELE; WELCHER, DORIS W.; AND MELLITS, E. DAVID. "Maternal Age and Intellectual Functioning of Offspring." *Johns Hopkins Med J* 128(6):347–61 Je '71. *
1395. MCKINNEY, JAMES D., AND CORTER, HAROLD M. "Flexibility Training With Educable Retarded Children." *J Sch Psychol* 9(4):455–61 w '71. * *(PA* 48:1711)
1396. MAXWELL, MICHAEL T. "The Relationship Between the Wechsler Intelligence Scale for Children and the Slosson Intelligence Test." *Child Study J* 1(3):164–71 sp '71. * *(PA* 48:1709)
1397. MILGRAM, NORMAN A. "IQ Constancy in Disadvantaged Negro Children." *Psychol Rep* 29(1):319–26 Ag '71. * *(PA* 47:2652)
1398. OAKLAND, THOMAS D.; KING, JOHN D.; WHITE, LINDA ANN; AND ECKMAN, ROBERT. "A Comparison of Performance on the WPPSI, WISC, and SB With Preschool Children: Companion Studies." *J Sch Psychol* 9(2):144–9 '71. * *(PA* 47:7563)
1399. O'GRADY, DONALD J.; BERRY, HELEN K.; AND SUTHERLAND, BETTY S. "Cognitive Development in Early Treated Phenylketonuria." *Am J Dis Children* 121(1):20–3 Ja '71. *
1400. PASEWARK, RICHARD A.; RARDIN, MAX W.; AND GRICE, JOHN E., JR. "Relationship of the Wechsler Pre-School and Primary Scale of Intelligence and the Stanford-Binet (L-M) in Lower Class Children." *J Sch Psychol* 9(1):43–50 '71. * *(PA* 47:5609)
1401. PHILLIPS, DORIS CAMPBELL. *An Exploratory Study of the Relationship Between Mothers' Individualization of Their Children and the Children's Developmental Progress.* Doctor's thesis, Washington University (St. Louis, Mo.), 1971. *(DAI* 32:2201A)
1402. PRASAD, R.; MUKHERJEE, A.; AND VARMA, S. K. "The Role of Intelligence Testing in the Assessment of Cerebral Palsy Children." *J Assn Physicians India* 19(10):715–7 O '71. *
1403. PROSSER, NANETTE S., AND CRAWFORD, VEDA B. "Relationship of Scores on the Wechsler Preschool and Primary Scale of Intelligence and the Stanford-Binet Intelligence Scale Form LM." *J Sch Psychol* 9(3):278–83 '71. * *(PA* 47:8634)
1404. QUAY, LORENE C. "Language Dialect, Reinforcement, and the Intelligence-Test Performance of Negro Children." *Child Develop* 42(1):5–15 Mr '71. * *(PA* 46:4660)
1405. RADIN, NORMA. "Maternal Warmth, Achievement Motivation, and Cognitive Functioning in Lower-Class Preschool Children." *Child Develop* 42(5):1560–5 N '71. * *(PA* 48:4724)
1406. SANDSTEAD, HAROLD H.; CARTER, JAMES P.; HOUSE, FAYE R.; MCCONNELL, FREEMAN; HORTON, KATHRYN B.; AND VANDER ZWAAG, ROGER. "Nutritional Deficiencies in Disadvantaged Preschool Children: Their Relationship to Mental Development." *Am J Dis Children* 121(6):455–63 Je '71. *
1407. SCHWARZ, ROBERT H., AND COOK, JOHN J. "Mental Age as a Predictor of Academic Achievement." *Ed & Train Mental Retard* 6(1):12–5 F '71. *
1408. SCHWARZ, ROBERT H., AND FLANIGAN, PATRICK J. "Evaluation of Examiner Bias in Intelligence Testing." *Am J Mental Def* 76(2):262–5 S '71. * *(PA* 47:9664)
1409. SILVERSTEIN, A. B. "Reliability and Constancy of a New Measure of Intelligence for Institutionalized Retardates." *Am J Mental Def* 76(2):257–8 S '71. * *(PA* 47:9514)
1410. SPENCE, ALLYN G.; MISHRA, SHITALA P.; AND GHOZEIL, SUSAN. "Home Language and Performance on Standardized Tests." *El Sch J* 71(6):309–13 Mr '71. * *(PA* 47:2655)
1411. SUNDEAN, DAVID A., AND SALOPEK, THOMAS F. "Achievement and Intelligence in Primary and Elementary

Stanford-Binet Intelligence Scale

Classes for the Educable Mentally Retarded." *J Sch Psychol* 9(2):150–6 '71. * *(PA* 47:7610)

1412. TAYLOR, JOHN F. "A Table for Predicting Retardate Mental Age Growth." *Am J Mental Def* 75(4):499–503 Ja '71. * *(PA* 46:3623)

1413. WELCHER, DORIS W.; MELLITS, E. DAVID; AND HARDY, JANET B. "A Multivariate Analysis of Factors Affecting Psychological Performance." *Johns Hopkins Med J* 129(1):19–35 Jl '71. *

1414. WIKOFF, RICHARD L. "Subscale Classification Schemata for the Stanford-Binet, Form L-M." *J Sch Psychol* 9(3):329–37 '71. * *(PA* 47:8931)

CUMULATIVE NAME INDEX

Abbott, R. F.: 753
Abel, T. M.: 1248
Abelson, H. H.: 1140
Abernethy, E. M.: 1094
Ables, B. S.: 1366
Aborn, M.: 477
Abt, I. A.: 1164
Achenbach, T. M.: 942, 1367
Ack, M.: 660
Ackerson, L.: 43
Adams, F. J.: 187
Aderman, M.: 921
Adkins, M. M.: 279
Adler, D. L.: 166
Adler, H. M.: 1164
Albert, K.: 1290
Alderdice, E. T.: 511
Alexander, S.: 870
Allan, M. E.: 280
Allen, J. C.: 971
Allen, L.: 433
Allen, M.: 920
Allen, M. K.: 240
Allen, R. D.: 1068
Alling, R. L.: 591
Alper, A. E.: 741
Alpern, G. D.: 943
Altmaier, C. L.: 1180
Altman, C. H.: 89
Altus, W. D.: 336
Altus, W. S.: 441
Amacher, P. L.: 1303
Anastasi, A.: 661, 869
Anderson, C. J.: 870
Anderson, E. E.: 241
Anderson, G. L.: 424, 478
Anderson, H. D.: 1212
Anderson, L. D.: 167
Anderson, S. F.: 241
Apgar, V.: 641, 736
Applebaum, A. P.: 831
Arlitt, A. H.: 1099
Armstrong, C. P.: 281
Armstrong, E. M.: 1161
Armstrong, H. C.: 732
Armstrong, J. G.: 871
Armstrong, R. J.: 1368–9
Arnold, F. C.: 563
Arthur, G.: 112, 461, 480
Asher, E. J.: 1133, 1213
Asher, P.: 1287
Atwell, C. R.: 113
Avery, G. T.: 23, 1066
Axelbaum, E. M.: 1214
Babcock, H.: 404
Babson, S. G.: 908, 1347
Bach, L. C.: 872
Bacon, A. M.: 368
Bailey, H. K.: 442
Bailey, L. L.: 574
Baker, C. T.: 547, 564, 579, 1301, 1311, 1313
Baker, H. J.: 1046
Baldwin, A. L.: 425–6
Baldwin, B. T.: 13, 1047, 1067
Baldwin, J. W.: 688
Balinsky, B.: 114; *exc,* 6:536
Ball, R. S.: 830
Ball, T. S.: 1336
Bannon, W. J.: 427, 895
Barabasz, A. F.: 909
Barclay, A.: 755, 804, 852, 886, 910, 1348
Barlow, F. P.: 1259
Barratt, E. S.: 602
Bartelme, P.: 1164
Bartley, S. H.: 701
Bateman, B.: 873
Battle, E. S.: 955
Baughman, E. E.: 874

Baumgarten, D. L.: 602
Bayley, N.: 443, 628, 944, 1232, 1256, 1295, 1299
Bean, K. L.: 200
Beard, R. M.: 777
Beck, E. C.: 934
Beck, E. J.: 603
Beckham, A. S.: 1194
Beechley, R. M.: 481
Beeson, M. F.: 137
Begg, T. L.: 613
Bellak, L.: 201
Beller, E. K.: 1342
Benger, K.: 875
Bennett, D. K.: 945
Benoit, E. P.: 588
Bensberg, G. J.: 462, 513, 1292
Benson, R. R.: 708
Benton, A. L.: 102, 202, 1333
Benton, J. G.: 810
Berger, A.: 127, 176, 242–3
Berger, M.: 946
Berger, S. E.: 1384
Bergman, R. L.: 1384
Berk, R. L.: 512
Berko, M. J.: 631–2
Berman, A. B.: 210
Berman, I. R.: 437
Bernreuter, R. G.: 103
Bernstein, L.: 744
Berry, H. K.: 1399
Bersoff, D. N.: 1370
Beverly, L.: 513
Biddle, A. E.: 1141
Bieri, J.: 1344
Bijou, S. W.: 298, 400, 1249, 1273
Birch, H. G.: 842, 914, 1337, 1382
Birch, J. W.: 479, 565
Birch, L. B.: *exc,* 6:536
Birkemeyer, F.: 762
Birns, B.: 1380
Black, D. B.: 805
Black, I. S.: 115
Blackburn, I.: 967
Blanchard, M. B.: 54
Blanchard, P.: 16
Blatt, B.: 712
Blauvelt, J.: 202
Bliesmer, E. P.: 566, 585
Block, Z.: 654
Blum, J. E.: 947
Boeker, H.: 1083
Bolton, I. A.: 371
Bond, E. A.: 161
Bond, J.: 1224
Bond, G. L.: 463
Bonfield, J. R.: 876
Borosage, V.: 877
Boruszak, R. J.: 548
Bovée, A. G.: 413
Boyd, H. F.: 588
Bozarth, D. C.: 1349
Bradley, C.: 1257
Bradway, K.: 1388
Bradway, K. P.: 172, 282–3, 299, 317–8, 401, 638, 662, 689, 1215
Brady, J. J.: 880, 916
Braen, B. B.: 1314
Bray, P. F.: 934
Brengelmann, J. C.: 663
Bridger, W.: 1380
Brigger, G.: 992
Brill, M.: 83
British Psychological Society, English Division of Professional Psychologists (Educational and Clinical): 709
Brittain, M.: 878
Brody, L.: 1250
Brody, M. B.: 128, 203, 244–5
Broman, S. H.: 985
Brooks, B. R.: 246
Brooks, F. D.: 39, 358, 1117, 1181
Broom, E.: 1165
Broom, M. E.: 1134
Broughton, E.: 920
Brown, A. W.: 143, 1262
Brown, D. L.: 1371
Brown, F.: 178, 247–8, 284, 300, 405, 1274
Brown, G. L.: 464, 1048
Brown, J.: 1356
Brown, R. R.: 147
Bruce, M.: 177
Bruch, C.: 1350
Bruch, C. B.: 1372
Bruininks, R. H.: 911, 948–9
Bryan, A. I.: 1208
Buck, C.: 1373
Buckingham, B. R.: 1015
Budoff, M.: 710, 834, 1374
Bugden, C. W.: 504
Buhler, C.: 105
Bunuan, J. S.: 912
Burchard, K. A.: 525
Burgemeister, B. B.: 1283, 1285
Burks, B. S.: 1142
Burnett, A.: 778
Burns, H. M.: 354
Burnside, L. H.: 71
Burson, G. E.: 806
Burt, C.: 9, 116, 249; *exc,* 1:B497, 2:1420, 3:293
Burton, A.: 444
Butler, A. J.: 511, 528
Butterfield, C. C.: 906
Butterfield, E. C.: 950
Byrd, E.: 647
Caldwell, H. H.: 1006, 1049
Caldwell, M. B.: 951
Calhoun, F. J.: 567
Callaway, B.: 952
Canady, H. G.: 1223
Candee, B.: 148
Cannell, C. F.: 214
Capobianco, R. J.: 763
Carleton, F. O.: 580
Carlson, J. J.: 337
Carlton, T.: 129, 250–2
Carmichael, L.: 1095
Carolan, P.: 804
Carpenter, C. C.: 1007
Carr, E. J.: 103
Carroll, H. A.: 1173
Carson, M. K.: 445
Cartee, J. K.: 546
Carter, C. O.: 648
Carter, J. P.: 1406
Casey, M. L.: 1118, 1143
Cassingham, C. C.: 135
Castell, J. H. F.: 709, 779
Cattell, P.: 48, 60, 90, 1174–5, 1178, 1182, 1195
Cattell, R. B.: 91; *exc,* 1:B497
Challman, A.: 178
Charles, C. M.: 61
Chase, H. W.: 1007
Chassell, J. R.: 876
Chassell, L. M.: 1030
Chassell, M. A.: 204, 412
Chesire, L. E.: 47
Childs, H. G.: 1, 4
Chipman, C. E.: 141, 1166
Chodorkoff, J.: 1323
Chun, R. W. M.: 891
Church, J. C.: 780
Churchill, W. D.: 807
Cieutat, V. J.: 781, 835
Cisler, L. E.: 1262
Clark, B.: 920
Clark, A.: 1277
Clark, E. T.: 947
Clark, J. H.: 441
Clark, S.: 259
Clark, W. M.: 1347
Clark, W. W.: 1016, 1050
Clarke, A. D. B.: 614, 709

Clarke, D. P.: 205
Clarke, F. R.: 465
Cleland, D. L.: 690
Close, R. L.: 301
Cobb, M. V.: 1051–2
Cochran, M. L.: 913, 953
Coffey, H. S.: 387
Cohen, B. D.: 514
Cole, L. W.: 1001
Cole, R.: 428
Collart, D. S.: 1354
Coller, A. R.: 964
Collier, M. J.: 514
Collins, A. L.: 168, 206, 730
Collins, J.: 1284
Collmann, R. D.: 615
Colloton, C.: 11
Colman, P. G.: 808
Colvin, S. S.: 1068
Conrad, H. S.: 54, 1258
Cook, J. J.: 1407
Cook, J. M.: 480
Cordiner, M. E.: 782
Cornell, E. L.: 20; *exc,* 3:293
Cornwell, A. C.: 914
Corter, H. M.: 1395
Costa, J.: 1327
Costello, J.: 954
Costello, T. W.: 388
Cowdery, K. M.: 1053
Cox, J. F.: 1176
Cox, T.: 1345
Crandall, V. C.: 955
Cravens, R. B.: 638
Crawford, J. M.: 476
Crawford, V. B.: 915, 1403
Crissey, O. L.: 1233
Croke, K.: 568
Cronbach, L. J.: 446
Cruickshank, W. M.: 420, 466
Cuneo, I.: 4–5
Cunningham, B. V.: 1209
Cupp, M. E.: 789
Cureton, E. E.: 549
Curr, W.: 586
Curtin, M. E.: 667
Cushman, C. L.: 138
Cutts, R. A.: 349
Dahlstrom, W. G.: 874
Darbes, A.: 664, 882
Darcy, N. T.: 408
Darsie, M. L.: 1119
Dashiell, J. F.: 1096
Dave, P. N.: 956
Davenport, C. B.: 1177
Davidson, H. P.: 1097, 1147
Davidson, J. F.: 550, 607
Davidson, M.: 92
Davis, A. J.: 150
Davis, D. R.: 608
Davis, E. A.: 207
Davis, F. B.: 117, 179, 208
Davis, R.: 238, 386
Davis, R. M.: 1247
Dawson, C. D.: 1054
Dawson, S.: 1186
Day, R.: 1288
Deahl, K.: 375
Dean, D. A.: 467
Dean, S.: 523
Dearborn, W. F.: 140, 1178
DeBurger, R. A.: 667
DeBusk, B. W.: 1069
DeCamp, J. E.: 1031
DeLapa, G.: 836
Demarest, R.: 414
Denny, C.: 667
Denny, E. C.: 515
Denum, D. C.: 754
Denworth, K. M.: 1144
Derner, G. F.: 477
Derrick, S. M.: 1017
Despert, J. L.: 338
Deutschberger, J.: 974
DeVoss, J. C.: 1098
Dibble, M. F.: 783
Dickie, J.: 954
Dickson, V.: 135
Dickson, V. E.: 1018
Dietsch, M. K.: 1145
Dill, J.: 964
Diller, L.: 481
Dillon, L. E.: 363
DiLorenzo, L. T.: 879–81, 916

Stanford-Binet Intelligence Scale

Dingman, H. F.: 937
Dobson, J. C.: 837
Dokecki, P. R.: 917
Dole, A. A.: 724
Doll, E. A.: 346, 995
Domino, G.: 785
Dougherty, M. L.: 359
Downey, J. E.: 996–7, 1002
Dragositz, A.: 308
Drash, P. W.: 1340, 1343
Dreger, R. M.: 575
Drillien, C. M.: 665
Duffett, J. W.: 918
Dulsky, S. G.: 1269
Duncan, J. O.: 532
Dunn, H. G.: 1357
Dunn, J. A.: 838
Dunn, O. J.: 854, 1339
Dunphy, D.: 1320
Dunsdon, M. I.: 516, 533–4, 569–70, 604, 648, 666
Durea, M. A.: 432
Durkin, D.: 957
Durling, D.: 52, 1158–9
Durrell, D. D.: 139, 1196
Dyke, R. G.: 752
Dysinger, D. W.: 768
Earhart, R. H.: 764
Earl, C. J. C.: 393; *exc*, 2:B1093
Eaton, H. T.: 1070
Eattell, E. A.: 495
Eaves, L. C.: 1357
Ebert, E.: 729
Ebert, E. H.: 209
Eckman, R.: 1398
Edmondson, M. B.: 1019
Edwards, A. J.: 711
Eells, W. C.: 1197, 1212
Eisenman, R.: 839, 882
Ellington, W.: 271
Elliott, R.: 1376
Ellis, N. R.: 1306
Elonen, A. S.: 429, 447
Elwood, M. I.: 76, 118, 376, 517
Emch, M. A.: 364
Emerson, P.: 920
Engelmann, S.: 958
English, H. B.: 389
English, R. A.: 919
Erickson, M. T.: 883
Eshleman, E. R.: 587
Espeseth, V. K.: 965
Estabrooks, G. H.: 1146
Estes, B. W.: 667, 784
Estes, R. E.: 959
Evans, M. L.: 551
Fagan, J.: 920
Falek, A.: 698, 715
Falk, R.: 1277
Farson, M. R.: 1198
Farthing, M.: 518
Faterson, H. F.: 752
Fay, L. C.: 463
Feifel, H.: 448, 468, 519
Feinberg, H.: 53, 77, 84
Feldman, D. H.: 948
Fendrick, P.: 1224
Ferguson, C.: 241
Ferinden, W. E.: 960
Fernald, M. R.: 180, 1099
Ferneau, L.: 369
Fernow, D. L.: 170
Fiedler, M.: 985
Fields, D. L.: 1377
Finley, C. J.: 725
Finley, K. H.: 1354
Firnhaber, E. P.: 636
Fisher, G. M.: 668, 686
Fisher, M. A.: 961
Fishman, S.: 1279
Fisichelli, V. R.: 1327
Fitt, A. B.: 535
Flanagan, J. C.: *exc*, 1:B497
Flanders, J. K.: 135
Flanigan, P. J.: 1408
Fleming, K.: 691
Fleming, V. V. D.: 253, 302
Flemming, C. W.: 1160
Flick, G. L.: 835
Flynn, E.: 319
Font, M. M.: 181

Ford, C. A.: 1167
Forehand, R.: 1378
Forlano, G.: 362
Francey, R. E.: 649
Francis, G. M.: 1324
Frandsen, A.: 1259
Frandsen, A. N.: 469, 482
Franken, R. E.: 861
Fraser, D.: 1351
Fraser, E. D.: *rev*, 6:536
Fraser, W. D.: 1352
Frasier, G. W.: 1020
Frazeur, H. A.: 321
Frede, M. C.: 917
Freedheim, D. K.: 1316
Freeman, F. N.: 1055, 1147; *exc*, 1:B497
Freeman, F. S.: 353, 470, 692, 1148
Freides, D.: *rev*, 7:425
French, L. A.: 1298
Fretwell, L. N.: 789
Friedline, C. L.: 210
Froehlich, G. J.: 413
Fromm, E.: 605
Fukuda, T.: 1100
Futterer, J. W.: 962
Gabet, Y.: 937
Gabler, E. R.: *exc*, 3:294
Galbreath, N.: 4
Gallagher, J. J.: 588, 637
Gannon, D. R.: 884
Garfunkel, F.: 712
Garrett, H. E.: 285; *exc*, 3:293
Garrett, J. F.: 398
Garrison, M.: 1312
Garrison, S. C.: 14, 622, 1032, 1101
Gaskins, J. R.: 669
Gates, A. I.: 1033, 1056, 1071, 1082–3, 1102, 1120
Gautney, D. B.: 917
Gaw, E. A.: 430
Gay, J. R.: 626
Gayton, W. F.: 963, 1379
Gehman, I. H.: 589
Gerlach, M.: 169
Gerstein, S.: 211
Gerver, J. M.: 1288
Gewirtz, J. L.: 431
Ghosh, S. P.: 1293
Ghozeil, S.: 1410
Gibson, D.: 1377
Gibson, F. J.: 536
Gifford, E.: 399
Gifford, E. V.: 293
Gill, M. R.: 581
Gillette, A. L.: 182, 212
Gioioso, J. V.: 921
Girdany, B. R.: 736
Gittelman, M.: 1337
Glanville, A. D.: 1234
Glenn, I.: 1057
Glenn, R. T.: 483
Glenn, W. D.: 1096
Glick, H. N.: 319
Godfrey, L. L.: 552
Goldberg, B.: 1169
Golden, M.: 1380
Goldenberg, S.: 733
Goldfarb, W.: 303
Goldman, R.: 111
Goldschmid, M. L.: 785
Goldstein, L. S.: 964
Goodenough, D. R.: 752
Goodenough, F. L.: 254, 1103; *exc*, 1:B497
Goodey, D. R.: 606
Gordon, D. A.: 1378
Gordon, K.: 15, 1008, 1072
Gordon, L. V.: 432
Gothberg, L. C.: 449
Goulet, L. R.: 755
Gourlay, N.: 586
Grabow, D. B.: 891
Gragg, D. B.: 187
Graham, D. D.: 670
Graham, V. T.: 1121, 1260
Granick, S.: 471, 1300
Gravem, H.: 968
Graves, K. B.: 1084
Gray, J.: 241
Gray, P. L.: 1073–4, 1085, 1122

Green, E.: 1257
Green, H. J.: 49
Greenberg, N. E.: 1343
Greene, E. B.: 36
Greene, K. B.: 1149
Greeson, L. E.: 1384
Gregg, R.: 1373
Grice, J. E.: 1400
Griffiths, R.: 96, 110, 625
Gross, F. L.: 983
Gross, M.: 1353
Gross, M. B.: 1358
Growdon, C. H.: 183, 213
Guiler, W. S.: 1058
Gurevitz, S.: 1296
Guthrie, G. M.: 506
Haag, C. H.: 745
Haan, N.: 765, 1325
Hafemeister, N.: 458
Hallowell, D. K.: 1150
Halpern, F.: 255
Hamilton, M. E.: 450
Hamlin, R.: 382
Hammill, D. D.: 840
Hanesian, H.: 859
Hanson, H. B.: 437
Hardy, J. B.: 1413
Hardy, M. C.: 1152
Harlow, J. E.: 607
Harman, H. H.: 1282
Harper, M.: 1373
Harriman, P. L.: 119, 1199
Harris, A. J.: 93, 106
Harris, D. B.: *exc*, 6:B396
Harrison, R. H.: 1374
Hart, H.: 1086
Harter, D. I.: 1104, 1143
Harter, S.: 1338
Hartman, B.: 693
Hartman, L. D.: 605
Hartson, L. D.: 409
Hatt, E.: 47
Haury, G.: 154
Havighurst, R. J.: 406, 411
Haw, A. B.: 1221
Haworth, M. R.: 702; *rev*, 5:413
Hay, E. N.: *exc*, 1:B497
Hayes, S. P.: 40, 286
Hayweiser, L.: 930
Heaton-Ward, W. A.: 671
Heckman, S. B.: 1087
Heilman, J. D.: 1200
Helme, W. H.: 1296
Henderson, N.: 1347
Henmon, V. A. C.: 354
Henry, J. A.: 184
Herrick, C. J.: 229
Herring, J. P.: 24–5, 1088
Hersh, J. B.: 1381
Hertzberg, O. E.: 1168
Hertzig, M. E.: 1382
Heston, J. C.: 214
Hewes, A.: 1089
Hicks, V. C.: 988
Higgins, C.: 639, 713
Higginson, J. B.: 482
Highfield, M. E.: 410
Hilden, A. H.: 78, 107, 451
Hildreth, G.: 30, 120–1, 215, 287, 1151, 1160
Hildreth, G. H.: 1105
Hill, H.: 1225
Hilty, D. P.: 162
Himelstein, P.: 809, 885
Hindley, C. B.: 694
Hinman, M. E. H.: 288
Hinton, R. T.: 1226, 1251
Hirsch, M. J.: 1315
Hirschenfang, S.: 672, 810
Hirshoren, A.: 922
Hirt, Z. I.: 320
Hiskey, M. S.: 616
Hittinger, J.: 241
Ho, D.: 714
Hoakley, Z. P.: 130, 146, 321
Hoch, P.: 1290
Hodgins, A. S.: 1359
Hoefer, C.: 1152
Hoffman, C. B.: 742
Hofmeister, A.: 965
Hogan, H. P.: 216
Hohman, L. B.: 1316
Holland, G. A.: 537

Holland, P. E.: 304
Hollingworth, L. S.: 372, 1123–4, 1135, 1173, 1228
Holowinsky, I.: 695
Holt, M.: 1089
Holzinger, K. J.: 1147
Honzik, M. P.: 433, 1235, 1261, 1354
Horne, B. M.: 741
Horton, K. B.: 1406
Houlihan, R. A. M.: 415
House, B. J.: 707
House, F. R.: 1406
Houser, J. D.: 989
Howard, J. L.: 841
Howard, J. O.: 923
Howard, L.: 135
Howell, A. A.: 394
Hsiao, H. H.: 1183
Hubbard, O. S.: 135
Huizinga, R. J.: 1383
Hultsch, C. L.: 315
Humphreys, L. G.: 966
Hunt, B. M.: 1317
Hunt, D.: 673
Hunt, W. A.: 434
Hunter, M.: 229
Huntley, R. M. C.: 648
Hurst, J. G.: 696
Hutt, M. L.: 347
Hutton, J. B.: 766
Ingram, T. T. S.: 967
Ireton, H.: 968
Irwin, O. C.: 840
Israel, H.: 114
Iversen, I.: 860
Jacobson, L. I.: 1384
Jacobson, S.: 960
James, A.: 256
James, E. B.: 160
Janke, L. L.: 406, 411
Jaramillo, S.: 810
Jarman, P.: 859
Jarvik, L. F.: 697–8, 715, 947
Jaspen, N.: 305
Jastak, J.: 452, 1236, 1252
Jeffress, S.: 187
Jenkins, C. D.: 786, 1321
Jenkins, M. D.: 1227, 1272
Jenkins, R. L.: 185, 1172, 1262
Jensen, J. A.: 1369
Jenson, G.: 767
Jewett, S. P.: 16
Jimenez, C.: 555
Joesting, J.: 1385
Joesting, R.: 1385
John, E.: 249
Johnson, A. P.: 170
Johnson, B.: 1059
Johnson, B. J.: 1106
Johnson, C. A.: 1386
Johnson, D. L.: 1386
Johnson, D. R.: 1298
Johnson, E. Z.: 520, 538
Johnson, G. O.: 591
Jones, A. M.: 1107, 1153
Jones, H. E.: 50, 54, 1232, 1235, 1258
Jones, H. G.: 590
Jones, L. V.: 435, 453, 484, 553
Jones, V. A.: 1108
Jongeward, P. A.: 924–5
Jordan, A. M.: 1075
Jordan, J. S.: 55
Jordan, T. E.: 1387
Justman, J.: 485, 544
Kaback, G. R.: 787
KaDell, M. B.: 650
Kallmann, F. J.: 698
Kamat, V. V.: 171
Kamii, C. K.: 926
Kandel, A.: 811
Kangas, J.: 908, 1388
Kangas, J. A.: 969
Kaplan, E.: 1201
Kaplan, O.: 289
Karadenes, M.: 1389
Kardos, M. S.: 554
Karelitz, R.: 1327
Karelitz, S.: 1327
Karnes, M. B.: 1359
Karp, S. A.: 752
Kaspar, J. C.: 798

Stanford-Binet Intelligence Scale

Kato, J. G.: 805
Katz, E.: 217, 571, 592, 617, 633–5, 1263
Kaunitz, R. M.: 377
Kavruck, S.: 257
Kawin, E.: *exc*, 1:B497
Keach, C. C.: 812
Kebbon, L.: 788
Keen, A. M.: 365, 1179
Keim, R. P.: 927
Keir, G.: 1278
Kendig, I.: 131
Kennedy, V.: 422
Kennedy, W.: 715a
Kennedy, W. A.: 674, 716, 776, 928
Kennedy-Fraser, D.: 322, 454
Kenny, J. T.: 663
Kent, G. H.: 21, 158; *exc*, 2:1420
Kent, N.: 608
Kepner, R. D.: 407
Keston, M. J.: 555
Kicklighter, R. M.: 813
Kidd, A. H.: 651, 699
Kidder, J. W.: 919
Kilburn, K. L.: 814
Killian, C. D.: 389
Kilman, B. A.: 668
Kimberlin, C. C.: 943
Kimbrell, D. L.: 815
Kinder, E. F.: 381–2
King, J. D.: 1398
Kirkpatrick, F. H.: *exc*, 3:293
Kittredge, W. B.: 1079
Klapper, Z. S.: 842
Klatskin, E. H.: 1328
Klebanoff, S. G.: 434
Klonoff, H.: 1357
Klugman, S. F.: 306
Knight, D.: 951
Knight, M. W.: 72
Knollin, H. E.: 4, 990, 1036
Knox, S.: 763
Kobler, F. J.: 560
Kodman, F.: 970
Kogan, K. L.: 456
Koh, T. H.: 843
Kohs, S. C.: 998
Kolb, L.: 1109
Koller, J. R.: 1390
Kolstoe, O. P.: 731
Konstans, D. J.: 652
Koppitz, E. M.: 844
Korner, A. F.: 429
Kovalinsky, T.: 960
Kreezer, G. L.: 172, 1289
Kroske, W. H.: 789
Krugman, J. I.: 485
Krugman, M.: 122, 485; *exc*, 2:1420
Kuhlmann, F.: 258
Kundu, R.: 845
Kureth, G.: 521, 539
Kurko, V. K.: 487
Kushner, R.: 308
Kutash, S. B.: 323
Kvaraceus, W. C.: 186, 218, 1264
Kyte, G. C.: 1237
Lacy, L. D.: 1125
Lacy, W. I.: 1003
Lair, C. V.: 940
Lambert, R. A.: 728
Lamp, R. E.: 886
Lamson, E. E.: 1243
Lane, H. A.: 1216
Lantz, B.: 593
Lantz, C. M. B.: 395
Larsen, M. J.: 971
Larsen, M. R. J.: 887
LaSalle, J.: 1071, 1082
Lawrence, E. M.: 1184
Laycock, S. R.: 259, 324
Layman, J. W.: 260, 383, 396, 1265
Leahy, A. M.: 1217
Leberfeld, D. T.: 734
Lebovitz, L.: 828
Lee, M. V.: 1185
Lehmann, I. J.: 643, 738
Lehmann, M. M.: 556
Leitch, M.: 440
Leithwood, K. A.: 1391

Lennox, W. G.: 730
Lessing, E. E.: 675
Levi, J.: 296
Levin, J.: 475, 491
Levine, D.: 768
Levinson, B. M.: 594, 609, 618, 644, 653–4, 743, 1307–8
Levinson, E. J.: 756, 1392
Levy, P.: 888
Lewis, D. G.: 1309
Lewis, J. F.: 929
Lewis, R.: 1393
Lewis, V.: 1334, 1340
Lidz, T.: 626
Lincoln, E. A.: 32, 62, 79, 85, 1060–1, 1154, 1218
Linde, L. M.: 854, 1339
Lindholm, B. W.: 769, 790
Lindner, R.: 674
Line, W.: 1201
Lively, M. L.: 329–30
Livingston, J. S.: 610, 619
Lobl, M.: 1394
Lodge, T.: 108
Long, H. H.: 140, 1219
Lore, J.: 870
Lorge, I.: 468, 1228
Lorr, M.: 219, 261
Louden, M. V.: 63–4
Lourie, D. K.: 384
Louttit, C. M.: 86
Lowden, G. L.: 20
Lowell, F. E.: 220
Lucker, W. G.: 949
Luckey, B.: 1156
Ludlow, H. E.: 494
Luh, C. W.: 366
Lumsden, J.: 595
Luong, C. K. M.: 889
Luszki, W. A.: 816
Lyman, B.: 4
Lytton, H.: 676
McAnulty, E. A.: 1155
McArthur, C. R.: 890
McBride, K.: 1158–9
McBride, K. E.: 1231
McCandless, B. R.: 345, 1273; *rev*, 4:358
McCloskey, E. P.: 223
McClure, W. E.: 1169, 1202
McConnell, F.: 1406
McCulloch, T. L.: 311, 572
McCullough, B. R.: 436, 469
McElwee, E. W.: 1187, 1220
McFadden, J. H.: 51, 367
Macfarlane, J. W.: 433
McFie, J.: 629, 677
McGee, E.: 561
McGrath, R. F.: 390
McHugh, G.: 290
McIntosh, R.: 736
McKay, B. E.: 402
MacKay, D. N.: 1376
McKerracher, D. W.: 817
McKinney, J. D.: 1395
McKinstry, E.: 241
Macmeeken, A. M.: 123
MacMurray, D.: 94
McNemar, Q.: 164, 264, 540, 627–8
Macomber, L.: 319
McRae, H.: 1270
MacRae, J. M.: 573
Madden, R.: 56
Madow, A. A.: 843
Madsen, I. N.: 26, 73
Magaret, A.: 351, 419, 472
Mahan, H. C.: 87
Maity, H.: 31
Maizlish, I. L.: 221, 262
Malamud, W.: 163
Mann, A.: 486
Mann, C. W.: 124
Mann, H. P.: 124
Manolakes, G.: 522, 562
Manuel, H. T.: 187, 379
Marine, E. L.: 41, 361
Marks, E. S.: 421
Marquart, D. I.: 574
Marschak, M.: 605
Marsden, R. E.: 1073–4, 1085, 1122, 1170
Marshall, A.: 846
Marshall, H.: 263, 628

Martin, A. H.: *exc*, 1:B497
Martin, F.: 1281
Martinson, B.: 222
Marx, B.: 360
Masling, J. M.: 1314
Mason, A. W.: 847, 967
Massari, D.: 930
Mateer, F.: 173, 621, 1004
Matheny, A. P.: 818
Mathews, J.: 1034
Matthew, J.: 1156
Matthews, C. G.: 891
Matyas, R. P.: 557, 589
Maurer, K. M.: 416
Maxfield, F. N.: 152, 1005; *rev*, 1:1062; *exc*, 1:B497, 3:293–4
Maxwell, A. E.: 640
Maxwell, J.: 655, 931; *exc*, 6:536
Maxwell, M. T.: 1396
May, W. T.: 611, 828, 862
Mayer, B. A.: 80–1, 153
Mayman, M.: 325, 339
Meeker, M.: 791
Meeker, M. M.: 718
Meeker, M. N.: 932
Meier, J. H.: 792
Mein, R.: 700
Meissler, G. R.: 972
Meister, R. K.: 191, 219, 230, 261, 422, 487
Mellits, E. D.: 1394, 1413
Mellone, M. A.: 526
Melton, K.: 814
Mensh, I. N.: 434
Meranski, S.: 1089
Mercer, M.: 870
Merrill, M. A.: 98–9, 109, 545, 657a, 1090, 1126
Merriman, C.: 1091
Meskin, J.: 1374
Meyer, M.: 930
Meyers, C. E.: 803
Michael, W. B.: 826
Michaels, J. J.: 155–6
Miezitis, S. A.: 892
Milgram, N. A.: 1397
Millard, M. S.: 1222
Miller, B.: 848
Miller, E.: 630
Miller, H.: 1240
Miller, I.: 660
Miller, J. O.: 973
Miller, L. R.: 291
Miller, V. C.: 558
Millham, J.: 1384
Minogue, B. M.: 1127, 1177
Miscevich, M. B.: 849
Mishra, S. P.: 1410
Mitchell, B. C.: 1147
Mitchell, D.: 1062, 1092
Mitchell, M. B.: 188, 224–5, 265, 292
Mitchell, R. J.: 793
Mittler, P.: 709
Mittler, P. J.: 779
Mohan, P. J.: 861
Monahan, J. E.: 1124, 1135
Money, J.: 1302, 1329, 1334, 1340, 1343
Moon, H.: 674
Mooney, R. F.: 1368–9
Moore, T.: 850
Morán, R. E.: 1319
Morgenthau, D. R.: 17
Moriarty, A.: 746
Morris, H. L.: 959
Moss, A.: 1380
Motter, M. E.: 241
Mowrer, W. M. C.: 65
Mueller, M. W.: 794–5, 893, 933
Muench, G. A.: 1275
Muhr, J. P.: 521
Mukherjee, A.: 1402
Mullen, F. A.: 266
Mumbauer, C. C.: 973
Mundy, L.: 640, 1310
Munson, G.: 174, 226
Murphy, M.: 1157, 1203
Mussen, P.: 523
Muzekari, L. H.: 851
Myers, C. R.: 293, 399

Nagler, E.: 881
Nakamura, H.: 747, 796
Nale, S.: 488
Nale, S. L.: 645
Narosny, E. H.: 1238
Nash, P. N.: 717
Neale, M. D.: *exc*, 6:536
Needham, N. R.: 307
Needham, W. E.: 934
Neely, J. H.: 591
Nelson, K. B.: 974
Nelson, T. M.: 701
Nelson, V.: 1301
Nelson, V. L.: 547, 564, 579, 1311
Nelson, W.: 674
Nemzek, C. L.: 66–7
Nevill, E. M.: *exc*, 1:B497
Nevins, F. A.: 267
New York Public Schools, Division of Tests and Measurements: 227
Newland, T. E.: 718
Newlyn, D.: 615
Nicholson, C. L.: 975
Noble, H.: 1022
Noller, P. A.: 493
Norman, R. D.: 543
Norman, R. M.: 110, 625
Norton, J. K.: 135, 1021
Nottingham, R. D.: 1239
Nunnally, J. C.: 770
Nurss, J. R.: 976
Nuttall, J. C.: 1357
Oakland, T. D.: 1398
Obelkevich, H.: 1188
Oblinger, B.: 350
O'Connor, G.: 937
O'Connor, N.: 476, 596
Odell, C. W.: 10, 1035
Oden, M. H.: 81, 628
Odoroff, M. E.: 258
Oexle, H. M.: 228
O'Grady, D. J.: 1399
O'Kelly, E.: 1360
Olivier, K.: 852
Oppel, W.: 727
Ordahl, G.: 4, 1076
Ordahl, L. E.: 4
Ordahl, V. E.: 417
Orgel, A. R.: 575
Otis, A. S.: 135, 1036
Outhit, M. C.: 1204
Page, H. A.: 982
Page, J. D.: 189, 1267
Pal, S.: 29
Palmer, A. B.: 771
Palmer, E. M.: 157, 163
Palmer, F. H.: 977, 980
Papania, N.: 559
Papurt, M. J.: 380
Parker, H. T.: 74
Parkyn, G. W.: 326
Parsley, K. M.: 678
Pasewark, R. A.: 1400
Pastovic, J. J.: 506
Paton, R.: 1335
Patterson, H. J.: 894
Payne, W. E.: 679
Pazeian, B.: 1297
Pearson, J. S.: 1303
Peatman, J. G.: 88
Peatman, L. B.: 88
Pedrini, D. T.: 864–6, 913, 978
Pedrini, L. N.: 978
Pegram, E. L.: 316
Penrose, L. S.: 1253, 1277
Perce, F. C.: 391
Perkins, R. E.: 57
Perry, H. W.: 611
Pessin, V.: 1320
Phillips, A.: 58
Phillips, C. J.: 772, 895
Phillips, D. C.: 1401
Phillips, E. L.: 437
Pickles, D. G.: 853
Pickup, K. T.: 719
Pierce, H. O.: 338, 438
Piercy, M. F.: 629
Pignatelli, M. L.: 268, 294
Pilliner, A. E. G.: 655
Piness, G.: 1240
Pinneau, S. R.: 657a, 680

Stanford-Binet Intelligence Scale

Pintner, R.: 269, 308, 1022
Piotrowski, Z. A.: 95
Plant, W. T.: 841, 896
Platt, J. J.: 882
Pollitt, E.: 1329
Porrata, E.: 870
Porteus, S. D.: 229, 352, 407, 1077
Portwood, P. F.: 620
Post, M.: 646
Poull, L. E.: 1037
Powell, J. A.: 507
Powell, M.: 678
Prager, D.: 190
Prasad, R.: 1402
Pratt, C. C.: 999
Prentice, N. M.: 1344
Price, A. C.: 500, 607
Pringle, M. L. K.: 719, 832, 1345
Proctor, W. M.: 1023-4, 1038
Prosser, N. S.: 1403
Purseglove, E. M.: 710
Putnam, T. J.: 1283, 1285
Pyle, W. H.: 987
Qualtere, T. J.: 466
Quay, L. C.: 1404
Qureshi, M. Y.: 681, 1330, 1341
Rabin, A. I.: 309
Radin, N.: 1405
Radin, N. L.: 926
Raleigh, W. H.: 524
Ramsey, P. H.: 979
Rand, G.: 1110
Randall, F. B.: 33
Rapaport, I.: 489
Rappaport, M. E.: 1210
Rappaport, S. R.: 541
Rardin, M. W.: 1400
Rasof, B.: 854, 1339
Rautman, A. L.: 270
Ray, J. B.: 497
Raybold, E.: 1111
Rebhun, A. M.: 1304
Redbird, H. M.: 757
Reed, H. R.: 1291
Rees, A. H.: 980
Reichard, J. D.: 1205
Reinhart, R. A.: 1331
Rellas, A. J.: 935
Reswick, J.: 572
Reymert, M. L.: 191, 230
Reynolds, M. C.: 1294
Rheingold, H. L.: 391
Rhinehart, J. B.: 68
Richards, B. F.: 748
Richards, B. W.: 576
Richards, T. W.: 271, 490, 1189-90
Richardson, C. A.: 18
Richardson, E. J.: 560
Richardson, M. W.: 192, 231
Richmond, W. V.: 131
Rider, R. V.: 727
Riggs, M. M.: 525
Riley, G.: 142
Risch, F.: 296
Roach, C. B.: 82
Robeck, M. C.: 773
Roberts, A. D.: 327-8
Roberts, C. S.: 1244
Roberts, D. M.: 819
Roberts, H. E.: 682
Roberts, J. A. F.: 96, 110, 455, 526, 534, 570, 604, 625, 666
Robinson, E. L.: 193
Robinson, M. S.: 1101
Robinson, N.: 839
Robinson, N. M.: 662
Robinson, S. J.: 1354
Robitaille, H. J.: 232
Roe, A.: 310, 1231
Roff, M.: 1268
Rogers, A. L.: 1158-9
Rohan, J. C.: 233
Rohrs, F. W.: 702
Roller, R. D.: 1138
Root, W. T.: 623, 1039, 1063, 1078
Rosanoff, A. J.: 624
Rosenberg, L. A.: 820
Rosenberg, M.: 523
Rosenfeld, G. B.: 630

Rosenfeld, L.: 1327
Rosenow, C.: 1025
Rosenzweig, S.: 456
Rothbart, H. B.: 1221
Rothney, J. W. M.: 97; rev, 1:1062
Rotman, C. B.: 758
Rottersman, L.: 473
Rowland, M. S.: 936
Ruch, F. L.: 1171
Ruch, G. M.: 1026
Rudolf, G. de M.: 439
Rugg, H.: 11
Rugg, L. S.: 1112
Rushton, C. S.: 720
Russell, C. A.: 855
Saam, T.: 1009
Sacks, E. L.: 527
Sadnavitch, J. M.: 616
Saffir, M. A.: 174, 226
Salopek, T. F.: 1411
Saltzman, S.: 194
Sampson, O. C.: 1318
Sánchez, G. I.: 75
Sandercock, M. G.: 528
Sanderson, R. E.: 814
Sandler, A. M.: 749
Sandler, J.: 749
Sandstead, H. H.: 1406
Sarason, E. K.: 340, 348, 418
Sarason, S. B.: 340, 348, 397, 418
Sartain, A. Q.: 341
Satter, G.: 561, 577
Sattler, J. M.: 797, 821-2, 856
Scarr, E. H.: 542
Schachter, F. F.: 641
Schafer, S.: 440
Schell, M.: 1206
Schena, R. A.: 721
Scherer, I. W.: 683
Schilling, M. E.: 155-6
Schnack, G. F.: 329-30
Schonell, F. E.: 1287
Schoonover, S. M.: 1305
Schott, E. L.: 45
Schramm, T. A.: 493
Schreffler, R. H.: 897
Schriefer, L.: 1059
Schulman, J. L.: 798
Schwartz, A. A.: 474
Schwarz, R. H.: 1407-8
Schwegler, R. A.: 1027
Scott, G. R.: 501
Scott, J.: 817
Scottish Council for Research in Education, Mental Survey Committee: 372
Scottish Council for Research in Education, Terman Revision Committee: 125
Scripture, M. K.: 1079
Seashore, H. G.: 457
Sedal, V. S.: 597
Seelye, B. J.: 857
Seidl, J. C.: 385
Sekyra, F.: 898
Sella, A. P.: 1355
Sen, R.: 1293
Serota, K. E.: 1136
Shakow, D.: 89, 93, 106, 111, 310, 329-30, 1222
Shane, J. F.: 799
Sharp, H. C.: 612
Shatus, E. L.: 1361
Shechtman, A. M.: 750
Sheldon, W. D.: 522, 562
Sheldon, W. H.: 1093
Sheverbush, R. L.: 858, 899
Shine, A.: 684
Shine, A. E.: 685
Shipe, D.: 900
Shipley, W. C.: 151
Shor, J.: 1279
Shotwell, A. M.: 311, 331, 668, 937
Siderits, M. A. T.: 823
Sievers, D. J.: 543
Sigel, I.: 859
Silberberg, M.: 860
Silberberg, N.: 860
Silverstein, A. B.: 686, 722, 774, 800, 824-5, 861, 938-9, 981, 1332, 1409; exc, 6:B396

Simmers, C. P.: 1362
Simmons, K.: 729
Simmons, P. W.: 1207
Sitkei, E. G.: 826
Sivers, C. H.: 639
Skaggs, E. B.: 7
Skalet, M.: 59
Skeels, H. M.: 78, 1229, 1245, 1286
Skene, D. M.: 159
Skodak, M.: 1286
Slaughter, D. T.: 1363
Sless, B.: 175
Sloan, W.: 349-50, 462, 1282, 1306
Slocombe, C. S.: 1137
Slutzky, J. E.: 544
Smart, R. C.: 801
Smith, C. S.: 827
Smith, F. W.: 1289
Smith, H.: 148
Smith, H. W.: 828, 862
Smith, M.: 378
Smith, M. P.: 1346
Smith, S. E.: 807
Smith, W. L.: 578
Smitter, F. W.: 1230
Snell, J.: 1089
Snider, S.: 1373
Sonneman, L. J.: 759
Sontag, L. W.: 547, 564, 579, 1301, 1311, 1313
Sontag, M.: 1355
Southern, M. L.: 896
Spache, G.: 272-3, 295, 312-3
Sparling, M. E.: 234
Spaulding, P. J.: 332, 342
Spearman, C.: exc, 1:B497
Spearman, L. H. O.: 723
Speer, G. S.: 195-6, 1266
Speevack, M.: 127, 176, 243
Spence, A. G.: 1410
Spiegel, H.: 1279
Spieth, P. E.: 760
Spoerl, D. T.: 1276
Spreen, O.: 1333
Stacey, C. L.: 475, 491, 580-1
Stackman, H.: 86
Stackman, H. A.: 64
Stalnaker, E. M.: 1138
Stanger, M.: 1160
Stanley, J. C.: 582-3; exc, 6:536
Stecher, L. I.: 13
Stein, Z.: 656
Steinbach, A. A.: 1211
Steiner, M. A.: 1191
Stenquist, J. L.: 19
Sternlicht, M.: 802
Stockwin, A. E.: 720
Stoke, S. M.: 69
Stormer, G. E.: 829
Stott, D. H.: 657, 687
Stott, L. H.: 830
Stott, M. B.: 132
Strachan, L.: 1026, 1128
Strauss, A. A.: 197, 222, 235
Street, R. F.: 274
Stromer, W. F.: 529
Strother, C. R.: 412
Stroud, M.: 820
Struhs, I.: 598
Stutsman, R.: 47
Sullivan, E. B.: 628
Sullivan, E. G.: 1240
Sullivan, E. T.: 46, 1129
Sullivan, R. A.: 901
Sundberg, N. D.: rev, 5:413
Sundean, D. A.: 1411
Sunne, D.: 1010, 1113
Susser, M.: 656
Sutherland, B. S.: 1399
Sweeny, M. E.: 47
Symonds, P. M.: 22
Tagiuri, R.: 343
Talbert, W.: 4
Tatham, C. B.: 724
Tatham, L. J.: 530, 607
Tavris, E.: 775
Taylor, G. A.: 1083, 1102
Taylor, H. C.: 736
Taylor, J. F.: 982, 1412
Teagarden, F. M.: 1064, 1254

Terman, L. M.: 1-6, 8, 98-9, 135, 545, 628, 657a, 990, 993, 1011, 1028, 1040
Teska, J. A.: 984, 1359
Theye, F.: 856
Thiesen, J. W.: 198
Thompson, C. W.: 351, 472, 638, 689
Thompson, E. M.: 37
Thompson, J. M.: 725
Thompson, M. M.: 761
Thompson, W. H.: 891
Thorndike, R. L.: 373, 1160, 1355
Throne, F. M.: 798
Thurstone, L. L.: 43, 1172
Thweatt, R. C.: 703
Thwing, E.: 968
Tiber, N.: 776
Tietze, C.: 626
Tilis, H. S.: 964
Tippett, J. S.: 622
Tizard, J.: 476
Tolley, J.: 907
Tomlinson, H.: 187, 275, 314
Toms, D. C.: 739
Toussaint, I. H.: 690, 751
Townsend, R. R.: 38
Trachtman, G. M.: 740
Trapp, C. E.: 160
Traxler, A. E.: exc, 1:B497
Triggs, F. O.: 546
Trost, H.: 4
Tuchman, S. B.: 902
Tuel, J. K.: 803
Tulchin, S. H.: 149
Turner, A. J.: 940
Turner, J.: 674
Uecker, A. E.: 1298
Updegraff, R.: 1192, 1245
Valett, R. E.: 726
Van Alstyne, D.: 1083
Vandenberg, S.: 900
Van de Riet, V.: 704, 715a, 716
Vander Zwaag, R.: 1406
Vane, J. R.: 831, 979
Varma, S. K.: 1402
Venables, P. H.: 596
Vernon, P. E.: 100-1; exc, 1:B497
Vick, G.: 241
Vignos, P. J.: 1322
Waddle, C.: 4
Waelsch, H.: 1290
Waggoner, R. W.: 1280
Wagner, W. K.: 509, 563
Wagoner, L. C.: 1161
Wakefield, H. E.: 890
Walcott, G. D.: 1029
Walker, G. W. R.: 805
Walker, K. P.: 983
Wall, W. D.: 832
Wallin, J. E. W.: 34, 44, 70, 133, 199, 315, 344, 355, 1012, 1041-3, 1065, 1080
Walters, F. C.: 27, 1139
Walton, D.: 584, 613
Warburton, F. W.: 599
Wariner, E. M.: 531
Warren, S. A.: 764
Washburn, M. F.: 1013
Washburne, C. W.: 1014
Washington, E. D.: 984
Waters, T. J.: 600
Watson, R. I.: 492
Weaver, A. S.: 863
Wechsler, D.: 114, 1130
Weeks, A. L.: 1044
Wegman, M.: 458
Weider, A.: 202, 236, 296, 493
Weil, W. B.: 660
Weinlander, M. M.: 737
Weinstein, B.: 403
Weise, P.: 658, 803
Weisenburg, T.: 1231
Weisgerber, C. A.: 521
Weisman, F.: 1045
Weisman, S. E.: 144
Weissmann, S.: 572
Weitzman, J.: 831
Welcher, D. W.: 1394, 1413
Wellman, B. L.: 316, 333, 345, 1193, 1241, 1245-6

Wells, D. G.: 864–6
Wells, F. L.: 35, 994, 1000, 1255; *rev*, 1:1062
Welsh, G. B.: 735
Wentworth, M. M.: 356–7
Werner, H.: 134, 197
Wesman, A. G.: 457
Wexberg, E.: 237
Whitacre, R. L.: 903
Whitcomb, M. A.: 334
White, D. T.: 714
White, G.: 1364
White, J. C.: 705, 715a, 716
White, L. A.: 904, 1398
White, M. L.: 276
White, R. R.: 772
Whitten, C. F.: 1323
Wiener, G.: 727
Wikoff, R. L.: 1414
Wilcock, J. C.: 833
Wile, I. S.: 238, 386, 1247
Wilk, W. S.: 706
Willerman, L.: 985
Williams, H. M.: 458, 1245
Williams, J. H.: 4, 991
Williams, J. R.: 833, 867
Williams, M.: 434
Williams, R. D. B.: 900
Wilner, C. F.: 28, 1081
Wilson, B. A.: 642
Wilson, C. A.: 47
Wilson, G. M.: 1114
Wilson, J. A. R.: 773
Wilson, M. T.: 392, 1271
Wilsoncroft, W. E.: 1336
Winn, E.: 1027
Winslow, C. N.: 982
Winter, W. N.: 502
Wise, J. H.: 905
Wiser, W. C.: 934
Wisler, M. L.: 374

Witkin, H. A.: 752
Witmer, L.: 87
Witty, P. A.: 1162, 1216
Wladkowsky, E.: 165
Wolf, R.: 593
Wolf, S. J.: 1242
Wolf, W. C.: 601
Woodall, C. S.: 145
Woods, E. L.: 1115
Woodward, W. M.: 709
Woodworth, R. S.: 1163
Wooley, H. T.: 1116
Woo-Sam, J.: 986
Worbois, G. M.: 277
Worcester, D. A.: 239
Worden, D. K.: 1322
Worthington, M. R.: 1131–2
Wrenn, C. G.: 459
Wright, C.: 278, 419
Wright, E. L.: 1365
Wright, R. E.: 126
Wrightstone, J. W.: 485, 544
Wu, T. M.: 366
Yater, A. C.: 910
Yates, L. G.: 868
Yen, S. M. Y.: 941
Yerkes, R. M.: 12, 136
Young, F. A.: 1326
Young, F. M.: 280
Zabin, D. H.: 370
Zeaman, D.: 707, 961
Zeidler, R.: 4
Zeigler, T. W.: 1280
Zemanek, D.: 1356
Zigler, E.: 906, 950
Zimmerman, F. T.: 1283, 1285
Zimmerman, I. L.: 986
Zingle, H. W.: 728
Zuk, G. H.: 659
Zunich, M.: 907

[526]

[Re Stanford-Binet Intelligence Scale] A Clinical Profile for the Stanford Binet Intelligence Scale (L-M). Ages 5 and over; 1965; title on profile is *A Profile for the Stanford Binet (L-M)*; an item classification system for use by school psychologists in analyzing and reporting performance in 6 categories: general comprehension, visual-motor ability, arithmetic reasoning, memory and concentration, vocabulary and verbal fluency, judgment and reasoning; Robert E. Valett; Consulting Psychologists Press, Inc. *

For additional information, see 7:426.

[527]

Stanford-Ohwaki-Kohs Block Design Intelligence Test for the Blind: American Revision of the Ohwaki-Kohs Test. Blind and partially sighted ages 16 and over; 1965–66; uses same testing materials as *The Ohwaki-Kohs Tactile Block Design Intelligence Test for the Blind*; Richard M. Suinn and William L. Dauterman; Western Psychological Services. *

For additional information, see 7:427.

[528]

Vane Kindergarten Test. Ages 4–6; 1968; VKT; 4 scores: perceptual motor, vocabulary, drawing a man, total; Julia R. Vane; Clinical Psychology Publishing Co., Inc. *

For additional information and reviews by Dorothy H. Eichorn and Marcel L. Goldschmid, see 7:428 (3 references).

REFERENCES THROUGH 1971

1–3. See 7:428.
4. POWERS, SANDRA MATTHEWS. *Long-Term Reliability and Predictive Validity of the Vane Kindergarten Test.* Doctor's thesis, University of Connecticut (Storrs, Conn.), 1970. (*DAI* 31:6411A)
5. D'ANGELO, R.; WALSH, J.; AND LOMANGINO, L. "IQs of Negro Head Start Children on the Vane Kindergarten Test." *J Clin Psychol* 27(1):82–3 Ja '71. * (*PA* 46:821)
6. JOHNSON, ROBERT E. L., JR. *Psycho-Social Correlates of Black Pre-School Children's Educational Progress.* Doctor's thesis, University of Oklahoma (Norman, Okla.), 1971. (*DAI* 32:4137A)
7. VANE, JULIA R. "Importance of Considering Background Factors When Evaluating the Effects of Compensatory Education Programs Designed for Young Children." *J Sch Psychol* 9(4):393–8 w '71. * (*PA* 47:11817)
8. VANE, JULIA R., AND DAVIS, WILLIAM M. "Factors Related to the Effectiveness of Preschool Programs With Disadvantaged Children." *J Ed Res* 64(7):297–9 Mr '71. *
9. WALSH, JOHN F., AND D'ANGELO, RITA. "IQs of Puerto Rican Head Start Children on the Vane Kindergarten Test." *J Sch Psychol* 9(2):173–6 '71. * (*PA* 47:7806)
10. WALSH, JOHN F.; D'ANGELO, RITA; AND LOMANGINO, LOUIS. "Performance of Negro and Puerto Rican Head Start Children on the Vane Kindergarten Test." *Psychol Sch* 8(4):357–8 O '71. * (*PA* 47:11641)

CUMULATIVE NAME INDEX

D'Angelo, R.: 5, 9–10
Davis, W. M.: 8
Eichorn, D. H.: *rev*, 7:428
Ellerman, R. A.: 2
Goldschmid, M. L.: *rev*, 7:428
Johnson, R. E. L.: 6
Lomangino, L.: 5, 10
Powers, S. M.: 4
Vane, J. R.: 1, 7–8
Wadley, J. A.: 2
Walsh, J.: 5
Walsh, J. F.: 9–10
Willis, D. J.: 3

[529]

Wechsler Adult Intelligence Scale. Ages 16 and over; 1939–55; WAIS; revision of Form I of *Wechsler-Bellevue Intelligence Scale*; 14 scores: verbal (information, comprehension, arithmetic, similarities, digit span, vocabulary, total), performance (digit symbol, picture completion, block design, picture arrangement, object assembly, total), total; David Wechsler; Psychological Corporation. (South African edition: Ages 18–59; 1969; National Institute for Personnel Research [South Africa]. British manual supplement: 1971; Peter Saville; NFER Publishing Co. Ltd. [England].) *

For additional information and reviews by Alvin G. Burstein and Howard B. Lyman, see 7:429 (538 references); see also 6:538 (180 references); for reviews by Nancy Bayley and Wilson H. Guertin, see 5:414 (42 references). For reference to reviews of an earlier edition, see 532. For excerpts from related book reviews, see 6:B503 (3 excerpts).

REFERENCES THROUGH 1971

1–42. See 5:414.
43–222. See 6:538.
223–762. See 7:429.
763. KALDEGG, A. "Migraine Patients: A Discussion of Some Test Results." *J Mental Sci* (England) 98:672–82 O '52. * (*PA* 27:6067)
764. WEST, ALICE A., III. *A Comparison of Subtest Scatter on the Wechsler-Bellevue Form I and the WAIS.* Master's thesis, University of Arizona (Tucson, Ariz.), 1956.
765. BAUER, ROBERT W., AND JOHNSON, DERWOOD E. "The Question of Deterioration in Alcoholism." Abstract. *J Consult Psychol* 21:296 Ag '57. * (*PA* 33:1669)
766. BEHRENS, BARBARA, AND MILES, GUY H. "A Test of 'Tendency to Analyze' for Use With College Men." *Proc Iowa Acad Sci* 64:508–13 '57. * (*PA* 33:3814)
767. THROP, JAMES L. *Scatter on the Wechsler Adult Intelligence Scale as a Measure of Personality Adjustment.* Master's thesis, University of Arizona (Tucson, Ariz.), 1957.
768. INGLIS, JAMES. "Learning, Retention, and Conceptual Usage in Elderly Patients With Memory Disorder." *J Abn & Social Psychol* 59:210–5 S '59. * (*PA* 34:3317)
769. JONES, NELSON F., JR. "The Validity of Clinical Judgments of Schizophrenic Pathology Based on Verbal Responses to Intelligence Test Items." *J Clin Psychol* 15:396–400 O '59. * (*PA* 36:1HI96J)
770. KENNEDY, WALLACE A.; SMITH, MARION; VAN DE RIET, HANNAH; VAN DE RIET, VERNON; SMITH, HERBERT; RAPP, DON; AND PAINE, R. W. "A Multidimensional Study of Mathematically Gifted Adolescents." *Child Develop* 31:655–66 D '60. * (*PA* 33:2FH55K)
771. MIRSKY, ALLAN F.; PRIMAC, DANIEL W.; MARSAN, COSIMO AJMONE; ROSVOLD, H. ENGER; AND STEVENS, JANICE R. "A Comparison of the Psychological Test Performance of Patients With Focal and Nonfocal Epilepsy." *Exp Neurol* 2:75–89 F '60. *
772. SHAPIRO, M. B.; KESSELL, R.; AND MAXWELL, A. E. "Speed and Quality of Psychomotor Performance in Psychiatric Patients." *J Clin Psychol* 16:266–71 Jl '60. * (*PA* 36:2HI66S)

773. WENDLAND, LEONARD V.; URMER, ALBERT H.; AND SAFFORD, H. WILLIAM. "The Intellectual Functioning of Postpoliomyelitic Patients." *J Clin Psychol* 16:179–81 Ap '60. * (PA 36:2HD79W)
774. SHNEIDMAN, EDWIN S. "The Case of El: Psychological Test Data." *J Proj Tech* 25:131–54 Je '61. * (PA 36:21K31S)
775. SPERBER, ZANWIL, AND ADLERSTEIN, ARTHUR M. "The Accuracy of Clinical Psychologists' Estimates of Interviewees' Intelligence." *J Consult Psychol* 25:521–4 D '61. * (PA 37:4969)
776. VASSILIOU, VASSO, AND HIMWICH, H. E. "Psychological Effects of Isocarboxazid and Nialamide on a Group of Depressed Patients." *J Clin Psychol* 17:319–20 Jl '61. * (PA 38:7581)
777. CARKHUFF, ROBERT R. "The Face Supplement: A Quick Index of Intelligence for Adult Subnormals." *J Clin Psychol* 18:346–7 Jl '62. * (PA 39:1721)
778. GRUEN, ARNO. "Psychologic Aging as a Pre-existing Factor in Strokes." *J Nerv & Mental Dis* 134:109–16 F '62. * (PA 37:965)
779. HERRON, WILLIAM G. "Abstract Ability in the Process-Reactive Classification of Schizophrenia." *J General Psychol* 67:147–54 Jl '62. * (PA 37:3691)
780. JENKINS, C. DAVID. "The Relation of EEG Slowing to Selected Indices of Intellective Impairment." *J Nerv & Mental Dis* 135:162–70 Ag '62. *
781. PEARL, DAVID. "Phenothiazine Effects in Chronic Schizophrenia." *J Clin Psychol* 18:86–9 Ja '62. * (PA 38:7573)
782. PIERCY, MALCOLM M., AND SMYTH, V. O. G. "Right Hemisphere Dominance for Certain Non-Verbal Intellectual Skills." *Brain* (England) 85:775–90 D '62. *
783. SCHULBERG, HERBERT C. "Insight, Authoritarianism and Tendency to Agree." *J Nerv & Mental Dis* 135:481–8 D '62. *
784. WYKE, MARIA. "An Experimental Study of Verbal Association in Dysphasic Subjects." *Brain* (England) 85:679–82 D '62. *
785. CLARK, MERVIN L.; RAY, THOMAS S.; AND RAGLAND, ROBERT E. "Chlorpromazine in Chronic Schizophrenic Women: Rate of Onset and Rate of Dissipation of Drug Effects." *Psychosom Med* 25:212–7 My–Je '63. * (PA 38:4397)
786. MULERO, RICARDO; IN COLLABORATION WITH J. WHITNEY KELLEY AND DONALD L. FAUTH. "The Effects of Valium on Psychological Testing." *Neb Med J* 48:499–505 S '63. *
787. SHAFFER, JOHN W.; FREINEK, WILFRIED R.; WOLF, SIDNEY; FOXWELL, NANCY H.; AND KURLAND, ALBERT A. "A Controlled Evaluation of Chlordiazepoxide (Librium) in the Treatment of Convalescing Alcoholics." *J Nerv & Mental Dis* 137:494–507 N '63. * (PA 39:5332)
788. WHEELER, LAWRENCE, AND REITAN, RALPH M. "Discriminant Functions Applied to the Problem of Predicting Cerebral Damage From Behavioral Tests: A Cross-Validation Study." *Percept & Motor Skills* 16:681–701 Je '63. * (PA 38:6415)
789. WHEELER, LAWRENCE; BURKE, CLETUS J.; AND REITAN, RALPH M. "An Application of Discriminant Functions to the Problem of Predicting Brain Damage Using Behavioral Variables." *Percept & Motor Skills* 16:417–40 Ap '63. * (PA 38:2991)
790. WOODS, JAMES E., AND MYERS, ROGER A. "A Comparison of IQ Scores on the Revised Beta Examination and the Wechsler Adult Intelligence Scale." *Rehabil Counsel B* 7:54–8 S '63. *
791. CARR, ARTHUR C. "Psychological Defect and Psychological Testing." *Int Psychiatry Clinics* 1:773–98 O '64. *
792. LEVITA, ERIC; RIKLAN, MANUEL; AND COOPER, IRVING S. "Cognitive and Perceptual Performance in Parkinsonism as a Function of Age and Neurological Impairment." *J Nerv & Mental Dis* 139:516–20 D '64. * (PA 39:10554)
793. McLEOD, H. N. "The Use of Information and Block Design Subtests of the W.A.I.S. as a Measure of Intelligence in Psychiatric Hospital Patients." *Ont Psychol Assn Q* (Canada) 17:60–1 su '64. *
794. OBERLEDER, MURIEL. "Effects of Psycho-Social Factors on Test Results of the Aging." *Psychol Rep* 14:383–7 Ap '64. * (PA 39:1390)
795. SPIETH, WALTER. "Cardiovascular Health Status, Age, and Psychological Performance." *J Gerontol* 19:277–84 Jl '64. *
796. TAYLOR, JAMES BENTLEY. "The Structure of Ability in the Lower Intellectual Range." *Am J Mental Def* 68:766–74 My '64. * (PA 39:1793)
797. WATSON, CHARLES G., AND CAHOON, D. D. "A Note on the Relationship Between the Revised Beta Examination and the Wechsler Adult Intelligence Scale." *Rehabil Counsel B* 8:47–9 D '64. *
798. BEARD, BELLE BOON. "Survival Traits: Adaptive Intelligence of Centenarians." *Proc Int Congr Gerontol* 6:233–6 '65. *
799. BLATT, SIDNEY J. Chap. 23, "The Wechsler Scales and Acting Out," pp. 242–51. In *Acting Out: Theoretical and Clinical Aspects*. By Lawrence Edwin Abt and Stuart L. Weissman. New York: Grune & Stratton, Inc., 1965. Pp. xiii, 336. *
800. BRENGELMANN, JOHANNES C., AND HILLMAN, WILLIAM A., JR. "Determinants of Learning in the Retardate: A Pilot Study." *Training Sch B* 61:156–62 F '65. * (PA 39:10570)
801. DIXON, JAMES C. "Cognitive Structure in Senile Conditions With Some Suggestions for Developing a Brief Screening Test of Mental Status." *J Gerontol* 20:41–9 Ja '65. *

802. GRAD, B.; KRAL, V. A.; AND CRAMER-AZIMA, F. "Correlations Between Salivary Sodium and Potassium Concentration and Memory Function in Elderly Persons, Normal and Psychotic." *Recent Adv Biol Psychiatry* 7:97–106 '65. *
803. KASWAN, JAQUES; HARALSON, SALLY; AND CLINE, RUTH. "Variables in Perceptual and Cognitive Organization and Differentiation." *J Personality* 33:164–77 Je '65. * (PA 40:2418)
804. LAWRENCE, RONALD M., AND LEICHMAN, NATHAN S. "Comparison of the Effects of Heparin Sodium, Xanthinol Niacinate (Complamin) and 2-Dimethyl-Aminoethanol (Deaner) in Institutionalized Geriatric Groups." *J Am Geriatrics Soc* 13:325–42 Ap '65. *
805. MACKIE, JAMES B., AND BECK, EDWARD C. "Relations Among Age, Intelligence, and Critical Flicker Fusion." *Percept & Motor Skills* 21:875–8 D '65. * (PA 40:4535)
806. SPREEN, OTFRIED, AND BENTON, ARTHUR L. "Comparative Studies of Some Psychological Tests for Cerebral Damage." *J Nerv & Mental Dis* 140:323–33 My '65. * (PA 40:700)
807. STEWART, HORACE F., JR., AND KEELER, CLYDE E. "A Comparison of the Intelligence and Personality of Moon-Child Albino and Control Cuna Indians." *J Genetic Psychol* 106:319–24 Je '65. * (PA 39:14888)
808. CORRELL, ROBERT E.; ROKOSZ, SAUNDRA; AND BLANCHARD, BRADFORD M. "Some Correlates of WAIS Performance in the Elderly." *J Gerontol* 21:544–9 O '66. *
809. FELIX, R., AND ARIELI, S. "The Pattern of the Human Hand." *Israel Ann Psychiatry* 4:30–42 sp '66. * (PA 41:656)
810. GRISWOLD, BARBARA B.; WILTSE, KERMIT T.; AND ROBERTS, ROBERT W. "Some Personality and Intellectual Correlates of Repeated Out-of-Wedlock Childbirth Among Welfare Recipients." *J Clin Psychol* 22:348–53 Jl '66. * (PA 40:11141)
811. LEVY, RUSSELL H., AND MOORE, WINSTON E. "Cross-Sectional Psychometric Evaluation of Court-Labelled Delinquent Boys." *J Correct Ed* 18:7–9 Jl '66. *
812. MACKIE, JAMES B., AND BECK, EDWARD C. "Relations Among Rigidity, Intelligence and Perception in Brain-Damaged and Normal Individuals." *J Nerv & Mental Dis* 142:310–7 Ap '66. * (PA 40:13429)
813. MAUPIN, EDWARD W., AND HUNTER, DIANE. "Digit Span as Measure of Attention: Attempted Validation Studies." *Psychol Rep* 18:457–8 Ap '66. * (PA 40:8398)
814. MEIER, MANFRED J., AND FRENCH, LYLE A. "Longitudinal Assessment of Intellectual Functioning Following Unilateral Temporal Lobectomy." *J Clin Psychol* 22:22–7 Ja '66. * (PA 40:4283)
815. NORDVIK, HILMAR. "Factor Analytical Research on Aging by the Wechsler Adult Intelligence Scale." *Proc Int Congr Gerontol* 6(sup):525–8 '66. *
816. PAREDES, ALFONSO; BAUMGOLD, JOHN; PUGH, LAWRENCE A.; AND RAGLAND, ROBERT. "Clinical Judgment in the Assessment of Psychopharmacological Effects." *J Nerv & Mental Dis* 142:153–60 F '66. * (PA 40:11294)
817. SATZ, PAUL. "Specific and Non-Specific Effects of Brain Lesions in Man." *J Abn Psychol* 71:65–70 F '66. * (PA 40:4292)
818. SIM, MYRE; TURNER, ERIC; AND SMITH, W. THOMAS. "Cerebral Biopsy in the Investigation of Presenile Dementia: 1, Clinical Aspects." *Brit J Psychiatry* 112:119–25 F '66. *
819. BLUNDELL, ELIZABETH. "A Psychological Study of the Effects of Surgery on Eighty-Six Elderly Patients." *Brit J Social & Clin Psychol* 6:297–303 D '67. * (PA 42:7707)
820. FALBERG, ROGER M. "The Psychological Evaluation of Prelingually Deaf Adults." *J Rehabil Deaf* 1:31–46 Jl '67. *
821. FISHER, JEROME, AND PIERCE, ROBERT C. "Dimensions of Intellectual Functioning in the Aged." *J Gerontol* 22:166–73 Ap '67. *
822. GRANICK, SAMUEL, AND FRIEDMAN, ALFRED S. "The Effect of Education on the Decline of Psychometric Test Performance With Age." *J Gerontol* 22:191–5 Ap '67. *
823. LEVITA, ERIC, AND RIKLAN, MANUEL. "Patterns of Psychological Function Before, After Unilateral, and After Bilateral Thalamic Surgery." *Percept & Motor Skills* 24:619–26 Ap '67. * (PA 41:9973)
824. LEVY, PHILIP. "The Correction for Spurious Correlation in the Evaluation of Short-Form Tests." *J Clin Psychol* 23:84–6 Ja '67. * (PA 41:5253)
825. LEVY, RUSSELL H. "Dimensions of Mental Retardation Among Wards of the Illinois Youth Commission." *J Correct Ed* 19:12–6 O '67. *
826. MONEY, JOHN, AND EPSTEIN, RALPH. "Verbal Aptitude in Eonism and Prepubertal Effeminacy—A Feminine Trait." *Trans N Y Acad Sci* 29:448–54 F '67. * (PA 41:16833)
827. RAMALINGASWAMI, P. "A Comparative Study on the Use of Block Design Test." *Indian J Psychol* 42(1–4):29–33 '67. *
828. SHIMKUNAS, ALGIMANTAS M.; GYNTHER, MALCOLM D.; AND SMITH, KATHLEEN. "Schizophrenic Responses to the Proverbs Test: Abstract, Concrete, or Autistic?" *J Abn Psychol* 72:128–33 Ap '67. * (PA 41:7605)
829. SUINN, RICHARD M. "The Theory of Cognitive Style: A Partial Replication." *J General Psychol* 77:11–5 Jl '67. * (PA 41:14063)
830. BARRINGTON, BYRON L. "Special Education Students—

Wechsler Adult Intelligence Scale

How Many Are Misplaced?" *J Learn Dis* 1:726-9 D '68. * (*PA* 45:6998)

831. BLOCK, J. BRADFORD. Chap. 13, "Hereditary Components in the Performance of Twins on the WAIS," pp. 221-8. In *Progress in Human Behavior Genetics*. Edited by Steven G. Vandenberg. Baltimore, Md.: Johns Hopkins Press, 1968. Pp. xi, 356. *

832. DE LUCA, JOSEPH N. "Motivation and Performance in Chronic Schizophrenia." *Psychol Rep* 22:1261-9 Je '68. * (*PA* 42:19082)

833. GOLDSTEIN, NORMAN P.; EWERT, JOSEPHINE C.; RANDALL, RAYMOND V.; AND GROSS, JOHN B. "Psychiatric Aspects of Wilson's Disease (Hepatolenticular Degeneration): Results of Psychometric Tests During Long-Term Therapy." *Am J Psychiatry* 124:1555-61 My '68. * (*PA* 42:12656)

834. LEWIS, VIOLA G.; MONEY, JOHN; AND EPSTEIN, RALPH. "Concordance of Verbal and Nonverbal Ability in the Adrenogenital Syndrome." *Johns Hopkins Med J* 122:192-5 Ap '68. *

835. LOEWER, H. D. "The Dependence of the Factorial Structure of Intelligence From the Level of Intelligence and From the Brain State." *Proc Inter Congr Appl Psychol* 16:707-12 '68. *

836. FREEMAN, JAMES; M'COMISKY, JAMES G.; AND BUTTLE, DEREK. "Student Selection: A Comparative Study of Student Entrants to Architecture and Economics." *Ed Sci* (England) 3(3):189-97 D '69. *

837. GIANNITRAPANI, DUILIO. "EEG Average Frequency and Intelligence." *Electroenceph & Clin Neurophysiol* (Netherlands) 27(5):480-6 N '69. * (*PA* 45:2021)

838. HALPERN, ANDREW S., AND EQUINOZZI, ARTHUR M. "Verbal Expressivity as an Index of Adaptive Behavior." *Am J Mental Def* 74(2):180-6 S '69. * (*PA* 44:5551)

839. HOLMES, DOUGLAS S. "Comment on Levy's Reply." *Psychol Rep* 24(3):936 Je '69. * (*PA* 44:707)

840. KEEVIL-ROGERS, PATRICIA, AND SCHNORE, MORRIS M. "Short-Term Memory as a Function of Age in Persons of Above Average Intelligence." *J Gerontol* 24(2):184-8 Ap '69. *

841. MANN, EDWARD T. "Use of the KTSA as a Technique for Assessing Intelligence and Psychodynamics in Drug Addicts." *Int J Symbol* 1(2):57-66 D '69. * (*PA* 45:10218)

842. MASICA, DANIEL N.; EHRHARDT, ANKE A.; AND LEWIS, VIOLA G. "IQ, Fetal Sex Hormones and Cognitive Patterns: Studies in the Testicular Feminizing Syndrome of Androgen Insensitivity." *Johns Hopkins Med J* 124(1):34-43 Ja '69. *

843. MONEY, JOHN, AND BRENNAN, JOHN G. "Achievement Versus Failure: Intelligence, Education and Career in Seven Female Transsexuals." *J Learn Dis* 2(2):76-81 F '69. * (*PA* 45:6641)

844. MYERS, SUSAN SLOAT. *Investigation of Creativity of Female Electronics Assemblers*. Master's thesis, Southern Methodist University (Dallas, Tex.), 1969.

845. RAFFEL, SHERMAN C.; SWINK, RICHARD; AND LAMPTON, T. D. "The Influence of Chlorphenesin Carbamate and Carisoprodol on Psychological Test Scores." *Curr Ther Res* 11(9):553-60 S '69. *

846. THETFORD, WILLIAM N., AND SCHUCMAN, HELEN. "Self-Choices, Preferences, and Personality Traits." *Psychol Rep* 25(2):659-67 O '69. * (*PA* 44:5171)

847. WEINBERG, H. "Correlation of Frequency Spectra of Averaged Visual Evoked Potentials With Verbal Intelligence." *Nature* (England) 224(5221):813-5 N 22 '69. *

848. ALEXANDER, SHIRLEY MAE. *A Study of Perceptual and Verbal Differentiation Among Male College Students*. Doctor's thesis, George Washington University (Washington, D.C.), 1970. (*DAI* 31:6887B)

849. BEACH, JOE EDWARD. *A Study of the Relationship of Intelligence and Academic Achievement of a Selected Group of Deaf Pupils*. Master's thesis, Mississippi State University (State College, Miss.), 1970.

850. BERRINGER, DALTON EARL. *An Examination of Geometric Errors in the WAIS Block Design Test and the Effects Upon Performance as a Function of Spatial Relations Ability*. Doctor's thesis, University of Northern Colorado (Greeley, Colo.), 1970. (*DAI* 31:6393A)

851. BOCK, R. DARRELL; VANDENBERG, STEVEN G.; BRAMBLE, WILLIAM; AND PEARSON, WRIGHT. "A Behavioral Correlate of Blood-Group Discordance in Dizygotic Twins." *Behav Genetics* 1(2):89-98 My '70. * (*PA* 47:10428)

852. GIANNITRAPANI, D. "WAIS I.Q. as Related to EEG Frequency Scores." Abstract. *Electroenceph & Clin Neurophysiol* (Netherlands) 28(1):102 Ja '70. *

853. GREEN, RUSSEL F., AND REIMANIS, GUNARS. "The Age-Intelligence Relationship—Longitudinal Studies Can Mislead." *Indus Gerontol* 6:1-16 su '70. * (*PA* 45:7981)

854. KIMBALL, CHASE P. "The Experience of Open Heart Surgery: 2, Determinants of Post-Operative Behavior." *Psychother & Psychosom* (Switzerland) 18(1-6):259-74 '70. * (*PA* 47:5515)

855. LABERTEAUX, THOMAS E. *A Comparison of Single and Multiple Stimuli Overinclusion Measures*. Doctor's thesis, St. Louis University (St. Louis, Mo.), 1970. (*DAI* 32:1216B)

856. LYNCH, WILLIAM JOHN. *The Performance of LSD Users on Certain Neuropsychological Tests*. Doctor's thesis, University of Tennessee (Knoxville, Tenn.), 1970. (*DAI* 31:5630B)

857. MEIER, MANFRED J. "Effects of Focal Cerebral Lesions on Contralateral Visuomotor Adaptation to Reversal and Inversion of Visual Feedback." *Neuropsychologia* (England) 8(3):269-79 Jl '70. * (*PA* 44:21410)

858. MILLER, LAURENCE RICHARD. *A Factor Analytic Study of Cognitive Variables in Congenitally Blind Individuals*. Doctor's thesis, Case Western Reserve University (Cleveland, Ohio), 1970. (*DAI* 32:248A)

859. PAGE, STEWART. "Examiner Effect, Expertise, and Intelligence Testing." *Ont Psychologist* (Canada) 2(3):181-4 '70. *

860. ROSS, DONALD R. "A Technique of Verbal Ability Assessment of Deaf Adults." *J Rehabil Deaf* 3(3):7-15 Ja '70. *

861. RUDOLPH, LINDA. *Correlates of the Slosson Intelligence Test, Wechsler Adult Intelligence Scale, ACT Scores and Grade Point Averages*. Master's thesis, Austin Peay State University (Clarksville, Tenn.), 1970.

862. TARNOPOL, LESTER. "Delinquency and Minimal Brain Dysfunction." *J Learn Dis* 3(4):200-7 Ap '70. * (*PA* 47:3517)

863. WAGNER, NATHANIEL N. "Malaysian Medical Students: Intellectual Performance and Ethnic Background." *Brit J Med Ed* 4(2):109-13 Je '70. *

864. WHITMAN, JAMES R. "Learning Impairment in Schizophrenic and Brain-Damaged Patients." *Percept & Motor Skills* 30(1):311-6 F '70. * (*PA* 46:9296)

865. BACKMAN, MARGARET E., AND STEINDLER, FRANCES M. "Cognitive Abilities Related to Attrition in a Collegiate Nursing Program." *Nursing Outl* 19(12):807-8 Jl '71. *

866. BACKMAN, MARGARET E., AND STEINDLER, FRANCES M. "Prediction of Achievement in a Collegiate Nursing Program and Performance on State Board Examinations." *Nursing Outl* 19(7):487 Jl '71. *

867. BEARDSLEY, JAMES V., AND PULETTI, FLAVIO. "Personality (MMPI) and Cognitive (WAIS) Changes After Levodopa Treatment: Occurrence in Patients With Parkinson's Disease." *Arch Neurol* 25(2):145-50 Ag '71. * (*PA* 48:1446)

868. BEN-YISHAY, YEHUDA; DILLER, LEONARD; MANDLEBERG, IAN; GORDON, WAYNE; AND GERSTMAN, LOUIS J. "Similarities and Differences in Block Design Performance Between Older Normal and Brain-Injured Persons: A Task Analysis." *J Abn Psychol* 78(1):17-25 Ag '71. * (*PA* 47:3261)

869. BETZ, ROGER CHARLES. *Predicting Rehabilitation Outcomes Through Selected Personal, Psychological and Program Variables*. Doctor's thesis, University of Northern Colorado (Greeley, Colo.), 1971. (*DAI* 32:3681A)

870. BOWERS, KENNETH S. "Sex and Susceptibility as Moderator Variables in the Relationship of Creativity and Hypnotic Susceptibility." *J Abn Psychol* 78(1):93-100 Ag '71. * (*PA* 47:2042)

871. BREWER, COLIN, AND PERRETT, LANCE. "Brain Damage Due to Alcoholic Consumption: An Air-encephalographic, Psychometric and Electroencephalographic Study." *Brit J Addict* 66(3):170-82 N '71. * (*PA* 48:5229)

872. BROWN, DON A. "Intelligence of Adult Illiterates." *Yearb Nat Read Conf* 19(1):94-8 '71. *

873. BUCKLEY, FELICITY. "Preliminary Report on Intelligence Quotient Scores of Patients With Turner's Syndrome: A Replication Study." *Brit J Psychiatry* 119(552):513-4 N '71. * (*PA* 48:3046)

874. CHAMBERS, JEAN FORBES. *Predicting the Academic Achievement Level of Deaf Students*. Doctor's thesis, University of Arizona (Tucson, Ariz.), 1971. (*DAI* 31:6396A)

875. CLARK, JACK MANNING. *The Prediction of Gain in Reading Among Adult Illiterates From an Analysis of Items on the Wechsler, Leiter and Davis-Eells Scales*. Doctor's thesis, State University of New York (Buffalo, N.Y.), 1971. (*DAI* 32:2512A)

876. COWDEN, JAMES E.; PETERSON, WILLIAM M.; AND PACHT, ASHER R. "The Validation of a Brief Screening Test for Verbal Intelligence at Several Correctional Institutions in Wisconsin." *J Clin Psychol* 27(2):216-8 Ap '71. * (*PA* 46:7125)

877. CULL, JOHN G., AND HARDY, RICHARD E. "Correlation Between the Immediate Test and the Wechsler Adult Intelligence Scale Verbal Scale in the Rehabilitation Setting." *J Psychol* 77(2):203-5 Mr '71. * (*PA* 46:1627)

878. DAVIS, WILLIAM E.; BECKER, BRUCE C.; AND DEWOLFE, ALAN S. "Categorization of Patients With Personality Disorders and Acute Brain Trauma Through WAIS Subtest Variations." *J Clin Psychol* 27(3):358-60 Jl '71. * (*PA* 47:5077)

879. DAVIS, WILLIAM E.; DIZZONNE, MICHAEL F.; AND DEWOLFE, ALAN S. "Relationships Among WAIS Subtest Scores, Patient's Premorbid History, and Institutionalization." *J Consult & Clin Psychol* 36(3):400-3 Je '71. * (*PA* 46:9377)

880. DEMERS, ROBERT G., AND HENINGER, GEORGE R. "Visual-Motor Performance During Lithium Treatment—A Preliminary Report." *J Clin Pharmacol* 11(4):274-9 Jl '71. * (*PA* 47:3169)

881. DEWOLFE, ALAN S. "Differentiation of Schizophrenia and Brain Damage With the WAIS." *J Clin Psychol* 27(2):209-11 Ap '71. * (*PA* 46:7073)

882. DEWOLFE, ALAN S.; BARRELL, ROBERT P.; BECKER, BRUCE C.; AND SPANER, FRED E. "Intellectual Deficit in Chronic Schizophrenia and Brain Damage." *J Consult & Clin Psychol* 36(3):197-204 Ap '71. * (*PA* 46:3117)

883. DICKSTEIN, LOUIS S., AND MACEVITT, MARJORIE. "Com-

prehension Subtest of the WAIS and Need for Approval." *Psychol Rep* 28(2):482 Ap '71. * (*PA* 46:6845)

884. DISPENZIERI, ANGELO; GINIGER, SEYMOUR; REICHMAN, WALTER; AND LEVY, MARGUERITE. "College Performance of Disadvantaged Students as a Function of Ability and Personality." *J Counsel Psychol* 18(4):298–305 Jl '71. * (*PA* 46:11687)

885. DONAHUE, DANIEL, AND SATTLER, JEROME M. "Personality Variables Affecting WAIS Scores." Abstract. *J Consult & Clin Psychol* 36(3):441 Je '71. * (*PA* 46:9041)

886. DUJOVNE, BEATRIZ E., AND LEVY, BERNARD I. "The Psychometric Structure of the Wechsler Memory Scale." *J Clin Psychol* 27(3):351–4 Jl '71. * (*PA* 47:5081)

887. FIELDS, FRANCIS R. J. "Relative Effects of Brain Damage on the Wechsler Memory and Intelligence Quotients." *Dis Nerv System* 32(10):673–5 O '71. * (*PA* 48:12023)

888. FIELDS, FRANCIS R. J. "Relative Effects of Brain Damage on the Wechsler Memory and Intelligence Quotients." *Newsl Res Psychol* 13(2):5–6 My '71. *

889. FIRETTO, ANTHONY C., AND DAVEY, HEATHER. "Subjectively Reported Anxiety as a Discriminator of Digit Span Performance." *Psychol Rep* 28(1):98 F '71. * (*PA* 46:5001)

890. FLICK, GRAD L., AND EDWARDS, KENNETH R. "Prediction of Lateralized Organic Brain Dysfunction With a Neuropsychological Test Battery: A Discriminant Function Analysis." *Newsl Res Psychol* 13(2):16–7 My '71. *

891. FREYMARK, BARRY A. *WAIS Block Design Performance as a Function of Amount of Exposure to Embedded Figures Tasks.* Master's thesis, Illinois State University (Normal, Ill.), 1971.

892. GEORGAS, JAMES G.; VASSILIOU, VASSO; AND KATAKIS, HARRIS. "The Verbal Intelligence of Athenians." *J Social Psychol* 83(2):165–73 Ap '71. * (*PA* 46:3084)

893. GOLDSTEIN, GERALD, AND SHELLY, CAROLYN H. "Field Dependence and Cognitive, Perceptual and Motor Skills in Alcoholics." *Q J Studies Alcohol* 32(1A):29–40 Mr '71. * (*PA* 46:7095)

894. GRANICK, SAMUEL. "Brief Tests and Their Interrelations as Intelligence Measures of Aged Subjects." Abstract. *Proc 79th Ann Conv Am Psychol Assn* 6(2):599–600 '71. * (*PA* 46:4727)

895. GRIFFITHS, A. W. "Prisoners of XYY Constitution: Psychological Aspects." *Brit J Psychiatry* 119(549):193–4 Ag '71. * (*PA* 47:7155)

896. GUERTIN, WILSON H.; LADD, CLAYTON E.; FRANK, GEORGE H.; RABIN, ALBERT I.; AND HIESTER, DOUGLAS S. "Research With the Wechsler Intelligence Scales for Adults: 1965–1970." *Psychol Rec* 21(3):289–339 su '71. * (*PA* 47:8926)

897. HANNINEN, HELENA. "Psychological Picture of Manifest and Latent Carbon Disulphide Poisoning." *Brit J Indus Med* 28(4):374–81 O '71. *

898. HARWOOD, ELSIE, AND NAYLOR, G. F. K. "Changes in the Constitution of the WAIS Intelligence Pattern With Advancing Age." *Austral J Psychol* 23(3):297–303 D '71. * (*PA* 48:2746)

899. HEDL, JOHN J., JR.; O'NEIL, HAROLD F., JR.; AND HANSEN, DUNCAN N. "Affective Nature of Computer-Based Testing Procedures." Abstract. *Proc 79th Ann Conv Am Psychol Assn* 6(2):535–6 '71. * (*PA* 46:5468)

900. HUNT, WILLIAM A., AND WALKER, RONALD E. "Cue Utilization in Diagnostic Judgment." *J Clin Psychol* 27(1):62–4 Ja '71. * (*PA* 46:1425)

901. IVINSKIS, ALGIS; ALLEN, STEPHEN; AND SHAW, ELVA. "An Extension of Wechsler Memory Scale Norms to Lower Age Groups." *J Clin Psychol* 27(3):354–7 Jl '71. * (*PA* 47:5087)

902. KAHN, MARVIN S. "Murderers Who Plead Insanity: A Descriptive Factor-Analytic Study of Personality, Social, and History Variables." *Genetic Psychol Monogr* 84(2):275–360 N '71. * (*PA* 49:990)

903. KANGAS, JON, AND BRADWAY, KATHERINE. "Intelligence at Middle Age: A Thirty-Eight-Year Follow-Up." *Develop Psychol* 5(2):333–7 S '71. * (*PA* 47:2985)

904. LEVENSON, MARVIN, AND NEURINGER, CHARLES. "Problem-Solving Behavior in Suicidal Adolescents." *J Consult & Clin Psychol* 37(3):433–6 D '71. * (*PA* 47:9261)

905. LEVINE, NIRA R. "Validation of the Quick Test for Intelligence Screening of the Elderly." *Psychol Rep* 29(1):167–72 Ag '71. * (*PA* 42:2717)

906. LIBB, J. WESLEY, AND COLEMAN, JOHN M. "Correlation Between the WAIS and Revised Beta, Wechsler Memory Scale and Quick Test in a Vocational Rehabilitation Center." *Psychol Rep* 29(3):863–5 D '71. * (*PA* 47:9410)

907. LOGOTHETIS, JOHN; HARITOS-FATOUROS, MARY; CONSTANTOULAKIS, MATHIOS; ECONOMIDOU, JOANNA; AUGOUSTAKI, OLGA; AND LOEWENSON, RUTH B. "Intelligence and Behavioral Patterns in Patients With Cooley's Anemia (Homozygous Betathalassemia); A Study Based on 138 Consecutive Cases." *Pediatrics* 48(5):740–4 N '71. *

908. LOGUE, PATRICK E., AND ALLEN, KATHE. "WAIS-Predicted Category Test Scores With the Halstead Neuropsychological Battery." *Percept & Motor Skills* 33(3):1095–6 D '71. * (*PA* 48:1463)

909. LORANGER, ARMAND W.; GOODELL, HELEN; MCDOWELL, FLETCHER; LEE, JOHN; AND SWEET, RICHARD D. "Cognitive Impairment in Parkinson's Syndrome." Abstract. *Proc 79th Ann Conv Am Psychol Assn* 6(1):463–4 '71. * (*PA* 46:5322)

910. MCCORMICK, CLARENCE C.; KLAPPAUF, JEANNIE; SCHNOBRICH, JANICE N.; AND HARVEY, JOHN. "Relationships Among Arrow-Dot IES Scores and Wechsler IQs and MMPI Scales for Hospitalized, Disturbed Adolescents." *Percept & Motor Skills* 33(3):1227–34 D '71. * (*PA* 48:3263)

911. MCKERRACHER, D. W. "Psychological Aspects of a Sex Chromatin Abnormality." *Can Psychologist* 12(2):270–81 Ap '71. * (*PA* 46:9096)

912. MILLHAM, JIM; JACOBSON, LEONARD I.; AND BERGER, STEPHEN E. "Effects of Intelligence, Information Processing, and Mediation Conditions on Conceptual Learning." *J Ed Psychol* 62(4):293–9 Ag '71. * (*PA* 47:220)

913. MISHRA, SHITALA P. "Wechsler Adult Intelligence Scale: Examiner vs Machine Administration?" *Psychol Rep* 29(3):759–62 D '71. * (*PA* 47:8928)

914. MOLISH, H. BARRY; KRAFT, IRVIN A.; AND WIGGINS, P. Y. "Psychodiagnostic Evaluation of the Heart Transplant Patient." *Seminars Psychiatry* 3(1):46–57 F '71. * (*PA* 49:7577)

915. MOSHER, LOREN R.; POLLIN, WILLIAM; AND STABENAU, JAMES R. "Identical Twins Discordant for Schizophrenia: Neurologic Findings." *Arch Gen Psychiatry* 24(5):422–30 My '71. * (*PA* 47:9365)

916. PAGE, STEWART. "On Wessler's 'Estimating IQ: Expertise or Examiner Effect?': Research and Discussion." *Percept & Motor Skills* 33(2):435–8 O '71. * (*PA* 47:7094)

917. PETERSEN, PAUL W. *Predicting Work Evaluation Results From the Wechsler Adult Intelligence Scale.* Doctor's thesis, Brigham Young University (Provo, Utah), 1971. (*DAI* 32:4454A)

918. PRINGLE, ROGER K., AND HAANSTAD, MARTIN. "Estimating WAIS IQs From Progressive Matrices and Shipley-Hartford Scores." *J Clin Psychol* 27(4):479–81 O '71. * (*PA* 47:8929)

919. ROYER, FRED L. "Information Processing of Visual Figures in the Digit Symbol Substitution Task." *J Exp Psychol* 87(3):335–42 Mr '71. * (*PA* 46:109)

920. ROYER, FRED L. "Information Processing of Visual Figures in the Digit-Symbol Substitution Task." *Newsl Res Psychol* 13(1):15–9 F '71. *

921. RUSSELL, ELBERT W. "Reexamination of Halstead's Biological Intelligence Factors." Abstract. *Proc 79th Ann Conv Am Psychol Assn* 6(1):461–2 '71. * (*PA* 46:5335)

922. SCHOFIELD, LARRY F., AND KUNCE, JOSEPH T. "The WAIS Adaptability Scale and Vocational Behavior." *J Voc Behav* 1(4):355–60 O '71. * (*PA* 48:5351)

923. SCHOOLER, CARMI, AND SILVERMAN, JULIAN. "Differences Between Correlates of Perceptual Style and Petrie Task Performance in Chronic and Acute Schizophrenics." *Percept & Motor Skills* 32(2):595–601 Ap '71. * (*PA* 46:11261)

924. SEITZ, FRANK C., AND BRAUCHT, GEORGE N. "Ammons' Quick Test as a Measure of Adult Intelligence in a Psychiatric Sample." *Psychol Rep* 29(2):356–8 O '71. * (*PA* 47:9302)

925. SHIMKUNAS, ALGIMANTAS M.; GROHMANN, MARY; AND ZWIBELMAN, BARRY. "Sources of Intellectual Inefficiency." *Psychol Rep* 29(3):747–54 D '71. * (*PA* 47:9374)

926. SHORE, CELIA; SHORE, HOWARD; AND PIHL, R. O. "Correlations Between Performance on the Category Test and the Wechsler Adult Intelligence Scale." *Percept & Motor Skills* 32(1):70 F '71. * (*PA* 46:3068)

927. SILVERSTEIN, A. B. "A Corrected Formula for Assessing the Validity of WAIS, WISC, and WPPSI Short Forms." *J Clin Psychol* 27(2):212–3 Ap '71. * (*PA* 46:6881)

928. SIMPSON, C. DENE, AND VEGA, ARTHUR. "Unilateral Brain Damage and Patterns of Age-Corrected WAIS Subtest Scores." *J Clin Psychol* 27(2):204–8 Ap '71. * (*PA* 46:7308)

929. SMITH, W. LYNN, AND LOWREY, J. B. "Differential Effects of Cyclandelate on Psychological Test Performance in Patients With Cerebral Vascular Insufficiency," pp. 69–73. In *Assessment in Cerebrovascular Insufficiency.* Edited by G. Stöcker and Others. Stuttgart, Germany: Georg Thieme Verlag, 1971. Pp. viii, 152. *

930. TOOMEY, TIMOTHY CHARLES. *The Effect of a Televised Model in Altering a Behavioral Correlate of Field Dependence and Field Independence.* Doctor's thesis, University of Georgia (Athens, Ga.), 1971. (*DAI* 32:4231B)

931. TOPPEN, J. T. "Underemployment: Economic or Psychological." *Psychol Rep* 28(1):111–22 F '71. * (*PA* 46:4762)

932. TRIESCHMANN, ROBERTA B., AND SAND, PATRICIA L. "WAIS and MMPI Correlates of Increasing Renal Failure in Adult Medical Patients." *Psychol Rep* 29(3):1251–62 D '71. * (*PA* 48:1559)

933. TSAI, LOH SENG, AND HAINES, RICHARD B. "Tsai Number-Joining Test Scores Correlated With College Students' Performance on WAIS and DAT." *Percept & Motor Skills* 33(1):35–44 Ag '71. * (*PA* 47:3643)

934. VEGA, ARTHUR, AND PARSONS, OSCAR A. "Lateralized Brain Damage and Differential Psychological Effects: Reply to Dr. Woo-Sam." *Percept & Motor Skills* 33(1):269–70 Ag '71. * (*PA* 47:3518)

935. WARRINGTON, ELIZABETH K.; LOGUE, VALENTINE; AND PRATT, R. T. C. "The Anatomical Localisation of Selective

Impairment of Auditory Verbal Short-Term Memory." *Neuropsychologia* (England) 9(4):377–87 D '71. * (*PA* 48:5435)
936. WEINSTOCK, CAMILDA, AND BENNETT, RUTH. "From 'Waiting on the List' to Becoming a 'Newcomer' and an 'Oldtimer' in a Home for the Aged: Two Studies of Socialization and Its Impact Upon Cognitive Functioning." *Aging & Hum Develop* 2(1):46–58 F '71. * (*PA* 48:8893)
937. WELLS, DONALD G., AND PEDRINI, DUILIO T. "Relationships Among Wechsler Adult Intelligence Scale, Goodenough-Harris, and Peabody Picture Vocabulary Tests With Institutionalized Retarded Adults." *Percept & Motor Skills* 33(1):227–32 Ag '71. * (*PA* 47:3549)
938. WILKIE, FRANCES, AND EISDORFER, CARL. "Intelligence and Blood Pressure in the Aged." *Sci* 172(3986):959–62 My 28 '71. * (*PA* 46:8804)
939. WILLNER, ALLEN E. "Abstraction, Associative Focusing, and Similarities Tests: Towards More Clinically Sensitive and Better Understood Tests." *Psychol Rep* 29(3):683–731 D '71. * (*PA* 47:8001)
940. WOO-SAM, JAMES. "Lateralized Brain Damage and Differential Psychological Effects: Parsons, *et al.*, Re-Examined." *Percept & Motor Skills* 33(1):259–62 Ag '71. * (*PA* 47:3519)

CUMULATIVE NAME INDEX

Abidin, R. R.: 431
Abram, H. S.: 605
Abrams, S.: 367
Abt, L. E.: 799
Adar, L. D.: 683
Adlerstein, A. M.: 775
Affleck, D. C.: 368
Air, D. H.: 698
Alexander, S.: 510
Alexander, S. M.: 848
Alimena, B.: 107
Allan, J. H.: 605
Allen, B. V.: 296
Allen, K.: 908
Allen, R. M.: 139
Allen, S.: 901
Allison, J.: 311, 508, 518
Alper, A. E.: 228
Alston, P. P.: 668
Altus, W. D.: *exc*, 6:B503
Anastasi, A.: 4, 108, 509
Anderson, C. J.: 510
Anderson, C. W. G.: 418
Anderson, H. E.: 432, 511
Andy, O. J.: 286
Anthony, R. J.: 723
Arieli, S.: 809
Armstrong, H. E.: 330, 387
Arnette, J. L.: 565
Asso, D.: 606–7
Augoustaki, O.: 907
Avery, C.: 512
Avery, C. D.: 599
Ax, A. F.: 513
Aylaian, A.: 140
Bachelis, L.: 105, 507
Backman, M. E.: 865–6
Baer, P.: 433
Baker, B. L.: 311, 688
Baker, J. A.: 344
Balinsky, B.: 5
Ballard, H. T.: 253
Bamford, J. L.: 513
Banaka, W. H.: 103
Barclay, A.: 187, 608
Barrell, R. P.: 882
Barrett, A. M.: 115
Barrington, B. L.: 830
Bartz, W. R.: 514
Bassett, J. E.: 609
Batcheldor, K. J.: 11
Bauer, R. W.: 765
Baumgold, J.: 816
Bayley, N.: 515–6; *rev*, 5:414
Beach, J. E.: 849
Beard, B. B.: 798
Beardsley, J. V.: 655, 867
Beardsley, K.: 109
Beck, A. T.: 141
Beck, E. C.: 654, 805, 812
Becker, B. C.: 878, 882
Behrens, B.: 766
Belden, B. R.: 689
Belden, E.: 564
Bell, A.: 237
Bennett, G. K.: 44
Bennett, R.: 936
Benson, R. R.: 178
Benton, A. L.: 12, 806
Benton, J. G.: 385
Ben-Yishay, Y.: 684–6, 868
Berger, L.: 246–7, 266, 310
Berger, S. E.: 912
Bergmann, K.: 437
Berke, N. D.: 434
Berkowitz, B.: 309
Berman, I.: 267–8
Bernstein, A.: 246–7, 266, 310
Bernstein, A. S.: 310
Bernstein, L.: 238
Berringer, D. E.: 850
Berry, R. A.: 369
Bersoff, D. N.: 687
Betz, R. C.: 869
Beverfelt, E.: 269
Bielefeld, M. O.: 517
Bingham, W. C.: 370, 611
Birch, H. G.: 461
Birnbaum, J.: 430
Birren, J. E.: 110–1, 142, 179, 248–50
Blackburn, H. L.: 12
Blanchard, B. M.: 808
Blatt, B.: 371
Blatt, S. J.: 311, 358, 377, 435, 443, 508, 518, 589, 626, 688, 799
Blazer, J. A.: 372
Block, J. B.: 831
Blocker, W. W.: 553
Bloom, B. L.: 54, 143
Bloor, B. M.: 533
Blumkoltz, F. P.: 321
Blundell, E.: 819
Bock, R. D.: 851
Bodwell, A.: 736
Bolton, N.: 373, 582
Bonner, M. W.: 519, 689
Boor, M.: 520
Borgatta, E. F.: 74
Botwinick, J.: 248, 250
Bourestom, N. C.: 521
Bowers, K. S.: 870
Bradway, K. H.: 903
Bradway, K. P.: 112, 144
Bramble, W.: 851
Braucht, G. N.: 924
Bray, P. F.: 654
Brengelmann, J. C.: 113, 800
Brennan, J. G.: 843
Brewer, C.: 871
Briggs, P. F.: 75, 496
Brigham, B. W.: 436
Brill, R. G.: 145
British Psychological Society, English Division of Professional Psychologists (Educational and Clinical): 180
Britton, P. G.: 373–4, 437, 583
Broman, H. J.: 635
Brooks, E. M.: 220
Brown, D. A.: 872
Brown, F.: 522, 594
Brown, L.: 544
Brown, O.: 438
Brown, R.: 732
Buckley, F.: 873
Budoff, M.: 439
Burgess, M. M.: 610, 690–1
Burke, C. J.: 789
Burke, H. R.: 370, 611
Burn, J.: 658
Burnand, G.: 440
Burstein, A. G.: *rev*, 7:429
Burton, D. A.: 523
Busse, E. W.: 16, 58, 244, 501, 758
Butler, A. J.: 270
Buttle, D.: 836
Byrne, A. V.: 431
Cahoon, D. D.: 797
Callens, C. J.: 612
Campo, R. E.: 251
Cancro, R.: 252
Canter, A.: 613
Carkhuff, R. R.: 777
Carlisle, A. L.: 312
Carr, A. C.: 791
Cartwright, D. S.: 274
Cartwright, J. L.: 524
Castell, J. H. F.: 180, 313
Cate, C. C.: 441
Chabassol, D. J.: 525
Chambers, J. F.: 874
Chambers, W. R.: 39
Chansky, N. M.: 375
Cherry, N.: 423
Clark, G. R.: 737
Clark, J. R.: 875
Clark, M. L.: 785
Clarke, A. D. B.: 180
Clayton, H.: 55
Cleeland, C. S.: 727
Clifton, S. W.: 595
Cline, R.: 803
Clore, G. L.: 181
Clower, R. P.: 415
Clum, G. A.: 526
Cochran, M. L.: 614, 692
Cohen, J.: 6, 13–4, 246–7, 266, 310
Cohen, L. D.: 16, 58, 116
Colarelli, N. J.: 713
Cole, D.: 7
Cole, S.: 492
Coleman, J. M.: 906
Colvin, C. R.: 696
Connor, M. W.: 527
Conrad, W. G.: 270
Conry, R.: 314
Constantoulakis, M.: 907
Cook, C.: 432, 511
Cook, R. A.: 114, 155
Coons, W. H.: 56, 693
Cooper, G. V.: 694
Cooper, I. S.: 792
Correll, R. E.: 808
Corsini, R. J.: 74
Coslett, S. B.: 315
Costa, L. D.: 146, 615
Cowden, J. E.: 876
Craddick, R. A.: 147, 182, 376
Craft, M.: 316
Craig, R. J.: 616
Cramer-Azima, F.: 802
Crandall, F. E.: 617
Crawford, P. L.: 229–30
Cronholm, B.: 528
Crookes, T. G.: 468, 695
Crown, S.: 607
Cull, J. G.: 696, 877
Cupp, M. E.: 340
Dahlgren, H.: 679
Dana, J. M.: 618
Dana, R. H.: 15, 618
Daniels, A.: 483
Darbes, A.: 76
Daroff, R. B.: 553
Dauterman, W.: 494
Davey, H.: 889
Davidson, J.: 280
Davidson, N. L.: 260
Davis, W. E.: 619–20, 697–8, 878–9
Dawes, R. M.: 397, 466, 722
de Lint, J.: 442
DeLuca, J.: 529
De Luca, J. N.: 832
Demers, R. G.: 880
De Milan, J.: 317
Den Broeder, J.: 272
Dennerll, R. D.: 271–2, 587
Dent, O. B.: 642
Desai, A. N.: 530
Desroches, H. F.: 253
Deutsch, M. R.: 597
DeVault, S.: 386
DeWolfe, A. S.: 698, 878–9, 881–2
Dickinson, T. C.: 531
Dickstein, L. S.: 377, 443, 621, 883
Diller, L.: 684–6, 868
Dingman, H. F.: 130
Dispenzieri, A.: 884
Dixon, J. C.: 801
Dizzone, M. F.: 697–8, 879
Doherty, M. A.: 378
Domino, G.: 532, 723
Donahue, D.: 885
Dooley, M. D.: 81
Doorbar, R. R.: 444
Doppelt, J. E.: 1–2, 8, 57
Doty, B. A.: 445
Downing, L. N.: 36
Doyle, E. D.: 318
Drake, W. E.: 679
Drewes, H. W.: 227
Duffey, M.: 610
Dujovne, B. E.: 886
Duke, R. B.: 446, 533
Duncan, D. F.: 699
Duncan, D. R.: 115
Dunn, J. A.: 534
Dunnette, M. D.: 32
Durward, M.: 560
Eber, H. W.: 447
Economidou, J.: 907
Edwards, G. A.: 379
Edwards, H. P.: 319
Edwards, K. R.: 890
Ehrhardt, A. A.: 842
Eisdorfer, C.: 16, 58, 116, 183–4, 244, 938
Eisenson, J.: 232
Elenewski, J. J.: 549
Elkin, L.: 535
Elwood, D. L.: 622, 700
Eme, R. F.: 623
Engelbart, E. S.: 464
Epstein, R.: 826, 834
Equinozzi, A. M.: 838
Ernhart, C. B.: 536, 701
Estes, B. W.: 153, 185
Evans, L.: 36, 45
Evans, R. B.: 186
Ewert, J. C.: 833
Falberg, R. M.: 820
Falek, A.: 195
Faterson, H. F.: 430
Fauth, D. L.: 786
Febiger, C. H.: 716
Feffer, M. H.: 240
Feinberg, M. R.: 273
Feldman, S. E.: 537
Felix, R.: 809
Fernald, P. S.: 702
Feshbach, S.: 141
Fidel, Y.: 608
Field, J. G.: 77
Fields, F. R. J.: 624, 762, 887–8
Fink, S. L.: 33, 325
Finnie, F. R.: 538
Firetto, A. C.: 757, 889
Fisher, C.: 550–1, 639
Fisher, G. S.: 539, 671
Fisher, G. M.: 59, 78–82, 99, 117–9, 130, 148–50, 173
Fisher, J.: 821
Fiske, D. W.: 274
Fitzhugh, K. B.: 275–6, 476
Fitzhugh, L. C.: 275–7
Fitzpatrick, P.: 620
Fleming, J. W.: 231
Flick, G. L.: 890
Flinn, D. E.: 254
Floor, L.: 580, 737
Flynn, W. F.: 380
Fogel, M. L.: 151, 277, 320–1
Foley, J. M.: 741
Ford, D. H.: 176
Foster, A.: 625
Fox, E.: 626
Foxwell, N. H.: 787
Francis, P. S.: 336
Frank, G. H.: 154, 383, 703, 896

Wechsler Adult Intelligence Scale

Frederickson, W. K.: 368
Freeburne, C. M.: 188
Freedman, S.: 540
Freeman, F. S.: 152
Freeman, J.: 836
Freinek, W. R.: 787
French, L. A.: 814
Fretwell, L. N.: 340
Freud, S. L.: 23
Freymark, B. A.: 891
Friedman, A. S.: 822
Friedman, E. C.: 187, 608
Friedman, J.: 381
Funkhouser, T. R.: 541
Gaitz, C.: 433
Gale, E. N.: 643
Gallagher, H. C.: 542
Gallaher, P. J.: 255
Gamewell, J.: 448
Gardner, M. S.: 83
Garfield, S. L.: 60
Gathercole, C. E.: 382
Gaver, K. D.: 73
Gayton, W. F.: 609
Geiser, R. L.: 120
Gendel, H.: 278
Gentry, W. D.: 577
Georgas, J. G.: 892
Gerdine, P. Van H.: 279
Gerstman, L.: 685–6
Gerstman, L. J.: 868
Giannell, A. S.: 188
Giannitrapani, D.: 837, 852
Gianturco, J.: 604
Gibeau, P. J.: 322
Gibson, J.: 449
Gilberstadt, H.: 450, 543
Gilman, R. H.: 451
Giniger, S.: 884
Gittinger, J. W.: 581
Glick, I. D.: 627
Goldfarb, N.: 628
Goldfarb, W.: 628
Goldman, B. A.: 84, 189–90
Goldman, R. K.: 143
Goldsamt, M.: 409
Goldstein, G.: 704, 893
Goldstein, N. P.: 833
Goldstein, S. G.: 452
Golland, J. H.: 705
Gonen, J. Y.: 544, 706
Gonen, Y.: 545
Goodell, H.: 909
Goodenough, D. R.: 430
Gordon, C.: 477
Gordon, W.: 685, 868
Gourevitch, V.: 240
Grad, B.: 802
Graham, E. E.: 34
Granick, S.: 191, 822, 894
Green, H. B.: 323
Green, R. F.: 309, 629, 853
Greenberg, G.: 16
Greenberg, I. M.: 707
Greenburg, H.: 691
Greenwood, D. I.: 324
Gressett, J. D.: 630
Griffith, R. M.: 35, 153
Griffiths, A. W.: 895
Grippaldi, R.: 717
Grisso, J. T.: 453
Griswold, B. B.: 810
Grohmann, M.: 925
Gross, F. L.: 756
Gross, J. B.: 833
Gross, R. B.: 713
Grossman, J. L.: 631
Grossman, J. S.: 325
Grossmann, K.: 147
Grotelueschen, A.: 454, 555, 708
Gruen, A.: 778
Guertin, W. H.: 154, 383, 896; rev, 5:414
Guyette, A.: 280
Gynther, M. D.: 828
Haanstad, M.: 918
Haas, A.: 686
Hahn, M.: 705
Haines, R. B.: 933
Hall, J. C.: 9, 17
Hall, W. E.: 605
Hallenbeck, C. E.: 325
Halpern, A. S.: 838

Hamlin, R. M.: 326
Hamlin, R. W.: 192
Hanna, G. S.: 546
Hänninen, H.: 897
Hannon, J. E.: 709
Hannum, T. E.: 410
Hansen, D. N.: 899
Haralson, S.: 803
Hardy, R. E.: 877
Hardyck, C.: 193
Harford, T.: 738
Haritos-Fatouros, M.: 907
Haronian, F.: 455
Hartlage, L. C.: 677
Hartman, B. O.: 254
Harvey, J.: 910
Harwood, B. T.: 456
Harwood, E.: 898
Haskell, S. H.: 327
Haugen, E. S.: 281
Hedl, J. J.: 899
Heilbrun, A. B.: 48
Heninger, G. R.: 880
Henning, J. J.: 328, 457
Herrans, L. L.: 632
Herrell, J. M.: 705
Herron, W. G.: 779
Hiester, D. S.: 383, 896
Higbee, W. R.: 384
Hillix, W. A.: 743
Hillman, W. A.: 800
Himelstein, P.: 18–20, 329
Himwich, H. E.: 776
Hirschenfang, S.: 85, 232, 385
Hirt, M. L.: 114, 155
Hodges, W. F.: 633
Hogan, T. P.: 425, 634
Hoggart, K.: 440
Holden, R. H.: 386
Hollender, J. W.: 635
Holmes, D. S.: 330, 387, 636, 839
Holmes, J. S.: 547
Holt, R. R.: 548
Holzman, P. S.: exc, 6:B503
Hooker, E.: 21
Hopper, C. L.: 727
Horne, B. M.: 228
Horowitz, F. D.: 388
Horwitz, M.: 615
House, B.: 546
Howard, M. T.: 521
Howard, W.: 49, 61
Howell, R. J.: 36
Hudson, J.: 366
Huff, F. W.: 282
Hughes, D.: 605
Hulicka, I. M.: 156
Hunt, W. A.: 86, 157, 283, 359, 389–90, 900
Hunter, D.: 813
Hunter, H.: 440
Hunter, R. C. A.: 133
Hustmyer, F. E.: 710
Hutton, G. H.: 716
Ilanit, N.: 239
Imre, P. D.: 194
Inglis, J.: 768
Ison, M. G.: 22
Ivanoff, J.: 641
Ivinskis, A.: 901
Jacobson, L. I.: 549, 912
Jambor, K. L.: 637
Jarvik, L. F.: 195
Jastak, J. F.: 284
Jastak, S. R.: 284
Jenkins, C. D.: 780
Jennings, C. L.: 256, 391
Johnson, D. E.: 765
Johnson, D. T.: 638
Johnson, J. J.: 285
Johnson, M. H.: 330, 387
Jones, H. G.: 10
Jones, N. F.: 62, 86, 769
Jones, R. E.: 192
Jones, R. L.: 158, 458
Jordheim, G. D.: 299
Jortner, S.: 711
Joslin, H. F.: 392
Jurjevich, R.: 197–8
Jurjevich, R. M.: 196, 459
Jurko, M. F.: 286
Kaback, G. R.: 331
Kahn, G. B.: 550–1, 639

Kahn, M.: 584–5
Kahn, M. W.: 332, 552, 902
Kaldegg, A.: 87, 763
Kamano, D.: 34
Kangas, J.: 903
Kangas, J. A.: 712
Kanter, H. M.: 640
Kaplan, M. L.: 713
Karlin, I. W.: 232
Karp, S. A.: 199
Karras, A.: 200
Karson, S.: 23
Kasper, S.: 37
Kassinove, H.: 714
Kastl, A. J.: 553
Kaswan, J.: 803
Katakis, H.: 892
Kaufman, H.: 641
Kaufman, H. I.: 460, 715
Kay, D. W. K.: 437
Keefe, K.: 719
Keefe, M. K.: 121
Keeler, C. E.: 807
Keevil-Rogers, P.: 840
Kelley, J. W.: 786
Kelly, F. D.: 554
Kelly, F. J.: 211
Kemp, D. E.: 94
Kendrick, D. C.: 287
Kennedy, W. A.: 88, 201, 333, 770
Kenny, J. T.: 113
Kern, F. E.: 432, 511
Kessell, R.: 772
Kettell, M. E.: 288
Kicklighter, R.: 709
Kilman, B. A.: 118
Kimball, C. P.: 854
Kimbreall, G. M.: 253
Kinzie, W. B.: 759
Kirchner, W. K.: 32
Kirschner, D.: 226
Kirtner, W. L.: 274
Kivitz, M. S.: 737
Klappauf, J.: 910
Klapper, Z. S.: 461
Klappersack, B.: 704
Kleemeier, R. W.: 244
Klein, D. F.: 576
Klein, E.: 246–7, 266, 310
Klett, W. G.: 50, 257, 601
Klonoff, H.: 716
Kløve, H.: 393, 400, 469
Knox, A. B.: 555
Knox, S. J.: 364
Knox, W. J.: 334, 717
Ko, Y. H.: 159
Kodanaz, A.: 690–1
Koestline, W. C.: 642
Kole, D. M.: 241, 335
Korotkin, A. L.: 234
Kraft, I. A.: 914
Kral, V. A.: 802
Kramer, E.: 336
Kraus, J.: 337–9, 394, 462, 556
Kraus, M. J.: 136
Krippner, S.: 289
Kroske, W. H.: 340
Kunce, J. T.: 718, 922
Kurland, A. A.: 787
Labak, A. S.: 463
L'Abate, L.: 160, 643
Laberteaux, T. E.: 855
Labrecque, J. M.: 161
Lacks, P. B.: 719
Ladd, C. E.: 63, 154, 290, 383, 896
Lampton, T. D.: 845
Lanfeld, E. S.: 122
Lasky, J. J.: 291
Lassman, F. M.: 464
Laver, A. B.: 202
Lawrence, R. M.: 804
Laywell, H. R.: 397, 466, 722
Lee, J.: 909
Legg, D.: 141
Lehmann, I. J.: 406
Leichman, N. S.: 804
Levenson, M.: 904
Leventhal, D. B.: 713
Levine, H. D.: 490
Levine, N. R.: 644, 905
Levinson, B. M.: 24–5, 38, 64–5, 89–90, 162, 203–4, 292–3, 341, 395, 645
Levita, E.: 792, 823
Levy, B. I.: 886
Levy, M.: 884
Levy, P.: 557, 646, 824
Levy, R. H.: 457, 558, 811, 825
Lewis, D. W.: 605
Lewis, F. W.: 559
Lewis, L. L.: 46
Lewis, V. G.: 834, 842
Lewis, W. M.: 720
Libb, J. W.: 906
Libowitz, J. M.: 396
Liebert, R. M.: 651
Light, M. L.: 39
Light, P.: 449
Lin, T. T.: 729–30
Lin, Y. G.: 587
Lindner, R.: 88
Lipton, R.: 409
Liroff, J. H.: 549
Little, A. J.: 562
Lo Cascio, R.: 138
Loewenson, R. B.: 907
Loewer, H. D.: 835
Logothetis, J.: 907
Logue, P. E.: 908
Logue, V.: 560, 607, 935
Looft, W. R.: 721
Loranger, A. W.: 66, 91, 909
Lordahl, D. S.: 549
Lore, J.: 510
Love, H. G. I.: 647
Lowe, C. M.: 465
Lowrey, J. B.: 929
Lucas, G.: 246, 266
Lund, R. D.: 561
Lundy, C. T.: 452
Luszki, M. B.: 397, 466, 722
Luszki, W. A.: 294, 342, 398
Lyman, H. B.: rev, 7:429
Lynch, W. J.: 856
Lynd, C.: 67
Lyons, T. J.: 454
McCarthy, D.: 123, 467, 723
McCormick, C. C.: 910
M'Comisky, J. G.: 836
McDermott, D.: 531
McDonald, C.: 648
McDonald, K. G.: 468
McDowell, F.: 909
MacEvitt, M.: 883
Mack, J. L.: 724
McKee, J. L.: 725
McKeever, W. F.: 124, 343
McKenzie, R. E.: 254
McKerracher, D. W.: 399, 562, 911
Mackie, J. B.: 258, 805, 812
McLelland, P. E.: 563
McLeod, H. N.: 125–7, 163, 793
McNemar, Q.: 26
McQuarrie, D.: 708
Majumdar, P. K.: 295
Majzoub, H. S.: 533
Malerstein, A. J.: 564
Maley, R. F.: 726
Mandleberg, I.: 684, 868
Mann, E. T.: 649, 841
Marks, E.: 176
Marmorston, J.: 186
Marsan, C. A.: 771
Marshall, R. J.: 167
Martin, W. E.: 728
Masica, D. N.: 842
Masser, E. V.: 565
Matarazzo, J. D.: 73, 296, 335
Matthews, C. G.: 393, 400, 469, 727
Maupin, E. W.: 813
Maxfield, K. E.: 128
Maxwell, A. E.: 92, 129, 772
Maxwell, J.: 27
May, P. R. A.: 343
Mayman, M.: 100
Meadow, A.: 453
Meer, B.: 344
Megargee, E. I.: 662
Meier, M. J.: 401, 650, 728, 814, 857
Meikle, S.: 566

Wechsler Adult Intelligence Scale

Meltzer, M. L.: 140, 612
Mendelson, M. A.: 386
Merbaum, M.: 676
Mercer, M.: 510
Merryman, P.: 433
Miele, J. A.: 51
Miles, G. H.: 766
Miller, D. R.: 130
Miller, J. M.: 734
Miller, L. R.: 858
Miller, M. H.: 232
Millham, J.: 912
Mills, D. H.: 402
Milstein, V.: 174
Minard, J.: 169
Miner, J. B.: 164
Mirsky, A. F.: 771
Mishra, S. P.: 913
Misiak, H.: 66, 91
Mittler, P.: 180
Mittler, P. J.: 313
Mogel, S.: 170, 205
Molish, H. B.: 914
Money, J.: 297, 826, 834, 843
Monroe, K. L.: 403
Moon, H.: 88
Moore, A. B.: 567
Moore, W. B.: 568
Moore, W. E.: 811
Morgan, D. W.: 404
Morledge, J.: 480
Morris, L. W.: 651
Morrison, D. F.: 111, 248–9
Morrison, M. M.: 71
Moses, J. L.: 652
Mosher, L. R.: 915
Moulton, R.: 352
Muehleman, T.: 584–5
Mulero, R.: 786
Mulhern, M.: 620
Murdy, W. G.: 242
Murray, J. B.: 471
Murray, S.: 370
Muskera, D. J.: 569
Myers, R. A.: 790
Myers, S. S.: 844
Nachmann, B.: 352
Nadel, R. S.: 653
Nadler, E. B.: 28
Nathan, P.: 243
Nathanson, I. A.: 367
Naylor, G. F. K.: 898
Needham, W. E.: 654
Neher, L. A.: 743
Neilsen, M. K.: 360
Nelson, L. A.: 235
Nelson, W.: 88
Neubert, J.: 531
Neuringer, C.: 43, 206, 655, 704, 904
Newland, T. E.: 472
Newton, G. M.: 345
Nickols, J.: 207, 259
Nickols, J. E.: 165
Nicolay, R. C.: 360
Nixon, W. L. B.: 560
Nordvik, H.: 269, 815
Norman, R. D.: 405
Norman, R. P.: 131
Nowakiwska, M.: 580
Nugent, G. R.: 533
Nunnally, J. C.: 298
Nyaard, M.: 269
Oberleder, M.: 473, 794
Obrist, W. D.: 244, 501, 758
Offer, D.: 672
Ogdon, D. P.: 474
Ogilvie, R. D.: 346
Okayama, M.: 650
Olin, T. D.: 29, 40
Olsen, I. A.: 299
O'Neil, H. F.: 899
O'Neil, W. M.: 166
Orgass, B.: 656
Orme, J. E.: 570
Overall, J. E.: 571
Pacht, A. R.: 876
Page, S.: 859, 916
Pagedar, R. M.: 261, 347
Paine, R. W.: 770
Palmore, E. B.: 657
Panton, J. H.: 93
Paredes, A.: 816
Parker, R. S.: 260

Parsons, O. A.: 94, 658, 678, 934
Pasricha, P.: 261, 347
Patrick, J. H.: 571
Patten, M. P.: 602
Pauker, J. D.: 208–9
Paul, M. E.: 475
Paulson, M. J.: 729–30
Payne, D.: 55
Payne, D. A.: 406
Peacock, E. P.: 56, 693
Peacock, W.: 620
Peak, D. T.: 572
Pearl, D.: 781
Pearson, P. R.: 695
Pearson, W.: 851
Peck, D. F.: 731
Pedrini, D. T.: 614, 937
Pelosi, J. W.: 573
Penzer, W. N.: 273
Perrett, L.: 871
Perry, J. D.: 128
Petersen, P. W.: 917
Peterson, W. M.: 876
Petrinovich, L. F.: 193
Pettit, D. E.: 348
Phillips, R. M.: 659
Pierce, R. C.: 210, 821
Pierce, R. M.: 574
Piercy, M.: 560
Piercy, M. M.: 782
Pihl, R. O.: 575, 926
Pishkin, V.: 42
Plant, W. T.: 52, 67, 314
Plante, M.: 222
Plotkin, R. R.: 505
Poeck, K.: 656
Poland, R. G.: 68
Pollack, M.: 576
Pollack, R. C.: 628
Pollin, W.: 915
Pool, D. A.: 732
Pool, K. B.: 23
Porrata, E.: 510
Porter, T. L.: 668
Powell, B. J.: 733
Powell, D. H.: 254
Prado, W. M.: 349
Pratt, R. T. C.: 560, 935
Prentice, N. M.: 211
Price, A. C.: 577
Primac, D. W.: 771
Prince, R. H.: 133
Pringle, R. K.: 918
Pugh, L. A.: 816
Puletti, F.: 867
Purdom, G. A.: 53
Quattlebaum, L. F.: 660
Quay, H. C.: 390, 417
Quereshi, M. Y.: 300, 578–9, 734–5
Quinlan, P.: 435
Rabin, A. I.: 154, 383, 896
Radcliffe, J. A.: 407
Raffel, S. C.: 845
Rafi, A. A.: 212
Ragland, R.: 816
Ragland, R. E.: 785
Ramalingaswami, P.: 350, 827
Ramer, J. C.: 356
Randall, R. V.: 833
Rapaport, G. M.: 167
Rapp, D.: 770
Ray, T. S.: 785
Reed, H. B. C.: 213
Reed, J. C.: 476
Reichman, W.: 884
Reimanis, G.: 853
Reitan, R. M.: 95, 213, 788–9
Reitz, W.: 365
Reitz, W. E.: 408, 428
Renear, K. R.: 661
Resch, J. A.: 401
Reznikoff, M.: 29
Rhone, D. E.: 268
Rhudick, P. J.: 477
Rice, W.: 278
Richard, W.: 483
Richman, J.: 478
Ricks, J. H.: 47
Riegel, K. F.: 168, 249
Riegel, R. M.: 168
Ries, H. A.: 330, 387
Riklan, M.: 792, 823

Risley, T. R.: 119
Ritter, W.: 615
Roberts, R. W.: 810
Robertson, J. P. S.: 11
Robertson, M. H.: 214
Robinson, N. M.: 112
Rochester, D. E.: 736
Rokosz, S.: 808
Rosen, M.: 580, 737
Rosenberg, E.: 714
Rosenquist, C. M.: 662
Rosenzweig, S. P.: 738
Rosicki, M.: 663
Ross, D.: 215
Ross, D. R.: 479, 860
Ross, R. T.: 480
Rosvold, H. E.: 771
Roth, R. J.: 667
Roth, R. M.: 216
Royer, F. L.: 919–20
Rubin, E. J.: 262
Rubin, J.: 127, 163
Rubino, C. A.: 739
Ruby, T. M.: 481
Rudolph, L.: 861
Rusalem, H.: 409
Russell, E. W.: 740, 921
Russell, J. A.: 607
Rustin, S. L.: 308
Saber-Motamedi, H.: 665
Safford, H. W.: 773
Sako, Y.: 450
Salisbury, L. H.: 546
Sand, P. L.: 932
San Diego, E. A.: 666, 741
Sannito, T. C.: 410, 757
Santos, B.: 233
Sarason, I. G.: 169
Saslow, G.: 296
Sattler, J. M.: 482, 667, 742–3, 885
Satz, P.: 170, 205, 483, 817
Saunders, D. R.: 69, 96–7, 122, 132, 455, 581
Savage, R. D.: 373–4, 437, 582–3
Saxe, E. L. G.: 411
Saxon, J. P.: 668
Schafer, R.: 98
Schalling, D.: 528
Schalon, C. L.: 412
Schiff, S.: 419
Schill, T.: 413, 520, 584–5
Schiro, F. M.: 467
Schnadt, F.: 349
Schnobrich, J. N.: 910
Schnore, M. M.: 840
Schofield, L. F.: 922
Schooler, C.: 669, 923
Schucman, H.: 586, 744, 755, 846
Schulberg, H. C.: 783
Schultz, W.: 397, 466, 722
Schwartz, M. L.: 283, 359, 414, 587
Schwartz, M. S.: 351
Schwartzman, A. E.: 133
Scott, J.: 399
Seashore, H. G.: 57
Segal, S. J.: 352
Segel, R. H.: 490
Seitz, F. C.: 924
Selecki, B. R.: 339, 462
Severinsen, K. N.: 588
Shaffer, J. W.: 171, 787
Shapiro, B.: 494
Shapiro, M. B.: 772
Shaw, D. J.: 301, 353, 400, 484–5
Shaw, E.: 901
Shaw, H. W.: 5
Shelly, C. H.: 893
Sherman, A. R.: 589
Shimkunas, A. M.: 745, 828, 925
Shinn, S. M.: 746
Shneidman, E. S.: 774
Shontz, F. C.: 33
Shore, C.: 926
Shore, H.: 926
Shotwell, A. M.: 59, 82, 118, 173
Siebert, L. A.: 217
Siegal, S. M.: 713

Siegel, L.: 597
Silverman, J.: 669, 923
Silverstein, A. B.: 81, 99, 119, 172–3, 218, 486–7, 590–2, 670–1, 747–9, 927
Sim, M.: 818
Simmons, H.: 70
Simpson, C. D.: 928
Simpson, R. L.: 593, 750
Sims, N. B.: 415
Sines, L. K.: 70
Singer, P. R.: 672
Singh, S. B.: 751
Singh, U. P.: 488, 673
Sinnett, K.: 100
Sinowitz, M.: 594
Sjorgren, D. D.: 489, 555
Small, J. G.: 174
Smart, R. G.: 354
Smith, A.: 201, 416
Smith, B. M.: 605
Smith, H.: 770
Smith, H. E.: 752
Smith, K.: 828
Smith, L. C.: 355
Smith, M.: 770
Smith, P. A.: 472
Smith, W. L.: 929
Smith, W. T.: 818
Smyth, V. O. G.: 782
Sokolov, S. L.: 272
Soltz, W. H.: 753
Song, A. Y.: 674
Song, R. H.: 674
Sorensen, M. A.: 595
Spaner, F. E.: 882
Spence, J. T.: 219, 304
Sperber, Z.: 775
Spielberger, C. D.: 633
Spieth, P. E.: 263
Spieth, W.: 142, 795
Sprague, R. L.: 417
Spreen, O.: 418, 806
Stabenau, J. R.: 915
Staker, J. E.: 223
Stallings, L.: 580
Stein, H.: 596
Stein, Z.: 101
Steinberg, M.: 490
Steindler, F. M.: 865–6
Steiner, F.: 264
Steinhelber, J. C.: 679
Steinman, W. M.: 491
Stern, M. R.: 182
Sternberg, D.: 419, 627
Sterne, D. M.: 30, 420, 675
Sternlicht, M.: 597
Stevens, J. R.: 174, 771
Stewart, H.: 492
Stewart, H. F.: 807
Stier, S. A.: 493
Stinson, P. J.: 71
Stone, L. A.: 356
Stotsky, B. A.: 134
Stratton, A. J.: 598
Straumanis, J. J.: 613
Streitfeld, J. W.: 599
Stricker, G.: 676
Sudimack, J. P.: 467
Suinn, R. M.: 494, 829
Susser, M.: 101
Sweet, R. D.: 909
Swenson, E. W.: 302
Swink, R.: 845
Sydiaha, D.: 495
Tangeman, P.: 676
Tarnopol, L.: 862
Taylor, C.: 324
Taylor, J. B.: 421, 796
Taylor, J. F.: 754
Tellegen, A.: 496
Temmer, H. W.: 357
Templer, D. I.: 497, 677
Thaler, V. H.: 498
Thetford, W. N.: 586, 744, 755, 846
Theye, F.: 482
Thomas, C. A.: 422
Thompson, C. W.: 144
Throp, J. L.: 767
Thune, J.: 423
Tine, S.: 423
Tolor, A.: 303
Toolson, R. N.: 499

Wechsler Adult Intelligence Scale

Toomey, T. C.: 930
Toppen, J. T.: 931
Trieschmann, R. B.: 932
Trudeau, P.: 714
Tsai, L. S.: 933
Tsushima, W.: 371
Tucker, L. R.: 402
Tuddenham, R. D.: exc, 6:B503
Tuma, A. H.: 343
Turner, E.: 818
Turner, J.: 88
Twain, D. C.: 220
Urmer, A. H.: 773
Vandenberg, S. G.: 851
Van De Riet, H.: 770
Van De Riet, V.: 770
Vassiliou, V.: 776, 892
Vaughan, H. G.: 146, 615
Veale, S. O.: 424
Vega, A.: 658, 678, 928, 934
Vellutino, F. R.: 425
Virmani, V.: 751
Vitale, J. H.: 679
Wachtel, P. L.: 358
Wagner, E. E.: 72, 102
Wagner, N. N.: 600, 863
Wagner, R. F.: 500
Wahler, H. J.: 175, 224
Waite, R. R.: 135
Walker, K. P.: 756
Walker, R. E.: 86, 157, 283, 304, 359-60, 378, 389-90, 623, 741, 757, 900
Walker, W.: 556
Wall, H. W.: 176
Wallace, W. L.: 1-2
Walsh, J.: 333
Wang, H. A.: 501
Wang, H. S.: 758
Wapner, S.: 280
Ward, W. D.: 326
Warren, S. A.: 136
Warrington, E. K.: 935
Wasden, R.: 682
Watkins, J. T.: 759
Watson, C. G.: 305, 361-3, 426, 601, 797
Watson, L. S.: 175
Watson, R. A.: 562
Webb, A. P.: 221, 265, 306
Wechsler, D.: 41, 225
Weinberg, H.: 847
Weiner, I. B.: 427
Weinstock, C.: 936
Weinstock, C. S.: 680
Weiss, A. D.: 248
Weiss, J.: 688
Weissman, S. L.: 799
Weleba, L.: 7
Wells, D. G.: 937

Weltman, R. E.: 106
Wendland, L. V.: 773
Werner, H.: 280
Werts, C. E.: 236
Wesman, A. G.: 3
Wessler, R. L.: 760
West, A. A.: 764
Wheeler, G. R.: 655
Wheeler, L.: 307, 788-9
White, J. G.: 364, 602
White, W. F.: 660
Whitman, J. R.: 864
Whitmyre, J. W.: 42, 624, 762
Wickstrom, M. L.: 681
Widlak, F. W.: 735
Wiener, G.: 31
Wiens, A. N.: 73, 103, 296
Wiggins, P. Y.: 914
Wilensky, H.: 131
Wilkie, F.: 938
Willcutt, H.: 201
Williams, J. R.: 502
Williams, R.: 492
Willner, A.: 365
Willner, A. E.: 428-9, 939
Wilson, J. D.: 603
Wiltberger, A. C.: 503
Wiltse, K. T.: 810
Winer, D.: 245
Winget, B. M.: 667, 742
Winter, G. D.: 504
Winter, K. S.: 562
Wirls, C. J.: 505
Wirth, G.: 506
Wiser, W. C.: 654
Witkin, H. A.: 430
Wittenborn, J. R.: 222
Woerner, M. G.: 576
Wolf, S.: 787
Wolff, B. B.: 104, 137
Wolff, R.: 682
Wolfson, W.: 105-6, 138, 507
Wolk, R. L.: 308
Wolter, D. J.: 214
Woods, J. E.: 790
Woodward, W. M.: 180
Woo-Sam, J.: 940
Worley, B.: 718
Wyke, M.: 784
Yamahiro, R. S.: 35
York, D. H.: 82
Young, J. R.: 761
Zeigler, M. L.: 176
Zerof, S. A.: 153
Ziegler, D. K.: 690-1
Zimet, C. N.: 508
Zimmerman, S. F.: 762
Zubek, J. P.: 237
Zung, W. W. K.: 604
Zwibelman, B.: 925
Zytowski, D. G.: 366

[530]

[Re Wechsler Adult Intelligence Scale] **Rhodes WAIS Scatter Profile.** Ages 16 and over; 1971; a form for profiling WAIS scores; Fen Rhodes; Educational and Industrial Testing Service. *

For additional information, see 7:430.

[531]

★[Re Wechsler Adult Intelligence Scale] **WAIS Test Profile.** Ages 16 and over; 1968–69; Consulting Psychologists Press, Inc. *

[532]

Wechsler-Bellevue Intelligence Scale. Ages 10 and over; 1939–47; W-B; 2 forms; David Wechsler; Psychological Corporation. (South African adaptation: National Institute for Personnel Research [South Africa].) *

a) FORM 1. 1939–47; out of print except for record form.

b) FORM 2. 1946–47; catalog states that "Form 2 is the retest instrument for the WAIS as well as for Form 1"; 14 scores: verbal (general information, general comprehension, digit span, arithmetic, similarities, vocabulary, total), performance (picture arrangement, picture completion, block design, object assembly, digit symbol, total), total; for a downward extension, see 533.

For additional information, see 6:539 (123 references); see also 5:415 (253 references); for reviews by Murray Aborn and William D. Altus, see 4:361 (250 references); for a review by Robert I. Watson, see 3:298 (119 references); for a review by F. L. Wells and excerpted reviews by Grace H. Kent and one other, see 2:1429 (2 references). For excerpts from related book reviews, see 6:B503 (3 excerpts), 5:B332 (2 excerpts), 4:362 (1 excerpt), 3:299 (7 excerpts), 3:300 (7 excerpts), 3:301 (5 excerpts), and 2:B1121 (10 excerpts).

REFERENCES THROUGH 1971

1–2. See 2:1429.
3–121. See 3:298.
122–371. See 4:361.
372–625. See 5:415.
626–748. See 6:539.
749. PETERSON, RACHEL. *The Use of the Wechsler-Bellevue Intelligence Scale With the Visually Handicapped.* Master's thesis, MacMurray College (Jacksonville, Ill.), 1944.
750. ALTUS, WILLIAM D. "Racial and Bi-Lingual Group Differences in Predictability and in Mean Aptitude Test Scores in an Army Special Training Center." *Psychol B* 42:310-20 My '45. * (PA 19:3049)
751. ALTUS, WILLIAM D., AND MAHLER, CLARENCE A. "The Significance of Verbal Aptitude in the Type of Occupation Pursued by Illiterates." *J Appl Psychol* 30:155-60 Ap '46. * (PA 20:3265)
752. WAGGONER, R. W., AND ZEIGLER, THORNTON WOODWARD. "Psychiatric Factors in Medical School Students Who Fail." *Am J Psychiatry* 103:369-76 N '46. * (PA 21:1671)
753. COLLINS, A. LOUISE, AND LENNOX, WILLIAM G. "The Intelligence of 300 Private Epileptic Patients." *Res Publ Assn Res Nerv & Mental Dis* 26:586-603 '47. *
754. SANDS, HARRY, AND PRICE, JERRY C. "A Pattern Analysis of the Wechsler-Bellevue Adult Intelligence Scale in Epilepsy." *Res Publ Assn Res Nerv & Mental Dis* 26:604-15 '47. *
755. ZIMMERMAN, FREDERIC T.; BURGEMEISTER, BESSIE B.; AND PUTNAM, TRACY J. "A Group Study of the Effect of Glutamic Acid Upon Mental Functioning in Children and Adolescents." *Psychosom Med* 9:175-83 My-Je '47. * (PA 21:3474)
756. BOWIE, CAROL C. "The Meaning of the Marriage Contract to 674 Negro Male Veterans." *Int J Sexol* 2:42-3 Ag '48. * (PA 26:6297)
757. ALTUS, WILLIAM D. "The Relationship of Intelligence and Years of Schooling When Literacy Is Held Constant." *J Consult Psychol* 13:375-6 O '49. * (PA 24:2757)
758. PETRIE, ASENATH. "Personality Changes After Pre-Frontol Leucotomy." *Brit J Med Psychol* 22:200-1 pts 3-4 '49. * (PA 25:2002)
759. PETRIE, ASENATH. "Preliminary Report of Changes After Prefrontal Leucotomy." *J Mental Sci* (England) 95:449-55 Ap '49. * (PA 24:278)
760. WHITEMAN, MORDECAI, AND WHITEMAN, DORIT B. "The Application of Cluster Analysis to the Wechsler-Bellevue Scale." *Delaware State Med J* 21:174-6 Ag '49. * (PA 25:483)
761. DIERS, WALLACE C., AND BROWN, CLINTON C. "Psychometric Patterns Associated With Multiple Sclerosis: 1, Wechsler-Bellevue Patterns." *Arch Neurol & Psychiatry* 63: 760-5 My '50. * (PA 25:4779)
762. GOLDSTEIN, M. J. "A Preliminary Evaluation of the Use of the Wechsler-Bellevue Adult Intelligence Scale in South Africa." *J Social Res* (South Africa) 1:220-6 D '50. * (PA 27:4256)
763. GURVITZ, MILTON S. *An Experimental Application of Wechsler-Bellevue Type Tests in an Attempt to Discriminate and Diagnose Psychopathic Personality Types Resident in a Penal Institution.* Doctor's thesis, New York University (New York, N.Y.), 1950. (DA 10:234)
764. KOGAN, WILLIAM SANFORD. "An Investigation Into the Relationship Between Psychometric Patterns and Psychiatric Diagnosis." *J General Psychol* 43:17-46 Jl '50. * (PA 25:6215)
765. RAPAPORT, DAVID. "Diagnostic Testing in Psychiatric Practice." *B N Y Acad Med* 26:115-25 F '50. * (PA 24:5250)
766. WEBER, GEORGE H. "Some Qualitative Aspects of an Exploratory Personality Study of 15 Juvenile Automobile Thieves." *Trans Kans Acad Sci* 53:548-56 '50. * (PA 25:7574)
767. CANTER, AARON HERMAN. "Direct and Indirect Measures of Psychological Deficit in Multiple Sclerosis: Part 1." *J General Psychol* 44:3-25 Ja '51. * (PA 25:7027)
768. CANTER, AARON HERMAN. "Direct and Indirect Measures of Psychological Deficit in Multiple Sclerosis: Part 2." *J General Psychol* 44:27-50 Ja '51. * (PA 25:7028)
769. CARSCALLEN, H. B.; BUCK, C. W.; AND HOBBS, G. E.

"Clinical and Psychological Investigation of Prefrontal Lobotomy in Chronic Schizophrenia." *Arch Neurol & Psychiatry* 65:206–20 F '51. * (*PA* 25:6996)

770. KANTOR, ROBERT E., AND BOYES, FREDERICK E. "Effects of a Supranormal Diet of Glutamic Acid on the Test Performance of Paretics." *Sci* 113:681–2 Je 15 '51. * (*PA* 26:1646)

771. KLINE, MILTON V. "Hypnosis and Age Progression: A Case Report." *J Genetic Psychol* 78:195–205 Je '51. * (*PA* 26:2613)

772. KRAL, V. A., AND DÖRKEN, HERBERT, JR. "Comparative Psychological Study of Hyperkinetic and Akinetic Extrapyramidal Disorders." *Arch Neurol & Psychiatry* 66:431–42 O '51. * (*PA* 26:2937)

773. LUCHINS, ABRAHAM S. "The Einstellung Test of Rigidity: Its Relation to Concreteness of Thinking." *J Consult Psychcl* 15:303–10 Ag '51. * (*PA* 26:6071)

774. MERCER, MARGARET, AND HECKER, ARTHUR O. "The Use of Tolserol (Myanesin) in Psychological Testing." *J Clin Psychol* 7:263–6 Jl '51. * (*PA* 26:926)

775. REED, HOMER R. "The Intelligence of Epileptics." *J Genetic Psychol* 78:145–52 Je '51. * (*PA* 26:2942)

776. STEISEL, IRA M. "The Relation Between Test and Retest Scores on the Wechsler–Bellevue Scale (Form I) for Selected College Students." *J Genetic Psychol* 79:155–62 D '51. * (*PA* 26:5633)

777. STEISEL, IRA M. "Retest Changes in Wechsler-Bellevue Scores as a Function of the Time Interval Between Examinations." *J Genetic Psychol* 79:199–203 D '51. * (*PA* 26:5634)

778. THOMPSON, CLARE WRIGHT. "Decline in Limit of Performance Among Adult Morons." *Am J Psychol* 64:203–15 Ap '51. * (*PA* 26:3489)

779. WILLENSON, DAVID. *Relation of Subtest Performance on the Wechsler-Bellevue Intelligence Scale to the Effects of Psychosurgery.* Master's thesis, Columbia University (New York, N.Y.), 1951.

780. BERGER, DAVID G. *The Emotional Reaction on Admission to a Tuberculosis Hospital.* Doctor's thesis, Michigan State College (East Lansing, Mich.), 1952. (*DA* 14:550)

781. CALDWELL, BETTYE MCDONALD, AND WATSON, ROBERT I. "An Evaluation of Psychologic Effects of Sex Hormone Administration in Aged Women: 1, Results of Therapy After Six Months." *J Gerontol* 7:228–44 Ap '52. * (*PA* 27:1874)

782. DILLER, LEONARD. "A Comparison of the Test Performances of Delinquent and Non-Delinquent Girls." *J Genetic Psychol* 81:167–83 D '52. * (*PA* 27:6658)

783. MENSH, IVAN N.; SCHWARTZ, HENRY G.; MATARAZZO, RUTH G.; AND MATARAZZO, JOSEPH D. "Psychological Functioning Following Cerebral Hemispherectomy in Man." *Arch Neurol & Psychiatry* 67:787–96 Je '52. * (*PA* 27:2167)

784. RAUB, EDWIN S.; MERCER, MARGARET; AND HECKER, ARTHUR O. "A Study of Psychotic Patients Assumed To Be Mentally Deficient on the Basis of School Progress and Social Adjustment." *Am J Mental Def* 57:82–8 O '52. * (*PA* 27:3704)

785. SUMMERSKILL, JOHN; SEEMAN, WILLIAM; AND MEALS, DONALD W. "An Evaluation of Postelectroshock Confusion With the Reiter Apparatus." *Am J Psychiatry* 108:835–8 My '52. * (*PA* 27:515)

786. DOUST, JOHN W. LOVETT; SCHNEIDER, ROBERT A.; TALLAND, GEORGE A.; WALSH, MICHAEL A.; AND BARKER, G. B. "Studies on the Physiology of Awareness: The Correlation Between Intelligence and Anoxemia in Senile Dementia." *J Nerv & Mental Dis* 117:383–98 My '53. * (*PA* 29:1258)

787. DOZIER, JUSTIN P., AND GETZ, S. B. "Problems Involved in the Placement of a Deaf Puerto Rican Child in an Educational Environment in the United States." *Am Ann Deaf* 98:260–7 Mr '53. * (*PA* 28:3253)

788. FLANARY, WOODROW. *A Study of the Possible Use of the Wechsler-Bellevue Scale in Diagnosis of Reading Difficulties of Adolescent Youth.* Doctor's thesis, University of Virginia (Charlottesville, Va.), 1953. (*DA* 14:1045)

789. MURPHY, MARY MARTHA. "Social Class Differences in Intellectual Characteristics of Alcoholics." *Q J Studies Alcohol* 14:192–6 Je '53. * (*PA* 28:2923)

790. STEVENSON, WILLIAM D. *Form II of the Wechsler-Bellevue Scale as a Predictor of Academic Success.* Master's thesis, University of Arizona (Tucson, Ariz.), 1953.

791. STRUCKETT, PAULINE B. A. "Effect of Prefrontal Lobotomy on Intellectual Functioning in Chronic Schizophrenia." *Arch Neurol & Psychiatry* 69:293–304 Mr '53. * (*PA* 28:1346)

792. VAN LENNEP, J. E. "Some Considerations Regarding the Clinical-Psychological Examination of Paranoid States." *Folia Psychiatrica Neurologica et Neurochirurgica Neerlandica* (Netherlands) 56:769–78 '53. *

793. WEXLER, MURRAY. *The Relationship Between Personality Organization and Electroshock: A Comparative Study of the Personality Characteristics of Psychotic Patients Who Improve or Do Not Improve From Electroshock Therapy.* Doctor's thesis, New York University (New York, N.Y.), 1953. (*DA* 14:2281)

794. CADMAN, WILLIAM H., MISBACH, LORENZ; AND BROWN, DONALD V. "An Assessment of Round-Table Psychotherapy." *Psychol Monogr* 68(13):1–48 '54. * (*PA* 29:7345)

795. CALDWELL, BETTYE MCDONALD, AND WATSON, ROBERT I. "An Evaluation of Sex Hormone Replacement in Aged Women." *J Genetic Psychol* 85:181–200 D '54. * (*PA* 29:7046)

796. CHANCE, JUNE; LOTSOF, ERWIN J.; PINE, IRVING; PATTERSON, RALPH M.; AND CRAIG, JAMES. "Effects of Cortisone on Psychiatric Patients." *Psychosom Med* 16:516–25 N–D '54. * (*PA* 29:6020)

797. CLARKE, A. D. B., AND CLARKE, A. M. "Cognitive Changes in the Feebleminded." *Brit J Psychol* 45:173–9 Ag '54. * (*PA* 29:4256)

798. COLGAN, CARROLL M. "Critical Flicker Frequence, Age, and Intelligence." *Am J Psychol* 67:711–3 D '54. * (*PA* 30:2126)

799. DUNHAM, RALPH E. "Factors Related to Recidivism in Adults." *J Social Psychol* 39:77–91 F '54. * (*PA* 28:8866)

800. GALLAHER, PHILLIP J. *The Influence of Sex Differences and Handedness on the Digit Symbol Subtest of the Wechsler-Bellevue.* Master's thesis, San Diego State College (San Diego, Calif.), 1954.

801. HEILBRUN, ALFRED B., JR. *The Localization of Cerebral Lesions by the Use of Psychological Tests.* Doctor's thesis, State University of Iowa (Iowa City, Iowa), 1954. (*DA* 14:1804)

802. HERNDON, C. NASH. "Intelligence in Family Groups in the Blue Ridge Mountains." *Eug Q* (England) 1:53–7 Mr '54. * (*PA* 28:8556)

803. HILER, EDWARD WESLEY. *An Investigation of Psychological Factors Associated With Premature Termination of Psychotherapy.* Doctor's thesis, University of Michigan (Ann Arbor, Mich.), 1954. (*DA* 14:712)

804. HOLZBERG, JULES D.; ALESSI, SALVATORE L.; AND TALKOFF, ALVIN. "Judgments of Premorbid Intellectual Functioning in Severely Impaired Psychiatric Patients." *J Clin Psychol* 10:219–24 Jl '54. * (*PA* 29:2793)

805. LEWINSKI, ROBERT J. "Variations in Mental Ability According to Month, Season, and Period of Birth." *J Genetic Psychol* 85:281–8 D '54. * (*PA* 29:6914)

806. MAILER, AUDREY B. "Effects on Mephenesin and Prenderol on Intellectual Functions of Mental Patients." *J Clin Psychol* 10:283–5 Jl '54. * (*PA* 29:2643)

807. REITAN, RALPH M. "Intelligence and Language Functions in Dysphasic Patients." *Dis Nerv System* 15:131–7 My '54. *

808. ROGERS, LAWRENCE S., AND TAYLOR, JAMES W. "Case Report on a Mental Hygiene Clinic Patient Tested Before and After Frontal Lobe Injury." *J Clin Psychol* 10:75–9 Ja '54. * (*PA* 28:7908)

809. RUBIN-RABSON, GRACE. "Correlates of the Non-Committal Test-Item Response." *J Clin Psychol* 10:93–5 Ja '54. * (*PA* 28:7546)

810. RUBIN-RABSON, GRACE. "Intelligence and Conservative-Liberal Attitudes." *J Psychol* 37:151–4 Ja '54. * (*PA* 28:7408)

811. UECKER, ALBERT E.; FRENCH, LYLE A.; AND JOHNSON, DAVID R. "Psychological Studies of Seven Epileptic Hemiparetics Before and After Hemispherectomy." *Arch Neurol & Psychiatry* 72:555–64 N '54. * (*PA* 29:6114)

812. BAYLEY, NANCY. "On the Growth of Intelligence." *Am Psychologist* 10:805–18 D '55. * (*PA* 30:6898)

813. GARDNER, M. J.; HAWKINS, H. M.; JUDAH, L. N.; AND MURPHREE, O. D. "Objective Measurement of Psychiatric Changes Produced by Chlorpromazine and Reserpine in Chronic Schizophrenia." *Psychiatric Res Rep* 1:77–83 Jl '55. * (*PA* 30:8411)

814. HOVEY, H. B., AND KOOL, KENNETH A. "Transient Disturbances of Thought Processes and Epilepsy." *Arch Neurol & Psychiatry* 74:287–91 S '55. * (*PA* 30:5102)

815. LEVINSON, BORIS M. "The Intelligence of Middle-Aged White Homeless Men in Receipt of Public Assistance." *Psychol Rep* 1:35–6 Mr '55. * (*PA* 30:2602)

816. LEVIT, HERBERT I. *A Study of the Effects of Electroconvulsive Therapy on Certain Psychological and Physiological Functions in Paranoid Schizophrenia.* Doctor's thesis, Temple University (Philadelphia, Pa.), 1955. (*DA* 15:1440)

817. MEYER, VICTOR, AND YATES, AUBREY J. "Intellectual Changes Following Temporal Lobectomy for Psychomotor Epilepsy: Preliminary Communication." *J Neurol Neurosurg & Psychiatry* (England) 18:44–52 F '55. * (*PA* 29:7775)

818. MORROW, ROBERT S., AND MARK, JOSEPH C. "The Correlation of Intelligence and Neurological Findings on Twenty-Two Patients Autopsied for Brain Damage." *J Consult Psychol* 19:283–9 Ag '55. * (*PA* 30:5112)

819. QUADFASEL, ANGELA FOLSOM, AND PRUYSER, PAUL W. "Cognitive Deficit in Patients With Psychomotor Epilepsy." *Epilepsia* (United States) 4:80–90 N '55. * (*PA* 30:8437)

820. TATERKA, JOHN H., AND KATZ, JOSEPH. "Study of Correlations Between Electroencephalographic and Psychological Patterns in Emotionally Disturbed Children." *Psychosom Med* 17:62–72 Ja–F '55. * (*PA* 29:7565)

821. BLANK, LEONARD, AND RAWN, MOSS L. "An Experimental Method to Measure Intellectual Functioning With Verbal and Motor Factors Minimal (1)." *J Psychol* 41:119–26 Ja '56. * (*PA* 30:8106)

822. HUNT, WILLIAM A., AND ARNHOFF, FRANKLYN N. "The Repeat Reliability of Clinical Judgments of Test Responses." *J Clin Psychol* 12:289–90 Jl '56. * (*PA* 31:6088)

823. PEYMAN, D. A. R. "An Investigation of the Effects of Group Psychotherapy on Chronic Schizophrenic Patients." *Group Psychother* 9:35–9 Ap '56. * (*PA* 33:4391)

824. Reitan, Ralph M. "Investigation of Relationships Between 'Psychometric' and 'Biological' Intelligence." *J Nerv & Mental Dis* 123:536–41 Je '56. * (*PA* 32:1345)
825. Seymour, John H. *Some Changes in Psychometric, Perceptual and Motor Performance as a Function of Sleep Deprivation.* Doctor's thesis, New York University (New York, N.Y.), 1956. (*DA* 16:2216)
826. Tallent, Norman. "Behavioral Control and Intellectual Achievement of Secondary School Boys." *J Ed Psychol* 47: 490–503 D '56. * (*PA* 32:4624)
827. West, Alice A., III. *A Comparison of Subtest Scatter on the Wechsler-Bellevue Form I and the WAIS.* Master's thesis, University of Arizona (Tucson, Ariz.), 1956.
828. Yates, Aubrey J. "The Rotation of Drawings by Brain-Damaged Patients." *J Abn & Social Psychol* 53:178–81 S '56. * (*PA* 32:3248)
829. Abrams, Julian. *Chlorpromazine in the Treatment of Chronic Schizophrenia: A Comparative Investigation of the Therapeutic Value of Chlorpromazine in Effecting Certain Psychological and Behavioral Changes in Chronic Schizophrenic Patients.* Doctor's thesis, New York University (New York, N.Y.), 1957. (*DA* 17:1589)
830. Olson, Ray Willard. *A Comparison of Mental Deterioration and Intellectual Functioning in Senescent and Brain-Damaged Subjects.* Doctor's thesis, University of Utah (Salt Lake City, Utah), 1957. (*DA* 17:1813)
831. Altrocchi, John, and Rosenberg, B. G. "A New Sorting Technique for Diagnosing Brain Damage." *J Clin Psychol* 14:36–40 Ja '58. * (*PA* 33:6202)
832. Blank, Leonard. "The Intellectual Functioning of Delinquents." *J Social Psychol* 47:9–14 F '58. * (*PA* 34:3237)
833. Bromley, Dennis B. "Some Effects of Age on Short Term Learning and Remembering." *J Gerontol* 13:398–406 O '58. * (*PA* 33:9786)
834. Eppley, Mary Vineita (Boots). *The Relationship of Personal Factors and Reading Performance to Academic Achievement of Selected Oregon State College Students.* Doctor's thesis, Oregon State University (Corvallis, Ore.), 1958. (*DA* 19:730)
835. Heilbrun, Alfred B., Jr. "Vocabulary Response as Related to Lateralization of Cerebral Lesion: An Investigation of 'Latent Aphasia.'" *J Abn & Social Psychol* 57:237–9 S '58. * (*PA* 33:10876)
836. Reitan, Ralph M. "Qualitative Versus Quantitative Mental Changes Following Brain Damage." *J Psychol* 46: 339–46 O '58. * (*PA* 34:3350)
837. Tanck, Roland H. "Psychologic Changes Induced by Reserpine Therapy on a Group of Severely Disturbed Psychotics." *J Nerv & Mental Dis* 126:353–9 Ap '58. * (*PA* 33:8581)
838. Fauls, John Thomas. *Superior Readers Versus Mediocre Readers: A Comparison of Ego Organizations.* Doctor's thesis, Florida State University (Tallahassee, Fla.), 1959. (*DA* 20:3376)
839. Foster, Arthur L. "A Note Concerning the Intelligence of Delinquents." *J Clin Psychol* 15:78–9 Ja '59. * (*PA* 34:3200)
840. Haber, Wilfred. *The Contribution of Selected Variables to Success or Failure in a Vocational Rehabilitation Evaluation.* Doctor's thesis, New York University (New York, N.Y.), 1959. (*DA* 20:4171)
841. Heilbrun, Alfred B., Jr. "Lateralization of Cerebral Lesion and Performance on Spatial-Temporal Tasks." *Arch Neurol* 1:282–7 S '59. * (*PA* 34:6461)
842. Levine, Murray; Spivack, George; Fuschillo, Jean; and Tavernier, Ann. "Intelligence, and Measures of Inhibition and Time Sense." *J Clin Psychol* 15:224–6 Ap '59. * (*PA* 35:4859)
843. Paolino, Albert F., and Friedman, Ira. "Intellectual Changes Following Frontal Lobe Procainization." *J Clin Psychol* 15:437–9 O '59. * (*PA* 36:1DC37P)
844. Riklan, Manuel; Weiner, Herman; and Diller, Leonard. "Somato-Psychologic Studies in Parkinson's Disease." *J Nerv & Mental Dis* 129:263–72 S '59. * (*PA* 34:6482)
845. Royo, D., and Martin, F. "Standardized Psychometric Tests Applied to the Analysis of the Effects of Anti-Convulsive Medication on the Intellectual Proficiency of Young Epileptics." *Epilepsia* (Netherlands) 1:189–207 D '59. *
846. Simmons, Audrey Ann. "Factors Related to Lipreading." *J Speech & Hearing Res* 2:340–52 D '59. * (*PA* 34:6510)
847. Smith, Aaron, and Kinder, Elaine F. "Changes in Psychological Test Performances of Brain-Operated Schizophrenics After 8 Years." *Sci* 129:149–50 Ja 16 '59. * (*PA* 34:4700)
848. Victor, Maurice; Talland, George A.; and Adams, Raymond D. "Psychological Studies of Korsakoff's Psychosis: 1, General Intellectual Functions." *J Nerv & Mental Dis* 128:528–37 Je '59. * (*PA* 34:4702)
849. Bortner, Morton, and Birch, Herbert G. "Perceptual and Perceptual-Motor Dissociation in Brain-Damaged Patients." *J Nerv & Mental Dis* 130:49–53 Ja '60. * (*PA* 35:6742)
850. Crokes, T. G., and Keller, Anna J. "Rorschach Card Rejection and IQ." *J Clin Psychol* 16:424–6 O '60. * (*PA* 37:3140)
851. Fitzhugh, Loren C.; Fitzhugh, Kathleen B.; and Reitan, Ralph M. "Adaptive Abilities and Intellectual Functioning in Hospitalized Alcoholics." *Q J Studies Alcohol* 21: 414–23 S '60. * (*PA* 35:6863)
852. Orchinik, C. W. "Some Psychological Aspects of Circumscribed Lesions of the Diencephalon." *Confinia Neurologica* (Switzerland) 20:292–310 '60. * (*PA* 35:2522)
853. O'Reilly, P. O., and Harrison, K. "The Gorham Proverbs Test." *Dis Nerv System* 21:382–5 Je '60. *
854. Phelps, Henry Beveridge. *Conceptual Ability and the Perception of Interaction in Movement by Elderly Persons.* Doctor's thesis, Columbia University (New York, N.Y.), 1960. (*DA* 21:2007)
855. Williams, Moyra. "The Effect of Past Experience on Mental Test Performance in the Elderly." *Brit J Med Psychol* 33:215–9 pt 2 '60. * (*PA* 36:4FI15W)
856. Brierley, Harry. "A Comparison of the Test Responses of Criminals and Mental Defectives." *Brit J Ed Psychol* 31: 212–4 Je '61. *
857. O'Brien, Cyril C. "Exceptional Tonal Memory and Intelligence." *Percept & Motor Skills* 12:282 Je '61. * (*PA* 36:2HD82O)
858. Tuck, James A. "Wechsler Verbal Scale Propensity in Psychopathic Patients." *Ont Psychol Assn Q* (Canada) 14:12–3 Mr '61. *
859. de Mille, Richard. "Intellect After Lobotomy in Schizophrenia: A Factor Analytic Study." *Psychol Monogr* 76(16):1–18 '62. * (*PA* 38:2784)
860. de Mille, Richard. "Intellectual Effects of Transorbital Versus Prefrontal Lobotomy in Schizophrenia: A Follow-Up Study." *J Clin Psychol* 18:61–2 Ja '62. * (*PA* 38:9042)
861. Doehring, Donald G., and Reitan, Ralph M. "Concept Attainment of Human Adults With Lateralized Cerebral Lesions." *Percept & Motor Skills* 14:27–33 F '62. * (*PA* 37:3531)
862. Fitzhugh, Loren C.; Fitzhugh, Kathleen B.; and Reitan, Ralph M. "Sensorimotor Deficits of Brain-Damaged SS in Relation to Intellectual Level." *Percept & Motor Skills* 15:603–8 D '62. * (*PA* 38:2983)
863. Laskowitz, David. "A Comparison of the Intellectual Performance of the Juvenile Addict With Standardization Norms." *J Correct Ed* 14:31–2 Ap '62. *
864. Peterson, Paul G. Chap. 4, "Intellectual Abilities and Social Attitudes," pp. 55–70, 219–25. In *Aging and Personality: A Study of Eighty-Seven Older Men.* By Suzanne Reichard and Others. New York: John Wiley & Sons, Inc., 1962. Pp. xv, 237. * (*PA* 37:2962)
865. Piercy, Malcolm M., and Smyth, V. O. G. "Right Hemisphere Dominance for Certain Non-Verbal Intellectual Skills." *Brain* (England) 85:775–90 D '62. *
866. Schein, Edgar H., and Singer, Margaret T. "Follow-Up Intelligence Test Data on Prisoners Repatriated From North Korea." *Psychol Rep* 11:193–4 Ag '62. * (*PA* 37:4877)
867. Sklar, Maurice. "Psychological Test Scores, Language Disturbances, and Autopsy Findings in Aphasia Patients." *Newsl Res Psychol* 4:65–79 Ag '62. *
868. Smith, Aaron. "Psychodiagnosis of Patients With Brain Tumors: The Validity of Hewson's Ratios in Neurological and Mental Hospital Populations." *J Nerv & Mental Dis* 135:513–33 D '62. *
869. Berger, Leslie; Bernstein, Alvin; Klein, Edward; Cohen, Jacob; and Lucas, Gerald. "Effects of Aging and Pathology on the Factorial Structure of Intelligence." *Newsl Res Psychol* 5:35–6 Ag '63. * (*PA* 38:8442)
870. Berkowitz, Bernard, and Green, Russel F. "Changes in Intellect With Age: 1, Longitudinal Study of Wechsler-Bellevue Scores." *Newsl Res Psychol* 5:2–4 My '63. *
871. Burke, Joan L.; Isaac, Donald M.; and Lafave, Hugh G. "Reappraisal of the Diagnosis of Mental Deficiency in Mental Hospitals." *J Clin Psychol* 19:359–61 Jl '63. * (*PA* 39:8369)
872. Green, Russel F., and Berkowitz, Bernard. "Changes in Intellect With Age: 2, Factorial Analysis of Wechsler-Bellevue Scores." *Newsl Res Psychol* 5:17–8 Ag '63. * (*PA* 38:8455)
8-3. Kramish, Arthur A. "Examining for Mental Deficiency at an Induction Center (W.W. II)." *Mental Retard* 1:95–6+ Ap '63. * (*PA* 38:8962)
874. Ostrow, Jeanne. *A Comparative Study of Certain Aspects of Intellectual Functioning in Achieving and Low-Achieving High School Students.* Doctor's thesis, University of Michigan (Ann Arbor, Mich.), 1963. (*DA* 25:617)
875. Sklar, Maurice. "Relation of Psychological and Language Test Scores and Autopsy Findings in Aphasia." *J Speech & Hearing Res* 6:84–90 Mr '63. * (*PA* 38:1201)
876. Berkowitz, Bernard. "Changes in Intellect With Age: 4, Changes in Achievement and Survival." *Newsl Res Psychol* 6:18–20 Ag '64. * (*PA* 39:4632)
877. Berkowitz, Bernard, and Green, Russel. "Changes in Intellect With Age: 3, The Relationship of Heterogeneous Brain Damage to Achievement in Older People." *Newsl Res Psychol* 6:36–7 F '64. * Also repeated 6:20–1 My '64. *
878. Broverman, Donald M. "Generality and Behavioral Correlates of Cognitive Styles." *J Consult Psychol* 28:487–500 D '64. * (*PA* 39:7680)
879. Fitzhugh, Kathleen B., and Fitzhugh, Loren C. "Patterns of Abilities in Relation to Abstraction Ability and

Age in Subjects With Longstanding Cerebral Dysfunction." *J Gerontol* 19:479-84 O '64. *

880. FITZHUGH, KATHLEEN B.; FITZHUGH, LOREN C.; AND REITAN, RALPH M. "Influence of Age Upon Measures of Problem Solving and Experiential Background in Subjects With Longstanding Cerebral Dysfunction." *J Gerontol* 19:132-4 Ap '64. * (PA 39:5632)

881. FITZHUGH, LOREN C., AND FITZHUGH, KATHLEEN B. "Relationships Between Wechsler-Bellevue Form I and WAIS Performances of Subjects With Longstanding Cerebral Dysfunction." *Percept & Motor Skills* 19:539-43 O '64. * (PA 39:8348)

882. GINETT, LYNDON E., AND MORAN, LOUIS J. "Stability of Vocabulary Performance by Schizophrenics." *J Consult Psychol* 28:178-9 Ap '64. * (PA 39:2675)

883. GREEN, RUSSEL F., AND BERKOWITZ, BERNARD. "Changes in Intellect With Age: 2, Factorial Analysis of Wechsler-Bellevue Scores." *J Genetic Psychol* 104:3-18 Mr '64. * (PA 39:5120)

884. HARROWER, MOLLY. *Appraising Personality: An Introduction to Projective Techniques, Revised Edition*, pp. 101-23. New York: Franklin Watts, Inc., 1964. Pp. xiv, 302. * (PA 39:7895)

885. JENKIN, NOEL; SPIVACK, GEORGE; LEVINE, MURRAY; AND SAVAGE, WILLIAM. "Wechsler Profiles and Academic Achievement in Emotionally Disturbed Boys." Abstract. *J Consult Psychol* 28:290 Je '64. * (PA 39:5926, title only)

886. JUEL-NIELSEN, NIELS. "Individual and Environment: A Psychiatric-Psychological Investigation of Monozygotic Twins Reared Apart." *Acta Psychiatrica Scandinavica Supplementum* (Denmark) 183:1-292 '64. *

887. KIRSCHNER, DAVID. "Differences in Gradients of Stimulus Generalization as a Function of 'Abstract' and 'Concrete' Attitude." *J Consult Psychol* 28:160-4 Ap '64. * (PA 39:2389)

888. KRAL, V. A.; GRAD, B.; CRAMER-AZIMA, F.; AND RUSSELL, L. "Biologic, Psychologic, and Sociologic Studies in Normal Aged Persons and Patients With Senile Psychosis." *J Am Geriatrics Soc* 12:21-37 Ja '64. *

889. LANSDELL, HERBERT, AND MIRSKY, ALLAN F. "Attention in Focal and Centrencephalic Epilepsy." *Exp Neurol* 9:463-9 Je '64. * (PA 39:5620)

890. LEVINSON, BORIS M. "The 'Beat' Phenomenon in Wechsler Tests." *J Clin Psychol* 20:118-20 Ja '64. * (PA 39:10133)

891. MATTHEWS, CHARLES G., AND FOLK, EARL D. "Finger Localization, Intelligence, and Arithmetic in Mentally Retarded Subjects." *Am J Mental Def* 69:107-13 Jl '64. * (PA 39:2525)

892. MATTHEWS, CHARLES G., AND MANNING, GEORGE C., JR. "Psychological Test Performances in Three Electroencephalographic Classifications of Mentally Retarded Subjects." *Am J Mental Def* 68:485-92 Ja '64. * (PA 39:2526)

893. MATTHEWS, CHARLES G., AND REITAN, RALPH M. "Correlations of Wechsler-Bellevue Rank Orders of Subtest Means in Lateralized and Non-lateralized Brain-damaged Groups." *Percept & Motor Skills* 19:391-9 O '64. * (PA 39:8354)

894. PRESTON, CAROLINE E. "Psychological Testing With Northwest Coast Alaskan Eskimos." *Genetic Psychol Monogr* 69:323-419 My '64. * (PA 39:4713)

895. REITAN, RALPH M. Chap. 14, "Psychological Deficits Resulting From Cerebral Lesions in Man," pp. 295-312. In *The Frontal Granular Cortex and Behavior: A Symposium*. Edited by J. M. Warren and K. Akert. New York: McGraw-Hill Co., 1964. Pp. x, 492. *

896. RIKLAN, MANUEL, AND LEVITA, ERIC. "Psychological Effects of Lateralized Basal Ganglia Lesions: A Factorial Study." *J Nerv & Mental Dis* 138:233-40 Mr '64. * (PA 39:4087)

897. SCHON, MARTHA. "Hypothyroidism: A Psychoendocrinological Evaluation." *Psychosomatics* 5:203-12 Jl-Ag '64. *

898. SEYBOLD, FRED R., AND PEDRINI, DUILIO T. "The Relation Between Wechsler-Bellevue Subtests and Academic Achievement Using Institutionalized Retardates." *Psychiatirc Q* 38:635-49 O '64. * (PA 39:12755)

899. SHIMOTA, HELEN E. "Reading Skills in Emotionally Disturbed, Institutionalized Adolescents." *J Ed Res* 58:106-11 N '64. *

900. SMITH, AARON. "Mental Deterioration in Chronic Schizophrenia." *J Nerv & Mental Dis* 139:479-87 N '64. *

901. SWENSON, EDWIN WAYNE. *A Comparison of the Wechsler-Bellevue, Form I, and the Wechsler Adult Intelligence Scale for a Population of Average Intelligence*. Master's thesis, University of Utah (Salt Lake City, Utah), 1964.

902. TAVRIS, EDWARD. "An Attempt to Distinguish Between 'Successful' and 'Unsuccessful' Separation Groups in a Hospital for Mentally Retarded Patients." *Training Sch B* 60:184-91 F '64. * (PA 39:5488)

903. BERKOWITZ, BERNARD. "Changes in Intellect With Age: 4, Changes in Achievement and Survival in Older People." *J Genetic Psychol* 107:3-14 S '65. *

904. BERKOWITZ, BERNARD, AND GREEN, RUSSEL F. "Changes in Intellect With Age: 5, Differential Changes as Functions of Time Interval and Original Score." *J Genetic Psychol* 107:179-92 D '65. * (PA 40:5284)

905. BURNETT, ALASTAIR. "Comparison of the PPVT, Wechsler-Bellevue, and Stanford-Binet on Educable Retardates." *Am J Mental Def* 69:712-5 Mr '65. * (PA 39:12715)

906. COHEN, EDWIN. "Examiner Differences With Individual Intelligence Tests." *Percept & Motor Skills* 20:1324 Je '65. * (PA 39:15316)

907. DE MILAN, JEAN. "Bilingualism and the Wechsler Vocabulary Scales." *J Clin Psychol* 21:298 Jl '65. * (PA 39:15346)

908. FITZHUGH, KATHLEEN B., AND FITZHUGH, LOREN C. "Effects of Early and Later Onset of Cerebral Dysfunction Upon Psychological Test Performance." *Percept & Motor Skills* 20:1099-100 Je '65. * (PA 39:15321)

909. FITZHUGH, LOREN C.; FITZHUGH, KATHLEEN B.; AND REITAN, RALPH M. "Adaptive Abilities and Intellectual Functioning of Hospitalized Alcoholics: Further Considerations." *Q J Studies Alcohol* 26:402-11 Je '65. * (PA 40:2900)

910. GREEN, RUSSEL F., AND BERKOWITZ, BERNARD. "Changes in Intellect With Age: 3, The Relationship of Heterogeneous Brain Damage to Achievement in Older People." *J Genetic Psychol* 106:349-59 Je '65. * (PA 39:14787)

911. HAMILTON, J., AND MCKENNA, B. "Sex Differences in the Wechsler Intelligence Tests." *Can Psychologist* 6a:353-7 O '65. *

912. HUNT, WILLIAM A.; SCHWARTZ, MELVIN L.; AND WALKER, RONALD E. "Judgmental Bias in the Differentiation of Process and Reactive Schizophrenia." *J Clin Psychol* 21:172 Ap '65. * (PA 39:12847)

913. KRAUS, J. "Discriminatory Power of the Wechsler-Bellevue Intelligence Scale Subtests Within the Range of Mental Defective Functioning." *Am J Mental Def* 69:571-4 Ja '65. * (PA 39:10129)

914. LANSDELL, H., AND URBACH, NELLY. "Sex Differences in Personality Measures Related to Size and Side of Temporal Lobe Ablations." Abstract. *Proc Ann Conv Am Psychol Assn* 73:113-4 '65. * (PA 39:14113)

915. POLLACK, MAX; KLEIN, DONALD F.; WILLNER, ARTHUR; BLUMBERG, ARNOLD; AND FINK, MAX. "Imipramine-Induced Behavioral Disorganization in Schizophrenic Patients: Physiological and Psychological Correlates." *Recent Adv Biol Psychiatry* 7:53-61 '65. *

916. PRADO, WILLIAM M., AND CANNON, ROBERT C. "Shipley-Hartford and Wechsler-Bellevue Intellectual Functioning: A Selection Screening Approach." *Psychol Rep* 16:853-6 Je '65. * (PA 39:15260)

917. PRADO, WILLIAM M., AND SCHNADT, FREDERICK. "Differences in WAIS—WB Functioning of Three Psychiatric Groups." *J Clin Psychol* 21:184-6 Ap '65. * (PA 39:12305)

918. REED, HOMER B. C., JR.; REITAN, RALPH M.; AND KLØVE, HALLGRIM. "Influence of Cerebral Lesions on Psychological Test Performances of Older Children." *J Consult Psychol* 29:247-51 Je '65. * (PA 39:12702)

919. RIKLAN, MANUEL; LEVITA, ERIC; AND COOPER, IRVING S. "Psychological Effects of Bilateral Subcortical Surgery for Parkinson's Disease." *J Nerv & Mental Dis* 141:403-9 O '65. * (PA 40:5052)

920. SPREEN, OTFRIED, AND BENTON, ARTHUR L. "Comparative Studies of Some Psychological Tests for Cerebral Damage." *J Nerv & Mental Dis* 140:323-33 My '65. * (PA 40:700)

921. BAILEY, MATTOX A. "Normalized Vocabulary Scores Equivalent to Wechsler-Bellevue Intelligence Quotient." *Newsl Res Psychol* 8:23-5 F '66. *

922. BATMAN, ROBERT H.; ALBEE, GEORGE W.; AND LANE, ELLEN A. "Intelligence Test Performance of Chronic and Recovered Schizophrenics." Abstract. *Proc 74th Ann Conv Am Psychol Assn* 1:173-4 '66. * (PA 41:6108)

923. BLACK, ALAN H., AND DAVIS, LEO J., JR. "The Relationship Between Intelligence and Sensorimotor Proficiency in Retardates." *Am J Mental Def* 71:55-9 Jl '66. * (PA 40:11420)

924. BLUNDELL, ELIZABETH. "Parietal Lobe Dysfunction in Subnormal Patients." *J Ment Def Res* (England) 10:141-52 Je '66. * (PA 41:1814)

925. BURNETT, ALASTAIR. "Borderline Intelligence: Some Problems and Implications." *Mental Retard* 4:3-8 Je '66. *

926. DAVIS, LEO J., JR., AND REITAN, RALPH M. "Methodological Note on the Relationship Between Ability to Copy a Simple Configuration and Wechsler Verbal and Performance IQs." *Percept & Motor Skills* 22:381-2 Ap '66. * (PA 40:8850)

927. DAVIS, LEO J., JR.; HAMLETT, IONA C.; AND REITAN, RALPH M. "Relationship of Conceptual Ability and Academic Achievement to Problem-Solving and Experiential Backgrounds of Retardates." *Percept & Motor Skills* 22:499-505 Ap '66. * (PA 40:9152)

928. GOLDBERG, LEWIS R., AND WERTS, CHARLES E. "The Reliability of Clinicians' Judgments: A Multitrait-Multimethod Approach." *J Consult Psychol* 30:199-206 Je '66. * (PA 40:8999)

929. GUERTIN, WILSON H.; LADD, CLAYTON E.; FRANK, GEORGE H.; RABIN, ALBERT I.; AND HIESTER, DOUGLAS S. "Research With the Wechsler Intelligence Scales for Adults: 1960-1965." *Psychol B* 66:385-409 N '66. * (PA 41:40)

930. HILER, E. WESLEY. "Prognostic Indicators for Children in a Psychiatric Hospital." *J Consult Psychol* 30:169-71 Ap '66. * (PA 40:6773)

931. HOROWITZ, FRANCES DEGEN. "The Relationship Between Wechsler Intelligence Quotients and Parsons Language-Sample Scores of Mentally Retarded Children." *J Genetic Psychol* 108:59–63 Mr '66. * (*PA* 40:10400)
932. HUNT, WILLIAM A.; QUAY, HERBERT C.; AND WALKER, RONALD E. "The Validity of Clinical Judgments of Asocial Tendency." *J Clin Psychol* 22:116–8 Ja '66. * (*PA* 40:4410)
933. MATTHEWS, CHARLES G.; FOLK, EARL D.; AND ZERFAS, PHILIP G. "Lateralized Finger Localization Deficits and Differential Wechsler-Bellevue Results in Retardates." *Am J Mental Def* 70:695–702 Mr '66. * (*PA* 40:6983)
934. PURDY, RUTH SANDERS. *The Developmental Process, the Inhibition Process, and the Production of Human Movement on the Kinget Drawing Completion Test.* Doctor's thesis, University of Oklahoma (Norman, Okla.), 1966. (*DA* 27:1680A)
935. REED, HOMER B. C., JR., AND FITZHUGH, KATHLEEN B. "Patterns of Deficits in Relation to Severity of Cerebral Dysfunction in Children and Adults." *J Consult Psychol* 30:98–102 Ap '66. * (*PA* 40:6963)
936. REITAN, RALPH M. "Diagnostic Inferences of Brain Lesions Based on Psychological Test Results." *Can Psychologist* 7a(4):368–83 '66. * (*PA* 41:2477)
937. RUBINO, CARL A. "Chronic Brain Damage and the Wechsler-Bellevue." *Ont Psychol Assn Q* (Canada) 19:64–9 su '66. *
938. SHANAN, JOEL; COHEN, MARGALITH; AND ADLER, EMIL. "Intellectual Functioning in Hemiplegic Patients After Cerebrovascular Accidents." *J Nerv & Mental Dis* 143:181–9 Ag '66. * (*PA* 41:4893)
939. SHARON (SINGER), SHLOMO. "Family Interaction With Schizophrenics and Their Siblings." *J Abn Psychol* 71:345–53 O '66. * (*PA* 40:13385)
940. SMITH, AARON. "Intellectual Functions in Patients With Lateralized Frontal Tumours." *J Neurol Neurosurg & Psychiatry* (England) 29:52–9 F '66. *
941. SMITH, AARON. "Verbal and Nonverbal Test Performances of Patients With 'Acute' Lateralized Brain Lesions (Tumors)." *J Nerv & Mental Dis* 141:517–23 N '66. * (*PA* 40:6964)
942. SPREEN, OTFRIED, AND ANDERSON, CHARLES W. G. "Sibling Relationship and Mental Deficiency Diagnosis as Reflected in Wechsler Test Patterns." *Am J Mental Def* 71:406–10 N '66. * (*PA* 41:1850)
943. DAVIS, LEO J., JR., AND REITAN, RALPH M. "Dysphasia and Constructional Dyspraxia Items, and Wechsler Verbal and Performance IQs in Retardates." *Am J Mental Def* 71:604–8 Ja '67. * (*PA* 41:6179)
944. HONZIK, MARJORIE P. "Prediction of Differential Abilities at Age 18 From the Early Family Environment." Abstract. *Proc 75th Ann Conv Am Psychol Assn* 2:151–2 '67. * (*PA* 41:13595)
945. KUNDU, RAMANATH. "A Comparison of Stanford-Binet and Wechsler-Bellevue Scales." *Indian Psychol R* 3:114–8 Ja '67. * (*PA* 41:8901)
946. REED, JAMES C., AND FITZHUGH, KATHLEEN B. "Factor Analysis of WB-1 and WAIS Scores of Patients With Chronic Cerebral Dysfunction." *Percept & Motor Skills* 25:517–21 O '67. * (*PA* 42:5964)
947. REED, JAMES C., AND REED, HOMER C., JR. "Concept Formation Ability and Non-Verbal Abstract Thinking Among Older Children With Chronic Cerebral Dysfunction." *J Spec Ed* 1:157–61 w '67. * (*PA* 41:12362)
948. ASKAR, A. M.; RAKHAWY, Y. T.; AND SHAALAN, M. "Conceptual Measurement as a Means of Assessing Therapeutic Changes in Schizophrenia." *J Egypt Med Assn* 51(1):1–17 '68. *
949. ASKAR, A. M.; SHAALAN, M.; AND RAKHAWY, Y. T. "The Stability of Vocabulary in Schizophrenics." *J Egypt Med Assn* 51(4):227–33 '68. *
950. BAYLEY, NANCY. "Behavioral Correlates of Mental Growth: Birth to Thirty-Six Years." *Am Psychologist* 23:1–17 Ja '68. * (*PA* 42:8705)
951. DRASH, PHILIP W.; GREENBERG, NANCY E.; AND MONEY, JOHN. Chap. 39, "Intelligence and Personality in Four Syndromes of Dwarfism," pp. 568–81. In *Human Growth, Body Composition, Cell Growth, Energy, and Intelligence.* Edited by Donald B. Cheek. Philadelphia, Pa.: Lea & Febiger, 1968. Pp. xxx, 781. *
952. KISSIN, BENJAMIN; ROSENBLATT, SIDNEY M.; AND MACHOVER, SOLOMON. "Prognostic Factors in Alcoholism." *Psychiatric Res Rep Am Psychiatric Assn* 24:22–43 Mr '68. * (*PA* 43:1099)
953. LANSDELL, HERBERT. "The Use of Factor Scores From the Wechsler-Bellevue Scale of Intelligence in Assessing Patients With Temporal Lobe Removals." *Cortex* (Italy) 4:257–68, S '68. * (*PA* 43:4325)
954. PEAK, DANIEL T. "Changes in Short-Term Memory in a Group of Aging Adults." *J Gerontol* 23:9–16 Ja '68. *
955. RAPAPORT, DAVID; GILL, MERTON M.; AND SCHAFER, ROY; EDITED BY ROBERT R. HOLT. Chap. 3, "The Wechsler-Bellevue Scale," pp. 71–160. In their *Diagnostic Psychological Testing, Revised Edition.* New York: International Universities Press, Inc., 1968. Pp. xi, 562. *
956. SCHUCMAN, HELEN, AND THETFORD, WILLIAM N. "Expressed Symptoms and Personality Traits in Conversion Hysteria." *Psychol Rep* 23:231–43 Ag '68. * (*PA* 43:7148)

957. WILLARD, LOUISA A. "A Comparison of Culture Fair Test Scores With Group and Individual Intelligence Test Scores of Disadvantaged Negro Children." *J Learn Dis* 1:584–9 O '68. * (*PA* 45:3968)
958. APPELBAUM, STEPHEN A.; COYNE, LOLAFAYE; AND SIEGAL, RICHARD S. "Change in IQ During and After Long-Term Psychotherapy." *J Proj Tech & Pers Assess* 33(3):290–7 Je '69. * (*PA* 43:14310)
959. ASKAR, A. M.; EL-GUNDY, T.; AND SHAHEEN, O. "Effect of Thioproperazine (Majeptil) on Some Wechsler Bellevue Subtests." *J Egypt Med Assn* 52(10):807–12 '69. *
960. BLUM, JUNE E. *Psychological Changes Between the 7th and 9th Decades of Life.* Doctor's thesis, St. John's University (Jamaica, N.Y.), 1969. (*DAI* 30:3854B)
961. BLUM, JUNE E., AND JARVIK, LISSY F. "Variations in Intellectual Decline as Indicators of Pathology: A Longitudinal Twin Study." Abstract. *Proc 77th Ann Conv Am Psychol Assn* 4(2):743–4 '69. * (*PA* 44:499)
962. HAMLIN, ROY M. "The Stability of Intellectual Function in Chronic Schizophrenia." *J Nerv & Mental Dis* 149(6):496–503 D '69. * (*PA* 44:8863)
963. JANSSEN, R. H. C.; WELMAN, A. J.; AND COLLA, P. "Wechsler-Bellevue Test and Brain-Damaged Patients." *Nederlands Tijdschrift voor de Psychologie en haar Grensgebieden* (Netherlands) 24(5):257–66 My–Je '69. * (*PA* 44:5517)
964. LANSDEL, H. "Verbal and Nonverbal Factors in Right-Hemisphere Speech: Relation to Early Neurological History." *J Comp & Physiol Psychol* 69(4):734–8 D '69. * (*PA* 44:2694)
965. SATTLER, JEROME M. "Effects of Cues and Examiner Influence on Two Wechsler Subtests." *J Consult & Clin Psychol* 33(6):716–21 D '69. * (*PA* 44:4171)
966. SERAFETINIDES, E. A. "Psychological Effects of Sudden Complete Hemianopia." *Percept & Motor Skills* 28(1):206 F '69. * (*PA* 43:11749)
967. WYSOCKI, BOLESLAW A., AND WYSOCKI, AYDIN C. "Cultural Differences as Reflected in Wechsler-Bellevue Intelligence (WBII) Test." *Psychol Rep* 25(1):95–101 Ag '69. * (*PA* 44:3623)
968. APPELBAUM, STEPHEN A.; COYNE, LOLAFAYE; AND SIEGAL, RICHARD S. "Routes to Change in IQ During and After Long Term Psychotherapy." *J Nerv & Mental Dis* 151(5):310–5 N '70. * (*PA* 45:10050)
969. BLUM, JUNE E.; JARVIK, LISSY F.; AND CLARK, EDWARD T. "Rate of Change on Selective Tests of Intelligence: A Twenty-Year Longitudinal Study." *J Gerontol* 25(3):171–6 Jl '70. *
970. BOLL, THOMAS J., AND REITAN, RALPH M. "Deficits in Adaptive Abilities in Parkinson's Disease." Abstract. *Proc 78th Ann Conv Am Psychol Assn* 5(2):549–50 '70. * (*PA* 44:19137)
971. CRANDALL, VIRGINIA C., AND BATTLE, ESTHER S. "The Antecedents and Adult Correlates of Academic and Intellectual Achievement." *Minn Symposia Child Psychol* 4:36–93 '70. *
972. DHAPOLA, T. S. "Some Observations on the Use of the W-B Intelligence Scale in India." *Indian Psychol R* 7(1):55–9 Jl '70. *
973. FRANK, GEORGE H. "The Measurement of Personality From the Wechsler Tests." *Prog Exp Pers Res* 5:169–94 '70. *
974. GREEN, RUSSEL F., AND REIMANIS, GUNARS. "The Age-Intelligence Relationship—Longitudinal Studies Can Mislead." *Indus Gerontol* 6:1–16 su '70. * (*PA* 45:7981)
975. HAMLIN, ROY M. "Intellectual Function 14 Years After Frontal Lobe Surgery." *Cortex* (Italy) 6(3):299–307 S '70. * (*PA* 46:1513)
976. HIRSCH, ERNEST A. *The Troubled Adolescent: As He Emerges From Psychological Tests.* New York: International Universities Press, Inc., 1970. Pp. xv, 645. *
977. LANSDELL, H. "Relation of Extent of Temporal Removals to Closure and Visuomotor Factors." *Percept & Motor Skills* 31(2):491–8 O '70. * (*PA* 45:6846)
978. MIGNONE, R. J.; DONNELLY, E. F.; AND SADOWSKY, DORIS. "Psychological and Neurological Comparisons of Psychomotor and Non-Psychomotor Epileptic Patients." *Epilepsia* (Netherlands) 11(4):345–59 D '70. *
979. OBUCHOWSKI, K.; ZIENKIEWICZ, H.; AND GRACZYKOWSKA-KOCZOROWSKA, A. "Psychological Studies in Pituitary Dwarfism." *Polish Med J* 9(5):1229–35 '70. * (*PA* 48:1554)
980. QUERESHI, M. Y., AND MILLER, JEFFREY M. "The Comparability of the WAIS, WISC, and WBII." *J Ed Meas* 7(2):105–11 su '70. * (*PA* 44:18711)
981. QUERESHI, M. Y., AND WIDLAK, FREDERIC W. "Perceptual Diversity as a Function of Intelligence." Abstract. *Proc 78th Ann Conv Am Psychol Assn* 5(1):379–80 '70. * (*PA* 44:18613)
982. REITAN, RALPH M. "Sensorimotor Functions, Intelligence and Cognition, and Emotional Status in Subjects With Cerebral Lesions." *Percept & Motor Skills* 31(1):275–84 Ag '70. * (*PA* 45:4773)
983. RUBINO, CARL A. "Psychometric Procedures and the Detection and Exploration of Behavioral Deficits Due to Cerebral Dysfunction in Man." *Can Psychologist* 11(3):239–60 Jl '70. * (*PA* 44:21180)
984. SCHUT, DIEN; BESIJN, J. W.; BOEKE, P. E.; AND ULEMAN, A. L. "Psychological Examination Before and After Stereotactic Operations in Parkinson Patients." *Psychiatria*

Neurologia Neurochirurgia (Netherlands) 73(5):375–86 S–O '70. * (*PA* 47:11421)

985. Woo-Sam, James. "Note on Wechsler Comprehension and Picture Arrangement Scores of Head-Injured Epileptics." *Percept & Motor Skills* 31(3):818 D '70. * (*PA* 45:10513)

986. Landsell, H. "A General Intellectual Factor Affected by Temporal Lobe Dysfunction." *J Clin Psychol* 27(2):182–4 Ap '71. * (*PA* 46:7303)

987. Reddy, Michael Joseph. *Interaction Testing in the Measurement Marital Disturbance.* Doctor's thesis, Ohio State University (Columbus, Ohio), 1971. (*DAI* 32:6659B)

988. Reitan, Ralph M., and Boll, Thomas J. "Intellectual and Cognitive Functions in Parkinson's Disease." *J Consult & Clin Psychol* 37(3):364–9 D '71. * (*PA* 47:9471)

989. Reitan, Ralph M., and Fitzhugh, Kathleen B. "Behavioral Deficits in Groups With Cerebral Vascular Lesions." *J Consult & Clin Psychol* 37(2):215–23 O '71. * (*PA* 47:9486)

990. Reitan, Ralph M.; Reed, James C.; and Dyken, Mark L. "Cognitive, Psychomotor, and Motor Correlates of Multiple Sclerosis." *J Nerv & Mental Dis* 153(3):218–24 S '71. * (*PA* 47:11420)

991. Woo-Sam, James; Zimmerman, Irla Lee; and Rogal, Richard. "Location of Injury and Wechsler Indices of Mental Deterioration." *Percept & Motor Skills* 32(2):407–11 Ap '71. * (*PA* 46:11364)

CUMULATIVE NAME INDEX

Aborn, M.: 269–70; *rev*, 4:361
Abrams, J.: 829
Abramson, H. A.: 548
Adams, N. A.: 408
Adams, R. D.: 848
Adcock, C. J.: 501
Adler, E.: 938
Aita, J. A.: 107
Albee, G. W.: 922
Alderdice, E. T.: 406
Alessi, S. L.: 804
Alexander, F. S.: 108
Alimena, B.: 333
Allen, L.: 166
Allen, R. M.: 109, 146–7, 189–91, 502, 564
Altrocchi, J.: 831
Altus, W. D.: 59, 80, 148, 192–4, 391, 750–1, 757; *rev*, 4:361; *exc*, 6:B503
Anastasi, A.: *exc*, 3:300
Andersen, A. L.: 258, 334
Anderson, C. W. G.: 942
Anderson, E. E.: 20
Anderson, S. F.: 20
Angers, W. P.: 528, 613, 731
Appelbaum, S. A.: 958, 968
Arenberg, D.: 633
Armitage, S. G.: 81, 107, 614
Armstrong, C. P.: 32
Armstrong, D. M.: 646
Armstrong, R. G.: 458
Arnhoff, F. N.: 822
Arnold, G. F.: 124
Askar, A. M.: 948–9, 959
Atkey, R. R.: 195
Atwell, C. R.: *exc*, 2:B1121
Azima, F. C.: 667
Bacon, C. S.: 503
Baggett, M. P.: 111
Bailey, M. A.: 921
Baldwin, A. L.: *exc*, 3:299
Balinsky, B.: 1, 3, 6, 18
Balthazar, E. E.: 687–8, 732–3
Barker, G. B.: 786
Barnett, I.: 259
Barrett, A. M.: 697
Barry, J. R.: 565
Batman, R. H.: 922
Battle, E. S.: 971
Bay, M. S.: 149
Bayley, N.: 196, 593, 812, 950
Beach, H. D.: 735
Becker, G. J.: 150
Beech, H. R.: 730
Bell, A.: 668
Bell, J. E.: 197
Belmont, L.: 434
Bensberg, G. J.: 260, 496
Benson, S.: 529
Benton, A. L.: 7–8, 920
Berger, D. G.: 780
Berger, L.: 869
Berk, R. L.: 407
Berkowitz, B.: 459, 734, 870, 872, 876–7, 883, 903–4, 910
Berks, M. D.: 149
Berman, I. R.: 181
Bernstein, A.: 869
Bernstein, L.: 620
Bernstein, R.: 460
Besijn, J. W.: 984
Biesheuvel, S.: 461, 647
Bilodeau, I. M.: 349
Binks, V. M.: 408
Birch, H. G.: 849
Birren, J. E.: 277–80, 335–6, 379, 392, 409
Black, A. H.: 923
Blackburn, A. R.: 303
Blake, R. R.: 151, 443–4
Blank, L.: 821, 832
Blatt, S. J.: 648
Blauvelt, J.: 8
Blum, J. E.: 960–1, 969
Blumberg, A.: 915
Blumberg, E.: 348
Blundell, E.: 924
Boehm, A. E.: 110
Boeke, P. E.: 984
Boll, T. J.: 970, 988
Bonier, R. J.: 689
Bortner, M.: 849
Bortner, R. W.: 737
Botwinick, J.: 336, 392, 462
Bowie, C. C.: 756
Bowman, K. M.: 163
Boyes, F. E.: 770
Brackbill, G. A.: 592
Bradway, K.: 529
Brecher, S.: 82
Breiger, B.: 566
Bressler, M. B.: 530
Bridges, C.: 649
Brierley, H.: 856
Brierley, J.: 730
Brody, A. B.: 261
Bromley, D. B.: 833
Brooks, L. E.: 126
Broverman, D. M.: 878
Brower, D.: 152
Brown, C. C.: 761
Brown, D. V.: 794
Brown, F.: 669
Brown, J. F.: 9
Brown, M. H.: 531–2, 594–5, 631
Brown, M. N.: 198
Brown, R. R.: 21
Bryan, G. E.: 531–3, 594–5, 631
Buck, C. W.: 769
Burgemeister, B. B.: 755
Burik, T. E.: 199, 262
Burke, J. L.: 871
Burnett, A.: 735, 905, 925
Burnham, C. A.: 200
Burns, W. H.: 708
Burton, A.: 201
Butler, A.: 504
Butler, A. J.: 406
Cadman, W. H.: 794
Calden, G.: 525
Caldwell, B. M.: 781, 795

Caldwell, M. B.: 567
Campbell, E. F.: 410
Campbell, J. C.: 650
Cannicott, R. G.: 349
Cannon, R. C.: 916
Canter, A. H.: 202, 270, 767–8
Caputo, D. V.: 736
Carment, D. W.: 505
Carp, A.: 153, 263
Carscallen, H. B.: 769
Carse, D.: 382
Cassel, R. H.: 708
Catterall, C. D.: 203
Chambers, W. R.: 618
Chance, J.: 796
Charles, D. C.: 557
Chesrow, E. J.: 204
Clark, E. T.: 969
Clark, J. H.: 154, 193–4, 205–6, 264–5
Clarke, A. D. B.: 797
Clarke, A. M.: 797
Clarke, F. R.: 383
Clarke, H. J.: 83
Clarke, W. V.: *exc*, 2:B1121
Cleveland, S. E.: 47
Cofer, C. N.: 132
Cohen, B.: 60, 127, 133
Cohen, D.: 134
Cohen, E.: 384, 906
Cohen, J.: 266, 337, 411–2, 534, 869
Cohen, M.: 938
Cole, D.: 418
Cole, E. M.: 111
Colgan, C. M.: 798
Colla, P.: 963
Collins, A. L.: 338, 753
Collins, J. J.: 527
Cook, M.: 506
Cook, R. A.: 690
Coon, G. P.: 86–8
Cooper, I. S.: 684, 919
Coppinger, N. W.: 737
Copple, G. E.: 155
Corotto, L. V.: 691
Corrie, C. C.: 507, 538
Corsini, R. J.: 413–4, 460, 463
Corter, H. M.: 415
Cortes, C. F.: 416
Cotzin, M.: 207, 267
Cowley, J. J.: 461
Coyne, L.: 958, 968
Coyne, W. J.: 799
Craddick, R. A.: 692
Craig, J.: 796
Cramer-Azima, F.: 888
Crandall, V. C.: 971
Crokes, T. G.: 850
Cronbach, L. J.: 208
Cronholm, B.: 738
Crookes, T. G.: 693
Crutchlow, E.: 108
Cummings, S. B.: 84, 117, 257
Cummins, J. F.: 695
Cureton, E. E.: *exc*, 3:299
Cutts, R. A.: 61, 77, 112
Daley, M. F.: 659
Dana, R. H.: 596
Darbes, A.: 694
Davidson, J. L.: 582
Davidson, K. S.: 268
Davis, J. C.: 96, 567, 597
Davis, L. J.: 923, 926–7, 943
Davis, P. C.: 417, 568
Deane, M. A.: 297
De Haan, H.: 368
DeLange, W. H.: 700
Delattre, L.: 418
Della Piana, G. M.: 540
Delli Colli, P.: 598
Demarest, R.: 128
DeMartino, M. H. A.: 464, 508
De Milan, J.: 907
de Mille, R.: 859–60
Denny, J. P.: 744
Denton, L. R.: 627
Derner, G. F.: 269–70
Desai, M. M.: 535
DeStephens, W. P.: 465
Devonshire, M. E.: 419
Dhapola, T. S.: 972
Diamond, S.: 113
Dibner, A. S.: 695

Diers, W. C.: 761
Diller, J. C.: 536
Diller, L.: 684, 782, 844
Doehring, D. G.: 696, 861
Donnelly, E. F.: 978
Doppelt, J.: 209
Dorcus, R. M.: 399
Dore, J. J.: 466
Dörken, H.: 467, 772
Doust, J. W. L.: 786
Dozier, J. P.: 787
Drash, P. W.: 951
Dubin, S. S.: 9, 156
DuBois, P. H.: 433
Duncan, D. R.: 697
Duncan, J. O.: 468
Dunham, R. E.: 799
Durea, M. A.: 157
Dyken, M. L.: 990
Dysinger, D. W.: 47
Edmonston, W. E.: 736
Edrington, T. C.: 271
Eglash, A.: 272
Ehrmann, J. C.: 559
Eisen, V. W.: 526
El-Gundy, T.: 959
Ellis, A.: 158
Engen, T.: 420
Eppley, M. V. (B.): 834
Erwin, E. F.: 273
Escalona, S. K.: 640
Estes, S. G.: 22, 85
Everett, E. G.: 569
Everson, R. R.: 393
Falek, A.: 715, 717
Farber, I. E.: 602
Fassett, K. K.: 413–4, 463
Fauls, J. T.: 838
Fellers, G. L.: 469
Ferguson, C.: 20
Fey, W. F.: 162
Ficca, S. C.: 274
Field, J. G.: 670
Fink, M.: 915
Finkelstein, M.: 421
Fishbein, S.: 372
Fisher, G. C.: 210, 615
Fisher, G. M.: 671, 698, 710, 748
Fisher, K. A.: 211
Fisher, S.: 275
Fitzhugh, K. B.: 699, 711–2, 719, 739, 851, 862, 879–81, 908–9, 935, 946, 989
Fitzhugh, L. C.: 699, 711–2, 739, 851, 862, 8-9–81, 908–9
Flanary, W.: 788
Flynn, J. J.: 509
Fogel, J.: 507, 538
Folk, E. D.: 891, 933
Forster, C. R.: 537
Fortson, C. B.: 570
Foster, A.: 135, 510
Foster, A. L.: 839
Foster, C.: 394
Foster, C. G.: 136
Foster, D. V.: 408
Fox, C.: 137, 277–80, 379
Frandsen, A. N.: 276
Frank, G. H.: 507, 538, 571, 575, 713, 929, 973
Franklin, J. C.: 62
Freeburne, C. M.: 740
Freeman, A. V.: 159–60
Freeman, F. S.: 281
French, G. E.: 167, 225
French, L. A.: 811
Friedman, I.: 843
Fry, L. M.: 572
Frye, U. C.: 573
Fulkerson, S. C.: 565
Fuschillo, J.: 842
Gainer, W. L.: 422
Gallagher, J. J.: 207, 267
Gallaher, P. J.: 800
Gardner, M. J.: 813
Garfield, S. L.: 114, 138, 161–2, 212, 672
Gaskill, P.: 599
Gaston, C. O.: 637, 700
Geertsma, R.: 555
Geil, G. A.: 63
Gerboth, R.: 282, 421
Germain, G. L.: 423

Gerstein, A. I.: 619
Gerstein, R. A.: 213
Getz, S. B.: 787
Giannell, A. S.: 740
Gibby, R. G.: 214, 268
Gibson, F. J.: 470
Giedt, H. M.: 424
Gilgash, C. A.: 600, 701
Gilhooly, F. M.: 215, 283-5
Gill, M.: 34, 54, 75
Gill, M. M.: 955
Gilliland, A. R.: 4, 33
Ginett, L. E.: 882
Glik, E. E.: 339
Glueck, E.: 286
Glueck, S.: 286
Goetzinger, C. P.: 601
Goldberg, L. R.: 928
Goldfarb, W.: 10, 48, 64
Goldman, G. D.: 287
Goldman, M.: 33, 540
Goldman, R.: 86-8
Goldstein, K.: 87
Goldstein, M. J.: 375, 762
Goldstein, N. N.: 11
Goldwasser, M. L.: 310
Goodstein, L. D.: 602
Goolishian, H. A.: 510, 574
Gorham, D. R.: 678
Gothberg, L. C.: 216
Goyne, J. B.: 635
Graczykowska-Koczorowska, A.: 979
Grad, B.: 888
Graham, E. E.: 425
Grajales, M. C.: 373
Grassi, J. R.: 288
Gray, C. V.: 217
Gray, J.: 20
Green, R.: 877
Green, R. F.: 734, 870, 872, 883, 904, 910, 974
Greenberg, N. E.: 951
Greenblatt, M.: 86-8
Greenbloom, G. C.: 289, 467
Greenwood, E. D.: 49
Griffith, R. M.: 616
Griffiths, J. S.: 426
Groves, M. H.: 340
Guertin, W. H.: 185, 357, 511, 575, 651, 713, 724, 763, 929
Gurvitz, M. S.: 65, 218, 290, 341-2, 427-8, 512, 763
Gutman, B.: 291
Guy, W.: 366
Haber, W.: 840
Hackman, R. B.: 164
Haggerty, A. D.: 471
Hall, J. C.: 603
Hall, K. R. L.: 429
Hallberg, M. C.: 539
Halperin, S. L.: 219
Halpern, F.: 23, 129
Halstead, H.: 66
Hamilton, J.: 911
Hamister, R. C.: 220
Hamlett, I. C.: 927
Hamlin, R. M.: 962, 975
Haner, C.: 253
Haner, C. F.: 376
Hanley, C.: 689
Hansen, F. W.: 116
Hanson, H. B.: 181
Harper, A. E.: 292-4
Harris, R.: 629
Harris, R. E.: 163
Harrison, K.: 681, 853
Harrower, M.: 430, 884
Harrower, M. R.: 343
Hauser, R. J.: 714
Havighurst, R. J.: 125
Haward, L. R. C.: 638
Hawkins, H. M.: 813
Hayden, S. J.: 344
Hayes, S. P.: 24, 295
Hays, W.: 296, 345
Heathers, L. B.: 439-40, 486
Hecht, I.: 221
Hecker, A. O.: 774, 784
Heilbrun, A. B.: 639, 673, 801, 835, 841
Heister, D. S.: 929
Helmick, J. S.: 431
Henning, R. L.: 472

Herman, K.: 666
Herndon, C. N.: 802
Herring, F. H.: 432
Herrmann, M.: 164
Hewson, L. R.: 222
Heyer, A. W.: 223
Hilden, A. H.: 224, 433
Hiler, E. W.: 617, 702, 803, 930
Hirsch, E. A.: 976
Hirt, M. L.: 690
Hittinger, J.: 20
Hobbs, G. E.: 769
Hoch, P. M.: 428
Hodgson, G. L.: 165, 395
Hoffman, M.: 108
Hollingsworth, B. H.: 513
Holt, R. R.: 640, 955
Holtzman, W. H.: 678
Holzberg, J. D.: 297, 371, 434, 804
Holzman, P. S.: *exc*, 6:B503
Honzik, M. P.: 166, 944
Hopkins, B.: 473, 490
Horlick, R. S.: 385
Horowitz, F. D.: 931
Horwitz, M.: 540
Hover, G. L.: 346
Hovey, H. B.: 814
Howard, W.: 641
Howell, I. L.: 7
Howell, R. J.: 380, 541-2
Hunt, W. A.: 167-8, 225, 822, 912, 932
Hunt, W. L.: 226
Inglis, J.: 576
Ipson, W. M.: 543
Isaac, D. M.: 871
Iscoe, I.: 516, 549
Israel, H.: 1, 18
Jackson, C. V.: 544
Jacobs, G. F.: 461
Janke, L. L.: 125
Janssen, R. H. C.: 963
Jarvik, L. F.: 715-7, 961, 969
Jastak, J.: 227, 298, 474, 612
Jenkin, N.: 885
Johnson, A. P.: 115, 708
Johnson, D. R.: 811
Johnson, L. C.: 228
Johnson, T. F.: 229
Judah, L. N.: 813
Judson, A. J.: 674
Juel-Nielsen, N.: 886
Jui, A. H.: 381
Kahn, J.: 230
Kahn, M. W.: 652
Kaldegg, A.: 299, 577
Kalinkowitz, B. N.: 169
Kallmann, F. J.: 715, 717
Kamman, G. R.: 545
Kandel, A.: 723
Kantor, R. E.: 245, 770
Karle, H.: 653
Karson, S.: 604
Kass, W.: 231
Katz, J.: 820
Kaufman, M. R.: 548
Keehn, J. D.: 605
Keller, A. J.: 850
Kelley, K.: 514
Kelly, F. J.: 745
Kendig, I.: *exc*, 2:B1121
Kent, G. H.: *exc*, 2:1429
Kinder, E. F.: 847
King, D. M.: 396
King, G. F.: 559
Kingsley, L.: 675
Kirschner, D.: 887
Kissin, B.: 952
Kitzinger, H.: 347-8, 483
Klebanoff, S. G.: 167-8
Klein, D. F.: 915
Klein, E.: 869
Klein, G. S.: 89, 170
Kline, M. V.: 771
Klonoff, H.: 397
Kløve, H.: 636, 654, 696, 718-9, 741, 918
Klugman, S. F.: 171
Knight, R. P.: 34
Knopf, I. J.: 475, 515
Knott, J. R.: 349
Knowles, J. B.: 655

Kogan, K. L.: 90, 240
Kogan, W. S.: 232, 300, 764
Kool, K. A.: 814
Korner, A. F.: 358
Kral, V. A.: 667, 772, 888
Kram, C.: 545
Kramer, E. J. J.: 547
Kramish, A. A.: 873
Krato, J. C.: 191
Kraus, J.: 343, 913
Kriegman, G.: 116
Kubala, A. L.: 565
Kundu, R.: 945
Kutash, S. B.: 67, 435
L'Abate, L.: 736
Ladd, A. H.: 301
Ladd, C. E.: 713, 929
Lafave, H. G.: 871
Landisberg, S.: 139
Lane, E. A.: 922
Lane, M. O'K.: 112
Langston, R. D.: 580
Lansdell, H.: 889, 914, 953, 964, 977, 986
Lansing, K. M.: 676
Laskowitz, D.: 720, 863
LaTourelle, C. W.: 91
Lawrence, R. M.: 302
Lawton, G.: *exc*, 2:B1121
Lee, F. J.: 540
Leiding, W. C.: 642
Leipold, W. D.: 705
Lennox, W. G.: 753
Levi, J.: 45, 68, 122
Levin, J.: 324
Levine, A.: 548
Levine, B.: 516, 549
Levine, B. D.: 476
Levine, J.: 303
Levine, L. S.: 172-3, 233, 386, 398
Levine, M.: 643, 842, 885
Levinson, B. M.: 815, 890
Levit, H. I.: 816
Levita, E.: 896, 919
Levitt, E. A.: 322
Levreault, L. P.: 517
Lewinski, R. J.: 35-6, 50, 69-70, 140, 174, 805
Liddicoat, R.: 647, 703, 721
Light, M. L.: 618
Lindzey, G. E.: 130
Lipton, M. B.: 350
Long, J. A.: 656
Lorge, I.: 715; *exc*, 3:300
Lotesta, P.: 350
Lotsof, E. J.: 796
Lott, W. J.: 550
Love, D. B.: 551
Love, L. R.: 477
Lozoff, M.: 34
Lubin, A.: 662
Luborsky, L.: 640
Lucas, G.: 869
Luchins, A. S.: 92, 478, 773
Luchins, E. H.: 478
McCarty, B. S.: 151
McCord, C. P.: *exc*, 3:299
McCreary, J. R.: 501
McCullough, M. W.: 304
McFarland, R. L.: 722
Macfarlane, J. W.: 166
McFie, J.: 626, 677, 704
McGee, E.: 523
Machover, S.: 37-8, 683, 952
McKeever, W. F.: 619
McKenna, B.: 911
McKenzie, R. E.: 351
McKinstry, E.: 20
McLean, O. S.: 479, 518
MacMullen, M. R.: 111
McNeal, B. F.: 305
McNeil, E. B.: 268
McNemar, Q.: 306; *exc*, 3:301
MacPhee, H. M.: 84, 117, 257
Madonick, M. J.: 118
Magaret, A.: 25, 39, 141, 175; *exc*, 3:301
Magaret, G. A.: 12
Mahler, C. A.: 751
Mahrer, A. R.: 620, 632, 665
Mailer, A. B.: 806
Mainord, W. A.: 480
Maizlish, I. L.: 26

Maksimczyk, W. J.: 481
Malos, H. B.: 436
Mandler, G.: 352, 437
Manne, S. H.: 723
Manning, G. C.: 892
Mariani, R. R.: 578
Mark, J. C.: 818
Markham, S.: 548
Markin, K. E.: 362
Marks, M. R.: 482
Markwell, E. D.: 483
Marshak, M. D.: 630
Martin, F.: 845
Martin, H.: 657
Martin, S. B.: 519
Masling, J.: 658
Matarazzo, J. D.: 783
Matarazzo, R. G.: 552-3, 783
Mattar, J. C.: 484
Matthews, C. G.: 724, 742, 891-3, 933
Maxwell, A. E.: 644
Mayman, M.: 71, 93, 353
Meals, D. W.: 785
Mech, E.: 485
Mee, E. A.: 438
Meer, B.: 554-5
Meier, L. D.: 377
Mendola, V. S.: 307
Mensh, I. N.: 167-8, 783
Mercer, M.: 234, 308, 774, 784
Merrill, R. M.: 439-40, 486
Meyer, M. M.: 235
Meyer, V.: 817
Mignone, R. J.: 978
Miller, J. M.: 980
Miller, J. S.: 428
Milne, G. G.: 579
Milstein, V.: 475, 515
Milton, E. O.: 51
Mindess, H.: 606
Mirsky, A. F.: 889
Misbach, L.: 794
Misselbrook, B. D.: *exc*, 3:300
Mitchell, M. B.: 27
Moldawsky, P. C.: 441
Moldawsky, S.: 441
Money, J.: 951
Monroe, J.: 354
Monroe, J. J.: 442
Moore, J. H.: 265
Moran, F. A.: 443-4
Moran, L. J.: 443-4, 678, 882
Morris, F.: 744
Morrison, D. H.: 687-8
Morrow, R. S.: 818
Morrow, W. R.: 640
Motter, M. E.: 20
Mundy, J. P.: 176
Mundy, L.: 644
Mundy-Castle, A. C.: 621, 679-80, 725
Murfett, B. J.: 475, 515
Murphree, O. D.: 813
Murphy, D. B.: 580
Murphy, K. P.: 607
Murphy, M. M.: 789
Murstein, B. I.: 705
Nelson, C. L.: 722
Nelson, G. K.: 680, 725
Nesvig, D.: 702
Neuringer, C.: 581, 743
Newman, J. R.: 561
Newton, B. W.: 399
Newton, R. L.: 309
Nichols, J. E.: 726
Norman, R. D.: 487, 493, 659
North, G. E.: 556
O'Brien, C. C.: 857
Obuchowski, K.: 979
O'Connor, J. P.: 236
O'Dell, P. L.: 387
Olch, D. R.: 177
Olson, R. W.: 830
O'Neill, J. J.: 582
Oppenheim, H.: 400
Oppenheim, S.: 68, 310
Orchinik, C. W.: 852
O'Reilly, P. O.: 681, 853
Ostrander, J. M.: 178
Ostrow, J.: 874
Owens, E. P.: 748
Page, K.: 311
Palmer, J. O.: 495

Wechsler-Bellevue Intelligence Scale

Paolino, A. F.: 843
Parker, J. W.: 608
Parker, M. M.: *exc*, 2:B1121
Parsons, O. A.: 633, 744
Parsons, P. A.: 710
Partington, J. E.: 21
Pascal, G. R.: 237
Patterson, C. H.: 94–5, 179–80, 488
Patterson, R. M.: 796
Payne, R. W.: 706
Peak, D. T.: 954
Pearl, D.: 614
Pedrini, D. T.: 898
Peixotto, H. E.: 312
Peters, J. S.: 682
Peterson, P. G.: 864
Peterson, R.: 749
Petrie, A.: 758–9
Peyman, D. A. R.: 823
Phelps, H. B.: 854
Phillips, E. L.: 181
Piercy, M. F.: 626
Piercy, M. M.: 865
Pine, I.: 796
Pizzat, F. J.: 445
Plant, W. T.: 583, 622, 645
Plumb, G. R.: 355, 557
Plumeau, F.: 683
Pollack, M.: 915
Pollens, B.: 356
Pool, K. B.: 604
Portnoy, B.: 363
Post, F.: 576
Powell, J. A.: 401
Prado, W. M.: 916–7
Prager, D.: 5
Prentice, N. M.: 745
Preston, C. E.: 894
Price, H. G.: 72
Price, J. C.: 754
Price, J. R.: 558
Pruyser, P. W.: 819
Ptacek, J. E.: 520
Purcell, C. K.: 446
Purcell, K.: 584
Purdy, R. S.: 934
Putnam, T. J.: 755
Puzzo, F.: 683
Puzzo, F. S.: 142
Quadfasel, A. F.: 819
Quay, H. C.: 932
Quereshi, M. Y.: 980–1
Rabin, A. I.: 13–4, 28–9, 40, 52–3, 73–4, 96, 357, 559, 575, 713, 929
Rabinovitz, A.: 107
Raine, L. M.: 378
Rakhawy, Y. T.: 948–9
Rakusin, J.: 239
Ramsay, R.: 574
Rapaport, D.: 9, 34, 41, 54, 56, 75, 353, 640, 765, 955
Rappaport, S. R.: 313, 489
Rashkis, H. A.: 97, 143
Raub, E. S.: 784
Rawn, M. L.: 821
Reddy, M. J.: 987
Reed, H. B. C.: 727, 746–7, 918, 935
Reed, H. C.: 947
Reed, H. R.: 775
Reed, J. C.: 946–7, 990
Reich, H.: 402
Reichard, S.: 41–2, 358
Reimanis, G.: 974
Reinitz, A. H.: 204
Reitan, R. M.: 107, 636, 660–1, 696, 699, 711–2, 724, 727, 739, 742, 746–7, 807, 824, 836, 851, 861–2, 880, 893, 895, 909, 918, 926–7, 936, 943, 970, 982, 988–90
Reitz, W.: *exc*, 2:B1121
Reynell, W. R.: 55
Reynolds, G. A.: 314
Rhoderick, W. A.: 521
Richards, T. W.: 447
Richardson, H.: 622
Richmond, W.: *exc*, 3:300
Riegel, K. F.: 728–9
Riegel, R. M.: 728–9
Riklan, M.: 684, 844, 896, 919
Rioch, M. J.: 662

Risch, F.: 45
Ritchie, J. E.: 501
Roberts, A. D.: 76
Roberts, A. O. H.: 721
Robinowitz, R.: 585
Robison, R. K.: *exc*, 5:B332
Rogal, R.: 991
Rogers, L. S.: 315–7, 359, 808
Rondberg, S. R.: 736
Rose, D. M.: 318
Rosenberg, B. G.: 831
Rosenblatt, S. M.: 952
Rosenthal, D.: 723
Rosenzweig, S.: 240
Rossi, A. M.: 722
Rossi, P. D.: 450
Roth, M.: 473, 490
Rothstein, H. J.: 491
Rousey, C. L.: 601
Royo, D.: 845
Rubin, H.: 492
Rubino, C. A.: 937, 983
Rubin-Rabson, G.: 586, 809–10
Rubinstein, E. A.: 182
Rudolf, G. de M.: 241–2
Russell, G. E.: 522
Russell, L.: 888
Sabeh, R.: 319
Sadowsky, D.: 978
Sanders, J. R.: 320
Sanderson, M. H.: 96
Sands, H.: 754
Sappenfield, B. R.: 119
Sarason, S. B.: 110, 352, 437
Sartain, A. Q.: 98
Satter, G.: 523, 560
Sattler, J. M.: 965
Saucer, R. T.: 737
Saunders, D. R.: 685
Savage, W.: 885
Sawrey, J. M.: 583
Scarborough, B. B.: 587
Schafer, R.: 42, 54, 56, 75, 99, 183, 243, 353, 955
Schalling, D.: 738
Schein, E. H.: 866
Scherer, I. W.: 244, 624
Schillo, R. J.: 403
Schlosser, J. R.: 245
Schmidt, A. G.: *exc*, 2:B1121
Schmidt, D. G.: 100
Schnadt, F.: 448, 917
Schneider, B.: 345
Schneider, R. A.: 786
Schneyer, S.: 609
Schofield, W.: 449
Schon, M.: 897
Schucman, H.: 956
Schut, D.: 984
Schwartz, H. G.: 783
Schwartz, M. L.: 912
Seaquist, M. R.: 565
Sears, R.: 184
Seashore, H.: 209
Seashore, H. G.: 255
Seeman, W.: 785
Segal, S. J.: 268
Senti, M. M.: 449
Serafetinides, E. A.: 966
Seybold, F. R.: 898
Seymour, J. H.: 825
Shaalan, M.: 948–9
Shaffer, L. F.: *exc*, 4:362, 5:B332
Shaheen, O.: 959
Shanan, J.: 938
Shannon, W.: 450
Shapiro, M. B.: 576, 730
Sharon (Singer), S.: 939
Shier, D. E.: 588
Shimota, H. E.: 899
Shneidman, E. S.: 451
Shoben, E. J.: 321
Shuttleworth, F. K.: *exc*, 2:B1121
Siddique, H.: 634
Siegal, R. S.: 958, 968
Sievers, D. J.: 493
Silver, C. E.: 388
Silverman, H.: 268
Silverstein, A. B.: 748
Simkin, J. S.: 360–1
Simmons, A. A.: 846
Simon, A.: 163

Simon, L. M.: 322
Simpson, M. M.: 141, 175
Sines, L. K.: 623
Singer, E.: 104, 230, 246
Singer, M. T.: 866
Sklar, M.: 867, 875
Slater, P.: 66, 730
Sloan, W.: 61, 77, 120, 185, 260, 496, 561
Smith, A.: 847, 868, 900, 940–1
Smith, A. E.: 247
Smith, J. B.: 663
Smykal, A.: 389
Smyth, V. O. G.: 865
Snider, H. L.: 49
Solomon, M.: 118
Somerset, H. C. A.: 501
Sorsby, F. B.: 248
Spache, G.: 186
Spaner, F. E.: 323
Spanier, S. W.: 524
Spitz, H.: 635
Spivack, G.: 842, 885
Spreen, O.: 920, 942
Springer, N. N.: 101
Stacey, C. L.: 324, 362–3, 524
Stanley, J. C.: 494
Stanton, J. M.: 249
Starer, E.: 325, 452
Stark, I.: *exc*, 3:301
Stead, L. S. G.: 404
Stefic, E. C.: 326
Stein, M. I.: 554–5
Steisel, I. M.: 78, 133, 776–7
Stenger, C. A.: 502, 564
Sternberg, T. H.: 399
Sternberg, U.: 635
Stevenson, W. D.: 790
Stewart, K. D.: 633
Stogdill, E. L.: *exc*, 3:299
Stone, C. P.: 102
Storrs, S. V.: 453
Stotsky, B. A.: 364, 454
Strange, F. B.: 495
Strong, P. N.: 664
Strother, C. R.: 57
Struckett, P. B. A.: 791
Sugarman, L.: 707
Sullivan, A.: 610
Sullivan, A. M.: 735
Sullivan, E. B.: 399
Summerskill, J.: 785
Sunukjian, H.: 275
Super, D. E.: 250
Swenson, E. W.: 901
Tagiuri, R.: 103, 131
Talkoff, A.: 804
Talland, G. A.: 786, 848
Tallent, N.: 826
Tamarin, S.: 350
Tamminen, A. W.: 365
Tanck, R. H.: 837
Taterka, J. H.: 820
Tatom, M. H.: 251
Tavernier, A.: 842
Tavris, E.: 902
Taylor, G. J.: 157
Taylor, J. W.: 433, 808
Teicher, M. I.: 104
Thaler, M.: 156, 589
Theaman, M.: 327
Thetford, W. N.: 956
Thompson, C. W.: 778
Thorne, G. D.: 558
Thornton, T. E.: 502, 564
Thorp, T. R.: 665
Thurston, J. R.: 525
Tillman, C. G.: 9
Todd, R. E.: 588
Tolor, A.: 590–1
Tooth, G.: 144
Topetzes, N. J.: 611
Torrance, P.: 187
Trehub, A.: 624
Triggs, F.: 408
Trist, C. L.: 15
Tuck, J. A.: 858
Tuddenham, R. D.: *exc*, 6:B503
Uecker, A. E.: 811
Uleman, A. L.: 984
Umberger, J. P.: 349
Urbach, N.: 914

Vanderhost, L.: 496
Vane, J. R.: 526
van Lennep, J. E.: 792
Van Vorst, R. B.: 43
Varvel, W. A.: *exc*, 2:B1121
Vaughn, C. L.: *exc*, 3:299
Vick, G.: 20
Victor, M.: 666, 848
Vistica, N. J.: 252
Vorhaus, P. G.: 455
Waggoner, R. W.: 752
Waldfogel, S.: 366
Walker, R. E.: 912, 932
Walsh, M. A.: 786
Walters, R. H.: 497
Ward, J. H.: 562
Warner, S. J.: 328
Watson, R. L.: 105, 367, 498, 781, 795; *rev*, 3:298
Webb, B.: 30
Webb, W. B.: 44, 121, 253, 313, 368, 376, 456
Weber, G. H.: 766
Wechsler, D.: 1–2, 16–8, 58, 68, 369
Weider, A.: 8, 19, 45, 123
Weiner, H.: 684, 844
Weisgerber, C. A.: 563
Wells, F. L.: 111; *rev*, 2:1429
Welman, A. J.: 963
Welsh, G. S.: 97, 254
Wentworth-Rohr, I.: 329
Wertheimer, M.: 519
Werts, C. E.: 928
Wesman, A.: 209
Wesman, A. G.: 255
West, A. A.: 827
Westbrook, C. H.: *exc*, 3:301
Westerhold, R.: 421
Wexler, M.: 793
Wheatley, M. M.: 374
Wheeler, E. T.: 145
Wheeler, J. I.: 370
Wheeler, W. M.: 330, 483
Whitcomb, M. A.: 79
White, E. E.: 666
White, P. T.: 741
Whiteman, D. B.: 760
Whiteman, M.: 331, 612, 760
Widlak, F. W.: 981
Wiggins, J. G.: 405
Wiggins, N. W.: 686
Wiley, L. N.: 332
Wilkins, W. L.: 370
Willard, L. A.: 957
Willenson, D.: 779
Williams, M.: 167–8, 855
Willner, A.: 915
Wilson, M. O.: 389
Winne, J. F.: 499
Wishner, J.: 188
Witt, E. L.: 390
Wittenborn, J. R.: 256, 371
Wittman, P.: 33
Wladkowsky, E.: 106
Wolfensberger, W. P.: 625
Wolff, S. J.: 500
Woolf, H.: *exc*, 3:300
Woo-Sam, J.: 985, 991
Wosika, P. H.: 204
Wright, C.: 39, 46
Wright, H. F.: 84, 117, 257
Wright, S. C.: 308
Wrightstone, J. W.: *exc*, 3:300
Wyatt, F.: 87
Wysocki, A. C.: 967
Wysocki, B. A.: 967
Yacorzynski, G. K.: 31
Yamahiro, R. S.: 616
Yates, A. J.: 628, 817, 828
Yeats, L. C.: 457
Young, F. M.: 520, 527
Zeaman, J. B.: 237
Zeigler, T. W.: 752
Zerfas, P. G.: 933
Ziebell, P. W.: 688
Zienkiewicz, H.: 979
Zimet, C. N.: 592
Zimmerman, F. T.: 755
Zimmerman, I. L.: 399, 991
Zimmerman, M. C.: 399
Zubek, J. P.: 668

Wechsler-Bellevue Intelligence Scale

[533]
Wechsler Intelligence Scale for Children. Ages 5–15; 1949; WISC; downward extension of Form 2 of *Wechsler-Bellevue Intelligence Scale;* 13–15 scores: verbal (information, comprehension, arithmetic, similarities, vocabulary, digit span [optional], total), performance (picture completion, picture arrangement, block design, object assembly, mazes [optional], coding, total), total; David Wechsler; Psychological Corporation. (Australian edition: 1968; manual by J. A. Radcliffe and F. E. Trainer; Australian Council for Educational Research [Australia]. British edition: 1971; manual supplement by Peter Saville; NFER Publishing Co. Ltd. [England].) *

For additional information and reviews by David Freides and R. T. Osborne, see 7:431 (518 references); for a review by Alvin G. Burstein, see 6:540 (155 references); for reviews by Elizabeth D. Fraser, Gerald R. Patterson, and Albert I. Rabin, see 5:416 (111 references); for reviews by James M. Anderson, Harold A. Delp, and Boyd R. McCandless, and an excerpted review by Laurance F. Shaffer, see 4:363 (22 references). For excerpts from related book reviews, see 7:B234 (2 excerpts).

REFERENCES THROUGH 1971

1–22. See 4:363.
23–133. See 5:416.
134–288. See 6:540.
289–807. See 7:431.
808. KARLSEN, BJÖRN. *A Comparison of Some Educational and Psychological Characteristics of Successful and Unsuccessful Readers at the Elementary School Level.* Doctor's thesis, University of Minnesota (Minneapolis, Minn.), 1954. (*DA* 15:456)
809. JORDAN, THOMAS E. "Psychological Findings in a Case of Von Recklinghausen's Disease and Hyperpituitarism." *J Clin Psychol* 12:389–91 O '56. * (*PA* 32:4470)
810. MONEY, JOHN. "Psychologic Studies in Hypothyroidism: Recommendations for Case Management." *Arch Neurol & Psychiatry* 76:296–309 S '56. * (*PA* 31:4827)
811. REBHUN, ALBERT M. "The Level-Sharpening Dimension as Manifested in Other Perceptual and Non-Perceptual Tasks." *Psychol Newsl* 7:43–6 Ja–F '56. * (*PA* 31:1767)
812. RICHARDS, T. W., AND HOOPER, SARA. "Brain-Injury at Birth (Cerebral Palsy) and Perceptual Responses During Childhood and Adolescence." *J Nerv & Mental Dis* 123:117–24 F '56. * (*PA* 31:8608)
813. SPACHE, GEORGE D. "Intellectual and Personality Characteristics of Retarded Readers." *Psychol Newsl* 9:9–12 S–O '57. * (*PA* 32:4526)
814. MURSTEIN, BERNARD I. "Personality and Intellectual Changes in Leukemia: A Case Study." *J Proj Tech* 22:421–6 D '58. * (*PA* 34:1401)
815. BECK, HARRY S. "A Comparison of Convulsive Organic, Non-Convulsive Organic, and Non-Organic Public School Children." *Am J Mental Def* 63:866–75 Mr '59. * (*PA* 34:1656)
816. BRAEN, BERNARD B., AND MASLING, JOSEPH M. "Intelligence Tests Used With Special Groups of Children." *Excep Children* 26:42–5 S '59. * (*PA* 35:2194)
817. HOHMAN, LESLIE B., AND FREEDHEIM, DONALD K. "A Study of IQ Retest Evaluations on 370 Cerebral Palsied Children." *Am J Phys Med* 38:180–7 O '59. *
818. SCHACTER, FRANCES F., AND APGAR, VIRGINIA. "Perinatal Asphyxia and Psychologic Signs of Brain Damage in Childhood." *Pediatrics* 24:1016–25 D '59. *
819. WINITZ, HARRIS. "Language Skills of Male and Female Kindergarten Children." *J Speech & Hearing Res* 2:377–86 D '59. * (*PA* 34:5895)
820. HAND, JACK, AND MARTIN, J. D. "An Abbreviated Form of the Wechsler Intelligence Scale for Children." *J Crim Law Criminol & Police Sci* 51:81 My–Je '60. *
821. JACKSON, PHILIP W.; GETZELS, JACOB W.; AND XYDIS, GEORGE A. "Psychological Health and Cognitive Functioning in Adolescence: A Multivariate Analysis." *Child Develop* 31:285–98 Je '60. * (*PA* 36:3FH85J)
822. KENNEDY, WALLACE A.; SMITH, MARION; VAN DE RIET, HANNAH; VAN DE RIET, VERNON; SMITH, HERBERT; RAPP, DON; AND PAINE, R. W. "A Multidimensional Study of Mathematically Gifted Adolescents." *Child Develop* 31:655–66 D '60. * (*PA* 36:2FH55K)
823. ELKIND, DAVID. "The Development of Quantitative Thinking: A Systematic Replication of Piaget's Studies." *J Genetic Psychol* 98:37–46 Mr '61. * (*PA* 35:6143)
824. GOODSTEIN, LEONARD D. "Intellectual Impairment in Children With Cleft Palates." *J Speech & Hearing Res* 4:287–94 S '61. * (*PA* 36:2JB87G)

825. CONVERSE, HAROLD D., AND COURTNEY, JOHN MICHAEL. "A Comparative Study of the Lorge-Thorndike Group Intelligence Tests With an Individual Intelligence Test." *J Res Services* 1:1–5 My '62. *
826. MORAN, ROBERTA E. "Observations and Recommendations on the Puerto Rican Version of the Wechsler Intelligence Scale for Children." *Pedagogía* (Puerto Rico) 10:89–98 Ja–Je '62. * (*PA* 37:1205)
827. SACKS, LENORA; FEINSTEIN, ALVAN R.; AND TARANTA, ANGELO. "A Controlled Psychologic Study of Sydenham's Chorea." *J Pediatrics* 61:714–22 N '62. *
828. WITHERSPOON, Y. T. "The Measurement of Indian Children's Achievement in the Academic Tool Subjects." *J Am Indian Ed* 1:5–9 My '62. *
829. CROOKES, T. G., AND GREENE, MARGARET C. L. "Some Characteristics of Children With Two Types of Speech Disorder." *Brit J Ed Psychol* 33:31–40 F '63. * (*PA* 38:1221)
830. HARITOS-FATOUROS, MARY. *A Study of the Wechsler Intelligence Scale for Children Applied to Greek School Children.* Master's thesis, University of London (London, England), 1963.
831. KRIPPNER, STANLEY. "Sociopathic Tendencies and Reading Retardation in Children." *Excep Children* 29:258–66 F '63. *
832. ORTAR, GINA. "Is a Verbal Test Cross-Cultural?" pp. 219–35. (*PA* 39:1753) In *Scripta Hierosolymitana: Studies in Education, Vol. 13.* Jerusalem, Israel: Magnes Press, 1963. Pp. viii, 264. *
833. ROBECK, MILDRED C. "Readers Who Lacked Word Analysis Skills: A Group Diagnosis." *J Ed Res* 56:432–4 Ap '63. *
834. SEMLER, IRA J., AND ISCOE, IRA. "Comparative and Developmental Study of the Learning Abilities of Negro and White Children Under Four Conditions." *J Ed Psychol* 54:38–44 F '63. * (*PA* 37:7996)
835. BARBEE, EUNICE W. *A Comparison of the Validity of Individual and Group Administration of Intelligence Tests With First Grade Pupils.* Master's thesis, Furman University (Greenville, S.C.), 1964.
836. LOVELL, K.; SHAPTON, D.; AND WARREN, N. S. "A Study of Some Cognitive and Other Disabilities in Backward Readers of Average Intelligence as Assessed By a Non-Verbal Test." *Brit J Ed Psychol* 34:58–64 F '64. * (*PA* 38:9233)
837. POLLITT, ERNESTO, AND MONEY, JOHN. "Studies in the Psychology of Dwarfism: 1, Intelligence Quotient and School Achievement." *J Pediatrics* 64:415–21 Mr '64. *
838. WRIGHT, HELEN C. *The Analysis of WISC Profiles and Bender-Gestalt Protocols of a Sample of Elementary School Children With Reading Disability.* Master's thesis, University of Arizona (Tucson, Ariz.), 1964.
839. BELL, D. A.; TAYLOR, W. C.; AND DOCKRELL, W. B. "A Ten Year Follow-Up of Low Birth Weight Infants: Intellectual Functioning." *Alberta J Ed Res* (Canada) 11:220–5 D '65. * (*PA* 40:7538)
840. CLEVELAND, SIDNEY E.; REITMAN, E. EDWARD; AND BREWER, EARL J., JR. "Psychological Factors in Juvenile Rheumatoid Arthritis." *Arthr & Rheum* 8:1152–8 D '65. *
841. CORAH, NORMAN L.; ANTHONY, E. JAMES; PAINTER, PAUL; STERN, JOHN A.; AND THURSTON, DONALD. "Effects of Perinatal Anoxia After Seven Years." *Psychol Monogr* 79(3): 1–34 '65. * (*PA* 39:9776)
842. DREW, ARTHUR L., AND NORTON, JAMES A. "A Study of the Inheritance of Measured Intelligence." *Recent Adv Biol Psychiatry* 7:171–82 '65. *
843. McBEATH, MARCIA. "The Effect of Pretest Interaction on a Perceptual Task." *Calif J Ed Res* 16:203–9 N '65. * (*PA* 40:4609)
844. RAJALAKSHMI, R., AND JEEVES, M. A. "Comparative Performance of Normals and Retardates of the Same Mental Age on Certain Psychological Tasks." *J Genetic Psychol* 106:39–43 Mr '65. * (*PA* 39:12748)
845. RUESS, AUBREY L. "A Comparative Study of Cleft Palate Children and Their Siblings." *J Clin Psychol* 21:354–60 O '65. * (*PA* 40:1880)
846. CAPOBIANCO, R. J. "Ocular-Manual Laterality and Reading in Adolescent Mental Retardates." *Am J Mental Def* 70:781–5 Mr '66. * (*PA* 40:6970)
847. EVANS, LIONEL. "A Comparative Study of the Wechsler Intelligence Scale for Children (Performance) and Raven's Progressive Matrices With Deaf Children." *Teach Deaf* (England) 64:76–82 Mr '66. *
848. FLOWER, RICHARD M.; VIEHWEG, RICHARD; AND RUZICKA, WILLIAM R. "The Communicative Disorders of Children With Kernicteric Athetosis: 2, Problems in Language Comprehension and Use." *J Speech & Hearing Disorders* 31:60–8 F '66. * (*PA* 40:9108)
849. GRIFFIN, DONALD CASSATT. *Admission Tests as Predictors of Gain in Reading in a Remedial School.* Master's thesis, University of California (Los Angeles, Calif.), 1966.
850. LEVY, RUSSELL H., AND MOORE, WINSTON E. "Cross-Sectional Psychometric Evaluation of Court-Labelled Delinquent Boys." *J Correct Ed* 18:7–9 Jl '66. *
851. MONEY, JOHN, AND LEWIS, VIOLA. "IQ, Genetics and Accelerated Growth: Adrenogenital Syndrome." *Johns Hopkins Med J* 118:365–73 My '66. *

852. MONEY, JOHN; WEINBERG, ROBERT S.; AND LEWIS, VIOLA. "Intelligence Quotient and School Performance in Twenty-Two Children With a History of Thyrotoxicosis." *B Johns Hopkins Hosp* 118:275–81 Mr '66. *

853. MONTGOMERY, G. W. G. "Differences in the Interrelationships of Non-Verbal Intelligence Test Scores, Educational Attainments and Residual Hearing in Selected and Unselected Populations." *Teach Deaf* (England) 64:29–33 Ja '66. *

854. ORPET, R. E., AND MEYERS, C. E. "Six Structure-of-Intellect Hypotheses in Six-Year-Old Children." *J Ed Psychol* 57:341–6 D '66. * (*PA* 41:1416)

855. PICKLES, DENNIS G. "The Wechsler Performance Scale and Its Relationship to Speech and Educational Response in Deaf Slow-Learning Children." *Teach Deaf* (England) 64:382–92 N '66. *

856. WILHELM, ROWENA. "Diagnostic Value of Test Score Differentials Found Between Measures of Visual and Auditory Memory in Severely Disabled Readers." *Acad Ther Q* 2:42–4 f '66. * (*PA* 40:13545)

857. EVERETT, GARY D. *An Analysis of the Performance of Children With Severe Articulation Problems and Children With Minimal Brain Dysfunction as Manifested on a Selected Battery of Tests.* Master's thesis, Texas Technological College (Lubbock, Tex.), 1967.

858. GITTELMAN, MARTIN, AND BIRCH, HERBERT G. "Childhood Schizophrenia: Intellect, Neurologic Status, Perinatal Risk, Prognosis, and Family Pathology." *Arch Gen Psychiatry* 17:16–25 Jl '67. * (*PA* 41:15552)

859. LEVY, RUSSELL H. "Dimensions of Mental Retardation Among Wards of the Illinois Youth Commission." *J Correct Ed* 19:12–6 O '67. *

860. MONEY, JOHN; DRASH, PHILIP W.; AND LEWIS, VIOLA. "Dwarfism and Hypopituitarism: Statural Retardation Without Mental Retardation." *Am J Mental Def* 72:122–6 Jl '67. * (*PA* 41:15732)

861. VANDENBERG, STEVEN G. "Hereditary Factors in Psychological Variables in Man, With a Special Emphasis on Cognition," pp. 99–133. In *Genetic Diversity and Human Behavior.* Viking Fund Publications in Anthropology No. 45. Edited by J. N. Spuhler. Chicago, Ill.: Aldine Publishing Co., 1967. Pp. xi, 291. *

862. BURNS, GARY W. *A Comparison of the Peabody Picture Vocabulary Test With the Stanford-Binet Intelligence Scale and With the Wechsler Intelligence Scale for Children.* Master's thesis, Sacramento State College (Sacramento, Calif.), 1968.

863. COHEN, S. ALAN. "Socially Disadvantaged Americans: Slow Learners." *Slow Learning Child* (Australia) 14:153–60 Mr '68. * (*PA* 42:19298)

864. DOMRATH, RICHARD P. "Constructional Praxis and Visual Perception in School Children." *J Consult & Clin Psychol* 32:186–92 Ap '68. * (*PA* 42:8174)

865. IRVINE, JAMES. *Correlates of Grade One Achievement.* Master's thesis, University of Alberta (Edmonton, Alta., Canada), 1968.

866. LEWIS, VIOLA G.; MONEY, JOHN; AND EPSTEIN, RALPH. "Concordance of Verbal and Nonverbal Ability in the Adrenogenital Syndrome." *Johns Hopkins Med J* 122:192–5 Ap '68. *

867. MALIN, A. J. "Adaptation of the Wechsler Intelligence Scale for Children." *J Rehabil Asia* (India) 9:19–20 O '68. *

868. MANN, LESTER; HAUGHEY, CHARLES; TREFSGAR, THEODORE F.; AND KEFFER, CHARLES E. "Achievement and Personality Measurements Associated With Progress in a Programmed Course in Decimals and Fractions at a Fifth Grade Level." *Scientia Paedagogica Experimentalis* (Belgium) 5(1):76–83 '68. * (*PA* 45:3108)

869. GRANDOVIC, MARGARET CLARK. *A Study of the Usefulness of the Bender Gestalt Test With Young Educable Retarded Children Using the Koppitz Procedures.* Doctor's thesis, Temple University (Philadelphia, Pa.), 1969. (*DAI* 32:1335A)

870. HONZIK, MARJORIE P.; COLLART, DONNA S.; ROBINSON, SAUL J.; AND FINLEY, KNOX H. "Sex Differences in Verbal and Performance IQ's of Children Undergoing Open-heart Surgery." *Sci* 164(3878):445–7 Ap 25 '69. * (*PA* 45:6906)

871. JOINER, LEE M.; ERICKSON, EDSEL L.; CRITTENDEN, JERRY B.; AND STEVENSON, VIVIAN M. "Predicting the Academic Achievement of the Acoustically-Impaired Using Intelligence and Self-Concept of Academic Ability." *J Spec Ed* 3(4):425–31 f '69. * (*PA* 44:15092)

872. MASICA, DANIEL N.; EHRHARDT, ANKE A.; AND LEWIS, VIOLA G. "IQ, Fetal Sex Hormones and Cognitive Patterns: Studies in the Testicular Feminizing Syndrome of Androgen Insensitivity." *Johns Hopkins Med J* 124(1):34–43 Ja '69. *

873. PARKER, JAMES. "Adapting School Psychological Evaluation to the Blind Child." *New Outl Blind* 63(10):305–11 D '69. * (*PA* 47:3654)

874. ROSENQUIST, CARL M., AND MEGARGEE, EDWIN I. *Delinquency in Three Cultures,* pp. 208–24. Austin, Tex.: University of Texas Press, 1969. Pp. xvi, 554. *

875. RUSCHIVAL, MARY LENA. *The Effectiveness of the Wechsler Preschool and Primary Scale of Intelligence in the Identification of Gifted Preschool Children.* Master's thesis, East Carolina University (Greenville, N.C.), 1969.

876. CARING, LILLIAN COTT. *The Relation of Cognitive Style, Sex and Intelligence to Moral Judgment in Children.* Doctor's thesis, New York University (New York, N.Y.), 1970. (*DAI* 31:7568B)

877. COHEN, LEO. "The Effects of Material and Non-Material Reinforcement Upon Performance of the WISC Block Design Subtest by Children of Different Social Classes: A Follow-up Study." *Psychol* 7(4):41–7 N '70. * (*PA* 46:2794)

878. CRONIN, ROBERT. "I Give I.Q. Tests Without Looking." *New Outl Blind* 64(5):142–7 My '70. * (*PA* 46:9446)

879. CROWN, PHYLLIS JO. *The Effects of Race of Examiner and Standard vs. Dialect Administration of the Wechsler Preschool and Primary Scale of Intelligence on the Performance of Negro and White Children.* Doctor's thesis, Florida State University (Tallahassee, Fla.), 1970. (*DAI* 32:232A)

880. DANGEL, HARRY LEWIS. *The Biasing Effect of Pretest Information on the WISC Scores of Mentally Retarded Children.* Doctor's thesis, Pennsylvania State University (University Park, Pa.), 1970. (*DAI* 32:233A)

881. EARLY, GEORGE H., AND SHARPE, THEODORE M. "Developing Perceptual-Motor Skills: Perceptual-Motor Training and Basic Abilities." *Acad Ther* 5(3):235–40+ sp '70. * (*PA* 44:19036)

882. EAVES, LINDA C.; NUTTALL, J. C.; KLONOFF, H.; AND DUNN, H. G. "Developmental and Psychological Test Scores in Children of Low Birth Weight." *Pediatrics* 45(1):9–20 Ja '70. * Correction: 45(5):886–7 My '70. *

883. FRETZ, BRUCE R.; JOHNSON, WARREN R.; AND JOHNSON, JULIA A. "Intellectual and Perceptual Motor Development as a Function of Therapeutic Play," pp. 475–80. In *Contemporary Psychology of Sport.* Proceedings of the Second International Congress of Sport Psychology, Washington, D.C., 1968. Chicago, Ill.: Athletic Institute, 1970. Pp. xix, 878. *

884. GARMS, JOE D. "Factor Analysis of the WISC and ITPA." *Psychol* 7(4):30–1 N '70. * (*PA* 46:3067)

885. HAFNER, LAWRENCE E., AND WEAVER, WENDELL W. "Correlates of Error Rate in the Pronunciation of WISC Vocabulary Items." *J Read Behav* 3(2):27–31 sp '70–71 ['71]. *

886. HARTMAN, ROBERT KINTZ. *An Investigation of the Incremental Validity of Human Figure Drawings in the Diagnosis of Learning Disabilities.* Doctor's thesis, University of Connecticut (Storrs, Conn.), 1970. (*DAI* 31:6403A)

887. JAYAGOPAL, RAJABATHER. *Problem Solving Abilities and Psychomotor Skills of Navajo Indians, Spanish Americans and Anglos in Junior High School.* Doctor's thesis, University of New Mexico (Albuquerque, N.M.), 1970. (*DAI* 31:5035A)

888. KAUFMAN, MARTIN JOEL. *Level, Shape and Dispersion as Relevant Variables in WISC Profiles of Minimally Brain-Injured Children.* Doctor's thesis, University of Texas (Austin, Tex.), 1970. (*DAI* 31:5888A)

889. LANEY, BILLIE JOHNSON. *A Comparative Study of Expressive and Comprehensive Vocabulary Development in Male and Female Kindergarten Children.* Doctor's thesis, East Texas State University (Commerce, Tex.), 1970. (*DAI* 31:4386A)

890. LEVINE, MAUREEN. *Psychological, Neuropsychological, and Educational Correlates of Reading Deficit: Etiological and Normative Comparison.* Master's thesis, Central Michigan University (Mt. Pleasant, Mich.), 1970.

891. McCONOCHIE, WILLIAM A. "Juvenile Delinquents: Relationship Between WISC Scores, Offenses, Race, Chronological Age and Residence." *Correct Psychologist* 4(3):103–10 N–D '70. * (*PA* 49:2685)

892. McNINCH, GEORGE HAAS WILEY. *The Relationships Between Selected Perceptual Factors and Measured First Grade Reading Achievement.* Doctor's thesis, University of Georgia (Athens, Ga.), 1970. (*DAI* 31:3965A)

893. MARCHI, JACK UGO. *Comparison of Selected Piagetian Tasks With the Wechsler Intelligence Scale for Children as Measures of Mental Retardation.* Doctor's thesis, University of California (Berkeley, Calif.), 1970. (*DAI* 31:6442A)

894. MAXWELL, MICHAEL T. *The Relationship Between the Wechsler Intelligence Scale for Children and the Slosson Intelligence Test.* Master's thesis, Eastern Montana College (Billings, Mont.), 1970.

895. MOENY, WILLIAM COWIN. *An Investigation of the Relationships Between Ocular-Motor Skill and Intelligence in Mentally Retarded and Normal Children.* Doctor's thesis, University of New Mexico (Albuquerque, N.M.), 1970. (*DAI* 31:5889A)

896. NEAVES, ALISON I. "To Establish a Basis for Prognosis in Stammering." *Brit J Dis Commun* 5(1):46–58 Ap '70. * (*PA* 46:5319)

897. OWEN, DAVID R., AND SINES, JACOB O. "Heritability of Personality in Children." *Behav Genetics* 1(3–4):235–48 Ag–N '70. * (*PA* 47:10446)

898. PAGE, STEWART. "Examiner Effect, Expertise, and Intelligence Testing." *Ont Psychologist* (Canada) 2(3):181–4 '70. *

899. RAJATASILPIN, ANUSITH; SUEPSAMAN, BANCHONG; AND YAMARAT, VALAITIP. "Intellectual Development and Its Relationship to the Nutritional Status Among School Children." *J Med Assn Thailand* 53(11):788–93 N '70. *

900. REBISH, DELLA. *Learning Ability as a Function of Verbal and Nonverbal Intelligence.* Doctor's thesis, Claremont Graduate School (Claremont, Calif.), 1970. (*DAI* 31:7609B)

901. REED, JAMES C. "The Deficits of Retarded Readers—Fact or Artifact?" *Read Teach* 23(4):347–52+ Ja '70. * (*PA* 45:2972)

902. Richards, Hyrum E., and Stone, David R. "The Learning and Transference of the Piagetian Concept of Conservation." *Mental Retard* 8(4):34–7 Ag '70. * (*PA* 48:1714)

903. Rosenberger, Peter B. "Visual Matching and Clinical Findings Among Good and Poor Readers." *Am J Dis Children* 119(2):103–10 F '70. * (*PA* 44:16376)

904. Rychlak, Joseph F. "Personality Factors in Self- and Peer-Evaluations of WISC Performance Intelligence Among Middle-Class Children." *J Spec Ed* 4(3):269–77 su–f '70. * (*PA* 46:6585)

905. Schneider, Judy H. *A Correlation Study Between Performance Scores of the Wechsler Intelligence Scale for Children and Experimental Preschool and School Age Scale of Intellectual Function With Deaf Children.* Master's thesis, Bowling Green State University (Bowling Green, Ohio), 1970.

906. Silberberg, Norman, and Feldt, Leonard S. "Intellectual and Perceptual Correlates of Reading Disabilities." *Skolepsykologi* (Denmark) 7(2):67–81 '70. * (*PA* 46:5502)

907. Simmers, Catherine Powell. *Cognitive Correlates of Attitudinal Rigidity.* Doctor's thesis, Case Western Reserve University (Cleveland, Ohio), 1970. (*DAI* 32:1348A)

908. Smith, Maxine McGowan. *Patterns of Intellectual Abilities in Educationally Handicapped Children.* Doctor's thesis, Claremont Graduate School (Claremont, Calif.), 1970. (*DAI* 31:6415A)

909. Wells, Clinton George. *A Comparative Study of Children Grouped by Three Basic Score Patterns on the Wechsler Intelligence Scale for Children.* Doctor's thesis, University of Northern Colorado (Greeley, Colo.), 1970. (*DAI* 31:6444A)

910. Wiener, Gerald. "The Relationship of Birth Weight and Length of Gestation to Intellectual Development at Ages 8 to 10 Years." *J Pediatrics* 76(5):694–9 My '70. *

911. Wyne, Marvin D.; Coop, Richard H.; and Brookhouse, Diane B. "Information Processing in Young Mildly Retarded Children." *Am J Mental Def* 75(3):371–5 N '70. *

912. Ables, Billie S. "The Use of the Draw-A-Man Test With Borderline Retarded Children Without Pronounced Pathology." *J Clin Psychol* 27(2):262–3 Ap '71. * (*PA* 46:7068)

913. Ackerman, Peggy T.; Peters, John E.; and Dykman, Roscoe A. "Children With Specific Learning Disabilities: Bender Gestalt Test Findings and Other Signs." *J Learn Dis* 4(8):437–46 O '71. * (*PA* 47:9714)

914. Ackerman, Peggy T.; Peters, John E.; and Dykman, Roscoe A. "Children With Specific Learning Disabilities: WISC Profiles." *J Learn Dis* 4(3):150–66 Mr '71. * (*PA* 47:9713)

915. Bagwell, Frances Imogene. *The Effects of a Selected Language Training Program on the Measured Verbal and Intellectual Ability of Educable Mentally Retarded Pupils.* Doctor's thesis, Texas Tech University (Lubbock, Tex.), 1971. (*DAI* 32:5064A)

916. Barron, Robert Charlton. *A Comparison of Patterns of Intellectual and Psycho-Linguistic Abilities Among First Graders With Average and Very Low Reading Ability.* Doctor's thesis, University of Minnesota (Minneapolis, Minn.), 1971. (*DAI* 32:1817B)

917. Bartin, Norma Gladys. *The Intellectual and Psycholinguistic Characteristics of Three Groups of Differentiated Third Grade Readers.* Doctor's thesis, State University of New York (Buffalo, N.Y.), 1971. (*DAI* 32:228A)

918. Bellamy, Edward Ellsworth. *A Study of Productive Thinking in Mentally Retarded Children.* Doctor's thesis, University of Illinois (Urbana, Ill.), 1971. (*DAI* 32:4411A)

919. Bergan, Alene; McManis, Donald L.; and Melchert, Paul A. "Effects of Social and Token Reinforcement on WISC Block Design Performance." *Percept & Motor Skills* 32(3):871–80 Je '71. * (*PA* 47:3622)

920. Bersoff, Donald N. "Short Forms of Individual Intelligence Tests for Children: Review and Critique." *J Sch Psychol* 9(3):310–20 '71. * (*PA* 47:8924)

921. Black, Bob Gene. *Determining the Predictive Value of Selected Measures for First Grade Reading Success.* Doctor's thesis, North Texas State University (Denton, Tex.), 1971. (*DAI* 32:3548A)

922. Black, F. William. "An Investigation of Intelligence as a Causal Factor in Reading Problems." *J Learn Dis* 4(3):139–42 Mr '71. * (*PA* 47:9695)

923. Boll, Thomas J. "Correlation of WISC With Motor Speed and Strength for Brain-Damaged and Normal Children." *J Psychol* 77(2):169–72 Mr '71. * (*PA* 46:1674)

924. Borreson, Paul M. *A Replication and Extension of Studies of the Relations Between Distractibility and the WISC Digit Span Test.* Master's thesis, University of Wisconsin (LaCrosse, Wis.), 1971.

925. Braff, Reba Gertrude. *Signal-to-Noise Speech Discrimination of Black and White Children With Varying Socio-Economic Backgrounds.* Doctor's thesis, University of Southern California (Los Angeles, Calif.), 1971. (*DAI* 32:3686B)

926. Burnes, Kay. "Clinical Assumptions About WISC Subtest Score and Test Behavior Relationships." Abstract. *J Consult & Clin Psychol* 36(2):299 Ap '71. * (*PA* 46:2633)

927. Bush, Wilma Jo. *A Comparative Study of the WISC Test Patterns of the Bright and Gifted Underachievers With the Test Patterns of Underachievers With Normal Intelligence.* Doctor's thesis, Texas Tech University (Lubbock, Tex.), 1971. (*DAI* 32:5066A)

928. Butler, Gary D. *The Performance of Sixth Grade Over and Underachievers on the Information, Arithmetic, Digit Span, and Coding Subtests of the Wechsler Intelligence Scale for Children.* Master's thesis, East Tennessee State University (Johnson City, Tenn.), 1971.

929. Cerbus, George, and Oziel, L. Jerome. "Correlation of the Bender-Gestalt and WISC for Negro Children." *Percept & Motor Skills* 32(1):276 F '71. * (*PA* 46:2703)

930. Clarke, Bryan R., and Leslie, Perry T. "Visual-Motor Skills and Reading Ability of Deaf Children." *Percept & Motor Skills* 33(1):263–8 Ag '71. * (*PA* 47:3463)

931. Cole, Spurgeon, and Hunter, Mildred. "Pattern Analysis of WISC Scores Achieved by Culturally Disadvantaged Children." *Psychol Rep* 29(1):191–4 Ag '71. * (*PA* 47:2647)

932. Creed, C. D., and Robinson, W. P. "Intelligence Test Scores in the Evaluation of a 'Use of Language' Programme for Infant School Children." *Res Ed* (England) 6:1–11 N '71. * (*PA* 48:12239)

933. Dahlke, Anita B. "Predicting True Reading Gains After Remedial Tutoring," pp. 81–102. In *Diagnostic Viewpoints in Reading.* Edited by Robert E. Leibert. Newark, Del.: International Reading Association, 1971. Pp. viii, 133. *

934. Dershowitz, Zachary. "Jewish Subcultural Patterns and Psychological Differentiation." *Int J Psychol* (France) 6(3):223–31 '71. * (*PA* 49:672)

935. Dreyer, Albert S.; Dreyer, Cecily A.; and Nebelkopf, Edwin B. "Portable Rod-and-Frame Test as a Measure of Cognitive Style in Kindergarten Children." *Percept & Motor Skills* 33(3):775–81 D '71. * (*PA* 48:710)

936. Duffy, Robert J., and Moore, Marcia Czyzewski. "The Relationship Between Intelligence and Gestural Behavior in a Mentally Retarded Population." *J Genetic Psychol* 119(2):195–202 D '71. * (*PA* 48:1508)

937. Durojaiye, M. O. A., and Such, M. "Predicting Educational Suitability of Children in an Assessment Unit." *J Exp Ed* 40(2):27–36 w '71. * (*PA* 47:11608)

938. Falk, Libby Janet. *A Profile of Learning Abilities and Behavioral Characteristics of Elementary School-Age Children With Phenylketonuria.* Doctor's thesis, Temple University (Philadelphia, Pa.), 1971. (*DAI* 32:1913A)

939. Feldman, Solomon E., and Sullivan, David S. "Factors Mediating the Effects of Enhanced Rapport on Children's Performance." Abstract. *J Consult & Clin Psychol* 36(2):302 Ap '71. * (*PA* 46:3726)

940. Finnerty, Richard J.; Soltys, John J.; and Cole, Jonathan O. "The Use of D-Amphetamine With Hyperkinetic Children." *Psychopharmacologia* (West Germany) 21(3):302–8 '71. * (*PA* 47:9150)

941. Freer, Frank J. *Visual and Auditory Perceptual Modality Differences as Related to Success in First Grade Reading Word Recognition.* Doctor's thesis, Rutgers—The State University (New Brunswick, N.J.), 1971. (*DAI* 32:6193A)

942. Friedman, Geraldine H. Probe. *A Comparative Study of Psychoeducational Test Scores of Emotionally Disturbed Children and Children With Learning Disabilities.* Doctor's thesis, St. Louis University (St. Louis, Mo.), 1971. (*DAI* 33:1043A)

943. Galdieri, Anthony August. *The Effect of Verbal Approval Upon the Performance of Middle- and Lower-Class Third-Grade Children on the Wechsler Intelligence Scale for Children.* Doctor's thesis, Ohio University (Athens, Ohio), 1971. (*DAI* 32:1270A)

944. Garner, John; Percy, Lynda M.; and Lawson, Tom. "Sex Differences in Behavioral Impulsivity, Intellectual Impulsivity, and Attainment in Young Children: OSCAR and WISC." *J Child Psychol & Psychiatry* (England) 12(4):261–71 D '71. *

945. Goffeney, Barbara; Henderson, Norman B.; and Butler, Bruce V. "Negro-White, Male-Female Eight-Month Developmental Scores Compared With Seven-Year WISC and Bender Test Scores." *Child Develop* 42(2):595–604 Je '71. * (*PA* 47:651)

946. Goldstein, Harris S., and Peck, Rosalind. "Cognitive Functions in Negro and White Children in a Child Guidance Clinic." *Psychol Rep* 28(2):379–84 Ap '71. * (*PA* 46:7556)

947. Grief, Ellen G. *An Analysis of the Performance of Children With Learning Disabilities on the Illinois Test of Psycholinguistic Abilities and the Wechsler Intelligence Scale for Children.* Doctor's thesis, University of Kansas (Lawrence, Kan.), 1971. (*DAI* 32:5638A)

948. Hannaford, Alonzo E. "Factors Affecting Motor and Cognitive Performance of the Educable Mentally Retarded." *Am Correct Ther* 25(4):105–10 Jl–Ag '71. *

949. Hardy, Miriam P.; Mellits, David; and Willig, Sharon N. "Reading: A Function of Language Usage." *Johns Hopkins Med J* 129(1):43–53 Jl '71. *

950. Heiss, Warren Esler. *Intersensory Integration and Intelligence in Learning Disabled Children.* Doctor's thesis, Yeshiva University (New York, N.Y.), 1971. (*DAI* 32:5639A)

951. Henderson, N. B.; Butler, B. V.; and Clark, W. M., Jr. "Relationships Between Selected Perinatal Variables and Seven-Year Intelligence." Abstract. *Proc 79th Ann Conv Am Psychol Assn* 6(1):139–40 '71. * (*PA* 46:2707)

952. HILDMAN, LEE K., AND LOWE, JAMES D., JR. "The Usefulness of Parental Occupation as a Criterion for Standardization of the WISC." *South J Ed Res* 5(3):120–9 Jl '71. * (*PA* 49:9933)

953. HINTON, GEORGE G., AND KNIGHTS, ROBERT M. "Children With Learning Problems: Academic History, Academic Prediction, and Adjustment Three Years After Assessment." *Excep Children* 37(7):513–9 Mr '71. * (*PA* 47:3663)

954. HOWELL, ROBERT WAYNE. *Evaluation of Cognitive Abilities of Emotionally Disturbed Children: An Application of Piaget's Theories.* Doctor's thesis, Southern Illinois University (Carbondale, Ill.), 1971. (*DAI* 32:5037A)

955. HUIZINGA, RALEIGH JAMES. *The Relationship of the Illinois Test of Psycholinguistic Abilities to the Stanford-Binet Form L-M and the Wechsler Intelligence Scale for Children.* Doctor's thesis, University of Arizona (Tucson, Ariz.), 1971. (*DAI* 32:3823A)

956. HUNTER, EDNA J., AND JOHNSON, LAVERNE C. "Developmental and Psychological Differences Between Readers and Nonreaders." *J Learn Dis* 4(10):572–7 D '71. * (*PA* 47:11671)

957. JERROLDS, BOB W.; CALLAWAY, BYRON; AND GWALTNEY, WAYNE. "A Comparative Study of Three Tests of Intellectual Potential, Three Tests of Reading Achievement, and the Discrepancy Scores Between Potential and Achievement." *J Ed Res* 65(4):168–72 D '71. * (*PA* 48:1647)

958. JOESTING, JOAN, AND JOESTING, ROBERT. "The Quick Test as a Screening Device in a Welfare Setting." *Psychol Rep* 29(3):1289–90 D '71. * (*PA* 48:992)

959. KAPPELMAN, MURRAY M.; LUCK, ELIZABETH; AND GANTER, ROBERT L. "Profile of the Disadvantaged Child With Learning Disorders." *Am J Dis Children* 121(5):371–9 My '71. *

960. KILLIAN, L. R. "WISC, Illinois Test of Psycholinguistic Abilities, and Bender Visual-Motor Gestalt Test ·Performance of Spanish-American Kindergarten and First-Grade School Children." *J Consult & Clin Psychol* 37(1):38–43 Ag '71. * (*PA* 47:1738)

961. KLONOFF, HARRY. "Factor Analysis of a Neuropsychological Battery for Children Aged 9 to 15." *Percept & Motor Skills* 32(2):603–16 Ap '71. * (*PA* 46:11508)

962. KLUEVER, RAYMOND. Chap. 8, "Mental Abilities and Disorders of Learning," pp. 196–212. In *Progress in Learning Disabilities, Vol. 2.* Edited by Helmer R. Myklebust. New York: Grune & Stratton, Inc., 1971. Pp. ix, 404. *

963. KOPPITZ, ELIZABETH MUNSTERBERG. *Children With Learning Disabilities: A Five Year Follow-Up Study.* New York: Grune & Stratton, Inc., 1971. Pp. xv, 218. *

964. LEHMAN, ELYSE BRAUCH, AND LEVY, BERNARD I. "Discrepancies in Estimates of Children's Intelligence: WISC and Human Figure Drawings." *J Clin Psychol* 27(1):74–6 Ja '71. * (*PA* 46:1427)

965. LEICHTMAN, SANDRA ROSE. *Correlates of Role-Taking and Communication Skill in Children.* Doctor's thesis, University of North Carolina (Chapel Hill, N.C.), 1971. (*DAI* 32:7314B)

966. LESSLER, KEN, AND GALINSKY, M. DAVID. "Relationship Between Slosson Intelligence Test and WISC Scores in Special Education Candidates." *Psychol Sch* 8(4):341–4 O '71. * (*PA* 47:9677)

967. LEVI, HELENE S., AND WELCHER, DORIS W. "Social Class and Race as Determinants of the Sex of Human Figures Drawn by Seven-Year-Olds." *Johns Hopkins Med J* 129(1):10–8 Jl '71. *

968. LEVINSON, ELIZABETH J. "The Modification of Intelligence by Training in the Verbalization of Word Definitions and Simple Concepts." *Child Develop* 42(5):1361–80 N '71. * (*PA* 48:4673)

969. LOGOTHETIS, JOHN; HARITOS-FATOUROS, MARY; CONSTANTOULAKIS, MATHIOS; ECONOMIDOU, JOANNA; AUGOUSTAKI, OLGA; AND LOEWENSON, RUTH B. "Intelligence and Behavioral Patterns in Patients With Cooley's Anemia (Homozygous Betathalassemia); A Study Based on 138 Consecutive Cases." *Pediatrics* 48(5):740–4 N '71. *

970. MCKINNEY, JAMES D., AND CORTER, HAROLD M. "Flexibility Training With Educable Retarded Children." *J Sch Psychol* 9(4):455–61 w '71. * (*PA* 48:1711)

971. MCNINCH, GEORGE. "Auditory Perceptual Factors and Measured First-Grade Reading Achievement." *Read Res Q* 6(4):472–92 su '71. * (*PA* 47:11769)

972. MCPROUTY, VIVIAN HELEN. *Piaget's Theory as the Basis for the Assessment of Reading Disability and Suggested Remediation Through an Adapted Science Curriculum.* Doctor's thesis, University of the Pacific (Stockton, Calif.), 1971. (*DAI* 32:2488A)

973. MATHENY, ADAM P., JR. "Comparability of WISC and PPVT Scores Among Young Children." *Excep Children* 38(2):147–50 O '71. * (*PA* 48:3673)

974. MATHER, LEONARD JOSEPH. *A Causal Comparative Study of Intellectual Functioning in Good and Poor Readers.* Doctor's thesis, Catholic University of America (Washington, D.C.), 1971. (*DAI* 32:1920A)

975. MEICHENBAUM, DONALD H., AND GOODMAN, JOSEPH. "Training Impulsive Children to Talk to Themselves." *J Abn Psychol* 77(2):115–26 Ap '71. * (*PA* 46:3785)

976. MIKLICH, DONALD R. "A Device to Facilitate Administering the Object Assembly Test." *Meas & Eval Guid* 4(2):115–6 Jl '71. *

977. MOORE, MARY, AND WELCHER, DORIS W. "A Descriptive Analysis of the Seven-Year Psychological Data." *Johns Hopkins Med J* 128(6):332–46 Je '71. *

978. MOORE, TELFORD IRA. *The Relationship Among Differentiated Cognitive Abilities, Field Dependency, Achievement, and Rated Classroom Behavior of Ninth Grade Junior High School Students.* Doctor's thesis, University of Southern California (Los Angeles, Calif.), 1971. (*DAI* 32:249A)

979. MYKLEBUST, HELMER R.; BANNOCHIE, MARGARET N.; AND KILLEN, JAMES R. Chap. 9, "Learning Disabilities and Cognitive Processes," pp. 213–51. In *Progress in Learning Disabilities, Vol. 2.* Edited by Helmer R. Myklebust. New York: Grune & Stratton, Inc., 1971. Pp. ix, 404. *

980. NEWMAN, ANABEL POWELL. *Longitudinal Study of Pupils Who Were Underachieving in Reading in First Grade.* Doctor's thesis, State University of New York (Buffalo, N.Y.), 1971. (*DAI* 32:2313A)

981. OAKLAND, THOMAS D.; KING, JOHN D.; WHITE, LINDA ANN; AND ECKMAN, ROBERT. "A Comparison of Performance on the WPPSI, WISC, and SB With Preschool Children: Companion Studies." *J Sch Psychol* 9(2):144–9 '71. * (*PA* 47:7563)

982. OLSHIN, DAVID. *The Relationship of Race and Social Class to Intelligence and Reading Achievement at Grades One and Five.* Doctor's thesis, Temple University (Philadelphia, Pa.), 1971. (*DAI* 32:1923A)

983. OROS, JAMES ALLAN. *Effects of Induced Anxiety on the Wechsler Intelligence Scale for Children.* Master's thesis, Illinois State University (Normal, Ill.), 1971.

984. OWEN, FREYA WEAVER; ADAMS, PAULINE AUSTIN; FORREST, THOMAS; STOLZ, LOIS MEEK; AND FISHER, SARA. "Learning Disorders in Children: Sibling Studies." *Monogr Soc Res Child Develop* 36(4):1–77 N '71. * (*PA* 48:12196)

985. PASEWARK, RICHARD A.; FITZGERALD, BERNARD J.; AND GLOECKLER, TED. "Relationship of Peabody Picture Vocabulary Test and Wechsler Intelligence Scale for Children in an Educable Retarded Group: A Cautionary Note." *Psychol Rep* 28(2):405–6 Ap '71. * (*PA* 46:7516)

986. PAUL, LEONARD MARC. *WISC and Bender as Predictors of Reading Performance in Children With Learning Disabilities.* Doctor's thesis, University of Pennsylvania (Philadelphia, Pa.), 1971. (*DAI* 32:1923A)

987. POLLEY, DALE. *The Relationship of the Channels of Communication of the Illinois Test of Psycholinguistic Abilities to the Wechsler Intelligence Scale for Children.* Doctor's thesis, University of Northern Colorado (Greeley, Colo.), 1971. (*DAI* 32:4194B)

988. PRICE, JAMES DAVID. *Analysis of Changes in Intelligence Test Scores of Mexican-American Youth Assigned to Special Classes in Relation to Jensen's Two-Level Theory of Mental Abilities.* Doctor's thesis, University of Arizona (Tucson, Ariz.), 1971. (*DAI* 32:3125A)

989. PROSSER, NANETTE S., AND CRAWFORD, VEDA B. "Relationship of Scores on the Wechsler Preschool and Primary Scale of Intelligence and the Stanford-Binet Intelligence Scale Form LM." *J Sch Psychol* 9(3):278–83 '71. * (*PA* 47:8634)

990. PYLE, ROBERT FORREST. *Shortening the Information, Arithmetic, and Picture Completion Subtests of the Wechsler Intelligence Scale for Children.* Doctor's thesis, University of Northern Colorado (Greeley, Colo.), 1971. (*DAI* 32:2408B)

991. REBISH, DELLA. "Mask of Competence." *Claremont Read Conf Yearb* 35:109–19 '71. *

992. REDMOND, NEIL JOSEPH. *Rorschach Correlates of Underachievement and Cognitive Deficits of Underachievers.* Doctor's thesis, St. John's University (Jamaica, N.Y.), 1971. (*DAI* 32:3015B)

993. RESNICK, ROBERT J., AND ENTIN, ALAN D. "Is an Abbreviated Form of the WISC Valid for Afro-American Children?" *J Consult & Clin Psychol* 36(1):97–9 F '71. * (*PA* 45:9973)

994. RITZINGER, FRANCES CONNOR. *Psychological and Physiological Differentiation in Children Six to Eleven Years of Age.* Doctor's thesis, Washington University (St. Louis, Mo.), 1971. (*DAI* 32:2409B)

995. ROBERTS, JEAN. *Intellectual Development of Children as Measured by the Wechsler Intelligence Scale for Children: United States.* U.S. Department of Health, Education, and Welfare Publication No. (HSM) 72-1004; Vital Health Statistics, Series 11, No. 107. Washington, D.C.: Government Printing Office, August 1971. Pp. v, 41. * (*PA* 48:2696)

996. ROBERTS, JEAN. "Intellectual Development of Children as Measured by the Wechsler Intelligence Scale for Children: United States." *Vital & Health Stat* Series 11(107):1–41 Ag '71. * (*PA* 48:2696)

997. ROBERTS, JEAN. "Intellectual Development of Children by Demographic and Socioeconomic Factors: United States." *Vital & Health Stat* Series 11(110):1–71 D '71. * (*PA* 48:7748)

998. ROURKE, B. P.; YOUNG, G. C.; AND FLEWELLING, R. W. "The Relationships Between WISC Verbal-Performance Discrepancies and Selected Verbal, Auditory-Perceptual, Visual-Perceptual, and Problem-Solving Abilities in Children With Learning Disabilities." *J Clin Psychol* 27(4):475–9 O '71. * (*PA* 47:9738)

999. ROURKE, BYRON P., AND TELEGDY, GABOR A. "Lateralizing Significance of WISC Verbal-Performance Discrepancies for Older Children With Learning Disabilities." *Percept & Motor Skills* 33(3):875-83 D '71. * (PA 48:1715)

1000. RUBINO, C. A.; KROCCO, D.; AND SHEA, M. "An Analysis of Right Hemispheric Deficits in the Moderately Retarded Child as Measured by the WISC and Leiter." *Ont Psychologist* (Canada) 3(2):85-95 '71. * (PA 47:9488)

1001. RUDEL, RITA G., AND TEUBER, H.-L. "Spatial Orientation in Normal Children and in Children With Early Brain Injury." *Neuropsychologia* (England) 9(4):401-7 D '71. * (PA 48:5446)

1002. RUSCHIVAL, M. LENA, AND WAY, JOHN GILBERT. "The WPPSI and the Stanford-Binet: A Validity and Reliability Study Using Gifted Preschool Children." Abstract. *J Consult & Clin Psychol* 37(1):163 Ag '71. * (PA 47:1586)

1003. SABATINO, DAVID A., AND BECKER, JOHN T. "Relationship Between Lateral Preference and Selected Behavioral Variables for Children Failing Academically." *Child Develop* 42(6):2055-60 D '71. * (PA 48:9861)

1004. SACHS, DAVID A. "WISC Changes as an Evaluative Procedure Within a Token Economy." *Am J Mental Def* 76(2):230-4 S '71. * (PA 47:9683)

1005. SAPIR, SELMA G. "Learning Disability and Deficit Centered Classroom Training." *Cognitive Studies* 2:324-38 '71. * (PA 49:1359, title only)

1006. SATTLER, JEROME M., AND MARTIN, SANDER. "Anxious and Nonanxious Examiner Roles on Two WISC Subtests." *Psychol Sch* 8(4):347-9 O '71. * (PA 47:11628)

1007. SCHWARZ, ROBERT H., AND COOK, JOHN J. "Mental Age as a Predictor of Academic Achievement." *Ed & Train Mental Retard* 6(1):12-5 F '71. *

1008. SCHWARZ, ROBERT H., AND FLANIGAN, PATRICK J. "Evaluation of Examiner Bias in Intelligence Testing." *Am J Mental Def* 76(2):262-5 S '71. * (PA 47:9664)

1009. SCOTT, RALPH, AND SATTEL, LUDWIG. "School and Home: Not Either-Or." *Merrill-Palmer Q* 17(4):335-45 O '71. *

1010. SEARLS, EVELYN FITCH. *WISC and WPPSI IQ's and Subtest Patterns Related to First Grade Reading Achievement.* Doctor's thesis, University of Miami (Coral Gables, Fla.), 1971. (*DAI* 32:6225A)

1011. SHELDON, HARRY JAY. *An Investigation of Syntactical Ability and Vocabulary Knowledge of First Graders as Related to Reading and Vocabulary Achievement as Measured by the Stanford Achievement Test.* Doctor's thesis, University of Iowa (Iowa City, Iowa), 1971. (*DAI* 32:1201A)

1012. SILVERSTEIN, A. B. "A Corrected Formula for Assessing the Validity of WAIS, WISC, and WPPSI Short Forms." *J Clin Psychol* 27(2):212-3 Ap '71. * (PA 46:6881)

1013. SMITH, NATHANIEL C., JR. "A Comparison of Short-Form Estimation Methods in the WISC in Juvenile Public Offenders." *J Clin Psychol* 27(1):77-9 Ja '71. * (PA 46:1476)

1014. SMITH, PHILIP A., AND MARX, RONALD W. "The Factor Structure of the Revised Edition of the Illinois Test of Psycholinguistic Abilities." *Psychol Sch* 8(4):349-56 O '71. * (PA 47:9666)

1015. SOUTHERN, MARA L., AND PLANT, WALTER T. "Differential Cognitive Development Within and Between Racial and Ethnic Groups of Disadvantaged Preschool and Kindergarten Children." *J Genetic Psychol* 119(2):259-66 D '71. * (PA 48:637)

1016. SPENCE, ALLYN G.; MISHRA, SHITALA P.; AND GHOZEIL, SUSAN. "Home Language and Performance on Standardized Tests." *El Sch J* 71(6):309-13 Mr '71. * (PA 47:2655)

1017. STEWART, JOE GLENN. *The Relationship of Selected Abilities to Gross Motor Performance of Educable Mentally Retarded Students.* Doctor's thesis, North Texas State University (Denton, Tex.), 1971. (*DAI* 32:6799A)

1018. SUNDEAN, DAVID A., AND SALOPEK, THOMAS F. "Achievement and Intelligence in Primary and Elementary Classes for the Educable Mentally Retarded." *J Sch Psychol* 9(2):150-6 '71. * (PA 47:7610)

1019. SURWILLO, W. W. "Digit Span and EEG Frequency in Normal Children." *Electroenceph & Clin Neurophysiol* (Netherlands) 31(1):93-5 Jl '71. * (PA 47:10315)

1020. SWADE, ROBERTA EDYTHE. *Relationship of the Block Design Subtest of the WISC to Reading Achievement.* Doctor's thesis, Temple University (Philadelphia, Pa.), 1971. (*DAI* 32:1927A)

1021. SWANSON, ELINOR, AND DEBLASSIE, RICHARD. "Interpreter Effects on the WISC Performance of First Grade Mexican-American Children." *Meas & Eval Guid* 4(3):172-5 O '71. * (PA 49:12095)

1022. SWEET, ROGER C., AND RINGNESS, THOMAS A. "Variations in the Intelligence Test Performance of Referred Boys of Differing Racial and Socioeconomic Backgrounds as a Function of Feedback or Monetary Reinforcement." *J Sch Psychol* 9(4):399-409 w '71. * (PA 48:1664)

1023. SWIZE, LYDIA MARIE. *The Relationship Between Performance on Piagetian Conservation Tasks and Intelligence and Achievement in Educable Mentally Retarded Children.* Doctor's thesis, University of Northern Colorado (Greeley, Colo.), 1971. (*DAI* 32:3806A)

1024. THOMAS, ALEXANDER; HERTZIG, MARGARET E.; DRYMAN, IRVING; AND FERNANDEZ, PAULINA. "Examiner Effect in IQ Testing of Puerto Rican Working-Class Children." *Am J Orthopsychiatry* 41(5):809-21 O '71. * (PA 47:11636)

1025. TIGAY, BARRY, AND KEMPLER, HYMAN L. "Stability of WISC Scores of Children Hospitalized for Emotional Disturbance." *Percept & Motor Skills* 32(2):487-90 Ap '71. * (PA 46:11229)

1026. VANCE, SANDRA B. *A Comparison of the Wechsler Intelligence Scale for Children and the Columbia Mental Maturity Scale With Mental Retardates.* Master's thesis, East Tennessee State University (Johnson City, Tenn.), 1971.

1027. VASA, STANLEY FRANK. *A Comparison of Selected Intelligence Scales With Bilingual Children.* Doctor's thesis, University of Nebraska (Lincoln, Neb.), 1971. (*DAI* 32:802A)

1028. WAGONSELLER, BILL R. *A Comparison of Intellectual Ability, Achievement Level, Self-Concept, and Behavior Problems Exhibited by Children Labeled as Learning Disabilities and Emotionally Disturbed.* Doctor's thesis, University of Kansas (Lawrence, Kan.), 1971. (*DAI* 32:5644A)

1029. WALLBROWN, FRED HAROLD. *A Validity Study of the Wallach-Kogan Creativity Test: The Prediction of Six Concurrent Criteria in Visual Art.* Doctor's thesis, Ohio State University (Columbus, Ohio), 1971. (*DAI* 32:6630B)

1030. WEINER, PAUL S. "The Cognitive Functioning of Language Deficient Children." *Cognitive Studies* 2:338-63 '71. *

1031. WEINER, PAUL S. "Stability and Validity of Two Measures of Intelligence Used With Children Whose Language Development Is Delayed." *J Speech & Hearing Res* 14(2):254-61 Je '71. * (PA 48:5419)

1032. WELCHER, DORIS W.; MELLITS, E. DAVID; AND HARDY, JANET B. "A Multivariate Analysis of Factors Affecting Psychological Performance." *Johns Hopkins Med J* 129(1):19-35 Jl '71. *

1033. WHITEHOUSE, DENNIS. "Psychological and Neurological Correlates of Seizure Disorders." *Johns Hopkins Med J* 129(1):36-42 Jl '71. *

1034. WILLS, I. H., AND BANAS, NORMA. "The Vulnerable Child: Prescriptive Teaching From WISC Patterns." *Acad Ther* 7(1):79-83 f '71. *

1035. WILSON, GERALDINE O. *The Difference in Approach to the Block Subtest of the Wechsler Intelligence Scale for Children and the Bender Visual-Motor Gestalt Test by Subjects With Organic Brain Dysfunction and Normal Subjects.* Master's thesis, Southern Connecticut State College (New Haven, Conn.), 1971.

1036. WITMER, J. MELVIN; BORNSTEIN, ALAN V.; AND DUNHAM, RICHARD M. "The Effects of Verbal Approval and Disapproval Upon the Performance of Third and Fourth Grade Children on Four Subtests of the Wechsler Intelligence Scale for Children." *J Sch Psychol* 9(3):347-56 '71. * (PA 47:9668)

1037. WRIGHT, LOGAN, AND JIMMERSON, STEVE. "Intellectual Sequelae of Hemophilus Influenzae Meningitis." *J Abn Psychol* 77(2):181-3 Ap '71. * (PA 46:3584)

CUMULATIVE NAME INDEX

Abercrombie, M. L. J.: 328
Ables, B. S.: 912
Abrams, J. C.: 87
Abrams, S.: 654
Ackerman, P. T.: 913-4
Adams, N. A.: 32, 84
Adams, P. A.: 984
Aderman, M.: 675
Ahmad, F. Z.: 431
Alexander, D.: 627
Alimena, B.: 9, 191
Allen, J.: 236
Allen, R. M.: 376
Allison, J.: 379
Allor, B. A.: 726
Alper, A. E.: 127, 163, 483
Altus, G. T.: 31, 48, 88, 106
Ames, L. B.: 213, 237, 329
Anastasi, A.: 192, 566
Anderson, C. W. K.: 473
Anderson, D. E.: 567
Anderson, M. H. E.: 533
Anderson, J. M.: rev, 4:363
Anderson, L. M.: 314
Anderson, R. P.: 419, 759
Ando, K.: 568
Anthony, E. J.: 841
Apgar, V.: 143, 818
Armstrong, J. G.: 569
Armstrong, R. G.: 89, 105
Arnold, F. C.: 90
Arnoult, J. F.: 633
Arnsfield, P.: 131
Ashlock, F.: 377
Ashlock, P. R.: 315
Atchison, C. O.: 91
Augoustaki, O.: 969
Auria, C.: 303

Ayers, M. A.: 583
Bacon, C. S.: 65
Bae, A. Y.: 570
Bagwell, F. I.: 915
Baird, R. K.: 727
Baker, B. L.: 379, 730
Balthazar, E. E.: 193
Banaghan, W. F.: 292
Banas, N.: 655, 1034
Bannochie, M. N.: 979
Barbee, E. W.: 835
Barclay, A.: 432, 519, 656, 807
Barnsley, R.: 593
Baroff, G. S.: 144
Bar-Or, O.: 728
Barratt, E. S.: 107, 113
Barrett, G. V.: 555
Barron, R. C.: 916
Bartin, N. G.: 917
Bartlett, C. J.: 221-2, 255
Barton, B.: 729
Bashaw, W. L.: 533, 642
Bastendorf, W. L.: 300
Battin, R.: 571
Baumann, K. S.: 657
Baumeister, A.: 221
Baumeister, A. A.: 194, 222, 255, 330, 433
Baumgarten, D. L.: 113
Bean, W. J.: 484
Beck, E. C.: 699, 706
Beck, F.: 572
Beck, H. S.: 92, 815
Becker, J. T.: 1003
Beldoch, M.: 256
Bell, D. A.: 839
Bell, D. B.: 759

Wechsler Intelligence Scale for Children

Bellamy, E. E.: 735, 918
Belluomini, H. M.: 223
Belmont, I.: 485-6
Belmont, L.: 434, 485-6
Beniskos, J. M.: 145
Bensberg, G. J.: 63
Benton, A. L.: 412
Berg, V.: 435
Bergan, A.: 919
Bergstein, V.: 728
Berlin, M. A.: 436
Berman, I.: 331
Bernstein, A. J.: 784
Bernstein, L.: 304
Bernstein, S.: 744
Bersoff, D. N.: 920
Bibb, J. J.: 332
Bierbryer, B.: 697-8
Binks, V.: 32, 84
Birch, H. G.: 224, 434, 485-6, 658, 858
Birkemeyer, F.: 333, 378
Birnbaum, J.: 479
Bjerring, J.: 664
Black, B. G.: 921
Black, F. W.: 922
Blakemore, J. R.: 49
Blatt, S. J.: 379, 730
Blommers, P.: 123
Bogan, S.: 615
Bogartz, W.: 131
Boll, T. J.: 923
Bornstein, A. V.: 487, 1036
Borreson, P. M.: 924
Bortner, M.: 224, 658
Boruszak, R. J.: 66
Bowles, F. L.: 573
Boydstun, J. A.: 551
Braen, B. B.: 816
Braff, R. G.: 925
Bransford, L. A.: 437
Bray, P. F.: 699
Breeskin, J.: 438
Brewer, E. J.: 840
Bridges, C.: 146
Bridges, C. C.: 159
Briggs, P. F.: 554
Bright, H. A.: 86
Brill, R. G.: 225
Brito, H.: 536
Brittain, M.: 574
Brockway, R. L.: 731
Brodt, A.: 488
Brodt, A. M.: 659
Brookhouse, D. B.: 911
Brooks, E. M.: 287
Brown, C.: 630
Brown, F.: 284
Browne, D. B.: 732
Bruce, P.: 93
Brunson, F. W.: 575
Buchman, M. D.: 334
Burch, C. W.: 576
Burks, H. F.: 93
Burnes, D. K. S.: 577
Burnes, K.: 733, 926
Burnett, C. W.: 631
Burns, G. W.: 862
Burns, L.: 1
Burns, R. C.: 164
Burstein, A. G.: rev, 6:540
Burt, C. 165
Burwell, E.: 374
Bush, W. J.: 927
Buskirk, E.: 728
Butler, A. J.: 42
Butler, B. V.: 679, 945, 951
Butler, G. D.: 928
Butler, K. G.: 489
Butterfield, E. C.: 578
Byrd, C.: 660
Caccavo, E.: 579
Cain, E. R.: 152
Caldwell, M. B.: 67, 580, 716
Callaway, B.: 957
Camp, B. W.: 439
Cannon, T. M.: 661
Capobianco, R. J.: 846
Caputo, D. V.: 257
Caring, L. C.: 876
Carleton, F. O.: 68, 94, 103
Carolan, P.: 432
Carr, D.: 738
Carson, A. S.: 166

Cartee, J. K.: 62, 84
Cate, C. C.: 490
Cerbus, G.: 929
Chain, R. U.: 581
Chalmers, J. M.: 134
Chambers, J. A.: 147
Chang, T. M. C.: 491
Chang, V. A. C.: 491
Chansky, N. M.: 765
Charry, L. B.: 492
Chawla, T. R.: 662
Chiappone, A. D.: 582
Chodorkoff, J.: 258
Chrisien, G.: 282
Christ, A. E.: 643
Christiansen, T.: 734
Chun, R. W. M.: 611
Churchill, J. A.: 380, 562, 583
Clark, W. M.: 951
Clarke, B. R.: 930
Clarke, F. R.: 2
Clarke, W. M.: 951
Clawson, A.: 226
Clements, G. R.: 381
Clements, S. D.: 307
Cleveland, S. E.: 840
Cohen, B. D.: 33
Cohen, J.: 148
Cohen, L.: 877
Cohen, S. A.: 863
Cohen, T. B.: 259
Cole, D.: 34
Cole, J. O.: 940
Cole, S.: 931
Cole, S. N.: 493
Coleman, J. C.: 260-1
Coleman, L.: 293
Collart, D. S.: 870
Collier, M. J.: 33
Comrey, A.: 131
Conklin, R. C.: 494
Connolly, J. K.: 584
Constantoulakis, M.: 969
Converse, H. D.: 316, 825
Cook, J. J.: 1007
Coop, R. H.: 911
Cooper, J. G.: 128
Corah, N. L.: 841
Cordiner, M. E.: 382
Corotto, L. V.: 195
Corter, H. M.: 970
Corwin, J. P.: 383, 495
Courtney, J. M.: 825
Coyle, F. A.: 384, 735
Craddick, R. A.: 440
Cramblett, H.: 707-8
Crawford, V. B.: 663, 989
Creed, C. D.: 932
Crittenden, J. B.: 871
Crockett, D.: 664
Crofts, I. E.: 108
Cronin, R.: 878
Crookes, T. G.: 829
Cropley, A. J.: 335
Crown, P. J.: 879
Cundick, B. P.: 736
Curtin, M. E.: 199
Dahlke, A. B.: 585, 933
Dangel, H. L.: 880
Darley, F. L.: 196
Davidson, J. F.: 69, 115
Davies, J.: 542
Davis, D. R.: 118
Davis, L. J.: 441, 496
Dawson, A.: 215
Deal, M.: 385
Dean, S.: 39
DeBlassie, R.: 1021
DeBruler, R. M.: 497
DeBurger, R. A.: 199
Delattre, L.: 34
Dell, D.: 536
Delp, H. A.: 50; rev, 4:363
De Marco, W.: 665
Den Broeder, J.: 336
Dennerll, R. D.: 336, 783
Denny, C.: 199
Denton, L. R.: 135
Dershowitz, Z.: 934
Di Nello, M.: 738
Di Nello, M. C.: 386
Dockrell, W. B.: 167, 494, 839
Domrath, R. P.: 864
Doppelt, J.: 6

Doris, R. E.: 95
Doubros, S. G.: 666
Drash, P. W.: 860
Drew, A. L.: 842
Drews, E. M.: 246
Dreyer, A. S.: 935
Dreyer, C. A.: 935
Dryman, I.: 1024
Dudek, S. Z.: 498, 586, 667-8, 758
Duff, M. M.: 587
Duffy, R. J.: 936
Dunham, R. M.: 1036
Dunn, H. G.: 882
Dunn, J. A.: 499-500
Dunsdon, M. I.: 96-7, 114, 197
Durojaiye, M. O. A.: 937
Dustman, R. E.: 706
Dwyer, R. C.: 442
Dyer, G. B.: 668
Dyke, R. G.: 313
Dykman, R. A.: 551, 913-4
Early, R. G. H.: 381
Eaton, A. E.: 417
Eaves, L.: 737
Eaves, L. C.: 882
Eckman, R.: 981
Economidou, J.: 969
Edmonston, W. E.: 257
Egeland, B.: 501, 669, 738
Egeland, B. R.: 443
Ehrhardt, A. A.: 462, 872
Eisenman, R.: 337
Ekwall, E. E.: 444
Elitcher, H.: 502
Elkind, D.: 823
Ellis, E.: 290
Enburg, R.: 198
Entin, A. D.: 993
Eppley, E. B.: 588
Epstein, R.: 524, 866
Erickson, E. L.: 871
Erikson, R. V.: 503
Ertl, J. P.: 670
Estes, B. W.: 51, 98, 199, 387
Estes, R. E.: 739
Evans, J.: 302
Evans, L.: 847
Everett, G. D.: 857
Exner, J. E.: 445
Fagert, C. M.: 589
Falk, L. J.: 938
Fast, R. E.: 504
Faterson, H. F.: 313, 479
Fedio, P.: 671
Fee, F.: 590
Feffer, M. H.: 309
Feinstein, A. R.: 827
Feldhusen, J. F.: 308
Feldman, S. E.: 939
Feldt, L. S.: 472, 634, 906
Ferinden, W. E.: 672
Fernald, P. S.: 505
Fernandez, P.: 1024
Fidel, Y.: 656
Field, J. G.: 168
Fillmore, A. R.: 82
Finley, C.: 149
Finley, C. J.: 129, 247-8, 286
Finley, K. H.: 870
Finnerty, R. J.: 940
Fisher, G. M.: 169, 175, 200
Fisher, S.: 984
Fitch, M. J.: 446
Fitzgerald, B. J.: 740, 985
Fitzgerald, M. C.: 482
Flanigan, P. J.: 1008
Flax, M. L.: 567
Fleeman, G. W.: 591
Fleming, J. M.: 506
Fleming, J. W.: 297, 673
Flewelling, R. W.: 998
Floor, L.: 628
Flower, R. M.: 848
Foley, M. V.: 447
Ford, J. B.: 388
Forrest, T.: 984
Foster, D.: 84
Foster, D. V.: 32
Frandsen, A. N.: 10
Fransella, F.: 389
Fraser, E. D.: rev, 5:416
Freedheim, D. K.: 817

Freeman, F. S.: 227
Freer, F. J.: 941
Freides, D.: rev, 7:431
Fretz, B. R.: 741, 883
Friedman, E. C.: 656
Friedman, G. H. P.: 942
Friedman, R.: 742
Friedrich, D.: 674
Frommelt, L. A.: 338
Frost, B. P.: 170, 228
Frost, R.: 228
Frostig, M.: 507, 592
Fuller, G. B.: 448, 674
Furth, H. G.: 390
Gaddes, W. H.: 593
Gage, G. E.: 391
Gainer, W. L.: 229-30, 392
Galdieri, A. A.: 943
Galinsky, M. D.: 966
Gallagher, J.: 179
Gallagher, J. J.: 201
Galvan, R. R.: 508
Ganter, R. L.: 959
Gardner, R. W.: 594-5
Garibay, C.: 393
Garms, J. D.: 743, 884
Garner, E. H.: 339
Garner, J.: 944
Garton, J.: 158
Gault, U.: 70
Gayton, W. F.: 744
Gehman, I. H.: 109
Gerver, D.: 389
Getzels, J. W.: 821
Geuting, M. P.: 298
Ghozeil, S.: 1016
Gibson, W. M.: 630
Gilbert, J. G.: 394
Gillingham, W. H.: 745
Gioioso, J. V.: 675
Gittelman, M.: 858
Glasser, A. J.: 509
Gloeckler, T.: 740, 985
Glowatsky, E.: 52
Goens, B. D.: 676
Goffeney, B.: 679, 945
Goldberg, J. S.: 667-8
Goldenberg, S.: 291
Goldstein, H. S.: 946
Golen, M. E.: 395
Golland, J. H.: 680
Goodenough, D. R.: 202, 313, 479
Goodman, J.: 975
Goodstein, L. D.: 824
Gourevitch, V.: 309
Goyen, J.: 691
Grabow, J. D.: 611
Grabow, J. M.: 205
Graham, C.: 262
Graham, E. E.: 35, 53
Grandovic, M. C.: 869
Graubard, P. S.: 510
Graves, G. R.: 317
Gray, E. A.: 354
Gredler, G. R.: 765
Green, H. B.: 396
Greene, M. C. L.: 829
Greenmun, R.: 397
Grief, E. G.: 947
Griffin, D. C.: 849
Grimaldi, J.: 746
Grisell, J.: 583
Gross, F. L.: 803
Grossberg, J. M.: 340
Grove, W. R.: 3
Guarino, E. A.: 205
Guthrie, G. M.: 15
Gwaltney, W.: 957
Haas, J.: 728
Hafner, A. J.: 171
Hafner, L. E.: 747, 885
Hagen, E. P.: 11, 36
Hall, L. P.: 677, 748
Hand, J.: 820
Hannaford, A. E.: 948
Hannon, J. E.: 749
Hardy, J. B.: 1032
Hardy, M. P.: 949
Haritos-Fatouros, M.: 830, 969
Harlow, J. F.: 115
Harper, P. A.: 649
Harris, A. J.: 596
Harris, B. R.: 498, 667

Wechsler Intelligence Scale for Children

Harris, H.: 750
Harris, R.: 137
Harte, M. L.: 449
Hartlage, L. C.: 751
Hartman, R. K.: 886
Haskell, S. H.: 398
Haughey, C.: 868
Haupt, T. D.: 376
Hawkins, W. F.: 255, 433, 674
Haworth, M. R.: 241
Hayden, B. S.: 721
Hayden, D. L.: 778–80
Hecht, P. J.: 399
Heiss, W. E.: 950
Hemberger, L. W.: 678
Henderson, N. B.: 679, 945, 951
Hendrix, R.: 71
Henning, J. J.: 511
Herndon, J. D.: 231
Herrell, J. M.: 680
Herron, W. G.: 711
Hershenson, D. B.: 512
Hertel, R. K.: 782
Hertzig, M. E.: 1024
Hewitt, P. S.: 681
Higginson, J. B.: 10
Hildman, L. K.: 952
Hillix, W. A.: 781
Himelstein, P.: 231
Hine, W. D.: 752–3
Hinton, G. G.: 953
Hirsch, E. A.: 754
Hirst, L. S.: 172
Hite, L.: 54
Hofmann, L. J.: 698
Hohman, L. B.: 817
Holland, G. A.: 55
Holland, W. R.: 173
Hollingsworth, B. H.: 72
Holloway, H. D.: 56, 73
Holroyd, J.: 400, 597
Holroyd, J. C.: 341
Holtzman, W. H.: 450
Hommel, R. W.: 598
Honzik, M. P.: 870
Hooper, S.: 812
Hopkins, K. D.: 203, 342, 451, 513
Horowitz, F. D.: 452
Houston, C.: 599–600
Howell, R. W.: 954
Hudson, F. G.: 700
Hueftle, M. K.: 514
Huelsman, C. B.: 755
Hughes, D. H.: 299
Hughes, R. B.: 401
Hughes, V. A.: 398
Huizinga, R. J.: 955
Hunt, D.: 204
Hunter, E. J.: 956
Hunter, M.: 931
Huntress, D. W.: 136
Hutton, J. B.: 343
Indow, T.: 139
Ingham, J. G.: 601
Irvine, J.: 865
Irwin, D. O.: 344, 453
Irwin, O. C.: 515
Iscoe, I.: 345, 469, 834
Ison, M. G.: 116
Iverson, I. A.: 712
Jackson, C. L.: 346
Jackson, E. M.: 602
Jackson, M. A.: 174
Jackson, P. W.: 821
Jacobson, A.: 796
Jacobson, F. N.: 516
Jacobson, S.: 672
James, P.: 269
Jaros, E.: 430
Jastak, J. F.: 347
Jastak, S. R.: 347
Jayagopal, R.: 887
Jeeves, M. A.: 418, 844
Jenkin, N.: 348
Jerrolds, B. W.: 957
Jillson, R. P.: 150
Jimmerson, S.: 1037
Joesting, J.: 958
Joesting, R.: 958
Johnson, C. I.: 682
Johnson, D. D.: 683
Johnson, D. L.: 618
Johnson, J. A.: 883
Johnson, L. C.: 956
Johnson, O. L.: 232
Johnson, W. R.: 883
Joiner, L. M.: 871
Jonckheere, J.: 328
Jones, G. T.: 517
Jones, R. L.: 630
Jones, R. W.: 376
Jones, S.: 151, 233
Jongeward, P. A.: 684–5
Jordan, T. E.: 809
Jurjevich, R.: 263–4
Justman, J.: 12
Kaback, G. R.: 402
Kahn, J. H.: 238
Kaiser, M. D.: 349
Kallos, G. L.: 205
Kalter, N.: 693
Kappelman, M. M.: 959
Kardos, M. S.: 74
Karlsen, B.: 808
Karp, S. A.: 202, 313, 686
Kaspar, J. C.: 249, 421, 425, 603
Kass, C. E.: 687
Kaufman, M. J.: 888
Kearney, J. E.: 688
Kearsley, R. B.: 417
Keffer, C. E.: 868
Kell, E. R.: 785
Keller, J. E.: 117
Kelly, F. J.: 273
Kempler, H. L.: 1025
Kennedy, W. A.: 822
Kent, N.: 118
Kern, K. C.: 692
Kicklighter, R.: 749
Killen, J. R.: 979
Killian, L. R.: 960
Kilman, B. A.: 175
Kimbrell, D. L.: 176
King, J. D.: 981
Kissel, S.: 454–5
Klahn, J. E.: 208
Klausmeier, H. J.: 308
Klonoff, H.: 664, 737, 882, 961
Kløve, H.: 470
Kluever, R.: 962
Knights, R. M.: 953
Knopf, I. J.: 57, 75
Knott, J. R.: 412
Kogan, N.: 428
Kolstoe, O. P.: 76, 289
Koos, E. M.: 350
Koppitz, E. M.: 130, 518, 963
Korst, J. W.: 515
Koutstaal, C. W.: 318
Kovalinsky, T.: 672
Kraft, I. A.: 571
Kralovich, A. M.: 77
Kranzler, G. D.: 474
Kriegman, G.: 403
Kriegman, L. S.: 403
Krippner, S.: 319, 351–2, 756, 831
Krocco, D.: 1000
Krugman, J. I.: 12
Krugman, M.: 12
Kureth, G.: 37, 58
L'Abate, L.: 257
LaDriere, L.: 677
La Driere, M. L.: 748
Lair, C. V.: 766
Laird, D. S.: 119
Lam, R. L.: 92
Lamp, R. E.: 519
Landrum, J. P.: 265
Laney, B. J.: 889
Larr, A. L.: 152
Larson, K. H.: 353
Lauber, M.: 123
Lauer, B. A.: 456
Lavos, G.: 234
Lavitt, J. A.: 520
Lawson, T.: 944
Lee, R.: 536
Lehman, E. B.: 964
Lehmann, M. M.: 78
Leichtman, S. R.: 965
Lerand, L. W.: 457
Leslie, P. T.: 930
Lessing, E. E.: 266, 757
Lessing, J. C.: 266
Lessler, K.: 401, 966
Lester, E. P.: 586, 667–8, 758
Lester, L. P.: 498
Levi, J.: 19
Levin, J.: 19
Levine, M.: 348, 890
Levinson, B. M.: 153–4, 177, 206, 301
Levinson, E. J.: 968
Levitt, E. E.: 186
Levy, B. I.: 964
Levy, P.: 604
Levy, R. H.: 511, 605, 850, 859
Lewis, F. D.: 759
Lewis, L. L.: 138
Lewis, V.: 851–2, 860
Lewis, V. G.: 866, 872
Lindsey, J. M.: 458, 534
Litaker, R. G.: 493
Littell, W. M.: 178
Livermore, G.: 734
Lockyer, L.: 689, 760
Loewenson, R. B.: 969
Logothetis, J.: 969
Loos, F. M.: 100
Loper, D. J.: 404
Lotsof, E. J.: 131
Lovell, K.: 354, 521, 836
Lovinger, R. J.: 596
Lovinger, S. L.: 761
Lowe, J. D.: 952
Lucito, L.: 179
Lucito, L. J.: 201
Luck, E.: 959
Luong, C. K. M.: 606
Lusienski, D. R.: 355
Luszki, W. A.: 356, 405
Lyle, J. G.: 607, 690–1
Lytton, H.: 608
McArthur, C. R.: 609
McBeath, M.: 843
McBrearty, J. F.: 13
McBride, J. W.: 337
McCandless, B. R.: rev, 4:363
McCarthy, D.: 207
McCauley, J. H.: 406
McConochie, W. A.: 891
McCulloch, T. L.: 99
McElhaney, M. L.: 459
McFie, J.: 762
McGraw, J. J.: 460
McGuire, L. S.: 451, 513
Machi, V. S.: 126
McHugh, A. F.: 267
McKenzie, A.: 593
McKerracher, D. W.: 610
McKinney, J. D.: 970
McLean, T. K.: 320
McLeod, J.: 407, 461, 522
McManis, D. L.: 919
McMenemy, R. A.: 415
McMullen, C. P.: 408
McNinch, G. H. W.: 892, 971
McPherson, M. W.: 254
McProuty, V. H.: 972
Mac Vicar, D. B.: 357
Mahan, T. W.: 268
Malin, A. J.: 409, 867
Mann, L.: 868
Marchi, J. U.: 893
Margach, C.: 692
Marks, J. B.: 208
Marley, A. D.: 358
Marsden, G.: 693, 763
Martin, A. W.: 79
Martin, J. D.: 820
Martin, S.: 1006
Marx, R. W.: 1014
Mascarenhas, J. C.: 666
Masica, D. N.: 872
Masling, J. M.: 816
Massey, J. O.: 410, 681
Matheny, A. P.: 973
Mather, L. J.: 974
Mathews, A.: 559
Matthews, C. G.: 132, 470, 611
Matyas, R. P.: 80, 109
Maxwell, A. E.: 155–6, 180, 209–10
Maxwell, M. T.: 894
Maycock, G. A.: 764
Mayer, R. W.: 140
Meeker, M. N.: 694
Megargee, E. I.: 874
Mehrotra, K. K.: 612–3
Meichenbaum, D. H.: 975
Meier, J. H.: 411
Melchert, P. A.: 919
Mellits, D.: 949
Mellits, E. D.: 1032
Meyers, C. E.: 854
Michael, W. B.: 203
Miele, J. A.: 141
Miezitis, S. A.: 614
Miklich, D. R.: 976
Milgram, N. A.: 390, 523
Miller, C. K.: 765
Miller, H. R.: 695
Miller, J. M.: 771
Milstein, V.: 57, 75
Mirsky, A. F.: 671
Mishra, S. P.: 1016
Moed, G.: 269
Moeny, W. C.: 895
Mogel, S.: 544
Mohan, P. J.: 281
Moller, H.: 181
Money, J.: 359, 462, 524, 810, 837, 851–2, 860, 866
Montgomery, G. W. G.: 853
Moon, W. H.: 766
Moore, D.: 627
Moore, M.: 977
Moore, M. C.: 936
Moore, T. I.: 978
Moore, W. E.: 850
Morán, R. E.: 826
Mordock, J. B.: 615
Morgan, C. E.: 294
Moriarty, A.: 594–5
Morledge, J.: 540
Morper, J.: 463
Morris, H. L.: 739
Morrison, D. H.: 193
Morrison, E. B.: 295
Morrison, J.: 321
Muehl, S.: 412
Muhr, J. P.: 37–8
Muir, N.: 758
Mukherjee, B. N.: 182
Mumpower, D. L.: 360
Munger, P. F.: 474
Munz, A.: 767
Murfett, B. J.: 57, 75
Murphy, L. J.: 120
Murstein, B. I.: 814
Mussen, P.: 39
Myers, C. E.: 769
Myklebust, H. R.: 979
Naar, R.: 413
Nale, S.: 14
Nalven, F. B.: 525, 616, 696–8
Namy, E.: 526
Naumann, T. F.: 391
Neaves, A. I.: 896
Nebelkopf, E. B.: 935
Needham, W. E.: 699
Neher, L. A.: 781
Nelson, C. C.: 142
Nelson, C. M.: 700
Nelson, D.: 757
Neuhaus, M.: 527
Neville, D.: 211
Newland, T. E.: 399, 528
Newman, A. P.: 980
Newman, J. R.: 100
Nickols, J.: 270, 464, 529
Nickols, M.: 270, 464
Nix, A. P.: 493
Noller, P. A.: 21
Norton, J. A.: 842
Nowakiwska, M.: 628
Nunnally, J. C.: 361
Nurss, J. R.: 768
Nuttall, J. C.: 882
Oakland, J. A.: 701
Oakland, T. D.: 981
O'Connell, A. W.: 322
Ogdon, D. P.: 183, 530
Oki, T.: 531
Oliver, D. E.: 354
Olshin, D.: 982
O'Neil, W. M.: 235
O'Neill, H. D.: 702
Oppel, W. C.: 649
Oros, J. A.: 983
Orpet, R. E.: 769, 854

Wechsler Intelligence Scale for Children

Orr, K. N.: 23
Ortar, G.: 832
Ortiz, K. K.: 617
Osborne, R. T.: 236, 271, 362, 414, 465, 532–4, 722; rev, 7:431
Osman, H. H.: 535
Otto, W.: 415, 599–600
Owen, D. R.: 897
Owen, F. W.: 984
Owens, K. D.: 416
Oziel, L. J.: 929
Page, S.: 898
Paine, R. W.: 822
Painter, P.: 841
Palmer, F. H.: 774
Parker, J.: 873
Pasework, R. A.: 536, 740, 985
Pastovic, J. J.: 15, 26
Paterra, M. E.: 272
Patterson, G. R.: rev, 5:416
Patteson, R. F.: 296
Paul, L. M.: 986
Pavlos, A. J.: 212
Peck, R.: 946
Pedersen, D. M.: 618
Pelz, K.: 237
Pelz, K. S.: 213
Penfold, D. J.: 45
Percy, L. M.: 944
Peters, J. E.: 307, 551, 913–4
Pickles, D. G.: 537, 855
Pickup, K. T.: 274
Pierce-Jones, J.: 345
Pihl, R. O.: 619
Pike, F.: 213, 237
Pinneau, S. R.: 214
Pitts, V. A.: 22
Plant, W. T.: 125, 1015
Pless, I. B.: 417
Polley, D.: 987
Pollie, D. M.: 171
Pollitt, E.: 837
Portnoy, B.: 7
Portwood, P. F.: 133
Post, J. M.: 770
Powell, K.: 747
Prentice, N. M.: 273
Price, A. C.: 24, 115
Price, J. D.: 988
Price, J. R.: 101
Pringle, M. L. K.: 274
Prosser, N. S.: 989
Puleo, V. T.: 616
Pyle, R. F.: 990
Quereshi, M. Y.: 363, 620–4, 771–2
Query, W. T.: 773
Rabin, A. I.: 166; rev, 5:416
Rabinowitz, J.: 805
Rachiele, L. D.: 59
Rachman, S.: 559
Rainwater, H. G.: 625
Rajalakshmi, R.: 418, 844
Rajatasilpin, A.: 899
Raleigh, W. H.: 40
Rapaport, I.: 16
Rapp, D.: 822
Rasof, B.: 261
Ravenette, A. T.: 238
Rebhun, A. M.: 811
Rebish, D.: 900, 991
Redmond, N. J.: 992
Reed, J. C.: 538, 626, 703–4, 901
Rees, A. H.: 774
Reger, R.: 215, 239, 310, 466
Reid, W. B.: 627
Reid, W. R.: 275, 467
Reidy, M. E.: 41
Reilley, R. R.: 705
Reitan, R. M.: 496, 704
Reitman, E. E.: 840
Resnick, R. J.: 993
Reswick, J.: 99
Rhodes, L. E.: 706
Rhone, D. E.: 331
Rice, D. B.: 775
Rich, C. C.: 419
Richards, H. E.: 902
Richards, T. W.: 812
Richardson, H. M.: 110
Rider, R. V.: 649
Rieker, G. A.: 720

Ringness, T. A.: 1022
Ritzinger, R. C.: 994
Robeck, M. C.: 184, 240, 364–5, 833
Roberts, J.: 995–7
Roberts, J. A. F.: 97, 114, 197
Robinowitz, R.: 111
Robinson, S. J.: 870
Robinson, W. P.: 932
Rockwell, G. J.: 539
Rogge, H. J.: 157
Rohrs, F. W.: 241
Rondberg, S. R.: 257
Rosen, M.: 628
Rosenberg, M.: 39
Rosenberger, P. B.: 903
Rosenquist, C. M.: 874
Rosier, F. N. G.: 776
Ross, R. T.: 540
Roth, R. J.: 710
Rottersman, L.: 4
Rourke, B. P.: 998–9
Rowley, V. N.: 198, 216, 276
Rubin, E. J.: 394
Rubino, C. A.: 777, 1000
Rudel, R. G.: 1001
Ruess, A. L.: 845
Ruschival, M. L.: 875
Russell, C. A.: 541
Rutter, M.: 689, 760
Ruzicka, W. R.: 848
Rychlak, J. F.: 904
Rymsza, J. S. D.: 629
Sabatino, D. A.: 630–1, 707–8, 778–80, 1003
Sachs, D. A.: 1004
Sacks, L.: 827
Safrin, R. K.: 311, 366
Sak, H. G.: 542
Salisbury, D. L.: 785
Salopek, T. F.: 1018
Salvati, S. R.: 185
Sandercock, M. G.: 42
Sandry, M.: 252
Sandstedt, B.: 367
Sapir, S. G.: 1005
Sattel, L.: 1009
Sattler, J. M.: 543, 710, 781, 1006
Satz, P.: 544
Savage, R. D.: 795
Savage, W.: 348
Sawa, H.: 217
Sawyer, R.: 368
Sawyer, R. I.: 420
Sawyer, R. N.: 536
Scallon, R. J.: 632, 711
Schachter, F. F.: 143, 818
Schafer, E. W. P.: 670
Schiff, D.: 721
Schneider, B.: 18
Schneider, J. H.: 905
Schoer, L. A.: 467
Scholl, G.: 60
Schonhorn, R.: 81
Schoonover, S. M.: 782
Schramm, T. A.: 21
Schubert, J. G.: 545, 601
Schulman, J. L.: 249, 421, 425, 603
Schwartz, L.: 186
Schwartz, M. L.: 783
Schwarz, R. H.: 1007–8
Schwebel, A. I.: 784
Schwitzgoebel, R. R.: 43
Scott, E. M.: 187
Scott, G. R.: 25
Scott, R.: 785, 1009
Scottish Council for Research in Education: 546
Searls, E. F.: 1010
Seashore, H.: 6
Seashore, H. G.: 5, 17
Sekyra, F.: 633
Sells, S. B.: 468
Semler, I. J.: 469, 834
Shaffer, J. W.: 242
Shaffer, L. F.: exc, 4:363
Shane, J. F.: 422
Shapiro, E.: 53
Shapton, D.: 836
Sharp, H. C.: 121
Sharpe, T. M.: 881
Shatswell, D. W.: 786

Shaw, D. J.: 470
Shea, M.: 1000
Shearburn, C.: 728
Shearer, P. D.: 471
Sheldon, H. J.: 1011
Sheldon, M. S.: 158
Shields, J. B.: 521
Shinedling, M. M.: 618
Shinagawa, F.: 277
Shipe, D. M.: 243
Shohen, S. S.: 323
Shore, M. F.: 244
Siebert, L. A.: 278
Siegenthaler, B. M.: 787
Siegman, A. W.: 245
Silberberg, M. C.: 712
Silberberg, N.: 634, 906
Silberberg, N. E.: 423, 472, 712
Silberman, L.: 686
Silverstein, A. B.: 279–81, 547–50, 635–9, 713, 788–90, 1012
Simmers, C. P.: 907
Simon, W. E.: 714
Simpson, R. L.: 640, 791–2
Simpson, W. H.: 159
Sines, J. O.: 897
Sinton, D. W.: 551
Skinner, J.: 728
Skripol, J. N.: 793
Sloan, W.: 18, 63
Slobodzian, E. B.: 641
Smith, A. A.: 542
Smith, B. S.: 218
Smith, E.: 536
Smith, H.: 822
Smith, L. M.: 82
Smith, M.: 822
Smith, M. M.: 908
Smith, N. C.: 715, 1013
Smith, P. A.: 528, 1014
Smith, R. E.: exc, 7:B234
Smith, T. A.: 580, 716
Snider, M.: 417
Sokolov, S. L.: 336
Solkoff, N.: 282, 369
Sollee, N. D.: 717
Soltys, J. J.: 940
Sonneman, L. J.: 324
Sosulski, M. C.: 102, 305
Southern, M. L.: 1015
Spache, G. D.: 813
Spearman, L. H. O.: 283
Spence, A. G.: 1016
Spivack, G.: 348
Spreen, O.: 473, 794
Springfield, L.: 660
Stacey, C. L.: 7, 19, 68, 94, 103
Stallings, L.: 628
Stanley, J. C.: 104
Stark, R.: 83
Stempel, E. F.: 61
Stern, J. A.: 841
Stevens, D. A.: 551
Stevenson, V. M.: 871
Stewart, J. G.: 1017
Stewart, R. R.: 795
Stoffel, C. M.: 160
Stolz, L. M.: 984
Stone, B.: 198
Stone, D. R.: 902
Stone, F. B.: 276
Stone, L. A.: 552
Stout, D. H.: 219
Strecker, R. V.: 718
Stroud, J. B.: 122–3
Stumpf, J. C.: 188
Such, M.: 937
Suepsaman, B.: 899
Sullivan, D. S.: 939
Sundean, D. A.: 1018
Surko, E. F.: 110
Surwillo, W. W.: 1019
Swade, R. E.: 1020
Swanson, E.: 1021
Swanson, M. S.: 796
Sweet, R. C.: 719, 1022
Swize, L. M.: 1023
Taft, L. T.: 486
Talbot, S. C.: 189
Talerico, M.: 284
Talkington, L. W.: 720

Talmadge, M.: 721
Tanyzer, H. J.: 312
Taranta, A.: 827
Tatham, L. J.: 44, 115
Tava, E. G.: 553
Taylor, J. F.: 797
Taylor, W. C.: 839
Teahan, J. E.: 246
Teigland, J. J.: 474
Telegdy, G. A.: 999
Tellegen, A.: 554
Teuber, H. L.: 1001
Theye, F.: 543
Theye, F. W.: 798
Thomas, A.: 1024
Thompson, B. B.: 285, 306
Thompson, G. M.: 27
Thompson, J.: 129, 149
Thompson, J. A.: 762
Thompson, J. M.: 247–8, 286
Thompson, W. H.: 611
Thompson, W. W.: 799
Thorne, G. D.: 101
Thornton, C. L.: 555
Thorpe, J. S.: 424
Throne, F. M.: 249, 421, 425, 603
Throne, J. M.: 28
Thurston, D.: 841
Tiahrt, H. G.: 732
Tigay, B.: 1025
Tillman, H. M.: 722
Tillman, M. H.: 475, 532, 556–7, 642
Townes, B.: 643
Tozier, L. L.: 644
Trainer, F. E.: 723
Trapp, E. P.: 302
Trefsgar, T. F.: 868
Trieglaff, A. L.: 558
Triggs, F.: 32
Triggs, F. O.: 62, 84
Trussell, W. D.: exc, 7:B234
Tryk, H. E.: 794
Turner, G. H.: 45
Turner, R. K.: 559
Tutt, M. L.: 370
Tuttle, L. E.: 371, 476
Twain, D. C.: 287
Tyson, M. H.: 645
Ufford, M. S.: 426
Vanbramer, P. J.: 724
Vance, S. B.: 1026
Vancini, J. P.: 646
Vandenberg, S. G.: 861
Vanderhost, L.: 63
Van De Riet, H.: 544, 822
Van De Riet, V.: 822
Vanderpool, J.: 427
Vasa, S. F.: 1027
Viehweg, R.: 848
Viitamäki, R. O.: 250, 372
Vogelsang, M. P.: 800
Volle, F. O.: 124
Wagner, E. E.: 801
Wagner, W. K.: 29, 90
Wagoner, O. L.: 802
Wagonseller, B. R.: 1028
Wakefield, H. E.: 609
Walker, C.: 325
Walker, H. A.: 112
Walker, K. P.: 803
Walker, R. E.: 659
Walker, R. N.: 329
Walker, W.: 795
Wallace, G.: 725
Wallach, M. A.: 428
Wallbrown, F. H.: 1029
Wapner, I.: 171
Ward, B. J.: 804
Ward, J.: 560, 590
Wariner, E. M.: 46
Warren, N. S.: 836
Warrington, E. K.: 561
Wasserberger, M.: 536
Wassing, H. E.: 429
Watson, R. A.: 610
Weaver, W. W.: 747, 885
Webb, A. P.: 288, 326, 373
Wechsler, D.: 8, 20, 64, 430
Weider, A.: 21, 64
Weinberg, R. S.: 852
Weinberg, S.: 805
Weiner, P. S.: 1030–1

Wechsler Intelligence Scale for Children

Weise, P.: 190
Weisgerber, C. A.: 37
Weiss, J.: 730
Weissmann, S.: 99
Welcher, D. W.: 967, 977, 1032
Wells, C. G.: 909
Wempen, E. H.: 251
Wendt, R. A.: 374
Wesman, A.: 6
Whatley, R. G.: 125
White, A. J.: 161
White, L. A.: 647, 981
Whitehouse, D.: 1033
Whitten, C. F.: 258
Wickham, W.: 631
Widlak, F. W.: 772
Widman, J. B.: 648
Wiechers, J. E.: 79
Wiener, G.: 649, 910
Wight, B. W.: 252, 269
Wilhelm, R.: 856
Wilk, W. S.: 253
Willard, L. A.: 650
Willerman, L.: 562, 583
Williams, J. M.: 220
Williams, R. J.: 126
Williams, R. L.: 493
Willig, S. N.: 949
Willis, J.: 806
Wills, I. H.: 655, 1034
Wilson, G. O.: 1035
Wilson, L.: 47
Wilson, W. T.: 744

Wiltberger, A. C.: 563
Winget, B. M.: 710
Winitz, H.: 162, 196, 819
Winkler, R. C.: 474
Winpenny, N.: 30
Winschel, J. F.: 327
Winters, S.: 686
Wiser, W. C.: 699
Wisser, R. E.: 478, 505
Witherspoon, Y. T.: 828
Witkin, H. A.: 313, 479
Witmer, J. M.: 1036
Wolf, C. W.: 651
Woody, R. H.: 375, 564, 652
Wright, F.: 400
Wright, H. C.: 838
Wright, L.: 1037
Wrightstone, J. W.: 12
Wunderlin, R. J.: 254
Wussler, M.: 807
Wyne, M. D.: 911
Xydis, G. A.: 821
Yalowitz, J. M.: 105
Yamarat, V.: 899
Young, F. L.: 85
Young, F. M.: 22, 86
Young, G. C.: 998
Yudin, L. W.: 480
Yule, W.: 565
Zagorin, S. W.: 757
Zedler, E. Y.: 481, 653
Zimmerman, I. L.: 509
Zlody, R. L.: 482

[534]
[Re Wechsler Intelligence Scale for Children] **California Abbreviated WISC.** Educable mentally retarded ages 8–13.5, intellectually gifted elementary school children; 1966; consists of 5 subtests of *Wechsler Intelligence Scale for Children;* 2 levels; Carmen J. Finley and Jack M. Thompson; Western Psychological Services. *

a) FORM 1. Educable mentally retarded ages 8–13.5; CAW-MR; 6 scores: information, picture arrangement, picture completion, block design, coding, total.
b) FORM 2. Intellectually gifted elementary school children; CAW-IG; 6 scores: information, picture arrangement, picture completion, block design, similarities, total.

For additional information and a review by A. B. Silverstein, see 7:432 (1 reference).

REFERENCES THROUGH 1971
1. See 7:432.

CUMULATIVE NAME INDEX
Bellamy, E. E.: 1   Silverstein, A. B.: rev, 7:432
Coyle, F. A.: 1

[535]
[Re Wechsler Intelligence Scale for Children] **Rhodes WISC Scatter Profile.** Ages 5–15; 1969; a form for profiling WISC scores; Fen Rhodes; Educational and Industrial Testing Service. *

For additional information, see 7:433.

[536]
★[Re Wechsler Intelligence Scale for Children] **WISC Mental Description Sheet.** Ages 5–15; 1970–71; a form for profiling WISC scores; 1971 form identical with form copyrighted 1970; no manual; John A. Blazer; Psychologists and Educators, Inc. *

[537]
★[Re Wechsler Intelligence Scale for Children] **WISC Test Profile.** Ages 5–15; 1968–69; Consulting Psychologists Press, Inc. *

[538]
Wechsler Preschool and Primary Scale of Intelligence. Ages 4–6.5; 1967, c1949–67; WPPSI; 8 of the 11 tests provide the same measures as the *Wechsler Intelligence Scale for Children* and approximately ⅓ of the total number of items are essentially the same; 13 or 14 scores: verbal (information, vocabulary, arithmetic, similarities, comprehension, sentences [optional], total), performance (animal house, picture completion, mazes, geometric design, block design, total), total; David Wechsler; Psychological Corporation. (British edition: 1971; manual supplement by Peter Saville; NFER Publishing Co. Ltd. [England].) *

For additional information, reviews by Dorothy H. Eichorn and A. B. Silverstein, and excerpted reviews by C. H. Ammons and O. A. Oldridge (with E. E. Allison), see 7:434 (56 references).

REFERENCES THROUGH 1971
1–56. See 7:434.
57. HARTMAN, ROBERT K. "The Wechsler Preschool and Primary Scale of Intelligence." *Dig Mental Retard* 5(2):107–9 w '68–69 ['69]. *
58. RUSCHIVAL, MARY LENA. *The Effectiveness of the Wechsler Preschool and Primary Scale of Intelligence in the Identification of Gifted Preschool Children.* Master's thesis, East Carolina University (Greenville, N.C.), 1969.
59. BOYD, MILLER WILLIAMS, JR. *A Factor Analysis of the Wechsler Preschool and Primary Scale of Intelligence.* Doctor's thesis, St. Louis University (St. Louis, Mo.), 1970. (*DAI* 32:1186B)
60. GUEST, KRISTIN ELIZABETH. *Relationships Among the Illinois Test of Psycholinguistic Abilities, Receptive and Expressive Language Tasks, Intelligence, and Achievement.* Doctor's thesis, University of Wisconsin (Madison, Wis.), 1970. (*DAI* 31:5845A)
61. KINNIE, ERNEST J. *The Influence of Nonintellective Factors on the IQ Scores of Middle- and Lower-Class Children.* Doctor's thesis, Purdue University (Lafayette, Ind.), 1970. (*DAI* 31:626oB)
62. LIVO, NORMA J. "Reading Readiness Factors and Beginning Reading Success." *Read Teach* 24(2):124–9+ N '70. * (*PA* 45:10960)
63. MUSGROVE, WALTER J. "Comparisons of Low Socioeconomic Black and White Kindergarten Children." *Acad Ther* 6(2):163–7 w '70. *
64. SHATUS, ERWIN L. "Validation of the Wechsler Preschool and Primary Scale of Intelligence With the Stanford-Binet, Form L-M, on Culturally Deprived Children." *South J Ed Res* 4(1):18–36 Ja '70 [My '71]. *
65. BERSOFF, DONALD N. "Short Forms of Individual Intelligence Tests for Children: Review and Critique." *J Sch Psychol* 9(3):310–20 '71. * (*PA* 47:8924)
66. FREER, FRANK J. *Visual and Auditory Perceptual Modality Differences as Related to Success in First Grade Reading Word Recognition.* Doctor's thesis, Rutgers—The State University (New Brunswick, N.J.), 1971. (*DAI* 32:6193A)
67. GORDON, GEORGE, AND HYMAN, IRWIN. "The Measurement of Perceptual-Motor Abilities of Head Start Children." *Psychol Sch* 8(1):41–8 Ja '71. * (*PA* 46:7777)
68. HAGIN, ROSA A.; SILVER, ARCHIE A.; AND CORWIN, CAROL G. "Clinical-Diagnostic Use of the WPPSI in Predicting Learning Difficulties in Grade 1." *J Spec Ed* 5(3):221–32 f '71. * (*PA* 48:12188)
69. HAYWOOD, NANCY ROBERTS. *The Wechsler Preschool and Primary Scale of Intelligence and Picture Motivation Scale as Predictors of Academic Achievement in First-Grade Children.* Master's thesis, George Peabody College (Nashville, Tenn.), 1971.
70. KINNIE, ERNEST J., AND STERNLOF, RICHARD E. "The Influence of Nonintellective Factors on the IQ Scores of Middle- and Lower-Class Children." *Child Develop* 42(6):1989–95 D '71. * (*PA* 48:8823)
71. KRUSEN, MARGARET MARY MORROW. *The Relationship of Physical Condition at Birth to Intellectual Functioning at Early School Age.* Doctor's thesis, University of Nebraska (Lincoln, Neb.), 1971. (*DAI* 32:2485A)
72. MATHENY, ADAM P., JR., AND BROWN, ANNE M. "Activity, Motor Coordination and Attention: Individual Differences in Twins." *Percept & Motor Skills* 32(1):151–8 F '71. * (*PA* 46:2639)
73. MOFFITT, P.; NURCOMBE, B.; PASSMORE, M.; AND MCNEILLY, A. "Intervention in Cultural Deprivation: The Comparative Success of Preschool Techniques for Rural Aborigines and Europeans." *Austral Psychologist* 6(1):51–61 Mr '71. * (*PA* 47:3795)
74. MUSGROVE, WALTER J., AND LAWSON, JOHN R. "A Comparison of Lower Class Negro and White Children on Three Standardized Tests." *J Negro Ed* 40(1):53–5 w '71. *
75. OAKLAND, THOMAS D.; KING, JOHN D.; WHITE, LINDA ANN; AND ECKMAN, ROBERT. "A Comparison of Performance on the WPPSI, WISC, and SB With Preschool Children:

Companion Studies." *J Sch Psychol* 9(2):144–9 '71. * (*PA* 47:7563)
76. OLSHIN, DAVID. *The Relationship of Race and Social Class to Intelligence and Reading Achievement at Grades One and Five.* Doctor's thesis, Temple University (Philadelphia, Pa.), 1971. (*DAI* 32:1923A)
77. PASEWARK, RICHARD A.; RARDIN, MAX W.; AND GRICE, JOHN E., JR. "Relationship of the Wechsler Pre-School and Primary Scale of Intelligence and the Stanford-Binet (L-M) in Lower Class Children." *J Sch Psychol* 9(1):43–50 '71. * (*PA* 47:5609)
78. PROSSER, NANETTE S., AND CRAWFORD, VEDA B. "Relationship of Scores on the Wechsler Preschool and Primary Scale of Intelligence and the Stanford-Binet Intelligence Scale Form LM." *J Sch Psychol* 9(3):278–83 '71. * (*PA* 47:8634)
79. ROBINSON, HALBERT B., AND ROBINSON, NANCY M. "Longitudinal Development of Very Young Children in a Comprehensive Day Care Program: The First Two Years." *Child Develop* 42(6):1673–83 D '71. * (*PA* 48:8827)
80. RUSCHIVAL, M. LENA, AND WAY, JOHN GILBERT. "The WPPSI and the Stanford-Binet: A Validity and Reliability Study Using Gifted Preschool Children." Abstract. *J Consult & Clin Psychol* 37(1):163 Ag '71. * (*PA* 47:1586)
81. SCHWARZ, ROBERT H., AND FLANIGAN, PATRICK J. "Evaluation of Examiner Bias in Intelligence Testing." *Am J Mental Def* 76(2):262–5 S '71. * (*PA* 47:9664)
82. SEARLS, EVELYN FITCH. *WISC and WPPSI IQ's and Subtest Patterns Related to First Grade Reading Achievement.* Doctor's thesis, University of Miami (Coral Gables, Fla.), 1971. (*DAI* 32:6225A)
83. SEITZ, ELAINE KELLER. *The Relationship Between Cognitive Abilities and Impulse Control in Project Headstart Children.* Doctor's thesis, New York University (New York, N.Y.), 1971. (*DAI* 32:6061B)
84. SILVERSTEIN, A. B. "A Corrected Formula for Assessing the Validity of WAIS, WISC, and WPPSI Short Forms." *J Clin Psychol* 27(2):212–3 Ap '71. * (*PA* 46:6881)
85. TAKACS, CAROL PAULA. *Comparison of Mental Abilities Between Lower Socioeconomic Status Five-Year-Old Negro and White Children on Individual Intelligence Measures.* Doctor's thesis, Kent State University (Kent, Ohio), 1971. (*DAI* 32:3806A)
86. YATER, ALLAN C.; BARCLAY, ALLAN; AND LESKOSKY, RICHARD. "Goodenough-Harris Drawing Test and WPPSI Performance of Disadvantaged Preschool Children." *Percept & Motor Skills* 33(3):967–70 D '71. * (*PA* 48:698)

CUMULATIVE NAME INDEX

Allen, M.: 25
Allison, E. E.: *exc*, 7:434
Ammons, C. H.: *exc*, 7:434
Bach, L. C.: 2
Barclay, A.: 19, 86
Berger, M.: 41
Bersoff, D. N.: 65
Birney, S. D.: 40
Bonfield, J. R.: 3
Boyd, M. W.: 59
Brittain, M.: 20
Broughton, E.: 25
Brown, A. M.: 72
Brudenell, G. A.: 21
Butler, S.: 41
Campanella, S.: 4
Clark, B.: 25
Corwin, C. G.: 68
Crawford, V. B.: 78
Cundick, B. P.: 42
Curry, D. R.: 22
Delaney, R. J.: 43
Dienstag, R.: 23
Dokecki, P. R.: 24
Eckman, R.: 75
Eichorn, D. H.: *rev*, 7:434
Emerson, P.: 25
Fagan, J.: 25
Flanigan, P. J.: 81
Frede, M. C.: 24
Freer, F. J.: 66
Fuller, B. L.: 5
Futterer, J. W.: 44
Garver, S. A.: 26
Gautney, D. B.: 24
Goens, B. D.: 27
Gordon, G.: 67
Graham, G. A.: 45
Green, R. M.: 28
Grice, J. E.: 77
Guest, K. E.: 60
Hagin, R. A.: 68
Handley, W. B.: 46
Hartman, R. K.: 57
Haywood, N. R.: 69
Herman, D. O.: 6
Hyman, I.: 67
Jones, E. L. H.: 47
Kavajecz, K. L. G.: 29
King, J. D.: 75
Kinnie, E. J.: 61, 70
Knoll, D. B.: 7
Kordinak, S. T.: 40
Krebs, E. G.: 30
Krusen, M. M. M.: 71
Lawson, J. R.: 74
Leskosky, R.: 86
Lichtman, M. V.: 31
Livo, N. J.: 32, 62
McNamara, J. R.: 33
McNeilly, A.: 73
McRae, J.: 8
Matheny, A. P.: 72
Meeker, M. N.: 34
Miezitis, S.: 38
Miller, L. E.: 33
Milliren, A. P.: 35
Moffitt, P.: 48, 73
Musgrove, W. J.: 63, 74
Nase, R. R.: 36
Newham, V.: 41
Newland, T. E.: 35
Nurcombe, B.: 48, 73
Oakland, T. D.: 75
O'Keefe, G. S.: 49
Oldridge, O. A.: *exc*, 7:434
Olshin, D.: 76
Pasewark, R. A.: 77
Passmore, M.: 73
Paul, G. T.: 9
Plant, W. T.: 10
Porterfield, C. L.: 33
Prosser, N. S.: 78
Rardin, M. W.: 77
Rellas, A. J.: 37
Richards, J. T.: 11, 50
Robinson, H. B.: 79
Robinson, N. M.: 79
Ruschival, M. L.: 58, 80
Schwarz, R. H.: 81
Searls, E. F.: 82
Seitz, E. K.: 83
Shatus, E. L.: 64
Shipe, D.: 38
Silver, A. A.: 68
Silverstein, A. B.: 1, 12–6, 39, 51–2, 84; *rev*, 7:434
Smith, R. A.: 17
Southern, M. L.: 10
Sternlof, R. E.: 70
Takacs, C. P.: 85
Taylor, V. C.: 53
Tizard, J.: 41
Vingoe, F. J.: 40
Wasik, B. H.: 54
Wasik, J. L.: 54
Way, J. G.: 80
White, L. A.: 18, 75
Woo-Sam, J.: 56
Works, M. N.: 55
Yater, A. C.: 19, 86
Yule, W.: 41
Zimmerman, I. L.: 56

[539]
★[Re Wechsler Preschool and Primary Scale of Intelligence] **WPPSI Test Profile.** Ages 4–6.5; 1968–69; Consulting Psychologists Press, Inc. *

[540]
Williams Intelligence Test for Children With Defective Vision. Blind and partially sighted ages 5–15; 1956; M. Williams; distributed by NFER Publishing Co. Ltd. [England]. *

For additional information and a review by T. Ernest Newland, see 6:541 (2 references).

REFERENCES THROUGH 1971

1–2. See 6:541.
3. WILLIAMS, M. "Superior Intelligence of Children Blinded From Retinoblastoma." *Arch Dis Childh* (England) 43:204–10 Ap '68. * (*PA* 42:17499)

CUMULATIVE NAME INDEX

Newland, T. E.: *rev*, 6:541   Williams, M.: 1–3

[Out of Print Since TIP I]

Alexander Performance Scale, 6:514 (1 review, 11 references); see also 4:334 (3 reviews, 2 excerpts)
Carl Hollow Square Scale, 3:273 (2 reviews, 5 references)
Children's Picture Information Test, 6:516 (2 reviews, 2 references)
Detroit Kindergarten Test, 3:274 (2 reviews, 1 reference)
Diagnostic Performance Tests, 6:519 (1 review, 1 reference)
Griffiths Mental Development Scale for Testing Babies From Birth to Two Years, 6:523 (2 reviews, 7 references)
Intelligence Tests for Children, 5:405 (2 reviews, 8 excerpts, 5 references)
Northwestern Intelligence Tests, 5:411 (2 reviews, 1 excerpt, 9 references)
Ontario School Ability Examination, 2:1411 (1 review, 2 references)
Pacific Infants Performance Scale, 7:416 (1 reference)
Performance Tests of Intelligence: A Series of Non-Linguistic Tests for Deaf and Normal Children, 3:290 (3 excerpts, 2 references)
Preliminary Test of Intelligence, 3:291
Randall's Island Performance Series, T:908
Tests of Mental Development, 2:1426 (4 reviews, 2 excerpts, 1 reference)
Van Alstyne Picture Vocabulary Test, 6:537 (3 reviews, 6 references)

SPECIFIC

[541]
★**Abstract Spatial Relations Test, Second Edition.** Bantu industrial workers with 0–12 years of education; ?–1969; ASRT; J. Kelmovitz (test); National Institute for Personnel Research [South Africa]. *

REFERENCES THROUGH 1971

1. GRANT, G. V. "Spatial Thinking: A Dimension in African Intellect." *Psychologia Africana* (South Africa) 13(2–3):222–39 O '70. *

CUMULATIVE NAME INDEX

Grant, G. V.: 1

[542]

Alternate Uses. Grades 6–16 and adults; 1960; revision of *Unusual Uses;* experimental form; spontaneous flexibility; for a downward extension, see 554i; Paul R. Christensen, J. P. Guilford, Philip R. Merrifield, and Robert C. Wilson; Sheridan Psychological Services, Inc. *

For additional information, see 6:542 (7 references).

REFERENCES THROUGH 1971

1–7. See 6:542.
8. MEADOW, ARNOLD, AND PARNES, SIDNEY J. "Evaluation of Training in Creative Problem-Solving." *J Appl Psychol* 43:189–94 Je '59. * (PA 34:5568)
9. MARKS, ALVIN; MICHAEL, WILLIAM B.; AND KAISER, HENRY F. "Comparison of Manual and Analytic Techniques of Rotation in a Factor Analysis of Aptitude Test Variables." *Psychol Rep* 7:519–22 D '60. * (PA 35:2792)
10. GARWOOD, DOROTHY SEMENOW. *Some Personality Factors Related to Creativity in Young Scientists.* Doctor's thesis, Claremont Graduate School (Claremont, Calif.), 1961. (DA 22:3273)
11. MCGUIRE, CARSON; HINDSMAN, EDWIN; KING, F. J.; AND JENNINGS, EARL. "Dimensions of Talented Behavior." *Ed & Psychol Meas* 21:3–38 sp '61. * (PA 36:1KH03M)
12. MALTZMAN, IRVING; SEYMORE, SIMON; AND LICHT, LEONARD. "Verbal Conditioning of Common and Uncommon Word Associations." *Psychol Rep* 10:363–9 Ap '62. * (PA 37:2450)
13. PENNY, R. K., AND MCCANN, B. "Application of Originality Training to the Mentally Retarded." *Psychol Rep* 11:347–51 O '62. * (PA 37:8161)
14. BARRON, FRANK. *Creativity and Psychological Health: Origins of Personal Vitality and Creative Freedom.* Princeton, N.J.: D. Van Nostrand Co., Inc., 1963. Pp. xi, 292. *
15. HAAS, MARY GERALDINE. *A Comparative Study of Critical Thinking, Flexibility of Thinking, and Reading Ability Involving Religious and Lay College Seniors.* Doctor's thesis, Fordham University (New York, N.Y.), 1963. (DA 24:622)
16. IRVINE, DAVID JAMES. *An Empirical Study of the Relationship Between Certain Pupil Characteristics and Selected Measures of Creativity.* Doctor's thesis, University of North Carolina (Chapel Hill, N.C.), 1963. (DA 25:4543)
17. CASTELLI, CHARLES DOMINIC. *An Exploration of the Relationship Between Teacher Creative Ability and Teacher-Pupil Classroom Behavior.* Doctor's thesis, State University of New York (Buffalo, N.Y.), 1964. (DA 25:3320)
18. FLEISCHER, GERALD. *The Effects of Anxiety Upon Tests of Creativity.* Doctor's thesis, State University of New York (Buffalo, N.Y.), 1964. (DA 25:5372)
19. GARWOOD, DOROTHY SEMENOW. "Personality Factors Related to Creativity in Young Scientists." *J Abn & Social Psychol* 68:413–9 Ap '64. * (PA 39:1729)
20. GRIFFIN, WILLIAM MAXWELL. *A Study of the Relationship of Certain Characteristics of High School Seniors to Effectiveness in Independent Study.* Doctor's thesis, Syracuse University (Syracuse, N.Y.), 1964. (DA 25:5787)
21. ISCOE, IRA, AND PIERCE-JONES, JOHN. "Divergent Thinking, Age, and Intelligence in White and Negro Children." *Child Develop* 35:785–97 S '64. * (PA 39:4589)
22. MCGLOTHLIN, WILLIAM H.; COHEN, SIDNEY; AND MCGLOTHLIN, MARCELLA S. "Short-Term Effects of LSD on Anxiety, Attitudes and Performance." *J Nerv & Mental Dis* 139:266–73 S '64. * (PA 39:7046)
23. RAINWATER, JANETTE MUNKITTRICK. *Effects of Set on Problem Solving in Subjects of Varying Levels of Assessed Creativity.* Doctor's thesis, University of California (Berkeley, Calif.), 1964. (DA 25:6753)
24. SEITZ, THEODORE LEE. *The Relationship Between Creativity and Intelligence, Personality, and Value Patterns in Adolescence.* Doctor's thesis, University of Denver (Denver, Colo.), 1964. (DA 25:3679)
25. WHITE, LOUISE ELIZABETH. *Creativity as a Function of Feelings of Self Worth.* Doctor's thesis, Vanderbilt University (Nashville, Tenn.), 1964. (DA 25:2619)
26. ABOU-GHORRA, I. M. "Dynamic Predictors of Production of Creative Novel Solutions in Counseling Among College Students." Abstract. *Proc Ann Conv Am Psychol Assn* 73:353–4 '65. * (PA 39:15850)
27. BACHELIS, LEONARD A. *Body-Field Perceptual Differentiation as a Variable in Creative Thinking.* Doctor's thesis, Yeshiva University (New York, N.Y.), 1965. (DA 26:3475)
28. DIXON, JAMES C. "Cognitive Structure in Senile Conditions With Some Suggestions for Developing a Brief Screening Test of Mental Status." *J Gerontol* 20:41–9 Ja '65. *
29. FELDHUSEN, JOHN F.; DENNY, TERRY; AND CONDON, CHARLES F. "Anxiety, Divergent Thinking, and Achievement." *J Ed Psychol* 56:40–5 F '65. * (PA 39:10771)
30. FLEISCHER, GERALD, AND COHEN, IRA S. "The Relationship Between Test Anxiety and Tests of Creativity." Abstract. *Proc Ann Conv Am Psychol Assn* 73:311–2 '65. * (PA 39:15458)
31. CORDER, BILLIE FARMER. *A Study of Shift in Set in Relation to Intelligence, Rigidity Measured as a Cognitive and Personality Variable, and Educational Set.* Doctor's thesis, University of Kentucky (Lexington, Ky.), 1966. (DAI 30:1861A)
32. EISENSTADT, J. MARVIN. "Problem-Solving Ability of Creative and Non-Creative College Students." *J Consult Psychol* 30:81–3 F '66. * (PA 40:4223)
33. FLAX, MORTON LEWIS. *The Stability of Relationships Between Creativity and Personality Variables.* Doctor's research study No. 1, Colorado State College (Greeley, Colo.), 1966. (DA 27:2857B)
34. GETZELS, J. W., AND CSIKSZENTMIHALYI, M. Chap. 15, "The Study of Creativity in Future Artists: The Criterion Problem," pp. 349–68. In *Experience, Structure and Adaptability.* Edited by O. J. Harvey. New York: Springer Publishing Co., Inc., 1966. Pp. ix, 406. *
35. HAYNES, CAROLYN R. *The Relationships of Performances of Seventh Grade Students on Measures of Creativity, Study Habits and Attitudes, Expressed Need for Counseling and Achievement.* Master's thesis, Texas A & M University (College Station, Tex.), 1966.
36. HELSON, RAVENNA. "Personality of Women With Imaginative and Artistic Interests: The Role of Masculinity, Originality, and Other Characteristics in Their Creativity." *J Personality* 34:1–25 Mr '66. * (PA 40:8830)
37. JANSSEN, CALVIN WAYNE. *Comparative Creativity Scores of Lower Socio-Economic Dropouts and Non-Dropouts.* Doctor's thesis, University of Tennessee (Knoxville, Tenn.), 1966. (DA 27:1659A)
38. MAHAL, BARBARA KRUEGER. *Achievement and Rigidity.* Doctor's thesis, Rutgers—The State University (New Brunswick, N.J.), 1966. (DA 27:1661A)
39. NICOLAY, GLEN C. *Relationship Between a Risk-Taking Questionnaire and Selected Personality Characteristics.* Doctor's thesis, Fordham University (New York, N.Y.), 1966. (DA 27:2142B)
40. RAY, WILBERT S. "Absence of Transfer in Unusual Uses Tests." *Psychol Rep* 18:237–8 F '66. * (PA 40:6644)
41. SMITH, ROBERT M., AND NEISWORTH, JOHN T. "Creative Thinking Abilities of Intellectually Superior Children in the Regular Grades." *Psychol Rep* 18:335–41 Ap '66. * (PA 40:8832)
42. BRUCH, CATHERINE BELL. *Cognitive Characteristics of Effectively Creative Teachers.* Doctor's thesis, University of California (Los Angeles, Calif.), 1967. (DA 28:3524A)
43. COMPTON, MARY FRANCES. *An Attempt to Foster Creative Thinking in Teachers.* Doctor's thesis, University of Florida (Gainesville, Fla.), 1967. (DA 29:164A)
44. GIVENS, PAUL R.; PINKARD, CAROLYN A.; AND RICH, THOMAS A. "Relationship of Personality Factors, Creativity and Academic Achievement Among High School Seniors." *Fla J Ed Res* 9:45–56 Ja '67. *
45. JACKSON, ROBERT LEON. *An Investigation of the Creative Growth Curves of University Students.* Doctor's thesis, East Texas State University (Commerce, Tex.), 1967. (DA 28:3508A)
46. JENKINS, JOHN MERVIN. *A Study of the Characteristics Associated With Innovative Behavior in Teachers.* Doctor's thesis, University of Miami (Coral Gables, Fla.), 1967. (DA 28:903A)
47. MANGAN, GORDON L. "Studies of the Relationship Between Neo-Pavlovian Properties of Higher Nervous Activity and Western Personality Dimensions: 3, The Relations of Transformation Mobility to Thinking Flexibility." *J Exp Res Personality* 2:117–23 My '67. * (PA 41:11907)
48. PANKOVE, ETHEL WASSERMAN. *The Relationship Between Creativity and Risk Taking in Fifth-Grade Children.* Doctor's thesis, Rutgers—The State University (New Brunswick, N.J.), 1967. (DA 28:1308A)
49. RIDLEY, DENNIS R., AND BIRNEY, ROBERT C. "Effects of Training Procedures on Creativity Test Scores." *J Ed Psychol* 58:158–64 Je '67. * (PA 41:10457)
50. SIDLE, ALLAN CHARLES. *Creativity and Delusional Thinking in Schizophrenics.* Doctor's thesis, Stanford University (Stanford, Calif.), 1967. (DA 28:353B)
51. SKAGER, R. W.; KLEIN, S. P.; AND SCHULTZ, C. B. "The Prediction of Academic and Artistic Achievement at a School of Design." *J Ed Meas* 4:105–17 su '67. *
52. SMITH, ROBERT M. "Creative Thinking Abilities of Educable Mentally Handicapped Children in the Regular Grades." *Am J Mental Def* 71:571–5 Ja '67. * (PA 41:6197)
53. WINDHOLZ, GEORGE, AND MCINTOSH, WILLIAM A. "Concurrent Validation of Guilford's Six Convergent Tests." *Ed & Psychol Meas* 27:393–400 su '67. * (PA 41:12843)
54. ADAMS, JOHN C., JR. "The Relative Effects of Various Testing Atmospheres on Spontaneous Flexibility, a Factor of Divergent Thinking." *J Creative Behav* 2:187–94 su '68. * (PA 43:5882)

Abstract Spatial Relations Test

55. ARMSTRONG, CARMEN LAPP GERBERDING. *Changes Evidenced in the Art Products of Elementary Education Majors Exhibiting the Characteristic of Flexibility.* Doctor's thesis, Indiana University (Bloomington, Ind.), 1968. (*DA* 29:1799A)

56. BROWN, STEPHEN W.; GUILFORD, J. P.; AND HOEFFNER, RALPH. "Six Semantic-Memory Abilities." *Ed & Psychol Meas* 28:691–717 au '68. * (*PA* 43:4427)

57. CRAVER, ANN APRIL. *Convergent and Divergent Creative Thinking as a Function of Stimulation.* Doctor's thesis, University of Georgia (Athens, Ga.), 1968. (*DA* 29:4842B)

58. EDWARDS, ARTHUR B. *An Analysis of the Creative Ability Levels of the Potential Dropout in the Average Mental Ability Range.* Doctor's thesis, University of Tennessee (Knoxville, Tenn.), 1968. (*DA* 29:3828A)

59. GETZELS, J. W., AND CSIKSZENTMIHALYI, M. "The Value-Orientations of Art Students as Determinants of Artistic Specialization and Creative Performance." *Studies Art Ed* 10:5–16 f '68. *

60. GIBSON, JAMES W.; KIBLER, ROBERT J.; AND BARKER, LARRY L. "Some Relationships Between Selected Creativity and Critical Thinking Measures." *Psychol Rep* 23:707–14 D '68. * (*PA* 43:9748)

61. HINTON, BERNARD L. "Environmental Frustration and Creative Problem Solving." *J Appl Psychol* 52:211–7 Je '68. * (*PA* 42:11701)

62. JANSSEN, CALVIN. "Comparative Creativity Scores of Lower Socio-Economic Dropouts and Non-Dropouts." *Psychol Sch* 5:183–4 Ap '68. * (*PA* 43:17498)

63. LETT, WARREN ROBERT. *Some Postulated Correlates of Creativity and Need Achievement.* Doctor's thesis, University of California (Berkeley, Calif.), 1968. (*DA* 29:1106A)

64. MANSKE, MARY E., AND DAVIS, GARY A. "Effects of Simple Instructional Biases Upon Performance in the Unusual Uses Test." *J General Psychol* 79:25–33 Jl '68. * (*PA* 42:16417)

65. STIMSON, ROGER C., JR. "Factor Analytic Approach to the Structural Differentiation of Description." *J Counsel Psychol* 15:301–7 Jl '68. * (*PA* 42:15457)

66. WHITE, KINNARD. "Anxiety, Extraversion-Intraversion, and Divergent Thinking Ability." *J Creative Behav* 2:119–27 sp '68. * (*PA* 42:17233)

67. WINDHOLZ, GEORGE. "The Relation of Creativity and Intelligence Constellations to Traits of Temperament, Interest, and Value in College Students." *J General Psychol* 79:291–9 O '68. * (*PA* 43:3998)

68. ALKER, HENRY A.; CARLSON, JULIA A.; AND HERMANN, MARGARET G. "Multiple-Choice Questions and Student Characteristics." *J Ed Psychol* 60(3):231–43 Je '69. * (*PA* 43:13299)

69. BLACKHURST, A. EDWARD; MARKS, CLAUDE H.; AND TISDALL, WILLIAM J. "Relationship Between Mobility and Divergent Thinking in Blind Children." *Ed Visually Handicapped* 1(2):33–6 My '69. * (*PA* 43:14813)

70. GRIMSLEY, WILLIAM GERALD. *The Relationship Between Creativity and Leader Behavior of School Superintendents.* Doctor's thesis, University of Missouri (Columbia, Mo.), 1969. (*DAI* 30:5193A)

71. GUILFORD, J. P., AND HOEFFNER, RALPH. "Comparisons of Varimax Rotations With Rotations to Theoretical Targets." *Ed & Pyschol Meas* 29(1):3–22 sp '69. * (*PA* 44:15668)

72. HAAG, RICHARD A., AND DAVID, KENNETH H. "The Latent Dimensionality of Several Measures of Creativity." *J General Psychol* 80(2):279–85 Ap '69. * (*PA* 43:11328)

73. LEHRER, ARNOLD CURTIS. *The Personality Correlates of Creativity in Undergraduates.* Doctor's thesis, Colorado State College (Greeley, Colo.), 1969. (*DAI* 31:397B)

74. OLIVE, HELEN. *Sibling Resemblances in Divergent Thinking.* Doctor's thesis, Columbia University (New York, N.Y.), 1969. (*DAI* 33:3289B)

75. ROELKE, PATRICIA LYNN. *Reading Comprehension as a Function of Three Dimensions of Word Meaning.* Doctor's thesis, Indiana University (Bloomington, Ind.), 1969. (*DAI* 30:5300A)

76. SIMPSON, DONALD JAMES. *The Effect of Selected Musical Studies on Growth in General Creative Potential.* Doctor's thesis, University of Southern California (Los Angeles, Calif.), 1969. (*DAI* 30:502A)

77. BARRON, FRANK. "Heredability of Factors in Creative Thinking and Judgment." *Acta Geneticae Medicae et Gemellologiae* (Italy) 19(1–2):294–8 Ja–Ap '70. *

78. DELLAS, MARIE. *Effects of Creativity Training, Defensiveness, and Intelligence on Divergent Thinking.* Doctor's thesis, State University of New York (Buffalo, N.Y.), 1970. (*DAI* 31:4540A)

79. FELDHUSEN, JOHN F.; TREFFINGER, DONALD J.; AND ELIAS, ROBERT M. "Prediction of Academic Achievement With Divergent and Convergent Thinking and Personality Variables." *Psychol Sch* 7(1):46–52 Ja '70. * (*PA* 44:11410)

80. HEUSSENSTAMM, FRANCES K. "Creativity and Alienation: An Exploration of Their Relationship in Adolescence." *Calif J Ed Res* 21(3):140–6 My '70. *

81. HINTON, BERNARD L. "Personality Variables and Creative Potential." *J Creative Behav* 4(3):210–7 su '70. *

82. LAKE, A. E., III, AND TEDFORD, W. H., JR. "Influence of Creativity on Formation of Subjective Units." *J General Psychol* 83(2):227–37 O '70. * (*PA* 45:2406)

83. LAMONTAGNE, CHARLES WARREN. *An Exploration of the Relationship of Creativity and Educational Administration.* Doctor's thesis, Boston University (Boston, Mass.), 1970. (*DAI* 31:2064A)

84. OLESON, D. S., AND ZUBEK, JOHN P. "Effect of One Day of Sensory Deprivation on a Battery of Open-Ended Cognitive Tests." *Percept & Motor Skills* 31(3):919–23 D '70. * (*PA* 46:358)

85. OWEN, STEVEN V.; FELDHUSEN, JOHN F.; AND THURSTON, JOHN R. "Achievement Prediction in Nursing Education With Cognitive, Attitudinal, and Divergent Thinking Variables." *Psychol Rep* 26(3):867–70 Je '70. * (*PA* 45:1361)

86. REESE, HAYNE W., AND PARNES, SIDNEY J. "Programming Creative Behavior." *Child Develop* 41(2):413–23 Je '70. * (*PA* 44:15509)

87. RICHMOND, BERT O. "Creativity: Its Relationship to the Counselor's Approach." *J Stud Pers Assn Teach Ed* 8(2):56–63 w '70. * (*PA* 44:19438)

88. SIMMS, JEANNE THOMAS. *An Investigation of the Differences Between Creative High Socio-Economic College Freshmen and Creative Low-Socio-Economic College Freshmen on Measures of Vocational Interests and Certain Motivational Factors.* Doctor's thesis, Catholic University of America (Washington, D.C.), 1970. (*DAI* 31:2693A)

89. ABRAHAM, CAROL. *The Relationship of Authoritarianism to Independence and Creativity Among College Students.* Doctor's thesis, New York University (New York, N.Y.), 1971. (*DAI* 32:6023B)

90. ANASTASI, ANNE, AND SCHAEFER, CHARLES E. "Note on the Concepts of Creativity and Intelligence." *J Creative Behav* 5(2):113–6 '71. * (*PA* 48:7724)

91. BYRNE, MARY ANN; FELDHUSEN, JOHN F.; AND KANE, ROBERT B. "The Relationships Among Two Cloze Measurement Procedures and Divergent Thinking Abilities." *Read Res Q* 6(3):378–93 sp '71. * (*PA* 47:3624)

92. MARINO, CHARLES. "Cross-National Comparisons of Catholic-Protestant Creativity Differences." *Brit J Social & Clin Psychol* 10(2):132–7 Je '71. *

93. RENNER, VIVIAN, AND RENNER, JOHN C. "Effects of a Creativity Training Program on Stimulus Preferences." *Percept & Motor Skills* 33(3):872–4 D '71. * (*PA* 48:1002)

94. SCHOEL, DORIS R., AND BUSSE, THOMAS V. "Humor and Creative Abilities." *Psychol Rep* 29(1):34 Ag '71. * (*PA* 47:2958)

95. SHAW, FILIZ. "Verbal Time Stress and Divergent Thinking." *J Ed & Psychol* (India) 29(1):41–4 Ap '71. *

96. SHEEHAN, PETER W. "Task Structure as a Limiting Condition of the Occurrence of the Treatment Effects of Simulation Instruction in Application of the Real-Simulating Model of Hypnosis." *Int J Clin & Exp Hyp* 19(4):260–76 O '71. * (*PA* 47:4066)

97. TAFT, RONALD. "Creativity: Hot and Cold." *J Personality* 39(3):345–61 S '71. * (*PA* 47:6804)

98. TISDALL, WILLIAM J.; BLACKHURST, A. EDWARD; AND MARKS, CLAUDE H. "Divergent Thinking in Blind Children." *J Ed Psychol* 62(6):468–73 D '71. * (*PA* 47:9708)

99. TUELLER, REX LAMAR. *The Use of Personality Traits in Predicting Doctoral Student Success at Utah State University.* Doctor's thesis, Utah State University (Logan, Utah), 1971. (*DAI* 32:3732A)

100. WADE, SERENA E. "Adolescents, Creativity, and Media: An Exploratory Study." *Am Behav Sci* 14(3):341–51 Ja '71. * (*PA* 46:8797)

101. WILLIAMSON, HELEN THORWORTH. *Tolerance of Ambiguity and Creativity Thinking in Elementary School Children: A Study of the Relationships Among Tolerance of Ambiguity, Intelligence, Training in Creative Thinking, and Flexibility of Concept Formation.* Doctor's thesis, New York University (New York, N.Y.), 1971. (*DAI* 32:6821A)

CUMULATIVE NAME INDEX

Abdel-Razik, T. M.: 6
Abou-Ghorra, I. M.: 26
Abraham, C.: 89
Adams, J. C.: 54
Alker, H. A.: 68
Anastasi, A.: 90
Armstrong, C. L. G.: 55
Bachelis, L. A.: 27
Barker, L. L.: 60
Barron, F.: 1, 7, 14, 77
Beittel, K. R.: 3
Birney, R. C.: 49
Blackhurst, A. E.: 69, 98
Brittain, W. L.: 3
Brown, S. W.: 56
Bruch, C. B.: 42
Busse, T. V.: 94
Byrne, M. A.: 91
Carlson, J. A.: 68
Castelli, C. D.: 17
Cohen, I. S.: 30
Cohen, S.: 22

Compton, M. F.: 43
Condon, C. F.: 29
Corder, B. F.: 31
Craver, A. A.: 57
Csikszentmihalyi, M.: 34, 59
David, K. H.: 72
Davis, G. A.: 64
Dellas, M.: 78
Denny, T.: 29
Dixon, J. C.: 28
Edwards, A. B.: 58
Eisenstadt, J. M.: 32
Elias, R. M.: 79
Feldhusen, J. F.: 29, 79, 85, 91
Flax, M. L.: 33
Fleischer, G.: 18, 30
Garwood, D. S.: 10, 19
Getzels, J. W.: 34, 59
Gibson, J. W.: 60
Givens, P. R.: 44
Griffin, W. M.: 20

Alternate Uses

Grimsley, W. G.: 70
Guilford, J. P.: 2, 56, 71
Haag, R. A.: 72
Haas, M. G.: 15
Haynes, C. R.: 35
Helson, R.: 36
Hermann, M. G.: 68
Heussenstamm, F. K.: 80
Hindsman, E.: 11
Hinton, B. L.: 61, 81
Hoepfner, R.: 56, 71
Irvine, D. J.: 16
Iscoe, I.: 21
Jackson, R. L.: 45
Janssen, C.: 62
Janssen, C. W.: 37
Jenkins, J. M.: 46
Jennings, E.: 11
Kaiser, H. F.: 4–5, 9
Kane, R. B.: 91
Kibler, R. J.: 60
King, F. J.: 11
Klein, S. P.: 51
Lake, A. E.: 82
Lamontagne, C. W.: 83
Lehrer, A. C.: 73
Lett, W. R.: 63
Licht, L.: 12
McCann, B.: 13
McGlothlin, M. S.: 22
McGlothlin, W. H.: 22
McGuire, C.: 11
McIntosh, W. A.: 53
Mahal, B. K.: 38
Maltzman, I.: 12
Mangan, G. L.: 47
Manske, M. E.: 64
Marino, C.: 92
Marks, A.: 4–5, 9
Marks, C. H.: 69, 98
Meadow, A.: 8
Michael, W. B.: 4–5, 9
Neisworth, J. T.: 41

Nicolay, G. C.: 39
Oleson, D. S.: 84
Olive, H.: 74
Owen, S. V.: 85
Pankove, E. W.: 48
Parnes, S. J.: 8, 86
Penney, R. K.: 13
Pierce-Jones, J.: 21
Pinkard, C. A.: 44
Rainwater, J. M.: 23
Ray, W. S.: 40
Reese, H. W.: 86
Renner, J. C.: 93
Renner, V.: 93
Rich, T. A.: 44
Richmond, B. O.: 87
Ridley, D. R.: 49
Roelke, P. L.: 75
Schaefer, C. E.: 90
Schoel, D. R.: 94
Schultz, C. B.: 51
Seitz, T. L.: 24
Seymore, S.: 12
Shaw, F.: 95
Sheehan, P. W.: 96
Sidle, A. C.: 50
Simms, J. T.: 88
Simpson, D. J.: 76
Skager, R. W.: 51
Smith, R. M.: 41, 52
Stimson, R. C.: 65
Taft, R.: 97
Tedford, W. H.: 82
Thurston, J. R.: 85
Tisdall, W. J.: 69, 98
Treffinger, D. J.: 79
Tueller, R. L.: 99
Wade, S. E.: 100
White, K.: 66
White, L. E.: 25
Williamson, H. T.: 101
Windholz, G.: 53, 67
Zubek, J. P.: 84

[543]
Benton Visual Retention Test, Revised Edition.
Ages 8 and over; 1946–55; BVRT; title on manual is *Revised Visual Retention Test;* Arthur L. Benton; distributed by Psychological Corporation. *

For additional information, see 6:543 (22 references); for a review by Nelson G. Hanawalt, see 5:401 (5 references); for reviews by Ivan Norman Mensh, Joseph Newman, and William Schofield of the original edition, see 4:360 (3 references); for an excerpted review, see 3:297.

REFERENCES THROUGH 1971

1–3. See 4:360.
4–8. See 5:401.
9–30. See 6:543.
31. KOLSTOE, OLIVER PAUL. *A Comparison of Mental Abilities of Bright and Dull Children Having the Same Mental Ages.* Doctor's thesis, State University of Iowa (Iowa City, Iowa), 1952. (*DA* 12:707)
32. STRUCKETT, PAULINE B. A. "Effect of Prefrontal Lobotomy on Intellectual Functioning in Chronic Schizophrenia." *Arch Neurol & Psychiatry* 69:293–304 Mr '53. * (*PA* 28:1346)
33. HEILBRUN, ALFRED B., JR. *The Localization of Cerebral Lesions by the Use of Psychological Tests.* Doctor's thesis, State University of Iowa (Iowa City, Iowa), 1954. (*DA* 14:1804)
34. WAHLER, HARRY JOE. *Analysis of the Performance of Brain-Damaged Patients on a Memory-For-Designs Test.* Doctor's thesis, State University of Iowa (Iowa City, Iowa), 1954. (*DA* 14:2406)
35. KAPLAN, HENRY KAY. *A Study of Relationships Between Handwriting Legibility and Perception Adjustment and Personality Factors.* Doctor's thesis, University of Wisconsin (Madison, Wis.), 1957. (*DA* 17:1950)
36. HEILBRUN, ALFRED B., JR. "Lateralization of Cerebral Lesion and Performance on Spatial-Temporal Tasks." *Arch Neurol* 1:282–7 S '59. * (*PA* 34:6461)
37. BENTON, A. L. "The Visual Retention Test as a Constructional Praxis Task." *Confinia Neurologica* (Switzerland) 22(2):141–55 '62. *
38. JENKINS, C. DAVID. "The Relation of EEG Slowing to Selected Indices of Intellective Impairment." *J Nerv & Mental Dis* 135:162–70 Ag '62. *
39. PEARL, DAVID. "Phenothiazine Effects in Chronic Schizophrenia." *J Clin Psychol* 18:86–9 Ja '62. * (*PA* 38:7573)
40. SEVERSON, ROGER ALFRED. *Some Nonreading Correlates of Reading Retardation.* Doctor's thesis, State University of Iowa (Iowa City, Iowa), 1962. (*DA* 23:2798)
41. BARNES, CHARLES MANLY. *Prediction of Brain Damage Using the Holtzman Inkblot Technique and Other Selected Variables.* Doctor's thesis, State University of Iowa (Iowa City, Iowa), 1963. (*DA* 24:4789)
42. HUBER, THEODORE G. *A Comparative Study of Visual Retention Between Deaf and Hearing Adolescents Using the Benton Visual Retention Test.* Master's thesis, University of Kansas (Lawrence, Kan.), 1963.
43. NICKOLS, JOHN. "Mental Deficit, Schizophrenia and the Benton Test." *J Nerv & Mental Dis* 136:279–82 Mr '63. * (*PA* 38:4615)
44. BENTON, ARTHUR L., AND SPREEN, OTFRIED. "Visual Memory Test Performance in Mentally Deficient and Brain-Deficient Patients." *Am J Mental Def* 68:630–3 Mr '64. * (*PA* 39:2494)
45. GOETZINGER, C. P., AND HUBER, T. G. "A Study of Immediate and Delayed Visual Retention With Deaf and Hearing Adolescents." *Am Ann Deaf* 109:297–305 My '64. * (*PA* 39:2443)
46. GRANT, THOMAS NICHOLAS. *The Effect of Narcotic Addiction on CFF, Digit Symbol and the Benton Visual Retention Test.* Master's thesis, Fordham University (New York, N.Y.), 1965.
47. KLONOFF, HARRY, AND KENNEDY, MARGARET. "Memory and Perceptual Functioning in Octogenarians and Nonagenarians in the Community." *J Gerontol* 20:328–33 Jl '65. *
48. SIMMS, LORRAINE G. *A Validation Study of Benton's Visual Retention Test as a Measure of Intelligence.* Master's thesis, North Carolina State University (Raleigh, N.C.), 1965.
49. SMITH, LAURENCE C., JR. "The Effects of Heat Stroke on Cognitive Functioning." *Proc Ann Conf Air Force Behav Sci* 11:130–42 Jl '65. *
50. SPREEN, OTFRIED, AND BENTON, ARTHUR L. "Comparative Studies of Some Psychological Tests for Cerebral Damage." *J Nerv & Mental Dis* 140:323–33 My '65. * (*PA* 40:700)
51. ALEXANDER, DUANE; EHRHARDT, ANKE A.; AND MONEY, JOHN. "Defective Figure Drawings, Geometric and Human, in Turner's Syndrome." *J Nerv & Mental Dis* 142:161–7 F '66. * (*PA* 40:11185)
52. BRENNER, MAY WOOLF, AND GILLMAN, SELMA. "Visuomotor Ability in Schoolchildren: A Survey." *Develop Med & Child Neurol* (England) 8:686–703 D '66. * (*PA* 41:4397)
53. CHANSKY, NORMAN M. "Measuring the Intelligence and Achievement of School Dropouts With the Benton Visual Retention Test." *Am J Mental Def* 71:191–5 S '66. * (*PA* 40:13186)
54. FJELD, STANTON P.; SMALL, IVER F.; SMALL, JOYCE G.; AND HAYDEN, MARY P. "Clinical, Electrical and Psychological Tests and the Diagnosis of Organic Brain Disorder." *J Nerv & Mental Dis* 142:172–9 F '66. * (*PA* 40:11285)
55. KLONOFF, HARRY, AND KENNEDY, MARGARET. "A Comparative Study of Cognitive Functioning in Old Age." *J Gerontol* 21:239–43 Ap '66. *
56. MONEY, JOHN; ALEXANDER, DUANE; AND EHRHARDT, ANKE. "Visual-Constructional Deficit in Turner's Syndrome." *J Pediatrics* 69:126–7 Jl '66. *
57. NICKOLS, JOHN. "Schizophrenic Deficit as a Function of the Test Materials." *J Clin Psychol* 22:77–9 Ja '66. * (*PA* 40:4465)
58. SHANAN, JOEL; COHEN, MARGALITH; AND ADLER, EMIL. "Intellectual Functioning in Hemiplegic Patients After Cerebrovascular Accidents." *J Nerv & Mental Dis* 143:181–9 Ag '66. * (*PA* 41:4893)
59. BENTON, A. L.; SPREEN, O.; FANGMAN, M. W.; AND CARR, D. L. "Visual Retention Test, Administration C: Norms for Children." *J Spec Ed* 1:151–6 w '67. * (*PA* 41:11175)
60. CHANSKY, NORMAN M. "Validity of the Benton Visual Retention Test." *Percept & Motor Skills* 24:1126 Je '67. * (*PA* 41:14437, title only)
61. EGELAND, BYRON; RICE, JAMES; AND PENNY, SUSAN. "Inter-Scorer Reliability on the Bender Gestalt Test and the Revised Visual Retention Test." *Am J Mental Def* 72:96–9 Jl '67. * (*PA* 41:15715)
62. OLIVER, J. E., AND RESTELL, MARY. "Serial Testing in Assessing the Effect of Meclofenoxate on Patients With Memory Defects." *Brit J Psychiatry* 113:219–22 F '67. * (*PA* 41:7456)
63. PETTIFOR, R. E. "The Effects of Unilateral Brain Damage on Performance on the Benton Visual Retention Test." *Alberta Psychologist* (Canada) 8(1):5–11 Ja '67. * (*PA* 41:10840)
64. SIMPSON, SEYMOUR AARON. *Perceptual Functions in Cerebral-Palsied Children.* Doctor's thesis, Yeshiva University (New York, N.Y.), 1967. (*DA* 28:508A)
65. TEMPLER, DONALD I. "Relation Between Immediate and Short-Term Memory and Clinical Implications." *Percept & Motor Skills* 24:1011–2 Je '67. * (*PA* 41:13086)
66. ALLEY, GORDON R. "Visual Retention Test, Administration C: Norms for Mentally Retarded Children." *Percept & Motor Skills* 27:438 O '68. * (*PA* 43:5776)
67. CRONHOLM, BÖRJE, AND SCHALLING, DAISY. "Cognitive Test Performances in Cerebrally Palsied Adults Without Men-

tal Retardation." *Acta Psychiatrica Scandinavica* (Denmark) 44(1):37–50 '68. * (*PA* 43:2937)
68. DOMRATH, RICHARD P. "Constructional Praxis and Visual Perception in School Children." *J Consult & Clin Psychol* 32:186–92 Ap '68. * (*PA* 42:8174)
69. LOEWER, H. D. "The Dependence of the Factorial Structure of Intelligence From the Level of Intelligence and From the Brain State." *Proc Inter Congr Appl Psychol* 16:707–12 '68. *
70. LOISELLE, ROBERT H.; YOUNG, KATHLEEN M.; AND MCDONALD, MARGARET A. "Four Common Tests of Brain Damage Compared." *Psychiatric Commun* 10(2):41–4 '68. *
71. RICE, JAMES A. "Form Equivalence of the Revised Visual Retention Test in Mental Retardates: An Extension." *J Psychol* 68:159–63 Ja '68. * (*PA* 42:7666)
72. TEMPLER, DONALD I. "Memory and Grade Point Average of College Students." *Psychol Rep* 22:944 Je '68. * (*PA* 42:14591)
73. WATSON, CHARLES G. "The Separation of NP Hospital Organics From Schizophrenics With Three Visual Motor Screening Tests." *J Clin Psychol* 24:412–4 O '68. * (*PA* 43:4168)
74. ALLEY, GORDON R. "Comparative Constructional Praxis Performance of Organically Impaired and Cultural-Familial Mental Retardates." *Am J Mental Def* 74(2):279–82 S '69. * (*PA* 44:5526)
75. DEE, HENRY LEE. *Visuoconstructive and Visuoperceptive Deficit in Patients With Unilateral Cerebral Lesions.* Doctor's thesis, University of Iowa (Iowa City, Iowa), 1969. (*DAI* 30:3383B)
76. HALL, JOSEPH CLARENCE. *A Comparative Study of Selected Measures of Intelligence as Predictors of First-Grade Reading Achievement in a Culturally Disadvantaged Population.* Doctor's thesis, Temple University (Philadelphia, Pa.), 1969. (*DAI* 31:1074A)
77. L'ABATE, LUCIANO, AND GALE, ELLIOT N. "Neurological Status and Psychological Functioning." *Percept & Motor Skills* 29(3):999–1007 D '69. * (*PA* 46:5330)
78. LANGE, UNA ANN. *Differential Performances of Minimally Brain-Damaged Boys and of Non-Brain-Damaged Boys on Selected Tests.* Doctor's thesis, University of Nebraska (Lincoln, Neb.), 1969. (*DAI* 30:2852A)
79. ORGASS, B., AND POECK, K. "Assessment of Aphasia by Psychometric Methods." *Cortex* (Italy) 5(4):317–30 D '69. * (*PA* 44:17125)
80. OWENS, RICHARD THOMAS. *A Study of the Performance of Minimally Brain-Damaged and Emotionally Disturbed Boys on Six Selected Psychological Tests.* Doctor's thesis, University of Nebraska (Lincoln, Neb.), 1969. (*DAI* 31:383B)
81. STERNE, DAVID M. "The Benton, Porteus and WAIS Digit Span Tests With Normal and Brain-Injured Subjects." *J Clin Psychol* 25(2):173–5 Ap '69. * (*PA* 43:14481)
82. VITALE, JOHN H.; STEINHELBER, JOHN C.; DRAKE, WILLIAM E., JR.; AND DAHLGREN, HELEN. "Psychological Dimensions of Cerebrovascular Insufficiency." *Percept & Motor Skills* 29(2):555–63 O '69. * (*PA* 44:3996)
83. BIDDER, T. G.; STRAIN, J. J.; AND BRUNSCHWIG, L. "Bilateral and Unilateral ECT: Follow-Up Study and Critique." *Am J Psychiatry* 127(6):737–45 D '70. * (*PA* 47:5329)
84. BURGESS, MICHAEL M.; KODANAZ, ALTAN; AND ZIEGLER, DEWEY K. "Prediction of Brain Damage in a Neurological Population With Cerebrovascular Accidents." *Percept & Motor Skills* 31(2):595–601 O '70. * (*PA* 45:6841)
85. BURGESS, MICHAEL M.; KODANAZ, ALTAN; ZIEGLER, DEWEY; AND GREENBURG, HOWARD. "Prediction of Brain Damage in Two Clinical Populations." *Percept & Motor Skills* 30(2):523–32 Ap '70. * (*PA* 46:7299)
86. DEE, H. L. "Visuoconstructive and Visuoperceptive Deficit in Patients With Unilateral Cerebral Lesions." *Neuropsychologia* (England) 8(3):305–14 Jl '70. * (*PA* 44:21403)
87. DEE, H. L., AND BENTON, A. L. "A Cross-Modal Investigation of Spatial Performances in Patients With Unilateral Cerebral Disease." *Cortex* (Italy) 6(3):261–72 S '70. * (*PA* 46:1677)
88. ADAMS, JERRY, AND RUSHTON, SUSAN Y. "Immediate and Delayed Responses From Memory in Brain-Damaged Patients." Abstract. *J Consult & Clin Psychol* 37(2):305 O '71. * (*PA* 47:9479)
89. BLAKE, MARION ELIZABETH. *A Hierarchical Presentation of Tasks in Visual Perception and Their Relationship to Reading Performance.* Doctor's thesis, State University of New York (Buffalo, N.Y.), 1971. (*DAI* 32:779A)
90. BRAFF, RHODA A. *Imagery, Activity Level, and Learning Modality Preference as Indications of Sensory-Motor Stage Behavior in Low-Income Kindergarten Children.* Doctor's thesis, New York University (New York, N.Y.), 1971. (*DAI* 32:5605A)
91. BREWER, COLIN, AND PERRETT, LANCE. "Brain Damage Due to Alcoholic Consumption: An Air-encephalographic, Psychometric and Electroencephalographic Study." *Brit J Addict* 66(3):170–82 N '71. * (*PA* 48:5229)
92. CRARY, HELEN L., AND RIDGWAY, ROBERT W. "Relationships Between Visual Form Perception Abilities and Reading Achievement in the Intermediate Grades." *J Exp Ed* 40(1):17–22 f '71. * (*PA* 47:9796)
93. FALCONER, A. D. "Measurement of Cognitive Function in Two Groups of Alcoholics." *J Alcoholism* (England) 6(4):118–23 w '71. *
94. FREER, FRANK J. *Visual and Auditory Perceptual Modality Differences as Related to Success in First Grade Reading Word Recognition.* Doctor's thesis, Rutgers—The State University (New Brunswick, N.J.), 1971. (*DAI* 32:6193A)
95. GLAISTER, BRIAN R. "An Ordinate Comparison Method of Calculating Brain Damage Probability." *Brit J Social & Clin Psychol* 10(4):367–74 D '71. * (*PA* 48:1489)
96. GOLDSMITH, R. W., AND BRENGELMANN, J. C. "Rotation of Brain-Damaged and Schizophrenic Subjects." *Archiv für die Gesamte Psychologie* (West Germany) 123:164–70 '71. *
97. HALL, JOSEPH C., AND CHANSKY, NORMAN M. "Relationships Between Selected Ability and Achievement Tests in an Economically Disadvantaged Negro Sample." *Psychol Rep* 28(3):741–2 Je '71. * (*PA* 46:11501)
98. HANNINEN, HELENA. "Psychological Picture of Manifest and Latent Carbon Disulphide Poisoning." *Brit J Indus Med* 28(4):374–81 O '71. *
99. KLONOFF, HARRY. "Factor Analysis of a Neuropsychological Battery for Children Aged 9 to 15." *Percept & Motor Skills* 32(2):603–16 Ap '71. * (*PA* 46:11508)
100. LACKS, PATRICIA BRILLIANT. "Revised Interpretation of Benton Visual Retention Test Scores." *J Clin Psychol* 27(4):481–2 O '71. * (*PA* 47:9205)
101. SHUKLA, T. R.; JHA, J.; AND MISRA, M. N. "The Diagnostic Usefulness of the Benton Revised Visual Retention Test of Brain Damage." *Psychol Studies* (India) 16(1):35–41 Ja '71. *

CUMULATIVE NAME INDEX

Adams, J.: 88
Adler, E.: 58
Alexander, D.: 51, 56
Alley, G. R.: 66, 74
Baer, P. E.: 14
Barclay, A.: 26
Barnes, C. M.: 41
Benton, A. L.: 1–3, 13, 16–7, 29, 37, 44, 50, 59, 87
Bidder, T. G.: 83
Blake, M. E.: 89
Boelling, G. M.: 18
Braff, R. A.: 90
Brengelmann, J. C.: 96
Brenner, M. W.: 52
Brewer, C.: 91
Brilliant, P. J.: 23
Brunschwig, L.: 83
Burgess, M. M.: 84–5
Canter, A.: 24
Carr, D. L.: 59
Castleton, B.: 9
Chansky, N. M.: 53, 60, 97
Chused, T. M.: 27
Cohen, M.: 37
Collins, N. T.: 2
Cooper, A.: 30
Crary, H. L.: 92
Cronholm, B.: 25, 67
Crookes, T. G.: 10
Dahlgren, H.: 82
Dee, H. L.: 75, 86–7
Domrath, R. P.: 68
Drake, W. E.: 82
Egeland, B.: 61
Ehrhardt, A.: 56
Ehrhardt, A. A.: 51
Falconer, A. D.: 93
Fangman, M. W.: 59
Fjeld, S. P.: 54
Fogel, M. L.: 16
Freer, F. J.: 94
Friedman, E. C.: 26
Friedman, W. H.: 27
Gale, E. N.: 77
Gillman, S.: 52
Glaister, B. R.: 95
Goetzinger, C. P.: 45
Goldsmith, R. W.: 96
Grant, T. N.: 46
Greenburg, H.: 85
Gynther, M. D.: 23
Hall, J. C.: 76, 97
Hanawalt, N. G.: *rev*, 5:401
Hänninen, H.: 98
Hayden, M. P.: 54
Heilbrun, A. B.: 11, 33, 36
Huber, T. G.: 42, 45
Hutton, R. D.: 18
Jenkins, C. D.: 38

Jha, J.: 101
Kaplan, H. K.: 35
Kennedy, M.: 47, 55
Klonoff, H.: 47, 55, 99
Kodanaz, A.: 84–5
Kolstoe, O. P.: 5, 31
L'Abate, L.: 18, 27, 77
Lachmann, F. M.: 6
Lacks, P. B.: 100
Lange, U. A.: 78
Leton, D. A.: 19
Loewer, H. D.: 69
Loiselle, R. H.: 70
McDonald, M. A.: 70
McGavren, M.: 17
Mathews, D. L.: 18
Matunas, M. I.: 12
Mensh, I. N.: *rev*, 4:360
Misra, M. N.: 101
Money, J.: 51, 56
Nash, J.: 7
Newman, J.: *rev*, 4:360
Nickols, J.: 43, 57
Oliver, J. E.: 62
Orgass, B.: 79
Owens, R. T.: 80
Pearl, D.: 39
Penny, S.: 61
Perrett, L.: 91
Pettifor, R. E.: 63
Poeck, K.: 79
Restell, M.: 62
Rice, J.: 61
Rice, J. A.: 71
Riddell, S. A.: 20
Ridgway, R. W.: 92
Rowley, V. N.: 14
Rushton, S. Y.: 88
Schalling, D.: 25, 67
Schnore, M. M.: 15
Schofield, W.: *rev*, 4:360
Severson, R. A.: 40
Shaffer, J. W.: 21
Shanan, J.: 58
Shukla, T. R.: 101
Silverstein, A. B.: 22, 28
Simms, L. G.: 48
Simpson, S. A.: 64
Small, I. F.: 54
Small, J. G.: 54
Smith, L. C.: 49
Spreen, O.: 13, 29, 44, 50, 59
Steinhelber, J. C.: 82
Sterne, D. M.: 81
Strain, J. J.: 83
Stricker, G.: 30
Struckett, P. B. A.: 32
Templer, D. I.: 65, 72
Vitale, J. H.: 82
Vogler, R. E.: 27

Wahler, H. J.: 8, 34
Watson, C. G.: 73
Wharton, L. H.: 4
Young, K. M.: 70
Ziegler, D. K.: 84–5

[544]

★**Biographical Inventory—Creativity.** "Adolescents and young adults"; 1970; BIC; 2 scores for boys: art-writing, mathematics-science; 2 scores for girls: art, writing; Charles E. Schaefer; Educational and Industrial Testing Service. *

REFERENCES THROUGH 1971

1. ANASTASI, ANNE, AND SCHAEFER, CHARLES E. "Biographical Correlates of Artistic and Literary Creativity in Adolescent Girls." *J Appl Psychol* 53(4):267–73 Ag '69. * (PA 43:15812)
2. SCHAEFER, CHARLES E. "'Onomatopoeia and Images': Further Evidence of Validity." *Percept & Motor Skills* 31(3): 786 D '70. * (PA 45:9979)

CUMULATIVE NAME INDEX

Anastasi, A.: 1
Schaefer, C. E.: 1–2

[545]

The Block-Design Test. Mental ages 5–20; [1919]; also called *Kohs' Block-Design Test;* modifications appear in *Arthur Point Scale of Performance Tests, New Guinea Performance Scales, Ohwaki-Kohs Tactile Block Design Intelligence Test for the Blind,* and *Pacific Design Construction Test;* S. C. Kohs; Stoelting Co. *

REFERENCES THROUGH 1971

1. DOLL, EDGAR A. "Intelligence Measurement: A Review." *J Ed Res* 11:218–9 Mr '25. *
2. RAYBOLD, EMMA. "An Experiment With Primary Intelligence Tests." *Ed Res B* (Los Angeles City Schools) 4:8 Je 15 '25. *
3. GRAHAM, VIRGINIA TAYLOR. "The Intelligence of Chinese Children in San Francisco." *J Comp Psychol* 6:43–71 F '26. * (PA 1:663)
4. STEIN, MARTIN L. "A Trial With Criteria of the MacQuarrie Test of Mechanical Ability." *J Appl Psychol* 11:391–3 O '27. * (PA 2:2964)
5. BROOM, EUSTACE. "The Validity of Four Individual Tests of Mental Ability." *Ed Res B* (Los Angeles City Schools) 8:9–10 Mr '29. *
6. LESTER, OLIVE P. "Performance Tests and Foreign Children." *J Ed Psychol* 20:303–9 Ap '29. * (PA 3:2889)
7. BROWN, A. JEAN. "An Enquiry Into the Standardization of the Kohs' Block-Design Test." *J Appl Psychol* 14:178–81 Ap '30. * (PA 4:3309)
8. EIGLER, PAULINE. "The Kohs Block Design Test." *Child Develop* 1:341–2 D '30. * (PA 5:2582)
9. HUTT, MAX L. "A Simplified Scoring Method for the Kohs Block-Design Tests." *Am J Psychol* 42:450–2 Jl '30. * (PA 4:4578)
10. PORTEUS, S. D.; WITH THE ASSISTANCE OF DORIS M. DEWEY AND ROBERT G. BERNREUTER. "Race and Social Differences in Performance Tests." *Genetic Psychol Monogr* 8:93–208 Ag '30. * (PA 4:4947)
11. WILE, IRA S., AND DAVIS, ROSE. "A Comparative Study of the Kohs Block Design Test." *Am J Orthopsychiatry* 1:89–103 O '30. * (PA 5:2593)
12. MCDONALD, JANE REGINA. *A Comparative Study of Deaf Children by Means of the Kohs Block Design Tests and Porteus Maze.* Master's thesis, Ohio State University (Columbus, Ohio), 1931.
13. KENT, GRACE H. "Modification of the Kohs Block Design Test." *J Appl Psychol* 18:578–98 Ag '34. * (PA 9:982)
14. AXELBAUM, ETHEL M. *Differences Between the Kohs and Stanford-Binet in a Group of Artistically Gifted Children.* Master's thesis, Columbia University (New York, N.Y.), 1935.
15. WILE, IRA S., AND DAVIS, ROSE. "The Use of the Kohs Test as an Indicator of Mental Confusion." Discussion by Rose Anderson. *Am J Orthopsychiatry* 6:1–17 Ja '36. * (PA 10:3586)
16. EARL, C. J. C. "The Performance Test Behavior of Adult Morons." *Brit J Med Psychol* 17:78–92 pt 1 '37. * (PA 12:1400)
17. GREENE, EDWARD B. "Practice Effects on Various Types of Standard Tests." *Am J Psychol* 49:67–75 Ja '37. * (PA 11:2482)
18. BENTON, ARTHUR L. "The Performance of Pre-School Children on the Kohs Block Design Test." *J Genetic Psychol* 53:231–3 Je '38. * (PA 13:2217)
19. NADEL, AARON B. *A Qualitative Analysis of Behavior Following Cerebral Lesions Diagnosed as Primarily Affecting the Frontal Lobes.* Archives of Psychology, No. 224. Washington, D.C.: American Psychological Association, April 1938. Pp. 60. * (PA 13:83)
20. BENTON, ARTHUR L. "The Performance of Young Adults on the Kohs Block Designs Test." Abstract. *Psychol B* 37:513 Jl '40. * (PA 14:5728, title only)
21. EARL, C. J. C. "A Psychograph for Morons." *J Abn & Social Psychol* 35:428–48 Jl '40. * (PA 14:5403)
22. PRICE, E. J. J. "The Nature of the Practical Factor (F)." *Brit J Psychol* 30:341–51 Ap '40.'* (PA 14:3783)
23. BENTON, ARTHUR L. "Application of Hutt's Revised Scoring of the Kohs Block Designs Test to the Performances of Adult Subjects." *Am J Psychol* 54:131–2 Ja '41. * (PA 15:1991)
24. BENTON, ARTHUR L. "A Study of the Performances of Young Adults on the Kohs Block Designs Test." *J Appl Psychol* 25:420–7 Ag '41. * (PA 15:5400)
25. BENTON, ARTHUR L., AND HOWELL, IRA L. "The Use of Psychological Tests in the Evaluation of Intellectual Function Following Head Injury: Report of a Case of Post-Traumatic Personality Disorder." *Psychosom Med* 3:138–51 Ap '41. * (PA 15:4206)
26. THOMSON, GODFREY H. "The Speed Factor in Performance Tests." *Brit J Psychol* 32:131–5 O '41. * (PA 16:368)
27. WECHSLER, DAVID. *The Measurement of Adult Intelligence, Second Edition,* pp. 93–6, 177–9. Baltimore, Md.: Williams & Wilkins Co., 1941. Pp. xi, 248. *
28. BENTON, ARTHUR L., AND PERRY, JAMES D. "Short Method of Administering the Kohs Block Designs Test." *Am J Orthopsychiatry* 12:231–3 Ap '42. * (PA 16:3322)
29. LIDZ, THEODORE; GAY, JAMES R.; AND TIETZE, CHRISTOPHER. "Intelligence in Cerebral Deficit States and Schizophrenia Measured by the Kohs Block Design Test." *Arch Neurol & Psychiatry* 48:568–82 O '42. * (PA 17:862)
30. YACORZYNSKI, G. K. "Degree of Effort: 2, Quality of Work and Time of Completion of Performance Tests." *J Exp Psychol* 30:342–4 Ap '42. * (PA 16:2635)
31. BRADFORD, E. J. G. "Performance Tests in the Diagnosis of Mental Deficiency." *Brit J Med Psychol* 19:394–414 pts 3–4 '43. * (PA 17:3783)
32. EBERT, ELIZABETH, AND SIMMONS, KATHERINE. *The Brush Foundation Study of Child Growth and Development: 1, Psychometric Tests.* Monographs of the Society for Research in Child Development, Vol. 8, No. 2, Serial No. 35. Washington, D.C.: the Society, National Research Council, 1943. Pp. xiv, 113. * (PA 18:3322)
33. GOLDFARB, WILLIAM. "Note on a Revised Block Design Test as a Measure of Abstract Performance." *J Ed Psychol* 36:247–51 Ap '45. * (PA 19:2392)
34. BRADFORD, E. J. G. "Selection for Technical Education: Parts I and II." *Brit J Ed Psychol* 16:20–31, 69–81 F, Je '46. * (PA 20:2887, 4881)
35. SARASON, SEYMOUR B., AND SARASON, ESTHER KROOP. "The Discriminatory Value of a Test Pattern With Cerebral Palsied, Defective Children." Abstract. *Am Psychologist* 1:288 Jl '46. * (PA 20:3668, title only)
36. LANDISBERG, SELMA. "A Personality Study of Institutionalized Epileptics." *Am J Mental Def* 52:16–22 Jl '47. * (PA 22:2267)
37. POTTER, ELMER H., AND SARASON, SEYMOUR B. "Color in the Rorschach and Kohs Block Designs." Abstract. *Am Psychologist* 2:269–70 Ag '47. * (PA 22:4391, title only)
38. SARASON, SEYMOUR B., AND POTTER, ELMER H. "Color in the Rorschach and Kohs Block Designs." *J Consult Psychol* 11:202–6 Jl–Ag '47. * (PA 22:205)
39. TOOTH, GEOFFREY. "On the Use of Mental Tests for the Measurement of Disability After Head Injury: With a Comparison Between the Results of These Tests in Patients After Head Injury and Psychoneurotics." *J Neurol Neurosurg & Psychiatry* (England) 10:1–11 F '47. *
40. BIESHEUVEL, S. Chap. 4, "Psychological Tests and Their Applications to Non-European Peoples," pp. 87–126. In *The Yearbook of Education, 1949.* London: Evans Brothers Ltd., 1949. Pp. xv, 660. *
41. FREUDENBERG, R. K., AND ROBERTSON, J. P. S. "Investigation Into Intellectual Changes Following Prefrontal Leucotomy." *J Mental Sci* (England) 95:826–41 O '49. * (PA 24:3833)
42. YELA, MARIANO. "Application of the Concept of Simple Structure to Alexander's Data." *Psychometrika* 14:121–35 Je '49. * (PA 24:1066)
43. ROGERS, BARBARA ELLEN. *An Investigation to Examine the Results of Kohs' Block Design Test When Used With Young Deaf Children.* Master's thesis, MacMurray College for Women (Jacksonville, Ill.), 1950.
44. TIZARD, J.; IN COLLABORATION WITH N. O'CONNOR AND J. M. CRAWFORD. "The Abilities of Adolescent and Adult High-Grade Male Defectives." *J Mental Sci* 96:888–907 O '50. * (PA 25:5421)
45. MANDLER, GEORGE, AND SARASON, SEYMOUR B. "Anxiety as a Factor in Test Performance." Abstract. *Am Psychologist* 6:341 Jl '51. *
46. SHAPIRO, M. B. "Experimental Studies of a Perceptual Anomaly: 1, Initial Experiments." *J Mental Sci* 97:90–110 Ja '51. * (PA 25:6220)
47. LIDZ, THEODORE; CARTER, JAMES D.; LEWIS, BERNARD I.; AND SURRATT, CAROLYN. "Effect of ACTH and Cortisone on

Mood and Mentation." *Psychosom Med* 14:363-77 S-O '52. * (*PA* 27:4457)

48. McFie, J., and Piercy, M. F. "Intellectual Impairment With Localized Cerebral Lesions." *Brain* (England) 75:292-311 S '52. * (*PA* 27:7649)

49. Mandler, George, and Sarason, Seymour B. "A Study of Anxiety and Learning." *J Abn & Social Psychol* 47:166-73 Ap '52. * (*PA* 27:2743)

50. Shapiro, M. B. "Experimental Studies of a Perceptual Anomaly: 2, Confirmatory and Explanatory Experiments." *J Mental Sci* (England) 98:605-17 O '52. * (*PA* 27:6085)

51. Shapiro, M. B. "An Experimental Investigation of the Block Design Rotation Effect: An Analysis of a Psychological Effect of Brain Damage." *Brit J Med Psychol* 27:84-8 pts 1 and 2 '54. * (*PA* 28:8947)

52. Yates, Aubrey J. "The Validity of Some Psychological Tests of Brain Damage." *Psychol B* 51:359-79 Jl '54. *

53. Lachmann, Frank Michael. *Perceptual-Motor Development in Children Retarded in Reading Ability.* Doctor's thesis, Northwestern University (Evanston, Ill.), 1955. (*DA* 15:1900)

54. Ray-Chowdhury, K. "Imagery and Performance Tests of Intelligence." *Indian Psychol B* 2:25-30 S '57. * (*PA* 37:4964)

55. Bilger, Robert C. "Limitations on the Use of Intelligence Scales to Estimate the Mental Ages of Children." *Volta R* 60:321-5 S '58. *

56. Gutekunst, Josef Grant. *The Prediction of Art Achievement of Art Education Students by Means of Standardized Tests.* Doctor's thesis, Temple University (Philadelphia, Pa.), 1959. (*DA* 20:3202)

57. Jayalakshmi, G. "Correlation of Tests of Psychomotor Ability With Intelligence and Non-motor Tests." *J Psychol Res* (India) 3:78-84 S '59. *

58. Taylor, A. J. W. "Social Isolation and Imprisonment." *Psychiatry* 24:373-6 N '61. * (*PA* 37:5462)

59. Warhapdande, N. R., and Khullar, B. M. P. "Factorial Analysis of Intelligence Tests." *Manas* (India) 10(2):89-100 '63. * (*PA* 38:10180)

60. Budoff, Milton, and Friedman, Martin. "'Learning Potential' as an Assessment Approach to the Adolescent Mentally Retarded." *J Consult Psychol* 28:434-9 O '64. * (*PA* 39:5651)

61. Coates, Gerald E. *Basic Components of Performance on the Block Design Test: A Validation Study.* Master's thesis, University of Chicago (Chicago, Ill.), 1964.

62. Larson, Richard K. *The Kohs Block Design Test as a Diagnostic Tool in the Area of Remedial Reading.* Master's thesis, Moorhead State College (Moorhead, Minn.), 1964.

63. Chatterjee, Neera. "A Comparison of Performance of Tribal and Non-Tribal Boys of Tripura (India) on Five Performance Tests." *J Psychol Res* (India) 9:151-8 S '65. * (*PA* 40:6561)

64. Kosc, Ladislav. "Kohs Test and Its Qualitative Analysis in Psychological Clinical Practice." *Studia Psychologica* (Czechoslovakia) 8(3):241-4 '66. *

65. Thune, Jeanne; Tine, Sebastian; and Cherry, Nancy. "Personality Characteristics of Successful Older Leaders." *J Gerontol* 21:463-70 Jl '66. *

66. Budoff, Milton. "Learning Potential Among Institutionalized Young Adult Retardates." *Am J Mental Def* 72:404-11 N '67. * (*PA* 42:7631)

67. Dawson, John L. M. "Cultural and Physiological Influences Upon Spatial-Perceptual Processes in West Africa, Part I." *Int J Psychol* (France) 2(2):115-28 '67. * (*PA* 41:15125)

68. Dawson, John L. M. "Cultural and Physiological Influences Upon Spatial-Perceptual Processes in West Africa, Part II." *Int J Psychol* (France) 2(3):171-85 '67. * (*PA* 43:5194)

69. Kessler, Michael R., and Kronenberger, Earl J. "Dogmatism and Perceptual Synthesis." *Percept & Motor Skills* 24:179-82 F '67. * (*PA* 41:8210)

70. Shrivastava, Radhika Pd. "Kohs Block Design Test Norms for Children." *Indian Psychol R* 4:68-70 Jl '67. *

71. De-Nour, Atara K.; Shaltiel, Judith; and Czaczkes, J. W. "Emotional Reactions of Patients on Chronic Hemodialysis." *Psychosom Med* 30:521-33 S-O '68. * (*PA* 43:8624)

72. Elkin, Lorne. "Predicting Performance of the Mentally Retarded on Sheltered Workshop and Non-Institutional Jobs." *Am J Mental Def* 72:533-9 Ja '68. * (*PA* 42:7638)

73. Kimball, Chase P. "The Experience of Open Heart Surgery: 2, Determinants of Post-operative Behavior." *Psychother & Psychosom* (Switzerland) 18(1-6):259-74 '70. * (*PA* 47:5515)

74. Berry, J. W. "Ecological and Cultural Factors in Spatial Perceptual Development." *Can J Behav Sci* 3(4):324-36 O '71. * (*PA* 47:8577)

CUMULATIVE NAME INDEX

Anderson, R.: 15
Axelbaum, E. M.: 14
Benton, A. L.: 18, 20, 23-5, 28
Bernreuter, R. G.: 10
Berry, J. W.: 74
Biesheuvel, S.: 40
Bilger, R. C.: 55
Bradford, E. J. G.: 31, 34
Broom, E.: 5
Brown, A. J.: 7
Budoff, M.: 60, 66
Carter, J. D.: 47
Chatterjee, N.: 63
Cherry, N.: 65
Coates, G. E.: 61
Crawford, J. M.: 44
Czaczkes, J. W.: 71
Davis, R.: 11, 15
Dawson, J. L. M.: 67-8
De-Nour, A. K.: 71
Dewey, D. M.: 10
Doll, E. A.: 1
Earl, C. J. C.: 16, 21
Ebert, E.: 32
Eigler, P.: 8
Elkin, L.: 72
Freudenberg, R. K.: 41
Friedman, M.: 60
Gay, J. R.: 29
Goldfarb, W.: 33
Graham, V. T.: 3
Greene, E. B.: 17
Gutekunst, J. G.: 56
Howell, I. L.: 25
Hutt, M. L.: 9
Jayalakshmi, G.: 57
Kent, G. H.: 13
Kessler, M. R.: 69
Khullar, B. M. P.: 59
Kimball, C. P.: 73
Kosc, L.: 64
Kronenberger, E. J.: 69
Lachmann, F. M.: 53
Landisberg, S.: 36
Larson, R. K.: 62
Lester, O. P.: 6
Lewis, B. I.: 47
Lidz, T.: 29, 47
McDonald, J. R.: 12
McFie, J.: 48
Mandler, G.: 45, 49
Nadel, A. B.: 19
O'Connor, N.: 44
Perry, J. D.: 28
Piercy, M. F.: 48
Porteus, S. D.: 10
Potter, E. H.: 37-8
Price, E. J. J.: 22
Raybold, E.: 2
Ray-Chowdhury, K.: 54
Robertson, J. P. S.: 41
Rogers, B. E.: 43
Sarason, E. K.: 35
Sarason, S. B.: 35, 37-8, 45, 49
Shaltiel, J.: 71
Shapiro, M. B.: 46, 50-1
Shrivastava, R. P.: 70
Simmons, K.: 32
Stein, M. L.: 4
Surratt, C.: 47
Taylor, A. J. W.: 58
Thomson, G. H.: 26
Thune, J.: 65
Tietze, C.: 29
Tine, S.: 65
Tizard, J.: 44
Tooth, G.: 39
Warhapdande, N. R.: 59
Wechsler, D.: 27
Wile, I. S.: 11, 15
Yacorzynski, G. K.: 30
Yates, A. J.: 52
Yela, M.: 42

[546]

*Christensen-Guilford Fluency Tests. Grades 7-16 and adults; 1957-73; 4 tests; Paul R. Christensen and J. P. Guilford; Sheridan Psychological Services, Inc. *

a) WORD FLUENCY.
b) IDEATIONAL FLUENCY I.
c) ASSOCIATIONAL FLUENCY I.
d) EXPRESSIONAL FLUENCY.

For additional information and reviews by J. A. Keats and Albert S. Thompson, see 6:544 (4 references).

REFERENCES THROUGH 1971

1-4. See 6:544.

5. Bereiter, Carl Edward. *Verbal and Ideational Fluency in Superior Tenth-Grade Students.* Doctor's thesis, University of Wisconsin (Madison, Wis.), 1959. (*DA* 20:2139)

6. Merrifield, P. R.; Guilford, J. P.; Christensen, P. R.; and Frick, J. W. "Interrelationships Between Certain Abilities and Certain Traits of Motivation and Temperament." *J General Psychol* 65:57-74 Jl '61. * (*PA* 36:2HD57M)

7. de Mille, Richard. "Intellect After Lobotomy in Schizophrenia: A Factor Analytic Study." *Psychol Monogr* 76(16):1-18 '62. * (*PA* 38:2784)

8. Irvine, David James. *An Empirical Study of the Relationship Between Certain Pupil Characteristics and Selected Measures of Creativity.* Doctor's thesis, University of North Carolina (Chapel Hill, N.C.), 1963. (*DA* 25:4543)

9. Locke, Edwin A. "Some Correlates of Classroom and Out-of-Class Achievement in Gifted Science Students." *J Ed Psychol* 54:238-48 O '63. * (*PA* 38:4649)

10. May, Lomax Louis. *A Study of the Relationships Between Achievement on a Complex Visual-Auditory Learning Task and Certain Selected Variables.* Doctor's thesis, University of Alabama (University, Ala.), 1963. (*DA* 25:1750)

11. Atkinson, Bea Henrietta. *The Relationship Between Problem-Solving Strategies and Measures of Convergent and Divergent Thinking in a Selelcted Group of Secondary School Pupils.* Doctor's thesis, University of Florida (Gainesville, Fla.), 1964. (*DA* 25:7070)

12. McGlothlin, William H.; Cohen, Sidney; and McGlothlin, Marcella S. "Short-Term Effects of LSD on Anxiety, Attitudes and Performance." *J Nerv & Mental Dis* 139:266-73 S '64. * (*PA* 39:7046)

13. Seitz, Theodore Lee. *The Relationship Between Creativity and Intelligence, Personality, and Value Patterns in Adolescence.* Doctor's thesis, University of Denver (Denver, Colo.), 1964. (*DA* 25:3679)

14. Bachelis, Leonard A. *Body-Field Perceptual Differentiation as a Variable in Creative Thinking.* Doctor's thesis, Yeshiva University (New York, N.Y.), 1965. (*DA* 26:3475)

15. Butler, Marjorie Johnson. *Criteria for Creativity in Counseling.* Doctor's thesis, University of Pittsburgh (Pittsburgh, Pa.), 1965. (*DA* 27:977B)
16. Castiglione, Lawrence Virgil. *The Relation of Intelligence to Selected Measures of Creativity.* Doctor's thesis, New York University (New York, N.Y.), 1965. (*DA* 27:1278B)
17. Flax, Morton Lewis. *The Stability of Relationships Between Creativity and Personality Variables.* Doctor's research study No. 1, Colorado State College (Greeley, Colo.), 1966. (*DA* 27:2857B)
18. Haynes, Carolyn R. *The Relationships of Performances of Seventh Grade Students on Measures of Creativity, Study Habits and Attitudes, Expressed Need for Counseling and Achievement.* Master's thesis, Texas A & M University (College Station, Tex.), 1966.
19. Janssen, Calvin Wayne. *Comparative Creativity Scores of Lower Socio-Economic Dropouts and Non-Dropouts.* Doctor's thesis, University of Tennessee (Knoxville, Tenn.), 1966. (*DA* 27:1659A)
20. John, Martha Adeline Tyler. *The Relationship of Symbolic Peer-Modeling to Ideational Fluency in Homogeneous and Heterogeneous Groups.* Doctor's thesis, Stanford University (Stanford, Calif.), 1966. (*DA* 27:2070A)
21. Smith, Robert M., and Neisworth, John T. "Creative Thinking Abilities of Intellectually Superior Children in the Regular Grades." *Psychol Rep* 18:335–41 Ap '66. * (*PA* 40:8832)
22. Givens, Paul R.; Pinkard, Carolyn A.; and Rich, Thomas A. "Relationship of Personality Factors, Creativity and Academic Achievement Among High School Seniors." *Fla J Ed Res* 9:45–56 Ja '67. *
23. Gray, James Joseph. *An Investigation of the Relationship Between Primary Process Thinking and Creativity.* Doctor's thesis, Fordham University (New York, N.Y.), 1967. (*DA* 28:5206B)
24. Jackson, Robert Leon. *An Investigation of the Creative Growth Curves of University Students.* Doctor's thesis, East Texas State University (Commerce, Tex.), 1967. (*DA* 28:3508A)
25. Jenkins, John Mervin. *A Study of the Characteristics Associated With Innovative Behavior in Teachers.* Doctor's thesis, University of Miami (Coral Gables, Fla.), 1967. (*DA* 28:903A)
26. Mangan, Gordon L. "Studies of the Relationship Between Neo-Pavlovian Properties of Higher Nervous Activity and Western Personality Dimensions: 4, A Factor Analytic Study of Extraversion and Flexibility, and the Sensitivity and Mobility of the Nervous System." *J Exp Res Personality* 2:124–7 My '67. * (*PA* 41:11908)
27. Smith, Robert M. "Creative Thinking Abilities of Educable Mentally Handicapped Children in the Regular Grades." *Am J Mental Def* 71:571–5 Ja '67. * (*PA* 41:6197)
28. Windholz, George, and McIntosh, William A. "Concurrent Validation of Guilford's Six Convergent Tests." *Ed & Psychol Meas* 27:393–400 su '67. * (*PA* 41:12843)
29. Anderson, Ronald Jude. *Divergent Thinking Within Superior, Average, and Retarded Subjects.* Doctor's thesis, University of Nebraska (Lincoln, Neb.), 1968. (*DA* 29:1126A)
30. Brown, Stephen W.; Guilford, J. P.; and Hoepfner, Ralph. "Six Semantic-Memory Abilities." *Ed & Psychol Meas* 28:691–717 au '68. * (*PA* 43:4427)
31. Edwards, Arthur B. *An Analysis of the Creative Ability Levels of the Potential Dropout in the Average Mental Ability Range.* Doctor's thesis, University of Tennessee (Knoxville, Tenn.), 1968. (*DA* 29:3828A)
32. Getzels, J. W., and Csikszentmihalyi, M. "The Value-Orientations of Art Students as Determinants of Artistic Specialization and Creative Performance." *Studies Art Ed* 10:5–16 f '68. *
33. Janssen, Calvin. "Comparative Creativity Scores of Lower Socio-Economic Dropouts and Non-Dropouts." *Psychol Sch* 5:183–4 Ap '68. * (*PA* 43:17498)
34. Lett, Warren Robert. *Some Postulated Correlates of Creativity and Need Achievement.* Doctor's thesis, University of California (Berkeley, Calif.), 1968. (*DA* 29:1106A)
35. Stimson, Roger C., Jr. "Factor Analytic Approach to the Structural Differentiation of Description." *J Counsel Psychol* 15:301–7 Jl '68. * (*PA* 42:15457)
36. Windholz, George. "The Relation of Creativity and Intelligence Constellations to Traits of Temperament, Interest, and Value in College Students." *J General Psychol* 79:291–9 O '68. * (*PA* 43:3998)
37. Blackhurst, A. Edward; Marks, Claude H.; and Tisdall, William J. "Relationship Between Mobility and Divergent Thinking in Blind Children." *Ed Visually Handicapped* 1(2):33–6 My '69. * (*PA* 43:14813)
38. Gray, James J. "The Effect of Productivity on Primary Process and Creativity." *J Proj Tech & Pers Assess* 33(3):213–8 Je '69. * (*PA* 43:14302)
39. Grimsley, William Gerald. *The Relationship Between Creativity and Leader Behavior of School Superintendents.* Doctor's thesis, University of Missouri (Columbia, Mo.), 1969. (*DAI* 30:5193A)
40. Guilford, J. P., and Hoepfner, Ralph. "Comparisons of Varimax Rotations With Rotations to Theoretical Targets." *Ed & Psychol Meas* 29(1):3–22 sp '69. * (*PA* 44:15668)
41. Haakonsen, Harry Olav. *An Investigation of the Relationships Between Selected Psychological Characteristics of Students and Performance in an Audio-Tutorial Genetics Program.* Doctor's thesis, Syracuse University (Syracuse, N.Y.), 1969. (*DAI* 31:63A)
42. Lehrer, Arnold Curtis. *The Personality Correlates of Creativity in Undergraduates.* Doctor's thesis, Colorado State College (Greeley, Colo.), 1969. (*DAI* 31:397B)
43. Olive, Helen. *Sibling Resemblances in Divergent Thinking.* Doctor's thesis, Columbia University (New York, N.Y.), 1969. (*DAI* 33:3289B)
44. Simpson, Donald James. *The Effect of Selected Musical Studies on Growth in General Creative Potential.* Doctor's thesis, University of Southern California (Los Angeles, Calif.), 1969. (*DAI* 30:502A)
45. Barron, Frank. "Heredability of Factors in Creative Thinking and Judgment." *Acta Geneticae Medicae et Gemellologiae* (Italy) 19(1–2):294–8 Ja–Ap '70. *
46. Oleson, D. S., and Zubek, John P. "Effect of One Day of Sensory Deprivation on a Battery of Open-Ended Cognitive Tests." *Percept & Motor Skills* 31(3):919–23 D '70. * (*PA* 46:358)
47. Reese, Hayne W., and Parnes, Sidney J. "Programming Creative Behavior." *Child Develop* 41(2):413–23 Je '70. * (*PA* 44:15509)
48. Simms, Jeanne Thomas. *An Investigation of the Differences Between Creative High Socio-Economic College Freshmen and Creative Low-Socio-Economic College Freshmen on Measures of Vocational Interests and Certain Motivational Factors.* Doctor's thesis, Catholic University of America (Washington, D.C.), 1970. (*DAI* 31:2693A)
49. Abraham, Carol. *The Relationship of Authoritarianism to Independence and Creativity Among College Students.* Doctor's thesis, New York University (New York, N.Y.), 1971. (*DAI* 32:6023B)
50. Byrne, Mary Ann; Feldhusen, John F.; and Kane, Robert B. "The Relationships Among Two Cloze Measurement Procedures and Divergent Thinking Abilities." *Read Res Q* 6(3):378–93 sp '71. * (*PA* 47:3624)
51. Tisdall, William J.; Blackhurst, A. Edward; and Marks, Claude H. "Divergent Thinking in Blind Children." *J Ed Psychol* 62(6):468–73 D '71. * (*PA* 47:9708)
52. Wade, Serena E. "Adolescents, Creativity, and Media: An Exploratory Study." *Am Behav Sci* 14(3):341–51 Ja '71. * (*PA* 46:8797)

CUMULATIVE NAME INDEX

Abdel-Razik, T. M.: 3
Abraham, C.: 49
Anderson, R. J.: 29
Atkinson, B. H.: 11
Bachelis, L. A.: 14
Barron, F.: 45
Bereiter, C. E.: 5
Blackhurst, A. E.: 37, 51
Brown, S. W.: 30
Butler, M. J.: 15
Byrne, M. A.: 50
Castiglione, L. V.: 16
Christensen, P. R.: 2, 4, 6
Cohen, S.: 12
Csikszentmihalyi, M.: 32
de Mille, R.: 7
Edwards, A. B.: 31
Feldhusen, J. F.: 50
Flax, M. L.: 17
Frick, J. W.: 2, 6
Getzels, J. W.: 32
Givens, P. R.: 22
Gray, J. J.: 23, 38
Grimsley, W. G.: 39
Guilford, J. P.: 1–2, 4, 6, 30, 40
Haakonsen, H. O.: 41
Haynes, C. R.: 18
Hoepfner, R.: 30, 40
Irvine, D. J.: 8
Jackson, R. L.: 24
Janssen, C.: 33

Janssen, C. W.: 19
Jenkins, J. M.: 25
John, M. A. T.: 20
Kane, R. B.: 50
Keats, J. A.: *rev*, 6:544
Lehrer, A. C.: 42
Lett, W. R.: 34
Locke, E. A.: 9
McGlothlin, M. S.: 12
McGlothlin, W. H.: 12
McIntosh, W. A.: 28
Mangan, G. L.: 26
Marks, C. H.: 37, 51
May, M. L.: 10
Merrifield, P. R.: 2, 6
Neisworth, J. T.: 21
Oleson, D. S.: 46
Olive, H.: 43
Parnes, S. J.: 47
Pinkard, C. A.: 22
Reese, H. W.: 47
Rich, T. A.: 22
Seitz, T. L.: 13
Simms, J. T.: 48
Simpson, D. J.: 44
Smith, R. M.: 21, 27
Stimson, R. C.: 35
Thompson, A. S.: *rev*, 6:544
Tisdall, W. J.: 37, 51
Wade, S. E.: 52
Windholz, G.: 28, 36
Zubek, J. P.: 46

[547]

Closure Flexibility (Concealed Figures). Industrial employees; 1956–65; revision of *Gottschaldt Figures;* L. L. Thurstone (test), T. E. Jeffrey (test), and Manpower Research and Development Division, Industrial Relations Center, University of Chicago (manual); the Center. * [The publisher has not replied to our four requests to check the accuracy of this entry.]

For additional information, see 7:435 (9 references); for a review by Leona E. Tyler, see 6:545 (4 references).

REFERENCES THROUGH 1971

1–4. See 6:545.
5–13. See 7:435.
14. LONG, ROBERT I. "Field-Articulation as a Factor in Verbal Learning and Recall." *Percept & Motor Skills* 15:151–8 Ag '62. * (*PA* 37:4375)
15. KARP, STEPHEN A. "Field Dependence and Occupational Activity in the Aged." *Percept & Motor Skills* 24:603–9 Ap '67. * (*PA* 41:10284)
16. DICKSTEIN, LOUIS S. "Field Independence in Concept Attainment." *Percept & Motor Skills* 27:635–42 O '68. * (*PA* 43:4803)
17. DAUGHERTY, ROBERT A., AND WATERS, THOMAS J. "Closure Flexibility, Field Dependence and Student Leadership." *Percept & Motor Skills* 29(1):256–8 Ag '69. * (*PA* 44:2341)
18. HASETH, KJELL; SHAGASS, CHARLES; AND STRAUMANIS, JOHN J. "Perceptual and Personality Correlates of EEG and Evoked Response Measures." *Biol Psychiatry* 1(1):49–60 Ja '69. * (*PA* 46:4440)
19. KEISER, THOMAS WILLARD. *Some Correlates of Perceptual Differentiation.* Doctor's thesis, Wayne State University (Detroit, Mich.), 1969. (*DAI* 32:3007B)
20. TARNOPOL, LESTER. "Delinquency and Minimal Brain Dysfunction." *J Learn Dis* 3(4):200–7 Ap '70. * (*PA* 47:3517)
21. LANGLEY, C. W. "Differentiation and Integration of Systems of Personal Constructs." *J Personality* 39(1):10–25 Mr '71. * (*PA* 46:4956)
22. RESNICK, HARVEY. *The Relationship of Client Cognitive Style to Counselor Verbal Style in a Counseling Analogue.* Doctor's thesis, Ohio State University (Columbus, Ohio), 1971. (*DAI* 32:3015B)

CUMULATIVE NAME INDEX

Baehr, M. E.: 11
Blewett, D. B.: 2
Brayer, R.: 4
Corter, H. M.: 1
Daugherty, R. A.: 6, 17
Dickstein, L. S.: 16
Froemel, E. C.: 11
Furcon, J. E.: 11
Gardner, R. W.: 12
Gordon, O.: 4
Gordon, O. J.: 3
Häseth, K.: 18
Karp, S. A.: 15
Keiser, T. W.: 19
Langley, C. W.: 21
Lewin, P. B.: 7
Lohrenz, L. J.: 12
Long, R. I.: 14
Mangan, G. L.: 8
Ohnmacht, F. W.: 9
Resnick, H.: 22
Scheibner, R. M.: 13
Shagass, C.: 18
Steinmetz, A.: 10
Straumanis, J. J.: 18
Tarnopol, L.: 20
Tikofsky, R.: 4
Tikofsky, R. S.: 3
Tyler, L. E.: *rev,* 6:545
Uhlmann, F. W.: 5
Waters, T. J.: 17
Weckowicz, T. E.: 2

[548]
Closure Speed (Gestalt Completion). Industrial employees; 1956–66; formerly called *Gestalt Completion: A Test of Speed of Closure;* L. L. Thurstone (test), T. E. Jeffrey (test), and Norman J. Kantor (manual); Industrial Relations Center, University of Chicago. * [The publisher has not replied to our four requests to check the accuracy of this entry.]

For additional information, see 7:436 (2 references); for a review by Leona E. Tyler, see 6:546 (3 references).

REFERENCES THROUGH 1971

1–3. See 6:546.
4–5. See 7:436.
6. HASETH, KJELL; SHAGASS, CHARLES; AND STRAUMANIS, JOHN J. "Perceptual and Personality Correlates of EEG and Evoked Response Measures." *Biol Psychiatry* 1(1):49–60 Ja '69. * (*PA* 46:4440)

CUMULATIVE NAME INDEX

Baehr, M. E.: 4
Bass, B. M.: 1–2
Coates, C. H.: 1
Coscarelli, J. E.: 5
Froemel, E. C.: 4
Furcon, J. E.: 4
Häseth, K.: 6
Karstendiek, B.: 2
McCarty, J. J.: 3
McCullough, G.: 2
Pruitt, R. C.: 2
Sanders, J. W.: 5
Shagass, C.: 6
Straumanis, J. J.: 6
Tyler, L. E.: *rev,* 6:546

[549]
Concept Assessment Kit—Conservation. Ages 4–7; 1968; CAKC; 2 editions; Marcel L. Goldschmid and Peter M. Bentler; Educational and Industrial Testing Service. *

a) FORMS A AND B. 13 scores: 2 scores (behavior, explanation) in each of 6 areas (2-dimensional space, number, substance, continuous quantity, weight, discontinuous quantity), total.

b) FORM C. 13 scores: 2 scores (behavior, explanation) in area (3 scores) and length (3 scores), total.

For additional information, a review by J. Douglas Ayers, and excerpted reviews by Rheta DeVries (with Lawrence Kohlberg), Vernon C. Hall (with Michael Mery), and Charles D. Smock, see 7:437 (5 references).

REFERENCES THROUGH 1971

1–5. See 7:437.
6. GOLDSCHMID, MARCEL L. "Role of Experience in the Acquisition of Conservation." Abstract. *Proc 76th Ann Conv Am Psychol Assn* 3:361–2 '68. * (*PA* 43:665, title only)
7. RARDIN, DONALD R., AND MOAN, CHARLES E. "Peer Interaction and Cognitive Development." *Child Develop* 42(6):1685–99 D '71. * (*PA* 48:8760)
8. SWIZE, LYDIA MARIE. *The Relationship Between Performance on Piagetian Conservation Tasks and Intelligence and Achievement in Educable Mentally Retarded Children.* Doctor's thesis, University of Northern Colorado (Greeley, Colo.), 1971. (*DAI* 32:3806A)
9. SWIZE, MYRON THEODORE. *Prediction of Piagetian Conservation for Second Grade Mexican-American and Anglo-American Children.* Doctor's thesis, University of Northern Colorado (Greeley, Colo.), 1971. (*DAI* 32:5624A)
10. WASIK, BARBARA H., AND WASIK, JOHN L. "Performance of Culturally Deprived Children on the Concept Assessment Kit—Conservation." *Child Develop* 42(5):1586–90 N '71. * (*PA* 48:4660)

CUMULATIVE NAME INDEX

Ayers, J. D.: *rev,* 7:437
Baker, E. A.: 4
Bentler, P. M.: 3, 5
DeVries, R.: *exc,* 7:437
Goldschmid, M. L.: 1–3, 6
Hall, V. C.: *exc,* 7:437
Kohlberg, L.: *exc,* 7:437
Mery, M.: *exc,* 7:437
Moan, C. E.: 7
Rardin, D. R.: 7
Smock, C. D.: *exc,* 7:437
Swize, L. M.: 8
Swize, M. T.: 9
Wasik, B. H.: 10
Wasik, J. L.: 10

[550]
★**Concept Attainment Test.** College and adults; 1959; CAT; J. M. Schepers; National Institute for Personnel Research [South Africa]. *

[551]
Consequences. Grades 9–16 and adults; 1958–62; 2 scores: originality, ideational fluency; the original 1958 single-form, 10-item test has been divided into two 5-item tests, Forms A-1 (first 5 items) and A-2 (last 5 items); no manual for the 5-item tests; P. R. Christensen, P. R. Merrifield, and J. P. Guilford; Sheridan Psychological Services, Inc. *

For additional information and a review by Goldine C. Gleser of the 10-item test, see 6:547 (13 references).

REFERENCES THROUGH 1971

1–13. See 6:547.
14. MARKS, ALVIN; MICHAEL, WILLIAM B.; AND KAISER, HENRY F. "Comparison of Manual and Analytic Techniques of Rotation in a Factor Analysis of Aptitude Test Variables." *Psychol Rep* 7:519–22 D '60. * (*PA* 35:2792)
15. GARWOOD, DOROTHY SEMENOW. *Some Personality Factors Related to Creativity in Young Scientists.* Doctor's thesis, Claremont Graduate School (Claremont, Calif.), 1961. (*DA* 22:3273)
16. McGUIRE, CARSON; HINDSMAN, EDWIN; KING, F. J.; AND JENNINGS, EARL. "Dimensions of Talented Behavior." *Ed & Psychol Meas* 21:3–38 sp '61. * (*PA* 36:1KH03M)
17. MERRIFIELD, P. R.; GUILFORD, J. P.; CHRISTENSEN, P. R.; AND FRICK, J. W. "Interrelationships Between Certain Abilities and Certain Traits of Motivation and Temperament." *J General Psychol* 65:57–74 Jl '61. * (*PA* 36:2HD57M)
18. BARRON, FRANK. *Creativity and Psychological Health: Origins of Personal Vitality and Creative Freedom.* Princeton, N.J.: D. Van Nostrand Co., Inc., 1963. Pp. xi, 292. *
19. IRVINE, DAVID JAMES. *An Empirical Study of the Relationship Between Certain Pupil Characteristics and Selected Measures of Creativity.* Doctor's thesis, University of North Carolina (Chapel Hill, N.C.), 1963. (*DA* 25:4543)

20. LOCKE, EDWIN A. "Some Correlates of Classroom and Out-of-Class Achievement in Gifted Science Students." *J Ed Psychol* 54:238-48 O '63. * (*PA* 38:4649)
21. WHITTEMORE, ROBERT GEORGE, JR. *Modification of Originality Responses in Academically Talented, Male University Freshmen.* Doctor's thesis, Arizona State University (Tempe, Ariz.), 1963. (*DA* 25:6403)
22. CASTELLI, CHARLES DOMINIC. *An Exploration of the Relationship Between Teacher Creative Ability and Teacher-Pupil Classroom Behavior.* Doctor's thesis, State University of New York (Buffalo, N.Y.), 1964. (*DA* 25:3320)
23. FLEISCHER, GERALD. *The Effects of Anxiety Upon Tests of Creativity.* Doctor's thesis, State University of New York (Buffalo, N.Y.), 1964. (*DA* 25:5372)
24. GARWOOD, DOROTHY SEMENOW. "Personality Factors Related to Creativity in Young Scientists." *J Abn & Social Psychol* 68:413-9 Ap '64. * (*PA* 39:1729)
25. GRIFFIN, WILLIAM MAXWELL. *A Study of the Relationship of Certain Characteristics of High School Seniors to Effectiveness in Independent Study.* Doctor's thesis, Syracuse University (Syracuse, N.Y.), 1964. (*DA* 25:5787)
26. MCGLOTHLIN, WILLIAM H.; COHEN, SIDNEY; AND MCGLOTHLIN, MARCELLA S. "Short-Term Effects of LSD on Anxiety, Attitudes and Performance." *J Nerv & Mental Dis* 139:266-73 S '64. * (*PA* 39:7046)
27. RAINWATER, JANETTE MUNKITTRICK. *Effects of Set on Problem Solving in Subjects of Varying Levels of Assessed Creativity.* Doctor's thesis, University of California (Berkeley, Calif.), 1964. (*DA* 25:6753)
28. RICHARDS, JAMES M., JR.; CLINE, VICTOR B.; AND NEEDHAM, WALTER E. "Creativity Tests and Teacher and Self Judgments of Originality." *J Exp Ed* 32:281-5 sp '64. * (*PA* 39:5135)
29. SEITZ, THEODORE LEE. *The Relationship Between Creativity and Intelligence, Personality, and Value Patterns in Adolescence.* Doctor's thesis, University of Denver (Denver, Colo.), 1964. (*DA* 25:3679)
30. BACHELIS, LEONARD A. *Body-Field Perceptual Differentiation as a Variable in Creative Thinking.* Doctor's thesis, Yeshiva University (New York, N.Y.), 1965. (*DA* 26:3475)
31. BUTLER, MARJORIE JOHNSON. *Criteria for Creativity in Counseling.* Doctor's thesis, University of Pittsburgh (Pittsburgh, Pa.), 1965. (*DA* 27:977B)
32. FELDHUSEN, JOHN F.; DENNY, TERRY; AND CONDON, CHARLES F. "Anxiety, Divergent Thinking, and Achievement." *J Ed Psychol* 56:40-5 F '65. * (*PA* 39:10771)
33. FLEISCHER, GERALD, AND COHEN, IRA S. "The Relationship Between Test Anxiety and Tests of Creativity." Abstract. *Proc Ann Conv Am Psychol Assn* 73:311-2 '65. * (*PA* 39:15458)
34. CROPLEY, A. J. "Creativity and Intelligence." *Brit J Ed Psychol* 36:259-66 N '66. * (*PA* 41:573)
35. EISENSTADT, J. MARVIN. "Problem-Solving Ability of Creative and Non-Creative College Students." *J Consult Psychol* 30:81-3 F '66. * (*PA* 40:4223)
36. FLAX, MORTON LEWIS. *The Stability of Relationships Between Creativity and Personality Variables.* Doctor's research study No. 1, Colorado State College (Greeley, Colo.), 1966. (*DA* 27:2857B)
37. HARDYCK, CURTIS D. "Personality Characteristics and Motor Activity: Some Empirical Evidence." *J Pers & Social Psychol* 4:181-8 Ag '66. * (*PA* 40:11183)
38. NICOLAY, GLEN C. *Relationship Between a Risk-Taking Questionnaire and Selected Personality Characteristics.* Doctor's thesis, Fordham University (New York, N.Y.), 1966. (*DA* 27:2142B)
39. SMITH, ROBERT M., AND NEISWORTH, JOHN T. "Creative Thinking Abilities of Intellectually Superior Children in the Regular Grades." *Psychol Rep* 18:335-41 Ap '66. * (*PA* 40:8832)
40. COMPTON, MARY FRANCES. *An Attempt to Foster Creative Thinking in Teachers.* Doctor's thesis, University of Florida (Gainesville, Fla.), 1967. (*DA* 29:164A)
41. CROPLEY, A. J. "Creativity, Intelligence, and Achievement." *Alberta J Ed Res* (Canada) 13:51-8 Mr '67. * (*PA* 41:15253)
42. GIVENS, PAUL R.; PINKARD, CAROLYN A.; AND RICH, THOMAS A. "Relationship of Personality Factors, Creativity and Academic Achievement Among High School Seniors." *Fla J Ed Res* 9:45-56 Ja '67. *
43. JACKSON, ROBERT LEON. *An Investigation of the Creative Growth Curves of University Students.* Doctor's thesis, East Texas State University (Commerce, Tex.), 1967. (*DA* 28:3508A)
44. MANGAN, GORDON L. "Studies of the Relationship Between Neo-Pavlovian Properties of Higher Nervous Activity and Western Personality Dimensions: 3, The Relations of Transformation Mobility to Thinking Flexibility." *J Exp Res Personality* 2:117-23 My '67. * (*PA* 41:11907)
45. SIDLE, ALLAN CHARLES. *Creativity and Delusional Thinking in Schizophrenics.* Doctor's thesis, Stanford University (Stanford, Calif.), 1967. (*DA* 28:353B)
46. SMITH, ROBERT M. "Creative Thinking Abilities of Educable Mentally Handicapped Children in the Regular Grades." *Am J Mental Def* 71:571-5 Ja '67. * (*PA* 41:6197)

47. ADAMS, JOHN C., JR. "The Relative Effects of Various Testing Atmospheres on Spontaneous Flexibility, a Factor of Divergent Thinking." *J Creative Behav* 2:187-94 su '68. * (*PA* 43:5882)
48. ANDERSON, RONALD JUDE. *Divergent Thinking Within Superior, Average, and Retarded Subjects.* Doctor's thesis, University of Nebraska (Lincoln, Neb.), 1968. (*DA* 29:1126A)
49. BOWERS, KENNETH. "Hypnosis and Creativity: A Preliminary Investigation." *Int J Clin & Exp Hyp* 16:38-52 Ja '68. * (*PA* 42:11537)
50. BROWN, STEPHEN W.; GUILFORD, J. P.; AND HOEPFNER, RALPH. "Six Semantic-Memory Abilities." *Ed & Psychol Meas* 28:691-717 au '68. * (*PA* 43:4427)
51. HINTON, BERNARD L. "Environmental Frustration and Creative Problem Solving." *J Appl Psychol* 52:211-7 Je '68. * (*PA* 42:11701)
52. LETT, WARREN ROBERT. *Some Postulated Correlates of Creativity and Need Achievement.* Doctor's thesis, University of California (Berkeley, Calif.), 1968. (*DA* 29:1106A)
53. ROGERS, MARTIN IRVING. *Self-Actualization as Process.* Doctor's thesis, Case Western Reserve University (Cleveland, Ohio), 1968. (*DAI* 30:4380B)
54. SHAPIRO, R. J. *Creative Research Scientists.* Psychologica Africana Monograph Supplement No. 4. Johannesburg, South Africa: National Institute for Personnel Research, 1968. Pp. 180. * (*PA* 43:923)
55. WHITE, KINNARD. "Anxiety, Extraversion-Intraversion, and Divergent Thinking Ability." *J Creative Behav* 2:119-27 sp '68. * (*PA* 42:17233)
56. BLACKHURST, A. EDWARD; MARKS, CLAUDE H.; AND TISDALL, WILLIAM J. "Relationship Between Mobility and Divergent Thinking in Blind Children." *Ed Visually Handicapped* 1(2):33-6 My '69. * (*PA* 43:14813)
57. GRIMSLEY, WILLIAM GERALD. *The Relationship Between Creativity and Leader Behavior of School Superintendents.* Doctor's thesis, University of Missouri (Columbia, Mo.), 1969. (*DAI* 30:5193A)
58. GUILFORD, J. P., AND HOEPFNER, RALPH. "Comparisons of Varimax Rotations With Rotations to Theoretical Targets." *Ed & Psychol Meas* 29(1):3-22 sp '69. * (*PA* 44:15668)
59. KLEIN, STEPHEN P.; FREDERIKSEN, NORMAN; AND EVANS, FRANKLIN R. "Anxiety and Learning to Formulate Hypotheses." *J Ed Psychol* 60(6):465-75 D '69. * (*PA* 44:3087)
60. KROP, HARRY. "Effects of Extrinsic Motivation, Intrinsic Motivation, and Intelligence on Creativity: A Factorial Approach." *J General Psychol* 80(2):259-66 Ap '69. * (*PA* 43:11332)
61. KROP, HARRY D.; ALEGRE, CECILIA E.; AND WILLIAMS, CARL D. "Effect of Induced Stress on Convergent and Divergent Thinking." *Psychol Rep* 24(3):895-8 Je '69. * (*PA* 44:218)
62. OLIVE, HELEN. *Sibling Resemblances in Divergent Thinking.* Doctor's thesis, Columbia University (New York, N.Y.), 1969. (*DAI* 33:3289B)
63. SCHNITZER, LEAH PALTIEL, AND STEWART, ROBERT A. C. "Originality and Personality Variables in High School Art Students." *Psychol* 6(1):36-9 F '69. * (*PA* 43:11334)
64. BARRON, FRANK. "Heredability of Factors in Creative Thinking and Judgment." *Acta Geneticae Medicae et Gemellologiae* (Italy) 19(1-2):294-8 Ja-Ap '70. *
65. BOWERS, KENNETH S., AND VAN DER MEULEN, SANDRA J. "Effect of Hypnotic Susceptibility on Creativity Test Performance." *J Pers & Social Psychol* 14(3):247-56 Mr '70. * (*PA* 44:8441)
66. DELLAS, MARIE. *Effects of Creativity Training, Defensiveness, and Intelligence on Divergent Thinking.* Doctor's thesis, State University of New York (Buffalo, N.Y.), 1970. (*DAI* 31:4540A)
67. FELDHUSEN, JOHN F.; TREFFINGER, DONALD J.; AND ELIAS, ROBERT M. "Prediction of Academic Achievement With Divergent and Convergent Thinking and Personality Variables." *Psychol Sch* 7(1):46-52 Ja '70. * (*PA* 44:11410)
68. FRUIN, DAVID JOHN. *Response Styles and Creativity.* Doctor's thesis, Johns Hopkins University (Baltimore, Md.), 1970. (*DAI* 31:4361B)
69. HINTON, BERNARD L. "Personality Variables and Creative Potential." *J Creative Behav* 4(3):210-7 su '70. *
70. LAMONTAGNE, CHARLES WARREN. *An Exploration of the Relationship of Creativity and Educational Administration.* Doctor's thesis, Boston University (Boston, Mass.), 1970. (*DAI* 31:2064A)
71. OLESON, D. S., AND ZUBEK, JOHN P. "Effect of One Day of Sensory Deprivation on a Battery of Open-Ended Cognitive Tests." *Percept & Motor Skills* 31(3):919-23 D '70. * (*PA* 46:358)
72. OWEN, STEVEN V.; FELDHUSEN, JOHN F.; AND THURSTON, JOHN R. "Achievement Prediction in Nursing Education With Cognitive, Attitudinal, and Divergent Thinking Variables." *Psychol Rep* 26(3):867-70 Je '70. * (*PA* 45:1361)
73. REESE, HAYNE W., AND PARNES, SIDNEY J. "Programming Creative Behavior." *Child Develop* 41(2):413-23 Je '70. * (*PA* 15509)
74. RENNER, VIVIAN. "Effects of Modification of Cognitive Style on Creative Behavior." *J Pers & Social Psychol* 14(3):257-62 Mr '70. * (*PA* 44:8435)

Consequences

75. RICHMOND, BERT O. "Creativity: Its Relationship to the Counselor's Approach." *J Stud Pers Assn Teach Ed* 8(2):56–63 w '70. * (*PA* 44:19438)
76. SMITH, I. LEON. "IQ, Creativity, and the Taxonomy of Educational Objectives: Cognitive Domain." *J Exp Ed* 38(4):58–60 su '70. * (*PA* 46:5688)
77. ABRAHAM, CAROL. *The Relationship of Authoritarianism to Independence and Creativity Among College Students.* Doctor's thesis, New York University (New York, N.Y.), 1971. (*DAI* 32:6023B)
78. ANASTASI, ANNE, AND SCHAEFER, CHARLES E. "Note on the Concepts of Creativity and Intelligence." *J Creative Behav* 5(2):113–6 '71. * (*PA* 48:7724)
79. BOWERS, KENNETH S. "Sex and Susceptibility as Moderator Variables in the Relationship of Creativity and Hypnotic Susceptibility." *J Abn Psychol* 78(1):93–100 Ag '71. * (*PA* 47:2042)
80. CROPLEY, A. J., AND CLAPSON, L. "Long Term Test-Retest Reliability of Creativity Tests." *Brit J Ed Psychol* 41(2):206–8 Je '71. * (*PA* 47:9640)
81. SMITH, I. LEON. "IQ, Creativity, and Achievement: Interaction and Threshold." *Multiv Behav Res* 6(1):51–62 Ja '71. * (*PA* 46:9753)
82. TISDALL, WILLIAM J.; BLACKHURST, A. EDWARD; AND MARKS, CLAUDE H. "Divergent Thinking in Blind Children." *J Ed Psychol* 62(6):468–73 D '71. * (*PA* 47:9708)
83. WADE, SERENA E. "Adolescents, Creativity, and Media: An Exploratory Study." *Am Behav Sci* 14(3):341–51 Ja '71. * (*PA* 46:8797)
84. WILLIAMS, JOHN D.; HARLOW, STEVEN D.; AND BORGEN, JEROME S. "Creativity, Dogmatism, and Arithmetic Achievement." *J Psychol* 78(2):217–22 Jl '71. * (*PA* 46:9760)

CUMULATIVE NAME INDEX

Abdel-Razik, T. M.: 10
Abe, C.: 9
Abraham, C.: 77
Adams, J. C.: 47
Alegre, C. E.: 61
Anastasi, A.: 78
Anderson, R. J.: 48
Asher, J. J.: 13
Bachelis, L. A.: 30
Barron, F.: 1, 11, 18, 64
Beittel, K. R.: 5
Berger, R. M.: 2
Blackhurst, A. E.: 56, 82
Borgen, J. S.: 84
Bowers, K.: 49
Bowers, K. S.: 65, 79
Brittain, W. L.: 5
Brown, S. W.: 50
Butler, M. J.: 31
Castelli, C. D.: 22
Christensen, P. R.: 2, 4, 17
Clapson, L.: 80
Cline, V. B.: 9, 12, 28
Cohen, I. S.: 33
Cohen, S.: 26
Compton, M. F.: 40
Condon, C. F.: 32
Cropley, A. J.: 34, 41, 80
Dellas, M.: 66
Denny, T.: 32
Eisenstadt, J. M.: 35
Elias, R. M.: 67
Evans, F. R.: 59
Feldhusen, J. F.: 32, 67, 72
Flax, M. L.: 36
Fleischer, G.: 23, 33
Frederiksen, N.: 59
Frick, J. W.: 17
Fruin, D. J.: 68
Garwood, D. S.: 15, 24
Givens, P. R.: 42
Gleser, G. C.: rev, 6:547
Griffin, W. M.: 25
Grimsley, W. G.: 57
Guilford, J. P.: 2–4, 17, 50, 58
Hardyck, C. D.: 37
Harlow, S. D.: 84
Hindsman, E.: 16
Hinton, B. L.: 51, 69
Hoepfner, R.: 50, 58
Irvine, D. J.: 19
Jackson, R. L.: 43
Jacobsen, T. L.: 13
Jennings, E.: 16
Kaiser, H. F.: 7–8, 14
Kettner, N. W.: 4
King, F. J.: 16
Klein, S. P.: 59
Krop, H.: 60
Krop, H. D.: 61
Lamontagne, C. W.: 70
Lett, W. R.: 52
Locke, E. A.: 20
McGlothlin, M. S.: 26
McGlothlin, W. H.: 26
McGuire, C.: 6, 16
Mangan, G. L.: 44
Marks, A.: 7–8, 14
Marks, C. H.: 56, 82
Merrifield, P. R.: 17
Michael, W. B.: 7–8, 14
Needham, W. E.: 12, 28
Neisworth, J. T.: 39
Nicolay, G. C.: 38
Oleson, D. S.: 71
Olive, H.: 62
Owen, S. V.: 72
Parnes, S. J.: 73
Pinkard, C. A.: 42
Rainwater, J. M.: 27
Reese, H. W.: 73
Renner, V.: 74
Rich, T. A.: 42
Richards, J. M.: 9, 12, 28
Richmond, B. O.: 75
Rogers, M. J.: 53
Schaefer, C. E.: 78
Schnitzer, L. P.: 63
Seitz, T. L.: 29
Shapiro, R. J.: 54
Sidle, A. C.: 45
Smith, I. L.: 76, 81
Smith, R. M.: 39, 46
Stewart, R. A. C.: 63
Thurston, J. R.: 72
Tisdall, W. J.: 56, 82
Treffinger, D. J.: 67
van der Meulen, S. J.: 65
Wade, S. E.: 83
White, K.: 55
Whittemore, R. G.: 21
Williams, C. D.: 61
Williams, J. D.: 84
Zubek, J. P.: 71

[552]

★**Consequences [NIPR].** Ages 15 and over; 1972; verbal creativity; H. E. Schmidt (manual); National Institute for Personnel Research [South Africa]. *

[553]

★**Creativity Attitude Survey.** Grades 4–6; 1971; CAS; Charles E. Schaefer; Psychologists and Educators, Inc. *

REFERENCES THROUGH 1971

1. SCHAEFER, CHARLES E., AND BRIDGES, CAROLYN I. "Development of a Creativity Attitude Survey for Children." *Percept & Motor Skills* 31(3):861–2 D '70. * (*PA* 45:9980)

CUMULATIVE NAME INDEX

Bridges, C. I.: 1   Schaefer, C. E.: 1

[554]

★**Creativity Tests for Children.** Grades 4–6; 1971; CTC; "divergent production abilities"; 10 tests; J. P. Guilford and others listed below; Sheridan Psychological Services, Inc. *

a) ADDING DECORATIONS. Identical with first half of *Decorations* (see 555); Arthur Gershon, Sheldon Gardner, and Philip R. Merrifield.

b) DIFFERENT LETTER GROUPS. Arthur Gershon.

c) HIDDEN LETTERS.

d) KINDS OF PEOPLE. Adaptation of *Possible Jobs* (see 573); Arthur Gershon.

e) MAKE SOMETHING OUT OF IT.

f) MAKING OBJECTS. Adaptation of adult test with the same title (see 562); Sheldon Gardner, Arthur Gershon, and Philip R. Merrifield.

g) NAMES FOR STORIES. Adaptation of *Plot Titles* (see 572).

h) SIMILAR MEANINGS. Adaptation of *Associational Fluency I* (see 546c); Philip R. Merrifield.

i) WHAT TO DO WITH IT. Adaptation of *Alternate Uses* (see 542); Philip R. Merrifield.

j) WRITING SENTENCES.

[555]

Decorations. Grades 9–16 and adults; 1963; "divergent production of figural implications" or "ability to add meaningful details"; Arthur Gershon, Sheldon Gardner, Philip R. Merrifield, and J. P. Guilford; Sheridan Psychological Services, Inc. *

For additional information, see 6:548 (1 reference).

REFERENCES THROUGH 1971

1. See 6:548.
2. MACKLER, BERNARD, AND SHONTZ, FRANKLIN C. "Life Style and Creativity: An Empirical Investigation." *Percept & Motor Skills* 20:873–96 Je '65. * (*PA* 39:15302)
3. MACKLER, BERNARD, AND SPOTTS, JAMES V. "Characteristics of Responses to Tests of Creativity: A Second Look." *Percept & Motor Skills* 21:595–9 O '65. * (*PA* 40:2880)
4. HEUSSENSTAMM, FRANCES K. "Creativity and Alienation: An Exploration of Their Relationship in Adolescence." *Calif J Ed Res* 21(3):140–6 My '70. *
5. OLESON, D. S., AND ZUBEK, JOHN P. "Effect of One Day of Sensory Deprivation on a Battery of Open-Ended Cognitive Tests." *Percept & Motor Skills* 31(3):919–23 D '70. * (*PA* 46:358)
6. RAIA, JAMES R., AND OSIPOW, SAMUEL H. "Creative Thinking Ability and Susceptibility to Persuasion." *J Social Psychol* 82(2):181–6 D '70. * (*PA* 45:6341)

CUMULATIVE NAME INDEX

Guilford, J. P.: 1   Raia, J. R.: 6
Heussenstamm, F. K.: 4   Shontz, F. C.: 2
Mackler, B.: 2–3   Spotts, J. V.: 3
Oleson, D. S.: 5   Zubek, J. P.: 5
Osipow, S. H.: 6

[556]

Feature Profile Test: Pintner-Paterson Modification. Ages 4 and over; [1917–23]; modification of *Knox-Kempf Feature Profile Test* ['14]; subtest of *Arthur Point Scale of Performance Tests* and *Performance Tests of Intelligence;* R. Pintner and D. G. Paterson; Stoelting Co.

REFERENCES THROUGH 1971

1. WECHSLER, DAVID. *The Measurement of Adult Intelligence, Second Edition*, pp. 98–100, 175–7. Baltimore, Md.: Williams & Wilkins Co., 1941. Pp. xi, 248. *

CUMULATIVE NAME INDEX

Wechsler, D.: 1

[557]

★**Gottschaldt Figures [NIPR].** Job applicants with at least 10 years of education; 1943–56; adaptation of U.S. Army Air Forces Test AC121; test in English and Afrikaans; no manual; National Institute for Personnel Research [South Africa]. *

[558]

Healy Pictorial Completion Tests. Ages 5 and over; [1914–21]; 2 tests; William Healy; Stoelting Co. *

a) TEST I. 1914; modification appears in *Arthur Point Scale of Performance Tests*.
b) TEST II. [1917–21]; subtest of *Arthur Point Scale of Performance Tests*.

REFERENCES THROUGH 1971

1. HEALY, WILLIAM. "A Pictorial Completion Test." *Psychol R* 21:189–203 My '14. *
2. PINTNER, RUDOLF, AND PATERSON, DONALD G. *A Scale of Performance Tests*, pp. 44–53, 122–6. New York: D. Appleton & Co., 1917. Pp. xi, 218. *
3. WALKER, MIRIAM A., AND WASHBURN, M. F. "The Healy-Fernald Picture Completion Test as a Test of the Perception of the Comic." *Am J Psychol* 30:304–7 Jl '19. *
4. GAULT, ROBERT H. "Picture Completion." *J Appl Psychol* 4:310–5 D '20. *
5. SKAGGS, E. B. "A Comparison of Results Obtained by the Terman Binet Tests and the Healy Picture Completion Test." *J Ed Psychol* 11:418–420a O '20. *
6. HEALY, WILLIAM. "Pictorial Completion Test II." *J Appl Psychol* 5:225–39 S '21. *
7. JOHNSON, BUFORD, AND SCHRIEFER, LOUISE. "A Comparison of Mental Age Scores Obtained by Performance Tests and the Stanford Revision of the Binet-Simon Scale." *J Ed Psychol* 13:408–17 O '22. *
8. MORGENTHAU, DOROTHY RUTH. "Some Well-Known Mental Tests Evaluated and Compared." *Arch Psychol* 52:1–54 My '22. *
9. PERRY, DORIS E. "Interpretations of the Reactions of the Feeble-Minded on the Healy Pictorial Completion Test II—Social Implications." *J Deling* 7:75–85 Mr '22. *
10. GAW, FRANCES. "A Study of Performance Tests." *Brit J Psychol* 15:374–92 Ap '25. *
11. JOHNSON, BUFORD J. *Mental Growth of Children in Relation to the Rate of Growth in Bodily Development: A Report of the Bureau of Educational Experiments, New York City*, pp. 123–5. New York: E. P. Dutton & Co., 1925. Pp. 160. *
12. MCCAULLEY, SELINDA. "One Hundred Non-Conformed Boys." *Psychol Clinic* 16:141–66 My–Je '25. * (*PA* 3:1607)
13. PASCHAL, FRANKLIN C., AND SULLIVAN, LOUIS R. "Racial Influences in the Mental and Physical Development of Mexican Children." *Comp Psychol Monogr* 3(14):1–76 O '25. * (*PA* 1:393)
14. JONES, GRACE L. *A Study of the Healy Completion Test II*. Master's thesis, Ohio Wesleyan University (Delaware, Ohio), 1926. *
15. WORTHINGTON, MYRTLE RAYMAKER. "A Study of Some Commonly Used Performance Tests." *J Appl Psychol* 10:216–27 Je '26. *
16. DORCUS, MILDRED DAY. "Analysis of Specific Responses of Children in the Healy Pictorial Completion Test II." *J Genetic Psychol* 35:574–86 D '28. * (*PA* 3:2436)
17. SCHIEFFELIN, BARBARA, AND SCHWESINGER, GLADYS C. *Mental Tests and Heredity: Including a Survey of Non-Verbal Tests*, pp. 148–50. New York: Galton Publishing Co., Inc., 1930. Pp. ix, 298. *
18. ECCLES, AUGUST M. "The Performance of Delinquent Boys on the Healy Completion Test II." *Training Sch B* 28:61–70 Je '31. * (*PA* 7:1981, title only)
19. LOUTTIT, C. M. "Test Performance of a Selected Group of Part-Hawaiians." *J Appl Psychol* 15:43–52 F '31. * (*PA* 5:4204)
20. SCOVILL, MARY SOPHIA. *A Comparative Study of the Performance of Normal and Feebleminded Subjects on the Healy Pictorial Completion Test II*. Master's thesis, Ohio State University (Columbus, Ohio), 1931. *
21. NOTTINGHAM, RUTH D. "A Psychological Study of Forty Unmarried Mothers." *Genetic Psychol Monogr* 19:157–228 My '37. * (*PA* 11:4670)
22. VERNON, P. E. "A Study of the Norms and the Validity of Certain Mental Tests at a Child Guidance Clinic: Part II." *Brit J Ed Psychol* 7:115–37 Je '37. * (*PA* 11:4827)
23. WILSON, FRANK T., AND FLEMING, CECILE WHITE. "Correlations of Performance Tests With Other Abilities and Traits in Grade I." *Child Develop* 8:80–8 Mr '37. * (*PA* 11:4814)
24. CARPENTER, RACHEL STANLEY. *What Value Has Healy's Picture Completion Test II as a Prognostic Test for Success in Geometry?* Master's thesis, Trinity College (Hartford, Conn.), 1938. *
25. HAMLIN, ROY, AND ABEL, THEODORA M. "Test Pattern of Mental Defectives Skilled in Weaving." *J Appl Psychol* 22:385–9 Ag '38. * (*PA* 13:1642)
26. MARSH, CHARLES JUDD. *Performance Test Abilities of Adults*. Doctor's thesis, Stanford University (Stanford, Calif.), 1938. *
27. HANFMANN, EUGENIA. "A Qualitative Analysis of the Healy Pictorial Completion Test II." *Am J Orthopsychiatry* 9:325–30 Ap '39. * (*PA* 13:5385)
28. WERNER, HENRY. "A Comparative Study of a Small Group of Clinical Tests." *J Appl Psychol* 24:231–6 Ap '40. * (*PA* 14:4775)
29. WOOD, LOUISE. "A New Picture Completion Test." *J Genetic Psychol* 56:383–409 Je '40. * (*PA* 15:576)
30. SCHWERIN, ERNA. *A Study of Comparative Reliability and Validity of the Healy Completion Test II and a Revised Form*. Master's thesis, Bowling Green State University (Bowling Green, Ohio), 1953.
31. SCHWERIN, ERNA, AND FITZWATER, MYLEN E. "Comparative Reliability and Validity of the Healy Completion Test II and a Revised Form." Abstract. *Am Psychologist* 9:468 Ag '54. *
32. SCHWERIN, ERNA, AND FITZWATER, MYLEN E. "Comparative Reliability and Validity of the Healy Completion Test II and a Revised Form." *J Clin Psychol* 10:248–51 Jl '54. * (*PA* 29:2475)
33. CLARK, KENNETH C. *The Healy Picture Completion Test II as an Indicator of Emotional Disorder in Elementary School Children*. Master's thesis, Fresno State College (Fresno, Calif.), 1956.
34. FITZPATRICK, CONSTANCE H. *A Study of the Performance of a Group of Mentally Retarded Children on the Healy Pictorial Completion Test II*. Master's thesis, Boston University (Boston, Mass.), 1957.
35. BILGER, ROBERT C. "Limitations on the Use of Intelligence Scales to Estimate the Mental Ages of Children." *Volta R* 60:321–5 S '58. *
36. JUDGE, CAROLE HESSE. *Thought Disorder in Parents of Schizophrenics*. Doctor's thesis, University of Minnesota (Minneapolis, Minn.), 1967. (*DA* 28:3473B)
37. MYKLEBUST, HELMER R.; BANNOCHIE, MARGARET N.; AND KILLEN, JAMES R. Chap. 9, "Learning Disabilities and Cognitive Processes," pp. 213–51. In *Progress in Learning Disabilities, Vol. 2*. Edited by Helmer R. Myklebust. New York: Grune & Stratton, Inc., 1971. Pp. ix, 404. *

CUMULATIVE NAME INDEX

Abel, T. M.: 25
Bannochie, M. N.: 37
Bilger, R. C.: 35
Carpenter, R. S.: 24
Clark, K. C.: 33
Dorcus, M. D.: 16
Eccles, A. M.: 18
Fitzpatrick, C. H.: 34
Fitzwater, M. E.: 31–2
Fleming, C. W.: 23
Gault, R. H.: 4
Gaw, F.: 10
Hamlin, R.: 25
Hanfmann, E.: 27
Healy, W.: 1, 6
Johnson, B.: 7
Johnson, B. J.: 11
Jones, G. L.: 14
Judge, C. H.: 36
Killen, J. R.: 37
Louttit, C. M.: 19
McCaulley, S.: 12
Marsh, C. J.: 26
Morgenthau, D. R.: 8
Myklebust, H. R.: 37
Nottingham, R. D.: 21
Paschal, F. C.: 13
Paterson, D. G.: 2
Perry, D. E.: 9
Pintner, R.: 2
Schieffelin, B.: 17
Schriefer, L.: 7
Schwerin, E.: 30–2
Schwesinger, G. C.: 17
Scovill, M. S.: 20
Skaggs, E. B.: 5
Sullivan, L. R.: 13
Vernon, P. E.: 22
Walker, M. A.: 3
Washburn, M. F.: 3
Werner, H.: 28
Wilson, F. T.: 23
Wood, L.: 29
Worthington, M. R.: 15

[559]

Hidden Figures Test. Grades 6–16; 1962–63; HFT; for research use only; flexibility of closure; 2 tests; Educational Testing Service (Atlanta Office). *

a) FORM CF-1. 1962–63; manual by John W. French, Ruth B. Ekstrom, and Leighton B. Price.
b) FORM 5. 1962.

For additional information, see 7:440 (31 references).

REFERENCES THROUGH 1971

1–31. See 7:440.
32. BOERSMA, FREDERIC J.; MUIR, WALTER; WILTON, KERI;

Feature Profile Test

AND BARHAM, RICHARD. "Eye Movements During Embedded Figure Tasks." *Percept & Motor Skills* 28(1):271–4 F '69. * (*PA* 43:11294)
33. EVANS, FREDERICK J. "Effects of Practice on the Validity of a Group-Administered Embedded Figures Test." *Acta Psychologica* (Netherlands) 29(2):172–80 Mr '69. * (*PA* 44:1634)
34. STRAUSS, MILTON E. "Cognitive Style and the Use of Incidental Cues in Problem Solving." *J Psychol* 73(1):69–74 S '69. * (*PA* 44:4548)
35. GREENFIELD, ADELAIDE. *Perceptual Style, Attitudes Toward Problem Solving, and Problem-Solving Performance.* Doctor's thesis, New York University (New York, N.Y.), 1970. (*DAI* 31:7571B)
36. MCDONAGH, JOHN MICHAEL. *The Relationship Between Familial Characteristics and Two Measures of Dependency.* Doctor's thesis, University of Oklahoma (Norman, Okla.), 1970. (*DAI* 32:542B)
37. ADCOCK, C. J., AND WEBBERLEY, M. "Primary Mental Abilities." *J General Psychol* 84(2):229–43 Ap '71. * (*PA* 46:4979)
38. BRILHART, BARBARA LIEB, AND BRILHART, JOHN K. "Field Independence and Academic Achievement of Engineering Students." *Percept & Motor Skills* 32(2):443–6 Ap '71. * (*PA* 46:11645)
39. COOPER, WALTER, AND ARMSTRONG, WAYNE. "Beginning Tennis Skill and Field Independence." *South J Ed Res* 5(2):114–9 Ap '71. *
40. DARGEL, RUSSELL, AND KIRK, ROGER E. "Manifest Anxiety, Field Dependency, and Task Performance." *Percept & Motor Skills* 32(2):383–93 Ap '71. * (*PA* 46:10865)
41. DINGMAN, ROBERT LEWIS. *A Study of Cognitive Style Differences as a Factor of Communications in School Counseling.* Doctor's thesis, Wayne State University (Detroit, Mich.), 1971. (*DAI* 32:6756A)
42. GRIEVE, TARRANCE DON, AND DAVIS, J. KENT. "The Relationship of Cognitive Style and Method of Instruction to Performance in Ninth Grade Geography." *J Ed Res* 65(3):137–41 N '71. * (*PA* 48:1927)
43. HOCHMAN, SIDNEY H. "Field Independence and Stroop Color-Word Performance." *Percept & Motor Skills* 33(3):782 D '71. * (*PA* 48:953)
44. HUCKABEE, MALCOM W., AND MC GOWN, W. P. "Differences Between Field Independent and Field Dependent Persons on the Stroop Color-Word Test: A Failure to Replicate." *J Clin Psychol* 27(2):226 Ap '71. * (*PA* 46:6888)
45. KAZELSKIS, RICHARD. "Field Independence and Serial Verbal Learning." *South J Ed Res* 5(1):31–8 Ja '71. *
46. PARLETT, T. A. A., AND AYERS, J. D. "The Modification of Criminal Personality Through Massed Learning by Programmed Instruction." *Can J Criminol & Correct* 13(2):155–65 Ap '71. *
47. RICHARDS, TERRY D. *The Effects of Cognitive Style Sets of Flexibility Upon Counselor Perception: Field Dependence and Repression-Sensitization in Relation to Empathic Accuracy.* Doctor's thesis, New York University (New York, N.Y.), 1971. (*DAI* 32:1865A)
48. FLEISHMAN, JOSEPH J., AND FINE, BERNARD J. "Note on Cognitive Factors Related to Factor B of the 16 PF Test." *Psychol Rep* 29(3):1075–7 D '71. * (*PA* 48:988)
49. FLEISHMAN, JOSEPH J., AND DUSEK, E. RALPH. "Reliability and Learning Factors Associated With Cognitive Tests." *Psychol Rep* 29(2):523–30 O '71. * (*PA* 47:7996)

CUMULATIVE NAME INDEX

Acker, M. B.: 5
Adcock, C. J.: 37
Anderson, C. C.: 2
Armstrong, W.: 39
Ayers, J. D.: 46
Barham, R.: 32
Barrett, G. V.: 10, 15, 23
Bartelt, C. A.: 16
Beckerle, G. P.: 3
Boersma, F. J.: 11, 32
Brigham, B. W.: 6
Brilhart, B. L.: 38
Brilhart, J. K.: 38
Brinton, G.: 17
Bryan, V.: 12
Cabe, P. A.: 10, 15, 23
Cline, V. B.: 1
Conklin, R. C.: 18
Cooper, W.: 39
Crego, C. A.: 24
Cropley, A. J.: 2, 4, 7
Dargel, R.: 40
Davis, J. K.: 8, 25, 42
Dingman, R. L.: 41
Dusek, E. R.: 49
Duvall, N. S.: 19
Erginel, A.: 20
Evans, F. J.: 33
Farr, R. S.: 13
Fine, B. J.: 48
Fleishman, J. J.: 48–9
Frederick, W. C.: 9
Graham, J.: 29
Greenfield, A.: 35
Grieve, T. D.: 42
Gruenfeld, L. W.: 26
Hochman, S. H.: 43
Huckabee, M. W.: 21, 44
Kazelskis, R.: 27, 45
Kirk, R. E.: 40
Klausmeier, H. J.: 25
Kohler, E. T.: 30
McDonagh, J. M.: 36
Mc Gown, W. P.: 44
McWhinnie, H. J.: 28
Mausner, B.: 29
Muir, W.: 32
Needham, W. E.: 1
Ohnmacht, F. W.: 30
Parlett, T. A. A.: 46
Richards, J. M.: 1
Richards, T. D.: 47
Rouleau, R. A.: 17
Sharp, E. Y.: 31
Strauss, M. E.: 34
Thornton, C. L.: 10, 15, 23
Titus, H. E.: 22
Weaver, W. W.: 30
Webberley, M.: 37
Weissenberg, P.: 26
Werbel, S. A.: 14
Wilton, K.: 32
Zingle, H. W.: 18

[560]

Higgins-Wertman Test: Threshold of Visual Closure. Ages 5–15; 1968; manual title is *Visual Closure Assessment;* 6 scores: initial closure, final closure, number of responses prior to final closure (whole and detail), perseveration, impotence; Conwell Higgins and Howard Wertman; Higgins-Wertman Associates. *

For additional information, see 7:441 (1 reference).

REFERENCES THROUGH 1971

1. See 7:441.
2. RUSCH, REUBEN R. "Note on the Validity of the Claim That Final Closure Is Related to Reading Achievement." *Percept & Motor Skills* 32(2):394 Ap '71. * (*PA* 46:11669)

CUMULATIVE NAME INDEX

Rusch, R. R.: 1–2

[560A]

Jensen Alternation Board. Ages 5 and over; 1959–60; JAB; learning age; Milton B. Jensen; Lafayette Instrument Co. *

For additional information, see 6:550 (2 references).

REFERENCES THROUGH 1971

1–2. See 6:550.
3. FLICK, GRAD L., AND WATKINS, ERNEST O. "Alternation Learning and Its Relationship to Intellectual Functioning in Primary Retardates." *Psychol Rep* 16:931–2 Je '65. * (*PA* 39:16045)
4. CHAPA, DOLORES G. *An Investigation of the Jensen Alternation Board, Social Maturity and Intelligence as Predictive Factors of Achievement in Retardates.* Master's thesis, Texas Woman's University (Denton, Tex.), 1966.
5. GATES, DONALD O. *The Relationship Between the Jensen Alternation Board and Objective Measures of Ability and Emotional Adjustment.* Doctor's thesis, University of Southern Mississippi (Hattiesburg, Miss.), 1966. (*DA* 28:339B)

CUMULATIVE NAME INDEX

Chapa, D. G.: 4
Flick, G. L.: 3
Gates, D. O.: 5
Jensen, M. B.: 1–2
Watkins, E. O.: 3

[561]

Kit of Reference Tests for Cognitive Factors, 1963 Revision. Various grades 6–16; 1954–63; previously called *Kit of Selected Tests for Reference Aptitude and Achievement Factors;* for research use only; groups of 2–5 tests measuring 24 (16 in the 1954 Kit) "of the better established factors in the cognitive area"; 4 of the 16 factors presented in the 1954 Kit have been dropped and 12 new factors added; "whereas the tests in the first Kit [1954] were usually exact copies of those used in earlier factor studies, most of the tests in the present edition have been newly adapted"; although most tests have been "adapted" or revised, the same titles are used in both the 1954 and 1963 Kits; unless otherwise indicated, all tests were prepared by the Educational Testing Service; tests compiled and manual written by John W. French, Ruth B. Ekstrom, and Leighton A. Price; Educational Testing Service (Atlanta Office) unless otherwise indicated. *

a) FACTOR CF: FLEXIBILITY OF CLOSURE. Grades 6–16; 1962; 3 tests.
  1) *Hidden Figures Test, Cf-1.*
  2) *Hidden Patterns Test, Cf-2.*
  3) *Copying Test, Cf-3. Out of print.*

b) FACTOR CS: SPEED OF CLOSURE. Grades 6–16; 1962; 2 tests.
  1) *Gestalt Completion Test, Cs-1.*
  2) *Concealed Words Test, Cs-2.*

c) FACTOR FA: ASSOCIATIONAL FLUENCY. Grades 6–16; 1957–62; 3 tests.

1) *Controlled Associations Test, Fa-1.* 1962. *Out of print.*
2) *Associational Fluency 1, Form A, [Fa-2].* See 546c; 1957; Paul R. Christensen and J. P. Guilford; Sheridan Psychological Services, Inc.
3) *Associations 4, Fa-3.* 1962; J. P. Guilford. *Out of print.*

d) FACTOR FE: EXPRESSIONAL FLUENCY. Grades 8–16; 1958–62; 3 tests.
1) *Expressional Fluency, [Fe-1].* See 546d; 1958; Paul R. Christensen and J. P. Guilford; Sheridan Psychological Services, Inc.
2) *Simile Interpretations, Fe-2.* 1962; J. P. Guilford. *Out of print.* For a revision consisting of the 4 items of this test plus 4 new items, see 579.
3) *Word Arrangement, Fe-3.* 1962; J. P. Guilford. *Out of print.*

e) FACTOR FI: IDEATIONAL FLUENCY. Grades 8–16; 1962; 3 tests. *Out of print.*
1) *Topics Test, Fi-1.*
2) *Theme Test, Fi-2.*
3) *Thing Categories Test, Fi-3.*

f) FACTOR FW: WORD FLUENCY. Grades 6–16; 1962; 3 tests. *Out of print.*
1) *Word Endings Test, Fw-1.*
2) *Word Beginnings Test, Fw-2.*
3) *Word Beginnings and Endings Test, Fw-3.*

g) FACTOR I: INDUCTION. Grades 8–16; 1962; 3 tests.
1) *Letter Sets Test, I-1.*
2) *Locations Test, I-2.*
3) *Figure Classification, I-3.*

h) FACTOR LE: LENGTH ESTIMATION. Grades 6–16; 1962; 3 tests.
1) *Estimation of Length Test, Le-1.*
2) *Shortest Road Test, Le-2. Out of print.*
3) *Nearer Point Test, Le-3.*

i) FACTOR MA: ASSOCIATIVE (ROTE) MEMORY. Grades 6–16; 1962; 3 tests. *Out of print.*
1) *Picture-Number Test, Ma-1.*
2) *Object-Number Test, Ma-2.*
3) *First and Last Names Test, Ma-3.*

j) FACTOR MK: MECHANICAL KNOWLEDGE. 1962; 3 tests. *Out of print.*
1) *Tool Knowledge Test, Mk-1.* Grades 6–16.
2) *Mechanical Information Test, Mk-2.* Grades 8–16.
3) *Electrical Information Test, Mk-3.* Grades 8–16.

k) FACTOR MS: MEMORY SPAN. Grades 6–16; 1962; 3 tests.
1) *Auditory Number Span Test, Ms-1. Out of print.*
2) *Visual Number Span Test, Ms-2. Out of print.*
3) *Auditory Letter Span Test, Ms-3.*

l) FACTOR N: NUMBER FACILITY. Grades 6–16; 1953–62; 3 tests; 1962 tests essentially the same as tests copyrighted 1953 except for an increase in items.
1) *Addition Test, N-1.*
2) *Division Test, N-2.*
3) *Subtraction and Multiplication Test, N-3.*

m) FACTOR O: ORIGINALITY. Grades 10–16; 1958–62; 3 tests. *Out of print.*
1) *Plot Titles, O-1.* 1962. For a 1969 reissued edition of this test with revised administration instructions, see 572.
2) *Symbol Production, O-2.* 1962.
3) *Consequences, O-3 [10-Item Edition].* 1958; P. R. Christensen, P. R. Merrifield, and J. P. Guilford. For a revision of this 10-item test into two 5-item tests, Forms A-1 (first 5 items) and A-2 (last 5 items), see 551.

n) FACTOR P: PERCEPTUAL SPEED. Grades 6–16; 1962; 3 tests.
1) *Finding A's Test, P-1.*
2) *Number Comparison Test, P-2. Out of print.*
3) *Identical Pictures Test, P-3.*

o) FACTOR R: GENERAL REASONING. 1955–62; 4 tests.
1) *Mathematics Aptitude Test, R-1.* Grades 6–12; 1962. *Out of print.*
2) *Mathematics Aptitude Test, R-2.* Grades 11–16; 1962.
3) *Ship Destination Test, [R-3].* See 457; 1955; Paul R. Christensen and J. P. Guilford; Sheridan Psychological Services, Inc.
4) *Necessary Arithmetic Operations Test, R-4.* Grades 6–16; 1962.

p) FACTOR RE: SEMANTIC REDEFINITION. Grades 10–16; 1962; 3 tests. *Out of print.*
1) *Gestalt Transformation, Re-1.*
2) *Object Synthesis, Re-2.* J. P. Guilford.
3) *Picture Gestalt, Re-3.* J. P. Guilford. For a revision, see *New Uses* (568).

q) FACTOR RS: SYLLOGISTIC REASONING. Grades 11–16; 1955–62; 3 tests.
1) *Nonsense Syllogisms Test, Rs-1.* 1962.
2) *Logical Reasoning, [Rs-2].* See 1761; 1955; Alfred F. Hertzka and J. P. Guilford; Sheridan Psychological Services, Inc.
3) *Inference Test, Rs-3.* 1962.

r) FACTOR S: SPATIAL ORIENTATION. 1947–62; 3 tests.
1) *Card Rotations Test, S-1.* Grades 8–16; 1962.
2) *Cube Comparisons Test, S-2.* Grades 8–16; 1962.
3) *Guilford-Zimmerman Aptitude Survey: Part 5, Spatial Orientation, [S-3].* See 1074; 1947; J. P. Guilford and Wayne S. Zimmerman; Sheridan Psychological Services, Inc.

s) FACTOR SEP: SENSITIVITY TO PROBLEMS. Grades 8–16; 1962; 3 tests. *Out of print.*
1) *Apparatus Test, Sep-1.* J. P. Guilford.
2) *Seeing Problems, Sep-2.* For a test published in 1969 consisting of the first 2 of the 4 problems in this test, see 577.
3) *Seeing Deficiencies, Sep-3.* J. P. Guilford.

t) FACTOR SS: SPATIAL SCANNING. Grades 6–16; 1962; 3 tests.
1) *Maze Tracing Speed Test, Ss-1.*
2) *Choosing a Path, Ss-2.*
3) *Map Planning Test, Ss-3.*

u) FACTOR V: VERBAL COMPREHENSION. 1962; 5 tests.
1) *Vocabulary Test, V-1.* Grades 7–12. *Out of print.*
2) *Vocabulary Test, V-2.* Grades 7–12.
3) *Wide Range Vocabulary Test, V-3.* Grades 7–16.
4) *Advanced Vocabulary Test, V-4.* Grades 11–16.
5) *Vocabulary Test, V-5.* Grades 11–16. *Out of print.*

v) FACTOR VZ: VISUALIZATION. Grades 9–16; 1962; 3 tests.
1) *Form Board Test, Vz-1.*
2) *Paper Folding Test, Vz-2.*
3) *Surface Development Test, Vz-3.*

w) FACTOR XA: FIGURAL ADAPTIVE FLEXIBILITY. Grades 11–16; 1962; 3 tests. *Out of print.*
1) *Match Problems 2, Xa-1.* For a 1963 test identical with this 1962 test except for change of title to *Match Problems*, see 564.
2) *Match Problems 5, Xa-2.* For a 1969 test identical with this 1962 test except for one new item, one revised item, and administration instructions, see 565.
3) *Planning Air Maneuvers, Xa-3.*

x) FACTOR XS: SEMANTIC SPONTANEOUS FLEXIBILITY. Grades 6–16; 1960–62; 3 tests.
1) *Utility Test, Xs-1.* 1962. *Out of print.* For a 1969 test identical with this 1962 test except for administration instructions, see 591.
2) *Alternate Uses, [Xs-2].* See 542; 1960; Paul R. Christensen, J. P. Guilford, Philip R. Merrifield, and

Kit of Reference Tests for Cognitive Factors

Robert C. Wilson; Sheridan Psychological Services, Inc.
3) *Object Naming, Xs-3.* 1962; J. P. Guilford. *Out of print.*
For additional information, see 6:551.

REFERENCES THROUGH 1971

1. BARRON, FRANK. "The Disposition Toward Originality." *J Abn & Social Psychol* 51:478–85 N '55. * (*PA* 31:2533)
2. MEADOW, ARNOLD, AND PARNES, SIDNEY J. "Evaluation of Training in Creative Problem-Solving." *J Appl Psychol* 43:189–94 Je '59. * (*PA* 34:5568)
3. GARDNER, RILEY W.; JACKSON, DOUGLAS N.; AND MESSICK, SAMUEL J. "Personality Organization in Cognitive Controls and Intellectual Abilities." *Psychol Issues* 2(4):i–x, 1–148 '60. * (*PA* 36:2HA49G)
4. MARKS, ALVIN; MICHAEL, WILLIAM B.; AND KAISER, HENRY F. "Comparison of Manual and Analytic Techniques of Rotation in a Factor Analysis of Aptitude Test Variables." *Psychol Rep* 7:519–22 D '60. * (*PA* 35:2792)
5. GARWOOD, DOROTHY SEMENOW. *Some Personality Factors Related to Creativity in Young Scientists.* Doctor's thesis, Claremont Graduate School (Claremont, Calif.), 1961. (*DA* 22:3273)
6. MERRIFIELD, P. R.; GUILFORD, J. P.; CHRISTENSEN, P. R.; AND FRICK, J. W. "Interrelationships Between Certain Abilities and Certain Traits of Motivation and Temperament." *J General Psychol* 65:57–74 Jl '61. * (*PA* 36:2HD57M)
7. DE MILLE, RICHARD. "Intellect After Lobotomy in Schizophrenia: A Factor Analytic Study." *Psychol Monogr* 76(16):1–18 '62. * (*PA* 38:2784)
8. OWEN, CRAMER. "An Investigation of Creative Potential at the Junior High Level." *Studies Art Ed* 3:16–33 sp '62. *
9. BARRON, FRANK. *Creativity and Psychological Health: Origins of Personal Vitality and Creative Freedom.* Princeton, N.J.: D. Van Nostrand Co., Inc., 1963. Pp. xi, 292. *
10. ATKINSON, BEA HENRIETTA. *The Relationship Between Problem-Solving Strategies and Measures of Convergent and Divergent Thinking in a Selected Group of Secondary School Pupils.* Doctor's thesis, University of Florida (Gainesville, Fla.), 1964. (*DA* 25:7070)
11. EDWARDS, ALLEN JACK, AND PARKS, PAULA. "Note on Normative Data of Tests Measuring Flexibility in Cognitive Processes." *Psychol Rep* 14:741–2 Je '64. * (*PA* 39:5116)
12. MOLOMO, RAYMOND R-S. *Two Spatial Factors in Two-Dimensional and Three-Dimensional Spatial Aptitude.* Master's thesis, University of Ottawa (Ottawa, Ont., Canada), 1964.
13. MORAN, LOUIS J.; KIMBLE, JAMES P., JR.; AND MEFFERD, ROY B., JR. "Repetitive Psychometric Measures: Equating Alternate Forms." *Psychol Rep* 14:335–8 Ap '64. * (*PA* 39:302)
14. RAINWATER, JANETTE MUNKITTRICK. *Effects of Set on Problem Solving in Subjects of Varying Levels of Assessed Creativity.* Doctor's thesis, University of California (Berkeley, Calif.), 1964. (*DA* 25:6753)
15. KELLY, FRANCIS J.; HUNKA, STEPHEN; AND CONKLIN, RODNEY. "Further Normative Data on Tests Measuring Flexibility in Cognitive Processes." *Psychol Rep* 17:683–6 D '65. * (*PA* 40:3575)
16. VINT, VIRGINIA HOLLISTER. *The Effect of Prior Convergent or Divergent Art Training on Subsequent Art Activity.* Doctor's thesis, Stanford University (Stanford, Calif.), 1965. (*DA* 26:914)
17. ANDERSON, C. C., AND CROPLEY, A. J. "Some Correlates of Originality." *Austral J Psychol* 18:218–27 D '66. * (*PA* 41:4572)
18. CROPLEY, A. J. "Creativity and Intelligence." *Brit J Ed Psychol* 36:259–66 N '66. * (*PA* 41:573)
19. EDWARDS, ALLEN JACK. "Reliability of Selected Tests of Flexibility in Cognitive Processes." *Psychol Rep* 19:1267–70 D '66. * (*PA* 41:3710)
20. JANSSEN, CALVIN WAYNE. *Comparative Creativity Scores of Lower Socio-Economic Dropouts and Non-Dropouts.* Doctor's thesis, University of Tennessee (Knoxville, Tenn.), 1966. (*DA* 27:1659A)
21. NEEDHAM, WALTER EVANS. *Intellectual, Personality and Biographical Characteristics of Southern Negro and White College Students.* Doctor's thesis, University of Utah (Salt Lake City, Utah), 1966. (*DA* 27:1609B)
22. SMITH, ROBERT M., AND NEISWORTH, JOHN T. "Creative Thinking Abilities of Intellectually Superior Children in the Regular Grades." *Psychol Rep* 18:335–41 Ap '66. * (*PA* 40:8832)
23. WAMPLER, JOE F. "Prediction of Achievement in College Mathematics." *Math Teach* 59:364–9 Ap '66. *
24. WEISS, DAVID J.; DAWIS, RENE V.; LOFQUIST, LLOYD H.; AND ENGLAND, GEORGE W. *Instrumentation for the Theory of Work Adjustment.* University of Minnesota, Industrial Relations Center Bulletin 44; Minnesota Studies in Vocational Rehabilitation 21. Minneapolis, Minn.: the Center, December 1966. Pp. viii, 85. *
25. BRAUND, ROBERT A. "Pilot Study of a Cognitive Restructuring Paradigm." *Psychol Rep* 20:275–9 F '67. * (*PA* 41:7919)
26. COMPTON, MARY FRANCES. *An Attempt to Foster Creative Thinking in Teachers.* Doctor's thesis, University of Florida (Gainesville, Fla.), 1967. (*DA* 29:164A)
27. CROPLEY, A. J. "Creativity, Intelligence, and Achievement." *Alberta J Ed Res* (Canada) 13:51–8 Mr '67. * (*PA* 41:15253)
28. EKSTROM, RUTH BURT. *A Comparison of Two Groups of Reference Tests Measuring Selected Perception and Closure Factors.* Doctor's thesis, Rutgers—The State University (New Brunswick, N.J.), 1967. (*DA* 28:1703A)
29. GRAY, JAMES JOSEPH. *An Investigation of the Relationship Between Primary Process Thinking and Creativity.* Doctor's thesis, Fordham University (New York, N.Y.), 1967. (*DA* 28:5206B)
30. JENKINS, JOHN MERVIN. *A Study of the Characteristics Associated With Innovative Behavior in Teachers.* Doctor's thesis, University of Miami (Coral Gables, Fla.), 1967. (*DA* 28:903A)
31. KARSTEN, MARY O'KEEFFE. *The Relationship of Tested Creative Abilities and Selected Factors of Academic Achievement, Intelligence, Sex, Socioeconomic Status, and Pupil Attitudes.* Doctor's thesis, University of Southern California (Los Angeles, Calif.), 1967. (*DA* 28:2557A)
32. LEMKE, ELMER A.; KLAUSMEIER, HERBERT J.; AND HARRIS, CHESTER W. "Relationship of Selected Cognitive Abilities to Concept Attainment and Information Processing." *J Ed Psychol* 58:27–35 F '67. * (*PA* 41:3959)
33. MANGAN, GORDON L. "Studies of the Relationship Between Neo-Pavlovian Properties of Higher Nervous Activity and Western Personality Dimensions: 3, The Relations of Transformation Mobility to Thinking Flexibility." *J Exp Res Personality* 2:117–23 My '67. * (*PA* 41:11907)
34. MILES, DAVID T. *An Experimental Investigation of Programed Creativity.* Doctor's thesis, Southern Illinois University (Carbondale, Ill.), 1967. (*DA* 28:2099A)
35. PLOGMAN, BERNARD EDWARD. *The Creative Relationship Between Art Teachers and Their Ninth Grade Art Students in Art Room Practices, Personality and Pencil Drawing in Catholic Schools.* Doctor's thesis, University of Cincinnati (Cincinnati, Ohio), 1967. (*DA* 28:3534A)
36. RICHARDS, JAMES M., JR. "Can Computers Write College Admissions Tests?" *J Appl Psychol* 51:211–5 Je '67. * (*PA* 41:10942)
37. RIDLEY, DENNIS R., AND BIRNEY, ROBERT C. "Effects of Training Procedures on Creativity Test Scores." *J Ed Psychol* 58:158–64 Je '67. * (*PA* 41:10457)
38. SIDLE, ALLAN CHARLES. *Creativity and Delusional Thinking in Schizophrenics.* Doctor's thesis, Stanford University (Stanford, Calif.), 1967. (*DA* 28:353B)
39. SKAGER, R. W.; KLEIN, S. P.; AND SCHULTZ, C. B. "The Prediction of Academic and Artistic Achievement at a School of Design." *J Ed Meas* 4:105–17 su '67. *
40. SMITH, ROBERT M. "Creative Thinking Abilities of Educable Mentally Handicapped Children in the Regular Grades." *Am J Mental Def* 71:571–5 Ja '67. * (*PA* 41:6197)
41. STOKER, H. W., AND KROPP, R. P. "Note on the Kit of Reference Tests." *Ed & Psychol Meas* 27:1171–2 w '67. * (*PA* 42:8944)
42. VERY, PHILIP S. "Differential Factor Structures in Mathematical Ability." *Genetic Psychol Monogr* 75:169–207 My '67. * (*PA* 41:10451)
43. WINDHOLZ, GEORGE, AND MCINTOSH, WILLIAM A. "Concurrent Validation of Guilford's Six Convergent Tests." *Ed & Psychol Meas* 27:393–400 su '67. * (*PA* 41:12843)
44. ADAMS, JOHN C., JR. "The Relative Effects of Various Testing Atmospheres on Spontaneous Flexibility, a Factor for Divergent Thinking." *J Creative Behav* 2:187–94 su '68. * (*PA* 43:5882)
45. ALZOBAIE, ABDUL JALIL; METFESSEL, NEWTON S.; AND MICHAEL, WILLIAM B. "Alternative Approaches to Assessing the Intellectual Abilities of Youth From a Culture of Poverty." *Ed & Psychol Meas* 28:449–55 su '68. * (*PA* 42:19264)
46. ANDERSON, RONALD JUDE. *Divergent Thinking Within Superior Average, and Retarded Subjects.* Doctor's thesis, University of Nebraska (Lincoln, Neb.), 1968. (*DA* 29:1126A)
47. BROWN, STEPHEN W.; GUILFORD, J. P.; AND HOEFFNER, RALPH. "Six Semantic-Memory Abilities." *Ed & Psychol Meas* 28:691–717 au '68. * (*PA* 43:4427)
48. BRYAN, VINCENT. *The Experimental Induction of Stress in Relation to Field Articulation.* Doctor's thesis, Yeshiva University (New York, N.Y.), 1968. (*DAI* 30:1354B)
49. EDWARDS, ARTHUR B. *An Analysis of the Creative Ability Levels of the Potential Dropout in the Average Mental Ability Range.* Doctor's thesis, University of Tennessee (Knoxville, Tenn.), 1968. (*DA* 29:3828A)
50. GIBSON, JAMES W.; KIBLER, ROBERT J.; AND BARKER, LARRY L. "Some Relationships Between Selected Creativity and Critical Thinking Measures." *Psychol Rep* 23:707–14 D '68. * (*PA* 43:9748)
51. HETRICK, SUZANNE H.; LILLY, ROY S.; AND MERRIFIELD, PHILIP R. "Figural Creativity, Intelligence, and Personality in Children." *Multiv Behav Res* 3:173–87 Ap '68. * (*PA* 42:15273)
52. JANSSEN, CALVIN. "Comparative Creativity Scores of Lower Socio-Economic Dropouts and Non-Dropouts." *Psychol Sch* 5:183–4 Ap '68. * (*PA* 43:17498)

53. WINDHOLZ, GEORGE. "The Relation of Creativity and Intelligence Constellations to Traits of Temperament, Interest, and Value in College Students." *J General Psychol* 79:291-9 O '68. * (*PA* 43:3998)
54. ANDERSON, HARRY E., JR.; WHITE, WILLIAM F.; AND STEVENS, JOHN C. "Student Creativity, Intelligence, Achievement, and Teacher Classroom Behavior." *J Social Psychol* 78(1):99-107 Je '69. * (*PA* 43:16427)
55. BLACKHURST, A. EDWARD; MARKS, CLAUDE H.; AND TISDALL, WILLIAM J. "Relationship Between Mobility and Divergent Thinking in Blind Children." *Ed Visually Handicapped* 1(2):33-6 My '69. * (*PA* 43:14813)
56. DICKSTEIN, LOUIS S. "Prospective Span as a Cognitive Ability." *J Consult & Clin Psychol* 33(6):757-60 D '69. * (*PA* 44:3616)
57. EDWARDS, ALLEN JACK. "Order Effects on Scores and Reliability Estimates Obtained With a Divergent-Thinking Task." *Psychol Rep* 24(2):610 Ap '69. * (*PA* 43:14999)
58. GARDNER, RILEY W., AND LOHRENZ, LEANDER J. "Some Old and New Group Tests for the Study of Cognitive Controls and Intellectual Abilities." *Percept & Motor Skills* 29(3):935-50 D '69. * (*PA* 46:4981)
59. GOODMAN, P.; FURCON, J.; AND ROSE, J. "Examination of Some Measures of Creative Ability by the Multitrait-Multimethod Matrix." *J Appl Psychol* 53(3):240-3 Je '69. * (*PA* 43:11327)
60. GRAY, JAMES J. "The Effect of Productivity on Primary Process and Creativity." *J Proj Tech & Pers Assess* 33(3):213-8 Je '69. * (*PA* 43:14302)
61. GRIMSLEY, WILLIAM GERALD. *The Relationship Between Creativity and Leader Behavior of School Superintendents.* Doctor's thesis, University of Missouri (Columbia, Mo.), 1969. (*DAI* 30:5193A)
62. GUILFORD, J. P., AND HOEPFNER, RALPH. "Comparisons of Varimax Rotations With Rotations to Theoretical Targets." *Ed & Psychol Meas* 29(1):3-22 sp '69. * (*PA* 44:15668)
63. KANDERIAN, SUAD SIROP. *Study of the Relationship Between School Achievement and Measures of Intelligence and Creativity for Students in Iraq.* Doctor's thesis, University of Southern California (Los Angeles, Calif.), 1969. (*DAI* 31:644A)
64. KARLINS, MARVIN; SCHUERHOFF, CHARLES; AND KAPLAN, MARTIN. "Some Factors Related to Architectural Creativity in Graduating Architecture Students." *J General Psychol* 81(2):203-15 O '69. * (*PA* 44:6775)
65. KLEIN, STEPHEN P.; FREDERIKSEN, NORMAN; AND EVANS, FRANKLIN R. "Anxiety and Learning to Formulate Hypotheses." *J Ed Psychol* 60(6):465-75 D '69. * (*PA* 44:3087)
66. SCHNITZER, LEAH PALTIEL, AND STEWART, ROBERT A. C. "Originality and Personality Variables in High School Art Students." *Psychol* 6(1):36-9 F '69. * (*PA* 43:11334)
67. STRAUSS, MILTON E. "Cognitive Style and the Use of Incidental Cues in Problem Solving." *J Psychol* 73(1):69-74 S '69. * (*PA* 44:4548)
68. VANDENBERG, STEVEN G. "A Twin Study of Spatial Ability." *Multiv Behav Res* 4(3):273-94 Jl '69. * (*PA* 44:356)
69. ALEXANDER, SHIRLEY MAE. *A Study of Perceptual and Verbal Differentiation Among Male College Students.* Doctor's thesis, George Washington University (Washington, D.C.), 1970. (*DAI* 31:6887B)
70. EL-ABD, HAMED A. "The Intellect of East African Students." *Multiv Behav Res* 5(4):423-33 O '70. * (*PA* 45:8037)
71. FRUIN, DAVID JOHN. *Response Styles and Creativity.* Doctor's thesis, Johns Hopkins University (Baltimore, Md.), 1970. (*DAI* 31:4361B)
72. GREENFIELD, ADELAIDE. *Perceptual Style, Attitudes Toward Problem Solving, and Problem-Solving Performance.* Doctor's thesis, New York University (New York, N.Y.), 1970. (*DAI* 31:7571B)
73. JOHNSON, MARIE LOUISE. *Black Adolescents' Nonstandard English and Its Relation to Intellectual Skills.* Doctor's thesis, Illinois Institute of Technology (Chicago, Ill.), 1970. (*DAI* 31:7573B)
74. KHAN, S. B. "Development of Mental Abilities: An Investigation of the 'Differentiation Hypothesis.'" *Can J Psychol* 24(3):199-205 Je '70. * (*PA* 45:5667)
75. MCDONAGH, JOHN MICHAEL. *The Relationship Between Familial Characteristics and Two Measures of Dependency.* Doctor's thesis, University of Oklahoma (Norman, Okla.), 1970. (*DAI* 32:542B)
76. OHNMACHT, FRED W.; WEAVER, WENDELL W.; AND KOHLER, EMMETT T. "Cloze and Closure: A Factorial Study." *J Psychol* 74(2):205-17 Mr '70. * (*PA* 44:12542)
77. PARLETT, T. A. A. *The Modification of Criminal Personality Through Massed Learning by Programmed Instruction.* Master's thesis, University of Victoria (Victoria, B.C., Canada), 1970.
78. REESE, HAYNE W., AND PARNES, SIDNEY J. "Programming Creative Behavior." *Child Develop* 41(2):413-23 Je '70. * (*PA* 44:15509)
79. SHARP, ELIZABETH YERXA. *The Relationship of Visual Closure to Speechreading Among Deaf Children.* Doctor's thesis, University of Arizona (Tucson, Ariz.), 1970. (*DAI* 31:2198A)
80. ADCOCK, C. J., AND WEBBERLEY, M. "Primary Mental Abilities." *J General Psychol* 84(2):229-43 Ap '71. * (*PA* 46:4979)
81. BALDWIN, THOMAS S. "Relationships Among Student Achievement and 'Pure Factors' of Intellect." *J Indus Teach Ed* 9(1):15-25 f '71. *
82. BRILHART, BARBARA LIEB, AND BRILHART, JOHN K. "Field Independence and Academic Achievement of Engineering Students." *Percept & Motor Skills* 32(2):443-6 Ap '71. * (*PA* 46:11645)
83. BYRNE, MARY ANN; FELDHUSEN, JOHN F.; AND KANE, ROBERT B. "The Relationships Among Two Cloze Measurement Procedures and Divergent Thinking Abilities." *Read Res Q* 6(3):378-93 sp '71. * (*PA* 47:3624)
84. COOPER, WALTER, AND ARMSTRONG, WAYNE. "Beginning Tennis Skill and Field Independence." *South J Ed Res* 5(2):114-9 Ap '71. *
85. DARGEL, RUSSELL, AND KIRK, ROGER E. "Manifest Anxiety, Field Dependency, and Task Performance." *Percept & Motor Skills* 32(2):383-93 Ap '71. * (*PA* 46:10865)
86. DINGMAN, ROBERT LEWIS. *A Study of Cognitive Style Differences as a Factor of Communications in School Counseling.* Doctor's thesis, Wayne State University (Detroit, Mich.), 1971. (*DAI* 32:6756A)
87. FLEISHMAN, JOSEPH J., AND DUSEK, E. RALPH. "Reliability and Learning Factors Associated With Cognitive Tests." *Psychol Rep* 29(2):523-30 O '71. * (*PA* 47:7996)
88. FLEISHMAN, JOSEPH J., AND FINE, BERNARD J. "Note on Cognitive Factors Related to Factor B of the 16 PF Test." *Psychol Rep* 29(3):1075-7 D '71. * (*PA* 48:988)
89. GRIEVE, TARRANCE DON, AND DAVIS, J. KENT. "The Relationship of Cognitive Style and Method of Instruction to Performance in Ninth Grade Geography." *J Ed Res* 65(3):137-41 N '71. * (*PA* 48:1927)
90. GUTHRIE, GEORGE M.; SINAIKO, H. WALLACE; AND BRISLIN, RICHARD. "Nonverbal Abilities of Americans and Vietnamese." *J Social Psychol* 84(2):183-90 Ag '71. *
91. HOCHMAN, SIDNEY H. "Field Independence and Stroop Color-Word Performance." *Percept & Motor Skills* 33(3):782 D '71. * (*PA* 48:953)
92. HUCKABEE, MALCOM W., AND MC GOWN, W. P. "Differences Between Field Independent and Field Dependent Persons on the Stroop Color-Word Test: A Failure to Replicate." *J Clin Psychol* 27(2):226 Ap '71. * (*PA* 46:6888)
93. KAZELSKIS, RICHARD. "Field Independence and Serial Verbal Learning." *South J Ed Res* 5(1):31-8 Ja '71. *
94. KORAN, MARY LOU. "Differential Response to Inductive and Deductive Instructional Procedures." *J Ed Psychol* 62(4):300-7 Ag '71. * (*PA* 47:1820)
95. KORAN, MARY LOU; SNOW, RICHARD E.; AND MCDONALD, FREDERICK J. "Teacher Aptitude and Observational Learning of a Teaching Skill." *J Ed Psychol* 62(3):219-28 Je '71. * (*PA* 46:9703)
96. LINKER, JERRY MAC. *The Interaction of Cognitive Factors, Visual Fidelity, and Learning Tasks in Learning From Pictures.* Doctor's thesis, University of Texas (Austin, Tex.), 1971. (*DAI* 33:144A)
97. MILLER, JEFFREY O. "Personality Factors and Perceptual Factors in Motor Performance." *ICHPER* 13:46-61 '71. *
98. OHNMACHT, FRED W., AND MCMORRIS, ROBERT F. "Creativity as a Function of Field Independence and Dogmatism." *J Psychol* 79(2):165-8 N '71. * (*PA* 47:6800)
99. PARLETT, T. A. A., AND AYERS, J. D. "The Modification of Criminal Personality Through Massed Learning by Programmed Instruction." *Can J Criminol & Correct* 13(2):155-65 Ap '71. *
100. RICHARDS, TERRY D. *The Effects of Cognitive Style Sets of Flexibility Upon Counselor Perception: Field Dependence and Repression-Sensitization in Relation to Empathic Accuracy.* Doctor's thesis, New York University (New York, N.Y.), 1971. (*DAI* 32:1865A)
101. RYBACK, RALPH S.; LEWIS, OLIVER F.; AND LESSARD, CHARLES S. "Psychobiologic Effects of Prolonged Bed Rest (Weightless) in Young Healthy Volunteers (Study II)." *Aerospace Med* 42(5):529-35 My '71. *
102. TISDALL, WILLIAM J.; BLACKHURST, A. EDWARD; AND MARKS, CLAUDE H. "Divergent Thinking in Blind Children." *J Ed Psychol* 62(6):468-73 D '71. * (*PA* 47:9708)
103. WILLIAMS, JOHN D.; HARLOW, STEVEN D.; AND BORGEN, JEROME S. "Creativity, Dogmatism, and Arithmetic Achievement." *J Psychol* 78(2):217-22 Jl '71. * (*PA* 46:9760)

CUMULATIVE NAME INDEX

Adams, J. C.: 44
Adcock, C. J.: 80
Alexander, S. M.: 69
Alzobaie, A. J.: 45
Anderson, C. C.: 17
Anderson, H. E.: 54
Anderson, R. J.: 46
Armstrong, W.: 84
Atkinson, B. H.: 10
Ayers, J. D.: 99
Baldwin, T. S.: 81
Barker, L. L.: 50
Barron, F.: 1, 9

Birney, R. C.: 37
Blackhurst, A. E.: 55, 102
Borgen, J. S.: 103
Braund, R. A.: 25
Brilhart, B. L.: 82
Brilhart, K. J.: 82
Brislin, R.: 90
Brown, S. W.: 47
Bryan, V.: 48
Byrne, M. A.: 83
Christensen, P. R.: 6
Compton, M. F.: 26
Conklin, R.: 15

Kit of Reference Tests for Cognitive Factors

Cooper, W.: 84
Cropley, A. J.: 17-8, 27
Dargel, R.: 85
Davis, J. K.: 89
Dawis, R. V.: 24
de Mille, R.: 7
Dickstein, L. S.: 56
Dingman, R. L.: 86
Dusek, E. R.: 87
Edwards, A. B.: 49
Edwards, A. J.: 11, 19, 57
Ekstrom, R. B.: 28
El-Abd, H. A.: 70
England, G. W.: 24
Evans, F. R.: 65
Feldhusen, J. F.: 83
Fine, B. J.: 88
Fleishman, J. J.: 87-8
Frederiksen, N.: 65
Frick, J. W.: 6
Fruin, D. J.: 71
Furcon, J.: 59
Gardner, R. W.: 3, 58
Garwood, D. S.: 5
Gibson, J. W.: 50
Goodman, P.: 59
Gray, J. J.: 29, 60
Greenfield, A.: 72
Grieve, T. D.: 89
Grimsley, W. G.: 61
Guilford, J. P.: 6, 47, 62
Guthrie, G. M.: 90
Harlow, S. D.: 103
Harris, C. W.: 32
Hetrick, S. H.: 51
Hochman, S. H.: 91
Hoepfner, R.: 47, 62
Huckabee, M. W.: 92
Hunka, S.: 15
Jackson, D. N.: 3
Janssen, C.: 52
Janssen, C. W.: 20
Jenkins, J. M.: 30
Johnson, M. L.: 73
Kaiser, H. F.: 4
Kanderian, S. S.: 63
Kane, R. B.: 83
Kaplan, M.: 64
Karlins, M.: 64
Karsten, M. O.: 31
Kazelskis, R.: 93
Kelly, F. J.: 15
Khan, S. B.: 74
Kibler, R. J.: 50
Kimble, J. P.: 13
Kirk, R. E.: 85
Klausmeier, H. J.: 32
Klein, S. P.: 39, 65
Kohler, E. T.: 76
Koran, M. L.: 94-5
Kropp, R. P.: 41
Lemke, E. A.: 32
Lessard, C. S.: 101

Lewis, O. F.: 101
Lilly, R. S.: 51
Linker, J. M.: 96
Lofquist, L. H.: 24
Lohrenz, L. J.: 58
McDonagh, J. M.: 75
McDonald, F. J.: 95
Mc Gown, W. P.: 92
McIntosh, W. A.: 43
McMorris, R. F.: 98
Mangan, G. L.: 33
Marks, A.: 4
Marks, C. H.: 55, 102
Meadow, A.: 2
Mefferd, R. B.: 13
Merrifield, P. R.: 6, 51
Messick, S. J.: 3
Metfessel, N. S.: 45
Michael, W. B.: 4, 45
Miles, D. T.: 34
Miller, J. O.: 97
Molomo, R. R-S.: 12
Moran, L. J.: 13
Needham, W. E.: 21
Neisworth, J. T.: 22
Ohnmacht, F. W.: 76, 98
Owen, C.: 8
Parks, J.: 11
Parlett, T. A. A.: 77, 99
Parnes, S. J.: 2, 78
Plogman, B. E.: 35
Rainwater, J. M.: 14
Reese, H. W.: 78
Richards, J. M.: 36
Richards, J. M.: 100
Ridley, D. R.: 37
Rose, J.: 59
Ryback, R. S.: 101
Schnitzer, L. P.: 66
Schuerhoff, C.: 64
Schultz, C. B.: 39
Sharp, E. Y.: 79
Sidle, A. C.: 38
Sinaiko, H. W.: 90
Skager, R. W.: 39
Smith, R. M.: 22, 40
Snow, R. E.: 95
Stevens, J. C.: 54
Stewart, R. A. C.: 66
Stoker, H. W.: 41
Strauss, M. E.: 67
Tisdall, W. J.: 55, 102
Vandenberg, S. G.: 68
Very, P. S.: 42
Vint, V. H.: 16
Wampler, J. F.: 23
Weaver, W. W.: 76
Webberley, M.: 80
Weiss, D. J.: 24
White, W. F.: 54
Williams, J. D.: 103
Windholz, G.: 43, 53

[562]

Making Objects. Grades 9–16 and adults; 1963; "divergent production of figural systems" or "figural expressional fluency"; for a downward extension, see 554f; Sheldon Gardner, Arthur Gershon, Philip R. Merrifield, and J. P. Guilford; Sheridan Psychological Services, Inc. *

For additional information, see 6:552 (1 reference).

REFERENCES THROUGH 1971

1. See 6:552.
2. SMITH, ROBERT M., AND NEISWORTH, JOHN T. "Creative Thinking Abilities of Intellectually Superior Children in the Regular Grades." *Psychol Rep* 18:335–41 Ap '66. * (*PA* 40: 8832)
3. FORD, ELEANOR DIANE. *The Relationship of Certain Socio-Cultural Factors Among Junior High School Students to Creativity in Art.* Doctor's thesis, North Texas State University (Denton, Tex.), 1967. (*DA* 28:3502A)
4. KARSTEN, MARY O'KEEFFE. *The Relationship of Tested Creative Abilities and Selected Factors of Academic Achievement, Intelligence, Sex, Socioeconomic Status, and Pupil Attitudes.* Doctor's thesis, University of Southern California (Los Angeles, Calif.), 1967. (*DA* 28:2557A)
5. SMITH, ROBERT M. "Creative Thinking Abilities of Educable Mentally Handicapped Children in the Regular Grades." *Am J Mental Def* 71:571–5 Ja '67. * (*PA* 41:6197)

6. ALZOBAIE, ABDUL JALIL; METFESSEL, NEWTON S.; AND MICHAEL, WILLIAM B. "Alternative Approaches to Assessing the Intellectual Abilities of Youth From a Culture of Poverty." *Ed & Psychol Meas* 28:449–55 su '68. * (*PA* 42:19264)
7. KANDERIAN, SUAD SIROP. *Study of the Relationship Between School Achievement and Measures of Intelligence and Creativity for Students in Iraq.* Doctor's thesis, University of Southern California (Los Angeles, Calif.), 1969. (*DAI* 31:644A)
8. SIMPSON, DONALD JAMES. *The Effect of Selected Musical Studies on Growth in General Creative Potential.* Doctor's thesis, University of Southern California (Los Angeles, Calif.), 1969. (*DAI* 30:502A)
9. OLESON, D. S., AND ZUBEK, JOHN P. "Effect of One Day of Sensory Deprivation on a Battery of Open-Ended Cognitive Tests." *Percept & Motor Skills* 31(3):919–23 D '70. * (*PA* 46:358)

CUMULATIVE NAME INDEX

Alzobaie, A. J.: 6
Ford, E. D.: 3
Guilford, J. P.: 1
Kanderian, S. S.: 7
Karsten, M. O.: 4
Metfessel, N. S.: 6

Michael, W. B.: 6
Neisworth, J .T.: 2
Oleson, D. S.: 9
Simpson, D. J.: 8
Smith, R. M.: 2, 5
Zubek, J. P.: 9

[563]

Manikin Test. Ages 2 and over; [1917]; subtest of *Merrill-Palmer Scale of Mental Tests* and *Arthur Point Scale of Performance Tests, Form 1;* R. Pintner; Stoelting Co.

REFERENCES THROUGH 1971

1. WECHSLER, DAVID. *The Measurement of Adult Intelligence, Second Edition,* pp. 98–100, 175–7. Baltimore, Md.: Williams & Wilkins Co., 1941. Pp. xi, 248. *

CUMULATIVE NAME INDEX

Wechsler, D.: 1

[564]

Match Problems. Grades 9–16 and adults; 1963; formerly called *Match Problems 2;* "divergent production of figural transformations" or "originality in dealing with concrete visual material"; identical with the 1962 *Match Problems 2* (see 561w1); Raymond M. Berger and J. P. Guilford; Sheridan Psychological Services, Inc. *

For additional information, see 6:554 (7 references).

REFERENCES THROUGH 1971

1–7. See 6:554.
8. GARWOOD, DOROTHY SEMENOW. *Some Personality Factors Related to Creativity in Young Scientists.* Doctor's thesis, Claremont Graduate School (Claremont, Calif.), 1961. (*DA* 22:3273)
9. OWEN, CRAMER. "An Investigation of Creative Potential at the Junior High Level." *Studies Art Ed* 3:16–33 sp '62. *
10. GARWOOD, DOROTHY SEMENOW. "Personality Factors Related to Creativity in Young Scientists." *J Abn & Social Psychol* 68:413–9 Ap '64. * (*PA* 39:1729)
11. RAINWATER, JANETTE MUNKITTRICK. *Effects of Set on Problem Solving in Subjects of Varying Levels of Assessed Creativity.* Doctor's thesis, University of California (Berkeley, Calif.), 1964. (*DA* 25:6753)
12. RICHARDS, JAMES M., JR.; CLINE, VICTOR B.; AND NEEDHAM, WALTER E. "Creativity Tests and Teacher and Self Judgments of Originality." *J Exp Ed* 32:281–5 sp '64. * (*PA* 39:5135)
13. FORD, ELEANOR DIANE. *The Relationship of Certain Socio-Cultural Factors Among Junior High School Students to Creativity in Art.* Doctor's thesis, North Texas State University (Denton, Tex.), 1967. (*DA* 28:3502A)
14. ARMSTRONG, CARMEN LAPP GERBERDING. *Changes Evidenced in the Art Products of Elementary Education Majors Exhibiting the Characteristic of Flexibility.* Doctor's thesis, Indiana University (Bloomington, Ind.), 1968. (*DA* 29:1799A)
15. BUSSE, THOMAS V. "Establishment of the Flexible Thinking Factor in Fifth-Grade Boys." *J Psychol* 69:93–100 My '68. * (*PA* 42:11690)
16. HINTON, BERNARD L. "Environmental Frustration and Creative Problem Solving." *J Appl Psychol* 52:211–7 Je '68. * (*PA* 42:11701)
17. LEHRER, ARNOLD CURTIS. *The Personality Correlates of Creativity in Undergraduates.* Doctor's thesis, Colorado State College (Greeley, Colo.), 1969. (*DAI* 31:397B)
18. HEUSSENSTAMM, FRANCES K. "Creativity and Alienation: An Exploration of Their Relationship in Adolescence." *Calif J Ed Res* 21(3):140–6 My '70. *
19. HINTON, BERNARD L. "Personality Variables and Creative Potential." *J Creative Behav* 4(3):210–7 su '70. *

20. OLESON, D. S., AND ZUBEK, JOHN P. "Effect of One Day of Sensory Deprivation on a Battery of Open-Ended Cognitive Tests." *Percept & Motor Skills* 31(3):919–23 D '70. * (*PA* 46:358)
21. ADCOCK, C. J., AND WEBBERLEY, M. "Primary Mental Abilities." *J General Psychol* 84(2):229–43 Ap '71. * (*PA* 46:4979)
22. ARBUTHNOT, JACK BRAEDEN. *Field Independence and Maturity of Moral Judgment, Critical Distinctive Feature Analysis, and Perceived Locus of Control.* Doctor's thesis, Cornell University (Ithaca, N.Y.), 1971. (*DAI* 32:2190A)

CUMULATIVE NAME INDEX

Abe, C.: 6
Adcock, C. J.: 21
Arbuthnot, J. B.: 22
Armstrong, C. L. G.: 14
Beittel, K. R.: 3
Berger, R. M.: 1
Brittain, W. L.: 3
Busse, T. V.: 15
Christensen, P. R.: 1
Cline, V. B.: 6–7, 12
Ford, E. D.: 13
Garwood, D. S.: 8, 10
Guilford, J. P.: 1–2
Heussenstamm, F. K.: 18
Hinton, B. L.: 16, 19
Kaiser, H. F.: 4–5
Lehrer, A. C.: 17
Marks, A.: 4–5
Michael, W. B.: 4–5
Needham, W. E.: 7, 12
Oleson, D. S.: 20
Owen, C.: 9
Rainwater, J. M.: 11
Richards, J. M.: 6–7, 12
Webberley, M.: 21
Zubek, J. P.: 20

[565]

Match Problems 5, [Revised Edition]. Grades 9–16; 1962–69; "divergent production of figural transformations"; 1969 test identical with test copyrighted 1962 (see 561w2) except for one new and one revised item; no manual; Philip R. Merrifield and J. P. Guilford; Sheridan Psychological Services, Inc. *

For additional information, see 6:551w2.

[566]

★Memory for Events. Grades 9–13; 1969; "memory for semantic systems"; J. P. Guilford; Sheridan Psychological Services, Inc. *

[567]

★Memory for Meanings. Grades 7–16; 1969; "memory for semantic units"; Ralph Hoepfner and J. P. Guilford; Sheridan Psychological Services, Inc. *

[568]

New Uses. Grades 10–16; 1962–69; "convergent production of semantic transformations"; revision of *Picture Gestalt* (see 561p3); Ralph Hoepfner and J. P. Guilford; Sheridan Psychological Services, Inc. *

[569]

★Pattern Relations Test. College graduates; 1968–69; PRT; abstract reasoning; test in English and Afrikaans; D. Daneel (test) and Delene Barker (manual); National Institute for Personnel Research [South Africa]. *

[570]

Perceptual Speed (Identical Forms). Grades 9–16 and industrial employees; 1956–66; L. L. Thurstone (test), T. E. Jeffrey (test), and Norman J. Kantor (manual); Industrial Relations Center, University of Chicago. * [The publisher has not replied to our four requests to check the accuracy of this entry.]

For additional information, see 7:444 (2 references); for a review by Leroy Wolins, see 6:556.

REFERENCES THROUGH 1971

1–2. See 7:444.
3. BILKA, LOISANNE PFEIFER. *An Evaluation of the Predictive Value of Certain Reading Readiness Measures as Related to Method of Instruction, Sex, and Mental Age.* Doctor's thesis, University of Pittsburgh (Pittsburgh, Pa.), 1970. (*DAI* 31:5922A)
4. BORDEAUX, ELIZABETH ANN. *Auditory and Visual Readiness Factors Related to Reading Achievement in First Grade Based on Three Methods of Instruction.* Doctor's thesis, University of North Carolina (Chapel Hill, N.C.), 1970. (*DAI* 31:5924A)

CUMULATIVE NAME INDEX

Baehr, M. E.: 2
Bilka, L. P.: 3
Bond, G. L.: 1
Bordeaux, E. A.: 4
Dykstra, R.: 1
Froemel, E. C.: 2
Furcon, J. E.: 2
Wolins, L.: rev, 6:556

[571]

Pertinent Questions. Grades 9–16 and adults; 1960; experimental form; conceptual foresight; Raymond M. Berger, J. P. Guilford, and P. R. Merrifield (manual); Sheridan Psychological Services, Inc. *

For additional information, see 6:557 (3 references).

REFERENCES THROUGH 1971

1–3. See 6:557.
4. LOCKE, EDWIN A. "Some Correlates of Classroom and Out-of-Class Achievement in Gifted Science Students." *J Ed Psychol* 54:238–48 O '63. * (*PA* 38:4649)

CUMULATIVE NAME INDEX

Christensen, P. R.: 3
Frick, J. W.: 3
Guilford, J. P.: 3
Kaiser, H. F.: 1–2
Locke, E. A.: 4
Marks, A.: 1–2
Merrifield, P. R.: 3
Michael, W. B.: 1–2

[572]

Plot Titles. Grades 9–16; 1962–69; PT; 2 scores: ideational fluency, originality; 1969 test identical with test copyrighted 1962 (see 561m1) except for administration instructions; for a downward extension, see 554g; Raymond M. Berger and J. P. Guilford; Sheridan Psychological Services, Inc. *

For additional information, see 6:551m1.

REFERENCES THROUGH 1971

1. BARRON, FRANK. "The Disposition Toward Originality." *J Abn & Social Psychol* 51:478–85 N '55. * (*PA* 31:2533)
2. MEADOW, ARNOLD, AND PARNES, SIDNEY J. "Evaluation of Training in Creative Problem-Solving." *J Appl Psychol* 43:189–94 Je '59. * (*PA* 34:5568)
3. MARKS, ALVIN; MICHAEL, WILLIAM B.; AND KAISER, HENRY F. "Comparison of Manual and Analytic Techniques of Rotation in a Factor Analysis of Aptitude Test Variables." *Psychol Rep* 7:519–22 D '60. * (*PA* 35:2792)
4. BARRON, FRANK. *Creativity and Psychological Health: Origins of Personal Vitality and Creative Freedom.* Princeton, N.J.: D. Van Nostrand Co., Inc., 1963. Pp. xi, 292. *
5. VINT, VIRGINIA HOLLISTER. *The Effect of Prior Convergent or Divergent Art Training on Subsequent Art Activity.* Doctor's thesis, Stanford University (Stanford, Calif.), 1965. (*DA* 26:914)
6. GUILFORD, J. P., AND HOEPFNER, RALPH. "Sixteen Divergent-Production Abilities at the Ninth-Grade Level." *Multiv Behav Res* 1:43–66 Ja '66. * (*PA* 41:1602)
7. HILL, ARTHUR H. "A Longitudinal Study of Attrition Among High Aptitude College Students." *J Ed Res* 60:166–73 D '66. *
8. JANSSEN, CALVIN WAYNE. *Comparative Creativity Scores of Lower Socio-Economic Dropouts and Non-Dropouts.* Doctor's thesis, University of Tennessee (Knoxville, Tenn.), 1966. (*DA* 27:1659A)
9. GRAY, JAMES JOSEPH. *An Investigation of the Relationship Between Primary Process Thinking and Creativity.* Doctor's thesis, Fordham University (New York, N.Y.), 1967. (*DA* 28:5206B)
10. JENKINS, JOHN MERVIN. *A Study of the Characteristics Associated With Innovative Behavior in Teachers.* Doctor's thesis, University of Miami (Coral Gables, Fla.), 1967. (*DA* 28:903A)
11. MANGAN, GORDON L. "Studies of the Relationship Between Neo-Pavlovian Properties of Higher Nervous Activity and Western Personality Dimensions: 3, The Relations of Transformation Mobility to Thinking Flexibility." *J Exp Res Personality* 2:117–23 My '67. * (*PA* 41:11907)
12. MILES, DAVID T. *An Experimental Investigation of Programed Creativity.* Doctor's thesis, Southern Illinois University (Carbondale, Ill.), 1967. (*DA* 28:2099A)
13. RIDLEY, DENNIS R., AND BIRNEY, ROBERT C. "Effects of Training Procedures on Creativity Test Scores." *J Ed Psychol* 58:158–64 Je '67. * (*PA* 41:10457)
14. WINDHOLZ, GEORGE, AND MCINTOSH, WILLIAM A. "Concurrent Validation of Guilford's Six Convergent Tests." *Ed & Psychol Meas* 27:393–400 su '67. * (*PA* 41:12843)
15. BROWN, STEPHEN W.; GUILFORD, J. P.; AND HOEPFNER, RALPH. "Six Semantic-Memory Abilities." *Ed & Psychol Meas* 28:691–717 au '68. * (*PA* 43:4427)
16. EDWARDS, ARTHUR B. *An Analysis of the Creative Ability Levels of the Potential Dropout in the Average Mental Ability*

Range. Doctor's thesis, University of Tennessee (Knoxville, Tenn.), 1968. (*DA* 29:3828A)
17. JANSSEN, CALVIN. "Comparative Creativity Scores of Lower Socio-Economic Dropouts and Non-Dropouts." *Psychol Sch* 5:183–4 Ap '68. * (*PA* 43:17498)
18. WINDHOLZ, GEORGE. "The Relation of Creativity and Intelligence Constellations to Traits of Temperament, Interest, and Value in College Students." *J General Psychol* 79:291–9 O '68. * (*PA* 43:3998)
19. ANDERSON, HARRY E., JR.; WHITE, WILLIAM F.; AND STEVENS, JOHN C. "Student Creativity, Intelligence, Achievement, and Teacher Classroom Behavior." *J Social Psychol* 78(1):99–107 Je '69. * (*PA* 43:16427)
20. GRAY, JAMES J. "The Effect of Productivity on Primary Process and Creativity." *J Proj Tech & Pers Assess* 33(3):213–8 Je '69. * (*PA* 43:14302)
21. GUILFORD, J. P., AND HOEPFNER, RALPH. "Comparisons of Varimax Rotations With Rotations to Theoretical Targets." *Ed & Psychol Meas* 29(1):3–22 sp '69. * (*PA* 44:15668)
22. SCHNITZER, LEAH PALTIEL, AND STEWART, ROBERT A. C. "Originality and Personality Variables in High School Art Students." *Psychol* 6(1):36–9 F '69. * (*PA* 43:11334)
23. FRUIN, DAVID JOHN. *Response Styles and Creativity.* Doctor's thesis, Johns Hopkins University (Baltimore, Md.), 1970. (*DAI* 31:4361B)

CUMULATIVE NAME INDEX

Anderson, H. E.: 19
Barron, F.: 1, 4
Birney, R. C.: 13
Brown, S. W.: 15
Edwards, A. B.: 16
Fruin, D. J.: 23
Gray, J. J.: 9, 20
Guilford, J. P.: 6, 15, 21
Hill, A. H.: 7
Hoepfner, R.: 6, 15, 21
Janssen, C.: 17
Jenkins, C. W.: 8
Jenkins, J. M.: 10
Kaiser, H. F.: 3
McIntosh, W. A.: 14
Mangan, G. L.: 11
Marks, A.: 3
Meadow, A.: 2
Michael, W. B.: 3
Miles, D. T.: 12
Parnes, S. J.: 2
Ridley, D. R.: 13
Schnitzer, L. P.: 22
Stevens, J. C.: 19
Stewart, R. A. C.: 22
Vint, V. H.: 5
White, W. F.: 19
Windholz, G.: 14, 18

[573]

Possible Jobs. Grades 6–16 and adults; 1963; "divergent production of semantic implications" or "ability to suggest alternative deductions"; for a downward extension, see 554d; Arthur Gershon and J. P. Guilford; Sheridan Psychological Services, Inc. *

For additional information, see 6:558 (1 reference).

REFERENCES THROUGH 1971

1. See 6:558.
2. HAYNES, CAROLYN R. *The Relationships of Performances of Seventh Grade Students on Measures of Creativity, Study Habits and Attitudes, Expressed Need for Counseling and Achievement.* Master's thesis, Texas A & M University (College Station, Tex.), 1966.
3. GRAY, JAMES JOSEPH. *An Investigation of the Relationship Between Primary Process Thinking and Creativity.* Doctor's thesis, Fordham University (New York, N.Y.), 1967. (*DA* 28:5206B)
4. WINDHOLZ, GEORGE. "The Relation of Creativity and Intelligence Constellations to Traits of Temperament, Interest, and Value in College Students." *J General Psychol* 79:291–9 O '68. * (*PA* 43:3998)
5. GRAY, JAMES J. "The Effect of Productivity on Primary Process and Creativity." *J Proj Tech & Pers Assess* 33(3):213–8 Je '69. * (*PA* 43:14302)
6. SIMPSON, DONALD JAMES. *The Effect of Selected Musical Studies on Growth in General Creative Potential.* Doctor's thesis, University of Southern California (Los Angeles, Calif.), 1969. (*DAI* 30:502A)
7. HEUSSENSTAMM, FRANCES K. "Creativity and Alienation: An Exploration of Their Relationship in Adolescence." *Calif J Ed Res* 21(3):140–6 My '70. *
8. OLESON, D. S., AND ZUBEK, JOHN P. "Effect of One Day of Sensory Deprivation on a Battery of Open-Ended Cognitive Tests." *Percept & Motor Skills* 31(3):919–23 D '70. * (*PA* 46:358)
9. SMITH, I. LEON. "IQ, Creativity, and the Taxonomy of Educational Objectives: Cognitive Domain." *J Exp Ed* 38(4):58–60 su '70. * (*PA* 46:5688)
10. SMITH, I. LEON. "IQ, Creativity, and Achievement: Interaction and Threshold." *Multiv Behav Res* 6(1):51–62 Ja '71. * (*PA* 46:9753)

CUMULATIVE NAME INDEX

Gray, J. J.: 3, 5
Guilford, J. P.: 1
Haynes, C. R.: 2
Heussenstamm, F. K.: 7
Oleson, D. S.: 8
Simpson, D. J.: 6
Smith, I. L.: 9–10
Windholz, G.: 4
Zubek, J. P.: 8

[574]

***Remote Associates Test.** High school, college and adults; 1967–71, c1959–71; RAT; "ability to think creatively"; 2 levels; Sarnoff A. Mednick and Martha T. Mednick; Houghton Mifflin Co. *

a) HIGH SCHOOL LEVEL. 1971.

b) COLLEGE AND ADULT LEVEL. 1967, c1959–67.

For additional information and reviews by Leonard L. Baird, George K. Bennett, and Philip E. Vernon of *b,* see 7:445 (100 references).

REFERENCES THROUGH 1971

1–100. See 7:445.
101. HOUSTON, JOHN P., AND MEDNICK, SARNOFF A. "Creativity and the Need for Novelty." *J Abn & Social Psychol* 66:137–41 F '63. * (*PA* 37:6699)
102. MCGLOTHLIN, WILLIAM H.; COHEN, SIDNEY; AND MCGLOTHLIN, MARCELLA S. "Short-Term Effects of LSD on Anxiety, Attitudes and Performance." *J Nerv & Mental Dis* 139:266–73 S '64. * (*PA* 39:7046)
103. MENDELSOHN, GERALD A., AND GRISWOLD, BARBARA B. "Differential Use of Incidental Stimuli in Probem Solving as a Function of Creativity." *J Abn & Social Psychol* 68:431–6 Mr '64. * (*PA* 39:740)
104. MENDELSOHN, GERALD A.; GRISWOLD, BARBARA B.; AND ANDERSON, MILTON L. "Individual Differences in Anagram-Solving Ability." *Psychol Rep* 19:799–809 D '66. * (*PA* 41:3943)
105. WHITTEMORE, ROBERT G., JR., AND HEIMANN, ROBERT A. "Modification of Originality Responses." *J Counsel Psychol* 13:213–8 su '66. * (*PA* 40:8833)
106. GALL, MEREDITH, AND MENDELSOHN, GERALD A. "Effects of Facilitating Techniques and Subject-Experimenter Interaction on Creative Problem Solving." *J Pers & Social Psychol* 5:211–6 F '67. * (*PA* 41:3953)
107. KLEIN, PETER, AND KELLNER, HAROLD. "Creativity in a Two-Choice Probability Situation." *J General Psychol* 76:193–200 Ap '67. * (*PA* 41:8394)
108. LAUGHLIN, PATRICK R. "Incidental Concept Formation as a Function of Creativity and Intelligence." *J Pers & Social Psychol* 5:115–9 Ja '67. * (*PA* 41:3958)
109. MCDONALD, DONALD C., JR., AND MARTIN, RANDALL B. "Word Association Training and Creativity." *Psychol Rep* 20:319–22 F '67. * (*PA* 41:6681)
110. DESIDERATO, OTELLO, AND SIGAL, SUSAN. "Associative Productivity as a Function of Creativity Level and Type of Verbal Stimulus." *Psychon Sci* 18(6):357–8 Mr 25 '70. * (*PA* 44:12581)
111. KORIAT, ASHER. *Creativity and the Structure of Memory.* Doctor's thesis, University of California (Berkeley, Calif.), 1970. (*DAI* 31:6242B)
112. WARREN, THOMAS FRANKLIN. *Creative Thinking Techniques: Four Methods of Stimulating Original Ideas in Sixth Grade Students.* Doctor's thesis, University of Wisconsin (Madison, Wis.), 1970. (*DAI* 31:5863A)
113. BOWERS, KENNETH S., AND KEELING, KENNETH R. "Heart-Rate Variability in Creative Functioning." *Psychol Rep* 29(1):160–2 Ag '71. * (*PA* 47:2468)
114. BURKE, RONALD J. "Correlates of the Ability to Fragment and Reorganize Stored Information." *J General Psychol* 84(2):183–9 Ap '71. * (*PA* 46:4255)
115. DACEY, JOHN S., AND MADAUS, GEORGE F. "An Analysis of Two Hypotheses Concerning the Relationship Between Creativity and Intelligence." *J Ed Res* 64(5):213–6 Ja '71. * (*PA* 46:4712)
116. DAVIS, GARY A., AND BELCHER, TERENCE L. "How Shall Creativity Be Measured? Torrance Tests, RAT, Alpha Biographical, and IQ." *J Creative Behav* 5(3):153–61 '71. *
117. DEL GAUDIO, ANDREW CHARLES. *Psychological Differentiation and Mobility as Related to Creativity.* Doctor's thesis, Fordham University (New York, N.Y.), 1971. (*DAI* 32:2393B)
118. ENRIQUEZ, VIRGILIO GASPAR. *Language and Originality: Recall of Postnominal Adjectives and Semantically Ill-Formed Sentences as a Function of the Structural Locus and Anomaly.* Doctor's thesis, Northwestern University (Evanston, Ill.), 1971. (*DAI* 32:5336A)
119. LEFCOURT, HERBERT M., AND TELEGDI, MELANIE SMITH. "Perceived Locus of Control and Field Dependence as Predictors of Cognitive Activity." *J Consult & Clin Psychol* 37(1):53–6 Ag '71. * (*PA* 47:903)
120. OHNMACHT, FRED W., AND MCMORRIS, ROBERT F. "Creativity as a Function of Field Independence and Dogmatism." *J Psychol* 79(2):165–8 N '71. * (*PA* 47:6800)
121. PERRONE, JAMES V. *An Investigation of Two Approaches to the Measurement of Creative Potential in College Students.* Doctor's thesis, St. John's University (Jamaica, N.Y.), 1971. (*DAI* 32:2989B)
122. PHILLIPS, VICTOR K., AND TORRANCE, E. PAUL. "Divergent Thinking, Remote Associations, and Concept Attainment Strategies." *J Psychol* 77(2):223–8 Mr '71. * (*PA* 46:361)
123. PIERS, ELLEN V., AND KIRCHNER, ELIZABETH P. "Pro-

ductivity and Uniqueness in Continued Word Association as a Function of Subject Creativity and Stimulus Properties." *J Personality* 39(2):264–76 Je '71. * (*PA* 47:210)

124. PIZAM, ABRAHAM. *Some Socio-Psychological Correlates of Innovation Within Industrial Suggestion Systems.* Doctor's thesis, Cornell University (Ithaca, N.Y.), 1971. (*DAI* 32:606B)

125. SCHOEL, DORIS R., AND BUSSE, THOMAS V. "Humor and Creative Abilities." *Psychol Rep* 29(1):34 Ag '71. * (*PA* 47:2958)

126. SUTER, BARBARA ANN. *Masculinity-Femininity in Creative Women.* Doctor's thesis, Fordham University (New York, N.Y.), 1971. (*DAI* 32:2411B)

127. TURNEY, JOHN R.; ROSEN, NED A.; AND CONKLYN, ELIZABETH D. "Early Identification of Managerial Potential in a Technical-Professional Organization." Abstract. *Proc 79th Ann Conv Am Psychol Assn* 6(2):481–2 '71. * (*PA* 46:5909)

128. WIRWICK-VAN DUSEN, MAXINE, AND HALL, ALFRED E. "Need for Associative Novelty: An Unreliable Effect." *J Exp Res Personality* 5(2):119–23 Je '71. * (*PA* 48:1004)

129. WORTHEN, BLAINE R., AND CLARK, PHILIP M. "Toward an Improved Measure of Remote Associational Ability." *J Ed Meas* 8(2):113–23 su '71. * (*PA* 46:10884)

CUMULATIVE NAME INDEX

Abney, C. W.: 68
Alegre, C. E.: 78
Anderson, C. C.: 26
Anderson, D. L.: 65
Anderson, M. L.: 104
Andrews, F. M.: 1, 19, 34, 48, 84
Antell, M. J.: 69
Arvidson, R. M.: 38, 51
Bader, L. J.: 85
Baird, L. L.: *rev,* 7:445
Becica, B.: 52
Belcher, T. L.: 116
Belloni, M.: 14
Bennett, G. K.: *rev,* 7:445
Berman, J. R.: 53
Bone, R. N.: 54
Bowers, K. S.: 113
Brody, E. B.: 86
Burgess, M. M.: 70
Burke, R. J.: 114
Busse, T. V.: 125
Butler, M. J.: 20
Castiglione, L. V.: 21
Cicirelli, J. S.: 87
Cicirelli, V. G.: 71, 87
Clark, P. M.: 129
Cohen, I. S.: 22
Cohen, S.: 102
Conklyn, E. D.: 127
Corlett, F.: 54
Craver, A. A.: 55
Cropley, A. J.: 26–7
Dacey, J. S.: 115
Damm, V. J.: 39, 88
Dana, R. H.: 32
Danks, J. H.: 28
Datta, L. E.: 9–10
David, K. H.: 74
Davis, G. A.: 116
Day, H. I.: 72
Del Gaudio, A. C.: 117
Desiderato, O.: 110
Doherty, M. A.: 62
Dolby, L. L. L.: 42
Duffey, M.: 70
Dunn, R. F.: 62
Easterbrook, C. M.: 11
Elenewski, J. J.: 59
Enriquez, V. G.: 118
Fishbein, M.: 14
Flanagan, M. L.: 40
Fleischer, G.: 12, 22
Freedman, J. L.: 23
Furcon, J.: 73
Gall, M.: 106
Gall, M. D.: 97
Gallup, H. F.: 40
Gamble, K. R.: 56
Gantz, B. S.: 29
Ginsburg, G. P.: 13, 57, 76, 89–90, 92–3
Glucksberg, S.: 28
Goodman, P.: 73
Gordon, G.: 84
Griswold, B. B.: 24, 33, 103–4
Guilliams, C. I.: 30
Haag, R. A.: 74
Hall, A. E.: 91, 128
Halpern, S. K.: 79
Ham, D. G.: 58
Harris, R.: 91
Heimann, R. A.: 105
Helin, W. C.: 65
Higgins, J.: 31, 41–2
Hippe, D. L.: 65
Hood, R. W.: 75–6, 89–90, 92–3
Houston, J. P.: 101
Jacobson, L. I.: 59
Jacoby, J.: 43, 60
Jenkins, A. H.: 4
Johnson, D. A.: 61
Jung, C. C.: 15
Kaplan, M.: 77
Kaplan, M. F.: 81
Karlins, M.: 44, 71
Kays, D.: 46
Keeling, K. R.: 113
Keillor, J. S.: 94
Kellner, H.: 56, 107
Kirchner, E. P.: 123
Klein, P.: 107
Koriat, A.: 111
Króp, H. D.: 78
Lahn, M.: 5
Langevin, R.: 72
Laughlin, P. R.: 62, 108
Lefcourt, H. M.: 119
Libby, W. L.: 95
Liroff, J. H.: 65
Listiak, R. L.: 65
Lordahl, D. S.: 59
Lucas, F. R.: 32, 45
Lynch, M. D.: 46–7
McDonald, D. C.: 109
McGaughey, M. V.: 63
McGlothlin, M. S.: 102
McGlothlin, W. H.: 102
McMorris, R. F.: 120
Madaus, G. F.: 115
Maltzman, I.: 14
Martin, R. B.: 109
Mednick, E. V.: 16
Mednick, M. T.: 3, 6, 15–6, 48, 79, 96
Mednick, S. A.: 2–3, 15–6, 64, 80, 101
Mendelsohn, G. A.: 33, 97, 103–4, 106
Moser, R. J.: 65
Ohnmacht, F. W.: 120
Olczak, P. V.: 81
Pelz, D. C.: 34
Perkins, S. A.: 35
Perrone, J. V.: 121
Phillips, V. K.: 122
Piers, E. V.: 123
Pizam, A.: 124
Rainwater, J. M.: 17
Rose, J.: 73
Rosen, N. A.: 127
Rossiter, J. R.: 36
Schlicht, W. J.: 65
Schoel, D. R.: 125
Schuerhoff, C.: 77
Shry, S. A.: 66
Sigal, S.: 110
Silber, D. E.: 96
Simon, L. R.: 82
Smith, I. L.: 98
Stock, W. H.: 67
Suter, B. A.: 126
Swink, E.: 47
Taft, R.: 36, 49
Telegdi, M. S.: 119
Tobias, S.: 83
Torrance, E. P.: 122
Tortorella, W. M.: 50
Treadwell, Y.: 99
Turney, J. R.: 127
Vernon, P. E.: *rev,* 7:445
Walker, H. E.: 7
Walker, J. L.: 65
Wardeska, B. C.: 100
Warren, T. F.: 112
White, L. E.: 18
Whittemore, R. G.: 8, 57, 105
Williams, C. D.: 78
Wirwick-Van Dusen, M.: 128
Worthen, B. R.: 129
Yahav, A. L.: 25
Zoob, I.: 37

[575]

The Rutgers Drawing Test. Ages 4–6, 6–9; 1952–69; RDT; Anna Spiesman Starr; the Author. *

For additional information and a review by Melvyn I. Semmel, see 7:446 (6 references); see also 6:559 (2 references).

REFERENCES THROUGH 1971

1–2. See 6:559.
3–8. See 7:446.

CUMULATIVE NAME INDEX

Balinky, J. L.: 4
Dudek, S. Z.: 5, 8
Goldberg, J. S.: 8
Harris, B. R.: 5, 8
Lester, E. P.: 8
Lester, L. P.: 5
Leton, D. A.: 2
Panther, E. E.: 6
Semmel, M. I.: *rev,* 7:446
Starr, A. S.: 1
Stevens, M. C.: 3
Yudin, L. W.: 7

[576]

★**Seeing Faults.** Ages 15 and over; 1971; verbal creativity; H. E. Schmidt (manual); National Institute for Personnel Research [South Africa]. *

[577]

*****Seeing Problems.** Grades 9–16; 1962–69; 1969 test identical with half of test copyrighted 1962 (see 56182) except for administration instructions; Philip R. Merrifield and J. P. Guilford; Sheridan Psychological Services, Inc. *

For additional information, see 6:551s2.

REFERENCES THROUGH 1971

1. DE MILLE, RICHARD. "Intellect After Lobotomy in Schizophrenia: A Factor Analytic Study." *Psychol Monogr* 76(16):1–18 '62. * (*PA* 38:2784)
2. ATKINSON, BEA HENRIETTA. *The Relationship Between Problem-Solving Strategies and Measures of Convergent and Divergent Thinking in a Selected Group of Secondary School Pupils.* Doctor's thesis, University of Florida (Gainesville, Fla.), 1964. (*DA* 25:7070)
3. ANDERSON, C. C., AND CROPLEY, A. J. "Some Correlates of Originality." *Austral J Psychol* 18:218–27 D '66. * (*PA* 41:4572)
4. CROPLEY, A. J. "Creativity and Intelligence." *Brit J Ed Psychol* 36:259–66 N '66. * (*PA* 41:573)
5. GUILFORD, J. P., AND HOEPFNER, RALPH. "Sixteen Divergent-Production Abilities at the Ninth-Grade Level." *Multiv Behav Res* 1:43–66 Ja '66. * (*PA* 41:1602)
6. HILL, ARTHUR H. "A Longitudinal Study of Attrition Among High Aptitude College Students." *J Ed Res* 60:166–73 D '66. *
7. NEEDHAM, WALTER EVANS. *Intellectual, Personality and Biographical Characteristics of Southern Negro and White College Students.* Doctor's thesis, University of Utah (Salt Lake City, Utah), 1966. (*DA* 27:1609B)
8. SMITH, ROBERT M., AND NEISWORTH, JOHN T. "Creative Thinking Abilities of Intellectually Superior Children in the Regular Grades." *Psychol Rep* 18:335–41 Ap '66. * (*PA* 40:8832)
9. CROPLEY, A. J. "Creativity, Intelligence, and Achievement." *Alberta J Ed Res* 13:51–8 Mr '67. * (*PA* 41:15253)
10. KARSTEN, MARY O'KEEFFE. *The Relationship of Tested Creative Abilities and Selected Factors of Academic Achievement, Intelligence, Sex, Socioeconomic Status, and Pupil Attitudes.* Doctor's thesis, University of Southern California (Los Angeles, Calif.), 1967. (*DA* 28:2557A)
11. SMITH, ROBERT M. "Creative Thinking Abilities of Educable Mentally Handicapped Children in the Regular Grades." *Am J Mental Def* 71:571–5 Ja '67. * (*PA* 41:6197)
12. BLACKHURST, A. EDWARD; MARKS, CLAUDE H.; AND TISDALL, WILLIAM J. "Relationship Between Mobility and Divergent Thinking in Blind Children." *Ed Visually Handicapped* 1(2):33–6 My '69. * (*PA* 43:14813)
13. GOODMAN, P.; FURCON, J.; AND ROSE, J. "Examination of Some Measures of Creative Ability by the Multitrait-Multi-

method Matrix." *J Appl Psychol* 53(3):240–3 Je '69. * (*PA* 43:11327)
14. GRIMSLEY, WILLIAM GERALD. *The Relationship Between Creativity and Leader Behavior of School Superintendents.* Doctor's thesis, University of Missouri (Columbia, Mo.), 1969. (*DAI* 30:5193A)
15. TISDALL, WILLIAM J.; BLACKHURST, A. EDWARD; AND MARKS, CLAUDE H. "Divergent Thinking in Blind Children." *J Ed Psychol* 62(6):468–73 D '71. * (*PA* 47:9708)

CUMULATIVE NAME INDEX

Anderson, C. C.: 3
Atkinson, B. H.: 2
Blackhurst, A. E.: 12, 15
Cropley, A. J.: 3–4, 9
de Mille, R.: 1
Furcon, J.: 13
Goodman, P.: 13
Grimsley, W. G.: 14
Guilford, J. P.: 5
Hill, A. H.: 6
Hoepfner, R.: 5
Karsten, M. O.: 10
Marks, C. H.: 12, 15
Needham, W. E.: 7
Neisworth, J. T.: 8
Rose, J.: 13
Smith, R. M.: 8, 11
Tisdall, W. J.: 12, 15

[578]

Seguin-Goddard Formboard. Ages 5–14; [1911]; modifications appear in *Arthur Point Scale of Performance Tests* and *Merrill-Palmer Scale of Mental Tests;* E. Seguin, H. H. Goddard, and N. Norsworthy; Stoelting Co.

REFERENCES THROUGH 1971

1. GAW, FRANCES. "A Study of Performance Tests." *Brit J Psychol* 15:374–92 Ap '25. *
2. WORTHINGTON, MYRTLE RAYMAKER. "A Study of Some Commonly Used Performance Tests." *J Appl Psychol* 10:216–27 Je '26. *
3. PORTEUS, S. D.; WITH THE ASSISTANCE OF DORIS M. DEWEY AND ROBERT G. BERNREUTER. "Race and Social Differences in Performance Tests." *Genetic Psychol Monogr* 8:93–208 Ag '30. * (*PA* 4:4947)
4. PORTEUS, STANLEY D. Chap. 21, "Tests of Temperament and Intelligence," pp. 351–77. In his *The Psychology of a Primitive People: A Study of the Australian Aborigine.* New York: Longmans, Green & Co., 1931. Pp. xvi, 438. * (*PA* 6:1168, title only)
5. PORTEUS, STANLEY D. Chap. 23, "Aboriginal Children's Intelligence," pp. 408–20. In his *The Psychology of a Primitive People: A Study of the Australian Aborigine.* New York: Longmans, Green & Co., 1931. Pp. xvi, 438. * (*PA* 6:1168, title only)
6. VANCE, THOMAS F. "The Effect of Size of Peg and Form Boards Upon the Performance Scores of Young Children." *Proc Iowa Acad Sci* 40:181–4 '33. * (*PA* 9:3048)
7. NOTTINGHAM, RUTH D. "A Psychological Study of Forty Unmarried Mothers." *Genetic Psychol Monogr* 19:157–228 My '37. * (*PA* 11:4670)
8. VERNON, P. E. "A Study of the Norms and the Validity of Certain Mental Tests at a Child Guidance Clinic: Part II." *Brit J Ed Psychol* 7:115–37 Je '37. * (*PA* 11:4827)
9. HAMLIN, ROY, AND ABEL, THEODORA M. "Test Pattern of Mental Defectives Skilled in Weaving." *J Appl Psychol* 22:385–9 Ag '38. * (*PA* 13:1642)
10. BERKO, MARTIN J. "Some Factors in the Perceptual Deviations of Cerebral Palsied Children." *Cerebral Palsy R* 15:3–4+ F '54. * (*PA* 28:7892)
11. TEUBER, HANS-LUKAS, AND WEINSTEIN, SIDNEY. "Performance on a Formboard-Task After Penetrating Brain Injury." *J Psychol* 38:177–90 Jl '54. * (*PA* 29:4573)
12. BILGER, ROBERT C. "Limitations on the Use of Intelligence Scales to Estimate the Mental Ages of Children." *Volta R* 60:321–5 S '58. *
13. REITAN, RALPH M. "Effects of Brain Damage on a Psychomotor Problem-Solving Task." *Percept & Motor Skills* 9:211–5 S '59. * (*PA* 34:6479)
14. MATTHEWS, CHARLES G., AND REITAN, RALPH M. "Psychomotor Abilities of Retardates and Patients With Cerebral Lesions." *Am J Mental Def* 66:607–12 Ja '62. * (*PA* 36:4JI07M)
15. REED, HOMER B. C., JR., AND REITAN, RALPH M. "The Significance of Age in the Performance of a Complex Psychomotor Task by Brain-Damaged and Non-Brain-Damaged Subjects." *J Gerontol* 17:193–6 Ap '62. * (*PA* 37:2961)
16. FAHMY, MOSTAFA. "Initial Exploring of the Intelligence of Shilluk Children: Studies in the Southern Sudan." *Vita Hum* (Switzerland) 7(3–4):164–77 '64. * (*PA* 39:7815)
17. KLATSKIN, ETHELYN HENRY. "Relationships of Deficits in Intelligence Test Performance of Preschool Children to Perinatal Experience." *J Consult Psychol* 28:228–33 Je '64. * (*PA* 39:4590)
18. MARSHALL, ANNE. *The Abilities and Attainments of Children Leaving Junior Training Centres.* London: National Association for Mental Health, 1967. Pp. i, 62. *
19. MEIER, MANFRED J., AND RESCH, JOSEPH A. "Behavioral Prediction of Short-Term Neurologic Change Following Acute Onset of Cerebrovascular Symptoms." *Mayo Clin Proc* 42:641–7 O '67. *
20. SANTORO, ROSEANN MARIE. *The Relationship of Reading Achievement to Specific Measures of Visual Perception, Visual-Motor Perception and Intelligence.* Doctor's thesis, Fordham University (New York, N.Y.), 1967. (*DA* 28:4010A)
21. BOURESTOM, NORMAN C., AND HOWARD, MARY T. "Behavioral Correlates of Recovery of Self-Care in Hemiplegic Patients." *Arch Phys Med & Rehabil* 49:449–54 Ag '68. *
22. COLE, SPURGEON; BURKHEIMER, G. J.; AND STEINBERG, JAY. "Validity of Seguin Formboard With Retarded Children." *Psychol Rep* 22:1143–4 Je '68. * (*PA* 42:19179)
23. MEIER, MANFRED J., AND OKAYAMA, MASAHIRO. "Behavior Assessment." *Geriatrics* 24(11):95–110 N '69. *
24. MEIER, MANFRED J. "Effects of Focal Cerebral Lesions on Contralateral Visuomotor Adaptation to Reversal and Inversion of Visual Feedback." *Neuropsychologia* (England) 8(3):269–79 Jl '70. * (*PA* 44:21410)
25. GORDON, GEORGE, AND HYMAN, IRWIN. "The Measurement of Perceptual-Motor Abilities of Head Start Children." *Psychol Sch* 8(1):41–8 Ja '71. * (*PA* 46:7777)

CUMULATIVE NAME INDEX

Abel, T. M.: 9
Berko, M. J.: 10
Bernreuter, R. G.: 3
Bilger, R. C.: 12
Bourestom, N. C.: 21
Burkheimer, G. J.: 22
Cole, S.: 22
Dewey, D. M.: 3
Fahmy, M.: 16
Gaw, F.: 1
Gordon, G.: 25
Hamlin, R.: 9
Howard, M. T.: 21
Hyman, I.: 25
Klatskin, E. H.: 17
Marshall, A.: 18
Matthews, C. G.: 14
Meier, M. J.: 19, 23–4
Nottingham, R. D.: 7
Okayama, M.: 23
Porteus, S. D.: 3–5
Reed, H. B. C.: 15
Reitan, R. M.: 13–5
Resch, J. A.: 19
Santoro, R. M.: 20
Steinberg, J.: 22
Teuber, H. L.: 11
Vance, T. F.: 6
Vernon, P. E.: 8
Weinstein, S.: 11
Worthington, M. R.: 2

[579]

Simile Interpretations [Sheridan Edition]. Grades 10–16; 1962–69; "divergent production of semantic systems"; consists of the 4 items in the 1962 test of the same title (see 561d2) plus 4 new items; Paul R. Christensen, J. P. Guilford, and Ralph Hoepfner; Sheridan Psychological Services, Inc. *

For additional information, see 6:551d2.

REFERENCES THROUGH 1971

1. GUILFORD, J. P., AND HOEPFNER, RALPH. "Sixteen Divergent-Production Abilities at the Ninth-Grade Level." *Multiv Behav Res* 1:43–66 Ja '66. * (*PA* 41:1602)

CUMULATIVE NAME INDEX

Guilford, J. P.: 1
Hoepfner, R.: 1

[580]

★**Similes Test.** Grades 4–16 and adults; 1971; ST; creativity; Charles E. Schaefer; Research Psychologists Press, Inc. *

REFERENCES THROUGH 1971

1. SCHAEFER, CHARLES E. "The Similes Test: A New Measure of Metaphorical Thinking." Abstract. *Proc 78th Ann Conv Am Psychol Assn* 5(1):169–70 '70. * (*PA* 44:18718)

CUMULATIVE NAME INDEX

Schaefer, C. E.: 1

[581]

★**Sketches.** Grades 9 and over; 1967; "divergent production of figural units" or "visual-figural fluency"; S. Gardner, A. Gershon, P. R. Merrifield, and J. P. Guilford; Sheridan Psychological Services, Inc. *

REFERENCES THROUGH 1971

1. GUILFORD, J. P., AND HOEPFNER, RALPH. "Sixteen Divergent-Production Abilities at the Ninth-Grade Level." *Multiv Behav Res* 1:43–66 Ja '66. * (*PA* 41:1602)

CUMULATIVE NAME INDEX

Guilford, J. P.: 1
Hoepfner, R.: 1

[582]

Subsumed Abilities Test. Ages 9 and over; 1957–63; 5 scores: recognition, abstraction, conceptualization, total (demonstrated abilities), potential abilities; Joseph R. Sanders; Martin M. Bruce, Ph.D., Publishers. *

For additional information and a review by Naomi Stewart, see 6:560.

REFERENCES THROUGH 1971

1. BRUCE, MARTIN M. "Normative Data Information Exchange, No. 11–14." *Personnel Psychol* 11:280 su '58. *
2. BRUCE, MARTIN M. "Normative Data Information Exchange, No. 11–15." *Personnel Psychol* 11:281 su '58. *

CUMULATIVE NAME INDEX

Bruce, M. M.: 1–2   Stewart, N.: *rev*, 6:560

[583]

★**Symbol Identities.** Grades 10 and over; 1967; "evaluation of symbolic units"; Ralph Hoepfner and J. P. Guilford; Sheridan Psychological Services, Inc. *

[584]

Symbol Series Test: I.B.P. Edition, 1968. Illiterate and semi-literate adults; 1969; abstract reasoning; G. V. Grant; National Institute for Personnel Research [South Africa]. *

For additional information, see 7:447.

[585]

★**Test of Concept Utilization.** Ages 4.5–18.5; 1972; TCU; 24 scores: 6 equivalence scores (color, shape, homogeneous function, abstract, stimulus bound, object bound), 2 relational scores (relational function, minor relational), 3 structure scores (total equivalence, total relational, total unilateral), 6 reality match scores (color, shape, homogeneous function, abstract, relational function, total), 2 concept articulation scores (acceptable mains, inferior mains), 4 qualitative scores (action, object qualities, infusions, creations), negations; Richard L. Crager and Ann J. Spriggs; Western Psychological Services. *

REFERENCES THROUGH 1971

1. CRAGER, RICHARD L., AND SPRIGGS, ANN J. "Development of Concept Utilization." *Develop Psychol* 1(4):415–24 Jl '69. * (*PA* 43:14117)

CUMULATIVE NAME INDEX

Crager, R. L.: 1   Spriggs, A. J.: 1

[586]

★**Test of Creative Potential.** Grades 2–12 and adults; 1973; TCP; Ralph Hoepfner and Judith Hemenway; Monitor. *

[587]

★**Thinking Creatively With Sounds and Words, Research Edition.** Grades 3–12, adults; 1973; TCSW; 2 tests; technical manual by Joe Khatena and E. Paul Torrance; Personnel Press. *
a) SOUNDS AND IMAGES. SI; Bert F. Cunnington and E. Paul Torrance.
b) ONOMATOPEIA AND IMAGES. OI; Joe Khatena.

REFERENCES THROUGH 1971

1. WHITTEMORE, ROBERT GEORGE, JR. *Modification of Originality Responses in Academically Talented, Male University Freshmen.* Doctor's thesis, Arizona State University (Tempe, Ariz.), 1963. (*DA* 25:6403)
2. WHITTEMORE, ROBERT G., JR., AND HEIMANN, ROBERT A. "Modification of Originality Responses." *J Counsel Psychol* 13:213–8 su '66. * (*PA* 40:8833)
3. KHATENA, JOE. "'Onomatopoeia and Images': Preliminary Validity Study of a Test of Originality." *Percept & Motor Skills* 28(1):335–8 F '69. * (*PA* 43:11331)
4. KHATENA, JOE. *The Training of Creative Thinking Strategies and Its Effects on Originality.* Doctor's thesis, University of Georgia (Athens, Ga.), 1969. (*DAI* 30:3324A)
5. TORRANCE, E. P. "Originality of Imagery in Identifying Creative Talent in Music." *Gifted Child Q* 13(1):3–8 sp '69. * (*PA* 43:14320)
6. KHATENA, JOE. "Note on Reliability and Validity of Onomatopoeia and Images." *Percept & Motor Skills* 31(1):86 Ag '70. * (*PA* 45:4282)
7. KHATENA, JOE. "Repeated Presentation of Stimuli and Production of Original Responses." *Percept & Motor Skills* 30(1):91–4 F '70. * (*PA* 46:9071)
8. KHATENA, JOE. "Training College Adults to Think Creatively With Words." *Psychol Rep* 27(1):279–81 Ag '70. * (*PA* 45:6340)
9. SCHAEFER, CHARLES E. "'Onomatopoeia and Images': Further Evidence of Validity." *Percept & Motor Skills* 31(3):786 D '70. * (*PA* 45:9979)
10. KHATENA, JOE. "Adolescents and the Meeting of Time Deadlines in the Production of Original Verbal Images." *Gifted Child Q* 15(3):201–4 f '71. * (*PA* 47:11651)
11. KHATENA, JOE. "Breaking Away From Perceptual Set and Statistical Infrequency in Production of Original Verbal Images." *Percept & Motor Skills* 32(3):958 Je '71. * (*PA* 47:2991)
12. KHATENA, JOE. "Children's Version of 'Onomatopoeia and Images': A Preliminary Validity Study of Verbal Originality." *Percept & Motor Skills* 33(1):26 Ag '71. * (*PA* 47:2992)
13. KHATENA, JOE. "Evaluation and the Creative Potential in Music." *Gifted Child Q* 15(1):19–22 sp '71. * (*PA* 47:11802)
14. KHATENA, JOE. "Production of Original Verbal Images by Children Between Ages 8 and 19 as Measured by the Alternate Forms of Onomatopoeia and Images." Abstract. *Proc 79th Ann Conv Am Psychol Assn* 6(1):187–8 '71. * (*PA* 46:2605)
15. KHATENA, JOE. "A Second Study Training College Adults to Think Creatively With Words." *Psychol Rep* 28(2):385–6 Ap '71. * (*PA* 46:6162)
16. KHATENA, JOE. "'Sounds and Images': Further Evidence of Validity of a Test of Originality." *Percept & Motor Skills* 32(3):850 Je '71. * (*PA* 47:2993)
17. KHATENA, JOE, AND TORRANCE, E. PAUL. "Attitude Patterns and the Production of Original Verbal Images: A Study in Construct Validity." *Gifted Child Q* 15(2):117–22 su '71. * (*PA* 47:9614)

CUMULATIVE NAME INDEX

Heimann, R. A.: 2   Torrance, E. P.: 5, 17
Khatena, J.: 3–4, 6–8, 10–7   Whittemore, R. G.: 1 2
Schaefer, C. E.: 9

[588]

The Time Appreciation Test. Ages 10 and over; 1943–46; test sheet title is *JNB Time Test;* John N. Buck; Western Psychological Services. *

For additional information and reviews by E. J. G. Bradford and Charles N. Cofer, see 3:266 (2 references).

REFERENCES THROUGH 1971

1–2. See 3:266.
3. COFER, CHARLES N., AND BIEGEL, MARK M. "A Study of the Kent and Buck Screen Tests of Mental Ability in Relation to Otis and Stanford Achievement Test Scores." *J Consult Psychol* 12:187–9 My–Je '48. * (*PA* 22:4943)
4. ENGLE, T. L., AND HAMLETT, IONA C. "The Use of the Time Appreciation Test as a Screening or Supplementary Test for Mentally Deficient Patients." *Am J Mental Def* 54:521–5 Ap '50. * (*PA* 25:410)
5. ENGLE, T. L., AND HAMLETT, IONA C. "Constancy of the I.Q. With Mentally Deficient Patients as Measured by the Time Appreciation Test." *Am J Mental Def* 56:775–6 Ap '52. * (*PA* 26:7081)
6. HAMMER, EMANUEL F. "Comparison of the Performances of Negro Children and Adolescents on Two Tests of Intelligence, One an Emergency Scale." *J Genetic Psychol* 84:85–93 Mr '54. * (*PA* 28:8659)
7. JOHNSON, EDWARD E. "Time Concepts as Related to Sex, Intelligence and Academic Performance." *J Ed Res* 57:377–9 Mr '64. *

CUMULATIVE NAME INDEX

Biegel, M. M.: 3   Hamlett, I. C.: 4–5
Bradford, E. J. G.: *rev*, 3:266   Hammer, E. F.: 6
Buck, J.: 1   Johnson, E. E.: 7
Cofer, C. N.: 3; *rev*, 3:266   Landisberg, S.: 2
Engle, T. L.: 4–5

[589]

Torrance Tests of Creative Thinking, Research Edition. Kgn through graduate school; 1966; TTCT; revision of *Minnesota Tests of Creative Thinking;* 2 tests; E. Paul Torrance; Personnel Press. *
a) VERBAL TEST. Test booklet title is *Thinking Creatively With Words;* 3 scores: fluency, flexibility, originality.

Subsumed Abilities Test

b) FIGURAL TEST. Test booklet title is *Thinking Creatively With Pictures;* 4 scores: fluency, flexibility, originality, elaboration.

For additional information, reviews by Leonard L. Baird and Robert L. Thorndike, and excerpted reviews by Ralph Hoepfner, John L. Holland, and Michael A. Wallach, see 7:448 (243 references).

REFERENCES THROUGH 1971

1-243. See 7:448.
244. FLEMING, ELYSE S., AND WEINTRAUB, SAMUEL. "Attitudinal Rigidity as a Measure of Creativity in Gifted Children." *J Ed Psychol* 53:81-5 Ap '62. * (*PA* 37:1918)
245. TORRANCE, E. PAUL. "Cultural Discontinuities and the Development of Originality of Thinking." *Excep Children* 29:2-13 S '62. * (*PA* 37:6707)
246. YAMAMOTO, KAORU. "Creativity and Sociometric Choice Among Adolescents." *J Social Psychol* 64:249-61 D '64. * (*PA* 39:7828)
247. CREEKMORE, FLORINE. *A Study of the Creative Thinking Abilities of Teachers and the Tested Creativity of Their Pupils.* Master's thesis, Central Washington College of Education (Ellensburg, Wash.), 1965.
248. HAVEN, GEORGE A., JR. "Creative Thought, Productivity, and the Self-Concept." *Psychol Rep* 16:750-2 Je '65. * (*PA* 39:15291)
249. LONG, BARBARA H., AND HENDERSON, EDMUND H. "Originality, Reading, and Arithmetic." *Percept & Motor Skills* 21:553-4 O '65. * (*PA* 40:2871)
250. MACKLER, BERNARD, AND SHONTZ, FRANKLIN C. "Life Style and Creativity: An Empirical Investigation." *Percept & Motor Skills* 20:873-96 Je '65. * (*PA* 39:15302)
251. TORRANCE, E. PAUL. *Rewarding Creative Behavior: Experiments in Classroom Activity.* Englewood Cliffs, N.J.: Prentice-Hall, Inc., 1965. Pp. xiii, 353. *
252. WODTKE, KENNETH H., AND WALLEN, NORMAN E. "The Effects of Teacher Control in the Classroom on Pupils' Creativity-Test Gains." *Am Ed Res J* 2:75-82 Mr '65. *
253. YAMAMOTO, KAORU. "A Note on Fifth-Grade Children's Vocational World and Creative Thinking." *Gifted Child Q* 9:187-91 w '65. * (*PA* 40:5254)
254. SMITH, ROBERT M., AND NEISWORTH, JOHN T. "Creative Thinking Abilities of Intellectually Superior Children in the Regular Grades." *Psychol Rep* 18:335-41 Ap '66. * (*PA* 40:8832)
255. CICIRELLI, VICTOR G. "Sibling Constellation, Creativity, IQ, and Academic Achievement." *Child Develop* 38:481-90 Je '67. * (*PA* 41:10210)
256. MCWHINNIE, HAROLD J. "Some Relationships Between Creativity and Perception in Sixth-Grade Children." *Percept & Motor Skills* 25:979-80 D '67. * (*PA* 42:8733)
257. PANEY, HENRY, AND HORROCKS, CAROL. "Creativity in a Troop of Low Average Intelligent Boy Scouts." *Adolescence* 2:231-41 su '67. * (*PA* 42:3962)
258. YAMAMOTO, KAORU. "Creativity and Unpredictability in School Achievement." *J Ed Res* 60:321-5 Mr '67. *
259. BUDOFF, MILTON; MESKIN, JOAN D.; AND KEMLER, DEBORAH. "Training Productive Thinking of EMRs: A Failure to Replicate." *Am J Mental Def* 73:195-9 S '68. * (*PA* 43:4371)
260. BURNHAM, RUTH ELIZABETH. *The Relationship Between the Intelligence Quotient and the Creative Ability of Second Grade Children in the Villa Park School System.* Master's thesis, Northern Illinois University (DeKalb, Ill.), 1968.
261. HADDON, F. A., AND LYTTON, HUGH. "Teaching Approach and the Development of Divergent Thinking Abilities in Primary Schools." *Brit J Ed Psychol* 38:171-80 Je '68. * (*PA* 42:17790)
262. PUGH, RICHARD C. "Tests for Creative Thinking—Potential for School Testing Programs." *B Sch Ed Ind Univ* 44(6):1-30 N '68. * (*PA* 46:5483)
263. COFFEY, FRANK HOLMES. *The Relationship of Intelligence to Creativity.* Master's thesis, Wisconsin State University (Oshkosh, Wis.), 1969.
264. KOONS, NANCY. *The Relationship Between E. Paul Torrance's Tests for Creativity in Art and Performance in Art Class.* Master's thesis, Millersville State College (Millersville, Pa.), 1969.
265. SHACKEL, D. S. J., AND LAWRENCE, P. J. "Improving Creativity Through Programmed Instruction." *N Zeal J Ed Studies* 4(1):41-56 My '69. *
266. TORRANCE, E. PAUL. "New Types of Items for Measuring the Creative Thinking Abilities," pp. 239-309. In *Developments in Educational Testing, Vol. I.* Edited by Karlheinz Ingenkamp. London: University of London Press Ltd., 1969. Pp. 446. *
267. ARCHAMBAULT, FRANCIS XAVIER, JR. *A Computerized Approach to Scoring Verbal Responses to the Torrance Tests of Creative Thinking.* Doctor's thesis, University of Connecticut (Storrs, Conn.), 1970. (*DAI* 31:6464A)
268. BATES, BRIAN C.; SUNDBERG, NORMAN D.; AND TYLER, LEONA E. "Divergent Problem Solving: A Comparison of Adolescents in India and America." *Int J Psychol* (France) 5(4):231-44 '70. * (*PA* 47:10696)
269. BURGESS, WILLIAM VANDER. *The Analysis of Teacher Creativity, Pupil Age, and Pupil Sex as Sources of Variation Among Elementary Pupils' Performances on Pre- and Post-Tests of Creative Thinking.* Doctor's thesis, University of California (Berkeley, Calif.), 1970. (*DAI* 32:747A)
270. JOSE, TERESITA A. "Convergent-Divergent Thinking Abilities and Risk-Taking in Children." *Philippine J Psychol* 3(1):22-35 Je '70. * (*PA* 49:11231)
271. MCDONALD, NORMA LEE HALE. *A Study of Creativity in Educable Mentally Retarded Children.* Doctor's thesis, University of Denver (Denver, Colo.), 1970. (*DAI* 31:4587A)
272. MARBURG, GALEN SANFORD. *The Relationship Between Classroom Climate and Creative Performance Among Fifth Grade Elementary School Children.* Doctor's thesis, University of Maryland (College Park, Md.), 1970. (*DAI* 31:6407A)
273. MAUL, TERRY LEE. *An Investigation of the Relationships Between Self-Actualization and Creative Thinking Processes.* Doctor's thesis, University of California (Berkeley, Calif.), 1970. (*DAI* 32:793A)
274. OVERSTREET, GEORGE CLARK. *A Study of Teacher Characteristics in Changing and Stable Schools.* Doctor's thesis, University of Kentucky (Lexington, Ky.), 1970. (*DAI* 32:796A)
275. RANZAU, MARIE-LOUISE. *Correlates of Creativity in Nursing Education.* Doctor's thesis, University of Texas (Austin, Tex.), 1970. (*DAI* 31:6715B)
276. SHIVELY, JOE E. *Evaluation of the Effects of Creativity Training Programs in the Elementary School.* Doctor's thesis, Purdue University (Lafayette, Ind.), 1970. (*DAI* 31:5215A)
277. SILVERBERG, ROBERT ALLAN. *The Relationship of Children's Perceptions of Parental Behavior to the Creativity of Their Children.* Doctor's thesis, New York University (New York, N.Y.), 1970. (*DAI* 31:6413A)
278. STEVENS, HOWARD LAMAR. *A Study of Creative and Causal Thinking Skills and Student-Faculty Perceptions in a Mexican Institution.* Doctor's thesis, University of Georgia (Athens, Ga.), 1970. (*DAI* 31:6416A)
279. WALTON, JOSEPH MOSES. *Predicting the Success of Prospective Teachers in an Urban Teacher Education Project.* Doctor's thesis, Ohio State University (Columbus, Ohio), 1970. (*DAI* 32:190A)
280. WARREN, THOMAS FRANKLIN. *Creative Thinking Techniques: Four Methods of Stimulating Original Ideas in Sixth Grade Students.* Doctor's thesis, University of Wisconsin (Madison, Wis.), 1970. (*DAI* 31:5863A)
281. WEISER, JOHN C. "Personality Variables Associated With Creativity in Prospective Female Teachers." *J Stud Pers Assn Teach Ed* 8(3):77-84 sp '70. * (*PA* 44:18682)
282. WONZER, ANN CUSHMAN. *A Study of the Relationships Among Creativity, Intelligence, and Achievement Measures Based on Longitudinal Data.* Doctor's thesis, University of Michigan (Ann Arbor, Mich.), 1970. (*DAI* 32:1205A)
283. ALSTON, DOROTHY JEAN. *A Comparison of Motor Creativity With Verbal Creativity and Figural Creativity of Black Culturally Deprived Children.* Doctor's thesis, University of North Carolina (Greensboro, N.C.), 1971. (*DAI* 32:2458A)
284. BELLAMY, EDWARD ELLSWORTH. *A Study of Productive Thinking in Mentally Retarded Children.* Doctor's thesis, University of Illinois (Urbana, Ill.), 1971. (*DAI* 32:4411A)
285. BERRETTA, SHIRLEY. *Comparative Effects of Play on Creative Thinking: The Immediate Influence of Art, Drama, and Playground Experiences on Children.* Doctor's thesis, University of Southern Mississippi (Hattiesburg, Miss.), 1971. (*DAI* 32:2981B)
286. BLOCKER, LARRY PAUL. *Effect of In-Service Training for Teachers on the Creative Production of Students.* Doctor's thesis, United States International University (San Diego, Calif.), 1971. (*DAI* 32:1952A)
287. CACHA, FRANCES BLACKHALL. *A Study of the Relation of Creative Thinking Abilities to Personality Factors and Peer Nominations of Fifth Grade Children.* Doctor's thesis, New York University (New York, N.Y.), 1971. (*DAI* 32:1329A)
288. CULLINA, JAMES JOSEPH. *The Effects of Ambiguous Visual Stimuli in Art Instruction on Divergent Thinking Abilities.* Doctor's thesis, Ball State University (Muncie, Ind.), 1971. (*DAI* 32:3085A)
289. DACEY, JOHN S., AND MADAUS, GEORGE F. "An Analysis of Two Hypotheses Concerning the Relationship Between Creativity and Intelligence." *J Ed Res* 64(5):213-6 Ja '71. * (*PA* 46:4712)
290. DAFFRON, MARTHA RUTH. *The Influence of Selective Factors on the Divergent Thinking Abilities of Fourth Grade School Children.* Doctor's thesis, Mississippi State University (State College, Miss.), 1971. (*DAI* 32:3780A)
291. DAVIS, GARY A., AND BELCHER, TERENCE L. "How Shall Creativity Be Measured? Torrance Tests, RAT, Alpha Biographical, and I.Q." *J Creative Behav* 5(3):153-61 '71. *
292. DILCHER, RONALD CLARENCE. *Relationships Among Independent Study, Divergent Thinking, Convergent Thinking, Attitudes and Achievement in General College Biology.* Doctor's thesis, State University of New York (Buffalo, N.Y.), 1971. (*DAI* 31:1743A)
293. DILL, JOHN RICHARD. *A Study of the Influence of Race of the Experimenter and Verbal Reinforcement on Creativity*

Torrance Tests of Creative Thinking

Test Performance of Lower Socioeconomic Status Black Children. Doctor's thesis, New York University (New York, N.Y.), 1971. (*DAI* 32:6071B)

294. EMRICK, CAROL SHAW. *Language Performance of Stuttering and Nonstuttering Children.* Doctor's thesis, University of Iowa (Iowa City, Iowa), 1971. (*DAI* 32:5509B)

295. FELDHUSEN, JOHN F.; TREFFINGER, DONALD J.; VAN MONDFRANS, ADRIAN P.; AND FERRIS, DONALD R. "The Relationship Between Academic Grades and Divergent Thinking Scores Derived From Four Different Methods of Testing." *J Exp Ed* 40(1):35–40 f '71. * (*PA* 47:9798)

296. FERENCE, CAMILLE. *Prediction of Creativity by Means of Interest Measures.* Doctor's thesis, Ohio State University (Columbus, Ohio), 1971. (*DAI* 32:3685A)

297. GREENE, JOHN FRANCIS. *Scoring Creativity Tests by Computer Simulation.* Doctor's thesis, University of Connecticut (Storrs, Conn.), 1971. (*DAI* 32:237A)

298. JOESTING, JOAN, AND JOESTING, ROBERT. "The Picture Interpretation Test and Its Relationship to the Stanford-Binet." *Psychol Rep* 29(3):1146 D '71. * (*PA* 48:1649)

299. KALTSOUNIS, BILL. "Differences in Creative Thinking of Black and White Deaf Children." *Percept & Motor Skills* 32(1):243–8 F '71. * (*PA* 46:3745)

300. KALTSOUNIS, BILL, AND STEPHENS, HOWARD G. "Learning Mathematics by Discovery: Implications for a Creative Child." *Percept & Motor Skills* 33(3):884–6 D '71. * (*PA* 48:1929)

301. KANITZ, HUGO EDWARD. *Predicting Effectiveness in Potential Teachers.* Doctor's thesis, Ohio State University (Columbus, Ohio), 1971. (*DAI* 32:1855A)

302. KEEN, CHARLES FLOYD. *A Study of Relationships Between Growth and Developmental Variables, Creativity, and Musicality.* Doctor's thesis, University of Michigan (Ann Arbor, Mich.), 1971. (*DAI* 32:3791A)

303. KELLENBERGER, LONNIE ROBERT. *Student Question-Asking Behavior in Grade Six Social Studies.* Doctor's thesis, University of Oregon (Eugene, Ore.), 1971. (*DAI* 32:4881A)

304. KHATENA, JOE. "Teaching Disadvantaged Preschool Children to Think Creatively With Pictures." *J Ed Psychol* 62(5):384–6 O '71. * (*PA* 47:5851)

305. LADNER, JUDITH LEE. *Enhancement of Productive Thinking in Institutionalized Mental Retardates.* Doctor's thesis, Fordham University (New York, N.Y.), 1971. (*DAI* 32:2401B)

306. LANDRY, RICHARD G. "The Factorial Orthogonality of the Torrance Tests of Creative Thinking and the Culture-Fair Intelligence Test." *Col Ed Rec Univ N Dak* 57(2):20–6 N '71. *

307. LANGGULUNG, HASAN. *A Cross-Cultural Study of the Child's Conception of Situational Causality in India, Western Samoa, Mexico, and the United States.* Doctor's thesis, University of Georgia (Athens, Ga.), 1971. (*DAI* 32:5040A)

308. LOW, HELEN E. *Identification of Gifted Mexican-American Children by Using the Torrance Tests of Creative Thinking.* Master's thesis, California State College (Long Beach, Calif.), 1971.

309. MAR'I, SAMI KHALIL. *Creativity of American and Arab Rural Youth: A Cross-Cultural Study.* Doctor's thesis, University of Wisconsin (Madison, Wis.), 1971. (*DAI* 31:6407A)

310. MEERBACH, JOHN CALVIN. *A Study of the Relationship of Creativity, Vocational Maturity and Vocational Choice Among Eighth Grade Students.* Doctor's thesis, University of Toledo (Toledo, Ohio), 1971. (*DAI* 32:3695A)

311. MITCHELL, BRUCE. "The Classroom Pursuit of Creativity: One Strategy That Worked." *J Res & Develop Ed* 4(3):57–61 sp '71. *

312. MOSIER, JACK ARTHUR. *A Study of Parent Occupational Expectations for Gifted and Average Children Compared With the Child's Occupational Goals and Creativity.* Doctor's thesis, Brigham Young University (Provo, Utah), 1971. (*DAI* 32:4297A)

313. OGLETREE, EARL. "A Cross-Cultural Examination of the Creative Thinking Ability of Public and Private School Pupils in England, Scotland, and Germany." *J Social Psychol* 83(2):301–2 Ap '71. * (*PA* 46:2836)

314. OGLETREE, EARL J. "Are Creativity Tests Valid in Cultures Outside the United States?" *J Res & Develop Ed* 4(3):129–30 sp '71. *

315. PHILLIPS, VICTOR K., AND TORRANCE, E. PAUL. "Divergent Thinking, Remote Associations, and Concept Attainment Strategies." *J Psychol* 77(2):223–8 Mr '71. * (*PA* 46:361)

316. RAMIREZ, JUDITH VALLA. "Effects of Tutorial Experiences on the Problem-Solving Behavior of Sixth-Graders." *Calif J Ed Res* 22(2):80–90 Mr '71. *

317. RENZULLI, JOSEPH S.; HARTMAN, ROBERT K.; AND CALLAHAN, CAROLYN M. "Teacher Identification of Superior Students." *Excep Children* 38(3):211–4+ N '71. * (*PA* 49:7941)

318. RICHARDS, P. N., AND BOLTON, N. "Type of Mathematics Teaching, Mathematical Ability and Divergent Thinking in Junior School Children." *Brit J Ed Psychol* 41(1):32–7 F '71. * (*PA* 46:9822)

319. RICHMOND, BERT O. "Creative and Cognitive Abilities of White and Negro Children." *J Negro Ed* 40(2):111–6 sp '71. * (*PA* 47:7566)

320. SPEEDIE, STUART M.; ASHER, J. WILLIAM; AND TREFFINGER, DONALD J. "Comment on 'Fluency as a Pervasive Element in the Measurement of Creativity.'" *J Ed Meas* 8(2):125–6 su '71. * (*PA* 46:10883)

321. STRUM, IRENE S. *The Relationship of Creativity and Academic Risk-Taking Among Fifth Graders.* Doctor's thesis, Fordham University (New York, N.Y.), 1971. (*DAI* 32:801A)

322. STUDER, MARILYN RITA. *The Relationship of Discovery Methods in Mathematics to Creative Thinking and Attitudes Toward Mathematics.* Doctor's thesis, Ohio State University (Columbus, Ohio), 1971. (*DAI* 32:3816A)

323. THORSEN, ERIC EDWARD. *The Heritability of "G" and Figural Divergent Thinking.* Doctor's thesis, Boston College (Chestnut Hill, Mass.), 1971. (*DAI* 32:1351A)

324. TORRANCE, E. PAUL. "Are the Torrance Tests of Creative Thinking Biased Against, or in Favor of 'Disadvantaged' Groups?" *Gifted Child Q* 15(2):75–80 su '71. * (*PA* 47:8656)

325. TORRANCE, E. PAUL. "Is Bias Against Job Changing Bias Against Giftedness?" *Gifted Child Q* 15(4):244–8 w '71. * (*PA* 48:5010)

326. TORRANCE, E. PAUL. "Stimulation, Enjoyment, and Originality in Dyadic Creativity." *J Ed Psychol* 62(1):45–8 F '71. * (*PA* 46:3079)

327. TURKNETT, ROBERT LAVALE. *A Study of the Differential Effects of Individual Versus Group Reward Conditions on the Creative Productions of Elementary School Children.* Doctor's thesis, University of Georgia (Athens, Ga.), 1971. (*DAI* 32:5625A)

328. TURNER, THOMAS NOEL. *A Correlational Study of Creative Verbal Behavior and Perception in the Elementary School.* Doctor's thesis, Pennsylvania State University (University Park, Pa.), 1971. (*DAI* 33:89A)

329. VAN MONDFRANS, ADRIAN P.; FELDHUSEN, JOHN F.; TREFFINGER, DONALD J.; AND FERRIS, DONALD R. "The Effects of Instructions and Response Time on Divergent Thinking Test Scores." *Psychol Sch* 8(1):64–71 Ja '71. * (*PA* 46:7464)

330. VAUGHAN, MARGERY, AND MYERS, R. E. "Examination of Musical Process as Related to Creative Thinking." *J Res Music Ed* 19(3):337–41 f '71. * (*PA* 48:5879)

331. WILLIAMS, ROBERT L. "Relationship of Class Participation to Personality, Ability, and Achievement Variables." *J Social Psychol* 83(2):193–8 Ap '71. * (*PA* 46:3721)

CUMULATIVE NAME INDEX

Aliotti, N. C.: 165, 204, 240
Allen, A.: 172
Alston, D. J.: 283
Amram, F. M.: 125
Anderson, R. E.: 7
Arasteh, J. D.: 126
Archambault, F. X.: 267
Asher, J. W.: 320
Bachtold, L. M.: 208
Bader, L. J.: 209
Bahlke, S. J. M.: 166
Bailey, J. T.: 210
Baird, L. L.: rev, 7:448
Barabasz, A. F.: 167
Barrish, B.: 211
Bates, B. C.: 268
Bates, O. E.: 243
Beck, E. J.: 17
Belcher, T. L.: 291
Beleff, N.: 127
Bellamy, E. E.: 284
Bellin, A. P.: 86
Benton, J. E.: 87
Beretta, S.: 285
Bilon, L. R.: 88
Bish, G. G.: 18
Blocker, L. P.: 286
Blockhus, W. A.: 8
Boersma, F. J.: 128
Bolton, N.: 318
Bolton, S. L.: 168
Bowers, J.: 169
Bradfield, R. H.: 129
Brewton, B. C.: 130
Broome, L. W.: 89
Bruininks, R. H.: 212
Budoff, M.: 259
Burgess, M. V.: 269
Burke, B. P.: 131
Burnham, R. E.: 260
Burstiner, I.: 213
Cacha, F. B.: 287
Callahan, C. M.: 317
Calvert, J. F.: 132
Carey, J. E.: 59
Cave, R. L.: 214
Cawley, J. F.: 90
Chase, D. V.: 90
Chimbidis, M. E.: 84
Cicirelli, J. S.: 215
Cicirelli, V. G.: 19, 39, 60, 170, 215, 255

Clark, P. M.: 216
Clarke, D. F.: 95
Claus, K. E.: 210
Coates, C.: 220
Coffey, F. H.: 263
Collins, D. R.: 61
Collins, M. T.: 61
Coone, J. G.: 133
Covington, N. R.: 134
Cox, O.: 171
Creekmore, F.: 247
Cullina, J. J.: 288
Cummings, S. P. N.: 91
Dacey, J.: 172
Dacey, J. S.: 289
Daffron, M. R.: 290
Dauw, D. C.: 40, 55, 62–5, 81, 92, 135
Davis, D. J.: 66, 173
Davis, G. A.: 291
Davis, O. L.: 41
Dent, P. A.: 174
Dever, W. T.: 20
Dewing, K.: 217–8
Dilcher, R. C.: 292
Dill, J. R.: 293
Duenk, L. G.: 67–8, 113
Dukes, B. M.: 21
Eastwood, G. R.: 42
Ellinger, B. D.: 22
Ellis, J. R.: 145
Elsom, B. F.: 175
Emrick, C. S.: 294
Even, R. L.: 9
Feldhusen, J. F.: 193, 242, 295, 329
Feldman, D. H.: 212
Felton, T. A.: 176
Ference, C.: 296
Ferris, D. R.: 295, 329
Fleming, E. S.: 244
Fletcher, K. R.: 93
Fortson, L. R.: 163
Frengel, B. A.: 85
Fretwell, L. N.: 13
Freyermuth, R. A.: 136
Frick, R. C.: 177
Fuqua, N. V.: 69
Gallagher, M. S.: 137
Gensemer, I. B.: 94
Gill, M. J.: 77
Glass, G. V.: 138

Goldman, R. J.: 23, 95
Gowan, J. C.: 43, 240
Greene, J. F.: 297
Grossman, M.: 219
Grossman, M. J.: 178
Grover, B. L.: 70
Guth, R. O.: 71
Haddon, F. A.: 261
Hadley, D. J.: 44
Hahn, M. S.: 96
Hamby, T. M.: 72
Hanson, D. E.: 24
Hart, A. M.: 3
Hartman, R. K.: 317
Harvey, O. J.: 220
Hatfield, R. C.: 139
Haven, G. A.: 25, 248
Henderson, E. H.: 249
Henrickson, P. R.: 2
Henson, J. P.: 97
Hicks, D.: 229
Hillery, M. C.: 179
Hine, W. W.: 98
Hoepfner, R.: *exc*, 7:448
Hoffmeister, J. K.: 220
Holland, J. L.: *exc*, 7:448
Holman, E. R.: 140
Horrocks, C.: 147, 257
Huguelet, P. W.: 73
Hurley, J. D.: 221
Ingmire, B. D.: 141
Irons, J. L.: 99
Irvine, F. R.: 142
Jennings, B. L.: 100
Joesting, J.: 298
Joesting, R.: 298
Johnson, C. M.: 143
Johnson, J. O.: 101, 180
Johnson, R. T.: 10
Jones, J. C.: 222
Jose, T. A.: 270
Juffer, V. M.: 181
Kaltsounis, B.: 182-3, 223-5, 299-300
Kanitz, H. E.: 301
Karioth, E. J.: 102
Karioth, J.: 226
Keen, C. F.: 302
Keenan, J. F.: 227
Kellenberger, L. R.: 303
Kelly, G. R.: 45
Kelson, F.: 46
Kemler, D.: 259
Kernaleguen, A. P.: 144
Ketcherside, W. J.: 11
Khatena, J.: 304
Kirsh, J. L.: 47
Kobayashi, M. J.: 184
Koons, N.: 264
Kuo, Y. Y.: 103-4
Ladner, J. L.: 305
Landry, R. G.: 228, 306
Langgulung, H.: 307
Lanier, P. E.: 105
Lawrence, P. J.: 265
Laynor, H. A.: 74
Leton, D. A.: 61
Lewis, R. B.: 13
Lichtman, M. V.: 185
Lindsey, J. F.: 229
Long, B. H.: 249
Low, H. E.: 308
Lucht, W. E.: 12
Lytton, H.: 261
McCormack, A. J.: 186
McCutcheon, N. S.: 187
McDaniel, S. W.: 106
McDonald, F. J.: 210
McDonald, N. L. H.: 271
MacDougall, M. J.: 75
McElvain, J. L.: 13
Mackler, B.: 107, 250
McWhinnie, H. J.: 188, 230, 256
Madaus, G.: 172
Madaus, G. F.: 108-9, 289
Many, W. A.: 145
Marburg, G. S.: 272
Mar'i, S. K.: 309
Martin, F.: 231
Maul, T. C.: 273
Mayhon, W. G.: 76
Mearig, J. S.: 26
Meerbach, J. C.: 310
Merryman, E. P.: 110

Meskin, J. D.: 259
Middents, G. J.: 111
Middleton, F. T.: 189
Mirels, H. L.: 216
Mitchell, B.: 311
Mitchell, B. M.: 112
Mosier, J. A.: 312
Moss, J.: 113
Myers, R. E.: 330
Neal, J. A.: 114
Neisworth, J. T.: 254
Nuttall, E. V.: 190
O'Bryan, K.: 128
Ogletree, E.: 313
Ogletree, E. J.: 314
Olson, D. R.: 77
Orlandi, L. R.: 191
O'Rourke, R. H.: 146
Osipow, S. H.: 234
Osman, M. H.: 115
Overstreet, G. C.: 274
Owens, R. E.: 27
Palermo, R. R.: 48
Paney, H.: 257
Pang, H.: 147
Paton, C. L.: 49
Paulus, D. H.: 148, 232
Perry, J. M.: 78
Pesci, M. L.: 233
Phatak, P.: 4
Philipp, J. A.: 116, 192
Phillips, V. K.: 315
Plogman, B. E.: 117
Pogue, B. C.: 28
Pollert, L. H.: 193
Pope, A. L.: 118
Porter, R. C.: 194
Pugh, R. C.: 262
Ragouzis, P. N.: 29
Raia, J. R.: 234
Raina, M. K.: 149, 195, 235-7
Rambo, F. L.: 30
Ramirez, M. V.: 316
Ranzau, M. L.: 275
Rappel, D.: 238
Ray, P. B.: 5
Reardon, B.: 77
Renzulli, J. S.: 148, 317
Richards, P. N.: 318
Richmond, B. O.: 319
Ripple, R. E.: 241
Rittmayer, J. F.: 150
Roderick, J. A.: 119, 151
Roderick, J. L.: 50
Rogers, D. W.: 120
Roughton, E. L.: 14
Rouse, S. T.: 15, 51
Rumley, E.: 77
Schmidt, R. H.: 152
Scott, L. E.: 52
Shackel, D. S. J.: 265
Shapiro, R. J.: 153
Sheldon, E.: 154
Sheldon, M. J. R.: 53
Sherwood, D. W.: 196
Shigaki, I. S.: 197
Shively, J. E.: 276
Shontz, F. C.: 107, 250
Silverberg, R. A.: 277
Smith, D. L.: 79
Smith, G. P.: 198
Smith, R. H.: 31
Smith, R. M.: 254
Soliman, A. M.: 121
Solomon, A. O.: 155
Speedie, S. M.: 320
Springer, T. A.: 199
Stafford, R. L.: 80
Steinmetz, C. S.: 156
Stephens, H. G.: 300
Stevens, H. L.: 278
Stevens, J. C.: 200
Stimeling, W. F.: 201
Strum, I. S.: 321
Stubbings, J. R.: 122
Studer, M. R.: 322
Sundberg, N. D.: 268
Thomas, S. B.: 242
Thompson, R. A.: 157
Thorndike, R. L.: *rev*, 7:448
Thorsen, E. E.: 323
Tibbetts, J. W.: 158
Torrance, E. P.: 1-2, 6, 43,

54-5, 81, 123, 159-63, 202-4, 239-40, 245, 251, 266, 315, 324-6
Treffinger, D. J.: 193, 241-2, 295, 320, 329
True, S.: 82
True, S. R.: 32
Tryk, H. E.: 164
Tucker, C. A.: 56
Turknett, R. L.: 327
Turner, T. N.: 328
Tyler, L. E.: 268
Van Mondfrans, A. P.: 193, 295, 329
Van Pelt, B. N.: 57
Vaughan, M.: 330
Walker, P. C.: 205
Wallace, H. R.: 33
Wallach, M. A.: *exc*, 7:448

Wallen, N. E.: 252
Walton, J. M.: 279
Warren, T. F.: 280
Weber, W. A.: 124
Weintraub, S.: 244
Weiser, J. C.: 281
Weltner, W. H.: 206
Werner, E. E.: 208
White, B. J.: 220
Williams, F. E.: 125
Williams, R. L.: 331
Wirth, J. W.: 83
Wodtke, K. H.: 16, 34, 252
Wonzer, A. C.: 282
Wood, R. H.: 207
Wu, J. J.: 240
Yamamoto, K.: 35-7, 41, 58, 84-5, 246, 253, 258
Yee, G. F.: 38

[590]

Two-Figure Formboard. Ages 4 and over; [1917]; modification appears in *Arthur Point Scale of Performance Tests*; R. Pintner; Stoelting Co.

[591]

*Utility Test. Grades 9-12; 1962-69; for research use only; 2 scores: divergent production of semantic units, divergent production of semantic classes; 1969 test identical with test copyrighted 1962 (see 561x1) except for administration instructions; Robert C. Wilson, Philip R. Merrifield, and J. P. Guilford; Sheridan Psychological Services, Inc. *

For additional information, see 6:551x1.

REFERENCES THROUGH 1971

1. GUILFORD, J. P., AND HOEPFNER, RALPH. "Sixteen Divergent-Production Abilities at the Ninth-Grade Level." *Multiv Behav Res* 1:43-66 Ja '66. * (PA 41:1602)
2. BRAUND, ROBERT A. "Pilot Study of a Cognitive Restructuring Paradigm." *Psychol Rep* 20:275-9 F '67. * (PA 41:7919)
3. GRAY, JAMES JOSEPH. *An Investigation of the Relationship Between Primary Process Thinking and Creativity.* Doctor's thesis, Fordham University (New York, N.Y.), 1967. (DA 28:5206B)
4. KARSTEN, MARY O'KEEFFE. *The Relationship of Tested Creative Abilities and Selected Factors of Academic Achievement, Intelligence, Sex, Socioeconomic Status, and Pupil Attitudes.* Doctor's thesis, University of Southern California (Los Angeles, Calif.), 1967. (DA 28:2557A)
5. MANGAN, GORDON L. "Studies of the Relationship Between Neo-Pavlovian Properties of Higher Nervous Activity and Western Personality Dimensions: 3, The Relations of Transformation Mobility to Thinking Flexibility." *J Exp Res Personality* 2:117-23 My '67. * (PA 41:11907)
6. PLOGMAN, BERNARD EDWARD. *The Creative Relationship Between Art Teachers and Their Ninth Grade Art Students in Art Room Practices, Personality and Pencil Drawing in Catholic Schools.* Doctor's thesis, University of Cincinnati (Cincinnati, Ohio), 1967. (DA 28:3534A)
7. ALZOBAIE, ABDUL JALIL; METFESSEL, NEWTON S.; AND MICHAEL, WILLIAM B. "Alternative Approaches to Assessing the Intellectual Abilities of Youth From a Culture of Poverty." *Ed & Psychol Meas* 28:449-55 su '68. * (PA 42:19264)
8. ANDERSON, RONALD JUDE. *Divergent Thinking Within Superior, Average, and Retarded Subjects.* Doctor's thesis, University of Nebraska (Lincoln, Neb.), 1968. (DA 29:1126A)
9. BROWN, STEPHEN W.; GUILFORD, J. P.; AND HOEPFNER, RALPH. "Six Semantic-Memory Abilities." *Ed & Psychol Meas* 28:691-717 au '68. * (PA 43:4427)
10. ANDERSON, HARRY E., JR.; WHITE, WILLIAM F.; AND STEVENS, JOHN C. "Student Creativity, Intelligence, Achievement, and Teacher Classroom Behavior." *J Social Psychol* 78(1):99-107 Je '69. * (PA 43:16427)
11. GRAY, JAMES J. "The Effect of Productivity on Primary Process and Creativity." *J Proj Tech & Pers Assess* 33(3): 213-8 Je '69. * (PA 43:14302)
12. KANDERIAN, SUAD SIROP. *Study of the Relationship Between School Achievement and Measures of Intelligence and Creativity for Students in Iraq.* Doctor's thesis, University of Southern California (Los Angeles, Calif.), 1969. (DAI 31:644A)
13. RYBACK, RALPH S.; LEWIS, OLIVER F.; AND LESSARD, CHARLES S. "Psychobiologic Effects of Prolonged Bed Rest (Weightless) in Young Healthy Volunteers (Study II)." *Aerospace Med* 42(5):529-35 My '71. *
14. WILLIAMS, JOHN D.; HARLOW, STEVEN D.; AND BORGEN, JEROME S. "Creativity, Dogmatism, and Arithmetic Achievement." *J Psychol* 78(2):217-22 Jl '71. * (PA 46:9760)

CUMULATIVE NAME INDEX

Alzobaie, A. J.: 7
Anderson, H. E.: 10
Anderson, R. J.: 8
Borgen, J. S.: 14
Braund, R. A.: 2
Brown, S. W.: 9
Gray, J. J.: 3, 11
Guilford, J. P.: 1, 9
Harlow, S. D.: 14
Hoepfner, R.: 1, 9
Kanderian, S. S.: 12
Karsten, M. O.: 4
Lessard, C. S.: 13
Lewis, O. F.: 13
Mangan, G. L.: 5
Metfessel, N. S.: 7
Michael, W. B.: 7
Plogman, B. E.: 6
Ryback, R. S.: 13
Stevens, J. C.: 10
White, W. F.: 10
Williams, J. D.: 14

[592]

Wechsler Memory Scale. Adults; 1945–63; 1962–63 tests are slight revisions of tests copyrighted 1945 and 1948; David Wechsler and Calvin P. Stone (Form 2); Psychological Corporation. *

For additional information, see 6:561 (9 references); for reviews by Ivan Norman Mensh and Joseph Newman, see 4:364 (6 references); for a review by Kate Levine Kogan, see 3:302 (3 references).

REFERENCES THROUGH 1971

1–3. See 3:302.
4–9. See 4:364.
10–18. See 6:561.
19. BERAN, MARIANNE; PERKINS, JOHN C.; AND SCOLLON, ROBERT W. "Psychological Studies on Patients Undergoing Nonconvulsive Electric-Stimulation Treatment." *Am J Psychiatry* 109:367–74 N '52. * (*PA* 27:5168)
20. CALDWELL, BETTYE MCDONALD, AND WATSON, ROBERT I. "An Evaluation of Psychologic Effects of Sex Hormone Administration in Aged Women: 1, Results of Therapy After Six Months." *J Gerontol* 7:228–44 Ap '52. * (*PA* 27:1874)
21. MENSH, IVAN N.; SCHWARTZ, HENRY G.; MATARAZZO, RUTH G.; AND MATARAZZO, JOSEPH D. "Psychological Functioning Following Cerebral Hemispherectomy in Man." *Arch Neurol & Psychiatry* 67:787–96 Je '52. * (*PA* 27:2167)
22. STRUCKTEL, PAULINE B. A. "Effect of Prefrontal Lobotomy on Intellectual Functioning in Chronic Schizophrenia." *Arch Neurol & Psychiatry* 69:293–304 Mr '53. * (*PA* 28:1346)
23. CALDWELL, BETTYE MCDONALD, AND WATSON, ROBERT I. "An Evaluation of Sex Hormone Replacement in Aged Women." *J Genetic Psychol* 85:181–200 D '54. * (*PA* 29:7046)
24. STANDLEE, LLOYD S. "Validity of Archimedes Spiral in Discriminating Memory Ability of Psychotics and of Normals." *Arch Neurol & Psychiatry* 71:648–50 My '54. * (*PA* 29:2839)
25. UECKER, ALBERT E.; FRENCH, LYLE A.; AND JOHNSON, DAVID R. "Psychological Studies of Seven Epileptic Heminarectics Before and After Hemispherectomy." *Arch Neurol & Psychiatry* 72:555–64 N '54. * (*PA* 29:6114)
26. MEYER, VICTOR, AND YATES, AUBREY J. "Intellectual Changes Following Temporal Lobectomy for Psychomotor Epilepsy: Preliminary Communication." *J Neurol Neurosurg & Psychiatry* (England) 18:44–52 F '55. * (*PA* 29:7775)
27. QUADFASEL, ANGELA FOLSOM, AND PRUYSER, PAUL W. "Cognitive Deficit in Patients With Psychomotor Epilepsy." *Epilepsia* (United States) 4:80–90 N '55. * (*PA* 30:8437)
28. SEYMOUR, JOHN H. *Some Changes in Psychometric, Perceptual and Motor Performance as a Function of Sleep Deprivation.* Doctor's thesis, New York University (New York, N.Y.), 1956. (*DA* 16:2216)
29. STONESIFER, FRED A. *Intellectual and Perceptual Performance of Defective Idiopathic Epileptics and Familial Mental Defectives.* Doctor's thesis, Pennsylvania State University (University Park, Pa.), 1956. (*DA* 17:400)
30. STENBACK, ASSER; VIITAMÄKI, R. OLAVI; AND KUKKONEN, SIMO. "Personality Changes in Electroconvulsive Treatment. A Study of the Effect of Three Successive Electroconvulsive Treatments With Special Reference to Spacing of Treatments." *Acta Psychiatrica et Neurologica Scandinavica* (Denmark) 32(3):345–59 '57. * (*PA* 33:1500)
31. DASTON, PAUL G. "Effects of Two Phenothiazine Drugs on Concentrative Attention Span of Chronic Schizophrenics." *J Clin Psychol* 15:106–9 Ja '59. * (*PA* 34:3050)
32. KRAL, V. A., AND WIGDOR, B. T. "Androgen Effect on Senescent Memory Function." *Geriatrics* 14:450–6 Jl '59. * (*PA* 34:5687)
33. SANTOS, BERTHA. *A Comparison of Memory and Learning Ability With Social Competence and Social Participation in Aged Senile Dements in a Mental Institution.* Doctor's thesis, New York University (New York, N.Y.), 1959. (*DA* 20:1441)
34. VICTOR, MAURICE; TALLAND, GEORGE A.; AND ADAMS, RAYMOND D. "Psychological Studies of Korsakoff's Psychosis: 1, General Intellectual Functions." *J Nerv & Mental Dis* 128:528–37 Je '59. * (*PA* 34:4702)
35. HUMPHRIES, CHARLES C. *Temporal Variability and Pre-Morbid Adjustment in Schizophrenia.* Doctor's thesis, University of Florida (Gainesville, Fla.), 1960. (*DA* 21:2003)

36. MIRSKY, ALLAN F.; PRIMAC, DANIEL W.; MARSAN, COSIMO AJMONE; ROSVOLD, H. ENGER; AND STEVENS, JANICE R. "A Comparison of the Psychological Test Performance of Patients With Focal and Nonfocal Epilepsy." *Exp Neurol* 2:75–89 F '60. *
37. NELSON, LOIS AUDREY. *A Study of Certain Cognitive Aspects of the Speech of Multiple Sclerotic Patients.* Doctor's thesis, University of Wisconsin (Madison, Wis.), 1960. (*DA* 21:1666)
38. ORCHINIK, C. W. "Some Psychological Aspects of Circumscribed Lesions of the Diencephalon." *Confinia Neurologica* (Switzerland) 20:292–310 '60. * (*PA* 35:2522)
39. WILLIAMS, MOYRA. "The Effect of Past Experience on Mental Test Performance in the Elderly." *Brit J Med Psychol* 33:215–9 pt 2 '60. * (*PA* 36:4FI15W)
40. BERKOWITZ, PEARL H. "Some Psychophysical Aspects of Mental Illness in Children." *Genetic Psychol Monogr* 63:103–48 F '61. * (*PA* 35:6452)
41. GUERRANT, JOHN; ANDERSON, WILLIAM W.; FISCHER, AMES; WEINSTEIN, MORTON R.; JAROS, R. MARY; AND DESKINS, ANDREW. Chap. 5, "Psychological Considerations," pp. 66–92. In their *Personality in Epilepsy.* Springfield, Ill.: Charles C Thomas, Publisher, 1962. Pp. xii, 112. *
42. PEARL, DAVID. "Phenothiazine Effects in Chronic Schizophrenia." *J Clin Psychol* 18:86–9 Ja '62. * (*PA* 38:7573)
43. ZUCKERMAN, MARVIN; ALBRIGHT, RICHARD J.; MARKS, CLIFFORD S.; AND MILLER, GERALD L. "Stress and Hallucinatory Effects of Perceptual Isolation and Confinement." *Psychol Monogr* 76(30):1–15 '62. * (*PA* 38:7226)
44. CAMERON, D. EWEN; SVED, S.; SOLYOM, L.; WAINRIB, B.; AND BARIK, H. "Effects of Ribonucleic Acid on Memory Defect in the Aged." *Am J Psychiatry* 120:320–5 O '63. * (*PA* 38:5511)
45. CARROLL, WAYNE R. "The Differentiation of Organic and Non-Organic Hospital Patients by Use of the Wechsler Memory Scale." *Newsl Res Psychol* 5:11 F '63. *
46. KRAL, V. A., AND WIGDOR, B. T. "Clinical and Psychological Observations in a Group of Well-Preserved Aged People." *Med Services J Can* 19:1–11 Ja '63. *
47. KRAL, V. A.; GRAD, B.; CRAMER-AZIMA, F.; AND RUSSELL, L. "Biologic, Psychologic, and Sociologic Studies in Normal Aged Persons and Patients With Senile Psychosis." *J Am Geriatrics Soc* 12:21–37 Ja '64. *
48. LEVITA, ERIC; RIKLAN, MANUEL; AND COOPER, IRVING S. "Cognitive and Perceptual Performance in Parkinsonism as a Function of Age and Neurological Impairment." *J Nerv & Mental Dis* 139:516–20 D '64. * (*PA* 39:10554)
49. SUEHS, JAMES ERNEST. *A Comparative Study of Brain-Damaged and Schizophrenic Subjects on Several Psychological Tests.* Doctor's thesis, University of Houston (Houston, Tex.), 1964. (*DA* 25:1347)
50. DIXON, JAMES C. "Cognitive Structure in Senile Conditions With Some Suggestions for Developing a Brief Screening Test of Mental Status." *J Gerontol* 20:41–9 Ja '65. *
51. GRAD, B.; KRAL, V. A.; AND CRAMER-AZIMA, F. "Correlations Between Salivary Sodium and Potassium Concentration and Memory Function in Elderly Persons, Normal and Psychotic." *Recent Adv Biol Psychiatry* 7:97–106 '65. *
52. KLONOFF, HARRY, AND KENNEDY, MARGARET. "Memory and Perceptual Functioning in Octogenarians and Nonagenarians in the Community." *J Gerontol* 20:328–33 Jl '65. *
53. MEER, BERNARD, AND BAKER, JANET A. "Reliability of Measurements of Intellectual Functioning of Geriatric Patients." *J Gerontol* 20:410–4 Jl '65. *
54. ZAMORA, EMIL L., AND KAELBLING, RUDOLF. "Memory and Electroconvulsive Therapy." *Am J Psychiatry* 122:546–54 N '65. * (*PA* 40:3046)
55. HOWARD, ALVIN R. "A Fifteen-Year Follow-Up With the Wechsler Memory Scale." *J Consult Psychol* 30:175–6 Ap '66. * (*PA* 40:6958)
56. HULICKA, IRENE M. "Age Differences in Wechsler Memory Scale Scores." *J Genetic Psychol* 109:135–45 S '66. * (*PA* 40:13204)
57. KLONOFF, HARRY, AND KENNEDY, MARGARET. "A Comparative Study of Cognitive Functioning in Old Age." *J Gerontol* 21:239–43 Ap '66. *
58. BAER, P.; MERRYMAN, P.; AND GAITZ, C. "Performance Deficit Related to Chronic Brain Syndrome, Schizophrenia and Age." *Gerontologist* 7(3, pt 2):37 S '67. * (*PA* 41:16721)
59. BOURESTOM, NORMAN C., AND HOWARD, MARY T. "Behavioral Correlates of Recovery of Self-Care in Hemiplegic Patients." *Arch Phys Med & Rehabil* 49:449–54 Ag '68. *
60. GILBERSTADT, HAROLD. "Relationships Among Scores of Tests Suitable for the Assessment of Adjustment and Intellectual Functioning." *J Gerontol* 23:483–7 O '68. *
61. GOLDSTEIN, NORMAN P.; EWERT, JOSEPHINE C.; RANDALL, RAYMOND V.; AND GROSS, JOHN B. "Psychiatric Aspects of Wilson's Disease (Hepatolenticular Degeneration): Results of Psychometric Tests During Long-Term Therapy." *Am J Psychiatry* 124:1555–61 My '68. * (*PA* 42:12656)
62. KAHN, EDWIN, AND FISHER, CHARLES. "Individual Differences and Amount of Rapid Eye Movement Sleep in Aged Adulthood." Abstract. *Psychophysiol* 4:393–4 Ja '68. * (*PA* 42:15311)

63. KAHN, EDWIN, AND FISHER, CHARLES. "The Relationship of REM Sleep to Various Measures in the Aged." Abstract. *Psychophysiol* 5:228–9 S '68. * *(PA* 43:14153*)*

64. KASTL, ALBERT J.; DAROFF, ROBERT B.; AND BLOCKER, W. WEBSTER. "Psychological Testing of Cerebral Malaria Patients." *J Nerv & Mental Dis* 147:553–61 D '68. * *(PA* 43:14654*)*

65. LEVY, RAYMOND. "The Clinical Evaluation of Unilateral Electroconvulsive Therapy." *Brit J Psychiatry* 114:459–63 Ap '68. * *(PA* 42:12248*)*

66. SCHAIE, K. W., AND STROTHER, C. R. "Limits of Optimal Functioning in Superior Old Adults." Discussion by Joseph H. Britton. *Interdiscipl Topics Gerontol* 1:132–53 '68. *

67. SCHAIE, K. WARNER, AND STROTHER, CHARLES R. "Cognitive and Personality Variables in College Graduates of Advanced Age," pp. 281–308. *(PA* 43:15628, title only) In *Human Aging and Behavior: Recent Advances in Research and Theory.* Edited by George A. Talland. New York: Academic Press Inc., 1968. Pp. xiii, 322. *

68. FOWLER, ROY S., JR. "A Simple Non-Language Test of New Learning." *Percept & Motor Skills* 29(3):895–901 D '69. * *(PA* 46:7301*)*

69. JACOBS, ELEANOR A.; WINTER, PETER M.; ALVIS, HARRY J.; AND SMALL, S. MOUCHLY. "Hyperoxygenation Effect on Cognitive Functioning in the Aged." Abstract. *Proc 77th Ann Conv Am Psychol Assn* 4(2):721–2 '69. * *(PA* 44:505*)*

70. JACOBS, ELEANOR A.; WINTER, PETER M.; ALVIS, HARRY J.; AND SMALL, S. MOUCHLY. "Hyperoxygenation Effect on Cognitive Functioning in the Aged." *New Engl J Med* 281(14): 753–7 O 2 '69. * *(PA* 44:7205*)*

71. KAHN, EDWIN, AND FISHER, CHARLES. "Some Correlates of Rapid Eye Movement Sleep in the Normal Aged Male." *J Nerv & Mental Dis* 148(5):495–505 My '69. * *(PA* 44:507*)*

72. RAFFEL, SHERMAN C.; SWINK, RICHARD; AND LAMPTON, T. D. "The Influence of Chlorphenesin Carbamate and Carisoprodol on Psychological Test Scores." *Curr Ther Res* 11(9):553–60 S '69. *

73. VITALE, JOHN H.; STEINHELBER, JOHN C.; DRAKE, WILLIAM E., JR.; AND DAHLGREN, HELEN. "Psychological Dimensions of Cerebrovascular Insufficiency." *Percept & Motor Skills* 29(2):555–63 O '69. * *(PA* 44:3996*)*

74. BIDDER, T. G.; STRAIN, J. J.; AND BRUNSCHWIG, L. "Bilateral and Unilateral ECT: Follow-Up Study and Critique." *Am J Psychiatry* 127(6):737–45 D '70. * *(PA* 47:5329*)*

75. CRONON, D.; BODLEY, P.; POTTS, L.; MATHER, MARCIA D.; GARDNER, R. K.; AND TOBIN, JEAN C. "Unilateral and Bilateral ECT: A Study of Memory Disturbance and Relief From Depression." *J Neurol Neurosurg & Psychiatry* (England) 33(5):705–13 O '70. * *(PA* 47:9139*)*

76. DAVIS, LEO J., JR., AND SWENSON, WENDELL M. "Factor Analysis of the Wechsler Memory Scale." Abstract. *J Consult & Clin Psychol* 35(3):430 D '70. * *(PA* 45:6577*)*

77. FLEMINGER, J. J.; DE L. HORNE, D. J.; AND NOTT, P. N. "Unilateral Electroconvulsive Therapy and Cerebral Dominance: Effect of Right- and Left-Sided Electrode Placement on Verbal Memory." *J Neurol Neurosurg & Psychiatry* (England) 33(3):408–11 Je '70. * *(PA* 47:9140*)*

78. CRARY, HELEN L., AND RIDGWAY, ROBERT W. "Relationships Between Visual Form Perception Abilities and Reading Achievement in the Intermediate Grades." *J Exp Ed* 40(1):17–22 f '71. * *(PA* 47:9796*)*

79. DUJOVNE, BEATRIZ E., AND LEVY, BERNARD I. "The Psychometric Structure of the Wechsler Memory Scale." *J Clin Psychol* 27(3):351–4 Jl '71. * *(PA* 47:5081*)*

80. FALCONER, A. D. "Measurement of Cognitive Function in Two Groups of Alcoholics." *J Alcoholism* (England) 6(4):118–23 w '71. *

81. FIELDS, FRANCIS R. J. "Relative Effects of Brain Damage on the Wechsler Memory and Intelligence Quotients." *Dis Nerv System* 32(10):673–5 O '71. * *(PA* 48:12023*)*

82. FIELDS, FRANCIS R. J. "Relative Effetcs of Brain Damage on the Wechsler Memory and Intelligence Quotients." *Newsl Res Psychol* 13(2):5–6 My '71. *

83. FLICK, GRAD L., AND EDWARDS, KENNETH R. "Prediction of Lateralized Organic Brain Dysfunction With a Neuropsychological Test Battery: A Discriminant Function Analysis." *Newsl Res Psychol* 13(2):16–7 My '71. *

84. IVINSKIS, ALGIS; ALLEN, STEPHEN; AND SHAW, ELVA. "An Extension of Wechsler Memory Scale Norms to Lower Age Groups." *J Clin Psychol* 27(3):354–7 Jl '71. * *(PA* 47:5087*)*

85. LIBB, J. WESLEY, AND COLEMAN, JOHN M. "Correlation Between the WAIS and Revised Beta, Wechsler Memory Scale and Quick Test in a Vocational Rehabilitation Center." *Psychol Rep* 29(3):863–5 D '71. * *(PA* 47:9410*)*

86. MOLISH, H. BARRY; KRAFT, IRVIN A.; AND WIGGINS, P. Y. "Psychodiagnostic Evaluation of the Heart Transplant Patient." *Seminars Psychiatry* 3(1):46–57 F '71. * *(PA* 49:7577*)*

87. SMALL, IVER F., AND SMALL, JOYCE G. "Electroencephalographic (EEG), Evoked Potential, and Direct Current (DC) Responses With Unilateral Electroconvulsive Treatment (ECT)." *J Nerv & Mental Dis* 152(6):396–404 Je '71. * *(PA* 47:11054*)*

88. SOMASUNDARAM, C. P.; KALIAPPAN, K. V.; AND POLNAYA, MEERA. "A Psychometric Study of Patients Disabled by Cerebrovascular Disease (A Preliminary Study of 54 Cases)." *Neurol India* 19(1):34–7 Mr '71. *

CUMULATIVE NAME INDEX

Adams, R. D.: 34
Albrecht, R.: 2
Albright, R. J.: 43
Allen, S.: 84
Alvis, H. J.: 69–70
Anderson, W. W.: 41
Baer, P.: 58
Baker, J. A.: 53
Barik, H.: 44
Beran, M.: 19
Berkowitz, P. H.: 40
Bidder, T. G.: 74
Blocker, W. W.: 64
Bloom, B. L.: 16
Bodley, P.: 75
Bourestom, N. C.: 59
Britton, J. H.: 66
Brunschwig, L.: 74
Caldwell, B. M.: 20, 23
Cameron, D. E.: 44
Carroll, W. R.: 45
Cohen, J.: 7
Coleman, J. M.: 85
Cooper, I. S.: 48
Cramer-Azima, F.: 47, 51
Crary, H. L.: 78
Cronon, D.: 75
Dahlgren, H.: 73
Daroff, R. B.: 64
Daston, P. G.: 31
Davis, L. J.: 76
de L. Horne, D. J.: 77
Deskins, A.: 41
Dixon, J. C.: 50
Drake, W. E.: 73
Dujovne, B. E.: 79
Edwards, K. R.: 83
Ewert, J. C.: 61
Falconer, A. D.: 80
Fanelli, G. C.: 5
Fields, F. R. J.: 81–2
Fischer, A.: 41
Fisher, C.: 62–3, 71
Fleminger, J. J.: 77
Flick, G. L.: 83
Fowler, R. S.: 68
French, L. A.: 25
Gaitz, C.: 58
Gardner, R. K.: 75
Gilberstadt, H.: 60
Girdner, J.: 2
Goldstein, N. P.: 61
Grad, B.: 47, 51
Gross, J. B.: 61
Guerrant, J.: 41
Herman, K.: 17
Horst, P.: 14
Howard, A. R.: 8, 11, 55
Howard, M. T.: 59
Hulicka, I. M.: 56
Humphries, C. C.: 35
Ivinskis, A.: 84
Jacobs, E. A.: 69–70
Jaros, R. M.: 41
Johnson, D. R.: 25
Kaelbling, R.: 54
Kahn, E.: 62–3, 71
Kaliappan, K. V.: 88
Kastl, A. J.: 64
Kennedy, M.: 52, 57
Klonoff, H.: 52, 57
Kogan, K. L.: rev, 3:302
Kraft, I. A.: 86
Kral, V. A.: 32, 46–7, 51
Kukkonen, S.: 30
Lampton, T. D.: 72
Levita, E.: 48
Levy, B. I.: 79
Levy, R.: 65
Libb, J. W.: 85
Marks, C. S.: 43
Marsan, C. A.: 36
Matarazzo, J. D.: 21
Matarazzo, R. G.: 21
Mather, M. D.: 75
Meer, B.: 53
Mensh, I. N.: 21; rev, 4:364
Merryman, P.: 58
Meyer, V.: 26
Miller, G. L.: 43
Mirsky, A. F.: 36
Molish, H. B.: 86
Nelson, L. A.: 37
Newman, J.: rev, 4:364
Nott, P. N.: 77
Orchinik, C. W.: 38
Parker, J. W.: 12
Pearl, D.: 42
Perkins, J. C.: 19
Polnaya, M.: 88
Potts, L.: 75
Primac, D. W.: 36
Pruyser, P. W.: 27
Quadfasel, A. F.: 27
Raffel, S. C.: 72
Randall, R. V.: 61
Ridgway, R. W.: 78
Riklan, M.: 48
Rosvold, H. E.: 36
Russell, L.: 47
Santos, D. J.: 33
Schaie, K. W.: 14, 66–7
Schwartz, H. G.: 21
Scollon, R. W.: 19
Seymour, J. H.: 28
Shaw, E.: 84
Shaw, J. H.: 18
Shontz, F. C.: 13
Silva, J. J.: 6
Small, I. F.: 87
Small, J. G.: 87
Small, S. M.: 69–70
Solyon, L.: 44
Somasundaram, C. P.: 88
Standlee, L. S.: 24
Stenbäck, A.: 30
Stevens, J. R.: 39
Stone, C. P.: 2–4
Stonesifer, F. A.: 29
Strain, J. J.: 74
Strother, C. R.: 14, 66–7
Struckett, P. B. A.: 22
Suehs, J. E.: 49
Sved, S.: 44
Swenson, W. M.: 76
Swink, R.: 72
Talland, G. A.: 34
Tobin, J. C.: 75
Uecker, A. E.: 25
Victor, M.: 17, 34
Viitamäki, R. O.: 30
Vitale, J. H.: 73
Wainrib, B.: 44
Walton, D.: 15
Watson, R. I.: 9, 20, 23
Wechsler, D.: 1
Weider, A.: 10
Weinstein, M. R.: 41
White, E. E.: 17
Wigdor, B. T.: 32, 46
Wiggins, P. Y.: 86
Williams, M.: 39
Winter, P. M.: 69–70
Yates, A. J.: 26
Zamora, E. L.: 54
Zuckerman, M.: 43

[593]

★**Willner Instance Similarities Test.** Adults; 1971; WIST; no manual; Allen E. Willner; Cognitive Test Center. *

REFERENCES THROUGH 1971

1. WILLNER, ALLEN E. "Crucial Flaw in Similarities Tests and a Remedy." Abstract. *Proc 76th Ann Conv Am Psychol Assn* 3:457–8 '68. * *(PA* 43:932, title only)

2. WILLNER, ALLEN E. "Abstraction, Associative Focusing, and Similarities Tests: Towards More Clinically Sensitive and Better Understood Tests." *Psychol Rep* 29(3):683–731 D '71. * (*PA* 47:8001)

CUMULATIVE NAME INDEX

Willner, A. E.: 1–2

[594]

Word Fluency. Industrial employees; 1959–61; Raymond J. Corsini and Measurement Research Division, Industrial Relations Center, University of Chicago; the Center. * [The publisher has not replied to our four requests to check the accuracy of this entry.]

For additional information and a review by James E. Kennedy, see 6:562.

REFERENCES THROUGH 1971

1. BLACKHURST, A. EDWARD; MARKS, CLAUDE H.; AND TISDALL, WILLIAM J. "Relationship Between Mobility and Divergent Thinking in Blind Children." *Ed Visually Handicapped* 1(2):33–6 My '69. * (*PA* 43:14813)

2. HEUSSENSTAMM, FRANCES K. "Creativity and Alienation: An Exploration of Their Relationship in Adolescence." *Calif J Ed Res* 21(3):140–6 My '70. *

CUMULATIVE NAME INDEX

Blackhurst, A. E.: 1
Heussenstamm, F. K.: 2
Kennedy, J. E.: *rev*, 6:562

Marks, C. H.: 1
Tisdall, W. J.: 1

[Out of Print Since TIP I]

Creative Ability Inventory, T:1138
Cube Construction Test, T:921
Fret Continuation Test, 7:438
Fret Repetition Test, 7:439
Mare and Foal Formboard, T:929
Meyer Finger Mazes, T:930
Nufferno Tests of Speed and Level, 6:555 (2 reviews, 7 references)
Stencil Design Tests I and II, 4:359 (2 reviews, 4 references)

Willner Instance Similarities Test

REPRINTED FROM *The First Mental Measurements Yearbook*

INTELLIGENCE—FIRST MMY

REVIEWS BY *Anne Anastasi, Psyche Cattell, W. D. Commins, Stuart A. Courtis, Henry Feinberg, John C. Flanagan, Louis D. Hartson, V. A. C. Henmon, Theos A. Langlie, Richard Ledgerwood, Francis N. Maxfield, Rudolf Pintner, John W. M. Rothney, David Segel, Arthur E. Traxler, Austin H. Turney, and F. L. Wells.*

GROUP

[1037]

American Council on Education Psychological Examination for College Freshmen, 1937 Edition. Grade 13; c1937; 9 earlier forms, 8 of which have the title *Psychological Examination for High School Graduates and College Freshmen;* a new form is scheduled for publication each August; published annually since 1924; 7¢ per test; 15¢ per specimen set; 2¢ per answer sheet for use with the special experimental edition scorable for the international test scoring machine; 60(65) minutes; L. L. Thurstone and T. G. Thurstone; American Council on Education.

Anne Anastasi, Columbia University. This is an intelligence test primarily designed for college freshmen, although it has also been successfully employed at the high school level in a number of private schools whose students are highly selected. New forms of the test have appeared yearly since 1924. The 1937 form consists of five tests requiring a total of 60 minutes. Essentially the same five tests have been employed for the past nine years, although the specific items differ from year to year. A machine-scoring form of the 1937 edition has also been prepared, but it is still in an experimental stage.

This test is admirably suited for large scale surveys on college populations. The relatively short time required, the ease of administration and scoring, and the very extensive norms available all increase the practical value of the test. The norms for each annual edition are regularly reported in the April issue of the *Educational Record.* The 1937 norms are based on reports submitted by 323 colleges and include the scores of 68,899 freshmen. In addition to total distributions, separate tabulations are also given for public and private institutions; coeducational, men's and women's schools; and four-year colleges, junior colleges, and teachers colleges. The test is also well adapted for use in prolonged follow-up studies, since equivalent scores for the last four annual editions are furnished in the manual.

A somewhat broader range of material is covered than is usually the case in tests of this type. The five tests include three verbal (completion, opposites, and artificial language), one numerical (arithmetic), and one spatial (analogies). The analogies and artificial language tests present fairly novel situations, whereas the other three tests involve material which has been more directly learned in the courts of specific school instruction. It should also be noted that separate percentile norms are given for each of the five tests. This makes possible a much more detailed analysis of the student's special abilities and disabilities, and is in keeping with the present trend towards the measurement of more specific and clearly defined segments of intelligence. The specific selection of tests can undoubtedly be improved in the light of recent research on mental organization in college populations, but the present examination represents a step in the right direction.

A study of the predictive value of the various tests in several colleges, using scholarship as a criterion, is reported in the *Educational Record* for April, 1927. Data on reliability and validity are also given in the 1931 manual. In view of the large body of data collected with this examination each year, it is unfortunate that the authors do not report similar analyses for the more recent forms. It would also seem desirable to include in the test manual itself, in concise form, whatever information may be available on the validity and prognostic value of the different parts of the examination, so that the test counsellor could more adequately interpret the student's performance.

David Segel, United States Office of Education. This examination is a scholastic aptitude test. It is being used extensively in liberal arts colleges, teachers colleges, and junior colleges, and to a small extent in technical schools and with high school seniors. The scores on the test are not translated into mental age scores or IQ equivalents. The examination attempts to cover the mental traits used in college work by using five different types of testing—i.e., completion, arithmetic, artificial language, analogies, and opposites. The three verbal parts of the examination—the completion, artificial language, and opposites—account for 66 per cent of the total possible points. This emphasis on the language factor is proper, since it is used mainly by colleges in which the curriculum is primarily concerned with the exercise of the language ability. However, it is highly probable that this emphasis on the language factor reduces its prognostic value for students in technical schools, engineering divisions of colleges, and for those majoring in the physical sciences, mathematics, and the accounting phases of economics.

That the subtests do actually discriminate between language and non-language factors has been shown by a study by Traxler. He correlated the language IQ's and non-language IQ's obtained on the *California Test of Mental Maturity* with the scores on the five subtests of the American Council Test. He found the following correlations in a one-grade range to be as follows:

Subtest	Language	Nonlanguage
Completion	.62	.29
Arithmetic	.39	.39
Artificial language	.55	.46
Analogies	.41	.45
Opposites	.61	.13

These results show that the subtests on completion, artificial language, and opposites are definitely related to the language IQ's on the California test. It might be well therefore, to separate the scores for the language tests and the non-language tests when using the test results for individual guidance.

This test furnishes, in general, as good a prognostication of success in college as high school grades. Where college students are drawn from a large number of high schools of varying size and efficiency the score on the test is superior in prognostic efficiency to marks received from these different schools. Apart from its intrinsic value as a predictive instrument, it is especially of value because of the norms which have been established on large numbers of students and because of the comparability of scores from year to year. The norms and comparability scores are published each year in the April number of the *Educational Record*.

[1038]

American Council on Education Psychological Examination for High School Students, 1937 Edition. Grades 9–12; c1937; 4 earlier forms, 3 of which have the title *Psychological Examination for Grade Nine to Twelve;* a new form is scheduled for publication each August; published annually since 1933; 5¢ per test; 10¢ per specimen set; quantity discounts; 60(65) minutes; L. L. Thurstone and T. G. Thurstone; American Council on Education.

V. A. C. Henmon, University of Wisconsin. This examination is modeled after the well-known and widely used *American Council Psychological Examination for High School Graduates and College Freshmen* and the content is similar except that the test items are easier and the artificial language test is omitted. The examination consists of four subtests: completion (55 items, 14 minutes), arithmetic (20 items, 20 minutes), analogies (29 items, 19 minutes), opposites (54 items, 7 minutes). The score is expressed by the median of the four percentile ranks or by the percentile rank of his gross score, the latter being indicated as preferable if a single index is desired. Frequency distributions and percentiles are given for each subtest and the gross score based on records of 84,248 pupils in grades 9–12 in 74 high schools for the 1936 examination. Since the 1937 edition is parallel in difficulty with the 1936 edition, the percentile ranks from the 1936 edition are recommended for use until the 1937 records are available. Reliability data are not given in the manual but the reliability may be expected to be high. The examination is certain to be widely used.

[1039]

Army Alpha Examination: First Nebraska Edition. High school, college, and adults; c1937; 1 form; $2.50 per 50 tests; $4.50 per 100 tests; 25¢ per specimen set; J. P. Guilford; Sheridan Supply Co.

W. D. Commins, Catholic University of America. This revision, in a single form, is based upon an item analysis of four earlier forms of the *Army Alpha*. The most diagnostic items were selected and items referring unnecessarily to military affairs or depending upon out-of-date information were eliminated.

The items are arranged in order of difficulty as empirically determined.

The make-up and scoring follow the plan of the original *Alpha*. The directions are given orally for each item in the directions test, also separately timed, and oral directions precede each of the subtests. This has often seemed to be one of the inconvenient features of the *Alpha*, especially when used with college and adult subjects.

Norms were apparently not recalculated from an administration of the present revision, as "the average level of difficulty for each test is the same as that for the original forms of the *Army Alpha*, and so the customary norms should, therefore, apply." Norms are given in terms of percentiles for the adult population. An estimated mental age and IQ may also be obtained from the same table. The norms for IQ are derived from a comparison of the percentile norms with those offered by Terman and Merrill for the distribution of IQ's in the American white population.

The manual contains no data on reliability or validity, presumably as high or higher than the original. The test should serve as a profitable research device or as a preferred substitute for the earlier *Alphas* when given in the original manner.

[1040]
Army Group Examination Alpha: Schrammel-Brannan Revision. Grades 4–16 and adults; c1936–38; 3 forms; $1.20 per 25 tests, postpaid; 25¢ per specimen set; quantity discounts; 40(45) minutes; H. E. Schrammel and C. V. Brannan; Bureau of Educational Measurements.

W. D. Commins, Catholic University of America. Three forms have been devised from the original five forms of the army test, with appropriate modification and the introduction of new items. The items have been individually equated from form to form. The eight subtests of the original *Alpha* have been retained. The scoring is easier, the responses being digits or a plus or minus placed in parantheses to the left of each item. The directions test has been reduced to printed directions, with only a total time limit, each item not being timed individually. Beyond the first few introductory remarks, oral directions have been eliminated, the test being largely self-administering. Even the time limits, 5 minutes for each subtest, are not rigid. The examiner merely records the time for the group at five-minute intervals, allowing a later return to earlier items not completed if time allows. The items are presumably in order of difficulty. Scoring is done by cardboard keys supplied with the test.

Grade, age, and a few occupational norms are supplied. The grade norms extend from the fourth grade through the elementary, high school, and college level. The number of cases for each grade averages around 700, with over 2000 college freshmen and about 300 for each of the other college years. Age norms extend from 8 to 25 and above. There is progressive increase in the median score up to age 17, after which the increase is irregular. The norms would seem to be best from ages 9 to 17, both on this point and on the number of cases. The tentative norms are based almost entirely on school and college groups, a fact evidently to be taken into consideration if the subjects to be tested are not students. The occupational norms are for C.C.C. Camps, General Electric Company applicants, police officers, student nurses, and public school teachers. These must be regarded as very tentative.

The mimeographed manual gives no data on reliability, which perhaps would be high, nor on validity, which would probably also be fairly good for the measurement of abstract intelligence or scholaptitude. The elimination of oral directions, the existence of three forms, and the modification for ease of scoring are appealing features of the test.

[1041]
Auditory Scale for Group Measurement of General Mental Ability. Grades 3–8, 7–12; c1936; 2 forms; 2 levels (grades 3–8: Test No. I; grades 7–12: Test No. II); $1 per manual (no other material needs to be purchased to administer this scale); (30) minutes; I. M. Gast; Edwards Brothers, Inc.

[1042]
California Test of Mental Maturity. Grades Kgn.–1, 1–3, 4–8, 7–10, 9–14; c1936–37; 1 form; 5 levels; $1.25 per 25 tests; 25¢ per specimen set of any one level; 90(100) minutes; E. T. Sullivan, W. W. Clark, and E. W. Tiegs; [California Test Bureau].
a) PRE-PRIMARY BATTERY. Grades Kgn.–1 (ages 4–7); c1937.
b) PRIMARY BATTERY. Grades 1–3; c1936.
c) ELEMENTARY BATTERY. Grades 4–8; c1936.
d) INTERMEDIATE BATTERY. Grades 7–10; c1937.
e) ADVANCED BATTERY. Grades 9–14; c1937.

W. D. Commins, Catholic University of America. This very interesting test purports to approach the measurement of ability to do school work in terms of the mental factors which statistical analysis has shown to be unique. It provides a M.A. and IQ based on the total test, comparable with other general intelligence tests, as well as a separate M.A. for the language and non-language divisions of the scale, but "its primary purpose is to make for each pupil a diagnostic evaluation of (his various) mental abilities. . . . The analytical comparison of the various sections of the test indicates a definite central factor, but yet a specificity for each test to justify its inclusion as a measure of a more or less unique factor."

Each battery is composed of 15 or 16 tests, classified into language and non-language tests. The first two tests for visual and for auditory acuity allow a rough classification of the pupils into low, average, and high. Visual acuity is measured by the identification of letters in decreasing size of print (or figures for the pre-primary and primary), auditory acuity by the marking of pictures corresponding to words read by the tester in the ordinary schoolroom tone of voice. The third test, one of motor coordination, consists in tracing an irregular pathway with pencil, giving a rough classification into low, average, and high. The remaining tests give numerical scores, each of which is convertible into definite age scores. These tests are divided into those for: (A) memory (immediate and delayed recall); (B) special relationships (sensing right and left, manipulation of areas, foresight in spatial situations); (C) reasoning (opposites, similarities, analogies, number series, numerical quantity, inference); and (D) vocabulary.

One is impressed with the great amount of pictured material in measuring processes which ordinarily are measured through language. The opposites and the analogies tests, for example, make use of pictures even in the advanced battery. Only four tests, delayed recall (based on a story read earlier), numerical quantity (arithmetic problems), inference (syllogistic reasoning), and vocabulary, are of the language variety. Even these, of course, have the printed language eliminated in the junior batteries.

The testing time takes about two hours, divisible into two or three sittings. Time limits for the separate tests are not rigid although they are suggested for the sake of convenience.

The material appears to be well scaled. The reliability of the total battery computed by the split-half method and corrected runs well above .90 for separate grades. The probable error of measurement is 3 to 5 months. Norms were determined on at least 300 pupils for each grade, with some grades represented by more. The pre-primary battery, for example, was standardized on over 500 cases. The reliabilities of the sub-divisions of the battery are also high. A "diagnostic profile" is provided on the first page of the test blank. Norms in terms of grade placement are also given. The manual of directions is very explicit and the scoring is easily done through a printed key.

As "there are no purely objective criteria or standards which correspond to the factors or abilities in terms of which conceptions of mentality are currently described," the validity of the diagnostic features of the test must perhaps await further study of its practical significance. Its breadth of material and the evident care given to its construction would recommend it at least as a worthy competitor of other general intelligence tests. Whether it may not be overloaded from a practical point of view with tests of certain "factors" for the sake of academic or logical consistency (e.g., the inclusion of the maze test in the advanced battery as a measure of "foresight in spatial situations"), only time can tell. The practical validation of the diagnostic features of a test such as the present one is a widely recognized need.

Rudolf Pintner, Columbia University. These four tests, spanning the whole range from kindergarten to senior high school, are built upon a uniform plan. The content of the sub-tests is supposed to measure the same functions at all levels. The novel feature of these tests, a feature not found in any other group test to the writer's knowledge, is the attempt to obtain a rough measure of visual acuity, auditory acuity and motor coordination. This is done in the first three subtests, called pretests. Visual acuity is measured by marking given forms or letters which become progressively smaller. The test is admittedly a rough one and is only meant to spot children with gross visual defect who would be handicapped by taking the rest of the test. The auditory test consists of marking well-known objects in a picture in order to

California Test of Mental Maturity

test whether the child can hear accurately oral directions as given in an ordinary schoolroom. The motor coordination test consists of very simple tracing along paths—horizontal, vertical and oblique. By means of these three pretests, children with marked physical handicaps may be detected, and, thus, the examiner will be made aware of the fact that their scores on the mental tests that follow are probably inadequate. This is a very interesting idea, and if it can be shown that these three pretests really function as intended, it may prove really useful. The manual of directions does not tell how successful these pretests are in spotting the physically handicapped nor does the present writer know of any study which shows this. Some work in this field is necessary. Assuming that the three pretests are useful for their intended purpose, it is questionable whether they ought to form an integral part of an intelligence battery. It might be more useful to have them separate, so that they may be given only when needed. They would be useless in many schools where all children are given thorough visual and auditory tests, and physical examinations. In any case it seems that they should be scored before the actual mental testing begins.

The content of the mental tests proper consists in each battery of two subtests for memory, immediate and delayed; three subtests of spatial relationships; subtests of reasoning, six for the two lower levels and seven for the two upper levels; one subtest of vocabulary. These are the factors or faculties or functions into which the authors group their subtests. Under the blanket concept of reasoning we note the common type of intelligence test material, e.g., opposites, analogies, similarities, inference and the like. The authors have presented no factor analysis up to the present time, and have grouped their tests on a common-sense basis, but they do give the impression that their tests are diagnosing various powers or functions of the mind, and this, it seems, is rather dangerous with our present uncertain knowledge of the factors that go to make up general intelligence.

Again the authors split up the 12 or 13 subtests into language and nonlanguage factors and compute a language and nonlanguage M.A. Under nonlanguage are grouped immediate memory (auditory memory); sensing right and left; manipulation of areas; maze tracing; pictorial opposites, similarities and analogies; number series; and numerical concepts. These tests are made up of pictures and numbers. They are nonverbal in content, but language is required to understand the oral or printed directions, and it would have been well if the authors had called them nonverbal in conformity with customary usage, leaving the term nonlanguage for tests that do not require a knowledge of the English language either printed or oral. These tests, therefore, cannot be used in testing foreign or deaf children. However, the use of so much nonverbal material in the upper levels (upper elementary and high school) is a decided novelty in mental testing and it is to be hoped that we shall soon have reports as to whether this nonverbal material is as adequate as the usual verbal material in giving a valid mental rating. In all likelihood it will not correlate as highly with school achievement, but that will be no drawback if it can be shown to be a good measure of general intelligence.

Reliabilities (split halves) are reported for all batteries for each grade separately and for groups of grades. In almost all cases they are in the nineties for the total score on the test. Norms for all levels are given.

In conclusion, therefore, we note that these tests represent a breaking-away from certain traditions in intelligence testing. They attempt to split up the concept of general intelligence and measure some of the factors that are supposed to make up the total, thus serving a diagnostic purpose. Furthermore, the authors introduce a large amount of nonverbal material right through the high school level. In addition, they include pretests for spotting physically handicapped cases. The authors are to be congratulated with reference to these innovations and it is to be hoped that work with these tests will justify their expectations.

Arthur E. Traxler, Educational Records Bureau, New York City. This test represents an attempt to utilize the contributions made by studies in factor analysis and to make a diagnostic measurement of mental functions. Each of the four batteries is designed to measure memory, spatial relations, reasoning, and vocabulary, and contains either fifteen or sixteen subtests, including samplings of verbal ability, mathematical ability, spatial relations, and logic.

The test is designed to measure power rather than rate, but one of the parts is to be timed exactly and time limits are suggested for the other parts. Each battery can be administered within two periods of approximately forty-five minutes each.

The test is characterized by the following unique features: (1) The first three tests, known as the pretests, are planned to measure visual acuity, auditory acuity and motor coordination, under group conditions. The purpose is to discover the pupils with gross defects which would prevent a fair measure of mental maturity. The results of the three pretests are kept separate from the other tests and are not used in finding the total mental factors. (2) A diagnostic profile is provided on the cover of the test booklet so that the score of the pupil in each test and each group of tests may be shown graphically in terms of mental age. (3) The test yields three intelligence quotients: an IQ for language factors and an IQ for nonlanguage factors, as well as the usual type of IQ based on total mental factors.

Reliability coefficients based on the scores of pupils in each grade from one through twelve are reported in the manual of directions for the various kinds of scores derived from the California test. Most of the coefficients for total mental factors are about .95. The reliability coefficients for both language factors and nonlanguage factors tend to be above .90. The majority of those for memory, spatial relations, reasoning, and vocabulary in the elementary and advanced batteries are close to .90. The corresponding coefficients for the primary battery tend to be somewhat lower, falling in most instances between .70 and .90.

A recent study of the scores made on the advanced battery of the California test by ninety-five boys in grades 8 and 9 of an independent school showed reliability coefficients that tended to be only a little lower than those reported by the publishers for all parts of the test except spatial relationships. In the case of the spatial relations part, the reliability found in this study was only .65, as compared with a reliability of .871 reported for Grade IX in the manual of directions. The discrepancy between these reliability coefficients suggests a need for further study of this point.

The same study indicated that the correlations between total mental factors on the California test and total scores on the *American Council on Education Psychological Examination* exceeded .70 and that the correlation of total mental factors with the *Kuhlmann-Anderson Test* was about .80. These correlations compare favorably with correlations usually found between tests of intelligence.

In this study, the correlations between language intelligence quotients and total scores on two reading tests were much higher than the correlations between nonlanguage intelligence quotients and scores on these two tests. The relatively low correlations of nonlanguage intelligence quotients with reading scores (approximately .35) indicates that reading ability has little influence on this part of the California test. If further study supports this inference, the California test should prove to be especially useful in measuring the intelligence of reading disability cases.

On the whole, the available evidence is favorable to the reliability, validity, and utility of the California test, but additional objective data about the test are needed.

Volta R 40:362 Je '38. * The tests utilize both language and nonlanguage situations. There are tests of vision, hearing, and motor co-ordination. This latter fact is of considerable importance, for, unusual among performance tests given to public school children, each series indicates a pretest to find out whether the children see well enough to take the remaining tests with fairness to themselves and whether they hear well enough to follow the spoken directions given. * Obviously, deaf or severely hard of hearing children would be eliminated at the outset, so the remaining tests of motor co-ordination, memory, spatial relationships, etc., do not apply to them, but any teacher would find a study of these tests interesting and valuable, especially as they are so arranged that anyone who studies the manual of directions will know how to give them.

[1043]

Dawson Mental Test. Ages 11–12; c1936; 2 forms; 3s.6d. per 25 tests; 1s. per manual; 6d. per single copy; 40(45) minutes; S. Dawson, George G. Harrap & Co., Ltd.

Human Factor 10:239 Je '37. * arranged in the cycle omnibus form * contains....80 items.... of the usual type of problems, * The scoring is entirely objective *

Mental Welfare 17:61–2 Ap '36. *Grace Rawlings.* * the writer has had no opportunity of administering the tests, * the general layout of the test is confusing for younger children and for the dull child * It is all to the good that Testees are not expected to keep solely to underlining and ringing correct answers. * The Teacher's Manual....is very inadequate. * We are not told within what range the tests are reliable, * A serious difficulty is the length of time that must be expended in scoring these tests. * no statistical data is offered on which the Tester can judge the validity, reliability, and standardization of these tests. * In short, these tests serve to increase the number of mediocre tests that are now on the market, without making any scientific contribution to the development of group testing of intelligence.

[1044]

Detroit Beginning First-Grade Intelligence Test, Revised. c1921–37; 1 form; nontimed (30) minutes; $1.10 per 25 tests; 70¢ per specimen set; A. M. Engel and H. J. Baker; World Book Co.

Psyche Cattell, Harvard University. This test is an extension and revision of an earlier form. It consists of an eight-page booklet of pictures which the child is to mark according to the directions given orally. For example: "Mark the largest cat." "Mark four things that lay eggs." "Mark the three things that are most alike." "Draw a line from the ball to the basket that will go over the top of the star."

The validity of the items was determined by comparing the percentage of passes in three groups of children, one bright, one average, and one dull. Only those items were included in the final test which showed a satisfactory increase in the percentage of passes from the dull to the bright group. One hundred and sixteen cases gave a correlation coefficient of .76 with the *Stanford Binet.* The reliability coefficient of the test obtained by the odd-even technique and corrected by the Spearman-Brown formula was .91.

The test is easy to administer and the directions for giving and scoring are on the whole clear. The child is frequently asked to "look at line No. .. (so-and-so) and put a mark...." Since many entering first grade pupils do not know the meaning of "number" or how to read numerals, it would probably have been better to name the first picture on the next row and ask the child to look at it rather than the numbers.

Mental age norms are given based on 10,000 first grade children and run from 3-5 to 9-2. How this range of mental ages was obtained is not made clear. It is not often, if ever, that children are admitted to first grade at the age of three and a half years; and if enough eight- and nine-year olds to obtain satisfactory norms were admitted, it is not likely that they would be typical first grade children.

Va Teach 19:38 F '38. *P. H.* * The test consists of a series of exercises using pictures of common objects which are to be marked in certain ways entirely by spoken directions. No reading or writing is required. The exercises vary one from another so as to indicate types of ability; and the different items in each exercise grow progressively more difficult so as to locate the stronger pupils.

[1045]

Gibson's Intelligence Tests. Ages 10–13; 3 forms (Tests Nos. 1, 2, and 3); 2s.6d. per 20 tests; 3d. per specimen set; quantity discounts; 35–50(45–60) minutes; Robert Gibson and Sons (Glasgow), Ltd.

[1046]

Junior School Grading Test. Age 7; p1937; 1 form; 4d. per test; 3s.6d. per 12 tests; 20s. per 100 tests; 9d. per handbook of instructions; 1s. per specimen set; 12(30) minutes; W. P. Alexander; University of London Press, Ltd.

[1047]

Kelvin Measurement of Mental Ability. Ages 8–14; 1 form; 2s.6d. per 20 tests; 3d. per specimen set; quantity discounts; 5(20) minutes; C. M. Fleming; Robert Gibson and Sons (Glasgow), Ltd.

[1048]

Kentucky General Scholastic Ability Test. Grades 11–13; p1937; a revision of the *Kentucky Classification Test* published in 1932; 1 form; 50(55) minutes; $3.50 per 100 tests; 10¢ per specimen set; E. J. Asher; Kentucky Cooperative Testing Service.

Richard Ledgerwood, Ohio State University. A revision of the *Kentucky Classification Test,* this test is designed to measure general ability to do school work at the upper high school and college levels. It requires one continuous working time of 50 minutes to administer and consists of 120 items in multiple-choice form, with four alternatives. Opposites, mathematics (arithmetic and algebra problems), synonyms, and proverb matching are represented in approximately equal numbers, items of the four kinds being interspersed in a cyclical order. The reliability of the test is not stated, but a validity of .60 to .70 is predicted on the basis of item validation against first-year college scholarship. No ready means of scoring performance separately on the four different kinds of task is provided. All items receive equal gross-score weight.

[1049]
Kuhlmann-Anderson Tests, Fourth Edition. Grades 1B, 1A, 2, 3, 4, 5, 6, 7–8, 9–12, c1927–33; 1 form; $1.25 per 25; 40¢ per specimen set; 40¢ per manual; 30(40–60) minutes; F. Kuhlmann and R. G. Anderson; Educational Test Bureau, Inc.

Psyche Cattell, Harvard University. The authors of the *Kuhlmann-Anderson Intelligence Tests* state that every precaution has been taken to obtain a high validity and reliability. However, no coefficients are reported, the authors claiming that such measures are more likely to be misleading than enlightening. Most psychologists would probably agree with some of the criticisms raised against these measures and only a few with others but almost all would like some objective evidence of the reliability and validity of the tests. None is given. The manual gives the impression that the test items have been selected, evaluated and put together with more than ordinary care and the resulting intelligence tests appear to be excellent, but some objective proof of their excellence would be helpful.

S. A. Courtis, University of Michigan. For those who accept conventional methods of mental measurement and desire to give serious consideration to the many problems involved, the Kuhlmann-Anderson tests are one of the best series on the market. The thirty-nine tests are organized into nine batteries of appropriate difficulty for the various grades. Each battery contains ten separate tests. Each item in each test has been standardized in terms of the mental development (mental age) required to pass it. The norms have been determined and redetermined from measurements of many thousands of children in various states. Adequate keys, score sheets, directions, and standards of interpretation are available. IQ's may be found in the conventional fashion, or a new measure called the per cent of average development may be derived from the scores expressed in units of mental growth. Each of the ten tests is scored independently of all the rest and the final estimate of the level of development attained is taken as the median of the ten scores. The tests may be used for individual testing as well as for mass measurement. It will be evident, therefore, that the tests embody many distinctive features.

One does not need to accept all the concepts and principles on which the tests are based to recognize the advantages of using instruments which have been carefully and consistently constructed. It is customary for makers of tests to conceal their troubles and difficulties and report only end products. In this case, however, every problem has been faced and the method of solution presented. For instance in the illustration of the use of the scoring device given in the manual (page 33) the mental ages of the child being tested, as given by the ten tests, range from six years eight months to nine years five months. The median age is seven years six months. That is, the average deviation of the various scores from the final estimate of ability is 8.3 months. Thus one can easily determine the reliability of his measurements, can compare the reliabilities of different children, and study the changes in reliability which take place under changed conditions. Similarly it is possible to appraise the operation of every solution adopted by the authors to see whether or not its adoption is justified. To one critically inclined some of these principles to be questioned are: the use of many short tests instead of one long one, the assumption that by giving in all grades tests of the same degree of difficulty in relation to development, one eliminates the effect of variations in effort, the advisability of using abstract meaningless tasks as tests instead of more intriguing content, forms, etc.

The use of a growth curve and developmental units of ability is a step in advance of current practice. It is to be regretted, however, that so short a step has been taken. For longitudinal studies of growth have shown very clearly that the assumption that "intelligence quotients below 100 tend to decrease and above 100 tend to increase as the child grows older," is only partially true. Whether an IQ tends to increase or decrease depends not upon its size but upon the relation of the individual's cycles of growth to the pattern of growth taken as average. The Heinis growth curve and personal constant are themselves inadequate for complete interpretation of a child's mental development. The device fails to take account of differences in starting points and maxima as well as in cycles of development. Nevertheless, its use will quickly reveal its defects and prepare one to take the remaining steps toward expressing a child's score in terms of his position and level of development on his own growth curve.

The most serious criticism of all is one which is fundamental to all tests and not peculiar to the Kuhlmann-Anderson series. It is failure to differentiate between performance and ability. Like all existing tests, these measure achievement only, then assume that differences in achievement correspond to differences in ability. Much evidence has accumulated which proves this assumption is false. At least the Kuhlmann-Anderson tests given year after year supply the evidence by which its truth or falsity may be established.

Austin H. Turney, University of Kansas. To those familiar with the work of Kuhlmann, the reception of the *Kuhlmann-Anderson Intelligence Tests* is not surprising. As in the case of his individual examination (the *Kuhlmann-Binet*) the utmost care was exercised in their development. The first edition appeared in 1927. Since then a second, third, and fourth have appeared. Of these only the third was unchanged. The actual work of developing these tests began in 1916. More than 30,000 children were examined with these tests during the years of their development and refinement.

The tests are for age six to maturity. The entire scale is divided into nine batteries, each one applicable for a given range. This is a unique and highly desirable arrangement since it permits a greater number of items applicable to a given range than in the case of those tests which with a single battery cover a wide range.

There is a total of thirty-nine "tests," each having, however, a number of items or "trials" as the authors call them. The separate batteries are in convenient booklets. Median mental ages are used and are readily determined by the examiner. Provision is made for use of mental growth units and the personal constant, a change that is much to be desired.

Not the least important item is the excellent manual containing brief but searching discussions of validity, reliability, and mental growth.

The reviewer has used these tests with entire satisfaction and considers them the most outstanding group scale available for use in the public schools.

[1050]

Northox Group Intelligence Test. Ages 11–12; p1933; 1 form; $1.10 per 25; 8¢ per instructions; 30¢ per key; 10¢ per sample test; 30(35) minutes; G. P. Williams; London: George G. Harrap and Co., Ltd. (Represented in Canada by Clarke, Irwin and Co., Ltd.)

Human Factor 7:415 N '33. * There is no information as to the principles on which the test has been constructed, and there are no norms with which an individual's score can be compared.

[1051]

Ohio State University Psychological Test, Form 20. Grades 9–16 and adults; p1937; 8 earlier forms (Forms 9, 10, 11, 12, 14, 17, 18, and 19) are available at reduced prices; 10¢ per test (tests can be used repeatedly, only answer pads need be purchased); 6¢ per extra answer pad (by using a stylus rather than a pencil, 3 identical records of a student's answers are made available); mimeographed manual, gratis; 10¢ per specimen set; quantity discount rates for state-wide testing purposes will be quoted on request; work-limit (power) test allowing unlimited time, approximately 2 to 3 hours is required; Herbert A. Toops; Ohio College Association Committee on Intelligence Tests for Entrance, Herbert A. Toops, chairman, Ohio State University.

Louis D. Hartson, Oberlin College. RELIABILITY. The reliability of the earlier form of the test, which was administered by the conventional time-limit method, has been checked for various intervals of time. This has been found to range from .93 for the interval of a week ($N = 14$), and .88 after four months ($N = 208$), to .81 over a period of three years ($N = 403$). In these cases different forms of the test were employed. When Form 17 was given on three successive Wednesdays to 33 students, the intercorrelations were: between the first and second trial, .935, and between the second and third trial, .949. These figures show that the examination is reasonably dependable.

VALIDITY. The coefficients representing the correlation between *O. S. U. Psychological Examination* scores and the first semester scholarship of entire freshman classes at

Oberlin have ranged between .429 and .696. This report covers a period of 12 years. During this time two factors have been introduced which have influenced the figures. For one thing the method of grading was changed, a ranking system being substituted for the conventional method. That this was an important factor is indicated by the fact that the correlation between high school and college records improved from .474 (classes of 1929–33) to .582 (1934–40) for the men, and from .411 to .488 for the women. The other factor was a shift from the time-limit to a modified work-limit method of administration. It is inferred that this factor is responsible for some improvement in the validities of test scores from the fact that reports from other colleges confirm those obtained in Oberlin. In Oberlin the improvement is represented by a rise from an average of .53 to one of .60, when the twelve-year period is divided on this basis. With one class both methods of administration were employed. The advantage in favor of the work-limit method was found to be .129. Comparisons made at Ohio University and Ohio Wesleyan also favor the work-limit method, although the report from Wittenberg gives higher figures for the time-limit method.

Another factor which should not be neglected in a review of experience with this examination is the method used for compiling the items for the more recent revisions. Each item has been selected after preliminary validation. Those items in the early forms which have the best record for predicting college scholarship have been supplemented by new items which are prevalidated by correlation with grades already on the books. By this procedure it has been possible to construct a test of 150 items with even higher validity than was formerly obtained with one of nearly twice the number of items. This seems particularly to be the case at Ohio State University where, in 1933–34, Form 18 gave first-quarter validities as follows: agriculture, .577; arts, .589; commerce, .526; education, .602; and engineering, .673.

In each of five times when both the O.S.U. examination and the test sponsored by the American Council on Education have been used at Oberlin, higher validities have been obtained from the O.S.U. test. This superiority, on the average, amounts to .074, when the mean figure for the O.S.U. test is .594.

Theos A. Langlie, Wesleyan University. The *Ohio State University Psychological Tests* (Forms 18, 19 and 20) are among the most valuable scholastic aptitude tests at the college level. This is true particularly because of the ease of administration (power test) and the ease of scoring. Reliability coefficients are represented to be in the .90's; validity coefficients are as high as .70. The validity of successive forms has been increased by item analysis so that the most recent forms are probably as good as can be expected. Attempts which the present critic has made to find other tests which will predict performance in special courses such as foreign languages, social studies, and the sciences have failed to yield additional tests which add to the predictive value of this test.

This test is most applicable to average institutions rather than to highly selective institutions. In the latter, notably Wesleyan University, the obtained distribution of scores is skewed in such a way that differentiation among the very superior is difficult. When used in admissions procedure, however, this limitation is unimportant since the differentiation of men of marginal ability is easily made.

When additional tests involving speed are administered to college freshmen, it is possible to select individuals who have sufficient ability to succeed when given adequate time. Generally, however, the slow students who make satisfactory scores on this test achieve satisfactorily in college.

It is to be hoped that special answer sheets for machine scoring will be made available with the test.

Rudolf Pintner, Columbia University. This is the 1937–38 form prepared by Toops for the Ohio College Association. It has been prescribed for teacher-training entrance in Ohio in 1937–38. It is the end result of continuous revision of the original test published in 1919. Practically every item has been subjected to validation and, since the validities reported for its predecessors are mostly in the sixties, we can assume that the validity of this form will be at least as high. The reliability is reported to be about .94. Norms based upon 6090 college freshmen are available.

The test consists of three subtests, as follows: (1) same and opposites; (2) analogies; (3) reading comprehension. All the items are multiple-choice (five choices) and the examinee indicates his choice by punching a hole in the appropriate box with a stylus. This pierces three answer sheets. The score is the number of correct items which can be easily identified by the coincidence of the punch hole in a white box on the rear sides of the several prescored answer sheets of the scoring pad. The author suggests that the examinee and two other students may score a given paper, thus checking each other's work and at the same time eliminating all expense of scoring. If scored in the office, two scorers may work independently, thus checking each other's work. Furthermore, the advantage of three answer sheets is that they may be used and kept by three different offices in the university. The use of a test blank by a student does not destroy the test because he makes all his answers on the answer pad. In this way the test blank itself can be used over again by replacing the answer pad.

The test is a work-limit test. It usually requires about two hours but slow workers take longer. It is, therefore, extremely useful for testing the occasional student who does not fit into a group. He can be tested at any time by himself because there are no time limits to keep.

This *Ohio State University Psychological Test* is now so well-known that further description is unnecessary. It is definitely one of the outstanding college tests in this country today. It has been constructed with infinite care. The norms which become available as soon as it has been given to large numbers of students in Ohio make the interpretation of its scores extremely easy. And in addition the user of the test has the constant help of the very illuminating Ohio College Association Bulletins which give the results of the testing under the auspices of that association.

[1052]

"Orton" Intelligence Test. Ages 10–14; 1 form; 2s.6d. per 20 tests; 3d. per specimen set; quantity discounts; 60(75) minutes; Robert Gibson and Sons (Glasgow), Ltd.

[1053]

Otis Quick-Scoring Mental Ability Tests. Grades 1–4, 4–9, 9–16; c1936–38; quantity discounts; the Beta and Gamma Tests are revisions and extensions of the Intermediate and Higher Examinations, respectively, of the *Otis Self-Administering Tests of Mental Ability;* A. S. Otis; World Book Co.

a) ALPHA TEST. Grades 1–4; c1936–38; 2 forms; may be given as either a verbal or as a non-verbal test; $1.15 per 25 tests; 25¢ per specimen set; 20(25) minutes for verbal or non-verbal.

b) BETA TEST. Grades 4–9; c1937; 2 forms (2 other forms are in preparation); 85¢ per 25 tests; 20¢ per specimen set; 30(35) minutes.

c) GAMMA TEST. Grades 9–16; c1937; 2 forms (2 other forms are in preparation); supplementary answer sheets are available for use with the International Business Machine Corporation scoring machine; 90¢ per 25 tests; 15¢ per specimen set; articulated machine scoring answer blanks in lots of 500–999, $1.40 per 100 blanks; 1000 to 2999, $1.20 per 100; 3000 to 4999, $1.05 per 100; 5000 and up, 95¢ per 100; prices for less than 500 machine scoring answer sheets quoted upon request; 30(35) minutes.

Psyche Cattell, Harvard University. These tests will probably find wide use on account of the ease and speed with which they may be administered and scored, and the comparatively short time limits of twenty and thirty minutes. However, the coefficients of reliability of the Alpha and Beta tests are rather low and that for the Gamma test, not high. The data for the Gamma test norms are adequate, but not those for the tentative norms for Alpha and Beta.

R. Pintner, Teachers College, Columbia University. [*Review of the Beta and Gamma Tests.*] These two new tests, together with the Alpha Test for grades 1 to 4 published in 1936, form a complete series from first grade to college. These tests constitute a revision and extension of the old and well-known *Otis Self-Administering Tests of Mental Ability.* The novel feature of the tests consists of the quick-scoring technique. All the items are of the multiple-choice technique with five choices, and the examinee indicates his choice by a mark in one of the five circles (Beta Test) or in one of the five vertical spaces (Gamma Test). The test booklets are so arranged that all the answers appear on one sheet, so that when the punched stencil is laid over the sheet, the scorer has merely to count the number of marks appearing through the punched holes of the stencil. No shifting of the stencil or turning over pages is necessary. The Gamma Test foreshadows the coming use of machine scoring. The examinee reacts just as he would to the special answer sheet required for machine scoring.

Each test consists of 80 items. The material consists of analogies, vocabulary, opposites, mixed sentences, reasoning, proverbs, and the like. Five or six nonverbal items appear in each form. The material then is the same in type as appears in so many of our group tests and, therefore, these tests are measuring what we usually refer to as general intelligence or verbal intelligence or scholastic ability.

The norms for Beta are based upon 16,242 cases; the norms for Gamma are tentative norms at the present time.

Reliability coefficients for Beta (Form A vs. Form B) range from .65 to .98 with an average of .79 for 12 coefficients for individual grades. For all grades combined the coefficient is .96. Odd-even reliabilities range from .79 to .90 for individual grades with an average of .86 for six coefficients. The probable error of a score is 2.7 points. Similar coefficients of reliability have not yet appeared for Gamma, but the Gamma test is reported to correlate about .86 with the Otis Self-Administering Higher Examination.

It would seem, therefore, that these new tests will fulfill adequately the uses for which they have been designed and will take the place of the older *Otis Self-Administering Tests,* which have proved so useful in the past. The quick-scoring technique will be a great boon to teachers and psychologists.

Sch 26:184 O '37. J. A. Long. * the name Otis is sufficient guarantee that neither reliability nor validity has been sacrificed. The tests have been prepared with great care. *

Va Teach 19:38 F '38. P. H. * really an extension of the popular Otis Self-Administering. * The quick-scoring feature should prove very popular.

[1054]

Psychological Examination: Prepared for the Teachers College Personnel Association, Form C—1938 Edition. Teachers college students; c1938; Form C, the fifth edition, replaces previous forms and editions; machine scorable; 60(70) minutes; $6 per 100 tests, nonconsumable; $1 per 100 answer sheets; Intelligence Test Committee of the Teachers College Personnel Association; C. F. Malmberg, the Committee, P. O. Box 66, Normal, Ill.

John C. Flanagan, Cooperative Test Service, New York City. [Review of Form B, 1937 Edition.] This examination was prepared by the Intelligence Test Committee of the Teachers College Personnel Association. Work was begun shortly after the organization of the Association in 1931, and Form A was published in 1934. Form B was first published in 1935 and these two have been reprinted, with minor changes, in alternate years. The examination being specifically treated in this review is the 1937 edition of Form B. This raises a point of some importance concerning the labelling of tests. Some authors and publishers refer to the various similar forms of a test which are practically the same in all respects except the specific content of the items as Form A, Form B, or Form 1936, Form 1937, etc. On the other hand, certain groups have adopted the procedure of labelling these similar forms as 1936 edition, 1937 edition, etc. This is likely to lead to considerable confusion unless the publishers' descriptions are very specific.

The 1937 edition of Form B of the *Teachers College Psychological Examination* contains exactly the same specific items as the 1935 edition in all parts. The only differences are (1) minor changes on the cover page, (2) a change of the number series items (Part II) from multiple-choice to completion form, and (3) a misprint, the insertion of an extra letter in the first item of the first part. As stated in the manual, the purpose of the committee responsible for the construction of the test was: "(1) To prepare an intelligence test that would be better adapted for teachers college use than the then-existing tests; (2) To establish norms on this intelligence test using only teachers college populations."

The principal purpose for which these tests are intended and for which they have been used is as a predictive measure of success in teachers college work. The two forms of the test have been used in the last four annual cooperative testing programs of the Teachers College Personnel Association. The annual reports of these programs have been competently prepared by Mr. J. D. Heilman. These reports provide a variety of information concerning the validity of this examination. One learns, for example, from Table III of the February 1938 Report that the correlation between Form A of this examination and the 1934 form of the *American Council on Education Psychological Examina-*

tion for a group of 326 entering freshmen at the Colorado State College of Education is .834. The scores on these two examinations are also correlated with the average of the grades received by these students for the first two quarters of college. The correlation with average grade for the *Teachers College Psychological Examination* is .576. For the *American Council on Education Psychological Examination* the corresponding correlation is .624.

The examination consists of six parts: vocabulary, number series, same-opposite, arithmetic reasoning, completion, and analogies. These parts are quite similar to the corresponding parts of the American Council examination. There are thus three verbal sections, two numerical sections, and an analogies section which has verbal, numerical, and geometric-figure items. The *time* allowed for each part is exactly 10 minutes. The time for reading the directions for each section is included in these time allowances, which gives an advantage to the individual who is familiar with the particular type of item. This is particularly true in the three sections which require detailed instructions of about half a page in length.

The Spearman-Brown reliability coefficient reported in the manual for this form is .957. Although the manual does not state whether the group used represented a single class, other evidence indicates that the spread of scores was about that to be found in the entering class of a single teachers college.

The items were selected on the basis of difficulty and discriminative value. However, the groups on which the preliminary tryout was made must have been much superior to the typical group since the median of the 5293 scores reported from 28 teachers colleges which used the test in the fall of 1937 was 62, or about 29% of 215, the maximum possible score. It is possible that this condition may also have been due to the introduction of a substantial speed factor in the final form which was not present in the experimental edition. The February 1936 Report states that the distribution of scores for teachers college entering freshmen has marked positive skewness indicating that the examination is too difficult for this group.

The *percentile norms* for entering freshmen in teachers colleges referred to above are reported in the *1938 Report of the Cooperative Testing Program of the Teachers College Personnel Association*. Norms are not reported for the separate parts nor for groups other than teachers college entering freshmen.

In summary, it may be said that this test has been shown to be a satisfactory one for the purpose intended. It is, however, not clearly a *better* test than others in the field. Thus the experience of this group in the construction of a psychological examination for entering college freshmen inclines one to wonder whether such organizations would not be rendering a greater contribution if they directed their energies toward the improvement and supplementing of available examination rather than duplicating the efforts of existing agencies.

[1055]
Ryburn Group Intelligence Tests. Ages 6–12; 1 form; 2s.6d. per 20 tests; 3d. per specimen set; quantity discounts; 100(120) minutes; H. V. Clark; Robert Gibson and Sons (Glasgow), Ltd.

[1056]
School Aptitude Test. Age 11; p1937; 1 form; 4d. per test; 5s. per 25 tests; 15s. for 100 tests; 1s. per handbook; 1s.6d. per specimen set (including the arithmetic and English tests in the Thanet Mental Tests series); 30(40) minutes; W. P. Alexander; University of London Press, Ltd.

INDIVIDUAL

[1057]
Animal Puzzles. Pre-school and kindergarten (mental ages, 4½ to 8 years); p1937; 2 forms; a nonlanguage performance test of mental capacity; individual; $1 for each form; (10) minutes; G. Hildreth; Psychological Corp.

[1058]
Detroit Tests of Learning Aptitude. Age 4 through adulthood; c1935–36; individual; 1 form; 10¢ per pupil's record booklet; 8¢ per booklet, 25 or more copies; $1 per examiner's book of pictorial material (nonconsumable); $2 per examiner's handbook; $3 per complete sample packet (including pictorial materials and handbook); H. J. Baker and B. Leland; Public School Publishing Co.

Anne Anastasi, Columbia University. The *Detroit Tests of Learning Aptitude* are an individual intelligence scale consisting of 19 separate tests. In administering the scale to any one subject, however, only from 9 to 13 tests are employed. The authors report that at the upper age levels, the test series requires about the same length of time as the *Stanford-Binet,* but at the younger ages it requires about

1½ times as long. The tests cover a fairly wide sampling of subject matter, including pictorial, verbal, and numerical materials. The mechanical layout of the material is good from the standpoint of facility of administration.

Probably the best feature of the scale is the fact that a separate mental age is obtained on each of the tests, the total score on the scale being the median of these mental ages. This of course makes possible a more specific analysis of the subject's abilities and disabilities. An individual profile may be obtained, to supplement the median mental age. The principle upon which such scoring techniques are based is fundamentally sound. Recent findings on the relationships of mental traits and the nature of intelligence suggest strongly that the use of lump scores derived from a heterogeneous collection of items is very inadequate and may be definitely misleading in certain cases. Further advantages of such a scoring device are the flexibility of the scale and the facility with which additions or substitutions may be made in the course of further research, without the necessity of revising the entire scale.

The chief fault of the scale is undoubtedly its inadequate and rather unsystematic standardization. The tests were apparently released prematurely for practical application. Thus the authors report that the order of difficulty of individual items within each test was determined on "approximately fifty *average* children at each age for which the material is suitable" (p. 19). The same statement is made in regard to the establishment of mental age norms for performance on each test (p. 22). These norms are reported in units of three months (pp. 144–51), a procedure which creates a rather misleading impression of accuracy, since only about 50 cases were employed within each *year* group. Similarly, a reliability of .959 is reported on only 48 cases retested after an interval of four or five months, and a correlation of .910 with the *Stanford-Binet* is given for 32 cases (age ranges are not stated for either correlation).

In regard to interpretation, the authors proceed far beyond the available data and seem to rely chiefly upon anecdotal and armchair methods. Two chapters of the examiner's handbook are devoted to a survey of the specific mental abilities involved in each of the tests (Chap. 2) as well as in each school subject (Chap. 3). No hint is given to the reader that such a differentiation and allocation of mental traits is based upon any data whatever. On page 8, for example, appears a table headed "The Tests and Specific Mental Faculties." The "mental faculties" listed are: (1) reasoning and comprehension, (2) practical judgment, (3) verbal ability, (4) time and space relationships, (5) number ability, (6) auditory attentive ability, (7) visual attentive ability, (8) motor ability. For each of the 19 tests in the scale, the authors have marked the specific "faculties" called into play. The whole presents the appearance of a table such as one might draw up as the result of an extensive factor analysis. But the reader looks in vain even for a single correlation or for any reference to data, published or unpublished, which might have suggested to the authors such a galaxy of "mental faculties" and their specific allocation to each test. The authors point out that "this is suggestive rather than final because knowledge of human behavior is at present largely both tentative and incomplete." It is to be hoped that the statements made by our fellow psychologists—however tentative—are based upon a somewhat more solid factual basis than is given in this manual. If the authors have actually identified the eight "faculties" listed above in populations ranging in age from four years through adulthood and have devised tests to measure such "faculties," even *tentatively,* they should be urged to publish these results without further delay. Such an epoch-making achievement would be eagerly welcomed.

It is regrettable that the general tone of the handbook which accompanies the tests is naive and slipshod. Some of the statements are loosely expressed, others are incorrect or utterly incomprehensible. On page 2, for example, the authors report that at the lower ages the Detroit tests require longer time to administer than the *Stanford-Binet* and then add: "This increase in testing time with improved reliability may disturb the somewhat prevalent idea that intelligence of young children improves under favorable environmental conditions. Such may be an idle will-o'-the-wisp arising merely from inadequate testing." Presumably the idea which the writers are trying to convey in these two sentences is that the

Detroit Tests of Learning Aptitude

rise in intelligence test score of young children upon improvement in environmental conditions, which has been reported by various investigators, may have been a chance rise attributable to the unreliability of the measuring instrument. This is based upon a misconception of the nature of test reliability. Chance errors may occur in *either* direction. A drop on retesting might be expected just as often as a rise. It should be added, incidently, that no reliability coefficients are reported to substantiate the assertion that, *for young children,* the longer Detroit test actually yields more reliable results than the *Stanford-Binet.*

Similarly, on page 19, the authors write: "Certain traditions and convictions have developed about the aristocracy of *high* correlations which are supposed to exist between various tests given to the same individuals. Any tests which did not fit into this elite family, having either *low* or actually negative correlations, have been frowned upon or even rejected as black sheep." It is well known, of course, that the customary procedure is just the reverse of that described in these sentences. As any textbook on test construction clearly states, one of the chief principles in the selection of tests for a battery is low intercorrelations among the component tests.

These statements are cited merely as illustrations. It is beyond the scope of this review to undertake a detailed analysis of the various assertions made in the handbook and of the assumptions underlying them. We wish only to emphasize the point that the practice of offering conclusions without at the same time furnishing the evidence, or some reference to a source wherein the evidence may be found, is one to be sincerely discouraged in scientific research.

Henry Feinberg, Mental Hygiene Clinic of the Jewish Social Service Bureau, Detroit, Mich. The *Detroit Tests of Learning Aptitude* are instruments describing the level of the several factors of intelligence of an individual. They consist of a battery of nineteen tests, examining a wide range of functions of intelligence, including reasoning and comprehension, practical judgment, verbal ability, time and space relationships, number ability, auditory attentive ability, visual attentive ability, and motor ability. The mental age range for the entire scale is from three to nineteen years. The tests are standardized to meet the need of the school child and they correlate well with his school achievement.

The *Detroit Tests of Learning Aptitude* differ in principle from other individual intelligence tests in the following manner: Less emphasis is placed on the test as a unit picture. More emphasis is placed on special abilities and disabilities. The factor of a basal age is omitted. While an IQ may be derived from the median of the mental ages at which each of the tests is passed, the tests lend themselves to a profile study describing each function of intelligence with greater clarity than is obtainable from the total picture. More is left to the judgment of the examiner than is true in other testing situations. Not all the tests need be given in order that one may obtain an adequate picture. A minimum of eleven tests is required and a maximum of thirteen to fifteen is prescribed.

The advantages of the *Detroit Tests of Learning Aptitude* are several. Materials used in administering the tests consist only of a comparatively small examiner's handbook, a booklet of pictorial material for several of the tests and a record booklet for each subject. In the administration of the examination the subject experiences a series of short tasks which begin at an easy level and continue until failure is reached. There is comparatively less feeling of failure than when a total failing year or level must be experienced at the end of many individual examinations. In relating the child's problem to the results of the examination the examiner is able, through the study of the profile obtained, to discuss the situation with the parents or the child in more acceptable and understandable language. For instance, lay people can more readily accept and understand a deficient number ability for which there is compensation by a superior auditory attentive ability than they can a resultant general score, such as an IQ, or mental age. The diversification and greater sampling of mental functions as indicated by the profile study clarify for the teacher the cause of the child's difficulty, revealing, at the same time, a comprehensive picture of his learning potentialities. In specific situations the teacher will know, for example, whether the visual or auditory approach tends to facilitate the learning process.

On the other hand, the standardization of

Detroit Tests of Learning Aptitude

the tests may be criticized on the basis that the tests have been standardized only on fifty children at each age level. Also, some criticism may be forthcoming from persons who would demand more exactitude in terms of IQ, rather than a general impression of a child's abilities. Finally, it may be said, that the utility of the *Detroit Tests for Learning Aptitude* is limited since they are chiefly suitable for children rather than for adults.

J Ed Psychol 27:258–62 Ap '36. D. A. Worcester and S. M. Corey. * The introductory discussions in the *Handbook* seem to have been written hastily, and with an organization that is sometimes baffling. * Part II, called "Diagnostic Interpretations," rightfully begins with the admonition that the *Detroit Tests of Learning Aptitude* do not measure everything, despite the nineteen separate scales. "Habits of industry, health, home environment, personality traits and many other factors all contribute their effects to the learning situation. The *Detroit Tests of Learning Aptitude* do not attempt to measure these other factors but chiefly that of the mental phases of learning" (p. 6).[1] After this auspicious beginning, however, the authors present a very clear tabular description of "the entire series of tests with specific abilities which are related to success in the given tests" (p. 8)—*without any supporting evidence.* * Part III of the manual is not in any sense a *profound* "Analysis of School Subjects." * Part IV of the manual, "Statistical Evaluations," is most interesting in its lack of statistical validity. * Apparently the test was standardized by comparison with itself. * According to the authors, sixteen of the nineteen sub-tests have been used in intercorrelation computations. Although this information could have been presented very readily in a table, with great benefit to anyone trying to understand the nature of the scales, such was not done. Rather, three very general summary paragraphs were given, the data in which were based on test results from "approximately one hundred children ages eight to twelve years" (p. 20). No probable errors were given nor any partial or multiple correlations. Actual reliability data are published for but one sub-test out of nineteen—"the auditory attention span for unrelated words had a reliability of +.78 on one hundred fifty average children at an interval of three months" (p. 21). For the tests as a whole, (p. 21) "the *Detroit Tests of Learning Aptitude* have had reliability determined for certain tests, but for the whole series of tests announcement will be made within a short time." ("America to the Fore!" Sell the test first; determine its reliability later.) It is also stated (pp. 21–22) that because certain other investigators found reliability coefficients ranging from +.78 to +.933 on tests *"somewhat similar"* (italics ours) "there is every reason to expect a reliability of +.80 or higher will be found." (A long step forward!) * Norms for the Detroit Tests were established with fifty children of average ability (IQ ninety to one hundred ten) for each age. "In some instances ten or more of the nineteen tests were given to the same children, in other instances only two or three tests" (p. 22). This technique makes it impossible to learn (from the Manual) the exact number of subjects upon which any one test item was standardized. No data are given which would enable the student to determine the range of scores for any *CA*. No correlations were reported with the *Binet Simon Scale* although the authors, confirmed in such practices apparently, state that "the results of the two tests are very closely comparable" (p. 24). In all fairness it should be noted that the tests here criticized have the appearance of being good tests. They are well put up, and their administration appears to have been very carefully worked out. It is therefore all the more difficult for the present writers to cloak their surprise that a test battery such as the Detroit Series is so prematurely published. Presumably it is an excellent measuring device, but so to conclude calls for more faith than judgment. Even a casual comparison of the standardization of the Detroit Scales with the pains taken by Terman and his associates causes one to wonder about the "capacity of benefit from experience." As was stated earlier, in this day and age one has reason to expect that a new scale, "a long step forward in intelligence testing!" might be standardized, and its reliability and validity determined, before final publication, but such hopes are probably naïve.

[1] The construction of the second sentence is rather maladroit, but the meaning is clear.

[1059]
Ontario School Ability Examination. Ages 3–15; c1936; "a performance test prepared more especially for use among children who are deaf, whose native tongue is other than English or who for any reason are lacking in language facility"; authorized by the Minister of Education for use in the schools of Ontario, Canada; 1 form; individual; $1.75 per box of testing materials; 90¢ per manual; 75¢ per 50 test blanks; 20–40 minutes; H. Amoss; Ryerson Press.

[1060]
Passalong Test: A Performance Test of Intelligence. Ages 8 and above; c1937; 1 form; individual; suitable for hearing and deaf cases; 21s. per box of blocks, cards, and manual; 1s.6d. per set of cards; 1s. per manual; (15) minutes; W. P. Alexander; University of London Press, Ltd.

[1061]
Record Blank for Pintner-Paterson Performance Tests: Short Scale. Ages 4–15; c1937; includes the following tests: Mare and Foal Picture Board; Seguin Form Board, Five Figure Board, Two Figure Board, Casuist Form Board, Manikin Test, Feature Profile Test (two parts), Ship Test, Picture Completion Test, and Cube Test; 5¢ per record blank; 35¢ per 15 record blanks; 50¢ per manual of directions; G. H. Hildreth and R. Pintner; Bureau of Publications.

Francis N. Maxfield, Ohio State University. Pintner and Paterson published their *Scale of Performance Tests* in 1917. Later Pintner collaborated with Spaid in arranging this *short scale,* in which five of the less satisfactory tests of the original scale were omitted and two, the Pintner manikin and the Knox-Kempf feature profile, were designated for alternate use. As far as the writer knows, no norms for using the "point scale" or the "year scale" methods of the complete scale were ever published. Scoring on the short scale was, therefore, limited to the median mental age and median percentile methods. For these scorings the norms of the original scale were used.

Unfortunately for careful clinical work, over-enthusiasm for the Binet-Simon method, and particularly for the Stanford revision, caused many who were called upon to make estimates of intelligence to ignore this Pintner-Paterson scale and other nonverbal tests except in dealing with subjects who did not speak English, or were illiterate, or were deaf. The bulky test material was inconvenient for the itinerant clinician and its use involved some capital outlay. Yet many mistakes made by those who have considered a Stanford-Binet test a psychological examination and the intelligence quotient thus obtained as *"the IQ"* first and last might have been avoided if they had made a wider sampling of mental traits by using such scales as this. An excellent statement of the function of such tests appeared in the manual (Chapter 1) for the *Cornell-Coxe Performance Ability Scale.* The use made of these same test materials in more recent scales (e.g., most of them use Pintner's manikin) bears witness to the significance of the work of the authors of this pioneer scale.

The authors of this recent manual for the Pintner-Paterson short scale have apparently made no revision of earlier norms. The elementary school children from whom the Pintner-Paterson norms for ages thirteen and fourteen were derived were selected downward, in that brighter children of these ages had passed on to higher grades. In five of the fourteen tables for the short scale the median scores for fourteen years are inferior to those for thirteen. The scale was, therefore, unsatisfactory for the brighter children of these ages. Rescoring their short scale performance on the Grace Arthur scale will frequently increase their mental age scores by several years.

Pintner and Paterson's use of the percentile method has received less attention than it has deserved. It is unfortunate that Arthur, Cornell, and Coxe give no measures of dispersion in the manuals for their respective scales—neither percentile tables nor standard deviations from which standard scores may be computed. That there is no suggestion of the use of any such measures in this manual is to be regretted.

The outstanding difficulty with the Pintner-Paterson method at any age has been the necessity for counting errors or moves. It is difficult to do this accurately, and counting interferes with careful observation of method. The definitions of errors and moves given in this manual will frequently lead to three different counts by as many observers for the same performance.

The "Seguin" form board, though that used by Spaid in his work on the short scale, is not self-corrective (the oblong may be placed in several recesses), as was that used by Goddard and by Sylvester, and is less satisfactory on that account, particularly as Sylvester's norms are used. The random placement of the blocks in the Healy pictorial completion test I is to be regretted. The directions for Pintner's modification of the Knox cube test are very unsatisfactory for an examiner not already familiar with the standard procedure.

A record blank on which the norms are printed makes reference to tables unnecessary. The final score is the median of thirteen mental ages. One is directed to derive a P.Q., or performance quotient, from this, but is not told what divisor to use in the case of adults. The manual will require a good deal of annotation if it is to be put into the hands of psychoclinicians not already familiar with standard Pintner-Paterson procedures.

[1062]

Revised Stanford-Binet Scale. Ages 2 years to adult; c1937; a revision of the Stanford-Binet Scale published in 1916; 2 forms (Forms L and M); $2 (7s.6d.) per 25 record booklets (12 pages); 60¢ (3s.6d.) per record form (4 pages); $1.75 (4s.6d.) per set of printed card material for either form; $8 (45s.) per box of test materials, including printed card material, for either form; Directions for Administering, 124 pages, in press; *Analysis of 6000 Stanford-Binet Tests,* in preparation; $2.25 (10s.6d.) per copy of the manual, *Measuring Intelligence;* L. M. Terman and M. A. Merrill; Houghton Mifflin Co. (London: George G. Harrap and Co., Ltd.)

Francis N. Maxfield, Ohio State University. Professors Lewis M. Terman and Maud A. Merrill, both of Stanford University, have collaborated in this new revision of the earlier (1916) *Stanford-Binet* scale. They have provided two complete and independent scales designated as Form L and Form M. A single manual, *Measuring Intelligence,* contains some account of the research on which the revision is based and clearly stated directions for giving and scoring both forms.

Terman's 1916 revision of the *Binet-Simon* scale had come to be almost universally used in the United States and has served as a model for revisions elsewhere published in numerous languages. It has been used extensively in research as well as in the applied fields of clinical psychology, psychiatry, vocational guidance, and education. The high correlation between scores obtained on this scale and ability for school work has been a factor in making its use particularly significant in dealing with children of school age.

Some changes in the new scales may be noted. Instead of 90 test items, each scale includes 129. The new scales begin at eighteen months instead of twenty-four and provide twelve tests per year instead of six for each year at the lower levels. Instead of twelve adult tests there are twenty-six. For years XI to XIV ten tests have been added. These changes give a wider range of sampling and extend the usefulness of the scale both downward and upward. Instead of a maximum adult IQ of 122 we have a maximum of 152.

In computing the IQ, ages from thirteen to sixteen are scaled downward by one-third of the excess of thirteen. To find the IQ of a fourteen-year-old child one divides his mental age score in months by 164, and for one of fifteen years by 172; for an "adult" (i.e., 16 years and over) he divides the mental age score in years by 15. Tables in the manual, however, obviate any calculation of IQ's, a frequent source of error in the old scale.

For reexamination, or where there is reason to suspect coaching, the alternate scale is used. Starred test items at each level provide an abbreviated scale.

The IQ in itself provides no close measure of deviation, except to show whether this score is above or below average. The authors provide a table from which standard scores may be derived. These may be translated into centile ranks for those who find standard scores difficult for teachers, social workers, and others who are not statistically minded.

Many who use the scales will wish that some greater degree of "serial testing" had been favored by the authors in their standardization. Their insistence that the person using these scales allow no deviation from the standard order of the test items is logical enough where the subject is emotionally stable and cooperative. As they themselves point out, in the case of preschool children, for example, where a negativistic attitude is sometimes encountered, or in the case of emotionally unstable adolescents and adults, one must not be too firmly bound by this ruling.

One can be sure that these new scales will replace the 1916 *Stanford-Binet*. They are based on extended careful research and their technological form is certainly superior. That scores in the form of mental ages and IQ's derived from them will have both greater validity and greater reliability is also certain. This will be particularly true in the case of adolescents and adults, for it was with them that scores derived from the earlier revision were so likely to be misleading.

Record Blank for Pintner-Paterson Performance Tests

J. W. M. Rothney, Harvard University. The new revision seems to have been made with due consideration to the possible objections of critics and the authors have therefore avoided many of the pitfalls that the maker of tests meets. Had the standardization procedure been continued so that a thousand cases were included at each age level the test might have been as perfect as the assumptions involved in this type of testing allow. The "sinking of shafts" and the "age-scale" techniques have proven to be useful in education and if the number of cases used in standardization proves to be adequate, we ought to have an instrument as valuable to the new education as the old test was to education in the period in which it has been used. Until results of carefully planned trials of the test are reported, however, we can judge the value only by the authors' reports concerning the construction of the test. We have reason to believe that results of trials will be excellent.

F. L. Wells, Boston Psychopathic Hospital. The Binet scales, of which the 1916 Stanford revision is perhaps the most widely known representative, should have done more to diffuse a social consciousness of the individual differences in mental powers than any other device in history. They have furnished the principal basis of such part as psychological techniques contribute, not without some confusion, to administrative regulations in this country. The present revision and extension of the 1916 scale has thus been awaited with interest as a genuine cultural event. Its structure is in the main similar to the old, but amplified and improved especially in the lower ranges, extending now to year 2. Improvements have been made in eliminating some of the more cumbrous items of the earlier version, and a number of good devices, new to the scale (and one not-so-good, "finding reasons"), are introduced. The two alternate forms are, judging from experience, good protection against fore-knowledge.

The original function of the Binet scale was as a gauge of proper school progress. For this function it is still reasonably suited; if clinical psychologists object that it is oververbalistic, the answer is that so is the curriculum. But circumstances often lead to its employment in a number of other ways, for which it was not specially intended, as for measurements of adult intellectual powers or for functions of personality adjustment; and in its final significance it has to be evaluated also from these standpoints. In general the scale ascends in merit as it approaches the earlier years. The contribution at the adult levels is doubtful, at grade school levels it is good of its kind; at preschool levels very good, save for the weakness inherent in Binet systems generally, lack of functional organization. They represent an embryonic, undifferentiated, mass reaction phase in psychometric development.

The earlier series and Form L of the present series are rather loaded with themata involving violence. This limits their usefulness in some clinical settings, as long since remarked.

From an editorial standpoint the present work is scarcely up to the standard of the previous. The manual is not organized to the best practical advantage, and much more art could have been used in the preparation of record forms, with reference to cues provided. The examples of passes and failures impress one as less critically chosen than those of the 1916 volume. The standards are lenient and suggest that various tests might well have been located at higher levels with more rigorous requirements. With no manual at hand, a safe rule for the writer's practice would be "when in doubt, pass it."

A considerable regret from the clinician's standpoint must still be that the series is so detached from events in the field of applied mental measurement during the past twenty years. The generously spent resources would have made a much more valuable contribution through a series of subtests, each strong enough to stand alone, fairly balanced among verbal and nonverbal functions, extending from early levels to something like average adult. The *Kuhlmann-Anderson Series,* the *Minnesota Preschool Scale* and other studies, such as those of David Wechsler, and the *Detroit Learning Aptitude Series,* have been pointing the way. The present writer recalls making an allied suggestion to Terman himself, at the end of 1923. With all sympathy for the sentiment that impels one to rebuild and refurbish an old faithful of a Model T, the more practical recourse is generally to a later machine.

Austral J Psychol and Philos 16:190–2 Ag '38. A. H. Martin. * The author insists on the administration of the tests seriatim, expressly objecting to the digit memory tests being given together * Surely if the test usage must so narrowly follow the method set out by this new revision the English version which magnificently changes dollars to shillings and pounds without justification of standardization in England is also unwarranted. * Most test workers, including the reviewer, will gratefully welcome and accept the new versions as a decided advance in the procedure of testing children.

Brit J Ed Psychol 8:205–6 Je '38. * the detailed instructions for the giving of the test ....become somewhat wearisome and it seems doubtful whether so much detailed instruction is worth while in view of the fact that there may be differences of opinion as to whether some of the answers are legitimate or not. The final result is probably the most elaborate and carefully planned set of intelligence tests based upon the Binet series * If....one abandons the too great an insistence upon the testing merely of a *general* element and recognises that specific abilities are important and inevitably present, the convenience of this type of test, giving a mental age and intelligence quotient so conveniently and readily, is undoubted. A serious weakness in the whole scheme, however, is the elaborate box of apparatus and its high cost. Incidentally, the warnings printed on the test material boxes against copying by exact reproduction or in a modified form, because of copyright, reads strangely in view of the fact that, of course, the great majority of the tests in the book are based upon intelligence tests used and devised by other workers, as, indeed, is inevitable in the development of intelligence testing. It is somewhat strange, by the way, that there is no reference to the extended standardisation for English children of the Binet Tests made by Professor Burt. * a remarkably extensive piece of research work and a notable contribution to intelligence testing.

Brit J Inebriety 35:201–2 Ap '38. * will be warmly welcomed....on both sides of the Atlantic *

Char and Pers 6:114–131 D '37. R. B. Cattell. * Recently a dispute arose at an inter-clinic meeting, representative of the child guidance clinics of England, concerning the best means of measuring intelligence. The present writer took the view that the Binet-Simon and its modifications constitute an obsolete instrument which ignores all that progress in the theory of mental testing which has been made in the last twenty years, and which should be replaced by more up-to-date measures of "g." The opposition was, for the most part, mute or expressed without any reference to the principles of scientific psychology, but the unexpressed resistances of the clinical psychologists soon received academic expression through the able championship of Dr. P. E. Vernon. Before dealing with Vernon's contentions, I will state the objections to the continued use of the Binet Test. They are: (1) That its component test items are frequently tests of scholastic attainment and life experience, rather than of "g." * (2) The test items are too few in number to give good reliability and fine grading. (3) It is inadequate at the higher mental ages. (4) Certain special factors play a rather large part in contributing to the total score, e.g., the "practical ability" of Alexander's research; "v" and almost certainly the "f" factor of "fluency of association" which is a matter of temperament rather than of cognitive ability. (5) That if, as most clinical psychologists concede, the test is not concerned with any one ability but a collection of abilities, the attachment of a single quantitative value to this hodgepodge is meaningless. (6) That is consequence of the contamination of "g" with scholastic attainment, the Binet does not give a scatter of intelligence quotients as wide as that which actually exists. * (7) The personal relationship which arises between tester and testee in this kind of test, and which is sometimes claimed to give greater reliability, is just as likely, in comparison with the impersonal group test situation, to introduce errors arising from shyness and other temperamental variations in the child, as to improve the reliability of the score. Furthermore, the examiner is also likely to be misled by unconscious attractions and hostilities and by the appearance and conduct of the child; for many items are such as cannot be scored with entire objectivity. * The prolonged worship of the Binet as a test of intelligence has left us with an encumbering heritage of erroneous conceptions, principally

Revised Stanford-Binet Scale

in matters concerning the distribution of intelligence, its development in the individual, and its role in society. * The expenditure of time and money over twenty years on improving, standardizing, and applying an instrument which was never rooted in adequate research has deflected a stream of valuable effort which should have gone to newer problems. This charge is made initially with regard to the influence of the Binet Test upon the progress of intelligence measurement, but it holds even more strongly with regard to the testing effects upon the growth of techniques for assessing temperament and character. * The intuitionist desires to know another personality directly, by empathy instead of in an objective fashion through the mediation of a mathematical formula of personality. * Intuition has an indispensable place in research, as a scaffolding under the shadow of which objective investigations may be built up; but propounded as an independent method of arriving at psychological knowledge, it would seem to be a pure illusion.

Char and Pers 6:99–113 D '37. P. E. Vernon. The appearance of the revised Stanford-Binet Test provides a good opportunity for ventilating the controversy between those who criticize this test as an antiquated and unreliable instrument which should give place to more modern and scientific techniques, and those who on the other hand persist in regarding it as the best psychological measuring instrument at their disposal. In a recent discussion, Dr. R. B. Cattell put forward the former view, but he was strongly opposed by many of the experienced Child Guidance Clinic psychologists who were present. Although I must not claim that my views are representative of those held by Clinic psychologists in general, yet I hope, in this article, to place our opposition upon a more systematic footing. The controversy would appear to result from a still more fundamental disagreement between those who favor what may be termed the *psychometric* and the *clinical* approaches to the study of personality. As I have indicated elsewhere, both approaches are legitimate and valuable, and they should reinforce rather than exclude one another. But the psychometric approach by itself is unable to satisfy the requirements of psychologists engaged in clinical work. I must discuss this point first, and will then hope to show that the Binet Test is a very successful compromise between the two approaches. * It has the flexibility and the control of the subjective situation characteristic of the clinical interview, but at the same time sufficient objective control to yield a reliable measure of ability. Binet's first scale was predominantly clinical; * In the Stanford revisions, especially in the most recent, Terman appears to have compromised further with psychometric standards, since the tests are somewhat less representative of everyday experiences, their application and scoring have been made more definite, and there has been a more elaborate study of the consistency of each test with the scale as a whole. But this mental maturity has never been regarded as a strictly unitary trait, although it is expressed in quantitative terms, and there is no reason why it should be so regarded. * the psychologist at a school or a child guidance clinic....does not want the best tests of g or of other factors, but rather tests which most nearly resemble the practical situations of daily life. * It seems doubtful whether this argument can ever be settled by discussion. * If the Binet Test was as inaccurate as its critics suggest, surely there would have been volumes of complaint during the past thirty-odd years from the parents, teachers, doctors, and other clinic workers, who are most affected by its diagnoses. Rather have the complaints been directed at the much more objective group tests. An experimental comparison of the relative validity of the two approaches will, I hope, one day be carried out. * In my view, the two approaches should be complementary rather than conflicting; for each type of worker could learn much from the other. * It is obvious that many of the component items of the test are affected by acquirements such as reading, arithmetic, etc., but there appears to be no good evidence that any other intelligence test of a predominantly verbal type is not also so affected. *

Childh Ed 14:36–7 S '37. E. Kawin. The long awaited revision of the Stanford-Binet Scales has at last appeared, * The new scales.... represent such distinct improvements and advantages over the earlier one that they should soon entirely supersede it and may justifiably be regarded as a new and very important contribution to educational procedures. * These carefully devised new instruments for the measurement of intelligence should prove of inestimable value and usefulness in the hands of thoroughly trained *psychologists* who are competent to administer, score, and interpret them with adequate appreciation of their significance and full awareness of their limitations.

Ed Forum 1:480–81 My '37. * It will serve admirably to guide school authorities in dealing with individual pupils. It will be no less helpful to research workers who now have at their disposal an instrument which will make it possible to refine and improve their statistical results. Every authority on testing will wish to own the book.

Ed Res B 16:192–3 O 20, '37. F. N. Maxfield. * One regrets that the "serial method" in such tests as repeating digits forward or backward, comprehension, and so on, is prohibited for all tests except the vocabulary in Form L. The authors give a brief and satisfactory account of their methods and results in the research on which these scales are based. They have set a high standard for painstaking thoroughness in test construction. It is not their fault that nine out of ten of those who use these scales will ignore this discussion, as users of the old Stanford-Binet have ignored the account of that revision published by Terman and his collaborators in 1917. The use of these scales will rapidly replace the older revision. What they will do to the....misuse of that revision remains to be seen, and in any case one can hardly hold the authors responsible for that. To the extent that they have made the scales more nearly foolproof, have extended their range of sampling, and have eliminated the chief source of arithmetical errors, the chance of misuse is reduced. Yet in the case of that great number of users who will continue to think of the Stanford-Binet intelligence quotient as "the IQ," and of giving this scale as a psychological examination, we may expect even less attention in individual cases to the necessity for the interpretation of test results in the light of the clinical history, and to the evaluation of other psychological factors outside the range of the sampling included in these scales.

El Sch J 38:387–88 Ja '38. F. N. Freeman. * The new scale evidently constitutes a marked advance over the old one. In addition to the essential improvements which have been mentioned, the form of the manual has been made more convenient and the instructions for giving and scoring have been made clearer. The scale is still an interview scale, and the scoring in many of the tests is based on a discriminative judgment of the response. The correct use of the scale, therefore, demands careful preparation and training. The general scores determined by competent testers, however, should not vary a great deal. It is the belief of the reviewer that this revision will have a long and productive career comparable to that of the first edition.

Harvard Ed R 8:130–33 Ja '38. J. C. Flanagan. * Certain facts concerning this standardization should be emphasized. A point of some significance is that it was based almost entirely on pre-school and school groups. * There is no indication that any individuals over eighteen years of age were tested. * The authors, assisted by Dr. McNemar, have departed from the usual procedures of reporting the accuracy of measurement of such scales. They very appropriately point out that a single reliability coefficient cannot adequately express the accuracy of measurement of I.Q.'s derived from these scales. The "errors of measurement and derived reliabilities" have therefore been reported for five I.Q. levels. The authors are to be strongly commended for this attempt to report the accuracy of measurement of their scales in a more precise manner. However, it is unfortunate that they have failed to provide what would be the most useful and precise description of the accuracy of their scales, namely, the standard errors of measurement of mental-age scores at various levels. They are also guilty of a few loose statements such as the following: "The probable error in terms of months of mental age is of course larger with older than with young children because of the increasing spread of mental-age scores as we go from younger to older groups" (p. 44). A statement pointing out the fact that the error in terms of mental age at any point on the scale depends only on the number of tests functioning at that level and their discriminating value would seem to be a much more adequate presentation of the facts. Perhaps a brief outline of the steps involved in trying to interpret the accuracy of the I.Q.'s derived for particular individuals will serve to

Revised Stanford-Binet Scale

clarify this point. First let us suppose the I.Q. obtained for a particular individual is 100. To interpret this from the data supplied by the authors we should consult their Table II and learn that an I.Q. from 90 to 109 has a standard error of measurement of 4.51. This might appear to be satisfactory, but let us further examine the situation for individuals having an I.Q. of 100 but who are placed at differing age levels. If the chronological age of such an individual is 100 months, we may deduce that the standard error of measurement in terms of mental age would be 4.51 months, for an error of 4.51 months in the mental age would produce an error of 4.51 points in the I.Q. at this chronological age. If, however, the individual was 150 months old, the error of measurement in terms of mental age which would produce an error of 4.51 points in the I.Q. would be 6.76 months. It is seen that Table II could only be a correct description of the situation if the error of measurement in terms of mental-age scores of any point on the scale were directly proportional to the mental age at that point. That this situation exists seems unlikely since there are the same number of tests, six, at each age level from VI to XIV and it is unreasonable to suppose that the tests at successive age levels are progressively less discriminatory. We are thus forced to the conclusion that it is impossible to determine the standard error of measurement of any particular I.Q. with the type of information represented in Table II. On the other hand, it is obvious that if standard errors of measurement were reported in terms of various ages, it would require merely a bit of simple arithmetic for anyone to determine the standard error of measurement of any I.Q. at any age level. Lest the foregoing discussion be interpreted as a major criticism of this book, it should be emphasized that its authors have rendered a real service to users of these and other such scales by pointing out certain common fallacies in the interpretation of the accuracy of a scale of this type. * The publication of this book is a milestone in the progress of the individual-testing of intelligence, and a careful reading of it is highly recommended. The painstaking efforts that are reported in its pages indicate that the many people for whom the Stanford Revision of the Binet-Simon intelligence scale has been an invaluable tool will find the new revision an even greater aid in the clinical and research work of the years to come.

Human Factor 11:368–70 O '37. C. Spearman. As nothing less than news of the world must rank the announcement that Terman's Stanford-Binet *Tests of Intelligence* have now been revised. Indeed, the author himself does not hesitate to claim that: * And of a truth this credit for fascination and popularity, large as it is, would appear to have been really attained and fully deserved, * More questionable, however, is their further claim that over and above its wide attractiveness, this series of tests: "....is at the same time based upon what we believe to be sound psychological theory." For what, we are bound to inquire, is then the essential nature of this theory which is thus said to supply the tests with their very foundation? On this crucial matter Terman has, in his original publication, been a little shy. * In point of fact Terman himself did subsequently supply at least as accredited a definition as could easily be found, when he declared that: "....an individual is intelligent in proportion as he is able to carry on abstract thinking" (*J. Ed. Psych.,* 1921). Unfortunately, however, his actual tests (1916) had shown no tendency to carry this definition into effect. * With lively interest, then, we turn to his new tests and examine how far this, his concept of intelligence, has now been further developed and fructified in the course of the subsequent twenty years of arduous investigation. To our surprise, it does not seem to have advanced at all, but instead to have receded into oblivion. This time, on the contrary, the first criterion of the validity of the Tests is said to consist of: "....the increase in the per cents, passing from one age to the next." But this criterion also seems to have never been seriously applied. Otherwise, indeed, there might have been introduced such tests as the correctness of spelling, the speed of reaction, or even the acquisition of teeth. * Above all, we must press for enlightenment as to how a number of different shafts can ever supply any justifiable *single* 'measurement.' * How,....shall we admit the claim to measure one single 'general level,' when the authors themselves positively state that no such thing exists? * The objection to setting up a single measure becomes still more acute in view of the fact that the authors find themselves obliged to introduce frequent exceptions. * If we hardly examine for ourselves how much the said Tests really do include, we certainly find much where the concept of intelligence is, to say the least of it, singularly strained. * In all the preceding respects, then, we seem forced to conclude that the new Tests fail to reveal any genuine advance beyond the old ones. Where, then, do they achieve notable progress? At any rate, in two important respects. First, the number of subjects used for standardization has been increased from 1,000 to 3,184. Secondly, the number of Tests has been increased from a single set containing 90, to two alternative sets containing respectively 199 and 209; * several technical defects in the older tests have been more or less overcome; in particular, many uses may be made of the two alternative sets; also more adequate catering has been made for children under five years of age. On the whole, those clinicians, teachers and industrialists, whose main requirement is that each test should be "a new adventure in which every step is interesting and meaningful," will find the new series even more serviceable than the old one. Less satisfaction will be found by those who want rather to keep abreast of modern research, who aim at obtaining all the most helpful information about the subjects tested; above all, who shrink from risking untold injury to children by registering them as "unintelligent" on the strength of tests whose real significance seems not even to be guessed at. For anything that the present authors tell us, such a stigma put on any one tested *may* be justified, or it *may not*.

J Ed [London] 70:54 Ja '38. Since the publication of Terman's *Measurement of Intelligence* the Stanford-Binet scale has been more widely used in England than any other individual intelligence test, and in spite of certain weaknesses, in the main it has proved unexpectedly well adapted for use with English children. * no English workers have produced so thorough a revision as the new one which comes from Stanford University. *

Mental Welfare 18:130 O '37. M. D. * One thing only is to be regretted with regard to this new volume....those extremely valuable chapters "The Uses of Intelligence" and "Sources of Error in Judging Intelligence," which preceded the description of the tests in the 1916 edition, have been omitted. * The descriptive advertisement and the price of this material lead one to expect a quality vastly superior to that actually supplied. * In the card material, the diagrammatic drawings are clear, but those intended to be realistic are surprisingly bad.

Mind 47:101–3 Ja '38. Cyril Burt. * despite its obvious defects, the scale devised by Binet and Simon nearly thirty years ago remains the standard method. In almost every civilised country these tests have been used; and their very simplicity has often led the practical worker to forget their admitted imperfections. * One welcome feature of the new revision is the reduction of the verbal element. The new tests for younger children consist largely of problems to be solved with the aid of beads, coloured cubes, diminutive objects, and other materials that appeal to the infant mind. Unfortunately, the special apparatus thus required is costly; * The data incidentally collected by this survey must be a mine of suggestive information; and, to the theorist, the most interesting chapter in the book is that which deals with a statistical analysis of the results. * On the I.Q. scale the average standard deviation proves to be about 17 points. This is rather higher than that obtained in earlier surveys; but a better test always yields a wider scatter, and it has long been suspected that the amount of individual variability within the total population has been under-estimated. The new figure, if confirmed, will be of great practical significance. * From the note to the English edition it would appear that, with Prof. Terman's approval, a number of verbal alterations have been made to adapt the instructions for workers in this country. Even so, however, many difficulties remain which only a systematic study by experimental methods can hope to eliminate. The most obvious defects are the Americanisms which are still left in the injunctions to be recited to the child. * In general, however, the wording of the old tests has been much improved; and the new tests greatly enhance the value of the scale. One or two, it is true, seem open to criticism. * Plans have already been proposed for a co-operative study of the new revision with a view to making it as valuable in Great Britain as it undoubtedly

Revised Stanford-Binet Scale

will be in America. In the past much injustice has been done by those who have assumed that a scale of tests standardised in one country could be forthwith adopted in another. * All who are engaged in intelligence-testing—whether teachers, doctors, or psychologists—will feel an immense debt of gratitude to Prof. Terman and his colleagues for their long and arduous research, and will be eager to congratulate them on the success with which they have managed to combine the requirements of a serviceable scale with the demands of scientific precision.

New Era 19:54–55 F '38. E. M. Nevill. With all their imperfections the Binet-Simon Tests are too valuable and too widely used to be easily discarded and those who are still enthusiastic about their value will welcome this timely, much altered and adapted revision. The task of revision has taken ten years, and the book leaves us in no doubt about the thoroughness of the work. There are certain verbal alterations in the English edition which will probably make slight differences to the norms. At present it will be necessary to use the American ones but it is to be hoped that the publication of British norms will be possible in the near future. * Although still subject to mistakes in scoring and leaving a good deal to the common sense of the examiner, the instructions are on the whole clearer and more uniform than before, so that there is little excuse for serious errors. * it is hoped that the greater expense involved will not limit the use of the tests too seriously. * No one must expect to begin the use of these new tests without undertaking some serious work on them. They demand even closer adherence to actual wording than before, although on the other hand they are easier in that the order in which they are given must never vary. It is quite possible to criticize details, especially the inclusion of some of the old as well as added absurdities of a gruesome kind, * There is no doubt that this revision is worth all the painstaking work which has been put into it and no psychologist will regret the added trouble entailed in mastering it if it be more accurate —as it undoubtedly is. * It should quickly supersede all previous revisions.

Personnel J 16:308 Ma '38. E. N. Hay. * Unfortunately, the Binet-Simon tests are designed particularly for the testing of children, and are not applicable to an industrial situation, * the time involved....makes it prohibitive for ordinary industrial use. Also, it is doubtful whether the material offered for the adult is of the sort which would hold his attention and call forth his best efforts, especially if he were under the strain of applying for a position. The book's value to the personnel man lies chiefly in its presentation of techniques for scoring and standardization. It throws new light on the problem which the test-compiler must face, not only when dealing with intelligence, but in setting up any psychological measure. If it does nothing else, it should lead the would-be psychologist to pause for careful consideration before setting up new tests of his own.

Psychiatric Q 11:517–8 Jl '37. * can be highly commended. *

Psychol B 34:605–9 O '37. F. L. Goodenough. As indicated by the title, this is essentially a manual for administering and scoring the revised edition of the famous Stanford-Binet tests with only a minimum amount of space devoted to the process of standardization which is to be described in a later publication. Four preliminary chapters, totaling 66 pages, precede the manual proper. Of these, the first three give a general description of the scale, pointing out the reasons why it is believed to be an improvement over the earlier edition, together with a brief account of the process of standardization and a statistical analysis of the results. * The authors defend this [the retention of the age-scale] on the ground of its clinical usefulness and the fact that all available statistical procedures for constructing an "equal-unit scale" rest upon the unproven assumption that intelligence is normally distributed. The mental-age scale, they point out, makes no such assumption, nor does it pretend to measure intelligence as linear distance is measured. * After a good deal of experience with scales of the "equal-unit" type, I am inclined to agree with this conclusion. There are, however, certain difficulties inherent in the mental-age unit which the authors point out and have attempted to overcome. * The work of revision required a ten-year period for its completion and will probably stand for many years as the most thorough-going example of test-construction that has ever been carried out.

Revised Stanford-Binet Scale

* Perhaps the most serious question that can be raised about the new scales is one that has been pointed out by the authors themselves. It is a well-known principle of test construction that the intelligence quotient is a valid interpretative measure only if the standard deviations of mental ages increase in proportion to age. This is equivalent to saying that the standard deviations of intelligence quotients must remain constant from age to age. In neither of the two forms of the revision does this appear to be the case. * Inasmuch as none of the possible explanations can be demonstrated to be true, the authors conclude that "in the lack of positive proof to the contrary, we are probably justified in assuming that the true variability is approximately constant from age to age." It is to be hoped that future findings will show that this assumption is warranted. * the authors' wording [on pp. 44–45] is somewhat unfortunate, though the meaning is apparent. * "A subject's fluctuation in mental age score will be proportional, not to the variability of his chronological age group but to the variability of his mental age group." Evidently what is meant here is the variability of the chronological age group to which the subject's mental age corresponds. Likewise the last column of Table 11 on p. 46 requires some interpretation. * [the reported reliability coefficients] would clearly not hold for the restricted ranges to which they are ascribed; their meaning is purely theoretical and can be expressed only in rather awkward terms prefaced by an "if" that does not hold good. If the standard deviation of IQ were as great for each of the various sub-groups as it is for the entire range (an obvious absurdity) then the reported reliability coefficients might actually be obtained. With the facts as they are, it would seem better to describe the stability of individual standing only in terms of the error of prediction without reference to correlation coefficients that are unsuitable for use with the data. * The instructions are exceptionally clear and sufficiently detailed to make it possible for any experienced examiner who will give sufficient attention to learning the rules to follow the standardized procedure without variation.

Sch R 45:549–50 S '37. A. E. Traxler. * Persons not actually engaged in administering the revised tests will be mainly interested in the first seventy-one pages, comprising Part I of the book. * It is probable that for some years to come *Measuring Intelligence* will be the chief guide to individual mental measurement in America. *

Teaching 10:141–2 Mr '38. * the authors are to be congratulated * In some tests words like *telephone* and *stove* are used. It is doubtful whether these words are equally suitable for children of rural areas.

Times Ed Sup 1159:255 Jl 17 '37. * Americanisms have been taken out of the text for the English edition, but some stay in: "Dirt" for "earth," " 'cause" for "because," "sick" for "ill," " 'til" for "till," "mad" for "angry," and so forth, give some of the tests an exotic look.

Univ Mich Sch Ed B 8:112 Ap '37. * Probably the most significant feature of the new revision is the replacement of the original scale by two, *

P. E. Vernon. *Year Book of Education, 1938,* London: Evans Brothers Ltd., 1938, pp. 27–34. There can be little doubt that Terman's [1916] Stanford revision of the Binet-Simon scale has been more widely used and has yielded results of greater value than any other psychological test. Admittedly, however, it possesses a number of defects, among the chief of which are: (1) It has not been restandardised in Britain; * (2) The scale is relatively inadequate at both ends. * (3) The method of calculating intelligence quotients among persons aged more than 12 years is highly artificial. * (4) Several of the component tests are unsatisfactory for one reason or another. * (5) There are too many loopholes for subjective bias and errors on the part of the tester, both in giving the test and in scoring the responses. * Psychologists have known that Terman was fully alive to these inadequacies, and that he was working on a new revision which should correct them as far as possible. * Those who are about to start learning the practice of individual testing should certainly use the new (1937) rather than the old (1916) revision. In spite of its greater elaborateness, it is much easier to apply and to score. But there is likely to be a good deal of inertia among those who are already experienced testers: they will naturally be unwilling to learn a whole new set of tests, and they may complain of the expense of purchasing the new material.

Revised Stanford-Binet Scale

* Of the 258 tests included in the two Forms, approximately one-half are either identical with tests in the old revision, or else directly developed out of old tests * The following tests in the old scale have been dropped altogether: sex; name and surname; comparison of weights (both levels); colour naming; age; a.m. or p.m.; naming coins (both levels); right and left; dictation; counting backwards; date; months; stamps; fables (both levels); clock reversals; president and king; code; physical relations. Few of these will be regretted; they certainly include the tests which have aroused most criticism. Of the new tests, more than half are duplicates or developments of the rest. Thus we are left with less than fifty entirely fresh tests, half of which fall within the 2–4½-year levels, half in the 5 to Superior Adult levels. The task of the experienced tester who wishes to learn the new scale is therefore not very onerous, especially if his or her testing is confined to children of school age. The fresh tests for 5 years and upwards are mainly based on the type of items used in group intelligence tests. * It is not possible yet to judge whether the scale will be successful in the individual testing of adults. It may still lack sufficient discriminatory power, and be too childish in content; though in both these respects it is much improved over the old revision. * The new pre-school tests are very different from the old, being specially chosen to arouse and hold the attention of the young. The majority are based either on naming, or on description of the use of various toy objects—spoon, engine, cat, doll, chair, etc. * In the present writer's opinion there is little to choose between the new Stanford tests and the Merrill-Palmer scale at these ages; but his practical experience is, of course, limited to the latter scale. The former possesses the advantage of continuity with the scale for children of school age; and in America (but not in Britain) it is probably better standardised. In general, much greater care has been taken in securing highly valid tests which will, to use Spearman's terminology, be strongly saturated with g. There is a slight disadvantage in this, namely that the tests tend to be somewhat more removed from children's everyday-life experiences, somewhat less natural and varied in content. * the directions for applying and scoring the tests....are still much less "fool-proof" or "mechanised" than the instructions and scoring in group tests, but they are more clear, definite and comprehensive than in any previous individual scale. We can claim, then, that the second, fourth, and fifth defects of the old revision have been very largely corrected in the new. * Our third criticism has been met in....[an] ingenious manner. * The standardisation of the scale for American children and adults was exceptionally thorough. * the test is highly reliable. * We have still to deal with the most vital question, namely the applicability of the scale in Britain. It is, of course, unstandardised in this country; but so also is the old revision. * Of more immediate concern is the translation of the scale; * Mere substitution of the nearest British equivalents for the American wording is insufficient; * Generally speaking, the alterations introduced into the English edition of the test material and instructions are adequate, and there is very little need, or excuse, for further modifications. The instructions for scoring have been treated much less carefully. These instructions consist largely of specimen responses which are either to be accepted or rejected. Often when the test itself has been translated, corresponding alterations have not been made in the acceptable responses; and those who do not possess the American edition may fail to realise that the responses quoted no longer apply. * Such errors are too numerous to be mentioned here in full. The only course which British testers can take is to keep in mind the American origin of the listed responses, and judge for themselves whether responses given by British children attain to, or fail to reach, an equivalent intellectual level. To conclude, then the tests themselves are almost all applicable as they stand in this country; but the scoring of responses will inevitably be somewhat more subjective and open to error, until such time as a thorough restandardisation is carried out, including the preparation of a completely new list of good and poor responses obtained from British children. At the same time we should remember that the old revision possesses the same defects to a still greater extent. In almost every respect the new scale is an improvement on the old *

Revised Stanford-Binet Scale

Reprinted from *The Second Mental Measurements Yearbook*

INTELLIGENCE — SECOND MMY

Reviews by Anne Anastasi, Rachel Stutsman Ball, Nancy Bayley, Robert G. Bernreuter, J. M. Blackburn, Andrew W. Brown, B. M. Castner, Raymond B. Cattell, James Drever, Jack W. Dunlap, August Dvorak, Howard Easley, Charles Fox, Henry E. Garrett, Florence L. Goodenough, J. P. Guilford, E. Patricia Hunt, A. M. Jordan, T. J. Keating, Truman L. Kelley, Grace H. Kent, F. Kuhlmann, W. Line, Herschel T. Manuel, Francis N. Maxfield, Myrtle Luneau Pignatelli, S. D. Porteus, C. Ebblewhite Smith, Percival Smith, C. Spearman, Florence M. Teagarden, Lorene Teegarden, Godfrey H. Thomson, Robert L. Thorndike, Robert C. Tryon, A. H. Turney, David Wechsler, F. L. Wells, Carroll A. Whitmer, D. A. Worcester, and Ll. Wynn Jones.

[1376]
Alexander Performance Scale. Ages 9 and over; 1935; individual; 1 form, 3 subtests; 12s. 6d. or $3.15 per manual; [2] (40-60) minutes; W. P. Alexander.
a) PASSALONG TEST. 1932-37; 21s. per box of blocks, cards, and manual; London: University of London Press, Ltd.
b) BLOCK DESIGN TEST. 1919-36; Drever and Collins' modification of Kohs' *Block Design Test* (using only Designs 1-3, 5, 7-9, and 14-16); 12s. 8d. per set of 16 color cubes; 6s. per 10 design cards; Edinburgh, Scotland: Andrew H. Baird, Scientific Instrument Maker.
c) CUBE CONSTRUCTION TEST. 1918-25; Gaw's modification of Doll's *Cube Construction Test*; 8s. 6d. per 26 cubes and 3 blocks; London: National Institute of Industrial Psychology.

REFERENCES
[1] ALEXANDER, W. P. "A New Performance Test of Intelligence." *Brit J Psychol* 23:52-63 Jl '32.
[2] ALEXANDER, WILLIAM PICKEN. *Intelligence, Concrete and Abstract*: A Study of Differential Traits. British Journal of Psychology Monograph Supplements, Vol. 6, No. 19. London: Cambridge University Press, 1935. Pp. x, 177. 12s. 6d. Paper.
[3] ALEXANDER, W. P. "Intelligence, Concrete and Abstract." *Brit J Psychol* 29:74 Jl '38.

J. M. Blackburn, *Lecturer in Social Psychology, London School of Economics.* In the pilot survey on 71 adults made before he finally chose the three tests to form his performance scale, Alexander found that the frequency distribution of scores on Kohs' *Block Design Test* was skewed at the bottom, indicating that the test was rather difficult for some of the subjects; that the distribution for the *Cube Construction Test* was skewed at the top, showing that it was on the easy side; and that the distribution for the *Passalong Test* approached the normal curve of error.

Alexander therefore came to the conclusion that a combination of the three tests met the principal requirements for a performance scale suitable for vocational and educational guidance between the ages of 14 and 18 years. The weakest subjects score positively on the scale while the strongest subjects are still well within the maximum score. He subsequently standardised this scale on four groups of subjects, totaling 374 cases, employing an alteration—and, in my opinion, a definite improvement on the methods of scoring Kohs' *Block Design Test* and the *Cube Construction Test*.

From my own experience I would say without hesitation that Kohs' *Block Design Test* is far more diagnostic for clinical purposes than either of the other two. The *Passalong Test* I have found to be scored on the lenient side. If this were its only defect it could be easily remedied, but in addition to this it depends too much on the chance factor. If a subject in one of the early subtests properly assimilates the significance of breaking down a rectangular vertical block composed of two square blocks into a rectangular horizontal block, he will gain an advantage, which is out of all proportion to the importance of this piece of "insight," over another subject who fails to see it until later, or who fails to see it at all. It is true that after the time limit for each subtest has expired, the experimenter demonstrates the solution to the subject, but this hardly affects the point at issue. Though I readily agree that the more intelligent subject will be likely to acquire the piece of knowledge more readily than the less intelligent, my argument is that it is unfortunate that so much may depend on the fact of its acquisition.

The *Cube Construction Test*, even with Alexander's improved method of scoring, I have never found to be satisfactory, except as a shock absorber. The careful, plodding subject is, in my experience, unduly penalised, and the impulsively quick subject gains many more chance successes than he deserves. As a shock absorber, however, the test has its place, and its next most useful purpose is in helping the experimenter to make some qualitative observations on a subject's temperamental qualities.

But neither of these tests approaches the importance of Kohs' *Block Design Test*. Alexander's method of scoring is a definite improvement on that of Drever and Collins and on that of Kohs, because it presents a *graduated* score for the designs on the basis of the time taken. It was a defect of the other methods—particularly of that suggested by Kohs—that so many points in a subject's score might turn on a second or two, the subject getting no points if he exceeded the time limit for the design, but—in one case—as many as 9 points if he took a few seconds less. For this reason, and because of the important observations about a subject's temperamental characteristics that may be made by a skilled clinician who watches the subject as he performs the test, I regard it as unfortunate that Alexander chose to use the Drever and Collins reduction in the number of designs from 16 to 10. Much more can be learnt about a subject who is given the full 16 designs, for there are more designs of the same type for the subject to become familiar with before he is suddenly shifted to a new type of design, and it is at this point that emotional stability or instability often betrays itself. In the 10-card test he is more directly oriented towards a sudden change of design, he does not lose his balance so readily when the type of design is altered, and so this information is frequently submerged. Consequently I would like to see the full Kohs' test of 16 designs, scored on Alexander's principles, employed as the *Alexander Performance Scale*.

[1377]

American Council on Education Psychological Examination for College Freshmen, Form 1939. Grade 13; 1939; a new form has been issued annually since 1924; 3 editions; 7¢ per test; 15¢ per specimen set; L. L. Thurstone and Thelma Thurstone; Washington, D. C.: American Council on Education.
a) HAND-SCORING EDITION. 37 (55-60) minutes.
b) PERFORATED MACHINE-SCORED EDITION. 33 (55-60) minutes.
c) SEPARATE ANSWER SHEET MACHINE-SCORED EDITION. 2¢ per machine-scorable answer sheet; 33 (55-60) minutes.

REFERENCES

1 THURSTONE, L. L. "Psychological Tests for College Freshmen." *Ed Rec* 6:69-83, 282-94 Ap, O '25.
2 NELSON, M. J., AND DENNY, E. C. "The Terman and Thurstone Group Tests as Criteria for Predicting College Success." *Sch and Soc* 26:501-2 O 15 '27.
3 OWENS, WILLIAM A. "On a Certain Value of the Thurstone (American Council on Education) Tests in Predicting Scholarship." *Ed Adm and Sup* 13:495-9 O '27.
4 THURSTONE, L. L. "Psychological Examinations for College Freshmen." *Ed Rec* 8:156-82 Ap '27.
5 KENT, R. A., AND SCHREURS, ESTHER. "Predictive Value of Four Specified Factors for Freshman English and Mathematics." *Sch and Soc* 27:242-6 F 25 '28.
6 STALNAKER, JOHN M. "American Council Psychological Examination for 1926 at Purdue University." *Sch and Soc* 27:86-8 Ja 21 '28.
7 THURSTONE, L. L. "Norms for the 1927 Psychological Examination." *Ed Rec* 9:102-7 Ap '28.
8 CONDIT, PHILIP M. "The Prediction of Scholastic Success by Means of Classification Examinations." *J Ed Res* 19:331-5 My '29.
9 KELLOGG, CHESTER E. "Relative Values of Intelligence Tests and Matriculation Examinations as Means of Estimating Probable Success in College." *Sch and Soc* 30:893-6 D 28 '29.
10 THURSTONE, L. L., AND THURSTONE, THELMA GWINN. "The 1929 Psychological Examination." *Ed Rec* 11:101-28 Ap '30.
11 FREEMAN, FRANK S. "Predicting Academic Survival." *J Ed Res* 23:113-23 F '31.
12 THURSTONE, L. L., AND THURSTONE, THELMA GWINN. "The 1930 Psychological Examination." *Ed Rec* 12:160-78 Ap '31.
13 THURSTONE, L. L., AND THURSTONE, THELMA GWINN. "The 1931 Psychological Examination." *Ed Rec* 13:121-36 Ap '32.
14 HUNSICKER, LILIAN. "A Comparison of Scores on Two College Freshman Intelligence Tests." *J Ed Res* 26:666-7 My '33.
15 RHINEHART, JESSE BATLEY. "An Attempt to Predict the Success of Student Nurses by the Use of a Battery of Tests." *J Appl Psychol* 17:277-93 Ap '33.
16 SEGEL, DAVID, AND GERBERICH, J. R. "Differential College Achievement Predicted by the American Council Psychological Examination." *J Appl Psychol* 17:637-45 D '33.
17 THURSTONE, L. L., AND THURSTONE, THELMA GWINN. "The 1932 Psychological Examination." *Ed Rec* 14:183-97 Ap '33.
18 WAITS, J. VIRGIL. "The Differential Predictive Value of the Psychological Examination of the American Council on Education." *J Exp Ed* 1:264-71 Mr '33.
19 JORGENSEN, C. "Analysis of Some Psychological Tests by the Spearman Factor Method." *Brit J Ed Psychol* 4:96-109 F '34.
20 MCCONNELL, T. R. "Change in Scores on the Psychological Examination of the American Council on Education from Freshman to Senior Year." *J Ed Psychol* 25:66-9 Ja '34.
21 THURSTONE, L. L., AND THURSTONE, THELMA GWINN. "The 1933 Psychological Examination." *Ed Rec* 15:161-75 Ap '34.
22 JONES, GEORGE A. A., AND LASLETT, H. R. "The Prediction of Scholastic Success in College." *J Ed Res* 29:266-71 D '35.
23 MOSIER, CHARLES I. "Group Factors in College Curricula." *J Ed Psychol* 26:513-22 O '35.
24 THURSTONE, L. L., AND THURSTONE, THELMA GWINN. "The 1934 Psychological Examination." *Ed Rec* 16:226-40 Ap '35.
25 DAVIES, J. EARL. "The Relative Effects of Two Kinds of Provision for Response upon the Validity of an Artificial Language Test." *J Ed Res* 29:593-5 Ap '36.
26 LIVESAY, T. M. "Racial Comparisons in Performance on the American Council Psychological Examination." *J Ed Psychol* 27:631-4 N '36.
27 THURSTONE, L. L., AND THURSTONE, THELMA GWINN. "The 1935 Psychological Examination." *Ed Rec* 17:296-317 Ap '36.
28 DRAKE, LEWIS E., AND HENMON, V. A. C. "The Prediction of Scholarship in the College of Letters and Science at the University of Wisconsin." *Sch and Soc* 45:191-4 F 6 '37.
29 LIVESAY, T. M. "Sex Differences in Performance on the American Council Psychological Examination." *J Ed Psychol* 28:694-702 D '37.
30 SCHMITZ, SYLVESTER B. "Predicting Success in College: A Study of Various Criteria." *J Ed Psychol* 28:465-73 S '37.
31 THURSTONE, L. L., AND THURSTONE, THELMA GWINN. "The 1936 Psychological Examination for College Freshmen." *Ed Rec* 18:252-73 Ap '37.
32 UPSHALL, C. C. "Contrast of the Upper and Lower 16 Per¢ent on the American Council Psychological Examination (Abstract)," pp. 45-6. In *The Role of Research in Educational Progress*: Official Report, American Educational Research Association, A Department of the National Education Association, New Orleans, Louisiana, February 20-24, 1937. Washington, D. C.: the Association, May 1937. Pp. 255. $1.50. Paper.
33 Educational Records Bureau. *1937 Fall Testing Program in Independent Schools*: Including a Study of the California Test of Mental Maturity, pp. 1-16. Educational Records Bulletin No. 22. New York: the Bureau, January 1938. Pp. x, 60. $1.50. Paper, lithotyped.
34 KOHN, HAROLD A. "Achievement and Intelligence Examinations Correlated with Each Other and with Teacher's Rankings." *J Genetic Psychol* 52:433-7 Je '38.
35 MCGEHEE, WILLIAM. "Freshman Grades and the American Council Psychological Examinations." *Sch and Soc* 47:222-4 F 12 '38.
36 THURSTONE, L. L., AND THURSTONE, THELMA GWINN. "The 1937 Psychological Examination for College Freshmen." *Ed Rec* 19:209-34 Ap '38.
37 BUTSCH, R. L. C. "Improving the Prediction of Academic Success through Differential Weighting." *J Ed Psychol* 30:401-20 S '39.

38 CURETON, EDWARD E. "Note on the Validity of the American Council on Education Psychological Examination." *J Appl Psychol* 23:306-7 Ap '39.
39 LIVESAY, T. M. "Does Test Intelligence Increase at the College Level?" *J Ed Psychol* 30:63-8 Ja '39.
40 SEDER, MARGARET. "The Reliability and Validity of the American Council Psychological Examination, 1938 Edition," pp. 51-8. In *1938 Fall Testing Program in Independent Schools and Supplementary Studies*. Educational Records Bulletin No. 26. New York: Educational Records Bureau, January 1939. Pp. x, 69. $1.00. Paper, lithotyped.
41 THURSTONE, L. L.; THURSTONE, THELMA GWINN; AND ADKINS, DOROTHY C. "The 1938 Psychological Examination." *Ed Rec* 20:263-300 Ap '39.
42 TRAXLER, ARTHUR. "Summary of Test Results, Fall 1938," pp. 1-21. In *1938 Fall Testing Program in Independent Schools and Supplementary Studies*. Educational Records Bulletin No. 26. New York: Educational Records Bureau, January 1939. Pp. x, 69. $1.00. Paper, lithotyped.
43 BARNETTE, W. LESLIE. "Norms of Business College Students on Standardized Tests: Intelligence, Clerical Ability, English." *J Appl Psychol* 24:237-44 Ap '40.
44 FLORY, CHARLES D. "The Intellectual Growth of College Students." *J Ed Res* 33:433-51 F '40.
45 SEDER, MARGARET. "The Reliability of the American Council on Education Psychological Examination, 1939 Edition," pp. 34-8. In *1939 Fall Testing Program in Independent Schools and Supplementary Studies*. Educational Records Bulletin No. 29. New York: Educational Records Bureau, January 1940. Pp. x, 50. $1.00. Paper, lithotyped.
46 SUPER, DONALD E. "The *A.C.E.* Psychological Examination and Special Abilities." *J Psychol* 9:221-6 Ap '40.
47 THOMSON, WILLIAM A. "Note on Retest Results on the ACE Psychological Examination for College Students." *J Ed Psychol* 31:229-33 Mr '40.
48 THURSTONE, L. L., AND THURSTONE, THELMA GWINN. "The American Council on Education Psychological Examinations, 1939 Editions," pp. 3-38. In *Psychological Examinations, 1939*. American Council on Education Studies, Series 5, Vol. 4, No. 2. Washington, D. C.: the Council, May 1940. Pp. v, 53. $0.25. Paper.

Jack W. Dunlap, Associate Professor of Educational Psychology, The University of Rochester. This examination is designed for use primarily in colleges. It provides two scores—a linguistic value based on the composite of the scores on the same-opposite test, the completion test, and the verbal analogies test; and a quantitative score based on the results on the arithmetic test, the number series test, and the tables or figure analogies test. Considerably more weight is attached to the linguistic score than to the quantitative score—roughly in the ratio two to one. This is not chance as is attested by the authors' statement, "In general, a scholastic aptitude test should be rather heavily saturated with language factors, since these represent scholarship." There is, therefore, some question as to the suitability of such an instrument for use in technical schools, such as the scientific and engineering schools. No evidence is offered as to the validity of the Q and L scores. Such evidence should be available to test users.

This test is put out in two forms, one for hand-scoring and one for machine-scoring. The forms are identical, with two exceptions: (*a*) the order for presentation of the tests; and (*b*) the substitution in the hand-scoring form of a "tables" test for the figure analogy test in the machine-scored edition. The shift from the figure analogies test to the "tables" test in the hand-scored edition will affect the comparability of the two tests, but this effect should be slight. The new test is ingenious and requires the subject to examine a series of simple facts and to deduce from them certain relationships. In its simplest form it consists of giving the total number and the number in class A, and requiring the subject to determine the number in class B.

The total time for administration of the test is fifty-two minutes for each form. On the machine-scored form, this is distributed as nineteen minutes for practice tests and thirty-three minutes for the testing, and on the hand-scored edition as fifteen minutes for practice tests and thirty-seven minutes for testing. The use of practice exercises is commendable, but personal experience indicates that the time devoted to these might be reduced to about two minutes, thus saving about seven minutes, which would allow the test proper to be lengthened. The amount of test time allowed seems inadequate to the reviewer, in view of the importance attached to the results by administrative officers and personnel workers. No evidence is submitted as to the reliability of the instrument. Some data are presented as to the validity of the 1938 forms, where it is shown that the examination correlates approximately .50 with the results of each of four six-hour examinations in introductory courses in biology, the humanities, physical sciences, and the social sciences.

Robert L. Thorndike, Associate Professor of Education, Columbia University. These new forms continue the series of annual tests for college freshmen prepared by the Thurstones since 1924. Like the earlier forms of the test, these forms are characterized by: (*a*) a variety of subtests, both verbal and quantitative in character; (*b*) norms from a large college population, reported fully and with various breakdowns; and (*c*) data on the comparability of successive forms.

The new forms show a number of changes. These include: (*a*) Preparation of a machine-scored form of the test, and rearrangement of the hand-scored form so that its format resembles that of the machine-scored form. (*b*) The introduction of practice exercises, upon which a substantial part of the total testing time is to be spent. (*c*) Certain changes in the subtests, as follows: the addition of a number series subtest to all the forms; the replacing of the artificial languages test in both 1939 forms by a verbal analogies test; and the replacing of the figure-analogies test in the handscored 1939 form by a tables test. (*d*) The provision, in all forms, for a *quantitative* and a verbal subscore.

The advantages of the machine-scored test from the point of view of efficiency of scoring can hardly be questioned. That it calls for more complicated instructions is suggested both in the volume of instructional material and by the provision of practice exercises. Some question might be raised as to the "efficiency" of a test which devotes 19 minutes to practice and 33 minutes to testing. Does the preliminary practice permit the actual test time to be used enough more effectively to give a more reliable and valid result for the total time expenditure?

The several changes in subtests cannot be judged in terms of information made available at this time.

The provision of separate quantitative and verbal scores is a first step in the direction of differential diagnosis with this test. Now that separate scores are available, research will be possible to determine the value of these subscores for differentiating between aptitude for literary and scientific curricula.

These tests represent, then, the continuation of a well-planned hour test for college students with certain new variations, the value of which remains to be determined by further research.

For reviews by Anne Anastasi and David Segel, see 1037.

[1378]
American Council on Education Psychological Examination for High School Students, Form 1939. Grades 9-12; 1939; a new form has been issued annually since 1933; 2 editions; 5¢ per test; 10¢ per specimen set; 33(60) minutes; L. L. Thurstone and Thelma Gwinn Thurstone; Washington, D. C.: American Council on Education.
a) HAND-SCORING EDITION.
b) MACHINE-SCORING EDITION. 2¢ per machine-scorable answer sheet.

REFERENCES

1 THURSTONE, L. L.; THURSTONE, THELMA GWINN; AND ADKINS, DOROTHY C. "The 1938 Psychological Examination." *Ed Rec* 20:263-300 Ap '39.
2 THURSTONE, L. L., AND THURSTONE, THELMA GWINN. "The American Council on Education Psychological Examinations, 1939 Editions," pp. 3-38. In *Psychological Examinations, 1939*. American Council on Education Studies, Series 5, Vol. 4, No. 2. Washington, D. C.: the Council, May 1940. Pp. v, 53. $0.25. Paper.
See also references for 1377.

A. H. Turney, Professor of Education, The University of Kansas. The use of the *American Council on Education Psychological Examination for College Students* is so widespread that a description of these tests would be superfluous. The figures [1] in the *Educational Record* for April, 1939, would seem to indicate that the *American Council on Education Psychological Examination for High School Students* is not so widely known. The high school tests are the same in form and content (not identical items, of course) and the manuals are in the same form. Both hand- and machine-scorable forms are available. There seems to be no reason why the high school forms are not as serviceable and valuable as the college forms.

The reviewer has used the latter for seven years, testing new students to the number of about ten thousand, and has been well satisfied with the results.

These two editions have separated the test into a language and a quantitative section, giving respectively an *L* and *Q* score and also a gross score. These may appeal to many users. The manual and scoring devices are simple yet entirely adequate. It seems only just to say that a very valuable service is being rendered by the makers and publishers of these tests.

For a review by V. A. C. Henmon, see 1038.

[1379]
Arthur Point Scale of Performance Tests. Ages 6 and over; 1925-30; 2 forms; $62.50 per complete testing outfit for Form I (No. 37047); $29.75 per set of four additional tests necessary for Form II; $1 per 25 record blanks for Form I (No. 44003); (35-90) minutes; Grace Arthur; Chicago, Ill.: C. H. Stoelting Co.

REFERENCES

1 ARTHUR, GRACE, AND WOODROW, HERBERT. "An Absolute Intelligence Scale: A Study in Method." *J Appl Psychol* 3:118-37 Je '19.
2 ARTHUR, GRACE. "A Standardization of Certain Opposites for Children of Grade School Age." *J Ed Psychol* 14:483-95 N '23.
3 ARTHUR, GRACE. "A New Point Performance Scale." *J Appl Psychol* 9:390-416 D '25.
4 ARTHUR, GRACE. "A Group Point Scale for the Measurement of Intelligence." *J Appl Psychol* 10:228-44 Je '26.
5 ARTHUR, GRACE. "An Attempt to Sort Children with Specific Reading Disability from Other Non-Readers." *J Appl Psychol* 11:251-63 Ag '27.
6 ARTHUR, GRACE. "The Re-Standardization of a Point Performance Scale." *J Appl Psychol* 12:278-303 Je '28.
7 RILEY, G. "Stanford Binet 'Indicators' of Mechanical Ability." *Psychol Clinic* 18:128-32 My-Je '29.
8 ARTHUR, GRACE. *A Point Scale of Performance Tests*: Vol. I, Clinical Manual, New York: Commonwealth Fund, 1930. Pp. ix, 82. $1.50. (London: Oxford University Press. 6s. 6d.)
9 BROWN, ANDREW W. "The Correlations of Non-Language Tests with Each Other, with School Achievement, and with Teachers' Judgments of the Intelligence of Children in a School for the Deaf." *J Appl Psychol* 14:371-5 Ag '30.
10 ARTHUR, GRACE. *A Point Scale of Performance Tests*: Volume II, The Process of Standardization. New York: Commonwealth Fund, 1933. Pp. xi, 106. $1.50. (London: Oxford University Press, 6s. 6d.)
10.1 MACKANE, KEITH. *A Comparison of the Intelligence of Deaf and Hearing Children*: A Study of the Reactions of Comparable Groups of Deaf and Hearing Children to Three Performance Scales and a Non-Language Test. Columbia University, Teachers College, Contributions to Education, No. 585.

Rudolf Pintner, faculty sponsor. New York: Bureau of Publications, the College, 1933. Pp. ix, 47. Out of print.
11 KNIGHT, MAXINE WISLER. "A Comparative Study of the Performance of Feeble-Minded and Juvenile Delinquents on the Arthur Performance Scale and the Stanford-Binet Test of Intelligence." *J Juvenile Res* 18:5-12 Ja '34.
12 MAHAN, HARRY C. "A Battery of Performance Tests: The Arthur Scale Revised." *J Appl Psychol* 18:645-55, 859, O, D '34.
13 HILDEN, ARNOLD H., AND SKEELS, HAROLD M. "A Comparison of the Stanford-Binet Scale, the Kuhlmann-Anderson Group Test, the Arthur Point Scale of Performance Tests, and the Unit Scales of Attainment." *J Exp Ed* 4:214-30 D '35.
14 HUMM, KATHRYN A. "The Applicability of the Grace Arthur Performance Scale to an Adolescent Group." *Psychol B* 32:538 O '35.
15 BISHOP, HELEN M. "Performance Scale Tests Applied to Deaf and Hard of Hearing Children." *Volta R* 38:447 Ag '36.
16 ARTHUR, GRACE. "The Predictive Value of the Kuhlmann-Binet Scale for a Partially Americanized School Population." *J Appl Psychol* 21:359-64 Ag '37.

Andrew W. Brown, Chief Psychologist, Institute for Juvenile Research, Chicago, Illinois; and Associate Professor of Psychology, University of Illinois. The *Arthur Point Scale of Performance Tests* is a restandardization of twelve of the formboards of the *Pintner-Paterson Performance Scale* and in addition the *Porteus Maze Test* and the *Block Design Test*. These fourteen tests are divided into two forms. The *Knox Cube Test,* the *Seguin Formboard,* the *Porteus Maze Test,* and the *Block Design Test*—the most discriminative tests—are included in both forms, but presented in a different way in each form. Two of the tests, the *Two-Figure Formboard* and the *Gwyn Triangle Test,* are given as practice tests and are not scored. The material and methods used in the construction of the test are clearly and systematically presented in Volume II.[10] Volume I is the clinical manual.[8]

Theoretically the scale has two distinct advantages over some of the other performance tests. First, it is a point scale and second, the various tests are weighted according to their "discriminative value." The tests which most sharply discriminate one age group from the other receive the greatest weight in the total score. The age norms for Form I are based upon the scores of 1,100 public school children of a good middle class "American" district. The norms for Form II are based upon scores of 535 of the same children who had already been tested on Form I.

The probable error of measurement between the IQ's on the two forms ranges from 4.52 at age six to 8.45 at age fourteen. There are norms for ages six to fifteen. In contrast to some of the verbal tests the material seems interesting and attractive to most children.

The scale in its present form is intended as a clinical instrument to be used by adequately trained clinicians in psychological and psychiatric clinics. As such it has fulfilled its purpose well, especially between the ages seven or eight and twelve or thirteen. It does not appear to work as well above this level as does the *Cornell-Coxe Performance Ability Scale*.

The primary value of the Arthur scale is its use with foreign children or those who come from homes where a foreign language is spoken or those with educationally impoverished environment or those with reading difficulties.

With one or two exceptions the tests can be given by pantomime directions, and although verbal directions were used in the standardization, the test results by pantomime would probably deviate little if any from those obtained by verbal directions. It can therefore be used effectively in the examination of deaf children.

The scale is a valuable clinical instrument. One is often surprised, after having inspected the growth curves in Pintner and Paterson's *A Scale of Performance Test,* that it works as well as it does. Frequently the results correspond more closely with clinical impressions and the child's history, than the results of verbal tests. Correlations ranging between .50 and .75 have been reported between this and the Stanford-Binet. Because of these relatively low correlations and because of its fairly high reliability the scale serves as a good supplement to verbal tests of the Binet type. The scale also gives the examiner an opportunity to observe the child under different conditions than those during a verbal test. The child's method of approach in a concrete situation, his insight, his motor coordination and his persistence in a task can be noted.

On the other hand the clinician must not take the results too seriously especially for older dull children. Tests such as the *Seguin Formboard,* the *Casuist Formboard,* and the *Mare and Foal Test* are for children at this level more tests of speed-of-motor-performance than tests of "intelligence." Frequently older dull children of juvenile court age make relatively high scores on the performance tests which are entirely discrepant with performance in school, in shop, in the community or with clinical impressions.

Carroll A. Whitmer, Assistant Professor of Psychology, The University of Pittsburgh. The *Arthur Scale of Performance Tests* is composed of the following individual tests:

Knox Cube Test, Seguin Formboard, Two-Figure Formboard (used only as a transition between the solid block board and the divided block board and not scored), *Casuist Formboard, Manikin and Feature Profile* (scored in series), *Mare and Foal Test, Pictorial Completion Test I, Porteus Maze Test* and the *Block Design Test*. Form II consists of the *Knox Cube Test, Seguin Formboard, Gwyn Triangle Test, Five-Figure Formboard, Glueck's Ship Test, Pictorial Completion Test II, Porteus Maze Test,* and *Block Design Test*.

The subjects used in standardizing Form I, after a preliminary period of experimentation, numbered 1,125 and ranged in age from five to fifteen. These subjects were chosen from a public school in a middle class "American" district. Out of this standardization group, 574 children with Kuhlmann or Stanford-Binet IQ's in an approximate range of 57-125 were used for the mental age norms.

The process involved in fitting each test into the scale and in standardizing the scale as a whole is described in detail in Volume II [10] accompanying the manual [8] for the tests. It is sufficient to say in review that each test takes its point score value from its capacity to discriminate between successive age levels and is used in the manner which yielded the highest discriminative value according to the formula employed. It is obvious that the experience reported in the standardization volume would be of definite value to any other worker who considers using any of these tests in a new scale. The author reports a probable error between the Kuhlmann-Binet IQ's and Form I of the Arthur scale of 4.97. The corresponding probable error between Form I and Stanford-Binet IQ's was 4.92.

Form II of the scale is less well standardized and according to the author would require more work before it could equal Form I in reliability. It is obvious to any one experienced in formboard use that retesting with any formboard or scale of formboards presents an almost insurmountable problem of dealing with practice effects. For that reason and after having observed some retest cases with Form II, the writer feels that the primary serviceability of the Arthur scale is in Form I.

A method of extrapolation of scores is presented for use in the case of the subject whose score falls outside the norms for the chronological ages 6.5 to 16.5 years inclusive. The author admits the relative inaccuracies of such procedures particularly in respect to the lower extension. In view of the fact that the subject who scores less than the points required for the 5½-year rating must certainly score below the norm on some tests, it would seem that that subject is relatively unmeasured. In practice we have found the scale less suitable than the *Merrill Palmer Scale of Mental Tests* for measuring the child of preschool age or the dull child who scores below the 7-year level.

Although the inaccuracies of the extrapolation for the brighter or older subject are admitted, we have found the method of extrapolation useful because of its possibility for use with the foreign speaking or deaf subject who under normal conditions would not be a logical subject for formboards.

The Arthur scale provides a means of interpreting the total point value obtained when one test is omitted from the scale. We have found this treatment of the score useful when the subject has had some specific experience with one of the tests.

As compared with the *Pintner-Paterson Performance Scale* we feel that the Arthur scale is better suited to the examination of school children because of its method of standardization. In comparison to other formboard scales it is relatively easy to administer and score. The directions for presenting the tests are simple and the scoring does not require the counting of moves or errors. All tests are scored on time or success in parts or as a whole. The author has used what seems to us a very awkward means of handling the child in the test situation in requiring him to turn his head or hide his eyes while the material of the test is being arranged. It would seem much more reasonable to arrange the material on the back of the boards before the subject appears, then the parts could be quickly slid onto the table and the board placed at the time the directions are being given, thus facilitating the administration process.

We have found the Arthur scale a very valuable supplement to the Binet type of test. In cases of deaf, foreign language speaking, or emotionally blocked subjects, the test provides a substitute which with qualitative observation plus the score gives a fair index of general mental level. We feel that the Arthur should be used as a *substitute* only when the Binet cannot be accurately done, but it certainly

Arthur Point Scale of Performance Tests

should be a part of the equipment of any well-equipped clinic for mental examinations of children.

J Ed Psychol 21:716-7 D '30. *Donald Snedden.* * The chief disadvantage of the scale as a whole is its inelasticity. Good age norms are available for the total point score, but not for the separate tests. This means that in case a test is "spoiled" an adjustment (that is not simple) has to be made to the incomplete total score. It seems to the reviewer that the advantages far outweigh the disadvantages and that the scale should have and will have a very wide clinical usefulness.

[1380]
Australian Council for Educational Research Non-Verbal Tests. Ages 9-14; 1936; 1s. per 25; 5d. per manual; 24 (40-45) minutes; Melbourne, Australia: Australian Council for Educational Research.

REFERENCES

1 MCINTYRE, G. A. *The Standardization of Intelligence Tests in Australia.* Australian Council for Educational Research, Educational Research Series, No. 54. Melbourne, Australia: Melbourne University Press, 1938. Pp. 82. 4s. Paper. (London: Oxford University Press, 1939. 4s.) (New York: G. E. Stechert & Co. $1.00.)

[1381]
Bristol Group Reasoning Tests. Ages 10½-14; 1926; 3 forms; 1s. 8d. per 25; 8d. per 25 practice sheets; 6d. per manual; 9d. per specimen set; nontimed (90) minutes; A. Barbara Dale; London: University of London Press, Ltd.

REFERENCES

1 DALE, A. BARBARA. "Group Tests in Reasoning Ability." *Brit J Psychol* 16:314-38 Ap '26.

Charles Fox, formerly Director of Training, University of Cambridge. This admirable test is based on Burt's individual test of reasoning, amplified and recast so as to be suitable for group testing. There are three equivalent forms of the test, each containing 15 items, and a practice test to act as a shock absorber. There is no time limit as speed is not of importance in testing reasoning; but one hour is sufficient to enable each testee to do all he is capable of doing. It is essential for reliability to emphasize the fact that there is no need to hurry, and to make arrangements accordingly in the testing room. The table of norms given in the manual of directions covers the age-range 10½ to 14 years for primary school children; but the tests can be applied up to 16 years at least. The construction and validation of the tests have been described by the author in the *British Journal of Psychology.*[1] There appears to be no difference in the standardization for English or American children; nor any appreciable sex differences. Objectivity of marking, which is a great difficulty in reasoning tests, is secured by allowing the testee to select by underlining among a number of alternatives. Much ingenuity has been displayed in the alternatives given, so that guessing is precluded.

Many individual or group tests include tests of reasoning as subtests, but there are few tests of reasoning alone, and the Bristol test is the best of them. The present reviewer has given a selection from these tests to brighter and duller classes of 12 years of age in a central school, and found a marked difference in average scores. He was able also to confirm the finding of the author of the tests that there is a correlation between the total class position of the testees and excellence in the tests. The tests are, therefore, useful for diagnostic purposes to get an estimate of general suitability for school work. The three alternative forms of equal difficulty provide a ready means of estimating the growth of ability over a prolonged period of time.

Percival Smith, Principal Assistant Organiser, Education Department, Birmingham, England. These tests have been very carefully constructed. The fact that they are based on an early test-scale prepared by Cyril Burt who has written an introductory note to the instructions is evidence that the tests may be accepted, within certain limits, as scientific and reliable. Dale, however, in overlooking Burt's statement that "the power to reason is *one of the most important* mental capacities," puts her claim too high when she asserts that one of her chief aims has been to "use as a measure of mental ability the fundamental process of reasoning." The tests are reasoning tests and the results should and no doubt do give a valuable and reliable assessment of one facet of mental ability.

The instructions are clear and thorough although minor criticisms might be made. For instance, it seems unwise to "provide each child with pen or pencil." It is preferable and usual for pencils only to be allowed in such tests.

Two tables of norms are supplied and two methods have been followed in their preparation. The first table gives the average score obtained by children from 10½ to 14 years of age at intervals of six months.

The second table gives the average score obtained by children in Standards IV, V, VI, and VII respectively. This second table at once dates the test as it is no longer the practice to grade children in English elementary schools in such a simple manner. As a rule children are graded according to their age in "year groups" and secondarily in streams according to their capacity. Although exact details are not supplied it would appear that the norms were prepared some 13 years ago. It is suggested that a useful purpose would be served by calculating up-to-date norms. These useful tests would then be of even greater value.

[1382]
California First-Year Mental Scale. Ages 1-18 months; 1933; individual; 1 form; $73.82 per complete testing outfit (No. 37018); $36.07 per testing outfit not including the crib, table, high chair, and mirror; 55¢ per manual; $1.12 per 25 record blanks; Nancy Bayley; Chicago, Ill.: C. H. Stoelting Co.

REFERENCES

1 BAYLEY, NANCY. *The California First-Year Mental Scale.* University of California, Syllabus Series No. 243; Institute of Child Welfare. Berkeley, Calif.: University of California Press, May 1933. Pp. 24. $0.50. Paper.

Florence L. Goodenough, Research Professor, Institute of Child Welfare, The University of Minnesota. The standardization of the *California First-Year Mental Scale* is unique in that it was based upon repeated examinations of the same group of infants who were tested at monthly intervals from 1 through 15 months and were again tested at 18 and at 21 months. The total number of cases was 61; the average number tested at each of the specified ages was 54, and the smallest number tested at any age was 46. Although this seems like a small group for normative purposes, the developmental changes in performance are probably more reliably established than they could have been by the use of much larger numbers selected by the usual cross-sectional method. Inasmuch as all the children came from the city of Berkeley, where, owing to the large proportion of families connected with the University of California the average intellectual level of the population has been shown to be above that of the country as a whole, it is probable that the standards given are somewhat above those for the infant population in general, particularly since the author states that the socio-economic status of the families was slightly higher, on the average, than even the Berkeley standards. However, it is obvious that such an error, if it exists, would operate equally at all ages at which the test was given. The test should therefore be relatively free from the irregularities not uncommonly met with in tests standardized on a cross-sectional basis in which it may chance that the children tested at one age are on the average truly inferior to those tested at another age.

The instructions for giving and scoring the test are clear and concise. Results may be expressed in terms of an absolute scale value derived by the Thurstone method, the sigma deviation from the mean of the age-group, or in mental age units. The use of the IQ or Developmental Quotient is not recommended since the standard deviations do not increase in proportion to age beyond the first few months.

Although the scale appears to provide a fairly accurate appraisal of the child's developmental status at time of testing, it does not afford a basis for predicting mental status after the period of infancy has passed. As a matter of fact, the author has shown that the correlations between individual test performance during the first year of life and standing on other recognized tests of intelligence after the age of three years show a low but consistently negative trend. This is in accordance with the findings of other investigators with tests designed for infants. A number of interesting theoretical questions are thereby raised, but a probable explanation appears to be that the content of the tests included in the infant scales may be psychologically so dissimilar from that of the tests used with older children that no clear-cut relationship could be expected. It should be noted that the tests used for infants are largely concerned with relatively simple motor and perceptual items of a kind that have never been found to correlate highly with intelligence at any age.

Perhaps at some time a future student of child development will be able to single out other aspects of infantile behavior that will provide more stable indications of his mental potentialities. On the other hand, it may be that the overt manifestations of that which we later call "intelligence" do not reach the threshold of perceptibility until after the period of infancy is past. In attempting to predict the later mental status of a child on the basis of his behavioral capacity during infancy, we may be in much the same case as if we were to attempt to predict the later growth of the beard of a male child at the same age. Except by inference from other known facts, no character can be predicted until its emergence has at least begun.

Although the writer has not lost hope that the first possibility may in time be realized, there is no use in blinding ourselves to the fact that the time is not yet come. In the meantime, it should be noted that the so-called mental tests for infants have done much to acquaint the scientific world with the normal course of certain aspects of behavioral growth during its early stages, but that thus far these tests have not proved to be useful instruments for the clinical prediction of later mental capacity.

[1383]
California Preschool Mental Scale. Ages 1½-6 years; 1934; individual; 1 form; $27.95 per testing outfit without manual, carrying case, or record blanks; $10 per carrying case; 75¢ per manual; 5¢ per record blank, 50 or more (the manual and record blanks must be ordered from the University of California Press, Berkeley, California); Adele S. Jaffa; Berkeley, Calif.: Joseph Dominion, 2734 Milvia St.

REFERENCES

1 JAFFA, ADELE S. *The California Preschool Mental Scale: Form A.* Foreword by Herbert R. Stolz. University of California, Syllabus Series, No. 251; Institute of Child Welfare. Berkeley, Calif.: University of California Press, November 1934. Pp. v, 66. $0.75. Paper.

B. M. Castner, Clinic of Child Development, Yale University. We have here a group of test situations, mostly borrowed from previously published scales, and arranged in developmental sequences under ten headings, some of which refer to important basic fields of behavior, such as "Language" and "Manual Facility," while others are simply descriptive categories, such as "Block-Building" and "Completion." The selection of tests is good, on the whole, and the normative placement of the individual items does not vary significantly from their original placement in the scales from which they were taken. The amount of testing material called for seems unnecessarily great, with many small items, difficult to keep in order.

Details of the standardization procedures are not given, nor is there any detailed presentation of results. The number of cases—there were about 2,000 tests on approximately 800 children—is relatively large as preschool standardization groups go. Since large groups representative of the general population are not available within this age range, as they are in the case of school children, it is particularly necessary to present details as to selection of subjects, conditions of testing, variability of response, and the like, in order that the results may be properly evaluated. It is conceded that a major group, which has furnished the basis for one method of scoring, is definitely superior.

Three methods of scoring are provided: (*a*) an "approximate" mental age and IQ score; (*b*) a sigma score; and (*c*) a profile score, in which the maturity levels indicated in the respective test categories are considered individually and collectively. The MA-IQ type of scoring for preschool children will not appeal to those who have sufficient experience, based upon follow-up study of many children over a period of several years, to know in how large a number of cases such measures can be seriously misleading. Unfortunately, it will appeal, because of its simplicity, to those who attempt to use the tests without a background of training and experience, and are likely to put precisely similar interpretations upon MA and IQ that they are accustomed to make in the case of school children. The sigma score would be expected to have more value, but is here based upon the results obtained in a superior group. The "profile" score has definite advantages over the other two types in that it encourages an analytic interpretation of the total performance, and emphasizes acceleration or retardation in specific fields of behavior, so commonly met with in preschool children, and so important for the proper understanding of the test results, particularly from the point of view of prognosis. The value of this method of scoring would be increased if the test-categories were better defined in terms of significant basic fields of behavior. It is unfortunate, too, that the profile scores have not been thoroughly studied, and are "offered principally as an interesting departure from traditional method." They are, even so, if applied with clinical judgment based upon adequate experience, better than either of the two other methods.

But the gravest defect in the scale, from the social as well as the clinical point of view, lies in the extremely brief and quite inadequate description of what are to be scored as "successes" in response to the individual items, and the omission of any discussion of the significance of qualitative variations from the prescribed responses. Much less than older persons do normal preschool children respond in the cut-and-dried way which might be expected from reading the brief statements given here; and interpretation of failures is often extremely difficult, even for the experienced examiner. There is little in this presentation to discourage the inexperienced tester from attempting developmental diagnosis on the basis of tests given according to formula and woodenly scored by a plus-and-minus rating, as has been done to the point of scandal in the case of older children. Within the preschool age range, the serious injustice that often results from such methods is certain to be even more frequent.

In summary, it may be said that this scale contains a good group of individual tests, probably well placed from the normative point of view, but inadequately standardized as a scale. Since none of the scoring methods are completely satisfactory, and since the discussion of the significance of test-responses is too brief to be clinically useful, most examiners will prefer to use one of the other available preschool scales in which the requirements are more adequately met. Further research, however, might convert this into a useful method for preschool study.

Florence L. Goodenough, Research Professor, Institute of Child Welfare, The University of Minnesota. The *California Preschool Mental Scale* was prepared especially for use in certain research projects at the University of California Institute of Child Welfare and has been little used elsewhere. The items were selected from a number of other published scales with some additions by the author. A distinctive feature of the test is the attempt to maintain psychological uniformity of content from age to age by dividing the items into ten categories, roughly described as (*a*) manual facility, (*b*) block-building, (*c*) drawing, (*d*) form discrimination, (*e*) spatial relations discrimination, (*f*) size and number discrimination, (*g*) language comprehension, (*h*) language facility, (*i*) immediate recall, (*j*) completions, with one or more tests in each category (with a few exceptions) included at each age level. The record booklet is prepared in the form of a profile chart by which the child's standing on each of the ten categories is shown separately. However, inasmuch as this standing is based upon so few tests that lie near the developmental level of any individual child, it is questionable whether the individual profiles can be said to have much clinical significance since the reliability of the separate point-determinations cannot be high. The author gives no data on this head. Undoubtedly, however, uniformity of test-meaning from age to age has been increased by this arrangement.

The instructions for scoring are needlessly complicated but the method itself is not difficult, once it has been worked through. A technique is devised whereby the child is not penalized for the accidental omission of items or for items that he refuses to attempt. Results may be expressed in the usual terms of mental age and intelligence quotient, in sigma units, or in a point score scaled according to the Thurstone technique.

The test items seem to have been very well selected both from the standpoint of children's interests and variety of content. The scale merits a wider use than it has received.

[1384]

California Test of Mental Maturity. Grades Kgn.-1, 1-3, 4-8, 7-10, 9-adults; 1936-39; 1 form, 3 editions; $1.25 per 25 copies of the regular edition; 75¢ per 25 copies of the short-form edition; 25¢ per specimen set of any one edition at any one level; 2¢ per machine-scorable answer sheet; (90) minutes for the regular edition; (45) minutes for the short-form editions; Elizabeth T. Sullivan, Willis W. Clark, and Ernest W. Tiegs; Los Angeles, Calif.: California Test Bureau.

a) PRE-PRIMARY BATTERY. Grades Kgn.-1; [*Regular Edition*]; *Pre-Primary S-Form*.

b) PRIMARY BATTERY. Grades 1-3; [*Regular Edition*]; *Primary S-Form*.

c) ELEMENTARY BATTERY. Grades 4-8; [*Regular Edition*]; *Elementary S-Form*; *Elementary S-Form: Machine Scoring Edition*.

d) INTERMEDIATE BATTERY. Grades 7-10; [*Regular Edition*]; *Intermediate S-Form*; *Intermediate S-Form: Machine Scoring Edition*.

e) ADVANCED BATTERY. Grades 9-adults; [*Regular Edition*]; *Advanced S-Form*; *Advanced S-Form: Machine Scoring Edition*.

REFERENCES

1 TIEGS, ERNEST W. "Breaking Down the I.Q." *Prog Ed* 13:603-5 D '36.

2 MAXFIELD, FRANCIS N. "California Test of Mental Maturity." *Ed Res B* 16:188-9 + O '37.

3 TRAXLER, ARTHUR E. "A Study of the California Test of Mental Maturity," pp. 49-60. In *1937 Fall Testing Program in Independent Schools*: Including a Study of the California Test of Mental Maturity. Educational Records Bulletin No. 22. New York: Educational Records Bureau, January 1938. Pp. x, 60. $1.50. Paper, lithotyped.

4 TRAXLER, ARTHUR E. "Some Correlation Data for the California Test of Mental Maturity," pp. 63-9. In *1938 Fall Testing Program in Independent Schools and Supplementary Studies*. Educational Records Bulletin No. 26. New York: Educational Records Bureau, January 1939. Pp. x, 69. $1.00. Paper, lithotyped.

5 TRAXLER, ARTHUR E. "Study of the California Test of Mental Maturity, Advanced Battery." *J Ed Res* 32:329-35 Ja '39.

Raymond B. Cattell, G. Stanley Hall Professor of Genetic Psychology, Clark University. This test has a regular and a short form and is available in hand-scored or machine-scored printings. However, since the same principles of construction are well observed throughout, it is possible to consider the merits of the test as a whole.

A plan of which most psychologists will approve is the breaking-up of the range of mental improvement into several ranges, each of two or three years' span. In this way the measurement is made finer by more items and the type of test is better adapted to the child's mental age. On the other hand, the tester needs to know beforehand, by some preliminary omnibus test, in what range of mental age any given child is likely to fall.

These tests are exceedingly well designed from the point of view of adaptation to school needs and the convenience of the teacher. All the data regarding consistencies, standardization, correlation with school progress, etc., that one could reasonably demand, are clearly presented in the handbook of instructions. In only one case is there some danger of misunderstanding, and then only by the test user not familiar with the statistical and psychological notions of the professional psychologist. This occurs in the table on "IQ's and Related Data as Shown by School Surveys" in which one finds opposite IQ 114, 99th percentile; and opposite IQ 85, 5th percentile. Many teachers will probably need to be emphatically warned that this is not the percentile distribution of individual IQ's, but of group medians (and how big are these groups?). In the same table, years of retardation in reading are set against IQ levels. That this relation depends on the absolute age of the pupil is not conspicuously suggested by the table.

An admirable feature of this test is the courageous manner in which the authors come out into the open regarding the purpose, principles, and theory of test design. They point to factor analysis as their foundation, but reject the two-factor theory of a general intellective power g in favor of a multiple-factor supposition. They are, of course, quite entitled to do this, since either of these theories fits the correlations, but it seems a little wayward deliberately to adopt the more complex rather than the more simple explanation, with special cause for doing so.

A possible reason for this behavior becomes evident when we come to the application of results. People having little acquaintance with intelligence test research, as is well known, like to pass beyond the mere IQ, possibly because they feel that a single index is a small return for so much labor of testing. They wish to elaborate their analysis of the child and will generalize, from particular test items, or even from the child's manner of answering or his handwriting, in a far-reaching way about temperament or special abilities. Every psychologist is familiar with the tendency in teachers or parents, but not all are willing to cater to it.

The authors evidently feel that this desire to find out more than about intelligence from an intelligence test alone is to be encouraged, for they write, "dealing only with mental ages and intelligence quotients obscures and ignores the separate important factors." They add, rightly, that independent special factors have been found in verbal and arithmetical fields and (incorrectly) in spatial performance but then proceed to speak as if the separate subtests in their test measure these factors and are independent. They offer a profile which "analyzes and summarizes the various factors which are measured by the test situations," and claim that this "reduces the 'mystery' which has surrounded the meaning of mental age and intelligence quotient." This attempt to produce for special consumption a "psychology without mystery" ends by appearing to the psychologist to be "mystery without psychology." No proof is offered that these subtests do, in fact, test independent factors or that one is justified in generalizing from them to performances in everyday life which happen to have the same verbal label.

A useful application of ingenuity in these tests is the introduction of tests of visual acuity and hearing at the beginning of the test. Most psychologists have known "mental defectives" who turn out only to be somewhat deaf.

Ingenuity is less happy in the use of terms; indeed, originality here seems to have become perverse. Why, for example, "Foresight in Spatial Situations," or why call the familiar and correctly described "Classifications" test a "Similarities" test? Why bring confusion and mystery into a very good intelligence test by departing from custom so far as to call it a "Mental Maturity" test? The term "maturity" in personality measurement has become increasingly associated with the notion of emotional maturity. Intelligence is not "maturity," otherwise we should count a child's teeth in assessing it, and it would continue in growth far beyond adolescence. It is to be hoped, both in the interests of their test and of avoiding dis-

California Test of Mental Maturity

ruption of clear discussion in psychology, that the authors will indicate by a better label that their test belongs to the category of intelligence tests.

F. Kuhlmann, Director of the Division of Examinations and Classification, State Department of Public Institutions, St. Paul, Minnesota. These tests include five batteries to cover the range from kindergarten to grade 14, inclusive. There is a long and short form, the long form requiring two sessions of about forty-five minutes each to give. In each battery there is a test on visual acuity, auditory acuity, and motor co-ordination. Following this the tests are grouped as tests of Memory, Spatial Relationships, Reasoning, and Vocabulary. The tests in these four groups are also classed as "Language Factors" tests, and "Nonlanguage Factor" tests. Age norms are given for each of these and for the total number of right responses on the whole battery, making it possible to compute seven sets of mental ages and corresponding IQ's. Profile scoring is provided for and recommended.

The outstanding features of these batteries are: first, the inclusion of tests on vision, hearing, and motor co-ordination, which, if defective, would invalidate the results on the other tests; second, the wealth of material included in each battery; third, the underlying theory on which the selection of the tests and construction of the batteries are based.

We do not believe there is much merit in labeling tests as regards functions measured, as the authors have done; first, because it cannot be done correctly by inspection; and second, because these labels are not of much value until we know also how these functions enter into school achievement in different school subjects. Also, when a battery is divided into several different measures the tests assigned to measure any particular function tend to become inadequate in number and range to do so reliably. It would be hazardous, indeed, to conclude from the score on two brief tests that a child has a poor memory, for example. It seems to be implied also that the child mind is simply the adult mind in miniature, so that tests should measure the same function at all ages. We believe the empirical and more usual procedure is better. This starts out experimentally to find tests of maximum discriminative capacity at each age, and regards the question of what functions are measured at any age by such tests as of minor importance. The authors' distinction between language factor and nonlanguage factor tests is also somewhat misleading. Language enters both, the real distinction being that in the former the child has to read test material, while in the latter he is told what to do with picture material and, with a few exceptions, no reading is involved.

The authors have probably built much better than they planned. The different tests in each battery probably measure a much greater variety of functions than they are intended to measure. They should have given more evidence that the tests are arranged in order of difficulty in each battery and that they are more or less equally spaced on the basis of difficulty. The increase in total raw score with increase in age does this only rather roughly. Outside of this, we believe the *unabbreviated* batteries are to be classed among the very best on the market for determining general levels of mental maturity. It is gratifying to see authors with the courage to offer tests that take more than a single class period to give and who do not attempt to get the maximum economy in time and dollars, by sacrificing everything necessary to attain this end.

Chicago Sch J 21:304 My-Je '40. D(avid) K(opel). [Review of the Short Form.] * Each test contains six sub-tests, of which three are designated as "non-language" and three as "language." It is claimed, quite reasonably, that this feature is particularly valuable in cases where reading or language difficulties may invalidate the results obtained from use of the ordinary group verbal test of intelligence. An unusual feature is the inclusion of a pretest of visual acuity. Since many items in each test consist of pictures and other symbols containing fine details, it is thought necessary to identify individuals suffering from gross visual defect for whom the test is therefore inappropriate.

For reviews by W. D. Commins, Rudolf Pintner, and Arthur E. Traxler see 1042.

[1385]
Carl Hollow Square Scale. Ages 10 and over; 1939; 1 form; $36.00 per testing outfit; (25-60) minutes; George P. Carl; Philadelphia, Pa.: Psychological Service, Institute of the Pennsylvania Hospital.

REFERENCES
1 CARL, GEORGE P. *Manual of Directions for the Carl Hollow Square Scale.* Philadelphia, Pa.: Psychological Service, Insti-

tute of the Pennsylvania Hospital, 1939. Pp. 30. Sold only with testing outfit. Mimeographed.
2 CARL, GEORGE P. "A New Performance Test for Adults and Older Children: The Carl Hollow Square Scale." *J Psychol* 7:179-99 Ja '39.

T. J. Keating, Research Fellow, The Training School at Vineland, New Jersey. The Carl Hollow Square Scale meets the need for a formboard test which has enough top to be useful for superior adults. The materials used—a frame and blocks—are well made and conveniently arranged in a portable wooden box. The blocks are so labeled that those used in a particular subtest—the scale is composed of twenty—may be easily identified.

Contrary to one's initial impression, administration is relatively easy. The time consumed is fairly long, twenty-five minutes or more. Scoring, which is based on time, moves, and a correction, is somewhat cumbersome. The effect of readministration is not indicated in the author's manual. The subtests do not appear to become increasingly difficult in a regular progression. The length of the scale acts as a corrective to this irregular progression; results may therefore be accepted with some assurance.

[1386]
Cattell Intelligence Tests, Revised Edition. Mental ages 4-8, 8-11, 11-15, 15 and over; 1930-35; 2s. for manual for Scales I-III; 6s. per specimen set; R. B. Cattell; London: George G. Harrap & Co., Ltd.
a) SCALE 0 (DARTINGTON SCALE). Mental ages 4-8; 1933; individual; 1 form; 6s. per 25; 6s. per set of cards; 2s. per manual; (45) minutes.
b) SCALE I (NON-VERBAL) REVISED. Mental ages 8-11; 1930-35; 2 forms; 6s. per 25; (45-50) minutes.
c) SCALE II, REVISED. Mental ages 11-15; 1930-35; 5s. per 25; 6s. per set of cards; 2 forms; 66(75) minutes.
d) SCALE III, REVISED. Mental ages 15 and over; 1930-35; 2 forms; 5s. per 25; 66(75) minutes.

REFERENCES
1 CATTELL, RAYMOND B., AND BRISTOL, HILDA. "Intelligence Tests for Mental Ages of Four to Eight Years." *Brit J Ed Psychol* 3:142-69 Je '33.
2 CATTELL, RAYMOND B. "Occupational Norms of Intelligence, and the Standardization of an Adult Intelligence Test." *Brit J Psychol* 25:1-28 Jl '34.
3 CATTELL, RAYMOND B. "Standardization of Two Intelligence Tests for Children." *Brit J Psychol* 26:263-72 Ja '36.

Godfrey H. Thomson, Professor of Education and Director of the Training Centre for Teachers, University of Edinburgh. These tests are in many ways excellent. The handbooks give full and clear directions, and give references to the articles in easily accessible journals where the ingenious standardisation of the tests is described. I do not think, however, that any reliabilities are given either in the handbooks or in the articles referred to. If there are any they are at least not given a prominent place. And there is one statement (that "Scale III is at the moment the most widely standardised of adult tests") which appears to be entirely unsupported. As I have no experience of Cattell's Scale 0 (for mental ages of 4-8 years) I shall in the remarks which follow speak only of his Scales I, II, and III.

The chief criticism I have to make of the handbook to these scales is that it does not warn the purchaser sufficiently that these tests have the peculiarity that they give a much wider scatter of intelligence quotients than is usual. My criticism, as I wish to make very clear, is not against this feature of Cattell's tests in itself, but against inadequate warning of the peculiarity. The only sentence in the handbook concerning this point is that "the scatter of IQ's is decidedly greater than on the Binet Test and in accordance with recent research," with a reference to an article[2] by Cattell. Even in that article, however, the purchaser, if he refers to it, will not easily find a quantitative statement of how much greater the Cattell scatter is than the Binet scatter. The standard deviation of Binet IQ's is about 15 or 16 points. In the article referred to, I find by calculations on Figures 7 and 8 a standard deviation of 27 points of Cattell IQ and on Figure 3 about 20 points. A calculation on Figure 5 in another article[3] of Cattell's, which refers to Scale IIA, gives a standard deviation of 21 points of Cattell IQ. Our experience at Moray House in giving tests to university graduates of about 22 years of age is that the excess of IQ over 100 needs to be reduced about two-thirds in order to be comparable with other tests.

In the diagram showing intelligence levels in various occupations, reproduced in the handbook, there is indirect evidence, for those familiar with vocational IQ's, of the wide scatter of Cattell IQ's. The average IQ of 90 elementary schoolteachers for example is given as 137, which is much higher than their average Binet IQ.

It is of course possible that Cattell is right in finding this scatter. In his 1934 article he quotes my own experience in finding higher standard deviations with group tests than with the Binet test. I did not, however, conclude that the Binet scatter was wrong, though I anticipated the rise from Terman's Californian 13 points to the Scottish Survey's 16 or 17 points. I have reread Cattell's articles on standardising his tests and find much to praise and nothing to criticise except the small number of cases on which some points depend, and the very daring way in which he multiplies up his actual 1,039 men on page 8 of his 1934 article to obtain a balanced population of 227,081. But I do not think his wide scatter of IQ's is explicable by these features. There should be, I think, further research on the lines he has indicated. Meanwhile, however, the handbook to his tests should more emphatically, and *quantitatively*, warn the purchaser that Cattell IQ's, if they are high, are too high, and if they are low, are too low, compared with most other measures of IQ.

[1387]

Chicago Non-Verbal Examination. Ages 7-adults; 1936-40; 1 form; individual; may be administered using either verbal or nonverbal directions; $1.50 per 25 tests; 60¢ per manual and keys; 10¢ per sample test; (40) minutes; A. W. Brown with the assistance of S. P. Stein and P. L. Rohrer; New York: Psychological Corporation.

REFERENCES

1 BROWN, ANDREW W. "The Development and Standardization of the Chicago Non-Verbal Examination." *J Appl Psychol* 24:36-47, 122-9 F, Ap '40.

Robert G. Bernreuter, Director of the Psycho-Educational Clinic and Associate Professor of Psychology, The Pennsylvania State College. The *Chicago Non-Verbal Examination* is intended to measure the nonverbal aspects of intelligence. It is a group test, composed of ten subtests, which may be administered either orally or by pantomime. It requires 25 minutes of actual working time, plus the time necessary for making the task clear in each of the subtests.

Reliability coefficients varying from .80 to .93 are reported by the author. They were obtained by both the split-half and the retest techniques, on groups with ranges of two and three years in chronological age, and two to six grades in school placement. As a consequence, the test is probably not reliable enough to use in comparing a child with his classmates within a single grade, but probably is reliable enough to compare him with the children in a wider range of grades.

Four criteria were used to determine the validity of the test: correlation with chronological age, comparison of normal and feebleminded children, the normality of the distribution of scores, and the correlation with other tests. So far as can be told by these criteria, the test seems to be reasonably valid. Furthermore, the types of items of which the ten subtests are composed are all well known and have been shown by previous investigators to be useful. However, the author has not made a multiple factor analysis of the intercorrelations of his subtests. Had he done so, the validity of the test as measures of Thurstone's primary abilities might have been disclosed. Lacking this information, it is impossible to say more than that the test measures the "nonverbal aspects of intelligence." Considered in the light of Thurstone's work, this is very nearly a meaningless phrase.

A total of over 6,000 cases, from age six to adulthood were tested during the process of standardization. Mental ages, percentile scores and so-called "modified standard scores" have been prepared for the test administered orally. The latter serve as a substitute for IQ's above 14 years and are reasonably similar, numerically, to IQ's obtained on the Revised Stanford-Binet. However, a comparison of the table for obtaining mental ages from raw scores with the one for obtaining percentile scores, discloses some discrepancies in the derived scores. If, for example, a child has a constant IQ at each age from 6 to 14, his percentile scores will vary unsystematically, sometimes as much as 20 points. If he has a constant percentile score, his IQ will vary unsystematically. Because of these characteristics, the norms must be treated as tentative.

Myrtle Luneau Pignatelli, Clinical Psychologist, Bellevue Psychiatric Hospital, New York, New York. The *Chicago Non-Verbal Examination* is a test purporting to measure general intelligence without the use of verbal symbols. It is especially suitable for those children who are deaf or are hard of hearing, who have reading difficulties, who come from environments where there is limited use of the English language, and in general those who have difficulty in manipulating verbal concepts. It will especially be useful in urban centers which have large foreign populations.

The author has selected for the battery, tests which can be administered by both verbal and pantomime directions. Using the verbal directions, the test can be applied to children from age 6 through the adult level, and with the nonverbal directions, to children of age 7 through the adult level. The tests include the following performances: (*a*) common digit-symbols test; (*b*) marking out what does not belong in a series of pictures or designs; (c) counting number of blocks in a pile; (d) selecting from a series of geometrical forms, two of which can be put together to make a given form; (e) selecting from a series of designs one of which is just like a given design; (f) arranging the parts of a picture to make a complete picture; (g) numbering pictures according to a certain sequence; (h) marking the thing that is wrong in each of a number of pictures; (i) selecting from a series of pictures, the one that goes with or is a part of a given picture; and (j) learning, of a more difficult type than that in a.

The norms for the tests were established on 1844 normal hearing children from the middle-economic class in Chicago. The sampling is held to be respresentative of children of elementary school age up to year 14. Norms are given for mental ages, percentile ranks, and modified standard scores for each age up to 14 years. For groups above 14 years, only percentile ranks and standard scores are available. Reliability obtained for both verbal and pantomime directions is between .80 and .90. Clinical use of the tests by the authors has shown its value for the child with language difficulty, and ratings are reported to compare favorably with Stanford-Binet rating in the middle IQ range.

The examination compares favorably with the *Pinter Non-Language Mental Test* and the *Revised Beta Examination* as an instrument for the measurement of general intelligence, although it covers a wider range of mental functions. The tests make demands on the powers of association, visualization, depth imagery, integrative perceptual capacity, momentary perceptive retentiveness for purposes of gestalt organization, social appercention, and judgment. The instrument shows how difficult it is to devise tests which do not make use of verbal concepts in some forms. Of the ten tests in the battery, only four appear entirely free of such concepts, while the remaining tests make wide demands on general information and knowledge of things associated with everyday life.

The directions are clear, but for some types of individuals, may not be readily grasped. The scoring is objective, and facilitated by the use of stencils. The pictures in some of the tests could be clearer and less detailed, though the printing is fairly distinct.

The examination will not be a good measure of general intelligence for persons with uncorrected visual difficulties or slow psychomotor reactions, but clinically it may prove to be a very good indicator of the efficiency of mental functioning in certain types of mental cases. It has possibilities for use as a research instrument, and from a practical standpoint, if used with individuals who are functioning up to capacity, it will tap, somewhat more thoroughly than other instruments of its type, the essential aspects of intelligence.

S. D. Porteus, Director of the Psychological Clinic and Professor of Clinical Psychology, University of Hawaii. This scale consists of ten subtests. Tests 1 and 10 are digit substitution tests, the former being much simpler than the latter. In Test 10 there are no less than twelve drawings which look like Chinese characters to be paired with digits. If the person is test-wise he can make a good score without much mental exercise by taking one form at a time throughout the series and putting the digit underneath it wherever it occurs. If he is not test-wise it is a rather difficult exercise in associating symbols arbitrarily. This, of course, is not the common use of symbols. Ordinarily symbols are used to shortcut reasoning processes as in algebra, but there is no exercise of memory required in remembering what the symbol stands for. Symbol substitution of the kind examined in the test is of little or no importance in our thinking. To weight it by including two tests of this nature in the series is unwise.

Test 2 is a test of the ability to see quickly the incongruous item in a pictured series. Unfortunately, some of the objects are so badly drawn that precious time is consumed by the effort to see what the drawing represents. The writer could not tell whether one item was a woman's hat or a handbag, and in another was confused in determining whether the picture represented a telegraph key or a patent can opener.

Test 3 is a cube counting test in which the cubes are drawn in most unnatural perspective. In my opinion, it should be declared unconstitutional as involving cruel and inhuman punishment of the subject. Anyone who can count those cubes without eyestrain has exceptional vision. Is the test one of cube counting or is it

Chicago Non-Verbal Examination

intended to examine persistence in the face of ocular distress?

Test 4 presents a task in recognizing space relationships, the task being to duplicate a given shape by selecting from a number the appropriate segments. This kind of visual ability is, of course, very useful in working out jigsaw puzzles, but the ordinarily intelligent person can get along with a very moderate degree of ability in this direction. The writer is aware of this fact because he usually does very poorly in this kind of exercise. Test 6 provides another trial of capacity to mentally manipulate pictured forms, while Test 5, like Test 3, sets a problem in matching complicated forms that is certainly hard on the eyes.

Test 7, arrangement of pictured events in proper time sequence, is one of the most interesting, but unfortunately as the test becomes more difficult the artist (*sic*) becomes more careless. This criticism applies chiefly to the last three sequences, which are annoyingly unintelligible. Among three psychologists who attempted the final sequence, there were four opinions as to the correct solution. It showed (*a*) a boy riding on a bicycle, (*b*) a man sitting on his hunkers looking at two roadside lunch wagons (or alternatively—by stretching your imagination and the man's legs—a person running towards a train), (*c*) a man receiving a telegram, (*d*) a man blowing his nose at what might be a death bed scene. All this is interesting but it could be anybody's guess whether the person died first or last in the sequence. Relatives must sometimes be sent for *after* a person's demise, especially if that person has been inconsiderate enough to die without warning.

Unfortunately, the artistry of Tests 8 and 9 is equally atrocious. In the latter the subject is shown an object and then he is supposed to select one of four others with which the first picture naturally belongs. For example, Item 5 shows a little boat with two seats (presumably to carry five persons) suspended from davits (with no mechanism for lowering the boat so that the only way to launch it would be to cut the ropes and let it fall into the sea). The unhappy testee is required to say whether this boat belongs with an ill-drawn yacht, a pleasure cruiser, a liner, or another steamship—all equally ill drawn. The right answer is, of course, that it goes with none of them—least of all the liner, which is scored correct. These may seem like picayune criticisms of trifles, but it is attention to details that the test is supposed to examine. One wonders whether the artist ever saw a ship.

Undoubtedly a great deal of ingenuity has gone into the making of this test, and one can assume that a psychologist of Andrew Brown's status will have done all the work necessary on validation and standardization. The test needs redrawing, for in its present form it offends again two prime requisites of a good test—namely, intelligibility and nonambiguity of the problem. If by increasing the size of the pictures and improving the drawings these objections can be obviated, then the scale may have a useful function.

[1388]
Cornell-Coxe Performance Ability Scale. Ages 4½-16; 1934; 1 form; individual; $26.95 per complete testing outfit (the testing outfit should be ordered from Ellen Wilson, 1013 N. Madison St., Rome, N. Y.); $1.50 per examination manual; [1] 90¢ per 25 individual record blanks; Ethel L. Cornell and Warren W. Coxe; Yonkers, N. Y.: World Book Co.

REFERENCES

[1] CORNELL, ETHEL L., AND COXE, WARREN W. *A Performance Ability Scale*: Examination Manual. Yonkers, N. Y.: World Book Co., 1934. Pp. iv, 88. $1.50.
[2] BRILL, MOSHE. "Performance Tests as Aids in the Diagnosis of Maladjustment." *J Genetic Psychol* 49:199-214 S '36.
[3] LINCOLN, HAZEL. "A Study of the Cornell-Coxe Performance Ability Scale with Superior Children." *J Genetic Psychol* 50:283-92 Je '37.

Francis N. Maxfield, Professor of Psychology, Psychological Clinic, The Ohio State University. This scale consists of a series of six nonverbal tests, with a seventh test which may be used as an alternate for Test 3. Test 2 is a modification of Kohs' *Block Design Test*. The other six were used in the *Army Performance Scale*. The material is less expensive than that required for the Pintner-Paterson or Arthur scales and less cumbersome. The directions for giving and scoring the tests (Chap. 5) are very clear and unequivocal. Coloring the sample block designs on page 71 will facilitate scoring. Speed as well as accuracy is scored in four tests. Raw scores on each test are translated into weighted scores, which are added to derive a point score for the scale. This is translated in turn into a mental age score.

As Thurstone pointed out years ago the concept of "mental age" is ambiguous. One may use, as most authors have done, the respective mean or median scores of successive age groups to determine his mental age score, or he may use the respective mean or median chronological ages of those making a series of scores. The authors of this scale profess (p. 33) a preference for the latter determination, but go on (p. 34) to use a compromise method for their own table of norms, so that the mental ages derived from the scale do not conform to either definition of mental age. The IQ, or "PIQ," is derived in the usual way, though directions are not given as to what one should use for a divisor in the case of a feebleminded adult with a mental age score of six years.

Scores in terms of mental age or IQ are often misleading or ambiguous because they do not indicate the degree of deviation of the score in question below or above the norm for the pupil's age group. If a boy of seven makes a mental age score of 7 years, 7 months on Form L of the *Revised Stanford-Binet Scale*, his IQ being 108, one can give this rating a standard score of 0.5, or a centile rank of 69. Unfortunately the authors of the Cornell-Coxe scale give no tables from which deviation within the pupil's age group may be determined.

The scale will be found most useful in testing children of elementary school age. Its use in differentiating different types among over-age children who test low on the Stanford-Binet is well illustrated in Chapters 3 and 4. With slight modification, the scale can be given to children who are deaf or who understand little English. For children over thirteen, it is not as satisfactory as the Arthur scale.

Chapter I, *Functions of a Performance Scale*, is a clear statement of the practical method of the clinical psychologist in his use of tests in general and of nonverbal or "performance" tests in particular. Psychologists and psychoclinicians of limited experience should reread this chapter every three months, and those of longer experience occasionally check their practice by it. Think how much unnecessary misunderstanding might have been avoided in some recent discussions of changes in intelligence if everyone had noted this sentence carefully. "We," the authors state, meaning not themselves but authors of tests in general, "have constructed tests on the theory that we could measure differences in intelligence by measuring differences in performance when experience and opportunity were the same, and then we have often proceeded to ignore the differences in experience and opportunity and considered that we had *bona fide* differences in intelligence." (p. 4)

Correlations: between original and retest scores made by 125 pupils on this scale, $r = .93$; between mental ages on the Stanford-Binet and on this scale (306 pupils from kindergarten through the eighth grade), $r = .79$; between CA and MA on this scale, $r = .78$.

Carroll A. Whitmer, Assistant Professor of Psychology, The University of Pittsburgh. The *Cornell-Coxe Performance Ability Scale* is composed of the following tests: Test 1, Manikin-Profile; Test 2, Block-Designs; Test 3, Picture-Arrangement; Test 4, Digit-Symbol; Test 5, Memory-for-Designs; Test 6, Cube Construction; and Test 7, Picture-Completion. Only six of the tests are used, Test 7 being a substitute for Test 3.

Detailed description of the tests and the procedure involved in the standardization of the tests is presented in the examination manual. The manual also includes a very good discussion of the functions of the performance scale as well as a discussion of interpretations illustrated by case studies.

The raw scores on the separate tests are computed on a combined time and accuracy basis and stated in points. The standardization process involved weighting the raw scores so that each test would contribute equally to the total raw score. The method used to achieve this end was to distribute the scores for each test on a 10 sigma base line. According to the authors: "In order to find a score on the Block-Designs Test equivalent to any sigma value, say 3.0, we determined from a statistical table the per cent of cases which should fall below this sigma value (2.28 per cent), then found this same per cent of our 306 cases (i.e., 7 cases), and calculated the score below which this number of cases fell (score 3.7). In a similar way we located every sigma value in terms of the test score." (p. 30) Arbitrary weights from 1 up were then assigned to the sigma values of the scores. The computed test score equivalent and the corresponding weights assigned for each test score were then plotted and a line of best fit adjusted to these data. The final weighted test scores were taken from the line of best fit.

The total battery score is the sum of the weighted score values for the six tests of the battery. Age norms for the total scores were read from a line drawn midway between the regression lines plotted first, upon the best fit for the means of chronological ages corresponding to each score, and, second, for the means of the scores corresponding to each chronological age.

According to the authors the validity of the battery is substantiated by its relationship to other test results (correlation with *National Intelligence Test*, .74 and with Binet, .79) and in the fact that the correlation with chronological age is .78. An indirect indication of validity is claimed in results shown by individual case analysis. The reliability of the battery is indicated by a correlation of .93 between the two performances of 125 children reexamined after an interval of 11 months.

In summarizing the standardization data the reviewer feels that 306 cases ranging in grade placement from kindergarten through eighth grade is a very questionable sampling. The manual does not include an adequate description of the standardization group with respect to age other than grade placement. Consequently, adequate age norms for performance on the separate tests are lacking.

For practical clinic purposes the Cornell-Coxe scale offers a variety of tests not found in the other performance scales. It is unfortunate that adequate age norms are not presented for the performance on the separate tests in order to allow the examiner some standard reference point for the child's performance.

The administration and scoring of the battery is somewhat more complicated than that of either the Arthur or the Pintner-Paterson scales. A special record blank which includes the Digit-Symbol Test and the tables for scoring conversions and norms as well as a record of performance on the other tests is provided for using the test. The need for the special blank increases the cost of using the test. The record blank would be improved if the locations for drawing the designs were not outlined. The subject frequently attempts to use the lines bounding the space provided and when not actually permitted to make them part of his drawing still uses them as guides.

In our experience we find that the scale fails to measure the average or superior child above 10 or 12 years of age because of its inadequacy in the upper range. We find also that the directions for the Pintner-Paterson and the Arthur scales are easier to explain to the deaf or non-English-speaking child.

For the experienced examiner the Cornell-Coxe scale provides a variety of material of interest to the child and a means of observing the qualitative aspects of his performance. We could recommend the battery with its present standardization as a supplement to rather than in place of either the Binet type of test or the other formboard batteries mentioned above.

See also B77 and B335.

[1389]

Dawson Mental Test. Ages 11-12; 1936; 2 forms; 3s. 6d. per 25; 6d. per test; 1s. per manual; 40(45) minutes; Shepherd Dawson; London: George G. Harrap and Co., Ltd.

Raymond B. Cattell, G. Stanley Hall Professor of Genetic Psychology, Clark University. The design of this test shows the throughness, common sense perspective and care over detail which characterised all the research enterprises of the late Shepherd Dawson.

The test is in omnibus form with a reasonably adequate number (80) of pass or fail items, and a working time (40 minutes) which is not too brief. The A and B forms are well designed in parallel, almost item for item, but it seems a mistake to supply only one norm table for both, on the assumption that they will coincide in difficulty over all ranges of performance.

There is no indication in the booklet as to the number or quality of the child populations used in standardization, nor is there any reference to articles in which these particulars might be found. That validity and consistency coefficients are overlooked is not so important; for consistency is meaningless without particulars of the dispersion of the population concerned, while validity as measured against a Binet test might in this case be an attempt to assess a good test against a less g saturated medley.

For the subtest forms mixed in this omnibus —opposites, classification, analogies, etc.—are all such as have been shown by many previous researches and factor analyses to have high g saturation for children of this age range (9 years and upwards). There has also been much care to avoid unusual words or words likely to belong only to a bigger vocabulary. Increasing difficulty has not been produced by the fallacious procedure of demanding more verbal education but by requiring nicer judgment among words and ideas known presumably to all children.

Nevertheless there is no research proof that every word is within the vocabulary of the youngest children taking the test. The reviewer's opinion is that the test attempts to measure too wide a range of mental age with one test form. It is probable too that the omnibus design, involving special instruction on each item or group of items is wasteful of testing time in comparison with the test constituted by half a dozen subtests, each having items graded in difficulty.

Percival Smith, Principal Assistant Organiser, Education Department, Birmingham, England. This mental test is prepared in the cycle omnibus style but not with the cycle omnibus system. Each alternative test consists of 80 questions of very varied types, including reasoning, analogies and numbers. The alternative tests appear very similar but it would be interesting to know whether the two have been correlated and if so what coefficient was obtained.

The test can apparently be applied to children between the ages of 9 and 18 years; at any rate the published table of norms gives scores for all ages between these limits. The reviewer finds it difficult to believe that the test can be reliable for such a wide age range. It is always wise when placing a mental test on the market to publish data in regard to its standardization. No doubt this test was given to a considerable number of children during its preparation and particulars are known as to its correlation with other mental measures. Such information would be helpful to teachers and others who desire to make use of the test.

The instructions allow 40 minutes for giving the test. The reviewer found that at the end of 25 minutes a girl of 17 had completed the test and had been through the answers a second time. The table of norms gives a mental age of 18 to a child getting a perfect score of 80. It is not usual for a group intelligence test to be constructed in such a way that a perfect score can be obtained.

For additional reviews, see 1043.

[1390]

Dearborn-Anderson Formboards 2 and 2b. Ages 5-10, 10 and over; 1916; 2 levels; also called *Formboard 2, Dearborn Formboard 2,* or *Reconstruction Puzzle*; Walter F. Dearborn and John E. Anderson.
a) FORMBOARD 2. Ages 10 and over; 8-depression board; $8.00; (8-20) minutes for first trial; Cambridge, Mass.: Psycho-Educational Clinic, Palfrey House, Harvard University.
b) FORMBOARD 2b. Ages 5-10; 4-depression board; $5; (5-10) minutes for first trial; Cambridge, Mass.: Psycho-Educational Clinic, Palfrey House, Harvard University. ($6.50 (No. 27165); Chicago, Ill.: C. H. Stoelting Co.)

REFERENCES

1 DEARBORN, W. F.; ANDERSON, J. E.; AND CHRISTIANSEN, A. O. "Form Board and Construction Tests of Mental Ability." *J Ed Psychol* 7:445-58 O '16.
2 DEARBORN, WALTER F.; SHAW, EDWIN A.; AND LINCOLN, EDWARD A. *A Series of Form Board and Performance Tests of Intelligence.* Harvard University, Harvard Monographs in Education, Series 1; Studies in Educational Psychology and Educational Measurement, No. 4. Cambridge, Mass.: Graduate School of Education, Harvard University, September 1923. Pp. 64. $1.00. Paper.
3 BRONNER, AUGUSTA F.; HEALY, WILLIAM; LOWE, GLADYS M.; AND SHIMBERG, MYRA E. *A Manual of Individual Mental Tests and Testing,* pp. 155, 229. Judge Baker Foundation Publication No. 4. Boston, Mass.: Little, Brown and Co., 1927. Pp. x, 287. $3.50.
4 SCHIEFFELIN, BARBARA, AND SCHWESINGER, GLADYS C. *Mental Tests and Heredity:* Including a Survey of Non-Verbal Tests, pp. 169-70. New York: Galton Publishing Co., Inc. 1930. Pp. ix, 298. Out of print.

Grace H. Kent, Psychologist, Danvers State Hospital, Hathorne, Massachusetts. Two formboards, published as Formboards 2 and 2*b*, are built to carry the same insets. These three insets are irregular quadrilateral blocks, markedly unlike in size and form but having certain dimensions in common. Each block can be matched against either of the others in any of five ways. There are many different ways of assembling these three blocks in a group; and thus it is possible to obtain the outlines for many irregular figures which are equal in area while differing widely in form. Board 2 has eight recesses thus outlined, and Board 2*b* has four.

The four-hole board, which is the more convenient both in size and in degree of difficulty, is used at Danvers State Hospital for a practice series of at least three trials. The board is presented as shown in the publisher's catalog illustration, with its three blocks in the upper left corner from the subject's point of view. The subject is informed that all three blocks can be fitted into each of the holes; and is instructed (in language appropriate to his mental level) to insert them in each recess, in a clockwise circle, without stopping until the blocks are back in the starting place. It is made clear that he is being timed for the whole circle, not for individual figures; and if he pauses after filling one recess he is hurried along to the completion of the circle. After the time is recorded for the first trial he is requested to try again and see if he can do it more quickly.

Dawson Mental Test

The number of trials need not be kept constant for different examiners nor for different subjects, but the third trial is perhaps the most significant one for the average subject. It may be expected that the first performance will be by trial and error. The mathematical nicety of construction—at all times a delight to the examiner—is usually lost on the subject at first; but his appreciation of it is frequently apparent in the later trials. Occasionally he carefully seeks the middle block for first placement in each recess, thus marking off clearly the exact positions for the other two blocks.

The reviewer would not wish to see this board standardized, because standardization would of necessity destroy its adaptability to the individual subject. The discriminative capacity of a single formboard is rarely wide enough to justify the effort and cost of standardization, and it is doubtful if norms would add anything important to the usefulness of this test.

The board is inexpensive, easily portable, and so simple that it can be made by hand from several layers of cardboard. (Not, however, from any published drawings seen recently by the reviewer.) Requiring very little time for presentation and very little space in the briefcase, it can be recommended as a convenient addition to the equipment of the traveling clinic.

[1391]

Dearborn Formboard 3. Ages 6 and over; 1916; also called *Construction Puzzle, Block Test,* or *Formboard 3*; individual; $10 (No. 27179); worklimit (10-20) minutes; Walter F. Dearborn; Chicago, Ill.: C. H. Stoelting Co. ($10; Cambridge, Mass.: Psycho-Educational Clinic, Palfrey House, Harvard University.)

REFERENCES

1 DEARBORN, W. F.; ANDERSON, J. E.; AND CHRISTIANSEN, A. O. "Form Board and Construction Tests of Mental Ability." J Ed Psychol 7:445-58 O '16.
2 DEARBORN, WALTER F.; SHAW, EDWIN A.; AND LINCOLN, EDWARD A. *A Series of Form Board and Performance Tests of Intelligence.* Harvard University, Harvard Monographs in Education, Series 1; Studies in Educational Psychology and Educational Measurement, No. 4. Cambridge, Mass.: Graduate School of Education, Harvard University, September 1923. Pp. 64. $1.00. Paper.
3 YOAKUM, CLARENCE S., AND YERKES, ROBERT M., EDITORS. *Army Mental Tests,* pp. 107-9, 122. Published with the authorization of the War Department. New York: Henry Holt and Co., 1920. Pp. xiii, 303. Out of print.
4 YERKES, ROBERT M., EDITOR. *Psychological Examining in the United States Army,* pp. 132-3, 152-3, 184-5, 191, 307, 400, and passim. Memoirs of the National Academy of Sciences, Vol. 15. Washington, D. C.: Government Printing Office, 1921. Pp. vi, 890. Out of print.
5 GAW, FRANCES. *Performance Tests of Intelligence,* pp. 24-7. Medical Research Council, Industrial Research Board, Report No. 31. London: H. M. Stationery Office, 1925. Pp. iv, 45. 2s. 6d. Paper.
6 BRONNER, AUGUSTA F.; HEALY, WILLIAM; LOWE, GLADYS M.; AND SHIMBERG, MYRA E. *A Manual of Individual Mental Tests and Testing,* pp. 123-4, 219-20. Judge Baker Foundation Publication No. 4. Boston, Mass.: Little, Brown, and Co., 1927. Pp. x, 287. $3.50.
7 WELLS, F. L. *Mental Tests in Clinical Practice,* pp. 129-31. Yonkers, N. Y.: World Book Co., 1927. Pp. x, 315. $2.16.
8 SCHIEFFELIN, BARBARA, AND SCHWESINGER, GLADYS C. *Mental Tests and Heredity:* Including a Survey of Non-Verbal Tests, pp. 170. New York: Galton Publishing Co., Inc. 1930. Pp. ix, 298. Out of print.

Grace H. Kent, Psychologist, Danvers State Hospital, Hathorne, Massachusetts. Of all the performance tests used in Danvers State Hospital, this formboard is the favorite. There are no norms that can be recommended, nor is there any published series of tasks in which full utilization of the test-possibilities of the board is even approached; but the construction of the board itself—so far as this reviewer is concerned—is absolutely beyond criticism.

The board contains nine recesses, one being a 2-inch square and another, a circle of 2-inch diameter. The other seven recesses are multiples either of these figures or of their component parts, in various combinations. The most distinctive inset is made by taking a semicircle of 1-inch radius out of one side of a 2-inch square. (The remaining portion of the square is referred to here as a "concave," for lack of a better name.) For the nine recesses there are twenty-one insets, as follows: five whole figures, including three squares, one circle and one double-concave; sixteen half-figures, consisting of six triangles, six semicircles and four concaves.

The smallest recess can be filled only by a single block of its own form; whereas the largest one can be filled by any one of at least eleven different combinations. The possibilities of setup for the entire board are practically innumerable, and the number of tasks to be included in a series is entirely optional. (The reviewer uses eight tasks of increasing difficulty, plus a demonstration task.)

The unit task, which serves as the basis for more complicated tasks, may be described as follows: The board is presented with one whole square on the outside, and with no vacant places in the board except a semicircle in one figure and its complementary "concave" in another figure. The subject is instructed to make a place for the square in the frame without making any more moves than are necessary. If he can spot a square filled with the blocks needed for these two openings, he can in three moves transfer these blocks to the appropriate vacant places and then insert the square in the place thus left vacant.

The distinctive feature of the test is that it permits an accurate move-count, thus making possible a scoring system which is not dependent upon speed. It is permissible, if desired, to record the time of performance as well as the number of moves; and to evaluate the achievement by two independent variables. But the reviewer prefers to measure the subject's speed of performance by some test which does not admit of being scored except by speed, and to assure the subject in advance that his performance on this test will not be timed. In the great majority of performance tests the slow worker is very heavily discriminated against. This test owes its unique value to the fact that it gives the slow worker a fair opportunity to show what he can do. As an untimed test, it is applicable even to the pathologically retarded patient.

Another very strong feature of the test is that a failure from the examiner's point of view is not usually apparent to the subject as a failure. The young child, interested primarily in filling the board, easily forgets that his moves are being counted. The subject who empties the board and replaces the blocks by trial and error is as a rule well satisfied with his performance. For him, it is a real achievement to complete the task of filling the board.

Although not quite essential, it is highly desirable to have a board for each task and to prepare the setup in advance of the examination. It is worth-while also to have a specially-built cabinet with a shelf for each board.

[1392]
Detroit Advanced First-Grade Intelligence Test.
Grades 1-2; 1925-28; 1 form; $1.10 per 25; 10¢ per specimen set; (30-35) minutes; Harry J. Baker; Yonkers, N. Y.: World Book Co.

A. M. Jordan, Professor of Educational Psychology, The University of North Carolina. The purpose of this test is to furnish an instrument for measuring the unclassified pupils of the first grade and those of the low second. Seven tests constitute the whole. In none of these tests is reading required. The recognition of printed numbers is demanded in all to designate position and in one to designate the number of items to be counted. The tests are the usual ones: marking drawings or objects from their names and from a description of them; discovering similarities; drawing in missing parts; recognizing one object among five others, recognizing parts of objects from their description, recognizing printed numerals up to 18 and then counting the designated number of objects. The test has developed through preliminary editions in mimeographed form. It uses the old Stanford-Binet technique of measuring tests against a high group, middle group, and low group which to say the least is open to question since the very division into higher, middle and lower was determined by a preliminary use of these very tests. The items are roughly scaled in each part of the test. The scoring is simple and quickly done. There are tables for transmuting these scores into letter grades for each six months from 5½ to 11 years. This is a distinct advantage. The letter ratings are based on 2,975 cases tested, curiously enough, in the year 1926. Approximate MA equivalents are also available. The reliability of the test with repeated measures of the same test is given as .94. The reviewer believes that the probable error of measurement should also be furnished with each test. This measure does not appear. The second testing produced a gain of 9 points. The correlation with Stanford-Binet MA's in the case of 46 unselected pupils was .85; but in the case of 227 mentally backward, .57.

The drawings except in two or three cases are easily recognizable. In one case the reviewer could not tell whether the picture was a ball, an orange, or some other unrecognizable object. Then, too, some of the directions seem at least a little fuzzy. For example, "Mark the part of the pail to carry it . . . and the part of the tea kettle where the water [*sic!*] comes out," or again, mark "the part of the face that talks" and "the part of the bee that helps him fly." These statements which seem confusing to an adult might not be so to a six-year old.

As a whole the test will fill a useful niche in the testing of young children.

[1393]
[**Detroit Intelligence Tests.**] Grades 2-4, 5-9, 9-16; 1924-34; 2 forms, 3 levels; $3.00 per 100; 15¢ per specimen set of any one level; Harry J. Baker; Bloomington, Ill.: Public School Publishing Co.
a) DETROIT PRIMARY INTELLIGENCE TEST. Grades 2-4; 1924-34; (30-35) minutes.
b) DETROIT ALPHA INTELLIGENCE TEST. Grades 5-9; 1924; (45-50) minutes.
c. DETROIT ADVANCED INTELLIGENCE TEST. Grades 9-16; 1924; 29(40) minutes.

REFERENCES
1 KUHLMANN, F. "The Kuhlmann-Anderson Intelligence Tests Compared with Seven Others." *J Appl Psychol* 12:545-94 D '28.
2 SEAGOE, M. V. "An Evaluation of Certain Intelligence Tests." *J Appl Psychol* 18:432-6 Je '34.

W. Line, Associate Professor of Psychology, University of Toronto. The series is of a

Dearborn Formboard 3

fairly traditional type. In form the tests are satisfactory, and the instructions appear to be adequate and clear. The standardization is based on a population sufficiently large to warrant confidence in their usefulness for general school purposes. The manual presents some evidence suggesting that the various sections of the test are less homogeneous than might be desired if the instrument is to be used beyond the local setting in which it was constructed. For that reason, local norms and reliabilities differ from those based on nation-wide data. Perhaps tests of the information type are partly responsible for this. Justification for the plan of interpreting results by subsections (e.g., under such captions as Memory, Reasoning, etc.) is not given, since detailed analysis of the results of the standardization is not given.

[1394]

Ferguson Formboards. Ages 4 and over; 1920; individual; $58.50 per set of 6 formboards (No. 37007); (10-40) minutes; George Oscar Ferguson, Jr.; Chicago, Ill.: C. H. Stoelting Co.

REFERENCES

1 FERGUSON, GEORGE OSCAR, JR. "A Series of Form Boards." *J Exp Psychol* 3:47-58 F '20.
2 MCFARLANE, MARGARET. *A Study of Practical Ability*, pp. 68-9. British Journal of Psychology Monograph Supplements. Vol. 3, No. 8. London: Cambridge University Press, 1925. Pp. viii, 75. 7s. Paper.
3 BRONNER, AUGUSTA F.; HEALY, WILLIAM; LOWE, GLADYS M.; AND SHIMBERG, MYRA E. *A Manual of Individual Mental Tests and Testing*, pp. 126-7, 220. Judge Baker Foundation Publication No. 4. Boston, Mass.: Little, Brown, and Co., 1927. Pp. x, 287. $3.50.
4 MACPHEE, E. D., AND BROWN, A. J. "An Inquiry into the Standardization of the Ferguson Form Boards." *J Ed Psychol* 21:24-36 Ja '30.
5 SCHIEFFELIN, BARBARA, AND SCHWESINGER, GLADYS C. *Mental Tests and Heredity*: Including a Survey of Non-Verbal Tests, pp. 166-7. New York: Galton Publishing Co., Inc. 1930. Pp. ix, 298. Out of print.
6 GARRETT, HENRY E., AND SCHNECK, MATTHEW R. *Psychological Tests, Methods, and Results*, Part 2, pp. 85-6. New York and London: Harper and Bros., 1933. Pp. x, 137, 235. $2.75; 10s. 6d.
7 PESCOR, M. J. "A Further Study of the Ferguson Form Board Test." *Pub Health Rep* 51:1195-1201 Ag 28 '36.
8 WILLIAMS, GRIFFITH W., AND LINES, JANET. "An Evaluation of the Ferguson Form Boards and the Derivation of New Age and Grade Norms: Part I, Procedure and Derivation of Norms." *J Appl Psychol* 21:556-71 O '37.
9 WILLIAMS, GRIFFITH W., AND LINES, JANET. "An Evaluation of the Ferguson Form Boards and the Derivation of New Age and Grade Norms: Part II, Presentation of Norms and Discussion." *J Appl Psychol* 21:673-87 D '37.
10 WOOD, LOUISE, AND KUMIN, EDYTHE. "A New Standardization of the Ferguson Form Boards." *J Genetic Psychol* 54:265-84 Je '39.
11 WERNER, HENRY. "A Comparative Study of a Small Group of Clinical Tests." *J Appl Psychol* 24:231-6 Ap '40.
12 FOWLER, H. L. "Report on Psychological Tests on Natives in the North-West of Western Australia." *Australian J Sci* 2:124-7 Ap '40.

Grace H. Kent, Psychologist, Danvers State Hospital, Hathorne, Massachusetts. This is a series of six tasks of increasing difficulty, each board having six somewhat irregular recesses fitted with insets. The first board has one block for each recess, and all the others have two for each. In Boards 3, 5, and 6 the two blocks for each recess are fitted together by matched beveled edges; and in Board 4 one block of each pair has a double bevel which fits into a groove in the other block. The tasks are essentially self-corrective, and can be presented without use of language.

The test was used by the reviewer in 1923, as an instrument for observation rather than for numerical results. The series marked an important advance over the detached form boards of the Pintner-Paterson scale; establishing beyond question the advantage of a graded series starting at the six-year level and leading up to a task discriminative at the adult level. The Ferguson series furnished the stimulus for the development of other performance test series having tasks graded in difficulty but similar in kind.

It is not, however, a strictly continuous series. The six tasks are quite varied in kind; (unavoidably so, inasmuch as it is almost impossible to increase the difficulty of a form-board series without introducing new principles of construction); and the six problems of a given task are also somewhat varied in nature. For example: one of the figures in Board 2 is an all-but-regular octagon having its diagonal dimensions slightly greater than the vertical and horizontal dimensions, divided diagonally into halves. No other figure of the board is divided diagonally into halves, and therefore there is nothing to suggest a diagonal placement for these two blocks. Almost any subject for whom the task is discriminative will try to insert the blocks in a vertical position, a placement which just barely misses being possible. Frequently the subject will make repeated attempts to insert the blocks either vertically or horizontally, apparently quite unable to accept the evidence that such placement is impossible. He may spend more time on this one figure than on the other five figures; may remove blocks correctly placed in other recesses, in his efforts to find a place for these blocks; may lose credit for the entire task because of his failure to solve this one problem; and occasionally may become so irritated by his failure as to react unfavorably to the rest of the examination. It seemed to the reviewer, when using the test, that this board offered material which might better have been used in two independent tasks.

What is measured by a test depending largely upon form perception is not easy to state, but there is no reasonable doubt concerning the value of the test. The lower end of the series appears to the observer to have some significance as a measure of mental capacity, but the upper end appears rather to be a test of mechanical aptitude. The form perception required for the performance of the first task is of so elementary a nature that it must almost of necessity be possessed by any person who has learned to dress himself; whereas the principles underlying the tasks at the upper end are rarely used except by engineers, skilled tradesmen and other technically trained persons. Experience in handling concrete materials is a strong factor in a subject's achievement. A dressmaker may achieve a high score, although women are generally weak in the test as compared with men. A cabinet maker of low achievement in language tests may spot the place for each block with almost unerring accuracy; while a university professor who has had comparatively little occasion to use his hands may startle the observer by the utter stupidity with which he attempts impossible placements.

The norms developed by the Judge Baker Foundation staff are much more adequate than those originally offered by Ferguson; but the value of the test is by no means dependent upon norms.

[1394.1]
Essential Intelligence Test. Ages 7-12; 1940; 1 form; 4d. per test; 3d. per test, 25 to 49 copies; 45(50) minutes; Fred J. Schonell and R. H. Adams; Edinburgh, Scotland: Oliver & Boyd, Ltd.

[1395]
Fiji Test of General Ability. Ages 9 and over; 1935; 1 form; 6d. per test; 1s. 6d. per manual; 27(60) minutes; Cecil W. Mann; Suva, Fiji: Government Printer.

REFERENCES
1 MANN, CECIL W. *Objective Tests in Fiji.* Suva, Fiji: Government Printer, 1937. Pp. i, 39. 1s. 6d. Paper.
2 MANN, CECIL W. "A Test of General Ability in Fiji." *J Genetic Psychol* 54:435-54 Je '39.

[1396]
General Intelligence Test for Africans. "African youths and adults who have received a certain amount of schooling"; 1932-37; 1 form; 25½(90) minutes; R. A. C. Oliver; Nairobi, Kenya Colony, East Africa: Government Printer.

REFERENCES
1 OLIVER, R. A. C. "The Adaptation of Intelligence Tests to Tropical Africa." *Oversea Ed* 4:186-91 '33.
2 OLIVER, R. A. C. "The Adaptation of Intelligence Tests to Tropical Africa II." *Oversea Ed* 5:8-13 '33.
3 OLIVER, RICHARD A. C. "Mental Tests in the Study of the African." *Africa* 7:40-6 Ja '34.
4 OLIVER, R. A. C. Chapter 15, "Mental Tests for Primitive Races," pp. 165-75. In *The Testing of Intelligence.* Edited by H. R. Hamley. London: Evans Brothers, Ltd., 1937. Pp. 175. 2s. 6d. Paper.

[1397]
Group Test of Intelligence, Advanced: Dominion Tests. High School and college; 1940; 2 forms; 2¢ per test in quantity; 15¢ per manual; 5¢ per sample test; 30(40-45) minutes; Toronto, Canada: Department of Educational Research, University of Toronto.

[1398]
Henmon-Nelson Test of Mental Ability. Grades 3-8, 7-12, 13-16; 1932-35; 2 forms, 3 levels; 75¢ per 25; single speciment set free; 30(35) minutes; V. A. C. Henmon and M. J. Nelson; Boston, Mass.: Houghton Mifflin Co.
a) ELEMENTARY SCHOOL EXAMINATION. Grades 3-8.
b) HIGH SCHOOL EXAMINATION. Grades 7-12.
c) INTELLIGENCE TEST FOR COLLEGE STUDENTS.

REFERENCES
1 DRAKE, LEWIS E., AND HENMON, V. A. C. "The Prediction of Scholarship in the College of Letters and Science at the University of Wisconsin." *Sch and Soc* 45:191-4 F 6 '37.
2 HENMON, V. A. C., AND NELSON, M. J. *The Measurement of Intelligence.* Educational Progress Bulletin, Vol. 13, No. 2. Boston, Mass.: Houghton Mifflin Co., September 1937. Pp. 21. Gratis. Paper.

Anne Anastasi, Assistant Professor of Psychology and Chairman of the Department of Psychology, Queens College. The three levels of this test, for elementary school, high school, and college, are closely similar in construction and administration. Each of the equivalent forms at each level consists of 90 items arranged in order of increasing difficulty. A wide variety of items is included, such as vocabulary, sentence completion, disarranged sentences, classification, logical selection, series completion, directions, analogies, anagrams, proverb interpretation, and arithmetic problems. Spatial, as well as verbal and numerical materials, are employed. The different types of items are not segregated but are arranged in a "scrambled" sequence. Administration is very simple, the examiner reading with the subjects the directions and sample exercises printed on each test. Scoring is by the Clapp-Young self-marking device and requires no key.

The validity of the tests was checked against scholastic achievement as well as against scores on other common intelligence tests. The authors report that for each of their tests the original selection of items was made by the method of contrasted- groups, i.e., "only such items as proved to differentiate between pupils of known superior and known inferior mental ability were retained." We are not told in what way the subject's superior or inferior ability was "known," but presumably the criterion was scholastic success. In some of the college groups, correlations are also reported between test scores and grades in various courses, as well as composite first term grades. The latter correlation was .60, the others ranging from

Ferguson Formboards

.46 to .60. These correlations compare fairly well with those obtained between most scholastic aptitude tests and college grades. Correlations between the Henmon-Nelson scores and scores on other well-known and widely-used group intelligence scales are also fairly high. Among the college groups, they range from .68 to .79. In the high school groups, they range from .77 to .88, and in the elementary school from .54 to .90. The number of subjects in each of the groups upon which these correlations were based was usually over 100, ranging from 57 to 554.

Reliability of the college form was determined by correlating the scores of 171 freshmen on Forms A and B. The correlation proved to be .89. For the other levels, reliability was found by the odd-even technique and the Spearman-Brown formula, but we are not told which of the three parallel forms of the test was employed in finding these correlations. Separate reliability coefficients are reported for each age and each grade. In the high school group, 100 cases were employed in finding each correlation, but no number is reported for the elementary school data. The reliabilities thus found are all high, being consistently in the upper .80's or in the .90's.

Percentile norms are reported for each grade in elementary and high school and for each of the four college classes. In the elementary and high school forms, tables of mental age equivalents are also included. Each of the three sets of norms was obtained on approximately 5,000 cases. In addition, the mental age equivalents for elementary and high school groups were subsequently checked on much larger samplings covering a wide geographical area. Further details regarding the selection of subjects are not given, except for the statement that the college students were drawn from colleges of different sizes and in different parts of the country. It would seem, in general, that the representativeness of the norms compares quite favorably with that found in the general run of intelligence tests.

The use of the mental age equivalent for point scores, as well as the use of percentile scores, are, of course, open to criticism. For a crude evaluation of the individual's relative standing in the group, however, such devices serve adequately. Similarly, the use of a single score based upon a hodgepodge of different types of items could be questioned, if one wanted a particularly fine or discriminative measure. But like other tests of its kind, this scale serves the practical purposes of (a) preliminary rapid exploration, and (b) rough classification of broad groups. It is interesting to note, in conclusion, that at the college level, the tests are described as a measure of "the aptitude of college students for academic work, or what has ordinarily been termed 'mental ability' or 'intelligence'." At the elementary and high school level, on the other hand, the prospective tester is told flatly and with no qualification that the tests measure mental ability. It is to be hoped that the distinction made by the authors in their manual is not a reflection on the relative psychological perspicacity of testers at the respective levels.

August Dvorak, Professor of Education, The University of Washington. These tests are designed to measure the mental ability of students in junior and senior high schools or in grades seven to twelve inclusive. Three forms of the test, which are identical in difficulty and construction, are available. Each form consists of ninety items arranged in order of increasing difficulty. Scoring is done in a remarkably short time, since the Clapp-Young self-marking device is employed. No scoring keys are necessary.

Two hundred fifty items were originally prepared and submitted to *experienced teachers* for their criticisms. The number was thus reduced to 202 items. These were divided into two forms and administered to about 500 students. The two forms of 90 items each were made from the items having the best predictive value. The tests were then printed in their present form and it is on the basis of the administration of this printed edition that the statistical data herein presented were derived.

In determining the validity of these intelligence tests, the authors secured correlation coefficients between IQ's of $r = .72$ to $r = .88$ for groups varying from 57 to 554 pupils to whom these tests and one of five other tests (Otis, Terman, American Council, Kuhlmann-Anderson, and Illinois) had been administered. It should be remembered that these coefficients were inflated by the common factor, chronological age, in both IQ's (spurious index correlation). Correlations between MA's and/or scores were $r = .78$ to .81. The validity of these tests may better be estimated when it is remembered that the alienation coefficient for $r = .80$ is $.60\sigma$.

The chief advantages of these tests lie in their ease of administration and scoring and that the relatively small number (90) of items require only 30 minutes of pupils' time. They may be an adequate measuring instrument for measuring intelligence if a low-cost (3¢ per pupil), 30-minute, quick-scoring test is desired.

Howard Easley, Assistant Professor of Educational Psychology, Duke University. These three tests are of the omnibus type. The materials of each test are very similar, consisting of, with minor variations, information, sentence completion, logical selection, classification, verbal analogies, number relations, anagrams, disarranged sentences, geometrical analogies, proverbs, word meaning, identifying family relationships, and arithmetic problems. Each test consists of 90 items, arranged in order of increasing difficulty. The validity of the individual items was determined by administering a much larger number of items to approximately 500 students and selecting the items which had the best predictive value.

The validity of the tests was determined by correlating these with a number of well-known tests. The correlations for the elementary test ranged from .54 to .92. Nine of the 19 correlations reported were above .80. The correlations for the high school test ranged from .72 to .88.

The reliability of the test for grades 3-8, determined by correlating odd-even halves, ranged from .89 to .94 for the separate age groups 8 to 14, and from .86 to .90 for the separate age groups 3 to 8. Similar reliability coefficients for the high school examination range from .91 to .94 for ages 12 to 17, and from .88 to .90 for grades 7 to 12.

For each of the lower grade tests mental age equivalents and the more important percentile points for the appropriate ages and grades are given; also tables for reading IQ directly from age and score. These tables are merely the result of computations of the MA divided by CA, and are unaffected by the varying significance of a given score made by children of different ages. It is not clear from the description in the manual whether the mental age equivalents represent the average scores made by children of certain ages, or the average ages of children who make certain scores.

The reliability of the college examination, determined by correlating the Form A scores with the Form B scores of 171 college freshmen, is reported as .89. The validity was determined by correlating the test with the *Psychological Examination for High School Graduates and College Freshmen* and the *Otis Self-Administering Test of Mental Ability.* In four studies in different institutions these correlations ranged from .68 to .79. The correlations between the test and grades earned in six subjects at Iowa State Teachers College ranged from .46 to .60. Thirteen important percentile points for each of the four college classes are given.

The content and standardization of these three tests seem as satisfactory as those of the better group tests of intelligence, but not strikingly more so. In two respects they have definite advantages—viz., price and mechanical features. They are almost completely self-administering and self-scoring. The scoring device (a carbon record) is simple and fool-proof, and has about the highest degree of convenience and perfection short of machine scoring.

J. P. Guilford, Professor of Psychology, The University of Southern California. An examination of these group tests and the manuals and scoring keys that accompany them impresses one immediately with the kind of care and expertness with which one wishes all tests were constructed.

The tests are appropriately entitled "Tests of Mental Ability" rather than "Tests of Intelligence" though the authors imply very clearly that "intelligence" is the important unity which they are measuring. This being the emphasis, it is fortunate that they include a variety of items which demand a variety of mental operations, thus touching many areas of mental ability sampled in so-called tests of intelligence. The kinds of items include: following directions; arithmetical problems; common sense (as in Army Alpha); word meaning; word opposites; and geometric analogies. These varieties are scrambled and rotated so that when taken in order an equal number of each kind will be attempted. It is fortunate that the attempt was made to keep the composition of the tests constant from lowest to highest ages, though in the elementary test the authors were less successful in this. To the extent that

Henmon-Nelson Test of Mental Ability

the content is uniform, the scores and IQ's will consequently have an unusual constancy of meaning at all ages.

As a preliminary to the preparation of every test form, many experimental items were tried out and an item analysis made, usually two times. As a consequence the highest validity and reliability that is now attainable was probably assured. At any rate, the reliability coefficients are typically up in the low .90's, even within the narrow ranges of ability provided by single age or grade groups. Validity coefficients, as indicated by correlations with the Stanford Revision, Otis, Terman, and Kuhlmann tests, are between the limits of .75 and .90 and are usually in the .80's. The various forms at the same level are equated for difficulty so that scores are directly comparable. Mental-age evaluations and IQ's can be computed even with the high school forms by those testers who prefer these measurements. Convenient tables are given for computing IQ's from mental ages in terms of months. The validity of the college form as an indicator of scholastic aptitude is as high as can now be obtained from so short a test, with coefficients ranging between .45 and .65 for both specific courses and general scholastic averages.

Every form makes use of the Clapp-Young self-marking system, with its carbon impressions, which makes the counting of correct responses a quick and easy mode of scoring. The print is quite legible except at the college level in which forms it is unduly crowded. Short practice exercises are provided for the testee before he begins the test proper. Norms are based upon 5,000 or more scores in every case, including in the standardizing population testees from various parts of the country.

Ed Res B 17:143-4 My '38. *Francis N. Maxfield.* * Standardization on five thousand pupils and checking on over two hundred thousand gives a basis for superior statistical treatment and data on which interpretation of test scores may be based. * The authors provide tables for translation of raw scores into mental-age scores and *I.Q.*'s, but commendably urge those who use these tests to substitute centile ranks for these measures, against which so many objections may be raised, particularly at the high-school level. *

[1399]
Herring Revision of the Binet-Simon Tests. Grades 1-12; 1922; individual; 1 form; $1.50 (5s.) per 25 individual record cards; $1.50 (4s. 6d.) per examination manual;[1] John P. Herring; Yonkers, N. Y.: World Book Co. (London: George G. Harrap & Co., Ltd.)

REFERENCES

1 HERRING, JOHN P. *Herring Revision of the Binet-Simon Tests*: Examination Manual, Form A. Yonkers, N. Y.: World Book Co., 1922. Pp. 56. $1.50. (London: George G. Harrap & Co., Ltd. 4s. 6d.)
2 WILNER, CHARLES F. "Mental Age Equivalents for a Group of Non-Reading Tests of the Herring Revision of the Binet-Simon Tests." *J Ed Psychol* 14:296-9 My '23.
3 AVERY, GEORGE T. "Comparison of Stanford and Herring Binet Revisions Given to First Grade Children." *J Ed Psychol* 15:224-8 Ap '24.
4 HERRING, JOHN P. "Avery's Comparison of the Stanford and Herring Revisions." *J Ed Psychol* 15:383-8 S '24.
5 HERRING, JOHN P. "Herring Revision of the Binet-Simon Tests." *J Ed Psychol* 15:172-9 N '24.
6 HERRING, JOHN P. *Herring Revision of the Binet-Simon Tests and Verbal and Abstract Elements in Intelligence Examinations.* Yonkers, N. Y.: World Book Co., 1924. Pp. 71. $0.60. Paper.
7 HERRING, JOHN P. "Reliability of the Stanford and the Herring Revision of the Binet-Simon Tests." *J Ed Psychol* 15:217-23 Ap '24.
8 WILNER, CHARLES F. "A Comparative Study of the Stanford and the Herring Revisions of the Binet-Simon Tests." *J Ed Psychol* 15:520-9 N '24.
9 REMMERS, H. H. "Systematic Differences in the Various Parts of the Herring Revision of the Binet-Simon Test When Applied to Normal Dull Adults." *J Ed Psychol* 20:622-7 N '29.
10 CARROLL, HERBERT A., AND HOLLINGWORTH, LETA S. "The Systematic Error of the Herring Binet in Rating Gifted Children." *J Ed Psychol* 21:1-11 Ja '30.
11 NEMZEK, CLAUDE L. "Is the IQ Constant?" *Peabody J Ed* 9:123-4 S '31.
12 GARRETT, HENRY E., AND SCHNECK, MATTHEW R. *Psychological Tests, Methods, and Results,* Part 2, pp. 11-2. New York and London: Harper and Bros., 1933. Pp. x, 137, 235. $2.75; 10s. 6d.
13 NEMZEK, CLAUDE L. "The Comparative Constancy of Stanford-Binet and Herring-Binet IQ's." *J Appl Psychol* 17:475-7 O '33.

Andrew W. Brown, Chief Psychologist, Institute for Juvenile Research, Chicago, Illinois; Associate Professor of Psychology, University of Illinois. The *Herring Revision of the Binet-Simon Tests* was constructed as an alternative form for the 1916 *Stanford Revision*. The contents of the two tests are therefore very similar. Their structure, however, is quite different. First, the Herring is a point scale rather than a mental age scale which according to most test theorists is an advantage. Second, it is divided into five groups of tests. These groups are accumulative, i.e., each group consists of each preceding group and eight or nine additional tests. At the end of each group are directions for the omission of certain tests in the next group. These omissions are determined by the score in Group A (the first group) and include those tests in which the examinee is certain to make either a perfect score or a zero score. The examinee is given full credit for the former and no credit for the latter. Mental age norms are available for each group of tests. The author, however, because of the small number of items advises against the use of these norms for the first two groups except as rough approximations.

The test is unusually easy to administer and to score. The examination manual is arranged so that the instruction for giving a test and the test itself are on the same page, e.g., in Test 3, Reproduction of Thought, the passage to be read by the subject and the instructions for giving and scoring are on the same page; the former facing the child, the latter, the examiner.

Although the test has a number of unique features it also has a number of limitations. First it is extremely verbal in nature. Eighteen of the thirty-eight are regarded by the reviewer as distinctly verbal. Four of these tests yielding a total of 55 points are "Reproduction of Thought" tests, which depend upon ability to read and comprehend the English language. This distinctly verbal aspect of the test, although in accord with Herring's general theory that intelligence is the ability to carry on abstract thinking, makes it of limited use in a clinic or school situation where there are a large number of children with reading difficulty or language handicaps.

A second limitation is that the test is poorly standardized in comparison with other individual tests. One hundred fifty four cases were used and the norms for the various age levels derived by statistical manipulation.[5] As a consequence the test results often do not give true mental ratings. Carroll and Hollingworth[10] have shown that the test rates gifted children about 17 points lower in terms of IQ than does the Stanford. They state further that "Invalidity rests with Herring-Binet, since when the criterion of subsequent scholastic success under conditions of full opportunity is applied, Herring-Binet makes, on the average, a minus error of prediction amounting to about eighteen points of discrepancy between IQ and EQ." Whether the same degree of invalidity exists at other levels of intelligence has not been determined. There is no evidence, however, to indicate that it does not. The very high correlations (.98 and .99) between the Herring and the Stanford reported by Herring and Wilner[8] (which, incidentally, have not been confirmed by other studies) do not necessarily indicate a close correspondence in individual scores.

The test has many original features which should be further developed, but until it is better standardized it has very limited use.

[1400]

Junior School Grading Test. Age 7 or entrants to the junior school; 1937; 1 form; 6s. 6d. per 25; 9d. per manual; 1s. per specimen set; 12(30) minutes; W. P. Alexander; London: University of London Press, Ltd.

E. Patricia Hunt, Vocational Psychologist, Education Office, Birmingham, England. This intelligence test for classifying seven-year-old pupils when they enter Junior Schools supplies a great need and should prove very valuable. It has been constructed by an expert of considerable experience and can be used without hesitation by those wanting a reliable test for seven-year olds. The general notes and instructions for giving and scoring are admirable, and due warning is given concerning any points on which the giver of the test might come to grief. The reviewer is strongly opposed to psychological tests being given by persons untrained in the technique of psychological testing, but, as yet, in many instances this cannot be avoided. Alexander has produced a test which can be given even by untrained persons with the expectation of achieving reliable results.

One criticism does arise in the reviewer's mind regarding the table of norms. A mental age of 57 months is assigned to children obtaining a score of 1. Surely anyone would hesitate to assign any value to a score of 1 on any test! At the other end of the scale a mental age of 150 months is assigned to the score of 90. This is the maximum total score, and in a sound intelligence test, as the reviewer judges this to be, no candidate should be able to achieve the maximum total score. Hence it seems redundant to assign a mental age to this score. It would appear that in this table of norms the author has allowed theoretical enthusiasm to override practical common sense. This criticism, however, must not be regarded as throwing any doubt on the reliability of the norms which, having been constructed by Alexander, can be accepted with full confidence.

[1401]

Kent-Shakow Formboard. Ages 6 to adult; 1928; 1 form, 2 models; revision of the *Worcester Formboard*; Grace H. Kent and David Shakow; Chicago, Ill.: C. H. Stoelting Co.; Worcester, Mass.: Sven G. Nilsson, 16 Maverick Road.
a) INDUSTRIAL MODEL. (20-40) minutes; Stoelting: $120; Nilsson: $45 including container and instructions.
b) CLINICAL MODEL. (15-30) minutes; Stoelting: $120; Nilsson: $40 including container and instructions.

REFERENCES

1 SHAKOW, DAVID, AND KENT, GRACE H. "The Worcester Formboard Series." *J Genetic Psychol* 32:599-611 D '25.
2 BRONNER, AUGUSTA F.; HEALY, WILLIAM; LOWE, GLADYS M.; AND SHIMBERG, MYRA E. *A Manual of Individual Mental*

Tests and Testing. pp. 174-5, 233-4. Judge Baker Foundation Publication, No. 4. Boston, Mass.: Little, Brown and Co., 1927. Pp. x, 287. $3.50.
  3 KENT, GRACE H., AND SHAKOW, DAVID. "Graded Series of Form Boards." *Personnel J* 7:115-20 Ag '28.
  4 SCHIEFFELIN, BARBARA, AND SCHWESINGER, GLADYS C. *Mental Tests and Heredity:* Including a Survey of Non-Verbal Tests, pp. 171-2. New York: Galton Publishing Co., Inc. 1930. Pp. ix, 298. Out of print.
  5 GROVE, WILLIAM R. "An Experimental Study of the Kent-Shakow Industrial Formboard Series." *J Appl Psychol* 19:467-73 Ag '35.
  6 BRILL, MOSHE. "Performance Tests as Aids in the Diagnosis of Maladjustment." *J Genetic Psychol* 49:199-214 S '36.
  7 EARL, C. J. C. "The Performance Test Behaviour of Adult Morons." *Brit J Med Psychol* 17:78-92 pt 1 '37.
  8 PATERSON, DONALD G.; SCHNEIDLER, GWENDOLEN, G.; AND WILLIAMSON, EDMUND G. *Student Guidance Techniques,* pp. 229-33. New York: McGraw-Hill Book Co., Inc., 1938. Pp. xviii, 316. $3.00. (London: McGraw-Hill Publishing Co., Ltd., 18s.)
  9 SHAKOW, DAVID, AND PAZEIAN, BESSIE. "Adult Norms for the K-S Clinical Formboards." *J Appl Psychol* 23:495-502 Ag '39.

Lorene Teegarden, Psychological Examiner, Public Schools, Cincinnati, Ohio. This formboard is made in a small size called the clinical board, and a larger size called the industrial formboard. The reviewer has used the industrial board only, in work with adults over sixteen years of age.

The board contains five holes or recesses into which are to be fitted eight sets of blocks presenting a graded series of tasks or problems. In each task the blocks for the five holes are cut by the same pattern, so that the pattern is presented five times in the five holes. This feature minimizes chance in solution, for although the blocks may be correctly placed by chance in one or two of the holes, this cannot happen for all the holes in any task.

The test possesses intrinsic interest for a wide range of age and ability. The blocks are sufficiently large to fit the adult hand, and while the simplest tasks can be completed by young children, the more difficult tasks offer a challenge to even the superior adult. Because of this interest, the test is valuable for establishing rapport with the adult applicant who may be a bit scornful or fearful of manipulative tests. The first five tasks can be completed by all adults except a few of very poor ability. The last three are too difficult for those who exceed certain time limits on the simpler tasks. The time required for the test is from 20 to 40 minutes, depending upon the ease and rapidity with which the subject works. Though the test has been used in several studies which have been reported, norms for general use have not yet been published.

Each task except the first is timed and scored by percentile rating or other method. The reviewer uses percentile ratings (unpublished) developed at the Cincinnati Employment Center, which are combined into two mean ratings, one for the simple tasks, and one for the complicated tasks of the series. These ratings may differ widely for a given individual. In addition to numerical ratings, the test yields information as to the subject's manner of work which should be recorded in the examiner's notes. Such qualitative data may relate to poise under difficulties, insight into the problem, adaptability and resourcefulness in varying the method and trying new methods, or rapidity of movement in handling objects.

Industrially the *Kent-Shakow Formboard* is useful for selecting workers for jobs involving complicated situations, especially those of a mechanical nature. Perhaps the most useful standards for industrial use will prove to be those developed by each industry in relation to its specific jobs. The test is valuable also for aid in guidance. It has a wider usefulness than the *Minnesota Spatial Relations Test* since it includes problems of a wide range of difficulty. In certain situations it should be supplemented by tests measuring manual or finger dexterity and eye-hand co-ordination.

[1402]
Kentucky General Scholastic Ability Test [1939 Revision]. Grades 10-13; 1937-39; a revision of the *Kentucky Classification Test (see 338)* ; 1 form; $3.50 per 100; 10¢ per specimen set; nontimed (30-80) minutes; E. J. Asher; Lexington, Ky.: Kentucky Cooperative Testing Service, University of Kentucky.

REFERENCES

  1 MCQUITTY, JOHN V. "Student Mortality in Relation to Scores on the Kentucky Classification Test." *Ky Personnel B* 19:1-2 My '37.
  2 ASHER, ESTON J. "The Reliability and Validity of the Kentucky General Scholastic and Kentucky English Tests." *Ky Personnel B* 21:1-2 S '38.
  3 BISHOP, HELEN. "A Study in Prediction and Mortality." *J Am Assn Col Registrars* 14:62-3 O '39.

For a review by Richard Ledgerwood of an earlier form, see 1048.

[1403]
Kingsway Intelligence Tests. 1939; a 29-page booklet of 15 practice tests; 7d. per pupils' edition; 10d. per teachers' edition with answers; London: Evans Brothers Ltd.

Scottish Ed J 23:273 *Ap* '40. The object of these Tests is to familiarise children, especially pupils sitting for special places in English secondary schools, with the usual type of Group Intelligence Tests, so that they may be able to show their full capacity when called upon to work them under examination conditions. Fifteen different sets of tests, containing twenty items each of different types, are given in the booklet. Much less practice than this is now believed to produce the maximum effect, and teachers coaching pupils through the whole fifteen sets may be wasting valuable time. The collection itself is quite satisfactory, although the correction might have been simplified.

[1404]
Kuhlmann-Anderson Intelligence Tests, Fourth Edition. Grades 1B, 1A, 2, 3, 4, 5, 6, 7-8, 9-12; 1927-39; 1 form, 9 levels; $1.25 per 25; 40¢ per manual; 25¢ per 100 individual record cards; 40¢ per specimen set; 15¢ per 25 copies of any single page for individual testing; (40-60) minutes; F. Kuhlmann and Rose G. Anderson; Minneapolis, Minn.: Educational Test Bureau, Inc.

REFERENCES

1 KUHLMANN, F. "A Median Mental Age Method of Weighting and Scaling Mental Tests." *J Appl Psychol* 11:181-98 Je '27.
2 KUHLMANN, F. "The Kuhlmann-Anderson Intelligence Tests Compared with Seven Others." *J Appl Psychol* 12:545-94 D '28.
3 KUHLMANN, F. "The Pearson Formula, and a Further Note on the Kuhlmann-Anderson Tests." *J Appl Psychol* 13:32-45 F '29.
4 KUHLMANN, F. "Effect of Degree of Difficulty on Operation of Intelligence Tests." *J Juvenile Res* 14:8-21 Ja '30.
5 STECKEL, MINNIE L. "The Restandardization of IQ's of Different Tests." *J Ed Psychol* 21:278-83 Ap '30.
6 CATTELL, PSYCHE. "The Heinis Personal Constant as a Substitute for the IQ." *J Ed Psychol* 24:221-8 Mr '33.
7 CHARLES, C. M. "A Comparison of the Intelligence Quotients of Three Different Mental Tests Applied to a Group of Incarcerated Delinquent Boys." *J Appl Psychol* 17:581-4 O '33.
8 KUHLMANN, F. "What the IQ Means Today." *Nation's Sch* 11:33-8 F '33.
9 BOYNTON, PAUL L. "A Reply to Professor Nemzek." *Peabody J Ed* 12:239-41 Mr '35.
10 HILDEN, ARNOLD H., AND SKEELS, HAROLD M. "A Comparison of the Stanford-Binet Scale, the Kuhlmann-Anderson Group Test, the Arthur Point Scale of Performance Tests, and the Unit Scales of Attainment." *J Exp Ed* 4:214-30 D '35.
11 NEMZEK, CLAUDE L. "A Note Concerning the Kuhlmann-Anderson Tests." *Peabody J Ed* 12:238-9 Mr '35.
12 BRADWAY, KATHERINE PRESTON, AND HOFFEDITZ, E. LOUISE. "The Basis for the Personal Constant." *J Ed Psychol* 28:501-13 O '37.
13 HALES, W. M. "Results of a Group Intelligence Re-test with a Reformatory Group." *J Juvenile Res* 21:181-7 Jl '37.
14 SPACHE, GEORGE. "The Use of the Kuhlmann-Anderson Intelligence Tests in Private Schools." *J Appl Psychol* 30:618-23 N '39.
15 ANDERSON, ROSE G. "Fifth Revision of Kuhlmann-Anderson Tests." *J Appl Psychol* 24:198-206 Ap '40.

Henry E. Garrett, Associate Professor of Psychology, Columbia University. This well-known test series was first published in 1927, and in its present revised form in 1933. The battery consists of 39 separate tests which contain from 5 to 28 items each. These tests have been assembled into 9 booklets and cover the ability-range from the first to the twelfth grades. The average chronological age of those children in the standardization group who passed 1, 2, 3, or more of the items of each test has been calculated; and the "median mental age" of a given child is the median of the "ages" which he earns on the tests. Since abilities of school children are relatively undifferentiated as compared to the abilities of adults, this is probably as satisfactory a method as any for obtaining the typical level at which a child functions.

The instruction manual which accompanies the tests contains explicit directions for giving and scoring the tests, as well as a 20-page description of the theory and methods employed in the construction of the scale. The directions are detailed and clear; but the theoretical introduction is badly written—it reads like a poor translation—and contains some astonishingly naive and inaccurate statements. In discussing validity criteria, for instance, the authors discard the usual methods. Instead, they propose to use the "discriminative capacity" of the tests—by which is meant the ability of a test to show—or not to show—steady and significant increases in score with age. Although much is made of the superiority of this technique over other methods in the advertising which describes the scale, the notion itself is not new and has nothing essentially to do with test validity. It is necessary, of course, that we compute the discriminative capacity of a test if we wish to know its difficulty and the age range over which the test is most effective. But since physical strength, motor agility, and emotional control (to mention a few), all increase with age, mere increase in score with age is no guarantee that a test is an adequate measure of intellect. The authors really admit this when they say (p. 9) : "we have depended on common sense analysis in the selection of tests." As practical people who know and have had wide experience with both children and tests the authors' scale is very probably a valid measure of intelligence—but not for the reasons which they and their publishers give.

Several curious statements regarding test validity appear on page 7 of the manual. In arguing against the need for obtaining validity correlations with such criteria as school marks, our authors say: "But it is conceded by psychologists that test scores themselves are a better criterion of intelligence than anything else available." It would be enlightening to know how "test scores" become criteria of intelligence in the first place; and what "psychologists" are willing to make so broad a concession. Again, with reference to validity, our authors write: "Too close an agreement between test scores and school marks is evidence that the tests are not entirely valid tests of intelligence, because school marks are not determined entirely by intelligence. From this example (*sic*), it is clear that a knowledge of

Kingsway Intelligence Tests

the amount of correlation between test scores and any other criteria may mislead instead of inform about the value of the tests." It is difficult to guess just what the authors are trying to say here. Should criterion correlations with school marks be low because school marks are not simon-pure measures of intelligence? If so, how low? And how high must test correlations with "any other criteria" be before they "mislead" instead of "inform"? Though admittedly fallible—if they were not we should not need intelligence tests—school marks constitute our best single criterion of that kind of intellectual activity which intelligence testers, since Binet, have attempted to measure. If our tests measure something radically different from that ability measured by school marks, then they are not useful estimates of the intellectual ability of school children, no matter what their discriminative capacity.

In introducing the topic of reliability, Kuhlmann and Anderson remark that: "The literature on this subject is in a badly muddled condition" (p. 10). Their subsequent discussion is the best exhibit they could offer of the truth of this statement. Apparently our authors have completely confused "goodness" of a test (validity) with consistency of test scores (reliability). They write: "If either circumstances or the children are different the second time they (*sic*) are given the same tests, the tests would be poor instead of good if they gave the same results. . . . In other words, close agreement between the first and second set of scores, and as expressed by the coefficient of correlation, may be evidence that the tests are poor instead of good." What our authors intend to say, apparently, is that high self-correlation is no guarantee of high reliability—*if* circumstances and children have changed between testings. What they really say is that high reliability does not necessarily imply high validity ("goodness"). The latter statement is, of course, true. But the former statement is true only if one can conceive of a test which would give more consistent retest results when circumstances are altered and children different (practised, coached, emotionally upset, etc.) than the same test would give when these factors have been rigidly controlled. A test may be highly reliable and not be a valid measure of intellect (e.g., the tapping test); and by the same token, a test may be a "good" measure of intellect (e.g., syllogisms) and still not show

"close agreement" on two successive occasions. Sameness of score is no measure of "goodness" or "poorness"; and goodness in a test does not necessarily lead to highly stable scores.

An interesting conception of the reliability coefficient is given by our authors on page 11. In contending that high reliability coefficients are evidence of a "good" test only when difficulty of items has been cared for, they write: "But high correlations also result when the tests are either too easy or too difficult, because all scores then tend to be the same. Perfect reliability would result if the tests were so easy that all children could easily get a maximum score on them any time, no matter what the circumstances, or if they were so difficult that no children could get above a zero score on them at any time." In the highly improbable (not to say absurd) situation in which children's scores are either all zero or all maximum on both test and retest, there is, of course, perfect agreement between test and retest scores. But a reliability coefficient in such a situation has no meaning—and would never be calculated outside of an insane asylum. In the more likely situation in which all scores—test and retest—show little spread and cluster around some common point, say the mean, the self-correlation approaches zero, not 1.00.

A final word may be said of our authors' use of the "Heinis growth units"—of which much is made. Heinis units are derived values obtained by fitting an arbitrarily selected exponential equation to certain poorly described data, gathered by Heinis from various sources. Our authors' data are so much superior to and more extensive than those used by Heinis that it is surprising that they did not derive "growth units" from their own test scores.

For reviews by Psyche Cattell, S. A. Courtis, and Austin H. Turney, see 1049.

[1405]

Leiter International Performance Scale. Ages 4 and over; 1936-40; 1 form; 68 nonlanguage tests which can be given without language or pantomime; $68 per testing outfit, including manual and 100 record blanks; $2 per manual; $2 per 100 record booklets; (30) minutes at the 6-year-old level and (90) minutes at the high school level; Russell Graydon Leiter; Santa Barbara, Calif.: the Author, 601 East Valerio St.

REFERENCES

1 LEITER, RUSSELL G. *The Leiter International Performance Scale.* University of Hawaii Bulletin, Vol. 15, No. 7; Research Publications, No. 13. Appendix by Stanley D. Porteus. Honolulu, Hawaii: the University, May 1936. Pp. 42. $0.30. Paper.
2 LEITER, RUSSELL GRAYDON. *The Leiter International Performance Scale*: Vol. 1, Directions for the Application and

[1406]

Merrill-Palmer Scale of Mental Tests. Ages 24-63 months; 1926-31; individual; 1 form; $46.60 per testing outfit (No. 37061); $1.50 per 25 record blanks (No. 44088); $2.45 per manual [5] (No. 46621) (the manual may be purchased directly from the publisher for $2.20); test purchasers having the following tests may save approximately $9.15: *Mare and Foal Test*: Pintner-Paterson, *Manikin Test*: Pintner, and the *Block Design Test*: Kohs; Rachel Stutsman; Chicago, Ill.: C. H. Stoelting Co.

REFERENCES

1 STUTSMAN, RACHEL. *Performance Tests for Children of Pre-School Age.* Genetic Psychology Monographs Vol. 1, No. 1. Worcester, Mass.: Clark University Press, January 1926. Pp. 67. $2.00. Paper.
2 STUTSMAN, RACHEL. *A Scale of Mental Tests for Preschool Children.* Unpublished Doctor's thesis, University of Chicago, 1928. Pp. 350.
3 WILSON, CHARLES A.; SWEENY, MARY E.; STUTSMAN, RACHEL; CHESIRE, LEONE E.; AND HATT, ELISE. *The Merrill-Palmer Standards of Physical and Mental Growth.* Detroit, Mich.: Merrill-Palmer School, 1930. Pp. ix, 121. $0.50. Paper.
4 KAWIN, ETHEL, AND HOEFER, CAROLYN, assisted by Edna Mohr, Maria G. Linder, and Marian W. Taylor. *A Comparative Study of a Nursery-School versus a Non-Nursery-School Group.* Chicago, Ill.: University of Chicago Press, 1931. Pp. 52. $0.75. Paper.
5 STUTSMAN, RACHEL. *Mental Measurement of Preschool Children*: With a Guide for the Administration of the Merrill-Palmer Scale of Mental Tests. Yonkers, N. Y.: World Book Co., 1931. Pp. xi, 368. $2.20.
6 DRISCOLL, GERTRUDE PORTER. *The Development Status of the Preschool Child as a Prognosis of Future Development.* Columbia University, Teachers College, Child Development Monographs, No. 13. New York: Bureau of Publications, the College, 1933. Pp. xiv, 111. $1.50.
7 GORDON, R. G. "The Merrill-Palmer Scale of Intelligence Tests for Pre-School Children Applied to Low-Grade Mental Defectives." *Brit J Psychol* 24:178-86 O '33.
8 MOWRER, WILLIE MAE C. "Performance of Children in Stutsman Tests." *Child Development* 5:93-6 Je '34.
9 STUTSMAN, RACHEL. "Factors to be Considered in Measuring the Reliability of a Mental Test, with Special Reference to the Merrill-Palmer Scale." *J Ed Psychol* 25:630-3 N '34.
10 BRISTOL, HILDA. "An English Norm for the Merrill-Palmer Performance Tests: Based on a Study of 530 Children between the Ages of Two and Six Years." *Brit J of Ed Psychol* 6:250-66 N '36.
11 OBERLIN, DIANA S. "Verbal and Manual Functions at the Preschool Level." *Del State Med J* 9:95-8 Ap '37.
12 WELLMAN, BETH L. *The Intelligence of Preschool Children as Measured by the Merrill-Palmer Scale of Performance Tests.* University of Iowa Studies, New Series No. 361; Studies in Child Welfare, Vol. 15, No. 3. Iowa City, Iowa: the University, October 1938. Pp. 150. Cloth, $1.35; paper, $1.00.
13 DEFORREST, RUTH. *A Study of the Prognostic Value of the Merrill-Palmer Scale of Mental Tests and the Minnesota Preschool Scale.* Unpublished master's thesis, University of Pittsburgh, 1939. Pp. 21.

Nancy Bayley, Research Associate, Institute of Child Welfare, University of California. The Merrill-Palmer scale has the handicap of all preschool scales which have been so far standardized: that is, its predictive value is very limited. Its merits must lie in any ability it may have to measure children's present intellectual capacities. It is one of the earlier tests for preschool children for which norms are based on an adequate sample of cases. (The scale was first published in 1926.) The norms are based on 631 cases ranging in age from 18 to 77 months, and secured from a variety of sources. These included kindergarten and first grade children from the public schools, children from child care agencies and health clinics, and children on the Merrill-Palmer nursery school waiting list. The test items are to a large extent nonlanguage, and they have been selected for their intrinsic interest to young children. Their outstanding merit is in the children's interest in performing most of the tasks set to them. On the other hand, a fault of the scale lies in its generous use of time-scores. The abilities of young children can not be adequately measured by speed of performance, because speed has not yet become a goal for them, and their shifting attention often alters the score in a way which obscures skill of manipulation and insight into the solution of a problem.

Although Stutsman claims r's of .79 between scores on her scale and the Stanford-Binet, she obtained these r's without partialling out chronological age, in an age range where her own data show a marked correlation between test performance and chronological age. Actually, the tests have been found by other investigators to have rather low relationship to Stanford-Binet IQ's. From these later investigations it is evident that the two tests do not measure the same array of abilities. A number of the items in the Merrill-Palmer scale test motor skills and co-ordinations rather than learning or insightful behavior. For these reasons, the scale should not be used as a substitute for the Binet type of tests, but it should rather be considered a supplementary measure.

Stutsman describes the processes of standardization in some detail, and in addition gives other material of value to the person who wishes information about preschool tests generally. This information includes a historical summary of preschool testing, short descriptions of other preschool scales, and a discussion of technics and problems of preschool testing. This latter discussion includes a section on the tendency of preschool children to refuse tests, with suggested ways of surmounting this difficulty. Stutsman also takes account of this tendency in her scoring, so that a child is not penalized for resistive behavior. Other sections deal with the effects of environment on test scores, sex differences, a guide for observing personality, and case studies which illustrate various factors which are relevant in judging a child's mental level.

B. M. Castner, Clinic of Child Development, Yale University. This is one of the better-

Leiter International Performance Scale

constructed preschool scales, its defects lying rather in the scope of its sampling of abilities, and in the limited age-range covered, than in details of the scale itself. The ages covered are from 18 to 77 months, with 6-month intervals; but Stutsman does not recommend use of the scale above 63 months or below 24 months. This seriously limits its clinical usefulness, particularly at the lower end. The age of referral of children is steadily dropping, and the examiner whose practice includes the ages below 2 years will by preference make use of a scale which is continuous from infancy upward, permitting the study of growth sequences through follow-up examinations in terms of a unitary group of tests.

No attempt has been made to group tests on the basis of specific fields of behavior. Such a grouping aids materially in the analytic interpretation of test results, and can be more definitely made in the preschool years than in the case of older children, whose behavior is more complexly integrated. It is particularly useful in bringing into relief, fields showing specific retardation or acceleration which may be overlooked in a more heterogeneous grouping of tests. This lack is partially, but not wholly, compensated for by a far better discussion of qualitative individual differences in response and their interpretation, than is sometimes found in manuals for preschool testing.

The range of abilities tested seems inadequate for a thorough clinico-developmental study of a child, although it will usually be roughly satisfactory when only an approximate general rating is desired. The important fields of postural, locomotor, and gross motor behavior, deviations which may greatly influence the total clinical picture, are untapped. Drawing, which has a high diagnostic value aside from its purely normative significance, could to advantage be extended beyond the three tests included. Items based upon personal-social behavior are omitted, although there is an excellent chapter on the significance of personality observations as made in the examination. Language—important not only in itself, but by reason of the vital part it plays in the gradual integration of the individual's total behavior—should be more extensively represented. The principal language test—the Action-Agent—is perhaps the best single test in the scale. The "Simple Questions," however, designed for the ages below 3 years, have not proved very satisfactory in clinical practice; they are often annoying to give, and the wide individual differences in response make the interpretation of failure difficult.

Details as to standardization methods and selection of subjects—problems offering peculiar difficulty in the case of preschool children—are fully and clearly presented. There is adequate tabular presentation of results, and the statistical treatment is satisfactory without going beyond limits justified by the nature of the material.

Scoring is provided for by any of three methods—standard deviation in terms of either MA or IQ, or on a percentile basis. Stutsman does not recommend the IQ method, because of the undetermined relationship of such a measure at this age to the IQ obtained on higher-age scales. The same objection applies in part to the use of MA; some such rating in terms of behavior maturity age is useful, but it would be desirable to use a term which does not carry with it so many connotations, some helpful but many misleading, acquired through its use in the case of school children and adults. It is, in fact, doubtful whether any strict numerical method of scoring a complete examination is justified at present below the age of 5 or 6 years, especially since there are no correction formulae for such factors as inattentiveness, temporary retardation in specific fields, lack of normal environmental experience, deviations caused by illness, personality complications, and others, which are more frequent and more pronounced in their effects during the preschool years, when development is more rapid and more easily disturbed in its manifestations, and when a difference of a few months or even weeks in the developmental rating looms much larger than in later years.

Florence L. Goodenough, Research Professor, Institute of Child Welfare, The University of Minnesota. The Merrill-Palmer tests for preschool children have been widely used in nursery schools and preschool behavior clinics throughout the country. Undoubtedly, their popularity with children has had a good deal to do with their popularity among clinicians since in many other respects they fall short of modern technical requirements in the field of mental measurement. The method of scoring with its emphasis upon speed of performance is hardly in accordance with present-day knowledge of the psychology of early childhood which has shown the very rudimentary concepts of time usually found among children of preschool age. On the other hand, the scale has so many excellent features that one can only hope that its author will at some future time see fit to prepare a revision which will preserve its good points while correcting those details that at present interfere with its usefulness.

In any test designed for young children, the intrinsic interest of the tasks and the materials is of first-rank importance. In this respect the Merrill-Palmer scale easily takes the lead. The tests have been selected on the basis of an intimate understanding of child psychology and are put up in gay-colored boxes which, piled where the child can see them, keep him in a state of happy anticipation as to what is coming next. The order of administration may be varied in whatever way seems best suited to the child's interests, thus permitting the examiner to seize upon a favorable moment for interjecting the more difficult or the less attractive items.

The tests are largely of the "performance" type but there are a small number of language tests, including a modification of the Woodworth and Wells Action-Agent test. Other tests include formboards, block building, peg boards, picture puzzles, copying simple designs, following directions, buttoning, etc. Since instructions are given verbally, some degree of language comprehension on the part of the child is presupposed; yet these instructions are so simple and obvious that a rough appraisal of the abilities of young deaf children can be had by giving certain parts of the test in pantomime. The use of the test with handicapped children or those unusually difficult to manage is greatly facilitated by an ingenious method of making allowance for omitted items or those which the child refuses to try so that the total score is not affected.

The most serious difficulty in the practical use of the test has been pointed out by its author. This is the fact that the standard deviations of scores do not increase in proportion to age throughout the age range for which the test is designed (18 to 66 months) but reach their maximum at three and one-half years and decrease thereafter. The result is that the test results are likely to be misleading when used by persons with little statistical sophistication. The use of intelligence quotients as a means of indicating the degree of brightness is ruled out for the reason just given; for example, an IQ of 166 at 45 months has the same meaning as one of 122 at 27 months. For this reason, norms are also given in terms of standard deviation units and percentiles but in such broad steps that interpolation must be made if fine units are desired. Such interpolation is, however, hardly warranted at the ages beyond four, since the decreasing variability of the scores at the later ages makes the significance of small differences decidedly questionable, especially when, as in this case, those differences depend largely upon speed of performance. A fundamental defect in the construction of a test cannot be wholly overcome by any statistical devices.

For children between the ages of 18 and 42 months the test is a valuable one. Thereafter its usefulness steadily decreases until, except for those intellectually backward, it becomes of little service for children who have passed the age of 54 months. In the hands of a skillful clinician it affords an excellent opportunity for observing personality characteristics. A useful guide for such observations together with a series of case studies is provided in the manual.

Florence M. Teagarden, Professor of Psychology, The University of Pittsburgh. After several years in which it has been used and compared with other preschool tests, this test must still be considered one of the best available. The careful standardization of the scale largely accounts for this fact. From 49 to 81 children at each six-month interval from 18 months through 77 months of chronological age constituted the standardization group, 300 girls and 331 boys in all. (It is to be noted, however, that Stutsman recommends the use of the scale for only those children 24 to 63 months of age.) The standardization group was selected from 20 widely different sources. Stutsman's evidence as to reliability and validity of the test is certainly as convincing as that given for most scales.

The entire scale includes 38 different tests. Sixteen of these score at only one point and are, therefore, called "all-or-none" tests. The remaining 22 tests have variable score values and score at 77 different points on the scale. In all there are thus 93 different items arranged in six-month intervals beginning at 18 to 23 months and running through 66 to 72 months. The tests require manipulation of body (opposition of thumb and fingers, standing on one foot and the like), language, and the use of such objects as ball, mirror, blocks, peg boards, scissors, paper and pencil, form boards, jigsaw puzzles, buttons, colors, manikin, etc. The commercialized material for the test is needlessly expensive and this prevents its being standard equipment in many testing centers where it should be found.

Ratings are secured by use of *score, mental age, standard deviation,* and *percentile rank.* In actual practice it sometimes happens that there is a slight discrepancy in the rating of a child by the use of one of these methods as compared with another. Stutsman does not recommend the use of the IQ technique for this test. There is also a "personality blank" which although almost entirely subjective in nature is suggestive as to items of behavior for which one should look in evaluating the reactions of preschool children. The provisions for scoring "omitted" and "refused" test items are exceedingly helpful even though one is sometimes in doubt as to whether a test item should be scored "refused" or "failed." Some of the items are "timed" tests. However one might wish that preschool children's responses need not be scored by the use of a stop watch, nevertheless there is probably no satisfactory substitute in making certain differentiations.

Mastery of the testing technique requires more time perhaps than is true of certain other tests but this may after all be a merit rather than otherwise. One has a feeling that Stutsman has been perfectly straightforward in her directions for administering and scoring. In her book there is none of the "esoteric" that one so often finds in manuals for testing infants and young children.

Several years use of the scale has demonstrated to the writer that children *like* the test and, as a rule, a skilled examiner has no difficulty in getting cooperative response from children to the test. In the hands of an expert the test has great value also in attempts to evaluate the intelligence of older children who for undetermined reasons are not talking.

An unpublished master's thesis by Ruth DeForrest [13] gives data on 170 children who were given Merrill-Palmer ratings while in nursery school and who were subsequently given the *Revised Stanford-Binet Scale.* Prediction of subsequent Binet IQ became less and less accurate the older the child at the time his Merrill-Palmer was secured. For the age range 24 to 63 months Revised Binet IQ could be predicted from Merrill-Palmer ratings 16 per cent better than by chance. For children 24 to 42 months of age when given the Merrill-Palmer, prediction of Binet IQ was 30 per cent better than by chance while it was only two per cent better than by chance for the 51 to 63 months age group. DeForrest also found that IQ's obtained by Merrill-Palmer were as reliable as the standard deviation which Stutsman very greatly prefers.

[1407]
Minnesota Preschool Scale. Ages 1½ to 6 years; 1932; 2 forms; individual; nontimed; $9.50 per testing outfit for a single form; 75¢ per 25 individual record blanks; Florence L. Goodenough, Josephine C. Foster, and M. J. Van Wagenen; Minneapolis, Minn.: Educational Test Bureau, Inc.

REFERENCES

1 MOWRER, WILLIE MAE C. "Intelligence Scales for Preschool Children." *Child Development* 4:318-22 D '33.
2 CURTI, MARGARET WOOSTER, AND STEGGERDA, MORRIS. "A Preliminary Report on the Testing of Young Maya Children in Yucatan." *J Comp Psychol* 28:207-24 O '39.
3 DEFORREST, RUTH. *A Study of the Prognostic Value of the Merrill-Palmer Scale of Mental Tests and the Minnesota Preschool Scale.* Unpublished master's thesis, University of Pittsburgh, 1939. Pp. 21.

Rachel Stutsman Ball, Psychologist, The Merrill-Palmer School, Detroit, Michigan. The *Minnesota Preschool Scale* is a well-organized, easily administered test for preschool children, consisting of 26 separate test items. The test is largely an adaptation of items chosen from earlier Binet materials, but includes some other original and perhaps more interesting additions. In producing a test scale which is compact and relatively inexpensive in price, the authors have profited wisely and well from earlier and cruder Binet test scales. The test has the advantage of giving language and non-language scores, thus eliminating the necessity when time is limited for more complex double testing procedures. The test blank is carefully and conveniently set up. It contains a section for recording test reactions that is a decided contribution to test record forms. There are two test forms, A and B, so set up as to have equivalent value for testing. This should have the advantage of decreasing the practice effect upon retesting if a different form is used.

The test is not sufficiently interesting or varied to be very satisfactory with many children under three years of age, particularly in clinic situations. The authors suggest that the scores for children under three should not be separated into verbal and nonverbal. There is no device for scoring omitted or refused tests and this lack makes for inaccuracy of scoring the responses of young children. Deaf children or those with other language problems such as foreign language handicaps and aphasia cannot be tested by the test. There is no plan for omitting easy test items, thus shortening testing time for older children. However, the test may be shortened for the younger ages by omitting similar more difficult items when others have been failed. The test is most suited for children from 3 to 5 years of middle ability ranges. It is inferior to the Stanford-Binet for older bright children because it does not offer sufficient range of difficulty to establish the upper limit of his ability.

The test was standardized on 900 children representing a cross section of different socio-economic levels in the city of Minneapolis. Each test form was given to 75 children. The raw point scores are converted into C-scores which in turn can be interpreted in terms of IQ equivalents, percentile scores, or standard deviation scores. For half-year age ranges the product moment correlation between the C-scores on the two forms with a 1- to 7-day interval varies at the different ages from .68 to .94 for the verbal scales, .67 to .92 for the nonverbal scales, and from .80 to .94 when verbal and nonverbal scales are combined.

The brief statement about the standardization in the test manual is hardly satisfying to those who wish to be thoroughly familiar with the test. The statistical competence of the authors of this test cannot be questioned, but one cannot help wishing that the long promised monograph giving details of the standardization procedures might soon be available.

Nancy Bayley, Research Associate, Institute of Child Welfare, University of California. Intelligence tests for preschool children must be used with precautions and reservations. Their value is exceptionally dependent on the skill of the examiner in getting the child willingly to put forth efforts in the desired directions. For this reason careful training and experience in dealing with young children are necessary before adequate test scores can be secured. Furthermore, even when the scores are reliable, it is problematic whether intelligence in such young children develops at predictable rates. The predictive value of preschool test scores has been found to be very uncertain, and hence emphasis should be placed, instead, on their evaluation of the child's present status.

The manual of directions for the Minnesota scale gives a summary of the procedures of standardization. The scale has been carefully standardized on 900 children, 100 at each of 9 half-year intervals. These cases were selected, on the basis of parents' occupation, to form a representative socio-economic cross section of the population. Two forms were administered on alternate days with careful procedures for determining practice effects. The reliability coefficient for a single scale is .89. The tests are arranged so that scores can be computed separately for verbal, nonverbal, and total items. The tests are scored in C-score absolute units, and tables are given for converting these into percentile ranks, standard deviation placements, and IQ equivalents. Although the method of obtaining a child's score of relative ability is somewhat more abstruse than is the computation of the IQ, it is statistically preferable, and IQ equivalents are available for those who wish them.

The test items used are in their general nature similar to the Binet tests, a number of them having been adapted from the Kuhlmann-Binet. The scale has been carefully assembled and, if one wishes to test at preschool levels the same functions as are measured in the Binet type of school-age test, it is one of the best of the preschool scales. It is sufficiently verbal in character to have some similarity to the tests more generally employed with older children. On the other hand, most of the items have intrinsic interest for young children. Another factor in favor of this scale is the omission of time-scores. At these early ages speed of performance is a very inaccurate measure of a child's ability because his attention often shifts, he has no notion of "working fast" as a goal, or if he does the very effort for speed often disturbs his co-ordinations and lowers his scores. The provision for the separate scoring of verbal and nonverbal items, in addition to giving information on relative abilities in different fields, takes care, in part, of the difficulty of obtaining scores for children who refuse some of the tests. Most refusals are among the verbal items, which tend to make the child self-conscious and more aware of the examiner's presence in the situation. For children who refuse to respond under these conditions

Minnesota Preschool Scale

the nonverbal score will often give a more adequate measure of mental status.

Florence M. Teagarden, Professor of Psychology, The University of Pittsburgh. The test was standardized on 100 children at each half-year age level from 18 months to 6 years, making 900 children in all. There are two alternate forms of the test, which permits of periodic examination if first one form and then the other is used. Each form contains items which together make up a "verbal" section and other items which constitute a "nonverbal" section. Reliability coefficients approximating .90 are quoted for the scale as a whole. No measures of validity are given in the manual which accompanies the test.

The test material, which is reasonable in price, comes in a box which is easy to carry. Much of the equipment is contained in a series of envelopes which are bound together and which carry abbreviated directions for administering the test. The child's folder, however, when ready to file is likely to be somewhat disorderly with its assortment of separate pieces of paper that have been used for "tracing," "folding," and the like.

There are 26 separate items in the scale and with few exceptions all must be given to each child. The result is that the test requires rather too much time for younger children, and even older preschool children tend to tire before the test is completed. There is no provision in the scoring for "omissions" or "refusals."

The statistical work of standardization and derivation of scoring units of equal difficulty at all points along the scale are merits not found in most preschool tests. For children over three years of age the verbal and nonverbal parts are scored separately. One finds for each child a verbal C-score, IQ equivalent, percentile, standard deviation, and mental age. Similar measures for the nonverbal section and for the total examination are also found. Obviously, the scoring becomes somewhat tedious. The scoring of separate test items is very difficult at places also. This is particularly true of the picture test where varying credit is given for nouns, verbs, and prepositions in the child's responses to pictures. The child's usage of the word is the basis of scoring, however, rather than grammatical classification. A page and a half of the manual is required for explaining these scoring directions, and experience shows that even then many questions arise on the scoring of this part of the test. Again in the scoring of a test requiring that the child trace a form with a pencil, difficulties arise. If the child's pencil *touches* the boundary, there is no penalty; if it crosses the boundary the distance between where his pencil leaves the line and where it returns to the line is measured and all such measurements are added. This procedure implies a statistical accuracy that the circumstances do not seem to warrant.

A commendable feature of the test is that it provides fore-exercises which are very fine for young children. In some instances, however, the amount of time spent on the fore-exercises is out of proportion to the value of the test item which they are meant to illustrate. Perhaps the greatest weakness of the test is that many preschool children do not care for it and become bored by the monotonous repetition and similarity of test items. The record blank provides space for entering sociological data about the parents, and personality and behavior data about the child.

Ruth DeForrest [3] found on 44 cases that the Minnesota total IQ and the Minnesota verbal IQ predicted Revised Stanford-Binet IQ with approximately the same degree of success as the Merrill-Palmer IQ.

[1408]

Modification of the Kent-Shakow Formboard. Adult males; 1937; 1 form; $25 per set of unpainted formboards made of masonite; 50¢ per blue print for those wishing to construct their own formboards; (15-30) minutes; William R. Grove; Pittsburgh, Pa.: William R. Grove, Behavior Clinic of the Criminal Court, County of Allegheny.

REFERENCES

[1] GROVE, WILLIAM R. *Modification of Kent-Shakow Formboard Series.* Unpublished doctor's thesis, University of Pittsburgh, 1937. Pp. iv, 70.
[2] GROVE, WILLIAM R. "An Experimental Study of the Kent-Shakow Industrial Formboard Series." *J Appl Psychol* 19:467-73 Ag '35.
[3] GROVE, WILLIAM R. "Modification of the Kent-Shakow Formboard Series." *J Psychol* 7:385-97 Ap '39.

[1409]

Moray House Test 10. Ages 10-12½; 1934; 2s. 9d. per 12; 17s. 6d. per 100; 1s. per 12 practice tests; 7s. per 100 practice tests; 6d. per manual; 9d. per specimen set; 45(60) minutes; Godfrey H. Thomson and colleagues; London: University of London Press, Ltd.

REFERENCES

[1] THOMSON, GODFREY H. "The Standardization of Group Tests and the Scatter of Intelligence Quotients: A Contribution to the Theory of Examining." *Brit J Ed Psychol* 2:92-112, 125-38 F, Je '32.

C. Ebblewhite Smith, Lecturer in the Department of Higher Degrees and Research, Institute of Education, University of London.

English test users have learned to place great value on the Moray House Tests. The *Moray House Test 10* is well up to the standard that Moray House has set itself and is perhaps the best English intelligence test for children of 11+. The idea of preceding the test proper by a ten-minute practice test is to be commended. The test is of satisfactory length and of suitably graded difficulty giving a very good spread of marks with 11-year-olds. Instructions to supervisors are practical and adequate.

Norms have been obtained with over 5,000 children from various English Counties, County Boroughs or Boroughs, the entire age group 10-6 to 11-6 being taken in each case. Scores have been adjusted for age and expressed as "standard scores" having a mean of 100 and a standard deviation of 15. This method constitutes a good compromise for obtaining IQ's when complete figures for norms cannot be obtained. This is an excellent test for its purpose.

[1410]
Northox Group Intelligence Test. Ages 11-12; 1933; 1 form; 3s. 6d. per 25; 3d. per test; 1s. per key; 2d. per manual; 30(35) minutes; G. Perrie Williams; London: George G. Harrap & Co., Ltd.

E. Patricia Hunt, Vocational Psychologist, Education Office, Birmingham, England. Each of the five subtests in this booklet is of a type recognised as suitable for testing general intelligence, viz: (*a*) pictorial observation, (*b*) pictorial classification, (*c*) pattern-completion, (*d*) substitution, and (*e*) arithmetic: missing digits. It is a pity, however, that some form of analogies test is not included as this is recognised as a most valuable test of *g*.

The subtests are well constructed. They are clearly set out, and each subtest contains one type of question only. The time limits, however, appear overgenerous and the reviewer doubts whether there are a sufficient number of items in each subtest to occupy the time allowed. This would need trying out, but if it is the case, it is a bad fault. Any test should be of such a length that the brightest candidate cannot succeed in completing it in the given time. Only in this way can a true estimate of the ability tested be obtained.

The absence of "practice" tests is a weak point. "Practice" tests should always be included to help the candidates to overcome initial nervousness and also to diminish any disparity among the candidates due to previous experience of, or coaching in intelligence tests. The whole test is entirely nonverbal and the reviewer thinks that it is more suitable for a younger age-group than 11-12 years.

The instructions are carefully worded and well set out. It would, however, be advisable to add to the "general instructions" a regulation that the printed instructions must be adhered to. No warning of this kind is included and the reviewer's personal experience provides many examples of untrained persons using tests and deviating considerably from the printed instructions.

It is unfortunate that the whole value of this test is vitiated by the absence of any norms. When the test has been given and scored the examiner is no wiser as to the intelligence rating of the candidates; all that has been obtained is a ranking within a particular group. The test, as an intelligence test, is therefore valueless. The author should have procured norms before publication; having failed in this, norms should have been procured as soon as possible after publication. The test was published in 1933. It is now 1939 and apparently published norms are still non-existent.

For an additional review, see 1050.

[1411]
Ontario School Ability Examination. Ages 3-15; 1936; "a performance test prepared more especially for use among children who are deaf, whose native tongue is other than English or who for any reason are lacking in language facility"; authorized by the Minister of Education for use in the schools of Ontario, Canada; 1 form; individual; $1.75 per box of testing materials; 90¢ per manual; [1] 75¢ per 50 test blanks; (20-40) minutes; H. Amoss; Toronto, Canada: Ryerson Press.

REFERENCES

[1] Amoss, Harry. *Ontario School Ability Examinations: A Performance Test Prepared More Especially for Use among Children Who Are Deaf, Whose Native Tongue Is Other than English or Who for Any Reason Are Lacking in Language Facility.* Toronto, Canada: Ryerson Press, 1936. Pp. ii, 54. $0.90.
[2] Morrison, W. J. "The Ontario School Ability Examination." *Am Ann Deaf* 85:184-9 Mr '40.

W. Line, Professor of Psychology, University of Toronto. In the manual,[1] Amoss presents his point of view regarding intelligence and its measurement, an account of the experimental work in establishing the scale, a description of the materials used, and detailed instructions for administering and scoring the tests.

The statement of point of view is of interest mainly as describing the general nature of the examination itself—which seeks to observe the three principles: (*a*) limitation of trial and error procedure; (*b*) progressions of increasingly complex situations, rather than scattered samplings; and (*c*) elimination of all special skills.

The experimental work involved preliminary tryouts with 31 backward and 8 average pupils of the Ontario School for the Deaf, 30 deaf pupils in the Day Classes of Toronto, and some 50 hearing children. Scaling of the selected test items was based on results obtained with an unspecified number of hearing pupils who had previously been examined by means of the Stanford Revision, and with deaf students who had taken the original form of the test. When administered to 288 deaf students (age range, 5 to 22), the examination gave a fairly normal distribution of intelligence quotients about the median 94. The 6-point shifting to the left agrees with results obtained when the IQ's of deaf and of hearing children were compared. The author has used the scale extensively in connection with the work of his staff in selecting candidates for special education in the Ontario schools.

The materials include adaptations of performance tests from Gesell, the Stanford Revision, Drever and Collins, Kohs, Knox, and Pintner, and some which the author his devised.

The instructions are clear. A few minor misprints (e.g., Series G-Weight Arrangement) are not likely to lead to confusion, since the corrections are fairly obvious.

The scale as a whole is easy to administer, although the more complex items in the tapping series will make demands on the examiner's skill.

The author, his staff, and other examiners have found the scale of great value in the Provincial Elementary Schools, in determining the school ability of "deaf children, retarded children, and children whose home language is other than English." As with all empirical instruments of this kind, adequate evaluation can be made only after extensive use.

[1412]
Otis Self-Administering Test: Adapted by Australian Council for Educational Research. Ages 9-15, 13-17; 4 forms, 2 levels; 6*d.* per 12; 5*d.* per manual; 30 (35-40) minutes; Melbourne, Australia: Australian Council for Educational Research.

[1413]
Otis Quick-Scoring Mental Ability Tests. Grades 1A-4, 4-9, 9-16; 1936-39; 3 levels; 2¢ per machine-scorable answer sheet; Arthur S. Otis; Yonkers, N. Y.: World Book Co. (London: George G. Harrap & Co., Ltd.)
a) ALPHA TEST. Grades 1A-4; 1936-38; 2 forms; may be given as a verbal or nonverbal test or both; 20(25) minutes for either verbal or nonverbal administration; $1.15 per 25; 25¢ per specimen set.
b) BETA TEST. Grades 4-9; 1937-39; 4 forms; 85¢ per 25 (Forms A and B); 90¢ per 25 machine-scorable tests (Forms CM and DM); 20¢ per specimen set; 30(35) minutes.
c) GAMMA TEST. Grades 9-16; 1937-39; 4 forms; 85¢ per 25 (Forms C and D); 90¢ per 25 machine-scorable tests (Forms AM and BM); 15¢ per specimen set; 30(35) minutes.

F. Kuhlmann, Director of the Division of Examinations and Classification, State Department of Public Institutions, St. Paul, Minnesota. The chief objective of these three batteries of tests seems to be economy in administration. This has been achieved to a considerable degree, except for Alpha which when given as a "verbal" is not self-administering. Quick scoring concerns the rapidity with which the number of right responses may be counted with the aid of a single cut-out stencil placed over the single test-sheet, except with Alpha in which the test material consists of a booklet of ten pages which must be scored two pages at a time. Deriving mental ages and intelligence quotients from the number of right responses is, on the whole, more involved than with most other tests.

Judged from inspection only, one would say that the choice of the different test items is ingenious and exceptionally well done, though lacking in variety, resulting in the reduction of the number of abilities measured by the battery. Where Otis uses a total of 80 or 90 trials in a battery some other tests use two or three times that number to cover the same range of mental levels.

In the reviewer's experience self-administering tests have not compared favorably with others, possibly largely because they do not keep the child motivated as well as tests do in which he is motivated anew with each successive test in the battery. A given type of question, such as opposites, recurs a number of times without others intervening. This removes some of the novelty which other tests continue to present throughout. Conceivably this may further reduce interest and motivation. When many children work with poor effort resulting age norms will be too low which in turn gives too high mental ages thereafter for those who work with good effort. This could account for the abnormally high variability in IQ's that he finds when they are computed in the usual way.

One is somewhat surprised at Alpha, which, though offered as a measure of general mental ability, consists, as a "nonverbal" test, entirely of recognition of similarities. Given as a "verbal" test it is almost equally limited in this respect.

The ages for which norms are given include a much larger range than the ages that are normal for the grades to which the tests were given to get norms. This makes the accuracy of these norms somewhat doubtful at both the lower and upper ends for each battery. All norm data were apparently obtained from volunteer contributions from schools using the tests, and are to be verified in the same manner. Nothing is said about the mental testers who gave the tests.

The need of arbitrarily allowing two months in mental age for every one point in raw score after age thirteen in Beta—instead of using the age norms unchanged—in order to keep the variability in IQ's down to what was found on a Binet scale suggests error elsewhere in the scale. Further, when raw scores exceed 70 they are increased by one to ten points to make the "IQ's more constant for a given individual than ordinary IQ's." For all three batteries the "IQ's" are not quotients, but are obtained by subtracting a child's raw score deviation from the age norm from 100, if the score is below the age norm, and adding this deviation to 100, if the raw score is above the age norm. The resulting measure may be as useful as true IQ's but it is unfortunate that the author suggests applying the term "IQ" to it. There is much arbitrary procedure in computing it. The difference is often considerable.

An attempt was apparently made to arrange the test questions in each battery in order of difficulty. This is a vital matter for any battery or scale, and some statistical evidence that this has been achieved should have been given. Without it one is not assured that the battery does not give results similar to what a Binet scale would give if it had a dozen or more tests for one age group, and only one or two for some other age group.

The reviewer has long contended that the range of abilities found in school children from grades 1 to 12 cannot be adequately measured by as few as three or four batteries that are brief enough for practical administrative purposes. When attempted, either the range of difficulty of test items is smaller than the existing range of abilities to be measured, or the number of test items is so small as to give a poor sampling of abilities at different levels, or there may be a compromise between these two faults. The Otis batteries represent such a compromise, but on the whole with more leaning toward small number of items than toward restricted range in difficulty of items.

Occupational Psychol 13:159 Ap '39. The intelligence tests of Dr. Otis are undoubtedly popular. * Scoring is an easy matter and can be accomplished with astonishing rapidity. We feel, however, that ease and rapidity are to some extent gained at the expense of the testee, who is, at any rate in the Beta and Gamma tests, asked to record his replies and manipulate his booklet in a rather involved fashion. Further, we are not convinced that all the items included in the tests are reasonable ones for intelligence, or "mental ability," tests. The norms quoted in the manuals of directions are for American children.

For reviews by Psyche Cattell and Rudolf Pintner, see 1053.

[1414]

Passalong Test: A Performance Test of Intelligence. Ages 8 and over; 1932-37; individual; 1 form; suitable for hearing and deaf cases; 21s. per box of blocks, cards, and manual; 1s. 6d. per set of cards; 1s. per manual; (10-15) minutes; W. P. Alexander; London: University of London Press, Ltd.

REFERENCES

1 ALEXANDER, W. P. "A New Performance Test of Intelligence." *Brit J Psychol* 23:52-63 Jl '32.
2 ALEXANDER, WILLIAM PICKEN. *Intelligence, Concrete and Abstract:* A Study of Differential Traits. British Journal of Psychology Monograph Supplements, Vol. 6, No. 19. London: Cambridge University Press, 1935. Pp. x, 177. 12s. 6d. Paper.
3 EARL, C. J. C. "The Performance Test Behaviour of Adult Morons." *Brit J Med Psychol* 17:78-92 pt 1 '37.
4 VERNON, P. E. "A Study of the Norms and the Validity of Certain Mental Tests at a Child Guidance Clinic." *Brit J Ed Psychol* 7:115-37 Je '37.
5 FOWLER, H. L. "Report on Psychological Tests on Natives in the North-West of Western Australia." *Australian J Sci* 2:124-7 Ap '40.

James Drever, Professor of Psychology, University of Edinburgh. This is a very interesting test, and, for general purposes, probably one of the best of the available performance tests. Its chief defect arises from the fact that the grading of difficulty is by no means uniform. The step between Test 3 and Test 4 is a very considerable one as compared with the step from 1 to 2 or from 2 to 3. The step between Tests 4 and 5 is approximately of the same difficulty as is the step from 5 to 6 and possibly that from 6 to 7. Again, however, we come to a more difficult step still between 7 and 8, a step

Otis Quick-Scoring Mental Ability Tests

which, if intelligently taken, makes that from 8 to 9 too easy. At the same time it must be freely admitted that Alexander deserves the greatest credit for his attempt at grading a test of this kind.

Like most performance tests trial and error with chance success may obtain an unmerited high score, but the *Passalong Test* is superior to most performance tests in this regard. As one of a battery of performance tests, with, say Kohs' *Block-Design Test*, Healy's *Pictorial Completion Test II*, and the *Cube Construction Test*—the *Passalong Test* merits further attention.

T. J. Keating, Research Fellow, The Training School at Vineland, New Jersey. This test consumes little time but appears to give fairly satisfactory results. It is quickly set up and quickly scored, the scoring being based on timing. A reasonable time is allowed the examiner for making qualitative observations. In this respect the test is superior to many others in the performance category, especially those requiring counting of moves.

The test is so designed that the goal set is easily comprehended by the subject, which makes it useful, for example, for testing the deaf. It has intrinsic appeal to subjects and is thus practically self-motivating. It could readily be adapted for blind subjects.

The scoring might be too liberal. A study of the results with 16 to 34 mentally deficient subjects showed that, in these cases at least, the median test age of the group on the *Passalong Test* was at least a year above the median test ages obtained on the 1916 *Stanford-Binet*, the *Vineland Social Maturity Scale* and the *Porteus Maze Test*. Further work with the test may explain this discrepancy, which is superficially explained by the known relative superiority of mentally deficient subjects on performance tests. The inclusion in the test manual of the scores obtained by the standardization group, arranged by age levels, would make possible comparative studies. The test seems too useful to be discarded without further study because of the supposed weakness of unduly generous norms. There are no data available on the practice effect of the test but it is felt on the basis of inspection of a few cases that this is not great.

Preliminary indications from a small number (16 to 34) of mentally deficient subjects suggests that the *Passalong Test* correlates low with the *Stanford-Binet* ($r = .21$), a point perhaps in its favor as a nonverbal test; moderately well with the nonverbal *Porteus Maze Test* ($r = .61$), and intermediately ($r = .47$) with the *Vineland Social Maturity Scale*.

Grace H. Kent, Psychologist, Danvers State Hospital, Hathorne, Massachusetts. This test is based upon a mechanical puzzle commonly known as a toy, developed here into a nine-task graded series. For each task a small tray holds several rectangular blocks of the sizes: 1×1 inch, 1×2 inches, or 2×2 inches; with an area of at least one square inch left open to permit the blocks to be moved in the tray without being lifted from it. Two opposite edges of the tray are painted red and blue, respectively; and the tray is invariably presented with blue blocks at the red edge and red blocks at the blue edge. The task is to slide each block to the edge of its own color, arranging the blocks according to a painted pattern which is kept before the subject.

Four trays of different sizes serve for the nine tasks, and the setup for each task can be prepared in a few seconds during the examination. The entire outfit is sufficiently compact to be carried in a briefcase and taken to the traveling clinic.

The test is one of absorbing interest, one which usually commands the spontaneous cooperation of the subject. For this reason it affords the examiner an unusual opportunity for observation. The task holds the subject's attention so completely that he is hardly aware of being observed.

The presentation is needlessly time-consuming, because the performance is to be continued until there have been two consecutive failures. Two nonconsecutive failures might safely be accepted as evidence that the subject has reached his limit, and a first failure on Task 8 might be accepted as final. A little time might be saved also by using Task 1 for demonstration only instead of for credit, the subject being permitted to perform it for practice.

The reviewer has not seen anyone solve Task 9 within the time limit. The interval between 8 and 9 is wider than between any other adjacent tasks, and yet these two tasks differ only in the arrangement of certain blocks. The first step in the solution of 9 is to change its setup to that of 8; but it more often happens that the subject changes the setup of 8 to that of 9, thereby destroying all likelihood of success. These two tasks are more tricky than is desirable in a test intended to measure "intelligence"; but the test could hardly have been made discriminative at the upper levels without involving some play of chance. The actual interference is slight, because failure by chance is more common than success by chance. Accidental failure is an accident which cannot easily happen to a subject who has grasped the principles of the test.

Evaluation is wholly in terms of speed, and some important factors are left unrecorded. The test could not be scored accurately by move-count, but it is worth while at least to record a subject's tendency to keep repeating a course of procedure which has already been proven fruitless.

The scoring system is notably weak as compared with the test itself. The weighting at the upper end is entirely inadequate, while at the lower end full credit is allowed for a one-minute performance of tasks requiring only a few seconds. The subject who scores one point on Task 8 is usually credited with five points each on the Tasks 3 to 7; but the single point which he achieves on the difficult task is more significant than the 25 points he has earned by rapid performance of the five easy tasks.

One who is dissatisfied with the scoring system is of course dissatisfied also with the norms; but even if there were no norms at all, the reviewer would eagerly adopt this test as an attractive and very valuable unit of a performance test battery.

For a review by J. M. Blackburn of the Alexander Performance Scale *which includes the* Passalong Test, *see 1376.*

[1415]

Personnel Test. Adults in business and industrial situations; 1939; an adaptation of the *Otis Self-Administering Tests of Mental Ability*: Higher Form by Arthur S. Otis; 3 forms; $5 per 100; 75¢ per specimen set; sale is restricted to technically qualified personnel workers in business and industry; 12(20) minutes; E. F. Wonderlic; Chicago, Ill.: the Author, 919 North Michigan Avenue.

REFERENCES

1 HOVLAND, CARL IVER, AND WONDERLIC, E. F. "A Critical Analysis of the Otis Self-Administering Test of Mental Ability —Higher Form." *J Appl Psychol* 23:367-87 Je '39.
2 WONDERLIC, E. F., AND HOVLAND, CARL IVER. "The Personnel Test: A Restandardized Abridgment of the Otis S-A Test for Business and Industrial Use." *J Appl Psychol* 23:685-702 D '39.

[1416]

Pintner General Ability Tests: Verbal Series. Grades kdgt.-2, 5-8, 9-12; 1923-39; 2 forms, 3 levels; $1.25 per 25; Yonkers, N. Y.: World Book Co. (London: George G. Harrap & Co., Ltd.)
a) PINTNER-CUNNINGHAM PRIMARY TEST. Grades kdgt.-2; 1923-39; 15¢ per specimen set; (25) minutes; Rudolf Pintner, Bess V. Cunningham, and Walter N. Durost.
b) PINTNER INTERMEDIATE TEST. Grades 5-8; 1931-39; a revision of the *Pintner Intelligence Test* published in 1931 by the Bureau of Publications, Teachers College, Columbia University; 20¢ per manual; 20¢ per specimen set; 45(55) minutes; Rudolf Pintner.
c) PINTNER ADVANCED TEST. Grades 9-12; 1938-39; 20¢ per manual; 20¢ per specimen set; 55(65) minutes; Rudolf Pintner.

REFERENCES

1 KIRKPATRICK, FORREST H., AND RUPP, ROBERT A. "The Pintner Test at the College Level." *J Ed Res* 33:357-9 Ja '40.

Am J Psychol 53:477-8 Jl '40. Roger M. Bellows. * Form A of the Primary Test is like the original Pintner-Cunningham Primary Mental Test except that the pictures have been redrawn and new items have been substituted for dated ones. * A well prepared manual of 16 pages for the Intermediate and Advanced Tests gives a description of the series, a brief but unusually adequate statement of the requirements of a good test, characteristics of statistical data and standardization of the series, and suggestions for interpretation and use of the tests. * Directions for administering and scoring which have been carefully edited are given in a separate manual. Sampling procedures as well as number of cases used in establishing the norms (the total is above 100,000 Ss) would seem to be satisfactory. Every child in the public schools in the appropriate grades of the coöperating communities took the test, and the authors believe they have eliminated Sampling errors which might arise from intracommunity selection. Communities were chosen which were widely different in size, socio-economic status, and geographic location. * Reliabilities for the total tests are high enough for group comparison but test performance must of course be interpreted with great caution when the purpose is individual diagnosis or orientation. * Reported statistical validity of the tests is very high. The Intermediate Test correlates 0.84 with total scores on the Metropolitan Achievement Tests for 168 cases in grade 5, and 0.79 for 209 cases in grade 7. Coefficients between the Pintner General Ability Tests and seven other psychological tests range from 0.71 for the Revised Stanford Binet to 0.87 for the Otis Group Intelligence Scale. The reviewer was favorably impressed, not only by the care used in the development of the tests, their elaborate standardization, and their detailed evaluation *before* publication, but also by the clear and conservative presentation of interpretative material in the manual. Repetition of such statements as the following quotation from the manual will do much to aid test users in general to appreciate limitations of adequate instruments of measurement—"success or failure must be interpreted in terms of variety of additional facts concerning the child."

Ed Res B 18:117-8 Ap '39. J. Wayne Wrightstone. * These tests follow the generally accepted ideas of exercises which should constitute a test of academic aptitude. Apparently no factor analysis of the components of academic aptitude, such as that proposed by Thurstone, has been applied to these tests. No correlations of these tests with other tests of academic aptitude or tests of academic achievement are supplied. * Inadequate data are provided in the Manual about the reliability and the validity of these tests, but it may be presumed that in both of these aspects, the tests are as good as most currently available tests of "verbal intelligence." Another inadequacy is the lack of explanation of the derivation and meaning of the so-called "standard scores" which are provided. Until psychological research has revealed more convincing evidence about the components of academic aptitude, the *Pintner General Ability Tests* may be recommended for use in schools. The apparent care in construction is noteworthy.

Ed Res B 19:60 Ja 17 '40. J. Wayne Wrightstone. [Review of the *Pintner-Cunningham Primary Test.*] The revision . . . has not included any radical departures from its previous edition. * The reliability coefficients of this test are high, approximating .88 in each grade for which it is designed to be used. An innovation in terms of scores is a standard-score scale which has been established for the series of batteries of the Pintner General Ability Test. This test in its previous form has been widely used in the primary grades to provide an index of academic aptitude and probably will continue to be used widely until other and better tests are constructed to replace it. Its main value is that it does provide an index of a primary-grade child's ability to deal with abstract symbols which correlate with ability to do verbal and number work efficiently in the early school grades.

[1417]

Progressive Matrices: A Perceptual Test of Intelligence. Mental ages 3 and over; 1938; individual; 1 form, 3 editions (this entry refers only to the published booklet edition; for information about the Board Form and the Portfolio Form *see* the article "Matrix Tests"[8]); 10*s*. 6*d*. per testing outfit; 3*s*. per 100 record forms; nontimed (20-60) minutes; prepared for the Research Department, Royal Eastern Counties' Institution, Colchester, England; J. C. Raven; London: H. K. Lewis & Co., Ltd.

REFERENCES

1 PENROSE, L. S., AND RAVEN, J. C. "A New Series of Perceptual Tests: Preliminary Communication." *Brit J Med Psychol* 16:97-104 pt 2 '36.
2 SPEARMAN, CH. E. "Measurement of Intelligence." *Scientia* 64:75-82 Ag '38.
3 DAVIDSON, MARSH. "Studies in the Application of Mental Tests to Psychotic Patients." *Brit J Med Psychol* 18:44-52 pt 1 '39.
4 MILLER, F. M., AND RAVEN, J. C. "The Influence of Positional Factors on the Choice of Answers to Perceptual Intelligence Tests." *Brit J Med Psychol* 18:35-9 pt 1 '39.
5 RAVEN, J. C. "The R.E.C.I. Series of Perceptual Tests: An Experimental Survey." *Brit J Med Psychol* 18:16-34 pt 1 '39.
6 RAVEN, J. C., AND WAITE, A. "Experiments on Physically and Mentally Defective Children with Perceptual Tests." *Brit J Med Psychol* 18:40-3 pt 1 '39.
7 SPEARMAN, C. " 'Intelligence' Tests." *Eug R* 30:249-54 Ja '39.
8 RAVEN, JOHN C. "Matrix Tests." *Mental Health* 1:10-8 Ja '40.

T. J. Keating, Research Fellow, The Training School at Vineland, New Jersey. The *Progressive Matrices*, a series of perceptual tests, qualifies as a desirable instrument in these practical respects: equipment is simple—only the booklet of matrices and a scoring sheet are needed; administration and scoring are easy; self-administration is possible; applicability is extended to deaf, aphasic, and foreign subjects; and readministration affects results but slightly.

Its useful range is limited to years nine to thirteen inclusive. (A formboard variation of the test is available for younger subjects.) The norms at year fourteen are less reliable than others, according to the authors. As an individual test it is time-consuming, especially with brighter subjects. If, however, an examiner's time needs to be spared, the subject may work alone. For subjects who appear to be perturbed by the presence of an examiner, working alone may be advantageous. No item analysis has been attempted, but it is apparent that Item E-8 is unsatisfactory.

[1418]

Psychological Examination, Form D—1939 Edition. Grades 12-13; 1935-39; 1 form (Form D replaces the five earlier editions); machine scorable; 50(60) minutes; Intelligence Test Committee of the Teachers College Personnel Association; Normal, Ill.: the Association, c/o C. F. Malmberg.

REFERENCES
Same as for 1280.

Howard Easley, Assistant Professor of Educational Psychology, Duke University. [Review of Form D.] Form D of this examination is the 1939 edition, Forms A, B, and C having appeared in 1934, 1935, and 1938. The major changes in the 1939 edition are the omission of the completion test, the addition of some number-series items, changing the form of the examination from the subtest type to the omnibus type, and, new since 1937, provision for machine scoring.

This test is prepared especially for use in teachers colleges, but, according to the manual "may be used alone for all purposes common to intelligence tests." The test material reveals, as one might expect, no selection with the view to its peculiar usefulness to teachers colleges. The norms (percentile ranks on Forms B and C) are based entirely on scores from teachers college freshmen. We may expect this test to do a better job of ranking students according to the abilities of teachers college students in general, no better job of ranking them among students of a given institution, and a poorer job of ranking them among college students in general, than is done by other college entrance psychological examinations with norms based on a wider selection of college students.

D. A. Worcester, Chairman of the Department of Educational Psychology and Measurements, The University of Nebraska. This is a fourth form of a psychological examination which has been prepared by a committee of the Teachers College Personnel Association.

The committee explains in detail the statistical procedures by which the items have been validated and presents reliable coefficients (which run from .720 to .920 for the various tests) for previous forms of the test. The committee presents evidence of the discriminative value of the test, and it can undoubtedly be used with confidence.

The content of the test is from six conventional fields, namely: vocabulary, number series, same-opposite, arithmetic reasoning, completion, and analogies. In justification of these fields the somewhat naive statement is made: "We recognize the fact that in recent studies arithmetic reasoning and number completion tests have not been found particularly valuable for predicting academic success. Language and number, however, are the two fundamental social arts that all must acquire. It was felt, therefore, that an intelligence test should include both these elements."

There are some who might argue that tests used more generally would offer a desirable possibility of comparison of students in teacher-training institutions with those in other colleges and universities. Whereas the content of this test does not show any observable internal evidence of being peculiar to the experience of those who are preparing to teach, it would perhaps be better to secure norms from non-teacher-training students and to use it more generally.

The reviewer has one serious question concerning the test. The instructions, including the sample exercises, are somewhat long and complicated, occupying about one and one-third pages. The time spent in familiarizing oneself with these instructions and practice exercises is included in the fifty-five minutes of working time allowed for the test. This would appear to be a significant advantage to the student who has had earlier experience with tests of this kind. There are two blank pages in the booklet, and it would seem desirable to have the instructions and sample exercises presented separately and then to have a uniform working time on the test proper.

Instead of giving zero scores to tests apparently marked according to some different plan, as is recommended, the booklet should be thrown out and the student treated as "not tested." The manual of instructions and the instructions in the test booklet need more careful editing.

For a review by John C. Flanagan, see 1054.

[1419]

Revised Beta Examination. Grades 3 and over; 1931-35; 1 form; $7 per 100; 25¢ per specimen set; (40-75) minutes; C. E. Kellogg assisted by N. W. Morton; New York: Psychological Corporation.

REFERENCES

1 YOAKUM, CLARENCE S., AND YERKES, ROBERT M., EDITORS. *Army Mental Tests,* pp. 79-92, 276-84, and passim. New York: Henry Holt and Co., 1920. Pp. xiii, 303. Out of print.
2 YERKES, ROBERT M., EDITOR. *Psychological Examining in the United States Army,* pp. 162-7, 235-58, 368-95, 466-8, and passim. Memoirs of the National Academy of Sciences, Vol. 15. Washington, D. C.: Government Printing Office, 1921. Pp. vi, 890. Out of print.
3 KELLOGG, C. E., AND MORTON, N. W. "Revised Beta Examination." *Personnel J* 13:94-100 Ag '34.
4 HORTON, SAMUEL P. *Relationships Among Nineteen Group Tests and Their Validity for Freshman Engineering Marks.* Human Engineering Laboratory, Technical Report, No. 46. Boston, Mass.: the Laboratory, 1939. Pp. viii, 141. $1.00. Paper, mimeographed.

S. D. Porteus, Director of the Psychological Clinic and Professor of Clinical Psychology, University of Hawaii. Of the tests that were either devised or assembled by the committee that worked on the Army examinations, the most unsatisfactory effort was, in the writer's opinion, the *Beta Performance Scale*. There was a hopeful assumption that it could serve as a substitute for *Army Alpha*, but this, in a clinical sense, it was not. I doubt very much if we can ever substitute a nonverbal for a verbal test, any more than we can substitute a musical test for one in mathematics. For the illiterate, the *Army Beta* provided a most inadequate appraisal of abilities.

One of the chief reasons for this lay in the choice of tests which put a premium on memory of one kind or another. In the revised Beta this choice of tests has been improved so that there is not the same emphasis on immediate memory for unrelated material. The scale, however, still suffers because some of its individual tests are limited to material that can be readily applied to groups.

Test 1, a form of maze test, was copied from the writer's earlier individual maze test, but the imitation was no flattery. The Beta form is scored on accuracy—with a time limit—which damns it completely as a measure of planning capacity, the only feature which, in my opinion, makes a maze test worth using. Obviously, speed can only be attained by sacrificing the time that should be taken for planning and preconsideration. In the second place, using the test as a group test robs the examiner of any opportunity to watch the subject at work and thus observe the characteristics that make for nonsuccess.

Test 2 is a substitution test which examines the subject's ability to make purely arbitrary associations between two sets of symbols such as digits and letter-like forms. The capacity tested would be valuable in code-writing or possibly to a mild degree in learning the vocabulary of a foreign language. I cannot see, however, that it has any particular function in our everyday thinking or behavior. In other words, it is a good test of an unimportant ability.

The third test is one in which the subject marks the faulty item in pictures arranged in series of fours. It was this test which, it must be confessed, roused the ire of the reviewer. The pictures are so small and ill-drawn as to be almost unintelligible, and in some cases the scoring is ambiguous. The first picture in Item 9 could be anything from a baby in a bath to a castle on a sea of vegetation. A picture in Item 11 shows a man using an axe to split wood, with his foot in such a position that there is grave danger that it will be badly cut—yet that is not, according to the key, the faulty item. The next picture shows a man pulling on a rope over a pulley that hangs unattached in the air—yet that, too, in the artist's conception, is correct! Item 13 has nothing wrong with it, although it shows a balance held down with a smaller weight—which, of course, often happens when heavy material is balanced against lighter. Items 18 and 19 are so unintelligible that they might qualify as tests of imagination, but of nothing else. Anything, apparently, will do for a mental test!

Test 4 is one of the well-known mental formboards—ingenious enough, but like Test 2, examining a capacity that seems of little importance. The next test is a rather simple missing-feature test, which seems to be overweighted in the scoring. Test 6 resolves itself into a visual rote memory test.

The best feature of the *Revised Beta Examination* is the opportunity that is given for fore-exercise. On the whole, the reviewer doubts the value of an attempt, no matter how painstaking, to revive a justly discarded performance scale such as the Beta.

David Wechsler, Chief Psychologist, Psychiatric Division, Bellevue Hospital, New York, New York. The test offered by the authors may be best described as a modification rather than a revision of the *Army Beta*. Of the seven tests originally constituting the *Army Beta* only Test 1 (Maze) is retained unaltered. Test 2 (Cube Analysis) and Test 3 (X-O Series) have been entirely omitted. Test 4 (Digit-Symbol) has been altered so that the subject writes the numbers instead of symbols. Test 5 (Number Checking) has been expanded to include pictures and symbols as well as numbers. Test 6 (Pictorial Completion) and 7 (Geometrical Construction) are kept in substantially the original form but have been lengthened. For the two tests omitted, the authors have substituted a new one (Picture Discrimination Test), so that the entire examination consists of six instead of seven tests. On the whole the modification of the examination seems to be an improvement on the old Beta. The Cube Counting and X-O series were the poorest of the original Beta examination.

The added new test, however, does not seem to be a very happy choice. The pictures are too miniscule and decidedly hard on the eyes. It also appears to be one of the tests that is still hard to get across in spite of the preliminary practice exercises.

The chief feature and most noteworthy contribution of the Kellogg-Morton revision is the elimination of the pantomime method of presentation and its replacement by the practice exercise. The pantomime method of presentation was laborious and costly, requiring an elaborate and expensive blackboard setup. It had the advantage of enabling the examiner to test the totally deaf as well as individuals who did not understand English at all. This advantage is largely lost by the revision, but is more than made up by the test's new features.

The revised Beta was standardized on Canadian children, ages 7 to 18 and grades 3 through 11. Mental age score equivalents and grade norms are available. Although standardized on Canadian children the norms appear applicable to corresponding American age groups. Thus, Morris Krugman of the Bureau of Child Guidance of the Board of Education of the City of New York informed the reviewer that data obtained from New York City school children furnished norms which do not deviate markedly from those furnished by the author. The test shows good reliability (.987) as measured by inter-test correlations (odd versus even items). The retest r, however, is relatively low showing only an r of .77 between first and second administrations of the test. The main shortcoming of the revision is its continued omission of any attempt to weight the different tests. Thus Test 1 (Maze) which is one of the best, contributes a possible maximum score of only 10 as against the possible maximum of 25 on the number-checking test which, in the reviewer's opinion, is one of the poorest tests of general intelligence. There is also the fact that while the author furnishes mental age equivalents for test scores, no distribution of MA's at different age levels is given. The result is that one is again confronted with a problem as to how to interpret IQ's obtained by dividing an MA by a CA for classification purposes. In this respect, however, the revised Beta sins no more than most other tests on the market.

In spite of certain merits the revised Beta lends itself to only limited application. Unlike the original Beta it does not seem to have been devised merely for the speedy testing of large groups of illiterates. Knowing the avidity of many clinicians for new instruments, one suspects that it may be used as a paper-and-pencil performance type of test as a substitute and shortcut for the Pintner-Paterson, the Grace Arthur, or similar scales. It is important therefore to point out that it cannot be so used. Except for Test 1, the revised Beta contains no test which can be classified as performance. Most of the remaining tests involve functions which measure very much the same things that verbal tests do except that the raw data furnished the subject is given in pictures and symbols and not in words. That this is so, is attested, for example, by the fact that the highest correlation furnished by the revised Beta was that obtained between it and the time and error scores of the Thurstone's *Examination in Clerical Work* (.81).

[1420]

Revised Stanford-Binet Scale. Ages 2 and over; 1937; a revision of the Stanford-Binet Scale published in 1916; 2 forms (Forms L and M); $2 (7s. 6d.) per 25 record booklets; 60¢ (3s. 6d.) per record form; $1.75 (4s. 6d.) per set of printed card material for each form; $8 (45s.) per testing outfit for each form; $2.25 (10s. 6d.) per copy of the manual; [99] $1.35 per abbreviated directions for administering; [98] Lewis M. Terman and Maud A. Merrill; Boston, Mass.: Houghton Mifflin Co. (London: George G. Harrap & Co., Ltd.)

REFERENCES

1 TERMAN, LEWIS M., AND CHILDS, H. G. "A Tentative Revision and Extension of the Binet-Simon Measuring Scale of Intelligence." *J Ed Psychol* 3:61-74, 133-43, 198-208, 277-89 F, Mr, Ap, My, '12.
2 TERMAN, LEWIS M. "Suggestions for Revising, Extending and Supplementing the Binet Intelligence Tests." *J Psycho-Asthenics* 18:20-33 S '13.
3 TERMAN, LEWIS M. *The Measurement of Intelligence*: An Explanation of and a Complete Guide for the Use of the Stanford Revision and Extension of *The Binet-Simon Intelligence Scale*. Boston, Mass.: Houghton Mifflin Co., 1916. Pp. xix, 362. $2.00. (London: George G. Harrap & Co., Ltd. 8s. 6d.)
4 TERMAN, LEWIS M.; LYMAN, GRACE; ORDAHL, GEORGE; ORDAHL, LOUISE ELLISON; GALBREATH, NEVA; AND TALBERT, WILFORD; ASSISTED BY HERBERT E. KNOLLIN, J. H. WILLIAMS, H. G. CHILDS, HELEN TROST, RICHARD ZEIDLER, CHARLES WADDLE, AND IRENE CUNEO. *The Stanford Revision and Extension of the Binet-Simon Scale for Measuring Intelligence*. Educational Psychology Monographs, No. 18. Baltimore, Md.: Warwick & York, Inc., 1917. Pp. v, 179. $2.58.
5 CUNEO, IRENE, AND TERMAN, LEWIS M. "Stanford-Binet Tests of 112 Kindergarten Children and 77 Repeated Tests." *J Genetic Psychol* 25:414-28 D '18.
6 TERMAN, LEWIS M. "The Vocabulary Test as a Measure of Intelligence." *J Ed Psychol* 9:452-66 O '18.
7 SKAGGS, E. B. "A Comparison of Results Obtained by the Terman Binet Tests and the Healy Picture Completion Test." *J Ed Psychol* 11:418-20a O '20.
8 TERMAN, L. M. *Condensed Guide for the Stanford Revision of the Binet-Simon Intelligence Test*. Boston, Mass.: Houghton Mifflin Co., 1920. Pp. 32. $1.00. (London: George G. Harrap & Co., Ltd. 4s. 6d.)
9 BURT, CYRIL. *Mental and Scholastic Tests*, pp. 68-72. London: P. S. King and Son, Ltd., 1921. Pp. xv, 432. 18s.
10 ODELL, C. W. "A Few Data on the Use of the Stanford Revision of the Binet-Simon Tests by Halves." *J Ed Res* 4:437-8 D '21.
11 RUGG, HAROLD, AND COLLOTON, CECILE. "Constancy of the Stanford-Binet I.Q. as Shown by Retests." *J Ed Psychol* 12:315-22 S '21.

Revised Beta Examination

12 YERKES, ROBERT M. EDITOR. *Psychological Examining in the United States Army.* pp. 172-82, 271-4, 397-9, 407-11, and passim. Memoirs of the National Academy of Sciences, Vol. 15. Washington, D. C.: Government Printing Office, 1921. Pp. vi, 890. Out of print.
13 BALDWIN, BIRD T., AND STECHER, LORLE I. "Additional Data from Consecutive Stanford-Binet Tests." *J Ed Psychol* 13:556-60 D '22.
14 GARRISON, S. C. "Additional Retests by Means of the Stanford Revision of the Binet-Simon Tests." *J Ed Psychol* 13:307-12 My '22.
15 GORDON, KATE. "Some Retests with the Stanford-Binet Scale." *J Ed Psychol* 13:363-5 S '22.
16 JEWETT, STEPHEN PERHAM, AND BLANCHARD, PHYLLIS. "Influence of Affective Disturbances on Responses to the Stanford Binet Test." *Mental Hyg* 6:39-56 Ja '22.
17 MORGENTHAU, DOROTHY RUTH. *Some Well-Known Mental Tests Evaluated and Compared.* Columbia University, Archives of Psychology, No. 52. New York: the University, 1922. Pp. 54. Paper. Out of print.
18 RICHARDSON, C. A. "Note on a Method of Estimating the True Stanford-Binet Intelligence Quotients of Adults." *Brit J Psychol* 12:383-4 Ap '22.
19 STENQUIST, JOHN L. "Constancy of the Stanford Binet-IQ as Shown by Retests." *J Ed Psychol* 13:54-6 Ja '22.
20 CORNELL, ETHEL L., AND LOWDEN, GLADYS L. "A Comparison of the Stanford and Porteus Tests in Several Types of Social Inadequacy." *J Abn and Social Psychol* 18:33-42 Ap-Je '23.
21 KENT, GRACE H. "A Combination Mental Test for Clinical Use." *J Appl Psychol* 7:246-57 S '23.
22 SYMONDS, PERCIVAL M. "A Second Approximation to the Curve of the Distribution of Intelligence of the Population of the United States, with a Note on the Standardization of the Stanford Revision of the Binet-Simon Scale." *J Ed Psychol* 14:65-81 F '23.
23 AVERY, GEORGE T. "Comparison of Stanford and Herring Binet Revisions Given to First Grade Children." *J Ed Psychol* 15:224-8 Ap '24.
24 HERRING, JOHN P. "Avery's Comparison of the Stanford and Herring Revisions." *J Ed Psychol* 15:383-8 S '24.
25 HERRING, JOHN P. "Reliability of the Stanford and the Herring Revision of the Binet-Simon Tests." *J Ed Psychol* 15:217-23 Ap '24.
26 MADSEN, I. N. "Some Results with the Stanford Revision of the Binet-Simon Tests." *Sch and Soc* 19:559-62 My 10 '24.
27 WALTERS, FRED C. "Language Handicap and the Stanford Revision of the Binet-Simon Tests." *J Ed Psychol* 15:276-84 My '24.
28 WILNER, CHARLES F. "A Comparative Study of the Stanford and the Herring Revisions of the Binet-Simon Tests." *J Ed Psychol* 15:520-9 N '24.
29 PAL, SATYAJIVAN. *The Tests of the Stanford Revision of the Binet-Simon Intelligence Scale*: Adapted for Use with Bengali Boys and Translated into the Bengali Language, with Notes on the Procedure. Foreword by M. West. Dacca University Bulletins, No. 5. Published for Dacca University. Bombay, India: Oxford University Press, 1925. Pp. iv, 55. Rs. 1-8.
30 HILDRETH, GERTRUDE. "Stanford-Binet Retests of 441 School Children." *J Genetic Psychol* 33:365-86 S '26.
31 MAITY, H. "A Report on the Application of the Stanford Adult Tests to a Group of College Students." *Indian J Psychol* 1:214-22 '26.
32 LINCOLN, EDWARD A. "The Reliability of the Stanford-Binet Scale and the Constancy of Intelligence Quotients." *J Ed Psychol* 18:621-6 D '27.
33 RANDALL, FLORENCE B. "A Study on the Constancy of the IQ." *Sch and Soc* 26:311-2 S 3 '27.
34 WALLIN, J. E. W. "A Further Note on Scattering in the Binet Scale." *J Appl Psychol* 11:143-54 Ap '27.
35 WELLS, F. L. *Mental Tests in Clinical Practice,* pp. 32-53. Yonkers, N. Y.: World Book Co., 1927. Pp. x, 315. $2.16.
36 GREENE, EDWARD B. "A Graphic Summary of the Stanford-Binet Test." *J Appl Psychol* 12:343-7 Je '28.
37 THOMPSON, E. M. "The Stanford Revision Vocabulary Test." *South African J Sci* 25:461-3 '28.
38 TOWNSEND, REBECCA P. "Tests of the Stanford Revision of the Binet-Simon Scale Most Frequently Failed by Children in Orthogenic Backward Classes." *Psychol Clinic* 17:200-3 N-D '28.
39 BROOKS, FOWLER D. "The Accuracy of the Abbreviated Stanford-Binet Scale." *Psychol Clinic* 18:17-20 Mr-Ap '29.
40 HAYES, SAMUEL P. "The New Revision of the Binet Intelligence Tests for the Blind." *Teach Forum* 2:2-4 N '29.
41 MARINE, EDITH LUCILE. *The Effect of Familiarity with the Examiner upon Stanford-Binet Performance.* Columbia University, Teachers College, Contributions to Education, No. 381. New York: Bureau of Publications, the College, 1929. Pp. v, 42. $1.50.
42 RILEY, G. "Stanford Binet 'Indicators' of Mechanical Ability." *Psychol Clinic* 18:128-32 My-Je '29.
43 THURSTONE, L. L., AND ACKERSON, LUTON. "The Mental Growth Curve for the Binet Tests." *J Ed Psychol* 20:569-83 N '29.
44 WALLIN, J. E. WALLACE. *A Statistical Study of the Individual Tests in Ages VIII and IX in the Stanford-Binet Scale.* Mental Measurements Monographs, No. 6. Baltimore, Md.: Williams & Wilkins Co., June 1929. Pp. vii, 58. $1.00. Paper.
45 SCHOTT, EMMETT L. "Variability of Mental Ratings in Retests of Neuropsychiatric Cases." *Am J Psychiatry* 87:213-27 S '30.
46 SULLIVAN, ELIZABETH T. "The Mental Development of Thirty-Three Ten Year Old Children." *J Juvenile Res* 14:27-33 Ja '30.
47 WILSON, CHARLES A.; SWEENY, MARY E.; STUTSMAN, RACHEL; CHESIRE, LEONE E.; AND HATT, ELISE. *The Merrill-Palmer Standards of Physical and Mental Growth.* Detroit, Mich.: Merrill-Palmer School, 1930. Pp. ix, 121. $0.50. Paper.
48 CATTELL, PSYCHE. "Constant Changes in the Stanford-Binet IQ." *J Ed Psychol* 22:544-50 O '31.
49 GREEN, HELEN J. *Qualitative Method for Scoring the Vocabulary Test of the New Revision of the Stanford-Binet.* Unpublished master's thesis, Stanford University, 1931.
50 JONES, HAROLD ELLIS. *The Pattern of Abilities among Adult and Juvenile Defectives.* University of California Publications in Psychology, Vol. 5, No. 2. Berkeley, Calif.: University of California Press, May 1931. Pp. 47-61. $0.25. Paper.
51 MCFADDEN, JOHN HOLMAN. *Differential Responses of Normal and Feebleminded Subjects of Equal Mental Age, on the Kent-Rosanoff Free Association Test and the Stanford Revision of the Binet-Simon Intelligence Test.* Mental Measurement Monographs, No. 7. Baltimore, Md.: Williams & Wilkins Co., February 1931. Pp. 85. $1.50. Paper.
52 DURLING, DOROTHY. "Note on the Comparative Reliability of the Stanford-Binet below the Age of Six." *J Appl Psychol* 16:331-33 Je '32.
53 FEINBERG, HENRY. "The Stanford Revision of the Binet-Simon Tests Compared with the Pintner-Paterson Short Performance Scale." *J Genetic Psychol* 40:486-99 Je '32.
54 JONES, H. E.; CONRAD, H. S.; AND BLANCHARD, M. B. *Environmental Handicap in Mental Test Performance.* University of California Publications in Psychology, Vol. 5, No. 3. Berkeley, Calif.: University of California Press, January 1932. Pp. 63-99. $0.40. Paper.
55 JORDAN, JOHN S. "Reliability of Stanford-Binet Intelligence Quotients Derived by Student Examiners." *J Ed Res* 26:295-301 D '32.
56 MADDEN, RICHARD. "A Note on the Eight and Nine Year Levels of Stanford-Binet." *Sch and Soc* 36:576 O 29 '32.
57 PERKINS, RUTH E. "A Study of the Relation of Brightness to Stanford-Binet Test Performance." *J Appl Psychol* 16:205-16 Ap '32.
58 PHILLIPS, ARTHUR. "An Analytical and Comparative Study of the Binet-Simon Test Responses of 1,306 Philadelphia School Children with an Attempt to Evaluate and Grade the Separate Tests." *Psychol Clinic* 21:1-38 Mr-My '32.
59 SKALET, MAGDA. "A Statistical Study of the Responses of a Group of Normal Children to the Individual Tests in the Stanford-Revision of the Binet-Simon Scale." *Psychol Clinic* 21:183-95 S-N '32.
60 CATTELL, PSYCHE. "Do the Stanford-Binet IQ's of Superior Boys and Girls Tend to Decrease or Increase with Age?" *J Ed Res* 26:668-73. My '33.
61 CHARLES, C. M. "A Comparison of the Intelligence Quotients of Three Different Mental Tests Applied to a Group of Incarcerated Delinquent Boys." *J Appl Psychol* 17:581-4 O '33.
62 LINCOLN, E. A. "Preliminary Report on the Stanford Binet IQ Changes of Superior Children." *J Exp Ed* 1:287-92 Mr '33.
63 LOUDEN, MARY V. "Relative Difficulty of Stanford-Binet Vocabulary for Bright and Dull Subjects of the Same Mental Level." *J Ed Res* 27:179-86 N '33.
64 LOUDEN, MARY V. "Relative Difficulty of Vocabulary Lists in the Stanford-Binet Scale." *J Ed Res* 26:601-7 Ap '33.
65 MOWRER, WILLIE MAE C. "Intelligence Scales for Preschool Children." *Child Development* 4:318-22 D '33.
66 NEMZEK, CLAUDE L. "The Comparative Constancy of Stanford-Binet and Herring-Binet IQ's." *J Appl Psychol* 17:475-7 Ag '33.
67 NEMZEK, CLAUDE L. "The Constancy of the IQ." *Psychol B* 30:143-68 F '33.
68 RHINEHART, JESSE BATLEY. "An Attempt to Predict the Success of Student Nurses by the Use of a Battery of Tests." *J Appl Psychol* 17:277-93 Ap '33.
69 STOKE, STUART M. "The Eight and Nine Year Levels of the Stanford-Binet Scale." *Sch and Soc* 37:459-61 Ap 8 '33.
70 WALLIN, J. E. WALLACE. "Further Data on Stanford-Binet VIII- and IX-Year Tests." *Psychol Clinic* 22:94-100 Je-Ag '33.
71 BURNSIDE, LENOIR H. "A Comparison of the Abbreviated and the Complete Stanford Revision of the Binet-Simon Scale." *Child Development* 5:361-7 D '34.
72 KNIGHT, MAXINE WISLER. "A Comparative Study of the Performance of Feeble-Minded and Juvenile Delinquents on the Arthur Performance Scale and the Stanford-Binet Test of Intelligence." *J Juvenile Res* 18:5-12 Ja '34.
73 MADSEN, I. N. "The Reliability and Validity of the Stanford-Binet Tests when Administered by Student Examiners." *J Ed Res* 28:265-70 D '34.
74 PARKER, H. T. "Fluctuations in the Intelligence Quotients of Subnormal Children." *J Juvenile Res* 16:163-8 Jl '34.
75 SÁNCHEZ, GEORGE I. "The Implications of a Basal Vocabulary to the Measurement of the Abilities of Bilingual Children." *J Social Psychol* 5:395-402 Ag '34.

76 ELWOOD, M. I. "A Statistical Study of Results of the Stanford Revision of the Binet-Simon Scale with a Selected Group of Pittsburgh School Children." *Pittsburgh Sch* 9:116-140 Mr '35.
77 FEINBERG, HENRY. "The Examinee Defines 'Shrewd,'" pp. 549-57. In *Papers of the Michigan Academy of Science, Arts and Letters*, Vol. 20: Containing Papers Submitted at the Annual Meeting in 1934. Edited by Eugene S. McCartney and Alfred H. Stockard. Ann Arbor, Mich.: University of Michigan Press, 1935. Pp. xv, 755. Cloth, $4.00; paper, $2.25.
78 HILDEN, ARNOLD H., AND SKEELS, HAROLD M. "A Comparison of the Stanford-Binet Scale, the Kuhlmann-Anderson Group Test, the Arthur Point Scale of Performance Tests, and the Unit Scales of Attainment." *J Exp Ed* 4:214-30 D '35.
79 LINCOLN, EDWARD A. "The Stanford Binet IQ Changes of Superior Children." *Sch and Soc* 41:519-20 Ap 13 '35.
80 MAYER, BARBARA A. "Negativistic Reactions of Preschool Children on the New Revision of the Stanford-Binet." *J Genetic Psychol* 46:311-34 Je '35.
81 ODEN, MELITA H., AND MAYER, BARBARA A. "A Study of the Effect of Varying the Procedure in the Ball and Field Test." *J Genetic Psychol* 46:335-48 Je '35.
82 ROACH, CORNELIA BELL. "A Discussion of the Six, Seven and Eight Year Levels of the Stanford-Binet Scale." *J Ed Res* 29:216-8 N '35.
83 BRILL, MOSHE. "A Comparison of the Abbreviated and the Complete Stanford Binet Scales." *Sch and Soc* 43:102-4 Ja 18 '36.
84 FEINBERG, HENRY. "The Examinee Defines 'Mellow.'" *J Ed Psychol* 27:179-92 Mr '36.
85 LINCOLN, EDWARD A. "Stanford-Binet IQ Changes in the Harvard Growth Study." *J Appl Psychol* 20:236-42 Ap '36.
86 LOUTTIT, C. M., AND STACKMAN, HARVEY. "The Relationship between Porteus Maze and Binet Test Performance." *J Ed Psychol* 27:18-25 Ja '36.
87 MAHAN, HARRY C., AND WITMER, LOUISE. "A Note on the Stanford-Binet Vocabulary Test." *J Appl Psychol* 20:258-63 Ap '36.
88 PEATMAN, LILLIE BURLING, AND PEATMAN, JOHN GRAY. "The Adequacy of the Shortened, Single-List Vocabulary Test of the Binet-Simon Tests (Terman Revision)." *J Ed Psychol* 27:161-72 Mr '36.
89 ALTMAN, CHARLOTTE HALL, AND SHAKOW, DAVID. "A Comparison of the Performance of Matched Groups of Schizophrenic Patients, Normal Subjects, and Delinquent Subjects on Some Aspects of the Stanford-Binet." *J Ed Psychol* 28:519-29 O '37.
90 CATTELL, PSYCHE. "Stanford-Binet IQ Variations." *Sch and Soc* 45:615-8 My 1 '37.
91 CATTELL, RAYMOND B. "Measurement versus Intuition in Applied Psychology." *Char and Pers* 6:114-31 D '37.
92 DAVIDSON, MARSH. "A Study of Schizophrenic Performance on the Stanford-Binet Scale." *Brit J Med Psychol* 17:93-7 pt 1 '37.
93 HARRIS, ALBERT J., AND SHAKOW, DAVID. "The Clinical Significance of Numerical Measures of Scatter on the Stanford-Binet." *Psychol B* 34:134-50 Mr '37.
94 MACMURRAY, DONALD. "A Comparison of the Intelligence of Gifted Children and of Dull-Normal Children Measured by the Pintner-Paterson Scale, as Against the Stanford-Binet Scale." *J Psychol* 4:273-80 O '37.
95 PIOTROWSKI, ZYGMUNT A. "Objective Signs of Invalidity of Stanford-Binet Tests." *Psychiatric Q* 11:623-36 O '37.
96 ROBERTS, J. A. F., AND GRIFFITHS, R. "Studies on a Child Population: II, Retests on the Advanced Otis and Stanford-Binet Scales, with Notes on the Use of a Shortened Binet Scale." *Ann Eug* 8:15-45 '37.
97 ROTHNEY, J. W. M. "The New Binet—A Caution." *Sch and Soc* 45:855-6 Je 19 '37.
98 TERMAN, LEWIS M., AND MERRILL, MAUD A. *Directions for Administering Forms L and M: Revision of the Stanford-Binet Tests of Intelligence.* Boston, Mass.: Houghton-Mifflin Co., 1937. Pp. v, 116. $1.35. Spiral binding.
99 TERMAN, LEWIS M., AND MERRILL, MAUD A. *Measuring Intelligence*: A Guide to the Administration of the New Revised Stanford-Binet Tests of Intelligence. Boston, Mass.: Houghton Mifflin Co., 1937. Pp. xiv, 461. $2.25. (London: George G. Harrap and Co., Ltd., 1939. 10s. 6d.)
100 VERNON, P. E. "The Stanford-Binet Test as a Psychometric Method." *Char and Pers* 6:99-113 D '37.
101 VERNON, P. E. "A Study of the Norms and the Validity of Certain Mental Tests at a Child Guidance Clinic." *Brit J Ed Psychol* 7:72-88 F '37.
102 BENTON, ARTHUR L. "Performances of School Children on the Revised Stanford-Binet and the Kent E-G-Y-Test." *J Genetic Psychol* 52:395-400 Je '38.
103 BERNREUTER, ROBERT G., AND CARR, EDWARD J. "The Interpretation of IQ's on the L-M Stanford-Binet." *J Ed Psychol* 29:312-4 Ap '38.
104 BOND, ELDEN A. "Some Verbal Aspects of the 1937 Revision of the Stanford-Binet Intelligence Test, Form L." *J Exp Ed* 6:340-2 Mr '38.
105 BUHLER, CHARLOTTE. "The Ball and Field Test as a Help in the Diagnosis of Emotional Difficulties." *Char and Pers* 6:257-73 Je '38.
106 HARRIS, ALBERT J., AND SHAKOW, DAVID. "Scatter on the Stanford-Binet in Schizophrenic, Normal, and Delinquent Adults." *J Abn and Social Psychol* 33:100-11 Ja '38.
107 HILDEN, A. H. "Training Kindergarten Teachers to Test Their Pupils on the Stanford-Binet Scale." *Sch and Soc* 48:123-4 Jl 23 '38.
108 LODGE, TOWNSEND. "Variation in Stanford-Binet IQ's of Pre-school Children According to the Months in Which Examinations Were Given." *J Psychol* 6:385-95 O '38.
109 MERRILL, MAUD A. "The Significance of IQ's on the Revised Stanford-Binet Scales." *J Ed Psychol* 29:641-51 D '38.
110 ROBERTS, J. A. F.; NORMAN, R. M.; AND GRIFFITHS, R. "Studies on a Child Population: IV, The Form of the Lower End of the Frequency Distribution of Stanford-Binet Intelligence Quotients and the Fall of Low Intelligence Quotients with Advancing Age." *Ann Eug* 8:319-36 '38.
111 SHAKOW, DAVID, AND GOLDMAN, ROSALINE. "The Effect of Age on the Stanford-Binet Vocabulary Score of Adults." *J Ed Psychol* 29:241-56 Ap '38.
112 ARTHUR, GRACE. "The Agreement of Kuhlmann-Binet and Stanford-Binet Ratings for 200 Cases." *J Appl Psychol* 23:521-4 Ag '39.
113 ATWELL, C. R. "Comparison of Vocabulary Scores on the Stanford-Binet and the Revised Stanford-Binet." *J Ed Psychol* 30:467-9 S '39.
114 BALINSKY, B., ISRAEL, H., AND WECHSLER, D. "The Relative Effectiveness of the Stanford-Binet and the Bellevue Intelligence Scale in Diagnosing Mental Deficiency." *Am J Orthopsychiatry* 9:798-801 O '39.
115 BLACK, IRMA SIMONTON. "The Use of the Stanford-Binet (1937 Revision) in a Group of Nursery School Children." *Child Development* 10:157-71 S '39.
116 BURT, CYRIL. "The Latest Revision of the Binet Intelligence Tests." *Eug R* 30:255-60 Ja '39.
117 DAVIS, FREDERICK B. *Table of Equivalence Values for Intelligence Quotients Derived from the 1916 and 1937 Revisions of the Stanford-Binet Scales.* Avon, Conn.: Avon Old Farms, 1939. Pp. 4. Privately distributed. Paper.
118 ELWOOD, MARY ISABEL. "A Preliminary Note on the Vocabulary Test in the Revised Stanford-Binet Scale, Form L." *J Ed Psychol* 30:632-4 N '39.
119 HARRIMAN, PHILIP LAWRENCE. "Irregularity of Successes on the 1937 Stanford Revision." *J Consulting Psychol* 3:83-85 My-Je '39.
120 HILDRETH, G. "Retests with the New Stanford-Binet Scale." *J Consulting Psychol* 3:49-53 Mr-Ap '39.
121 HILDRETH, GERTRUDE. "Comparison of Early Binet Records with College Aptitude Test Scores." *J Ed Psychol* 30:365-71 My '39.
122 KRUGMAN, MORRIS. "Some Impressions of the Revised Stanford-Binet Scale." *J Ed Psychol* 30:594-603 N '39.
123 MACMEEKEN, A. M. *The Intelligence of a Representative Group of Scottish Children.* Publications of the Scottish Council for Research in Education, [No.] 15. International Examinations Inquiry. London: University of London Press, Ltd., 1939. Pp. xvi, 144. 5s.
124 MANN, CECIL W., AND MANN, HELENE POWNER. "An Analysis of the Results Obtained by Retesting Juvenile Delinquents." *J Psychol* 8:133-41 Jl '39.
125 Scottish Council for Research in Education, Terman Revision Committee, D. KENNEDY-FRASER, CONVENER. *Modifications Proposed for British Use of the Revised Stanford-Binet Tests of Intelligence in Measuring Intelligence* by LEWIS M. TERMAN and MAUD A. MERRILL published by George G. Harrap & Company, Ltd., 1937. Edinburgh, Scotland: the Council, January 1939. Pp. iv, 16, i, 11. Paper, mimeographed.
126 WRIGHT, RUTH E. "A Factor Analysis of the Original Stanford-Binet Scale." *Psychometrika* 4:209-20 S '39.
127 BERGER, ARTHUR, AND SPEEVACK, MORRIS. "An Analysis of the Range of Testing and Scattering among Retarded Children on Form L of the Revised Stanford Binet." *J Ed Psychol* 31:39-44 Ja '40.
128 BRODY, M. B. "A Note of the Use of the 1937 Revision of the Stanford Binet Vocabulary List in Mental Hospital Patients." *J Mental Sci* 86:532-3 My '40.
129 CARLTON, THEODORE. "Performances of Mental Defectives on the Revised Stanford-Binet, Form L." *J Consulting Psychol* 4:61-5 Mr-Ap '40.
130 HOAKLEY, Z. PAULINE. "A Comparison of the Results of the Stanford and Terman-Merrill Revisions of the Binet." *J Appl Psychol* 24:75-81 F '40.
131 KENDIG, ISABELLE, AND RICHMOND, WINIFRED V. *Psychological Studies in Dementia Praecox*, pp. 10-18, 49-85, and passim. Ann Arbor, Mich.: Edwards Brothers, Inc., 1940. Pp. x, 211. $0.50. Paper, lithotyped.
132 STOTT, M. BOOLE. "The Relation between Intelligence and Proficiency in Binet-Simon Testing." *Brit J Ed Psychol* 10:135-42 Je '40.
133 WALLIN, J. E. WALLACE. "The Results of Multiple Binet Re-Testings of the Same Subjects." *J Exceptional Children* 6:211-22 Mr '40.
134 WERNER, HENRY. "A Comparative Study of a Small Group of Clinical Tests." *J Appl Psychol* 24:231-6 Ap '40.

Eug R 30:255-60 Ja '39. Cyril Burt. Nearly twenty-five years ago, when the Binet-Simon tests were first coming into vogue, I endeavoured to examine, in two articles in this *Review*, their merits and limitations as a means of measuring innate intelligence. * Terman's new revision is now at length available; and those whose work entails the assessment of intelligence are inquiring whether the new version is, as it claims to be, genuinely superior to the older versions, and whether it has successfully eliminated the defects that had become obvious in the first scale without destroying any of the merits. A large committee, comprising all the leading educational psychologists in Great Britain, together with representatives or members of every body or institution engaged in mental tests, has been set up to work through the wording of the new revision, test by test, and to check the age standardizations on the basis of extensive experiments all over the country. A provisional "translation" (if I may so call it) is now available, and may be obtained from the Psychological Department, University College, London, for private experimental use. Thanks to the prompt cooperation of teachers, psychologists and medical officers, a large mass of data has already come to hand; and it may be of interest to summarize briefly the chief conclusions that emerge from a first preliminary survey of the results. * As regards the chief practical purpose of the scale—the diagnosis of dull and defective children—there seems little question that the new revision is decidedly more efficient than the old. As regards the wording and the age-assignments of the numerous tests that have been retained, the new revision frequently accepts the modifications proposed in the former London version. The principle of "internal grading," too, which was advocated in this Review, has been far more freely used—notably, in the vocabulary test. Many of the problems, however, are entirely new; and here the American age-assignments and even the American wording seem often far from appropriate to English children. * In the revised scale, most of the poorer tests that figured in the original scale (e.g., "Suggestion," "Months," "Age," "Sex," "Surname") have silently been dropped. The newer tests inserted in their place are based on accepted psychological principles; nevertheless those principles have really been derived more from group testing than from individual examinations. An intensive item analysis for each test separately is thus an urgent requisite. Such an investigation, however, will call for a long and patient research. * As I pointed out in my original examination of the scale, its difficulties and defects arise largely from the adoption of the plan of "external" instead of "internal grading." This plan proves convenient for the practical examiner; but makes it far from easy to test the tests themselves. With "internally graded" tests we can arrange the persons tested in order according to their ability in each test, and so correlate the tests with each other or with an independent criterion in the ordinary way. With "externally graded" tests, we can only say whether each person passes or fails, and so at best estimate the correlation between test and intelligence from fourfold tables by a "coefficient of colligation" or the like—never a very satisfactory procedure. * With an externally graded scale, like the Binet-Simon series, everything turns upon the relative difficulty of the test-problems. The standardization of each problem in terms of a mental age assumes that the order of difficulty is constant for the two sexes, for different social classes, for different ages, for different types of child, and above all for different localities. Thus, if a child repeats four numbers backwards, Terman would give him a mental age of 9; if he repeats six numbers forwards, i.e., in the order in which they have been recited to him, he would get a mental age of 10. Now with London children it is found that the latter test is actually easier than the former. And so with many other tests: the order of difficulty is often reversed. Worse still, when we experiment with the scale as a whole, there seems to be no fixed order at all: what is easier for one child may be harder for another. Indeed, the early critics of the scale were constantly pointing out how no two editors of Binet's scale ever agreed over the relative difficulty of the several tests. The orders of difficulty seem to vary with different examiners as well as with different examinees. At the very outset, therefore, in examining the validity of the whole proposal, the task of the psychologist must be to compare these different orders, and see whether they vary so widely as to invalidate the very foundations of the scale. * Now the original Binet scale had a heavy verbal bias; and such a bias is particularly hard upon the mentally defective child, who, as every teacher knows, is better at practical things than he is at reading, writing, spelling, and rational conversation. This defect in Binet's own series has, of course, not escaped

Revised Stanford-Binet Scale

Professor Terman: and, indeed, the chief difference between the former Terman series and the new is that, whereas the former was still overweighted with verbal tests, the new is, if anything, overweighted with practical or manual tests. * the question is this: how much of the total "variance" (i.e., of the variations in performance due to any and every type of cause) is attributable to a single general factor common to all children, and how much is due to specific and irrelevant factors—sex, social opportunity, school teaching, and above all perhaps qualitative difference in mental type? The data that have already been received enable us to give some first provisional answer to this question. * The figures ... are so far based on but comparatively few cases: but, so far as they go, they indicate that the new scale is appreciably more reliable than the old. But far more numerous data are needed. * the whole diagnostic value of the scale turns on the way we shall ultimately answer this preliminary question: how far is our order of difficulty trustworthy and how far is that order —and consequently our whole scheme of age-assignments—liable to be disturbed by wholly irrelevant conditions? With a little ingenuity we may perhaps turn the defect into a merit, and even ultimately make the scale to do two things at once: measure the child's general intelligence with a rough but reasonable degree of accuracy and at the same time throw side-lights on the kind as well as on the nature and extent of the special abilities or the special defects that he displays.

Psychol Rec 1:409-32 N '37. Grace H. Kent. "Suggestions for the Next Revision of the Binet-Simon Scale." * The new Stanford-Binet scale is of course a much stronger test than the 1916 edition, especially quantitatively. On the qualitative side it should be mentioned with approval that the blood-curdling absurdities of the older edition have given place to statements which are emotionally neutral and yet interesting; also that the memory test has been greatly improved by substituting a single sentence of suitable length for two sentences combined in one task. It is especially with reference to the set-up of the scale that the authors have failed to take advantage of the contributions published since 1916. * The basic construction of the Binet-Simon scales— the age-grade or year-scale method used by Binet and followed by Terman—is needlessly cumbersome and uneconomical as compared with a scoring system in which the responses are evaluated by points. Unconditional acceptance or rejection of a response is unfair to the subject whose response just barely misses being acceptable. * Within the year-scale system, the subject matter of the Stanford-Binet scale is used with unnecessary wastefulness. When a child responds correctly to only three of the five absurdity questions, he of course fails to achieve ten-year credit on that item [referring to the 1916 edition]; but might he not be given nine-year credit for three acceptable responses, and possibly eight-year credit for two responses? * The year-scale method is essentially an uneconomical scoring system for a subject of whatever age, because each examination includes so many items which add nothing to its adequacy. It is strictly required that the examination be carried low enough in the scale to yield six correct responses at a given age-level; and that it be carried high enough to elicit six consecutive failures. Thus there are at least twelve items (some of them multiple items requiring considerable time for presentation) which are frankly non-discriminative for the particular subject examined * It is not for the purpose of shortening the examination that the non-discriminative material should be reduced to the minimum, but rather to gain time for the use of additional tests not included in the scale. * Furthermore, the time thus wasted in a psychometric examination is much worse than wasted. The typical clinical subject over ten years of age is usually sensitive about being brought to a clinic at all. The items which are most annoying to a self-conscious child or adolescent are these questions at the upper and lower ends of his natural range. * it is nothing less than inhuman to use a larger amount of inappropriate material than is necessary to the adequacy of the examination. * A thoroughgoing revision of the Binet-Simon scale is too costly a project to be undertaken more than once or twice in a generation; also, the standardization requires so many years that there is time for items to lose something of their significance before the test is ready to be used. We cannot depend upon such a scale as Stanford-Binet without being forced to make considerable use of outdated material. * The great need of the clinic is a test system that can be adapted to the individual subject. * It is impossible that the Stanford-Binet scale or any other inflexible system should be suitable for cases of unusual types. * The climax of complexity is reached in the new Stanford-Binet, with all the rigidity of the earlier form still retained. If each item . . . which admits of being graded in difficulty had been made up in the form of an independent graded series, discriminative for the range of mental levels for which it is appropriate, the resulting collection of tests would offer a wealth of material sufficiently varied to contain something suitable for almost any subject who can be tested at all. This scale contains the raw material for a remarkably adequate system, but it is given us in a form which renders it inconvenient in all cases, wasteful of time in all cases, and invalid—in varying degrees—in a very large proportion of clinical cases. It is in the clinic that we are especially in need of a flexible test that can be adapted to the individual subject; but the test which has been individually standardized for clinical use has been made so inflexible that it is almost exceptional to have a subject for whom it can be used with satisfactory validity. * * * Of all the items included in the Stanford-Binet scale, the one which seems to the writer most strikingly to fall short of its possibilities is the vocabulary test. In the first place, 100 words (or 50 words) selected by rule from a dictionary of 18,000 words do not afford a large enough sampling to justify a conjectural estimate of the subject's total vocabulary, nor is such estimate of any use in determining the subject's "mental age." * If we require the subject to give an oral definition . . . there would be many advantages in using words which admit of being defined by the person who recognizes them—words which would elicit more uniform responses and which would permit more uniform evaluation. In the second place, the plan of having the words orally defined by the subject at all is open to serious objections: 1. It involves the personal equation of the examiner both in presenting the words and in scoring the results. 2. The request to define a word is unduly annoying to a large proportion of subjects; and the succession of failures with which the series is usually brought to a close makes it an instrument of torture to the extremely sensitive subject. 3. It measures the subject's willingness to attempt a definition, not invariably his actual ability to offer an acceptable response. Subjects differ widely in respect to the standards of certainty which seem to them to justify a response. It is sometimes the highly intelligent person who is most reluctant to offer anything short of a definition worthy of the dictionary, and who will decline to answer at all rather than attempt a crude explanation which does not satisfy his own standard of definition. * 4. For the typical clinical subject (as opposed to the school children upon whom tests are standardized) the request to define a word seems unnatural and wholly remote from everyday experience. We use words at all times, but only rarely have occasion to define them. * * * It is recommended that language test material be developed according to the method used by Pintner and Paterson for a group of performance tests. Any item which can be graded in difficulty may be developed into a graded series and standardized as an independent unit. Each unit should be so graded as to cover the entire range of mental levels for which it can appropriately be used; but for economy of presentation, the standardization should be for overlapping sections rather than for the series as a whole * If independent norms be published for each section, the non-discriminative material to be used in a given examination may be reduced to a negligible quantity. When sufficient test-units have been thus developed and standardized, an examiner may make up a battery by selecting for each case such units as are individually suited to the subject. The examination will be custom-made to fit each subject, instead of the subject being held responsible for fitting the test. The battery of tests used in a given examination will yield a series of independent ratings, the median of which may be placed on record for reference. When a one-figure numerical rating is required, this median rating is the figure to be reported. *

J Ed Psychol 30:594-603 N '39. M. Krugman. "Some Impressions of the Revised Stanford-Binet Scale." * For this paper, the writer approached the evaluation of Form L of the new scale by four different methods: (1) Impressions of ten psychologists of the Bureau of Child Guidance on eight specific questions were obtained. (2) An examination of one thousand two hundred cases was made for the complaint that frequently we cannot be certain, after obtaining a basal and a final year, that the child has been adequately measured. (3) A study of ninety clinic cases, in which both the old and the new scales were administered to the same children, was made. (4) A study was made of surveys conducted in four schools in widely separated areas of the city, surveys in which individual examinations were administered to entire grades. In these schools the old and the revised scales were administered at different times and random samplings of their populations were obtained by examining one or all of the first three grades. There were one thousand three hundred sixty-one children to whom the old Stanford-Binet scale had been administered, and four hundred three who were given Form L. * In conclusion, the experience at the Bureau of Child Guidance with Form L of the Revised Stanford-Binet scale would indicate that it is much superior to the old scale statistically; that it is better standardized and better validated, as a whole; that it eliminates successfully many of the objections to the old by including new lower levels, extending the upper, and filling in the gaps; that the lower levels no longer give results that seem too high, and the upper levels, results that seem too low; that the dispute over using thirteen, fourteen, fifteen or sixteen for maximum CA for adults has finally been settled; that, on the one hand, preschool and very dull kindergarten and first-grade children can now be examined without the use of an additional preschool battery, and, on the other hand, the superior adolescents can be reached; that directions have, in general, been simplified; that, in the main, it is a much more refined psychological scale, but, apparently, so much attention has been paid to these refinements in the process of revision, that some of the old weaknesses in content were not eliminated, and others have crept in. These are some of the weaknesses: (1) Longer time required for administration—twenty-five to thirty per cent more time, on the average. (2) Emphasis on verbal material still present, possibly to a greater extent, especially in middle and upper levels. (Admitted by Terman.) (3) Years VIII and XI seem especially poor in this respect. (4) Rote memory still seems emphasized too much at the upper levels. (5) Possibly because of refinements, there is considerably more scatter on the new scale.

(6) A single basal or final year is not as conclusive as it was on the old scale. (7) In attempting to simplify directions, confusion to the child has resulted on some tests. (8) Scoring directions and criteria are sometimes not clear. (9) Many tests seem misplaced for New York City children. (10) Many situations and many words seem unfair to New York City children. (11) Much of the content is unsuited to clinic children who show emotional disturbances. (12) For clinic work, more flexibility in administration would be desirable. Since in the year-by-year testing, the easy material is presented all at one time, and the difficult material at another, consecutive failure introduces an additional emotional stress. All in all, then, Form L of the new scale seems to be a better constructed instrument, much superior to the old for survey purposes, and possibly even for clinical purposes, but with many shortcomings which, if corrected, would make it much more satisfactory for clinic use.

For reviews by Francis N. Maxfield, J. W. M. Rothney, and F. L. Wells, see 1062. Also see B497.

[1421]
Ryburn Group Intelligence Tests for Senior Children. Ages 10-14; 1940; 1 form; 3s. per 20; 5s. per 50; 60(65) minutes; H. V. Clark; Glasgow, Scotland: Robert Gibson & Sons, Ltd.

[1422]
School Aptitude Test: Thanet Mental Tests. Age 11; 1 form; 5s. per 25; 1s. per handbook; 1s. 6d. per specimen set, including the arithmetic and the English tests in the same series; 30(40) minutes; W. P. Alexander; London: University of London Press, Ltd.

C. Ebblewhite Smith, Lecturer in the Department of Higher Degrees and Research, Institute of Education, University of London. For many English children, the Entrance Scholarship Examination taken at the age of 11 plus, constitutes a hurdle which must be successfully negotiated if they wish to proceed to higher education. Competition is keen, and with the whole future career of the child depending upon the result of this one examination it behooves examiners to make it as reliable and as valid an instrument as present day knowledge of examining and testing will allow. The three Thanet Mental Tests are together designed to perform the function of the Entrance Scholarship Examination. The *School Aptitude Test* is an intelligence test; the other two tests are minimum essential tests of English and of the fundamentals of arithmetic.

Most weight in the examination is placed on the results of the *School Aptitude Test* which is largely a verbal intelligence test, of the self-administering type, comprising 75 items and taking 30 minutes working time.

What is it that causes the author to believe that on the basis of this 30-minute group test fine distinctions having far-reaching importance can be drawn between individuals? Is the test more than usually reliable? We are given no clue in the handbook. Is the test very valid? We are not told in the handbook of any measures taken to compare test scores with an outside criterion or of any measures taken to ensure item validity. Indeed, one has reason to believe that the item validity of some of the types of item used will not be high. Perhaps the special merit of the test in the author's eyes is that it measures g and v in equal proportions (*sic*). One would wish to see some reference to the experimental work by means of which such a result was obtained. There is some evidence that g and v have in the past been measured in about equal proportions in English Secondary School Examinations but is there any reason for perpetuating this? How does Alexander propose to distinguish the child with low g and high v from the child with high g and low v? It is always difficult to interpret the results of a test designed to measure several mental factors at the same time. A test which measures g and v in equal proportions for 11-year-olds of average mental age will measure g and v in different proportions for 11-year-olds of superior intelligence. The effect of familiarity with intelligence test material will be to change the relative proportion of g and v measured by the test. In the test here reviewed, insufficient preliminary practice material is given.

Surely the payment of one shilling for the test handbook should entitle the purchaser to learn something of the standardization of a test. Beyond a somewhat casual reference to the fact that norms have been obtained on five thousand cases no other mention is made of standardization. One would like to know how the cases were chosen, apart from this information the graphs given on pages 8 and 9 are meaningless.

The test is simple to administer and the instructions are good. The scoring is simple and speedy.

This test will be useful as a survey test for obtaining a distribution of mental ages over a wide range, but in the absence of further information from the author one would hesitate to use it as a major factor in making individual selection for competitive scholarships.

[1423]
Southend Group Test of Intelligence. Ages 10½-13; 1939; 1 form; 6s. per 25; 9d. per handbook; non-timed (40-60) minutes; selected from tests originated by William Stephenson; London: George G. Harrap & Co., Ltd.

Scottish Ed J 23:273 Ap 19 '40. The characteristic feature of this Group Test is that whereas half the sections are of the verbal type, the other half consists exclusively of comparisons of shapes. * No information is given as to the population on whom the Test was standardised. What validity the Test has, if any, is likewise not disclosed.

[1424]
Terman Group Test of Mental Ability. Grades 7-12; 1920; 2 forms; $1.20 (6s.) per 25; 20¢ (2s.) per specimen set; 27(40) minutes; Lewis M. Terman; Yonkers, N. Y.: World Book Co. (London: George G. Harrap & Co., Ltd.)

REFERENCES

1 BRIGHT, IRA J. "The Intelligence Examination For High-School Freshmen." *J Ed Res* 4:44-55 Je '21.
2 FRANZEN, RAYMOND. "Attempts at Test Validation." *J Ed Res* 6:145-58 S '22.
3 AVERY, GEORGE T. "A Study of the Binet and Terman Intelligence Tests, with Eleven-Year-Old Children." *J Ed Res* 7:429-33 My '23.
4 HINES, HARLAN C. *A Guide to Educational Measures*, pp. 96-104. Boston, Mass.: Houghton Mifflin Co., 1923. Pp. xxiii, 270. $1.90.
5 JORDAN, A. M. "The Validation of Intelligence Tests." *J Ed Psychol* 14:348-66, 414-28 S, O '23.
6 MILLER, W. S. "The Variation and Significance of Intelligence Quotients Obtained from Group Tests." *J Ed Psychol* 15:359-66 S '24.
7 WILSON, J. H. "Comparison of Certain Intelligence Scales." *Brit J Psychol* 15:44-63 Jl '24.
8 BROOKS, FOWLER D. "The Accuracy of Intelligence Quotients from Pairs of Group Tests in the Junior High School." *J Ed Psychol* 18:173-86 Mr '27.
9 GUILER, W. S. "The Predictive Value of Group Intelligence Tests." *J Ed Res* 16:365-74 D '27.
10 NELSON, M. J., AND DENNY, E. C. "The Terman and Thurstone Group Tests as Criteria for Predicting College Success." *Sch and Soc* 26:501-2 O 15 '27.
11 SYMONDS, PERCIVAL M. *Ability Standard for Standardized Achievement Tests in the High School.* New York: Bureau of Publications, Teachers College, Columbia University, 1927. Pp. x, 91. $1.05.
12 KUHLMANN, F. "The Kuhlmann-Anderson Intelligence Tests Compared with Seven Others." *J Appl Psychol* 12:545-94 D '28.
13 COLE, ROBERT D. "A Conversion Scale for Comparing Scores on Three Secondary School Intelligence Tests." *J Ed Res* 20:190-8 O '29.
14 KEFAUVER, GRAYSON N. "Need of Equating Intelligence Quotients Obtained from Group Tests." *J Ed Res* 19:92-101 F '29.
15 MILLER, W. S. "Variation of IQ's Obtained from Group Tests." *J Ed Psychol* 24:468-74 S '33.
16 TURNEY, AUSTIN H., AND FEE, MARY. "The Comparative Value for Junior High School Use of Five Group Mental Tests." *J Ed Psychol* 24:371-9 My '33.
17 MOORE, HERBERT, AND TRAFTON, HELEN. "Equating Test Scores." *J Ed Psychol* 25:216-9 Mr '34.
18 SEAGOE, M. V. "An Evaluation of Certain Intelligence Tests." *J Appl Psychol* 18:432-6 Je '34.
19 FINCH, F. H. "Equating Intelligence Quotients from Group Tests." *J Ed Res* 28:589-92 Ap '35.
20 MITCHELL, CLAUDE. "Prognostic Value of Intelligence Tests." *J Ed Res* 28:577-81 Ap '35.
21 WILSON, J. H. "The Exactness of 'g' as Determined by Certain Intelligence Tests." *Brit J Psychol* 26:93-8 Jl '35.

22 FINCH, F. H., AND ODOROFF, M. E. "The Reliability of Certain Group Intelligence Tests." *J Appl Psychol* 21:102-6 F '37.
23 PATERSON, DONALD G.; SCHNEIDLER, GWENDOLEN G.; AND WILLIAMSON, EDMUND G. *Student Guidance Techniques*, pp. 56-8. New York: McGraw-Hill Book Co., Inc., 1938. Pp. xviii, 316. $3.00. (London: McGraw-Hill Publishing Co., Ltd. 18s.)
24 BISHOP, HELEN. "A Study in Prediction and Mortality." *J Am Assn Col Registrars* 14:62-3 O '39.
25 KEYS, NOEL. "The Value of Group Test IQ's for Prediction of Progress beyond High School." *J Ed Psychol* 31:81-93 F '40.

Anne Anastasi, Assistant Professor of Psychology and Chairman of the Department of Psychology, Queens College. Both forms of this test consist of ten subtests: (*a*) information; (*b*) best answer, including interpretation of proverbs and questions of fact; (*c*) word meaning, and opposites test; (*d*) logical selection; (*e*) arithmetic reasoning; (*f*) sentence meaning, each sentence containing a single term or concept whose understanding determines the response; (*g*) analogies; (*h*) mixed sentences; (*i*) classifications; and (*j*) number series completion. Administration and scoring are very simple. Directions are printed at the top of each subtest and the examiner reads these with the subjects. Sample items are also included in all the tests except arithmetic reasoning, a fact which insures much better understanding of procedure. The omission of samples in the arithmetic reasoning test is understandable in view of the familiarity of this task to the subjects.

Percentile norms are reported for each grade from 7 to 12 inclusive. These norms are based upon a total of 41,241 white children, the number varying from approximately four to ten thousand for each grade level. The subjects were drawn chiefly from city schools, about two-thirds of them being from California and the remainder being chiefly from the Middle West. These restrictions should, of course, be borne in mind in any attempt to use the test with other groups. A table is also provided for transmuting the raw scores into mental age equivalents. No further data regarding the construction or standardization of the test are furnished in the manual.

One could, of course, take issue with the use of percentile scores which do not represent a scale of equal units. Similarly, the practice of estimating mental ages from scores on a test which is not standardized in terms of age levels is open to question. The content of the test, furthermore, is highly overweighted with verbal material for a test which purports to measure "mental ability." These are criticisms, however, which could be leveled against the large majority of intelligence tests. As traditional "intelligence tests" go, this scale has much to commend it. It will serve more or less adequately for purposes of rough classification and especially in the classification of school children, to which its author specifically refers in the manual. Since this function seems to have been uppermost in the author's mind, it would perhaps have been more accurate to have labeled the test a measure of scholastic aptitude rather than general mental ability.

For any problem requiring very accurate measurement or fine discrimination, such a test would be unsuited, as would any test which attempts to measure in a single score such a composite and ill-defined characteristic as "general intelligence." Undoubtedly, tests of separate aptitudes will gradually replace the general intelligence tests for this purpose. It should be noted in this connection that the author himself is quite cautious and explicit in describing the use of his test. Thus, for example, he calls attention in the manual to the fact that a score on such a test should serve chiefly as a "point of departure for further study" of the individual, and he emphasizes the need of supplementing such a score with other data.

Howard Easley, Assistant Professor of Educational Psychology, Duke University. This test consists of ten subtests, with separate directions for each, namely: Information, Best Answer, Word Meaning, Logical Selection, Arithmetic, Sentence Meaning, Analogies, Mixed Sentences, Classification, and Number Series. Such an arrangement hardly seems justified, because (*a*) the part scores are of little use. No norms for them are given, and no indication of their significance. (*b*) Even if they measure different aspects of mental ability they can hardly do it well with so small numbers of items, 11 to 20, in the various subtests. The 370 items in the two forms were selected from an original list of 886. Each item was required to distinguish between children of known brightness and children of known dullness. The total working time is twenty-seven minutes, and the whole test is supposed to be administered "easily within a school period of thirty-five minutes." Experience indicates, however, that this time is about the absolute minimum, and that forty minutes is practically required.

The scoring is objective and simple, but time

consuming compared to the more recent economical devices. Each test is on a separate page, and five different answer strips are required.

Percentile grade scores, based on 41,241 cases, and mental age equivalents, based on 1,422 cases, are given. The mental age equivalents involve an error common to many such norms, due to failure to take account of the regression of mental age on scores. "If a pupil obtains a score of 49, his mental age is 138 months, since 49 is the average of the scores obtained by pupils who are 138 months old" (Manual, p. 11). It would be more nearly correct to give as the mental age equivalent for a score of 49 the average age of pupils who made scores of 49.

This was a good test when it was first published in 1920, both in terms of its intrinsic and relative values. There were no other group tests which were unmistakably better. It is not certain that other more recent tests do a better job of measuring mental ability, but many of them do it more economically and conveniently. Many improvements have been made, especially in the mechanics of testing, since 1920; but this test remains in its original form.

[1425]
Test of General Knowledge. Ages 14 and over; 1938; a disguised intelligence test; 1 form; $3 per 20; specimen sets obtainable on approval; 23½(30) minutes; Eugene J. Benge; Philadelphia, Pa.: Management Service Co.

REFERENCES
1 BENGE, EUGENE J. "Tests in Selecting Employes." *Soc Adv Mgmt J* 3:72-5 Mr '38.

[1426]
Tests of Mental Development. Ages 3 months and over; 1939; 1 form; individual; $6.80 per testing outfit including the necessary materials for 25 examinations; $1.60 per manual; $2.75 per carrying case; F. Kuhlmann; Minneapolis, Minn.: Educational Test Bureau, Inc.

REFERENCES
1 PORTER, E. H., JR. "A Method of Organizing Test Materials of the Kuhlmann Tests of Mental Development." *J Appl Psychol* 24:92-5 F '40.

Grace H. Kent, Psychologist, Danvers State Hospital, Hathorne, Massachusetts. The raw material for this scale is taken from many sources, especially the Binet and Stanford-Binet scales, the Kuhlmann-Anderson tests, the Gesell tests, and the Buehler tests.

The children employed as subjects for standardization were from the public schools of certain carefully-selected Minnesota towns. Preschool children were selected from the birth registries as being exactly of the ages desired and were examined in their homes by appointment. Less than one per cent of the parents refused to permit the examination. In each case the child's feeding time and sleeping time were ascertained in advance, in order to avoid all danger of finding a child hungry or sleepy. The discriminative capacity of the scale starts at four to six months. The standardization for children of school age includes 140 cases for each year, and for preschool children about 106 for each year.

The tests form a continuous series of increasing difficulty and are not grouped according to age levels; but the presentation is similar to that of the Binet scale, in that the examination is to be carried far enough upward to exclude any chance of further success and far enough downward to exclude possibility of failure.

The scale is constructed on the Heinis mental growth curve. Passing scores for tests are located at every third point in the growth curve, and each test is placed at the level at which it is passed by fifty per cent. The tests are scored in terms of mental growth values, and the Percent of Average (P.A.) is recommended as a substitute for the IQ.

The reviewer believes the lower end to be the most valuable part of the scale, because of the scarcity of properly standardized test material for infants. The toys included in the outfit are exceptionally attractive as compared with the materials of most preschool tests. Some of the pictures for preschool levels are excellent, but it is to be regretted that others are too small and very poorly proportioned. In one series of pictures intended for the six-year level, the potato and pumpkin and radish are so nearly equal in size as to be confusing to the mature subject. One member of our psychological department mistook the radish for a beet, and another thought it was a turnip.

The scoring system, based largely upon speed, is too complicated to be described in the space allowed here. The author states that the scale is not more difficult of presentation than its predecessors and that the scoring is "easier because more objective." It may be easy to one who has mastered it, but to the beginner it seems very much like trying to read a strange language without having a dictionary at hand. There ought to be a one-page index to the abbreviations used in the manual, many of which are far from being self-explanatory;

and there is serious need also of a general index.

The inherent weakness of the composite scale, which can be used only as a whole, is indicated by the author's instructions for evaluating the achievement of the child who suffers from some special handicap. Each test apparently affected by the handicap is to be scored *minus* with an interrogation point, and the child is to be given credit for half the tests thus scored. But if the various tests had been evaluated independently, as in the Kuhlmann-Anderson series, there would be no need of taking liberties with the results in order to be fair to the child, inasmuch as any particular test affected by the handicap could be omitted. It is highly disappointing to find the author of a flexible school test reverting to the composite scale when developing a new test for individual examination.

The manual of instructions is for the most part rather heavy reading matter, but there is one chapter which can be recommended for careful study on the part of every clinical examiner who uses mental tests—the fifth chapter, on the conduct of a clinical examination.

Francis N. Maxfield, Professor of Psychology, Psychological Clinic, The Ohio State University. One would hardly expect a snapshot photograph of the Norris dam, even if the man behind the camera had some knowledge of engineering and economics, to be a very significant item in a discussion of power control or of hydraulic engineering. This scale of Kuhlmann's rests on such a broad basis of author-experience and both theoretical and practical research that anything more than a snapshot would be presumptious within the limits of this review and in light of the recency of publication.

In that many of the test items in the scale are not found in the Binet-Simon scale of 1911 or in early revisions and translations, including Kuhlmann's own, some will hesitate to call this scale the "Kuhlmann-Binet," yet it is clearly in the Binet tradition in many of its theoretical and practical aspects. Yet the author himself frequently speaks of the "Binet method" in contrast with his own. A preliminary list of one hundred twenty-one tests prepared in 1933 was given to some 15,000 persons ranging in age from three months to sixty years. Thirteen test items discarded and nineteen retained as "supplementary tests" left eighty-nine for the final scale.

The directions for administering the scale are an improvement on those in Kuhlmann's 1922 manual. Test materials are packed in a carrying case, but are still cumbersome and inconvenient. E. H. Porter,[1] an assistant at Ohio State University, has devised a convenient arrangement of the many-sized cards and the directions for the tests in which they are used which should be put out by the publishers as a "condensed guide." For the time-limit tests taken over from the Kuhlmann-Anderson series, critical scores for scoring when the full time is taken should be written in a third line, as below.

For example, Test 73 (p. 167):

Scoring

M.U. — 312 — 330 — 375 — 399
R/T — .039 — .054 — .088 — .105
Critical score
when T = 120"   5   7   11   13

The most common source of error in psychometric work done by assistants lies in arithmetical calculation. The author endeavors to eliminate these errors by including in the appendix one hundred twenty pages of tables from which most results may be read.

Kuhlmann abandons age grouping of tests, assumes the validity of Heinis's mental growth curve, and has at least one test scoring at every third point on this curve from 21 to 528. The scale is scored in points on this curve. The score may be translated into a mental age score or an IQ. Heinis's P.C. (personal constant) is rechristened "P.A.," or "percent of average," and is recommended for prediction. Scores for speed, accuracy, and variability for test items No. 71 and following add to the list, so that each full use of the scale yields seven scores. The author raises statistical objections to the use of standard scores or centile ranks. He rejects the assumption of a normal surface of distribution for measures of intelligence. Yet his own distributions of P.A. values for five different age groups in Table 30 do not indicate marked skewness. The probable errors of these "percents" of average, taken as half the interquartile distance, are small (about .07) for psychometric values and relatively uniform for age groups six to fourteen. The clinician dealing with an individual case is interested in degree of deviation from average as well as status

(M.U.) and prediction (P.A.). Forgetting nice points as to skewness and the doubtful validity of extreme values, the clinician should set up tables from which deviations may be read more readily than from Tables 28 and 30.

The use of the 1916 Stanford-Binet became so nearly universal in this country that the revised Stanford-Binet will go ahead with some of that momentum, as well as on its own merits. Nine out of ten of those that use it give little thought to the theoretical questions discussed so ably by Kuhlmann. Even if they give his scale a trial, they will be prejudiced from the start, not only by their previous experience, but by the uniform cards, the convenient Directions for Administering, and the dual forms of the Terman-Merrill revision. Kuhlmann's scale will not find extensive use unless his publishers make it easier for the clinician to discover its merits.

Myrtle Luneau Pignatelli, Clinical Psychologist, Bellevue Psychiatric Hospital, New York, New York. The scale, *Tests of Mental Development,* recently standardized by Kuhlmann, differs essentially from the older type of Binet scale. The author feels that in using experience gained with thousands of problem cases as well as normal individuals, a more solid foundation was established for the scale as a whole. Only those tests were chosen which had: (a) discriminative capacity with age, (b) variety in make-up, (c) freedom from practice effect and coaching, (d) freedom from variable training, (e) objectivity in scoring, (f) and the right degree of difficulty of separate items or trials.

The scale has 89 tests and 19 supplementary ones. The levels extend from 3 months of age through the superior adult. Final norms were obtained in Minnesota on 3,000 white non-selected public school and preschool children down to the age of three months. Instead of age-level scoring, the test items are placed at equally spaced distances on the Heinis mental growth curve. The norms for each test represent 50 percentile scores, and are expressed in terms of scale or mental units. The 89 tests of the scale represent Heinis scale numerical values ranging from 21 to 528 mental units. Mental growth values after the age of 16 are assumed values, and have been extended to a level equivalent to a mental age of 45 years.

Outstanding features of the scale, are: (a) the ingenuity of its author in devising the tests, (b) the demands that the instrument makes on the "power" of mentality under examination, (c) the technique of administering the scale seems more detailed and it makes more demands on the testing judgment of the examiner, than other similar scales, (d) the scoring of the tests at many levels permits the measurement of mental traits by degrees, (e) the inclusion of paper and pencil tests which can be given to subjects in small groups, (f) the stress on the time factor throughout the scale, with time as well as accuracy entering into the scoring of all tests at the upper levels, (g) the use of P.A. (percent of average) instead of the IQ, and in addition, scoring for mental age, mental level (M.U.), speed, accuracy and variability, (h) the use of many tables for computations and for the converting of scores.

On first acquaintance, the scale seems very difficult. Experienced examiners, however, will find it interesting and easy to master. A thorough understanding of the theoretical basis of the scale and the concepts introduced therein, as well as a mastery of technique are essential. Inexperienced examiners and students will need special training in order to use the instrument intelligently, as it makes greater demands on psychological background and clinical technique, than other instruments of its kind. Time for giving the test runs from 30 minutes to over an hour, depending on the age of the subject. The examiner must use his judgment as to what constitutes adequate testing, as there are no established critical points, such as basal age and upper limit.

There is only one form of the scale, but practise effect is not great after a lapse of several months. Kuhlmann's idea to add supplementary tests to the scale to be used with individuals who have special handicaps, would add to its usefulness. The test manual is unusually good, though it is unfortunate that an index was omitted, and that data were not given on problem cases. Information for scoring is adequate, with the exception of a few tests which need additional scoring data.

Characteristics of the scale which will limit its use are the following: (a) the extensive material which must be handled during the process of a single examination; (b) the complicated procedure associated with scoring and obtaining final ratings; (c) the demand which the tests make on perception and reading will make it unfeasible for reading disability cases, illiterate adults and persons who have visual defects.

The test content is not as familiar as that of the *Revised Stanford-Binet Scale,* and the test is not so generally applicable to adults who come to clinics, as the *Wechsler-Bellevue Intelligence Scale,* but it offers new avenues of approach to the measurement of mentality, which will be challenging to those psychologists who can appreciate its possibilities as a clinical instrument.

F. L. Wells, Psychologist, Department of Hygiene, Harvard University. This work is based in large part on the Kuhlmann-Binet series, but the metamorphosis is too great to be classed as a "revision." The number of separate tests, 89 plus 19 alternates, is comparable to the Binet systems, but the year level division is done away with, and a scale in units of mental growth is substituted. It can of course be transmuted into the more familiar terms of mental age and IQ.

The feature of essential distinction in this scale is actually its foundation on the Heinis "Personal Constant," here known as "percent of average," P.A. This is offered as a measure of considerably greater reliability than the conventional IQ, and the data on pp. 85-92 would seem to justify this. The IQ has long been under fire from various quarters, and probably survives for reasons other than scientific. The superiority claimed for the new measure raises serious question as to the advisability of reworking other psychometric procedures in its terms.

The standpoint from which the writer desires to discuss the work especially is its internal methodology. Here, as in other ways, it occupies a position between the Binet systems and the *Wechsler-Bellevue Intelligence Scale* and *Detroit Tests of Learning Aptitude;* on the whole nearer the Binet. The main issue is between a large number of disparate procedures, each aimed at a single or narrow range of developmental levels, and a much smaller number, each covering a considerable range of developmental levels. Kuhlmann is clearly a partisan of variety, in the Binet tradition. The background of the present writer definitely favors the other policy, as embodied originally in the performance scales, and now very effectively in the Bellevue. It is probably a matter of differential interests; Kuhlmann's being primarily in the juvenile and defective areas, the present writer's in the adult of normal or superior intellectual functions (cf., the earlier and later portions of the present scale). Here one lays stress on the better understanding that accrues to each procedure, in respect to both administration and evaluation. One acquires a feel for a wide range of response adequacies, both quantitative and qualitative, that is not approached with numerous discrete items of the Binet type.

Naturally there are limits to which this can be carried. Procedure for infant and preschool ages cannot be adapted to the superior adult, as Kuhlmann points out very forcibly. But this only brings into question the wisdom of organizing test series to cover so wide a range. It has official advantages, where one is administratively concerned with large numbers, as Kuhlmann presumably is. Whether the skilled examiner gets as good an understanding through such means, is another matter.

Though it is many years since Gesell set an example of differential categories for the early ages, development in this direction has been relatively slow. The *Minnesota Preschool Scale* and the *Wechsler-Bellevue Intelligence Scale* make specific distinctions of verbal and nonverbal accomplishments. Many users should find it convenient similarly to reorganize the upper levels of the present scale, for which its resources are ample. In series like the Bellevue and Detroit, individual test procedures may be strong enough to acquire notable intrinsic significance, as is also incidentally the case here. But the technology continues largely under the spell of a global figure of some sort, which heavily masks the status in such disparate functions as e.g., vocabulary range, abstracting power, and imaginative richness.

On the other hand, a real advance is made in the special consideration given to speed and error, apart from age level scores. The discussion of this point is very pertinent, though one may find it difficult to go along with all the reasoning. The Kuhlmann-Binet test gave more than usual recognition to these factors, but made too much attempt to get them into a single score. Here they are treated more analytically, as they should be.

Kuhlmann apparently feels that the existing

Tests of Mental Development

variety of test devices is reasonably satisfactory, at any rate it has not appeared necessary to strive for novelty in this respect. Borrowings from other systems are freely acknowledged. The underlying viewpoint requires somewhat more rigidity in response patterns than is usual in most clinical methods; in the name of objectivity, as little as possible is left to "qualitation." This may account for the absence of problems in the "absurd sentence" or "comprehension" class. Such restrictions might be a liability in work with problem cases, unless qualitation is supplied from elsewhere, as, of course, it can be. To purposes essentially educational the new scale is well adapted, either as a basic procedure, or as an alternate to whatever already has the prestige of use.

Aside from the necessary juvenile content at times, the material includes effective elements for aphasia examination; the writer has elsewhere commented on the usefulness from this standpoint of certain Kuhlmann-Anderson procedures. Items of the present scale especially suggesting themselves are the tests numbered 23, 26, 28, 32 (in principle), 33, 35, 39, 40, 42, 45, 55, 67, 73, 74, and 19s.

Range for range the new scale seems easier to learn than the Stanford-Binet, less easy than the Detroit, more foolproof than either, so far as scoring goes. Administrative convenience is impertinent to judge without experience in giving, but here it probably does not differ greatly in the early ages from the revised Stanford-Binet; at the later ages it looks more cumbrous. This is owing to considerations of material; its recording system is distinctly preferable. In respect to convenience it cannot properly be compared with Bellevue or Detroit, because of their smaller age ranges; the Detroit, however, seems the only procedure that has really exerted itself in this direction. Two suggestions may be offered on this point, towards facilitating the diffusion of the present device. (a) Make the record blank available in sheet rather than card form. (b) Put Chapter VI of the manual, together with such portions of the Appendix as are not functions of simple arithmetic, in a separate spiral binder, possibly somewhat condensed.

All in all, the present offering probably represents the best instrument available over a fairly wide area, denoted as follows: (a) where it is desired to represent the intelligence function by a single figure; (b) for healthy individuals up to say fourteen years of age; and (c) for individuals with intelligence defect.

J Consulting Psychol 3:128-30 Jl-Ag '39. *Gertrude Hildreth.* * departs radically in scoring and item selection from the classic Binet type test. From our first preliminary experience with the scale it appears to constitute a marked step in advance over the 1922 Kuhlmann revision. Any attempt to make a complete appraisal at this time would be premature. The scale needs an extensive tryout in order to determine its advantages and possible limitations. * For the most part the materials are simple in character and at the younger age levels capitalize the child's interest in natural play materials. The first tests requiring response to printed verbal symbols come at age eight years, six months. This may work a hardship on the very gifted child of six who has not yet learned to read, but there is no actual reading test in the sense of deriving thought from consecutive content until near the end of the scale. Objectivity in scoring is increased by the inclusion of multiple choice items throughout the scale. * [the] scaling scheme makes the whole scale more flexible than the traditional Binet scale, for any separate test, such as a form board, that is standardized and scaled in the same way may be admitted into the scale at any point. Furthermore, there is the practical advantage that the examiner need not go through any set number of tests before he concludes that no more items would be passed or failed. * We find that Item 53, memory for pictured objects, has diagnostic value in beginning stages of reading, but this capacity in no way invalidates the test. Our preliminary experience with the scale indicates that the child has somewhat less opportunity for verbal response than on other Binet revisions. On the other hand, a premium is placed on the subject's ability and tendency to listen to verbal instructions, and to give sustained mental effort while doing so. * We have found that for the young, bright child some of the items that must be used are not intrinsically very interesting. Certain items are rather tedious and require close attention to directions that must be read verbatim from the manual. Young gifted children may also be at some disadvantage in responding to tests that are closely timed. Handling the large

Tests of Mental Development

quantity of paper and card material will require considerable practice to insure efficiency. We use a large notebook with manila pockets to hold the materials, numbered according to the test items, and arranged in proper sequence. The toys and materials for the infant and nursery levels are conveniently handled in a small container. One must learn from experience where to begin the test and how far up or down in the scale to go in order to complete the test. It is important to score the test as much as possible while it is being given so that two testing sessions need not be necessary. * The new scale contains considerable material that entails response to spatial relations, geometrical in character. This material is advantageous because it requires no verbal response, but it seems to narrow somewhat the subject's repertory of responses. It is impossible to give the test properly unless one is completely free of all distractions. The timing must be done precisely with a stop watch. All computations should be checked twice for accuracy. Carelessness will vitiate the ultimate rating obtained. On the whole, the separate items can be scored with a minimum of deliberation. The examiner will, however, puzzle over how to score some items; he will be uncertain at some points what to consider a "pass" or "fail." Each examiner will need to develop his own scoring standards for doubtful items through practice with the test. Fortunately the items in which this need arises are comparatively few in number. There appear to be some slight irregularities in the placement of sub-items within tests, and even of total test items. The blank could be improved upon, for school testing purposes at least, by omitting some of the squares now provided for scoring and leaving space at the top for note-taking. Although at first glance the scale appears to be rather formidable and intricate, there are no intrinsic difficulties that do not yield to faithful study and practice. One advantage of the scale is that it will not be readily coached. Furthermore, few but serious clinical workers will be apt to develop expertness with the scale, and the casual testing done by untrained persons that has so frequently brought testing into disrepute will be eliminated. In the hands of qualified workers it will prove to be a highly reliable, stable, and accurate mental measurement scale.

Tests of Mental Development

Loyola Ed Digest 15:11-2 O '39. *Austin G. Schmidt.* * Particularly gratifying to the reviewer is the author's forthright rejection of the coefficient of reliability, which he brands as useless and even misleading. It is indeed true that the importance of the coefficient of reliability has been grossly overemphasized. Virtue has been attached to high reliability, as if the fact that a test consistently did the same thing was proof of its validity. Dr. Kuhlmann's wide experience and scientific background are a sufficient guarantee of the merit of these tests. * an important contribution in the field of mental measurement.

[1427]

Tests for Primary Mental Abilities, Experimental Edition, 1938. High school and college; 1938; 1 form, 3 parts; 40¢ per set of 3 parts, 5 to 39 sets; 25¢ per set, 40 or more; $1 per specimen set; 153(270) minutes; L. L. Thurstone; Washington, D. C.: American Council on Education.

REFERENCES

1 THURSTONE, L. L. "The Factorial Isolation of Primary Abilities." *Psychometrika* 1:175-82 S '36.
2 THURSTONE, L. L. "A New Conception of Intelligence." *Ed Rec* 17:441-50 Jl '36.
3 THURSTONE, L. L. "A New Concept of Intelligence and a New Method of Measuring Primary Abilities." *Ed Rec* 17: Sup 10:124-38 O '36.
4 THURSTONE, L. L. *Primary Mental Abilities.* Psychometric Society, Psychometric Monograph No. 1. Chicago, Ill.: University of Chicago Press, 1938. Pp. ix, 121. $2.00. Paper. (London: Cambridge University Press. 9s.)
5 THURSTONE, L. L. *Primary Mental Abilities*: This Supplement Contains the Experimental Psychological Tests that Were Used in the Factorial Analysis Described in the Monograph. Supplement to Psychometric Monograph No. 1. Published for the Psychometric Society. Chicago, Ill.: University of Chicago Press, 1938. Pp. 274. Paper, lithotyped. Out of print.
6 SHANNER, WILLIAM M. "A Report on the Thurstone Tests of Primary Mental Abilities," pp. 54-60. In *1939 Achievement Testing Program in Independent Schools and Supplementary Studies.* Educational Records Bulletin No. 27. New York: Educational Records Bureau, June 1939. Pp. xiii, 76, 11. $1.50. Paper, lithotyped.
7 STALNAKER, JOHN M. "Primary Mental Abilities." *Sch and Soc* 50:868-72 D 30 '39.
7.1 WRIGHT, RUTH E. "A Factor Analysis of the Original Stanford-Binet Scale." *Psychometrika* 4:209-20 S '39.
8 CRAWFORD, A. B. "Some Observations on the Primary Mental Abilities Battery in Action." *Sch and Soc* 51:585-92 My 4 '40.
9 STALNAKER, JOHN M. "Results from Factor Analysis: With Special Reference to 'Primary Mental Abilities.'" *J Ed Res* 33:698-704 My '40.
10 ADKINS, DOROTHY C. "The Relation of Primary Mental Abilities to Vocational Choice," pp. 39-53. In *Psychological Examinations, 1939.* American Council on Education Studies, Series 5, Vol. 4, No. 2. Washington, D. C.: the Council, May 1940. Pp. v, 53. $0.25.

Henry E. Garrett, Associate Professor of Psychology, Columbia University. This unique examination has as its purpose the measurement of seven primary mental abilities or "factors." These seven factors are designated by capital letters and may be described as follows: P, perceptual ability; N, numerical ability; V, verbal ability; S, spatial-visualizing ability; M, memory; I, induction or generalizing ability; and D, deductive or reasoning ability. The test battery consists of three booklets which comprise a total of 16 separate tests. Many of these tests cover familiar ground (same-opposite, arithmetic, completion, number series) but many are original in content or in form (marks, cards, number patterns, figures). Fore-exercises are provided; and the tests are timed individually, the whole examination requiring about four hours. An examinee's standing in each of the seven abilities is summarized graphically by an individual profile.

The seven primary abilities measured by the test battery were identified by Thurstone through the application of his centroid method of factor analysis to the intercorrelations of 56 tests administered to 240 college freshmen. A "primary mental ability" may be defined as a function which cuts across many mental operations, and is involved to a greater or lesser degree in various tasks, much as physical strength or visual acuity is involved in many different activities. In the present study, the seven primary abilities are assumed to be independent. It is theoretically possible to think of the fundamental mental traits as being unique; and practically it is much easier to calculate factors which are statistically uncorrelated. But it may be remarked that the assumption of independence of factors is not necessary to factor theory. Comments upon the test may be grouped conveniently under several heads.

IDENTIFICATION OF FACTORS. Derivation of factors by any method of analysis from a table of correlations involving 56 tests and more than 1,500 coefficients is a huge task. Cut-and-fit and approximation methods as well as arbitrary decisions as to what factor weights should be considered significant are, therefore, a practical necessity; but as a result the identity of several of the postulated factors becomes doubtful. The two factors I and D may be artifacts and are certainly not definitely established; while factor P is probably what other investigators have called "mental speed." The four factors, V, N, M, and S have been so consistently found by other workers in a variety of experimental setups that their identity seems reasonably sure. The present study of Thurstone verifies and extends earlier work.

INDEPENDENCE OF FACTORS. While it was undoubtedly convenient for Thurstone to assume orthogonality (statistical independence) among factors in the present study in order to analyze mathematically a correlational matrix involving so many coefficients, from the psychological point of view the assumption of unique factors has its drawbacks. Words, numbers, and geometrical figures are all symbols; and it is hard to conceive of independent brain and neural structures underlying V, N, and S. It is easier, perhaps, to think of speed (synaptic resistance) or of memory (cortical retentiveness) as being independent functions; though even here strict independence seems far fetched. Considerable experimental work with factors indicates that, if not zero, the intercorrelations of V, N, S, and M are not high—probably from .20 to .30. Hence, it is not likely that the assumption of independence among mental factors in the present study introduces any great error.

TEST. In administering the *Tests for Primary Mental Abilities* to graduate and professional students, the reviewer noted several minor criticisms of the test as a practical instrument. The fore-exercises are nearly all too long; many of the tests are interesting and challenging, but several are so obviously of the puzzle type that students are either amused or bored —a bad test attitude in either case; the memory tests are too short, too superficial, and rely too much upon the factor of confusion; and the battery as a whole is too long.

These shortcomings in the test as well as other criticisms are to be expected in a new instrument. The test is certainly a step in the right direction—that is, toward the differentiation and measurement of certain essential mental traits. From both the theoretical and practical points of view such an approach is vastly superior to that taken by makers of omnibus tests who hope by averaging scores on a hodgepodge of functions to obtain, finally, a measure of some worth-while ability.

Truman L. Kelley, Professor of Education, Harvard University. The experimental and statistical analysis of mental life into a number of independent factors is the modern equivalent of the philosophical endeavors of earlier times to typify men and to assign different activities to fundamentally different psychological categories. It is the reviewer's belief that these typological psychologies are discredited because, like phrenology, palmistry, and astrology, they were built upon hypotheses pure and undefiled and not upon demonstrable and proven individual differences.

This modern attempt by Thurstone differs

from the just mentioned earlier attempts in that he gets mental factors from the findings of contemporary experimental and mental factor psychologists, verifying and supplementing these by his own experimental investigations. In short, his mental factors are not purely hypothetical, but are demonstrable and capable of measurement by means of objective measuring devices.

Though this is altogether an improvement in methodology over that of the armchair analysts, it still seems to the reviewer to be essentially weak in that the mental factors thus enumerated may be trivial. That there are demonstrable individual differences of a certain sort is no guarantee that they are important. The reviewer agrees with the viewpoints of Thorndike, Tryon, and Thomson that, due to the infinite variety of genetic structure and of psychological associative process, real and provable individual differences of infinite multiplicity are to be expected. If this is so it is not sufficient that Thurstone have evidence that his mental traits exist in demonstrably different amounts from subject to subject. He certainly should be called upon to show that they differentiate individuals in respects that are important in academic, vocational, and avocational living if he proposes them as essential rubrics, which he does in using the title "Primary Mental Abilities."

There seems to be a serious hiatus in his argument for he calls them "primary" and then admits that he does not know whether they serve any function. He writes: "It is too early in these investigations to make any definite statements about the particular combinations of abilities that are called for by each vocation . . . Before attempting to give individual vocational advice, it is well to recall that a man might be a success in accounting without being quick in adding a column of figures, that he might be a success in some phase of engineering or architecture without being superior in the factor S [space] which may be involved in design, and that he might be a success in law without being superior in the verbal factors." That Thurstone makes these hedging statements is highly commendable in view of the known facts about his measures, but that he needs to make them signifies that the issuance of the tests for public consumption is premature. As it is, the public is overwhelmed with tests. The crucial weakness of the test movement today is not primarily paucity of good tests, but lack of widely-known, sound, and helpful interpretative techniques. The *Tests for Primary Mental Abilities* not only cannot be interpreted in a sound and helpful manner by lay users, they cannot be so interpreted by experts. They would seem to but further confuse a market already surfeited with meaningless or bewildering measures.

Though the reviewer believes this to be the case with the battery entire he would, nevertheless, readily grant that certain of the seven measures are more important and more interpretable than certain others. Without documenting the accumulated evidence it seems believable that four of the seven abilities—number, verbal, space, and memory—are serviceably independent and it seems certain that two of these are widely important in forecasting academic and vocational differences. If these four stood alone and if the measures did not have grievous technical shortcomings the battery would be highly promising.

The shortcomings are, first: The use of speeded tests for functions never before ascertained to be speed functions—perception, number, verbal, space, memory, induction, and reasoning. The tests are so timed that no subjects are expected to finish them within the time limits set, thereby making speed a function of each and every one. This raises the reliability coefficients, which are high as reported, but it lowers the purity of the measures. It introduces a correlation between the tests, which the author acknowledges, but does not use, nor does he note that it is largely due to a common speed factor. The most obvious measure to be gotten from these seven is one of "mental speed," but no scoring for such is provided.

The second serious technical shortcoming is that an inadequate scoring formula is employed throughout—the score being the number of "rights." The correct formula for multiple-choice tests is $R - W/(n - 1)$, where R is the number of rights; W, the number of wrongs; and n, the number of options. It is particularly important that this formula be used if many subjects do not attempt all the items, otherwise a mere marking at random will increase a person's score.

A third serious shortcoming lies, not in the tests, but in the record sheet provided, which omits any place for recording "sex"—a trait far more important than any of the seven constituting the battery.

The reviewer is aware of the severity of his criticisms, but is constrained not to temper them because of his knowledge of the history of the general-intelligence-test movement. The analytical outlook and the temperate claims of Binet quickly gave way in his followers to the general-intelligence fetish, which has blighted the study of individual mental differences for nearly a generation and is still the source of befuddlement of sincere but nonanalytical teachers and counselors. If the use of analytical mental measures is not to follow a similar course it is necessary that pragmatic values and not wishful thinking—even though introduced in so inconspicuous a manner as in the selection of the original tests to be subjected to factor analysis—be the basis of trait analysis.

If this battery of "Primary Mental Abilities" is recognized as an initial attempt to accomplish a very difficult task, for which we can be very grateful to the author, and if it leads to an investigative attitude rather than to one of trust and confidence in this as yet uncharted realm it will prove an important stepping stone in the transition from reliance upon "general intelligence" to knowledge and use of "analytical and independent mental measures."

C. Spearman, Professor of Psychology, The University of London. [Joint review of the *Tests for Primary Mental Abilities* and the English version of the *Otis Quick-Scoring Mental Tests* (*see* 1413).] Here are two recent works of the highest interest, partly by the renown of their authors, partly by their intrinsic merits, and again by the extraordinary contrast between them.

To begin with, the test of Otis is above all things practical. At the start, indeed, and particularly in the development of group testing, this author displayed remarkable originality. But afterwards, he seems to have settled down to groping after improvement of detail; he has sought above all to supply the needs of ordinary teachers. Thurstone, at the other extreme, has from first to last been theoretical and original. His present work is the crown of a long series of fundamental and inspiring researches.

This contrast between them comes strikingly to expression in the fact that, whereas the test of Otis can be completed in twenty minutes, that of Thurstone requires the intolerable amount of twelve hours. Again, the Otis test is drawn up in three separate versions, each carefully adapted for a different age group—7-10, 10-15, and 15-18. With Thurstone, on the other hand, the point seems to find little if any consideration. He takes into account exclusively the application of the tests to university students. The opposite occurs in respect to the nature of the ability tested. For here it is Otis who is content with one single value; he simply follows the old and still almost universal custom of throwing all the test scores into one indiscriminating pool and so measure one single "general ability." Thurstone, instead, reintroduces the venerable doctrine that the mind is made up of several "primary mental abilities," each of them is determined by two or three different tests taken to be "fairly heavily saturated" with it. These abilities are: Perception, Number, Verbal, Space, Memory, Induction, and Reasoning. As for the elsewhere almost universally admitted "general" ability, this now completely vanishes.

Of these two new tests, undoubtedly that of Thurstone is the more open to criticism. For he is the daring pioneer, a role full of honour, but also of danger. One objection that might be raised is that we have to await indications of his faculties being really serviceable to practical teachers, psychiatrists, and industrialists. More dubious still is the question as to whether such workers in the field of applied psychology will ever be able to dispense with the said "general ability" or at least something akin. But I must venture to suggest something yet worse. In general, I myself yield to nobody with respect to Thurstone's admirable contributions to statistical psychology. But I have been forced to the conclusion that in his present study he has at last gone quite astray. The paradoxical absence of any general factor in this analysis I have been obliged to attribute to a grave fault of method. (*See* my article, "Thurstone's Work Re-worked," *J Ed Psychol* 30:1-16 Ja '39.) And this conclusion has been immediately confirmed by the reappearance of the general factor in another study [7,1] made by the same School.

On the whole, then, the chief value of Thurstone's tests would seem to lie, not so much in application as rather in stimulation.

Godfrey H. Thomson, Professor of Education and Director of the Training Centre for

Teachers, University of Edinburgh. It is seldom that tests can be published with so thorough and complete a scientific backing as these. The manual of instructions [4] is clear and almost beyond criticism and the references to articles and books justifying the standardisation and significance of the tests are complete, except that the study at the Hyde Park School, Chicago, has not yet been published, though it is promised "in the near future." The estimated reliabilities of the tests are given, and their estimated "validity," defined as the estimated correlation between the score and a pure test of the relative primary factor. But since it is the function of a critic to be critical, let me see what minor faults I can descry.

There is nowhere an explicit statement that the tests are intended for young adults. That has either to be known by the reader from his previous acquaintance with Thurstone's articles, or deduced from the reference to high schools and from the use of the word "students" for those taking the test.

The whole interpretation of the tests depends, of course, on the user's acceptance of Thurstone's theory of simple structure and primary factors. It is perhaps too much to expect the manual to explain that other systems exist and to give references to adverse articles by workers who disagree.

As a "test technician" I am myself most troubled by two things. The first is the absence of any information by which I can check the estimated reliabilities and validities. I am not even quite sure what the estimated validity exactly is.

The second point is concerned with the "compromise which was made in adapting the tests for practical use." The manual is to be commended for making quite clear what that compromise is, and what the ideal but very laborious method would be. My first reaction, however, was one of great disappointment that Thurstone, after all the spade-work he has done towards measuring these primary abilities as accurately as possible, should have descended to the crude plan of offering the sum of the raw scores in a couple of tests as the measure of each factor.

And this brings me back to the first point. For to know how much has been lost by this compromise I would need to be sure of what the "estimated validity" means. In his *Primary Mental Abilities* [4] one can calculate (though he does not give them explicitly) the determinable part of each factor as estimated from the whole battery of 57 tests, by post-multiplying Table 7 (p. 98) by Table 3 (p. 96). Thus, for example, one finds the determinate part of the P factor there to be .616, and of the N factor to be .825. If the squares of the "estimated validities" in the present tests are to be compared with these quantities, they are .65 squared and .63 squared, or .423 and .397, indicating a very considerable loss of "validity" by the compromise of simplicity. And if this comparison is not the proper one to make, then I criticise the manual for not making perfectly clear what is meant by "estimated validity." Possibly, however, these criticisms might have been unnecessary had the Hyde Park School article appeared. Yet I do not really think so. These tests of primary mental abilities are a new departure along a pioneer track. The manual accompanying them ought to have been, in part, a summary of their theoretical justification, to be read, of course, with the assumption that the relevant articles in the journals were known.

But having now done my duty as a critic I would like to conclude by saying, without any implication that I am subscribing to Thurstone's theories, that I should be very proud to have produced these tests and this manual.

Robert C. Tryon, Associate Professor of Psychology, The University of California. The reviewer is frankly defeatist regarding the theory that there exist a few important functional, primary unities in human behavior and that factor analysis provides the means of discovering them. This test which purports to measure seven such primary traits as isolated by Thurstone's factor method requires, in the reviewer's mind, restricted use. The troubling thought is that the test—developed by such an eminent and brilliant authority and bolstered by an awe-inspiring mathematics—may set a new tradition of a few faculties of the mind, just at the time psychologists are showing some signs of recovering from the pall of the IQ doctrine.

In his manual of instructions, the author does indeed urge caution, recommending the use of the test only in schools employing a competent psychologist. But competence in evaluating these "primary traits" requires a grounding in factor theory; one should, for example, be conversant with Thomson's *Fac-*

torial Analysis of Human Ability, in which Thurstone's arbitrary assumptions are set off against a variety of others which could equally well be made. Probably not a handful of school psychologists have such a training.

The intent of the test is to measure several important *functions*, but the author admits uncertainty regarding the psychological nature of these. Factor P "*seems* to be a perceptual ability," "those who excel in [factor V] . . . are *probably* verbally-minded in their thinking," "it *seems reasonable* to expect" that ability S refers to visualization; "factor M can be *tentatively* named the ability to memorize," "the hypothesis that the factor I is associated with [inductive thinking] . . . *seems plausible*," "factor D *seems* to represent facility in formal reasoning." [Words italicized by the reviewer.]

What is clearly wanted is convincing evidence of the psychological validity of these abilities. The manual presents the "estimated validity" of each type of ability score, which is a composite of two or more subtests. But validity is defined as "the estimated correlation between the composite score and a pure test of the primary factor." One not familiar with factor logic might suppose that this means a correlation between the test score and a superlatively constructed experimental or empirical criterion. But its real meaning is geometric, to wit: the projection of the test on a primary trait vector which, as such, is not experimentally determined. The primary trait vectors are *theoretical* abilities inferred from the intercorrelations between the tests and governed by the assumptions of Thurstone's factor methods.

Taken at face value, furthermore, all of the validities of the seven measures are discouragingly low, being of the order .6. As an illustration of the inadequacy of this value, the variance of the measure of Reasoning (D) as scored in the experimental sample of subjects is only about 36 per cent determined by the pure reasoning factor and 64 per cent by factors having nothing to do with reasoning. These other nonreasoning factors would correlate as high as .8 with the D scores. Individual diagnosis of a trait is precarious where the diagnostic score is only about a third determined by a pure measure of the trait and where the pure measure itself is a theoretical and undefined continuum.

The test is an interesting and ingenious research instrument to be used by factor-trained psychologists. The reviewer believes that years of research will be necessary before the test can be shown to possess practical value in vocational counseling.

J Ed Res 33:698-704 My '40. John M. Stalnaker. "Results from Factor Analysis." * The most striking characteristic of the tests, obvious from inspection, is that they are all short speed tests. Manual dexterity in operating a pencil and speed of reaction are of unquestioned importance in almost all the tests. Speed is so important, and the tests are so brief, that slight errors in timing must assume major importance. The test results would differ greatly for various age groups. Adults, on the average, cannot work at the speed demanded—such as in the "same-opposites" test in which twenty items per minute are offered and then the response word may be the same or the opposite of the stimulus word. In using machine-scorable sheets some subjects, it has been found, blacken the space between the lines very carefully. Such a person will be found deficient in all primary mental abilities. There is evidence that a very different factor pattern would emerge if these tests were given without time limits. Although speed is certainly of primary significance in these tests, no factor or primary mental ability of speed has been found. That it has not may be a reflection on or limitation of the method of analysis used. Does it make psychological sense to ignore speed? * To summarize: the mathematical theory underlying factor analysis techniques will doubtless be perfected in time so that factor analysis will be recognized as a powerful mathematical tool. Its application to the results of valid tests given to various but known types of populations may yield data of value for a better understanding of the functioning of the mind and for purposes of practical educational guidance. At the moment, however, the greatest need seems to be for vastly improved basic tests, tests developed with but one object in view—a thorough and dependable measure of certain types of ability. Such tests will require more time from the candidates; some of the tests may be more difficult to score; all of them will require great care in construction. Until such tests are used as a source for the primary data, positive conclusions from any system of factor analysis must be viewed as conjecture. To Mr. Thurstone we are all indebted for stimulating interest in this problem by offering the experimental edition of his tests, tests which he personally advocates be restricted at this time to experimental purposes and to group not to individual interpretation. One can but hope that a like amount of intelligence, energy, and industry will be devoted, by him and by others, to producing tests of the high quality necessary to make the results from mathematical analyses of test data of practical significance, not alone for basic theoretical studies, but also for the use of those who are merely "faithful workers in the vineyards."

Sch and Soc 50:868-72 D 30 '39. John M. Stalnaker. "Primary Mental Abilities." * Of practical importance is the question of the value of this particular set of tests for individual diagnosis and guidance. Even if the theory on which the tests are based were beyond question, there is still the problem of how thoroughly it has been applied and how well prepared the present series is. The analysis here reported throws some light on the question. In spite of the enormous amount of research which directly or indirectly has gone into the preparation of the present set of tests and the careful editing to which they have been subjected, the results obtained with one group of candidates do not support in full the theory of the seven primary abilities. Speed, although not recognized as a "factor," appears to be of utmost importance. The time allowed for each test is brief, and the resulting individual scores, therefore, are not as dependable as if longer tests had been used. The tests could be materially improved by the elimination of items of low validity, by arranging the items in order of difficulty and by adjusting the time limits. It will be interesting to observe the relationship found for university freshmen between the test scores of a perfected set of tests, tests given without time limits, and also to note the factors which may be postulated to account for the correlations thus obtained. Although tests given by the amount-limit method usually require more careful preparation than those given under very short time limits, such care and attention may be justified if a theory of primary mental abilities is to be established. A definite arrangement of the items according to difficulty may be desirable if time limits, even generous ones, are to be used. Longer tests may yield scores sufficiently dependable for individual diagnosis. The present experimental edition is an interesting and stimulating initial attempt. The psychologists, the personnel and guidance groups, will all undoubtedly eagerly await a revision and improvement of these tests. The present tests are more useful in suggesting new lines of experimentation, needed developments and points of weakness, than they are in yielding data useful for individual diagnosis or guidance.

Sch and Soc 51:585-92 My 4 '40. A. B. Crawford. "Some Observations on the Primary Mental Abilities Battery in Action." * Now that the Thurstone Primary Mental Abilities battery has been made generally available in readily scorable form, many personnel officers and educational authorities in schools and colleges alike are eager to learn how it can be utilized to serve practical problems of student orientation and guidance. A recently published analysis [6] . . . of current experience with this battery at one of the larger independent secondary schools in the East is . . . of timely interest. * With due appreciation of the care and completeness with which Mr. Shanner has marshalled and presented his data, I venture to question certain of the associated comments and conclusions. * The concluding paragraph of Mr. Shanner's report is as follows:

A comparison of the three different types of profiles suggests that groups selected upon the basis of academic achievement may differ significantly with respect to their mental abilities. In so far as the Thurstone *Tests for Primary Mental Abilities* are capable of accurately defining these abilities, we may use the tests for guidance purposes and for predicting performance on various achievement tests. The battery of tests is satisfactorily reliable and the intercorrelations for the ability scores are sufficiently low to indicate considerable independence of mental factors measured, even though they are not so low as one should desire. Although there should be additional refinement and improvement of the tests and further research concerning the interpretation of the results, the available evidence indicates that the tests in their present form unquestionably constitute a valuable addition to the field of aptitude testing.

Though Mr. Shanner has put us in his debt by the careful analysis and complete presentation of his data, I cannot find justification therein for these conclusions. He is, of course, entitled, with all proper respect, to his own opinions. Those of a different nature here presented are doubtless open to considerable criticism in turn. Yet, with no intention to be arrogant, I submit (*a*) that, to quote Mr. Shanner again, if "groups selected upon the basis of academic achievement" do really "differ significantly with respect to their mental abilities" (as is altogether likely), such difference is *not* revealed by this particular trial of the tests in question; and (*b*) that intercorrelations as reported in the study are *not* "sufficiently low to indicate considerable independence of mental factors measured," although they certainly *are* "not so low as one should desire." That "the tests in their present form unquestionably constitute a valuable addition to the field of aptitude testing" I sincerely hope and believe; but this demonstration of their diagnostic powers is unconvincing. The results thus reported appear, at least to the present writer, distinctly less encouraging than had been hoped for, when the long-awaited primary ability measures became generally available. Having offered some suggestions as to why they may not have operated, in the situation so carefully analyzed by Mr. Shanner, as their author had reason to expect, I still maintain faith in their ultimate importance as significant contributions not only to psychological theory, but to practical guidance needs as well. That the desired objectives were not satisfactorily realized in this early trial should but serve as a challenge to further experiment. * Thurstone . . . has been under continued pressure to make at least some preliminary form of the P. M. A. battery available for field experimentation and immediate use. That he has consented to do so, even though the present composite instruments admittedly do not satisfy his standards of "purity," represents, under the circumstances, a generous concession which should be duly appreciated. Yet the current battery bears the Primary Mental Abilities label and generally is regarded as measuring the traits so designated. Its imperfections in this respect are less widely recognized than its objectives. * Obviously, however, this one administration and the resultant analyses herein discussed neither prove nor disprove the value of Professor Thurstone's battery. They do distinctly indicate the need for further investigation of how these measures, conceived in scientific purity, can meet realistic educational and human demands. *

See also B503 and B1099.

[1428]
Unit Scales of Aptitude. Grades 4-5, 6-7, 8-9, 10-12; 1934-38; 2 forms; $1.00 per 25; 25¢ per specimen set; (50-60) minutes; M. J. Van Wagenen; Minneapolis, Minn.: Educational Test Bureau, Inc.

Herschel T. Manuel, Professor of Educational Psychology, The University of Texas, and Director of Research, Texas Commission on Coordination in Education. This test is designed to yield measures of five "significant mental functions"—rate of comprehension of simple paragraphs, perception of relations (verbal analogies), reading vocabulary, composition vocabulary, and range of general information. The five together provide an "index of verbal competence," which is roughly comparable to the intelligence quotient. The difference between the reading vocabulary and the composition vocabulary test is illustrated by the following examples, respectively: (*a*) *commence* begin keep on stop rest delay; (*b*) He put up a *brave* fight prudent discreet uncouth inglorious valiant. In the first the stimulus word is supposed to be more difficult than the responses; in the second this is reversed.

The test bears evidence of careful work. The mechanical arrangement of the test booklet is satisfactory for hand scoring. With the exception of the first test (rate of comprehension), in which a cross-out technique is used, pupil responses are indicated by writing numbers in conveniently aligned blanks. The publication of the test in four divisions, each for a group of grades, avoids the bulkiness sometimes found in tests covering a wide range.

Although the manual of directions is fairly extensive and detailed, it seems to offer unnecessary difficulty to the reader. Perhaps the C-score is itself a difficult concept, but one feels that the explanation is not as clear as it might be. The use of terms with meanings that are unexpected (at least to the reviewer) is a possible source of difficulty. Verbal analogies, for example, bear the name "*perception* of relations." "Percent placement" turns out to be based, not upon the frequency of the score as one might expect, but upon the scale itself. It is simply a score for an age group scaled in terms of P.E. with a median of fifty. Thus a "percent placement" of 10 is a score of −4 P.E. This is 10 per cent "of the way between the lowest and highest cases among a representative thousand." Another possible criticism is that the number of different numerical measures used in interpreting scores seems rather formidable.

The test as a whole is probably a fairly satisfactory basis for an index of general ability such as is obtained from a short verbal group test of intelligence. Reading, vocabulary, analogies, and general information are acceptable components of such a test. The total score could be made more useful, however, by including in the individual profile an index of the level of total ability as well as an index of relative standing.

The most serious questions to be raised by this reviewer center around the five analytic measures, the "significant mental functions," which the test is said to measure. Perhaps the question of reliability—measuring five functions in 45 minutes—may be passed with the observation that a second form of the test might be administered to make the measures more stable if one had use for this particular analysis. Too, one should not lightly discourage any analysis that may prove to be useful. Factor analysis is too young for anyone to know just what analyses will be most useful. It is safe, however, to observe that nothing which the reviewer has found in the test material or elsewhere makes clear the specific use which a teacher may make of the separate measures. "Just how difficult content he knows and understands in each of the functions measured can be readily seen"—but what then? In verbal analogies, for example, what useful information would a high score give the teacher which would not be given much more reliably by the test as a whole?

[1429]

Wechsler-Bellevue Intelligence Scale. Age 10 and over; 1939; individual; $12.50 per outfit of testing material (not including the manual); $3.50 per manual; 75¢ per 25 record blanks; David Wechsler; New York: Psychological Corporation.

REFERENCES

1 BALINSKY, B.; ISRAEL, H.; AND WECHSLER, D. "The Relative Effectiveness of the Stanford-Binet and the Bellevue Intelligence Scale in Diagnosing Mental Deficiency." *Am J Orthopsychiatry* 9:798-801 O '39.
2 WECHSLER, DAVID. *The Measurement of Adult Intelligence.* Baltimore, Md.: Williams & Wilkins Co., 1939. Pp. ix, 229. $3.50. (London: Baillière, Tindall, and Cox. 16s.)

F. L. Wells, Psychologist, Department of Hygiene, Harvard University. This series is by a considerable margin the best available procedure for adults, in a clinical setting. The writer will here discuss it from the standpoint not of general organization, which may be left to reviews of Wechsler's book, but of technical matters having special concern for a workaday user, as the writer has for some time had the good fortune to be. Naturally this involves mention, if not enumeration, of real or fancied flaws in detail. In important features, the scale's status is as above set forth; as it deserves great use, it can also bear minute scrutiny without captiousness.

To begin with, the question of the preceding president will obviously vary in difficulty according to the length of the current incumbency. The "pints" question is an interesting one suggesting that its relative value may have something to do with the misleading association furnished by "quart" (quarter, fourth). The writer does not like the use of the word "obtain"; too high-brow for a question so early in the series. The standard answer to the thermometer question is also of a high level for so early a position, and since the test may be often given in general hospital surroundings, attention should be paid to response in terms of clinical thermometers. "Average height" again seems rather complicated from a vocabulary standpoint for its position in the series. The writer has always favored formulating an information question in the simplest possible terms (e.g., What does rubber come from? About how tall are American women mostly?) even if it involves a recasting of norms. Few things are so disturbing to an examinee's attitude as a question with an unintelligible or even very unfamiliar expression in it. The airplane, North Pole, and United States population questions are specially interesting for their distribution of erroneous answers. The instructions for certain items should make clearer what is the limit of tolerance in the responses; as in, e.g., apocrypha, habeas corpus.

In the comprehension subtest the first question would probably benefit by specifying a "new" (uncancelled) stamp. The scoring of the leather question seems needlessly cumbrous. The second alternate involves rather too many variables to be satisfactory from the standpoint of intelligence, whatever might be its significance for an evaluation of personality. Comprehension questions in general give good insights into the examinee's intellectual processes, but it is hard to set up satisfactory scoring criteria for them. The present questions illustrate dependence on attitude and background; cf., urban and rural background to the "forest" question.

Digit span hardly calls for comment. The most meaningful of the verbal subtests is surely Similarities. The directions are particularly well found. But it is impossible to avoid repeating the criticism that more levels of credit should be recognized, and especially given a wide spread. As to specific items, wood and alcohol make trouble on account of the "wood alcohol" association, and Wechsler must have somehow escaped wrestling with dialect pronunciations of "poem."

Among the arithmetical questions the sugar problem has seemed placed a little late in the series. It is embarrassing to raise invidious questions of commercial ethics, but so much complication has arisen over the prescribed wording of the making change problems, that the word "should" appears preferable to "will." As on other grounds, "get back" is preferable to "receive." (Also in Item 8 of the same, "how much did it cost new" rather than ". . . was it worth new.")

The organization of performance tests always presents greater difficulty than obtains with language content. A more distinctive name than "picture completion" might have been found for the first listed. It is not clear whether there has been a studied inclusion of misleads in such items as the hinge on the door (knobs are hardly more "important" than hinges), the discontinuous cane in the sunset, and the missing antennae of the ship.

Picture arrangement is an excellent testing device, limited by its cumbrousness. (The Bellevue series could have spared itself much of this by printing, as it could easily have done, each one of its pictures on a separate 3 × 5 card.) Cultural difficulties enter, e.g., the taxi outside an urban environment. It has been objected that in the holdup situation the A, B, D, C order is too reasonable to be scored zero, especially since the outmoding of prison "stripes."

The block design series is probably the strongest of the performance subtests. One could wish that more use had been made of the principle, which could well include three-dimensional models. The object-assembly test is cumbrous for what it distinctively contributes, and pencil-and-paper tests, even though nonverbal, seem out of place in a strictly "performance" scale. Fortunately the scale is not a tightly closed system and it is perhaps not too much to hope that the performance scale may be amplified into a manipulative (e.g., block design) and non-manipulative (e.g., digit-symbol) series.

An alternate subtest has been added, a vocabulary test of the Terman type (other words) being taken for the purpose; probably as wise a choice as available. Notation would be easier with double and single credits, as elsewhere, rather than single and half.

That very important and often neglected feature of a test series, the record form, is only moderately well designed. In addition to some rearrangement of material, the writer would prefer to have most of the rulings omitted; they cramp eye movements as well as size of writing, and disregard the consideration that little or nothing may need recording on one item, with a long note on the next.

Special mention should also be made of age norms, tracing the gradual decline of performance after early adult years. In terms of mental age this is some 20 per cent between ages 20 and 60 (pp. 56, 196).[2] Although little cited here, perhaps the strongest feature of the scale is its structure, which can serve as a model, in its facility of comparison between records of different well-constructed subtests. For the author of a treatment of Army Alpha from this standpoint, Wechsler lays less stress on this feature than might be anticipated. The chief use of global scores is administrative.

Arch Neurology and Psychiatry 43:614 Mr '40. * a clear presentation * provides a scale which is simple to give and is reliable. *

Psychol B 37:251-4 Ap '40. Grace H. Kent. * The book opens with a ten-page chapter on the nature of intelligence, which is defined as "the aggregate or global capacity of the individual to act purposefully, to think rationally and to deal effectively with his environment." No question is raised by the author concerning the measurability of intelligence as thus defined. The need for a test system intended specifically for study of adult intelligence as opposed to juvenile intelligence is stated in a way which must strike a responsive chord in every clinical examiner who has had occasion to present the Binet scale to a mature subject of average or superior achievement. * In spite of his opposition to the IQ as we know it, the author considers "Intelligence Quotient" too happy a term to be discarded. In his standardization of the Bellevue tests he presents the norms, as determined by standard deviation procedure, in tables by means of which the weighted scores can be converted directly into what he calls the "IQ." This use of the term, as applied to something entirely different from what we understand by it, is likely to be misleading. The strongest feature of the system is the selection of cases for standardization. The norms are based upon scores obtained from 1750 subjects ranging in age from seven to seventy, selected out of 3500 subjects to whom the tests had been presented, the selection being a sampling based upon the occupational distribution of the country's adult white population, as indicated by the 1930 census. The adult subjects were divided into age groups by five-year intervals, the number of cases in a group ranging from 50 subjects in the later fifties to 195 subjects in the later twenties. The collection of such a mass of data is a marvelous achievement. The scale consists of ten test units (plus one alternate), each unit having a wide range of discriminative capacity. Correlations and intercorrelations have been calculated for all possible combinations, and the units are ranked in value according to their correlation with the scale as a whole. The scores have been so weighted as to make the numerical values approximately uniform for the eleven units. Three tables of norms are based upon these weighted scores: one for ten tests, one for five language tests, and one for five performance tests. The student who is not too scrupulous about manipulations of results will be able to obtain approximate ratings from other combinations. Most of the tests are modified forms of tests already in use. The strongest unit of the scale is "Similarities," a series of 12 pairs beginning with *orange—banana* and ending with *fly—tree*. Following Binet, Dr. Wechsler has apparently given more careful attention to criteria for standardization than to criteria for selection of test items. He includes Memory Span for Digits, although acknowledging it to be a weak test as a measure of intelligence. Furthermore, he combines digits forwards and digits backwards under one score, allowing the same credit for five digits forwards as for five digits backwards. He uses also the Symbol-Digit test, observing that the scores show a marked decline with advancing age, but making no mention of visual strain as a possible explanation of this decline. In the tests called "Picture Arrangement" and "Picture Completion," he has used pictures which are too small and too sketchy to be easily understood. It appears that the value of a test, for him, is statistical rather than psychological. The text is carelessly written. "Like" is used as a conjunction, and "where" as a relative pronoun. Throughout the book the author refers to himself as "we," as if the work were a joint product. His irregular use of the "editorial we" is at times misleading, especially when he uses "we" as including (apparently) the small group of students who assisted in making the examinations or the larger group of psychologists who may be expected to use the test in the future. Some of the test materials are contained in six pasteboard boxes, each of which has the name *Bellevue Intelligence Test* blazoned on the cover. Before placing these boxes on the table in full view of the subject, the examiner would do well to cover the offensive labels with something in code. Clinical examiners who are relatively satisfied with some form of the Binet-Simon scale for examination of children will welcome a test which is intrinsically better adapted to adult interests and which is adequately standardized for adults. To this extent, the Bellevue scale will meet a need that has been keenly felt for more than twenty years. It does not, however, show any such advance over the Binet scale as might be expected as a result of our collective experience in the use of tests for a full generation. Students engaged in the development of tests for individual study can learn much from Dr. Wechsler's plan of standardization. The table by means of which a score can be converted directly into the IQ (or its equivalent, preferably under some other name) marks a very important advance over the current method of deriving the IQ. If all tests were thus standardized, the public demand for a one-figure rating could be satisfied honestly and without distortion of results. But the "mental age," although it lends itself to gross abuse, need not be wholly discarded. Many students, with full appreciation of Dr. Wechsler's contribution to higher standards of accuracy in evaluation of test results, will be disappointed because he has made it difficult to derive a satisfactory "mental age" from the scores of his tests. So long as this way of expressing results is so nearly universal, the "mental age" is indispensable as a common denominator. It is a mistake for any author of tests to assume that others will wish to adopt his system as a whole and use it exactly as he himself uses it. Some of us prefer a flexible system to any composite scale. If Dr. Wechsler had included a table of true

Wechsler-Bellevue Intelligence Scale

"mental age" norms for the ages seven to seventeen, not for this three scales, but for each individual unit, the Bellevue tests would be incomparably more useful and would presumably see much wider service. A full-size textbook is too large to be used conveniently as a manual of instructions for test presentation. The third part of this book, containing the instructions and norms, might better have been separated from the reference material in the first two parts. For the convenience of the examiner it is to be hoped that the author will publish additionally a compact booklet or pamphlet containing only what is needed for the daily use of the tests. It is strongly urged that he offer norms (for each unit individually) in the form of simple decile scores for each age group, unweighted and wholly free from mathematical manipulation. He has in his possession much material which would be invaluable to clinical examiners.

See also B1121.

[1430]

"West Riding" Tests of Mental Ability. Ages 9-14; 1925; 2 parts; 6s. 6d. per 25 test booklets; 1s. 9d. per 25 answer sheets; 6d. per manual; 1s. per specimen set; 55(65) minutes; T. P. Tomlinson; London: University of London Press, Ltd.
a) SET Y.
b) SET Z. For use only with examinees who have taken Set Y on the day previous to taking Set Z.

Ll. Wynn Jones, Senior Lecturer in Experimental Psychology, University of Leeds. Each set consists of eight subtests: Test A, Instructions; Test B, Word Meaning; Test C, Arithmetic; Test D, Analogies; Test E, Incongruities; Test F, Logical Selection; Test G, Jumbled Sentences; and Test H, Classification. These tests were standardised by Tomlinson in preparation for an M.Ed. thesis entitled *A Group Scale of Mental Ability* which was approved by the University of Leeds in June, 1923.

In the main Tomlinson based his statistical evaluation of the tests on the Spearman technique. For each subtest the reliability and the correlation with the central intellective factor or g are high, whether for city, rural, or small town children. The reliability of the scale as a whole is as high as .95. Some of the subtests, however, cannot be marked as quickly as the more modern forms. Thus in the analogies test Tomlinson decided that the form which requires the testee to find the correct answer was more valid than the more modern form of underlining one of five given words and therefore adopted it. This also applies to the incongruities test where the testee has to express his answer in words. The word meaning test, the logical selection test, and the classification test were new, at least in the form in which Tomlinson used them.

In the Examiners' Manual there is a table giving the mental age equivalents, so that an approximate value for the IQ of each testee may be obtained. In one rural school Tomlinson found the average IQ of the native children to be 82.5, a standard deviation of 15.3, and a range of 58 to 110. These figures may be compared with the corresponding figures given by Burt for a Warwickshire Village, viz., 81.6, 15.7, and 38 to 112. The distribution of IQ's in an average city school was found to agree very closely with the normal distribution given by Terman. Tomlinson himself points out in his thesis that the word meaning test, the incongruities test, and the classification test have little distributing value for the lower 25 per cent of the 9-year-old children tested. This means that the tests are not effective for mental ages below 7. This, of course, is partly due to the fact that any group test of a literary nature would tend to correlate highly at low mental ages with scholastic attainments in reading and writing. Coefficients of correlation were obtained with teacher's estimates of .84 at age 12 and of .71 at age 13. There was a greater range of g in the rural schools where there was a high percentage of low as well as of high IQ's. Godfrey Thomson refers to the migration of the more intellectual elements of rural districts to the city. Tomlinson mentions the migration of the lesser intellectual elements from the villages to a neighbouring township which offers abundance of employment of an unskilled nature. In some cases there has been immigration of higher intellectual elements into villages on the outskirts of big towns and is probably one of the factors operating to provide Thomson with his highest IQ's in such localities.

[1430.1]

Word-Number Test of Scholastic Aptitude. Grades 4-8, 9-16; 1939-40; 1 form, 2 levels; $1.75 per 30; $1.50 per 100 machine-scorable answer sheets; 10¢ per specimen set; 30(35-40) minutes; H. T. Manuel, James Knight, J. A. Floyd, and R. C. Jordon; Austin, Texas: Steck Co.
a) FORM X. Grades 4-8.
b) FORM A. Grades 9-16.

INTELLIGENCE — THIRD MMY

REVIEWS BY *Anne Anastasi, James M. Anderson, Brent Baxter, Nancy Bayley, Marion A. Bills, Harold H. Bixler, E. J. G. Bradford, H. E. Brogden, Emily T. Burr, Cyril Burt, Psyche Cattell, Charles N. Cofer, John Cohen, W. D. Commins, Raleigh M. Drake, W. G. Emmett, George A. Ferguson, John C. Flanagan, Charles D. Flory, Henry E. Garrett, Florence L. Goodenough, J. P. Guilford, James R. Hobson, Carl I. Hovland, Grace H. Kent, Kate Levine Kogan, Frederic Kuder, Charles R. Langmuir, Irving Lorge, Stanley S. Marzolf, L. S. Penrose, Walter C. Shipley, Patrick Slater, Florence M. Teagarden, Robert L. Thorndike, William W. Turnbull, F. T. Tyler, Ruth W. Washburn, Robert I. Watson, David Wechsler, Beth L. Wellman, F. L. Wells, Carroll A. Whitmer, D. A. Worcester.*

GROUP

[214]
★**Academic Aptitude Test: Non-Verbal Intelligence.** Grades 7-16 and adults; 1944; 1 form; $2.50 per 25; 10¢ per manual; 50¢ per specimen set; 26(35) minutes; Andrew Kobal, J. Wayne Wrightstone, and Karl R. Kunze; Acorn Publishing Co.

[215]
★**Academic Aptitude Test: Verbal Intelligence.** Grades 7-16 and adults; 1943-45; 1 form; $2.50 per 25; 10¢ per manual; 50¢ per specimen set; 40(45) minutes; Andrew Kobal, J. Wayne Wrightstone, and Karl R. Kunze; Acorn Publishing Co.

Marion A. Bills, Assistant Secretary, Aetna Life Insurance Company, Hartford, Connecticut. This test is made up of three time-limit subtests which are set up to measure separately (*a*) information, (*b*) mental alertness, (*c*) comprehension of relations. Its purpose is to differentiate between those persons capable of continuing with academic work and those not capable.

Norms for the various school grades have been carefully set up by adequate testing. Grades correspond closely with individual tests of mental alertness. Tests on a small group of employed persons show about the expected correspondence with position and employee ratings. Suggestions for interpretation are clearly given.

The advantages of the test are that the subtests may be scored separately, and the test is difficult enough to differentiate at the higher levels of ability. A disadvantage of the test is that the individual timing of subsections makes it necessary for a person to be in attendance during the entire time of the test.

[216]

★Adaptability Test. Grades 9-12 and adults; 1942-43; preliminary manual; Forms A, B; $1.85 per 25; 50¢ per specimen set, postpaid; 15(20) minutes; Joseph Tiffin and C. H. Lawshe; Science Research Associates.

REFERENCES

1. LAWSHE, C. H., JR., AND THORNTON, G. R. "A Test Battery for Identifying Potentially Successful Naval Electrical Trainees." *J Appl Psychol* 27:399-406 O '43. * (PA 18:265)
2. TIFFIN, JOSEPH, AND LAWSHE, C. H., JR. "The Adaptability Test: A Fifteen Minute Mental Alertness Test for Use in Personnel Allocation." *J Appl Psychol* 27:152-63 Ap '43. * (PA 17:3556)
3. SARTAIN, A. Q. "Relation Between Scores on Certain Standard Tests and Supervisory Success in an Aircraft Factory." *J Appl Psychol* 30:328-32 Ag '46. * (PA 21:250)

Anne Anastasi, Associate Professor of Psychology, Fordham University, New York, New York. Designed with special reference to its use as an employment aid, this test attempts to furnish a quick estimate of "general mental ability" by means of a wide variety of items. It is self-administering and consists of 35 items in spiral omnibus arrangement. In form, the items are either of the multiple-choice variety, or they are questions which can be answered with a letter or number. In content, they are predominantly verbal and cover an exceptionally heterogeneous sampling of familiar types. The test is hand-scored from a key. Two equivalent forms, A and B, are available. Percentile and standard score norms are given for four samplings (612 industrial female applicants, 200 Navy electrical trainees, 86 clerical employees, and 43 Purdue seniors) as well as for all four combined. The manual is in preliminary mimeographed form and contains a number of printing errors, including the omission of words, numbers, and one entire graph!

The 70 items comprising Forms A and B were chosen from an original compilation of 120, 60 of which were administered to Navy trainees and 60 to engineering students. Item analyses were made against total scores, only those items being kept which yielded a difference of 1 σ or more between the performance of the best quarter and the poorest quarter of the group. Reliability coefficients, computed on the same four groups employed for the norms (cf. above), range from .60 to .90 by the split-half method and from .79 to .93 by the retest method. Validity was checked against supervisors' ratings for the clerical employees and against mean grades for the Navy trainees. In both groups, reliable differences in mean test scores were found between the contrasted criterion subgroups.

The *Adaptability Test* illustrates the value of item analysis in yielding a short test, the reliability and validity of which may be as high as, or even higher than, those of a longer test. Since, however, the strength of such a test derives so largely from the definitiveness of the original item analysis, it is regrettable that such a restricted sampling was employed for this purpose (i.e., Navy electrical trainees and engineering students, N not stated). The discriminative value of specific items may be quite different even for the remaining types of subjects included in the norms, not to mention other types of workers to whom the test may be applied. It would seem, furthermore, that a slightly greater number of items would have been desirable, especially in view of the excessive heterogeneity of content. The test contains, for example, only one or two items of certain types. In discussing the interpretation of scores, the authors rightly stress the need for finding anew, within each industrial concern, the "effective ranges" of scores for specific job types. They appear, however, to lay undue emphasis upon a hierarchy of jobs in terms of scores on this test and do not call sufficient attention to the importance of special aptitudes in the higher level jobs of a predominantly nonverbal nature. For example, office clerks and skilled tradesmen are listed within the same score range without reference to the fact that a low score on this particular test is a more serious occupational handicap for the clerk than for the skilled tradesman. The chief advantages of this test are its brevity and good "face validity" in a plant situation, many items being expressed in terms relevant to an industrial environment.

Marion A. Bills, Assistant Secretary, Aetna Life Insurance Company, Hartford, Connecticut. This 15-minute test consists of 35 items on vocabulary, arithmetic, and logic arranged in order of increasing difficulty. Experimentation by the authors seems to have proved that the test will differentiate between clerical workers who should be employed for complicated work and those who should be employed for simple routine work only. The advantages of the test are that it is simple, short, and easily administered. The disadvantages are: (*a*) Separate scores on vocabulary, arithmetic, and logic cannot be used. This is, of course, an inherent defect in all time-limit spiral tests. (*b*) Some of the questions seem to be of the puzzle type rather than straight arithmetic or reasoning and might therefore be resented.

[217]

American Council on Education Psychological Examination for College Freshmen. 1924–47; new form issued annually; IBM; separate answer sheets must be used; $2 per 25 tests; 50¢ per 25 machine-scorable answer sheets; 50¢ per specimen set; 38(65) minutes; L. L. Thurstone and Thelma Gwinn Thurstone; Educational Testing Service.

REFERENCES

1-48. *See* 40:1377.
49. Stalnaker, John M. *A Statistical Study of Some Aspects of the Purdue Orientation Testing Program.* Bulletin of Purdue University, Vol. 28, No. 6; Studies in Higher Education VIII. Lafayette, Ind.: Division of Educational Reference, the University, February 1928. Pp. 68. Paper. $0.20. *
50. Gerberich, J. R. "Validation of a State-Wide Educational Guidance Program for High-School Seniors." *Sch & Soc* 34: 606-10 O '31. * (*PA* 6:1622)
51. Holcomb, G. W., and Laslett, H. R. "A Prognostic Study of Engineering Aptitude." *J Appl Psychol* 16:107-15 Ap '32. * (*PA* 7:4722)
52. Fritz, Ralph A. "Predicting College Marks and Teaching Success for Students in a Teachers College." *J Appl Psychol* 17:439-46 Ag '33. * (*PA* 8:600)
53. Taylor, H. R. "The Effect of Time Interval on the Reliability of ACE Psychological Examination Scores." Abstract. *Psychol B* 32:545-6 O '35. * (*PA* 10:655, title only)
54. Wagner, Mazie Earle, and Strabel, Eunice. "Predicting Success in the College Physical Sciences." *Sci Ed* 19:4-9 F '35. * (*PA* 10:2997)
55. Clements, Dollie. *The Correlation Between the Grade Made on A.C.E. Psychological Examination and the Grade Made by Arts and Sciences Freshmen First Semester.* Unpublished master's thesis, Texas Technological College, 1936.
56. Brooks, Esther. "The Value of Psychological Testing." *Am J Nursing* 37:885-90 Ag '37. *
57. Peiser, Walter Gilbert. *The Prognosis Value of the American Council on Education Psychological Examination.* Unpublished doctor's thesis, Louisiana State University, 1937. (*Abstracts of Theses . . . 1937*, 1938, pp. 18-20.)
58. Quaid, Thomas Dell Doma. *A Study in the Prediction of College Freshman Marks.* Unpublished doctor's thesis, University of Oklahoma, 1937. Pp. xii, 151. (*Abstracts of Theses . . . 1937*, 1939, pp. 20-2.)
59. Wagner, Mazie Earle, and Strabel, Eunice. "Predicting Performance in College English." *J Ed Res* 30:694-9 My '37. * (*PA* 11:3912)
60. Bryan, Alice I., and Perl, Ruth E. "A Comparison of Woman Students Preparing for Three Different Vocations." *J Appl Psychol* 22:161-8 Ap '38. * (*PA* 13:2673)
61. Creutzer, Willard A. *A Study of the Relationship Between Grades Made in Introductory Psychology and Scores Made on the American Council on Education Psychological Examination.* Unpublished master's thesis, University of Pittsburgh, 1938. (*Abstracts of Theses . . . 1938*, pp. 416-7.)
62. Pratt, Karl C. "Intelligence as a Determinant of the 'Functional' Value of Curricular Content." *J Ed Psychol* 29: 44-9 Ja '38. * (*PA* 12:4371)
63. Quaid, T. D. D. "A Study in the Prediction of College Freshman Marks." *J Exp Ed* 6:350-75 Mr '38. * (*PA* 12:6106)
64. Eckermann, Arthur C. *An Attempt to Devise an Inventory to Indicate the Difference Between American Council on Education Test Score and College Grades.* Unpublished master's thesis, Baylor University, 1939.
65. Lott, Hiram V. *A Comparative Study of Five Criteria for Predicting Achievement in Freshman History in the Junior Division at Louisiana State University.* Unpublished master's thesis, Louisiana State University, 1939. (*Abstracts of Theses . . . 1939*, 1940, p. 45.)
66. Martinson, Melvin P. *Predictive Value of the Thurstone Psychological Examination.* Unpublished master's thesis, University of Montana, 1939. Pp. ii, 168.
67. Niemela, Weston A. *Study of Value of American Council on Education Psychology Examination.* Unpublished master's thesis, State College of Washington, 1939. Pp. 28.
68. Sisk, Henry Lybran. *A Multiple Factor Analysis of Mental Abilities in the Freshman Engineering Curriculum.* Unpublished doctor's thesis, Cornell University, 1939. (*Abstracts of Theses . . . 1939*, 1940, pp. 86-7.)
69. Varnado, Gladys R. *A Further Study of the Predictive Value of Various Criteria on Achievement in Freshman Mathematics at Louisiana State University for the Session 1938-1939.* Unpublished master's thesis, Louisiana State University, 1939. (*Abstracts of Theses . . . 1939*, 1940, p. 197.)
70. Bolton, Euri Belle. "Placement Tests in the Guidance Program of College Students." *Peabody J Ed* 17:379-88 My '40. * (*PA* 14:6192)
71. Gearan, John S. *The Reliability of the American Council on Education Psychological Examination.* Unpublished master's thesis, Massachusetts State Teachers College, Fitchburg, 1940. Pp. 54.
72. Greene, Edward B. "Predicting the Student's Success." *J Higher Ed* 11:252-6 My '40. * (*PA* 14:5199)
73. Kirkpatrick, Forrest H. "Four Mental Tests and Freshman Marks." *J Higher Ed* 11:38-9 Ja '40. * (*PA* 14:3215)
74. Leaf, Curtis T. "Prediction of College Marks." *J Exp Ed* 8:303-7 Mr '40. * (*PA* 14:4739)
75. Manuel, H. T.; Adams, F. J.; Jeffress, Sylvia; Tomlinson, Helen; and Gragg, D. B. "The New Stanford-Binet at the College Level." *J Ed Psychol* 31:705-9 D '40. * (*PA* 15:2838)
76. Rarick, Harold J. *Professional Prognostic Value of College Objective Testing With Special Reference to the Bernreuter Personality Inventory and Thurstone's Psychological Examination for College Freshmen.* Unpublished master's thesis, Ball State Teachers College, 1940. Pp. 62.
77. Remmers, H. H., and Geiger, H. E. "Predicting Success and Failure of Engineering Students in the Schools of Engineering in Purdue University," pp. 10-9. In *Studies in Engineering Education.* Purdue University, Division of Educational Reference, Studies in Higher Education, [No.] 38. Lafayette, Ind.: the Division, May 1940. Pp. 33. Paper. $0.35. *
78. Ruedisili, Chester H. "The Relation Between the Subtests of the American Council Psychological Examination, High School Rank, and Four-Year College Subject Grades." Abstract. *Psychol B* 73:573 O '40. * (*PA* 15:547, title only)
79. Traxler, Arthur E. "What Is a Satisfactory I.Q. for Admission to College?" *Sch & Soc* 51:462-4 Ap 6 '40. * (*PA* 14:4273)
80. Addison, Eleanor M. *The Predictive Value of Q and L Scores on the American Council on Education Psychological Examination at the College Freshman Level.* Unpublished master's thesis, Brown University, 1941. Pp. 30.
81. Beaman, Gale C. *The Relationship Between Ability as Measured by the A.C.E. Psychological Examination and Achievement in the Social Studies.* Unpublished master's thesis, University of Kansas, 1941.
82. Froehlich, Gustav J. "Academic Prediction at the University of Wisconsin." *J Am Assn Col Reg* 17:65-76 O '41. *
83. Gifford, Dorothy W. *The Predictive Value of Q and L Scores on the A.C.E. Psychological Examination at the Secondary Level.* Unpublished master's thesis, Brown University, 1941. Pp. 27.
84. Greene, Paul C. "Some Relationships Between Placement Scores and Scholastic Rating." *Proc Iowa Acad Sci* 48: 361-6 '41. * (*PA* 16:2867)
85. Langsam, Rosalind Streep. "A Factorial Analysis of Reading Ability." *J Exp Ed* 10:57-63 S '41. * (*PA* 16:1187)
86. MacPhail, Andrew H., and Foster, Laurence S. "New Data for Placement Procedures." *J Chem Ed* 18:235 My '41. * (*PA* 15:4016)
87. Mason, C. T., and Wilkins, T. B. "Entrance Examinations and Success in College." *J Negro Ed* 10:54-8 Ja '41. * (*PA* 15:3161)
88. Morrow, Robert S. "An Experimental Analysis of the Theory of Independent Abilities." *J Ed Psychol* 32:495-512 O '41. * (*PA* 16:2209)
89. Peterson, B. H. "Can You Predict Who'll Be Able to Go to College." *Sch Executive* 61:26-7 N '41. * (*PA* 16:1202)
90. Schlesser, G. E., and Roberts, R. C. "Selection and Predicting Success in Medical Schools." *J Assn Am Med Col* 16: 282-92 S '41. * (*PA* 16:2079, title only)
91. Schrader, Everett N. *The Predictive Capacity and Validity of the Sub-Tests in the American Council on Education*

Psychological Examinations. Unpublished master's thesis, University of Kansas, 1941.

92. SHANNER, WILLIAM M., AND KUDER, G. FREDERIC. "A Comparative Study of Freshman Week Tests Given at the University of Chicago." *Ed & Psychol Meas* 1:85-92 Ja '41. * (PA 15:2814)

93. SMITH, JOSEPHINE M. "The Prognostic Value of Entrance Tests in a Junior College." *J Ed Psychol* 32:584-92 N '41. * (PA 16:2888)

94. STEVENS, WILLIAM CHARLES. *The Predictive Value of the 1938 American Council on Education Psychological Examination.* Unpublished master's thesis, Vanderbilt University, 1941. (Abstracts of Theses 1941, p. 70.)

95. STOPHER, EMMET C. "The Freshman Testing Program." *J Higher Ed* 12:159-62 Mr '41. * (PA 15:4420)

96. THURSTONE, L. L., AND THURSTONE, THELMA GWINN. *Psychological Examinations, 1940 Norms.* American Council on Education, [Council Staff Reports, Series 5, No. 3]. Washington, D. C.: the Council, [May, 1941]. Pp. [28]. Paper. $0.10. *

97. TRAXLER, ARTHUR E. "The American Council Psychological Examination: Intercorrelations of Scores on the 1938, 1939, and 1940 College Freshman Editions," pp. 69-74. In *1941 Achievement Testing Program in Independent Schools and Supplementary Studies.* Educational Records Bureau. Educational Records Bulletin No. 33. New York: the Bureau, June 1941. Pp. x, 76. Paper, lithotyped. $1.50. * (PA 15:4388)

98. ANDERSON, EDWARD E.; ANDERSON, SARAH FERRALL; FERGUSON, CAROLINE; GRAY, JEAN; HITTINGER, JANE; McKINSTRY, ELEANORE; MOTTER, MARY ELIZABETH; AND VICK, GALE. "Wilson College Studies in Psychology: I, A Comparison of the Wechsler-Bellevue, Revised Stanford, and American Council on Education Tests at the College Level." *J Psychol* 14:317-26 O '42. * (PA 17:981)

99. BRYAN, ALICE I. "Grades, Intelligence and Personality of Art School Freshmen." *J Ed Psychol* 33:50-64 Ja '42. * (PA 16:3186)

100. HARRISON, MARY R. "Intelligence Scores of Prospective Teachers in a Liberal-Arts College." *Sch & Soc* 56:416-20 O 31 '42. * (PA 17:684)

101. HEILMAN, J. D., AND CONGDON, NORA A. "The Influence of College Activities on Intelligence Test Scores." *Ed Adm & Sup* 28:448-56 S '42. * (PA 17:2174)

102. HUNTER, E. C. "Changes in Scores of College Students on the American Council Psychological Examination at Yearly Intervals During the College Course." *J Ed Res* 36:284-91 D '42. * (PA 17:2178)

103. JOHNSON, A. P. *The Prediction of Scholastic Achievement for Freshman Engineering Students at Purdue University.* Purdue University, Division of Educational Research, Studies in Engineering Education II. Lafayette, Ind.: the Division, May 1942. Pp. 22. Paper. $0.35. * (PA 16:5020)

104. JOHNSON, A. P. *The Relationship of Test Scores to Scholastic Achievement for 244 Engineering Freshmen Entering Purdue University in September, 1939.* Unpublished doctor's thesis, Purdue University, 1942.

105. MACPHAIL, ANDREW H. "Q and L Scores on the ACE Psychological Examination." *Sch & Soc* 56:248-51 S 19 '42. * (PA 17:315)

106. NELSON, CHARLES W. "Testing the Influence of Rural and Urban Environment on A.C.E. Intelligence Test Scores." *Am Sociol R* 7:743-51 D '42. * (PA 17:3611)

107. OBERHEIM, GRACE M. "The Prediction of Success of Student Assistants in College Library Work." *Ed & Psychol Meas* 2:379-85 O '42. * (PA 17:1364)

108. RAINIER, RUTH NEELY; REHFELD, FLORENCE WASHBURN; AND MADIGAN, MARIAN E. "The Use of Tests in Guiding Student Nurses." *Am J Nursing* 42:679-82 Je '42. * (PA 16:5029)

109. SCHNEIDLER, GWENDOLEN G., AND BERDIE, RALPH F. "Educational Hierarchies and Scholastic Survival." *J Ed Psychol* 33:199-208 Mr '42. * (PA 16:4181)

110. SHUEY, AUDREY M. "A Comparison of Negro and White College Students by Means of the American Council Psychological Examination." *J Psychol* 14:35-52 Jl '42. * (PA 16:4474)

111. STALNAKER, ELIZABETH M. "A Four Year Study of the Freshman Class of 1935 at the West Virginia University." *J Ed Res* 36:100-18 O '42. * (PA 17:974)

112. THURSTONE, L. L., AND THURSTONE, THELMA GWINN. *Psychological Examinations, 1941 Norms.* American Council on Education Studies, Vol. 6; Council Staff Reports, Series 5, No. 4. Washington, D. C.: the Council, May 1942. Pp. iii, 42. Paper. $0.10. *

113. TRAXLER, ARTHUR E. "Intelligence Quotients Derived from American Council Psychological Examination, College Freshman Edition," pp. 44-50. In *1941 Fall Testing Program in Independent Schools and Supplementary Studies.* Educational Records Bureau, Educational Records Bulletin, No. 35. New York: the Bureau, January 1942. Pp. xiv, 57. Paper. $1.00. * (PA 16:2055)

114. BARNES, MELVIN W. "Gains on the ACE Psychological Examination During the Freshman-Sophomore Years." *Sch & Soc* 57:250-2 F 27 '43. * (PA 17:2155)

115. BARNES, MELVIN W. "The Relationship of the Study of Mathematics to Q-scores on the ACE Psychological Examination." *Sch Sci & Math* 43:581-2 Je '43. * (PA 17:3942)

116. BRADLEY, WILLIAM ARTHUR, JR. "Correlates of Vocational Preferences." *Genetic Psychol Monogr* 28:99-169 N '43. * (PA 18:597)

117. MCGEHEE, WILLIAM. "The Prediction of Differential Achievement in a Technological College." *J Appl Psychol* 27:88-92 F '43. * (PA 17:2893)

118. THURSTONE, L. L., AND THURSTONE, THELMA GWINN. *Psychological Examination for College Freshmen, 1942 Norms.* American Council on Education Studies, Vol. 7; Council Staff Reports, Series 5, No. 6. Washington, D. C.: the Council, May 1943. Pp. v, 32. $0.10. *

119. TRAXLER, ARTHUR E. "Some Comments on 'The Prediction of Differential Achievement in a Technological College'." *J Appl Psychol* 27:176-9 Ap '43. * (PA 17:3603)

120. WELBORN, E. L. "A Study in Changes in Scores on the American Council Psychological Examination During a Three-Year Period." Abstract. *Proc Ind Acad Sci* 52:180 '43. * (PA 18:1255, title only)

121. WOERNER, EDITH MARIE. *High School and American Council of Education Test Rank of University of Nebraska Freshmen as Compared With Their Academic Achievement.* Unpublished master's thesis, University of Nebraska, 1943.

122. FOX, WILLIAM H. *An Analytical Study of January-February (1943) Entering Freshmen at Indiana University.* Bulletin of the School of Education, Indiana University, Vol. 20, No. 1. Bloomington, Ind.: Indiana University Bookstore, January 1944. Pp. 46. Paper. $0.50. * (PA 18:3880)

123. MARSHALL, M. V. "Predicting Success in Freshmen English." *Col Engl* 5:219-21 Ja '44. *

124. THURSTONE, L. L., AND THURSTONE, THELMA GWINN. *Psychological Examination for College Freshmen, 1943 Norms.* American Council on Education Studies, Vol. 8; Council Staff Reports, Series 5, No. 8. Washington, D. C.: the Council, June 1944. Pp. v, 28. Paper. $0.10. *

125. ROLFE, J. F. "The Measurement of Teaching Ability: Study Number Two." *J Exp Ed* 14:52-74 S '45. * (PA 20:1268)

126. ROSTKER, L. E. "The Measurement of Teaching Ability: Study Number One." *J Exp Ed* 14:6-51 S '45. * (PA 20:1269)

127. THURSTONE, L. L., AND THURSTONE, THELMA GWINN. *Psychological Examination for College Freshmen, 1944 Norms.* American Council on Education Studies, Vol. 9; Council Staff Reports, Series 5, No. 9. Washington, D. C.: the Council, May 1945. Pp. v, 29. Paper. $0.10. *

128. TRAXLER, ARTHUR E. "The Correlation Between Two Tests of Academic Aptitude." *Sch & Soc* 61:383-4 Je 9 '45. * (PA 19:3197)

129. WEBER, EDMUND G. "Equating High-School Intelligence Quotients with College Aptitude Test Scores." *J Ed Psychol* 30:443-6 O '45. * (PA 20:1703)

130. WEINTRAUB, RUTH G., AND SALLEY, RUTH E. "Graduation Prospects of an Entering Freshman." *J Ed Res* 39:116-26 O '45. * (PA 20:572)

131. CRAWFORD, ALBERT B., AND BURNHAM, PAUL S. "The American Council Psychological Examination," pp. 90-101. In *Forecasting College Achievement: A Survey of Aptitude Tests for Higher Education: Part I, General Considerations in the Measurement of Academic Promise.* New Haven, Conn.: Yale University Press, 1946. Pp. xxi, 291. $3.75. * (London: Oxford University Press, 1946. 25s.) (PA 20:4331)

132. EMBREE, R. B., JR. "Note on the Estimation of College Aptitude Test Scores From IQ's Derived From Group Intelligence Tests." *J Ed Psychol* 37:502-4 N '46. * (PA 21:1677)

133. FULLER, ELIZABETH MECHEM. "The Use of Measures of Ability and General Adjustments in the Preservice Selection of Nursery School-Kindergarten-Primary Teachers." *J Ed Psychol* 37:321-34 S '46. * (PA 21:1640)

134. MANDELL, MILTON M., AND ADKINS, DOROTHY C. "The Validity of Written Tests for the Selection of Administrative Personnel." *Ed & Psychol Meas* 6:293-312 aut '46. * (PA 21:905)

135. SARTAIN, A. Q. "A Comparison of the New Revised Stanford-Binet, the Bellevue Scale, and Certain Group Tests of Intelligence." *J Social Psychol* 23:237-9 My '46. * (PA 21:309)

136. THURSTONE, L. L., AND THURSTONE, THELMA GWINN. *Psychological Examination for College Freshmen, 1945 Norms.* American Council on Education Studies, Vol. 10; Council Staff Reports, Series 5, No. 10. Washington, D. C.: the Council, May 1946. Pp. iii, 34. Paper. $0.10. *

137. VOTAW, DAVID F. "A Comparison of Test Scores of Entering College Freshmen as Instruments for Predicting Subsequent Scholarship." *J Ed Res* 40:215-8 N '46. * (PA 21:1304)

138. VOTAW, DAVID F. "Regression Lines for Estimating Intelligence Quotients and American Council Examination Scores." *J Ed Psychol* 37:179-81 Mr '46. * (PA 20:3339)

139. BERG, IRWIN AUGUST. "A Study of Success and Failure Among Student Nurses." *J Appl Psychol* 31:389-96 Ag '47. *

140. FLORENCE LOUISE, SISTER M. "Mental Growth and Development at the College Level." *J Ed Psychol* 38:65-82 F '47. * (PA 21:2930)

141. LONIGAN, MARY A. *The Effectiveness of the Otis, the A.C.E. and the Minnesota Speed of Reading Tests for Predicting Success in College.* Unpublished master's thesis, Boston University, 1947. Pp. 49.

142. SLAYMAKER, R. R. "Admission Test Procedure." *J Eng Ed* 37:402-13 Ja '47. * (PA 21:1661)

143. THOMPSON, LOUISE M., AND HAINES, ELEANOR M. "The Relation of College Aptitude Scores to Performance in College Courses." *Can J Psychol* 1:37-40 Mr '47. * (PA 21:3277)

W. D. Commins, Associate Professor of Psychology, The Catholic University of Amer-

ica, Washington, D. C. This is perhaps the test that one is likely to recommend to anyone who is looking for a "good" intelligence test to give to a group of college freshmen. It may be administered in an hour's time and may be scored conveniently through the use of stencils or by machine. Another feature that is likely to appeal to the general user of tests is to be found in its wide use throughout the country. Although the data on the norms and the relative ranking of different types of colleges are not available for each yearly edition until well into the school year, the authors always try beforehand to make the scores experimentally equivalent. The large list of colleges submitting test records to the authors for the purpose of setting up norms is made up, for the great part, of smaller institutions; and while the range of ability in these is considerable, it would be interesting to have many of the larger institutions also represented. Each test is preceded by a practice exercise of the same kind. This is not only desirable on general grounds but is definitely reassuring to the giver of the test if he has doubts about the homogeneity of his group or about their being "test-wise." The division of the score into a Q (quantity or number) partial score and an L (language or verbal) score, with appropriate norms, is a refinement that may be useful on occasion but needs considerable study before its full significance is apparent.

The later yearly editions have improved in general over the early ones in a number of mechanical features as well as in the dropping of the artificial language test. It would seem, however, that the study of the individual items might be carried further. This might be in the direction of the "mental functions" that are supposedly tested by the items constituting each subtest. The psychologist would like the test material to be homogeneous in this respect and is not always satisfied with the exclusive use of a "factor analysis" approach and the disregarding of some kind of "qualitative" analysis. Thus, some items in the completion test of the present edition seem to plumb one's familiarity with relatively uncommon words, as "gill" and "gobbler," while other items seem aimed more at an understanding of the object whose name is sought. This is not the kind of thing that is seriously reflected in the objectively determined validity of a mental test, particularly if used for educational purposes; but because of the wide general acceptability of the present test, it might become the basis for still further "psychological" improvement.

J. P. Guilford, Professor of Psychology, The University of Southern California, Los Angeles, California. This is a member of a series of examinations of like content that have been designed for measuring aptitude at the college level. It is evidently constructed with the usual high quality of workmanship exhibited by all forms of the series.

Its predecessors have commonly shown somewhat lower validities for the prediction of over-all academic achievement than its chief rival, the *Ohio State University Psychological Test*. In this fact there is comparative strength as well as weakness. By incorporating a wider variety of functional content, the ACE test covers a somewhat more diverse list of abilities. This avoids the overweighting of one fundamental resource (verbal ability) to the neglect of others that may be relatively more important in specialized curricula and courses. It is time that the specific aptitudes, in terms of distinct abilities, become much more generally recognized in various academic areas and receive appropriate weights. Academic-aptitude tests should not be restricted to verbal ability, though this may be central, but should be extended to cover all significant qualities. This goal requires optimal assessment of achievement in each type of course, aimed at genuine objectives in those courses. Too often, final grades and achievement examinations reflect a preponderance of verbal variance when the objectives of training really do not. A vicious circle of circumstances has brought to the fore measurements of verbal talent in both aptitude and achievement tests.

This line of thought leads directly to a demand for a more comprehensive battery of "primary-ability" tests. The authors of the examination under discussion are known to be most sympathetic to this point of view. We are therefore led to the conclusion that the present form of the examination is some kind of a compromise with popular demand. To the reviewer it is an unsatisfactory compromise, for the reasons that follow.

The tests in the "linguistic" part of the examination seem to be most heavily saturated with verbal-factor variance. The "quantitative"

American Council on Education Psychological Examination for College Freshmen part is a conglomerate factorially. Besides measuring numerical facility, this part also probably measures three kinds of reasoning as well as other factors to a small degree. It probably would select students with good reasoning abilities, but validity studies might well fail to show this fact because of the manner in which achievement is assessed.

It should be unnecessary, in view of the last paragraph, to use six parts in order to derive two part scores. A vocabulary test would suffice for the linguistic or verbal score. The number-series test could be dispensed with in the "quantitative" part, since it probably adds nothing unique in the way of factors.

Each of the six parts is separately timed. It is the reviewer's belief, without any definitive proof for it, that the factors measured, except for the numerical, should be assessed by means of power tests.

The norms given for these examinations are very extensive, being obtained on a nation-wide scale and covering different types of colleges. The smaller institution is probably overweighted in this.

The authors wisely warn against attempts to make mental-age and IQ equivalents out of the total scores.

For reviews by Anne Anastasi, Jack W. Dunlap, David Segel, and Robert L. Thorndike of earlier forms, see 38:1037 and 40:1377.

[218]
American Council on Education Psychological Examination for High School Students. Grades 9-12; 1933-47; new form issued annually; IBM; separate answer sheets must be used; $2 per 25 tests; 50¢ per 25 machine-scorable answer sheets; 50¢ per specimen set; 35(65) minutes; L. L. Thurstone and Thelma Gwinn Thurstone; Educational Testing Service.

REFERENCES

1-2. *See* 40:1378.
3. KOHN, HAROLD A. "Achievement and Intelligence Examinations Correlated With Each Other and With Teacher's Rankings." *J Genetic Psychol* 52:433-7 Je '38. * (*PA* 13:181)
4. WILMOT, WILBUR GEORGE. *Predictive Significance of A.C.E. Psychological Examinations in High School.* Unpublished master's thesis, University of Oregon, 1938.
5. WOODY, CLIFFORD. *The Sophomore and Freshman Testing Program in the Accredited High Schools of Michigan, 1939.* University of Michigan, School of Education, Bureau of Educational Reference and Research, Bulletin No. 152. Ann Arbor, Mich.: the School, September 1, 1939. Pp. viii, 160. Paper. $0.75. *
6. SARASON, SEYMOUR BERNARD. *The Effects of Training on Four Intelligence Tests.* Unpublished master's thesis, Clark University, 1940. (*Abstracts of Dissertations . . . 1940,* pp. 113-4.)
7. LIVESAY, T. M. "Test Intelligence and Future Vocation of High School Seniors in Hawaii." *J Appl Psychol* 25:679-86 D '41. * (*PA* 16:939)
8. THURSTONE, L. L., AND THURSTONE, THELMA GWINN. *Psychological Examinations, 1940 Norms.* American Council on Education, [Council Staff Reports, Series 5, No. 3.] Washington, D. C.: the Council, [May, 1941]. Pp. [28]. Paper. $0.10. *
9. WOODY, CLIFFORD, AND GATIEN, RAOUL. *The Sophomore and Freshman Testing Program in the Accredited High Schools of Michigan, 1942.* University of Michigan, School of Education, Bureau of Educational Reference and Research, Bulletin No. 155, Ann Arbor, Mich.: the School, March 15, 1943. Pp. x, 197. Paper. $1.25. * (*PA* 18:1258)
See also references for 217.

Carl I. Hovland, Professor of Psychology and Chairman of the Department, Yale University, New Haven, Connecticut. The Thurstones have continued their important contribution to scholastic aptitude testing at the high school level with the 1946 edition of the *American Council on Education Psychological Examination for High School Students.*

In the current edition only one form has been prepared, the answer sheet for which can be either hand- or machine-scored. The two forms, one for machine-scoring and one for hand-scoring, used in previous years caused difficulties with respect to the comparability of norms for the two forms. For hand-scoring, a time-saving scoring board is described, manufactured, and distributed by C. H. Stoelting.

Four types of material are used: (*a*) same-opposite, (*b*) completion, (*c*) arithmetic reasoning, and (*d*) number series. The scores for the first two can be combined to obtain an L-score, indicative of linguistic ability, and the latter two, to give a Q-score for quantitative ability. It is suggested that this breakdown into two factors may be useful in counseling.

The yearly revision of the tests makes it difficult to prepare a maximally useful accompanying manual. Reliabilities and norms cannot be provided at the time the manual is prepared. This may cause considerable inconvenience to small high schools using the tests. Preliminary norms are prepared as soon as cooperating schools send in their data, but heavy bias in selection operates as to which schools submit their data. In recent editions this bias was reduced by getting a somewhat more complete sample of a smaller universe, specifically the state of Illinois. But even here the authors state: "There is also evidence that the schools reporting are not a random sampling of high schools so that the norms based on their reports would not be reliable." (Report of Norms on 1944 Psychological Examination for High School Students.)

No data are available concerning the reliability of the current test. On this point we must rely on data from analogous tests prepared by the same authors and upon their general reputation as careful workers. One would estimate the reliability to be reasonably high, but it would be most helpful if data on reliability were routinely supplied in some form by all constructors of tests.

Validity is based on the a priori relevance of the material to scholastic aptitude and the similarity of the tests to others which have been validated in school situations. The tests have been used in various factor analyses aimed at determining primary mental abilities, and the subdivision of the content into linguistic and quantitative subtests is supported by such analyses. The authors are modest in stating the value of their tests: "While the scores do show roughly the mental alertness of the student, they should not be thought of as measuring mentality with high accuracy. The scores are roughly indicative of the level of mental alertness of the student, but they should not be taken so seriously as to exclude other evidences of intelligence and talent in individual cases." (Manual of Instructions, 1946 Edition.)

For reviews by V. A. C. Henmon and A. H. Turney of earlier forms, see 38:1038 and 40:1378.

[219]

★Army General Classification Test: First Civilian Edition. Grades 9-16 and adults; 1947; commonly called *AGCT*; IBM; Forms AH (hand scored), AM (machine scored); separate answer pads or answer sheets must be used; 45¢ per hand-scored test booklet; $1.65 per 25 hand-scored answer pads; 75¢ per specimen set (Form AH); 35¢ per machine-scored test booklet; $2.35 per 100 machine-scorable answer sheets; $1 per set of machine-scoring keys; 40(55) minutes; Science Research Associates.

REFERENCES
1. *The Inductee's Mental Test.* New York: Arco Publishing Co., 1942. Pp. 31. Paper. $0.25. *
2. *Full-Length Practice Examinations for U.S. Army-Navy Classification Tests: Especially Applicable for Those Desiring a Grade High Enough to Enable Them to Enter Officer Candidate School.* Milwaukee, Wis.: Pergande Publishing Co., 1943. Pp. 99. Lithotyped. $1.65. *
3. *Practice for the Soldier's I.Q. Test.* Cincinnati, Ohio: Practice Publishing Co., 1943. Pp. 65. Paper. $1.00. *
4. BILLETER, PAUL EDWARD. "Predicting Success in Training Army Stenographers." *J Bus Ed* 19:13-4 O '43. *
5. ADJUTANT GENERAL'S OFFICE, CLASSIFICATION AND REPLACEMENT BRANCH, PERSONNEL RESEARCH SECTION. "The Army General Classification Test." *Psychol B* 42:760-8 D '45. * (PA 20:1658)
6. CONOVER, DAVID M. *Certain Relationships Obtaining Between the Army General Classification Test and the Mechanical Aptitude Test and Several Variables.* Unpublished master's thesis, University of Southern California, 1945.
7. HARRELL, THOMAS W., AND HARRELL, MARGARET S. "Army General Classification Test Scores for Civilian Occupations." *Ed & Psychol Meas* 5:229-39 su '45. * (PA 20:2865)
8. CHRISTENSEN, THOMAS E. "Dictionary Classification of the A.G.C.T. Scores for Selected Civilian Occupations." *Occupations* 25:97-101 N '46. * (PA 21:884)
9. HARRELL, THOMAS W. "Army General Classification Test Results for Air Forces Specialists." *Ed & Psychol Meas* 6:341-9 au '46. * (PA 21:893) Abstract *Am Psychol* 1:292-3 Jl '46. *
10. DUNCAN, ACHESON J. "Some Comments on the Army General Classification Test." *J Appl Psychol* 31:143-9 Ap '47. * (PA 21:2798)
11. JENSEN, MILTON B., AND ROTTER, JULIAN B. "The Value of Thirteen Psychological Tests in Officer Candidate Screening." *J Appl Psychol* 31:212-22 Je '47. * (PA 21:4107)
12. STEWART, NAOMI. "A.G.C.T. Scores of Army Personnel Grouped by Occupation." *Occupations* 26:5-41 O '47. * (PA 22:1894)
13. STEWART, NAOMI. "Relationship Between Military Occupational Specialty and Army General Classification Test Standard Score." *Ed & Psychol Meas* 7:677-93 w '47. *
14. WAR DEPARTMENT, ADJUTANT GENERAL'S OFFICE, PERSONNEL RESEARCH SECTION. "The Army General Classification Test: With Special Reference to the Construction and Standardization of Forms 1a and 1b." *J Ed Psychol* 38:385-420 N '47. * (PA 22:1943)

J Consult Psychol 11:339 N-D '47. * Two formats are supplied: IBM machine scoring, and a self-scoring form in a bound booklet of 18 step-down sheets employing a replaceable pin-punch answer sheet similar to the familiar Kuder. Planned as a test of adult learning ability, it uses three types of items, arranged in spiral-omnibus form. Verbal comprehension is measured by vocabulary, quantitative reasoning by arithmetic problems, and spatial thinking by block counting. No part scores are obtained. The reliability of the total score is about .95. Information is given concerning its correlations (.27 to .40) with success in several army training courses. Interpretation is effected by converting raw scores to AGCT standard scores and percentiles. A chart gives the mean and range of scores for each of 125 civilian occupations. The occupational data may be misinterpreted dangerously by poorly trained users, as no indication is given of the much higher predictive value of the test for some occupations than for others. The manual's statement that scores "will indicate aptitude for learning the majority of civilian occupations" seems unjustified in the light of known low validities. Let us hope that this test will escape many of the abuses that the Army Alpha suffered after World War I!

[220]

Army Group Examination Alpha and revisions.
a) ARMY GROUP EXAMINATION ALPHA. Grades 5-16 and adults; released by the War Department for general use in 1919; Forms 5, 6, 7, 8, 9; $1.20 per 25, postpaid; 25¢ per specimen set, postpaid; 22¼ (35-40) minutes; manual revised in 1939 by H. E. Schrammel and E. R. Wood; prepared by the Psychology Committee of the National Research Council; Bureau of Educational Measurements, Kansas State Teachers College of Emporia.
b) BUREAU TEST VI, MENTAL ALERTNESS. Grades 9-16 and adults; 1920-29; 15(20) minutes; out of print.
c) REVISION OF ARMY ALPHA EXAMINATION. Grades 9-16 and adults; 1925-35; Forms A, B; $2.50 per 25, postpaid; 35¢ per specimen set, postpaid; 21⅔ (35-40) minutes; revision by Elsie O. Bregman; Psychological Corporation.
d) SCOVILL CLASSIFICATION TEST. Adults; 1927; 2 parts (Part I is nonverbal, Part II is verbal); $3.75 per 25 copies of Part I, postpaid; $2.70 per 25 copies of Part II, postpaid; 35¢ per specimen set of both parts, postpaid; (30) minutes for Part I; (20) minutes for Part II; prepared by the Scovill Manufacturing Co.; Psychological Corporation.

e) REVISED ALPHA EXAMINATION, FORMS 5 AND 7. Grades 9-12 and adults; 1932-33; Forms 5, 7; $2.50 per 25, postpaid; 35¢ per specimen set, postpaid; 21½(30) minutes; revision by F. L. Wells; Psychological Corporation.

f) REVISED ALPHA EXAMINATION FORM 6, SHORT FORM. Grades 9-16 and high-grade adults; 1933; a short form of the experimental edition of Revised Alpha Examination, Form 6, consisting of subtests 2, 4, 7, and 8; $1.50 per 25, postpaid; 35¢ per specimen set, postpaid; 13½(20) minutes; revision prepared under the supervision of C. R. Atwell and F. L. Wells; Psychological Corporation.

g) ARMY ALPHA EXAMINATION: FIRST NEBRASKA EDITION. Grades 9-16 and adults; 1937; revision of Army Group Examination Alpha; $2.25 per 25; 40¢ per specimen set; 22¼(35) minutes; revision prepared by J. P. Guilford; Sheridan Supply Co.

h) ARMY GROUP EXAMINATION ALPHA: SCHRAMMEL-BRANNAN REVISION. Grades 7-16 and adults; 1936-38; Forms A, B, C; $1.30 per 25, postpaid; 25¢ per specimen set, postpaid; 40(45) minutes; revision by H. E. Schrammel and Christine V. Brannan; Bureau of Educational Measurements, Kansas State Teachers College of Emporia.

i) MODIFIED ALPHA EXAMINATION FORM 9. Grades 7-12 and adults; 1941; separate answer sheets must be used; $4.00 per 25, postpaid; $1.25 per 50 answer sheets, postpaid; 35¢ per specimen set, postpaid; 24(35) minutes; revision by F. L. Wells; Psychological Corporation.

REFERENCES

1. TERMAN, L. M. "The Use of Intelligence Tests in the Army." *Psychol B* 15:177-87 Je '18. *
2. CHURCH, H. V. "Results of Intelligence Tests at the University of Illinois: Alpha Tests Given to Students." *Sch & Soc* 9:542-6 My 3 '19. *
3. FILLER, MERVIN G. "A Psychological Test—Preliminary Survey." *Sch & Soc* 10:208-9 Ag 16 '19. *
4. HUNTER, H. T. "Intelligence Tests At Southern Methodist University." *Sch & Soc* 10:437-40 O 11 '19. *
5. MADSEN, I. N., AND SYLVESTER, R. H. "High School Students' Intelligence Ratings According to the Army Alpha Test." *Sch & Soc* 10:407-10 O 4 '19. *
6. ROBERTS, GEORGE L., AND BRANDENBURG, G. C. "The Army Intelligence Tests At Purdue University." *Sch & Soc* 10:776-8 D 27 '19. *
7. WALCOTT, GREGORY D. "Mental Testing at Hamline University." *Sch & Soc* 10:57-60 Jl 12 '19. *
8. ANDERSON, JOHN E. "Intelligence Tests of Yale Freshmen." *Sch & Soc* 11:417-20 Ap 3 '20. *
9. BRIDGES, J. W. "The Correlation Between College Grades and the Alpha Intelligence Tests." *J Ed Psychol* 11:361-7 O '20. *
10. BURTT, H. E., AND ARPS, G. F. "Correlation of Army Alpha Intelligence Test With Academic Grades in High Schools and Military Academies." *J Appl Psychol* 4:289-93 D '20. *
11. JONES, EDWARD S. "The Army Tests and Oberlin College Freshmen." *Sch & Soc* 11:389-90 Mr 27 '20. *
12. MADSEN, I. N. "The Army Intelligence Test as a Means of Prognosis in High School." *Sch & Soc* 11:625-7 My 22 '20. *
13. MADSEN, I. N. "High School Students' Intelligence Ratings According to the Army Alpha Test." *Sch & Soc* 11:298-300 Mr 6 '20. *
14. NOBLE, ELLIS L., AND ARPS, GEORGE F. "University Students' Intelligence Ratings According to the Army Alpha Test." *Sch & Soc* 11:233-7 F 21 '20. *
15. RUCH, G. M., AND STRACHAN, LEXIE. "Intelligence Ratings by Group Scales and by the Stanford Revision of the Binet Tests." *J Ed Psychol* 11:421-9 N '20. *
16. VAN WAGENEN, M. J. "Some Results and Inferences Derived From the Use of the Army Tests at the University of Minnesota." *J Appl Psychol* 4:59-72 Mr '20. *
17. WEBB, L. W. "Ability in Mental Tests in Relation to Reading Ability." *Sch & Soc* 11:567-70 My 8 '20. *
18. WENTWORTH, MARY M. "Army Alpha Tests and Teachers' Estimates in Hollywood High School." *Sch & Soc* 12:58-60 Jl 10 '20. *
18a. YOAKUM, CLARENCE S., AND YERKES, ROBERT M., EDITORS. *Army Mental Tests*, pp. 79-92, 276-84, and passim. New York: Henry Holt and Co., 1920. Pp. xiii, 303. Out of print. *
19. BENSON, C. E. "The Results of the Army Alpha Test in a Teacher-Training Institution." *Ed Adm & Sup* 7:348-9 S '21. *
20. BILLS, M. A. "A Test for Use in the Selection of Stenographers." *J Appl Psychol* 5:372-7 D '21. *
21. DAVIS, HOMER. "Army Alpha and Students' Grades: Illustrating the Value of the Regression Equation." *Sch & Soc* 14:223-7 S 24 '21. *
22. DECAMP, J. E. "Studies in Mental Tests: Army Alpha, Thurstone IV, and Binet-Simon (SR)." *Sch & Soc* 14:353-8 O 1 '21. *
23. HANSEN, C. F., AND REAM, M. J. "The Predictive Value of Short Intelligence Tests." *J Appl Psychol* 5:184-5 Je '21. *
24. LUFKIN, H. M. "Report of the Use of the Army Alpha Test in Rural Schools." *Sch & Soc* 13:27-30 Ja 1 '21. *
25. PETERSON, H. A., AND KUDERNA, J. G. "Army Alpha in the Normal Schools." *Sch & Soc* 13:476-80 Ap 16 '21. *
25a. YERKES, ROBERT M., EDITOR. *Psychological Examining in the United States Army*, pp. 162-7, 235-58, 368-95, 466-8, and passim. Memoirs of the National Academy of Sciences, Vol. 15. Washington, D. C.: Government Printing Office, 1921. Pp. vi, 890. Out of print. *
26. JORDAN, A. M. "Correlations of Four Intelligence Tests With Grades." *J Ed Psychol* 13:419-29 O '22. *
27. STONE, CHARLES LEONARD. "The Significance of Alpha in Colleges." *J Ed Psychol* 13:298-302 My '22. *
28. VITELES, MORRIS S. "A Comparison of Three Tests of 'General Intelligence'." *J Appl Psychol* 6:391-402 D '22. *
29. JORDAN, A. M. "The Validation of Intelligence Tests." *J Ed Psychol* 14:348-66, 414-28 S, O '23. *
30. MCGEOCH, JOHN A. "Some Results From Three Group Intelligence Tests." *Sch & Soc* 17:196 F 17 '23. *
31. RUCH, G. M., AND KOERTH, WILHELMINE. "'Power' vs. 'Speed' in Army Alpha." *J Ed Psychol* 14:193-208 Ap '23. *
32. BINGHAM, W. V., AND DAVIS, W. T. "Intelligence Test Scores and Business Success." *J Appl Psychol* 8:1-22 Mr '24. *
33. MILLER, W. S. "The Variation and Significance of Intelligence Quotients Obtained From Group Tests." *J Ed Psychol* 15:359-66 S '24. *
34. MANSON, GRACE E. "Personality Differences in Intelligence Test Performance." *J Appl Psychol* 9:230-55 S '25. *
35. OWENS, WILLIAM A. "On a Certain Value of the Thurstone (American Council on Education) Tests in Predicting Scholarship." *Ed Adm & Sup* 13:495-9 O '27. *
36. STEIN, MARTIN L. "A Trial With Criteria of the MacQuarrie Test of Mechanical Ability." *J Appl Psychol* 11:391-3 O '27. * (*PA* 2:2964)
37. JONES, ALFRED H. "The Prognostic Value of the Low Range Army Alpha Scores." *J Ed Psychol* 20:539-41 O '29. * (*PA* 4:409)
38. KELLOGG, CHESTER E. "Relative Values of Intelligence Tests and Matriculation Examinations as Means of Estimating Probable Success in College." *Sch & Soc* 30:893-6 D 28 '29. * (*PA* 4:856)
39. WOODALL, CHAS. S. "The Army Alpha Test Applied to Mental Defectives." *J Psycho-Asthenics* 34:82-99 '29. * (*PA* 4:4366)
40. HENDRICKSON, GORDON. "A Useful Abbreviation of Army Alpha." *Sch & Soc* 33:467-8 Ap 4 '31. * (*PA* 5:3303)
41. HALES, NORA M. *An Advanced Test of General Intelligence: A Report on the Revision, Extension, and Standardization of a Form of the American Army Examination Alpha.* Foreword by A. H. Martin. Australian Council for Educational Research, Educational Research Series, No. 11. Melbourne, Australia: Melbourne University Press, 1932. Pp. 64. Paper. 3s. 6d. * (*PA* 7:376)
42. WECHSLER, DAVID. "Analytic Use of the Army Alpha Examination." *J Appl Psychol* 16:254-6 Je '32. * (*PA* 7:4210)
43. WELLS, F. L. "Army Alpha—Revised." *Personnel J* 10:411-7 Ap '32. * (*PA* 6:3032)
44. ATWELL, CHARLES R., AND WELLS, F. L. "Army Alpha Revised—Short Form." *Personnel J* 12:160-3 O '33. * (*PA* 8:1844)
45. CONRAD, H. S.; JONES, H. E.; AND HSIAO, H. H. "Sex Differences in Mental Growth and Decline." *J Ed Psychol* 24:161-9 Mr '33. * (*PA* 7:4177)
46. MILLER, W. S. "Variation of IQ's Obtained From Group Tests." *J Ed Psychol* 24:468-74 S '33. * (*PA* 8:662)
47. NEMZEK, CLAUDE L. "Intelligence Testing at the College Level." *J Ed Res* 26:617-8 Ap '33. * (*PA* 7:4196)
48. POND, MILLICENT, AND BILLS, MARION A. "Intelligence and Clerical Jobs Held: Two Studies of Relation of Test Scores to Job Held." *Personnel J* 12:41-56 Je '33. * (*PA* 7:4734)
49. ACHILLES, P. S., AND SCHULTZ, R. S. "Characteristics of Life Insurance Salesmen." *Personnel J* 12:260-3 F '34. * (*PA* 8:2217)
50. JORGENSEN, C. "Analysis of Some Psychological Tests by the Spearman Factor Method." *Brit J Ed Psychol* 4:96-109 F '34. * (*PA* 8:4318)
51. MOORE, HERBERT, AND TRAFTON, HELEN. "Equating Test Scores." *J Ed Psychol* 25:216-9 Mr '34. * (*PA* 8:3827)
52. FINCH, F. H. "Equating Intelligence Quotients From Group Tests." *J Ed Res* 28:580-92 Ap '35. * (*PA* 9:3920)
53. LORGE, IRVING. "A Table of Percentile Equivalents for Eight Intelligence Tests Frequently Used With Adults." *J Appl Psychol* 20:392-5 Je '36. * (*PA* 10:5552)
54. ATWELL, C. R. "Relationship of Scores and Errors on the Army Alpha Test." *J Appl Psychol* 21:451-5 Ag '37. * (*PA* 12:961)
55. BAKER, CLYDE WILLIAM. *Schrammel-Brannan Revision of Army Alpha Test, Validity.* Unpublished master's thesis, Kansas State Teachers College of Emporia, 1937. Pp. 33. (*An Annotated Bibliography of Dissertations . . . 1929-1939*, 1939, p. 30.)
56. DAVIDSON, CHARLES M. "Analysis of Clerical Tests." *Personnel J* 16:95-8 S '37. * (*PA* 11:5916)

57. Davidson, Charles M. "Evaluation of Clerical Tests." *Personnel J* 16:57-64 Je '37. * (PA 11:4713)
58. Finch, F. H., and Odoroff, M. E. "The Reliability of Certain Group Intelligence Tests." *J Appl Psychol* 21:102-6 F '37. * (PA 11:4818)
59. Schmitz, Sylvester B. "Predicting Success in College: A Study of Various Criteria." *J Ed Psychol* 28:465-73 S '37. * (PA 12:538)
60. Davidson, Charles M. "Permanency of Mental Alertness Measures." *J Appl Psychol* 22:307-10 Je '38. * (PA 12:6667)
61. Guilford, J. P. "A New Revision of the Army Alpha Examination and a Weighted Scoring for Three Primary Factors." *J Appl Psychol* 22:239-46 Je '38. * (PA 12:6668)
62. Macvaugh, Gilbert S. "Regression Formula to Predict Educational Ages From Revised Alpha Scores." *J Appl Psychol* 22:275-81 Je '38. * (PA 12:6670)
63. Hartman, A. A. "A Comparison of the Ratings of Mentally Retarded Prisoners on Army Alpha and Stanford-Binet." *J Appl Psychol* 23:608-11 O '39. * (PA 14:1106)
64. Macvaugh, Gilbert S. "Centile and T-Scale Norms for Revised Alpha Examination, Form 5." *J Appl Psychol* 23:720-2 D '39. * (PA 14:2641)
65. Failor, Leona Mae. *An Evaluation of Intelligence Tests Used in Industrial Schools and Reformatories.* Unpublished doctor's thesis, University of Nebraska, 1940. (*Abstracts of Doctoral Dissertations* . . ., 1940, pp. 59-65.)
66. Hay, Edward N., and Blakemore, Arline M. "Comparison of Otis and Alpha Test Scores Made by Bank Clerks." *J Appl Psychol* 26:850-1 D '42. * (PA 17:2917)
67. Mitrano, Anthony J. "The Relationship Between Age and Test Performance of Applicants to a Technical-Industrial High School." *J Appl Psychol* 26:482-6 Ag '42. * (PA 17:2498)
68. Bennett, George K. "Distribution of Scores From Revisions of Army Alpha." *J Appl Psychol* 27:150-1 Ap '43. * (PA 17:3607)
69. Hay, Edward N. "Predicting Success in Machine Bookkeeping." *J Appl Psychol* 27:483-93 D '43. * (PA 18:1677)
70. Wells, Frederic L., and Savage, Beatrice M. "Normative Data for Consultative Use of a Modified Alpha Procedure." *J Consult Psychol* 7:171-8 Jl-Ag '43. * (PA 17:4286)
71. Morgan, W. J. "Some Remarks and Results of Aptitude Testing in Technical and Industrial Schools." *J Social Psychol* 20:19-29 Ag '44. * (PA 19:556)
72. Demand, J. W. "Correlations Between Scores on the Modified Alpha Examination Form 9 and Grades in Various High School Subjects." *Trans Kan Acad Sci* 47:417-8 '45. *
73. Rabin, A. I., and Weinik, H. M. "The Nebraska Army Alpha Revision and the Comparative Strength of Factors *V*, *N*, and *R* in Nursing Students." *J General Psychol* 34:197-202 Ap '46. * (PA 20:4385)
74. Sartain, A. Q. "A Comparison of the New Revised Stanford-Binet, the Bellevue Scale, and Certain Group Tests of Intelligence." *J Social Psychol* 23:237-9 My '46. * (PA 21:309)
75. Sartain, A. Q. "Predicting Success in a School of Nursing." *J Appl Psychol* 30:234-40 Je '46. * (PA 20:4350)

For a review by W. D Commins of the Army Alpha Examination: First Nebraska Edition, see 38:1039. For a review by W. D. Commins of the Army Group Examination Alpha: Schrammel–Brannan Revision, see 38:1040.

[221]

★[Benge Employment Tests.] Adults; 1942; 1 form; 2 levels; $3 per introductory set including 10 tests, postpaid; 5¢ per extra test, postpaid; introductory sets may be ordered on approval; Eugene J. Benge; Management Service Co.
a) EMPLOYMENT TEST, FORM B. Adults with an eighth-grade education or less; 12(20) minutes.
b) BASIC EMPLOYMENT TEST. Adults with more than an eighth-grade education; 22(30) minutes.

Brent Baxter, *Director of Personnel Research, Chesapeake and Ohio Railway Company, Cleveland, Ohio.* This pair of tests was designed for industrial and business use in measuring intelligence; they are the outgrowth of service to industrial clients.

The test items resemble those of most group verbal intelligence tests. The author reports that "The Basic Test correlates with Otis Advanced between .80 to .85." The items are classified as memory, numbers, vocabulary, spatial perception, and reasoning, with a profile chart being made for these aspects. No data are available to the reviewer on the interrelationship of these parts or on their reliability or validity. For Form B there are only ten possible items on each factor; this suggests that the part scores are not likely to be too reliable. The different kinds of items are arranged in spiral order, which makes the scoring more complicated and subject to error.

The test manual provides no data for the evaluation of the tests. A personal letter from the test author suggests that a great deal of data has been collected for many years but that it has never been assembled. But, "we have made no reliability studies of the Basic test whatsoever." It would appear that the tests can be sold in industry without offering any scientific statistical data, a reflection upon industry and test salesmen rather than upon the tests.

It is understood that these tests are usually sold as part of a management service, and it is therefore assumed that normally more help on interpretation and use is given to the test user than is offered in the manual. The manual merely suggests that the tests be tried out locally to see if they discriminate between better and poorer workers. Then local "job standards" for rejecting potential failures should be set up. No help is given for establishing these job standards.

Decile norms are given for "usual applicants." Such a generality can certainly lead to wide errors, especially since the test author privately writes that for the *Basic Employment Test* the norms are for a sampling of "clerical, supervisory, and executive positions in industry." No provision is made for the wide variety of skilled and semiskilled positions. The manual also suggests a change in time limits without changing the norms.

Without data an adequate over-all evaluation of the tests cannot be made. On the surface they appear similar to other intelligence tests in industrial use. Their only unique feature is the attempted measurement of five separate factors. While these factors are probably properly evaluated, is worth considering in industry. not reliably measured, this kind of approach,

Marion A. Bills, Assistant Secretary, Aetna Life Insurance Company, Hartford, Connecicut. BASIC EMPLOYMENT TEST. This test consists of 100 items of five types—information, arithmetic, vocabulary, spatial perception, and reasoning—arranged in cyclic order. The directions are clear except that no examples are given of the spatial perception types of item. The author assumes that the different types of items may be scored separately, thereby giving a profile of the individual's ability. This practice is questionable since the testee may have devoted much more time to some types of items than to others. Some of the items are of the puzzle type which might well increase this hazard. No validating data are given, and the author sounds warning that each company should give the test to workers of proved ability and set up its own standards.

The advantages of the test are that it is a short, self-administering test which avoids being resented by an applicant as an intelligence test because of its name. For jobs where spatial relations are essential, the test would have an advantage over tests not including this type of item. The test has the disadvantage of all time-limit spiral tests in that individual types of ability cannot be accurately scored separately.

EMPLOYMENT TEST, FORM B. This test consists of 50 items of the same five types but much less difficult. No questions of the puzzle type are included. The test is a simple, self-administering, short, very easy mental alertness test which is not immediately recognized as an intelligence test. Disadvantages of the test are that it should not be scored for the various types of items, since the time devoted to any one type is not known and that it is too easy to discriminate between people of fair to good mental alertness, regardless of education.

[222]
★California Capacity Questionnaire. Grades 7–16 and adults; 1941–42; IBM; an abbreviated adaptation of *California Test of Mental Maturity*; Forms A, B; Elizabeth T. Sullivan, Willis W. Clark, and Ernest W. Tiegs; California Test Bureau.
a) HAND SCORING EDITION. 1941; $1.20 per 25; 35¢ per specimen set; 30(40) minutes.
b) MACHINE SCORING EDITION. 1942; 6¢ per test; 2¢ per machine-scorable answer sheet; 35(45) minutes.

Anne Anastasi, Associate Professor of Psychology, Fordham University, New York, New York. This 30-minute, self-administering test yields verbal, nonverbal, and total IQ's for ages 11 up. Its two equivalent forms are available in hand-scoring as well as IBM machine-scoring editions. The 132 items comprising each form are grouped into seven subtests administered with a single over-all time limit of 30 minutes. Some effort has been made to equalize the distribution of content throughout the test, the different types of items (with the exception of right-left orientation) recurring at least twice in successive subtests with increasing difficulty level. It is doubtful, however, whether this expedient has allowed adequately for the use of a single over-all time limit. A subject who is poor in right-left orientation, for example, may spend so much time on the more difficult items of Test 1 as to be seriously handicapped on the other types of items —or one who experiences difficulty with the manipulation of areas in Test 3 may never reach some of the later vocabulary items in which he might have excelled. The effect of the present arrangement of items is therefore to minimize any existing difference between the subject's ability in the verbal and nonverbal parts, which are scored separately. In reference to mechanical layout, it might be noted that some of the pictures used in the spatial items are very small and indistinct, a few being difficult to recognize.

MA equivalents for verbal, nonverbal, and total raw scores are furnished, but no information is given about the size or composition of the groups from which these mental age norms were derived. The use of the MA and the IQ in a test which is not an age scale is open to criticism. There are certain well-known statistical conditions which an intelligence test must meet in order to yield a constant IQ, conditions which most group scales fail to meet. The authors give no indication that the present test meets these conditions. Moreover, since this test is oriented in large part toward adult testing, the IQ is especially unsuitable. The table of norms gives MA's ranging up to 32 years! It is also rather startling to find percentile equivalents for the IQ's. One wonders why such percentiles are not computed directly from the raw scores.

Spearman–Brown reliability coefficients of .925 for the total test, .900 for verbal subscores, and .703 for nonverbal subscores were found on "320 persons" whose ages and other characteristics are not stated. The correlation between verbal and nonverbal subscores (presumably on the same group?) is .45. The items of the present test were chosen from the much longer and more comprehensive *California Test of Mental Maturity,* Intermediate and Advanced Series. In discussing validity, the authors report a correlation of .835 between the present test and the *California Short-Form Test of Mental Maturity* (N = 121). The present test correlates .821 (N = 129) with the *Kuhlmann-Anderson Intelligence Test.* These correlations are difficult to evaluate since the characteristics of the subjects are unknown. Among children, for example, the large general factor usually found at the lower age levels may result in high correlations between tests which among older groups yield low, negligible correlations. For the proper interpretation of the given correlations, the degree of homogeneity of the group should also be known.

No further data on validity are discussed in the manual. General references are made to the "exacting tryout" of items in all parts of the country as well as to the sampling of aptitudes which were identified through factor analysis. None of these data, however, are presented either in the present manual or in those of the earlier forms. Nor are specific references to the literature cited. The general vagueness and ambiguity of sources is also illustrated by a table (p. 6) showing the expected percentile ranks in such basic skills as reading comprehension and arithmetic fundamentals in relation to median IQ for the class or school. In giving the derivation of this table, the authors state only that it is "based upon over 100 school surveys and 48,000 individual measurements." In the absence of any statement to the contrary, the reader may well be left with the impression that these data were obtained with the present test. The identical table, however, is printed in the manual of the earlier *California Tests of Mental Maturity* with the identical explanation. Finally, the authors' effort to sample the various mental "factors" uniformly may have resulted in an instrument of lower validity than the usual predominantly verbal intelligence test. There is a growing realization that verbal ability plays a major part in many of the practical achievements which intelligence tests try to predict. For maximum validity, therefore, the tests themselves may have to be overloaded with verbal ability.

Emily T. Burr, Director, Guidance Bureau, Inc., New York, New York. This test, devised in response to the need for a short, easily administered, and dependable measure of mental ability, is a welcome addition to the testing field. It takes but 30 minutes and is self-administering, thus satisfying the first two requirements. Another of its distinct advantages is the fact that it is possible to derive separate mental ages in the area of language and nonlanguage ability. This is of significant value when a counselor is seeking to ascertain an individual's assets so that suitable educational and vocational advice may be offered.

The questionnaire is composed of tests to determine perceptual ability, memory, spatial orientation, logical reasoning and inference, mathematical reasoning, and practical ideas. It thus reveals a wide sampling of abilities that are basic to the understanding of relationships and situations.

Besides statements regarding the validation of the tests, the manual includes interesting and helpful lists of jobs that may be performed by persons of very superior, superior, high average, low average, and inferior ability. These lists give the counselor pertinent and most valuable information that always proves enlightening in a practical discussion with the applicant who is trying to decide for what occupation he should aim. This factual material, however, must be used wisely and with discrimination. Test results alone cannot solve a guidance problem. Physique, health, age, training, experience, appearance, and interest are among the essential characteristics to be checked.

As the demand for scientific aid in the selection of employees in industry increases, such tests as these will become more and more valuable. For this highly specialized purpose, it is desirable that critical scores be determined by means of careful, thorough research. We shall profit by knowing the minimum score which will enable a man to make good on a particular aspect of a certain occupation. As data regarding success or failure on a job is tabulated and checked with the results of tests administered to that individual previously, we shall have at our disposal a large amount of fundamental knowledge about tests that will greatly facilitate our guidance service.

This questionnaire, standardized after years of careful and extensive research, is a fitting

California Capacity Questionnaire

tool to be used for such a survey. Large numbers of persons from all social and economic levels, living in various sections of the United States have taken part in its formation, so that it appears to be based on the responses of people throughout the country as a whole.

Credit for this excellent piece of practical research must be given to Dr. Ernest W. Tiegs, formerly Dean of University College and Professor of Education at the University of Southern California; to Dr. Elizabeth T. Sullivan, Senior Educational Psychologist of the Los Angeles Schools; and to Willis W. Clark, Research and Guidance Consultant, Los Angeles. These three are among the most experienced and best qualified psychologists who could have undertaken the task. One cannot but have faith in the effectiveness and validity of their results.

[223]

California Test of Mental Maturity. Grades kgn-1, 1-3, 4-8, 7-10 and adults, 9-adults; 1936-46; 1 form; 35¢ per specimen set of any one edition at any one level; 3¢ per answer sheet for the highest three levels; Elizabeth T. Sullivan, Willis W. Clark, and Ernest W. Tiegs; California Test Bureau.
a) CALIFORNIA TEST OF MENTAL MATURITY: 1946 REVISION. 1936-46; $2 per 25; (90) minutes.
b) CALIFORNIA SHORT-FORM TEST OF MENTAL MATURITY. 1938-42; $1.20 per 25; 6¢ per copy of machine-scoring edition for the highest three levels; (45) minutes.
c) CALIFORNIA INTELLIGENCE TEST: LANGUAGE SECTION. 1942-43; same as language section in *California Test of Mental Maturity;* 1943; $1.20 per 25; 6¢ per copy of machine-scoring edition for the highest three levels; (45-50) minutes.
d) CALIFORNIA INTELLIGENCE TEST: NON-LANGUAGE SECTION. 1942-43; same as nonlanguage section of *California Test of Mental Maturity;* $1.50 per 25; 6¢ per copy of machine-scoring edition for the highest three levels; (45-50) minutes.

REFERENCES

1-5. See 40:1384.
6. McDONALD, DAVID. *The Relation Between Test Intelligence and Test Achievement in Grade Six.* Unpublished doctor's thesis, University of Oregon, 1938. (*Graduate Theses . . . 1932-42,* 1946, pp. 29-31.)
7. FAILOR, LEONA MAE. *An Evaluation of Intelligence Tests Used in Industrial Schools and Reformatories.* Unpublished doctor's thesis, University of Nebraska, 1940. (*Abstracts of Doctoral Dissertations . . . , 1940,* pp. 59-65.)
8. BAILEY, ALBERT ERNEST. *The Relative Validity of Ten Different Intelligence Tests.* Unpublished doctor's thesis, University of Washington, 1942. (*Abstracts of Theses . . . 1942,* 1943, p. 189.)
9. NELSON, A. GORDON. *The Value of Certain Tests of Differentiated Abilities for the Diagnosis and Prognosis of Achievement.* Unpublished doctor's thesis, New York University, 1943. Pp. 168. (*Abstracts of Theses . . . [School of Education] 1943,* pp. 149-55.)
10. STRANG, RUTH. "Relationships Between Certain Aspects of Intelligence and Certain Aspects of Reading." *Ed & Psychol Meas* 3:355-9 w '43. * (*PA* 18:2606)
11. WOODY, CLIFFORD. *Guidance Implications From Measurements of Achievements, Aptitudes and Interests.* University of Michigan, School of Education, Bureau of Educational Reference and Research, Bulletin No. 156. Ann Arbor, Mich.: the School, September 1, 1944. Pp. viii, 162. Paper. $1.25. * (*PA* 20:573)
12. KNEZEVICH, STEPHEN J. "The Constancy of the IQ of the Secondary School Pupil." *J Ed Res* 39:506-16 Mr '46. * (*PA* 20:3329)
13. ORDAHL, VIDA ELLISON. *An Intercomparison of the Otis Self-Administered Test of Mental Ability, Intermediate Form A; the Stanford-Binet Intelligence Scale, Form-L; and the California Test of Mental Maturity, Elementary S-Form.* Unpublished master's thesis, University of Southern California, 1946.
14. BOLTON, FLOYD B. "Value of Several Intelligence Tests for Predicting Scholastic Achievement." *J Ed Res* 41:133-8 O '47. * (*PA* 22:2327)
15. ONARHEIM, JAMES. "Scientific Selection of Sales Engineers." *Personnel* 24:24-34 Jl '47. *

Henry E. Garrett, Professor of Psychology, Columbia University, New York, New York. These tests consist of five batteries designed to cover the range of mental ability from kindergarten to college. Each battery contains sixteen subtests described as measuring memory, spacial relations, reasoning, and vocabulary, as well as tests of visual and auditory acuity and of motor coordination. Age norms are supplied from which MA's and IQ's may be determined for the language and nonlanguage tests separately and for the test battery as a whole. A diagnostic profile permits one to appraise the relative strengths and weaknesses of the examinee in the various subtest groups.

Several comments *pro* and *con* may be offered with regard to this test battery: (*a*) Information concerning the test is quite complete; directions for administering and scoring, data on reliability, age norms, relations to tests of school progress, and the like are adequate. (*b*) The pictorial tests are clear and well designed. (*c*) The tests of visual and auditory acuity and of motor coordination are undoubtedly useful additions to the examination.

Criticisms of the test may be summarized as follows: (*a*) The authors offer no evidence to show that their test batteries are so constructed as to fulfill the conditions of IQ constancy. The IQ, thought of as a developmental ratio, has little or no meaning when used with adults and is always suspect when calculated from group tests. It would have been far better if some other type of score had been employed. (*b*) No evidence is offered to show that the particular "factors" ostensibly measured by the subtests are independent or quasi-independent variables. If they are, the total score (IQ), of course, has no meaning. Use of the term "mental factor" to describe a test group is in a sense a misnomer as the term "factor" has come to be identified with an ability-cluster located through factor analysis. (*c*) The test user must remember that the labeling of groups of tests as measures of logical reasoning, spacial relations, and the like is very often simply a common sense divination as to probable function. Such classifications may be practically useful but other groupings might be proposed with as much justification. The authors should provide more evidence as to the validity of their categories than a few references to factor studies. (*d*) The authors state that it is their desire to break down the IQ into its component parts. This is a laudable ambition. But it is doubtful whether two tests of memory are sufficient to give a valid measure of memory and whether there are enough subtests in the other groupings to provide an adequate basis for differential judgment. The score derived from the test battery as a whole is probably the most valid measure of mental level which the tests yield.

Am J Psychiatry 97:993 Ja '41. W. Line. [Review of *California Short-Form Test of Mental Maturity.*] * The standardization appears to be indicative rather than final, and the claims for the tests are based partly upon factor analysis. The subdivision into Language and Non-Language categories would seem to be most pertinent at the lower level, and should everywhere be used with caution. The manuals give clear directions, and reflect the authors' point of view on the nature of intellectual development. This point of view, called a multiple-factor theory of intelligence, is not sufficiently elaborated to be harmful. The tests themselves will probably prove to be quite useful, particularly at the intermediate level, and under circumstances that normally give reliable results.

J Consult Psychol 11:156 My-Je '47. The chief features of this test are its analysis into language and nonlanguage abilities, and into five factors (memory, spatial relationships, logical reasoning, numerical reasoning, and vocabulary), on all of which useful scores can be obtained. * A pretest detects children whose visual and auditory acuity, and motor coordination, might be so handicapped as to influence the results. * Validity is chiefly inferred, but a correlation of .88 with the Stanford–Binet Test is stated, for an unspecified level and range. * The large amount of nonverbal material, even at the higher levels, is a distinctive and commendable feature of this test.

For reviews by Raymond B. Cattell, W. D. Commins, F. Kuhlmann, Rudolf Pintner, and Arthur E. Traxler, and excerpts from reviews by David Kopel and one other, see 38:1042 and 40:1384.

[224]
Carnegie Mental Ability Tests: Clapp-Young Self-Marking Tests. Grades 9-16; 1932; Form A; separate answer booklets must be used; $2.75 per 25 sets of test and answer booklets; 90¢ per 25 answer booklets; 12¢ per specimen set, postpaid; 65(90) minutes; Glen U. Cleeton; Houghton Mifflin Co.

REFERENCES

1. FISHER, HOWARD R. *A Study in Prediction of Success in College Chemistry.* Unpublished master's thesis, University of Arizona, 1940. Pp. 34. (*Abstracts of Theses . . . 1940, 1941*, pp. 27-8.)
2. CRAWFORD, JOHN EDMUND. *Measurement of Some Factors Upon Which is Based Achievement in Elementary Machine Detail Drafting.* Unpublished doctor's thesis, University of Pittsburgh, 1941. (*Abstracts of Theses . . . 1941, 1942*, pp. 85-93.)
3. GARRETT, WILEY S. "The Number Relations Section of the Carnegie Mental Ability Tests Treated as a Power Test." *Ed & Psychol Meas* 7:309-18 su '47. * (PA 22:1097)

W. D. Commins, Associate Professor of Psychology, The Catholic University of America, Washington, D. C. Although the manual for this test does not give all the information desirable for its evaluation, such as the character of and number in the groups employed in its standardization, the reported coefficients of validity (based on scholastic records in college) and of reliability are high, the former ranging from .50 to .70 and the latter being .95. It would appear, however, from the nature of the test that it is heavily loaded with science and mathematics items and would perhaps find its chief use in predicting scholarship in engineering schools.

The time required for administration probably runs close to two hours, which would probably make it less available for general college use. It enjoys, however, the Clapp–Young self-marking feature, making for ease of scoring.

Although each item was checked against scholarship records of students before being chosen for the test, it does not seem that the items have been sufficiently well scaled. Certain items in the latter part of a subtest are not obviously of greater difficulty than those appearing in the earlier part. The information items seem at times to be largely "verbal," such as "the toad is a mammal," or "the larynx functions in speech," and would apparently need reworking. A fresh revision of the test would improve it considerably.

Separate scores are obtainable on the Word Relations Test and on the Number Relations Tests, a feature of definite utility at times. The inclusion of two tests of High School Information probably increases the accuracy of predicting college grades when the academic background of the students is similar, but would be of more doubtful value when a large variety of high schools is represented.

Robert L. Thorndike, Associate Professor of Education, Teachers College, Columbia University, New York, New York. This test was developed for the specific purpose of predicting academic achievement. The purpose should perhaps be defined even more narrowly than that as prediction of academic success in the freshman year of a pre-engineering curriculum. It is reported that each test item was retained only if it individually yielded some discrimination between individuals at different levels of academic achievement as defined above. The test has, therefore, primarily a pragmatic rather than a theoretical basis. This pragmatic interest has led to the combining of subtests of the more general "aptitude" type with tests covering information specifically taught in school courses. It is the contention of the author of the test that a combination of the two types of material permits a better prediction of academic achievement than either taken alone. This may be true,* but one may still question the desirability of combining into a single test both types of items. However, the author does provide separate norms for the verbal, number, and information sections, so that these parts may be treated separately. The eight subtests may be characterized as follows: (1) disarranged sentences, (2) verbal analogies, (3) mixed synonyms and antonyms, (4) number series, (5) numerical computations, (6) arithmetic reasoning, (7) information, academic in character (multiple choice), (8) information, academic in character (true-false).

The test appears to place quite a premium upon speed. This may result in a more valid test of academic promise within a given time limit, though no evidence is presented to support this. From the theoretical point of view, it means that this test, like many others, is in unknown mixture a measure of speed and level of mental functioning. The speed element has the one specific effect of making the reported odd-even reliability coefficients (for an unspecified type of group) spuriously high.

The "Manual" for this test consists of a single sheet printed on both sides. This sheet contains instructions for administering and timing the nine subtests, all material on norms, all material on statistical analyses of reliability and validity, together with descriptive and promotional material on the construction of the tests. The critic finds this rather meager, particularly with regard to the rationale, development, and statistical constants of the test.

The form of the test appears satisfactory, and use of the Clapp–Young type of answer sheet permits of efficient scoring.

[225]
★Chicago Tests of Primary Mental Abilities. Ages 11-17; 1941-47; revision of *Tests for Primary Mental Abilities*; L. L. Thurstone and Thelma Gwinn Thurstone.
a) SIX BOOKLETS EDITION. 1941; IBM; $6 per set of 6 subtests; $1 per set of memory cards; $2 per set of scoring stencils; $1 per specimen set; $1.25 per 25 of any one of the following subtests: Number, Verbal Meaning, Space, Word Fluency, and Reasoning; 65¢ per 25 of the subtest Memory; (240) minutes; Science Research Associates.
b) SINGLE BOOKLET EDITION. 1943; $3.75 per 25; $1 per set of memory cards; 75¢ per set of scoring stencils; 75¢ per 14 profile cards; $2.75 per specimen set; (120) minutes; Science Research Associates.
c) SRA PRIMARY MENTAL ABILITIES. 1947-48; a shortened version of the Single Booklet Edition; IBM; Forms AH (hand scored), AM (machine scored); separate answer pads or answer sheets must be used; 43¢ per hand-scored test booklet with answer pad; $1.65 per 25 hand-scored answer pads; 35¢ per machine-scored test booklet; $2.35 per 100 machine-scorable answer sheets; $2 per set of machine-scoring keys; 45¢ per 25 profile sheets; 75¢ per specimen set; 25(45) minutes; Science Research Associates.

REFERENCES

1-10. *See* 40:1427.
11. BERNREUTER, ROBERT G. "Primary Ability Tests Applied to Engineering Freshmen." Abstract. *Psychol B* 36:548-9 Jl '39. * (*PA* 13:6449, title only)
12. CAIN, LEO FRANCIS. *The Relation of Primary Mental Abilities Factors to the Academic Achievement of College Students.* Unpublished doctor's thesis, Stanford University, 1939. (*Abstracts of Dissertations . . . 1939-40*, 1940, pp. 23-30.)
13. DRISCOLL, ANITA MARY. *The Relation of Thurstone's Primary Mental Factors to Success in Various School Subjects.* Unpublished master's thesis, Fordham University, 1939. (*Dissertations . . . , 1940*, p. 94.)
14. FARRELL, MARIE LUCILLE. *The Relation of Thurstone's Primary Mental Factors to General Intelligence and Cognitive Ability.* Unpublished master's thesis, Fordham University, 1939. (*Dissertations . . . , 1940*, pp. 98-9.)
15. GOODMAN, CHARLES M. *A Study of the Thurstone Primary Mental Abilities Test.* Unpublished master's thesis, Pennsylvania State College, 1939. Pp. 48.
16. TREDICK, VIRGINIA DICKEY. *The Thurstone Primary Mental Abilities Tests and a Battery of Vocational Guidance Tests as Predictors of Academic Success.* Unpublished master's thesis, Pennsylvania State College, 1939.
17. ADKINS, DOROTHY C. "The Relation of Primary Mental Abilities to Preference Scales and to Vocational Choice." Abstract. *Psychol B* 37:456-7 Jl '40. * (*PA* 14:5392, title only) Also in *Psychometrika* 5:316 D '40. *
18. ADKINS, DOROTHY C., AND KUDER, G. FREDERIC. "The Relation of Primary Mental Abilities to Activity Preferences." *Psychometrika* 5:251-62 D '40. * (*PA* 15:2259)
19. BALL, FRED J. *A Study of the Predictive Values of the Thurstone Primary Mental Abilities as Applied to Lower Division Freshmen.* Unpublished master's thesis, Pennsylvania State College, 1940. Pp. 25.
20. HARRELL, WILLARD, AND FAUBION, RICHARD. "Correlations Between 'Primary Mental Abilities' and Aviation Maintenance Courses." Abstract. *Psychol B* 37:578 O '40. * (*PA* 15:447, title only)

---

* The test author's study which undertakes to document this point appears, unfortunately, to suffer from a mathematical error, so that a reported multiple correlation of .605 for an intelligence and an achievement test is found to be only .513 when computations are checked. The achievement test alone gives a correlation of .511. These are the only data reported sufficiently completely to permit checking.

21. MOFFIE, D. J. "A Nonverbal Approach to the Thurstone Primary Mental Abilities." Abstract. *Psychol B* 37:446-7 Jl '40. * (*PA* 14:5426, title only)
22. MOFFIE, DANNIE J. *A Non-Verbal Approach to the Thurstone Primary Mental Abilities.* Unpublished doctor's thesis, Pennsylvania State College, 1940. Pp. 57. (*Abstracts of Doctoral Dissertations . . . 1940,* 1941, pp. 313-21.)
23. SCHAEFER, WILLIS C. "The Relation of Test Difficulty and Factorial Composition Determined From Individual and Group Forms of Primary Mental Abilities Tests." Abstract. *Psychol B* 37:457 Jl '40. * (*PA* 14:5739, title only) Also in *Psychometrika* 5:316-7 D '40. *
24. THURSTONE, L. L. "Experimental Study of Simple Structure." *Psychometrika* 5:153-68 Je '40. * (*PA* 14:4357)
25. THURSTONE, THELMA G. "Primary Mental Abilities of Children." Abstract. *Psychol B* 37:446 Jl '40. * (*PA* 14:5776, title only)
26. BERNREUTER, ROBERT G., AND GOODMAN, CHARLES H. "A Study of the Thurstone Primary Mental Abilities Tests Applied to Freshman Engineering Students." *J Ed Psychol* 32:55-60 Ja '41. * (*PA* 15:3137)
27. COOMBS, CLYDE H. "A Factorial Study of Number Ability." *Psychometrika* 6:161-89 Je '41. *
28. ELLISON, MARY LOU, AND EDGERTON, HAROLD A. "The Thurstone Primary Mental Abilities Tests and College Marks." *Ed & Psychol Meas* 1:399-406 O '41. * (*PA* 16:1162)
29. GOODMAN, CHARLES H. *Ability Patterns of Engineers and Success in Engineering School.* Unpublished doctor's thesis, Pennsylvania State College, 1941. Pp. 91. (*Abstracts of Doctoral Dissertations . . . 1941,* 1942, pp. 321-7.)
30. HARRELL, WILLARD, AND FAUBION, RICHARD. "Primary Mental Abilities and Aviation Maintenance Courses." *Ed & Psychol Meas* 1:59-66 Ja '41.* (*PA* 15:2746)
31. PANKASKIE, MARGARET. *Factors in Reading Achievement at the College Level.* Unpublished doctor's thesis, University of Iowa, 1941. (*Doctoral Dissertations . . . 1940 and 1941,* 1944, pp. 336-47.)
32. ROBINSON, J. BEN, AND BELLOWS, ROGER M. "Characteristics of Successful Dental Students." *J Am Assn Col Reg* 16:109-22 Ja '41. * (*PA* 15:2810)
33. SHANNER, WILLIAM M., AND KUDER, G. FREDERIC. "A Comparative Study of Freshman Week Tests Given at the University of Chicago." *Ed & Psychol Meas* 1:85-92 Ja '41. * (*PA* 15:2814)
34. STUIT, D. B., AND LAPP, C. J. "Some Factors in Physics Achievement at the College Level." *J Exp Ed* 9:251-3 Mr '41. * (*PA* 15:4421)
35. THURSTONE, L. L., AND THURSTONE, THELMA GWINN. *Factorial Studies of Intelligence.* Psychometric Society, Psychometric Monograph No. 2. Chicago, Ill.: University of Chicago Press, 1941. Pp. v, 94. Paper. $1.50. * (London: Cambridge University Press. 9s.) (*PA* 15:3743)
36. THURSTONE, THELMA G. "Primary Mental Abilities of Children." *Ed & Psychol Meas* 1:105-16 Ap '41. * (*PA* 15:4466)
37. TRAXLER, ARTHUR E. "Stability of Scores on the Primary Mental-Abilities Tests." *Sch & Soc* 53:255-6 F 22 '41. * (*PA* 15:2399)
38. VAN VOORHIS, WALTER R. *The Improvement of Space Perception Ability by Training.* Unpublished doctor's thesis, Pennsylvania State College, 1941. Pp. 116. (*Abstracts of Doctoral Dissertations . . . 1941,* 1942, pp. 229-36.)
39. YUM, K. S. "Primary Mental Abilities and Scholastic Achievements in the Divisional Studies at the University of Chicago." *J Appl Psychol* 25:712-20 D '41. Abstract *Psychol B* 38:552 Jl '41. * (*PA* 16:1709)
40. HESSEMER, MARIANNE. *The Thurstone Primary Mental Abilities Tests in a Study of Academic Success in the School of Chemistry and Physics.* Unpublished master's thesis, Pennsylvania State College, 1942.
41. JOHNSON, A. P. *The Prediction of Scholastic Achievement for Freshman Engineering Students at Purdue University.* Purdue University, Division of Educational Research, Studies in Engineering Education II. Lafayette, Ind.: the Division, May 1942. Pp. 22. Paper. $0.35. * (*PA* 16:5020)
42. JOHNSON, A. P. *The Relationship of Test Scores to Scholastic Achievement for 244 Engineering Freshmen Entering Purdue University in September, 1939.* Unpublished doctor's thesis, Purdue University, 1942.
43. McELWEE, AGNES R. *The Effect of Training on Verbal Ability.* Unpublished doctor's thesis, Pennsylvania State College, 1942. Pp. 146. (*Abstracts of Doctoral Dissertations . . . 1942,* 1943, pp. 229-37.)
44. MOFFIE, DANNIE J. "A Non-Verbal Approach to the Thurstone Primary Mental Abilities." *J General Psychol* 27:35-61 Jl '42. * (*PA* 16:5046, title only)
45. REINING, HENRY, JR., AND STROMSEN, KARL E. "Mental Abilities and Personality Traits." *Personnel Adm* 5:14-8 S '42. *
46. STUIT, DEWEY B., AND HUDSON, HARRY H. "The Relation of Primary Mental Abilities to Scholastic Success in Professional Schools." *J Exp Ed* 10:179-82 Mr '42. * (*PA* 16:3311)
47. WHITE, ISABELLA WADDELL. *The Use of Certain Tests in the Prediction of Academic Success as Applied to Students of Home Economics.* Unpublished doctor's thesis, Pennsylvania State College, 1942. Pp. 100. (*Abstracts of Doctoral Dissertations . . . 1942,* 1943, pp. 214-219.)
48. GOODMAN, CHARLES H. "Factorial Analysis of Thurstone's Seven Primary Abilities." *Psychometrika* 8:121-9 Je '43. * (*PA* 17:3713)
49. GOODMAN, CHARLES H. "A Factorial Analysis of Thurstone's Sixteen Primary Mental Abilities Tests." *Psychometrika* 8:141-51 S '43. * (*PA* 18:326)
50. CLARK, MAMIE PHIPPS. *Changes in Primary Mental Abilities With Age.* Archives of Psychology, No. 291. Washington, D. C.: American Psychological Association, Inc., May 1944. Pp. 30. Paper. $0.80. * (*PA* 19:341)
51. GOODMAN, CHARLES H. "Prediction of College Success by Means of Thurstone's Primary Abilities Tests." *Ed & Psychol Meas* 4:125-40 su '44. * (*PA* 19:542)
52. SHANNER, WILLIAM M. *Primary Mental Abilities and Academic Achievement.* Unpublished doctor's thesis, University of Chicago, 1944. Pp. 130. (*PA* 22:462, title only)
53. THURSTONE, L. L. "Testing Intelligence and Aptitude." *Hygeia* 23:32-6+ Ja '45. * (*PA* 19:2068)
54. THURSTONE, LOUIS L. "Testing Intelligence and Aptitudes." *Pub Personnel R* 6:22-7 Ja '45. * (*PA* 19:1360)
55. CRAWFORD, ALBERT B., AND BURNHAM, PAUL S. Chap. 6, "Unitary Traits and Primary Abilities," pp. 170-215. In *Forecasting College Achievement: A Survey of Aptitude Tests for Higher Education: Part I, General Considerations in the Measurement of Academic Promise.* New Haven, Conn.: Yale University Press, 1946. Pp. xxi, 291. $3.75. * (London: Oxford University Press, 1946. 25s.) (*PA* 20:4331)
56. FRUCHTER, BENJAMIN. *A Factorial Study of Fluency Based on Thurstone's Primary Mental Abilities Battery.* Unpublished master's thesis, University of Southern California, 1946.
57. THURSTONE, L. L. "Theories of Intelligence." *Scientific Mo* 62:101-12 F '46. * (*PA* 20:2296)
57a. GUETZKOW, HAROLD, AND BROZEK, JOSEF. "Intellective Tests for Longitudinal Experiments on Adults." *Am J Psychol* 60:350-66 Jl '47. * (*PA* 22:199)
57b. HAVIGHURST, ROBERT J., AND BREESE, FAY H. "Relation Between Ability and Social Status in a Midwestern Community: III, Primary Mental Abilities." *J Ed Psychol* 38:241-7 Ap '47. * (*PA* 22:619)
58. HOBSON, JAMES R. "Sex Differences in Primary Mental Abilities." *J Ed Res* 41:126-32 O '47. * (*PA* 22:2062)
59. TOWNSEND, AGATHA. "A Report on the Chicago Tests of Primary Mental Abilities," pp. 39-48. In *1946 Fall Testing Program in Independent Schools and Supplementary Studies.* Educational Records Bulletin No. 47. New York: Educational Records Bureau, February 1947. Pp. x, 58. Paper, lithotyped. $1.50. * (*PA* 21:2497)
60. JACOBS, ROBERT. "The Reliability and Intercorrelation of the Scores on the SRA Primary Mental Abilities Test," pp. 49-58. In *1947 Fall Testing Program in Independent Schools and Supplementary Studies.* Educational Records Bulletin, No. 49. New York: Educational Records Bureau, February 1948. Pp. xii, 69. Paper, lithotyped. $1.50. *

Cyril Burt, Professor of Psychology, University College, London, England. [Review of the 1941 and 1943 editions.] Judged from the practical standpoint, the construction and arrangement of these tests seem admirable. The test material has been most carefully selected and prepared; and the explanations given to examiners regarding administration, scoring, and interpretation are simple, lucid, and easy to apply.

The theoretical basis for the tests, however, will naturally evoke criticism from those who do not entirely accept Professor Thurstone's view on mental factors. Attempts to devise tests for intellectual abilities have been based on three alternative hypotheses: (*a*) that the measurement of "general" intelligence is of supreme importance (Spearman, Binet, most British group tests); (*b*) that the use of "a single index" for "general" intelligence does not "differentiate kinds of intelligence" and should therefore be replaced by tests measuring a number of primary abilities (Thurstone); (*c*) that *both* the "general factor" of intelligence *and* specialized "group factors," like verbal, numerical, manual abilities, etc., should be measured (Burt).

The object of the Chicago tests is to assess "independent factors of the mind." Six factors are provisionally chosen as most readily identifiable and measurable: (*a*) number, (*b*) verbal meaning, (*c*) word fluency, (*d*) space, (*e*) inductive reasoning, (*f*) rote memory. An endeavour has been made to devise tests "in which there is a heavy saturation of a primary factor and in which other factors are minimized." The marks obtained by each examinee are to be plotted in the form of an individual "profile," which, it is suggested, will be of value for educational and vocational guidance. The ultimate aim thus resembles that set out in this reviewer's 1917 Report to the London Education Authority on "The Distribution and Relations of Mental Abilities," where such special abilities as the arithmetical, manual or mechanical, and verbal (of two types) were reported and the pupil's varying levels in a battery of standardized tests was exhibited by means of individual "psychographs."

CRITICISMS. (*a*) *Omission of General Factor*. To most British psychologists the omission of a separate measurement for "intelligence" (i.e., innate, general, cognitive ability) will seem a serious defect, since in the past our assessments of pupils for backward classes, central schools, secondary schools, etc., have been based chiefly on written tests for "intelligence" (supplemented by estimates of special abilities and disabilities and by individual testing where necessary). In the Chicago Tests the presence of a general factor seems indicated by the positive intercorrelations between the primary abilities (.15 to .55); and its similarity to "intelligence" is attested by the relative magnitudes of the factor-loadings for the several tests (highest for reasoning, decidedly high for the verbal abilities—possibly because there is so large a verbal element in most of the tests —low for memory and the space factor). It probably includes a marked element of speed and may underrate those whose capabilities are exhibited more freely in practical or manual problems. The authors recognize the presence of this "second order general factor" and its "psychological interest"; and presumably a measure of it, if required, could be obtained by taking a simple (or better a weighted) total of the six scores.

In this country we find that, with pupils of 11 to 13, the general factor of "intelligence" will account for far more of the total variance than the specialized factors and that (save for exceptional cases) estimates of the latter have a low reliability at these earlier years and do not yield very safe indications of the way such special aptitudes or interests may develop at or after puberty. This seems to be in agreement with the experience of the authors, who note that at the ages concerned (11 to 17) the correlations "are higher than the correlations between primary factors for adults" and consider it "now an interesting question to determine whether such correlations with still younger children will reveal, perhaps even more strongly, a second-order general factor." British psychologists would reply that the evidence available has already confirmed this anticipation.

(*b*) *Assessment of Special Abilities*. The attempt to measure special abilities, however, is of great interest and should be particularly instructive to British users in view of the present plans (enjoined by the recent Education Act) to allocate pupils, at the age of 11 *plus*, to different types of schools according to their special aptitudes. There can be little doubt that the six abilities selected by the Chicago Tests are of great importance both for school success and for vocational guidance; and, to judge by our own limited experience, this set of tests appears to assess them (at any rate with older pupils) far more effectively than any other existing set of group tests.

Nevertheless, I believe that the assessment of special abilities or aptitudes is far more difficult than the assessment of general intelligence. The following seem to be some of the more obvious difficulties and drawbacks. (*i*) Even with the fuller version, the "composite score" for each primary ability has fairly high saturations (often as much as .57 or .58) for other abilities, as well as for the particular ability which it is intended to measure. Hence, the tests are not sufficiently "pure" to dispense with the need for regression equations, if we are to obtain an adequate appraisal of the separate factors. (*ii*) These saturations or "validities" supply only a theoretical validation, based on a hypothetical interpretation of the factors involved: they do not give correlations with independent criteria. However, it is stated that "teachers, etc., have expressed their satisfaction with the profile plotted for each child";

Chicago Tests of Primary Mental Abilities

and confirmatory evidence is found in the fact that "students in linguistic subjects excel in V and W; science students typically excel in the space factor, and have high or average N; and it is expected that accountants will have high scores in N." (*iii*) Few school psychologists would, I fancy, be satisfied with an assessment of general intelligence reached after a composite test lasting for much less than an hour; can we therefore be satisfied with an assessment of these more elusive special aptitudes, which has been based on a couple of tests each lasting about five minutes only? (*iv*) The only relevant score for pupils to be selected for technical or trade schools would be that given by the space factor; no attempt is made to assess manual or mechanical aptitudes, so far as they involve motor or kinaesthetic components.

However, no tests can pretend to be either perfect or final. The authors emphasize that their tests are necessarily provisional and will be enlarged and improved in the light of further experience and research. There can, I think, be little question that, in the hands of suitably trained teachers or psychologists, they will yield helpful information that could not be obtained so rapidly by any other means; and those who consider them inadequate by themselves will still find them suggestive as a preliminary to a more intensive study of selected individuals discovered by their means. Above all, they should stimulate the critic to produce something better if he can, and will provide him with a model of conscientious and systematic research and of lucid and frank presentation.

James R. Hobson, Director of Child Placement, Public Schools, Brookline, Massachusetts. [Review of the 1943 edition.] This series of tests does in a measure what every teacher charged with the guidance of adolescent youth has long felt needed to be done, namely, provides measures of differentiated abilities which have educational importance and vocational implications.

The six primary factors measured by this battery may be identified as: N, Numerical Facility; V, Verbal Comprehension; S, Spacial Orientation; W, Word Fluency; R, Inductive Reasoning; and M, Visual Rote Memory.

The manual of instructions accompanying the shortened single booklet edition of these tests is quite complete but does not present any new information about, or any additional aids in, the interpretation of the tests. The tables of age norms in the 1941 manual have been replaced by a profile of age scores and a profile of percentile ranks on the back of the test booklet in the 1943 single booklet edition.

There is one error on page 9 of the manual in Part I, Section 7, in which reference is made to the five tests dropped from the 1941 edition to leave twelve remaining tests in the 1943 edition. Actually six tests were dropped and eleven remain. Another minor criticism of the manual of the 1943 edition is the fact that all of the coefficients of reliability and validity quoted refer to the longer 1941 edition. This fact is pointed out in an inconspicuous footnote. In any event, it is impossible to determine how the elimination of more than one-third of the tests in the 1941 edition has affected these important considerations in test selection.

However, these criticisms are minor compared to the criticisms of the tests themselves which the writer has recorded over the past five years as a result of administering one edition or the other to about 3,500 eighth- and ninth-grade pupils. For purposes of clarity and emphasis these criticisms will be enumerated as follows:

(*a*) To begin with, a premium appears to have been placed upon speed rather than power in five of the six abilities measured. This is defensible perhaps in the cases of N and W because facility is frankly the thing which is being measured and speed is certainly a function of facility. The tests of Verbal Comprehension are not so highly speeded as the tests of Spacial Orientation and Inductive Reasoning. The practical and vocational usefulness of extreme speed in the latter two primary abilities is open to question.

(*b*) A second criticism is that there is no evidence that the test items in V, S, and R are arranged in order of difficulty as they should be if any attempt is to be made to measure power. As a matter of fact, a purely subjective survey of the test items involved raises a question as to whether the items in these six tests could be scaled satisfactorily for the entire age range of the battery.

(*c*) The norms developed for this test are in terms of age scores and percentile ranks based upon Chicago children. This reviewer cannot understand how sex differences in the primary abilities could have been ignored when

Chicago Tests of Primary Mental Abilities

sex was one of the variables taken into consideration in the factorial analyses in "The Eighth-Grade Experiment." As a result of administering this series of tests to about 2,000 eighth-grade and 1,500 ninth-grade pupils, the writer has found markedly significant sex differences at these ages in all abilities except Numerical Facility and has since the first year of administration reported results in terms of separate sex percentile ranks in which the same raw score shows a percentile difference of as much as 15 points between the sexes.

(d) The results obtained by this reviewer from the original data referred to above show a definite and consistent increase in mean performance from grade eight to grade nine in all abilities except Memory in which no increase was found. This would seem to indicate that this ability may not increase after age thirteen and one-half years and that increased age norms above that age are at variance with the facts.

(e) Again, the writer questions the choice of media for the measurement of R and M. The use of letter series and letter groupings as the vehicle for measuring inductive reasoning is, in the entirely subjective opinion of this reviewer, responsible for the significantly higher mean rating of girls than boys in this ability. This result is contrary to published results in comparative problem-solving ability and the observed superiority of boys in academic subjects in which inductive reasoning is an important tool. In measuring memory, the ability to remember the first name when the last name is given would appear to be a rather sterile one so far as academic or vocational values are concerned. The ability to recall more meaningful and related material would appear to be more significant educationally and vocationally.

(f) Finally, the Science Research Associates who publish and distribute the single booklet edition have rendered a real disservice to the cause of evaluation and guidance in making machine scoring of the 1943 edition impossible. (The 1941 edition is machine scorable.) Test publishers will have to learn that, with clerical labor as scarce, expensive, and often unreliable as it is, schools are going to turn in larger numbers to the use of the IBM scoring machine. If the use of such a machine is decided upon, substitution is sure to be made in the cases of those instruments not adaptable for machine scoring, in which case exclusively hand-scored batteries of tests will not prove to be as profitable as anticipated. If test publishers do not wish to publish a machine-scored edition, they should so arrange the physical make-up of their tests as to permit the use of standard IBM answer sheets and stencils.

The fact that a great deal of criticism, mostly constructive, has been leveled at this series of tests by outstandingly competent reviewers as well as by practical consumers, such as the writer, is more or less beside the point. These tests are trail blazers which, while quite useful and usable in their present stage of development, can be counted on to be constantly improved because of the eminence of their authorship and the society under whose auspices they were developed.

F. L. Wells, Psychologist, Department of Hygiene, Harvard University, Cambridge, Massachusetts. [Review of 1941 Edition.] This test series is a recasting of the 1938 Experimental Edition (*see* 40:1427), subtests of which were somewhat different and generally more difficult. Among those eliminated from the older series are those termed Arithmetic, Mechanical Movements, Number Series, Number Patterns, and Marks. Among the accessions the more distinctive are those termed Three-Higher, Letter Series, and Pedigrees. The announced range is 11–17 years, which should make it serviceable up to at least the upper ten per cent of adult population, possibly higher, with a reduction of time limits. Aside from factorial considerations, it impresses this writer as easily the best designed series adapted to mass testing within this range.

Tests having the quality of these and their immediate predecessors raise a question whether clinicians are not missing a useful clinical approach. Such tests do not, of course, replace the more qualitative and projective methods, from Bellevue to Rorschach; but they are able to supplement the latter more effectively than can be realized by those who confine their observations essentially to free-answer procedures. The above-mentioned 1938 series has lent itself very well to this use, and the present gives similar promise. The approach must of course be a wholly eclectic one among subtests, and some procedural changes may be needed to adapt those chosen for individual use. It may thus be necessary to determine normative data for the specific uses. Neither is machine scoring suited to clinical functions, if for no other reason than that it commonly omits account of errors and "skips"; but separate answer sheets are easily adaptable.

There is said to be a wide-spread illusion that the authors have put forward these tests as for *the* primary mental abilities. No such pretense is made; but it is put forward that from among an indefinite number of "primary abilities" certain ones have been isolated, for which the names Number, Verbal Meaning, Space, etc., are here appropriate. This can be conceded; though it is an unfortunate circumstance that names like these denote so much broader functions than are subsumed in the tests concerned. It is very reasonable to expect that research will isolate other and further "primary" abilities in these various areas, and the authors themselves so indicate.

One limitation, already hinted at, will be difficult to overcome. There is practically complete dependence on multiple-choice technique, and whoever uses this in parallel with free-answer procedure, soon learns that they do not record the same abilities. Some concession to this fact is embodied in a curiously hybrid role assigned to the present "Word-Fluency" procedures. In effect, these are very simplified projection tests; a large part of whose meaning is still qualitative, may even be affectively determined. The tests in question well exemplify a consideration above mentioned ("broader functions"), in that fluency (*a*) consists not merely, or so much, in the setting down of discrete language symbols, as in organizing them into a meaningful *Gestalt;* (*b*) is very much a function of social situations, and of speech or writing. In any case, certain modifications of the tasks in respect to initial letters and number of letters might prove desirable with general use.

For reviews by Henry E. Garrett, Truman L. Kelley, C. Spearman, Godfrey H. Thomson, and Robert C. Tryon, and excerpts from reviews by A. B. Crawford and John M. Stalnaker, see 40:1427.

[226]
Cole-Vincent Group Intelligence Tests for School Entrants. Grades kgn-1; 1924–28; 1 form; $1.20 per 25; 25¢ per set demonstration cards; 40¢ per specimen set; (20–30) minutes; Lawrence W. Cole and Leona E. Vincent; Bureau of Educational Measurements, Kansas State Teachers College of Emporia.

Ruth W. Washburn, Consultant in Child Development, Shady Hill School, Cambridge, Massachusetts. When it was first published in 1924, this should have been considered one of the good tests for the determination of a child's readiness for the work of the kindergarten and first grade. By its use the teacher could learn about a child's understanding of language and his ability to follow verbal directions, the development of his perception of form with special reference to likenesses and differences, and, most important, his ability to translate through his hand what he saw with his eye. Even though its standardization was based on the scores of 1,171 pupils whose Stanford–Binet mental ages were known, further detailed scientific work in the field of developmental readiness has made the norms of this test of questionable value. Parts of this test are very difficult even for well-developed five and six year old children; for example, Test 8 in which 12 geometric figures of increasing difficulty are copied. Established norms for the Porteus maze test suggest that Test 9, a blind alley test, is also very difficult for candidates for the first grade.

The promotion policy based on the findings of the test ("a plan which is very satisfactory arranges for the pupils of highest ability to complete three grades in two years by means of mid-year promotions") has for some time been abandoned in many school systems. Experience has proved that it is a rare child with a mental age of five years and two months who can carry on the work and the life of the first grade.

[227]
★**Cotswold Mental Ability Test.** Ages 10–11; 1947; 2 forms (Series 1, 2); 6s. per 20; 1s. per manual; 6d. per single copy; 40(50) minutes; C. M. Fleming (manual) and J. W. Jenkins; Robert Gibson & Sons (Glasgow), Ltd.

[228]
★**Culture-Free Test.** Mental ages 12 and over; 1944–46; 1 form; $4.00 per 25, postpaid; 35¢ per specimen set, postpaid; (80–90) minutes; Raymond B. Cattell; Psychological Corporation.

REFERENCES
1. CATTELL, RAYMOND B. "A Culture-Free Intelligence Test I." *J Ed Psychol* 31:161–79 Mr '40. * (PA 14:4768)
2. FEINGOLD, SOLOMON NORMAN. *A Culture Free Intelligence Test: Evaluation of Cultural Influence on Test Scores.* Unpublished master's thesis, Clark University, 1940. (*Abstracts of Dissertations . . . 1940*, pp. 108-10.)
3. SARASON, SEYMOUR BERNARD. *The Effects of Training on Four Intelligence Tests.* Unpublished master's thesis, Clark University, 1940. (*Abstracts of Dissertations . . . 1940*, pp. 113-4.)
4. CATTELL, RAYMOND B.; FEINGOLD, S. NORMAN; AND SARASON, SEYMOUR B. "A Culture-Free Intelligence Test: II, Evaluation of Cultural Influence on Test Performance." *J Ed Psychol* 32:81-100 F '41. * (PA 15:4042)

L. S. Penrose, Galton Professor of Eugenics, University College, London, England. The new test is a revision, which follows very closely the draft prepared under the title of *A Culture-Free Test of Intelligence* in 1940. There are now six parts: I, classifications; II, reflections; III, series completions; IV, matrices (2 × 2); V, matrices (3 × 3); and VI, incomplete matrices (3 × 3). A set of mazes, originally included, was found to be valueless and was deleted. Each part consists of a set of items arranged in order of difficulty. The test is essentially untimed, in that ample time, in all 80 to 90 minutes, is allowed for completion. Although the material is pictorial and nonverbal, the instructions for the test are given verbally and are planned so that groups of subjects can be tested simultaneously. Some norms for high school students are provided with the manual of directions.

The test is scored by adding up the total number of items correctly answered; 72 is the maximal score. In its original form, performance on the *Culture-Free Test* was found to be correlated highly with the Binet IQ ($r = .66$ to .87). The new test has been compared with the *Army Alpha* and the *Minnesota Paper Formboard,* and correlations varying from .32 to .71 have been obtained. Intercorrelations between the parts of the test itself proved to be rather surprisingly low, varying from .12 between Parts I and II to .63 between Parts III and IV. As with all other intelligence tests, scores are found to improve after training, but the author considers that the errors in measurement caused in this way are less in the *Culture-Free Test* than in tests involving scholastic training.

The test material consists of problems of the type known as "perceptual," which are believed to measure Spearman's general factor of intelligence more accurately than any other type. Moreover, ability to do perceptual problems is said to be free from the influence of cultural and educational training. However, it is impossible to get away entirely from differences in performance due to familiarity or unfamiliarity of subjects with test situations in general. Some children are more predisposed than others by training to accept a test as worthy of serious and prolonged attention. Any pencil-and-paper test is only relatively culture-free. Furthermore, to deal with linguistically handicapped or deaf subjects, the instructions would have to be modified—though this should not present serious difficulty.

The construction of perceptual tests needs to be carried out with great accuracy in order to avoid secondary solutions which are as reasonable as the primarily intended solutions. In the case of Item 8 of Part I of the present test, the author has actually had to admit two reasonable possibilities. Tests using classifications and series completions are commonly inaccurately constructed, and the subject's task is partly to discover what has been in the mind of the examiner. Part II is free from such ambiguities. So also are Parts IV and V, which are similar to the series of *Progressive Matrices,* which has been very widely used in England during the war in connection with personnel selection. Part VI ingeniously combines the ideas of matrix completion and series completion but may not be absolutely free from ambiguity; Item 4 is not very well drawn.

Tests relatively free from cultural bias are needed for many purposes, for genetical studies and for comparing groups with different cultural backgrounds in anthropological studies. They are also of practical value in the estimation of intelligence of immigrants. The present test has the advantage of covering a wide range of ability and, when adequate norms are available and minor errors corrected, should prove useful, provided that plenty of time is available for the examination.

Walter C. Shipley, Professor of Psychology, Wheaton College, Norton, Massachusetts. This is a nonverbal, group intelligence test suitable for testing over the mental-age range from about twelve years to superior adulthood. Like Raven's *Progressive Matrices,* it is designed to measure Spearman's "G" factor in highly saturated form and to be relatively uninfluenced by verbal or cultural factors. It is composed of 72 abstract perceptual items of the multiple-choice type, divided into six parts: classifications, pool reflections, series, and three series of matrices. The first part requires the identification of two figures out of a group of six which do not embody the same principle as the other four; the second requires the identification of figures as they would appear if inverted; the third, the identification of the figure which continues a series started by three others; the last three parts each require the selection of a figure which will complete a sequential pattern; and in the very last part, portions of the pattern are omitted and must virtually be reconstructed mentally before completion is possible. Within each part the items are arranged in order of difficulty.

The test requires from 80 to 90 minutes to administer and can be scored in a minute or two. While there are time limits for each part, these are so liberal as to render the test one of power rather than speed. Norms, expressed in percentile equivalents, are available for high school freshmen (N = 1,009) and high school seniors (N = 918). The self-correlation of the test, Spearman–Brown adjusted, is reported for 121 high school freshmen to be .88.

The test has much to commend it. Research with it in an earlier form has shown it to be relatively uninfluenced by cultural factors and to be highly saturated with a general intellectual factor. The reviewer finds it difficult, however, in view of a striking basic similarity between this and Raven's *Progressive Matrices* (first published in 1938), to make any general recommendation of one over the other. For many purposes they would appear to be virtually interchangeable. Both appear to fill an urgent need for a highly discriminating, non-verbal, culture-free test of general intelligence.

David Wechsler, Chief Psychologist, Psychiatric Division, Bellevue Hospital, New York, New York. The title of this test is misleading for, apart from the arbitrariness of the author's definition of culture, there is little evidence to show that the test is free from over-all cultural influences, however defined. Actually, Dr. Cattell's test is a nonverbal (paper and pencil) scale, consisting largely of visuo-perceptual items. In its latest form, it consists of 6 subtests: classifications, pool reflections, series, and three separate matrices tests modeled after Raven's *Progressive Matrices*. Originally it also contained a Maze Test which was deleted because it discriminated poorly between senior and junior high school students who were used as criteria in differentiating test items. The test was standardized on approximately 1,000 high school freshmen and 1,000 high school seniors, and the norms available are in terms of percentile ranks for these two groups, irrespective of age.

Apart from the constricted population used in its standardization, the most serious limitation of the *Culture-Free Test* is its restricted subject (content) range. It consists, as already mentioned, exclusively of visual perceptual items, and while the abstract reasoning involved differs from test to test, the role of the capacity for the visuo-perceptual organization is much overworked. It is for this reason that the *Culture-Free Test* may be expected to be a less effective test of intelligence than the Kellogg–Morton *Revised Beta Examination* or the *Chicago Non-Verbal Examination* which have a broader range. For this reason too, the time required for its administration is much too long, to wit, 80 to 90 minutes. This is more than double the time required for the Kellogg–Morton scale. Nevertheless, the correlations of the *Culture-Free Test* with other intelligence tests are of about the same order as those obtained between the latter and other nonverbal scales (e.g., *Army Beta*), namely, r's from .50 to .60. No important sex differences were obtained except in the case of one correlation with the *Revised Minnesota Paper Formboard* which is .32 for the boys and .64 for the girls (high school freshmen).

J Consult Psychol 11:282 S-O '47.

[229]

★**Duplex Series of Ability Tests.** Ages 10-11, 11-12, 12-13, 13-14; 1947; 1 form, 4 levels; 10s. 6d. per 25 copies of Test No. 1 (ages 10-11) or Test No. 2 (ages 11-12); 12s. 6d. per 25 copies of Test No. 3 (ages 12-13); 15s. per 25 copies of Test No. 4 (ages 13-14); 2s. 6d. per manual; 5s. 9d. per specimen set; Frank M. Earle; George G. Harrap & Co. Ltd.

[230]

Essential Intelligence Test. Ages 7-11 and reading ages of 7½ or more; 1940-46; manual and publisher's catalog refer to the test as *Essential Junior Intelligence Test;* 1 form; 5d. per test; 25-49, 4d. each; 1s. per manual; 45(55) minutes; Fred J. Schonell and R. H. Adams; Oliver & Boyd Ltd.

[231]

Group Test of Learning Capacity: The Dominion Tests. Grades kgn-1, 4-6, 7-9, 9-12; 1934-46; formerly called *Group Test of Intelligence;* Forms A, B; prepared by Department of Educational Research, University of Toronto; Vocational Guidance Centre, Ontario College of Education, University of Toronto.
a) PRIMARY. Grades kgn-1; 1944-46; $1.20 per 30; 30¢ per specimen set; 33(65) minutes.
b) JUNIOR. Grades 4-6; 1940-41; 65¢ per 25; 30¢ per specimen set; 25(45) minutes.
c) INTERMEDIATE. Grades 7-9; 1934; 95¢ per 25; 30¢ per specimen set; 37(50) minutes.
d) ADVANCED. Grades 9-12; 1939-40; 65¢ per 25; 30¢ per specimen set; 30(45) minutes.

REFERENCES
1. PHILLIPS, ALEXANDER J. "Comparison of Methods of Calculating Mental Age Equivalents." *J Ed Psychol* 34:152-65 Mr '43. * (PA 18:328)

F. T. Tyler, Professor of Psychology and Education, The University of British Columbia, Vancouver, Canada. The Advanced forms are of the omnibus, self-administering type; the forms at the three earlier levels contain subtests which are separately timed. Total testing requires from 45 to 60 minutes, varying with the level. The manual includes complete directions for administering and scoring the tests. As the form in which the answers are presented does not lend itself to speed or accuracy of scoring, users will need to prepare their own scoring keys.

Mental age equivalents are presented for all tests. The authors prepared their own norms for the Primary form and used the *National Intelligence Test* and the *Terman Group Test of Mental Ability* to determine mental age equivalents for scores on their other tests.

Reliability coefficients, obtained by the equivalent-forms method, are usually reported by both grades and levels. The reliability coefficient for the Intermediate form, .95, is based on 1,000 students in one (unspecified) grade. For the other levels, coefficients range from .81 to .92. The numbers of subjects used in determining reliability ranged from 41 to 186, except for the Primary form, for which 933 first grade pupils were used.

The probable errors of scores, when reported, were very consistent, ranging from 2.5 to 3.0, except for grade 1 where the P.E. of an individual score on each form was 4.5 IQ points. The standard deviations of scores ranged from 9.36 to 13.38; variabilities of IQ's were not reported except for grade 1, where the standard deviation was 17.5. The mean IQ was reported only for grade 1, where it was 108.3. In the absence of more complete data it is difficult to determine the comparability of IQ's at different grade levels. IQ's are of the well-known ratio type.

The manuals, though not all equally complete, are comparable to those for most group tests. They do, however, fall short of the standards set up by R. W. B. Jackson and G. A. Ferguson in their *Studies on the Reliability of Tests* (*see* 952). The relationship between subtests is not indicated at all. Incomplete data are given on item validities, although certain manuals indicate that the items in the final form were selected from a much larger number after a study of item validity.

[232]

★Inductive Reasoning Test. Grades 9-12 and adults; 1946; IBM; 1 form; 50¢ per 25 machine-scorable test-answer sheets; 25¢ per key; 35¢ per specimen set, postpaid; 20(25) minutes; G. Bernard Baldwin; Educational Test Bureau.

Charles R. Langmuir, Director, New York Office, Educational Testing Service, New York, New York. This test consists of 40 number-series items printed on one side of an IBM-type answer sheet. One-third of the page is used for directions and practice exercises. While the directions are read, the test items are upside down. Upon the starting signal, the page is turned end for end. The arrangement is convenient and practical.

The details of the item form, variety, and range of difficulty are best shown by reproducing Items 1, 11, and 40:

							10	11	12	13	14
[1]	7	8	9	10	11	....	::	::	::	::	::
							15	4	20	16	8
[11]	7	49	6	36	5	25.....	::	::	::	::	::
							40	41	47	43	51
[40]	17	19	23	29	31	37.....	::	::	::	::	::

Two answers are required to each item. "Score is the number of items in which *both* choices are correct." No other scoring information is given. The catalog description indicates hand or machine scoring. The space provided for recording the score was not designed for use in machine scoring. This defect can be overlooked since the requirement of two correct marks for each item makes machine scoring impossible.

All the information available about the test, including directions for administering, the method of item selection, the method and results of determining reliability and validity of the test, and the report of norms, is presented in a one-page manual (582 words of text).

Norms are limited to a table of scores equivalent to the 1st, 2nd, 16th, 50th, 84th, 97th, and 99th percentiles in the four high school grades. Score distributions are not reported. There is no information about the students forming the norms group other than grade placement in unidentified schools.

The test will interest experimenters and teachers who want a brief, easily administered, and easily scored number-series test as a measure of power in number factor. This reviewer recommends that users disregard the so-called norms, investigate the need for increasing the time limit, verify the scoring key, and then accumulate interpretive data from local experience.

In fourteen items the alternatives are so chosen that the series can be marked correctly for three or more spaces, as in Item 1. Should the student be marked wrong on "inductive reasoning" when he correctly extends the series beyond two entries? The choice of a rule for scoring these items may have a considerable effect on the validity of the scores.

The scoring key is an *International Test Scoring Machine* key form punched by hand. Users would be wise to verify the key. In the key reviewed, the answers to Item 40 were given as 47 and 51. This reviewer, in consultation with 13 literate advisors, was forced to ascribe the obscurity of the item to defects in both the problem and the key.

J Consult Psychol 11:156 My-Je '47

[233]

★Junior Scholastic Aptitude Test. Grades 7-9; 1935–45; Forms DR, ER, FR; charges include test materials, scoring, and reporting of results; all test materials, used and unused, must be returned; $1 per individual; 86(105) minutes; prepared by the Bureau of Research (A. L. Lincoln, chairman), Secondary Education Board, Milton, Mass.; distributed and scored by the Educational Records Bureau.

REFERENCES

1. TRAXLER, ARTHUR E. "A Study of the Junior Scholastic Aptitude Test," pp. 61-75. In *1939 Achievement Testing Program in Independent Schools and Supplementary Studies*. By Educational Records Bureau. Educational Records Bulletin No. 27. New York: the Bureau, June 1939. Pp. xiii, 76, 11. $1.50. Paper, lithotyped. (*PA* 14:4774)
2. TRAXLER, ARTHUR E. "A Study of the Junior Scholastic Aptitude Test." *J Ed Res* 35:16-27 S '41. * (*PA* 15:5392)
3. TOWNSEND, AGATHA. "The Use of Results From the Junior Scholastic Aptitude Test," pp. 34-9. In *1943 Fall Testing Program in Independent Schools and Supplementary Studies*. Educational Records Bulletin, No. 39. New York: Educational Records Bureau, January 1944. Pp. xii, 48. Paper, lithotyped. $1.00. * (*PA* 18:1910)

[234]

Kentucky General Ability Test. Grades 12-13; 1946; a revision of the *Kentucky General Scholastic Ability Test;* Form 46; 8¢ per test including scoring service; 5¢ per test without scoring service; 30(35) minutes; E. J. Asher; revised by P. L. Mellenbruch; Kentucky Cooperative Testing Service, University of Kentucky.

REFERENCES

1-3. See 40:1402.

For a review by Richard Ledgerwood of an earlier form, see 38:1048.

[235]

Kingsway Intelligence Tests. 1939; a 29-page booklet of 15 practice tests; 7d. per pupils' edition; 10d. per teachers' edition; Evans Brothers Ltd.

J Ed (London) 72:394 Ag '40. Controversy still rages around the use and interpretation of the results of group tests of intelligence. Where two different, but equivalent, forms of a group intelligence test are given successively to the same group of children, the gain of the second test over the first may be as high as twenty per cent. Gains of this size have been found in the American Army Tests, and in others. Any teacher can buy Intelligence Tests, coach his pupils in them, and they will obtain a consequent increase in the scores on subsequent tests of the same type. Questions of all the common types used in Intelligence Tests of the Entrance Examination are obtainable in the Kingsway Intelligence Tests. Nothing could be more foolish or cruel to the borderline scholarship child than the use of such books. The child thus coached may manage to "pass" the Intelligence Test at the expense of a more intelligent child who has not had such coaching. But the result will be that he will spend a miserable four years trying to live up to his intelligence score, attempting work that is far too difficult for him, and becoming a drag on the school. Admittedly, this kind of coaching is now done in many schools, but those teachers who do it show a complete lack of understanding of examinations. They too frequently regard the examiner as a foe to be outwitted rather than as a friend with whom co-operation is necessary. Some even consider training in intelligence tests to be training in intelligence. This is not so. The candidate who is test-sophisticated has learnt to recognize the instructions, and has acquired more efficient methods of working than the child who comes new to the test, but this is not to say that he is more intelligent. Those who have prepared and used intelligence tests know that they are sensitive instruments easily rendered invalid by mishandling. Their successful use depends on the standardization of the conditions under which they are used. Where some testees are familiar with tests and others are not, the test results become entirely invalid and, under such conditions, it would be well to abandon them altogether. It would be a pity to have to do this now, at a time when a number of county authorities are coming to depend on the Intelligence Test in the County Entrance Examination.

For an additional review, see 40:1403.

[236]

Kuhlmann-Anderson Intelligence Tests, Fifth Edition. Grades 1B, 1A, 2, 3, 4, 5, 6, 7-8, 9-12; 1927-42; 1 form; 9 levels; $1.50 per 25 of any one level; 50¢ per manual; $1 per specimen set, postpaid; 15¢ per pad of

25 of any one subtest for individual testing; (40-60) minutes; F. Kuhlmann and Rose G. Anderson; Educational Test Bureau.

REFERENCES

1-15. *See 40:1404.*
16. KELLY, PRICE ORVILLE. *Comparative Validity and Reliability of Four Intelligence Tests in the Ninth Grade.* Unpublished master's thesis, University of Kentucky, 1933. Pp. 63. (*Theses in Education . . . , 1937*, pp. 18-9.)
17. NEMZEK, CLAUDE L. "Intelligence Testing at the College Level." *J Ed Res* 26:617-8 Ap '33. * (*PA* 7:4196)
18. ADKINS, DOROTHY C. "The Effects of Practice on Intelligence Test Scores." *J Ed Psychol* 28:222-31 Mr '37. * (*PA* 11:3629)
19. ADKINS, DOROTHY C. "The Efficiency of Certain Intelligence Tests in Predicting Scholarship Scores." *J Ed Psychol* 28:129-34 F '37. * (*PA* 11:3391)
20. BERSON, P. M. *Optimum Use of Reading Tests and of Non-Visual-Verbal and Visual-Verbal Subtests of the Kuhlmann-Anderson Intelligence Test in Indicating the Rate of Progress through the Primary Grades.* Unpublished master's thesis, College of the City of New York, 1937. Pp. 43.
21. CAVELL, ANGELO CIAVARELLA. *A Study of the Kuhlmann-Anderson Tests Administered to Inmates of the Western State Penitentiary.* Unpublished master's thesis, University of Pittsburgh, 1937. (*Abstracts of Theses . . . 1937*, pp. 454-5.)
22. ALLEN, MILDRED M. *Prediction of Academic Success of Elementary School Pupils by Means of Kuhlmann-Anderson Test.* Unpublished doctor's thesis, New York University, 1940. Pp. 128.
23. BRUCE, MYRTLE. *Factors Affecting Intelligence Test Performance of Whites and Negroes in the Rural South.* Archives of Psychology, No. 252. Washington, D. C.: American Psychological Association, Inc., July 1940. Pp. 99. Paper. $1.50. * (*PA* 15:4591)
24. KOSLOW, SYDNEY. "Reading Readiness and Reading Achievement in First Grade." *J Exp Ed* 9:154-9 D '40. * (*PA* 15:2379)
25. HARTSON, L. D., AND SPROW, A. J. "The Value of Intelligence Quotients Obtained in Secondary School for Predicting College Scholarship." *Ed & Psychol Meas* 1:387-98 O '41. * (*PA* 16:1174)
26. SPACHE, GEORGE. "Deriving Language and Non-Language Measures of Intelligence From the Kuhlmann-Anderson Intelligence Tests." *J Ed Psychol* 32:673-80 D '41. * (*PA* 16:2907)
27. TRAXLER, ARTHUR E. "Comparison Between I.Q.'s on the New Edition of the Kuhlmann-Anderson Intelligence Tests and Binet I.Q.'s," pp. 27-32. In *1940 Fall Testing Program in Independent Schools and Supplementary Studies.* Educational Records Bulletin, No. 31. New York: Educational Records Bureau, January 1941. Pp. xi, 41. Paper, lithotyped. $1.00. * (*PA* 15:3580)
28. TRAXLER, ARTHUR E. "I.Q.'s Obtained on the New Edition of the Kuhlmann-Anderson Tests and on the Binet Scale." *El Sch J* 41:614-7 Ap '41. * (*PA* 16:1238)
29. BAILEY, ALBERT ERNEST. *The Relative Validity of Ten Different Intelligence Tests.* Unpublished doctor's thesis, University of Washington, 1942. (*Abstracts of Theses . . . 1942*, 1943, p. 189.)
30. CARLTON, THEODORE. "A Comparison of the Kuhlmann-Anderson Intelligence Test With the Revised Stanford-Binet, Form L." *J Genetic Psychol* 60:85-98 Mr '42. * (*PA* 16:3822)
31. KUHLMANN, F., AND ODOROFF, M. E. "Verification of the Heinis Mental Growth Curve on Results With the Stanford-Binet Tests." *J Psychol* 13:355-64 Ap '42. * (*PA* 16:3824)
32. MULLEN, FRANCES A. "Comparison of the Revised Kent Emergency Battery With the Revised Stanford-Binet and the Kuhlmann-Anderson Tests." Abstract. *Psychol B* 39:591 O '42. * (*PA* 17:716, title only)
33. ALLEN, MILDRED M. "Relationship Between Kuhlmann-Anderson Intelligence Tests and Academic Achievement in Grade IV." *J Ed Psychol* 35:229-39 Ap '44. * (*PA* 18:3902)
34. ALLEN, MILDRED M. "Relationship Between Kuhlmann-Anderson Intelligence Tests in Grade 1 and Academic Achievement in Grades 3 and 4." *Ed & Psychol Meas* 4:161-8 su '44. * (*PA* 19:535)
35. HOLLAND, PATTIE E. *The Intelligence of Rural Children as Measured by the Kuhlmann-Anderson Intelligence Test and the Stanford-Binet Scale.* Unpublished master's thesis, University of Virginia, 1944.
36. TOWNSEND, AGATHA. "Some Aspects of Testing in the Primary Grades," pp. 51-4. In *1944 Achievement Testing Program in Independent Schools and Supplementary Studies.* Educational Records Bulletin, No. 40. New York: Educational Records Bureau, June 1944. Pp. xii, 58. Paper, lithotyped. $1.50. * (*PA* 18:3907)
37. ALLEN, MILDRED M. "Relationship Between the Indices of Intelligence Derived From the Kuhlmann-Anderson Intelligence Tests for Grade I and the Same Tests for Grade IV." *J Ed Psychol* 36:252-6 Ap '45. * (*PA* 19:2387)
38. CHAPANIS, ALPHONSE, AND WILLIAMS, W. C. "Results of a Mental Survey With the Kuhlmann-Anderson Intelligence Tests in Williamson County, Tennessee." *J Genetic Psychol* 67:27-55 S '45. * (*PA* 20:575)
39. WIMBERLY, STAN E. "A Systematic Error in Kuhlmann-Anderson Mental Ages." *J Ed Psychol* 37:193-218 Ap '46. * (*PA* 21:311)
40. ANDERSON, ROSE G. "Wimberly's Criticisms of Kuhlmann-Anderson Tests." *J Ed Psychol* 38:45-50 Ja '47. * (*PA* 21:3283)

W. G. Emmett, Lecturer in Experimental Education, University of Edinburgh, Edinburgh, Scotland. These tests were first published in 1927. In the present edition, the level of difficulty of some of the items has been raised to allow more headroom for the brighter candidates. There are 39 tests in all, 10 for each grade from grade 1 to maturity, 6 or 7 tests being common to successive grades. There is little to criticise about the subject matter of the tests; it might be said that the method of answering 11 of the earlier tests by making a dot on a picture or diagram is somewhat hazardous, but doubtless the authors have satisfied themselves that accurate marking is not imperiled. The instructions for marking and scoring are clear, and aids for computing a measure of brightness are provided.

The norms are based on the scores of some 30,000 children. They are given for each test in terms of mental age corresponding to each point of score obtained. The median of the mental ages from the several tests within a grade is taken as the best estimate of the mental age of the candidate. From this point two courses of expressing the brightness of a candidate are available. First, the mental age may be converted into an intelligence quotient, the maximum chronological age to be used as divisor being 186 months. The authors, although allowing this method, are strongly critical of its use. They prefer a measure based on Heinis's growth curve, the mental age being expressed as a percentage of average development. If the IQ unit is adopted, the resulting standard deviation of the quotients given by the test should be quoted, in order to determine the size of the unit. It is well known that the standard deviation depends on the test material and may vary from 13 up to perhaps 25. The authors unfortunately do not give the information.

The Heinis's growth scale seems a more rational method of measuring brightness, if the scale is constructed from well-substantiated data. Best of all, however, in the reviewer's opinion is a scale of standard scores, centered round 100 with a constant standard deviation such as 15, determined by agreement among psychologists and educationalists. Individuals would then be rated in standard units above or below the average performance of others of the same age.

The authors have quaint and unacceptable notions about the validity and reliability of mental tests. They say, "Test scores themselves are a better criterion of intelligence than anything else available." This sounds very like, 'Heads I win, tails you lose.' There seems little point in giving an intelligence test if it is not to predict a criterion. However, if there be virtue in measuring intelligence for its own sake, the measure should be as accurate as possible, that is, the reliability coefficient of the test should be high. But surprisingly the authors say, "close agreement between the first and second set of scores and (sic) as expressed by the coefficient of correlation may be evidence that the tests are poor instead of good." We are left wondering.

On the whole, the authors appear to have produced a reasonably good set of tests, presumably by somewhat empirical methods.

Stanley S. Marzolf, Professor of Psychology, Illinois State Normal University, Normal, Illinois. The preparation of the first edition of these tests was begun by the late Dr. Kuhlmann in 1916 with a view to conserving for group use as many of the desirable features of an individual test as possible. Dr. Anderson, who joined in this task in 1920, has been responsible for organizing the instructions for the tests and for the testing involved in preliminary trials for the first and subsequent revisions.

Thirty-nine tests, each containing from 6 to 72 items, are to be used in batteries suitable for the age or grade of the person tested. When used as an individual test, it is recommended that 14 tests constitute a battery; for group use, 10 are sufficient. Booklets containing the tests suitable to a given grade are available. For use as an individual test, pads of the separate tests are available. The total time required for administration is approximately 45 minutes. Mental age credit depending upon the number of items correctly answered is given separately for each subtest. The median mental age of all subtests given, neglecting zero and maximum scores, indicates the general level of mental development. An alternative method of scoring is strongly recommended by the authors, namely, the use of Mental Units and PA (per cent of average development). Mental Units have been computed using the Heinis growth curve data and are assignable in accordance with the number of items of the subtest passed. The ratio of the median number of mental units attained to the average number for a given CA is the PA.

The fifth revision was undertaken chiefly to increase the range of possible mental ages. The maximum "mental age" obtainable is now 40. as compared with 30-5 for the fourth edition. The maximum CA to be used in computing IQ's is now 15-6 rather than 16. The higher mental ages obtainable are due principally to added trials in 16 tests. Tests considered dependent upon specific school training do not appear in booklets below grade 3. The 25th printing, which appeared in 1942, contains norms which call for some downward revision of the maximum mental ages, since in nearly all cases the median MA of unselected ages from 6 to 16 was one or two months higher than expected.

The directions for administering the tests are clear and specific, and scoring is entirely objective. Some minor alterations in phrasing must be made when the test is used individually. Perhaps the biggest source of possible error in the use of these tests by the classroom teacher is the timing. Time intervals of 10, 15, and 20 seconds are quite common at the lower levels. At the upper levels, time limits up to 3 minutes occur. Time limits at the lower levels are quite ample, since speed is not intended to be a significant factor.

The standardization groups have been selected from supposedly representative communities of the North Central and Middle Atlantic states. Repeated revision and the use of over 5,000 subjects for the final revision have produced mental age norms which are doubtless quite dependable.

Mental Units and PA represent a commendable and straightforward attack upon the recognized inequality of mental age units, though the data Kuhlmann has accepted for the growth function could readily be improved upon. Doubtless the principal reason PA has not challenged the IQ more successfully is the weight of tradition and custom which had accumulated by the time PA was proposed. Kuhlmann's lead in this direction deserves more attention than it has received.

The manual does not include validity coefficients. In the opinion of the authors such coefficients are misleading since a suitable criterion is not available. School marks cannot be used because they are contaminated by other factors than intelligence, such as health, diligence, teacher proficiency, and the like. While it is true that school marks do not constitute a perfectly desirable criterion, we have a right to expect an intelligence test to show some relation to them. Certainly, correlations of the order of .60 have been found with sufficient frequency to cause us to view with suspicion any test with a validity coefficient much below this level. In fact, correlations of this magnitude have been found for this test (28, 34), and the publishers quote from two unpublished University of Washington dissertations to the effect that these tests ranked high in validity when compared with other tests. No competent person is likely to find these studies misleading, the authors' manual notwithstanding.

In the final analysis, the validity of these tests rests upon the informed judgment of the authors. It is their claim that "chronological age is used as the criterion of what the tests propose to measure." As it stands this statement is absurd, since measures of height, weight, or degree of ossification would each meet this criterion. The authors' wide experience and their knowledge of the experience of others with kinds of test items has undoubtedly enabled them to develop a good test. Manipulations involving chronological age provide a derived scale for quantifying responses; they do nothing to enhance the validity. The authors are explicit in admitting use of common-sense judgment as the basis for ruling out tests which depend upon training, but they are not explicit in admitting the use of such judgment in accepting tests which do not depend upon school training.

Reliability coefficients are respected even less than validity coefficients. For the authors, the reliability which scores from these tests possess arises from careful scaling of difficulty, the care with which directions have been formulated, and the use of the median mental age method of scoring. Maybe so, but we still wonder what degree of reliability has resulted from these efforts.

These tests are probably much better than the authors' reasoning about validity and reliability would lead one to expect. They will continue to be widely used, largely because of their brevity. Perhaps, the best reason for their continued use is that they are relatively less dependent upon reading skill than are most other group tests.

For reviews by Psyche Cattell, S. A. Courtis, *Henry E. Garrett, and Austin H. Turney, of an earlier edition, see 38:1049 and 40:1404.*

[237]

Laycock Mental Ability Test. Grades 4-10; 1933-35; 5¢ per test; 25-499 copies, 4¢ each; 5¢ per manual; 5¢ per key; 32½(40) minutes; S. R. Laycock; University of Saskatchewan Bookstore.

George A. Ferguson, Assistant Professor of Psychology, McGill University, Montreal, Canada. This test, published in 1933, provides a measure of the mental ages and resulting intelligence quotients of school children from grades 4 to 8. It consists of seven subtests of the more commonly used types of test material: classification, verbal analogies, figure analogies, opposites, inference, number series, and sentence completion.

The items included in the present final form of the test were selected from three previous experimental drafts, the number of items being progressively reduced from an original 550 to the present 168. Items were initially selected from the original draft on the basis of their ability to discriminate between different mental age groups, mental ages determined by the *National Intelligence Test* serving as the criterion. The author reports a correlation of .83 with the *National Intelligence Test* (N = 40, grade 4 pupils) and a correlation with teachers' judgments of ability of .63 (N = 49, grade 8 pupils). Other items of validation data are presented.

The test norms are based on 7,500 public school children in grades 3 to 8, selected from both rural and urban schools in seven provinces of Canada and 1,000 high school children selected from schools in the province of Saskatchewan.

Although this test contains nothing unique in format, test material, or methodology of construction, very considerable care and labour have been exercised in its development and in the procuring of various forms of validation data. Its norms are based on a broad and representative sample of the Canadian school population, and it serves as a satisfactory instrument for appraising the mental level of school children within the age range specified.

F. T. Tyler, Professor of Psychology and Education, The University of British Columbia, Vancouver, Canada. The *Laycock Mental Ability Test* sets out to measure Spearman's general factor, "*g*," by means of seven subtests involving the eduction of relations and correlates. The author points out that "Tests of Information" have not been used. Nevertheless, such an item as "Subservient people are apt to be—aristocratic, conceited, proud, deferential" requires the testee to *manipulate* information. Still, the author seems to assume that all individuals taking the test have had equal opportunity to acquire the information called for by the item. This is the case with most of the present mental ability tests. The author gives no data on the extent to which the test is measuring "*g*" or on the relationships existing among the seven subtests.

The 550 items with which the author started were reduced to 168 by eliminating, first, all the items which failed to show an increase in percentage passing with increase in mental ages obtained from the *National Intelligence Test*. The tests went through three revisions, but no other factor used in eliminating items is indicated. The tests were validated by correlating with teachers' judgments, other intelligence test scores, and average school marks. The median correlations were .67, .81, and .59, respectively, in small groups of 30 to 40 students. These correlations are typical of those found when other tests are used, but the groups used are rather small for validation.

Reliability is indicated by means of coefficients of correlation. The test-retest correlation for 40 pupils after a six month's interval was .80; the split-half reliability for 195 students chosen at random from the 8,500 pupils in public and high schools used in making the norms was .95. These results are typical of those reported by other test makers.

Test scores from 20 to 155 are changed to mental ages in order to compute the usual ratio type of IQ. The maximum divisor is 15, and CA's of children beyond 13 years of age are adjusted in a manner similar to that used to compute *Revised Stanford–Binet* IQ's. The maximum IQ obtainable at age 12 is 153; this is reduced to 122 at age 16.

The method of indicating responses, namely, underlining the choice, is not too well chosen.

Mental age norms are based on 8,500 students in all grades from 3 through 11. Samples for the elementary school subjects were selected from seven Canadian provinces; all high school students were in Saskatchewan schools. The average numbers of students per grade level are somewhat small as compared with numbers used by many other test makers.

Judged by the recommendations of R. W. B. Jackson and G. A. Ferguson in *Studies on the Reliability of Tests* (*see* 952) more information is to be desired. Insufficient data on reliability and item validity are presented. The numbers of cases used in some of the studies were inadequate. On the other hand, data presented in the manual compare favourably with those for many other tests of mental ability.

[238]
Mental Alertness Test: George Washington University Series, Revised Form. Grades 12-13; 1926–30; $10 per 100; 15¢ per specimen set, postpaid; 50(60) minutes; L. Omwake, S. Doran, F. Crowley, and H. Peterson, Center for Psychological Service, George Washington University.

J. P. Guilford, Professor of Psychology, The University of Southern California, Los Angeles, California. This test has so many faults that one is relieved to find that the copyright date is 1930 rather than 1947.

To be more specific, some now well-recognized rules of good test construction have been violated. (*a*) In the first three parts, the "Rights — Wrongs" scoring formula is used, without any specific instructions regarding guessing and penalties for wrong responses at the beginning of each part, and apparently without recognition of the fact that all examinees will have had ample time to complete each part. (*b*) The several parts have one over-all time limit. This is sound practice if the time is sufficiently liberal to allow every examinee to attempt all items. If there are slow examinees who do not even attempt items in part 5, however, and if part 5 is functionally different from other parts (it probably is not in this examination), the total scores for slow examinees would be somewhat different in meaning from those of rapid examinees. (*c*) Scores for parts 4 and 5 are weighted 5 and 2 times, respectively. One would like to see reasons for this given in the test manual. (*d*) Part 4 contains only five items and hence must be quite unreliable. By virtue of its unusual weight it would tend to lower the reliability of the total score.

The total score is apparently heavily weighted with verbal-ability variance. All the parts, except part 4, would also have their heaviest variance in that same factor. In part 3 we find an attempt to measure memory for content of prose material. This is a rather novel feature in

Laycock Mental Ability Test

scholastic aptitude tests and one that deserves to be validated. The aim of part 3 probably miscarries to a large extent, however, because the prose material is sufficiently familiar that many examinees could make a fair score without having read the specific material.

In spite of these shortcomings, the test can still have a substantial degree of scholastic-aptitude validity, because of the probably heavy weighting with the verbal factor and the correspondingly great emphasis on this factor in measures of academic achievement. No data on reliability or validity are given in the test manual, or on intercorrelations of parts.

The norms given with the test are highly inadequate. It is merely stated that they pertain to college freshmen, but information as to how many, what sex, and what college is not given. Centile equivalents are given only over the range from the 10th to the 90th centile. This restriction of range is considerable, since the scale distance under the normal curve is as great from the 90th to the 99th centile as it is from the 50th to the 90th.

[239]

★Mill Hill Vocabulary Scale. Ages 4½ and over; 1943; Forms I, II; 12s. 6d. per 50 of either form; also for use with the complementary test, *Progressive Matrices* (see 258); J. C. Raven; H. K. Lewis & Co., Ltd.

REFERENCES

1. RAVEN, J. C., AND WALSHAW, J. B. "Vocabulary Tests." *Brit J Med Psychol* 20:185-94 pt 2 '44. * (PA 19:2059)
2. HIMMELWEIT, H. T. "The Intelligence-Vocabulary Ratio as a Measure of Temperament." *J Personality* 14:93-105 D '45. * (PA 20:3705)
3. EYSENCK, H. J. *Dimensions of Personality*, pp. 123-5. A record of research carried out in collaboration with H. T. Himmelweit and W. Linford Rees with the help of M. Desai, W. D. Furneaux, H. Halstead, O. Marum, M. McKinlay, A. Petrie, and P. M. Yap. Foreword by Aubrey Lewis. London: Kegan Paul, Trench, Trubner & Co. Ltd., 1947. Pp. xi, 308. 25s. * (PA 22:210)

David Wechsler, Chief Psychologist, Psychiatric Division, Bellevue Hospital, New York, New York. The *Mill Hill Vocabulary Scale* is a wide-range vocabulary test standardized by the authors on an English population, ages 4½ through adulthood. It has two forms which can be used individually or as a group test. Each form in turn is divided into two parts. The first part of each requires the subject to define the words either verbally or by writing them out; the second part, administered only to the subject who can read, is a multiple-choice vocabulary test in which the subject selects the nearest synonym (1 of 6) to the stimulus word.

Results for both forms are given in percentiles for different ages. Scoring makes use of both qualitative and quantitative criteria, but only the latter are used to obtain the subject's test score. Test-retest correlations between Forms 1 and 2 as a whole are in the "neighborhood of .97"; between the oral definitions parts, .95 and for the synonym selection parts "in the neighborhood of .9." A method is furnished for converting the quantitative scores into MA equivalents without, however, any validation of the technique employed.

The 88 words which comprise the two vocabulary lists were taken from the *Concise Oxford Dictionary* supplemented by synonyms from *Roget's International Thesaurus*. In spite of the excellent criteria and statistical procedures used, the net result, as in the case of other vocabulary lists, is to furnish median scores which discriminate only modestly between successive age levels. Thus the differences between successive median age scores (4½ to 14 inclusive) is on the average only about two words. On the other hand, the author's norms show a very marked jump from the median 14-year score to that of the average adult. The difference between these two age levels is much greater than those found by American authors (Terman, Wechsler). On the Mill Hill list (88 words) the jump is from 38 to 55; on the Terman list (45 words) from 16 to 20; on the Wechsler list (42 words) from 20 to 25.

The authors originally presented their vocabulary test as a measure of verbal ability rather than of general intelligence and were opposed to combining it with other tests to give a single measure of intelligence. In their latest manual, however, they state that it was designed as a "complement" to Raven's *Progressive Matrices* (see 258), "both Scales (being) constructed to cover as nearly as possible the whole range of intellectual development from infancy to maturity." This claim is unsupported and would be difficult to prove. The *Mill Hill Vocabulary Scale* is nevertheless an excellent test measuring in a rather good way the same factors which may be said to be measured by other vocabulary tests. Comparative norms on an American population would be very desirable.

[240]

★Moray House Picture Intelligence Test 1. Ages 78-103 months; 1944; 12s. 6d. per 25; 8d. per manual; 1s. 4d. per specimen set, postpaid; 25(75) minutes; Margaret A. Mellone under the supervision of Godfrey H. Thomson and an Advisory Committee of Edinburgh Headmasters and Infant School Mistresses; University of London Press Ltd.

REFERENCES

1. MELLONE, MARGARET A. "An Investigation Into the Relationship Between Reading Ability and I.Q. as Measured by a Verbal Group Intelligence Test." *Brit J Ed Psychol* 12:128-35 Je '42. * (*PA* 16:3968)
2. MELLONE, MARGARET A. "A Factorial Study of Picture Tests for Young Children." *Brit J Psychol* 35:9-16 S '44. * (*PA* 19:271)

[241]

[Moray House Tests of Intelligence.] Ages 10-12.0 or 10-12.5; 1934-37; 5 forms; withdrawn from publication in 1947; 45(60) minutes; Moray House Tests 10, 11a, 13, and 20 by Godfrey H. Thomson and colleagues; University of London Press Ltd.
a) MORAY HOUSE TEST 10. Ages 10-12.5; 1934.
b) MORAY HOUSE TEST 11A. Ages 10-12.0; 1934.
c) MORAY HOUSE TEST 13. Ages 10-12.0; 1935.
d) MORAY HOUSE TEST BJ. Ages 10-12.5; 1937.
e) MORAY HOUSE INTELLIGENCE TEST 23. Ages 10-12.0; no date; Alexander S. Mowat and William G. Emmett in consultation with Godfrey H. Thomson.

REFERENCES

1. RODGER, ALLAN G. "The Application of Six Group Intelligence Tests to the Same Children, and the Effects of Practice." *Brit J Ed Psychol* 6:291-305 N '36. * (*PA* 11:1521)
2. THOMSON, GODFREY H. *What Are Moray House Tests?* London: University of London Press Ltd., [no date]. Pp. 8. Paper. 6d. *

Patrick Slater, Chief Research Officer at the Social Survey and Honorary Psychometric Psychologist at St. Thomas's Hospital, London, England. All children educated by local education authorities under the English Ministry of Education undergo an examination between the ages of eleven and twelve; their performance is used in deciding what kind of secondary education would be best for them. English and arithmetic are the obligatory subjects, but nearly all authorities use an intelligence test as well. Most authorities employ a psychologist, and it is frequently one of his (or her) duties to prepare the test. But others make use of the Moray House tests, which are specially prepared for this purpose by a team of psychologists working under the direction of Professor Godfrey Thomson. According to Thomson, the number of children to whom these tests are given is of the order of 400,000 per annum.

"In carrying out this work," Thomson writes, "the makers of Moray House tests have themselves got much satisfaction and pleasure, and perhaps some reputation and, in the case of the younger, material for degree theses and the like. But they have not made any money out of it: for from the beginning all fees and royalties have been paid into a fund (nowadays administered by trustees) which is devoted to the furtherance of research in education and particularly to research into the improvement of tests."

Meticulous care thus goes into the preparation of the tests, and they are pre-eminently suitable for children of normal mental ability aged from ten to twelve. After some 20,000 children have been tested, permanent conversion tables are set up, giving the IQ corresponding to a given score on each test, and the test is thereafter supplied to Directors of Education only, for use in their areas, and under promise that adequate care will be taken to preserve secrecy. A few of the tests which have served a large number of authorities in this way have been released to the general public, among them the tests enumerated here.

They consist of problems of types used since the beginning of this century in verbal tests of intelligence—directions, analogies, classification, sentence completion, series completion, jumbled sentences, deciphering codes, and miscellaneous problems including some arithmetic. There are no sections; problems of all kinds are presented one after the other in their order of difficulty. Any teacher can administer them after studying the manual of directions. Perhaps in view of their extensive circulation more attention to simplifying scoring methods, e.g., by mechanical means, would be justifiable.

For the age groups and the purpose intended, no better tests are published in the British Isles. But they do not measure intelligence independently of other aptitudes, for success in them depends also on special abilities in the use of words and numbers. Particular precautions are necessary if they are to be introduced into experiments involving factor analysis, and generally speaking they are unsuitable for this purpose.

[242]

Multi-Mental Scale. Grades 3-16; 1925-30; Forms 1, 2; $1.45 per 100; 25¢ per specimen set; 20(30) minutes; William A. McCall; Bureau of Publications, Teachers College, Columbia University.

REFERENCES

1. MCCALL, WILLIAM A., AND HIS STUDENTS. "The Multi-Mental Scale." *Teach Col Rec* 27:109-20 O '25. *
2. MCCALL, WILLIAM A.; ROBINSON, CLARA; STRIBLING, FRANCES; LERCHE, MARIE; HUTCHINGS, MABEL; LONG, ELIZABETH; GARRISON, N. L.; LONG, JOHN A.; BARTHELMESS, HARRIET M.; MORRISON, NELLIE C.; OESCHLER, HAZEL; SARTORIUS, I. C.; FALK, RITA; LAZAR, MAE; OWEN, REBA; DODGE, AMY B.; MOFFAT, GRACE W.; SCHUH, BELL; KAO, KYUIN SAN; AND OPPERMANN, ALICE F. "Construction of Multi-Mental Scale." Summary. *Teach Col Rec* 27:394-415 Ja '26. *
3. COMMINS, W. D. "A Comparison of Intelligence Tests." *Sch & Soc* 27:298-300 Mr 10 '28. * (*PA* 2:2340)
4. WITTY, PAUL A., AND TAYLOR, J. F. "Some Results of the Multi-Mental Test." *J Ed Psychol* 20:299-302 Ap '29. * (*PA* 3:2895)
5. LAUDERBACH, J. C., AND HAUSE, ENID. "On the Reliability and Validity of Derived Scores Yielded by the McCall Multi-Mental Scale." *J Appl Psychol* 16:322-3 Je '32. * (*PA* 7:4187)
6. KELLY, PRICE ORVILLE. *Comparative Validity and Reliability of Four Intelligence Tests in the Ninth Grade.* Unpublished master's thesis, University of Kentucky, 1933. Pp. 63. (*Theses in Education . . .*, 1937, pp. 18-9.)
7. TURNEY, AUSTIN H., AND FEE, MARY. "The Comparative Value for Junior High School Use of Five Group Mental Tests." *J Ed Psychol* 24:371-9 My '33. * (*PA* 7:5570)
8. PHILLIPS, ALEXANDER J. "Further Evidence Regarding Weighted Versus Unweighted Scoring of Examinations." *Ed & Psychol Meas* 3:151-5 su '43. * (*PA* 18:1925)

Moray House Picture Intelligence Test 1

D. A. Worcester, *Chairman, Department of Educational Psychology and Measurements, The University of Nebraska, Lincoln, Nebraska.* This scale, published in 1925, consists of 100 groups, each of five words one of which is to be crossed out as not belonging with the others. While the type of response is the same for each item, at least 16 different mental sets are required. The subject is not told but must "divine" the necessary point of view in each case. Each word in the group is calibrated for its degree of correctness. Great care was given to the choice of the items and the statistical treatment was much more thorough than was usually given to tests at that time. The scale was validated against several of the best intelligence and achievement tests then in use.

It is hard to convince users, however, that a 20-minute test can "be used with equal success from grade three through the university" and that it will yield grade scores from 1.4 to 30 with age equivalents from 6.9 to 38. It is doubtful, too, that many psychologists at present will agree that, for the calculation of IQ's, 20 years (CA) should be used as the maturation point for intelligence. One wonders if the authors still hold to this age, but no revision of the manual has been put forward. The scoring key was based on the responses of 250 pupils, and the adult user is warned that disagreements as to the weighting will be due to his sophistication. Since the scale is to be used with adults as well as with children, it would seem that some adults could have been well used in the standardization. The idea of the scale is good but revision is needed.

[243]
★Non-Language Multi-Mental Test. Grades 2 and over; 1942; Forms A, B; $3.85 per 100; 25¢ per specimen set; 30(40) minutes; E. L. Terman, William A. McCall, and Irving Lorge; Bureau of Publications, Teachers College, Columbia University.

REFERENCES
1. TERMAN, E. L. *The Development and Application of National Education Survey Techniques With Special Emphasis on Criteria for Measuring Intelligence Internationally.* Unpublished doctor's dissertation, New York University, 1930.

Carroll A. Whitmer, *Director of Special Education, Public Schools, Pittsburgh, Pennsylvania.* According to the manual, this test is designed to give an estimate of the intelligence of children and adults who do not speak English or who are deaf or illiterate. It is administered by simple verbal directions or pantomime. Scoring is done by a marked copy, and the score is the number of correct responses.

The authors made an original tryout of this type of material on 149 WPA employees who were also given *Otis Self-Administering Tests of Mental Ability* and found that the two tests measured a common function. The standard scores obtained in this testing were averaged and used as a criterion score for the selection of the 120 items used in the two forms of the final test. Each form is composed of three cycles of twenty items arranged in order of difficulty.

The norms for the test were obtained from statistical treatment of the scores of 2,531 New York City school children in grades 3 through 8, selected for socio-economic background and intelligence. The table of mental age equivalents in the manual ranges from 33 months to 236 months. Scores at the extremes (above 47, MA 173 months, and below 20, MA 72 months) have been extrapolated. Grade equivalents are also given for grade 1.5 to 8.5. Grade equivalents below grade 3.4 are extrapolated.

The reliability of the test for grades 3 through 8, estimated by the Kuder–Richardson reliability formula, is .86 and .90 for the separate forms and .94 for both forms. The authors recommend using both forms.

"In essence, the test requires the same type of intelligence performance among its pictorial symbols as is required among more conventional verbal symbols. The kinds of relationship required are of the form of relations of opposites, of similar pairs, of part to whole, of whole to parts, and of sequences." This generalization quoted from the manual may be interpreted to represent a quite different assumption from that usually used in the justification of non-language tests. Overlapping abilities are usually admitted, but it is generally assumed that the ability to work with nonverbal symbols represents another type of intelligent performance.

A 30-minute group test composed of 60 items which purports to differentiate mental age from 33 months to 236 months assumes almost miraculous discriminative power. One point of score determines a mental age difference of three to six months.

The motivation of the young or dull subject in a test which has all the practice exercises at the beginning of the test period is questionable, particularly in a test which uses pantomime directions and has items arranged in difficulty cycles.

This test may be a serviceable instrument for rough survey, but any of the tests standardized

[244]

Ohio State University Psychological Test. Grades 9-16 and adults; 1919-47; separate answer sheets must be used; prepared by Herbert A. Toops for the Ohio College Association.

a) FORM 21. 1920-41; 45¢ per test booklet with answer pad; $1.80 per 25 answer pads; 75¢ per specimen set; work limit (90) minutes; Science Research Associates.

b) FORM 23. 1920-47; IBM; test booklets may be either rented or purchased; 4¢ rental charge per test booklet; 5¢ per used test booklet; 8¢ per new test booklet; 3½¢ per answer pad for stylus marking (nonmachine-scorable); ⅓¢ per pin stylus; 2¢ per stylus; 3¢ per machine-scorable answer sheet; 6¢ per electrographic pencil; 5¢ per hand-scoring stencil; scoring service for machine-scorable answer sheets is available at 3¢ per test plus postage; earlier forms available include Form 19 (1935), Form 20 (1937), Form 21 (1941), and Form 22 (1943); work limit (120) minutes; Ohio College Association.

REFERENCES

1. GUILER, W. S. "The Predictive Value of Group Intelligence Tests." *J Ed Res* 16:365-74 D '27. * (*PA* 2:1094)
2. SOUTH, EARL B., AND CLARK, GENEVIEVE Y. "Some Uses of Psychological Tests in Schools of Nursing." *Am J Nursing* 29:1495-1501 D '29. * (*PA* 4:1740)
3. BYRNS, RUTH K. "Scholastic Aptitude and Freshman Achievement." *Sch & Soc* 35:713-8 My 21 '32. * (*PA* 6:3745)
4. REUSSER, W. C.; BRINEGAR, VAUGHN; AND FRANK GUY. "Predicting Success in First-Year College Chemistry." *Sch & Soc* 40:197-200 Ag 11 '34. * (*PA* 8:5664)
5. GUNNING, IRA CURTIS. *The Relation of Aptitude to Academic Progress.* Unpublished master's thesis, University of Oklahoma, 1935. Pp. vii, 47. (Abstracts of Theses . . . 1935, 1937, p. 116.)
6. HARTSON, L. D. "Does College Training Influence Test Intelligence?" *J Ed Psychol* 27:481-91 O '36. * (*PA* 11:1480)
7. QUAID, THOMAS DELL DOMA. *A Study in the Prediction of College Freshman Marks.* Unpublished doctor's thesis, University of Oklahoma, 1937. Pp. xii, 151. (Abstracts of Theses . . . 1937, 1939, pp. 20-2.)
8. SELOVER, ROBERT B., AND PORTER, JAMES P. "Prediction of the Scholarship of Freshman Men by Tests of Listening and Learning Ability." *J Appl Psychol* 21:583-8 Ag '37. * (*PA* 12:2137)
9. STUIT, DEWEY B. "Differential Characteristics of Superior and Inferior Students." *Sch & Soc* 46:733-6 D 4 '37. * (*PA* 12:1640)
10. KOHN, HAROLD A. "Achievement and Intelligence Examinations Correlated With Each Other and With Teachers's Rankings." *J Genetic Psychol* 52:433-7 Je '38. * (*PA* 13:181)
11. QUAID, T. D. D. "A Study in the Prediction of College Freshman Marks." *J Exp Ed* 6:350-75 Mr '38. * (*PA* 12:6106)
12. SAUM, ANNA LOIS. "The Relative Significance of Time as a Factor in Tests of Ability at the College Level." *J Appl Psychol* 22:192-210 Ap '38. * (*PA* 13:2750)
13. STUIT, DEWEY B. "Fluctuations in the Correlation Between Psychological Test Scores and University Grades." *J Exp Ed* 6:343-5 Mr '38. * (*PA* 12:6110)
14. GREENE, J. E., AND STATON, THOMAS F. "Predictive Value of Various Tests of Emotionality and Adjustment in a Guidance Program for Prospective Teachers." *J Ed Res* 32:653-9 My '39. * (*PA* 13:4211)
15. TOOPS, HERBERT A. *The Evolution of the Ohio State University Psychological Examination.* Ohio College Association Bulletin, No. 113. Columbus, Ohio! the Association, Ohio State University, March 20, 1939. Pp. 2287-2311:2. Paper, mimeographed. $0.15. *
16. BECK, ROLAND L. "Predicting Success in College English." *Col Engl* 1:541-4 Mr '40. *
17. BERNARD, HAROLD W. "Some Relationships of Vocabulary to Scholarship." *Sch & Soc* 51:494-6 Ap 13 '40. * (*PA* 14:4236)
18. CAHOW, ARTHUR C. "Relationships of Test Scores of Education College Freshmen to Grades in Selected Courses." *J Exp Ed* 8:284-9 Mr '40. *
19. KIRKPATRICK, FORREST H. "Four Mental Tests and Freshman Marks." *J Higher Ed* 11:38-9 Ja '40. * (*PA* 14:3215)
20. LADIEU, GLORIA BERTHA. *Predicting Academic Success: A Critical Evaluation of the Relation Between Achievement in College and Various Predictive Measures.* Unpublished master's thesis, Tulane University, 1940. (Abstracts of Theses . . . 1940, pp. 78-9.)
21. HARTSON, L. D., AND SPROW, A. J. "The Value of Intelligence Quotients Obtained in Secondary School for Predicting College Scholarship." *Ed & Psychol Meas* 1:387-98 O '41. * (*PA* 16:1174)
22. STOPHER, EMMET C. "The Freshman Testing Program." *J Higher Ed* 12:159-62 Mr '41. * (*PA* 15:4420)
23. HESTON, JOSEPH C. "The Use of Non-Verbal Tests in the Prediction of Academic Success." *J Ed Psychol* 33:608-14 N '42. * (*PA* 17:2488)
24. LOWRIE, KATHLEEN HARRIET. *Factors Which Relate to the Extra-Curricular Performance of College Women.* Unpublished doctor's thesis, University of Iowa, 1942.
25. HARTSON, L. D. "School Marks vs. Mental Tests in Rating Secondary Schools: A Second Study." *Sch & Soc* 57:80-3 Ja 16 '43. * (*PA* 17:1349)
26. GARRETT, WILEY S. "Ohio State Psychological Examination: An Instrument for Predicting Success in College." *Occupations* 22:489-95 My '44. * (*PA* 18:3286)
27. KRUEGER, A. FREDERIC. *The Ohio State University Psychological Examination, Form 20.* Unpublished master's thesis, Butler University, 1945.
28. CARTER, W. R. *The Missouri College Aptitude Testing Program.* University of Missouri Bulletin, Vol. 47, No. 24; Education Series, No. 40. Columbia, Mo.: the University, August 20, 1946. Pp. 72. Paper. * (*PA* 21:3260)

J. P. Guilford, Professor of Psychology, The University of Southern California, Los Angeles, California. [Review of Form 21.] This well-known examination has gone through numerous revisions, and in these revisions some of the most exacting test-construction procedures have been employed. Its three parts have survived repeated item-analysis and validity studies. With a reported validity coefficient of .68 (against the criterion of "Point Hour Ratio"), the total score would seem to offer the best predictions now available for an over-all academic-aptitude instrument at the college level. It is wisely set up as a power test, all students being permitted to attempt all 150 items. The reliability estimate ($N = 300$) is .93.

Part 3, a reading comprehension test, may be interpreted on the basis of separate norms provided. The author should have presented data on intercorrelations of the three parts, however, so that the user can judge whether the separate scoring of part 3 is justified. Owing to the high degree of verbal-factor variance that seems evident in all parts, one would expect very high intercorrelations. No estimate of reliability of part 3 scores is provided.

In spite of the unusually high validity coefficient, which probably rests on the fact that verbal ability is by far the greatest contributor to average scholastic achievement as measured, it is time to question whether other qualities that are really important, particularly in the more specialized curricula and courses, should not receive more consideration. The Ohio examination, while achieving its unequalled validity, may be the result of a vicious circle which has overstressed verbal ability in education. In order to gain more light on this point, we need measures of achievement that are more in line with genuine objectives. It will then probably be found by the same procedures by which the

Ohio test has been brought to its present degree of refinement that a much more varied content is desirable, both for the selection of students and for their guidance. It is time for us to think more in terms of academic aptitudes than of academic ability. It is time for us to validate tests less often against grade-point averages and more often against specific course achievement properly measured.

The norms provided with the test are based upon samples of adequate size, though not representing the national scope that is true of the *American Council on Education Psychological Examination.* Norms are conveniently given for each year of high school as well as for college freshmen.

The printing format of the test booklet is largely determined by the convenient pinhole scoring system, but something might still be done to avoid the extremely long lines of print, a feature that psychological studies have condemned as a reading handicap. There is no evidence that this affects the value of the test results, but it is a matter of reading comfort.

For reviews by Louis D. Hartson, Theos A. Langlie, and Rudolf Pintner of Form 20, see 38:1051.

[245]

★**Oral Directions Test: An Intelligence Test on Phonograph Records.** Adults; 1945–46; 2 styles of vinylite recordings; each record set includes manual, plastic-covered key, and 100 answer sheets; $16 per transcription record (33⅓ rpm) set; $17 per standard record (78 rpm) set; $4 per 100 answer sheets; 28(35) minutes; Charles R. Langmuir; Psychological Corporation.

Charles D. Flory, Rohrer, Hibler and Replogle, New York, New York. This test purports to be a measure of the general intelligence of adults, and especially of adults in industrial situations. The major features of this test are simplicity of administration, range of coverage, and ease of scoring.

The *Oral Directions Test* is unique in that both directions and questions are given by phonograph reproductions. The recordings are available in two styles: (*a*) the Transcription Record which is a double-faced, 16-inch disk to be reproduced at 33⅓ rpm, and (*b*) the Standard Records, consisting of four double-faced, 12-inch records for use on a standard phonograph. In the standard model the test is broken by natural pauses so that the records can be changed without disturbing the continuity of thought for the subjects. Both styles of recording are made on vinylite discs, which are practically permanent. Directions are provided so that the test can be given from printed script, but this procedure defeats one of the major advantages of the test.

The items are intended to fit an unselected adult population but in some instances favor the city dweller. The author contends that "illiterates can be tested in the same group with high school graduates without embarrassment to the examiner or the applicant." The range of difficulty among the items suggests the possibility of using this instrument in a screening procedure preparatory to the application of more rigorous classification techniques.

The test is composed of only 30 items, but through weighted scoring a maximum of 58 points can be earned. The scorer is instructed to memorize the key, which can be done very quickly. The weights per item vary from 1 to 10, with 23 items receiving only one point.

This test, because of its uniqueness, should be given further experimental use. There are several points, however, at which critical users will undoubtedly raise questions. Few psychologists will agree with the author when he says, "Any available office worker is qualified to administer the test." The attitude of subjects is important even when a test is self-administering. Desirable attitudes for reliable test results are not produced by "any office worker."

The norms have been established by testing 768 Army enlisted men who were selected as representative of all enlisted men. A table of general population equivalents was devised by comparing the *Oral Directions Test* scores with the *Revised Alpha Examination,* Form 5 scores for these 768 men. It is evident from the equivalent scale that the *Oral Directions Test* discriminates less well at the upper intelligence levels than it does at the lower levels. The spread in points for the upper 50 per cent is only 11 while the spread for the lower 50 per cent is 24 points. Logic also leads to questions about norms in which half of the people tested in an industrial group were in the lowest 30 per cent of the general population and the average for those who graduated from high school was only slightly above the 30th percentile on the equivalent scale. These results suggest need for more typical standardizing data.

This test seems to the reviewer to be heavily weighted with the perceptual aspects of intelligence and relatively light on judgment items. It is therefore possible that the test has greater industrial application to special jobs than as a general screening test. Only research can answer this question. The tempo is so slow in places that brighter subjects consider the tasks tedious. The complexity is likely, however, to cause some unselected adults to lose interest or to answer at random in an unsupervised situation.

It seems likely that an examiner who has thirty minutes of testing time will prefer, in most situations, a test with more items and items which will probe more facets of intellectual competence.

Irving Lorge, Professor of Education, and Executive Officer, Institute of Psychological Research, Teachers College, Columbia University, New York, New York. The subtitle for this test is "An Intelligence Test on Phonograph Records." Basically, the test is an orally administered omnibus-form intelligence test. The item types include simple directions, figure recognition, digit span, memory for detail, number completion, and comprehension. Among the items are several requiring spatial orientation and direction. Such items seem to cause a special difficulty to corrected left-handers.

The manual suggests that the test may be given without phonograph records by a trained examiner, but implies that the records will be superior to such administration. There can be no doubt that the record controls the stimuli and the timing, yet there may be some difficulties with the recording. First, the record is spoken by a male whose lower register may not be understood by older women. Second, occasional misunderstandings may affect the reliability and validity of the test, e.g. the different meanings for "blocks" in Item 14 (where "streets" or "squares" would be the preferred localism), the enunciation of the letter "N" in Item 20, and the confusion of "X" and "J" in Item 18. Such possible auditory disadvantages, however, will be relatively small for a young adult group provided that the amplification system is adequate.

The idea of an orally administered intelligence test is not new. As a matter of fact, the first test of the *Army Group Examination Alpha* is an orally administered directions test. The oral administration has the advantage of controlling time on each question so that candidates are not penalized by spending too much time on any single question. The test can be given to a wide range of ability without undue ennui on the part of able candidates or undue frustration in duller people.

The reliability of the test is reported on the basis of the correlation of first half by second half as .81. The manual suggests that the first half of the test may be given as a short form. As such, the test would be basically a rough screening test with a rather large standard error. The total test would have a reliability of about .9.

The validity is reported on the basis of the correlation of the *Oral Directions Test* with Wells' *Modified Alpha Examination Form 9*. The correlation for various samples hovers about .84.

The norms are reported on the basis of the method of equal centiles. The author had available data for a representative sample of enlisted men on the *Army General Classification Test* and Wells' *Revised Alpha Examination, Form 5*. Since the relationships between Wells' Forms 5 and 9 were available, the author produced norms for a specified sample of the population. Since the norms were produced as a first approximation under the stress of a war situation, it is hoped that the author and publisher will produce a better set of normative data soon. The test undoubtedly will show sex and age differences. Since the enlisted population is truncated at the low end of the ability continuum, and truncated on age, the currently available norms do not represent the general population. Auxiliary norms for a specialized group of clients in a community advisory service center are also given.

The relationship of the test score to age and sex is given in terms of mean differences between semidecades for men and women. As may be expected with an auditory speed test, significant differences exist between age groups. There is a significant age decrement. The manual, however, does not suggest any correction for age nor does it suggest any clinical evaluation of lower scores in older groups. Sex differences are reported. These, however, cannot be evaluated adequately, since there is no evidence as to the representativeness of the sampling of successive age groups. Some of the poorer performances of the older women may be attributable to the fact that older women do not understand male speech patterns as well as men or younger women.

The test is simple to give and fairly easy to score. Except for possible minor misunderstandings of the speech pattern, the test should be fairly adequate for large scale screening projects.

William W. Turnbull, Secretary of the Board and Head of the Test Construction Department, College Entrance Examination Board, Princeton, New Jersey. DESCRIPTION. This test is subtitled "An Intelligence Test on Phonograph Records," and was designed as "a test of general mental ability which would be simple, valid, and practical for use in testing adult groups." The complete test, both directions and questions, has been recorded on unbreakable discs. It consists of thirty items, some of which are subdivided, affording a total of 58 scorable units. The subject's task is to listen to each question, remember it, solve it, and record the answer. The questions sample a wide variety of abilities. Memory plays a large part in almost all questions, but ability to follow complex verbal directions, spatial reasoning, number facility, and ability to concentrate are also important.

SCORING. All questions are answered by writing a symbol, number, or word in a specified position on the answer sheet; and thus the test cannot be scored by machine or with a stencil. The scoring key consists of an answer sheet, on which the correct answers and rules for scoring variations have been overprinted in red, which is sheathed in celluloid—an excellent protective device.

NORMS. Percentile equivalents of raw scores are given to provide norms for the general population, as represented by a controlled sample of 768 Army enlisted men. Further norms are given for 258 male applicants for vocational and educational guidance at a community advisory service center. More extensive norms are obviously needed, and will no doubt be gathered as the test finds wider application.

VALIDITY. Correlations in the low .80's have been established between scores on this test and scores (total, verbal, and numerical) on the *Modified Alpha Examination,* Form 9. The population included over 2,500 adult men and women, whose mean scores on the ODT fell between the 20th and 30th percentiles of the norms for the general population. When given to a group of some 3,000 adult applicants for employment in a war plant, the test showed a total score difference of approximately one standard deviation (12 raw score points) between applicants whose education had extended to grade 8 or below (mean score at 13th percentile), and those who had attended high school (mean score at 34th percentile); and a raw score difference of 7 points between the high school group and those who had attended college (mean score at 59th percentile). It is unfortunate that both studies were made with groups whose mean ability was markedly below average, since the question of the test's validity for the general population is thereby left in doubt. Since the test seems to be most discriminating at the lower levels, the reported validity may well exceed the actual validity for the general population.

RELIABILITY. The reliability is estimated (by controlled split-half technique with 737 cases) as .93, which is excellent in view of the unspeeded nature of the test. The corresponding standard error of measurement is 3.3 raw score points, compared with a raw score standard deviation of 12 points. It should be noted that the mean score of the population on which the reliability is based fell below the 35th percentile. Thus for the general population the reliability, like the validity, is probably lower than the figure reported.

MANUAL. The manual is well set up, and gives adequate information concerning the construction and standardization of the test, and about the studies on which reliability and validity figures are based, as well as full directions for giving and scoring the examination. A copy of the script accompanies the manual.

EVALUATION. This test seems likely to serve its purpose very well when applied to a relatively low-level group. It is doubtful if it is difficult enough for effective use with a group of above-average ability. The norms show a spread of 24 raw score points between the 5th and 50th percentiles, but of only 11 points between the 50th and 95th percentiles. The test material itself shows every evidence of careful preparation. The recording is distinct, the directions clear, the items unequivocal. The presentation on records has a considerable degree of face validity for use with adults at low ability levels, since in most work situations their instructions will be given orally. The oral feature is advantageous also in testing memory. One of the objects in recording the test is to standardize the wording and timing of the directions, and so to avoid errors of administration in these respects. Against this advantage will have to be counted the differences which will be introduced by varying excellence of play-back equipment and by differences in room acoustics.

J Consult Psychol 11:282 S-O '47.

[246]
O'Rourke General Classification Test, Senior Grade, 1942 Edition. Grades 12-13 and adults; 1927–42; Form L; $3.25 per 50, postpaid; 25¢ per specimen set, postpaid; 40(55) minutes; L. J. O'Rourke; Psychological Institute.

REFERENCES
1. DAVIDSON, CHARLES M. "Analysis of Clerical Tests." *Personnel J* 16:95-8 S '37. * (PA 11:5916)
2. DAVIDSON, CHARLES M. "Evaluaton of Clerical Tests." *Personnel J* 16:57-64 Je '37. (PA 11:4713)
3. LAWSHE, C. H., JR., AND THORNTON, G. R. "A Test Battery for Identifying Potentially Successful Naval Electrical Trainees." *J Appl Psychol* 27:399-406 O '43. * (PA 18:265)

Marion A. Bills, Assistant Secretary, Aetna Life Insurance Company, Hartford, Connecticut. This 40-minute mental alertness test consists of 105 items of eight types, two of which are vocabulary, two of logic, one of arithmetic of the problem type, one information, one spelling, and one grammar. Each type becomes more difficult as the test progresses, the different types appearing in cycles. The directions are clearly given, the norms are based on approximately three thousand males.

Its advantages are that it is easily administered and contains enough variety of items so that a person of high school level has a chance to demonstrate ability.

Its disadvantages are that the various types of ability cannot be scored separately, and the mixture of different types of items might confuse the less mentally alert.

[247]
Otis Classification Test, Revised. Grades 4-8; 1923-41; Forms R, S, T; consists of an achievement test and an intelligence test (the *Otis Quick-Scoring Mental Ability Tests, Beta Test*); $1.70 per 25; 35¢ per specimen set, postpaid; 60(70) minutes; Arthur S. Otis; World Book Co.

REFERENCES
1. BANKER, HOWARD J. "Correlation Studies of the Student's Ability Index." *J Ed Res* 20:31-7 Je '29. * (PA 3:4621)
2. SARGENT, RUTH F. "The Otis Classification Test—Form A, Part II." *Teachers Forum* 4:30-3 N '31. * (PA 6:918)
3. THOMPSON, MILTON D. "The Intelligence of 567 Prisoners Confined in the Kentucky State Reformatory." *J Appl Psychol* 24:628-32 O '40. * (PA 15:987)

Ed Res B 21:186-8 S 16 '42. William J. Jones. The manual....contains more figures, tables, and charts for determining indexes, norms, and various types of ages than for any other test known to the present writer. The test, which is a combination mental-ability and achievement test, yields not only raw and standard scores, but also MA, EA, IQ, EQ, CI, PR, AR, IE, and MEA! For those who revel in statistical gymnastics, the possibilities of the interpretative charts included in the manual are well-nigh limitless. The 80 items comprising the mental ability test (Part I) are the same as those in the widely used Otis Quick-Scoring Mental Ability Tests. The material consists of opposites, analogies, proverbs, vocabulary, reasoning, mixed sentences, similarities, and the like. The achievement test of 115 items (Part II) is largely made up of items dealing with language, arithmetic, geography, history and civics, physiology and hygiene, music, and general information which were included in the original Otis Classification Test, published for the first time twenty years ago. * It can almost be said that the test is self-administering and self-scoring; it is so practicable. It is necessary merely to pass out the booklets, allow the pupils time to study the first page with a minimum of directions, and then let them go ahead and take the test, allowing thirty minutes for each of the two parts. * One of the important assumptions upon which the test is based is that innate mental ability and achievement based on school training are different, and can be measured separately. Part I is therefore designed to rule out or hold constant the influence of the school by including only "elements of their environment that are common to all children," while Part II is made up of items which depend on "knowledge gained in school." Due to the fact that the reported coefficients between Parts I and II average .79, it seems unnecessary, even unwise, to figure out the relationships between scores on the separate parts (as suggested in the manual) since the magnitude of the r shows that they measure the same ability to a large extent. Dependable interpretations cannot be drawn from the resultant spurious relationships. In this connection it is interesting to note that in compiling the test norms it was necessary to make up fictitious mental ages for certain scores in order to have a "more nearly uniform correspondence between mental ages and scores." Because of this, the manual recommends determining the intelligence quotient by addition or subtraction, instead of division. For the reasons just mentioned, it would be better not to take the recommended statistical manipulations too seriously. The total score which the test yields, however, is a worth-while index which can be used along with other criteria by those who sometimes find it desirable to classify pupils.

[248]
Otis General Intelligence Examination: Designed Especially for Business Institutions. Applicants for clerical and executive positions; 1920; 1 form; $1.20 per 25; 35¢ per specimen set, postpaid; nontimed (40) minutes; Arthur S. Otis; World Book Co.

Frederic Kuder, Professor of Psychology, Duke University, Durham, North Carolina. As a collector's item this test (copyright date, 1920) is of interest. Adequate evidence of its worth, however, is conspicuously lacking. For example, there are no data on the reliability of the test given in the manual. Validity was determined by correlating scores of 100 clerks with the combined ratings of "intelligence." Correcting for attenuation in the criterion, a coefficient of .73 resulted. The size of this sample, derived from a single business concern, and the dubiety of the criterion measure make this less than sufficient demonstration of validity by present-day standards. Norm tables are not titled to show the number of cases on which they are based. Finally, no bibliography is provided in the manual to permit the test user access to information concerning empirical studies of the test.

The test bears considerable resemblance to the newer *Otis Self-Administering Tests of Mental Ability.* Many of the items are similar to those incorporated in the latter test. However, there are also several items so ambiguous in construction as to lack reliability entirely. Significantly, these items do not occur in the later well-validated tests.

This test thus stands in the same relation to the well-established tests of general ability as the crystal set to the frequency modulation radios—it might deliver, but the consistency and quality of performance is doubtful. It cannot compete with the *Wonderlic Personnel Test* nor its lineal descendants, the *Otis Self-Administering Tests of Mental Ability* and the *Otis Quick-Scoring Mental Ability Tests.*

[249]
Otis Quick-Scoring Mental Ability Tests. Grades 1.5-4, 4-9, 9-16; 1936-39; IBM for grades 4 and over; 2 to 4 forms; 3 levels; Arthur S. Otis; World Book Co.
a) ALPHA TEST. Grades 1.5-4; 1936-38; Forms A, B; $1.50 per 25; 35¢ per specimen set, postpaid; 20(25) minutes.
b) BETA TEST. Grades 4-9; 1937-39; IBM; revision of *Otis Self-Administering Tests of Mental Ability, Intermediate Examination;* Forms A, B, CM, DM; $1.00 per 25 (Forms A, B); $1.30 per 25 machine-scorable tests (Forms CM, DM); 35¢ per specimen set, postpaid; 70¢ per 25 machine-scorable answer sheets; 20¢ per machine-scoring key; 30(35) minutes.
c) GAMMA TEST. Grades 9-16; 1937-39; IBM; revision of *Otis Self-Administering Tests of Mental Ability, Higher Examination;* Forms AM, BM, C, D; $1.10 per 25 (Forms C, D); $1.35 per 25 machine-scorable tests (Forms AM, BM); 35¢ per specimen set, postpaid; 70¢ per 25 machine-scorable answer sheets; 20¢ per machine-scoring key; 30(35) minutes.

REFERENCES
1. BAILEY, ALBERT ERNEST. *The Relative Validity of Ten Different Intelligence Tests.* Unpublished doctor's thesis, University of Washington, 1942. (*Abstracts of Theses . . . 1942,* 1943, p. 189.)
2. PREISCHE, WALTER A. *The Relationship of Certain Measurable Factors to Success in Secondary-School Physics.* Unpublished doctor's thesis, New York University, 1944. (*Abstracts of Theses . . .* [School of Education] 1944, pp. 217-21.)
3. SHUMAN, JOHN T. *An Investigation Into the Value of Certain Tests in the Selection and Upgrading of Personnel in Aircraft Engine and Propeller Industries.* Unpublished doctor's thesis, Pennsylvania State College, 1944. Pp. 251. (*Abstracts of Doctoral Dissertations . . . 1944,* 1945, pp. 160-76.)
4. BININGER, MARY LEE. *A Study on the Prediction of Success in an Engineering College.* Unpublished master's thesis, Clark University, 1945. (*Abstracts of Dissertations . . . 1945,* pp. 20-21.)
5. SHUMAN, JOHN T. "The Value of Aptitude Tests for Factory Workers in the Aircraft Engine and Propeller Industries." *J Appl Psychol* 29:156-60 Ap '45. * (*PA* 19:2346)
6. SHUMAN, JOHN T. "The Value of Aptitude Tests for Supervisory Workers in the Aircraft Engine and Propeller Industries." *J Appl Psychol* 29:185-90 Je '45. * (*PA* 19:3138)
7. WEBER, EDMUND G. "Equating High-School Intelligence Quotients With College Aptitude Test Scores." *J Ed Psychol* 36:443-6 O '45. * (*PA* 20:1703)
8. PUGH, GLADYS S. "Summaries From 'Appraisal of the Silent Reading Abilities of Acoustically Handicapped Children.'" *Am Ann Deaf* 91:331-49 S '46. * (*PA* 21:290)
9. BOLTON, FLOYD B. "Value of Several Intelligence Tests for Predicting Scholastic Achievement." *J Ed Res* 41:133-8 O '47. *

Frederic Kuder, Professor of Psychology, Duke University, Durham, North Carolina. ALPHA TEST. These picture tests appear attractive enough to gain and hold the attention of a jaded seven-year old. By an ingenious plan, it is possible to use these tests for both nonverbal and verbal testing, using the same items and test blanks. The author of the tests recommends that both tests be given for increased reliability.

From the standpoint of convenience of administration the Alpha tests combine the features of self-administration with rapid scoring by means of a hand stencil for the nonverbal test. The verbal tests require the recitation of test items by the teacher or examiner. The amount or quality of reading skill of the examinees does not affect their test scores. Multiple-choice items composed of series of pictures graduated in difficulty from familiar, concrete objects to more abstract "geometrics" make up the test content.

Unlike the Beta and Gamma Tests, these are not revisions of the *Otis Self-Administering Tests of Mental Ability* but the method of determining item inclusion is the same, i.e., per cent of "passes" by groups of students making rapid progress against those making slow school progress. Further evidence of validity is offered in reports of correlation of the Alpha Tests with the Primary Examination (sic) and Grade Placement, the biserial coefficients being .65 and .86, respectively, with total score.

Reliability for total score is reported as .81, computed from total scores of Form A and Form B, for grade range of 2 to 3. This reliability is not impressively high; however, considered with regard to the high variability of performance in young children, the limited sampling of abilities and the narrow range of grades, the reliability appears acceptable for group prediction or appraisal. The reliability compares favorably with other nonlanguage tests for about the same grade range: *Haggerty Intelligence Examination,* Delta I, reliability reported as .79; *Chicago Non-Verbal Examination,* coefficients ranging from .80 to .93; *Pintner–Cunningham Primary Test* as .89 and .93 (N = 22 and 23). It would be indeed hazardous to attempt prediction and control in the individual case from information derived from these test scores, but the reliability seems adequate for group comparisons.

Scores may be reported in terms of "IQ's" and "MA's" with norms based on nearly 18,000 cases of school children.

Since test scores will be influenced by visual acuity, especially the discernment of differences among the "geometrics," a welcome addition to the tests would be some simple determination of eye efficiency such as is provided on the *California Test of Mental Maturity.*

BETA TEST. These revisions of the *Otis Self-Administering Tests of Mental Ability* are designed for either machine scoring or hand scoring by means of a stencil.

The reliability, as computed by the correlation of comparable forms, yields a combined coefficient of .96, based on grades 4 to 9, inclusive. However, it is observed that the reliability coefficient for the grade levels taken separately is an average coefficient of .79. Therefore, the accuracy of measurement for any individual examinee is considerably less than might be inferred from the coefficient of .96.

The only advantage these tests offer over the *Otis Self-Administering Tests* is that of rapid scoring. Where a small group of papers, 25 to 50, is to be hand-scored the gain is small indeed and must be balanced against the increased time required for oral instructions. Furthermore, the answer sheets of Forms CM and DM require rather complex manipulation and may result in lowering of scores for the less test-wise members of the group.

The tests would be improved if practice responses were made on the answer sheet proper rather than in an analogous, but not identical, manner. Moreover, a more specific check of the accuracy of sample responses would increase the assurance of both the examiner and the examinee that the method of response is understood. The writer has in mind the well-known American Council examinations wherein "doing" and demonstrating are effected on the answer sheet proper. A further flaw in the design of Forms CM and DM is the procedure of giving the oral instructions with the test material exposed to the roving eye. The examiner may control the actual marking of the answer sheet in advance of the "Go" signal, but it would not be possible to control the reading of items by the student who requires little or no instruction. Since these disadvantages do not occur in Forms A and B of the Beta series, it is believed that they offer forms preferable to Beta CM and DM. Forms A and B do not, however, permit machine scoring.

Neither these tests nor the Self-Administering group instruct the examinee concerning the advisability of guessing on doubtful test items. This question frequently arises in practice, particularly among the test sophisticates aware that various methods of counting "wrongs" exist. The absence of any definite instruction in this matter may result in the test measuring other factors in addition to test content. The majority of well-constructed tests in the field are explicit on this point. Since there is no information provided in the manual on this matter, it is recommended that, in the interest of comparability of scores, the examiner urge against guessing.

For reviews by Psyche Cattell, F. Kuhlmann, Rudolf Pintner, and C. Spearman, and excerpts from reviews by J. A. Long and one other, see 38:1053, 40:1413, and 40:1427.

Otis Self-Administering Tests of Mental Ability. Grades 4-9, 9-16; 1922–28; Forms A, B, C, D; $1 per 25 of either level; 35¢ per specimen set, postpaid; 30(35) minutes or 20(25) minutes; Arthur S. Otis; World Book Co.
a) INTERMEDIATE EXAMINATION. Grades 4-9.
b) HIGHER EXAMINATION. Grades 9-16.

REFERENCES

1. McGeoch, John A. "Some Results From Three Group Intelligence Tests." *Sch & Soc* 17:196 F 17 '23. *
2. Miller, W. S. "The Variation and Significance of Intelligence Quotients Obtained From Group Tests." *J Ed Psychol* 15:359-66 S '24. *
3. Brooks, Fowler D. "The Accuracy of Intelligence Quotients From Pairs of Group Tests in the Junior High School." *J Ed Psychol* 18:173-86 Mr '27. * (*PA* 1:1453)
4. Cushman, C. L. "A Study of the Reliability of Mental Tests as Used in Oklahoma City." *J Appl Psychol* 11:509-11 D '27. * (*PA* 2:2944)
5. Guiler, W. S. "The Predictive Value of Group Intelligence Tests." *J Ed Res* 16:365-74 D '27. * (*PA* 2:1094)
6. Lange, Irene Dunn. *The Value of the Otis Self-Administering Test of Mental Ability as a Means of Predicting the Success of Pupils in Junior High School.* Unpublished master's thesis. University of Chicago, 1927.
7. Odell, C. W. "An Attempt at Predicting Success in the Freshman Year at College." *Sch & Soc* 25:702-6 Je 11 '27. * (*PA* 1:2078)
8. Bass, Hyman. *An Attempt to Improve the Directional Scoring of the Otis Self-Administering Test.* Unpublished master's thesis, College of the City of New York, 1928. Pp. 44.
9. Kuhlmann, F. "The Kuhlmann-Anderson Intelligence Tests Compared With Seven Others." *J Appl Psychol* 12:545-94 D '28. * (*PA* 3:1751)
10. Cole, Robert D. "A Conversion Scale for Comparing Scores on Three Secondary School Intelligence Tests." *J Ed Res* 20:190-8 O '29. * (*PA* 4:439)
11. South, Earl B., and Clark, Genevieve Y. "Some Uses of Psychological Tests in Schools of Nursing." *Am J Nursing* 29:1495-1501 D '29. * (*PA* 4:1740)
12. Broom, M. Eustace. "How Constant is the IQ Yielded by the Otis Self-Administering Test of Mental Ability." *J Ed Res* 22:53-5 Je '30. * (*PA* 4:3725)
13. Cattell, Psyche. "Comparability of I.Q.'s Obtained From Different Tests at Different I.Q. Levels." *Sch & Soc* 31:437-42 Mr 29 '30. * (*PA* 4:2561)
14. Cattell, Psyche. "IQ's and the Otis' Measure of Brightness." *J Ed Res* 22:31-5 Je '30. * (*PA* 4:3726)
15. Steckel, Minnie L. "The Restandardization of IQ's of Different Tests." *J Ed Psychol* 21:278-83 Ap '30. * (*PA* 4:3313)
16. Taylor, Don H. "The Selection of Printers' Apprentices." *Voc Guid Mag* 8:281-8 Mr '30. * (*PA* 4:3624)
17. Cattell, Psyche. "Why Otis' 'IQ' Cannot be Equivalent to the Stanford-Binet IQ." *J Ed Psychol* 22:599-603 N '31. * (*PA* 6:906)
18. Gordon, Hans C. *The Specific Nature of Achievement and the Predictive Value of the IQ: An Investigation of the Limitations Placed Upon the Predictive Values of Otis IQ's by the Variation in the Achievement of Twelfth Grade Students in Their Different Subjects.* Unpublished doctor's thesis, University of Pennsylvania, 1931. Pp. 147.
19. Miles, Catharine Cox. "The Otis S-A as a Fifteen-Minute Intelligence Test." *Personnel J* 10:246-9 D '31. * (*PA* 6:915)
20. Miles, Catharine Cox, and Miles, Walter R. "The Correlation of Intelligence Scores and Chronological Age From Early to Late Maturity." *Am J Psychol* 44:44-78 Ja '32. * (*PA* 6:2044)
21. Nemzek, Claude L. "Intelligence Testing at the College Level." *J Ed Res* 26:617-8 Ap '33. * (*PA* 7:4196)
22. Torgerson, T. L., and Aamodt, Geneva P. "The Validity of Certain Prognostic Tests in Predicting Algebraic Ability." *J Exp Ed* 1:277-9 Mr '33. * (*PA* 7:4145)
23. Turney, Austin H., and Fee, Mary. "The Comparative Value for Junior High School Use of Five Group Mental Tests." *J Ed Psychol* 24:371-9 My '33. * (*PA* 7:5570)
24. Miles, Catharine Cox. "Influence of Speed and Age on Intelligence Scores of Adults." *J General Psychol* 10:208-10 Ja '34. * (*PA* 8:5687)
25. Moore, Herbert, and Trafton, Helen. "Equating Test Scores." *J Ed Psychol* 25:216-9 Mr '34. * (*PA* 8:3827)
26. Stevens, S. N., and Wonderlic, E. F. "The Relationship of the Number of Questions Missed on the Otis Mental Tests and the Ability to Handle Office Detail." *J Appl Psychol* 18:364-8 Je '34. * (*PA* 8:6083)
27. Traxler, Arthur E. "Reliability, Constancy, and Validity of the Otis IQ." *J Appl Psychol* 18:241-51 Ap '34. * (*PA* 8:5273)
28. Copeland, Herman A. "Some Characteristics of Three Tests Used to Predict Clerical Success." *J Appl Psychol* 20:461-70 Ag '36. * (*PA* 11:421)
29. Krueger, William C. F. "Note Concerning Group Influence Upon Otis S.-A. Test Scores." *J Ed Psychol* 27:554-5 O '36. * (*PA* 11:1518)
30. Lorge, Irving. "A Table of Percentile Equivalents for Eight Intelligence Tests Frequently Used With Adults." *J Appl Psychol* 20:392-5 Je '36. * (*PA* 10:5552)
31. Chapanis, Alphonse. "A Note on the Validity and Difficulty of Items in Form A of the Otis Self-Administering Test of Mental Ability." *J Exp Ed* 5:246-8 Mr '37. * (*PA* 11:3922)
32. Copeland, Herman A. "Validating Two Tests for Census Enumeration." *J Appl Psychol* 21:230-2 Ap '37. * (*PA* 11:4712)
33. Harris, Albert J. "The Relative Significance of Measures of Mechanical Aptitude, Intelligence, and Previous Scholarship for Predicting Achievement in Dental School." *J Appl Psychol* 21:513-21 O '37. * (*PA* 12:2113)
34. Flottman, Edward Albert. *The Prediction of High School Success From Achievement Tests.* Unpublished master's thesis, University of Washington, 1938. (*Abstracts of theses* ..., 1938, pp. 79-81.)
35. Balinsky, B., and Stone, Irving R. "A New Method of Finding the Intelligence Quotient on Otis Self-Administering Tests, Higher Examination." *J Social Psychol* 10:459-65 N '39. * (*PA* 14:1620)
36. Cohen, Edith R. *A Comparison of the Revised Terman Scale and the Otis Higher Examination.* Unpublished master's thesis, Columbia University, 1939.
37. Hovland, Carl Iver, and Wonderlic, E. F. "A Critical Analysis of the Otis Self-Administering Test of Mental Ability —Higher Form." *J Appl Psychol* 23:367-87 Je '39. * (*PA* 13:5941)
38. Seidenfeld, Morton A. "Some Psychometric Observations of the Tuberculous Patients in a National Institution: I. The Otis Self-Administering Test of Mental Ability." *J General Psychol* 21:447-55 O '39. * (*PA* 14:358)
39. Tiffin, Joseph, and Greenly, R. J. "Employee Selection Tests for Electrical Fixture Assemblers and Radio Assemblers." *J Appl Psychol* 23:240-63 Ap '39. * (*PA* 13:4840)
40. Wonderlic, E. F., and Hovland, Carl Iver. "The Personnel Test: A Restandardized Abridgment of the Otis S-A Test for Business and Industrial Use." *J Appl Psychol* 23:685-702 D '39. * (*PA* 14:2649)
41. Failor, Leona Mae. *An Evaluation of Intelligence Tests Used in Industrial Schools and Reformatories.* Unpublished doctor's thesis, University of Nebraska, 1940. (*Abstracts of Doctoral Dissertations* ..., 1940, pp. 59-65.)
42. Harrell, Willard. "Testing Cotton Mill Supervisors." *J Appl Psychol* 24:31-5 F '40. * (*PA* 14:3709)
43. Johnson, A. P. "A Study of One Company's Criteria for Selecting College Graduates." *J Appl Psychol* 24:253-64 Je '40. * (*PA* 14:6165)
44. Redmond, Mary, and Davies, F. R. J. *The Standardization of Two Intelligence Tests.* New Zealand Council for Educational Research, Educational Research Series, No. 14. Wellington, New Zealand: Whitcombe & Tombs Ltd., 1940. Pp. xv, 129. 7s. 6d. * (London: Oxford University Press, 1941. 7s. 6d.) (*PA* 15:2841)
45. Baxter, Brent. "An Experimental Analysis of the Contributions of Speed and Level in an Intelligence Test." *J Ed Psychol* 32:285-96 Ap '41. * (*PA* 16:362)
46. Blum, Milton L., and Candee, Beatrice. "The Selection of Department Store Packers and Wrappers With the Aid of Certain Psychological Tests: Study II." *J Appl Psychol* 25:291-9 Je '41. * (*PA* 15:4336)
47. Crooks, William R., and Ferguson, Leonard W. "Item Validities of the Otis Self-Administering Tests of Mental Ability for a College Population." *J Exp Ed* 9:229-32 Mr '41. * (*PA* 15:4432)
48. Goldfarb, William. *An Investigation of Reaction Time in Older Adults and Its Relationship to Certain Observed Mental Test Patterns.* Columbia University, Teachers College, Contributions to Education, No. 831. Irving Lorge and Rudolf Pintner, faculty co-sponsors. New York: Bureau of Publications, the College, 1941. Pp. ix, 76. $1.60. * (*PA* 15:4615)
49. Riker, Britten L., and Gaudet, Frederick J. "The Use of Some Tests in the Prediction of Legal Aptitude." *J Appl Psychol* 25:313-22 Je '41. * (*PA* 15:4414)
50. Bailey, Albert Ernest. *The Relative Validity of Ten Different Intelligence Tests.* Unpublished doctor's thesis, University of Washington, 1942. (*Abstracts of Theses* ... 1942, 1943, p. 189.)
51. Baxter, Brent. "On the Equivalence of Time-Limit and Work-Limit Methods." *Am J Psychol* 55:407-11 Jl '42. * (*PA* 16:5040)
52. Blair, Glenn Myers, and Kamman, James F. "Do Intelligence Tests Requiring Reading Ability Give Spuriously Low Scores to Poor Readers at the College Freshman Level?" *J Ed Res* 36:280-3 D '42. * (*PA* 17:2207)
53. Hay, Edward N., and Blakemore, Arline M. "Comparison of Otis and Alpha Test Scores Made by Bank Clerks." *J Appl Psychol* 26:850-1 D '42. * (*PA* 17:2017)
54. Hay, Edward N., and Blakemore, Arline Mance. "Testing Clerical Applicants." *J Appl Psychol* 26:852-5 D '42. * (*PA* 17:2854)
55. McGehee, William, and Moffie, D. J. "Psychological Tests in the Selection of Enrollees in Engineering, Science, Management, Defense Training Courses." *J Appl Psychol* 26:584-6 O '42. * (*PA* 17:2186)
56. Older, H. J. "A Note on the Twenty-Minute Time Limit of the Otis S-A Tests When Used With Superior High School Students." *J Appl Psychol* 26:241-4 Ap '42. * (*PA* 16:4203)
57. Ames, Viola. "Factors Relating to High-School Achievement." *J Ed Psychol* 34:229-36 Ap '43. * (*PA* 17:4252)
58. Crider, Blake. "A School of Nursing Selection Program." *J Appl Psychol* 27:452-7 O '43. * (*PA* 18:281)
59. Hay, Edward N. "Predicting Success in Machine Bookkeeping." *J Appl Psychol* 27:483-93 D '43. * (*PA* 18:1877)
60. Forlano, George, and Kirkpatrick, Forrest H. "Intelligence and Adjustment Measurements in the Selection of Radio Tube Mounters." *J Appl Psychol* 29:257-61 Ag '45. * (*PA* 20:283)

61. NIEMI, GEORGE M. *An Analysis of Data From Retesting 1024 Students With the Otis Self-Administering Test of Mental Ability.* Unpublished master's thesis, University of Oregon, 1945.
62. SARTAIN, A. Q. "The Use of Certain Standardized Tests in the Selection of Inspectors in an Aircraft Factory." *J Consult Psychol* 9:234-7 S-O '45. * (PA 20:1241)
63. SHULTZ, IRVIN T., AND BARNABAS, BENTLEY. "Testing for Leadership in Industry." *Trans Kan Acad Sci* 48:160-4 S '45. * (PA 20:896)
64. TRAXLER, ARTHUR E. "The Correlation Between Two Tests of Academic Aptitude." *Sch & Soc* 61:383-4 Je 9 '45. * (PA 19:3197)
65. FLEMMING, EDWIN G., AND FLEMMING, CECILE WHITE. "A Qualitative Approach to the Problem of Improving Selection of Salesmen by Psychological Tests." *J Psychol* 21:127-50 Ja '46. * (PA 20:1636)
66. ORDAHL, VIDA ELLISON. *An Intercomparison of the Otis Self-Administered Test of Mental Ability, Intermediate Form-A; the Stanford-Binet Intelligence Scale, Form-L; and the California Test of Mental Maturity, Elementary S-Form.* Unpublished master's thesis, University of Southern California, 1946.
67. SARTAIN, A. Q. "A Comparison of the New Revised Stanford-Binet, the Bellevue Scale, and Certain Group Tests of Intelligence." *J Social Psychol* 23:237-9 My '46. * (PA 21:309)
68. SARTAIN, A. Q. "Relation Between Scores on Certain Standard Tests and Supervisory Success in an Aircraft Factory." *J Appl Psychol* 30:328-32 Ag '46. * (PA 21:250)
69. SARTAIN, A. Q. "A Note on Otis S.-A. Test Scores Made by Candidates for Supervisory Positions in an Aircraft Factory." *J Social Psychol* 24:253-4 N '46. * (PA 21:1681)
70. CASE, HARRY W. "Selection of Aircraft Engineering Draftsmen and Designers." *J Appl Psychol* 31:583-8 D '47. *
71. THORNDIKE, ROBERT L. "The Prediction of Intelligence at College Entrance From Earlier Test." *J Ed Psychol* 38:129-48 Mr '47. * (PA 22:861)

Frederic Kuder, Professor of Psychology, Duke University, Durham, North Carolina. For purposes of prediction of school and college success these tests compare favorably with other measures of general ability. Recent studies have indicated a high relationship between the *American Council on Education Psychological Examinations* and the *Otis Self-Administering Tests,* with the latter test showing as high, or higher, relationship to college grades. There is some evidence to indicate that when the IQ's on the Otis and the familiar individual intelligence tests are compared, the IQ's of the Otis will correspond more closely with those of the Wechsler-Bellevue than those of the Stanford-Binet. (The IQ's for the three tests are, of course, computed on the basis of different postulates.)

The Otis tests are among the easiest and most economical to administer and score of all the general ability tests. A consideration of these factors of cost and administrative ease brings to mind the *Wonderlic Personnel Test.* This "restandardized abridgment of the Otis S-A test" was standardized on employees and some student groups. It may be given as a speed test (12 minutes) or a power test. The reliability of this shorter test is somewhat lower than that of the *Otis Self-Administering Tests.* Correlations between the Wonderlic and the Otis are not as high as between various forms of the Otis tests. A good feature of the *Wonderlic Personnel Test* is the correction of score to allow for the reduced speed of older adults. Wonderlic furnishes a table for adding points, according to age, to the scores of examinees more than thirty years old. The use of the Otis tests in adult counseling centers suggests the need for deriving similar norms for various age levels of the population, since current norms are based on young people presumably working at optimum functioning level. The current norms do not permit the comparison of adults in one age group with adults in other age groups which have experienced a greater or less amount of the known diminution of mental alertness as measured by a speed test.

The procedure of administering the Higher Examination on a 20-minute basis with scores transmuted into terms of 30-minute scores, according to a table in the manual, has stimulated some research into the accuracy of such conversions. The results of these experiments are not entirely conclusive but generally imply that the conversions are not applicable to all age and ability groups. In addition to the inaccuracies of measurement obtained on the 20-minute basis, there may be inadequate measurement where certain types of items are grouped near the end of the test and are unlikely to be attempted by examinees tested at the 20-minute rate. For example, in the Higher Examination, there are three or four questions based on a geometric figure, presumably designed to measure some factor related to space perception; these items all appear near the end of the test, and only there. It is thus likely that this particular function would not be tested because the examinee's time ran out before he reached the items.

The manual is more comprehensive than most in describing procedures of standardization, various methods of interpreting scores, devices for wide and varied application in schools, and even some elementary instruction in statistical techniques. It is, however, seriously deficient in bibliography. The increasing use of tests, with consequent stimulus to research, indicates the need for a list of references to be incorporated in the manual.

[251]

★**Perception of Relations Scales.** Adults; 1944–46; 1 form; $1 per 25; nontimed (30-60) minutes; Educational Test Bureau.
a) PERCEPTION OF RELATIONS SCALES. 1944; 25¢ per specimen set; M. J. Van Wagenen.

b) ADVANCED PERCEPTION OF RELATIONS SCALES. 1946; IBM; 25¢ per specimen set; Lindsey R. Harmon and M. J. Van Wagenen.

Charles D. Flory, Rohrer, Hibler and Replogle, New York, New York. "The Perception of Relations Scales are designed to provide a quick, simple, valid means of predicting the learning ability of adults, particularly in personnel work where a complete testing program is impractical." These tests are intended by the author to be a short intelligence test, a screening instrument to be used with adults in industry or education.

The tasks provided require an understanding of the relationship between two elements that are given and the detection of a similar relationship between a third given element and one of five possible choices. There are sixty items scaled in difficulty. The relationships involve time, place, identity, integral parts, quality, and cause. The difficulty of the relationship presented is intended to exceed the difficulty of the vocabulary or information required for solution of the item.

The performance of 18-year-old men and women has been used as a basis for determining norms. The raw scores of 1,000 subjects were scaled so that raw scores can be transmitted directly into per cent placement, standard scores, or percentile rank. The scales cover approximately ten probable errors. The advanced scales arranged by Van Wagenen and Harmon are similar in form and content to the original scales but are more difficult. In the original and simpler scales, the middle score for 18-year-old subjects is the 50th percentile while on the advanced scales, the middle item was answered correctly by only 10 per cent of the 18-year-old group. The authors therefore feel that the advanced scales are well adapted to use with students above the secondary level and at the supervisory-executive levels in industry.

These scales are practically self-administering. They can be given individually or in groups. The scoring can be done manually in less than one minute per test. The advanced scales are also arranged for machine scoring. The scales are given as a power test rather than a speed test. The time suggested is about thirty minutes but wide variation occurs with rapid workers finishing in half the suggested time or less and the slowest workers requiring more than twice the suggested time. This feature is a definite handicap in large-scale industrial testing where the measurement of intelligence is only one part of a selection or placement test battery.

Meager data are supplied concerning the standardization and validation of these scales. The statement is made that validation results from the use of outside criteria but no hints are given concerning these criteria. The items are purported to discriminate both from grade to grade and between pupils varying in ability within each grade. None of the statistical evidence supporting these contentions is to be found in the manual. The norms are reported as tentative.

The test is intended for adults but standardized on 18-year-old subjects. The assumption is made that gains in ability to sense the types of relationships involved have stabilized by age eighteen. Ability to handle analogies in contrast to vocabulary proficiency does appear to reach its peak in the late teens but there must be some decline in the ability to perceive relationships during adulthood. This point has not been treated in the interpretative data accompanying these scales.

Analogies have long been used in the measurement of intelligence, but these scales have the weakness of any single-type test such as vocabulary, memory, or number as an index of intellectual competence. Research has yet to demonstrate whether the short intelligence test should sample a single aspect of intellectual functioning or seek to sample the various abilities that compose intelligent action.

[252]

★Personnel Classification Test [Henderson]. Adults; 1946; IBM; 1 form; separate answer sheets must be used; $20 per 100; $2 per 100 machine-scorable answer sheets; 35¢ per scoring stencil; 25¢ per single copy; 25¢ per manual; Robert W. Henderson; the Author, University Personnel Service, University of Kentucky, Lexington, Kentucky.

Brent Baxter, Director of Personnel Research, Chesapeake and Ohio Railway Company, Cleveland, Ohio. This test appears to have been been published prematurely as far as being a standardized test is concerned. The test has two parts, verbal ability and arithmetical ability, but there is no data about their reliability, relationship, or validity. The norms, based on 100 persons of an atypical group, are quite inadequate. No studies of the validity of the test are available. A single reliability coefficient based on an unspecified group is given.

A system of adjusting total scores for the length of time used to complete the test is offered, but it is based on "rule of thumb" developed from the scores of 25 people.

Therefore, in its present form this test is not an effective contribution to industrial testing. As the author collects future evidence, however, he may then be able to offer a useful tool. At present, it represents only a typical-looking group of items on vocabulary, general information, and arithmetic ready for evaluation.

John C. Flanagan, Professor of Psychology, The University of Pittsburgh, Pittsburgh, Pennsylvania. According to the manual, this test was designed to measure mental ability in an employment or work situation. There is no time limit and the test is designed to be used with a standard five-choice answer sheet. The first part contains approximately 100 items, with alternate items testing information and word knowledge. The second section of the test is composed of 25 problems "selected to measure practical arithmetical ability."

Although no time limit is used in administering this test, a table is provided for allowing speed credit or demerit points in accordance with the number of minutes required to complete the test. This table is to be used only if it is desired "to determine the speed score."

The norms presented were determined from 100 clients of a private employment agency. Ages ranged from 17 to 50. Eighty per cent were high school graduates, 17 per cent were college graduates. One half were men. The manual states: "They represent many occupations and should not be considered as typical of any one employee group." It is stated that the norms are illustrative and that "after a sampling has been made, local norms [should] be established that will be representative of the group being studied."

The manual also states the odd-even reliability of the test in one study was .91. The number of cases included in this study and the results for other studies are not presented.

The test items are short and appear likely to differentiate between individuals with varying amounts of vocabulary information and arithmetical skill. However, they do not seem to be quite so carefully edited as some in the better published tests of this type. For example, one of the items states: "Which substance will not conduct electricity?", and the answer given is "rubber." Although there should be no difficulty in identifying this as the intended answer, it would be more accurate to say that it is a poor conductor of electricity rather than that it is *not* a conductor of electricity. Similarly, an item regarding mercury gives the answer that it is a liquid, and other choices are "gas" and "solid." It would be more accurate to state that under ordinary conditions of pressure and temperature mercury is a liquid.

One misprint was noted; one of the options for "thyroid" was printed as "figament." Presumably "ligament" was intended.

The arithmetic items include not only questions which require arithmetical computations but also questions measuring an understanding of numbers, such as, "Which is the smaller fraction?", and, "25 divided by zero equals."

In conclusion, it may be stated that this set of items will tend to differentiate people on much the same basis as many currently published tests of general intelligence. The fact that it has been designed for use without time limits represents a possible advantage, but since usable norms have not been provided, the test user could as easily utilize other test materials and develop his own norms for the no-time-limit situation. The items tend to be somewhat more practical than academic; and the test should prove useful to persons interested in obtaining a combined measure of vocabulary, information, and arithmetical abilities for general classification purposes.

[253]

★**Personnel Classification Test [Wesman].** Grades 8-16 and adults; 1947; Forms A, B; $1.50 per 25, postpaid; 35¢ per specimen set, postpaid; 28(35) minutes; Alexander G. Wesman; Psychological Corporation.

J Consult Psychol 11:340 N-D '47. Intended primarily for industrial and business use, this short general ability test yields three scores: verbal, numerical and total. Part I consists of 40 multiple-choice verbal analogies items, in which the first and fourth terms of the analogy must be chosen, with the second and third terms given. Part II contains 20 arithmetic computation items. Reliabilities range from .77 for 93 college freshmen, to .92 for 97 life insurance salesmen. Norms are supplied for several educational and occupational groups. "Validity" is indicated by the correspondence of test scores with educational level and with another group intelligence test, and by data showing a relationship to supervisors' ratings of chain store clerks. The manual stresses the value of the separate verbal and numerical scores for occupational placement.

[254]

★**Pintner General Ability Tests: Non-Language Series.** Grades 4-9; 1945; may be administered in pantomime; Forms K, L; $2.30 per 25; 15¢ per pantomime directions; 35¢ per specimen set, postpaid; 50(60) minutes; Rudolf Pintner; World Book Co.

Carroll A. Whitmer, Director of Special Education, Public Schools, Pittsburgh, Pennsylvania. The nonlanguage series of the *Pintner General Ability Tests* was projected to parallel the author's verbal series as closely as possible in "mechanics of standardization and general structure." The advanced form has not been published.

The intermediate test consists of six sections, namely, figure dividing, reverse drawings, pattern synthesis, movement sequence, manikin, and paper folding. Although the total working time on the test is 50 minutes, the directions are quite elaborate and include practice exercises for each section of the tests. The author recommends that the test be administered in two sittings. The test is hand scored with a cutout stencil.

The manual of directions gives a detailed discussion of construction and standardization of the tests and the interpretation of scores.

The test items were selected for their discriminative power. The scores for over 6,000 children in the four yearly age groups from 9½ to 13½ were used in the standardization. The children were selected by taking all the members of three consecutive school grades in eleven communities from different sections of the United States.

Reliability data for the two forms of the test are presented as split-half correlations of .858 and .890 corrected by the Spearman-Brown formula and probable errors of measurement of 4.1 and 3.7. The standard deviations of median scores are 16.0 and 16.4.

A full-page discussion of the validity of the test is given in the manual in terms of the uses for which the test is recommended. These are "as a supplement to the Pintner Verbal Test in order to get a better measurement of all-round mental ability"; as a measure of the type of mental skill which functions in school and life situations involving shop work, drafting, and vocations of a mechanical nature; and as a substitute for verbal tests in measuring the hard-of-hearing, deaf, and foreign-language-speaking. Some statistical evidence is presented in defense of the validity of the test for the last-mentioned purpose, but research is recommended for the establishment of the validity of the test for the second purpose stated.

Five different end scores may be obtained from the raw score on this test. The first of these, the subtest standard score, is not recommended for separate use with present evidence. The other end scores are median standard score, mental age, deviation IQ, and percentile rank. The use of these various scores is discussed in the manual.

It is gratifying to the reviewer to find a test manual as detailed as this one and a nonlanguage test which is as well constructed as this one. It appears to be the best test in its field, but like all group tests which cover a wide age range, it should prove most efficient in the middle of the age range for which it is intended.

[255]

Pintner General Ability Tests: Verbal Series. Grades kgn-2, 2-4, 4-9, 9+; 1923-46; 20¢ per manual; World Book Co.
a) PINTNER-CUNNINGHAM PRIMARY TEST. Grades kgn-2; 1923-46; Forms A, B, C; $1.45 per 25; 35¢ per specimen set; Rudolf Pintner, Bess V. Cunningham, and Walter N. Durost.
b) PINTNER-DUROST ELEMENTARY TEST. Grades 2.5-4.5; Scales 1 (requires no reading) and 2 (requires reading) may be used separately or together; Forms A, B; $2.00 per 25 Scale 1; $1.60 per 25 Scale 2; 35¢ per specimen set; (45) minutes per scale; Rudolf Pintner and Walter N. Durost.
c) PINTNER INTERMEDIATE TEST. Grades 4.5-9.5; 1931-42; revision of *Pintner Intelligence Test*; Forms A, B; $1.70 per 25; 35¢ per specimen set; $1.20 per 25 machine-scorable answer sheets; 45(55) minutes; Rudolf Pintner.
d) PINTNER ADVANCED TEST. Grade 9 and above; 1938-42; Forms A, B; $1.70 per 25; 35¢ per specimen set; $1.20 per 25 machine-scorable answer sheets; Rudolf Pintner.

REFERENCES

1. PINTNER, R., AND CUNNINGHAM, BESS V. "The Problem of Group Intelligence Tests for Very Young Children." *J Ed Psychol* 13:465-72 N '22. *
2. HIRSCH, NATHANIEL D. MTTRON. "A Study of Natio-Racial Mental Differences." *Genetic Psychol Monogr* 1:231-406 My & Jl '26. * (PA 2:179)
3. PINTNER, RUDOLF. "The Pintner-Cunningham Primary Test." *J Ed Psychol* 18:52-8 Ja '27. * (PA 1:977)
4. KUHLMANN, F. "The Kuhlmann-Anderson Intelligence Tests Compared With Seven Others." *J Appl Psychol* 12:545-94 D '28. * (PA 3:1751)
5. SANGREN, PAUL V. "Comparative Validity of Primary Intelligence Tests." *J Appl Psychol* 13:394-412 Ag '29. * (PA 3:4324)
6. PORTER, M. POWELL, AND LAUDERBACH, J. CALVIN. "On the Constancy of the IQ." *Sch & Soc* 33:675-6 My 16 '31. * (PA 5:3570)
7. SEAGOE, M. V. "An Evaluation of Certain Intelligence Tests." *J Appl Psychol* 18:432-6 Je '34. * (PA 8:6140)

8. WALKER, ELLIS WOODS. *The Predictive Value of the Pintner-Cunningham Primary Mental Test: A Follow-up Study.* Unpublished master's thesis, Birmingham-Southern College, 1935. Pp. 57.
9. GRANT, ALBERT. "A Comparison of the Metropolitan Readiness Tests and the Pintner-Cunningham Primary Mental Test." *El Sch J* 38:118-26 O '37. * (*PA* 15:3195)
10. GRANT, ALBERT. "The Comparative Validity of the Metropolitan Readiness Tests and the Pintner-Cunningham Primary Mental Tests." *El Sch J* 38:599-605 Ap '38. * (*PA* 12:4990)
11. GATES, ARTHUR I. "A Further Evaluation of Reading Readiness Tests." *El Sch J* 40:577-91 Ap '40. * (*PA* 15:3581)
12. KIRKPATRICK, FORREST H., AND RUPP, ROBERT A. "The Pintner Test at the College Level." *J Ed Res* 33:357-9 Ja '40. * (*PA* 14:2132)
13. BAILEY, ALBERT ERNEST. *The Relative Validity of Ten Different Intelligence Tests.* Unpublished doctor's thesis, University of Washington, 1942. (*Abstracts of Theses . . . 1942,* 1943, p. 189.)

Stanley S. Marzolf, Professor of Psychology, Illinois State Normal University, Normal, Illinois. Four batteries of subtests make up this series. The primary battery (of which Form A is a slightly modified version of the original *Pintner–Cunningham Primary Test*) consists of seven subtests, each involving responses to pictorial materials. The elementary battery is made up of two parts or scales which are published in separate booklets. The first part, Picture Content, has six subtests composed entirely of pictures. Scale 2, Reading Content, also has six parts, namely vocabulary, number sequence, analogies, opposites, logical selection, and arithmetic reasoning. Separate norms are available for these two scales. The Intermediate and Advanced Tests have eight subtests each, namely those included in the elementary battery and, in addition, a classification test and a best-answer test. Both the Intermediate and Advanced Tests are adapted for use of a hand-scoring stencil or for machine scoring. Except for the Primary Test, standard score norms are provided for all subtests, and the general level of ability is the median of the subtest scores. Mental-age equivalents of standard scores are provided. Ratio IQ's may be computed in the usual way, but the use of deviation IQ's is urged. In addition to the usual instruction manual provided with each battery, a Manual for Interpreting the Intermediate and Advanced Tests is obtainable.

This last-named manual is very complete and satisfactory. It contains material which will be profitable to the users of the primary and elementary batteries also. It explains the functions which intelligence tests may serve, describes the standardization procedures, reports subtest intercorrelations, explains standard scores, gives norms, and describes the procedure for computing IQ's.

According to this manual, a valid intelligence test for school use must sample a broad range of the effects of the child's total environment so as to assist in predicting future school achievement. This practical approach defines intelligence as that which enables a child to do school work, yet is not dependent upon the school experience itself. Validity is to be tested by logical analysis of the items, intercorrelations between the subtests, and correlations with school achievement.

Whether a variety of abilities has been sampled is determined by intercorrelations of the subtests of the intermediate and advanced batteries. The median intercorrelation for the former is .58 and for the latter, .43. However, when the contribution of the vocabulary test is partialled out these medians drop to .30 and .24 respectively. No subtest intercorrelation data are given for the Primary and Elementary Tests. The Picture Content and the Reading Content scales of the latter correlate .70 approximately.

Some data on correlation with achievement are given. For 168 fifth-grade children, a correlation with total scores on the *Metropolitan Achievement Test* of .84 was found. For 209 seventh-grade children the correlation was .785. At the college level, test scores were found to correlate .59 with grades in all courses, .77 with the *Cooperative English Test,* and .56 with the *Cooperative General Achievement Test* (12). Correlations with other intelligence tests range from .71 (Binet) to .87 (Otis). The Primary Test was found to correlate .63 with reading test scores of first-grade pupils. No data are given for the most recently developed battery, the elementary.

Lack of perfect correlation with school achievement is explained on the basis that the "tests are not supposed to be measuring identical abilities." In view of the purported aim of the tests it would be more to the point to make specific mention of such factors as the fallibility of school marks, differences in previous school training, and differences in motivation which doubtless account for part of achievement variance.

Frequent reference is made to the comparability of scores at one level with those at another. It is claimed that the scores are comparable because the subtests have been selected to make this possible. Emphasis of this point had better be delayed until factor analysis studies give empirical evidence for it.

Pintner General Ability Tests: Verbal Series

The reliabilities obtained by the split-half and interform methods for the various batteries are, in the majority of cases, in excess of .90. Sources of reliability data are given in all instances.

Standardization has been based on "approximately 100,000 tests from widely separated parts of the country." Further collection of scores for normative purposes is now in progress.

The computation of deviation IQ's is amply explained and illustrated. For the Intermediate and Advanced Tests a monograph which facilitates computation of IQ's and centile equivalents is provided.

This series is one of the best available for school use. The tests are easy to give and score. Raw scores are easily converted to a normative form. The same score system, standard score, mental age, and deviation IQ, is used throughout the series. The attempt to make the tests comparable at all grade levels is commendable, even though empirical evidence that this has been accomplished is lacking.

D. A. Worcester, Chairman, Department of Educational Psychology and Measurements, The University of Nebraska, Lincoln, Nebraska. The above tests constitute a series running from the kindergarten age to maturity. Norms on the advanced test are given for MA's to 21, but apparently the standardization was on public school pupils.

The primary test, originally published in 1923 was revised in 1938, though the changes required for this "thorough revision" seem to have been very few. Seven subtests, all using pictures or drawings are included, involving common observation, aesthetic comparison, associated objects, discrimination of size, picture parts, picture completion, and dot drawing. The test requires detailed instructions and accurate timing, in seconds, on many items. This may account for the fact that in some instances children secure higher scores on this than on some other tests; inexperienced testers are likely to allow a little more than the stated times.

The elementary test is in two parts, one entirely of pictures, the other employing reading. The parts are meant to be as nearly as possible equivalent, but inspection suggests that they are by no means wholly so. Correlations between them are substantial but not high. The attempt is to measure on this test the same elements as are included in the intermediate and advanced tests. The administration of the test is quite complicated; there are many, detailed oral instructions each with its separate timing. Like the primary test, good results necessitate an examiner not only experienced in testing but in handling groups of children. Some of the pictures are not as clear as is desirable.

The intermediate and advanced tests each have eight subtests. All are timed but with limits so liberal, intentionally, that they are not to be considered as speed tests. The materials of the tests are on the whole of the kind that one finds in most of the conventional intelligence tests.

Each test of the series has received careful statistical treatment and the statistical findings are given in the manuals. Norms for the tests are articulated with each other, making possible comparable measures at the various age levels. Scores may be interpreted in almost any way which the user may wish: standard scores, ratio or deviation IQ's, percentile ranks, mental ages, or grade equivalents. Machine scoring is available for the intermediate and the advanced tests. While the task of administering these tests is somewhat greater than that for some of the tests constructed more recently, there is evidence that they have been constructed with care and may be employed with good results.

For excerpts from reviews by Roger M. Bellows and J. Wayne Wrightstone, see 40:1416.

[256]

Pintner Non-Language Primary Mental Test. Grades kgn-2; 1929-30; $2.20 per 25; 30¢ per specimen set; Rudolf Pintner; Bureau of Publications, Teachers College, Columbia University.

REFERENCES

1. PINTNER, RUDOLF. "Results Obtained with the Non-Language Group Test." *J Ed Psychol* 15:473-83 N '24. *
2. BROWN, ANDREW W. "The Correlations of Non-Language Tests With Each Other, With School Achievement, and With Teachers' Judgments of the Intelligence of Children in a School for the Deaf." *J Appl Psychol* 14:371-5 Ag '30. * (PA 5:880)
3. PINTNER, R. "A Group Intelligence Test Suitable For Younger Deaf Children." *J Ed Psychol* 22:360-3 My '31. * (PA 5:3569)
4. PINTNER, RUDOLF. "The Influence of Language Background on Intelligence Tests." *J Social Psychol* 3:235-40 My '32. * (PA 6:3793)
5. SENOUR, A. C. "Necessity for Use of a Non-Language Mental Test in Group Intelligence Testing." *J Ed Res* 27:435-41 F '34. * (PA 8:2816)
6. GARTH, THOMAS R., AND SMITH, OWEN D. "The Performances of Full-Blood Indians on Language and Non-Language Intelligence Tests." *J Abn & Social Psychol* 32:376-81 O-D '37. * (PA 12:3064)

Psyche Cattell, Clinical Psychologist, Lancaster, Pennsylvania. This test was devised for use in testing the intelligence of kindergarten and first- and second-grade children in situations where a test which requires no knowledge of written or spoken language is desired. All the directions are given in pantomime. The children's responses consist of marking or completing pictures and diagrams in the record booklet.

The data regarding the validity and reliability given in the mimeographed manual of directions are somewhat meager, making it difficult to evaluate the tests. Mental-age norms are given for ages 4 9/12 to 9 7/12 years, but the number of cases on which they are based is not reported. The lowest norm given is for only two correct responses, and the highest, for a perfect score. Obviously a mental-age norm which is based on a near-zero score or a near-perfect one cannot be a reliable measure of ability. No distribution of scores is given to aid the examiner in determining within what range the scores will give a reasonably reliable mental-age measure.

Correlating the odd and even items and correcting for the length of the test gave a reliability coefficient of .90 for the first-grade and .86 for second-grade children. A validity coefficient obtained by correlating the mental ages of 80 kindergarten children on this test and on the Stanford–Binet is .61. Using this test and the *Pintner–Cunningham Primary Test,* the coefficient was only .51, even though the range here included three school grades. No information regarding the distribution of children within these grades is given, nor any information regarding the socio-economic level of the groups.

Carroll A. Whitmer, Director of Special Education, Public Schools, Pittsburgh, Pennsylvania. The purpose of this test is to provide a means of testing children with all types of language background, from good or poor homes, without permitting language facility to influence the test results. The directions for the test are given entirely in pantomime. The examiner must not use any verbal supplement to the pantomime.

The manual warns that this test is much more difficult to administer than the ordinary test with verbal directions and recommends that the examiner rehearse the directions two or three times before attempting to give the test. It is the reviewer's experience that it takes many more than two or three practice rehearsals to become proficient in administering test directions to five- and six-year-olds in deaf-mute style when they are not accustomed to that type of performance.

The arrangement of test material for this test is quite similar to that used in the older *Pintner–Cunningham Primary Test*. This type of arrangement with large figures and a small number of items on a page has a great advantage over the crowded page so frequently seen in paper-and-pencil tests intended for young children. The appropriate responses to be made by the child are done with a large pencil and do not require finer co-ordinations than should be reasonably expected of children beginning school.

The score on the test is the number of correct responses. Raw scores are converted to mental ages by the use of a table in the manual. Mental ages on the test range from 4 years 9 months (raw score 2) to 9 years 4 months (raw score 74). IQ's are computed in the usual manner. It is immediately apparent that the test has little range at the low end. Even though the test is suitable for children in the age range of 4.5 to 5.5, the test does not measure the younger kindergarten child whose ability is much below average. Nor does it measure the six-year-old whose mental retardation is more than a year.

The test manual presents very little statistical data. Split-half reliabilities of .90 for 111 first-grade children and .86 for 129 second-graders are presented without mention of whether or not a correction formula was used. The evidence for validity offered in the manual consists of correlations of .61 with Stanford–Binet mental ages for 80 kindergarten children, .78 for 28 other cases not identified, and .51 with Pintner–Cunningham mental ages of 154 children in kindergarten to third grade.

The scores from this test should be used with great caution because the test samples a very limited range of a very limited kind of ability. The many uncontrolled variables in the administration of a group test at the primary level become even more significant when a strange form of test administration is used. The test may serve a good purpose as a rough screen when a large number of children of the type for which it is intended must be examined quickly. Certainly, individual testing with more comprehensive tests would be desirable if any important decisions depended upon the test results.

[257]

★Profion Dealltwriaeth Cyfaddasiad Cymbraeg. Ages 7-10; 1946; a Welsh edition of the *Ryburn Group Intelligence Tests for Junior Children,* 1936; 6s. per 20; 1s. per manual; 4d. per single copy; 30(40) minutes; H. V. Clark; Robert Gibson & Sons (Glasgow) Ltd.

[258]

Progressive Matrices: A Perceptual Test of Intelligence, 1938. Ages 6 and over; 1938-43; 1 form; £8 8s. per 25; 1s. 6d. per key and norms; 3s. 5d. per 100 record forms; 15s. per specimen set; (60) minutes; J. C. Raven; H. K. Lewis & Co., Ltd.

REFERENCES

1-8. See 40:1417.
9. RAVEN, JOHN C. "Standardization of Progressive Matrices, 1938." *Brit J Med Psychol* 19:137-50 pt 1 '41. * (*PA* 16:790)
10. RAVEN, J. C. "Testing the Mental Ability of Adults." *Lancet* 242:115-7 Ja 24 '42. * (*PA* 16:2496)
11. BRADFORD, E. J. G. "Performance Tests in the Diagnosis of Mental Deficiency." *Brit J Med Psychol* 19:394-414 pts 3-4 '43. * (*PA* 17:3783)
12. EYSENCK, H. J. "Neurosis and Intelligence." *Lancet* 245:362-3 S 18 '43. * (*PA* 18:475)
13. HALSTEAD, H. "An Analysis of the Matrix (Progressive Matrices) Test Results on 700 Neurotic (Military) Subjects, and a Comparison With the Shipley Vocabulary Test." *J Mental Sci* 89:202-15 Ap '43. * (*PA* 17:3794)
14. HARDING, D. W. "Prognostic Tests for Students of Architecture." *Occupational Psychol* 17:126-31 Jl '43. * (*PA* 18:290)
15. EDHOLM, O. G., AND GIBSON, Q. H. "Examination Results and an Intelligence Test." *Lancet* 247:294-6 Ag '44. * (*PA* 19:2362)
16. EYSENCK, H. J. "The Effect of Incentives on Neurotics, and the Variability of Neurotics as Compared With Normals." *Brit J Med Psychol* 20:101-3 Ap '44. * (*PA* 18:2795)
17. EYSENCK, MARGARET DAVIES. "A Study of Certain Qualitative Aspects of Problem Solving Behaviour in Senile Dementia Patients." *J Mental Sci* 91:337-45 Jl '45. * (*PA* 20:395)
18. HALSTEAD, H., AND SLATER, PATRICK. "An Experiment in the Vocational Adjustment of Neurotic Patients." *J Mental Sci* 92:509-15 Jl '45. * (*PA* 21:281)
19. EYSENCK, H. J. *Dimensions of Personality,* pp. 111-28. A record of research carried out in collaboration with H. T. Himmelweit and W. Linford Rees with the help of M. Desai, W. D. Furneaux, H. Halstead, O. Marum, M. McKinlay, A. Petrie, and P. M. Yap. Foreword by Aubrey Lewis. London: Kegan Paul, Trench, Trubner & Co. Ltd., 1947. Pp. xi, 308. 25s. * (*PA* 22:210)
20. SLATER, PATRICK. "The Association Between Age and Score in the Progressive Matrices Test." *Brit J Psychol, Stat Sect* 1:64-9 O '47. *
21. VERNON, P. E. "The Variations of Intelligence With Occupation, Age, and Locality." *Brit J Psychol, Stat Sect* 1:52-63 O '47. *

Walter C. Shipley, Professor of Psychology, Wheaton College, Norton, Massachusetts. This is a nonverbal intelligence test designed to measure Spearman's "G" factor (eduction of relations). It comprises sixty untimed multiple-choice problems, each consisting of a design or "matrix" from which a part has been removed. The testee examines the matrix and chooses the correct part for completing it. The easier problems draw principally on discrimination; the more difficult ones, on reasoning by analogy. The problems are divided into five series, each developing a different theme, with twelve problems to a series arranged in order of difficulty. Choices are recorded on a separate answer sheet so that the test booklets can be used over and over again. Norms, expressed in percentiles, are based on data from 1,407 children and 3,665 men. Statistical data on reliability are not given.

The test has much to commend it. Since the content is limited to highly abstract material which is largely foreign either to the classroom or to everyday experience, it is highly probable that what is being measured relates more directly to "native" abstract intelligence and less to academic achievement, educational opportunity, or cultural background than is the case with most tests of general intelligence. Striking attestation to its probable value is the fact that in World War II, a more difficult form of the test was administered by the British as a first sieve for all naval candidates and as a part of their standard army battery applied at primary training centers.

In many ways this test is resembled by Cattell's *Culture-Free Test.* Because of the rather striking similarity between the two with respect to both rationale and content, the reviewer finds it difficult to recommend one over the other. For many purposes they would appear to be virtually interchangeable. The present test, however, seems to require less time to administer, and to be applicable over a somewhat wider range. Both appear to fill an urgent need for a highly discriminating, nonverbal and culture-free test of general intelligence.

David Wechsler, Chief Psychologist, Psychiatric Division, Bellevue Hospital, New York, New York. This test consists of a graded series of logically designed patterns (matrices) serving to measure what the author variously calls "innate eductive ability," "eductive intelligence," or simply "eduction." Eventually, however, they are offered as a test of general intelligence and as such will be reviewed in this article.

The Matrices are divided into 5 sets, each involving a somewhat different principle but all requiring the subject to supply a missing part to a design by choosing one of six possible inserts. The "themes" of the successive sets or subtests are: (a) continuous patterns, (b) figure analogies, (c) progressive alteration of patterns, (d) permutations of figures, and (e) resolution of figures into constituent parts. In an earlier form of the test, the first two subtests were put out as formboards (intended for use with young children), but as now available all items are contained in a 6-page printed booklet.

The *Progressive Matrices* may be administered as either a group or an individual test with percentile norms available for each of the subtests as well as for the test as a whole. There are also separate norms, as are seemingly necessary, for the individual as against the group form of the test. The age range is from 6 to 13½ years (individual form) and from 8 to 14 (group form), with a single adult group. The adult group is made up exclusively of males (British soldiers).

In appraising the *Progressive Matrices* it seems well to emphasize three points. In the first place the *Progressive Matrices* are one of the few or relatively few new tests that have come from psychological laboratories in the last fifteen years. By new I mean contextually different. The second important point is that the Matrices do seem to be excellent tests of intelligence. I use the word seem, because the author, while claiming high correlations with other tests of intelligence including the Stanford–Binet, has only published one coefficient of correlation (.60), that obtained with the *Mill Hill Vocabulary Scale*. The last point is that the *Progressive Matrices* present what may be called the first comprehensive attempt to measure intelligence in terms of a single intellectual function, to wit, that of visual perception.

The main limitation of the *Progressive Matrices* is that they attempt to measure general intelligence (or even eductive ability) through a single modality of performance. To this there are serious theoretical objections; but leaving these aside there still remains the practical consideration that there is no test, no matter how excellent, but that certain individuals may fail to do justice to themselves because they simply are not good in doing the test or type of task used. The *Progressive Matrices* are no exception. A second limitation of the test is that it has a rather low ceiling. Considering that there are 60 items, the mean test score for each age group (age 12 and above) increases negligibly or not at all; the average adult score is the same as that of subjects at age 14. Findings of the *Progressive Matrices* are thus in line with results obtained with most other sensory and perceptual motor tests which, at higher levels at least, turn out to be relatively undifferentiating. There is yet another problem which will confront the author, and that is the probable rapid decline of scores on the test with ages beginning with adulthood. It is possible that the identical scores obtained for average adults and the 14-year-olds are due to the fact that the adult group included a considerable number of subjects whose scores already showed this age decline.

The above strictures notwithstanding, the *Progressive Matrices* should be a welcome addition to psychometrics because they constitute a real contribution to the field.

For a review by T. J. Keating, see 40:1417.

[259]
Revised Beta Examination. Grades 3 and over; 1931–46; 1 form; a French edition is also available; $3.50 per 25, postpaid; 35¢ per specimen set, postpaid; 15(45-60) minutes; 1946 restandardization by Robert M. Lindner and Milton Gurvitz; C. E. Kellogg assisted by N. W. Morton; Psychological Corporation.

REFERENCES

1-4. See 40:1419.
5. BENNETT, GEORGE K., AND FEAR, RICHARD A. "Mechanical Comprehension and Dexterity." *Personnel J* 22:12-7 My '43. * (PA 17:2843)
6. KLUGMAN, SAMUEL F. "Test Scores and Graduation." *Occupations* 21:389-93 Ja '43. * (PA 17:1354)
7. McMURRY, ROBERT N., AND JOHNSON, DALE L. "Development of Instruments for Selecting and Placing Factory Employees." *Adv Mgmt* 10:113-20 S '45. * (PA 19:3473)
8. LINDNER, ROBERT M., AND GURVITZ, MILTON. "Restandardization of the Revised Beta Examination to Yield the Wechsler Type of IQ." *J Appl Psychol* 30:649-58 D '46. * (PA 21:1680)
9. BENNETT, GEORGE K., AND WESMAN, ALEXANDER G. "Industrial Test Norms for a Southern Plant Population." *J Appl Psychol* 31:241-6 Je '47. * (PA 21:4095)

Raleigh M. Drake, Professor of Psychology and Head of the Department, Kent State Univerity, Kent, Ohio. There is a real need for a group non-verbal general intelligence test which can be given to illiterate adults. In spite of the amount of work which has been devoted to the Army Beta, including the present restandardization, this test does not fulfill this need adequately, although it may do about as well as most other tests made for the same purpose.

No changes of any kind have been made in the test section. The only significant modifications are confined to assigning equal weights to the six subtests and to constructing a new table of norms by employing Wechsler's method of computing IQ's. The authors (Lindner and Gurvitz) of the 1946 restandardization report an r of .92 between Beta IQ's and Wechsler IQ's for 192 male prisoners. If this were typical, and if the reliability could be taken as satisfactory, the test would be very valuable since it can be given to groups at a great saving of time and money over individual tests.

Many items are ambiguous, as pointed out by Porteus in an earlier review (40:1419). This is true of Test 3, Item 11 in which one is required to select the one wrong item out of four presented—at least three of the items are equally wrong. Items 18 and 20 in the same section are poor because of unclear detail in the drawings. In Test 6, the last item in the pictorial similarities is drawn differently but is scored as being the same. Some of the pictorial items depend upon information about, or experience with, tools, which makes them inappropriate for women. This fact should be kept in mind in connection with the comments that follow because the Army Beta was specifically constructed for males and no attempt has been made to adapt it for use with the opposite sex.

The reviewer gave the *Revised Beta Examination* to a group of college women and found the following: (a) A reliability coefficient of .30 (N = 116) by correlating the odd subtests with the even subtests. Kellogg and Morton report .90, or better, by odd-even items and by subtests 1, 2, and 3 with subtests 4, 5, and 6. Because the subtests are very dissimilar in content, and the odd-even method accentuates this dissimilarity, it is to be expected that lower self-reliabilities would be found when they are correlated with one another than when odd-even items are correlated; but unless it can be shown that each subtest is a valid measure of general intelligence, we must require that the parts of the total be consistent with one another. Test 4 (geometrical forms) is similar to the now well-known *Revised Minnesota Paper Formboard Test* and is no longer considered a good test of general intelligence. Test 6 (number and picture checking) is essentially the same as the *Minnesota Vocational Test for Clerical Workers*, which is definitely not an intelligence test. What the Army Beta does seem to measure well is the ability for close observation. Success in Test 1 (maze tracing), Test 3 (detecting missing parts of pictures), Test 5 (drawing in missing parts of pictures), and Test 6 (similarities) depends upon quick visual observation, an important factor in general intelligence but hardly as important as the overloading given it in the present test (i.e., four out of six subtests are of this nature). The remaining two subtests, (Tests 2 and 4, number substitution and geometrical forms), have not been very successful measures of intelligence. The reliability is low also because the range for each subtest is from the third grade to the adult level, according to the publisher's catalog, so there can only be one or two items which are really critical at each age or ability level, which in effect makes each subtest very short. Actually, each subtest requires only from one and one-half to four minutes working time. (b) These considerations may account for the low reliability found in the reviewer's group and for the low correlations found when the Beta was correlated with other tests of mental ability, an r of .58 being obtained with the *Henmon–Nelson Test of Mental Ability* (raw scores), an r of .30 with the *Otis Self-Administering Test of Mental Ability* (raw scores), and an r of .23 between Beta IQ's and Otis IQ's. (c) The average IQ for the group on the Army Beta was 111.06, and for the Otis IQ it was 111.45. The average difference between IQ's on the two tests was 9.4 points, and the standard deviations were 9.6 and 10.5 respectively. Considering the difficulty of obtaining IQ's for ages over 16, the two tests agree rather well; and if the r of .92 between the Beta and the Wechsler–Bellevue reported is representative, we may conclude that the Beta yields a usable IQ score, considering the purpose for which it is intended that it be used, i.e., illiterate male adults. (d) Using a long, reliable, and finely scaled final examination in general psychology, Otis, Henmon–Nelson, and Beta raw scores yielded r's of .57, .34, and .19 respectively. This low r (.19) for the Beta, together with the low reliability found for our group of women, indicates that, for our group at least, the test is much inferior to other group tests available. This is partly due to the restricted range and the high level of talent for our group, besides the fact that the test is not intended for use with women.

The 1946 restandardization was based on 1,225 male white adult prisoners at the U.S. Federal Penitentiary at Lewisburg, Pennsylvania with sampling controlled to represent the educational and socio-economic distribution found in the 1940 census. The norms are presented in convenient tables so that for a given weighted score the computed IQ can be determined for ages 16 to 59 inclusive. The authors wisely warn against assuming that the Beta IQ's are equivalent to Stanford–Binet IQ's or even to Wechsler IQ's, but it is doubtful if such a warning will be heeded for there is no practical way of differentiating them. The test will find its greatest usefulness in cases of illiteracy where

Walter C. Shipley, Professor of Psychology, Wheaton College, Norton, Massachusetts. This is not a new test but rather a new and radically different standardization of a well-known and widely used instrument, the *Revised Beta Examination,* prepared by Kellogg and Morton, intended—like the *United States Army Group Examination Beta* from which it was derived—to serve as a measure of general intellectual ability for persons who are relatively illiterate or who are non-English speaking.

The restandardization, while introducing only minor refinements in administrative and raw-scoring procedures, involves a very significant change in the general procedure for computing the IQ. This procedure is patterned directly after that originated and employed by Wechsler for computing IQ's for the *Wechsler–Bellevue Intelligence Scale.* The procedure involves (*a*) converting the raw scores on the separate parts of the test to weighted scores so that each part contributes equally to the total score—a method which readily lends itself both to the plotting of meaningful profiles and to proration in case parts of the test must be omitted—and (*b*) allowing, in computing the IQ, for the fact of decreasing performance (raw score) with age.

The standardization sample on which the norms are based comprised 1,225 white male adult prisoners at the United States Federal Penitentiary at Lewisburg, Pennsylvania. While the criticism might well be made that a prison population is not a typical cross-sectional adult sample, this objection is in a large measure mitigated by the facts that (*a*) the population was carefully selected so that education and socio-economic status were in proportion to the distributions for white male adults in the 1940 census and (*b*) the group was composed of individuals considered as improvable offenders, i.e., lawbreakers, rather than criminals.

Although the reviewer has not had occasion to use the new procedure, he feels that the application of the Wechsler refinements to the scoring of the Beta Examination is a highly desirable step and thoroughly recommends it.

other superior tests are inappropriate and when interpreted in a liberal manner as being only a rough approximation to the conventional IQ.

For reviews by S. D. Porteus and David Wechsler, see 40:1419.

Revised Beta Examination

[260]
★**Scale of Nonverbal Mental Ability.** Ages 10-12; 1947; 1 form; £3 10s. per 100; 9s. per 12; 10d. per single copy; 6d. per table of norms; 10d. per booklet of answers; 30(35) minutes; J. W. Jenkins; National Foundation for Educational Research in England and Wales.

[261]
★**SRA Non-Verbal Classification Form.** Grades 9-12 and adults; 1946–47; preliminary manual; IBM; Form AH (hand scoring); Form AM (machine scoring); 10(15) minutes; Robert N. McMurry and Dale L. Johnson; Science Research Associates.
a) FORM AH. $1.90 per 25; 50¢ per specimen set.
b) FORM AM. $1.30 per 25; $2.35 per 100 machine-scorable answer sheets; 50¢ per scoring key.

J Consult Psychol 11:340 N-D '47. This is a brief nonverbal intelligence test of 60 items. The items are all of one form (to select the "most different" one of five pictures), but involve two types of tasks: pictured logical relationships, and geometrical relationships. The format, scoring methods, and interpretative tables are uniform with the SRA *Verbal Form* ... and a common manual serves the two tests. The reliability is stated as .85. The test will be a useful supplement to verbal mental ability tests.

[262]
★**SRA Verbal Classification Form.** Grades 9-12 and adults; 1946–47; an abbreviated edition of the *Thurstone Test of Mental Alertness* which is an abbreviated adaptation of the *American Council on Education Psychological Examination for High School Students*; IBM; preliminary manual; Form AH (hand scoring); Form AM (machine scoring); 15(20) minutes; Science Research Associates.
a) FORM AH. $1.90 per 25; 50¢ per specimen set.
b) FORM AM. $1.30 per 25; $2.35 per 100 machine-scorable answer sheets; 50¢ per set of scoring keys.

[263]
★**Terman-McNemar Test of Mental Ability.** Grades 7-12; 1942; revision of *Terman Group Test of Mental Ability*, 1920; IBM; Forms C, D; separate answer sheets need not be used; $1.50 per 25; 35¢ per specimen set, postpaid; 85¢ per 25 machine-scorable answer sheets; 20¢ per stencil for scoring answer sheets; 40(45) minutes; Lewis M. Terman and Quinn McNemar; World Book Co.

REFERENCES

1-25. See 40:1424.
26. JORDAN, A. M. "Correlations of Four Intelligence Tests With Grades." *J Ed Psychol* 13:419-29 O '22. *
27. WILLARD, DUDLEY W. "Native and Acquired Mental Ability as Measured by the Terman Group Test of Mental Ability." *Sch & Soc* 16:750-6 D 30 '23. *
28. MILLER, W. S. "The Variation and Significance of Intelligence Quotients Obtained From Group Tests." *J Ed Psychol* 15:359-66 S '24. *
29. O'BRIEN, F. P. "Mental Ability With Reference to Selection and Retention of College Students." *J Ed Res* 18:136-43 S '28. * (PA 3:478)
30. KAULFERS, WALTER VINCENT. "Effect of the IQ on the Grades of One Thousand Students of Foreign Languages." *Sch & Soc* 30:163-4 Ag 3 '29. * (PA 3:4281)
31. KEFAUVER, GRAYSON N. "Relationship of the Intelligence Quotient and Scores on Mechanical Tests With Success in Industrial Subjects." *Voc Guid Mag* 7:198-203+ F '29. * (PA 3:1637)

32. SCUDDER, KENYON J. "The Predictive Value of General Intelligence Tests in the Selection of Junior Accountants and Bookkeepers." *J Appl Psychol* 13:1-18 F '29. * (*PA* 3:2449)
33. KLEIN, ADOLPH. "I.Q.'s Compared With Achievement." *B High Points* 12:3-5 F '30. * (*PA* 4:2825)
34. MCCUEN, THERON L. "Predicting Success in Algebra." *J Ed Res* 21:72-4 Ja '30. * (*PA* 4:1362)
35. STEDMAN, MELISSA BRANSON. "Factors Influencing School Success in Bookkeeping." *J Appl Psychol* 14:74-82 F '30. * (*PA* 4:4556)
36. TOZER, GEORGE E. "A Statistical Prediction of High-School Success for Purposes of Educational Guidance." *J Ed Res* 22:399-402 N '30. * (*PA* 5:2049)
37. HANSKE, CARL F. "The Correlation Between Scores on Objective Tests in Chemistry and Terman Intelligence Quotients." *J Ed Res* 23:49-54 Ja '31. * (*PA* 5:2543)
38. PINTNER, RUDOLF. "The Influence of Language Background on Intelligence Tests." *J Social Psychol* 3:235-40 My '32. * (*PA* 6:3793)
39. KELLY, PRICE ORVILLE. *Comparative Validity and Reliability of Four Intelligence Tests in the Ninth Grade*. Unpublished master's thesis, University of Kentucky, 1933. Pp. 63. (*Theses in Education* . . ., 1937, pp. 18-9.)
40. COHEN, EDITH R. *A Comparison of the Revised Terman Scale and the Otis Higher Examination*. Unpublished master's thesis, Columbia University, 1939.
41. RHOADES, FORDYCE LAUREN. *An Evaluation of Measures for the Prediction of Success in Instrumental Music Study*. Unpublished master's thesis, University of Washington, 1939. (*Abstracts of Theses* . . ., 1939, pp. 224-6.)
42. KEYS, NOEL. "The Value of Group Test IQ's for Prediction of Progress Beyond High School." *J Ed Psychol* 31:81-93 F '40. * (*PA* 14:3741)
43. MORGAN, FRANK. *The Reliability of the Terman Group Test in Predicting Academic Success in the North Texas State Teachers College*. Unpublished master's thesis, North Texas State Teachers College, 1940.
44. BENNETT, MARY WOODS. "Factors Influencing Performance on Group and Individual Tests of Intelligence: I, Rate of Work." *Genetic Psychol Monogr* 23:237-318 My '41. * (*PA* 15:5399)
45. HARTSON, L. D., AND SPROW, A. J. "The Value of Intelligence Quotients Obtained in Secondary School for Predicting College Scholarship." *Ed & Psychol Meas* 1:387-98 O '41. * (*PA* 16:1174)
46. BAILEY, ALBERT ERNEST. *The Relative Validity of Ten Different Intelligence Tests*. Unpublished doctor's thesis, University of Washington, 1942. (*Abstracts of Theses* . . . 1942, 1943, p. 189.)
47. MCRAE, HUGH. "The Inconstancy of Group Test I.Q.'s." *Brit J Ed Psychol* 12:59-70 F '42. * (*PA* 16:2905)
48. TYLER, F. T. "Analysis of the Terman-McNemar Tests of Mental Ability." *Ed & Psychol Meas* 5:49-58 sp '45. * (*PA* 20:347)
49. BENNETT, MARY WOODS. "Factors Influencing Performance on Group and Individual Tests of Intelligence: II, Social Facilitation." *J Ed Psychol* 37:347-58 S '46. * (*PA* 21:1674)
50. BOLTON, FLOYD B. "Value of Several Intelligence Tests for Predicting Scholastic Achievement." *J Ed Res* 41:133-8 O '47. * (*PA* 22:2327)

Carl I. Hovland, Professor of Psychology and Chairman of the Department, Yale University, New Haven, Connecticut. The authors are to be commended on the thoroughness of this revision and restandardization of the *Terman Group Test of Mental Ability* first published in 1920.

The test consists of 162 items arranged in seven subtests: (*a*) Information, (*b*) Synonyms, (*c*) Logical Selection, (*d*) Classification, (*e*) Analogies, (*f*) Opposites, and (*g*) Best Answer. The number of items in each subtest is too small to provide separate scores, so no norms for the separate subtests have been prepared by the authors. Four and five alternative multiple-choice items have replaced the two-choice items. Provision has been made for scoring by means either of a perforated key sheet or by machine methods.

The new tests eliminate the arithmetical and numerical subtests used in the original forms. This was done because factor analysis had indicated that these did not scale with the other subtests; this revision makes the scores of different individuals "lie along the same continuum." The result is that the test is primarily one of *verbal* intelligence and may be somewhat inadequate as a measure of general intelligence. The alternative would have been to strengthen the quantitative portion and thus obtain two scores, one verbal and one quantitative, as in the Thurstone *American Council on Education Psychological Examination for High School Students.*

The arrangement of the items of each subtest in order of increasing difficulty and the "ample time allowance" should make this more a power than a speed test, but no data bearing on this point are presented.

The construction appears to have been done very carefully and systematically. The item analysis was based on 1,200 pupils in the 7th and 11th grades. The comparability of the old and new tests was tested on a sample of 1,400 cases, grades 7 to 12, and that of the two forms of the new test on a sample of 1,500 pupils in grades 7, 9, and 11.

The norms appear to be extremely well standardized, based on a 10 per cent sample of results from 148 communities in 33 states. Data are available for interpreting the results in terms of normalized standard scores, mental ages, percentile ranks, and "deviation IQ's." The latter requires that the difference be found between the obtained standard score and the average standard score for other individuals of the same age. This difference is then interpreted from a table in terms of IQ. This IQ is thus not a quotient like the usual IQ but is a general measure of brightness. Because the use of a separate answer sheet affects performance on the test, particularly at the lower ages, separate norms are given for interpretation when the separate answer sheet is used. This seems to complicate matters, but one wonders how often this point is neglected in other standardizations.

The Manual of Directions is unusually complete and useful. It makes a fairly good compromise between the simplification required for nonstatistically minded test users and the sophistication expected by research users of tests.

The reliability of .96 reported for age 14 (and said to vary only slightly for other ages) is very satisfactory. Reliability has been analyzed in terms of split-half correlation, inter-form correlation, and the probable error of measurement.

It is a criticism of the entire test-making business that we have no adequate theoretical formulation of intelligence against which we can measure practical tests to determine validity. It is regrettable that such outstanding test constructors as Terman and McNemar have to say, "The best evidence of the validity of the Terman test is to be found in its successful use over the period of years since the test was first issued. Many instances may be cited where the Terman test has been used with great success in guidance and administration." The validity of the new test is measured by the correlation of .91 between it and the original Terman test.

Robert L. Thorndike, Associate Professor of Education, Teachers College, Columbia University, New York, New York. This test is a revision of the *Terman Group Test of Mental Ability* which has been one of the standard instruments for testing at the junior and senior high school levels for 25 years. The revision undertakes to incorporate into the test the advances which were made both in the theory and in the mechanics of mental measurement between 1920 and 1940.

In content, the chief change in the new form is its restriction entirely to verbal materials. All problems involving numerical or quantitative thinking have been excluded. This has had the effect both of narrowing and of purifying the function measured; that is, the test becomes a better measure of a more restricted segment of human ability. The choice was one which was deliberately made in constructing the test and one which can certainly be defended. However, the user should realize that it is *verbal* intelligence which he is assessing. For a number of purposes it may be desirable to supplement this test with some other measure specifically aimed at *quantitative* mental operations.

The superficial form of the examination has been modernized so as to permit more efficient testing and scoring. The present form consists entirely of multiple-choice items. It permits either hand scoring, using a superimposed stencil, or machine scoring.

In the norms of this test, an effort is made to bridge the gap between the IQ, with its long tradition and wide popular acceptance and meaning, and the statistically more acceptable standard score. The "deviation intelligence quotient" is the index of brightness preferred by the authors. This is essentially a standard score with mean for the age group set at 100 and standard deviation of any age group set at 16. Thus, the numerical values have very nearly the same meaning, in terms of degree of excellence, as the IQ's on the *Revised Stanford–Binet*. However, the ambiguities of quotient indices, which become meaningless as adulthood is reached, are avoided. This type of compromise index is probably the most satisfactory for use in school testing at the present time.

The item analyses underlying the selection of items for the test and the extensive testing to establish norms bear witness to careful and thorough work in the test's construction. The testing to establish norms was on a truly imposing scale. No indication is given, however, to support the representativeness of the 200 communities in which testing was carried out to establish norms. It is to be hoped that they were as adequate qualitatively as they were quantitatively. The homogeneity of the content and the care in construction appear between them to have yielded a test of quite satisfactory reliability.

All in all, this test appears to be a professional and workmanlike successor to the *Terman Group Test.*

For reviews by Anne Anastasi and Howard Easley of the original edition, see 40:1424.

[264]
★Tests of Primary Mental Abilities for Ages 5 and 6. 1946; also called *SRA Primary Mental Abilities for Ages 5 and 6;* 1 form; $2.35 per 25; 50¢ per specimen set; (60) minutes; Thelma Gwinn Thurstone and L. L. Thurstone; Science Research Associates.

REFERENCES
1. THURSTONE, THELMA GWINN. *Play and Learn: The Red Book: Learning to Think Series.* Chicago, Ill.: Science Research Associates, 1947. Pp. 80. Paper. $0.55. *
2. THURSTONE, THELMA GWINN. *Teacher's Manual for Play and Learn: The Red Book: Learning to Think Series.* Chicago, Ill.: Science Research Associates, 1948. Pp. iii, 75. Paper. $0.50. *

See also references for 225.

Florence L. Goodenough, Research Professor, Institute of Child Welfare, University of Minnesota, Minneapolis, Minnesota. With the publication of these tests, the Thurstones have extended their work on the factor analysis of mental ability to the early childhood level. Their view of intelligence as a molecular rather than a molar trait is exemplified in the definition given on page ii of the Examiner's Manual, where they state, "Intelligence may be defined as the composite of abilities for acquiring knowledge of various types." This obviously calls for a multiple rather than a unitary type of appraisal.

After presenting this definition, they proceed to a brief overview of the primary abilities isolated in their previous work with adolescents and young adults. This discussion includes a few curious statements. For instance on page ii it is said that "word fluency involves the ability to think of isolated words with little concern for their meaning. It is important . . . in occupations requiring creative writing or reporting." Some "creative writing," it is true, seems based on this principle! And of the "space factor" it is noted (p. iii) that "the fact that young children have had no specific training in this factor suggests that it is fundamental to the child's intelligence." As stated, this argument is not easy to grasp though what is probably meant is that whatever ability along this line the child may show is the result of innate ability to profit by the casual experiences of everyday life rather than of formal instruction.

In devising the new battery, seventy tests, "all of the known types of tests for children of this age were included—the current intelligence, reading readiness, arithmetic readiness, and other measures of learning ability," together with a number of newly devised tests, were administered to 200 children in kindergarten and first grade. On the basis of a factor analysis, five factors, identified as Verbal-Meaning (V), Perceptual-Speed (P), Quantitative (Q), Motor (M), and Space, (S) were isolated. Mental age norms for each of the five factors separately, and for V, P, Q, and S combined, were derived from approximately 1,200 Chicago school children from five to eight years old. By extrapolation, standards for ages three to nine years were added.

Approximately 35 items are provided for each of the five abilities. These consist entirely of pictures to be marked by the children. The pictures would have been improved in some instances by the omission of confusing small details and greater emphasis upon the salient features. Some of the items may be criticized on the ground that they are likely to fall outside the experience of young children from rural areas or small towns. There are others for which the choice of a "right" answer seems questionable, e.g., one on page 5 where a padlock is to be chosen in response to the question, "If you do not have a key, which one will lock the door?" The picture of a doorknob below which is a keyhole that might well belong to a Yale lock seems to me an equally sensible choice.

The instructions for administering and scoring the tests are clear and sufficiently detailed. One or two typographical errors were noted. The word "driving" in place of "diving" on page 8 might lead to confusion since it is a part of the examiner's instructions to the children, though not one of the scored items. No data are presented with respect to the self-correlations of the tests, their intercorrelations, or their agreement with other criteria.

[265]

★**Thurstone Test of Mental Alertness.** Grades 9-16 and adults; 1943; an abbreviated adaptation of the *American Council on Education Psychological Examination for High School Students;* preliminary manual; IBM; 1 form; 2 editions; 40(50) minutes; Thelma Gwinn Thurstone and L. L. Thurstone; Science Research Associates.

a) HAND-SCORED EDITION, FORM AH. $1.85 per 25; 60¢ per set of scoring folders; 50¢ per specimen set, postpaid.
b) MACHINE-SCORED EDITION, FORM AM. IBM; $3 per 25 machine-scorable test-answer booklets; $2 per set of scoring keys.

REFERENCES

1. MAHER, HOWARD, AND FIFE, ISABELLE E. "A Biological-Pharmaceutical Checker Selection Program." *J Appl Psychol* 31:469-76 O '47. * (PA 22:3665)

Anne Anastasi, Associate Professor of Psychology, Fordham University, New York, New York. This is a short adaptation of the *American Council on Education Psychological Examination,* designed for use with high school and general adult populations. It is virtually self-administering, all the necessary instructions appearing on the test booklet. The test proper, consisting of 70 five-response and 28 four-response multiple-choice items, has a single, over-all time limit of 20 minutes. The total testing time, including the instructions and 11 practice problems which precede the test proper, is estimated as 25 minutes. The items are presented in spiral omnibus arrangement and include: word definitions, same-opposite, arithmetic reasoning, and number-series completion. Besides a total score, the test yields an L-score (Linguistic Ability) and a Q-score (Quantitative Thinking), based upon the two former and the two latter types of items, respectively. The layout of the test is exceptionally compact, all the items of the test proper being printed on the two sides of a single sheet which is detachable for scoring.

The test is available in a hand-scoring as well as an IBM machine-scoring form. Convenient transparent stencils are furnished for hand scoring. For the benefit of those planning to use the test, it might be added parenthetically that the instructions on the scoring stencils ought to read, "Place the test in the (L- or Q-) stencil folder so that the page number of the test coincides with the page number of the stencil." If one follows the present instructions to place the test paper "so that the lower edge of the paper is at the fold of the stencil," the markings on test and stencil will not correspond—at least, they failed to do so in the specimen examined by the present reviewer! Percentile norms on 3,820 high school students attending nine high schools in scattered parts of the country are given for total as well as for L- and Q-scores. Separate percentiles are reported for each of the four years of high school.

No correlations between scores on this short form and on the long forms of the *American Council on Education Psychological Examination* are reported, nor are reliability or validity coefficients of the present form given. The present adaptation may be somewhat more difficult than the original because of the scrambled arrangement of items which necessitates a constant shifting of mental set on the part of the examinee. To this should be added the fact that the specific instructions for each item are omitted in the test proper, having been given only in the practice problems. Thus the subject must first recognize the type of item and recall the corresponding instructions, before he can proceed with the item in the usual way. The unduly high difficulty level of the test is reflected in the distribution of scores. For example, although a "chance" score on this test would correspond to approximately 21 correct items, the lowest percentile in the 9th, 10th, 11th, and 12th grades extends down to 12, 14, 18, and 22 items correct, respectively. These represent in effect zero scores. The differentiation among the four high school classes, moreover, was not very great, the differences in median scores between successive classes being 6½, 6, and 3½ items, respectively, out of 98. These relatively small inter-class differences may suggest that the test is not sufficiently sensitive to individual differences at the high school level, since its unduly high difficulty level tends to dilute the scores with a large element of guessing or "chance" performance. It should be noted that if the test is actually too difficult for high school students, then its difficulty level is all the more inappropriate for unselected adult populations, whose average education falls considerably short of high school graduation. It is unfortunate that norms are furnished only for a high school population. The principal advantages of this test are its brevity, ease of administration, ease of scoring, and compactness, in each of which the test represents a high degree of efficiency.

Emily T. Burr, Director, Guidance Bureau, Inc., New York, New York. This test is an abbreviated adaptation of the *American Council on Education Psychological Examination for High School Students*. The adaptation is arranged more compactly, requires less time, and is easier to administer and score. Inasmuch as the results of these tests correlate highly with actual classroom standing, they are immensely useful in the analysis of the individual pupil's progress.

[266]

★**Time Appreciation Test.** Ages 10 and over; 1946; formerly called *JNB Time Test;* nontimed (10) minutes; 1¢ per form sheet; 25¢ per manual (reprint of John N. Buck's, "The Time Appreciation Test," *Journal of Applied Psychology* 30:388-98 August 1946); John N. Buck; Steward's Office, Lynchburg State Colony, Colony, Virginia.

REFERENCES
1. BUCK, JOHN. "The Time Appreciation Test." *J Appl Psychol* 30:388-98 Ag '46. * (PA 21:305)
2. LANDISBERG, SELMA. "A Personality Study of Institutionalized Epileptics." *Am J Mental Def* 52:16-22 Jl '47. * (PA 22:2267)

E. J. G. Bradford, Senior Lecturer in Education, The University of Sheffield, Sheffield, England. The name of this test is unfortunate since it is not a test of time sense or of time appreciation, but is based on a sampling of the knowledge about time that might be acquired in school, through conversation, or by reading. A similar series of questions could be devised by sampling the subject matter related to weight or to distance. In spite of the restricted field of sampling, the resulting estimate of mental age obtained is usually within one year for people of about normal intellectual level, somewhat closer for subnormals, and less close for those above normal. About half the questions can be answered by morons and borderlines, i.e., the lowest 10 per cent of the population, leaving the remaining 15 or 16 questions for differentiating the remaining 90 per cent of the population. Obviously, the best field for the application of the test is the subnormal. With a few modifications needed to make the test suitable for use in England, the *Time Appreciation Test* was found to give results roughly one year higher than other tests, including the *Kent E-G-Y Test*.

Boredom or offence would be avoided if a start were made with Item 13, followed by Items 15 and 17, and then straight on to Item 22. Should any errors be made in answering these four items, the examination might be restarted with Item 1. Otherwise the subject might be given full credit for the first 22 items.

In the reviewer's opinion, the test would be improved if the Kent plan of dividing the series into sections were adopted. In such a form it could be used to advantage as a supplement or alternative to the *Kent E-G-Y Test*, and would be valuable in giving more precision to the range of mental ages above 14 years.

Charles N. Cofer, Associate Professor of Psychology, University of Maryland, College Park, Maryland. This test is designed as a "screen" or "emergency" device to allow rapid determination of intellectual level. It is composed of 30 items relating to knowledge of holidays, temporal terms, and temporal units and to present orientation. It is designed for either individual or group administration, has no time limit, and requires 10 minutes or less to give. The test is applicable to subjects whose chronological age is 10 years or more, and it yields adult IQ's from 30 to 123 and MA's from 4½ to 18½. It appears to be an interesting and potentially valuable test, and the author is to be commended for his brief but perceptive remarks on its interpretative use. Questions concerning its standardization, however, prevent unqualified endorsement of it at the present time.

Information given concerning the standardization groups is very meager. The first norms were developed on 675 white Virginians by group administration. Although the norms developed on this group were established by "chronological selection" (1, p. 389), no data are given as to the number and kind of subjects available at the ages 8 to 23 years represented in this group. These norms "were later amended in certain instances" in view of the data obtained from individual examination of 350 additional whites. The range in educational and chronological age of the latter group was wider than for the first group, and the intelligence of the second group had been determined by the use of standard intelligence tests. No data are given to describe the second group more adequately than the first, and the method of "amendment" of the initial norms is not described.

Test-retest reliability was determined on small and unrepresentative groups (student nurses and psychiatric and mentally defective patients). Group administration yielded a reliability coefficient of .80, and individual administration a coefficient of .96. Directions for scoring the test appear to be adequate. The items are not arranged in strict order of difficulty; all of them must be presented to each patient, an inconvenience not present in the Kent Scales which are designed also as screen tests.

Correlations are reported between the *Time Appreciation Test* and the *Revised Stanford-Binet Scale*, the *Wechsler-Bellevue Intelligence Scale*, and the *Otis Quick-Scoring Mental Ability Test*. These data, obtained from seven relatively small groups which, for the most part, contained defectives and epileptics, show the test to have fairly high "validity" (range of r from .67 to .88). The range of intellectual level in these groups was fairly wide.

On the whole, the reviewer is well impressed with the potentialities of this test as a screen device. The criticisms made arise largely from the inadequate presentation by the author of standardization data and methods and from the difficulty that any single investigator must face in making his standardization and validity studies on large and representative samples from more than a local population.

[267]
★**V.G.C. Intelligence Indicator.** Grades 3-8, 7-12; 1943; an adaptation of the *Henmon-Nelson Tests of Mental Ability* (40:1398); Forms A, B; 2 levels; separate answer sheets must be used; $2.25 per 25 of either level; 40¢ per 25 answer sheets for either level; 25¢ per specimen set of either level; specimen set must be purchased to obtain the manual; 30(35) minutes; adaptation by M. D. Parmenter; Vocational Guidance Centre.

[268]
★**Willis-Smith Advanced Mental Test.** Grades 8-12; 1939; 1 form, 2 parts (Forms A, B); 5¢ per set of both forms; 100(115) minutes; C. B. Willis and H. E. Smith; Institute of Applied Art, Ltd., Edmonton, Alberta, Canada.

Harold H. Bixler, Director of Research and Guidance, Public Schools, Atlanta, Georgia. Although this test is listed as including Forms A and B, this statement is somewhat misleading inasmuch as both forms must be given in order to compute an IQ. The purpose, say the authors, is that the forms may be given on successive days, using one period each day. This test is compiled by Canadian authors, and presumably the norms are based on Canadian students.

This test is of the self-administering type and resembles the *Otis Self-Administering Tests of Mental Ability* very much. Like the Otis test, the items include vocabulary, number series, analogies, and arithmetic problems.

Neither in the test manual nor in the publisher's catalog are there given any data about the validity or reliability of the test. One might guess that the test would be reliable because of the length of testing time, that is, 100 minutes. The test is probably adapted for the grades for which it is advertised, i.e., grades 7 to 12 inclusive. The test yields an IQ.

The test is probably not as good as other mental tests for the high school grades, such as the *Otis Quick-Scoring Mental Ability Test*, the *Terman–McNemar Test of Mental Ability*, and the *Pintner General Ability Tests*.

F. T. Tyler, Professor of Psychology and Education, The University of British Columbia, Vancouver, Canada. This test consists of Forms A and B, *both* of which must be administered before the IQ can be computed. Each form contains 80 items and is of the omnibus, self-administering type. Both completion and multiple-choice types of items are used.

The manual discusses three points—administration, scoring, and computation of IQ's. Scoring rules are described, and a convenient scoring key is provided. IQ's are determined from a graph which has ages from 13½ to 18 on the horizontal axis and scores from 4 to 136 on the vertical axis. IQ's for the ages and scores indicated are read directly from the graph. The authors state that "scores [sic] above 136 can be estimated from the amount by which they exceed 136." Apparently this means that IQ's can be computed for scores above 136 by determining the amount by which the score exceeds 136. How this is done is not at all clear.

It is to be noted that since the manual of directions gives no information beyond that just described, there are no data on such factors as validity, item validity, reliability, sample used in preparing the test, uses of the test results, etc.

Willis-Smith Advanced Mental Test

[269]
Wonderlic Personnel Test. Adults; 1939–42; Forms A, B, D, E, F; Forms D, E, and F are adapted for business use from the *Otis Self-Administering Tests of Mental Ability,* Higher Form; $6 per 100; $4 per special introductory package containing 10 copies of each form; 12(20) minutes; E. F. Wonderlic; the Author, 750 Grove St., Glencoe, Ill.

REFERENCES

1-2. See 40:1415.
3. CARLSON, WALTER A. "Intelligence Testing of Flying Cadet Applicants: A Report on Psychometric Measurement." *J Aviat Med* 12:226-9 S '41. * (PA 16:305)
4. WRIGHT, JAMES H., AND LAING, DONALD M. "The Time Factor in the Administration of the Wonderlic Personnel Test." *J Appl Psychol* 27:316-9 Ag '43. * (PA 18:274)
5. BOLANOVICH, D. J. "Selection of Female Engineering Trainees." *J Ed Psychol* 35:545-53 D '44. * (PA 19:1010)
6. WONDERLIC, E. F. "How to Use the Personnel Tests." *Personnel Dig* 1:19-23 su '44. *
7. MCMURRY, ROBERT N., AND JOHNSON, DALE L. "Development of Instruments for Selecting and Placing Factory Employees." *Adv Mgmt* 10:113-20 S '45. * (PA 19:3473)
8. JENSEN, MILTON B., AND ROTTER, JULIAN B. "The Value of Thirteen Psychological Tests in Officer Candidate Screening." *J Appl Psychol* 31:312-22 Je '47. * (PA 21:4107)
9. THOMPSON, CLAUDE EDWARD. "Selecting Executives by Psychological Tests." *Ed & Psychol Meas* 7:773-8 w '47. *

H. E. Brogden, Research Psychologist, Personnel Research Section, The Adjutant General's Office, Washington, D. C. The *Wonderlic Personnel Test* is a short (50 items), rapidly administered (12-minute time limit) general intelligence test. Forms D, E, and F are adaptations of the Otis for industrial use. Forms A and B, developed subsequently, are similar but include a greater variety of item content. Percentile norms based on industrial populations are presented in the manual. The directions, format, and scoring precedures offer little room for criticism in view of the intended use of the test.

Reliabilities, determined by correlation between forms, are reported as ranging from .82 to .94. The figure .93 is said to result after correction for homogeneity of the population. Slightly higher corrected odd-even coefficients are also quoted. It might be noted in passing that the odd-even coefficient is not applicable to time-limit tests such as the Wonderlic and that considerable positive bias can usually be expected to result from its use. In all, the above quoted figure of .93 appears possibly to be an overestimate. The reliability is in any event sufficiently high that an increase in length would not appear justifiable in expectation of any resulting increase in validity.

Use of a general intelligence test might be criticized from the viewpoint of the factor analysts. If, however, the presence of a general factor among adults is admitted—and the reviewer does not believe that its existence has been disproved—this criticism could not be regarded as serious. Since the test contains a considerable variety of pertinent content, it is probably a reasonably good measure of *G*. With the exception, possibly, of a heavy verbal bias, it is also probably not heavily loaded with group factors other than *G*. It is realized that, from the strictly pragmatic viewpoint of the average personnel director, the factor structure of the general content of the test is not important in relation to the primary consideration of validity. Even though the test were a composite of a number of unrelated variables, high validity is still quite possible since criteria are probably themselves composites of a number of unrelated activities. Knowledge of factor structure may, however, be useful in predicting validity or lack of it in various possible applications.

While the manual is commendably cautious —although not too informative—in discussing the validity of the test, the write-up entitled "A Summary of Experiences With the Wonderlic Personnel Test" leaves the definite impression that the Wonderlic test can be used in predicting success in almost any type of industrial work. To the reviewer this impression is undesirable. There is sufficient evidence in the literature to indicate that a general intelligence test cannot be expected to show high validity in general industrial use. Limitations in the use of a general intelligence test should be discussed. It might help if validity were considered in relation to particular jobs or job areas so that waste motion on the part of those personnel managers not acquainted with the testing field could be avoided. Probably, for example, emphasis on usefulness of a general intelligence test in predicting success in clerical work and ability to absorb training and on its general lack of usefulness for predicting success in routine assembly-line types of jobs would be appropriate even though no more restrictive statements were attempted.

In general, if a measure of general intelligence is desired for industrial selection, the Wonderlic seems adequate and can probably be more cheaply and conveniently administered than most competing tests.

Charles D. Flory, Rohrer, Hibler and Replogle, New York, New York. Many testmakers have, in the interest of reliability, extended the testing time beyond practical limits. Wonderlic was among the first to take an accepted intelligence testing instrument and scale it down to twelve minutes with little loss in reliability. The *Wonderlic Personnel Test* was originally a restandardization and revision of the *Otis Self-Administering Tests of Mental Ability*. The format was retained in the revision but the content was reduced by eliminating those items with the least predictive value in an industrial situation. These tests originally were available in two forms, subsequently a third was added, and recently two more have been provided. The publicity concerning these tests sometimes mentions four and sometimes five forms, but the reviewer has seen five forms, A, B, D, E, and F. Statements by the author that "there are four equal and similar forms" and that "the new forms A and B are exactly equivalent to . . . forms D and F" seem slightly exaggerated. The correlations reported for one test taken immediately following another range from .82 to .94. These results suggest "similar" but hardly "exactly equivalent" forms.

The *Personnel Test* has been used widely in industry, and therefore has norms based upon more than 35,000 subjects. The author wisely recommends the use of percentiles in interpreting results for the adult population. He also cautions against the use of psychological data by those who are untrained in the field.

These tests are weakest in two areas, format and content. The print is so small and the items so variable in type and arrangement that uninitiated subjects become confused in taking the test. The items are also strongly academic in flavor since they follow the Otis pattern. These conditions make the tests of limited value for individuals in the lowest two deciles of intelligence and for individuals with little schooling.

The contention that the name of the tests conceals their purpose is probably incorrect and also of doubtful value. There is little value to be gained by subterfuge in industrial situations. The brightest subjects know better and are critical of the ruse. Subjects of less insight care little about labels but react strongly to attitudes in the group. The competent psychologist has little trouble examining applicants except when a defensively incompetent person is encountered. These instances are rare enough to be insignificant.

These tests have many uses where a quick measure of intelligence is desired. A test of this length is more likely to meet the needs of industrial personnel directors than the typical intelligence tests which are from two to five times as long. These tests are easy to administer and can be scored manually in less than one minute. Minimum scores have been established for more than twenty-five different vocations.

Irving Lorge, Professor of Education, and Executive Officer, Institute of Psychological Research, Teachers College, Columbia University, New York, New York. The *Wonderlic Personnel Test* is a 50-item omnibus-type intelligence test prepared for 12-minute time limit administration. The items for Forms D, E, and F were selected from the *Otis Self-Administering Tests of Mental Ability:* Higher Examination. The general approach was to normalize the distribution of item difficulties for adult groups with an average difficulty at fifty per cent subject to a triple check on item validity. The validation was based on the differentiation of each item between "successful and unsuccessful industrial employees," on the differentiation of each item between "good and poor school records" of college students, and on the biserial correlation coefficients of each item using the total score as a criterion (2). Forms A and B "were developed with the same formula which was used in developing Forms D, E, and F."

The reliability of the test is reported in the manual, on the basis of comparable forms, as ranging from .82 to .94 and, on the basis of equivalent halves raised by Spearman–Brown prophecy formula, as ranging from .88 to .94. In a study, however, Wright and Laing (4) report the reliability on equivalent halves for Form D as .87 on 318 cases, for Form E as .70 for 88 cases and for Form F as .81 for 116 cases with the comment "The reliability of this test varies with the different forms and is not as high as it might be."

The validity is considered to be demonstrated by the reporting of the correlation with the original Otis test as ranging from .81 to .87, and the statement, without evidence, "This test has been shown to be a valid instrument in determining success on a number of different jobs." Furthermore, a table in the manual on "Minimum Scores on Personnel Test for Various Occupations" implies a relationship between test score and job success. While the author suggests "These minimum scores are not presented as final critical scores, but merely to guide the research worker," the average user may be confused since he is supposed to be the practical business man.

The item types are like those of the Army Alpha: analogies, geometric figures, arithmetic reasoning, directions, disarranged sentences, logical inference, proverbs, opposites, similarities, etc. Forms D, E, and F are well arranged for writing the appropriate answer between parentheses; forms A and B, however, while continuing the same arrangement do not provide enough room for reporting the complete answer.

Forms D, E, and F are not completely independent since some of the items are repeated in several forms. Item 50, for example, occurs in each form. The overlap, moreover, is particularly disconcerting since a number of mathematicians to whom the item was given, neither agree with each other nor with the key. Item 50 apparently puts an artificial ceiling on the test. Forms A and B are not printed as well as the earlier forms. In my opinion, older people would be penalized by the over-black appearance of the test and the small type for the proverbs and clerical matching items.

The keys are of simple strip variety. Scoring is fairly easy. There would be an advantage to include the right answer for Item 50 of Form B (the answer is 650).

The author suggests that the test can be given either with a 12-minute time limit or as a power test in unlimited time. Unfortunately, the manual provides no data for interpreting the unlimited time scores. Wright and Laing report the correlation between a 12-minute and a 24-minute time limit score as .944 which is not surprising since on the average over ninety per cent of the 24-minute score is the 12-minute score. Their evidence, moreover, does not justify the failure to report power norms.

The time limit norms are based on about 37,000 cases. While the norms are categorized separately by highest grade reached, the samples are not well defined as to their representativeness. The practical business man does not know with what to compare employees' scores.

The author suggests the use of an age correction ranging from 3 points at age 30-39 to 11 points at age 60-69. The latter allowance exceeds the average eighth grade norm.

This is a simple self-administering test of intelligence which for its short time limit may give fair group results, but which lacks sufficient reliability for individual appraisal. The author overclaims the validity of the test and further makes an arcanum of test construction by stating ". . . it was scientifically constructed following a very complicated formula."

The norms could be improved by specifying with scientific accuracy the population of which the sample is supposed to be representative.

INDIVIDUAL

[270]
Alexander Performance Scale: A Performance Scale for the Measurement of Practical Ability. Ages 8-18; 1935-46; individual; 1 form; £9 7s. per testing outfit; 2s. per 50 record sheets; (40-50) minutes; W. P. Alexander; Thomas Nelson and Sons Ltd.

REFERENCES

1-3. See 40:1376.
4. AMIN, D. L. "Differences Among the Deaf and Hearing Children." *Indian J Psychol* 21:91-2 pts 1-4 '46. *

John Cohen, Lecturer, University of Leeds, Leeds, England. This is a performance scale for measuring practical ability, based on W. P. Alexander's well-known study *Intelligence, Concrete and Abstract* (Cambridge Unversity Press, 1935). The scale comprises three tests—the *Passalong Test* (devised by Alexander himself), Kohs' *Block Design Test,* and the *Cube Construction Test*—and is specially designed for children between 11 and 16 years of age. It can, however, be used, though not so effectively, with children 2 or 3 years younger than 11 and older than 16. Testing time is about 40 minutes.

The scale was published to meet the need, created by the English Education Act of 1944, for allocating all children at 11+ to one of three forms of secondary education, viz., (a) literary or humanistic, (b) scientific, and (c) technical or practical. It is to test aptitudes for the third type, i.e., technical and practical education, that the scale is primarily intended. In addition to its use in allocating for secondary education, the scale can also be usefully employed for ascertaining educationally retarded children, for classifying pupils *within* secondary schools, for child and vocational guidance, for selecting apprentices, and with the deaf and partially deaf. The tests are attractively designed and convenient to handle in compact form. There can be no doubt that they will be extensively employed in the next few years in large numbers of English schools.

The scores on the three component tests yield a Practical Ability Ratio (i.e., a ratio of practical to chronological age) distributed like Binet IQ's with a mean of 100 and a standard deviation of 15. The pupil's PAR, as Alexander suggests, should be noted on the primary school record form together with mental and attainment ratios and ratings of personality. This scale is the most up-to-date of its kind in England and is a marked advance on the Collins and Drever performance scale, which is too complex for wide use in schools.

The mean intercorrelation, corrected for attenuation, of the three component tests is .78. The scale as a whole has a correlation of about .8 with "g" and about .7 with the practical factor ("F"). The reliability coefficient, computed from successive testings, is of the order .8.

The record sheets accompanying the tests are unusually simple and convenient to use, and the Instruction Book is a model of conciseness and clarity. Altogether the scale is very strongly recommended, though further validation work is doubtless desirable and would add to the discriminative and predictive worth of what promises to be a first-rate testing device.

Schoolmaster 151:395 My 8 '47. G. W. * Attention is drawn especially to the handbook of instructions. The first half contains a clear description of the tests and how to administer them. The purposes for which the scale can be used are clearly outlined. The second half relates the use of the scale to general educational theory. Particularly illuminating are its references to school records and its analysis of the considerations determining the allocation of children at 11 plus to different types of secondary education. * A valid instrument for measuring practical ability is of great importance to educationists. During recent years considerable evidence for the validity of the Alexander Performance Scale has been produced. It is with confidence that the scale is recommended for a thorough trial.

Times Ed Sup 1670:206 My 3 '47. This is a battery of tests for measuring practical as distinct from academic or verbal ability. The most important purpose of the scale is to select children for secondary education of a technical kind; and the most appropriate time to apply it is at the end of the primary school course. * The test material is supplied in a well-made wooden box about a foot long, 8 in. wide, and 3 in. deep. * The price of the apparatus seems a little alarming, but it must be borne in mind that one box is enough for a school and that the material will last for many years. The important question is: Does the test fulfil its purpose? There is good reason for thinking that it does. Dr. Alexander has carefully tried out the scale for the last 10 years, and has been able to provide norms of performance for the various ages, and to fix a level above which he contends that a technical training is indicated. Success at a technical school is in his opinion assured if the child's practical ability ratio is 120 or over in a scale where the average is 100 and the standard deviation 15. * Among the other purposes for which it is claimed that the Alexander scale can be used, besides the allocation of pupils at 11 plus to appropriate secondary schools, the following may be mentioned: the testing of the deaf and the partially deaf, child guidance, vocational guidance, and the selection of apprentices.

For a review by J. M. Blackburn, see 40: 1376. For reviews by James Drever, T. J. Keating, and Grace H. Kent of the Passalong Test, *see 40:1414. See also 36:B3 and 38:B293.*

[271]

[Arthur] Point Scale of Performance Tests. Ages 4½ or 5½ through superior adults; 1925–47; individual; 2 forms; (45-90) minutes; Grace Arthur.
a) FORM I. Ages 5½ through superior adults; 1925–43; C. H. Stoelting Co.
b) REVISED FORM II. Ages 4½ through superior adults; 1947; all prices include postage; $2.50 per *Knox Cube Test*, Arthur Revision; $15 per *Seguin Formboard*, Arthur Revision; $3 per *Stencil Design Test I*; $10.50 per set of 14 pads of the *Porteus Maze Test*, Arthur revision; $20.50 per *Healy Picture Completion Test II*; $2.50 per 100 score sheets; $2.50 per 100 score cards; $2.25 per manual; $49 per complete testing outfit without carrying case; $3.75 extra for carrying case; Psychological Corporation.

REFERENCES

1-16. See 40:1379.
17. DEAHL, KATHARINE. *The Arthur Performance Scale and the Stanford Binet: An Examination of One Hundred Sixty-nine Ten-Year-Old Children.* Unpublished master's thesis, Stanford University, 1934.
18. HUMM, KATHRYN A. *Applicability of the Arthur Performance Scale to an Adolescent Group.* Unpublished master's thesis, University of Southern California, 1935.
19. DITOLLA, EUGENIA E. *A Comparative Study of Performance Tests.* Unpublished master's thesis, Fordham University, 1939. (*Dissertations . . .,* 1940, pp. 97-98.)
20. BRUCE, MYRTLE. *Factors Affecting Intelligence Test Performance of Whites and Negroes in the Rural South.* Archives of Psychology, No. 252. Washington, D. C.: American Psychological Association, Inc., July 1940. Pp. 99. Paper. $1.50. * (PA 15:4591)
21. SARASON, SEYMOUR BERNARD. *The Effects of Training on Four Intelligence Tests.* Unpublished master's thesis, Clark University, 1940. (*Abstracts of Dissertations . . . 1940,* pp. 113-4.)
22. ARTHUR, GRACE. "An Experience in Testing Indian School Children." *Mental Hyg* 25:188-95 Ap '41. * (PA 15:3481)
23. BIJOU, SIDNEY W. "An Experimental Analysis of Arthur Performance Quotients." *J Consult Psychol* 6:247-52 S-O '42. * (PA 16:5041)
24. BURCHARD, EDWARD M. L., AND MYKLEBUST, HELMER R. "A Comparison of Congenital and Adventitious Deafness With Respect to Its Effect on Intelligence, Personality, and Social Maturity: Part I, Intelligence." *Am Ann Deaf* 87:140-54 Mr '42. * (PA 17:75)

24a. ARTHUR, GRACE. *A Point Scale of Performance Tests: Vol. I, Clinical Manual, Second Edition.* New York: Commonwealth Fund, 1943. Pp. xi, 64. $1.50. * (PA 18:1539)
25. ARTHUR, GRACE. "A Non-Verbal Test of Logical Thinking." *J Consult Psychol* 8:33-4 Ja-F '44. * (PA 18:2286)
26. HAVIGHURST, ROBERT J., AND HILKEVITCH, RHEA R. "The Intelligence of Indian Children as Measured by a Performance Scale." *J Abn & Social Psychol* 39:419-33 O '44. * (PA 19:475)
27. WALLIN, J. E. WALLACE, AND HULTSCH, CATHARINE L. "The Pathognomonic Significance of Psychometric Patterns." *Am J Mental Def* 48:269-77 Ja '44. * (PA 18:2983)
28. ABEL, THEODORA M. "The Relationship Between Academic Success and Personality Organization Among Subnormal Girls." *Am J Mental Def* 50:251-6 O '45. * (PA 20:2883)
29. CAPWELL, DORA F. "Performance of Deaf Children on the Arthur Point Scale." *J Consult Psychol* 9:91-4 Mr-Ap '45. * (PA 19:2398)
30. ROBERTS, A. DUDLEY. "Intelligence and Performance Test Patterns Among Older Mental Defectives." *Am J Def* 49:300-3 Ja '45. * (PA 19:3386)
31. SHOTWELL, ANNA M. "Arthur Performance Ratings of Mexican and American High-Grade Mental Defectives." *Am J Mental Def* 49:445-9 Ap '45. * (PA 20:170)
32. PATTERSON, R. MELCHER. "The Significance of Practice Effect Upon Readministration of the Grace Arthur Performance Scale to High Grade Mentally Deficient Children." *Am J Mental Def* 50:393-401 Ja '46. * (PA 20:4381)
33. SARASON, SEYMOUR B., AND SARASON, ESTHER KROOP. "The Discriminatory Value of a Test Pattern in the High Grade Familial Defective." *J Clin Psychol* 2:38-49 Ja '46. * (PA 20:1940)
34. FRAZEUR, HELEN A., AND HOAKLEY, Z. PAULINE. "Significance of Psychological Test Results of Exogenous and Endogenous Children (Arthur Point Scale)." *Am J Mental Def* 51:384-88 Ja '47. * (PA 22:367)
35. SARASON, SEYMOUR B., AND SARASON, ESTHER KROOP. "The Discriminatory Value of a Test Pattern With Cerebral Palsied, Defective Children." *J Clin Psychol* 3:141-7 Ap '47. * (PA 21:3029)

J Consult Psychol 11:224 Jl-Ag '47. * A notable feature of the selection of subtests is the elimination of the complex, speeded, form boards that were once the core of performance testing, which recent research has shown to reward rapid trial and error, rather than planned response. *Form II* has two primary uses, as a retest for children of school age who have been examined with *Form I,* and as a first test for use with pre-school children, in connection with the forthcoming Arthur adaptation of the Leiter International Performance Scale. The convenient spiral-bound manual gives clear descriptions of the tests, directions for administration and scoring, and tables for obtaining MA's from each test and from the entire scale. *

For reviews by Andrew W. Brown and Carroll A. Whitmer and an excerpt from a review by Donald Snedden, see 40:1379. See also 36: B19, 38:B304, and 40:B830.

[272]

★**Canadian Intelligence Examination.** Ages 3-16; 1940; a modification of the 1916 *Stanford Revision of the Binet-Simon Intelligence Scale;* individual; 1 form; 45¢ per set of test materials; $1 per manual; 75¢ per 50 record forms; Harry Amoss and Charles G. Stodgill; Ryerson Press.

REFERENCES

1. STOTHERS, C. E. "The Use of the Canadian Intelligence Test." *Sch* 30:920-3 Je '42. *

Sch 30:946+ Je '42. *C(lara) B(lacklock).* For some time there has been an urgent need for an individual intelligence test published in Canada and standardized on norms obtained in Canada. American tests are both expensive and difficult to obtain. Experience with these Canadian tests proves them to be of interest and enjoyment to students. They have somewhat more originality than various tests that are definitely based on a revision of the Binet. Undoubtedly the inclusion of a greater number of mathematical tests gives a more complete picture and a fairer chance to the not-too-articulate person. The clarity, general plan, and set-up of the manual makes it decidedly helpful to the administrator. The administering and scoring requires approximately the same time as the Binet test and the results prove to be practically the same. Keen interest is felt in a further report which Dr. Stothers, Inspector of Auxiliary Classes, is preparing, including comparative results of a series of Binet Tests and Canadian Intelligence Examinations given to a wide range of groups throughout the province last year. A standardized Canadian test will certainly be most welcome to all interested in this field of study.

Understanding the Child 9:34 Ja '41. It will be of considerable interest to teachers in Canada to know that at last there has been prepared an individual test of general intelligence of the Binet–Simon type, designed particularly for use with Canadian children. The Canadian Intelligence Examination is based largely on the Terman, Kuhlmann, and Gesell tests, but original items have been devised and included. The chief points of difference from the Stanford revision are that the language of instruction used in the presentation of the various problems has been simplified; the acceptable responses have been more rigorously defined; and an attempt has been made to reduce the weighting heretofore given to acquired literary skills by the inclusion of more mathematical and constructional problems. In order to avoid local and literary expressions, the word list in the vocabulary test has been selected from language common to both urban and rural communities in Canada rather than from the dictionary. The materials necessary for the administration of the test are simple and easily procured at little expense. The simplicity of the arrangement of the test items shortens the time usually required to administer an individual intelligence examination. The test has been standardized chiefly in Ontario, but it is probable that it will prove more applicable to Canadian school children anywhere in the Dominion than the present revisions of the Binet test currently sold in the United States.

[273]

Carl Hollow Square Scale. Ages 10 and over; 1939–45; individual; 1 form; $42 per testing outfit, postpaid; (25-60) minutes; George P. Carl; Psychological Service, Institute of the Pennsylvania Hospital, 111 North 49th St., Philadelphia 30, Pa.

REFERENCES

1-2. See 40:1385.
3. LINCOLN, EDWARD A. "The Reliability of the Lincoln Hollow Square Form Board and a Comparison of Hollow Square Scores With Stanford Binet Mental Ages." *J Appl Psychol* 15:79-81 F '31. * (PA 5:4334)
4. ESTES, STANLEY G. "A Study of Five Tests of 'Spatial' Ability." *J Psychol* 13:265-71 Ap '42. * (PA 16:3771)
5. HALSTEAD, H., AND SLATER, PATRICK. "An Experiment in the Vocational Adjustment of Neurotic Patients." *J Mental Sci* 92:509-15 Jl '45. * (PA 21:281)

Grace H. Kent, Visiting Professor of Psychology, The University of Miami, Coral Gables, Florida. This test might appropriately have been named the "Bevel-Edge Formboard Series." It differs from the *Lincoln Hollow Square* in the use of beveled edges, and from the *Ferguson Formboards* in that the beveled edge is used systematically and consistently. It is an exquisite piece of apparatus, one which apparently must have required years of preliminary experimentation. It can be said of the standardization also that it represents a vast amount of labor. Each of the 1,500 subjects was given a very thorough examination, and the norms are based upon correlation with other tests.

The recess into which the blocks are to be fitted is a hole about 4¾ inches square. There are twenty tasks, all except two requiring four blocks apiece. For each task the edges of the blocks which touch the frame are perpendicular, but the matchings within the square invariably involve the fitting together of two beveled edges. There are 29 blocks, no two alike, whose basic forms are rectangular, triangular, trapezoidal and somewhat irregular. Each block is numbered, and the four blocks needed for a given task are selected by their labels. The entire outfit, including a well-built container, is so compact that it can be carried in a briefcase.

A very strong feature of the test is its attractiveness to the subject. The problem is one of absorbing interest to the subject who is able to grasp the significance of the beveled edge; and his interest is well sustained throughout a series of increasing difficulty.

This reviewer regards the test as a masterpiece, and has nothing but the highest praise for the basic idea and for the way in which it has been worked out in the apparatus. All criticisms here expressed relate wholly to the way in which the test has been used.

The formula for presentation includes nearly 500 words to be read aloud to the subject, and the reading occupies at least three minutes. This is not only a waste of time; it is also somewhat irritating to a subject who comprehends the task and who is impatient to get the new toy into his hands. Even a highly trained subject finds it difficult to listen attentively to the instructions. For the average subject it should be sufficient to show the performance of a demonstration task, explaining that the straight edge of any block should always be placed at the edge of the square. One whose performance of the first task shows that he has failed to follow this demonstration may safely be considered an unsuitable subject for the test.

Each task is evaluated by points, based upon an arbitrary combination of the time record and the move count. The score is modified further by additional points bonus for completing a task within a "sub-limit" in respect to time or moves, or by penalty for going beyond an upper limit in time or number of moves. The computation of results is somewhat complicated, and it takes the examiner about thirty minutes to evaluate the record.

The final score is the sum of the points earned in all the tasks. The score for male subjects has been found to be 31 points less than the IQ by the Stanford–Binet scale, and for female subjects it was 39 points less than the Stanford–Binet IQ. Accordingly, the author derives an IQ for a male subject by adding 31 points to his score, and for a female subject by adding 39 points. The "mental age," if desired, is derived from the IQ by reckoning backwards.

To the reviewer this method of evaluation seems neither justifiable nor necessary. What we call "intelligence," however defined, is a factor in the performance of any test, as it is also a factor in the performance of such household tasks as cooking and dishwashing. It is natural that any two tests should show a moderately high correlation, but it does not follow that they measure the same thing. To consider the Carl test a special aptitude test does not imply any disparagement. The aptitude test has an important place in the clinical study of adolescent children, especially with reference to vocational guidance; and it is not essential that such a test yield an IQ.

It is at the lower age levels and lower mental levels that formboard tests are most useful in the clinic. The very simple formboard, dealing with form-experience so elementary as to be universal among normal children of school age, may rank almost with the language test in its measurement of what we wish to measure by our so-called "intelligence tests"; but as we go higher in the difficulty scale, we deal increasingly with form-experience which is far from universal and which our subject may or may not have had. The tridimensional formboard is at the upper end of the formboard scale. The mechanical engineer may be expected to achieve a high score, and so also may the cabinetmaker who left school before reaching instruction in geometry; whereas the professional man who deals chiefly with words and abstractions may show amazing stupidity in his failure to recognize the most obvious similarities and differences in form.

Most formboard tests (including those developed by the reviewer) involve so many factors that it is impossible to say what is measured by them. The strength of an aptitude test depends largely upon the success with which some one particular factor is isolated and measured; but this single aptitude, however well measured, cannot fairly be used as an index to a subject's mental capacity in general.

As a means of measuring the subject's aptitude for dealing with beveled edges, the *Carl Hollow Square* is a superb instrument. Let it be standardized and used for just exactly what it is, and it should rank very high in serviceability. It cannot be recommended for routine clinical use. There are a few clinics in which time is allowed for an exhaustive study of a subject's special aptitudes, but they are exceptional. For the clinic in which the psychometric examination is crowded into one hour, this test is too limited in scope to yield results commensurate with the time required for its presentation.

Whatever defects may be found in the author's methods of presentation, recording, and standardization, the test itself can be unconditionally recommended for use in the industries; and it seems to be especially rich in potential value for the boys' vocational school. On the

Carl Hollow Square Scale

chance that some student will see its possibilities and undertake its standardization as an aptitude test, the following suggestions are offered for its use:

a) The presentation should be adapted to the comprehension of the subject. It is far more important that it be natural and informal than that it be uniform for all subjects. One of the "extra" tasks may be used frankly for demonstration, the subject to be given whatever help he requires for its solution. Any subject who then fails to solve the first task of the series within a reasonable time limit should be excused from further work with this test. He may be given a little help in completing this one task, after which he should be given a task which is easily within his reach. The *Lincoln Hollow Square,* because of its superficial similarity to the Carl test, would be a very good formboard to have at hand for the purpose of easing over a failure.

b) Time limits for the various tasks should not be too liberal. There are enough tasks to make the test abundantly discriminative at any level, even if some tasks are scored as failures. When the time limit of a task is reached, the subject may be shown the solution and then given the next task. He will not be wholly deprived of its practice-effects on the remaining tasks.

c) In the face of the author's confidence in his system of scoring the results, the reviewer recommends that the move count be omitted and that the score be based wholly upon the time record. This plan will permit the examiner to take notes on the subject's mode of procedure, and the author concedes the value of supplementary qualitative observations.

The fundamental objection to the move count, except in a test designed specifically with reference to an accurate move count, is that it is too subjective to be trustworthy. The movements which a subject may make are too varied in kind to be accurately defined. There is no opportunity for deliberation concerning a hair-splitting distinction, and no check on a move that has been recorded or left unrecorded. While the examiner is trying to decide what to do with some particular half-move, the subject continues to make more and more moves. It is true that the highly practised examiner may be able to establish his own criteria for evaluating the moves, but it does not follow that two experienced examiners would agree as to their criteria.

The subject who tries to work rapidly is likely to make unnecessary moves, and the one who concentrates upon economy of moves is almost sure to take more time than is needed. There is an irreconcilable interference between the two variables. Scoring them both in terms of one or the other is an attempt to get something for nothing, and is almost in the class with the perpetual-motion concept. Any formboard which permits an accurate move count should be scored wholly in terms of moves, and the subject should be informed that he is not being timed; whereas the test which does not permit an objective move count may better be evaluated wholly in terms of speed.

The Carl test is almost in a class by itself in respect to the essential fairness with which it may be scored by speed. As there are only four placements required in any given task, there is little opportunity for serious confusion. The same principle runs through the series, and there are enough tasks to offset the effects of chance. Almost any subject is likely to have accidental difficulty with some task, possibly with one of the easier tasks in the early part of the series; but his speed score on the series as a whole will furnish a reasonably fair index to his aptitude in the matching of beveled edges. When the test is used for study of this aptitude and not as an intelligence test, the move count is as unnecessary as it is inaccurate.

It is recommended that the time records in seconds be totaled for the several tasks, and that this figure be accepted as the final score, exactly as it stands. The stopwatch should be used openly as a means of letting the subject know that he is being timed. There is no need of instructing him to work rapidly.

d) It is suggested that the norms be relative rather than absolute. Standardization for a selected group of subjects is a much simpler process than is the development of norms intended to be generally applicable. Only within the age limit for compulsory school attendance is it easy to find a representative sampling of the population; and the standardization of tests for adults and adolescents presents inherent difficulties. It is much easier to standardize a test for a given industry or for a given school; and the norms thus obtained may be used with reservations for individual study of a person belonging to the same selected group. The

Carl Hollow Square Scale

norms for the group may be expressed in decile or quintile or quartile scores, according to the range of scores and the number of subjects.

e) The norms, in whatever form offered, should be worked out independently for several different levels of achievement. The subject who can barely complete two or three tasks within the time limit should not be required to struggle through the entire series for the sake of obtaining a score. A given set of records can be used for the establishment of as many levels of norms as are needed, with preferably not over three tasks for the lowest level. The intervals between consecutive levels should be small enough so that no subject need be required to continue after two failures. There should be definite rules for bringing the performance to a conclusion as soon as the subject appears to have reached his limit; and a frank failure should invariably be followed by a formboard task easy enough to insure success. The examination should always leave the subject with a sense of achievement rather than a sense of failure.

For a review by T. J. Keating, see 40:1385.

[274]
Detroit Kindergarten Test. Kgn entrants; 1921–25; individual; 1 form; $1.40 per 25; 35¢ per specimen set; (7-12) minutes; Harry J. Baker and H. J. Kaufmann; World Book Co.

REFERENCES
1. GASKILL, HAROLD V. "Language Responses and Intelligence: I, Verbalization and Intelligence." *J Genetic Psychol* 58:407-17 Je '41. * (PA 16:99)

Psyche Cattell, Clinical Psychologist, Lancaster, Pennsylvania. The *Detroit Kindergarten Test* is designed for a short individual intelligence test for children entering kindergarten. The test consists of a booklet of pictures which the examiner marks according to the child's responses to his instructions.

Percentile curves based on 895 cases and age norms based on over 5,000 kindergarten pupils are given for ages 3 0/12 years to 7 6/12 years. The lowest norm is based on a score of two, and the highest, on a perfect score. Obviously mental age norms at the extremes of the possible range of scores cannot be reliable. In general, as the authors point out, the younger children attending a kindergarten are more intelligent than the average child, whereas the older ones are below average, and therefore the norms are "necessarily somewhat hypothetical except for about the age of five years." The authors do not, however, state what if any measures have been taken to correct for the atypical sampling of the younger and older age groups. No information on reliability and validity is reported.

The items for the test appear to have been carefully selected; the directions for giving and scoring the tests are simply written in language that can be understood and followed by an intelligent teacher; the test can be administered in less than half the time required for the Stanford–Binet; and it requires considerably less training on the part of the examiner than such a test as the Stanford–Binet.

It is unfortunate that a test with the above advantages should not report data on reliability and validity and that unselected groups at the upper and lower age levels could not have been obtained for the standardization.

From the inadequate information offered, it appears probable that this test should not be used for obtaining mental ages or intelligence quotients, but that it might well prove of value in classifying kindergarten children into percentile ranks.

Ruth W. Washburn, Consultant in Child Development, Shady Hill School, Cambridge, Massachusetts. The publication of this test in 1922 has been followed by so much excellent work in the field that the test has little left to recommend it save the short time necessary for its administration as an individual test (7 to 12 minutes). Though the norms for ages 3 years 0 months to 7 years 6 months are based on total scores of 5,069 pupils and "partly upon Binet mental ages of 102 pupils," the authors of the test felt that norms were so difficult to obtain as to make them "necessarily somewhat hypothetical except for the age of about five years where they are fairly reliable." Had the test been standardized more recently the norms could have been more reliably established by using the test in conjunction with some of the excellent tests for preschool children now available.

A major criticism of the test is that the young child is given no chance to use a pencil or other concrete material, so nothing is learned of the development of eye-hand coordinations, so important in kindergarten and preprimary work.

Carl Hollow Square Scale

[275]

Detroit Tests of Learning Aptitude. Ages 4 and over; 1935–39; individual; 1 form; $4.20 per testing outfit; 10¢ per record booklet; Harry J. Baker and Bernice Leland; Public School Publishing Co.

REFERENCES

1. WORCESTER, D. A., AND COREY, STEPHEN M. "In Criticism of the Detroit Tests of Learning Aptitude." *J Ed Psychol* 27:258-62 Ap '36. * (PA 10:6004)

F. L. Wells, Psychologist, Department of Hygiene, Harvard University, Cambridge, Massachusetts. The earlier edition of the *Detroit Tests of Learning Aptitude* (DTLA) was reviewed in the 1938 edition of this *Yearbook* (38:1058). The present revision cites further experience with its use (12,000 cases) with some minor evaluative changes resulting therefrom. Only slight procedural alterations have been made; no change was observed in the pictorial material. Thus, it is not clear that the presentation of the series now offered materially *alters* the pertinence of the judgments given in the earlier reviews. But in a "forced choice," clinicians would be generally well advised to prefer a test series organized by, for example, Grace H. Kent with 500 cases to one organized by machinery with 50,000. The sort of criticism above directed at the DTLA applied with considerable force to the original *Kent E-G-Y Test;* yet for its dimensions there has never been so useful a procedure in clinical psychometrics. The clinical value of a test is too much a qualitative function, and too much a function of the background the examiner brings to it, to be properly assessable in terms of experience-tables of whatever magnitude.

As in the original edition, the norms are in the common terms of age level, uniformly at intervals of three months. Such age symbolism is undeniably specious, but its lucidity causes it variously to persist. A more rational procedure would be to cite for somewhat less frequent age intervals mean scores with sigmas; this would give, with little added effort, a much clearer idea of where an individual stands with reference to his own developmental group.

Like other tests, the DTLA is limited in the age range to which it is most appropriate. Its chief usefulness is in the grade-school years. At both extremes it has effective competitors, but also the persistent advantage of physical convenience. Indeed, the layout has received uniform commendation, and no better is known to have been achieved; but there should be a worth-while gain in spiral binding for the Examiner's Handbook also. This would greatly facilitate learning, as well as accurate use of the detailed scoring data, at all levels of practically attainable skill. Everyone, except the beginner with such tests, should learn not to be dependent on printed record forms. Comparatively little of the DTLA record booklet is expendable as such, and the regular user might well effect economies of cost and space and, with practice, of time, with ordinary ruled paper.

The subtests of the series embody well-tried devices, such as absurdities and "comprehension," and others less well known but ingenious, as pictorial opposites and disarranged pictures. The most widely useful single subtest has seemed to be verbal opposites. Like other series of similar organization, the DTLA is not a closed system. The clinician should feel quite free to brigade selections from its subtests with others from the Wechsler–Bellevue, the Kuhlmann–Anderson, and the like. In this way certain quantitative and spatial underemphases of the DTLA can be compensated; for with all concessions to the penetrating review of these matters recently contributed by Garrett, this series also puts a good many of its eggs in the verbal basket.

For reviews by Anne Anastasi and Henry Feinberg and an excerpt from a review by D. A. Worcester and S. M. Corey of an earlier edition, see 38:1058.

[276]

Gesell Developmental Schedules. Ages 4-60 weeks; 1925-40; individual; also called *Gesell Maturity Scale, Gesell Norms of Development, Gesell Tests, Preschool Child Development Scale, Preschool Child Test, Yale Psycho-Clinic Developmental Schedules, Yale Tests of Child Development,* and other variations; Arnold Gesell and others.
a) 1925 SERIES. 1925; manual (Gesell's *The Mental Growth of the Preschool Child*) is out of print; testing materials (listed in publisher's catalog as *Pre-School Child Test*)—C. H. Stoelting Co.
b) 1938 SERIES. 1925-38; manual (Gesell, Thompson, and Amatruda's *The Psychology of Early Growth*)—Macmillan Co.; testing materials (listed in publisher's catalog as *Gesell Maturity Scale*)—Marietta Apparatus Co.
c) 1940 SERIES. 1925-41; manual (Gesell, Halverson, Thompson, Ilg, Castner, Ames, and Amatruda's *The First Five Years of Life*)—Harper & Brothers testing materials must be assembled by examiner; 60¢ per specimen set of printed materials and record forms—Psychological Corporation.

REFERENCES

1. GESELL, ARNOLD. *The Mental Growth of the Preschool Child: A Psychological Outline of Normal Development From Birth to the Sixth Year, Including a System of Developmental Diagnosis.* New York: Macmillan Co., 1925. Pp. x, 447. Out of print. *

2. GESELL, ARNOLD. "Monthly Increments of Development in Infancy." *J Genetic Psychol* 32:203-8 Je '25. *
3. GESELL, ARNOLD. "The Diagnosis of Mental Defect in Early Infancy." *J Psycho-Asthenics* 33:211-8 '28. * (PA 3:732)
4. GESELL, ARNOLD. *Infancy and Human Growth.* New York: Macmillan Co., 1928. Pp. xix, 418. Out of print. * (PA 3:886)
5. GESELL, ARNOLD. *The Guidance of Mental Growth in Infant and Child.* New York: Macmillan Co., 1930. Pp. xi, 322. Out of print. * (PA 5:1999)
6. ALDRICH, CECELIA G., AND DOLL, EDGAR A. "Comparative Intelligence of Idiots and Normal Infants." *J Genetic Psychol* 39:227-57 Je '31. * (PA 6:520)
7. STECKEL, MINNIE L. "Items of Gesell's Developmental Schedule Scaled." *J Ed Psychol* 23:99-103 F '32. * (PA 6:2047)
8. BROWN, CLARENCE W.; BARTELME, PHYLLIS; AND COX, GERTRUDE M. "The Scoring of Individual Performance on Tests Scaled According to the Theory of Absolute Scaling." *J Ed Psychol* 24:654-62 D '33. * (PA 8:2807)
9. SYMMES, EDITH F. "An Infant Testing Service as an Integral Part of a Child Guidance Clinic." *Am J Orthopsychiatry* 3:409-30 O '33. * (PA 8:740)
10. GESELL, ARNOLD. *Atlas of Infant Behavior: A Systematic Delineation of the Forms and Early Growth of Human Behavior Patterns,* Two Volumes. Limited edition. Illustrated with 3,200 Action Photographs. New Haven, Conn.: Yale University Press, 1934. Pp. 921. Loose-leaf. $25.00. (London: Oxford University Press. Pp. 922. £5 10s.) (PA 9:449)
11. GESELL, ARNOLD, AND THOMPSON, HELEN; ASSISTED BY CATHERINE STRUNK AMATRUDA. *Infant Behavior: Its Genesis and Growth.* New York: McGraw-Hill Book Co., Inc., 1934. Pp. viii, 343. $3.00. * (London: McGraw-Hill Publishing Co. Ltd. 18s.) (PA 9:3024)
12. CURTI, MARGARET W.; MARSHALL, FRANCES BOTKIN; AND STEGGERDA, MORRIS; WITH THE ASSISTANCE OF ETHEL M. HENDERSON. "The Gesell Schedules Applied to One-, Two-, and Three-Year-Old Negro Children of Jamaica, B. W. I." *J Comp Psychol* 20:125-56 O '35. * (PA 10:1063)
13. GESELL, ARNOLD, AND THOMPSON, HELEN; ASSISTED BY CATHERINE STRUNK AMATRUDA. *The Psychology of Early Growth: Including Norms of Infant Behavior and a Method of Genetic Analysis.* New York: Macmillan Co., 1938. Pp. ix, 290. Out of print. * (PA 12:3211)
14. NELSON, VIRGINIA LAFAYETTE, AND RICHARDS, T. W. "Studies in Mental Development: I, Performance on Gesell Items at Six Months and Its Predictive Value for Performance on Mental Tests at Two and Three Years." *J Genetic Psychol* 52:303-25 Je '38. * (PA 13:610)
15. RICHARDS, T. W., AND NELSON, VIRGINIA LAFAYETTE. "Studies in Mental Development: II, Analysis of Abilities Tested at the Age of Six Months by the Gesell Schedule." *J Genetic Psychol* 52:327-31 Je '38. * (PA 13:615)
16. ANDERSON, L. DEWEY. "The Predictive Value of Infancy Tests in Relation to Intelligence at Five Years." *Child Develop* 10:203-12 S '39. * (PA 13:6507)
17. GESELL, ARNOLD; AMATRUDA, CATHERINE S.; CASTNER, BURTON M.; AND THOMPSON, HELEN. *Biographies of Child Development: The Mental Growth Careers of Eighty-Four Infants and Children: A Ten-Year Study From the Clinic of Child Development at Yale University.* New York: Paul B. Hoeber, Inc., 1939. Pp. xvii, 328. Out of print. (PA 13:3325)
18. NELSON, VIRGINIA LAFAYETTE, AND RICHARDS, T. W. "Studies in Mental Development: III, Performance of Twelve-Months-Old Children on the Gesell Schedule and Its Predictive Value for Mental Status at Two and Three Years." *J Genetic Psychol* 54:181-91 Mr '39. * (PA 13:5388)
19. RICHARDS, T. W., AND NELSON, VIRGINIA L. "Abilities of Infants During the First Eighteen Months." *J Genetic Psychol* 55:299-318 D '39. * (PA 14:2170)
20. GESELL, ARNOLD; HALVERSON, HENRY M.; THOMPSON, HELEN; ILG, FRANCES L.; CASTNER, BURTON M.; AMES, LOUISE BATES; AND AMATRUDA, CATHERINE S. *The First Five Years of Life: A Guide to the Study of the Preschool Child.* From the Yale Clinic of Child Development. New York: Harper & Brothers, 1940. Pp. xiii, 393. $4.00. * (PA 14:3804)
21. NELSON, VIRGINIA, AND RICHARDS, T. W. "Fels Mental Age Values for Gesell Schedules." *Child Develop* 11:153-7 S '40. * (PA 15:1090)
22. GESELL, ARNOLD, AND AMATRUDA, CATHERINE S. *Developmental Diagnosis: Normal and Abnormal Child Development: Clinical Methods and Practical Applications.* New York: Paul B. Hoeber, Inc., 1941. Pp. xiii, 447. $6.50. * (PA 15:4836)
23. AMES, LOUISE BATES. "The Gesell Incomplete Man Test as a Differential Indicator of Average and Superior Behavior in Preschool Children." *J Genetic Psychol* 62:217-74 Je '43.* (PA 18:905)
24. AMES, LOUISE BATES, AND ILG, FRANCES L. "Variant Behavior as Revealed by the Gesell Developmental Examination." *J Genetic Psychol* 63:273-305 D '43. * (PA 18:1267)
25. AMES, LOUISE BATES. "Free Drawing and Completion Drawing: A Comparative Study of Preschool Children." *J Genetic Psychol* 66:161-5 Je '45. * (PA 19:3521)
26. GESELL, ARNOLD, AND AMES, LOUISE B. "The Development of Handedness." *J Genetic Psychol* 70:155-75 Je '47. * (PA 22:231)
27. GESELL, ARNOLD, AND AMES, LOUISE B. "The Infant's Reaction to His Mirror Image." *J Genetic Psychol* 70:141-54 Je '47. * (PA 22:232)
28. MEAD, MARGARET. "On the Implications for Anthropology of the Gesell-Ilg Approach to Maturation." *Am Anthropol* 49:69-77 Ja-Mr '47. * (PA 21:3664)

Nancy Bayley, Lecturer in Psychology and Research Associate, Institute of Child Welfare, University of California, Berkeley, California. The *Gesell Developmental Schedules* have been widely used and copied since their appearance in 1925. Because in their early form the procedures, scoring, and standardization were very incompletely described, efforts to use the tests have resulted in a variety of adaptations, all independently standardized, with each author interpreting them differently and establishing his own specific methods of giving and scoring essentially the same testing situations and materials.

Recently, in a series of books, Gesell (with various collaborators) has published revisions of the tests with very full descriptions. *The Psychology of Early Growth* (13) describes the normative sample and presents in great detail the methods and behavior norms for the first year; *The First Five Years of Life* (20) among other things includes directions for the developmental tests from one through five years; and *Developmental Diagnosis* (22) gives directions for administering, scoring, and interpreting the tests from four weeks through three years. It is not possible to get all of the information about the tests and their standardization from any single book; and in each book, the organization of the directions and the forms for recording the child's behavior are different. *Developmental Diagnosis* is probably the most practical to use as a testing manual. The record forms developed in this book are less complicated (though one may question the advisability of their emphasis on "key" ages), and the directions are better organized for exploring the behavior of a given child in a testing situation. However, even in this book, the specific directions for administering the tests are in an entirely different section from the descriptions of characteristic behavior to be expected and scored.

The "normative sample" on whom the tests were standardized consists of 107 children (49 boys and 58 girls) selected to represent a homogeneous middle-class background (on the basis of the Barr rating scale). These children were tested repeatedly, so that there were at least 26 children and usually about 35 tested at each of 20 age levels from four weeks through five years.

The descriptions of characteristic behavior, developmental trends in behavior, and techniques for eliciting the desired behavior at different levels of development are very superior. They evidence much experience, careful observation, and good clinical insight in these matters. The test materials are very suitable for their purposes and by now are well known to anyone at all familiar with infant tests. The complicated equipment of crib, photographic dome, one-way vision screen, etc., though important for research, are not essential for the tests, and practical alternatives are indicated.

The tests are arranged to give a general impression of a child's maturity of performance. Many characteristic types of behavior which may or may not occur are listed, and there is no attempt to have equal numbers of items at successive age levels. In scoring the *Gesell Developmental Schedules,* the items of behavior are rated plus or minus, according to whether or not they occur, and then the highest age at which plus signs are predominant is determined by inspection and called the developmental age. The developmental age may be modified by the tester's judgment about the general quality of a child's performance. It may be further qualified by a plus or minus, to indicate whether the average performance is somewhat above or below the assigned age level. A developmental quotient, or DQ, may then be computed by the same method as the IQ (i.e., 100 × DA/CA).

Gesell's insistence on the superiority of his method of scoring, and his claims for predicting later intelligence from these scores in infancy, appear to rest on several confusions combined with a failure to make any careful quantitative test of the relation between the children's scores made in infancy and later.

As for the scores, Gesell repeatedly insists that it is a mistake to give a numerical score to an infant's pattern of behavior by some form of counting items. But what he fails to realize is that such a numerical score always falls at the most representative level of a child's behavior if the items are arranged approximately in their developmental sequence. Therefore, a "clinical appraisal," which is not too influenced by factors other than the child's actual maturity of behavior, gives essentially the same results. The main differences are that such appraisals are more subjective and less amenable to statistical treatment. Furthermore, no qualified tester depends solely on the numerical test score in interpreting a child's performance; the qualifying factors are considered *in addition to* the test score.

The insistence on the superiority of the DQ over the IQ is supported only by emotionally toned words and phrases to the effect that the DQ *unlike* the IQ may be used as a starting point in diagnosis, that it is not "limited to a single inclusive formula" but can be computed independently for the various fields of behavior, making possible better judgments about a child's real developmental status. (He does not even mention other methods of indicating relative performance.) A better justification for the use of the term *developmental quotient* is that in infancy the most important factor in determining individual differences in performance is variation in *rates of maturing.*

However, he fails to note that as the general process of maturing slows down, this factor loses ground rapidly to innate differences in capacity (and environmental factors) which eventually become paramount after all individuals have reached maturity. As there is no logical necessity for rates of maturing to be related to eventual individual differences, it becomes important to test whether or not this is so. This Gesell fails to do. He continues to hold, by assertion and a few selected illustrative cases, that the DQ remains relatively constant and that both feeble-mindedness (simple amentia) and intellectual superiority can be diagnosed in infancy. But there is nowhere any quantitative evaluation of the extent to which the children in the normative sample (or others) remain in the same diagnostic classification, and no recognition that other investigators have consistently found that these early behavior scores have little relation to scores made after three or four years. (See, for example, the tests of P. Cattell, Goodenough, and Bayley.)

Florence M. Teagarden, Professor of Psychology, The University of Pittsburgh, Pittsburgh, Pennsylvania. One is confronted with selecting from the dozen or more books put out by Dr. Gesell and his collaborators those that will most nearly clarify for the clinical psychologist the actual procedures used by Dr. Gesell. Books and motion pictures have rather clearly demonstrated Dr. Gesell's approach to the child and his handling of his own test materials. Nowhere, however, has any one been able to discover how Dr. Gesell uses his normative data for a quantified appraisal of an individual child. The following review attempts to compare his descriptions of examining and appraising infants as described in the three most recent of his books in this field, namely: *The Psychology of Early Growth* (13), *The First Five Years of Life* (20), and *Developmental Diagnosis* (22).

In *The Psychology of Early Growth* Gesell and Thompson give *maturity level summaries* for ages 4, 6, 8, 12, 16, 20, 24, 28, 32, 36, 40, 44, 48, 52, and 56 weeks. These summaries list developmental sequences critical for each age level (short and less detailed summaries are also given in an appendix for ages 15 months through 66 months). The summaries through the 56 weeks level include items on head control, arm-hand posture, leg-foot posture, body-posture and progression, regard, prehension, language and social development, and adaptive behavior. There are differing numbers of items in these different categories and at different ages. In this respect the summaries do not constitute a "scale" as scales are ordinarily constructed. The summaries, however, are fairly clear-cut and are rather easily used by anyone who has had experience in the infant field. The writer has been using them extensively for a number of years and has enjoyed the possibility of comparing a child's development in the different fields mentioned above. This is true even though one may not see the need, or indeed the wisdom, of using Gesell's very elaborate "analytic development schedule" provided in this volume. This is a very time-consuming method of finding indications of "more maturity" and "less maturity" than the "two distinctive and adjacent age levels from which to reckon deviations." One must in the end work out his own method of scoring, recording, and summarizing the child's behavior in respect to these summaries.

In *The First Five Years,* Dr. Gesell gives descriptive accounts of the behavior of infants of 4, 16, 28, and 40 weeks and of 1 year of age. These descriptions conform fairly closely to the corresponding age level summaries in *Psychology of Early Growth*. No discussion is given, however, in *The First Five Years* as to clinical use for appraisal purposes. Dr. Gesell also gives similar descriptions of behavior of children of 18 months, 2 years, 3 years, 4 years and 5 years. At still another place in this volume Dr. Gesell begins a technique which he develops further in the text discussed below, that is, to give in parallel columns the percentage of children performing each behavior item at two or three successive age levels. No method of computing final scores or measures is given, however.

Developmental Diagnosis by Gesell and Amatruda is the most recent volume dealing with infant measurement. Again behavior items are given which represent motor, adaptive, language, and personal-social development. Beginning at 4 weeks, pictures and descriptions are given of development at succeeding 12-week intervals through 12 months; likewise, for 18, 24, and 36 months. The gaps between these levels, however, are supplied through additional charts of parallel columns. For example, where 16 weeks is the *key age,* comparison is shown of the 12 weeks and of the 20 weeks levels. In this volume, too, Gesell provides for a *Developmental Quotient* or DQ derived by dividing *maturity age* by *chronological age.* "A distinctive DQ can be derived for each of the four major fields of behavior or for specific functions like prehension, locomotion, manipulation, etc." "In any field of behavior the child's maturity level is at that point where the aggregate of + signs changes to an aggregate of − signs. If the + and − signs are so irregularly distributed that this point of change becomes a band or zone of change, the maturity level must be thought of as a zone with a basal level." The usual confusion of Gesell's books occurs in this volume also since "growth trend charts" give almost but not quite the same comparisons as those just described. This volume then, in short, gives more clearly the Gesell method of infant measurement and appraisal than any of his previous publications.

One cannot call the behavior inventories a *scale*. The number of items differs from one category to another and from one age to another. This is not a weakness of the method so much as it is an evidence of our inability to break down infant behavior into small segments. One may not care to use a *developmental quotient* for an infant. What is of more importance for practical clinical purposes is to be able to distinguish those phases of an infant's behavior which partake of what we shall later in his life call "intelligence" or "social behavior" from those which are "gross motor" in nature. When a clinician is faced with the task of making repeated appraisals of an infant's development with a view of determining "suitability for adoption," for example, he realizes the contribution that Dr. Gesell has made and at the same time the enormous amount of knowledge and sagacity still to be developed.

[277]

★[Re Gesell Developmental Schedules.] GESELL, ARNOLD, AND AMATRUDA, CATHERINE S. **Developmental Diagnosis: Normal and Abnormal Child Development: Clinical Methods and Practical Applications.** New York: Paul B. Hoeber, Inc., 1941. Pp. xiii, 447. $6.50. * (PA 15:4836)

Am J Mental Def 46:430 Ja '42. I. N. K. * this work is the first of its kind to give the practitioner quantitative measures for the evalulation of defective children.

Am J Orthopsychiatry 12:372 Ap '42. Margaret T. Wilson. This book....is principally addressed to pediatricians and family physicians. Child psychologists can use it advantageously. A thorough treatise on the developments in childhood, its value is increased because it includes both normal, and abnormal child development. Deviations such as the amentias, endocrine and convulsive disorders, cerebral injuries, sensory defects, prematurity and precocity are noted in special chapters devoted to each. A new diagnostic technique is evident, and the last quarter of the book can be used as a manual for these tests. The content of the test items is not entirely new, but their arrangement is. The practicability of this method in diagnosis and the interpretation of findings is exemplified in many case studies. Developmental diagnosis requires study of the major fields in development, considered to be the *motor, adaptive, language,* and *personal-social behavior.* These four fields develop interdependently while they also parallel each other. This test of behavior the authors consider as logical as any of the functional tests of clinical neurology. Rate of development is expressed by the *developmental quotient* (D.Q.) which *represents the proportion of normal development present at any given age.* The advantage of this expression over the intelligence quotient is that it can be used for each one of the four fields and is therefore more adaptable as a device. The trend of growth is divided into zones or key ages from 4 weeks to 36 months. An interesting distinction is made between permanent and temporary patterns in behavior and this is one of the keynotes of diagnosis for prognosis. In addition, the total symptom complex of each individual case must be considered, and the many ramifications that are so often coincident, such as environmental influences. An additional advantage of the book is the inclusion of a section on *arrangements for hospitals and institutions,* and *clinical cinematography.* Any child psychologist who must examine cases for adoption should not be without this book.

Am J Psychiatry 99:470 N '42. Milton H. Firestone. * a compilation of previous publications by the authors, and although much broader in scope confines itself to diagnostic and prognostic procedures. They have had an unusual opportunity for research with both normal and abnormal children in the infant and preschool age groups and have very ably condensed their results to furnish a guide to the understanding of growth in all of its aspects. * Special attention is called to a new term in psychological parlance, the Developmental Quotient, which is technically computed in a manner similar to the Intelligence Quotient but is distinct from it. The Developmental Quotient evaluates the child from an integrated total picture, taking into account behavior in its widest meaning as the standard rather than measuring the so-called intelligence which is a part function. This fact is important, because recognition of the D.Q. at an early age may make it possible to predict the rate of growth with accuracy, the D.Q. being a constant factor —i.e., a D.Q. of 50 at age 3 will indicate that the child will be 50 per cent developed at age 6 or at any other age selected. Furthermore, it is possible to determine the D.Q. of any specific aspect of major behavior in the motor, adaptability, language or personal-social spheres, which makes it a flexible device. * An interesting use of the cinema to study behavior of children is introduced. *

Am J Psychol 55:611-2 O '42. Edgar A. Doll. The able authors of many publications on infant development and clinical pediatrics have collected and reformulated herein much valuable material on normal and abnormal child development. How much of it is new and original will depend on the reader's familiarity with the work of others in the same fields. The treatment is essentially clinical and is directed primarily to neurologists and pediatricians. * One is inclined to deprecate the heavy claims of the publishers on jacket and advertising circular, and to commiserate the authors on the professional embarrassments these must have caused them. Let us hope, too, that such ingenuous publisher's enthusiasm will not mislead the unsophisticated student. The well-known four-aspect Yale schedules of early child development (birth to five years) are presented with explicit clarity but without material evidence on normative versus clinically significant deviation. The developmental quotient is reaffirmed as essentially constant and predictive without much regard for evidence to the contrary, and only a minimum of comment on delayed development and delayed retardation. The clinical difficulties of forecasting the course of development in endogenous versus exogenous cases, and the individual vagaries of predictability so seldom anticipated yet often encountered, are only lightly emphasized. As material on the experience, point of view, and working methods of one laboratory the volume is helpfully illuminating, so illuminating indeed that one could wish that the treatment were more representative of the field of developmental diagnosis as a whole. The authors have performed a genuine service in bringing the normative and developmental points of view of clinical and child psychology to medical attention. A larger function might have been served had more comprehensive reference to other methods and standpoints been offered—some supportive, some elaborative, and some contradictory, the more so because of the authors' high prestige, skill in formulation, extended clinical orientation, and especially their position as intermediaries between clinical child psychology and clinical pediatrics.

J Am Med Assn 118:259 Ja 17 '42. * The second part of the book deals with defects and deviations of development. This is a most valuable section, which will be appreciated by physicians who tend to be baffled by problems of mental retardation. Differential diagnosis, in terms of the author's use of the developmental quotient, is succinctly dealt with, and an etiologic classification of developmental defects and deviations is offered. Mental retardation, endocrine and convulsive disorders are discussed diagnostically. A chapter on special sensory handicaps is particularly informative. A discussion of clinical aspects of child adoption presents an excellent point of view with which all physicians should be familiar. * It is recommended that all medical students and youthful physicians read the small section entitled "Imparting a Diagnosis" (p. 312). Here some important mental health considerations in dealing with retarded children are stressed. * This book may be warmly recommended to pediatricians and physicians. It offers comprehensive and well organized information about infants and children. The authors state specifically that they are chiefly concerned with the maturity and organization of the neuromotor system; with developmental neurology. This approach, most useful as it is, results in less emphasis on some psychologically and psychiatrically important aspects of child development. The intense focusing of interest on the conduct of the infant is not paralleled or supplemented by equally full consideration of his primary relationships with the mother and other members of the family. These considerations are not neglected in the book but are not sufficiently brought into focus to give as fully rounded a picture of the early development of the child as the rich material of the book might permit. A word of caution also is in order. It would be easy to gain the impression that the use of the developmental schedules and the conduct of the developmental examination is a simple matter and that any physician without particular preparation might apply them in his office practice. As a matter of fact, if authentic use of Dr. Gesell's developmental norms is to be made, the physician should be carefully schooled and practiced in the conduct of the examination, and the greatest care and meticulousness exercised. Successful use of the examination, particularly for prognostic purposes, requires closest attention to very minor deviations in the infant's responses. The use of the refined tool Dr. Gesell has developed calls for skill and precision, and therefore training in its use. The volume is well printed, the language throughout is clear, simple and concise, and there are abundant photo tracings.

J Consulting Psychol 6:272–3 S-O '42. Helen L. Koch. * Since no new basic data are being presented, those crudities of standardization and quantification which obtained in the case of the findings reported previously, still obtain. Simplification of presentation is achieved by the use of charts, phototracings, and by tabular arrangements which make it easy to get both horizontal and vertical views of the behavior complex Gesell is trying to analyze. The behavior picture, furthermore, is sketched in detail only for what have been called key ages —4, 16, 28, and 40 weeks and 12, 18, 24, and 36 months. The physician is encouraged to compute a Developmental Quotient for his child patient, or even several quotients. In the derivation of these he is allowed much liberty. Unfortunately, Gesell gives no hint of the effect upon the magnitude of the D.Q. of such factors as test composition, statistical artifacts, or standardization procedures. One is told that "in uncomplicated cases we assume the rate will remain more or less constant throughout the whole cycle of behavior growth." (P. 114) The California, Fels Foundation and Harvard results, for example, whether because of the nature of mental growth or the instruments used to reveal it, would scarcely support this statement unless the terms "uncomplicated" and "more or less" are stretched seriously. Since the average physician has no training in psychometrics, statistics, child psychology, or allied disciplines and since, furthermore, his judgments are likely to reflect themselves promptly in recommendations for the treatment of his patient, the writer wonders if both the physician and his patient might not fare better if the former employed some one adequately trained to make and evaluate the behavior determinations just as in the case of blood chemistry analyses, etc. * In spots the content of the volume resembles that of a text on differential diagnosis, though the treatment of particular disorders and symptoms is scarcely sufficiently thorough and detailed to justify this classification. The volume apparently aims rather to inform the physician of how children with various defects—birth injuries, lesions of specific areas of the nervous system, sensory handicaps, convulsive disorders, endocrine anamolies and amentia—may be expected to perform when faced with the tasks around which Gesell's normative schedules have been built. Consistent with this objective, the authors seldom mention any contributions of other workers to the problems considered or provide any substantial evaluation of controversial theories as to the causation of any of the disorders discussed. Since the writer is limited to a very brief review, she will simply list a few out of a considerably larger number of statements which she believes are due some challenging. (1) "*Formed* connections have been made between nerve fibers and muscle fibers. A behavior pattern has taken place. All behavior patterns both in prenatal and postnatal life take shape in a comparable manner." (P. 4.) (Is not this at best, even if the particular wording is ignored, an oversimplification not necessary in a medical text?) (2) "The D.Q., unlike the I.Q., is not limited to a single inclusive formula. A distinctive D.Q. can be derived for each of the four major fields of behavior; for specific functions like prehension, locomotion, manipulation, etc. This makes the D.Q. an adaptable device. The I.Q. registers changes in the growing complex of behavior. Fluctuations in a general D.Q. or in specific D.Q.'s denote intrinsic and extraneous factors which are subject to interpretation." (P. 115.) (3) "In some of its manifestations precocity may be regarded as a form of *environmental acceleration*. It may reflect a disproportionate emphasis on verbal behavior; but such an overstimulation can scarcely produce primary acceleration. It is more in the nature of excessive specification and overorganization." (P. 272.) (Since "primary" in the text is used to mean genetic, Line 4, in effect, offers proof by definition.) (4) "Well-defined speech prior to the first birthday, however dependent on models for imitation, can scarcely be ascribed to environmental forcing. It represents an inherent growth characteristic, biologically determined." (P. 273.) (Evidence? Of course, for anything the organism does it must have the necessary structure, but this consideration does not illuminate the problem of individual differences which is implied.) The format of the volume is good. Type and margins are large; punctuating devices numerous.

J Ed Res 35:226–7 N '41. Carter V. Good. * another of the important contributions by Gesell and his associates * While....addressed primarily to the physician, it contains much of value to educational and psychological workers * much of the background material on which the new book is based has appeared elsewhere, addressed more directly to workers in education and psychology. *

J Nerv & Mental Dis 101:89 Ja '45. A(rthur) N. F(oxe). * the fruit of many years of industrious work and collecting of data on the infant and child. The authors' work in this field is already well known and here they add to the accomplishment. The value of having norms is undisputed. They are presented one after the other for each age period in the child. As stated by the authors, the volume should be very helpful to the pediatrician and general practitioner. *

J Speech Disorders 11:247–8 S '46. Warren H. Gardner. Speech pathologists are interested in the development and maturation of the normal and abnormal child, especially as these relate to the acquisition or lack of average speech. They seek to learn the causes of deviations in speech development. *Development Diagnosis* is replete with hints, suggestions and diagnostic indications of abnormal development that leave little doubt of possible implications with speech deviations. Normal total integrated functioning of behavior is presented in many stages of development together with retarded or halted stages. * A most interesting chapter on sensory handicaps presents the correlation of such deviations to behavior responses, for example, the relation of deafness to quality and degree of vocalization, visual attention, social adaptations, and emotional behavior. Throughout the discussions the presence or absence of speech or stages of its development reveals the significance of growth deviations to speech defects. An interesting chapter entitled 'Environmental Retardation' points to the tragedy of institutionalized children or those with unfortunate backgrounds together with symptoms of their misfortune. Speech deviations often are among these symptoms. This book should be on the 'must' list of collateral reading in speech pathology, and should be on the desk of every speech specialist.

Psychosom Med 5:108 Ja '43. Alfred A. Washburn. Many of us who have watched with admiration the painstaking studies of Dr. Gesell and his group at the Yale Clinic of Child Development have hoped for a book from Dr. Gesell's pen which would present the gist of his work in a form such that it might be applied by the busy practitioner to the everyday problems of child care. "Developmental Diagnosis" is a delightful and fascinating answer to this hope. Presented with clarity and simplicity, with a choice of words and illustrations inimitably Gesell's, it should furnish both an ideal text for medical students and an indispensable reference book for the young practitioner. Nearly every one dealing with children might read "Developmental Diagnosis" with both pleasure and profit. The four chapters of Part I are concerned with the principles and methods of establishing a developmental diagnosis. * The simplicity of this presentation should appeal to busy practitioners or welfare workers who must have such material in a form easily and pleasantly available if they are to make good use of it. The growth of behavior is made to stand out, as it should, as an integral part of the essential unity of the developing organism. Part II contains Chapters V-XVII, dealing with the diagnosis of defects and deviations of development. * Although there were moments when I found Gesell a little too rigid and dogmatic for my point of view yet I found a store of wisdom and kindliness in every chapter. * The discussion of cerebral injuries is thought-provoking. * In his discussion of special sensory handicaps and of child adoption Gesell demonstrates the depth of his understanding of human nature during its early years of development. And in his chapter on environmental retardation he balances nicely the genetic and environmental forces. * Part III closes the volume with the emphasis on treatment in two brief and concise chapters, "Diagnosis and Guidance" and "Developmental Supervision." Here he presents the form for a preliminary behavior inventory which is surely brief and simple enough to be of value to even the busiest of clinicians. * In order to make the book of maximum use to those readers who wish to follow the study of developmental diagnosis in their own work the authors have included 84 pages of appendices. Here may be found detailed descriptions, charts and tables which cover the techniques and equipment of the examination, of charting growth trends, and of making cinema studies.

Q R Biol 17:92–3 Mr '42. A series of publications on the pioneer work of Gesell and his co-workers has preceded this book. *Developmental Diagnosis,* which is destined to become a classic, has the advantage over these earlier books in that it is much more inclusive as regards subject matter. It also gives the most concise and workable presentation to date of the Gesell clinical testing material. * Chapter III, by far the longest in the book, is the most basic in that it "integrates the developmental tests, the behaviour characteristics, and the growth trends of the behaviour patterns for the period from 4 weeks to 3 years. This chapter is organized for convenient reference and is illustrated with over a hundred photo-tracings of normative behaviour patterns." * an excellent working index.

Gesell Developmental Schedules

[278]

[*Re* Gesell Developmental Schedules.] GESELL, ARNOLD; AMATRUDA, CATHERINE S.; CASTNER, BURTON M.; AND THOMPSON, HELEN. **Biographies of Child Development: The Mental Growth Careers of Eighty-Four Infants and Children: A Ten-Year Study From the Clinic of Child Development at Yale University.** New York: Paul B. Hoeber, Inc., 1939. Pp. xvii, 328. Out of print. * (*PA* 13: 3325)

Am J Psychiatry 97:996–8 Ja '41. W. Line. * The interested reader will find in each case history a considerable amount of fascinating and definitely stimulating material. Insofar as any comprehensive thesis emerges, it is that later development can be predicted, along certain potentials at least, with a degree of accuracy that is indeed encouraging—provided that the predictions are based upon discerning observations. Even individuality often shows itself in infancy significantly for prediction purposes, and, again, along some lines more than others. So that, on the whole, the report gives considerable evidence of the validity and solidarity of the objective observational approach to the field of child development. In addition to the general thesis, almost every page of the book reflects some challenging tentative suggestions * The aim of dynamic psychology, as expressed by Allport, for example, is to be increasingly able to predict what can be accomplished with an individual, rather than what he (because of physical or mental constitution) will become. This point of view is in marked contrast with that of the volume under review—not in being contrary, of course, but only in being complementary. It is one, however, to which the whole field of child study must give increasing attention.

J Consulting Psychol 5:90 Mr-Ap '41. Elizabeth E. Lord. In *Biographies of Child Development* we are shown the practical application of the testing techniques described in the earlier books by Gesell. A familiarity with these earlier books, more particularly with *The Mental Growth of the Pre-School Child* and *Infancy and Human Growth* would seem to be a prerequisite for a vivid, meaningful appreciation of these biographies, since "the analytic appraisal of maturity" is obtained through the clinical use of the Gesell schedules. For the clinical psychologist concerned with the appraisal and prediction of mental growth these studies are of special interest. *

J Genetic Psychol 58:221–4 Mr '41. Livingston Welch. * Examples of biographical analysis that should remain as classics are to be found in this book. The cases under discussion are limited to 84 and these have been carefully selected from many thousands. * Apart from any specific interest in predictability, much is to be gained by a careful study of a great number of the biographies of atypical cases. * Both the clinical material and theoretical discussions are the most interesting products that so far have come from the Clinic of Child Development at Yale. They constitute invaluable contributions to child psychology and psychiatry.

Nature 145:140 Ja 27 '40. * The primary aim of the authors is to assess the prognostic value of the normative criteria used at the Yale Clinic of Child Development. The book is carefully written and may be recommended to psychologists in Great Britain.

For additional reviews, see 40:B913.

[279]

[*Re* Gesell Developmental Schedules.] GESELL, ARNOLD; HALVERSON, HENRY M.; THOMPSON, HELEN; ILG, FRANCES L.; CASTNER, BURTON M.; AMES, LOUISE BATES; AND AMATRUDA, CATHERINE S. **The First Five Years of Life: A Guide to the Study of the Preschool Child.** From the Yale Clinic of Child Development. New York: Harper & Brothers, 1940. Pp. xiii, 393. $4.00. * (London: Methuen & Co. Ltd., 1941. 21s.) (*PA* 14:3804)

Am J Dis Children 60:1009 O '40. * This authoritative work....probably gives the most accurate picture of physical and intellectual growth which has appeared. * Like all of the books by Gesell and his associates, this book is written in a very direct style, the terminology is easily understood and it is interesting throughout. It should be read by every one working with children.

Am J Phys Anthrop 27:171–2 Je 29 '40. A(leš) H(rdlička). * Dealing only with the White American child and that of a restricted locality, it is of but secondary interest to anthropology; and it gives but little attention to the numerous highly interesting behaviors reminiscent of human ancestry. But it includes....many tests and observations which shed considerable light on child mentality. How much more valuable would all this have been had it included some racial—at least the Negro—and other group comparisons, made by the same methods and same observers. But perhaps that is reserved for a further endeavor.

Am J Pub Health 30:1125–6 S '40. Richard A. Bolt. There is no book of which this reviewer is aware that gives a more complete picture of the normal growth and development of the preschool child in so compact a form as this.... volume * The care with which the material has been selected out of twenty years of fundamental research is evident on every page. We have here not only the results of carefully planned scientific observations but also a philosophy and methods which should point the way to productive future studies. The task "is to get a better appreciation of the individual ways in which individual preschool children mature." We grasp the central concept of this illuminating volume when we realize in its own words that "The *total child* ceases to be an academic abstraction as soon as we try to ascertain the grouping of his behavior traits and the trends of his growth career." The contributors to this volume have preserved a remarkable unity of purpose in presenting a great diversity of material. * This reviewer having a keen interest in photography is especially impressed with the pictorial illustrations covering twenty-one pages. * The section on Examination Records and Arrangements should prove very helpful to all those actually interested in growth and development of preschool children. A list of 142 selected references completes the volume. Here is a book that cannot be too highly recommended.

Brit J Ed Psychol 11:236 N '41. C. W. V(alentine). * The first part....by Dr. Gesell.... provides an up-to-date survey of the results of the large amount of research that has gone on now for many years at the Yale Clinic. After general discussion of the nature of mental growth, Gesell turns to a detailed study of the first year of life, giving typical descriptions of the behaviour and accomplishments of the infant at one, four, six, nine, and twelve months of age. Of course, there are, at these stages, enormous individual variations; but Gesell attempts to draw a recognizable picture of the 'average' child of these periods. The next chapter gives similar sketches of typical behaviour at eighteen months, two years, three years, four and five years. These are all valuable in that they are more than the itemized results of specific tests, though they are based to a very considerable extent upon tests and observations on specific points. Part II....gives more detailed, specialized accounts of certain aspects of development. Thus Dr. Halverson first writes on motor development, including walking and prehension. Dr. Helen Thompson provides a long chapter on 'adaptive behaviour,' including drawing and number concepts. Dr. Castner deals with language development and others collaborate on personal and social behaviour, including play activities, developmental detachment, and so forth. All these form valuable supplements to the more general unified descriptions given in Part I. In Part III the chief section deals with what is called the 'development examination.' As usual, Dr. Gesell avoids confining his tests to those of general intelligence. The book concludes with schedules of the standard tests. It is useful to have a revised list of these according to the latest results obtained at the Yale Clinic. * even for those who are familiar with the numerous publications of Dr. Gesell and others of the Yale Clinic, this further general summary and survey forms a most useful and important contribution to the study of the pre-school child.

J Ed (London) 74:134–6 Mr '42. J. W. Jenkins. * an admirable guide to the study of behaviour development in young children. It is a book which all nursery-school teachers and clinicians should consult. Dr. Gesell edits the book....and gives a preliminary outline of the process of development from birth to the sixth year. The terminology he uses is, in general, non-technical, his style is attractive and well suited to his subject. It is designed to appeal to a wide circle of readers, and many parents will find much to interest them in these pages. The use of a pictorial survey is a characteristic feature and shows children of various ages performing both individually and collectively. The second section, which is contributed by Dr. Gesell's collaborators, is an objective study of behaviour development in four major fields— motor characteristics, adaptive, language, and personal-social behaviour. Full details are given of the standardized procedures followed by the research workers and, as far as possible, they describe their technique for enlisting the co-operation of the more wayward infants. The experimental method as a whole is dominated by a liberal and humane application of psychological principles. It is difficult to overestimate the value of this work, and one cannot help feeling that funds should be available in this country for clinics to be set up, similar to the Yale Clinic, in which child guidance work could be supplemented and research organized into the behaviour development of children at these early formative stages. Finally, in the last section the conduct of the developmental examination is considered. The object is to diagnose a child's behaviour level in the four fundamental categories treated in section two. This is done by matching the performance of an individual child with a series of schedules which are derived from an intensive study of a 'normative group' of children. This group was small and represents a fairly homogeneous sample of children under 6 years of age. It is clear, from a study of these schedules, that in a number of cases the variability in performance is considerable and it is to be expected that with an unselected population this would be even greater. It seems desirable that some further investigation should be made into the age distribution of children responding in a way considered typical of an age group. As these schedules are more widely used it may be found necessary to give a more specific measure of this variability. The results are stated as percentages and when interpreting these results the size of the groups involved must be borne in mind. The percentage scale is liable to mislead when used with such small numbers of children. These are very minor criticisms which merely concern the form in which the results are presented. There can be no question of the great significance and value of this work to child study, and should these schedules require some slight modification in the light of further research it is doubtful whether the differences made will seriously affect diagnosis.

Psychoanalytic Q 10:475–8 Jl '41. Ives Hendrick. To all students of the development of mind and personality, a new book by Arnold Gesell is of special interest. His life work has become one of the important cornerstones of our knowledge of how the infant becomes a child. * There is a cleanness about both the technique and conceptual vision of Gesell which is seldom muddied by work from other fields. He can frequently refer to the importance of social and environmental factors which he has not intensively studied without being sidetracked by the work of those who have. This perfectionist individualism has contributed both to the clarity of his work, and also to his scientific isolation. The psychoanalyst will be the first to point out that Gesell has studied only the building material and not the carpentry of the individual's personality development. Gesell himself says in the book we are reviewing (p. 13): 'Environment determines the occasion, the intensity, and the correlation of many aspects of behavior; but it does not engender the basic progressions of behavior development. These are determined by inherent, maturational mechanisms.' Freud's own reiterated views of the importance of constitution refer more especially to the hereditary determination of drives and 'choice of neurosis' than to the effectors which Gesell especially studies; but there is no essential contradiction. The analyst can find in Gesell's results much empirical material for checking his own inductions concerning infantile development, and especially the rudiments of the ego. The importance of such factors as fantasy, pleasure and pain, object relationships, and identification in determining the eventual selection and configuration of potentialities in the development of personality are vaguely recognized by Gesell, but not intensively studied. But morphology and physiology are none the less fundamental because they are not the whole story. The First Five Years of Life....will not become a basic book in child psychology only because it is essentially a restatement of those methods, results and fundamental concepts which were definitively presented in The Mental Growth of the Preschool Child (Macmillan, 1925) and Infancy and Human Growth (Macmillan, 1928). The new book does not present a basically new research, as did Feeding Behavior of Infants, by Gesell and Ilg (Yale University Press, 1937), nor is it a new technique of clinical reporting as was the detailed photographic manual, An Atlas of Human Behavior (Yale University Press, 1934). Some of the unity and literary effectiveness of the earlier books are sacrificed to the advantages of collaboration with his associates. It gains chiefly from the amplification and refinement of many details in consequence of the work of the intervening years and from the reiterated emphasis on the clinical viewpoint and depreciation of laboratory quantification for its own sake. * There is a bibliography and an excellent index.

Q R Biol 15:509 D '40. * beautiful photographic illustrations * probably the most authoritative and comprehensive work on a subject in which the work of the author and his group have been greatly responsible for such progress as has been made.

Univ Mich Sch Ed B 12:32 N '40. * The book is detailed and authoritative, replete with illustration and example, and written in clear, nontechnical style. It will be an important reference in psychology and a source of much specific background for prospective teachers of nursery groups.

For additional reviews, see 40:B914.

[280]

[*Re Gesell Developmental Schedules.*] GESELL, ARNOLD, AND THOMPSON, HELEN; ASSISTED BY CATHERINE STRUNK AMATRUDA. **The Psychology of Early Growth: Including Norms of Infant Behavior and a Method of Genetic Analysis.** New York: Macmillan Co., 1938. Pp. ix, 290. Out of print. * (*PA* 12 3211)

Brit Med J 4046:182 Jl 23 '38. * important book of reference * Thanks to this work we are beginning to obtain a very fair idea of what the normal infant can do at various ages and how far deviations from the normal are to be regarded as non-pathological. It is only by establishing this norm that we can study abnormalities with intelligence and discover what conditions in infancy may be recoverable and what must be regarded as inevitably permanent handicaps. The medical man who is concerned with the diagnosis and prognosis of injuries and developmental defects in infancy will find a wealth of material in this volume which will serve him in very good stead in controlling his own observations.

For additional reviews, see 40:B916.

[281]

★Infant Intelligence Scale. Ages 3-30 months; 1940; a downward extension of the *Revised Stanford-Binet Scale;* individual; $45 per testing outfit, postpaid; 90¢ per 25 record forms, postpaid; $4.00 per manual (*The Measurement of Intelligence of Infants and Young Children* by Psyche Cattell); (20-40) minutes; Psyche Cattell; Psychological Corporation.

REFERENCES

1. CATTELL, PSYCHE. *The Measurement of Intelligence of Infants and Young Children.* New York: Psychological Corporation, 1940. Pp. 274. $4.00, postpaid. * (*PA* 15:2397)
2. CATTELL, PSYCHE. "Intelligence of Infants and Its Measurement." *Trans N Y Acad Sci, Series II* 3:162-71 Ap '41. * (*PA* 15:4041)

Florence M. Teagarden, Professor of Psychology, The University of Pittsburgh, Pittsburgh, Pennsylvania. The research from which the test was developed was conducted at the School of Public Health of Harvard University. The "standardization is based on 1,346 examinations made on 274 children at the ages of three (months), six, nine, twelve, eighteen, twenty-four, thirty, and thirty-six months." As is usually true in the construction of a new scale, currently existing scales provided some of the material for test items. "A study of the reliability and validity coefficients and of the individual IQ curves gives indications that the tests from about fifteen months on have nearly as high reliability and predictive value as do most intelligence tests for children of school age." Most clinicians will probably agree with Dr. Cattell that the scale at the lower levels, where prediction is not high, *nevertheless* is "of considerable assistance in appraising an infant."

The testing materials, nearly all of which are again available, are relatively simple and inexpensive. They come packed in a convenient container. What is of even greater importance is that the materials appeal to infants and young children. Some of them are familiar to those who have had experience with earlier infant tests. Directions for administering and scoring are, for the most part, clear and definite.

The testing begins at the two-month level, each of the five test items at this level being given .2 month (two-tenths month) credit. Two alternate test items are also provided at this level. This plan is carried out for each month through the twelve-month level. At that point two months are grouped together. For example, at the thirteen and fourteen months level there are five items, each item carrying .4 month (four-tenths month) credit. Beginning at the thirty-one-month level the test is the same as the corresponding levels of the *Revised Stanford Binet Scale,* Form L. The test runs through the four-year level.

Cattell's *Infant Intelligence Scale* is a great comfort to a clinician who wants to add some quantifying data to his own observations, infant behavior inventories, and hunches. The test does not permit an analytical breakdown into the various functions or mental operations displayed by the infant. Such a breakdown is a merit of the different Gesell standardizations. Of course an experienced clinician can make his own analysis of the baby's Cattell performance, but there is no provision for quantifying or recording separately skill in gross motor abilities, prelanguage ability, social characteristics, and so on.

The answer at which the clinician arrives by the use of the Cattell scale is a "mental age" to tenths of a month! One may not care to avail himself of the IQ technique for which the test thus provides. One may wish that some discrepancies in age placement between the manual, the test-blank items, and the test recording spaces could be eliminated (as they no doubt will be). Nevertheless, the *Infant Intelligence Scale* is a valuable clinical adjunct in the field of infant and preschool testing.

Beth L. Wellman, Professor of Child Psychology, Iowa Child Welfare Research Station, The State University of Iowa, Iowa City, Iowa. Cattell's scale represents an assembly of a large number of test items very well adapted to infants in terms of motivation and interest. The procedures are clearly described, and the manual is well documented with photographic illustrations.

Selection of test items to be included in the scale was mostly made from the Gesell array. Many items, however, were summarily dismissed, without trial, as those "which were thought to be unduly influenced by home training or to depend mainly on large muscular control" (1, p. 23). It is difficult for the reviewer to grasp the rationale of omitting items influenced by home training, since if this procedure were to be followed in other tests at older ages such items as vocabulary, making change, and many others would be eliminated. With the objective of eliminating items dependent on large muscular control the reviewer is heartily in accord, since the usual finding at all ages is lack of relationship between muscular control and intelligence. However, inspection of the items included in the Cattell scale leads one to feel that a good many items did creep in, nevertheless, that were mainly motor in character. For example, such items as hand preference, lifts head, lifts chest, head erect and steady, appear highly questionable. Cattell made no item analysis or validation of items except to give per cent passing by age. It is unfortunate that the work of Richards and Nelson * on the Gesell items appeared too close to the time of the publication of the Cattell scale for the results to be utilized.

The avowed purpose of the Cattell scale was that it was "so constructed as to constitute an extension downward of Form L of the Stanford–Binet tests" (1, p. 24). In spite of the fact that the test items were placed in such a manner as to bring the median IQ's as close as possible to that obtained with the Stanford–Binet at three years, the scores at the youngest ages failed to correlate to any appreciable degree. The correlation of the score at 3 months with Form L at 36 months was .10, at 6 months .34, and at 9 months .18. From 12 months on the correlations ranged from .56 to .83. Thus, if validity is to be judged in terms of correlation with later measures, this scale is of doubtful validity below 12 months, and the scale did not meet its main purpose for the first year of life.

It is unfortunate that the author showed a complete unawareness throughout of the work of Kuhlmann and the fact that he had published a scale in 1922 (revised in 1939) extending through infancy. While Cattell's scale has a larger number of items, it remains to be seen whether the selection of items was more adequate.

Cattell's standardization group was not large (274 children), and she makes no claim that they represented a random sample.

Sch & Soc 54:475–6 N 22 '41. Norma V. Scheidemann. * This scale represents an enormous task painstakingly carried out. It is a definite improvement over all other infants tests now available. Because of its many advantages it is by far the most usable device for testing infants and should prove to be of inestimable value to clinical and research psychologists who are competent to administer and interpret intelligence tests with due regard to their significance and full awareness of their limitations. Even psychologists not specifically concerned with mental measurement will be impressed with the amount of objectivity and scientific accuracy the author has found possible to incorporate in this scale. It is the reviewer's belief that the Cattell scale will become the standard instrument for testing infants; that it will attain a prestige among infant scales comparable to that attained by the Stanford–Binet among intelligence scales for older children.

★[Re Infant Intelligence Scale.] CATTELL, PSYCHE. **The Measurement of Intelligence of Infants and Young Children.** New York: Psychological Corporation, 1940. Pp. 274. $4.00. * (*PA* 15:2397)

Am J Orthopsychiatry 11:607 Jl '41. Helen Speyer. * a test which many psychologists engaged in testing infants and young children will welcome * is so constructed that it constitutes a downward extension of Form L of

---

* Nelson, Virginia L., and Richards, T. W. "Studies in Mental Development: I, Performance on Gesell Items at Six Months and Its Predictive Value for Performance on Mental Tests at Two and Three Years." *J Genetic Psychol* 52:303-25 Je '38.
Nelson, Virginia L., and Richards, T. W. "Studies in Mental Development: III, Performance of Twelve-Months-Old Children on the Gesell Schedule, and Its Predictive Value for Mental Status at Two and Three Years." *J Genetic Psychol* 54:181-91 Mr '39.
Richards, T. W., and Nelson, Virginia L. "Studies in Mental Development: II, Analysis of Abilities Tested at the Age of Six Months by the Gesell Schedule." *J Genetic Psychol* 52:327-31 Je '38.
Richards, T. W., and Nelson, Virginia L. "Abilities of Infants During the First Eighteen Months." *J Genetic Psychol* 55:299-318 D '39.

the Stanford–Binet. This gives it a tremendous advantage over other preschool tests, since it provides a simple scale with which a child may be examined from infancy to maturity. One error in re-testing is thus eliminated, as results obtained on different scales will not need to be compared and equated. * Statistical findings are clearly presented. Chapter 3, which gives instructions for administering the examination, is especially fine and shows that Dr. Cattell is well aware of some of the difficulties involved in the clinical use of preschool tests. Some delightful illustrations of infants' responses to test situations will help an examiner in scoring. This scale fills a definite need and many of us will look forward to widespread use and early confirmation of its value.

Am J Psychol 58:153 Ja '45. T. L. McCulloch. * Apparent errors of item-placement are numerous. According to the tables, e.g. all 18-month items are more difficult than any regular items placed at 20 and 22 months. Other types of error throughout the book are of relatively minor importance. Validity and reliability are reported as being very low at lower age-levels, but acceptable at higher levels. The author stresses the importance of not attaching too great significance to scores from the scale alone. Most of the test-items offer great promise of usefulness, but, because of irregular placements at in-between ages, results from administration of the present scale should be treated with even greater reserve than is liberally recommended by the author.

J Appl Psychol 25:366–7 Je '41. C. M. Louttit. * Cattell gives valuable suggestions for examining young children and warns against using the scale as an instrument of precision. The quantitative characteristics of the scale make it valuable for research purposes. However, its relatively low validity (r = .10 between 3 and 36 months, and .71 between 2 years and 3 years) makes individual prediction hazardous unless experienced clinical judgment supports the test score. This new scale appears to be a useful addition to present instruments. Its value can only be proved by use.

Psychol B 38:900 N '41. Rachel Stutsman Ball. A rare degree of insight into the nature of young children and into the requirements of a satisfactory test for them has been combined in this new scale with a highly practicable organization of the materials and methods of testing. * Some of the outstanding merits of this scale are: (1) The test age levels are set at each month for children from two to twelve months, for two-month levels from twelve to eighteen months, and for three-month intervals from eighteen to thirty months. This offers the potentiality of much greater accuracy in testing than earlier scales with greater intervals between age levels. (2) There are five items at each age level, with at least one alternate and often more. (3) The scoring of the scale is easily understood, since it follows the same method used in the Stanford–Binet scale. (4) Certain of the Stanford–Binet items are intermingled with the items from other sources at the ages twenty-two to thirty months to facilitate the supplemental use of the scale with the Stanford–Binet scale. (5) The scale avoids time limits and timed tests. (6) The test scale needs to be administered in no definite order, and it has been standardized so that the child may be held on the mother's lap during the test if it seems desirable. (7) The examination takes from twenty to thirty minutes. (8) The standardization is based on 1346 examinations on 274 children. (9) The directions for test administration are clearly and fully given with illustrative photographs for each test. (10) The author has given a helpful analysis of the adjustments and points of view necessary in testing infants and young children. * There is no exact statement of the criteria used for the placement of tests at the different age levels, although a table is given showing the per cent passing each test at all the significant age levels. Whatever method was used, apparently there needed to be considerable realignment of the items during the course of the standardization. * There is a tacit assumption that correlation with another test evaluates the validity of the test. The split-half method was used to determine reliability, which method some might question with material of this type. The test results upon which the scale was standardized are used to determine the predictive value of the scale. * While this meagerness of statistical treatment is disappointing to those who realize its significance and danger, this fact should not be allowed to detract from this really valuable contribution to the mental measurements of young children.

[283]
★**Intelligence Tests for Young Children.** Ages 2-8; 1945; individual; requires only such apparatus

"that can readily be found or made in the school or home"; 4s. per manual; (30) minutes; C. W. Valentine; Methuen & Co. Ltd.

REFERENCES
1. WAKELAM, B. B. "The Application of a New Intelligence Test in an Infant School and the Prediction of Backwardness." *Brit J Ed Psychol* 14:142-50 N '44. * (PA 19:1355)
2. VALENTINE, C. W. *Intelligence Tests for Young Children.* London: Methuen & Co. Ltd., 1945. Pp. xii, 67. 4s. * (Cleveland, Ohio: Sherwood Press. $1.50.) (PA 19:3520)

Brit J Ed Psychol 15:105 Je '45. C. Burt. For long there has been an urgent need for some simple scale of intelligence tests for use with younger children in this country. The best known scales, such as the Terman–Merrill revision or the Binet tests, require apparatus that is at once bulky and expensive; and, further, they have been constructed and standardized for American rather than for British children. * The author has selected from various well-known scales those tests which are of recognized validity and at the same time easy and interesting to apply; but in addition he has devised some extremely ingenious and attractive tests of his own. The clear and detailed instructions make the procedure perfectly comprehensible even to those with little or no formal training in the technique of mental testing, and include suggestive comments which could be read with advantage even by experienced testers at child guidance clinics. The construction, standardization and different uses of the tests are fully described in an Appendix; and the discussion incidentally brings out several pressing problems, which deserve the attention of future research workers. The amount of useful and instructive matter here packed into one small volume makes it a miracle of condensation; and the whole is based on a unique combination of common sense, scientific insight and a life-long study of the problems of early childhood. A word of gratitude is due to the publishers for the excellent production under war-time conditions.

Brit J Psychol 36:106 Ja '46. * for the use principally of teachers and those who are not expert intelligence testers. * An excellent selection of both verbal and performance tests has been made; they are taken from Burt's revision of the Binet–Simon tests, the Terman–Merrill and Merrill–Palmer scales; some of the Gesell items are included; and the author has added some of his own. He also discusses the selection, use and standardization of the tests, and gives a very useful set of instructions and description of procedure. The whole forms an exceptionally valuable testing scale, consisting of items likely to be interesting and attractive to children and well designed to show up every facet of their intelligence. For certain of the biographical items relating to the younger children, which are taken from Gesell, the tester might have to rely on hearsay evidence; but these items are well worth including since they are such good indicators of the child's general maturity. If one point of criticism may be offered, it is that the scoring of mental age is rather involved, owing to the fact that the number of tests, and hence their score value, differs at different ages. Perhaps in a second edition the author could simplify this—and also extend the scale for older children, including tests difficult enough for the controversial 11+ group.

[284]

★Kent Series of Emergency Scales. Ages 5-7, 6-8, 6.5-10, 9-14; 1932–46; also called *E-G-Y Scales;* individual; 1 form; 4 levels; 60¢ per manual; Grace H. Kent; Psychological Corporation.
a) SCALE A. Ages 5-7; 1944–46; formerly called *Andover School-Entrance Test;* $1.75 per 100, postpaid.
b) SCALES B AND C. Ages 6-8, 6.5-10; 1946; $1.75 per 100, postpaid.
c) SCALE D. Ages 9-14; 1932–46; revision of *Emergency Test* or *Kent E-G-Y Test;* $1.75 per 100, postpaid.

REFERENCES
1. KENT, GRACE H. *Oral Test for Emergency Use in Clinics.* Mental Measurement Monographs, Serial No. 9. Baltimore, Md.: Williams and Wilkins Co., January 1932. Pp. i, 50. Paper. Out of print. * (PA 6:1654)
2. KENT, GRACE H. "Written Tests for the Clinic." *J Genetic Psychol* 44:49-68 Mr '34. * (PA 8:4785)
3. McINTIRE, J. THOMAS, AND HOFFEDITZ, E. LOUISE. "Comparative Study of the Kent Emergency Test With Feebleminded Subjects." *Training Sch B* 33:22-6 Ap '36. * (PA 10:4281)
4. ELWOOD, MARY I.; BURCHARD, EDWARD M. L.; AND TEAGARDEN, FLORENCE M. "An Evaluation of the Kent Oral Emergency Test." *J Appl Psychol* 21:75-84 F '37. * (PA 11:4817)
5. TEAGARDEN, FLORENCE M. "A Method of Interpolating Kent Oral Emergency Test Scores Into Mental Age Years and Months." *J Appl Psychol* 21:468-73 Ag '37. * (PA 12:965)
6. BENTON, ARTHUR L. "Performances of School Children on the Revised Stanford-Binet and the Kent E-G-Y Test." *J Genetic Psychol* 52:395-400 Je '38. * (PA 13:566)
7. HOGAN, HELENA P. "Comparison of Stanford-Binet and Kent Oral Emergency Scores." *J Genetic Psychol* 58:151-9 Mr '41. * (PA 15:4044)
8. RUDOLF, G. DE M. "The Development of Knowledge in the Mental Defective Based on Kent's Oral Test." *Brit J Med Psychol* 18:338-43 F '41. * (PA 15:3027)
9. SLOAN, WILLIAM, AND SHARP, AGNES A. "A Note on Interpolation of Kent Oral Emergency Test Scores Into Mental Age Years and Months." *J Appl Psychol* 25:592-4 O '41. * (PA 16:1236)
10. SPRINGER, N. NORTON. "Kent Oral Emergency and Stanford-Binet Tests Applied to Adolescent Delinquents." *Am J Orthopsychiatry* 11:292-9 Ap '41. * (PA 15:4328)
11. KENT, GRACE H. "Emergency Battery of One-Minute Tests." *J Psychol* 13:141-64 Ja '42. * (PA 16:2493)
12. KOENIG, FRANK J., AND SMITH, JOHN. "A Preliminary Study Using a Short Objective Measure for Determining Mental Deficiency in Selective Service Registrants." *J Ed Psychol* 33:443-8 S '42. * (PA 17:985) Also in *Mil Surg* 91:442-6 O '42. * (PA 17:713)
13. LEWINSKI, ROBERT J. "A Qualitative Analysis of the Kent Oral Emergency Test as a Clinical Instrument in the Examination of Naval Recruits." *J Appl Psychol* 26:316-31 Je '42. * (PA 16:4202)
14. MULLEN, FRANCES A. "Comparison of the Revised Kent Emergency Battery With the Revised Stanford-Binet and the Kuhlmann-Anderson Tests." Abstract. *Psychol B* 39:591 O '42. * (PA 17:716, title only)

15. KENT, GRACE H. "Tentative Norms for Emergency Battery." *J Psychol* 15:137-49 Ja '43. * (PA 17:1378)
16. LEWINSKI, ROBERT J. "Performances of Naval Recruits on the Kent Oral Emergency Test and the Verbal Battery of the Bellevue-Wechsler Adult Intelligence Scale." *Am J Orthopsychiatry* 13:138-40 Ja '43. * (PA 17:2209)
17. MULLEN, FRANCES A. "Comparison of the Revised Kent Emergency Tests With the Revised Stanford-Binet and the Kuhlmann-Anderson Tests." *J Psychol* 15:151-63 Ja '43. * (PA 17:1380)
18. GREENWOOD, EDWARD D.; SNIDER, HERVON L.; AND SENTI, MILTON M. "Correlation Between the Wechsler Mental Ability Scale, Form B, and Kent Emergency Test (E-G-Y) Administered to Army Personnel." *Am J Orthopsychiatry* 14:171-3 Ja '44. * (PA 18:2984)
19. HUNT, WILLIAM A., AND OLDER, HARRY J. "Psychometric Scatter Pattern as a Diagnostic Aid." *J Abn & Social Psychol* 39:118-23 Ja '44. * (PA 18:2227)
20. KENT, GRACE H. "The 'Andover' School-Entrance Test." *J Ed Psychol* 35:108-19 F '44. * (PA 18:2965)
21. LEWINSKI, ROBERT J. "Notes on the Original and Revised Kent Scales in the Examination of Naval Recruits." *J Ed Psychol* 35:554-8 D '44. * (PA 19:1060)
22. RAUTMAN, ARTHUR L. "Performance of Mental Defectives on the Revised Stanford-Binet and the Kent E-G-Y Tests." *J Appl Psychol* 28:329-35 Ag '44. * (PA 18:3905)
23. WHEELER, JOHN A.; WILLIAMS, STANLEY B.; DRUMMOND, WILLIAM A.; AND HARRIS, JOHN D. "Experiences in the Use of the Kent Battery." *U S Naval Med B* 43:44-5 Jl '44. *
24. KENT, GRACE H. "Additional Norms for Emergency Battery." *J Genetic Psychol* 67:17-26 S '45. * (PA 20:577)
25. MILES, DWIGHT W.; WILKINS, WALTER L.; LESTER, DAVID W.; AND HUTCHENS, WENDELL H. "The Efficiency of a High-Speed Screening Procedure in Detecting the Neuropsychiatrically Unfit at a U. S. Marine Corps Recruit Training Depot." *J Psychol* 21:243-68 Ap '46. * (PA 20:3288)
26. BONGIOVANNI, ALFRED M. "Psychometric Examinations Aboard a Destroyer." *U S Naval Med B* 47:27-32 Ja-F '47. * (PA 21:2773)

Charles N. Cofer, Associate Professor of Psychology, University of Maryland, College Park, Maryland. For fifteen years the Kent E-G-Y Scales have served a real need, found especially in the military services during the war, for a rapid and adequate means of roughly evaluating an individual's intellectual ability. In this revision, the valuable features of the earlier forms have been preserved, and the scales seem to be stronger than before.

The new scales contain many more questions than did the old forms. There are four scales in the revision as compared to three in the 1932 edition, and the new scales cover the age range from 5 to 14 years. The use of independent norms for each scale and the overlapping of each scale with the ones above and below it are important and valuable features. The content of the questions is varied and would appear to have interest value for almost any English-speaking subject. The reviewer's extensive experience with the old forms of the scales leads him to recommend them highly as clinical instruments for rough evaluations; indeed, in a few cases they have given a more satisfactory index of the patient's ability, as seen independently in his occupational and social history, than have elaborate psychometric devices.

There are, however, serious limitations in the standardization and other methodological aspects of the development of the scales. Since Dr. Kent is fully aware of these limitations and discusses them briefly in the manual, it seems unnecessary to mention them further here. Dr. Kent justifies the presentation of the scales in terms of their use as rough, approximate, screen devices not designed to supplant the formal tests. In the hands of competent and experienced clinicians the scales would not, in most cases, be used unwisely. However, they are apparently so simple and easy to administer and require so little material for administration that untrained, careless, or irresponsible persons are easily able to use them and may do serious harm through attaching great significance to the mental ages obtained. This reviewer has seen often enough psychiatrists, social workers, and others regard any mental age as being as fixed as the patient's chronological age. This type of occurrence points to the need for even more careful evaluation of sampling, reliability, standardization, and validity for the simple techniques than perhaps for the more elaborate devices.

A number of studies have been reported which showed the old scales to give good agreement with results from the Stanford–Binet, Wechsler–Bellevue, etc. E-G-Y scores have sometimes been found to vary with some constancy above or below scores obtained from one or another of such psychometric devices. It would add to the usefulness of the present scales if such data were available, and a revision of the manual might include such evidence at least for the old scales. A more complete description of standardization groups and processes than is given would likewise be valuable.

[285]
Linfert-Hierholzer Scale for Measuring the Mental Development of Infants During the First Year of Life. Ages 30-152, 153-365 days; 1928; individual; out of print; Harriette-Elise Linfert and Helen M. Hierholzer; Catholic University of America Press.

REFERENCES
1. FURFEY, PAUL HANLEY. "The Relation Between Socio-Economic Status and Intelligence of Young Infants as Measured by the Linfert-Hierholzer Scale." *J Genetic Psychol* 35:478-80 S '28. * (PA 3:1360)
2. LINFERT, HARRIETTE-ELISE, AND HIERHOLZER, HELEN M. *A Scale for Measuring the Development of Infants During the First Year of Life.* Catholic University of America, Studies in Psychology and Psychiatry, Vol. 1, No. 4. Washington, D. C.: Catholic University of America Press, 1928. Paper. $1.25. (PA 3:2359)
3. CONGER, J. A. *An Evaluation of the Linfert Scale for Measuring the Mental Development of Infants.* Unpublished master's thesis, University of Minnesota, 1930. Pp. 30.
4. MUEHLENBEIN, J. M. *The Validation of the Hierholzer Scale.* Unpublished master's thesis, Catholic University of America, 1931. Pp. 25.
5. FURFEY, PAUL HANLEY, AND MUEHLENBEIN, JOSEPHINE. "The Validity of Infant Intelligence Tests." *J Genetic Psychol* 40:219-23 Mr '32. * (PA 6:3783)
6. ANDERSON, L. DEWEY. "The Predictive Value of Infancy Tests in Relation to Intelligence at Five Years." *Child Develop* 10:203-12 S '39. * (PA 13:6507)

Nancy Bayley, Lecturer in Psychology and Research Associate, Institute of Child Welfare, University of California, Berkeley, California. This is one of the early scales for measuring infant intelligence, and its value is now primarily historical. It is derived in part from the 1925 Gesell tests. The scale is notable, not only because it is one of the first efforts to describe carefully the administration and scoring of infants' responses to a varied selection of standardized test situations, but also because it includes statistical evaluations of the reliability and validity of numerical scores based on test items passed. The sample of infants tested was selected to be a representative cross-section of the American white urban population, using Chapman–Sims socio-economic scores as a criterion. A total of 300 infants (50 each at months 1, 2, 4, 6, 9, and 12) were tested. The materials are simple, including colored balls, a ring, feathers, cubes, teaspoon, colored pictures, etc. The tests have been divided into two series. Series I, comprising 29 tests, applies to infants 1 through 5 months: Series II, comprising 35 tests, is applicable to infants aged 6 through 12 months.

There may be some question as to the suitability of calling these tests scales of "mental" development because of their inclusion of varied types of behavior. The items in Series I are for the most part tests of sensory perception, gross motor coordinations, and simple reflex reactions. About one third of the items in Series II are of gross bodily coordinations, such as standing and walking. About a fifth involve language comprehension and use. The others test adaptive responses or learning as evidenced in simple games and habit training (the latter often depending on the mother's report).

Test scores are the per cent passed of the total number of items given (usually the number in a series). The means for each age were plotted and found to show essentially straight-line progression within each series. Smoothed age norms for each series were read from the plots.

The split-half reliability of the tests (with Spearman–Brown correction) was calculated for each age. These r's range from .70 to .88 and average .81. In testing validity, the scores at each age were correlated with the parents' Chapman–Sims scores. The average of these r's is .06. There were no significant differences in the scores of groups divided on the basis of number of siblings, of breast or bottle feeding, of health or of dentition.

It is interesting to note that in a later study (5) the infants' scores at 6, 9 and 12 months were found to have low negative correlations (of $-.11$, $-.32$ and $-.20$ respectively) with their scores on the Stanford–Binet at four years.

[286]

Minnesota Preschool Scale. Ages 1.5-6; 1932-40; individual; Forms A, B; $14.50 per testing outfit of either form; $1 per 25 record blanks; $1 per specimen set of sample blank and manual, postpaid; Florence L. Goodenough, Katharine M. Maurer, and M. J. Van Wagenen; Educational Test Bureau.

REFERENCES

1-3. See 40:1407.
4. GOODENOUGH, FLORENCE L., AND MAURER, KATHARINE M. *The Mental Growth of Children From Two to Fourteen Years: A Study of the Predictive Value of the Minnesota Preschool Scales.* University of Minnesota, Institute of Child Welfare, Monograph Series, No. 20. Minneapolis, Minn.: University of Minnesota Press, 1942. Pp. xv, 130. Out of print. * (PA 16: 4562)
5. MAURER, KATHARINE M. *Intellectual Status at Maturity as a Criterion for Selecting Items in Preschool Tests.* University of Minnesota, Institute of Child Welfare Monograph Series, No. 21. Minneapolis, Minn.: University of Minnesota Press, 1946. Pp. ix, 166. Lithotyped. $2.50. * (London: Oxford University Press. 15s. 6d.) (PA 21:286)

Beth L. Wellman, Professor of Child Psychology, Iowa Child Welfare Research Station, The State University of Iowa, Iowa City, Iowa. The materials for this test are compact and very conveniently arranged in Manila envelopes bound together in a booklet with attached instructions. In general, they are attractive to children, although not particularly colorful or artistically appealing. The 1940 manual is an improvement over that of 1932 in the following respects: presentation of test procedures and scoring, greater detail on scoring, and consolidation of several tables into one for translating score points into C-scores, per cent placement and IQ equivalents.

Theoretically it would be an advantage to compute separate verbal and nonverbal IQ's, for which the scale provides, if the term nonverbal could be clarified. This the authors have not been able to do, either in the manual or in subsequent publications. No help is given the examiner on how to interpret the two scores. Curiously enough, the nonverbal items do not extend below 2 years 6 months, the very ages at which verbal responses are most difficult to elicit and at which negativism and resistance are most frequently encountered.

Although two forms of the test are available, Forms A and B, the manual states that both should be administered whenever anything of real importance is to be determined from the score. This, of course, obviates one of the chief advantages of alternate forms, that of interchangeability.

Little information is given about the standardization group. In the 1932 manual there was promised a future monograph which, so far as the reviewer has been able to ascertain, has never appeared. The size of the standardization group (900 cases, ages 1½ to 6 years) appears adequate. The main bases of selection were occupation of father and sex. All of the children were urban and from one section of the country.

In their 1942 publication (4) the authors state that the computations of C-scores and IQ equivalents were based on a wrong table of standards, but the correct values have not been published.

The maximum IQ equivalent that is provided for at any age is 152; this maximum will be confusing to those accustomed to dealing with IQ's on the Binet tests ranging from 150 to 200. That the scale lacks sufficiently difficult items to sample the abilities of bright children older than about 3½ years is shown by the table of score points necessary to obtain the maximum IQ equivalent of 152 (or 100 per cent placement). On the verbal scale these are, at ages 3-6, 4-0, 4-6, 5-0, and 5-6, respectively: 71, 74, 76, 78, and 79 points out of a possible 80. Out of a possible 55 on the nonverbal they are: 48, 51, 53, 55 (at 5-0 where a perfect score is required). Since it is not at all uncommon for younger children to obtain IQ's of 150, the implications are, to note only two: (a) groups of superior children at 5 years are likely to show considerably lower IQ's than groups similarly sampled at 3 years; (b) the test should be used with great caution in a study of IQ changes.

For reviews by Rachel Stutsman Ball, Nancy Bayley, and Florence M. Teagarden of the original edition, see 40:1407.

[287]
★[Re Minnesota Preschool Scale.] GOODENOUGH, FLORENCE L., AND MAURER, KATHARINE M. **The Mental Growth of Children From Two to Fourteen Years: A Study of the Predictive Value of the Minnesota Preschool Scales.** University of Minnesota, Institute of Child Welfare, Monograph Series, No. 20. Minneapolis, Minn.: University of Minnesota Press, 1942. Pp. xv, 130. Out of print. (PA 16:4562)

Am J Psychol 58:151–2 Ja '45. Willard C. Olson. * Interesting questions for further investigation grow out of the study. Is there a difference in rate of maturing and stabilization of status in girls? Would improvement in the predictive value of tests for young children be brought about by means of an item-analysis in which terminal rather than initial status is used as one of the criteria for selection? To what extent is early differential success in tests according to type-of-content predictive of similar specialization at a later time? Answers to these and similar questions are being sought in further work. The monograph should be studied and pondered by the clinician and by the student of the testing methods.

Brit J Ed Psychol 16:102 Je '46. C. W. V(alentine). * The whole research provides a valuable piece of evidence, with special reference, of course, to the Minnesota tests. The authors, however, do not, I think, attach sufficient importance to the need for giving to young children under five years three or four re-testings within a few months of each other to allow for varying moods and fluctuations and newly developing abilities.

Brit J Psychol 34:79 Ja '44. * describes first the preparation of new scales of verbal and nonverbal intelligence test, each with alternative scales, for pre-school children aged 2-5 years. * The second part....deals with the testing, re-testing and follow-up over a twelve-year period of about 500 children. The main result that emerged was that although re-tests of children ages 3-4 years after periods up to one year showed a fair reliability, yet even then the average shift was 10 I. Q. points, and shifts of 20 points were not uncommon. Prediction of mental status at later periods, up to the time of college entrance, was extremely uncertain. Nevertheless, characteristic sex differences emerged at very early ages, and also differences between those who excelled on the verbal scales, and those who excelled on the non-verbal. One would like to know if there were any consistent relationships between the type of fluctuation or shift in mental development as demonstrated by the test results, and the children's personality characteristics. It is to be hoped that the authors will continue their valuable investigations to include the study of such qualitative relationships, and thus throw more light on individual differences in mental development.

El Sch J 43:372–3 F '43. Gustav J. Froehlich. * Among the desirable features of the monograph one might mention the graphic presentations of individual patterns of growth. These demonstrate clearly the fallibility of mental estimates based on a single test administration. The appendix giving "I.Q.-Equivalents for the Merrill–Palmer Tests," the relatively adequate bibliography, and the frequent cross-references to related investigations are also noteworthy. In general....shows many evidences of care, thought, and meticulous research. On the other hand, one might question the continuity of the sampling. We are told that "in spite of the changes in its personnel, . . . the general character of our group has not shifted greatly in the course of the twelve-year period" (p. vii), but this statement is not backed up with sufficient objective evidence. The statistician may be somewhat disturbed by the arbitrariness resorted to in the derivation of the scale values for the Minnesota Preschool Scales. This weakness has been recognized by the authors, but their argument that relative rather than absolute values are of primary concern in this study is well taken. This monograph is not a textbook; it is highly theoretical. Only the professional worker in the field of mental measurement will find in it much of value for him. The casual student and the general reader in educational psychology and child guidance will find little to interest him.

J Consulting Psychol 7:207–8 Jl-Ag '43. Nancy Bayley. * Part I....summarizes the historical background of tests for young children, and then describes briefly the Minnesota Preschool Scales. * In Part II....scores on the Minnesota scales are compared with retests on the same scale after elapsed intervals of one and two years, and with retests at various intervals on other scales: the Merrill–Palmer, both revisions of the Stanford–Binet, the Arthur Point Scale, and the American Council on Education College Entrance Examinations. Correlations between tests increase with increasing age at the time of first testing. However the tendency (reported by others) for *r*'s to decrease with increasing intervals between tests was found for some tests but not consistently. The Merrill–Palmer test showed the lowest relation to the Minnesota, all *r*'s being positive but low. Correlations with the Arthur scale are somewhat higher, but still lower than with the Stanford–Binet. In neither Merrill–Palmer nor Arthur scales is there any consistent change in the correlation as the interval between tests increases. This lack of agreement with other studies is puzzling. However, the authors do not make clear to what extent the same cases enter into the *r*'s between different tests at different ages, nor whether the number of previous tests per child has been controlled in the *r*'s for prediction. If the cases used in each *r* are in large part different, or have unequal amounts of testing experience, then the failure to get consistently decreasing *r*'s with increasing intervals between tests may be due, at least to some extent, to these variations in the sample. * This book makes an important contribution to our knowledge of the values and limitations of several widely used intelligence tests. In general the authors' results from repeated tests of the same children corroborate those of other studies which have shown low predictability of later intelligence from preschool tests. They further point to the areas in which prediction may be improved, and indicate fields for valuable future research on the processes of mental growth.

[288]
★[*Re* Minnesota Preschool Scale.] MAURER, KATHARINE M. **Intellectual Status at Maturity as a Criterion for Selecting Items in Preschool Tests.** University of Minnesota, Institute of Child Welfare Monograph Series, No. 21. Minneapolis, Minn.: University of Minnesota Press, 1946. Pp. ix, 166. Lithotyped. $2.50. * (London: Oxford University Press. 15s. 6d.) (*PA* 21:286)

J Consult Psychol 11:155 My-Je '47. This study makes a direct attack upon a psychological problem of long standing: the low correlation of measures of intellect at preschool ages with those obtained later. * provides valuable source material for future test construction.

Times Ed Sup 1657:58 F 1 '47. * lucidly written * The investigation revealed that only half the pre-school test items possessed long-term predictive value. Equally significant is the inference that the best predictors are those tests involving perception. It is not surprising, therefore, to find in this study further evidence of "a constant core of mental functioning." In other words, the truth may be that aptitude tests for the under-sevens are reliable, in the non-technical sense, to the extent to which they measure "g." Careful analysis of individual test items is essential if comparative "purity" of the "g" saturation is to be obtained.

[289]
★**Nebraska Test of Learning Aptitude for Young Deaf Children: A Non-Verbal Individual Scale**

Especially Devised for Deaf and Hard of Hearing Children From Four to Ten Years of Age. 1941; individual; 1 form; $42 per testing outfit; $1.75 per 100 sets of blanks and record forms; (50-60) minutes; Marshall S. Hiskey; distributed by the Psychological Corporation.

REFERENCES

1. HISKEY, MARSHALL S. *A Non-Verbal Test of Learning Aptitude (Especially Adapted for Young Deaf Children)*. Unpublished doctor's thesis, University of Nebraska, 1940. (*Abstracts of Doctoral Dissertations . . .*, 1940, pp. 77-84.)
2. HISKEY, MARSHALL S. "A New Performance Test for Young Deaf Children." *Ed & Psychol Meas* 1:217-32 Jl '41. * (*PA* 15:5405)
3. HISKEY, MARSHALL S. "A Nonverbal Test of Learning Aptitude for Young Deaf Children." Abstract. *Psychol B* 38:712 O '41. * (*PA* 16:338, title only)

[290]

Performance Tests of Intelligence: A Series of Nonlinguistic Tests for Deaf and Normal Children, Third Edition. Ages 5-6, 7-16; 1928–44; individual; Sets A (Ages 5-6), B (Ages 9-16); £23 for Set A materials; £14 2s. 3d. for additional materials needed for Set B; 5s. per manual; manual must be ordered from Oliver and Boyd Ltd.; test materials must be ordered from A. H. Baird, Instrument Maker, Lothian St., Edinburgh, Scotland; James Drever and Mary Collins.

REFERENCES

1. MACKANE, KEITH. *A Comparison of the Intelligence of Deaf and Hearing Children: A Study of the Reactions of Deaf and Hearing Children to Three Performance Scales and a Non-Language Test.* Columbia University, Teachers College, Contributions to Education, No. 585. Rudolf Pintner, faculty sponsor. New York: Bureau of Publications, the College, 1933. Pp. ix, 47. Out of print. *
2. DREVER, JAMES, AND COLLINS, MARY. *Performance Tests of Intelligence: A Series of Non-Linguistic Tests for Deaf and Normal Children, Third Edition.* Edinburgh, Scotland: Oliver and Boyd Ltd., 1946. Pp. 59. 5s. *

For excerpts from three reviews, see 36:B87.

[291]

★**Preliminary Test of Intelligence: A Brief Test of Adult Intelligence Designed for Psychiatric Examiners.** Adults; 1947; individual; 1 form; the test and instructions for administration, scoring, and interpretation are presented in *American Journal of Psychiatry* 103:785-92 May 1947; no materials need be purchased; (5-15) minutes; Margaret Keller, Irvin L. Child, and Frederich C. Redlich.

[292]

Revised Stanford-Binet Scale. Ages 2 and over; 1937; a revision of the *Stanford-Binet Scale* published 1916; Forms L, M; individual; $12 per testing outfit for each form; $2.50 per 25 record booklets for each form; 80¢ per 25 abbreviated record forms; $1.75 per abbreviated directions for administering; $2.25 per set of printed card material for each form; $3.00 per manual (98); Lewis M. Terman and Maud A. Merrill; Houghton Mifflin Co.

REFERENCES

1-134. See 40:1420.
135. TERMAN, LEWIS M.; ASSISTED BY ARTHUR S. OTIS, VIRGIL DICKSON, O. S. HUBBARD, J. K. NORTON, LOWRY HOWARD, J. K. FLANDERS, AND C. C. CASSINGHAM. "A Trial of Mental and Pedagogical Tests in a Civil Service Examination for Policemen and Firemen." *J Appl Psychol* 1:17-29 Mr '17. *
136. YERKES, ROBERT M. "The Binet Versus the Point Scale Method of Measuring Intelligence." *J Appl Psychol* 1:110-22 Je '17. *
137. BEESON, M. F. "Intelligence at Senescence." *J Appl Psychol* 4:219-34 Je-S '20. *
138. CUSHMAN, C. L. "A Study of the Reliability of Mental Tests as Used in Oklahoma City." *J Appl Psychol* 11:509-11 D '27. * (*PA* 2:2944)
139. DURRELL, DONALD D. *The Effect of Special Disability in Reading on Performance on the Stanford Revision of the Binet-Simon Test.* Unpublished master's thesis, State University of Iowa, 1927.
140. DEARBORN, WALTER F., AND LONG, HOWARD H. "On Comparing IQ's at Different Age Levels on the Same Scale." *J Ed Res* 18:265-74 N '28. * (*PA* 3:970)
141. CHIPMAN, CATHERINE E. "The Correspondence of School Achievement and Industrial Efficiency With Mental Age as Determined by the Stanford-Binet." *Psychol Clinic* 18:21-8 Mr-Ap '29. * (*PA* 3:4267)
142. RILEY, G. "Stanford Binet 'Indicators' of Mechanical Ability." *Psychol Clinic* 18:128-32 My-Je '29. * (*PA* 4:1429)
143. BROWN, ANDREW W. "The Change in Intelligence Quotients in Behavior Problem Children." *J Ed Psychol* 21:341-50 My '30. * (*PA* 4:4576)
144. WEISMAN, SARA E. "Case Studies of the Relationship Between High-School Achievement and Educational Counselling." *J Ed Res* 21:357-63 My '30. * (*PA* 4:4070)
145. WOODALL, CHAS. S. "Analysis of I. Q. Variability." *J Psycho-Asthenics* 36:247-62, discussion 262-6 '31. * (*PA* 6:3274)
146. HOAKLEY, Z. PAULINE. "The Variability of Intelligence Quotients." *J Psycho-Asthenics* 37:119-46, discussion 146-8 '32. * (*PA* 7:2667)
147. BROWN, RALPH R. "The Time Interval Between Test and Re-Test in Its Relation to the Constancy of the Intelligence Quotient." *J Ed Psychol* 24:81-96 F '33. * (*PA* 7:3094)
148. CANDEE, BEATRICE, AND SMITH, HELEN. "Relation Between Vocational and Other Interests and the Type of Performance on the Stanford-Binet Tests." Abstract. *Psychol B* 30:570 O '33. * (*PA* 8:1363, title only)
149. TULCHIN, SIMON H. "The Evaluation of Psychological Test Results." *Am J Orthopsychiatry* 3:349-54 Jl '33. * (*PA* 7:4909)
150. DAVIS, ALONZO J. "Personality, Parent Intelligence and 'Scatter' on the Stanford-Binet." *J Juvenile Res* 18:175-8 Jl '34. * (*PA* 8:5992)
151. SHIPLEY, WALTER C. "Stanford-Binet Test Scattering as Related to IQ in Clinical Cases." Abstract. *Psychol B* 31:684-5 N '34. * (*PA* 9:1273, title only)
152. MAXFIELD, FRANCIS N. "Substitutes for the 'I.Q.'" *J Psycho-Asthenics* 40:147-56 '35. * (*PA* 10:1698)
153. MAYER, BARBARA A. "Negativistic Reactions of Preschool Children on the New Revision of the Stanford-Binet." Abstract. *Psychol B* 32:541-2 O '35. * (*PA* 10:652, title only)
154. HAURY, GERTRUDE. *An Analysis of the Responses of Normal and Delinquent Individuals to Certain Test Items of the Stanford-Binet Scale and the Pintner-Paterson Scale.* Unpublished master's thesis, University of Kansas, 1936.
155. MICHAELS, JOSEPH J., AND SCHILLING, MARGARET E. "An Attempt to Determine the Degree of Anti-Social Behavior in Psychopathic Personalities and Its Correlation With the Porteus Maze and Binet-Simon Tests." *Am J Orthopsychiatry* 6:397-405 Jl '36. * (*PA* 11:407)
156. MICHAELS, JOSEPH J., AND SCHILLING, MARGARET E. "The Correlations of the Intelligence Quotients of the Porteus Maze and Binet-Simon Tests in Two Hundred Neuropsychiatric Patients." *Am J Orthopsychiatry* 6:71-4 Ja '36. * (*PA* 10:3560)
157. PALMER, ELEANOR MARGARET. *A Study of Intellectual Deterioration in a Series of Schizophrenics and Organic Brain Diseases.* Unpublished doctor's thesis, University of Iowa, 1936.
158. KENT, GRACE H. "Suggestions for the Next Revision of the Binet-Simon Scale." *Psychol Rec* 1:409-33 N' 37. * (*PA* 12:2662)
159. SKENE, DOROTHY MARGARET. *Serial Testing Versus Nonserial Testing of the 1937 Revision of the Stanford-Binet.* Unpublished master's thesis, Columbia University, 1937.
160. TRAPP, CARL E., AND JAMES, EDITH B. "Comparative Intelligence Ratings in the Four Types of Dementia Praecox." *J Nerv & Mental Dis* 86:399-404 O '37. * (*PA* 12:3016)
161. BOND, ELDEN A. "Some Verbal Aspects of the 1937 Revision of the Stanford-Binet Intelligence Test, Form L." *J Exp Ed* 6:340-2 Mr '38. * (*PA* 12:6113)
162. HILTY, DOROTHY PAULINE. *Differential Responses of Epileptics and Nonepileptics to Items of the 1916 Stanford-Binet Scale.* Unpublished master's thesis, Ohio State University, 1938. Pp. 32.
163. MALAMUD, WILLIAM, AND PALMER, ELEANOR M. "Intellectual Deterioration in the Psychoses." *Arch Neurol & Psychiatry* 39:68-81 Ja '38. *
164. MCNEMAR, QUINN. "The Equivalence of the General Factors Found for Successive Levels on the New Stanford Revision." Abstract. *Psychol B* 35:657 N '38. * (*PA* 13:1727, title only)
165. WLADKOWSKY, EDITH. "A Preliminary Study of Mental Growth After the Age of Fourteen Years in an Institution for Mental Defectives." *J Psycho-Asthenics* 43:181-7 '38. * (*PA* 13:2582)
166. ADLER, DANIEL LESLIE. *Types of Similarity and the Substitute Value of Activities at Different Age Levels.* Unpublished doctor's thesis, University of Iowa, 1939.
167. ANDERSON, L. DEWEY. "The Predictive Value of Infancy Tests in Relation to Intelligence at Five Years." *Child Develop* 10:203-12 S '39. * (*PA* 13:6507)
168. COLLINS, ANNA LOUISE. *Analysis of Stanford-Binet Test Responses in Three Types of Mental Disorder.* Unpublished doctor's thesis, Boston University, 1939.
169. GERLACH, MARJORIE. "A Study of the Relationship Between Psychometric Patterns and Personality Types." *Child Develop* 10:269-78 D '39. * (*PA* 14:2475)
170. JOHNSON, ANNA P., AND FERNOW, DOROTHY L. "Comparison of Results of Stanford-Binet and Performance Tests

Given at the Dixon State Hospital." *J Psycho-Asthenics* 44: 103-9 '39. * *(PA 14:3549)*

171. KAMAT, V. V. "Sex Differences Among Indian Children in the Binet-Simon Tests." *Brit J Ed Psychol* 9:251-6 N '39. * *(PA 14:3084)*

172. KREEZER, GEORGE L., AND BRADWAY, KATHERINE P. "The Direct Determination of the Probable Error of Measurement of Binet Mental Age." *J Ed Res* 33:197-214 N '39. * *(PA 14:1108)*

173. MATEER, FLORENCE. "Differential Syndromes in Stanford Binet Failures." Abstract. *Psychol B* 36:507-8 Jl '39. * *(PA 13:6276, title only)*

174. MUNSON, GRACE, AND SAFFIR, MILTON A. "A Comparative Study of Retest Ratings on the Original and the Revised Stanford Binet Intelligence Scales." Abstract. *Psychol B* 36:524-5 Jl '39. * *(PA 13:6518, title only)*

175. SLESS, BERNARD. *A Comparative Study of the 1916 Stanford-Binet Intelligence Test and the 1937 Stanford-Binet (Form L) Intelligence Test on the College Level.* Unpublished master's thesis, Temple University, 1939. Pp. 36.

176. BERGER, ARTHUR, AND SPEEVACK, MORRIS. "An Analysis of the Range of Testing and Scattering Among Retarded Children on Form L of the Revised Stanford Binet." *J Ed Psychol* 31:39-44 Ja '40. * *(PA 14:3247)*

177. BRUCE, MYRTLE. *Factors Affecting Intelligence Test Performance of Whites and Negroes in the Rural South.* Archives of Psychology, No. 252. Washington, D. C.: American Psychological Association, Inc., July 1940. Pp. 99. Paper. $1.50. * *(PA 15:4591)*

178. CHALLMAN, ALAN, AND BROWN, FRED. "Binet Testing by Kindergarten Teachers as a Mental Hygiene Measure." *Sch & Soc* 52:668-72 D '40. * *(PA 15:1537)*

179. DAVIS, FREDERICK B. "The Interpretation of IQ's Derived From the 1937 Revision of the Stanford-Binet Scales." *J Appl Psychol* 24:595-604 O '40. * *(PA 15:1087)*

180. FERNALD, MABEL R. "A Comparative Study of Scatter on the Original and the Revised Stanford-Binet Scales by the Use of Retest Data." Abstract. *Psychol B* 37:510 Jl '40. * *(PA 14:5732, title only)*

181. FONT, MARION MCKENZIE. "The 1937 Stanford-Binet Scale as a Technique in the Diagnosis of Schizophrenia." Abstract. *Psychol B* 37:547 O '40. * *(PA 15:253, title only)*

182. GILLETTE, ANNETTE L. "The Accumulation of Some Data From Clinical Material on the Revised Binet, Form L." Abstract. *Psychol B* 37:512 Jl '40. * *(PA 14:5733, title only)*

183. GROWDON, C. H. "Is the Revised Stanford-Binet Scale Really an Age Scale?" Abstract. *Psychol B* 37:512 Jl '40. * *(PA 14:5734, title only)*

184. HENRY, JANET ALLYN. *A Comparison of Intelligence Test Scores as Measured by the Old and New Stanford-Binet Tests.* Unpublished master's thesis, State University of Iowa, 1940.

185. JENKINS, R. L. "Considerations Relative to the Selection of an Index of Intelligence." *J Ed Psychol* 31:527-40 O '40. * *(PA 15:1993)*

186. KVARACEUS, W. C. "Pupil Performances on the Abbreviated and Complete New Stanford-Binet Scales, Form L." *J Ed Psychol* 31:627-30 N '40. * *(PA 15:2837)*

187. MANUEL, H. T.; ADAMS, F. J.; JEFFRESS, SYLVIA; TOMLINSON, HELEN; AND GRAGG, D. B. "The New Stanford-Binet at the College Level." *J Ed Psychol* 31:705-9 D '40. * *(PA 15:2838)*

188. MITCHELL, MILDRED B. "Irregularities of University Students on the Revised Stanford-Binet." Abstract. *Psychol B* 37:511-2 Jl '40. * *(PA 14:5737, title only)*

189. PAGE, JAMES D. "The Effect of Nursery School Attendance Upon Subsequent IQ." *J Psychol* 10:221-30 O '40. *(PA 15:1121)*

190. PRAGER, DANIEL. *The Performance of Adult Mental Patients on the Revised Stanford-Binet, Form L, and the Bellevue Adult Intelligence Scales.* Unpublished master's thesis, University of Iowa, 1940.

191. REYMART, MARTIN L., AND MEISTER, RALPH K. "A Comparison of the Original and Revised Stanford-Binet Intelligence Scales." Abstract. *Psychol B* 37:572 O '40. * *(PA 15:570, title only)*

192. RICHARDSON, M. W. "The Logic of Age Scales." Abstract. *Psychol B* 37:513 Jl '40. * *(PA 14:5638, title only)*

193. ROBINSON, ELEANOR L. *A Comparison of Ratings on the 1916 and the 1937 Revisions of the Stanford-Binet Intelligence Scale at the First Grade Level.* Unpublished master's thesis, Pennsylvania State College, 1940. Pp. 33.

194. SALTZMAN, SARA. "The Influence of Social and Economic Background on Stanford-Binet Performance." *J Social Psychol* 12:71-81 Ag '40. * *(PA 15:571)*

195. SPEER, GEORGE S. "The Problem of Pseudo-Feeblemindedness: A Reply." *J Ed Psychol* 31:693-8 D '40. * *(PA 15:2639)*

196. SPEER, GEORGE S. "Range of Success on the Revised Stanford-Binet Examination." Abstract. *Psychol B* 37:572 O '40. * *(PA 15:573, title only)*

197. STRAUSS, ALFRED A., AND WERNER, HEINZ. "Qualitative Analysis of the Binet Test." *Am J Mental Def* 45:50-5 Jl '40. * *(PA 15:574)*

198. THIESEN, JOHN W. *A Tentative Scale for Differentiating Behavior Problem Children From Normals on the Revised Stanford-Binet.* Unpublished master's thesis, Columbia University, 1940.

199. WALLIN, J. E. W. "The Results of Multiple Binet Retestings of the Same Subjects: The Educational Implications of Variation of Test Performance." *J Genetic Psychol* 57:345-91 D '40. * *(PA 15:2400)*

200. BEAN, KENNETH L. "Negro Responses to Certain Intelligence Test Items." *J Psychol* 12:191-8 O '41. * *(PA 16:1055)*

201. BELLAK, LEOPOLD. "A Possible Dynamic Explanation of Variability in the I.Q." *J Abn & Social Psychol* 36:106-9 Ja '41. * *(PA 15:2537)*

202. BENTON, ARTHUR L.; WEIDER, ARTHUR; AND BLAUVELT, JEAN. "Performances of Adult Patients on the Bellevue Intelligence Scales and the Revised Stanford-Binet." *Psychiatric Q* 15:802-6 O '41. * *(PA 16:3821)*

203. BRODY, M. B. "The 1916 Stanford Binet Vocabulary Test Revised for Rapid Routine Practice." *J Mental Sci* 87:88-95 Ja '41. * *(PA 15:2832)*

204. CHASSELL, MARIAN A. *The Effect of the Interpolation of Performance Test Items on Stanford-Binet Scores.* Unpublished master's thesis, University of Iowa, 1941.

205. CLARKE, DANIEL P. "Stanford-Binet Scale 'L' Response Patterns in Matched Racial Groups." *J Negro Ed* 10:230-8 Ap '41. * *(PA 15:3491)*

206. COLLINS, A. LOUISE. "Psychometric Records of Institutionalized Epileptics." *J Psychol* 11:359-70 Ap '41. * *(PA 15:3401)*

207. DAVIS, EDITH A. "The Concept of 'Highest Binet Attainment' Applied to Unselected Clinical Cases." *J Ed Psychol* 32:697-703 D '41. * *(PA 16:2903)*

208. DAVIS, FREDERICK B. "The Derivation of Three Subscores from the 1937 Revision of the Stanford-Binet Scales." *J Consult Psychol* 5:287-91 N-D '41. * *(PA 16:782)*

209. EBERT, ELIZABETH H. "A Comparison of the Original and Revised Stanford-Binet Scales." *J Psychol* 11:47-61 Ja '41. * *(PA 15:2398)*

210. FRIEDLINE, CORA L., AND BERMAN, ABRAHAM B. "A Critical Analysis of Sub-Tests in the Terman-Merrill Revised Stanford-Binet Intelligence Scale, Forms L and M." *J Psychol* 11:279-84 Ap '41. * *(PA 15:3189)*

211. GERSTEIN, SAMUEL. "A Suggestion for a Revision of the Revised Stanford-Binet Examination Applied to Adults." *J Psychol* 12:225-6 O '41. * *(PA 16:784)*

212. GILLETTE, ANNETTE L. "Relative Difficulty of Tests Within Each Year Level of Revised Stanford-Binet, Form L, Years Six Through Twelve." *J Psychol* 12:125-38 Jl '41. * *(PA 15:5402)*

213. GROWDON, C. H. "The Revised Stanford-Binet Scale Applied as a Point Scale." *J Appl Psychol* 25:660-71 D '41. * Abstract *Psychol B* 38:593 Jl '41. * *(PA 16:1713)*

214. HESTON, JOSEPH C., AND CANNELL, CHARLES F. "A Note on the Relation Between Age and Performance of Adult Subjects on Four Familiar Psychometric Tests." *J Appl Psychol* 25:415-9 Ag '41. * *(PA 15:5004)*

215. HILDRETH, GERTRUDE. "Evaluating the Mental Status of Partially Seeing Children." *Teach Col Rec* 43:211-23 D '41. * *(PA 16:1737)*

216. HOGAN, HELENA P. "Comparison of Stanford-Binet and Kent Oral Emergency Scores." *J Genetic Psychol* 58:151-9 Mr '41. * *(PA 15:4044)*

217. KATZ, EVELYN. "The Constancy of the Stanford-Binet IQ From Three to Five Years." *J Psychol* 12:159-81 O '41. * *(PA 16:1233)*

218. KVARACEUS, W. C. "The Extent of Stanford-Binet I.Q. Changes of Mentally Retarded School Children." *J Ed Res* 35:40-2 S '41. * *(PA 15:5155)*

219. LORR, MAURICE, AND MEISTER, RALPH K. "The Concept of Scatter in the Light of Mental Test Theory." *Ed & Psychol Meas* 1:303-10 Jl '41. * *(PA 15:5406)*

220. LOWELL, FRANCES E. "A Study of the Variability of IQ's in Retests." *J Appl Psychol* 25:341-56 Je '41. * *(PA 15:4158)*

221. MAIZLISH, I. LEON. "A Comparison of the Complete and Abbreviated Stanford-Binet and of Clusters of Items Within the Test for Adult Offenders." Abstract. *Psychol B* 38:592-3 Jl '41. * *(PA 15:5407, title only)*

222. MARTINSON, BETTY, AND STRAUSS, ALFRED A. "A Method of Clinical Evaluation of the Responses to the Stanford-Binet Intelligence Test." *Am J Mental Def* 46:48-59 Jl '41. * *(PA 16:788)*

223. MCCLOSKEY, ETHEL P. *A Study of the Relation of the New Stanford-Binet Test and the Kuhlmann Tests of Mental Development.* Unpublished master's thesis, University of Texas, 1941.

224. MITCHELL, MILDRED B. "Irregularities of University Students on the Revised Stanford-Binet." *J Ed Psychol* 32:513-22 O '41. * *(PA 16:2494)*

225. MITCHELL, MILDRED B. "The Revised Stanford-Binet for Adults." *J Ed Res* 34:516-21 Mr '41. * *(PA 15:2839)*

226. MUNSON, GRACE, AND SAFFIR, MILTON A. "A Comparative Study of Retest Ratings on the Original and Revised Stanford-Binet Intelligence Scales." *Am J Mental Def* 45:565-71 Ap '41. * *(PA 15:4434)*

227. NEW YORK PUBLIC SCHOOLS, DIVISION OF TESTS AND MEASUREMENTS. *A Supplementary Guide for Scoring the Revised Stanford-Binet Intelligence Scale, Form L.* Divisional Bulletin No. 1. New York: the Division, Bureau of Reference, Research and Statistics, Board of Education of the City of New York, May 1941. Pp. 27. Paper. $0.15. * *(PA 16:363)*

228. OEXLE, HELEN M. *The Effect of Certain Interruptions on Test Performance on the 1937 Revision of the Stanford-Binet Scale.* Unpublished master's thesis, University of Iowa, 1941.

Revised Stanford-Binet Scale

229. PORTEUS, STANLEY D.; WITH THE ASSISTANCE OF MARY HUNTER AND COLIN J. HERRICK. *The Practice of Clinical Psychology*, pp. 11-38. New York: American Book Co., 1941. Pp. ix, 579. $5.00. * (PA 15:4248)
230. REYMART, MARTIN L., AND MEISTER, RALPH K. "A Comparison of the Original and Revised Stanford Binet Intelligence Scales." *Ed & Psychol Meas* 1:67-76 Ja '41. * (PA 15:2842)
231. RICHARDSON, M. W. "The Logic of Age Scales." *Ed & Psychol Meas* 1:25-34 Ja '41. * (PA 15:2844)
232. ROBITAILLE, H. J. *An Attempt at the Factorial Analysis of the Revised Stanford-Binet Scale*. Unpublished master's thesis, Catholic University of America, 1941.
233. ROHAN, J. C. "A Study of the Binet and Cattell Systems of Intelligence Testing in a Colony for Mental Defectives." *J Mental Sci* 87:192-207 Ap '41. * (PA 15:3190)
234. SPARLING, MARGARET E. "Intelligence of Indian Children: The Relationship Between Binet and Porteus Scores." *Am J Mental Def* 46:60-2 Jl '41. * (PA 16:819)
235. STRAUSS, ALFRED A. "Enriching the Interpretation of the Stanford-Binet Test." *J Excep Child* 7:260-4, 280-1 Ap '41. * (PA 15:4047)
236. WEIDER, ARTHUR. *A Comparative Study of the Performance of Psychopathic Adults on the Revised Stanford-Binet, Form L, and the Bellevue Intelligence Scale*. Unpublished master's thesis, Columbia University, 1941.
237. WEXBERG, ERWIN. "Testing Methods for the Differential Diagnosis of Mental Deficiency in a Case of Arrested Brain Tumor." *Am J Mental Def* 46:39-45 Jl '41. * (PA 16:369)
238. WILE, IRA S., AND DAVIS, ROSE. "A Study of Failures on the Stanford Binet in Relation to Behavior and School Problems." *J Ed Psychol* 32:275-84 Mr '41. * (PA 16:360)
239. WORCESTER, D. A. "Differences Among Examiners Using Stanford-Binet Tests With Subjects of Various Levels of Age and Intelligence." Abstract. *Psychol B* 38:711 O '41. * (PA 16:370, title only)
240. ALLEN, MARK K. "A Comparison Between Test Scores on the Original and the Revised Stanford-Binet Intelligence Scales Administered to a Group of Retarded and Mentally Deficient Subjects." *Am J Mental Def* 46:501-7 Ap '42. * (PA 16:3820)
241. ANDERSON, EDWARD E.; ANDERSON, SARAH FERRALL; FERGUSON, CAROLINE; GRAY, JEAN; HITTINGER, JANE; MCKINSTRY, ELEANORE; MOTTER, MARY ELIZABETH; AND VICK, GALE. "Wilson College Studies in Psychology: I, A Comparison of the Wechsler-Bellevue, Revised Stanford, and American Council on Education Tests at the College Level." *J Psychol* 14:317-26 O '42. * (PA 17:981)
242. BERGER, ARTHUR. "Test Construction and IQ Constancy." *J Excep Child* 8:109-11+ Ja '42. * (PA 16:4691)
243. BERGER, ARTHUR, AND SPEEVACK, MORRIS. "An Analysis of the Range of Testing and Scattering Among Retarded Children on Form M of the Revised Stanford-Binet Scale." *J Ed Psychol* 33:72-5 Ja '42. * (PA 16:3323)
244. BRODY, M. B. "The Measurement of Dementia." *J Mental Sci* 88:317-27 Ap '42. * (PA 16:3324)
245. BRODY, M. B. "A Psychometric Study of Dementia." *J Mental Sci* 88:512-33 O '42. * (PA 17:1178)
246. BROOKS, BERNICE R. *A Study of the Relation of the New Stanford-Binet and the Kuhlmann Tests of Mental Development*. Unpublished master's thesis, University of Texas, 1942.
247. BROWN, FRED. "A Comparison of the Abbreviated and the Complete Stanford-Binet Scales." *J Consult Psychol* 6:240-2 S-O '42. * (PA 16:5042)
248. BROWN, FRED. "The Minneapolis Kindergarten Binet Testing Program: An Experiment in Applied Psychology." *J Consult Psychol* 6:142-8 My-Je '42. * (PA 16:3325)
249. BURT, CYRIL, AND JOHN, ENID. "A Factorial Analysis of Terman Binet Tests: Part I." *Brit J Ed Psychol* 12:117-27 Je '42. * (PA 16:4199)
250. CARLTON, THEODORE. "A Comparison of the Revised Stanford-Binet, Form L, With the Kuhlmann Tests of Mental Development." *J Genetic Psychol* 61:47-54 S '42. * (PA 17:982)
251. CARLTON, THEODORE. "A Comparison of the Revised Stanford-Binet, Form L, With the Kuhlmann Tests of Mental Development: II, Performances of Mentally Defective Children." *J Appl Psychol* 26:159-67 Ap '42. * (PA 16:4200)
252. CARLTON, THEODORE. "The Effect of Chronological Age on Revised Stanford-Binet Vocabulary Score at the Moron and Imbecile Levels." *J Genetic Psychol* 61:321-6 D '42. * (PA 17:983)
253. FLEMING, VIRGINIA VAN DYNE. "A Study of Stanford-Binet Vocabulary Attainment and Growth in Children in the City of Childhood, Mooseheart, Illinois, as Compared With Children Living in Their Own Homes." *J Genetic Psychol* 60:359-73 Je '42. * (PA 16:4580)
254. GOODENOUGH, FLORENCE L. "Studies of the 1937 Revision of the Stanford-Binet Scale: I, Variability of the IQ at Successive Age-Levels." *J Ed Psychol* 32:241-51 Ap '42. * (PA 17:984)
255. HALPERN, FLORENCE. "A Comparison of the Revised Stanford L and the Bellevue Adult Intelligence Test as Clinical Instruments." *Psychiatric Q Sup* 16:206-11 Jl '42. * (PA 20:3328)
256. JAMES, ANNETTE. *An Analysis of the Revised Stanford-Binet in Terms of Reading Readiness Criteria*. Unpublished master's thesis, Claremont Colleges, 1942. Pp. 119.
257. KAVRUCK, SAMUEL. "A Study of the Relation of Retardation in Reading to Test Performance on the Revised Stanford-Binet, (Form L)." *J Ed Res* 36:221-3 N '42. * (PA 17:1725)
258. KUHLMANN, F., AND ODOROFF, M. E. "Verification of the Heinis Mental Growth Curve on Results With the Stanford-Binet Tests." *J Psychol* 13:355-64 Ap '42. * (PA 16:3824)
259. LAYCOCK, SAMUEL R., AND CLARK, STANLEY. "The Comparative Performance of a Group of Old-Dull and Young-Bright Children on Some Items of the Revised Stanford-Binet Scale of Intelligence, Form L." *J Ed Psychol* 33:1-12 Ja '42. * (PA 16:3328)
260. LAYMAN, JAMES W. "IQ Changes in Older-Age Children Placed for Foster Home Care." *J Genetic Psychol* 60:61-70 Mr '42. * (PA 16:3837)
261. LORR, MAURICE, AND MEISTER, RALPH K. "The Optimum Use of Test Data." *Ed & Psychol Meas* 2:339-48 O '42. * (PA 17:1379)
262. MAIZLISH, I. LEON. "A Comparison of the Stanford-Binet and Bellevue-Wechsler Scales for Adult Offenders." Abstract. *Psychol B* 39:472 Jl '42. * (PA 16:5045, title only)
263. MARSHALL, HELEN. "The Clinical Interpretation of Markedly Divergent Performance on Repeated Tests, Form L and Form M, Stanford-Binet: A Case Study." *Am J Mental Def* 46:351-3 Ja '42. * (PA 16:2689)
264. MCNEMAR, QUINN. *The Revision of the Stanford-Binet Scale: An Analysis of the Standardization Data*. Introductory chapter by Lewis M. Terman. Boston, Mass.: Houghton Mifflin Co., 1942. Pp. ix, 189. $3.50. * (London: George G. Harrap & Co. Ltd., 1942. 15s.) (PA 16:3329)
265. MITCHELL, MILDRED B. "Performance of Mental Hospital Patients on the Wechsler-Bellevue and the Revised Stanford Binet, Form L." *J Ed Psychol* 33:538-44 O '42. * (PA 17:1604)
266. MULLEN, FRANCES A. "Comparison of the Revised Kent Emergency Battery With the Revised Stanford-Binet and the Kuhlmann-Anderson Tests." Abstract. *Psychol B* 39:591 O '42. * (PA 17:716, title only)
267. NEVINS, F. A. *Analysis of Results of the Revised Stanford-Binet test of Intelligence for General and Classroom Use*. Unpublished master's thesis, Stanford University, 1942.
268. PIGNATELLI, MYRTLE LUNEAU. "A Comparative Study of Mental Functioning Patterns of Problem and Nonproblem Children Seven, Eight, and Nine Years of Age." Abstract. *Psychol B* 39:440-1 Jl '42. * (PA 16:5062, title only)
269. PINTNER, R. "Intelligence Testing of Partially-Sighted Children." *J Ed Psychol* 33:265-72 Ap '42. * (PA 17:987)
270. RAUTMAN, ARTHUR L. "Relative Difficulty of Test Items of the Revised Stanford-Binet: An Analysis of Records From a Low Intelligence Group." *J Exp Ed* 10:183-94 Mr '42. * (PA 16:3330)
271. RICHARDS, T. W., AND ELLINGTON, WILLIS. "Objectivity in the Evaluation of Personality" *J Exp Ed* 10:228-37 Je '42. * (PA 17:1742)
272. SPACHE, GEORGE. "Serial Testing with the Revised Stanford-Binet Scale, Form L, in the Test Range II-XIV." *Am J Orthopsychiatry* 12:81-6 Ja '42. * (PA 16:2906)
273. SPACHE, GEORGE. "The Short Form of the Revised Stanford-Binet Scale, Form L, Test Range II-XIV." *J Consult Psychol* 6:102-4 Mr-Ap '42. * (PA 16:2499)
274. STREET, ROY F. "I.Q. Changes of Exceptional Children." *J Consult Psychol* 6:243-6 S-O '42. * (PA 17:356)
275. TOMLINSON, HELEN. *An Analysis of the Performance of Negro Children on the Revised Stanford-Binet Tests*. Unpublished doctor's thesis, University of Texas, 1942.
276. WHITE, MARIAN L. "Mental Age Norms for Vocabulary Scores in the 1937 Stanford-Binet." *Psychol Rec* 5:157-69 Ap '42. * (PA 17:719)
277. WORBOIS, G. M. "Changes in Stanford-Binet IQ for Rural Consolidated and Rural One-Room School Children." *J Exp Ed* 11:210-4 D '42. * (PA 17:3606)
278. WRIGHT, CLARE. "A Modified Procedure for the Abbreviated Revised Stanford-Binet Scale in Determining the Intelligence of Mental Defectives." *Am J Mental Def* 47:178-84 O '42. * Abstract *Psychol B* 39:610 O '42. * (PA 17:989)
279. ADKINS, MARGARET M. "General Intellectual Ability," pp. 446-68. In *Physique, Personality and Scholarship: A Cooperative Study of School Children*. By R. Nevitt Sanford, Margaret M. Adkins, R. Bretney Miller, Elizabeth A. Cobb, and others. Monographs of the Society for Research in Child Development, Vol. 7, No. 1, Serial No. 34. Washington, D. C.: the Society, National Research Council, 1943. Pp. ix, 705. Paper, lithotyped. $2.50. * (PA 17:4319)
280. ALLAN, MARY ELIZABETH, AND YOUNG, FLORENE M. "The Constancy of the Intelligent Quotient as Indicated by Retests of 130 Children." *J Appl Psychol* 27:41-60 F '43. * (PA 17:2631)
281. ARMSTRONG, CLAIRETTE P. "Tests as Diagnostic Aids in Clinical Practice." *Am J Mental Def* 47:270-6 Ja '43. * (PA 17:3260)
282. BRADWAY, KATHERINE P. "Comparison of Standard and Wide-Range Testing on the Stanford-Binet." *J Consult Psychol* 7:179-190 Jl-Ag '43. * (PA 17:3977)
283. BRADWAY, KATHERINE P. "Factors Associated With IQ Changes in Children." Abstract. *Psychol B* 40:582 O '43. * (PA 18:333, title only)
284. BROWN, FRED. "The Significance of the IQ Variability in Relation to Age on the Revised Stanford-Binet Scale." *J Genetic Psychol* 63:177-81 S '43. * (PA 18:906)

285. GARRETT, HENRY E. "The Standardization of the Terman-Merrill Revision of the Stanford-Binet Scale: A Special Review." *Psychol B* 40:194-201 Mr '43. *

286. HAYES, SAMUEL P. "A Second Test Scale for the Mental Measurement of the Visually Handicapped: The Interim Hayes-Binet Intelligence Tests for the Blind, 1942 Revision." *Outlook for Blind* 37:37-41 F '43. * (*PA* 17:3609)

287. HILDRETH, GERTRUDE. "Stanford Binet Retests of Gifted Children." *J Ed Res* 37:297-302 D '43. * (*PA* 18:1541)

288. HINMAN, MARGARET E. H. "Items of the Binet Test as a Prediction of Reading Ability." Abstract. *Brit J Ed Psychol* 13:164 N '43. * (*PA* 18:1260, title only)

289. KAPLAN, OSCAR. "Mental Decline in Older Morons." *Am J Mental Def* 47:277-85 Ja '43. * (*PA* 17:3127)

290. McHUGH, GELOLO. *Changes in I.Q. at the Public School Kindergarten Level.* American Psychological Association, Psychological Monographs, Vol. 55, No. 2, Whole No. 250. Washington, D. C.: the Association, Inc., 1943. Pp. vi, 34. Paper. $0.75. * (*PA* 18:327)

291. MILLER, LEO R. "Some Results of Retesting Elementary-School Pupils With the Stanford Revision of the Binet-Simon Test." *J Ed Psychol* 34:237-41 Ap '43. * (*PA* 17:4284)

292. MITCHELL, MILDRED B. "The Revised Stanford-Binet for University Students." *J Ed Res* 36:507-11 Mr '43. * (*PA* 17:3262)

293. MYERS, C. ROGER, AND GIFFORD, ELIZABETH V. "Measuring Abnormal Pattern on the Revised Stanford-Binet Scale (Form L)." *J Mental Sci* 89:92-101 Ja '43. * (*PA* 17:2518)

294. PIGNATELLI, MYRTLE LUNEAU. "A Comparative Study of Mental Functioning Patterns of Problem and Non-Problem Children, Seven, Eight, and Nine Years of Age." *Genetic Psychol Monogr* 27:69-162 My '43. * (*PA* 17:3273)

295. SPACHE, GEORGE. "The Vocabulary Tests of the Revised Stanford-Binet as Independent Measures of Intelligence." *J Ed Res* 36:512-6 Mr '43. * (*PA* 17:3263)

296. WEIDER, ARTHUR; LEVI, JOSEPH; AND RISCH, FRANK. "Performances of Problem Children on the Wechsler-Bellevue Intelligence Scales and the Revised Stanford-Binet." *Psychiatric Q* 17:695-701 O '43. * (*PA* 18:624)

297. "Some Independent-School Distributions and Percentiles for Intelligence Quotients on the Terman-Merrill Revision of the Stanford-Binet Scale," pp. 46-8. In *1943 Fall Testing Program in Independent Schools and Supplementary Studies.* Educational Records Bulletin, No. 39. New York: Educational Records Bureau, January 1944. Pp. xii, 48. Paper, lithotyped. $1.00. * (*PA* 18:1920)

298. BIJOU, SIDNEY W. "Behavior Efficiency as a Determining Factor in the Social Adjustment of Mentally Retarded Young Men." *J Genetic Psychol* 65:133-45 S '44. * (*PA* 19:459)

299. BRADWAY, KATHERINE P. "IQ Constancy on the Revised Stanford-Binet From the Preschool to the Junior High School Level." *J Genetic Psychol* 65:197-217 D '44. * (*PA* 19:1056)

300. BROWN, FRED. "An Experiment in 'Preventive Testing' in the Kindergarten." *Mental Hyg* 28:450-5 Jl '44. * (*PA* 19:242)

301. CLOSE, RUTH L. "Abilities Measured by Paper-Cutting Tests (Stanford-Binet, 1937 Revision)." *Occupations* 22:308-10 F '44. * (*PA* 18:2288)

302. FLEMING, VIRGINIA VAN DYNE. "A Study of the Subtests in the Revised Stanford-Binet Scale, Forms L and M." *J Genetic Psychol* 64:3-36 Mr '44. * (*PA* 18:2289)

303. GOLDFARB, WILLIAM. "Adolescent Performance in the Wechsler-Bellevue Intelligence Scales and the Revised Stanford-Binet Examination, Form L." *J Ed Psychol* 35:503-7 N '44. * (*PA* 19:1058)

304. HOLLAND, PATTIE E. *The Intelligence of Rural Children as Measured by the Kuhlmann-Anderson Intelligence Test and the Stanford-Binet Scale.* Unpublished master's thesis, University of Virginia, 1944.

305. JASPEN, NATHAN. "A Note on the Age-Placement of Binet Tests." *Psychol B* 41:41-3 Ja '44. * (*PA* 18:1922)

306. KLUGMAN, SAMUEL F. "The Effect of Money Incentive Versus Praise Upon the Reliability and Obtained Scores of the Revised Stanford-Binet." *J General Psychol* 30:255-69 Ap '44. * (*PA* 18:3649)

307. NEEDHAM, NORMA R. "A Comparative Study of the Performance of Feebleminded Subjects on the Goodenough Drawing, the Goldstein-Scheerer Cube Test, and the Stanford-Binet." *Am J Mental Def* 49:155-61 O '44. * (*PA* 19:2774)

308. PINTNER, RUDOLF; DRAGOSITZ, ANNA; AND KUSHNER, ROSE. *Supplementary Guide for the Revised Stanford-Binet Scale (Form L).* Applied Psychology Monographs of the American Psychological Association, No. 3. Stanford University, Calif.: Stanford University Press, 1944. Pp. 135. Cloth, $2.25; paper, $1.50; lithotyped. * (*PA* 19:578)

309. RABIN, ALBERT I. "The Relationship Between Vocabulary Levels and Levels of General Intelligence in Psychotic and Non-Psychotic Individuals of a Wide Age-Range." *J Ed Psychol* 35:411-22 O '44. * (*PA* 19:421)

310. ROE, ANNE, AND SHAKOW, DAVID. "Intellectual Functions in Alcoholic Psychoses." *Q J Studies Alcohol* 4:517-22 Mr '44. * (*PA* 18:2820)

311. SHOTWELL, ANNA M., AND McCULLOCH, T. L. "Accuracy of Abbreviated Forms of the Revised Stanford-Binet Scale With Institutionalized Epileptics." *Am J Mental Def* 49:162-4 O '44. * (*PA* 19:3196)

312. SPACHE, GEORGE. "The Abbreviated Stanford-Binet Scale in a Superior Population." *J Ed Psychol* 35:314-8 My '44. * (*PA* 18:3906)

313. SPACHE, GEORGE. "Methods of Predicting Results of Full Scale Stanford-Binet." *Am J Orthopsychiatry* 14:480-2 Jl '44. * (*PA* 19:273)

314. TOMLINSON, HELEN. "Differences Between Pre-School Negro Children and Their Older Siblings on the Stanford-Binet Scales." *J Negro Ed* 13:474-9 fall '44. * (*PA* 19:582)

315. WALLIN, J. E. WALLACE, AND HULTSCH, CATHARINE L. "The Pathognomonic Significance of Psychometric Patterns." *Am J Mental Def* 48:269-77 Ja '44. * (*PA* 18:2983)

316. WELLMAN, BETH L., AND PEGRAM, EDNA LEE. "Binet IQ Changes of Orphanage Preschool Children: A Re-Analysis." *J Genetic Psychol* 65:239-63 D '44. * (*PA* 19:1061)

317. BRADWAY, KATHERINE P. "An Experimental Study of Factors Associated With Stanford-Binet IQ Changes From the Preschool to the Junior High School." *J Genetic Psychol* 66:107-28 Mr '45. * (*PA* 19:1584)

318. BRADWAY, KATHERINE P. "Predictive Value of Stanford-Binet Preschool Items." *J Ed Psychol* 36:1-16 Ja '45. * (*PA* 19:1814)

319. GLICK, H. N.; FLYNN, ELIZABETH; AND MACOMBER, LOIS. "Some Comparisons Between the Original and the Revised Stanford-Binet Scales." *J Ed Psychol* 36:177-83 Mr '45. * (*PA* 19:2391)

320. HIRT, ZOE ISABELLE. "Another Study of Retests With the 1916 Stanford-Binet Scale." *J Genetic Psychol* 66:83-105 Mr '45. * (*PA* 19:1585)

321. HOAKLEY, Z. PAULINE, AND FRAZEUR, HELEN A. "Significance of Psychological Test Results of Exogenous and Endogenous Children." *Am J Mental Def* 50:263-71 O '45. * (*PA* 20:2939)

322. KENNEDY-FRASER, D. *The Terman-Merrill Intelligence Scale in Scotland.* Publications of the Scottish Council for Research in Education, [No.] 23. London: University of London Press, Ltd., 1945. Pp. viii, 47. Paper. 1s. * (*PA* 12:2393)

323. KUTASH, SAMUEL B. "A Comparison of the Wechsler-Bellevue and the Revised Stanford-Binet Scales for Adult Defective Delinquents." *Psychiatric Q* 19:677-85 O '45. * (*PA* 20:3330)

324. LAYCOCK, S. R. "Researches in the Revised Stanford-Binet Scale of Intelligence, Form L." *B Can Psychol Assn* 5:35-6 Ap '45. * (*PA* 19:2772)

325. MAYMAN, MARTIN. "Review of the Literature on 'Scatter,'" pp. 548-58. In *Diagnostic Psychological Testing: The Theory, Statistical Evaluation, and Diagnostic Application of a Battery of Tests,* Vol. I. By David Rapaport with the collaboration of Merton Gill and Roy Schafer. Chicago, Ill.: Year Book Publishers, Inc., 1945. Pp. xi, 573. $6.50. * (*PA* 20:929)

326. PARKYN, G. W. "The Clinical Significance of IQ's on the Revised Stanford-Binet Scale." *J Ed Psychol* 36:114-8 F '45. * (*PA* 19:1818)

327. ROBERTS, A. DUDLEY. "Intelligence and Performance Test Patterns Among Older Mental Defectives." *Am J Mental Def* 49:300-3 Ja '45. * (*PA* 19:3386)

328. ROBERTS, A. D. "Some I.Q. Changes on the Stanford-Binet, Form L." *Am J Mental Def* 50:134-6 Jl '45. *

329. SCHNACK, GEORGE F.; SHAKOW, DAVID; AND LIVELY, MARY L. "Studies in Insulin and Metrazol Therapy: I, The Differential Prognostic Value of Some Psychological Tests." *J Personality* 14:106-24 D '45. * (*PA* 20:3669)

330. SCHNACK, GEORGE F.; SHAKOW, DAVID; AND LIVELY, MARY L. "Studies in Insulin and Metrazol Therapy: II, Differential Effects on Some Psychological Functions." *J Personality* 14:125-49 D '45. * (*PA* 20:3669)

331. SHOTWELL, ANNA M. "Arthur Performance Ratings of Mexican and American High-Grade Mental Defectives." *Am J Mental Def* 49:445-9 Ap '45. * (*PA* 20:170)

332. SPAULDING, PATRICIA J. "Comparison of 500 Complete and Abbreviated Revised Stanford Scales Administered to Mental Defectives." *Am J Mental Def* 50:81-8 Jl '45. * (*PA* 20:2503)

333. WELLMAN, BETH L. "IQ Changes of Preschool and Nonpreschool Groups During the Preschool Years: A Summary of the Literature." *J Psychol* 20:347-68 O '45. * (*PA* 20:582)

334. WHITCOMB, MARIAN A. "A Comparison of Social and Intellectual Levels of 100 High-Grade Adult Mental Defectives." *Am J Mental Def* 50:257-62 O '45. * (*PA* 20:2850)

335. "Revised Independent-School Distributions and Percentile Ratings for Intelligence Quotients on the Terman-Merrill Revision of the Stanford-Binet Scale," pp. 64-6. In *1945 Fall Testing Program in Independent Schools and Supplementary Studies.* Educational Records Bulletin, No. 44. New York: Educational Records Bureau, January 1946. Pp. xiii, 66. Paper, lithotyped. $1.00. * (*PA* 20:2096)

336. ALTUS, WILLIAM D. "The Validity of the Terman Vocabulary for Army Illiterates." *J Consult Psychol* 10:268-76 S-O '46. * (*PA* 21:1307)

337. CARLSON, JESSIE J. "Psychosomatic Study of Fifty Stuttering Children: Round Table: III, Analysis of Responses on the Revised Stanford-Binet." *Am J Orthopsychiatry* 16:120-6 Ja '46. * (*PA* 20:2509)

338. DESPERT, J. LOUISE, AND PIERCE, HELEN OEXLE. "The Relation of Emotional Adjustment to Intellectual Function." *Genetic Psychol Monogr* 34:3-56 Ag '46. * (*PA* 21:928)

339. MAYMAN, MARTIN. "An Analysis of Scatter in Intelligence Test Results: A Review of the Literature." *Trans Kan Acad Sci* 48:429-44 Mr '46. * (*PA* 20:2923)

340. SARASON, SEYMOUR B., AND SARASON, ESTHER KROOP. "The Discriminatory Value of a Test Pattern in the High Grade Familial Defective." *J Clin Psychol* 2:38-49 Ja '46. * *(PA 20:1940)*
341. SARTAIN, A. Q. "A Comparison of the New Revised Stanford-Binet, the Bellevue Scale, and Certain Group Tests of Intelligence." *J Social Psychol* 23:237-9 My '46. * *(PA 21:309)*
342. SPAULDING, PATRICIA J. "Retest Results on the Stanford L With Mental Defectives." *Am J Mental Def* 51:35-42 Jl '46. * *(PA 21:491)*
343. TAGIURI, R. "Comparison of Results Obtained From the Wechsler-Bellevue Vocabulary Test With Those From the Stanford-Binet Vocabulary Test Using a Population of Normal Subjects and Mental Patients." Abstract. *B Can Psychol Assn* 6:101 O-D '46. * *(PA 21:920, title only)*
344. WALLIN, J. E. W. "A Comparison of the Stanford 1916 and 1937 (Form L) Test Results With Those From the Arthur Performance Scale (Form I) Based on the Same Subjects." *J Genetic Psychol* 69:45-55 S '46. * *(PA 21:921)*
345. WELLMAN, BETH L., AND MCCANDLESS, BOYD R. *Factors Associated With Binet IQ Changes of Preschool Children.* American Psychological Association, Psychological Monographs, Vol. 60, No. 2, Whole No. 278. Washington, D. C.: the Association, Inc., 1946. Pp. iii, 29. Paper. $0.75. * *(PA 21:1103)*
346. DOLL, EDGAR A. "Note on the Age Placement of Year-Scale Tests." *J Consult Psychol* 11:144-7 My-Je '47. * *(PA 22:198)*
347. HUTT, MAX L. "A Clinical Study of 'Consecutive' and 'Adaptive' Testing With the Revised Stanford-Binet." *J Consult Psychol* 11:93-103 Mr-Apr '47. * *(PA 21:3631)*
348. SARASON, SEYMOUR B., AND SARASON, ESTHER KROOP. "The Discriminatory Value of a Test Pattern With Cerebral Palsied, Defective Children." *J Clin Psychol* 3:141-7 Ap '47. * *(PA 21:3029)*
349. SLOAN, WILLIAM, AND CUTTS, RICHARD A. "Test Patterns of Mental Defectives on the Revised Stanford-Binet Scale." *Am J Mental Def* 51:394-6 Ja '47. * *(PA 22:374)*
350. SLOAN, WILLIAM, AND OBLINGER, BARBARA. "Diagnostic Value of Picture Anomalies and Verbal Absurdities for Institutional Adjustment." *Am J Mental Def* 51:532-4 Ja '47. * *(PA 22:375)*
351. THOMPSON, CLARE WRIGHT, AND MAGARET, ANN. "Differential Test Responses of Normals and Mental Defectives." *J Abn & Social Psychol* 42:285-93 Jl '47. * *(PA 22:1240)*

For reviews by Francis N. Maxfield, J. W. M. Rothney, and F. L. Wells and excerpts from reviews by Cyril Burt, R. B. Cattell, C. J. C. Earl, J. C. Flanagan, F. N. Freeman, F. L. Goodenough, E. N. Hay, E. Kawin, Grace H. Kent, M. Krugman, A. H. Martin, E. M. Nevill, C. Spearman, A. E. Traxler, P. E. Vernon, and eleven others, see 38:1062, 38:B497, 40:1420, and 40:B1093. See also 293 and 294.

[293]
★[*Re* Revised Stanford-Binet Scale.] MCNEMAR, QUINN. **The Revision of the Stanford-Binet Scale: An Analysis of the Standardization Data.** Introductory chapter by Lewis M. Terman. Boston, Mass.: Houghton Mifflin Co., 1942. Pp. ix, 189. $3.50. * (London: George G. Harrap & Co. Ltd. 15s.) *(PA 16:3329)*

Brit J Ed Psychol 14:112 Je '44. This book reports an extensive statistical analysis of the data obtained in the standardization of the new Terman–Merrill tests. Professor Terman writes the first chapter, which forms an admirable introduction to the rest of the book. * There are many detailed tables which will be of special interest to statisticians.

Ed Res B 22:51-2 F '43. *Francis N. Maxfield.* * In 1917 Terman published an account of the data on which his 1916 Stanford–Binet scale was based. Unfortunately little attention was paid to this publication. It contained a great deal of material that was significant for research, and still more significant for the clinical interpretation of psychometric scores. The Stanford–Binet scale outran all competitors, and its popularity was a major factor in causing the psychometric method not only to outrun the method of clinical case studies, but to a considerable extent to supplant this method. More careful attention to Terman's 1917 publication might well have prevented some of the misinterpretations of Stanford–Binet scores that became current. * It will be unfortunate if McNemar's statistical analysis of Terman and Merrill's data is similarly ignored. The author's concise summary (Chap. XII) can be read in ten minutes and will serve the reader's purpose better than any statement the reviewer can make here.

J Consulting Psychol 7:60-1 Ja-F '43. *Ethel L. Cornell.* The long awaited statistical analysis of the standardization data of the revision of the Stanford–Binet Scale has been compressed into a small volume, but one that will reward close study. The material that has been selected for the volume has been carefully chosen and admirably presented to clarify some of the clinical, as well as statistical, questions that have been raised. * A clearer realization of the difficulties of both construction and adequate statistical analysis of such an age-scale raises some question in the reviewer's mind as to whether psychologists will not soon discover a way to preserve the clinical advantages of this type of test while securing an instrument with more statistical flexibility. * The chapter dealing with the shape of I.Q. distributions at different ages is perhaps of most general interest. * About a quarter of the book is devoted to a discussion of factor analysis. Dr. McNemar has done a superb job of condensing an enormous amount of material and of presenting it so that it is readable both by the statistical and the nonstatistical minded. * The book is one that should be accessible for ready reference by all users of the revised scale, and should be carefully studied by critics of the scale.

Occupational Psychol 17:204-6 O '43. *Cyril Burt.* In standardizing their latest revision.... Terman and his colleagues arranged for the tests to be given to 3,184 persons—roughly speaking, 100 boys and 100 girls at each age from 6 to 14, and 50 at each age above and below that level. The inquiry is thus almost as extensive as that on which the standardization of the British revision of the tests was based some twenty years ago * By far the longest and most instructive chapter is that which deals with the factorial analysis of the several tests. Prof. Terman, in his introduction to Dr. McNemar's account, observes that 'the Binet Scale has often been criticized because of its great variety of brief, disconnected tests—a 'motley array,' as Spearman has somewhat scornfully described them." It was, however, originally designed to test a 'general factor' of intelligence. That being so, it is astonishing that so few investigators have attempted either to demonstrate that there is, in point of fact, a 'general factor' running through all the tests, or to measure the amount which that factor contributes to the total variance. In this country, we have, on a somewhat limited scale, endeavoured to factorize the correlations between the tests both in the earlier and in the later revisions. We found a general factor contributing 42 per cent of the variance, and at least two subsidiary factors contributing about 12 per cent and 16 per cent respectively. Dr. McNemar's results are almost identical. He finds that on an average "the first common factor accounts for about 40 per cent of the variance of the tests" and "the second factor for 5 to 11 per cent, and the third for 4 to 7 per cent." His evidence suggests that the general factor is nearly the same at different ages. And he concludes that the tests may fairly be said to measure general intelligence, and "not a hodgepodge of abilities, as some have suggested." To discover the nature of the subsidiary factors he relies on a rough graphic procedure. They seem to differ at different ages; the more conspicuous are apparently a 'verbal,' a 'numerical,' a 'memory,' a 'problem,' and (at the earlier ages) a 'motor' factor. These are almost exactly the same as were obtained by British investigators with a somewhat different procedure, namely, a 'group-factor analysis.' * those familiar with reports of Binet surveys undertaken in this country will note that.... there is a remarkable correspondence between the results obtained from the American data and the English. That of itself should greatly strengthen the confidence felt in the methods now available for measuring the intelligence of children of school age. This brief summary by no means exhausts the interesting problems discussed in Dr. McNemar's book. The whole series of studies constitutes by far the most extensive, thorough, and up-to-date analysis of data obtained by means of the Binet tests; and should provide a model for future investigators.

Occupations 22:70 O '43. Forrest H. Kirkpatrick. * McNemar's statistical analysis of Terman and Merrill's data is highly significant and must not be ignored. His concise summary (Chap. XII) can be read in ten minutes and adequately reports the study. *

Psychol B 40:194–201 Mr '43. Henry E. Garrett. * McNemar....is certainly to be commended for the compact and succinct form in which the material is presented. * Various psychometricians, as our author notes, have held that an item is correctly placed when assigned to that age level at which just 50 per cent of the subjects pass it; and mathematically this would seem to be reasonable. McNemar, however, vigorously condemns reliance upon the 50 per cent criterion. He lists three "considerations" (p. 87) to explain why higher percents are necessary in the New Revision. These are (1) "the fact that it is simply impossible otherwise to construct an age scale of the Binet type that will yield mean mental ages equal to mean chronological ages"; (2) "the fact that the location and grouping of items at a given level is mainly one of convenience which facilitates testing and scoring";....and (3) "the fact that the individuals of any age group encounter items which are actually of 50 per cent difficulty for their age group even though the items placed at their own age levels may be less difficult." It is not immediately obvious that either (2) or (3) of these considerations is directly relevant to the issue of test placement, while (1) is simply a flat pronouncement of what scale standardization may have shown to be true without showing why this is true. Terman's explanation of the allocation of tests in the Old Revision is much more clarifying (*Stanford revision of the Simon–Binet Scale,* 1917, pp. 154–155) than is the present discussion. The rapid rise of the age progress curve in the early years and the resulting drastic changes in percents passing, plus the increase in spread at the later ages, are apparently the crux of the matter. * Essentially the allocation of test items to specific age levels boils down to a cut-and-fit process. The authors could have saved themselves much space by saying so at the outset. * Fourteen separate factor analyses were then made (using Thurstone's centroid method) * a strong first factor is conspicuous in all 14 tables. This factor accounts for the intercorrelations of the items and for from 35–50 per cent of the variance of the battery. * The fact that such a diversity of test items can be assembled to yield a general factor—even when carefully chosen so to do—is strong evidence (it seems to the reviewer) for the existence of such a general factor in mental activity as Spearman has long urged. * In Chapter XI (*Units of Measurement*), McNemar drops the role of expositor to express positive opinions upon several of the persistent problems which confront the testmaker. * A standard score, he writes (p. 158), is simply a linear transformation of raw scores into SD–units; such a transformation (he points out) does not change the form of the distribution nor equalize the units of the test. This is entirely true, but is not directly relevant to the problem of scaling test scores into "truly equal units" (the phrase is Thorndike's). I cannot agree with McNemar that there are "a surprisingly large number of psychologists 'who claim' that the use of the standard-score method will yield units which are equal or 'truly equal' (p. 157)." * I think that McNemar has confused standard-scores with T-scores,—at least so far as equal unit scaling is concerned. T-scaling converts the percents achieving each score into equivalent SD–positions along the baseline of the normal curve. No assumption is made regarding the distribution of raw scores, but the true distribution of ability measured by the test is assumed to be normal. The distribution of calculated T-scores will have the same form as that of the original scores; only in the ideal normal distribution assumed for the trait are the T-scores normally distributed. SD–units along the baseline of the normal curve (upon which our T-scores will fall at irregular intervals) are mathematically equal or in Thorndike's words "truly equal." The point should be stressed, perhaps, that the units on *any* scale are equal *only* with respect to certain defined criteria. Psychologists have done too much breast-beating over the great advantage possessed by the physicist in having scales with equal units and a true zero. To be sure, the much-vaunted "cgs" scale does possess many advantages, among them that of having equal units; but these units are equal with respect to certain criteria,—not all. The Weber–Fechner Law has shown that an inch added to a man's nose is not *perceptually* the same as an inch added to his height, and the same number of pounds or of seconds is often psychologically quite unequal. The same situation holds even more truly of other physical scales. * McNemar (p. 159) in his example showing that pounds are unequal to T-scale units exhibits clearly the confusion which arises when systems of measurement are compared which are set up on different criteria and are not directly commensurable. The scaled scores of the psychologist are "truly equal" with respect to a defined criterion of performance on the assumption of normality in the trait. That such scales are useful and efficient experience has amply shown. Closely related to his discussion of equal units is McNemar's criticism of Thorndike's demonstration that intellect in man is normally distributed. McNemar contends that since Thorndike scaled his tests into equal units by means of the normal curve, it is not surprising that distributions expressed in these derived units should turn out to be normal. He writes: (p. 17) "Thorndike has only demonstrated the obvious; a normal curve can be produced by assuming it in advance." It may be noted that Terman has also made essentially the same criticism (*Measuring Intelligence,* p. 25): he calls it "lifting oneself over the fence by one's bootstraps." This criticism, I feel, is not only superficial and incorrect, but coming from such sources is liable to do real harm. It may be pointed out, in the first instance, that Thorndike fully understood the "circularity" objection advanced by McNemar. In Chapters II, VIII, and Appendix III of his *Measurement of Intelligence* (1927), he states explicitly that a normal distribution of test scores might arise in lieu of other causes from (1) the fact that the test was constructed with the normal hypothesis definitely in mind; and (2) from chance errors, the scores of all subjects being the same. To meet the first difficulty, Thorndike employed two procedures. First, he scaled the score distributions for several well known tests (Otis, Alpha, National, are examples) into "truly equal" units by means of the normal curve. The normal distribution was selected for scaling (others were considered, see Chapter II) because the distributions of scores in the school grades employed as standardization groups were bell-shaped and not noticeably skewed. Distributions of scores, expressed in

Revised Stanford-Binet Scale

terms of corrected units, were then demonstrated to be normal for new and different groups taken at various age levels. It is important to note that the scaling procedures corrected the units of the test (lengthened or compressed them) but did not *force* the new distributions into the normal form. As a second procedure, Thorndike showed that a test scored in truly equal units derived from Grade VI will return a normal distribution for Grade IX. He argues that while a test-maker might conceivably select his items so as to return a normal distribution for a given group, it is too much to expect him to repeat for other and quite different groups. To meet the second difficulty, Thorndike averaged four to five repetitions of the same test before scaling, on the hypothesis that the mean of several determinations would be largely free from chance error. One may offer valid objections to certain details of Thorndike's procedure. I am not entirely convinced that he has really demonstrated intellect to be distributed in strictly normal fashion, and I agree with McNemar that his use of the Chi-Square test is dubious. But I feel sure that Thorndike has shown intellect in man (as measured by standard tests) to be essentially symmetrical and bell-shaped, and at least to be approximately normal. And this demonstration is not invalidated by the rather shallow charge of circularity. In summarizing the material in this monograph, I should like to express the opinion that the New Revision is the most useful and is certainly the best constructed instrument for measuring the intelligence of children which we now possess. It represents an achievement of first rank; and one of which all psychologists, no matter what their persuasion, may well be proud.

[294]

★[*Re* Revised Stanford-Binet Scale.] PINTER, RUDOLF; DRAGOSITZ, ANNA; AND KUSHNER, ROSE. **Supplementary Guide for the Revised Stanford-Binet Scale (Form L).** Applied Psychology Monographs of the American Psychological Association, No. 3. Stanford, Calif.: Stanford University Press, 1944. Pp. 135. Cloth, $2.25; paper, $1.50; lithotyped. * (*PA* 19:578)

Clearing House 19:458–60 Mr '45. E(arl) R. G(abler). * a necessary supplement to.... *Measuring Intelligence*, by Terman and Merrill * As one who has given many Binets, it seems that this monograph is a veritable gold mine of definitive information for the examiner. The responses are sufficient in number and variety to fit the range of pupil performance. By good organization the material is made easily accessible and usable.

Ed Res B 25:55–6 F 13 '46. Francis N. Maxfield. Terman and Merrill's revised Stanford–Binet scale (1937) seems likely to maintain the popularity of Terman's earlier revision (1916) as an individual test of intelligence. One reason for the very general adoption of these scales has been the fact that the authors' manuals in both cases have given fuller directions for scoring the various test items than were provided by the authors of other revisions. More than half of the one hundred twenty-nine test items of either Form L or Form M of the revised Stanford–Binet scale can be scored as rigidly as the stencil-scoring of a group test. In the other sixty test items there is a flexibility characteristic of Binet's method that may elicit responses that are not scored so readily. Pintner and his collaborators have prepared this manual to supplement the directions given by Terman and Merrill for scoring responses to test items of the latter type in Form L. Actual responses taken from several thousand test records are scored plus, minus, or "Q," as in the Terman–Merrill manual. A notable original feature is a listing of responses in categories according to type, thus emphasizing the principle underlying the scoring. On the whole, the scoring will commend itself. As the authors have purposely chosen many items on the borderline between plus and minus scoring, most experienced examiners will disagree with an occasional scoring. For example, in S. A. I, 6, the examiner asks, "What is the principal way in which melting and burning are alike?" One subject says, "Both break down a substance." Another says, "Both make whatever is melted or burned disintegrate." Why should one of these be scored minus and the other plus? The scoring of the first figure on page 27 is clearly in error. But, in general, this "supplementary guide" is excellent, and the emphasis on underlying principles is particularly commendable.

[295]

★**Stencil Design Test.** Ages 6 and over; 1944–45; individual; 1 form; 2 levels; $3 per set of testing materials and 25 record forms for either level, postpaid; 75¢ per 25 record forms for either level, postpaid; 35¢ per set of manuals; Grace Arthur; Psychological Corporation.
a) STENCIL DESIGN TEST I.
b) STENCIL DESIGN TEST II.

REFERENCES
1. ARTHUR, GRACE. "A Non-Verbal Test of Logical Thinking." *J Consult Psychol* 8:33-4 Ja-F '44. * (*PA* 18:2286)
2. BOULGER, CATHERINE, AND ARTHUR, GRACE. "An Unpublished Design Test." *J Consult Psychol* 8:31-2 Ja-F '44. * (*PA* 18:2287)

James M. Anderson, Instructor in Clinical Psychology, University of Rochester, Rochester, New York. Although intended as a subtest for the alternate forms of the *Arthur Point Scale of Performance Tests,* this ingenious series of tasks will undoubtedly find much wider use. Form I consists of 20 geometrically symmetrical designs in color to be reproduced by using varying numbers of the 18 paper stencils of various colors and shapes. Form II is similar to Form I except that the designs are in black and white and they are reproduced by superimposing varying numbers of the 12 paper stencil shapes, each of which is provided in both dark blue and yellow. Both the designs and the stencils are 3 by 3 inches so that it is possible to reproduce exactly the design, which remains before the subject.

These tests seem to have universal appeal and they usually command spontaneous interest. There appears to be some unevenness in the scale of difficulty, but it is not marked. The range of difficulty is quite broad with a very high ceiling (some graduate students experience difficulty), and, unfortunately, the lower level is of such difficulty as to prevent its use with most preschool subjects.

There are two mechanical weaknesses of the test associated with the present material used for the stencils. Since they are made of paper, they are subject to very rapid deterioration. The bending experienced after a few uses is sufficient to give the reproduction a three-dimensional effect (as many as 5 stencils are needed for some designs). This was bothersome to some subjects.

The use of dark blue and yellow stencils for the reproduction of the black and white designs of Form II seems to facilitate the reversal of figure and ground in the reproductions. These reversals are scored as being correct. It would be interesting to see if reversals are as common with black and white stencils.

Form II is noticeably more difficult than Form I, apparently because of the absence of colors which give a clue as to the successive stencils to be used for successive layers in evolving the designs.

The theoretically possible time limit of approximately 83 minutes for each form might possibly be prohibitive, especially if the tests are to be included in a battery of performance items.

Some of the subjects observed by this reviewer evolved a "system" of proceeding from the center of the design outward. Once the "system" was grasped, the nature of the task seemed to change radically, and the time required for the test seemed to be a function of how early the "system" became apparent. This may not be a serious weakness, but it seems well to point out that the tests do not seem to test the same function(s) for all individuals.

The present scoring system which uses pass or fail within the 4-minute time limit for each design appears to be too crude. Such an intrinsically fine instrument deserves a more discriminating scoring system if it is to achieve its maximum usefulness.

Tentative norms, in terms of CA (by whole-year steps) and number of designs passed, are available for Form I. There are no published norms for Form II.

[296]
Van Alstyne Picture Vocabulary Test for Preschool Children. Ages 3-4; 1929; 1 form; individual; out of print; (15) minutes; Dorothy Van Alstyne; Public School Publishing Co.

REFERENCES
1. VAN ALSTYNE, DOROTHY. *The Environment of Three-Year-Old Children: Factors Related to Intelligence and Vocabulary Tests.* Columbia University, Teachers College, Contributions to Education, No. 366. New York: Bureau of Publications, the College, 1929. Pp. 108. Out of print. (*PA* 4:386)

Ruth W. Washburn, Consultant in Child Development, Shady Hill School, Cambridge, Massachusetts. The publisher's catalog states: "This test is valuable not only for testing the vocabulary comprehension of normal children, but is also especially recommended as a substitute for a mental test with shy or negativistic children, or with those who have retarded speech development." For these purposes it has excellent features in that no oral response is necessary and the scoring is objective. The child either does or does not point to the correct picture, one of four, on each of forty-five cards presented serially.

The standardization of the test is, however, based on its use with a small group of eighty children whose age range was only seven months (33 to 39, inclusive), a group in which the average IQ was high (114). The cultural background of the children in the group was so similar as to make the test of improbable value for other cultural groups. For example,

Stencil Design Test

a word such as "chipmunk" is rarely known by children in urban communities.

The basis for the selection of the test words represented by pictures was good. On each card there is, first, at least one word of an equal level of frequency with the test word; second, at least one word associated with the test word in life situations such as "socks-shoes"; and third, at least one word with a sound similarity, of the first letter, with that of the test word. The drawing throughout the test is of very amateur quality. In some instances the drawing is so poor as to make failure to identify the picture understandable.

[297]
★Visual Retention Test for Clinical Use. Adults; 1946; individual; $2 per manual (no other materials are required); (4) minutes; Arthur L. Benton; Psychological Corporation.

REFERENCES
1. BENTON, ARTHUR L. "A Visual Retention Test for Clinical Use." *Arch Neurology & Psychiatry* 54:212-6 S '45. * (PA 20:2917)

J Consult Psychol 11:225 Jl-Ag '47. The Visual Retention Test is a clinical supplement to the more common auditory memory span test. Each of the alternative forms, A and B, consists of seven cards containing designs of increasing complexity. Administration, which requires only four minutes, follows the usual procedure of a memory-for-designs test, a ten-second exposure, and an untimed reproduction. Normative data are given for 160 adults, mostly men, and children's norms are in process of compilation. Data indicate a rough correspondence of scores with levels of intelligence. Clinical use with patients suffering from cerebral injury indicates the diagnostic value of the test in relation to aphasia, and also suggests implications similar to those of the Bender Gestalt test. The spiral-bound manual contains information on administration and interpretation, specimens for scoring, and the 14 plates for Forms A and B.

[298]
Wechsler-Bellevue Intelligence Scale. Ages 10-70; 1939-46; individual; postpaid prices; $1.10 per 25 record blanks for either form; David Wechsler; Psychological Corporation.
a) FORM I. 1939; $11.25 per set of materials including 25 record blanks; $2.60 per manual, *The Measurement of Intelligence*.
b) FORM II. 1946; $12.75 per set of testing materials including 25 record blanks and manual.

REFERENCES
1-2. See 40:1429.
3. BALINSKY, BENJAMIN. *An Analysis of the Mental Factors of Various Age Groups From Nine to Sixty.* Unpublished doctor's thesis, New York University, 1940. Pp. 44. (*Abstracts of Theses . . . [School of Education] 1940*, pp. 157-9.)
4. GILLILAND, A. R. "Differential Functional Loss in Certain Psychoses." Abstract. *Psychol B* 37:439 Jl '40. * (PA 14:5535, title only)
5. PRAGER, DANIEL. *The Performance of Adult Mental Patients on the Revised Stanford-Binet, Form L, and the Bellevue Adult Intelligence Scales.* Unpublished master's thesis, University of Iowa, 1940.
6. BALINSKY, BENJAMIN. "An Analysis of the Mental Factors of Various Age Groups From Nine to Sixty." *Genetic Psychol Monogr* 23:191-234 F '41. * (PA 15:3723)
7. BENTON, ARTHUR L., AND HOWELL, IRA L. "The Use of Psychological Tests in the Evaluation of Intellectual Function Following Head Injury: Report of a Case of Post-Traumatic Personality Disorder." *Psychosom Med* 3:138-51 Ap '41. * (PA 15:4206)
8. BENTON, ARTHUR L.; WEIDER, ARTHUR; AND BLAUVELT, JEAN. "Performances of Adult Patients on the Bellevue Intelligence Scales and the Revised Stanford-Binet." *Psychiatric Q* 15:802-6 O '41. * (PA 16:3821)
9. BROWN, J. F.; RAPAPORT, DAVID; TILLMAN, CARL-GUSTAF; AND DUBIN, S. SANFORD. "An Analysis of Scatter in a Test Battery Used in Clinical Diagnosis." Abstract. *Psychol B* 38:715 O '41. * (PA 16:781, title only)
10. GOLDFARB, WILLIAM. *An Investigation of Reaction Time in Older Adults and Its Relationship to Certain Observed Mental Test Patterns.* Columbia University, Teachers College, Contributions to Education, No. 831. Irving Lorge and Rudolf Pintner, faculty co-sponsors. New York: Bureau of Publications, the College, 1941. Pp. ix, 76. $1.60. * (PA 15:4615)
11. GOLDSTEIN, NATHAN N. "The I.Q. in Clinical Practice." *Delaware State Med J* 13:135-8 Je '41. *
12. MAGARET, GRETCHEN ANN. *Differences in Intellectual Functioning Among Normal, Paretic, and Schizophrenic Adults.* Unpublished doctor's thesis, Stanford University, 1941. (*Abstracts of Dissertations . . . 1940-41*, 1941, pp. 219-22.)
13. RABIN, ALBERT I. "Psychometric Patterns as an Aid in Differential Diagnosis (Schizophrenia vs. Manic Depressive)." Abstract. *Psychol B* 38:536 Jl '41. * (PA 15:5175, title only)
14. RABIN, ALBERT I. "Test-Score Patterns in Schizophrenia and Non-Psychotic States." *J Psychol* 12:91-100 Jl '41. * (PA 15:5174)
15. TRIST, E. L. "Short Tests of Low-Grade Intelligence, III." *Occupational Psychol* 15:120-32 Jl '41. * (PA 16:1721)
16. WECHSLER, DAVID. "The Effect of Alcohol on Mental Activity." *Q J Studies Alcohol* 2:479-85 D '41. * (PA 16:1554)
17. WECHSLER, DAVID. *The Measurement of Adult Intelligence, Second Edition.* Baltimore, Md.: Williams & Wilkins Co., 1941. Pp. xi, 248. * (London: Baillière, Tindall, and Cox.) (PA 16:1239) For latest edition, see (58) below.
18. WECHSLER, DAVID; ISRAEL, HYMAN; AND BALINSKY, BENJAMIN. "A Study of the Sub-Tests of the Bellevue Intelligence Scale in Borderline and Mental Defective Cases." *Am J Mental Def* 45:555-8 Ap '41. * (PA 15:4436)
19. WEIDER, ARTHUR. *A Comparative Study of the Performance of Psychopathic Adults on the Revised Stanford-Binet, Form L, and the Bellevue Intelligence Scale.* Unpublished master's thesis, Columbia University, 1941.
20. ANDERSON, EDWARD E.; ANDERSON, SARAH FERRALL; FERGUSON, CAROLINE; GRAY, JEAN; HITTINGER, JANE; MCKINSTRY, ELEANORE; MOTTER, MARY ELIZABETH; AND VICK, GALE. "Wilson College Studies in Psychology: I, A Comparison of the Wechsler-Bellevue, Revised Stanford, and American Council on Education Tests at the College Level." *J Psychol* 14:317-26 O '42. * (PA 17:981)
21. BROWN, RALPH R., AND PARTINGTON, J. EDWIN. "The Intelligence of the Narcotic Drug Addict." *J General Psychol* 26:175-9 Ja '42. * (PA 16:2265)
22. ESTES, STANLEY G. "A Study of Five Tests of 'Spatial' Ability." *J Psychol* 13:265-71 Ap '42. * (PA 16:3771)
23. HALPERN, FLORENCE. "A Comparison of the Revised Stanford L and the Bellevue Adult Intelligence Test as Clinical Instruments." *Psychiatric Q Sup* 16:206-11 '42. * (PA 20:3328)
24. HAYES, SAMUEL P. "Alternative Scales for the Mental Measurement of the Visually Handicapped." *Outlook for Blind* 36:225-30 O '42. * (PA 17:1749)
25. MAGARET, ANN. "Parallels in the Behavior of Schizophrenics, Paretics, and Pre-Senile Non-Psychotics." *J Abn & Social Psychol* 37:511-28 O '42. * (PA 17:865)
26. MAIZLISH, I. LEON. "A Comparison of the Stanford-Binet and Bellevue-Wechsler Scales for Adult Offenders." Abstract. *Psychol B* 39:472 Jl '42. * (PA 16:5045, title only)
27. MITCHELL, MILDRED B. "Performance of Mental Hospital Patients on the Wechsler-Bellevue and the Revised Stanford Binet, Form L." *J Ed Psychol* 33:538-44 O '42. * (PA 17:1604)
28. RABIN, A. I. "Differentiating Psychometric Patterns in Schizophrenia and Manic-Depressive Psychosis." *J Abn & Social Psychol* 37:270-2 Ap '42. * (PA 16:2697)
29. RABIN, A. I. "Wechsler-Bellevue Test Results in Senile and Arteriosclerotic Patients." Abstract. *Psychol B* 39:510 Jl '42. * (PA 16:5047, title only)
30. WEBB, BERNARD. "The Use of the Wechsler-Bellevue Intelligence Test in the Study of Mental Deterioration." Abstract. *Proc Iowa Acad Sci* 49:450-1 '42. * (PA 17:2756, title only)
31. YACORZYNSKI, G. K. "Degree of Effort: II, Quality of Work and Time of Completion of Performance Tests." *J Exp Psychol* 30:342-4 Ap '42. * (PA 16:2635)

32. ARMSTRONG, CLAIRETTE P. "Tests as Diagnostic Aids in Clinical Practice." *Am J Mental Def* 47:270-6 Ja '43. * (PA 17:3260)

33. GILLILAND, A. R.; WITTMAN, PHYLLIS; AND GOLDMAN, MEYER. "Patterns and Scatter of Mental Abilities in Various Psychoses." *J General Psychol* 29:251-60 O '43. * (PA 18:1540)

34. KNIGHT, ROBERT P.; GILL, MERTON; LOZOFF, MILTON; AND RAPAPORT, DAVID. "Comparison of Clinical Findings and Psychological Tests in Three Cases Bearing Upon Military Personnel Selection." *B Menninger Clinic* 7:114-28 My '43. * (PA 17:4241)

35. LEWINSKI, ROBERT J. "Intertest Variability of Subnormal Naval Recruits on the Bellevue Verbal Scale." *J Abn & Social Psychol* 38:540-4 O '43. * (PA 18:907)

36. LEWINSKI, ROBERT J. "Performances of Naval Recruits on the Kent Oral Emergency Test and the Verbal Battery of the Bellevue-Wechsler Adult Intelligence Scale." *Am J Orthopsychiatry* 13:138-40 Ja '43. * (PA 17:2209)

37. MACHOVER, SOLOMON. "Cultural and Racial Variations in Patterns of Intellect: Performance of White and Negro Criminals on the Bellevue Adult Intelligence Scale." Abstract. *Teach Col Rec* 45:52-4 O '43. * (PA 18:433, title only)

38. MACHOVER, SOLOMON. *Cultural and Racial Variations in Patterns of Intellect: Performance of Negro and White Criminals on the Bellevue Adult Intelligence Scale.* Columbia University, Teachers College, Contributions to Education, No. 875. Percival M. Symonds, faculty sponsor. New York: Bureau of Publications, the College, 1943. Pp. v, 91. $1.60. * (PA 17:2831)

39. MAGARET, ANN, AND WRIGHT, CLARE. "Limitations in the Use of Intelligence Test Performance to Detect Mental Disturbance." *J Appl Psychol* 27:387-98 O '43. * (PA 18:171)

40. RABIN, ALBERT I. "A Short Form of the Wechsler-Bellevue Test." *J Appl Psychol* 27:320-4 Ag '43. * (PA 18:320)

41. REICHARD, SUZANNE, AND RAPAPORT, DAVID. "The Role of Testing Concept Formation in Clinical Psychological Work." *B Menninger Clinic* 7:99-105 My '43. * (PA 17:4153)

42. REICHARD, SUZANNE, AND SCHAFER, ROY. "The Clinical Significance of the Scatter on the Bellevue Scale." *B Menninger Clinic* 7:93-8 My '43. * (PA 17:4285)

43. VAN VORST, ROBERT B. "An Evaluation of Test Performances of a Group of Psychopathic Delinquents." Abstract. *Psychol B* 40:583 O '43. * (PA 18:192, title only)

44. WEBB, WILSE BERNARD. *A Study of the Clinical Applications of the Wechsler-Bellevue Intelligence Test.* Unpublished master's thesis, University of Iowa, 1943.

45. WEIDER, ARTHUR; LEVI, JOSEPH; AND RISCH, FRANK. "Performances of Problem Children on the Wechsler-Bellevue Intelligence Scales and the Revised Stanford-Binet." *Psychiatric Q* 17:695-701 O '43. * (PA 18:624)

46. WRIGHT, C. *The Nature of the Decline of Performance Abilities in Adult Morons as Compared With That of Normal Adults.* Unpublished doctor's thesis. Stanford University. 1943.

47. CLEVELAND, SIDNEY E., AND DYSINGER, DON W. "Mental Deterioration in Senile Psychosis." *J Abn & Social Psychol* 39:368-72 Jl '44. * (PA 18:3743)

48. GOLDFARB, WILLIAM. "Adolescent Performance in the Wechsler-Bellevue Intelligence Scales and the Revised Stanford-Binet Examination, Form L." *J Ed Psychol* 35:503-7 N '44. * (PA 19:1058)

49. GREENWOOD, EDWARD D.; SNIDER, HERVON L.; AND SENTI, MILTON M. "Correlation Between the Wechsler Mental Ability Scale, Form B, and Kent Emergency Test (E-G-Y) Administered to Army Personnel." *Am J Orthopsychiatry* 14:171-3 Ja '44. * (PA 18:2984)

50. LEWINSKI, ROBERT J. "Discriminative Value of the Sub-Tests of the Bellevue Verbal Scale in the Examination of Naval Recruits." *J General Psychol* 31:95-9 Jl '44. * (PA 19:576)

51. MILTON, E. OHMER, JR. "A Difficulty Encountered When Comparing Drug Addict Scores on the Wechsler-Bellevue Scale With Norms of the Scale." *J General Psychol* 30:271-3 Ap '44. *

52. RABIN, ALBERT I. "Fluctuations in the Mental Level of Schizophrenic Patients." *Psychiatric Q* 18:78-91 Ja '44. * (PA 18:1730)

53. RABIN, ALBERT I. "Test Constancy and Variation in the Mentally Ill." *J General Psychol* 31:231-9 O '44. * (PA 19:579)

54. RAPAPORT, DAVID; WITH THE COLLABORATION OF ROY SCHAFER AND MERTON GILL. "The Bellevue Scale," pp. 28-121. In their *Manual of Diagnostic Psychological Testing: I. Diagnostic Testing of Intelligence and Concept Formation.* Preface by Karl Menninger. Review Series, Vol. 2, No. 2. New York: Josiah Macy, Jr. Foundation, 1944. Pp. xiii, 239. Paper, lithotyped. Out of print. * (PA 19:3105)

55. REYNELL, W. R. "A Psychometric Method of Determining Intellectual Loss Following Head Injury." *J Mental Sci* 90:710-9 Jl '44. * (PA 19:423)

56. SCHAFER, R., AND RAPAPORT, D. "The Scatter: In Diagnostic Intelligence Testing." *Char & Pers* 12:275-84 Je '44. * (PA 19:580)

57. STROTHER, C. R. "The Performance of Psychopaths on the Wechsler-Bellevue Test." *Proc Iowa Acad Sci* 51:397-400 '44. * (PA 20:2924)

58. WECHSLER, DAVID. *The Measurement of Adult Intelligence, Third Edition.* Baltimore, Md.: Williams & Wilkins Co., 1944. Pp. vii, 258. $3.50. * (PA 19:815)

59. ALTUS, WILLIAM D. "The Differential Validity and Difficulty of Subtests of the Wechsler Mental Ability Scale." *Psychol B* 42:238-49 Ap '45. * (PA 19:2388)

60. COHEN, BERTRAM. *Validity of the Short Form of the Wechsler-Bellevue on Four Psychiatric Groups.* Unpublished master's thesis, University of Iowa, 1945.

61. CUTTS, RICHARD A., AND SLOAN, WILLIAM. "Test Patterns of Adjusted Defectives on the Wechsler-Bellevue Test." *Am J Mental Def* 50:98-101 Jl '45. * (PA 20:1903)

62. FRANKLIN, JOSEPH CHARLES. "Discriminative Value and Patterns of the Wechsler-Bellevue Scale in the Examination of Delinquent Negro Boys." *Ed & Psychol Meas* 5:71-85 sp '45. * (PA 20:264)

63. GEIL, GEORGE A. "A Clinically Useful Abbreviated Wechsler-Bellevue Scale." *J Psychol* 20:101-8 Jl '45. * (PA 19:3518)

64. GOLDFARB, WILLIAM. "Note on a Revised Block Design Test as a Measure of Abstract Performance." *J Ed Psychol* 36:247-51 Ap '45. * (PA 19:2302)

65. GURVITZ, MILTON S. "An Alternate Short Form of the Wechsler-Bellevue Test." *Am J Orthopsychiatry* 15:727-32 O '45. * (PA 20:1276)

66. HALSTEAD, H., AND SLATER, PATRICK. "An Experiment in the Vocational Adjustment of Neurotic Patients." *J Mental Sci* 92:509-15 Jl '45. * (PA 21:281)

67. KUTASH, SAMUEL B. "A Comparison of the Wechsler-Bellevue and the Revised Stanford-Binet Scales for Adult Defective Delinquents." *Psychiatric Q* 19:677-85 O '45. * (PA 20:3330)

68. LEVI, JOSEPH; OPPENHEIM, SADI; AND WECHSLER, DAVID. "Clinical Use of the Mental Deterioration Index of the Bellevue-Wechsler Scale." *J Abn & Social Psychol* 40:405-7 O '45. * (PA 20:579)

69. LEWINSKI, ROBERT J. "The Psychometric Pattern: I, Anxiety Neurosis." *J Clin Psychol* 1:214-21 Jl '45. * (PA 19:3519)

70. LEWINSKI, ROBERT J. "The Psychometric Pattern: II, Migraine." *Psychiatric Q* 19:368-76 Jl '45. * (PA 19:3376)

71. MAYMAN, MARTIN. "Review of the Literature on 'Scatter,'" pp. 548-58. In *Diagnostic Psychological Testing: The Theory, Statistical Evaluation, and Diagnostic Application of a Battery of Tests,* Vol. I. David Rapaport with the collaboration of Merton Gill and Roy Schafer: Chicago, Ill.: Year Book Publishers, Inc., 1945. Pp. xi, 573. $6.50. * (PA 20:929)

72. PRICE, HELEN GERTRUDE. *The Interrelationship Among Wechsler-Bellevue I.Q.'s, Reading Achievement, and College Grades.* Unpublished master's thesis, University of Iowa, 1945.

73. RABIN, ALBERT I. "Psychometric Trends in Senility and Psychoses of the Senium." *J General Psychol* 32:149-62 Ja '45. * (PA 19:1708)

74. RABIN, ALBERT I. "The Use of the Wechsler-Bellevue Scales With Normal and Abnormal Persons." *Psychol B* 42:410-22 Jl '45. * (PA 20:344)

75. RAPAPORT, DAVID; WITH THE COLLABORATION OF MERTON GILL AND ROY SCHAFER. Chap. 2. "The Bellevue Scale," pp. 44-318, 394-5, 515-22. In their *Diagnostic Psychological Testing: The Theory, Statistical Evaluation, and Diagnostic Application of a Battery of Tests,* Vol. I. Chicago, Ill.: Year Book Publishers, Inc., 1945. Pp. xi, 573. $6.50. * (PA 20:929)

76. ROBERTS, A. DUDLEY. "Intelligence and Performance Test Patterns Among Older Mental Defectives." *Am J Mental Def* 49:300-3 Ja '45. * (PA 19:3386)

77. SLOAN, WILLIAM, AND CUTTS, RICHARD A. "Test Patterns of Defective Delinquents on the Wechsler-Bellevue Test." *Am J Mental Def* 50:95-7 Jl '45. * (PA 20:1944)

78. STEISEL, IRA MURRAY. *The Effect of Practice on the Various Sub-Tests of the Wechsler-Bellevue Intelligence Tests.* Unpublished master's thesis, University of Iowa, 1945.

79. WHITCOMB, MARIAN A. "A Comparison of Social and Intellectual Levels of 100 High-Grade Adult Mental Defectives." *Am J Mental Def* 50:257-62 O '45. * (PA 20:2850)

80. ALTUS, WILLIAM D. "The Comparative Validities of Two Tests of General Aptitude in an Army Special Training Center." *J Appl Psychol* 30:42-4 F '46. * (PA 20:2494)

81. ARMITAGE, STEWART G. *An Analysis of Certain Psychological Tests Used for the Evaluation of Brain Injury.* Psychological Monographs, Vol. 60, No. 1, Whole No. 277. Washington, D. C.: American Psychological Association, Inc., 1946. Pp. iii, 48. Paper. $1.25. *

82. BRECHER, SYLVIA. "The Value of Diagnostic Signs for Schizophrenia on the Wechsler-Bellevue Adult Intelligence Test." *Psychiatric Q Sup* 20:58-64 pt 1 '46. * (PA 21:1866)

83. CLARKE, HELEN JANE. "The Diagnosis of a Patient With Limited Capacity." *J Personality* 15:105-12 D '46. * (PA 21:3001)

84. CUMMINGS, S. B.; MACPHEE, H. M.; AND WRIGHT, H. F. "A Rapid Method of Estimating the IQ's of Subnormal White Adults." *J Psychol* 21:81-9 Ja '46. * (PA 20:1710)

85. ESTES, STANLEY G. "Deviations of Wechsler-Bellevue Subtest Scores From Vocabulary Level in Superior Adults." *J Abn & Social Psychol* 41:226-8 Ap '46. * (PA 20:3929)

86. GOLDMAN, ROSALINE; GREENBLATT, MILTON; AND COON, GAYLORD PALMER. "Use of the Bellevue-Wechsler Scale in Clinical Psychiatry: With Particular Reference to Cases With Brain Damage." *J Nerv & Mental Dis* 104:144-79 Ag '46. * (PA 21:471)

87. GREENBLATT, MILTON; GOLDMAN, ROSALINE; AND COON, GAYLORD P. "Clinical Implications of the Bellevue-Wechsler Test: With Particular Reference to Brain Damage Cases." Discussion by Frederick Wyatt, Kurt Goldstein, and others. Proceedings of the Boston Society of Psychiatry and Neurology.

J Nerv & Mental Dis 104:438-42 O '46. * (*PA* 21:307, title only)
88. GREENBLATT, MILTON; GOLDMAN, ROSALINE; AND COON, GAYLORD P. "Clinical Implications of the Bellevue-Wechsler Test, With Particular Reference to Cases of Injury to the Brain." Abstract. *Arch Neurol & Psychiatry* 56:714, discussion 714-7 D '46. * (*PA* 21:1467, title only)
89. KLEIN, GEORGE S. "The Differentiation of Schizophrenics and Normals on the Bellevue-Wechsler Intelligence Test by Means of a Multiple Correlation Technique." Abstract. *Am Psychol* 1:263-4 Jl '46. * (*PA* 20:3644, title only)
90. KOGAN, KATE LEVINE. "The Diagnosis of a Patient With Organic Defect." *J Personality* 15:113-20 D '46. * (*PA* 21:3025)
91. LATOURELLE, CURTIS WILBUR. *A Study of the Relationship of the Subtest Deviations on the Wechsler-Bellevue Intelligence Scale and Scores of the Minnesota Multiphasic Personality Inventory.* Unpublished master's thesis, University of Southern California, 1946.
92. LUCHINS, A. S. "On Certain Misuses of the Wechsler-Bellevue Scales." *J Consult Psychol* 10:109-11 Mr-Ap '46. * (*PA* 20:4380)
93. MAYMAN, MARTIN. "An Analysis of Scatter in Intelligence Test Results: A Review of the Literature." *Trans Kan Acad Sci* 48:429-44 Mr '46. * (*PA* 20:2923)
94. PATTERSON, C. H. "A Comparison of Various 'Short Forms' of the Wechsler-Bellevue Scale." *J Consult Psychol* 10:260-7 S-O '46. * (*PA* 21:1313)
95. PATTERSON, C. H. "The Wechsler-Bellevue Scale as an Aid in Psychiatric Diagnosis." *J Clin Psychol* 2:348-53 O '46. * (*PA* 21:1121)
96. RABIN, A. I.; DAVIS, J. C.; AND SANDERSON, M. H. "Item Difficulty of Some Wechsler-Bellevue Subtests." *J Appl Psychol* 30:493-500 O '46. * (*PA* 21:628)
97. RASHKIS, HAROLD A., AND WELSH, GEORGE S. "Detection of Anxiety by Use of the Wechsler Scale." *J Clin Psychol* 2:354-7 O '46. * (*PA* 21:1122)
98. SARTAIN, A. O. "A Comparison of the New Revised Stanford-Binet, the Bellevue Scale, and Certain Group Tests of Intelligence." *J Social Psychol* 23:237-9 My '46. * (*PA* 21:309)
99. SCHAFER, ROY. "The Expression of Personality and Maladjustment in Intelligence Test Results." *Ann N Y Acad Sci* 46:609-23, discussion 623 Jl 30 '46. * (*PA* 20:4913)
100. SCHMIDT, DAVID G. "Levels of Intelligence of Prison Inmates." *Am J Mental Def* 51:63-6 Jl '46. * (*PA* 21:561)
101. SPRINGER, N. NORTON. "A Short Form of the Wechsler-Bellevue Intelligence Test as Applied to Naval Personnel." *Am J Orthopsychiatry* 16:341-4 Ap '46. * (*PA* 20:3933)
102. STONE, CALVIN P. "Characteristic Losses and Gains in Scores on the Wechsler Memory Scales as Applied on Psychotic Patients Before, During, and After a Series of Electro-Convulsive Shocks." Abstract. *Am Psychol* 1:245 Jl '46. * (*PA* 20:3681, title only)
103. TAGIURI, RENATO. *Comparison of Results Obtained From the Wechsler Bellevue Vocabulary Test With Those From the Stanford-Binet Vocabulary, Using a Population of Normal Subjects and Mental Patients.* Unpublished master's thesis, McGill University, [1946?]. Abstract *B Can Psychol Assn* 6:101 O-D '46. * (*PA* 21:920, title only)
104. TEICHER, MORTON I., AND SINGER, ERWIN. "A Report on the Use of the Wechsler-Bellevue Scales in an Overseas General Hospital." *Am J Psychiatry* 103:91-3 Jl '46. * (*PA* 21:155)
105. WATSON, ROBERT I. "The Use of the Wechsler-Bellevue Scales: A Supplement." *Psychol B* 43:61-8 Ja '46. * (*PA* 20:2130)
106. WLADKOWSKY, EDITH. "Personality and Diagnostic Evaluation by Means of Non-Projective Techniques." Discussion by F. L. Wells and Roy Schafer. *Ann N Y Acad Sci* 46:625-32, discussion 638-40 Jl 30 '46. * (*PA* 20:4687)
107. AITA, J. A.; ARMITAGE, S. G.; REITAN, R. M.; AND RABINOVITZ, A. "The Use of Certain Psychological Tests in the Evaluation of Brain Injury." *J General Psychol* 37:24-44 Jl '47. *
108. ALEXANDER, FRANCES S.; CRUTEHLOW, EILEEN; AND HOFFMANN, MARY. "A Selective Survey of the Wechsler-Bellevue Section of Rapaport's *Diagnostic Psychological Testing*." *Can J Psychol* 1:111-5 S '47. * (*PA* 22:709)
109. ALLEN, ROBERT M. "The Test Performance of the Brain Injured." *J Clin Psychol* 3:225-30 Jl '47. * (*PA* 22:422)
110. BOEHM, ALICE E., AND SARASON, SEYMOUR B. "Does Wechsler's Formula Distinguish Intellectual Deterioration From Mental Deficiency?" *J Abn & Social Psychol* 42:356-8 Jl '47. * (*PA* 22:1272)
111. COLE, EDWIN M.; BAGGETT, MIRIAM P.; AND MACMULLEN, MARJORIE R. "Mental and Performance Testing of Neurologic Patients." Discussion by F. L. Wells. Abstract. *Arch Neurol & Psychiatry* 58:104-7 Jl '47. * (*PA* 22:1334, title only)
112. CUTTS, RICHARD A., AND LANE, MARGERY O'KELLEY. "The Effect of Hospitalization on Wechsler-Bellevue Subtest Scores by Mental Defectives." *Am J Mental Def* 51:391-3 Ja '47. * (*PA* 22:363)
113. DIAMOND, SOLOMON. "The Wechsler-Bellevue Intelligence Scales and Certain Vocational Aptitude Tests." *J Psychol* 24:279-82 O '47. * (*PA* 22:1264)
114. GARFIELD, SOL L. "A Note on Patterson's Article, 'The Wechsler-Bellevue Scale as an Aid in Psychiatric Diagnosis'." *J Clin Psychol* 3:198-200 Ap '47. * (*PA* 21:3119)
115. JOHNSON, ANNA P. "Measuring Mental Deterioration by the 'Differential Test Score Method'." *Am J Mental Def* 51:389-90 Ja '47. * (*PA* 22:426)
116. KRIEGMAN, GEORGE, AND HANSEN, FRANK W. "VIBS: A Short Form of the Wechsler-Bellevue Intelligence Scale." *J Clin Psychol* 3:209-16 Jl '47. * (*PA* 22:36)
117. MACPHEE, H. M.; WRIGHT, H. F.; AND CUMMINGS, S. B., JR. "The Performance of Mentally Subnormal Rural Southern Negroes on the Verbal Scale of the Bellevue Intelligence Examination." *J Social Psychol* 25:217-29 My '47. * (*PA* 22:1610)
118. MADONICK, M. J., AND SOLOMON, MARIAN. "The Wechsler-Bellevue Scale in Individuals Past Sixty." *Geriatrics* 2:34-40 Ja-F '47. * (*PA* 21:2297)
119. SAPPENFIELD, BERT R. "Rapid Method for Placement of Wechsler Object Assembly Pieces." *J Clin Psychol* 3:301 Jl '47. * (*PA* 22:204)
120. SLOAN, WILLIAM. "Validity of Wechsler's Deterioration Quotient in High Grade Mental Defectives." *J Clin Psychol* 3:287-8 Jl '47. * (*PA* 22:373)
121. WEBB, WILSE B. "A Note on the Rabin Ratio." *J Consult Psychol* 11:107-8 Mr-Ap '47. * (*PA* 21:3636)

Robert I. Watson, Associate Professor of Medical Psychology, Department of Neuropsychiatry, Washington University School of Medicine, St. Louis, Missouri. This individually administered point scale is particularly suitable for appraising selected verbal and performance abilities of adolescents and adults. Two forms are available, the second appearing in the early part of 1946. Since the first form is deservedly rather familiar, but the second not as well known, some attention will be devoted to a comparison of the two.

Both forms contain eleven subtests, all suitable and applicable throughout the age range covered by the scale. The six of these which Wechsler classifies as verbal tests are titled: general information, general comprehension, digit span forward and backward, arithmetic, similarities, and vocabulary. Originally it was assumed that the vocabulary test was unfair for illiterates and persons with a language handicap. Consequently, the normative tables for the derivation of a verbal IQ were designed on the assumption that five verbal tests, not six, would be used in many instances. Prorating is therefore necessary if one follows the current recommendation of Wechsler to administer all six verbal tests. The so-called performance scale includes picture arrangement, picture completion, block design, object assembly, and digit symbol. The sum of the weighted scores of this group of tests yields a performance IQ and, in combination with the weighted scores of the verbal group, makes possible the derivation of a full-scale IQ. All three IQ's are found for a given individual by point score entry into tables appropriate to the chronological age group within which he falls. This makes irrelevant any procedure calling for the intermediate step of the derivation of a mental age.

Personal experience in a military setting

demonstrated again and again a clinical validity superior, for example, to that demonstrated by the *Revised Stanford–Binet Scale*, which had a tendency to yield IQ's customarily interpreted as demonstrating mental deficiency in many individuals who could not be said clinically to be functioning at that level. The verbal material is couched in language suitable for the chronological ages and the culture of the individuals under consideration, with the exception of the picture arrangement subtest, which proved too sophisticated for the average recruit tested. It also appeared easier to prepare nonclinically trained psychologists to administer this device correctly and with acumen than was the case with certain measures involving the mental age approach.

The only information available in the literature, as yet, on the standardization of Form II as an alternate form appears in the introduction to the manual for this form. Essentially the only data supplied are to the effect that norms are based on 1,000 male adults, 18 to 40; that preliminary comparison shows a "high correlation" between the scales; that there is a mean difference of less than 2 points between the full scale scores; and that there is only a "small difference" in retest scores in the subtests, except that in Form II the comprehension subtest is "a little harder" and object assembly is "a little easier." There is no reason to doubt that this is a fair summary; nevertheless, an opportunity to examine the data on which these conclusions are based should be available.

The directions for Forms I and II are deceptively alike, but close scrutiny will show a considerable number of minor changes in wording. Most of these changes exhibit at least a greater surface clarity, but for the sake of these changes one must pay the price of learning two sets of directions differing so slightly and yet so pointedly that a certain amount of confusion and irritation inevitably results.

The Form II test material boxes revive the original Form I practice, later abandoned, of having the word "intelligence" prominently displayed on the cover with the consequent "mental paralysis" that overcomes some subjects when faced with this ominous word. The reason for this revival is not readily apparent.

In contrast to the measures using the mental age method of calculating IQ's, each Wechsler–Bellevue subtest yields at all levels of functioning a point score which is possible of conversion to a weighted score. Each weighted subtest score is a discrete measure capable of direct comparison with the scores for other subtests. This has made almost inevitable two prominent trends of research interest. There has appeared a plethora of abbreviated forms based upon the selection of three to six subtests, from the sum of the weighted scores of which an attempt would be made to derive a total score corresponding to that for the entire scale. Also, there has been considerable attention paid to the rationale or meaning of the mental abilities measured by the subtests and their relative standards of functioning either within an individual or a diagnostic grouping. A shorthand of sign patterns for various diagnostic groups derived from the absolute and relative magnitude of the weighted scores on the various subtests was an accompaniment of this latter trend. Wechsler himself has shown a commendable caution in regard to both trends, pointing out that the use of shorter forms depends upon the objectives of the examiner in using the test and that the diagnostic features are to be interpreted with careful attention to all other sources of data.

In the opinion of the reviewer, the *Wechsler–Bellevue Intelligence Scale* yields a more complete and valid picture of the intellectual functioning of an adolescent or adult than does any other single measure of intelligence. Only at the extremes, idiots and imbeciles on the one hand and very superior adults on the other, do other measures possibly make available a richer, more complete picture of the general functioning ability of the individual.

For review by F. L. Wells, see 40:1429. See also 299, 300, 301, and 40:B1121.

[299]
[*Re* Wechsler-Bellevue Intelligence Scale.] WECHSLER, DAVID. **The Measurement of Adult Intelligence.** Baltimore, Md.: Williams & Wilkins Co., 1939. Pp. ix, 229. * (London: Baillière, Tindall, and Cox.) (*PA* 13:5389) For latest edition, *see* 301.

Am J Psychol 54:154 Ja '41. Edward E. Cureton. * The tests appear to have been reasonably well selected, and the directions are clear. * Nearly all the cases used in standardizing the scale were obtained in and near New York City. The method of selection probably gives approximately correct *averages* at the various ages, but there is some evidence that the *variabilities* were not well controlled. As a result the interpretation of the IQ's is somewhat doubtful except where they are close to 100. On the other hand, adjustments for changes in average intelligence from 16 to 60 remove one major cause of error in previous scales. The work is marred by numerous statistical errors. In attempting to insert a theoretical foundation under what is obviously an empirical structure the author bogs down badly in factor theory. He confuses the standard error of the mean with the standard error of estimate (p. 135), proposes to measure the mental deterioration (with age) of individuals by a method that seems logical (p. 65) but ignores the fact that the tests would need to be much more reliable than any now in existence, computes coefficients of variation from scores based on an arbitrary zeropoint (p. 123), and assuming that standard scores are scaled scores, presents a skew distribution of IQ's (p. 129) which probably proves only that the tests possess inadequate numbers of hard items. Since the empirical work is apparently good and the scale fills a real need, it will probably be used widely during the next few years in spite of its technical shortcomings.

Ed Res B 20:238 N 12 '41. Emily L. Stogdill. * The book is one that will be included in any training program for psychologists especially those who plan to work with the older age groups. The chapter on "The Problem of Mental Deterioration" is a particularly significant one. The chapters on "The Nature of Intelligence" and on "The Need for an Adult Intelligence Scale" are of general interest also * should be known at least by name to all teachers interested in tests and personnel work *

J Abn & Social Psychol 35:598-9 O '40. Alfred L. Baldwin. * Not only does the book make a practical contribution by introducing an intelligence test designed for adults, but it makes a theoretical contribution as well. In his discussion of the nature of intelligence the author exposes implicit assumptions which, lying beneath current terminology, are misleading and inconvenient if not, indeed, theoretically incorrect. * Wechsler indicates that he wishes to define intelligence entirely in terms of a normal distribution of individuals of the same age as the individual being tested. * Although he may be quite correct in his preference for this definition of intelligence, his is not necessarily the only definition. Current procedure in standardization of tests is clearly based on other assumptions either explicitly or implicitly, and proponents might well find justification for expecting that the distribution of IQ's would spread with an increase in age. This difference in basic assumptions is not an adequate basis for a criticism of current test procedure unless there is some empirical demonstration of the superiority of the new definition. The import of the author's other criticisms, however, is independent of the answer to this question, and we are grateful that this important question in test methodology has been brought to the surface for discussion. *

J Higher Ed 12:499-500 D '41. Emily L. Stogdill. * an interesting combination of theoretical and practical considerations of the problem of intelligence testing, especially at the adult level. Everyone concerned with the education or the clinical treatment of adolescents and adults should be familiar with the book and the test. It will be an important reference book in the training of psychologists and social workers. The first two chapters deal with the theoretical considerations underlying the concept of intelligence, and its measurement in adult years. The need for a new test is clearly shown. The third chapter discusses the concept of mental age and the intelligence quotient. The statistical considerations involved in the problem are presented quite clearly. * the author forcefully expresses his position on the tendency of some medical men to relegate intelligence examinations to what he calls "apersonal psychometrics." * For many readers Chapter VI on the problem of mental deterioration will be the most significant. In the past, much that has been written on this topic was unscientific. Studies in the last decade are revealing that much that has passed as deterioration is actually not in this category at all. The whole field is newly re-opened for consideration; this book is a contribution to clarity of thinking in this area. * Chapter X on limitations and special merits of the scale will be of importance to persons using the scale, rather than to the general reader. * The Bellevue scale requires about an hour each to give and score. Its items are chosen with reference to the adults' vocabulary, which will make it more acceptable to them than the Binet tests which have been so widely used to determine the level of intelligence. The practice of using group tests of intelligence with young adults and college students, however, is well intrenched, and has the added advantage of greater speed in giving and scoring, and of widely standardized norms. For these reasons, it is probable that this test will have a somewhat restricted usage, particularly with groups which are already accustomed to the use of the older measure (Binet) or the group-test scores. It would seem rather evident that this test is destined to be an important one in the history of work with adults, and for this reason, the book is one which should be known to all adult educationists and clinical psychologists.

J Social Psychol 12:229–39 Ag '40. Charles L. Vaughn. * This work is extremely important and needs to be considered carefully because he has accumulated a mass of test data by individual examination of adults, and because he has constructed an intelligence scale which purports to do with adults what the *Stanford Revision of the Binet–Simon Intelligence Scales* has done with children. * Wechsler's most significant contribution to theoretical, and perhaps to applied, psychology is to be found in his chapter on the "Problem of Mental Deterioration," because it is in this chapter that he discusses the data from his study which bear upon the important topic "Variation of Scores on Different Tests with Age." * Because of the number and types of subjects and the variety of tests that he has used, Wechsler's study will stand as a landmark in this field. * presents some suggestive ideas about the measurement of mental deterioration, but because of the difficulties involved, Wechsler makes no definite commitments on this topic. * Wechsler's chapter on the "Nature of Intelligence" is perhaps his poorest. It is not an exceptionally lucid review of divergent standpoints on the subject; one gets the impression that he has attempted to reconcile the irreconcilable. * The norms are based upon examinations of 1751 adults and children in various occupational and educational groups of New York State, principally of New York City. Wechsler has apparently surmounted quite well the difficulty of obtaining adult subjects, so frequently mentioned by others. * Although the adult subjects were not selected on the basis of their educational attainment, the percentages of U. S. population and Bellevue adults in the respective educational categories agree rather well; there are, however, relatively more cases at the upper educational levels among the Bellevue group than in the total population. One would expect Bellevue *IQ*'s to be lower than they should be for this reason; but the error involved is probably not a large one. Holding age constant, Wechsler has attempted to represent each occupational group according to the percentages of total white population in each occupational category of the U. S. Census of 1930. However, because of the predominantly urban character of his population, it was necessary to substitute for the rural groups not available certain urban occupational groups which might have a mean intelligence rating of the same order. He took mean scores of the various occupational groups represented in the U. S. Army draft. "Thus we found that barbers, bakers and teamsters could be substituted for farmers, and that other missing occupational representatives could be similarly replaced" (p. 111). Though this procedure is an ingenious solution to a difficult problem, it raises the question as to whether his distribution represents that of the total population. This question cannot be answered until data are accumulated from other parts of the country. Another similar criticism is that most of the children used for standardization came from the public schools of the City of New York, Yonkers, and unspecified New Jersey cities; he did, however, obtain some subjects from institutions for the feebleminded. Wechsler insists upon using *IQ*'s, although I believe that theoretical and practical purposes would be as well served by other methods of expressing brightness. * There is a glaring omission of the distributions of scores by age groups from this book. Certain facts would indicate that his distributions are not normal. * Except for the omission of Vocabulary in the original scale and the inclusion of Object Assembly, the subtests are well chosen. * The seven primary abilities isolated by Thurstone (*number, visualizing, memory, word facility, verbal relations, perceptual speed,* and *induction*), as well as certain other abilities, are pretty well represented. *Word facility per se* does not appear to be as well represented as the others; the author realizes that he was mistaken in not including the Vocabulary Test in his original battery. Intertest correlations are substantial, but are low enough to indicate that different abilities are being measured by the subtests. Whether the author has selected the subtests

Wechsler-Bellevue Intelligence Scale

with the lowest possible intercorrelations and highest possible correlations with the criterion, is difficult to determine. Although it is desirable to select tests thus, one is confronted by a number of insurmountable practical problems in attempting to select tests in this manner; and probably no one has abided by the letter of this rule in test construction. Wechsler has used a crude item selection technique, but he does not present details of the work; and his criterion appears to be intelligence ratings from other tests. Regarding the correlations between the subtests and the total scale, Wechsler is not clear, for he gives two different impressions of his procedure. * Unfortunately, the author has given no differential weighting to the subtests even though they do not correlate equally well with the remaining tests. The reliability of the scale is fairly high, but still somewhat lower than that of the Stanford–Binet. * The correlation between two groups of four tests ($N = 355$, ages 20–34) was .90 when corrected. In discussing these procedures the author leaves an unfavorable impression by such misuse of terms as this: "When corrected for attenuation by the Spearman–Brown formula, the correlations . . ." (p. 126). Obviously he is using the Spearman–Brown correction for double-length and not the correction formula for attenuation. * Although the verbal and performance scales are not equivalent, there does seem to be a closer agreement between them than there is between other verbal and performance scales, and for this reason can be more readily substituted for each other when the need arises. * Wechsler is properly enthusiastic about the validity of the scales. * The correlation for 75 cases (ages 14-16) between Bellevue and Stanford–Binet IQ's is 82 ± .026. This correlation is fairly high, and shows that the two tests measure about the same thing. It does not tell how closely Binet and Bellevue IQ's correspond. * On the surface, at least, the Bellevue scale appears to be better for commitment purposes with adults than does the Stanford–Binet. In using the test we meet with the same major objection that Wechsler has; namely, Bellevue IQ's seem too high for older persons. This situation is most likely due to the fact that the Bellevue IQ takes into account the decline in test performance of persons after maturity. In connection with the validation of this test a question arises, which is raised by all tests of intelligence with which I am familiar. Instead of assembling a test upon the basis of some general, ill-defined conception of intelligence, going through an elaborate standardizing procedure, and then trying to find out what a test will do, why not first set up specific quantitative criteria, formulate questions which would seem to test intelligence, and then proceed to construct the scale by using the better item selection techniques, such as those of Horst? * Record sheets and test materials for the Bellevue Scales may be purchased from the Psychological Corporation. A most careless job has been done on the record sheets. In comparing them with the manual, one finds numerous reversals of items on the subtests and other errors, which, although of probably no great importance, are annoying when one uses the record form. Possibly unjustly, this situation casts a shadow on the whole test, causing one to wonder whether the buried details of the test construction work have been attended to as well as they should have been. The test materials on the other hand have been carefully designed. Materials for the *Object Assembly Test* are a definite improvement over those in the Pintner–Paterson *Performance Test*. The Picture Arrangement cards meet with much less resistance among adults than do those of the Cornell–Coxe *Performance Ability Scale*. This situation is partly due to the fact that the Cornell–Coxe is so difficult. The materials are relatively inexpensive, and the parts can be purchased separately in case of breakage. It would be well, however, if a manual with tables were forthcoming, as it is necessary to purchase the whole book in order to obtain the manual contained in one-third. Rather than attempt to elaborate in detail upon every item of the Bellevue tests, I have prepared a table which shows the extent to which Conrad's *desiderata* of a valid general intelligence test are satisfied by the Bellevue scales. Table 1 contains this information. In looking over this table, one is struck by the large number of criteria which are fulfilled by these scales in comparison with those doubtfully satisfied or not satisfied. However, some of the most important criteria either are not met or are doubtfully met by these scales. Variations in IQ's, for example, may merely represent inadequacies in the statistical procedures; the latter cannot be fully evaluated without certain data which Wechsler does not present. Adequate statistical procedures in themselves, on the other hand, do not insure a constant *IQ*. Much research will be needed before we can have some assurance that the Bellevue *IQ* is constant. For clinical purposes, the Bellevue Intelligence Scales will have certain limitations as well as merits. They require only about an hour to give and score, and adult subjects are more favorably inclined to their content than to that of tests designed for children. The test will probably not be as popular as the Stanford–Binet, however, for several reasons. The Binet is particularly useful for committing children to institutions for the feebleminded and for ability grouping in the public schools. The Bellevue tests are not likely to have extensive usage in the educational field, except perhaps in adult education. Group tests are much less time-consuming for college students, who fall in the age group for which the Bellevue tests were designed, and group tests of intelligence are probably not much less valuable than individual tests for personnel and guidance work among high school graduates. Use of the results in court work as evidence for commitment will not be as extensive as that of the Stanford–Binet results, primarily because there are fewer mentally defective adults than children who have not been committed, and because in many states it is quite difficult to get adults committed. Courts will undoubtedly prove reticent about accepting results from this test unsupported by other psychometric data, until it has had widespread application. In the meantime it would be well to present results from other tests in conjunction with those from the Bellevue Scales. Clinics which examine adults and older adolescents should have this test in their repertoire; and it should be a standard item for study in the graduate training program for clinical psychologists. Despite several questions about the test, principally about the constancy of the *IQ* obtained from it, the test appears to be the best individual adult intelligence examination on the market. It will prove to be a valuable supplement to the Stanford–Binet intelligence examination for adolescents and should eventually supersede it for adults. The performance scale appears to have been worked out better than most performance tests which are designed to measure general intelligence, but the fact that it has not been standardized on foreign language and Negro groups limits the test where it would be most useful. The book, *The Measurement of Adult Intelligence,* should prove useful as collateral material in teaching courses in intelligence testing, test construction, mental growth and decline, and abnormal psychology. The chapter on the "Problem of Mental Deterioration" cannot be overlooked in any study of mental growth and decline.

Psychiatric Q 15:593–4 Jl '41. * The first portion of this book is a lucid though cursory dissertation on the nature of intelligence with especial reference to its range, its aberrations, and its chronological changes in the adult. A discussion of this kind, augmented as it is by practical considerations, constitutes an excellent prologue to the second division of the book. * To the psychiatrist, the chapter on mental deterioration, another unsettled problem, will prove interesting. * The book is....no exhaustive treatise on intelligence but makes a good manual for administration of the test and subsequent interpretation of the scores. It merits recognition, and the scales should fill a definite need.

Psychoanalytic Q 11:111–2 Ja '42. Clinton P. McCord. * The chapters dealing with the nature of intelligence, the classification of intelligence and the concepts of mental age and mental deficiency constitute especially fine summaries of certain theoretical and practical considerations in clinical psychology which deserve to be better understood by psychiatrists who are too often handicapped because their training in psychology has been limited in both extent and character. In the last part of the book is given The Manual of the Bellevue Intelligence Tests....followed by a concise exposition of the special statistical methods which were used to treat the material and to make the necessary corrections in the process of standardization. This is followed by a series of carefully prepared tables of intelligence quotients for the various age levels and for both performance and verbal scales. The footnotes throughout are to the point and most illuminating. * At every point the author reveals that he is in touch with the work and accomplishments of other important investigators in this special field, and his evaluations exhibit a remarkable and refreshing degree of objectivity. Dr. Wechsler's book represents a piece of painstaking research, well tabulated, concisely reported, and with valuable practical implications for any psychiatrist whose training has afforded a certain degree of mastery of the techniques of clinical psychology. It should also be directly or indirectly useful to judges, juries, educators and lay executives.

For additional reviews, see 40:B1121.

[300]

★[*Re* Wechsler-Bellevue Intelligence Scale.] WECHSLER, DAVID. **The Measurement of Adult Intelligence, Second Edition.** Baltimore, Md.: Williams & Wilkins Co., 1941. Pp. xi, 248. * (London: Baillière, Tindall, and Cox.) (*PA* 16:1239) For latest edition, *see* 301.

Am J Orthopsychiatry 14:553 Jl '44. Henriette Woolf. * essentially the same as the original published in 1939, except for the addition of a chapter titled "Diagnostic and Clinical Features." In this the author formulates subtest patterns that are typical of the organic, the schizophrenic, the neurotic, the adolescent psychopath, and the mental defective. The material is based on clinical observation rather than extensive statistical validation. The method is not intended as a psychometric shortcut to psychiatric diagnosis but as a differential aid of value in proportion to the skill and experience of the examiner. There is a discussion of the personality patterns reflected by the various tests and illustrative cases are given. The preface comments on the changes in wording of some test questions and states that new examples have been added to the scoring directions for three tests. Detailed comparison of the two editions revealed six simple changes in directions and approximately the same number of scoring additions. The appendix now has tables of means and standard deviations for ages seven to forty-nine and a formula for calculating IQ's between the ages of sixty and eighty.

Am J Psychol 55:608–9 O '42. Anne Anastasi. * One may....question the wisdom of using the term IQ to refer to a ratio whose derivation is basically different from that of the traditional IQ. * Approximately the first third of the book contains a discussion of underlying theoretical problems involved in the construction of the scale, such as the nature of intelligence, mental decline and the problems encountered in adult testing, and the concept of mental deficiency. It is perhaps unfortunate that the reader should be introduced to the excellent piece of work which this book represents through the chapter on the nature of intelligence. In this chapter, for instance, the writer presents Spearman's two-factor theory as though it were the universally accepted theory of trait relationship, the reader receiving no hint of controversy or discrepant results in this connection. A number of statements in the chapter appear, furthermore, to be a combination of circular reasoning and wishful thinking. Thus Wechsler writes (p. 8), "but as regards the demonstration of the existence of 'g' as a common factor, there seems to be no possibility of doubt. Psychometrics, without it, loses its basic prop." (p. 8). Hypostatization is found in his contention that "we may say that 'g' is a psychomathematical quantity which measures the mind's capacity to do intellectual work" (p. 8). Wechsler's own bias towards a single general factor is illustrated further in the book, when he outlines the various possibilities for treating marked discrepancies between verbal and performance scores. The possibilities he presents are: to accept the verbal IQ; to accept the performance IQ; and to average the two—he ignores completely the fourth possibility of retaining both as two independent measures! In a pessimistic critique of test-validation, Wechsler writes, "teachers' judgments which were first condemned were now used as supporting criteria for the validity of tests" (p. 130). This involves a basic confusion between *follow-up judgments* based upon observation of behavior over a long period of time, which should serve as criterion ratings for test validation, and *judgments from first impressions,* which the tests are designed to replace. On page 27 Wechsler presents a graph which shows a definitely curvilinear relationship between standard scores on the Wechsler–Bellevue Scale and chronological age between 7 and 17. From such data he concludes that "any method of calculating IQ's which assumes a linear relationship between chronological age and mental age cannot possibly give constant values for any considerable portion of the growth period." This involves a confusion between original test-score and mental age. If mental age is determined in the customary way, *i.e.,* by the performance of the majority of subjects at each chronological age, then the relationship between mental age and chronological age must be linear, the mental-age unit automatically shrinking to adjust for the decreasing progress at the upper ages. In conclusion, it may be said that the chief merit of Wechsler's book is to be found in its presentation of a well-constructed and carefully standardized scale which represents a very valuable contribution to adult intelligence testing. The author's excursions into psychological and testing theory, on the other hand, are open to criticism at many points and frequently weaken, rather than strengthen, his discussion of the test.

J Assn Am Med Col 17:64 Ja '42.

J Consulting Psychol 7:167–8 My-Je '43. Irving Lorge. The second edition....is not materially changed from the first. The primary change is the inclusion of a chapter on the clinical factors of the Wechsler–Bellevue intelligence scales and their diagnostic application. * Wechsler undoubtedly has made a significant contribution to clinical practice in the organization of well-known tests into a composite scale. Clinically applied, the scale has considerable diagnostic as well as measurement value. The clinical usefulness of this test, of course, will depend on the examiner's familiarity with the test and with the meaning of the test scores from various populations. Basically, however, the point of origin is the basic philosophy of the test. Wechsler defines intelligence as "the aggregate or global capacity of the individual to act purposefully, to think rationally, to deal effectively with his environment." In this sense, *global* is intended to characterize the individual's behavior as a whole. * The first question that can be asked of the scales might be: Is the test measuring a unitary function? * In order to interpret Dr. Wechsler's contribution, an independent analysis of Dr. Balinsky's data was made, using the Hotelling component analysis. * In the age-9 group, the first factor accounts for approximately 44 per cent of the total variance; in the 12-year group, 41 per cent; in the 15-year group, 31 per cent; in the 25-29-year group, 27 per cent; in the 35-44-year group, 38 per cent and in the 50-59-year group, 50 per cent. These findings seem to corroborate those of Jones and Conrad that various sub-tests make differential contributions to the total score as a person grows older. It is particularly important to recognize that in some age groups only about one quarter of the total variance is accounted for in the first factor, whereas in the other age groups almost one half of the total variance is accounted for in the first factor. If intelligence is to be considered as a global whole, one would certainly expect that the relative contribution of a general factor such as *g* should make approximately the same contribution in all age groups. This, Wechsler's scale undoubtedly does not make. Since Dr. Wechsler implies that "Professor Spearman's generalized proof of the two-factor theory of human abilities constitutes one of the great discoveries of psychology," it should also be recognized that Dr. Wechsler's scale is not a two-factor scale by any means. It is a multi-factor scale, in which the factors are inconsistent from age group to age group. * Wechsler's scale not only is not a test, but also is not a test of consistent factors. Combinations of the various factors into a total test-scale must be very difficult to interpret, partly because we do not know the genetic variation in subtest scores nor the genetic variation in factor scores. The clinician, therefore, must interpret cautiously the implication of the test score in terms of the age of the person. Undoubtedly, Dr. Wechsler's scale raises once more the important question of content and form in intelligence scales. * Wechsler purposely mixes up measures of speed and of power. The mixture....raises the important problem of what it is that the scales are measuring. Are they measuring the ability to learn, the ability to adjust in the world or the efficiency of behavior? As a person grows older, reaction time declines, visual and auditory acuity decline. Such physiological and sensory changes, in combination with the psychological adoption of tempo may penalize older persons on speed tests. Insofar as they do penalize a person, the interpretation of an intelligence test score becomes complicated. Is the test measuring fundamentally physiological changes or an adopted tempo or is it measuring intellectual power to adjust to the world? Dr. Wechsler's test measures neither well. The number of factors derived at each age level suggests that he is measuring many different things simultaneously. This measurement of many different things simultaneously is not global intelligence, even though a single score may be used to represent a person's position. The test will reflect variation in educational opportunity. In tests of information, of arithmetic and even of comprehension, the environment and educational background of the person undoubtedly influence his test score. It seems, therefore, that a general appraisal of Dr. Wechsler's scale is that he has made a significant contribution in pooling the ten or eleven tests he has used, but that he has not yet solved the problem of measurement of adult intelligence either globally or differentially. It is unfortunate that the many contributions to the measurement of adult intelligence that have been made available since 1937 have not been incorporated into Dr. Wechsler's book. It is more unfortunate that some of the typographical errors in the first edition were not corrected in the second. Certainly the Williams and Wilkins Company are not to be congratulated on the second edition. The printing of tables, particularly, does not reflect favorably on a house whose printing is to be *"sans tache."*

J Higher Ed 13:396–7 O '42. J. Wayne Wrightstone. * timely and important * This is the best and most carefully constructed of the present scales for measuring adult intelligence. * Several sections of Mr. Wechsler's volume are of general interest and value. These include his discussions of the need for an adult-intelligence scale which recognizes that test performance varies with age, revision of concepts of mental age and intelligence quotient as applied to adults, concept of mental deficiency, and preliminary uses of the scale for diagnostic and clinical purposes. Certain biases or prejudices of the author are implicit, especially in his discussion of the nature of intelligence where he seems unduly to favor and present the theories of Spearman and Thorndike and to dismiss those of Thurstone, Kelley, and others. Certain shortcomings, also, should be mentioned. The norms, for example, should be accepted as tentative until checked by use among more unselected geographical and cultural groups than were originally used. The formula for predicting intelligence quotients for various age-groups needs to be checked and refined upon unselected samples. The diagnostic and clinical features need to be checked carefully and to be accepted critically by trained examiners until the validity of such diagnosis has been more fully demonstrated. This volume will be of particular interest to students of tests and measurements, to psychologists and psychiatrists in hospitals and correctional institutions for adults, and to clinical workers in colleges or in industries.

Occupational Psychol 16:92–4 Ap '42. B. D. Misselbrook. This important contribution to the literature of mental testing is still insufficiently known in this country. It has a dual claim to prominence.—First, on account of much original and valuable information and some very pertinent criticism contained in it; secondly, as probably the last of the scales. Wechsler has produced a work of compromise, and in so doing has indirectly shown the inadequacy of a scale. Something is offered to those who are interested in the battery as opposed to the scale, by the provision of separate verbal and performance I.Q.'s, and by the presence of tables giving the means and standard deviations for the sub-tests. In a short chapter on the clinical features of the scale, which appears in the second edition, patterns of performance are also considered. But the real estimate of the 'global capacity' intelligence is to be found in the I.Q.'s for the full scale. Wechsler accepts Spearman's demonstration of the existence of 'g,' but maintains that a test which endeavours to measure 'g' exclusively is a poor test of intelligence. Other 'salient factors' must be included, and by these he means principally the 'X' and 'Z' factors of W. P. Alexander. Reference is also made to the 'functional unities' of Alexander, but we are given no information on the factorial content of the sub-tests; this might have been of particular interest in the case of the performance tests. Psychologists who would be in agreement about the importance of the 'X' and 'Z' factors, and who, in fact, regard the performance at any test as the reaction of the total personality, will find little information about the nature of the clinical data to be obtained from the individual tests provided. Many of the tests, e.g. Comprehension, Similarities, Block Designs, do provide such data; but it is its analysis, and the construction of tests for the detailed study of aspects of a reaction, which are now most required. This is too large a project for one man or one book. The book contains important facts on the decline of mental efficiency with increasing age, and on those tests which 'hold up' with age and those which do not. The analysis of the meaning of the M.A. and the I.Q., particularly when used in assessing adult intelligence, is excellent. It can be recommended to psychiatrists. The Bellevue Scale I.Q.'s are calculated by a new and more valid method. It is, however, to be regretted that the term was not abandoned. Wechsler has not merely complained of the inadequacy of the existing material for clinical use with adults; he has given a lead by producing something else. Unfortunately it is a lead in the wrong direction. Although it may be useful to obtain English norms for certain of the sub-tests for immediate use, a standardization of the full scale is undesirable. The alternative is for psychologists working in the clinical field in this country to collaborate to produce an adequate battery.

Psychiatric Q 16:610 Jl '42. * The new edition has given the author an opportunity to add a chapter on the clinical features and diagnostic applications of the scale. In addition, other changes have been made in the text which add to clearness and ease of understanding on the part of the subject being tested. * presents, in a readable form, all that is worthwhile in both theoretical and practical aspects of mental deficiency. During the present generation, much advancement has been made in the study of this subject and interest is steadily developing. There is much yet to be done in this field and Wechsler does not hesitate to point out what is lacking in attempts which are being made in various directions for perfecting the art of intelligence testing in the case of the subnormal, the average and those more gifted children and adults who are often in need of guidance.

Psychiatry 5:454–6 Ag '42. Winifred Richmond. * Chapter Three is an excellent discussion of the concepts of mental age and the intelligence quotient * One's personality functions in everything that he does, and he may succeed or fail on tests not because he lacks learning ability or the capacity to comprehend, but because of traits or habits or temperamental qualities which help or hinder the function of his intelligence. The process of merely getting an I.Q. ignores this fact, and may do grave injustice to a child classified on that basis alone —as is still the practice in many places. The inclusion of performance tests in the Bellevue scale does something to remedy the situation, and gives the subject a chance at practical concrete situations as well as bringing out certain modes of behavior in attacking such tasks. In the chapter on "Diagnostic Features" the author discusses the use of his test in pathological cases. On the whole it is an excellent presentation and any psychologist at all capable of examining such cases ought not to be misled by the tables and illustrative cases into thinking it is easy to diagnose psychiatric conditions by means of 'signs.' But one feels that the author does not stress sufficiently the fact that psychoses occur at all levels of intelligence, down to the imbecile at least, and that the degree of intelligence possessed by the subject may influence an intelligence test as much as, or even more, than the type of mental disorder. Many cases, even of dementia præcox, can pass excellent intelligence tests, with little indication of abnormal functioning; and there are no tests of this type that will discover the non-institutional psychopath—and often enough the institutional one as well. Nothing is more revealing to the institution-trained psychologist than to be set to examining "normal" people. He finds all the peculiarities he has been accustomed to find in his pathological cases, if not in such number or such great degree, at least enough to show him that the tests are not yet specific for any particular mental state. They can offer leads, but are not yet refined enough for differential diagnosis. When the Manual of Instructions is reached, one will find that the poor placing of instructions, norms, criteria, and so on which made the first edition difficult to use has been remedied. One is obliged to turn pages here and there and turn back again in scoring and in interpreting. Something could be done in rearranging the individual tests on the blanks to make the order correspond to that in the book, but surely instructions for scoring should be gathered together in one place, and not scattered about throughout the test presentation or placed after the tables of weighted scores. Perhaps a word about experience with the Bellevue tests is in order. For normal people, nurses, attendants, and others who must be examined, they were found to be very useful, giving considerable information about the kind and degree of the subject's intelligence, and being less time-consuming than some other tests. For neurotics they are also useful, especially for the more intelligent. For psychotics, except the convalescents and those not very sick, they are not so useful. The verbal portion of the scale is overweighted with tests of abstraction, there are no memory tests except the repetition of digits, and the performance tests are fatiguing to many patients. Nor has it proved very reliable with patients of low intelligence; it rates them higher than, by other criteria, they are known to be. Nevertheless, one feels that the Wechsler-Bellevue test is on the right track. The fetish of the I.Q. is disposed of, the growth and decline of intelligence with age is taken into account, and the combination of verbal and performance tests in one scale is a time-saver for the busy psychologist.

Q R Biol 17:283 S '42.

[301]

★[*Re* Wechsler-Bellevue Intelligence Scale.] WECHSLER, DAVID. **The Measurement of Adult In-**

telligence, Third Edition. Baltimore, Md.: Williams & Wilkins Co., 1944. Pp. vii, 258. $2.50. * (PA 19:815)

Am J Psychol 58:420–2 Jl '45. *Quinn McNemar.* There is no evidence in this edition that the author has profited from the critical reviews of the first edition by Cureton (this JOURNAL, 54, 1941, 154) and of the second edition by Anastasi (*ibid.*, 55, 1942, 608–609). The present reviewer, who agrees with, and recommends to the reader, all the criticisms set forth by Cureton and by Anastasi, will confine his attention to the two main changes made in this third edition. These are concerned with a method of measuring mental deterioration and the use of 'signs' and interest variability in clinical work. It is proposed that mental deterioration can be measured on the basis of the difference between an individual's scores on four *Hold* subtests versus four *Don't Hold* (decline more with age) subtests, allowance being made for normal decline. The difference is expressed as a percentage, with the 'hold' score as a base or divisor, "in order to take into account the absolute magnitude" (p. 65) of the scores being compared. This false notion of 'absolute' leads to percentages varying as widely as 20 per cent to 80 per cent for deteriorations which would be judged equal on a standard-score basis. But this is not our major criticism. Suppose a 52-year-old with a 'hold' score of 36 (average for his age-group) has a 'don't hold' score of 22 (9 points below his age average). His deterioration would be 39 per cent, which becomes 25 per cent when allowance is made for normal decline with age. Does this really represent deterioration? If so, from what unknown earlier level of functioning? Straightforward consideration of the correlation (*circa* .74) between 'hold' and 'don't hold' scores, and their standard deviations (*Circa* 9.3), leads to the interesting fact that 7 per cent of normals with no deterioration whatever except normal decline would show as large a loss by merely maintaining their relative positions as of age 20. If a 52-year-old scored 36 on the 'hold' and 31 on the 'don't hold' tests, no loss other than normal decline would be inferred; *but* for all that the clinician can tell this 31 may have represented a 19-point loss, since the patient's score on the 'don't hold' tests could easily have been 50 at age 20, even though his score at that time was average on the 'hold' tests. Such are possible outcomes of Wechsler's differential-test-score method for measuring mental deterioration without knowledge of previous functioning. For clinical and diagnostic use, the author has elaborated a system of *signs* which depend upon an individual's intertest variability. When a subtest score deviates more than a specified number of points from the individual's mean subtest score, it is said to be 'significant.' The required amount of deviation varies with the magnitude of the total score which implies that the scattergrams for total score versus subtests are heteroscedastic. The same deviation is required for all ten subtests despite the fact that typically their correlations with total score range from the .50s into the .70s. Surely a deviation of 2 points for Object Assembly cannot possibly have the same significance as a 2-point deviation for Block Design (*r*'s of .409 and .714 respectively, ages 20–34). Furthermore, what is the real significance of, for example, a 2-point deviation accompanying total scores of 80-110? Since the standard deviation of the distribution for any subtest is approximately 3.00, it follows that the standard errors of estimate, or normal variations of subtest scores for a given total score, will range from 2.0 to 2.5. Thus a deviation as great as 2 points will occur 32 (or more) per cent of the time as a matter of normal variation, hence it seems gratuitous to claim 'significance' therefor. Wechsler next proposes to utilize certain of the 'significant' deviations as *signs* for use in clinical diagnosis. It is to be hoped that such usage can be objectively validated instead of being based on that vague thing called 'clinical experience,' which Wechsler (p. 157) crawls behind in discussing the well-controlled experiment of Magaret and Wright (*J. Appl. Psychol.*, 27, 1943, 387-398). The findings of these investigators concerning the lack of large intertest variability for schizophrenics is rejected because it is not in agreement with his 'own observations' and the 'clinical experience' of others. This discrepancy is attributed to the method used by Magaret and Wright for calculating intertest variability, which he properly—considering his misunderstanding of the method—argues should have been done differently. Then he proposes a method of calculating intertest variability which is the exact method they used, so he has unwittingly placed himself in the position of having to accept their findings, or else again take cover in the clinical foxhole.

J Am Med Assn 127:739 Mr 24 '45. One of

the most serious criticisms of earlier editions of this well-known and accepted battery of intelligence tests devised for adults rather than for children was that the tests given were not standardized on a sufficient number of persons. This situation has now been corrected to some extent, but the type of cases used leads to statistical misinterpretations. In addition there are some defects in the author's concepts of test formation, particularly the idea that there is such a thing as mental alertness that can be measured. Wechsler argues that his test is a good measure of intelligence because experience has shown it to be so, and the experience of the reviewer is that this is not an acceptable statement. In many instances the test results are too high when weighted against the psychiatric evaluation. The fact that the test is weighted for adults causes the author to make certain concessions which are not acceptable: the slightly deteriorated or elderly adult reacts higher than his actual mental function. Mental defectives are also rated higher than they would be on other tests, and most clinical psychiatric evaluations indicate that the Wechsler examination rates defective persons too high. The test procedure and the criteria for evaluating the answers are included in the book. For the skilled examiner who can select tests effectively to suit various problem individuals, the Wechsler test is a very satisfactory one. For general use the psychiatrist might well be cautious in accepting results obtained by any but the most highly trained clinical psychologist.

Personnel Adm 8:23 S '45. Irma Stark. * The Wechsler–Bellevue Scale has made psychological history. Since its first appearance, users of the Scale have recorded in volume and with enthusiasm its value as a clinical instrument. The literature, collectively reviewed, indicates that the Scale has accomplished for adult intelligence testing what the Binet has done in the field of child testing. In addition, it is the first such scale which provides a scientific basis for analyzing the behavior of an individual in terms of those elements which are characteristic of psychological disorders. Although the book is indispensable to clinical psychologists, psychiatrists, teachers of psychology and psychiatric social workers, it has value too for those personnel workers engaged either in test construction, test administration, or individual placement and rehabilitation. * Although the Wechsler–Bellevue Intelligence Scales will undoubtedly have most usefulness in those agencies where individual diagnosis and treatment are the primary concern, such as in Veterans' Facilities, there is much in the book, in the excellent introductory section, in the careful discussion of the standardizing techniques and in the test items themselves that can offer leads for more scientific personnel administration and merit examination test construction.

Psychol B 42:186–7 Mr '45. Ann Magaret. * Chapter 6 outlines a method for determining quantitatively....the degree of a subject's mental deterioration. Based on the assumption that abilities which do not decline with age in normal subjects are those least affected by deteriorative processes in psychosis, the method involves comparing a subject's mean score on the tests which hold up with age with his mean score on tests which do not hold up with age. * Whether the assumption that deterioration in psychiatric disorders follows that in senility is justified can be determined only through the application of Wechsler's technique to psychotic groups and comparison of clinical with psychometric findings. With the exception of one case study, however, no test of this assumption is reported. Chapter 11, Diagnostic and Clinical Features, summarizes the author's impressions concerning the significance of a patient's relative performance on single subtests of the scale in the differential diagnosis of neurosis, organic brain disease, schizophrenia, psychopathy, and mental deficiency. * Tables are given showing patterns of subtest scores for various clinical syndromes. The reader is told what constitutes a significant variation from subtest to subtest, and is provided with "rules of thumb" for determining diagnostically important variations, but evidence for the validity of such rules is not reported. Despite the facts outlined in Chapter 6, age is apparently not considered in this method of diagnosis. The validity of differential diagnosis must depend upon demonstration of correspondence between inter-test variations and particular psychiatric disorders, preferably with large groups of carefully diagnosed patients, age controlled. No such analysis is presented by the author, who depends rather upon informal clinical experience in correlating pattern with syndrome. A cursory inspection of recent research on the use of the scale in diagnosis (as listed in Wechsler's bibliography) reveals that the impressionistic data found in the author's diagnostic tables are occasionally at variance with reported research results. Despite this fact, and despite Wechsler's own statement that "the data . . . are not intended, nor can they be used as psychometric shortcuts to psychiatric diagnosis" (158), there are general statements throughout this chapter which strongly tempt the hurried psychometrician to succumb to such short cuts. For example, "The correlations are sufficiently high to be of value in vocational guidance . . ." (146); "The inconsistency here is what definitely shows this case to be schizophrenic" (163). * A convenient method of obtaining IQ's for subjects between the ages of 60 and 80 is offered. * Psychological examiners may regret the continued absence of precise statements of subtest reliabilities, and of indications of practice effects, and will recognize the repetition of minor awkwardnesses of instructions. The thesis of the major revisions, it seems to the reviewer is that an examiner administering the Wechsler–Bellevue Scale to a single patient may obtain considerable information besides a measurement of general intelligence. Clinicians would agree that this is true of any standardized situation in which a patient is observed. In a scale which finds as wide application as the Wechsler–Bellevue, however, it seems essential that those cues which the examiner uses in assaying the patient be made explicit through the reporting of exact research results wherever possible. Unless this is done systematically by the authors and users of standard scales, the diagnosis of mental deterioration or psychiatric disorder from intelligence test results will remain inspired guesswork.

Q R Biol 20:106–7 Mr '45. C. Hart Westbrook. * One outstanding value of the Bellevue Scale is that it enables clinicians to measure and score separately by the Verbal and the Performance Scales the two distinct groups of abilities or capacities, verbal and performance, which in some other widely used tests are measured by single scale and indicated by a composite score. * Another value of the book is that the extension of the Scale to mental levels higher than those measured by any other but Thorndike's CAVD Scales makes possible the mental measurement of persons up to the age of 60 years, and by a process of extrapolation, "without serious error by the use of some simple multipliers which take care of the age factor," of those between 60 and 80 years. * Wechsler has completely revised the table of "signs" for different clinical entities revealed by the tests and has elaborated a new quantitative method for the determination of mental deterioration. These changes will render the book much more valuable to the clinician, both for his own records and in his interpretation of the results for the guidance of other members of the clinic in their final diagnosis and in treatment and disposition of difficult cases. Alterations in the scoring of certain subtests and in the use of scores of subtests for further analysis of the mental deterioration or improvement of the subject constitute another improvement in the Scale. * Chapter 11, on Diagnostic and Clinical Features, should be especially valuable, as it contains tables of test characteristics of the clinical groups, followed by comments on the groups and illustrative cases, each accompanied by a tabulation of the scores made on the subtests of both Verbal and Performance scales and the respective I.Q.'s. * In view of the well-adapted materials used and the evidences of standardization, validity, and reliability presented by the author, it seems that the new edition of the Bellevue Scale should prove to be highly reliable and valid for general use as well as for the special use intended with returning soldiers in the problems of their rehabilitation.

[302]

★**Wechsler Memory Scale.** Adults; 1945; individual; Forms 1, 2; $1.75 per 50 record forms, postpaid; 50¢ per manual, postpaid; 60¢ per specimen set, postpaid; David Wechsler; Psychological Corporation.

REFERENCES

1. WECHSLER, DAVID. "A Standardized Memory Scale for Clinical Use." *J Psychol* 19:87-95 Ja '45. * (*PA* 19:1186)
2. STONE, CALVIN P.; GIRDNER, JOHN; AND ALBRECHT, RUTH. "An Alternate Form of the Wechsler Memory Scale." *J Psychol* 22:199-206 O '46. * (*PA* 21:919)
3. STONE, CALVIN P. "Losses and Gains in Cognitive Functions as Related to Electro-Convulsive Shocks." *J Abn & Social Psychol* 42:206-14 Ap '47. * (*PA* 21:2938)

Kate Levine Kogan, Clinical Psychologist, 154 Chesterfield Road, Pittsburgh 13, Pennsylvania. This simple, concise measure of memory function has already proved to be a valuable addition to the available clinical techniques. Administration time is brief, directions are clear, and scoring criteria are objective. Perhaps its most important use is in conjunction with the Wechsler-Bellevue intelligence scale, since the memory quotient is designed to be directly comparable to the intelligence quotient. Use of the test permits intra-individual comparison of the patient's memory impairment with his loss in other intellectual functions rather than only a comparison with a general average or norm. Thus, it is possible to distinguish accurately between the kind of memory impairment which is merely one aspect of generalized mental inefficiency and that which represents a specific decrement in memory function. Certain other measures have had a somewhat similar goal. The *Hunt–Minnesota Test for Organic Brain Damage,* for example, is based on the relation between vocabulary level and scores on two types of immediate memory tasks. However, since vocabulary level is commonly accepted as being a better indication of native endowment prior to the onset of illness than it is a measure of functioning level, a different picture is obtained. The *Wechsler Memory Scale,* in conjunction with the intelligence scale, allows for a broader analysis of specific mental interference at the time of examination. Furthermore, allowance is made for memory variations with age.

The test material is sufficiently varied to provide qualitative observations which may have additional value. One can distinguish, for example, cases in which remote memory, data of personal identification, and extremely familiar, well-learned patterns are retained in contrast to faulty performance with the formation of new learning associations; such findings often provide confirmatory evidence of disturbances of attention and concentration. One can compare retention of meaningful material and rote memory. Finally, one can isolate specific disturbance in the area of space-form perception and visual memory. These features make the test findings especially helpful in problems involving differential diagnosis.

The test was designed for use with adults only, and the scoring involves the addition of certain constants to the raw score in order to equate scores at different age levels above twenty years. The test author has stated in a personal communication to the writer several years ago that the test might prove to be useful with adolescents by employing the same age-correction unit established for the 20- to 24-year group. This has not been subjected to experimental verification, but the practice has seemed to yield meaningful and consistent results with adolescents.

Because of its advantages over other similar techniques, this scale is appropriate to a wide variety of research studies. However, the lack of an alternate or parallel form has been felt, especially for those experimental designs which require a "test-retest" method. One group of investigators has recently proposed an alternate form which was designed to provide equivalent material for each of the test items (2). This has been published so recently that there has not been sufficient time for widespread use. However, if it proves to be an accurately equated alternate form it will extend the sphere of usefulness of the Wechsler Memory Scale even further.

REPRINTED FROM *The Fourth Mental Measurements Yearbook*

INTELLIGENCE—FOURTH MMY

REVIEWS BY *Murray Aborn, William D. Altus, James M. Anderson, Gwen F. Arnold, Benjamin Balinsky, Charlotte Banks, George K. Bennett, Robert G. Bernreuter, E. J. G. Bradford, W. D. Commins, William M. Cruickshank, Edward E. Cureton, John T. Dailey, Frederick B. Davis, Harold A. Delp, Robert G. Demaree, Jerome E. Doppelt, Raleigh M. Drake, Walter N. Durost, W. G. Emmett, George A. Ferguson, John C. Flanagan, H. M. Fowler, Henry E. Garrett, William R. Grove, J. P. Guilford, Alice W. Heim, Edwin R. Henry, Carl I. Hovland, Gertrude Keir, William S. Kogan, Jane Loevinger, C. M. Louttit, Boyd R. McCandless, Louis L. McQuitty, Herschel T. Manuel, James Maxwell, Ivan Norman Mensh, Joseph Newman, Stanley D. Nisbet, E. A. Peel, M. L. Kellmer Pringle, Willis C. Schaefer, William Schofield, F. J. Schonell, William B. Schrader, Gladys C. Schwesinger, Harold G. Seashore, David Segel, Naomi Stewart, Charles A. Stickland, Erwin K. Taylor, Mildred C. Templin, David V. Tiedeman, W. D. Wall, F. W. Warburton, George Westby, and Dael Wolfle.*

GROUP

[267]

★**A.C.E.R. Adult Test (B40).** Ages 13 and over; 1940; 1 form; no data on reliability and validity; no description of normative population; 2s. 9d. per 10; 6d. per manual; 1s. per specimen set; cash orders postpaid within Australia; 55(65) minutes; Australian Council for Educational Research. *

REFERENCES

1. COOK, P. H. "Criteria for the Selection of Personnel Officers." *B Ind Psychol & Personnel Prac* 2:28–37 Je '46. * (*PA* 20:4761)
2. HOHNE, H. H. "The Prediction of Academic Success." *Austral J Psychol* 1:38–42 Je '49. *

[268]

★**A.C.E.R. General Ability Test: Advanced M.** Ages 13 and over; 1948; 3 scores: linguistic, quantitative, total; 2 parts; 1 form; no data on reliability and validity; no description of normative population; 2s. 4d. per 10 of any one part; 6d. per set of scoring keys; 6d. per manual; 1s. 6d. per specimen set; cash orders postpaid within Australia; Australian Council for Educational Research. *

a) SECTION L. 1 score: linguistic; 15(25) minutes.
b) SECTION Q. 1 score: quantitative; 20(30) minutes.

[269]

★**A.C.E.R. General Test A.** Ages 10–14; 1938; 1 form ['38]; no data on reliability and validity; no description of normative population; mimeographed manual ['38]; 2s. 6d. per 10; 3d. per key; 6d. per manual; 1s. per specimen set; cash orders postpaid within Australia; 30(40) minutes; Australian Council for Educational Research. *

For related reviews, see 3:1110 and 40:B1005.

[270]

★**A.C.E.R. General Test C.** Ages 10–14; 1939; 1 form ['39]; no data on reliability and validity; no description of normative population; mimeographed manual ['39]; 2s. 6d. per 10; 3d. per key; 6d. per manual; 1s. per specimen set; cash orders postpaid within Australia; 35(45) minutes; Australian Council for Educational Research. *

[271]

★**A.C.E.R. Junior A.** Ages 9–11; 1946; 1 form; no data on reliability and validity; no description of normative population; 4s. per 10; 6d. per key; 6d. per manual; 1s. 5d. per specimen set; cash orders postpaid within Australia; 30(40) minutes; Australian Council for Educational Research. *

[272]
A.C.E.R. Non-Verbal Test. Ages 10–14; 1936; 1 form; manual ['36]; 3s. 9d. per 10; 6d. per set of keys; 2s. per manual; 2s. 10d. per specimen set; cash orders postpaid within Australia; 24(40–45) minutes; Australian Council for Educational Research. *

REFERENCES
1. McINTYRE, G. A. *The Standardization of Intelligence Tests in Australia.* Australian Council for Educational Research, Educational Research Series, No. 54. Melbourne, Australia: Melbourne University Press, 1938. Pp. 82. Paper. (London: Oxford University Press, 1939.) (New York: G. E. Stechert & Co.)
2. REDMOND, MARY, AND DAVIES, F. R. J. *The Standardization of Two Intelligence Tests.* New Zealand Council for Educational Research, Educational Research Series, No. 14. Wellington, New Zealand: Whitcombe & Tombs Ltd., 1940. Pp. xv, 129. (London: Oxford University Press, 1941.) (*PA* 15:2841)

F. J. SCHONELL, *Professor of Education and Head of the Department, University of Queensland, St. Lucia, Brisbane, Queensland.*

This is a nonverbal test, suitable for children between the ages of 10 and 14, a group for whom a suitable nonverbal group test is very badly needed. The test consists of four subtests—similarities, geometrical relations, analogies, and time sequence—with a total of only 56 items.

Validity coefficients of the test were derived from correlations with the *Stanford-Binet Scale* (.63), with the *Otis Self-Administering Test of Mental Ability* (.74), and with the Tasmanian Education Department's *General Ability Test* (.68). None of these validity coefficients is really sufficiently high to give users very great confidence in the test. Although research has shown that the specific verbal factors in verbal group tests and the specific spatial factor in nonverbal tests tend to reduce the size of correlation coefficients between the two types of test, if both types of test purport to give an indication of general intellectual ability we are justified in expecting higher validity coefficients.

It may well be that validity has been reduced by having only four subtests covering 56 items, and it would be interesting to see what validity coefficient would result from an expansion to subtests covering 100 items. Reliability on a split half method using the Spearman-Brown prophecy formula gave a correlation of .85.

The test has been exceptionally well standardised, and most effective statistical analysis has been done to provide users with effective interpretative instruments. The only point I would make here relates to the corrections—of somewhat doubtful value and validity I feel—that have been worked out for children in three types of schools somewhat arbitrarily divided into A-class schools with over 200 pupils, B-class with 50 to 200, and C-class with under 50 pupils. One would have thought that each child should be assessed in comparison with members of his own age or grade group irrespective of school, even although there may be evidence of different levels in schools of different size or type. The test is excellently provided with good, clear drawings, an important element in nonverbal tests.

There are interesting interstate norms and comparisons between city and country children, the latter bearing out the now generally accepted difference between city and rural school children; in this case city children are superior by roughly four points of IQ.

In general, this test has such excellent possibilities that one would like to see it extended to 100 items with a possible improvement in validity so that schools and research departments would then have at their disposal a most valuable measuring instrument.

[273]
★**A.C.E.R. Test L.** Ages 13 and over; 1943; 1 form; a practice exercise must precede administration of test; no data on reliability and validity; no description of normative population; 3s. 6d. per 10; 6d. per manual; 11d. per specimen set; cash orders postpaid within Australia; 50(70) minutes; Australian Council for Educational Research. *

[274]
Academic Aptitude Test: Non-Verbal Intelligence: Acorn National Aptitude Tests. Grades 7–16 and adults; 1943–44; 4 scores: spatial relations, physical relations, graphic relations, total; 1 form, '44; no norms for part scores; $2.75 per 25; 25¢ per manual ('44); 50¢ per specimen set; postage extra; 26(45) minutes; Andrew Kobal, J. Wayne Wrightstone, and Karl R. Kunze; Acorn Publishing Co. *

WILLIAM B. SCHRADER, *Assistant Director, Department of Statistical Analysis, Educational Testing Service, Princeton, New Jersey.*

This 57-item test is designed to provide part scores for physical, spatial, and graphic relations as well as a total score for "non-verbal intelligence." Each part seems too short to have satisfactory reliability; the pictorial test of physical relations, in particular, includes only 17 items, 8 of which offer only two choices. No statement about guessing is provided in the instructions. If, as is likely, the parts of the test differ in factorial composition, the total score is difficult to interpret without evidence on the relative contribution of each part.

In spite of its brevity, this test may prove useful in supplementing other information about a person. Such usefulness would depend on validation of a much wider scope than the two studies of validity cited in the manual. In the first study, it was found that in grades 7–9 "slow" sections did less well on the test than students in "normal" sections. In the second study, it was found that professionals engaged in engineering, architecture, and designing did somewhat better than professionals in social science fields. No evidence that sex or age was considered in the latter study is given, though both might well be important in this type of test.

The items published were selected from a larger group on the basis of test-retest comparisons. Half of the professional-technical norm group made four or fewer errors, and one fifth of the group made no errors; this provides some indirect evidence that the items are not ambiguous or defective.

Total score norms based on a total of 4,109 pupils are provided for grades 7 through 12; separate norms for boys and girls are not provided. The gain in test score for grades 8 through 11 amounts to about four raw score points.

The sections on interpretation and use go considerably beyond available evidence in interpreting test performance. In particular, the statement that a score at or below the 30th percentile "should disqualify a student for technical work" is surely unwarranted without an extensive study of validity. The manual discusses the prediction of success in engineering but does not mention the evidence, long available from the studies of Thorndike and Thurstone, that mathematical ability is of outstanding value in predicting success in engineering school. Instead, much stress is placed on "ambition," "diligence," and the nonverbal test score.

The authors of this test have made a contribution by developing and publishing a brief test embracing the following potentially useful item types: figure analogies, size estimation, pictorial physical relations, and paper formboard. Until further validation data are made available, the test is likely to be useful primarily to persons equipped to make their own validation studies. If used cautiously, however, this test may be useful in counseling and selection as a supplement to other information.

[275]
*Academic Aptitude Test: Verbal Intelligence: Acorn National Aptitude Tests.** Grades 7–16 and adults; 1943–50; 4 scores: general information, mental alertness, comprehension of relations, total; 1 form, '50 —same as test copyrighted in 1943 except for slight changes; $2.50 per 25; 15¢ per manual ('45); 50¢ per specimen set; postage extra; 40(45) minutes; Andrew Kobal, J. Wayne Wrightstone, and Karl R. Kunze; Acorn Publishing Co. *

WILLIAM B. SCHRADER, *Assistant Director, Department of Statistical Analysis, Educational Testing Service, Princeton, New Jersey.*

According to the authors, this test is primarily useful for estimating academic promise of secondary school and first year college students and for predicting success in business positions which require "a high degree of mental alertness and ability to handle complex situations intelligently." The authors envisage a broader range of possible usefulness: normative data are given for each of the four years of college, for administrative and executive employees, and for professionals.

The test is printed in distinctive (Gothic) type. Except that the letter "j" looks a bit odd in this type when used to designate an answer option, the material is quite legible. However, the possibilities of print and layout to aid the test administrator are not well utilized. Thus, some of the "sections," which are not separately timed, are headed in the same type as "tests," which are separately timed. Test III (separately timed) does not begin on a new page. Printed instructions to keep the students going at the end of a page or section are not used. No statement about guessing appears in the printed (or oral) instructions.

The manual makes it clear that considerable work was done in developing the test. The 140 items in the final test were selected from a total of 1,050 items on the basis of "discriminative power." A reliability coefficient of .97 was obtained by one of the Kuder-Richardson formulas. The size and grade range of the group are not reported, and no mention is made of the possibility that the reliability coefficient may have been increased by the speededness of the test. A validity coefficient of .82, using IQ's on various tests as a criterion, is reported for a group of students in grades 9–12. A validity study based on "employees in administrative and executive positions" yielded a coefficient of .59 with "overall employment rating." A clear description of the employee groups and of the criterion measures used would make the results more useful.

The section on interpretation of scores is distinctly below the standard set by the rest of the manual; in this section the problem of using the test scores in guidance is seriously oversimplified.

Much stress is laid on the three part scores of Information, Mental Alertness, and Comprehension of Relations. Separate norms are given for each part for grades 9–12, but no intercorrelations are reported. It seems likely that these three parts are too highly similar in the abilities measured to have much differential value. (The fact that the 10th to 90th percentile range of the total score agrees quite closely with the sum of the 10th to 90th percentile ranges of the part scores also indicates high intercorrelations of parts.)

The reported norms give the deciles and the 1st and 99th percentiles. For grades 7–12, norms for each grade were based on at least 500 students in both city and rural high schools in several states. The groups for the other norms given are less clearly defined. If the norm group for college students is reasonably typical, the test is too easy to be efficient for use with college students. The 1st percentile for first year college students corresponds to a score of 78 of a possible 140. For professionals, the 1st percentile is at 101 and the 80th percentile is at 140. However, a reasonably good spread of performance is shown by the "executive and administrative employees," especially for the lower half of the distribution.

This test is based upon a substantial amount of test development. It seems to be best adapted for use in high school (especially junior high school) and for selection in business positions requiring high school training.

For a review by Marion A. Bills, see 3:215.

[276]
★**Akron Classification Test.** Grades 11–16 and adults; 1950; 1 form; $4 per 50; 35¢ per specimen set; postpaid; nontimed (10–45) minutes; Robert W. Henderson and Francis J. Werner; Robert W. Henderson, 940 Eighth St., N.E., Massillon, Ohio. *

ERWIN K. TAYLOR, *Director, Personnel Research Institute, Western Reserve University, Cleveland, Ohio.*

This test claims to be a measure of "scholastic aptitude." It was constructed on the basis of an item analysis sample of 120 college students and against an internal criterion. Evidence for its validity is limited to its correlation with other tests. Samples in all instances are grossly inadequate. Three sets of norms are presented in the manual: "general population" norms based on 53 cases, the college norms on 180 upper classmen, and "non-college" norms on 76 cases.

In the opinion of this reviewer, this test is faulty in its construction; its standardization is grossly inadequate and its validation non extant. We can imagine no set of circumstances under which its use could possibly be justified.

[277]
★**American Council on Education Psychological Examination for College Freshmen.** Grade 13; 1924–50; 3 scores: quantitative, linguistic, total; IBM; Editions 1946, 1947, 1948, 1949; Editions 1933–45 out of print; no data on reliability and validity in manual; manual ('50); $2.50 per 25; separate answer sheets must be used; 90¢ per 25 IBM answer sheets; 25¢ per set of scoring stencils; cash orders postpaid; 50¢ per specimen set, postpaid; 38(65) minutes; 1947 and earlier editions by L. L. Thurstone and Thelma Gwinn Thurstone; later editions prepared by publisher from materials developed by the Thurstones; Cooperative Test Division, Educational Testing Service. *

REFERENCES

1–48. See 40:1377.
49–143. See 3:217.
144. SEYMOUR, OLIVER J. *The Predictive Value of the Thurstone Psychological Examination.* Master's thesis, University of Arkansas (Fayetteville, Ark.), 1928. Pp. 90.
145. TOLL, CHARLES H. "Scholastic Aptitude Tests in Amherst College." *Sch & Soc* 28:524–8 O 27 '28. * (*PA* 3:512)
146. ROSENSTEIN, J. L. "Intelligence Test Ratings and Trainability of Nurses." *Psychol Clinic* 21:260–7 D–F '32–33. * (*PA* 8:569)
147. SCHULTZ, RICHARD S. "The Relation of General Intelligence, Motor Adaptability, and Motor Learning to Success in Dental Technical Courses." *Psychol Clinic* 21:226–34 D–F '32–33. * (*PA* 8:572)
148. WAITS, JOHN VIRGIL. *The Differential Predictive Value of the Psychological Examination of the American Council on Education.* Master's thesis, Alabama Polytechnic Institute (Auburn, Ala.), 1932.
149. MCLAUCHLIN, JAMES ARGYLE. *A Comparative Study of the Reliability and Validity of the Artificial Language Test in the American Council Psychological Examination, 1931 and 1932 Editions.* Master's thesis, Oklahoma Agricultural and Mechanical College (Stillwater, Okla.), 1933. Pp. 35.
150. WARREN, ELMER CHAPMAN. *The 1929 American Council on Education Psychological Examination and Its Relations to the First Semester, Freshman Year Scholarship of the Class of 1933 at a Northeastern College of Liberal Arts.* Master's thesis, Boston University (Boston, Mass.), 1933. Pp. 56.
151. HANCHEY, GORDON B. *The Value of High School Grades and Psychological Examination Scores in Predicting First Term Freshman Grades in College.* Master's thesis, East Texas State Teachers College (Commerce, Tex.), 1937. (*Graduate Studies ....1937–1938*, 1938, p. 16.)
152. BENEZET, LOUIS T. *A Study of Mental Types as Indicated by the American Council on Education Psychological Examination for 1938.* Master's thesis, Reed College (Portland, Ore.), 1939. Pp. 73.
153. LAWRENCE, WILLIAM A. *An Evaluation of Achievement in the Various Colleges of the Louisiana State University with Special Reference to Certain Aspects of the Junior Division.* Doctor's thesis, Louisiana State University (University, La.), 1939. (*Abstracts of Theses....1939–1940*, 1941, pp. 10–11.)
154. LAYCOCK, S. R., AND HUTCHEON, N. B. "A Preliminary Investigation into the Problem of Measuring Engineering Aptitude." *J Ed Psychol* 30:280–8 Ap '39. * (*PA* 13:5899)
155. SHERMAN, ORPHA. "A Comparative Study of the A.C.E. Test and the Iowa Silent Reading Test." *Proc Iowa Acad Sci* 46:291–3 '39. *
156. SISK, HENRY L. "A Multiple Factor Analysis of Mental Abilities in the Freshman Engineering Curriculum." *J Psychol* 9:165–77 Ap '39. * (*PA* 14:3759)
157. THOMSON, WILLIAM A. "Retest Results on the A.C.E. Psychological Examination." Abstract. *Psychol B* 36:636 O '39. * (*PA* 14:593, title only)
158. ALLISON, GLENN, AND BARNETT, ALBERT. "Freshman Psychological Examination Scores as Related to Size of High Schools." *J Appl Psychol* 24:651–2 O '40. * (*PA* 15:1011)
159. LAUGHLIN, WILLIAM PATRICK. *Changes of Intelligence Scores of College Students Over a Period of Approximately Four Years.* Doctor's thesis, University of Minnesota (Minneapolis, Minn.), 1940. (*Summaries of Ph.D. Theses*, 1949, pp. 92–4.)
160. CROW, CECILIA BACHRACH. *The Predictive Value of College Admissions Data.* Master's thesis, Southern Methodist

University (Dallas, Tex.), 1941. (*Abstracts of Theses....1941*, pp. 61-3.)
161. LANGSAM, ROSALIND STREEP. *A Factorial Analysis of Reading Ability.* Doctor's thesis, New York University (New York, N.Y.), 1941. (*Abstracts of Theses....[School of Education] October 1940-June 1941*, 1941, pp. 153-6.)
162. RUEDISILI, C. H. "Differential Prediction of College Achievement in the College of Letters and Science of the University of Wisconsin." Abstract. *Psychol B* 38:553 Jl '41. * (PA 15:5387, title only)
163. RUEDISILI, CHESTER HENRY. *Differential Prediction of College Achievement in the College of Letters and Science at the University of Wisconsin.* Doctor's thesis, University of Wisconsin (Madison, Wis.), 1941. (*Summaries of Doctoral Dissertations...., July, 1940-June, 1941*, 1942, pp. 265-7.)
164. LIVESAY, T. M. "Racial Comparisons in Test-Intelligence." *Am J Psychol* 55:90-5 Ja '42. * (PA 16:2001)
165. SHEFFIELD, EDWARD F. "Achievement of Evening College Students." *J Am Assn Col Reg* 17:319-24 Ap '42. *
166. SHUEY, AUDREY M. "Differences in Performance of Jewish and Non-Jewish Students on the American Council Psychological Examinations." *J Social Psychol* 15:221-43 My '42. * (PA 16:4475)
167. SMITH, MADORAH E. "The Effect of Bilingual Background on College Aptitude and Grade Point Ratios Earned by Students at the University of Hawaii." *J Ed Psychol* 33:356-64 My '42. * (PA 17:1369)
168. THOMPSON, R. B. "Predictive Criteria for Selecting A.S.T. Students." *J Am Assn Col Reg* 19:492-500 Jl '44. * (PA 18:3867)
169. WEBER, CHRISTIAN O. "Old and New College Board Scores and Grades of College Freshmen." *J Am Assn Col Reg* 20:70-5 O '44. * (PA 19:570)
170. BAILEY, H. W., AND DALLENBACH, KARL M. "A Study of Selective Procedures and Educational Achievement of ASTP Trainees Processed by the STAR Unit at the University of Illinois." *Am J Psychol* 58:1-24 Ja '45. * (PA 19:1556)
171. SMITH, FRANCIS F. "The Use of Previous Record in Estimating College Success." *J Ed Psychol* 36:167-76 Mr '45. * (PA 19:2377)
172. BERG, IRWIN AUGUST. "A Study of Success and Failure Among Student Nurses." Abstract. *Am Psychol* 1:249-50 Jl '46. * (PA 20:3872, title only)
173. FOX, WILLIAM H. *An Analysis of Different Methods Used in the Prediction of General University Achievement.* Doctor's thesis, Indiana University (Bloomington, Ind.), 1946. (*Studies in Education....1945-1949*, 1950, pp. 28-31.) (PA 25:7106, title only)
174. JONES, RONALD DEVALL. "The Prediction of Teaching Efficiency from Objective Measures." *J Exp Ed* 15:85-99 S '46. * (PA 21:606)
175. LINS, LEO JOSEPH. "The Prediction of Teaching Efficiency." *J Exp Ed* 15:2-60 S '46. * (PA 21:610)
176. WELBORN, ERNEST L. "The Quality of Students Attending Teachers Colleges." *J Ed Res* 39:668-70 My '46. * (PA 20:4355)
177. DAUGHTREY, JOHN PATRICK. *An Evaluation of the American Council Examination at the University of North Carolina.* Master's thesis, University of North Carolina (Chapel Hill, N.C.), 1947. (*Research in Progress, October, 1945-December, 1948*, 1949, pp. 96-7.) (PA 24:6539, title only)
178. GOULD, GEORGE. "The Predictive Value of Certain Selective Measures." *Ed Adm & Sup* 33:208-12 Ap '47. *
179. HESTON, JOSEPH C. "The Graduate Record Examination vs. Other Measures of Aptitude and Achievement." *Ed & Psychol Meas* 7:618-30 au '47. * (PA 22:3210)
180. LANIGAN, MARY A. "The Effectiveness of the Otis, the A.C.E. and the Minnesota Speed of Reading Tests for Predicting Success in College." *J Ed Res* 41:289-96 D '47. * (PA 22:2748)
181. LONG, LOUIS, AND PERRY, JAMES D. "Entrance Examinations at the City College of New York." *Ed & Psychol Meas* 7:765-72 w '47. * (PA 23:310)
182. THORNDIKE, ROBERT L. "The Prediction of Intelligence at College Entrance From Earlier Test." *J Ed Psychol* 38:129-48 Mr '47. * (PA 22:861)
183. BREDT, CARL V. *An Evaluation of the Q- and L-Scores of the A.C.E. for the Educational Guidance of College Freshmen.* Doctor's thesis, University of Texas (Austin, Tex.), 1948.
184. COOPRIDER, H. A., AND LASLETT, H. R. "Predictive Values of the Stanford Scientific and the Engineering and Physical Science Aptitude Tests." *Ed & Psychol Meas* 8:683-7 w '48. * (PA 24:1488)
185. EVANS, M. CATHARINE. "Differentiation of Home Economics Students According to Major Emphasis." *Occupations* 27:120-5 N '48. * (PA 23:4410)
186. FEIL, MADELEINE HOFFMAN. *A Study of Leadership and Scholastic Achievement in Their Relation to Prediction Factors.* Doctor's thesis, Ohio State University (Columbus, Ohio), 1948. (PA 23:363, title only) (*Abstracts of Dissertations....Summer Quarter 1948-49*, 1950, pp. 151-5.) (PA 24:6522, title only)
187. HAVENS, VIRGINIA. "A Prediction of Law School Achievement From High-School Rank, Reading Test Scores, Psychological Test Scores, and Average Grade in Pre-Law Courses." *J Ed Psychol* 39:237-42 Ap '48. * (PA 23:1463)
188. HESTON, JOSEPH C. "The Graduate Record Examination vs. Other Measures of Aptitude and Achievement." *J Ed Res* 41:338-47 Ja '48. * (PA 22:3210)

189. MILLIGAN, E. E.; LINS, L. JOSEPH; AND LITTLE, KENNETH. "The Success of Non-High-School Graduates in Degree Programs at the University of Wisconsin." *Sch & Soc* 67:27-9 Ja 10 '48. * (PA 22:2749)
190. MUNROE, RUTH L. "Academic Success and Personal Adjustment in College," pp. 30-42. In *Exploring Individual Differences: A Report of the 1947 Invitational Conference on Testing Problems*, New York City, November 1, 1947. Henry Chauncey, Chairman. American Council on Education Studies, Vol. 12, Series 1, No. 32. Washington, D.C.: the Council, October 1948. Pp. vii, 110. Paper. *
191. PORTENIER, LILLIAN G. "Predicting Success in Introductory Psychology." Abstract. *J Colo-Wyo Acad Sci* 3:61 Mr '48. *
192. PORTENIER, LILLIAN G. "Predicting Success in Introductory Psychology." *Ed & Psychol Meas* 8:117-26 sp '48. * (PA 22:3730)
193. REMMERS, H. H., AND GAGE, N. L. *The Abilities and Interests of Pharmacy Freshmen.* The Pharmaceutical Survey, Monograph No. 1. Reprinted from *The American Journal of Pharmaceutical Education* Vol. 12, No. 1, January 1948. Washington, D.C.: American Council on Education, [1948]. Pp. 65 plus 13 inserts. Paper. * (PA 22:4107)
194. ROBERTS, S. O. "Socio-Economic Status and Performance on the ACE of Negro Freshman College Veterans and Non-Veterans, From the North and South." Abstract. *Am Psychol* 3:266 Jl '48. * (PA 22:5572, title only)
195. SHUEY, AUDREY M.; ASSISTED BY SALLY HILBUN AND NATALYN J. HOLLOCK. "Improvement in Scores on the American Council Psychological Examination From Freshman to Senior Year." *J Ed Psychol* 39:417-26 N '48. * (PA 23:2916)
196. THOMANN, DON F. "Relationships Between the High School and College Editions of the American Council on Education Psychological Examination and Their Relative Value in Predicting College Achievement." *Col & Univ* 23:217-33 Ja '48. * (PA 22:4631)
197. THORNDIKE, ROBERT L. "Growth of Intelligence During Adolescence." *J Genetic Psychol* 72:11-5 Mr '48. * (PA 22:4837)
198. *College Preparatory Testing Program: A Guide to the Use of Tests and Interpretation of Results.* Princeton, N.J.: Cooperative Test Division, Educational Testing Service, [1949]. Pp. 30. Paper. *
199. *Report on the 1948 National College Freshman Testing Program.* Princeton, N.J.: Cooperative Test Division, Educational Testing Service, [1949]. Pp. 28. Paper. *
200. BARNETTE, W. LESLIE, JR. *Occupational Aptitude Patterns of Counseled Veterans.* Doctor's thesis, New York University (New York, N.Y.), 1949. Pp. viii, 385. * (PA 24:362, title only)
201. BLANCHARD, HOWARD L. *A Comparison of Teachers' Marks With an Actual Battery of Aptitude Test Percentile Scores.* Doctor's "Field Study No. 1," Colorado State College of Education (Greeley, Colo.), 1949. (*Abstracts of Field Studies....1949*, 1950, pp. 12-5.)
202. BORG, WALTER R. "A Study of the Relationship Between General Intelligence and Success in an Art College." *J Ed Psychol* 40:434-40 N '49. * (PA 24:3378)
203. DAVENPORT, K. S. "The Influence of Mathematics Training on Achievement in Chemistry of First-Year Students in Home Economics," pp. 7-16. (PA 25:2652) In *Student Achievement and Instructor Evaluation in Chemistry.* Edited by H. H. Remmers. Purdue University, Division of Educational Reference, Studies in Higher Education [No.] 66. Lafayette, Ind.: the Division, July 1949. Pp. 26. Paper. *
204. DAY, JAMES FRANCIS. *Achievement of Freshman Students at Visalia College.* Doctor's thesis, Stanford University (Stanford, Calif.), 1949. (*Abstracts of Dissertations....1949-50*, 1950, pp. 306-10.)
205. FUSFELD, IRVING S. "On the ACE Psychological Examination." *Sch & Soc* 70:117-8 Ag 20 '49. * (PA 26:2427)
206. GERLACH, HARRY M. "The Attendance Record and Scholastic Aptitude Test Scores of Students Dropped for Poor Scholarship." *Col & Univ* 24:370-3 Ap '49. *
207. HAUSER, LUELLEN J. MUNN. "A Comparative Study of the Intelligence of University Freshmen Enrolled in Business and Liberal Art Schools." *J Ed Res* 43:49-57 S '49. * (PA 24:2089)
208. HORRALL, BERNICE MOODY. "Relationships Between College Aptitude and Discouragement-Buoyancy Among College Freshmen." *J Genetic Psychol* 74:185-243 Je '49. * (PA 24:2090-1)
209. JACOBS, ROBERT. "Public School Testing Project: First Report," pp. 66-72. (PA 23:3446) In *1948 Fall Testing Program in Independent Schools and Supplementary Studies.* Educational Records Bulletin, No. 51. New York: the Bureau, January 1949. Pp. xiii, 72. Paper, lithotyped. *
210. KAHN, HARRIS, AND SINGER, ERWIN. "An Investigation of Some of the Factors Related to Success or Failure of School of Commerce Students." *J Ed Psychol* 40:107-17 F '49. * (PA 24:2062)
211. OSBORNE, R. TRAVIS; SANDERS, WILMA B.; AND GREENE, JAMES E. "The Differential Prediction of College Marks by A.C.E. Scores." Abstract. *Am Psychol* 4:286-7 Jl '49. * (PA 23:6446, title only)
212. OWENS, WILLIAM A., AND OWENS, WILLIAM A., JR. "Some Factors in the Academic Superiority of Veteran Students." *J Ed Psychol* 40:499-502 D '49. * (PA 24:3390)
213. POWELL, DAVIS BRYAN, JR. *An Educational and Occu-*

pational Survey of One Hundred North Carolina High School Seniors Who Ranked at the Ninety-Ninth Percentile on the American Council on Education Psychological Examination, 1947, High School Edition, Which Was Administered to All Accredited White High Schools in the State During the State-Wide Testing Program on January 21, 1948. Master's thesis, University of North Carolina (Chapel Hill, N.C.), 1949. (Research in Progress, January, 1949–December, 1949, 1950, pp. 187–8.) *(PA 25:5691, title only)*

214. REMMERS, H. H.; ELLIOTT, D. N.; AND GAGE, N. L. "Curricular Differences in Predicting Scholastic Achievement: Applications to Counseling." *J Ed Psychol* 40:385–94 N '49. * *(PA 24:3407)*

215. REMMERS, H. H., AND GAGE, N. L. "Student Personnel Studies of the Pharmaceutical Survey." *Am J Pharm Ed* 13: 6–126 Ja '49. * *(PA 23:1004)*

216. RINSLAND, HENRY D. "The Prediction of Veterans' Success From Test Scores at the University of Oklahoma," Part 1, pp. 59–72. In *The Sixth Yearbook of the National Council on Measurements Used in Education, 1948–1949*. Fairmont, W.Va.: the Council, Fairmont State College, 1949. Pp. v, 140 (variously numbered). Paper, mimeographed. *

217. SALLEY, RUTH E., AND WEINTRAUB, RUTH G. "Student Records of Entrance and Graduation." *Sch & Soc* 69:404–6 Je 4 '49. * *(PA 26:1719)*

218. SILVEY, HERBERT M. *Change in Status of Iowa State Teachers College Students as Revealed by Repeating Placement Tests*. Iowa State Teachers College, Research Report No. 58. Cedar Falls, Iowa: Bureau of Research, the College, July 20, 1949. Pp. 27. Paper, lithotyped. *

219. STAPLETON, MARY R. *The Differential Prognostic Value of Certain Measures as Criteria for the Educational Guidance of Entering Freshman Women*. Doctor's thesis, New York University (New York, N.Y.), 1949. *(Abstracts of Theses.... [School of Education] October 1948–June 1949*, 1950, pp. 137–40.)

220. SUPER, DONALD E. *Appraising Vocational Fitness By Means of Psychological Tests*, pp. 114–24. New York: Harper & Brothers, 1949. Pp. xxiii, 727. * *(PA 24:2130)*

221. TREUMANN, MILDRED JENKINS, AND SULLIVAN, BEN A. "Use of the Engineering and Physical Science Aptitude Test as a Predictor of Academic Achievement of Freshman Engineering Students." *J Ed Res* 43:129–33 O '49. * *(PA 24:2804)*

222. TRITES, DAVID KEIGHTLEY. *Correlation of Item Responses on the A.C.E. Psychological Examination With First Quarter Grades in Engineering Courses*. Master's thesis, Iowa State College (Ames, Iowa), 1949.

223. WALLACE, W. L. "Differential Predictive Value of the ACE Psychological Examination." *Sch & Soc* 70:23–25 Jl 9 '49. * *(PA 24:2097)*

224. WHEELER, LESTER R. "Summary of a Study of the Intelligence of University of Miami Freshmen." *J Ed Res* 43: 307–8 D '49. * *(PA 24:3899)*

225. WHEELER, LESTER R., AND WHEELER, VIOLA D. "The Relationship Between Reading Ability and Intelligence Among University Freshmen." *J Ed Psychol* 40:230–8 Ap '49. * *(PA 24:2837)*

226. WILLETT, G. W. "Reliability of Test Scores on Seven Tests." *J Ed Res* 43:293–8 D '49. * *(PA 24:3900)*

227. WRENN, C. GILBERT. "Potential Research Talent in the Sciences: Based on Intelligence Quotients of Ph.D's." *Ed Rec* 30:4–22 Ja '49. *

228. ZWILLING, VIRGINIA T. *The Prediction of Grades in Freshman English From a Battery of Tests of Mental Ability, Interests and Aptitudes Administered to Students Entering a Liberal Arts College*. Doctor's thesis, Fordham University (New York, N.Y.), 1949. *(Dissertations..., 1949*, pp. 62–5.)

229. *College Preparatory Testing Program, 1950: A Guide to the Use of the Tests and the Interpretation of Results*. Princeton, N.J.: Cooperative Test Division, Educational Testing Service, [1950]. Pp. 30. Paper. *

230. *Report on the 1949 National College Freshman Testing Program*. Princeton, N.J.: Cooperative Test Division, Educational Testing Service, [1950]. Pp. 22. Paper. *

231. ALTUS, WILLIAM D. "Personality Correlates of Q-L Differentials on the A.C.E. for College Women." Abstract. *Am Psychol* 5:462 S '50. * *(PA 25:4556, title only)*

232. BASIUL, WALTER JOSEPH. *A Study of the Efficiency of Sub-Scores of the American Council on Education Psychological Examination in the Differential Prediction of College Grades*. Master's thesis, Clark University (Worcester, Mass.), 1950. *(Abstracts of Dissertations and Theses, 1951*, pp. 155–6.)

233. BERDIE, RALPH F., AND SUTTER, NANCY A. "Predicting Success of Engineering Students." *J Ed Psychol* 41:184–90 Mr '50. * *(PA 24:6056)*

234. BERKSHIRE, ROGER, AND FLEET, DONALD. "College Junior Norms for 1947 A.C.E. and Minnesota Clerical Tests." *Occupations* 29:30–1 O '50. * *(PA 25:3417)*

235. BISCHOF, LEDFORD JULIUS. *Relationships of General Aptitude Test Battery Scores With Scores on the ACE Psychological Examination for College Freshmen*. Doctor's thesis, Indiana University (Bloomington, Ind.), 1950. *(Thesis Abstract Series....1950*, 1951, pp. 5–11.) *(PA 25:7103, title only)*

236. BROMLEY, ANN, AND CARTER, GERALD C. "Predictability of Success in Mathematics." *J Ed Res* 44:148–50 O '50. * *(PA 25:5630)*

237. BROTHERS, WILBUR LEO. *The Relationship of Certain Factors to Effectiveness in Student Teaching in the Secondary Schools*. Doctor's thesis, Indiana University (Bloomington, Ind.), 1950. *(Thesis Abstract Series....1950*, 1951, pp. 12–8.)

238. BROWN, HUGH S. "Differential Prediction by the ACE." *J Ed Res* 44:116–21 O '50. * *(PA 25:5683)*

239. COCHRAN, SAMUEL W., AND DAVIS, FREDERICK B. "Predicting Freshman Grades at George Peabody College for Teachers." *Peabody J Ed* 27:352–6 My '50. *

240. EMBREE, ROYAL B., JR. "A Longitudinal Study of Performance on the Henmon-Nelson Test of Mental Ability, the Differential Aptitude Tests, and the American Council on Education Psychological Examination for College Freshmen." Abstract. *Am Psychol* 5:352 Jl '50. * *(PA 25:1276, title only)*

241. FURST, EDWARD J. "Relationship Between Tests of Intelligence and Tests of Critical Thinking and of Knowledge." *J Ed Res* 43:614–25 Ap '50. * *(PA 25:1621)*

242. GRANT, WILLIAM VANCE, JR. *The Comparative Value of the General Aptitude Test Battery and the American Council on Education Psychological Examination in Predicting the Quality Point Averages of a Group of Florida State University Students*. Master's thesis, University of Florida (Gainesville, Fla.), 1950.

243. JACKSON, ROBERT. "The Selection of Students for Freshman Chemistry by Means of Discriminant Functions." *J Exp Ed* 18:209–14 Mr '50. * *(PA 25:2032)*

244. JACOBS, ROBERT. "A Study of the Need for Special Norms on Scholastic Aptitude and Mechanics of English Tests for College Preparatory Students in Public Schools," pp. 52–66. *(PA 24:3895)* In *1949 Fall Testing Program in Independent Schools and Supplementary Studies*. Educational Records Bulletin, No. 53. New York: Educational Records Bureau, January 1950. Pp. xiii, 70. Paper, lithotyped. *

245. KOLASA, BLAIR JOHN. *The Relationship Between Bilingual Background and Performance on the L Subtest of the American Council on Education Psychological Examination*. Master's thesis, University of Pittsburgh (Pittsburgh, Pa.), 1950.

246. LINS, L. J. "Probability Approach to Forecasting University Success With Measured Grades as the Criterion." *Ed & Psychol Meas* 10:386–91 au '50. * *(PA 25:3405)*

247. MACHEN, LORELLE HORING. *The Relationship of A.C.E. Q, L, and Total Scores to College Grades and Achievement*. Master's thesis, Catholic University of America (Washington, D.C.), 1950. *(PA 25:4080, title only)*

248. MARTIN, FREDERICK M. "The Prognostic Value of Significantly Different Q and L Scores of the A.C.E. Psychological Examination at the College Level." Abstract. *Am Psychol* 5:471 S '50. * *(PA 25:4852, title only)*

249. MARTIN, HENRY JOHN. *A Comparison of the Composite Ability Index of College Freshmen With Grades Earned in Different Courses and Departments of Instruction at Indiana University*. Doctor's thesis, Indiana University (Bloomington, Ind.), 1950. *(Thesis Abstract Series....1950*, 1951, pp. 86–90.)

250. OSBORNE, R. TRAVIS; SANDERS, WILMA B., AND GREENE, JAMES E. "The Differential Prediction of College Marks by ACE Scores." *J Ed Res* 44:107–15 O '50. * *(PA 25:5689)*

251. PIERCE-JONES, JOHN, AND TYLER, FRED T. "A Comparison of the A.C.E. Psychological Examination and the Culture-Free Test." *Can J Psychol* 4:109–14 S '50. * *(PA 25:3422)*

252. PRED, GORDON DAVID. "An Analysis of Orientation Test Results in the Purdue Technical Institute Courses," pp. 36–63. In *Motives and Aptitudes in Education: Four Studies*. Edited by H. H. Remmers. Purdue University, Division of Educational Reference. Studies in Higher Education, No. 74. Lafayette, Ind.: the Division, December 1950. Pp. iii, 63. Paper. *

253. SANDERS, MERRITT WILLIAM. *The Prediction of Academic Success Among University Freshmen in a School of Education*. Doctor's thesis, New York University (New York, N.Y.), 1950. Abstract: *Microfilm Abstracts* 11:63–4 no 1 '51. * *(PA 26:2430, title only)*

254. SCHLESSER, GEORGE E. "Gains in Scholastic Aptitude Under Highly Motivated Conditions." *J Ed Psychol* 41:237–42 Ap '50. * *(PA 25:3409)*

255. SHUEY, AUDREY M. "Choice of Major Subject as Related to American Council Examination Score and College Grades." *J Ed Psychol* 41:292–300 My '50. * *(PA 25:3392)*

256. SMITH, D. D., AND TRIGGS, FRANCES O. "Educational Successes and Failures of Students With High 'Q' and Low 'L' on the American Council on Educational Psychological Examination." Abstract. *Am Psychol* 5:353–4 Jl '50. * *(PA 25: 1283, title only)*

257. TRAVERS, ROBERT M. W., AND WALLACE, WIMBURN L. "Inconsistency in the Predictive Value of a Battery of Tests." *J Appl Psychol* 34:237–9 Ag '50. * *(PA 25:6480)*

258. WILEY, LLEWELLYN N. "Equating Scores on Three Intelligence Tests." Abstract. *Am Psychol* 5:467 S '50. * *(PA 25:4600, title only)*

259. *Report on the 1950 National College Freshman Testing Program*. Princeton, N.J.: Cooperative Test Division, Educational Testing Service, [1951]. Pp. 32. Paper. *

260. BAILEY, DONALD W., AND BRAMMER, LAWRENCE M. "Variability in A.C.P.E. Scores From Freshman to Junior and Senior Years." *Calif J Ed Res* 2:159–64 S '51. *

261. BARNETTE, W. LESLIE, JR. *Occupational Aptitude Patterns of Selected Groups of Counseled Veterans*. American Psychological Association, Psychological Monographs: General and Applied, Vol. 65, No. 5, Whole No. 322. Washington, D.C.: the Association, Inc., 1951. Pp. v, 49. Paper. * *(PA 26:2794)*

262. BELMAN, H. S., AND EVANS, R. N. "Selection of Students for a Trade and Industrial Educational Curriculum." *J Ed Psychol* 42:52–8 Ja '51. * *(PA 25:6486)*

263. BERDIE, RALPH; DRESSEL, PAUL; AND KELSO, PAUL. "Relative Validity of the Q and L Scores of the ACE Psychological Examination." *Ed & Psychol Meas* 11:803–12 w '51. *
264. BISCHOF, LEDFORD J. *Relationships of General Aptitude Test Battery Scores with Scores on the A.C.E. Psychological Examination for College Freshmen*. Doctor's thesis, Indiana University (Bloomington, Ind.), 1951.
265. BURACK, MARVIN. "The Relationship of Social Status and Intelligence to Retention and Progress at the Junior College Level." Abstract. *Am Psychol* 6:369–70 Jl '51. *
266. CARLIN, LESLIE ORVILLE. *A Comparison of the College Marks by Subject Made by 312 of the June, 1950 Graduating Seniors at Central Michigan College of Education With Their Battery of Guidance Tests and Inventory Percentile Scores*. Doctor's "Field Study No. 2," Colorado State College of Education (Greeley, Colo.), 1951. (*Abstracts of Field Studies....1951, 1952,* pp. 15–20.)
267. FARBER, ROBERT HOLTON. *Guidance Implications of the Freshman Testing Program at DePauw University*. Doctor's thesis, Indiana University (Bloomington, Ind.), 1951. (*Thesis Abstract Series....1951,* 1952, pp. 37–42.)
268. KNICKERBOCKER, K. L. "Placement of Freshmen in First-Quarter English." *J Higher Ed* 22:211–5+ Ap '51. * (*PA* 26:520)
269. LUKER, ALBERT G. *Scholastic Aptitude and Scholastic Achievement at a College of Education*. Doctor's "Field Study No. 2," Colorado State College of Education (Greeley, Colo.), 1951. (*Abstracts of Field Studies....1951,* 1952, pp. 103–6.)
270. SILVEY, HERBERT M. "Changes in Test Scores After Two Years in College." *Ed & Psychol Meas* 11:494–502 au '51. *
271. SMOTHERMAN, THURMAN EDWIN. *The Significance of Discrepancies Between Quantitative and Linguistic Abilities for Scholastic Success and College Adjustment*. Doctor's thesis, University of Missouri (Columbia, Mo.), 1951. Abstract: *Microfilm Abstracts* 11:618–20 no 3 '51. (*PA* 26:1720, title only)
272. TRIGGS, FRANCES ORALIND. "Educational Successes and Failures of Students With High 'L' and Low 'Q' on the American Council on Education Psychological Examination." Abstract. *Am Psychol* 6:295–6 Jl '51. *
273. WALLACE, W. L. "Differential Predictive Value of the ACE Psychological Examination." *Sch & Soc* 70:23–5 Jl 9 '51. * (*PA* 26:2432)
274. WALLACE, W. L. "The Prediction of Grades in Specific College Courses." *J Ed Res* 44:587–97 Ap '51. * (*PA* 26:5838)
275. WHEELER, LESTER R., AND WHEELER, VIOLA D. "The Intelligence of Music Students." *J Ed Psychol* 42:223–30 Ap '51. * (*PA* 26:2433)
276. WOODS, ROY C. "How Reliable Are National Norms When Applied to Specific Geographical Areas," pp. 17–25. In *The Eighth Yearbook of the National Council on Measurements Used in Education, 1950–51*. Fairmont, W.Va.: the Council, Fairmont State College, 1951. Pp. vii, 58. Paper, mimeographed. *

For reviews by W. D. Commins and J. P. Guilford of the 1946 Edition, see 3:217; for reviews by Jack W. Dunlap and Robert L. Thorndike of the 1939 Edition, see 40:1377; for reviews by Anne Anastasi and David Segel of 1937 Edition, see 38:1037.

[278]

*American Council on Education Psychological Examination for High School Students. Grades 9–12; 1933–52; 3 scores: quantitative, linguistic, total; IBM; Editions 1946, 1947, 1948; Editions 1933–45 out of print; manual ['52]; $2.50 per 25; separate answer sheets must be used; 90¢ per 25 IBM answer sheets; 25¢ per set of scoring stencils; cash orders postpaid; 25¢ per specimen set, postpaid; 35(65) minutes; 1947 and earlier editions by L. L. Thurstone and Thelma Gwinn Thurstone; 1948 Edition prepared by publisher from materials developed by the Thurstones; Cooperative Test Division, Educational Testing Service. *

REFERENCES

1–2. See 40:1378.
3–9. See 3:218.
10. MUNTYAN, MILOSH. "A Study of the Re-Test Factor in the Illinois Statewide High School Testing Program." *J Ed Res* 41:183–92 N '47. * (*PA* 22:2750)
11. THOMANN, DON F. "Relationships Between the High School and College Editions of the American Council on Education Psychological Examination and Their Relative Value in Predicting College Achievement." *Col & Univ* 23:217–33 Ja '48. * (*PA* 22:4631)

For a review by Carl I. Hovland of the 1946 Edition, see 3:218; for a review by A. H. Turney of the 1939 Edition, see 40:1378; for a review by V. A. C. Henmon of the 1937 Edition, see 38:1038.

[279]

The Army Alpha Examination: First Nebraska Revision. Grades 6–16 and adults; 1937; a revision of *Army Group Examination Alpha* (see 281); 4 scores: verbal character, numerical computation, relationships, total; 1 form; no data on reliability; $3.75 per 25, postage extra; 50¢ per specimen set, postpaid; 22¼ (35) minutes; J. P. Guilford; Sheridan Supply Co. *

REFERENCES

1–4. See 3:220 (61, 66, 69, 73).
5. GUILFORD, J. P. *Psychometric Methods,* pp. 491–510. New York: McGraw-Hill Book Co., 1936. Pp. xvi, 566. *

ROBERT G. DEMAREE, *Assistant Professor of Psychology; and* LOUIS L. MCQUITTY, *Professor of Psychology; University of Illinois, Urbana, Illinois.*

DESCRIPTION OF THE TEST. This revision is patterned after the original forms of the Army Alpha with eight subtests: 1, Directions; 2, Arithmetical Problems; 3, Practical Judgment; 4, Synonym-Antonym; 5, Disarranged Sentences; 6, Number Series Completion; 7, Analogies; and 8, Information. It is a time-limit test with answers recorded in the test booklet.

PURPOSE OF THE TEST. In view of the college sample upon which this revision was based, the most appropriate use is in connection with counseling and guidance activities for persons at the college level. However, the publishers state that it is appropriate for subjects from the sixth grade to the adult level.

ADMINISTRATION. Each of the subtests is separately timed and administered. Oral instructions must be given by the examiner for each item of the Directions test. The manual offers no suggestions as to the rapidity with which examiners should read these instructions, some of which are tongue twisters. Examiner differences in administering this portion may lower the validity somewhat.

FACTOR SCORES. As reported by Guilford (5) in 1936, the scores on the eight subtests of the revised form were intercorrelated for 108 freshmen who were entering a college of engineering and who were homogeneous as to sex and age. Factor analysis resulted in three factors. Multiple regression weights were established for predicting the score of a person on each factor from the scores on the subtests most highly related to that factor. Tests 3, 4, 5 and 8 enter into prediction of the score on V, the verbal factor. Tests 2 and 6 are weighted on N, the numerical-computation factor, and tests 1 and 7 give scores on R, the factor interpreted as grasping and using relationships.

In only tests 2, 4 and 7 did the three factors account for over half of the variance in the test scores. The least amount of variance accounted for by the three factors was 38 per cent in the case of test 1. There is no basis for knowing to what extent the unaccounted variance in each subtest is due to abilities which are unique to the subtest or is due to unreliability. No information is available as to the reliability of any of the part scores or even of the total score.

A table of percentile norms, based upon 243 University of Nebraska students, is given for scores on factors V, N and R, and the total score. The manual offers no suggestions as to the range of applicability of these norms; it would be hazardous, to say the least, to apply them to groups which differ from the standardization groups with respect to age or education.

The endeavor to provide more parsimonious and yet more meaningful scores on the subtests by relating them to scores on factors is noteworthy. However, the factors V, N and R as revealed by this test are defined very broadly within their respective realms. Many refinements of these factors, and of tests to measure them, have been put forth in the past decade. Even apart from the fact that we do not have information as to the dependability of differences in scores on V, N and R, other tests are currently available which have more to offer for diagnostic use in counseling and guidance or for making other differential predictions. The *Differential Aptitude Test* is one of these.

DISTRIBUTIONS AND NORMS. The table given in the manual for converting total scores into percentile and mental age norms is based upon data from World War I, using the initial forms of Army Alpha. The statement is made that "The average level of difficulty for each test is the same as that for the original forms of Army Alpha, and so the customary norms should therefore apply." This conclusion is clearly unwarranted, since it is known that the distribution of scores on a test is not only a function of the difficulties of the items but is also a function of the inter-item correlations. The latter may have differed quite considerably between this revision and the initial forms of the Army Alpha. That these norms are of doubtful applicability has been questioned in empirical studies (73).

OVERALL EVALUATION. This test undoubtedly represented a significant contribution at the time of its release, but it does not compare favorably with other tests presently available and appropriate for use at the college level.

The use of the test outside of the college level is not recommended unless separate standardization is planned; the norms and predicted factor scores would be of questionable applicability for any population not comparable to college-level students.

For a review by W. D. Commins, see 38:1039.

[280]
*Army General Classification Test, First Civilian Edition.** Grades 9–16 and adults; 1947–48; also called AGCT; IBM; 2 editions; 1 form, '47—identical to Form 1a ('40) of the Army Edition; revised manual ('48); separate answer pads or answer sheets must be used; 75¢ per specimen set of any one edition; cash orders postpaid; 40(55) minutes; Science Research Associates, Inc. *
a) FORM AH (HAND SCORING EDITION). 49¢ per test and answer pad; $1.80 per 25 answer pads.
b) FORM AM (MACHINE SCORING EDITION). 39¢ per test; $2.90 per 100 IBM answer sheets; $1 per set of scoring keys.

REFERENCES

1–14. See 3:219.
15. THOMPSON, R. B. "Predictive Criteria for Selecting A.S.T. Students." *J Am Assn Col Reg* 19:492–500 Jl '44. * (PA 18:3867)
16. BAILEY, H. W., AND DALLENBACH, KARL M. "A Study of Selective Procedures and Educational Achievement of ASTP Trainees Processed by the STAR Unit at the University of Illinois." *Am J Psychol* 58:1–24 Ja '45. * (PA 19:1556)
17. HARRELL, THOMAS W. "Army Classification Test Results for Air Forces Specialists." Abstract. *Am Psychol* 1:292–3 Jl '46. * (PA 20:3802, title only)
18. BITTNER, REIGN H. "The Army General Classification Test," pp. 45–55. (PA 21:4174) In *New Methods in Applied Psychology*. Edited by George A. Kelly. Proceedings of the Maryland Conference on Military Contributions to Methodology in Applied Psychology Held at the University of Maryland, November 27–28, 1945 Under the Auspices of the Military Division of the American Psychological Association. College Park, Md.: University of Maryland, 1947. Pp. viii, 301. Lithotyped. *
19. ALTUS, WILLIAM D. "A Note on Group Differences in Intelligence and the Type of Test Employed." *J Consult Psychol* 12:194–5 My–Je '48. * (PA 22:4833)
20. TUDDENHAM, READ D. "Soldier Intelligence in World Wars I and II." *Am Psychol* 3:54–6 F '48. * (PA 22:2954)
21. ALTUS, WILLIAM D. "The Height and Weight of Soldiers in Association With Scores Earned on the Army General Classification Test." *J Social Psychol* 29:201–10 My '49. * (PA 24:99)
22. AYLESWORTH, HOWARD CLARENCE. *A Survey of the Army General Classification Test Used in World War II.* Master's thesis, University of Virginia (Charlottesville, Va.), 1949.
23. BRADLEY, GLADYCE H. "A Review of Educational Problems Based on Military Selection and Classification Data in World War II." *J Ed Res* 43:161–74 N '49. * (PA 24:3860)
24. KIRKPATRICK, JAMES J., AND CURETON, EDWARD E. "Vocabulary Item Difficulty and Word Frequency." *J Appl Psychol* 33:347–51 Ag '49. * (PA 24:2234)
25. SUPER, DONALD E. *Appraising Vocational Fitness By Means of Psychological Tests*, pp. 124–32. New York: Harper & Brothers, 1949. Pp. xxiii, 727. * (PA 24:2130)
26. DUBOIS, PHILIP H., AND WATSON, ROBERT I. "The Selection of Patrolmen." *J Appl Psychol* 34:90–5 Ap '50. * (PA 25:2076)
27. GLASER, ROBERT. "Predicting Achievement in Medical School." *J Appl Psychol* 35:272–4 Ag '51. * (PA 26:3046)
28. GLASER, ROBERT. "The Validity of Some Tests for Predicting Achievement in Medical School." Abstract. *Am Psychol* 6:298 Jl '51. *
29. TAMMINEN, A. W. "A Comparison of the Army General Classification Test and the Wechsler Bellevue Intelligence Scales." *Ed & Psychol Meas* 11:646–55 w '51. *

JOHN T. DAILEY, *Technical Director, Research Division, Bureau of Naval Personnel, Washington, D.C.*

According to the 1950 SRA catalog, "This test is designed as a measure of general learning ability. Administered to more than 12 million soldiers during the war, it is probably the most widely used test ever constructed. Developed by a distinguished staff of Army psychologists, it presents three types of problems: *vocabulary* to measure the verbal factor, *arithmetic word problems* to measure the number and reasoning factors, and *block counting* to measure the space factor." However, according to the Staff, Personnel Research Section writing in 1947, "The first two forms were constructed under considerable pressure, by an insufficient and shifting staff, and on the basis of data which were recognized as inadequate in several respects" (*14*). According to the same source, Forms 1a and 1b, of which Form 1a became the civilian edition, were administered to less than one million cases and were replaced by Forms 1c and 1d shortly before Pearl Harbor. In other words, the civilian AGCT is *not* the AGCT that was administered throughout World War II.

In regard to the standardization of the AGCT, it should be pointed out that, while the various versions of it have been administered to 12 million soldiers as stated, the test was not standardized on this large group or even on any representative sample of it. Instead, each successive form of the AGCT has been scaled by tying it into the previous forms all the way back to Form 1a. This has been accomplished by equating scores on the new forms to scores on the earlier forms given previously to the same subjects, thus equating retest scores to initial test scores.

Form 1a was standardized on a group of 3,790 soldiers and 606 CCC enrollees tested in September 1940. This group forms the basis for the entire superstructure of Army standard score scales from that date onward. An attempt was made to stratify a sample from this group on the basis of age, education, and area of origin but was only partially successful because these three variables fail to account for a large enough proportion of the variance on the AGCT and because the soldiers and CCC enrollees were apparently not representative of young men of the same age, education and area of origin in the general population. At any rate, when Forms 1a and 1b were actually administered to representative samples of inductees they yielded standard score distributions with a decided negative skew and with a mean score significantly greater than 100. Various attempts have been made since to adjust the Army standard score scale to make it representative of the general male population of military age, but it has never been possible to draw such a straightforward sample to form a revised basis for the Army standard score scale. As a result it is still largely a matter of conjecture as to what is the AGCT mean and variance of the general population. In view of this fact, it would appear that the early version of the AGCT released to the public domain would have little to recommend it to the civilian user in preference to many of the similar commercial tests now on the market.

The later forms of the AGCT were well constructed tests and accomplished well the purpose for which they were constructed: to serve as instruments to enable relatively untrained personnel to screen huge numbers of inductees in terms of their intellectual aptitude. The AGCT represented a compromise between a comprehensive classification battery suitable for maximum efficiency of differential classification and the traditional group intelligence test of the 1920s. In 1940 the military psychologists had the know-how to construct such a comprehensive classification battery but operational limitations such as the amount of testing time available prevented its construction and use. Since the end of World War II, both the Army and the Air Force have adopted such batteries.

For an excerpt from a review, see 3:219.

[281]

Army Group Examination Alpha. Grades 5–16 and adults; 1919–39; released by the War Department for general use in 1919; Forms 5 ('19), 6 ('19), 7 ('19), 8 ('19), 9 ('19); no data on reliability; revised manual ('39); $1.20 per 25; 25¢ per specimen set; postpaid; 22¼ (35–40) minutes; manual by H. E. Schrammel and E. R. Wood; prepared by the Psychology Committee of the National Research Council; Bureau of Educational Measurements, Kansas State Teachers College of Emporia. *

REFERENCES

1–75. See 3:220.
76. BREGMAN, ELSIE OSCHRIN. "On Converting Scores on the Army Alpha Examination Into Percentiles of the Total Population." *Sch & Soc* 23:695–6 My 29 '26. *
77. TOLL, CHARLES H. "Scholastic Aptitude Tests in Amherst College." *Sch & Soc* 28:524–8 O 27 '28. * (*PA* 3:512)
78. FRYER, DOUGLAS, AND SPARLING, E. J. "Intelligence and Occupational Adjustment." *Occupations* 12:55–63 Je '34. *
79. HOLLINGWORTH, LETA S., AND KAUNITZ, RUTH M. "The Centile Status of Gifted Children at Maturity." *J Genetic Psychol* 45:106–20 S '34. * (*PA* 9:451)
80. GUILFORD, J. P. *Psychometric Methods,* pp. 491–510. New York: McGraw-Hill Book Co., Inc., 1936. Pp. xvi, 566. * (*PA* 10:6010)
81. ALPER, THELMA G., AND BORING, EDWIN G. "Intelligence-Test Scores of Northern and Southern White and Negro

Recruits in 1918." *J Abn & Social Psychol* 39:471–4 O '44. * (PA 19:455)
82. GARRETT, HENRY E. "Comparison of Negro and White Recruits on the Army Tests Given in 1917–1918." *Am J Psychol* 58:480–95 O '45. * (PA 20:855)
83. MONTAGU, M. F. ASHLEY. "Intelligence of Northern Negroes and Southern Whites in the First World War." *Am J Psychol* 58:161–88 Ap '45. * (PA 19:2299)
84. MARCUSE, F. L., AND BITTERMAN, M. E. "Notes on the Results of Army Intelligence Testing in World War I." *Sci* 104:231–2 S 6 '46. * (PA 21:204)
85. STONE, CALVIN P. "Losses and Gains on the Alpha Group Examination as Related to Electroconvulsive Shocks." *J Comp Physiol & Psychol* 40:183–9 Je '47. * (PA 21:4372)
86. PASTORE. NICHOLAS. "A Fallacy Underlying Garrett's Use of the Data of the Army Alpha and Beta Tests—A Comment." Letter. *Sci Mo* 69:279–80 O '49. * (PA 24:1145)
87. OWENS, WILLIAM A., JR. "The Effects of a Thirty-Year Age Increment Upon Individual and Trait Differences in Intelligence." Abstract. *Am Psychol* 6:398 Jl '51. *

JOHN T. DAILEY, *Technical Director, Research Division, Bureau of Naval Personnel, Washington, D.C.*

Nearly 35 years after its development, a reexamination of this test reveals a rather startling conformity between many features of the Army Alpha and much of current test theory. For example, one practice which many test theorists now strongly urge is the use of numerous short subtests in a test battery or omnibus test rather than a restricted number of long subtests. The original Army Alpha is a perfect example of such a test with eight short subtests administered in a combined testing time of only 40 to 50 minutes. In this respect the Army Alpha strongly resembles the currently employed General Aptitude Test Battery of the United States Employment Service. As a matter of fact, all of the currently employed comprehensive classification batteries bear many points of resemblance to the Army Alpha and contain many subtests identical with, or closely similar to, some of the subtests in it. When examined from the point of view of modern factor theory, the various subtests of the Army Alpha appear to cover fairly well most of the factors in the intellectual domain, although the factorial purity of some of the subtests could be improved upon. In fact, the Army Alpha, with the deletion of items now obsolete in content, could well form the nucleus of a modern type of comprehensive classification battery. If supplemented with measures of the various perceptual, spatial, mechanical, and motor factors, it could do a fairly good job of predicting differential success in a wide variety of vocational and military specialties. It would appear that the builders of the original Army Alpha built even more wisely than they realized.

While the Army Alpha is an admirable pioneering product with many features in accordance with the latest testing theory, it still has many obsolete features that limit its utility as an omnibus test of general intellectual aptitude. For one thing, even in the revised forms, it fails to give sufficient differentiation at the lowest literate levels because it does not use an adequate formula to correct for chance success. In a highly speeded test such as the Army Alpha with some multiple choice items, it is impossible to interpret low scores below or near the mean chance score that would occur if subjects guessed at each multiple choice item. For the Schrammel-Brannan revision this mean chance score is approximately 59 and falls near the 15th percentile for the CCC norms. The test scores for the lowest 15 per cent of such a population would not seem to be interpretable. Those revised forms that fail to time each subtest separately are even less appropriate for administration to low aptitude subjects. In such a case it is possible for one slow worker to plod along and bog down on an early subtest while another shops around for easy items or else responds to all the multiple choice items first.

The highly speeded nature of the test is also objectionable in a test designed to be administered to low as well as high aptitude subjects. Most modern test theorists lean toward the use of a more adequate allotment of working time in order to allow most subjects to respond to all items. If such a test is in spiral omnibus form, it may legitimately be given under relatively unspeeded conditions, without separate timing of subparts, and be scored rights only, thus becoming more nearly self-administering.

However, if the Army Alpha were to be revised in light of the above principles, the scores could no longer be employed with the original norms. Thus the Army Alpha, even in revised form, is not generally recommended except in cases where a prime desideratum is to be able to compare the test performance of the subjects with the norms for World War I soldiers.

WILLIS C. SCHAEFER, *Institute for Research in Human Relations, Washington, D.C.*

The *Army Group Examination Alpha* and its revisions have a long history of research application and practical usefulness, and this record of service will undoubtedly continue on into the future. While there is an extensive bibliography of relevant research references, none of this background material is referred to in the brief manual. This is unfortunate since for many users of the test the manual is the only reference for test interpretation which is directly available. This reviewer believes that a real service could be performed for users of the *Revised Alpha Examination* by the extension of the manual to include a list of selected references and a systematic summary of the findings of greatest practical value in the use of the test. Certainly the test publishers recognize the desirability of providing readily available background interpretive material for effective test usage as evidenced by their excellent manual for the *Differential Aptitude Tests*.

The use of this test involves several practical considerations. For one thing, the test is not self-administering. It requires careful oral presentation of all instructions and strict adherence to time limits for eight subtests, thus making it necessary to limit the test group in size to one in which there will be no hearing problems and in which effective supervisory control can be maintained without difficulty. Then, the test is set up for hand scoring only. While this may be a relatively rapid clerical process for small group administration, it can be quite unwieldy if large groups are involved. Probably most important, no normative or intercorrelational data are contained in the manual for subtest scores either singly or combined; hence, the user must do his own research for general or specific comparative group performances. If part scores are not to be used, then considering the administrative difficulties of subtest time limits, some single time limit spiral-omnibus test form would appear to be justified. Part scores are no end in themselves simply because they were historically available and persist as a result of the general usefulness of their sum total in correlating with other general intelligence tests or work criteria.

Test norms are presented in terms of centile ranks separately for high school boys and girls, freshmen and seniors, and for army enlisted men. The brief explanation of the derivation of these norms contained in the manual is neither adequate nor clear. The implication that the norms presented apply to high school boys and girls in general is not justified, nor is the heading "General Adult Population (Men)" for normative data based on scores of the 768 army enlisted men mentioned above, even though these cases were selected on the basis of scores on the *Army General Classification Test* "to be representative of all enlisted men." With the limited space available, the section on acknowledgments to schools cooperating in the latest standardization might profitably be condensed to allow for the provision of more useful interpretative data as, for example, occupation equivalents in terms of more useful centile rank distributions such as are provided for the AGCT.

The *Revised Alpha Examination,* Forms 5 and 7, are equivalent forms of a general intelligence test which has demonstrated usefulness in a wide variety of situations over a long period of time. The present usefulness of this test depends largely on the user's knowledge of background applications relevant to his problem. Since its original development, newer tests have been produced which are equally reliable and valid, as well as easier to administer and to score singly or in large group situations. For those situations in which specific subtest scores are desirable, newer tests with better rationale and greater experimental evidence for the specific parts are also available.

[282]

*California Test of Mental Maturity and Adaptations. Grades kgn–1, 1–3, 4–8, 7–10 and adults, 9–16 and adults; 1936–51; 5 levels (Pre-Primary, Primary, Elementary, Intermediate, and Advanced); 5 editions; IBM for grades 4 and over; postage extra; 35¢ per specimen set of any one level of any one edition, postpaid; Elizabeth T. Sullivan, Willis W. Clark, and Ernest W. Tiegs; California Test Bureau.

a) CALIFORNIA TEST OF MENTAL MATURITY. Grades kgn–1, 1–3, 4–8, 7–10 and adults, 9–16 and adults; 1936-51; 19 scores: 11 subtests (not listed here), verbal concepts, and combined scores of memory, spatial relations, logical reasoning, numerical reasoning, total mental, language, nonlanguage; 1 form, '51; manuals ('51); $2.75 per 25 of any one level; separate answer sheets may be used for grades 4 and over; 4¢ per IBM answer sheet; 7¢ per Scoreze answer sheet; 60¢ per set of stencils for machine scoring of answer sheets of any one level; 40¢ per set of stencils for hand scoring of answer sheets of any one level; Pre-Primary: 50(70) minutes; Primary: 65(85) minutes; Elementary, Intermediate, and Advanced: 84–92(100–105) minutes.

b) CALIFORNIA SHORT-FORM TEST OF MENTAL MATURITY. Grades kgn–1, 1–3, 4–8, 7–10 and adults, 9–16 and adults; 1938–50; 13 scores: 6 subtests (not listed here), verbal concepts, and combined scores of spatial relations, logical reasoning, numerical reasoning, total mental, language, nonlanguage; S-Form ('50); manuals ('50); $1.75 per 25 of any one level; separate answer sheets may be used for grades 4 and over; 4¢ per IBM answer sheet; 7¢ per Scoreze answer sheet; 40¢ per set of stencils for machine scoring of answer sheets of any one level; 20¢ per set of stencils for hand scoring of answer sheets of any one level; Pre-Primary: 20(40) minutes; Primary: 42(60) minutes; Elementary: 47(60) minutes; Intermediate: 51(60) minutes; Advanced: 52(60) minutes.

c) CALIFORNIA TEST OF MENTAL MATURITY: LANGUAGE SECTION. Grades kgn–1, 1–3, 4–8, 7–10 and adults, 9–16 and adults; 1942–51; formerly called *California Intelligence Tests, Language Section;* 5 scores: 4 subtests (not listed here), total language; 1 form, '51; $1.50 per 25 of any one level; separate answer sheets may be used for grades 4 and over; 4¢ per IBM answer sheet; 7¢ per Scoreze answer sheet; 20¢ per set of stencils for machine scoring of answer sheets of any one level; 20¢

per set of stencils for hand scoring of answer sheets of any one level; Pre-Primary: 20(28) minutes; Primary: 26(34) minutes; Elementary, Intermediate, and Advanced: 40–41(46) minutes.

d) CALIFORNIA TEST OF MENTAL MATURITY: NON-LANGUAGE SECTION. Grades kgn–1, 1–3, 4–8, 7–10 and adults, 9–16 and adults; 1942–51; formerly called *California Intelligence Tests: Non-Language Section;* 12 scores: 8 subtests (not listed here), memory, and combined scores of spatial relationships, reasoning, total nonlanguage; 1 form, '51; manual ('51); $1.75 per 25 of any one level; separate answer sheets may be used for grades 4 and over; 4¢ per IBM answer sheet; 7¢ per Scoreze answer sheet; 40¢ per set of stencils for machine scoring of answer sheets of any one level; 20¢ per set of stencils for hand scoring of answer sheets of any one level; Spanish editions for grades 7–10 and adults, 9–16 and adults available at same prices; Pre-Primary: 30(42) minutes; Primary: 39(51) minutes; Elementary, Intermediate, and Advanced: 48–51 (54–59) minutes.

e) CALIFORNIA CAPACITY QUESTIONNAIRE. Grades 7–16 and adults; 1941–42; an abbreviated adaptation of *California Test of Mental Maturity* (1936–39); 3 scores: nonlanguage, language, total; 2 editions; Forms A, B; manual ['42]; $1.50 per 25 of any one edition, postage extra.

1) *Hand Scoring Edition.* 1941; 30(40) minutes.
2) *Machine Scoring Edition.* 1942; 2¢ per IBM answer sheet; 20¢ per machine scoring stencil; 20¢ per hand scoring stencil; postage extra; 35(45) minutes.

REFERENCES

1–5. See 40:1384.
6–15. See 3:223.
16. COFFEY, HUBERT STANLEY. *A Study of Certain Mental Functions and Their Relation to Changes in the Intelligence of Preschool Children.* Doctor's thesis, University of Iowa (Iowa City, Iowa), 1938.
17. NOLAN, ESTHER GRACE. "Reading Difficulty Versus Low Mentality." *Calif J Sec Ed* 17:34–9 Ja '42. (PA 16:2468)
18. BARNOWE, THEODORE JOSEPH. *The Influence of Scoring Technique and Construction on the Validity of Mental Tests.* Doctor's thesis, University of Washington (Seattle, Wash.), 1946. (*Abstracts of Theses....1945–1946,* 1946, pp. 11–2.)
19. CHURCH, ALFRED M. "The Standardized Testing Program Summary Report: Territorial Public Schools, 1946–47." *Hawaii Ed R* 36:49+ O '47. * (PA 22:4627)
20. DAVIS, W. ALLISON, AND HAVIGHURST, ROBERT J. "The Measurement of Mental Systems: Can Intelligence Be Measured?" *Sci Mo* 66:301–16 Ap '48. * (PA 22:3381)
21. DEJMEK, FRANK W. "A Study of Relationships Among Scores on the Minnesota Paper Form Board-Revised Series AA, the Non-Language Section of the California Test of Mental Maturity, and Test 2 of the Non-Language Section of the California Test of Mental Maturity." *J Ed Res* 42:307–11 D '48. * (PA 23:3647)
22. EVANS, M. CATHARINE. "Differentiation of Home Economics Students According to Major Emphasis." *Occupations* 27:120–5 N '48. * (PA 23:4410)
23. HERRMANN, MAY, AND HACKMAN, ROY B. "Distributions of Scores on the Wechsler-Bellevue Scales and the California Test of Mental Maturity at a V.A. Guidance Center." *J Appl Psychol* 32:642–8 D '48. * (PA 23:3648)
24. SCHELLENBERG, ERNEST DAVID. *A Study of the Relationship of the Progressive Achievement Tests and the California Mental Maturity Subtests.* Master's thesis, University of Southern California (Los Angeles, Calif.), 1948.
25. STEIN, HARRY L. "On Establishing Norms in a Large City System." *J Exp Ed* 16:192–5 Mr '48. * (PA 20:5348)
26. BAILEY, HELEN K. "A Study of the Correlations Between Group Mental Tests, the Stanford-Binet, and the Progressive Achievement Test Used in the Colorado Springs Elementary Schools." *J Ed Res* 43:93–100 O '49. * (PA 24:2825)
27. CLARK, JERRY H. "An Investigation of Certain Relationships Between the California Test of Mental Maturity and the Wechsler-Bellevue Intelligence Scale." *J General Psychol* 41:215. Jl '49. * (PA 24:2597)
28. CLARK, WILLIS W. "The Differentiation of Mental Abilities at Various Age Levels." Abstract. *Am Psychol* 4:291 Jl '49. * (PA 23:6071, title only)
29. CLARK, WILLIS W. "The Differentiation of Mental Abilities at Various Age Levels," Part 1, pp. 23–9. In *The Sixth Yearbook of the National Council on Measurements Used in Education, 1948–1949.* Fairmont, W.Va.: the Council, Fairmont State College, 1949. Pp. v, 140 (variously numbered). Paper, mimeographed. *
30. RINSLAND, HENRY D. "The Prediction of Veterans' Success From Test Scores at the University of Oklahoma," Part 1,

pp. 59–72. In *The Sixth Yearbook of the National Council on Measurements Used in Education, 1948–1949.* Fairmont, W.Va.: the Council, Fairmont State College, 1949. Pp. v, 140 (variously numbered). Paper, mimeographed. *
31. CARLSON, HILDING B., AND HENDERSON, NORMAN. "The Intelligence of American Children of Mexican Parentage." *J Abn & Social Psychol* 45:544–51 Jl '50. * (PA 25:915)
32. MANSON, MORSE P. "The Measurement of Intelligence of One Hundred Two Male Paraplegics." *J Consult Psychol* 14:193–6 Je '50. * (PA 25:506)
33. NAIR, RALPH KENNETH. *Predictive Value of Standardized Tests and Inventories in Industrial Arts Teacher Education.* Doctor's thesis, University of Missouri (Columbia, Mo.), 1950. Abstract: *Microfilm Abstracts* 10:77–8 no 3 '50. * (PA 25:4862, title only)
34. WILEY, LLEWELLYN N. "Equating Scores on Three Intelligence Tests." Abstract. *Am Psychol* 5:467 S '50. * (PA 25:4600, title only)
35. WINANS, J. MERRITT. "Measuring I.Q. Changes of High School Students." *Calif J Ed Res* 1:56–9 Mr '50. *
36. ELIAS, JACK Z. *Non-Intellective Factors in Certain Intelligence and Achievement Tests: An Analysis of Factors in Addition to the Cognitive Entering Into the Intelligence and Achievement Scores of Children at the Sixth Grade Level.* Doctor's thesis, New York University (New York, N.Y.), 1951. Abstract: *Microfilm Abstracts* 11:558–60 no 3 '51. * (PA 26:1495, title only)
37. PLUMB, GALEN R. *The Evaluation of the Mental Characteristics of a Reformatory Population as Revealed by the Wechsler-Bellevue Intelligence Scale and the California Test of Mental Maturity.* Doctor's thesis, University of Nebraska (Lincoln, Neb.), 1951.
38. ROSILDA, M. "Is an I.Q. an Index to Algebra Ability?" *J Ed Res* 44:391–93 Ja '51. * (PA 25:8258)
39. STRAUS, MURRAY A. "Mental Ability and Cultural Needs: A Psychocultural Interpretation of the Intelligence Test Performance of Ceylon University Entrants." *Am Sociol R* 16:371–5 Je '51. *

J Consult Psychol 15:516 D '51. Laurance F. Shaffer. [Review of the *California Short-Form Test of Mental Maturity, 1950 S-Form.*] The revision of this group mental ability test places more stress on the differential aptitudes measured, and less on the total MA and IQ. The test for each stage of maturity consists of seven parts, presumably comparable from level to level because of similar content. Scores are obtained for total mental factors, language factors, nonlanguage factors, spatial relationships, logical reasoning, numerical reasoning, and verbal concepts. Total score reliabilities range from .92 to .95, and part-score reliabilities from .81 to .95, being generally higher at the upper age levels. The subtest intercorrelations, mainly from the .20's to the .40's, give some support to the differential interpretation of the profiles. Norms are based on very large groups that were controlled with respect to age and school progress. No evidence is given, however, about the geographic or socioeconomic distribution of the normative subjects. Validity is defended in terms of high correlation with the Stanford-Binet, but the exact coefficient is not stated. No data are presented on the test's relationships to subsequent school achievement or to other appropriate criteria. In these respects, the information given in the manuals falls short of meeting desirable professional standards.

For a review by Henry E. Garrett and excerpts from reviews of the California Test of

Mental Maturity, *see 3:223;* for reviews by Anne Anastasi and Emily T. Burr of the California Capacity Questionnaire, *see 3:222;* for reviews by Raymond B. Cattell, F. Kuhlmann, *and an excerpt from a review of the* California Test of Mental Maturity, *see 40:1384;* for reviews by W. D. Commins, Rudolf Pintner, Arthur E. Traxler, *and an excerpt from a review of the* California Test of Mental Maturity, *see 38:1042.*

[283]

*Chicago Non-Verbal Examination. Ages 6 and over; 1936–47; may be administered orally or in pantomime; 1 form, '36; manual ['47]: $3.45 per 25; $1.20 per manual and scoring keys; $1.25 per specimen set; postpaid; (40) minutes; Andrew W. Brown with the assistance of Seymour P. Stein and Perry L. Rohrer; Psychological Corporation. *

REFERENCES

1. Brown, Andrew W. "The Development and Standardization of the Chicago Non-Verbal Examination." *J Appl Psychol* 24:36–47, 122–9 F, Ap '40.

For reviews by Robert G. Bernreuter, Myrtle Luneau Pignatelli, and S. D. Porteus, see 40: 1387.

[284]

★Classification Test for Industrial and Office Personnel. Adults; 1943–49; Forms A ('47—revision of 1943 form), B ('47); mimeographed manual ['47]; norms ('49); $2 per 25, postage extra; 50¢ per specimen set, postpaid; 10(15) or 15(20) minutes; Jay L. Otis, Evelyn Katz (A), Robert W. Henderson (A), Mary Aiken (A), David J. Chesler (B), and Gardner E. Lindzey (B); Personnel Research Institute, Western Reserve University. *

REFERENCES

1. Otis, Jay L., and Chesler, David J. "A Short Test of Mental Ability." *J Appl Psychol* 33:146–50 Ap '49. * (PA 24:16)

[285]

★College Entrance Examination Board Scholastic Aptitude Test. Candidates for college entrance; 1926–51; available only in College Entrance Examination Board Admissions Testing Program (see 526); 2 scores: verbal, mathematical; 180(210) minutes; prepared by the Staff of Educational Testing Service; program administered by Educational Testing Service for the College Entrance Examination Board. *

REFERENCES

1. Moore, Herbert, and Trafton, Helen. "Equating Test Scores." *J Ed Psychol* 25:216–9 Mr '34. * (PA 8:3827)
2. Dickter, M. Richard. "The Relationship Between Scores on the Scholastic Aptitude Test and College Marks in Chemistry." *J Exp Ed* 6:40–5 S '37. * (PA 12:2102)
3. Dickter, Morris Richard. *The Relationship Between Scores on the Scholastic Aptitude Test and Marks in Mathematics and Science.* Doctor's thesis, University of Pennsylvania (Philadelphia, Pa.), 1937. Pp. 57.
4. Dickter, M. Richard. "The Relationship Between Scores on the Scholastic Aptitude Test and College Grades in Mathematics." *J Ed Psychol* 29:363–73 My '38. * (PA 13:519)
5. Virene, Edgar Paul. *A Factor Analysis of the Scholastic Aptitude Test.* Philadelphia, Pa.: University of Pennsylvania, 1940. Pp. vii, 36. Paper. *
6. Shanner, William M., and Kuder, G. Frederic. "A Comparative Study of Freshman Week Tests Given at the University of Chicago." *Ed & Psychol Meas* 1:85–92 Ja '41. * (PA 15:2814)
7. Weber, Christian O. "Old and New College Board Scores and Grades of College Freshmen." *J Am Assn Col Reg* 20:70–5 O '44. * (PA 19:570)
8. Peixotto, Helen E. "Relationship of College Board Examination Scores and Reading Scores for College Freshmen." *J Appl Psychol* 30:406–11 Ag '46. * (PA 21:289)
9. Stalnaker, Ruth C., and Stalnaker, John M. "The Effect on a Candidate's Score of Repeating the Scholastic Aptitude Test of the College Entrance Examination Board." *Ed & Psychol Meas* 6:495–503 w '46. * (PA 21:2496)
10. Thorndike, Robert L. "The Prediction of Intelligence at College Entrance From Earlier Test." *J Ed Psychol* 38:129–48 Mr '47. * (PA 22:861)
11. Conrad, Herbert S., and Miller, Joseph M. "Institutional Standards as a Factor in the Validity of a Scholastic Aptitude Test." Abstract. *Am Psychol* 3:260 Jl '48. * (PA 22:5567, title only)
12. Seltzer, Carl C. "Academic Success in College of Public and Private School Students: Freshman Year at Harvard." *J Psychol* 25:419–31 Ap '48. * (PA 22:4606)
13. Stalnaker, John M. "Results of the Pepsi-Cola Finalists on the College Board Test." *Sch & Soc* 68:110–1 Ag 14 '48. * (PA 24:3409)
14. Frederiksen, Norman. "Predicting Mathematics Grades of Veteran and Nonveteran Students." *Ed & Psychol Meas* 9:73–88 sp '49. * (PA 24:5745)
15. Pearson, Richard. "Testing the Board's Tests." *Col Bd R* 9:111–4 D '49. * (PA 24:2833)
16. Traxler, Arthur E. "A Note on the Correlation of the Secondary Education Board Junior Scholastic Aptitude Test With the College Entrance Examination Board Scholastic Aptitude Test," pp. 63–5. (PA 23:3453) In *1948 Fall Testing Program in Independent Schools and Supplementary Studies.* Educational Records Bulletin, No. 51. New York: Educational Records Bureau, January 1949. Pp. xii, 72. Paper, lithotyped. *
17. Johnson, A. Pemberton. "College Board Mathematical Tests and the Pre-Engineering Inventory Predict Scholastic Success in Colleges of Engineering." Abstract. *Am Psychol* 5:353 Jl '50. * (PA 25:1279, title only)
18. Mollenkopf, W. G. "Slow—But How Sure?" *Col Board R* 11:147–51 Je '50. * (PA 25:3421)
19. Myers, R. C., and Schultz, D. G. "Predicting Academic Achievement With a New Attitude-Interest Questionnaire—I." *Ed & Psychol Meas* 10:654–63 w '50. * (PA 25:6474)
20. Schultz, Douglas G. "The Comparability of Scores From Three Mathematics Tests of the College Entrance Examination Board." *Psychometrika* 15:369–84 D '50. * (PA 25:6415)
21. Traxler, Arthur E. "A Further Study of Relationship Between the SEB Junior Scholastic Aptitude Test and the CEEB Scholastic Aptitude Test," pp. 48–51. (PA 24:3898) In *1949 Fall Testing Program in Independent Schools and Supplementary Studies.* Educational Records Bulletin, No. 53. New York: Educational Records Bureau, January 1950. Pp. xiii, 70. Paper, lithotyped. * (PA 24:3894)
22. Dyer, Henry S. "The Scholastic Aptitude Test—Items, Scores, and Coaching." *Col Board R* 15:235–9 N '51. *

Frederick B. Davis, *Professor of Education, and Director of the Educational Clinic, Hunter College, New York, New York; and Director, Test Research Service, Bronxville, New York.* [Review of Forms XSA2-Z$_5$, XSA1$_4$, YSA1$_{12}$, ZSA1$_1$, ZSA2$_3$.]

This test includes five 30-minute speeded sections. Three of these appear to measure principally word knowledge and reasoning ability in verbal materials, and two of them principally knowledge of arithmetic, algebra, and elementary geometry plus ability to reason in quantitative terms. The items in all of the sections show evidence of careful construction and editing. However, to the reviewer they lack originality and interest. The passages on which the reading items are based seem dull and, in general, poorly written. The difficulty of the items based on them often seems to derive from the muddiness of the passages rather than from the necessity for close reasoning or sensitiveness to implications on the part of the examinee. In all types of verbal items, the examinee who has a well-rounded assortment of clichés will do well to consider them in selecting his answers.

As in the case of most tests, some faulty items can be found. One poorly edited item, referring to a load of baled hay, asks, "If each bale averages 110 pounds, how many bales of hay are there in his load?" Naturally, one cannot get an average weight for a single bale except by weighing it more than once. What is meant is, "If the bales average 110 pounds each, how many bales are there in his load?" A number of items are faulty in that the keyed answer is not so nearly correct as could probably be provided. This fault is pointed up by the fact that the directions ask the examinee to mark the one correct answer, to choose "the correct completion" or "the *one* correct completion." The usual directions to select the best answer would be better.

Otherwise, the directions seem satisfactory except, perhaps, for their treatment of the problem of guessing. They encourage shrewd guessing "since a shrewd guess is more often right than wrong," but continue, "Do not, however, waste time in haphazard guessing." This sentence implies that the scores are corrected for chance success; unless this is true, time spent in "haphazard guessing" is far from wasted—a fact widely known among high school students and almost universally known among preparatory school students especially coached to take the College Board examinations.

Reliability and validity data have been obtained for the test. The reliability data available to the reviewer were computed by methods that may yield spuriously high coefficients for speeded tests like most sections of the *Scholastic Aptitude Test*. However, it seems safe to say that the reliability coefficients of the verbal and quantitative scores are so much higher than their validity coefficients that the reliabilities could vary considerably without appreciably affecting the test's effectiveness for predicting academic success.

The validity data indicate that this test is about as useful for predicting academic success as a test of its limited scope can be. Tests that have been commercially available for twenty years are about equally useful. Any unique merit in using the *Scholastic Aptitude Test* lies in the fact that one can be reasonably sure that the examinees will not have had access to it beforehand and that it will be administered and scored with scrupulous care and accuracy.

[286]
★**College Transfer Test.** Candidates for college junior year entrance; 1950–51; formerly called *College Ability Test*; 2 scores: verbal comprehension and English expression, quantitative reasoning; test administered five times annually (December, January, March, May, August) at centers established by Educational Testing Service; application form and bulletin of information may be obtained from Educational Testing Service; fee, $6 per student; fee includes scoring service and reporting of scores to any three designated colleges; scores not reported to examinees; $1 per additional report; 180(210) minutes; test administered by Educational Testing Service for the College Entrance Examination Board. *

REFERENCES
1. ENGELHART, MAX D. "Examinations to Facilitate Transfer of Junior College Graduates to Senior Colleges." *Jun Col J* 20:332–6 F '50. *

[287]
Culture-Free Test. Grades 9–16 and adults; 1944–47; 1 form, '44; manual ['47]; $4 per 25; 35¢ per specimen set; postpaid; 72(80) minutes; Raymond B. Cattell; Psychological Corporation. *

REFERENCES
1–4. See 3:228.

RALEIGH M. DRAKE, *Professor of Psychology and Head of the Department, Kent State University, Kent, Ohio*:

There is no doubt that a culture-free test is needed. The elimination of the influences of training and environment would make scores from intelligence tests much more meaningful than they are at present when a score is made up of unknown proportions of innate capacity and environmental effects. This test is made entirely of nonverbal materials. Mental ability is measured by the amount and goodness of eduction of relations among the nonverbal symbols presented. That most of the common cultural influences are eliminated is obvious. Even the directions can be given in pantomime if necessary. Very little validity and reliability data are given. Correlations with the Army Alpha run from .50 to .60 for four groups of high school students. A reliability coefficient, based on only one high school freshman class numbering 121, is given as .88. Percentile norms are given for high school freshmen and high school seniors based on 1009 and 918 cases respectively. Since the test is appropriate for levels through the adult, more norms would be very desirable.

The reviewer has given the test to various groups during the past five years. For a group of college seniors and graduate students at Kent State University, it correlated .84 ($N = 28$) with the *Wechsler-Bellevue Intelligence Scale*; .83 with the *Army General Classification Test*;

College Entrance Examination Board Scholastic Aptitude Test

.84 with the *Otis Self-Administering Test of Mental Ability;* .44 (N = 49) with the *Miller Analogies Test,* which is a rather high level verbal reasoning test; .13 (N = 25) with the *KSU Graduate Qualifying Examination,* a 210-minute comprehensive examination covering the various fields of psychology; and, for specific courses, .11 (N = 22) with Systems, .19 (N = 24) with Learning Theory, .31 (N = 62) with Mental Tests, .31 (N = 25) with Social, and .45 (N = 35) with Statistics.

Correlation matrices including this test indicate that it is measuring very little of the memory factor, which is more prevalent in verbal tests, but that it correlates with what appear to be the eductive factors measured by other intelligence tests.

It does not correlate as well (.36) with high school grades as does the Henmon-Nelson (.80) or the Otis (.62), nor as well (.36) with teachers' ratings of intelligence as does the Henmon-Nelson (.71) or the Otis (.71). The difference could be accounted for by the absence of the memory and verbal factors in the Cattell and their presence in the two verbal tests, and by the usual overemphasis in school on verbal and memory factors as represented by school grades and teacher ratings of intelligence. Since its high correlations with various recognized intelligence tests indicate that it is measuring mental energy (general intelligence) as usually defined, the low correlations with grades may not be a serious drawback. In fact, its use in school might be a distinct advantage in that it would emphasize relation finding (eduction), reasoning, constructive thinking, and problem solving, rather than memory. If teachers would think of intelligence in these terms, they might emphasize the attitudes and techniques conducive to logical thinking. The Learning To Think Series by Thelma Thurstone is an attempt in this direction.

A communication from C. M. Bhatia, director of the Bureau of Psychology for the State of Uttar Pradesh, Allahabad, India, tells how the test was used for selecting applicants for government service. Only Matrices I and II were given. Correlations with two other intelligence tests were .62 and .59 (N = 228). He says, "The use of Cattell's test thus appears to us to be perfectly justified in our present group." He is not, however, sure that the test is one hundred per cent culture free. He suggests that giving it to rural illiterate masses might indicate how free it is of culture and training. A. Edwin Harper, Jr., psychologist at Ewing Christian College in Allahabad, India, has given the whole test to 56 college students and reports the following:

Test was administered to First and Second-Year College students, and correlated with marks in two-year course in General and Educational Psychology (which is ⅕ of their college work). Sigma is almost identical with Cattell's, but Mean is at his 10th percentile. Distribution is normal, not skewed. Correlation with two-year average marks is .416 ± .07. The large number not finishing suggests that this test is *not* "essentially an untimed test" for our group. It is also cumbersome to administer as instructions often take 10 to 15 minutes, before understood.

At least this test can be given to literate-illiterate, educated-uneducated, and to other groups of widely varying cultural backgrounds; it provides a means for studying the effects of racial, cultural, and educational influences on mental ability test scores and perhaps even of obtaining some evidence concerning these influences on the constitutional factors responsible for mental capacity. In view of the widesweeping claims and poor experimental evidence in the Iowa Studies and in the Schmidt report, it is evident that the respective roles of nature and nurture have never been adequately evaluated and that the true relationship between an IQ, any other score on a mental ability test, and real mental ability (energy) has not been clearly conceived, let alone even approximately determined. A wealth of revealing research results awaits the intensive use of this and other similar relatively nonverbal and culture-free tests.

For reviews by L. S. Penrose, Walter C. Shipley, and David Wechsler, see 3:228.

[288]
*[Detroit Intelligence Tests.] Grades 2–4, 5–9, 9–16; 1924–42; 3 levels; $4.20 per 100 of any one level, postage extra; 18¢ per specimen set of any one level, postpaid; Harry J. Baker; Public School Publishing Co. *

a) DETROIT PRIMARY INTELLIGENCE TEST. Grades 2–4; 1924; Forms C, D; no data on validity; 30 (35) minutes.

b) DETROIT ALPHA INTELLIGENCE TEST. Grades 4–8; 1924–42; Forms S ('41—a revision of Form M), T ('42—a revision of Form R); manual ('41); 45(50) minutes.

c) DETROIT ADVANCED INTELLIGENCE TEST. Grades 9–16; 1924–42; Forms V ('25), W ('24); no data on validity; revised manual ('42); 40(45) minutes.

REFERENCES
1. KUHLMANN, F. "The Kuhlmann-Anderson Intelligence Tests Compared with Seven Others." *J Appl Psychol* 12:545–94 D '28.
2. SEAGOE, M.V. "An Evaluation of Certain Intelligence Tests." *J Appl Psychol* 18:432–6 Je '34.

For a review by W. Line, see 40:1393.

[289]
*Duplex Series of Ability Tests. Ages 10, 11, 12, 13; 1947–50; 6 scores: verbal ability, logical reasoning, numerical reasoning, spatial relationships, nonlanguage factors, total; 4 levels; 3s. 6d. per revised manual ('50); 7s. per specimen set of any one level; purchase tax (British purchasers only) and postage extra; Frank M. Earle; George G. Harrap & Co. Ltd. *

a) NO. 1. Age 10; 1 form, '47; 12s. 6d. per 25; nontimed (60) minutes.
b) NO. 2. Age 11; 1 form, '47; 12s. 6d. per 25; nontimed (80) minutes.
c) NO. 3. Age 12; 1 form, '50; 17s. 6d. per 25; nontimed (90) minutes.
d) NO. 4. Age 13; 1 form, '50; 20s. per 25; nontimed (180) minutes.

REFERENCES
1. EARLE, F. M. "The Significance of Ability Differences at Eleven-plus." *Occupational Psychol* 21:193–202 O '47. * (PA 22:1562)
2. EARLE, F. M. "Use of the Duplex Tests in Selection for Secondary Education." Abstract. *Adv Sci* 7:95 My '50. *

W. G. EMMETT, *Reader in Educational Research, University of Edinburgh, Edinburgh, Scotland.*

These tests were constructed to give guidance in selecting children for different types of secondary school, and in particular for different courses within such schools. The issue of 1950 differs from that of 1947 only in some alterations to Tests 3 and 4, and in the amendment of answers and norms in the manual.

Test No. 1, suitable for 10-year-olds, starts with 20 easy practice items forming Part I. Part II contains 50 verbal items of types common in intelligence tests, while Part III has 50 arithmetical and spatial items. Marking is objective, except for Items 21 to 30 of Part II, where the marker is likely to meet difficulty, especially in cases of bad spelling. Percentile norms are given, indicating a median raw score of 49 with a standard deviation of 19. The test is thus of a suitable order of difficulty; the spread of scores is not very high.

Test No. 2, for 11-year-olds, has 70 verbal items of usual type in Part I and 50 arithmetical and spatial items in Part II. Marking of scripts should proceed without much difficulty though the lay-out of the answers in the manual is certainly not helpful. Half marks are awarded here and there for partially correct answers, and some items receive 2 marks and some 3. The maximum possible score is 145, with a median of 68 and standard deviation of about 26. Economy of effort and time on the part of both children and markers is best achieved when test scores give a standard deviation of from 20 to 25 points for every 100 points of raw score. From this aspect the test is not highly discriminative.

Test No. 3, for 12-year-olds, contains 90 verbal items in Part I and 75 arithmetical, spatial and mechanical items in Part II. Instructions to the children in one or two places are liable to be misinterpreted, and quite a few of the answers given in the key cannot be accepted as unique, or even as correct. The maximum possible score is 196; the median score is 80 and the standard deviation is 34. For a similar test of 100 items the standard deviation would be about 17, showing relatively poor discrimination. The 99th percentile score is only 148; several items must therefore be too difficult for children aged 12 and 13.

Test No. 4, for 13-year-olds, is divided into four sections. Section A of 100 items tests attainments in English; Section B is a mixed bag containing verbal classification items, analogies, reasoning and general knowledge, 90 items in all. These are followed by 25 arithmetical problems and 35 spatial items in Section Ç. Then comes Section D with 35 geometrical items, 50 mechanical and 15 spatial items of three dimensions. Some items receive two marks, others three; the maximum possible score for all 350 items is 395. Marking must be a laborious process, and in some items the marker's judgment must be exercised. The test leaves the impression that much of it is too difficult for children of 13, even of grammar school standard. This is confirmed by a median score for boys of 134 (out of 395) and a 99th percentile score for boys of 285. The standard deviation of raw scores is 52, corresponding to 13 for an equivalent test of 100 items; only a very low discrimination is thus attained.

Considerable ingenuity in the construction of items is evident, but it is obvious that many items would not be present if they had been subjected to the scrutiny of preliminary trial. To allow unlimited working time must cause difficulties of administration.

The reviewer has been in correspondence with the author about statistics missing from the manual. Norms were based on 1,000 unselected children in each age group from an English county borough; as the mean IQ in different boroughs may vary by as much as 10 points the basis of standardisation is not very secure. Percentile norms are given for each test, and for each broad type of item within each test; mental age and IQ norms are given for test total scores. Reliability coefficients are not available.

As the main purpose of the tests was to classify

children for different courses in the secondary schools, the validity of different groups of items was ascertained by forming contingency tables comparing the numbers of children who would have been placed in certain courses on the basis of their test scores with the numbers actually taking such courses, it being assumed that the children have been correctly placed by the school staff. Agreement between the test results and teachers' placings on a five-point scale occurred in from 80 to 90 per cent of the cases.

In general, tests of this type should serve a most useful purpose. The tests under review, however, should undergo considerable revision and should be substantiated with more statistical information before they can be recommended.

STANLEY D. NISBET, *Professor of Education, University of Glasgow, Glasgow, Scotland.*

These tests are designed for educational guidance during the period of transition from the primary to the secondary school. Earle has for long insisted (*1, 2*) that the prevalent British practice of making a sharp division, about the age of 11, into two groups (those fit to go to a Grammar or Senior Secondary school and those who are to go to a Modern or Junior Secondary school) largely on the basis of all-round general ability is absurdly oversimplified and in fact fundamentally unsound. His emphasis has always been on special aptitudes as opposed to general mental ability, and his tests have been devised to give profiles rather than single total scores. He claims that the tests can predict, with fair accuracy, the type of secondary school course in which a pupil is likely to be most successful, but his classification, unlike the usual dichotomy, has as many as 15 different types and levels of course. The Duplex tests represent his latest attempt to provide a battery which can be used to guide pupils into the courses most appropriate for them.

The directions given in the manual for using the tests are naturally more complicated than those for tests with a more limited aim, since the classification depends essentially on profiles of subtest scores. The necessary figures are nevertheless clearly and definitely presented in tabular form. The tests have been carefully constructed, and the provision of separate sets for each age group makes for finer discrimination, and takes account of psychological differences between the younger and the older children.

I believe these tests are very valuable, but not so much, at their present stage of development, for regular routine use in schools as for research workers, including heads of schools who are experimenting with more scientific ways of classifying, or at least giving guidance to, pupils embarking on their secondary education. I am convinced that Earle's approach is the right one and look forward to the time when tests of this kind may be confidently recommended for general application: that is why I hope research workers will use these tests extensively. I hesitate, however, to recommend them for general use because I am not satisfied that the process of validation and refinement is yet complete. Admirable as have been Earle's earlier experimental trials, the numbers he has been dealing with are too small to admit of adequate standardization or follow-up. The final determination of the best test profiles for each type of course will have to be made as the result of numerous and complex follow-up investigations. The reliability both of tests and of subtests must be accurately assessed, in order to let users know the standard errors of individual scores; and many item analysis studies will have to be made and reported. At present I do not feel that the profiles given can be surely enough established for general acceptance (for instance, the negative weighting of nonverbal subtests in selecting pupils for "linguistic" courses would require more investigation), though they are obviously on the right lines; reliability coefficients are not given in the manual, and it is probable that the tables of percentiles, especially for small subtests of 10 or 15 items, give a false impression of the stability of the raw scores. I have doubts, too, about a few individual items and should like to see new item analyses carried out on them. Finally, there is no indication in the manual of the size and composition of the standardizing groups on which the norms for the Duplex tests were drawn up.

To sum up, therefore, I believe these tests represent an important contribution to research in the scientific educational guidance of children entering the secondary schools, but I am not convinced that they are ready yet to be issued for general use in the schools.

Occupational Psychol 22:161–2 Jl '48. P. E. V(ernon). * The manual....does not give as much information as one would like on the principles of construction * By 13 years, although g is still the main source of individual differences in abilities, additional types of ability—probably influenced by interests and temperament—may be distinguished, the main ones being: (*A*) Knowledge of words and comprehension of sentences. (*B*) Reasoning—seeing relations between objects and ideas, recognizing and describing attributes of persons and things. (*C*) Recognizing relations between, and carrying out operations with, (i) numbers, (ii) shapes. (*D*) Comprehending the structure and functions of shapes, mechanical and other objects, and carrying out operations with them. Among younger children abilities are less specialized. *A* and *B* tend to coalesce, also *C* and *D*, and *g* is relatively more predominant, so that only very tentative diagnoses can be made before 12 years. For each of the main kinds of secondary course—two or one language, scientific, technical, commercial, and general with or without a practical bent—there exists an optimum range of scores on *g* (*i.e.* the test as a whole) and on one or more of the sets of sub-tests corresponding to these ability types. How successfully do the four batteries of tests achieve these aims? If this review appears somewhat critical, it should not be regarded as depreciating Dr. Earle's ingenious and pioneering approach to an extremely difficult problem. As an overworked headmaster he should be congratulated for having progressed so far in a field which needs years of full-time research in a large number of schools. In the first place the reviewer is doubtful, in the absence of factorial evidence, whether these particular four types are really self-consistent and distinctive. Number abilities tend to be more closely linked with verbal than with spatial and mechanical among average adults, and only coalesce into a scientific factor at very superior levels. American research also indicates that geometry ability does *not* depend on *k*. Secondly, it is well known that ability structure depends to a large extent on the teaching or training received. Thus the classification reached in a Scottish multilateral school may or may not apply to different educational systems. (That the tests may retain their prognostic value under different conditions has, however, been indicated by research reported in Dr. Earle's 1944 book.) Thirdly, it is not always easy to see the connexion between some of the sub-tests and the abilities at which they are aimed. Thus printed Directions items occur in the 10+ and 12+ tests of *CD*-type abilities. No doubt it is convenient to have different batteries for each age group, but the later tests do not always develop clearly from earlier ones. Thus Mechanical Comprehension items, and arranging graded objects in order, occur at 12+ but are omitted at 13+. The writer would prefer to see the (approximately) 30 different types of items from all four batteries all tried out on 11 to 13-year-olds, factorized, and followed up by multiple correlation technique. Each such sub-test would be better given with a time limit. The present batteries have no limits and last up to 60, 80, 90 and 180 minutes, respectively. But the writer knows of no evidence that untimed tests are more prognostic than timed among children, and wonders whether the *D* items at the end of the 13+ battery receive a fair share of the children's zest under untimed conditions. Lastly, there are several minor defects, indicative of hurried construction. The range of difficulty in the sub-tests varies enormously; the 50th percentile scores fall anywhere from 0 per cent. to 75 per cent. correct. There is a misprint in one test which has to be corrected in the Manual, and two footnotes on p. 43 of the Manual are omitted altogether. In occasional instances the scoring is unclear (*e.g.* Do items 61 to 63 in Test 3, Part II, receive 3 or 4 marks in all?), and in many cases it is unnecessarily elaborate. Some of the items have "open" answers, where doubtfully correct alternatives might be given. Others tend to be "tricky." This makes one wonder whether full item-analysis has been carried out, since such items are usually shown thereby to possess poor validity. The arrangement of the sub-tests is far from convenient; a great deal of searching is needed to determine which sets of items are supposed to represent which types of ability. Surely it would have been possible to demarcate them clearly by letters or numerals. The reviewer's conclusion then is that the Duplex Tests provide admirably varied and promising material for a thorough investigation of classification at 11 to 13+, rather than a finished product. Nevertheless it is greatly to be hoped that psychologists and qualified teachers (overcoming their scruples at having to pay 7*d*. to 10*d*. for each test paper) will try out this material, since it is only by collection of results on a large scale under diverse conditions that further progress can be made.

[290]

*The Essential Intelligence Test. Ages 7–12; 1940–49; title on manuals is *Essential Junior Intelligence Test;* Forms [A] ('40), B ('49), C ('48); distribution of Form B is restricted; Form A manual ['40]; Form B manual ['49]; 25–49 copies, 5½*d*. each; 6*d*. per

Duplex Series of Ability Tests

single copy; 1s. 6d. per manual; postage extra; 45(55) minutes; Fred J. Schonell and R. H. Adams; Oliver & Boyd Ltd. *

F. W. WARBURTON, *Lecturer in Educational Psychology, University of Manchester, Manchester, England.*

This is a verbal test of general intelligence for children between the ages of 7 and 11 plus. The authors claim that it also gives valid results with dull or backward pupils of 11 years or more, provided that their reading age is at least 7½ years. It seems likely, however, to be more useful within the middle range of ages than at the extremes.

There are 100 questions, most of which are multiple choice, but in some cases a single word, letter, or number has to be written by the child.

Particular attention has been given to the attractiveness of the test items, and the layout of the questions is excellent. Instructions to the children and to the tester are clear and contain some valuable advice on testing method. The children are introduced to a book of "puzzles" and are told, amongst other things, that there are no catches (an important point) and that spelling mistakes will not count. The tester is told to begin by working out the test himself, to encourage a spirit of enjoyment throughout the test session, and is warned against divulging IQ's to the class.

The back page of the booklet is used for practice. The tester works through 11 typical questions orally with the class. Help to individual children is presumably not allowed.

Scores are converted into mental ages from which IQ's can be obtained. The dangers inherent in this method are largely avoided, since the standardisation sample gives a very close fit to a normal distribution and has a standard deviation of 16.1, which means that IQ's are fairly strictly comparable, in the statistical sense, with those given by the Binet and the widely used Moray House tests. The mean IQ is 103.1, however, so that some error is introduced by this method of obtaining IQ's. This is not likely to be due to the sample chosen for the standardization, as the authors state that careful consideration of the groups chosen make up for limitations in the number of children tested (3,200). No details of this sample are given in the handbook. A stencil to facilitate marking would be an improvement.

The reported split-half reliability coefficient of .92 is based on an inadequate group of only 66 pupils, confined to the 11-year-old age group. The manual also reports a reliability coefficient of .92 based upon retesting an unspecified group of pupils after an interval of one year. One thus suspects that the test is reliable.

There are two parallel forms of the test. Form A is on general sale; Form B is on the "secret" list and is meantime for sale only to education authorities. The two forms correlate .95. Form B was standardized on 7,759 pupils, and has a test-retest reliability after an interval of three months of .92. Form B is distinctly more difficult than Form A (presuming that equivalent groups were used for standardising the two forms).

There is a shortage in Britain of good intelligence tests for the age range 7 to 11. This test has already done a great deal to bridge the gap. The authors have achieved very well the purpose for which the test was designed.

[291]

★**Figure Reasoning Test: A Non-Verbal Intelligence Test.** Ages 10 and over; 1949; 1 form; 3s. 6d. per test, postage extra; separate answer sheets must be used; answer sheets must be duplicated by test purchaser; 30(40) minutes; John C. Daniels; Crosby Lockwood & Son Ltd. *

REFERENCES

1. DANIELS, JOHN C. *Study in the Variability of Intelligence Tests.* Master's thesis, Durham University (Durham, England), 1948.

E. J. G. BRADFORD, *Senior Lecturer in Education, The University of Sheffield, Sheffield, England.*

This test could best be described as a variant of the *Progressive Matrices:* indeed, some of the matrices are practically identical, but the new test is intended to differentiate more accurately among the higher ranges of intelligence. The author claims that his test is highly reliable and heavily saturated with the intelligence factor, but unfortunately no experimental data are offered in support of these claims. Distributions of raw scores, means, and standard deviations of each age group would have given more confidence to psychologists who wished to use the test, than do the tables of standard scores which are all expressed in terms of a standard deviation of 15 per cent.

An item validation was carried out on the original version of the test; the result was not impressive. Although the author rejected items giving a correlation of less than .25 with the criterion because they were below the 1 per cent level of significance, half the remaining 45 items gave a correlation of less than .35. An item whose correlation with the criterion is definitely not due to chance is not necessarily a satisfactory measure of the variable which the criterion represents. The test would have been a better instrument of measurement if it had been constructed from only 20 of the more valid items. This would have meant scrapping Items 40 to 45, the very ones which, presumably, were intended to differentiate the higher intelligences.

Items 4, 7, 12-4, 17 and 26 all give validity correlations above .55. The reviewer is of the opinion that a close examination of the characteristics of these matrices would well repay the author or anyone else who wished to improve the test.

Since the validation of the original version of the test was carried out, one of the examples and nine of the items have been modified. One is left to wonder what effect such modifications have had.

The instructions for administering the test might satisfy a practising schoolmaster but hardly a psychologist. If followed literally, some groups of children might, by proffered solutions and by many questions, get more tuition than other groups who were shy or dull.

If, instead of applying the complete test to thousands of additional children, fresh norms were calculated from, say, 15 or 20 items with the highest validity coefficients, a really valuable addition might be made to the present very limited number of good nonverbal tests.

JAMES MAXWELL, *Principal Lecturer in Psychology, Moray House, Edinburgh, Scotland.*

This test, described as a "new non-verbal Intelligence Test," is constructed on principles similar to those of Raven's *Progressive Matrices.* Each of the 45 items consists of a 3 × 3 square set of diagrams, with the last one missing. The subject selects the missing diagram from a choice of six. Six practice items are given, and the need for adequate explanation is stressed in the instructions. The order of items is a compromise between logical sequence and degree of difficulty.

Norms for ages 10 to 16 and for adults are given in the form of standard scores. These are derived from a population of English secondary school children (4,500 cases) adjusted to give the prevailing proportions of different types of secondary schools. In such a population there will be a tendency to selection bias with the older and younger children, and though some allowance has been made for this, it is likely that the norms for ages 12 to 15 will be the most reliable. Data are being collected for more broadly based norms.

The split half reliability of the test is .96, and retest after a year's interval gave a reliability of the order of .7. Both of these must be considered as satisfactory. In a factorial analysis of eight miscellaneous tests of scholastic and intellectual ability the general factor loading of the test was of the order of 0.85, with an additional nonverbal factor present.

The test is produced in a small, sturdy booklet; the diagrams are, in general, boldly drawn, though at times the paper is not quite opaque enough. The norms, instructions for administration, answer key and specimen answer sheet are all printed on one folded sheet; a small booklet would be an improvement. The cost of 3/6 per test is not, we suppose, excessive as these things go nowadays, and the booklet can be used more than once.

The test appears to be a fairly useful general purpose test of intelligence but without specific value in any field. With so wide an age range, no high degree of discrimination is likely. The items in the test also have a wide range of difficulty, the earlier items being very easy; but the last, even with the answer key available, gave the reviewer considerable difficulty.

Brit J Ed Psychol 20:206 N '50. * a nonverbal group test which....has forty-five items and is designed for use with subjects over the age of ten years. Each item consists of two completed series of three diagrams each and a third incomplete series which can be finished by discovering the relationships which exist between the drawings in the completed series. The answer is selected from six possible solutions. Standardisation was on 4,500 secondary school children and norms are given in the form of standard scores having a mean of 100 and a standard deviation of 15. By extrapolation the norms have been extended beyond the school range to include a rating for adults. There is also a table showing a special classification based on a grammar school population, but this will probably be of little use outside the area where it was standardised as in the population given here 30 per cent. of the pupils score less than 108 and the distribution has been given an artificial normality which would seem to be hardly justified. The test is easy to administer and very quick and easy to mark. Answers are written on a separate sheet of paper so that the test booklet can be

Figure Reasoning Test

used over and over again. It is a great pity that it has been printed on rather transparent paper which allows one subtest to interfere with another. The binding, too, could be improved.

[292]

Goodenough Intelligence Test. Grades kgn–3; 1926; also called *Draw-a-Man;* 1 form; $1 per 25 children's drawing sheets, postage extra; $3.12 per manual, *Measurement of Intelligence by Drawings* (see *1* below), postpaid; specimen set not available; nontimed (10) minutes; Florence L. Goodenough; World Book Co.

REFERENCES

1. GOODENOUGH, FLORENCE L. *Measurement of Intelligence by Drawings.* Yonkers, N.Y.: World Book Co., 1926. Pp. xiii, 177. *
2. GOODENOUGH, FLORENCE L. "A New Approach to the Measurement of the Intelligence of Young Children." *J Genetic Psychol* 33:185–211 Je '26. *
3. YEPSEN, LLOYD N. "The Reliability of the Goodenough Test." Abstract. *Tr Sch B* 25:62 Je '28. * (*PA* 2:3153)
4. YEPSEN, LLOYD N. "The Reliability of the Goodenough Drawing Test With Feebleminded Subjects." *J Ed Psychol* 20:448–51 S '29. *
5. WILLIAMS, MARION L. "The Growth of Intelligence as Measured by the Goodenough Drawing Test." *J Appl Psychol* 14:239–56 Je '30. * (*PA* 4:5139)
6. DYETT, E. G. *The Goodenough Drawing Scale Applied to College Students.* Master's thesis, Columbia University (New York, N.Y.), 1931.
7. EGGERS, M. M. *Comparison of Army Alpha and Goodenough Drawings in Delinquent Women.* Master's thesis, Columbia University (New York, N.Y.), 1931.
8. LEVY, L. R. *The Function of the Goodenough Drawing Scale in the Study of High School Freshmen.* Master's thesis, Columbia University, (New York, N.Y.), 1931.
9. HILDRETH, GERTRUDE. "Mental Ability Measured by Verbal and Non-Verbal Tests." *Teach Col Rec* 34:134–42 N '32. * (*PA* 7:1178)
10. McELWEE, EDNA WILLIS. "The Reliability of the Goodenough Intelligence Test Used With Sub-Normal Children Fourteen Years of Age." *J Appl Psychol* 16:217–8 Ap '32. * (*PA* 7:4193)
11. MANUEL, H. T., AND HUGHES, LOIS S. "The Intelligence and Drawing Ability of Young Mexican Children." *J Appl Psychol* 16:382–7 Ag '32. *
12. TELFORD, C. W. "Test Performance of Full and Mixed-Blood North Dakota Indians." *J Comp Psychol* 14:123–45 Ag '32. * (*PA* 7:712)
13. COHEN, D. N. *The Goodenough Drawing Scale Applied to 13-Year-Old Children.* Master's thesis, Columbia University (New York, N.Y.), 1933.
14. GITLITZ, HARRY B. *The Goodenough Drawing Scale Applied to 14-Year-Old Children.* Master's thesis, Columbia University (New York, N.Y.), 1933.
15. McELWEE, EDNA WILLIS. "Profile Drawings of Normal and Subnormal Children." *J Appl Psychol* 18:599–603 Ag '34. * (*PA* 9:1008)
16. BERRIEN, F. K. "A Study of the Drawings of Abnormal Children." *J Ed Psychol* 26:143–50 F '35. * (*PA* 9:2778)
17. BRILL, MOSHE. "The Reliability of the Goodenough Draw a Man Test and the Validity and Reliability of an Abbreviated Scoring Method." *J Ed Psychol* 26:701–8 D '35. * (*PA* 10:2729)
18. DATTA, ANATHNATH. "Drawings of Children." *Indian J Psychol* 10:179–82 O '35. * (*PA* 10:5559)
19. HINRICHS, WILLIAM ERNEST. *The Goodenough Drawing in Relation to Delinquency and Problem Behavior.* Archives of Psychology, No. 175. New York: Archives of Psychology, Columbia University, 1935. Pp. 130. * (*PA* 9:4712)
20. MENZEL, EMIL W. "The Goodenough Intelligence Test In India." *J Appl Psychol* 19:615–24 O '35. * (*PA* 10:3761)
21. WILLIAMS, J. HAROLD. "Validity and Reliability of the Goodenough Intelligence Test." *Sch & Soc* 41:653–6 My 11 '35. * (*PA* 9:5371)
22. ISRAELITE, JUDITH. "A Comparison of the Difficulty of Items for Intellectually Normal Children and Mental Defectives on the Goodenough Drawing Test." *Am J Orthopsychiatry* 6:494–503 O '36. * (*PA* 11:1321)
23. BRILL, MOSHE. "A Study of Instability Using the Goodenough Drawing Scale." *J Abn and Social Psychol* 32:288–302 O–D '37. * (*PA* 12:3028)
24. McCARTHY, DOROTHEA. "A Study of the Reliability of the Goodenough Drawing Test of Intelligence." Abstract. *Psychol B* 34:759–60 N '37. * (*PA* 12:1660, title only)
25. SMITH, FRANKLIN O. "What the Goodenough Intelligence Test Measures." Abstract. *Psychol B* 34:760–1 N '37. * (*PA* 12:1663, title only)
26. BOEHNCKE, FRIEDA CAROLINE. *A Comparative Study of the Goodenough Drawing Test and the Leiter International Performance Scale.* Master's thesis, University of Southern California (Los Angeles, Calif.), 1938.
27. FINGERT, HYMAN H.; KAGAN, JULIA R.; AND SCHILDER, PAUL. "The Goodenough Test in Insulin and Metrazol Treatment of Schizophrenia." *J General Psychol* 21:349–65 O '39. * (*PA* 14:322)
28. BENDER, LAURETTA. "The Goodenough Test (Drawing A Man) in Chronic Encephalitis in Children." *J Nerv & Mental Dis* 91:277–86 Mr '40. * (*PA* 15:841)
29. OAKLEY, C. A. "Drawings of a Man by Adolescents." *Brit J Psychol* 31:37–60 Jl '40. * (*PA* 14:4800)
30. SPOERL, DOROTHY TILDEN. "The Drawing Ability of Mentally Retarded Children." *J Genetic Psychol* 57:259–77 D '40. * (*PA* 15:2427)
31. CHASE, JANE MUSTARD. "A Study of the Drawings of a Male Figure Made by Schizophrenic Patients and Normal Subjects." *Char & Pers* 9:208–17 Mr '41. * (*PA* 15:3400)
32. SPRINGER, N. NORTON. "A Study of the Drawings of Maladjusted and Adjusted Children." *J Genetic Psychol* 58:131–7 Mr '41. * (*PA* 15:4081)
33. DENNIS, WAYNE. "Performance of Hopi Indian Children on the Draw-a-Man Test." Abstract. *Psychol B* 39:578 O '42. * (*PA* 17:449, title only)
34. DENNIS, WAYNE. "The Performance of Hopi Children on the Goodenough Draw-a-Man Test." *J Comp Psychol* 34:341–8 D '42. * (*PA* 17:1254)
35. RUSSELL, ROGER W. "The Spontaneous and Instructed Drawings of Zuñi Children." *J Comp Psychol* 35:11–5 F '43. * (*PA* 17:1664)
36. GEIL, GEORGE A. "The Use of the Goodenough Test for Revealing Male Homosexuality." *J Crim Psychopath* 6:307–13 O '44. * (*PA* 19:1692)
37. HAVIGHURST, ROBERT J., AND JANKE, LEOTA LONG. "Relations Between Ability and Social Status in a Midwestern Community: I, Ten-Year-Old Children." *J Ed Psychol* 35:357–68 S '44. * (*PA* 19:476)
38. McCARTHY, DOROTHEA. "A Study of the Reliability of the Goodenough Drawing Test of Intelligence." *J Psychol* 18:201–16 O '44. * (*PA* 19:270)
39. NEEDHAM, NORMA R. "A Comparative Study of the Performance of Feebleminded Subjects on the Goodenough Drawing, the Goldstein-Scheerer Cube Test, and the Stanford-Binet." *Am J Mental Def* 49:155–61 O '44. * (*PA* 19:2774)
40. BERDIE, RALPH F. "Measurement of Adult Intelligence by Drawings." *J Clinical Psychol* 1:288–95 O '45. * (*PA* 20:574)
41. McHUGH, GELOLO. "Changes in Goodenough IQ at the Public School Kindergarten Level." *J Ed Psychol* 36:17–30 Ja '45. * (*PA* 19:1816)
42. McHUGH, GELOLO. "Relationship Between the Goodenough Drawing a Man Test and the 1937 Revision of the Stanford-Binet Test." *J Ed Psychol* 36:119–24 F '45. * (*PA* 19:1817)
43. MOTT, SINA M. "Muscular Activity As an Aid in Concept Formation." *Child Dev* 16:97–109 Mr–Je '45. * (*PA* 20:595)
44. WHITE, MABEL FRANCES RODGER. *A Study of the Performance of Epileptic, Feeble-Minded, and Normal Children on the Goodenough Intelligence Test.* Master's thesis, University of Iowa (Iowa City, Iowa), 1945.
45. HAVIGHURST, ROBERT J.; GUNTHER, MINNA KOROL; AND PRATT, INEZ ELLIS. "Environment and the Draw-a-Man Test: The Performance of Indian Children." *J Abn & Social Psychol* 41:50–63 Ja '46. * (*PA* 20:2120)
46. ROSENZWEIG, SAUL. "The Dynamics of an Amnesic Personality." *J Personality* 15:121–42 D '46. * (*PA* 21:3062)
47. SHRIMALI, P. L. "The Standardization of the Goodenough Intelligence Test for India." Abstract. *Proc 34th Indian Sci Congr, Delhi,* 1947 34:9 '46. *
48. McCURDY, HAROLD GRIER. "Group and Individual Variability on the Goodenough Draw-a-Man Test." *J Ed Psychol* 38:428–36 N '47. * (*PA* 22:2155)
49. DARKE, ROY A., AND GEIL, GEORGE A. "Homosexual Activity: Relation of Degree and Role to the Goodenough Test and to the Cornell Selectee Index." *J Nerv & Mental Dis* 108:217–40 S '48. * (*PA* 23:839)
50. GEIL, GEORGE A. "The Goodenough Test as Applied to Adult Delinquents." *J Clin Psychopath* 9:62–82 Ja '48. *
51. SEARS, RICHARD. "Castration Anxiety in an Adult as Shown by Projective Tests." Abstract. *Am Psychol* 3:281 Jl '48. * (*PA* 22:5371, title only)
52. BIRCH, JACK W. "The Goodenough Drawing Test and Older Mentally Retarded Children." *Am J Mental Def* 54:218–24 O '49. * (*PA* 24:2668)
53. FIEDLER, FRED E., AND SIEGEL, SAUL M. "The Free Drawing Test as a Predictor of Non-Improvement in Psychotherapy." *J Clin Psychol* 5:386–9 O '49. * (*PA* 24:3749)
54. ROSENZWEIG, SAUL; WITH THE COLLABORATION OF KATE LEVINE KOGAN. *Psychodiagnosis: An Introduction to Tests in the Clinical Practice of Psychodynamics,* pp. 39–43. New York: Grune & Stratton, Inc., 1949. Pp. xii, 380. * (*PA* 23:3761)
55. STONESIFER, FRED A. "A Goodenough Scale Evaluation of Human Figures Drawn by Schizophrenic and Non-Psychotic Adults." *J Clin Psychol* 5:396–8 O '49. * (*PA* 24:3813)
56. D'ANGELO, RITA Y. *A Comparison of White and Negro Pre-School Children in Goodenough I.Q. and Language Development.* Master's thesis, Fordham University (New York, N.Y.), 1950.

57. GOODENOUGH, FLORENCE L., AND HARRIS, DALE B. "Studies in the Psychology of Children's Drawings: II 1928–1949." *Psychol B* 47:369-433 S '50. * (PA 25:2456)
58. JOHNSON, A. P.; ELLERD, ARTHUR A.; AND LAHEY, THOMAS H. "The Goodenough Test as an Aid to Interpretation of Children's School Behavior." *Am J Mental Def* 54:516-20 Ap '50. * (PA 25:364)
59. OCHS, ELEANORE. "Changes in Goodenough Drawings Associated With Changes in Social Adjustment." *J Clin Psychol* 6:282-4 Jl '50. * (PA 25:1852)
60. ROTTERSMAN, LEON. *A Comparison of the IQ Scores on the New Revised Stanford-Binet, Form L, The Wechsler Intelligence Scale for Children, and the Goodenough "Draw a Man" Test at the Six Year Age Level.* Master's thesis, University of Nebraska (Lincoln, Neb.), 1950.

NAOMI STEWART, *Educational Testing Service, Princeton, New Jersey.*

Although the recent literature pertaining to the Draw-A-Man test reflects considerable interest in its possible uses for the study of personality, this test, as developed and standardized by Goodenough, is primarily a measure of intelligence and most appropriately evaluated on its merits as such.

During the 25 years the test has been in existence, a number of studies have confirmed that it compares favorably in test-retest reliability with most group tests of intelligence applicable in the same age range. It also compares favorably in validity, as demonstrated on the basis of its correlations with the Stanford-Binet within the age groups for which it was designed, while yet possessing the advantage of being nonverbal in character. However, any test whose major interpretation must depend on certain assumptions concerning its score distribution within various subgroups of the population cannot help but lose in value as these assumptions lose in accuracy. This test is no exception.

The raw score, which gives the number of points out of a possible total of 51 on which a given drawing has received credit, is not ordinarily used directly. Raw scores are converted into "mental ages," and the ratio between the subject's mental age and his chronological age is then taken as his Goodenough IQ. The table for converting raw scores into mental age equivalents derives from the norms for ages 3–13 published by Goodenough in 1926. These were based on 2,306 children, age 4–10, in grades appropriate to their age, drawn almost entirely from schools in four cities in New Jersey and in New York City. Norms were obtained by smoothing mean raw scores for the children at each age from 4 to 10, and then extrapolating downward to age 3 and upward to age 13. The values found by smoothing and extrapolating were then verified, without any change, on data for 1,445 additional children of normal grade for their age, mainly in the 6–12 age range, and drawn from schools in three other localities. The drawings of 1,876 children who were accelerated or retarded in grade placement were also obtained and examined in the course of the standardization, bringing the entire number of cases involved to the total of 5,627 which is sometimes cited, although not all of this total number actually entered into the means on which the norms were based.

Have the mental age equivalences thus established remained unchanged for 25 years? This seems unlikely in light of the startling changes found to have occurred during the period between World War I and World War II with respect to the distribution of scores among the general population on such tests as the Army Alpha—as revealed, for example, in data by Tuddenham [1] which show a rise of 50 points in median Alpha score during that time. Apart from the fact that the Draw-A-Man age norms are now 25 years old, a check on their accuracy would seem to be worthwhile, considering that even at the time of their original publication certain investigators (*13, 14*) questioned whether the norms for ages 10 and above were not unduly high.

A norms verification study would also provide opportunity for checking upon possible changes in validity of any of the 51 scoring points used in the Goodenough scale. With the wide dissemination of comic books among present-day moppets, the drawing instruction provided for them on television, etc., it is not unlikely that the development of certain drawing features no longer proceeds along the same lines as at the time of the original study. Here, too, apart from the possible effects of influences of this sort, certain investigators (*6–8*) have taken issue with some of the original scoring points on grounds that they penalize subjects who draw full-face rather than profile figures, and that this penalty is unwarranted, reducing the differentiation afforded by the instrument.

These suggestions are not intended to imply any fundamental defect in the test or in its basic scoring rationale. The Goodenough Draw-A-Man test is undoubtedly a most valuable instrument and as such is well worth the effort required to keep it fully up-to-date.

[1] Tuddenham, Read D. "Soldier Intelligence in World Wars I and II." *Am Psychol* 3:54-6 F '48. * (PA 22:2954)

[293]

★Graduate Record Examinations Aptitude Test. Senior year college through graduate school and candidates for graduate school; 1949–51; available only in Graduate Record Examinations programs (see 527); 2 scores: verbal ability, quantitative ability; 180 (220) minutes; prepared by the Staff of Educational Testing Service; Educational Testing Service. *

REFERENCES

1. SAUM, JAMES A. "The Graduate Record Examination and Its Application in the Stanford School of Education." Abstract. *Calif J Ed Res* 2:183 S '51. *
2. STAFFORD, JOHN W. "The Prediction of Success in Graduate School." Abstract. *Am Psychol* 6:298 Jl '51. *

J. P. GUILFORD, *Professor of Psychology, University of Southern California, Los Angeles, California.*

This test was designed to predict success of students in graduate work. But nowhere in the manual, or in other literature accompanying the tests, is there a discussion of the nature of aptitude for graduate study. The content of the test and its "verbal" and "quantitative" scores indicate that aptitude at the graduate level is virtually the same as that at the undergraduate level where similar tests have been used for many years. Graduate-school catalogs commonly state that it is not enough for the student to earn good grades in courses and that graduate work stresses skills in independent scholarship and research. Although common practice in graduate work may belie such statements, the fact remains that aptitude tests should be aimed at something more than grade getting.

It is to the credit of the publisher of this test that criteria other than grades have been used in the validation of its graduate tests—ratings of seminar and research performances. No validation data have as yet been reported for this particular test. From earlier validations of a verbal score in a number of universities and subject fields, we find indications of what to expect from the verbal score in this test. The correlations with grades ranged from −.19 to .67, with a median of .32. The correlations with ratings ranged from .14 to .77, with a median of .34.

The manual is extremely explicit and detailed with respect to procedure for administration of the test. There are norms, based upon samples of adequate size. There is very little other information of the kind we usually expect in manuals.

From information provided the reviewer but not published generally, it can be reported that reliabilities (Kuder-Richardson 20) of the scores are high (verbal, .97 and .95; quantitative, .89 and .93; in Forms X and Y, respectively). Intercorrelations of verbal and quantitative scores are sufficiently low (about .50) to justify differential predictions. No indications are given as to what differential predictions can be made or as to their margins of error. The quantitative part was found to be highly speeded (only 25 and 17 per cent completed the part), but the test is essentially a power test in spite of this fact. Other parts are less speeded. More time, however, might well be given to the more speeded parts.

Although the items in the verbal part are somewhat varied in form (synonyms, antonyms, analogies, sentence completion, and reading comprehension), the prevailing variance in the score is probably that of the verbal comprehension factor. If only one score is to be given, it might as well be based upon a vocabulary test. If other factors, probably reasoning, are believed to be important, it would be desirable to bring them out strongly in other types of tests and to give them separate scores so they can be weighted independently.

One or two minor technical points concerning items might be mentioned. In the reading comprehension items the alternative answers are generally about as long as the stem of the item; the item and the answers read much like a series of true-false items. This raises the question whether it might not be just as well to substitute five true-false items for each five-choice item (with more than one true statement in five, of course). There is also the question, applying to any multiple choice test, whether five choices are enough better than four to justify the extra printing and time. Stated otherwise, would the time and space devoted to fifth responses not be better devoted to additional items?

The standard scale originally adopted for the Graduate Record Examinations has a mean of 500 and a standard deviation of 100. This has probably been justified at some time and some place, but it seems a presumptuous exhibition of refinement of measurement, for even with reliabilities as high as these, errors of measurement are appreciable in the raw scores and are multiplied many times over in going to the standard scale.

In summary, this test aims at the selection of graduate students in the same ways in which we select undergraduate students. Its scores show high to very high reliabilities. The two forms have undergone considerable refined statistical study, the results of which have not yet been included in the manual. No information concerning validities of these forms is given, but similar verbal scores have demonstrated substantial value in predicting grades and ratings in some situations. It is urged that improvements will depend very much upon progress in understanding and arriving at criteria of success in graduate work which go considerably beyond course grades.

CARL I. HOVLAND, *Sterling Professor of Psychology, Yale University, New Haven, Connecticut.* [Review of Forms XGR and YGR.]

This newly developed scholastic ability test for use in the selection of students for graduate school is the successor to the Verbal Factor and Mathematics subtests in the Profile Test series of the Graduate Record Examinations, and accordingly yields two scores, one for verbal ability and one for quantitative ability. The verbal ability portion of the test includes vocabulary definition, verbal reasoning, and reading comprehension questions, and the test of quantitative ability contains items on arithmetical reasoning, algebraic problems, and the interpretation of graphs and descriptive data.

Administration and scoring of the tests are kept under careful control. The tests can be taken only at centers established by the Educational Testing Service, but a substantial number of these have been set up here and abroad. Scores on the test are reported both to the individual and to the graduate schools specified by the applicant. Although the tests are kept highly confidential, arrangements are available for graduate faculties considering their use to inspect them under appropriate conditions of control.

Two forms of the test are available, Forms XGR and YGR. These are in the process of development and are not parallel forms with respect to content or timing. No data appear to be available with respect to their relative difficulty determined from matched samples. Scores are determined to some extent by speed. The proportion of candidates completing the test varies from 17 per cent for the quantitative portions of Form YGR to 80 per cent for the vocabulary comprehension portion of Form XGR.

RELIABILITY. The reliability of the verbal portion of the tests is very satisfactory considering the rather narrow range of ability represented by college graduates applying to graduate schools. The odd-even reliability is .97 for XGR and .95 for YGR. These results are based on samples of 500 candidates for admission to graduate schools. Slightly lower reliabilities have been obtained for the quantitative portions of the examination (.89 for Form XGR and .93 for Form YGR).

VALIDITY. Since the test is so new, there are as yet no validation data available, but arrangements have been made by the Educational Testing Service to secure information on this problem from a number of institutions. The similarity of the verbal reasoning items to those of the *Miller Analogies Test* and the vocabulary items to those of the earlier Verbal Factor subtests of the GRE makes it appear likely, however, that the new test will be of real value in graduate student selection. Similarly the fact that the methods and procedures used in developing the mathematics portion of the Profile Test were closely followed in the construction of the present Quantitative subtest makes the new test appear promising. In the twenty-odd studies of the original Mathematics test in the Profile Test series, a median correlation of about .40 was obtained between test score and grades in graduate school. The predictive value of the new test may be expected to vary greatly for different fields of specialization and for different institutions, with their varying admissions policies and criteria for success.

Unfortunately no manual is yet available describing the technical aspects of the construction of the test. It is hoped that one will soon be forthcoming, and that it will contain full information on reliability, difficulty and discrimination of items, intercorrelations between subtests, correlation with other tests, validation studies based on survival in school and (hopefully) postschool success, the contribution of speed vs. power, and other technical information to permit proper evaluation. The Educational Testing Service has done an outstanding job of preparing manuals for examiners and for supervisors. They clearly state the policies and procedures governing the standardized administration of the tests.

SUMMARY. This test appears to have been developed in a careful and competent manner. Both subtests have an adequate reliability, particularly in the light of the narrow range found among candidates for graduate school. The test is so new that no satisfactory data are yet available concerning its validity, but the similarity of content to that of earlier forms in the Profile

[294]

*Group Test of Learning Capacity: Dominion Tests. Grades kgn–1, 4–6, 7–9, 9–12 and adults; 1934–50; formerly called *Group Test of Intelligence;* 4 levels; 25¢ per manual for any one level; postage extra; prepared by the Department of Educational Research, Ontario College of Education, University of Toronto; distributed by Vocational Guidance Centre. *
a) PRIMARY. Grades kgn–1; 1934–50; Forms A ('44), B ('44); a practice exercise ('44) must precede administration of test; manual ('46); revised norms ('50); $1.50 per 25; 35¢ per specimen set; practice exercise: (20) minutes; test: (45) minutes.
b) JUNIOR. Grades 4–6; 1940–41; Forms A ('40), B ('40); manual ('41); $1 per 25; 35¢ per specimen set; 25(45) minutes.
c) INTERMEDIATE. Grades 7–9; 1934–50; 2 editions; Forms A, B.
  1) [*Original Edition.*] 1934; $1.50 per 25; 35¢ per specimen set; 37(50) minutes.
  2) (*1950 Edition, Omnibus Type*). 1950; $1 per 25; 45¢ per specimen set; 30(45) minutes.
d) ADVANCED. Grades 9–12 and adults; 1939–40; Forms A ('39), B ('39); manual ('40); $1 per 25; 45¢ per specimen set; 30(45) minutes.

REFERENCES

1. PHILLIPS, ALEXANDER J. "Comparison of Methods of Calculating Mental Age Equivalents." *J Ed Psychol* 34:152–65 Mr '43. * (*PA* 18:328)
2. *Selection and Training of Shorthand Students in Ontario Secondary Schools.* A study conducted by The Shorthand Survey Committee of The Ontario Commercial Teachers' Association and The Department of Educational Research, Ontario College of Education, University of Toronto. Toronto, Canada: Sir Isaac Pitman & Sons (Canada) Ltd., 1949. Pp. vii, 68. Paper. *
3. YULE, D. L. G. *A Study of the Relationship Between Reading Ability and Performance on the Dominion Group Test of Learning Capacity.* Master's thesis, University of Toronto (Toronto, Canada), 1950. Pp. 53.

W. G. EMMETT, *Reader in Educational Research, University of Edinburgh, Edinburgh, Scotland.*

PRIMARY. Each form of this test contains four separately timed sections with 54 items in all. Emphasis is laid on the necessity that all children should understand what they have to do; the layout of the test items and the admirable instructions for administration certainly comply with this requirement. One feels uncertain whether items such as joining dots to reproduce a given pattern, or finding from a random arrangement of drawings those which appear in a given picture, measure "learning capacity" efficiently, and no supporting correlations with criteria are given to dispel one's doubts. The correlation between Forms A and B based on 933 cases was .85, a reasonable figure for a short test for such young children. Norms are given in terms of mental ages for each point of raw score; the revised norms of 1950 based on 1,800 Ontario children give a mean IQ 8.1 points below the earlier norms of 1946, based on 933 cases. The original publication of the test was obviously premature.

JUNIOR. This test has five separately timed sections, containing 81 well chosen verbal and arithmetical items of established types. The instructions contain one flaw: in the first three sections the moment at which the children are to start work is not clear. Correlations between the parallel forms vary from .83 to .92 for different grades from 3 to 7, and the standard deviation of raw scores within each grade is about 12. These figures denote rather poor discrimination. A higher reliability coefficient (.95) and standard deviation (17.5) resulted from pooling the data for the five grades, but no great reliance can be placed on the figures as the spread of age and ability in the samples is not quoted.

INTERMEDIATE (ORIGINAL EDITION). The tests are in eight separately timed sections, comprising arithmetical problems, opposites, "does not belong," analogies, number series, reasoning, sentence completion and syllogisms. The items have obviously been carefully chosen and should give a good measure of general intelligence. The sections, which are of unequal length, are weighted so as to give approximately the same maximum score for each. Standard deviations of raw scores are not quoted, but the reliability coefficient of .95 for 100 cases of one grade only suggests adequate dispersion. Mental age norms are based, as far as one can judge, on 5,000 pupils from all parts of Canada; we are not told how these children were selected. The only clue given to the validity of the test is its correlation with Spearman's "g," .93, apparently an internal criterion and therefore of no great value. The nature of the items, however, should ensure the usefulness of the test.

INTERMEDIATE (1950 EDITION, OMNIBUS TYPE). This is a test of 75 questions without internal timing. Thirty minutes are allowed for working. It is constructed for Grades 7, 8 and 9, and appears in two parallel forms, A and B. It comprises opposites, analogies, number series, arithmetic problems, "does not belong," synonyms and a few of miscellaneous type. There are 14 number series items and 19 arithmetical problems, undue proportions which probably favour boys. Mental age norms based on the scores of 3,300 pupils are provided. The standard deviation of raw scores was about 13.5, a low figure for a 75-item test. The correlation between the two forms of the test was .93 for 391 children, a figure higher than the standard deviation of raw scores would lead one to expect. It may have been increased by a wide age range, but we are not told.

ADVANCED. There are 75 items in each form, presented without internal timing. They were selected by elimination of unsuitable items from an original 486. The items are mostly verbal of standard type; 14 items are "number series," a rather excessive proportion of the whole test, especially as their solution depends largely on previous experience with this type. Reliability coefficients run from .81 to .90 and standard deviations of raw scores from 9.5 to 13.4 for grades 9 to 13 taken separately; the discrimination is therefore not particularly good.

GENERAL CRITICISMS. The errors associated with individual scores are given in terms of the old-fashioned "probable error," while standard deviations are employed for dispersions of raw scores. The authors quote the stability of the probable errors of individual *raw scores* from one grade to another with satisfaction. But it is obvious from their data that this stability results from a low reliability coupled with a low standard deviation of the score distribution in one case and opposite conditions in another case. The relevant statistic should be the standard (or probable) error of the individual IQ, which refers the errors of measurement to the same scale; the reviewer believes that marked differences would then be noted.

All correlations are based on children within certain grades and cannot be interpreted without knowledge of the spread of ability and age in the particular grade, which is not available. Where standardization has been effected by a comparison with other intelligence tests, the regression line has been taken as expressing the relation between the two tests; it is probable that this relation would be better expressed by the major axis of the elliptical frequency contours.

In the reviewer's opinion the use of mental age norms is to be deprecated, for they yield different standard deviations of IQ and therefore different scales with different tests. This may occur even within the same test, as for example the *Revised Stanford-Binet Scale,* where the SD of IQ for six-year-olds is 12.5 and for 12-year-olds 20.0. There is much to be said for the establishment of an international scale based on standardised scores with a mean of 100 and an agreed SD at, say, 15. The position at present is chaotic. The authors of the tests give no clue as to the scale on which the resulting IQ's are measured.

In general, the tests are well constructed, the instructions are on the whole excellent, and marking is entirely objective. However, more statistical information should be available before the tests can be recommended with confidence.

For a review by F. T. Tyler, see 3:231.

[295]
★Group Test 33 (Intelligence): National Institute of Industrial Psychology. Ages 14 and over; 1923–46; 1 form ['23]; no data on reliability, validity, and normative population in manual; data available on request; revised manual ('46); 3s. 8d. per 12; 1s. per single copy; 1s. per manual; postage extra; 29(35) minutes; Cyril Burt; National Institute of Industrial Psychology. *

REFERENCES
1. FARMER, E. AND CHAMBERS, E. G. *The Prognostic Value of Some Psychological Tests.* Medical Research Council, Industrial Health Research Board Report, No. 74. London: H. M. Stationery Office, 1936. Pp. 41. Paper.
2. VERNON, PHILIP E., AND PARRY, JOHN B. *Personnel Selection in the British Forces.* London: University of. London Press Ltd., 1949. Pp. 324. * (PA 24:776)

[296]
★Group Test 36 [Intelligence]: National Institute of Industrial Psychology. Ages 10–14; 1937–45; 1 form ['37]; no data on reliability, validity, and normative population in manual; data available on request; mimeographed manual ['37]; norms ['45]; 6s. 9d. per 12; 1s. 6d. per single copy; 1s. per manual; postage extra; 20(30) minutes; National Institute of Industrial Psychology. *

[297]
★Group Test 70 [Nonverbal Intelligence]: National Institute of Industrial Psychology. Ages 14 and over; 1939–50; 2 tests; no data on reliability, validity, and normative population in manual; data available on request; norms ['50]; postage extra; National Institute of Industrial Psychology. *
a) GROUP TEST 70/1. 1950; 1 form ['50]; 4s. 6d. per 12; 1s. per single copy; 1s. 3d. per manual; 5(10) minutes.
b) GROUP TEST 70/23 [REVISED EDITION]. 1939–50; 1 form ['46—same as test copyrighted in 1943]; manual ['46]; 21s. per 12; 1s. 9d. per single copy; separate answer sheets must be used; 1s. 2d. per 12 answer sheets; 1s. per manual; 13(20) minutes.

REFERENCES
1. SLATER, PATRICK. "Tests for Selecting Secondary and Technical School Children." *Occupational Psychol* 15:10–25 Ja '41. * (PA 15:3177)
2. MILLS, L. F. *The Properties of a Space Test.* Bachelor's thesis, University of Edinburgh (Edinburgh, Scotland), 1947.
3. VERNON, P. E. "The Structure of Practical Abilities." *Occupational Psychol* 23:81–96 Ap '49. * (PA 23:5313)
4. VERNON, PHILIP E., AND PARRY, JOHN B. *Personnel Selection in the British Forces.* London: University of London Press Ltd., 1949. Pp. 324. * (PA 24:776)
5. "The Human Problems of the Building Industry: Guidance, Selection and Training." *Occupational Psychol* 24:96–104 Ap '50. * (PA 24:5914)

GEORGE WESTBY, *Head of the Psychological Laboratory, University College of Hull, Hull, England.*

GROUP TEST 70/1. This test is described by Vernon and Parry, on the basis of experience in the British Armed Forces as "a very simple but surprisingly effective test" *(4)*, an entirely justified description in view of the fact that it has a single principle and is easily administered in ten minutes including the pretest practice (the actual scored test has a time limit of five minutes).

The principle is that five standard figures numbered from 1 to 5 composed of two lines bisecting each other at various angles are given; and the testee has to number correctly as many as possible of the part figures (printed in the test booklet below the key figures). Practice on two sets of figures using the same key is given beforehand. Factor analysis suggests that this test is loaded with "g" or relational thinking to about the same degree as Raven's *Progressive Matrices 1938,* namely .78 (Matrices .79) with a small spatial-perceptual factor. If a P or perceptual speed factor exists one would certainly except it in such a test, although Vernon's Services analyses showed no evidence of it. In addition, capacity for continuous high-pressure concentration and ability quickly to memorize the key figures seems, a priori, to be involved. Little work has been reported with the test, however, and considerable further experimentation with it seems desirable. If this is an almost pure "g" test as factor analysis suggests, then a speed factor in any mental testing seems to be more than doubtful, yet Armed Services scores for Matrices used as a timed test and N.I.I.P. *Group Test 70* were proved to correlate most highly with visual signalling, radar, and antiaircraft jobs of a perceptual type.

The absence of data on reliability is remarkable (none is reported by Vernon and Parry even from their experience in the Services), but it is presumably not high. Norms for the general population of young adults issued by the N.I.I.P. (1950) are based on scores of a stratified sample of 1,000. Percentiles for school ages (unpublished) have been established for restricted use and are based on 5,500 cases. The test has also yielded percentiles for other special groups, such as "Higher Level Executives," but these again have not been released as yet since the N.I.I.P. uses the test extensively in its commissions in industry and vocational guidance. No validatory studies are available. The likeliest future for this test, which is certainly intriguing, is in a comprehensive battery; it is certainly too brief to be used alone, and the test principle involves processes which are almost certainly more complex than the apparent simplicity of the task and would bear careful research investigation.

GROUP TEST 70/23. This test, composed of 53 non verbal items simply constructed geometrically and based in the main on Matrix principles, is again remarkable for its economy of time, taking in all about 25 minutes (13 minutes only of test time) to administer. Here again the test is highly loaded with "g" or relational thinking and a small visuo-spatial factor. Here again, also unfortunately there is a total lack of data on reliability and validity. The norms issued by the N.I.I.P. are based on 2,454 cases from the Institute's industrial work and 5,147 school cases done by vocational guidance sections. Separate norms are given for unselected young male adults and adolescents and for Grammar School boys from 14.0 to 16.0. Again the Institute has established useful special norms which it cannot yet release.

The principle and construction of the test seem excellent; it is safeguarded like *Group Test 70/1* by adequate pretest practice, but the absence of necessary data will handicap its wide dissemination until, no doubt, it is superseded by better tests at the N.I.I.P. We shall then be allowed the benefit of its use with necessary safeguards and knowledge of which we are at the moment deprived.

[298]
★**Group Test 90A [Intelligence]:** National Institute of Industrial Psychology. Adults; 1948; 1 form ['48]; no data on reliability, validity, and normative population in manual; data available on request; mimeographed manual; 4s. 6d. per 12; 1s. per single copy; 9d. per manual; postage extra; 20(30) minutes; National Institute of Industrial Psychology. *

[299]
*****The Henmon-Nelson Tests of Mental Ability: The Clapp-Young Self-Marking Tests.** Grades 3–8, 7–12, 12–16; 1931–50; IBM for grades 7–12; 3 levels; postage extra; 30(35) minutes; V. A. C. Henmon and M. J. Nelson; Houghton Mifflin Co. *
a) ELEMENTARY SCHOOL EXAMINATION. Grades 3–8; 1931–46; Forms A ('31), B ('32), C ('32); revised manual ('46); $1 per 25; 28¢ per specimen set, postpaid.
b) HIGH SCHOOL EXAMINATION. Grades 7–12; 1931–50; IBM; 2 editions; revised manual ('46).
  1) [*Clapp-Young Self-Marking Edition.*] Forms A ('31), B ('32), C ('35); $1 per 25.
  2) [*Machine Scoring Edition.*] Forms A ('50, c'31), C ('48, c'35); $1.50 per 50; separate answer sheets must be used; $1 per 50 IBM answer sheets; 20¢ per machine scoring stencil; 28¢ per specimen set, postpaid.
c) INTELLIGENCE TEST FOR COLLEGE STUDENTS. Grades 12–16; 1931–32; Forms A ('31), B ('32); manual ('32); $1 per 25; 25¢ per specimen set, postpaid.

REFERENCES
1. BOND, ELDEN A. "A Method of Selecting Subnormal Children for a Vocational School." *J Juvenile Res* 21:188–92 Jl '37. * (PA 12:503)
2. DRAKE, LEWIS E., AND HENMON, V. A. C. "The Prediction of Scholarship in the College of Letters and Science at the University of Wisconsin." *Sch & Soc* 45:191–4 F 6 '37.

3. HENMON, V. A. C., AND NELSON, M. J. *The Measurement of Intelligence.* Educational Progress Bulletin, Vol. 13, No. 2. Boston, Mass.: Houghton Mifflin Co., September 1937. Pp. 21. Paper.
4. MORRIS, CHARLES M. "An Experimental Analysis of Certain Performance Tests." Abstract. *Psychol B* 34:716–7 N '37. * (*PA* 12:1661, title only)
5. ALTENEDER, LOUISE E. *The Value of Intelligence, Personality, and Vocational-Interest Tests in a Guidance Program.* Doctor's thesis, New York University (New York, N.Y.), 1938. Pp. 130. (*Abstracts of Theses*....[*School of Education*] 1938, pp. 41–4.)
6. CHRIST, AUSTIN F. *The Relation of Mental Test Ratings to Achievement of High-School Pupils.* Master's thesis, Lawrence College (Appleton, Wis.), 1938. Pp. 105.
7. EMERICK, LUCILLE MAE. *Predicting Success in Music Education for Adults.* Doctor's thesis, New York University (New York, N.Y.), 1938. Pp. 239. (*Abstracts of Theses*....[*School of Education*] 1938, pp. 101–5.)
8. BECKHAM, ALBERT SIDNEY. "The Intelligence of a Negro High School Population in a Northern City." *J Genetic Psychol* 54:327–36 Je '39. * (*PA* 14:400)
9. ALTENEDER, LOUISE E. "The Value of Intelligence, Personality, and Vocational Interest Tests in a Guidance Program." *J Ed Psychol* 31:449–59 S '40. * (*PA* 15:1480)
10. FAILOR, LEONA MAE. *An Evaluation of Intelligence Tests Used in Industrial Schools and Reformatories.* Doctor's thesis, University of Nebraska (Lincoln, Neb.), 1940. (*Abstracts of Doctoral Dissertations*....1940, pp. 59–65.)
11. FAILOR, LEONA MAE. "An Evaluation of Intelligence Tests Used in Industrial Schools and Reformatories." Abstract. *Psychol B* 38:711 O '41. * (*PA* 16:364, title only)
12. FROEHLICH, GUSTAV J. "Academic Prediction at the University of Wisconsin." *J Am Assn Col Reg* 17:65–76 O '41. *
13. HARTSON, L. D., AND SPROW, A. J. "The Value of Intelligence Quotients Obtained in Secondary School for Predicting College Scholarship." *Ed & Psychol Meas* 1:387–98 O '41. * (*PA* 16:1174)
14. BAILEY, ALBERT ERNEST. *The Relative Validity of Ten Different Intelligence Tests.* Doctor's thesis, University of Washington (Seattle, Wash.), 1942. (*Abstracts of Theses*....1942, 1943, p. 189.)
15. DEMAND, J. W. "Correlations Between Scores on the Modified Alpha Examination Form 9 and Grades in Various High School Subjects." *Trans Kans Acad Sci* 47:417–8 '45.*
16. HARTSON, L. D. "Influence of Level of Motivation on the Validity of Intelligence Tests." *Ed & Psychol Meas* 5:273–83 au '45. * (*PA* 20:2500)
17. HULT, ESTHER. "Study of Achievement in Educational Psychology." *J Exp Ed* 13:174–90 Je '45. * (*PA* 19:3494)
18. KNEZEVICH, STEPHEN J. "The Constancy of the IQ of the Secondary School Pupil." *J Ed Res* 39:506–16 Mr '46. * (*PA* 20:3329)
19. LINS, LEO JOSEPH. "The Prediction of Teaching Efficiency." *J Exp Ed* 15:2–60 S '46. * (*PA* 21:610)
20. BUSHONG, GEORGE E. *College Entrance Examinations.* Master's thesis, Southern Methodist University (Dallas, Tex.), 1947. (*Abstracts of Theses*....1946, 1947, p. 10.)
21. DAVIS, W. ALLISON, AND HAVIGHURST, ROBERT J. "The Measurement of Mental Systems: Can Intelligence Be Measured?" *Sci Mo* 66:301–16 Ap '48. * (*PA* 22:3381)
22. HAAS, LEONARD. "Four Year Studies of the Freshman Classes of 1936 and 1940 at the Eau Claire State Teachers College." *J Ed Res* 42:54–61 S '48. * (*PA* 23:2917)
23. FROOK, W. F. "A Statistical Study of 224 Senior Students Graduated in June, 1949." *J Ed Res* 43:101–9 O '49. * (*PA* 24:2806)
24. ALLEN, ROBERT M., AND BESSELL, HAROLD. "Intercorrelations Among Group Verbal and Non-Verbal Tests of Intelligence." *J Ed Res* 43:394–5 Ja '50. * (*PA* 24:4841)
25. EMBREE, ROYAL B., JR. "A Longitudinal Study of Performance on the Henmon-Nelson Test of Mental Ability, the Differential Aptitude Tests, and the American Council on Education Psychological Examination for College Freshmen." Abstract. *Am Psychol* 5:352 Jl '50. * (*PA* 25:1276, title only)

H. M. FOWLER, *Associate Professor of Educational Research, University of Toronto, Toronto, Ontario, Canada.*

Soon after the first world war, test constructors, following the lead of Binet and Terman, concerned themselves with measuring that difficult-to-define capacity which we call general intelligence. In the last 20 or 30 years, however, there has been a trend toward attempting to construct tests which could give an analytical picture of mental ability. The California Tests of Mental Maturity, for example, were designed to give both a verbal and a nonverbal intelligence quotient. Carrying this trend for mental analysis even further, the factor theorists have been trying to isolate, and eventually measure, the primary mental abilities.

The *Henmon-Nelson Tests of Mental Ability* belong to the class of group intelligence tests which yield a single global score, an overall estimate of general intelligence; having no part tests, they are not diagnostic and they provide no measure of specifics. In the manual, the authors say "a wide variety of types of questions is used, thus furnishing a test of many kinds of ability." But the 90 items of Form A of the test for elementary grades include at least 52 items which are strictly verbal—vocabulary, word classification, verbal analogy, anagrams, and sentence completion. The items may be different in form, but the function being measured would appear to be almost entirely verbal comprehension. At all three levels, these tests are patently measures of that highly verbal component sometimes called "general intelligence" but perhaps more aptly labelled "scholastic aptitude."

Each of the three elementary and three high school forms have 90 items arranged in order of increasing difficulty in spiral omnibus form and printed on two sides of a two-page, 10" by 12", answer booklet. The inside pages of the sealed booklet are reserved for the special Clapp-Young self-marking device. The two college forms are similar but are printed on 8½" by 11" pages. The paper on which the tests are printed is inferior and the printing is rather small, especially for certain items such as geometrical analogies which become unduly ambiguous when not clearly printed in large figures. The space allowance for marking the items is none too generous, and this may unfairly handicap students with poor eyesight.

For those who prefer a single score measure of intelligence, the *Henmon-Nelson Tests of Mental Ability* have some definite advantages: their administration is simple, they can be scored quickly, and, most important, as far as one can judge from the available evidence, they *do* measure scholastic aptitude, particularly at the lower levels where verbal comprehension is perhaps a more important constituent of school success than is either originality or initiative. Worthy of praise, too, is the manner in which the tests were constructed in the first place; the items were selected rather carefully and only those which survived rigorous statistical tests were included in the final forms. This reviewer's chief complaint is that the Henmon-Nelson tests are now showing signs of wear. The inadequacy of some of the information given in the manuals and the lack of other information give the impression that the authors are not applying to the tests the constant revision which is necessary to keep them at their full effectiveness. Although the Henmon-Nelson tests were soundly constructed for a specific, if somewhat narrow, purpose originally, and although it would be too much to say that they have outlived their usefulness, one feels that they now need a norm adjustment, an overhaul of the manuals, and certain other changes and improvements to bring them back to par.

Perhaps most important in the upkeep of an intelligence test is constant attention to repair or renewal of the norms. Are the Henmon-Nelson intelligence quotients and mental ages too high, as is commonly averred? The manuals for the elementary and high school tests show that for reasonably large groups the mean mental ages and the mean IQ's of the Henmon-Nelson agree fairly closely with the corresponding averages obtained on other group tests of intelligence, but some recent investigations indicate that the Henmon-Nelson does give mental ability estimates which are too high. For example, Knezevich reports that the average Henmon-Nelson IQ for a group of forty-eight students was about three points higher than the average for the same students on the *California Test of Mental Maturity,* a test which is reputed to give rather high estimates (*18*). But this small, though statistically significant, difference could be accounted for in terms of practice effect or changes in the students since the Henmon-Nelson was given about a month after the California test. This reviewer made a comparison of the Henmon-Nelson with the *Dominion Group Test of Learning Capacity,* Intermediate (Omnibus Type) by using mental ratings obtained on the two tests from 70 grade 9 pupils in a small Ontario town. Although this group is too small to provide final conclusions, the comparison provided a check of the Henmon-Nelson norms against mental age equivalents recently obtained on a large representative Ontario group (June 1950). The correlations between IQ's and between mental ages, .88 and .70 respectively, suggest that the two tests are comparable, a conclusion which is reinforced by an inspection of the tests. They are both omnibus type tests yielding one overall measure of general intelligence, their content is highly verbal, and their items are similar in form and appearance. Nevertheless, the average mental ages were quite different: the Henmon-Nelson gave an average of 187 months compared with 184 months given by the Dominion despite the fact that the Henmon was given *first*. The Henmon-Nelson IQ's also averaged about three points higher than the Dominion IQ's. Although these results are not conclusive, they do support the view that the Henmon-Nelson norms, at least for the high school test, are out of line for use today in Ontario schools.

In fairness to the authors and publishers of the Henmon-Nelson tests, it must be said that the reported norms are based on a very large number of cases—for the elementary test, "220,000 pupils from every state and parts of Canada," and for the High School Test, "about 300,000 pupils in widely separated areas of the United States." Unfortunately this is all the information that is given in the manuals. In a letter to the reviewer one of the authors states: "Each year users send in many thousand scores and these are tabulated every two years and compared with the norms. When variations are found, a complete study is made and norms are corrected as necessary." A statement of what the authors are doing to keep the norms up-to-date should appear in the manuals, which at present do not even give the date of the last norm revision. This would correct any impression that the norms are completely outmoded. Even so, it is questionable whether checking norms by means of scores obtained almost at random by solicitation can take the place of a planned attempt to restandardize the test under controlled conditions.

The Henmon-Nelson gives two sets of norms, a table of mental age equivalents which can be used to convert raw scores to intelligence quotients, and a table in which the percentile ranks of the raw scores are reported by grades. The authors deserve praise for giving percentile norms as well as mental age equivalents. Intelligence quotients obtained on a carefully standardized test are probably not too misleading in the lower grades, but their use for students over the age of 14 can be seriously challenged. Mursell[1] has criticised the Henmon-Nelson for presenting percentile norms by grade groups.

[1] Mursell, James L. *Psychological Testing, Revised Edition,* pp. 154–5. New York: Longmans, Green & Co., 1949. Pp. xvi, 488. * (PA 25:190)

He argues that the meaning of "grade six" shows such variation from one locality to another that to use grade norms is to define the unknown in terms of something equally unknown. This reviewer believes that teachers find grade norms definitely helpful; the differences in grades from one place to another may be smaller than Mursell suggests. Data recently collected by the Department of Educational Research on the *Dominion Group Test of Learning Capacity,* Junior, suggest that, for the lower grades at least, the between-province differences for grades 3 to 7 are not large. There is, however, the difficulty that age groups do not coincide with grade groups, particularly in the upper grades where there may be a considerable disparity between the two. It would seem to be useful, and in keeping with the original conception of the purpose of mental measures, to report percentile norms by age groups as well as by grade groups.

Of less import than the suspicion which attaches to the norms, but still significant, are limitations and weaknesses of the manuals. These are four-page booklets which give descriptions of the tests, directions for administering and scoring them, and data for interpreting the scores. Neither in appearance nor in content do these manuals measure up to the best psychological test manuals of the present day. In the first place, too much is crowded into too few pages; since the inner pages are taken up with a table for reading intelligence quotients directly from raw scores, only the outer two pages are left for the description of the tests, the administration directions, and a number of tables containing data which may be used for interpreting scores. It may be advantageous to cut a teacher's manual to the minimum, but certain information should not be omitted. The Henmon-Nelson manuals have practically no description of the norm groups or reliability groups, so that the reader is unable to decide how applicable the norms may be or how much confidence he may place in the reliability estimates. Criticism may be levelled at the authors not only for their sins of omission but also for the way in which they have presented some of the material that *is* included in the manuals. The use of the split half procedure for estimating the reliability of a 30-minute test is particularly reprehensible, especially since no other reliability estimates are given, and the critical ratio technique described by the authors in difficult technical language definitely "dates" the statistics. The use of outmoded statistics in the manuals is unfortunate because it serves to undermine the reader's confidence in the validity of the tests for use today. The table for converting raw scores to intelligence quotients directly without reference to the mental age equivalents table will be warmly welcomed by the busy teacher. However, it is impossible to decide from an inspection of this table whether the authors have determined by research the age of arrest of mental growth for the Henmon-Nelson tests or have simply followed the Stanford-Binet precedent in adjusting chronological age divisors.

In designing an elementary test for grades 3 to 8 and a high school test for grades 7 to 12, the authors of the Henmon-Nelson tests have attempted, in the opinion of this reviewer, to cover greater age ranges than can efficiently be tested by single group tests of general intelligence. The percentile norms show that the ceiling of the elementary test is too low for eighth-grade children and that the floor is too high for third-grade children. The elementary test works best for grades 4 to 7 and its use should be confined to those grades. Still better, the authors might provide separate tests for grades 3–5, grades 6–8, and grades 9–12.

In summary, it may be said that the Henmon-Nelson tests still rank among the better group tests of general intelligence despite the fact that they have now been on the market for about 20 years. Although the tests provide only overall estimates of intelligence, they can still be recommended to those who want a quickly and fairly cheaply obtained rough measure of that highly verbalized factor sometimes called scholastic aptitude. They are inappropriate for use in clinical situations in which diagnosis is desired, and they will probably give but poor assessments of the mental ability of children with language or reading difficulty or of children who are not verbally inclined. The tests appear to have most usefulness in the elementary school where they are particularly valuable in predicting school success. Because of the apparent lack of a continuous and concerted research program, the tests now give every sign of being in need of repair and renewal although they were well constructed originally. It is claimed, and evidence can be found to support the view, that the norms are now out of line, with the result that an unduly high proportion of above average intelligence quotients is being obtained by testwise children.

Henmon-Nelson Tests of Mental Ability

The manuals need to be revised to bring them up to date and to include some vital information which is now lacking. Other suggested changes are the addition of percentile norms by age groups and the provision of three separate tests for the junior, intermediate, and high school grades.

For reviews by Anne Anastasi, August Dvorak, Howard Easley, and J. P. Guilford and an excerpt from a review by Francis N. Maxfield, see 40:1398.

[300]
★**The IPAT Culture Free Intelligence Tests.** Ages 4–8, 8–adults, 14–superior adults; 1933–50; title on test booklet is *Test of g: Culture Free;* IBM for ages 8–adults and 14–superior adults; 50¢ per manual ['50] for any one level; cash orders postpaid; R. B. Cattell and A. K. S. Cattell (2, 3); Institute for Personality and Ability Testing. *
a) SCALE 1. Ages 4–8; 1933–50; identical to the *Cattell Intelligence Tests, Scale O: Dartington Scale* (see 40:1386a) published by George G. Harrap & Co. Ltd.; individual; 1 form, '50; $2.80 per 25; 25¢ per scoring key; $3 per set of cards for classification test; 55¢ per specimen set; (30) minutes.
b) SCALE 2. Ages 8–adults; 1949–50; IBM; Forms A ('49), B ('49); $2.50 per 25; $4.60 per 25 sets of both forms; 70¢ per specimen set; separate answer sheets may be used; $1.50 per 50 IBM answer sheets; design for machine scoring stencil included in manual; 25¢ per stencil for hand scoring of answer sheets for any one form; 14(30) minutes.
c) SCALE 3. Ages 14–superior adults; 1950; Forms A, B; prices same as for Scale 2; 14(30) minutes.

REFERENCES
1. PIERCE-JONES, JOHN, AND TYLER, FRED T. "A Comparison of the A.C.E. Psychological Examination and the Culture-Free Test." *Can J Psychol* 4:109–14 S '50. * (PA 25:3422)
2. CATTELL, RAYMOND B. "Classical and Standard Score IQ Standardization of the I.P.A.T. Culture-Free Intelligence Scale 2." *J Consult Psychol* 15:154–9 Ap '51. * (PA 26:6255)

RALEIGH M. DRAKE, *Professor of Psychology and Head of the Department, Kent State University, Kent, Ohio.*

This test has the same purpose as Cattell's original *Culture-Free Test* published in 1944 by the Psychological Corporation. It differs in that it is shorter and more convenient to give and in that it is available in three levels. Scale 1 is not really culture-free because it consists of relation-finding among culture-bound pictorial materials with rather specific verbal directions. Within our own culture, however, it is relatively free of the verbal and ordinary schooling factors. Scale 2 and Scale 3 are the same in effect as the 1944 edition except that the subtest Pool Reflections is replaced by a subtest called Conditions which is a more complex relation-finding test and which should, therefore, be a better measure of mental capacity. All three scales can be administered in groups, and the cost is reasonable. The provision of answer sheets would have been desirable for Scales 2 and 3.

The wide range of ability from the feeble-minded to the superior adult, the availability of two equivalent forms, and the freedom from memory and training factors make it a very valuable measure of mental energy. The mimeographed manuals (there is a manual for each scale) give little data on reliability and validity but references to published data are given. Both reliability and validity are about as high as one could hope for with such tests.

The reviewer has given Scale 2 to the third and fourth grades in a summer school where about 50 per cent of the students were making up failures or low grades of the year before; r's of .56 and .36 ($N = 28$) respectively were obtained with the *Revised Stanford-Binet Scale* and the *Stanford Achievement Tests*. The Cattell r of .36 with the *Stanford Achievement Test* is 11 points higher than is the Stanford-Binet r of .25. In another study, of ten different groups from high school to college, the Cattell r's (Scale 3) with grade point averages ranged from .37 to .91, with an average of .51 ($N = 8$–49 per group); the r's between the *Otis Self-Administering Tests of Mental Ability* and grade point averages ranged from zero to .92, with an average of .35 for the same groups. For the same ten groups, the correlation of Cattell with Otis averaged .73, with a range of .34 to .90. For a college group of 32 students the Cattell correlated .59 with the *American Council on Education Psychological Examination*. In view of the facts that (*a*) school training would have practically no direct influence on the Cattell scores and yet the Cattell correlates higher (on the average) than the Otis with school success and (*b*) that the Cattell correlates an average of .73 with other recognized tests of general ability, it would appear that a test which is almost culture-free has many advantages over the usual culture-bound tests. Its advantages should be recognized as a possible way of equating all subjects for past subject-matter-training effects and thus obtaining a more accurate score representing each subject's innate ability. Used together with a test having a high saturation of verbal ability, it might reveal much more concerning a particular individual than does the usual global score of general ability.

Scale 1 was standardized on only 117 children, with 20 being the largest for any year. It is therefore very tenuous. Since at this age a difference of one or two scale points, as well as one or two months' variation in age, makes a great difference in the resulting IQ, the reliability of the scale is not very high. No evidence of reliability is given.

Scale 2 is standardized on 713 pupils in two midwestern university towns and 2,584 pupils in an industrial city in England. The SD of the *Culture-Free Test* is 24, a considerably higher figure than the *Revised Stanford-Binet Scale* SD which averages 16 (range 12–20). It should be noted that IQ's which are very distant from the mean will not be comparable between distributions which vary in SD.

Scale 3 is standardized on 886 high school pupils and 600 students from three different colleges and universities. For the same reason as for Scale 2, IQ's some distance from the mean will be much higher or much lower than those usually obtained. For this reason too, all IQ's calculated from these scales must not be taken as necessarily the same as Stanford-Binet or Wechsler-Bellevue IQ's. No actual comparisons are given with other tests.

GLADYS C. SCHWESINGER, *Senior Clinical Psychologist, California Youth Authority, Ventura, California.*

This test consists of three scales each appropriate to different age and intelligence levels. Directions for administering and scoring each of the three scales are fully and clearly given in the separate test manuals which also include discussion of what the test measures, structure of the test in relation to purpose, and essential and peripheral standardization tables. No information is presented in the manuals on the reliability of the present scales. These tests have higher validity for low cultural or intelligence levels than do other tests, while for highly cultured groups, tests charged with scholastic skills show a higher saturation of general ability. However, on the average, the culture free test is highly valid for all situations. Thomson (40: 1386) called attention to the wider scatter (SD's of 20 to 27) of the *Cattell Intelligence Tests* (which include Scale 1 of *Test of g*) as compared with the standard deviations of the Binet (SD's of 15 to 16), a fact of which test users should be aware, and one which should be made subject to more research. This scatter means that the Scale 1 IQ's may be either too high or too low, assuming Binet as a standard!

The purpose of the Cattell test is, as its name implies, to have an instrument free of cultural influence, and one which can more readily be applied to different kinds and degrees of culture throughout the world. The underlying principle is *perceptual* rather than *apperceptual*, thus doing away with a dependence on particular cultural associations—and incidentally also meeting the proverbial anthropologist's objections to most of our intelligence tests that similar objects are invested with different meanings in different cultures. Geometrically rather than pictorially meaningful material is used as the substance of the subtests, with general ability for any individual being detected according to the level of complexity of relations he can handle. Perceptual appreciation attracted English psychologists about 1937–1938 and during World War II became the standard for their wholesale testing program. In this respect, the United States is technically behind Oxford and other English universities dealing with intelligence measurement.

These tests do not require reading ability, while a section of Scale 1 and all of Scales 2 and 3 do not require pictorial recognition of objects of our culture. They are designed to measure general mental capacity, Spearman's "g," the second order factor behind Thurstone's primary abilities. Precise technical data on the relative "g" saturation of the various kinds of subtests are not yet available. However, although not enough data have been assembled to allow for vagaries of sampling, etc., studies by Rimoldi in Thurstone's laboratory in Chicago already show that general intelligence, that is, second order factor measurement in these tests, is rather strongly weighted in the reasoning factor in Thurstone's first order abilities. The fourth subtest in the IPAT series of scales is entirely new and has not yet been properly evaluated among perceptual tests, but the others have about the same saturation on whatever is common to the subtests.

The tests are interesting to children and primitive peoples, and for the latter should be administered on an individual basis, with minimum needed motivation being provided for by the field worker. Younger children increase more in test sophistication on these tests than do older children, while within one age group, increase in test sophistication is slightly less for the lower IQ's. Repeated exposure to the tests, however, would result in a greater overall advance for the dull than for the bright.

The particular contribution of these tests is

that they are as saturated with "*g*" as are any tests, and that they are free of the scholastic aspect of culture. In other words, they are as free of culture as any performance test, and as full of "*g*" as verbal intelligence tests like the Binet, ACE, etc. The perceptual type test represents an entirely new tool for intelligence testing, a radical departure introduced by Spearman two decades ago, which is now well appreciated in England, although still failing to catch the interest and imagination of American psychometrists.

[301]

★Kentucky Classification Battery. Grades 9–11, 12–13; 1948–51; 4 scores: general ability, English, mathematics, total; 2 levels (labeled Forms 1L and 2); Kentucky norms only; tests rented rather than sold; rental fee, 24¢ per student; rental service includes rental of booklet, answer sheet, electrographic pencil, and scoring and reporting results; specimen sets available on loan basis only; 90(105) minutes; Lysle W. Croft, Robert D. North, Ordie U. Davis, and Howard B. Lyman; Kentucky Cooperative Counseling and Testing Service. *
a) LOWER LEVEL. Grades 9–11; 1951; Form 1L; no data on reliability and validity; no manual; no norms; directions for administering ['51].
b) [UPPER LEVEL.] Grades 12–13; 1948–50; a battery consisting of revisions of *Kentucky General Ability Test* (see 3:234), *Kentucky English Test* (see 3:132), and *Kentucky Mathematics Test* (see 3:311); Form 2 ('50—a revision of Form 1); reliability and validity data for Form 1 only; manual ('50); earlier editions by E. J. Asher, T. E. McMullen, and P. L. Mellenbruch.

REFERENCES

1–3. See 40:1402.
4. DAVIS, H. L. "The Utilization of Potential College Ability Found in the June, 1940, Graduates of Kentucky High Schools." *J Am Assn Col Reg* 18:14–22 O '42. * (PA 17:2166)

DAVID V. TIEDEMAN, *Lecturer on Education, Harvard University, Cambridge, Massachusetts.* [A review of Upper Level Form 2.]

This battery is in three sections, General Ability, English Fundamentals, and Mathematics. Thirty, 25, and 35 minutes are allotted to each section respectively. The test authors' claim that the time limits are long enough to allow most students to complete all of the items seems reasonable.

Although this test is called a "classification battery" the authors completely ignore any potential for classification which the test may possess. No information concerning problems like those of vocational or curricular classification has been given by the authors.

The battery "is designed for the dual purpose of evaluating high school achievement at the twelfth grade level and estimating aptitude for academic work at the college freshman level." It is doubtful that many English teachers would wish to evaluate the English achievement of their students by means of a 45-item, 25-minute test of grammar. The 45-item, 35-minute mathematics section contains a fair sample of the concepts which are frequently taught in an introductory algebra course, but none of the concepts of geometry, trigonometry, or advanced algebra are included. Thus, these two sections and the General Ability section, which by definition would not be recommended for evaluating high school achievement, fall far short of providing a valid framework for "evaluating high school achievement at the twelfth grade level."

The purpose which the test can probably serve best is that of "estimating aptitude for academic work at the college freshman level." However, at the present time, the degree to which the test fulfills even this purpose is unknown. We are told that the correlation between total scores of a random sample of 100 students on Form 1 of the battery and grade-point standing at the end of the first year at the University of Kentucky was .63. That is all well and good, but the important question of how the new Form 2 correlates with grade-point standing remains unanswered.

The reliability of Form 2 also remains indeterminate. It would be nice if the authors' hopes for high reliability were realized but perhaps we should postpone using the test until the facts are clear.

A few of the items in the General Ability Section can be answered without too great a knowledge of the words concerned. For instance, in looking for the opposite of "benevolence" as is called for in Item 14, one might choose the correct option, "malevolence," because it is the only option with a suffix like that of "benevolence." A similar criticism may be leveled at Item 17 where "heterogeneous" is the correct opposite of "homogeneous" and at Item 21 where "heinous" is the correct synonym for "atrocious." In the mathematics section Items 113 and 127 may prove confusing because the exponents are not raised sufficiently.

In taking the test, the reviewer found himself at one time recording answers in the wrong places on the answer sheet. The authors of the test would have done well to leave space after questions 15, 30, 45, 75, 90, 120, and 135 and to admonish the student to verify his position on the answer sheet at those places.

In discussing the administration of the battery, the authors state, "It is desirable that the administrator be a person who has had experience in giving group examinations and who appreciates the necessity for carefully controlled conditions, especially with respect to seating, timing, and giving directions." With the poor instructions for administering the test which the manual contains experience is not only desirable, it is downright necessary.

Percentile ranks associated with part and total scores are given. Ranks are reported for two groups, 8,042 cases which were taken from throughout the state of Kentucky, and 775 entering students at the University of Kentucky, fall 1950. In using the ranks for this latter group, it must be remembered that the rank refers to the percentage of the group who made poorer scores on the *test* and not to the percentage of the group who did poorer in *college*.

At the time this review was written the only evidence concerning the utility of Form 2 of the *Kentucky Classification Battery* was that it is one of a family of tests that have been reliable and have had some validity for prediction of success in academic work at the college freshman level. However, in a strict sense, the battery at present is a "classification battery" with no information as to what it classifies and how well it does so; it is a battery that was constructed to increase the reliability of a former test but the reliability of the present test is unknown; it is a battery which is recommended for use in evaluating achievement at the high school level, and all that it includes for such a purpose is some English grammar and some algebra; it is a battery for estimating aptitude for college work and yet its validity for this purpose is unknown. The authors would have done well to withhold release of the battery until some information concerning *this specific test* were known.

[302]

*Kuhlmann-Anderson Intelligence Tests, Sixth Edition.** Grades kgn, 1, 2, 3, 4, 5, 6, 7–8, 9–12; 1927–52; 9 levels (labeled K, A, B, C, D, E, F, G, and H); 1 form, '52—same as 1942 edition; directions for administering ('52); handbook ('52); master manual ('52); $2.25 per 25 of any one level; 100 or more, $2 per 25 of any one level; $1.50 per master manual; postage extra; $1 per specimen set (does not include master manual), postpaid; (30–45) minutes; F. Kuhlmann and Rose G. Anderson; Personnel Press, Inc. * (Formerly published by Educational Test Bureau, Educational Publishers, Inc.)

REFERENCES

1–15. See 40:1404.
16–40. See 3:236.
41. SAWYER, CLIFFORD R. *A Comparison of the Detroit and Kuhlmann-Anderson Intelligence Tests as Applied in the Grand Forks Public Schools.* Master's thesis, University of North Dakota (Grand Forks, N.D.). 1931. Pp. 60.
42. MURPHY, LAURA WHITE. "The Relation Between Mechanical Ability Tests and Verbal and Non-Verbal Intelligence Tests." *J Psychol* 2:353–66 '36. * (*PA* 11:3928)
43. GIBBONS, CHARLES C. "A Comparison of Kuhlmann-Anderson Test Scores and Teachers' Estimates." *Sch & Soc* 47:710–2 My 28 '38. *
44. SEAGOE, MAY V. "Prediction of Achievement in Foreign Languages." *J Appl Psychol* 22:632–40 D '38. * (*PA* 13:2725)
45. GENTRY, DOROTHY E. *An Attempt to Predict Scholarship From a Variety of Objective Tests: College Ability Test, Nelson-Denny Reading Test, Kuhlmann-Anderson Intelligence Test, and English Placement Test.* Master's thesis, Ohio University (Athens, Ohio), 1943. Pp. 33. (*Abstracts of Masters' Theses....1943*, 1944, pp. 36–7.)
46. HARTSON, L. D. "Influence of Level of Motivation on the Validity of Intelligence Tests." *Ed & Psychol Meas* 5:273–83 au '45. * (*PA* 20:2500)
47. BARNOWE, THEODORE JOSEPH. *The Influence of Scoring Technique and Construction on the Validity of Mental Tests.* Doctor's thesis, University of Washington (Seattle, Wash.), 1946. (*Abstracts of Theses....1945–1946*, 1946, pp. 11–2.)
48. TILTON, J. W. "The Relation Between IQ and Trait Difference as Measured by Group Intelligence Tests." *J Ed Psychol* 38:343–52 O '47. * (*PA* 22:2066)
49. DAVIS, W. ALLISON, AND HAVIGHURST, ROBERT J. "The Measurement of Mental Systems: Can Intelligence Be Measured?" *Sci Mo* 66:301–16 Ap '48. * (*PA* 22:3381)
50. BAILEY, HELEN K. "A Study of the Correlations Between Group Mental Tests, the Stanford-Binet, and the Progressive Achievement Test Used in the Colorado Springs Elementary Schools." *J Ed Res* 43:93–100 O '49. * (*PA* 24:2825)

HENRY E. GARRETT, *Professor of Psychology, Columbia University, New York, New York.*

The 1952 edition of the Kuhlmann-Anderson tests represents the sixth edition of this well known test series first published in 1927. As before the test battery consists of 39 tests, each test with 6 to 24 items or trials. The tests cover the ability range from the first grade through high school; Booklet K is for kindergarten and grade one, and Test Booklets A to H cover the first grade through the high school. Tests have been arranged in order of difficulty based upon the median chronological age of children able to pass half of the trials and no more. The total scale is arranged in 9 separate booklets, each with its own instructions and scoring key. All booklets but two contain 10 tests so that each battery includes a few of the tests found in the next higher level as well as a few in the next lower level. In this way the 9 booklets constitute overlapping measures of the total scale of 39 tests. A child's score is the median of the mental ages earned on the tests administered to him. The abilities of school children are relatively undifferentiated, at least as compared with adults. Hence the median mental age is a satisfactory way of determining the level at which a child typically functions in tests of this sort.

Instructions for administering the tests are clear and easy to follow, and the discussions of validity and reliability are far more satisfactory than was true in former editions. Validity is defined in terms of discriminative capacity, that is, of the ability of tests to detect differences in mental development over the age range covered. While the tests are given under timed conditions they seem to be primarily measures of power. Statistical evidence indicates little difference between timed and untimed scores from grades 3 to 9. It seems clear, also, that the test battery is able to differentiate satisfactorily among children who are old-for-grade, young-for-grade, and on-grade.

The reliability of the test is high in terms of the split half coefficient and the standard error of a score (5.5 points of IQ) compares favorably with the same error of measurement in the 1937 Stanford-Binet.

The reviewer can find very little to criticize in the construction and development of these test batteries. One statement on page 10 is, perhaps, subject to qualification. Our authors state that when a subtest has a very high correlation with another subtest in the battery, both may be measuring the same thing and hence one at least is superfluous. On the other hand, they state that if the intercorrelations are low or negative, the subtests may be measuring different abilities and hence do not belong in the same battery. They conclude from this that moderate intercorrelations are to be sought for in that they imply overlap but not identity. The reviewer would agree with these statements though he would point out that high correlation between two subtests and the low correlation of one of them with the criterion may be desirable if the second test is "suppressing" part of the non-valid variance of the first test. Better evidence that the battery is measuring a homogeneous ability (called "intelligence") might have been forthcoming had a factor analysis been made of overlapping test batteries, much as was done by McNemar and by Jones with the 1937 Stanford-Binet.

The tests provide a measure of mental age as well as of IQ, and it is concerning this latter measure that the reviewer is most dubious. Test data reported in Table 11, page 27 of the manual, indicate that the standard deviations of the IQ distributions at different chronological age levels vary from approximately 10 to 16. This means that some part at least of the variability in IQ upon retest can be attributed to differences in IQ variability from one age level to another. It would probably be advisable for our authors not to use the term IQ at all. If they feel that they must, their IQ's should be labeled "Kuhlmann-Anderson IQ's" to distinguish them from Stanford-Binet IQ's.

In general the format of the test is good although it seems to the reviewer that some of the picture items in the early age batteries are rather small for young children. For the kindergarten and first grade child accustomed to large drawings, several of the picture items in Tests 3 and 4 may not be entirely clear.

The authors, as in earlier editions of these tests, provide mental growth unit equivalents for trials passed in each of the 39 tests of the scale. Heinis Mental Growth Units, although they seem to work surprisingly well, are subject to definite qualifications as was indicated by this reviewer in his discussion of the 4th edition of the Kuhlmann-Anderson tests (see 40:1404). Apparently the authors do not make as much of this feature in scoring their tests as they did in earlier editions.

DAVID SEGEL, *Specialist in Tests and Measurements, Office of Education, Federal Security Agency, Washington, D.C.*

These tests are the same as those of the Fifth Edition. What is changed besides the publisher are: (*a*) a redesignation of the test booklets to indicate their level by letter (for particular ages) rather than by grade; (*b*) revision of the general directions for administering and scoring to make them simpler and easier to follow; and (*c*) the development of new statistical evidence on the validity and reliability of the tests.

The *Kuhlmann-Anderson Intelligence Tests* have been in part unique in (*a*) the use of median mental age scores on separate tests to arrive at the mental age of the pupil, thus obtaining IQ's less affected by extreme scores on any subtest caused by some particular extraneous influence; and (*b*) the use of a greater number of separate booklets for varying levels of competence which make tests better adapted to the different groups of pupils. It also has somewhat less verbal material than most group intelligence tests.

The claim for validity rests on (*a*) data showing that the intercorrelations among the subtests and the correlations between the subtests and the total test are neither high nor low which the authors interpret as meaning that the tests are independent enough to add to the intelligence measure but not so independent that it is measuring something else entirely; (*b*) on statistics showing considerable variation in average score as among groups of retarded pupils, on-grade pupils, and accelerated pupils; and (*c*) on the progressive increase in pupils attaining a larger number of correct answers through the grades.

In general, these are acceptable statistical indices concerning intelligence tests for the purposes for which such tests are now used in schools. The reliability of the tests at various age levels shows that the results may be used in the guidance of individual pupils. The reliability coefficients were found to be .91 for grade 3, .88 for grade 5, .92 for grade 7, and .95 for grade 9. The standard errors of measurement of about six IQ points indicate considerable stability.

These tests are among the best as all-round group intelligence tests that give an overall mental age and only one caution need be made. As the authors themselves emphasize, the subtests should not be used as measures of this or that mental function and the profile of trials passed should not be used for guidance purposes. The profile may, however, be examined for possible erratic test performance.

For a review by Henry E. Garrett of the fourth edition, see 40:1404; for reviews by Psyche Cattell, S. A. Courtis, and Austin H. Turney of the fourth edition, see 38:1049.

[303]
*The Mill Hill Vocabulary Scale.** Ages 4–14, 11–14, 14 and over; 1943–48; 3 levels; 2 editions; manual ('48); 15s. per 50 of any one level; 2s. 6d. per manual; 17s. 6d. per specimen set including 5 copies of each form and a specimen set of the complementary *Progressive Matrices (1938)* (see 314); purchase tax (British purchasers only) and postage extra; nontimed (15–20) minutes; J. C. Raven; H. K. Lewis & Co., Ltd. *

a) JUNIOR. Ages 11–14; Forms 1 ('48), 2 ('48).
b) SENIOR. Ages 14 and over; Forms 1 ('48), 2 ('48).
c) ORAL DEFINITIONS FORM. Ages 4 and over; consists of all words in both forms of the junior and senior levels; individual; 1 form ('48).

REFERENCES
1–3. See 3:239.
4. FOULDS, G. A., AND RAVEN, J. C. "Intellectual Ability and Occupational Grade." *Occupational Psychol* 22:197–203 O '48. * (PA 23:1961)
5. FOULDS, G. A., AND RAVEN, J. C. "Normal Changes in the Mental Abilities of Adults as Age Advances." *J Mental Sci* 94:133–42 Ja '48. * (PA 22:4882)
6. RAVEN, J. C. "The Comparative Assessment of Intellectual Ability." *Brit J Psychol* 39:12–9 S '48. * (PA 24:1063)
7. SLATER, PATRICK. "Comment on 'The Comparative Assessment of Intellectual Ability.'" *Brit J Psychol* 39:20–1 S '48. * (PA 24:1065)
8. FOULDS, G. A. "Variations in the Intellectual Activities of Adults." *Am J Psychol* 62:238–46 Ap '49. * (PA 24:1716)
9. FOULDS, G. A. "Variations in the Intellectual Activities of Adults: Their Assessment and Significance," pp. 61–2. Abstract. In *Proceedings and Papers of the Twelfth International Congress of Psychology Held at the University of Edinburgh, July 23rd to 29th, 1948.* Edinburgh, Scotland: Oliver and Boyd Ltd., 1950. Pp. xxviii, 152. Paper. *
10. PETRIE, ASENATH, AND POWELL, MURIEL B. "The Selection of Nurses in England." *J Appl Psychol* 35:281–6. * (PA 26:3090)

For a review by David Wechsler, see 3:239.

[304]
*Miller Analogies Test.** Candidates for graduate school; 1926–50; Form H ('50); Form G ('47) discontinued, but available for special purposes approved by publisher; manual ('47); supplementary manual ('50); distribution is restricted and the test is administered only at specified licensed testing centers; details may be obtained from publisher; 50(55) minutes; W. S. Miller; Psychological Corporation. *

REFERENCES
1. LOVEGREN, LEVI ALTON. *Students in the Lowest Decile of Miller's Analogies Test.* Doctor's thesis, University of Minnesota (Minneapolis, Minn.), 1936. Pp. 118.
2. DUGAN, WILLIS E. *A Study of the Miller Analogies Test With Graduate Students in Education.* Master's thesis, University of Minnesota (Minneapolis, Minn.), 1939. Pp. 117.
3. COOK, WALTER W. "Predicting Success of Graduate Students in a College of Education." *Sch & Soc* 56:192–5 S 5 '42. * (PA 17:299)
4. FULLER, ELIZABETH MECHEM. "The Use of Measures of Ability and General Adjustments in the Preservice Selection of Nursery School-Kindergarten-Primary Teachers." *J Ed Psychol* 37:321–34 S '46. * (PA 21:1640)
5. KENDALL, WILLIAM E., AND HAHN, MILTON E. "The Use of Tests in the Selection of Medical Students by the College of Medicine of Syracuse University." Abstract. *Am Psychol* 2:297 Ag '47. * (PA 21:4650, title only)
6. JENSEN, RALPH E. *Predicting Scholastic Achievement of First-Year Graduate Students.* Doctor's thesis, University of Pittsburgh (Pittsburgh, Pa.), 1949. (*Abstracts of Doctoral Dissertations....1949,* 1950, pp. 305–13.) (PA 23:2992, title only)
7. WRENN, C. GILBERT. "Potential Research Talent in the Sciences: Based on Intelligence Quotients of Ph.D's." *Ed Rec* 30:4–22 Ja '49. *
8. ZAGORSKI, HENRY JOSEPH. *A Pattern Analysis of the Miller Analogies Test.* Master's thesis, University of Pittsburgh (Pittsburgh, Pa.), 1949. (PA 24:390, title only)
9. BRADFIELD, ANNE FREDERIKSEN. *Predicting the Success in Training of Graduate Students in School Administration.* Doctor's thesis, Stanford University (Stanford, Calif.), 1950. (*Abstracts of Dissertations....1949–50,* 1950, pp. 294–7.)
10. KELLY, E. LOWELL, AND FISKE, DONALD W. "The Prediction of Success in the VA Training Program in Clinical Psychology." *Am Psychol* 5:395–406 Ag '50. * (PA 25:2183)
11. TRAVERS, ROBERT M. W., AND WALLACE, WIMBURN L. "The Assessment of the Academic Aptitude of the Graduate Student." *Ed & Psych Meas* 10:371–9 au '50. * (PA 25:3414)
12. DOPPELT, JEROME E. "Difficulty and Validity of Analogies Items in Relation to Major Field of Study." *J Appl Psychol* 35:30–3 F '51. * (PA 25:7076)
13. GLASER, ROBERT. "Predicting Achievement in Medical School." *J Appl Psychol* 35:272–4 Ag '51. * (PA 26:3046)
14. GLASER, ROBERT. "The Validity of Some Tests for Predicting Achievement in Medical School." Abstract. *Am Psychol* 6:298 Jl '51. *
15. KELLY, E. LOWELL, AND FISKE, DONALD W. *The Prediction of Performance in Clinical Psychology.* Ann Arbor, Mich.: University of Michigan, 1951. Pp. xv, 311. Lithotyped. *
16. WEBSTER, EDWARD C.; WINN, ALEXANDER; AND OLIVER, JOHN A. "Selection Tests for Engineers: Some Preliminary Findings." *Personnel Psychol* 4:339–62 w '51. * (PA 26:6572)

J. P. GUILFORD, *Professor of Psychology, University of Southern California, Los Angeles, California.*

Forms G and H of this test are culminations of about 25 years of development, aimed at measuring scholastic aptitude at the graduate level. Very extensive item analyses have gone into the preparation of both forms. The manual is carefully prepared, with a few oversights to be mentioned later.

The reliability of Form G (odd-even) was estimated to be .92 to .93. Form H correlated .83 to .90 with Form G in three groups of graduate students.

Practical validity for Form G is indicated by several procedures. With grades in 24 education courses at Minnesota the median correlation was .55. At three other universities, 12 correlations with grades and grade-point averages had a median of .35. At Minnesota and Syracuse, correlations with 15 part scores on comprehensive masters' examinations had a median of about .40. In the clinical training program at the University of Michigan, the mean scores on four groups—"completed the Ph.D.," "still in training," "voluntarily dropped," and "dismissed"—were 78, 72, 69, and 62, respectively. Centile norms are given for 13 different graduate and professional school groups, with number of cases ranging from 70 to 1,084. The same norms apply to Form H, with minor corrections.

The most important criticism that one can offer for this test is that it was not based upon any explicitly stated philosophy of education at the graduate level. Scholastic aptitude at the graduate level is not even defined in the manual. The operational definition, as indicated by the emphasis upon course grades in validation studies, is whatever course grades indicate. Those of us who train students beyond the M.A. level well know that there are often great discrepancies in both directions between grade getting abilities and capacities for independent thinking and research.

The indications are that the *Miller Analogies Test* is almost entirely a measure of the verbal comprehension factor. When we aim a test at predicting grade getting, we are likely to come out with such a measure. Even at the graduate level, courses emphasize concept formation and the highly verbal student surpasses. The correlations of the test with the Verbal Factor part of the *Graduate Record Examination* clustered about .75 to .80. Its correlation with a vocabulary test (reported by R. R. G. Watt in a personal communication) was .86.

Some minor technical details occurred to the reviewer as he tried the items. Unlike standard analogies tests, the four alternative answers may come at any one of the four positions, not always at the fourth position, as is customary. No explanation for this is given in the manual; it would have to be a good one to outweigh the risk of confusion this practice entails. Some analogies are *very* loose. On the one hand, this may irk the examinee who demands tighter logic. On the other hand, it may encourage accepting wrong loose analogies in other items. The alternative answers are not always of the same part of speech in an item. This sometimes serves as an irrelevant cue for elimination of wrong answers. On rare occasions more than one item hinges on knowing the meaning of a certain word or principle. This extra source of interdependence of items may add to the apparent reliability of scores without adding to effective measurement.

In summary, it can be said that this test has been prepared with the careful use of the technical procedures now available to test makers, overlooking a few minor defects of item writing and editing. It has shown substantial value in predicting "scholarship at the graduate level" as indicated by grades in courses and comprehensive examinations. Its very strong component of verbal comprehension variance assures that outcome. A thorough study of what it takes to make a successful graduate student beyond the master's level will show much room for supplementary predictive aids. The user of this test should give special attention to the statement on the cover of the manual: "for use as one factor in the *selection of graduate students*." The reviewer would add a recommendation that if a fixed minimum qualifying score is used at all, it be not too high. We do not yet have the information needed to say what such a score should be. The reviewer would also add the ungracious suggestion that a good vocabulary test would probably do as well and do it more efficiently.

CARL I. HOVLAND, *Sterling Professor of Psychology, Yale University, New Haven, Connecticut.*

Development of the *Miller Analogies Test* was begun over 25 years ago by W. S. Miller as an aid in selecting students for graduate work at the University of Minnesota. As a result of interest on the part of other institutions, the test has been made available more generally through licensed centers by the Psychological Corporation.

The test consists simply of 100 analogy problems in verbal form. Thus it lends itself readily to self-administration and to group testing. It can be easily scored by hand or by IBM equipment. Nearly all students complete the test within the time limit of 50 minutes. A nearly perfect correlation has been found between scores with a 50-minute time limit and with a 90-minute limit. The items are arranged in order of difficulty and the score is the number of items correct.

Two forms are currently in print. Form G, developed by Miller on the basis of two earlier forms, is now restricted for special uses. Form H, prepared by Miller and the staff of the Psychological Corporation, is being extensively used at present. Work is underway on Form J. Considerable care appears to have been exercised to make the types of items used in Forms H and J closely comparable in difficulty and content area to the original form. Nevertheless Form H is slightly more difficult than Form G. The publishers recommend that two points be added to Form H scores in the range from 30 to 70 to permit use of the percentile equivalent tables developed for Form G. At no point does the 2-point difference in raw score change the percentile values by more than five points. The two forms have approximately equivalent standard deviations and correlate .89.

RELIABILITY. The reliability of Form G appears to be satisfactorily high considering the narrow range of ability represented by graduate school applicants. The data presented in the manual show odd-even reliabilities of about .93 (corrected for length by the Spearman-Brown formula). So far, similar information has not been released for Form H although such data must now be available in considerable profusion. It appears to the reviewer that many institutions will be working with more restricted ranges than those used by Miller in his computation of the reliability coefficient, and appropriate consideration must be given this fact in their interpretation of test-retest results.

CORRELATION WITH OTHER TESTS. A considerable body of information is available on the correlation of the Miller test with other tests, but no systematic factor analysis of its components appears to be available. Since successful performance on the test requires knowledge of vocabulary and familiarity with the content of courses in science and the humanities in addition to reasoning ability, it is not surprising that it correlates with both the Verbal Aptitude (about .80) and Quantitative Aptitude (about .60) portions of the *Graduate Record Examination*, with the *Ohio State University Psychological Examination* (.82), with the *Terman Concept Mastery Test* (.73), and with a variety of tests of knowledge of school subjects (about .50–.80). (Data from manual and mimeographed memorandums prepared by the publisher.)

VALIDITY. The main data on validity are those bearing on the correlation between Miller tests scores and performance in various graduate courses. In a variety of courses in education at the University of Minnesota, correlations with course grades were predominantly in the range from about .40 to .60. Somewhat similar data are reported elsewhere for grades in chemistry, psychology, biology, and language. A recent study of Glaser (*13*) indicates a correlation of .38 between Miller scores and first year grades in medical school. The data on validity are probably of necessity rather fragmentary and scattered since as Miller points out:

> One must expect that the validity will vary from school to school, from course to course, and from year to year. It depends in part on the factors which go into graduate school marks, the number of applicants for admission to a school or department, and the relevance of the ability measured by the test to the qualities required by courses for which it is predicting.

The data from the studies reported in the literature are often difficult to interpret because rarely is information presented on the reliability of the criterion.

Significant data are being accumulated on the relation between Miller scores and survival in graduate school. The most comprehensive data currently available are those of Kelly and Fiske (*15*) obtained in connection with the selection of clinical psychologists in the Veterans Administration training program. The test battery was administered to a large group of students selected for training, and the result compared with careful follow-up data. The data indicate a clear relationship between Miller scores and the completion of graduate training. Trainees who subsequently completed their studies and obtained the Ph.D. averaged 77.6 (SD = 8.4) while those who were dismissed from the program averaged only 62.4 (SD = 13.7). The difference in means is highly significant ($t = 5.9$).

SUMMARY. The Miller test appears to be a carefully constructed instrument for use in a very difficult area of selection where the criterion itself is far from satisfactory. The reliability is adequate even for the narrow range of ability typically involved and a large number of studies indicate that the test has considerable predictive value for academic success at the graduate school level. The limiting of the use of the test to licensed centers is an important safeguard for its proper use.

[305]

*Modified Alpha Examination Form 9. Grades 7-12 and adults; 1941-51; 3 scores: numerical, verbal, total; Form 9 ('42); revised manual ('51); supplementary norms ['47]; $4 per 25; separate answer sheets must be used; $1.50 per 50 answer sheets; 35¢ per specimen set; postpaid; 24(35) minutes; revision by F. L. Wells; Psychological Corporation. *

REFERENCES

1-3. See 3:220 (68, 70, 72).
4. EIMICKE, VICTOR W., AND FISH, HERMAN L. "A Preliminary Study of the Relationships Between the Bernreuter Personality Inventory and Performances on the Army Alpha Examination and the George Washington Social Intelligence Test." *J Psychol* 25:381-7 Ap '48. * *(PA* 22:4418)
5. SELTZER, CARL C. "Academic Success in College of Public and Private School Students: Freshman Year at Harvard." *J Psychol* 25:419-31 Ap '48. * *(PA* 22:4606)
6. MURRAY, JOHN E. "An Analysis of Geometric Ability." *J Ed Psychol* 40:118-24 F '49. * *(PA* 24:2066)
7. ALLEN, ROBERT M., AND BESSELL, HAROLD. "Intercorrelations Among Group Verbal and Non-Verbal Tests of Intelligence." *J Ed Res* 43:394-5 Ja '50. * *(PA* 24:4841)
8. EIMICKE, VICTOR WILLIAM. *A Study of the Effect of Intensive Sales Training Experience Upon the Measured Abilities and Personality Characteristics of Salesman-Candidates.* Doctor's thesis, New York University (New York, N.Y.), 1951. Abstract: *Microfilm Abstracts* 11:951-2 no 4 '51.

DAEL WOLFLE, *Director, Commission on Human Resources and Advanced Training, 2101 Constitution Ave., N.W., Washington, D.C.*

This test has been changed from the original Alpha format in a number of respects. It is in a reusable booklet with a separate (hand scored) answer sheet. Antiquated items have been revised. The eight subtests are: addition, following directions, arithmetic problems, verbal analogies, number series, mixed-up sentences, highest common divisor, and same or opposite words. With four verbal and four numerical sections, verbal and numerical scores as well as the total score are obtained.

The old trusting attitude that examinees would not look at the test items until time to start the test is partly gone. But not entirely; a person getting the idea of a test form quickly can, on some parts, solve a number of the items while the examiner is reading the directions.

The reliability is indicated by correlations of from .87 to .92, with scores on *Revised Alpha Examination, Forms 5 and 7*. Correlations with several other variables are given. For example, correlations with *Otis Self-Administering Tests of Mental Ability* run from .64 to .79. Numerical, verbal, and total score norms are given for boys and girls combined in each of grades 7-12. There are also norms for adult men applying for executive positions and for four groups of "male engineering personnel of a large airplane company" and for these four groups combined.

We now demand more information about a test's construction, item analysis, and validation than the author and publisher have provided. There is, however, a wealth of information about the original *Army Group Examination Alpha* and its various revisions not found in the manuals; that literature can provide anyone who is interested with much more extensive information about this still good test than that which is available concerning all but a few of its successors.

[306]

*****Moray House Picture Intelligence Test 1.** Ages 78-102 months; 1944-48; 1 form ['44]; manual ('48); 20s. per 25; 1s. per single copy; 1s. 3d. per manual; 1s. 9d. per specimen set; postage extra; 25(75) minutes; Margaret A. Mellone under the supervision of Godfrey H. Thomson and an Advisory Committee of Edinburgh Headmasters and Infant School Mistresses; University of London Press Ltd. *

REFERENCES

1. MELLONE, MARGARET A. "An Investigation Into the Relationship Between Reading Ability and I.Q. as Measured by a Verbal Group Intelligence Test." *Brit J Ed Psychol* 12:128-35 Je '42. * *(PA* 16:3968)
2. MELLONE, MARGARET A. *A Factorial Study of Picture Tests for Young Children.* Doctor's thesis, University of Edinburgh (Edinburgh, Scotland), 1943.
3. MELLONE, MARGARET A. "A Factorial Study of Picture Tests for Young Children." *Brit J Psychol* 35:9-16 S '44. * *(PA* 19:271)
4. EMMETT, W. G. "Evidence of a Space Factor at 11+ and Earlier." *Brit J Psychol, Stat Sect* 2:3-16 Mr '49. * *(PA* 23:4509)
5. HUGHES, H. O. "Intelligence Test Surveys of 7+ Age Groups." *Ed R* 1:181-9 Je '49. *

GERTRUDE KEIR, *Lecturer in Psychology, University College, London, England.*

The test consists of nine nonverbal subtests: Directions, Doesn't Belong, Completion, Absurdities, Sequence, Reversed Similarities, Always Has, Analogies, and Series. The drawings are well spaced, and clear, though in some there is a little too much detail for children of this age. There are practice items for all the nine subtests with the exception of Directions. Each subtest is timed.

The manual gives very complete and clear directions to the teacher for the administration of the test. The examiner's instructions for each subtest do not suffer from lengthiness more than is usual in group tests for young children. The manual also contains directions for scoring, an answer key, and tables for the conversion of raw scores into IQ's. The user is warned that the IQ's are not computed by means of mental age, and so are not comparable to the IQ's of the Binet test. In the 1948 edition of the manual the IQ's differ by about one point from those given in the original manual, being based on a more representative sample, hence those using the test should see that they use this, or later, manuals. For the convenience of clinical psychologists who "frequently require a measure of a child's brightness in terms of mental ages" a table of mental age norms is given at the end of the manual. "The figures have been extrapolated graphically outside the range 6 years 9 months to 7 years and 10 months and therefore become less secure towards the extremes."

The test has been constructed with great care. It consists of the most discriminative items from three trial batteries given to more than 600 children.

The manual states that "the test shows a bias in favour of boys," the average superiority of the boys being about 2½ points of IQ. This sex bias has not been confirmed by later statistics gathered by W. G. Emmett. Further scores for 2,289 boys and 2,150 girls of complete age groups gives the mean for boys 57.56 and for girls 57.54 (SD about 20). The reliability coefficient, obtained by the Kuder-Richardson formula 20 from a random sample of 250 scripts of 5,415 Edinburgh children, is .96. Using Thurstone's centroid method, the author carried out a factorial analysis on the results of an early form of the test applied to 414 boys and girls. This form consisted of 14 subtests, of which 9 were retained for the final version. The results of boys and girls were analysed separately. A general factor was found to be present in both. A second factor, a space factor, appeared in the boys' results in addition to specifics; this was not found in the girls' results, only general and specifics being present. The test appears to have good reliability and a fairly good degree of validity. The size of the correlations between this test and other group tests of intelligence, lower than might be deemed altogether satisfactory, is no doubt due to the age of the children tested and also to the fact that spatial ability appears to be measured by it to some extent. Nevertheless, it is among the best group tests of intelligence in this country for younger children.

M. L. KELLMER PRINGLE, *Lecturer in Education, and Acting Deputy Head, Remedial Education Centre, University of Birmingham, Birmingham, England.*

Designed to test intelligence at the transition stage when children move from the infant to the junior school, the test is being widely used in this country as it is the only group test for this young age group produced by trained and experienced educationists. It consists of nine subtests each of which has a number of items (varying from 8 to 15). With the exception of the first one, all subtests are preceded by three practice items for which no score is given, while all correct items receive one point; except for the first and last subtest, all the items are of the multiple choice type.

In view of the age of the children for whom the test is intended, it is an important advantage that neither reading nor writing is required; the instructions are given orally by the "supervisor" (to use Mellone's term), and to solve the various problems, patterns, designs or pictures are to be ticked, crossed out, or encircled. According to the general instructions in the manual, no more than 30 children should be tested at one time and two adults should be present, one to read out the instructions, the other to supervise the children's work. In the writer's experience 30 is too large a number with such young children. Copying is very easy and liberal spacing out is needed; 15 to 20 children would seem the maximum number.

The first subtest, Directions, not only contains some rather poorly drawn pictures (the ring and the house for instance are neither typical nor representative of the child's own world) but also seems psychologically unsound, since it tends to arouse in some children anxiety at the beginning of the test. Being asked to draw lines across a page which looks neat and tidy with competently drawn pictures goes right against the usual training given at school where defacing and scribbling in printed books is frowned upon. As none of the other subtests are based on this manner of response, there seems to be no reason why this test should not be replaced by one similar to the other eight subtests.

The test has been standardised on a total sample of 8,107 children aged between 6 years 9 months to 7 years 10 months, one group being children from Edinburgh and another from some English mining and country areas. The intelligence quotients derived from this test are so arranged as to have an average of 100 with a standard deviation of 15. They differ from the Binet IQ's in that not being based on the usual calculation from chronological and mental ages, the IQ conversion tables are not self-consistent if interpreted in terms of mental age.

Only the scantiest statistical data are offered despite the fact that the test has been widely used over the past six years or so in many parts of England and Scotland. The reliability coefficient, "calculated from an answer pattern drawn up from a random sample of 250 scripts from the complete year group of 5,415 Edinburgh children," is given as .96. Correspondingly, the standard error of the IQ is 3.1 which is smaller than that of most group tests but larger than the standard error of individual tests. Considering the high variability of performance with

Moray House Picture Intelligence Test 1

young children and the narrow age range, it is fairly moderate. No data are given for the validity of the test or for its correlation and intercorrelation with other tests.

It is stated in the manual that it must not be assumed on the evidence of this test alone (or of any group test) that an IQ of less than 70 necessarily implies that the child is mentally defective. But surely it ought to be stressed even more that group tests are unreliable with young children, and that they often give a serious underestimate of intelligence not only with the dull, but with the emotionally disturbed, the sensitive, the discouraged, or excitable child. This test can be considered a useful tool for predicting a child's readiness to respond to more formal methods of teaching. A low result should be accepted only as an indication that a child is not ready for such an approach but the reason for this must be found through individual tests and case study procedure.

[307]

*Non-Verbal Test. Ages 10–11; 1947–51; title on test booklet is *A Scale of Non-Verbal Mental Ability;* 2 forms (listed below); use of the practice exercise, *Preliminary Practice Test 1* ['50], is optional; revised manual ['51]; 70s. per 100; 9s. per 12; 10d. per single copy; 25s. per 100 practice exercises; 3s. 6d. per 12; 4d. per single copy; 2s. 9d. per manual; postage extra; practice exercise: 10(15) minutes; test: 30(35) minutes; J. W. Jenkins and D. M. Lee (II); National Foundation for Educational Research in England and Wales. *

a) NON-VERBAL TEST I. 1947.
b) NON-VERBAL TEST II. 1948.

REFERENCES

1. MILLS, L. F. *The Properties of a Space Test.* Bachelor's thesis, University of Edinburgh (Edinburgh, Scotland), 1947.
2. PEEL, E. A. "Symposium on Selection of Pupils for Different Types of Secondary Schools: VI. Evidence of a Practical Factor at the Age of Eleven." *Brit J Ed Psychol* 19:1–15 F '49. *
3. SCOTT, G. C. "Measuring Sudanese Intelligence." *Brit J Ed Psychol* 20:43–54 F '50. * (*PA* 25:316)

E. A. PEEL, *Professor of Education and Head of the Department, University of Birmingham, Birmingham, England.*

These parallel scales of nonverbal ability may be applied according to two procedures, I and II. In the first procedure the test is applied without preliminary practice in similar material, and in the second a practice test is given and the instructions for the main test are presented orally. The second procedure is to be preferred.

Scale I was devised by the late J. W. Jenkins as a measure of nonverbal intelligence. It has been used extensively in England and where applied by research workers in a mixed battery of verbal, nonverbal, pictorial and spatial tests, has generally come out as a measure of pure *g*.

Thus when the results of such batteries are analysed by Thurstone's centroid method and the unrotated factors examined, the communality of Jenkins' test appears to be almost completely explicable in terms of the first factor. Its loading in the second bipolar factor is usually very near to zero. The test is therefore to be recommended as a useful reference test where problems relating to different qualities of intelligence are being investigated. It is to be deprecated that the publishers of this test do not present some of the interesting factorial information concerning the test.

The test is composed of five separately timed subtests making up an overall time of 30 minutes. Jenkins used the mathematico-logical principles of classification, ordered sequence and analogy, and applied them to nonverbal pattern material. Subtests 1 and 3 use the device of like and unlike as a test of the principle of classification; Subtests 2 and 4 utilise the familiar device of ordered sequence; and Subtest 5, the analogy. These are familiar enough concepts but the main feature of the Jenkins test is that they lead to high *g* saturation and negligible or insignificant *k* loadings.

When used without practice tests the instructions at the head of each subtest have to be read by the testee. These are brief but admit the possibility of verbal interference, and it would be preferable if they were orally presented by the tester. The key is much smaller than the test booklet and is difficult to relate to the test. Instructions and information about the test are provided separately. Norms are provided over the age range 10:0–12:11, and there is a marked gradient in the scores with respect to age. For example, the standardised score of 100 at 10:0 is equivalent to a raw score of 28, and at 12:11 to a raw score of 45. The test is therefore discriminative with regard to age. The standardisation is based on a mean of 100 and a standard deviation of 15, and the scores are therefore roughly equivalent to IQ scores.

It would be advantageous if the information about the test, instructions, key and norms, were all given in a single test manual of the same size as the test booklet. The possibility of sex differences is not discussed and the norms are based on a mixed population of boys and girls. The test reliability is .95 by the split half method, but no test validity is given either in terms of other tests of intelligence or independent estimates of general intellectual ability. As in the case of the relationship of the test to other tests of intelligence there is much material available about the relationship of this test to outside estimates of intelligence and the publishers might well have produced some of this information to guide the would-be user of the test. For all that, the test is to be recommended as a measure of *g*. It should not, however, be used to measure spatial ability or practical ability. In this respect the title may be a little misleading.

Scale II was devised by Lee and Jenkins as a parallel form of the first issue and embodies the same logical principles. It may be administered according to either procedure, that is, with or without practice material. The new test manuals now printed are a great improvement and the key is of the same size as the test booklet. This makes for rapid, easy scoring of the test. Reliability of the test is .92 and the two parallel forms correlate to the extent of .87. As in the case of the first test no information is given about the relation of the test to other published tests of intelligence and also no correlations are given between the test and independent estimates of intellectual ability. Norms are given over the same age range and standardised to the same basis as the first form. The second form is not so discriminative with regard to age. At 10:0 the standardised score of 100 is equivalent to 22 points of raw score, and at 12:11 to 38 points. This gradient, however, makes fair discrimination with regard to age. The norms are based on a mixed population, but the authors might well have given some indication of the sex differences of the test, particularly in view of the accumulating evidence that this type of material may show significant differences. In spite of these criticisms both forms of the test are to be recommended as useful for research workers investigating mental ability and for routine grading of children on the basis of non-verbal general ability. For school selection purposes the material should be supplemented by verbal material.

The review excerpt presented in the first printing of The Third Mental Measurements Yearbook *(3:260) is a review of the* SRA Non-Verbal Classification Form.

[308]

*****Ohio State University Psychological Test.** Grades 9–16 and adults; 1919–50; 2 scores: reading, total; IBM; Forms 18 ('33), 20 ('37), 21 ('40), 22 ('43), 23 ('47), 24 ('50); forms are successive revisions, not parallel forms; separate answer pads or answer sheets must be used; 6¢ per answer pad; 5¢ per IBM answer sheet (Forms 21, 22, 23 only); 5¢ per scoring stencil; postage extra; worklimit (120) minutes; Herbert A. Toops; Ohio College Association. *
a) FORM 24. 10¢ per test and answer pad or IBM answer sheet.
b) FORMS 18, 20, 21, 22, 23. 7¢ per new test; 2¢ per used test. (Form 21 also published in 2 editions by Science Research Associates, Inc.: Form AH (hand scoring edition): 49¢ per test and answer pad; $2.15 per 25 answer pads; Form AM (machine scoring edition): 39¢ per test; $2.90 per 100 IBM answer sheets; 50¢ per scoring stencil; 75¢ per specimen set; cash orders postpaid.)

REFERENCES

1–28. See 3:244.
29. HARDIN, ROBERT ALLEN. *A Study of the Maturity of High School Seniors, Junior College, and University Students as Measured by the Ohio State University Psychological Test and the Pressey Interest-Attitude Test.* Doctor's thesis, University of Nebraska (Lincoln, Neb.), 1935.
30. MAJOR, C. L. "The Percentile Ranking on the Ohio State University Psychological Test as a Factor in Forecasting the Success of Teachers in Training." *Sch & Soc* 47:582–4 Ap 30 '38. * *(PA* 12:4361)
31. LAUGHLIN, WILLIAM PATRICK. *Changes of Intelligence Scores of College Students Over a Period of Approximately Four Years.* Doctor's thesis, University of Minnesota (Minneapolis, Minn.), 1940. (*Summaries of Ph.D. Theses,* 1949, pp. 92–4.)
32. GENTRY, DOROTHY E. *An Attempt to Predict Scholarship From a Variety of Objective Tests: College Ability Test, Nelson-Denny Reading Test, Kuhlmann-Anderson Intelligence Test, and English Placement Test.* Master's thesis, Ohio University (Athens, Ohio), 1943. Pp. 33. (*Abstracts of Masters' Theses....1943,* 1944, pp. 36–7.)
33. THOMPSON, R. B. "Predictive Criteria for Selecting A.S.T. Students." *J Am Assn Col Reg* 19:492–500 Jl '44. * *(PA* 18:3867)
34. HARTSON, L. D. "Influence of Level of Motivation on the Validity of Intelligence Tests." *Ed & Psychol Meas* 5:273–83 au '45. * *(PA* 20:2500)
35. SHARP, HEBER CANNON. *A Comparative Analysis of the Ohio State Psychological Scores of the Yearly Groups of University of Utah Freshmen.* Master's thesis, University of Utah (Salt Lake City, Utah), 1945.
36. PAULSEN, GAIGE B. "The Intellectual Demands of the Various Curriculi in a University." Abstract. *Am Psychol* 2:422 O '47. * *(PA* 12:1386, title only)
37. COOPRIDER, H. A., AND LASLETT, H. R. "Predictive Values of the Stanford Scientific and the Engineering and Physical Science Aptitude Tests." *Ed & Psychol Meas* 8:683–7 w '48. * *(PA* 24:1488)
38. HERTEL, J. P., AND DI VESTA, FRANCIS J. "An Evaluation of Five Factors for Predicting the Success of Students Entering the New York State College of Agriculture." *Ed & Psychol Meas* 8:389–95 au '48. * *(PA* 23:4412)
39. INGRAM, LOIS M. *The Prediction of Scholastic Success From a Variety of Measures of Ability and Achievement.* Master's thesis, Ohio University (Athens, Ohio), 1948. Pp. 31. (*Abstracts of Masters' Theses....,* 1948, pp. 66–7.)
40. PORTENIER, LILLIAN G. "Predicting Success in Introductory Psychology." *Ed & Psychol Meas* 8:117–26 sp '48. * *(PA* 22:3730)
41. PORTENIER, LILLIAN G. "Predicting Success in Introductory Psychology." Abstract. *J Colo-Wyo Acad Sci* 3:61 Mr '48. *
42. DI VESTA, FRANCIS J.; WOODRUFF, ASAHEL D.; AND HERTEL, JOHN P. "Motivation as a Predictor of College Success." *Ed & Psychol Meas* 9:339–48 au '49. * *(PA* 26:2985)
43. MACDONALD, GORDON LUNDY. *Predicting Collegiate Survival From Pre-Admission Data.* Doctor's thesis, New York University (New York, N.Y.), 1949. Abstract: *Microfilm Abstracts* 10:42–4 no 1 '50. * *(PA* 24:6063, title only)
44. RINSLAND, HENRY D. "The Prediction of Veterans' Success From Test Scores at the University of Oklahoma," Part 1, pp. 59–72. In *The Sixth Yearbook of the National Council on Measurements Used in Education, 1948–1949.* Fairmont, W.Va.: the Council, Fairmont State College, 1949. Pp. v, 140 (variously numbered). Paper, mimeographed. *
45. UHRBROCK, RICHARD STEPHEN. "Construction of a Selection Test for College Graduates." *J General Psychol* 41:153–93 O '49. * *(PA* 24:4874)
46. WRENN, C. GILBERT. "Potential Research Talent in the Sciences: Based on Intelligence Quotients of Ph.D's." *Ed Rec* 30:4–22 Ja '49. *
47. JAMES, RICHARD WARREN. *Selection of Graduate Students: (1) The Adequacy of Certain Measures for Differentiating Between Two Groups of Master Candidates (2) The Value of These Measures in Prognosing Graduate Academic Achievement.* Doctor's thesis, New York University (New York, N.Y.), 1950. Abstract: *Microfilm Abstracts* 11:53–4 no 1 '51. * *(PA* 24:2428, title only)

48. PORTENIER, LILLIAN G. "Mental Ability Ratings of Honor Students." *J Ed Psychol* 41:493-9 D '50. * (*PA* 25:5666)
49. RYAN, SULER ELDON. *Some Characteristics of the 1948 Freshman Class at the University of Missouri and the Relation of These Characteristics to Academic Success.* Doctor's thesis, University of Missouri (Columbia, Mo.), 1950. Abstract: *Microfilm Abstracts* 10:84-5 no 3 '50. * (*PA* 25:4828, title only)
50. SABEH, RAYMOND. *Comparisons of the Wechsler-Bellevue Adult Intelligence Scale With the Ohio State Psychological Examination in Predicting Academic Success for College Freshmen.* Master's thesis, Ohio University (Athens, Ohio), 1950. Pp. 40. (*Abstracts of Masters' Theses....*, 1950, p. 126.)
51. CARTER, W. R. *The Missouri College Aptitude Testing Program.* University of Missouri Bulletin, Vol. 52, No. 30; Education Series, No. 40. Columbia, Mo.: the University, October 20, 1951. Pp. 76. Paper. * (*PA* 26:3043)

GEORGE A. FERGUSON, *Professor of Psychology, McGill University, Montreal, Canada.* [Review of Form 24]

This test, which is widely known and used, has been revised many times since work was first initiated on it in 1919. Few, if any, tests have been the object of more careful, prolonged, and continuous study. Further, a number of important contributions to psychological test theory have accompanied its development. Its authors over the past 30 years have employed the most exacting technical procedures in the development of new forms. Form 24 is not markedly dissimilar in format and content from a number of earlier forms. Three subtests comprise the test: same-opposites, word relationships, and reading comprehension. There are 150 items in all. No time limit is specified. The test is of the power-limit or power type. This, the authors contend, provides a much more accurate evaluation of a student's scholastic potentiality than similar time-limit tests. The test is self-marking, the testee employing a pin stylus to record his answers on an answer sheet. A score is obtained by simply adding up the right answers. IBM answer sheets and scoring may also be employed.

Percentile norms for total scores and subtests separately are available based on a sample of 3,799 freshmen in Ohio colleges. Norms are available also for Ohio high school freshmen, sophomores, juniors, and seniors.

The unusual technical effort expended in the development of this test has yielded dividends in terms of increased validity. Recent forms of the tests are reported to have correlations with a criterion of scholastic performance consistently of the order .60 with an occasional coefficient greater than .70. No reliability data are reported for Form 24. The reliability of Form 21 (N = 300) is .93.

This test emphasizes verbal ability which is of undoubted importance in scholastic achievement. My impression is that the authors have approached a limit in the prediction possible with this type of test material. It is probable that future technical improvements, however exacting, will not result in an appreciable increase in validity. This test serves as an excellent illustration of what can be accomplished by the rigorous appliance of sound technical procedures. It illustrates, likewise, the limitations of that accomplishment. A correlation of .70 with a criterion, which is high for tests of this class, still leaves about 50 per cent of the criterion variance unaccounted for. The technology that has evolved around the construction and use of mental tests, however rigorously applied, can carry us only so far in the prediction of human behavior. Progress in this area will to a considerable extent depend on the development of new types of test material which define properties of human behavior radically different from those defined by many of the more widely used types of tests. These observations are in no way intended to imply criticism of the present test, which clearly stands out as a model of technical excellence among tests of this class.

For a review by J. P. Guilford of Form 21, see 3:244; for reviews by Louis D. Hartson, Theos A. Langlie, and Rudolf Pintner of Form 20, see 38:1051.

[309]
*Oral Directions Test: An Intelligence Test on Phonograph Records.** Grades 6-12 and adults; 1945-50; also called O.D.T.; 1 form, '45; revised manual ('50); 3 types of vinylite recordings: standard 78 rpm (four 12-inch records), transcription 33⅓ rpm (one 16-inch record), "LP" microgroove 33⅓ rpm (one 12-inch record); each record set includes manual, plastic-covered key, and 100 answer sheets; $18 per standard record set; $17 per transcription record set; $12 per microgroove record set; $4 per 100 answer sheets; postpaid; 28(35) minutes; Charles R. Langmuir; Psychological Corporation. *

REFERENCES
1. SEASHORE, HAROLD G. "Psychological Testing With Phonograph Recordings." Abstract. *Am Psychol* 1:248 Jl '46. * (*PA* 20:3932, title only)

For reviews by Charles D. Flory, Irving Lorge, and William W. Turnbull, see 3:245.

[310]
★**Otis Employment Tests.** Applicants for employment; 1943, c1922; identical to Forms A and B of *Otis Self-Administering Tests of Mental Ability* (see 3:250) except for manual and cover page; 2 levels; Forms A, B; no data on reliability and validity in manual (for data presented elsewhere by the author, see manual for *Otis Self-Administering Tests of Mental Ability*); $1.60 per 25 of any one level, postage extra; 35¢ per specimen set, postpaid; 30(35) minutes; Arthur S. Otis; World Book Co. *
a) TEST I. Applicants for jobs requiring a grammar school level of ability.

b) TEST II. Applicants for jobs requiring a high school level of ability.

[311]

★**P.C. Verbal Capacity Sampler.** Male adults (ages 20 and over); 1950–51; Form AH ('51); preliminary manual ('51); $1.25 per 25; 25¢ per scoring stencil; 25¢ per manual; 75¢ per specimen set; postpaid; 5(10) minutes; Byron B. Harless and Gerald P. Bodily; Psychological Counseling, Inc., Tampa, Fla. *

[312]

★**Pattern Perception Test.** Ages 6 and over; 1943; 1 form; no data on reliability and validity; no manual; mimeographed directions for administering ['43]; mimeographed directions for self-administering ['43]; 30s. per 100, postage extra; 1s. per specimen set, postpaid; 30(40) minutes; L. S. Penrose; Galton Laboratory, University College, Gower St., London W.C.1, England. *

REFERENCES

1. PENROSE, L. S. "An Economical Method of Presenting Matrix Intelligence Tests." *Brit J Med Psychol* 20:144–6 pt 2 '44 (issued F '45). * (PA 19:2067)
2. PENROSE, L. S. "The Pattern Perception Test: Experimental Results." *Brit J Med Psychol* 20:339–43 pt 4 '46. * (PA 21:2800)
3. PETRIE, ASENATH, AND POWELL, MURIEL B. "The Selection of Nurses in England." *J Appl Psychol* 35:281–6 Ag '51. * (PA 26:3090)

ALICE W. HEIM, *Medical Research Council Applied Psychology Research Unit, Psychological Laboratory, University of Cambridge, Cambridge, England.*

This is a paper and pencil intelligence test consisting of 64 items. These are preceded by a set of eight examples which the tester explains and answers for the subject. Each problem consists of a row of five diagrams; the subject is instructed to find four diagrams in each row which form a perfect pattern (or matrix) and to strike out the odd one. The problems are arranged in eight sets of graded difficulties. In each set they begin with an elementary presentation of a theme which is subsequently developed. In some problems, the matrix of four consists of two more or less closely related pairs of diagrams.

The score is the number of correct answers given. It is unnecessary to penalise wrong answers or to adjust for correct guesses since low scoring subjects were found to answer the difficult problems correctly in much less than 20 per cent of cases. Evidently failure to grasp the principle, especially for the harder questions in this test, results in the choice of a wrong answer more often than would be expected by chance.

The test has very wide application since it effects discrimination at both ends of the intelligence scale (i.e., among mental defectives on the one hand and among university students or army officer candidates on the other). Its correlations with other standard intelligence tests range from .73 (with a random sample of 597 army males) to .43 (with 67 medical students). The reviewer has no information as to its test-retest consistency. (*1*)

Some interesting differences have been found (*1*) with respect to individual test items in the scores of male and female subjects and of normal and psychotic subjects. These differences suggest (*a*) that whilst men tend to excel on items requiring rotation and superimposition for their solution, women do better on those in which (to quote the author of the test) "the pattern itself is intriguing"; (*b*) that distinctions between psychotic and normal thinking, exemplified in test results, do not necessarily require a verbal test for their detection. Psychotic subjects were found to do relatively well on items which involved rotation or reflection of figures or mere counting and to do relatively poorly on items requiring "common sense or constructive thought." (*1*)

The main weakness of Pattern Perception as a test of general intelligence lies in its having only one "bias": not only is every problem diagrammatic in nature but the form of the subject's task is exactly the same throughout the test. This inevitably results in certain subjects scoring "unduly" high and others scoring "unduly" low marks. Furthermore, the lack of variety makes difficult the production of those discrepant scores which, in mixed tests, often prove illuminating.

A further criticism derives from the theoretical basis of the construction of the problems. It is an extremely ingenious system based on combination theory; but as a direct result of this the subject may acquire, or fail to acquire, a knack which seems to the reviewer still more specific than that required by most "pure" intelligence tests. It is perhaps the logical rather than the psychological outcome of attempting to assess mental calibre by means of one homogeneous measure. For example, some of the problems require four of the diagrams to be recognised as two pairs, the fifth being extra because it is unpaired. But in many such items, one of the members of a pair is, for instance, the only diagram of the five which is all black. It may be argued that all blackness as the criterion should be rejected since another of the paired diagrams is all white. This is indeed always the case in such questions. In the reviewer's opinion, however, this point should be brought out during the preliminary examples. These examples contain no illustration of the particular type of problem criticised above; they are all therefore easier than the items on the last pages of the test proper. Finally, the subject does not complete these examples on his own account. These seem to the writer to constitute serious weaknesses of the test.

Pattern Perception is however an exceptionally welcome test because of its unique suitability for subjects of every range of intelligence.

[313]

★**The Peel Group Test of Practical Ability.** Ages 8–14; 1951; for selecting "children who might benefit from a technical craft, or art school education"; nonlanguage; 1 form ['51]; manual ['51]; 7s. 6d. per 25; 6d. per single copy; 1s. 3d. per manual; purchase tax (British purchasers only) and postage extra; 25(30) minutes; E. A. Peel; Thomas Nelson & Sons Ltd. *

REFERENCES

1. LAMBERT, CONSTANCE M. "Symposium on Selection of Pupils for Different Types of Secondary Schools: VII, A Survey of Ability and Interest at the Stage of Transfer." *Brit J Ed Psychol* 19:67–81 Je '49. *
2. PEEL, E. A. "Symposium on Selection of Pupils for Different Types of Secondary Schools: VI, Evidence of a Practical Factor at the Age of Eleven." *Brit J Ed Psychol* 19:1–15 F '49. *

GEORGE WESTBY, *Head of the Psychological Laboratory, University College of Hull, Hull, England.*

This is a novel and economical pencil and paper test consisting of 54 perceptual items in the form of well designed and printed black and white patterns, mainly but not exclusively geometrical (some organic configurations are included) and arranged in three subtests X, Y, Z requiring 10, 5, and 10 minutes respectively to administer. In each of the X and Z items there is an imperfection in the "Gestalt" or "Structure" and the task of the testee is first to discover the law of the configuration or pattern-principle, then observe the fault and mark it with a cross in the test booklet, a task which may well involve some special ability beyond simple perceptual discrimination and comprehension of relations of similarity. Subtest Y is a simple matching test. The testee compares a correct with a faulty pattern where both are printed side by side and again marks the imperfection with a cross. It would be interesting to know how this item correlates with the two other subtests and with total score in view of what seems "a priori" to be a significant difference in the tasks.

The test designer observed in 1949 that an aesthetic factor seemed to be involved in some nonverbal tests and hazarded a guess that the measurement of this along with the spatial factor might be relevant for some selection problems. This led to the construction of the test now published with the claim that it measures "sensitive reaction to form and pattern" and that this enters into "all technical and craft operations." Further, that "high correlations are attained with success in woodwork, metalwork, technical drawing and art school design, indicating that the test is a true technical measure." Correlations given (without, however, any data of populations), are .5 to .6 with woodwork and technical drawing, .68 with art school drawing, and .42 with art school design. Correlations with the *Alexander Performance Scale,* an individual test with much the same purpose, are given as between .4 and .6, and with verbal tests, as between .5 and .7, but again no information is given as to the populations from which these coefficients were obtained. The reliability is given as .86 which is around the minimum for a good mental test, but again the method used to arrive at this is not indicated. There is no published information as to the correlations of the test with other superficially similar tests which claim only to measure relational thinking by means of visual perceptual tasks such as Raven's *Progressive Matrices,* the Cattell *Culture-Free Test,* or the British N.I.I.P. *Group Tests 70.* Such a comparison would enable an assessment to be made of the special claim of this test to be measuring something new.

The main uses claimed for the test are: (*a*) To help in the selection from among British primary school children aged 10.3 to 11.2, those likely to benefit from a technical, craft, or art school training, at the point when a transfer is made to secondary education. (*b*) To show whether pupils between the ages of 12.3 and 14.0 already receiving academic secondary education should be transferred to technical, craft, or art school. (*c*) To provide some guidance in the choice of *vocation* after leaving school. With these ends in view a thorough standardization of the test to a mean of 100 and SD of 15 involving some 15,000 children has made available the following adequate and independent norms: (*a*) Norms for each sex separately, in the age group 10.3 to 11.2, the usual age range for selection for secondary education in British schools. (It is worthy of note that no sex differences appeared.) (*b*) Norms for a mixed group of 15,000 aged from 12.3 to 14.0, the transfer group. (*c*) Norms for a mixed group of about 1,000 in the age group 8.6 to 9.6. The last group was selected with the hope of using the test to assess the emergence of "special abilities" in the early school years, presumably for research or guidance purposes as there is no need for selection at this stage.

Any assessment of a new and relatively untried instrument must obviously be provisional, but it seems doubtful whether the loading of the "k" or "f" or any spatial or "practical" factor, or of any special "aesthetic" factor, or of any P or "perceptual speed" factor will be large enough to implement its purpose. Reports by Vernon and Parry [1] suggest that a nonverbal test of relational thinking along with suitably designed measures of mechanical and practical interest (through what may be largely a test of mechanical information and attainment along lines of the Bennett *Test of Mechanical Comprehension*), along with an arithmetic test for technical entrance would provide the most satisfactory method of attaining the ends outlined above, insofar as psychological tests can play a part.

In the absence of much more explicit and adequate data of validation, any programme as economical as this test must remain in the reviewer's opinion incautiously optimistic and calculated once again to weaken the recovering reputation of the mental tester among educationists who are able to assess psychometric claims without prejudice.

[314]

*Progressive Matrices. Ages 5–11, 6 and over, 11 and over; 1938–51; nonlanguage; 3 levels; separate answer sheets must be used; purchase tax (British purchasers only) and postage extra; J. C. Raven; H. K. Lewis & Co., Ltd. *

a) PROGRESSIVE MATRICES (1938): SETS A, B, C, D, AND E. Ages 6 and over; 1938–50; 1 form, '38; 168s. per 25; 7s. 6d. per 25 answer sheets; 2s. 6d. per manual ('50); 17s. 6d. per specimen set including 5 copies of each form of the complementary *Mill Hill Vocabulary Scale* (see 303); nontimed (60) minutes.

b) COLOURED PROGRESSIVE MATRICES (1947): SETS A, Ab, AND B. Ages 5–11; 1947–51; 1 form, '47; 168s. per 25; 7s. 6d. per 25 answer sheets; 2s. 6d. per manual ('51); 17s. 6d. per specimen set including 5 copies of each form of the complementary *Crichton Vocabulary Scale* (see 337); nontimed (30) minutes; also distributed by George G. Harrap & Co. Ltd.

c) PROGRESSIVE MATRICES (1947): SETS I AND II. Ages 11 and over (especially with above average intelligence)'; 1943–47; 2 editions; 1 form, '47; no data on reliability and validity.

1) *Set I*. For use either as a practice test for Set II or as a rough screening test; no norms; 50s. per 25; 5s. per test; (10) minutes.

2) *Set II*. For use either as "a test of intellectual capacity" when used without a time limit or as "a test of intellectual efficiency" when used with a time limit ("usually of 40 minutes"); distribution is restricted to registered users who after signing an agreement and paying an annual service fee may borrow tests for indefinite periods at 150s. per set of 25 tests or for 4 weeks at 20s. per set of 25 tests; 7s. 6d. per 100 record forms; specimen set not available.

REFERENCES

1-8. See 40:1417.
9-21. See 3:258.
22. SLATER, PATRICK. "Scores of Different Types of Neurotics on Tests of Intelligence." *Brit J Psychol* 35:40-2 Ja '45. * (PA 19:966)
23. OXLADE, M. "An Experiment in the Use of Psychological Tests in the Selection of Women Trainee Telephone Mechanics." *B Ind Psychol & Personnel Practice* 2:26-32 Mr '46. * (PA 20:4838)
24. "Raven's Intelligence Test." Editor's reply to query. *Brit Med J* 4506:766 My 17 '47. * Reply by John C. Raven: *Brit Med J* 4510:872 Je 14 '47. *
25. MILLS, L. F. *The Properties of a Space Test.* Bachelor's thesis, University of Edinburgh (Edinburgh, Scotland), 1947.
26. FOULDS, G. A., AND RAVEN, J. C. "Intellectual Ability and Occupational Grade." *Occupational Psychol* 22:197-203 O '48. * (PA 23:1961)
27. FOULDS, G. A., AND RAVEN, J. C. "Normal Changes in the Mental Abilities of Adults as Age Advances." *J Mental Sci* 94:133-42 Ja '48. * (PA 22:4882)
28. RAVEN, J. C. "The Comparative Assessment of Intellectual Ability." *Brit J Psychol* 39:12-9 S '48. * (PA 24:1063)
29. RIMOLDI, H. J. A. "A Note on Raven's Progressive Matrices Test." *Ed & Psychol Meas* 8:347-52 au '48. * (PA 23:4258)
30. RIMOLDI, H. J. A. "Study of Some Factors Related to Intelligence." *Psychometrika* 13:27-46 Mr '48. * (PA 22:3382)
31. RUDOLF, G. DE M. "The Kent and Other Tests Used on the Same Subjects." *J Mental Sci* 44:452-8 Ap '48. * (PA 23:1295)
32. SLATER, PATRICK. "Comment on 'The Comparative Assessment of Intellectual Ability.'" *Brit J Psychol* 39:20-1 S '48. * (PA 24:1065)
33. TRACHT, VERNON S. "Preliminary Findings on Testing the Cerebral Palsied With Raven's 'Progressive Matrices.'" *J Excep Child* 15:77-9 | Ap '48. * (PA 24:733)
34. CASSEL, ROBERT H. "Qualitative Evaluation of the Progressive Matrices Tests." *Ed & Psychol Meas* 9:233-41 su '49. * (PA 24:184)
35. FOULDS, G. A. "Variations in the Intellectual Activities of Adults." *Am J Psychol* 62:238-46 Ap '49. * (PA 24:1716)
36. JASTAK, JOSEPH. "Problems of Psychometric Scatter Analysis." *Psychol B* 46:177-97 My '49. * (PA 24:188)
37. KEIR, GERTRUDE. "The Progressive Matrices as Applied to School Children." *Brit J Psychol, Stat Sect* 2:140-50 N '49. (PA 24:3213)
38. NOTCUTT, BERNARD. "The Distribution of Scores on Raven's Progressive Matrices Test." *Brit J Psychol* 40:68-70 D '49. * (PA 24:5809)
39. VERNON, P. E. "The Structure of Practical Abilities." *Occupational Psychol* 23:81-96 Ap '49. * (PA 23:5313)
40. VERNON, PHILIP E. "Occupational Norms for the 20-Minute Progressive Matrices Test." *Occupational Psychol* 23:58-9 Ja '49. * (PA 23:3935)
41. VERNON, PHILIP E., AND PARRY, JOHN B. *Personnel Selection in the British Forces.* London: University of London Press Ltd., 1949. Pp. 324. * (PA 24:776)
42. FOULDS, G. A. "Variations in the Intellectual Activities of Adults: Their Assessment and Significance," pp. 61–2. Abstract. In *Proceedings and Papers of the Twelfth International Congress of Psychology Held at the University of Edinburgh, July 23rd to 29th, 1948.* Edinburgh, Scotland: Oliver & Boyd Ltd., 1950. Pp. xxviii, 152. Paper. *
43. FOULDS, G. A., AND RAVEN, J. C. "An Experimental Survey With Progressive Matrices (1947)." *Brit J Ed Psychol* 20:104-10 Je '50. * (PA 25:1094)
44. HALSTEAD, H. "Abilities of Male Mental Hospital Patients." *J Mental Sci* 96:726-33 Jl '50. * (PA 25:2598)
45. HEIM, A. W., AND WALLACE, J. G. "The Effects of Repeatedly Retesting the Same Group on the Same Intelligence Test." *Q J Exp Psychol* 2:19-32 F '50. * (PA 25:6938)
46. OLÉRON, P. "A Study of the Intelligence of the Deaf." *Am Ann Deaf* 95:179-95 Mr '50. * (PA 24:6018)
47. SINHA, UMA. "A Study of the Reliability and Validity of the Progressive Matrices Test." Master's thesis, University of London (London, England), 1950. Abstract: *Brit J Ed Psychol* 21:238-9 N '51. * (PA 26:4812, title only)
48. TIZARD, J.; IN COLLABORATION WITH N. O'CONNOR AND J. M. CRAWFORD. "The Abilities of Adolescent and Adult High-Grade Male Defectives." *J Mental Sci* 96:888-907 O '50. * (PA 25:5421)
49. VERNON, P. E. "An Application of Factorial Analysis to the Study of Test Items." *Brit J Psychol, Stat Sect* 3:1-15 Mr '50. * (PA 24:4982)
50. BANKS, CHARLOTTE, AND SINHA, UMA. "An Item-Analysis of the Progressive Matrices Test." *Brit J Psychol, Stat Sect* 4:91-4 Je '51. * (PA 26:2738)
51. HOLDEN, RAYMOND H. "Improved Methods in Testing Cerebral Palsied Children." *Am J Mental Def* 56:349-53 O '51. * (PA 26:2184)
52. MOORE, B. G. R., AND PEEL, E. A. "Predicting Aptitude

---
[1] Vernon, Philip E., and Parry, John B. *Personnel Selection in the British Forces.* London: University of London Press Ltd., 1949. Pp. 324. * (PA 24:776)

for Dentistry." *Occupational Psychol* 25:192–9 Jl '51. * (*PA* 26:3675)
53. O'CONNOR, N., AND TIZARD, J. "Predicting the Occupational Adequacy of Certified Mental Defectives." *Occupational Psychol* 25:205–11 Jl '51. * (*PA* 26:3487)

CHARLOTTE BANKS, *Department of Psychology, University College, London, England.* [A review of Sets A, Ab, and B.]

This edition of *Progressive Matrices* is usually known as the "Coloured Matrices." It has been specially adapted for use with children of 5 to 11 years of age. This has been done by interposing, between Sets A and B of the 1938 scale, a new set of problems Ab, of approximately the same difficulty as those in A or B, and by reproducing a large number of the items in brilliant colours. Thus, of the total of 36 items, only 12 are, in fact, new. This version of the test is presented in both booklet and board form, though it may be purchased only in the booklet form; the board form can only be borrowed from the Crichton Royal Department of Psychological Research "for a limited period," and only "for certain experimental purposes." The owner of the test claims that "for the majority of routine purposes, when coloured grounds are used, the Book and Board forms of the test give practically the same results."

The Coloured Matrices have been produced in order that a wider dispersion of scores may be obtained from children of this age range than was obtainable with the 1938 edition of the test. Thus, a great deal depends on the efficacy, for this purpose, of the 12 new items in Set Ab. Unfortunately, no item analysis, and, still more important, no measures of scatter have yet been published. It is not possible, therefore, to state whether or not the coloured version does in fact fulfill the main purpose for which it has been designed. However, comparison of the scores given at the end of the manual to the coloured edition, with published figures obtained with the 1938 edition, suggests that the range and standard deviation of total scores for the age range of 5 to 9 may not be appreciably greater for the 1947 version. Insertion of the twelve new items, Set Ab, would seem to have raised the mean scores, but not to have increased the scatter to any great extent.

Norms in percentile form are given separately for the book and board versions of the test; those for the book form are based on results of approximately 600 children, for the board form on the results of about half this number. "For practical purposes," the percentile figures are classified into five grades, ranging from Grade I or "intellectually superior," the top five per cent, to Grade V or "intellectually defective," the bottom five per cent.

Reliability coefficients are quoted only for the results of children under 7 and children aged 9. With the children under 7, we are told, both forms of the test "have, so far, shown a low re-test reliability in the neighbourhood of 0.65. * By the age of 9, the re-test reliability of both.... has been found to increase to at least 0.80." The tests were repeated after an interval of two months, and the numbers of children tested were small: "groups of only 35 to 100." The author claims that, with children under 7, both forms of the test correlate about .5 with the *Crichton Vocabulary Scale* and the *Revised Stanford-Binet Scale;* and, with children aged 9, about .65 with these two other tests.

Detailed and helpful instructions are given in the manual for administration of the test, which may be given as a group, individual, or self-administered test. When given with the *Crichton Vocabulary Scale,* the two tests together usually take about half an hour to complete. The author also claims that the test is suitable, not only for use with children, but also with "persons who are for any reason mentally sub-normal or impaired," and with those "suffering from partial paralysis, deafness or defective speech." However, no results for groups such as these have been published.

W. D. WALL, *Reader in Education, University of Birmingham, Birmingham, England.* [Review of Sets A, Ab, and B.]

This is a development of the *Progressive Matrices (1938)* in a form suitable for children and for mental defectives. This new test contains additional problems to those in sets A and B of the original version, all the problems are presented in colour to make them more attractive, and the whole can be given individually either in booklet or in board form. For most children over the age of eight, the author claims, the test can be fairly satisfactorily used as a self-administered or group test.

The rationale of the test, like that of others of the series, is that it tests, with a series of increasingly difficult pattern completion problems, the "intellectual capacity to form comparisons and reason by analogy."

Administration and scoring, either as an individual or as a group test, is simple; and in the writer's experience the problems are attractive to children—especially in board form. It is, however, important to realise that the test is still experimental and that too great a dependency cannot as yet be placed upon the norms, nor indeed upon the general reliability of the test for use with very young children or low grade defectives. The norms given in the handbook accompanying the test are based only upon 608 Scottish children for the book form (age range 5–11, roughly 50 per 6-months age group), and on 291 Scottish children for the board form (age range 5–10, roughly 32 per 6-months age group). Reliability with young children is not high (test-retest .65 with children under seven). The author claims, however, a test-retest reliability of .9 over the whole range of development for which the test is constructed but states frankly that this is based on relatively small groups.

Clinically, the author claims, the test will differentiate clearly between different degrees of intellectual deficiency or impairment. In association with the *Crichton Vocabulary Test,* he suggests that it can be used to assess intellectual deterioration.

The test is likely to be a valuable adjunct in the clinical study of young children, defectives, cases of deterioration, and possibly—though much research is required here—in the differential diagnosis of cerebral injury. It can, however, be regarded as an adjunct only; even with the addition of a vocabulary scale, it is not a substitute for more thorough measurement and diagnosis.

GEORGE WESTBY, *Head of the Psychological Laboratory, University College of Hull, Hull, England.*

PROGRESSIVE MATRICES (1938), SETS A, B, C, D, E. The concerted attack by Spearman, Burt, and the British "g" school of factor analysis upon the empirically composed heterogeneous test as developed by Binet and his American followers secured its first indubitably spectacular success in Raven's *Progressive Matrices (1938)* developed in his work with Penrose with mental defectives at the Colchester Institution. Here was a test simple to administer, usually enthralling, and universally acceptable to dull and clever, child and adult, friendly and suspicious alike, claiming to provide a "measure of a person's capacity to form comparisons, reason by analogy and develop a logical method of thinking regardless of previously acquired information." Moreover, the testee need not have it presented as an "intelligence test," and he need not work under time pressure, valuable assets indeed in clinical work with disturbed personalities. All subjects seem to derive motivation from the built-in training in each set of tasks. A highly intelligent schizoid subject described it as "like a crossword puzzle with shapes, but it gets more difficult and interesting instead of getting simpler and boring."

A generation should be time enough to assess even a test as original and as far reaching as this, especially now that clinics have amassed considerable experience, and data are to hand from the testing in British Armed Forces in the Second World War. Unfortunately, the test seems to have been little worked in the U.S.A., an unjustifiable neglect of an unusual contribution of which even Raven's British critics may feel inclined to complain, for there is no doubt in this reviewer's mind that the method developed by Raven is capable of the finest refinement in testing practice.

The test is described in the current (1950) manual as follows: "P.M. 1938 is a non-verbal test of a person's capacity at the time of the test to apprehend figures presented for his perception [Spearman's Principle of Experience], see relations between them [Spearman's Eduction of Relations], and conceive the correlative figures completing the systems of relations presented [Spearman's Eduction of Correlates]."

Sixty well drawn "matrices" or patterns are divided into five sets (A, B, C, D, and E) of 12 problems each and are well printed in strong covered booklets which can be used again and again. Each matrix is a network of logical relations between simple and more complex visual forms, mainly of geometrical design; and each matrix has a "gap" which has to be filled by indicating on the printed score sheet the number of the correct choice from the alternatives printed below the matrix. The relations within the matrix usually allow of more than one mode of analysis of the problem. The aim of the test designer was to produce five sets of items progressively graded in difficulty both between and within sets and of sufficient range of complexity to discriminate in a short testing time (about 45 minutes at the 50th percentile) a sample of the general population in Raven's words "from infancy to maturity." This is an ambitious project which one is not surprised to find has been placed in better perspective by the designer himself, by his own subsequent development out of PM 1938 of the two more specialized 1947 tests.

Factor analysis in the Services suggests that the test is an almost pure "g" test with a small loading of some spatial perceptual factor and the latest data for its reliability agree exactly with the figure of .88 which Services testing revealed, adequate perhaps, but certainly to be improved and not supporting the original claims of the designer. Slater's probit analysis and indeed Raven's own admission show that too many easy items have resulted in a markedly skew distribution; and a recent study suggests that too many poor items and a low general factor between the five sets (despite apparent homogeneity) militate against very high validity. The crucial test, however, for any selective instrument is the external criterion; and the weakness of a theoretically based "g" test is usually just that it claims to measure a psychological "thing" rather than to predict successful behavior in some more or less special social situation. The author warns us against taking the test as one of "general intelligence," but has nevertheless himself proceeded on some such basis to draw what appear to be inappropriate conclusions about "The Development and Decline of *Mental Ability*" (reviewer's italics) and specifically describes his five rough screening grades as "intellectually superior" (at or above the 95th percentile), "definitely above average in intellectual capacity" (between the 75th and 95th percentiles), "intellectually average" and "definitely below the average in intellectual ability" (at or below the 25th percentile), and "intellectually defective" (at or below the 5th percentile).

Without accepting in detail the supporting argument, it is certainly better as Raven has aimed in his test design, "to evaluate an adult's ability in terms of the percentage frequency with which a similar degree of ability is found to occur amongst people of the same age." This is another way of formulating Wechsler's well known claim that intelligence be defined in terms of the normal distribution of individuals of the same age group as the testee.

An important claim is made that the score pattern, that is, discrepancies between actual and expected scores on each of the five sets for a given total score, "have considerable psychological significance," but there is still no data published to support this clinical claim after 15 years experience with the test. It is clear that the streamlined nature of the test, which is one of its special features, limits its usefulness as compared with the *Wechsler-Bellevue Intelligence Scale* in providing appreciable information of a clinical nature for score profiles.

Now our hypotheses on the nature of intelligence, our preferences for "oligarchic," "hierarchic," or "democratic" theories, need not entirely determine our evaluation of this test. It is quite evident that reliable, carefully constructed, and standardized intelligence tests devised upon the most diverse theoretical bases range a given population in much the same order. But even if we accept the psychological reality of a unitary and general "g" factor of relational thinking, it does not seem entirely permissible to assume that geometrical matrices are entirely culture free in our geometry ridden machine civilization. It is even more likely that cultural factors might account for group differences in respect of "abstraction-tolerance" within our own western societies. This would be expected from the apparent differential decline in intelligence between those adults whose jobs make no demands on abstract relational thinking and those whose jobs do. It might be well to use the test with greater scepticism about its freedom from practice and cultural influences. Unfortunately, as the designer may well answer, it is impossible here in the sphere of mental testing, as elsewhere, to find the "neutral non-sense-syllables" which would provide the perfect counters to manipulate, and Raven may be said to have done as well as is possible to avoid effects of previous learning and established attitudes. It might, however, be well to consider a programme of tailoring the test to the testee as shown in case history and interview wherever this is possible and practicable as it is sometimes in clinical work. There is much to be said for the common practice in guidance work in Great Britain of using the test with a good mixed scale or verbal test. It is certainly imperative at the very least to use the Matrices, as the designer suggests, with a vocabulary test such as his *Mill Hill Vocabulary Scale*. This reviewer would stress the above considerations rather than the reason advanced by Raven for this practice, viz., that vocabulary is a "measure of present mental functioning" as against the normally untimed Matrices score which he claims measure "mental capacity." The graceful will o' the wisp of "innate capacity" is perhaps even more enticing in the geometrical jungle, but recently published re-

Progressive Matrices

sults of the Heim's experiments at Cambridge and other evidence seems to suggest that considerable gain in scores may be expected in well motivated repeated testing in PM 1938 without any knowledge of results. Moreover, it does not seem possible to draw a clear-cut logical distinction between capacity to reason by analogy as in the PM 1938 and capacity to recall information by finding a word similar in meaning to a given word. The relational thinking here is no less evident than in some of the simpler items in the PM 1938; it is merely that the counters are different, verbal instead of perceptual.

Whatever weight is given to the above criticisms, the test must be considered as having opened a most important exploratory path in purely nonverbal testing and to have established a special place for itself in Great Britain as a highly convenient rough grading instrument for the mass testing of adults as used in the British armed forces with a 20-minute time limit. It is a pity that in devising the new tests it has not been found possible to improve the test further by better grading of the items, but it may still be recommended warmly to our American friends.

PROGRESSIVE MATRICES (1947), SETS I, II. This test is a forthright attempt to develop out of PM 1938 an instrument which will discriminate usefully a population of testees within the top quarter of a sample of the population. The construction of the new test and the way in which it is presented reveal a spirit both critical and empirical, this latter especially welcome perhaps in view of the traditional theoretical approach of pure "g" test construction. (*Progressive Matrices (1947), Sets A, Ab, B,* is a similar attempt to deal with the lowest quarter.) If we must deplore the fact that it has not yet been found possible to improve the PM 1938 to anywhere near the limit of its possibilities, the designer is to be congratulated upon the development of these three refinements of the original test, each of more limited aim, but each distinctly promising and frankly and scientifically presented. The first two tests which constitute Parts I and II of PM 1947 are based upon PM 1938 and an earlier version of the high level test first drafted in 1943 for use in British War Office Selection Boards. The final 1947 version is composed of items very similar to the 1938 test and is published with the claim that it provides "a means of assessing all the ordinal, analytical and integral operations involved in the higher thought processes"

and that it "differentiates clearly between people of even superior ability." In so far as "speed of accurate intellectual work" (as Raven defines "Mental Efficiency") is a factor in any training, the test is designed, when given with a time limit of 40 minutes, to distribute scores normally and provide useful information concerning "a person's probable rate of progress and success in any course of study." Raven, however, also suggests that since mental efficiency so defined varies with health and practice, it is most important to be able to obtain "a more valid estimate of a person's real capacity for intellectual activity under normal conditions where clarity of thought and accuracy of judgment, rather than speed of work during a fixed period of time, are important." This alternative purpose of the test may be achieved, he claims, by giving it without time limit.

Part I consists of 12 matrices designed to cover in method all the different types of problems the testee will meet in the 48 problems of Part II. It is essentially a pretest training, but it is held to be in itself a useful quick test (10 minutes) for rough grading the normal population into those below the 10th percentile, those above the 90th percentile, and those between these limits. The items of Part II are probably rightly claimed to be of such difficulty "that no one of even outstanding intellectual capacity ["efficiency" surely?] solves them all in less than half an hour." Estimated norms only are available as yet for Part II; for ages 11.6–12.6 above the 75th percentile, for ages 13–30 above the 50th percentile, for ages 30–40 above the 75th percentile only. The difficulty of establishing accurate norms around the 95th percentile is emphasized, but in due course it is hoped to establish reliable norms for the 95th percentile to the 50th.

Useful prepublication work on the internal consistency, reliability, and validity of the test, based on the testing of 1,844 school children and adults is reported in some detail in the manual, a commendable but rare feature in the initial publication of a test. Unsatisfactory correlations between percentages of passes and total scores appear in a few tests and an alternative key or a "cook," as the chess problemist might describe it, appears in connection with problem 46.

Four problems are placed too high, four are too low, and minor improvements in respect of the groups of alternatives might be made in re-

Progressive Matrices

spect of ten of the items. Test-retest reliability is unsatisfactory below 11 years at .76, not good at 12.6 years at .86, but with adults of more than average ability Raven's claim is again high at .91.

No really satisfactory conclusions as to validity are possible on the basis of school children aged 10–13 years, (the only studies reported besides the data on university undergraduates which do not bear directly on the question), but the author is no doubt well aware of this inadequacy, though we must impatiently await further validatory evidence. It should be added that the figures given for the distribution of scores among university students suggest an approximately normal distribution about a mean of 33–34 right out of 48 items with a standard deviation of about four and no ceiling effects.

There can be no doubt that this is a valuable new instrument of research and the inclusion of critical analysis in the first edition speaks well for the scientific conscience of the designer and is a good augury for its future development. There is undoubted need for an acceptable, practical, reliable, and valid test for predicting high level intelligent behavior as required in university education and in technical and managerial situations. This reviewer, however, is not satisfied that it is the best plan in tackling this problem to set out by isolating "g" intelligence, defined as relational thinking, from the other requirements of complex social-intelligent behavior evidenced in the above situations for which we are selecting. It seems that if "g" tests must be supplemented in high level entry selection in the Armed Forces and the Civil Service in order to ensure right choice (*41*), it is equally likely that we shall need some sort of battery or conceivably a portmanteau test using a variety of problem "counters" for manipulation (e.g., verbal, numerical, and pictorial besides geometrical) and also perhaps tests of memory functioning with different counters as well as tests of special interests. The 1947 Matrices, it would seem, ought to evolve an even more stripped and streamlined model to take its place in such a battery. In this respect, it has the advantage in its simplicity of administration and construction over the Heim Ah5 with a similar aim. It is also perhaps more easily pruned down to say a 30-minute testing time. On the other hand, and this may very well be a crucial defect, it tests with only one set of counters and so covers less of the ideal testing breadth at this level. At present and until adequate validating data are available for both tests, it is impossible to know whether either is superior.

PROGRESSIVE MATRICES (1947) SETS A, AB, B. This test is designed to disperse the scores of children from 3 to 10 years of age or of the mentally defective or impaired. An extra set of items is introduced to link Sets A and B of the 1938 scale by problems of intermediate difficulty, and most of the problems are printed in colour to make the task more attractive to young children although in the reviewer's experience this was scarcely necessary and may be a distracting and irrelevant stimulus. The test can also be used in a formboard version which does seem to serve the requirement of an activity method for the more efficient testing of preschool children. It can easily be given without verbal instructions. The test designer himself is rightly sceptical of the predictive value of tests of children below the age of 6, but is moderately sanguine about the Board Form of the Matrices. It is recommended especially for the qualitative information it may give by "rendering visible the process of approximations by trial and error." Warning is given that for judging mental deficiency as legally defined in Great Britain it must be supplemented by tests of attainment.

The norms at present available for this test are unsatisfactory, being based upon only 291 Dumfries school children, and it is not shown how these few cases are distributed over the age range from five to ten years. Regional differences established during Services testing placed Glasgow and Scotland lowest of the main British geographical areas and although there are pitfalls in drawing conclusions from these figures, Raven himself expects that norms for a general population of English children will probably be higher. However, with the establishment of regional differences among adults, the question naturally arises whether for some selection purposes the logical continuation is not to construct norms regional to the population from which selection is made. This is not so much a criticism of this test as of the tacit assumption of most testing programmes.

In general conclusion, a word of appreciation on the part of the many British users of the Matrices Tests seems appropriate. The development of these instruments by the Psychological Research Department of the Crichton Royal is a fruitfully specialized piece of work which ought to be known more widely in America. In the opinion of this reviewer, the complicated and

Progressive Matrices

intimidating arrangements made for the safeguarding (in itself a laudable object) of the PM 1947, Set II do not encourage such wide recognition; this is a pity. The annual loan charge seems excessively high besides being highly questionable in principle.

For reviews by Walter C. Shipley and David Wechsler of the 1938 edition, see 3:258; for a review by T. J. Keating of the 1938 edition, see 40:1417.

[315]

*Revised Alpha Examination, Forms 5 and 7. Grades 9–12 and adults; 1932–51; Forms 5 ('32), 7 ('33); revised manual ('51); $3 per 25; 35¢ per specimen set; postpaid; 21½(30) minutes; revision by F. L. Wells; Psychological Corporation. *

REFERENCES

1–7. See 3:220(43, 53, 54, 62, 64, 65, 67)
8. Cox, K. J. "Aptitude Testing in Industry." *B Can Psychol Assn* 5:99–102 D '45. * (*PA* 20:2035)
9. Bluett, C. G. "Pictures of the Mind." *J Rehabil* 13:4–10 Je '47. * (*PA* 21:3630)
10. Tuddenham, Read D. "Soldier Intelligence in World Wars I and II." *Am Psychol* 3:54–6 F '48. * (*PA* 22:2954)
11. Gurvitz, Milton Solomon. *An Experimental Application of Wechsler-Bellevue Type Tests in an Attempt to Discriminate and Diagnose Psychopathic Personality Types Resident in a Penal Institution.* Doctor's thesis, New York University (New York, N.Y.), 1949. Abstract: *Microfilm Abstracts* 10:234–5 no 3 '50. *

Dael Wolfle, *Director, Commission on Human Resources and Advanced Training, 2101 Constitution Ave., N.W., Washington, D.C.*

This test consists of eight parts: addition, arithmetic problems, common sense questions, same or opposite words, mixed-up sentences, number series, verbal analogies, and following directions. Several of these item forms are rarely used now. A few of the individual items are ambiguous, for example:

> If it rains when you are starting to go for a doctor, what should you do? 1, stay at home. 2, take a raincoat. 3, wait until it stops raining.

Some are out of date, for example:

> A dealer bought some used cars for $1000. He sold them for $1,200, making $20 on each car. How many cars were there?

Directions and test items appear on the same page. An examinee who gets the idea of a test form quickly can solve a number of the items while the examiner is reading the directions. Answers are to be written in the test booklet. Thus the booklet cannot be re-used and the tests must be scored by hand.

By current standards, the statistical information given in the test manual is quite inadequate. "About nine hundred high school freshmen were given both Modified Alpha Examination Form 9 and one of these tests," according to the manual. Percentile norms for high school freshman boys and girls were set by formula on the basis of Form 9 and norms for high school senior boys and girls obtained by extrapolation, also on the basis of Form 9 norms. That is all the information given about the norms.

The Personnel Research Section of the Adjutant General's Office during World War II administered Revised Form 5 to "768 Army enlisted men selected on the basis of Army General Classification Test scores to be representative of all enlisted men. The correlation of scores on Alpha 5 and AGCT for this population is .90." The correlation of .90 indicates that the test would still serve fairly well the military classification purposes for which it was developed. Although AGCT has long since deservedly replaced Alpha, this correlation is a tribute to the pioneers who devised the World War I test.

There are many newer tests and tests more specifically designed for special purposes. These can be used in most testing programs. But Alpha will always be the test to use in showing students how our group testing developments started. And if one wants to use it practically, under appropriate conditions it is still a good test.

[316]

Revised Alpha Examination Form 6, Short Form. Grades 9–16 and high-grade adults; 1933; a short form of the experimental edition of *Revised Alpha Examination, Form 6*, consisting of subtests 2, 4, 7, and 8; Form 6, Short Form; no data on reliability and validity; no description of normative population; $1.65 per 25; 35¢ per specimen set; postpaid; 13½ (20) minutes; revision prepared under the supervision of C. R. Atwell and F. L. Wells; Psychological Corporation. *

REFERENCES

1. Atwell, Charles R., and Wells, F. L. "Army Alpha Revised—Short Form." *Personnel J* 12:160–3 O '33. * (*PA* 8:1844)

Edwin R. Henry, *Personnel Research Advisor, Employee Relations Department, Standard Oil Company (New Jersey), New York, New York.*

This test may be "easier and shorter to administer and score" but there are no data to indicate that it is "more appropriate for educational and business use," nor that it is any less "out of date" than original Army Alpha. Norms for the general population start at 50th percentile (N is not given) and those for high school freshmen and seniors were derived from another test.

Dael Wolfle, *Director, Commission on Human Resources and Advanced Training, 2101 Constitution Ave., N.W., Washington 25, D.C.*

Revised Form 6 of the Army Alpha is a shortened version consisting of only four tests: problems, same or opposite words, following directions, and analogies. This form is intended for use with high grade adults and high school students. In format, method of administration, and scoring, it resembles *Revised Alpha Examination, Forms 5 and 7*. Percentile norms for high school freshmen and seniors are given with no more explanation than "as derived from Modified Alpha Examination Form 9." Even greater trust is shown in the method of securing general population norms. Those norms (for scores from the 50th to the 99th percentile) are presented simply "as obtained by F. L. Wells." No other statistical information is given in the manual.

[317]

*Revision of Army Alpha Examination. Grades 7–16 and adults; 1925–47; Forms A ('46), B ('35); manual ('47); no data on reliability; $3 per 25; 35¢ per specimen set; postpaid; 21⅔(35–40) minutes; revision by Elsie O. Bregman; Psychological Corporation. *

REFERENCES

1. LORGE, IRVING. "A Table of Percentile Equivalents for Eight Intelligence Tests Frequently Used With Adults." *J Appl Psychol* 20:392–5 Je '36. * (PA 10:5552)
2. BITTNER, REIGN H., AND WORCESTER, D. A. "The Selection of Men for the Nebraska Safety Patrol." *J Consult Psychol* 3:57–64 Mr–Ap '39. * (PA 13:3829)
3. HARTMAN, A. A. "A Comparison of the Ratings of Mentally Retarded Prisoners on Army Alpha and Stanford-Binet." *J Appl Psychol* 23:608–11 O '39. * (PA 14:1106)

EDWARD E. CURETON, *Professor of Psychology, The University of Tennessee, Knoxville, Tennessee.*

The manual states that:

Each revision of the *Army Alpha Examination*, Form A and Form B, is a combination of the five forms of Alpha used in the United States Army during World War I. The questions best for general use have been selected by order-of-merit method. To make these revisions more suitable for use with civilians than any of the original forms, items addressed particularly to men recruits have been excluded and military terms modified. Otherwise the revisions are identical with the original forms. The revised examinations are constructed to be of average difficulty of the original *Army Alpha* and to yield average scores.

The statistical data on which these statements rest are not given in the manual. Taking them at face value, the test is still essentially the original *Army Group Examination Alpha*. The World War I Army norms are given in the manual, along with norms for grades 7–12 inclusive (N's 1372 to 4126), freshmen at Ohio State University and at the College of the City of New York, and student nurses. Norms are given for total scores and also for total scores omitting the administratively troublesome Directions Test (Test 1). Most of these norms are out of date, and the author rightly mistrusts an attempt (reported in the manual) to equate the scores on this test indirectly to those of the *Army General Classification Test* of World War II.

The manual gives no data on reliability or validity. Since more recent group intelligence tests are more convenient to administer and are provided with more modern interpretative aids, we may conclude that this test, in common with the earlier revisions of Army Alpha which tried to preserve the original World War I norms, is now less useful than these more recent tests, even though it probably measures about the same combination of abilities with about the same reliability.

EDWIN R. HENRY, *Personnel Research Advisor, Employee Relations Department, Standard Oil Company (New Jersey), New York, New York.*

If one has need for a form of Army Alpha different from the originals, this is probably as good as any. According to the manual the reliabilities should be better than the originals but no data are presented. Norms for grades 7–12 were collected before 1931, those for college freshmen at Ohio State, before 1926. Norms for freshmen at CCNY and for student nurses are undated. The author draws attention to possible changes in norms since hers were collected.

[318]

*SRA Non-Verbal Form. Grades 9–12 and adults; 1946–47; formerly called *SRA Non-Verbal Classification Form*; preliminary school edition; IBM; 2 editions; 1 form, '47; manual ('47); 50¢ per specimen set of any one edition; cash orders postpaid; 10(15) minutes; prepared by Robert N. McMurry and Company; Science Research Associates, Inc. *

a) FORM AH (HAND SCORING EDITION). $2.65 per 25.
b) FORM AM (MACHINE SCORING EDITION). $2.65 per 25; $2.90 per 100 IBM answer sheets; 50¢ per set of scoring keys.

W. D. COMMINS, *Associate Professor of Psychology, Catholic University of America, Washington, D.C.*

A nonverbal "objective index of student intelligence" might seem at first glance to have much to recommend it. Unfortunately, serious criticisms can be made of all tests of this kind. We scarcely know whether "student intelligence" has anything of practical value left over after "verbal" intelligence has been subtracted. It is possible to think of some ideal "intelligence" without academic associations, but in practice we commonly find that the available nonverbal test is basically not so different from the verbal variety. The present test, for example, based as it is upon the classification of pictured objects and figures, contains many examples of a principle of classification that is strongly academic. Many studies suggest that our ordinary nonverbal tests are not less, but actually more, influenced by cultural factors than are verbal tests. The manual of the present test gives no validity data bearing on the "purpose of the SRA forms," measuring ability to learn, career aptitude, school course aptitude, college caliber, etc., and where the nonverbal test might be successful in these respects, it probably duplicates the verbal kind but measures ability with a typically lower reliability. The time limit of the present test, 10 minutes, seems unduly short for an adequate measure of intelligence, and other available nonverbal tests offer a greater variety of items.

The present reviewer doubts the value of nonverbal tests in general. Research is needed to tell us what they actually measure and to give us concrete validity data. Instead of using the *SRA Non-Verbal Form* as "a re-check on those students scoring below Percentile 25 on the *Verbal Form*," as the manual recommends, it would be better, in the opinion of the reviewer, to depend on the best group verbal and individual tests to improve the accuracy of measurement within the school situation.

For an excerpt from a review, see 3:261 (in the first printing of The Third Mental Measurements Yearbook, *the excerpt is incorrectly listed under 3:260).*

[319]

*SRA Verbal Form. Grades 9–12 and adults; 1946–47; formerly called *SRA Verbal Classification Form;* an abbreviated edition of *Thurstone Test of Mental Alertness* (see 3:265) which is an abbreviated adaptation of *American Council on Education Psychological Examination for High School Students,* 1940 Edition; preliminary school edition; 3 scores: quantitative, linguistic, total; IBM; 2 editions; 1 form, '47; manual ('47); 50¢ per specimen set of any one edition; cash orders postpaid; 15(20) minutes; Thelma Gwinn Thurstone and L. L. Thurstone; Science Research Associates, Inc. *

a) FORM AH (HAND SCORING EDITION). $2.65 per 25.
b) FORM AM (MACHINE SCORING EDITION). $2.65 per 25; $2.90 per 100 IBM answer sheets; 50¢ per set of scoring keys.

W. D. COMMINS, *Associate Professor of Psychology, Catholic University of America, Washington, D.C.*

This test has a number of features that would recommend its use for class sectioning, personnel selection, or other survey purposes when convenience and speed are desirable. It is self-administering, has a short time limit of 15 minutes, is easy to score, and the items are clearly phrased. For many group comparisons, it would seem adequate. There are, however, some features of the test, its standardization, and published norms that would incline one to doubt its ability to discriminate between individuals in many cases that would have educational and practical significance. The time limit of 15 minutes seems unduly short, not necessarily for the test as it stands, but as a feature of any adequate test of intelligence. The Q and L scores, separately derived for "quantitative" and "linguistic" intelligence, can scarcely be accepted at the present time as offering any practical distinction. The value of the age norms, from 12 to 17 inclusive, is difficult to estimate when all the manual tells us is that "500 representative students at each of the age levels" were employed to furnish the data. Whether they were representative as students or as age groups should be known to the user of the test.

The amount of mental growth shown by this test between the ages of 14 and 15 is presented as being about one third as great as that between 15 and 16. This would be a very peculiar and anomalous finding if the standardization groups were representative of age. They might, of course, represent student years, but it would be well to have the facts on this, as well as on the scaling of the items and the steps separating them.

The use of the "standard deviation" method of finding the IQ should make the user of this test very careful in his comparison of the IQ so found with an IQ calculated in the Binet manner. Thus, a 12-year-old child who would receive an IQ of 114 according to the method of the manual would obtain an IQ of 125 if we computed his MA from the conversion table in the manual and divided it by his CA. The reliability coefficients as published are high, but since we do not know the range of ability used in the calculation, it would be more meaningful if we were given the standard error of measurement. Further work on scaling of the items and on obtaining and reporting evidence of validity seems desirable.

WILLIS C. SCHAEFER, *Institute for Research in Human Relations, Washington, D.C.*

The *SRA Verbal Form* (as well as the *SRA Non-Verbal Form*) is a test designed "to furnish an objective index of student intelligence" which is "sometimes called the ability to learn, to solve problems, to foresee and plan, to use initiative, to think quickly and creatively." It is noted that neither the term "test" nor "intelligence" appears in the title, nor, for that matter, does the term "intelligence" appear anywhere in the test booklet. This practice in test construction of avoiding words which may provoke emotional attitudes to the detriment of some students' performance in the testing situation is an example of a small consideration which may be of marked practical consequence for fair evaluation.

The excellent overall appearance of both test and manual in terms of content, typography, format, and usefulness is understandable in terms of the long experience of the Thurstones in test construction and the modern publishing standards of Science Research Associates. The page of fore-exercises presents adequate instructions and practice for self-administration. The test is designed in spiral-omnibus form consisting of blocks of seven items; each cycle or block contains two same-opposite, one arithmetic-reasoning, two vocabulary-recall, and two number-series items. Items increase in difficulty throughout the test. A total of 84 items with a strict 15 minute time limit makes this a speed test for which students are warned that they are "not expected to finish in the time allowed." While the four item types would permit separate part scores, only language (L) and quantitative (Q) subscores are computed following the practice with ACE from which this form was developed. The sum of these two part scores is the "index of intelligence" raw score. Both hand and machine scored forms are identical in content, thus utilizing the same normative tables and interpretations. The hand scoring form utilizes a carbon transfer to a precoded answer sheet which greatly simplifies scoring. In fact since carbon marks cannot be duplicated by direct pencil, and since the carbon marks cannot be easily erased, this form may be scored by the person tested minimizing any possible cheating. The direct equivalence in interchangeability of these two forms is a very useful feature in the practical situation. In addition, the availability of the supplemental *SRA Non-Verbal Form* for cases in which there are reading difficulties, or for cases scoring very low and requiring recheck, makes this group of test forms widely useful as a series of coordinated measuring instruments.

Normative data for part, total scores, and Non-Verbal Form converting directly to centile ranks, quotient ranks (IQ equivalents), and stanine ranks are very effectively presented in a single table. Score equivalents are presented separately for each chronological age group from 12 through 17 and over. This manner of presenting extensive standardization data in a relative simple format for maximum usefulness is recommended as a model for test publishers. The basis for this standardization, unfortunately, is limited in manual presentation to the statement that the "Conversion Table was prepared from scores made by 500 representative students at each of the age levels. It furnishes the range of general intelligence found in a typical cross-section of the student population." It seems desirable to demand that test standardization data include specific characteristics of the groups which are sampled. A general statement which implies representative sampling of *the* (entire) student population when it may in fact be only a sample of those students who happened to take a particular examination in 1940 does not meet the high standards which test publishers speak about for themselves.

An additional feature of broad general usefulness in interpreting general intelligence test scores is the inclusion in the test manual of a Job Chart showing the average and interquartile range of centile scores for 150 major occupational groups. While these data were obtained on a different test, the *Army General Classification Test,* in World War II, the equivalence of centile ranks for these two tests may reasonably be assumed as a working hypothesis in test score interpretation. It would be desirable for this hypothesis to be clearly pointed out in the manual together with some estimate of the correlation between these two tests.

In general the *SRA Verbal Form* is an excellent test, well constructed, self-administering, simple scoring, and broadly useful. Where a short form (20 minutes) estimate of general intelligence with possible part scores for linguistic and quantitative abilities is desired, the test can be highly recommended for general use.

[320]

*Scovill Classification Test. Adults; 1927-47; an adaptation of *Army Group Examination Alpha* ('19) and *Army Group Examination Beta* ('20); 2 parts; 1 form; no data on reliability and validity; norms ('39) —publishers recommend the use of local norms; manual ['47]; 35¢ per specimen set; postpaid; prepared by Scovill Manufacturing Co.; Psychological Corporation. *

a) PART I. Illiterates and literates; can be administered in pantomime; $4.25 per 25; (30) minutes.
b) PART II. Literates; $3.30 per 25; (20) minutes.

REFERENCES

1. POND, MILLICENT, AND BILLS, MARION A. "Intelligence and Clerical Jobs Held: Two Studies of Relation of Test Scores to Job Held." *Personnel J* 12:41–56 Je '33. * (PA 7:4734)

ROBERT G. BERNREUTER, *Director, The Psychological Clinic, and Professor of Psychology, The Pennsylvania State College, State College, Pennsylvania.*

This is an early test which was based upon the original Army Alpha and Army Beta and brought up to date by more recent norms. The manual presents norms for populations ranging from 1,924 to 1,939. Of the seven scored parts, four are from the Beta (picture completion, number checking, digit symbol, and paper formboard) and three are from the Alpha (arithmetic reasoning, synonym-antonym, verbal analogies). The eighth unscored part is a test of hand coordination. The final score is the average of the converted scores on each part of the test, which permits any combination of the verbal or nonverbal tests to be used. For the convenience of the administrator the tests are published in two separate booklets. Normally only the first booklet is used with illiterate subjects; both booklets are used for those who can read and write.

No attempt has been made to make the administration of the nonverbal tests any easier than it was for the original Army Beta. Demonstration boards must be locally made for use with the four nonverbal tests. This arrangement permits the use of pantomime instructions with only a minimum of verbal instructions but requires awkward equipment and a considerable amount of practice on the part of the administrator in order to give the tests in a standardized manner.

The manual does not give any data on reliability and validity. However, the well known validity of the original parts of the Army Alpha and Beta apply to this test also.

The norms provided in the manual are based upon large industrial populations from one company only and cover jobs which are not described. Consequently the recommended procedure of constructing local norms for each new industrial user must be followed.

The *Scovill Classification Test* is an adaptation of the original Army Alpha and Army Beta but it is no improvement over the original tests. No attempt has been made to utilize the knowledge of test construction which has been developed since 1918. As a consequence this test can be recommended for use only in industrial concerns where local norms have already been constructed. Other industrial concerns which are now initiating testing programs will undoubtedly prefer to use some of the newer tests that are now available.

EDWARD E. CURETON, *Professor of Psychology, The University of Tennessee, Knoxville, Tennessee.*

This test is composed largely of items from the Army Alpha and Beta tests of World War I. One booklet, designed to be used with both literate and nonliterate subjects, contains picture completion, number checking, digit-symbol substitution, paper form board, and cross-out tests (the last an almost pure motor-speed test). A second booklet, for literate subjects only, includes arithmetic reasoning, same-opposite, and verbal analogies tests.

The applicability of the number checking, digit-symbol substitution, and cross-out tests as indicators of general intelligence is open to question, but they may still be useful as indicators of performance on particular jobs.

No data on reliability or validity are given in the manual. Normative data are confined to samples from one company and are presented (aside from one table) only in somewhat cryptically labelled graphs. The test may still be valuable, however, to those who wish to conduct their own validity studies and prepare their own norms. Few other tests include so wide a range of subtest types in a single battery.

Test authors should study the directions for administration given in the manual for this test. They are models of simplicity, clarity, and adherence to the basic principles of group test administration.

[321]

★**The Simplex Group Intelligence Scale.** Ages 9 and over; 1922–39; 1 form, '39; no data on reliability; manual ('34); tentative norms; 8*s*. 6*d*. per 25; 1*s*. 3*d*. per scoring stencil; 1*s*. 3*d*. per manual; 3*s*. per specimen set; purchase tax (British purchasers only) and postage extra; 90(95) minutes; C. A. Richardson; George G. Harrap & Co. Ltd. *

[322]

*[**The Simplex Junior Intelligence Tests.**] Ages 7–14; 1932–51; 2 forms (listed below); purchase tax (British purchasers only) and postage extra; 45(50) minutes; C. A. Richardson; George G. Harrap & Co. Ltd. *

a) THE SIMPLEX JUNIOR INTELLIGENCE SCALE. 1932; 6*s*. per 25; 6*d*. per single copy; 8*d*. per manual.
b) THE SIMPLEX JUNIOR 'A' INTELLIGENCE TEST. 1951; 35*s*. per 100; 6*d*. per single copy; 1*s*. per manual.

REFERENCES
1. KEIR, GERTRUDE. "The Progressive Matrices as Applied to School Children." *Brit J Psychol, Stat Sect* 2:140–50 N '49. (*PA* 24:3213)
2. WILSON, JAMES T. "A Consideration of the Ability for Algebra Shown by Secondary School Entrants." Bachelor's thesis, Glasgow University (Glasgow, Scotland), 1949. Abstract: *Brit J Ed Psychol* 20:65–6 F '50. * (*PA* 25:570, title only)

[323]
Southend Group Test of Intelligence. Ages 10.5–13; 1939; 1 form; no data on reliability and validity; no description of normative population; 7s. 6d. per 25; 10d. per handbook; postage extra; selected from tests originated by William Stephenson; George G. Harrap & Co. Ltd. *

REFERENCES
1. PEEL, E. A. "Symposium on Selection of Pupils for Different Types of Secondary Schools: VI, Evidence of a Practical Factor at the Age of Eleven." *Brit J Ed Psychol* 19:1–15 F '49. *

GERTRUDE KEIR, *Lecturer in Psychology, University College, London, England.*

This test is "designed to grade normal children who are about to enter the Senior School * It is not suitable for children who are markedly dull and backward." It consists of eight subtests, four verbal and four nonverbal, each verbal subtest being followed by its nonverbal equivalent. Each subtest is preceded by a teacher's demonstration on the blackboard. The tests fall only into two types, classification and analogies. The test as a whole suffers from a certain monotony and the number of mental processes involved is limited.

The manual contains instructions for the administration of the test, a key to answers and scoring (laid out in a somewhat involved way) and tables for the conversion of scores into mental ages and IQ's. It gives no details as to test construction and standardisation procedures.

The test items, selected from tests already devised, were arranged in order of difficulty and administered to the entire school population of Southend between the ages of 10½ and 13 years. "The scores are medians of each of the monthly age groups * The S.D. in terms of crude scores lies at between 8 and 9 points. * The upper limits of mental age were assessed by comparing scores after application of this test and the 1938 revision of the Binet Scale to the same subjects." [1] The reliability of the test is said to be .93 (split half method). No information is available as to whether this is the corrected figure, nor is there any on the sample on which the study of reliability was carried out. The author states that "Factor analysis suggests it discriminates more on the non-verbal items than the verbal." [1] The test correlates .7 both

[1] Personal communication.

with Jenkin's *Non-Verbal Test* and with Raven's *Progressive Matrices*. The size of the sample used in the correlational studies is unknown. Details of the results of item analysis are not available.

The scanty information regarding the construction, standardisation, reliability, and validity of this test should make one hesitate to use it as a valid and reliable measure of intelligence.

For an excerpt from a review, see 40:1423.

[324]
★Terman-McNemar Test of Mental Ability. Grades 7–12; 1941–49; a revision of *Terman Group Test of Mental Ability* (see 40:1424); IBM; Forms C ('41), D ('41); manual ('49); $1.90 per 25; 35¢ per specimen set, postpaid; separate answer sheets may be used; 85¢ per 25 IBM answer sheets; 20¢ per stencil for scoring answer sheets; postage extra; 40(45) minutes; Lewis M. Terman and Quinn McNemar; World Book Co. *

REFERENCES
1–25. See 40:1424.
26–50. See 3:263.
51. TRASTER, STELLA. *A Study of the Significance of the Scattering of the Scores of the 10 Subtests of the Terman Group Intelligence Tests—Form B in Relation to Psychopathic Tendency in 102 Students of the Fredonia, Kansas High School.* Master's thesis, University of Kansas (Lawrence, Kan.), 1927.
52. TOLL, CHARLES H. "Scholastic Aptitude Tests in Amherst College." *Sch & Soc* 28:524–8 O 27 '28. * (*PA* 3:512)
53. TRIGG, CHARLES WILDERMAN. *An Analysis of Individual Responses to the Items of the Terman Group Tests, Form A.* Master's thesis, University of Southern California (Los Angeles, Calif.), 1931. Pp. 132.
54. RICHARDSON, H. D. "The Intelligence Quotient and Secondary-School Guidance." *Sch R* 43:49–59 Ja '35. *
55. MURPHY, LAURA WHITE. "The Relation Between Mechanical Ability Tests and Verbal and Non-Verbal Intelligence Tests." *J Psychol* 2:353–66 '36. * (*PA* 11:3928)
56. HARTSON, L. D. "Influence of Level of Motivation on the Validity of Intelligence Tests." *Ed & Psychol Meas* 5:273–83 au '45. * (*PA* 20:2500)
57. TILTON, J. W. "The Relation Between IQ and Trait Difference as Measured by Group Intelligence Tests." *J Ed Psychol* 38:343–52 O '47. * (*PA* 22:2066)
58. BLUMENFELD, WALTER. "Intelligence Examinations in Peru With the Lima Revision of Terman's Group Test." *J Genetic Psychol* 73:251–67 D '48. * (*PA* 23:3106)
59. DAVIS, W. ALLISON, AND HAVIGHURST, ROBERT J. "The Measurement of Mental Systems: Can Intelligence Be Measured?" *Sci Mo* 66:301–16 Ap '48. * (*PA* 22:3381)
60. BAYLEY, NANCY. "Consistency and Variability in the Growth of Intelligence From Birth to Eighteen Years." *J Genetic Psychol* 75:165–96 D '49. * (*PA* 24:4511)
61. YELA, MARIANO. "Application of the Concept of Simple Structure to Alexander's Data." *Psychometrika* 14:121–35 Je '49. * (*PA* 24:1066)
62. LENNON, ROGER T. *A Comparison of Results of Three Intelligence Tests.* Test Service Notebook, No. 11. Yonkers, N.Y.: World Book Co., [1951]. Pp. 4. Paper. *

For reviews by Carl I. Hovland and Robert L. Thorndike, see 3:263; for reviews by Anne Anastasi and Howard Easley of the original edition, see 40:1424.

[325]
★Tests of General Ability: Cooperative Inter-American Tests. Grades 1–3, 4–7, 8–13; 1950; IBM for grades 4 and over; 3 levels; 2 editions; English edition: Forms AE, BE; Spanish edition: Forms AS, BS; tentative norms; $2.50 per 25; 50¢ per series manual; cash orders postpaid; 50¢ per specimen set, postpaid; prepared under the auspices of the Committee on Modern Languages of American Council on Education, Herschel T. Manuel, Director of Test Con-

struction; Cooperative Test Division, Educational Testing Service. *

a) PRIMARY LEVEL. Grades 1–3; 2 scores: oral vocabulary, total; nontimed (30–40) minutes.

b) INTERMEDIATE LEVEL. Grades 4–7; 3 scores: nonverbal, verbal, total; IBM; separate answer sheets must be used; 90¢ per 25 IBM answer sheets; 30¢ per set of stencils for scoring answer sheets; 34(50) minutes.

c) ADVANCED LEVEL. Grades 8–13; 3 scores: nonverbal, verbal, total; IBM; separate answer sheets must be used; 90¢ per 25 IBM answer sheets; 30¢ per set of stencils for scoring answer sheets; 34(50) minutes.

REFERENCES

1. STOVALL, FRANKLIN L. *An Evaluation of Three Non-Verbal Tests of Mental Ability.* Master's thesis, University of Texas (Austin, Tex.), 1942.
2. MCCRANIE, JOSEPHINE. *A Study of Four Inter-American Tests Applied to High School Seniors.* Master's thesis, University of Texas (Austin, Tex.), 1944.
3. KELLEY, FRANCES. *A Study of the Inter-American Tests at the High School Level.* Master's thesis, University of Texas (Austin, Tex.), 1945.
4. WILLHAUK, RALPH C. *A Study of Inter-American Tests in Relation to the Stanford-Binet.* Master's thesis, University of Texas (Austin, Tex.), 1946.
5. ZACCARIA, MICHAEL ANGELO. *An Item Analysis of the Advanced Inter-American Tests of General Ability.* Master's thesis, University of Texas (Austin, Tex.), 1946.
6. DUNHAM, CHARLES V. *A Study of the Inter-American Tests of General Ability With Special Reference to Children Aged Seven and Eight.* Doctor's thesis, University of Texas (Austin, Tex.), 1947.
7. STOVALL, FRANKLIN L. *A Study of Scaled Scores With Special Reference to the Inter-American Tests.* Doctor's thesis, University of Texas (Austin, Tex.), 1947.
8. FIFE, ROBERT HERNDON, AND MANUEL, HERSCHEL T. *The Teaching of English in Puerto Rico,* pp. 171–313, 337–410. Prepared for the American Council on Education. San Juan, P.R.: Department of Education Press, 1951. Pp. xix, 410. *

RALEIGH M. DRAKE, *Professor of Psychology and Head of the Department, Kent State University, Kent, Ohio.*

With the large number of general mental ability tests available nowadays, one must ask what justifies the appearance of a new series on the market. The only claim that this series legitimately has is the fact that it offers identical tests in English and Spanish from the primary level to the level of the first year in college. There is no evidence stated, implied, or evident that any improvement has been contributed to the field of intelligence testing.

Most of the test content is of nonverbal material. Scoring directions mention verbal and nonverbal scores, but the norms in the manual do not provide any means of interpreting or comparing them. In fact, in spite of the fact that the tests have been given to 6,000 pupils in Mexico, 20,000 pupils in Puerto Rico, and 10,000 pupils in the United States, the only norms data consist of "approximate medians" for grades one to twelve. These medians are based on the results of testing done in 1943 with preliminary forms of the tests which were later revised but not given again. The original medians have since been adjusted for changes made in final forms of the tests.

There is in the manual considerable discussion of validity in general and of the steps that were taken to insure the validity of all the tests in the Inter-American battery. The statement is made that in the construction of the several tests "an exercise which did not discriminate satisfactorily (between high scorers and low scorers) was rejected or revised." No statistical data are offered to substantiate this statement, and no correlations with other tests, with grades, or with ratings are reported. The meaning of reliability is also discussed in the manual, but not one reliability coefficient is presented; it would seem that for tests administered as early as 1943 ample data would have been provided before this for extensive studies of both reliability and validity.

The authors have tried to select test items which, since they are either nonverbal or verbal analogies employing identical concepts in both languages and identical mental processes, are apparently free from cultural influences. However, whether the content of the tests is actually culture free is questionable. If it is, and if the tests are equivalent in difficulty for both language groups, then, according to the medians provided, children in the United States are superior in general ability to children in Mexico and Puerto Rico, and children in Mexico are superior to children in Puerto Rico. One wonders whether the tests are actually equivalent, whether children in the United States *are* superior in intelligence to children in Mexico and Puerto Rico, whether the sampling was equivalent for the three groups, whether the motivation was different for the three groups, whether other cultural factors are involved, or whether the differences may be due to a combination of several of these factors with each one contributing an unknown proportion to the total effect. No mention is made in the manual of the wide national differences in the scores of the children tested so far, or of the problems of interpretation posed by these differences.

It is to be regretted that these tests, already given to a total of 36,000 subjects, have an accompanying manual which offers so little of what one needs to know if the tests are to be used, and the results interpreted, intelligently. The manual states only that the norms are "extremely approximate and will be replaced as soon as it is feasible." It is hoped that more adequate norms will be supplied, and that these tests will be subjected to many critical studies to determine their usefulness. If it is found that their content is relatively culture free and that satisfactory validity and reliability can be demonstrated, there is no obvious reason why the tests should not be offered in German, Chinese, or any other language, and so ultimately fulfill a purpose far beyond that for which they were intended. But all that rests upon research that is to come. For the present, these tests can only be used with extreme caution.

WALTER N. DUROST, *Director, Test Service and Advisement Center, Dunbarton, New Hampshire.*

In order to "accent the positive" this reviewer would like to state initially that, while fully aware of the difficulties involved, he believes heartily in the type of international test development represented by the Inter-American series. The fact that the committee was aware of these difficulties is clearly stated in the manual and at other appropriate places. This is about as much as one can say, however, for the material provided by the publishers for the reviewer's use. Direct correspondence with Herschel T. Manuel, chairman of the committee responsible for the construction of the test, brought additional information.[1] The availability of this information does not free the publishers from the responsibility which is solely theirs for publishing the tests for general use without adequate supporting information. If experimental editions are to be made available for further study (and these must be considered experimental at the present time), due cautions and restrictions on their use should be exercised by the publishers.

Validity. Validity is never general: it is always specific to the situation in which a test is to be used, and data presented can be generalized only on logical, not statistical, grounds. The evidence in this case indicates that great care was taken to secure parallelism in Spanish and English editions from the point of view of vocabulary, intrinsic difficulty of the concepts involved, etc. This care should do much to heighten the meaningfulness of comparisons from one language group to another. However, the ultimate usefulness of the instruments calls for their validation in both Spanish and English speaking situations following along lines already established by the series of masters and doctoral studies being carried out at the University of Texas.

From the point of view of validity, it seems clear that these tests are superior to tests currently available in the United States for measuring mental ability for Spanish-English groups. Unfortunately, little specific evidence has been made available concerning the validity statistics obtained at the time of test construction, such as distributions of the phi coefficients which were computed or even distributions of difficulty values in English or Spanish, or both.

Some data have been made available concerning the subsequent use of the test. In a study by Dunham (6) intercorrelations of the parts of the Primary test are reported to fall between .23 and .55; and intercorrelations of the parts of the Intermediate test, between .28 and .57. Correlations of total scores (for the Primary test presumably) with the *Otis Quick-Scoring Test of Mental Ability* were from .69 to .76; with Binet mental ages, from .42 to .71. Otis scores are reported to correlate with Binet mental ages between .51 and .71. Since the implication is that several values were computed without clear-cut definition of what all the variables are, these data are not so valuable as they might be. However, it would appear that they are typical of other similar correlations in the literature. The same investigator reports split half reliability coefficients of between .69 and .94 on single age groups. Nothing is said about correcting the test intercorrelations for attenuation, so presumably the values reported are uncorrected.

In another study by Willhauk (4) the Intermediate test was correlated with the Binet on the basis of the results of 50 fifth and sixth grade pupils in Austin, Texas. The correlation with the Binet was .75; with school marks the correlation was .58.

In another study by McCranie (2) Form BE of the Advanced test was given to 212 Louisiana high school seniors. This investigator found a split half reliability coefficient of .88 on this group. She also found a correlation of .35 with high school marks. Correlations with other tests in the Inter-American series are reported as follows: with Reading, .51; with Natural Sciences, .47; with Social Studies, .56.

In still another study, Kelley (3) reports correlations between .40 and .64 for the Advanced test with the subject matter tests in the series. She also reports correlations between .26 and

---

[1] The most pertinent information came from Chapters 10 and 11 of *The Teaching of English in Puerto Rico* (8) by Robert H. Fife and Herschel T. Manuel, graciously made available, in manuscript form, by Pablo Roca, Director, Division of Research and Statistics, Department of Education, Government of Puerto Rico.

.29 with total school marks but a correlation of .44 with algebra marks alone.

One can best summarize the reported information on the correlation of scores on the *Tests of General Ability* with achievement measures of various types by saying that they fall within the typical range of such values. They provide no basis for thinking that these tests are any better than other widely used intelligence measures for measuring learning capacity in the typical American school.

RELIABILITY. The manual gives no statistical evidence on reliability for the present tests, saying "Because the Cooperative Inter-American Tests are being offered for general use for the first time, reliability statistics are not available at present." This is inexcusable from the point of view of good publishing practice, but the situation is somewhat retrieved by the availability of data on the earlier experimental editions even though these editions were somewhat different in content. Pertinent data from Table 26 of the Fife and Manuel report indicate that the within-grade reliability coefficients range from .86 to .93. The nature of the grade groups or the number of cases on which these reliability coefficients were based is not available. However, other reports of reliability contained in the same study on more clearly identified groups are consistent with the information given. One can conclude that the tests probably are about "run-of-the-mill" with respect to reliability.

NORMS. The normative data provided in the manual are of little practical usefulness. This means that the interpretation of the scores, for the present at least, must be based upon local distributions. So long as the interpretation is concerned only with variations within the population tested, this is not necessarily bad, but it must be considered a weakness in the tests with respect to good publishing standards.

MECHANICAL DETAILS. One would be happy indeed if he were able to say that mechanically the tests are all that they should be. Instead, the writer feels that the art work is not very good and that sometimes the intent of the picture is very hard indeed to determine. Even granting that the primary purpose in a test of this sort is representation, there is need for great care to prevent confusion of meaning. Larger type size could have been used for the printed sections of the test without increasing the amount of space required.

Nothing is done to simplify the use of the separate answer sheet in spite of the fact that it will normally be used with populations not generally testwise. Cycling the numbering of response spaces through a cycle of ten digits instead of five would be helpful. For example, it would be better if the numbering of the alternatives for Item 1 ran 1 2 3 4 5; for Item 2, 6 7 8 9 10; for Item 3, 1 2 3 4 5; for Item 4, 6 7 8 9 10; etc. This simple device tends to break up the possibility of an individual misplacing his answers by one set of answer spaces and thus having all of his answers scored as chance responses.

Nothing is done to make the scoring keys, which are designed primarily for machine scoring, easy to use for hand scoring. The inclusion of guide arrows for positioning the answer key over the answer sheet would greatly improve this situation.

CONCLUSION. At the present time, one must conclude that there is very little about the tests as presented in the materials available which would argue in favor of their use in this country in place of widely used standardized intelligence measures. However, their continued use with populations of bilingual children at the borders of English- and Spanish-speaking countries is certainly desirable. Even though the results may not be so immediately useful as they might be, the tests undoubtedly represent the best that is available for use in Spanish-speaking countries. With the task of making good tests for use in a unique situation having been carried so far, it would appear only reasonable that the work be carried to the point where it will receive the professional recognition which it deserves. It is to be hoped that much additional research will be forthcoming to implement further the use of these tests, and that the publishers will do what is necessary to secure more adequate reliability, validity, and normative information.

[326]

*Thurstone Test of Mental Alertness.** Grades 9–12 and adults; 1943–48; an abbreviated adaptation of *American Council on Education Psychological Examination for High School Students,* 1940 Edition; 3 scores: quantitative, linguistic, total; IBM; 2 editions; 1 form, '43; manual ('48); 50¢ per specimen set of any one edition; cash orders postpaid; 20(25) minutes; Thelma Gwinn Thurstone and L. L. Thurstone; Science Research Associates, Inc. *

a) FORM AH (HAND SCORING EDITION). $1.85 per 25; 60¢ per set of scoring folders.

b) FORM AM (MACHINE SCORING EDITION). $3 per 25 IBM test-answer booklets; $2 per set of scoring keys.

REFERENCES

1. HACKNEY, KENNETH URBAN. *Prediction of College Success From Scores on Achievement Tests and Tests of General Mental*

Ability. Master's thesis, Southern Methodist University (Dallas, Tex.), 1947. (*Abstracts of Theses....1946,* 1947, p. 69.)
2. MAHER, HOWARD, AND FIFE, ISABELLE E. "A Biological-Pharmaceutical Checker Selection Program." *J Appl Psychol* 31:469–76 O '47. * (*PA* 22:3665)
3. BORG, WALTER R. "Some Factors Relating to Art School Success." *J Ed Res* 43:376–84 Ja '50. * (*PA* 24:4811)

For reviews by Anne Anastasi and Emily T. Burr, see 3:265.

[327]

V.G.C. Intelligence Indicator. Grades 3–8, 7–12; 1943; an adaptation of *Henmon-Nelson Tests of Mental Ability* (see 299); 2 levels; Forms A, B; preliminary manual, revised; $1.95 per 25 of any one level; separate answer sleeves must be used; 40¢ per 25 answer sleeves for any one level; 10¢ per manual for any one level; 85¢ per specimen set of any one level; postage extra; available only to Canadian schools; 30(35) minutes; adaptation by M. D. Parmenter; Vocational Guidance Centre. *

GEORGE A. FERGUSON, *Professor of Psychology, McGill University, Montreal, Canada.*

These tests are an adaptation of the *Henmon-Nelson Tests of Mental Ability.* The 90 test items in each form are identical with those of the Henmon-Nelson and include vocabulary, sentence completion, verbal analogies, figure analogies, and the like. They differ, however, in format, method of administration, and scoring.

The test forms are printed on heavy cardboard. The testee records his answers on a separate cardboard answer sheet or sleeve which is fitted over the test form and subsequently inserted into a plastic sleeve for scoring purposes. The format and the scoring method are ingenious and should have application to other types of tests. My impression is, however, that this test does not represent an improvement, in terms of ease of scoring, over the original forms of the Henmon-Nelson which used the Clapp-Young scoring system with its carbon impressions. The advantage of this test over the Henmon-Nelson resides in economy. The test forms are of substantial manufacture and may be used many times. In testing fairly large numbers of individuals, the cost would work out at very roughly a little more than half the cost involved in using the original Henmon-Nelson forms.

Tables of mental age equivalents for given raw scores are provided. All data relating to the Henmon-Nelson such as norms, reliability information, correlations with other tests and the like, are presumed to be directly applicable to the *V.G.C. Intelligence Indicator.* There is no reason to doubt this presumption. The differences in format between the Henmon-Nelson and the present test should have little or no bearing on the performance of subjects. On the whole I prefer the format of the Henmon-Nelson. If, however, economy is a consideration, then the *V.G.C. Intelligence Indicator* is recommended.

For a review by H. M. Fowler of the Henmon-Nelson Tests of Mental Ability, *see 299; for reviews by Anne Anastasi, August Dvorak, Howard Easley, and J. P. Guilford and an excerpt from a review of the* Henmon-Nelson Test of Mental Ability, *see 40:1398.*

[328]

★**Verbal and Non-Verbal Test.** Ages 10–11, 12–13; 1951; 2 levels; 1 form ['51]; a practice exercise, entitled *Verbal and Non-Verbal Practice Test I,* must precede administration of test; manual ['51]; 90s. 6d. per 100 sets of test and practice exercise for any one level; 12s. 6d. per 12 sets of any one level; 1s. 2d. per single set of any one level; postage extra; practice exercise: nontimed (10–15) minutes; test: 40(45) minutes; National Foundation for Educational Research in England and Wales. *
a) VERBAL AND NON-VERBAL TEST I. Ages 12–13; no data on reliability.
b) VERBAL AND NON-VERBAL TEST II. Ages 10–11; no data on reliability and validity.

[329]

★**Verbal Intelligence Test.** Grades 12–16 and applicants for executive positions; 1948–50; formerly called *Verbal Intelligence Test for Business Executives;* 1 form '50—same as test copyrighted in 1948; manual ('49); supplementary manual ['50]; no data on reliability; $2.50 per 25; 50¢ per specimen set; sample test free to qualified test users; cash orders postpaid; 20 (25) minutes; William J. Morgan and Antonia Morgan; Aptitude Associates. *

WILLIAM B. SCHRADER, *Assistant Director, Department of Statistical Analysis, Educational Testing Service, Princeton, New Jersey.*

This vocabulary test is designed to be acceptable in form and content to well educated adults. The items are printed across the center spread of a 4-page booklet in clear, blue, 12-point type. The front cover is used for identifying information, and the back cover presents an adequate set of instructions. The words which constitute the test do not appear to be excessively rare, pedantic, or technical. On the whole, this test should make a favorable impression on the person taking it.

Five items, each of which includes 10 words to be matched by a synonym or antonym from a list of 12 words, comprise the test. The total possible score is 50. In four of the items, each key word is substantially different in meaning from the other key words; the last item, however, has one alternative (No. 7) which is synonymous with two key words and with one alternative. This would seem to require an excessively subtle discrimination for a test of this kind. The test does not seem to be arranged in order of difficulty.

The 3-page manual published in 1950 is well adapted to the proposed uses of the test. Clear and sufficiently detailed instructions for administration and scoring are provided. Norms for each decile and for the 95th and 99th percentiles are presented for two samples: 312 high school graduates and 575 college graduates. Both norms groups are based on adults aged 20 to 49. It is regrettable that the authors described the samples as "random"; a few words about how the samples were obtained would have been far more helpful. Although a more precise statement of the limitations of the norms would be desirable, the data should have considerable value if used with common sense.

Superior performance by college graduates as compared with high school graduates and reasonably high (.67 to .84) correlation coefficients with the *Henmon-Nelson Test of Mental Ability* and the V score of Thorndike's CAVD are offered as evidence of validity. These correlation coefficients indicate at least fair reliability for the test, but no direct evaluation of reliability is presented. The absence of sex differences and age differences in performance within the groups studied, as reported in the manual, is a finding of some interest. The statistical studies are presented in a condensed but acceptable style; one hopes that a fuller technical account will be published.

Since this test is pitched at a fairly high difficulty level, and since vocabulary has often proved to be a useful predictor of certain kinds of success, this test has considerable potential value. Its usefulness would be increased if the method used in its construction were specified and if studies of its validity for particular uses in business and industry were available.

[330]

★**Verbal Test I.** Ages 10–11; 1951; 1 form; a practice exercise, entitled *Preliminary Practice Test for Verbal Test* ['51], must precede administration of test; no data on reliability and validity; manual ['51]; 50s. per 100 sets of test and practice exercise; 7s. per 12 sets; 8d. per single set; 1s. 6d. per manual; postage extra; practice exercise: 10(15) minutes; test: 50(55) minutes; I. Macfarlane Smith and J. Darroch; National Foundation for Educational Research in England and Wales. *

[331]

*****Wesman Personnel Classification Test.** Grades 8–16 and adults; 1946–51; 3 scores: verbal, numerical, total: Forms A ('46), B ('47); revised manual ('51);

$1.65 per 25; 35¢ per specimen set; postpaid; 28(35) minutes; Alexander G. Wesman; Psychological Corporation. *

REFERENCES

1. ABT, LAWRENCE EDWIN. "A Test Battery for Selecting Technical Magazine Editors." *Personnel Psychol* 2:75–91 sp '49. * (PA 23:5099)
2. PORUBEN, ADAM, JR. "A Test Battery for Actuarial Clerks." *J Appl Psychol* 34:159–62 Je '50. * (PA 25:3995)
3. GILBERT, HARRY B. *An Evaluation of Certain Procedures in the Selection of Camp Counselors Based on Objective Test Data as Predictive of Practical Performance.* Doctor's thesis, New York University (New York, N.Y.), 1951. Abstract: *Microfilm Abstracts* 11:953–4 no 4 '51.

JOHN C. FLANAGAN, *President, American Institute for Research; and Professor of Psychology, University of Pittsburgh, Pittsburgh, Pennsylvania.*

The first part of this test consists of verbal analogies items of the form *"blank* is to water as eat is to *blank."* Four options are provided for each of the two blanks, and the correct response is found by selecting both the number corresponding to the key word in the first series, *drink* (2), and also the letter corresponding to the key word in the second series, *food* (C). The author points out that this design provides for reasoning through analogy, perception of relationships, a wide variety of subject matter and a very small chance of getting the item correct by guessing because of the double series. He concludes this discussion with the statement, "The net effect of these advantages is a more efficient, more accurate measure of verbal reasoning ability than is obtained by other types of verbal tests." No experimental evidence is provided to substantiate this statement. Perhaps the author meant to offer this as a hypothesis. However, it appears unmodified in the 1951 revision of the manual as well as the 1948 edition.

The second part of the test contains 20 items. These involve the addition, subtraction, multiplication, and division of integers, decimals, and fractions. Percentage, square root, and ratios are also included. The items stress "the use of numerical concepts,....the ability to perceive relationships and to operate with ingenuity," rather than "sheer figure-handling speed." The zero correlation reported between the total score and the numbers score of the *Minnesota Clerical Test* tends to indicate success in this regard.

Throughout the test the items appear to be of good quality and only a very few appeared to this reviewer as somewhat ambiguous.

The manual states "The test is essentially a measure of power rather than of speed." One high school senior was given the test using the standard time limits. He read 33 of the 40 items

Verbal Intelligence Test

in the Verbal Part in the 18 minutes allowed, answering 31 of them and getting 3 wrong. On the Numerical Part he completed 19 out of 20 in the time limit with 18 correct. He answered the remaining 7 items on Part I and the 1 item on Part II in an additional 4 minutes getting 4 of them right. This is a change of slightly more than half a standard deviation in his total score. This one case, of course, does not prove the test is not a power test for most of those who take it. It does suggest that the author might do well to supply a more quantitative and objective statement than the sentence quoted at the beginning of this paragraph about the extent to which speed is a factor for those tested.

Norms are provided for six groups of students, three groups of employees, and eight groups of applicants. These groups vary in size from 93 to 1,476. The median size is about two hundred. A paragraph description of each of the 17 groups is provided. This information should be of value to test users. Certainly more of this type of normative information for tests of this type is needed, and the author and publisher should be commended for this detailed information. However, it would be useful in many cases to know a little more about the groups. In trying to interpret the score obtained for the high school senior mentioned above, it was useful to know how he compared with seniors in a New York high school. The high schools of New York vary greatly in the quality of their students, and there is no hint as to whether this is one of the better or worse ones. Similarly, it is valuable to be able to compare his score with "freshmen men in a small New England college of average standing." This point of reference seems a little vague. The mean score for this group is only a point and a half higher than the mean for applicants to nursing schools.

The discussions of the reliability and validity of the test in the manual are comprehensive and competent. The test is shown to have a correlation of about .70 with the Otis and Wonderlic intelligence tests. Although this can probably be accepted as typical, the failure to provide means and standard deviations for the groups concerned makes it difficult to estimate the effects of the variability of the groups on these coefficients.

In general the average scores increase with educational and occupational level. The data appear convincing on this point. However, the reader is given no information as to how the seventeen groups were selected.

Reliability data are provided for a large number of groups using split half methods and for two groups using alternate forms. The reliability coefficients for the same groups are only slightly higher when split half procedures are used than when alternate forms are correlated. This suggests that speed was not a large factor in determining the scores in these two groups. The reliability coefficients for total scores computed in single grade ranges are in the low .80's.

Forms A and B are said to be equivalent. The author reports that these forms "showed very similar cumulative percentile distributions and high test-retest reliability coefficients." It would be helpful if he had reported either the distributions or means and standard deviations by which someone else might get an idea of what he regards as "very similar."

In conclusion it appears that Wesman has provided a test which should be useful in many situations. He has not provided evidence that it is better than similar available tests. It appears that it may be almost as difficult to show superiority for one "intelligence" test over another as it is to show superiority for a particular brand of soap or cigarettes. In spite of this competitive situation the general quality of the technical data supplied with the *Wesman Personnel Classification Test* is excellent. It is hoped that authors and publishers will continue to improve their test manuals so that factual data will completely replace the type of claims so typical of commercial advertising.

ERWIN K. TAYLOR, *Director, Personnel Research Institute, Western Reserve University, Cleveland, Ohio.*

The title of this test implies to this reviewer that it was constructed primarily for use in the selection and placement of personnel in business and industry. The 1951 revision of the manual contains a lengthy discussion on the validity of intelligence tests. It is prefaced by the statement "in the final analysis, its [an intelligence test] validity rests on the validity of the basic philosophy underlying the test and the extent to which the test's content faithfully exemplifies that philosophy."

This reviewer takes a point of view diametrically opposed to that expressed in the foregoing paragraph. Tests are marketed neither as examples of basic philosophies nor to provide mental gymnastics, but rather to provide devices for prediction in a given area. This prediction may concern academic achievement or occupational success, among many other things. The test consequently has no such things as abstract "validity." It is valid for this, that, or the other purpose. If it is independent in a correlational sense of the criterion for a specific situation, a test, regardless of how good a measure of "intelligence" it is, is useless for that purpose. This correlational relationship, as the manual appropriately notes, may be of a product-moment, biserial, or tetrachoric nature, as the situation requires. It may even be that a curvilinear relationship between the test and the criterion exists, although appearances of these in the available literature are so rare as to render them inconsequential.

The test manual presents three types of "validity" evidence. First it considers the relationship of PCT to the *Otis Self-Administering Tests of Mental Ability*, the *Otis General Intelligence Examination*, and the *Wonderlic Personnel Test*. These correlations on six samples of between 100 and 200 cases range from .68 to .84. Secondly, it is demonstrated that the mean score on each of the parts, and the total, increases for populations of successively higher educational achievement. The same relationship is demonstrated for a number of vocational groups. Finally five validity studies on industrial populations are summarized. In three of these, validities are expressed in correlational terms and are of a magnitude adequate to justify consideration of the test on an experimental basis in situations where measures of verbal and numerical ability appear to hold promise of validity.

The reliability of the test appears to be adequate for any use for which it might prove valid. The manual provides norms for 11 vocational groups ranging in size from 116 to 1,496 cases. Norms are also presented for six student populations. The size of these varies from 93 to 436.

In summary, this instrument seems to be an excellent *experimental* intelligence test. Its use for *research* purposes, where measurement of verbal and numerical facility is indicated, is recommended. Its validity has not, in this writer's opinion, been firmly established for any purpose, and there are no circumstances in which it would appear that its operational use, without a specific validation study, could be justified.

For an excerpt from a review, see 3:253.

Wesman Personnel Classification Test

[332]
★"West Yorkshire" Group Test of Intelligence. Ages 7.5–15; 1940; 2 forms ['40]; no data on validity; no description of normative population; 9d. per manual for any one form; 2s. 3d. per specimen set; postage extra; J. P. Tomlinson; University of London Press Ltd. *
a) FORM W. 9s. 3d. per 25 sets of test and answer sheet; 7d. per single set of test and answer sheet; separate answer sheets must be usd; 1s. 3½d. per 12 answer sheets; 57(70) minutes.
b) FORM X. 12s. per 25; 8d. per single copy; 60(70) minutes.

[333]
Word-Number Test of Scholastic Aptitude. Grades 4–8, 9–16; 1939–40; 3 scores: verbal, quantitative, total; IBM; 2 levels; 1 form, '40—same as test copyrighted in 1939; no norms for part scores; manual ('40); tentative norms; $2.50 per 30 of any one level; separate answer sheets may be used; 1½¢ per IBM answer sheet; 25¢ per specimen set; postpaid; 30(35–40) minutes; H. T. Manuel, James Knight, J. A. Floyd, and R. C. Jordan; Steck Co. *
a) FORM X. Grades 4–8.
b) FORM A. Grades 9–16.

JANE LOEVINGER, *Research Associate in Psychology, Washington University, St. Louis, Missouri.*

This test is an excellent example of a psychological test. The accompanying manual is straightforward and explicit in describing what the test purports to accomplish and what evidence exists as to how well it fulfills its purposes.

Stress is laid on the fact that the test measures present ability. "The relative contributions of heredity and environment, if ascertained at all, must be discovered by supplementary study." A number of practical illustrations are given of situations in which the test can be useful for educational and vocational guidance.

Data on reliability and validity of the test are presented with clarity. Reliability is described in terms of forms correlated, nature of the groups tested, and number of cases. A significant omission is the time interval between testings for these coefficients. Standard deviations might well have been included also. Corrected odd-even correlations for single grade, with 100 cases in each grade but one, range from .82 to .95. Form X tends to have higher odd-even coefficients than Form A.

Data on validity include a number of correlations of .7 and .8 with other recognized tests of intelligence, and a correlation of .4 with first-semester grade-points of 51 college freshmen. These correlations would also be more meaningful if accompanied by standard deviations and a statement concerning time intervals between tests.

Concerning grade norms for Form X, the test booklet states, "The norms for grade 8 have been adjusted upward on the basis of results with Form A." The precise reason for this adjustment and how it was accomplished should have been stated.

As to content, one might question the inclusion of "to demise" in Form A. The reviewer has failed to find a college professor familiar with the expression, and it seems to be uncommon even among lawyers. One item in Form X is also open to question. The first wrong alternative for "to observe" is given as "keep." There is, however, one usage of keep, perhaps colloquial, in which the words are equivalent: to keep a holiday is to observe a holiday. With these small exceptions, the content of the test appears to be unambiguous and well chosen.

The two forms of this test deserve wide use in view of the excellence of the content and the clearness of the supporting data. One can only hope that the modesty with which the claims for this test are presented will not lead test users to prefer tests with more pretentious but less well documented claims.

INDIVIDUAL

[334]

Alexander Performance Scale: A Performance Scale for the Measurement of Practical Ability. Ages 8–18; 1935–46; individual; 3 tests; 1 form; manual ('46); 147s. per set of testing materials; 2s. per 50 record sheets; purchase tax (British purchasers only) and postage extra; (40–50) minutes; W. P. Alexander; Thomas Nelson and Sons Ltd. *

a) THE PASSALONG TEST. 1932–37; may be administered alone as a quick measure of practical ability; (15) minutes.
b) KOH'S BLOCK DESIGN TEST. 1919–36.
c) CUBE CONSTRUCTION TEST. 1918–25.

REFERENCES

1–3. See 40:1376.
4. See 3:270.
5. DREW, L. J. "An Investigation Into the Measurement of Technical Ability." *Occupational Psychol* 21:34–48 Ja '47. * (PA 21:2020)
6. HOOD, H. BLAIR. "A Preliminary Survey of Some Mental Abilities of Deaf Children." *Brit J Ed Psychol* 19:210–9 N '49. * (PA 24:3355)
7. LAMBERT, CONSTANCE M. "Symposium on Selection of Pupils for Different Types of Secondary Schools: VII. A Survey of Ability and Interest at the Stage of Transfer." *Brit J Ed Psychol* 19:67–81 Je '49. *
8. YELA, MARIANO. "Application of the Concept of Simple Structure to Alexander's Data." *Psychometrika* 14:121–35 Je '49. * (PA 24:1066)

CHARLES A. STICKLAND, *Psychologist, Harperbury Hospital, Hertfordshire, England.*

This performance scale consists of three tests, the *Passalong Test*, a shortened version of Kohs' *Block Design Test* (similar to that used in the Drever-Collins *Performance Tests of Intelligence*), and the *Cube Construction Test*. It has much to recommend it. Each of the tests contains a series of items graded in order of difficulty, and the score is thus not so subject to chance effects as are scales containing tests that are single items. The test materials are attractively coloured and supplied in a box convenient for actual administration of the test. The three subtests themselves have proved quite useful in other contexts apart from the scale.

The criticisms that can be made are on points of detail rather than on the scale as a whole.

a) It has been pointed out elsewhere that with some subjects difficulty is experienced in the *Block Design Test* when there is a changeover from a 4-block to a 9-block design and from a 9-block design to a 16-block design. In these cases the score may be influenced by an emotional reaction against the abrupt change. The inclusion of 6-block and 12-block designs would help to overcome this.

b) The scoring of the *Cube Construction Test* represents an advance over the usual method with respect to speed only or to accuracy only; i.e., the score is based on time taken and on the number of blocks correct. One wonders, however, whether a similar method could not be developed for the *Block Design Test*. It quite often happens that the majority of a design is completed within a time limit, but no score is given because the result is not perfect.

c) The description of the scoring of the *Cube Construction Test* is made rather confusing by the choice of words concerned. A simplification could be introduced by calling the "full" time-score the "actual" time-score and the so-called "actual" time-score (which has no real existence) the "corrected" time-score. Apart from minor points such as these, the scale, principally designed to measure the practical ability of children between the ages of 11 and 16, can be well recommended.

For a review by John Cohen and excerpts from reviews, see 3:270; for a review by J. M. Blackburn, see 40:1376; for reviews by James Drever, T. J. Keating, and Grace H. Kent of the Passalong Test, *see 40:1414; for related reviews, see 38:B293 and 36:B3.*

[335]

Arthur Point Scale of Performance Tests. Ages 4.5 or 5.5 to superior adults; 1925–47; individual; 2 forms; (45–90) minutes; Grace Arthur. *

a) FORM I. Ages 5.5 to superior adults; 1925–43; 10 tests; $78 per complete set of testing materials; postage extra; C. H. Stoelting Co.

b) REVISED FORM II. Ages 4.5 to superior adults; 1947; 5 tests; $60 per complete set of testing materials including manual and 100 score sheets; $3.50 per 100 score sheets; $3.50 per 100 score cards; $2.50 per manual; $4.50 per carrying case (when ordered with complete set); postpaid; Psychological Corporation. *

1) *Knox Cube Test, Arthur Revision.* $3.60 per test.
2) *Sequin Form Board, Arthur Revision.* $22 per test.
3) *Arthur Stencil Design Test I.* $3 per test.
4) *Porteus Maze Test, Arthur Printing.* $11.50 per complete set of 14 pads.
5) *Healy Picture Completion Test II.* $22.50 per test.

REFERENCES

1–16. See 40:1379.
17–35. See 3:271.
36. WISLER, MAXINE L. *A Comparative Study of Performance of Feebleminded and Juvenile Delinquents on the Arthur Performance Scale and the Stanford-Binet Test of Intelligence.* Master's thesis, Claremont Colleges (Claremont, Calif.), 1933. Pp. 73.
37. SEIDL, JULIUS C. *The Effect of Bilingualism on the Measurement of Intelligence.* Doctor's thesis, Fordham University (New York, N.Y.), 1937. (*Dissertations....*1938, pp. 22–4.)
38. BIJOU, SIDNEY W. "A Genetic Study of the Diagnostic Significance of Psychometric Patterns." *Am J Mental Def* 47:171–7 O '42. * (*PA* 17:939)
39. PATTERSON, R. MELCHER. "Analysis of Practice Effect on Readministration of the Grace Arthur Scale in Relation to Academic Achievement of Mentally Deficient Children." *Am J Mental Def* 52:337–41 Ap '48. * (*PA* 22:4953)
40. HAMILTON, MILDRED E. "A Comparison of the Revised Arthur Performance Tests (Form II) and the 1937 Binet." *J Consult Psychol* 13:44–9 F '49. * (*PA* 23:3751)
41. ROSENZWEIG, SAUL; WITH THE COLLABORATION OF KATE LEVINE KOGAN. *Psychodiagnosis: An Introduction to Tests in the Clinical Practice of Psychodynamics,* pp. 34–9. New York: Grune & Stratton, Inc., 1949. Pp. xii, 380. * (*PA* 23:3761)
42. ARTHUR, GRACE. "The Relative Difficulty of Various Tests for Sixty Feebleminded Individuals." *J Clin Psychol* 6:276–9 Jl '50. * (*PA* 25:1883)
43. ARTHUR, GRACE. "Some Factors Contributing to Errors in the Diagnosis of Feeblemindedness." *Am J Mental Def* 54:495–501 Ap '50. * (*PA* 25:405)
44. BENSBERG, GERARD J., AND SLOAN, WILLIAM. "A Study of Wechsler's Concept of 'Normal Deterioration' in Older Mental Defectives." *J Clin Psychol* 6:359–62 O '50. * (*PA* 25:8073)
45. COOK, JOHN MUNSON, AND ARTHUR, GRACE. "Intelligence Ratings for 97 Mexican Children in St. Paul, Minn." *J Excep Child* 18:14–5+ O '51. *
46. MCBREARTY, J. F. *A Comparison of the WISC with the Arthur Performance Scale, Form I, and Their Relationship to the Progressive Achievement Tests.* Master's thesis, Pennsylvania State College (State College, Pa.), 1951.
47. WATSON, ROBERT I. *The Clinical Method in Psychology,* pp. 278–312. New York: Harper & Brothers, 1951. Pp. xii, 779. *

WILLIAM R. GROVE, *Chief, Clinical Psychology Service, Veterans Administration Hospital, Palo Alto, California.*

It is impossible to review this scale adequately without relating its history of development through the years. It is a notable and proud history of painstaking research that documents the professional life of Grace Arthur, a clinical psychologist of distinction.

In my student days the contribution of Binet held the center of the stage in the embryonic field of clinical psychology. At that time the Stanford-Binet (1916) was the tool par excellence of the clinician. But discerning psychologists of those days realized that the Binet told only part of the story. A child's abilities could not always be adequately assessed by a test that relied so heavily upon verbal responses alone. There were subjects who had a specific disability or handicap in the verbal area—such as deaf children, those who spoke a language other than English, or those with severe speech defects as in cerebral palsy—for whom the Stanford-Binet was entirely unsuitable.

And so we were taught to supplement the Binet rating on a child by administering nonverbal tests called performance tests. Such tests typically involved the use of such materials as formboards, pencil mazes, blocks, and other paraphernalia of a similar sort. Using these, we presented the subject with a variety of tasks and problems believed to test his general intelligence. Such tests were often validated by using the Binet as a criterion. In the early days there was a profusion of performance tests from which the psychologist could select. Each was separately standardized, and there was no way to be sure of the comparability of the norms. Then various workers began to assemble groups of performance tests into test batteries intended to be used together. The *Arthur Point Scale of Performance Tests* was one of the better of these batteries.

The Arthur scale consisted of two forms. Form II as originally standardized was designed for retest purposes only, and the norms for it were applicable only to those subjects who had already been tested with Form I. Although Form I proved fairly satisfactory from the first, Form II was less so because its standardization was less adequate and it had several technical weaknesses. It was never extensively used and was eventually discarded.

The *Arthur Point Scale of Performance Tests, Revised Form II* (1947) is a thorough revision and restandardization. In many ways it is an entirely new scale. It consists of five subtests, each separately standardized, combined into a single point scale.

The scale is not one that can be used by an untrained person. The examiner needs to be thoroughly versed in the administration of individual tests in a clinical setting. In addition, in order to manage the examination smoothly and adequately, he must have specific experience in the use of the test materials. The materials provided are of excellent quality and are convenient and easy to use. Directions for administration are entirely adequate. The clinical "bugs" have been worked out by an author who has devoted years of study to the efficient management of such examinations. Instructions for scoring are easy to follow. The tasks presented are intrinsically interesting to children, and, in our experience, easily stimulate adequate effort.

Norms are based upon "the scores of 968 pupils from the same middle-class 'American' district used in standardizing *Form I*." An effort was made to have the selection of these children representative and not biased by fortuitous selective factors. In spite of this care, Arthur believes that Form I is slightly easier than the Revised Form II. This she accounts for by the high motivation that was characteristic of the children used in the restandardization.

In my judgment, the reliability of the scale as a whole is probably fairly high, although the test manual does not present adequate data on this point.

The question of the basic validity of the scale is less clear. Arthur relies for evidence of validity upon the "discriminative value" of each subtest at successive age levels and upon "the agreement of ratings obtained from the *Revised Form II*, with those obtained from *Form I* and with those obtained from the Binet scale." In my opinion such evidence is inconclusive and unsatisfactory. This scale is now in need of rigorous validation studies. Arthur presents "Some Notes on the Use of the Scale" in the test manual that are helpful and suggestive. These could well be used as a basis for further validation studies. In correspondence, Arthur has indicated that she has other unpublished validity data.

In closing, we should note that Arthur has recently completed an adaptation and restandardization of the *Leiter International Performance Scale* which she recommends for use with the Arthur Scale, Revised Form II "to reinforce the measurement of the ability of preschool children." This should prove a welcome addition, for, in our experience, the Arthur scale in both forms is too difficult for adequate measurement of dull preschool children.

For reviews by Andrew W. Brown and Carroll A. Whitmer, see 40:1379; for excerpts from reviews, see 3:271 and 40:1379; for related reviews, see 40:B830, 38:B304, and 36:B19.

[336]

*Canadian Intelligence Examination, 1947 Revision. Ages 3–16; 1940–47; a modification of the 1916 *Stanford Revision of the Binet-Simon Intelligence Scale;* individual; 1 form, '47; no data on reliability; 60¢ per set of test materials; $1.50 per manual ('47); $1 per 50 record forms; cash orders postpaid; nontimed (25–45) minutes; Harry Amoss, Charles G. Stogdill, and Carman E. Stothers; Ryerson Press. *

GWEN F. ARNOLD, *Assistant Professor of Education, University of Wisconsin, Madison, Wisconsin.*

This test, published in 1940 and revised in 1947, is basically a revision of the original *Stanford-Binet Scale*. The revision was undertaken, according to the authors, "to iron out certain existing discrepancies [in the *Stanford-Binet Scale*] and to adjust the content more precisely to the needs of both rural and urban [Canadian] communities." The major changes indicated are these:

a) "Language of instruction used in the presentation of various problems has been simplified." In many instances, this appears at face value to have also simplified the task, as compared with the task in the Stanford-Binet.

b) "Attempt has been made more vigorously to define acceptable responses."

c) "Certain tests in which the element of chance seemed unduly involved have been dropped." These revisions are commendable since they attempt to eliminate two of the weaknesses of the Binet Scale—chance success and subjectivity of scoring.

d) "With a view to the avoidance of local and literary expressions, the word list in the vocabulary test has been selected from conversational language common to both rural and urban communities rather than from a dictionary." While there are advantages in utilizing conversational vocabulary, there is the possibility of less precise differentiation in the higher levels of intelligence.

e) "To reduce the weighting heretofore given acquired literary skills, more mathematical and constructional problems have been introduced." This has greatly increased the nonverbal aspects of the scale, a questionable result, since it tends to reduce its value as a predictive measure of academic aptitude (if this is one of the purposes for which the scale is to be used) It might have been more advantageous to maintain the verbal aspects and to use the *Ontario School Ability Examination,* from which the authors have borrowed a number of items, as a supplementary test if an estimate of nonverbal abilities was desired.

f) "Partial answers have been allowed credits for the purpose of obtaining a more finely graded result as well as for the purpose of eliminating overleniency in the interpretation of responses." The need for partial credits is one that has been recognized for some time by psychologists who have used the Binet scale. The actual value of the credits set here can only be determined through use of the scale.

g) "The mean age of mental maturity has been fixed at 15 instead of 16. This change was made in consideration of the fact that practically all retests of children at 16 and 17 who had been previously tested at 8–13 showed a falling off in the intelligence quotient. The use of 180 as a maximum denominator largely rectifies this diminution and tends to keep the I.Q. constant." In his 1937 revision of the Binet scale, Terman also established 15 as the mean age of subjects 15 years and older.

The Canadian scale was found to have a correlation of .92 with the *Stanford-Binet Scale* when administered to 1,099 children of Canadian school population in grades 1 to 8 inclusive. This would indicate that while this scale is radically revised, it gives highly comparable results with the Stanford-Binet. The scale has proved satisfactory in measuring the intelligence and the school ability of normal, English-speaking Canadian children between the ages of 3 and 16, superior children between the ages 3 and 14, and subnormal children above age 4.

This scale is well standardized and can be used as a substitute test for the *Stanford-Binet Scale* in Canada. The same cultural and vocabulary differences which necessitated the preparation of the Canadian scale would preclude its general application for children in the United States, however; with these considerations in mind it might be used on occasion as an alternate scale for Stanford-Binet.

For excerpts from reviews, see 3:272.

[337]

*The Crichton Vocabulary Scale. Ages 4–11; 1950; individual; 1 form; 15s. per 50; 2s. 6d. per manual; 17s. 6d. per specimen set including 12 tests and a specimen set of the complementary *Coloured Progressive Matrices* (1947) (see 314); purchase tax (British purchasers only) and postage extra; nontimed (15–20) minutes; J. C. Raven; H. K. Lewis & Co., Ltd. (Also distributed by George G. Harrap & Co. Ltd.) *

CHARLOTTE BANKS, *Department of Psychology, University College, London, England.*

The *Crichton Vocabulary Scale,* designed specifically for use with the *Coloured Progressive Matrices,* "is constructed to cover as nearly as possible the same range of intellectual development," namely, that from age 5 to age 11. Indeed, the author claims that it is "suitable for use with persons of sub-normal intelligence, as well as for *all children* [reviewer's italics] under 11 years of age."

The test consists of two series or sets of words, which the child has to explain, each set being arranged in an approximate order of difficulty. The words in Set 1 are identical with the first 40 words in the *Mill Hill Vocabulary Scale*. Those in Set 2 are nearly all new, and have been chosen as being roughly equivalent to the words in Set 1, although "towards the end, the words of Set Two are slightly more difficult to explain than the equivalent words of Set One."

The scale is given as an individual test. When testing young children the words are read to them, one by one, by the tester. Children over 10, however, may read the words aloud to the tester, explaining them as they go.

Although the two series are claimed to be "equivalent," norms are given only for the results of the two sets added together. These norms are based on the results of 608 children, and are in the form of percentile points, which are given for each half year of age from 4½ to 11. It is recommended that, as in the case of the Coloured Matrices, the percentiles should be interpreted in terms of five grades, ranging from Grade I or "verbally superior," the top five per cent, to Grade V or "verbally defective," the bottom five per cent.

Test-retest reliability coefficients are given in the manual, but only for age 6, age 9, and for the years 5 to 10 inclusive. These are as follows: for year 6, $r = .87$; for year 9, $r = .95$; and for the years 5 to 10, $r = .98$. The final figure is, of course, spuriously high, and it is also very probable that memory plays a considerable part in raising the figure at age 6 and age 9. These correlations are based on a very small number of children. Only 35 children were tested at ages 6 and 9, and only 60 over the whole range from 5 to 10—that is, 10 children at each year.

Correlations between this scale and both the *Coloured Progressive Matrices* and the *Revised Stanford-Binet Scale* are also given for the same children. These are: between the Crichton Scale and the Coloured Matrices, at age 6, $r = .53$, at age 9, $r = .65$, and for the ages 5 to 10 inclusive, $r = .94$; between the Crichton Scale and the Stanford-Binet, at age 6, $r = .84$, and at age 9, $r = .79$.

Careful instructions are given for using the

test, and examples of acceptable and unacceptable replies to each word are provided, since, as with all open answer tests of this type, the marking is largely subjective.

The *Crichton Vocabulary Scale* and the *Coloured Progressive Matrices* are sold together as a single set, and a single record form is supplied on which the results of both tests may be entered for each child. Raven claims that:

> While the Matrices Test indicates a person's present capacity for intellectual activity whatever knowledge he has acquired, the Vocabulary Test provides an index of his general cultural attainments. By using the Matrices and Vocabulary Tests together instead of a single verbal test of general intelligence, a child's present capacity for intellectual activity and his acquired fund of verbal information can be assessed separately. As a result, it is possible to estimate more accurately both the validity of the assessments made and the psychological significance of any discrepancy between the two.

It is perhaps unfair to point out that it is hardly an advantage to give two tests together in order that what they both measure may then be assessed separately. Raven has not clearly stated what he means. In any case, few modern psychologists would content themselves, in assessing a child's intelligence, with a purely verbal test, as Raven seems to suggest. There is no doubt, however, that in publishing a test of vocabulary to supplement the *Coloured Progressive Matrices,* the author is meeting a widely recognised demand, although many psychologists would probably agree that the addition of a vocabulary test adds more information about general intelligence than about cultural attainments. For example, in the *Revised Stanford-Binet Scale,* vocabulary shows a consistently high biserial correlation with total test score, from age 6 to the superior adult level.

Until some systematic results are obtainable, it is impossible to assess the "validity of the assessments made" by these two tests. Raven suggests, in the manual, some interesting conclusions which may be drawn in cases where there is a wide discrepancy between the Vocabulary and Matrices scores. These, however, appear to be based on casual observation rather than on any systematic analysis.

W. D. WALL, *Reader in Education, University of Birmingham, Birmingham, England.*

This scale of 80 words for oral presentation to children up to the age of 11 is a development of the *Mill Hill Vocabulary Scale.* It is intended to be used in association with *Progressive Matrices (1947) Sets A, Ab, and B,* and the two are claimed by the author to be an adequate measure of intelligence. Differences between matrix score and vocabulary score, he holds, indicate differences between the child's present capacity for intellectual activity and his acquired fund of verbal information.

This claim should be accepted with some caution. In the handbook to the test, the author gives norms of performance based on 608 children between 4 and 11 years. If my calculations are correctly derived from his data, none of the single increments of score for each half-year group constitutes a significant difference. The same applies to the norms for *Progressive Matrices.* Hence, differences in level between the two tests would have to be considerable to be significant statistically and therefore worth evaluating diagnostically.

A further point is worth making here. In groups of narrow age range, the correlation of vocabulary and matrix scores is relatively low (.53 for 6½ year olds, .65 for 9½ year olds). Hence, observed discrepancies between status on the two tests may well be regression phenomena merely.

Reliability data are given the handbook, and again the exiguousness of the sampling suggests caution. For 35 children of 6½, the test-retest correlation is .87; for 35 children of 9½, it is .95; and for 60 children from 5 to 10 years, .98. In themselves these figures are satisfactory; most of us, however, would regard them as inconclusive evidence that the test can be accepted as anything but an experimental tool.

All this indicates that although the test is promising and convenient in form for clinical work, much research upon it has still to be done. In the meantime, it is a useful supplement or alternative to the vocabulary scales in such batteries as the *Revised Stanford-Binet Scale* or the *Wechsler Intelligence Scale for Children.*

[338]

★Curtis Classification Form. Grades 12–16 and adults; 1951; a disguised intelligence test administered as an interview; individual; Forms A, B; Form A recommended for selection purposes, Form B for clinical use; $3.75 per 100, cash orders postpaid; specimen set free to qualified test users; (10) minutes; James W. Curtis; Science Research Associates, Inc. *

HAROLD G. SEASHORE, *Director, Test Division, The Psychological Corporation, New York, New York.*

This test consists of 15 questions which are

asked of the examinee in the manner of an employee interview. It is supposed to foster rapport and to prevent resentment or "blocking"; nervousness and attempts to "beat the test" are said to be virtually eliminated.

Rating the mental abilities of individuals from the content of interviews has been common practice for many years, with good and bad results. Curtis' test is an attempt to formalize the procedure by providing a scoring method for 10 of the 15 questions asked. The interviewing itself is intended to be informal. Some of the questions are highly structured and presumably the examiner should ask them just as printed; for example, "What is your height?" After recording the reported height, the examiner states the height (as printed on the form) of the average person of appropriate sex and then asks, "Exactly how much above (or below) average is your height?" The reply to this mental arithmetic problem is recorded. After recording the response of the person to a question about the specific type of work in which he is interested, the examiner asks, "In general, what are the most important advantages of that type of work?" The answer to this question is scored 2, 1, or 0 points, according to the criteria mentioned in the manual.

As noted above, Forms A and B are recommended for different purposes. Although the difference in use of the two forms is iterated several times in the manual, the rationale is not given. Six of the 10 scored questions are identical or essentially the same. Perhaps the reason that Form B is not usable in personnel selection is that it contains questions on religion; these are illegal in many places and in bad taste in most.

The reviewer also wonders why the question "What was the highest level of school you completed?" is not scored when level of school attainment is an obvious basis for an estimate of intelligence, one that has been used informally so long that it is almost a classical basis for a first estimate. The manual gives no information regarding the selection of the items or the method for evaluating their contribution to the total score.

The scoring key presents criteria for evaluating each question on the 2, 1, or 0 basis, but evidence is lacking concerning the objectivity of the scoring, a matter of utmost importance in view of the brevity of the test. The manual does point out that with 33 cases given without careful study of the manual, correlation between Curtis scores and Wechsler IQ's was only .74. The standardization is based on 500 individuals, about half of each sex, in the age range of 15 to 61; apparently there was an approximately equal number in each of the five-year intervals from ages 15 to 50. The author states that a correction for chronological age proved superfluous.

Norms for interpretation are presented (a) as ranges of scores which differentiate stated levels of intelligence, (b) as an expectancy table in which the test scores are on one axis and the percentages of persons expected to equal or exceed IQ's of 125, 105, 90, and 70 are on the other; and (c) in terms of suggested job levels for persons with certain scores, this being a dubious extrapolation from *Army General Classification Test* data.

The author estimates that the reliability of the test is at least .80; odd-even values of .76 and .77, for A and B, are given. He asserts that when Form C is ready, test-retest reliability will be obtained; considering the similarity of the Forms A and B, one may ask why this study has not been possible.

The basic validity data for the Curtis test reside in its correlation with the *Wechsler-Bellevue Intelligence Scale*, Form I. This correlation is reported as being .89, $N = 120$. The correlation of Curtis scores with IQ's from either the Wechsler or the *California Capacity Questionnaire* is given as .86, $N = 250$. In the light of the reliability of this short test, these values are so high as to be suspect, a criticism anticipated and remarked upon by the author.

The reviewer feels that Curtis has attempted to fill an important gap in testing. A method for quick determination of mental ability in a natural interview situation is needed. One only wishes that there were more evidence of critical item analysis and that the rationale of the content were established.

[339]

★**The FR-CR Test.** Adults; 1949; a memory test for use in evaluating brain injury; individual; 1 form; memory selections included in manual; $3 per 100 record sheets; $1 per manual (reprinted from *Psychol Service Center J* 1:52–61 S '49); postage extra; (3–5) minutes; Russell Graydon Leiter; Psychological Service Center Press. *

REFERENCES

1. INTERNATIONAL PSYCHOLOGICAL SERVICE CENTER. "The FR-CR Test With Quantitative Scores and a Qualitative Check List for Clinical Use in the Evaluation of Brain Injury." *Psychol Service Center J* 1:52–61 S '49. * (PA 24:2918)

Curtis Classification Form

WILLIAM S. KOGAN, *Chief Psychologist, Veterans Administration Hospital;* and KATE LEVINE KOGAN, *Clinical Psychologist, 6034 44th Ave., N.E.; Seattle, Washington.*

The publishers of this brief memory test, consisting of one paragraph, claim that it is a useful addition to the psychologist's armamentarium. This is to be questioned for several reasons. (*a*) It duplicates in type of material and method of scoring a part of the *Wechsler Memory Scale.* The latter has the advantage of more extensive standardization and a varied sampling of different forms of behavior involving memory. The FR-CR is too brief and limited a sample of behavior from which to obtain clinical impressions. (*b*) Although several inferences are made concerning the usefulness of the test in eliciting qualitative clinical material effective in delineating individuals with organic brain defect, the only substantiating material presented in the test manual is one reference to the literature; this states in general terms that it was found to be "fairly sensitive" to such things as circumstantiality, blocking, pseudoprofundity, and so forth. It would seem that an experienced clinician would be in a position to obtain this material from tests useful in other ways as well. (*c*) It is inferred that the addition of a controlled recall section makes possible the evaluation of personality organization. The test manual notes that this addition was made 15 years ago, but comments further in another place that a shortage of time made it impossible to evaluate the hypothesis. (*d*) Although reservations are made concerning the practice, provision is made for the calculation of an MA and IQ. It is interesting to note in this connection that the FR-CR is termed a useful addition to the verbal section of the Wechsler-Bellevue with implied equivalence to Wechsler IQ's, yet the FR-CR has been standardized against the *Revised Stanford-Binet,* whose IQ scores are known to deviate from those of the Wechsler-Bellevue in specific ways.

Because this test is new the reviewers arranged to have it administered experimentally to a series of adult veterans by three examiners. They were in agreement that although the test was brief and easy to use, it did not provide information or elicit behavior which was not secured by procedures already in routine use.

In summary the publishers of the FR-CR test infer that this 3- to 4-minute sample of behavior is probably useful in eliciting information concerning intellectual level, personality organization, and organic brain impairment. Poorly supported inferences are an unfortunate basis for the publication of a test procedure for general use.

[340]

★**Full-Range Picture Vocabulary Test.** Ages 2 and over; 1948; individual; Forms A, B; no data on reliability and validity with test (for data presented elsewhere by the authors, see *1–9* below); no manual; $5 per set of testing materials; separate answer sheets must be used; $1.10 per 25 answer sheets; $4 per 100; postage extra; nontimed (10–15) minutes; Robert B. Ammons and Helen S. Ammons; Southern Universities Press. *

REFERENCES

1. AMMONS, ROBERT B., AND AMMONS, HELEN S. "The Full-Range Picture Vocabulary Test." Abstract. *Am Psychol* 4:267–8 Jl '49. * (PA 23:6202, title only)
2. AMMONS, ROBERT B., AND HOLMES, JAMES CLIFFORD. "The Full-Range Picture Vocabulary Test: III, Results for a Preschool-Age Population." *Child Develop* 20:5–14 Mr '49. * (PA 24:2226)
3. AMMONS, ROBERT B., AND HUTH, RICHARD W. "The Full-Range Picture Vocabulary Test: I, Preliminary Scale." *J Psychol* 28:51–64 Jl '49. * (PA 24:424)
4. COPPINGER, NEIL WILSON. *The Full-Range Picture Vocabulary Test: A Normative Study of Southern Negro Children.* Master's thesis, Tulane University (New Orleans, La.), 1949. (*Abstracts of Theses 1949,* p. 86.)
5. AMMONS, ROBERT B., AND AGUERO, ABELARDO. "The Full-Range Picture Vocabulary Test: VII, Results for a Spanish-American School-Age Population." *J Social Psychol* 32:3–10 Ag '50. * (PA 25:3806)
6. AMMONS, ROBERT B.; ARNOLD, PAUL R.; AND HERMANN, ROBERT S. "The Full-Range Picture Vocabulary Test: IV, Results for a White School Population." *J Clin Psychol* 6:164–9 Ap '50. * (PA 24:6134)
7. AMMONS, ROBERT B.; LARSON, WILLIAM L.; AND SHEARN, CHARLES R. "The Full-Range Picture Vocabulary Test: V, Results for an Adult Population." *J Consult Psychol* 14:150–5 Ap '50. * (PA 24:5601)
8. AMMONS, ROBERT B., AND MANAHAN, NEIL. "The Full-Range Picture Vocabulary Test: VI, Results for a Rural Population." *J Ed Res* 44:14–21 S '50. * (PA 25:3154)
9. AMMONS, ROBERT B., AND RACHIELE, LEO D. "The Full-Range Picture Vocabulary Test: II, Selection of Items for Final Scales." *Ed & Psychol Meas* 10:307–19 su '50. * (PA 25:5821)
10. HOLDEN, RAYMOND H. "Improved Methods in Testing Cerebral Palsied Children." *Am J Mental Def* 56:349–53 O '51. * (PA 26:2184)

WILLIAM D. ALTUS, *Associate Professor of Psychology and Chairman of the Department, Santa Barbara College, University of California, Santa Barbara, California.*

One may infer from the publications of Ammonses that they wished to construct a multiple choice picture vocabulary test which would measure the same functions as does the vocabulary section of the 1937 Stanford-Binet. They have reported data which indicates that the two forms of the picture vocabulary test correlate quite well with this criterion. In their discussion of the standardization of the picture test in the mimeographed sheet which accompanies the test, the authors report an *r* of .95 with the Stanford-Binet vocabulary test. This correlation coefficient, based on an N of 44, looks spuriously high when one considers that two fallible instruments are involved. However, the correlations reported for samples of a rural population (*8*) and a bilingual, Spanish speaking group (5) run in the .80's. These latter figures appear to be more reasonable and conservative and doubtless represent the relative validity of the picture test when the vocabulary section of the Stanford-Binet is used as the criterion. When the criterion is changed to the vocabulary subtest of the *Wechsler-Bellevue Intelligence Scale,* the same sort of correlations emerge for a sample of the adult population, .86 for Form A of the picture vocabulary test and .85 for Form B (7).

Although the number of words involved in the picture vocabulary test is relatively small, the reliability is quite adequate, a finding which is not surprising in the area of vocabulary testing. For an adult sample, the authors report an r of .93 between Forms A and B. For the standardizing groups, the median odd-even reliability for the various age levels is .81 (6). The coefficient for the full range of talent came to the spuriously high figure of .987. Reliability would seem to be sufficiently taken care of; the correlations reported in the preceding paragraph for "validity" would be prima facie evidence of fairly adequate reliability anyway.

The authors have, then, constructed a test based on pictures, which measures approximately the same factor or factors which underlie the respective vocabulary tests of Terman and of Wechsler. In order for it to be acceptable for anything except research purposes, the authors must show that their test can serve certain groups of people or certain desired ends more effectively than can the criterion tests which have been used in deriving the new one. The authors have not yet done this. They emphasize the speed with which the test may be administered, saying that "it takes only fifteen minutes or less to administer." If the authors wish the picture vocabulary to supplant the Stanford-Binet vocabulary, this "fifteen minutes or less" is much too slow. During World War II, the writer was chief psychologist in an Army training center through which over 15,000 adult male illiterates passed. All of these who could speak English were given the Stanford-Binet vocabulary test. Those who administered this test had to study the acceptable and unacceptable responses in the Terman-Merrill manual until they could score the individual answers of illiterates plus or zero without writing down the answers. The average time for administering the Terman vocabulary test in this fashion was *three* minutes, not "fifteen or less." Thus, the criterion test against which the authors validated this new one is much more efficient in terms of time of administration—if the person administering the Stanford-Binet vocabulary is properly and thoroughly trained in its use. This point would not be made were it not that the authors in their publications and in the mimeographed sheet which accompanies this test make much of the rapidity with which the test may be given.

Ammons and Agüero note in one article that Spanish speaking American children of Mexican ancestry do considerably poorer on the picture vocabulary test than do monoglot Americans of the same chronological age. Similar findings have been reported numerous times by many psychologists, including the writer whose conclusions were based on his work with Army illiterates. The picture vocabulary test suffers the same limitations as do other personally administered vocabulary tests when they are given to certain bilingual groups. Setting up new norms for deficient bilinguals, as the Ammonses propose for those of Mexican ancestry, does not improve the efficacy or usefulness of the test.

WILLIAM M. CRUICKSHANK, *Director, Education for Exceptional Children, School of Education, Syracuse University, Syracuse, New York.*

This test, designed to give a rapid estimate of verbal comprehension, has been in use for only two years and as yet has not met the crucial test of clinical experimentation. It consists of 16 plates each with four separate cartoon-like drawings on it. The testee is asked to indicate by word or gesture which of the four pictures best illustrates the meaning of a given word. Approximately 80 words are used in each of the two parallel forms which cover the range of verbal abilities from early infancy to the superior adult level. Items are given an approximate age placement, but this is only intended to facilitate the mechanical aspect of testing since the test is actually a point scale.

The test meets a need felt by clinicians working in the field of the mental testing of persons with speech handicaps since it is essentially nonverbal in the sense that the testee need not say a word during the performance. The cartoon-like nature of the drawings should have an intrinsic interest value for children. Also, as the author mentions, it is very easy to administer. The author reports that proficient examiners were able to test three or four children an hour with both this test and the Stanford-Binet or Wechsler vocabulary.

Admirable also is the designers' thorough and meaningful standardization procedure. The limitation of a circumscribed geographical sample from around the Denver area and from a rural area of Nebraska does not appear to be a serious handicap. A careful breakdown of the standardization population made it possible to include in the final norms an adequate sample of rural subjects. Then too, 80 Spanish-American and 80 Negro children have been included in the final standardization norms. The author rejected items for the final scale if they showed inadequate discrimination in per cent passing between successive age levels, regional bias, sex differences in difficulty, ambiguity of denotation, or poor discrimination at one age level even though the same item was satisfactory at another level.

For Form A of the final scale, the correlation with the Stanford-Binet vocabulary raw score was .91 and for Form B it was .93. Since Stanford vocabulary scores have a correlation of .81 with the mental age of their scale as a whole, the validity of the Ammons as a measure of verbal intelligence is not as outstanding as the correlation might suggest since it is twice removed. Taking this into account, however, the scale still offers a satisfactory estimate of the desired verbal comprehension. The total score on the test can be transcribed into mental age scores at the younger levels and percentiles at the adult level.

The present reviewer considers this test valuable as a quick verbal intelligence screening device in industry and in the armed services and as a means of testing persons seriously handicapped by a speech defect or by upper extremity disabilities.

[341]
*Gesell Developmental Schedules. Ages 4 weeks to 6 years; 1925-49; individual; also called *Gesell Maturity Scale, Gesell Norms of Development, Gesell Tests, Preschool Child Development Scale, Preschool Child Test, Yale Psycho-Clinic Developmental Schedules, Yale Tests of Child Development,* and other variations; (20-40) minutes; Arnold Gesell and others.
a) 1925 SERIES. 1925; the authors consider the 1925 Series out of date and superseded by the 1940 Series (see *c* below); manual, *The Mental Growth of the Preschool Child* (see *1* below) is out of print; $65 per set of testing materials (listed in publisher's catalog as *Pre-School Child Test*), postage extra; C. H. Stoelting Co.
b) 1938 SERIES. 1925-38; manual, *The Psychology of Early Growth* ('38—see *13* below), out of print; test materials out of print; Marietta Apparatus Co.
c) 1940 SERIES. 1925-49; manuals: *The First Five Years of Life* ('40—see *20* below) and *Developmental Diagnosis,* Second Edition ('47—see *31* below); $68.50 per set of testing materials; 80¢ per specimen set of printed materials and record forms; 50¢ per revised general instructions booklet ('49); postage extra; Psychological Corporation. *

REFERENCES
1–28. See 3:276.
29. KASAMBI, KAMALA. "Suggestions for Improving the Technique of Child Testing." *Indian J Psychol* 11:191-200 Jl-O '36. * (*PA* 11:2483)
30. GERSTEIN, REVA APPLEBY. "An Analysis of Infant Behavioural Development." Abstract. *B Can Psychol Assn* 5:73-5 O '45. * (*PA* 20:938, title only)
31. GESELL, ARNOLD, AND AMATRUDA, CATHERINE S. *Developmental Diagnosis: Normal and Abnormal Child Development: Clinical Methods and Pediatric Applications,* Second Edition. New York: Paul B. Hoeber, Inc., 1947. Pp. xvi, 496. * (*PA* 22:230)
32. ESCALONA, SIBYLLE. "The Predictive Value of Psychological Tests in Infancy; A Report on Clinical Findings." Abstract. *Am Psychol* 3:281 Jl '48. * (*PA* 22:5366, title only)
33. ESCALONA, SIBYLLE. "The Use of Infant Tests for Predictive Purposes." *B Menninger Clinic* 14:117-28 Jl '50. * (*PA* 25:5387)

For reviews by Nancy Bayley and Florence M. Teagarden, see 3:276; for related reviews, see 3:277-80 and 40:B912-6.

[342]
★The Immediate Test: A Quick Verbal Intelligence Test. Adults; 1951; individual; orally administered; 1 form; $1 per 25, postage extra; 25¢ per specimen set, postpaid; (5) minutes; Raymond J. Corsini: Sheridan Supply Co. *

REFERENCES
1. CORSINI, RAYMOND. "The Immediate Test." *J Clin Psychol* 7:127-30 Ap '51. * (*PA* 25:7778)

JEROME E. DOPPELT, *Assistant Director, Test Division, The Psychological Corporation, New York, New York.*

This is a vocabulary test consisting of 66 words grouped into 11 sections. Each section corresponds to a "mental year," with years 10 through 20 represented. The score on the test is the number of words below the basal year plus the words actually defined correctly by the subject. This raw score may be converted to MA or IQ by means of a table printed on the test. There is no scoring key. It is simply suggested that the examiner ask himself, "Does the subject know what the word means?"

Since the determination of the MA or IQ is ultimately dependent on the proper allocation of words to mental years, the procedure used to assign the words is of considerable importance. However, the manual is woefully inadequate on this point. It is stated that the difficulty of words was determined by noting "the percent of passing individuals at each mental age." The numbers and kinds of cases are not given. A journal article cited as a reference gives a rather confusing picture of several different difficulty analyses. One of these studies was apparently made with 104 subjects distributed over at least eight mental age levels. One can only say that the number of cases at each mental age must have been remarkably small.

All of the statistical data are based on male prison populations. The test-retest reliability is reported as .90, and correlations with other tests such as Otis, Terman List and Wechsler-Bellevue range from .77 to .91. Unfortunately, the author does not give means and standard deviations either on the other tests or on his own test, so the reader is left to wonder about the effects of range on the correlation coefficients. Before these coefficients are accepted, further verification of the findings based on other populations, preferably with means and standard deviations given, should be obtained.

The reviewer finds great difficulty in accepting the author's statement that vocabulary "is less affected by culture than most kinds of material." This difficulty is enhanced by finding words like 'borsht" and "fid" in the test. One can hardly accept these words as "culture-free."

There are a number of inconsistencies in the short manual. It is stated that the test should be announced in a manner that does not mention "intelligence" or "test." Yet at the top of the list of words, which the subject is permitted to see if he wishes, is the subtitle, "A Quick Verbal Intelligence Test." There is also a certain inconsistency between the statement that the test "is a laboratory technique and requires proper administrative procedures" and the subjective scoring system.

In the reviewer's opinion, there is nothing in the manual which would justify confidence either in the mental age equivalents or the IQ's obtained from this test.

IVAN NORMAN MENSH, *Assistant Professor of Medical Psychology, Washington University Medical School, St. Louis, Missouri.*

This test is described by its author as a quick verbal intelligence test—"an emergency clinical instrument." Consisting of 66 words, six at each age level from 10 through 20 and ranging in difficulty from "zebra" to "gecko," the test is a vocabulary measure designed as an age scale. Mental age and IQ values are immediately available on the single-sheet form on which the subject's identifying data and responses are recorded. The two-page manual consists of brief statements on the advantages of a vocabulary test as a measure of intellectual status; a description of the test; its construction in terms of word selection, difficulty, discriminating power of the individual words, validity, and reliability; and directions for administration and scoring. The author suggests that, according to the data from the standardization samples, which were male reformatory and prison inmates, *The Immediate Test* is suitable for adults with IQ's between 75 and 125. The standardization samples had also been administered the Otis, the Terman vocabulary, Form L of the Stanford-Binet, and Forms I and II of the Wechsler-Bellevue. With N's of 50 to 300 the correlations of *The Immediate Test* with the criterion tests range from .77 to .91 for 12 samples. Test-retest reliability on 137 prisoners is reported as .90.

Unlike many brief tests, this rapid measure is not an abbreviated technique derived from a parent test but was specifically designed as a short test. Thus there are no previous data available on which to judge the merits of Corsini's vocabulary scale. Only cross validation on samples other than those used in the standardization can provide adequate demonstration of the validity and reliability of the scale for other elements of our test population. The test has been introduced so recently that this necessary evidence has not yet been accumulated. Finally, one caution recognized and mentioned by the test author should be stressed. He states that the simplicity of administration of the scale suits it to the needs of workers without training in psychometrics, "but its simplicity ought not to be confused with the great difficulty of adequately determining intelligence." There is danger in the evaluation of intelligence by untrained individuals who do not recognize the limitations of brief measures sampling a single area of intellectual functioning.

[343]
*Intelligence Tests for Children. Ages 2–11; 1945–50; formerly called *Intelligence Tests for Young Children*; 1 form; requires only such apparatus "that can readily be found or made in the school or home"; 5s. per manual ('50—same as the 1948 edition [see 3 below]); (30) minutes; C. W. Valentine; Methuen & Co. Ltd.

REFERENCES
1. WAKELAM, B. B. "The Application of a New Intelligence Test in an Infant School and the Prediction of Backwardness." *Brit J Ed Psychol* 14:142–50 N '44. * (PA 19:1355)
2. VALENTINE, C. W. *Intelligence Tests for Young Children, First and Second Editions.* London: Methuen & Co. Ltd., 1945, 1946. Pp. xii, 67. * (PA 19:3520) [The second edition is a reprinting of the first edition.]
3. VALENTINE, C. W. *Intelligence Tests for Children, Third and Fourth Editions.* London: Methuen & Co. Ltd., 1948, 1950. Pp. xiii, 81. * (PA 25:4596) [The fourth edition is a reprinting of the third edition.]

For excerpts from reviews, see 345; for excerpts from reviews of an earlier edition, see 344 and 3:283.

Immediate Test

[344]

[*Re* Intelligence Tests for Children.] VALENTINE, C. W. **Intelligence Tests for Young Children, First and Second Editions.** London: Methuen & Co. Ltd., 1945, 1946. Pp. xii, 68. * (*PA* 19:3520) [The second edition is a reprinting of the first edition.] For latest edition, see 345.

Lancet 249:80 Jl 21 '45. Professor Valentine has done the educationists a good service by collecting together a number of standard tests for young children, adding to them some new tests, and making a new scale of tests. These range from tests for children of eighteen months to children of eleven years, and they are meant to be given by teachers. They call for only the simplest equipment and his hope is that in this way every child will be tested three times in the years from his nursery school up to his entry into the senior school. In a sense, it is "utility" intelligence testing. The reader is given a clear idea of what a test situation should be like, what are the necessary safeguards to be observed, and the commoner pitfalls and misconceptions are as honestly faced as they can be in the brief space of so small a book as this. The instructions, both for giving the test and for scoring it, are clear and concise. They are nevertheless not entirely unambiguous; and here and there the author rather breezily disposes of the need for absolute standardisation. He wisely makes the point that at the very young end of the scale, the rapport is all-important, and in his readiness to approximate and subsequently correct at a later test, he probably underestimates the high degree of accuracy obtainable by an expert working with say the Gesell material. He will, however, be able to add to his knowledge of the young child, and, wisely used, these tests should go far to prevent any failure in *early* recognition of marked deviations from normal ability.

Nature 156:349 S 22 '45. John Cohen. * Although the scale is intended chiefly for teachers, it is also meant for the use of that *rara avis,* an "intelligent parent," eager to weigh the native talent of his offspring. Apart from four new tests, all the material is borrowed, often with slight modifications, from Burt, Gesell, Stutsman and from the Merrill-Palmer and Terman-Merrill scales. In many cases new age assignments have been given. As in the Binet scale, the tests are scored on a pass-fail principle, and all test items are given equal weight, though no evidence is offered that they deserve it. A practical advantage is the simplicity of the apparatus required. The reader may be surprised not to find in a book of this kind, where the emphasis is upon intellectual ability, any reference to the work of Dr. Charlotte Bühler, for Dr. Bühler's aim is to judge the degree of maturity attained by the child's personality as a whole, including its cognitive aspects. A few of the "tests," for example, bowel and bladder control, are scarcely tests at all in the sense of sampling responses in a standardized situation, for success in them depends on habits acquired under varied conditions of training. Without further evidence, one cannot therefore regard them as indexes of basic ability. The validity of the "sentence completion" test at age six is also questionable, since it requires the highly specific ability to use two prepositions. One intriguing point is the author's statement (p. 10) that he found a "very close correspondence between very early tests (at only 12 or even 6 months) with tests of intelligence at 10 years and later." One would like to know precisely which tests were given at the age of six months to obtain such good predictions of later ability. * Prof. Valentine admits that the age assignments are not altogether satisfactory, especially in the very early years. Thus the "action agent" test at age three requires the infant to know the meaning of such words as "gallops," "aches," "explodes," "roars," etc. This surely deserves a higher age assignment than the Binet test in which the child is required to point to its nose, eyes, mouth, hair and knee, or the one in which the child has to put on his shoes. Some brief experiments by the reviewer confirm this view. Nevertheless, the scale may be warmly recommended for further experimentation and clinical use. It may be justified as a device for roughly gauging the general ability of young children, the estimates improving in accuracy as the child grows older. Much careful work is, however, needed, as the author would doubtless agree, before all the tests could claim a sound theoretical foundation.

For an additional review, see 3:283.

[345]

*[*Re* Intelligence Tests for Children.] VALENTINE, C. W. **Intelligence Tests for Children, Third and Fourth Editions.** London: Methuen & Co. Ltd., 1948, 1950. Pp. xiii, 81. 5s. * (*PA* 25:4596) ["I have added tests for the ages of 12, 13, 14, and 15, which should provide ample material for the bright 11-year-olds and the average 12- or 13-year-olds."—Preface to the Third Edition. The fourth edition is a reprinting of the third edition which is a revision of *Intelligence Tests for Young Children.*]

Brit J Ed Psychol 18:169 N '48. C(yril) B(urt). * In its original form the book sought to provide a variety of simple and interesting tests for children from the ages of 1½ to 11. The new edition includes tests for older children up to the age of 15. Thus the book can now be used for testing pupils of 11 plus who are being selected for an appropriate type of secondary education; and the addition of problems for higher mental ages makes it possible to examine brighter children at the age of transference. One feature of the original series has appealed particularly to teachers in these post-war years; it dispensed with all elaborate apparatus that might require to be imported from abroad or purchased at some expense. Most of the test-material needed was furnished by the book itself in the shape of pictures or diagrams. For the rest nothing was required except a little simple apparatus such as can easily be found or made in the school or at home. This admirable principle has been preserved in selecting new tests for the higher ages. They include problems of well-established types, such as Reasoning, Analogies, Absurdities, together with Performance Tests including Mazes; but the mazes and other diagrams are printed in the book itself, and nothing else is wanted but cards cut to the appropriate shapes, and occasionally a pencil and paper. In the past, many of the test-scales produced for school pupils have been constructed either by laboratory psychologists with little or no teaching experience, or by teachers not very familiar with modern scientific principles for standardizing such tests. Professor Valentine's tests have a double advantage; they can claim the scientific merits of a scale that is constructed by one who is a leading educational psychologist; at the same time they show a first-hand practical appreciation of the needs of the teacher in the classroom.

Brit J Psychol, Gen Sect 39:172 Mr '49. S. J. F. P(hilpott). * an enlarged edition of a well-known and valued book. The additional material consists of tests for children beyond the 11-year range. As the author notes in his preface, it is nowadays advisable to have tests available for assessing the bright youngsters likely to be entering Grammar Schools or Technical High Schools. By the addition of tests up to the 15-year level enough material has been given adequately to stretch the brighter 11-year olds and of course the more ordinary children at a higher level. Full instructions are given with all necessary diagrams. The tests involve little other apparatus and none which cannot easily be found in school.

J Ed (London) 80:700 D '48. E. M. Bartlett. * contains little that is new, but is a collection of well-standardized individual tests, from other scales, for children to the ages of 15. This book in its turn may be "dangerous." Prof. Valentine is himself aware of the danger, as is indicated in his remark in the preface that "for a precise assessment of a child's intelligence quotient the expert tester is needed," but his own suggestion that the scale can be used by teachers and even by an "intelligent parent" may open the way to all sorts of abuse, especially as it seems generally true that the less one knows about the theory of intelligence the greater one's faith in the result of a single test.

Scottish Ed J 31:757 D 24 '48. In a July 1946 issue of this *Journal* Emeritus Professor Valentine's new battery of intelligence tests was welcomed as a useful alternative to the Terman-Merrill scales. By adding tests for the ages 12, 13, 14 and 15, Prof. Valentine has in the new enlarged edition still further increased the usefulness of the original work.

For reviews of the first edition, see 344 and 3:283.

[346]
Kent Series of Emergency Scales. Ages 5–7, 6–8, 7–10, 9–14; 1932–46; also called E-G-Y Scales; individual; 4 levels; 1 form, '46; $2.50 per 100 of any one level (Scales B and C are combined); 60¢ per manual ('46—contains the four scales); postpaid; (15) minutes; Grace H. Kent; Psychological Corporation. *
a) SCALE A. Ages 5–7. 1944–46; formerly called *Andover School-Entrance Test.*
b) SCALES B AND C. Ages 6–8, 7–10; 1946.
c) SCALE D. Ages 9–14; 1932–46; a revision of *Emergency Test* (also called *Kent E-G-Y Test*).

REFERENCES

1–26. See 3:284.
27. HUNT, W. A.; WITTSON, C. L.; HARRIS, H. I.; SOLOMON, P.; AND JACKSON, M. M. "Psychometric Procedures in the Detection of the Neuropsychiatrically Unfit." *U S Naval Med B* 41:471–80 Mr '43. *
28. DEMAREST, RUTH. "Differences in Results on Five Standard Tests Administered to Anglo-American and Spanish-American 7th Grade Boys." Abstract. *Am Psychol* 1:244 Jl '46. * (*PA* 20:3928, title only)
29. COFER, CHARLES N., AND BIEGEL, MARK M. "A Study of the Kent and Buck Screen Tests of Mental Ability in Relation to Otis and Stanford Achievement Test Scores." *J Consult Psychol* 12:187–9 My–Je '48. * (*PA* 22:4943)
30. HUNT, WILLIAM A.; KLEBANOFF, SEYMOUR G.; MENSH, IVAN N.; AND WILLIAMS, MEYER. "The Validity of Some Abbreviated Individual Intelligence Scales." *J Consult Psychol* 12:48–52 Ja–F '48. * (*PA* 22:3032)
31. KNOTT, JOHN R., AND CANNICOTT, RICHARD G. "The Application of Brief Tests of Intelligence in the Psychiatric Clinic." Abstract. *Am Psychol* 3:365 Ag '48. * (*PA* 23:777, title only)
32. RUDOLF, G. DE M. "The Kent and Other Tests Used on the Same Subjects." *J Mental Sci* 44:452–8 Ap '48. * (*PA* 23:1295)
33. WRIGHT, H. F.; MACPHEE, H. M.; AND CUMMINGS, S. B., JR. "The Relationship Between the Kent EGY and the Bellevue

Verbal Scale." *J Abn & Social Psychol* 44:223-30 Ap '49. * (PA 23:5533)
34. KNOTT, JOHN R.; CANNICOTT, RICHARD G.; UMBERGER, JOHN P.; AND BILODEAU, INA McD. "Brief Tests of Intelligence in the Psychiatric Clinic." *J Clin Psychol* 7:123-6 Ap '51. * (PA 25:8099)

IVAN NORMAN MENSH, *Assistant Professor of Medical Psychology, Washington University Medical School, St. Louis, Missouri.*

Kent's manual for her series opens with a statement which immediately defines her goals in devising the test. She has carefully stated that the E-G-Y was offered "as a preliminary measure....useful in helping the examiner to decide at what mental level to start the more formal examination; and occasionally it may serve to indicate how exhaustive an examination is required." Introduced in 1932, revised in 1942, and increased by three new scales with additional norms added in 1944 and 1945, the Kent Series were widely used during World War II. The press of military and naval demands often required a brief, "simple and informal mental test" as a screening device in selection of recruits. In this setting the Kent tests were extremely valuable as a step beyond the initial screening of group intelligence measures, providing a clinical tool for face to face examining of suspected mental defectives.

In actual practice, when used with service personnel the Kent Series have shown correlations of .73 and .74 with the Wechsler-Bellevue Verbal Scale and the Stanford-Binet, respectively, both in the U.S. and in England. These correlations have led various investigators (e.g., Wright, MacPhee, and Cummings (*33*) and Rudolf (*32*)) to conclude that the E-G-Y does not sufficiently discriminate levels of mental functioning and cannot be used in place of longer tests. Against these studies are those by Hunt, Wittson, Harris, Solomon, and Jackson (*27*), Lewinski (*13, 16, 21*), Cofer and Biegel (*29*), and others. Hunt, for example, reported that predictions of Wechsler-Bellevue mental age from Kent E-G-Y performance showed an average error of six months or less. It should be recalled that Kent did not intend the E-G-Y as another test, but rather as a preliminary measure. With this specific goal in mind, the arguments against the Kent Series seem to have less weight.

Finally, unlike many, if not most, test authors, Kent has devoted a significant portion of her manual to "Suggestions for Further Development." She points out that she "is not prepared to carry its development further, but is hoping that it will be taken up by some younger person."

The critical thinking about test construction which has gone into Kent's suggestions for further development can well serve as a model for other authors.

This method of using the available material—the arrangement of questions covering a wide range of difficulty in overlapping scales which carry independent norms—is believed to be a more important contribution than any actual test-material offered by the writer. Almost any particular question is likely to lose its significance with the passage of time, and probably the best of scales should be brought up to date and restandardized at intervals of not over twenty years; but the system here proposed is capable of indefinite expansion. This set-up of scales is one which effects the maximal usefulness of every question and the minimal use of inappropriate questions, while at the same time permitting the utmost economy of time.

For a review by Charles N. Cofer, see 3:284.

[347]

★**The Leiter Adaptation of Arthur's Stencil Design Test.** Adults; 1945-49; a subtest of *Leiter-Partington Adult Performance Scale* (see 350); individual; 1 form, '49; manual ('49); $3 per set of stencils and designs; $3 per 100 record cards; $3 per 100 qualitative check lists for evaluating brain injury; $1 per manual; manual and record cards same as for *Leiter-Partington Adult Performance Scale;* postage extra; (25-30) minutes; Russell Graydon Leiter; Psychological Service Center Press. *

REFERENCES
1. ADJUTANT GENERAL'S OFFICE, CLASSIFICATION AND REPLACEMENT BRANCH, PERSONNEL RESEARCH SECTION. "The New Army Individual Test of General Ability." *Psychol B* 41:532-8 O '44. * (PA 19:581)

J Consult Psychol 14:162 Ap '50. *Laurance F. Shaffer.* This upward revision of the stencil design test is substantially the "shoulder patches" item of the *Army Individual Test.* As a measure of ability in male adults, it shows a correlation with the Revised Stanford-Binet of .62. Norms, in terms of MA and IQ are for adult young men only. An interesting clinical check list (by Neal Watson) calls attention to observations of ability to shift, synthesize, plan, and analyze, that may be useful indicators of brain injury.

[348]

★**The Leiter Adaptation of the Painted Cube Test.** Adults (especially with IQ's over 110); 1941-49; a variation of *Imaged Cube Test* which appeared about 1900; a subtest of *Leiter-Partington Adult Performance Scale* (see 350); individual; 1 form, '49; manual ('49); $6 per set of 24 cubes; $3 per set of model cards; $3 per 100 record cards; $1 per manual; manual and record cards same as for *Leiter-Partington Adult Performance Scale;* postage extra; nontimed (10-15) minutes; author of original test not known; adaptation by Russell Graydon Leiter; Psychological Service Center Press. *

REFERENCES
1. ADJUTANT GENERAL'S OFFICE, CLASSIFICATION AND REPLACEMENT BRANCH, PERSONNEL RESEARCH SECTION. "The New Army Individual Test of General Ability." *Psychol B* 41:532-8 O '44. * (PA 19:581)

J Consult Psychol 14:162 Ap '50. *Laurance F. Shaffer.* Although some versions of the cube-assembly tests are about 50 years old, the present compact and useful form was devised by Leiter in 1941, and served as a part of the *Army Individual Test.* The revision differs from the well-known World War I form by using colored pictures of cube assemblies as the models, instead of solid blocks. Data on 256 male veterans show that the test correlates .57 with the Revised Stanford-Binet, and that it has superior discrimination at the upper IQ levels, above 110. Norms are available only for adult young men.

[349]

*Leiter International Performance Scale. Ages 2–18; 1936–48; individual; 54 tests which can be given without language or pantomime; 1 form, revised, '48; revised manual ('48); test materials are in three trays: Tray 1 (tests for years 2–7), Tray 2 (tests for years 8–12), Tray 3 (tests for years 14–18); $27.50 per tray; $3 per 100 record cards; $3 per manual; $8 per carrying case; postage extra; (30–60) minutes; Russell Graydon Leiter; Psychological Service Center Press. *

REFERENCES

1. LEITER, RUSSELL G. *The Leiter International Performance Scale.* University of Hawaii Bulletin, Vol. 15, No. 7; Research Publications, No. 13. Appendix by Stanley D. Porteus. Honolulu, Hawaii: the University, May 1936. Pp. 42. Paper. (*PA* 10:6018)
2. BOEHNCKE, FREIDA C. *A Comparative Study of the Goodenough Drawing Test and The Leiter International Performance Scale.* Master's thesis, University of Southern California (Los Angeles, Calif.), 1938.
3. CRAIG, ANNE L. *A Study of the Performance of Mexican Children on the Leiter International Performance Scale.* Master's thesis, University of Southern California (Los Angeles, Calif.), 1938.
4. LEITER, RUSSELL GRAYDON. *A Comparative Study of the General Intelligence of Caucasian, Chinese, and Japanese Children as Measured by the Leiter International Performance Scale.* Doctor's thesis, University of Southern California (Los Angeles, Calif.), 1938. (*Abstracts of Dissertations....1938*, 1939, pp. 25–9.)
5. BENEFIEL, ROBERT C. *A Study of the Responses of Mentally Retarded Children on the Leiter International Performance Scale.* Master's thesis, University of Southern California (Los Angeles, Calif.), 1939.
6. DARBY, HAROLD E. *The General Intelligence of American-Born Japanese Children in California as Measured by the Leiter International Performance Scale.* Master's thesis, University of Southern California (Los Angeles, Calif.), 1940.
7. GOULARD, STANLEY ELLSWORTH. *The General Intelligence of American-Born Japanese Children in California Measured by the Leiter International Performance Scale.* Master's thesis, University of Southern California (Los Angeles, Calif.), 1940.
8. LEITER, RUSSELL GRAYDON. *The Leiter International Performance Scale: Vol. 1, Directions for the Application and Scoring of Individual Tests.* Santa Barbara, Calif.: Santa Barbara State College Press, 1940. Pp. ix, 95. (*PA* 14:3780)
9. MOLINO, HENRY SAMUEL. *The Leiter International Performance Scale as a Contribution to Educational Anthropology.* Master's thesis, University of Southern California (Los Angeles, Calif.), 1940.
10. DEAN, CORINNE CALOYTHA. *A Study of the Performance of Negro Children on the Leiter Performance Scale.* Master's thesis, University of Southern California (Los Angeles, Calif.), 1941.
11. PORTEUS, STANLEY D.; WITH THE ASSISTANCE OF MARY HUNTER AND COLIN J. HERRICK. *The Practice of Clinical Psychology,* pp. 200–6. New York: American Book Co., 1941. Pp. ix, 579. *
12. WILLIAMS, RUTH MARGARET. *A Clinical Examination of the Leiter International Performance Scale.* Master's thesis, University of Southern California (Los Angeles, Calif.), 1941.
13. MICHEA, CLAUDE ANGUS. *The Intelligence of Nine- and Ten-Year-Old Mexican Children Measured by the Leiter International Performance.* Master's thesis, University of Southern California (Los Angeles, Calif.), 1942.
14. EARLE, ELIZABETH S. *The Use of the Leiter International Performance Scale in India.* Master's thesis, Ohio State University (Columbus, Ohio), 1943.
15. ARNOLD, GWEN FREUND. *A Study of the Mental Abilities of the Cerebral Palsied.* Doctor's thesis, University of Wisconsin (Madison, Wis.), 1945. (*Summaries of Doctoral Dissertations....July, 1943 to June, 1947,* 1949, pp. 401–2.)
16. MADELEY, CHARLOTTE BOEHNCKE. *A Study of the Leiter International Performance Scale as a Measure of General Intelligence of Caucasian High School Pupils.* Master's thesis, University of Southern California (Los Angeles, Calif.), 1945.
17. "Report on the Status of the Arthur Adaptation and the 1948 Revision of the Leiter International Performance Scale." *Psychol Service Center J* 1:1–7 Ja '49. * (*PA* 23:5514)
18. ARTHUR, GRACE. "The Arthur Adaptation of the Leiter International Performance Scale." *J Clin Psychol* 5:345–9 O '49. * (*PA* 24:3733)
19. GOULARD, LOWELL JACK. *A Study of the Intelligence of Eleven- and Twelve-Year-Old Mexicans by Means of the Leiter International Performance Scale.* Master's thesis, University of Southern California (Los Angeles, Calif.), 1949.
20. LEITER, RUSSELL GRAYDON. "Caucasian Norms for the Leiter International Performance Scale." *Psychol Service Center J* 1:136–8 D '49. * (*PA* 25:1792)
21. MATTHEWS, JACK, AND BIRCH, JACK W. "The Leiter International Performance Scale: A Suggested Instrument for Psychological Testing of Speech and Hearing Clinic Cases." *J Speech & Hearing Disorders* 14:318–21 D '49. * (*PA* 25:6977)
22. BESSENT, TRENT E. "A Note on the Validity of the Leiter International Performance Scale." *J Consult Psychol* 14:234 Je '50. * (*PA* 25:355)
23. TATE, MIRIAM E. *A Study of the Performance of Selected Groups of Five-Year-Olds on the Leiter International Performance Scale.* Doctor's thesis, University of Iowa (Iowa City, Iowa), 1950.
24. BIRCH, JANE R., AND BIRCH, JACK W. "The Leiter International Performance Scale as an Aid in the Psychological Study of Deaf Children." *Am Ann Deaf* 96:502–11 N '51. *
25. GLENN, ROBERT T. *A Comparison of Intelligence Quotients Derived by the Leiter International Performance Scale and the 1937 Stanford Revision of the Binet.* Master's thesis, University of Pittsburgh, (Pittsburgh, Pa.), 1951.

GWEN F. ARNOLD, *Assistant Professor of Education, University of Wisconsin, Madison, Wisconsin.*

This nonverbal mental age scale for measuring intelligence, published in 1940, was used comparatively little until the last five years because of its unavailability during the war years. The scale consists of 68 standardized items, four at each age level, ranging in difficulty from the 2-year to the 18-year level. The author suggests that its greatest usefulness is for children between the ages of 5 and 12. It is unfortunate that the standardization data have not yet been published. However, the author states that the standardization and location of items in the scale followed the procedure used by Terman in the *Revised Stanford-Binet Scale.* He further states that while the items in this scale are in no way adaptations or modifications of the Binet tests, they may be considered of equal value at each year level despite the difference in the basic assumptions regarding the indices of intelligence. While Terman believes that the amount of information a child acquires through incidental learning is an index of brightness, Leiter built his scale on the principle that the ability to cope with new situations is a truer indication of intelligence. In both scales the mental age is the total number of months of credit earned. The intelligence quotient is the ratio MA/CA. Leiter uses a chronological age of 156 months for anyone thirteen years and older. This in itself defines the upper limits of the test's usefulness.

The scale utilizes the common test technique of matching, ranging from simple pairing of like colors and objects to the more complex relationships of designs, genus, analogies, etc. The instructions are given in pantomime and, since the materials are unique, the influence of coaching and previous experience are minimized. The items at the lower levels are sufficiently easy and the technique of administration is such as to provide opportunities for learning to take place during the testing.

The advantages of this test as a clinical instrument are many. It is useful with children who have hearing, speech, and multiple handicaps, as well as with non-English speaking children. It is extremely interesting to children. While manipulation of materials is at a minimum, it provides activity for the young child which fosters attention. The minimal recording allows the examiner to observe the child's approach to problem solving and his emotional reactions while working. These observations are frequently more significant than the score itself. Timed items are negligible, thus making it a power rather than a speed test. It has some value in diagnosing brain damage. It can be adapted for use with the multiply handicapped.

The greatest practical disadvantage of this scale is the amount of material which must be handled. The cost is also high.

The level of difficulty of tests at years two and three seems to be too high for these ages. In the experience of the reviewer, the total score in the preschool ranges of the test averages 10 IQ points lower when compared with other scales.

The all-or-none aspect of the scoring, while it lends itself to greater objectivity in scoring, penalizes the child who may comprehend the nature of the task but who for other reasons does not accurately complete the total task. A partial score would be more definitive. With only four items at each age level, a failure exacts great penalty and lends itself to misinterpretation of the overall estimate of a child's ability by the non-technically trained person.

From observations made during test administration the reviewer questions the validity of the following items in the scale. *Year V, Test 1, Genus:* Many children match the items on the basis of color rather than genus. While this may have been intended as part of the discriminative value of the test, it frequently fails in this purpose. *Year V, Test 3, Clothing:* The pictures of clothing are so outmoded and disproportionate that many children of this age fail, not because of lack of comprehension of the task, but because the pictured items are misleading. *Year VI, Test 2, Pattern Completion:* This is most baffling to children of this age level. The author, too, has noticed this. In general, the six year tests seem to have a steep incline in difficulty level. *Year X, Test 1, Recognition of Footprints:* This item seems rather inappropriate for our culture and does not seem to have any discriminative value. *Year XII, Test 2, Similarities:* The use of real objects and materials and pictured objects to be matched with pictured objects is unduly confusing and does not conform with the other items in the scale since this technique is not otherwise employed. *Year XII, Test 3, Recognition of Facial Expression:* This was an unfortunate choice of item to measure intelligence since its unreliability has been shown in other types of studies.

Arthur also recognized the inadequate standardization at the two and three year levels and in her revision of the scale has modified it so that a basal age of two years yields a mental age equivalent of two years six months. The writer has found in rechecking tests on this basis that the results are more nearly equivalent to other test results. Similarity of results does not of itself prove adequacy or validity of a test. However, there are clinical situations where the Leiter scale, to date, is the only administrable measure, and the examiner must make recommendations on the basis of it. In the hands of nonclinically trained persons the prediction of a subject's potential could be unfortunate.

The reviewer has used this scale for six years, both for experimental and diagnostic purposes. She feels that despite some of its inadequacies, it is a good clinical instrument. She prefers it for clinical diagnosis rather than as a test to be used widely in public school situations as a measure of general intelligence.

J Consult Psychol 13:386 O '49. Laurance F. Shaffer. * Although the scale seems to be a stimulating and original contribution to the measurement of ability with nonlanguage tasks, full clinical acceptance still awaits the publication of data concerning its standardization.

[350]
★**Leiter-Partington Adult Performance Scale.** Adults; 1938–50; individual; 3 tests (also listed separately); revised manual ('50—reprinted from *Psychol Service Center J* 1:139–71 D '49); $30 per com-

plete set of testing materials including 100 record cards and 200 qualitative check lists for evaluating brain injury; $3 per 100 record cards; $3 per 100 qualitative check lists; postage extra; (35-45) minutes; Russell Graydon Leiter and John E. Partington; Psychological Service Center Press. *

a) PARTINGTON'S PATHWAYS TEST. 1938-49; for prices, see 355.
b) THE LEITER ADAPTATION OF THE PAINTED CUBE TEST. 1941-49; for prices, see 348.
c) THE LEITER ADAPTATION OF ARTHUR'S STENCIL DESIGN TEST. 1945-49; for prices, see 347.

REFERENCES

1. ADJUTANT GENERAL'S OFFICE, CLASSIFICATION AND REPLACEMENT BRANCH, PERSONNEL RESEARCH SECTION. "The New Army Individual Test of General Ability." *Psychol B* 41:532-8 O '44. * (PA 19:581)
2. ARMITAGE, STEWART G. *An Analysis of Certain Psychological Tests Used for the Evaluation of Brain Injury.* American Psychological Association, Psychological Monographs, Vol. 60, No. 1, Whole No. 277. Washington, D.C.: the Association, Inc., 1946. Pp. iii, 48. Paper. *
3. LEITER, RUSSELL GRAYDON, AND PARTINGTON, JOHN E. "Manual for the Leiter-Partington Adult Performance Scale." *Psychol Service Center J* 1:139-71 D '49. * (PA 25:1382)
4. WEAVER, HERBERT B.; WITH THE ASSISTANCE OF ROGER C. BROWN AND LOUIS H. DOERMAN. "The Leiter-Partington Adult Performance Scale at the College Level." *Psychol Service Center J* 2:182-8 S '50. *

HAROLD A. DELP, *Coordinator of Educational Activities, The Training School, Vineland, New Jersey.*

DESCRIPTION OF TESTS. (*a*) *Pathways.* Pathways I, with a practice and a test pathway, includes circled numbers which are to be connected in order. Pathways II, also with a practice and a test, includes numbers and alphabet to be connected alternately. (*b*) *Stencil Designs.* Test is composed of a practice design and nine test designs. Materials include 19 round stencils in 6 colors, adapted from Arthur. (*c*) *Painted Cubes.* The test has an innovation in the use of three printed cards picturing the piles of cubes to be made. Individual wooden cubes are painted red on one or more sides with the other sides white. Cards vary in number of cubes and tiers illustrated.

GENERAL COMMENTS. The authors criticize both the *Revised Stanford-Binet Scale* and the *Wechsler-Bellevue Intelligence Scale* when used for adults. They claim the L-P was devised to fill certain vacuums and to satisfy necessary characteristics for adult testing. Wechsler is criticized for his use of conventional items. Yet both the cube and stencil tests are adaptations of older tests.

The manual contains no real data on validity. Its main argument is based on the correlation with the *Revised Stanford-Binet Scale,* although admitting the S-B is not applicable to adults. Correlation between the tests is .78. The authors imply that for validity a test must "produce results that are commensurate with expert judgment of the mental ability." No evidence is given even at the subjective level that this is obtained. The authors believe that the L-P is "as reliable and valid as the performance section of the Wechsler-Bellevue Scale." No data concerning the relation to the Wechsler are described or referred to.

Despite the lack of specific evidence to substantiate claims, there seems to be some truth in the statements. Personal use by this reviewer plus an informal study have shown relatively high agreement for the majority of cases between L-P and Wechsler full scale results. The relationship with the Wechsler performance score was still better.

According to the authors, Pathways and Stencil Design offer best discrimination at mental levels of average and below (IQ's 65-110), while Painted Cubes is best at superior and above (IQ's 110-about 145). The scale as a whole is interesting and easily administered to adults. Administration time is relatively short (about 45 minutes as a maximum). Norms range in MA from about 8-0 to 19-0 and in IQ from 65 to 145 for subtests and total score. Times for completion of items are converted to raw scores and then into MA and IQ. Chronological age of 13-0 is used as the age of mental maturity (maximum divisor).

Norms are based on "256 unselected male World War II veterans between the ages of 19 and 36 who had been given the 1937 Revision of the Stanford-Binet Scale." Approximate normal distribution on S-B scores is taken to imply adequacy of sample. Socio-economic, occupational, and other background of the sample are not given. Even though "unselected," the sample seems entirely too small for developing adequate norms. The authors freely caution against the use for individuals not similar to the standardization population. They also mention the limitation of any single subtest as a measure of general intelligence. It is doubtful that the three subtests together are adequate to cover the area.

The authors state that "two of the three tests [*Pathways and Stencil Designs*] composing the scale have been found to be useful in evaluation of brain injury." While the considerations involved in the analysis of brain injury seem consistent with other such lists and characteristics, there are no data in the manual to validate the above statement directly. One article is referred to which is used as the basis, even though the arguments on the pathways are by implication only.

SUMMARY. The *Leiter-Partington Adult Performance Scale* is composed of three subtests, each complete in itself and interesting to adults. MA and IQ scores are given for each part and for the total score. The scale appears subjectively to produce satisfactory results, but reliability and validity are not completely substantiated by the data given. The norm population seems too small and too restricted to be compared with a general population. Accuracy is a prerequisite, with credit based on a time score. Clinical and diagnostic values are claimed but with inadequate validation.

HERSCHEL MANUEL, *Professor of Educational Psychology, and Director, Testing and Guidance Bureau, University of Texas, Austin, Texas.*

The *Leiter-Partington Adult Performance Scale* consists of three subtests: *Partington's Pathways Test,* the *Leiter Adaptation of Arthur's Stencil Design Test,* and the *Leiter Adaptation of the Painted Cube Test.* In the first of the subtests the subject marks with pencil two irregular pathways, one indicated by circles bearing the numbers 1 to 25 and the other indicated by numbers and letters alternately. The second subtest requires the building up of various designs by superimposing circular pieces of colored paper, all of which, except the ones to be used as the foundation, have cut-out portions. The third subtest consists of assembling small cubes to make blocks with painted sides like the stimulus pictures. Directions are given by pantomime illustrating the procedure.

Each subtest is scored separately on the basis of the time required for successful completion of each part. Maximum time limits beyond which no credit is allowed are prescribed for the several parts of the Stencil Design and Painted Cubes tests. Raw scores are converted into mental ages and intelligence quotients by reference to tables provided in the manual. The IQ's are based upon a divisor of 13 in contrast with the 15 used in the *Revised Stanford-Binet Scale.* A total mental age or intelligence quotient is found by simple summation of the raw scores on the three subtests and reference to a conversion table.

A version of the three tests was used as the performance portion of the *Army Individual Test* constructed for the measurement of general mental ability. Probably the most significant difference in the two series was in the use of verbal directions in the Army and the use of pantomime in the present series. The evaluation of the tests by the Personnel Research Section, AGO (*1*), is quite definite and unequivocal: The *Army Individual Test* "is valid and it is practical * It contains both verbal and nonverbal materials which contribute equally to the variance of the total score." The intercorrelations of the three performance tests vary from .43 to .60, and the correlation of the total weighted performance score with the score on the *Army General Classification Test* is .74.

Intercorrelations reported in the manual for the Leiter-Partington scale are .45 for Pathways and Cubes, .50 for Stencils and Pathways, and .63 for Stencils and Cubes. The correlation of the total score with the Stanford-Binet is .78.

Weaver used the Leiter-Partington scale with 50 male and 50 female college sophomores and compared the results (with a few exceptions) with the results of the *American Council on Education Psychological Examination* administered at the beginning of the freshman year (*4*). No significant sex differences on the performance tests were found. The Pathways Test gave a wide distribution of scores but lacked sufficient ceiling. The distributions on the other two tests were good. Correlations of the total Leiter-Partington score and the ACE were: L score, .18; Q score, .45; and total score, .24. Weaver thinks that the Leiter-Partington scale measures something "quite different from scholastic aptitude as measured by the ACE, and should prove a valuable supplement to tests of the verbal-symbolic type."

Armitage used the Army Version of Partington's Pathways under the name Trail Making and the Army version of the *Leiter Adaptation of the Arthur Stencil Design Test* under the name Shoulder Patches in comparing cases of brain injury with normal or neurotic cases having no history of brain injury (*2*). Although there was considerable overlapping of the scores of the two groups mean scores on both tests were higher for the control group. The manual of the Leiter-Partington scale contains suggestions for obtaining "qualitative data" for use in the evaluation of brain injury.

In the reviewer's opinion the clinician may add the *Leiter-Partington Adult Performance Scale* to his equipment with confidence that he will have a useful instrument. Its coverage is obviously limited, but this is true of many tests from which helpful information may be obtained.

It is probable that factor analysis would add interpretative information of considerable interest.

J Consult Psychol 15:88 F '51. Laurance F. Shaffer. The L-P Performance Scale consists of the three nonverbal subtests of the Army Individual Test developed during World War II: the pathways test, a stencil design test employing round patterns, and a painted cube assembly test. The reliability of the whole scale is not given, but its correlation with the Revised Stanford Binet is .78 in a group of 256 adult males. The intercorrelations of the three subtests range from .45 to .69. Tables of norms give adult MA's and IQ's for each subtest separately and for the battery. Since the materials are novel and do not seem childish, the scale offers a useful addition to resources for the nonverbal examination of adults. The manual discusses qualitative observations obtained from the tests that may have values in psychological diagnosis.

[351]

Minnesota Preschool Scale. Ages 1.5–6; 1932–40; 3 scores: verbal, non-verbal, total; individual; Forms A ('32), B ('32); manual ('40); $14.50 per set of testing materials needed by examiner; $1.25 per 25 record blanks; postage extra; $1 per specimen set, postpaid; nontimed (10–30) minutes; Florence L. Goodenough, Katharine M. Maurer, and M. J. Van Wagenen; Educational Test Bureau, Educational Publishers, Inc. *

REFERENCES

1–3. See 40:1407.
4–5. See 3:286.
6. COFFEY, HUBERT STANLEY. *A Study of Certain Mental Functions and Their Relation to Changes in the Intelligence of Preschool Children.* Doctor's thesis, University of Iowa (Iowa City, Iowa), 1938. (*Programs Announcing Candidates for Higher Degrees 1938.*)
7. DE FOREST, RUTH. "A Study of the Prognostic Value of the Merrill-Palmer Scale of Mental Tests and the Minnesota Preschool Scale." *J Genetic Psychol* 59:219–23 S '41. * (*PA* 16:1231)

For a review by Beth L. Wellman, see 3:286; for reviews by Rachel Stutsman Ball, Nancy Bayley, and Florence M. Teagarden, see 40:1407; for related reviews, see 352 and 3:287–8.

[352]

[*Re Minnesota Preschool Scale.*] MAURER, KATHARINE M. **Intellectual Status at Maturity as a Criterion for Selecting Items in Preschool Tests.** University of Minnesota, Institute of Child Welfare Monograph Series, No. 21. Minneapolis, Minn.: University of Minnesota Press, 1946. Pp. ix, 166. Lithotyped. $2.50. * (London: Oxford University Press. 20s) (*PA* 21:286)

El Sch J 48:167–9 N '47. Lee J. Cronbach. * introduces a basically different method of item selection—one which has much to commend it. Items are tested, not to see whether they have certain theoretically desirable characteristics when given, but to determine whether they predict ultimate mental ability. She takes advantage of data accumulated over the years by the Minnesota Institute, which permit one to re-examine, at maturity, young people tested originally below the age of six. Maurer tested a superior, selected group of 226 persons at the age of sixteen or later with the Wells Revision of Army Alpha Test. Binet records were also used for fifty adolescents. The results are striking—even astonishing—in the light of the complacency with which some items have been accepted for years as measures of "intelligence." Among Maurer's group nonverbal items were generally predictive, while many verbal items had little or no relation to standing at maturity. The author points out that verbal items are peculiarly subject to special experience and even coaching by persons who wish children to show impressive "development." If the general-factor hypothesis is accepted—and Maurer's data support this view—these nonverbal items are evidently a better measure of g at earlier ages than are many verbal tests. At later ages, verbal tests are heavily saturated with g, according to long-standing evidence. Among the items which have highly predictive value are imitative drawing, block-building, form discrimination, digit span, mutilated pictures, picture puzzles, vocabulary, and opposites. Since few of these tests depart in any way from the standard conception of mental ability, the import of this study is to point out certain types of items for discarding, rather than to draw attention to new forms. A standard preschool test, believed to contain only good items, was the original basis of the study. Yet twelve of the original twenty-nine item-forms were found to be inadequate predictors. It is to be hoped that this study may lead some ingenious worker to invent superior item types to replace those lost. *

J Ed (London) 80:700+ D '48. C. M. Fleming. * a scholarly analysis * Greater predictive value is indicated for items such as imitative drawing, block building, discrimination of form, memory for digits, knowledge of word opposites, comprehension of directions, than for items of the type of aesthetic comparisons, paper folding, or the naming of familiar objects. It is possible to agree that there is in this some evidence of a constant core of mental functioning, in the sense that what is commonly described as intelligence is manifested in a candidate's adaptability to what, at the age in question, is something of a novel situation. In view of the extent of the disparities covered by correlations even so high as +.7 or +.8, it seems, however, dangerous to claim that these findings give promise that we shall yet succeed in predicting terminal intellectual status from pre-school testing. This book, in its concentration on the search for stability and its lack of allowance for the influence of later experiences, comes near to being one of those of which it may fairly be said that to continue such educational research for a means of effecting a neat and final classification of pupils at a specified age is to remain within the intellectual framework of the nineteenth century. The more recent emphasis on educability, rather than on fixity, and on flexibility rather than stability, is the fruit of those more adequate studies of mental performing which offer not a single retesting after ten to sixteen years, but cumulative recording and annual measurements. From such continued observations of the details of personal growth, one is led to an admission of variability and to an awareness that each individual follows a pattern of his own in relation to the average of his group. Prediction at any age is hazardous, and it is dangerous to claim that what an individual does do to-day provides a full indication of what he can do at some future date.

J Ed Res 41:314–5 D '47. Nancy Bayley. * The study as a whole is very carefully done, and the implications of the results and the theoretical discussion are very important additions to our knowledge of intelligence and its growth. It may be noted, however, that in its present state prediction from this shortened test remains very poor. The great value of this research is that it points the way to the type of test items which should be devised and added to those already known to be predictive, in the hope of developing a test battery which will predict mature intelligence at an early age. It is hoped that data now available from other longitudinal studies will be similarly analyzed. From such analyses we may eventually learn the extent to which the growth of intellectual factors is consistent in individual children.

Occupational Psychol 22:217–8 O '48. H. J. Eysenck. * A good deal of complacency has accompanied the inculcation of a belief in the "constancy of the IQ" into educational psychologists. This belief is in no way justified. Correlations between test and retest on the Binet are notoriously low when several years have intervened between test and retest; in a survey of published material the present reviewer found that after an interval of ten years Binet retests correlated only about .52 with original tests. A value of this kind represents an improvement over chance guessing of only 14 per cent. Clearly then intelligence tests of the Binet type leave much to be desired in terms of predictive efficiency. Matters are even worse when we turn to pre-school tests; here correlations of test with later retest are lower still, and may even become negative for very young age-groups. For this reason, psychologists have given up the use of pre-school tests for predictive purposes, although the practice still lingers in some backwaters. * Detailed figures are given regarding the predictive value of each item in the scales. These should be of immense value to those interested in the use and interpretation of pre-school scales. One weakness in an otherwise scholarly and thorough study is the method of validation, in which prediction coefficients derived from part of the total group of subjects are applied to another part of the group. While obviously such validation is essential, the method used by Maurer is probably the most inefficient which could have been devised under the circumstances, and indeed leaves the question at issue largely unsettled. Even in view of the natural limitations of the study in terms of number of subjects, its importance can hardly be overrated. The problems raised are of such importance to psychology that one can only hope that a large-scale study using thousands rather than hundreds of subjects will soon be inaugurated. And as one further point, one would like the same method used on tests other than pre-school tests; the problem of prediction is no less urgent with the older child than with the four-year old, and the application of similar methods should go far to dispel the present false optimism which still enshrouds so many educational psychologists, while substituting a more firmly grounded factual belief.

Psychol B 44:578–9 N '47. Quinn McNemar. * A grand total of about 700 biserial correlations, between Alpha scores and the Preschool Scale items, were computed on 180 cases subdivided into nine age groups according to age at time of their preschool test (N's varied from 9 to 33). The records of 46 cases (every fifth) were held for "validating" the "predictive" scale made up of the subtests selected on the basis of the item analysis. Two points lead the reviewer to question the accuracy of the statistical analysis. With sizable standard errors (up to .30), it is very doubtful that the 400 *r*'s under .40 (200 under .20) would all be on the positive side of zero; yet no negative biserial values are reported. About one-tenth of the 700 given standard errors, for biserials, are erroneously low. On the basis of the item biseral *r*'s, 17 of the 29 subtests of each form were retained as "predictive." These 17 represent about 75% of the 224 scoring items per form. The preschool test blanks of the 46 validating cases were rescored on these selected items, and the correlations of Alpha with selected tests were compared with the correlations yielded by all the preschool subtests. With *r*'s based on N's of 3 to 8 per age group, the results are inconclusive: it cannot be said that the scores based on selected tests are any more predictive than scores based on all the tests. This lack of conclusiveness also holds for the findings based on a supplementary validation group with Stanford-Binet IQ's at ages 11 to 15 taken as measures of near terminal intelligence. A better procedure would have been to choose on the basis of the item analysis the best half of the items as predictive, with the remaining half as nonpredictive, then to compare the validity of the predictive versus that of the nonpredictive tests, instead of the predictive versus the total. The difficulty of eliminating the age factor so as to have a validity coefficient based on all 46 cases could be overcome by rescoring a sufficient number of typical Minnesota Preschool Test blanks as a basis for standard scores, at each age level, for the predictive items. These standard scores could then be correlated with later Alpha standing, also expressed as standard scores by age level. This monograph represents an enormous amount of work on a very important, and likely fruitful, line of research. Far more cases will be required for checking the reasonable hypothesis that preschool scales contain "dead wood" as far as the prediction of terminal intelligence is concerned.

For additional reviews, see 3:288.

[353]
Nebraska Test of Learning Aptitude for Young Deaf Children: A Non-Verbal Individual Scale Especially Devised for Deaf and Hard of Hearing Children from Four to Ten Years of Age. Ages 4–10; 1941; individual; 1 form; $52 per set of testing materials and 100 record forms; $1.75 per 100 record forms; $1.75 per 100 completion-of-drawings blanks; $1.75 per manual; postpaid; (50–60) minutes; Marshall S. Hiskey; distributed by Psychological Corporation. *

REFERENCES

1–3. See 3:289.
4. THOMURE, EUGENE. *A Comparative Study of the Results of the Nebraska Test of Learning Aptitude for Young Deaf Children With Results of Other Learning Aptitude Tests Given in the Kendall School for the Deaf.* Master's thesis, Gallaudet College (Washington, D.C.), 1950–51. (PA 26:1825, title only)

MILDRED C. TEMPLIN, *Associate Professor, Institute of Child Welfare, University of Minnesota, Minneapolis, Minnesota.*

This test is constructed specifically for young deaf and hard of hearing children and has been standardized on such a group. The following criteria were among those against which the items in the preliminary scale were selected: (*a*) similarity to school tasks of the deaf child, (*b*) possibility of nonverbal measurement, (*c*) instructions that can be pantomimed, (*d*) correlation with accepted criteria of intelligence and learning ability, (*e*) objective scoring, and (*f*) nontimed scores. In an item analysis those items showing the greatest increase in percentage passing from age to age were retained. In the final scale there are 124 test items arranged according to difficulty under 11 types of measurement: memory for colored objects, bead stringing, pictorial associations, block building, memory for digits, completion of drawings, pictorial identification, paper folding, visual attention span, puzzle blocks, and pictorial analogies. The instructions for each item are pantomimed, no item is a "speed test," and practice items are presented for the various types of measures.

The split half reliability of the test, corrected by the Spearman-Brown formula, is .963. The validity rests largely on the method of selection of items for the preliminary scale and on the item analysis for the selection of items for the final scale. No attempt was made to establish validity through correlation with other tests since "there is no existing test which would have been an acceptable criterion." The relation between the total test score and each of the 11 test parts is reported in coefficients ranging from .63 to .84 for the age groups 4 to 7 and 8 to 10 years.

The results of the test are expressed as a learning age (LA) which is interpreted similarly to the MA except that the LA indicates the performance of the average *deaf* child. The learning quotient (LQ), while presented, must be used cautiously.

A short form of the test, including five types of measures which are most highly correlated with the total test score, can be administered in about 30 minutes. On the standardization group the correlations between the five parts and the total test are .94 for both the 4 to 7 and the 8 to 10 age groups.

The test is attractive and interesting to children; since it was constructed and standardized for deaf children, it has a special value.

[354]

★Northwestern Intelligence Tests. Ages 4–12 weeks, 13–36 weeks; 1949–51; a revision of *Gilliland-Shotwell Intelligence Scale* ('43) by A. R. Gilliland and Anna M. Shotwell; individual; 2 levels; 1 form; $2 per 25 test record sheets for any one level; other test materials may be purchased from A. R. Gilliland, Northwestern University, Evanston, Ill.; 40¢ per specimen set of test record sheet and manual for any one level; postpaid; (20–30) minutes; A. R. Gilliland; Houghton Mifflin Co. *

a) TEST A. Ages 4–12 weeks; 1949.
b) TEST B. Ages 13–36 weeks; 1951.

REFERENCES

1. GILLILAND, A. R., AND MORGAN, J. J. B. "A Test for Measuring the Mentality of Infants." Abstract. *Psychol B* 38: 595 Jl '41. * (*PA* 15:5403, title only)
2. SHOTWELL, ANNA M., AND GILLILAND, A. R. "A Preliminary Scale for the Measurement of the Mentality of Infants." *Child Develop* 14:167–77 S '43. * (*PA* 18:908)
3. DRUMMOND, MARY D., AND GILLILAND, A. R. "The Validation of the Gilliland-Shotwell Infant Intelligence Scale." Abstract. *Am Psychol* 1:464 O '46. * (*PA* 21:624, title only)
4. GILLILAND, A. R. "An Intelligence Test for Early Infancy." Abstract. *Am Psychol* 2:302 Ag '47. * (*PA* 21:4661, title only)
5. BERKS, MARY DEE DRUMMOND. *New Data in the Development of the Gilliland-Shotwell Intelligence Scale.* Master's thesis, Northwestern University (Evanston, Ill.), 1948.
6. GILLILAND, A. R. "Environmental Influences on Infant Intelligence Test Scores." Abstract. *Am Psychol* 3:265 Jl '48. * (*PA* 22:5367, title only)
7. GILLILAND, A. R. "The Measurement of the Mentality of Infants." *Child Develop* 19:155–8 S '48. * (*PA* 23:5519)
8. GILLILAND, A. R. "Environmental Influence on Infant Intelligence Test Scores." *Harvard Ed R* 19:142–6 su '49. * (*PA* 24:3106)
9. GILLILAND, A. R. "Socio-Economic Status and Race as Factors in Infant Intelligence Test Scores." *Child Dev* 22: 271–3 D '51. *

MILDRED C. TEMPLIN, *Associate Professor, Institute of Child Welfare, University of Minnesota, Minneapolis, Minnesota.*

The 40 test items in the present revision of the *Northwestern Infant Intelligence Test* (NIIT) are based on a study of 276 complete infant tests. They were selected according to four criteria: (*a*) the test items have definite instructions for giving and scoring, (*b*) they require relatively simple equipment, (*c*) they measure adaptation to the physical and social environment rather than maturation, and (*d*) they show an increasing percentage of babies passing from week to week. The raw score for the test is the total number of items passed. An IQ can be computed for any age. It should be noted that the test items in the earlier forms were made up from items used by other infant test authors, primarily Gesell, from some modification of other infant test items, and from items devised by Gilliland and Shotwell after noting signs of development in comparing the behavior of younger and older babies.

The odd-even reliability coefficients, corrected by the Spearman-Brown formula, range between .79 and .94 for each week between 4 and 11. The coefficient for the total age range is .84. The validity of the test has been considered in several ways. The age-grade progress of the individual items and of the test as a whole is one of the criteria used in the construction of the test. The results of the tests of 72 inmates of the Lincoln State School and Colony, Lincoln, Illinois are reported as approximate to expectation for various groups of feebleminded children. The mean difference between the IQ measured on the NIIT and the Cattell test or the Kuhlmann-Binet is 3.8 points for 29 children. Although no quantitative results are reported, "several of the normal infants who were tested by one of the earlier forms of the test have been given the Stanford-Binet Tests later. While the numbers are too small for statistical analysis, the results thus far have shown high predictive value for the early tests." (7) It is probable that the real value of the NIIT rests upon the quantified evidence which will accumulate as the results of the many tests of the same children as infants are compared with their test results in later years.

J Consult Psychol 13:385 O '49. Laurance F. Shaffer. Because of the need, especially of adoption agencies, for a test for very young infants, a scale of 40 items was developed drawn in part from the work of Gesell, Cattell and Buehler and in part from original observations. The observations emphasize responses showing adaptation to the physical and social environment rather than growth or maturation. * There is some evidence of good agreement with other infant tests.

[355]

★Partington's Pathways Test. Adults (especially with IQ's between 65 and 110); 1938–50; formerly called *Distributed Attention;* a subtest of *Leiter-Partington Adult Performance Scale* (see 350); individual; can be given in pantomime; 1 form, '49; revised manual ('50); $9 per set of pads for 100 examinations; $3 per 100 record cards; $3 per 100 qualitative check lists for evaluating brain injury; $1 per manual; manual and record cards same as for *Leiter-Partington Adult Performance Scale;* postage extra; (3–5) minutes; John E. Partington and Russell Graydon Leiter; Psychological Service Center Press. *

REFERENCES

1. ADJUTANT GENERAL'S OFFICE, CLASSIFICATION AND REPLACEMENT BRANCH, PERSONNEL RESEARCH SECTION. "The New Army Individual Test of General Ability." *Psychol B* 41:532–8 O '44. * (*PA* 19:581)

GEORGE K. BENNETT, *President, The Psychological Corporation, New York, New York.*

When this test was originally developed it was

called "Distributed Attention." A slightly modified version used by the U.S. Army was called "Trail Making." The present test differs from its predecessors in having two parts, each of which is prefaced by both a demonstration and a practice test. The task consists of drawing a pencil line to intercept sequentially each of 25 labeled circles printed on an 8½ by 11 inch page. In Part I the circles are numbered; in Part II the series runs: 1, A, 2, B, and so on. The examiner's demonstration upon a miniature practice test is followed by at least one practice run, and if necessary several, on the fore-exercise to insure the subject's familiarity with the process. Score points are awarded in a roughly linear relationship to speed on each of the two real trials. On Part I, the maximum of 20 points is earned if the route is traced in under 40 seconds while only 2 points are granted to a subject who requires 110 seconds or more. On Part II the corresponding limits are 45 seconds and 145 seconds. No credit is given on either part if an error is made and left without prompt and spontaneous correction.

Although this test is available for separate use, it is one of the three parts of the *Leiter-Partington Adult Performance Scale,* the manual for which serves also for each of the component tests. This manual clearly indicates that the Pathways test is regarded by the authors as a test of general intelligence suitable for use with adults with IQ's of 60 to 140. Table III of the manual gives MA and IQ equivalents for scores. This designation appears to have two foundations. The first is that the test meets the authors' requirements of yielding speed scores, containing inherently motivating material, and not resembling childish activities. The second is that when the test was administered to "256 unselected male World War II veterans between the ages of 19 and 36" who had also taken the Stanford-Binet, a correlation of .68 was obtained. It should be noted that this was the same group as that from which the time zones for point values were established. As a consequence the coefficient of .68 is probably an overestimate. Through the courtesy of the publisher an as yet unpublished article by H. Weaver entitled "The Leiter-Partington Adult Performance Scale at the College Level" has been made available in manuscript. Correlation with the *American Council on Education Psychological Examination* L score is reported as .12; and with Q score, as .62. The correlation with total is not given.

Subjects were an unspecified number (less than 100) of University of Cincinnati sophomores who had been tested on ACE while freshmen. The distribution of Pathways test scores is severely skewed.

A qualitative checklist permits the examiner to make a record of his observations of the subject's planning, method, and reaction to errors. This is supplemented by a series of questions to be asked after testing is completed. The manual reports that the checklist and inquiry have been designed with reference to the findings of Stewart G. Armitage in relation to brain-injured subjects. No data are offered in support, although journal references are given.

The reviewer feels that it would be highly unfortunate if the *Partington's Pathways Test,* on the basis of present evidence, were to be taken seriously as a measure of intelligence. The performance itself is a simple tracing operation of very brief duration in which a sort of perceptual-motor speed is the controlling factor. Although tables of MA and IQ equivalents are given, these are based upon a single group of veteran counseling candidates. No report of reliability is given and, unless the Weaver study is so regarded, there is no validation upon a second group. It would appear to be highly hazardous to use the results of this test in its present stage of development as a basis for any decisions affecting an individual. Later experimentation may confirm or contradict the faith of the publishers which at present would seem to rest largely on uncritical optimism.

J Consult Psychol 13:386 O '49. Laurance F. Shaffer. The Pathways Test is a performance task using printed forms. In Part I the subject draws a line to irregularly placed circles numbered 1, 2, 3, etc., in sequence, and in Part II to similar circles in the order 1, A, 2, B, 3, C, etc. Although an *r* of .68 with the 1937 Stanford Binet is reported for 256 adult males, the test is not intended to be a comprehensive measure of intelligence. The author regards it as a measure of a complex of speed, eye-hand coordination, alertness and distributed attention. Norms are given in terms of MA and IQ, for adult males only.

[356]
★Porteus Maze Test, Vineland Revision. Ages 3 and over; 1914–50; 2 scores: qualitative, quantitative; individual; 1 maze for each of the 12 years 3–12, 14, and adult I; 1 form, '33; manual, *The Porteus Maze Test and Intelligence* ('50—see *50* below) replaces *The Maze Test and Mental Differences* ('33—see *22*

below) and *Qualitative Performance in the Maze Test* ('42—see 33 below); $1 per 100 of any one test; $4.10 per manual; specimen set not available; postpaid; nontimed (15-60) minutes; Stanley D. Porteus; Psychological Corporation. *

REFERENCES

1. PORTEUS, S. D. "Mental Tests for the Feebleminded: A New Series." *J Psycho-Asthenics* 19:200-13 Je '15.
2. PORTEUS, S. D. "Motor-Intellectual Tests for Mental Defectives." *J Exp Pedagogy* 3:127-35 Je '15.
3. CUNNINGHAM, K. S. "Binet and Porteus Tests Compared: Examination of One Hundred School Children." *J Ed Psychol* 7:552-6 N '16. *
4. PORTEUS, S. D. "Mental Tests With Delinquents and Australian Aboriginal Children." *Psychol R* 24:32-42 Ja '17. *
5. PORTEUS, S. D. "The Measurement of Intelligence: Six Hundred and Fifty-Three Children Examined by the Binet and Porteus Tests." *J Ed Psychol* 9:13-31 Ja '18. *
6. BURT, CYRIL. "The Porteus Maze-Tests," pp. 242-56. In his *Mental and Scholastic Tests*. Preface by Robert Blair. London: Staples Press Ltd., 1921. Pp. xv, 432. *
7. MORGENTHAU, DOROTHY RUTH. *Some Well-Known Mental Tests Evaluated and Compared*. Archives of Psychology, No. 52. New York: Archives of Psychology, Columbia University, 1922. Pp. 54. Paper. *
8. PORTEUS, S. D. "Temperament and Mentality in Maturity, Sex and Race." *J Appl Psychol* 8:57-74 Mr '24. *
9. GAW, FRANCES. *Performance Tests of Intelligence*. Medical Research Council, Industrial Fatigue Research Board, Report No. 31. London: H. M. Stationery Office, 1925. Pp. iv, 45. Paper. *
10. GAW, FRANCES. "A Study of Performance Tests." *Brit J Psychol* 15:374-92 Ap '25. *
11. WORTHINGTON, MYRTLE RAYMAKER. "A Study of Some Commonly Used Performance Tests." *J Appl Psychol* 10:216-27 Je '26. *
12. LESTER, OLIVE P. "Performance Tests and Foreign Children." *J Ed Psychol* 20:303-9 Ap '29. * (*PA* 3:2889)
13. POULL, LOUISE E., AND MONTGOMERY, RUTH P. "The Porteus Maze Test as a Discriminative Measure in Delinquency." *J Appl Psychol* 13:145-51 Ap '29. * (*PA* 3:3280)
14. PETERSON, JOSEPH, AND TELFORD, C. W. "Results of Group and Individual Tests Applied to the Practically Pure-Blood Negro Children on St. Helena Island." *J Comp Psychol* 11:115-44 D '30. * (*PA* 5:1576)
15. PORTEUS, S. D.; WITH THE ASSISTANCE OF DORIS M. DEWEY AND ROBERT G. BERNREUTER. "Race and Social Differences in Performance Tests." *Genetic Psychol Monogr* 8:93-208 Ag '30. * (*PA* 15:4947)
16. FRY, H. R., AND PULLEINE, R. H. "The Mentality of the Australian Aborigine." *Austral J Exp Biol & Med Sci* 8:153-67 Je 16 '31. *
17. HICKS, J. ALLAN, AND RALPH, DOROTHY W. "The Effects of Practice in Tracing the Porteus Diamond Maze." *Child Develop* 2:156-8 Je '31. * (*PA* 5:4595)
18. LOUTTIT, C. M. "Test Performance of a Selected Group of Part-Hawaiians." *J Appl Psychol* 15:43-52 F '31. * (*PA* 5:4204)
19. MCDONALD, JANE REGINA. *A Comparative Study of Deaf Children by Means of the Kohs Block Designs and Porteus Maze*. Master's thesis, Ohio State University (Columbus, Ohio), 1931.
20. TELFORD, C. W. "Test Performance of Full and Mixed-Blood North Dakota Indians." *J Comp Psychol* 14:123-45 Ag '32. * (*PA* 7:712)
21. KARPELES, LOTTA M. "A Further Investigation of the Porteus Maze Test as a Discriminative Measure in Delinquency." *J Appl Psychol* 16:427-3 Ag '32. * (*PA* 7:3993)
22. PORTEUS, STANLEY D. *The Maze Test and Mental Differences*. Vineland, N.J.: Smith Printing and Publishing House, 1933. Pp. ix, 274. *
23. LOUTTIT, C. M., AND STACKMAN, HARVEY. "The Relationship Between Porteus Maze and Binet Test Performance." *J Ed Psychol* 27:18-25 Ja '36. * (*PA* 10:3211)
24. EARL, C. J. C. "The Performance Test Behaviour of Adult Morons." *Brit J Med Psychol* 17:78-92 pt 1 '37. * (*PA* 12:1400)
25. MORRIS, CHARLES M. "An Experimental Analysis of Certain Performance Tests." Abstract. *Psychol B* 34:716-7 N '37. * (*PA* 12:1661, title only)
26. PORTEUS, S. D. *Primitive Intelligence and Environment*. New York: Macmillan Co., 1937. Pp. ix, 325. * (London: Macmillan & Co., Ltd.) (*PA* 11:4677)
27. VERNON, P. E. "A Study of the Norms and the Validity of Certain Mental tests at a Child Guidance Clinic, Part II." *Brit J Ed Psychol* 7:115-37 Je '37. * (*PA* 11:4827)
28. PORTEUS, S. D. "The Validity of the Porteus Maze Test." *J Ed Psychol* 30:172-8 Mr '39. * (*PA* 13:4917)
29. ZECKEL, A., AND KOLK, J. J. VAN DER. "A Comparative Intelligence Test of Groups of Children Born Deaf and of Good Hearing, by Means of the Porteus Test." *Am Ann Deaf* 84:114-23 Mr '39. * (*PA* 14:248)
30. HESTON, JOSEPH C., AND CANNELL, CHARLES F. "A Note on the Relation Between Age and Performance of Adult Subjects on Four Familiar Psychometric Tests." *J Appl Psychol* 25:415-9 Ag '41. * (*PA* 15:5004)
31. PORTEUS, STANLEY D.; WITH THE ASSISTANCE OF MARY HUNTER AND COLIN J. HERRICK. *The Practice of Clinical Psychology*, pp. 152-9. New York: American Book Co., 1941. Pp. ix, 579. * (*PA* 15:4248)
32. SPARLING, MARGARET E. "Intelligence of Indian Children: The Relationship Between Binet and Porteus Scores." *Am J Mental Def* 46:60-2 Jl '41. * (*PA* 16:819)
33. PORTEUS, S. D. *Qualitative Performance in the Maze Test*. New York: Psychological Corporation, 1942. Pp. ii, 55. * (*PA* 17:718)
34. HAVIGHURST, ROBERT J., AND JANKE, LEOTA LONG. "Relations Between Ability and Social Status in a Midwestern Community: I, Ten-Year-Old Children." *J Ed Psychol* 35:357-68 S '44. * (*PA* 19:476)
35. PORTEUS, S. D. "Medical Applications of the Maze Test." *Med J Austral* 31:558-60 Je 17 '44. * (*PA* 20:3660, title only)
36. PORTEUS, STANLEY D., AND KEPNER, RICHARD DEMONBRUN. "Mental Changes After Bilateral Pre-Frontal Lobotomy." *Genetic Psychol Monogr* 29:3-115 F '44. * (*PA* 18:2455)
37. WRIGHT, CLARE. "The Qualitative Performance of Delinquent Boys on the Porteus Maze Test." *J Consult Psychol* 8:24-6 Ja-F '44. * (*PA* 18:2209)
38. ARNOLD, GWEN FREUND. *A Study of the Mental Abilities of the Cerebral Palsied*. Doctor's thesis, University of Wisconsin (Madison, Wis.), 1945. (*Summaries of Doctoral Dissertations....July, 1943 to June, 1947*, 1949, pp. 401-2.)
39. PORTEUS, S. D. "Porteus Maze Tests: Applications in Medical and Allied Fields." *Brit J Med Psychol* 20:267-70 O '45. * (*PA* 20:1282)
40. PORTEUS, S. D. "Q-Scores, Temperament, and Delinquency." *J Social Psychol* 21:81-103 F '45. * (*PA* 19:1553)
41. SANDERSON, MARGARET H. "Performance of Fifth, Eighth, and Eleventh Grade Children in the Porteus Qualitative Maze Tests." *J Genetic Psychol* 67:57-65 S '45. * (*PA* 20:580)
42. PORTEUS, STANLEY D., AND PETERS, HENRY N. "Maze Test Validation and Psychosurgery." *Genetic Psychol Monogr* 36:3-86 Ag '47. * (*PA* 22:1101)
43. PORTEUS, S. D., AND PETERS, H. N. "Psychosurgery and Test Validity." *J Abn & Social Psychol* 42:473-5 O '47. *
44. BURT, CYRIL. *Handbook of Tests for Use in Schools, Second Edition*, pp. 98-110. London: Staples Press Ltd., 1948. Pp. xvi, 110. *
45. PHILLIPS, E. LAKIN; BERMAN, ISABEL R.; AND HANSON, HAROLD B. *Intelligence and Personality Factors Associated With Poliomyelitis Among School Age Children*. Monographs of the Society for Research in Child Development, Vol. 12, No. 2, Serial No. 45. Evanston, Ill.: Child Development Publications, the Society, 1948. Pp. vii, 60. Paper, lithotyped. *
46. CARSON, MARGARET K. *A Comparative Study of the Stanford-Binet Form L, and the Porteus Composite Binet*. Master's thesis, University of Hawaii (Honolulu, Hawaii), 1949. (*PA* 26:1768, title only)
47. FISHER, SEYMOUR, AND SUNUKJIAN, HELEN. "Intellectual Disparities in a Normal Group and Their Relationship to Emotional Disturbance." *J Clin Psychol* 6:288-90 Jl '50. * (*PA* 25:1786)
48. LANDIS, CARNEY, AND ERLICK, DWIGHT. "An Analysis of the Porteus Maze-Test as Affected by Psychosurgery." *Am J Psychol* 63:557-66 O '50. * (*PA* 25:4788)
49. PORTEUS, S. D. "Thirty-Five Years' Experience With the Porteus Maze." *J Abn & Social Psychol* 45:396-401 Ap '50. * (*PA* 25:5876)
50. PORTEUS, STANLEY D. *The Porteus Maze Test and Intelligence*. Palo Alto, Calif.: Pacific Books, 1950. Pp. vi, 194. * (*PA* 25:1105)
51. TIZARD, J.; IN COLLABORATION WITH N. O'CONNOR AND J. M. CRAWFORD. "The Abilities of Adolescent and Adult High-Grade Male Defectives." *J Mental Sci* 96:888-907 O '50. * (*PA* 25:5421)
52. FOULDS, G. A. "Temperamental Differences in Maze Performance: Part I, Characteristic Differences Among Psychoneurotics." *Brit J Psychol, Gen Sect* 42:209-17 Ag '51. * (*PA* 26:4005)
53. PETERS, HENRY N., AND JONES, FRANCIS D. "Evaluation of Group Psychotherapy by Means of Performance Tests." *J Consult Psychol* 15:363-7 O '51. * (*PA* 26:7149)
54. PORTEUS, S. D. "Recent Research on the Porteus Maze Test and Psycho-Surgery." *Brit J Med Psychol* 24:132-40 Je '51. * (*PA* 26:1056)
55. TIZARD, J. "The Porteus Maze Test and Intelligence: A Critical Survey." *Brit J Ed Psychol* 21:172-85 N '51. * (*PA* 26:4813)
56. WATSON, ROBERT I. *The Clinical Method in Psychology*, pp. 302-10. New York: Harper & Brothers, 1951. Pp. xii, 779. *

C. M. LOUTTIT, *Assistant to the Provost, University of Illinois, Urbana, Illinois.*

Since its original publication in 1915 the *Porteus Maze Test* has been widely used by itself and as part of the *Arthur Point Scale of Performance Tests*. Based upon the extent of use alone, the instrument has apparently been found acceptable by clinical psychologists. However, there are still questions unanswered as to the meaning, reliability, and validity of the Maze Test performance.

Originally Porteus (1915) offered the Maze as a test supplementary to the *Stanford-Binet Scale* which would sample such nonverbal aspects of ability as prudence and forethought. In subsequent publications the tendency has been to emphasize the usefulness of the Maze in revealing "planning and foresight" in dealing with an essentially simple concrete situation. Correlations with the Binet of the order of .60 indicate appreciable communality between the abilities required on the two tests. Maze performance also requires abilities in common with other types of performance tests. Finally, there appears to be a third requirement, probably adequately expressed in "planning and foresight," for successful Maze performance. This type of analysis of the Maze Test rests in large measure on logic and intuition—there has been a surprising lack of rigorous experimental analysis of a test which is so widely used.

The nature of the Maze Test makes use of the usual measures of reliability questionable. Administration of the graded series of Mazes, designated by year levels, always begins at year V or below and proceeds until a specified criterion of failure is met. An element in success is ability to profit from experience, i.e., a learning factor. Because of this, test-retest correlations may be expected to be high because of learning and not because of consistency of test measurement. Split half methods of estimating reliability are not applicable at all because scores on parts of the total series completed are meaningless. That the Maze Test is reliable in a statistical sense has been intuitively accepted, but not adequately demonstrated.

Consideration of validity immediately raises the question of a criterion. From earlier discussion it is evident that performance on Binet-type or performance tests are not adequate criteria for validating the Maze as a measure of "planning and foresight." There have been no attempts of which the reviewer is aware to devise special situations involving these traits against which validity might be measured. The most promising evidence comes from studies contrasting the performance of delinquents and nondelinquents, adjusted and maladjusted feebleminded and delinquents, pre- and post-lobotomy patients, and various social groups. Evidence from such studies is consistent in showing that the less well adjusted have poorer Maze performance than the better adjusted groups. In spite of consistency in the findings they are open to serious methodological questions because "adjusted" and "maladjusted" have usually not been carefully defined.

The Maze Tests were standardized on an age level basis. The Maze age score (and its derived Maze IQ) is based upon a success-failure performance on the series. This all-or-none type of scoring takes no account of qualitative differences in subjects' performance. Everyone who has used the Maze Tests to any extent recognizes that subjects earning the same Maze age scores may exhibit wide variation in the details of their performance. In 1942 Porteus published a study of results with a method of scoring performance in terms of quality of line and accuracy of successful drawing. This scoring method showed significant difference between delinquent and nondelinquent children and between criminal and noncriminal adults. This qualitative scoring adds to the clinical usefulness of the test, but more extensive investigation is needed.

In summary it may be said that the *Porteus Maze Tests* have been widely used and therefore have apparently found usefulness in psychological clinics. Nevertheless, there has not been adequate study of the test to establish it on a firm technical base. For those of us who have found the test meaningful intuitively, there would be much value in knowing that adequate investigation had established its reliability, validity, and specific significance.

GLADYS C. SCHWESINGER, *Senior Clinical Psychologist, California Youth Authority, Ventura, California.*

The Maze Test began between 1912 and 1914 when Porteus contributed to the intelligence testing movement by offering this test of "prudence and foresight." His first papers were published simultaneously in England and America in 1915, with subsequent generalized accounts appearing in 1919, 1924, 1933, and the most recent in 1950. The last publication, *The Porteus Maze Test and Intelligence,* carries a bibliography of 91 titles, attesting to the intense study which the Maze Test has undergone at the hands of its author and many other investigators. During these 35 years, the Maze patterns and methods of scoring went through some minor changes, but the design of the test is essentially the same. The tests have been republished and standardized in several foreign languages. Recently an alternative procedure for adults has been arranged by Peters. A second series standardized against the original series, with the new one to be scored so as to diminish or eliminate practice effect, is now being developed by Porteus.

Methods of validation have progressively changed from correlation with scores from other mental tests through judgments and ratings of educational, industrial, and social sufficiency, quality of adjustment in the community, adaptability of the test in widely differing environments, to the most recent and dramatic checking of Maze Test results against the effects of psychosurgery. From this new approach more significant research on Maze Test validity has been done within the last 10 years than in the previous 25, with new vistas open to what is now recognized as a highly sensitive testing instrument.

Correlation coefficients between Maze Test and innumerable well known tests of intelligence have all been positive, suggesting a high degree of "g" saturation. In Porteus' own opinion, this reflects the common factor, planning capacity, present in all tests of intelligence. Males do better than females in nearly all environments, this being attributed to the fact that environment puts less stress on males than on females. The Maze Test also has the distinction of being able to tap emotional and temperamental factors which do not affect performance in other tests to the same degree.

Maze Tests show a fairly high correlation with Stanford-Binet for subjects relatively homogeneous as to education and training. In nonschool situations, however, with heterogeneous adults, the correlation is not so very high. This latter moderate correlation shows that when scholastic aptitude is ruled out, the two tests measure different things. Burt found that the nonlinguistic mazes proved a better measure of practical intelligence than did the Binet-Simon which carried advantages for the verbally glib. But when the Maze Tests were applied to criminals, delinquents, and socially maladjusted subjects their scores ran lower, making it even clearer that the Maze tested temperamental qualities such as prudence and emotional control as well as mental capacity. By 1941 this realization led to Porteus' devising a supplementary method of scoring responses on the Maze Test. In addition to obtaining a *quantitative* measure of mental ability (for which the units of measurement are scaled by years and half-years of age with a test age or test quotient being obtained) the psychologist can now simultaneously derive a *qualitative* measure of temperament and emotional control (scored by error points, with a critical score of 29 for normal males, and 31 for females, with the average Q score for delinquents 50 for males and 54 for females). The total weighted error scores range from 0 to 150 and more points. Responses on this qualitative scale of errors include: cutting corners, crossing lines, lifting pencil, making wavy lines, going in the wrong direction, and being penalized for mistakes on the tests for years V and VI in the regular series. It should be repeated that the qualitative measure does not serve to replace the quantitative measure but to supplement it.

As a high Q (i.e., qualitative) score marks an inferior effort, with the reverse being true for the test age score on the quantitative scale, negative correlations are to be expected to indicate corresponding relationships. For delinquent girls, $r = -.40$; for criminals, $r = -.37$, showing that the more intelligent individuals tend to be more exact and careful, but not so much so as to indicate that intelligence is an important factor in *quality* of Maze performance. Critical scores obtained for these various groups show relatively small overlapping. Objective scoring on both qualitative and quantitative scales must still be accompanied by careful observation and notetaking during the clinical interview.

Social status is reflected in Maze Test response, with children in higher social grades doing better than those in the lower grades, both being an expression of greater prudence, forethought, and planning capacity. The Maze Test has been widely used in studies of national-racial differences as they are independent of language disabilities, cultural disadvantages, and educational inequalities, points which invalidate findings of mental comparisons obtained by other standard tests, especially if the performance of the white race is made the standard of comparison.

With two quite differently discriminating scales in one test instrument, the *Porteus Maze Test* is packed with value for any clinic repertoire of tests. With the new and startling checks on validity derived through use of the Maze Tests on lobotomized and topectomized patients the Mazes have shown their superiority over other intelligence tests in correlating with that core of the intelligence process known as planning capacity. With the nonlanguage character of the Mazes, and with the universality of their interest and appeal, the Maze Test is still one of the very few which can be employed in many widely varying environments and different linguistic groups. With the additional light they throw on mental reactions in mentally retarded children, already tested by other instruments, their use before any final diagnosis of mental deficiency is made is strongly indicated; and certainly so before any commitments to institutions for the feebleminded are recommended. The Maze Test should be routine in any psychological clinic dealing with children, for it is a very useful and very discriminating instrument.

For related reviews, see 357, 38:B453, and 36:B210.

[357]

★[*Re* Porteus Maze Test.] PORTEUS, STANLEY D. **The Porteus Maze Test and Intelligence.** Palo Alto, Calif.: Pacific Books, 1950. Pp. vi, 194. $4.00. (*PA* 25:1105)

Am J Psychol 64:322 Ap '51. Madison Bentley. The author of a clever and widely employed instrument of examination explains "why a test devised in 1914 should be written about at length in 1950." Although Porteus allows the main sanction to rest upon its recent usefulness in modifications of "intelligence" through lobotomy and other surgical insults to the brain, wrought for diagnosis, relief and recovery, he might have laid weight also upon the later advances in the conception and determination of intelligence and in the author's long-continued researches at Vineland and in Honolulu.

J Consult Psychol 14:417–8 O '50. Laurance F. Shaffer. As the author says in his Preface, "1914 seems a very long time ago" when the Porteus Maze Tests were first devised. Since that time, however, they have been the subject of continued research, much of it in the past decade. Although there were books about the maze test in 1919, 1924, and 1933, the author has no need to apologize for still another. Porteus reports the origin and development of the test, and the results of studies in many areas: feeblemindedness, industrial applications, racial differences, delinquency, brain surgery, and organic brain defects. The data are stated clearly and fairly, but the comments often depart from cold science toward a personal and autobiographical flavor with more than a trace of contentiousness. A complete manual for the administration and scoring of the test, and for quantitative and qualitative interpretation, is included. Regret must be expressed that, in determining the age-score ratio or test quotient, Porteus continues to tinker with the chronological age in order to adjust to variations in test difficulty at different age levels. It would have been far more rational to provide a conversion table to turn test ages into true performance ages. Small shortcomings, however, do not conceal the value of the maze test. It is one of the great original contributions to psychometrics of the first half of the century. The present volume replaces all others as a sufficient manual for the test, which should continue in wide use.

J Ed Psychol 41:502–3 D '50. Lee J. Cronbach. * The book is more than a manual for the test, although it includes instructions for testing, scoring guides, and similar clinical helps. Porteus discusses use of the test in clinical diagnosis, and the implications of changes in performance following lobotomy. He presents a qualitative score which has been found to differentiate delinquents from control groups. Both of these will have interest for some practicing psychologists, although it appears that the test is best treated as an opportunity for observing the subject rather than by any objective scoring of the product. Two chapters on differences among racial groups collect much material previously published in scattered sources, and express the author's view that such differences on the Maze reflect constitutional factors. The book is most of all a personal history, recounting the long period when Porteus' contributions were, in his opinion, over-shadowed by the Stanford-Binet. This retelling of our tribal conflicts is not without interest, but Porteus' anecdotes, quotations from early sources, and retracing of the path by which we have modified our interpretation of the Binet test seem lacking in present-day relevance. His advocacy of the Maze Test as a clinical tool is well-warranted, but he seems to distinguish inadequately between what the Maze measures and "planning" as a general trait. The strongly-felt opinions Porteus drops are in turn intriguing and stimulating, amusing, and outrageous. The book is a lively memento of a psychological pioneer.

Psychol B 48:529–30 N '51. D. A. Worcester. The thesis of this book is that the Porteus Maze Test is an indispensable member of a battery of tests for the evaluation of intelligence. * Porteus considers several definitions of intelligence and finds in most of them, although he has to strain a little now and then to do so, the common element of planning. He comes, then, to his own definition of intelligence as "Capacity for making planned responses to an increasing range of relevant stimuli." While such tests as the Binet or the Wechsler are important for measuring, in part, this planning capacity, they are not adequate for the entire task—missing the mark especially with respect to "certain capacities or traits of a practical nature essential to social efficiency." Citations in this connection are made of several accounts of instances in which persons of low IQ's have not exhibited feeblemindedness in the sense of being unable to get along acceptably in their social and economic environments. The Maze is most helpful in the identification of such individuals. The Maze, too, has exceptional value in the estimation of differences of intelligence among racial groups, which must always be evaluated in light of the problems and the environment of the racial group studied. The Qualitative Score, which has been used since 1942, has been shown to separate from the normal those with tendencies towards delinquency. The reviewer finds it very difficult to evaluate, on the basis of the information given in the manual, a performance according to this qualitative score. Wavy lines are supposed to be significant, but there is no good description of "wavy." Examples are given, but these do not show what could be accepted in contrast with what could not. Evidence for the above claims has been presented before. The new, and for Porteus the final, proof of the value of the Maze comes through brain surgery. The Maze appears to be sensitive to changes in the capacity for planning as commonly observed in lobotomized patients but which are not revealed by such tests as the Binet or the Wechsler. The results of several studies are given. The Maze "has the best claims to being considered a 'frontal brain' test." Although Porteus is sharply critical of the limitations of widely-used tests of intelligence and of the statements of test users, he states clearly that these tests must always be used along with the Maze. One detects a rather plaintive note permeating the book. This is understakable in one who for 35 years has been working assiduously with a test of his own making, has seen it used in many studies in many parts of the world, but who still has not seen it accepted as having the primary value he believes it to possess. Porteus is somewhat repetitious and there are a few instances of careless proofreading. The book is, however, interesting and challenging. Allowing a little for the author's bias, those engaged in clinical practice should read it.

[358]

Revised Stanford-Binet Scale. Ages 2 and over; 1937; a revision of *Stanford-Binet Scale* ('16); individual; Forms L, M; $16 (95s. 7d.) per complete set of testing materials for any one form; $2.25 (8s. 2d.) per set of printed card material for any one form; $2.80 (10s. 10d.) per 25 record booklets for any one form; $1 (5s. 9d.) per 25 abbreviated record forms for any one form; $3.75 (12s. 6d.) per manual, *Measuring Intelligence;* $2 per abbreviated directions for administering; postpaid; (30–90) minutes; Lewis M. Terman and Maud A. Merrill; Houghton Mifflin Co. (English distributor: George G. Harrap and Co., Ltd.) *

REFERENCES

1–134. See 40:1420.
135–351. See 3:292.
352. PORTEUS, S. D. "Mental Tests With Delinquents and Australian Aboriginal Children." *Psychol R* 24:32–41 Ja '17. *
353. FREEMAN, FRANK S. "A Comparison of IQ's Obtained With Dearborn Group Tests and the Stanford Revision." *J Ed Psychol* 14:441–3 O '23. *
354. HENMON, V. A. C., AND BURNS, HELEN M. "The Constancy of Intelligence Quotients With Borderline and Problem Cases." *J Ed Psychol* 14:247–50 Ap '23. *
355. WALLIN, J. E. WALLACE. "The Consistency Shown by Intelligence Ratings Based on Standardized Tests and the Teacher's Estimates." *J Ed Psychol* 14:231–46 Ap '23. *
356. WENTWORTH, MARY M. "Two Hundred Cases of Dementia Praecox Tested by the Stanford Revision." *J Abn & Social Psychol* 18:378–84 Ja '24. *
357. WENTWORTH, MARY M. *Individual Differences in the Intelligence of School Children.* Harvard Studies in Education, Vol. 7. Cambridge, Mass.: Harvard University Press, 1926. Pp. xiii, 162. *
358. BROOKS, FOWLER D. "The Accuracy of Intelligence Quotients From Pairs of Group Tests in the Junior High School." *J Ed Psychol* 18:173–86 Mr '27. * (*PA* 1:1453)
359. DOUGHERTY, MARY L. "What Changes the I.Q.?" *El Sch J* 29:114–21 O '28. * (*PA* 3:972)
360. MARX, BARBARA. *A Study of the First Fifty Words of the Stanford-Binet Vocabulary.* Master's thesis, Stanford University (Stanford, Calif.). 1928.
361. MARINE, EDITH LUCILE. *The Effect of Familiarity With the Examiner Upon Stanford-Binet Test Performance.* Doctor's thesis, Columbia University (New York, N.Y.), 1929.
362. FORLANO, GEORGE. *Item Validity Analysis of the Ninth Year Level of the Stanford-Binet Tests.* Master's thesis, College of the City of New York (New York, N.Y.), 1930. Pp. 15.
363. DILLON, LOUISE ELINOR. *A Statistical Analysis of the Individual Tests in Years 8, 9, and 10 of the Stanford-Binet Scale.* Master's thesis, Catholic University of America (Washington, D.C.), 1931. Pp. 52.
364. EMCH, M. A. *A Study of Scatter in the Stanford-Binet.* Master's thesis, University of Illinois (Urbana, Ill.), 1931.
365. KEEN, ANGELINA MYRA. *An Analysis of the Specific Effect of Practice on Retests With the Stanford Binet.* Master's thesis, Stanford University (Stanford, Calif.), 1931.
366. LUH, C. W., AND WU, T. M. "A Comparative Study of the Intelligence of Chinese Children on the Pintner Performance and the Binet Tests." *J Social Psychol* 2:402–8 Ag '31. * (*PA* 6:784)
367. MCFADDEN, J. H. *Differential Responses of Normal and Feebleminded Subjects of Equal Mental Age, on the Kent-Rosanoff Free Association Test and the Stanford Revision of the Binet-Simon Intelligence Test.* Doctor's thesis, University of North Carolina (Chapel Hill, N.C.), 1931.
368. BACON, ARLEIGHN MAE. *A Study of the Factors of Social Adjustment Related to the Test Findings on the Stanford-Binet Test and Healy Picture Completion Test II.* Master's thesis, Smith College (Northampton, Mass.). 1932.
369. FERNEAU, LELAH. *Alternate Tests for Stanford-Binet.* Master's thesis, Ohio State University (Columbus, Ohio), 1932. Pp. 50.
370. ZABIN, DOROTHY H. *The Relation of the Pintner-Patterson Performance Tests to the Stanford Revision of the Binet Scale: a Comparison of Four Tests on the Pintner-Paterson Performance Scale With the Stanford Revision of the Binet-Simon Test in an Effort to Analyze the Component Parts of Present Day Intelligence Tests.* Master's thesis, Columbia University (New York, N.Y.), 1932.
371. BOLTON, INA A. *The Diagnosis of the Relative Difficulty*

of the Test Elements of the Stanford-Binet Scale for Feebleminded and Normal Individuals of the Same Mental Age Levels. Master's thesis, University of Kansas (Lawrence, Kan.), 1933. Pp. 113.

372. SCOTTISH COUNCIL FOR RESEARCH IN EDUCATION, MENTAL SURVEY COMMITTEE. *The Intelligence of Scottish Children: A National Survey of an Age-Group.* Publications of the Scottish Council for Research in Education, [No.] 5. London: University of London Press, Ltd., 1933. Pp. x, 160. *(PA 8:666)*

373. THORNDIKE, ROBERT L. "The Effect of the Interval Between Test and Retest on the Constancy of the I.Q." *J Ed Psychol* 24:543–9 O '33. * *(PA 8:667)*

374. WISLER, MAXINE L. *A Comparative Study of Performance of Feebleminded and Juvenile Delinquents on the Arthur Performance Scale and the Stanford-Binet Test of Intelligence.* Master's thesis, Claremont Colleges (Claremont, Calif.), 1933. Pp. 73.

375. DEAHL, KATHARINE. *The Arthur Performance Scale and the Stanford Binet: An Examination of One Hundred Sixtynine Ten-Year-Old Children.* Master's thesis, Stanford University (Stanford, Calif.), 1934.

376. ELWOOD, MARY ISABEL. *A Statistical Study of Results of the Stanford Revision of the Binet-Simon Scale With a Selected Group of Pittsburgh School Children.* Doctor's thesis, University of Pittsburgh (Pittsburgh, Pa.), 1934.

377. HOLLINGWORTH, LETA S., AND KAUNITZ, RUTH M. "The Centile Status of Gifted Children at Maturity." *J Genetic Psychol* 45:106–20 S '34. * *(PA 9:451)*

378. SMITH, MILTON. *The Chronological Age Limits Used for Determining an Intelligence Quotient on the Stanford Revision of the Binet-Simon Scale.* Master's thesis, Columbia University (New York, N.Y.), 1934.

379. MANUEL, H. T. *Spanish and English Editions of the Stanford-Binet in Relation to the Abilities of Mexican Children.* University of Texas Bulletin, No. 3532. Austin, Texas: University of Texas, August 22, 1935. Pp. 63. Paper. * *(PA 10:1093)*

380. PAPURT, MAXWELL J. "Administering the Stanford-Binet in Correctional Institutions." *Consulting Psychologist* 2:13 D '35. *

381. KINDER, E. F. "Variations in Performance on Sub-tests of the Stanford-Binet Scale of a Group of Letchworth Village Subjects Retested Over a Six-Year Period." Abstract. *Psychol B* 33:604–5 O '36. * *(PA 11:496, title only)*

382. KINDER, ELAINE F., AND HAMLIN, ROY. "Consistency in Test Performance Pattern of Mentally Subnormal Subjects." *J Psycho-Asthenics* 42:132–7 '37. * *(PA 12:1427)*

383. LAYMAN, JAMES W. "A Comparative Study of the Intellectual Performance of Mentally Ill Patients and Normal Subjects." Abstract. *Psychol B* 34:717–8 N '37. *

384. LOURIE, DORIS K. *A Comparison of the Stanford Revisions of the Binet-Simon Scale.* Master's thesis, New York University (New York, N.Y.), 1937. Pp. 80.

385. SEIDL, JULIUS C. *The Effect of Bilingualism on the Measurement of Intelligence.* Doctor's thesis, Fordham University (New York, N.Y.), 1937. (Dissertations...., 1938, pp. 22–4.)

386. WILE, IRA S., AND DAVIS, ROSE. "A Study of the Basal Age With Reference to Its Meaning for School Adjustment." *Am J Orthopsychiatry* 7:441–55 O '37. * *(PA 12:1664)*

387. COFFEY, HUBERT STANLEY. *A Study of Certain Mental Functions and Their Relation to Changes in the Intelligence of Preschool Children.* Doctor's thesis, University of Iowa (Iowa City, Iowa), 1938.

388. COSTELLO, TIMOTHY W. *Relative Performance of Behavior Problem Boys on the Stanford-Binet and Cornell-Coxe Performance Scales.* Master's thesis, Fordham University (New York, N.Y.), 1939. (Dissertations...., 1940, p. 96.)

389. ENGLISH, HORACE B., AND KILLIAN, CARL D. "The Constancy of the I.Q. at Different Age Levels." *J Consult Psychol* 3:30–2 Ja–F '39. * *(PA 13:2411)*

390. MCGRATH, RICHARD F. *A Study of Scatter in the 1937 Stanford-Binet Intelligence Tests.* Master's thesis, Fordham University (New York, N.Y.), 1939. (Dissertations...., 1940, p. 100.)

391. RHEINGOLD, HARRIET L., AND PERCE, FRANCES C. "Comparison of Ratings on the Original and the Revised Stanford-Binet Intelligence Scales at the Borderline and Mental Defective Levels." *J Psycho-Asthenics* 44:110–9 '39. * *(PA 14:3784)*

392. WILSON, MARGARET T. *A Comparison of the 1937 Revision of the Stanford-Binet With the Vineland Social Maturity Scale.* Master's thesis, Fordham University (New York, N.Y.), 1939. (Dissertations...., 1940, pp. 103–4.)

393. EARL, C. J. C. "A Psychograph for Morons." *J Abn & Social Psychol* 35:428–48 Jl '40. * *(PA 14:5403)*

394. HOWELL, ANABEL ALBY. *A Clinical Comparison of the 1916 and 1937 Stanford-Binet Tests.* Master's thesis, University of Southern California (Los Angeles, Calif.), 1940.

395. LANTZ, C. M. BEATRICE. *Some Dynamic Aspects of Success and Failure as Evidenced by Intelligence Test Responses, Verbal, Behavioral, and Personality Variations of Nine-Year-Old Boys.* Doctor's thesis, Stanford University (Stanford, Calif.), 1940. (Abstracts of Dissertations....1939–40, 1940, pp. 162–4.)

396. LAYMAN, JAMES W. "IQ Changes in Older-Age Children Placed for Foster-Home Care." Abstract. *Psychol B* 37:443 Jl '40. * *(PA 14:5420, title only)*

397. SARASON, SEYMOUR BERNARD. *The Effects of Training on Four Intelligence Tests.* Master's thesis, Clark University (Worcester, Mass.), 1940. (Abstracts of Dissertations....1940, pp. 113–4.)

398. GARRETT, JAMES FRANCIS. *School Achievement as Related to the Subdivisions of the Stanford-Binet Intelligence Test.* Doctor's thesis, New York University (New York, N.Y.), 1941. Pp. 110. *(Abstracts of Theses....[School of Education] 1941,* pp. 129–32.)

399. GIFFORD, ELIZABETH, AND MYERS, C. R. "Re-scoring the Stanford-Binet." Abstract. *B Can Psychol Assn* 1:29 Ap '41. * *(PA 15:3608, title only)*

400. BIJOU, SIDNEY W. "A Genetic Study of the Diagnostic Significance of Psychometric Patterns." *Am J Mental Def* 47:171–7 O '42. * *(PA 17:939)*

401. BRADWAY, KATHERINE PRESTON. *An Experimental Study of Factors Associated With Stanford-Binet IQ Changes From the Preschool to the Junior High School Level.* Doctor's thesis, Stanford University (Stanford, Calif.), 1942. (Abstracts of Dissertations....1941–42, 1942, pp. 130–2.)

402. MCKAY, B. ELIZABETH. "A Study of I.Q. Changes in a Group of Girls Paroled From a State School for Mental Defectives." *Am J Mental Def* 46:496–500 Ap '42. * *(PA 16:3610)*

403. WEINSTEIN, BENJAMIN. "Stanford-Binet Intelligence Test Type Performance by a Rhesus Monkey." Abstract. *Psychol B* 39:471–2 Jl '42. * *(PA 16:4731, title only)*

404. BABCOCK, HARRIET. "The Bottleneck in Psychology as Illustrated by the Terman Vocabulary Test." *Psychol R* 50:244–54 Mr '43. * *(PA 17:2237)*

405. BROWN, FRED. "An Experimental and Critical Study of the Intelligence of Negro and White Kindergarten Children." *J Genetic Psychol* 65:161–75 S '44. * *(PA 19:583)*

406. HAVIGHURST, ROBERT J., AND JANKE, LEOTA LONG. "Relations Between Ability and Social Status in a Midwestern Community: I, Ten-Year-Old Children." *J Ed Psychol* 35:357–68 S '44. * *(PA 19:476)*

407. PORTEUS, STANLEY D., AND KEPNER, RICHARD DEMONBRUN. "Mental Changes After Bilateral Pre-Frontal Lobotomy." *Genetic Psychol Monogr* 29:3–115 F '44. * *(PA 18:2455)*

408. DARCY, NATALIE T. *The Effect of Bilingualism Upon the Measurement of the Intelligence of Children of Pre-School Age.* Doctor's thesis, Fordham University (New York, N.Y.), 1945. (Dissertations...., 1945, pp. 11–9.)

409. HARTSON, L. D. "Influence of Level of Motivation on the Validity of Intelligence Tests." *Ed & Psychol Meas* 5:273–83 au '45. * *(PA 20:2500)*

410. HIGHFIELD, M. E. *The Diagnostic Significance of the Terman-Merrill Scale.* Master's thesis, University of London (London, England), 1945.

411. JANKE, LEOTA LONG, AND HAVIGHURST, ROBERT J. "Relations Between Ability and Social Status in a Mid-Western Community: II, Sixteen-Year-Old Boys and Girls." *J Ed Psychol* 36:499–509 N '45. * *(PA 20:1999)*

412. STROTHER, C. R., AND CHASSELL, M. A. "The Effect of Interpolation of Performance Test Items on Stanford-Binet Scores." *Proc Iowa Acad Sci* 52:271–3 '45. *

413. BOVÉE, ARTHUR GIBBON, AND FROEHLICH, GUSTAV J. "Some Observations on the Relationship Between Mental Ability and Achievement in French." *Mod Lang J* 26:333–6 O '46. *

414. DEMAREST, RUTH. "Differences in Results on Five Standard Tests Administered to Anglo-American and Spanish-American 7th Grade Boys." Abstract. *Am Psychol* 1:244 Jl '46. * *(PA 20:3928, title only)*

415. HOULIHAN, RITA A. M. *An Experimental Attempt to Develop a New Form of the Stanford-Binet Intelligence Test for Retarded Readers.* Master's thesis, Fordham University (New York, N.Y.), 1946.

416. MAURER, KATHARINE M. "Mental Evaluation of Cerebral Palsied Children." Abstract. *Am Psychol* 1:288–9 Jl '46. * *(PA 20:3959, title only)*

417. ORDAHL, VIDA ELLISON. *An Intercomparison of the Otis Self-Administered Test of Mental Ability, Intermediate Form-A; the Stanford-Binet Intelligence Scale, Form-L; and the California Test of Mental Maturity, Elementary S-Form.* Master's thesis, University of Southern California (Los Angeles, Calif.), 1946.

418. SARASON, SEYMOUR B., AND SARASON, ESTHER KROOP. "The Discriminatory Value of a Test Pattern With Cerebral Palsied, Defective Children." Abstract. *Am Psychol* 1:288 Jl '46. * *(PA 20:3668, title only)*

419. WRIGHT, CLARE, AND MAGARET, ANN. "Differential Test Responses of Normal and Mentally Defective Subjects: Some Theoretical Considerations." Abstract. *Am Psychol* 1:465 O '46. * *(PA 21:630, title only)*

420. CRUICKSHANK, WILLIAM M. "Qualitative Analysis of Intelligence Test Responses." *J Clin Psychol* 3:381–6 O '47. * *(PA 22:4428)*

421. MARKS, ELI S. "Sampling in the Revision of the Stanford-Binet Scale." *Psychol B* 44:413–34 S '47. * *(PA 22:1009)*

422. MEISTER, R. K., AND KENNEDY, VIRGINIA. "An Evaluation of a Short Administration of the Revised Stanford Binet." Abstract. *Am Psychol* 2:424 O '47. * *(PA 22:1218, title only)*

423. "Revised Independent-School Percentile Ratings for Intelligence Quotients Derived From the Terman-Merrill Revision of the Stanford-Binet Scale," pp. 68–9. In *1947 Fall Testing Program in Independent Schools and Supplementary Studies.* Educational Records Bulletin, No. 49. New York: Educational Records Bureau, February 1948. Pp. xii, 69. Paper, lithotyped. * *(PA 22:3281, 3644, 3648–9)*

424. ANDERSON, GLADYS LOWE. "Projective Interpretation of the Stanford-Binet in a Clinical Training Program." Abstract. *Am Psychol* 3:284 Jl '48. * *(PA* 22:5417, title only)
425. BALDWIN, ALFRED L. "The Relative Difficulty of Stanford-Binet Items and Their Relation to I.Q." *J Personality* 16:417-30 Je '48. * *(PA* 23:2226)
426. BALDWIN, ALFRED L. "Variation in Stanford-Binet I.Q. Resulting From an Artifact of the Test." *J Personality* 17: 186-98 D '48. * *(PA* 25:3156)
427. BANNON, W. J. *An Examination of the Performance of a Group of 251 Scottish Children on Age-Level XIII of the Terman-Merrill Revision of Stanford-Binet Scale.* Bachelor's thesis, Glasgow University (Glasgow, Scotland), 1948. Abstract: *Brit J Ed Psychol* 19:221-2 N '49. *
428. COLE, RAYMONDE. "An Item-Analysis of the Terman-Merrill Revision of the Binet Tests." *Brit J Psychol, Stat Sect* 1:137-51 N '48. * *(PA* 23:4814)
429. ELONEN, ANNA S., AND KORNER, ANNELIESE FRIEDSAM. "Pre- and Post-Operative Psychological Observations on a Case of Frontal Lobectomy." *J Abn & Social Psychol* 43:532-43 O '48. * *(PA* 23:1821)
430. GAW, ESTHER ALLEN. "Testing Sixth Grade Children of El Salvador With the Stanford-Binet (1937)." Abstract. *Am Psychol* 3:342 Ag '48. * *(PA* 23:710, title only)
431. GEWIRTZ, JACOB L. "Studies in Word-Fluency: I, Its Relation to Vocabulary and Mental Age in Young Children." *J Genetic Psychol* 72:165-76 Je '48. * *(PA* 23:1275)
432. GORDON, L. V., AND DUREA, M. A. "The Effect of Discouragement on the Revised Stanford-Binet Scale." *J Genetic Psychol* 73:201-7 D '48. * *(PA* 23:3215)
433. HONZIK, M. P.; MACFARLANE, J. W.; AND ALLEN, L. "The Stability of Mental Test Performance Between Two and Eighteen Years." *J Exp Ed* 17:309-24 D '48. * *(PA* 23:4819)
434. HUNT, WILLIAM A.; KLEBANOFF, SEYMOUR G.; MENSH, IVAN N.; AND WILLIAMS, MEYER. "The Validity of Some Abbreviated Individual Intelligence Scales." *J Consult Psychol* 12:48-52 Ja-F '48. * *(PA* 22:3032)
435. JONES, LYLE V. *A Factor Analysis of the Revised Stanford-Binet at Four Age Levels.* Master's thesis, University of Washington (Seattle, Wash.), 1948. *(PA* 24:3212)
436. MCCULLOUGH, BETSEY R. *The Effects of Serial Testing Upon the Results of the Stanford-Binet Tests of Intelligence.* Master's thesis, Utah State Agricultural College (Logan, Utah), 1948.
437. PHILLIPS, E. LAKIN; BERMAN, ISABEL R.; AND HANSON, HAROLD B. *Intelligence and Personality Factors Associated With Poliomyelitis Among School Age Children.* Monographs of the Society for Research in Child Development, Vol. 12, No. 2, Serial No. 45. Evanston, Ill.: Child Development Publications, the Society, 1948. Pp. vii, 60. Paper, lithotyped. *
438. PIERCE, HELEN OEXLE. "Errors Which Can and Should Be Avoided in Scoring the Stanford-Binet Scale." *J Genetic Psychol* 72:303-5 Je '48. * *(PA* 23:1292)
439. RUDOLF, C. DE M. "The Kent and Other Tests Used on the Same Subjects." *J Mental Sci* 44:452-8 Ap '48. * *(PA* 23:1295)
440. SCHAFER, SARAH, AND LEITCH, MARY. "An Exploratory Study of the Usefulness of a Battery of Psychological Tests With Nursery School Children." *Am J Psychiatry* 104:647-52 Ap '48. * *(PA* 23:813)
441. ALTUS, WILLIAM S., AND CLARK, JERRY H. "Some Sectional Differences Among Negro and White Illiterate Soldiers." *J Social Psychol* 30:97-104 Ag '49. * *(PA* 24:2499)
442. BAILEY, HELEN K. "A Study of the Correlations Between Group Mental Tests, the Stanford-Binet, and the Progressive Achievement Test Used in the Colorado Springs Elementary Schools." *J Ed Res* 43:93-100 O '49. * *(PA* 24:2825)
443. BAYLEY, NANCY. "Consistency and Variability in the Growth of Intelligence From Birth to Eighteen Years." *J Genetic Psychol* 75:165-96 D '49. * *(PA* 24:4511)
444. BURTON, ARTHUR. "The Use of Psychometric and Projective Tests in Clinical Psychology." *J Psychol* 28:451-6 O '49. * *(PA* 24:2505)
445. CARSON, MARGARET K. *A Comparative Study of the Stanford-Binet Form L, and the Porteus Composite Binet.* Master's thesis, University of Hawaii (Honolulu, Hawaii), 1949. *(PA* 26:1768, title only)
446. CRONBACH, LEE J. Chap. 6, "The Binet Scale and Its Descendants," pp. 101-39. In his *Essentials of Psychological Testing.* New York: Harper & Brothers, 1949. Pp. xiii, 475. * *(PA* 24:647)
447. ELONEN, ANNA S. *A Comparison of Two Tests of Intelligence Administered to Adults.* American Psychological Association, Psychological Monographs: General and Applied, Vol. 63, No. 11, Whole No. 306. Washington, D.C.: the Association, Inc., 1949. Pp. iii, 35. Paper. * *(PA* 25:2452)
448. FEIFEL, HERMAN. "Qualitative Differences in the Vocabulary Responses of Normals and Abnormals." *Genetic Psychol Monogr* 39:151-204 My '49. * *(PA* 24:178)
449. GOTHBERG, LAURA C. "A Comparative Study of the Stanford-Binet Old Form Test and Wechsler-Bellevue, Verbal-, Performance-, and Full-Scale, as Shown in the Results of Unselected Employees." *Am J Mental Def* 53:497-503 Ja '49. * *(PA* 23:3216)
450. HAMILTON, MILDRED E. "A Comparison of the Revised Arthur Performance Tests (Form II) and the 1937 Binet." *J Consult Psychol* 13:44-9 F '49. * *(PA* 23:3751)
451. HILDEN, ARNOLD H. "A Longitudinal Study of Intellectual Development." *J Psychol* 28:187-214 Jl '49. * *(PA* 24:520)
452. JASTAK, JOSEPH. "Problems of Psychometric Scatter Analysis." *Psychol B* 46:177-97 My '49. * *(PA* 24:188)
453. JONES, LYLE V. "A Factor Analysis of the Stanford-Binet at Four Age Levels." *Psychometrika* 14:299-331 D '49. * *(PA* 24:3212)
454. KENNEDY-FRASER, DAVID. Chap. 4, "Individual Testing," pp. 49-67. In *The Trend of Scottish Intelligence: A Comparison of the 1947 and 1932 Surveys of the Intelligence of Eleven-Year-Old Pupils.* Preface by Godfrey Thomson. Sponsored by The Population Investigation Committee and The Scottish Council for Research in Education. Publications of the Scottish Council for Research in Education [No.] 30. London: University of London Press Ltd., 1949. Pp. xxviii, 151. * *(PA* 25:2303)
455. ROBERTS, JOHN A. FRASER. Chap. 8, "Comparison of the 1947 and 1932 Individual Test Results," pp. 119-39. In *The Trend of Scottish Intelligence: A Comparison of the 1947 and 1932 Surveys of the Intelligence of Eleven-Year-Old Pupils.* Preface by Godfrey Thomson. Sponsored by The Population Investigation Committee and The Scottish Council for Research in Education. Publications of the Scottish Council for Research in Education [No.] 30. London: University of London Press Ltd., 1949. Pp. xxviii, 151. * *(PA* 25:2303)
456. ROSENZWEIG, SAUL; with the collaboration of KATE LEVINE KOGAN. *Psychodiagnosis: An Introduction to Tests in the Clinical Practice of Psychodynamics,* pp. 14-24. New York: Grune & Stratton, Inc., 1949. Pp. xii, 380. * *(PA* 23:3761)
457. WESMAN, ALEXANDER G., AND SEASHORE, HAROLD G. "Frequency vs. Complexity of Words in Verbal Measurement." *J Ed Psychol* 40:395-404 N '49. * *(PA* 24:3393)
458. WILLIAMS, H. M.; HAFEMEISTER, NORMAN; AND WEGMAN, MARGARET. "An Analytical Study of Scores on Stanford-Binet, Revised Army Beta, and School Achievement Tests." *Am J Mental Def* 53:617-20 Ap '49. * *(PA* 24:2687)
459. WRENN, C. GILBERT. "Potential Research Talent in the Sciences: Based on Intelligence Quotients of Ph.D's." *Ed Rec* 30:4-22 Ja '49. *
460. "1949 Revision, Independent-School Percentile Ratings for Intelligence Quotients Derived From the Terman-Merrill Revision of the Stanford-Binet Scale," pp. 69-70. In *1949 Fall Testing Program in Independent Schools and Supplementary Studies.* Educational Records Bulletin, No. 53. New York: Educational Records Bureau, January 1950. Pp. xiii, 70. Paper, lithotyped. * *(PA* 23:3894)
461. ARTHUR, GRACE. "The Relative Difficulty of Various Tests for Sixty Feebleminded Individuals." *J Clin Psychol* 6:276-9 Jl '50. * *(PA* 25:1883)
462. BENSBERG, GERARD J., AND SLOAN, WILLIAM. "A Study of Wechsler's Concept of 'Normal Deterioration' in Older Mental Defectives." *J Clin Psychol* 6:359-62 O '50. * *(PA* 25:8073)
463. BOND, GUY L., AND FAY, LEO C. "A Comparison of the Performance of Good and Poor Readers on the Individual Items of the Stanford-Binet Scale, Forms L and M." *J Ed Res* 43:475-9 F '50. * *(PA* 25:550)
464. BROWN, GILBERT L. "On the Constancy of the I.Q." *J Ed Res* 44:151-3 O '50. * *(PA* 25:5172)
465. CLARKE, F. R. *A Comparative Study of the Wechsler Intelligence Scale for Children and the Revised Stanford-Binet Intelligence Scale, Form L, in Relation to Scholastic Achievement of a 5th Grade Population.* Master's thesis, Pennsylvania State College (State College, Pa.), 1950.
466. CRUICKSHANK, WILLIAM M., AND QUALTERE, THOMAS J. "The Use of Intelligence Tests With Children of Retarded Mental Development: I, Comparison of the 1916 and 1937 Revisions of the Stanford-Binet Intelligence Scales; II, Clinical Considerations." *Am J Mental Def* 54:361-81 Ja '50. * *(PA* 24:3780)
467. DEAN, DOUGLAS A. *A Factor Analysis of the Stanford-Binet and SRA Primary Mental Abilities Battery at the First Grade Level.* Doctor's thesis, Pennsylvania State College (State College, Pa.), 1950. *(Abstracts of Doctoral Dissertations....1950,* 1951, pp. 394-7.) *(PA* 26:2174, title only)
468. FEIFEL, HERMAN, AND LORGE, IRVING. "Qualitative Differences in the Vocabulary Responses of Children." *J Ed Psychol* 41:1-18 Ja '50. * *(PA* 24:4519)
469. FRANDSEN, ARDEN N., AND MCCULLOUGH, BETSEY R. "Serial Versus Consecutive Order Administration of the Stanford-Binet Intelligence Scales." *J Consult Psychol* 14:316-20 Ag '50. * *(PA* 25:2455)
470. FREEMAN, FRANK S. *The Theory and Practice of Psychological Testing,* pp. 121-50, 328-34. New York: Henry Holt & Co., 1950. Pp. xxiii, 518. * (London: Sir Isaac Pitman & Sons, Ltd., 1951.) *(PA* 24:4344)
471. GRANICK, SAMUEL. *Intellectual Performance Related to Emotional Instability in Children.* Doctor's thesis, Columbia University (New York, N.Y.), 1950. Abstract: *Microfilm Abstracts* 10:61-3 no 2 '50. *(PA* 25:227, title only)
472. MAGARET, ANN, AND THOMPSON, CLARE WRIGHT. "Differential Test Responses of Normal, Superior and Mentally Defective Subjects." *J Abn & Social Psychol* 45:163-7 Ja '50. *
473. ROTTERSMAN, LEON. *A Comparison of the IQ Scores on the New Revised Stanford-Binet, Form L, The Wechsler Intelligence Scale for Children, and the Goodenough "Draw a Man" Test at the Six Year Age Level.* Master's thesis, University of Nebraska (Lincoln, Neb.), 1950.
474. SCHWARTZ, ARTHUR A. "Some Interrelationships Among

Four Tests Comprising a Test Battery: A Comparative Study." *J Proj Tech* 14:153–72 Je '50. * (*PA* 25:4592)
475. STACEY, CHALMERS L., AND LEVIN, JANICE. "Performance of Retarded Individuals on Stanford-Binet and Wechsler-Bellevue Intelligence Scales." *Am J Mental Def* 55:123–31 Jl '50. * (*PA* 25:2542)
476. TIZARD, J.; IN COLLABORATION WITH N. O'CONNOR AND J. M. CRAWFORD. "The Abilities of Adolescent and Adult High-Grade Male Defectives." *J Mental Sci* 96:888–907 O '50. * (*PA* 25:5421)
477. ABORN, MURRAY, AND DERNER, GORDON F. "IQ Variability in Relation to Age on the Revised Stanford-Binet." *J Consult Psychol* 15:231–5 Je '51. * (*PA* 26:6244)
478. ANDERSON, GLADYS L. Chap. 20, "Qualitative Aspects of the Stanford-Binet," pp. 581–603. In *An Introduction to Projective Techniques*. Edited by Harold H. Anderson and Gladys L. Anderson. New York: Prentice-Hall, Inc., 1951. Pp. xxiv, 720. *
479. BIRCH, JACK W. *An Investigation of the Utility of Certain Short Forms of the Terman-Merrill Revision of the Stanford-Binet Tests of Intelligence*. Doctor's thesis, University of Pittsburgh (Pittsburgh, Pa.), 1951.
480. COOK, JOHN MUNSON, AND ARTHUR, GRACE. "Intelligence Ratings for 97 Mexican Children in St. Paul, Minn." *J Excep Child* 18:14–5+ O '51. *
481. DILLER, LEONARD, AND BEECHLEY, ROBERT M. "The Constancy of the Altitude: A Note." *J Clin Psychol* 7:191–3 Ap '51. * (*PA* 25:8080)
482. FRANDSEN, ARDEN N., AND HIGGINSON, JAY B. "The Stanford-Binet and the Wechsler Intelligence Scale for Children." *J Consult Psychol* 15:236–8 Je '51. * (*PA* 26:6268)
483. GLENN, ROBERT T. *A Comparison of Intelligence Quotients Derived by the Leiter International Performance Scale and the 1937 Stanford Revision of the Binet*. Master's thesis, University of Pittsburgh (Pittsburgh, Pa.), 1951.
484. JONES, LYLE V. *Primary Mental Abilities in the Stanford-Binet, Age 13*. University of Chicago, Psychometric Laboratory [Report] No. 71. Chicago, Ill.: the Laboratory, June 1951. Pp. 19. Paper, lithotyped. *
485. KRUGMAN, JUDITH I.; JUSTMAN, JOSEPH; WRIGHTSTONE, J. WAYNE; AND KRUGMAN, MORRIS. "Pupil Functioning on the Stanford-Binet and the Wechsler Intelligence Scale for Children." *J Consult Psychol* 15:475–83 D '51. *
486. MANN, ARTHUR. "The Problem of Testing the Defective Delinquent." *Am J Mental Def* 56:411–8 O '51. * (*PA* 26:2301)
487. MEISTER, RALPH K., AND KURKO, VIRGINIA KENNEDY. "An Evaluation of a Short Administration of the Revised Stanford-Binet Intelligence Examination." *Ed & Psychol Meas* 11:489–93 au '51. *
488. NALE, STANLEY. "The Childrens-Wechsler and the Binet on 104 Mental Defectives at the Polk State School." *Am J Mental Def* 56:419–23 O '51. * (*PA* 26:2191)
489. RAPAPORT, I. *A Comparison of Performance on the Wechsler Intelligence Scale for Children and the Revised Stanford-Binet Scale*. Master's thesis, University of Pittsburgh (Pittsburgh, Pa.), 1951.
490. RICHARDS, T. W. "Mental Test Performance as a Reflection of the Child's Current Life Situation: A Methodological Study." *Child Develop* 22:221–33 S '51. *
491. STACEY, CHALMERS L., AND LEVIN, JANICE. "Correlation Analysis of Scores of Subnormal Subjects on the Stanford-Binet and Wechsler Intelligence Scale for Children." *Am J Mental Def* 55:590–7 Ap '51. * (*PA* 25:7541)
492. WATSON, ROBERT I. Chap. 9, "Revised Stanford-Binet Tests of Intelligence," pp. 221–3. In his *The Clinical Method in Psychology*. New York: Harper & Brothers, 1951. Pp. xii, 779. *
493. WEIDER, ARTHUR; NOLLER, PAUL A.; AND SCHRAMM, THEODORE A. "The Wechsler Intelligence Scale for Children and the Revised Stanford-Binet." *J Consult Psychol* 15:330–3 Ag '51. * (*PA* 26:6303)

BOYD R. MCCANDLESS, *Director, Iowa Child Welfare Research Station, State University of Iowa, Iowa City, Iowa.*

It may safely be predicted that the average clinical psychologist of the reviewer's generation has given hundreds of Stanford-Binets, both Forms L and M. He could probably recite the test while asleep. Since the literature on the tests is tremendous, this review is quite frankly impressionistic and summative. One or two trends (particularly in clinical practice) which have emerged in the past few years are pointed out.

Though universally used, the Stanford-Binet is annoying both to the tester and, as standardly administered, to the subject. The academic and verbal bias of the items, the uneven distribution of "pure" verbal, reality testing, and performance items from one year level to another (with the consequent tendency to double basal ages and ceilings) are disadvantages. The time required to administer the test is unpredictable. The standard procedure of leaving the subject with a string of at least six successive failures is distressing to all concerned. The academic nature of the materials and questions is embarrassing when the tester is confronted with a "dead end kid" or dull adult. Because of the nature of some of the items it is almost as disconcerting to test the only child, the orphan, or the extremely superior preschool child. The test is extremely weak for adults and much of its equipment out of date for small children. Its fairness to the urban Eastern, the rural, the academically retarded, or the minority group child is questionable. The Stanford-Binet is so verbally weighted that a performance scale must be administered in addition for valid assessment. Certain responses, as to the proverbs, are very hard to peg as far as correctness is concerned. The MA scale is cumbersome. The organization of the text does not give comparable behavior for comparison of one IQ or CA level with another, as does a point scale.

Some of these disadvantages, particularly leaving a child with a flat sense of failure, may be eliminated by serial testing (tests of same type at different levels given together) which does not seem seriously to affect the predictive efficiency of the test. This trend seems to be a healthy one.

One advantage of the Stanford-Binet over, for example, the *Wechsler Intelligence Scale for Children* is that "we know what we are doing." This advantage is not inherent (although its relatively good standardization population and the tremendous amount of effort, experience, and intelligence which went into its items certainly are major factors) but lies in the tremendous amount of research which has gone into the scale and its prediction coefficients. These coefficients (mainly for academic achievement) are at the present time, however, no better for groups than are the group tests. Many children (e.g., the reading retardate or the rebel against school) who are penalized by a group test are also penalized by the verbal, academic Stanford-Binet.

However, the Stanford-Binet presents a wide

Revised Stanford-Binet Scale

range of situations in which a child may be placed. Much is learned of his personality, stress resistance, power to concentrate, etc., that no group test can give. As an instrument, it lends itself well to "projective" use, a real advantage for the clinician.

In general, the Stanford-Binet plus a performance test, in the hands of a good clinician, is a combination which is remarkably predictive and informative. However, if the *Wechsler Intelligence Scale for Children,* which is more interesting and up to date and is a point scale with all the advantages thereof, lives up to some of the tentative indications of its academic prediction efficiency, the *Revised Stanford-Binet Scale* is likely to decline sharply in popularity. The reviewer, however, will continue to use the test routinely, if for no other reason than the great body of research which buttresses it. Forms L and M present real advantages (although M, with its lack of the vocabulary, so rich in projective material, seems to the reviewer weaker) in routine, repeated service, and research testing. For the clinician, it may be advisable to add the vocabulary to the Form M.

For reviews by Francis N. Maxfield, J. W. M. Rothney, and F. L. Wells, see 38:1062; for excerpts from reviews, see 40:1420; for related reviews, see 3:293–4, 40:B1093, and 38:B497.

[359]

*Stencil Design Test. Ages 4 or 6 to superior adults; 1944–47; individual; 2 forms, '44—listed below; manuals ('47); $3.50 per set of testing materials and 25 record sheets for any one form; 90¢ per 25 record sheets for any one form; 35¢ per manual for any one form; postpaid; (20–25) minutes; Grace Arthur; Psychological Corporation. *
a) STENCIL DESIGN TEST I. Ages 4 to superior adults; a subtest of *Arthur Point Scale of Performance Tests, Revised Form II* (see 335).
b) STENCIL DESIGN TEST II. Ages 6 to superior adults; tentative norms.

REFERENCES

1. ARTHUR, GRACE. "A Non-Verbal Test of Logical Thinking." *J Consult Psychol* 8:33–4 Ja–F '44. * (PA 18:2286)
2. BOULGER, CATHERINE, AND ARTHUR, GRACE. "An Unpublished Design Test." *J Consult Psychol* 8:31–2 Ja–F '44. * (PA 18:2287)
3. LEITER, RUSSELL GRAYDON. "The Leiter Adaptation of Arthur's Stencil Design Test." *Psychol Service Center J* 1:62–8+ S '49. * (PA 24:2920)
4. WATSON, NEAL. "A Qualitative Check List for the Clinical Use of the Leiter Adaptation of Arthur's Stencil Design Test in the Evaluation of Brain Injury." *Psychol Service Center J* 1:69–70 S '49. * (PA 24:3350)

BENJAMIN BALINSKY, *Assistant Professor of Psychology, The City College, New York, New York.*

The *Stencil Design Test I* is part of the Revised Form II of the *Arthur Point Scale of Performance Tests* and may be used by itself as a separate. *Stencil Design Test II* is not included in the Scale but is also administered as a separate. Both tests are individually administered. In devising the Revised Form II of the Point Scale, the *Stencil Design Test* was developed as an alternate to the *Kohs Block Design Test* because the latter showed practice effect upon repetition.

The *Stencil Design Tests* are challenging and provocative of sustained interest for both children and adults. They require the reproduction of designs by means of colored stencils. Test I consists of 20 designs and 18 colored stencils used to reproduce the designs. Test II also consists of 20 designs but has 24 colored stencils with which to reproduce them. Test II is more difficult than Test I and the tests are not equivalent forms.

Both Test I and Test II involve form, color, and depth (building stencils one over another). In Test I the colors serve as clues but in Test II the designs are in black and white while the stencils are either yellow or blue. Although reversals of color are not considered as errors (black and white may be represented by either yellow on blue or blue on yellow), the colors must necessarily be treated in an abstract manner. The examinee is not guided by the colors as in Test I. This additional factor may account in part for the greater difficulty of Test II over Test I.

Neither test can be said to be well standardized. The norms for Test I are based altogether on 968 cases for age groups four to fifteen. For Test II the norms are described as tentative. They are based on only 421 pupils all of whom had experience working on Test I before they did Test II.

Scores for both tests are in terms of chronological age in years. For younger children no provision is made for months although it is well known that growth in the younger ages is too rapid to be precisely measured by so wide a unit as a year. In the manual for Test I, IQ's are calculated on the basis of the score made on Test I. In the light of the incomplete standardization, this should not be done. Also a test employing a single type of measure cannot be considered to ascertain the IQ in the way that a test utilizing several kinds of measures does. If the IQ is to be used at all, it must be considered only as a means of making comparisons between results on the *Stencil Design Test* and other tests and this quite roughly.

The scoring method can probably be improved. The score is the number of designs completed within the time limit of four minutes each. The test author indicates inclusion of time credits if they should prove to increase the discriminate value of the test. This reviewer would also like to see a recheck of the order of presentation of the cards. They were placed in order of difficulty but it seems that some are out of order.

The reliabilities of the *Stencil Design Tests* have apparently not been calculated. Revised Form II of the Point Scale of which *Stencil Design Test I* is part has been compared with Form I of the Point Scale to give a rather crude measure of reliability.

As for the validity of the tests, evidence is available that the *Stencil Design Test I* distinguishes the highest and lowest quarters of certain classes in mechanical drafting and architectural drafting. Other single cases are cited to show the value of the test. Test II is assumed to have similar validity.

It would be important to design more validation studies and also to determine more clearly what the tests measure. Factor analysis would be useful in regard to the latter. It could be that the tests are measuring different functions at different age groups.

There is a mechanical defect that can be easily remedied. The stencils are too thin, are hard to grasp and pick up, and bend easily.

The time the test takes is supposed to average between 20 and 25 minutes. But the time would depend upon whom you are testing. If you happen to have selected groups, the average may be less or more than 25 minutes. However, the possibilities for qualitative observations of behavior of the examinee often make any extra time seem worthwhile. The Design tests would also be useful for testing the deaf and those whose command of English is limited by foreign birth or incomplete education.

The *Stencil Design Tests* have, on the whole, excellent potential. The material is interesting, the tests apparently have validity in measuring abilities that go into drafting, and they provide media for observing behavior. With further and more complete standardization, the tests should prove very worthwhile.

For a review by James M. Anderson, see 3:295.

*Visual Retention Test for Clinical Use. Ages 8 and over; 1946-50; individual; 2 editions; $2 per manual ('46); postpaid; Arthur L. Benton. *
a) DRAWING TYPE. 1946; Forms A, B; no materials required other than manual; (4) minutes; Psychological Corporation.
b) MULTIPLE CHOICE TYPE. 1950; 1 form (includes all test items from Forms A and B of Drawing Type); no data on reliability and validity in manual (for data presented elsewhere by the author, see *3*); test free to qualified users; (5) minutes; the Author, Department of Psychology, State University of Iowa, Iowa City, Iowa.

REFERENCES
1. BENTON, ARTHUR L. "A Visual Retention Test for Clinical Use." *Arch Neurol & Psychiatry* 54:212-6 S '45. * (PA 20:2917)
2. BENTON, ARTHUR L., AND COLLINS, NANCY T. "Visual Retention Test Performance in Children: Normative and Clinical Observations." *Arch Neurol & Psychiatry* 62:610-7 N '49. * (PA 25:5327)
3. BENTON, ARTHUR L. "A Multiple Choice Type of the Visual Retention Test." *Arch Neurol & Psychiatry* 64:699-707 N '50. * (PA 25:5593)

IVAN NORMAN MENSH, *Assistant Professor of Medical Psychology, Washington University Medical School, St. Louis, Missouri.*

Designed for clinical examination of patients, this test was developed as a brief technique to supplement auditory-vocal digit span tests in studying immediate memory. The manual lists several advantages of the test: it is brief (4 minutes); the sensorimotor components (visual-motor) involved are different from those of auditory-vocal digit span tests; the material to be retained is of a nonsymbolic nature (abstract designs rather than numbers, letters, words, or pictures); the test is less "interpersonal" than auditory-vocal digit span tests; the degree of difficulty is such that normal persons rarely do poorly; and equivalent forms are available. Normative data are given in the manual for 34 normal subjects and 126 patients in five diagnostic groups; and in an article (*2*) for 245 school children. Two forms are available with 7 cards each. These provide alternates for test-retest situations, frequently helpful in following the course of recovery or of deterioration in patients suffering from brain pathology.

In using any brief test such as this, one must decide whether brevity is worth the narrowing of range of response of the subjects. In the original setting of the test, the premium was worth its cost in range because of the rapidity afforded in screening patients in a Naval hospital. Further, Benton indicates the need for studying age and sex differences, neither of which have yet been reported in the literature by him or others. Norms of adult performance would be useful from a sample less highly selected than naval personnel, and it is hoped that the author's post-World War II experiences with the test will provide published information on performance of other adult samples. The children's norms are tentative, and it is from clinical observation rather than statistical analysis that several diagnostic conclusions are drawn. These trends, however, may be significant in diagnosis; they indicate that mentally defective children perform on the test in accordance with their mental age, and mentally superior children in accordance with chronological age. Brain injured children and "a proportion" of children with reading disabilities (intelligence within average range, as were the brain injured) make significantly defective performances. Such trends could be extremely valuable for diagnosis, particularly if further data showed them to be statistically significant and if they were found in other comparable tests. Cross comparisons of visual-motor tests constitute a needed area of research in the undeveloped field of psychodiagnosis in organic pathology.

JOSEPH NEWMAN, *Clinical Psychologist, Veterans Administration Hospital, Canandaigua, New York.*

The *Visual Retention Test for Clinical Use* is a performance test of immediate memory designed to supplement the auditory-vocal digit span test. The test consists of seven cards bearing geometrical designs roughly graded in difficulty, ranging from one simple figure to three complex figures on one card. The subject is required to reproduce the design or designs after he has looked at the card for 10 seconds. Each drawing is scored as correct or incorrect, the maximum score being seven. Two equivalent forms exist.

The test has been applied to children and normative data are provided. A multiple choice type of the *Visual Retention Test* has also appeared. This form is suitable for use with subjects who have motor deficits of such a nature as to preclude or impair significantly the ability to draw.

The test was standardized on 160 cases, most of them patients in a naval hospital, all male but five. This number is rather small for an age spread of 17 to 51 years. The only additional data we have on this group concern age, IQ, and diagnosis. There are no data on education, socioeconomic status, or occupation, data which would seem to be necessary information concerning any standardization group. We would also like to know the influence of age upon test performance, if any. A close correlation between intelligence level and performance on the *Visual Retention Test* is reported but no coefficient is given. For a test of this type, a rather low correlation with intelligence would seem desirable.

A reliability coefficient of .71 is reported for the drawing type of the *Visual Retention Test*. The method of calculation is not given. The multiple choice type has a reliability coefficient of .76 by the split half method. These coefficients are rather low for tests purporting to differentiate among individuals. The somewhat higher coefficient reported for the multiple choice type is probably a reflection of the fact that this test is longer than the drawing type.

Benton informs us that the test is relatively insensitive to emotional influences. It is difficult to conceive of any human production, particularly one such as this, to be free of emotional influence. Anastasi and Foley in studies of drawings by various groups of adults have found that reproduction of stimuli reflect disturbances in perception, in intellectual ability, and in emotional balance.

By limiting his scoring technique to correct or incorrect, Benton places restrictions upon the sensitivity of his instrument in addition to the theoretical point whether such dichotomous grouping adequately describes any human expression. This fact comes out clearly both with the multiple choice type and with the drawing form where, in 50 per cent of the patients tested, impairment was not demonstrated. To explain this failure, Benton finds it necessary to take a rather difficult theoretical position—that the test "failed" only if one assumes that behavioral impairment consequent to cerebral injury is always of a general nature. He holds that variety not unity of behavioral defects prevails. Without entering into the relative merits of this position, it hardly seems that varied expression alone would account for so great a discrepancy.

The *Visual Retention Test* would have greater sensitivity if the scoring technique were expanded. This can be seen by comparison to very similar instruments described by Sharp [1] and by Kendall and Graham.[2] These investigators found that their instruments differentiated among various diagnostic groups.

[1] Sharp, Agnes A. "The Diagnostic Significance of a Visual Memory Drawing Test." *J Abn & Social Psychol* 44:517–27 O '49. * (*PA* 24:2225)
[2] Kendall, Barbara S., and Graham, Frances K. "Further Standardization of the Memory-for-Designs Test on Children and Adults." *J Consult Psychol* 12:349–54 S–O '48. * (*PA* 23:1773)

The *Visual Retention Test for Clinical Use* has some usefulness as part of a battery of tests to investigate memory defect. In the last analysis one can take the position of Benton himself that "no single test method is likely to achieve very impressive efficiency" in differentiating impaired and unimpaired patients. However, this should not prevent us from sharpening our tools.

WILLIAM SCHOFIELD, *Associate Professor, Departments of Psychiatry and Psychology, University of Minnesota, Minneapolis, Minnesota.*

This little exercise was devised to fill a gap in the battery of functions generally included in the clinical examination of patients. Specifically, it was designed to round out the evaluation of memory as customarily based on auditory digit span. The author sought to design a test which would have the brevity and administrative facility of the digit span test while involving distinctly different functions. Accordingly, his "memory for designs" test involves vision on the sensory side and drawing in the motor aspect. Furthermore, since the digits of the auditory test are "symbolic," it was desired that the material of the visual test be nonsymbolic. This latter aim seems to have been fairly well accomplished through the use of simple, abstract geometrical designs (squares, circles, etc.) for the retention material. It seems unjustified, however, to assume without reservation that digits are always "symbolic" and geometric designs "nonsymbolic." In discussing auditory digit span, the manual points out that this is not a pure measure of memory function but appears to tap factors of attention as much as those of retention. Similar comments regarding the "psychology" of the *Visual Retention Test* would be appropriate but do not appear.

The directions for administration are not sufficiently explicit and detailed; consequently, administration probably proceeds in a far less standardized fashion than is desirable. Directions to the subject are only suggested and not directly stated in quotation form. Thus, some examiners might instruct subjects to draw "exactly" what they have seen; others might follow the tenor of the manual and tell the subject to "draw what he has seen." Marked differences in performances might stem from such variation in instruction, such differences being more a reflection of personality than of differences in retentive ability. The subject is not instructed to study each card for the full 10-second exposure unless he begins to draw the first design before 10 seconds have elapsed. With perverse exactness, the manual then gives a direct quotation to be given the subject in explaining the necessity of looking at the card for the full exposure. Finally, the manual states: "The patient's performances may be praised." This seems a particularly ill advised permissiveness regarding the potentially exhortatory behavior of an examiner giving a test in which attention, concentration, and effort are so important to successful performance.

Normative data are presented in the form of distributions of scores on both forms of the test for 155 males and 5 females (!), most of whom were patients in a Naval hospital. Of this number, 34 were diagnosed as "normal." The distributions are given in terms of five levels of intelligence, "superior" through "moron" as established by the Wechsler-Bellevue IQ's of the subjects. Such normative data encourage one to think of this exercise as a test of general intelligence; the author further encourages this with a misleading statement that: "a close correlation between intelligence level and performance on the visual retention test is evident." The median scores of the "average" and "superior" groups are identical and differ by only a single point, on a 7-point scale, from the median score of the "dull average group"! It is difficult to see how a test with such an obviously limited range of difficulty can be expected to correlate closely with general intellectual level. No reliability data are reported. The two forms appear to be well equated. Validity, aside from relationship to Wechsler-Bellevue IQ's, is given only by informal reference to clinical cases.

In view of the author's expressed purpose of providing a supplement to the auditory digit span test and his implication, with two case reports, that disparities between auditory and visual retention have clinical import, it is unfortunate that he does not report the observed relationships between these two functions in his norm group, since auditory digit span would be readily available from his Wechsler examinations. In a sample of 16 patients with known organic pathology and positive evidence of intellectual impairment, nine (56 per cent) made scores below the average on the *Visual Retention Test*. In combination with auditory digit span, these data helped to establish the relative generality or specificity and gross magnitude of any retention defect.

The idea underlying the *Visual Retention Test* is good. As it stands, it provides a quick and convenient technique for clinical screening of *gross* defect in visual retention. It would be greatly improved by better standardization, with particular attention to more explicit directions for administration; increase in the range of difficulty; better normative data, especially in terms of age and sex variables; and careful validation against good clinical criteria. Even then, it should not be used as a brief examination for general intelligence.

Persons interested in this type of instrument should review the work of Sharp [1] and of Graham and Kendall.[2]

For an excerpt from a review, see 3:297.

[361]
*Wechsler-Bellevue Intelligence Scale. Ages 10–70; 1939–47; 3 scores: verbal, performance, total; individual; 2 forms; $1.50 per 25 record blanks for any one form; postpaid; (40–60) minutes; David Wechsler; Psychological Corporation. *
a) FORM I. 1939–47; $16.50 per set of test materials and 25 record blanks ('47); $3.65 per manual, *The Measurement of Adult Intelligence, Third Edition* ('44).
b) FORM II. 1946–47; $18 per set of testing materials, 25 record blanks ('47), and manual ('46); $2.25 per manual.

REFERENCES

1-2. See 40:1429.
3-121. See 3:298.
122. LEVI, JOSEPH. *A Psychometric Pattern of the Adolescent Psychopathic Personality.* Doctor's thesis, New York University (New York, N.Y.), 1943. (*Abstracts of Theses....* [School of Education] *October 1943–June 1944,* 1944, pp. 65–8.)
123. WEIDER, ARTHUR. "Effects of Age on the Bellevue Intelligence Scales in Schizophrenic Patients." *Psychiatric Q* 17:337–46 Ap '43. * (*PA* 17:3613)
124. ARNOLD, GWEN FREUND. *A Study of the Mental Abilities of the Cerebral Palsied.* Doctor's thesis, University of Wisconsin (Madison, Wis.), 1945. (*Summaries of Doctoral Dissertations....July, 1943 to June, 1947,* 1949, pp. 401–2.)
125. JANKE, LEOTA LONG, AND HAVIGHURST, ROBERT J. "Relations Between Ability and Social Status in a Mid-Western Community: II, Sixteen-Year-Old Boys and Girls." *J Ed Psychol* 36:499–509 N '45. * (*PA* 20:1999)
126. BROOKS, LEAH E. *The Application of the Hunt-Minnesota Test for Organic Brain Damage and the Wechsler-Bellevue Test to Psychotic Patients Before and After Shock Therapy.* Master's thesis, Fordham University (New York, N.Y.), 1946.
127. COHEN, BERTRAM. "Validity of a Short Form of the Wechsler-Bellevue on Four Psychiatric Groups." Abstract. *Am Psychol* 1:464 O '46. * (*PA* 21:240, title only)
128. DEMAREST, RUTH. "Differences in Results on Five Standard Tests Administered to Anglo-American and Spanish-American 7th Grade Boys." Abstract. *Am Psychol* 1:244 Jl '46. * (*PA* 20:3928, title only)
129. HALPERN, FLORENCE. "Studies of Compulsive Drinkers: Psychological Test Results." *Q J Stud Alcohol* 6:468–79 Mr '46. * (*PA* 20:274*)
130. LINDZEY, GARDNER E. "Four Psychometric Techniques Useful in Vocational Guidance." *J Clin Psychol* 2:157–60 Ap '46. * (*PA* 20:3899)
131. TAGIURI, R. "Comparison of Results Obtained From the Wechsler-Bellevue Vocabulary Test With Those From the Stanford-Binet Vocabulary Test Using a Population of Normal Subjects and Mental Patients." Abstract. *B Can Psychol Assn* 6:101 O–D '46. * (*PA* 21:920, title only)
132. COFER, CHARLES N. "Psychological Test Performance Under Hyoscine: A Case of Post-Infectious Encephalopathy." *J General Psychol* 36:221–8 Ap '47. * (*PA* 22:3028)

[1] Sharp, Agnes A. "The Diagnostic Significance of a Visual Memory Drawing Test." *J Abn & Social Psychol* 44:517–27 O '40. * (*PA* 24:2225)
[2] Graham, Frances K., and Kendall, Barbara S. "Performance of Brain-Damaged Cases on a Memory-for-Designs Test." *J Abn & Social Psychol* 41:303–314 Jl '46. * (*PA* 20:4616)

133. COHEN, BERTRAM, AND STEISEL, IRA M. "An Evaluation of the Various Short Forms of the Wechsler-Bellevue Test." *Proc Iowa Acad Sci* 54:221–6 '47. * (*PA* 23:5518)
134. COHEN, DAVID. *Wechsler-Bellevue Test Score Patterns in Anxiety State and Situation Reaction Due to Combat.* Master's thesis, University of Pittsburgh (Pittsburgh, Pa.), 1947.
135. FOSTER, AUSTIN. "Age and the Wechsler-Bellevue Scattergraph." *J Clin Psychol* 3:396–7 O '47. * (*PA* 22:4419)
136. FOSTER, CHARLES GRAHAM. *A Study of the Wechsler-Bellevue Intelligence Scale as a Vocational Guidance Indicator of Engineering Aptitude.* Master's thesis, University of Southern California (Los Angeles, Calif.), 1947.
137. FOX, CHARLOTTE. "Factor in Intelligence Testing in Later Maturity." *J Gerontol* 2:344–6 O '47. *
138. GARFIELD, SOL L. "An Appraisal of Wechsler-Bellevue Scatter Patterns in Schizophrenia." Abstract. *Am Psychol* 2:425 O '47. * (*PA* 22:1233, title only)
139. LANDISBERG, SELMA. "A Personality Study of Institutionalized Epileptics." *Am J Mental Def* 52:16–22 Jl '47. * (*PA* 22:2267)
140. LEWINSKI, ROBERT J. "The Psychometric Pattern: III, Epilepsy." *Am J Orthopsychiatry* 17:714–22 O '47. * (*PA* 22:1836)
141. MAGARET, ANN, AND SIMPSON, MARY. "A Comparison of Two Measures of Deterioration in Psychotics." Abstract. *Am Psychol* 2:425 O '47. * (*PA* 22:1312, title only)
142. PUZZO, FRANK S. *A Study of the Psychometric Signs of Anxiety in the Wechsler-Bellevue Intelligence Scale and the Rorschach Test.* Master's thesis, Fordham University (New York, N.Y.), 1947.
143. RASHKIS, HAROLD A. "The Psychometric Analysis of a Diagnostic Problem." *Am J Orthopsychiatry* 17:529–32 Jl '47. * (*PA* 22:711)
144. TOOTH, GEOFFREY. "On the Use of Mental Tests for the Measurement of Disability After Head Injury: With a Comparison Between the Results of These Tests in Patients After Head Injury and Psychoneurotics." *J Neurol Neurosurg & Psychiatry* 10:1–11 F '47. *
145. WHEELER, ERMA T. *A Study of Certain Aspects of Personality as Related to the Electroencephalogram.* Doctor's thesis, University of Pittsburgh (Pittsburgh, Pa.), 1947. (*Abstracts of Doctoral Dissertations....,* 1948, pp. 183–96.) (*PA* 22:5361)
146. ALLEN, ROBERT M. "A Note on the Use of the Bellevue-Wechsler Scale Mental Deterioration Index With Brain Injured Patients." *J Clin Psychol* 4:88–9 Ja '48. * (*PA* 22:5439)
147. ALLEN, ROBERT M. "The Test Performance of the Brain Diseased." *J Clin Psychol* 4:281–4 Jl '48. * (*PA* 23:284)
148. ALTUS, WILLIAM D. "A Note on Group Differences in Intelligence and the Type of Test Employed." *J Consult Psychol* 12:194–5 My–Je '48. * (*PA* 22:4833)
149. BAY, MARGARET S., AND BERKS, MARY D. "Comprehension, Similarities, and Digit Symbols of the Wechsler Bellevue Scale Used in a Court Clinic." Abstract. *Am Psychol* 3:365+ Ag '48. * (*PA* 23:743, title only)
150. BECKER, GEORGE J. *The Relationship Between the Thurstone SRA Primary Mental Abilities Tests and the Wechsler Bellevue Intelligence Test.* Master's thesis, Fordham University (New York, N.Y.), 1948.
151. BLAKE, ROBERT R., AND MCCARTY, BILLY S. "A Comparative Evaluation of the Bellevue-Wechsler Mental Deterioration Index Distributions of Allen's Brain Injured Patients and of Normal Subjects." *J Clin Psychol* 4:415–8 O '48. * (*PA* 23:5703)
152. BROWER, DANIEL. "The Relations of Visuo-Motor Conflict to Personality Traits and Cardio-Vascular Activity." *J General Psychol* 38:69–99 Ja '48. * (*PA* 22:3383)
153. CARP, ABRAHAM. *Psychological Test Performance and Insulin Shock Therapy.* Doctor's thesis, Stanford University (Stanford, Calif.), 1948. (*Abstracts of Dissertations....1947–48,* 1948, pp. 180–3.) (*PA* 23:354, title only)
154. CLARK, JERRY H. "Intelligence Test Results Obtained From a Specific Type of Army A.W.O.L." *Ed & Psychol Meas* 8:677–82 w '48. * (*PA* 24:1322)
155. COPPLE, GEORGE ELLIS. *Senescent Decline on the Wechsler-Bellevue Intelligence Scale.* Doctor's thesis, University of Pittsburgh (Pittsburgh, Pa.), 1948. (*Abstracts of Doctoral Dissertations....1948,* 1949, pp. 227–36.) (*PA* 23:357, 24:1117; title only)
156. DUBIN, S. S., AND THALER, M. "A Preliminary Survey of Psychological Test Results Given to Schizophrenic Patients Before and After Treatment." Abstract. *J Colo-Wyo Acad Sci* 3:59 Mr '48. *
157. DUREA, M. A., AND TAYLOR, G. J. "The Mentality of Delinquent Boys Appraised by the Wechsler-Bellevue Intelligence Tests." *Am J Mental Def* 52:342–4 Ap '48. * (*PA* 22:5048)
158. ELLIS, ALBERT. "The Relationship Between Personality Inventory Scores and Other Psychological Test Results." *J Social Psychol* 28:287–9 N '48. * (*PA* 23:2705)
159. FREEMAN, A. V. *Scatter in Schizophrenia: A Study of Intraindividual Variability on the Wechsler-Bellevue Scale.* Doctor's thesis, Columbia University (New York, N.Y.), 1948.
160. FREEMAN, ALBERT VINCENT. "Wechsler-Bellevue 'Scatter' in Schizophrenics and Normal Controls." Abstract. *Am Psychol* 3:280–1 Jl '48. * (*PA* 22:5510, title only)
161. GARFIELD, SOL L. "A Preliminary Appraisal of Wechsler-Bellevue Scatter Patterns in Schizophrenia." *J Consult Psychol* 12:32–6 Ja–F '48. * (*PA* 22:3139)

162. GARFIELD, SOL L., AND FEY, WILLIAM F. "A Comparison of the Wechsler-Bellevue and Shipley-Hartford Scales as Measures of Mental Impairment." *J Consult Psychol* 12:259-64 Jl-Ag '48. * (*PA* 23:1289)

163. HARRIS, ROBERT E.; BOWMAN, KARL M.; AND SIMON, ALEXANDER. "Studies in Electronarcosis Therapy: III, Psychological Test Findings." *J Nerv & Mental Dis* 107:371-6 Ap '48. * (*PA* 22:4448)

164. HERRMANN, MAY, AND HACKMAN, ROY B. "Distribution of Scores on the Wechsler-Bellevue Scales and the California Test of Mental Maturity at a V.A. Guidance Center." *J Appl Psychol* 32:642-8 D '48. * (*PA* 23:3648)

165. HODGSON, GERALD L. "An Analysis of Subtests in the Wechsler-Bellevue Verbal Scale (Form I) Administered to 139 Delinquent Mexican Boys." Abstract. *Am Psychol* 3:343 Ag '48. * (*PA* 23:755, title only)

166. HONZIK, M. P.; MACFARLANE, J. W.; AND ALLEN, L. "The Stability of Mental Test Performance Between Two and Eighteen Years." *J Exp Ed* 17:309-24 D '48. * (*PA* 23:4819)

167. HUNT, WILLIAM A.; FRENCH, ELIZABETH G.; KLEBANOFF, SEYMOUR G.; MENSH, IVAN N.; AND WILLIAMS, MYER. "Further Standardization of the CVS Individual Intelligence Scale." *J Consult Psychol* 12:355-9 S-O '48. * (*PA* 23:1682)

168. HUNT, WILLIAM A.; KLEBANOFF, SEYMOUR G.; MENSH, IVAN N.; AND WILLIAMS, MYER. "The Validity of Some Abbreviated Individual Intelligence Scales." *J Consult Psychol* 12:48-52 Ja-F '48. * (*PA* 22:3032)

169. KALINKOWITZ, BERNARD NATHAN. *An Attempt to Differentiate Paranoid Schizophrenic Patients From Brain-Damaged Patients by Use of Psychological Test Procedures.* Doctor's thesis, New York University (New York, N.Y.), 1948. Abstract: *Microfilm Abstracts* 9:175-6 no 2 '49. * (*PA* 24:4197, title only)

170. KLEIN, GEORGE S. "An Application of the Multiple Regression Principle to Clinical Prediction." *J Genetic Psychol* 38:159-79 Ap '48. * (*PA* 23:1291)

171. KLUGMAN, SAMUEL F. "The Effect of Placement of the Digits Test in the Wechsler-Bellevue Intelligence Scale." *J Consult Psychol* 12:345-8 S-O '48. * (*PA* 23:1774)

172. LEVINE, LOUIS S. "Wechsler's Signs in the Differential Diagnosis of Schizophrenia." Abstract. *Am Psychol* 3:345 Ag '48. * (*PA* 23:875, title only)

173. LEVINE, LOUIS SAMUEL. *Wechsler's Signs in the Diagnosis of Schizophrenia.* Master's thesis, Stanford University (Stanford, Calif.), 1948.

174. LEWINSKI, ROBERT J. "Vocabulary and Mental Measurement: A Quantitative Investigation and Review of Research." *J Genetic Psychol* 72:247-81 Je '48. * (*PA* 23:1179)

175. MAGARET, ANN, AND SIMPSON, MARY M. "A Comparison of Two Measures of Deterioration in Psychotic Patients." *J Consult Psychol* 12:265-9 Jl-Ag '48. * (*PA* 23:1407)

176. MUNDY, JOHN PRICE. *The Immediate Effect of Alcohol on Intelligence as Measured by the Wechsler-Bellevue.* Master's thesis, University of Virginia (Charlottesville, Va.), 1948. Pp. iii, 142.

177. OLCH, DORIS R. "Psychometric Pattern of Schizophrenics on the Wechsler-Bellevue Intelligence Test." *J Consult Psychol* 12:127-36 My-Je '48. * (*PA* 22:5067)

178. OSTRANDER, JESSIE M. "A Report on Rorschach and Wechsler-Bellevue Records of a Man After the Removal of Tumor From the Frontal Lobes." *Rorsch Res Exch & J Proj Tech* 12:65-71 no 1 '48. * (*PA* 23:4950)

179. PATTERSON, C. H. "A Further Study of Two Short Forms of the Wechsler-Bellevue Scale." *J Consult Psychol* 12:147-52 My-Je '48. * (*PA* 22:4952)

180. PATTERSON, C. H. *Using the Wechsler-Bellevue Intelligence Scales in Counseling.* Preface by D. N. Wiener. Minneapolis, Minnesota: In-Service Training Section, Personnel Division, VA Regional Office, 1948. Pp. ii, 34. Paper, dittoed. *

181. PHILLIPS, E. LAKIN; BERMAN, ISABEL R.; AND HANSON, HAROLD B. *Intelligence and Personality Factors Associated With Poliomyelitis Among School Age Children.* Monographs of the Society for Research in Child Development, Vol. 12, No. 2, Serial No. 45. Evanston, Ill.: Child Development Publications, the Society, 1948. Pp. vii, 60. Paper, lithotyped. *

182. RUBINSTEIN, ELI A. "A Note on Recording Block Design Performance on the Wechsler-Bellevue Scales." *J Clin Psychol* 4:307-8 Jl '48. * (*PA* 23:169)

183. SCHAFER, ROY. *The Clinical Application of Psychological Tests: Diagnostic Summaries and Case Studies.* Foreword by David Rapaport. The Menninger Foundation Monograph Series, No. 6. New York: International Universities Press, Inc., 1948. Pp. 346. * (London: George Allen & Unwin Ltd., 1949.) (*PA* 23:778)

184. SEARS, RICHARD. "Castration Anxiety in an Adult as Shown by Projective Tests." Abstract. *Am Psychol* 3:281 Jl '48. * (*PA* 22:5371, title only)

185. SLOAN, WILLIAM, AND GUERTIN, WILSON H. "A Comparison of H-T-P and Wechsler-Bellevue IQ's in Mental Defectives." *J Clin Psychol* 4:424-6 O '48. * (*PA* 23:5532)

186. SPACHE, GEORGE. "Scoring Qualitative Responses on the Wechsler-Bellevue Scale." *Am J Orthopsychiatry* 18:360-3 Ap '48. * (*PA* 22:5437)

187. TORRANCE, PAUL. "Getting More Than an I.Q. From Testing Elementary-School Children." *El Sch J* 48:550-6 Je '48. * (*PA* 23:2418)

188. WISHNER, JULIUS. "Rorschach Intellectual Indicators in Neurotics." *Am J Orthopsychiatry* 18:265-79 Ap '48. * (*PA* 22:4427)

189. ALLEN, ROBERT M. "An Analysis of the Comparative Evaluation of Allen's Brain Injured Patients and of Normal Subjects." *J Clin Psychol* 5:422-3 O '49. * (*PA* 24:3823)

190. ALLEN, ROBERT M. "A Comparison of the Test Performances of the Brain-Injured and the Brain-Diseased." *Am J Psychiatry* 106:195-8 S '49. * (*PA* 24:3323)

191. ALLEN, ROBERT M., AND KRATO, JOHN C. "The Test Performance of the Encephalopathic." *J Mental Sci* 95:369-72 Ap '49. * (*PA* 24:294)

192. ALTUS, WILLIAM D. "Adjustment and Subtest Variation on the Army Wechsler for the Mentally Limited." *J General Psychol* 40:167-76 Ap '49. * (*PA* 24:3206)

193. ALTUS, WILLIAM D., AND CLARK, JERRY H. "Some Sectional Differences Among Negro and White Illiterate Soldiers." *J Social Psychol* 30:97-104 Ag '49. * (*PA* 24:2499)

194. ALTUS, WILLIAM D., AND CLARK, JERRY H. "Subtest Variation on the Wechsler-Bellevue for Two Institutionalized Behavior Problem Groups." *J Consult Psychol* 13:444-7 D '49. * (*PA* 24:3283)

195. ATKEY, RICHMOND R. *An Empirical Validation of the Wechsler-Bellevue Test for Mental Deterioration.* Master's thesis, University of Toronto (Toronto, Canada), 1949. Pp. 14.

196. BAYLEY, NANCY. "Consistency and Variability in the Growth of Intelligence From Birth to Eighteen Years." *J Genetic Psychol* 75:165-96 D '49. * (*PA* 24:4511)

197. BELL, JOHN ELDERKIN. "The Case of Gregor: Psychological Test Data." *Rorsch Res Exch & J Proj Tech* 13:155-205 no 2 '49. * (*PA* 24:2589)

198. BROWN, M. N. "A Critique of the Wechsler-Bellevue System of Weighted Scores." *J Clin Psychol* 5:170-3 Ap '49. * (*PA* 24:1881)

199. BURIK, THEODORE E. *Investigation of the Learning Involved in the Digit Symbol Subtest of the Wechsler-Bellevue Intelligence Scale.* Master's thesis, Fordham University (New York, N.Y.), 1949.

200. BURNHAM, CATHARINE A. "A Study of the Degree of Relationship Between Rorschach H% and Wechsler-Bellevue Picture Arrangement Scores." *Rorsch Res Exch & J Proj Tech* 13:206-9 no 2 '49. * (*PA* 24:2594)

201. BURTON, ARTHUR. "The Use of Psychometric and Projective Tests in Clinical Psychology." *J Psychol* 28:451-6 O '49. * (*PA* 24:2595)

202. CANTER, A. H. *Direct and Indirect Measures of Psychological Deficit in Multiple Sclerosis.* Doctor's thesis, Columbia University (New York, N.Y.), 1949.

203. CATTERALL, CALVIN D. "Reading Pupils Through the Wechsler-Bellevue Intelligence Tests," pp. 136-41. In *Claremont College Reading Conference, Fourteenth Yearbook, 1949: Conference Theme: The Problems and Techniques Involved in Reading Social Relationships.* Claremont, Calif.: Claremont College Curriculum Laboratory, 1949. Pp. viii, 191. Paper. *

204. CHESROW, EUGENE J.; WOSIKA, PAUL H.; AND REINITZ, ARTHUR H. "A Psychometric Evaluation of Aged White Males." *Geriatrics* 4:169-77 My-Je '49. * (*PA* 24:540)

205. CLARK, JERRY H. "An Investigation of Certain Relationships Between the California Test of Mental Maturity and the Wechsler-Bellevue Intelligence Scale." *J General Psychol* 41:21-5 Jl '49. * (*PA* 24:2597)

206. CLARK, JERRY H. "Subtest Variation on the Wechsler-Bellevue for Two Institutionalized Behavior Problem Groups." Abstract. *Am Psychol* 4:395 S '49. * (*PA* 24:1882, title only)

207. COTZIN, MILTON, AND GALLAGHER, JAMES J. "Validity of Short Forms of the Wechsler-Bellevue Scale for Mental Defectives." *J Consult Psychol* 13:357-65 O '49. * (*PA* 24:2672)

208. CRONBACH, LEE J. Chap. 7, "Mental Diagnosis: The Wechsler Test," pp. 140-60. In his *Essentials of Psychological Testing.* New York: Harper & Brothers, 1949. Pp. xiii, 475. * (*PA* 24:647)

209. DOPPELT, JEROME; SEASHORE, HAROLD; AND WESMAN, ALEXANDER. "The Standardization of the Wechsler Mental Ability Scale." Abstract. *Am Psychol* 4:240 Jl '49. * (*PA* 23:6207, title only)

210. FISHER, GRANVILLE C. *Significant Differences in Sub-Test Scores on the Wechsler-Bellevue Scale of Subjects With General Paresis.* Doctor's thesis, University of Chicago (Chicago, Ill.), 1949. Pp. 47.

211. FISHER, KENNETH ALLEN. "Changes in Test Performance of Ambulatory Depressed Patients Undergoing Electro-Shock Therapy." *J General Psychol* 41:195-232 O '49. * (*PA* 24:4722)

212. GARFIELD, SOL L. "An Evaluation of Wechsler-Bellevue Patterns in Schizophrenia." *J Consult Psychol* 13:279-87 Ag '49. * (*PA* 24:1340)

213. GERSTEIN, REVA A. "A Suggested Method for Analyzing and Extending the Use of Bellevue-Wechsler Vocabulary Responses." *J Consult Psychol* 13:366-70 O '49. * (*PA* 24:2603)

214. GIBBY, ROBERT G. "A Preliminary Survey of Certain Aspects of Form II of the Wechsler-Bellevue Scale as Compared to Form I." *J Clin Psychol* 5:165-9 Ap '49. * (*PA* 24:1886)

215. GILHOOLY, FRANCIS M. *An Investigation of the Relationship Between Variability and Ability on the Wechsler-Bellevue Intelligence Scale.* Master's thesis, Fordham University (New York, N.Y.), 1949.

216. GOTHBERG, LAURA C. "A Comparative Study of the Stanford-Binet Old Form Test and Wechsler-Bellevue, Verbal-,

Performance-, and Full-Scale, as Shown in the Results of Unselected Employees." *Am J Mental Def* 53:497–503 Ja '49. * (*PA* 23:3216)

217. GRAY, CONSTANCE V. *An Investigation of the Shipley-Hartford and Wechsler-Bellevue Scales and Measures of Deterioration.* Master's thesis, University of Toronto (Toronto, Canada), 1949. Pp. 35.

218. GURVITZ, MILTON SOLOMON. *An Experimental Application of Wechsler-Bellevue Type Tests in an Attempt to Discriminate and Diagnose Psychopathic Personality Types Resident in a Penal Institution.* Doctor's thesis, New York University (New York, N.Y.), 1949. Abstract: *Microfilm Abstracts* 10:234–5 no 3 '50. *

219. HALPERIN, SIDNEY L. "A Study of the Personality Structure of the Prisoner in Hawaii." Abstract. *Rorsch Res Exch & J Proj Tech* 13:243 no 2 '49. * (*PA* 24:2707, title only)

220. HAMISTER, RICHARD C. "The Test-Retest Reliability of the Wechsler-Bellevue Intelligence Test (Form I) for a Neuropsychiatric Population." *J Consult Psychol* 13:39–43 F '49. * (*PA* 23:3752)

221. HECHT, IRVING. *The Differentiation of Certain Psychosomatic Groups in Terms of Psychometric Patterns: An Evaluation of the Wechsler-Bellevue Intelligence Scale and of the Rorschach Projective Technique to Differentiate Among the Ulcer, Colitis, and Hypertension Groups.* Doctor's thesis, New York University (New York, N.Y.), 1949. Abstract: *Microfilm Abstracts* 10:148–9 no 2 '50. (*PA* 25: 361, title only)

222. HEWSON, LOUISE R. "The Wechsler-Bellevue Scale and the Substitution Test as Aids in Neuropsychiatric Diagnosis." *J Nerv & Mental Dis* 109:158–83, 246–66 F, Mr '49. * (*PA* 23:4378)

223. HEYER, ALBERT W., JR. "'Scatter Analysis' Techniques Applied to Anxiety Neurotics From a Restricted Culturo-Educational Environment." *J General Psychol* 40:155–66 Ap '49. * (*PA* 24:3307)

224. HILDEN, ARNOLD H. "A Longitudinal Study of Intellectual Development." *J Psychol* 28:187–214 Jl '49. * (*PA* 24: 520)

225. HUNT, WILLIAM A., AND FRENCH, ELIZABETH G. "Some Abbreviated Individual Intelligence Scales Containing Nonverbal Items." *J Consult Psychol* 13:119–23 Ap '49. * (*PA* 23: 4822)

226. HUNT, WILSON L. "The Relative Rates of Decline of Wechsler-Bellevue 'Hold' and 'Don't-Hold' Tests." *J Consult Psychol* 13:440–3 D '49. * (*PA* 24:3210)

227. JASTAK, JOSEPH. "Problems of Psychometric Scatter Analysis." *Psychol B* 46:177–97 My '49. * (*PA* 24:188)

228. JOHNSON, LENNART C. "Wechsler-Bellevue Pattern Analysis in Schizophrenia." *J Consult Psychol* 13:32–3 F '49. * (*PA* 23:3842)

229. JOHNSON, THOMAS F. "Some Needs in Research With the Wechsler-Bellevue Scale." *J General Psychol* 41:33–6 Jl '49. * (*PA* 24:2606)

230. KAHN, HARRIS, AND SINGER, ERWIN. "An Investigation of Some of the Factors Related to Success or Failure of School of Commerce Students." *J Ed Psychol* 40:107–17 F '49. * (*PA* 24:2062)

231. KASS, WALTER. "Wechsler's Mental Deterioration Index in the Diagnosis of Organic Brain Disease." *Trans Kans Acad Sci* 52:66–70 '49. * (*PA* 23:5713)

232. KOGAN, W. S. *An Investigation Into the Relationship Between Psychometric Patterns and Psychiatric Diagnosis.* Doctor's thesis, University of Pittsburgh (Pittsburgh, Pa.), 1949. (*Abstracts of Doctoral Dissertations....1949*, 1950, pp. 314–22.) (*PA* 29:2994, title only)

233. LEVINE, LOUIS S. "The Utility of Wechsler's Patterns in the Diagnosis of Schizophrenia." *J Consult Psychol* 13:28–31 F '49. * (*PA* 23:3844)

234. MERCER, MARGARET. "Diagnostic Testing in Two Cases of Schizophrenic Depression." *J Psychol* 28:147–60 Jl '49. * (*PA* 24:712)

235. MEYER, MORTIMER M. "Integration of Test Results With Clinical Observations: A Diagnostic Case Study." *Rorsch Res Exch & J Proj Tech* 13:325–40 S '49. * (*PA* 24:3202)

236. O'CONNOR, JAMES P. *The Wechsler-Bellevue Intelligence Scales as an Index of Deterioration in Psychoneurotics.* Master's thesis, Catholic University of America (Washington, D.C.), 1949. (*PA* 24:835, title only)

237–8. PASCAL, GERALD R., AND ZEAMAN, JEAN B. "A Note on the Validity of Wechsler-Bellevue Scatter." *Am J Psychiatry* 105:840–2 My '49. * (*PA* 24:1205)

239. RAKUSIN, JOHN. *The Analysis of Scatter on the Wechsler-Bellevue Adult Intelligence Scale in a Group of Adjusted and a Group of Maladjusted College Students.* Master's thesis, Pennsylvania State College (State College, Pa.), 1949. (*PA* 24: 5559, title only)

240. ROSENZWEIG, SAUL; WITH THE COLLABORATION OF KATE LEVINE KOGAN, *Psychodiagnosis: An Introduction to Tests in the Clinical Practice of Psychodynamics*, pp. 24–32. New York: Grune & Stratton, Inc., 1949. Pp. xii, 380. * (*PA* 23:3761)

241. RUDOLF, G. DE M. "Comparison of the Intelligence Quotient With Behaviour." *J Mental Sci* 95:703–5 Jl '49. * (*PA* 24: 1944)

242. RUDOLF, G. DE M. "Re-Testing of the Intelligence Quotient and the Social Age." *J Mental Sci* 95:696–702 Jl '49. * (*PA* 24:1945)

243. SCHAFER, ROY. "Wechsler-Bellevue Scale and Word Association Test: The Case of Gregor: Interpretation of Test Data: Symposium Presented at American Psychological Association Meeting, Denver, 1949." *Rorsch Res Exch & J Proj Tech* 13:434–8 D '49. (*PA* 24:3734)

244. SCHERER, ISIDOR W. "The Psychological Scores of Mental Patients in an Individual and Group Testing Situation." *J Clin Psychol* 5:405–8 O '49. * (*PA* 24:3740)

245. SCHLOSSER, JOHN R., AND KANTOR, ROBERT E. "A Comparison of Wechsler's Deterioration Ratio in Psychoneurosis and Schizophrenia." *J Consult Psychol* 13:108–10 Ap '49. * (*PA* 23:4831)

246. SINGER, ERWIN. *Personality Structure of Chronic Alcoholics.* Doctor's thesis, New York University (New York, N.Y.), 1949. Abstract: *Microfilm Abstracts* 10:153–4 no 2 '50. (*PA* 25:448, title only)

247. SMITH, ARTHUR E. *A Comparison of the SRA Primary Mental Abilities Test With the Wechsler-Bellevue Intelligence Scale.* Master's thesis, Illinois State Normal University (Normal, Ill.), 1949. (*PA* 24:382, title only)

248. SORSBY, FELMAN B. *A Briefer Method for the Wechsler-Bellevue Vocabulary Sub-Test.* Master's thesis, University of Pittsburgh (Pittsburgh, Pa.), 1949. (*PA* 23:3003, title only)

249. STANTON, JOHN M. *An Investigation of the Validity of the Mental Deterioration Index of the Wechsler-Bellevue Scale in Indicating Organic Brain Pathology.* Master's thesis, Fordham University (New York, N.Y.), 1949.

250. SUPER, DONALD E. *Appraising Vocational Fitness By Means of Psychological Tests*, pp. 142–6. New York: Harper & Brothers, 1949. Pp. xxiii, 727. * (*PA* 24:2130)

251. TATOM, MARY H. *Relationships Between Wechsler-Bellevue Sub-Test Scores and Certain Rorschach Test Factors in Clinical Patients.* Master's thesis, Catholic University of America (Washington, D.C.), 1949. (*PA* 24:842, title only)

252. VISTICA, NICHOLAS J. *Scatter Analysis on the Wechsler-Bellevue Scale as an Indicator of the Personality Adjustment of Normal Subjects.* Master's thesis, Fordham University (New York, N.Y.), 1949.

253. WEBB, WILSE B., AND HANER, CHARLES. "Quantification of the Wechsler-Bellevue Vocabulary Sub-Test." *Ed & Psychol Meas* 9:693–707 w '49. * (*PA* 26:2761)

254. WELSH, GEORGE S. "A Note on Scoring Wechsler-Bellevue Subtests." *J Clin Psychol* 5:421–2 O '49. * (*PA* 24: 3744)

255. WESMAN, ALEXANDER G., AND SEASHORE, HAROLD G. "Frequency vs. Complexity of Words in Verbal Measurement." *J Ed Psychol* 40:395–404 N '49. * (*PA* 24:3393)

256. WITTENBORN, J. R. "An Evaluation of the Use of Bellevue-Wechsler Subtest Scores as an Aid in Psychiatric Diagnosis." *J Consult Psychol* 13:433–9 D '49. * (*PA* 24:3220)

257. WRIGHT, H. F.; MACPHEE, H. M.; AND CUMMINGS, S. B., JR. "The Relationship Between the Kent EGY and the Bellevue Verbal Scale." *J Abn & Social Psychol* 44:223–30 Ap '49. * (*PA* 23:5533)

258. ANDERSEN, A. LLOYD. "The Effect of Laterality Localization of Brain Damage on Wechsler-Bellevue Indices of Deterioration." *J Clin Psychol* 6:191–4 Ap '50. * (*PA* 26:6474)

259. BARNETT, IRVING. "The Use of Z Scores in Equating the Wechsler-Bellevue Subtests." *J Clin Psychol* 6:184–8 Ap '50. * (*PA* 24:6347)

260. BENSBERG, GERARD J., AND SLOAN, WILLIAM. "A Study of Wechsler's Concept of 'Normal Deterioration' in Older Mental Defectives." *J Clin Psychol* 6:359–62 O '50. * (*PA* 25:8073)

261. BRODY, ABRAHAM BARNET. *A Factorial Study of Intellectual Functioning in Normal and Abnormal Adults.* Doctor's thesis, Columbia University (New York, N.Y.), 1950. Abstract: *Microfilm Abstracts* 11:445–6 no 2 '51. (*PA* 26:2171, title only)

262. BURIK, THEODORE E. "Relative Roles of the Learning and Motor Factors Involved in the Digit Symbol Test." *J Psychol* 30:33–42 Jl '50. * (*PA* 25:1089)

263. CARP, ABRAHAM. "Performance on the Wechsler-Bellevue Scale and Insulin Shock Therapy." *J Abn & Social Psychol* 45:127–36 Ja '50. * (*PA* 24:4719)

264. CLARK, JERRY H. "The Relationship of Wechsler-Bellevue Patterns to Psychiatric Diagnosis of Army Prisoners." *Am Psychol* 5:462 S '50. * (*PA* 25:4712, title only)

265. CLARK, JERRY H., AND MOORE, JAMES H. "The Relationship of Wechsler-Bellevue Patterns to Psychiatric Diagnosis of Army and Air Force Prisoners." *J Consult Psychol* 14:493–5 D '50. * (*PA* 26:1020)

266. COHEN, JACOB. *A Comparative Analysis of the Factors Underlying Intelligence Test Performance of Different Neuropsychiatric Groups Multiple Factor Analyses of the Wechsler-Bellevue Intelligence Scale Performance of Schizophrenic, Psycho-Neurotic and Brain-Damaged Groups.* Doctor's thesis, New York University (New York, N.Y.), 1950. Abstract: *Microfilm Abstracts* 10:313–5 no 4 '50. * (*PA* 25:4721, title only)

267. COTZIN, MILTON, AND GALLAGHER, JAMES J. "The Southbury Scale: A Valid Abbreviated Wechsler-Bellevue for Mental Defectives." *J Consult Psychol* 14:358–64 O '50. * (*PA* 25:4563)

268. DAVIDSON, KENNETH S.; GIBBY, ROBERT G.; MCNEIL, ELTON B.; SEGAL, STANLEY J.; AND SILVERMAN, HERBERT. "A Preliminary Study of Negro and White Differences on Form I of the Wechsler-Bellevue Scale." *J Consult Psychol* 14:489–92 D '50. * (*PA* 26:846)

269. DERNER, GORDON F., AND ABORN, MURRAY. "An Administration Board for the Wechsler-Bellevue Object Assembly Subtest." *J Consult Psychol* 14:71–2 F '50. * (*PA* 24:3929)

270. DERNER, GORDON F.; ABORN, MURRAY; AND CANTER,

Aaron H. "The Reliability of the Wechsler-Bellevue Subtests and Scales." *J Consult Psychol* 14:172–9 Je '50. * (PA 25:358)

271. Edrington, Thomas Craighead. *The Wechsler-Bellevue Test in Relation to the Demonstrated Academic Performance of the Naval R.O.T.C. Midshipmen in Tulane University.* Master's thesis, Tulane University (New Orleans, La.), 1950. (*Abstracts of Dissertations and Theses 1950,* pp. 118–9.)

272. Eglash, Al. "Validation of the Wechsler 'Shoes' Item." *J Abn & Social Psychol* 45:733–4 O '50. * (PA 25:2451)

273. Erwin, Edmond Francis. *Objective and Projective Measures of Withdrawal Behavior.* Doctor's thesis, Columbia University (New York, N.Y.), 1950. Abstract: *Microfilm Abstracts* 11:418–9 no 2 '51. (PA 26:2275, title only)

274. Ficca, Sylvester C. *Relationship of "Autonomic" Blood Pressure Pattern Types of Subject's Performance on the Wechsler-Bellevue and the Rorschach Test.* Doctor's thesis, Pennsylvania State College (State College, Pa.), 1950. (*Abstracts of Doctoral Dissertations....1950,* 1951, pp. 398–400.) (PA 26:2177, title only)

275. Fisher, Seymour, and Sunukjian, Helen. "Intellectual Disparities in a Normal Group and Their Relationship to Emotional Disturbance." *J Clin Psychol* 6:288–90 Jl '50. * (PA 25:1786)

276. Fox, Charlotte, and Birren, James E. "The Differential Decline of Subtest Scores of the Wechsler-Bellevue Intelligence Scale in 60–69-Year-Old Individuals." *J Genetic Psychol* 77:313–7 D '50. * (PA 25:4465)

277. Fox, Charlotte, and Birren, James E. "The Differential Decline of Wechsler Subtest Scores in 60–69 Year Old Individuals." Abstract. *Am Psychol* 5:467 S '50. * (PA 25:4466, title only)

278. Fox, Charlotte, and Birren, James E. "Intellectual Deterioration in the Aged: Agreement Between the Wechsler-Bellevue and the Babcock-Levy." *J Consult Psychol* 14:305–10 Ag '50. * (PA 25:2344)

279. Fox, Charlotte, and Birren, James E. "The Measurement of Intellectual Deterioration in the Aged." Abstract. *Am Psychol* 5:364 Jl '50. * (PA 25:980, title only)

280. Frandsen, Arden N. "The Wechsler-Bellevue Intelligence Scale and High School Achievement." *J Appl Psychol* 34:406–11 D '50. * (PA 25:4849)

281. Freeman, Frank S. *The Theory and Practice of Psychological Testing,* pp. 152–69, 334–42. New York: Henry Holt & Co., 1950. Pp. xxiii, 518. * (London: Sir Isaac Pitman & Sons, Ltd., 1951.) (PA 24:4344)

282. Gerboth, Renate. "A Study of the Two Forms of the Wechsler-Bellevue Intelligence Scale." *J Consult Psychol* 14:365–70 O '50. * (PA 25:4566)

283. Gilhooly, Francis M. "Correction of 'The Relationship Between Variability and Ability on the Wechsler-Bellevue.'" *J Consult Psychol* 14:329 Ag '50. * (PA 25:2613)

284. Gilhooly, Francis M. "The Relationship Between Variability and Ability on the Wechsler-Bellevue." *J Consult Psychol* 14:46–8 F '50. * (PA 24:4114)

285. Gilhooly, Francis M. "Wechsler-Bellevue Reliability and the Validity of Certain Diagnostic Signs of the Neuroses." *J Consult Psychol* 14:82–7 Ap '50. * (PA 24:5867)

286. Glueck, Sheldon, and Glueck, Eleanor. *Unraveling Juvenile Delinquency.* Foreword by Erwin N. Griswold. New York: Commonwealth Fund, 1950. Pp. xv, 399. (London: Oxford University Press.) * (PA 25:2578)

287. Goldman, George David. *An Investigation of the Similarities in Personality Structure of Idiopathic Epileptics, Hysterical Convulsives, and Neurological Patients.* Doctor's thesis, New York University (New York, N.Y.), 1950. Abstract: *Microfilm Abstracts* 11:176–7 no 1 '51. * (PA 26:368, title only)

288. Grassi, Joseph R. "Impairment of Abstract Behavior Following Bilateral Prefrontal Lobotomy." *Psychiatric Q* 24:74–88 Ja '50.* (PA 24:6478)

289. Greenbloom, Grace C. *The Psychological Investigation of Senile Dementia: The Wechsler-Bellevue Adult Intelligence Scale.* Master's thesis, University of Toronto (Toronto, Canada), 1950. Pp. 30.

290. Gurvitz, Milton S. "The Wechsler-Bellevue Test and the Diagnosis of Psychopathic Personality." *J Clin Psychol* 6:397–401 O '50. * (PA 25:8093)

291. Gutman, Brigette. "The Application of the Wechsler-Bellevue Scale in the Diagnosis of Organic Brain Disorders." *J Clin Psychol* 6: 195–8 Ap '50. * (PA 24:6479)

292. Harper, A. Edwin, Jr. *Differential Patterns in Schizophrenia on the Wechsler-Bellevue Intelligence Test.* Allahabad, U.P., India: the Author, Ewing Christian College, 1950. Pp. ix, 71. * (PA 26:439)

293. Harper, A. Edwin, Jr. "Discrimination Between Matched Schizophrenics and Normals by the Wechsler-Bellevue Scale." *J Consult Psychol* 14:351–7 O '50. * (PA 25:4727)

294. Harper, A. Edwin, Jr. "Discrimination of the Types of Schizophrenia by the Wechsler-Bellevue Scale." *J Consult Psychol* 14:290–6 Ag '50. * (PA 25:2599)

295. Hayes, Samuel P. Chap. 7, "Measuring the Intelligence of the Blind," pp. 77–96. (PA 26:496) In *Psychological Diagnosis and Counseling of the Adult Blind:* Selected Papers From the Proceedings of the University of Michigan Conference for the Blind. 1947. Edited by Wilma Donahue and Donald Dabelstein. New York: American Foundation for the Blind, Inc., 1950. Pp. vii, 173. * (PA 26:493)

296. Hays, William. "A Comparison of Scatter Patterning for Mental Defectives on the Wechsler Forms I and II." *Am J Mental Def* 55:264–8 O '50. * (PA 25:2527)

297. Holzberg, Jules D., and Deane, Maurice A. "The Diagnostic Significance of an Objective Measure of Intratest Scatter on the Wechsler-Bellevue Intelligence Scale." *J Consult Psychol* 14:180–8 Je '50. * (PA 25:362)

298. Jastak, Joseph. "An Item Analysis of the Wechsler-Bellevue Tests." *J Consult Psychol* 14:88–94 Ap '50. * (PA 24:5870)

299. Kaldegg, A. "The Wechsler Test in Clinical Practice: Comparison of Psychiatric and Psychosomatic Disorders With a Control Population." *J Mental Sci* 96:908–22 O '50. * (PA 25:5341)

300. Kogan, William S. "Wechsler Patterns and Psychiatric Diagnosis: A Re-evaluation Through a New Approach." Abstract. *Am Psychol* 5:471 S '50. * (PA 25:4576, title only)

301. Ladd, Alexander Hackett. *The Differential Predictive Value of the Wechsler-Bellevue Scale for Certain Areas of Teacher Preparation.* Doctor's thesis, Indiana University (Bloomington, Ind.), 1950. (*Thesis Abstract Series....1950,* 1951, pp. 62–8.) (PA 25:7112, title only)

302. Lawrence, Ray Margaret. *An Investigation of Selected Physical, Psychological and Sociological Factors Associated With Migraine and Psychogenic Headache.* Doctor's thesis, New York University (New York, N.Y.), 1950. Abstract: *Microfilm Abstracts* 11:171–2 no 1 '51. *

303. Levine, Jacob, and Blackburn, Alan R. "Intelligence Test Scores of Newly Blinded Soldiers." *J Consult Psychol* 14:311–5 Ag '50. * (PA 25:2638)

304. McCullough, Milton W. "Wechsler-Bellevue Changes Following Prefrontal Lobotomy." *J Clin Psychol* 6:270–3 Jl '50. * (PA 25:1999)

305. McNeal, Benjamin F. *The Prediction of Psychiatric Diagnosis by Signs Derived From Scatter on the Wechsler-Bellevue Adult Intelligence Scale.* Doctor's thesis, University of Pennsylvania (Philadelphia, Pa.), 1950.

306. McNemar, Quinn. "On Abbreviated Wechsler-Bellevue Scales." *J Consult Psychol* 14:79–81 Ap '50. * (PA 24:5872)

307. Mendola, Vincent S. *An Investigation of Intra-Individual Variability of a Group of Schizophrenics on the Wechsler-Bellevue Scale.* Master's thesis, Fordham University (New York, N.Y.), 1950.

308. Mercer, Margaret, and Wright, S. C. "Diagnostic Testing in a Case of Latent Schizophrenia." *J Proj Tech* 14:287–96 S '50. * (PA 25:4733)

309. Newton, Richard L. "A Comparison of Two Methods of Administering the Digit Span Test." *J Clin Psychol* 6:409–12 O '50. * (PA 25:8105)

310. Oppenheim, Sadi, and Goldwasser, Miriam L. "Psychological Report of the Cyprus Psychiatric Mission." *J Proj Tech* 14:245–61 S '50. * (PA 25:4547)

311. Page, Kay. *Use of the Wechsler-Bellevue Scale of Adult Intelligence.* Master's thesis, Chico State College (Chico, Calif.), 1950.

312. Peixotto, Helen E. "Wechsler-Bellevue Sub-Test Patterns: A Note of Caution." *J Clin Psychol* 6:188–90 Ap '50. * (PA 24:6359)

313. Rappaport, Sheldon R., and Webb, Wilse B. "An Attempt to Study Intellectual Deterioration by Premorbid and Psychotic Testing." *J Consult Psychol* 14:95–8 Ap '50. * (PA 24:5975)

314. Reynolds, Gerald A. *Investigation of Possible Relationships of the Object Assembly Subtest of the Wechsler-Bellevue Intelligence Scale.* Master's thesis, Fordham University (New York, N.Y.), 1950.

315. Rogers, Lawrence S. "A Comparative Evaluation of the Wechsler-Bellevue Mental Deterioration Index for Various Adult Groups." *J Clin Psychol* 6:199–202 Ap '50. * (PA 24:6484)

316. Rogers, Lawrence S. "Differences Between Neurotics and Schizophrenics on the Wechsler-Bellevue Scale." Abstract. *J Colo-Wyo Acad Sci* 4:64 O '50. * (PA 25:5517, title only)

317. Rogers, Lawrence S. "A Note on Allen's Index of Deterioration." *J Clin Psychol* 6:203 Ap '50. * (PA 24:6485)

318. Rose, Dorian Mabyl. *Personality, Psychiatric and Behavioral Patterns in Schizophrenia.* Doctor's thesis, Clark University (Worcester, Mass.), 1950. (*Abstracts of Dissertations & Theses....1950,* pp. 40–4.) (PA 25:5518, title only)

319. Sabeh, Raymond. *Comparisons of the Wechsler-Bellevue Adult Intelligence Scale With the Ohio State Psychological Examination in Predicting Academic Success for College Freshmen.* Master's thesis, Ohio University (Athens, Ohio), 1950. Pp. 40. (*Abstracts of Masters' Theses....,* 1950, p. 126.)

320. Sanders, Joseph Robert. *Verbal Concept Formation in Relation to Personal Adjustment.* Doctor's thesis, Columbia University (New York, N.Y.), 1950. Abstract: *Microfilm Abstracts* 11:431–3 no 2 '51. (PA 26:2006, title only)

321. Shoben, Edward Joseph. Jr. "The Wechsler-Bellevue in the Detection of Anxiety: A Test of the Rashkis-Welsh Hypothesis." *J Consult Psychol* 14:40–5 F '50. * (PA 24:4182)

322. Simon, Loron M., and Levitt, Eugene A. "The Relation Between Wechsler-Bellevue I.Q. Scores and Occupational Area." *Occupations* 29:23–5 O '50. * (PA 25:3246)

323. Spaner, Fred E. *An Analysis of the Relationship Between Some Rorschach Test Determinants and Subtest Scores on the Wechsler Bellevue Adult Scale.* Doctor's thesis. Purdue University (Lafayette, Ind.), 1950. (PA 24:4038, title only)

324. Stacey, Chalmers L., and Levin, Janice. "Performance of Retarded Individuals on Stanford-Binet and Wechsler-

Wechsler-Bellevue Intelligence Scale

Bellevue Intelligence Scales." *Am J Mental Def* 55:123–31 Jl '50. * (*PA* 25:2542)

325. STARER, EMANUAL. *An Analysis of the Type and Direction of Aggression and Sources of Frustration as Shown by the Results of the Rozenzweig Picture-Frustration Study, Rorschach Findings, and Case History for a Group of Anxiety Neurotic and a Group of Paranoid Schizophrenic Patients.* Doctor's thesis, New York University (New York, N.Y.), 1950. Abstract: *Microfilm Abstracts* 11:178–9 no 1 '51. * (*PA* 26:2342, title only)

326. STEFIC, EDWARD C. *Factors Affecting the "Negative Deterioration" Index on the Wechsler-Bellevue Scales of Psychoneurotics.* Master's thesis, Catholic University of America (Washington, D.C.), 1950. (*PA* 25:4109, title only)

327. THEAMAN, MILTON. *The Performance of Post-Traumatics, Post-Traumatic Epileptics, and Idiopathic Epileptics on Psychological Tests: A Study of the Relative Influence of Symptom and Etiology Upon Psychological Performance.* Doctor's thesis, New York University (New York, N.Y.), 1950. Abstract: *Microfilm Abstracts* 10:232–3 no 3 '50. *

328. WARNER, SAMUEL J. "The Wechsler-Bellevue Psychometric Pattern in Anxiety Neurosis." *J Consult Psychol* 14:297–304 Ag '50. * (*PA* 25:2620)

329. WENTWORTH-ROHR, IVAN. *A Study in the Differential Diagnosis of Idiopathic and Symptomatic Epilepsy Through Psychological Tests.* Doctor's thesis, New York University (New York, N.Y.), 1950. Abstract: *Microfilm Abstracts* 11:180–1 no 1 '51. * (*PA* 26:2374, title only)

330. WHEELER, WILLIAM MARSHALL. "The Internal Structure of Three Clinical Instruments." Abstract. *Am Psychol* 5:470 S '50. * (*PA* 25:4599, title only)

331. WHITEMAN, MORDECAI. "Altitude as a Reference Point in Scatter Analysis." *J Clin Psychol* 6:160–4 Ap '50. * (*PA* 24:6361)

332. WILEY, LLEWELLYN N. "Equating Scores on Three Intelligence Tests." Abstract. *Am Psychol* 5:467 S '50. * (*PA* 25:4600, title only)

333. ALIMENA, BENJAMIN. "Norms for Scatter Analysis on the Wechsler Intelligence Scales." *J Clin Psychol* 7:289–90 Jl '51. * (*PA* 26:904)

334. ANDERSEN, A. LLOYD. "The Effect of Laterality Localization of Focal Brain Lesions on the Wechsler-Bellevue Subtests." *J Clin Psychol* 7:149–53 Ap '51. * (*PA* 25:8219)

335. BIRREN, JAMES E. "A Factorial Analysis of the Wechsler-Bellevue Adult Intelligence Scale Given to an Elderly Population." Abstract. *Am Psychol* 6:398–9 Jl '51. *

336. BOTWINICK, JACK, AND BIRREN, JAMES E. "The Measurement of Intellectual Decline in the Senile Psychoses." *J Consult Psychol* 15:145–50 Ap '51. * (*PA* 26:6419)

337. COHEN, JACOB. "A Factor-Analytic Comparison of Intelligence Test Performance of Different Neuropsychiatric Groups." Abstract. *Am Psychol* 6:334–5 Jl '51. *

338. COLLINS, A. LOUISE. "Epileptic Intelligence." *J Consult Psychol* 15:392–9 O '51. * (*PA* 26:7179)

339. GLIK, E. E. "A Comparison of Recall and Recognition Types of Measurement on Verbal Items, and Their Implications for Deterioration Testing." *J Clin Psychol* 7:157–62 Ap '51. * (*PA* 25:8226)

340. GROVES, MARION H. *Some Relationships Between Certain Types of Mental Aberration and the Abilities Measured by the Wechsler-Bellevue Scale.* Doctor's thesis, University of Chicago (Chicago, Ill.), 1951.

341. GURVITZ, MILTON S. *The Dynamics of Psychological Testing: A Formulation and Guide to Independent Clinical Practice.* Foreword by Joseph S. A. Miller. New York: Grune & Stratton, Inc., 1951. Pp. xv, 396. * (*PA* 26:4007)

342. GURVITZ, MILTON S. "The Hillside Short Form of the Wechsler Bellevue." *J Clin Psychol* 7:131–4 Ap '51. * (*PA* 25:8092)

343. HARROWER, M. R., AND KRAUS, JANE. "Psychological Studies on Patients With Multiple Sclerosis." *AMA Arch Neurol & Psychiatry* 66:44–57 Jl '51. * (*PA* 26:1643)

344. HAYDEN, SPENCER J. *The Educational Significance of Wechsler-Bellevue Test Scatter Attained by College Students of Superior, Average and Inferior Academic Achievement.* Doctor's thesis, Fordham University (New York, N.Y.), 1951.

345. HAYS, WILLIAM, AND SCHNEIDER, BERNARD. "A Test-Retest Evaluation of the Wechsler Forms I and II With Mental Defectives." *J Clin Psychol* 7:140–3 Ap '51. * (*PA* 25:8095)

346. HOVER, GERALD LESLIE. *An Investigation of Differences in Intellectual Factors Between Normal and Neurotic Adults.* Doctor's thesis, University of Michigan (Ann Arbor, Mich.), 1951. Abstract: *Microfilm Abstracts* 11:423–4 no 2 '51. (*PA* 26:2348)

347. KITZINGER, HELEN. Chap. 20, "Wechsler-Bellevue Scale," pp. 211–9. In *Thematic Test Analysis.* By Edwin S. Shneidman with the collaboration of Walther Joel and Kenneth B. Little. Foreword by Henry A. Murray. New York: Grune & Stratton, Inc., 1951. Pp. xi, 320. * (*PA* 26:3422)

348. KITZINGER, HELEN, AND BLUMBERG, EUGENE. *Supplementary Guide for Administering and Scoring the Wechsler-Bellevue Intelligence Scale (Form I).* American Psychological Association, Psychological Monographs: General and Applied, Vol. 65, No. 2, Whole No. 319. Washington, D.C.: the Association, Inc., 1951. Pp. v, 20. Paper. * (*PA* 26:6872)

349. KNOTT, JOHN R.; CANNICOTT, RICHARD G.; UMBERGER, JOHN P.; AND BILODEAU, INA MCD. "Brief Tests of Intelligence in the Psychiatric Clinic." *J Clin Psychol* 7:123–6 Ap '51. * (*PA* 25:8099)

350. LIPTON, M. B.; TAMARIN, S.; AND LOTESTA, P. "Test Evidence of Personality Change and Prognosis by Means of the Rorschach and Wechsler-Bellevue Tests on 17 Insulin-Treated Paranoid Schizophrenics." *Psychiatric Q* 25:434–44 Jl '51. * (*PA* 26:5755)

351. MCKENZIE, RICHARD E. "A Study of the Wechsler-Bellevue Intelligence Scale and the VIBS Short Form in an Institute for the Mentally Deficient." *Am J Mental Def* 56:174–6 Jl '51. * (*PA* 26:2188)

352. MANDLER, GEORGE, AND SARASON, SEYMOUR B. "Anxiety as a Factor in Test Performance." Abstract. *Am Psychol* 6:341 Jl '51. *

353. MAYMAN, MARTIN; SCHAFER, ROY; AND RAPAPORT, DAVID. Chap. 19, "Interpretation of the Wechsler-Bellevue Intelligence Scale in Personality Appraisal," pp. 541–80. In *An Introduction to Projective Techniques.* Edited by Harold H. Anderson and Gladys L. Anderson. New York: Prentice-Hall, Inc., 1951. Pp. xxiv, 720. *

354. MONROE, JACK. *A Statistical Analysis of Intra-Individual Scatter on the Wechsler-Bellevue Intelligence Scale.* Doctor's thesis, Purdue University (Lafayette, Ind.), 1951.

355. PLUMB, GALEN R. *The Evaluation of the Mental Characteristics of a Reformatory Population as Revealed by the Wechsler-Bellevue Intelligence Scale and the California Test of Mental Maturity.* Doctor's thesis, University of Nebraska (Lincoln, Neb.), 1951.

356. POLLENS, BERTRAM. *The Relationship Between Psychological Data and Prognosis in Psychotherapy.* Doctor's thesis, New York University (New York, N.Y.), 1951. Abstract: *Microfilm Abstracts* 11:750–2 no 3 '51. (*PA* 26:1515, title only)

357. RABIN, ALBERT I., AND GUERTIN, WILSON H. "Research With the Wechsler-Bellevue Test: 1945–1950." *Psychol B* 48:211–48 My '51. * (*PA* 26:930)

358. REICHARD, SUZANNE. "Some Contributions of Psychological Tests to Therapeutic Planning." Discussion by Anneliese F. Korner. *Am J Orthopsychiatry* 21:532–41, discussion 541–2 Jl '51. * (*PA* 26:3445)

359. ROGERS, LAWRENCE S. "Differences Between Neurotics and Schizophrenics on the Wechsler-Bellevue Scale." *J Consult Psychol* 15:151–3 Ap '51. * (*PA* 26:6285)

360. SIMKIN, JAMES S. "An Investigation of Differences in Intellectual Factors Between Normal and Schizophrenic Adults." Abstract. *Am Psychol* 6:335 Jl '51. *

361. SIMKIN, JAMES SOLOMON. *An Investigation of Differences in Intellectual Factors Between Normal and Schizophrenic Adults.* Doctor's thesis, University of Michigan (Ann Arbor, Mich.), 1951. Abstract: *Microfilm Abstracts* 11:448–9 no 2 '51. (*PA* 26:2340, title only)

362. STACEY, CHALMERS L., AND MARKIN, KARL E. "A Study of the Differential Responses Among Three Groups of Subnormals on the Similarities Sub-Test of the Wechsler Intelligence Scale." *Am J Mental Def* 56:424–8 O '51. * (*PA* 26:2264)

363. STACEY, CHALMERS L., AND PORTNOY, BERNARD. "A Study of the Differential Responses on the Vocabulary Sub-Test of the Wechsler-Bellevue Intelligence Scale." *J Clin Psychol* 7:144–8 Ap '51. * (*PA* 25:8112)

364. STOTSKY, BERNARD ALEXANDREVICH. *Factors in Remission of Schizophrenics: A Comparative Study of Personality and Intellectual Variables Among Schizophrenics.* Doctor's thesis, University of Michigan (Ann Arbor, Mich.), 1951. Abstract: *Microfilm Abstracts* 11:758–9 no 3 '51. (*PA* 26:1618, title only)

365. TAMMINEN, A. W. "A Comparison of the Army General Classification Test and the Wechsler Bellevue Intelligence Scales." *Ed & Psychol Meas* 11:646–55 w '51. *

366. WALDFOGEL, SAMUEL, AND GUY, WILLIAM. "Wechsler Bellevue Subtest Scatter in the Affective Disorders." *J Clin Psychol* 7:135–9 Ap '51. * (*PA* 25:8114)

367. WATSON, ROBERT I. Chap. 8, "The Wechsler-Bellevue Intelligence Scale," pp. 154–220. In his *The Clinical Method in Psychology.* New York: Harper & Brothers, 1951. Pp. xii, 779. *

368. WEBB, WILSE B., AND DE HAAN, HENRY. "Wechsler-Bellevue Split-Half Reliabilities in Normals and Schizophrenics." *J Consult Psychol* 15:68–71 F '51. * (*PA* 26:6455)

369. WECHSLER, DAVID. Sect. 6, "The Wechsler-Bellevue Scale," pp. 23–39. In *Military Clinical Psychology.* Department of the Army Technical Manual TM 8-242; Department of the Air Force Manual AFM 160-45. Washington, D.C.: U.S. Government Printing Office, 1951. Pp. iv, 197. Paper. *

370. WHEELER, JOHN I., JR., AND WILKINS, WALTER L. "The Validity of the Hewson Ratios." *J Consult Psychol* 15:163–6 Ap '51. * (*PA* 26:6306)

371. WITTENBORN, J. R., AND HOLZBERG, J. D. "The Wechsler-Bellevue and Descriptive Diagnosis." *J Consult Psychol* 15:325–9 Ag '51. * (*PA* 26:6309)

MURRAY ABORN, *Instructor in Psychology, Michigan State College, East Lansing, Michigan.*

Since its introduction in 1939, the *Wechsler-Bellevue Intelligence Scale* has been awarded a widespread clinical usage rivaled by few other psychological instruments. Primarily, the test was welcomed as providing a much needed adult intelligence scale; one that included a more extensive sampling of adult age levels than was accounted for in the *Revised Stanford-Binet Scale,* and one that replaced the method of maintaining a fixed chronological age in the computation of adult IQ's with a method designed to accommodate the expected decline in intelligence with age.

Additionally responsible for its rapid recognition was the appearance of a scale for measuring intelligence seemingly possessing theoretical substance as well as practical applicability. According to Wechsler, the test presents the opportunity of obtaining a measure of the individual's "global" intelligence (i.e., his overall level of efficiency in functioning as a whole organism) along with the configuration of those elements, "not entirely independent but qualitatively differentiable" from one another, that compose this global entity. Wechsler contends that the ideal test of intelligence involves the measurement of some universal, common factor akin to Spearman's "g," any number of group factors something in the nature of Alexander's "functional unities," and such concomitant nonintellective factors as motivation, persistence, etc. that enter into all human measurement. He suggests, a priori, that his test is so equipped. The eleven diversified subtests divided into a Verbal and a Performance scale and combined into a Full scale offer, on the face of it, precisely the kind of practical situation adaptable to this rather enigmatic theoretical context. But aside from such controversy as may exist over the merits and shortcomings of Wechsler's theoretical position, numerous factor analyses have demonstrated that theory and practice certainly have not been reconciled in the Wechsler-Bellevue.

Clinical psychologists were particularly enthusiastic over the diagnostic potentialities inherent in its differential yet ostensibly homogeneous composition. On the basis of a small number of cases, Wechsler compiled several tables illustrating the typical test patterns of a few gross diagnostic categories. These were based upon an analysis of subtest scores by the method of counting or integrating *signs* (i.e., the degree of deviation of individual subtest scores from the mean subtest score). The method was to yield a system of pathognomonics based upon intratest patterns, a concept not far removed from the notion of *scatter analysis* on the Stanford-Binet. Close examination of the author's system reveals inconsistencies in the technique per se. For subtests within the range of normal intelligence the number of weighted score points constituting a "significant" deviation from the mean subtest score is less than the size of the standard deviation of the weighted score conversion scale. Since what might be termed *scatter* ordinarily varies with the magnitude of the IQ, what is and what is not "significant" becomes rather arbitrary and tends to confound the very meaning of the pathognomonics so derived. While in all fairness to Wechsler it should be pointed out that he has cautioned against the type of diagnosis accomplished by comparing individual test results against the tables of *signs,* the inclusion of these tables in his book could hardly be said to discourage such practices.

Judging from the research literature, the diagnostic significance of subtest score configurations has proved to be a favorite bone of contention. Beginning with the claims set forth by Wechsler, psychological journals have been deluged with an interminable flow of studies supporting, expanding, and rejecting the diagnostic implications of pattern analysis. Most of the "typical patterns," "indices," and "signs" have not proved reliable with either groups or individuals. In many instances, test patterns have not been found sufficiently diagnostic to permit their use in differentiating between schizophrenic and normal subjects (Garfield, *161*) and one investigator termed the clinical application of one of the more popular indices "dangerous" (Webb, *121*). As for the problem of making the even finer discriminations necessary for the diagnosis of nosological subtypes, Brecher (*82*) found that Wechsler-Bellevue *signs* were able to make differential diagnosis between five types of schizophrenia only 13 per cent better than chance. In general, the whole question of disorder-resistant and disorder-susceptible intellectual functions has not yet been satisfactorily resolved and the method of deviation from the mean of the subtest scores is a statistical concept whose clinical application lacks logical reinforcement. Specifically in the case of the Wechsler-Bellevue, it is not by any means certain that the reliability of the subtests could support a system of pathognomonics even if the concept were demonstrably valid. It would not be unfair to say that whatever enthusiasm was initially generated by the pathognomonic possibilities of this test has been considerably dimmed in recent years.

Wechsler-Bellevue Intelligence Scale

Wechsler offers estimates of the reliability of the scales on the basis of two studies. The first consists of intersubtest correlations in a method analogous to the split half technique. Eight subtests were selected and divided into two groups of four. The reliability coefficient so obtained is given as .90, after "correction for attenuation." The subtests in each group seem to have been selected in favor of obtaining optimal correlation with each other. Object Assembly, which correlates lowest with the other subtests of the scales, was omitted from the study. If subtests which had shown low correlation with each other were used, the derived coefficient would have been lower. As a matter of fact, there is some question as to whether this method really constitutes a valid reliability study in a test designed to measure specific intellectual functions as well as general intelligence. If the test had been divided in half by items rather than by subtests, the results would be more relevant. It follows that the fairly high correlation between Verbal and Performance IQ's, also offered as evidence of reliability, must be regarded as equally unsuitable.

A second study employing test-retest at varying intervals with 52 subjects yielded a reliability coefficient of .94 for the Full scale. No reliability coefficients for the subtests are given, but Derner, Aborn, and Canter (*270*) report average test-retest coefficients ranging from .62 to .88 for 158 normal subjects retested at well controlled intervals.

In discussing the validity of his instrument, Wechsler acknowledges all the usual difficulties inherent in the general problem of validating an intelligence test. He comments that the validity of an intelligence scale cannot be established directly and that indirect methods by way of correlations with such usual criteria as other measures of intelligence, teacher ratings, and psychiatric recommendations are, in turn, notably unsatisfactory. Having thus deplored these criteria, he proceeds to argue that their pertinence in the appraisal of any new test cannot be denied (p. 129). He furnishes evidence of agreement between Wechsler-Bellevue IQ's and the scores of several other tests, teacher ratings, and case study data. Aside from such validation, the author concludes that the instrument has been put to the pragmatic test and proved itself to be a "good" one. Strange as it may seem, in view of the ambiguities involved in arguing from both sides of the fence, the latter claim appears to be the most sensible and the one most substantiated in clinical experience.

The directions for administering many of the subtests bear clarification; the procedures for administration, specificity. For example, if a subject exceeds the time limit in completing Object Assembly does he receive credit for what he has done within the time limit? In Block Design, does "pausing to make clear to the subject how two half designs can be put together to make a solid patch of color" (p. 184) mean that the examiner is to explain it *verbally?* In Comprehension and Similarities the test manual calls for a reduction in score on those items where a subject "contaminates" his response. In practice, decisions on "contamination" are frequently difficult to make. Sometimes a subject will give inferior responses in an effort to elaborate his first and best response. Is this to lower his IQ? Many clinicians have difficulty in accepting the scoring rationale of these two subtests altogether. The proposition that a subject will always give the "best" response of which he is capable *spontaneously* is not a very sound one. In view of the fact that Wechsler implies the examiner may not always seek to improve a subject's response by querying (pp. 171, 181; footnotes pp. 172, 193) these subtest scores may often reflect what the subject has done, not what he can do. The ability to think "abstractly" or in the most general terms may be reasonable evidence of high intelligence, but it is too subject to educational and environmental influences to be measured in a perfunctory manner.

Recent years have seen increasing criticism leveled at the Wechsler-Bellevue. The normative population, sampling techniques, theoretical basis, diagnostic utility, and the structure of the test itself have been carefully picked apart and found wanting. The effect has been destructive, but the value of this test has been considerably enhanced by a recognition of what it is not and what it cannot do. Handled with judgment and a cognizance of its limitations, this test, as an instrument for measuring adult intelligence, is so superior to anything else available for that purpose that it remains a highly important psychological tool.

WILLIAM D. ALTUS, *Associate Professor of Psychology and Chairman of the Department, Santa Barbara College, University of California, Santa Barbara, California.*

Before making any comments on this widely

used intelligence test, the writer would like to present his credentials. He has administered the Wechsler, taught it, and has done research with it for a period of 12 years. Time does not, however, confer infallibility, despite the subjective feeling tone of the one who makes pronouncements.

The Wechsler tests, Forms I and II, lack an adequate ceiling for the quite bright. Probably the top five per cent, surely the top two or three per cent, is not adequately tested. Since clinical practice deals much less frequently with the very able, probably this point is not so adverse as it might otherwise sound.

The validation studies on test patterning, which Wechsler stresses in his manual, have been like the fable of the mountain in labor: Only a mouse-size bit of verified data remains. In the writer's opinion, the efficient little digit symbol subtest has shown an unspecified amount of overlap with what J. McV. Hunt calls "mental deficit," though its general responsiveness to most types of deviant behavior leaves it differentially undiagnostic. It also seems likely that the juvenile offender and the adult criminal do relatively better on performance subtests than on verbal ones, in about two cases out of three, say. It may well be that lack of attendance at school, or application therein, affects the verbal scores of this particular group—if it is incontrovertibly shown that this pattern is a genuine one, as the writer feels it to be. Factor analytic studies of the subtest intercorrelations of clinical groups at various age levels, matched with normal controls might lead the way out of the statistical morass into which the pattern validation studies have fallen.

In the writer's opinion, the object assembly subtest could very profitably be left out of the test altogether. Its very shortness precluded either marked validity or reliability. It is somewhat cumbersome to administer and, for its length, somewhat time consuming. If this test were dropped from the scale, the arithmetic subtest could be appreciably lengthened, thus increasing the reliability of this excellent short test. This would leave a total of six verbal subtests (vocabulary to be included as a regular part of the scale) and only four performance subtests. Our civilization awards its prizes much more frequently to those who are able in dealing with verbal concepts; in that sense, a 6 to 4 weighting of verbal and performance tests should increase the validity of the scale, which presently confers equal weights to the two types of test materials.

The writer doubts that the skewness Wechsler finds in his distribution of IQ's is any closer to "reality" (if general ability ever proves to be completely commensurate) than is the normal distribution curve hypothesized by Terman and others. It may well be, however, that there is greater asymmetry at the lower than at the upper part of the IQ curve, i.e., more dull subjects in certain IQ ranges than will be found at a corresponding place on the upper end of the curve. Birth injuries, disease processes, and post-natal trauma could readily account for the differential.

To summarize: (a) the Wechsler needs more "top"; (b) a greater emphasis on verbal subtests seems desirable; (c) for whatever reason, the "pattern" studies of the Wechsler in terms of clinical diagnosis, while not completely futile, have proved unrewarding.

For a review by Robert I. Watson, see 3:298; for a review by F. L. Wells and excerpts from reviews, see 40:1429; for related reviews, see 362, 3:299–301 and 40:B1121–2.

[362]

★[Re Wechsler-Bellevue Intelligence Scale.] **Plumb IQ Slide Rule for use with the Wechsler-Bellevue Intelligence Scale.** Ages 15 and over; 1948; $1 per copy, postpaid; G. R. Plumb; Psychological Corporation. *

J Consult Psychol 13:148 Ap '49. Laurance F. Shaffer. * If large numbers of Wechsler's are handled, the use of the device is perhaps more rapid than are the conventional tables.

[363]

★**Wechsler Intelligence Scale for Children.** Ages 5–15; 1949; a downward extension of *Wechsler-Bellevue Intelligence Scale;* also called WISC; 12 subtests [information, comprehension, arithmetic, similarities, vocabulary, digit span (optional), picture completion, picture arrangement, block design, object assembly, mazes (optional), coding] yielding 3 scores: verbal, performance, total; individual; 1 form; $22 per complete set of testing materials, manual, and 25 record forms; $2 per 25 record forms; $1.20 per 25 WISC Maze Tests, an alternate subtest which may be used in place of Coding; $3.50 per carrying case (when ordered with complete set); postpaid; (40–60) minutes; David Wechsler; Psychological Corporation. *

REFERENCES

1. BURNS, L. *A Correlation of Scores on the Wechsler Intelligence Scale for Children and the California Test of Personality Obtained by a Group of 5th Graders.* Master's thesis, Pennsylvania State College (State College, Pa.), 1950.
2. CLARKE, F. R. *A Comparative Study of the Wechsler Intelligence Scale for Children and the Revised Stanford-Binet Intelligence Scale, Form L, in Relation to Scholastic Achievement of a 5th Grade Population.* Master's thesis, Pennsylvania State College (State College, Pa.), 1950.
3. GROVE, WILLIAM R. "Mental Age Scores for the Wechsler

Intelligence Scale for Children." *J Clin Psychol* 6:393-7 O '50. * (*PA* 25:8089)
4. ROTTERSMAN, LEON. *A Comparison of the IQ Scores on the New Revised Stanford-Binet, Form L, The Wechsler Intelligence Scale for Children, and the Goodenough "Draw a Man" Test at the Six Year Age Level.* Master's thesis, University of Nebraska (Lincoln, Neb.), 1950.
5. SEASHORE, HAROLD G. "Differences Between Verbal and Performance IQ's on the Wechsler Intelligence Scale for Children." Abstract. *Am Psychol* 5:319 Jl '50. * (*PA* 25:1111, title only)
6. SEASHORE, HAROLD; WESMAN, ALEXANDER; AND DOPPELT, JEROME. "The Standardization of the Wechsler Intelligence Scale for Children." *J Consult Psychol* 14:99-110 Ap '50. * (*PA* 24:5881)
7. STACEY, CHALMERS L., AND PORTNOY, BERNARD. "A Study of the Differential Responses on the Vocabulary Sub-Test of the Wechsler Intelligence Scale for Children." *J Clin Psychol* 6:401-3 O '50. * (*PA* 25:8113)
8. WECHSLER, DAVID. "Intellectual Development and Psychological Maturity." *Child Develop* 21:44-50 Mr '50. * (*PA* 25:2970)
9. ALIMENA, BENJAMIN. "Norms for Scatter Analysis on the Wechsler Intelligence Scales." *J Clin Psychol* 7:289-90 Jl '51. * (*PA* 26:904)
10. FRANDSEN, ARDEN N., AND HIGGINSON, JAY B. "The Stanford-Binet and the Wechsler Intelligence Scale for Children." *J Consult Psychol* 15:236-8 Je '51. * (*PA* 26:6268)
11. HAGEN, ELIZABETH P. "A Factor Analysis of the Wechsler Intelligence Scale for Children." Abstract. *Am Psychol* 6:297 Jl '51. *
12. KRUGMAN, JUDITH I.; JUSTMAN, JOSEPH; WRIGHTSTONE, J. WAYNE; AND KRUGMAN, MORRIS. "Pupil Functioning on the Stanford-Binet and the Wechsler Intelligence Scale for Children." *J Consult Psychol* 15:475-83 D '51. * (*PA* 26:7003)
13. McBREARTY, J. F. *A Comparison of the WISC with the Arthur Performance Scale, Form I, and Their Relationship to the Progressive Achievement Tests.* Master's thesis, Pennsylvania State College (State College, Pa.), 1951.
14. NALE, STANLEY. "The Childrens-Wechsler and the Binet on 104 Mental Defectives at the Polk State School." *Am J Mental Def* 56:419-23 O '51. * (*PA* 26:2191)
15. PASTOVIC, JOHN J., AND GUTHRIE, GEORGE M. "Some Evidence on the Validity of the WISC." *J Consult Psychol* 15:385-6 O '51. * (*PA* 26:7008)
16. RAPAPORT, I. *A Comparison of Performance on the Wechsler Intelligence Scale for Children and the Revised Stanford-Binet Scale.* Master's thesis, University of Pittsburgh (Pittsburgh, Pa.), 1951.
17. SEASHORE, HAROLD G. "Differences Between Verbal and Performance IQs on the Wechsler Intelligence Scale for Children." *J Consult Psychol* 15:62-7 F '51. * (*PA* 26:6292)
18. SLOAN, WILLIAM, AND SCHNEIDER, BERNARD. "A Study of the Wechsler Intelligence Scale for Children With Mental Defectives." *Am J Mental Def* 55:573-5 Ap '51. * (*PA* 25:7475) Correction: 56:473 O '51. *
19. STACEY, CHALMERS L., AND LEVIN, JANICE. "Correlation Analysis of Scores of Subnormal Subjects on the Stanford-Binet and Wechsler Intelligence Scale for Children." *Am J Mental Def* 55:590-7 Ap '51. * (*PA* 25:7541)
20. WECHSLER, DAVID. "Equivalent Test and Mental Ages for the WISC." *J Consult Psychol* 15:381-4 O '51. * (*PA* 26:7016)
21. WEIDER, ARTHUR; NOLLER, PAUL A.; AND SCHRAMM, THEODORE A. "The Wechsler Intelligence Scale for Children and the Revised Stanford-Binet." *J Consult Psychol* 15:330-3 Ag '51. * (*PA* 26:6303)
22. YOUNG, FLORENE M., AND PITTS, VIRGINIA A. "The Performance of Congenital Syphilitics on the Wechsler Intelligence Scale for Children." *J Consult Psychol* 15:239-42 Je '51. * (*PA* 26:6492)

JAMES M. ANDERSON, *Assistant Professor of Psychology, Occidental College, Los Angeles, California.*

This test was standardized on 2,200 white American children, 100 boys and 100 girls at each of the 11 age levels from 5 to 15. The children were selected on the basis of age (within 1½ months of their midyear), rural-urban residence, father's occupation, geographic area, and the presence or absence of suspected feeblemindedness. The sample used was fairly representative of the 1940 census with respect to the above criteria. The selection of cases shows that much greater attention was paid to the necessity of securing a representative sample than in Wechsler's earlier work,[1] with which the author assumes that the user will be familiar.

The construction of an alternate form of a test should be an integral part of the original work of constructing and standardizing a test and not an afterthought if the two instruments are to be truly parallel. Since there is no mention of a proposed alternate form for WISC, we can suppose that such a form has not been planned. The publication of this scale seems unwise before an alternate form is available.

In reviewing the *Wechsler-Bellevue Intelligence Scale* in *The Third Mental Measurements Yearbook,* Watson wrote, "The directions for Forms I and II are deceptively alike, but close scrutiny will show a considerable number of minor changes in wording. Most of these changes exhibit at least a greater surface clarity, but for the sake of these changes one must pay the price of learning two sets of directions differing so slightly and yet so pointedly that a certain amount of confusion and irritation inevitably results." These same comments apply to the WISC. Only now, for those who use all three instruments, the confusion is doubly compounded. A little thought to this problem would have added considerably to the insurance that the examiner would "follow the directions in the manual exactly." Such confusion detracts considerably from the ease of administration on the part of examiners experienced with the adult forms.

Not only do the directions of the WISC differ from those for the Wechsler-Bellevue, Form II, but they also differ within the WISC itself "for Subjects under 8, and older suspected mental defectives" and "for Subjects 8 and older, not suspected mental defectives." These double directions hold for Similarities, Picture Arrangement, Block Design, Coding, and Mazes. In addition, the test material itself is entirely different for these two groups on Coding. For the older subjects the Digit Symbol test of the Wechsler-Bellevue, Form II is used while for the younger subjects a different test is employed.

It is well known that the alteration of instructions or procedure changes the nature of the task required of the subject by some unknown amount. This is the primary reason for insistence upon strict adherence to standardized directions. The fact that the changes in directions in the WISC are intentional does not vitiate the

[1] Wechsler, David. *The Measurement of Adult Intelligence, Third Edition.* Baltimore, Md.: Williams & Wilkins Co., 1944. Pp. vii, 258. * (*PA* 19:815)

objection to such changes. There is sufficient uncontrollable error inherent in every instrument without confounding it in some unknown degree with error that could be controlled.

The more mathematically facile reader will probably enjoy trying to reconcile Table IX in the WISC with the corresponding table of clinical ratings for IQ equivalents on page 8 of the manual for Wechsler-Bellevue, Form II. In his earlier work (58), Wechsler comments upon Terman's IQ classifications of intelligence, in part, "The first thing that strikes us is that the limiting second cipher of each new class is a zero. Thus the category borderline begins at 70 IQ, the category dull-normal at 80 IQ, the category average at 90 IQ, and so on. It is difficult to conceive of any statistical procedure which would give such neat correspondence. * the actual chance of each of them beginning with zero is only....one in 10,000,000." However, when we examine Table IX in the WISC manual, we find that borderline begins at 70 IQ, dull normal at 80 IQ, average at 90 IQ, and so on.

On page 4 of the manual we find, "the mean (100) and standard deviation (15) which have been chosen will give IQ's which, on the whole, are fairly close numerically to IQ's of other well-standardized tests like the Stanford-Binet. This will make comparison with IQ's of other scales, at least at the numerical level, a not too unreasonable procedure." Despite a reminder to make individual interpretations in terms of each test, this statement may encourage such comparisons.

Also in the manual we find that, "The WISC consists of twelve tests." However, the norms are based upon results from 10 tests. "It is permissible to give all tests; indeed in clinical situations, their inclusion is strongly advised because of the qualitative and diagnostic data they add." This practice should be discouraged rather than encouraged. Admittedly, more tests give more data but what the data mean is anybody's guess. Wechsler attempts no interpretation and gives no hint as to the "diagnostic" value of this data. If the tests were omitted in establishing the IQ tables because of low correlations with the other tests, the practice of assigning IQ's based upon the results of 12 tests from norms based upon 10 tests is highly suspect. Including inferior material and prorating to find an IQ would, in part, result in increased variability, decreased reliability, and an invalidation of the published correlations based upon 5 verbal and 5 performance tests. It would be more judicious to employ the group of tests upon which the norms are based and to prorate when fewer tests are used.

Coefficients of reliability and standard errors of measurement are reported for ages 7½, 10½, 13½. The same measures for the other ages, particularly at the lower levels, would be of interest and importance to the serious user of this test. It is hoped that these will appear in the publication which Wechsler promises will appear at a later date. The reliability for Coding (called Digit Symbol previously) is based upon the correlation of results on two different tests, the nonidentity of which is indicated by the reported r of .60 (incorrectly given as a coefficient of reliability). These comments hold also for the Digit Span test where the results on digits forward were correlated with the results on digits backward. It should also be pointed out that corrected odd-even reliability (the method used here for the most part) in general tends to be higher than reliability based upon the method of parallel forms.

Wechsler, in criticizing the Stanford-Binet in his book (58), suggests that tests intended for children are unsuited for use with adults. The rationale by which his material, originally intended for adults, is now suitable for children is conspicuous by its absence. Although adults do not object to the serial presentation of such items as the repetition of digits forward and backward, children seem to tire of these items rapidly. The serial presentation of items is in marked contrast to the variation of tasks on the Stanford-Binet which seems to be an important factor in eliciting the best efforts of the child.

There is considerable doubt in this reviewer's mind as to the applicability of this scale for the age range for which it is intended. Aside from objections on rational grounds, inspection of the tables of Scaled Score Equivalents discloses that zero raw scores are the equivalent of as much as 5 units of scaled score. Since the standard deviation of each test is set at 3 units in the scaling procedure, this is an amazing value to assign to no performance on a test and apparently results from the particular statistical approach employed. Inspection of the table for age 5–0 through 5–3 shows that a zero real performance on all tests yields scaled scores which when prorated and converted give a Verbal IQ of 57, a Performance IQ of 55, and a Full Scale IQ of 52. (Note that the Full Scale IQ is lower than either the Verbal or Performance IQ's.)

A zero scaled score cannot be earned until

Wechsler Intelligence Scale for Children

the age 6–8 through 6–11 and here only on one test. Not until we reach the norms for 12–0 through 12–3 do we find that credit is no longer given for zero performance. Nothing could more clearly indicate the inapplicability of this material for the younger age groups. One must go up to year 7, for instance, before a zero score on vocabulary yields a zero scaled score.

While the computational procedure for arriving at an IQ for the Stanford-Binet makes it sufficiently easy to arrive quickly at an IQ below 30 (the lowest tabled for the Stanford-Binet), many psychometrists may despair of calculating WISC IQ's below those tabled. The limits of the tabled IQ's are: Verbal 45–155, Performance 44–156, Full Scale 46–154. The possibility of having scaled scores reach zero before the IQ's do was undoubtedly one factor in not extending the table further.

Since the standardization was done on children within 1½ months of their midyear (excepting the feeble-minded cases where a more generous criterion applied), it is difficult to see how Wechsler can arrive at norms for every 4-month period and be consistent with his earlier objection to interpolation and extrapolation of scores and his insistence that a person's results be compared with norms based upon results of testing persons of his own age. Another questionable procedure is that of disregarding the days in computing a child's CA, e.g., a child whose age is 5 years, 3 months, and 28 days is given a CA of 5–3. This procedure was not employed in standardizing the test—reason enough for questioning its adoption as part of the standard procedure in using the test. One wonders about the efficiency of a scale so coarse that almost a month's difference in age is not reflected in the IQ, particularly at the lower ages.

The manual is of a convenient size and easy to handle. However, the use of bold-face type in the directions instead of the customary italics makes the reading of directions to the subject difficult. The scoring sheet gives adequate space for recording answers. Except for one arithmetic card, as far as this reviewer can tell, all of the material of Wechsler-Bellevue, Form II (exclusive of that in the manual) is used in the WISC. Had the material been published on separate cards as originally, instead of in spiral bindings, issuance of a master kit for the Wechsler-Bellevue, Form II and the WISC would not only be feasible but would effect a considerable savings for the purchaser. Separate cards would make the necessary shuffling an easy matter. (Some easier material has been added and could be issued separately to supplement the kits of those who already own the Wechsler-Bellevue, Form II.)

In summary, despite a conscientious job of trying to secure a representative sample for standardization, the inherent weaknesses of this test make it an unsatisfactory instrument which, in the field of testing children, cannot compare with the more adequate Stanford-Binet.

HAROLD A. DELP, *Coordinator of Educational Activities, The Training School, Vineland, New Jersey.*

Wechsler has followed his adult scale with this scale for children. It is based on the same philosophy of global intelligence and the inadequacy of the MA concept as the adult scale. The *Wechsler Intelligence Scale for Children* (WISC as it is usually called) is an extension of Form II of the adult scale, with additions and adaptations to permit use with children down through 5 years. It is useful for children from 5 through 15 years and better than the adult scale for the top of this range.

The manual warns against assuming that knowledge on the adult scale is transferable. WISC has different directions and different scoring standards. In addition it is pointed out that the same test items or materials may have different meanings for adults and children.

The standardization sample is much more adequate than for the adult scale. It included 100 boys and 100 girls at each age level (5 through 15), with distribution as to area of the country, urban-rural proportion, and parental occupations being based on 1940 U.S. census. Only white children were included in the sample.

The manual contains data on intercorrelations, as well as on reliability coefficients and standard errors, for all subtests and totals. Unlike the adult scale, raw scores for subtests on WISC are used to enter age tables from which Scaled Scores are obtained. One table converts all total Scaled Scores to IQ's. Scaled Scores have been derived so that a mean Scaled Score of 10 and a standard deviation of 3 are obtained at each age and for each subtest. Mean IQ is 100 and standard deviation is set at 15 IQ points. Thus, IQ's do not vary from age to age unless actual test performance varies with respect to peers.

Primary advantages include the following:

(*a*) WISC is modern in construction and standardization. (*b*) Test is easily administered. (*c*) It requires less time than most scales giving as complete results. (*d*) Materials are interesting to children. (*e*) Spiral manual is easily handled and contains clear directions and tables. (*f*) There are good norms derived from good statistical bases. (*g*) Both Verbal and Performance IQ's as well as Full Scale IQ are available, allowing differentiation in these basic areas of intelligence. (*h*) IQ's are directly comparable for various ages. (*i*) WISC provides better than most tests for clinical observations of subject's behavior. (*j*) It has future possibilities for clinical diagnosis from both quantitative and qualitative points.

Primary disadvantages include the following: (*a*) Evidence indicates the test may be too difficult for lower age brackets to be comparable with other tests (especially Stanford-Binet). (*b*) MA's desired by many clinicians are not directly considered (Wechsler gives data for obtaining age data in recent article, see *20*). (*c*) WISC is not effective for subjects at either end of the intelligence distribution (outside of IQ range 45–155). (*d*) Scoring of certain verbal items includes considerable subjectivity. (*e*) Few data are available for children in terms of other tests (validity claimed seems based on acceptance of adult scales). (*f*) Implied values from interpretations of subtests are not substantiated in the manual by directions or explanations for interpretation (only basic statistical or percentile interpretation is discussed).

BOYD R. MCCANDLESS, *Director, Iowa Child Welfare Research Station, Iowa City, Iowa.*

The WISC, as it seems to have been popularly labeled within the first few months of its publication, is sufficiently similar to the adult Wechsler-Bellevue to give the clinician a comfortable feeling of security as he approaches it. It is a 12-subtest point scale, divided as in the adult form into verbal and performance batteries, which can be summed and translated into a total IQ. The tests are similar to the adult Wechsler with certain exceptions.

The deviation IQ is used. (Children's scores are based on norms from other children of their age level.) This will be disconcerting to the Stanford-Binet habitue, since it tends to limit the occurrence of extremely high and extremely low IQ's.

The manual, which was the only source of information about the test known to the writer until mid-1950, when Seashore (*17*) began publishing supplementary material, is efficiently arranged and is self-contained. It gives certain rather sparse information on the sample (geographic, urban-rural, father's occupation data as compared with the 1940 U.S. Census) and tables of intercorrelations, reliabilities, and standard errors of measurement for the subtests and for the Verbal, Performance, and Full Scale IQ's.

During the first year of the test's life, the user was left not knowing the test's predictive value for other criteria. The most glaring deficiencies have been lack of published relationships with the classic *Revised Stanford-Binet Scale* and lack of knowledge of the test's predictive efficiency for school success. Such prediction, perhaps regrettably, *must* be known for a scale covering, as the WISC does, the ages of 5 through 15 years.

However, from mid-1950 on, Seashore, Wesman and Doppelt (*6*) and Seashore (*17*) have published more detailed data with reference to the standardization sample. A good job of standardization has been done. One hundred boys and 100 girls at each age level, 5 through 15 years, form the sample, 2,200 in all. Of these, 55 were nonrepresentationally selected (in terms of census data) from institutions for the mentally defective or special classes. Only white children were used. In general, the geographical selection and occupational selection of subjects is good. The reviewer questions the urban-rural sampling (skewed towards urban and small town "rural"). For some reason or another, the girls in the sample tend to test slightly lower than boys. Performance-verbal differences, mean IQ's and variability by age, etc. are remarkably even.

From early 1951 on, certain relationship and validational studies have begun to appear, although only a few have been published at the time of writing this review. Sloan and Schneider (*18*) reporting on 40 "familial or undifferentiated" mentally defective boys and girls, report r's of .79 and .76 with the *Arthur Point Scale of Performance Tests,* Form I, and the Stanford-Binet Form L respectively for the WISC Full Scale; .83 and .64 for WISC Performance Scale; and .47 and .75 for the WISC Verbal Scale. Considering the small number of cases these are not particularly unsatisfactory. Mean IQ's and standard deviations for the *Arthur*

Point Scale of Performance Tests, Form I, the Stanford-Binet Form L, and the WISC Full, Verbal, and Performance Scales were 64.9, 12.1; 56.3, 4.8; 59.7, 6.2; 64.6, 12.7; and 58.3, 9.5.

Stacey and Levin (19), reporting on 70 subnormals, find the Stanford-Binet Form L and the WISC Full, Verbal, and Performance mean IQ's and standard deviations to be 65.2, 7.21; 66.1, 8.5; 66.6, 7.0; and 71.6, 10.9, respectively. WISC Full Scale correlated .68 with the Stanford-Binet; WISC Verbal Scale correlated .69.

Cohen and Collier,[1] for from 49 to 53 normal 6, 7, and 8 year olds, report mean Arthur Performance Form II, Stanford-Binet Form L, and WISC Full, Verbal and Performance IQ's and standard deviations of 94.7, 16.4; 104.8, 15.1; 99.8, 14.6; 98.5, 14.3; and 101, 14.5. In their study, WISC Full, Verbal, and Performance IQ's correlate .85, .82, and .80 respectively with the Form L Stanford-Binet; and show etas of .80, .77 and .81 with the Arthur Performance Form II.

Magdsick and Blitz[2] report for an N of 64 first grade children an overall correlation of .53 for WISC Full IQ and teachers' marks, and of .76 with reading grades. The Stanford-Binet used in the same study shows a correlation with reading grades of .75.

To summarize, evidence begins to appear that the WISC is a pretty good test, though it possesses certain disadvantages. Among the major ones are: insufficient data about *what* it predicts, temptation to do elaborate pattern analyses on subjects' scores, some urban-rural inequity in the standardization sample, no Negro children in the sample, and a dubious mentally defective sample with consequent variable results with defectives.

Its positive virtues are its "up-to-dateness," the fact that an examiner can predict the time it will take to give a test, its real interest value for children, the fact that all children go through a comparable battery of all the available tests, plus the tentative indication that it can do the job of academic prediction so necessary for a test for the ages 5 through 15. The standardization sample is basically a good one, and the manual relatively compact. Some of the ambiguities of the adult Wechsler about assignment of weighted responses are present, and the appendix of acceptable responses is less complete than for the Stanford-Binet.

But at this point, the WISC seems a good and useful addition to the clinical armamentarium. Its final place depends, of course, on research.

J Consult Psychol 13:453–4 D '49. Laurance F. Shaffer. * The standardization is a radical departure from that of previous intelligence tests for children. The MA is discontinued entirely. Raw scores for the subtests are transmuted into standard scores by separate tables for each year level, and then into deviation IQ's with a mean of 100 and a standard deviation of 15. While a standardization that compares each child with others of his own age has long been desired, the lack of any means for expressing intelligence as a growth function will seem a shortcoming to many. The norming of the test on 2200 boys and girls of wide geographic distribution was carefully done and fully reported. On the other hand, evidences of the validity of the test as a whole, its subtests, or its items, are conspicuously missing from the manual. The value of the test for predicting common-sense criteria such as school progress or other evidences of adjustment remains to be established by future research. With its verbal and performance IQ's obtainable from one uniformly standardized scale, and its interesting possibilities for subtest analysis, the WISC undoubtedly will be used widely by clinicians, and will be evaluated by a wealth of studies.

[364]

Wechsler Memory Scale. Adults; 1945; individual; Forms 1, 2; $2.50 per 50 record forms and set of cards for subtest on visual reproduction; 50¢ per manual (reprinted from *J Psychol* 19:87–95 Ja '45); 60¢ per specimen set; David Wechsler and Calvin P. Stone (Form 2 only); Psychological Corporation. *

REFERENCES

1–3. See 3:302.
4. STONE, CALVIN P. "Characteristic Losses and Gains in Scores on the Wechsler Memory Scales as Applied on Psychotic Patients Before, During, and After a Series of Electro-Convulsive Shocks." Abstract. *Am Psychol* 1:245 Jl '46. * (PA 20:3681, title only)
5. FANELLI, GLORIA C. *An Evaluation and Comparison of the Wechsler Memory Scale and the Hunt-Minnesota Test for Organic Brain Damage.* Master's thesis, Fordham University (New York, N.Y.), 1948.
6. SILVA, JOSEPH J. *The Use of the Wechsler Memory Scale in Differential Diagnosis.* Master's thesis, Fordham University (New York, N.Y.), 1949.
7. COHEN, JACOB. "Wechsler Memory Scale Performance of Psychoneurotic, Organic, and Schizophrenic Groups." *J Consult Psychol* 14:371–5 O '50. * (PA 25:4654)
8. HOWARD, ALVIN R. "Diagnostic Value of the Wechsler Memory Scale With Selected Groups of Institutionalized Patients." *J Consult Psychol* 14:376–80 O '50. * (PA 25:4730)
9. WATSON, ROBERT I. *The Clinical Method in Psychology,* pp. 349–53. New York: Harper & Brothers, 1951. Pp. xii, 779. *

---

[1] Cohen, Bertram D., and Collier, Mary E. "The Relationship of the Wechsler Intelligence Scale for Children to Some Other Intelligence Tests." Paper read before 1951 Midwestern Psychological Association.
[2] Magdsick, Winifred K., and Blitz, Leroy L. "An Evaluation of the Wechsler Intelligence Scale for Children at the First Grade Level." Paper read before 1951 Midwestern Psychological Association.

IVAN NORMAN MENSH, *Assistant Professor of Medical Psychology, Washington University Medical School, St. Louis, Missouri.*

This memory scale was developed as "a rapid, simple, and practical memory examination.... for clinical purposes." The seven subtests are designed to sample personal and current information, immediate orientation to time and place, mental control, immediate recall of logical material, memory span for digits, reproduction of simple geometric figures from memory, and three-trial learning of paired words. The manual indicates such advantages as brevity, standardization on 200 normal adults, allowance for memory variation with age, and comparability of memory quotients with intelligent quotients, making possible the study of memory impairment as compared with deficits in other intellectual functions.

The availability of a memory quotient (MQ) corrected for age and thereby comparable to a subject's intelligence quotient is a significant diagnostic aid. However, the procedure for calculating MQ's is based upon the norm group, age 25–50, a range which limits the use of the conversion table even though age corrections through 64 are given in the table. Extrapolation above age 50 may be faulty; the study of memory and of other intellectual performances among the aged has been both limited and controversial, principally because of the size and lack of comparability of the samples studied. Wechsler cautions that, because of the empirical method of deriving them, the memory quotient equivalents provided in his manual are only approximate. Interpretation of MQ's in psychological practice should include this caution. A useful check may be provided by comparing the IQ–MQ deviation with the Deterioration Index of the *Wechsler-Bellevue Intelligence Scale* from which the IQ is computed.

Repeated testing to evaluate the degree and rate of impairment or of recovery of function is frequently of diagnostic value. Alternate forms are needed therefore, and Stone, Girdner, and Albrecht (*2*) have introduced an alternate form of the *Wechsler Memory Scale*. This second form is based on data from 87 subjects who were tested with both forms. Although there was little change in total score from one form to the other, the subtests had little differentiating value among the samples of student nurses, hospital patients, and college students. Thus far reports by other workers have not been published so that it is not known to what extent Form 2 is equivalent to the original form. A lack of published reports on its use also characterizes the *Wechsler Memory Scale* itself, although communication with a number of clinical psychologists confirms the reviewer's high opinion of it as a technique useful in the studying of deficit in certain areas of memory functioning. Responses of subjects to both the *Wechsler-Bellevue Intelligence Scale* and the *Wechsler Memory Scale* provide diagnostically rich data for psychological study.

JOSEPH NEWMAN, *Clinical Psychologist, Veterans Administration Hospital, Canandaigua, New York.*

This scale was devised to provide a simple and rapid measure of memory function. The directions are clear and the scoring criteria are adequate except for the test of Visual Reproduction (memory for designs) where scoring examples might profitably be added to the manual, obviating the necessity to go back to the original sources of the designs in the case of neophytes. The administration takes, on the average, 15 minutes. The total raw score is corrected for age, and the corrected score is translated into a Memory Quotient (MQ) equivalent. The MQ was designed to be directly comparable to the Wechsler-Bellevue intelligence quotient, and this is the most useful feature of the *Wechsler Memory Scale*.

The test was standardized on "approximately 200 normal subjects, ages 25 to 50, both men and women," an inadequate number for so wide an age range. Further data include only Wechsler-Bellevue IQ. We would want to have further data on education, occupation, and socioeconomic status. Another serious shortcoming is the lack of reliability data for either form. An estimated reliability coefficient of about .83 for clinical populations, based on the correlation between Form II and the Revised Alpha Examination Form 8, is presented. There is question, too, of the equivalence of Forms I and II. In devising Form II, Stone and his associates assembled "similar items previously equated for difficulty in other researches." The authors recognize the need for further experimental work to determine the actual comparability of the two forms. Data concerning the effects of practice are also needed. These deficiencies place limitations on the usefulness of the *Wechsler Memory Scale*.

The test is designed for use with a clinical population. It makes possible the comparison of memory efficiency with other aspects of intellectual function as measured by the Wechsler-Bellevue. Presumably, one should be able to distinguish between cases in which there is a specific memory defect, frequently found in conjunction with organic brain disease, and cases in which memory impairment is one aspect of a generalized intellectual inefficiency, such as may occur in a functional psychosis. In other words, performance on the *Wechsler Memory Scale* may provide diagnostic information. Wechsler thinks the scale is "useful in detecting special memory defects in individuals with specific organic brain injuries." Available research does not bear out this contention. Cohen studied the differentiating power of the scale among groups of "psychoneurotics," "organics," and "schizophrenics," and did not obtain any significant results.[1] Howard, on the other hand, found that the scale will discriminate between matched groups when the brain damage is of a gross nature.[2]

The value of the *Wechsler Memory Scale* as a diagnostic instrument has not been established; the situation as to memory functioning in general is still as Klebanoff[3] found it—inconsistent and contradictory. This limitation diagnostically is shared to a greater or lesser extent by all psychometric instruments. The scale's greatest usefulness is as an indicator of memory efficiency in comparison to the Wechsler-Bellevue. It can provide "clinical insights" as to personality reactions which may aid in the diagnostic process. As Rabin and Guertin have remarked in their review of the Wechsler-Bellevue, almost any test employed by a skillful clinician and insightful worker may prove an "aid in differential diagnosis."[4]

For a review by Kate Levine Kogan, see 3:302.

[1] Cohen, Jacob. "Wechsler Memory Scale Performance of Psychoneurotic, Organic, and Schizophrenic Groups." *J Consult Psychol* 14:371–5 O '50. * (*PA* 25:4654)

[2] Howard, Alvin R. "Diagnostic Value of the Wechsler Memory Scale With Selected Groups of Institutionalized Patients." *J Consult Psychol* 14:376–80 O '50. * (*PA* 25:4730)

[3] Klebanoff, Seymour G. "Psychological Changes in Organic Brain Lesions and Ablations." *Psychol B* 42:585–623 N '45. * (*PA* 20:649)

[4] Rabin, Albert I., and Guertin, Wilson H. "Research With the Wechsler-Bellevue Test: 1945–1950." *Psychol B* 48:211–48 Ap '51. *

REPRINTED FROM *The Fifth Mental Measurements Yearbook*

INTELLIGENCE — FIFTH MMY

REVIEWS BY C. J. Adcock, Charlotte E. K. Banks, Nancy Bayley, Cyril Burt, Lee J. Cronbach, John T. Dailey, Reginald R. Dale, John C. Daniels, Frederick B. Davis, Raleigh M. Drake, Walter N. Durost, Norman Eagle, George A. Ferguson, Joshua A. Fishman, John P. Foley, Jr., Hanford M. Fowler, Elizabeth D. Fraser, Frank S. Freeman, Gustav J. Froehlich, Eugene L. Gaier, Henry E. Garrett, Wilson H. Guertin, J. P. Guilford, Nelson G. Hanawalt, Mary Haworth, Alfred B. Heilbrun, Jr., A. W. Heim, Duncan Howie, Cyril J. Hoyt, J. A. Keats, D. Welty Lefever, Roger T. Lennon, John Liggett, James Lumsden, James Mainwaring, William B. Michael, T. R. Miles, John E. Milholland, G. A. V. Morgan, Louis C. Nanassy, Charles O. Neidt, John Nisbet, Raymond C. Norris, Gerald R. Patterson, E. A. Peel, D. A. Pidgeon, A. E. G. Pilliner, M. L. Kellmer Pringle, Albert I. Rabin, James H. Ricks, Jr., Cyril A. Rogers, Arthur B. Royse, C. Sanders, I. David Satlow, William B. Schrader, William Sloan, I. Macfarlane Smith, Julian C. Stanley, Naomi Stewart, Norman D. Sundberg, Calvin W. Taylor, Erwin K. Taylor, Florence M. Teagarden, W. Wesley Tennyson, David V. Tiedeman, Leona E. Tyler, F. W. Warburton, Alexander G. Wesman, John M. Willits, R. Winterbourn, and Alfred Yates.

GROUP

[295]

★**A.C.E.R. Advanced Tests AL and AQ.** College and superior adults; 1953–55; 1 form ['53]; 2 tests; mimeographed manual ['55]; 3s. per 10 tests; 6d. per scoring key ['54]; 4s. 6d. per manual; 5s. 3d. per specimen set; postpaid within Australia; manual by D. Spearritt; Australian Council for Educational Research. *
a) TEST AL. Linguistic; 1 form ['53]; 25(35) minutes.
b) TEST AQ. Quantitative; 1 form ['54]; 30(40) minutes.

DUNCAN HOWIE, *Professor of Psychology, The University of New England, Armidale, Australia.*

These tests are designed as high level intelligence tests to discriminate levels of general ability in students who are completing secondary education or entering university or similar tertiary education. Although the subtests appear as separates, with AL a test of ability to reason with linguistic material and AQ a test of ability to reason with quantitative material mainly of an arithmetical nature, they are intended not as measures of distinct abilities but as two approaches to a measure of general alertness from two differing media. There are 28 items in Test AL, ranging over analogies, opposites, letter series, and proverb types of problems. Test AQ consists of 25 items, comprising number series, number matrices, and arithmetical problems.

The manual gives a quite comprehensive account of the development of the test with completely adequate instructions for its administration at a level suited to teachers or others who have had the usual sort of elementary training in testing. A brief but valuable technical supplement gives the basic statistical data for the more expert.

The direct data for standardization are from 500 students (309 first year students in teachers colleges in Victoria and 191 seniors in a single high school). Provisional norms could have been drawn from these data for the guidance of those interested in using the test in relation to its objectives, for example, for comparing groups of students of comparable age and educational level. The publishers, however, adopted a more elaborate and more indirect procedure. Scores from AL-AQ were indirectly standardized against scores from the *A.C.E.R. Higher Test M*. This in turn was directly standardized at the 18 years plus level, but indirectly standardized at the 13–14 year levels against another A.C.E.R. test. Further, ML-MQ IQ's between the ages of 14 and 18 were arrived at by interpolation. In these circumstances, the IQ norms given in the AL-AQ manual for each 3-month age interval from 15.0 to 18.9 could appear misleadingly authoritative.

The publishers are careful to point out that these IQ's, derived by means of normalized standard scores for each age interval with mean at 100 and standard deviation of 15 points, are not to be confused with Binet type IQ's. The possibility of such confusion in itself raises a question as to whether anything is gained by perpetuating the by no means illuminating IQ concept at these later age and higher ability levels. The publishers' justification would appear to be that, recognizing that educationalists in general are still so sold on the IQ, it was thought advisable, as they put it, "to conform with current practice." In view of the danger that these indices can so easily be considered without reference to the conditions under which they were obtained, and bearing in mind the indirect nature of the standardization, it is unfortunate that the publishers have seen fit to pay so much respect to current practice or current prejudice.

Evidence of validity is confined to correlations between AL and a standardized A.C.E.R. English achievement test and between AQ and a similarly standardized A.C.E.R. mathematics test. Intercorrelations are reported for three groups of men and three groups of women in teachers colleges in three states. For the men the means of the correlations are: AL and English, .54; AQ and mathematics, .66. The respective means for the women are .65 and .70. The implications of these correlations would appear to be that AL-AQ correlates with measures of abilities which are of importance in academic achievement. Presumably, as the subtests are not designed as measures of distinct abilities, the differences between the relationships with verbal and mathematical tests are not being advanced as justification for using AL as a test of verbal ability and AQ as a test of mathematical ability. It would, however, have been of interest if correlations between AL and mathematics and AQ and English had been given. As the purpose of AL-AQ is to discriminate general ability levels in higher educational groups, one would wish to see further evidence of its validity in this respect, e.g., its relation to success or failure in senior high school, teachers college, or university work.

There is an increasingly acute need in Australia for an adequately standardized test with clear evidence of validity for selection and guidance at higher secondary and tertiary levels. The AL-AQ combination is a promising step in this direction and is, in fact, the best available Australian test for these purposes. It must be recognized, though, that the information from it should be used tentatively because its standardization implies no more than a basis of comparison and its validity remains to be shown. The data for direct standardization and evidences of the degree of the test's validity will accrue if it is used, as it deserves to be used, sufficiently extensively and intensively in research programmes in student selection and guidance.

[296]

***A.C.E.R. Advanced Test B40.** Ages 13 and over; 1940–53; title on test is *Adult Test (B40)*; 1 form ['40]; mimeographed manual ['53]; 5s. per 10 tests; 2s. per manual; 2s. 6d. per specimen set; postpaid within Australia; 55(65) minutes; Australian Council for Educational Research. *

REFERENCES

1. Cook, P. H. "Criteria for the Selection of Personnel Officers." *B Ind Psychol & Personnel Prac* 2:28–37 Je '46. * (PA 20:4761)
2. Hohne, H. H. "The Prediction of Academic Success." *Austral J Psychol* 1:38–42 Je '49. *
3. Hohne, H. H. *Success and Failure in Scientific Faculties of the University of Melbourne.* Melbourne, Australia: Australian Council for Educational Research, 1955. Pp. vii, 129. * (PA 31:3787)

C. SANDERS, *Professor of Education and Dean of the Faculty, University of Western Australia, Nedlands, Australia.*

Mental tests should meet the dictates of recognisable validity, sound construction and standardisation, acceptable reliability, and serviceable usage. If the *A.C.E.R. Advanced Test B40* is rated on the extent of its usage during and since the war, then it qualifies, in terms of its catalogue description, as a test of "general ability (intelligence)" for students in colleges and universities—at least in Australia.

Test B40 is designed to discriminate among students aged 15 years and over. When the A.C.E.R. moved into test construction at this level, it began by adapting the *Otis Self-Administering Tests of Mental Ability* to Australian conditions. This enabled Otis Higher C to be used in standardising Test B40, the first major Australian test of the advanced type.

Test B40 contains 77 verbal and quantitative items. Its directions are simple, its administration is straightforward, and its marking is reasonably easy. By means of conversion tables the raw scores from the test can be converted to IQ's on a range varying from 85 to 145.

The IQ as a measure of ability is well entrenched in Australia even though in "advanced" tests of the B40 type it is largely a misnomer, being more accurately a quantitative index or estimate of scholastic aptitude. On this assumption, and despite acceptance of the test by qualified people in Australia, B40 has not yet graduated beyond the experimental stage. For example, in a restandardisation of Otis Higher C by the A.C.E.R. some years ago, the conclusion was reached that the original Australian norms were too low and that the B40 IQ's, based on the Otis Higher C norms, were underestimated by about 3 points at the lower end of the range and 5 points at the upper end. In consequence, a reexamination of the B40 norms is to be undertaken. Meantime, the manual, containing directions, norms, and scoring key, remains tentative, and is supplied in duplicated form with the printed tests.

Although the original reliability and validity studies were based on only 74 cases, a split-half reliability coefficient of .89 and a validity coefficient of .80 with Otis Higher C were obtained. The test was widely employed during the war to assess various student groups as well as applicants for the public services, and the results it produced at that time were accepted as reasonably reliable.

Despite its present defects, including its tentative standardisation and impermanent manual, the *A.C.E.R. Advanced Test B40* is a useful comparative instrument for assessing groups of college and university students. However, in using it for such purposes the point should be kept in mind that the results it so far has produced may be somewhat conservative.

[297]
*A.C.E.R. Higher Test M. Ages 13 and over; 1944–55; formerly called *A.C.E.R. General Ability Test: Advanced M;* 3 scores: linguistic, quantitative, total; 1 form ['48]; 2 parts; revised mimeographed manual ['55]; 3s. per 10 tests; 9d. per scoring key; 6s. 6d. per manual; 7s. 6d. per specimen set; postpaid within Australia; manual by D. Spearritt; Australian Council for Educational Research. *
a) [PART ML.] Linguistic; 15(25) minutes.
b) [PART MQ.] Quantitative; 20(30) minutes.

C. SANDERS, *Professor of Education and Dean of the Faculty, University of Western Australia, Nedlands, Australia.*

Like its more advanced counterpart, *A.C.E.R. Advanced Tests AL and AQ,* Higher Test M yields two scores, L and Q, which can be taken separately or together. Part ML consists of linguistic or verbal relation items, and Part MQ of quantitative or number relation items. The comprehensive manual of directions gives substantial information about the history of the test and the various ways in which it may be employed. Each of the scores and the total score can be converted to estimates of IQ.

The test has been standardised in various ways and, although imperfection is easier to attain than perfection, the impression gained is that the work in general has been competently and ingeniously performed, and that the test and its subtests are reasonably valid and reliable. However, at the upper end of the scale the norms are based entirely on males—service trainees in one state—and adjustments have had to be made to allow for the performance of females.

Considerable information is given as to the interrelations of Test M, and its subparts L and Q, with other measures. A correlation of .63 is reported between L and Q. This, in the circumstances, is rather high, and indicates internal overlap to a greater extent than apparently is present in tests AL-AQ, between which the correlation is stated to be .45. However, ML-MQ correlates .76 with AL-AQ and .84 with the *A.C.E.R. Intermediate Test D.* Part ML correlates .66 with AL and Part MQ .73 with AQ. These latter coefficients are fairly good in view of the fact that tests AL and AQ are designed for a population aged 15 years and over.

The results of a factor analysis of ML-MQ and other variables are reported and interesting occupational norms in terms of raw scores are provided. As far as occupational differences are concerned, farmers and university students produced the widest variations. Farmers yielded mean 15.47, SD 7.2, on ML, and mean 15.24, SD 7.5, on MQ. The figures for university students were: ML—mean 31.0, SD 3.3; MQ—mean 30.84, SD 5.0.

As an experimenter among university students, the reviewer confesses a partiality towards the approach to mental testing adopted by the A.C.E.R. in its preparation of tests ML-MQ and AL-AQ. At a meeting of the

Australian and New Zealand Association for the Advancement of Science held at Brisbane in 1951, he pointed out, in a paper dealing with omnibus tests of the Advanced N type, how differences between groups of individuals who are verbally or nonverbally minded are concealed in total raw scores, or under the canopy of the IQ's obtained from raw scores. On this point he emphasised the opinion that reported differences in the mean IQ's of men and women students at the college and university level were probably due "in greater measure to the nature of the tests themselves and to the social and educational background of the sexes" than to other causes.

In the construction of the present tests, the A.C.E.R. seems to have paid some attention to the sort of criticism just mentioned. Tests of the ML-MQ type, despite difficulties in construction and some deficiencies in standardisation, have the advantage of variety and flexibility, and avoid the need to employ a test battery when such a procedure is inconvenient. Moreover, in the Australian context, the best scholastic predictors at the higher levels have been found to be tests of verbal relation and number relation, rather than other tests. However, the intrinsic worth of ML-MQ and AL-AQ will not be fully known until they have been more widely employed than so far has been the case.

[298]

★A.C.E.R. Intermediate Tests C and D. Ages 10–14.0; 1939–53; 1 form; 2 tests; 3s. 9d. per 10 tests; postpaid within Australia; Australian Council for Educational Research. *

a) TEST C. 1939–53; formerly called *A.C.E.R. General Test C;* 1 form ['52]; mimeographed manual ['53]; 4s. per manual; 6d. per scoring key; 4s. 9d. per specimen set; 35(45) minutes.
b) TEST D. 1947–51; 1 form ['47]; 3s. 6d. per manual ['51]; 1s. per scoring key; 4s. 9d. per specimen set; 30(50) minutes.

REFERENCES
1. DUNN, S., AND SPEARRITT, D. "A Comparative Study of the Reliability of Some Verbal and Non-Verbal Intelligence Tests." *Austral J Psychol* 7:169–74 D '55. * (PA 31:1030) •
2. DUNN, S. S., AND BROWNLESS, V. T. "Differences in Test and Retest Responses of a Group of Children to a Verbal and a Non-Verbal Test." *Austral J Psychol* 8:84–7 Je '56. * (PA 31:7910)

JAMES LUMSDEN, *Lecturer in Psychology, University of Western Australia, Nedlands, Australia.*

These tests are designed to assess the general aptitude for school work of children in Australian schools. Normalized standard score norms, called "IQ's" (mean 100, SD 15), are provided for the age range 10.0–14.0 years but the authors point out that the norms at the extremes of the range may be inaccurate. Norms for Test D are based on 300 to 600 subjects at each 6-month age interval. Norms for Test C were obtained by indirect standardization from Test D for the upper ages and from the *A.C.E.R. Junior B Test* for the lower ages. Indirect standardization is not theoretically valid, but the experience of test users indicates that marked variations in "IQ" from one test to the other are not more frequent than usual.

The items are of the well tried Otis type: verbal analogies, number series, letter series, vocabulary, arithmetical problems. Item discrimination between high and low scorers on the original item pool was used to select items for the final test. Quarrying the recognized item types in this way is unlikely to produce a great test but it will rarely produce a bad one.

The reliability coefficients for Test D, as determined by test-retest, split-half, and Kuder-Richardson methods, range from .91 to .96. Validity has been determined by correlation with standardized reading and arithmetic achievement tests. The resulting coefficients (for a slightly restricted sample) range from .21 to .70, indicating that Test D can be expected to predict the results in formal school subjects with reasonable accuracy. No direct evidence concerning its validity for educational guidance or placement is given, but it can be inferred to be high. Reliability and validity data are provided with adequate supporting explanation in the manual for Test D but similar data are not given for Test C.

It is not clear whether Test C is intended to be strictly parallel to Test D. The method of norming and the omission of details about validity for Test C would suggest that this is so, but the correlation between the tests (given to a restricted sample on the same occasion) is only .81. One would expect some explanation from the authors concerning its lowness; however, their only statement is that the value "would almost certainly be lower than the immediate test-retest coefficient for Test C."

Intermediate Test D is a first rate test. Work by the reviewer indicates that it has no superior in Australia for educational prediction. The manual is a model achieving a nice balance between brevity, clarity, and technical completeness. The manual for Intermediate Test C is quite unsatisfactory and rather gives the impression that the test was hurriedly prepared to provide an alternative when the use of Intermediate Test D was undesirable.

[299]
*A.C.E.R. Junior A Test. Ages 8.6–12.0; 1946–53; formerly called *General Test T*; 1 form ['46]; [revised] mimeographed manual ['53]; 6s. per 10 tests; 1s. 6d. per scoring key; 2s. 6d. per manual; 4s. 6d. per specimen set; postpaid within Australia; 30(40) minutes; Australian Council for Educational Research. *

R. WINTERBOURN, *Professor of Education, The University of Auckland, Auckland, New Zealand.*

This group test consists of 75 items, including the usual analogies, problems, similarities, best reasons, substitutions, arithmetic, and sequence arrangement types. Twenty-one of the items are nonverbal, mostly pictorial. These occur at intervals throughout the test, thus possibly helping to sustain the interest of the less verbally inclined children. At the same time, some users of the test have claimed that certain of these items are so attractive that they tend to distract the attention of some children. This is, of course, a subjective opinion. Another criticism is that the test, printed on seven foolscap-sized pages with the 75 items arranged without a break, may appear rather formidable to some children.

Since the test is intended for use with young children (although norms are provided for ages 8-6 to 12-0, the test is said to be most useful within the age range 9–11) directions are very clear and full, and are related to suitable practice examples. Scoring keys and easily read conversion tables are provided.

The test has been standardized so that the mean IQ for each age group is 100 and the SD 15. The standard error of measurement suggests reasonable limits of IQ variation. It is recommended that each score be interpreted in terms of an IQ range instead of being represented by a single IQ. This is a useful lesson for those teachers and others who still tend to think in terms of a rigidly fixed IQ. No IQ's are given beyond 135. It is claimed that the test discriminates satisfactorily among average and poorer than average children beyond 11 years of age but not among the brighter ones.

Certain possible shortcomings and limitations are apparent, but they are not of a major nature. The test's overall usefulness as an aid to grouping and classifying in schools has been demonstrated by its popularity for many years.

[300]
*A.C.E.R. Junior B Test. Ages 8.6–12.0; 1948–49; title on test is *General Ability Test: A.C.E.R. Junior B*; 1 form ['48]; mimeographed manual ['49]; no data on reliability and validity; no norms; distribution restricted; 5s. 3d. per 10 tests; 6d. per scoring key; 6s. 6d. per manual; 7s. 6d. per specimen set; postpaid within Australia; 35(60) minutes; Australian Council for Educational Research. *

REFERENCE
1. DUNN, S., AND SPEARRITT, D. "A Comparative Study of the Reliability of Some Verbal and Non-Verbal Intelligence Tests." *Austral J Psychol* 7:169–74 D '55. * (*PA* 31:1030)

R. WINTERBOURN, *Professor of Education, The University of Auckland, Auckland, New Zealand.*

Unlike the Junior A Test, this verbal group test of 65 items is broken down into five subtests, each with its own time limit. This arrangement overcomes one of the minor criticisms leveled at Junior A, i.e., that the test may appear quite formidable to some pupils. A further related point is that the practice examples are also broken into two groups, one being given before the first three subtests and the other before the last two. The subtests cover synonyms, problems, analogies, number series, and arithmetical problems.

Norms cover the ages 8-0 to 12-0. As for Junior A, there is an upper limit of 135 IQ. Easily used keys and conversion tables are supplied.

Validity coefficients ranging from .67 to .77 have been obtained between Junior B and the *A.C.E.R. Junior Non-Verbal Test*. Between Junior B and Intermediate Test D, correlations ranging from .75 to .85 have been obtained.

Test-retest and Kuder-Richardson reliability data are reported for the complete test and for the separate subtests. Retesting of 160 fifth grade Melbourne children after one week yielded a total score *r* of .86; retesting of 107 children after one year yielded a total score *r* of .88.

A Thurstone centroid analysis ($n = 152$ fifth grade Victorian children) of the intercorrelations found between Junior B and the A.C.E.R. arithmetic and reading achievement tests revealed loadings of .82 on what is called a general ability factor and .31 on a factor "which appears to be a reasoning factor of some kind."

This test has many features to commend it. It measures up quite well to the standard of test construction established by the A.C.E.R., a standard which is by no means reached by all test constructors. It should be apparent that the test's merit lies in the field of grouping and classifying rather than in that of individual assessment.

[301]

★A.C.E.R. Junior Non-Verbal Test. Ages 8.6–12.0; 1949–53; 1 form ['49]; [revised] mimeographed manual ['53]; 10s. per 10 tests; 1s. per scoring key; 3s. 6d. per manual; 5s. 6d. per specimen set; postpaid within Australia; 34(60) minutes; manual by D. Spearritt; Australian Council for Educational Research. *

REFERENCE
1. DUNN, S., AND SPEARRITT, D. "A Comparative Study of the Reliability of Some Verbal and Non-Verbal Intelligence Tests." *Austral J Psychol* 7:169–74 D '55. * (PA 31:1030)

D. A. PIDGEON, *Senior Officer, Test Services, National Foundation for Educational Research in England and Wales, London, England.*

This test is composed of 60 items which are divided into four separately timed subtests of 15 items each—time sequences, block series, diagrammatic analogies, and matrices. Each subtest is preceded by a page of practice examples illustrating the principle involved in that particular subtest; all instructions are given orally. The test is printed on rather cumbersome foolscap paper and the heavy type used does not give a particularly pleasing appearance.

Exceptional care was taken over the construction of the test, the choice of the four item types employed being based on research findings. A battery of nonverbal tests was given to a group of 167 fourth grade children in five Melbourne schools and the results submitted to factor analysis. The item types finally selected were those with high loadings on the general factor and negligible loadings on the verbalisation factor, thus producing items that presumably depend little on verbal ability for their solution.

The test has been well standardised on an effectively random sample of children attending all types of schools from the whole of Australia. The reliability coefficients quoted (average approximately .90) are not so high as might be desired, probably due in part to the fact that the test contains only 60 items. The manual, however, suggests that test results should be recorded in terms of an "IQ range," determined from the probable error of measurement, the value of which is given for three levels of raw score. In evidence of the test's validity, correlations ranging from .60 to .81 are quoted both with a verbal test and with another nonverbal test. The mean of the correlations with eight arithmetic and reading tests given to 152 Victorian fifth grade children is .34. No evidence, however, is provided on the value of the test for predicting future school work, or on the possible results of remedial education.

There is no doubt that this is a well made test, but, in the light of recent research, one is bound to question its value for educational guidance. The evidence from research disagrees with the implication in the manual that remedial work is possible only with children whose nonverbal scores are significantly above their scores on a verbal test and not with those unfortunates who obtain low scores on both types of test. If, as the manual states, "a verbal test cannot be expected to give a satisfactory assessment of the general ability of children who are handicapped by poor ability in reading," then it is an unwarranted assumption to think that a nonverbal test will do instead. The results of factorial analyses indicate clearly that nonverbal tests such as this measure group or specific factors of their own besides "g," and it is difficult to see why the ability to discover relationships among pictorial or other nonverbal materials should predict school work which is, for the most part, verbal.

If an adequate reason can be found for obtaining a reliable measure of the "nonverbal" ability of young school children, this test will provide that measure; as an indication of the ability of children to reason, within the context of the usual school subjects, it is difficult to see how it, or any other nonverbal test of a similar type, can replace a verbal one. Certainly, as an indication of a child's potential for learning school work, the scores on this test should be used with extreme caution, if at all.

[302]

★APT Performance Test. Adults; 1954–57; Forms A, B ('54); 2 tests; manual ['57]; distribution restricted to clients; $4 per 50 tests; specimen set available upon request; postpaid; 5(10), 10(15) minutes for verbal, quantitative tests; Bentley Barnabas; Associated Personnel Technicians. *

[303]

*Academic Aptitude Test: Non-Verbal Intelligence: Acorn National Aptitude Tests. Grades 7–16 and adults; 1943–57; 4 scores: spatial relations, physical relations, graphic relations, total; 1 form ('57, identical with test copyrighted in 1944); directions sheet ('43); no norms for part scores; $3.75 per 25 tests; 25¢ per manual ('44); 50¢ per specimen set; postage extra; 26(45) minutes; Andrew Kobal, J. Wayne Wrightstone, and Karl R. Kunze; Acorn Publishing Co. *

For a review by William B. Schrader, see 4:274.

[304]

*Academic Aptitude Test: Verbal Intelligence: Acorn National Aptitude Tests.** Grades 7–16 and adults; 1943–52; 4 scores: general information, mental alertness, comprehension of relations, total; 1 form ('52, identical with test copyrighted in 1943 except for minor changes); directions sheet ('43); $3.75 per 25 tests; 25¢ per manual ('45); 50¢ per specimen set; postage extra; 40(45) minutes; Andrew Kobal, J. Wayne Wrightstone, and Karl R. Kunze; Acorn Publishing Co. *

For a review by William B. Schrader, see 4:275; for a review by Marion A. Bills, see 3:215.

[305]

*Adaptability Test.** Job applicants; 1942–54; Forms A, B ('42); revised manual ('54); $2.45 per 20 tests; 50¢ per specimen set; postage extra; 15(20) minutes; Joseph Tiffin and C. H. Lawshe; Science Research Associates. *

REFERENCES

1–3. See 3:216.
4. KAHN, D. F. *An Analysis of Factors Related to Life Insurance Selling.* Doctor's thesis, Purdue University (Lafayette, Ind.), 1948. (PA 24:2884)
5. PRED, GORDON D. *A Comparison of the Test Performance of "Good" and "Poor" Industrial Supervisors.* Master's thesis, Purdue University (Lafayette, Ind.), 1948.
6. STROMBERG, ELEROY L. "Testing Programs Draw Better Applicants." *Personnel Psychol* 1:21–9 sp '48. * (PA 22:4157)
7. GIESE, WILLIAM JAMES. "A Tested Method for the Selection of Office Personnel." *Personnel Psychol* 2:525–45 w '49. * (PA 24:4278)
8. HADLEY, J. M., AND KAHN, D. F. "A Comment on Wallace's Note on 'Factors Related to Life Insurance Selling.'" *J Appl Psychol* 33:359–62 Ag '49. * (PA 24:2882)
9. KAHN, D. F., AND HADLEY, J. M. "Factors Related to Life Insurance Selling." *J Appl Psychol* 33:132–40 Ap '49. * (PA 24:357)
10. LAWSHE, C. H. "How Can We Pick Better Supervisors?" *Personnel Psychol* 2:69–73 sp '49. * (PA 23:5071)
11. WALLACE, S. RAINS, JR. "A Note on Kahn and Hadley's 'Factors Related to Life Insurance Selling.'" *J Appl Psychol* 33:356–8 Ag '49. * (PA 24:2884)
12. POE, WESLEY A., AND BERG, IRWIN A. "Psychological Test Performance of Steel Industry Production Supervisors." *J Appl Psychol* 36:234–7 Ag '52. * (PA 27:3794)
13. ROSENSTEEL, RICHARD K. *A Validation of a Test Battery and Biographical Data for the Selection of Machine Operator Trainees.* Master's thesis, Bowling Green State University (Bowling Green, Ohio), 1953.
14. PATTON, WENDELL M., JR. "Studies in Industrial Empathy: III, A Study of Supervisory Empathy in the Textile Industry." *J Appl Psychol* 38:285–8 O '54. * (PA 29:6378)
15. ALBRIGHT, LEWIS E. "Validity Information Exchange, No. 9-44: D.O.T. Code 0-66.93, Seed Analyst." *Personnel Psychol* 9:522–3 w '56. *
16. ALBRIGHT, LEWIS EDWIN. *The Development of a Selection Process for an Inspection Task.* Doctor's thesis, Purdue University (Lafayette, Ind.), 1956. (DA 16:2201)

JOHN M. WILLITS, *Business and Industrial Psychologist, 566 Everett Ave., Palo Alto, California.*

"Designed to measure....adaptability or mental alertness" in job applicants—to differentiate rapid learners from other persons better suited to simple, routine jobs—this test is itself an example of adaptation—to the time pressures so typical in employment offices. In 20 minutes it can be made to yield a composite measure of several "factors" of intelligence, derived from Thurstone's analysis. This spiral-omnibus test's 35 items would be judged to sample at least two verbal factors, two numerical factors, and one spatial factor. Thus it averages, at most, only seven items per factor! And yet data in the manual indicate this single, composite measure to be reasonably reliable (with coefficients clustering around .8) and probably valid, to a degree, for many jobs in business and industry.

Let us assume that, like very many employment managers today, we are still having to settle for only 20 minutes' testing time in which to measure mental ability. Does this test represent the *best* available use of that amount of time?

In reply we may ask: "How specific are the demands of the different job openings, in terms of intelligence factors utilized?" For the differential placement of applicants, we would do well to weigh the feasibility of measuring *several separate* factors in the allotted 20 minutes. In that time, the *Short Employment Tests* would yield three separate measures—verbal knowledge, computational speed and accuracy, and visual-perceptual speed and accuracy—with at least as much reliability and validity. Or, from the 10 factored tests of the newly published *Employee Aptitude Survey,* we could assemble literally dozens of different 3-test batteries, each requiring only 20 minutes but each tailored to the requirements of a different job or family of jobs—again with no loss statistically.

The 8-page revised manual for the *Adaptability Test* makes specific mention of the *Technical Recommendations for Psychological Tests and Diagnostic Techniques,* and it reflects many of those recommendations. This manual states clearly the use for which the test is intended. It indicates, though rather obscurely (by the designation "Level B" and a fragmentary quote from the reference just mentioned), the required qualifications for administering and using the test. It describes very briefly, yet clearly, the procedures of administering, scoring, and interpreting. It discusses the essential topics of item selection, comparability of forms, reliability (by two methods), and validity (both intrinsic and predictive). It stresses the importance of accumulating local norms and setting local cutting scores. And it warns that this test presumably measures only a portion of the significant factors in success on any given job.

The manual reports that items "were retained on the basis of an internal consistency item analysis," but it gives little information on the method of analysis or the size of the resulting coefficients. Validity correlations ranging from .73 to .79 are reported with three other mental tests: Ohio State, Otis Self-Administering, and Wonderlic. The latter two of these resemble the *Adaptability Test* in pattern and in length.

Predictive validity of the test is indicated by means of expectancy tables for four employee populations, but three of these populations are only vaguely described. There are no data on ranges of age, education, experience, etc. Confidence limits are reported for all four tables, but score means and sigmas are not. The validating criteria are described in some detail, but there is no mention of the adequacy or the reliability of these criteria, which are chiefly ratings. Nor is there mention of the possibility of criterion contamination by test results.

Equivalence of the two forms is supported by data on average discrimination values and difficulty levels for one population, and by score means and sigmas for four other populations. Two of these populations are too small for this purpose (n's of about 20 and 40), and it is not surprising that their means and sigmas vary widely.

Reliability evidence is apparently based on the same four populations, with neither the populations nor the testing conditions being adequately described. Though the manual specifically recommends "retesting of doubtful cases," there are no data on stability of retest scores nor on time elapsed between alternate forms reliability runs. Sigmas of score distributions are given for the reliability samples, but means are not. (Such means, if estimated from those of the form equivalence data, appear to vary widely.) There are no data on the error of measurement at different score levels. In justification of its split-half reliability data, the manual states that "this test is essentially a power test," but no data support this statement.

Norms, both in percentiles and in sigma units, are given for 12 populations, with adequate supporting statistics on their score distributions but with only minimal qualitative descriptions of their characteristics. Population sizes range from 32 to 6,000, with three n's below 50 and six over 600. Three of the largest normative populations are each composed of several potentially unlike subgroups, e.g., applicants of one firm combined with present employees of another firm in a different industry. No data are presented to justify such groupings. The manual merely states that the "jobs are similar" and that the score distributions of the subgroups either showed "no significant difference" or that "there was a significant but not a practical difference."

The *Adaptability Test* undertakes to measure a composite of several intelligence factors in a single score, within a short time limit demanded by many employment situations today. But several such factors can now be measured separately in as little time and with as much precision. The test manual is well planned, touching on most of the topics currently deemed essential—but touching rather lightly on many of them. There are numerous gaps in supporting statistical evidence and in the essential qualitative descriptions of normative populations. The test is now 16 years old, and the current manual is four. More of the needed data doubtless will be found in the manual's next edition.

For reviews by Anne Anastasi and Marion A. Bills, see 3:216.

[306]
★**Advanced Personnel Test.** High-level employees in business; 1926–52; Form H ('52, identical with Form H of *Miller Analogies,* copyrighted in 1950); no data on reliability and validity when used in business; no business norms; distribution restricted and test administered at specified licensed testing centers; details may be obtained from publisher; examination fee, $1; 50(55) minutes; W. S. Miller; Psychological Corporation. *

For a review by John T. Dailey, see 352; for reviews by J. P. Guilford and Carl I. Hovland, see 4:304.

[307]
★**Advanced Test N.** Ages 15 and over; 1951–52; title on manual is *General Test N;* 1 form ['51]; mimeographed manual ['52]; no data on reliability and validity; distribution restricted; 6s. per 10 tests; 1s. 9d. per manual; 2s. 3d. per specimen set; postpaid within Australia; 50(65) minutes; Australian Council for Educational Research. *

A. E. G. PILLINER, *Lecturer in Education, University of Edinburgh, Edinburgh, Scotland.*

The item construction in this test bears witness to the painstaking thoroughness and technical skill that has come to be associated with the tests issued by the Australian Council for Educational Research. There is an almost complete absence of ambiguity, which is a noteworthy achievement with items of this quite high level of difficulty.

The test proper is preceded by a practice test in two parts. The first consists of seven items to which the answers are given, together with explanations of the reasoning by which these answers are reached. In the second, there are 15 items, presented without answers, which the testees work through at approximately the same rate as that required in the test proper. Five and 10 minutes, respectively, are allowed for the two parts of the practice test.

For the test proper, which consists of 76 items, the time allowance is 50 minutes. The items include analogies, number series, classification, 3 x 3 matrices, and problems of various kinds. More than half of the test is verbal, about one quarter is nonverbal, and the rest is numerical. The various item types are scattered throughout the test rather than being grouped together. This means that a separate instruction has to be given with many items, so that the test is rather long in relation to the number of items it contains. What advantages the constructors claim for this way of ordering the items is not known.

There appears to be no manual of instructions. Instead, four mimeographed sheets are supplied, providing instructions for administration, norms, and the answer key. While each of these is clear in itself, the general effect is one of inadequacy. No information is given about reliability or validity, and we are not told what purpose the test is intended to serve. These omissions are unfortunate, since the result of entering the conversion table with a given raw score is a single "approximate IQ," the interpretation of which is puzzling since it is derived from a test with very mixed content. It would be useful to have a validity coefficient, or at least to know the views of the test constructors who, presumably, had in mind some particular purpose for which the "approximate IQ" resulting from performance on this heterogeneous test was thought to have sufficient validity.

No direct information is presented about the group of testees who worked the test for standardisation purposes. We are told, however, that the test was normed against Form C of the Higher Examination of the *Otis Self-Administering Tests of Mental Ability,* so that the IQ's from the two tests are approximately comparable. In the absence of reliability and validity data for *Advanced Test N,* it would have been useful to quote its correlation with Otis Higher C. Since the standardisation group must have worked both tests, this correlation should be available.

The test is difficult in terms of the Otis Higher C population on which the norms are indirectly based. For testees of 18 plus, a raw score of 25 gives an approximate IQ of 100. Thus there is ample headroom and good discrimination in the upper ability levels, though, in the absence of validity coefficients, what this discrimination means cannot be assessed. For testees between 13 and 18, age allowances are provided, those for the younger testees being startlingly large. A 13-year-old testee with a raw score of 11 or 12, for example, obtains an IQ of about 100. For young testees, therefore, responses made at random may give sizeable, though quite meaningless, IQ's.

To sum up: *A.C.E.R. Advanced Test N* is a heterogeneous collection of unusually well constructed items which will undoubtedly challenge even high ability testees. The reliability of the test and its general purpose supported by validity data are not given. IQ's obtained with it for younger testees should be accepted with reserve.

This reviewer has little doubt that this test will prove a useful instrument to those whose concern it is to measure adult ability, especially at its upper level, once the A.C.E.R. has expanded the somewhat meagre information at present available about the test.

C. SANDERS, *Professor of Education and Dean of the Faculty, University of Western Australia, Nedlands, Australia.*

In view of the complete lack of information about the purpose, construction, standardization, reliability, validity, and limitations of *Advanced Test N,* it is difficult to recommend it. The accompanying 4-page manual tells us nothing at all about the test, its development, or its intended uses. The directions to supervisors are set out on the first page of the manual; two further pages contain tables to convert raw scores to IQ's in a range from IQ 77 (5 items correct) to IQ 140 (70 items correct); and the last page provides the scoring key.

The test contains 76 items consisting of analogies, opposites, meanings, codes, number series, arithmetical problems, matrices, and space-form items. Test N is, therefore, a conglomerate type of measure. It is described as a "general" test; this presumably means a test of general ability rather than a test for general use. In construction, it resembles a "general aptitude" test produced by the A.C.E.R. during the war and subsequently discontinued after trial.

One assumes that it remains listed because there is a certain demand for it by Australian public service and similar authorities. But far more information about the test should be supplied to justify its inclusion in the standard catalogue of the A.C.E.R., even though its sale is reported to be "restricted."

[308]
*American Council on Education Psychological Examination for College Freshmen. Grade 13; 1924–54; 3 scores: quantitative, linguistic, total; IBM; Editions 1947, 1948, 1949, 1952, 1954; manual ('50); no data on reliability and validity; norms: 1947 Edition ('48), 1948 Edition ('49), 1949 Edition ('50), 1952 Edition ('53), 1954 Edition ('55); separate answer sheets must be used; $2.95 per 25 tests; $1 per 25 IBM answer sheets; 50¢ per set of scoring stencils; postage extra; 38(65) minutes; 1947 and earlier editions by L. L. Thurstone and Thelma Gwinn Thurstone; later editions prepared by publisher from materials developed by the Thurstones; Cooperative Test Division, Educational Testing Service. *

REFERENCES

1–48. See 40:1377.
49–143. See 3:217.
144–276. See 4:277.
277. DODSON, MARY H. *A Study in Shorthand and Typewriting Prognosis.* Master's thesis, University of Kentucky (Lexington, Ky.), 1943.
278. SOLOMON, LEWIS E. *Some Relationships Between Reading Ability and Degree of Academic Success in College.* Doctor's thesis, University of Colorado (Boulder, Colo.), 1944.
279. GUINN, MARY P. *Aids for the Prognosis of Success in Typewriting.* Master's thesis, Kansas State Teachers College (Pittsburg, Kan.), 1948.
280. SILVER, CHARLES E. *A Comparison of the Scores Made by College Reading Problem Cases on the California Short-form Test of Mental Maturity and Form I of the Wechsler-Bellevue Scales.* Master's thesis, Bowling Green State University (Bowling Green, Ohio), 1950.
281. VEON, DOROTHY H. *The Relationship of Learning Factors Found in Certain Modern Foreign-Language Aptitude Tests to the Prediction of Shorthand Achievement in College.* Stillwater, Okla.: Division of Commerce, Oklahoma Agricultural and Mechanical College, 1950. Pp. 74. *
282. BERNER, WILLIAM. *An Evaluation of the Freshman Testing Program at Southern Methodist University.* Master's thesis, Southern Methodist University (Dallas, Tex.), 1951.
283. HANSON, ANNA J. *An Analysis of "Drop Out" Students at Montana State University.* Master's thesis, Montana State University (Missoula, Mont.), 1951
284. HUFFMAN, WARREN J. *Personality Variations Among Men Preparing to Teach Physical Education.* Doctor's thesis, University of Illinois (Urbana, Ill.), 1951. *(DA 12:28)*
285. PETERSON, LEANDER H. *A Study of the Relative Validity of Q, L, and Total Scores of the American Council on Education Psychological Examination for Entering Freshmen.* Master's thesis, Chico State College (Chico, Calif.), 1951.
286. WELSH, MARY L. *A Comparison of Two Psychological Examinations in Predicting Academic Success of Ohio University Students.* Master's thesis, Ohio University (Athens, Ohio), 1951.
287. *Final Report on the 1951 National College Freshman Testing Program.* Princeton, N.J.: Cooperative Test Division, Educational Testing Service, [1952]. Pp. i, 27. *
288. ALTUS, WILLIAM D. "Personality Correlates of Q-L Variability on the ACE." *J Consult Psychol* 16:284–91 Ag '52. * *(PA 27:4237)*
289. ANGOFF, WILLIAM H. "Equating of the ACE Psychological Examinations for High School Students." Abstract. *Am Psychol* 7:287 Jl '52. *
290. BARRETT, DOROTHY M. "Differential Value of Q and L Scores on the ACE Psychological Examination for Predicting Achievement in College Mathematics." *J Psychol* 33:205–7 Ap '52. * *(PA 26:7231)*
291. BERDIE, RALPH F., AND LAYTON, WILBUR L. "Predicting Success in Law School." *J Appl Psychol* 36:257–60 Ag '52. * *(PA 27:3839)*

292. BOLTON, EURI BELLE. "Predictive Value for Academic Achievement of the A.C.E. Psychological Examination Scores." *Peabody J Ed* 29:345–60 My '52. *
293. CARRILLO, LAWRENCE W., JR., AND REICHART, ROBERT R. "The Use of a 'Caution Factor' to Increase the Predictive Value of the A.C.E. Examination for Students of Engineering." *J Ed Res* 45:361–8 Ja '52. * *(PA 27:2989)*
294. FREDERIKSEN, NORMAN, AND SCHRADER, W. B. "The ACE Psychological Examination and High School Standing as Predictors of College Success." *J Appl Psychol* 36:261–5 Ag '52. * *(PA 27:3786)*
295. FREEHILL, MAURICE F. "Student Self-Estimates as Guidance in Selecting Courses." *Col & Univ* 27:233–42 Ja '52. *
296. FRENCH, JOHN W.; TUCKER, LEDYARD R.; NEWMAN, SIDNEY H.; AND BOBBITT, JOSEPH M. "A Factor Analysis of Aptitude and Achievement Entrance Tests and Course Grades at the United States Coast Guard Academy." *J Ed Psychol* 43:65–80 F '52. * *(PA 26:7233)*
297. HANNA, JOSEPH V. "Use of Speed Tests in Guidance." *Occupations* 30:329–31 F '52. *
298. ISAACSON, LEE E. "Predictors of Success for Cooperative Occupational Education Classes in Kansas City, Missouri, High Schools." Abstract. *Am Psychol* 7:379 Jl '52. *
299. JOHNSON, GORDON. *An Analysis of Six Theories as to the Origin of Delinquent Behaviour.* Master's thesis, University of British Columbia (Vancouver, B.C., Canada), 1952.
300. KRATHWOHL, DAVID R.; EWING, T. N.; GILBERT, W. M.; AND CRONBACH, LEE J. "Prediction of Success in Architecture Courses." Abstract. *Am Psychol* 7:288–9 Jl '52. *
301. LIEN, ARNOLD JUEL. "A Comparative-Predictive Study of Students in the Four Curricula of a Teacher Education Institution." *J Exp Ed* 21:81–219 D '52. *
302. NEWMAN, SIDNEY H.; FRENCH, JOHN W.; AND BOBBITT, JOSEPH M. "Analysis of Criteria for the Validation of Selection Measures at the United States Coast Guard Academy." *Ed & Psychol Meas* 12:394–407 au '52. * *(PA 27:6159)*
303. O'NEAL, CHARLES E., AND COTTLE, WILLIAM C. "A Comparison of Freshman Entrance Scores for Successful and Unsuccessful Football Scholarship Candidates at the University of Kansas." *Univ Kans B Ed* 7:21–3 N '52. *
304. RASMUSSEN, ELMER M. *A Study of the Changes in Tested General Intelligence of Students Between the Freshman and Senior Years as Measured by the ACE Psychological Examination for College Freshmen.* Doctor's thesis, University of Nebraska (Lincoln, Neb.), 1952.
305. ROESEL, HILDE A. *The Value of the American Council on Education Psychological Examination in Assessing the Scholastic Potential of Entering Freshmen.* Master's thesis, East Tennessee State College (Johnson City, Tenn.), 1952.
306. SLATER, MARGARET M. *The Meaning of A.C.E. Scores of Students at Bowling Green State University.* Master's thesis, Bowling Green State University (Bowling Green, Ohio), 1952.
307. TRAXLER, ARTHUR E. "Reliability and Validity of the Scores on the Six Parts of the American Council on Education Psychological Examination." *Ed Rec B* 58:71–8 F '52. * *(PA 26:7238)*
308. WEISS, IRVING. "Prediction of Academic Success in Dental School." *J Appl Psychol* 36:11–4 F '52. * *(PA 26:7296)*
309. WILLIAMS, JOHN E., AND GERKEN, C. D'A. "'Verbal Factor' and 'Number Factor'—A Study of Two Tests." *Proc Iowa Acad Sci* 59:397–401 '52. * *(PA 28:6599)*
310. ANDERSON, ROSE G. "Do Aptitudes Support Interests?" *Personnel & Guid J* 32:14–7 S '53. * *(PA 28:4495)*
311. ANDERSON, SCARVIA B. "Prediction and Practice Tests at the College Level." *J Appl Psychol* 37:256–9 Ag '53. * *(PA 28:6583)*
312. ARN, ELMER H. R. *The Prediction of Academic Success in Ten Selected Science Areas at the University of Washington.* Doctor's thesis, University of Washington (Seattle, Wash.), 1953. *(DA 13:495)*
313. BENTZ, V. J. "A Test-Retest Experiment on the Relationship Between Age and Mental Ability." Abstract. *Am Psychol* 8:319–20 Ag '53. *
314. CARLIN, LESLIE C. "A Longitudinal Comparison of Freshman-Senior Standing." *J Ed Res* 47:285–90 D '53. * *(PA 28:6586)*
315. COLEMAN, WILLIAM. "An Economical Test Battery for Predicting Freshman Engineering Course Grades." *J Appl Psychol* 37:465–7 D '53. * *(PA 29:1562)*
316. DERIDDER, LAWRENCE M. "Relation Between Gross Scores on the A.C.E. and Academic Success." *J Ed Res* 46:353–8 Ja '53. * *(PA 28:1558)*
317. DRAKE, L. E., AND THOMAS, W. F. "Forecasting Academic Achievement in the College of Engineering." *J Eng Ed* 44:275–6 D '53. * *(PA 29:1564)*
318. DURNALL, EDWARD J., JR. "A Testing Program for Junior College for Women." *Jun Col J* 23:261–7 Ja '53. *
319. HALE, PETER P. "ACE Results of 72 Public Law 16 Teacher Trainees." *Sch & Soc* 77:41–3 Ja 17 '53. *
320. HARDAWAY, CHARLES. "Orientation Tests and Freshman Scholarship." *Teach Col J* 25:10–1 O '53. *
321. HENDRIX, O. R. "Predicting Success in Elementary Accounting." *J Appl Psychol* 37:75–7 Ap '53. * *(PA 28:1479)*
322. HERKE, MARY L. *The Value of Three Measures in Predicting Academic Success for Graduate Students of Bowling*

Green State University. Master's thesis, Bowling Green State University (Bowling Green, Ohio), 1953.

323. JOHNSON, A. PEMBERTON. "Counseling Engineering Freshmen." *Ed & Psychol Meas* 13:133-44 sp '53. * (PA 28:1566)

324. KERN, DONALD W. *The Prediction of Academic Success of Freshmen in a Community College.* Doctor's thesis, New York University (New York, N.Y.), 1953. (DA 15:85)

325. LINS, L. J., AND PITT, HY. "The 'Staying Power' and Rate of Progress of University of Wisconsin Freshmen." *Col & Univ* 29:86-99 O '53. *

326. MALLOY, J. P. *The Prediction of College Achievement With the Life Experience Inventory.* Doctor's thesis, University of Nebraska (Lincoln, Neb.), 1953.

327. MANUEL, HERSCHEL T. "Expectancy Tables for Predicting Academic Success." *Yearb Nat Council Meas Used Ed* 10: 66-72 '53. *

328. MERRILL, REED M., AND HEATHERS, LOUISE B. "A Comparison of the Wechsler-Bellevue and ACE Tests on a University Counseling Center Group." *J Consult Psychol* 17:63-6 F '53. * (PA 28:1570)

329. MILAM, OTIS H. *A Study of the Relationship Between High School Grades, American Council on Education Psychological Examination for College Freshmen Scores, a Combination of the Two, and Grades Earned During the First Semester at Marshall College.* Master's thesis, Marshall College (Huntington, W.Va.), 1953.

330. MORTVEDT, AUDREY R. *Relative Effectiveness of a Local English Test, the ACE L-Score, Cumulative Grade Average, and the Cooperative General Culture Test in the Selection of Upper-Class Regent's Scholarship Winners.* Master's thesis, University of Nebraska (Lincoln, Neb.), 1953.

331. SAMENFELD, HERBERT W. "Predicting College Achievement." *J Higher Ed* 24:432-3 N '53. * (PA 28:6595)

332. SATZ, MARTIN A. *The Relationship Between Eleven Independent Variables and Academic Performance in Nine Social Science Areas at the University of Washington.* Doctor's thesis, University of Washington (Seattle, Wash.), 1953. (DA 14:635)

333. SCHWINGER, WILLIAM A. *The Predictive Efficiency of the ACE Test for Sociology 1 in the College of Nursing at Niagara University.* Master's thesis, Niagara University (Niagara Falls, N.Y.), 1953.

334. SEVERANCE, KATHERINE M. *The ACE and the Purdue English Placement Tests as Predictors of Academic Success at Baylor University.* Master's thesis, Baylor University (Waco, Tex.), 1953.

335. SOIKA, GEORGE R. *Effect of Warm-Up on Performance of the ACE Q-L Subtests.* Doctor's thesis, George Peabody College for Teachers (Nashville, Tenn.), 1953.

336. SOPER, MERWIN E. *The Value of the ACE Psychological Examination and the Purdue Pegboard Test of Manual Dexterity in Predicting High School Typewriting Grades.* Master's thesis, Drake University (Des Moines, Iowa), 1953.

337. SWENSON, LLOYD G. *An Investigation of the Areas Measured by Selected Psychological and Sociological Instruments.* Doctor's field study, Colorado State College of Education (Greeley, Colo.), 1953.

338. TOWNSEND, AGATHA. "A Study of the American Council on Education Psychological Examination, 1952 Edition." *Ed Rec B* 60:53-60 F '53. * (PA 28:1577)

339. WARD, WILLIAM D. *An Investigation of the Predictability of Academic Success of the A.C.E. and Certain Factors Measured by the Johnson Temperament Analysis.* Doctor's thesis, Bradley University (Peoria, Ill.), 1953. (DA 13:518)

340. WEBB, SAM C., AND MCCALL, JOHN N. "Predictors of Freshman Grades in a Southern University." *Ed & Psychol Meas* 13:660-3 w '53. * (PA 28:6598)

341. ANDERSON, MARY R., AND STEGMAN, ERWIN J. "Predictors of Freshman Achievement at Fort Hays Kansas State College." *Ed & Psychol Meas* 14:722-3 w '54. * (PA 29:7952)

342. BASS, BERNARD M., AND COATES, CHARLES H. "Validity Information Exchange, No. 7-082: R.O.T.C. Cadets." *Personnel Psychol* 7:553-4 w '54. *

343. BOLTON, EURI BELLE. "The Predictive Value of the Columbia and the Michigan Vocabulary Tests for Academic Achievement." *Peabody J Ed* 32:9-21 Jl '54. * (PA 29:7954)

344. CASEY, JOHN E. *An Investigation of the Effect of Increasing the Homogeneity of Response Patterns on the General Culture Test on Its Correlation With the American Council on Education Psychological Examination and the Interpretation of Data Test.* Doctor's thesis, Indiana University (Bloomington, Ind.), 1954.

345. CHAPPELL, TOLAN L.; CALLIS, ROBERT; RENZAGLIA, GUY A.; AND SPOHRER, MYRON A. "The Differential Prediction of Achievement at the University of Missouri." *Ed & Psychol Meas* 14:724-5 w '54. * (PA 29:7955)

346. DI VESTA, FRANCIS J. "Subscore Patterns on ACE Psychological Examination Related to Educational and Occupational Differences." *J Appl Psychol* 38:248-52 Ag '54. * (PA 29:6268)

347. FITZGIBBON, THOMAS J. *The Prediction of Academic Success of Freshmen at Bradley University.* Doctor's thesis, Bradley University (Peoria, Ill.), 1954. (DA 14:1170)

348. FREEHILL, MAURICE F. "The Co-operative English Test in Academic Counseling." *Col & Univ* 29:244-52 Ja '54. *

349. FRITZ, MARTIN F. "Q and L Difference Scores on the A.C.E. Test." *Proc Iowa Acad Sci* 61:356-7 '54. * (PA 30:3458)

350. GRAHAM, WARREN R. "Identification and Prediction of Two Training Criterion Factors." *J Appl Psychol* 38:96-9 Ap '54. * (PA 29:1798)

351. GUAZZO, EUGENE J., JR. *Predicting Academic Success of Architecture Students.* Master's thesis, Alabama Polytechnic Institute (Auburn, Ala.), 1954.

352. HANER, CHARLES F. "Wonderlic, Wesman P.C.T., and A.C.E.: A Comparison of Three Group Intelligence Tests." *Proc Iowa Acad Sci* 61:358-60 '54. * (PA 30:3460)

353. HENDRIX, O. R. "'A Note' Acknowledged." *J Appl Psychol* 38:9 F '54. * (PA 29:1451)

354. HOERRES, MARY ANN, AND O'DEA, J. DAVID. "Predictive Value of the A.C.E." *J Higher Ed* 25:97 F '54. * (PA 28:8079)

355. HOLT, WELDON G. *Relationships Between the ACE and the Wesman Personnel Classification Test.* Master's thesis, University of Kansas (Lawrence, Kan.), 1954.

356. HOYT, DONALD P., AND NORMAN, WARREN T. "Adjustment and Academic Predictability." *J Counsel Psychol* 1:96-9 su '54. * (PA 29:3043)

357. JACOBS, ROBERT. "A Note on 'Predicting Success in Elementary Accounting.'" *J Appl Psychol* 38:7-8 F '54. * (PA 29:1456)

358. LEE, PHYLLIS J. *The Effectiveness of a Test Battery in Predicting Chemistry Grades.* Master's thesis, Alabama Polytechnic Institute (Auburn, Ala.), 1954.

359. MALECKI, GERALD S. *Effectiveness of the College Entrance Board Scholastic Aptitude Test, American Council on Education Psychological Examination, and High School Average for Predicting First Semester Scholarship at Fordham College.* Master's thesis, Fordham University (New York, N.Y.), 1954.

360. MARTIN, RICHARD R. *An Investigation of the Effectiveness of an Entrance Test Battery for Predicting Success in Law School.* Doctor's thesis, Temple University (Philadelphia, Pa.), 1954. (DA 16:575)

361. MURRAY, THOMAS. *An Analysis of First Year Chemistry Marks at the University of Scranton in Relation to High School Chemistry Marks, High School Quintile Standings and American Council on Education Test Scores.* Master's thesis, University of Scranton (Scranton, Pa.), 1954.

362. ROGO, ROBERT A. *The Relationship of Scores of the Diagnostic Reading Tests: Survey Section and the American Council on Education Psychological Examination, to First Semester Freshman Honor Point Averages for Students in the College of Arts and Sciences at the University of Detroit.* Master's thesis, University of Detroit (Detroit, Mich.), 1954.

363. SCHMITZ, ROY M., AND HOLMES, JOHN L. "Relationship of Certain Measured Abilities to Freshman Engineering Achievement," pp. 32-42. (PA 29:1584) In *Selection and Counseling of Students in Engineering.* Edited by Wilbur L. Layton. Minnesota Studies in Student Personnel Work, No. 4. Minneapolis, Minn.: University of Minnesota Press, 1954. Pp. iv, 89. *

364. SEASHORE, HAROLD. "Tenth Grade Tests as Predictors of Twelfth Grade Scholarship and College Entrance Status." Comment by David V. Tiedeman. *J Counsel Psychol* 1:106-15 su '54. * (PA 29:3054)

365. SEIGLE, WILLIAM F. "Prediction of Success in College Mathematics at Washburn University." *J Ed Res* 47:577-88 Ap '54. * (PA 29:2982)

366. SKARD, ØYVIND; AURSAND, INGER MARIE; AND BRAATEN, LEIF J. "Development and Application of Tests for University Students in Norway: A Report on Parts of a Research Project." *Psychol Monogr* 68(12):1-54 '54. * (PA 29:7971)

367. SPRING, LAURENCE E. *The American Council on Education Psychological Examination for College Freshmen as a Predictive Measure for Student Selection in Five Curriculums at the Buffalo State Technical Institute.* Master's thesis, University of Buffalo (Buffalo, N.Y.), 1954.

368. STONE, JOICS B. "Differential Prediction of Academic Success at Brigham Young University." *J Appl Psychol* 38:109-10 Ap '54. * (PA 29:3057)

369. WASHBURNE, NORMAN F., AND ANDREW, DEAN C. "Relation of Scholastic Aptitude to Socioeconomic Status and to a Rural-to-Urban Continuum." *J Appl Psychol* 38:113-5 Ap '54. * (PA 29:3059)

370. AHMANN, J. STANLEY. "Prediction of the Probability of Graduation of Engineering Transfer Students." *J Exp Ed* 23:281-8 Je '55. * (PA 30:3451)

371. ANDERSON, LEONE; RANKIN, RICHARD; RICHARDSON, JOY; SASSENRATH, JULIUS; AND THOMAS, JULIUS. "Differential Methods of Solving Selected Problems on the ACE Psychological Examination." *J Exp Ed* 24:133-40 D '55. * (PA 31:8803)

372. BAKER, PAUL C. *Experiments in Variable Selection for Prediction of Academic Achievement.* Doctor's thesis, Purdue University (Lafayette, Ind.), 1955. (DA 15:2565)

373. BERTRAND, JOHN R. "Relation Between High School Average Grade and Academic Achievement of Agricultural Students, Agricultural and Mechanical College of Texas." *Col & Univ* 30:166-81 Ja '55. * (PA 31:3771)

374. BOLIN, BYRON J. "A Comparison of Raven's Progressive Matrices (1938) With the ACE Psychological Examination and the Otis Gamma Mental Ability Test." Abstract. *J Consult Psychol* 19:400 O '55. *

375. CHAPMAN, HAROLD M. "The Prediction of Freshman

Achievement From a Combination of Test Scores and High School Grades." Abstract. *Am Psychol* 10:373 Ag '55. *

376. CHAPMAN, HAROLD M. *The Prediction of Freshman Scholarship From a Combination of Standardized Test Scores and High School Grades.* Doctor's thesis, University of Houston (Houston, Tex.), 1955. (*DA* 15:1201)

377. COLLINS, CHARLES C. *The Relationship of Breadth of Academic Interest to Academic Achievement and Academic Aptitude.* Doctor's thesis, Stanford University (Stanford, Calif.), 1955. (*DA* 15:1782)

378. DUNGAN, EARL W. *An Evaluation of the Orientation Test Battery at Dickinson State Teachers College for Purposes of Prediction and Counseling.* Doctor's field study, Colorado State College of Education (Greeley, Colo.), 1955.

379. GRATER, HARRY, AND THALMAN, W. A. "A Statistical Analysis of the Relationship Between American Council on Education Psychological Examination Ratings and Grade-Point Averages." *J Ed Res* 49:07–10 D '55. * (*PA* 30:7759)

380. HAYNES, JERRY O. *Some Predictive Factors of Academic Success in Two Curricula of a Land-Grant College.* Master's thesis, Alabama Polytechnic Institute (Auburn, Ala.), 1955.

381. JACKSON, ROBERT A. "Prediction of the Academic Success of College Freshmen." *J Ed Psychol* 46:296–301 My '55. * (*PA* 30:6333)

382. KLUGH, HENRY B., AND BENDIG, A. W. "The Manifest Anxiety and ACE Scales and College Achievement." Abstract. *J Consult Psychol* 19:487 D '55. *

383. KRAMAR, EDWARD J. J. *The Relationships of the Wechsler-Bellevue and A.C.E. Intelligence Tests With Performance Scores in Speaking and the Brown-Carlsen Listening Comprehension Test.* Doctor's thesis, Florida State University (Tallahassee, Fla.), 1955. (*DA* 15:2599)

384. MALLOY, JOHN. "The Prediction of College Achievement With the Life Experience Inventory." *Ed & Psychol Meas* 15:170–80 su '55. * (*PA* 30:3462)

385. MALLOY, JOHN P.; WYSOCKI, BOLESLAW; AND GRAHAM, LEO F. "Predicting Attrition-Survival in First Year Engineering." *J Ed Psychol* 46:217–21 Ap '55. * (*PA* 30:1624)

386. MELTON, RICHARD S. "Differentiation of Successful and Unsuccessful Premedical Students." *J Appl Psychol* 39:397–400 D '55. * (*PA* 30:7769)

387. MULLINS, CECIL J. "The Effect of Reading Ability on Two Standardized Classification Tests." *J Ed Psychol* 46:189–92 Mr '55. * (*PA* 30:1627)

388. MUTH, MARTHA JEAN. *Attitude Toward Mathematics as a Function of the Discrepancy Between Q and L Scores of the A.C.E.* Master's thesis, University of Florida (Gainesville, Fla.), 1955.

389. NAPP, FREDERICK P. *Forecasting Scholastic Achievement at Eastern New Mexico University on the Basis of Scores on the American Council on Education Psychological Examination.* Master's thesis, Eastern New Mexico University (Portales, N.M.), 1955.

390. PAUK, WALTER J. *An Analysis of Certain Characteristics of Above-Average and Below-Average Male and Female Readers at the Ninth-Grade Level.* Doctor's thesis, Cornell University (Ithaca, N.Y.), 1955. (*DA* 16:285)

391. POUNDS, RALPH L. "Prediction of Academic Success at the University of Cincinnati, Teachers College: Progress Report II." *Yearb Nat Council Meas Used Ed* 12(pt 2):12–31 '55. *

392. REILLY, WILLIAM J. *The Efficiency of the A.C.E. in Predicting English One and Two Grades in the College of Arts and Sciences at Niagara University.* Master's thesis, Niagara University (Niagara Falls, N.Y.), 1955.

393. ROYER, J. EVERETT. *Selection and Use of Certain Factors Significant in Predicting Achievement of Students in First-Semester Accounting at the University of Miami, 1950-1953.* Doctor's thesis, Indiana University (Bloomington, Ind.), 1955.

394. SCHULZ, R. E., AND CALVIN, ALLEN D. "A Failure to Replicate the Finding of a Negative Correlation Between Manifest Anxiety and ACE Scores." *J Consult Psychol* 19:223–4 Je '55. * (*PA* 30:2919)

395. SHEA, JOSEPH AUGUSTINE. *Predictive Value of Various Combinations of Standardized Tests and Subtests for Prognosis of Teaching Efficiency.* Catholic University of America, Educational Research Monograph, Vol. 19, No. 6. Washington, D.C.: Catholic University of America Press, Inc., June 1, 1955. Pp. xi, 44. *

396. SUPEAU, GERALD A. *Norms and Correlations of Scores Between the A. C. E. Psychological Examinations and Freshman Grades Received in History One and Two in the College of Arts and Sciences of Niagara University From 1948 to 1953.* Master's thesis, Niagara University (Niagara Falls, N.Y.), 1955.

397. TRAXLER, ARTHUR E. "Comparative Value of Certain Mental Ability Tests for Predicting School Marks in Two Independent Schools." *Ed Rec B* 65:65–75 F '55. * (*PA* 29:7976)

398. TRAXLER, ARTHUR E. "Relationship of Certain Predictive Measures to Achievement in First-Year French and Latin." *Ed Rec B* 66:73–7 Jl '55. * (*PA* 30:5181)

399. ANDERSON, RODNEY E. *The Use of Entrance Tests in the Differential Prediction of Freshman College Achievement, and the Effect of an Item Analysis on the Efficiency of the Predictive Batteries.* Doctor's thesis, Indiana University (Bloomington, Ind.), 1956. (*DA* 16:2344)

400. ANNESER, ROBERT. *An Evaluation of Scholastic Aptitude in Predicting Senior Level Achievement at Ohio University.* Master's thesis, Ohio University (Athens, Ohio), 1956.

401. BEAVER, ALMA P. "Psychometric Data and Survival in a College of Nursing." *Psychol Rep* 2:223–6 Je '56. * (*PA* 31:1738)

402. BOYER, LEE E., AND KOKEN, JAMES E. "Admissions Test as Criteria for Success in College." *J Ed Res* 50:313–5 D '56. * (*PA* 32:2095)

403. BOYER, ROSCOE A. *A Study of the Academic Success of Undergraduate Students as Identified by Aptitude Test Profiles.* Doctor's thesis, Indiana University (Bloomington, Ind.), 1956. (*DA* 15:89)

404. BRAGG, EMMA W. "A Study of Student Withdrawal at 'W.U.'" *J Ed Psychol* 47:199–202 Ap '56. *

405. CAPELLINI, JOHN, JR. *Norms and Relative Validity of the A.C.E. in Prediction of Scholastic Accomplishment of Freshmen in the College of Business Administration at Niagara University in the Fall Semester of 1955-1956.* Master's thesis, Niagara University (Niagara Falls, N.Y.), 1956.

406. FRICK, J. W., AND KEENER, HELEN E. "A Validation Study of the Prediction of College Achievement." *J Appl Psychol* 40:251–2 Ag '56. * (*PA* 31:6674)

407. HENDERSON, HAROLD L. "Prediction of Academic Success." *Psychol Rep* 2:321–2 S '56. * (*PA* 31:3784)

408. KEELER, HAROLD J. *Predicting Teacher Effectiveness of Graduates of the State University of New York Teachers Colleges.* Doctor's thesis, Cornell University (Ithaca, N.Y.), 1956. (*DA* 17:545)

409. NORTH, ROBERT D. "A Comparison of the Cooperative School and College Ability Tests: College Ability Test, and the American Council Psychological Examination: Reliabilities, Intercorrelations, and Correlations With the Diagnostic Reading Tests." *Ed Rec B* 67:65–72 F '56. * (*PA* 31:3800)

410. POLLARD, JAMES R. *The Significance of Quantitative and Linguistic Abilities for Academic Performance and High School Adjustment.* Doctor's thesis, University of Missouri (Columbia, Mo.), 1956. (*DA* 16:2089)

411. SMITH, GEORGE B. *Who Should Be Eliminated? A Study of Selective Admission to College.* University of Kansas Publications, Kansas Studies in Education, Vol. 7, No. 1. Lawrence, Kan.: School of Education, the University, December 1956. Pp. 28. Paper. *

412. TRAXLER, ARTHUR E. "Should *SCAT* Scat *ACE?* A Comparison Between the Cooperative School and College Ability Tests, Form 1A, and the American Council on Education Psychological Examination, 1948 College Freshman Edition, as to Difficulty and Value for Predicting School Marks." *Ed Rec B* 67:51–63 F '56. * (*PA* 31:3817)

413. VAN DER JAGT, E. R., AND MESNER, D. M. "Predictability of Success in College Courses, by Accelerating and Non-Accelerating Students as Measured by Scores Made by Entering Freshmen on A.C.E. and Cooperative Reading Test." *Sci Ed* 40:327–32 O '56. *

414. WEBB, SAM C. "The Prediction of Achievement for First Year Dental Students." *Ed & Psychol Meas* 16:543–8 w '56. *

415. WINING, MARY H. *Prediction of First Year Mathematics Grades at Central Washington College of Education With the ACE Psychological Examination.* Master's thesis, Central Washington College of Education (Ellensburg, Wash.), 1956.

416. ANGOFF, WILLIAM H. "The 'Equating' of Non-Parallel Tests." *J Exp Ed* 25:241–7 Mr '57. *

417. BRICE, MARSHALL M. "A Comparison of Subjective Predictions With Objective Predictions of College Achievement." *Col & Univ* 32:347–53 sp '57. *

418. CHANSKY, NORMAN M., AND BREGMAN, MARTIN. "Improvement of Reading in College." *J Ed Res* 51:313–7 D '57. *

419. GOWAN, J. C. "Intelligence, Interests, and Reading Ability in Relation to Scholastic Achievement." *Psychol Newsl* 8:85–7 Mr–Ap '57. * (*PA* 32:3346)

420. HENDERSON, HAROLD L. "Predictors of Freshmen Grades in a Long Island College." *Ed & Psychol Meas* 17:623–7 w '57. *

421. HEWER, VIVIAN H. "Vocational Interest-Achievement-Ability Interrelationships at the College Level." *J Counsel Psychol* 4:234–8 fall '57. *

422. HOLT, WELDON G.; OTTMAN, DONALD K.; AND COTTLE, WILLIAM C. "Evidenced Relationships Between the 'ACE' and the Wesman Personnel Classification Test." *J Ed Res* 51:71–7 S '57. *

423. KIM, KI SUK. *The Use of Certain Measurements of Academic Aptitude, Study Habits, Motivation, and Personality in the Prediction of Academic Achievement.* Doctor's thesis, Louisiana State University (Baton Rouge, La.), 1957. (*DA* 18:150)

424. KLUGMAN, SAMUEL F. "Agreement Between Two Tests as Predictors of College Success." *Personnel & Guid J* 36:255–8 D '57. *

425. LARSEN, TORA M. *A Study of the Student Personnel Records at East Carolina College as Relates to Prediction in Elementary Accounting.* Doctor's thesis, University of Minnesota (Minneapolis, Minn.), 1957. (*DA* 18:1304)

426. LOWRY, CARMEN E. *The Prediction of Academic Success in a Private Liberal Arts College for Negroes.* Doctor's thesis, University of Texas (Austin, Tex.), 1957. (*DA* 17:2500)

427. MANUEL, HERSCHEL T. "Aptitude Tests for College Admission." *Yearb Nat Council Meas Used Ed* 14:20–7 '57. *

428. NORTH, ROBERT D. "A Further Report on the Cooperative College Ability Test." *Ed Rec B* 69:60–2 F '57. * (*PA* 32:2119)

429. STONE, SOLOMON. *The Contribution of Intelligence, In-*

terests, Temperament and Certain Personality Variables to Academic Achievement in a Physical Science and Mathematics Curriculum. Doctor's thesis, New York University (New York, N.Y.), 1957. (*DA* 18:669)

430. ALTUS, WILLIAM D. "Q-L Variability, MMPI Responses, and College Males." *J Consult Psychol* 22:367–71 O '58. *

431. BARRETT, RICHARD S. "The Process of Predicting Job Performance." *Personnel Psychol* 11:39–57 sp '58. *

432. BERRY, CHARLES A., AND JONES, ARLYNNE L. "The Predictive Value of the Tests of the National Freshman Testing Program for Grambling College Freshmen." *Negro Ed R* 9:23–33 Ja '58. *

433. EVENSON, A. B., AND SMITH, D. E. "A Study of Matriculation in Alberta." *Alberta J Ed Res* 4:67–83 Je '58. *

434. GOWAN, J. C. "Intercorrelations and Factor Analysis of Tests Given to Teaching Candidates." *J Exp Ed* 27:1–22 S '58. *

435. MOORE, CHARLES W. *Some Relationships Between Standardized Test Scores and Academic Performance in the College of Business Administration of the University of Houston.* Doctor's thesis, University of Houston (Houston, Tex.), 1958. (*DA* 19:356)

436. PHILLIPS, JOHN C. "Normative Data Information Exchange, No. 11-6." *Personnel Psychol* 11:271 su '58. *

437. SOPCHAK, ANDREW L. "Prediction of College Performance by Commonly Used Tests." *J Clin Psychol* 14:194–7 Ap '58. *

438. SPILKA, B., AND KIMBLE, GLORIA. "Personality Correlates of Q-L Differentials on the ACE." Abstract. *J Consult Psychol* 22:142 Ap '58. *

439. VINCENT, LEWIS. "A Comparison of the Quantitative Items of the A.C.E. Psychological With Similar Items in the Cooperative School and College Abilities Tests." *Yearb Nat Council Meas Used Ed* 15:144–9 '58. *

HANFORD M. FOWLER, *Professor of Education, University of Toronto, Toronto, Ontario, Canada.*

Whereas the *Cooperative School and College Ability Tests* (SCAT) may be likened to a lusty newborn infant, still unproved but crying for research attention, the *American Council on Education Psychological Examination for College Freshmen* (ACE) should be considered a venerable gentleman of demonstrated worth who is now looking forward to an early retirement. Undoubtedly, ACE is one of the oldest and most respected psychological instruments on the market. Its continued use by many institutions across the country attests its value and its usefulness. Evidence of the great research interest in ACE may be found in the large number of references to it in the research literature. But like all members of an older generation, worthy and respected though they may be, ACE must soon give way to other younger, more modern, possibly more vigorous, instruments. No doubt many will prefer to remain with ACE as long as it is available and will regret its passing.

Although ACE seems destined to be superseded by SCAT, it is quite different from SCAT in a number of ways. Primarily, ACE is a psychological test of mental abilities and not a measure of "school-learned abilities," as is SCAT. This reviewer must confess that although he suspects there are differences between the two, the exact nature of these differences escapes him. Probably the best way to get at least a superficial knowledge of what ACE measures is to examine the test itself.

According to the manual, which has not been revised since 1950, "the examination consists of the six tests that have been used for several years." These are: arithmetical reasoning, 20 items; figure analogies, 30 items; number series, 30 items; same-opposite, 50 items; completion (vocabulary), 30 items; and verbal analogies, 40 items. The first three subtests make up the Q-score or quantitative score; the last three, the L-score or linguistic score.

The latest edition of ACE (1954), like earlier editions, is accompanied by a norms bulletin which is separate from the manual. This bulletin gives a list of the colleges which reported scores to the Cooperative Test Division and the results of the statistical analyses of these scores. The norms data consist of mean scores of individual colleges and universities and percentile ranks corresponding to the Q, L, and total scores. Also included in the bulletin are equivalent scores for the 1948, 1949, 1952, and 1954 college editions.

Strong features of the ACE are: its authorship and sponsorship (the Thurstones, who were the original authors, are well known for their work in the factorial analysis of psychological tests, and the Cooperative Test Division provides as good a sponsorship as can be found in the country); its use of the Q and L scores which, although they may not be factorially pure, provide at least the elements of a differential guidance along the lines of what appear to be the two chief correlates of success in high school and college; its good construction and sound, if somewhat conservative, treatment of mechanical features, such as printing, and format; the adequate statistical treatment; and the reporting service which has kept users informed of results currently being obtained by colleges across the country.

On the other hand, the weaknesses of ACE outnumber the strengths, and some of them are serious. Before these are discussed, it might be pointed out that in the last ten years or so there has been a considerable decline in the number of institutions using ACE and in the number of students whose scores were reported. In 1947, 293 colleges reported scores of 65,276 freshmen, whereas in 1954 these numbers had dropped to 186 and 26,603. It would be interesting to determine why so many colleges have stopped using ACE. Some, perhaps because of increasing awareness of weaknesses in ACE, may have decided to use another test, possibly SCAT after it became available.

Adverse criticism of ACE may be applied to the following aspects of the test: weaknesses in the norms; relatively low validity; absence of reporting of criterion statistics such as reliability and validity estimates; limitations in possible score interpretation; and deficiencies in basic characteristics of a good college aptitude test such as a convenient length of administration time and a suitable difficulty level. Other complaints which have been voiced by Berdie and others (*263*) relate to deficiencies in the Q score, to the adulterated nature of the part scores, and to the extensive overlap between the part scores as evidenced by reported high correlations between L and Q.

Those who believe that the worth of an aptitude test depends upon how adequately its scores can be interpreted in an individual situation will undoubtedly be unhappy about the norms for ACE. In the first place, no attempt has been made to present what might be called national norms. The norming samples, consisting of colleges who have reported scores, are accidental, not planned. The test user must feel very insecure about the norms, especially if he finds it difficult to identify the position of his own institution in the doubtful classification of colleges on which the norms are based. Secondly, there is no attempt to provide data, or instructions, which might help users to construct local norms. Surely the essence of usefulness of a standardized test is the provision of information which will make the test readily interpretable and abundantly meaningful in the local situation! Possibly soundly constructed national norms, if they were available, would provide some users with all the yardsticks they need; some users would prefer local norms; others might like both. ACE provides neither.

The validity of ACE has been questioned for some time. In particular, the Q scores have failed to measure up under the relentless scrutiny of the research worker. More serious than the low validity which has been reported frequently is the lack of consistency in the reported validity coefficients. Scientists are concerned more by inconsistent results than by consistently unsatisfactory results; in the latter case at least they know what to do. Berdie, Dressel, and Kelso (*263*) report that "correlations with total point average vary from .25 to .66. Within any particular subject area there is marked variation from .08 to .44." Studies such as this lead us to conclude that the validity of ACE is an uncertain quantity for institutions generally. The new user is forced to embark upon a time-consuming preliminary study to demonstrate validity in the local situation.

No reference is made in any of the norms bulletins to reliability estimates or validity estimates. This omission appears to be inexcusable in a modern test which has advanced well beyond the experimental stages. No doubt many studies have been completed. The publishers should summarize and present the salient features of these results. In a study designed to equate scores of the 1952 and 1954 editions, summary statistics are presented for a group of 511 students from one school system, but these results can hardly be considered representative of any large group of colleges.

Because of the lack of adequate norms, and for other reasons, it is not possible to get a clear-cut interpretation of the meaning of the Q and L scores. In the first place, it is difficult to believe that the sum of scores of three tests, which on the surface at least appear to be quite dissimilar, can reflect the type of homogeneity or psychological purity which makes test interpretation easy. Also, the content of the tests is not directly related to the content of the typical college curriculum. Perhaps most distressing is the absence of any sort of conversion score or standardized score to render the scores meaningful; reliance upon raw scores and uncertain norms is an open invitation to misuse of the scores. The absence of any kind of profile and of warnings about possible misinterpretations, such as the common mistake of considering scores as points rather than as intervals, contribute to the general picture of inadequacy.

Other deficiencies limiting the usefulness of ACE are the absence of comparable forms, the single difficulty level, and the amount of time it takes for administration. There are very few exceptions to the rule that all good tests require comparable forms if for no other reason than to provide double testing and an average of scores to reduce errors of measurement. The fact that ACE has only one difficulty level is particularly serious in a country which has a wide divergence of university standards. It has been said that the graduates of some American universities can just barely meet the entrance requirements of others. If this is so, it is obvious that ACE cannot be suitable for all institutions. Administration time is another factor which should be given careful consideration. Even though it is granted that validity is the ultimate criterion of a test's value, validity has little more than academic interest if a test is not used. ACE requires 58 minutes to administer after the general instructions have been read and all preliminary preparations have been completed. In these days of 50-minute college periods a test has to be really good before the layman is convinced that it is worth an hour or more of testing time.

All things considered, it must be concluded that ACE has pretty well outlived its usefulness. Its disadvantages greatly outweigh its advantages. This is not to deny that many colleges have made good use of the test, and may still find it useful. Much depends upon the individual situation. Those who have developed local norms, and have evidence of validity in the local situation, can rest content. But as a college aptitude test for general use ACE is lacking too much in too many ways. Fortunately what appears to be a worthy substitute (SCAT) is now available.

WILLIAM B. MICHAEL, *Director, The Testing Bureau, and Professor of Psychology and Education, University of Southern California, Los Angeles, California.*

Resembling in many respects the forms prepared for high school students, the *American Council on Education Psychological Examination for College Freshmen* (ACE) consists of six subtests. From the 120 items in the three subtests Completion, Same-Opposite, and Verbal Analogies a verbal score is obtained, and from the 80 items in the subtests Arithmetic, Figure Analogies, and Number Series a quantitative score is derived. Neither the verbal nor the quantitative section approximates factorial purity—a fact that is supported not only by a correlation of .54 between the two parts for a large sample of examinees (reported in a pamphlet upon norms and equating procedures accompanying the 1954 edition of the examination), but also by an inspection of the diversified content of the items themselves. Simply stated, the instrument furnishes an indication of general scholastic aptitude in which verbal reasoning and numerical abilities are primarily required.

Widely used by colleges for purposes of admission, placement, and guidance, the various forms of the examination offer satisfactorily reliable part and total scores. In addition, normative data in terms of percentile ranks have been carefully prepared for each of the forms and are issued routinely to authorized testing personnel. Other commendable features are found in the relative ease of administration, the simplicity of scoring, and the existence of numerous practice items at the beginning of each subtest.

From a negative standpoint the lack of validity data in the manual and in the bulletins containing normative information cannot be overlooked. Another limiting characteristic would appear to be the predominance of a speed factor, especially in the instance of the sections yielding a quantitative score. Since the items are arranged in order of difficulty, it might be anticipated, particularly for parts contributing to the quantitative score, that much validity might be lost in view of the fact that several of the more difficult items capable of discriminating between potentially bright and dull students would not be reached by examinees of either ability level. Thus, the scores realized would fail to distinguish in a too adequate fashion important amounts of individual differences in ability. Concerning the speed factor in this test, it was informally reported about five years ago by a discussant in the audience of a professional meeting of measurement workers that when the verbal and quantitative scores were combined in a regression equation to predict success in an engineering curriculum in a college in upstate New York, a negative (suppressor) weight for the quantitative scores arose. When the time limits were extended at the discretion of the examiner to approximate power conditions, substantial increments in predictive validity coefficients occurred.

It is interesting to note that both the *Cooperative School and College Ability Test* (SCAT), recently developed by the Cooperative Test Division of the Educational Testing Service more or less as a substitute for the ACE series, and the *College Qualification Test* (CQT), lately prepared by the Psychological Corporation, contain items that reflect somewhat more specific types of learning experiences in the high school curriculum than do the ACE forms. Moreover, both the SCAT and the CQT more nearly approximate the readily defensible power condition than do the rather speeded ACE counterparts. Since the interpretative materials and statistical data in the manual and in the special bulletins for the SCAT are unusually complete and, likewise, since the manual for the CQT is excellent in virtually every respect, one may anticipate that the ACE college series will soon be displaced, even though the examination, assured of a prominent position in the history of psychological testing, has been a reliable and serviceable instrument upon which many meaningful normative data have been collected.

For reviews by W. D. Commins and J. P. Guilford of an earlier edition, see 3:217; for reviews by Jack W. Dunlap and Robert L. Thorndike, see 40:1377; for reviews by Anne Anastasi and David Segel, see 38:1037.

[309]
*American Council on Education Psychological Examination for High School Students. Grades 9-12; 1933-54; 3 scores: quantitative, linguistic, total; IBM; Editions 1946, 1947, 1948, 1953; manual ['54]; no data on validity; separate answer sheets must be used; $3.25 per 25 tests; $1 per 25 IBM answer sheets; 50¢ per set of scoring stencils; postage extra; 35(65) minutes; 1947 and earlier editions by L. L. Thurstone and Thelma Gwinn Thurstone; later editions prepared by publisher from materials developed by the Thurstones; Cooperative Test Division, Educational Testing Service. *

REFERENCES

1-2. See 40:1378.
3-9. See 3:218.
10-11. See 4:278.
12. LAYTON, WILBUR L. "The Relation of Ninth Grade Test Scores to Twelfth Grade Test Scores and High School Rank." *J Appl Psychol* 38:10-1 F '54. * (PA 29:1570)

WILLIAM B. MICHAEL, *Director, The Testing Bureau, and Professor of Psychology and Education, University of Southern California, Los Angeles, California.*

Although the last annual release of the *American Council on Education Psychological Examination for High School Students* (ACE) was in 1953, various annual forms of the test are still being widely used. Two parts, Same-Opposites (consisting of 50 antonym-synonym multiple choice items) and Completion (made up of 60 items in which a definition of a word is followed by five letters, one of them being the initial letter of the word desired), furnish a verbal, or linguistic, score. The other two parts, Arithmetic (including 20 thought problems cast in multiple choice form) and Number Series (containing 30 different sequences of seven numbers each followed by five alternative numbers, one of which continues correctly the pattern formed by the series), yield a quantitative score. Despite the appearance of several competitive instruments during the past few years, including the sequel to ACE, the *Cooperative School and College Ability Test* (SCAT), ACE is still a highly useful and, even by today's improved procedures of test construction and standardization, a noteworthy test reflecting the high level of workmanship that the Thurstones employed in the building of initial forms and that the Cooperative Test Division of the Educational Testing Service continued after 1948.

Among many of the positive features of the various forms that are reported in the manual are the high reliabilities of the total scores (between .89 and .93) and the relatively high reliabilities for the part scores (between .87 and .92 for the verbal section and between .75 and .91 for the much shorter quantitative section), the presentation of tables of equivalent scores and percentile ranks for each of the various forms, a detailed description of the composition of the sample from which norms were derived, and additional statistical data regarding grade-to-grade shifts in mean and variability of scores, and the magnitudes of the standard errors of measurement for 8th and 12th grade groups. Additional advantages of the series include ease of administration and of scoring.

On the somewhat less positive side has been the lack of any mention in the manual as to the predictive validity, or, for that matter, to any kind of validity of the examination. It would seem that since such a large number of high school counselors and administrators have employed this test as a basis for placement and for prognostication of scholastic success either in a high school college preparatory program or in subsequent college work, certain information pertaining to validity either would have been reported within the body of the manual itself or would have been cited in a set of references to various appropriate journal articles, bulletins, or reports. In terms of the interest that the Thurstones have exhibited for a factorial approach to the study of intelligence, it has been somewhat disconcerting, perhaps, to note from the intercorrelations between scores on the verbal and quantitative sections the lack of factorial purity of the subtests—a circumstance that is apparent from an inspection of the nature of the items themselves. It would appear that a rather general measure of scholastic aptitude, or symbolic thinking, embracing verbal comprehension, word fluency, general reasoning, and numerical facility, has been achieved that, with the probable exception of the test in arithmetic, does not indicate specific attainment, or achievement, in high school courses.

Another characteristic of the test that is of concern to many, including the reviewer, has been the importance of speed of response to the realization of a high score. Since speed is such a decisive factor in the examination, it would seem desirable that examinees be advised somewhat more emphatically in the directions regarding the importance of working as rapidly as possible, of not spending too much time on any one item, and of not diverting attention to checking or double checking their work as they progress through each subtest. In light of some informal and not too well controlled observations that the reviewer made a number of years ago involving the analysis of responses on answer sheets of several small groups of high school seniors (residing for the most part in neighborhoods of middle socioeconomic level), it seemed that an increment of perhaps 25 per cent in working time on each test part would lead to the situation in which almost 90 per cent of the items in the two verbal sections would be attempted and perhaps 70 per cent of the items on the two quantitative parts would be tried. Of course, what is needed is a series of empirical validation studies in which not only mental set regarding speed of response is varied, but also different amounts of time are allowed for various parts of the examination.

It is interesting to compare briefly some of the characteristics of ACE and SCAT. It would appear that the latter test tends to reflect to a slightly greater extent the examinee's educational development and classroom experiences rather than the more generalized aspects of scholastic aptitude found in ACE. Although it is reasonable to hypothesize that the approach followed in SCAT might lead to somewhat higher predictive validities, comparative studies, which undoubtedly are forthcoming, are needed. In taking both tests, the reviewer noted that for SCAT, as compared with ACE, the significance of the speed factor was less (but still present); that the directions, content of the items, and layout appeared less threatening; and that the items were less difficult and more closely related to one's everyday reading and learning experiences. There is no doubt that the manual for SCAT is decidedly easier to interpret and that the normative procedures—especially in view of the introduction of confidence intervals—are much more meaningful than those reported for the ACE forms. In addition, tables are available for equating ACE scores to those of SCAT. Moreover, an excellent Technical Report containing detailed information upon reliability, validity, equating procedures, and normative data is available and will be augmented from time to time.

In summary, it may be said that the *American Council on Education Psychological Examination for High School Students* is a satisfactorily reliable instrument for which considerable normative information is available. However, the lack of validity data and the element of undue speed required for attainment of a high score pose reservations concerning its use. In view of the existence of other competitive instruments such as SCAT, for which considerable data upon reliability, validity, norms, and equating procedures are already available and for which an excellent manual replete with interpretative data exists, it seems only a matter of a few years before the ACE series will cease to be used.

For a review by Carl I. Hovland of an earlier edition, see 3:218; for a review by A. H. Turney, see 40:1378; for a review by V. A. C. Henmon, see 38:1038.

[310]
Army General Classification Test, First Civilian Edition. Grades 9–16 and adults; 1940–48; also called AGCT; IBM; 1 form ('47, identical with Form 1a ('40) of the Army Edition); 2 editions; revised manual ('48); separate answer pads or sheets must be used; $10.80 per 20 tests; 75¢ per specimen set of either edition; postage extra; 40(50) minutes; original test prepared by Personnel Research Section, The Adjutant General's Office, War Department; Science Research Associates. *
a) [HAND SCORING EDITION.] 1947–48; Form AH ('47); $2.35 per 20 answer pads.
b) [MACHINE SCORING EDITION.] 1947–48; IBM; Form AM ('47); $5 per 100 IBM answer sheets; $1 per set of scoring stencils.

REFERENCES
1–14. See 3:219.
15–29. See 4:280.
30. JOHNSON, RALPH H., AND BOND, GUY L. "Reading Ease of Commonly Used Tests." *J Appl Psychol* 34:319–24 O '50. * (PA 26:299)
31. MASON, CHARLES F. *Intelligence and Mental Illness.* Doctor's thesis, Purdue University (Lafayette, Ind.), 1950. (DA 15:2296)
32. FERSON, REGIS F. *The Probabilities of Success in Trade Training as Estimated by Standardized Tests.* Doctor's thesis, University of Pittsburgh (Pittsburgh, Pa.), 1951.
33. FRUCHTER, BENJAMIN. "Orthogonal and Oblique Solutions of a Battery of Aptitude, Achievement and Background

Variables." *Ed & Psychol Meas* 12:20–38 sp '52. * (*PA* 27:6180)
34. FULK, BYRON E., AND HARRELL, THOMAS W. "Negro-White Army Test Scores and Last School Grade." *J Appl Psychol* 36:34–5 F '52. * (*PA* 26:6925)
35. BERNARD, JACK. *Selection of Technical School Students: An Investigation of the Relationship Between Certain Personality Characteristics, Interests and Abilities, and Success in a Radio and Television Curriculum.* Doctor's thesis, New York University (New York, N.Y.), 1954. (*DA* 15:631)
36. CHAPPELL, TOLAN L.; CALLIS, ROBERT; RENZAGLIA, GUY A.; AND SPOHRER, MYRON A. "The Differential Prediction of Achievement at the University of Missouri." *Ed & Psychol Meas* 14:724–5 w '54. * (*PA* 29:7955)
37. DUBOIS, PHILLIP H., AND WATSON, ROBERT I. "Validity Information Exchange, No. 7-075:D.O.T. Code 2-66.23, Policeman." *Personnel Psychol* 7:414–7 au '54. *
38. GLASER, ROBERT, AND JACOBS, OWEN. "Predicting Achievement in Medical School: A Comparison of Preclinical and Clinical Criteria." *J Appl Psychol* 38:245–7 Ag '54. * (*PA* 29:6271)
39. BARNETTE, W. LESLIE, JR. "Diagnostic Features of the AGCT." *J Social Psychol* 42:241–7 N '55. * (*PA* 31:1019)
40. CHAPPELL, TOLAN L. "Note on the Validity of the Army General Classification Test as a Predictor of Academic Achievement." *J Ed Psychol* 46:53–5 Ja '55. * (*PA* 29:8993)
41. MULLINEAUX, JEWEL E. "An Evaluation of the Predictors Used to Select Patrolmen." *Pub Personnel R* 16:84–6 Ap '55. *
42. PATTERSON, CECIL H. *Test and Background Factors Related to Drop-Outs in an Industrial Institute.* Doctor's thesis, University of Minnesota (Minneapolis, Minn.), 1955. (*DA* 15:1024)
43. OTTERNESS, WILLIAM B.; PATTERSON, C. H.; JOHNSON, R. H.; AND PETERSON, LENNIS R. "Trade School Norms for Some Commonly Used Tests." *J Appl Psychol* 40:57–60 F '56. * (*PA* 31:3803)
44. PATTERSON, C. H. "The Prediction of Attrition in Trade School Courses." *J Appl Psychol* 40:154–8 Je '56. * (*PA* 31:6680)
45. WOLINS, LEROY, AND PERLOFF, ROBERT. "The Factorial Composition of AGCT 'Subtests' Along With College Aptitude Items and High School Grades." Abstract. *Am Psychol* 11:449 Ag '56. *
46. BARRETT, RICHARD S. "The Process of Predicting Job Performance." *Personnel Psychol* 11:39–57 sp '58. *

For a review by John T. Dailey, see 4:280; see 3:219 (1 excerpt).

[311]

★**The Business Test.** Clerical workers; 1952–56; Form A ['52]; mimeographed manual ['56]; no data on reliability; no norms; $2.50 per 25 tests; 35¢ per specimen set; postage extra; 10(15) or (10–25) minutes; Edward N. Hay; Aptitude Test Service. *

LOUIS C. NANASSY, *Professor of Business Education, Montclair State College, Upper Montclair, New Jersey.*

This is a verbal test of mental ability or quickness of learning, with the emphasis placed on perceiving relationships and solving problems. It consists of 35 items, mostly multiple choice, of a nonquantitative, nonmathematical nature, using a simple vocabulary; it may be used as either an untimed or a timed test.

According to the manual, the test was designed to overcome the disadvantage of some similar tests which, by reason of having many difficult words, penalize good workers, particularly foremen, whose education may not be high. Also according to the manual, a high proportion of clerical jobs require no particular vocabulary, so the test is also suitable for use in the selection of clerical employees.

Clear and concise directions are given for administering and scoring the test. It requires only a short period of time to take—10 to 25 minutes at the most. The test papers may be collected at the end of the 10 minutes; or, as an alternate procedure, at the end of 10 minutes the applicant may draw a line under the last item completed and then continue working until all items are completed. If only one score is desired, the 10-minute score is claimed to be sufficient.

For validation of the test, 67 clerical supervisors and 98 operating foremen of seven gas companies were tested. On the basis of the results, it was concluded that even if a company used no other tests to assist in determining who should be promoted from the ranks into the management organization, this short test, easy to obtain and easy to use, could make a significant contribution.

Perhaps the title *Business Test* is a misnomer. The items have little relationship to business situations and processes. In effect, the test is a simple intelligence test, with possible usefulness in evaluating people in numerous lines of work.

JAMES H. RICKS, JR., *Assistant Director, Test Division, The Psychological Corporation, New York, New York.*

When a test reaches the age of 6 years (as indicated by its copyright date) with neither reliability data nor anything approaching adequate norms in its manual, it can claim the serious attention of reviewers and prospective users only if some important, even though still hypothetical, virtue distinguishes it from its competitors. The distinctions which this test appears to possess are few and the evidence for them is scant. Three specific differences from "the typical intelligence test" are cited in the manual:

a) "There are no quantitative or mathematical items." This is true, but verbal mental ability scores uncontaminated by quantitative material may be obtained in short times from such tests as the *Short Employment Tests* and the *Thurstone Test of Mental Alertness.*

b) "It does not require an extensive vocabulary." Probably true, so far as inspection indicates, but not supported by reference to any evidence such as the Thorndike-Lorge frequency counts. The statement is equally applicable to the verbal score on the *Wesman Personnel Classification Test.* And neither argument nor evidence is adduced in support of the idea that verbal intelligence is better measured for employment purposes by analogies and other "reasoning" items than by a straight vocabulary test.

c) "It is designed to be used either as an untimed or a timed test." This statement is no less true of the *Wonderlic Personnel Test,* but its implications deserve further examination. It is not stated what elements of design qualify a test to be used on both a timed and an untimed basis. Presumably the difficulty range of the items is relevant to its use without time limit, but no information on item difficulties is provided.

Operationally, such a statement as the third one must mean that a score obtained within a time limit or a score obtained with unlimited time may be used. Actually, the manual suggests recording three scores, viz., the total time required, the number right in 10 minutes, and the total number of items answered correctly. In one of the validation studies, the score used is the sum of the second and third of these, equivalent to twice the number of points earned in 10 minutes plus the number earned after that limit (neither rationale nor data are offered in defense of this procedure). And in the recommended "Selection Scores" table offered in lieu of norms, there is no indication as to *which* of the four types of score was used!

In support of the test's usefulness, the information obtained from the manual plus two letters to the publisher consists of a correlation coefficient of .80 with the *Wonderlic Personnel Test* and a report indicating that supervisors rated "Best" by their superiors average higher than those rated "Middle" who in turn average higher than those rated "Poorest." No indications of the overlap among the groups nor of the significance of the differences are provided.

The manual observes that "some of the well known tests are familiar to applicants because they are so widely used." *The Business Test* may well continue to enjoy its advantage on this count.

[312]

★**California Analogies and Reasoning Test.** Grades 10–13; 1958; IBM; Forms A, B; $4.20 per 35 tests; separate answer sheets may be used; 5¢ per IBM answer sheet; 20¢ per set of hand and machine scoring stencils; postage extra; 50¢ per specimen set, postpaid; 40(50) minutes; Claude Mitchell; California Test Bureau. *

[313]

*****California Short-Form Test of Mental Maturity.** Grades kgn–1, 1–3, 4–8, 7–9, 9–13, 10–16 and adults; 1938–57; 7 scores: spatial relationships, logical reasoning, numerical reasoning, verbal concepts, language, nonlanguage, total; IBM for grades 4 and over; 1957 S-Form ('57); 6 levels; manual ('57) for each level; supplement ['50]; technical report ('57); $3.15 per 35 tests; separate answer sheets may be used in grades 4 and over; 4¢ per IBM answer sheet; 7¢ per Scoreze answer sheet; 20¢ per hand scoring stencil; 40¢ per machine scoring stencil; postage extra; 50¢ per specimen set of any one level, postpaid; Elizabeth T. Sullivan (except *e*), Willis W. Clark, and Ernest W. Tiegs; California Test Bureau. *

a) PRE-PRIMARY. Grades kgn–1; S-Form ('57); (29–40) minutes.
b) PRIMARY. Grades 1–3; S-Form ('57); (42–55) minutes.
c) ELEMENTARY. Grades 4–8; S-Form ('57); 47–49(60) minutes.
d) JUNIOR HIGH. Grades 7–9; S-Form ('57); 51–52(65) minutes.
e) SECONDARY. Grades 9–13; S-Form A ('57); 52–53(65) minutes.
f) ADVANCED. Grades 10–16 and adults; S-Form ('57); 52–53(65) minutes.

REFERENCES

1. SILVER, CHARLES E. *A Comparison of the Scores Made by College Reading Problem Cases on the California Short-form Test of Mental Maturity and Form I of the Wechsler-Bellevue Scales.* Master's thesis, Bowling Green State University (Bowling Green, Ohio), 1950.
2. LEACH, KENT W. "Intelligence Test Scores of Michigan Ninth-Grade Pupils." *Univ Mich Sch Ed B* 24:6–9 O '52. *
3. POE, WESLEY A., AND BERG, IRWIN A. "Psychological Test Performance of Steel Industry Production Supervisors." *J Appl Psychol* 36:234–7 Ag '52. * (*PA* 27:3794)
4. RALEIGH, WILLIAM H. *A Study of the Relationships of Academic Achievement in Sixth Grade With the Wechsler Intelligence Scale for Children and Other Variables.* Doctor's thesis, Indiana University (Bloomington, Ind.), 1952.
5. TAYLOR, EDWARD A. "Some Factors Relating to Social Acceptance in Eighth-Grade Classrooms." *J Ed Psychol* 43:257–72 My '52. * (*PA* 27:3770)
6. BREGOLI, ELMO J. *An Item Analysis of the Vocabulary Sub-Test of the California Short-Form Test of Mental Ability.* Master's thesis, Boston College (Chestnut Hill, Mass.), 1953.
7. O'NEIL, WILLIAM J. *An Item Analysis of the Numerical Quantity Section, Test 6, of the California Short-Form Test of Mental Ability.* Master's thesis, Boston College (Chestnut Hill, Mass.), 1953.
8. COWNE, LESLIE. "A Study of the California Short Form Test of Mental Maturity." *Ed Rec B* 62:67–75 F '54. * (*PA* 28:8070)
9. BLIESMER, EMERY P. "A Comparison of Results Obtained With Various Types of Capacity Tests Used With Retarded Readers." *Yearb Nat Council Meas Used Ed* 12(pt 1):60–2 '55. *
10. NORTH, ROBERT D. "The California Short-Form Test of Mental Maturity: Further Reliability and Correlation Data." *Ed Rec B* 65:59–64 F '55. * (*PA* 29:7307)
11. FOWLER, WILLIAM L. *A Comparative Analysis of Pupil Performance on Conventional and Culture-Controlled Mental Tests.* Doctor's thesis, University of Michigan (Ann Arbor, Mich.), 1956. (*DA* 17:91)
12. MITCHELL, JAMES V., JR. "A Comparison of the Factorial Structure of Cognitive Functions for a High and Low Status Group." *J Ed Psychol* 47:397–414 N '56. *
13. FOWLER, WILLIAM L. "A Comparative Analysis of Pupil Performance on Conventional and Culture-Controlled Mental Tests." *Yearb Nat Council Meas Used Ed* 14:8–19 '57. *
14. KLUGMAN, SAMUEL F. "Agreement Between Two Tests as Predictors of College Success." *Personnel & Guid J* 36:255–8 D '57. *
15. MOULY, GEORGE J., AND EDGAR, MARY. "Equivalence of IQ's for Four Group Intelligence Tests." *Personnel & Guid J* 36:623–6 My '58. *

CYRIL BURT, *Emeritus Professor of Psychology, University of London, London, England.*

This is an abridgement of the earlier *California Test of Mental Maturity,* and is described as "an instrument for appraising mental development or mental capacity." The whole scale comprises six booklets of increasing difficulty designed to cover the entire range of school grades from the preprimary to the adult level. Each booklet contains seven subtests which sample four main areas of mental activity (termed "mental factors"): spatial relations, logical reasoning, numerical reasoning, and verbal concepts.

The results obtained are intended to serve both normative and analytical purposes. The norms are given in terms of mental ages and IQ's; the analysis is effected by means of individual profiles, constructed graphically, which provide mental ages and IQ's for the four "factors" and for the language and nonlanguage sections of the test. In general, both the items and the format of the new 1957 edition remain much as before. But the content of the various subtests has been checked and revised, the norms have been evaluated afresh, and additional data on reliability and validity have been incorporated in the manuals (which now extend to 28 or 32 pages).

The items selected for the several levels and the resulting norms have been carefully articulated, in the hope that the IQ's both for the test as a whole and for the language and nonlanguage components will prove comparable when the pupil passes from the more elementary stages to the later levels. To check the articulation, correlations (analogous to reliability coefficients based on "parallel forms") have been computed by applying tests for adjacent levels to the same groups.

The variety of content and the high proportion of nonverbal problems even at the upper levels are commendable features. The directions for administering and scoring the tests are lucid and complete. The material presented (pictures, diagrams, and reading matter) is, on the whole, clearly printed, though the type size is rather small in the booklet for the youngest children. On the other hand, the discussions of methods to be used for calculating the various IQ's and for constructing the individual profiles seem needlessly long and overelaborate. An examiner who requires a detailed explanation of the meaning of "IQ" would scarcely be prepared to follow the detailed steps for converting the raw test data into a profile with 16 linear scales. Most teachers would probably prefer a short practical manual giving essential instructions for administering the particular test they intended to use and a separate introductory pamphlet explaining the theoretical basis of the whole series and summarizing the evidence for the reliability and validity of the different levels. This would avoid much of the repetition in the present manuals.

In the original form, the conceptual framework for the *California Test of Mental Maturity* was that of the Stanford-Binet scale. The fuller version has been in use for over 20 years. The experience and the mass of data thus accumulated have been freely utilized in progressively improving the shortened series. The outcome is one of the best sets of group tests at present available. The reliability has been assessed by various methods. With the Kuder-Richardson formula 21 the reliability of the total scores varies between .87 and .89 at most grade levels, but at the secondary stage (as one might expect) it is appreciably higher. The validity coefficients consist of observed and corrected correlations with the Stanford-Binet and WISC, and with group intelligence tests. They vary far more widely, averaging about .75. But correlations of this nature are not very informative.

The intercorrelations between the measurements for the four "mental factors" are positive at every stage, and usually range from .30 to .60 (without correction for selection), except for those between "spatial relationships" and "verbal concepts," which are far lower. Evidently a general cognitive factor dominates the picture. This supports the authors' claim that the test, taken as a whole, provides an excellent instrument for assessing general "capacity." But to state that it also measures "development" and to designate it as a test of "maturity" seems tantamount to adopting two alternative interpretations of "intelligence" which are not altogether consistent. Certainly there is very little evidence for claiming that it may likewise be used to measure distinct mental processes.

To begin with, the mere fact that similar types of tests are repeated stage after stage does not guarantee that the same special aptitudes are being assessed throughout the child's school life or that these particular types of tests really depend on the same mental factors or functions at different ages. At the preprimary stage the tests yielding the highest reliability (.66) are the subtests for spatial relationships; at the secondary stage they are the subtests for verbal concepts (.92). Such a result, together with what is already known about the progressive differentiation of mental capacities, seems merely to imply that for the younger ages the best measures of general capacity are to be obtained with nonverbal material and for the older with verbal problems. Specialization is usually a relatively late phenomenon; and even with older children the chief value of nonverbal tests is to counteract any special disabilities that might otherwise impair the value of the test as a whole.

In any case, two or three subtests, lasting in all for only 7 to 15 minutes, would scarcely suffice to yield a reliable and valid assessment for the so-called special "factors." Indeed, the reliability coefficients recorded for the separate assessments are nearly all fairly low (.50 to .75, but higher for the secondary group); much of this must really be reliability as measures of general capacity. Moreover, little or nothing is actually known as to how these particular "factors" would affect different types of school work. No doubt, in a few exceptional cases, especially at the later stages, the construction of a differential profile for some particular pupil will prove informative. But, from the practical standpoint of the teacher, the names given to the factors and the detailed instructions for their measurement in terms of separate mental ages or IQ's might encourage him to fancy that he can extract far more information out of the test results than is actually the case. These minor criticisms, however, in no way affect the general merits of the test as a whole.

For reviews of the California Test of Mental Maturity *and its adaptations, see 4:282, 3:223, 40:1384, and 38:1042.*

[314]

*California Test of Mental Maturity, 1957 Edition. Grades kgn–1, 1–3, 4–8, 7–9, 9–13, 10–16 and adults; 1936–57; 8 scores: memory, spatial relationships, logical reasoning, numerical reasoning, verbal concepts, language, nonlanguage, total; IBM for grades 4 and over; 1 form ('57); 6 levels; manual ('57) for each level; supplement ['50] technical report ('57); $5.25 per 35 tests; separate answer sheets may be used in grades 4 and over; 4¢ per IBM answer sheet; 7¢ per Scoreze answer sheet; 40¢ per set of hand scoring stencils; 60¢ per set of machine scoring stencils; postage extra; 50¢ per specimen set, postpaid; Pre-Primary: 48(70) minutes; Primary: 67(90) minutes; Elementary: 84–88(110) minutes; Junior High School: 88–90(115) minutes; Secondary: 90–(115) minutes; Advanced: 90–92(115) minutes; Elizabeth T. Sullivan, Willis W. Clark, and Ernest W. Tiegs; California Test Bureau. *

REFERENCES

1–5. See 40:1384.
6–15. See 3:223.
16–39. See 4:282.
40. ARNOLD, E. REX. *The Diagnostic Possibilities of the California Test of Mental Maturity.* Master's thesis, North Texas State College (Denton, Tex.), 1948.
41. CARL, PAULINE M. *California's Test of Mental Maturity as a Means of Detecting Cases of Reading Disability.* Master's thesis, Kansas State Teachers College (Pittsburg, Kan.), 1948.
42. JACKSON, B. J. *The Relationship Between Certain Mental Characteristics and Achievement.* Master's thesis, North Texas State College (Denton, Tex.), 1948.
43. AMERICAN GAS ASSOCIATION, PERSONNEL COMMITTEE. *Personnel Testing in the Gas Industry.* New York: the Association, January 1952. Pp. 10. *
44. BOGER, JACK H. "An Experimental Study of the Effects of Perceptual Training on Group I.Q. Test Scores of Elementary Pupils in Rural Ungraded Schools." *J Ed Res* 46:43–52 S '52. * (*PA* 27:5414)
45. CLARK, WILLIS W. "Evaluating School Achievement in Basic Skills in Relation to Mental Ability." *J Ed Res* 46:180–91 N '52. * (*PA* 27:6149)
46. DRISCOLL, JUSTIN A. *Factors in Intelligence and Achievement: A Study of the Factor Pattern Resulting From Analysis of the Scores of Boys in Junior Year of High School on Intelligence and Achievement Tests.* Catholic University of America, Educational Research Monographs, Vol. 16, No. 7. Washington, D.C.: Catholic University of America Press, Inc., June 15, 1952. Pp. viii, 56. * (*PA* 27:3330)
47. WELCH, W. BRUCE. *An Examination of the Usability of Selected Standardized Tests of Mental Ability and Achievement for College Groups With Atypical Socio-Economic Status.* Doctor's thesis, Indiana University (Bloomington, Ind.), 1952.
48. CLARK, WILLIS W. "Sex Differences in Mental Abilities Among Students of High Intelligence." *Calif J Ed Res* 5:90–3 Mr '54. * (*PA* 28:8559)
49. HAMMER, EMANUEL F. "Comparison of the Performances of Negro Children and Adolescents on Two Tests of Intelligence, One an Emergency Scale." *J Genetic Psychol* 84:85–93 Mr '54. * (*PA* 28:8659)
50. SCHWELLENBACH, JOHN A. "An Experiment in Predicting the Ability of Eighth Grade Students to Work Simple Algebra Problems." *Calif J Ed Res* 5:36–41 Ja '54. * (*PA* 28:7998)
51. SHELDON, WILLIAM D., AND MANOLAKES, GEORGE. "A Comparison of the Stanford-Binet, Revised Form L, and the California Test of Mental Maturity (S-Form)." *J Ed Psychol* 45:499–504 D '54. * (*PA* 29:7318)
52. SWEENEY, FRANCIS J. "Intelligence, Vocational Interests and Reading Speed of Senior Boys in Catholic High Schools of Los Angeles." *Calif J Ed Res* 5:159–65 S '54. * (*PA* 29:4656)
53. ALTUS, GRACE T. "Relationships Between Verbal and Nonverbal Parts of the CTMM and WISC." *J Consult Psychol* 19:143–4 Ap '55. * (*PA* 30:1008)
54. COMREY, ANDREW L., AND HIGH, WALLACE S. "Validity of Some Ability and Interest Scores." *J Appl Psychol* 39:247–8 Ag '55. * (*PA* 30:5278)
55. MCCALL, JOHN R. *Sex Differences in Intelligence: A Comparative Factor Study.* Washington, D.C.: Catholic University of America Press, Inc., 1955. Pp. viii, 65. * (*PA* 30:4171)
56. MANOLAKES, GEORGE, AND SHELDON, WILLIAM D. "The Relation Between Reading-Test Scores and Language-Factors Intelligence Quotients." *El Sch J* 55:346–50 F '55. * (*PA* 29:8918)
57. MARSHALL, THOMAS A. *Analysis of Predictive Value for Pupils in a Single Third Grade From Scores Based on the California Test of Mental Maturity.* Master's thesis, Fresno State College (Fresno, Calif.), 1955
58. SMITH, THOMAS WOOD, AND CAFFREY, JOHN. "Comprehension of Written Language (Reading) and Oral Language (Auding) as Related to 'Cultural Bias' on the Davis-Eells Games and the California Test of Mental Maturity." Abstract. *Am Psychol* 10:382–3 Ag '55. *
59. ALTUS, GRACE T. "Some Correlates of the Davis-Eells Tests." *J Consult Psychol* 20:227–32 Je '56. * (*PA* 31:6053)
60. BLIESMER, EMERY P. "A Comparison of Results of Various Capacity Tests Used With Retarded Readers." *El Sch J* 56:400–2 My '56. * (*PA* 31:5140)
61. CALIFORNIA TEST BUREAU, DIVISION OF PROFESSIONAL SERVICES; WITH THE ASSISTANCE OF JAMES C. COLEMAN. *California Test of Mental Maturity: Summary of Investigations Number Three.* Hollywood, Calif.: California Test Bureau, 1956. Pp. 30. * (*PA* 31:7287)
62. GALLAGHER, JAMES J.; BENOIT, E. PAUL; AND BOYD, HERBERT F. "Measures of Intelligence in Brain Damaged Children." *J Clin Psychol* 12:69–72 Ja '56. * (*PA* 30:5093)
63. MARSHALL, THOMAS A. *Analysis of Predictive Value for Pupils in a Single Third Grade From Scores Based on the California Test of Mental Maturity.* Master's thesis, Fresno State College (Fresno, Calif.), 1956.
64. SHANNER, WILLIAM M. "Relationships Between Norms for Mental Maturity and Achievement Tests." *Calif J Ed Res* 7:15–21 Ja '56. * (*PA* 30:7775)
65. SMITH, THOMAS WOOD. *Auding and Reading as Sources of Cultural Bias in the Davis-Eells Games and the California Test of Mental Maturity.* Doctor's thesis, University of Southern California (Los Angeles, Calif.), 1956.

California Short-Form Test of Mental Maturity

66. SMITH, THOMAS WOOD. "Comparison of Test Bias in the Davis-Eells Games and the CTMM." *Calif J Ed Res* 7:159–63 S '56. * (*PA* 31:6135)
67. TATE, MERLE W., AND VOSS, CHARLOTTE E. "A Study of the Davis-Eells Test of Intelligence." *Harvard Ed R* 26: 374–87 fall '56. * (*PA* 32:1347)
68. McHUGH, ANN F. *An Investigation of the Reliability and Concurrent Validity of Two Levels of the California Test of Mental Maturity, Short Form.* Doctor's thesis, Fordham University (New York, N.Y.), 1957.
69. NICHOLSON, ALICE. *Background Abilities Related to Reading Success in First Grade.* Doctor's thesis, Boston University (Boston, Mass.), 1957.
70. OWEN, JASON CAMILLOUS. *A Study of the Prognostic Value of Certain Measures of Intelligence and Listening Comprehension With a Selected Group of Elementary Pupils.* Doctor's thesis, University of Missouri (Columbia, Mo.), 1957. (*DA* 19:484)
71. TOPETZES, NICK JOHN. "A Program for the Selection of Trainees in Physical Medicine." *J Exp Ed* 25:263–311 Je '57. *
72. COOPER, JAMES G. "Predicting School Achievement for Bilingual Pupils." *J Ed Psychol* 49:31–6 F '58. *
73. NICHOLSON, ALICE. "Background Abilities Related to Reading Success in First Grade." *J Ed (Boston)* 140:7–24 F '58. *

FRANK S. FREEMAN, *Professor of Psychology, Cornell University, Ithaca, New York.*

The 1957 edition of this group test of intelligence is an improved version of earlier editions, but it is unchanged in respect to underlying structure and basic psychological rationale. "The major effort of this revision," state the manuals, "has been devoted to a re-evaluation and improvement of the norms, with special attention given to the articulation of successive levels."

As in all previous editions, the types of subtests included at all age levels are based upon the original psychological analysis, by one of the test's authors,[1] of the operations involved in the Stanford-Binet scale. It is to be noted that this was not a factorial analysis; yet the derived "mental factors" are strikingly similar to the statistically derived factors utilized in the tests of "primary mental abilities" which followed some years later.

Technically, there is much to recommend this sequence of scales. The authors provide a considerable amount of useful data in the manuals. The standardization population appears to be quite satisfactory as to numbers (25,000 originally, "checked against 100,000 additional cases"), geographic distribution, and stratification. At each level, tables are given showing percentage contribution of variance to language, nonlanguage, and total scores of each "mental factor" (memory, spatial relations, logical reasoning, numerical reasoning, and verbal concepts). From these tables the qualified user may draw his own inferences and better interpret individual test profiles. The data on reliability are as complete and as satisfactory as those generally found with the sounder tests—high coefficients for total score and for the two major divisions, language and non-language, and moderate to high coefficients for individual subtests. Anyone planning to use these scales should examine the reliability tables since the coefficients are not uniform for all age and grade levels. Still another type of reliability study, presented in place of alternate forms data, is given in a discussion of "articulation." The procedure here was to test "one and two school grades below and one and two grades above the recommended grade levels for the various tests. The equivalent Language and Non-Language raw scores for the level of the test being articulated were then computed for each consecutive Language and Non-Language raw score of the test level being used within its recommended range. The design of these studies specified that the raw scores coincide, test for test, within one standard error of measurement on either test." No data are presented to show the actual approximation to coincidence obtained, though we may assume, presumably, that the stated criterion of correspondence was satisfied.

Intercorrelations among subtests are given at each level. These range from very low (e.g., between spatial relationships and verbal concepts) to moderately high (e.g., between memory and verbal concepts), thus indicating various degrees of communality and independence of mental operations being tested by the several parts.

Instructions for administering and scoring are clear. Tables for converting scores into percentile ranks, mental ages, and estimated grade equivalents are quite satisfactory. The profiles are well designed.

The manuals state that these tests yield a "normal distribution of intelligence quotients, with a mean of 100 and a standard deviation of 16 for the unselected general population." However, the "Summary of Investigations Number Three" provides tables of *median* IQ's and standard deviations for grade levels, but not for age levels. Nor do the manuals or the "Summary" state explicitly the method used in deriving the mean (or median) of 100 IQ and the SD of 16. By experimental testing of the standardization population and item analysis? By the deviation IQ technique? In the "Summary" there is a suggestion, however, that the latter method was employed.

[1] SULLIVAN, ELIZABETH T. "Psychographic Representation of Results of the Stanford Revision of the Binet-Simon Tests." *J Delinquency* 10:284–5 Ja '26.

The major criticism of the technical information available for these scales has to do with data on their validity. The "Summary" lists five criteria.

a) Intercorrelations with other intelligence tests, both group and individual. On the whole, the coefficients resulting from these validating studies, which were carried out by investigators other than the authors of the scales, are satisfactory or even high, especially in the case of the Stanford-Binet and the Wechsler scales. But these tables of intercorrelations and their explications do not always provide essential statistical data such as probable (or standard) errors of the coefficients, number of subjects used, range of ages and of grades, and range of ability. But the "Summary" does include a bibliography which provides the sources from which the intercorrelations were obtained.

b) Correlations with achievement tests. These coefficients compare very favorably with those obtained with other tests, but here again some essential indices are lacking, much as in (*a*) above. Where grade levels are given, they are, for the most part, 7 and higher. Since these scales are intended for use beginning in the kindergarten, and primarily for educational guidance and placement, it is highly desirable to have data on reliability and validity (especially in terms of school achievement and prediction) separately at every age and grade level.

c) Intercorrelations among parts of the test itself. These have already been commented on above.

d) Distinguishing between "different kinds of mental maturity." This criterion has been studied in terms of intercorrelations between language and nonlanguage sections of the scales. The correlations are in the neighborhood of .5 and .6, indicating that these two principal sections are measuring abilities which are markedly similar in some respects but, at the same time, different in others. This criterion has also been studied in terms of correlations with arithmetic and reading achievement test results. As would be expected, the language sections correlate much higher (.50–.82) than do the nonlanguage sections (.26–.36).

e) Factor analytic evaluation. A table of factor loadings, based on the Thurstone centroid method and expressed in terms of percentages, indicates that the language factors, from preprimary through the advanced level, contribute from about 37 to 48 per cent of total common factor variance, while the nonlanguage factors contribute from about 53 to 62 per cent.

On the whole, these 1957 scales provide fuller and more significant standardization and evaluative data than did their predecessors; hence, they are more valuable than the earlier editions. But more data on them are needed to demonstrate the extent to which they are valid in educational selection, prediction, and guidance at each of the several age and grade levels. Data are needed, also, regarding validity and reliability of the tests when used with groups of individuals at each of the several levels of ability—that is, with the mentally deficient, the slow, the average, the superior, and the gifted. It has long been known that a test does not necessarily yield equally sound results at all levels along the scale of mental ability. When these additional data are supplied, the value of these scales will be enhanced.

JOHN E. MILHOLLAND, *Associate Professor of Psychology, and Chief, Evaluation and Examinations Division, Bureau of Psychological Services, University of Michigan, Ann Arbor, Michigan.*

The physical and practical aspects of this test are particularly appealing. The booklets seem to be sturdy enough to withstand repeated use, almost all the pictures are clear, and the general format is conducive to accurate following of directions by testees. Directions for administering are well written and easy for the tester to follow, scoring is simple for any of the three methods of registering answers, and provisions for collating results and recording normative equivalents are well organized. For handy filing, the back page of the test booklet or answer sheet contains a profile of subscores as well as the record of all raw scores and pupil information data.

The various levels of the tests were articulated in standardization by giving two tests to each school grade. One was the regular test for that grade, the other, the test for the level immediately below or above. The results of this procedure were taken account of in the norming so that IQ's and mental ages for successive levels would be comparable.

Another basis for comparability was produced by adjusting the norms to obtain a normal distribution of IQ's with a standard deviation of 16 at each level. Thus, a person who maintains the same relative position in the group will have a constant IQ.

The manuals give reliability coefficients and standard errors of measurement for certain single grades as well as for certain grade ranges for each of the six levels of the test. Three different methods of estimating reliability were used at various places: the split-half correlation, stepped up by the Spearman-Brown formula; Kuder-Richardson formula 21; and the Rulon split-half formula. All these are equivalence estimates and tend to be spuriously high if the test is speeded. The subtests are in fact timed, but the authors assert in the directions for administration that the test is a power test and that the time limis are "ample for examinees to reach the effective limits of their abilities." No data on the degree of speededness are presented in the manuals, and we can only hope that speededness has not seriously inflated the reliabilities.

For the total score, the single grade reliabilities for grades 1, 2, 5, 8, 12, and college freshmen are all above .90. For the language score, based on four subscores, these single grade reliabilities range from .80 to .95, with a median of .89; for the nonlanguage score, based on seven or eight subscores, the range is .83 to .96, median .91. The five subscores (memory, spatial relationships, logical reasoning, numerical reasoning, and verbal concepts), perseveratingly called "factors" by the authors, have reliabilities ranging from .55 to .92; 10 of the 30 are below .80. We are probably safe in saying that the language, nonlanguage, and total scores are sufficiently reliable for describing individual pupils; the subscores generally are not.

The manuals state that the original *California Tests of Mental Maturity* were designed to correlate with the Stanford-Binet. Herein, it is said, lies one of the chief claims for validity. One study is cited in which this correlation is .88, and the claim is made that several other studies have yielded even higher values. Correlations with a number of other intelligence tests are also reported.

The manuals do not report data on the relation between the CTMM and school achievement. This is rather odd, since the WXYZ series of the *California Achievement Tests* is supposed to have been anchored to the CTMM. Some correlations of an earlier edition of the test with school grades and with previous forms of the *California Achievement Tests* are, however, reported in a 1956 publication (*61*). These are in the usual ranges, .50 to .70, with an occasional higher one. The language, nonlanguage, and total scores of the CTMM seem, then, to exhibit satisfactory validities against intelligence and achievement measures.

For more than 20 years, reviewers in this *Yearbook* and elsewhere have criticized the authors of the CTMM for using the term "factors" for scores derived from tests whose development was not based on factor analyses. The authors have shown no disposition to discontinue the practice, possibly because they may have some claim to chronological priority in the use of the word. It is nonetheless unfortunate that the confusion continues. In the present series of manuals, explanations are given that the factors about which the CTMM were built are "logical constructs based on assumptions about higher mental processes, e.g., numerical reasoning, rather than the mathematical factors of a factor analytic method." It is further asserted that, although the entire series has been submitted to numerous factor analyses, "the mathematical factors have not proved as meaningful nor as practically useful as the original logical constructs, the 'mental factors.'" Concrete evidence is, however, lacking as to the meaning and practical usefulness of the "factors." Opinions are given, it is true, as to the importance of certain "factors" in certain areas of endeavor, but no factual information is presented for the use of the subscores. Nevertheless, throughout the manuals the impression is left that the unique and most valuable feature of the test is the availability of a profile of "factor" scores. The only validation of the "factors" appears in the manual for the junior high level and consists of a table of correlations between CTMM subscores and appropriate scores on the *Holzinger-Crowder Uni-Factor Tests* and on the *SRA Primary Mental Abilities*. For example, intercorrelations between CTMM and PMA subscores are as follows (the second figure in each case is the coefficient corrected for range and attenuation): Verbal Concepts and PMA Verbal Meaning, .69 (.89); Verbal Concepts and PMA Word-Fluency, .33 (.47); Spatial Relationships and PMA Space, .32 (.77); Logical Reasoning and PMA Reasoning, .46 (.92); Numerical Reasoning and PMA Number, .27 (.51). These data may be used either to support the construct validity of the CTMM "factors" or to attack the authors' position that the CTMM "factors" are more meaningful than factor-analytic ones.

There does seem to be sufficient research available to warrant the use of separate language and nonlanguage scores from the test.

To summarize, the test is an excellent and usable test of general intelligence and has real value for comparing an individual's verbal and nonverbal abilities. However, as long as the authors persist in emphasizing the use of the "factor" scores in the face of lack of research evidence, the use of the CTMM by classroom teachers should be discouraged unless they are sophisticated enough not to be taken in by the "Diagnostic Profile" or are supervised by someone who is.

See 4:282 (1 excerpt); for a review by Henry E. Garrett of an earlier edition, see 3:223 (2 excerpts); for reviews by Raymond B. Cattell and F. Kuhlmann, see 40:1384 (1 excerpt); for reviews by W. D. Commins, Rudolph Pintner, and Arthur E. Traxler, see 38:1042.

[315]
Cattell Intelligence Tests. Mental ages 4–8, 8–11, 11–15, 15 and over; 1930–52; 4 levels; no data on reliability and validity; Scales 1–3: manual, third edition ('52); 10s. per 25 tests; 6d. per single copy; 7s. 6d. per complete specimen set; postage extra; R. B. Cattell; George G. Harrap & Co. Ltd. *
a) SCALE O (DARTINGTON SCALE). Mental ages 4–8; 1933; identical with Scale 1 of *IPAT Culture Free Intelligence Test*; individual; 1 form; 63s. 6d. per set of 50 tests, cards, and manual; (45) minutes.
b) SCALE 1 (NON-VERBAL), NEW EDITION, REVISED. Ages 8–11; 1930–52; Forms A, B ('35); (45) minutes.
c) SCALE 2, NEW EDITION, REVISED. Mental ages 11–15; 1930–35; Forms A, B ('35); (90) minutes.
d) SCALE 3, NEW EDITION, REVISED. Mental ages 15 and over; 1930–35; Forms A ('35), B ('30); (90) minutes.

REFERENCES
1–4. See 3:228.
5. ROHAN, J. C. "A Study of the Binet and Cattell Systems of Intelligence Testing in a Colony for Mental Defectives." *J Mental Sci* 87:192–207 Ap '41. * (*PA* 15:3190)
6. HALSTEAD, H., AND CHASE, V. E. "Review of a Verbal Intelligence Scale on Military Neurotic Patients." *Brit J Med Psychol* 20:195–201 pt 2 '44 (issued F '45). * (*PA* 19:2066)
7. SLATER, PATRICK. "Scores of Different Types of Neurotics on Tests of Intelligence." *Brit J Psychol* 35:40–2 Ja '45. * (*PA* 19:966)
8. SMITH, CHRISTINA A. *Mental Testing of Hebridean Children in Gaelic and English.* With "A Statistical Analysis" by D. N. Lawley. Publications of the Scottish Council for Research in Education, [No.] 27. London: University of London Press, Ltd., 1948. Pp. 42. *
9. UHRBROCK, RICHARD STEPHEN. "Construction of a Selection Test for College Graduates." *J General Psychol* 41:153–93 O '49. * (*PA* 24:4874)
10. CATTELL, RAYMOND B. "The Fate of National Intelligence: Test of a Thirteen-Year Prediction." *Eug R* 42:136–48 O '50. * (*PA* 25:2896)
11. FITT, A. B., AND ROGERS, C. A. "The Sex Factor in the Cattell Intelligence Tests, Scale III." *Brit J Psychol* 41:186–92 D '50. * (*PA* 25:8085)
12. TIZARD, J.; IN COLLABORATION WITH N. O'CONNOR AND J. M. CRAWFORD. "The Abilities of Adolescent and Adult High-Grade Male Defectives." *J Mental Sci* 96:888–907 O '50. * (*PA* 25:5421)
13. MOORE, B. G. R., AND PEEL, E. A. "Predicting Aptitude for Dentistry." *Occupational Psychol* 25:192–9 Jl '51. * (*PA* 26:3675)

I. MACFARLANE SMITH, *Lecturer in Education, University of Durham, Newcastle, England.*

This series of intelligence tests was first published in 1930. There were originally three scales, Scale 1 for mental ages 8–11, Scale 2 for mental ages 11–15, and Scale 3 for mental ages 15 and over. Scale O for mental ages 4–8, an individual test, was published in 1933 as the *Dartington Scale*.

The *Dartington Scale* has not been revised. It consists of eight subtests, totaling 96 pass or fail items—Substitution (pictorial), Line's Test, Mazes, Selecting Named Objects, Following Directions, Wrong Pictures, Riddles, and Similarities (pictorial and diagrammatic). The content is reasonably appropriate for young children, being varied, interesting, and attractive and not overweighted with verbal or scholastic material. But the standardization is scarcely adequate, the norms being based on the scores of only 117 children, of which 20 was the largest group for any year. The sample was of approximately average ability according to the Binet and other scales.

Scales 1, 2, and 3, which are group tests, were revised in 1935. Considerable alterations were made as a result of the experience gained in the intervening five years. Preliminary practice sheets were introduced. These are probably of value as "shock-absorbers," but since the time allowed for practice is only 5 minutes, the sheets are scarcely sufficient to counteract the effects of differences in test sophistication, which is one of the reasons given for providing practice tests. Scale 1 was made entirely nonverbal, replacing the previous Scale 1 which was predominantly verbal. Though somewhat more difficult to administer, this test is now much fairer to children coming from widely differing educational environments. In Scales 2 and 3 various items were improved and time allowances were revised. Thus, in Scale 3 two subtests were shortened by 1 minute, and one subtest by 2 minutes.

The new scales have been extensively standardized, Scale 1 on more than 6,000 children, Scale 2 on 7,500 children, and Scale 3 on more than 3,000 adults. Each scale is available in two forms, parallel in construction and equal in difficulty. The manual contains very adequate tables of norms, but no data on reliability or validity. It also contains a statement of the aims and guiding principles which were followed in constructing the tests. One of these was to diminish the effects of verbal facility as far as was compatible with the retention of high g saturation. Yet, in spite of this declared aim, the tests for the two upper scales are almost entirely verbal in form. Of the possible marks for Scales 2 and 3, totaling 151 in each, only 8 are for nonverbal items. Hence, both these scales give a very great advantage to subjects possessing high verbal ability. It would seem very desirable to alter the title of the tests for Scales 2 and 3 to "verbal intelligence test" or simply "verbal test." This is all the more necessary since the manual contains a section headed "The Meaning of the Results" which is misleading when applied to Scales 2 and 3. The section includes a quotation from Spearman in which the meaning of general ability or g is explained. Cattell then writes, "The above discussion helps us more clearly to interpret the results of the tests. They measure this pure general ability." If the tests for Scales 2 and 3 were called verbal tests, there would be less likelihood of the scores being interpreted as measures of general ability or g. Also, there is much to be said for following Spearman's lead and dropping the term "intelligence" altogether from the titles of all tests of ability. This policy was adopted in 1950 by the National Foundation for Educational Research in England and Wales, and more recently by Moray House.

Apart from stating that the items were arranged in order of increasing difficulty, the manual provides no information about the methods of test construction or item analysis employed. A recent paper by R. T. Green [1] suggests that the methods of item analysis and selection have not been entirely satisfactory. According to Green:

> An item analysis of a well-established intelligence test [Cattell IIIA] using data provided by highly intelligent subjects shows that not only are some items poor indicators of intelligence as measured by the test as a whole, but that other items are good indicators of lack of intelligence. It is suggested that this defect....is inherent in the original selection of the officially correct items on subjective a priori grounds.

No doubt this criticism could be made of many other widely used intelligence tests, constructed about or before 1930.

[1] GREEN, R. T. "An Item Analysis of the Cattell IIIA Intelligence Scale." Abstract. *B Brit Psychol Soc* (35):A17 My '58. *

Cattell must be commended for having provided a wide range of test material covering mental ages from 4 upwards, and for having secured very adequate standardization data for his Scales 1, 2, and 3. The tests have been very widely used and the main criticism,[2] voiced from time to time, that the IQ's have not been comparable with those obtained from other tests, has been due to the fact that the standard deviation of the IQ's has been in the region of 25. Cattell has consistently maintained that this high standard deviation is the correct one. It is a matter for regret that psychologists have not been able to agree on this matter since so many British users of tests have now become accustomed to the lower standard deviation of 15 employed by N.F.E.R. and Moray House.

For a review by Godfrey H. Thomson, see 40:1386.

[316]

Chicago Non-Verbal Examination. Ages 6 and over; 1936-47; administered orally or in pantomime; 1 form ('36); $3.50 per 25 tests; $1.20 per set of manual ['47] and scoring keys; $1.25 per specimen set; postpaid; 25(40–50) minutes; Andrew W. Brown, Seymour P. Stein, and Perry L. Rohrer; Psychological Corporation. *

REFERENCES

1. BROWN, ANDREW W. "The Development and Standardization of the Chicago Non-Verbal Examination." *J Appl Psychol* 24:36–47, 122–9 F, Ap '40. * (*PA* 14:3774, 4767)
2. BROWN, ANDREW W., AND COTTON, CAROL B. "A Study of the Intelligence of Italian and Polish School Children From Deteriorated and Non-Deteriorated Areas of Chicago as Measured by the Chicago Non-Verbal Examination." *Child Develop* 12:21–30 Mr '41. * (*PA* 15:3486)
3. JOHNSON, ELIZABETH HUGHES. "The Effect of Academic Level on Scores From the Chicago Non-Verbal Examination for Primary Pupils." *Am Ann Deaf* 92:227–33 My '47. *
4. ALLEN, ROBERT M., AND BESSELL, HAROLD. "Intercorrelations Among Group Verbal and Non-Verbal Tests of Intelligence." *J Ed Res* 43:394–5 Ja '50. * (*PA* 24:4841)
5. EWING, R. M. *The Standardization of the Chicago Non-Verbal Examination on English-Speaking School Children Living in Nova Scotia.* Master's thesis, Acadia University (Wolfville, N.S., Canada), 1950. Pp. 79.
6. LAVOS, GEORGE. "The Chicago Non-Verbal Examination: A Study in Re-Test Characteristics." *Am Ann Deaf* 95:379–86 S '50. *
7. ROPER, GEORGE E. *Study of the Use of the Chicago Non-Verbal Examination in a Rural Psychiatric Clinic.* Master's thesis, Acadia University (Wolfville, N.S., Canada), 1952. Pp. 59.
8. NEWLAND, T. ERNEST, AND LAWRENCE, WILLIAM C. "Chicago Non-Verbal Examination Results on an East Tennessee Negro Population." *J Clin Psychol* 9:44–7 Ja '53. * (*PA* 27:7718)
9. LAVOS, GEORGE. "Interrelationships Among Three Tests of Non-Language Intelligence Administered to the Deaf." *Am Ann Deaf* 99:303–13 My '54. * (*PA* 29:4596)
10. LEVINE, BERT, AND ISCOE, IRA. "The Progressive Matrices (1938), the Chicago Non-Verbal, and the Wechsler Bellevue on an Adolescent Deaf Population." *J Clin Psychol* 11:307–8 Jl '55. * (*PA* 30:3334)

RALEIGH M. DRAKE, *Professor of Psychology, Kent State University, Kent, Ohio.*

This test was designed to minimize the English language factor in testing children from

[2] This point has been very fully discussed by Godfrey H. Thomson in *The 1940 Mental Measurements Yearbook.*

age 6 through the adult level. It is not a culture free test in which most environmental influences have been eliminated. On the contrary, it is very much culture bound and would be inappropriate in cultures dissimilar to ours. Even in the United States not all of the pictorial objects would be equally familiar to children in different parts of the country and some pictures are now out of date. A more serious feature is that many of the pictures are so small and vaguely drawn that the picture object or meaning is difficult to determine.

The test has been standardized with both verbal and pantomime directions. The standardization group numbered 3,778 with verbal directions and 2,260 with pantomime directions, respectable numbers for tests constructed in 1936. Although the sample was all from Chicago or nearby schools, reasonable attention was given to representativeness; in this respect, the test should be equal to most other general ability tests.

The reliability of .89 (split-half, corrected) reported for a group of 334 children aged 8 to 13 inclusive seems to be spuriously high, considering that the test correlates above .70 with age for a group with a similar age range. Since it is a point scale attempting to cover an extremely wide age range, most of the items are either too easy or too difficult for the average testee, a factor which in effect reduces the length of the test and therefore its reliability. Validity data show correlations of from .51 with mental ages on the *Kuhlmann-Anderson Intelligence Test* with chronological age constant, to .67 with IQ's on the *Otis Self-Administering Tests of Mental Ability* with an age range from 8 to 15 years. With age partialled out, this would probably be reduced to about .50. Correlations with the Stanford-Binet are not reported, although data from at least two groups were available showing average IQ's from the two tests to be almost identical. Although the averages were almost the same, there was an average difference in individual scores of 9.0 in one group and 7.3 in the other.

Since SD's for ages 6 to adult vary from 17.6 to 22.2, compared to 12.5 to 19 for the Stanford-Binet, there is a general tendency for the Chicago IQ equivalents (reported as standard scores in the manual) to run higher for scores above the mean and lower for scores below the mean. The farther the score is from the mean the greater is this tendency. Therefore, IQ's obtained from either test would have to vary considerably from those obtained from the other. A similar variability would occur if the same child were to be retested several times at different ages. Likewise, the IQ's (standard scores) from the test given with verbal directions are not directly comparable to scores resulting from the use of pantomime directions, SD's at various ages averaging almost 3 points higher under the latter procedure. On the average, there is about a 7-months' difference between MA's derived from the same raw score under the two types of directions. The separate standardization takes care of some of this variability, but not all. The test was never given to the same group under both types of directions and no direct comparison of scores is therefore possible. If the test with pantomime directions is to be used for testing the deaf and for non-English speaking children, which is reported as its main function, this rather large nonequivalence either to the verbal directions form or to the Stanford-Binet or any other test could be a serious disadvantage. Other tests also suffer from this same variability, of course, which is a common source of error in interpreting all converted IQ's.

Considering the demands made upon it (one test is expected to measure sensitively a complex ability like intelligence from age 6 to the adult level in 25 minutes of working time and 80 test items, plus two substitution tests), the results are not too disappointing. Nonetheless, the test is in need of considerable restandardizing, lengthening, and redrawing before it can be depended upon for individual diagnosis.

For reviews by Robert G. Bernreuter, Myrtle Luneau Pignatelli, and S. D. Porteus, see 40: 1387.

[317]
★**Classification Test 40-A.** Job applicants; 1957; 1 form; preliminary mimeographed manual; no data on reliability; no norms; separate answer sheets must be used; PPA member agency: 10–49 tests, 54¢ each; others, 68¢ each; $2 per specimen set; postpaid; 50-(60) minutes; Public Personnel Association. *

[318]
*College Entrance Examination Board Scholastic Aptitude Test.** Candidates for college entrance; 1926–58; for more complete information, see 599; 2 scores: verbal, mathematical; IBM; 180(240) minutes; program administered by Educational Testing Service for the College Entrance Examination Board. *

REFERENCES
1–22. See 4:285.
23. MYERS, ROBERT COBB. "Biographical Factors and Aca-

demic Achievement: An Experimental Investigation." *Ed & Psychol Meas* 12:415-26 au '52. * (*PA* 27:6158)
24. NEWMAN, SIDNEY H.; FRENCH, JOHN W.; AND BOBBITT, JOSEPH M. "Analysis of Criteria for the Validation of Selection Measures at the United States Coast Guard Academy." *Ed & Psychol Meas* 12:394-407 au '52. * (*PA* 27:6159)
25. PRESTON, RALPH C., AND BOTEL, MORTON. "The Relation of Reading Skill and Other Factors to the Academic Achievement of 2048 College Students." *J Exp Ed* 20:363-71 Je '52. * (*PA* 27:2967)
26. ALLISON, ROGER B., JR. "Comparison of Reading Comprehension Items and Verbal Items From the Scholastic Aptitude Test." Abstract. *Am Psychol* 8:311 Ag '53. *
27. DYER, HENRY S. "Does Coaching Help?" *Col Board R* (19):331-5 F '53. * (*PA* 28:1559)
28. WEBB, SAM C., AND MCCALL, JOHN N. "Predictors of Freshman Grades in a Southern University." *Ed & Psychol Meas* 13:660-3 w '53. * (*PA* 28:6598)
29. MALECKI, GERALD S. *Effectiveness of the College Entrance Board Scholastic Aptitude Test, American Council on Education Psychological Examination, and High School Average for Predicting First Semester Scholarship at Fordham College.* Master's thesis, Fordham University (New York, N.Y.), 1954.
30. OLSEN, MARJORIE A., AND SCHRADER, WILLIAM B. "A Comparison of Item Types in the College Board Scholastic Aptitude Test." Abstract. *Am Psychol* 9:445 Ag '54. *
31. PEARSON, RICHARD. "Equating the Scholastic Aptitude Test." *Col Board R* (23):449-50 My '54. *
32. SEASHORE, HAROLD. "Tenth Grade Tests as Predictors of Twelfth Grade Scholarship and College Entrance Status." Comment by David V. Tiedeman. *J Counsel Psychol* 1:106-15 su '54. * (*PA* 29:3054)
33. BOYD, JOSEPH D. *The Relative Prognostic Value of Selected Criteria in Predicting Beginning Academic Success at Northwestern University.* Doctor's thesis, Northwestern University (Evanston, Ill.), 1955. (*DA* 15:1780)
34. FRENCH, JOHN W. "An Answer to Test Coaching: Public School Experiment With the SAT." *Col Board R* (27):5-7 fall '55. * (*PA* 32:2107)
35. PARRES, JOHN G. *Prediction of Academic Success in the Undergraduate Schools of the University of Pennsylvania.* Doctor's thesis, University of Pennsylvania (Philadelphia, Pa.), 1955. (*DA* 15:2105)
36. COLLEGE ENTRANCE EXAMINATION BOARD. *A Description of the College Board Scholastic Aptitude Test.* Princeton, N.J.: Educational Testing Service, 1956. Pp. 64. * (*PA* 31:1745)
37. LEVINE, RICHARD L., AND ANGOFF, WILLIAM H. "The Effect of Practice on Scores on the Scholastic Aptitude Test of the College Entrance Examination Board." Abstract. *Am Psychol* 11:423 Ag '56. *
38. ANGOFF, WILLIAM H. "The 'Equating' of Non-Parallel Tests." *J Exp Ed* 25:241-7 Mr '57. *
39. EVENSON, A. B., AND SMITH, D. E. "A Study of Matriculation in Alberta." *Alberta J Ed Res* 4:67-83 Je '58. *
40. FEENEY, MARY MARTHA. *Scores on SAT-V and Survey of Study Habits and Attitudes as Predictors of Achievement in a College for Women.* Master's thesis, Fordham University (New York, N.Y.), 1958.
41. FRENCH, JOHN W. "Validation of New Item Types Against Four-Year Academic Criteria." *J Ed Psychol* 49:67-76 Ap '58. *
42. GUMMERE, JOHN F. "Scholastic Aptitude Test Scores of SEB Member Schools." *Sch & Soc* 86:197-8 Ap 26 '58. *

JOHN T. DAILEY, *Program Director, American Institute for Research, Washington, D.C.*

This test consists of five sections, each with a 30-minute time limit. The first three, containing mixtures of completion items, opposites, analogies, and paragraph comprehension exercises, are scored together as a verbal subtest; the last two, designated as Arithmetic Reasoning, although they include considerable algebra and elementary geometry, are scored as a mathematical subtest. Standard scores are available separately for the two subtests.

While a considerable number of applicants will not finish within the time allowed, the manual suggests that the test is essentially unspeeded because the items are arranged in order of difficulty. Several analyses indicate that the tests do appear for the most part to lack "speededness" since most of the items omitted seem to be beyond the level of the candidate. The two subscores are of adequate reliability to be used separately, the reported reliabilities being in the vicinity of .90. Standard errors of measurement are given for raw and scaled scores.

A tremendous amount of normative and analytical data regarding the test are published in the manuals. In addition, there are a very large number of validity studies for different schools with many different kinds of groups and criteria. The usual pattern of validities is found against course grades. Particular attention is given to the problem of test-retest effect and to the susceptibility of the test to "cram schools." Studies indicate it is relatively "cram resistant."

The large amount of normative data available in the manuals is probably the most valuable aspect of the test. For example, the *1957 Supplement to College Board Scores No. 2* contains 32 pages of norms for various types of candidates. Results are shown separately for public schools and independent schools, and for all schools, for preliminary and final candidates; boys and girls; students in liberal arts, engineering, and other curricula; transfer students; and college sophomores.

The test is essentially a conventional, general abstract "intelligence" test at the bright adult level. This can probably be said with equal truth of any of its competitors. It does a very effective job of estimating liberal arts scholarship potential and should be interpreted as just that and used accordingly in deciding on admission of a given applicant. The primary value of the test lies in the availability of annual forms, adequate security, and extremely voluminous normative and analytical statistical data.

For a review by Frederick B. Davis of earlier forms, see 4:285.

[319]
★**College Placement Test.** College entrants; 1957; 3 scores: verbal, quantitative, total; IBM; Form 1 ['57]; preliminary manual; $1 per student when scored by publisher; separate answer sheets must be used; $9.80 per 20 tests; $5 per 100 IBM answer sheets; 50¢ per either hand or machine scoring stencil; 35¢ per manual; $1.50 per specimen set; postage extra; 180-(200) minutes; Science Research Associates.*

GUSTAV J. FROEHLICH, *Assistant Director, Bureau of Institutional Research, University of Illinois, Urbana, Illinois.*

The *College Placement Test* is a power test of scholastic ability, designed to be administered in one session of 3 hours or less. It is similar in form and content to a number of currently available group intelligence tests for high school seniors and college freshmen. The test consists of 150 multiple choice items. The first half yields a verbal score; the last half, a quantitative score.

The verbal part is essentially a reading test consisting of 37 verbal relations items (synonyms, antonyms, analogies, sentence completions) and 38 paragraph comprehension questions based on reading passages from college social studies and biological sciences materials. The quantitative part of the test has 38 items involving the interpretation of various tables, graphs, figures and charts, and a 37-item high school mathematics reasoning test including algebra and geometry.

CPT scores, when used in conjunction with the interpretative data given in the test manual, yield useful predictions of college success. Hence, this test is essentially a guidance instrument which can be helpful to both college admissions officers and high school counselors in advising those who have college aspirations. It is not a "placement" test in the sense that it would provide a direct basis for assignment to advanced courses or to noncredit remedial courses.

The internal validity of the test is apparent. The content and language of the test items appear to be consistent with college performance situations. Reading passages, tables, graphs, figures, and charts are such as one would expect to find in college textbooks and references. The construction, analysis, and refinement of the test items were undertaken by three individuals whose competence as test construction specialists is unquestioned. All of the items were pretested on appropriate experimental groups and were selected on the basis of their difficulty level and internal consistency. The items are presented in the test in approximate order of difficulty and are arranged in blocks of similar item types.

The test shows a high positive correlation ($r = .68$, based on 590 cases) with the *Army General Classification Test*. The CPT has also demonstrated factorial validity, yielding measures of three separate factors of intelligence—general, language (more appropriately called reading comprehension), and quantitative ability.

Research studies have shown the feasibility of establishing equivalencies between total raw scores on the CPT and standard scores on the AGCT; and similarly, with standard scores on the *Selected Service College Qualification Test*. These equivalencies, along with percentile norms, are shown in the manual. Tentative equivalencies between raw V and Q scores and standard V and M scores, respectively, on the *Scholastic Aptitude Test* of the College Entrance Examination Board program are also shown in the manual, but further confirmation studies are necessary before these part score equivalences can be accepted as having been established.

From the percentile norms it can be inferred that the CPT has a great amount of "ceiling" (the 99th percentile for college freshmen begins at a total raw score of 118, out of a possible 150). As a matter of fact, as of the date of the manual, no perfect score had been recorded. On the other hand, the test probably has an inadequate "floor" for some college groups. There are a number of instances of record where the total raw score has been found to be below 30, the "chance" score on a 150-item five choice test.

It is the contention of its publishers, and rightly so, that the predictive validity of the CPT must be established for each different type of college and university—ideally for each institution separately. To this end the publishers have expressed a willingness to cooperate in such studies with any college or university interested to do so. To date, there have been only a limited number of such studies, but the results warrant the statement that the predictive validity of the test is as good as, or better than, most other currently available single predictive indices of overall academic success in college.

It has been shown that for Purdue University the total score on the CPT correlates .57 with freshman grade-point index, as compared with a correlation of .40 between high school rank and grade-point index. As a matter of fact, each one of the subtests was found to have a higher zero order correlation with grade-point index than the .40 found for high school rank. The Purdue study also showed that the test has a higher predictive validity than the *Purdue Orientation Tests*—a battery of three tests constructed especially for use on the Purdue campus.

Available studies of the reliability of CPT scores show total score reliabilities to be in the low .90's, V and Q score reliabilities in the middle .80's, and coefficients for the four different subtests ranging from the low .70's to the high .80's. The verbal relations subtest (Items 1–28) consistently shows the lowest subtest reliability. Taking into account the fact that the population tested to obtain the above reliability coefficients is a relatively homogeneous one, and also the fact that the inflationary effect of speed is entirely eliminated, it appears that adequate reliability has been demonstrated.

The test is entirely objective and provides for the use of a separate electrographic answer sheet. A special scoring stencil enables the answer sheet to be either machine or hand scored with a minimum of effort. Directions for administration and scoring are clear, concise, and adequate.

The only real objection this reviewer has is with respect to the format and choice of type for Items 29 through 66. These pages are too crowded, and the type for the reading passages is too small. The layout is conducive to unnecessary mental fatigue, and may prove to be an unnecessary stumbling block to those having even a minor visual deficiency. Similarly, the explanatory materials under the weather map and the detail in the airline schedule are hard to read.

The *College Placement Test* can provide useful predictions of college success in a variety of institutions when used by trained counselors and guidance personnel who are conscious of the pitfalls inherent in the use of any predictive index which is significantly better than a chance guess, but is still subject to considerable statistical "error." Its predictive validity has been demonstrated for a limited number of institutions; but further studies for a larger number of schools should be made. At the same time additional studies to determine the predictive efficiency of this test when used in combination with high school rank are in order. Finally, the validity of the V and Q score as predictive indices for specific curricular areas should be explored further.

DAVID V. TIEDEMAN, *Associate Professor of Education, Harvard University, Cambridge, Massachusetts.*

The *College Placement Test* is a power test which most college students are reported to finish in less than 2 hours. The verbal section consists of an approximately equal number of vocabulary items (synonyms, antonyms, analogies, and sentence completions) and of questions regarding comprehension of written material. Paragraphs are similar to textbook material encountered in several areas of college study. The quantitative section consists of an approximately equal number of items requiring the interpretation of data (tables, graphs, figures, and charts) and of items requiring quantitative reasoning of an algebraic and geometric kind when formulas are supplied. There are 75 items in each section. Perhaps it is this small number of items that makes the split-half reliability coefficients of the section scores only about .87 in a sample of college students. The standard error of measurement of each score is not reported.

The paragraph comprehension items and the data interpretation items are representative of the tasks facing college students in their courses. But the inclusion of these types of item material gives the factor structure of the test a peculiar cast. The reported factor analysis of four subscores (derived by scoring separately the two types of verbal material and the two types of quantitative material) indicates a definite "general" factor in all four tests with subsidiary Q (quantitative ability) and L (language ability) factors. But Q is more oriented by the data interpretation subtest than by the arithmetic reasoning subtest, and paragraph comprehension has a slight loading on the Q factor. L, on the other hand, is primarily oriented by paragraph comprehension; verbal relations and data interpretation have equal but secondary loadings on this factor. Thus, some caution should surround placing the V and Q scores of this test in the same system as the L and Q scores of the *American Council on Education Psychological Examination* and the V and N scores of the *College Qualification Tests*.

The manual treats in some detail (e.g., intercorrelations, multiple correlations, and factor analysis) four subscores which are not recommended for general use. This suggests that two verbal subtest scores and two quantitative subtest scores may have been under consideration at some time during the development of the test but that the four subtests were finally judged to be too interdependent to warrant separation into more than two sections.

With the "general" factor running through the CPT so definitely, it is somewhat surprising to find that the few predictive validity coefficients reported for the total score do not press nearer to .60 more frequently than they do. For the most part, validity coefficients for the total score run from .40 to .57.

The publishers have taken great pains to tie the CPT total score in with standard scores of the *Army General Classification Test* and with standard scores of the *Selective Service College Qualification Test*. The CPT is well anchored to a generally understood median of the AGCT and of the SSCQT. There is one trouble, however. CPT and AGCT are reported to correlate to the extent of only .68 in one sample. The standard error of estimating an AGCT score from a CPT score is 73 per cent of the standard deviation of the AGCT scores in this case. Thus, the CPT does not give a very good estimate of an AGCT score even though equi-percentile points are very well equated. The correlation of CPT and SSCQT is not reported. This does not matter so much for the purpose of selection as it does for the purpose of counseling.

The manual presents a table for converting V and Q scores on this test into equivalent V and M scores on the *Scholastic Aptitude Test*. Correlations between supposedly similar scores on the CPT and SAT are not reported; interpretation of the table of equivalencies should await the report of such correlations.

The manual for the CPT was designated as "preliminary" as of September 1957. In these circumstances, it is advisable for colleges to experiment with the test before making it operational. With the CPT, experimentation may proceed either independently or in collaboration with the publisher since the test is offered either for sale in the usual manner or as part of a service including scoring, development of local norms, and planning of local validity studies. Since the V and Q scores of the test are of seeming relevance for study in college, the test is likely to have at least some predictive validity in most colleges, as is suggested by the several predictive validity studies already reported.

Until the results of such experimentation are made available by the publisher or others, this test is of little or no help to a high school pupil in relation to his planning of college attendance. The reviewer would not yet make application of experience with the AGCT, the SSCQT, the ACE, or the SAT to the interpretation of scores on the CPT in individual cases. The translation of experience with these tests into the scores of the CPT is probably justifiable if the purpose is selective admission to college.

[320]

★**College Qualification Tests.** Candidates for college entrance; 1955-58; also called CQT; 6 scores: verbal, numerical, science information, social science information, total information, total; IBM; Forms A, B ('56); 2 editions; manual ('57); supplement ('58); distribution of Form B restricted to colleges and universities; separate answer sheets must be used; postpaid; George K. Bennett, Marjorie G. Bennett, Wimburn L. Wallace, and Alexander G. Wesman; Psychological Corporation. *
a) COMBINED BOOKLET EDITION. $5 per 25 tests; $3.50 per 50 IBM answer sheets; 60¢ per specimen set; 80(105) minutes.
b) SEPARATE BOOKLET EDITION. $2.50 per 25 tests; $1.90 per 50 IBM answer sheets; 90¢ per specimen set.
  1) *Test V.* Verbal; 15(25) minutes.
  2) *Test N.* Numerical; 35(45) minutes.
  3) *Test I.* 3 scores: science information, social science information, total; 30(40) minutes.

GUSTAV J. FROEHLICH, *Assistant Director, Bureau of Institutional Research, University of Illinois, Urbana, Illinois.*

The *College Qualification Tests* are a series of three ability tests developed for use by college admissions officers and guidance personnel. High school counselors may also find the test data helpful in advising those who want to go on to college.

Test V, Verbal, consists of 75 vocabulary items—50 synonyms and 25 antonyms. Test N, Numerical, contains 50 items, drawing on arithmetic, algebra, and geometry. It is aimed at conceptual skill in simple mathematics, not at computational or clerical speed. Test I, Information, has 75 items and yields, in addition to the overall information score, a separate science information score (based on 38 items drawn from the fields of biology, chemistry, and physics), and a separate social studies information score (based on 37 items drawn from the fields of economics, geography, government, and history).

Even though the tests are timed, they apparently function as power tests in that the time limits seem to be generous enough to permit all those who actually have college ability to attempt all of the items.

Everywhere throughout the test booklets and the manual there is evidence of careful planning, rigid adherence to the principles of good test construction, and adequate experimentation and research prior to putting the tests on the market. The mechanics of the tests—format, wording, type, and directions—are well executed.

It is the contention of the authors and publishers, and rightly so, that the approach to meaningful norms is through specific identification of the institutions and the individuals which make up the norms sample. Thus, a number of different sets of norms are in order, broken down not only by sex, but by type of institution and by curriculum. To this end, in addition to general percentile norms for college freshmen given separately for men and women, the manual contains the special sets of norms for freshmen in different types of colleges and universities and for freshmen in different types of curricula.

The most important single characteristic of a test is its validity. The *College Qualification Tests* were developed to serve as predictors of academic success in college courses. The elaborate table of validity coefficients reported (correlations between raw test scores and first semester college grade-point averages) indicates that the tests can serve a useful purpose by yielding estimates of probable success in the first semester of college which are significantly better than chance guesses. Furthermore, it is immediately evident from this table that the validity of the tests varies from one institution to another. Hence, it is suggested that each college which plans to use the tests extensively should develop its own set of norms. One factor which strongly influences test validity thus determined is the reliability of course grades; this, we know, varies considerably from institution to institution and from curriculum to curriculum within a given institution.

The manual reports both reliability coefficients and standard errors of measurement based upon a sampling of students whose score means and variances are comparable to those of the normative population. The reliabilities are adequate—in the middle .90's for the total score and from the high .70's through the low .90's for the subtests. No data are shown for the more homogeneous populations represented in the several special sets of norms.

The verbal and numerical tests are similar to those found in a number of currently available group intelligence tests at the freshman college level. The information test represents the conviction of the authors that a measure of educational background which the student brings to college will be indicative of his future learning and will be a more effective predictive index than high school grades, which are subject to considerable unreliability. Some justification for this is evident from the fact that a number of the validity coefficients reported for the information subtests are higher than those usually reported for rank in high school class.

The *College Qualification Tests* are well constructed instruments. They should be useful to college admission officers and high school counselors.

A. E. G. Pilliner, *Lecturer in Experimental Education, University of Edinburgh, Edinburgh, Scotland.*

For general layout and clarity of presentation of items, this pair of parallel tests is outstandingly good. Scoring, by whichever method is chosen, is simple. The manual is not only explicit in stating the purpose of the tests and in detailing the considerations which have guided the constructors in their work, but also presents a wealth of statistical information by the study of which the extent of their success in achieving their goals can be assessed. The instructions for administration are a model of clarity and conciseness.

The basic principles were laid down by an advisory committee of psychologists and educationists, "having responsibility for the college student at the time of entrance," who listed a number of requirements to be met in constructing tests to be used for selecting college students. Their main points are: (*a*) the tests should be broadly predictive of college success and suitable for many curricula; (*b*) they should stress power rather than speed; (*c*) they should serve several purposes, namely, selection, placement, and counseling; (*d*) comparability of tests should be ensured by having them normed on the same population; (*e*) the times and places of their administration should be at the discretion of the colleges using them; and (*f*) for reasons of security, the use of at least one form of the tests should be restricted to the colleges.

It may be said at once that the tests do in fact meet many of these requirements. The manual indicates that the committee's points (*d*), (*e*), and (*f*) have been successfully covered. By working through the tests himself, this reviewer was able to confirm their point (*b*). With regard to point (*a*), the validity coefficients published in profusion in the manual demonstrate that, provided one accepts first semester grade-point averages as an adequate criterion of college success, the tests predict as well as might be expected in a variety of different situations. This reviewer must, however, record his agreement with Guilford, who, discussing a previous test published by the Psychological Corporation, wrote, "Those of us who train students beyond the M.A. level know well that there are often great discrepancies in both directions between grade-getting abilities and capacities for independent thinking and research" (see 4:304).

With regard to point (c), this reviewer, while sympathising with the constructors' intention to make the tests multipurpose, must confess to some doubts as to the success likely to be achieved. For selection purposes, subject to what has been said about the adequacy of the present criterion, the tests appear to be efficient. For the kindred tasks of placement and counseling, the evidence is less convincing. Short of an *ad hoc* experiment which, while easy to design could scarcely be carried out in a democratic country, it is difficult to see how really convincing evidence could be obtained in relation to one specific test or battery of tests. We can never know what a student's grades might have been in a group of studies other than that he has in fact undertaken. Nevertheless, something might emerge indirectly from a comparison of the grade scores of students who had accepted advice based on their performances on the several parts of this series with the grade scores of students who had not done so.

As for psychometric quality: (a) The tables of norms in the manual show that each form successfully exercises discrimination over the whole range of already accepted students tested —no mean achievement within a total testing time of 80 minutes. The tests, that is, possess the first prerequisite of a selection instrument. (b) Having regard to the nature of the groups tested, reliability (internal consistency) is high, ranging from .95 for the verbal test to .80 for the social studies subtest, with .97 overall. So far as they go, these figures are satisfactory, but it would have been useful to know also the parallel-forms reliability. (c) Validity, as already mentioned, is reasonably high. The mean of the 24 validity coefficients based on total score is .55. (d) The intercorrelations among the parts range from .71 for verbal and social studies to .45 for numerical and social studies. (e) CQT correlates quite well with other scholastic aptitude tests, for example, .78 with the ACE and .82 with SCAT.

Few institutions using these tests will fail to find among the 11 sets of percentile norms (8 of these for men and women separately) that most appropriate to their requirements. Even so, test users are rightly urged to develop their own local norms which, to quote from the manual, "are, of course, more important for a particular school than are any published norms."

To sum up: the presentation of these tests and of their manual is technically excellent. So far as their limited objective of predicting grade-point averages goes, they are at least the equal of other tests having the same purpose. They should prove useful in selecting college students, but the claim that they can assist in counseling and placing in courses needs (and, it is hoped, will receive) confirmation.

DAVID V. TIEDEMAN, *Associate Professor of Education, Harvard University, Cambridge, Massachusetts.*

Test V consists of 75 vocabulary items requiring identification of synonyms or antonyms. The V score correlates highly with the L score of the *American Council on Education Psychological Examination* (ACE) and with the verbal score of the *Cooperative School and College Ability Tests* (SCAT).

Test N consists of 50 items requiring application of arithmetical, algebraic, and geometrical concepts. The N score correlates highly with the quantitative score of the SCAT, but the correlation of the CQT-N score with the ACE-Q score is only around .55.

Test I, Information, consists of 38 questions of a "scientific" nature and 37 questions of a "social studies" nature. Each of these tests correlates reasonably well with its counterpart in the *Cooperative General Achievement Test*, Form XX. Study of Test I reveals, however, that the subject does not have to reason very much with the concepts of either science or social studies to answer the questions. He will either have the answer to a question at his fingertips or not. The science items demand information accumulated in biology, chemistry, and physics. The social studies items demand information of an economic, geographical, legal, or political nature. Amount of information in

College Qualification Tests

either science or social studies correlates with first semester grade average as well as V or N scores do. Because of the relatively high correlation of scores of information about science and social studies with scores of either V or N, however, scores on these tests of information will add very little to the predictive efficiency of V and N scores. In addition, the slight variation of the average score in science and social studies information according to the degree program in which a freshman is enrolled suggests that these scores of science and social studies information will not be terribly useful in advising about degree programs. The scores are, of course, relevant for assessing the amount of information a student has stockpiled in each of these areas and hence *may* be indicative of interest in the area. But perhaps it might be easier and more valid to ask directly about interest in the fields. Hence the reviewer is of the opinion that Test I is not too useful.

Statistics on Forms A and B are reasonably comparable but the reviewer is more concerned about the "somewhat more perceptible" difference in averages for the total score of Test I than are the authors. In the first place, the difference in averages on the two forms is significant in the case of both men and women. The averages do not differ only randomly. Secondly, the difference in averages for men is 1.5 points, for women 1.8 points. Since the standard deviations for the two forms are similar in the data for either men and women, these differences indicate that the Form B distribution is almost everywhere 1.5 points above the Form A distribution for men and 1.8 points above the Form A distribution for women. The consequences of these circumstances can be illustrated in terms of the general norms for college freshmen. For men, in the percentile range from 5 to 95 inclusive, there are four percentile rank classes which are designated by a single score on Test I. The percentile rank of a score on Form B which should really be in one of these percentile rank classes will actually appear to be 5 percentile ranks higher. The same advantage of 5 percentile ranks will be associated with approximately one half of the scores in the 11 percentile rank classes which are defined by 2 raw score points and with approximately one third of the scores in the 4 percentile rank classes defined by 3 raw score points. The situation is even worse in the data for women. Finally, the differences in average scores of Forms A and B for Test I are between four and five tenths of the standard error of measurement for a score obtained either by a man or by a woman. This is too great an eliminable bias to leave in the interpretation of a true score on either Form A or B of Test I. In the case of Test I, scores on either form are not "directly comparable with scores earned on the other form." This does not negate the other conclusion that any differences "are still small enough so that averages based on combined scores yield sufficiently representative data to warrant merging the distributions."

Test V, Test N, Test I, and total scores are quite reliable. The science and social studies scores, however, are less reliable as the manual warns.

The CQT are offered to colleges for the purposes of selective admissions, placement in sections, and counseling. Since the CQT scores correlate with first semester grade average in several colleges to as high a degree as one usually obtains for such tests, a college would probably increase its pool of desired students by using the tests for the purpose of selective admissions *provided* the college considered its circumstances like the specified circumstances of the 14 colleges for which data are briefly reported. The manual provides no information of relevance for sectioning classes except for those colleges which have previously sectioned classes on the basis of the ACE or SCAT. The manual provides norms for freshmen *intending* to study for the A.B. or B.S. degree or to study in programs of business, education, engineering, technical fields, or nursing. Therefore, the tests are of some slight use in counseling with regard to the competition a student might face under several alternatives. However, the distributions of scores for those pursuing the several alternatives overlap too much to permit fine distinctions of this kind. The extensive norms and the completeness with which data on predictive validity are reported mean that the CQT are an important source of information in counseling with regard to ability to pursue collegiate study.

The CQT will be sold to high schools. Although norms are extensive and based on large numbers of cases, high school counselors should realize that only the 37 institutions listed in the manual are represented. In addition, counselors must rely upon their own prototypes of these institutions because no characteristics of an educational kind are associated with the norms save for the test scores themselves.

Psychometrically the tests are quite sound. Technically, the manual, test booklet, answer sheet, and scoring stencil are fine. Adequate time limits are provided for each test. Many mistakes will be made in getting the science and social studies scores in Test I by hand. In addition, the reviewer does not consider Test I to be very useful. Nevertheless, the CQT are ready for use by anyone capable of understanding the cautions the publisher explicitly incorporates throughout the manual. An informed person can immediately use these tests for any purpose for which they are offered, viz., selective admission to college, placement of students in sections (provided the ACE or SCAT was formerly used for this purpose), and counseling of high school students about college intentions and, to a slight degree, of college students about degree programs.

[321]

★**Concept Mastery Test.** Grades 15–16 and graduate students; 1956, c1950; IBM; Form T ('56); manual ('56); separate answer sheets must be used; $3 per 25 tests; $1.90 per 50 IBM answer sheets; 35¢ per specimen set; postpaid; (35–45) minutes; Lewis M. Terman; Psychological Corporation. *

REFERENCES

1. THORNDIKE, ROBERT L. "An Evaluation of the Adult Intellectual Status of Terman's Gifted Children." *J Genetic Psychol* 72:17–27 Mr '48. * (PA 22:4836)
2. BAYLEY, NANCY, AND ODEN, MELITA H. "The Maintenance of Intellectual Ability in Gifted Adults." *J Gerontol* 10:91–107 Ja '55. * (PA 30:2583)
3. BARTHOL, RICHARD P., AND KIRK, BARBARA A. "The Selection of Graduate Students in Public Health Education." *J Appl Psychol* 40:159–63 Je '56. * (PA 31:6666)
4. TAYLOR, DONALD W. "Variables Related to Creativity and Productivity Among Men in Two Research Laboratories." In *The Identification of Creative Scientific Talent.* Edited by Calvin W. Taylor. Salt Lake City, Utah: University of Utah Press, 1958.

J. A. KEATS, *Senior Lecturer in Psychology, University of Queensland, Brisbane, Australia.*

Perhaps the most interesting point about the *Concept Mastery Test* is that it is a by-product of Terman's extensive studies of gifted children and of these same children in adult life. The test is a high level verbal test for adults. It is untimed, but usually takes about 40 minutes to complete.

The test contains two types of items. In the first part are standard synonym-antonym items which rely for their difficulty on rather unusual vocabulary. Those in the second part are items of the analogy type, but this form is used with number items as well as verbal problems covering general knowledge and relationships between terms. The title "concept mastery" seems too broad to cover such restricted content. Coverage of what the reviewer understands by this title would require a battery of tests and the result would not be summarized in a single score. Terman concedes this point but claims that the test gives as good an indication of a person's ability to deal with abstract concepts as can be obtained in this limited time. In such circumstances, it would seem better to choose a more precise title.

The correlation between the two parts is .76 for the subjects of the Stanford Gifted Study for whom the test was intended. This figure is probably not very much below what the parallel forms reliability of either part computed separately would be; thus, a single score is justified. Reliability was found to lie between .86 and .94 using a parallel form of the test. With the gifted subjects, similar figures were obtained after a lapse of 12 years.

The test distinguishes clearly between adults of different educational levels and has shown the usual validity for such tests as predictors of success in university courses. Correlations between CMT and a number of other tests are provided in the manual.

Because of the two simple forms of presenting the problems, the need for complicated and detailed instructions is largely removed. Directions to be stressed deal entirely with the requirements for machine scoring and not with explanation of item forms.

Norms in the form of percentile ranks in 5 per cent intervals are provided for four groups of subjects. However, those based on the gifted subjects are the only norms obtained from a sample of more than 200 cases. Thus, the only satisfactory norms from the point of view of stability are for a rather special group. This lack of suitable norms limits the usefulness of the test.

It is interesting to note how many of the gifted subjects obtained high scores on a test requiring a wide background of information and knowledge of rare words. However, the claim that the test is "a measure of ability to deal with abstract ideas" needs further substantiation. The test may have value as a selection and guidance instrument, but the prospective user would have to carry out more preliminary standardization and validation work than would be required if he were to use some other tests currently available.

College Qualification Tests

CALVIN W. TAYLOR, *Professor of Psychology, University of Utah, Salt Lake City, Utah.*

Since no intellectual test was available that met the needs of Terman's follow-up studies of the gifted, the *Concept Mastery Test* was devised to reach into the stratosphere of adult intelligence by use of synonyms, antonyms, and verbal analogy items. From data presented in the manual, it would seem that the test served its purpose well.

In the follow-up studies Form A was administered in 1939–40 and Form T (earlier called Form B) in 1951–52. Form T, which is now being marketed, was designed to match all except the most difficult items in the earlier Form A and to extend the scale downward, making it suitable for wider use as a selection and a counseling tool. The items are arranged in order of difficulty and use concepts from a variety of fields.

The new claims for Form T are that it is suitable for testing college juniors and seniors, graduate students, and adults who are being considered for research, executive, and other unusually demanding jobs. Percentile norms are presented solely for specially selected groups and for one group of graduate students, with only means and standard deviations presented for college juniors and seniors. There is little doubt, however, that a wide variability in scores would occur on juniors, seniors, or graduate students.

Although the test deals with verbal concepts and abstractions, the examinee merely has to recognize such concepts, not to produce them. The author readily admits that this test does not tap all the kinds of intellect. He has stated that some aspects of intelligence, such as creative intelligence or the ability to make new mental constructs, are so elusive that man has been unable so far to map or quantify them adequately.

Donald Taylor (4) found that Form T correlated only .11 with undergraduate grades in the last two years and failed to correlate significantly with any supervisory ratings in research laboratories for creativity, productivity, originality, quality of work, or quantity of work. The test correlated at least moderately with the Owens-Bennett *Test of Mechanical Comprehension*, the *Test for Productive Thinking*, and the *Test for Selecting Research Personnel*, the highest correlation being with the least valid part of the last test. Every score from the above three tests had significant validities with the supervisor's creativity rating, while the *Concept Mastery Test* failed to have a significant validity. Apparently, the *Concept Mastery Test* is better in earlier academic situations and tends to lose some validity against later criteria. The main positive evidence known to the reviewer of the test's validity for the newly advertised purposes, as distinct from the Terman study purposes, is indirect evidence through its correlates. The evidence of validity for the initial purposes may or may not be very highly related to its new uses on advanced students and for predicting certain criteria of job success.

In summary, from its careful construction and from direct and indirect evidence, the *Concept Mastery Test* is apparently an excellent test for its initial purpose of measuring, at a high level and over a wide range, the ability to recognize (not necessarily produce) verbal concepts and abstractions. However, the available evidence casts some doubt on whether or not it works nearly as well in predicting upper division and graduate success and productivity and creativity on the job in science and other high level fields.

[322]

★**Cooperative School and College Ability Tests.** Grades 4–6, 6–8, 8–10, 10–12, 12–14; 1955–57; also called SCAT; 3 scores: verbal, quantitative, total; IBM; 5 levels (labeled forms); directions for administering ('57); record blank ('57); separate answer sheets must be used; $3.95 per 20 tests; $1 per 20 IBM answer sheets; 45¢ per scoring stencil; 40¢ per 20 profiles ('57); $1.25 per specimen set; postage extra; 70(95) minutes; Cooperative Test Division, Educational Testing Service. *

a) SCHOOL ABILITY TEST. Grades 4–6, 6–8, 8–10, 10–12; 2 forms, 4 levels.
  1) [*Level 5.*] Grades 4–6; Forms 5A, 5B ('56).
  2) [*Level 4.*] Grades 6–8; Forms 4A, 4B ('56).
  3) [*Level 3.*] Grades 8–10; Forms 3A, 3B ('56).
  4) [*Level 2.*] Grades 10–12; Forms 2A, 2B ('55).

b) COLLEGE ABILITY TEST. Grades 12–14; 4 forms.
  1) [*Level 1.*] Grades 12–14; Forms 1A, 1B, 1C, 1D ('55); Forms 1C and 1D available only by special arrangement for use with students in college.

REFERENCES

1. NORTH, ROBERT D. "A Comparison of the Cooperative School and College Ability Tests: College Ability Test, and the American Council Psychological Examination: Reliabilities, Intercorrelations, and Correlations With the Diagnostic Reading Tests." *Ed Rec B* 67:65–72 F '56. * (PA 31:3800)
2. TRAXLER, ARTHUR E. "Should SCAT Scat ACE? A Comparison Between the Cooperative School and College Ability Tests, Form 1A, and the American Council on Education Psychological Examination, 1948 College Freshman Edition, as to Difficulty and Value for Predicting School Marks." *Ed Rec B* 67:51–63 F '56. * (PA 31:3817)
3. MANUEL, HERSCHEL T. "Aptitude Tests for College Admission." *Yearb Nat Council Meas Used Ed* 14:20–7 '57. *
4. NORTH, ROBERT D. "A Further Report on the Cooperative College Ability Test." *Ed Rec B* 69:60–2 F '57. * (PA 32:2119)
5. EVENSON, A. B., AND SMITH, D. E. "A Study of Matriculation in Alberta." *Alberta J Ed Res* 4:67–83 Je '58. *

6. GREMILLION, BENEDICT JOSEPH. "The Cooperative School and College Ability Test as a Screening Instrument for the Mathematics Proficiency Examination." *J Social Psychol* 47: 149-51 F '58. *
7. VINCENT, LEWIS. "A Comparison of the Quantitative Items of the A.C.E. Psychological With Similar Items in the Cooperative School and College Abilities Tests." *Yearb Nat Council Meas Used Ed* 15:144-9 '58. *

FREDERICK B. DAVIS, *Professor of Education, and Director, Educational Clinic, Hunter College, New York, New York; and Director, Test Research Service, Bronxville, New York.*

The *Cooperative School and College Ability Tests* (SCAT) are intended primarily to aid in estimating the capacity of students in grades 4–14 to undertake additional schooling. Four operational skills are measured: Part 1, getting the meaning of isolated sentences (15 minutes); Part 2, performing numerical computations rapidly (20 minutes); Part 3, associating meanings of isolated words (10 minutes); Part 4, solving arithmetic problems (25 minutes). Parts 1 and 3 are combined to obtain a verbal score, Parts 2 and 4 to obtain a quantitative score, and all four parts to obtain a total aptitude score. The total score is influenced a little more by the verbal than by the quantitative parts.

The design of the test is such that it is likely to be moderately useful for many educational purposes but not especially useful for any one particular purpose. For predicting school grades, it is likely to be less accurate than previous grades in the same subject; for comparing school achievement in any given subject with potential capacity in that subject, it is likely to be less revealing than a test of basic psychological traits; for comparing the verbal and numerical or the verbal and quantitative reasoning aptitudes of one individual, it is likely to be less sensitive and less analytic than a pair of highly specialized tests.

Some interesting data regarding the predictive validity of the test are now available. In grades 9 and 11 the average correlations of SCAT verbal scores with English grades, of SCAT quantitative scores with mathematics grades, and SCAT total scores with grades in social studies and in science are about .50 to .55. In grade 7 analogous correlations (based on smaller samples) run as high as .65 to .70. Teachers of fifth grade in seven different schools rated pupils at the end of the academic year in defined verbal and quantitative abilities. The correlations of these ratings with SCAT verbal and quantitative scores were about .70 if the data from one school, which yielded markedly atypical results, are excluded. In all of these studies the SCAT scores were obtained at the beginning of the school year and the grades or ratings at the end of the school year. The SCAT scores were not made known in the schools during the year.

Directions for administration are provided in a neat 12-page brochure. All forms of the test at each of the five levels are given with the same time limits, answer sheets, and directions (with minor additions for the Level 5 tests, which have more answer spaces than items in Parts 1 and 3). There are advantages in this standardization of materials. If the test is given in one session, the directions recommend a 5-minute recess after Part 2. Since only one side of one answer sheet is used, a student who obtains helpful information during the recess can improve his score by changing answers and filling in spaces he left blank. To prevent this, the directions state: "It is preferable that groups of students going to the rest room be accompanied by a proctor in order to prevent discussion of specific test topics." There is no mention of this problem in the directions for giving the test in two sessions, although under these circumstances almost all students can obtain information enabling them to improve their scores. The boldest, most sophisticated, and least conscientious will avail themselves of this opportunity to the greatest extent. Recognition of this tends to engender in many students, parents, and educators unfavorable attitudes toward testing.

The scoring of SCAT is straightforward, but the need for locating and deleting (by erasure or the use of scotch tape) all multiple answer marks makes it tedious. Moreover, the recommended procedures will not cope with the practice (common among sophisticated examinees) of placing inconspicuous dots in one or more answer spaces for a given item in addition to blackening one of the spaces heavily. The best practical way of handling the problem of multiple marking is to include a correction for chance success in the scoring. This eliminates the need for scanning answer sheets prior to hand scoring and reduces the amount of scanning needed prior to machine scoring to the relatively simple matter of cleaning messy answer sheets. It also reduces greatly the likelihood that an examinee who spends the last few moments making marks at random to all the items he has not read will thereby improve his score. As a result, another source of unfavorable attitudes toward testing in students, parents, and educators is removed. Unfortunately, a correction for chance success is not used in scoring SCAT.

Considerable effort has been devoted to making possible the meaningful interpretation of scores. The degree of success attained rests mainly on the utility of the converted scores, the percentile bands, and the norms. Three scales have been developed, one for all verbal scores, one for all quantitative scores, and one for all total-aptitude scores. Thus, verbal converted scores are serviceably equivalent regardless of the form or level used; similarly, quantitative and total-aptitude converted scores. However, converted scores in verbal, quantitative, and total aptitude are not comparable with one another. Consequently, comparison of a given student's verbal and quantitative converted scores is conveniently possible only by converting them, in turn, into percentile ranks in an appropriate reference group. In practice, this is done by using the individual score norms to plot the student's percentile bands on the SCAT Student Profile. Some test users may feel that, since all the converted scores are not comparable, the conversion of raw scores directly to percentile bands (or percentile ranks) would be more economical of time and sacrifice little in ease of interpretation.

Percentile bands replace the more familiar percentile ranks for reporting SCAT scores. For example, a ninth grade student who obtains a quantitative converted score of 283 has a percentile band of 29–55. This method of reporting scores certainly emphasizes the lack of precision in some test scores. Whether it is more useful to test users than the reporting of percentile ranks with the standard error of measurement in terms of percentiles at various percentile ranks is doubtful. Each percentile band was obtained by laying off on both sides of the middle of a score category one standard error of measurement and taking the two points thus defined as the ends of the band. However, the resulting bands are not 68 per cent confidence intervals; the chances that a student's true aptitude standing is included by his percentile band are less than 68 out of 100 by an amount that cannot be exactly determined from the data. One reason for this is that the standard errors of measurement are spuriously small because they are based on reliability coefficients of *speeded* tests computed by Kuder-Richardson formula 20. In accordance with the basic plan of SCAT, the degree of speededness is greater for the quantitative than for the verbal parts. Data in the Technical Report indicate that at some grade levels as few as 48 per cent complete Part 2 and 60 per cent Part 4, and Parts 1 and 3 are completed by as few as 65 per cent and 80 per cent, respectively. Quite a different impression is given test users by the statement in the Directions for Administering and Scoring: "The subtests are relatively unspeeded; all but the slowest students can complete them in the time limits allowed." Examinees may also get an erroneous mind-set from the following sentence in the general directions: "If you work at average speed you will have plenty of time to read and answer all of the questions."

The SCAT Student Profile makes possible a comparison of a student's verbal and quantitative percentile bands. If the standard errors of measurement had been obtained by a more appropriate procedure and were the same for the two scores being compared, the technique recommended on the profile for identifying differences between verbal and quantitative scores that may be regarded as indicative of true differences in aptitude standing would so identify differences significant at the 16 per cent level, or better. In practice, the recommended technique so identifies some differences that do not meet this standard.

The samples on which the fall percentile norms are based were carefully constructed to be representative of students in grades 4–14, in American schools and colleges willing to participate in testing programs. It is rare to find normative groups that so well conform to their characterizations.

Other aids for interpreting scores are provided, including norms for school averages, tables of comparable scores for SCAT and the high school (1953) and college (1952) editions of the *American Council on Education Psychological Examinations,* and probability tables for estimating verbal and mathematics scores on the *College Entrance Examination Board Scholastic Aptitude Test* of students with specified SCAT converted scores.

Finally, it may be said that the items in SCAT are, in general, well written and well edited.

Cooperative School and College Ability Tests

HANFORD M. FOWLER, *Professor of Education, University of Toronto, Toronto, Ontario, Canada.*

The *Cooperative School and College Ability Tests* (SCAT) were designed "to aid in estimating the capacity of a student to undertake the next higher level of schooling." The two functions chosen for measurement, verbal and quantitative, presumably relate closely to skills which are essential to success in school and college.

Although the SCAT series resembles the *American Council on Education Psychological Examination* (ACE) in a number of ways, SCAT is strictly not a replacement for ACE. For one thing, the five levels of SCAT extend from the second year at college down through grade 4. ACE is for college freshmen and high school students only. There are other differences with respect to the tests themselves and the way in which they were developed. It is unlikely that the two series measure the same elements. On the other hand, the general purpose of the tests is probably the same. Those who have found usefulness in ACE may expect to find the same type of utility in SCAT.

The purpose of ACE is to measure what has been called scholastic aptitude or general intelligence; the authors of SCAT make no direct reference to intelligence but prefer to consider their tests measures of "school-learned abilities." They claim that SCAT measures "specific developed abilities rather than abstract, hard-to-explain psychological traits." However, in practice, SCAT will probably be used in much the same way as ACE has been used: for identifying the overachiever and the underachiever; for counseling the individual student; for comparing average abilities of different groups of students; and so on.

In outward appearance and attractiveness SCAT is as good as any test which this reviewer has seen. The series appears in attractive 7½ by 10½ inch booklets with clear printing, well spaced items, and a pleasing use of colour; the separate answer sheets have an equally attractive format. To assist the administration of the tests, no less than three manuals are provided: one contains directions for administering and scoring; one gives information, directions and illustrations to help in interpreting the scores; and one describes the procedure followed in the various experimental and norms programmes and gives statistical information describing the characteristics of SCAT and its relationships with ACE and with the *Scholastic Aptitude Test* (SAT). And there is even more to come! The publishers promise supplements in which will be reported the results of various studies now being conducted to determine predictive validity. All of this is very impressive, but it costs money. The test consumer who must pay the shot has a right to ask what value is being received for prices which are inflated far beyond those of the good old days of the 5-cent test. How does SCAT measure up with respect to validity, reliability, and standardization?

VALIDITY. No studies as yet have been reported which provide evidence of the predictive validity of SCAT; no evidence is available in the manual. Readers of the manual must infer their own estimates of validity from information relating to the construction of the test, which indeed is detailed and complete, and from fragmentary evidence of the concurrent validity of the test. Such inferences lack the conviction of data-based estimates. Fortunately, information on predictive validity of SCAT will be published in a forthcoming supplement, a draft of which has been made available to the writer. The results reported in the supplement are definitely favourable. Certainly the reported validity coefficients are at least as high as, and occasionally considerably higher than, similar coefficients reported for other tests of this type. We must conclude that on the evidence presently available SCAT shows promise of being an efficient measure of future scholastic success. Some of the coefficients in the lower grades, above .80 in a few cases, impressed this reviewer as being almost suspiciously high. However, the coefficients of the higher grades are generally lower than those in the lower grades. Two other considerations must be kept in mind: (*a*) when numbers are very small, as they were in a number of schools, high coefficients turn up with surprising regularity even if samples are drawn from a population in which the true relationship is zero; (*b*) great variation in the results appeared from school to school, which means that individuals are faced with the necessity of investigating the validity of the tests in their own local situations.

RELIABILITY. To the extent that validity depends upon reliability, the prospects for SCAT are good. Kuder-Richardson (formula 20) estimates of reliability for the total score are at least .95 in all grades; the reliabilities of the verbal scores are at least .92 in all grades; and the reliabilities of the quantitative scores are .90 or greater in three of the five grades (5, 7, 9, 11 and 13) used in the reliability study, the lowest estimate being .88 in grade 5. Readers who are more familiar with between-forms estimates of reliability should not be overimpressed by the size of the reported coefficients for two reasons: (*a*) consistency estimates as given by the Kuder-Richardson formula 20 tend to be considerably higher than between-forms estimates of reliability; (*b*) the reliability for an individual school at a particular grade level would tend to be lower than those reported for the heterogeneous experimental sample. The manual which gives no between-forms comparisons says that "the results should characterize the B forms reasonably well, since the A and B forms are very similar in content"; it promises more information on the equivalence of forms "as soon as there are sufficient data based on the administration of two forms of SCAT to the same students."

NORMS. A characteristic of modern standardized test construction is the care with which the norms are produced. The days of accidental sampling are definitely past. The development of SCAT provides no exception to this enlightened trend. Great care was taken to obtain a truly representative national sample in developing norms by grade for the interpretation of scores of individual students in grades 4 through 14, and school mean norms for the interpretation of mean scores of administrative groups of students in grades 4 through 12. Since only 12 students per school were tested at the college level it was not considered advisable to publish mean norms for grades 13 and 14.

Despite the use of the most modern statistical procedures to ensure representativeness, national norms have value only to the extent that they add required meaning in score interpretation. Much depends upon the way the test scores are going to be used. Are nationwide comparisons profitable? In general, the most meaningful test score interpretation involves a state or local community comparison rather than a national comparison based on results obtained from a large, despairingly heterogeneous, group. Local norms are more valuable than national norms for many test users. In the Manual for Interpreting Scores SCAT recognizes this trend by providing detailed instructions for the construction of local norms.

Evidence of the need for local norms is provided by the results of the administration of SCAT in 1956 to 8,852 Ontario students in grade 13 as part of the Atkinson Study of the Utilization of Student Resources (Department of Educational Research, Ontario College of Education). Large discrepancies appear between the Ontario results and the norms reported in the manual for 1,134 students in 97 colleges tested in the fall of the grade 14 year (it is assumed that Ontario grade 13, which leads to senior matriculation, would correspond to the first college year of universities which have junior matriculation admissions policies). At the extreme upper ends of the distributions the differences are not great, but at the middle and at the lower ends of the distributions the differences are so large that the use of the American norms would be completely unsuitable for this group. It is true that Ontario students in grade 13 are generally considered to be a highly selected group, but the fact remains that Ontario norms would be required for interpreting the scores of Ontario students in the Ontario situation. Indeed, for this particular group the efficiency of the test is seriously reduced by the marked piling up of scores at the top ends of the distributions. The distribution of the verbal scores is reasonably satisfactory, but the quantitative scores and, as a result, the total scores, show a very marked negative skew. The mathematical items are much too easy for this group. Additional evidence that the numerical items do not provide sufficient ceiling for top level students is contained in the Technical Report which says that "it should be noted that the quantitative sections of levels 1, 2 and 3 are so similar as to warrant considering them alternate forms."

STRONG POINTS. Among the excellent features of SCAT are: the use of equated conversion scores (not intelligence quotients) which permit comparison of scores not only from form to form but also from level to level—a feature which teachers in the elementary and secondary schools will find particularly attractive; the provision of profiles to assist score interpretation; the emphasis through the use of percentile bands upon the fallibility of test scores; and the lack of speededness in the subtests which makes it possible for all but the slowest students to complete them in the time limits allowed. In

Cooperative School and College Ability Tests

general, the technical recommendations for psychological tests which have been endorsed by the American Psychological Association, the American Educational Research Association, and the National Council on Measurements Used in Education have been followed.

SOME WEAKNESSES. Besides weaknesses in the national norms and limitations uncovered by the validity study, there are other deficiencies in SCAT. In the first place, a number of doubts are raised by the quantitative score: in the upper grades the items are apparently too easy, at least for superior students; in the first semester of grade 4 they are too difficult. The validity study shows disturbingly high intercorrelation coefficients between the quantitative score and the verbal score, particularly in the lower grades. One wonders whether the quantitative subtests are indispensable and whether their omission would greatly reduce the effectiveness of the test. A second matter of concern is the amount of time that is required to administer SCAT. Those who hoped that ACE would be replaced by a test which could be administered in a single college period are doomed to disappointment; it takes two full college periods to administer SCAT. Thus, the lack of speededness in the subtests has been obtained only at a considerable sacrifice in another direction.

USES OF SCAT. In accordance with the modern conception that a test is a tool to assist in the solution of an educational problem, rather than just a toy or a device for tagging a student, one may say that any test has value to the extent that it is used meaningfully in the schools. Reference has already been made to some possible uses of SCAT; the publishers suggest seven ways in which the individual test results can be used and four ways to employ results from classes, grades, departments, schools, and other groups. But SCAT measures ability only; it is not a measure of achievement in the ordinary sense of that word. Teachers and counselors are well aware that diagnosis and the proper choice of remedial treatment depend upon knowledge of student ability *and* student achievement. Users of SCAT will welcome the appearance of the *Sequential Tests of Educational Progress* (STEP) which are reviewed in another part of this Yearbook. SCAT-STEP should prove to be a useful team. STEP indicates a student's achievement and SCAT indicates his ability to achieve. The fact that the norming population for SCAT includes exactly the same students as the norming population for STEP greatly increases the value of the team for purposes of score interpretation.

SUMMARY. Undoubtedly, SCAT is a superior test series. It clearly shows the result of careful planning, an excellent experimental programme, and the use of sound, up-to-date statistical procedures. It is the type of test that could hardly be produced without the cooperation of many individuals, the assistance of technical experts, and the backing of a well financed organization blessed with all the necessary facilities for the construction of a nationally standardized instrument. There is certainly room for improvement; changes will no doubt be introduced as more data on the usefulness, as well as the limitations, of the test become available. At the moment it is relatively untried. It is tempting to commit oneself to a definite prediction of a rosy future for this test; but scientific caution warns that the data are for the most part still not in.

JULIAN C. STANLEY, *Professor of Education, University of Wisconsin, Madison, Wisconsin.*

This series of well standardized "scholastic aptitude" tests will be especially useful to those teachers and administrators who want to compare Mary's scores in grade 8, say, with Henry's in grade 9, or Henry's on Level 5A with his own later scores on Level 3B. A single common score scale for all levels, forms, and subtests (verbal and quantitative) makes such comparisons possible. Furthermore, through the norms, scores on the *Cooperative School and College Ability Tests* (SCAT) can be compared with scores on the *Sequential Tests of Educational Progress* (STEP) of the same publisher.

Each form has four parts yielding separate verbal, quantitative, and total scores. Part 1 contains 25 or 30 incomplete sentences, for each of which one word must be supplied from among the five options offered. Part 2 consists of 25 arithmetic computation items. "None of these" is the fifth option for every one of the items in this part. Part 3 has 25 or 30 vocabulary items of the definition recognition type. Part 4 contains 25 arithmetic reasoning items. By alternating A, B, C, D, E with F, G, H, J, K, as option labels, the authors help prevent purely clerical slips. If a student looks up from

Item 16 in the booklet with, say, G in mind as the correct answer, he cannot mark Item 15 or Item 17 by mistake because neither will have a G among the options.

The verbal raw score is the sum of the raw scores on Parts 1 and 3. The quantitative raw score is the sum of the raw scores on Parts 2 and 4. The total raw score is simply the sum of the raw scores on all four parts. No correction for chance is employed. Raw scores may be changed to "converted scores" by reference to a simple table on the back of the appropriate scoring stencil. Percentile rank equivalents of converted scores appear in the Manual for Interpreting Scores; these are expressed as bands, to emphasize the standard error of measurement of the scores and to facilitate intra- and inter-individual score comparisons.

Grades for which the various levels are recommended overlap intentionally. Because format, instructions, time limits, and answer sheets are identical for all levels and forms, testers are encouraged to use several levels simultaneously for testing a given group. The least able students, as judged by prior information, can be handed a lower level than the average students, who in turn may receive a lower level than the brightest students.

The hitherto standard procedure of retesting the lowest and highest scorers on a test can largely be avoided by careful advance determination of the optimum level for each testee. For a test with plenty of "floor" and "ceiling" for everyone, we aim, as a rule of thumb, for levels such that each testee will get about half the items right, corrected for chance. For 100 5-option items this would be a number-right score of 60 if all 100 items were marked. On Level 5A such a total score yields a converted score of 254, not far above the median of the grade 5 norms near the beginning of the school year. Roughly, we may assume that a given level is most suitable for average students at the beginning of the midgrade for which it is specified: Level 5 for grade 5, Level 4 for grade 7, Level 3 for grade 9, etc.

Oddly, instructions concerning "guessing" for SCAT differ from those for STEP, which encourage the student to try every item. The SCAT booklet states: "You may answer questions even when you are not perfectly sure that your answers are correct. Your score will be the number of correct answers you mark." Undoubtedly, testees will interpret the words "per- fectly sure" in various ways, depending upon their gambling propensities. Some will mark every item, even though they do not know much. Others will omit all but the ones about which they are virtually certain. Caution versus recklessness sometimes produces anomalous individual results. For example, sheer chance marking of the 50 quantitative items of Level 5A should yield, on the average, a converted score equivalent to the 21–40th percentile band for grade 4, while not marking the questions at all yields the 0–21st band. STEP avoids this common source of test invalidity by do-guess instructions (but thereby, of course, may increase chance variance); only force of habit seems to have prevented the authors of SCAT from utilizing a similar procedure.

Though the test items appear to have been constructed at least as carefully as were those in competing tests, quite a few of them would have benefited appreciably from the personal ministrations of a meticulous editor. The reviewer found a considerable number of not-quite-ideal stems and options in the verbal sections of the highest levels (1C and 1D). Quantitative items and the verbal items below Levels 1C and 1D seem better edited.

The Manual for Interpreting Scores and the Technical Report are both excellent. The former gives the typical test administrator considerable help, while the latter supplies further technical information that both he and the more statistically trained user will appreciate.

No comparable-forms reliability coefficients are available yet for SCAT. Kuder-Richardson (formula 20) coefficients vary from .88 for the quantitative raw score of Level 5A for fifth graders tested in the norms program to .96 for the total raw score of Level 4A in grade 7. As the Technical Report cautions, these figures are usually overestimates for individual schools, which are invited to compute their own estimates of reliability and are shown how to do so.

Since much of the rationale and standardization of SCAT is similar to that of STEP, the reader interested in SCAT is hereby encouraged to consult the STEP reviews in this volume also.

Overall, the 12 synchronized members of the SCAT series, each with two subtests, represent a new application and downward extension of the *American Council on Education Psychological Examination* and other scholastic aptitude tests with which Educational Testing

Cooperative School and College Ability Tests

Service has had much experience. They provide verbal, quantitative, and total scores based much more on power than speed. Test users who desire other intellective scores, such as nonlanguage or spatial, must supplement SCAT. Those who want a carefully devised, well standardized series of intelligence tests that can be used flexibly over many grades and related via norms to the STEP achievement test series should give the *Cooperative School and College Ability Tests* careful consideration.

[323]

★**Cotswold Junior Ability Tests.** Ages 8–9; 1949–51; Forms A ['49], B ['51]; no data on validity; 11s. per 20 tests; 6½d. per single copy; 1s. per manual; postage extra; C. M. Fleming; Robert Gibson & Sons (Glasgow), Ltd. *
a) JUNIOR MENTAL ABILITY A. Form A ['49]; manual ['49]; 30(40) minutes.
b) JUNIOR MENTAL ABILITY B. Form B ['51]; manual ['51]; 35(45) minutes.

[324]

*****Cotswold Measurement of Mental Ability.** Ages 10–12.5; 1947–54; title on manual is *Cotswold Measurement of Ability*; Series 1 and 2 entitled *Cotswold Mental Ability Test*; 6 forms: labeled Series 2 ['47], 3 ['50], 4 ['50], 5 ['52], 6 ['53], 7 ['54]; incomplete norms for Series 2–5; 7s. per 20 tests; 5½d. per single copy; 1s. per manual (dates as for tests) for any one series; postage extra; Series 2–5: 35(45) minutes; Series 6–7: 30(40) minutes; C. M. Fleming (except test booklet for Series 2) and J. W. Jenkins (Series 2); Robert Gibson & Sons (Glasgow), Ltd. *

A. W. HEIM, *Medical Research Council, Psychological Laboratory, University of Cambridge, Cambridge, England.*

The six Cotswold tests (Series 2-7) are broadly similar in form. They have a preliminary practice page for which 5 minutes are allowed; the practice items are identical throughout the six series. Each test consists of five subtests with verbal or numerical biases, each of them having a time limit of either 5 or 10 minutes. Most questions are multiple choice, the child being asked to underline the correct solution among the five presented.

The principal item types employed consist of analogies, classification items, series, and arithmetical and verbal problems involving deductive reasoning and instruction following. In Series 2, 3, and 4, one subtest consists of a simple table showing the number of children in three school classes who, for instance, sing, dance, and paint. The subject is asked eight questions whose answers demand interpretation of the table. The questions become progressively harder and the eighth question struck the reviewer as ambiguous. Apart from this, the problem seems admirably suitable for test purposes and a welcome change from the hackneyed, often artificial, type of test problem.

Series 5 and 6 include subtests which require the child to copy contrived foreign-looking words and phrases. In the reviewer's opinion this is a retrogressive step: the task assesses accuracy only—and is as demanding of the scorer as of the subject! The traditional virtues of objectivity and speed of marking are largely lost with such items.

In general, the method of scoring is not ideal. Since in several of the subtests the subject is required to *underline* his solution, the correct answers naturally come in different positions all over the page. In the marking key for the more recent tests, these solutions are printed in positions which correspond to their place on the test paper. Even so, scoring must still be slower than is desirable.

The most serious criticism of the test booklets concerns the preliminary practice sheet. There is no indication that this has to be *correctly* completed by *all* subjects before they embark on the test proper. This implies that children who are most in need of preliminary examples—the slow starters, the nervous, and those lacking in test sophistication—will gain the least benefit. Moreover, there are in the practice sheet no examples of "double analogies" nor of table interpretations. The reviewer feels strongly that the child should meet in the test proper only the types of problem with which he has familiarised himself in preliminary examples.

There are several individual items, notably (and inevitably) among the classification problems, whose cogency is questionable, despite the statement in the manuals that "the correctness of each response was determined after analysis of pupils' replies, and ambiguous questions were discarded." Furthermore, a few problems are misleadingly worded, e.g., those in Series 2, 3, and 4 that ask such things as "Which is the *first* letter of the alphabet which occurs only once in the word ECCENTRICITY?" (Reviewer's italics.)

Each series has its own manual containing directions for general procedure and oral instructions, marking keys for the five subtests, tables of standardised scores, and notes on the background of the tests, their construction, standardisation, validity, and reliability. These notes are overbrief. The explanation of the standardised scores is rendered needlessly difficult by careless errors in several of the manuals.

Apart from these objections, however, and the regrettable lack of any diagrammatic or pictorial items, the tests are well thought out and agreeably varied and the instructions in the manuals are clearly expressed. It is useful to have six almost parallel tests within the 10–12 age range.

[325]

★Daneshill Intelligence Test. Ages 9.5–11.5; 1950–51; 1 form ['51]; 8s. 6d. per 25 tests; 6d. per single copy; 1s. per manual ('50); postage extra; 45(60) minutes; R. MacDonald; University of London Press Ltd. *

A. W. HEIM, *Medical Research Council, Psychological Laboratory, University of Cambridge, Cambridge, England.*

The preface to the manual informs the reader that the test "is the result of a project arising out of discussions and lectures on the assessment of children's abilities during the period 1948–50 in Daneshill Training College. * It formed the growing point for the course in Educational Psychology." That this project proved useful for the students in training is readily believable. It would, however, be surprising if the exercise had resulted in a wholly satisfactory test of intelligence. There are, in effect, a good many criticisms to make, both of the test proper and of the manual.

To consider the latter first, the information given on test standardisation is quite inadequate. It is not clear how many children of what ages were used; for test reliability, only the split-half technique was employed—with an unspecified number of cases. There are literally no data at all on the validation of the test against an external criterion. It is not even clear whether the test was retested after having been altered in the light of item analysis findings.

Tables for converting scores into IQ's are presented for ages 10-0 to 10-11. Earlier in the manual, however, is a note stating that "by extrapolation the table may be extended to include the ages 9:6 to 11:6." This procedure consists of adding (or subtracting) one year to the age and adding (or subtracting) 6 from the IQ then found. No explanation is offered of this system but a warning is given that "such extrapolation must not be carried beyond the ages 9:6, 11:6."

The test booklet consists of 95 items, the vast majority of which score one point if correctly answered. The theoretical maximum test score is 100 marks. The questions cover verbal or numerical series, analogies, codes, classifications, directions, mixed (true-false) sentences, and reasoning problems. There are no preliminary examples for the subject to work through and the child is told to "ask no questions." The wording of some of the test problems is ambiguous, as, for example, in the problems which say, "A certain number is out of place in each of the following." The offending number is in fact one that has no place in the given set of numbers at all. Finally, there is some rather slipshod thinking in the actual problems themselves, notably in the classification questions and in the so-called "sames" and "opposites."

The reviewer would suggest that the training of students and the publishing of tests should be kept separate or, at the least, that tests arising in the course of student training should be allowed more than two years in which to mature.

F. W. WARBURTON, *Lecturer in Educational Psychology, University of Manchester, Manchester, England.*

This test is the outgrowth of a project concerning the assessment of children's abilities which was carried on during the period 1948–1950 in Daneshill Training College. The purpose of the project was to give students in training "some insight into the methods employed for measuring intelligence," and "a knowledge of statistical techniques applied to psychological investigations." These two objects were no doubt fulfilled, but they scarcely justify the publication of this rather amateurish test.

The general instructions to the children are clear, but no practice test is provided. The explanations preceding the individual sections are sometimes unambiguous, for example: "Look at this mixed sentence. Men fat are all. True. False. The sentence when rearranged is not true so FALSE has been underlined. Do the same in the following." In another section, no instruction is given.

The test is entitled "intelligence test" although it includes a few items which would usually be found in attainment tests, such as arithmetical sums and geographical comparisons. The key contains a typographical error in which "give" instead of "girl" is listed as the answer. The correct response to "What word begins with D and means the opposite of ADMIRE" is given as "Dislike." "Despise" might well be acceptable. The manual contains adequate instructions to supervisors. Conversion tables for ages 10-0 to 10-11, based on the analysis of as many as 5,078 scripts, are provided. The authors suggest that the tables may be extended to include the ages of 9-6 to 11-6 by extrapolation, a risky procedure. The reliability coefficient is fairly satisfactory. Unfortunately, no validities are given.

The 150 items were selected from an original pool of 300 items. There 150 items were given a trial on a group of 312 children from primary schools in Nottinghamshire. The test was refined on the basis of an analysis of the items in terms of "success and difficulty." (Unfortunately, indices of consistency were apparently not included among the selection criteria.) The resulting new edition of the test was tried out on a similar group of 127 children.

The Daneshill test clearly cannot supplant tests published by Moray House and the National Foundation for Educational Research, or Schonell's *Essential Intelligence Test*.

[326]

★Davis-Eells Test of General Intelligence or Problem-Solving Ability. Grades 1-2, 3-6; 1953, c1952-53; title on test is *Davis-Eells Games*; Form A ('53) ; 2 levels; directions for administering ('53) ; 85¢ per manual ('53) ; postage extra; 35¢ per specimen set of either level, postpaid; Allison Davis and Kenneth Eells; World Book Co. *

a) PRIMARY. Grades 1-2; $4.35 per 35 tests; (60) minutes in 2 sessions for grade 1; (90) minutes in 3 sessions for grade 2.

b) ELEMENTARY. Grades 3-6; $4.80 per 35 tests; (100-120) minutes in 2 sessions.

REFERENCES

1. SURRATT, CAROLYN. *Cultural Factors in Children's Solutions of Verbal Problems*. Master's thesis, University of Chicago (Chicago, Ill.), 1946.
2. ATAULLAH, KANIZ. *Cultural Influences on Children's Solution of Verbal Problems*. Doctor's thesis, University of Chicago (Chicago, Ill.), 1950.
3. HESS, ROBERT D. *An Experimental Culture-Fair Test of Mental Ability*. Doctor's thesis, University of Chicago (Chicago, Ill.), 1950.
4. GLADSTEIN, GERALD A. *Cultural Factors in an Experimental Test of Intelligence*. Master's thesis, University of Chicago (Chicago, Ill.), 1951.
5. WEISS, MARCIA. *The Validity of Non-Verbal Problems From a Culture-Fair Test for Middle and Lower-Class School Children*. Master's thesis, University of Chicago (Chicago, Ill.), 1952.
6. EELLS, KENNETH. "Some Implications for School Practice of the Chicago Studies of Cultural Bias in Intelligence Tests." *Harvard Ed R* 23:284-97 fall '53. *
7. STENQUIST, JOHN L., AND LORGE, IRVING. "Implications of Intelligence and Cultural Differences; As Seen by a Test-User; As Seen by a Test-Maker." *Teach Col Rec* 54:184-93 Ja '53. * (*PA* 27:6423)
8. GEIST, HAROLD. "Evaluation of Culture-Free Intelligence." *Calif J Ed Res* 5:209-14 N '54. * (*PA* 29:5291)
9. RICHIE, ALICE. "A Comparison of the Kuhlmann-Anderson With the Davis-Eells Intelligence Tests in a Fifth Grade." Abstract. *Calif J Ed Res* 5:186 S '54. *
10. ANGELINO, HENRY, AND SHEDD, CHARLES L. "An Initial Report of a Validation Study of the Davis-Eells Tests of General Intelligence or Problem-Solving Ability." *J Psychol* 40:35-8 Jl '55. * (*PA* 30:2854)
11. CAFFREY, JOHN, AND SMITH, THOMAS WOOD. "Preliminary Identification of Some Factors in the Davis-Eells Games." Abstract. *Am Psychol* 10:453-4 Ag '55. *
12. COLEMAN, WILLIAM, AND WARD, ANNIE W. "A Comparison of Davis-Eells and Kuhlmann-Finch Scores of Children From High and Low Socio-Economic Status." *J Ed Psychol* 46:465-9 D '55. * (*PA* 31:3779)
13. JUSTMAN, JOSEPH, AND ARONOW, MIRIAM. "The Davis-Eells Games as a Measure of the Intelligence of Poor Readers." *J Ed Psychol* 46:418-22 N '55. * (*PA* 31:3791)
14. MACRAE, JOHN M. "A Comparison of Davis-Eells and Stanford-Binet Scores at Different Socio-Economic Levels." Abstract. *Calif J Ed Res* 6:133 My '55. *
15. PAPANIA, NED; ROSENBLUM, SIDNEY; AND KELLER, JAMES E. "Responses of Lower Social Class, High-Grade Mentally Handicapped Boys to a 'Culture Fair' Test of Intelligence—The Davis-Eells Games." *Am J Mental Def* 59:493-8 Ja '55. * (*PA* 29:7494)
16. ROSENBLUM, SIDNEY; KELLER, JAMES E.; AND PAPANIA, NED. "Davis-Eells ('Culture-Fair') Test Performance of Lower-Class Retarded Children." *J Consult Psychol* 19:51-4 F '55. * (*PA* 29:8722)
17. SAWREY, JAMES M. "The Predictive Effectiveness of Two Non-Verbal Tests of Intelligence Used in the First Grade in the Santa Clara County Schools." Abstract. *Calif J Ed Res* 6:133 My '55. *
18. SMITH, THOMAS WOOD, AND CAFFREY, JOHN. "Comprehension of Written Language (Reading) and Oral Language (Auding) as Related to 'Cultural Bias' on the Davis-Eells Games and the California Test of Mental Maturity." Abstract. *Am Psychol* 10:382-3 Ag '55. *
19. ALEXANDER, ETHEL B. *A Study of the Davis-Eells Test of General Intelligence and Problem-Solving Ability in Selected Elementary Schools in Greensboro, North Carolina*. Master's thesis, Agricultural and Technical College (Greensboro, N. C.), 1956.
20. ALTUS, GRACE T. "Some Correlates of the Davis-Eells Tests." *J Consult Psychol* 20:227-32 Je '56. * (*PA* 31:6053)
21. FOWLER, WILLIAM L. *A Comparative Analysis of Pupil Performance on Conventional and Culture-Controlled Mental Tests*. Doctor's thesis, University of Michigan (Ann Arbor, Mich.), 1956. (*DA* 17:91)
22. LEVINSON, BORIS M. "Note on the Davis Eells Test of General Intelligence." *Psychol Rep* 2:242 S '56. * (*PA* 31:3048)
23. LUDLOW, H. GLENN. "Some Recent Research on the Davis-Eells Games." *Sch & Soc* 84:146-8 O 27 '56. * (*PA* 31:7947)
24. RUSSELL, IVAN L. "The Davis-Eells Test and Reading Success in First Grade." *J Ed Psychol* 47:269-70 My '56. * (*PA* 32:2125)
25. SMITH, THOMAS WOOD. *Auding and Reading as Sources of Cultural Bias in the Davis-Eells Games and the California Test of Mental Maturity*. Doctor's thesis, University of Southern California (Los Angeles, Calif.), 1956.
26. SMITH, THOMAS WOOD. "Comparison of Test Bias in the Davis-Eells Games and the CTMM." *Calif J Ed Res* 7:159-63 S '56. * (*PA* 31:6135)
27. TATE, MERLE W., AND VOSS, CHARLOTTE E. "A Study of the Davis-Eells Test of Intelligence." *Harvard Ed R* 26:374-87 fall '56. * (*PA* 32:1347)
28. ZWEIBELSON, I. "Test Anxiety and Intelligence Test Performance." *J Consult Psychol* 20:479-81 D '56. * (*PA* 32:1659)
29. CLARK, GLYNN E. *A Comparison of the Performance of Selected Pupils on the Davis-Eells Test and the Otis Test of Mental Ability*. Doctor's thesis, Washington University (St. Louis, Mo.), 1957. (*DA* 17:807)
30. FOWLER, WILLIAM L. "A Comparative Analysis of Pupil Performance on Conventional and Culture-Controlled Mental Tests." *Yearb Nat Council Meas Used Ed* 14:8-19 '57. *
31. FRANDSEN, ARDEN N., AND GRIMES, JESSE W. "Age Discrimination in Intelligence Tests." *J Ed Res* 51:229-33 N '57. *
32. KNIEF, LOTUS M. *An Investigation of the Cultural Bias Issue in Intelligence Testing*. Doctor's thesis, State University of Iowa (Iowa City, Iowa), 1957. (*DA* 17:1951)
33. LOVE, MARY I., AND BEACH, SYLVIA. "Performance of Children on the Davis-Eells Games and Other Measures of Ability." *J Consult Psychol* 21:29-32 F '57. * (*PA* 32:952)
34. COOPER, JAMES G. "Predicting School Achievement for Bilingual Pupils." *J Ed Psychol* 49:31-6 F '58. *
35. RUESS, AUBREY L. "Some Cultural and Personality Aspects of Mental Retardation." *Am J Mental Def* 63:50-9 Jl '58. *
36. STILLWELL, LOIS. *A Study of the Davis-Eells Games: A Group Test of Intelligence for Use in the Elementary Schools*. Master's thesis, Kent State University (Kent, Ohio), 1958.

CYRIL BURT, *Emeritus Professor of Psychology, University of London, London, England*.

This is a group intelligence test in pictorial form. No reading is required. The directions, expressed in colloquial language, are read by an examiner called the "game leader." To break tension, the solving of the problems is preceded by 3 minutes of physical exercise (waving arms or patting stomach and head), and letting the pupils "laugh as much as they wish," and throughout the test the "atmosphere" is to be kept "relaxed."

The material is based on a conception of general intelligence as "the sum total of the skills of thinking, work habits, and other factors which determine how well any given individual will be able to solve important kinds of intellectual problems that face him in life." The items have been selected so as to cover a wide variety of tasks which will "parallel the real-life problems of children more closely than most intelligence-test items in the past." The problems are often exceedingly ingenious. The pictures are drawn in semihumorous style, and are usually about 2½ or 3 inches square: the size is thus larger than is commonly adopted, and therefore should impose no handicap even on children with relatively poor vision. The whole procedure is "child oriented"; and, as the type of test material, the method of administration, and the title on the pupil's booklet all imply, the pupils are meant to regard their task rather as a game than as a formal test or school examination.

Tables are appended enabling the user to convert scores to IQ's. The authors, however, prefer the phrase "Index of Problem Solving Ability (I.P.S.A.)" as less vague, less misleading, and more meaningful than the older term. Two types of reliability coefficient are reported: (a) a split-half coefficient, which yields a reliability averaging about .82 for grades 2 to 6, and somewhat less for grade 1; and (b) a coefficient of stability, assessed by giving the test a second time to the same group after an interval of a couple of weeks: this was apparently possible for two grades only, and yielded a coefficient of .72 for grade 2 and .90 for grade 4.

The authors contend that the validity of the test is best "indicated by a careful analysis of its nature and of the nature of the problem-solving ability which it seeks to measure," not by the usual statistical comparison with scores from other tests, since these may actually be less effective than the test to be evaluated. The principle is excellent, but its practical consequences are not very successfully fulfilled. The definition stating the results of the analysis is far too loose for scientific purposes. "Intelligence" in the technical sense is ordinarily regarded as a mental capacity; and the phrase "skills of thinking" is at once too narrow and too broad to specify its nature with precision. The child's work habits and the other factors affecting his efficiency —his emotional attitudes, the effort he makes, and so on—call rather for separate assessment. The mere fact that the analysis of the test appears to correspond with the analysis of the capacity tested cannot of itself guarantee the test's validity: the ideal criterion would be the accuracy with which it predicts the subsequent performances of the child in the fields defined; failing that, the next best standard would be the assessments of a teacher, known to be a competent judge, who has systematically observed each child's progress and performance in the past. It is curious that American investigators make far less use of teachers' opinions than British.

An inspection of the actual material raises doubts as to whether the tasks presented are in fact as varied, as realistic, and as important as was intended. Experience and results already gained with similar pictorial tests indicate that, with increasing age, the scores obtained tend more and more to depend on special aptitudes, special experience, and special interest; indeed, with older children, a purely pictorial test yields as one-sided an assessment as a purely verbal test with the younger.

Presenting tests as games is an excellent device with the younger and duller pupils. But with British children aged 9 and upwards better results are secured when tests of intelligence are given quite frankly as an internal examination in which every pupil is expected to take the problems seriously and do his utmost to answer even the more difficult problems. To insist that the tests should be preceded by amusing exercises during which pupils are encouraged to "laugh as much as they wish" and that the problems should be tackled in a state of relaxation is scarcely likely to ensure that they do their best. Indeed, on making an actual trial, the reviewer finds that with British pupils this method of approach tends to reduce the reliability to .60 or less. The test material assumes a familiarity with the conventions of the strip cartoon (e.g., musical notation to represent sounds emerging from a child's mouth); and is thus bound to handicap the less sophisticated children from rural areas. The stylized exaggerations and would-be comicality of the drawings, amounting at times almost to caricature, tend to induce a mood of frivolity and frequently to obscure the real nature of the problem.

These criticisms apply far more strongly to some items than to others. If, as a provisional criterion, we take the total score for the test as a whole, preliminary trials would seem to indicate that the component items differ widely in validity, and that the grading in difficulty is very uneven. There appears, therefore, to be an urgent need for a more thorough item analysis before the test can be regarded as having reached a final or a satisfactory form.

RALEIGH M. DRAKE, *Professor of Psychology, Kent State University, Kent, Ohio.*

This reviewer is very much in favor of culture free, culture fair performance and other such tests which attempt to get a more direct measurement of mental capacity, mental potential, mental energy, or intelligence. To the extent that scores are influenced by environmental and training factors, our tests are subject to error and equivocal interpretation. The purpose of the *Davis-Eells Games* is to eliminate one of these spurious factors—socioeconomic differences and inequities. The original data report that this purpose was accomplished, but replications done elsewhere fail to verify these results (*10, 15, 20, 23, 33*).

A recent study (*36*) which this reviewer supervised, obtained similar results. The *California Test of Mental Maturity* was compared directly with the Davis-Eells on two groups, one a high socioeconomic group and the other a low socioeconomic group. The Davis-Eells consistently gave lower IPSA-scores (these are really IQ scores and are as directly equivalent to IQ's as are scores on any of the numerous tests which try to convert their scores to IQ's) than did the CTMM, but the Davis-Eells showed as much difference between the high and low socioeconomic groups as did the CTMM. This indicates that the Davis-Eells is not achieving anything in the way of an advantage as far as culture fairness is concerned. In view of the fact that the IQ's are approximately 7.5 points lower, it would appear that the Davis-Eells is culturally unfair to all subjects to about this extent. The reliability computed for this study is reported as .79. This is not so high as the reliability reported for CTMM or other tests. Validity was checked in two schools against the individual ratings of seven different teachers:

Teacher	1	2	3	4	5	6	7
Davis-Eells	.16	.49	.53	.42	.68	.63	.40
CTMM	.77	.73	.86	.93	.70	.71	.60

Correlations with the arithmetic test of the *Iowa Tests of Basic Skills* gave .41 and .51 for two groups while the CTMM gave r's of .61 and .67 for the same two groups. Correlations with the *California Reading Test* gave .36 and .41 for these same groups, while the CTMM gave .71 and .69, respectively. Thus, as a predictive instrument, the Davis-Eells is less valid than the CTMM with two criteria, teacher's ratings and scores on standardized achievement tests.

Another study (*34*) with native Indian children in Guam produced very similar results. Here the average IQ (IPSA) was about 16.6 points lower than with the CTMM. Most studies report that IQ's obtained with the Davis-Eells run lower than those obtained with other tests, and the test differentiates as much between high and low socioeconomic groups as do the general verbal tests which it was intended to improve upon. Some children in the Guam study had scores on the Davis-Eells as much as 51 points below their scores on the CTMM. If the Davis-Eells scores alone had been used, serious misclassification or interpretation of an individual child might have resulted. It appears that in attempting to eliminate socioeconomic influences, a significant portion of the test's intended capacity to discriminate differences in intelligence has been partialled out.

Additional comments are that it is difficult to administer because it requires a great deal of oral directions and as much as 90 minutes of working time (grade 2). Scoring is slow and tedious. Several items have strong emotional loadings: (*a*) a boy being spanked by his father, (*b*) three tough boys lying in wait to beat up another boy, (*c*) a boy being spanked for breaking a window, and (*d*) a girl crying because she thinks she hasn't a Christmas present. The directions for administering the arithmetical reasoning problem are not entirely clear to all children, with the result that some miss all of this section. A severe strain is put upon the attention span of young children. There is one favorable aspect—children like the test because of its gamelike nature.

J. P. GUILFORD, *Professor of Psychology, University of Southern California, Los Angeles, California.*

The purpose of this test as stated by the authors is "to measure fairly and accurately as possible the ability of children to solve problems of a kind interesting and important to them." The specification of "fairly" refers to the conviction of the authors that most tests of intelligence are biased in favor of children from the higher socioeconomic levels. In the selection of items considerable attention was given to ensure that they were equally within the sphere of experience of all groups.

This criterion was largely responsible for eliminating all need for reading on the part of examinees, the items being presented pictorially and the instructions for each item being given orally. Pictorial material also lends itself to intrinsic interest. An effort is made to maintain a "game" atmosphere throughout the test. Although the test can be given to groups of children, the long oral instructions make administration very cumbersome. The test is inefficient in view of the time it takes for the levels of reliability achieved (about .8 for split-half estimates and .7 and .9 for test-retest estimates in grades 2 and 4).

There are 47 items in a 16-page booklet at the primary level and 62 items in a 20-page booklet at the elementary level. One kind of item asks the child to make a judgment as to what is going on in a picture in which usually two or more individuals are in some kind of interaction. This would seem to this reviewer to measure something in the area of social intelligence, mainly ability for social cognition. Another kind of item shows three similar scenes in each of which a child is attempting to perform a task, the examinee being asked to say which child is acting most wisely. This would seem to measure an ability to evaluate behavior; hence it is also in the area of social intelligence, and possibly in the area of concrete intelligence, too, since objects are dealt with as well as individuals. In other kinds of items abilities more like those involved in conventional intelligence tests appear to be tested. In items involving coins and the counting of sums of money, probably some numerical facility is measured and possibly some foresight in dealing with symbols. Other items are essentially verbal analogies presented in pictorial form. The objects involved are so familiar that probably little verbal comprehension is measured, but the ability to see relationships between concepts should be assessed.

If this reviewer's guesses are correct, we have here a measure of something rather different from the usual intelligence test. Correlations with several forms of the *Otis Quick-Scoring Mental Ability Tests* are in the region of .4 to .6. Correlations with scholastic achievement tests are mostly in the range of .1 to .5, depending upon the subject.

The authors insist that the test measures problem solving ability. There is no empirical evidence presented to support this contention. Items were chosen for the supposed purpose merely by expert inspection. Except for the items involving coins, the items seem to this reviewer to be not so much in the nature of problems calling for solution as situations calling for cognition. Cognitions play their parts in solving problems, but more important is productive thinking. The latter seems to be of little importance in answering the items of this test. Perhaps the authors should have defined problem solving in an unusually broad sense. The term is likely to be interpreted more narrowly by the test user.

The test was obviously developed with great care and industry. The items went through several analytical studies. Norms are based upon large and well selected samples, except for the fact that no rural children were included.

Raw scores are transformed into the familiar IQ scale, but the authors properly urge that a scale score not be interpreted as a conventional IQ, that is, as to psychological meaning. It is unfortunate, for this and for other reasons mentioned earlier, that the term "general intelligence" appears in the title of the test. In fact, the entire title seems inappropriate.

In view of the efforts to achieve comparable scores for children of all socioeconomic groups, it is unfortunate that the authors do not present some comparative scores obtained from those different groups. It would not be surprising to find some differences after all. Such differences would probably be small, for in the area of social intelligence, which the reviewer believes to be stressed in the test, the social groups should be much more alike than they are on verbal intelligence.

For related reviews, see B140.

[327]
★Deeside Picture Puzzles. Ages 6.5–8.5; 1956–58; 1 form ('56); 15s. per 25 tests; 8d. per single copy; 3s. 6d. per manual ('58); postage extra; 25.5(75) minutes; W. G. Emmett; George G. Harrap & Co. Ltd. *

CHARLOTTE E. K. BANKS, *Lecturer in Psychology, University College, London, England.*

This test has been designed to measure the ability of children between the ages of 6-6 and 8-6. It contains 100 items in seven sections, with problems in following directions, classification, picture series, perception of mirror images and simple relations, and number series. It thus covers a slightly wider sample of cognitive processes than the N.F.E.R. *Picture Intelligence Test I.*

With the exception of attempts to draw sea, rivers, and mountains, the drawings are very clear and unambiguous, though peculiarly unaesthetic to the adult eye. The author has drawn up an excellent teachers' handbook, giving directions for administering and scoring, data concerning reliability, and suggestions for the use of the conversion table and norms.

The test was standardised on a complete year-group of 9,951 children between the ages of 7-1 and 8-2. Standard scores are given in the conversion table for each month between the ages of 6-6 and 8-6. The scores are based on norms having a mean of 100 and a standard deviation of 15. Mental ages are also given for the use of clinical psychologists. Intelligence quotients for children younger than 6-6 years and older than 8-6 years may be found by extrapolation, using a simple formula provided in the handbook.

The reliability of the test, determined by Ferguson's formula 29, is given as .97. The 100 items in the test were chosen from an original set of 250 items on the basis of item analysis. Little information, however, seems to be available about the validity of the test.

M. L. KELLMER PRINGLE, *Lecturer in Education, and Deputy Head, Department of Child Study, University of Birmingham, Birmingham, England.*

This recently designed test is closely similar to the *Moray House Picture Intelligence Test,* though it is in some aspects inferior to it. Of its seven sections, Following Directions, Doesn't Belong, Sequences, Matching, Mirror Images, Analogies, and Series, six are identical with six of the nine Moray House subtests; however, the layout of the latter is clearer and more generous. A number of the drawings in the Deeside test have too much detail for children of the age for which the test is intended, and a high proportion of the items (32 out of a total of 100) consist of educational symbols, such as letters, numbers, and clockfaces. The title of the test is thus rather misleading since a third of its content probes children's readiness to cope with reading and number work. For example, in Section 1 the following instructions are given: "There are five numbers. Put a cross on the number that is smaller than all but the third number" or "There are five sums. Put a cross on the sum that is wrong [i.e., five addition sums, the wrong one being 7 and 9 makes 17]." Or "Put crosses on the *two* words [out of a total of six words] which are spelt wrong." Similarly, in Section 2 an odd number has to be picked from among four even ones, and, from among six small clockfaces, the one showing a half hour instead of the full hour has to be crossed out. In the matching section, the logic of some items is rather unconvincing.

The Teacher's Handbook gives clear directions for administering and scoring the test.

Though quite a useful and well standardised addition to the available nonverbal tests for this age group, this reviewer fails to see that as a new test it has any special merits or purpose. Both the Moray House and the N.F.E.R. picture intelligence tests are superior in design and layout and at least equally well standardised. If the author of the *Deeside Picture Puzzles* is deliberately aiming at exploring the early stages of children's educational attainments, it is nowhere explicitly stated. This would constitute a departure from other tests of this type, in which case some interpretative guidance should be given to its users. Lastly, it is regrettable that the old label "mentally defective" for IQ's below 70 should be perpetuated in the Teacher's Handbook when the term "educationally subnormal" is officially (and with beneficial effects) current in our educational system.

[328]
★Detroit General Intelligence Examination. Grades 7–12; 1938–54; consists of 8 of the 10 subtests used to get an intelligence score in the *Detroit General Aptitudes Examination;* Form A ('54, identical with subtests copyrighted in 1938); revised manual ('54); $3.25 per 25 tests; 65¢ per specimen set; postpaid; 31(45) minutes; Harry J. Baker and Paul H. Voelker; Public School Publishing Co. *

[329]

*[Detroit Intelligence Tests.] Grades 2–4, 5–8, 9–16; 1924–56; 3 levels; $2.75 per 25 tests; 40¢ per specimen set of any one level; postpaid; Harry J. Baker; Public School Publishing Co. *

a) PUBLIC SCHOOL PRIMARY INTELLIGENCE TEST. Grades 2–4; 1954–56; revision of *Detroit Primary Intelligence Test;* Forms A, B ('54, identical with Forms C, D copyrighted in 1924 except for minor changes); manual ('56); (45) minutes.

b) DETROIT ALPHA INTELLIGENCE TEST. Grades 4–8; Forms S, T ('54, same as tests published in 1941); revised manual ('54); 32(45) minutes.

c) DETROIT ADVANCED INTELLIGENCE TEST. Grades 9–16; 1924–42; Forms V, W ('25); manual ('42); 29(40) minutes.

REFERENCES

1–2. See 4:288.
3. SAWYER, CLIFFORD R. *A Comparison of the Detroit and Kuhlmann-Anderson Intelligence Tests as Applied in the Grand Forks Public Schools.* Master's thesis, University of North Dakota (Grand Forks, N.D.), 1931. Pp. 60.
4. KELLY, PRICE O. *Comparative Validity and Reliability of Four Intelligence Tests in the Ninth Grade.* Master's thesis, University of Kentucky (Lexington, Ky.), 1933. Pp. 63.
5. NEMZEK, CLAUDE L., AND DE HEUS, JOHN H. "The Prediction of Academic and Non-Academic Marks in Junior High Schools." *Sch & Soc* 50:670–2 N 18 '39. * (*PA* 14:1598)
6. BAILEY, ALBERT E. *The Relative Validity of Ten Different Intelligence Tests.* Doctor's thesis, University of Washington (Seattle, Wash.), 1942.
7. MILLER, LYLE L. *An Analysis of the Predictive Values of the Section of the Detroit Advanced Intelligence Test.* Master's thesis, University of Southern California (Los Angeles, Calif.), 1944.
8. BARNOWE, THEODORE J. *The Influence of Scoring Technique and Construction on the Validity of Mental Tests.* Doctor's thesis, University of Washington (Seattle, Wash.), 1946.
9. CARLILE, A. B. "Predicting Performance in the Teaching Profession." *J Ed Res* 47:641–68 My '54. * (*PA* 29:3063)
10. FOWLER, WILLIAM L. *A Comparative Analysis of Pupil Performance on Conventional and Culture-Controlled Mental Tests.* Doctor's thesis, University of Michigan (Ann Arbor, Mich.), 1956. (*DA* 17:91)
11. FOWLER, WILLIAM L. "A Comparative Analysis of Pupil Performance on Conventional and Culture-Controlled Mental Tests." *Yearb Nat Council Meas Used Ed* 14:8–19 '57. *

For a review by W. Line, see 40:1393.

[330]

★The Dominion Group Test of Intelligence. Ages 13 and over; 1945; adaptation of Form B of the advanced level of *Group Test of Learning Capacity: The Dominion Tests* for Australian use; Form B ['45]; mimeographed manual ['45]; 5s. per 10 tests; 1s. per scoring key; 2s. per manual; 3s. 6d. per specimen set; postpaid within Australia; 30(45) minutes; Australian Council for Educational Research. *

[331]

★Doppelt Mathematical Reasoning Test. Graduate students and employees; 1958, c1954; IBM; Form A ('54); manual ('58); distribution restricted and test administered only at specified licensed testing centers; details may be obtained from publisher; 50(60) minutes; Jerome E. Doppelt; Psychological Corporation. *

[332]

★Easel Age Scale. Grades kgn–1; 1955; 1 form; $3.75 per set of testing materials; no formal testing time since paintings are produced during regular class sessions; Beatrice Lantz; California Test Bureau. *

NAOMI STEWART, *Formerly Staff Associate, Educational Testing Service, Princeton, New Jersey.*

The *Easel Age Scale* is a valuable new tool for understanding young children and deserves to be widely accepted. With the use of the scale, free tempera (calcimine) paintings produced by kindergarten and primary grade children in the course of their ordinary classroom activity can be scored in such a way as to yield reliable and valid measures of the children's mental maturity. The children are not subjected to any of the stresses that are sometimes involved in "taking a test." In fact, it is essential to the validity of the results that the children be under no strain and that each child feel free to paint as and what he wishes.

All that is required is an easel (or several), large paper (approximately 18 by 24 inches) of newsprint quality, long handled brushes with bristles around ¾ inches wide and 1 or 1½ inches long, paints in six designated colors, and —most important—a classroom atmosphere in which easel painting of a free character is a normal part of the day's activity. The teacher simply dates each picture as the child produces it and puts it away for scoring at her leisure.

The *Easel Age Scale* recognizes that children often produce paintings that are primarily expressions of their feelings and not attempts to express their ideas. Such paintings are not representative of a child's mental and physical maturity, and are not suitable for scoring. The manual gives a number of carefully developed criteria for identifying paintings of this nature —called "Q," for questionable, paintings—and 12 illustrations in full color which exemplify various features of "Q" productions. Teachers are urged to study each child's easel paintings and score the *best* of the paintings done during each period of observation. Paintings that qualify for scoring are rated independently on four separate counts: form, detail, meaning, and relatedness. The manual gives clear directions for rating each of these dimensions and also provides two dozen full color samples of children's paintings, for each of which is given its rating on form, detail, meaning, and relatedness, its easel score and the corresponding easel age, and the chronological age of the child who produced the painting.

The easel score, which is the sum of the four separate ratings, has a very satisfactory test-retest reliability (.95) and a surprisingly high scoring reliability (.94), even when used by comparatively inexperienced raters. The score converts to an easel age that correlates rather closely with mental ages derived from such instruments as the *Goodenough Intelligence Test,* the *Pintner-Cunningham Primary Test,* and the *California Test of Mental Maturity.*

Throughout the manual, emphasis is placed on using the scale in a developmental context. As already indicated, safeguards are included to make sure that only representative paintings are scored by the teacher. In addition, teachers are urged to maintain growth records on each child, making a minimum of three evaluations a year, based on paintings produced at the beginning, middle, and end of the year. In this context, and in light of the careful directions and illustrations for scoring the paintings, even inexperienced teachers should be able to obtain valid results.

In addition to its value as a measure of the mental maturity of young children, the *Easel Age Scale,* as the manual clearly explains and illustrates, has the important advantage of increasing the teacher's understanding of the child as a whole. The scale should undoubtedly be in the possession of every kindergarten and primary grade teacher who has, or can arrange for, facilities for making easel painting part of the regular class activity.

FLORENCE M. TEAGARDEN, *Emeritus Professor of Psychology, University of Pittsburgh, Pittsburgh, Pennsylvania.*

The author describes the *Easel Age Scale* as a "rating scale for studying the growth and adjustment of kindergarten and primary grade children, as well as somewhat older mentally retarded children." Over 10 years went into this study, involving the examination of more than 6,000 pictures painted at the easel by children of ages 4 to 9 in the Los Angeles area. Unfortunately, the statistical treatment does not reflect anything like the number of paintings studied. Further statistical studies are, however, promised. The author's claim for the reliability of the scale is based upon a study of pictures by 37 children who made two or more paintings within a month in 1945. The test-retest coefficient of reliability was found to be .95. The validity of the scale was determined by comparing pictures made by 112 children and their ratings on the *Goodenough Intelligence Test.*

Directions for administering the scale require that the rater examine a picture first to determine whether the child has primarily expressed his feelings and emotions rather than ideas. Such paintings of emotions are called "Q" (Questionable) because from them one cannot necessarily determine the child's maturity. No data are given as to the validation of the assumption of "emotions." Twelve samples are given of Q pictures. Certainly in a few of these the clinician can recognize some of the usual diagnostic signs, such as great use of color, restrictions within boundaries, meticulous detail, and the like. However, since no data are given as to the age, intelligence, or other evidences of emotionality for the children who made the samples, one might feel hesitant to discard a painting as a Q painting from these meager details.

If the person using the scale decides that a picture is not a Q picture, then he proceeds to examine and score it for each of these items in order: Form, on a 7-point scale; Detail, on a 7-point scale; Meaning (to the adult), on an 8-point scale; and Relatedness (beginning of depth perception) on an 8-point scale. The highest possible score in each of these categories is assigned pictures in which recognizable objects are portrayed in action. Twenty-four pictures are scored as samples.

Norms are based on analysis of the paintings of 1,329 children ranging in chronological age from 4-6 to 9-6. We are not told how the raw scores were converted into easel age equivalents. At some places along the normative scale an increase of a single raw point raises the easel age equivalent by 3 months; in some places by 2 months; and in some places by 1 month. The possible raw scores run from 2 through 30, with easel age equivalents from below 4-0 through 8-6 plus.

The progression of mental ability and representative drawing in a more or less *para passu* manner is an intriguing subject to the clinical and research psychologist. The author has added more material to the field. Her attempt to measure form, detail, meaning, and relatedness—each leading ultimately to representation of action—is good. The reproduced paintings are interesting. The reported statistics do not add greatly to the value of the study.

*The Essential Intelligence Test. Ages 7-12; 1940-52; c1940-48; title on manuals is *Essential Junior Intelligence Test;* Forms [A] ('40), B ('49); Form A manual ['40], Form B manual ['49]; revised norms ['52] for Form B; 25-49 tests, 5d. each; 6d. per single copy; 1s. 6d. per manual for either form; postage extra; 45(60) minutes; Fred J. Schonell and R. H. Adams; Oliver & Boyd Ltd. *

R. WINTERBOURN, *Professor of Education, The University of Auckland, Auckland, New Zealand.*

Form A of this verbal test of general intelligence has now been in use for 18 years, Form B for almost 10 years. During this time the two forms have been very widely applied, particularly in Great Britain, but also in other countries, notably Australia and New Zealand. It can fairly be said that they have withstood the test of time.

Face validity appears to be good. The 100 items are grouped in 18 sections, thus avoiding what must be for some children the formidable appearance of an unbroken sequence of a large number of items. Eleven practice items familiarize the child with all types of questions he will find. They are worked through orally with the examiner. Directions to both children and examiner are clear. The aim is to create a puzzle solving attitude in the former.

Item types include sentence completions (multiple choice and the filling of gaps), recognition of similarities, differences, and opposites, number and letter sequence completions, arithmetical problems, and other problems.

Because of the increasing test sophistication of British children, a restandardization is about to be carried out in Great Britain. An Australian standardization of Form A is now available.

A recently calculated split-half reliability coefficient (208 children, ages unspecified) is .94 (communication from the author). A split-half coefficient of .92 based on a small group of 66 11-year-olds and a test-retest coefficient of .92 (retest after one year on an unspecified group) were reported earlier for Form A. An intercorrelation of .95 is reported between Forms A and B.

The tests have measured up quite well to statistical evaluation and practical use in schools. Articles appearing in the *British Journal of Educational Psychology* from time to time, referring to the use of these tests along with others, indicate that they have proved to be satisfactory means of assessing general intelligence. One suspects that they are more valid for children in the middle and higher age groups than for 7- and 8-year-olds. It is to be hoped that more precise statistical data will be made available to confirm or reject this suspicion.

For a review by F. W. Warburton, see 4:290.

[334]

★**General Verbal Practice Test G1.** Ages 10–11; 1954; to be given at least 3 weeks before administering a verbal intelligence test in order to equalize coaching effects; 1 form ['54]; distribution restricted to directors of education; 4s. 6d. per 12 tests; 6d. per single copy; 6d. per manual ['54]; postage extra; 45(50) minutes; published for National Foundation for Educational Research in England and Wales; Newnes Educational Publishing Co. Ltd. *

[335]

Goodenough Intelligence Test. Grades kgn–3; 1926; also called *Draw-a-Man;* 1 form; $1.50 per 35 children's drawing sheets; $3.25 per manual (see *1* below); postage extra; specimen set not available; (10) minutes; Florence L. Goodenough; World Book Co. *

REFERENCES

1–60. See 4:292.
61. PETERSON, JOSEPH, AND TELFORD, C. W. "Results of Group and Individual Tests Applied to the Practically Pure-Blood Negro Children on St. Helena Island." *J Comp Psychol* 11:115–44 D '30. * (PA 5:1576)
62. TSAO, D. F. *A Comparative Study of Drawing Ability in English Children in the Goodenough Scale.* Master's thesis, University of London (London, England), 1935.
63. MAURER, KATHARINE M. "Measuring Leadership in College Women by Free Association." Abstract. *Am Psychol* 2:334 Ag '47. *
64. BEYER, FRANCES N. *The Goodenough Measurement of Intelligence Used in a Comparison of the Test Results of the Deaf Children and the Normal Hearing Children.* Master's thesis, MacMurray College for Women (Jacksonville, Ill.), 1949.
65. BENDER, LAURETTA. "The Goodenough Test (Drawing a Man) in Chronic Encephalitis in Children." *J Child Psychiatry* 3:449–59 O '51. *
66. ANSBACHER, H. L. "The Goodenough Draw-A-Man Test and Primary Mental Abilities." *J Consult Psychol* 16:176–80 Je '52. * (PA 27:5141)
67. BRITTON, JOSEPH H. "Influence of Social Class Upon Performance on Draw-A-Man Test." Abstract. *Am Psychol* 7:304 Jl '52. *
68. COBB, KATHARINE. "Measuring Leadership in College Women by Free Association." *J Abn & Social Psychol* 47:126–8 Ja '52. * (PA 26:6178)
69. DEJESÚS, CRUZ. *A Study of the Language Development and Goodenough I.Q. of Puerto Rican Preschool Children in New York.* Master's thesis, Fordham University (New York, N.Y.), 1952.
70. MCHUGH, ANN F. *The Effect of Preceding Affective States on the Goodenough Draw-A-Man Test of Intelligence.* Master's thesis, Fordham University (New York, N.Y.), 1952.
71. MARQUIS, DOROTHY P.; SINNETT, E. ROBERT; AND WINTER, WILLIAM D. "A Psychological Study of Peptic Ulcer Patients." *J Clin Psychol* 8:266–72 Jl '52. * (PA 27:6072)
72. ANASTASI, ANNE, AND DEJESÚS, CRUZ. "Language Development and Nonverbal IQ of Puerto Rican Preschool Children in New York City." *J Abn & Social Psychol* 48:357–66 Jl '53. * (PA 28:2471)
73. GLOWATSKY, EDWARD. "The Verbal Element in the Intelligence Scores of Congenitally Deaf and Hard of Hearing Children." *Am Ann Deaf* 98:328–35 My '53. * (PA 28:7921)
74. HANVIK, LEO J. "The Goodenough Test as a Measure of Intelligence in Child Psychiatric Patients." *J Clin Psychol* 9:71–2 Ja '53. * (PA 27:7773)
75. JOHNSON, GRANVILLE B., JR. "Bilingualism as Measured by a Reaction-Time Technique and the Relationship Between a Language and a Non-Language Intelligence Quotient." *J Genetic Psychol* 82:3–9 Mr '53. * (PA 27:7648)
76. PAPAVASSILIOU, I. TH. "The Validity of the Goodenough Draw-A-Man Test in Greece." *J Ed Psychol* 44:244–8 Ap '53. * (PA 28:2663)
77. REICHENBERG-HACKETT, WALLY "Changes in Goodenough Drawings After a Gratifying Experience." Discussion by Esther Katz Rosen. *Am J Orthopsychiatry* 23:501–17 Jl '53. * (PA 28:2667)
78. TUSKA, SHIRLEY A. *Developmental Concepts With the Draw-A-Person Test at Different Grade Levels.* Master's thesis, Ohio University (Athens, Ohio), 1953.
79. BLISS, MONTE, AND BERGER, ANDREW. "Measurement of Mental Age as Indicated by the Male Figure Drawings of the Mentally Subnormal Using Goodenough and Machover Instructions." *Am J Mental Def* 59:73–9 Jl '54. * (PA 29:4253)
80. BRITTON, JOSEPH H. "Influence of Social Class Upon Performance on the Draw-A-Man Test." *J Ed Psychol* 45:44–51 Ja '54. * (PA 28:7208)

81. Harris, Robert E., and Fisher, Jerome. "Closure Phenomena (Prägnanz) in Social Interaction." Abstract. *Am Psychol* 9:390–1 Ag '54. *
82. Haward, L. R. C., and Roland, W. A. "Some Inter-Cultural Differences on the Draw-A-Man Test: Goodenough Scores." *Man* 54:86–8 Je '54. *
83. Doris, Robert E. *The Relationship of the Goodenough Draw-A-Man Test to the Wechsler Intelligence Scale for Children: A Study With Mentally Retarded Children in Fresno County, California.* Master's thesis, Fresno State College (Fresno, Calif.), 1955.
84. Gunzburg, Herbert C. "Scope and Limitations of the Goodenough Drawing Test Method in Clinical Work With Mental Defectives." *J Clin Psychol* 11:8–15 Ja '55. * (*PA* 29:7280)
85. Haward, L. R. C., and Roland, W. A. "Some Inter-Cultural Differences on the Draw-A-Man Test: Part II, Machover Scores." *Man* 55:27–9 F '55. *
86. Haward, L. R. C., and Roland, W. A. "Some Inter-Cultural Differences on the Draw-A-Man Test: Part III, Conclusion." *Man* 55:40–2 Mr '55. *
87. Norman, Ralph D., and Midkiff, Katherine L. "Navaho Children on Raven Progressive Matrices and Goodenough Draw-A-Man Tests." *Southw J Anthrop* 11:129–36 su '55. * (*PA* 30:4426)
88. Bailey, Robert B. *A Study of Predicting Academic Success in Elementary School Reading From Projective Tests.* Doctor's thesis, University of Oklahoma (Norman, Okla.), 1956. (*DA* 16:1397)
89. Brenner, Anton, and Morse, Nancy C. "The Measurement of Children's Readiness for School." *Papers Mich Acad Sci, Arts & Letters* 41:333–40 '56. *
90. Murphy, Mary Martha. "A Goodenough Scale Evaluation of Human Figure Drawings of Three Non-Psychotic Groups of Adults." *J Clin Psychol* 12:397–9 O '56. * (*PA* 32:4199)
91. Dennis, Wayne. "Performance of Near Eastern Children on the Draw-A-Man Test." *Child Develop* 28:427–30 D '57. *
92. Herron, William G. *The Effect of Preceding Affective States on the Goodenough Drawing Test of Intelligence.* Master's thesis, Fordham University (New York, N.Y.), 1957.
93. Hunt, Betty, and Patterson, Ruth M. "Performance of Familial Mentally Deficient Children in Response to Motivation on the Goodenough Draw-A-Man Test." *Am J Mental Def* 62:326–9 S '57. *
94. Jones, Allan W., and Rich, Thomas A. "The Goodenough Draw-A-Man Test as a Measure of Intelligence in Aged Adults." *J Consult Psychol* 21:235–8 Je '57. *

For a review by Naomi Stewart, see 4:292.

[336]
*The Graduate Record Examinations Aptitude Test. College seniors and graduate students; 1949–58; for more complete information, see 599; 2 scores: verbal, quantitative; IBM; 150(170) minutes; Educational Testing Service. *

REFERENCES

1–2. See 4:293.
3. Saum, James A. *Selection Techniques and Their Application in the Stanford School of Education.* Doctor's thesis, Stanford University (Stanford, Calif.), 1951.
4. Crosby, Donald W. "The Development of a Test of Academic Aptitude for Superior College Students." Abstract. *Calif J Ed Res* 4:185–6 S '53. *
5. Schultz, Margaret K., and Angoff, William H. "The Development of New Scales for the Aptitude and Advanced Tests of the Graduate Record Examinations." Abstract. *Am Psychol* 8:430 Ag '53. *
6. Manuel, Herschel T. "A Study of an Examination for Admission to Candidacy for the Doctorate in Education." *Yearb Nat Council Meas Used Ed* 11:15–8 '54. *
7. Schultz, Margaret K., and Angoff, William H. "The Development of New Scales for the Aptitude and Advanced Tests of the Graduate Record Examinations." *J Ed Psychol* 47:285–94 My '56. * (*PA* 32:2127)
8. Capps, Marian P., and DeCosta, Frank A. "Contributions of the Graduate Record Examinations and the National Teacher Examinations to the Prediction of Graduate School Success." *J Ed Res* 50:383–9 Ja '57. * (*PA* 32:937)
9. Robinson, Donald W. "A Comparison of Two Batteries of Tests as Predictors of First Year Achievement in the Graduate School of Bradley University." *Yearb Nat Council Meas Used Ed* 15:118–27 '58. *

John T. Dailey, *Program Director, American Institute for Research, Washington, D.C.* [Review of Form EGR.]

This is a test of general scholastic ability suitable for use at the college senior or graduate school level. It is designed to accompany the Advanced Tests, which are comprehensive achievement tests in 16 different fields of study, and the Area Tests for the social sciences, humanities, and material sciences. The first part of the Aptitude Test consists of verbal reasoning questions (opposites, analogies, and completion) plus paragraph reading comprehension. These together make up the verbal score. The second part of the test includes various kinds of quantitative mathematical materials, such as questions on arithmetic reasoning, on algebraic problems, and on the interpretation of graphs, diagrams, and descriptive data. These give the quantitative score. Scores are reported as 3-digit scaled scores with the third digit always a zero. This is necessary since one raw score point represents 10 or more points of scaled score.

The reliability of each part of the test is reported as .92, which is adequate for the two parts of the test to be used separately when desired.

In content the test parallels most other scholastic aptitude tests from the junior high school level up. Essentially, it measures verbal reasoning ability, vocabulary-reading comprehension, and arithmetic achievement. Statistics quoted in the manual indicate that the test correlates substantially with the specific advanced tests. Validities are not available in the manual. They would, perhaps, be superfluous since the pattern of validities of this test should be highly predictable; at any rate, validity figures should be about the same as those obtained with any similar test commonly used at the graduate school level.

Extremely voluminous normative material is supplied in several manuals. Normative data are available for a large number of categories of applicants. Results on the Aptitude Test are reported separately for those subjects taking each of 16 advanced tests. As always, those taking the education test score lowest of all. It is of interest to note that psychologists, who are one of the highest scoring groups on the *Miller Analogies Test,* score at about the median for the various groups on the Aptitude Test. Exploring the reasons for this might prove interesting.

In summary, the Aptitude Test is an adequately constructed and well calibrated test of general scholastic potential that should be useful when used in combination with the Area

Tests and the Advanced Tests. It will be of less utility when used alone, becoming then only another general scholastic aptitude test although specifically slanted in terms of difficulty level for a high level school or graduate student population.

For reviews by J. P. Guilford and Carl I. Hovland of Forms XGR and YGR, see 4:293. For a review by Harold Seashore of the entire series, see 601.

[337]

★Group Selective Test No. 1. Ages 10–12.0; [1940]; 1 form; no data on reliability and validity; out of print; 31(45) minutes; M. M. Lewis; University of London Press Ltd. *

T. R. MILES, *Lecturer in Psychology, University College, Bangor, Wales.*

The instruction manual contains no details as to where or how this test was standardised, no reliability coefficient, and no record of any attempt at validation by means of external criteria. Its avowed purpose is to grade children "according to their ability to profit by higher education of the type which, at present, is provided in secondary schools"; but as to its effectiveness we are told only that in both urban and rural districts it has been found to give "satisfactory" results. Such a claim is far too vague to be convincing; in addition, the evaluative word "profit" brings in issues other than psychological ones. Whether a child has "profited" by his education can be determined only if there is broad agreement as to what is "profitable." This raises social and moral questions on which the psychologist, as such, has no special authority to pronounce.

With regard to individual items, the layout and explanation in the first part (Changing Patterns) seem to me very unsatisfactory; words and diagrams are interspersed in such a way that some of the time one has to read vertically instead of horizontally, and even then the result is anything but plain English. The reviewer is also uneasy about Part 4 (Reasoning), where on two occasions the correct answer is given as "I cannot tell," the data being insufficient for any conclusion to be drawn. "No answer possible" might perhaps have been a preferable formula. A notice at the top of the page says, "Underline *I cannot tell,* if that is your answer"; but is this cryptic remark sufficient to reassure the very conscientious child? Reluctance to say "I cannot tell" may vary according to a child's temperament and training; ability to overcome this reluctance is not purely a cognitive task.

A more serious criticism might perhaps be levelled at some of the items in Part 5. Each item contains five pictures, four of which tell a coherent story. The pictures are to be numbered in the correct order, the fifth being left blank. Far too many of these stories, it seems to the reviewer, are suggestive of what may be called a "bourgeois" background; they are taken from events in the social life of the British upper-middle classes—running water from a tap, parcels arriving by post, an elegant lady with an umbrella, and, above all, a boy having a bath and then going to bed in pyjamas. Has not the author overlooked the fact that at least some of the children taking the test may have no running water in their houses, let alone a bathroom, and that the use of pyjamas, even nowadays, may not be by any means universal? Part 5 seems to exemplify the danger that upper-middle class test setters may inadvertently overload tests with upper-middle class items.

One further caution should be given. When verbal and performance scores are discrepant, users of the test would do well to consider each in isolation; it may not always be meaningful to sum the two. A specific ability on the performance side is not unknown, and there may be children, particularly those suffering from the syndrome known as dyslexia or developmental aphasia (involving, briefly, failure to recognise words at sight and failure of spatial orientation), who show high reasoning ability but are quite at a loss when it comes to grasping the spatial relationships in some nonverbal items.

In general, I am hesitant to recommend the widespread use of this test. To investigate a child's powers of reasoning and abstraction by the occasional use of some such test may well be informative; but a simple numerical score, based on the number of "correct" answers, should not, by itself, be given much weight when major decisions about a child's future are involved. Since it is far from clear precisely what tests of this kind are supposed to be measuring (if indeed they are a measure of anything at all), it is dangerous to take for granted that they measure it efficiently.[1]

[1] Since this review was prepared the publisher has indicated that the test is now out of print.

[338]

★**Group Test 75.** Ages 12–13; 1957; 1 form ['57]; mimeographed manual ['57]; no data on reliability and validity; separate answer sheets must be used; 27s. per 12 tests; 1s. 6d. per 12 answer sheets; 2s. 3d. per set of scoring key and manual; 2s. 3d. per specimen set; postage extra; 20(35) minutes; National Institute of Industrial Psychology. *

[339]

***Group Tests 33 and 33B.** Ages 14 and over; 1923–56; forms 33 ['23]; 33B ['56]; mimeographed manuals [form 33, '50; form 33B, '56]; no data on reliability and validity; 5s. per 12 tests; 1s. 3d. per manual; 1s. per specimen set; postage extra; 29(35) minutes; National Institute of Industrial Psychology. *

REFERENCES

1–2. See 4:295.
3. MITCHELL, J. H. "An Experiment in the Selection of Sales Managers." *Occupational Psychol* 12:308–318 au '38. * (*PA* 13:500)
4. HOLLIDAY, FRANK. "An Investigation Into the Selection of Apprentices for the Engineering Industry." *Occupational Psychol* 14:69–81 Ap '40. * (*PA* 14:3710)
5. SLATER, PATRICK. "Some Group Tests of Spatial Judgment or Practical Ability." *Occupational Psychol* 14:40–55 Ja '40. * (*PA* 14:2644)
6. HOLLIDAY, FRANK. "A Further Investigation Into the Selection of Apprentices for the Engineering Industry." *Occupational Psychol* 15:173–84 O '41. * (*PA* 16:732)
7. HOLLIDAY, FRANK. "A Survey of an Investigation Into the Selection of Apprentices for the Engineering Industry." *Occupational Psychol* 16:1–19 Ja '42. * (*PA* 16:2823)
8. HOLLIDAY, FRANK. "The Relation Between Psychological Test Scores and Subsequent Proficiency of Apprentices in the Engineering Industry." *Occupational Psychol* 17:168–85 O '43. * (*PA* 18:1835)
9. ORTON, R., AND MARTIN, D. R. "Psychiatric Screening of Medical Students." *Lancet* 255:321–3 Ag 28 '48. *
10. TOZER, A. H. D., AND LARWOOD, H. J. C. "An Analysis of Intelligence Test Scores of Students in a University Department of Education." *Brit J Psychol* 44:347–58 N '53. * (*PA* 28:6597)
11. TOZER, A. H. D., AND LARWOOD, H. J. C. "The Changes in Intelligence Test Score of Students Between the Beginning and End of Their University Courses." *Brit J Ed Psychol* 28:120–8 Je '58. *

[340]

Group Test 90A. Adults; 1947–48; 1 form ['48]; no data on reliability and validity; mimeographed manual ['48]; 5s. per 12 tests; 1s. per single copy; 1s. 6d. per manual; postage extra; 20(30) minutes; National Institute of Industrial Psychology. *

JOHN LIGGETT, *Lecturer in Applied Psychology, University of Durham, Newcastle, England.*

This paper and pencil test of verbal intelligence consists of four separate sets of problems, each set requiring 5 minutes of working time. The first set employs items requiring the correct synonym or antonym of a given word to be selected from among five alternatives; the second requires the selection of correct "analogies" from among five possible choices; the third consists of jumbled sentences whose meaning (when the sentences are mentally rearranged) can be completed by only one of five given words; the last consists of straightforward sentences whose meaning can be completed by only one of five given words. There is supervised practice for each subtest.

Norms are given for ages 20–25 for an unselected group and for subjects who had previously attended a secondary grammar school. Information on distributions of scores up to 60 years of age is supplied on request to the publisher. This supplementary information shows that the test has been administered to 7,000 temporary civil servants, aged 20–60 years, drawn from all educational levels. These subjects were to some extent a selected group in that they had been displaced from their ordinary occupations by the upheaval of the war years. Results are subdivided according to level of school orginally attended. The figures show that the decline of scores with age is a perfectly linear one. No norms have been compiled for children of school age since the test has been mainly used for industrial purposes. The lack of norms for children is unfortunate since the test is a competently produced one with good item variety, and it is easy to administer and score. It should find considerable usefulness as a measure of verbal ability in normal subjects.

[341]

*****Group Test of Learning Capacity: Dominion Tests.** Grades kgn–1, 4–6, 7–9, 10–12 and adults; 1934–56; formerly called *Group Test of Intelligence*; 2 forms; 4 levels; 45¢ per specimen set of primary, intermediate, or advanced level; postage extra; Department of Educational Research, Ontario College of Education, University of Toronto; distributed by Guidance Centre. *

a) PRIMARY. Grades kgn–1; 1934–56; Forms A, B ('56); administration of both forms is recommended; revised manual ('56); norms ('50); $1.80 per 25 tests; (50) minutes in 2 sessions.
b) JUNIOR. Grades 4–6; 1940–56; Forms A, B ('56); revised manual ('56); norms ('52); $1.20 per 25 tests; 35¢ per specimen set; 25(45) minutes.
c) INTERMEDIATE. Grades 7–9; 1934–56; 2 editions.
  1) *Subtest Edition.* 1934–56; Forms A, B ('34); revised manual ('56); norms ('52); $1.80 per 25 tests; 37(50) minutes.
  2) *Omnibus Edition.* 1950–56; Forms A, B ('50); revised manual ('56); norms ('52); $1.20 per 25 tests; 30(45) minutes.
d) ADVANCED. Grades 10–12 and adults; 1939–55; Forms A, B ('39); revised manual ('55); norms ('54); $1.20 per 25 tests; 10¢ per scoring key; 30(45) minutes.

For a review by W. G. Emmett, see 4:294; for a review by F. T. Tyler, see 3:231.

[342]

*****The Henmon-Nelson Tests of Mental Ability, Revised Edition.** Grades 3–6, 6–9, 9–12; 1931–58; previous edition (see 4:299) still available; Forms A ('57), B ('58); 3 levels; manual ('57) for each level; $3 per 35 tests; 42¢ per specimen set of any one level; postage extra; 30(35) minutes; Tom A. Lamke and M. J. Nelson; Houghton Mifflin Co. *

REFERENCES

1-25. See 4:299.
26. DODSON, MARY H. *A Study in Shorthand and Typewriting Prognosis.* Master's thesis, University of Kentucky (Lexington, Ky.), 1943.
27. JOHNSON, RALPH H., AND BOND, GUY L. "Reading Ease of Commonly Used Tests." *J Appl Psychol* 34:319-24 O '50. * (PA 26:299)
28. BARBE, WALTER, AND GRILK, WERNER. "Correlations Between Reading Factors and IQ." *Sch & Soc* 75:134-6 Mr 1 '52. *
29. LIEN, ARNOLD JUEL. "A Comparative-Predictive Study of Students in the Four Curricula of a Teacher Education Institution." *J Exp Ed* 21:81-219 D '52. *
30. TURNER, G. H., AND PENFOLD, D. J. "The Scholastic Aptitude of Indian Children of the Caradoc Reserve." *Can J Psychol* 6:31-44 Mr '52. * (PA 26:6935)
31. JUSTMAN, JOSEPH, AND WRIGHTSTONE, J. WAYNE. "A Comparison of Pupil Functioning on the Pintner Intermediate Test and the Henmon-Nelson Test of Mental Ability." *Ed & Psychol Meas* 13:102-9 sp '53. * (PA 28:1567)
32. SMITH, VAUGHN E. *Correlation Between the Intelligence Quotients as Determined by the Henmon-Nelson Tests of Mental Ability and Achievement of Two Hundred and Fifty Graduates From Tony High School, Tony, Wisconsin.* Master's thesis, Wisconsin State College (Superior, Wis.), 1953.
33. CARLILE, A. B. "Predicting Performance in the Teaching Profession." *J Ed Res* 47:641-68 My '54. * (PA 29:3063)
34. RANDALL, ROGERS E. "Correlation of Henmon-Nelson Tests of Mental Ability With the National Achievement General Science Test." *Sch Sci & Math* 54:635-6 N '54. *
35. LAMKE, TOM ARTHUR. "The Revision of the Henmon-Nelson Test of Mental Ability." *Yearb Nat Council Meas Used Ed* 12(pt 1):78-80 '55. *
36. FOWLER, WILLIAM L. *A Comparative Analysis of Pupil Performance on Conventional and Culture-Controlled Mental Tests.* Doctor's thesis, University of Michigan (Ann Arbor, Mich.), 1956. (DA 17:91)
37. LAMKE, TOM ARTHUR. "The Standardization of the Henmon-Nelson Revision." *Yearb Nat Council Meas Used Ed* 13:42-4 '56. *
38. MITCHELL, JAMES V., JR. "A Comparison of the Factorial Structure of Cognitive Functions for a High and Low Status Group." *J Ed Psychol* 47:397-414 N '56. *
39. FOWLER, WILLIAM L. "A Comparative Analysis of Pupil Performance on Conventional and Culture-Controlled Mental Tests." *Yearb Nat Council Meas Used Ed* 14:8-19 '57. *

D. WELTY LEFEVER, *Professor of Education, University of Southern California, Los Angeles, California.*

CHANGES PRODUCED BY THE REVISION. In this revision of the *Henmon-Nelson Test of Mental Ability* a number of the weaknesses of the earlier edition have been remedied. The tests are much more attractive in typography, design, and quality of paper used. The items are more easily read, the provision for recording the responses is less confusing to the eye, and the manual is more complete and helpful. The revision retains the outstanding virtue of quick and easy scoring through the use of the Clapp-Young self-marking device which requires no separate scoring key. The pupil's responses are recorded on the reverse side of the test page by the action of a carbon backing. When the scorer removes the perforated edging and pulls the carbon backing away, the correct responses are clearly indicated.

In the revised edition, the range of grade levels from 3 through 12 has been assigned to three batteries (3-6, 6-9, 9-12), in place of the former two batteries (3-8, 7-12). This change has greatly improved the matching of item difficulty with the range of ability of the pupils at each grade level.

TEST CONTENT. The content of this edition is substantially the same as that of the original tests. Items from the earlier edition were revised and retained or discarded in accordance with an item analysis based on a national sample which included 77 communities in 24 states.

Each test is composed of a scrambled sequence of 90 five-choice items arranged in order of difficulty without regard to the exact character of the items. As a number of critics have remarked regarding the earlier edition, the test contains a "hodge-podge" of item types including vocabulary, sentence completion, word classification, logical selection, disarranged sentences, interpretation of proverbs, verbal analogies, mixed spelling, series completion, design analogies, and arithmetic reasoning. The content is heavily weighted with items measuring various types of verbal ability. However, the history of mental testing has indicated substantial correlations between such test content and scholastic success.

AUTHORS' RATIONALE FOR THE TEST. A potential user of the *Henmon-Nelson Tests of Mental Ability* must answer an important question for himself: Will a relatively short test (90 items in 30 minutes) carrying a heavy verbal emphasis and yielding a single score serve the purposes for which an intelligence test is being administered? Several pages in the manuals are devoted to the rationale underlying the authors' approach to this problem. According to the authors, research findings support the position that "factored" tests or multiscore tests have not predicted scholastic success any better than tests producing a single global score. Subtests in multiscore batteries which apparently have little to do with success in a given subject matter field often yield higher correlations with grades in that field than do the subtests which, because of the nature of their content, ought to be the best predictors. This reviewer finds considerable merit in the interpretation of background research presented in the manual. If a single predictor of school success is needed which can be given in less than a class period and scored with a minimum of time and effort, serious consideration should be given the Henmon-Nelson test. On the other hand, if guidance involving some differentiation among aptitudes is required and if a profile showing the strengths and weaknesses of each counselee is desired, a more complex test battery will be more appropriate. A test yielding a single score may not offer much diagnostic help leading to remedial instruction. In selecting such a test, however, the correlations reported between the subtests and appropriate criteria of success (such as grades) should be examined with care to be sure that a sufficient gain in predictive power is likely to counterbalance the greater cost in material, student time, and scoring time, and the greater expertness required for interpretation.

EVIDENCE FOR VALIDITY. The manual for each test summarizes the data available concerning the validity and reliability of the revised tests. The correlations reported as measures of validity are remarkably similar for the three grade levels.

Evidence for congruent validity is presented in the form of correlations with several well known tests of intelligence. The median coefficient for all levels is .76; the range is .50 to .84. Theoretically, these correlations should be discounted somewhat because of the presence of a common factor, chronological age. However, test manuals reporting correlations between mental ages or raw scores as well as IQ's (such as those for the *Lorge-Thorndike Intelligence Tests* and the *Differential Aptitude Tests*) do not support this suggestion.

Concurrent validity is rather well established by correlations between Henmon-Nelson IQ's and achievement test scores and between IQ's and teachers' grades. The median coefficient for total achievement battery scores versus IQ is .79 (range, .64 to .85). Average grades and IQ produced a median r of .60, with a range of .09 to .74.

In the light of the authors' contention that a single score will predict scholastic success as well as a more elaborate battery, perhaps the most interesting evidence of validity is the series of correlations between Henmon-Nelson IQ's and achievement test scores or teachers' grades for separate subject matter areas. Following are the medians of the correlations reported at the various grade levels: IQ and reading scores, .76; IQ and arithmetic or mathematics scores, .65; IQ and work-study scores, .72; IQ and science scores, .69. Teachers' grades and IQ's produced these median coefficients: English or reading, .64; mathematics, .53; science, .71. These correlations show a fairly homogeneous predictive potential for diverse areas of academic achievement. Since all of these data were obtained after the revision was completed, the number and quality of validity measures reported seems praiseworthy.

EVIDENCE FOR RELIABILITY. The reliability of the revised tests is reported in terms of odd-even correlations for each grade level and form. Correlations between Form A and Form B are given for grades 3, 6, and 12. The evidence for reliability is definitely satisfactory since the coefficients are consistently within the range of acceptable values. The median of the 24 odd-even reliability coefficients reported is .94; the range of values is .90 to .97. The six interform correlations range from .87 to .94, with a median of .91. The differences in reliability coefficients produced by the two approaches seem to demonstrate the presence, to some degree at least, of a speed factor. If further research should indicate that the scores of some pupils are affected by the present time limit, this reviewer would urge that more time be allowed. Too much concern has been given in some quarters to convenience and expediency at the possible sacrifice of the full value that tests can give.

STANDARDIZATION PROCEDURES. The authors deserve special commendation for the excellent plan for determining the norms of the test. They have achieved the rare distinction of clearly defining the population on which the norms are based and of selecting the norming sample in a way that permits an estimate to be made of the sampling error. Cluster sampling was employed and 250 school systems were selected at random from a master file in the Bureau of the Census after 8 strata for size of system and 48 strata representing the several states had been set up. Within each system, a school was selected at random; and within the school, a classroom in the range of grades 3–6. Then classrooms were selected for the 6–9 and 9–12 ranges because they represented the classrooms into which the children tested in the 3–6 range would go as they progressed through school. More than 96 per cent of the classrooms selected by the sampling process actually participated in the study. This is a remarkable achievement in itself and gives the norming sample employed unusual significance.

Tables are furnished in the manuals so that raw scores can be translated into percentile ranks by grade level groups, into mental ages, into grade equivalents, and into deviation IQ's. In the first edition of the manual a number of inconsistencies in IQ values occurred as the authors endeavored to obtain satisfactory articulation between successive test levels. The grade equivalent scale inadvertently slipped out of position during the process of producing better articulation. These discrepancies are being remedied and will undoubtedly be corrected by the time this review is published.

DIFFICULTY OF THE TESTS. In general the level of item difficulty appears to be satisfactory except for some evidence of insufficient ceiling for the 3–6 and the 6–9 tests. In order for a student aged 12 years 6 months (the age at which a raw score equivalent of a grade placement at the middle of grade 6 yields an average IQ and thus, apparently, the average CA for the middle of grade 6) to have an IQ of 130, 87 items would need to be answered correctly. This would leave only three more items for possible "ceiling." With an IQ of 140, only one item would be "left." A similar check on the norms for the middle of the ninth grade and the 6–9 test indicates that at this average CA, an IQ of 130 requires 85.5 correct answers while an IQ of 140 calls for 89. On the other hand, the 9–12 test requires only 79 items right for an IQ of 130 at a CA of 204 months, while an IQ of 140 is based on 83 right answers. Thus, the 9–12 test apparently allows the gifted pupil more opportunity to answer one more item correctly.

The scoring key shows no evidence of a "response bias." The correct answer is distributed among the response positions approximately equally.

More detailed suggestions for the use of test results, prepared for each grade level, would be valuable. Perhaps a special manual on the use of intelligence test measures would be more appropriate than more bulky examiners' manuals.

SUMMARY. The revised edition of the *Henmon-Nelson Tests of Mental Ability* represents a distinct improvement over the earlier edition. It is greatly improved in format, in the usefulness of the examiners' manuals, in the evidence for validity, and especially in the care with which the standardization was conducted. For many purposes a relatively short intelligence test yielding a single score will be satisfactory. As the basis for predicting success in academic subjects, the Henmon-Nelson offers reliable help. It may not be as valuable in diagnosing special problems in learning, in vocational counseling, or in working with the mentally retarded. The heavy emphasis on verbal content may produce results somewhat unfair to the nonacademic student. The potential user of an intelligence test should assess his objectives with care before deciding which type of test is best for him.

LEONA E. TYLER, *Professor of Psychology, University of Oregon, Eugene, Oregon.*

The revision of these widely used tests exemplifies the application of the newest technology of mental measurement to one of our oldest testing problems. The aim was to produce short, self-administering, easily scored instruments that would have maximum predictive validity in school situations. The effort was eminently successful, and the complete, clearly written manuals for the different grade levels present us with the evidence we need for evaluating and interpreting the results.

The reader cannot fail to be impressed with the care that was taken in (*a*) selecting items and matching them so that the different forms and levels would be truly equivalent, (*b*) sampling the total school population in a way that would insure that the norms would be truly representative of this population, and (*c*) collecting and reporting evidence of several different kinds with regard to reliability and validity. Scores can be expressed as mental ages, as percentiles, or as deviation IQ's equated to those on the Stanford-Binet. The grade equivalents of the raw scores are also reported. Any teacher should be able to administer and score the tests. Any educator with a moderately complete background in measurement and statistics should be able to interpret scores correctly.

The most serious question that is likely to be raised with regard to it is whether it does not imply adherence to a theory that intelligence is a single, unitary trait after factor analysis has made such a theory untenable. During the 1940's and the 1950's the trend has been toward batteries based on factor analysis and away from single-score tests. In the manual the authors face this problem and examine the usefulness of single measures of academic ability as compared with profiles of separate factors. The evidence they assemble indicates that the single-score test still does a better job in the school situation than the multiple factor tests do—and with a much smaller investment of testing time. What best predicts school success in any of the special subject areas seems to be whatever it is that the different factors have in common rather than what is distinctive about them. If this general intellectual capacity is what we wish to measure, then it would seem advantageous to measure it directly.

The revised Henmon-Nelson tests are carefully planned, carefully constructed, readily interpretable instruments designed to do one thing and do it well. They should find widespread acceptance in elementary and secondary schools.

J Consult Psychol 22:241 Je '58. *Laurance F. Shaffer.* * The content....is based on an extensive item analysis of the older tests, and the equivalence of the Forms A and B is well established. The....manuals....give impressively favorable data about reliability, congruent validity with other tests, and concurrent and predictive validity with achievement measures. * The standardization is a model of precise method, using a predetermined sample of 250 classrooms stratified by state and size of school system. The manual closes with a persuasive argument for the use of omnibus tests, rather than of tests with factor scores, for the prediction of school achievement. In all, the revised Henmon-Nelson impresses the reviewer as a scholarly example of the best in test construction, and as a remarkably efficient instrument for its length.

For a review by H. M. Fowler of the previous edition, see 4:299; for reviews by Anne Anastasi, August Dvorak, Howard Easley, and J. P. Guilford, see 40:1398 (1 excerpt).

[343]

*IPAT Culture Free Intelligence Test. Ages 4-8, 8-13 and average adults, grades 10-16 and superior adults; 1933-58; title on test is *Test of g: Culture Free*; 3 levels; cash orders postpaid; Raymond B. Cattell and A. K. S. Cattell (2, 3); Institute for Personality and Ability Testing. *

a) SCALE 1. Ages 4-8; 1933-50; identical with the *Cattell Intelligence Tests, Scale O: Dartington Scale*; individual in part; 1 form ('50); mimeographed manual ['50]; no data on reliability; $3.50 per 25 tests; $3 per set of cards for classification test; 25¢ per scoring key; 50¢ per manual; 75¢ per specimen set; (30) minutes.

b) SCALE 2. Ages 8-13 and average adults; 1949-58; Forms A ('57), B ('56); $3.30 per 25 tests; separate answer sheets may be used; $1.80 per 50 answer sheets; 50¢ per hand scoring key; $1.20 per manual ['58]; $1.75 per specimen set; 14(30) minutes.

c) SCALE 3. Grades 10-16 and superior adults; 1950; Forms A, B; mimeographed manual ['50]; no data on reliability; prices same as for Scale 2; 14(30) minutes.

REFERENCES

1-2. See 4:300.
3. GIBSON, Q. H. "Intelligence Tests and University Careers of Medical Students." *Lancet* 255:323-4 Ag 28 '48. *
4. CORDOVA, F. A. *A Comparison of the Performance of a Bilingual Group on a "Culture Free" Test Administered in English and in Spanish.* Master's thesis, Fordham University (New York, N.Y.), 1951.
5. SCHWARTZ, IRVING H. *A Validation Study of the Culture-Free Intelligence Test (A Measure of "G"), Scale 3.* Master's thesis, University of Florida (Gainesville, Fla.), 1951.
6. ANASTASI, ANNE, AND CORDOVA, FERNANDO A. "Some Effects of Bilingualism Upon the Intelligence Test Performance of Puerto Rican Children in New York City." *J Ed Psychol* 44:1-19 Ja '53. *
7. BENSBERG, GERARD J., AND SLOAN, WILLIAM. "The Use of the Cattell Culture Free Test With Mental Defectives." *Am J Mental Def* 59:499-503 Ja '55. * (PA 29:7476)
8. CATTELL, RAYMOND B. "A Note on Dr. Sloan's Evidence Regarding the Value of Culture-Free Intelligence Tests." *Am J Mental Def* 59:504-6 Ja '55. * (PA 29:7480)
9. KEEHN, J. D., AND PROTHRO, E. TERRY. "Non-Verbal Tests as Predictors of Academic Success in Lebanon." *Ed & Psychol Meas* 15:495-8 w '55. * (PA 30:7765)
10. MARQUART, DOROTHY I., AND BAILEY, LOIS L. "An Evaluation of the *Culture Free Test* of Intelligence." *J Genetic Psychol* 86:353-8 Je '55. * (PA 30:6905)
11. FOWLER, WILLIAM L. *A Comparative Analysis of Pupil Performance on Conventional and Culture-Controlled Mental Tests.* Doctor's thesis, University of Michigan (Ann Arbor, Mich.), 1956. (DA 17:91)
12. FOWLER, WILLIAM L. "A Comparative Analysis of Pupil Performance on Conventional and Culture-Controlled Mental Tests." *Yearb Nat Council Meas Used Ed* 14:8-19 '57. *
13. COOPER, JAMES G. "Predicting School Achievement for Bilingual Pupils." *J Ed Psychol* 49:31-6 F '58. *

I. MACFARLANE SMITH, *Lecturer in Education, University of Durham, Newcastle, England.*

This series of intelligence scales has the same aims as Cattell's original *Culture-Free Test* published in 1944: (*a*) to ensure the highest possible validity, (*b*) to ensure freedom from contamination by cultural learning effects, and (*c*) to provide adequate reliability.

The same principles of test construction have been employed in all three scales, though Scale 1 is not so exactly comparable as Scales 2 and 3, for only half of its eight subtests can be described as "culture free." Scales 2 and 3 each consist of four subtests involving different types of relation eduction. The first three subtests are of familiar types—series, classification, and matrices, but the fourth subtest, called Conditions, involves a novel type of "topological" reasoning.

Many of the criticisms made in *The Fourth Mental Measurements Yearbook* have been met in the most recent edition of the tests and manuals. Thus, answer sheets have been provided for Scales 2 and 3. Also, the latest edition of the manual for Scale 2 contains full information about the test, including data on validity and reliability and very comprehensive tables of norms to suit the requirements of different types of user. Data on validity are presented in the form of saturations with Thurstone's second order general ability factor or Spearman's "g." Correlations with "g" for the four subtests are .53, .68, .89, and .99. Data on reliability are presented in two ways. Immediate test-retest correlations on the full test were .82 and .85 on American and British samples, respectively. Consistency coefficients (split-half, corrected to full length) are reported as .70, .86, .87, and .92 for "four different groups." Since the actual testing time for one form alone is 14 minutes for Scales 2 or 3, the figures for validity and reliability are probably as high as could be expected. Thus, when sufficient time is available, it is desirable to give both forms. There is a useful device for testing groups containing individuals at different levels of test sophistication. Form A can be regarded as a training run; the score is based on Form B only. (The norms for Form B are applicable only when Form A has been given first.)

Scale 1 was standardized on only 117 children, 20 being the largest group for any age. These were selected as being "approximately of average ability according to the Binet and other scales." Scale 2 was standardized on 4,328 pupils, sampled from various regions of the United States and Britain. Scale 3 was standardized on 886 school pupils and 600 students from three universities or colleges. Thus, the standardization of Scale 2 is much more satisfactory than that of Scale 1 or Scale 3.

Attention has frequently been drawn to the fact that the standard deviation of IQ's obtained from Cattell's tests is very much higher than that of IQ's obtained from most other tests. This difference has sometimes created difficulty and misunderstanding when it has been necessary to compare scores on Cattell's tests with scores obtained on other tests. The new manual for Scale 2 should be helpful in this connection since the authors have provided tables of norms based on different standard deviations. One table gives the ordinary or classical IQ based on the actual sigma of 24.4 points of IQ. Another gives a normalized standard score based on a sigma of 24. A third gives a normalized standard score based on a sigma of 16. The third table makes it possible to compare readily the results of the culture free tests with IQ's obtained from many other tests. (British users have become accustomed to a standard deviation of 15 which is used both by the National Foundation for Educational Research and by Moray House.) The manual also contains tables giving percentiles for scores obtained when the tests are administered both with and without a time limit. These tables of norms are a valuable addition to the information provided in previous manuals.

Many psychologists have criticised the term "culture free" on the ground that it is not possible to produce an intelligence test which is entirely culture free. In the most recent manual, the authors have gone some way towards meeting this criticism by introducing the term "culture fair" as an alternative, which many will find more acceptable. Certainly there are grounds for claiming that the tests are relatively culture fair, for no significant differences were discovered in the performances of American, Australian, French, and British samples. On the other hand, norms were slightly different in some other countries, but it is possible that these differences were due to sampling artefacts. A striking finding is that when the tests were given twice to a complete age-group of 10 years in a city of 300,000 (retest interval, 14 years), no significant difference was obtained either in mean or standard deviation. This result contrasts with that obtained with other tests, e.g., the Binet test which, when used in the Scottish survey, showed an increase of 2.28 points of IQ over a period from 1932 to 1947.

The authors have to be commended for devising and developing these tests which have been shown to be relatively free from the influence of cultural factors. For this reason alone, the tests are likely to find many applications. On theoretical grounds, they are probably more effective tests of "g" than other culture fair tests such as *Progressive Matrices,* which put the whole emphasis on one particular type of subtest. On the other hand, the Cattell culture free tests necessitate more careful administration and timing than *Progressive Matrices,* which is normally given without a time limit.

For reviews by Raleigh M. Drake and Gladys C. Schwesinger, see 4:300.

[344]

*Jenkins Non-Verbal Test. Ages 10–14.0; 1949–53; adaptation of *Non-Verbal Test I* for Australian use; title on test is *A Scale of Non-Verbal Mental Ability;* 1 form ['49]; manual ['53]; 10s. per 10 tests; 1s. per scoring key; 3s. 6d. per manual; 5s. 6d. per specimen set; postpaid within Australia; 24(45) minutes; Australian Council for Educational Research. *

REFERENCES

1–3. See 4:307.
4. DUNN, S., AND SPEARRITT, D. "A Comparative Study of the Reliability of Some Verbal and Non-Verbal Intelligence Tests." *Austral J Psychol* 7:169–74 D '55. * (PA 31:1030)

5. DUNN, S. S., AND BROWNLESS, V. T. "Differences in Test and Retest Responses of a Group of Children to a Verbal and a Non-Verbal Test." *Austral J Psychol* 8:84–7 Je '56. * (PA 31:7910)

For a review by Cyril A. Rogers, see 356; for a review by E. A. Peel of the original edition, see 4:307.

[345]

*Junior Scholastic Aptitude Test, Revised Edition.** Grades 7–9; 1935–59; 2 scores: verbal, numerical; IBM; Forms A, B, C ('57); manual ('59); separate answer sheets must be used; tests rented only; $1 per student, postage extra; fee includes scoring and reporting service; 60(80) minutes; Secondary Education Board (original edition); Geraldine Spaulding (revised edition); Educational Records Bureau. *

REFERENCES

1–3. See 3:233.
4. TRAXLER, ARTHUR E. "Twelve Years of Experience With the Junior Scholastic Aptitude Test." *Ed Rec B* 59:79–92 Jl '52. * (PA 27:2996)
5. TRAXLER, ARTHUR E., AND TOWNSEND, AGATHA. "Relationship of Differences Between Verbal and Numerical Aptitude to Differences in Achievement in English and Mathematics." *Ed Rec B* 61:61–5 Jl '53. * (PA 28:4865)
6. TRAXLER, ARTHUR E. "Comparative Value of Certain Mental Ability Tests for Predicting School Marks in Two Independent Schools." *Ed Rec B* 65:65–75 F '55. * (PA 29:7976)
7. TRAXLER, ARTHUR E. "Relationship of Certain Predictive Measures to Achievement in First-Year French and Latin." *Ed Rec B* 66:73–7 Jl '55. * (PA 30:5181)
8. SPAULDING, GERALDINE "A Brief Account of the Preparation of New Editions of the Junior Scholastic Aptitude Test." *Ed Rec B* 70:71–3 Jl '57. *
9. SPAULDING, GERALDINE. "A Preliminary Report on the Reliability of the Revised Edition of the Junior Scholastic Aptitude Test." *Ed Rec B* 71:55–6 F '58. *
10. SPAULDING, GERALDINE. "Reliability and Other Data on the Revised Edition of the Junior Scholastic Aptitude Test, Forms A, B, and C." *Ed Rec B* 72:75–9 Jl '58. *

[346]

★**Kelvin Measurement of Ability in Infant Classes.** Ages 5–8; 1935; 1 form ['35]; 9s. per 20 tests; 5½d. per single copy; 6d. per manual ['35]; postage extra; administration time not reported; C. M. Fleming; Robert Gibson & Sons (Glasgow), Ltd. *

[347]

★**The Kingston Test of Intelligence.** Ages 10–12; 1953–54; 1 form ('53); practice sheet ['53]; 10s. per 25 tests; 6d. per single copy; 2s. 6d. per manual ('54); postage extra; 33(78) minutes; M. E. Highfield; George G. Harrap & Co. Ltd. *

A. W. HEIM, *Medical Research Council, Psychological Laboratory, University of Cambridge, Cambridge, England.*

This group test consists of a preliminary practice sheet (for which 30 minutes are allowed) and a test booklet consisting of five separate sections. Each section has a different maximum score and a different time limit. The five sections are as follows: numerical series, verbal analogies, diagrammatic analogies, classification of a kind, and arrangement (of three words) "in order of size or intensity." Sections 2, 3, and 4 are made up of questions of the multiple choice type, each accompanied by four solutions from which the correct one is to be chosen.

In the reviewer's opinion, this test is unsatisfactory from several points of view. For many of the multiple choice problems the "correct" solution is quite indefensible. This is true especially of the two sets of analogies, which contain some very odd reasoning. Section 4, described above as "classification," consists of 16 statements of the following form: "Honey is always useful, desirable, plentiful, of value." (The illustrations in this review are drawn from the preliminary practice sheet.) The subject is instructed to "underline the word which may be *sometimes* true but is not *always* so." There are three objections to this problem: (*a*) The question is expressed in a confusing and misleading manner. (*b*) Its form is in fact different from that used in the test proper. (*c*) In so far as the statement has any meaning, "desirable" would be as good (and bad) an answer as "plentiful"—the intended solution.

The deviser's logic has again let him down in the word arrangement section. Here the subject is asked to arrange in order words whose meanings often differ in *kind* as well as in *degree*. There are some factual errors in addition to logical errors, e.g., "The River is *still,* rushing, slow, rippling" (reviewer's italics). Cogent reasoning is lacking to at least as great an extent in the diagrammatic questions. It is felt that many items in this test might well penalise the brighter and more thoughtful child.

The only information given on validation is as follows: "The test was validated internally by item analysis, and a check on its discriminatory value was made by applying it to grammar school and secondary modern populations." The first of these assertions is not validation at all; the second, as it stands, gives virtually no information.

The layout of the test is appalling; the paper is of poor quality; the test booklet can be used once only; the marking key is so arranged that the scorer shall combine maximum time with minimum accuracy. The test might be useful for a psychologist wishing to conduct investigations on experimental neurosis in children.

[348]

Kuhlmann-Anderson Intelligence Tests, Sixth Edition. Grades kgn, 1, 2, 3, 4, 5, 6, 7–8, 9–12; 1927–52; 9 levels (labeled booklets K, A, B, C, D, E, F, G, and H); 1 form ('52, the same as 1942 edition); directions for administering ('52); handbook ('52); master manual ('52); $2.40 per 25 tests of any one level; 35¢ per handbook (free with first order); $2.50 per master manual; postage extra; $1 per specimen set (does not include master manual), postpaid; 25–30

(40–45) minutes; F. Kuhlmann and Rose G. Anderson; Personnel Press, Inc. *

REFERENCES

1–15. See 40:1404.
16–40. See 3:236.
41–50. See 4:302.
51. JOHNSON, RALPH H., AND BOND, GUY L. "Reading Ease of Commonly Used Tests." *J Appl Psychol* 34:319–24 O '50. * (PA 26:299)
52. SPAULDING, GERALDINE. "The Effects on the Kuhlmann-Anderson Intelligence Test Results of Changing From the 1940 Mental Age Norms to the Revised 1942 Norms." *Ed Rec B* 60:61–7 F '53. * (PA 28:1574)
53. RICHIE, ALICE. "A Comparison of the Kuhlmann-Anderson With the Davis-Eells Intelligence Tests in a Fifth Grade." Abstract. *Calif J Ed Res* 5:186 S '54. *
54. BLIESMER, EMERY P. "A Comparison of Results Obtained With Various Types of Capacity Tests Used With Retarded Readers." *Yearb Nat Council Meas Used Ed* 12(pt 1):60–2 '55. *
55. CANTONI, LOUIS J. "High School Tests and Measurements as Predictors of Occupational Status." *J Appl Psychol* 39:253–5 Ag '55. * (PA 30:4722)
56. HINKELMAN, EMMET ARTHUR. "Relationship of Intelligence to Elementary School Achievement." *Ed Adm & Sup* 41:176–9 Mr '55. * (PA 30:1622)
57. LEON, JOHN F. *An Experimental Study Comparing Matched Bilingual and Monolingual Groups on the Kuhlmann-Anderson Intelligence Test in Fifth Grade of One School in East Los Angeles.* Master's thesis, University of Southern California (Los Angeles, Calif.), 1955.
58. TRAXLER, ARTHUR E. "Comparative Value of Certain Mental Ability Tests for Predicting School Marks in Two Independent Schools." *Ed Rec B* 65:65–75 F '55. * (PA 29:7976)
59. TRAXLER, ARTHUR E. "Relationship of Certain Predictive Measures to Achievement in First-Year French and Latin." *Ed Rec B* 66:73–7 Jl '55. * (PA 30:5181)
60. BLIESMER, EMERY P. "A Comparison of Results of Various Capacity Tests Used With Retarded Readers." *El Sch J* 56:400–2 My '56. * (PA 31:5140)
61. NORTH, ROBERT D. "Relationship of Kuhlmann-Anderson IQ's and Stanford Achievement Test Scores of Independent School Pupils." *Ed Rec B* 68:53–60 Jl '56. * (PA 31:8837)
62. LOVE, MARY I., AND BEACH, SYLVIA. "Performance of Children on the Davis-Eells Games and Other Measures of Ability." *J Consult Psychol* 21:29–32 F '57. * (PA 32:952)
63. NASH, PHILIP G. "Comparison of IQ's Derived From Two Different Tests." *Calif J Ed Res* 8:23–6 Ja '57. * (PA 32:954)
64. TRAXLER, ARTHUR E. "Some Data on the Lorge-Thorndike Intelligence Tests Among Independent School Pupils." *Ed Rec B* 69:63–9 F '57. * (PA 32:2131)
65. NORTH, ROBERT D. "The Interpretation of Otis Quick-Scoring Mental Ability Test IQ's in Relation to Kuhlmann-Anderson IQ's, ACE Scores, and Independent School Norms." *Ed Rec B* 71:47–54 F '58. *

For reviews by Henry E. Garrett and David Segel, see 4:302; for reviews by W. G. Emmett and Stanley S. Marzolf of an earlier edition, see 3:236; for a review by Henry E. Garrett, see 40:1404; for reviews by Psyche Cattell, S. A. Courtis, and Austin H. Turney, see 38:1049.

[349]

★**Kuhlmann-Finch Tests.** Grades 1, 2, 3, 4, 5, 6, 7–9, 10–12; 1951–57; IBM for grades 4–12; 1 form ('57, identical with tests copyrighted in 1951 or 1952); 8 levels (Tests 1, 2, 3, 4, 5, 6; Junior High School Test; Senior High School Test); manual, second edition ('56); $2.95 per 25 tests; separate answer sheets may be used in grades 4–12; $2.40 per 50 IBM scorable answer sheets; 25¢ per hand or machine scoring stencil; $1.25 per manual; postage extra; $1.50 per complete specimen set, postpaid; 25(40), 30(45) minutes for grades 1–9, 10–12; Frank H. Finch; American Guidance Service, Inc. *

REFERENCES

1. COLEMAN, WILLIAM, AND WARD, ANNIE W. "A Comparison of Davis-Eells and Kuhlmann-Finch Scores of Children From High and Low Socio-Economic Status." *J Ed Psychol* 46:465–9 D '55. * (PA 31:3779)
2. FRANDSEN, ARDEN N., AND GRIMES, JESSE W. "Age Discrimination in Intelligence Tests." *J Ed Res* 51:229–33 N '57. *
3. MOULY, GEORGE J., AND EDGAR, MARY. "Equivalence of IQ's for Four Group Intelligence Tests." *Personnel & Guid J* 36:623–6 My '58. *

WALTER N. DUROST, *Director of Educational Services, Pinellas County Public Schools, Clearwater, Florida.*

Evidence concerning the validity of the *Kuhlmann-Finch Tests* is very meager. Briefly stated, the argument is that low intercorrelations among subtests coupled with a gain in score with increase in age constitute sufficient evidence of validity for a test of intelligence. True, if a test does not show gains in score through the age range where growth is obviously to be expected, then it cannot be a measure of mental ability. However, the reverse is not necessarily true. That the given test measures intelligence and not some other growth parameter rests solely on the face validity of the test, not increase in score with age.

In the manual for the *Kuhlmann-Finch Tests* much is made of the fact that this test is true to the tradition established by the work of Kuhlmann, who died in 1941. In the years since Kuhlmann was making his important and noteworthy contributions to mental measurement, it has become increasingly evident that measures of intelligence must demonstrate validity for something and not validity in general. For the most part, such tests are used to predict school learning capacity. This capacity measure is desirable in order that such things as the following may be accomplished: (*a*) the identification of slow learning and talented children for whom curriculum modification is needed; (*b*) the detection of children with mental potential not being realized in their school output; and (*c*) the determination of a community's capacity to reach or exceed national achievement test norms. In fairness to these tests, it must be said that few extant intelligence tests provide more convincing and definitive evidence of their usefulness along the lines indicated.

There is much that is left to be inferred from the information given in the manual concerning scaling procedures. The use of the deviation IQ is a positive step forward and one which the earlier *Kuhlmann-Anderson Intelligence Tests*, still widely used, would do well to emulate.

Insufficient evidence is presented to permit evaluation of the standardization of the test. Apparently the normative group was a stratified sample, but the bases for stratification seem to be the opinions of "such agencies as those operating statewide testing programs." No information is given as to conditions of participation in the standardization program.

Reliability information is reasonably adequate and the authors are to be commended for giving reliability information for separate single-year ranges. However, the reliability population was "a systematically drawn unused subsample of that [national standardization] group." This means that a substantial increase in heterogeneity must surely have arisen because the cases came from many different communities widely distributed geographically.

While using the median of subtest scores as the test average is an admirable technique devised many, many years ago, it works best for hand scored tests. Because of the need to get subtest scores for each of the five tests included, the test is very time-consuming to score by machine.

This is the worst looking test published by a major test publisher which the reviewer has ever seen. The art work is poor, and the printing off color, blurred, and oftentimes almost illegible. The IBM answer sheet enclosed with the material sent for review is a locally printed sheet which could not conceivably score accurately in an IBM test scoring machine. The use of a separate booklet for each grade is good for the first two or three grades, but is a waste of time and effort beyond grade 3.

The intent in publishing these tests, obviously, was to compete with or replace the good but ancient Kuhlmann-Anderson. There have been improvements by way of simplification of administration and the adoption of a more modern method of obtaining an index of brightness, but these gains are offset by obvious shortcomings in other areas.

HENRY E. GARRETT, *Professor Emeritus of Psychology, Columbia University, New York, New York.*

This is a battery of eight test booklets planned to cover the range of intelligence from grade 1 through high school. Each booklet contains five subtests. The first two booklets, intended for the first two grades, contain only nonverbal material—pictures and diagrams; the third booklet has one verbal test and four nonverbal tests; and the other five booklets have three of the five subtests in verbal form. The format of the tests follows that of the Kuhlmann-Anderson tests. Pictures and diagrams are well drawn, and the material is interesting and clear. The tests are timed, but are essentially power tests.

Validity is said to be a matter of test rationale and to depend upon certain principles in the selection and placement of test items. Most of these procedures are well known: increase in percentage passing with age, low inter r's and high criterion r's, homogeneity of test material over the age range, freedom of test items from specific training, objectivity in directions and scoring, and power rather than speed. For the K-F tests the main criterion appears to have been regular increase in per cent passing with age. When tests are well chosen and have been studied experimentally and item analyzed, as these have, this criterion is probably sufficient.

The K-F tests are well standardized. The original standardization sample consisted of approximately 10,000 children. In this and subsequent testing, the range of difficulty in each test was found to be suitable and the discriminative power of the items high. Boys and girls did about equally well on the tests. In one group of 197 13-year-olds, the correlations of test scores with an index of cultural status ranged from .19 to .27 for various types of test material. This is taken as evidence that the tests are not simply the products of culture. No correlations with criteria are given, as the author believes the tests to be validated sufficiently through their method of construction.

Evidence for reliability is found in the fact that the tests do not show increases in score under unlimited time, and in the high split-half correlations. Within-age reliability coefficients for ages 6–17 range from .86 to .92 for samples of from 110 to 250 pupils.

Norms for the K-F tests are in terms of median MA's and IQ's. The median MA is the chronological age corresponding typically to the median of the five point scores earned on the subtests. The IQ is a deviation or standard score in a distribution with a mean of 100 and a standard deviation of 16. Percentile ranks corresponding to standard score IQ's are provided. The median MA is an acceptable index of general level when the subtests correlate highly so that an average is based upon composite measures of a common ability. The manual reports intercorrelations for Test 6 ranging from .16 to .56, with a median of about .40. A median MA from these tests is, then, acceptable only as a rough index of general ability. A weighted composite of the five subtest scores in terms of a measured general factor would have been better—at least theoretically.

The rules offered in the manual for determining the median MA and the deviation IQ are unnecessarily confusing. In the paragraph on finding the MA, for example, the X marking the median score on the sample profile is mentioned as being referred to in the paragraph "immediately above"; the reference is in the paragraph following; on the sample record chart the IQ is never actually located; and the girl in the illustration is referred to variously as Mary Joan L—and Mary J. Smith. It is interesting to note that while the Heinis growth units are mentioned in the manual, probably in deference to Kuhlmann, they are not actually used.

As a supplement to group verbal tests or the Stanford-Binet, the *Kuhlmann-Finch Tests* are undoubtedly useful over the range of elementary and high school grades. They correspond closely to the *Kuhlmann-Anderson Intelligence Tests,* and are virtually alternate forms. The tests should have greatest value as measures of general level. They are not designed to be used in differential diagnosis of scholastic strengths and weaknesses.

CHARLES O. NEIDT, *Professor of Educational Psychology and Measurements and Chairman of the Department, University of Nebraska, Lincoln, Nebraska.*

The tests consist of five types of items divided into eight sequential levels with no duplication of content. The eight levels are presented in separate test booklets. Each of the five subtests in the eight booklets contains from 20 to 24 items. Performance on the tests is expressed as "standard IQ" and as mental age. The "standard IQ" is based upon the median score on the five subtests. Age units paralleling the Heinis mental growth unit curve were used in constructing the tests.

Evidence of the validity of these tests has been assembled following Kuhlmann's rationale that intercorrelations among subtests should be neither high nor low, tests should include items which will discriminate between the levels of ability found at successive ages, and test scores should be free from cultural influence. Data supporting these contentions are presented in the manual along with differences between median standard scores of adjacent age groups.

Reliability of the tests is based upon split-half estimates, correlations between scores from the administration of adjacent booklets, and retesting after a 6-month interval. The reliability coefficients reported are relatively high for a 25-minute test. Although the subtests are timed, speed is not an important factor in performance on these tests.

The standard deviation of the IQ's yielded by the tests is 16. Since most derived IQ's have a standard deviation of 15, some variation in interpretation of results will be necessary for test users who have become accustomed to interpretation based upon a standard deviation of 15. Fifteen would have been a better choice than 16 for the standard deviation.

In the section of the manual entitled "Relationships to Other Tests," means and standard deviations obtained from administering the Kuhlmann-Finch and the Kuhlmann-Anderson tests to two samples are shown. Whereas these data demonstrate similarity of the two overall distributions of IQ's, they can hardly be said to demonstrate relationship. Correlation would have been a more appropriate technique for showing relationship between the two series of scores.

The directions for administering and scoring the tests are clearly stated, and the general format of the tests is good. The organization of the manual could be improved by more effective grouping of the data presented. Tables 2 and 3 in the manual appear twice. There is little question that the content of these tables contributes to understanding the tests, but repetition of the material seems unnecessary.

In summary, the *Kuhlmann-Finch Tests* are based upon extensive item analysis data and are highly usable in terms of the availability of booklets for each grade level and their ease of administration and scoring. A less favorable aspect of these tests is the paucity of standardization cases at the lower age levels.

[350]

★**The Lorge-Thorndike Intelligence Tests.** Grades kgn–1, 2–3, 4–6, 7–9, 10–12; 1954–57; IBM for grades 4–12; Forms A, B ('54); 5 levels; Levels 3–5: 2 tests (nonverbal, verbal), 2 editions (consumable, reusable) of each test; manual ('57) for each level; technical manual ('57); Levels 1–2: $3 per 35 tests; Levels 3–5: $2.40 per 35 tests, separate answer sheets must be used with re-usable edition, $1.20 per 35 IBM answer sheets, 21¢ per hand scoring stencil; 12¢ per technical manual; 60¢ per specimen set of any one level; postage extra; Spanish directions available for nonverbal batteries; Irving Lorge and Robert L. Thorndike; Houghton Mifflin Co. *

a) LEVEL 1, NONVERBAL BATTERY. Grades kgn–1; (35) minutes in 2 or 3 sessions.
  b) LEVEL 2, NONVERBAL BATTERY. Grades 2–3; (35) minutes.
  c) LEVEL 3. Grades 4–6; IBM.
   1) *Verbal Battery*. 34(44–49) minutes.
   2) *Nonverbal Battery*. 27(37–42) minutes.
  d) LEVEL 4. Grades 7–9; IBM.
   1) *Verbal Battery*. 34(44–49) minutes.
   2) *Nonverbal Battery*. 27(37–39) minutes.
  e) LEVEL 5. Grades 10–12; IBM.
   1) *Verbal Battery*. 34(44–49) minutes.
   2) *Nonverbal Battery*. 27(37–39) minutes.

REFERENCES

1. ROSNER, BENJAMIN. *Community Socioeconomic Status in Mental Organization.* Doctor's thesis, Columbia University (New York, N.Y.), 1955.
2. KNIEF, LOTUS M. *An Investigation of the Cultural Bias Issue in Intelligence Testing.* Doctor's thesis, State University of Iowa (Iowa City, Iowa), 1957. (*DA* 17:1951)
3. NORTH, ROBERT D. "A Preliminary Report on the Reliability of the Lorge-Thorndike Intelligence Tests, Level 4, Verbal Battery, and Correlations With IQ's on the Otis Quick-Scoring Mental Ability Tests." *Ed Rec B* 69:71–2 F '57. * (*PA* 32:2120)
4. OWEN, JASON C. *A Study of the Prognostic Value of Certain Measures of Intelligence and Listening Comprehension With a Selected Group of Elementary Pupils.* Doctor's thesis, University of Missouri (Columbia, Mo.), 1957. (*DA* 19:484)
5. TRAXLER, ARTHUR E. "Some Data on the Lorge-Thorndike Intelligence Tests Among Independent School Pupils." *Ed Rec B* 69:63–9 F '57. * (*PA* 32:2131)
6. TRAXLER, ARTHUR E. "A Further Note on the Reliability of the Lorge-Thorndike Intelligence Tests With Independent School Pupils." *Ed Rec B* 71:57–8 F '58. *

FRANK S. FREEMAN, *Professor of Psychology, Cornell University, Ithaca, New York.*

This 1957 version of the *Lorge-Thorndike Intelligence Tests* is among the best group tests available, from the point of view of the psychological constructs upon which it is based and that of statistical standardization.

These scales utilize test materials that are both verbal and nonverbal in character in the three highest levels, but are entirely nonverbal in the two lowest (kindergarten and grades 1–3). The authors' position, however, is that both types of materials test "abstract intelligence," defined as "ability to work with ideas and relationships among ideas." Although the authors are not concerned with presenting or insisting upon a formal definition of intelligence, they do state that the following mental processes are descriptive of intelligent behavior and are sampled by their tests: (*a*) dealing with abstract and general concepts; (*b*) interpretation and use of symbols; (*c*) dealing with relationships among concepts and symbols; (*d*) flexibility in the organization of concepts and symbols; (*e*) utilizing one's experience in new patterns; and (*f*) utilizing "power" rather than speed in working with abstract materials. (It is noteworthy that, in this description of intelligent behavior, Lorge and Thorndike have, wisely the reviewer believers, utilized the views and theories of the late distinguished psychologists, Lewis M. Terman and C. Spearman.)

The statistical methods and analyses used in selecting individual items and in developing the scales as a whole are thoroughly presented in the manual. To begin with, each item was correlated (biserial or a value estimated from Flanagan's table) with scores on the subtest of which it is a part. For all the items finally retained, the median correlations range from .43 to .70, most of them (46 of 58 coefficients) being between .43 and .59. Although these coefficients are far from unity, they are high enough to warrant the conclusion that a sufficient number of items, thus positively correlated, will provide a satisfactory sampling of the psychological operations common to all of them.

The standardization population consisted of 136,000 children in 44 communities in 22 states. The communities were selected on the basis of "a composite of factors which have been found to be related to the measured intelligence of children in the community." These factors were: per cent of adult illiteracy, number of professional workers per thousand in the population, per cent of home ownership, and median home rental value. By these means, it was possible to obtain an appropriate stratified sample of American communities which were rated socio-economically as very high, high, average, low, and very low. With few exceptions, all pupils from the kindergarten through high school were tested in each community.

The composite distribution of scores from this large and representative sample population was used for the determination of IQ equivalents for each age group in terms of the familiar and widely used deviation IQ. The authors followed the now widely accepted practice of assuming a mean IQ of 100 and a standard deviation of 16 IQ points. Unlike some other current scales, the steps used in arriving at the deviation IQ's for each age group are fully presented in the manual for these tests.

Having obtained data from communities of varied and specified socio-economic levels, Lorge and Thorndike are able to present a valuable table of median IQ's for each age group within each of these five levels. Separate medians are given for the verbal and for the nonverbal scales. The value of this table would be enhanced if an index of dispersion were also given for each age and type of community.

Even so, however, these data are valuable not only in showing community differences but also in revealing the fact that both the verbal and the nonverbal IQ's exhibit the same general pattern in relation to community levels. That is, almost without exception, the higher the community's socio-economic rating, the higher are the median IQ's at each of the age levels. This fact has an important bearing on the contention of some educators and psychologists that verbal tests of intelligence are "culturally unfair" to individuals in the lower socio-economic groups.

Evidence of reliability of the scales is presented in several ways. Alternate forms correlate rather well (.76 to .90) at all levels, but the verbal scales for levels 3, 4, and 5 yield the highest coefficients, namely: .90, .86, and .86. All of these coefficients are the more significant since, in each instance, they were computed on the population of a single grade. Thus they were computed in accordance with a very desirable statistical practice, one which does not yield spuriously high reliability coefficients. The odd-even reliabilities are very high (.88 to .94), with one exception (Level 2, nonverbal, $r = .59$). About this the authors say: "At this level, an *odd-even* reliability coefficient is really not meaningful, since there is a systematic alternation between geometric and pictorial items in subtests 2 and 3." In that case, it seems to the reviewer that this method should not have been used at this level, especially since inspection of the test items shows that a different and more appropriate adaptation of the split-half technique could have been devised.

Standard errors of measurement in terms of IQ points are given as an additional and highly desirable estimate of the tests' reliabilities. The data of this table are useful, showing the SE to be within a reasonable number of points, especially in the middle score range and, more particularly, in the case of the verbal scales. The value of this table of standard errors of measurement is somewhat vitiated, however, by the fact that the data are based upon "only a modest number of cases" at each of the score levels, with the actual findings "smoothed by fitting a curve by eye to the observed points." The standard errors, therefore, must for the present be accepted as tentative estimates.

The validity of an intelligence test, it is well recognized, is more difficult to evaluate and demonstrate than is its reliability. The manual of the Lorge-Thorndike scales presents only a modest number of statistics on validity, and, in addition, a better than ordinary (as far as test manuals are concerned) discussion of what the authors call "rational" validity. This, presumably, is validity which cannot be demonstrated by statistics derived from experimental or empirical findings, but which the prospective user is asked to accept on the basis of "a rational analysis of what [psychological processes and test materials] should appropriately be included" in the tests.

Under rational validity the authors include "content" validity and "construct" validity. The first of these is what used to be called disparagingly, "face" validity, that is, a rational analysis of *materials* appropriate for inclusion in a test. This analysis will determine what particular types of items shall be used. Basically, every test author must begin this way, but he must go well beyond content validity as a criterion. Such a criterion, after all, will insure only the appropriateness of what might be called the raw materials. These have to be organized and refined in order to test the mental processes to be evaluated. Furthermore, the long history of intelligence testing provides all psychologists with abundant information regarding the most useful types of test materials with which to start.

The second type of rational validity, called "construct" validity, refers to the mental *processes* utilized by the test. The question is: Do these tested processes "correspond well with the concept or construct which the test is designed to measure"? In other words, does the test measure and evaluate intelligence by means of operations that are consistent with the test authors' definition and analysis of what intelligent behavior is? The Lorge-Thorndike construct and analysis are given earlier in this review.

It is clear that the answer to the question of whether a psychological test is valid with regard to content and construct will depend upon the psychological insights of qualified and expert judgment. This is reasonable. But the ultimate, the basic, value of a test of intelligence (or of any other psychological test) is its "functional" validity. The question here is, how well does it work in situations for which it is intended? How well does it select, differentiate, and predict? The manual of the Lorge-Thorndike scales provide only very meager data in answer to these questions, namely, a correlation of .67 between these tests (given at the beginning of grade 9) and the "average achievement" of 214 pupils at the end of the grade. In itself, this correlation is highly satisfactory, but more studies of "predictive" validity are needed throughout the grade ranges of the scales.

Another answer to the foregoing questions is found in what the authors call "concurrent" validity, that is, "correlation of test scores with other types of measures obtained before or at the same time that the test is given." As evidence of this type of validity, one study is cited: the correlation between Lorge-Thorndike IQ's and Stanford grade-equivalents in reading was .87, while that between IQ and average grade equivalents in arithmetic was .76 for 171 sixth grade pupils. These are encouraging findings; more such data are needed covering the entire grade range.

There are still other data on validity—correlations with other tests ("congruent" validity) and intercorrelations of subtests, though the latter data are not cited under the caption validity. Lorge-Thorndike test scores were correlated with those of four other group tests, as well as with the Stanford-Binet and the WISC. With few exceptions, the coefficients were .60 or higher (46 coefficients out of 52). Thus, all of the tests used will yield rankings that correspond reasonably well. With one exception correlations with the Stanford-Binet and the WISC were quite high (.63, .54, .71, .77). These are especially noteworthy because two of the coefficients (.63 and .54) were based on first grade children only while the other two were found with children in grades 7–9. In each instance, however, the number of cases was very small. The reviewer believes that in all studies of congruent validity too much emphasis is placed upon correlation coefficients and too little (almost none) upon the distribution, mean, and standard deviation of differences in ratings (MA's and IQ's) obtained with the tests employed. Reports on congruent validity would be much more meaningful and significant if this deficiency were corrected.

Intercorrelations among subtests of a scale should be given as evidence of its validity, perhaps, indirectly, of its construct validity; for unless the correlation coefficients support the concept or concepts upon which the test is presumably constructed, it cannot be said that the test exhibits construct validity, although the correlations in themselves do not necessarily demonstrate such validity. In the case of the Lorge-Thorndike scales, construct validity requires that the subtest intercorrelations be quite marked. Intercorrelations among the subtests range from .30 (number series with vocabulary) to .70 (sentence completion with vocabulary). Eight (of 21) intercorrelations are .50 or higher; five are in the .40's; six in the .30's; and two in the .20's. It appears, therefore, that we may infer that the extent of mental processes common to the subtests is appreciable in most instances, moderate in a few, and very limited in at least two. However, when the verbal and nonverbal batteries are taken as a whole and these two major divisions are correlated (each correlation being restricted to a single grade), the coefficients are much more convincing, ranging from .54 to .70, all but two being in the .60's.

On the whole, the Lorge-Thorndike series is among the sounder group instruments available, from the point of view of psychological insights (with regard to both content and concepts of intelligence) shown in selecting and developing the materials, and from the point of view of statistical analysis of the standardization data. The major deficiency, so far as available data are concerned, is the lack of adequate data on predictive and concurrent validity.

JOHN E. MILHOLLAND, *Associate Professor of Psychology, and Chief, Evaluation and Examinations Division, Bureau of Psychological Services, University of Michigan, Ann Arbor, Michigan.*

This test is admirable for the clarity with which its objective is stated and for the restraint exercised in the claims made for what it will do. It is frankly labeled an intelligence test, and we are told that it is a test of abstract intelligence, defined as "the ability to work with ideas and the relationships among ideas." There is, of course, no precise objective criterion for this definition, so one is forced to rely upon indirect evidence, inspection of the items, and the professional reputations of the authors for the assessment of this kind of validity. All three lines of evidence are confirmatory.

The suggestions made in the manual for the use of the results are reasonable and practical and do not rely upon exorbitant claims for what the test is measuring. The authors recommend administering both the verbal and nonverbal batteries in grades for which both are available, and state that "the functions are sufficiently similar so that, for most pupils, it will be appropriate to average the I.Q.'s from the two batteries to yield a single more comprehensive and more reliable estimate of intellectual ability. However, in about 25 per cent of cases, the two forms will yield I.Q.'s differing by as much as 15 points. In these cases, the difference may have practical significance in relation to a pupil's reading level, school achievement, or vocational planning."

With the possible exceptions of Word Knowledge and Arithmetic Reasoning, the subtest titles simply describe the types of items they contain. This should certainly reduce any temptation to try to interpret subtest scores, and, in keeping with this point of view, the authors present no subtest norms. It is gratifying to see that they do not expect to provide more than one usable score in 27 to 35 minutes of working time.

The standardization sample included more than 136,000 children in 44 communities in 22 states. Since participation by a community was on a volunteer basis, some bias may remain in the norms. Reliabilities are estimated by alternate forms correlations within single grades. This procedure tends to produce estimates which are lower than split-half estimates because of daily fluctuations in pupil performance and because any degree of speededness in the test inflates split-half estimates. The alternate forms reliabilities for the various levels and batteries range from .76 to .85. For comparison, split-half (odd-even) reliabilities of the tests are also given. With two exceptions the estimates are all above .90. One exception is .59 for a test in which there was systematic alternation of item types. One wonders why in this case items were not taken in units of two.

The examiner's manuals seem to be especially well adapted for use by classroom teachers. They contain directions for administration, suggestions for using the test, and tables of norms. The two paragraphs explaining the use of the standard error of measurement should probably be expanded. As they stand, these paragraphs might be more confusing than helpful to a great many teachers.

The details of construction, standardization, and validation of the tests are contained in the technical manual. Much of this information should be at hand in any testing program, and the reviewer hopes that at least one technical manual accompanies every test order filled by the publishers. Parts of it are excellent, and some information given (on item-test correlations and mean IQ's by socio-economic levels, for example) is frequently not found in test manuals. Despite these strengths, the technical manual leaves much to be desired. Some of the data seem to have been hastily or ill-advisedly collected and inadequately analyzed. The odd-even reliabilties, which are presumably given for comparison with the alternate-forms reliabilities which the authors advocate, are based on samples different from the ones on which the alternate-forms reliabilities were computed. There are some correlations reported with Stanford-Binet scores which are based on 20 cases (with extremely restricted range) and 34 cases, and one with WISC based on 39 cases. In the factor analysis reported, the reliabilities were used as communality estimates, yet the obtained communalities for three of the seven tests differed from the reliabilities by .12. These discrepancies may not have materially altered the factor loadings, but certainly iteration would have made the analysis neater. Also in connection with the factor analysis, a report of the multiple r between the verbal and nonverbal factors and the appropriate subtests would have provided useful evidence bearing on validity.

The formula on page 9, incidentally, is for the complement of the reliability, not the reliability.

The Lorge-Thorndike tests should be accorded a place among the best of our group intelligence tests. They are well designed, easily administered and scored, and, what is especially noteworthy, the uses recommended for them are reasonable and defensible.

D. A. PIDGEON, *Senior Officer, Test Services, National Foundation for Educational Research in England and Wales, London, England.*

The authors of this series of tests have attempted the commendable task of providing, for a wide age range, measures of "abstract intelligence" defined as "the ability to work with ideas and the relationships among ideas." To say that they have produced a number of excellent tests does not mean that they have necessarily succeeded in their task. Nevertheless, one may be impressed by the way the tests have been presented in a compact series arranged to suit the most fastidious of test users.

Apart from the examiner's manual supplied for each test level, a technical manual is provided giving detailed information on such points as item selection, norming, reliability, and validity. It is difficult to find fault with the construction of the tests, and, clearly, considerable care was taken to norm them on a sample that fully represented the complete United States population of children falling within the tests' age range. The norms are presented in a variety of ways—as grade percentiles, grade equivalents, age equivalents, and IQ equivalents, the last named assuming a population mean of 100 and a standard deviation of 16. Since the "IQ's" are not derived from any consideration of mental age, it seems a pity that the term "intelligence quotient" has been retained even if qualified by the word "equivalent." It also seems a pity that some agreement, preferably international, could not be made to standardise the value adopted for the standard deviation. English test users, for example, are now becoming familiar with normalised scores having a mean of 100 and an SD of 15.

Standard errors of measurement calculated from the differences between scores on Forms A and B show, as might be expected, that somewhat greater precision is obtained at intermediate score levels, hence it is recommended that users retest with a lower or higher level test if the scores obtained fall below or above stated values. Alternate-forms reliability coefficients range from about .79 for the tests of Levels 1 and 2, which use pictorial material, to about .87 for the verbal tests of Levels 3, 4, and 5. These values can be regarded as satisfactory, if rather on the low side.

No test, however reliably constructed and normed, is of value unless it can also be shown to serve adequately the purpose for which it is intended. The technical manual devotes nearly four pages to the question of validity and yet gives little direct evidence that is specifically related to the uses suggested for the tests, namely, "Formation of Class Groups," "Grouping within Class," "Setting Standards of Expectancy for the Individual Pupil," "Educational Guidance," and "Vocational Guidance." One of the reasons for this may be the confusion existing about what the tests are really measuring. Although, in the section on construct validity, the authors imply that they have taken an operational approach to the definition of "intelligence" and although, in discussing the selection of items, they state that their tests "have been designed to measure reasoning ability," in discussing the uses of the tests they use the words "intelligence," "scholastic aptitude," and "general mental ability" indiscriminately to imply some mental function that controls or limits the scholastic performance of pupils.

Certainly, for separating children into relatively homogeneous ability groups, a single test which correlates highly with most attainments is of positive value; correlations with reading and average arithmetic grade equivalents (.87 and .76, respectively) derived from the *Stanford Achievement Test,* indicate that the Lorge-Thorndike tests will adequately serve this purpose. But, for "setting standards of expectancy," tests are needed which will predict future scholastic performance. Only one study is cited, based on 214 cases and giving a correlation of .67 between Lorge-Thorndike (Level 4) given at the beginning of the ninth grade and average achievement at the end of the ninth grade. The manual does not state whether actual achievement at the beginning of the grade predicts end-of-year achievement any better or worse than this.

The test user is also encouraged to use the nonverbal battery with the retarded reader, since, it is argued, this procedure will enable an estimate to be obtained of mental ability which is "uninfluenced by specific disability in reading." However, no evidence is supplied to support this statement, and, since factorial studies have clearly demonstrated that nonverbal tests measure specific or group factors of their own besides "g," one may well doubt their value for predicting ability to read, or indeed for predicting any scholastic performance. Again, it is stated elsewhere that the difference between performance on the verbal and nonverbal batteries "may be useful in revealing significant facts about reading achievement, school progress, or vocational prospects." However, the manuals do not state what these facts are, nor is any evidence supplied to enable the test user to make his own judgment.

It should be made clear that, in this reviewer's opinion, this is an excellent series of tests, well designed and constructed, admirably printed and presented, and equipped with highly satisfactory norms. It can also be said that the tests provide reliable measures of verbal reasoning and nonverbal reasoning. In their use, however, extreme caution should be taken to see that the scores are only interpreted in this way and that no assumptions are made about their measuring mental capacity. It is to be hoped that the authors will subsequently provide evidence more directly relevant to the uses they suggest for the tests, especially uses relating to the prediction of achievement.

[351]

★Manchester General Ability Test (Senior) 1. Ages 13–15; 1952; 1 form ['52]; practice test ['52]; no data on validity; 10s. 6d. per 25 tests; 7d. per single copy; 2s. per 25 practice tests; 1d. per single copy; 9d. per manual ['52]; postage extra; 45(60) minutes; Stephen Wiseman; University of London Press Ltd. *

A. E. G. PILLINER, *Lecturer in Education, University of Edinburgh, Edinburgh, Scotland.*

The constructors of the *Manchester General Ability Test* have paid Moray House tests the compliment of rather closely following their layout, both in test and manual. Since MGAT is designed for use in English secondary schools, this similarity is an advantage to those testees and testers to whom the pattern of tests like the Moray House tests is familiar.

The MGAT covers the ages of 14 and 15, thus spanning a gap in the existing range of tests in current use in England. According to the manual, it is "more appropriately to be used in the secondary grammar school and the upper ability levels of the secondary modern school" since it provides "a measure of ability in the verbal and academic field." We are not told, however, what specific purpose it is intended to serve in measuring this ability, that is, to what use the quotients obtained with it are to be put in the schools.

The constructors are to be congratulated on the instructions for administration, which are admirably lucid. Those for markers, while equally clear and designed to minimise scoring errors, are possibly a little too rigid. Many of the test items are answered by inserting a number in brackets at the end of the item line. Since in most of the other tests currently used in Great Britain the correct response is underlined, it may happen that some children, accustomed to the latter method of answering, will inadvertently use it here also. If they do so, they cannot receive credit since the instructions state quite specifically: "No credit should be allowed for answers other than those appearing here." This is not only unduly "tough" but conceivably may reduce the reliability and validity of the test also.

Standardisation is based on the performance of an approximately complete English county authority age group of 4,175 children. British custom is followed in arranging the conversion table to give standardised scores ("quotients") with a mean of 100 and a standard deviation of 15. Users of the test are rightly warned that quotients so obtained are not strictly comparable with Binet-type quotients, but wrongly informed that the quotients from this test are comparable with those derived from other group tests of intelligence having the same standard deviation. With the same test, the mean quotients of complete year groups of children, each from a different English authority, range from 94 to 106 approximately. Age allowance varies also among authorities. Only if the different tests have been standardised on the same year group of children does one achieve strict comparability of quotients.

A study of the conversion table reveals that at the median age for the standardisation group the raw scores at the 15th, 50th, and 84th percentiles are approximately 10, 23, and 40, respectively. These figures suggest that the test is too difficult. While "headroom" is always desirable, there is probably too much here. The highest raw score against which an entry occurs in the unextrapolated portion of the table is 81. We are not told the raw score standard deviation (a defect which should be corrected) but the figures suggest that it is not high, so that discrimination will be adversely affected in some parts at least of the raw score range. On the other hand, there is a raw score range of 20 between the 84th and 97.5th percentiles, so that in this region discrimination will be good. Nevertheless, it would seem that the all-round measuring quality of the test would be improved by easing it by some 12–15 raw score points.

Internal consistency coefficients of .95 ("boosted" split-half) and .93 (Kuder-Richardson) are quoted. These are low for a test of this kind, and appear to confirm the view that the test is too difficult. Unfortunately, no test-retest reliability coefficients are reported.

One purpose of the short preliminary test provided is to give the children practice "in doing particular types of questions which might be unfamiliar to them." This purpose is scarcely achieved since (*a*) the mode of presentation of some of the item types in the practice test differs from that of the corresponding item types in the test proper, and (b) one item in the practice test has no counterpart in the test proper. The main virtue of the preliminary test, its effect as a "shock absorber," remains, but its items should be recast.

Approximately two thirds of the 100 items in the test proper, for which the time allowed is an uninterrupted 45 minutes, are conventional in type. Same and opposites, straight analogies, series, insertion of missing figures in multiplication sums, and classifications are all included. In addition, there are some items based on rectangular tables which, while differing in detail, are generally similar in that the child must grasp the whole problem presented by each table in order to answer the items based on it. The construction of these tables and items shows considerable ingenuity. A set of anagrams which the child has to solve with the help of a brief description (GERNE is a colour) is included.

In constructing tests for children younger than those for whom this test is intended, it is usual to follow the principle of grading the blocks of items and the items within the blocks from easy to difficult. While the item order is decided in most cases by some such statistical measure of difficulty as proportion passing, the experienced test constructor usually has a fairly good a priori notion of what the outcome of the statistical evidence will be. It is arguable that it is less important, with tests for older testees, to adhere to this principle, though this reviewer would maintain that it is a sound rule in general. An a priori impression derived in the absence of statistical evidence is that some of the early items in the test proper are more difficult than some of the later items. For instance, Items 1–8, in which the testee has to discover either a synonym or an antonym of a given word, appear to be among the most difficult items in the test, making considerable demands on vocabulary. A child weak in this respect might suffer discouragement which could affect adversely his performance on the remainder of the test.

Synonym-antonym items, intended to trap the unwary testee, succeed only too frequently in enmeshing the unvigilant test constructor. The flexibility of the English language is such that, given the right contexts, many words can mean "nearly the same as" or "nearly the opposite of" a given word. With items designed for more mature or high ability testees the danger of this kind of ambiguity is increased. Testees with the highest awareness of the possibilities suffer most. It is not enough to attempt to resolve ambiguities by the greater frequency of choice of one particular alternative. If a single testee can see a response legitimately alternative to that popularly chosen, the item needs modifying. These reflections are prompted by the fact that with the possible exception of one item, the writers of the synonym-antonym items in MGAT appear to have avoided the trap successfully. The exception is Item 1, in which the given word is PERMIT and among the alternative responses appear the words ALLOW and DENY. The synonym is certainly valid, and will be most frequently chosen, but may there not be a small minority of testees who, while seeing the synonym ALLOW, will also see DENY as a possible antonym? "To deny entry" is certainly the opposite of "to permit entry."

There is a minor defect in the preamble to Items 9–15. It begins, "In the table below, some numbers appear once only, some twice...." In the table only one number appears once only. This inaccuracy may confuse some testees.

Items 16–22, based on a rectangular table which must be completed from given clues, seem admirable if one admits the principle that the trick of completing the table must be mastered before any of the items can be answered successfully. An item analysis might well indicate a tendency towards an "all or none" response to this set. The wording of Item 20, which reads, "How much less did Peter earn?" is defective in that it relates back to the previous item, "What were Stanley's earnings for the week?" which is disconcerting.

The letter series, Items 37–48, presents no unusual features with the exception of Item 45: A, C, F, J, O, ( ) ( ). In order to complete this successfully, one must start again at the beginning of the alphabet, a situation which is not covered by the instructions.

In the instructions for the final set of items the testee is told first that "in each of the following questions there are three items which are alike in some way," and next that he must "find out which are the three which go together." This is unfortunate, since "alike" and "go together" do not necessarily mean the same, and the double-barreled attempt to clarify the instructions may have the opposite effect. A cup,

Manchester General Ability Test (Senior) 1

a plate, and a saucer are alike in that all three are made of porcelain, or that all three are containers. On the other hand a cup, a saucer, and a spoon are also alike in that they go together to constitute the set of utensils customarily employed in drinking tea. (All four objects are named in Item 92.)

It was stated earlier that the test includes a set (eight items) of anagrams. These appear to be open to criticism on two grounds, one particular and minor, the other general and major. The first relates to a discrepancy between the layout of the instructional example: "GERNE is a colour. Answer (GREEN)"; and that of the test items: MERMAN is a tool. Write it correctly here (   ). Why not repeat in the test items the layout in the example, thus avoiding the questionable "it"? More seriously, is the inclusion of items of this type desirable? What aspect of general ability do they test? Is not the "seeing" which leads to their rapid solution rather a specialized ability? It is clear from the special instructions preceding these items ("Do not spend too much time on these questions") that the test constructors are aware that these items are time consuming for these testees who do not "see" the solution rather quickly. How will such testees interpret the warning?

There are few tests which are beyond criticism, and, apart from the last one most of the criticisms made here are of a minor nature and can be taken into account in later editions. The general impression of this reviewer is that the test, as a whole, is good. Most of its material has a priori validity, the instructions in general are clear and concise, and, above all, working through it is more enjoyable than is the case with too many objective tests. If its a priori validity is confirmed by follow-up studies, this test is recommended to those requiring estimates of the general ability of testees of the age range it is designed to cover.

[352]

*Miller Analogies Test. Candidates for graduate school; 1926–52; Forms G ('47), H ('50), J ('52); Form H is also published under the title *Advanced Personnel Test* for use in business; revised manual ('52); supplement to manual ('56); distribution restricted and test administered at specified licensed testing centers; details may be obtained from publisher; 50(55) minutes; W. S. Miller; Psychological Corporation. *

REFERENCES

1–16. See 4:304.
17. CURETON, EDWARD E.; CURETON, LOUISE W.; AND BISHOP, RUTH. "Prediction of Success in Graduate Study of Psychology at the University of Tennessee." Letter. *Am Psychol* 4:361–2 Ag '49. *
18. STAFFORD, JOHN W. "The Prediction of Success in Graduate School." Abstract. *Am Psychol* 6:298 Jl '51. *
19. STREIT, L. ROBERT. *A Comparison of Miller Analogies Test Scores With Undergraduate and Graduate Grade-Point Averages of Graduate Students.* Master's thesis, Southern Methodist University (Dallas, Tex.), 1951.
20. BERDIE, RALPH F., AND LAYTON, WILBUR L. "Predicting Success in Law School." *J Appl Psychol* 36:257–60 Ag '52. * (PA 27:3839)
21. COCKRUM, LOGAN V. "Predicting Success in Training for the Ministry." *Relig Ed* 47:198–202 My–Je '52. *
22. STROWIG, RONALD W. *Predictive Values of the Miller Analogies Test for Master's Degree Students in Education.* Doctor's thesis, Stanford University (Stanford, Calif.), 1952.
23. FAHEY, GEORGE L. "Discriminatory Capacity of the University of Pittsburgh Examination Among Graduate Students in Psychology." *Am Psychol* 8:204–6 My '53. *
24. JENSON, RALPH E. "Predicting Scholastic Achievement of First-Year Graduate Students." *Ed & Psychol Meas* 13:322–9 su '53. * (PA 28:4833)
25. TRONCA, WILLIAM F. *A Study of the Validity and Reliability of Forms H and J of the Miller Analogies Test.* Master's thesis, Fordham University (New York, N.Y.), 1953.
26. WATTERS, G. V., AND PATERSON, D. G. "Miller Analogies Test Scores and Ratings of PhD's in Psychology." *Am Psychol* 8:89–90 F '53. * (PA 28:227)
27. DURNALL, EDWARD J., JR. "Predicting Scholastic Success for Graduate Students in Education." *Sch & Soc* 80:107 O 2 '54. * (PA 30:3456)
28. GLASER, ROBERT, AND JACOBS, OWEN. "Predicting Achievement in Medical School: A Comparison of Preclinical and Clinical Criteria." *J Appl Psychol* 38:245–7 Ag '54. * (PA 29:6271)
29. BUCKTON, LAVERNE, AND DOPPELT, JEROME E. "Freshman Tests as Predictors of Scores on Graduate and Professional School Examinations." *J Counsel Psychol* 2:146–9 su '55. * (PA 30:3453)
30. HOUNTRAS, P. T. *Factors Associated With the Academic Achievement of Foreign Graduate Students at the University of Michigan.* Doctor's thesis, University of Michigan (Ann Arbor, Mich.), 1955.
31. MEER, BERNARD, AND STEIN, MORRIS I. "Measures of Intelligence and Creativity." *J Psychol* 39:117–26 Ja '55. * (PA 29:9102)
32. MEER, BERNARD; STEIN, MORRIS I.; AND GEERTSMA, ROBERT. "An Analysis of the Miller Analogies Test for a Scientific Population." *Am Psychol* 10:33–4 Ja '55. * (PA 30:3658)
33. WARD, JOE H., JR. "Use of Electronic Computers in Psychological Research." Letter. *Am Psychol* 10:826–7 D '55. *
34. ARMSTRONG, HUBERT C. "The Prediction of Success in Graduate School Based on Undergraduate Records and the Miller Analogies Test." Abstract. *Calif J Ed Res* 7:129 My '56. *
35. HOUNTRAS, PETER T. "The Use of the Miller Analogies Test in Predicting Graduate Student Achievement." *Col & Univ* 32:65–70 fall '56. *
36. BRAMS, JEROME MARTIN. *The Relationship Between Personal Characteristics of Counseling Trainees and Effective Communication in Counseling.* Doctor's thesis, University of Missouri (Columbia, Mo.), 1957. (DA 17:1510)
37. HYMAN, SIDNEY R. "The Miller Analogies Test and University of Pittsburgh PhD's in Psychology." *Am Psychol* 12:35–6 Ja '57. * (PA 32:947)
38. SMITH, L. M. "Correlates of the Miller Analogies Test." *Sch & Soc* 85:286–7 O '57. *
39. DUNNETTE, MARVIN D., AND KIRCHNER, WAYNE K. "Validation of Psychological Tests in Industry." *Personnel Adm* 21:20–7 My–Je '58. *
40. FELDMAN, MARVIN J. "A Comparison of Miller Analogy Test Scores." *J Counsel Psychol* 5:149–50 su '58. *
41. PETERSON, TED T. *Selecting School Administrators: An Evaluation of Six Tests.* Doctor's thesis, Stanford University (Stanford, Calif.), 1958. (DA 19:262)
42. PEPINSKY, HAROLD N. "A Comparison of Miller Analogy Test Scores." *J Consult Psychol* 5:149–50 su '58. *
43. ROBINSON, DONALD W. "A Comparison of Two Batteries of Tests as Predictors of First Year Achievement in the Graduate School of Bradley University." *Yearb Nat Council Meas Used Ed* 15:118–27 '58. *
44. VOTAW, DAVID F. "Validity of Estimates of Success in Graduate School Based on Miller Analogies Test Scores." *Yearb Nat Council Meas Used Ed* 15:150–6 '58. *

JOHN T. DAILEY, *Program Director, American Institute for Research, Washington, D.C.*

The *Miller Analogies Test* is designed to measure scholastic aptitude at the graduate level. One of the earliest tests of its kind, it has in its several forms enjoyed steadily increasing use over a period of more than thirty years.

Considerable statistical data are furnished in the manual regarding the test. Alternate form reliabilities range between .85 and .89 for sizable samples of senior and graduate students; odd-even reliabilities, of course, run higher. The correlations between the test and the subject matter tests among the Graduate Record Examinations are for the most part between .75 and .80. The test also correlates in the low .80's with the Verbal factor in the Graduate Record Examinations.

It might, therefore, be concluded that the test has nothing to offer over and above a good vocabulary test; and yet, close examination of the test and analysis of available validity data seem to contraindicate this. The test itself is pitched at such a high difficulty level that it probably has more ceiling than any other test of its kind. For a highly selected group, such as graduate students, this could have a very positive effect in maximizing reliability and validity. The high ceiling on the test is a compounding of highly abstruse subject matter plus often very complex analogies. It is not likely that either a straight subject matter or a straight vocabulary test could have as much discrimination at extremely high levels. Some penalty is, however, paid for these advantages. Psychologically and educationally the test is extremely loosely structured and is a hodgepodge of subject matter from practically all fields, making it a very difficult test to interpret psychologically or educationally.

The manual reports the results of several validity studies. As is usual for tests of this sort, fairly high validity coefficients are found against measures of scholastic achievement. Relatively little data are available regarding the validity of this test as compared with other good predictive tests; however, some studies indicate that the test may offer validity over and above that offered by a combination of other commonly used tests, by course grades, or by other criteria. As always happens with tests of this type, the validity becomes progressively lower as one departs farther and farther from course grades as criteria.

The manual gives normative data for several groups of students in various subject matter fields. Of special interest is a 1956 supplement to the manual which reports several studies involving graduate students in education. Here, various institutions show tremendous variation in score distribution, and all show markedly lower scores for education students than those reported in the manual for students in other areas of graduate study. Of all groups for whom norms are provided, the psychologists score highest. This may be a function of greater operational use of the test in selection of the students in the normative group. It could also be influenced by the balance of subject matter in the test.

This test is undoubtedly subjected to the tightest security control for any test of its kind. The manual states that the test should not be used in mass testing situations and should be given only in small groups with highly trained proctors; the same manual, however, points out that the test is practically self-administering. Close examination of the test and the available statistics indicate that the test should be about as self-administering as anything in its field. The extreme emphasis on security should be a minus factor in the value of the test for most consumers.

The *Miller Analogies Test* is a well constructed test of general academic scholarship potential with a difficulty pitched at a high graduate student level. Its high difficulty level, together with its loading with highly abstruse subject matter, probably allows for greater validity than is likely for other criteria of academic graduate scholarship. However, the nature of this contribution has not been adequately explored and the excessive security of the test make its exploration more difficult.

[353]
*Moray House Intelligence Tests. Ages 8.5–10.5, 10–12, 12–14, 13.5–17.5; 1930–58; 4 levels; distribution restricted to education authorities; 2s. 9d. per 25 practice tests for *b* or *c*; postage extra; Department of Education, University of Edinburgh; University of London Press. *
a) MORAY HOUSE JUNIOR REASONING TEST 2 FOR NINE-YEAR-OLDS. Ages 8.5–10.5; 1947-58; former tests in series called *Moray House Junior Intelligence Tests;* 1 form ['58]; 13s. per 25 tests; 8d. per single copy; 1s. 6d. per manual ['58]; 45(104) minutes in 2 sessions.
b) MORAY HOUSE VERBAL REASONING TEST 61. Ages 10–12; 1930–58; former tests in series called *Moray House Intelligence Tests;* 1 form ['58]; 9s. 6d. per 25 tests; 6d. per single copy; 1s. 6d. per manual ['58]; practice test: 10(15) minutes; test: 45(50) minutes.
c) MORAY HOUSE VERBAL REASONING TEST (ADV.) 10. Ages 12–14; 1940–56; 1 form ['56]; prices same as for *b* above; practice test: 10(15) minutes; test: 45(50) minutes.
d) MORAY HOUSE ADULT TEST 1. Ages 13.5–17.5; 1952; title on test is *Intelligence Test (Adult) 1;* 1 form ['52]; prices same as for *b* above; 45(50) minutes.

REFERENCES

1-2. See 3:241.
3. THOMSON, G. H. "The Distribution of Intelligence Among University and College Students." *Brit J Ed Psychol* 15:76-9 Je '45. * (*PA* 20:333)
4. DEMPSTER, J. J. B. "Symposium on the Effects of Coaching and Practice in Intelligence Tests: III, Southampton Investigation and Procedure." *Brit J Ed Psychol* 24:1-4 F '54. * (*PA* 28:8718)

For a review by Patrick Slater of earlier forms, see 3:241.

[354]

*New Rhode Island Intelligence Test. Ages 3-6; 1923-55; identical with *Rhode Island Intelligence Test* ('23) except for slight changes in some drawings; 1 form ('55, combination of Forms A and B of original edition); no manual; directions for administering ('55); tentative norms; $2.15 per 25 tests; 25¢ per specimen set; postpaid; [30] minutes in 2 sessions; original test by G. E. Bird and Clara R. Craig; new edition by G. E. Bird and G. L. Betts; Public School Publishing Co. *

REFERENCES

1. TOWN, CLARA HARRISON. "A Mass Mental Test for Use With Kindergarten and First Grade Children." *J Appl Psychol* 6:89-112 Je '22. *
2. BIRD, GRACE E. "An Intelligence Test for Children From Three to Six." Abstract. *Psychol B* 20:97-8 F '23. *
3. BIRD, GRACE E. "The Rhode Island Intelligence Test." *J Ed Res* 8:397-403 D '23. *
4. POULL, LOUISE E. "Clinical Values of the Rhode Island Intelligence Test and the Town Picture Game." *J Appl Psychol* 11:68-72 F '27. *
5. SANGREN, PAUL V. "Comparative Validity of Primary Intelligence Tests." *J Appl Psychol* 13:394-412 Ag '29. * (*PA* 3:4324)
6. HUGGETT, A. J. "An Experiment in Reading Readiness." *J Ed Res* 32:263-70 D '38. *

RAYMOND C. NORRIS, *Associate Professor of Psychology, George Peabody College for Teachers, Nashville, Tennessee.*

The directions for administering the test indicate that the two parts (forms) are to be administered at separate sittings and the two MA estimates averaged before establishing the ratio IQ. The parts are apparently made as nearly parallel as possible by having directly equivalent items in the two forms. For instance, while Part 1 contains comparisons of pairs of objects calling for the identification of the bigger, faster, colder, heavier, etc., the items in Part 2 call for identification of the smaller, slower, warmer, lighter, etc. Each part consists of six subtests dealing with properties and qualities of common objects, identification of missing parts, recognition of family members, identification of common household and sports activities, identification of stereotypes, and ability to make discriminations among similar and different patterns.

All items consist of line drawings of people or objects to be marked over by the subject. While the quality of the drawings is not high and some pictures appear dated, it seems likely that any child familiar with the concepts can make a response.

Available norms are sketchy and based on a sample of unknown size and character. Local norms would have to be established before either the mental age or intelligence quotient scores could be interpreted.

[355]

★New South African Group Test. Ages 8-11, 10-14, 13-18; 1931-56; 3 scores: verbal, nonverbal, total; IBM; Forms A, B ['55]; 3 levels; mimeographed manual ['55]; mimeographed supplement ('56); separate answer sheets must be used; 43s. 2d. per 100 tests; 5s. 10d. per 100 IBM answer sheets; 7d. per scoring stencil; 1s. 6d. per manual; specimen set not available; postage extra; Afrikaans edition available; 70(75) minutes; National Bureau of Educational and Social Research under the auspices of South African Psychological Association; National Bureau of Educational and Social Research. *

a) JUNIOR. Ages 8-11.
b) INTERMEDIATE. Ages 10-14.
c) SENIOR. Ages 13-18.

[356]

*Non-Verbal Tests. Ages 8 to 11-0, 10 to 12-11, 10 to 11-11, 12 to 13-11; 4 levels; postage extra; published for National Foundation for Educational Research in England and Wales; Newnes Educational Publishing Co. Ltd. *

a) NON-VERBAL TESTS 1-2. Ages 10 to 12-11; 1947-51; title on test is *A Scale of Non-Verbal Mental Ability*; 2 forms; use of the practice exercise, *Preliminary Practice Test 1* ['50], is optional; no data on validity; distribution is restricted to directors of education; 8s. 6d. per 12 tests; 10d. per single copy; 3s. per 12 practice exercises; 4d. per single copy; 2s. 9d. per manual; practice exercise: 10(15) minutes; test: 30(35) minutes.

1) *Non-Verbal Test 1.* 1947-51; test ['49]; revised manual ['51]; provisional norms ['51] for administration with practice exercise for ages 10-2 to 11-1 only; Welsh ['54], Arabic ['48], and Hindi ['57] editions available; J. W. Jenkins.
2) *Non-Verbal Test 2.* 1948-51; test ['49]; revised manual ['51]; provisional norms for administration with practice exercise for ages 10-3 to 11-2 only; English-Welsh and Welsh-English editions ['58] available; D. M. Lee and J. W. Jenkins.

b) NON-VERBAL TEST 3. Ages 10 to 11-11; 1953-58; 1 form ['53]; separate answer sheets must be used; 16s. 6d. per 12 tests; 1s. 6d. per single copy; 1s. 6d. per 12 answer sheets; 1s. per revised manual ['58]; 50(60) minutes; I. Macfarlane Smith (manual), B. Calvert (test).

c) NON-VERBAL TEST 4. Ages 12 to 13-11; 1951; 1 form ['51]; no data on reliability and validity; 7s. 6d. per 12 tests; 8d. per single copy; 1s. per manual ['51]; 40(50) minutes.

d) NON-VERBAL TEST 5. Ages 8 to 11-0; 1953-57; 1 form ['53]; revised manual ('57); 10s. 6d. per 12 tests; 1s. per single copy; 1s. per manual; Hindi edition (no date) available; 20(40) minutes; D. A. Pidgeon.

REFERENCES

1-3. See 4:307.
4. JONES, W. R. "The Language Handicap of Welsh-Speaking Children: A Study of Their Performance in an English Verbal Intelligence Test in Relation to Their Non-Verbal Mental Ability and Their Reading Ability in English." *Brit J Ed Psychol* 22:114-23 Je '52. * (*PA* 27:2197)

CYRIL A. ROGERS, *Senior Lecturer in Psychology, University College of Rhodesia and Nyasaland, Salisbury, Southern Rhodesia.* [Review of Tests 1–3.]

These three tests have been designed to furnish a measure of nonverbal intelligence within the age range of 10–12 years. Practice exercises are included with each of the tests, and the directions for administration are outlined clearly and are easy to follow. The norms are logically arranged and simple to read.

Non-Verbal Test 1 employs five separately timed subtests embodying different principles of classification, ordered sequence, and nonverbal analogy. The norms, which straddle a range of from 10-0 to 12-11, have been standardised with a mean of 100 and a standard deviation of 15 points; they are therefore statistically, although not necessarily psychologically, the equivalent of IQ scores. There are two procedures for administering the test, the first without preliminary practice exercises and the second with practice exercises which can be administered within 15 minutes.

Apart from mentioning the size and age range of the sample, no information is given on the group which furnished norms for the first procedure. However, it is given that the provisional norms for the second procedure are based on an urban sample of 842 boys and 777 girls. The manual shows that there is a small sex difference in mean raw scores which favours the girls, but whether or not this is significant is not indicated. The test reliability, as determined by the split-half technique, was found to be .95, although the sample on which this was based is not described. Neither are there any data given to indicate validity.

A Welsh version of the test has been prepared and an inspection of the norms shows that children tested through the medium of the Welsh language obtain considerably lower scores than do English children tested in English. An Arabic version has been employed in the Sudan, but Scott's (3) findings indicate that such adaptations are of little value when compared with tests developed on the spot. No norms are available for the Arabic adaptation.

Non-Verbal Test 2 was designed as a parallel form of Test 1 although the correlation between the two is not given in the manual. Certainly the norms established for Test 2 (using practice exercises) indicate that it is either considerably more difficult than Test 1, or else the sampling has been fundamentally different. The first explanation seems the more likely, but, in the absence of descriptive data, one cannot be sure. Sex differences in mean score are more marked on Test 2 than Test 1, but the significance of these is not explored. As with the first test, no information is given concerning the relation of the scale to other well established tests of intelligence, nor are factorial studies cited which may throw some light on its validity. The publisher's test catalogue reports a reliability coefficient of .92 established on retesting 861 children after an interval of one week. This information should be given in the test manual.

Non-Verbal Test 3, originally planned for use with Maori children, contains 96 carefully designed items requiring the completion of a pattern within a square, or the completion of a series of diagrams or numerals. The manual claims that the test may be used: (*a*) to discover children "whose intelligence does not find adequate expression through verbal channels," (*b*) to test children who are having reading or other linguistic difficulties, and (*c*) to investigate the "intellectual capacities" of children in widely differing cultural groups. No evidence is given in the manual in support of these claims. Although the test probably has validity for the first two uses, its validity in widely differing cultural groups must be questioned.

The only validation reported on an external criterion is a correlation of .81 with Raven's *Progressive Matrices* based upon 86 pupils. No information on reliability is presented in the manual where it should be. The publisher's test catalogue reports an unidentified reliability coefficient of .95. Neither of these correlation coefficients can be interpreted properly without further information about the groups tested and identification of the statistical formulas employed. Provisional norms for each month from 10-6 to 12-0 years are presented without explanation as to their meaning. From information published elsewhere,[1] it appears that the norms are normalized scores with a mean of 100 and a standard deviation of 15. Yet it seems unlikely that such norms can be very well founded when they are presented separately for each of 19 age groupings and there were only 413 children tested in the normative group. Be-

[1] PIDGEON, D. A.; AND YATES, ALFRED. "The Use of Tests in the Classroom (5)." *B Nat Found Ed Res* (7):6–11 Mr '56. *

cause of the small sample and the lack of information about the normative group and the standardised scores, these provisional norms are of questionable value.

CONCLUSION. It is surprising that the National Foundation for Educational Research is willing to publish tests with so little information about their construction, reliability, validity, norming, and limitations. Although some of this information can be gleaned from other sources, it is essential that it be included in the manuals to the tests. As they stand, it is difficult to conceive of manuals which could be less complete. Until the information is readily available, these nonverbal tests cannot be recommended for general use in schools. Further studies are needed to demonstrate their usefulness in particular situations. Such studies should be made or reported by the publisher.

For a review by E. A. Peel of the original edition, see 4:307.

[357]

★**Nufferno Tests of Speed and Level.** Mental ages 11 and over; 1956; 5 tests; 4s. 6d. per 25 sheets; 15s. per set of level cards; 2s. 6d. per specimen set; postage extra; W. D. Furneaux; distributed by National Foundation for Educational Research in England and Wales. *

a) NUFFERNO SPEED TESTS. 5 scores: speed (stressed or unstressed), speed range, speed slope, stress speed-gain, accuracy; 2 tests; 7s. per manual ['56].
  1) *Nufferno Sheet 1: Test GIS/14E.36.* Mental ages 11–15; Forms A(1), A(2) on 1 sheet; (15) minutes.
  2) *Nufferno Sheet 2: Test GIS/14E.36.* Mental ages 13 and over; Forms A(2), B(1); (20) minutes.

b) NUFFERNO LEVEL TESTS. 3 tests; 5s. per manual ['56.]
  1) *Nufferno Level Test Cards: Test IL/2(AB)36.* Mental ages 11 and over; individual; 2 scores: personal level, situation level; 1 form ['56]; (40) minutes.
  2) *Nufferno Sheet 3: Test GL/2C.46.* Adults with IQ's 100 and over; 1 form ['56]; (40) minutes.
  3) *Nufferno Sheet 4: Test GL/3A.35.* Mental ages 11 and over; 1 form ['56]; (40) minutes.

REFERENCES
1. BLEWETT, D. B. "An Experimental Study of the Inheritance of Intelligence." *J Mental Sci* 100:922–33 O '54. * (PA 29:6909)
2. FURNEAUX, W. D. "The Nufferno Tests." *B Nat Found Ed Res Engl & Wales* (6):32–6 N '55. *
3. SHAPIRO, M. B., AND NELSON, E. H. "An Investigation of the Nature of Cognitive Impairment in Co-operative Psychiatric Patients." *Brit J Med Psychol* 28:239–56 pt 4 '55. * (PA 30:6185)

JOHN LIGGETT, *Lecturer in Applied Psychology, University of Durham, Newcastle, England.*

In the *Nufferno Tests of Speed and Level* an ingenious attempt has been made to assess separately the many different mental operations (such as speed, persistence, and accuracy) which contribute to intelligence test performance. The basic material is of conventional type (Thurstone letter series items), but there are several novel features in the mode of administration and in the treatment of results.

For the individual form of the level test, the material is a pack of cards of playing card size, each with a single letter series problem printed on it. The pack is divided into several sections each of which contains a group of problems whose difficulty steadily increases from very easy to very difficult. The individual cards are presented until two successive failures are made. The remaining (i.e., the more difficult) cards in that group are then discarded and a second cycle is begun. This too, is discontinued when the problems become too difficult. The number of these more or less equivalent cycles which are presented depends on the time available for testing and the reliability of measurement which is required. The scoring system is such that the maximum score possible is the same no matter how few or how many cycles have been completed and so it is perfectly possible for the slow, persistent but accurate worker to obtain a higher score than one who is fast but lacks persistence. In addition to discarding the "too difficult" items, the "too easy" items are also omitted from the second and subsequent cycles. The omission of too easy and too difficult items is very easily made by observing a simple system involving code letters and numbers printed on the back of the cards. These omissions, in addition to saving time, have the effect of equalising such motivational factors as discouragement.

In the group form of the level test, printed forms are used instead of "playing cards," but the problems are of the same letter series type and are arranged in the same cyclic form employed in the individual method.

The speed tests also employ letter series items, but all the items within a given form are of approximately equal difficulty. The total testing time is broken into a number of short timed periods or subsections. If the majority of answers within any subsection turn out to be wrong, that period is ignored for scoring purposes since, as the author explains, only times associated with correct responses should be taken into account. A scoring system is employed which gives maximum weighting to those subsections having the greatest proportion of correct answers. The speed tests may be administered under two different conditions —either unstressed (at the subject's own comfortable rate) or stressed (when the subject is asked to perform as quickly as possible and a stop watch is prominently displayed). Several methods of dealing with the speed scores are described in the manual in which the author presents his views on the theoretical aspects of speed measurement. According to the author, speed measurement cannot be made easily with little expenditure of time. "Strictly speaking," he says, "it calls for the use of specialised apparatus, in the laboratory." The author, however, "has found it possible....to devise a method for obtaining true speed scores, without special equipment, under group-test conditions, and without great loss of accuracy. Both testing and scoring, however, make special demands." He goes on to say that "testing requires the continuous active participation of the invigilator during the whole time that testing is in progress, and scoring requires a knowledge of how to use a table of logarithms." Certainly the schedule of instructions is a formidable one.

The manual summarises results obtained on both speed and level tests by a large number of normal and abnormal subjects. These results suggest that the tests may prove very useful in educational selection and in differential diagnosis. Psychotics have shown, for example, abnormal slowness on the speed tests, whereas neurotics have shown no such slowness. Interesting data is presented comparing speed under stressed and unstressed conditions. University students seeking psychological help showed a slower speed under stressed conditions, whereas normal subjects showed an increase of speed. Impressive normative data are presented for the level tests for groups such as normal adult males, university students, and school children from various types of schools.

There are unfortunate defects in the manual in spite of its attractive and useful looseleaf format. Explanations of procedure are not as clear as they could be. This is all the more unfortunate since the tests involve relatively complicated procedures and rest on much close theoretical argument. A great deal of searching backwards and forwards through the pages could have been avoided by a little repetition of procedural instructions. Convenience in use is more important than brevity in a manual. The presentation of the author's "Theory of Speed and Accuracy Measurements" could be improved. A number of theoretical concepts are introduced with scant explanation or justification. Some of the references are difficult of access and an important one has yet to appear. The status of the theory on which these tests rest can, of course, be established only by time, controversy, and much empirical work. But there can be little doubt that the Nufferno tests will come to occupy an important place in the equipment of psychologists, both clinical and educational. The tests are original, pointed, and skillfully designed. They are an important contribution to cognitive measurement.

E. A. PEEL, *Professor of Education, University of Birmingham, Birmingham, England.*

THE SPEED TESTS. The basic ideas underlying these tests are sound and the attempt to disengage speed, accuracy, and persistence is helpful. The tests are designed to measure speed and accuracy under stressed and unstressed conditions. Stress is brought about by telling the subject to work as fast as he can. The tests may be given individually or to groups. The essential technique in the speed tests is to count up the time devoted to successful solution of the items. These are composed of letter series to be completed by the next letter required. Times are converted to their logarithms and tables of percentile scores are provided, for both speed and accuracy, for groups of university students, normal adults, neurotics, and schizophrenics.

Accuracy of testing is measured by standard errors of estimates. A table in the manual gives correlations between different scores (speed, accuracy, etc.) after correction for reliability. The more technically minded reader might also like to see the reliabilities and the raw correlations between the tests.

The theoretical foreword and the tests themselves form a useful contribution in the field of ability testing, particularly in teasing out two variables which intelligence testers are usually content to leave undisturbed. But what an exercise is provided in the pages given over to descriptions and instructions! Here the reader needs to be tough minded indeed, for he is tossed like a shuttlecock backwards and forwards from page to page, from one set of symbols to another. The author has a penchant for never finally clearing up any particular point at any one place. The whole booklet is littered far too much with numerico-literal symbols. This part of the booklet really ought to be simplified if it is to be workable for less vigorous readers.

THE LEVEL TESTS. The author first discusses the interrelation of speed, accuracy, and continuance (persistence), and then takes up more fully the relationship between persistence and intelligence scores. We are given to understand that the personal level score is a measure of the level of intelligence at a constant level of subjective difficulty. The Nufferno concept of personal level of intelligence as the way in which persistence is affected by the test seems to be meaningful in the test situation. It is measured individually by Test IL/2(AB)36 by giving a series of short cycles of items of increasing difficulty so that items of similar difficulty appear in different cycles. The purpose is to ensure that the testee is asked to do only items that are neither too easy nor too hard for him. The items are not speeded; the author claims that under these conditions the persistent, accurate worker may obtain more marks than one who works fast, but lacks persistence.

A group test GL/3A.35 provides a similar measure in group test form. The items consist of letter series problems.

The author provides tables of norms for adults, university students, and school pupils for both individual and group tests, but he has not provided norms for abnormal groups. The instructions take less out of the reader than those for the speed tests. However, the author would also do well here to streamline them a little and perhaps use a simpler system of test nomenclature. The author's concept of personal level requires more attention from research workers. These tests should be tried out, particularly at the research level, in order to verify his findings. They could also be of use in individual cases where the usual intelligence tests have produced anomalous results.

[358]

★The Ohio Penal Classification Test. Penal institutions; 1952–54; 5 scores: block counting, digit-symbol, number series, memory span, total; Forms F ('54, women), PP ('52, men); manual ('52); separate answer sheets must be used; $1.95 per 20 tests; $1 per 20 answer sheets; $1 per specimen set (must be purchased to obtain manual); postage extra; 14.5(25–35) minutes; DeWitt E. Sell; Psychometric Affiliates. * (Form PP is also sold for industrial use under the title *Ohio Classification Test* with a 1957 copyright; manual by the original author, Robert W. Scollay, and Leroy N. Vernon.)

NORMAN EAGLE, *School Psychologist, Public Schools, Fort Lee, New Jersey.*

The Ohio Classification Tests are group administered, nonverbal, paper and pencil measures of adult mental ability. There are two "forms" of the *Ohio Penal Classification Test* (for use in prisons), and one "form" of the *Ohio Classification Test* (for use in industry). Each test is composed of four subtests. The first three subtests are identical for all forms; Form PP of the OPCT and the single form of OCT are identical throughout. Test 1 consists of counting blocks in a pile perceived at an oblique angle; it is supposed to measure spatial perceptive aptitude and reasoning capacity. Test 2 is an original digit-symbol task purporting to measure perception and associative learning speed. Test 3, requiring the completion of 20 number series arranged in order of increasing difficulty, is designed to measure number facility and reasoning. Test 4 consists of 10 drawings of common objects whose names the subject is required to write, from recall, after a brief exposure; this test is supposed to measure "both apperception and memory."

The purpose of the tests, as stated in the manual, is to provide a group test of adult mental ability "which would circumvent as far as possible the verbal factors in general intelligence which are overemphasized in widely used group intelligence tests and which would emphasize altitude or power rather than speed." The authors hope, in this way, to avoid penalizing the "uncultured and uneducated" for their verbal deficiencies. In removing the verbal factor, however, the authors have restricted the interpretation of what their tests measure to something less, or more specific, than general intelligence. The intellectual areas tapped are spatial and numerical reasoning, and visual associative learning and memory. The justification for such an excision of general intelligence would lie in showing that this test can predict success at certain tasks with greater facility than can more highly verbal tests. Unfortunately, this is not demonstrated by the evidence reported. In addition, all of the subtests are by no means power tests. Thus, there is considerable doubt as to whether the objectives of the tests have been realized.

The manuals for the two tests are practically

identical, the principal difference being in the more extensive interpretative data given in the manual for the OCT. The directions for administration leave much to be desired. On both the OCT and the OPCT, Test 1 is completely exposed while the examiner gives rather lengthy instructions for taking it. Examinees who finish Test 1 in the OCT early may gain some advantage from the fact that the digit symbols of Test 2 are clearly exposed. In this same test the directions call for turning "to" Test 3, whereas actually what is required is to invert the page. The directions for the digit-symbol test in both tests are, in the opinion of this reviewer, inadequate. Not all of the samples are exhausted in the practice, a situation which may lead to uncertainty as to where to begin the test. Test 4 suffers from not having a definite time interval during which the figures are exposed, as well as from failing to take into account the wide range of attention which may be present. This test is also qualitatively scored in that examinees may call the objects by different names, requiring scorer judgment and interpretation. Only little assistance is given by the manual on this problem. For these reasons, as well as the fact that this test correlates only .36 with the sum of the standard scores of the other three subtests, it probably would be better to exclude this test in favor of one drawing more on reasoning capacity.

The standardization population on which the test statistics are based consisted of 550 prisoners ranging in age from 17 to 30 years, with a mean of 23 years, and a white-Negro ratio of 7 to 3. The test was also administered to 107 ninth grade boys, and the mean scores of the two groups compared. The manual states in one place that the difference between these scores is *not* significant at the 2 per cent level of confidence; in another place it is admitted that the difference obtained *is* significant at the 5 per cent level. Also provided are standard score percentile norms for women factory workers ($n = 40$), male factory workers ($n = 100$), factory workers being considered for higher positions ($n = 65$), sales and managerial applicants ($n = 162$), "middle management men" ($n = 44$), graduate engineers ($n = 22$), and upperclass scientific and technical students ($n = 93$). No further information on the composition of these groups is given. While the provision of norms for these special groups demonstrates that the authors are aware of the inapplicability of the original norms to other than a selected prison population, the small size of most of these groups and the complete lack of identifying information still leaves the interpretation of nonprison population scores in doubt.

The manual states that "the 4 subtests of the *Ohio Classification Test* have already been extensively 'judged' by 'experts' to measure intelligence." There is no further elaboration, though some substantiation or reference would seem to be called for after such a declaration. The manual reports a correlation (presumably product-moment) of .79 between the OCT and Wechsler-Bellevue full scale for 155 prisoners, and a rank order correlation of .93 between these tests based on only 10 prisoners. However, correlations with other tests, including the *Minnesota Paper Form Board Test* and the *American Council on Education Psychological Examination for College Freshmen*, based on nonprison groups show relationships of a much lower order. One table in the manual shows the relationship between mean OCT standard scores and years of schooling; however, the interpretation of this relationship as evidence for test validity is clouded by indications that schooling affects IQ scores. A correlation of .34 is reported between OCT scores and average rate of salary increase, and it is claimed that this "is significant at the 1% level." This may be true, but it means that the correlation is significantly different from *zero correlation*, and in itself does not indicate a high degree of relationship. Further correlations are provided with merit rankings and average hourly earnings of industrial workers, but the numbers of subjects involved are so small as not to merit further comment. A test-retest reliability of .87, with a standard error of measurement of 5.76 IQ points, is reported for a prison sample of 138. Again, we do not know the range of scores or composition of the group upon which these statistics are based.

The *Ohio Penal Classification Test* may serve some function as a group test in the specific situation out of which it developed and for which it was designed, though the absence of the verbal factor may reduce its predictive ability in certain occupational areas, even within the prison setting. For nonprison situations the test does not seem to be applicable in its present form. In any case, the manuals and the test booklet for the *Ohio Classification Test* should be completely overhauled and the manuals printed in a type which can be read without the aid of a magnifying glass.

[359]

*Ohio State University Psychological Test. Grades 9–16 and adults; 1919–58; 4 scores: same-opposites, analogies, reading comprehension, total; IBM; Forms 18 ('33), 19 ('35), 20 ('37), 21 ('40), 22 ('43), 23 ('47), 24 ('50), 25 ('54), 26 ('58); mimeographed instructions and norms published separately as Ohio College Association Bulletins and Ohio High School Bulletins; high school norms for Forms 18–24 for total score only; college norms for Form 22 for reading comprehension and total score only; no norms for grades 14–16 or adults; separate answer sheets or pads must be used; high school prices: 5¢ per test booklet (Forms 23–26), 5¢ per answer pad, 5¢ per IBM answer sheet (Forms 21–26 only); college prices: 10¢ per test booklet (Forms 23–26), 8¢ per test booklet (Forms 18–22), 6¢ per answer pad, 6¢ per IBM answer sheet (Forms 21–26 only); 5¢ per IBM scoring stencil for both levels; postage extra; instructions and norms bulletins free; specimen set free to qualified school personnel; scoring service available at 4¢ per answer sheet, postage extra; (120) minutes; Herbert A. Toops; Ohio College Association. * (Form 21 also published in 2 editions by Science Research Associates: Forms AH (hand scoring edition), AM (machine scoring edition); $9.80 per 20 tests of either edition; $2.35 per 20 answer pads; $5 per 100 IBM answer sheets; 75¢ per specimen set; postage extra.)

REFERENCES

1–28. See 3:244.
29–51. See 4:308.
52. KIRK, HARRY A. *The Relation Between Intelligence Rating and Achievement in Shorthand and Typing.* Master's thesis, Kent State University (Kent, Ohio), 1942.
53. EDBERG, GEORGE. *The Validity of High School General Educational Development Tests and the Ohio Psychological (Form 21) Test in Predicting Chances of College Success for Students Who Have Had Less Than a High School Education.* Master's thesis, University of North Dakota (Grand Forks, N.D.), 1948.
54. JOHNSON, RALPH H., AND BOND, GUY L. "Reading Ease of Commonly Used Tests." *J Appl Psychol* 34:319–24 O '50. * (PA 26:299)
55. LAYTON, WILBUR L. *Factors Associated With Grades in the First Course in Psychology.* Doctor's thesis, Ohio State University (Columbus, Ohio), 1950.
56. WELSH, MARY L. *A Comparison of Two Psychological Examinations in Predicting Academic Success of Ohio University Students.* Master's thesis, Ohio University (Athens, Ohio), 1951.
57. HANNA, JOSEPH V. "Use of Speed Tests in Guidance." *Occupations* 30:329–31 F '52. *
58. NEWMAN, SLATER E.; DUNCAN, CARL P.; BELL, GRAHAM B.; AND BRADT, KENNETH H. "Predicting Student Performance in the First Course in Psychology." *J Ed Psychol* 43:243–7 Ap '52. * (PA 27:3178)
59. HENDRIX, O. R. "Predicting Success in Elementary Accounting." *J Appl Psychol* 37:75–7 Ap '53. * (PA 28:1479)
60. JENKINS, JAMES J. "Some Measured Characteristics of Air Force Weather Forecasters and Success in Forecasting." *J Appl Psychol* 37:440–4 D '53. * (PA 29:1642)
61. KINZER, JOHN R., AND KINZER, LYDIA GREENE. "Predicting Grades in Advanced College Mathematics." *J Appl Psychol* 37:182–4 Je '53. * (PA 28:3209)
62. SAMENFELD, HERBERT W. "Predicting College Achievement." *J Higher Ed* 24:432–3 N '53. * (PA 28:6595)
63. CARLILE, A. B. "Predicting Performance in the Teaching Profession." *J Ed Res* 47:641–68 My '54. * (PA 29:3063)
64. CASH, WILLIAM L., JR. *Relation of Personality Traits to Scholastic Aptitude and Academic Achievement of Students in a Liberal Protestant Seminary.* Doctor's thesis, University of Michigan (Ann Arbor, Mich.), 1954. (DA 14:630)
65. CONNER, HAROLD T. *An Investigation of Certain Factors for the Selection and Guidance of Prospective Students Entering a School of Public Health.* Doctor's thesis, University of North Carolina (Chapel Hill, N.C.), 1954.
66. HOYT, DONALD P., AND NORMAN, WARREN T. "Adjustment and Academic Predictability." *J Counsel Psychol* 1:96–9 su '54. * (PA 29:3043)
67. KINZER, JOHN R., AND KINZER, LYDIA GREENE. "Some Bases for Predicting Marks in Advanced Engineering Mathematics." *Ed Res B* 33:13–8 Ja 13 '54. *
68. SCHMITZ, ROY M., AND HOLMES, JOHN L. "Relationship of Certain Measured Abilities to Freshman Engineering Achievement," pp. 32–42. (PA 29:1584) In *Selection and Counseling of Students in Engineering.* Edited by Wilbur L. Layton. Minnesota Studies in Student Personnel Work, No. 4. Minneapolis, Minn.: University of Minnesota Press, 1954. Pp. iv, 89. *
69. BOYD, JOSEPH D. *The Relative Prognostic Value of Selected Criteria in Predicting Beginning Academic Success at Northwestern University.* Doctor's thesis, Northwestern University (Evanston, Ill.), 1955. (DA 15:1780)
70. CHAHBAZI, PARVIZ. "The Prediction of Achievement in a College of Agriculture." *Ed & Psychol Meas* 15:484–6 w '55. * (PA 30:7754)
71. LAYTON, WILBUR L. "Construction of a Short Form of the Ohio State University Psychological Examination." *Yearb Nat Council Meas Used Ed* 12(pt 1):81–5 '55. *
72. MUNGER, PAUL F., AND GOECKERMAN, ROBERT W. "Collegiate Persistence of Upper- and Lower-Third High School Graduates." *J Counsel Psychol* 2:142–5 su '55. * (PA 30:3416)
73. ALLUISI, EARL A. "Maintaining Test Validity by Selectively Scoring a Short Form." *Psychol Rep* 2:57–8 Mr '56. * (PA 31:65)
74. ANNESER, ROBERT. *An Evaluation of Scholastic Aptitude in Predicting Senior Level Achievement at Ohio University.* Master's thesis, Ohio University (Athens, Ohio), 1956.
75. BOYER, LEE E., AND KOKEN, JAMES E. "Admissions Test as Criteria for Success in College." *J Ed Res* 50:313–5 D '56. * (PA 32:2095)
76. CHAHBAZI, PARVIZ. *Prediction of Achievement in New York State College of Agriculture at Cornell University.* Doctor's thesis, Cornell University (Ithaca, N.Y.), 1956. (DA 17:562)
77. HOUK, CLIFFORD C. *An Investigation of the Relationship Between General Chemistry 3 at Ohio University and Various Measures of Achievement.* Master's thesis, Ohio University (Athens, Ohio), 1956.
78. HEWER, VIVIAN H. "Vocational Interest-Achievement-Ability Interrelationships at the College Level." *J Counsel Psychol* 4:234–8 fall '57. *
79. RICHARDS, JAMES M., JR. "The Prediction of Academic Achievement in a Protestant Theological Seminary." *Ed & Psychol Meas* 17:628–30 w '57. *
80. STACKHOUSE, HENRY A. *An Analysis of Factors Associated With the Use of the Ohio State Psychological Test Administered Under Two Different Conditions in the Missouri College Aptitude Testing Program.* Doctor's thesis, University of Missouri (Columbia, Mo.), 1957. (DA 17:2925)

CYRIL J. HOYT, *Associate Professor of Education, and* W. WESLEY TENNYSON, *Assistant Professor of Education, University of Minnesota, Minneapolis, Minnesota.*

The *Ohio State University Psychological Test* is a verbal test of scholastic ability based upon college grade level as a criterion. This test is comprised of three subtests for which centile norms are available for each of grades 9 through 12, and for college freshmen. The subtests consist of 30 same-or-opposite items, 60 word analogy items, and 60 reading comprehension items based on ten paragraphs. The subject matter of the reading paragraphs may be classified as six passages concerned with natural science and mathematics, two concerned with social science material, and two consisting of literary descriptions. All items of the test are of the multiple choice variety with five suggested responses.

Form 25, a worklimit or power test requiring approximately two hours for its administration, includes 78 items from Form 23 selected for having the highest correlations with one year cumulative point-hour ratios for approximately 4,000 college freshmen. These 78 items are currently in use at the University of Minnesota as a time limit test known as the *Minnesota Scholastic Aptitude Test*. The other 72 items of Form 25 are new items which have been selected for their high correlations with the ability to earn high college grades.

The items of OSUPT were given careful trials and study before they were incorporated in the published form. Distractors for items were formulated by college students responding to the items presented in completion form. Those student-supplied answers which showed negative correlations with the criterion of college grade-point average were used as distractors in a multiple choice tryout form. Such selection of distractors helped to assure the testmaker that no alternative responses were so near to the correct choice that the item's correlations with the criterion were lowered by the inclusion of the distractors. Application of these item analysis techniques has resulted in high validity on a limited set of items, and a general avoidance of validity retrogression, common among tests which have been in use for a period of time.

At Ohio State University, in 1952–53, Form 24 showed a correlation of .58 with first semester grades of 1,158 freshmen of both sexes; and in 1953–54, a correlation of .60 for 1,491 freshmen. The corresponding correlations for Form 25 were not available to the reviewers, though previous experience with other forms would indicate that this magnitude can be expected for this latest revision. No information is given on the magnitude of the correlations of the subtest scores with the criterion. Reliability coefficients were not provided on Form 25; however, the test authors report a satisfactory level of reliability of the total score on earlier forms.

Percentile norms for Form 25 are based upon 1,346 ninth graders, 826 tenth graders, 1,578 eleventh graders, 3,164 twelfth graders, and an unstated number of college freshmen. The secondary school norms were derived from the 1954–55 Ohio High School Intelligence Test Survey. The college norms are tentative.

The OSUPT has been refined over the years by means of repeatedly applying item selection procedures based upon a general ability to earn college grades regardless of any specialization in the college curriculum. This seems in keeping with the idea of continuing general education, at least through the 14th year. Technical

Ohio State University Psychological Test

and other schools will probably find it advantageous to supplement the OSUPT with tests of quantitative reasoning and other special ability tests.

As a test designed to measure college aptitude, the *Ohio State University Psychological Test* is particularly useful in providing accurate differentiations in ability in the upper half of the general high school senior population from which most college freshmen are drawn. Form 25 benefits from the exacting test construction procedures employed in the development of earlier forms. It should serve well its intended purpose.

For a review by George A. Ferguson of Form 24, see 4:308; for a review by J. P. Guilford of Form 21, see 3:244; for reviews by Louis D. Hartson, Theos A. Langlie, and Rudolf Pintner of Form 20, see 38:1051.

[360]

★**An Orally Presented Group Test of Intelligence for Juniors.** Ages 8–11; 1952; 1 form; 3s. 6d. per manual, postage extra; (75–100) minutes in 5 sessions; J. Cornwell; Methuen & Co. Ltd. *

REFERENCES

1. CORNWELL, J. *The Construction, Standardisation, and Validation of an Orally Presented Group Test of Intelligence for Children Between the Ages of Eight and Eleven.* Master's thesis, University of Birmingham (Birmingham, England), 1950.
2. CORNWELL, J. "An Orally Presented Group Test of Intelligence for Juniors." *Ed R* 3:212–21 Je '51. *

ELIZABETH D. FRASER, *Lecturer in Psychology, University of Aberdeen, Aberdeen, Scotland.*

This unpretentious little book presents a rather unusual type of group test designed for children between 8 and 11 years of age, and intended to be given by teachers in the classroom situation. It is administered orally, the teacher writing the sample items on the blackboard and demonstrating, also on the board, the method of recording answers. The child writes his answers on a simple sheet of ruled paper. The whole procedure resembles an ordinary classroom lesson rather than a special test occasion. This is claimed to have two advantages: (*a*) it arouses no "test-anxiety" and (*b*) the oral presentation makes each item a separate challenge to the child, possibly resulting in a more sustained effort throughout the test, especially in the case of easily distracted pupils.

The test consists of five short subtests of the verbal type, each containing 20 items. Subtest 1 involves the recognition of same and opposite word relations; subtest 2 requires the child to say whether a given statement is always true, always false, or sometimes true and sometimes false; subtest 3 consists of items requiring a kind of riddle-solving with a choice of answers, for example, "What often falls but is never damaged? Is it fruit, glass, a chimney, or snow?"; subtest 4 is composed of the familiar pick-out-the-one-that-is-different items; and subtest 5 involves the carrying out of simple instructions, e.g., "Put three crosses side by side on the line and draw a ring round the middle one." The subtests take 15 or 20 minutes each to administer. It is intended that they should be given on separate occasions in order to maintain concentration and avoid fatigue.

The preliminary work (*1*) on the development of the test has been admirably done and is a model for other test constructors to follow. The original test of 270 items in nine subtests was first tried out on a representative sample of 300 children aged 7 to 12. As a result of this trial the instructions were tightened up, timing was adjusted, the clearly unsuitable items were eliminated, and the remainder of the items were arranged in order of difficulty. A second tryout on a similar group of 600 children led to an analysis of the internal validity of each item, the selection of the most discriminating items, a further revision of the order of difficulty, and the calculation of correlations among the subtests. The five most satisfactory subtests, each containing the 20 most satisfactory items, were thus selected, and the test in this form was finally given to a standardisation sample of 4,150 children aged 8 to 12 in a representative sample of Birmingham schools. Norms are given in the form of IQ's, but are in fact based on standard scores with mean 100 and SD 16.5 (SD of Stanford-Binet, Form L, at 10 years of age).

The standardisation sample, in spite of its size, cannot be regarded as completely adequate since it is drawn entirely from a very large industrial city and contains no rural children at all. More widespread application of the test is obviously required.

The reliability quoted for the test (a split-half correlation based on 200 children in the 10–11 age group) is very high—.95. It must be remembered, however, that, on this occasion, the test was administered by training college students with some knowledge of the theory and practice of mental testing and some appreciation of the pitfalls of an orally presented test. One might expect a somewhat lower figure when the test is given by relatively unsophisticated teachers.

The only data available on validity are correlations with two other well known tests. The correlation with the *Simplex Junior Intelligence Test* (n = 200 Birmingham children aged 9–11) is .91. With a much smaller group of 50 children of indeterminate composition, the correlation with the Stanford-Binet was .85.

The aim of the author has been to provide a test which is easily given by teachers in the classroom setting and which will enable them to make a preliminary classification of children into groups broadly homogeneous with respect to intelligence. It is also intended to aid in the assessment of children who are backward readers, and who may be penalised in the more usual written tests of intelligence. Carefully administered and properly interpreted, the test may prove of considerable use and great interest to enquiring teachers. The reviewer would suggest, however, that the author might find a shorter and less unwieldy title for his test.

[361]
*Otis Quick-Scoring Mental Ability Tests. Grades 1.5–4, 4–9, 9–16; 1936–54; tests for grades 4 and over are revisions of *Otis Self-Administering Tests of Mental Ability;* IBM for grades 4–16; 3 levels; separate answer sheets may be used with Forms AM, BM, CM, DM; $1.25 per 35 IBM answer sheets; 20¢ per machine scoring stencil; postage extra; 35¢ per specimen set of any one level, postpaid; Arthur S. Otis; World Book Co. * For latest edition and references, see 362.
a) ALPHA TEST. Grades 1.5–4; 1936–39; the same test booklet may be used to administer the verbal test, non-verbal test, or both; 3 scores: non-verbal, verbal, total; Forms A ('36), B ('38); manual ('39); $3.20 per 35 tests; 20(25), (30) minutes for non-verbal, verbal.
b) BETA TEST. Grades 4–9; 1937–54; IBM; Forms A ('37), B ('39), CM ('39), DM ('39); manuals (A and B, '37; CM and DM, '54); $2.30 per 35 tests (Forms A, B) $2.80 per 35 tests (Forms CM, DM); 30(35) minutes.
c) GAMMA TEST. Grades 9–16; 1937–54; IBM; Forms AM ('37), BM ('37), C ('39), D ('39); manuals (AM and BM, '54; C and D, '39); $2.30 per 35 tests (Forms C, D); $2.80 per 35 tests (Forms AM, MM); 30(35) minutes.

For a review by Frederic Kuder, see 3:249; for reviews by F. Kuhlmann and C. Spearman, see 40:1413 and 40:1427; for reviews by Psyche Cattell and R. Pintner, see 38:1053 (2 excerpts).

[362]
*Otis Quick-Scoring Mental Ability Tests, New Edition. Grades 1.5–4, 4–9, 9–16; 1936–54; previous edition (see 361) still available; IBM for grades 4 and over; 3 levels; manual ('54) for each level; sep-

arate answer sheets may be used in grades 4 and over; $1.25 per 35 IBM answer sheets; 20¢ per machine scoring stencil; postage extra; 35¢ per specimen set of any one level, postpaid; Arthur S. Otis; World Book Co. *

a) ALPHA SHORT FORM. Grades 1.5–4; 1936–54; Form AS ('52); $2.70 per 35 tests; (35) minutes.

b) BETA TEST. Grades 4–9; 1937–54; IBM; Forms EM, FM ('54); $2.80 per 35 tests; 30(35) minutes.

c) GAMMA TEST. Grades 9–16; 1937–54; IBM; Forms EM, FM ('54); $2.80 per 35 tests; 30(35) minutes.

REFERENCES

1–9. See 3:249.
10. KERR, GEORGE. "Aptitude Testing for Secondary Courses: An Essay in Control Under War-Time Difficulties." *Occupational Psychol* 16:73–8 Ap '42. * (PA 16:3290)
11. WITTENBORN, J. R., AND LARSEN, R. P. "A Factorial Study of Achievement in College German." *J Ed Psychol* 35: 39–48 Ja '44. * (PA 18:2613)
12. DAVIS, W. ALLISON, AND HAVIGHURST, ROBERT J. "The Measurement of Mental Systems: Can Intelligence Be Measured?" *Sci Mo* 66:301–16 Ap '48. * (PA 22:3381)
13. PEEL, E. A. "Symposium on Selection of Pupils for Different Types of Secondary Schools: VI, Evidence of a Practical Factor at the Age of Eleven." *Brit J Ed Psychol* 19:1–15 F '49. *
14. ALLEN, ROBERT M., AND BESSELL, HAROLD. "Intercorrelations Among Group Verbal and Non-Verbal Tests of Intelligence." *J Ed Res* 43:394–5 Ja '50. * (PA 24:4841)
15. HURD, ARCHER W. *Factors Influencing Student Success in Medical Education, Exhibits 614–7.* Richmond, Va.: Bureau of Educational Research and Service, Medical College of Virginia, August 1950. Pages not numbered.
16. BARNETTE, W. LESLIE, JR. "Occupational Aptitude Patterns of Selected Groups of Counseled Veterans." *Psychol Monogr* 65(5):1–49 '51. * (PA 26:2794)
17. BARRON, EMERSON M., AND DONOHUE, H. H. "Psychiatric Aide Selection Through Psychological Examinations: A Preliminary Report of the Screening of Applicants at the Arkansas State Hospital." *Am J Psychiatry* 107:859–65 My '51. * (PA 27:697)
18. LENNON, ROGER T. *A Comparison of Results of Three Intelligence Tests.* Test Service Notebook, No. 11. Yonkers, N.Y.: World Book Co., [1951]. Pp. 4. *
19. PURDY, BENJAMIN F. *A Study of Certain Tests and Personal History Factors as Predictors of Job Success for a Group of Clerical Workers.* Master's thesis, Southern Methodist University (Dallas, Tex.), 1951.
20. BOGER, JACK H. "An Experimental Study of the Effects of Perceptual Training on Group I.Q. Test Scores of Elementary Pupils in Rural Ungraded Schools." *J Ed Res* 46:43–52 S '52. * (PA 27:5414)
21. FRUCHTER, BENJAMIN. "Orthogonal and Oblique Solutions of a Battery of Aptitude, Achievement and Background Variables." *Ed & Psychol Meas* 12:20–38 sp '52. * (PA 27:6180)
22. SLUTZKY, JACOB E.; JUSTMAN, JOSEPH; AND WRIGHTSTONE, J. WAYNE. "The Use of a Group Intelligence Test as a Screening Device for the Selection of Mentally Retarded Children for Placement in Special Classes." *Am J Mental Def* 57: 106–8 Jl '52. * (PA 27:3776)
23. ANDERSON, SCARVIA B. "Prediction and Practice Tests at the College Level." *J Appl Psychol* 37:256–9 Ag '53. * (PA 28:6583)
24. CROUCH, MILDRED S. *The Relative Value of the Differential Aptitude Tests and the Otis Quick-Scoring Mental Ability Test for Predicting Scholastic Success.* Master's thesis, Tennessee Agricultural and Industrial University (Nashville, Tenn.), 1953.
25. RIDLEY, WALTER N. *Prognostic Values of Freshman Tests Used at Virginia State College.* Doctor's thesis, University of Virginia (Charlottesville, Va.), 1953. (DA 14:1042)
26. DELANCY, ELMER O. *A Study of Three Psychological Tests as Related to Reading Achievement in Grade One American School Reading Readiness Test, Form A; SRA Primary Mental Abilities, Primary Form; Otis Quick-Scoring Mental Ability Tests, Alpha Test: Form A.* Doctor's thesis, Pennsylvania State University (University Park, Pa.), 1954.
27. "Comparison Between Terman IQ's and Otis IQ's for a Group of Independent School Boys." *Ed Rec B* 66:78–9 Jl '55. * (PA 30:5235)
28. BARNES, PAUL J. "Prediction of Achievement in Grades 1 Through 4 From Otis Quick-Scoring Mental Ability Tests: Alpha Short Form." *Ed & Psychol Meas* 15:493–4 w '55. * (PA 30:7750)
29. BOLIN, BYRON J. "A Comparison of Raven's Progressive Matrices (1938) With the ACE Psychological Examination and the Otis Gamma Mental Ability Test." Abstract. *J Consult Psychol* 19:400 O '55. *
30. MITCHELL, JAMES V., JR. "A Comparison of the Factorial Structure of Cognitive Functions for a High and Low Status Group." *J Ed Psychol* 47:397–414 N '56. *
31. ZWEIBELSON, I. "Test Anxiety and Intelligence Test Performance." *J Consult Psychol* 20:479–81 D '56. * (PA 32:1659)
32. "A Note on Comparison of Correlations With Grades of Otis IQ's and Terman IQ's in an Independent School for Boys." *Ed Rec B* 69:73–4 F '57. *
33. CLARK, GLYNN E. *A Comparison of the Performance of Selected Pupils on the Davis-Eells Test and the Otis Test of Mental Ability.* Doctor's thesis, Washington University (St. Louis, Mo.), 1957. (DA 17:807)
34. LENNON, ROGER T., AND SCHUTZ, RICHARD E. *A Summary of Correlations Between Results of Certain Intelligence and Achievement Tests.* Test Service Notebook, No. 18. Yonkers, N.Y.: World Book Co., 1957. Pp. 4. *
35. LONG, JAMES R. *Academic Forecasting in the Technical-Vocational High School Subjects at West Seattle High School.* Doctor's thesis, University of Washington (Seattle, Wash.), 1957. (DA 17:1951)
36. NICHOLSON, ALICE. *Background Abilities Related to Reading Success in First Grade.* Doctor's thesis, Boston University (Boston, Mass.), 1957.
37. NORTH, ROBERT D. "A Preliminary Report on the Reliability of the Lorge-Thorndike Intelligence Tests, Level 4, Verbal Battery, and Correlations With IQ's on the Otis Quick-Scoring Mental Ability Tests." *Ed Rec B* 69:71–2 F '57. * (PA 32:2120)
38. SPEER, GEORGE S. "Validity Information Exchange, No. 10-13: D.O.T. Code 0-88.31, Ship Pilot." *Personnel Psychol* 10:201 su '57. *
39. WELLMAN, F. E. "Differential Prediction of High School Achievement Using Single Score and Multiple Factor Tests of Mental Maturity." *Personnel & Guid J* 35:512–7 Ap '57. * (PA 32:4631)
40. MOULY, GEORGE J., AND EDGAR, MARY. "Equivalence of IQ's for Four Group Intelligence Tests." *Personnel & Guid J* 36:623–6 My '58. *
41. NICHOLSON, ALICE. "Background Abilities Related to Reading Success in First Grade." *J Ed (Boston)* 140:7–24 F '58. *
42. NORTH, ROBERT D. "The Interpretation of Otis Quick-Scoring Mental Ability Test IQ's in Relation to Kuhlmann-Anderson IQ's, ACE Scores, and Independent School Norms." *Ed Rec B* 71:47–54 F '58. *

D. WELTY LEFEVER, *Professor of Education, University of Southern California, Los Angeles, California.*

The new edition of the *Otis Quick-Scoring Mental Ability Tests* includes a shorter form of the Alpha Test (grades 1–4), in which the number of items has been reduced from 180 to 90, two new forms of the Beta Test (grades 4–9), and two revised forms of the Gamma Test (high school and college). The Beta and Gamma tests were developed from the Intermediate and Higher Examinations, respectively, of the *Otis Self-Administering Tests.*

The Alpha Short Form is composed of 45 sets of four pictorial forms, representing objects or designs. Each set of four pictures is treated as a nonverbal item, in which the pupil marks the picture which does not belong logically in the group, because it differs in kind, as a rabbit among domestic fowl, or because it differs in design or pattern. The same 45 items are transformed into a verbal test by requiring the pupil to follow such teacher-read directions as: "Mark the drawing that is just below the chain with the oval-shaped links."

As stated in the manual for each of the three tests, the purpose seems highly abstract and somewhat out of step with a modern definition of intelligence: "to measure mental ability—thinking power or the degree of maturity of the mind." However, in the Beta and Gamma manuals the definition is given a more operational character by the qualification that "any test which involves the use of language can measure mental ability only to the extent to which we may assume that pupils of the same age have had approximately the same opportunity to learn * In a given community in which all children have (such) opportunities, it is reasonable to assume that a pupil who progresses rapidly in school and learns much has a greater mental ability for his age than one who progresses less rapidly and learns less." This reviewer has no quarrel with such an assumption but he does object to the use of pupil acceleration and retardation as the direct criterion for selecting items for a mental ability test. The manuals for the Alpha Short Form and for the parent tests of Beta and Gamma indicate that in the construction of the preliminary editions two contrasting groups were employed in the validation, a "good group" and a "poor group." Twenty or more years ago school progress may have furnished a fairly meaningful criterion for judging intelligence, but this is no longer true because of marked changes in promotional policies in many school systems. Certainly the statement made in the Beta and Gamma manuals that "the actual rate of progress of pupils through school is the most appropriate criterion of the....test" cannot be justified.

The present reviewer is also unhappy with the use of the term "validity" in this quotation from the Gamma manual: "The validity of each item of the Higher Examination was investigated by finding the biserial coefficient of correlation between the item and the total score on the test." Such correlations are measures of internal consistency and should be considered primarily indicators of reliability.

In content, the Beta and Gamma tests parallel closely the parent tests. The self-administering approach is maintained. The directions for answering sample items are read by the pupils. The examiner explains the rather detailed instructions for manipulating the answer sheet.

The Beta and Gamma tests each yield a single score which summarizes the 80 items, including word meaning, verbal analogies, scrambled sentences, interpretation of proverbs, logical reasoning, number series, arithmetic reasoning, and design analogies. More than two thirds of the 80 items of the Beta Test measure some form of verbal competence. There is considerable evidence in the literature on group intelligence tests indicating that a single score reflecting a considerable emphasis on the use of verbal symbols will predict school success about as well as a more complex pattern of scores.

School personnel in using such a "single-variable" test of scholastic aptitude should guard against an oversimplified interpretation of this score for even the academically oriented pupil, and should be especially cautious in applying the test findings to children with clinical problems or to those who need remedial help in reading and in the language arts. The abilities of the pupil whose interests and talents are distinctly along "nonbookish" lines may be incorrectly appraised by this type of test.

Split-half reliability coefficients are reported for one of the new forms of each test. For Alpha the odd-even coefficients are .87 and .88 for two samples. The median grade level coefficient for Form EM of Beta is .93, the coefficients ranging from .84 to .95. For Form EM of Gamma split-half reliabilities of .92, .91, and .92 are reported for grades 10, 11, and 12, respectively. These data seem to indicate a satisfactory level of reliability. However, some evidence of a speed factor is shown in the fact that the median of 12 correlations between two older forms of Beta, A versus B, was only .80. The author accounts for the considerably higher odd-even coefficients on the grounds of the instability of the pupils. Since no data are given regarding the time interval between the administration of the two forms, it is difficult to disprove his contention; however, the most probable reason appears to be the necessity for completing 80 items in 30 minutes.

The size of the standard error of measurement reported for apparently the same sample of data differs in the Beta and Gamma manuals. Reference is made in each manual to 465 pupils in grades 4–9, but in the Beta manual the error of measurement is reported as 4.0 points while in the Gamma manual the value is 3.0 points.

The standardization of the new forms of each of the three tests is apparently based chiefly on comparisons with the earlier forms of the tests. The statements in the manuals are vague; no clear definition is given of the nature of the normative population nor of the normative sample. There are few facts given to support the author's statement that "the norms should not be thought of as necessarily representative of any particular section of the country but rather as representative of the country as a whole."

A count of the number of times the correct answer is assigned to each response position reveals a distinct response bias for the Beta and Gamma tests. For example, in Beta the correct answer is in the "a" position only 3 times out of an expected 16 times. The chi square value for Beta responses is 25.4; the similar chi square for Gamma is 15.4. Both values result in the rejection of the hypothesis of equal assignment of correct answers to the five possible response positions at well beyond the one per cent level.

In addition to the rather vague and incomplete account of the manner in which the norms were derived for the new forms, the most serious weaknesses of the revised tests appear to be the lack of percentile norm tables of any description and the failure to furnish normative data on the comparability of the two new forms for each level. The manuals are very brief. More detailed suggestions for teachers, counselors, and supervisors on the applications of the tests to instructional and guidance problems would be helpful. More recent evidence concerning the validity of Gamma is to be desired, as well as more extensive recent data for the predictive power of both Beta and Gamma tests.

Most of the above criticisms have been directed at the amount of information furnished the user of the tests rather than against the quality or value of the tests themselves. The *Otis Quick-Scoring Mental Ability Tests,* as the title implies, do furnish a short and easily scored indicator of scholastic aptitude. Such a measure, if interpreted with care, can be useful to both teacher and counselor by revealing within fairly broad limits of accuracy the probable level of academic achievement for a majority of pupils.

ALFRED YATES, *Senior Research Officer, National Foundation for Educational Research, London, England.*

This new series comprises three tests: the Alpha Short Form is designed for grades 1–4; Beta, suitable for grades 4–9, is a revision of the Intermediate Examination of the *Otis Self-Administering Tests of Mental Ability;* and Gamma, intended for high schools and colleges, is a revision of the Higher Examination of the older series.

The avowed purpose of the tests is to measure mental ability defined as "thinking power or the degree of maturity of the mind." The author states that in making up the tests the aim has been to choose items which depend as little as possible on schooling, except that in the Beta and Gamma tests questions on vocabulary and arithmetic reasoning, recognised as being largely measures of achievement, are included.

A number of specific applications of the tests are suggested. The first of these is to discover which pupils are capable of doing better school work than they are doing and to discover which pupils may be attempting work beyond their capacity. In the light of recent evidence concerning the distribution of achievement ratios or of the differences between tests of ability and achievement, it would seem that this application of the test should be treated with some reserve. A high score on a test of this kind does not necessarily imply that a pupil can be expected to distinguish himself in some particular branch of school work. For this purpose—and indeed for several of the other purposes listed in the manuals accompanying the tests—standardised tests of attainment in the various school subjects would seem to be more serviceable.

In certain circumstances, however, tests such as the ones included in this series can be used with advantage. If it is required, for example, to segregate pupils into relatively homogeneous groups for teaching, administrative, or research purposes, tests of this kind can afford a satisfactory rough classification. They would be especially advantageous in circumstances in which little is known about the pupils' previous attainments or at the outset of a new type of course, when knowledge of previous attainments is not necessarily predictive of the likelihood of success.

The reliability coefficients quoted for these tests are not strikingly high. The quoted values vary according to the test examined and the grade of the children concerned. For the Alpha test coefficients of .87 and .88 (split-half, with the Spearman-Brown correction) are reported for two samples of third grade pupils. The standard error for this test is 4 points. In other words, the "true score" of one child in 20 is likely to depart from his obtained score by more than plus or minus 8 points of standardised score. It is clear, therefore, that the results of applying such a test should be interpreted cautiously. The coefficients quoted for the Beta test average .91, and the standard error is again quoted as 4 points. The comparable figures for the Gamma test are .88 and 3 points, respectively.

The evidence concerning the validity of the test for predictive purposes is somewhat slender. It is indeed doubtful whether, for the normal purposes of classification and guidance within a school, teachers are likely to find the tests more serviceable than measures of attainment and their own judgments of their pupils' progress. The tests are obviously serviceable instruments, however, for the purposes of coarse classification when this has to be carried out without access to relevant information about children's previous educational progress.

For a review by Frederic Kuder of the previous edition, see 3:249; for reviews by F. Kuhlmann and C. Spearman, see 40:1413 and 40:1427; for reviews by Psyche Cattell and R. Pintner, see 38:1053 (2 excerpts).

[363]

Otis Self-Administering Tests of Mental Ability. Grades 4–9, 9–16; 1922–29; Forms A ('22), B ('22), C ('28), D ('29); 2 levels: intermediate examination, higher examination; manual ('28); interpretation chart ('22); no data on reliability for Forms C and D; $2.25 per 35 tests, postage extra; 35¢ per specimen set, postpaid; 20(25) or 30(35) minutes; Arthur S. Otis and Thomas N. Barrows (D, intermediate C); World Book Co. * For later editions, see 361–2.

REFERENCES

1–71. See 3:250
72. Isaacs, Archie. *Evaluation of the Items of the Otis Self-Administering Test in Terms of High-School English Marks.* Master's thesis, College of the City of New York (New York, N.Y.), 1928. Pp. 60.
73. Toll, Charles H. "Scholastic Aptitude Tests in Amherst College." *Sch & Soc* 28:524–8 O 27 '28. * (PA 3:512)
74. Dessotnekoff, Nathan. *The Improvement of the Otis S.A. Intelligence Test and Marks in High School English.* Master's thesis, College of the City of New York (New York, N.Y.), 1929. Pp. 19.
75. Riess, Bernard. *The Otis Self Administering Test as a Predictive Measure of Success in High School.* Master's thesis, College of the City of New York (New York, N.Y.), 1929.
76. Seagoe, May V. "Prediction of Achievement in Foreign Languages." *J Appl Psychol* 22:632–40 D '38. * (PA 13:2725)
77. Teepe, Elizabeth A. *"Speed" and "Power" on a Test of Mental Ability as Related to Age and Sex of Subject.* Master's thesis, George Washington University (Washington, D.C.), 1938. Pp. 40.
78. Garrison, K. C. "The Use of Psychological Tests in the Selection of Student-Nurses." *J Appl Psychol* 23:461–72 Ag '39. * (PA 13:6426)
79. Achard, F. H., and Clarke, Florence H. "You Can Measure the Probability of Success as a Supervisor." *Personnel* 21:353–73 My '45. *
80. Hartson, L. D. "Influence of Level of Motivation on the Validity of Intelligence Tests." *Ed & Psychol Meas* 5:273–83 au '45. * (PA 20:2500)
81. Cook, P. H. "Criteria for the Selection of Personnel Officers." *B Ind Psychol & Personnel Prac* 2:28–37 Je '46. * (PA 20:4761)
82. Oxlade, M. "An Experiment in the Use of Psychological Tests in the Selection of Women Trainee Telephone Mechanics." *B Ind Psychol & Personnel Prac* 2:26–32 Mr '46. * (PA 20:4838)
83. Walker, K. F., and Oxlade, M. N. "A Tentative Battery of Tests for the Selection of Women for Cotton Textile Spinning." *B Ind Psychol & Personnel Prac* 2:6–27 Je '46. * (PA 20:4871)
84. Kushner, Rose Estrin. *The Relationship Between Content of an Adult Intelligence Test and Intelligence Test Score as a Function of Age.* Columbia University, Teachers College, Contributions to Education, No. 933. New York: Bureau of Publications, the College, 1947. Pp. vii, 59. * (PA 22:621)
85. Lanigan, Mary A. "The Effectiveness of the Otis, the A.C.E. and the Minnesota Speed of Reading Tests for Predicting Success in College." *J Ed Res* 41:289–96 D '47. * (PA 22:2748)
86. Freeman, Kenneth H. "Predicting Academic Success in Admissions Work." *Jun Col J* 19:33–5 S '48. *
87. Oxlade, M. N. "Selection Tests for Power-Sewing Machine Operators." *B Ind Psychol & Personnel Prac* 4:26–36 Je '48. * (PA 23:1486)
88. Abt, Lawrence Edwin. "A Test Battery for Selecting Technical Magazine Editors." *Personnel Psychol* 2:75–91 sp '49. * (PA 23:5099)
89. Rosenzweig, Saul; with the collaboration of Kate Levine Kogan. *Psychodiagnosis: An Introduction to Tests in the Clinical Practice of Psychodynamics,* pp. 32–3. New York: Grune & Stratton, Inc., 1949. Pp. xii, 380. * (PA 23:3761)
90. Wightwick, Beatrice. *The Effect of Retesting on the Predictive Power of Aptitude Tests.* Doctor's thesis, New York University (New York, N.Y.), 1949.
91. Yela, Mariano. "Application of the Concept of Simple Structure to Alexander's Data." *Psychometrika* 14:121–35 Je '49. * (PA 24:1066)
92. Zakolski, F. C. "Studies in Delinquency: I, Personality Structure of Delinquent Boys." *J Genetic Psychol* 74:109–17 Mr '49. * (PA 23:4925)
93. Edmonson, Lawrence D. *Comparative Analyses of a Test Battery Used for the Prediction of Scholastic Success at the University of Missouri.* Doctor's thesis, University of Missouri (Columbia, Mo.), 1949. (Microfilm Abstr 9:64)
94. Super, Donald E. *Appraising Vocational Fitness By Means of Psychological Tests,* pp. 107–14. New York: Harper & Brothers, 1949. Pp. xxiii, 727. * (PA 24:2130)
95. Holmes, Frank J. "Validity of Tests for Insurance Office Personnel." *Personnel Psychol* 3:57–69 sp '50. * (PA 24:5490)
96. Johnson, Ralph H., and Bond, Guy L. "Reading Ease of Commonly Used Tests." *J Appl Psychol* 34:319–24 O '50. * (PA 26:299)
97. Poruben, Adam, Jr. "A Test Battery for Actuarial Clerks." *J Appl Psychol* 34:159–62 Je '50. * (PA 25:3995)
98. Bair, John T. "Factor Analysis of Clerical Aptitude Tests." *J Appl Psychol* 35:245–9 Ag '51. * (PA 26:3067)
99. Oxlade, M. N. "Further Experience With Selection Tests for Power-Sewing Machine Operators." *B Ind Psychol & Personnel Prac* 7:27–37 Mr '51. * (PA 25:7713)
100. Vaccaro, Joseph J. *A Study of Psychological Factors That Contrast the Most and Least Efficient Psychiatric Aids in a Mental Hospital.* Doctor's thesis, Fordham University (New York, N.Y.), 1951.
101. Case, Harry W. "The Relationship of Certain Tests to Grades Achieved in an Industrial Class in Aircraft Design." *Ed & Psychol Meas* 12:90–5 sp '52. * (PA 27:6106)
102. Johnson, Gordon. *An Analysis of Six Theories as to the Origin of Delinquent Behaviour.* Master's thesis, University of British Columbia (Vancouver, B.C., Canada), 1952. Pp. 190.
103. Moffie, Dannie J., and Milton, Charles R. "The Relationship of Certain Psychological Test Scores to Academic Success in Chemical Engineering." Abstract. *Am Psychol* 7:379–80 Jl '52. *
104. Bruce, Martin M. "The Prediction of Effectiveness as a Factory Foreman. *Psychol Monogr* 67(12):1–17 '53. * (PA 28:5019)
105. Johnson, Granville B., Jr. "Bilingualism as Measured by a Reaction-Time Technique and the Relationship Between a Language and a Non-Language Intelligence Quotient." *J Genetic Psychol* 82:3–9 Mr '53. * (PA 27:7648)
106. Seashore, Harold G. "Validation of Clerical Testing in Banks." *Personnel Psychol* 6:45–56 sp '53. * (PA 28:1670)
107. Bruce, Martin M. "Validity Information Exchange, No. 7-004: D.O.T. Code 0-97.61, Manager, Sales." *Personnel Psychol* 7:128–9 sp '54. *
108. Bruce, Martin M. "Validity Information Exchange, No. 7-076: D.O.T. Code 5-91.101, Foreman II." *Personnel Psychol* 7:418–9 au '54. *
109. Hanes, Bernard, and Halliday, R. W. "Unfavorable Conditions in Intelligence Testing." *J Genetic Psychol* 85:151–4 S '54. * (PA 29:5708)
110. Seashore, Harold. "Tenth Grade Tests as Predictors of Twelfth Grade Scholarship and College Entrance Status." Comment by David V. Tiedeman. *J Counsel Psychol* 1:106–15 su '54. * (PA 29:3054)
111. Barbe, Walter B. "Reading Improvement and Group Intelligence Test Scores." *Sch & Soc* 82:72–3 S 3 '55. * (PA 30:4550)
112. Bruce, Martin M. "Normative Data Information Exchange, No. 30." *Personnel Psychol* 9:541–2 w '56. *

113. BEAMER, GEORGE C., AND BONK, EDWARD C. "Reliability of Mental Ability Tests." *J Counsel Psychol* 4:322 w '57. *
114. BRICE, MARSHALL M. "A Comparison of Subjective Predictions With Objective Predictions of College Achievement." *Col & Univ* 32:347–53 sp '57. *
115. BRUCE, MARTIN M. "Validity Information Exchange, No. 10-3: D.O.T. Code 1-86.11, Salesmen, Commercial Equipment and Supplies." *Personnel Psychol* 10:77–8 sp '57. *
116. DU MAS, FRANK M. "A Manifest Structure Analysis of the Otis Intelligence Test." Abstract. *Am Psychol* 12:429–30 Jl '57. *
117. GUNNELL, DOROTHY C., AND NUTTING, RUTH E. "Prediction of Achievement in Schools of Nursing." *Calif J Ed Res* 8:184–91 S '57. *
118. HECHT, ROBERT, AND BRUCE, MARTIN M. "Normative Data Information Exchange, No. 10-40." *Personnel Psychol* 10:532 w '57. *
119. LAWRENCE, P. J. "Contributions to Intelligence Testing and the Theory of Intelligence: III, A Study of Cognitive Error Through an Analysis of Intelligence Test Errors." *Brit J Ed Psychol* 27:176–89 N '57. *
120. SAUNDERS, WM. J., JR. "Normative Data Information Exchange, No. 10-26." *Personnel Psychol* 10:360 au '57. *
121. SAUNDERS, WM. J., JR. "Normative Data Information Exchange, No. 10-27." *Personnel Psychol* 10:361 au '57. *
122. SHAH, SALEEM A. *An Investigation of Predictive Ability in Hospital Personnel and University Students.* Doctor's thesis, Pennsylvania State University (State College, Pa.), 1957. (*DA* 18:288–9)
123. DU MAS, FRANK M., AND MACBRIDE, KING. "A Manifest Structure Analysis of the Otis S-A Test of Mental Ability, Higher Examination: Form B." *J Appl Psychol* 42:269–72 Ag '58. *

For a review by Frederic Kuder, see 3:250.

[364]
*Personnel Research Institute Classification Test.** Adults; 1943–54; formerly called *Classification Test For Industrial and Office Personnel;* Forms A ('47, revision of 1943 form), B ('47); revised manual ('54); $3 per 25 tests; 50¢ per specimen set; cash orders postpaid; 15(20) minutes; Jay L. Otis, Evelyn Katz (A), Robert W. Henderson (A), Mary Aiken (A), David J. Chesler (B), and Gardner E. Lindzey (B); Personnel Research Institute. *

[365]
★**Personnel Research Institute Factory Series Test.** Applicants for routine industrial positions; 1950–56; Form B ('50); mimeographed manual ('56); no data on validity; $3 per 25 tests; 35¢ per specimen set; cash orders postpaid; 10(15) or 15(20) minutes; Jay L. Otis and Alfred H. Exton; Personnel Research Institute. *

[366]
★**Personnel Tests for Industry.** Trade school and adults; 1945–54; 3 tests; 35¢ per specimen set including manual for *Oral Directions Test;* postpaid; Psychological Corporation. *
a) PTI-VERBAL TEST. 1952–54; Forms A ('52), B ('52); preliminary manual ['54]; $1.70 per 25 tests; 5(15) minutes; Alexander G. Wesman.
b) PTI-NUMERICAL TEST. 1952–54; Forms A ('52), B ('52); preliminary manual ['54]; $1.70 per 25 tests; 20(25) minutes; Jerome E. Doppelt.
c) PTI-ORAL DIRECTIONS TEST. 1945–54; Form S ('54); preliminary manual ['54]; 2 types of recordings: LP microgroove 12-inch record (33⅓ rpm), tape recording (3.75 ips); $12 per set of scoring key, 100 answer sheets, manual, and either record or tape recording; $4 per 100 answer sheets; Spanish edition on tape available; (15) minutes; Charles R. Langmuir.

ERWIN K. TAYLOR, *President, Personnel Research and Development Corporation, Cleveland, Ohio.*

The PTI is a short, low-level intelligence battery of which three tests have been published at the time of this writing. These are a 5-minute Verbal Test, a 20-minute Numerical Test, and a 15-minute Oral Directions Test.

"The content of the tests," according to the manual, "was selected so as to appear reasonable to adult applicants and employees." In the writer's opinion, the items of the verbal and the numerical tests seem somewhat less academic in their terminology than is true of many available intelligence tests. On the other hand, it cannot be said that the PTI has achieved this objective to a markedly greater degree than a number of others on the market.

VERBAL TEST. With a time limit of 5 minutes for 50 items, one might question the publisher's claim that this is primarily a power rather than a speed test. The items covered are synonyms, information, classification, and "recognition of essentials." By the latter, we presume that the publisher means such items as "A team always has (A) equipment, (B) uniforms, (C) schedules, (D) members." Two forms of the test are available, and judging from the means and sigmas on nine populations (ranging in size from $n = 33$ to $n = 171$), an excellent job of equating the forms has been done.

Alternate form reliabilities range from .73 to .92. Normative data are presented for six industrial and three educational samples. These range in size from 80 to 237. The normative data are characterized by wide variation from sample to sample. The means of the groups vary from 15.8 for applicants for factory jobs in a southern textile mill to 37.1 for mechanical apprentices in an Ohio paper mill. The first percentile of the latter group is equivalent to the 72nd percentile of the former group. The manual, which shows admirable restraint in all respects, remarks, "It is generally recognized that the most appropriate norms are those which the test user develops from the testing of his own groups. The norms given in manuals are useful primarily as general reference points until local norms are developed." Save for the fact that this precludes small organizations from using tests, as well as rendering the use of tests questionable for positions that do not exist in large numbers, this advice seems sound.

The validity data presented are somewhat more extensive than those found in most manuals, even though they are not too impressive. Most of the data, unfortunately, are derived from training rather than job performance criteria. However, the test does show enough promise to justify its use on an experimental basis for the selection of low-level production workers. The reader should note, however, that the test has a rather low ceiling and is not likely to discriminate well among graduates of a four-year academic high school. No relationship with age is provided in the manual, but considering the speed factor, the reviewer would venture to predict that a rather substantial negative correlation exists.

NUMERICAL TEST. Each form of the Numerical Test consists of 30 open-ended items. The testees are required to calculate and write in the correct answer. The items are a combination of the arithmetic reasoning and number skills so that the testee needs first to determine the arithmetic process or processes appropriate to the problem and then to do the necessary computations correctly. Either of these processes will of course, if improperly done, yield an incorrect answer. The correlations between the two tests for nine populations ranged from .73 to .92. Normative data are available on the same populations as for the Verbal Test.

The comments above with reference to the Verbal Test are equally pertinent here. In Form B of the Numerical Test, Items 2 and 7 employ similar numerical values so that the answer to one provides a clue to the answer to the other. In Item 17 of this form, a contractor estimates that he will pay 65 per cent for labor, 10 per cent for overhead, and the remainder of a contract for material. The absence of a profit margin divests this item of reality—either that or this is a type of contractor completely unfamiliar to the writer. Item 29 in this form requires the computation of the area of a rhomboid. Knowledge of geometry, as well as an inference with reference to what may be a right angle, is needed to solve it.

ORAL DIRECTIONS TEST. This, like a television movie, is a truncated re-release of a longer version originally published in 1946. The test contains 39 scorable items. It is available either on a 12-inch long playing record or on a 300-foot standard magnetic tape to be played at the rate of 3¾ inches per second. A unique feature of the tape is the recording of the test on both tracks so that it may be used without rewinding. A special answer sheet is provided on which the examinee records his responses. The writer listened to the test from the magnetic tape recording. He found this to be of excellent quality, clarity, and auditory comprehensibility. With adequate sound reproducing equipment and good testing facilities, its use in a group testing situation should present no problems.

Like the other tests in the battery, the Oral Directions Test has a quite low ceiling and appears to be suitable for use only with populations whose socioeconomic and educational status would be expected to fall below the general population average. While the normative data are presented for nine populations, five male and four female, varying in number from 23 to 522, only five percentile points are presented. Since only one form of the test is available, only split-half reliabilities are reported. These range from .82 to .94. The test is paced rather than timed, therefore the usual objections to split-half reliability for timed tests do not apply in this case. No validation data with reference to this form of the test are given in the preliminary manual. The test is, however, undoubtedly of value in getting a rough estimate of the intelligence of semiliterates and of individuals with educational handicaps.

The entire battery is characterized by its low ceiling and the simplicity of its items. It is appropriate, therefore, primarily as a rejection device for rather low level positions in either factory or office.

For reviews by Charles D. Flory, Irving Lorge, and William W. Turnbull of the original edition of the Oral Directions Test, *see 3:245.*

[367]
★Picture Intelligence Test 1. Ages 7 to 8-1; 1955; 1 form ['55]; no data on validity; 10s. per 12 tests; 1s. per single copy; 1s. per manual; postage extra; 22(45) minutes; Joan E. Stuart; published for the National Foundation for Educational Research in England and Wales; Newnes Educational Publishing Co. Ltd. *

CHARLOTTE E. K. BANKS, *Lecturer in Psychology, University College, London, England.*

This 60-item test consists of problems in classification, picture series, and perception of simple relations. The test is entirely in pictures, with no writing of any kind. The drawings, although sometimes rather difficult for adults to decipher, are nevertheless fairly simple, and presumably suitable for children of this age.

There is an excellent manual giving detailed instructions for the administration and scoring of the test and also data on reliability, standardisation, and use of the tables which are provided for the purpose of converting raw scores into standard scores.

The test was originally constructed for testing 8-year-old children in the Population Investigation Committee's sample—a sample of children born in the first week of March 1946. Unfortunately, the results of this survey have not been published. The test has also been used for testing the 7–8 year age group in the National Survey in 1955. Again, the results of this survey are unfortunately not yet in print, but the reviewer understands from a private communication that the norms obtained scarcely differed from those given in the published manual.

The sample on which the test was standardised consisted of 4,350 children between the age of 6-9 and 8-3 in an urban and a rural area of Great Britain. It is on these results that the norms are based. Mental ages are not used. Each child's score is converted to a standard score and compared with those of children of his own age. The standard scores for each age group have a mean of 100 and a standard deviation of 15, thus corresponding in mean and spread to intelligence quotients as generally understood.

Reliability, calculated by Kuder-Richardson formula 20, is given as .92. Unfortunately, there seem to be no data available for assessing the validity of the test.

M. L. KELLMER PRINGLE, *Lecturer in Education, and Deputy Head, Department of Child Study, University of Birmingham, Birmingham, England.*

The test is designed for a narrow age band, namely the first year in the junior school. In contrast to other so-called picture tests, it really does consist of pictures only; neither patterns, letters, nor numbers are introduced. Moreover, the design and layout of the pictures are excellent: they are boldly and clearly drawn, well spaced out, and devoid of fussy detail which tends to be confusing to young children. The test has three sections: the first contains 15 items of the "doesn't belong" type; the second is made up of 20 items of the "sequence" and "series" type; and the third has 25 analogy items. Throughout, the items are of the multiple choice type. Each section has a separate, clearly marked practice page and the end of each section is indicated clearly. Perhaps the only drawback is that this very clarity facilitates copying; this point is stressed in the manual.

The directions for the administration of the tests are commendably brief and concise, and teachers will be appreciative of the fact that the total working time occupies just one school period. The manual also contains a well set out answer key and a table for the conversion of raw scores into standardised scores. These have been arranged so as to have a mean of 100 and a standard deviation of 15. It is explained that the standardised scores are similar to IQ's in their numerical distribution, but differ from them in that they are not arrived at through consideration of mental age. "Each child is assessed by comparing him with a representative sample of children of exactly the same age."

The test has been constructed with care. The most discriminative items and the most satisfactory method of administration were determined after preliminary drafts had been given three tryouts. It would have been of interest to know the number of children involved in the preliminary trials. For the final standardisation, the test was administered to 4,350 children between the ages of 6-9 and 8-3 in two areas, one urban and the other rural. The reliability coefficient, obtained by the Kuder-Richardson formula 20 from a random sample of 200 scripts, is .92. No data are given concerning the test's validity or its correlation with other tests.

The only serious criticism is for sins of omission. Nowhere is there a warning that a score of less than 70 does not necessarily mean that the child is educationally subnormal. Neither is there any indication that the author is aware of the unreliability of a nonverbal group test for predicting long term educable capacity for such young children, particularly if a child be emotionally disturbed or in any other way atypical. Lastly, in view of the fact that the National Foundation for Educational Research has during the past two or three years been reframing test design and rethinking test policy, it is surprising that there is no indication in the manual of the purpose for which this test was designed.

There is little doubt, however, that *Picture Intelligence Test 1* is carefully constructed, attractively designed, well laid out, and easy to administer. In addition, having been recently standardised, it must be considered one of the best nonverbal group tests of intelligence available in this country for children 7 to 8 years of age.

[368]
Pintner General Ability Tests: Verbal Series. Grades kgn–2, 2–4, 4–9, 9–12 and over; 1923–46; IBM for grades 4 and over; 4 levels; 35¢ per specimen set of any one level; separate answer sheets may be used for grades 4 and over; $1.70 per 35 IBM answer sheets; 40¢ per set of matching scoring stencils; postage extra; Rudolf Pintner, Bess V. Cunningham (*a*), and Walter N. Durost (*a, b*); World Book Co. *

a) PINTNER-CUNNINGHAM PRIMARY TEST. Grades kgn–2; 1923–46; Forms A ('38, revision of *Pintner-Cunningham Primary Mental Test*, '23), B ('39), C ('46); manual ('46); $3.05 per 35 tests; (20–25) minutes.

b) PINTNER-DUROST ELEMENTARY TEST. Grades 2–4; 1940–41; 3 scores: picture content (Scale 1), reading content (Scale 2), total; Forms A ('40), B ('41); manual ('41); $4.20 per 35 tests of Scale 1; $3.25 per 35 tests of Scale 2; (45) minutes per scale.

c) PINTNER INTERMEDIATE TEST. Grades 4–8; 1931–42; a revision of *Pintner Intelligence Test* ('31); IBM; Forms A ('38), B ('39); directions for administering ('42); interpretation manual ('39); $3.55 per 35 tests; 25¢ per interpretation manual; 45(55) minutes.

d) PINTNER ADVANCED TEST. Grades 9–12 and over; 1938–42; IBM; Forms A ('38), B ('39); directions for administering ('42); interpretation manual ('39); $3.55 per 35 tests; 25¢ per interpretation manual; 55(65) minutes.

REFERENCES

1–13. See 3:255.
14. KIRKPATRICK, FORREST H. "Four Mental Tests and Freshman Marks." *J Higher Ed* 11:38–9 Ja '40. * (*PA* 14:3215)
15. TILTON, J. W. "The Relation Between IQ and Trait Difference as Measured by Group Intelligence Tests." *J Ed Psychol* 38:343–52 O '47. * (*PA* 22:2066)
16. JORDAN, A. M. "Efficiency of Group Tests of Intelligence in Discovering the Mentally Deficient." *H Sch J* 31:73–94 Mr–Ap '48. *
17. LENNON, ROGER T. "The Relation Between Intelligence and Achievement Test Results for a Group of Communities." *J Ed Psychol* 41:301–8 My '50. * (*PA* 25:3391)
18. LENNON, ROGER T. *A Comparison of Results of Three Intelligence Tests.* Test Service Notebook, No. 11. Yonkers, N.Y.: World Book Co., [1951]. Pp. 4. *
19. DARCY, NATALIE T. "The Performance of Bilingual Puerto Rican Children on Verbal and on Non-Language Tests of Intelligence." *J Ed Res* 45:499–506 Mr '52. * (*PA* 27:1827)
20. DRISCOLL, JUSTIN A. *Factors in Intelligence and Achievement: A Study of the Factor Pattern Resulting From Analysis of the Scores of Boys in Junior Year of High School on Intelligence and Achievement Tests.* Catholic University of America, Educational Research Monographs, Vol. 16, No. 7. Washington, D.C.: Catholic University of America Press, Inc., June 15, 1952. Pp. viii, 56. * (*PA* 27:3330)
21. JUSTMAN, JOSEPH, AND WRIGHTSTONE, J. WAYNE. "A Comparison of Pupil Functioning on the Pintner Intermediate Test and the Henmon-Nelson Test of Mental Ability." *Ed & Psychol Meas* 13:102–9 sp '53. * (*PA* 28:1567)
22. MCCALL, JOHN R. *Sex Differences in Intelligence: A Comparative Factor Study.* Washington, D. C.: Catholic University of America Press, Inc., 1955. Pp. viii, 65. * (*PA* 30:4171)
23. LENNON, ROGER T., AND SCHUTZ, RICHARD E. *A Summary of Correlations Between Results of Certain Intelligence and Achievement Tests.* Test Service Notebook, No. 18. Yonkers, N.Y.: World Book Co., 1957. Pp. 4. *

For reviews by Stanley S. Marzolf and D. A. Worcester, see 3:255; see 40:1416 (3 excerpts).

[369]
★Primary School Verbal Intelligence Test 1. Ages 8 to 10–6; 1953–58; adaptation of *A.C.E.R. Junior A* and *A.C.E.R. Junior B*; 1 form ['53]; revised manual ('58); 5s. 6d. per 12 tests; 6d. per single copy; 1s. per manual; postage extra; 30(40) minutes; D. A. Pidgeon; published for the National Foundation for Educational Research in England and Wales; Newnes Educational Publishing Co. Ltd. *

JOHN NISBET, *Lecturer in Education, University of Aberdeen, Aberdeen, Scotland.*

The demands of selection for secondary education in Britain have ensured a plentiful supply of group tests of intelligence for the 10–12 age range. Less attention has been given to the age range 8–10, and this test should be welcomed as providing a soundly constructed measure for this younger group. The data given in the manual, though brief, are sufficient to show that the construction and standardisation (based on a sample of over 6,000) have been thoroughly and competently done. In technical aspects of construction, the test appears to satisfy the highest standards.

Three criticisms, however, make the reviewer hesitate to give an unqualified recommendation for its use.

Firstly, the test assumes a mastery of reading. Obviously, group tests should not be used with backward readers at this age level. At age 8–0, the child scoring at the mean on this test has only 20 items right out of 85, and norms given for lower raw scores at this age (for example, a score of 4 equals a standardised IQ-like score of 81) have little significance because of reading difficulties. But even at later ages and higher levels of ability, reading skill will influence score to an extent which is hardly justified by the implications of the title "verbal intelligence." Therefore, users should be cautious in interpreting the meaning of "verbal intelligence" applied to a score in this test. The print, however, is larger and clearer than in other tests constructed in England and hitherto available for this age range, such as the *Essential Intelligence Test* and *Simplex Junior Intelligence Tests.*

Secondly, the child who is familiar with tests will have a marked advantage on this test. The back page of the test booklet is a practice sheet with 11 items which are to be worked and checked under the teacher's supervision in the first 10 minutes. Once the practice test has been done, there are no worked examples in the test proper. The types of item are not grouped in sections but are mixed throughout the test, so that an analogy may be followed by a coding item, with a reasoning problem following that. The child must therefore retain the examples of the practice test clearly in mind throughout. Speed of working counts heavily, for only 30 minutes are allowed for the 85 items. The competitive setting in which intelligence tests have frequently been used has influenced some teachers to devote classroom time to coaching for objective tests. The form of this test is liable to encourage such coaching. A longer practice session, detailed instructions, worked examples throughout the test, and a more generous time limit would be necessary to minimise the advantage of the "sophisticated" child.

Finally, almost all the items are in multiple choice form, where each alternative is numbered and the child writes the number of the correct answer in a space at the end of the line. This seems to introduce an undesirable complication, apparently only for ease of marking. (The instructions add that if a child underlines the correct answer instead of writing the number, he is not to be penalised.)

On balance, the test is to be recommended as a measure of educational aptitude, provided that the user remembers that it is more affected by the teaching and training which has preceded it than are similar verbal intelligence tests constructed for older age groups.

F. W. WARBURTON, *Lecturer in Educational Psychology, University of Manchester, Manchester, England.*

This test was constructed "with a view to supplying teachers with an up-to-date verbal intelligence test for use in primary school." It is intended to be suitable for the age range 8 to 11. The present conversion table covers the age range 8-0 to 10-6 only, an omission which should be rectified by now, as the test was first published in 1953.

Most of the items were taken from the Junior A and Junior B tests of the Australian Council for Educational Research which have already been satisfactorily analysed. After a trial the 71 items considered most suitable were selected from these tests and combined with 14 original items to make an 85-item test.

The conversion table is based on the scores of a very large sample of 6,419 children. Lawley's method was used to give standardised scores with mean of 100 and standard deviation of 15. These scores are similar to intelligence quotients in their numerical distribution, but, as the manual points out, they differ in that they are not arrived at through consideration of mental age.

Satisfactory content validities have been obtained. Unfortunately, test-retest reliabilities have not been obtained, but Kuder-Richardson formula 20 gives a value of .97 (n = 330). The standard error of the scores is 2.5, a very satisfactory result.

This test has already been used in a large number of individual schools, and three or four authorities give it to all children as part of their record card programme. There would appear to be no reason why it should not be used more extensively with advantage. It gives every indication of being a useful addition to the rather small number of reliable mental tests available in Britain and of providing the up-to-date verbal intelligence test that the author claims it to be.

[370]

***Progressive Matrices.** Ages 5 and over; 1938–56; 3 levels; postage extra (postpaid); J. C. Raven; H. K. Lewis & Co. Ltd. * (U.S. distributor: Psychological Corporation.)

a) PROGRESSIVE MATRICES (1938), 1956 REVISION. Ages 6 and over; 1938–56; title on test is *Standard Progressive Matrices: Sets A, B, C, D, and E;* 1 form ('56, identical with test copyrighted in 1938 except for change in one item and order of items); revised manual ('56); no norms for individual administration for ages 14 and over; separate answer sheets must be used; 168s. ($12.50) per 25 (10) tests; 7s. 6d. ($1.50) per 25 (50) answer sheets; 20s. per scoring key; 7s. 6d. per 50 record booklets (no date); 3s. 6d. (75¢) per manual; 17s. 6d. ($2.25) per specimen set; (60) minutes.

b) COLOURED PROGRESSIVE MATRICES (1947), 1956 REVISION. Ages 5–11 and mental patients and senescents; 1947–56; individual, ages 5–8; 1 form ('56, subtest Sets A and B same as subtest Sets A and B of the *Progressive Matrices, 1938* except for color); revised manual ('56); record booklet (no date); separate answer sheets must be used for group administration; 189s. ($13.50) per 25 (10) tests; $1.50 per 50 answer sheets; 5s. (75¢) per manual; 18s. 6d. ($2.60) per specimen set; [30] minutes; also distributed by George G. Harrap & Co. Ltd.

c) PROGRESSIVE MATRICES (1947). Ages 11 and over; 1943–47; 2 editions; 1 form ('47); 7s. 6d. per 50 record booklets (no date); no data on reliability and validity.

1) *Set 1.* For use either as a practice test for Set 2 or as a rough screening test; no norms; 50s. per 25 tests; 5s. ($2.50) per specimen set; (10) minutes.

2) *Set 2.* For use either as "a test of intellectual capacity" when used without a time limit or as "a test of intellectual efficiency" when used with a time limit ("usually of 40 minutes"); distribution is restricted to registered users who after signing an agreement and paying an annual service fee may borrow tests for indefinite periods at 150s. per set of 25 tests or for 4 weeks at 20s. per set of 25 tests; 7s. 6d. per 100 record forms; specimen set not available; 147s. per 25 tests; 15s. per single copy; [40] minutes.

REFERENCES

1–8. See 40:1417.
9–21. See 3:258.
22–53. See 4:314.
54. ESHER, F. J. S. "Short Tests of Low-Grade Intelligence: II." *Occupational Psychol* 15:112–9 Jl '41. * (PA 16:1712)
55. SLATER, PATRICK. "Tests for Selecting Secondary and Technical School Children." *Occupational Psychol* 15:10–25 Ja '41. * (PA 15:3177)
56. SLATER, PATRICK, AND BENNETT, ELIZABETH. "The Development of Spatial Judgment and Its Relation to Some Educational Problems." *Occupational Psychol* 17:139–55 Jl '43. *
57. GIBSON, Q. H. "Intelligence Tests and University Careers of Medical Students." *Lancet* 255:323–4 Ag 28 '48. *
58. ORTON, R., AND MARTIN, D. R. "Psychiatric Screening of Medical Students." *Lancet* 255:321–3 Ag 28 '48. *
59. HEIM, A. W. "Learning in Intelligence Test Performance." Abstract. *Q B Brit Psychol Soc* (3):120–1 Ja '49. * Reply by John C. Raven: (3):197–8 Jl '49. * Rebuttal by A. W. Heim: (3):219–20 O '49. *
60. KLONOFF, HARRY. *An Exploratory Study and Analysis of the Wechsler-Bellevue Intelligence Scale and the Raven Progressive-Matrices*. Master's thesis, University of Toronto (Toronto, Ont., Canada), 1951.
61. TAIBL, RAYMOND MARTIN. *An Investigation of Raven's "Progressive Matrices" as a Tool for the Psychological Evaluation of Cebebral Palsied Children*. Doctor's thesis, University of Nebraska (Lincoln, Neb.), 1951.
62. DESAI, MAHESH. "The Test-Retest Reliability of Progressive Matrices Test." *Brit J Med Psychol* 25:48–53 pt 1 '52. * (PA 27:1177)
63. JOHNSON, ELIZABETH Z. "Sex Differences and Variability in the Performance of Retarded Children on Raven, Binet and Arthur Tests." *J Clin Psychol* 8:298–301 Jl '52. * (PA 27:5981)
64. JOHNSON, ELIZABETH Z. "The Use of the Rorschach Prognostic Scale With Raven's Progressive Matrices to Predict Playtherapy Progress Among Retarded Children." Abstract. *J Proj Tech* 16:385 S '52. *
65. LINGWOOD, JOAN. "Test Performances of ATS Recruits From Certain Civilian Occupations." *Occupational Psychol* 26:35–46 Ja '52. * (PA 26:6567)
66. O'CONNOR, N. "The Prediction of Psychological Stability and Anxiety-Aggressiveness From a Battery of Tests Administered to a Group of High Grade Male Mental Defectives." *J General Psychol* 46:3–17 Ja '52. * (PA 27:2055)
67. TURNER, G. H., AND PENFOLD, D. J. "The Scholastic Aptitude of Indian Children of the Caradoc Reserve." *Can J Psychol* 6:31–44 Mr '52. * (PA 26:6935)
68. WILSON, LOLITA. *A Comparison of the Raven Progressive Matrices (1947) and the Performance Scale of the Wechsler Intelligence Scale for Children for Assessing the Intelligence of Indian Children*. Master's thesis, University of British Columbia (Vancouver, B.C., Canada), 1952.
69. BROMLEY, D. B. "Primitive Forms of Response to the Matrices Test." *J Mental Sci* 99:374–93 Jl '53. * (PA 28:4101)
70. HOPKINS, BARBARA, AND ROTH, MARTIN. "Psychological Test Performance in Patients Over Sixty: I, Paraphrenia, Arteriosclerotic Psychosis and Acute Confusion." *J Mental Sci* 99:451–63 Jl '53. * (PA 28:4655)
71. JOHNSON, ELIZABETH Z. "The Clinical Use of Raven's Progressive Matrices to Appraise Potential for Progress in Play Therapy: A Study of Institutionalized Mentally and Educationally Retarded Children." Discussions by Anna S. Elonen and Thorleif G. Hegge. *Am J Orthopsychiatry* 23:391–405 Ap '53. * (PA 28:2865)
72. JOHNSON, ELIZABETH Z. "Individual Patterns of Emotional Functioning in Children of Comparable I.Q.'s—Implications for Education." *Am J Mental Def* 57:681–6 Ap '53. * (PA 28:1187)
73. JOHNSON, ELIZABETH Z. "Klopfer's Prognostic Scale Used With Raven's Progressive Matrices in Play Therapy Prognosis." *J Proj Tech* 17:320–6 S '53. * (PA 28:4363)
74. LEVINE, BERT D. *The Progressive Matrices 1938 and Its Relationship With Certain Subtests of the Wechsler-Bellevue Intelligence Scale*. Master's thesis, University of Texas (Austin, Tex.), 1953.
75. ROTH, MARTIN, AND HOPKINS, BARBARA. "Psychological Test Performance in Patients Over Sixty: I, Senile Psychosis and the Affective Disorders of Old Age." *J Mental Sci* 99:439–50 Jl '53. * (PA 28:4671)
76. SYDOW, DONALD W. *A Psychometric Differentiation Between Functional Psychotics and Non-Psychotics With Organic Brain Damage*. Doctor's thesis, University of Minnesota (Minneapolis, Minn.), 1953. (DA 13:1267)
77. ALLEBACH, NANCY L. *Raven's Colored Matrices and Tests of Primary Mental Abilities With Young Children*. Master's thesis, Pennsylvania State University (State College, Pa.), 1954.
78. GABRIEL, K. R. "The Simplex Structure of the Progressive Matrices Test." *Brit J Stat Psychol* 7:9–14 My '54. * (PA 29:2445)
79. LEVINE, BERT, AND ISCOE, IRA. "A Comparison of Raven's Progressive Matrices (1938) With a Short Form of the Wechsler-Bellevue." Abstract. *J Consult Psychol* 18:10 F '54. *
80. MARTIN, ANTHONY W., AND WIECHERS, JAMES E. "Raven's Colored Progressive Matrices and the Wechsler Intelligence Scale for Children." *J Consult Psychol* 18:143–4 Ap '54. * (PA 29:2457)
81. RICHARDSON, ELIZABETH J., AND KOBLER, FRANK J. "Testing the Cerebral Palsied." *Excep Child* 21:101–3+ D '54. * (PA 29:6108)
82. SATTER, GEORGE, AND MCGEE, EUGENE. "Retarded Adults Who Have Developed Beyond Expectation: Part I, Intellectual Functions." *Training Sch B* 51:43–55 My '54. * (PA 29:2662)
83. BOLIN, BYRON J. "A Comparison of Raven's Progressive Matrices (1938) With the ACE Psychological Examination and the Otis Gamma Mental Ability Test." Abstract. *J Consult Psychol* 19:400 O '55. *
84. BOLTON, FLOYD B. "Experiments With the Raven's Progressive Matrices—1938." *J Ed Res* 48:629–33 Ap '55. * (PA 30:1013)
85. CRAWFORD, AGNES. "An Analysis of Children's Wrong Answers on Raven's Progressive Matrices Test, 1938." Abstract. *B Brit Psychol Soc* (26):2 inset My '55. *
86. DESAI, MAHESH M. "The Relationship of the Wechsler-Bellevue Verbal Scale and the Progressive Matrices Test." Abstract. *J Consult Psychol* 19:60 F '55. *
87. GREEN, MEREDITH W., AND EWERT, JOSEPHINE C. "Normative Data on Progressive Matrices (1947)." *J Consult Psychol* 19:139–42 Ap '55. * (PA 30:1026)
88. JORDAN, THOMAS E. *The Utility of the Coloured Progressive Matrices*. Doctor's thesis, Indiana University (Bloomington, Ind.), 1955. (DA 15:1554)
89. KEEHN, J. D., AND PROTHRO, E. TERRY. "Non-Verbal Tests as Predictors of Academic Success in Lebanon." *Ed & Psychol Meas* 15:495–8 w '55. * (PA 30:7765)
90. LEVINE, BERT, AND ISCOE, IRA. "The Progressive Matrices (1938), the Chicago Non-Verbal, and the Wechsler Bellevue on an Adolescent Deaf Population." *J Clin Psychol* 11:307–8 Jl '55. * (PA 30:3334)
91. NORMAN, RALPH D., AND MIDKIFF, KATHERINE L. "Navaho Children on Raven Progressive Matrices and Goodenough Draw-a-Man Tests." *Southw J Anthrop* 11:129–36 su '55. * (PA 30:4426)
92. SATTER, GEORGE. "Retarded Adults Who Have Developed Beyond Expectation: Part III, Further Analysis and Summary." *Training Sch B* 51:237–43 F '55. * (PA 29:7498)
93. STACEY, CHALMERS L., AND CARLETON, FREDERICK O. "The Relationship Between Raven's Colored Progressive Matrices and Two Tests of General Intelligence." *J Clin Psychol* 11:84–5 Ja '55. * (PA 29:7321)
94. STACEY, CHALMERS L., AND GILL, MARIE R. "The Relationship Between Raven's Colored Progressive Matrices and Two Tests of General Intelligence for 172 Subnormal Adult Subjects." *J Clin Psychol* 11:86–7 Ja '55. * (PA 29:7322)
95. WALTON, D. "The Validity and Interchangeability of Terman-Merrill and Matrices Test Data." *Brit J Ed Psychol* 25:190–4 N '55. * (PA 30:7233)
96. WAMBA, DONALD E., AND MARZOLF, STANLEY S. "Use of Eye Movements as a Response Indicator in Testing the Physically Handicapped." *J Clin Psychol* 11:405–7 O '55. * (PA 30:6007)
97. BARRATT, ERNEST S. "The Relationship of the Progressive Matrices (1938) and the Columbia Mental Maturity Scale to the WISC." *J Consult Psychol* 20:294–6 Ag '56. * (PA 31:7893)
98. CASTETTER, JOELLEN S. *An Empirical Investigation of the Item Characteristics, Validity, and Reliability of Raven's Progressive Matrices Test (1938)*. Master's thesis, Indiana University (Bloomington, Ind.), 1956.
99. CURR, W., AND GOURLAY, N. "Differences Between Testers in Terman-Merrill Testing." *Brit J Stat Psychol* 9:75–81 N '56. *
100. GWYNNE JONES, H. "Comments on 'The Validity and Interchangeability of Terman-Merrill and Matrices Test Data' by D. Walton." *Brit J Ed Psychol* 26:141 Je '56. * (PA 31:6086)
101. KNEHR, CHARLES A. "Progressive Matrices Findings Associated With Cerebral Histopathology." *Percept & Motor Skills* 6:249–54 D '56. * (PA 31:6098)
102. STRUHS, ISABEL. *The Relation Between the Raven Progressive Matrices Test and the Stanford-Binet in a Group of Gifted Children*. Master's thesis, Fordham University (New York, N.Y.), 1956.
103. BUCKLOW, MAXINE, AND DOUGHTY, PATRICIA. "The Use of Aptitude Tests in Clerical Employment: The Selection of Accounting Machinists." *Personnel Pract B* 13:35–44 S '57. *
104. GASKILL, P. Chap. 9, "Tests of Ability and Attainments: Pilot Experiments in Selection and Guidance," pp. 188–212. In *Educational Guidance and the Deaf Child*. Edited by A. W. G. Ewing. Manchester, England: Manchester University Press, 1957. Pp. xiii, 345. *
105. HALL, JULIA C. "Correlation of a Modified Form of Raven's Progressive Matrices (1938) With the Wechsler Adult Intelligence Scale." *J Consult Psychol* 21:23–6 F '57. * (PA 32:267)
106. JORDAN, THOMAS E., AND BENNETT, CARSON M. "An Item Analysis of the Coloured Progressive Matrices (1947)." *J Consult Psychol* 21:222 Je '57. *
107. ORME, J. E. "Non-Verbal and Verbal Performance in Normal Old Age, Senile Dementia, and Elderly Depression." *J Gerontol* 12:408–13 O '57. *
108. QUALTERE, THOMAS J. *An Investigation of the Relation-*

ship Between Visual Figure-Background Disturbance and Performance on Raven's Progressive Matrices Test in Cerebral Palsy Children. Doctor's thesis, Syracuse University (Syracuse, N.Y.), 1957. (DA 17:1708)
109. RAVEN, JOHN C. "The 1956 Revision of the Matrices Tests." Abstract. B Brit Psychol Soc (32):3 inset My '57. *
110. SULLIVAN, ARTHUR. "Measurement of Intelligence in Different Environments." B Maritime Psychol Assn 6:18–23 D '57. *
111. WYSOCKI, BOLESLAW A. "Assessment of Intelligence Level by the Rorschach Test as Compared With Objective Tests." J Ed Psychol 48:113–7 F '57. *
112. BURKE, HENRY R. "Raven's Progressive Matrices: A Review and Critical Evaluation." J Genetic Psychol 93:199–228 D '58. *
113. KASPER, SIDNEY. "Progressive Matrices (1938) and Emotional Disturbance." Abstract. J Consult Psychol 22:24 F '58. *
114. SPERRAZZO, GERALD, AND WILKINS, WALTER L. "Further Normative Data on the Progressive Matrices." J Consult Psychol 22:35–7 F '58. *
115. TUDDENHAM, READ D.; DAVIS, LOUIS; DAVISON, LESLIE; AND SCHINDLER, RICHARD. "An Experimental Group Version for School Children of the Progressive Matrices." Abstract. J Consult Psychol 22:30 F '58. *

For reviews by Charlotte Banks, W. D. Wall, and George Westby, see 4:314; for reviews by Walter C. Shipley and David Wechsler of the 1938 edition, see 3:258; for a review by T. J. Keating, see 40:1417.

[371]

★**Proverbs Test.** Grades 5–16 and adults; 1954–56; 2 scores: abstract, concrete; general manual ('56); clinical manual ('56); $4.50 per set of 10 tests of all forms, cards, manuals and scoring keys; postage extra; specimen set not available; Donald R. Gorham; Psychological Test Specialists. *

a) BEST ANSWER FORM. 1 form ('56); separate answer sheets must be used; $2.50 per 25 tests; $2.50 per 100 answer sheets; (20–40) minutes.

b) [CLINICAL FORM.] Forms 1 ('54), 2 ('56), 3 ('56); individual; $1 per 25 tests; (10–30) minutes.

REFERENCES

1. GORHAM, DONALD R. "A Proverbs Test for Clinical and Experimental Use." Psychol Rep 2:1–12 sup 1 '56. * (PA 31:1037)
2. GORHAM, DONALD R. "Use of the Proverbs Test for Differentiating Schizophrenics From Normals." J Consult Psychol 20:435–40 D '56. * (PA 32:1849)
3. POUNDERS, C. J. A Study of the Proverbs Test as a Measure of the Abstract Level of Concept Formation. Master's thesis, Baylor University (Waco, Tex.), 1956.
4. ELMORE, CLYDE M., AND GORHAM, DONALD R. "Measuring the Impairment of the Abstracting Function With the Proverbs Test." J Clin Psychol 13:263–6 Jl '57. *

EUGENE L. GAIER, *Assistant Professor of Psychology, Louisiana State University, Baton Rouge, Louisiana.*

In the *Proverbs Test,* the subject either freely explains the meaning of each of 12 proverbs (individual Forms 1–3) or selects the best explanation among four presented choices for each of 40 items (group multiple-choice form). According to the author, the test makes use of "the universal appeal of proverbs to all age levels and to the mentally disturbed as well as to normal populations....[and] effectively taps verbal comprehension, particularly in the area of abstraction."

The presented norms are based on a standardization procedure with a series of samples totaling 1,345 children and adults. Scores equivalent to educational levels from the fifth grade through college are presented, as well as tentative norms for the clinical use of the test in the evaluation of schizophrenia.

The validity coefficients, based on correlations with other tests of "known" factorial content, indicate that the *Proverbs Test* is a measure of verbal comprehension.

Three principal uses of the test have been reported (clinical evaluation, clinical research, and screening and survey) and the author states that it can be used as a "rapid objective method for the appraisal of level of abstract verbal functioning" as well as an index of verbal functioning during psychotherapy. It is also indicated to be a sensitive measure of temporary intellectual impairment associated with severe emotional disturbance or schizophrenic disorganization.

Although industrial and counseling psychologists may find that the group form will provide a short and rapidly scored measure of verbal abstraction, it would be best to exercise caution in interpreting these scores as definitive measures of all that is claimed in the manual. The test is very short, the measures of reliability are based on small mixed samples (especially the Air Force enlistees), and the validity measures appear overinterpreted. As an ancillary index of verbal abstraction or gross differentiation of normals and schizophrenics, the individual forms should yield rich qualitative materials.

ALFRED B. HEILBRUN, JR., *Assistant Professor of Psychology, State University of Iowa, Iowa City, Iowa.*

This test seeks to measure the subject's verbal comprehension ability by requiring him to define the meaning of proverbs. Two modes of presentation are available. The clinical test consists of three parallel forms with 12 proverbs each. Scoring samples are provided to aid in evaluating the quality of the free responses on a 3-point abstractness scale. The multiple choice test contains 40 items and both an abstract and a concrete score are derived. Correlations between the clinical and multiple choice tests range from .81 when a single clinical form is used to .90 when the three are combined. These figures compare favorably to the tests' respective reliability coefficients (clinical test, .79, .88, .92 using one, two, and all three forms;

multiple choice test, .88), suggesting that it is as safe to interchange the two modes of testing as to rely on inferences from either.

The *Proverbs Test* has some potential merit as a verbal comprehension measure. This task probably holds more intrinsic interest than most intellectual tests. The multiple choice form has been administered to a substantial range of subjects from the fifth grade level (about 10 years of age) through college seniors with increasing mean scores and normal score distributions at each level increment resulting.

Certain aspects of the scoring procedures need clarification, however. Concerning the clinical form, Gorham states that the scoring system was derived *empirically* using certain a priori principles "as the author attempted to evaluate the answers of the original normative population." This would seem more like a judgmental derivation and one in which only one judge determined the scoring weights. In defining these a priori principles the manual stipulates: "Rationality of the abstractions was not considered; bizarre or autistic conceptions were given the same value as more usual responses as long as they met the criteria of converting the concrete symbolism of the proverb into concepts." Yet an examination of the 114 scoring samples of "adequate" responses fails to provide a single example of such irrational responses. Thus the examiner is left with the problem of how to score obviously incorrect yet conceptualized responses. Finally, the "validity" of the scoring values for each item was determined by the point biserial correlation of that item with scores on the total item pool. It should be pointed out that this procedure is better described as an internal consistency check rather than validation (i.e., correlation with an external criterion). A minimal correlation of .35 was selected as the criterion for item inclusion which means that an item could account for only about 12 per cent of the total item pool variance and still be retained.

Other questions which should be raised concern the operations involved in demonstrating the test's diagnostic utility. Starting with Goldstein's notion that the "abstract attitude" is impaired in schizophrenia, the performances of 100 hospitalized chronic schizophrenics were compared with those of 100 Air Force enlistees. These groups were matched in pairs on the basis of sex, education, and intelligence. Matching for intellectual level was attempted by pairing performance on the Word Knowledge Test of the Airman Classification Battery. Since vocabulary tests have been shown to be relatively insensitive to intellectual impairment in schizophrenia, such a measure would appear to be a poor estimate of present functional intelligence in the psychotic group. The effect of using a vocabulary test for matching would be systematically to match normals with less functionally intelligent schizophrenics. To the extent that performance on the *Proverbs Test* is negatively correlated with age at older age levels, the failure to match for age and the likelihood that the chronic schizophrenic group was older on the average than the normal group would also tend to increase spuriously the discriminative power of the test.

It also seems important to note the failure to control for the hospitalization variable. The effects of presumably prolonged institutionalization (the schizophrenics are described as chronic) should tend to depress performance on psychometric tasks because of altered motivational, attentional, and interest levels. Again, spuriously high discrimination would result.

Considering the above criticisms, the finding that classification on the basis of the most effective cutting score leads to only 77.5 per cent discrimination between basic airmen and hospitalized chronic schizophrenics does not lend confidence to the test's diagnostic use at the present time.

As a promising beginning, the *Proverbs Test* warrants further refinement and more rigorous investigation of its clinical or research utility.

[372]
★**Purdue Non-Language Test.** Grades 9–12 and adults; 1957–58; Forms A, B ('57); preliminary manual ('58); $1.75 per 20 tests; 30¢ per specimen set; postage extra; 25(30) minutes; Joseph Tiffin, Alin Gruber, and Kay Inaba; Science Research Associates. *

[373]
*__Quick-Scoring Test of Learning Capacity: Dominion Tests.__ Grades 7–9, 10 and over; 1934–58; quick scoring edition of *Group Tests of Learning Capacity: Dominion Tests;* Forms A, B ('58); 2 levels; preliminary manual ('58) for each level; separate answer sheets must be used; $1.75 per set of 25 tests, 25 answer sheets, and manual; $1 per 50 answer sheets; 10¢ per scoring key; 75¢ per complete specimen set of either level; postage extra; 30(40) minutes; Department of Educational Research, Ontario College of Education, University of Toronto; distributed by Guidance Centre. *
a) INTERMEDIATE. Grades 7–9; 1958.
b) ADVANCED. Grades 10 and over; 1955–58; revised norms ('55).

[374]

★**Reasoning Tests for Higher Levels of Intelligence.** College entrants; 1954; 1 form; group norms only; 8d. per test; 2s. per manual ['54]; postage extra; 55(60) minutes; C. W. Valentine; Oliver & Boyd Ltd. *

REGINALD R. DALE, *Lecturer in Education, University College of Swansea, Swansea, Wales.*

Designed especially for use in the selection of entrants to universities and teachers' training colleges, this test provides an assessment of general "reasoning ability" at a high level. Section A has 4 items involving inductive reasoning; Section B consists of 12 items of symbolic logic based partly on problems set in old logic papers, all the suggested solutions from which the candidate must choose being provided by the author. It is primarily a power test, the time limit being liberal. The items have a touch of humour reminiscent of the author, and students appear to enjoy attempting the problems; this is an important merit if other motivation is lacking.

A determined attempt is made to validate the test by using such criteria as the degree results of students and comparison of test results with a hierarchy of student groups. The validation outcome is good enough to give confidence to users, though neither the author nor the reviewer will be satisfied until further testing provides still larger numbers and wider representation in the subgroups. Two principal difficulties are apparent here. First, many subgroups, varying in sex, university and training college background, and intelligence level are essential. Second, the degree criterion is a difficult one, as the standard of a First Class Honours degree, for example, is inclined to vary from one university department to another. None the less, the difference between the means for First and Second Class Honours graduates is significant at the two per cent level, between Second and Third Class at the five per cent level, and between Second Class and Pass graduates at the one per cent level.

With regard to norms, the author claims that as his purpose is "to provide a college or university department with a further basis on which to select entrants, all each will need will be comparative estimates among its own applicants. Hence there is no absolute necessity for a wise standardisation and absolute norms." The provision of the present group norms is certainly sufficient to make the test valuable, but its value would be considerably increased if national norms could be provided for training college students of both sexes and for graduates in different faculties or faculty subgroups. There is evidence, for example, that a higher level of g is needed for success in physical science and mathematics than for success in literary subjects in the arts faculty, and there are other differences of this kind.

A split-half reliability coefficient reported for one group of men is .83. This figure is depressed by the fewness of the items and by the highly selected nature of the group.

This test is a welcome and praiseworthy attempt to break away from the conventional approaches in this area. As a pioneer effort, it achieves undoubted success. Like all pioneer efforts, it will in due course be improved upon. It will undoubtedly be widely used in Great Britain; its experimental use in the United States is recommended for cross-fertilisation purposes, even though there are at present no American norms. Those who use this test for selection will naturally bear in mind the importance for some subjects of those special abilities which have little weight in the test. Nor is it decrying the test to remind educationists that, among the highly selected applicants for university entry in Great Britain, temperamental factors and motivation are even more important than a further assessment of "reasoning ability," useful though this is for the border zone.

[375]

Revised Beta Examination. Grades 7–12 and adults; 1931–57; revision of *Army Group Examination Beta* ('20); nonlanguage; 1 form ('35); 2 editions; revised manual ('57); $4.20 per 25 tests; 35¢ per specimen set; postpaid; French edition available; 15(30) minutes; 1946 revision by Robert M. Lindner and Milton Gurvitz; D. E. Kellogg and N. W. Morton; Psychological Corporation. *

REFERENCES

1–4. See 40:1419.
5–9. See 3:259.
10. MURPHY, LAURA WHITE. "The Relation Between Mechanical Ability Tests and Verbal and Non-Verbal Intelligence Tests." *J Psychol* 2:353–66 '36. * (*PA* 11:3928)
11. MORTON, N. W. "Mental Age Norms for Revised Beta Examination." Abstract. *B Can Psychol Assn* 1:10–1 D '40. *
12. ROSS, LAURENCE W. "Results of Testing Machine-Tool Trainees." *Personnel J* 21:363–7 Ap '43. * (*PA* 17:2459)
13. WILLIAMS, H. M.; HAFEMEISTER, NORMAN; AND WEGMAN, MARGARET. "An Analytical Study of Scores on Stanford-Binet, Revised Army Beta, and School Achievement Tests." *Am J Mental Def* 53:617–20 Ap '49. * (*PA* 24:2687)
14. ZAKOLSKI, F. C. "Studies in Delinquency: I, Personality Structure of Delinquent Boys." *J Genetic Psychol* 74:109–17 Mr '49. * (*PA* 23:4925)
15. ELIAS, JACK Z. *Non-Intellective Factors in Certain Intelligence and Achievement Tests: An Analysis of Factors in Addition to the Cognitive Entering Into the Intelligence and Achievement Scores of Children at the Sixth Grade Level.* Doctor's thesis, New York University (New York, N.Y.), 1951. (*Microfilm Abstr* 11:558)
16. YERBURY, EDGAR C.; HOLZBERG, JULES D.; AND ALESSI, SALVATORE L. "Psychological Tests in the Selection and Place-

ment of Psychiatric Aides." *Am J Psychiatry* 108:91–7 Ag '51. *

17. BLUETT, CHARLES G. "Normative Data for the Alpha-Beta-Gregg Battery." *J Clin Psychol* 8:237–45 Jl '52. * *(PA* 27:5857)

18. KNAPP, WILLIAM. *A Study of the Quality of Slowness of Two Groups of Psychotic Patients as Demonstrated by Performance on the Revised Beta Examination.* Doctor's thesis, Western Reserve University (Cleveland, Ohio), 1952.

19. MOORE, JOSEPH E., AND ROSS, LAURENCE W. "The Changing of Mental Test Norms in a Southern Industrial Plant." *J Appl Psychol* 37:16–7 F '53. * *(PA* 28:1625)

20. LAVOS, GEORGE. "Interrelationships Among Three Tests of Non-Language Intelligence Administered to the Deaf." *Am Ann Deaf* 99:303–13 My '54. * *(PA* 29:4596)

21. LAVOS, GEORGE. "Sex Differences on the Revised Beta Examination." *J Consult Psychol* 18:375–6 O '54. * *(PA* 29:5714)

22. STOTSKY, BERNARD A. "Vocational Tests as Measures of Performance of Schizophrenics in Two Rehabilitation Activities." *J Clin Psychol* 12:236–42 Jl '56. * *(PA* 31:6447)

23. WOODS, WALTER A., AND TOAL, ROBERT. "Subtest Disparity of Negro and White Groups Matched for IQs on the Revised Beta Test." *J Consult Psychol* 21:136–8 Ap '57. *

For reviews by Raleigh M. Drake and Walter C. Shipley, see 3:259; for reviews by S. D. Porteus and David Wechsler, see 40:1419.

[376]

★**SRA College Classification Tests.** College entrants; 1958; 6 scores: English usage, mathematics usage, social studies reading, natural science reading, word usage, composite; IBM; Form A ('58); manual ('58); separate answer sheets must be used; tests rented only; $1 per student; fee includes scoring and reporting service; 170(200) minutes; Science Research Associates. *

[377]

★**SRA Tests of Educational Ability.** Grades 4–6, 6–9, 9–12; 1957–58; 5 scores (4 in grades 6–12): language, reasoning, quantitative, total, nonreading total (grades 4–6); 1 form, 3 levels; separate answer sheets must be used; $7 per 20 tests of any one level; $6 per 100 IBM answer sheets; 50¢ per scoring stencil; 35¢ per manual; $1 per revised technical supplement ('58); $2 per specimen set of any one level; postage extra; L. L. Thurstone and Thelma Gwinn Thurstone; Science Research Associates. *

a) GRADES 4–6. 1958; manual ('58); 26(52) minutes.
b) GRADES 6–9. 1958; manual ('58); 42(67) minutes.
c) GRADES 9–12. 1957–58; manual ('57); 27(45) minutes.

JOSHUA A. FISHMAN, *Director of Research, College Entrance Examination Board, New York, New York.* [Review of test for grades 9–12.]

This is the first test in what is planned as a five-test series covering the range of school grades from kindergarten through grade 12. It is a group test designed to provide an estimate of aptitude for current school work, and requires a test administrator for the reading of instructions and for the accurate timing of its four parts. The test consists of 110 items, which are subdivided as follows: 20 word grouping items (find the word that does *not* belong with the other four); 30 synonyms; 30 letter-series items (what letter should come next in this series: abx, cdx, efx, ghx?) taken from *SRA Primary Mental Abilities* for ages 11–17; and 30 number-judgment items. The first two item types, though separately timed, are combined to yield an L (language) score. The letter-series items yield an R (reasoning) score, and the number-judgment items, a Q (quantitative) score. A total score is also derived from all 110 items. The test is nicely printed, in reusable booklets with heavy paper covers. The answer sheet and the scoring stencil are both designed for either hand or machine scoring. A manual of directions and a separate technical supplement are available. The answer sheet permits a direct translation of raw scores into percentile ranks and AQ's ("ability quotients"), the latter being standard scores similar to deviation IQ's except that their comparison is with other pupils at the same *grade* (rather than *age*) level.

Some users may find unsatisfactory the directions in the manual which caution that the person administering the test "should be thoroughly familiar....with principles of group testing," without implying what these principles might be or what sources might be used in order that one might become familiar with these principles. The manual makes embarrassed mention of error of measurement without specifying its magnitude for this test. All in all, however, the manual, answer sheet, scoring stencil, and the explanatory sections of the test are at appropriate levels of clarity and readability. The relatively minor lapses such as those indicated above (as well as the fact that the instructions may seem to some to imply a correction for guessing although there is none) can be corrected easily in future editions.

The publishers emphasize that the test was constructed so as to maximize the short term prediction of academic grades. Due to this emphasis on an external, global criterion, item selection was necessarily less concerned both with internal consistency and with differential prediction. As a result, the reliability of the test is somewhat *lower* (in the .80's for the part scores and in the middle or high .80's for the total score) and the intercorrelations among the parts are *higher* (.63 between Q and L, and .65 between Q and R) than might have been attained had other criteria been kept to the fore. An impressive array of validity studies is reported in which intercorrelations between the TEA and other tests (intelligence, educational development, educational achievement) as well as between TEA scores and school marks are shown. The general conclusions from the validity studies would seem to be that the test as a whole and particularly the L section is as good a predictive instrument as one might seek of the 45–50 minute variety. The R and Q sections, however, do not seem to be functioning particularly well, there being several instances where the L section correlates higher with course grades and with scores on other tests—instances where one would expect the other sections to excel. The R and Q sections are, of course, serving face validity functions and adding to the entire test length and to the improved reliability and validity that accompanies greater length.

Although the test was not designed for differential purposes, both the technical supplement and the manual of directions defend the differential interpretation of part scores when they are at least 20 percentile points apart. The advisability of such interpretations seems open to question in view of the somewhat low part score reliabilities and validities (particularly the validities of Q and R) and the high intercorrelations among part scores. In any case, the advisability of differential interpretations should be demonstrated via appropriately designed studies rather than merely persuasively argued. The norming of the TEA was accomplished by equipercentile equating of its raw scores to the 1957 revised norms for the *Iowa Tests of Educational Development*. This stopgap approach to norms should also be improved upon, particularly in the light of the fact that the correlations between these two tests are not convincingly high (.71 for L, .51 for R, .62 for Q), nor are they as high as between the TEA and other tests cited by the publisher.

No special claim is made by the publisher as to the suitability of the TEA for college guidance or selection purposes. There would seem to be no reason to prefer it for such purposes to the 3-hour *SRA College Placement Test,* the Psychological Corporation's 80-minute *College Qualification Test* or the Educational Testing Service's 70-minute *Cooperative School and College Ability Tests.* For educational guidance and evaluation purposes in grades 9–12 the TEA seems generally inferior to Forms 1A and 2A of SCAT in conjunction with reliability, part score intercorrelations, and norming. Nevertheless, the TEA seems to be a quite adequate instrument for estimating current academic ability of a global nature. Various desirable technical improvements in future editions, as well as the preparation of a parallel form, would greatly enhance the substantial value which it already possesses.

WILLIAM B. MICHAEL, *Director, The Testing Bureau, and Professor of Psychology and Education, University of Southern California, Los Angeles, California.* [Review of test for grades 9–12.]

Designed to furnish a means for estimating a student's current ability to do high school work, the *SRA Tests of Educational Ability* (abbreviated as TEA) yield a total score and three part scores in subtests designated as Language (L), Reasoning (R), and Quantitative (Q). Although the total time for administration of the examination is expected to approximate 45 minutes, the short total working time of only 27 minutes (which, from the standpoint of the manual's stated preference for a power condition, might better have been 30 or 32 minutes) is distributed in the following manner: 10 minutes for Language which consists of two parts—word-grouping, a 20-item verbal test of a reasoning nature requiring 4 minutes and vocabulary, a 30-item synonym test taking 6 minutes; 6 minutes for Reasoning, a 30-item letter series test taken from the *SRA Primary Mental Abilities;* and 11 minutes for Quantitative, which is made up of 30 multiple choice items involving numerical skills and judgments concerning numerical relationships.

The content of the easy-to-read manual is directed primarily toward the problems of planning for a test session, of administering and scoring the examination, and of forming profiles and interpreting test results. To obtain information regarding validity, reliability, the intercorrelations of test parts, and the development of normative data, one is required to consult the carefully prepared technical supplement that was issued November 1957. Even though the technical supplement is clearly written, detailed in its coverage, and judiciously modest in its tone, the data upon which one must formulate judgments regarding reliability and validity are somewhat meager in view of the limited number of different high schools employed (five in the Chicago area), the possible lack of representativeness of these schools, the number of grade levels considered (usually only the 9th and 12th grades), and the size of

SRA Tests of Educational Ability

each of the samples involved (varying between 16 and 214 depending upon the subject or cluster of subjects with the grades of which scores on subtests were correlated). Although the publishers probably intend to release additional reliability and validity data as they become available and to revise the norms periodically, one cannot help but conclude that the release of TEA was somewhat premature.

Considering the data reported as tentative, it would appear that the reliabilities of the part scores (averaging about .80 or slightly above) and the total score (approximating .90) are satisfactory, although the estimates for the single form were based on internal consistency approaches for which the control of the speed factor was not entirely defensible. Initial concurrent validity data are quite promising with respect to the extent of correlation of the scores of each of the subtests with grades in specific courses and with total grade average, as well as with scores on other tests such as parts of the *Iowa Tests of Educational Development,* the *SRA Achievement Series,* and the Kuhlmann-Anderson mental age score.

Although some degree of differential predictability is apparent in the validity coefficients of the three parts with respect to different high school courses, it would appear, as stated in the technical supplement, that other test batteries developed primarily in a factor-analytic setting would tend to attain a higher degree of differential efficiency, for the authors have intended and contended that the TEA score is, essentially, a predictor of general achievement. (Additional evidence pertaining to the general nature of TEA is apparent in the reported intercorrelations of .57, .63, and .65 between L and R, L and Q, and R and Q part scores, respectively.)

Nevertheless, the normative data are portrayed as profiles containing the three part scores (L, R, and Q) and the total score at each of four grade levels in terms both of percentile ranks and of an ability quotient in which the mean is 100 and the standard deviation is 15. Through use of Flanagan's equipercentile method of equating, score standards for TEA were supposedly made comparable with those of ITED, which along with TEA, was administered in 1957 to 300 students at each grade level from 9 to 12 in two public high schools judged (on the basis of previous ITED performance) to be of average level (one in Texas and the other in Pennsylvania). Although the reviewer is optimistic of the eventual utility of the instrument in light of the initial validity data reported and in view of the previous excellent work of the Thurstones with experimental versions of the tests in TEA, he would feel much more comfortable if the standardization had already been carried out on a large number of samples representative of different geographical areas, of different types of educational programs, and of different philosophies of education—samples in which boys and girls were always treated separately.

In summary, TEA offers the advantages of being a conveniently administered, readily scored, and (potentially) easily interpreted device for prediction of high school achievement. However, until additional data concerning reliability and validity are obtained, until several parallel forms are devised, and especially until the standardization process is extended to diversified samples of high school boys and girls throughout the United States, the degree of confidence that can be placed in the interpretation of the scores will be somewhat less than that which can be given to other competitive instruments currently available.

E. A. PEEL, *Professor of Education, University of Birmingham, Birmingham, England.* [Review of test for grades 9–12.]

The purpose of these three tests is to provide an estimate of students' current potentiality for school success. For this purpose the authors have chosen short timed tests of language, reasoning, and number work. The first is made up of a 4-minute test of choosing the unlike word from sets of five words and a 6-minute vocabulary test using multiple choice technique. The reasoning test, timed to six minutes, consists of items requiring the completion of letter series, and the third test is one of number and simple arithmetical computation requiring 11 minutes. The whole test is accompanied by a comprehensive manual of directions and a technical supplement providing statistical and psychometric information of value to the specialist. The layout of the answer sheets and the marking stencil is good.

For use as a predicting device, the subtests are better combined to give a total measure. Inspection of the correlations between the subtests and teacher grades readily demonstrates that the language and quantitative (arithmetic) tests do not differentiate markedly between allied school subjects. This is perhaps not surprising in tests of such similar format even though the language and quantitative tests clearly make use of elements of attainment as well as ability. On the whole, the quantitative subtest seems, by casual inspection of the subscore versus grades correlations, to predict mathematical subject grades less well than the language test predicts language subject grades. This is a tendency often noticed in English 11+ selection and it seems that we have yet to devise a satisfactory number and space test to predict secondary school mathematical achievement. These opinions are confirmed by inspecting a shorter table where median correlations are set out. Here we see, in the case of 12 correlations with mathematics and science grades, that the language subtest is superior to both the reasoning and quantitative subtests in predicting mathematics and science achievement. The reliability figures given include some correlations which are perhaps rather low for this kind of test, although no doubt they are affected by the homogeneity of the sample of persons tested and the shortness of the tests.

All the material and information is so efficiently set out that instances to criticise are rare, but it might help the routine worker if, in the two sections on page three of the manual devoted to a description of the three subtests, the subtests were mentioned in the same order as used in the scheme of testing, and if the two parts of the language test were given in the same order as in the test itself. In the technical supplement, it would help the specialist if some standard deviations were given. This would apply particularly to those who wish to use this test outside the United States. The whole question of correlation is so bound up with homogeneity and distribution of scores that we need more than comments through the text that this or that group was more or less homogeneous.

In spite of these criticisms, the tests as a whole should provide a useful single predictor of secondary school potentiality, both for research work and for routine guidance.

[378]

*SRA Verbal Form. Ages 12 and over; 1946–56; formerly called *SRA Verbal Classification Form;* abbreviated adaptation of *Thurstone Test of Mental Alertness* which is an abbreviated adaptation of *American Council on Education Psychological Examination for High School Students,* 1940 Edition; 3 scores: quantitative, linguistic, total; Forms A ('47), B ('55);

manual, second edition ('56); $2.75 per 20 tests; 50¢ per specimen set; postage extra; 15(25) minutes; Thelma Gwinn Thurstone and L. L. Thurstone; Science Research Associates. *

[379]

★The Scholarship Qualifying Test. Juniors and seniors seeking college scholarships; 1956–58; test administered annually in October at participating secondary schools; 2 scores: verbal, quantitative; IBM; supervisor's manual ('57); examination fee, $1; fee includes the reporting of scores; scores for juniors reported only to secondary schools; 120(140) minutes; program administered by Educational Testing Service for the College Entrance Examination Board. *

LEE J. CRONBACH, *Professor of Education and Psychology, University of Illinois, Urbana, Illinois.* [Review of Form FSQ.]

The growing national awareness of the wasted talent of young people who cannot afford higher education has led to establishment of dozens of scholarship programs. Fair comparison of candidates requires a standard and unfamiliar test, and since the same pupil is eligible for numerous scholarships, a unified testing service for many if not all programs has become a necessity. A new form of the *Scholarship Qualifying Test,* prepared by the Educational Testing Service under the sponsorship of the College Entrance Examination Board, is given throughout the country each fall. A small fee is charged pupils, except for a limited number of top candidates named by the principal. Seniors who take the test are considered for about 20 different scholarship programs. Test scores are returned to the school for guidance purposes.

Form FSQ (1957) consists of 60 verbal items (sentence completion, analogies, reading comprehension) and 50 quantitative items (arithmetic reasoning, data interpretation). Nearly all students finish the verbal part, but over half fail to complete the quantitative items. Omissions are numerous, indicating that poor performance reflects unwillingness to try mathematical items as much as it does the effect of the time limit. As its purpose requires, the test is quite difficult, difficulty being attained mostly by subtlety. In the verbal section, words are rarely more unfamiliar than "prosaic" and "synopsis." But each multiple choice item contains numerous plausible, near-correct answers, and the student who is unwilling to make painstaking comparisons will fare badly. The reading section includes difficult adult reading material, and the comprehension questions are penetrating. A pupil with facility in commonplace algebra, ability to comprehend intricate problems, and patience in carrying out successive steps can earn a high score in the quantitative section. Very few items require geometric knowledge or specialized algebraic skills.

A primary requisite in a scholarship test is that it have a healthy effect on student attitudes and on the curriculum. This test stands up well on both counts. A student who fails to qualify for an award will have little excuse to offer save that others did better work. The questions are patently fair. If parents demand that the school do something to increase their son's chance of winning an award, the best "cramming" would be that sort of training in reading and reasoning which will also make him a better college prospect. (In this respect, the test by another publisher which replaced the SQT in the 1958 National Merit Scholarship testing is inferior. Some items in the new test call for knowledge of crammable grammatical rules, and the use of uncommon words in its verbal section makes almost reasonable the conduct of the reviewer's young acquaintance who prepared for the competition by reading through a dictionary.) The SQT seems to require more persistence and thoughtfulness than most mental tests, but no college teacher will regret having students of the sort who take this test in stride. The test is designed for steady pacers. The intuitive, nonconformist hare, darting here and there after brilliant ideas, will be left behind, but so will the drudging tortoises of academic life.

An unpublished memorandum prepared by Frances Swineford provides technical data on the test. Scores are reported for each section on a scale from 10 (chance) to 70 (perfect). Scaled scores for one year are equated to those from previous years. The argument for a distinctive scale is that, in a test not applied to a representative sample, standard scores would be of little use. The difficulty of the test is indicated by the fact that the midpoint of the verbal range comes at the 83rd percentile for the 256,000 pupils taking the test. The distribution is skewed, providing best discrimination in the upper portions of the range. Only one pupil in the entire sample earned a perfect verbal score, which suggests that the authors have been clever beyond necessity in concealing their correct answers. The test reliability is around .90 —a respectable figure, especially since a second test is generally used to select final scholarship winners. Here if ever, however, is a test for which one needs a separate report of the standard error of measurement in each portion of the range instead of an overall reliability. The test surely measures less accurately in the lower part of the range than elsewhere.

There are some risks in the system which this test represents. Principals find that the pupils they nominate to take the test without charge are often outscored by pupils who volunteer and pay a fee. There is need to make sure that all possible winners do take the test. A different problem arises from the application of the test to pupils who perform badly. Literally thousands of pupils who take the test earn chance-level scores on one or both sections. Such a discouraging experience is unprofitable for all concerned. Could not a short practice booklet profitably be used in the school both to prepare pupils for the items to be used and to help determine who should take the test?

For use in guidance, schools are provided with a booklet giving a brief summary of the meaning of the test, including a scale for making conversions to the scales of the *Scholastic Aptitude Test* and *Cooperative School and College Ability Tests*. It is better to return test scores to the school than to waste the information obtained. The recent announcement that the test will be opened to juniors indicates an apparent intention to feature the test for guidance purposes. This will require a more extensive manual reporting correlational information, particularly on the differential validity or significance, if any, of the separate subtest scores. Though the SQT appears excellent for separating the very best college prospects from the merely very good, no guidance program should use this as its principal test; other tests suited to the wider range of college-bound students or to the entire student body will give more useful information.

Roger T. Lennon, *Director, Division of Test Research and Service, World Book Company, Yonkers, New York.* [Review of Forms ESQ and FSQ.]

In October 1956, the Educational Testing Service initiated for the College Entrance Examination Board administration to high school seniors of the *Scholarship Qualifying Test* (SQT). SQT had as its primary aim the selection of students "to be given further consideration for the award of scholarships"; and, secondarily, provision of information useful in the educational guidance of students. In 1956 and 1957 SQT was used as the preliminary selection instrument in the National Merit Scholarship Program. Scores of examinees were reported to the various scholarship programs in which the examinees were participating and to the examinees' high schools; the respective scholarship programs made such use of the scores as they saw fit. In 1956, 166,581 examinees took SQT, in 1957, 255,887, and in 1958 well over 300,000. Beginning in 1959 the SQT is to be replaced by the *Preliminary Scholastic Aptitude Test* of the College Entrance Examination Board.

The first two forms of the *Scholarship Qualifying Test,* ESQ and FSQ, accessory materials, and information (exceptionally detailed in many respects) concerning technical characteristics of the tests have been made available to the reviewer, and form the basis for the comments which follow. Forms ESQ and FSQ are parallel forms in every important detail, and the comments pertain equally to both.

GENERAL DESCRIPTION. SQT yields two scores, Verbal and Quantitative, the former based on a 60-item subtest and the latter on a 50-item subtest, each subtest requiring 60 minutes' testing time. The 60 verbal items are divided equally among analogies, double definitions, and reading comprehension items; the quantitative section comprises 30 arithmetic reasoning and 20 data-interpretation items. The test is completely objective; all items are multiple choice, five-option items, with responses recorded on an IBM answer sheet. From the standpoint of content, SQT blazes no new trails but sticks to tried-and-true types of material for prediction of college success.

The reading comprehension part of the verbal subtest consists of four selections, ranging in length from about 200 to 400 words, each selection followed by from four to six questions. The content is largely drawn from scientific sources, presumably of a kind that college students will have to read. Questions assess ability to locate information, to draw inferences, to relate elements of information, and to understand the explicit information given. Item validity data, in the form of biserial correlations, presented in the technical report, both for the reading and the other parts of the verbal subtest, indicate a satisfactory degree of internal consistency, very few of the reported values falling below .30.

The quantitative subtest is fundamentally an arithmetic reasoning test, supplemented by exercises on interpretation of charts and tables; it makes few demands on mathematical skills acquired in any secondary level mathematics courses. Data in the technical report indicate that the quantitative section as a whole is rather more difficult than might be desired, and likewise appears to have more of a speed component than this reviewer would consider optimum for the purposes. Item validity data do, however, indicate that most of the items in the quantitative subtest have satisfactory discriminative capacity.

On the basis of a careful reading of a large proportion of the individual items, this reviewer judges them to be, on the whole, clear, unambiguous, and well written. The instructions to the examinees likewise seem entirely adequate, and the general directions for administration of the program, for maintenance of security of materials, etc., conform to the College Entrance Examination Board's customary high standards in these respects.

RELIABILITY. Kuder-Richardson formula 20 estimates of reliability are presented for both Form ESQ and Form FSQ, for all sections of the test, for the V score, the Q score, and total score. Estimates are reported for three independent populations chosen to represent different parts of the range of scores. The median estimate of reliability of the V score is approximately .87, of the Q score approximately .84, and of the total score .91—somewhat low, perhaps, for tests of this length and lower than might be hoped for, in view of the importance of the decisions made on the basis of the results.

INTERPRETIVE INFORMATION. The primary purpose of SQT, the identification of potential recipients of scholarships, may be achieved with little or no normative data, a mere ranking of candidates being sufficient for the purposes of most scholarship programs. For realization of the guidance values of SQT, however, additional interpretive information is called for. Such interpretive, or normative, data are provided in the form of percentile ranks corresponding to V and Q scores for the total group tested; tables indicating scores on ETS' *Scholastic Aptitude Test* and ETS' *Cooperative School and College Ability Tests* corresponding to SQT scores; and estimated percentile ranks for a representative national sample of 12th grade students, based on equating of SQT to SCAT. Additionally, a bulletin that accompanied reports of 1956 examination results to schools presented estimates of probability of admission to certain CEEB colleges corresponding to selected SQT scores. These data on equivalent scores on SAT and SCAT are presented with appropriate expressions of caution and with emphasis on the point that the conversions are not exact; it is pointed out that the estimated SAT or SCAT equivalent is not to be regarded with the same confidence as if it were derived directly from the test in question.

For educational guidance purposes it is also suggested, though again with appropriate reservations, that the counselor consider relative performance on the verbal and quantitative scores. Since correlations averaging slightly more than .60 are reported between the V and Q scores, the differential validity power of the two measures is probably quite limited. Interpretation of such differences is clouded also by systematic sex differences on both the V and the Q tests.

VALIDITY. The treatment of validity in the published material accompanying the test is indeed scant. The bulletin for the 1957 test asserts that, "The Verbal and Quantitative scores are measures of aptitude for learning verbal and quantitative types of material involved in many college courses. Such measures have been found to be useful and reliable in predicting success in academic work"; and this, as far as this reviewer could note, is the only reference to validity in the materials. Inasmuch as SQT was first administered in 1956 to students who did not complete their first year in college until June 1958, it was, obviously, impossible to obtain empirical predictive validity data in time for inclusion in any of the materials seen; but one would have felt more comfortable had the material included data on the correlation between SQT and other measures concerning whose predictive worth there are research findings—particularly when such correlations must have been available. In the absence of predictive data the reviewer must base his opinion as to the validity of SQT as a predictor of college success on consideration of the content of the test and its surface resemblance to other instruments whose predictive validity is better known. On this tenuous basis, the reviewer considers SQT to be of about the same order of predictive validity as, say, SAT, ACE, or the Ohio State psychological examination.

The validity of SQT for purposes other than identification of scholarship award winners—that is, for guidance purposes in the high school—is likewise entirely presumptive in character. The reviewer judges SQT to be no better for high school guidance purposes than measures of similar abilities in widespread use in high school and probably less valuable for these purposes than the better of the multifactor batteries.

Is SQT a fair and efficient instrument for the identification of worthy recipients of college scholarship assistance? This is a question not to be answered solely, and perhaps not even primarily, on the basis of the technical characteristics of the test. What types of high school students should society seek to encourage through scholarship aid to pursue their education? Is the notion of a single selection instrument for all scholarship candidates, regardless of the type of collegiate program they may be interested in pursuing, a sound approach? Does the SQT type of instrument, minimizing the influence of specific attainment in any high school course, have harmful consequences on the motivation of high school students? These are the types of questions that come quickly to mind as ones that must be answered before a satisfactory answer can really be offered to the opening question in this paragraph. Pending answers to these larger questions, this reviewer concludes that SQT does a reasonably effective job of identifying high school students having the ability to "succeed" in college, when that success is measured by conventional criteria, such as grade-point average or end-of-course examinations.

[380]

★Scholastic Mental Ability Tests. Grades kgn–1, 2–3, 4–9; 1953–54; various titles used by publisher; for Catholic schools; IBM for grades 4–9; 3 levels; 2 editions; 50¢ per specimen set of any one level of either edition; postage extra; Oliver F. Anderhalter; Scholastic Testing Service, Inc. *

a) LONG FORM. Grades kgn–1, 2–3, 4–9; 1953–54; 1 form; 3 levels.

1) *Pre-Primary Test.* Grades kgn–1; 1954; Form A; $3.50 per 35 tests; (50–60) minutes.

2) *Primary Test.* Grades 2–3; 1953–54; 6 scores: linguistic, non-linguistic, total, logical reasoning, numerical reasoning, fluency; Form A ('53); manual ('54); $3.25 per 35 tests; (50–60) minutes.

3) *Elementary Test.* Grades 4-9; 1954; scores same as for Primary Test; IBM; Form A; $3.50 per 35 tests; separate answer sheets may be used; $1.75 per 35 IBM scorable answer sheets; 24¢ per set of scoring stencils; 36(60) minutes.

b) SHORT FORM. Grades 2-3, 4-9; 1955; 2 levels.
1) *Primary Test.* Grades 2-3; Short Form A; $2.60 per 35 tests; (30-40) minutes.
2) *Elementary Test.* Grades 4-9; IBM; Short Forms A, B; $3 per 35 tests; $1.75 per 35 IBM scorable answer sheets; 12¢ per scoring stencil; 26(35) minutes.

WALTER N. DUROST, *Director of Educational Services, Pinellas County Public Schools, Clearwater, Florida.*

The *Scholastic Mental Ability Tests* are intended for use in Catholic parochial schools only. This was determined only after a diligent search of the manuals for the several levels of this series. Why an *intelligence* test for parochial schools only? The argument runs somewhat as follows.

Intelligence tests administered to a national cross-sectional group are not appropriately administered to parochial school children because such populations may be selected groups, and may have had instruction differing in quality and kind. Such factors would obviously influence intelligence test results. The author presents evidence that in at least one midwestern diocese the less able children (children below 90 IQ) tend to drop out of the parochial school population and, presumably, return to public school. If it were claimed that the test was designed to be paired with a valid measure of parochial school achievement standardized on the same group, this argument would bear considerable weight with the writer. No such evidence seems to be present.

As to validity, the argument is made that the construct validity of a test is to a considerable extent established if it can be shown that there is a gain in raw score from one age to a successively higher age group. This comparison is made in age groups differing by three months, and it is shown that there are consistent differences in mean raw score. That there would be similar differences in any other physical measure taken for similarly differing age groups is not mentioned. This argument for establishing the validity of a mental ability measure falls down completely unless it is demonstrated on logical grounds that the subtests do in fact measure mental traits which are largely independent of school instruction rather than some other phase of the individual's development. From this point of view, it would be very hard to justify the validity of using, as this test does, an arithmetic reasoning test which might be taken from any standardized achievement test.

Under concurrent validity, correlations are given with the Kuhlmann-Anderson and Otis Alpha tests, these being .75 and .78, respectively, for small single grade populations. There is no evidence that these are corrected for attenuation, and it would be the writer's judgment that these correlations are "run of the mine" for intercorrelations of intelligence measures at this grade level.

In one manual at least, the validity of the mental tests is discussed in terms of the nomenclature adopted for the evaluation of tests in the APA *Technical Recommendations for Psychological Tests and Diagnostic Techniques.* For example, the content validity of the picture classification test at the primary level is defended on the basis that a survey of currently marketed intelligence tests indicate that a similar subtest is found in 75 per cent of these tests, and that picture similarities tests have "long been recognized as containing a large amount of 'g' factor, or general intelligence." The defense of the content validity of the other tests at the primary level is similarly vague.

Throughout the discussion of the construction and standardization of the tests, phrases such as "research has long pointed to the fact that," "this test is a valuable measure of 'mental alertness,'" and "similarities tests have long been recognized as containing a large amount of general intelligence" appear. There is no documentation of these claims.

Assuming that someone in a position of authority in a parochial school system wishes seriously to consider this test for use in his school, the question is whether it is a good test from other points of view. It is not exactly a bad test, but one does not have to search too diligently to find things to criticize about the items themselves or about the procedures used in scaling and norming the test.

For example, Item 11 in the primary level picture arrangement test shows a sequence having to do with baseball. The artwork in this illustration is extremely bad, and the figures are very hard to distinguish. Regardless of this, it seems improbable that children in the second and third grade, especially girls, would know enough about baseball to arrange the pictures in correct sequence. This undoubtedly explains why this sequence is next to last in this particular test. Many other pictures in this test are so poorly drawn that their meaning is ambiguous.

In Primary Short Form A, Test 3 is a verbal classification test. There is one sample question plus five other examples, answers to which are given to the children taking the test. In all five of these examples the right answer is in the fourth or last position. It is also in the fourth or last position in 4 of the remaining 10 items in the actual test. It would hardly seem that this could occur by chance allocation of correct answer positions, especially since not a single item has the correct answer in the first position.

Other ambiguous or incorrect items were noted throughout the tests. While a majority of the items seem to be fairly satisfactory as well as one can tell without having the item statistics at hand, each subtest examined had one or two items that were open to serious criticism. The manuals leave much to be desired by way of explicit description of what was actually done in the construction of these tests. For example, each of the manuals states that "tetrachoric coefficients of correlation were computed, based on the relation of test item to total score of the test. This index is a measure of the item reliability, and was used since increasing the reliability of the test should tend also to improve the validity." It is hoped that "the test" refers to each *subtest* separately, but there is no indication that this is true. Furthermore, such indices are hardly reliability coefficients of individual items, but rather measures of the extent to which the item discriminates between more able and less able individuals, which is evidence of validity of a sort.

The mechanics of the test (scoring, layout on the page, etc.) are reasonably adequate. The answer sheet is evidently a locally printed sheet. The copy which came in the specimen set used for review would not score accurately in the test scoring machine available. The spacing between the answer spaces is just a very small amount too large, a type of deviation that is cumulative from the bottom to the top of the sheet as it is inserted in the machine.

The authors are to be commended for abandoning the ratio IQ, which certainly is outmoded, in favor of the deviation IQ, but no attempt has been made to adjust for changes in the standard deviation of standard scores from age to age.

ALEXANDER G. WESMAN, *Associate Director, Test Division, The Psychological Corporation, New York, New York.*

These tests are offered as intelligence tests yielding mental age and IQ for linguistic, nonlinguistic, and total ability, and separate scores for logical reasoning, numerical reasoning, and fluency at the primary and elementary levels; only nonlinguistic MA and IQ are provided for the preprimary level.

The preprimary test consists of five pictorial subtests dealing with object naming, identification of object characteristics, identification of missing elements, following oral directions, and object classification. The total number of items is 77.

The primary test consists of seven subtests: picture classification, picture arrangement, number series, classification (verbal), word and sentence formation, arithmetic reasoning, and vocabulary (synonyms). There are 112 items. A short form, which omits the picture arrangement section, is also available.

The elementary test is composed of seven subtests: picture similarities, picture arrangement, number series, inference (syllogisms), word arrangement, arithmetic reasoning, and vocabulary. A short form eliminates the picture and word arrangement tests. The numbers of items are 145 and 110, respectively.

In some ways, it would be easier to review this series one level at a time. Comparison of the manuals for the three levels simultaneously (or, for that matter, of the regular and short form manuals at a single level) reveals startling inconsistencies and leads to confusion. This is especially so since much of the content in any one manual is clearly intended to describe the entire series. For example, the elementary manual (long form) reports "no item was retained which yielded an average tetrachoric coefficient of less than .30." The elementary manual (short form) says "no item was retained if the average coefficient obtained from the several grades taking each item fell below .25." The preprimary manual says "the index of brightness used in the Scholastic Test of Mental Ability is the conventional 'quotient' IQ." The primary manual discusses the limitation imposed by the slackening of intelligence in the teens (how many teenagers are in grades 2 and 3?) and

Scholastic Mental Ability Tests

concludes, "the Scholastic Mental Ability Test uses a deviation IQ rather than a quotient IQ." The elementary manual (long form) states that 13,642 children entered into the norms determination; one must read the short form manual to learn that all these students were attending Catholic elementary schools.

The above contradictions and omissions are not isolated; additional instances abound. The net impression on the reader is that the manuals were prepared at different times by someone who changed his mind and failed to correct or amend what had been written earlier.

RELIABILITY. The author's treatment of reliability is both unorthodox and confusing. The preprimary manual states that "coefficients are reported for separate grade levels as well as for the combined group." The latter coefficients are not presented, which is just as well. In the regular edition primary and elementary manuals both "single-year" and "year-span" coefficients are reported. The former are the medians of the coefficients obtained for each grade; the year-span coefficients are based on all grades combined. In the short form manual for the primary level, coefficients are shown for each grade, but not for the combined group; the short form elementary manual reports the median and range of single-grade coefficients as well as interform reliability for grades 4, 6, and 8 and for these three grades combined.

Except for the interform reliability mentioned above, all coefficients are based on split-half correlation. With the preprimary and primary tests such estimates, when based on a single grade, may be reasonable. However, the elementary test is used to cover grades 4 to 9. We are informed that the test is primarily a power test (the evidence to support this claim is dubious). The absence of speededness is a necessary condition if split-half reliability coefficients are to be justifiable. Since the time limits for fourth grade and ninth grade students are the same, it seems clear that either the test has a large speed component with fourth grade students or ninth grade students finish in a fraction of the allotted time. Thus, one must conclude either that inappropriate coefficients of reliability are reported for (at least) the fourth grade, or that the test is a poor instrument at the ninth. One might be able to select a horn of this dilemma if data concerning the standard deviations were reported for the samples on which reliability coefficients were computed.

The presentation of reliability coefficients based on a sample of pupils from all six grades combined is unfortunate. The scholastic aptitude of fourth grade pupils is not ordinarily compared with that of ninth graders; the effect of presenting coefficients for combined groups is merely to delude the unwary reader into overestimating the reliability of the instrument.

VALIDITY. The material offered to document the validity of the test is poorly organized. Coefficients of correlation with well known instruments such as the Otis, Kuhlmann-Anderson, and Terman-McNemar tests appear in the manuals for the short forms, but not in the manuals for the regular forms. Means and standard deviations accompany some of the coefficients, but are unfortunately absent in places where they are vital to understanding. For example, the same coefficient is reported with Terman-McNemar scores for grade 6 students and for students in grades 5, 6, and 7 combined; a single standard deviation figure is given, presumably for the combined group, but not for the single-grade group.

The only evidence of predictive validity is a series of five coefficients with reading and achievement tests as criteria. With only 9 months intervening between the predictor and criteria, and with objective test scores rather than teacher grades being predicted, the predictive validity must be regarded as undistinguished.

There is discussion of construct and content validity, but no evidence to convince an informed reader.

TIME LIMITS. One of the fascinating features of the series is the casual attitude with respect to time limits. At several points in the preprimary directions the examiner is told to allow "about 5 seconds" for each item. In the primary manual we find "allow 5 to 10 seconds." This kind of informality is hardly consistent with standardized test procedures.

USES OF THE TESTS. The flavor of the manuals is epitomized for this reviewer by the statements offered in the preprimary manual on how to use the test. "Should a pupil be unusually bright or dull, or mischievous, or unusual in any respect, intelligence tests give information not possible through other means." "The results of the tests should assist the counselor in advising the pupil concerning the selection of suitable courses in school work, and concerning the selection of occupations within his ability level." Note that this manual is intended for use with kindergarten and first grade pupils!

SUMMARY. The *Scholastic Mental Ability Tests* were developed primarily for use in Catholic schools. Aside from the restriction of the standardization population to such schools, there is nothing to make the use of the tests more appropriate in Catholic schools than in any others. The manuals are largely uninformative if not outright bewildering. Until there is a better organized, more consistent, more convincing, more informative set of manuals offered for this series, Catholic schools (and non-Catholic schools) would do far better to use instruments such as the Metropolitan Readiness, Pintner, Kuhlmann-Anderson, or Thorndike-Lorge tests—to name but a few.

[381]
★**Schrammel General Ability Test.** Grades 9 and over; 1953–55; based in part upon the *Army Group Examination Alpha* and revisions; IBM; Forms A ('53), B ('55), C ('56); manual ('55); no data on reliability and validity for Form C; no norms for grades 14–16; no norms for Form C; $1.50 per 25 tests; separate answer sheets may be used; 85¢ per 25 IBM answer sheets; 30¢ per set of either hand or machine scoring stencils; postage extra; 35¢ per specimen set, postpaid; 50(60) minutes; H. E. Schrammel; Bureau of Educational Measurements. *

HENRY E. GARRETT, *Professor Emeritus of Psychology, Columbia University, New York, New York.*

This general ability test is an adaptation and revision of the *Army Group Examination Alpha* which was used widely in World War I. First revised and published with norms for public schools in 1920, the present tests have passed through several revisions to reach their current form. The examination is planned to be an entrance and placement test for college freshmen. It also provides norms for, and is said to have usefulness in, evaluating candidates for graduate school entrance. In the reviewer's opinion, however, the test is too limited in range and difficulty for the latter purpose.

The test contains 150 multiple choice items subdivided into five parts of 25–40 items each. Part 1 is vocabulary; Part 2, number series completion; Part 3, verbal analogies; Part 4, information; and Part 5, arithmetic problems. Each part is allotted 10 minutes of working time, but an examinee may continue on with the next section if he finishes one before time is called. The test is one of both speed and power, but the difficulty level is not very high. The format gives the impression of being crowded. There are too many items on a page and this makes reading difficult. The important parts of the directions could be made to stand out more. An examiner must search through the printed directions and could easily miss an important detail.

A single correlation coefficient of .65 between test scores and the one-year grades of 110 college freshmen is offered as evidence of validity. Reference is made to validity data obtained with previous editions. In view of the mass of material available on Army Alpha, the present test, which is much like Army Alpha, can probably be taken as having validity in the college screening situation. As implied above, its validity for use with advanced students is questionable.

Reliability coefficients for groups of high school seniors and college freshmen range from .87 to .94. These compare favorably with coefficients derived from comparable group tests of intelligence.

Nearly 12,000 high school students and 2,400 college freshmen and graduate students contributed to the norms. Separate percentile norms are presented for each high school grade, for college freshmen, and for graduate students (small groups). In addition to the percentile ranks, "IQ's" may be read from a table for raw scores ranging from "less than 56" to 150. These IQ's are said to "parallel very closely" Stanford-Binet IQ's. The author does not explain the derivation of his IQ's. Presumably they are deviation (standard) scores in a distribution with mean 100 and SD 16. The reviewer was unable completely to verify this. More detail here would clarify the procedure.

This is an intelligence test of mostly verbal materials and is not of a very high level of difficulty. According to the author, it is intended for use in classifying and sectioning entering students and also in individual counseling. The test should be useful in screening and selection but less valuable in individual guidance. It is neither comprehensive enough nor varied enough in content for other than a very preliminary approach to vocational or educational guidance. Its use above the college freshman level is not recommended.

[382]
★**Schubert General Ability Battery.** Grades 12–16 and adults; 1946–53; 5 scores: vocabulary, analogies,

arithmetic problems, syllogisms, total; 1 form ('46); revised mimeographed manual ('53); 1-99 tests, 15¢ each, postage extra; 16(25) or 32(40) minutes; Herman J. P. Schubert; the Author, 500 Klein Road, Route 2, Buffalo 21, N.Y. *

WILLIAM B. SCHRADER, *Director, Statistical Analysis, Educational Testing Service, Princeton, New Jersey.*

This test provides a measure of general ability based on vocabulary (50 items), verbal analogies (35 items), arithmetic problems (15 items), and logical reasoning (15 items). It is intended to be suitable for use in industry as well as in educational situations. It is well printed, although one spelling error slipped through in Item 24 of Part 1. The manual contains much relevant information.

With respect to test development, the author does not make it clear why he chose the particular item types used nor how he arrived at the relative weight given each part in determining the total score. Considerable stress is placed on the role of item analysis in developing the test, but the particular method of analysis used is not described. The items seem to be well written, except that Items 10 and 12 of the verbal analogies part tend to give each other away. Two serious flaws in the manual are that the directions give the candidate no information concerning whether a correction for guessing is made, and that there is no indication as to whether the candidates are to be informed in advance about the time limit for each part.

A discussion of score interpretation must take note of the fact that the test may be administered in several ways. Specifically, if 4-minute time limits are used for each part, the author regards this as a speeded test; if 8-minutes are allowed for each part, the author regards it as a power test. No data on per cent finishing the test within either time limit are reported. The author suggests that there are advantages to be gained by comparing the performance of a person who takes the test under both time limits, noting such things as amount of tension due to inner conflict, perseverance, and caution. It is unfortunate that this dual time limit approach to interpretation is recommended by the author without any specific evidence.

No data are given on the reliability of part scores; and since the author estimates the reliability of the total score by an internal consistency method, the only useful reliability coefficients reported are for the 8-minute time limit. These are .86 for 68 high school senior boys and .93 for 143 high school senior girls. The fact that two of the part scores contain only 15 items each and that some stress is placed on part scores in score interpretation make the need for part score reliability data acute. The development of a parallel form would make it possible to supply these data.

A number of interesting norms tables are presented. The adult-male table is based on 461 cases described as randomly selected from the adult-male population of the Great Lakes region. No statement is made, however, as to how the sample was obtained. High school norms are based on results in a single school; norms for college entrants, on results in a single university; and norms for graduate students in education, also on results in a single university. The distributions indicate that the tests are reasonably suitable in difficulty for these groups. Norms for the 4-minute time limit are given for factory workers, foremen, executives, store managers, wholesale salesmen, and office clerks. However, since these samples were evidently obtained independently of each other, comparisons across occupations must be made with caution. In the absence of reliability data for these scores, much of the value of the norms is lost as far as individual score interpretation is concerned.

Several correlational studies relating scores to high school and college grades and to scores on other tests are reported. The two verbal parts show reasonably high correlations with other tests and with appropriate course grades. Arithmetic, when given with a 4-minute time limit, yielded a disappointingly low coefficient (.25) with college mathematics grades. Results for the logical reasoning part are difficult to evaluate, but the evidence so far available is not encouraging. Total scores seem to show moderate correlations with other tests and with college grades on the basis of the limited evidence given.

On the whole, this test is well made and should be useful in industrial applications. It is fair to say, however, that the superstructure of interpretation has gone beyond the foundation of empirical studies, with the consequent danger that unwarranted interpretations of individual performance will be made. The inclusion of a logical reasoning section appears to be the only original feature of this test, and the brevity of this part seems likely to limit its differential value.

[383]

★**Ship Destination Test.** Grades 9 and over; 1955-56; general reasoning; IBM; Form A ('55); separate answer sheets must be used; $2 per 25 tests; 10¢ per single copy; 3¢ per IBM answer sheet; 50¢ per scoring stencil; 25¢ per manual ('56); postage extra; 15(20) minutes; Paul R. Christensen and J. P. Guilford; Sheridan Supply Co. *

REFERENCE

1. HILLS, JOHN R. "Factor-Analyzed Abilities and Success in College Mathematics." *Ed & Psychol Meas* 17:615-22 w '57. *

C. J. ADCOCK, *Senior Lecturer in Psychology, Victoria University of Wellington, Wellington, New Zealand.*

This test is based on factorial studies of reasoning ability. According to the manual, in two studies it had the highest loading of the tests analysed on the general reasoning factor (.51 and .56). It is a disguised arithmetical reasoning test but has practically no loading on the number factor.

In evaluating a test of this kind, two distinct questions must be kept in mind. The first relates to the authenticity and importance of the factor measured; the second, to the efficiency of the test in measuring this factor. With regard to the former we have to note that the general reasoning factor was first found by Thurstone among his primary mental abilities when it was named "restrictive reasoning." Zimmerman [1] made a new orthogonal rotation of the same data and found the reasoning factor in more clearly defined form which corresponded with the Army Air Force's "general reasoning" and was so named. Ahmavaara [2] has developed a technique of "transformation analysis" by means of which he has been able to make direct comparisons of factors found in different analyses. Making a comprehensive survey in this way, he found general reasoning to be a factor of the "second certainty class" with a mean variance value of .35. (For comparison, the number factor has a mean variance of .85.) The later work of Guilford would possibly raise this figure somewhat.

Naive users of the *Ship Destination Test* should be quite clear that general reasoning is not by any means a measure of general intelligence, nor is it even a general measure of reasoning capacity. This latter is probably manifested in three chief forms: verbal (deduction), analogical, and arithmetical. It is the last which is measured by the present test. It has a loading (.36) also on a factor involving the ability to handle complicated procedures, and one wonders whether the relative importance of these factors may not vary with level of ability in the same way that a simple intelligence test becomes largely a function of perceptual speed when administered to superior subjects. In working the test, one gets the impression that the ability to maintain a multiple set is very important. Some indication of the degree to which personality factors may have loadings on the test would also be useful. The handling of several variables under speed conditions is likely to be emotionally disturbing for some people.

VALIDITY. The only real measure of validity with this type of material is construct validity, based on the factor analysis. There is no pure criterion with which one can correlate it. It is interesting, however, to check on the predictive capacity for various purposes. According to the manual, the test results correlated significantly with course grades ($n = 116$) in nautical astronomy (.36), physics (.40), geometry and calculus (.39), algebra and trigonometry (.25), and descriptive geometry (.26). One industrial validity figure (.55) is reported, based on correlation of rank order of performance of 20 operations analysts in an aircraft manufacturing organization. If such coefficients are further confirmed, the test will certainly merit inclusion in diagnostic batteries.

TEST STRUCTURE. The test is ingenious in form. It provides a large number of items with the minimum of descriptive material. The homogeneous nature of the items favours a high level of reliability. By Kuder-Richardson formula 21, this ranges from .86 to .95. The saturation with other factors is kept to a minimum.

There appear, however, to be one or two weaknesses with regard to structure. The instructions require the subject to calculate the time required for a ship to travel between two stated points under certain conditions of wind and current. The quickest route is not asked for and the testee may, therefore, assume that routes which are spatially equivalent will require similar time. Unfortunately, this is not always so (e.g., Items 49, 50, 54, 56, and 57),

[1] ZIMMERMAN, WAYNE S. "A Revised Orthogonal Rotational Solution for Thurstone's Original Primary Mental Abilities Test Battery." *Psychometrika* 8:77-93 Mr '53. *
[2] AHMAVAARA, YRJÖ. *On the Unified Factor of Mind,* pp. 130-2. Helsinki, Finland: Finnish Academy of Science and Letters, 1957. Pp. 176. *

and a wrong answer is possible despite formal compliance with the instructions. The difficulty arises with regard to the allowances to be made for changes of direction. If the testee understands that complete reversal of direction should be avoided if possible and that no turns should be made until essential, ambiguous solutions will be avoided. Instructions to this affect, however, would probably change the norms and modify factorial composition. Some further research might raise both reliability and validity.

SUMMARY. This test is a useful addition to our tests of special abilities. Reliability and validity merit its inclusion in a comprehensive aptitude battery. It is probably the best available measure of the factor involved, but testers should be careful not to confuse the general reasoning ability with intelligence.

[384]

★The Simplex GNV Intelligence Tests. Ages 11–12.0; 1952–57; title on tests is, say, for form 1, *The Simplex Intelligence Test GNV 1;* forms 1 ('52), 2 ('54), 3 ('54), 4 ('55), 5 ('56), 6 ('57); manual for each form (dates as for tests); no data on reliability and validity; distribution of forms 4–6 restricted to Educational Committees; 9s. per 25 tests; 6d. per single copy; 1s. per manual; postage extra; 60(70) minutes; C. A. Richardson; George G. Harrap & Co. Ltd. *

REFERENCES

1. SHUTTLEWORTH, CLIFFORD W. "Tests of Technical Aptitude." *Occupational Psychol* 16:175–82 O '42. *
2. NISBET, JOHN D. "Contributions to Intelligence Testing and the Theory of Intelligence: IV, Intelligence and Age: Retesting With Twenty-Four Years' Interval." *Brit J Ed Psychol* 27:190–8 N '57. *

[385]

The Simplex Group Intelligence Scale. Ages 10 and over; 1922–39; 1 form ('34); no data on reliability; tentative norms; 12s. 6d. per 25 tests; 2s. 6d. per scoring stencil; 1s. 3d. per manual ('39); 4s. 3d. per specimen set; postage extra; 90(95) minutes; C. A. Richardson; George G. Harrap & Co. Ltd. *

JAMES MAINWARING, *Formerly Lecturer in Psychology and Music, Dudley Training College, Birmingham, England.*

One of the early intelligence tests, and using still earlier test material, the Simplex scale has survived over 15 reprints. It consists of 26 subtests of six questions each. They are divided into two similar groups of 10 subtests each and a more difficult group of 6 subtests. Each group includes various classifications, analogies, and vocabulary tests. The data are verbal and numerical. No pictorial material is included except that used in a reversed similarity test. The third group of subtests includes a memory test, requiring the recognition of 6- to 8-digit numbers printed in reverse, and a rather difficult vocabulary test. This last subtest hardly seems consistent with one of the stated aims of the test, that is, "it is directed to the estimation of the child's *natural mental endowment,* which is independent of teaching."

The test has two other specific aims. The first is to avoid the necessity of more than the briefest preliminary directions, and to achieve this "the tests are so worded and arranged as to provide their own instructions." The second is to avoid interruption of the test. For this reason, individual subtests are not timed, and subjects who complete the series before the allotted 90 minutes have a page on which to express their views of the test. This page is not scored.

The choice of this very comprehensive test will depend on how much significance is attached to the absence of the time factor and the absence of pictorial data in an instrument designed to assess relative inherent mental capacity.

[386]

[The Simplex Junior Intelligence Tests.] Ages 7–14; 1932–51; 2 forms; postage extra; 45(50) minutes; C. A. Richardson; George G. Harrap & Co. Ltd. *
a) THE SIMPLEX JUNIOR INTELLIGENCE SCALE. 1932; test ['32]; 6s. per 25 tests; 6d. per single copy; 8d. per manual.
b) THE SIMPLEX JUNIOR 'A' INTELLIGENCE TEST. 1950–51; title on test is *The Simplex Junior 'A' Test;* test ('50); no data on reliability and validity; 9s. per 25 tests; 6d. per single copy; 1s. per manual ('51).

REFERENCES

1–2. See 4:322.
3. CURR, W., AND GOURLAY, N. "Differences Between Testers in Terman-Merrill Testing." *Brit J Stat Psychol* 9:75–81 N '56. * (*PA* 32:1617)

ARTHUR B. ROYSE, *Lecturer in Psychology, The University of Hull, Hull, England.*

These are alternate forms, each comprising 100 completion type items. Items were rather arbitrarily chosen, some from existing tests, no particular novelty being claimed or achieved.

The chief claims made are that the tests are easily administered, are suitable for all children from 7 to 14, are valid measures of general intelligence, and are thoroughly standardised. The first two claims are obviously valid and, in these respects, the tests compare favourably with similar tests. Although it is possible that the second two claims are also valid, evidence to support them is not sufficiently rigorous.

Test-retest reliability for the first test is good (.95) but no measure is given for the Junior A, reliability apparently being assumed on the basis that they are alternate forms. This latter claim, however, is not based on correlation between scores but on the less reliable criterion of reasonable comparability of mental ages for identical raw scores. Validity for the Junior Intelligence Scale is claimed solely on the basis of a correlation of .93 with teacher estimates of intelligence. No attempt has been made to establish content validity either by item analysis or by demonstration of correlations or comparison of factor patterns with other intelligence tests. No follow-ups have been made and no attempt has been made to show effective prediction of variables other than teacher estimates.

Standardisation was thorough in that the whole relevant school population of a large English urban area—some 12,000 children—was used. Unfortunately, the only norms given are mental ages corresponding to 5-point intervals of raw score. As neither means and standard deviations nor percentile ranks for each age group are given, it is difficult, in the absence of knowledge of correlations with similar tests, to compare the resultant IQ's with IQ's from other tests.

In all, this is just one more intelligence test which presents no new features and which, although offering the virtues of ease of administration and wide applicability, is not sufficiently validated. As a result, major difficulties are encountered both in attaching precise meaning to the obtained IQ's and in utilising the IQ's for comparative or predictive purposes.

[387]

Sleight Non-Verbal Intelligence Test. Ages 6–10; 1931; 1 form; no data on reliability; tentative norms; 15s. per 25 tests; 8d. per single copy; 1s. per manual; postage extra; 20(75) minutes; George F. Sleight; George G. Harrap & Co. Ltd. *

JOHN C. DANIELS, *Lecturer in Education, University of Nottingham, Nottingham, England.*

The reviewer has used this test frequently with 7- and 8-year-old groups, and, unfortunately, is far from satisfied about its validity and reliability when given under ordinary classroom conditions. Children of this age, since they are naturally cooperative and relatively strange to the necessary, though alien, rigour of group test procedure, need a great deal of unobtrusive but thorough supervision or they will either not produce their best work or, alternatively, produce the freely offered work of other children.

Group testing, especially when such complicated instructions as accompany this test have to be given, is quite unsuitable for young children. It is recognized, however, that often the shortage of time available for testing may seem to indicate a group test as the only possibility. When given by teachers with little testing experience, however, the results are often quite useless. For this reason, both retest reliability and validity are to be doubted, in spite of the author's claim that "only tests of proved reliability have been included."

M. L. KELLMER PRINGLE, *Lecturer in Education, and Deputy Head, Department of Child Study, University of Birmingham, Birmingham, England.*

The test was first published in 1931 and, though it has been reprinted several times, it has been neither revised nor restandardised. This is all the more regrettable as it is still widely used in this country. Moreover, there are several signs betraying its age. Some of the drawings have an old fashioned air about them, especially the cars, lorries, and articles of clothing. It is still argued in the manual that both "genius" and subnormality can be detected by the use of this nonverbal group test as early as "the upper infant class and the lower junior school classes." And it is claimed that "most existing tests depend on the child's power to read and write," which is no longer true.

The test consists of 10 nonverbal subtests, all of which are preceded by practice items. Each subtest is timed. The layout of the test is rather cramped, particularly for subtests 2, 6, and 8; the individual pictures should be larger and the number of rows of pictures per page needs to be reduced. In the reviewer's experience, young and dull children tend to become confused even on the practice items; this is made worse by the fact that no numbers or letters are attached to the rows so that the examiner cannot give additional guidance to those who have lost their places. The simplified instructions for testing lower age groups or backward classes are useful, but for such children the total testing time required (though two sittings can be used with younger children) seems rather excessive (about 75 minutes; slightly longer with infant classes, provided the examiner "is perfectly familiar with the instructions"). To facilitate marking, the scoring key could be set out more clearly and systematically, especially for subtests 2, 3, 5, and 6.

On the back of the test's title page is a form "for the entry of additional particulars which may be relevant to the examiner," especially to one "investigating special cases of backwardness, etc." Though still useful, nowadays this portion is rarely filled in because some form of record card has been adopted by most local authorities and its completion by schools is obligatory.

The most serious criticisms must be leveled against the lack of information regarding the construction, standardisation, and reliability of the test. In the manual it is merely stated that "only tests of proved reliability in the measurement of intelligence have been included" and that "the items originally devised for the various tests were in the first place treated experimentally." However, no details are given about the numbers of items devised and tried out, nor about the number of children involved. Again, it is not stated what criteria were used in calculating coefficients of item discriminating power. All that is said is that "the data resulting from this preliminary survey was used to eliminate items which were not diagnostic, and to range the remainder in order of difficulty." The information on the standardisation is similarly vague and inadequate. Neither the mean nor the standard deviation nor reliability values are stated, the possibility of sex differences is not discussed, and no test validity is given either in terms of other tests of intelligence or of independent estimates of general ability. And perhaps most serious of all, the norms are still described as being "only tentative" in the current manual reprinted in 1957.

In view of this lack of information and the age of the test itself, one must be very hesitant in using it as a valid and reliable measure of intelligence.

[388]
★The Southend Test of Intelligence. Ages 10–12; 1953; 1 form; 10s. per 25 tests; 6d. per single copy; 2s. 6d. per manual; postage extra; 30(60) minutes in 2 sessions; M. E. Hebron and W. Stephenson (test); George G. Harrap & Co. Ltd. *

JAMES MAINWARING, *Formerly Lecturer in Psychology and Music, Dudley Training College, Birmingham, England.*

An analysis of a group of representative standard intelligence tests, comprising over 1,000 questions, reveals that 75 per cent of the questions depend essentially on two mental processes: the eduction of some relation or principle of classification, and the arrangement, selection, or rejection of items in accordance with this educed principle. The Southend test has the merit of isolating these two processes in five sharply graduated tests, three of classification and two of analogies. In three of the tests the processes are further isolated by being applied to shapes and patterned groups, in which the principle of relationship has to be sought very deliberately.

The manual is commendably clear, comprehensive, and concise. The construction and standardization of the test are described in less than a hundred words.

A practice period of 30 minutes, followed by a break of 15 minutes, helps to counteract the possibility that some testees may have had previous experience with similar tests while others have not. Each test is timed by a stop watch. Five minutes are allowed for the first and second tests together, for the third test, and for the fourth; the fifth is allotted 15 minutes.

Except for the possible criticism that the test should have included questions in which the aforementioned processes are applied to numerical data, the Southend test has everything to recommend it.

[389]
*Test of Word-Number Ability. Grades 10–16; 1939–57; Form K formerly called *Word-Number Test of Scholastic Aptitude,* Form A; 3 scores: word, number, total; IBM; Forms K, L ('55); manual ('57); college norms for entering freshmen only; tentative high school norms; distribution of Form L restricted to colleges; separate answer sheets must be used; $2.50 per 30 tests; 3½¢ per IBM answer sheet; 30¢ per set of scoring stencils; 25¢ per specimen set; cash orders postpaid; 40(50) minutes; H. T. Manuel, James Knight (K), J. A. Floyd (K), R. C. Jordan (K), Lulu Vinson (L), Marjorie L. Bagley (L), and B. F. Johnson, Jr. (L); Steck Co. *

REFERENCE
1. MANUEL, HERSCHEL T. "Aptitude Tests for College Admission." *Yearb Nat Council Meas Used Ed* 14:20–7 '57. *

I. DAVID SATLOW, *Chairman, Department of Accounting and Distributive Education, Thomas Jefferson High School, Brooklyn, New York.*

This test is a revision and extension of the *Word-Number Test of Scholastic Aptitude* for high school and college. It is designed to measure ability in two areas: verbal and numerical. The test is set up attractively in an 8-page booklet, and consists of two 20-minute parts.

Part 1 presents 90 multiple response vocabulary and analogy items, judiciously distributed in alternating groups of five questions. The vocabulary questions require the selection of a word having a meaning similar to or related to that of a given word or phrase. The analogy questions call for selecting a fourth word which bears the same relation to the third word that the second bears to the first. In the words of the manual, the framers of the test hope to provide "a partial measure of the extent and richness of vocabulary, the ability to see relations between concepts presented by words, and the ability to reason with verbal materials."

Part 2 consists of 45 questions designed to measure abilities to deal with fractions, decimals, and per cents in simple functional situations, to do some elementary algebra, and to apply mathematical reasoning.

Two forms of the test have been issued—Form K, usable at either senior high school or college, and Form L, which is available to colleges only. Both forms are similar as to scope of content and range of difficulty. According to the manual, the only reason for restricting the distribution of Form L is "to make it possible for a college to use the test without repeating a form already administered to the same students in high school."

Even though the guidance values of these tests are, in the opinion of this reviewer, the most significant aspect, one can well conceive of individual schools desiring to use test results for purposes of comparison with other groups. For such institutions, the published norms may prove of value.

JOHN M. WILLITS, *Business and Industrial Psychologist, 566 Everett Ave., Palo Alto, California.*

This test and its manual appear well suited to their assigned task: educational and vocational guidance in senior high school and college. The test yields part scores on two mental ability factors, verbal ability and numerical ability. These scores and their weighted total are reported to correlate about .8 with widely used college aptitude tests, and about .6 with grades of college freshmen. Odd-even reliabilities (corrected) are in the vicinity of .9.

The manual is almost a model in form and content. But its greatest strength is related to its chief weakness, and both its strength and its weakness apparently result from its being designed for users with minimal experience in testing. The manual's strength lies in the clarity and completeness of its text. One assumes, though specific statement is not found, that it was written primarily for secondary school officials or teachers who are not highly expert in test administration and interpretation. Its paragraphs teem with homely advice and suggestions on unglamorous but essential points that have long been routine to "old hands" in testing, e.g., proper atmosphere of a testing session, equipment and procedures for accurate timing, other duties of examiners during a testing session, control of the close of a session, how to score tests accurately, why a correction for guessing, why the Spearman-Brown formula, obtained scores and errors of estimate, limitations of "national" norms and of other normative samples as reported, uses of local norms, and factors other than mental ability in educational guidance. The 13-page manual clearly and convincingly discusses all these and numerous other extremely practical considerations for the tyro in testing—matters basic to the sound utilization of tests, and thus not replaceable by any amount of test theory or statistical lore. There is consistent emphasis throughout the manual on restraint and caution and on limitations and precautions consonant with the test's conservative title.

But the manual's weakness seems to derive from its very unity of purpose. If written mainly for test users with minimal experience in testing, its authors seem to feel, why should our manual include statistical data that would tax their comprehension? Thus, in the manual's five tables of correlation coefficients there is nary a mean nor a sigma! For all of the four tables of norms, the reader who wants means or sigmas must estimate them from percentiles. Sample sizes are omitted from one of these tables of norms, and also from a very usable expectancy table which shows test scores in relation to college freshman grades. This latter table also reveals nothing about confidence limits for its data. Statistical data such as these should be included for the users who can interpret them, even though many others may choose or may have to ignore them.

The manual makes no mention of correlation between the test's two part scores, nor of the reasoning behind the unequal weighting of part scores in the total score. One of the test's two forms is restricted to use at the college level to permit retesting at that level without duplication. But, though stability of scores is men-

Test of Word-Number Ability

tioned, no test-retest data or other statistics on stability are offered.

The various normative groups, all student populations, are adequately described for the most part, but there is no mention of sex distribution or of sex differences in score. The latter question is significant, particularly in relation to scores on the numerical part. One fourth of the numerical items require basic algebra. With algebra currently an elective in many high schools and more colleges, we may anticipate that fewer girls than boys elect it—and that, in consequence, there is considerable sex difference in scores on Part 2 of the test.

The norms for college freshmen have been equated, via the "national" norms of the *American Council on Education Psychological Examination for College Freshmen,* to distributions of student scores in a composite of some 269 colleges in various parts of the United States. The high school normative population was sampled from 15 schools all located in one state (Texas), but well distributed as to size of school and location within the state.

In summary, the *Test of Word-Number Ability,* true to its title, is modestly competent in its field of high school and college guidance, educational and vocational. Its manual is very well tailored to the needs of test users who are less than expert in test administration and interpretation, but it omits most of the supporting statistical evidence necessary for a critical evaluation of the correlations and norms which it reports.

For a review by Jane Loevinger of an earlier edition, see 4:333.

[390]

★**Tests AH4 and AH5.** Ages 10 and over, 13 and over; 1955–56; 1 form, 2 levels; separate answer sheets must be used; postpaid within U.K.; A. W. Heim; distributed by the National Foundation for Educational Research in England and Wales. *

a) TEST AH4: GROUP TEST OF INTELLIGENCE. Ages 10 and over; 1955; 1 form ['55]; no norms for age 10; 12s. per 25 tests; 4s. per 25 answer sheets; 1s. 6d. per set of scoring key and manual ['55]; 2s. 6d. per specimen set; 20(30–45) minutes.

b) TEST AH5: GROUP TEST OF HIGH-GRADE INTELLIGENCE. Ages 13 and over; 1956; 1 form ['56]; 17s. per 25 tests; 5s. per 25 answer sheets; 2s. per set of scoring key and manual ['56]; 3s. 3d. per specimen set; 40(60–70) minutes.

REFERENCES

1. HEIM, A. W. "An Attempt to Test High-Grade Intelligence." *Brit J Psychol* 37:70–81 Ja '47. * (PA 21:2036)
2. HEIM, A. W., AND BATTS, V. "Upward and Downward Selection in Intelligence Testing." *Brit J Psychol* 39:22–9 S '48. * (PA 24:1060)
3. HEIM, A. W. "Learning in Intelligence Test Performance." Abstract. *Q B Brit Psychol Soc* (3):120–1 Ja '49. * Reply by John C. Raven: (3):197–8 Jl '49. * Rebuttal by A. W. Heim: (3):219–20 O '49. *
4. CANE, V. R., AND HEIM, A. W. "The Effects of Repeated Retesting: III, Further Experiments and General Conclusions." *Q J Exp Psychol* 2:182–97 pt 4 '50. *
5. HEIM, A. W., AND WALLACE, J. G. "The Effects of Repeatedly Retesting the Same Group on the Same Intelligence Test." *Q J Exp Psychol* 2:19–32 F '50. * (PA 25:6938)
6. WALLACE, JEAN G. "The Intelligence Testing of University Staff and Students." Abstract. *Q B Brit Psychol Soc* 1:285–6 Ja '50. *
7. WALLACE, JEAN G. "Results of a Test of High-Grade Intelligence Applied to a University Population." *Brit J Psychol, Gen Sect* 43:61–9 F '52. * (PA 26:7239)
8. WATTS, KATHLEEN P. "Influences Affecting the Results of a Test of High-Grade Intelligence." *Brit J Psychol* 44:359–67 N '53. * (PA 28:5659)
9. WATTS, KATHLEEN P. "The Effect of a University Training in Mathematics on the Scores in an Intelligence Test." *Brit J Ed Psychol* 24:32–7 F '54. * (PA 28:9048)
10. HEIM, A. W. "Adaptation to Level of Difficulty in Intelligence Testing." *Brit J Psychol* 46:211–24 Ag '55. * (PA 30:5748)
11. WATTS, KATHLEEN P. "Intelligence Test Performance From 11 to 18: A Study of Grammar School Girls." *Brit J Ed Psychol* 28:112–9 Je '58. *

GEORGE A. FERGUSON, *Professor of Psychology, McGill University, Montreal, Canada.* [Review of Test AH4.]

This test is a measure of general intelligence for adults and for children over 10 years of age. It is divided into two parts. Part 1 consists of 65 items of the common verbal and numerical type, opposites, analogies, number series, following directions, arithmetic problems, and synonyms. Part 2 is an assortment of nonverbal items, figure analogies, figure series, superimpositions, sames, and subtractions. The author is concerned with the adjustment of the subject to the testing situation, and much emphasis is placed on the proper completion of the preliminary practice exercises. Time limit for each part is 10 minutes. Separate answer sheets, not adapted to machine scoring, are used. Scoring is done with a marking key.

The test manual provides norms based on three groups: (a) 3,407 industrial subjects, (b) 726 university students, and (c) groups of school children, ages 11 to 16. No conversion tables to percentiles or normalized standard scores are provided. A 5-point letter grade system based on the percentages 10, 20, 40, 20, 10 is used. Although norms for university students are given, the test is not suitable as a test of intelligence at the university level because the items are too easy. The mean score reported for university students is 96. A peculiarity of the normative data given in the manual is that the mean score for adults is 47, whereas the mean score for 11-year-old grammar school children is 60. Indeed, the average adult is not much above the 10th percentile for the 11-year-old group. This may mean, contrary to the claim in the manual, that the adult group used in the standardization is not representative of the adult population.

Test-retest reliability with one-month interval between testings is .92. Indications are that the test conforms to accepted standards of reliability and discriminatory capacity for average or below average groups.

While AH4 appears to be a fairly well constructed and useful test, it has few distinguishing features, if any, which would commend it in preference to numerous other group tests of intelligence. In many respects it is perhaps no better and no worse than many other tests. In the testing of school children in Britain, it has no characteristics which would recommend it in preference to the thoroughly standardized Moray House tests of intelligence. The nonverbal part has nothing to commend it, other perhaps than variety, in preference to the *Progressive Matrices*. It is improbable that AH4 will have much application in North America where many not dissimilar tests are available. An incidental observation is that the art work in Part 2 is amateurish, a fault which probably does not detract from the merits of the test as a measure of intelligence.

J. A. KEATS, *Senior Lecturer in Psychology, University of Queensland, Brisbane, Australia.* [Review of Test AH5.]

This is a general intelligence test to be used "with selected, highly intelligent [adult] subjects." It is claimed by the author that most intelligence tests discriminate between such subjects mainly on the basis of the speed with which they can do the items. Presumably, the present test is not intended to be speeded and, if not, should be a more valid measure of intelligence.

The test consists of two separately timed parts. Part 1 consists of verbal analogies, number series, ordering words according to meaning, and recognizing double meanings for one word. This part may be expected to be a good measure of academic aptitude. Some ingenious devices are used to obtain difficult and discriminating items which do not require knowledge of out of the way terms. Item 35 seemed to the reviewer to be unfortunate in that the correct answer (as keyed) could be obtained by the "clang" "manner is to matter" response.

Part 2 consists of diagram items in the form of clock problems, reversed and rotated figure problems, and problems requiring recognition of patterns and common characteristics. These items are similar to those in standard "nonverbal" tests which are usually regarded as good measures of general ability. The items involving the recognition of patterns seem very time-consuming to the reviewer and may well introduce an element of speed into this part.

The correlation between these two parts has been computed on five occasions with resulting coefficients of .49, .50, .52, .52, and .62. The reviewer does not agree that "it is satisfactory that the association is in fact always positive and significant." Such low correlations are hardly in keeping with the claim that "marked discrepancy between a subject's Part 1 score and his Part 2 score is unusual." The fact that these correlations are much lower than the reliability of either part suggests that the parts are measuring different attributes.

There has been a great deal of empirical work done with this test. The retest reliability with at least several months' interval between testing has been examined many times. For selected adults this measure was never less than .80, and in the majority of occasions a value greater than .90. was obtained. These figures indicate that reasonably stable attributes are being measured. The figures for the separate parts are not much smaller than this.

As might be expected, validity studies are confined to correlations with other intelligence tests and to predictions of academic success. The coefficients reported in the manual range from .27 to .54 for various prediction criteria. These values do not seem to be much if at all higher than values obtained with other tests. None of the six studies reported gives the validities for the two parts. This omission is the more surprising since separate norms and reliability coefficients are provided. In view of the relatively low correlation between the parts it is not impossible that one of the parts alone is contributing most of the validity. Correlations with other tests of general intelligence lie mainly in the range .55 to .65.

Again, separate correlations for the two parts are not provided. No estimate of the effect of practice is given although the data for such an estimate must have been available from the reliability studies. It is well known that performance on items of the kind used in Part 2 is influenced to a considerable extent by practice.

The manual also contains details for the testing procedure, standard instructions, and norms which have been established for three well defined groups by means of very adequate samples. Five letter ratings are provided: A, B, C, D, and E. These ratings correspond to the top 10 per cent, the next 20 per cent, the middle 40 per cent, the next 20 per cent, and the bottom 10 per cent, respectively. Scores corresponding to these ratings would have been estimated more accurately by some method such as that of Keats [1] which provides for smoothing the raw frequency distribution.

AH5 has been very thoroughly prepared according to a certain theoretical position concerning the nature of abilities. Whether or not a particular worker agrees with this position, he would probably not agree with a practice which leads to less precision in prediction—the practice of including items of Part 2 with those of Part 1 in a single score. This could lead to a lowering of the efficiency of prediction. The prospective user would probably be better served by treating the two parts as separate tests.

The test seems to have wide application for testing adults of high ability in English-speaking countries.

[391]

*Thurstone Test of Mental Alertness, Revised Edition.** Grades 9–12 and adults; 1943–53; abbreviated adaptation of *American Council on Education Psychological Examination for High School Students*, 1940 Edition; 3 scores: quantitative, linguistic, total; Forms A ('52), B ('53); manual, third edition ('52); separate answer pads must be used; $9.80 per 20 tests; $2.15 per 20 answer pads; 75¢ per specimen set; postage extra; 20(25) minutes; Thelma Gwinn Thurstone and L. L. Thurstone; Science Research Associates. *

JOSHUA A. FISHMAN, *Director of Research, College Entrance Examination Board, Inc., New York, New York.*

This is a 1952 revision of the 1943 instrument reviewed in *The Third Mental Measurements Yearbook*. The 1952 revision, like the 1943 edition, is virtually self-administering, except for an 11-item practice section and a few clarifying instructions. The test now has 126 items, or an increase of 28 over the 1943 version. As in the 1943 edition the items are arranged in spiral order and in order of increasing difficulty. The item types, as before, are word definitions, same-opposite, arithmetic, and number series completion. The test yields an L(inguistic) score, derived from the first two item types, a Q(uantitative) score, derived from the second two item types, and a total score.

The examiner's manual now presents percentile rank norms for a variety of occupational groups as well as for high school students. The high school norms reported are for the same 3,820 pupils in nine high schools that served in norming the 1943 edition. The number of cases in each of the four high school years is not reported although separate norms are given for each year. In some instances the norming populations seem to be either insufficient in size or restricted in location; in others, desirable information concerning the populations is not reported. In addition, the norms for all but business executives and stockmen-and-clerical workers are reported only up to the 90th percentile. This seems to be due to the fact that the new 126-item edition was administered only to these two groups. For the other groups, norms developed from administrations of the 1943 edition are presented and the claim is advanced that they may be used as good estimates of the eventual norms for the revised test. Inasmuch as the revised forms contain 28 items more than the earlier edition, the publishers admit that this will cause a difference in the "upper end of the scale." For this reason, all percentile tables based on results from the earlier edition are reported up to the 90th percentile only. More complete norms based on the revised test were promised when the 1952 version first appeared. If these have been compiled, they have not yet been released. All in all, the norms produce a makeshift impression.

The reliability and validity data presented are also far from the highest professional standards. Reliability coefficients are given for the 1943 version only. Although correlations between the 1943 and 1952 versions are reported, as well as correlations between the 1943 version and the college form of the *ACE Psychological Examination* (a surprisingly low .68), no reliability findings or estimates for the 1952 version proper are given. In view of the fact that the latter is more than 25 per cent longer than the former, it is probable that its reliability is as great as or slightly greater than that reported for the former, namely, .95 for split-halves corrected by the Spearman-Brown formula. On the other hand, it is questionable whether this is the proper method for estimat-

---

[1] KEATS, J. A. *A Statistical Theory of Objective Test Scores.* Melbourne, Australia: Australian Council for Educational Research, 1951. Pp. viii, 48.

ing reliability for such a highly speeded test. The validity findings are reported in a manner which makes it unclear whether they pertain to the 1943 or the 1952 version. The studies are largely based upon "t-tests" for the significance of the differences between mean TMA scores of groups (pertinent to the norm populations) that have been rated "good" or "poor" on "general effectiveness," "cooperation," and "sales mindedness." The differences reported are significant at the .05 level or better. "Accuracy," "ability to work under pressure," and "cooperation" ratings are related to TMA scores via biserial correlations, and the average of 8-months' sales for managers of small retail stores is related to TMA scores via the Pearson product moment correlation. With the exception of the biserial between "cooperation" and TMA (for 27 clerical workers), the other correlations are significantly greater than zero at the .01 level. On the other hand, the TMA failed to discriminate between "good" and "poor" retail store employees on "sales ability" and only the Q score did so on ratings for "customer service." A number of these validity studies are based on a very small sample (n's of 17, 19, 22, 23, and 27 are the lowest that are reported while the highest are 232, 173, and 169) and, in the absence of any data on the test's standard error of measurement, it is difficult to venture any opinion concerning the practical significance of the differences between means that prove to be statistically significant. The publishers summarize the section on the validity studies described above with the statement "It appears that the *Thurstone Test of Mental Alertness* has validity in predicting on-the-job success in positions which require flexibility, versatility, and resources for solving problems. Where such performance expectations do not exist, the TMA does not prove to be discriminating." The reviewer feels that none of the criterion ratings employed are clearly indicative of on-the-job flexibility, versatility, and resources for solving problems but that they are all rather easily seen as related to conformity with the expectations of the rater. The publishers seem to have concluded that the TMA is a test of mental alertness because it is named such. They then consider any variable significantly related to test performance as being a result of (or an aspect of) some type of mental alertness. Thus they claim that "the difference....between a cooperative and a non-cooperative employee is to a major degree a difference in adaptiveness and versatility," or that "*sales ability* [for managers of small retail stores] is highly related to mental flexibility and versatility as measured by the *Thurstone Test of Mental Alertness*." The trouble with all of this is not only that the distinctions between cognitive and noncognitive aspects of flexibility, adaptiveness, versatility, etc., are lost, but that the direct relevance of the TMA to even the cognitive aspects of these characteristics is never seriously probed. Finally, no evidence is presented concerning the validity of the TMA in any educational setting. For educational guidance purposes there certainly seems to be no reason to prefer the TMA to either the 60-minute *ACE Psychological Examination for High School Students,* the 75-minute *Cooperative School and College Ability Tests,* or the 45-minute *SRA Test of Educational Ability.*

To summarize, the principal advantages of this test remain, as in 1943, its brevity, ease of administration, ease of scoring, and compactness. Its greatest shortcoming is in the area of the meaning of its scores. Both the norms and the validity data are inadequate and the conceptual rationale for the test is unclear. The publishers claim that the TMA was "designed to measure an individual's capacity for acquiring new knowledge and skills." This claim is modest enough but the evidence advanced in support of its realization is unnecessarily oblique. It is certainly unacceptable to rest one's claim that this is a test of mental alertness on the observation that "like electricity, 'mental alertness' is easier to measure than to define or explain." The publishers venture the definition that "mental alertness" refers to "the kind of thinking flexibility and versatility an individual possesses that makes it possible for him to adjust to new situations." Although they are free to define this construct as they see fit, they have not demonstrated that the test is clearly related to the construct, however it may be defined.

For reviews by Anne Anastasi and Emily T. Burr of an earlier edition, see 3:265.

[392]

★**The Tomlinson Junior School Test.** Ages 7–12.0; 1953; 1 form; no data on reliability and validity; test booklets not required since the test is orally presented using black board examples; 2s. per 25 answer sheets; 1s. 6d. per manual; postage extra; [80-90] minutes; T. P. Tomlinson; University of London Press Ltd. *

JOHN C. DANIELS, *Lecturer in Education, University of Nottingham, Nottingham, England.*

This test has been designed primarily for classifying "the children of the 7–8 years age-group on their transfer to the junior school." It is a test for "streaming" children in the junior school, though it can, apparently, also be used at the 11–12 years age level for streaming in the secondary modern school.

Its special attraction is its cheapness, a quality stemming from the fact that the testee "expends" only one quarto size answer sheet for writing down the answers to about 120 questions. Each test question is read orally by the tester to the children, though before the testing session the teacher has to prepare five fairly substantial sets of "blackboard material." The test is given in two sections. In form, Section 2 is a replication of Section 1. Each section contains eight subtests with the following titles: Obeying Instructions, Definitions, Number Series, Opposites, Reasoning, Classification, Selection, and Analogies. When the reviewer gave the test to about 40 ten-year-olds, the total testing time added up to 2 hours 2 minutes—a formidable period for tester and tested. All the test items consist of questions of the classical intelligence test type, but they have been so carefully selected from the point of view of item consistency that the reviewer found no quarrel with the interpretation of any items. This is a record for this type of test.

The scores are converted directly into what the manual calls "IQ's." In the conversion table, IQ's are given only for scores at 10-point intervals, which makes it necessary to interpolate for practically every child's score. This makes this part of the testing unnecessarily cumbersome. Indeed, it is not made clear whether these "IQ's" once obtained are IQ's in the strict sense or standardized scores. No standard deviation for an unselected population is given.

No doubt this test will give reliable scores if properly administered, but the validity of tests given in this way is open to some doubt.

[393]

*Verbal and Non-Verbal Test 1. Ages 12 to 13-11; 1951–53; 1 form ['51]; either 54–item *Practice Test 1* ['51] or 22-item *Practice Test 1A* should precede administration of test by 1 week; no data on validity; 8s. 6d. per 12 tests; 9d. per single copy; 5s. per 12 copies of *Practice Test 1*; 6d. per single copy; 2s. 6d. per 12 copies of *Practice Test 1A*; 3d. per single copy; 2s. 6d. per manual ['51]; postage extra; practice test: [10–15] minutes; test: 40(45) minutes; published for National Foundation for Educational Research in England and Wales; Newnes Educational Publishing Co. Ltd. *

T. R. MILES, *Lecturer in Psychology, University College, Bangor, Wales.*

Although the manual gives detailed instructions for the administration and marking of this test, the crucial issues on the theoretical side receive no discussion at all. This seems to the reviewer a serious omission. By implication, the authors clearly want us to regard this test as a test of intelligence (whatever that means), but we are left completely in the dark as to what theoretical basis, if any, they had in mind in constructing it. Do they believe, for instance, that Spearman's application of factorial analysis to the study of intelligence constitutes a major scientific discovery? The existence of g or other factors is neither an agreed truth which can be taken for granted, nor an agreed blind alley comparable to, say, phlogiston; but one looks in vain in the manual for either an expression of acceptance or an unambiguous disclaimer. In the absence of any universally accepted theoretical basis for the study of intelligence, users of this test would be wise, in the reviewer's opinion, to treat the results as a general guide rather than as an accurate measure of some identifiable character trait. Those who are not statistically minded should also remember that, although the test is said to have a Kuder-Richardson reliability coefficient of .98, this figure relates to the consistency of item scores within the test. It does not and cannot mean—except by a verbal quibble—that the test is to that extent *a reliable measure of intelligence.*

A further difficulty is this. It is apparently assumed either that the administrator, the test situation, and all words and diagrams in the test booklet are emotionally neutral to the child, or else that emotional influences do not seriously affect performance on cognitive tasks. One continually wants to know whether the test was supervised by the child's regular teacher, whether the supervisor showed signs of worry at conforming strictly to the timetable, whether the child thought of the situation as a "special occasion," whether the test contains any words or symbols which in a free association test would have produced "blockage," and so on. Some brief reference to such problems should surely have been included; the absence of any such reference confirms one's general impression that those responsible for test construction have not, for the most part, taken such problems seriously enough.

A third general problem which this test has failed to solve is that of alternative methods of classification. In Test 1, for instance, the child has to delete the odd word from groups of four words, e.g., "milk butter cheese water." In some cases, the most suitable method of classification does not admit of serious dispute, but this is not invariably so. Thus in Item 6 ("eiderdown quilt blanket pillow"), the correct answer is given as pillow, presumably since it does not cover us, whereas the others do; but why not blanket, since it is the only one that is not padded? In Item 9 ("rosy red crimson scarlet"), the correct answer is given as rosy (the only adjective derived directly from a noun?), but why not red (the genus word), as opposed to the others which are species of red? It is hard to see, in general, by what right anyone can claim that his particular method of classification is the only correct one.

Apart from these three general difficulties, the reviewer's only other adverse criticisms are minor ones. The complete test is perhaps on the long side, with the result that there is too much of a premium on speed. Knowledge that the game commonly known as "tennis" should strictly be called "lawn tennis" (Test 5, Item 9) seems to the reviewer an unfair requirement, and he should certainly question the assumption that the word "quilt" (Test 1, Item 6) is universally known. There is a misprint on page 1 ("If your pencil points breaks"), and when the child is told on page 2 and elsewhere to underline "the words that are 'different,'" the use of inverted commas around "different" seems to the reviewer incorrect. Dark type or italics would provide the requisite emphasis.

On the credit side, mention should be made in particular of the fact that the instruction manual for this test (and for others in the same series) is addressed primarily to the teacher, who must therefore share the responsibility for assessing the results. It is very desirable, in my opinion, that the psychologist should take the teacher into his confidence in this way; the more the psychologist can be looked upon as a *consultant* rather than as a suspect authority figure, the better for everyone.

Other commendable features in this test are (a) that the problem of practice and coaching is squarely faced, and (b) that the somewhat unsatisfactory concept of "mental age" is no longer used in the scoring. As regards (a), two preliminary practice tests are available which are to be given a week or so beforehand. The teacher is required to go through all the different kinds of items with the class so that the general principles in each type of test are understood and the need for speed is appreciated. As for (b), the familiar procedure is adopted of converting the raw scores, with an allowance for age, into standard scores with mean 100 and standard deviation 15. A child's score is thus primarily an indication of his position in relation to other children of the same age.

This review has concentrated mainly on what the reviewer takes to be the defects of this test, but it would be unfair to conclude without paying tribute to the painstaking work which has clearly gone into its construction. The reviewer's main worry is a general one. Although he does not dispute the value of *individual* intelligence tests, such as those of Terman and Wechsler, as a standardised form of interview, he has some doubts as to whether, in view of the difficulties already mentioned, large scale multiplication of *group* intelligence tests justifies the amount of labour involved. There are so many profitable paths which psychological research can follow that one has to be all the more careful in trying to avoid the blind alleys.

[394]
★**Verbal Capacity Sampler.** Male adults; 1950–52; Form AH ('51); mimeographed manual ('52); 10¢ per test; 25¢ per scoring stencil; 25¢ per manual; 35¢ per specimen set; postage extra; 5(10) minutes; Byron B. Harless and Gerald P. Bodily (test); Gerald P. Bodily (manual); Byron Harless & Associates, Inc. *

[395]
*Verbal Intelligence Test. Grades 12–16 and applicants for executive positions; 1948–51; formerly called *Verbal Intelligence Test for Business Executives*; 1 form ('50, identical with test copyrighted in 1948); manual ('49); supplement ('51); no data on reliability; $2.50 per 25 tests; 50¢ per specimen set; cash orders postpaid; 20(25) minutes; William J. Morgan and Antonia Morgan; Aptitude Associates. *

JOHN P. FOLEY, JR., *President, J. P. Foley and Company, Inc., New York, New York.*

This test is printed in blue ink on the inside spread of a folded booklet, the front of the booklet providing space for identifying personal data and the back of the booklet containing the instructions as well as a sample exercise. In each of five sets of items, two columns of words are given. Column A consists of 10 words, Column B of 12 words. For each of the 10 words in Column A the subject is to select the word in Column B which is either most nearly similar or most nearly opposite in meaning. The number of the chosen word is then placed in the appropriately numbered answer space. The total possible score is thus 50.

The scoring sheet provided to the test user consists of a regular test booklet with correct answers overprinted in red. Instructions and norms are provided in a 2-page lithoprinted sheet carrying a 1949 copyright and in a 3-page lithoprinted supplement carrying a 1951 copyright. The 1949 sheet presents decile norms on 259 business executives, ranging in age from 23 to 48 years, with a median age of 36. Annual salaries within the group ranged from $4,500 to $12,000, with a median of $7,400. The group is said to constitute a "representative sample" and to have been "selected from a wide variety of business and industrial concerns." In the 1951 instructions and norms, two normative tables are supplied, one giving percentile equivalents of the scores made by a "random sample" of 312 high school graduates, aged 20 to 49, and the other the percentile equivalents of scores made by a "random sample" of 575 college graduates, ranging in age from 20 to 49.

No reliability data whatever are reported. Data relating to validity are inadequate. The following evidences of validity are claimed or reported: (a) Significantly higher scores are obtained by college graduates than by high school graduates. (b) Correlations with the *Henmon-Nelson Test of Mental Ability* for 334 unspecified cases ranged from .67 to .84 in four studies, although no information is provided on the range of ability or on other group characteristics that might affect these correlations. (c) A correlation of .83 with the V score on the Thorndike CAVD is reported for 43 unspecified cases. (d) Executives earning higher salaries are said to obtain higher test scores, although no supporting data are cited. There are no references given to published reports of any of these studies.

From the 1949 sheet of instructions and norms one learns that the *Verbal Intelligence Test* is designed for business executives. It would seem that most of the validation procedures utilized are not particularly relevant to industrial criteria. In the 1951 "manual," the test is described as "a test of mental ability for adults." This is misleading in the sense that only verbal ability of a limited nature is tested. The elementary nature of the instructions for administration and scoring suggests that the test is designed for use by psychologically untrained and unsophisticated persons. It is thus all the more liable to misuse and misinterpretation. The authors deserve credit, however, for calling attention to the fact that, in the selection of applicants for executive responsibilities, "many factors must be considered such as work attitudes, interests, vocational history, specialized training and education as well as the results of aptitude tests." It is also true, of course, that such factors must be considered in the selection of clerks, typists, administrative assistants, and all other types of personnel.

On the whole, the data relating to norms, reliability, and validity are clearly inadequate in the case of this test. Use of the instrument should be predicated upon local investigation of its validity and reliability, as well as upon the collection of local norms. It would be difficult, however, to justify the use of this test when other instruments, such as certain forms of the *Wonderlic Personnel Test,* are already available for rapid screening purposes.

For a review by William B. Schrader, see 4:329.

[396]

★**Verbal Test (Adv.) 1, 2, and 3.** Ages 12 to 13-11; 1954–58; forms 1 ['54], 2 ['57], 3 ['58]; no data on validity; distribution restricted to directors of education; 8s. 3d. per 12 tests; 9d. per single copy; 1s. 6d. per 12 practice tests; 2d. per single copy; 1s. 7d. per manual; postage extra; practice test: 10(15) minutes; D. A. Pidgeon; published for National Foundation for Educational Research in England and Wales (*a*); Newnes Educational Publishing Co. Ltd. *

a) VERBAL TEST (ADV.) 1. 1954–55; practice test ['54]; manual ('55); 50(60) minutes.
b) VERBAL TEST (ADV.) 2. 1957; practice test ['57]; manual ('57); 45(55) minutes.
c) VERBAL TEST (ADV.) 3. 1958; practice test ['58]; manual ('58); 45(55) minutes.

[397]

***Verbal Tests 1–2, 4–8.** Ages 10–11; 1951–58; 7 forms; no data on reliability for form 4; no data on validity; distribution restricted to directors of education; 6s. 6d. per 12 tests; 7d. per single copy; 1s. 3d. per 12 practice tests (dates same as for tests except 7B); 2d. per single copy; 1s. 7d. per manual; postage extra; form 1: 50(75) minutes; forms 2, 4–7: 45(65) minutes; I. Macfarlane Smith (*a–d*) and M. A. Brimer (*e*); published for National Foundation for Educational Research in England and Wales; Newnes Educational Publishing Co. *

a) VERBAL TEST 1. 1951–53; form 1 ['51]; manual ('53).
b) VERBAL TEST 2. 1952–53; form 2 ['52]; manual ['53]; no norms for ages 11-7 to 11-11.

c) VERBAL TEST 4. 1953; form 4 ['53]; manual ['53]; norms ['54].
d) VERBAL TEST 5. 1954–55; form 5 ['54]; manual ('55); no norms for ages 11-6 to 11-11.
e) VERBAL TEST 6. 1955–57; form 6 ['55]; manual ('57).
f) VERBAL TEST 7. 1957–58; forms 7A ['57], 7B ['57]; practice test ['58] for form 7B; manual (7A, '57; 7B, '57).
g) VERBAL TEST 8. 1957–58; forms 8A ['57], 8B ['58]; manual (8A, '58; 8B, '58).

[398]
Vocabulary Tests. Ages 10–15; 1931–35; 1 form ['31]; 5 tests; manual ('35, same as manual copyrighted in 1931); no data on reliability; 4s. 6d. per 25 copies of any one test; 3d. per single copy; 2s. per manual; postage extra; 50(60) minutes per test 1 day apart; Frank Watts; University of London Press Ltd. *
a) VOCABULARY TEST NO. 1, 100 COMMON NAMES.
b) VOCABULARY TEST NO. 2, 100 COMMON CLASS NAMES.
c) VOCABULARY TEST NO. 3, 100 COMMON VERBS.
d) VOCABULARY TEST NO. 4, 100 COMMON ADJECTIVES (LIST A).
e) VOCABULARY TEST NO. 5, 100 COMMON ADJECTIVES (LIST B).

JOHN NISBET, *Lecturer in Education, University of Aberdeen, Aberdeen, Scotland.*

The items in the first three of this series of 100-item tests are open questions; those in the last two are a type of multiple choice item. Norms are in the form of average scores (both sexes together) at each age from 10 through 15. The standardisation groups, which are not precisely described, vary in number from 2,857 for Test 1 to 1,898 for Test 3. No data on construction are given. Instructions are very brief, and the key gives few alternatives for answers to the open-ended questions. The tests are difficult, the average score, except on Test 1, reaching the 50 per cent correct mark only at about age 15.

The author suggests that the tests "will provide measures of intelligence similar to those obtained by the ordinary type of intelligence tests," and he himself has used them in his basic research on the relation of vocabulary to general mental growth in adolescence.[1] However, the tests seem unsuited for use as measures of general ability or even as measures of vocabulary for several reasons—their length, the inadequacy of instructions for administration and scoring, and the vagueness of data on construction and standardisation. Also, a number of the items are surprisingly dated. For example, Item 59 in Test 2: Common Class Names, asks "What do we call carbolic powder, Condy's fluid and chloride of lime?"

[1] WATTS, A. F. *The Language and Mental Development of Children.* London: George G. Harrap & Co. Ltd., 1944. Pp. 354.

The tests would require revision of certain out of date terminology and new item analysis and standardisation before they could be accepted as a useful vocabulary assessment at a fairly advanced level. They could be used more appropriately as teaching aids to help focus pupils' attention on the finer point of verbal expression, rather than as tests.

[399]
Wesman Personnel Classification Test. Grades 8–16 and adults; 1946–51; 3 scores: verbal, numerical, total; Forms A ('46), B ('47); revised manual ('51); $1.70 per 25 tests; 35¢ per specimen set; postpaid; 28(35) minutes; Alexander G. Wesman; Psychological Corporation. *

REFERENCES

1–3. See 4:331.
4. GILBERT, HARRY B. "The Use of Tests and Other Objective Data in the Selection of Camp Counselors." Abstract. *Am Psychol* 7:369 Jl '52. *
5. WILLIAMS, JOHN E., AND GERKEN, C. D'A. "'Verbal Factor' and 'Number Factor'—A Study of Two Tests." *Proc Iowa Acad Sci* 59:397–401 '52. * (PA 28:6599)
6. HANER, CHARLES F. "Wonderlic, Wesman P.C.T., and A.C.E.: A Comparison of Three Group Intelligence Tests." *Proc Iowa Acad Sci* 61:358–60 '54. * (PA 30:3460)
7. HOLT, WELDON G. *Relationships Between the ACE and the Wesman Personnel Classification Test.* Master's thesis, University of Kansas (Lawrence, Kan.), 1954.
8. PERRINE, MERVYN WILLIAM. "The Selection of Drafting Trainees." *J Appl Psychol* 39:57–61 F '55. * (PA 30:1725)
9. BAIER, DONALD E., AND DUGAN, ROBERT D. "Normative Data Information Exchange, No. 2." *Personnel Psychol* 9:265–6 su '56. *
10. BAIER, DONALD E., AND DUGAN, ROBERT D. "Tests and Performance in a Sales Organization." *Personnel Psychol* 9:17–26 sp '56. * (PA 31:5169)
11. HOLT, WELDON G.; OTTMAN, DONALD K.; AND COTTLE, WILLIAM C. "Evidenced Relationships Between the 'ACE' and the Wesman Personnel Classification Test." *J Ed Res* 51:71–7 S '57. *

For reviews by John C. Flanagan and Erwin K. Taylor, see 4:331; see 3:253 (1 excerpt).

[400]
Wonderlic Personnel Test. Adults; 1939–45; Forms D and F are adaptations, for business and industrial use, of *Otis Self-Administering Tests of Mental Ability, Higher Form;* Forms A ('42), B ('42), D ['39], F ['39]; manual ('45); $8 per 100 tests and manual; 50¢ per manual; postage extra; 12(20) minutes; E. F. Wonderlic; Wonderlic Personnel Test Co. *

REFERENCES

1–2. See 40:1415.
3–9. See 3:269.
10. JACOBSEN, CARLYLE F. "Interest and Attitude as Factors in Achievement in Medical School." *J Assn Am Med Col* 21:152–9 My '46. *
11. LINDZEY, GARDNER E. "Four Psychometric Techniques Useful in Vocational Guidance." *J Clin Psychol* 2:157–60 Ap '46. * (PA 20:3899)
12. ROBERTS, WILLIAM H. "Test Scores and Merit Ratings of Graduate Engineers." Abstract. *Am Psychol* 1:284 Jl '46. *
13. FISKE, DONALD W. "Validation of Naval Aviation Cadet Selection Tests Against Training Criteria." *J Appl Psychol* 31:601–14 D '47. * (PA 22:2770)
14. CHESLER, DAVID J. "The Wonderlic Personnel Test as a Predictor of Scores on the American Council on Education Examination." *J Clin Psychol* 4:82–5 Ja '48. * (PA 22:5566)
15. CAPWELL, DORA F. *Psychological Tests for Retail Store Personnel.* Pittsburgh, Pa.: Research Bureau for Retail Training, University of Pittsburgh, 1949. Pp. 48. * (PA 25:3449)
16. GLASER, ROBERT. "A Methodological Analysis of the Inconsistency of Response to Test Items." *Ed & Psychol Meas* 9:727–39 w '49. * (PA 26:2747)
17. KNAUFT, EDWIN B. "A Selection Battery for Bake Shop Managers." *J Appl Psychol* 33:304–15 Ag '49. * (PA 24:2850)
18. LINDZEY, GARDNER. "Remarks on the Use of the Won-

derlic Personnel Test as a 'Pre-Test.'" *J Clin Psychol* 5:100–2 Ja '49. * (PA 23:5522)
19. DOUB, BETTY ALLEN. "Better Clerks Can Be Hired With Tests." *Personnel J* 29:102–3 Jl–Ag '50. * (PA 25:2074)
20. DULSKY, STANLEY G., AND KROUT, MAURICE H. "Predicting Promotion Potential on the Basis of Psychological Tests." *Personnel Psychol* 3:345–51 au '50. * (PA 25:3452)
21. HAY, EDWARD N. "A Warm-Up Test." *Personnel Psychol* 3:221–3 su '50. * (PA 25:2078)
22. HOLMES, FRANK J. "Validity of Tests for Insurance Office Personnel." *Personnel Psychol* 3:57–69 sp '50. * (PA 24:5490)
23. HOLMES, FRANK J. "Validity of Tests for Insurance Office Personnel, II." *Personnel Psychol* 3:217–20 su '50. * (PA 25:2079)
24. MILLER, RICHARD B. "Reducing the Time Required for Testing Clerical Applicants." *Personnel J* 28:364–6 Mr '50. * (PA 24:4872)
25. WECHSLER, IRVING R. "The Personal Factor in Labor Mediation." *Personnel Psychol* 3:113–32 su '50. * (PA 25:2089)
26. BLAKEMORE, ARLINE. "Reducing Typing Costs With Aptitude Tests." *Personnel J* 30:20–4 My '51. * (PA 25:7749)
27. HAY, EDWARD N. "Mental Ability Tests in Clerical Selection." *J Appl Psychol* 35:250–1 Ag '51. * (PA 26:3071)
28. LANEY, ARTHUR R., JR. "Validity of Employment Tests for Gas-Appliance Service Personnel." *Personnel Psychol* 4:199–208 su '51. * (PA 26:1735)
29. MEYER, HERBERT H. "Factors Related to Success in the Human Relations Aspect of Work-Group Leadership." *Psychol Monogr* 65(3):1–29 '51. * (PA 25:7132)
30. AMERICAN GAS ASSOCIATION, PERSONNEL COMMITTEE. *Personnel Testing in the Gas Industry.* New York: the Association, January 1952. Pp. 10. *
31. HAY, EDWARD N. "Some Research Findings With the Wonderlic Personnel Test." *J Appl Psychol* 36:344–5 O '52. * (PA 27:5446)
32. JENNINGS, EUGENE EMERSON. "The Motivation Factor in Testing Supervisors." *J Appl Psychol* 37:168–9 Je '53. * (PA 28:3330)
33. SEASHORE, HAROLD G. "Validation of Clerical Testing in Banks." *Personnel Psychol* 6:45–56 sp '53. * (PA 28:1670)
34. "Validity Information Exchange, No. 7-094: D.O.T. Code 7-80.120, Beginner Mechanics." *Personnel Psychol* 7:572 w '54. *
35. BASS, BERNARD M.; KARSTENDIEK, BARBARA; MCCULLOUGH, GERALD; AND PRUITT, RAY C. "Validity Information Exchange, No. 7-024: D.O.T. Code 2-66.01, 2-66.11, 2-66.12, 2-66.23, Policemen and Detectives, Public Service." *Personnel Psychol* 7:159–60 sp '54. *
36. GROHSMEYER, FREDERICK A., JR. *Validation of Personnel Tests for a Paper Mill.* Doctor's thesis, Purdue University (Lafayette, Ind.), 1954. (DA 14:1796)
37. HANER, CHARLES F. "Wonderlic, Wesman P.C.T., and A.C.E.: A Comparison of Three Group Intelligence Tests." *Proc Iowa Acad Sci* 61:358–60 '54. * (PA 30:3460)
38. HAY, EDWARD N. "Comparative Validities in Clerical Testing." *J Appl Psychol* 38:299–301 O '54. * (PA 29:6351)
39. KNAUFT, EDWIN B. "Validity Information Exchange, No. 7-070: D.O.T. Code 0-72.21, Manager, Retail Food." *Personnel Psychol* 7:405–6 au '54. *
40. MCCARTY, JOHN J. "Validity Information Exchange, No. 7-077: D.O.T. Code 5-92.621, (Foreman II)." *Personnel Psychol* 7:420–1 au '54. *
41. MCCARTY, JOHN J.; WESTBERG, WILLIAM C.; AND FITZPATRICK, EUGENE D. "Validity Information Exchange, No. 7-091: D.O.T. Code 5-92.621, (Foreman II)." *Personnel Psychol* 7:568–9 w '54. *
42. RUSMORE, JAY, AND MARTIN, FRED. "Validity Information Exchange, No. 7-053: D.O.T. Code 1-37.34, Clerk-Typist." *Personnel Psychol* 7:289 su '54. *
43. SKARD, ØYVIND; AURSAND, INGER MARIE; AND BRAATEN, LEIF J. "Development and Application of Tests for University Students in Norway: A Report on Parts of a Research Project." *Psychol Monogr* 68(12):1–54 '54. * (PA 29:7971)
44. WESTBERG, WILLIAM C.; FITZPATRICK, EUGENE D.; AND MCCARTY, JOHN J. "Validity Information Exchange, No. 7-073: D.O.T. Code 1-37.32, Typist." *Personnel Psychol* 7:411–2 au '54. *
45. WESTBERG, WILLIAM C.; FITZPATRICK, EUGENE D.; AND MCCARTY, JOHN J. "Validity Information Exchange, No. 7-074: D.O.T. Code 1-37.32, Typist." *Personnel Psychol* 7:413 au '54. *
46. WESTBERG, WILLIAM C.; FITZPATRICK, EUGENE D.; AND MCCARTY, JOHN J. "Validity Information Exchange, No. 7-087: D.O.T. Code 1-37.32, Typist." *Personnel Psychol* 7:561–2 w '54. *
47. YOUNG, MARY B. *The Predictive Value of the Wonderlic Personnel Test and the Minnesota Clerical Test in the Selection of Clerical and Telephone Sales Workers.* Master's thesis, Boston University (Boston, Mass.), 1954.
48. BARNABAS, BENTLEY. "The Apt Performance Tests for Screening in Business Situations." *Trans Kans Acad Sci* 58:419–23 '55. *
49. BARNABAS, BENTLEY. "A Study of Speed-Power and Verbal-Quantitative Scores for the Personnel Test." *Trans Kans Acad Sci* 58:111–4 '55. *
50. CUOMO, SYLVIA, AND MEYER, HERBERT H. "Validity Information Exchange, No. 8-19: D.O.T. Code 6-78.632, Floor Assembler." *Personnel Psychol* 8:270 su '55. *
51. FITZPATRICK, EUGENE D., AND MCCARTY, JOHN J. "Validity Information Exchange, No. 8-35: D.O.T. Code 9-00.91, Assembler VII (Electrical Equipment)." *Personnel Psychol* 8:501–4 w '55. *
52. HARDING, F. D. "Validity Information Exchange, No. 8-23: D.O.T. Code 1-18.84, Collection Clerk." *Personnel Psychol* 8:378 au '55. *
53. HARRISON, ROSS; HUNT, WINSLOW; AND JACKSON, THEODORE A. "Profile of the Mechanical Engineer: 1, Ability." *Personnel Psychol* 8:219–34 su '55. * (PA 30:5414)
54. WEAVER, HERBERT B., AND BONEAU, C. A. "Equivalence of Forms of the Wonderlic Personnel Test: A Reliability Study." Abstract. *Am Psychol* 10:473 Ag '55. *
55. GOLDHOR, HERBERT. "Validity Information Exchange, No. 9-33: D.O.T. Code 1-20.01, Librarian Assistant." *Personnel Psychol* 9:378 au '56. *
56. KUSHMAR, HOWARD S., AND CANFIELD, ALBERT A. "Validity Information Exchange, No. 9-32: D.O.T. Code 1-18.63, Order Clerk-Clerical 11 (Telephone)." *Personnel Psychol* 9:375–7 au '56. *
57. MCCARTY, JOHN J., AND FITZPATRICK, EUGENE D. "Validity Information Exchange, No. 9-26: D.O.T. Code 5-92.621, (Foreman II)." *Personnel Psychol* 9:253 su '56. *
58. WALKER, FRANCIS C. "Normative Data Information Exchange, No. 3." *Personnel Psychol* 9:267 su '56. *
59. WEAVER, H. B., AND BONEAU, C. A. "Equivalence of Forms of the Wonderlic Personnel Test: A Study of Reliability and Interchangeability." *J Appl Psychol* 40:127–9 Ap '56. * (PA 31:6143)
60. MCCARTY, JOHN J. "Normative Data Information Exchange, No. 10-19." *Personnel Psychol* 10:241 su '57. *
61. MCCARTY, JOHN J. "Normative Data Information Exchange, No. 10-28." *Personnel Psychol* 10:362 au '57. *
62. MCCARTY, JOHN J. "Validity Information Exchange, No. 10-14: D.O.T. Code 1-33.01, Secretary." *Personnel Psychol* 10:202–3 su '57. *
63. MCCARTY, JOHN J. "Validity Information Exchange, No. 10-15: D.O.T. Code 1-33.01, Secretary." *Personnel Psychol* 10:204–5 su '57. *
64. ALBRIGHT, LEWIS E.; GLENNON, J. R.; AND SMITH, WALLACE J. "Normative Data Information Exchange, No. 11-8." *Personnel Psychol* 11:273 su '58. *
65. BARRETT, RICHARD S. "The Process of Predicting Job Performance." *Personnel Psychol* 11:39–57 sp '58. *
66. BRIDGMAN, C. S.; SPAETHE, M.; AND DIGNAN, F. "Validity Information Exchange, No. 11-21: D.O.T. Code 8-09.11, Sliced-Bacon Scaler; 8-09.11, Sliced-Bacon Packer, II." *Personnel Psychol* 11:264–5 su '58. *
67. GLENNON, J. R.; SMITH, WALLACE J.; AND ALBRIGHT, LEWIS E. "Normative Data Information Exchange, No. 11-7." *Personnel Psychol* 11:272 su '58. *
68. PHILLIPS, JOHN C. "Normative Data Information Exchange, No. 11-9." *Personnel Psychol* 11:274 su '58. *

For reviews by H. E. Brogden, Charles D. Flory, and Irving Lorge, see 3:269.

INDIVIDUAL

[401]
*Benton Visual Retention Test, Revised Edition. Ages 8 and over; 1946–55; individual; Forms C, D, E ('55); $4.50 per set of test materials, 50 record blanks ('55), and manual ('55), postpaid; 5(10) minutes; Arthur L. Benton; distributed by Psychological Corporation. *

REFERENCES

1–3. See 4:360.
4. WHARTON, LYLE H. *Effect of Stress-Produced Anxiety on Rorschach, Draw-A-Person, and Visual Performance.* Doctor's thesis, State University of Iowa (Iowa City, Iowa), 1953. (DA 13:1268)
5. KOLSTOE, OLIVER P. "A Comparison of Mental Abilities of Bright and Dull Children of Comparable Mental Ages." *J Ed Psychol* 45:161–8 Mr '54. * (PA 29:2270)
6. LACHMANN, FRANK M. *Perceptual-Motor Development in Children Retarded in Reading Ability.* Doctor's thesis, Northwestern University (Evanston, Ill.), 1955. (DA 15:1900)
7. NASH, JOHN. "The Diagnosis of Brain Damage by Psychological Techniques: A Review of the Literature and Present Status." *B Maritime Psychol Assn* 4:32–46 '55. * (PA 30:8440)
8. WAHLER, H. J. "A Comparison of Reproduction Errors Made by Brain-Damaged and Control Patients on a Memory-For-Designs Test." *J Abn & Social Psychol* 52:251–5 Mr '56. * (PA 31:3571)

NELSON G. HANAWALT, *Professor of Psychology, Douglass College, Rutgers University, New Brunswick, New Jersey.*

The manual states that this is "a clinical and research instrument designed to assess memory, perception and visuomotor functions." This statement is somewhat misleading since the test is one of memory for designs, not of memory in general. Memory in general becomes more and more difficult to assess by any single method or material after the age of 6 years as witnessed by the decreasing intercorrelations of memory tests with increasing age up to the adult level. Also, it is difficult to see how this is a perceptual test, since there is no mechanism to separate memory and perception unless Administration C, which does not measure memory at all, is also given. There is a good possibility that this test (as well as other memory for designs tests) could be improved by using Administration C (copying the design) as the learning method and taking the measurement of error of memory from the copies rather than from the stimulus figures. This method would give a much better measure of what the subject saw (perception) as distinguished from what he remembered, and would assist greatly in separating these two functions from drawing and motor ability.

A number of criticisms of the first edition of this test, reported in *The Fourth Mental Measurements Yearbook,* have been met in the new edition. The test now has 10 designs in place of 7. Better standardization for a normal population is indicated, but not at all adequately described, in the manual. Unfortunately, much of the data one would wish to have at hand in considering a test is not in the manual. One is referred to the American Documentation Institute for such things as population description, number of subjects, sex differences, statistical methods, reliability of the test, and the correlation among the three different forms of the test. For instance, a correlation of about .7 is reported between scores on the test and intelligence, but no indication is given as to the number or character of cases or the kind of "standard intelligence scales" used.

The new error scoring system introduced in this edition appears to add little to the previous, and still used, "number correct" score. Wahler (*8*) has published an analysis of "error" scores, comparing normal and brain damaged cases. In none of the different types of error was there a significant difference of proportion in the two groups, although several types of error were suggestive for further study. Copying the designs in the learning period would help eliminate some of the problems encountered in this work, such as the difficulty of not knowing whether the subject saw the peripheral figures which he did not reproduce. Size differences of peripheral and central figures also appear to be a promising lead. Copying the designs in the learning period would help determine whether this was a perceptual or a memory factor. Rotational errors are still another promising lead, but the test as designed does not separate the perceptual from the memory factors. Obviously a bizarre drawing is an important bit of evidence. Having the subject draw the design in the learning period would enable one to tell whether the subject saw the bizarre figure in the stimulus or whether it was entirely a matter of memory. The delayed recall test which Benton promises for the future also would appear to be a good addition to the test. In short, it is possible that better distinction beween perceptual, memory, and motor factors would help make a more precise distinction between normal and brain damaged cases.

The author admits that the validity of the test for diagnosing brain injury (the real purpose of the test) is not well established in this difficult field. His claim that, if the appropriate cutoff is used, the test will pick out 40 to 50 per cent of the brain damaged cases and include only about 4 per cent of normals, is about the same as that made for other memory for design tests. This reviewer tried the test on a small sample of 22 delinquent youths at the New Jersey Diagnostic Center. The 9 female and 13 male subjects ranged in age from 8 to 18 years, with a median age of 12.5. Wechsler-Bellevue IQ's ranged from 72 to 124, with a median of 95.5. Only the new error scoring was used. When scores were equated for age and intelligence according to the tables in the manual, only one subject did better than expected, 6 were within normal expectation, 2 were questionable, 3 were suggestive of brain damage, and 10 gave strong indication of brain damage. There were no obviously bizarre responses. One might conclude from the distribution of scores alone that the sample was drawn from a brain damaged population. In fact, the distribution was almost identical with that for Benton's sample of 100 brain injured patients, of whom 43 per cent were reported to have scored borderline or normal and 57 per cent defective. In the reviewer's sample 41 per cent were borderline or normal and 59 per cent defective. Although the correlations were positive, he found no significant correlations of "good memory" with either IQ or reading test score. The scoring instructions were found to be adequate and clear.

It is quite possible that the above sample of delinquents had a higher percentage of brain damage than the normal population, but it was a sample of the usual type of delinquents whose Wechsler-Bellevue scores were available, and not a sample of neurological cases. Most of the subjects were below their expected reading level. The above study is not a criticism of Benton's test in particular, but rather a criticism of all tests of memory for design as being specifically related to brain damage. There is no indication at present that any of the psychological tests for brain damage can separate out the neurological factors from the general environmental-developmental factors in test performance for most subjects (7). Certain striking cases keep hope alive and this is as it should be.

The revised edition of the *Benton Visual Retention Test* is an improvement over the first edition, but it is still in an experimental stage. It is probably as good as any of the three or four tests of this type which are currently being used to diagnose brain damage.

For reviews by Ivan Norman Mensh, Joseph Newman, and William Schofield of the original edition, see 4:360; see 3:297 (1 excerpt).

[402]
★**Columbia Mental Maturity Scale.** Mental ages 3–12; 1954; 2 scores: MA, IQ; individual; 1 form; $34 per examiner's kit including 100 record blanks; $1.10 per 100 record blanks; $4.75 per carrying case; postage extra; (15–30) minutes; Bessie B. Burgemeister, Lucille Hollander Blum, and Irving Lorge; World Book Co. *

REFERENCES

1. STROTHER, C. R. "Evaluating the Intelligence of Children Handicapped by Cerebral Palsy." *Crippled Child* 23:82–3 '45.
2. MILLER, ELSA, AND ROSENFELD, G. B. "The Psychological Evaluation of Children With Cerebral Palsy and Its Implication in Treatment." *J Pediatrics* 41:613–21 '52.
3. MILL, CYRIL R., AND TURNER, CHARLES J. "The Measurement of Primary Mental Abilities by the Columbia Mental Maturity Scale." Abstract. *J Consult Psychol* 19:472 D '55. *
4. ROSENBLUM, JEROME. *The Intellectual Evaluation of the Cerebral Palsied With the Columbia Mental Maturity Scale.* Master's thesis, University of North Carolina (Chapel Hill, N.C.), 1955.
5. BARRATT, ERNEST S. "The Relationship of the Progressive Matrices (1938) and the Columbia Mental Maturity Scale to the WISC." *J Consult Psychol* 20:294–6 Ag '56. * (PA 31:7893)
6. CANTER, ARTHUR. "The Use of the Columbia Mental Maturity Scale With Cerebral Palsied Children." *Am J Mental Def* 60:843–51 Ap '56. * (PA 31:5019)
7. GUSLOFF, RICHARD F. *Comparability of Columbia Mental Maturity Scale Quotients.* Master's thesis, Illinois State Normal University (Normal, Ill.), 1956.
8. JOHNSON, G. ORVILLE; NEELY, JAMES H.; AND ALLING, ROGER L. "A Comparison of the 1937 Revision of the Stanford-Binet (Form L) and the Columbia Scale of Mental Maturity." *Excep Child* 22:155–7+ Ja '56. * (PA 31:3562)
9. LANTZ, BEATRICE, AND WOLF, RUTH. "The Columbia Mental Maturity Scale and the Stanford-Binet Test with Cerebral Palsied Children." *Calif J Ed Res* 7:183–5 S '56. * (PA 31:6521)
10. TAYLOR, EDWARD A. "The Columbia Mental Maturity Scale as a Screening Test for Special Classes." Abstract. *Calif J Ed Res* 7:131 My '56. *
11. MAY, W. THEODORE, AND PERRY, HAROLD W. "The Relationship Between the Stanford-Binet (Form L) Vocabulary and the Columbia Mental Maturity Scale in a Group of Mentally Retarded Children." *Am J Mental Def* 62:330–3 S '57. *
12. SHONTZ, FRANKLIN C. "Evaluation of Intellectual Potential in Hemiplegic Individuals." *J Clin Psychol* 13:267–9 Jl '57. *
13. COOPER, JAMES G. "Predicting School Achievement for Bilingual Pupils." *J Ed Psychol* 49:31–6 F '58. *

[403]
*****Detroit Tests of Learning Aptitude.** Ages 3 and over; 1935–55; 20 scores: pictorial absurdities, verbal absurdities, pictorial opposites, verbal opposites, motor speed and precision, auditory attention span (for unrelated words, for related syllables), oral commissions, social adjustment A, visual attention span (for objects, for letters), orientation, free association, memory for designs, number ability, social adjustment B, broken pictures, oral directions, likenesses and differences, total; individual; 1 form ('35); manual ('35); revised record booklet ('39); supplementary norms ('55); no data on reliability for part scores except for auditory attention span for unrelated words; $6.50 per set of test materials; $3.60 per 25 record booklets; postpaid; (60–95) minutes; Harry J. Baker and Bernice Leland; Public School Publishing Co. *

For a review by F. L. Wells, see 3:275; for reviews by Anne Anastasi and Henry Feinberg of an earlier edition, see 38:1058 (1 excerpt).

[404]
★**The Griffiths Mental Development Scale for Testing Babies From Birth to Two Years.** 1951–55; individual; 6 scores: locomotor, personal-social, hearing and speech, eye and hand, performance, total; 1 form ('54); revised record booklet ('55); tentative norms; test materials sold only to persons taking author's lecture course; 495s. fee for course and set of test materials; 20s. per manual ('54, see 2 below), postage extra; (20–40) minutes; Ruth Griffiths; the Author, Child Development Research Centre, 47 Hollycroft Ave., London, N.W. 3, England. *

REFERENCES

1. GRIFFITHS, R. "A New Approach to the Assessment of General Mental Development in Infancy," pp. 68–70. Abstract. In *Proceedings and Papers of the Twelfth International Congress of Psychology Held at the University of Edinburgh, July 23rd to 29th, 1948.* Edinburgh, Scotland: Oliver and Boyd Ltd., 1950. Pp. xxviii, 152. *
2. GRIFFITHS, RUTH. *The Abilities of Babies: A Study in Mental Measurement.* London: University of London Press Ltd., 1954. Pp. x, 229. * (PA 29:76)
3. GRIFFITHS, RUTH. "Testing the Very Young." Abstract. *B Brit Psychol Soc* (29):40–1 My '56. *

NANCY BAYLEY, *Chief, Section on Child Development, Laboratory of Psychology, National Institute of Mental Health, National Institutes of Health, Public Health Service,*

United States Department of Health, Education, and Welfare, Bethesda, Maryland.

This is a carefully considered, well worked out British scale in which the author has made use of other infant scales (mostly from the United States) as a basis for her first selections of items and their age placements. After the preliminary selections and fairly extensive pretesting and observation of infants, she grouped the tests into five scales: locomotor, personal-social, hearing and speech, eye and hand, and performance. Items were arranged in the order of increasing difficulty and selected in such a way that there are three for each week during the first year and two for each week during the second year. They are equally distributed into the five categories, with 31 items in each for the first year and 21 in each for the second. The scale thus contains a total of 260 items, 52 for each scale category.

In the final standardization sample, 571 infants were selected to give an occupational distribution of fathers similar to that used by Goodenough. The number of cases at each month ranged from 16 to 31. Sixty babies were given a second test after an average interval of 30 weeks (range, 7 to 70 weeks). By counting each item in the first year as one third of a week and in the second year as one half of a week, Griffiths obtains a cumulative point score that is a mental age, and from this computes a ratio IQ or "GQ" (general intelligence quotient). Because the standard deviations of these GQ's were so large during the first eight months, an adjustment was applied for these ages by adding 8 weeks to both the MA and CA before computing the IQ. By this procedure, the SD's of the GQ's at all ages are approximately 12 points, and the average SD for the total sample is 12.1 points. By an appropriate pro-rating of mental age units to items within each of the five categories, quotients for them may be derived in the same way. With an SD of just 12 points, the range of quotients is rather restricted: for the total population of 571 infants Griffiths found the scores to range "between a little over 60 and a little below 140." As a test of validity, the author gives the correlation between first and second test of 60 cases, which is .87. For this *r* there is no control either of the ages of the subjects or the time interval between tests.

In addition to detailed directions for giving and scoring the tests and some excellent recommendations about the general procedures, there are chapters concerned with interpretation of the test results, including "Profile Studies of Normal Infants," and "Differential Diagnosis of Mental Handicap in Special Cases." Although the author several times cautions against accepting as final, scores for a single test on the young infants, she is optimistic about the scores' general usefulness both in predicting later levels of intelligence and in the diagnostic use of the five category profiles. She does say, however, that more studies need to be made to test both general prediction and the reliability and validity of the profiles. She makes use of individual cases to illustrate points. Where changes occur on repeat tests, they are usually attributed to intervening therapy or other specific conditions. In fact, the predictive usefulness of both the general quotient and the category quotients cannot be known until more systematic studies have been made on test-retest comparisons.

The scale impresses the reviewer as a very good, well worked out test of the developmental status of English children. The number of cases studied at any one age seems small, but care is evident in the preliminary trials and means by which items were selected; and this has resulted in a clear stable progression of scores with age. The test should not be applied to children in other countries, however, without some necessary adaptations. Both test materials and the language and idiomatic phrasing of the test procedures are in many instances peculiarly English. Although there is no statement to this effect in the text of the book, those who have tried to buy the testing materials have been told that Dr. Griffiths will sell them only to persons who have been trained by her in their use.

[405]

*Intelligence Tests for Children. Ages 1.5–15; 1945–58; formerly called *Intelligence Tests for Young Children;* individual; 1 form ('53); no data on reliability; 8s. 6d. per manual (see 5 below); postage extra; 7s. 6d. per set of test materials; (30–45) minutes; C. W. Valentine; Methuen & Co. Ltd. *

REFERENCES

1-3. See 4:343.
4. VALENTINE, C. W. *Intelligence Tests for Children, Fifth Edition.* London: Methuen & Co., Ltd., 1953. Pp. xiii, 84. *
5. VALENTINE, C. W. *Intelligence Tests for Children, Sixth Edition.* London: Methuen & Co. Ltd., 1958. Pp. xiii, 87. *

ELIZABETH D. FRASER, *Lecturer in Psychology, University of Aberdeen, Aberdeen, Scotland.*

Although elaborate and expensive apparatus does not necessarily add to the value of a test, it does have one advantage, especially in the case of individual tests of intelligence: it tends to keep the test in the hands of people who are competent to administer it and to interpret the results correctly and with due caution. In this test, Valentine dispenses with all but the very minimum of apparatus and recommends the test for teachers and even for "the intelligent parent who knows nothing of intelligence tests." This could be unwise even if the content of the test were new. But Valentine has constructed the test largely from items appearing in other tests, some of which, e.g., the Terman-Merrill revision of the Binet Scale, are in constant use by psychologists. The widespread application of the Valentine test in the hands of untrained people might well invalidate the later work of more competent testers.

The test claims to cater to children from 1½ to 15 years of age. It follows the pattern of the Stanford-Binet in that it has a set of tasks (varying in number from 6 to 10) to be performed at each age level. Instructions are given concerning the administration of the tests, the scoring of items, and the calculation of IQ.

On the question of standardisation, however, very little information is given. Although the items are derived from other tests, some of them well standardised and validated, these items were originally given in a different context. Moreover, Valentine has altered the presentation and the scoring of many of them before incorporating them in his test. Ideally, each item and certainly each test as a whole should have been tried out on a large representative sample of children. In fact, the sample was neither very large nor possibly very representative of British children. It consisted of 414 children aged between four and eight, who "were nearly all in unselected Infant and Junior Schools, almost all in or near Birmingham, except for a group of about 25 who were in a rural area. Of the Birmingham Schools, one was in a poor district and provided about 175 of the children. (Thirteen decidedly subnormal children in this school were not included in the results.) Three schools were in suburban districts and provided about 65 children. The remainder of about 150 were in fairly average schools, about a score being in Nursery Schools." No tryout of the tests for children up to 15 (tests introduced in the third edition and extended in the present edition) is reported by Valentine, and no reliability figures are quoted for the test as a whole at any age.

To sum up, the reviewer doubts the wisdom of publishing tests of this kind designed for unskilled testers, yet using material similar to or identical with that found in other tests used routinely by trained people. Even if this objection were disallowed, much work on standardisation would have to be done before the tests could be recommended.

G. A. V. MORGAN, *Senior Psychologist, North Wales Child Guidance Clinics, Denbighshire, North Wales.*

This set of individual tests of ability is clearly a grandchild of the Binet family and has the advantages and defects of the original. Many items are in fact adapted from the Burt and Stanford revisions of the Binet. Nevertheless, it must be judged not as a new revision, but as a compendium of tests for practical use by teachers.

This scale is not likely to be acceptable to the educational psychologist as a substitute for the WISC or traditional Terman-Merrill. It may, however, meet a need one sometimes feels, in brief preliminary testing of the very young and dull child, for items linking the Gesell and Merrill-Palmer type of "developmental" assessments with the introductory items of a Binet scale. It seems simpler, though less systematic for this purpose, than the Cattell scale.

The tests are varied and interesting in content, with some ingenious new items. They sample the usual range of functions forming the composite "general ability" which is useful to the clinician despite its factorial complexity. Verbal bias is about as heavy as in the Terman-Merrill.

The great weakness of this scale is its standardization. Items adapted from existing Binet revisions have age placements agreeing with the originals for ages 3-6 to 9. Actual trials of items on children between 5 and 7 confirmed, on the whole, the appropriateness of placement. For tests for ages 1-6 to 3-0, the author correctly remarks that he cannot feel the same confidence. Here, items from Gesell, Merrill-Palmer, and Terman-Merrill scales follow their original age placement, but the new scaling has not been empirically checked. The scale is least trustworthy for ages 11 to 15. In extending the scale upward, the author has adapted several tests, Burt's and Ballard's verbal reasoning tests among them, but has reported no restandardization for these items. One cannot feel happy about their placement according to original findings since (*a*) the original standardizations are about 40 years old, with no guarantee that they were representative even then, and (*b*) the tests have been considerably modified, e.g., adapted from written to oral form.

Elsewhere, too, modifications have been made in items, but no evidence is given to show the effect on item placement or discrimination.

Whilst sympathizing with the difficulties of standardizing an individual scale widely, one must criticize the weaknesses of the tryout sample. Restricted to ages 5 to 8, it was drawn from a small number of schools in the single city of Birmingham. The standardization cannot be regarded as representative.

Unfortunately, no measure of the test's reliability is quoted. It should be possible to derive a Kuder-Richardson estimate from the standardization data. In the hands of an experienced tester, the reliability of score should be as high —at least between the ages of 3 and 11—as for the Stanford scales.

An excellent feature of the test is the inclusion of 10 items at each age level up to 3 and 8 at each age level from 3-6 to 8. This widens the sampling of items and should improve reliability. By using starred items forming 50 per cent of each group, one can quickly establish the child's approximate level before testing in detail.

Predictive validity of the scale must be presumed to be similar to that of mental age scales which it resembles.

Two points of policy adopted by the author appear controversial. He implies that testers may use material (e.g., pictures) *"similar"* to that described in the manual or construct their own material according to brief specifications. This seems to leave the way open to unnecessary variations in standard. Normative samples of correct and incorrect responses to items are not given on the grounds that (as in the Terman-Merrill manual) these are usually overelaborate and possibly indefensible. Omitting scoring samples certainly simplifies instructions, but it may open the door to personal interpretations by individuals, especially teachers, likely to vary widely in testing experience and skill.

From the practical point of view, one would recommend that the test materials requiring manipulation be stronger (thick cardboard or thin plywood). The present ones are flimsy. It would also be more convenient if envelopes containing test material were assembled in a looseleaf booklet similar to that of the Terman-Merrill test.

Valentine, with his wide knowledge of the psychology of early childhood, has succeeded in producing a simple and varied scale for individual administration. It has marked weaknesses in standardization. Nevertheless, it should enable the skillful teacher to make a broadly correct assessment of the ability of pupils between 5 and 10 whilst observing them as individuals. Thus, it covers a period when group tests are inappropriate or can well be supplemented. The Valentine tests are not acceptable as a substitute for the educational psychologist's chief tools, but they may be a useful auxiliary for rapid "screening" of young children.

See 4:344 (2 excerpts), 4:345 (4 excerpts), and 3:283 (2 excerpts).

[406]

★**The Leiter Adult Intelligence Scale.** Adults; 1956–57; includes *The FR-CR Test, Partington's Pathways Test, The Leiter Adaptation of Arthur's Stencil Design Test,* and *The Leiter Adaptation of the Painted Cube Test;* 3 scores: language, nonlanguage, total; individual; 1 form ['56]; $29 per set of test materials; $5 per 100 record booklets ['57]; $2 per manual ['56]; postage extra; (40–60) minutes; Russell Graydon Leiter; C. H. Stoelting Co. *

REFERENCE

1. LEITER, RUSSELL GRAYDON. "The Leiter Adult Intelligence Scale." *Psychol Service Center J* 3:1–52 D '51. *

[407]

★**Leiter International Performance Scale: Arthur Adaptation.** Ages 2–12; 1952–55; individual; may be administered by pantomime; 1 form ['52]; test materials consist of Trays 1 and 2 (ages 2–12) of the *Leiter International Performance Scale;* manual ('52); $130 per set of test materials, 100 record blanks, carrying case, and manual; $5 per 100 record blanks ['55]; $4 per manual; postage extra; (30–60) minutes; Grace Arthur; C. H. Stoelting Co. * For references, see 408.

[408]

*****Leiter International Performance Scale.** Ages 2–18; 1936–52; individual; 1 form ('48); manual in 2 parts: Parts 1 ('48), 2 ('50, see 27 below); $187.50 per set of test materials, 100 record blanks, carrying case, and manual; $5 per 100 record blanks ('48); postage extra; specimen set not available; [30–60] minutes; Russell Graydon Leiter; C. H. Stoelting Co. *

REFERENCES

1–25. See 4:349.
26. LEITER, RUSSELL G. *Performance Tests for Measuring Native Intelligence.* Master's thesis, University of Southern California (Los Angeles, Calif.), 1929.
27. LEITER, RUSSELL GRAYDON. "Part II of the Manual for

the 1948 Revision of the Leiter International Performance Scale." *Psychol Service Center J* 2:259–343 D '50. *
28. ARNOLD, GWEN F. "A Technique for Measuring the Mental Ability of the Cerebral Palsied." *Psychol Service Center J* 3:171–8 S '51. *
29. BENSBERG, GERARD J., AND SLOAN, WILLIAM. "Performance of Brain-Injured Defectives on the Arthur Adaptation of the Leiter." *Psychol Service Center J* 3:181–4 S '51. *
30. ARTHUR, GRACE. *The Arthur Adaptation of the Leiter International Performance Scale.* Washington, D.C.: Psychological Service Center Press, 1952. Pp. viii, 73. *
31. BEVERLY, LOUISE, AND BENSBERG, GERARD J. "A Comparison of the Leiter, the Cornell-Coxe and Stanford-Binet With Mental Defectives." *Am J Mental Def* 57:89–91 Jl '52. * (*PA* 27:3620)
32. TATE, MIRIAM E. "The Influence of Cultural Factors on the Leiter International Performance Scale." *J Abn & Social Psychol* 47:497–501 Ap '52. * (*PA* 27:2763)
33. EVANS, MILDRED L. *A Comparison of the Performance of Mentally Defective Children on the Leiter International Performance Scale and the Stanford-Binet.* Master's thesis, Pennsylvania State University (State College, Pa.), 1954.
34. BURNS, PEARL PRATT. *The Value of the Leiter Scale in Testing Mexican-American Children.* Master's thesis, University of Southern California (Los Angeles, Calif.), 1955.
35. ORGEL, ARTHUR R., AND DREGER, RALPH MASON. "A Comparative Study of the Arthur-Leiter and Stanford-Binet Intelligence Scales." *J Genetic Psychol* 86:359–65 Je '55. * (*PA* 30:6907)
36. BIRCH, JANE R., AND BIRCH, JACK W. "Predicting School Achievement in Young Deaf Children." *Am Ann Deaf* 101:348–52 S '56. * (*PA* 31:6634)
37. GALLAGHER, JAMES J.; BENOIT, E. PAUL; AND BOYD, HERBERT F. "Measures of Intelligence in Brain Damaged Children." *J Clin Psychol* 12:69–72 Ja '56. * (*PA* 30:5093)
38. PEISNER, EARL FREDERICK. *The Validity of the Leiter International Performance Scale in Measuring the Intelligence of Selected Superior Children.* Doctor's thesis, Oregon State College (Corvallis, Ore.), 1956.
39. SHARP, HEBER C. "A Comparison of Slow Learner's Scores on Three Individual Intelligence Scales." *J Clin Psychol* 13:372–4 O '57. *
40. ALPER, A. E. "A Comparison of the Wechsler Intelligence Scale for Children and the Arthur Adaptation of the Leiter International Performance Scale With Mental Defectives." *Am J Mental Def* 63:312–6 S '58. *
41. COOPER, JAMES G. "Predicting School Achievement for Bilingual Pupils." *J Ed Psychol* 49:31–6 F '58. *
42. SHARP, HEBER C. "A Note on the Reliability of the Leiter International Performance Scale 1948 Revision." *J Consult Psychol* 22:320 Ag '58. *

For a review by Gwen F. Arnold, see 4:349 (1 excerpt); for a related review, see 40:B989.

[409]

*Nebraska Test of Learning Aptitude. Ages 4–10; 1941–55; standardized for both hearing and deaf children; individual; 1 form ('41); revised manual ('55); record blank ['41] with norms for deaf children, record blank ['55] with norms for hearing children; $52 per set of test materials including an aluminum carrying case, postage extra; (50–60) minutes; Marshall S. Hiskey; the Author, 5640 Baldwin, Lincoln, Neb. *

REFERENCES

1–3. See 3:289.
4. See 4:353.
5. LUDLOW, MARJORIE E. *A Comparison of the Nebraska Test of Learning Aptitude for Young Deaf Children and Form L of the Revised Stanford-Binet.* Master's thesis, Pennsylvania State College (State College, Pa.), 1942.
6. MACPHERSON, JANE GAERTNER. *A Comparison of Scores of Deaf and Hearing Children on the Hiskey Test of Learning Ability and on Performance Scales.* Master's thesis, Washington University (St. Louis, Mo.), 1945.
7. PERRY, JUNE A. *A Comparative Study of the Ontario and Nebraska Tests for the Deaf.* Master's thesis, Wisconsin State College (Milwaukee, Wis.), 1947.
8. DAVIS, KATHRYN A. *A Study of the Performance of Hearing Children and Deaf Children on the Nebraska Test of Learning Aptitude for Young Deaf Children.* Master's thesis, Southern Illinois University (Carbondale, Ill.), 1952.
9. ROSS, GRACE. "Testing Intelligence and Maturity of Deaf Children." *Excep Child* 20:23–4+ O '53. * (*PA* 28:4794)
10. WALSH, ROSALINE. *The Prognostic Value of the Merrill-Palmer Mental Tests and the Nebraska Test of Learning Aptitude for Pre-School Deaf Children.* Master's thesis, University of Buffalo (Buffalo, N.Y.), 1954.
11. HISKEY, MARSHALL S. "A Study of the Intelligence of Deaf and Hearing Children Through a Comparison of Performances on the Separate Standardizations of the Nebraska Test of Learning Aptitude." *Am Ann Deaf* 101:329–39 S '56. * (*PA* 31:6544)
12. HISKEY, MARSHALL S. "Norms for Children With Hearing for the Nebraska Test of Learning Aptitude." *J Ed Res* 51:137–42 O '57. *

WILLIAM SLOAN, *Superintendent, State Colony and Training School, Pineville, Louisiana.*

This is a revision of a test originally published in 1941. The primary additions are instructions and norms for hearing children. Also, the materials have been somewhat streamlined and are not so bulky. There are still 11 types of tests using 124 individual parts. However, they fit compactly into an easily carried case.

Present norms on deaf children are apparently based on the 1941 data. The test was standardized on 466 deaf children from ages 4 to 10. Except for the four year group (10 children), the number at each age ranged from 42 to 117. All the subjects were residents of schools for the deaf in several midwestern states. With few exceptions all the children in each school who fell within the ages 4 to 10 were included in the sample. Since the norms were obtained on institutionalized deaf children, the question must be raised concerning the possible deviation in intelligence of this sample from the total population. No data on this point are included. An item analysis yields correlations ranging from .63 to .84 for each group of items with the entire scale, i.e., part-whole correlations. Split-half reliability is reported as .96.

Validity is based mainly upon per cent passing at varying ages. For the deaf, no outside criterion is used. The author's reluctance to use "mental age" is understandable, since he feels this may lead to false comparisons with Binet MA's. However, his calling the score on this test a "learning age" is less clear since no evidence is adduced which would indicate a meaningful relationship to any of a variety of "learning" tasks. This is in spite of his assertion that the items involve tasks similar to those which a deaf child must perform in school. Curiously enough, a correlation of .829 between Nebraska and Binet scores on 380 hearing children is reported. Hiskey says in the manual, "If one accepts the Stanford-Binet as a useable criterion, this correlation is evidence of high validity and indicates that the *Nebraska Test of Learning Aptitude* can be used with confidence as a measure of intelligence."

The total score on the test is the median of the scores on the subtests taken. This has some advantages. Chance successes and failures, or accidental "spoiling" of an item will not invalidate the whole test. Also, special disabilities (e.g., motor disorders) are not unduly penalized if a few items are omitted. The instructions for pantomime administration are thorough. A few practice sessions will make the test relatively easy to administer for the experienced psychometrician. Abbreviated versions of the test are described but are not recommended if the entire scale can be given. Since a median score is used, the fewer the number of items on which it is based, the greater the possibility of errors. Separate directions and norms for hearing children are included along with an easily used record blank and simple instructions for obtaining the median "learning age." The materials are colorful and attractive to children and have much of the flavor of a game.

This test is a useful addition to the clinician's tools but more evidence needs to be forthcoming on its relation to other tests used with deaf children, such as the Arthur, Ontario, Chicago Non-Verbal, etc. Also, the question of "mental age" or "learning age" should be resolved on the basis of experimental evidence. In the meantime, it is felt to be a valuable instrument in shedding light on children with special problems, e.g., hearing, motor disability, speech defects, foreign language, or other communication problems.

For a review by Mildred C. Templin of an earlier edition, see 4:353.

[410]

★**Non-Verbal Intelligence Tests for Deaf and Hearing Subjects.** Ages 3–16; 1939–58; 2 forms ('58, Scales P, Q); $80 (572s.) per set of testing materials, manual, and 100 scoring forms; $3.50 (26s.) per manual ('58); $1.50 (10s.) per 100 scoring forms; postage extra; Dutch and German editions available; (45) minutes; J. Th. Snijders and N. Snijders-Oomen; J. B. Wolters, Groningen, Holland. *

[411]

The Northwestern Intelligence Tests: For Measuring Adaptation to the Physical and Social Environment. Ages 13–36 weeks; 1943–51; revision of *Gilliland-Shotwell Intelligence Scale* ('43) by A. R. Gilliland and Anna M. Shotwell; individual; 1 form (labeled Test B); Test A (ages 4–12 weeks) is out of print; $2.80 per set of 35 record blanks ('51) and manual ('51); 40¢ per specimen set; postage extra; (20–30) minutes; A. R. Gilliland; Houghton Mifflin Co. *

NANCY BAYLEY, *Chief, Section on Child Development, Laboratory of Psychology, National Institute of Mental Health, National Institutes of Health, Public Health Service, United States Department of Health, Education, and Welfare, Bethesda, Maryland.*

Each of these tests contains 40 items, arranged approximately in order of difficulty. The items cover, in general, the same behaviors that are to be found in other tests of infant development, but they utilize slightly different test materials and criteria for passing or failing. There is a strong component of motor coordinations, ranging from degrees of finger-thumb opposition to sitting and crawling. There are tests of visual and auditory reactivity, vocalizations, and of social responsiveness, as tested by interactions with adults. Some items would be classed as adaptive.

Although there are some interesting items that have not been included in other scales (e.g., "feels cardboard" and "moves head in flight movement" from cotton held against nose), the directions for giving and scoring are often ambiguous and difficult to follow.

The standardization was made on a large sample, 1100 infants for Test A and 214 for Test B. But over half of the first sample was composed of infants in institutions. The Test B sample is more in line with accepted usage, though it still includes a proportionately large number (36 of 214) of institutional infants. Until we have better information about the environmental effects of institutions on the development of infants, the scores of such infants are not appropriate for setting up norms.

Computation of the IQ appears to be based on a rule of thumb method that results in a normal distribution of IQ's with mean of 100, SD 14. The derivation of this method is not given.

Split-half reliability for Test A, corrected by the Spearman-Brown formula, is .84. Some validation was attempted for the scale but it is not described except to say that "in general a close agreement has been found" with a few Cattell and Stanford-Binet tests. A mean difference of 3.8 IQ points was found between Test A and these other tests, but the ages at testing and the numbers tested are not given. The Test B population is described as having a mean IQ of 100, SD 16.

Since Gilliland's death there apparently has been nothing further done with the test standardization. The printed forms still give the author as a source for securing test equipment.

The test, as it stands, may be used as a basis for further standardization or research, but it does not seem to this reviewer to be in a form that can be recommended for general application.

For a review by Mildred C. Templin, *see 4:354 (1 excerpt).*

[412]

*The Porteus Maze Test. Ages 3 and over; 1914–55; individual; 2 scores: quantitative, qualitative; 1 form; 3 editions and 1 supplement; Stanley D. Porteus. *

a) VINELAND REVISION. Ages 3 and over; 1914–21; 1 form ('21); 13 mazes: years 3–12, 14, adult 1, 2; manual ['21]; $11 per set of manual and 100 mazes of any one level; 90¢ per 100 copies of any one maze; postage extra; (15–60) minutes; C. H. Stoelting Co.

b) VINELAND REVISION: NEW SERIES. Ages 3 and over; 1914–50; 1 form ('33); 12 mazes: years 3–12, 14, adult 1; $11.50 per set of 100 copies of each maze; $4.10 per manual ('50, see 50 below); $1.15 per 100 mazes of any one level; (15–60) minutes; Psychological Corporation.

c) PORTEUS MAZE EXTENSION. Ages 14 and over; 1953–55; for use only as a supplement to the *Vineland Revision: New Series*; 1 form ('53); 8 mazes: years 7–12, 14, adult; no adult norms; $7.75 per set of 100 copies of each maze; $2.10 per manual ('55, see 74 below); $1.15 per 100 mazes of any one level; (25) minutes; Psychological Corporation.

d) BRITISH EDITION. Ages 3 and over; 1914–52; 1 form ('52, same as the *Vineland Revision: New Series* copyrighted in 1933 except for format); 12 mazes: years 3–12, 14, adult 1; 5s. per 100 mazes of any one level; 5s. per 100 score sheets ('52); 6s. per manual ('52); postage extra; [15–60] minutes; George G. Harrap & Co. Ltd. *

REFERENCES

1–56. See 4:356.
57. JARRETT, R. FITZROY. "Some Observations on Social Capacity: Application of the Porteus Maze Tests to 100 Borstal Lads." *Lancet* 211:1059–60 N 20 '26. *
58. MCDONALD, JANE REGINA. *A Comparative Study of Deaf Children by Means of the Kohs Block Designs and Porteus Maze.* Master's thesis, Ohio State University (Columbus, Ohio), 1931.
59. GRAJALES, M. C. *Porteus' Qualitative Maze Test as a Measure of Delinquency.* Master's thesis, Fordham University (New York, N.Y.), 1945.
60. ARNOLD, GWEN F. "A Technique for Measuring the Mental Ability of the Cerebral Palsied." *Psychol Service Center J* 3:171–8 S '51. *
61. FOULDS, G. A. "Temperamental Differences in Maze Performance: Part II, The Effect of Distraction and of Electroconvulsive Therapy on Psychomotor Retardation." *Brit J Psychol, Gen Sect* 43:33–41 F '52. * (*PA* 26:7159)
62. DOCTER, RICHARD FLOYD. *Delinquent vs. Non-Delinquent Performance on the Porteus Qualitative Maze Test.* Master's thesis, Stanford University (Stanford, Calif.), 1952.
63. MYATT, MARY FRANCES. *A Study of the Relationship Between Motivation and Test Performance of Patients in a Rehabilitation Ward.* Doctor's thesis, University of Minnesota (Minneapolis, Minn.), 1952. (*DA* 12:339)
64. O'CONNOR, N. "The Prediction of Psychological Stability and Anxiety-Aggressiveness From a Battery of Tests Administered to a Group of High Grade Male Mental Defectives." *J General Psychol* 46:3–17 Ja '52. * (*PA* 27:2055)
65. PORTEUS, S. D. *The Porteus Maze Test Manual.* London: George G. Harrap & Co., Ltd., 1952. Pp. 64. *
66. PORTEUS, S. D. "A Survey of Recent Results Obtained With the Porteus Maze Test." *Brit J Ed Psychol* 22:180–8 N '52. * (*PA* 27:5158)
67. SYDOW, DONALD WAYNE. *A Psychometric Differentiation Between Functional Psychotics and Non-Psychotics With Organic Brain Damage.* Doctor's thesis, University of Minnesota (Minneapolis, Minn.), 1953. (*DA* 13:1267)
68. DOCTER, RICHARD F., AND WINDER, C. L. "Delinquent vs. Nondelinquent Performance on the Porteus Qualitative Maze Test." *J Consult Psychol* 18:71–3 F '54. * (*PA* 28:8865)
69. FOULDS, G. A. "Comment on Professor Porteus' Paper: 'Maze Test Qualitative Aspects.'" *Brit J Med Psychol* 27:252 pt 4 '54. *
70. PORTEUS, S. D. "Maze Test Qualitative Aspects." *Brit J Med Psychol* 27:72–9 pts 1 and 2 '54. * (*PA* 28:8730)
71. SATTER, GEORGE, AND MCGEE, EUGENE. "Retarded Adults Who Have Developed Beyond Expectation: Part I, Intellectual Functions." *Training Sch B* 51:43–55 My '54. * (*PA* 29:2662)
72. SMALL, KALMAN. *Planning as a Non-Intellective Component of Intelligent Behavior.* Doctor's thesis, Columbia University (New York, N.Y.), 1954. (*DA* 14:1814)
73. MINSKI, LOUIS, AND DESAI, MAHESH M. "Aspects of Personality in Peptic Ulcer Patients: A Comparison With Hysterics." *Brit J Med Psychol* 28:113–34 Je '55. * (*PA* 30:3268)
74. PORTEUS, STANLEY D. *The Maze Test: Recent Advances.* Palo Alto, Calif.: Pacific Books, 1955. Pp. 71. * (*PA* 30:1051)
75. SATTER, GEORGE. "Retarded Adults Who Have Developed Beyond Expectation: Part III, Further Analysis and Summary." *Training Sch B* 51:237–43 F '55. * (*PA* 29:7498)
76. BENNETT, HOWARD J. "The Shipley-Hartford Scale and the Porteus Maze Test as Measures of Functioning Intelligence." *J Clin Psychol* 12:190–1 Ap '56. * (*PA* 31:4669)
77. PORTEUS, S. D. "Porteus Maze Test Developments." *Percept & Motor Skills* 6:135–42 Je '56. *
78. PURCELL, KENNETH. "A Note on Porteus Maze and Wechsler-Bellevue Scores as Related to Antisocial Behavior." *J Consult Psychol* 20:361–4 O '56. * (*PA* 31:7960)
79. STOTSKY, BERNARD A.; SACKS, JOSEPH M.; AND DASTON, PAUL G. "Predicting the Work Performance of Psychiatric Aides by Psychological Tests." *J Counsel Psychol* 3:193–9 fall '56. * (*PA* 31:8251)
80. AARONSON, BERNARD S. "The Porteus Mazes and Bender Gestalt Recall." *J Clin Psychol* 13:186–7 Ap '57. * (*PA* 32:2882)
81. FOOKS, GILBERT, AND THOMAS, ROSS R. "Differential Qualitative Performance of Delinquents on the Porteus Maze." *J Consult Psychol* 21:351–3 Ag '57. *
82. PORTEUS, S. D. "Maze Test Reactions After Chlorpromazine." *J Consult Psychol* 21:15–21 F '57. * (*PA* 32:735)
83. PORTEUS, S. D., AND BARCLAY, JOHN E. "A Further Note on Chlorpromazine: Maze Reactions." *J Consult Psychol* 21:297–9 Ag '57. *
84. GIBBENS, T. C. N. "The Porteus Maze Test and Delinquency." *Brit J Ed Psychol* 28:209–16 N '58. *

For reviews by C. M. Louttit *and* Gladys C. Schwesinger, *see 4:356; for related reviews, see 4:357, 38:B453, and 36:B210.*

[413]

Revised Stanford-Binet Scale. Ages 2 and over; 1916–37; revision of *Stanford-Binet Scale* ('16); individual; Forms L ('37), M ('37); manual ('37); $22 (105s.) per set of test materials; $4.20 (12s. 6d.) per 35 (25) record booklets ('37) of either form; $2.10 (5s.) per 35 (25) abbreviated record booklets ('37) for either form; $4.50 (12s. 6d.) per manual; postage extra; (30–90) minutes; Lewis M. Terman and Maud A. Merrill; Houghton Mifflin Co. (English distributor: George G. Harrap & Co. Ltd.) *

REFERENCES

1–134. See 40:1420.
135–351. See 3:292.
352–493. See 4:358.
494. LUDLOW, MARJORIE E. *A Comparison of the Nebraska Test of Learning Aptitude for Young Deaf Children and Form L of the Revised Stanford-Binet.* Master's thesis, Pennsylvania State College (State College, Pa.), 1942.
495. EATTELL, ELEANOR A. *The Terman-Merrill Intelligence Scale in Testing Institutionalised Epileptics.* Master's thesis, University of London (London, England), 1945.
496. HIGHFIELD, MIRIAM E. *The Diagnostic Significance of the Terman-Merrill Scale.* Master's thesis, University of London (London, England), 1945.
497. RAY, JOSEPH BLAND. *An Analysis of the Differential Performance on the Stanford-Binet Scale, Form L, of Mental Defective and Normal Children.* Master's thesis, University of Oklahoma (Norman, Okla.), 1949.
498. CLARKE, F. R. *A Comparative Study of the WISC and Revised Stanford-Binet, Form L, in Relation to Scholastic Achievement on a Fifth Grade Population.* Master's thesis, Pennsylvania State University (State College, Pa.), 1950.
499. DEAN, DOUGLAS ARTHUR. *A Factor Analysis of the Stanford-Binet and SRA Primary Mental Abilities Battery at the First Grade Level.* Doctor's thesis, Pennsylvania State College (State College, Pa.), 1950.
500. PRICE, ARTHUR COOPER. *A Preliminary Study in Statistical Comparison of the Revised Stanford-Binet Intelligence Test Form L With the Wechsler Intelligence Scale for Children Using the Ten Year Age Level.* Master's thesis, University of Florida (Gainesville, Fla.), 1950.

501. SCOTT, GORDON R. *A Comparison Between the Wechsler Intelligence Scale for Children and the Revised Stanford-Binet Scales.* Master's thesis, Southern Methodist University (Dallas, Tex.), 1950.
502. WINTER, WILLIAM NELSON. *An Investigation of the Relationship Between Scatter on the Stanford-Binet Test and Adjustment to Society by Children of Average Intelligence.* Master's thesis, University of Maryland (College Park, Md.), 1950.
503. BIRCH, JACK WILLARD. *An Investigation of the Utility of Certain Short Forms of the Terman-Merrill Revision of the Stanford-Binet Tests of Intelligence.* Doctor's thesis, University of Pittsburgh (Pittsburgh, Pa.), 1951.
504. BUGDEN, C. W. *The Stanford-Binet and the Wechsler Intelligence Scale for Children: A Correlational Study.* Master's thesis, Dalhousie University (Halifax, N.S., Canada), 1951. Pp. 32. *
505. GLENN, ROBERT THOMAS. *A Comparison of Intelligence Quotients Derived by the Leiter International Performance Scale and the 1937 Stanford Revision of the Binet.* Master's thesis, University of Pittsburgh (Pittsburgh, Pa.), 1951.
506. PASTOVIC, JOHN J., AND GUTHRIE, GEORGE M. "Some Evidence on the Validity of the WISC." *J Consult Psychol* 15:385-6 O '51. * (PA 26:7008)
507. POWELL, JOAN A. *A Comparison of the Stanford-Binet (1937 Revision, Form L) and Wechsler Intelligence Scale for Children at Different Age and Intellectual Levels.* Master's thesis, University of British Columbia (Vancouver, B.C., Canada), 1951. Pp. 63. *
508. RAPAPORT, IRENE. *A Comparison of Performance on the Wechsler Intelligence Scale for Children and the Revised Stanford-Binet Scale.* Master's thesis, University of Pittsburgh (Pittsburgh, Pa.), 1951.
509. WAGNER, WINIFRED K. *A Comparison of Stanford-Binet Mental Ages and Scaled Scores on the Wechsler Intelligence Scale for Children for Fifty Bowling Green Pupils.* Master's thesis, Bowling Green State University (Bowling Green, Ohio), 1951.
510. "1951 Norms for Independent-School Populations on the Terman-Merrill Revision of the Stanford-Binet Scale." *Ed Rec B* 58:85-6 F '52. *
511. ALDERDICE, E. T., AND BUTLER, A. J. "An Analysis of the Performance of Mental Defectives on the Revised Stanford-Binet and the Wechsler-Bellevue Intelligence Scale." *Am J Mental Def* 56:608-14 Ja '52. * (PA 26:4872)
512. BERK, ROBERT L. "Coaching in an Institution for Defective Delinquents: An Evaluation by Means of the Critical Incident Technique." *Am J Mental Def* 56:615-21 Ja '52. *
513. BEVERLY, LOUISE, AND BENSBERG, GERARD J. "A Comparison of the Leiter, the Cornell-Coxe and Stanford-Binet With Mental Defectives." *Am J Mental Def* 57:89-91 Jl '52. * (PA 27:3620)
514. COHEN, BERTRAM D., AND COLLIER, MARY J. "A Note on the WISC and Other Tests of Children Six to Eight Years Old." *J Consult Psychol* 16:226-7 Je '52. * (PA 27:5145)
515. DENNY, E. C. "Stanford-Binet Testing and Re-Testing." *Yearb Nat Council Meas Used Ed* 9:37-41 '52. *
516. DUNSDON, M. I. *An Application of the Myers-Gifford Response Pattern Scoring Scheme to the Terman-Merrill Records of Children.* Doctor's thesis, University of London (London, England), 1952.
517. ELWOOD, MARY ISABEL. "Changes in Stanford-Binet IQ of Retarded Six-Year-Olds." *J Consult Psychol* 16:217-9 Je '52. * (PA 27:5233)
518. FARTHING, MADELINE. *A Factor Analysis of the Revised Stanford-Binet at Two Age Levels.* Doctor's thesis, University of California (Berkeley, Calif.), 1952.
519. FEIFEL, HERMAN. "An Analysis of the Word Definition Errors of Children." *J Psychol* 33:65-77 Ja '52. * (PA 26:6266)
520. JOHNSON, ELIZABETH Z. "Sex Differences and Variability in the Performance of Retarded Children on Raven, Binet and Arthur Tests." *J Clin Psychol* 8:298-301 Jl '52. * (PA 27:5981)
521. KURETH, GENEVIEVE; MUHR, JEAN P.; AND WEISGERBER, CHARLES A. "Some Data on the Validity of the Wechsler Intelligence Scale for Children." *Child Develop* 23:281-7 D '52. * (PA 28:954)
522. MANOLAKES, GEORGE, AND SHELDON, WILLIAM D. "A Comparison of the Grace Arthur Revised Form II, and the Stanford-Binet, Revised Form L." *Ed & Psychol Meas* 12:105-8 sp '52. * (PA 27:5886)
523. MUSSEN, PAUL; DEAN, SANFORD; AND ROSENBERG, MARGERY. "Some Further Evidence on the Validity of the WISC." *J Consult Psychol* 16:410-1 O '52. * (PA 27:5891)
524. RALEIGH, WILLIAM H. *A Study of the Relationships of Academic Achievement in Sixth Grade With the Wechsler Intelligence Scale for Children and Other Variables.* Doctor's thesis, Indiana University (Bloomington, Ind.), 1952.
525. RIGGS, MARGARET M., AND BURCHARD, KATHRYN A. "Intra-Scale Scatter for Two Kinds of Mentally Defective Children." *Training Sch B* 49:36-44 Mr '52. * (PA 27:523)
526. ROBERTS, J. A. FRASER, AND MELLONE, MARGARET A. "On the Adjustment of Terman-Merrill I.Q.'s to Secure Comparability at Different Ages." *Brit J Psychol, Stat Sect* 5:65-79 Je '52. * (PA 27:2759)
527. SACKS, ELINOR L. "Intelligence Scores as a Function of Experimentally Established Social Relationships Between Child and Examiner." *J Abn & Social Psychol* 47:354-8 Ap '52. * (PA 27:2761)
528. SANDERCOCK, MARIAN G., AND BUTLER, ALFRED J. "An Analysis of the Performance of Mental Defectives on the Wechsler Intelligence Scale for Children." *Am J Mental Def* 57:100-5 Jl '52. * (PA 27:3640)
529. STROMER, WALTER F. "An Adaptation of the Stanford-Binet Test of Intelligence, Form M, for Use by a Blind Examiner." Abstract. *J Colo-Wyo Acad Sci* 4:77 O '52. *
530. TATHAM, LOUISE JEANETTE. *Statistical Comparison of the Revised Stanford-Binet Intelligence Test—Form L With the Wechsler Intelligence Scale for Children Using the Six and One-Half Year Level.* Master's thesis, University of Florida (Gainesville, Fla.), 1952.
531. WARINNER, ELLEN M. *A Comparison of Test Performance of Dull Children on the Revised Stanford-Binet and the Wechsler-Intelligence Scale for Children.* Master's thesis, University of Chicago (Chicago, Ill.), 1952.
532. DUNCAN, JOHN O. "Correlation Between the Wechsler-Bellevue and Stanford-Binet Vocabulary Lists." *Med Tech B* 4:45-7 Mr-Ap '53. * (PA 28:4348)
533. DUNSDON, M. I. "A Comparison of Terman Merrill Scale Test Responses Among Large Samples of Normal Maladjusted and Backward Children." *J Mental Sci* 99:72031 O '53. * (PA 28:6004)
534. DUNSDON, M. I., AND ROBERTS, J. A. FRASER. "The Relation of the Terman-Merrill Vocabulary Test to Mental Age in a Sample of English Children." *Brit J Stat Psychol* 6:61-70 N '53. *
535. FITT, A. B. *The Stanford-Binet Scale: Its Suitability for New Zealand.* New Zealand Council for Educational Research, Studies in Education Series No. 14. Christchurch, New Zealand: Whitcombe & Tombs Ltd., 1953. Pp. 32. *
536. GIBSON, FREDERICK J. *Correlation Study of the 1937 Revision of the Stanford-Binet Scale, Form L, With the Performance Items of the Wechsler-Bellevue Intelligence Scale, Adult, Form I.* Master's thesis, Boston College (Chestnut Hill, Mass.), 1953.
537. HOLLAND, GLEN A. "A Comparison of the WISC and Stanford-Binet IQ's of Normal Children." *J Consult Psychol* 17:147-52 Ap '53. * (PA 28:2638)
538. JOHNSON, ELIZABETH Z. "Individual Patterns of Emotional Functioning in Children of Comparable I.Q.'s—Implications for Education." *Am J Mental Def* 57:681-6 Ap '53. * (PA 28:1187)
539. KURETH, GENEVIEVE. *Correlation of the Subtests of the Wechsler Intelligence Scale for Children With the Revised Stanford-Binet For Five and Six Year Olds.* Master's thesis, University of Detroit (Detroit, Mich.), 1953.
540. MCNEMAR, QUINN. "Note on Elwood's Study of IQ Changes." *J Consult Psychol* 17:153 Ap '53. * (PA 28:2653)
541. RAPPAPORT, SHELDON R. "Intellectual Deficit in Organics and Schizophrenics." *J Consult Psychol* 17:389-95 O '53. * (PA 28:6365)
542. SCARR, ELIZABETH H. "Changes in Terman-Merrill I.Q.s With Dull Children: A Test of the Roberts-Mellone Adjustments." *Brit J Stat Psychol* 6:71-6 N '53. * (PA 28:7548)
543. SIEVERS, DOROTHY J., AND NORMAN, RALPH D. "Some Suggestive Results in Psychometric Testing of the Cerebral Palsied With Gesell, Binet, and Wechsler Scales." *J Genetic Psychol* 82:69-90 Mr '53. * (PA 27:7974)
544. SLUTZKY, JACOB E.; JUSTMAN, JOSEPH; AND WRIGHTSTONE, J. WAYNE. "Screening Children for Placement in Special Classes for the Mentally Retarded: A Preliminary Report." *Am J Mental Def* 57:687-90 Ap '53. * (PA 28:1528)
545. TERMAN, LEWIS M., AND MERRILL, MAUD A. "1937 Stanford-Binet Scales," pp. 510-21. (PA 27:7798) In *Contributions Toward Medical Psychology: Theory and Psychodiagnostic Methods, Vol. II.* Edited by Arthur Weider. New York: Ronald Press Co., 1953. Pp. xi, 459-885. *
546. TRIGGS, FRANCES ORALIND, AND CARTEE, J. KEITH. "Pre-School Pupil Performance on the Stanford-Binet and the Wechsler Intelligence Scale for Children." *J Clin Psychol* 9:27-9 Ja '53. * (PA 27:7800)
547. BAKER, C. T.; NELSON, V. L.; AND SONTAG, L. W. "General Versus Specific Areas of Ability in IQ Change." Abstract. *Am Psychol* 9:325 Ag '54. *
548. BORUSZAK, RUBY J. *A Comparative Study to Determine the Correlation Between the IQ's of the Revised Stanford Binet Scale, Form L, and the IQ's of the Wechsler Intelligence Scale for Children.* Master's thesis, Wisconsin State College (Milwaukee, Wis.), 1954.
549. CURETON, EDWARD E. "Mental Age Equivalents for the Revised Stanford-Binet Vocabulary Test." *J Consult Psychol* 18:381-3 O '54. * (PA 29:5696)
550. DAVIDSON, JACK FREDERICK. *A Preliminary Study in Statistical Comparison of the Revised Stanford-Binet Intelligence Test Form L With the Wechsler Intelligence Scale for Children Using the Fourteen Year Level.* Master's thesis, University of Florida (Gainesville, Fla.), 1954.
551. EVANS, MILDRED L. *A Comparison of the Performance of Mentally Defective Children on the Leiter International Performance Scale and the Stanford-Binet.* Master's thesis, Pennsylvania State University (State College, Pa.), 1954.
552. GODFREY, L. LARUE. *The Stanford-Binet Intelligence Scale in Appraising Reading Readiness.* Master's thesis, Utah State Agricultural College (Logan, Utah), 1954.
553. JONES, LYLE V. "Primary Abilities in the Stanford-

Binet, Age 13." *J Genetic Psychol* 84:125–47 Mr '54. * (PA 28:8725)

554. KARDOS, M. SERAPHIA. *A Comparative Study of the Performance of Twelve-Year-Old Children on the WISC and the Revised Stanford-Binet, Form L, and the Relationship of Both to the California Achievement Tests.* Master's thesis, Marywood College (Scranton, Pa.), 1954.

555. KESTON, MORTON J., AND JIMENEZ, CARMINA. "A Study of the Performance on English and Spanish Editions of the Stanford-Binet Intelligence Test by Spanish-American Children." *J Genetic Psychol* 85:263–9 D '54. * (PA 29:7290)

556. LEHMANN, MARGARET M. *The Basis of Teacher's Choice Between Two Intelligence Tests in an Elementary School.* Master's thesis, Ohio University (Athens, Ohio), 1954.

557. MATYAS, R. P. *A Longitudinal Study of the Revised Stanford-Binet and the WISC.* Master's thesis, Pennsylvania State University (State College, Pa.), 1954.

558. MILLER, VELMA J. *A Critical Analysis of Standardized Vocabulary Tests to Determine Those Most Valid for Use With the Macmillan Readers.* Master's thesis, Bowling Green State University (Bowling Green, Ohio), 1954.

559. PAPANIA, NED. "A Qualitative Analysis of the Vocabulary Responses of Institutionalized, Mentally Retarded Children." *J Clin Psychol* 10:361–9 O '54. * (PA 29:4272)

560. RICHARDSON, ELIZABETH J., AND KOBLER, FRANK J. "Testing the Cerebral Palsied." *Except Child* 21:101–3+ D '54. * (PA 29:6108)

561. SATTER, GEORGE, AND MCGEE, EUGENE. "Retarded Adults Who Have Developed Beyond Expectation: Part I, Intellectual Functions." *Training Sch B* 51:43–55 My '54. * (PA 29:2662)

562. SHELDON, WILLIAM D., AND MANOLAKES, GEORGE. "A Comparison of the Stanford-Binet, Revised Form L, and the California Test of Mental Maturity (S-Form)." *J Ed Psychol* 45:499–504 D '54. * (PA 29:7318)

563. ARNOLD, FRANK C., AND WAGNER, WINIFRED K. "A Comparison of Wechsler Children's Scale and Stanford-Binet Scores for Eight- and Nine-Year Olds." *J Exp Ed* 24:91–4 S '55. * (PA 30:8121)

564. BAKER, CHARLES T.; SONTAG, LESTER W.; AND NELSON, VIRGINIA L. "Specific Ability in IQ Change." *J Consult Psychol* 19:307–10 Ag '55. * (PA 30:4169)

565. BIRCH, JACK W. "The Utility of Short Forms of the Stanford-Binet Tests of Intelligence With Mentally Retarded Children." *Am J Mental Def* 59:462–84 Ja '55. * (PA 29:7258)

566. BLIESMER, EMERY P. "A Comparison of Results Obtained With Various Types of Capacity Tests Used With Retarded Readers." *Yearb Nat Council Meas Used Ed* 12(pt 1): 60–2 '55. *

567. CALHOUN, FRANKLIN J. *The Florida State-Binet Intelligence Scale for the Physically Handicapped.* Doctor's thesis, Florida State University (Tallahassee, Fla.), 1955. (DA 15: 1254)

568. CROKE, KATHERINE. *A Comparative Study of the Revised Stanford-Binet Intelligence Scale for Children, and the Vineland Maturity Scale.* Master's thesis, Wisconsin State College (Milwaukee, Wis.), 1955.

569. DUNSDON, M. I. "The Application of Vocabulary Tests to a Large Sample of Children." Abstract. *B Brit Psychol Soc* (26):22 inset My '55. *

570. DUNSDON, M. I., AND ROBERTS, J. A. FRASER. "A Study of the Performance of 2,000 Children on Four Vocabulary Tests: I, Growth Curves and Sex Differences." *Brit J Stat Psychol* 8:3–15 My '55. * (PA 30:3363)

571. KATZ, ELIAS. "Can the Mental Abilities of the Cerebral Palsied be Measured?" *Calif J Ed Res* 6:3–8 Ja '55. * (PA 29:7766)

572. MCCULLOCH, THOMAS L.; RESWICK, JOSEPH; AND WEISSMANN, SERENA. "Studies of Word Learning in Mental Defectives: II, Relation to Scores on Digit Repetition, the Stanford-Binet, M, and the WISC Verbal Scale." *Am J Mental Def* 60: 140–3 Jl '55. * (PA 30:4797)

573. MACRAE, JOHN M. "A Comparison of Davis-Eells and Stanford-Binet Scores at Different Socio-Economic Levels." Abstract. *Calif J Ed Res* 6:133 My '55. *

574. MARQUART, DOROTHY I., AND BAILEY, LOIS L. "An Evaluation of the *Culture Free Test* of Intelligence." *J Genetic Psychol* 86:353–8 Je '55. * (PA 30:6905)

575. ORGEL, ARTHUR R., AND DREGER, RALPH MASON. "A Comparative Study of the Arthur-Leiter and Stanford-Binet Intelligence Scales." *J Genetic Psychol* 86:359–65 Je '55. * (PA 30:6907)

576. RICHARDS, B. W. "Intelligence Survey of a Mental Deficiency Institution." *Brit J Med Psychol* 28:267–70 pt 4 '55. *

577. SATTER, GEORGE. "Psychometric Scatter Among Mentally Retarded and Normal Children." *Training Sch B* 52:63–8 Je '55. * (PA 30:3078)

578. SMITH, WILLIAM L. *The Establishment of a Grade Reading Level by the Stanford-Binet Intelligence Test.* Master's thesis, Utah State Agricultural College (Logan, Utah), 1955.

579. SONTAG, L. W.; BAKER, CHARLES T.; AND NELSON, VIRGINIA L. "Personality as a Determinant of Binet Performance." *Inter-Am Congr Psychol* 1:291–7 '55. *

580. STACEY, CHALMERS L., AND CARLETON, FREDERICK O. "The Relationship Between Raven's Colored Progressive Matrices and Two Tests of General Intelligence." *J Clin Psychol* 11:84–5 Ja '55. * (PA 29:7321)

581. STACEY, CHALMERS L., AND GILL, MARIE R. "The Relationship Between Raven's Colored Progressive Matrices and Two Tests of General Intelligence for 175 Subnormal Adult Subjects." *J Clin Psychol* 11:86–7 Ja '55. * (PA 29:7322)

582. STANLEY, JULIAN C. "A Note Concerning Brown's 'On the Constancy of the I.Q.'" *J Ed Res* 48:545–7 Mr '55. * (PA 30:1062)

583. STANLEY, JULIAN C. "Statistical Analysis of Scores From Counterbalanced Tests." *J Exp Ed* 23:187–207 Mr '55. * (PA 30:1919)

584. WALTON, D. "The Validity and Interchangeability of Terman-Merrill and Matrices Test Data." *Brit J Ed Psychol* 25:190–4 N '55. * (PA 30:7233)

585. BLIESMER, EMERY P. "A Comparison of Results of Various Capacity Tests Used With Retarded Readers." *El Sch J* 56:400–2 My '56. * (PA 31:5140)

586. CURR, W., AND GOURLAY, N. "Differences Between Testers in Terman-Merrill Testing." *Brit J Stat Psychol* 9:75–81 N '56. *

587. ESHLEMAN, EDITH R. "Detroit Beginning First Grade Test Compared With Stanford Binet." *J Ed Res* 49:543–6 Mr '56. * (PA 31:5144)

588. GALLAGHER, JAMES J.; BENOIT, E. PAUL; AND BOYD, HERBERT F. "Measures of Intelligence in Brain Damaged Children." *J Clin Psychol* 12:69–72 Ja '56. * (PA 30:5093)

589. GEHMAN, ILA H., AND MATYAS, RUDOLPH P. "Stability of the WISC and Binet Tests." *J Consult Psychol* 20:150–2 Ap '56. * (PA 31:6082)

590. JONES, H. GWYNNE. "Comments on 'The Validity and Interchangeability of Terman-Merrill and Matrices Test Data' by D. Walton." *Brit J Ed Psychol* 26:141 Je '56. * (PA 31: 6086)

591. JOHNSON, G. ORVILLE; NEELY, JAMES H.; AND ALLING, ROGER L. "A Comparison of the 1937 Revision of the Stanford-Binet (Form L) and the Columbia Scale of Mental Maturity." *Excep Child* 22:155–7+ Ja '56. * (PA 31:3562)

592. KATZ, ELIAS. "The Pointing Scale Method: A Modification of the Stanford-Binet Procedure for Use With Cerebral Palsied Children." *Am J Mental Def* 60:838–42 Ap '56. * (PA 31:5029)

593. LANTZ, BEATRICE, AND WOLF, RUTH. "The Columbia Mental Maturity Scale and the Stanford-Binet Test With Cerebral Palsied Children." *Calif J Ed Res* 7:183–5 S '56. * (PA 31:6521)

594. LEVINSON, BORIS M. "Note on the Davis Eells Test of General Intelligence." *Psychol Rep* 2:242 S '56. * (PA 31:3048)

595. LUMSDEN, J. "Revised Stanford-Binet Norms." *Austral J Psychol* 8:174–9 D '56. * (PA 32:271)

596. O'CONNOR, N., AND VENABLES, P. H. "A Note on the Basal Level of Skin Conductance and Binet I.Q." *Brit J Psychol* 47:148–9 My '56. * (PA 31:4374)

597. SEDAL, V. S. *The Stanford-Binet With Nine to Ten Year Old Children Whose Knowledge of English Is Inadequate.* Master's thesis, University of Toronto (Toronto, Ont., Canada), 1956.

598. STRUHS, ISABEL. *The Relation Between the Raven Progressive Matrices Test and the Stanford-Binet in a Group of Gifted Children.* Master's thesis, Fordham University (New York, N.Y.), 1956.

599. WARBURTON, F. W. "The Roberts-Mellone Corrections for Terman-Merrill I.Q.s." Abstract. *B Brit Psychol Soc* (28): 71 Ja '56. *

600. WATERS, THOMAS J. "Qualitative Vocabulary Responses in Three Etiologies of Mental Defectives." *Training Sch B* 53: 151–6 O '56. * (PA 31:8274)

601. WOLF, WILLIAM CHARLES, JR. *The Relationship Between Intelligence and Reading Success of Selected Elementary School Children.* Master's thesis, Ohio University (Athens, Ohio), 1956.

602. BARRATT, ERNEST S., AND BAUMGARTEN, DORIS L. "The Relationship of the WISC and Stanford-Binet to School Achievement." Abstract. *J Consult Psychol* 21:144 Ap '57. *

603. BECK, ELIZABETH J. *Item Analysis of Stanford-Binet Performance of Institutional Children in Comparison With the Standardization.* Master's thesis, Fordham University (New York, N.Y.), 1957.

604. DUNSDON, M. I., AND ROBERTS, J. A. FRASER. "A Study of the Performance of 2,000 Children on Four Vocabulary Tests: II, Norms, With Some Observations on the Relative Variability of Boys and Girls." *Brit J Stat Psychol* 10:1–16 My '57. *

605. FROMM, ERIKA; HARTMAN, LENORE DUMAS; AND MARSCHAK, MARIAN. "Children's Intelligence Tests as a Measure of Dynamic Personality Functioning." *Am J Orthopsychiatry* 27: 134–44 Ja '57. * (PA 32:1621)

606. GOODEY, D. J. *The Diagnostic Uses of the Reading Test of the Stanford-Binet Intelligence Scale.* Master's thesis, Utah State University (Logan, Utah), 1957.

607. HARLOW, JUSTIN E., JR.; PRICE, ARTHUR COOPER; TATHAM, LOUISE J.; AND DAVIDSON, JACK F. "Preliminary Study of Comparison Between Wechsler Intelligence Scale for Children and Form L of Revised Stanford Binet Scale at Three Age Levels." *J Clin Psychol* 13:72–3 Ja '57. *

608. KENT, NORMA, AND DAVIS, D. RUSSELL. "Discipline in the Home and Intellectual Development." *Brit J Med Psychol* 30:27–33 pt 1 '57. * (PA 32:3997)

609. LEVINSON, BORIS M. "Re-Evaluation of the Revised Stanford-Binet Form L Vocabulary as a Test of Intelligence for the Kindergarten and Primary School Child." Abstract. *Am Psychol* 12:380 Jl '57. *

Revised Stanford-Binet Scale

610. LIVINGSTON, JEROME STANLEY. *An Evaluation of a Photographically Enlarged Form of the Revised Stanford-Binet Intelligence Scale for Use With the Partially Seeing Child.* Doctor's thesis, New York University (New York, N.Y.), 1957. (*DA* 18:1866)
611. MAY, W. THEODORE, AND PERRY, HAROLD W. "The Relationship Between the Stanford-Binet (Form L) Vocabulary and the Columbia Mental Maturity Scale in a Group of Mentally Retarded Children." *Am J Mental Def* 62:330–3 S '57. *
612. SHARP, HEBER C. "A Comparison of Slow Learner's Scores on Three Individual Intelligence Scales." *J Clin Psychol* 13:372–4 O '57. *
613. WALTON, D., AND BEGG, T. L. "Cognitive Changes in Low-Grade Defectives." *Am J Mental Def* 62:96–102 Jl '57. *
614. CLARKE, A. D. B. "The 1937 Revision of the Stanford-Binet Scale—A Critical Appraisal." *B Brit Psychol Soc* (35): 11–3 My '58. *
615. COLLMANN, R. D., AND NEWLYN, D. "Changes in Terman-Merrill IQs of Mentally Retarded Children." *Am J Mental Def* 63:307–11 S '58. *
616. HISKEY, MARSHALL S., AND SADNAVITCH, JOSEPH M. "Minimizing Exaggerated Changes in Binet Ratings of Retarded Children." *Excep Child* 25:16–20 S '58. *
617. KATZ, ELIAS. "The 'Pointing Modification' of the Revised Stanford-Binet Intelligence Scales, Forms L and M, Years II Through VI: A Report of Research in Progress." *Am J Mental Def* 62:698–707 Ja '58. *
618. LEVINSON, BORIS M. "Reevaluation of the Revised Stanford-Binet Scale, Form L Vocabulary as a Test of Intelligence for the Kindergarten and Primary School Child." *J Genetic Psychol* 93:237–48 D '58. *
619. LIVINGSTON, JEROME S. "Evaluation of Enlarged Test Form Used With the Partially Seeing." *Sight-Saving R* 28:37–9 sp '58. *
620. PORTWOOD, PETER F. "Progress Report on the Sheffield E.S.N. Study." Abstract. *B Brit Psychol Soc* 34:61 Ja '58. *

MARY R. HAWORTH, *Assistant Professor of Psychology, Michigan State University, East Lansing, Michigan.*

Twenty-one years elapsed between the appearance of the original Stanford-Binet scale in 1916 and the revision by Terman and Merrill in 1937. An equally long interval of time has now passed, making a further revision imperative. Some of the pictures and objects (e.g., woodburning stoves and steam engines) are so out of date as to unduly penalize all but the brighter child with an interest in historical oddities. The current TV and space conscious culture has "juggled" vocabulary items into new positions in the hierarchy of difficulty, so that a longer presentation is often necessary to secure the required sequence of failures. Sweeping postwar population shifts, the higher standard of living, and possible changes in the general educational level of the nation all suggest that the original normative data may not adequately represent the population today.

In spite of its old fashioned tinge and the healthy competition of another now widely used child test (*Wechsler Intelligence Scale for Children*), the Stanford-Binet continues to serve as the standard and generally accepted criterion against which other tests are validated. Most comparative studies of the WISC and the Stanford-Binet attest to the latter's greater discriminative value at both the higher and lower mental levels. It is still the best available instrument for adequately measuring the intellectual abilities of children below school age and of mentally defective children and adults with mental levels below six or seven years. The lowest possible IQ on the WISC is 46 and the lowest "mean test age" is five years, two months. This means that a mentally defective child of that level would have to be 11 years of age before the most minimal testing could be accomplished. The Stanford-Binet, on the other hand, will yield mental ages as low as two years. Consequently a discrimination can be made between custodial, trainable, and educable cases at a much earlier age.

With the WISC coming into more widespread use with children, certain advantages and disadvantages of the Stanford-Binet, as an age scale, should be pointed out. While the same intellectual functions may not be tapped at each age level, any individual child will have an opportunity to confront a suitable variety of tasks over the usual span of several year levels. The alternate form of the Stanford-Binet is a distinct advantage. The all-or-none method of scoring is essential to the Stanford-Binet's schema and is not only easier to master but also more objective than the varying degrees of credit allowed throughout the WISC. Nevertheless, valuable qualitative data may be overlooked when responses are not scored for different levels of success.

The length of administration for the Stanford-Binet varies widely and may put too great a strain on a child for the little additional information that may be gained in establishing an accurate upper limit. In the process, the child could conceivably be subjected to as many as 11 consecutive failures, while on a point scale his failures would be scattered throughout the test.

The fluctuation in the standard deviations of the Stanford-Binet at different age levels, with the consequent variation in the meaning of the IQ, is a concept not easily grasped by some users of the test. But for any individual child, rate of mental growth from test to retest, and the relationship of his own mental age to his own chronological age have very real meaning in terms of present expectations and educational placement quite irrespective of his relative position among his peers.

An age scale is necessarily postulated on the assumption of a fairly regular and progressive increase in mental growth. Recent reports of longitudinal studies [1] suggest that such regularity is no more to be expected for intellectual development than for gains in height or weight. This maturational phenomenon might not have been detected but for age scales serving as the yardsticks against which to measure each child's idiosyncratic mental growth pattern. Point scales will not readily yield discriminating data concerning the unevenness of development, since the performance of each child is measured against that of his age group in terms of a predetermined and uniform mean and standard deviation at each age level. To refer back to the raw scores achieved at successive ages by each child would be inadequate since there is no provision in a point scale for equal, or proportionate, increments of increase from year to year, either within each subtest or for the scale as a whole.

There are no separate verbal and performance scales on the Stanford-Binet, but short forms of either type can be derived at the lower age levels. At least four items not requiring speech from the subject can be located at each half-year or year level through the first six years. A somewhat shorter scale of items requiring no speech on the part of either the subject or the examiner can be used with the deaf. The blind can be tested through all age levels by combining verbal items from Forms L and M (Interim Hayes-Binet). Recently a "pointing scale" (592) has been extracted for use with cerebral palsied children which employs only items requiring the subject to point to the correct response.

The administration and scoring of the present form of the test would be greatly facilitated if each test item in the manual were followed by its scoring criteria. The rationale and qualitative aspects for all the items could then be placed in a separate section.

It is highly unlikely that the perfect intelligence test will ever be devised. In the meantime, testing must be done and evaluations must be made. Some variation of the Binet-type test will probably continue to be the tool that best meets this clinical need.

NORMAN D. SUNDBERG, *Director, University Child Guidance Clinic and Associate Professor*

[1] BAYLEY, NANCY. "Individual Patterns of Development." *Child Develop* 27:45–74 Mr '56.
CORNELL, ETHEL L., AND ARMSTRONG, CHARLES M. "Forms of Mental Growth Patterns Revealed by Reanalysis of the Harvard Growth Data." *Child Develop* 26:169–204 S '55.

of Psychology, University of Oregon, Eugene, Oregon.

The grand old test has had to bow to an upstart. There is no doubt that the *Wechsler Intelligence Scale for Children* has usurped much of the field of individual intelligence testing of children. However, there is a lot of kick in the old Stanford-Binet yet. The appearance of WISC has precipitated a number of studies comparing the two tests which lead to the following conclusions: (*a*) Correlations between WISC and Stanford-Binet range from the .60's to .90's. (*b*) The WISC Verbal Scale, as expected, correlates more highly with the Stanford-Binet than the Performance Scale. (*c*) WISC IQ's tend to run a few points lower than Stanford-Binet IQ's except at the lowest levels, and they do not disperse as widely. These findings may be caused partly by the fact that the Stanford-Binet mean was intentionally set a little above 100 to correct for the urban sampling bias; also, the WISC standard deviation was set at 15 whereas the average Stanford-Binet standard deviation is 16.4. The differences are larger than might be expected for these reasons, but still they are not large enough to alter most practical judgments. Both tests predict school achievement about equally well.

An informal survey of psychologists in several clinics and school systems leads the reviewer to hypothesize that the WISC is definitely much more popular than the Stanford-Binet. The WISC probably accounts for at least 75 per cent of the individual intelligence testing of children. It is almost exclusively used for children from grades 3–8 and above this age the adult Wechsler tests predominate. On the other hand, the Stanford-Binet is still preferred with (*a*) young children, i.e., preschoolers or first graders, (*b*) children suspected of being considerably retarded, and (*c*) very gifted children. Frequent complaints about the Stanford-Binet concern the outmoded items, the lack of a performance score, and the awkwardness of the nonserial item arrangement.

What about the Stanford-Binet in the future? It was 21 years between the 1916 and 1937 versions; at this writing 21 more years have gone by. Fortunately some of the deficiencies are being corrected. Through the kindness of Merrill, the reviewer has had the opportunity to learn more about Form L-M which will probably be published by the time this Yearbook comes off the press. It is not a new scale

Revised Stanford-Binet Scale

nor a restandardization: it is a combination of the best items from Forms L and M. These are the items which display all four of the following characteristics: a substantial correlation with the rest of the scale, an increase in per cent passing with increasing age, proper location, and no discernible effect from cultural changes. Two thirds of these items are in the present Form L. Item modification has been kept to a minimum. The vocabulary has been rearranged in order of difficulty as determined by results on more than 5,000 cases tested in the 1950's, such words as "Mars" and "juggler," for example, now coming earlier in the test. IQ tables will incorporate corrections for inequalities in standard deviations at different ages. These changes will meet several of the criticisms of the test. Many psychologists will see it as unfortunate that the serial order of presentation of items could not have been instituted more broadly, thereby enhancing the efficiency and ease of administration. Undoubtedly there will be criticisms of the reordering of items without a restandardization; further research will be needed to check whether these changes will affect norms. Desirable as a large scale revision of the test would have been, there is a great deal of value in the intention of this Form L-M: to bring the Stanford-Binet up to date while still keeping it equivalent to the 1937 form, thus preserving the basic meaning of the test over the years. If this goal is achieved, the new version will be especially valuable for use in long range follow-up studies of the future. The reviewer's guess is that this test, which reflects the genius of Terman, will be standing as a memorial to him for several more decades to come.

A word about the Stanford-Binet in relationship to the whole field of psychological assessment. It is undoubtedly true that there will continue to be a great need for general intelligence tests like the Stanford-Binet. However, such tests are becoming less and less the dominating figures they once were. The *Zeitgeist* calls on psychologists to help with the making of decisions on a wider and wider variety of situations. The purposes for which tests are used vary so much that validity is no longer the simple matter it was once thought to be. We often expect too much of any single measure. In any important decision we use a complex combination of information data. Perhaps the limitations of the Stanford-Binet and other tests stem more from our ignorance of criterion situations and decision making processes than from test construction per se. It is against the decision matrix of the school and the clinic that the Stanford-Binet must be evaluated. Individual studies in separate situations are woefully inadequate for grasping the larger meaning and usefulness of tests. It would seem appropriate for test publishers and professional organizations to take it as their responsibility to collect, collate, and distribute information on intelligence tests, as is being done with some interest and personality tests. This need is particularly important with regard to interpretation and application of tests. Test manuals should be issued from time to time which give much more attention to the "pay-off" end of testing, rather than emphasizing just the beginning.

For a review by Boyd R. McCandless, see 4:358; see 40:1420 (3 excerpts); for reviews by Francis N. Maxfield, J. W. M. Rothney, and F. L. Wells, see 38:1062; for related reviews, see B149, 3:293–4, 40:B1093, and 38:B497.

[414]

*Wechsler Adult Intelligence Scale. Ages 16 and over; 1939–55; revision of Form I of *Wechsler-Bellevue Intelligence Scale;* individual; 14 scores: verbal (information, comprehension, arithmetic, similarities, digit span, vocabulary), performance (digit symbol, picture completion, block design, picture arrangement, object assembly), total; 1 form ['55]; $21 per set of test materials, 25 record booklets ('55), and manual ('55); $1.70 per 25 record booklets; 80¢ per 25 supplementary [record] sheets ('55); $2.75 per manual; postpaid; (40–60) minutes; David Wechsler; Psychological Corporation. *

REFERENCES

1. DOPPELT, JEROME E., AND WALLACE, WIMBURN L. "The Performance of Older People on the Wechsler Adult Intelligence Scale." Abstract. *Am Psychol* 10:338–9 Ag '55. *
2. DOPPELT, JEROME E., AND WALLACE, WIMBURN L. "Standardization of the Wechsler Adult Intelligence Scale for Older Persons." *J Abn & Social Psychol* 51:312–30 S '55. * (PA 30:4320)
3. WESMAN, ALEXANDER G. "Standardizing an Individual Intelligence Test on Adults: Some Problems." *J Gerontol* 10:216–9 Ap '55. * (PA 30:1923)
4. ANASTASI, ANNE. "Age Changes in Adult Test Performance." *Psychol Rep* 2:509 D '56. * (PA 31:4016)
5. BALINSKY, BENJAMIN, AND SHAW, H. WESTCOTT. "The Contribution of the WAIS to a Management Appraisal Program." *Personnel Psychol* 9:207–9 su '56. * (PA 31:8949)
6. COHEN, JACOB. "A Comparative Factor Analysis of WAIS Performance for Four Age Groups Between Eighteen and Eighty." Abstract. *Am Psychol* 11:449 Ag '56. *
7. COLE, DAVID, AND WELEBA, LOIS. "Comparison Data on the Wechsler-Bellevue and the WAIS." *J Clin Psychol* 12:198–9 Ap '56. * (PA 31:4675)
8. DOPPELT, JEROME E. "Estimating the Full Scale Score on the Wechsler Adult Intelligence Scale From Scores on Four Subtests." *J Consult Psychol* 20:63–6 F '56. * (PA 31:3024)
9. HALL, JULIA C. "Two Degrees of Overt Psychiatric Disturbance and Differences Among Subtest Scores of the Wechsler Adult Intelligence Scale (WAIS)." Abstract. *Am Psychol* 11:357 Ag '56. *
10. JONES, H. GWYNNE. "The Evaluation of the Significance of Differences Between Scaled Scores on the WAIS: The Perpetuation of a Fallacy." *J Consult Psychol* 20:319–20 Ag '56. * (PA 31:7928)

11. ROBERTSON, J. P. S., AND BATCHELDOR, K. J. "Cultural Aspects of the Wechsler Adult Intelligence Scale in Relation to British Mental Patients." *J Mental Sci* 102:612–8 Jl '56. * (*PA* 31:7965)
12. BLACKBURN, HAROLD L., AND BENTON, ARTHUR L. "Revised Administration and Scoring of the Digit Span Test." *J Consult Psychol* 21:139–43 Ap '57. *
13. COHEN, JACOB. "A Factor-Analytically Based Rationale for the Wechsler Adult Intelligence Scale." *J Consult Psychol* 21:451–7 D '57. *
14. COHEN, JACOB. "The Factorial Structure of the WAIS Between Early Adulthood and Old Age." *J Consult Psychol* 21:283–90 Ag '57. *
15. DANA, RICHARD H. "A Comparison of Four Verbal Subtests on the Wechsler-Bellevue, Form I, and the WAIS." *J Clin Psychol* 13:70–1 Ja '57. *
16. EISDORFER, CARL; BUSSE, EWALD W.; COHEN, LOUIS D.; AND GREENBERG, GEORGE. "The WAIS Performance of a Piedmont Aged Sample." Abstract. *Am Psychol* 12:374–5 Jl '57. *
17. HALL, JULIA C. "Correlation of a Modified Form of Raven's Progressive Matrices (1938) With the Wechsler Adult Intelligence Scale." *J Consult Psychol* 21:23–6 F '57. * (*PA* 32:267)
18. HIMELSTEIN, PHILIP. "A Comment on the Use of the Abbreviated WAIS With Homeless Men." *Psychol Rep* 3:440 S '57. * (*PA* 32:4178)
19. HIMELSTEIN, PHILIP. "A Comparison of Two Methods of Estimating Full Scale IQ From an Abbreviated WAIS." *J Consult Psychol* 21:246 Je '57. *
20. HIMELSTEIN, PHILIP. "Evaluation of an Abbreviated WAIS in a Psychiatric Population." *J Clin Psychol* 13:68–9 Ja '57. *
21. HOOKER, EVELYN. "The Adjustment of the Male Overt Homosexual." *J Proj Tech* 21:18–31 Mr '57. * (*PA* 32:3083)
22. ISON, M. GAIL. "The Effect of 'Thorazine' on Wechsler Scores." *Am J Mental Def* 62:543–7 N '57. *
23. KARSON, SAMUEL; POOL, KENNETH B.; AND FREUD, SHELDON L. "The Effects of Scale and Practice on WAIS and W-B I Test Scores." *J Consult Psychol* 21:241–5 Je '57. *
24. LEVINSON, BORIS M. "The Socioeconomic Status, Intelligence, and Psychometric Pattern of Native-Born White Homeless Men." *J Genetic Psychol* 91:205–11 D '57. *
25. LEVINSON, BORIS M. "Use of the Abbreviated WAIS With Homeless Men." *Psychol Rep* 3:287 Je '57. * (*PA* 32:4189)
26. MCNEMAR, QUINN. "On WAIS Difference Scores." *J Consult Psychol* 21:239–40 Je '57. *
27. MAXWELL, EILEEN. "Validities of Abbreviated WAIS Scales." *J Consult Psychol* 21:121–6 Ap '57. *
28. NADLER, EUGENE B. "Prediction of the Sheltered Shop Work Performance of Individuals With Severe Physical Disability." *Personnel & Guid J* 36:95–8 O '57. *
29. OLIN, TOM D., AND REZNIKOFF, MARVIN. "The Use of Doppelt's Short Form of the Wechsler Adult Intelligence Scale With Psychiatric Patients." *J Consult Psychol* 21:27–8 F '57. * (*PA* 32:500)
30. STERNE, DAVID M. "A Note on the Use of Doppelt's Short Form of the WAIS With Psychiatric Patients." Abstract. *J Consult Psychol* 21:502 D '57. *
31. WIENER, GERALD. "The Effect of Distrust on Some Aspects of Intelligence Test Behavior." *J Consult Psychol* 21:127–30 Ap '57. *
32. DUNNETTE, MARVIN D., AND KIRCHNER, WAYNE K. "Validation of Psychological Tests in Industry." *Personnel Adm* 21:20–7 My–Je '58. *
33. FINK, STEPHEN L., AND SHONTZ, FRANKLIN C. "Inference of Intellectual Efficiency From the WAIS Vocabulary Subtest." *J Clin Psychol* 14:409–12 O '58. *
34. GRAHAM, E. E., AND KAMANO, D. "Reading Failure as a Factor in the WAIS Subtest Patterns of Youthful Offenders." *J Clin Psychol* 14:302–5 Jl '58. *
35. GRIFFITH, RICHARD M., AND YAMAHIRO, ROY S. "Reliability-Stability of Subtest Scatter on the Wechsler-Bellevue Intelligence Scales." *J Clin Psychol* 14:317–8 Jl '58. *
36. HOWELL, ROBERT J.; EVANS, LAVON; AND DOWNING, LESTER N. "A Comparison of Test Scores for the 16–17 Year Age Group of Navaho Indians With Standardized Norms for the Wechsler Adult Intelligence Scale (Arizona and New Mexico)." *J Social Psychol* 47:355–9 My '58. *
37. KASPER, SIDNEY. "Progressive Matrices (1938) and Emotional Disturbance." Abstract. *J Consult Psychol* 22:24 F '58. *
38. LEVINSON, BORIS M. "Cultural Pressure and WAIS Scatter in a Traditional Jewish Setting." *J Genetic Psychol* 93:277–86 D '58. *
39. LIGHT, MORTON L., AND CHAMBERS, WILLIAM R. "A Comparison of the Wechsler Adult Intelligence Scale and Wechsler-Bellevue II With Mental Defectives." *Am J Mental Def* 62:878–81 Mr '58. *
40. OLIN, TOM D. "The Use of Age-Scaled Scores on the Determination of IQ Equivalents on the Wechsler Adult Intelligence Scale." *Psychol Newsl* 9:154–9 Mr–Ap '58. *
41. WECHSLER, DAVID. *The Measurement and Appraisal of Adult Intelligence*, Fourth Edition. Baltimore, Md.: Williams & Wilkins Co., 1958. Pp. ix, 297. *
42. WHITMYRE, JOHN W., AND PISHKIN, VLADIMIR. "The Abbreviated Wechsler Adult Intelligence Scale in a Psychiatric Population." *J Clin Psychol* 14:189–91 Ap '58. *

Wechsler Adult Intelligence Scale

NANCY BAYLEY, *Chief, Section on Child Development, Laboratory of Psychology, National Institute of Mental Health, National Institutes of Health, Public Health Service, United States Department of Health, Education, and Welfare, Bethesda, Maryland.*

This is a revision and restandardization of Form I of the *Wechsler-Bellevue Intelligence Scale.* The Psychological Corporation has collaborated with Wechsler in carrying out a large scale testing of a nationwide sample of 1,700 adults selected to match the 1950 United States census. The sampling procedure for the principal sample took into account occupation, age, sex, education, urban-rural, geographic, and racial variables. The entire testing program appears to have been carried out with great care, not only for the sample tested but also for the testing procedures, including the use of experienced testers who were carefully supervised in order to insure that their testing procedures would be comparable. An additional sample of 475 older persons (persons 60 years of age and over) was also included in the testing.

The tests themselves have been changed primarily in the direction of adding more ceiling, thus increasing the range in scores of some of the subtests, and of clearing up ambiguities both in test items and in their scoring. There is evidence that the changes in the new form have been made on the basis of wide experience with the original scale, including the suggestions that have been made in the many published reports on its use.

The resulting scale is an all-round improvement of a good instrument. The reliabilities both of the subtests and the total scales have been improved, and the upper range of IQ's has been extended about 10 points. Thus the scale is more discriminating among the highly intelligent, as well as being a more generally satisfactory and reliable instrument.

It is interesting to note that in the WAIS the curve of intelligence by age is somewhat different than in the 1939 Wechsler-Bellevue. In the new scale the scores start lower at 16 years, gain their maximum a little later, and remain high from 20 to 34 years, with a more gradual decline with age after 34. These differences may be the result of both a generally improved instrument and a better standardization sample.

WILSON H. GUERTIN, *Clinical Psychologist. Veterans Administration Hospital, Knoxville, Iowa.*

While critically reviewing the new *Wechsler Adult Intelligence Scale* one might be struck by the absence of a brief, explicit statement as to what the test is designed to do. However, workers in mental measurement are so familiar with the Wechsler intelligence scales that it suffices to describe the present revision in terms of its differences from its noble ancestors.

Only a few readers will need the orientation that the WAIS is designed to be a broad-sampling, wide range of ability, individual test of adult intelligence. Norms are provided for ages from 16 to 75 and for IQ's ranging from 45 to 159 for the young adult.

Six verbal and five performance areas are sampled by subtests to provide a point-scale indication of intelligence. Raw scores on the various subtests are converted directly into standard scores in order to facilitate intercomparisons. Thus, the various subtests provide indices of impairment from sensory, motor, and other special disabilities. Missing subtest scores are easily prorated to provide full scale estimates of IQ when special disabilities make it desirable to omit some of the subtests. Brief forms of the test are easily obtained by giving a few subtests and prorating the ones omitted. Wechsler persists in asserting that subtest score patterns may provide useful diagnostic indicators.

The WAIS is a revision of the original *Wechsler-Bellevue Intelligence Scale*. Only the vocabulary subtest is entirely new. A few new items have been added to the other subtests. Troublesome and ambiguous items in the W-B have been replaced. All of the subtests except Digit Span have been lengthened slightly. However, the overall change in content is not great. Some changes in administration and scoring have been made. The spiral-bound, large-type manual of directions seems serviceable and convenient. The quality of the test material is comparable to that of earlier issues.

Wechsler reports a full scale reliability of .97. Tables in his new book show reliability for the WAIS subtests to be greater than those for the W-B on 9 of the 11 subtests. However, comparison of the coefficients of reliability is hazardous since they came from two samples.

Several small sample studies of agreement between the WAIS and the W-B are reported. Full scale scores seem to be significantly higher for the W-B by 3 or 4 IQ points. In the old age range the differences are likely to be greater. The differences are attributable to differences in the standardization samples used with the two tests. Wechsler, quite justifiably, places more confidence in the more adequate WAIS standardization.

Correlation between the WAIS and the *Revised Stanford-Binet Scale* was .85. Correlation with Raven's *Progressive Matrices* was .72. In the latest revision of Wechsler's book (*39*) there are no data showing the relation between the Wechsler scales and external criteria such as school success, although such data were included in the previous edition. Such criteria are weak and it would appear that Wechsler has come to depend upon the traditional acceptance of his instruments rather than external criteria of validity. Wechsler is not alone in thinking that the care taken in construction of a test and its underlying rationale are often the best evidence that it will be effective in measuring what it purports to measure.

Wechsler admits being unable to present convincing evidence for the effectiveness of his deterioration measures and for the diagnostic strength of subtest pattern analysis. Over the years the positive diagnostic studies have been repeatedly offset by the negative findings of other researchers. Wechsler's ideas for evaluating psychiatric pathology continue to be intriguing even though weakly supported by research. Arbitrary psychiatric diagnoses and classificatory systems as well as poor sampling techniques continue to plague us and obscure small but real systematic differences.

The WAIS standardization sample of 2,175 individuals is twice that used for the W-B. Furthermore, the careful selection of a stratified sample appears to have produced a sample quite representative of the American population. The variables controlled were age, sex, urban-rural, location, race, occupation, and education. This represents a marked improvement over the W-B standardization sampling. One is encouraged to accept these new norms unconditionally for general clinical application.

Factor analytic discussion of the WAIS is included in Wechsler's latest revision. It would appear that the factorial constitution of the subtests is quite simple. The major factors seem to be a verbal and a nonverbal factor. In addition, there is a memory factor.

The 577-item bibliography in Wechsler's book is testimony to the amount of research interest in the scales. The WAIS is still quite new but what has been demonstrated with the W-B should, in time, be demonstrated to hold true for the WAIS, also, since they differ so little from one another. The W-B has been viewed rather critically by a few writers but seldom, if ever, have they compared the instrument unfavorably with other adult intelligence measures.

The WAIS is a clear improvement over the earlier, well received Wechsler scales. For the time being, at least, the WAIS stands alone with very little competition. It can be expected to take its place as a paragon of intelligence tests and will serve as a criterion of validity for nearly all newly proposed measures of intelligence.

For reviews by Murray Aborn and William D. Altus of an earlier edition, see 4:361; for a review by Robert I. Watson, see 3:298; for a review by F. L. Wells, see 40:1429 (2 excerpts); for related reviews, see 4:362, 3:299–301, and 40:B1121.

[415]

Wechsler-Bellevue Intelligence Scale. Ages 10 and over; 1939–47; individual; 2 forms; $1.70 per 25 record booklets ('47) of either form; postpaid; (40–60) minutes; David Wechsler; Psychological Corporation. * For revised edition, see 414.
a) FORM 1. 1939–47; out of print except for record forms and some replacement parts.
b) FORM 2. 1946–47; catalog states that "Form 2 is the retest instrument for the WAIS as well as for Form 1"; 14 scores: verbal (general information, general comprehension, digit span, arithmetic, similarities, vocabulary), performance (picture arrangement, picture completion, block design, object assembly, digit symbol), total; $19 per set of test materials, 25 record booklets ('47), and manual ('46); $2.25 per manual.

REFERENCES

1–2. See 40:1429.
3–121. See 3:298.
122–371. See 4:361.
372. FISHBEIN, SILVIA. *An Evaluation of the Wechsler-Bellevue Intelligence Tests for Use on the College Level.* Master's thesis, Temple University (Philadelphia, Pa.), 1941.
373. GRAJALES, M. C. *Porteus' Qualitative Maze Test as a Measure of Delinquency.* Master's thesis, Fordham University (New York, N.Y.), 1945.
374. WHEATLEY, MABEL MARIE. *Primary Mental Abilities of Deaf Children.* Doctor's thesis, University of Maryland (College Park, Md.), 1947.
375. GOLDSTEIN, M. J. "Standardisation for South Africa of the Wechsler-Bellevue Adult Intelligence Scale." *B Nat Inst Personnel Res* 1:3–7 N '48. *
376. HANER, CHARLES F., AND WEBB, WILSE B. "Quantification of the Wechsler-Bellevue Vocabulary." *Proc Iowa Acad Sci* 55:323–8 '48. *
377. MEIER, LORAINE D. *A Critical Analysis of Scores, Accumulated From the Presentation of the Wechsler-Bellevue Intelligence Scale to Adolescent and Adult Deafened Individuals.* Master's thesis, Washington University (St. Louis, Mo.), 1948.
378. RAINE, LOIS MARGARET. *An Investigation of Changes in Performance Level With Repetition on the Wechsler-Bellevue Intelligence Scale.* Master's thesis, University of Colorado (Boulder, Colo.), 1948.
379. FOX, CHARLOTTE, AND BIRREN, JAMES E. "Some Factors Affecting Vocabulary Size in Later Maturity: Age, Education, and Length of Institutionalization." *J Gerontol* 4:19–26 Ja '49. *
380. HOWELL, ROBERT J. *An Analysis of the California Capacity and Wechsler Bellevue Intelligence Tests.* Master's thesis, University of Utah (Salt Lake City, Utah), 1949.
381. JUI, ALICE HONG-ZOEN. *The Use of Wechsler-Bellevue With the Hard of Hearing Pupils.* Master's thesis, MacMurray College for Women (Jacksonville, Ill.), 1949.
382. CARSE, DOROTHY. *A Study of the Relationships Between the Wechsler-Bellevue Intelligence Scale and the Kuder Preference Record-Personal.* Master's thesis, North Texas State College (Denton, Tex.), 1950.
383. CLARKE, F. R. *A Comparative Study of the WISC and Revised Stanford-Binet, Form L, in Relation to Scholastic Achievement on a Fifth Grade Population.* Master's thesis, Pennsylvania State University (State College, Pa.), 1950.
384. COHEN, EDWIN. "Is There Examiner Bias on the Wechsler-Bellevue?" *Proc Okla Acad Sci* 31:150–3 '50. * (*PA* 27:417)
385. HORLICK, REUBEN S. *The Relationships of Psychometric Test Scores to Personality Disorders.* Doctor's thesis, New York University (New York, N.Y.), 1950.
386. LEVINE, L. S. *Psychometric Patterns in Psychiatric Diagnosis.* Doctor's thesis, Stanford University (Stanford, Calif.), 1950.
387. O'DELL, PERRY L. *Psychometric Patterns of the Wechsler-Bellevue Intelligence Scale Subtests as an Indicator of Schizophrenic Syndromes.* Master's thesis, North Texas State College (Denton, Tex.), 1950.
388. SILVER, CHARLES E. *A Comparison of the Scores Made by College Reading Problem Cases on the California Short-form Test of Mental Maturity and Form I of the Wechsler-Bellevue Scales.* Master's thesis, Bowling Green State University (Bowling Green, Ohio), 1950.
389. SMYKAL, A., AND WILSON, M. O. "Wechsler-Bellevue Subtest Score Changes Resulting From Electric Convulsive Therapy." *Proc Okla Acad Sci* 31:148–9 '50. * (*PA* 27:589)
390. WITT, EUGENE LESTER, JR. *A Study of the Relation of Form Perception in Color on the Rorschach Ink Blot Test and Performance on the Wechsler-Bellevue Block Design Subtest.* Master's thesis, Southern Methodist University (Dallas, Tex.), 1950.
391. ALTUS, WILLIAM D. "The Relation of Intelligence to Adjustment." Abstract. *Am Psychol* 6:490 S '51. *
392. BOTWINICK, JACK, AND BIRREN, JAMES E. "Differential Decline in the Wechsler-Bellevue Subtests in the Senile Psychoses." *J Gerontol* 6:365–8 O '51. * (*PA* 26:4134)
393. EVERSON, RICHARD REESE. *Senescent Decline on the Wechsler-Bellevue in Relation to Organic Brain Damage, Schizophrenia, and Psychoneurosis.* Master's thesis, University of Pittsburgh (Pittsburgh, Pa.), 1951.
394. FOSTER, CHARLES. *W-B Data as Indices of Aptitude for Law and Engineering—A Contribution to Vocational Counseling.* Doctor's thesis, University of Southern California (Los Angeles, Calif.), 1951.
395. HODGSON, GERALD L. "The Psychometric Pattern of the Mexican Delinquent." Abstract. *Am Psychol* 6:499 S '51. *
396. KING, DORIS MARIE. *A Comparative Study of the Wechsler-Bellevue Scores of Negro and White Prison Inmates.* Master's thesis, Southern Methodist University (Dallas, Tex.), 1951.
397. KLONOFF, HARRY. *An Exploratory Study and Analysis of the Wechsler-Bellevue Intelligence Scale and the Raven Progressive-Matrices.* Master's thesis, University of Toronto (Toronto, Ont., Canada), 1951.
398. LEVINE, LOUIS S. "The Diagnostic Utility of Qualitative Responses to Wechsler-Bellevue Test Items." Abstract. *Am Psychol* 6:499–500 S '51. *
399. NEWTON, BERNAUR W.; ZIMMERMAN, IRLA LEE; SULLIVAN, ELLEN B.; DORCUS, ROY M.; STERNBERG, THOMAS H.; AND ZIMMERMAN, MURRAY C. "An Evaluation of the Psychological Processes of the Neurosyphilitic: II. The Wechsler-Bellevue Scale." Abstract. *Am Psychol* 6:500 S '51. *
400. OPPENHEIM, HENRY. *Diagnostic Limitations of the Adult Wechsler-Bellevue Intelligence Scale in Cerebral Pathology.* Master's thesis, University of North Carolina (Chapel Hill, N.C.), 1951.
401. POWELL, JOAN A. *A Comparison of the Stanford-Binet (1937 Revision, Form L) and Wechsler Intelligence Scale for Children at Different Age and Intellectual Levels.* Master's thesis, University of British Columbia (Vancouver, B.C., Canada), 1951.
402. REICH, H. *The Applicability of Regression Equations to the Bellevue Adult Scale in Diagnosis of Schizophrenia.* Master's thesis, Brooklyn College (Brooklyn, N.Y.), 1951.
403. SCHILLO, RICHARD J. *Wechsler-Bellevue Results of Normals and Neurotics With Obsessive-Compulsive Features.* Master's thesis, Catholic University of America (Washington, D.C.), 1951.
404. STEAD, LUCY SASSCER GORE. *A Comparative Study of Schizophrenic Signs on the Rorschach and the Wechsler-Bellevue.* Master's thesis, Stanford University (Stanford, Calif.), 1951.
405. WIGGINS, JACK G., JR. *A Comparative Study of the Performances of Prison Inmates on a Group and on an Individual Intelligence Test.* Master's thesis, Southern Methodist University (Dallas, Tex.), 1951.
406. ALDERDICE, E. T., AND BUTLER, A. J. "An Analysis of the Performance of Mental Defectives on the Revised Stanford-

Binet and the Wechsler-Bellevue Intelligence Scale." *Am J Mental Def* 56:608–14 Ja '52. * (*PA* 26:4872)

407. BERK, ROBERT L. "Coaching in an Institution for Defective Delinquents: An Evaluation by Means of the Critical Incident Technique." *Am J Mental Def* 56:615–21 Ja '52. *

408. BINKS, VIRGINIA M.; FOSTER, DESMOND V.; ADAMS, NICHOLAS A.; AND TRIGGS, FRANCES. "The Relationship of Reading Skills as Learned in Grades 4–College Freshman Years to Verbal and Performance Scores on an Individual Intelligence Test." Abstract. *Am Psychol* 7:376–7 Jl '52. *

409. BIRREN, JAMES E. "A Factorial Analysis of the Wechsler-Bellevue Scale Given to an Elderly Population." *J Consult Psychol* 16:399–405 O '52. * (*PA* 27:5771)

410. CAMPBELL, ELIZABETH FLETCHER. *The Effects of Colour in the Wechsler-Bellevue Block Design Subtest and in the Rorschach.* Master's thesis, University of Western Ontario (London, Ont., Canada), 1952.

411. COHEN, JACOB. "A Factor-Analytically Based Rationale for the Wechsler-Bellevue." *J Consult Psychol* 16:272–7 Ag '52. * (*PA* 27:4251)

412. COHEN, JACOB. "Factors Underlying Wechsler-Bellevue Performance of Three Neuropsychiatric Groups." *J Abn & Social Psychol* 47:359–65 Ag '52. * (*PA* 27:2818)

413. CORSINI, RAYMOND J., AND FASSETT, KATHERINE K. "The Validity of Wechsler's Mental Deterioration Index." *J Consult Psychol* 16:462–8 D '52. * (*PA* 28:936)

414. CORSINI, RAYMOND J., AND FASSETT, KATHERINE K. "Wechsler-Bellevue Age Patterns for a Prison Population." Abstract. *Am Psychol* 7:402 Jl '52. *

415. CORTER, HAROLD M. "Factor Analysis of Some Reasoning Tests." *Psychol Monogr* 66(8):1–31 '52. * (*PA* 27:4995)

416. CORTES, CARLOS F. *The Use of the Wechsler-Bellevue Scale With Spanish-Speaking Students.* Master's thesis, University of Wyoming (Laramie, Wyo.), 1952.

417. DAVIS, PAUL C. *A Factor Analysis of the Wechsler-Bellevue Intelligence Scale, Form I, in a Matrix With Reference Variables.* Doctor's thesis, University of Southern California (Los Angeles, Calif.), 1952. (Abstract: *Am Psychol* 7:296)

418. DELATTRE, LOIS, AND COLE, DAVID. "A Comparison of the WISC and the Wechsler-Bellevue." *J Consult Psychol* 16:228–30 Je '52. * (*PA* 27:5147)

419. DEVONSHIRE, MARION E. *An Experimental Study of Abbreviated Forms of the Wechsler-Bellevue With a Group of Dull Normals.* Master's thesis, University of Texas (Austin, Tex.), 1952.

420. ENGEN, TRYGG. *A Comparison of Performance on the Wechsler-Bellevue Intelligence Scale and Success in the Engineering College.* Master's thesis, University of Detroit (Detroit, Mich.), 1952.

421. FINKELSTEIN, MELVILLE; GERBOTH, RENATE; AND WESTERHOLD, RUTH. "Standardization of a Short Form of the Wechsler Vocabulary Subtest." *J Clin Psychol* 8:133–5 Ap '52. * (*PA* 27:1956)

422. GAINER, WILLIAM L. *A Study of the Ability of the Wechsler-Bellevue Sub-Tests to Discriminate Between the Mental Levels of Delinquent Negro Boys.* Master's thesis, College of the Pacific (Stockton, Calif.), 1952.

423. GERMAIN, GEORGE L. *The Use of Z Scores in Place of the Regular Weighted Scores on the Wechsler-Bellevue Intelligence Scale, Form I.* Master's thesis, University of Detroit (Detroit, Mich.), 1952.

424. GIEDT, HELEN MOORE. *The Influence of Aphasia on Wechsler-Bellevue Scatter Patterns.* Doctor's thesis, University of Southern California (Los Angeles, Calif.), 1952.

425. GRAHAM, E. ELLIS. "Wechsler-Bellevue and WISC Scattergrams of Unsuccessful Readers." *J Consult Psychol* 16:268–71 Ag '52. * (*PA* 27:4564)

426. GRIFFITHS, JACK STEWART. *The Effect of Experimentally Induced Anxiety on Certain Subtests of the Wechsler-Bellevue.* Doctor's thesis, University of Kentucky (Lexington, Ky.), 1952. (*DA* 18:655)

427. GURVITZ, MILTON S. "Some Defects of the Wechsler-Bellevue." *J Consult Psychol* 16:124–6 Ap '52. *

428. GURVITZ, MILTON S., AND MILLER, JOSEPH S. A. Chap. 11, "Some Theoretical and Practical Aspects of the Diagnosis of Early and Latent Schizophrenia by Means of Psychological Testing," pp. 189–207. (*PA* 27:571) Discussion by Paul H. Hoch, pp. 215–6. In *Relation of Psychological Tests to Psychiatry.* Edited by Paul H. Hoch and Joseph Zubin. New York: Grune & Stratton, 1952. Pp. viii, 301. *

429. HALL, K. R. L. "Conceptual Impairment in Depressive and Organic Patients of the Pre-Senile Age Group." *J Mental Sci* 98:256–64 Ap '52. * (*PA* 27:572)

430. HARROWER, MOLLY. *Appraising Personality: The Use of Psychological Tests in the Practice of Medicine,* pp. 81–97. New York: W. W. Norton & Co., Inc., 1952. Pp. xvii, 197. * (*PA* 27:6532)

431. HELMICK, JOHN S. "Reliability or Variability?" *J Consult Psychol* 16:154–5 Ap '52. * (*PA* 27:2727)

432. HERRING, FRED H. "An Evaluation of Published Short Forms of the Wechsler-Bellevue Scale." *J Consult Psychol* 16:119–23 Ap '52. * (*PA* 27:2728)

433. HILDEN, ARNOLD H.; TAYLOR, JAMES W.; AND DUBOIS, PHILIP H. "Empirical Evaluation of Short W-B Scales." *J Clin Psychol* 8:323–31 O '52. * (*PA* 27:5876)

434. HOLZBERG, JULES D., AND BELMONT, LILLIAN. "The Relationship Between Factors on the Wechsler-Bellevue and Rorschach Having Common Psychological Rationale." *J Consult Psychol* 16:23–9 F '52. * (*PA* 27:1966)

435. KUTASH, SAMUEL B. "Interpretation of Jay's Wechsler-Bellevue Scale: The Case of Jay: Interpretations and Discussion." *J Proj Tech* 16:445–9, discussion 444–5, 462–73 D '52. * (*PA* 28:2678)

436. MALOS, HERBERT BERNARD. *Some Psychometric Evaluations of Epilepsy.* Doctor's thesis, University of Minnesota (Minneapolis, Minn.), 1952. (*DA* 12:396)

437. MANDLER, GEORGE, AND SARASON, SEYMOUR B. "A Study of Anxiety and Learning." *J Abn & Social Psychol* 47:166–73 Ap '52. * (*PA* 27:2743)

438. MEE, ELIZABETH ANN. *A Psychometric Study of Diffuse and Focal Cerebral Pathology Groups.* Doctor's thesis, University of Minnesota (Minneapolis, Minn.), 1952. (*DA* 12:338)

439. MERRILL, REED M., AND HEATHERS, LOUISE B. "Centile Scores for the Wechsler-Bellevue Intelligence Scale on a University Counseling Center Group." *J Consult Psychol* 16:406–9 O '52. * (*PA* 27:5890)

440. MERRILL, REED M., AND HEATHERS, LOUISE B. "Deviations of Wechsler-Bellevue Subtest Scores From Vocabulary Level in University Counseling-Center Clients." *J Consult Psychol* 16:469–72 D '52. * (*PA* 28:961)

441. MOLDAWSKY, STANLEY, AND MOLDAWSKY, PATRICIA CORCORAN. "Digit Span as an Anxiety Indicator." *J Consult Psychol* 16:115–8 Ap '52. * (*PA* 27:2747)

442. MONROE, JACK J. "The Effects of Emotional Adjustment and Intelligence Upon Bellevue Scatter." *J Consult Psychol* 16:110–4 Ap '52. * (*PA* 27:2748)

443. MORAN, L. J.; MORAN, F. A.; AND BLAKE, R. R. "An Investigation of the Vocabulary Performance of Schizophrenics: I, Quantitative Level." *J Genetic Psychol* 80:97–105 Mr '52. * (*PA* 27:581)

444. MORAN, L. J.; MORAN, F. A.; AND BLAKE, R. R. "An Investigation of the Vocabulary Performance of Schizophrenics: II, Conceptual Level of Definitions. *J Genetic Psychol* 80:107–132 Mr '52. * (*PA* 27:582)

445. PIZZAT, FRANK J. *Factor Analysis Patterns on the Wechsler-Bellevue Test of Adult Intelligence: Their Effectiveness in Discriminating Clinical Groups.* Doctor's thesis, University of Pittsburgh (Pittsburgh, Pa.), 1952.

446. PURCELL, CLAIRE KEPLER. "The Relationship Between Altitude—I.Q. Discrepancy and Anxiety." *J Clin Psychol* 8:82–5 Ja '52. * (*PA* 27:1978)

447. RICHARDS, T. W. "Personality of the Convulsive Patient in Military Service." *Psychol Monogr* 66(14):1–23 '52. * (*PA* 27:7364)

448. SCHNADT, FREDERICK. "Certain Aspects of Wechsler-Bellevue Scatter at Low IQ Levels." *J Consult Psychol* 16:456–61 D '52. * (*PA* 28:967)

449. SCHOFIELD, WILLIAM. "Critique of Scatter and Profile Analysis of Psychometric Data." *J Clin Psychol* 8:16–22 Ja '52. * (*PA* 27:1979)

450. SHANNON, WALTER, AND ROSSI, PHILIP D. "Suggestions for Efficient Presentation of the Wechsler-Bellevue Object-Assembly Sub-Test." *J Clin Psychol* 8:413–5 O '52. * (*PA* 27:5902)

451. SHNEIDMAN, EDWIN S. "The Case of Jay: Psychological Test and Anamnestic Data." *J Proj Tech* 16:297–345 S '52. * (*PA* 28:2676)

452. STARER, EMANUEL. "Aggressive Reactions and Sources of Frustration in Anxiety Neurotics and Paranoid Schizophrenics." *J Clin Psychol* 8:307–9 Jl '52. * (*PA* 27:5979)

453. STORRS, SIBYLL VIOLET. *An Evaluative Comparison of the United States Employment Service General Aptitude Test Battery and the Wechsler Bellevue Intelligence Scale.* Master's thesis, University of Florida (Gainesville, Fla.), 1952.

454. STOTSKY, BERNARD A. "A Comparison of Remitting and Nonremitting Schizophrenics on Psychological Tests." *J Abn & Social Psychol* 47:489–96 Ag '52. * (*PA* 27:2898)

455. VORHAUS, PAULINE G. "Case Study of an Adolescent Boy With Reading Disability." *J Proj Tech* 16:20–41 Mr '52. * (*PA* 27:650)

456. WEBB, WILSE B. "Corrections for Variability: A Reply." *J Consult Psychol* 16:156 Ap '52. *

457. YEATS, LEWIS CLIFFORD. *The Wechsler-Bellevue Adult Intelligence Scale as an Instrument for Predicting the Effects of Prefrontal Lobotomy.* Master's thesis, University of Western Ontario (London, Ont., Canada), 1952.

458. ARMSTRONG, RENATE GERBOTH. "A Comparison of the Comprehension Subtests of the Wechsler Bellevue Intelligence Scale, Forms I and II." *J Clin Psychol* 9:172–6 Ap '53. * (*PA* 28:2611)

459. BERKOWITZ, BERNARD. "The Wechsler-Bellevue Performance of White Males Past Age 50." *J Gerontol* 8:76–80 Ja '53. * (*PA* 28:657)

460. BERNSTEIN, RACHEL, AND CORSINI, RAYMOND J. "Wechsler-Bellevue Patterns of Female Delinquents." *J Clin Psychol* 9:176–9 Ap '53. * (*PA* 28:2963)

461. BIESHEUVEL, S.; JACOBS, G. F.; AND COWLEY, J. J. "Maladjustments of Military Personnel." *J Nat Inst Personnel Res* 5:138–68 D '53. *

462. BOTWINICK, JACK. "Wechsler-Bellevue Split-Half Subtest Reliabilities: Differences in Age and Mental Status." *J Consult Psychol* 17:225–8 Je '53. * (*PA* 28:2619)

463. CORSINI, RAYMOND J., AND FASSETT, KATHERINE K. "Intelligence and Aging." *J Genetic Psychol* 83:249–64 D '53. * (*PA* 28:7317)

464. DeMartino, Hugo A. *The Wechsler-Bellevue Intelligence Scale as a Predictor of Success in a College of Engineering.* Master's thesis, University of Detroit (Detroit, Mich.), 1953.

465. DeStephens, William P. "Are Criminals Morons?" *J Social Psychol* 38:187-99 N '53. * (*PA* 28:6294)

466. Dore, John J., Jr. *Performance on the Wechsler-Bellevue Intelligence Scale and Success in the College of Arts and Sciences at the University of Detroit.* Master's thesis, University of Detroit (Detroit, Mich.), 1953.

467. Dörken, Herbert, Jr., and Greenbloom, Grace C. "Psychological Investigation of Senile Dementia: II, The Wechsler-Bellevue Adult Intelligence Scale." *Geriatrics* 8:324-33 Je '53. * (*PA* 28:2359)

468. Duncan, John O. "Correlation Between the Wechsler-Bellevue and Stanford-Binet Vocabulary Lists." *Med Tech B* 4:45-7 Mr-Ap '53. * (*PA* 28:4348)

469. Fellers, Gloria L. *A Response-Category Analysis of Wechsler-Bellevue Intelligence Scale, Form I, Vocabulary Responses.* Master's thesis, Bowling Green State University (Bowling Green, Ohio), 1953.

470. Gibson, Frederick J. *Correlation Study of the 1937 Revision of the Stanford-Binet Scale, Form L, With the Performance Items of the Wechsler Bellevue Intelligence Scale, Adult, Form I.* Master's thesis, Boston College (Chestnut Hill, Mass.), 1953.

471. Haggerty, Arthur D. "The Intellectual Functioning of a Post-Institutional Group." *J Genetic Psychol* 83:303-6 D '53. * (*PA* 28:7816)

472. Henning, Richard L. *An Investigation of Sex Differences on the Weighted Subtest Scores of the Wechsler-Bellevue Intelligence Scale for Adults, Form I.* Master's thesis, Bowling Green State University (Bowling Green, Ohio), 1953.

473. Hopkins, Barbara, and Roth, Martin. "Psychological Test Performance in Patients Over Sixty: I, Paraphrenia, Arteriosclerotic Psychosis and Acute Confusion." *J Mental Sci* 99:451-63 Jl '53. * (*PA* 28:4655)

474. Jastak, Joseph. "Ranking Bellevue Subtest Scores for Diagnostic Purposes." *J Consult Psychol* 17:403-10 D '53. * (*PA* 28:7530)

475. Knopf, Irwin J.; Murfett, Betty J.; and Milstein, Victor. "A Comparative Study of the Wechsler-Bellevue Form I and the WISC." Abstract. *Am Psychol* 8:380 Ag '53. *

476. Levine, Bert D. *The Progressive Matrices 1938 and Its Relationship With Certain Subtests of the Wechsler-Bellevue Intelligence Scale.* Master's thesis, University of Texas (Austin, Tex.), 1953.

477. Love, Leonore Rice. *An Analysis of Wechsler-Bellevue Items Score for Assessing the Clinical Significance of Variability of Performance.* Doctor's thesis, University of California (Los Angeles, Calif.), 1953.

478. Luchins, Abraham S., and Luchins, Edith H. "Effects of Varying the Administration of the Digit Symbol Subtest of the Wechsler-Bellevue Intelligence Scale." *J General Psychol* 49:125-42 Jl '53. * (*PA* 28:6039)

479. McLean, Orison S. *Divergent Scores on the Wechsler-Bellevue Intelligence Scale as Indicators of Learning Ability Among Institutionalized Subjects.* Doctor's thesis, University of Kentucky (Lexington, Ky.), 1953.

480. Mainord, Willard A. "Some Effects of Sodium Amytal on 'Deteriorated' Schizophrenics." *J Consult Psychol* 17:54-7 F '53. * (*PA* 28:1329)

481. Maksimczyk, Walter J. *A Comparison of Performance on the Wechsler-Bellevue Intelligence Scale and Success in a College of Commerce and Finance.* Master's thesis, University of Detroit (Detroit, Mich.), 1953.

482. Marks, Melvin R. "A Criticism of the Use of the Wechsler-Bellevue Scale as a Diagnostic Instrument." *J General Psychol* 49:143-52 Jl '53. * (*PA* 28:6045)

483. Markwell, Earl D., Jr.; Wheeler, William M.; and Kitzinger, Helen. "Changes in Wechsler-Bellevue Test Performance Following Prefrontal Lobotomy." *J Consult Psychol* 17:229-31 Je '53. * (*PA* 28:2744)

484. Mattar, J. C. *A Study of the Performance of Multiple Sclerosis Patients on the Wechsler-Bellevue.* Master's thesis, University of Ottawa (Ottawa, Ont., Canada), 1953.

485. Mech, Edmund. "Item Analysis and Discriminative Value of Selected Wechsler-Bellevue Subtests." *J Ed Res* 47:241-60, 260a-260b D '53. * (*PA* 28:6046)

486. Merrill, Reed M., and Heathers, Louise B. "A Comparison of the Wechsler-Bellevue and ACE Tests on a University Counseling Center Group." *J Consult Psychol* 17:63-6 F '53. *

487. Norman, Ralph D. "Sex Differences and Other Aspects of Young Superior Adult Performance on the Wechsler-Bellevue." *J Consult Psychol* 17:411-8 D '53. * (*PA* 28:7541)

488. Patterson, C. H. *The Wechsler-Bellevue Scales: A Guide for Counselors.* Springfield, Ill.: Charles C Thomas, Publisher, 1953. Pp. viii, 146. * (*PA* 28:2664)

489. Rappaport, Sheldon R. "Intellectual Deficit in Organics and Schizophrenics." *J Consult Psychol* 17:389-95 O '53. * (*PA* 28:6365)

490. Roth, Martin, and Hopkins, Barbara. "Psychological Test Performance in Patients Over Sixty: I, Senile Psychosis and the Affective Disorders of Old Age." *J Mental Sci* 99:439-50 Jl '53. * (*PA* 28:4671)

491. Rothstein, Harvey Jones. *A Study of the Qualitative Aspects of the Wechsler-Bellevue Intelligence Scale.* Doctor's thesis, Columbia University (New York, N.Y.), 1953. (*DA* 14:1813)

492. Rubin, Harold. "A Quantitative Study of the H-T-P and Its Relationship to the Wechsler-Bellevue Scale." Abstract. *Am Psychol* 8:426-7 Ag '53. *

493. Sievers, Dorothy J., and Norman, Ralph D. "Some Suggestive Results in Psychometric Testing of the Cerebral Palsied With Gesell, Binet, and Wechsler Scales." *J Genetic Psychol* 82:69-90 Mr '53. * (*PA* 27:7974)

494. Stanley, Julian C. "Why Wechsler-Bellevue Full-Scale IQ's Are More Variable Than Averages of Verbal and Performance IQ's." *J Consult Psychol* 17:419-20 D '53. * (*PA* 28:7553)

495. Strange, Frank B., and Palmer, James O. "A Note on Sex Differences on the Wechsler-Bellevue Tests." *J Clin Psychol* 9:85-7 Ja '53. * (*PA* 27:7796)

496. Vanderhost, Leonette; Sloan, William; and Bensberg, Gerard J., Jr. "Performance of Mental Defectives on the Wechsler-Bellevue and the WISC." *Am J Mental Def* 57:481-3 Ja '53. * (*PA* 27:6629)

497. Walters, Richard H. "Wechsler-Bellevue Test Results of Prison Inmates." *Austral J Psychol* 5:46-54 Je '53. * (*PA* 29:1219)

498. Watson, Robert I. "Wechsler-Bellevue Intelligence Scale for Adolescents and Adults," pp. 530-44. (*PA* 27:7802) In *Contributions Toward Medical Psychology: Theory and Psychodiagnostic Methods, Vol. II.* Edited by Arthur Weider. New York: Ronald Press Co., 1953. Pp. xi, 459-885. *

499. Winne, John F. "An Alternate Form of the Series Completion Test." *J Clin Psychol* 9:321-7 O '53. * (*PA* 28:4405)

500. Wolff, Sidney J. "Clinical Application of the Wechsler-Bellevue Intelligence Scale for the Clinical Psychology Technician." *Med Tech B* 4:49-51 Ja-F '53. *

501. Adcock, C. J.; McCreary, J. R.; Ritchie, J. E.; and Somerset, H. C. A. "An Analysis of Maori Scores on the Wechsler-Bellevue." *Austral J Psychol* 6:16-29 Je '54. * (*PA* 29:5524)

502. Allen, Robert M.; Thornton, Thomas E.; and Stenger, Charles A. "Ammons and Wechsler Test Performances of College and Psychiatric Subjects." *J Clin Psychol* 10:378-81 O '54. * (*PA* 29:4022)

503. Bacon, Coleen Shaner. *A Comparative Study of the Wechsler-Bellevue Intelligence Scale for Adolescents and Adults, Form I, and the Wechsler Intelligence Scale for Children at the Twelve-Year Level.* Master's thesis, University of North Dakota (Grand Forks, N.D.), 1954.

504. Butler, Alfred. "Test-Retest and Split-Half Reliabilities of the Wechsler-Bellevue Scales and Subtests With Mental Defectives." *Am J Mental Def* 59:80-4 Jl '54. * (*PA* 29:4040)

505. Carment, D. W. *Differences in the Behavior Patterns and in the Wechsler-Bellevue Test Performances Between Psychopaths With Normal Electroencephalograms and Psychopaths With Abnormal Electroencephalograms.* Master's thesis, University of Toronto (Toronto, Ont., Canada), 1954.

506. Cook, Murray. *The Relationship Between Susceptibility to Secondary Motivation and Test Performance in Schizophrenics.* Doctor's thesis, New York University (New York, N.Y.), 1954. (*DA* 18:2197)

507. Corrie, C. C.; Fogel, J.; and Frank, G. H. "A Critique on Research With the Wechsler-Bellevue Test in Differential Psychodiagnosis." Abstract. *Am Psychol* 9:350-1 Ag '54. *

508. DeMartino, Hugo A. "The Wechsler-Bellevue Intelligence Scale as a Predictor of Success in a College of Engineering." *Papers Mich Acad Sci, Arts & Letters* 39:459-65 '54. *

509. Flynn, James J. *Rorschach and Wechsler-Bellevue Changes Following Electric Shock Therapy in the Aged.* Doctor's thesis, Loyola University (Chicago, Ill.), 1954.

510. Goolishian, H. A., and Foster, Austin. "A Note on Sex Differences on the Wechsler-Bellevue Test." *J Clin Psychol* 10:298-9 Jl '54. * (*PA* 29:2447)

511. Guertin, Wilson H. "The Effect of Instructions and Item Order on the Arithmetic Subtest of the Wechsler-Bellevue." *J Genetic Psychol* 85:79-83 S '54. * (*PA* 29:5706)

512. Gurvitz, Milton S. "An Experimental Evaluation of Judgment as Measured by the Comprehension Subtest of the Wechsler-Bellevue." Abstract. *Am Psychol* 9:386-7 Ag '54. *

513. Hollingsworth, Berneice H. *An Investigation of the Correlation Between the Wechsler Intelligence Scale for Children and the Durrell-Sullivan Reading Capacity Test.* Master's thesis, University of Denver (Denver, Colo.), 1954.

514. Kelley, Eileen. *A Study of the Relative Contributions of the Eleven Subtests to the Full Scale Wechsler-Bellevue Score.* Master's thesis, Bowling Green State University (Bowling Green, Ohio), 1954.

515. Knopf, Irwin J.; Murfett, Betty J.; and Milstein, Victor. "Relationships Between the Wechsler-Bellevue Form I and the WISC." *J Clin Psychol* 10:261-3 Jl '54. * (*PA* 29:2449)

516. Levine, Bert, and Iscoe, Ira. "A Comparison of Raven's Progressive Matrices (1938) With a Short Form of the Wechsler-Bellevue." Abstract. *J Consult Psychol* 18:10 F '54. *

517. Levreault, Lionel P. *Diagnosis of Idiopathic Epilepsy by Means of the Wechsler-Bellevue Scattergram.* Master's thesis, Ohio University (Athens, Ohio), 1954.

518. McLean, Orison S. "Divergent Scores on the Wechs-

ler-Bellevue Scale as Indicators of Learning Ability." *J Clin Psychol* 10:264–6 Jl '54. * (*PA* 29:2161)
519. MARTIN, STEPHAN B., AND WERTHEIMER, MICHAEL. "A Bibliography of Recent Work on the Wechsler-Bellevue." *Psychol Newsl* 6:10–38 S–O '54. * (*PA* 31:3053)
520. PTACEK, JAMES E., AND YOUNG, FLORENCE M. "Comparison of the Grassi Block Substitution Test With the Wechsler-Bellevue in the Diagnosis of Organic Brain Damage." *J Clin Psychol* 10:375–8 O '54. * (*PA* 29:4082)
521. RHODERICK, WAYNE A. *An Item Analysis of Wechsler-Bellevue Intelligence Scale, Form I Subtests.* Master's thesis, College of the Pacific (Stockton, Calif.), 1954.
522. RUSSELL, GEORGE E. "Wechsler-Bellevue Vocabulary Subtest Items: Revised Order of Words." *Med Tech B* 5:143–8 Jl–Ag '54. * (*PA* 29:950)
523. SATTER, GEORGE, AND MCGEE, EUGENE. "Retarded Adults Who Have Developed Beyond Expectation: Part I, Intellectual Functions." *Training Sch B* 51:43–55 My '54. * (*PA* 29:2662)
524. STACEY, CHALMERS L., AND SPANIER, S. WILLIAM. "Differential Responses Among College Students on the Vocabulary Subtest of the Wechsler Intelligence Scale." *J Ed Psychol* 45:29–35 Ja '54. * (*PA* 28:7552)
525. THURSTON, JOHN R., AND CALDEN, GEORGE. "Intelligence Factors in Irregular Discharge Among Tuberculosis Patients." Abstract. *J Consult Psychol* 18:404 D '54. *
526. VANE, JULIA R., AND EISEN, VIRGINIA W. "Wechsler-Bellevue Performance of Delinquent and Nondelinquent Girls." *J Consult Psychol* 18:221–5 Je '54. * (*PA* 29:2753)
527. YOUNG, FLORENE M., AND COLLINS, JOHN J. "Results of Testing Negro Contact-Syphilitics With the Wechsler-Bellevue Intelligence Scale." *J Social Psychol* 39:93–8 F '54. * (*PA* 28:8929)
528. ANGERS, W. P. *A Psychometric Study of Institutionalized Epileptics on the Wechsler-Bellevue.* Doctor's thesis, University of Ottawa (Ottawa, Ont., Canada), 1955.
529. BRADWAY, KATHERINE, AND BENSON, STANLEY. "The Application of the Method of Extreme Deviations to Rapaport's Wechsler-Bellevue Data." *J Clin Psychol* 11:285–91 Jl '55. * (*PA* 30:2859)
530. BRESSLER, MILDRED BLOOM. *A Study of an Aspect of Concept Formation in Brain-Damaged Adults With Aphasia.* Doctor's thesis, New York University (New York, N.Y.), 1955. (*DA* 16:568)
531. BROWN, MORONI H., AND BRYAN, G. ELIZABETH. "The Interpretation of the Wechsler-Bellevue Intelligence Scale in Terms of Altitude Scores." Abstract. *Am Psychol* 10:431 Ag '55. *
532. BROWN, MORONI H., AND BRYAN, G. ELIZABETH. "Sex Differences in Intelligence." *J Clin Psychol* 11:303–4 Jl '55. * (*PA* 30:2860)
533. BRYAN, GERALDINE E. *A Study of the Performance of Adolescents With Diagnosed Brain Damage on the Wechsler-Bellevue Intelligence Scale, Form One.* Master's thesis, University of Utah (Salt Lake City, Utah), 1955.
534. COHEN, JACOB. "The Efficacy of Diagnostic Pattern Analysis With the Wechsler-Bellevue." *J Consult Psychol* 19:303–6 Ag '55. * (*PA* 30:4557)
535. DESAI, MAHESH M. "The Relationship of the Wechsler-Bellevue Verbal Scale and the Progressive Matrices Test." Abstract. *J Consult Psychol* 19:60 F '55. *
536. DILLER, JULIET C. "A Comparison of the Test Performances of Male and Female Juvenile Delinquents." *J Genetic Psychol* 86:217–36 Je '55. * (*PA* 30:7485)
537. FORSTER, CECIL R. *The Relationship Between Test Achievement and Success in Training of a Selected Group of Tuberculosis Patients.* Doctor's thesis, New York University (New York, N.Y.), 1955. (*DA* 15:1201)
538. FRANK, G. H.; CORRIE, C. C.; AND FOGEL, J. "An Empirical Critique of Research With the Wechsler-Bellevue in Differential Psychodiagnosis." *J Clin Psychol* 11:291–3 Jl '55. * (*PA* 30:2877)
539. HALLBERG, MARGARET C. *A Study of the Characteristics of Mentally Competent Offenders as Revealed by Vocabulary Scatter on the Wechsler-Bellevue Intelligence Scale (Form 1).* Master's thesis, University of Alberta (Edmonton, Alta., Canada), 1955.
540. HORWITZ, MURRAY; DELLA PIANA, GABRIEL M.; GOLDMAN, MORTON; AND LEE, FRANCIS J. "Veridicality of Attitudes Toward Authority and Effects on Learning." Abstract. *Am Psychol* 10:336 Ag '55. *
541. HOWELL, ROBERT J. "Changes in Wechsler Subtest Scores With Age." *J Consult Psychol* 19:47–50 F '55. * (*PA* 29:8429)
542. HOWELL, ROBERT J. "Sex Differences and Educational Influences on a Mental Deterioration Scale." *J Gerontol* 10:190–3 Ap '55. * (*PA* 30:2887)
543. IPSON, WILLIAM M. *The Relationship Between the Critical Frequency of Flicker and Performance on the Wechsler-Bellevue Intelligence Scale.* Master's thesis, University of Utah (Salt Lake City, Utah), 1955.
544. JACKSON, C. V. "Estimating Impairment on Wechsler Bellevue Subtests." *J Clin Psychol* 11:137–43 Ap '55. * (*PA* 30:1030)
545. KAMMAN, GORDON R., AND KRAM, CHARLES. "Value of Psychometric Examinations in Medical Diagnosis and Treatment." *J Am Med Assn* 158:555–60 Ja 18 '55. * (*PA* 31:1044)
546. KELLEY, EILEEN. *A Study of the Relative Contributions of the Eleven Subtests to the Full Scale Wechsler-Bellevue Score.* Master's thesis, Bowling Green State University (Bowling Green, Ohio), 1955.
547. KRAMAR, EDWARD JOHN JOSEPH. *The Relationships of the Wechsler-Bellevue and A.C.E. Intelligence Tests With Performance Scores in Speaking and the Brown-Carlsen Listening Comprehension Test.* Doctor's thesis, Florida State University (Tallahassee, Fla.), 1955. (*DA* 15:2599)
548. LEVINE, A.; ABRAMSON, H. A.; KAUFMAN, M. R.; AND MARKHAM, S. "Lysergic Acid Diethylamide (LSD-25): XVI, The Effect on Intellectual Functioning as Measured by the Wechsler-Bellevue Intelligence Scale." *J Psychol* 40:385–95 O '55. * (*PA* 30:6904)
549. LEVINE, BERT, AND ISCOE, IRA. "The Progressive Matrices (1938), the Chicago Non-Verbal and the Wechsler-Bellevue on an Adolescent Deaf Population." *J Clin Psychol* 11:307–8 Jl '55. * (*PA* 30:3334)
550. LOTT, W. J. *Characteristics of High Standing University Students on the Wechsler-Bellevue Adult Intelligence Scale.* Master's thesis, University of Alberta (Edmonton, Alta., Canada), 1955.
551. LOVE, DEBORAH B. *Brain Damage and Wechsler-Bellevue.* Master's thesis, Howard University (Washington, D.C.), 1955.
552. MATARAZZO, RUTH G. "The Relationship of Manifest Anxiety to Wechsler-Bellevue Subtest Performance." Abstract. *J Consult Psychol* 19:218 Je '55. *
553. MATARAZZO, RUTH GADBOIS. *The Effect of Anxiety Level Upon Motor Learning, Level of Aspiration, and Wechsler-Bellevue Subtest Performance.* Doctor's thesis, Washington University (St. Louis, Mo.), 1955. (*DA* 15:877)
554. MEER, BERNARD, AND STEIN, MORRIS I. "Measures of Intelligence and Creativity." *J Psychol* 39:117–26 Ja '55. * (*PA* 29:9102)
555. MEER, BERNARD; STEIN, MORRIS I.; AND GEERTSMA, ROBERT. "An Analysis of the Miller Analogies Test for a Scientific Population." *Am Psychol* 10:33–4 Ja '55. * (*PA* 30:3658)
556. NORTH, GEORGE E. *The Rorschach Intellectual Indices: An Investigation of Relationships Between Rorschach and the Wechsler-Bellevue Tests.* Master's thesis, University of Utah (Salt Lake City, Utah), 1955.
557. PLUMB, GALEN R., AND CHARLES, DON C. "Scoring Difficulty of Wechsler Comprehension Responses." *J Ed Psychol* 46:179–83 Mr '55. * (*PA* 30:1049)
558. PRICE, JOHN R., AND THORNE, GARETH D. "A Statistical Comparison of the WISC and Wechsler-Bellevue, Form I." *J Consult Psychol* 19:479–82 D '55. * (*PA* 30:7221)
559. RABIN, A. I.; KING, G. F.; AND EHRMANN, J. C. "Vocabulary Performance of Short-Term and Long-Term Schizophrenics." *J Abn & Social Psychol* 50:255–8 Mr '55. * (*PA* 30:1361)
560. SATTER, GEORGE. "Retarded Adults Who Have Developed Beyond Expectation: Part III, Further Analysis and Summary." *Training Sch B* 51:237–43 F '55. * (*PA* 29:7498)
561. SLOAN, WILLIAM, AND NEWMAN, J. ROBERT. "The Development of a Wechsler-Bellevue II Short Form." *Personnel Psychol* 8:347–53 au '55. * (*PA* 30:7838)
562. WARD, JOE H., JR. "Use of Electronic Computers in Psychological Research." Letter. *Am Psychol* 10:826–7 D '55. * (*PA* 30:6510)
563. WEISGERBER, CHARLES A. "A Note on Diamond's Method of Scoring the Wechsler-Bellevue Intelligence Scale for Vocational Aptitude." *J Clin Psychol* 11:311 Jl '55. * (*PA* 30:3591)
564. ALLEN, ROBERT M.; THORNTON, THOMAS E.; AND STENGER, CHARLES A. "The Full-Range Picture Vocabulary Test Compared With Two Short Forms of the Wechsler Scale." *J Ed Res* 50:133–7 O '56. * (*PA* 32:933)
565. BARRY, JOHN R.; FULKERSON, SAMUEL C.; KUBALA, ALBERT L.; AND SEAQUIST, MAURICE R. "Score Equivalence of the Wechsler-Bellevue Intelligence Scales, Forms I and II." *J Clin Psychol* 12:57–60 Ja '56. * (*PA* 30:4553)
566. BREIGER, BORIS. "The Use of the W-B Picture Arrangement Subtest as a Projective Technique." Abstract. *J Consult Psychol* 20:132 Ap '56. *
567. CALDWELL, MARK B., AND DAVIS, JULIAN C. "A Short Form of the Wechsler-Bellevue Intelligence Scale Form II for a Psychotic Population." *J Clin Psychol* 12:402–3 O '56. * (*PA* 32:4168)
568. DAVIS, PAUL C. "A Factor Analysis of the Wechsler-Bellevue Scale." *Ed & Psychol Meas* 16:127–46 sp '56. * (*PA* 31:6072)
569. EVERETT, EVALYN G. *A Comparative Study of Paretics, Hebephrenics, and Paranoid Schizophrenics on a Battery of Psychological Tests.* Doctor's thesis, New York University (New York, N.Y.), 1956. (*DA* 16:1502)
570. FORTSON, CHARLES B. *A Study of the Comparability of Forms I and II of the Wechsler-Bellevue Intelligence Scale When Used With Clinically Normal Negro Adults.* Master's thesis, Atlanta University (Atlanta, Ga.), 1956.
571. FRANK, GEORGE H. "The Wechsler-Bellevue and Psychiatric Diagnosis: A Factor Analytic Approach." *J Consult Psychol* 20:67–9 F '56. * (*PA* 31:3032)
572. FRY, LOIS M. "A Predictive Measure of Work Success for High Grade Mental Defectives." *Am J Mental Def* 61:402–8 O '56. *
573. FRYE, U. CASSIAN. *The Relevancy of the SRA Primary Mental Abilities Test and the SRA Reading Record to Ninth*

Grade Achievement in a Catholic Boys' High School. Master's thesis, St. Louis University (St. Louis, Mo.), 1956.

574. GOOLISHIAN, H. A., AND RAMSAY, ROSE. "The Wechsler-Bellevue Form I and the WAIS: A Comparison." *J Clin Psychol* 12:147–51 Ap '56. * (PA 31:4691)

575. GUERTIN, WILSON H.; FRANK, GEORGE H.; AND RABIN, ALBERT I. "Research With the Wechsler-Bellevue Intelligence Scale: 1950–1955." *Psychol B* 53:235–57 My '56. * (PA 32:492)

576. INGLIS, J.; SHAPIRO, M. B.; AND POST, F. "'Memory Function' in Psychiatric Patients Over Sixty, the Role of Memory in Tests Discriminating Between 'Functional' and 'Organic' Groups." *J Mental Sci* 102:589–98 Jl '56. * (PA 31:7926)

577. KALDEGG, A. "Psychological Observations in a Group of Alcoholic Patients With Analysis of Rorschach, Wechsler-Bellevue and Bender Gestalt Test Results." *Q J Studies Alcohol* 17:608–28 D '56. * (PA 32:648)

578. MARIANI, ROSE RAMSAY. *A Comparison of a Projective Test Battery With Its Component Tests.* Doctor's thesis, University of Houston (Houston, Tex.), 1956. (DA 16:1506)

579. MILNE, G. G. "Deterioration and Over-Learning." *Austral J Psychol* 8:163–73 D '56. *

580. MURPHY, DONALD B., AND LANGSTON, ROBERT D. "A Short Form of the Wechsler-Bellevue and the Army Classification Battery as Measures of Intelligence." Abstract. *J Consult Psychol* 20:405 O '56. *

581. NEURINGER, CHARLES. *A Statistical Comparison of the Wechsler-Bellevue Intelligence Scale, Form I and the Wechsler Adult Intelligence Scale for a College Population.* Master's thesis, University of Kansas (Lawrence, Kan.), 1956.

582. O'NEILL, JOHN J., AND DAVIDSON, JOANN L. "Relationship Between Lipreading Ability and Five Psychological Factors." *J Speech & Hearing Dis* 21:478–81 D '56. * (PA 31:4907)

583. PLANT, WALTER T., AND SAWREY, JAMES M. "A Preliminary Review of the Data for 1,000 College Undergraduates Individually Tested With the Wechsler-Bellevue Scale, Form 1." Abstract. *Calif J Ed Res* 7:130 My '56. *

584. PURCELL, KENNETH. "A Note on Porteus Maze and Wechsler-Bellevue Scores as Related to Antisocial Behavior." *J Consult Psychol* 20:361–4 O '56. * (PA 31:7960)

585. ROBINOWITZ, RALPH. "Performances of Hospitalized Psychiatric Patients on the Kent Emergency Test and the Wechsler-Bellevue Intelligence Scale." *J Clin Psychol* 12:199–200 Ap '56. * (PA 31:4711)

586. RUBIN-RABSON, GRACE. "Item Order and Difficulty in Four Verbal Subtests of the Bellevue-Wechsler Scale." *J Genetic Psychol* 88:167–74 Je '56. *

587. SCARBOROUGH, B. B. "Some Mental Characteristics of Southern Colored and White Venereal Disease Patients as Measured by the Wechsler-Bellevue Test." *J Social Psychol* 43:313–21 My '56. *

588. SHIER, DAVID A. *An Exploratory Study of the Use of the Wechsler-Bellevue and the Rotter Tests to Determine Common Personality Patterns for Retarded Readers.* Master's thesis, Sacramento State College (Sacramento, Calif.), 1956.

589. THALER, MARGARET. "Relationships Among Wechsler, Weigl, Rorschach, EEG Findings, and Abstract-Concrete Behavior in a Group of Normal Aged Subjects." *J Gerontol* 11:404–9 O '56. * (PA 31:5871)

590. TOLOR, ALEXANDER. "A Comparison of the Bender-Gestalt Test and the Digit-Span Test as Measures of Recall." *J Consult Psychol* 20:305–9 Ap '56. * (PA 31:7979)

591. TOLOR, ALEXANDER. "The Wechsler-Bellevue Scale in Clinical Diagnosis: Some Aspects of Its Use in Clinical Diagnosis." *U S Armed Forces Med J* 7:192–9 F '56. * (PA 31:1071)

592. ZIMET, CARL N., AND BRACKBILL, GLEN A. "The Role of Anxiety in Psychodiagnosis." *J Clin Psychol* 12:173–7 Ap '56. * (PA 31:4722)

593. BAYLEY, NANCY. "Data on the Growth of Intelligence Between 16 and 21 Years as Measured by the Wechsler-Bellevue Scale." *J Genetic Psychol* 90:3–15 Mr '57. *

594. BROWN, MORONI H., AND BRYAN, G. ELIZABETH. "The Altitude Quotient as a Measurement of Intellectual Potential." *J Clin Psychol* 13:137–40 Ap '57. * (PA 32:2654)

595. BRYAN, G. ELIZABETH, AND BROWN, MORONI H. "A Method for Differential Diagnosis of Brain Damage in Adolescents." *J Nerv & Mental Dis* 125:69–72 Ja–Mr '57. *

596. DANA, RICHARD H. "A Comparison of Four Verbal Subtests on the Wechsler-Bellevue, Form I, and the WAIS." *J Clin Psychol* 13:70–1 Ja '57. *

597. DAVIS, JULIAN C. "The Scatter Pattern of a Southern Negro Group on the Wechsler-Bellevue Intelligence Scale." *J Clin Psychol* 13:298–300 Jl '57. *

598. DELLI COLLI, PASCAL. *The Rationale of the Wechsler-Bellevue Picture Arrangement Subtest, Form I.* Master's thesis, University of Ottawa (Ottawa, Ont., Canada), 1957.

599. GASKILL, P. Chap. 9, "Tests of Ability and Attainments: Pilot Experiments in Selection and Guidance," pp. 188–212. In *Educational Guidance and the Deaf Child.* Edited by A. W. G. Ewing. Manchester, England: Manchester University Press, 1957. Pp. xiii, 345. *

600. GILGASH, CURTIS A. "Effects of Thorazine on Wechsler Scores of Adult Catatonic Schizophrenics." *Psychol Rep* 3:561–4 D '57. *

601. GOETZINGER, C. P., AND ROUSEY, C. L. "A Study of the Wechsler Performance Scale (Form II) and the Knox Cube Test With Deaf Adolescents." *Am Ann Deaf* 102:388–98 N '57. *

602. GOODSTEIN, LEONARD D., AND FARBER, I. E. "On the Relation Between A-Scale Scores and Digit Symbol Performance." *J Consult Psychol* 21:152–4 Ap '57. *

603. HALL, JULIA C. "Reliability (Internal Consistency) of the Wechsler Memory Scale and Correlation With the Wechsler-Bellevue Intelligence Scale." *J Consult Psychol* 21:131–5 Ap '57. *

604. KARSON, SAMUEL, AND POOL, KENNETH BRYNER. "The Abstract Thinking Abilities of Mental Patients." *J Clin Psychol* 13:126–32 Ap '57. * (PA 32:3023)

605. KEEHN, J. D. "Repeated Testing of Four Chronic Schizophrenics on the Bender-Gestalt and Wechsler Block Design Tests." *J Clin Psychol* 13:179–82 Ap '57. * (PA 32:3167)

606. MINDESS, HARVEY. "Psychological Indices in the Selection of Student Nurses." *J Proj Tech* 21:37–9 Mr '57. * (PA 32:2908)

607. MURPHY, K. P. Chap. 11, "Tests of Abilities and Attainments: Pupils in Schools for the Deaf Aged Twelve," pp. 252–77. In *Educational Guidance and the Deaf Child.* Edited by A. W. G. Ewing. Manchester, England: Manchester University Press, 1957. Pp. xiii, 345. *

608. PARKER, JAMES W. "The Validity of Some Current Tests for Organicity." *J Consult Psychol* 21:425–8 O '57. *

609. SCHNEYER, SOLOMON. "A Short Form of the Wechsler-Bellevue Scale, Form II, for Alcoholic Outpatients." *Q J Studies Alcohol* 18:382–7 S '57. *

610. SULLIVAN, ARTHUR. "Measurement of Intelligence in Different Environments." *B Maritime Psychol Assn* 6:18–23 D '57. *

611. TOPETZES, NICK JOHN. "A Program for the Selection of Trainees in Physical Medicine." *J Exp Ed* 25:263–311 Je '57. *

612. WHITEMAN, MARTIN, AND JASTAK, JOSEPH. "Absolute Scaling of Tests for Different Age Groupings of a State-Wide Sample." *Ed & Psychol Meas* 17:338–46 au '57. *

613. ANGERS, WILLIAM P. "A Psychometric Study of Institutionalized Epileptics on the Wechsler-Bellevue." *J General Psychol* 58:225–47 Ap '58. *

614. ARMITAGE, STEWART G., AND PEARL, DAVID. "Wechsler Bellevue Changes Over Time." *J Clin Psychol* 14:22–4 Ja '58. *

615. FISHER, GRANVILLE C. "Selective and Differentially Accelerated Intellectual Dysfunction in Specific Brain Damage." *J Clin Psychol* 14:395–8 O '58. *

616. GRIFFITH, RICHARD M., AND YAMAHIRO, ROY S. "Reliability-Stability of Subtest Scatter on the Wechsler-Bellevue Intelligence Scales." *J Clin Psychol* 14:317–8 Jl '58. *

617. HILER, E. WESLEY. "Wechsler-Bellevue Intelligence as a Predictor of Continuation in Psychotherapy." *J Clin Psychol* 14:192–4 Ap '58. *

618. LIGHT, MORTON L., AND CHAMBERS, WILLIAM R. "A Comparison of the Wechsler Adult Intelligence Scale and Wechsler-Bellevue II With Mental Defectives." *Am J Mental Def* 62:878–81 Mr '58. *

619. McKEEVER, WALTER F., AND GERSTEIN, ALVIN I. "Validity of the Hewson Ratios: Investigation of a Fundamental Methodological Consideration." Abstract. *J Consult Psychol* 22:150 Ap '58. *

620. MAHRER, ALVIN R., AND BERNSTEIN, LEWIS. "A Proposed Method for Measuring Potential Intelligence." *J Clin Psychol* 14:404–9 O '58. *

621. MUNDY-CASTLE, A. C. "Electrophysiological Correlates of Intelligence." *J Personality* 26:184–99 Je '58. *

622. PLANT, WALTER T., AND RICHARDSON, HAROLD. "The IQ of the Average College Student." *J Counsel Psychol* 5:229–31 fall '58. *

623. SINES, LLOYD K. "Intelligence Test Correlates of Shipley-Hartford Performance." *J Clin Psychol* 14:399–404 O '58. *

624. TREHUB, ARNOLD, AND SCHERER, ISIDOR W. "Wechsler-Bellevue Scatter as an Index of Schizophrenia." *J Consult Psychol* 22:147–9 Ap '58. *

625. WOLFENSBERGER, WOLF P. "Construction of a Table of the Significance of the Difference Between Verbal and Performance IQ's on the WAIS and the Wechsler-Bellevue." *J Clin Psychol* 14:92 Ja '58. *

For reviews by Murray Aborn and William D. Altus, see 4:361; for a review by Robert I. Watson, see 3:298; for a review by F. L. Wells, see 40:1429 (2 excerpts); for related reviews, see B332, 4:362, 3:299–301, and 40:B1121.

[416]
Wechsler Intelligence Scale for Children. Ages 5–15; 1949; downward extension of Form 2 of *Wechsler-Bellevue Intelligence Scale;* also called WISC; individual; 15 scores: verbal (information, comprehension, arithmetic, similarities, vocabulary, digit span-optional), performance (picture completion, picture arrangement, block design, object assembly, mazes-

optional, coding), total; 1 form; record booklet (revised slightly in 1958 but dated 1949); $22 per set of test materials, 25 record booklets, and manual; $2.10 per 25 record booklets; $1.20 per 25 WISC Maze Tests, an alternate subtest which may be used in place of Coding; $2.50 per manual; postpaid; (40-60) minutes; David Wechsler; Psychological Corporation. *

REFERENCES

1-22. See 4:363.
23. ORR, KENNETH N. *The Wechsler Intelligence Scale for Children as a Predictor of School Success.* Master's thesis, Indiana State Teachers College (Terre Haute, Ind.), 1950.
24. PRICE, ARTHUR COOPER. *A Preliminary Study in Statistical Comparison of the Revised Stanford-Binet Intelligence Test Form L With the Wechsler Intelligence Scale for Children Using the Ten Year Age Level.* Master's thesis, University of Florida (Gainesville, Fla.), 1950.
25. SCOTT, GORDON R. *A Comparison Between the Wechsler Intelligence Scale for Children and the Revised Stanford-Binet Scales.* Master's thesis, Southern Methodist University (Dallas, Tex.), 1950.
26. PASTOVIC, JOHN JOSEPH. *A Validation Study of the Wechsler Intelligence Scale for Children at the Lower Age Level.* Master's thesis, Pennsylvania State College (State College, Pa.), 1951.
27. THOMPSON, GRACE M. "W. I. S. C. Patterns of a Selective Sample of Dull Bilingual Children." Abstract. *Am Psychol* 6:493-4 S '51. *
28. THRONE, JOHN MARSHALL. *A Short Form of the Wechsler-Bellevue Intelligence Test for Children.* Master's thesis, University of Florida (Gainesville, Fla.), 1951.
29. WAGNER, WINIFRED K. *A Comparison of Stanford-Binet Mental Ages and Scaled Scores on the Wechsler Intelligence Scale for Children for Fifty Bowling Green Pupils.* Master's thesis, Bowling Green State University (Bowling Green, Ohio), 1951.
30. WINPENNY, NAOMI. *An Investigation of the Use and the Validity of Mental Age Scores on the Wechsler Intelligence Scales for Children.* Master's thesis, Pennsylvania State College (State College, Pa.), 1951.
31. ALTUS, GRACE THOMPSON. "A Note on the Validity of the Wechsler Intelligence Scale for Children." *J Consult Psychol* 16:231 Je '52. * (*PA* 27:5140)
32. BINKS, VIRGINIA M.; FOSTER, DESMOND V.; ADAMS, NICHOLAS A.; AND TRIGGS, FRANCES. "The Relationship of Reading Skills as Learned in Grades 4-College Freshman Years to Verbal and Performance Scores on an Individual Intelligence Test." Abstract. *Am Psychol* 7:376-7 Jl '52. *
33. COHEN, BERTRAM D., AND COLLIER, MARY J. "A Note on the WISC and Other Tests of Children Six to Eight Years Old." *J Consult Psychol* 16:226-7 Je '52. * (*PA* 27:5145)
34. DELATTRE, LOIS, AND COLE, DAVID. "A Comparison of the WISC and the Wechsler-Bellevue." *J Consult Psychol* 16:228-30 Je '52. * (*PA* 27:5147)
35. GRAHAM, E. ELLIS. "Wechsler-Bellevue and WISC Scattergrams of Unsuccessful Readers." *J Consult Psychol* 16:268-71 Ag '52. * (*PA* 27:4564)
36. HAGEN, ELIZABETH P. *A Factor Analysis of the Wechsler Intelligence Scale for Children.* Doctor's thesis, Columbia University (New York, N.Y.), 1952. (*DA* 12:722)
37. KURETH, GENEVIEVE; MUHR, JEAN P.; AND WEISGERBER, CHARLES A. "Some New Data on the Validity of the Wechsler Intelligence Scale for Children." *Child Develop* 23:281-7 D '52. * (*PA* 28:954)
38. MUHR, JEAN P. *Validity of the Wechsler Intelligence Scale for Children at the Five and Six Year Level.* Master's thesis, University of Detroit (Detroit, Mich.), 1952.
39. MUSSEN, PAUL; DEAN, SANFORD; AND ROSENBERG, MARGERY. "Some Further Evidence on the Validity of the WISC." *J Consult Psychol* 16:410-1 O '52. * (*PA* 27:5891)
40. RALEIGH, WILLIAM H. *A Study of the Relationships of Academic Achievement in Sixth Grade With the Wechsler Intelligence Scale for Children and Other Variables.* Doctor's thesis, Indiana University (Bloomington, Ind.), 1952.
41. REIDY, MARY ELIZABETH. *A Validity Study of the Wechsler-Bellevue Intelligence Scale for Children and Its Relationship to Reading and Arithmetic.* Master's thesis, Catholic University of America (Washington, D.C.), 1952.
42. SANDERCOCK, MARIAN G., AND BUTLER, ALFRED J. "An Analysis of the Performance of Mental Defectives on the Wechsler Intelligence Scale for Children." *Am J Mental Def* 57:100-5 Jl '52. * (*PA* 27:3640)
43. SCHWITZGOEBEL, ROLAND R. *The Predictive Value of Some Relationships Between the Wechsler Intelligence Scale for Children and Academic Achievement in Fifth Grade.* Doctor's thesis, University of Wisconsin (Madison, Wis.), 1952.
44. TATHAM, LOUISE JEANETTE. *Statistical Comparison of the Revised Stanford-Binet Intelligence Test—Form L With the Wechsler Intelligence Scale for Children Using the Six and One-Half Year Level.* Master's thesis, University of Florida (Gainesville, Fla.), 1952.
45. TURNER, G. H., AND PENFOLD, D. J. "The Scholastic Aptitude of Indian Children of the Caradoc Reserve." *Can J Psychol* 6:31-44 Mr '52. * (*PA* 26:6935)
46. WARINNER, ELLEN M. *A Comparison of Test Performance of Dull Children on the Revised Stanford-Binet and the Wechsler-Intelligence Scale for Children.* Master's thesis, University of Chicago (Chicago, Ill.), 1952.
47. WILSON, LOLITA. *A Comparison of the Raven Progressive Matrices (1947) and the Performance Scale of the Wechsler Intelligence Scale for Children for Assessing the Intelligence of Indian Children.* Master's thesis, University of British Columbia (Vancouver, B.C., Canada), 1952.
48. ALTUS, GRACE T. "W.I.S.C. Patterns of a Selective Sample of Bilingual School Children." *J Genetic Psychol* 83:241-8 D '53. * (*PA* 28:7207)
49. BLAKEMORE, JOHN R. *A Comparison of Scores of Negro and White Children on the Wechsler Intelligence Scale for Children.* Master's thesis, College of the Pacific (Stockton, Calif.), 1953.
50. DELP, HAROLD A. "Correlations Between the Kent Egy and the Wechsler Batteries." *J Clin Psychol* 9:73-5 Ja '53. * (*PA* 27:7764)
51. ESTES, BETSY WORTH. "Influence of Socioeconomic Status on Wechsler Intelligence Scale for Children: An Exploratory Study." *J Consult Psychol* 17:58-62 F '53. * (*PA* 28:940)
52. GLOWATSKY, EDWARD. "The Verbal Element in the Intelligence Scores of Congenitally Deaf and Hard of Hearing Children." *Am Ann Deaf* 98:328-35 My '53. * (*PA* 28:7921)
53. GRAHAM, E. ELLIS, AND SHAPIRO, ESTHER. "Use of the Performance Scale of the Wechsler Intelligence Scale for Children With the Deaf Child." *J Consult Psychol* 17:396-8 O '53. * (*PA* 28:6449)
54. HITE, LORAIN. *Analysis of Reliability and Validity of the Wechsler Intelligence Scale for Children.* Doctor's thesis, Western Reserve University (Cleveland, Ohio), 1953.
55. HOLLAND, GLEN A. "A Comparison of the WISC and Stanford-Binet IQ's of Normal Children." *J Consult Psychol* 17:147-52 Ap '53. * (*PA* 28:2638)
56. HOLLOWAY, HAROLD DAVID. *Effects of Training Upon, and Relationships Between, Two Standard Child Intelligence Tests.* Doctor's thesis, State University of Iowa (Iowa City, Iowa), 1953. (*DA* 13:884)
57. KNOPF, IRWIN J.; MURFETT, BETTY J.; AND MILSTEIN, VICTOR. "A Comparative Study of the Wechsler-Bellevue Form I and the WISC." Abstract. *Am Psychol* 8:380 Ag '53. *
58. KURETH, GENEVIEVE. *Correlation of the Subtests of the Wechsler Intelligence Scale for Children With the Revised Stanford-Binet for Five and Six Year Olds.* Master's thesis, University of Detroit (Detroit, Mich.), 1953.
59. RACHIELE, LEO D. *A Comparative Analysis of Ten Year Old Negro and White Performance on the Wechsler Intelligence Scale for Children.* Doctor's thesis, University of Denver (Denver, Colo.), 1953.
60. SCHOLL, GERALDINE. "Intelligence Tests for Visually Handicapped Children." *Excep Child* 20:116-20+ D '53. * (*PA* 28:6455)
61. STEMPEL, ELLEN FLAUM. "The WISC and the SRA Primary Mental Abilities Test." *Child Develop* 24:257-61 S-D '53. * (*PA* 29:4089)
62. TRIGGS, FRANCES ORALIND, AND CARTEE, J. KEITH. "Pre-School Pupil Performance on the Stanford-Binet and the Wechsler Intelligence Scale for Children." *J Clin Psychol* 9:27-9 Ja '53. * (*PA* 27:7800)
63. VANDERHOST, LEONETTE; SLOAN, WILLIAM; AND BENSBERG, GERARD J., JR. "Performance of Mental Defectives on the Wechsler-Bellevue and the WISC." *Am J Mental Def* 57:481-3 Ja '53. * (*PA* 27:6629)
64. WECHSLER, DAVID, AND WEIDER, ARTHUR. "Wechsler Intelligence Scale for Children," pp. 522-9. (*PA* 27:7804) In *Contributions Toward Medical Psychology: Theory and Psychodiagnostic Methods, Vol. II.* Edited by Arthur Weider. New York: Ronald Press Co., 1953. Pp. xi, 459-885. *
65. BACON, COLEEN S. *A Comparative Study of the Wechsler-Bellevue Intelligence Scale for Adolescents and Adults, Form I, and the Wechsler Intelligence Scale for Children at the Twelve-Year Level.* Master's thesis, University of North Dakota (Grand Forks, N.D.), 1954.
66. BORUSZAK, RUBY J. *A Comparative Study to Determine the Correlation Between the IQ's of the Revised Stanford Binet Scale, Form L, and the IQ's of the Wechsler Intelligence Scale for Children.* Master's thesis, Wisconsin State College (Milwaukee, Wis.), 1954.
67. CALDWELL, MARCUS B. *An Analysis of Responses of a Southern Urban Negro Population to Items on the Wechsler Intelligence Scale for Children.* Doctor's thesis, Pennsylvania State University (University Park, Pa.), 1954.
68. CARLETON, FREDERICK O., AND STACEY, CHALMERS L. "Evaluation of Selected Short Forms of the Wechsler Intelligence Scale for Children (WISC)." *J Clin Psychol* 10:258-61 Jl '54. * (*PA* 29:2438)
69. DAVIDSON, JACK FREDERICK. *A Preliminary Study in Statistical Comparison of the Revised Stanford-Binet Intelligence Test Form L With the Wechsler Intelligence Scale for Children Using the Fourteen Year Level.* Master's thesis, University of Florida (Gainesville, Fla.), 1954.
70. GAULT, UNA. "Factorial Patterns of the Wechsler Intelligence Scales." *Austral J Psychol* 6:85-9 Je '54. * (*PA* 29:5704)
71. HENDRIX, RUBY. *A Study of the Revision of the Wechsler Intelligence Scale With Particular Reference to Laymen's Concepts of Intelligence.* Master's thesis, University of Texas (Austin, Tex.), 1954.

72. HOLLINGSWORTH, BERNEICE H. *An Investigation of the Correlation Between the Wechsler Intelligence Scale for Children and the Durrell-Sullivan Reading Capacity Test.* Master's thesis, University of Denver (Denver, Colo.), 1954.
73. HOLLOWAY, HAROLD D. "Effects of Training on the SRA Primary Mental Abilities (Primary) and the WISC." *Child Develop* 25:253–63 D '54. * (PA 29:7284)
74. KARDOS, M. SERAPHIA. *A Comparative Study of the Performance of Twelve-Year-Old Children on the WISC and the Revised Stanford-Binet, Form L, and the Relationship of Both to the California Achievement Tests.* Master's thesis, Marywood College (Scranton, Pa.), 1954.
75. KNOPF, IRWIN J.; MURFETT, BETTY J.; AND MILSTEIN, VICTOR. "Relationships Between the Wechsler-Bellevue Form I and the WISC." *J Clin Psychol* 10:261–3 Jl '54. * (PA 29:2449)
76. KOLSTOE, OLIVER P. "A Comparison of Mental Abilities of Bright and Dull Children of Comparable Mental Ages." *J Ed Psychol* 45:161–8 Mr '54. * (PA 29:2270)
77. KRALOVICH, ANNE M. *The Effect of Bilingualism on Intelligence Test Scores as Measured by the Wechsler Intelligence Scale for Children.* Master's thesis, Fordham University (New York, N.Y.), 1954.
78. LEHMANN, MARGARET M. *The Basis of Teacher's Choice Between Two Intelligence Tests in an Elementary School.* Master's thesis, Ohio University (Athens, Ohio), 1954.
79. MARTIN, ANTHONY W., AND WIECHERS, JAMES E. "Raven's Colored Progressive Matrices and the Wechsler Intelligence Scale for Children." *J Consult Psychol* 18:143–4 Ap '54. * (PA 29:2457)
80. MATYAS, R. P. *A Longitudinal Study of the Revised Stanford-Binet and the WISC.* Master's thesis, Pennsylvania State University (State College, Pa.), 1954.
81. SCHONHORN, ROBERT. "A Comparative Study of the Differences Between Adolescent and Child Male Enuretics and Non-Enuretics as Shown by an Intelligence Test." *Psychol Newsl* 6:1–9 S–O '54. * (PA 31:3369)
82. SMITH, LOUIS M., AND FILLMORE, ARLINE R. "The Ammons FRPV Test and the WISC for Remedial Reading Cases." Abstract. *J Consult Psychol* 18:332 O '54. *
83. STARK, ROSEMARY. *A Comparison of Intelligence Test Scores on the Wechsler Intelligence Scale for Children and the Wartegg Drawing Completion Test With School Achievement of Elementary School Children.* Master's thesis, University of Detroit (Detroit, Mich.), 1954.
84. TRIGGS, FRANCES ORALIND; CARTEE, J. KEITH; BINKS, VIRGINIA; FOSTER, DESMOND; AND ADAMS, NICHOLAS A. "The Relationship Between Specific Reading Skills and General Ability at the Elementary and Junior–Senior High School Levels." *Ed & Psychol Meas* 14:176–85 sp '54. * (PA 28:8005)
85. YOUNG, F. L. *The Reliability and Validity of the Wechsler Intelligence Scale for Children as Applied to British School Children of Primary School Age.* Master's thesis, University of London (London, England), 1954.
86. YOUNG, FLORENE M., AND BRIGHT, HOWARD A. "Results of Testing 81 Negro Rural Juveniles With the Wechsler Intelligence Scale for Children." *J Social Psychol* 39:219–26 My '54. * (PA 29:4094)
87. ABRAMS, JULES C. *A Study of Certain Personality Characteristics of Non-Readers and Achieving Readers.* Doctor's thesis, Temple University (Philadelphia, Pa.), 1955. (DA 16:377)
88. ALTUS, GRACE T. "Relationships Between Verbal and Nonverbal Parts of the CTMM and WISC." *J Consult Psychol* 19:143–4 Ap '55. * (PA 30:1008)
89. ARMSTRONG, RENATE GERBOTH. "A Reliability Study of a Short Form of the WISC Vocabulary Subtest." *J Clin Psychol* 11:413–4 O '55. * (PA 30:5972)
90. ARNOLD, FRANK C., AND WAGNER, WINIFRED K. "A Comparison of Wechsler Children's Scale and Stanford-Binet Scores for Eight- and Nine-Year Olds." *J Exp Ed* 24:91–4 S '55. * (PA 30:8121)
91. ATCHISON, CALVIN O. "Use of the Wechsler Intelligence Scale for Children With Eighty Mentally Defective Negro Children." *Am J Mental Def* 60:378–9 O '55. * (PA 30:6079)
92. BECK, HARRY S., AND LAM, ROBERT L. "Use of the WISC in Predicting Organicity." *J Clin Psychol* 11:154–8 Ap '55. * (PA 30:1202)
93. BURKS, HAROLD F., AND BRUCE, PAUL. "The Characteristics of Poor and Good Readers as Disclosed by the Wechsler Intelligence Scale for Children." *J Ed Psychol* 46:488–93 D '55. * (PA 31:3777)
94. CARLETON, FREDERICK O., AND STACEY, CHALMERS L. "An Item Analysis of the Wechsler Intelligence Scale for Children." *J Clin Psychol* 11:149–54 Ap '55. * (PA 30:1018)
95. DORIS, ROBERT E. *The Relationship of the Goodenough Draw-A-Man Test to the Wechsler Intelligence Scale for Children: A Study With Mentally Retarded Children in Fresno County, California.* Master's thesis, Fresno State College (Fresno, Calif.), 1955.
96. DUNSDON, M. I. "The Application of Vocabulary Tests to a Large Sample of Children." Abstract. *B Brit Psychol Soc* (26):22 inset My '55. *
97. DUNSDON, M. I., AND ROBERTS, J. A. FRASER. "A Study of the Performance of 2,000 Children on Four Vocabulary Tests: I, Growth Curves and Sex Differences." *Brit J Stat Psychol* 8:3–15 My '55. * (PA 30:3363)
98. ESTES, BETSY WORTH. "Influence of Socioeconomic Status on Wechsler Intelligence Scale for Children: Addendum." *J Consult Psychol* 19:225–6 Je '55. * (PA 30:2872)
99. MCCULLOCH, THOMAS L.; RESWICK, JOSEPH; AND WEISSMANN, SERENA. "Studies of Word Learning in Mental Defectives: II, Relation to Scores on Digit Repetition, the Stanford-Binet, M, and the WISC Verbal Scale." *Am J Mental Def* 60:140–3 Jl '55. * (PA 30:4797)
100. NEWMAN, J. ROBERT, AND LOOS, FRANK M. "Differences Between Verbal and Performance IQ's With Mentally Defective Children on the Wechsler Intelligence Scale for Children." Abstract. *J Consult Psychol* 19:16 F '55. *
101. PRICE, JOHN R., AND THORNE, GARETH D. "A Statistical Comparison of the WISC and Wechsler-Bellevue, Form I." *J Consult Psychol* 19:479–82 D '55. * (PA 30:7221)
102. SOSULSKI, MICHAEL C. *A Comparison of the Performance of Matched Pairs Old-Dull and Young-Bright Children on Some Items of the Wechsler Intelligence Scale for Children.* Master's thesis, University of Saskatchewan (Saskatoon, Sask., Canada), 1955.
103. STACEY, CHALMERS L., AND CARLETON, FREDERICK O. "The Relationship Between Raven's Colored Progressive Matrices and Two Tests of General Intelligence." *J Clin Psychol* 11:84–5 Ja '55. * (PA 29:7321)
104. STANLEY, JULIAN C. "Statistical Analysis of Scores From Counterbalanced Tests." *J Exp Ed* 23:187–207 Mr '55. * (PA 30:1919)
105. YALOWITZ, JEROME M., AND ARMSTRONG, RENATE GERBOTH. "Validity of Short Forms of the Wechsler Intelligence Scale for Children (WISC)." *J Clin Psychol* 11:275–7 Jl '55. * (PA 30:2937)
106. ALTUS, GRACE T. "A WISC Profile for Retarded Readers." *J Consult Psychol* 20:155–6 Ap '56. * (PA 31:6568)
107. BARRATT, ERNEST S. "The Relationship of the Progressive Matrices (1938) and the Columbia Mental Maturity Scale to the WISC." *J Consult Psychol* 20:294–6 Ag '56. * (PA 31:7893)
108. CROFTS, IRENE E. *A Comparison of Urban and Rural Responses to the Wechsler Intelligence Scale for Children.* Master's thesis, University of Manitoba (Winnipeg, Man., Canada), 1956.
109. GEHMAN, ILA H., AND MATYAS, RUDOLPH P. "Stability of the WISC and Binet Tests." *J Consult Psychol* 20:150–2 Ap '56. * (PA 31:6082)
110. RICHARDSON, HELEN M., AND SURKO, ELISE F. "WISC Scores and Status in Reading and Arithmetic of Delinquent Children." *J Genetic Psychol* 89:251–62 D '56. *
111. ROBINOWITZ, RALPH. "Learning the Relation of Opposition as Related to Scores on the Wechsler Intelligence Scale for Children." *J Genetic Psychol* 88:25–30 Mr '56. * (PA 31:4710)
112. WALKER, HARRY A. *The Wechsler Intelligence Scale for Children as a Diagnostic Device.* Master's thesis, Utah State Agricultural College (Logan, Utah), 1956.
113. BARRATT, ERNEST S., AND BAUMGARTEN, DORIS L. "The Relationship of the WISC and Stanford-Binet to School Achievement." Abstract. *J Consult Psychol* 21:144 Ap '57. *
114. DUNSDON, M. I., AND ROBERTS, J. A. FRASER. "A Study of the Performance of 2,000 Children on Four Vocabulary Tests: II, Norms, With Some Observations on the Relative Variability of Boys and Girls." *Brit J Stat Psychol* 10:1–16 My '57. *
115. HARLOW, JUSTIN E., JR.; PRICE, ARTHUR COOPER; TATHAM, LOUISE J.; AND DAVIDSON, JACK F. "Preliminary Study of Comparison Between Wechsler Intelligence Scale for Children and Form L of Revised Stanford Binet Scale at Three Age Levels." *J Clin Psychol* 13:72–3 Ja '57. *
116. ISON, M. GAIL. "The Effect of 'Thorazine' on Wechsler Scores." *Am J Mental Def* 62:543–7 N '57. *
117. KELLER, JAMES E. "The Relationship of Auditory Memory Span to Learning Ability in High Grade Mentally Retarded Boys." *Am J Mental Def* 61:574–80 Ja '57. * (PA 32:3046)
118. KENT, NORMA, AND DAVIS, D. RUSSELL. "Discipline in the Home and Intellectual Development." *Brit J Med Psychol* 30:27–33 pt 1 '57. * (PA 32:3997)
119. LAIRD, DOROTHY S. "The Performance of Two Groups of Eleven-Year-Old Boys on the Wechsler Intelligence Scale for Children." *J Ed Res* 51:101–7 O '57. *
120. MURPHY, L. J. Chap. 10, "Tests of Abilities and Attainments: Pupils in Schools for the Deaf Aged Six to Ten," pp. 213–51. In *Educational Guidance and the Deaf Child.* Edited by A. W. G. Ewing. Manchester, England: Manchester University Press, 1957. Pp. xiii, 345. *
121. SHARP, HEBER C. "A Comparison of Slow Learner's Scores on Three Individual Intelligence Scales." *J Clin Psychol* 13:372–4 O '57. *
122. STROUD, J. B. "The Intelligence Test in School Use: Some Persistent Issues." *J Ed Psychol* 48:77–86 F '57. *
123. STROUD, JAMES B.; BLOMMERS, PAUL; AND LAUBER, MARGARET. "Correlation Analysis of WISC and Achievement Tests." *J Ed Psychol* 48:18–26 Ja '57. * (PA 32:4623)
124. VOLLE, FRANK O. "A Proposal for 'Testing the Limits' With Mental Defectives for Purposes of Subtest Analysis of the WISC Verbal Scale." *J Clin Psychol* 13:64–7 Ja '57. *
125. WHATLEY, RUTH G., AND PLANT, WALTER T. "The Stability of W.I.S.C. IQ's for Selected Children." *J Psychol* 44:165–7 Jl '57. *
126. WILLIAMS, ROBERT J., AND MACHI, VINCENT S. "An Analysis of Interperson Correlations Among Thirty Psychotics." *J Abn & Social Psychol* 55:50–7 Jl '57. *

127. ALPER, A. E. "A Comparison of the Wechsler Intelligence Scale for Children and the Arthur Adaptation of the Leiter International Performance Scale With Mental Defectives." *Am J Mental Def* 63:312–6 S '58. *
128. COOPER, JAMES G. "Predicting School Achievement for Bilingual Pupils." *J Ed Psychol* 49:31–6 F '58. *
129. FINLEY, CARMEN J., AND THOMPSON, JACK. "An Abbreviated Wechsler Intelligence Scale for Children for Use With Educable Mentally Retarded." *Am J Mental Def* 63:473–80 N '58. *
130. KOPPITZ, ELIZABETH MUNSTERBERG. "Relationships Between the Bender Gestalt Test and the Wechsler Intelligence Test for Children." *J Clin Psychol* 14:413–6 O '58. *
131. LOTSOF, ERWIN J.; COMREY, ANDREW; BOGARTZ, W.; AND ARNSFIELD, P. "A Factor Analysis of the WISC and Rorschach." *J Proj Tech* 22:297–301 S '58. *
132. MATTHEWS, CHARLES GEORGE. *Differential Performances of Non-Achieving Children on the Wechsler Intelligence Scale.* Doctor's thesis, Purdue University (Lafayette, Ind.), 1958. (DA 19:878)
133. PORTWOOD, PETER F. "Progress Report on the Sheffield E.S.N. Study." Abstract. *B Brit Psychol Soc* 34:61 Ja '58. *

ELIZABETH D. FRASER, *Lecturer in Psychology, University of Aberdeen, Aberdeen, Scotland.*

In the WISC, as in the Wechsler adult scales, the concept of mental age is abandoned, a step deplored by many who stress the developmental aspect of intelligence, but hailed by those who have long objected to the defects and inconsistencies of this method of arriving at intelligence quotients.

In WISC, a child's performance is compared not with that of children older or younger than himself, but only with that of his own age group: the IQ given him is simply a convenient way of expressing his score in terms of the mean and standard deviation of his peers. This method has certain clear advantages. In the first place, it ensures equal means and standard deviations (100 and 15 respectively) at all ages—in contrast to the Stanford-Binet where SD's range from 12.5 at age 6 to 20.0 at age 12. With equal SD's direct comparison of IQ's of children of different ages is a much simpler affair. In the second place, it is particularly useful in the upper age levels, where the mental age concept begins to break down, and hypothetical mental ages of 22 years and over have previously had to be called into play.

On the other hand, this system throws great onus on the standardisation sample at each age level, especially in the case of the two extremes tested by the WISC, the 5-year-old and the 15-year-old groups. If a child's performance is to be related to that of a sample of his age group, then that sample must be adequate in number and fully representative; further, the sampling of his and their performance on the test must be adequate.

On the first count, there is good reason to believe that the WISC standardisation samples are as a whole a fair cross section of white American children—the manual provides a moderate amount of information about the selection of the sample—but with only 100 boys and 100 girls in each age group the sampling of very bright and very dull children at any one level must necessarily be somewhat scanty. In the Stanford-Binet, with much the same size of sample at each age, for the purposes of norms the numbers are supplemented by those in the age groups above and below.

On the second count, it appears from the manual that in the lowest age groups and especially in the duller members of these age groups, the sampling of test performance is far from adequate. A child of 5-0 to 5-3 does not have to perform at all in order to secure an IQ of 57 on the Verbal Scale and one of 55 on the Performance Scale. Even for an IQ of 80 on the Verbal Scale, a very small sample of his ability is tested. By contrast, the Stanford-Binet at this age taps a much wider range of performance.

The reliability coefficients quoted for the WISC are commendably high, .88 at age 7½, .96 at 10½ and again at 13½ for the Verbal Scale, and .86 at 7½, .89 at 10½ and .90 at 13½ for the Performance Scale, giving overall coefficients .92, .95, and .94 at those ages for the full scale. These are corrected split-half coefficients.

No validity figures for the test are quoted in the manual, and for information on this vital point and on the correlations between WISC and other tests, the user must refer to the rapidly growing literature, which contains many reports of relatively small scale investigations, which in general suggest that WISC and Stanford-Binet correlate fairly highly (.8 plus) and differ little in their ability to predict academic attainment.

The WISC has several very attractive features. It is easy to give, the material is compact and very accessible, and the testing time varies much less than in the Stanford-Binet. These are important practical points for those engaged in routine testing. WISC has the advantage of two scores, Verbal and Performance, and discrepancies between these scores may be of great value to the clinician and to the school.

For use in Great Britain, many items in the WISC are inappropriate as they stand, and a working party of the British Psychological Society has suggested a number of alterations based on the combined testing experience of some of its members. These amendments have been generally adopted, but so far have not been fully standardised. A great deal of work remains to be done on the development of norms before the test can be unreservedly recommended for British children.

To sum up: For testing children who are not outstandingly bright or markedly dull, the WISC is a convenient, reliable instrument which uses up-to-date material intrinsically interesting to the child; for very young children, and for children at the extreme ranges of intelligence, this reviewer still recommends the Stanford-Binet.

GERALD R. PATTERSON, *Assistant Professor of Psychology, University of Oregon, Eugene, Oregon.*

This instrument undoubtedly represents one of the major contributions to the field of intelligence testing with children in the last two decades. Although the standardization is limited to the white population, attention given to obtaining a representative sample makes this one of the better standardized individual tests. Equally rigorous attention has been given to some aspects of reliability with split-half coefficients in the .80's and .90's reported for the verbal and performance sections, and reliabilities in the .90's for the full scale. Needed, however, is information on test-retest consistency over varying lengths of time. This close attention to many of the problems of test construction, plus the use of up-to-date, inherently interesting materials makes it probable that this will be one of the main tools in the psychologists' armamentarium.

One of the features that is particularly appealing is the amount of information available for decision making when using scaled data from 12 subtests. This procedure is consistent with Wechsler's assumption that he is measuring not only a general g factor but in addition a set of unspecified group factors. Factor analytic studies of both his previous scales for adults, and the present test for children, indicate that at best only a few dimensions are being tapped (*36, 70*). If the subtests on the WISC did, in fact, measure different factors, perhaps we would have an even better contribution to the psychologist in search of more information about his client.

To some extent the work initiated with the adult scales on patterning has carried over to the children's scale, and with the same equivocal results (*34, 35, 48, 106*). For those tending to psychologize the WISC subtest in the same fashion applied to the adult scales, it should be noted that the scales are related but not equivalent. Although the relationship between IQ's on the adult and children's forms is high, all of the assumptions of equivalence are not met (*75, 101*). The assumption of equivalence is even more tenuous when comparing subtests; here only a few of the correlations reach the .70 range (*101*).

The order of items within subtests correlates very well with a ranking of the items in order of difficulty in a research report by Carleton (*94*). However, in spite of the fact that order is maintained, several clinicians, including the writer, have noted that there seem to be abrupt shifts in some of the subtests from easy to rather difficult material. Research supports this impression showing that the distribution of item difficulty is in general bimodal; that is, the items tend to be either easy or difficult with inadequate sampling of moderately difficult items (*94*).

Within a short span of time, the scale has been subjected to a variety of samples and clinical groups including the deaf (*53*), organics (*92*), Negroes (*91*), and mentally defective children (*42, 46, 63, 100*). Although only one study [1] involving cross-cultural comparisons was noted, it will be surprising if others are not made.

An impressive number of studies have been aimed at validating the WISC particularly as it relates to other measures of intelligence. Respectable relationships have been shown with such tests as *Progressive Matrices* (*79, 103, 107*), *California Test of Mental Maturity* (*88*), *SRA Primary Mental Abilities* (*61*), *Arthur Point Scale of Performance Tests* (*33*), *Full-Range Picture Vocabulary Test* (*82*), and with school achievement (*31, 39, 41*).

With the exception of the age group 5-7 years, the relationship between the Stanford-Binet and the WISC is reported consistently in the range .70 to .90 (*46, 55, 90, 115*). Harlow and others (*115*) with 30 6½-year-olds, and Triggs (*62*) with 46 5-year-olds, report lower relationships (.48 to .64). These findings perhaps reflect a tendency for many psychologists to use the Stanford-Binet at the lower age

---

[1] ORTAR, G. "Yitsuv mivhan Wechsler liladim b'Israel." *M'gamot* 4:87-100 '52-53. (*PA* 28:2662)

levels and the WISC for children seven years and older.

As might be expected, the Verbal and Full Scale IQ's on the WISC generally correlate higher with the Stanford-Binet than do the Performance IQ's. Within the average and high ranges of intelligence, one typically finds higher Binet than WISC scores. The discrepancies are particularly marked for the younger age groups and at the higher levels of intelligence (*37, 62, 115*). On the basis of a slightly smaller standard deviation used for the WISC, one would predict some discrepancies particularly at the extremes in intelligence. However, the discrepancies should not be of the magnitude reported nor should they necessarily vary as a function of age. It should be noted that at these younger ages the standard deviation on the Binet is actually smaller, leading to predictions which are directly opposite to results obtained in the literature. This problem merits further consideration, meanwhile calling for cautious interpretation of results at certain age levels and ranges of intellectual functioning.

The WISC, with some exceptions, is technically a satisfying instrument. The preliminary evidence now available indicates that the test will probably satisfy the major requirements of internal consistency, reliability, and validity. Presenting the psychologist with scaled information about the child's functioning in several areas is certainly a step in the right direction. What we need at this point is an individual test that provides information from factorially independent areas of intellective functioning. Such a test would serve the dual purpose of providing a variety of independent sources of information about the individual child and probably have greater predictive utility for many areas of behavior.

ALBERT I. RABIN, *Professor of Psychology and Director of Psychological Clinic, Michigan State University, East Lansing, Michigan.*

This "downward extension" of the *Wechsler Adult Intelligence Scale,* the adequacy of its standardization, and some of its advantages and disadvantages, were reviewed with a high degree of competence in *The Fourth Mental Measurements Yearbook.* Although, psychometrically, it was considered (and still is) a well standardized and thoughtfully devised test, some of the reviewers felt that the final place of WISC would be determined by the research done with it. A fair amount of research data is now available.

The problem of validity has been attacked primarily through correlation with older, standardized intelligence tests. High correlations with the Wechsler-Bellevue Form I were obtained ($r = .87$) by Delattre and Cole (*34*) and Price and Thorne (*101*). However, correlations were insufficient to meet the criteria for test "equivalence" (*101*). Correlations between WISC and W-B with defectives are somewhat lower: .72, .54, and .77 on the Full, Verbal, and Performance Scales, respectively (*63*). The WISC Verbal mean IQ was found to be significantly higher than that of the W-B. In a similar comparison, Knopf and others (*75*) obtained a higher total WISC IQ as well. An analysis of the subtest correlations further supports the thesis of dissimilarity between the two tests. Generally, the equivalence of the two tests in *individual* cases is very much to be doubted.

WISC correlations with the time honored Stanford-Binet are quite high (*37*). Yet, despite this fact, sizable discrepancies (5 to 13 points) between the IQ's of 5- and 6-year-olds have been noted. The WISC IQ's tend to be the lower ones. Especially of questionable validity are Picture Arrangement and Coding with children at the lower age range. Although Holland (*55*) found no relationship between age and IQ discrepancies, Harlow and others (*115*) obtained lower correlations with 6-year-olds as compared with ages 10 and 14. Most studies report higher Verbal IQ correlations with the Binet than for Performance IQ's.

Barratt and Baumgarten (*113*) report that the Verbal and Full Scales compare well with the Binet in their prediction of achievement in reading and arithmetic. Estes (*51*) also reports similar r's (.50's and .60's) with achievers and nonachievers. High r's between the WISC and a variety of other tests such as *Progressive Matrices, California Test of Mental Maturity* and *Columbia Mental Maturity Scale* are also reported in the literature.

The flexibility of the WISC as a research tool has stimulated a good deal of research with special clinical groups (organics, feebleminded, etc.), ethnic (Negro, Mexican) and socioeconomic classes. It probably will continue to be employed as a research tool because of its advantages as a point-scale; it will, like its W-B predecessor, be used to some extent "clinically" as a tool for diagnosis and description of non-intellective factors as well. However, the chief desideratum still remains—that of further investigation of the reliability and validity of this instrument. More longitudinal studies such as the ones reported by Estes (which cast some doubt on the reliability of the WISC) and school achievement prediction studies are needed for the better scientific delineation of this test.

For the present it may be stated that although, in general, the WISC measures the same thing as the Wechsler-Bellevue and the Stanford-Binet, its sensitivity and discrimination at the lower end of the age range (5-6 years) and at the higher end (14-15 years) are inferior to those of the time honored instruments. Serious difficulties in diagnosis of mental deficiency and discrimination within that category are noted. Probably a refinement of the scale, especially at the lower end, would add greatly to its usefulness. Also, more research will aid in establishing the place of this test more solidly as a psychometric and clinical tool.

For reviews by James M. Anderson, Harold A. Delp, and Boyd R. McCandless, see 4:363 (1 excerpt).

REPRINTED FROM *The Sixth Mental Measurements Yearbook*

INTELLIGENCE — SIXTH MMY

REVIEWS BY *J. Stanley Ahmann, Lewis E. Albright, James M. Anderson, Mary C. Austin, Andrew R. Baggaley, Ralph F. Berdie, L. B. Birch, Donald B. Black, Morton Bortner, John E. Bowers, Alvin G. Burstein, W. V. Clemans, Paul C. Davis, Jerome E. Doppelt, N. M. Downie, S. S. Dunn, Marvin D. Dunnette, Walter N. Durost, Dorothy Eichorn, George A. Ferguson, Warren G. Findley, Elizabeth D. Fraser, Robert L. French, Gustav J. Froehlich, James R. Glennon, Goldine C. Gleser, Bert A. Goldman, Russel F. Green, Mary R. Haworth, A. W. Heim, John R. Hills, C. B. Hindley, Marshall S. Hiskey, Marjorie P. Honzik, John E. Horrocks, Lloyd G. Humphreys, John D. Hundleby, Frank B. Jex, H. Gwynne Jones, J. A. Keats, James E. Kennedy, J. S. Lawes, D. Welty Lefever, Philip M. Levy, John Liggett, Howard B. Lyman, Boyd R. McCandless, Melvin R. Marks, William B. Michael, T. R. Miles, John E. Milholland, T. Ernest Newland, John Nisbet, Stanley Nisbet, David A. Payne, Douglas A. Pidgeon, Ellen V. Piers, A. E. G. Pilliner, S. Rachman, Benjamin Rosner, Arthur B. Royse, David G. Ryans, H. J. Sants, William B. Schrader, Richard E. Schutz, Julian C. Stanley, Naomi Stewart, Abraham J. Tannenbaum, Erwin K. Taylor, Albert S. Thompson, Leona E. Tyler, Wimburn L. Wallace, Norman E. Wallen, Emmy E. Werner, Warren W. Willingham, Leroy Wolins, Frank B. Womer, and Wayne S. Zimmerman.*

GROUP

[432]

★A.C.E.R. Higher Tests. Ages 13 and over; 1944–59; formerly called *A.C.E.R. General Ability Test: Advanced M*; 3 scores: linguistic, quantitative, total; 2 forms; 2 parts; mimeographed manual ('59, 36 pages); 3s. 6d. per 10 tests of either part; 1s. 6d. per key; 6s. 6d. per manual; 8s. 6d. per specimen set of either part; postpaid within Australia; D. Spearritt (original manual), M. L. Clark (revised manual), and B. Christeson (form W); Australian Council for Educational Research. *
a) FORMS ML AND WL [LINGUISTIC]. 2 forms: ML ['48], WL ['59], (4 pages); 15(25) minutes.
b) FORMS MQ AND WQ [QUANTITATIVE]. 2 forms: MQ ['48], WQ ['59], (4 pages); 20(30) minutes.

REFERENCES
1. MASON, P. L., AND CASEY, D. L. "The Use of Psychological Tests for Selecting Tabulating Machine Operators." *Personnel Prac B* 16:39–41 S '60. * (*PA* 35:4063)

For a review by C. Sanders, see 5:297.

[433]

★A.C.E.R. Intermediate Test A. Ages 10-0 to 14-0; 1938–61; test essentially the same as *A.C.E.R. General Test A* ['38]; 1 form ['61, 4 pages]; mimeographed manual ['61, 23 pages]; no description of normative population; 3s. 6d. per 10 tests; 1s. 6d. per key; 6s. 6d. per manual; 8s. 6d. per specimen set; postpaid within Australia; 30(50) minutes; Australian Council for Educational Research. *

For excerpts from related book reviews, see 3:1110 and 40:B1005.

[434]

★A.C.E.R. Junior A Test. Ages 8.5–12.0; 1946–58; formerly called *General Test T;* 1 form ['46, 8 pages]; mimeographed manual ['58, 18 pages]; 6s. per 10 tests; 3s. per key; 7s. 6d. per manual; 11s. 3d. per specimen set; postpaid within Australia; 30(40) minutes; Australian Council for Educational Research. *

For a review by R. Winterbourn, see 5:299.

[435]

★A.C.E.R. Junior B Test. Ages 8.5–12.0; 1948–58; 1 form ['48, 8 pages]; manual ('58, 29 pages); not available to government schools; 6s. per 10 tests; 6d. per key; 9s. 6d. per manual; 10s. 9d. per specimen set; postpaid within Australia; 35(60) minutes; Australian Council for Educational Research. *

REFERENCES
1. DUNN, S., AND SPEARRITT, D. "A Comparative Study of the Reliability of Some Verbal and Non-Verbal Intelligence Tests." *Austral J Psychol* 7:169–74 D '55. * (*PA* 31:1030)

For a review by R. Winterbourn, see 5:300.

[436]

★A.C.E.R. Test W.N.V. Ages 13-6 to 16-11; 1960; for research use only; pictorial general ability test; 1 form ['60, 4 pages]; mimeographed manual ['60, 9 pages]; tentative norms; 9s. per 10 tests; 1s. 6d. per key; 2s. 6d. per manual; 5s. per specimen set; postpaid within Australia; 15(25) minutes; Australian Council for Educational Research. *

[437]

★Academic Alertness "AA": Individual Placement Series (Area I). Adults; 1957–59; 7 scores: general knowledge, arithmetic, vocabulary, reasoning ability, logical sequence, accuracy, total; Forms A, B, ('57, 6 pages); preliminary manual ('59, 15 pages); no data on reliability; no description of normative population; separate answer sheets must be used; $20 per 25 tests; $1 per 25 answer sheets; 50¢ per key; $2.50 per specimen set; postpaid; 20(25) minutes; J. H. Norman; the Author. *

[438]

American Council on Education Psychological Examination for College Freshmen. Grade 13; 1924–54; 3 scores: quantitative, linguistic, total; IBM; Editions 1949, 1952, 1954, (14 pages); manual ('50, 7 pages); norms booklet (27–32 pages) for each edition: 1949 Edition ('50), 1952 Edition ('53), 1954 Edition ('55); separate answer sheets must be used; $4 per 25 tests; $1 per 25 IBM answer sheets; 25¢

per set of scoring stencils; postage extra; $1 per specimen set, cash orders postpaid; 38(65) minutes; 1947 and earlier editions by L. L. Thurstone and Thelma Gwinn Thurstone; later editions prepared by publisher from materials developed by the Thurstones; Cooperative Test Division. * (Withdrawn November 1964.)

REFERENCES

1–48. See 40:1377.
49–143. See 3:217.
144–276. See 4:277.
277–439. See 5:308.

440. SPANEY, EMMA. "Personality Tests and the Selection of Nurses." *Nursing Res* 1:4–26 F '53. *
441. JONES, WILLIAM ALTEN. *The Adequacy of Certain Measures Used in the Selection of Freshman State and Merit Scholarship Recipients at Indiana University.* Doctor's thesis, Indiana University (Bloomington, Ind.), 1955. (*DA* 15:1553)
442. JEX, FRANK B. *University of Utah Studies in the Prediction of Academic Success.* University of Utah Research Monographs in Education, Vol. 1, No. 1. Salt Lake City, Utah: the University, July 1957. Pp. ix, 51. *
443. SALTZGAVER, L. DUANE. *An Investigation of the A.C.E. Psychological Examination Percentile Rankings Made by Freshmen Students Who Have Entered the College of Education at the University of Maryland in Alternate Years From 1947 to 1955.* Master's thesis, University of Maryland (College Park, Md.), 1957.
444. SCARF, ROBERT C. "Differential Scores and Unstable Personality." *J Ed Psychol* 48:268–72 My '57. * (*PA* 33:2190)
445. WILLIAMS, CECIL L. *A Study of the Relative Effectiveness of the ACE Psychological Examination and the School and College Ability Test in Predicting First Semester Grade Point Averages.* Master's thesis, University of Kansas (Lawrence, Kan.), 1957.
446. BELAI, LOUISA. "A Comparative Study of the Results of Standardized Tests and Achievement at a Liberal Arts College for Women." *J Ed Res* 52:94–100 N '58. * (*PA* 33:11014)
447. GREHL, PAUL F. *Relative Predictive Value of ACE Psychological Examination for Freshmen, Science-Mathematics Students at Niagara University for the Years 1948, 1949, and 1950.* Master's thesis, Niagara University (Niagara University, N.Y.), 1958.
448. HVISTENDAHL, J. K. "Language Ability as a Factor in 'Cloze' Scores." *Journalism Q* 35:353–4 su '58. *
449. METZGER, STANLEY MILES. *A Study of Selected Characteristics of the Male Graduates and Scholastic Drop-Outs of the 1951 Freshman Class Entering State University of New York Teachers College at Cortland.* Doctor's thesis, Syracuse University (Syracuse, N.Y.), 1958. (*DA* 19:2020)
450. RILEY, ROBERT C. "Comparison of Results of AIA Achievement Test and ACE Psychological Examination." *Acctg R* 33:128–30 Ja '58. *
451. RILEY, ROBERT C., AND LOVE, JEAN O. "The Predictive Value of College Test Scores." *J Higher Ed* 29:393–5+ O '58. *
452. SPIELBERGER, CHARLES D. "On the Relationship Between Manifest Anxiety and Intelligence." *J Consult Psychol* 22:220–4 Je '58. * (*PA* 35:4898)
453. SPILKA, BERNARD. "Numerical-Verbal Ability Differentials: A Theory and Research Program." *Psychol Newsl* 10: 48–55 N-D '58. * (*PA* 33:9351)
454. STINSON, PAIRLEE J. "A Method for Counseling Engineering Students." *Personnel & Guid J* 37:294–5 D '58. * (*PA* 36:2KI94S)
455. WEBBER, VIVIENNE L., AND LEAHY, DOROTHY M. "Home Economics Majors Compared With Other Majors in Education on A.C.E. Test." *Calif J Ed Res* 9:74–9 Mr '58. * (*PA* 33:9053)
456. WIGGINS, NEWTON W. *The Predictive Ability of the Total and Partial Raw Scores of the A.C.E. Psychological Examination, the Cooperative English Tests, and High School Marks in Determining the Scholastic Success of Prospective Freshmen at Western Illinois University.* Master's thesis, Western Illinois University (Macomb, Ill.), 1958.
457. AKAMINE, TOSHIO. *A Study of High School Students' Records and Certain Test Scores as Prediotors of Academic Achievement at the State College of Washington.* Doctor's thesis, State College of Washington (Pullman, Wash.), 1959. (*DA* 20:955)
458. BLACK, D. B. "A Comparison of the Performance on Selected Standardized Tests to That on the Alberta Grade XII Departmental Examination of a Select Group of University of Alberta Freshmen." *Alberta J Ed Res* 5:180–90 S '59. * (*PA* 34:6559)
459. BROAD, ELMER J. *An Investigation of the Relative Effectiveness of the American Council on Education Psychological Examination and the School and College Ability Test in Predicting College Grade Point Averages.* Master's thesis, San Francisco State College (San Francisco, Calif.), 1959.
460. BURKETT, BILLIE. *The ACE Psychological Examination as a Predictor of Academic Success.* Master's thesis, Howard Payne College (Brownwood, Tex.), 1959.

461. CHARLES, DON C., AND PRITCHARD, SALLY ANN. "Differential Development of Intelligence in the College Years." *J Genetic Psychol* 95:41–4 S '59. *
462. DEIGNAN, FRANK J. "Two-Year Changes on the ACE by Students in a College of Art and Architecture." *J Psychol* 47:223–30 Ap '59. * (*PA* 34:6565)
463. EINSPAHR, MARTIN HARLEY. *The Construction and Validation of Scales for Predicting Academic Success in College.* Doctor's thesis, University of Houston (Houston, Tex.), 1959. (*DA* 20:3366)
464. GUTEKUNST, JOSEF GRANT. *The Prediction of Art Achievement of Art Education Students by Means of Standardized Tests.* Doctor's thesis, Temple University (Philadelphia, Pa.), 1959. (*DA* 20:3202)
465. HENDERSON, HAROLD L., AND MASTEN, SHERMAN H. "Six Predictors of College Achievement." *J Genetic Psychol* 94:143–6 Mr '59. * (*PA* 36:4KL43H)
466. HENDERSON, NORMAN B., AND MALUEG, EVELYN. "The Predictive Value of the American Council on Education Psychological Examination for College Freshmen." *Calif J Ed Res* 10:157–66 S '59. * (*PA* 34:8400)
467. KING, PAUL; NORRELL, GWEN; AND ERLANDSON, F. L. "The Prediction of Academic Success in a Police Administration Curriculum." *Ed & Psychol Meas* 19:649–51 w '59. * (*PA* 34:6166)
468. LEAHY, DOROTHY M. "Reading Ability of College Home Economics Students." *Calif J Ed Res* 10:42–8 Ja '59. * (*PA* 34:2106)
469. LEPLEY, WILLIAM M. "Predicting Success in Nurses Training." *J Psychol* 48:121–4 Jl '59. * (*PA* 34:6169)
470. MEYER, BURTON. "An Analysis of the Results of Pre-Nursing and Guidance, Achievement, and State Board Test Pool Examinations." *Nursing Outlook* 7:538–41 S '59. *
471. OBST, FRANCES. "A Study of Selected Psychometric Characteristics of Home Economics and Non-Home Economics Women at the University of California, Los Angeles." *Calif J Ed Res* 10:180–4+ S '59. * (*PA* 34:7957)
472. PETERSON, MARTHA ELIZABETH. *An Evaluation of Relationships Between Test Data and Success as a Residence Hall Counselor.* Doctor's thesis, University of Kansas (Lawrence, Kan.), 1959. (*DA* 21:3364)
473. STACK, SHIRLEY ELLEN. *A Study of the Relationships Between Prospective Teachers' Scores on the Chicago Certification Examination and on Standardized Ability and Achievement Tests.* Doctor's thesis, Northwestern University (Evanston, Ill.), 1959. (*DA* 20:2160)
474. STUCKY, MILO O., AND ANDERSON, KENNETH E. *A Study of Persistence in College Attendance in Relation to Placement-Test Scores and Grade-Point Averages.* University of Kansas, School of Education, Kansas Studies in Education, Vol. 9, No. 2. Lawrence, Kan.: the School, April 1959. Pp. 58. *
475. STUCKY, MILO O., AND ANDERSON, KENNETH E. "A Study of the Relationship Between Entrance-Test Scores and Grade-Point Averages and Length of Stay in College." *Yearb Nat Council Meas Used Ed* 16:164–70 '59. *
476. WEEKS, JAMES S. "The Predictive Validity of A.C.E. and S.C.A.T." *Personnel & Guid J* 38:52–4 S '59. *
477. BLACK, DONALD B. "The Prediction of Freshman Success in the University of Alberta From Grade XII Departmental Results." *Alberta J Ed Res* 6:38–53 Mr '60. *
478. DANSKIN, DAVID G., AND HOYT, DONALD P. "A Study of Some Potential Selective Admissions Criteria." *Col & Univ* 36:68–78 f '60. *
479. DARBES, ALEX. "Relationships Among College Students Scores on ACE, Otis, and WAIS Tests." *Proc W Va Acad Sci* 32:214–6 D '60. * (*PA* 36:3KK14D)
480. GOWAN, J. C. "Intercorrelations of the American Council Psychological Examination With Other Types of Tests." *J Ed Res* 54:157–9 D '60. *
481. GOWAN, JOHN C. "Intercorrelations of the California Psychological Inventory and the Guilford-Zimmerman Temperament Survey With Intelligence as Measured by the ACE." *Calif J Ed Res* 11:213–5 N '60. * (*PA* 35:4856)
482. JUOLA, ARVO E. "Predictive Validity of Five College-Level Academic Aptitude Tests at One Institution." *Personnel & Guid J* 38:637–41 Ap '60. * (*PA* 35:2791)
483. LANG, MARY JANE. *The Relationship Between Certain Psychological Tests and Shorthand Achievement at Three Instructional Levels.* Doctor's thesis, University of Missouri (Columbia, Mo.), 1960. (*DA* 21:2632)
484. MARCHES, JOSEPH R. "An Empirical Study of Performance in Mathematics and Performance on Selected Entrance Examinations." *J Ed Res* 53:181–7 Ja '60. * (*PA* 35:7087)
485. MARKWARDT, FREDERICK CHARLES, JR. *Pattern Analysis Techniques in the Prediction of College Success.* Doctor's thesis, University of Minnesota (Minneapolis, Minn.), 1960. (*DA* 21:2990)
486. MAXWELL, MARTHA JANE. *An Analysis of the California Psychological Inventory and the American Council on Education Psychological Test as Predictors of Success in Different College Curricula.* Doctor's thesis, University of Maryland (College Park, Md.), 1960. (*DA* 21:549)
487. MILLER, ROBERT E. "Selection of Engineering Students for an Abbreviated Mathematics Sequence." *Personnel & Guid J* 39:224–5 N '60. *

488. VINEYARD, EDWIN E., AND BAILEY, ROBERT B. "Interrelationships of Reading Ability, Listening Skill, Intelligence, and Scholastic Achievement." *J Develop Read* 3:174–8 sp '60. * (*PA* 35:1274)

489. WELNA, CECILIA THERESA. *A Study of Reasons for Success or Failure in College Mathematics Courses.* Doctor's thesis, University of Connecticut (Storrs, Conn.), 1960. (*DA* 21:1811)

490. WOLPIN, MILTON, AND GARFIELD, SOL L. "Continuance in Medical School as Related to ACE Scores." *J Med Ed* 35:999–1002 N '60. *

491. BARNHART, E. L., AND ANDERSON, KENNETH E. *A Study of the Relationships Between Grade-Point Averages, Placement-Test Scores, Semester Hours Earned, and Area of Major Interest for the Group Who Entered the University of Kansas in the Fall of 1954.* University of Kansas, School of Education, Kansas Studies in Education, Vol. 11, No. 1. Lawrence, Kan.: the School, January 1961. Pp. 36. *

492. CLYDE, ROBERT BURDETTE. *An Empirical Comparison of the School and College Ability Tests and the American Council on Education Psychological Examination.* Doctor's thesis, University of Southern California (Los Angeles, Calif.), 1961. (*DA* 22:151)

493. COOLEY, JOHN C. "A Study of the Relation Between Certain Mental and Personality Traits and Ratings of Musical Abilities." *J Res Music Ed* 9:108–17 f '61. *

494. IVANOFF, JOHN M. "The Use of Discriminant Analysis for Predicting Freshman Probationary Students at One Midwestern University." *Ed & Psychol Meas* 21:975–86 w '61. *

495. MCADAMS, HENRY EDWARD. *The Prediction of General and Differential Achievement in Two Samples of Junior College Students.* Doctor's thesis, University of Southern California (Los Angeles, Calif.), 1961. (*DA* 22:3524)

496. OMMEN, DUANE F. *A Statistical Study of the Relationship of the American Council on Education Psychological Examination Scores and High School Rank to Future College Success.* Master's thesis, South Dakota State College (Brookings, S.D.), 1961.

497. ROTH, ROBERT M., AND GILBERT, JEAN. "AF: A New Approach to the Concept of Achievement." *J Ed Res* 55:90–2 O '61. *

498. THOMSEN, STEPHEN J. "Academic Achievement and Institutional Testing Program Scores: A Longitudinal Study of One Class at a Liberal Arts College." *Proc W Va Acad Sci* 33:120–3 N '61. * (*PA* 36:5KL20T)

499. WITHERSPOON, ROBERT PAUL. *A Comparison of the Temperament Trait, Interest, Achievement, and Scholastic Aptitude Test Score Patterns of College Seniors Majoring in Different Fields at the Arkansas State Teachers College.* Doctor's thesis, University of Arkansas (Fayetteville, Ark.), 1961. (*DA* 22:1091)

500. ZUCKOWSKY, LEO MARK. *The Efficiency of SCAT and Other Selected Variables in Predicting Success in the Various Lower Division College Curricula.* Doctor's thesis, University of Notre Dame (Notre Dame, Ind.), 1961. (*DA* 22:2297)

501. ATKINSON, JOHN ALLEN. *Factors Related to the Prediction of Academic Success for Disabled Veterans in a Four Year College Engineering Program.* Doctor's thesis, University of Denver (Denver, Colo.), 1962. (*DA* 23:2786)

502. BERDIE, RALPH F.; LAYTON, WILBUR L.; HAGENAH, THEDA; AND SWANSON, EDWARD O. *Who Goes to College? Comparison of Minnesota College Freshman, 1930–1960.* Minneapolis, Minn.: University of Minnesota Press, 1962. Pp. vii, 56. *

503. CAMPBELL, JOEL T.; OTIS, JAY L.; LISKE, RALPH E.; AND PRIEN, ERICH P. "Assessments of Higher-Level Personnel: 2, Validity of the Over-All Assessment Process." *Personnel Psychol* 15:63–74 sp '62. * (*PA* 37:3908)

504. CASH, W. L., JR. "Predictive Efficiency of Freshman Entrance Tests." *J Psychol Studies* 13:111–6 Je '62 [issued F '64]. *

505. CRISTANTIELLO, PHILIP D. "Attitude Toward Mathematics and the Predictive Validity of a Measure of Quantitative Aptitude." *J Ed Res* 55:184–6 D–Ja '62. *

506. DARLEY, JOHN G. *Promise and Performance: A Study of Ability and Achievement in Higher Education.* Berkeley, Calif.: Center for Study of Higher Education, University of California, 1962. Pp. vii, 191. *

507. GILLESPIE, HORACE FORD. *The Construction and Validation of Scales for Predicting Academic Success in College in Specified Subject Matter Areas.* Doctor's thesis, University of Houston (Houston, Tex.), 1962. (*DA* 23:1576)

508. GREENWOOD, ROBERT LEROY. *The Prediction of Academic Success in the Technical Curricula of Community Colleges: An Investigation of the Prediction of Academic Success in the Chemical, Electrical, and Mechanical Curricula of Three Community Colleges in New York State.* Doctor's thesis, New York University (New York, N.Y.), 1962. (*DA* 23:898)

509. JONES, REGINALD L., AND SIEGEL, LAURENCE. "The Individual High School as a Predictor of College Academic Performance." *Ed & Psychol Meas* 22:785–9 w '62. * (*PA* 37:7189)

510. LONGENECKER, E. D. "Perceptual Recognition as a Function of Anxiety, Motivation, and the Testing Situation." *J Abn & Social Psychol* 64:215–21 Mr '62. * (*PA* 38:1723)

511. RALSTON, NANCY C. "The Advanced Placement Program in the Cincinnati Public Schools." *Personnel & Guid J* 40:557–60 F '62. * (*PA* 36:5KB57R)

512. ROHRS, DENNIS KERLIN. *Predicting Academic Success in a Liberal Arts College Music Education Program.* Doctor's thesis, State University of Iowa (Iowa City, Iowa), 1962. (*DA* 23:2937)

513. SUPER, DONALD E., AND CRITES, JOHN O. *Appraising Vocational Fitness by Means of Psychological Tests, Revised Edition*, pp. 109–18. New York: Harper & Brothers, 1962. Pp. xv, 688. * (*PA* 37:2038)

514. WHITESIDE, OSCAR R. *The Cooperative Algebra Test and the ACE Psychological Quantitative Test as Predictors of Mathematical Success for Engineering Success for Engineering Majors at Arlington State College.* Master's thesis, Texas Christian University (Ft. Worth, Tex.), 1962.

515. ANGOFF, WILLIAM H. "Can Useful General-Purpose Equivalency Tables Be Prepared for Different College Admission Tests?" *Personnel & Guid J* 41:792–7 My '63. *

516. ANGOFF, WILLIAM H. "Can Useful General-Purpose Equivalency Tables Be Prepared for Different College Admissions Tests." *Proc Inv Conf Testing Probl* 1962:57–73 '63. * (*PA* 38:3187)

517. BOWMAN, ALDEN E.; COBERLY, R. L.; LUCAS, DONALD; AND WHALEY, EARL R. "Selection and Performance of Scholarship Hall Award Winners." *J Col Student Personnel* 4:220–6+ Je '63. *

518. COROTTO, LOREN V. "The Prediction of Success in Initial College Mathematics Courses." *J Ed Res* 56:268–71 Ja '63. *

519. DURFLINGER, GLENN W. "Academic and Personality Differences Between Women Students Who Do Complete the Elementary Teaching Credential Program and Those Who Do Not." *Ed & Psychol Meas* 23:775–83 w '63. *

520. DURFLINGER, GLENN W. "Personality Correlates of Success in Student-Teaching." *Ed & Psychol Meas* 23:383–90 su '63. * (*PA* 38:1427)

521. EYDE, LORRAINE D., AND WALDROP, ROBERT S. "Predictors of Scores on an Employment Counselor Selection Battery." *Ed & Psychol Meas* 23:799–805 w '63. *

522. GIANNELL, A. STEVEN, AND FREEBURNE, CECIL M. "The Comparative Validity of the WAIS and the Stanford-Binet With College Freshmen." *Ed & Psychol Meas* 23:557–67 au '63. * (*PA* 38:6057)

523. JONES, KENNETH J. "Predicting Achievement in Chemistry: A Model." *J Res Sci Teach* 1:226–31 S '63. *

524. KAMMANN, RICHARD A. "Aptitude, Study Habits, and Reading Improvement." *J Develop Read* 6:77–86 w '63. *

525. KING, DONALD THOMAS. *A Comparison of a College Generation of Rural and Nonrural Students in Selected Colleges of Arkansas With Respect to Academic Success and Number of Semesters of Undergraduate Study Completed.* Doctor's thesis, University of Arkansas (Fayetteville, Ark.), 1963. (*DA* 24:626)

526. MACK, LAURENCE L. "Examining the Efficiency of Predictors Presently Being Used at the University of Alberta." *Alberta J Ed Res* 9:100–10 Je '63. *

527. MORICE, HERBERT OSCAR. *The Predictive Value of the High School Grade Point Average and a Select Group of Standardized Tests for Junior College Achievement.* Doctor's thesis, University of Houston (Houston, Tex.), 1963. (*DA* 24:1482)

528. MORRISON, JACK. "The Comparative Effectiveness of Intellective and Non-Intellective Measures in the Prediction of the Completion of a Major in Theater Arts." *Ed & Psychol Meas* 23:827–30 w '63. *

529. NORTH, ROBERT D. "Results of the ERB Public School Norms Project, 1962–63." *Ed Rec B* 84:72–4 Jl '63. *

530. OSBORN, LYNN R. "An Analysis of the Relationship Between Speech Performance and Performance on Written Examinations of Course Content in a Beginning College Speech Course as Reflected in Assigned Grades." *Univ Kans B Ed* 17:68–71 F '63. *

531. POWERS, GLENN F., AND WITHERSPOON, PAUL. "ACE Scores as a Possible Means of Predicting Success in General College Physics Courses." *Sci Ed* 47:416 O '63. *

532. SASSENRATH, JULIUS M., AND FATTU, NICHOLAS A. *Relationships Among Factors Obtained for Elementary and Secondary Student Teachers.* Bulletin of the School of Education, Indiana University, Vol. 39, No. 5. Bloomington, Ind.: Bureau of Educational Studies and Testing, the School, September 1963. Pp. vii, 34. * (*PA* 38:6666)

533. TAULBEE, GEORGE C., SR. *Construction and Validation of a Scale for Predicting Graduation From a College of Optometry.* Doctor's thesis, University of Houston (Houston, Tex.), 1963. (*DA* 24:387)

534. WILLIAMS, JOHN E., AND JOHNSTON, ROBERT A. "The Area Tests of the Graduate Record Examination as a Partial Criterion of Academic Success." *J Exp Ed* 32:95–100 f '63. *

535. ZIMMERER, ANN MORGAN. *A Study of Selected Variables for Predicting Success in a College of Engineering.* Doctor's thesis, University of Houston (Houston, Tex.), 1963. (*DA* 24:842)

For reviews by Hanford M. Fowler and William B. Michael, see 5:308; for reviews by

W. D. Commins and J. P. Guilford of the 1946 Edition, see 3:217; for reviews by Jack W. Dunlap and Robert L. Thorndike of the 1939 Edition, see 40:1377; for reviews by Anne Anastasi and David Segel of the 1937 Edition, see 38:1037.

[439]

★**American School Intelligence Test.** Grades kgn–3, 4–6, 7–9, 10–12; 1961–63; tests for grades 4–12 "developed from the *Illinois General Intelligence Scale*" (1920–26) which was designed for grades 3–8; IBM for grades 4–12; 4 levels; 2 editions (self-marking, machine scorable) for grades 4–12; separate answer sheets must be used with machine scorable edition; $3.20 per 35 tests for grades kgn–3, 4–6, or 7–9; $3.60 per 35 tests for grades 10–12; $1.75 per 35 IBM answer sheets; 25¢ per scoring stencil for answer sheets; 50¢ per specimen set of any one level; postage extra; (55–65) minutes; Willis E. Pratt, M. R. Trabue, Rutherford B. Porter, and George A. W. Stouffer, Jr.; Bobbs-Merrill Co., Inc. *
a) PRIMARY BATTERY. Grades kgn–3; self-marking Forms D, E, ('63, 8 pages); manual ('63, 25 pages).
b) INTERMEDIATE BATTERY. Grades 4–6; self-marking Forms D, E, ('61, 4 pages); machine scorable Forms DM, EM, ('61, 4 pages); separate manuals (identical except for directions) for self-marking edition (18 pages) and machine scorable edition (16 pages) of this level and advanced level below.
c) ADVANCED BATTERY. Grades 7–9; details same as for intermediate level.
d) HIGH SCHOOL BATTERY. Grades 10–12; self-marking Forms D, E, ('63, 4 pages); machine scorable Forms DM, EM, ('63, 4 pages); manual ('63, 15 pages) for both editions.

REFERENCES

1. HOFFORTH, ROGER A. *An Investigation of the Validity of the American School Intelligence Tests.* Master's thesis, Indiana State College (Terre Haute, Ind.), 1961. (Abstract: *Teach Col J* 33:45)

DAVID A. PAYNE, *Assistant Professor of Education, Syracuse University, Syracuse, New York.*[1]

These tests, available at four levels with two forms each, are designed to cover the range of mental ability from kindergarten through grade 12.

The tests for grades 4–12 "have been developed from the *Illinois General Intelligence Scale,* published in 1926," which was designed for use in grades 3 through 8. They are intended to include "samplings....of the types of mental abilities" commonly possessed by American students. For the three upper levels these abilities, called "factors," are: analogies, arithmetic problems, sentence vocabulary, nonverbal analogies, "sentence ingenuity," "arithmetic ingenuity," and synonyms and antonyms. Each of the three upper level tests is composed of 110 five-choice items apparently arranged in order of difficulty without regard to the exact character of the items. Tables are provided for conversion of single raw scores to MA's, IQ's, and percentile ranks. No attempt is made to obtain or use part scores representing differential abilities. No theoretical or empirical rationale for the selection of these "factors," which are the same rubrics included in the older test of 38 years ago, is presented. The statement, "a survey was first made of all the currently used intelligence tests to determine which of these factors were measured in such tests," is the only justification offered for the item content and type utilized in the tests. The reviewer believes the use of the word "factor" is somewhat inappropriate since apparently no factor analysis has been made of the ASIT.

At the primary level the abilities sampled are grouped in the test according to the following categories: comprehension, similarities, picture completion, series completion, "form" (object completion), arithmetic, discrimination, and opposites. These tests, which are composed of 77 items, again yield only a single score for conversion to MA, IQ, or percentile rank.

Some statistical data regarding the tests are furnished in the manuals. Alternate form reliability coefficients range between .85 and .92 for samples of from 120 to 222 pupils. Of interest is the fact that the high school and the primary level tests, which were reportedly administered within a single grade, give higher reliability coefficients than do the intermediate and advanced tests for which testing was done in a three-grade span. Some confusion exists about the nature of the sample used to study the equivalence reliability for the primary level test. The coefficient is reported for 145 first grade students, with standard deviations of 18 and 20 for Forms D and E, respectively. Other within-grades data indicate SD's half as large for the same level groups. The equivalent forms reliability estimate was probably based on a grades kindergarten–3 sample. Since one would expect greater variability across grades, the intermediate and advanced level reliability estimates are probably spuriously high. The coefficients for the intermediate and advanced tests would have been lower if they had been computed within a single grade. Even so, these coefficients are relatively high for alternate form reliabilities. Odd-even reliabilities, which are given for the primary and high school tests, run higher of course. The

---

[1] The reviewer wishes to acknowledge with thanks the assistance of Dr. Eric F. Gardner in the preparation of this review.

authors should be commended for presenting with each reliability coefficient, standard errors of measurement along with appropriate descriptive statistics.

The validity of an intelligence test, as is well recognized, is more difficult to evaluate and demonstrate than its reliability. No attempt is made in the manuals to present a discussion of what is sometimes called "rational" validity as was done so well in the Lorge-Thorndike manual. Only the statement that the items "were developed and pretested with great care" is offered. However, some information about concurrent validity—erroneously called by the authors construct or congruent (?) validity—is reported. Correlations, obtained from small samples, between the various batteries of the *American School Intelligence Test* and other intelligence tests such as the Stanford-Binet, WISC, WAIS, CTMM, and PMA are presented. These correlations are amazingly high, being in many instances as high as one of the reliability coefficients. Estimates of validity were made also by comparing test scores with school success. Correlations between ASIT IQ's obtained from the primary, intermediate, and advanced tests and scores on the *American School Achievement Tests* are reported as .92, .82, and .84, respectively for samples of 64–215 cases. Correlations between each of the batteries and school grades are .81, .75, .65, and .76, respectively. Although these coefficients are relatively high, they were obtained from rather small samples ($n = 45$ to 215) in specific situations over a period of years.

Test norms are presented in terms of mental age, IQ, percentile ranks, and stanines. Percentile ranks and stanines are presented for each form by age, but mental age is tabled without respect to form. No within-grade normative data are provided. Special emphasis is given to the use of the MA and "ratio" IQ for interpretative purposes despite the increasing amounts of research data which bear upon the variable rate of mental ability development as it interacts with psychometric scale characteristics. Such practice appears to be inconsistent with present knowledge. Detailed, but in a few instances somewhat inexact, descriptions of these norms are provided. Considering the studies which had been done relating the achievement test batteries and the intelligence test batteries, it is surprising to the reviewer that no expectancy tables are provided. These would have greatly facilitated the interpretation of resulting scores. Efforts were made to obtain a representative sample of the children attending school in the United States. It is reported that the children were selected on a randomized basis and stratified with respect to geographical location, size of community, school enrollment, and grade assignment. Efforts were made also to take into account socioeconomic status, race, and other factors of cultural significance. Although the impossibility of obtaining a truly representative sample is well known, the concern of the authors to take into account variables known to be related to intelligence is commendable. In the selection of a normative sample, research has shown that the number of pupils included is secondary to the number of classrooms represented. Over 300 classrooms, over 10,000 pupils, and schools in more than 70 school systems were used at each of the four levels. Over 35 states are represented. The participating communities are listed in the manuals.

Numerous interpretive problems are associated with ASIT scores. Although reasonable guidelines are provided for interpreting relative position of examinees with respect to the norms (percentile ranks and stanines), no attempt is made to show how scores can be used in actual educational settings. Answers to such questions as, "What can I say about the nature of the intelligence indicated by scores on this test," are not offered. Nine potential uses of the ASIT are listed in the manuals under the heading "Nature and Purposes of Intelligence Tests." Nowhere in the manuals are methods described whereby the uses can be made operational. Furthermore, the user is given little help in understanding the technical data. Coefficients of all types abound, but the user is left to his own devices to determine their significance. Occasionally misleading statements bearing upon interpretation are found, e.g., the standard error of measurement "is a more significant predictor of reliability than the correlation coefficients."

In conclusion, the *American School Intelligence Test* represents the adaptation and modification of earlier efforts to devise an omnibus single score measure of "academic brightness" which was undertaken initially at the time this concept was so popular. In providing such a measure it compares reasonably well with other group intelligence tests. It does not, however, provide separate verbal and quantitative measures as do many others, nor do the authors take advantage of their opportunity to provide concurrent standardization of intelligence and achievement scores. Obviously, it has little value for differential academic prediction, where multiscore measures of general academic ability might better be used. In spite of the reviewer's generally favorable impression of the care taken in developing this test he is unable to note any unique contribution. The tests do look promising as single score tests, but, even here, more data are needed before recommendations for use can be made. Information bearing upon construct and predictive validity, equivalence-stability reliability, and within-grades normative data, together with detailed examples of specific applications of test data, are requested.

FRANK B. WOMER, *Associate Professor of Education, and Test Consultant, Bureau of School Services, The University of Michigan, Ann Arbor, Michigan.* [Review of Intermediate and Advanced Batteries.]

The *American School Intelligence Test* (ASIT), new in 1961, is based upon the *Illinois General Intelligence Scale,* published in 1926. The tests show their ancestry in purpose, design, and items. They are spiral omnibus tests, and are designed for ease of use in securing a single "global" IQ.

The tests are designed to sample "the types of mental abilities involved in learning most of the materials commonly taught in American schools." An inspection of test items supports this assertion. The inspection, however, does not lend support to the authors' assertion that these tests are measuring "seven factors" of intelligence. The claim of measuring seven factors is made because seven item types are utilized. Item types such as analogies, arithmetic problems, sentence vocabulary, nonverbal analogies, sentence ingenuity, arithmetic ingenuity, and synonyms and antonyms may be defended in a "global" intelligence test, but should not be labeled "factors."

EDITING. The tests represent the poorest job of editing this reviewer has seen. The following examples are taken from the teacher's manuals for the edition utilizing carbon-type test-answer sheets. (*a*) In the table of contents every chapter except one is wrong in its pagination, and all tables are paged incorrectly. For example, Chapter 7, "Technical Data," is listed as beginning on page 27; the manual has 18 pages. These errors have been corrected in the manual for the IBM answer sheet edition. (*b*) In the tables of contents of both manuals, each chapter and table is identified by a Roman numeral. In the manuals each is identified by an Arabic number. (*c*) The directions for administration state that "approximately 55 minutes" of actual testing time is "suggested." At no place is an exact time limit stated. (*d*) Directions for administration end with the examiner asking pupils if they have any questions. There are no directions to "Begin Work" and no directions to "Stop Working." (*e*) Mental and chronological ages are printed in six-month intervals in the table of IQ's. No mention is ever made of whether to interpolate or use the nearest six month age. (*f*) A cover sheet for each specimen set says that the tests "were standardized among students in each of the 50 states." In the manual it is stated that "thirty-five states....were represented in the sample." If one counts the states as they are listed, 35 are named but a footnote for 3 of them says "Scores not tabulated."

RELIABILITY. Alternate-form reliabilities of .846 and .862 are claimed. These certainly are satisfactory. However, a claimed standard error of 1.087 for Form D intermediate level raw scores, when the standard deviation is 16.196 and the reliability .846, is a little difficult to fathom. This must be an error in computation. In the reliability tables all four reported standard errors of raw scores are 1.21 or less with SD's 16, 17, 14, and 14, and r's .864 and .862. Standard errors of IQ's also are reported in the validity tables. They run from 1.63 to 5.33 (for a situation in which 35.77 is the standard deviation). They obviously are in error.

VALIDITY. The principal claims of validity are made on the basis of concurrent evidence. Relationships between the ASIT and other intelligence tests are about .72 and .70 with *SRA Primary Mental Abilities,* .84 and .82 with the *California Short-Form Test of Mental Maturity,* and .67 with WISC. These indices are as high as one would expect to find generally. However, group mean IQ's vary by +2.5, −8.5, −6.3, +9, and +21 points in the five possible comparisons. More disturbing than the mean differences are the comparative SD's. For the five comparisons the differences in SD run +17.36 (PMA), +4.11 (CTMM-S), +4.73 (CTMM-S), +22.36 (WISC), and +12.17 (PMA). An intelligence test yielding standard deviations running 22 points higher than the WISC and 12 or 17 points higher than the PMA, or even 4 points higher than the CTMM-S (in a situation suggesting a homogeneous group) is subject to serious question.

Two comparisons are made with the *American School Achievement Tests* (r's of .82 and .84). Again, the standard deviations of IQ's are high (29.52 and 27.81). Two comparisons are made with school grades (r's of .75 and .65) and the IQ standard deviations are 32.12 and 28.21. Whatever the IQ scale is for the ASIT, it is not the conventional one with mean 100 and standard deviation 16. In connection with the latter point, it is interesting to note that the ASIT uses the ratio IQ rather than the deviation IQ. All major intelligence tests have shifted to the deviation IQ.

STANDARDIZATION. The ASIT were standardized in 1961 along with the *American School Achievement Tests*, the intermediate and advanced levels of which were restandardized. It is claimed that this conforms to "a general trend or pattern." Presumably a test user can use both the intelligence test and the achievement tests and then make some judgment as to whether a pupil is working up to capacity. It is true that this same procedure is used by other authors and publishers, but before a test user decides to make such comparisons he should look carefully at the correlations between the tests. The ASIT and ASAT correlate .82 and .84 whereas the ASIT's reliabilities are given as .85 and .86. This suggests that the ASAT are so closely related to the ASIT that they could reasonably be considered alternate forms. Under such circumstances, comparisons for assessing under- or over-achievement are highly suspect.

The manuals state that "the same national sampling yielded normative data for both tests." Yet an inspection of the names of communities participating in the ASIT sample yields the names of 14 cities (excluding those with "scores not tabulated") that do not appear in the norm group for the intermediate level ASAT. (Four of the 14 names do appear in the norm group for the advanced level.) Whether this is another case of poor editing or whether the two tests, in actuality, were normed on different samples cannot be determined from the manuals.

CONCLUSION. This reviewer cannot imagine a situation in which he would care to use the *American School Intelligence Test*. Many of the statistics presented in the manuals are either incorrect or misleading, and the editorial work on the manuals is the poorest seen by the reviewer. It is a shame that a test with reasonably good face validity should have been treated so poorly. The test user seeking an easily administered intelligence test yielding a single IQ should look to the *Henmon-Nelson Tests of Mental Ability* or the *Otis Quick-Scoring Mental Ability Tests*.

[440]

★**Analysis of Relationships.** Grades 12–16 and industry; 1960; manual subtitle is *A Test of Mental Ability;* 1 form (4 pages); mimeographed preliminary manual (6 pages); tentative norms; $2.75 per 25 tests; $1 per manual and key; $1.25 per specimen set; postage extra; (30–60) minutes; Edwin E. Ghiselli; Consulting Psychologists Press, Inc. *

REFERENCES
1. GHISELLI, EDWIN E. "The Relationship Between Intelligence and Age Among Superior Adults." *J Genetic Psychol* 90:131–42 Je '57. *
2. GHISELLI, EDWIN E. "Intelligence and Managerial Success." *Psychol Rep* 12:898 Je '63. * (PA 38:6759)

GUSTAV J. FROEHLICH, *Director, Bureau of Institutional Research, University of Illinois, Urbana, Illinois.*

The *Analysis of Relationships* purports to measure "the same type of general intellectual abilities that are ordinarily measured by intelligence tests"; but the author makes no attempt to define or explain the term "general intellectual abilities." As a matter of fact, this reviewer, after studying the materials available to him, has the very strong impression that this test project is far from finished—that whatever unique merit there might be in the use of items involving a response based on ability to analyze an implied relationship among sets of terms, statements, and numbers, has not been demonstrated.

The test, consisting of 40 multiple choice questions, is a conglomerate arrangement of items involving number series, vocabulary, proverbs, and arithmetic. These 40 items were selected, according to the author, from an original pool of 120 such items on the basis of (*a*) "the best distribution of responses among the incorrect alternatives," (*b*) "the highest correlations with total test score," (*c*) "the highest correlations with college grades and with scores on the *Otis Self-Administering Test of Mental Ability,*" and (*d*) their ability to discriminate among individuals, "even at the higher occupational and educational levels." This reviewer can only guess at the degree to which these criteria are operative. Adequate evidence, both statistical and descriptive, is lacking in the published materials available.

Evidence of the validity of the total test score is limited to three simple tables. The first table gives seven different correlations with school grades, ranging from .65 for the average of four years of high school work (the same correlation was also found for the first two years of college work) to .25 for first semester college freshman grades. This low correlation, however, is based on a sample of only 37 cases.

The second table of validity coefficients consists of nine coefficients showing "occupational validity." All those with a numerical value of better than .60 are based on samples of less than 40. The other coefficients range from .31 to .22, all except one again being based on very small samples.

The third set of validity coefficients are correlations with other tests. They range from .78 for the *Otis Self-Administering Tests of Mental Ability* (based on 127 cases) to .35 with an unidentified vocabulary test (based on 36 cases).

Evidence of the reliability of the total test score is limited to a single table of 12 odd-even coefficients, ranging from .90 (for 123 high school seniors) to .70 (for 30 clerical workers).

The table of percentile norms attempts to differentiate among lower division, upper division, and graduate college students, as well as among management personnel, salesmen, line supervisors, clerical workers, and skilled workers. These norms are not too meaningful on a nation-wide basis. All cases for the university student classifications are based on students from only one institution—the University of California at Berkeley. The other categories are based on very small samples.

The test booklet is a four-page expendable booklet, clearly printed with clearly stated and adequate directions. Hand scoring must be used; but the arrangement of the items in the booklet and the available scoring key make this a relatively simple task.

At best the *Analysis of Relationships* is a short, easily administered, untimed, group intelligence test. It may be useful when a gross measure of mental ability must be obtained quickly. It should not, however, be used routinely for guidance purposes.

WIMBURN L. WALLACE, *Director, Professional Examinations Division, The Psychological Corporation, New York, New York.*

The only description of the test provided in the manual is that it is "designed to measure the same type of general intellectual abilities that are ordinarily measured by intelligence tests....[and to] yield finer discriminations at the higher levels of ability." The manual goes on to say that the test has been used successfully with students and industrial personnel but fails to say for what purpose. No suggestions on the interpretation of scores are offered. Evaluation of the test is difficult in the absence of statements concerning its intended use and purpose and comments concerning the meaning of results.

The *Analysis of Relationships* is a short omnibus test. Its 40 items are divided more or less equally among the following five types: proverbs, analogies, arithmetic problems, number series, and word knowledge.

Reliability estimates are reported on 12 groups of students and employed personnel. Odd-even, split-half coefficients, adjusted by the Spearman-Brown formula, range from .70 to .90 with a median of .82. These values are rather low, especially for discriminations among individuals. The lack of a second form of the test eliminates the possibility of any alternate form reliability estimates.

As evidence of validity, three sets of correlation coefficients between scores on the test and external criteria are presented: (*a*) seven correlations between scores and average grades in high school or college range from .25 to .65, and are all concurrent validities; (*b*) nine correlations between scores and job or rating criteria in industry range from .22 to .76, but all the groups in which job proficiency ratings were used as the criterion measure comprised fewer than 40 individuals; hence, they were rather small for stable evidence; (*c*) six correlations between scores on this and other tests included highs of .70 with the *California Test of Mental Maturity* and .78 with the *Otis Self-Administering Tests of Mental Ability;* however, the remaining correlations indicate relatively low relationships which cannot be interpreted because the other tests were identified only as "arithmetic," "vocabulary," etc. For none of the correlation coefficients is the mean or standard deviation for either variable provided. This serious omission frustrates meaningful interpretation of the coefficients reported. It should also be noted that no predictive validation is described.

Mention of sex differences on the test is based on four small groups of students and employed persons in which the men tended to score about .6 point higher than the women. Although means and standard deviations are again lacking for these groups, it is very dubious that this small difference warrants the general conclusion that "the scores of males are slightly superior to those of females." At any rate, no separate norms are provided for the two sexes.

Similarly, statements about age differences in scores are insufficiently supported by data. Average scores of students and employed persons in different age brackets are compared, but groups of 50, 31, 11, and 6 persons in the four age ranges above 39 are much too small for even tentative indications about age differences in test performance.

Tables of norms are provided for three levels of college students and five categories of employed personnel. The collegiate norms were based solely on students at the Berkeley campus of the University of California. At least some of the employed groups are atypical, such as those of foremen and skilled workers which contained over half with some college education. Four of the five industrial norm groups comprise fewer than 100 persons. The 32 line supervisors in the smallest group hardly constitute an adequate number for even preliminary norms tables. Estimates for general population norms are derived from equivalencies with Otis and CTMM scores. They appear rather unrealistic in comparison with the other norms, in that the medians for all the student, managerial, sales, and clerical groups fall above the 90th percentile of the general population norms. No mean or standard deviation is provided for any norm group, but some indication of the restricted dispersion of scores can be inferred from the fact that the semi-interquartile range is only about three points in each of the seven norm groups.

SUMMARY. The *Analysis of Relationships* is a short test of mental ability containing an assortment of five general types of items. Lack of alternate forms is unfortunate. Reliability of the test borders on the inadequate, especially for individual discriminations. Evidence of validity is sketchy and erratic and is as yet insufficient in extent or description to provide a basis for evaluating the effectiveness of the test. No means or standard deviations are supplied with any of the coefficients or norms tables in the manual. The norms, based on university student groups and some personnel in employed categories, should be considered highly tentative in view of the questionable sampling and atypical composition of those groups. Statements on the purpose and uses of the test, as well as aids in interpretation of scores documented with relevant data, are needed in subsequent editions of the manual. Until these deficiencies are remedied, the test should be considered only for experimental use. Future assessment of potential utility will depend on the development and availability of the needed information about the test.

[441]
*Army General Classification Test, First Civilian Edition.** Grades 9–16 and adults; 1940–60; also called AGCT; IBM; 1 form ('47, identical with the 1940 Form 1a of the Army edition); 2 editions; revised manual ('60, 19 pages); technical report ('60, 31 pages); separate answer pads or sheets must be used; $10.80 per 20 tests; 60¢ per technical report; 75¢ per specimen set of either edition; postage extra; 40(50) minutes; test by Personnel Research Section, the Adjutant General's Office, War Department; Science Research Associates, Inc. *

a) [HAND SCORING EDITION.] 1947–60; Form AH ('47, 19 pages); $2.40 per 20 answer pads.

b) [MACHINE SCORING EDITION.] 1947–60; IBM; Form AM ('47, 12 pages); $5 per 100 IBM answer sheets; $1 per set of scoring stencils.

REFERENCES

1–14. See 3:219.
15–29. See 4:280.
30–46. See 5:310.
47. LeShan, Lawrence; Marvin, Sidney; and Lyerly, Olga. "Some Evidence of a Relationship Between Hodgkin's Disease and Intelligence." *A.M.A. Arch Gen Psychiatry* 1:477–9 N '59. * (*PA* 34:5584)
48. Darley, John G. "The Basis for Equivalent Scores on the Annual Editions of the American Council on Education Psychological Examination (ACE), 1941 to 1954," pp. 170–83. In his *Promise and Performance: A Study of Ability and Achievement in Higher Education.* Berkeley, Calif.: Center for Study of Higher Education, University of California, 1962. Pp. vii, 191. *
49. Griffith, Richard M.; Estes, Betsy Worth; and Zerof, Selwyn A. "Intellectual Impairment in Schizophrenia." *J Consult Psychol* 26:336–9 Ag '62. * (*PA* 38:4604)
50. Super, Donald E., and Crites, John O. *Appraising Vocational Fitness by Means of Psychological Tests,* Revised Edition, pp. 120–8. New York: Harper & Brothers, 1962. Pp. xv, 688. * (*PA* 37:2038)
51. Kent, Eric G.; Price, A. Cooper; and Anderson, Richard J. "The Performance of Patients With Organic Brain Impairment and Unimpaired Patients on the Army General Classification Block Counting Test." *J Gerontol* 18:180–1 Ap '63. * (*PA* 38:4547)

BERT A. GOLDMAN, *Associate Professor of Education, and Associate, Counseling Service, State University of New York at Albany, Albany, New York.*

The 1960 revised manual and technical report contain data which suggest the early version of the AGCT, released for civilian consumption in 1947, may be used as a test of general mental ability, scholastic aptitude (high school, college, and graduate school), trade school success, success in industrial training programs, and perhaps to a limited extent in the identification of mental illness, as well as an indicator of cultural background. A test of such extensive applicability would truly be a psychometric Goliath! However, John T. Dailey came to a much different conclusion in the *Fourth Mental Measurements Yearbook:* "it would appear that the early version of the AGCT released to the public domain would have little to recommend it to the civilian user in preference to many of the similar commercial tests now on the market." The following review supports Dailey's 1953 appraisal by strongly suggesting that there is little, if any, evidence in the revised manual or technical report to justify a more favorable conclusion.

Nothing is provided in the way of new reliability studies. Though the reliability coefficients are commendable, the majority falling in the .90's, they appear to be the same correlations based upon studies of military personnel reported in the old manual. In addition, a single test-retest study over a one-year interval showing the average gain in raw score to be 4.42 is gleaned from a small, select group—75 per cent of an original group of 59 war veterans in one trade school.

Norms for two of the four high school grades are derived by interpolation, instead of being collected by actually administering the AGCT. Norms for college graduates are based upon converted academic aptitude test scores (names not mentioned), rather than on actual AGCT scores. The two sets of norms for university freshmen were collected from very select groups and show wide discrepancies—a raw score of 90, for example, equaling the 20th percentile in one set and the 60th percentile in the other. Trade school norms are included, but no mention is made of the curriculum of the one school upon which they are based.

Adult male norms appear to be identical to those provided in the 1948 manual, with the exception that in the latest listing the raw scores are grouped in intervals. Each interval is presented with the middle standard score and percentile for the interval instead of separately listing each raw score with its corresponding standard score and percentile as is true of the 1948 presentation.

Nothing new is presented in the way of occupational norms. The same classical chart devised by Stewart almost 20 years ago appears in both the manual and technical report. How well do these norms apply to today's general civilian population when 20 years ago there was concern that Stewart's sample was not representative of the population because it did not include women, non-whites, officers, or those who did not take the AGCT because of deferment, rejection, and discharge? Then too, how well represented are those occupations with relatively few subjects who may or may not have been successful men in the civilian job they *claimed* they held before induction?

At first glance, the 10 pages of validity data contained in the technical report appear impressive. Upon closer scrutiny the data seem to be a catch-as-catch-can collection of correlations derived from a study by SRA's professional staff, old military studies, unpublished dissertations, published articles, and in addition what is referred to as personal communication. Such a conglomeration offers little in the way of a detailed, systematic effort to validate the many uses claimed for the AGCT.

The technical report contains four pages of studies involving a multitude of ratings for various military trainee courses of World War II fame. This research offers little, if any, value to present-day civilian consumers of the AGCT. Such data merely pad the pages!

The technical report asserts that each part of the test measures specific factors. No data are presented to show that such assertions are founded upon statistical analysis. On the contrary, two part score intercorrelation studies included in the technical report strongly suggest that the three types of items are far from measuring separate factors.

AGCT standard scores based upon a mean of 100 and a standard deviation of 20, when used as intelligence test results, may mislead naïve individuals to believe they are dealing with IQ's.

Army General Classification Test

Included in the technical report is an informative table, compiled by the Army Personnel Research Section during World War II, containing indices of difficulty and discrimination for each item in Form 1A of the AGCT. Although the item analysis published almost two decades ago suggests that many arithmetic items are too easy for the general population, no changes have been made in the test. Also, five block counting items, along with eight vocabulary items, appear to be poor discriminators. It would also be helpful to know whether biserial or point biserial coefficients were used to determine discrimination indices, since the former are usually larger.

Apart from the statistical analysis, cursory reading of the items indicates that changes are in order for dated expressions, such as 2 packs of cigarettes for 25 cents, milk selling for 9 cents per quart, and 5½ pounds of meat costing 10 cents per pound. Also, the answer to block counting item 120 is given as 10. Where is the tenth block hidden?

In sum, this reviewer recommends that the publishers conduct a complete set of validity and reliability studies of the AGCT. New and complete norms are needed, in addition to a revision of several of the items. Until systematic and comprehensive data are provided, this reviewer would prefer to use those instruments which are supported by such data.

HOWARD B. LYMAN, *Associate Professor of Psychology, University of Cincinnati, Cincinnati, Ohio.*

This is still the same test reviewed critically by John T. Dailey in the *Fourth Mental Measurements Yearbook*. His comments are still pertinent, in spite of a new technical report and a new examiner's manual, both published in 1960.

The new manual contains little beyond directions for administering and scoring. Less than seven pages are devoted to norms, uses, validity, reliability, and the like. Of these, two pages are used in presenting Stewart's classic study of AGCT scores by previous civilian occupations of World War II white enlisted men; however, Stewart's name is mentioned nowhere in the manual, nor is any date given for her study of nearly 20 years ago. One could easily assume that these scores had been obtained recently and, except for a parenthetical statement in small type, that they had been obtained from civilians.

Percentile norms are given for ninth, tenth, eleventh, and twelfth grade boys and girls, and for adult males; no further description of these groups is given in the manual.

The technical report (of 31 pages) is a little better. Some effort is made to state the number of subjects involved, type of statistic used, etc.; however, even here the publisher uses many vague phrases, such as "at various intervals" (this phrase describing a test-retest reliability coefficient). In a table, "The AGCT as a Predictor of High School Achievement," SRA fails to mention the time lag between testing and collection of criterion data (to assure us that these are coefficients of *predictive,* rather than *concurrent,* validity).

The report suggests that "meaningful data may be gleaned from an analysis of these [part] scores," but gives little supportive evidence; there are no part score norms, no consideration of part score reliabilities, etc.

Neither the manual nor the report cautions the test user to guard against overgeneralization of Stewart's World War II occupations study; nor does either source mention that most World War II soldiers were tested on forms other than Form 1a (which became the First Civilian Edition). Previous editions of the MMY contained these criticisms.

It is surprising that such an old test has not been more adequately reported. SRA does little to warn the unsophisticated test user against possible misuse or overinterpretation. The large number of omitted or vague statements does much to argue against the use of the AGCT. Either the publishers did not realize that the points should have been made more clear, or they deliberately left the points unclear; in either instance, most test users probably will want to consider selecting a test which comes closer to meeting the APA Technical Recommendations.

For a review by John T. Dailey, see 4:280; see also 3:219 (1 excerpt).

[442]

California Analogies and Reasoning Test. Grades 10–13; 1958; IBM; Forms A, B, (10 pages); manual (16 pages); $4.20 per 35 tests; separate answer sheets may be used; 5¢ per IBM answer sheet; 20¢ per scoring stencil; postage extra; 50¢ per specimen set, postpaid; 40(50) minutes; Claude Mitchell; California Test Bureau. *

JOHN R. HILLS, *Director, Testing and Guidance, The University System of Georgia, Atlanta, Georgia.*

The *California Analogies and Reasoning Test* (CART) is described by the publisher as a scholastic aptitude test, for grades 10 to 13, whose nature and difficulty make it particularly effective with the more able students. The publisher claims that the analogies items, based on content in natural science, mathematics, social science, English, and literature, call upon reasoning power, knowledge of terms, recognition of relationships, and analytical skill. Since the various subject matters appear in random order, the publisher claims that the score reflects adaptability as well as breadth and accuracy of knowledge.

This analogies test surely does use content from the named subjects, and in about equal amounts, but the reviewer could find no substantiation for claims that reasoning power, analytical skill, or adaptability influence the scores. It appears to the writer that the test measures primarily diffuse knowledge of miscellaneous information and terms. Few items could be "figured out" if at least one of the specific terms in the analogy was not known or recognized. Often knowledge about one term was sufficient to determine the correct answer. Such content may, however, be a sound basis from which to make predictions about school grades, i.e., to measure scholastic aptitude.

Is the test particularly effective with more able students? They may enjoy taking it, but the resulting measures will not be very good. The test doesn't have enough top except at the tenth grade. Both the limited set of norms provided and the table of item difficulties (a very commendable feature in a test manual!) reveal the preponderance of items which are answered correctly by the bulk of twelfth grade students. If a tenth grader gets fewer than 20 of the 101 items correct, he is below the first percentile.

The test should be easy to use. The score is the number right with no correction for guessing. The same key is used for both forms, which appear to be sound alternates in content, difficulty, etc. The items are not tricky. Only one error was found, that being an equating of "alliteration" and "rhyming."

As to technical details, reliabilities quoted for Form A appear adequate, ranging from .88 to .94; none are given for Form B. While correlations are reported between CART scores and scores from several other aptitude tests (for example, the *California Short-Form Test of Mental Maturity,* the *American Council on Education Psychological Examination,* and the *Miller Analogies Test*), the school user will be most interested in the validity of the CART scores for predicting school and college grades. Here the data are not as "extensive" as one might be led to believe from the publisher's catalog. They are based on students from five different secondary schools and one college of undesignated type or location. There is no indication of the proportions of male and female students in the groups; apparently the data were not treated separately by sex. The largest group on which prediction of grades was studied was 168. However, from these limited data it appears that validities for school grade prediction in the .50's can be expected, which is about the usual validity for scholastic aptitude tests.

The norms, as mentioned above, are limited. The manual gives a brief description of some procedure by which the CART norms were supposed to be made representative of a national sample by giving both the CART and the *California Short-Form Test of Mental Maturity* to about 800 students. That description was not at all clear to the reviewer after several readings. In fact, he was left wondering why he should not choose the *California Short-Form Test of Mental Maturity* in the first place for whatever purpose he had in mind in considering CART. Even if further inquiry revealed that the CART norms truly represented unselected national groups at the designated grade levels, it is severely handicapping that males and females are not presented separately. Table 3 in the manual leads one to believe that this test generally favors males. This is very unusual for a test so heavily loaded with verbal material. Certainly separate norms for the sexes are necessary. Other tests for similar purposes often give far more extensive norms and validity information, as for example, the *College Qualification Tests* or the *Cooperative School and College Ability Tests*. While these two tests take longer to administer and thus may not directly compete with CART, there is no justification for the shorter test having available so much less adequate interpretive material.

In summary, the *California Analogies and*

Reasoning Test may not be a bad choice as a predictor of school grades. As with any such tests, local specific validity studies provide the answer to this question. The best the publisher can do is provide data indicating that the local validities are likely to be of useful magnitude. The CART has good alternate forms (neither of them is "secure"), is easy to use, and simple to score. Its most serious weaknesses are that it is too easy for able students and its normative data are minimal. Potential users should consider such tests as the *Otis Quick-Scoring Mental Ability Tests* and the *California Short-Form Test of Mental Maturity* as likely alternate choices for predicting academic grades from about the same amount of testing time.

WIMBURN L. WALLACE, *Director, Professional Examinations Division, The Psychological Corporation, New York, New York.*

The *California Analogies and Reasoning Test* (CART) is a general mental ability test intended for use in grades 10–13. Each of the two forms of the test contains 101 items in the form of analogies, the first half in the stem and the second half in the options. Content is drawn from science, social studies, mathematics, and English. Since most of the items depend on specific factual knowledge, claims in the manual that the test involves reasoning power and a number of primary verbal abilities are not substantiated.

The reliability of CART is probably satisfactory, but the estimates of it reported in the manual are insufficient evidence. Coefficients computed by the Kuder-Richardson formula 21 range from .88 to .94 for Form A, but this method is inappropriate with timed tests. One retest coefficient of .93 is reported for a group of 64 twelfth grade students, but the sample is so small and isolated that it can hardly be considered sufficient. In the "validity" section of the manual, an alternate-form coefficient of .82 is reported based on 307 twelfth grade students tested on Forms A and B with a one-week interval between the testings. This would appear to be a more meaningful reliability coefficient than the others reported.

Validity data are extremely meager. Students in five high schools were tested during their senior year and their CART scores were correlated with overall grade averages for their last one, two, three, or four years. One group of 85 college freshmen (which obtained a mean CART score lower than the means of two of the five high school groups), was tested during the freshman year and their scores were correlated with first semester grade averages. These concurrent validity coefficients against academic criteria ranged from .30 to .59. Some correlations with other tests are reported. The tables include a gratuitous list of coefficients corrected for range of the other test and for attenuation on both tests. For four groups of students in grades 10, 11, and 13, coefficients of correlation between scores on CART and scores on scholastic aptitude tests range from .51 with ACE to .76 with SCAT. For two small groups of students in grades 12 and 13, correlations with parts of the Cooperative English and General Achievement tests tended to run higher than those with academic ability tests. Although these two samples of 49 and 59 students do not provide adequate basis for generalizations, a closer relationship of CART with achievement tests than with aptitude tests would not be surprising in view of the content of CART.

A table of percentile and standard score norms for each grade 10–13 appears in the manual. The explanation of the derivation of these norms is so beclouded that it would be meaningless to most users. Number of cases, distribution by sex, mean score, and standard deviation are not given for any of the four norm groups. There is a surprisingly large jump in the scores from grades 10 to 11, then only small increases from grades 11 to 12 to 13. No mention is made of sex differences in performance on the CART nor of justification for providing only combined sex norms.

The section of the manual entitled "Uses of Test Results" is rather pretentious in view of the limited research on the efficacy of the test. In the suggested applications to counseling and selection situations, there are repeated references to prediction of later performance in spite of the fact that there is no evidence at all contained in the manual on the predictive validity of the test. Such statements as the following are hardly sophisticated aids to the interpretation of test results:

> The greatest values will be realized from the percentiles or standard scores developed from local distributions of scores, either for high school or college groups. The real purpose and value of such a percentile or standard score is in helping students understand their potentialities with reference to a specific situation. This is particularly true if constructively presented to those whose abilities to succeed are seem-

ingly precluded or to those who tend to under-estimate their abilities. In either case, the expectancy concept inherent in the data is a positive approach that can reduce feelings of frustration and failure in some and can build up confidence in others.

SUMMARY. CART is a 101-item test designed to assess general scholastic ability. The items are in the form of analogies and appear to depend on specific information in science, social studies, mathematics, and English rather than on reasoning ability. Although the manual suggests that CART is usable for educational counseling in grades 10–13, evidence of validity for this purpose is as yet too meager to justify such application. Either more extensive standardization or clarification of the derivation and adequacy of the present norms is needed. At least until these deficiencies in validity and normative data are remedied, the CART cannot be recommended over other readily available tests which are designed for the same purpose and have much superior documentation of their essential characteristics and function.

J Consult Psychol 23:471 O '59. Edward S. Bordin. * The studies offered to support its predictive validity are less than adequate because they are based on samples tested either concurrently with the collection of criterion data (academic grades) or where the grades had already been earned. Thus, there is evidence to support the test's value for concurrent validity or for postdiction, but none for prediction.

J Counsel Psychol 7:53–4 su '60. Gordon V. Anderson. * According to its title, this is an analogies and reasoning test; it would be hard to prove or disprove the correctness of this. It is the feeling of the present reviewer, however, that very few of the items require the kind of reasoning ability usually considered necessary for solving analogies. * Altogether, more than two-thirds of the items are simple matching exercises, and most of them are so constructed that a correct answer will result from knowledge of only one of the two pairs. The analogies form of question is usually expected to require the testee to make use of information which he possesses. It is not normally used to merely check the presence or absence of that information. When a test has been constructed to do a particular job, perhaps to quibble over face validity is picayune. The CART is offered as a test of scholastic ability, so it should be judged on the basis of its predictive validity. Unfortunately, up to the present time no data are available for such a judgment. * Whether the CART measures aptitude or achievement, the score pattern is clearly related to educational level. Careful study of the test and of the statistical data reported in the manual lead to the conclusion here that it is a rough measure of general culture or educational development. There are no data to support its use for prediction purposes. On the plus side, it can be said that the test is well printed, it is easy to administer and interesting to take. The manual is well prepared, but the erroneous bias that it has proven usefulness as a prediction instrument could mislead naive counselors and is likely to irritate the more sophisticated ones.

[443]
*California Short-Form Test of Mental Maturity, 1963 Revision. Grades kgn–1.5, 1–3, 3–4, 4–6, 6–7, 7–9, 9–12, 12–16 and adults; 1938–64; 7 scores: logical reasoning, numerical reasoning, verbal concepts, memory, language total, nonlanguage total, total; IBM, NCS, and Grade-O-Mat for grades 4 and over; 8 levels; profile (date same as for test, 1 page) for each level; series guide to interpretation ('64, 38 pages) for this and test 444; $4.20 per 35 tests for Levels 0–1H; 10¢ per scoring key; $4.90 per 35 tests for Levels 2–5; separate answer sheets or cards may be used at Levels 2–5; 5¢ per IBM answer sheet; 20¢ per hand scoring stencil; 80¢ per set of machine scoring stencils; 9¢ per Scoreze answer sheet; 3¢ per Cal-Card; 20¢ per hand scoring stencil for Cal-Cards; 4¢ per set of Grade-O-Mat scorable punch-out cards; 6¢ per stylus; 6¢ per backing pad; 2¢ per profile; see 671 for prices of NCS answer sheets; 50¢ per guide to interpretation; tape recorded directions for administration of Levels 2–5 available at $5.95; postage extra; $1 per specimen set of any one level; $6.95 per specimen set of any one level (Levels 2–5) with tape; postpaid; Elizabeth T. Sullivan, Willis W. Clark, and Ernest W. Tiegs; California Test Bureau. *
a) LEVEL 0. Grades kgn–1.5; 1 form ('62, 11 pages); manual ('63, 49 pages); 34(39) minutes.
b) LEVEL 1. Grades 1–3; 1 form ('62, 12 pages); manual ('63, 52 pages); 41(46) minutes.
c) LEVEL 1H. Grades 3–4; 1 form ('62, 10 pages); manual ('64, 55 pages); 42(47) minutes.
d) LEVEL 2. Grades 4–6; 1 form ('61, 11 pages); manual ('63, 59 pages); 43(48) minutes.
e) LEVEL 2H. Grades 6–7; 1 form ('61, 11 pages); manual ('63, 60 pages); 41(46) minutes.
f) LEVEL 3. Grades 7–9; 1 form ('61, 11 pages); manual ('63, 57 pages); 41(46) minutes.
g) LEVEL 4. Grades 9–12; 1 form ('61, 11 pages); manual ('63, 53 pages); 39(45) minutes.
h) LEVEL 5. Grades 12–16 and adults; 1 form ('61, 11 pages); manual ('63, 47 pages); 39(45) minutes.

REFERENCES

1–15. See 5:313.
16. STACK, SHIRLEY ELLEN. *A Study of the Relationships Between Prospective Teachers' Scores on the Chicago Certification Examination and on Standardized Ability and Achievement Tests.* Doctor's thesis, Northwestern University (Evanston, Ill.), 1959. (*DA* 20:2160)

17. GUNDERSEN, RICHARD O., AND FELDT, LEONARD S. "The Relationship of Differences Between Verbal and Nonverbal Intelligence Scores to Achievement." J Ed Psychol 51:115-21 Je '60. * (PA 35:3981)
18. KOO, GLADYS Y. A Study of the Stability of Test-Retest IQ Scores Derived From the California Short Form Tests of Mental Maturity. Master's thesis, University of Hawaii (Honolulu, Hawaii), 1960.
19. MACARTHUR, R. S. "The Coloured Progressive Matrices as a Measure of General Intellectual Ability for Edmonton Grade III Boys." Alberta J Ed Res 6:67-75 Je '60. * (PA 36:2HD67M)
20. WARREN, PHYLLIS A. "A Mental Maturity Test as One Criterion for Admission to an American School Abroad." Personnel & Guid J 39:197-202 N '60. * (PA 35:3966)
21. WOLINS, LEROY; MACKINNEY, A. C.; AND STEPHANS, PAUL. "Factor Analyses of High School Science Achievement Measures." J Ed Res 54:173-7 Ja '61. * (PA 35:7129)
22. CLEGG, HERMAN D., AND DECKER, ROBERT L. "The Evaluation of a Psychological Test Battery as a Selective Device for Foremen in the Mining Industry." Proc W Va Acad Sci 34:178-82 N '62. *
23. DREW, ALFRED STANISLAUS. The Relationship of General Reading Ability and Other Factors to School and Job Performance of Machinist Apprentices. Doctor's thesis, University of Wisconsin (Madison, Wis.), 1962. (DA 23:1261)
24. MCDONNELL, M. W. "The Prediction of Academic Achievement of Superior Grade Three Pupils." Alberta J Ed Res 8:111-8 Je '62. * (PA 37:3886)
25. MACARTHUR, R. S., AND ELLEY, W. B. "The Reduction of Socioeconomic Bias in Intelligence Testing." Brit J Ed Psychol 33:107-19 Je '63. * (PA 38:4271)
26. NELSON, MARVEN O., AND EDELSTEIN, GERALD. "Raven Progressive Matrices, Non-Language Multi-Mental Test, and California Test of Mental Maturity: Intercorrelations." Psychol Rep 13:46 Ag '63. * (PA 38:6061)

JULIAN C. STANLEY, *Professor of Educational Psychology, and Director, Laboratory of Experimental Design, University of Wisconsin, Madison, Wisconsin.*

At the time this review was prepared (late March 1964), the Guide to Interpretation and Technical Report were not available to the reviewer, though the Examiner's Manuals for all but Level 1H were. Thus most technical questions can only be asked, not answered. A discussion of the norms must also await the appearance of these two accessories.

This 1963 revision (the tests themselves were copyrighted in 1961 or 1962) requires about 40 minutes of actual test-marking time, including several minutes for the tester to read a story to the examinees, compared with about 50 minutes for all but the lowest level of the previous version. This reduction in testing time in an attempt to fit the Short Form within a single school period was effected partly by reducing the number of items (e.g., from 145 to 120 in the highest level) and partly by reducing the time per item (14 per cent increase in speededness for the highest level, from 2.8 items per minute to 3.1).

Of the seven subtests, one (Delayed Recall) is completely new, whereas "Tests 1 through 6 include from 40 to 60 per cent new items [at Level 5; the percentage of new items ranges from 16 to 73 for subtests at other levels]. The 'core items' are those selected as the most efficient from the 1957 Edition." No criterion of efficiency is mentioned, though presumably it will be discussed in the Technical Report.

The eight levels, from preprimary to advanced, differ considerably in content but far less in format. In order to cover them all carefully, the reviewer sought the help of several persons well versed in teaching, testing, and measurement.[1] From his study of their critiques and the forms, he will note certain pervasive aspects and some specificities.

The most general observation is that the tests are intended primarily for students tested by their teachers. Directions for administering the various levels are for the most part clear, simple, and detailed. It seems likely that a conscientious teacher with little or no formal training in measurement can administer the CTMM S-Form adequately. He will of course need some training in order to interpret the results, however; the profile on the back of the test booklet bombards him with 12 raw scores from this one test. Some of these scores are expressible as percentile ranks, two kinds of standard scores, standard score IQ's, MA's, and an ISI (Intellectual Status Index, which "reflects the examinee's performance in relation to a national norm population for his *grade* placement").

The materials come separately designed for the various grade levels in reasonably convenient form. Failure to include even the simplest statistical evidence of reliability and validity in the Examiner's Manuals seems unfortunate, however. The less-than-one-page "Interpretation and Use of Results" part of the manuals, where the significance of intra-individual differences is considered, provides criteria for guarding against overinterpreting small and moderate differences between factor scores or section scores for the same person, but if material this complex can be presented in the Examiner's Manuals, then more basic aspects of reliability could have been included also.

This leads us to consider the statements in the Examiner's Manual that:

Factor analysis by the Thurstone centroid method produced four discrete factors, which form major interpretive units of the 1963 *Short-Form*. The composition of Factor 1, Logical Reasoning, has been considerably revised in the new *Short-Form*. For-

[1] He thanks the following persons for their assistance: Ronald D. Anderson, Patricia M. Davis, Frank H. Fox, William E. Hauck, Nora Hubbard, Yakub R. Namek, Louis A. Pingel, Andrew C. Porter, Robert M. Pruzek, Yoshiyuki Matsuura, D. G. Woolpert, and Patricia A. Woolpert.

merly, this factor consisted of two tests, Similarities and Inferences. In the 1963 Revision, the Inferences test has been removed and the Analogies and Opposites tests have been added to the factor.

Other changes were made, too, and new factor analyses were done to justify changes made in the subtests whose scores are summed to yield factor scores.

The two greatest weaknesses of the 1963 S-Form appear to be lack of care in editing items and poor quality of the art work. Nearly all of my collaborators pointed out defective items. For example, at the higher grade levels the sample item for Test 1, Opposites, consists of five drawings of men's hats. The stem is a drawing of a new light colored banded felt "city" hat with creased crown. Four options are given for its "opposite": an old appearing dark banded (straw?) city hat with creased crown; a new light colored unbanded felt "ten-gallon" hat with creased crown; a battered (old?) dirty looking banded felt city hat with creased crown; and a new light colored banded felt city hat with uncreased crown. Directions that the teacher reads to pupils for this *sample* item are:

> Look at the pictures of hats in the first row....The first picture shows a man's new hat. Look at the other pictures of hats in the same row. Find the picture that is the *opposite* of the first picture—the one with a difference. * The old hat is the correct answer because it is the opposite of the new hat.

Perhaps examinees unerringly perceive that of the six (at least) dichotomous concepts embodied in this sample item, which can generate 64 options, the relevant concept is oldness versus newness, but surely a less complex example could easily have been constructed.

Certain items of Test 1, Opposites, were mentioned by several of my collaborators as being defective conceptually and artistically. This subtest's quality varies somewhat from level to level, so the prospective user should study the particular level in which he is interested. At the highest level (Level 5), for example, he will want to scrutinize items 4, 5, 6, 11, and 15 (of 15 items) carefully for keying and ready intelligibility of drawings.

Test 2, Similarities, depends heavily on drawings, 7 for each of the 15 items at the five upper levels, 5 for each of 8–13 items at the three lowest levels. Some of these are easily interpreted, whereas others are indistinct, partly because of excessive blackness and lack of contrast in the printing.

Test 3, Analogies, also consists entirely of pictures, to which the same cautions apply.

Test 4, Numerical Values, involves counting of pictured objects at the lower grade levels (Levels 0 and 1), number series at Level 1H, and making change at the higher grade levels. The format for the latter is ingenious, but it results at Level 4 (grades 9–12) in 18 of the 60 distractors' being virtually ineffective because they can be eliminated quickly by noting that they do not contain the specified number of coins (e.g., an item calling for use of 7 coins to make 15 cents has two options that include only 6 coins, thereby making the question essentially a two-option item). Apparently, the constructors were trying to make this type of item easy enough for Level 4, because at Level 5 (grades 12 through adult) only two items (48 and 55) have options that can be eliminated in this way.

Test 5, Number Problems, features the familiar CTMM arithmetical reasoning items at the higher grade levels, but only 10 of them. Some of these would have benefited by editing. At Level 5, for example, the pilot flying the airmail and carrying 50 gallons of gasoline as fuel (item 65) is outdated. In items 61 and 69 the social context causes a logical fallacy; for example, "Jim *says* his age is one-fourth of his uncle's, and that their ages together total 40 years. How many years difference *is* there between Jim's and his uncle's age?" (Italics mine.) Isn't it time that we dropped from the stems of test items this groping at dialogue, especially at the higher grade levels? The same point is covered, without distraction, by "Jim is one fourth as old as his uncle, and their ages together total 40 years."

In Test 6 verbal comprehension is tested by the typical one-word stem, four-option (three-option at Level 1H) vocabulary item at Levels 1H and up. Directions are "Mark the number of the word that means the same or about the same as the first word." The 25 items at Level 5 are illustrative of the need for more careful selection and editing. Two of them are military terms, "bivouac" and "trajectory." One of the distractors for "bivouac" is the difficult word "coloratura," whereas the other options are the relatively simple nouns "party," "revision," and "encampment." Likewise, item 73, "predicament," has as one of its distractors "mantua"! It would be helpful to see an item analysis of these items and others in the CTMM S-Form.

California Short-Form Test of Mental Maturity

The first item on the Level 5 vocabulary test has as its stem "inefficient" and as the keyed option "incompetent," the only one of the four options having the prefix "in." Also, how nearly synonymous are these two words?

Item 76, "whimsical," has as the keyed response "fanciful," with distractors "accurate," "weighty," and "fashionable." It seems likely that the structural similarity between stem and key will make this item too easy and perhaps less discriminating than it would be with a different answer or with distractors more like the stem.

Use of "issue" in item 92 to mean "offspring" seems rather quaint in 1963, this being the twelfth meaning of "issue" in the *American College Dictionary* and probably more familiar to our grandparents than to our children.

Some of the distractors are not the same part of speech as the stem—for example, "digit" (which also occurs as a distractor in item 82) for "vex," "hangman" for "vigilant," and "sorry" for "articulation." For item 81 the stem is "tangent," which may be either a noun or an adjective; one must search the options "blend," "agent," "sensing," and "touching" to decide which part of speech is intended. The authors may have had an explicit rationale for varying the part of speech, but again it would be helpful to study item analyses and to try the items with options homogeneous with respect to part of speech.

The seventh and final test is Delayed Recall. A short story is read to the examinees before they begin Test 1, and they are asked questions about it after they complete Test 6. It is of course difficult to keep the stimulus, the reading of the story, constant from class to class. Also, it is not easy to find stories containing material so novel for the examinee that he cannot answer some of the questions without having heard the story. Furthermore, answering the questions at all but the two lowest levels requires considerable reading, so sheer memory is not all that is tested.

The reviewer administered the 25 items of Test 7 of Level 5 to a bright adult and an above average 15-year-old girl, *without* reading the story to them. They scored 17 and 13, respectively, the 69th and 46th percentiles for their age groups. Both 17 and 13 are significantly greater than the chance expected value of $25/4 = 6¼$.

Of the four factor scores three (numerical reasoning, verbal concepts, and memory) are based on only 25 items each at the higher five levels and 8–25 items each at the lower three levels. The other (logical reasoning) is based on 45 at the higher levels and 23–41 at the lower levels. In the absence of the Technical Report, the California Test Bureau has provided a "Reliability Report" and an apparently subsequent technical memo to show various characteristics of the four factor scores. The two reports have quite different statistics, generally much more favorable in the memo. For example, at Level 2 the factor score Kuder-Richardson formula 21 coefficients of equivalence change from .80, .84, .87, and .82 in the report to .87, .88, .91, and .81 in the memo, thereby making the language, nonlanguage, and total score K-R 21 coefficients rise from .90, .84, and .93 to .94, .89, and .95. The memo contains no explanation of these changes, nor does it refer to the reliability report. It is not clear from the memo just how heterogeneous the groups on whom the K-R 21's were computed were. It seems unlikely, however, that in a typical school the K-R 21 coefficients would be nearly as high as above. We cannot determine, either, to what extent the coefficients are inflated by speededness of the tests. Because there are no comparable forms of any of the S-Form levels, coefficients of equivalence and stability (i.e., comparable form reliability coefficients) cannot be computed. However, in its Technical Memo No. 5, the CTB staff compares scores from the 1957 and 1963 S-Forms at four levels. The correlations between total score IQ's for these two versions are .81, .76, .74, and .72. The time interval between the two testings is not specified.

A comment about the test booklets themselves: Words in them are readily legible, but (as noted above) figures do not always reproduce well. The format is in general attractive and effective, except at the lower grade levels where some pictures are too small and indistinct. The booklet cover seems unduly flimsy, tending to tear and shred easily.

EVALUATION. Overall, the reviewer feels that the CTMM S-Form is most useful at kindergarten through about the third grade (Levels 0 and 1) and progressively less useful in the higher grades. Its emphasis on nonverbal material, perhaps appropriate for children learning to read, is disproportionate at the higher levels. A simpler rationale, such as verbal versus quantitative as in the SCAT, SAT, and the GRE Aptitude Test, seems preferable from grade 4 upward. At the junior and senior high school levels one also has carefully prepared verbal tests such as the Terman-McNemar and multi-factor tests such as the APT and DAT to consider. Variety in testing throughout the school life of pupils is probably more important than attempted continuity via different levels of a given publisher's tests. Local norms within a school system can make comparisons from one test to another feasible. By the tenth or eleventh grade "external" programs (e.g., PSAT, NMSQT, CEEB, and ACT) have taken the majority of the *scholastic* aptitude and achievement testing load off the schools.

For a review by Cyril Burt of the 1957 edition, see 5:313; see also 4:282 (1 excerpt); for reviews of the regular edition, see 5:314, 3:223, 40:1384, and 38:1042.

[444]
*California Test of Mental Maturity, 1963 Revision. Grades 4–6, 7–9, 9–12, 12–16 and adults; 1936–64; 1957 edition (see 5:314) still available; 8 scores: logical reasoning, spatial relationships, numerical reasoning, verbal concepts, memory, language total, non-language total, total; IBM; 1 form ('61, 19 pages); 4 levels; manual ('64, 53–66 pages) for each level; series guide to interpretation ('64, 38 pages) for this and test 443; profile ('61, 1 page) for each level (also contained on back of test booklet and back of answer sheet); no data on reliability and validity of revised long form; $7 per 35 tests; separate answer sheets may be used; 10¢ per set of IBM answer sheet-profiles; 40¢ per set of hand scoring stencils; 80¢ per set of machine scoring stencils; 18¢ per set of Scoreze answer sheets; 50¢ per guide to interpretation; postage extra; $1 per specimen set of any one level, postpaid; Elizabeth T. Sullivan, Willis W. Clark, and Ernest W. Tiegs; California Test Bureau. *

a) LEVEL 2. Grades 4–6; 83(93) minutes.
b) LEVEL 3. Grades 7–9; 83(93) minutes.
c) LEVEL 4. Grades 9–12; 81(91) minutes.
d) LEVEL 5. Grades 12–16 and adults; 81(91) minutes.

REFERENCES

1–5. See 40:1384.
6–15. See 3:223.
16–39. See 4:282.
40–73. See 5:314.
74. KREBS, STEPHEN O. *A Study of the I.Q. Consistency, Internal Consistency and Correlations With Certain Academic Grades of the California Test of Mental Maturity (Short Form).* Master's thesis, Michigan State University (East Lansing, Mich.), 1957.
75. BARRY, CHARLES A., AND JONES, ARLYNNE L. "A Study of the Performance of Certain Freshman Students." *J Ed Res* 52:163–6 Ja '59. * (*PA* 34:2088)
76. CHAMBERS, JACK A. "Preliminary Screening Methods in the Identification of Intellectually Superior Children." *Excep Child* 26:145–50 N '59. * (*PA* 35:3249)
77. KING, PAUL; NORRELL, GWEN; AND ERLANDSON, F. L. "The Prediction of Academic Success in a Police Administration Curriculum." *Ed & Psychol Meas* 19:649–51 w '59. * (*PA* 34:6166)
78. KORTMEYER, HOWARD A. *A Statistical Study of the Relationship of the California Test of Mental Maturity Scores of South Dakota High School Freshmen to Future Academic Success.* Master's thesis, South Dakota State College (Brookings, S.D.), 1959.
79. CASSEL, RUSSELL N., AND STANCIK, EDWARD J. "Factorial Content of the Iowa Tests of Educational Development and Other Tests." *J Exp Ed* 29:193–6 D '60. *
80. CLYMER, THEODORE, AND BRENDEMUEHL, FRANK L. "A Study of the Validity of the California Test of Mental Maturity, Elementary, Non-Language Section." *Yearb Nat Council Meas Used Ed* 17:123–9 '60. *
81. JACOBS, RONALD E. "A Comparison of Tests: The Primary Mental Abilities: The Pintner Mental Abilities: The California Test of Mental Abilities." *Sch Counselor* 8:12–8 O '60. *
82. OSBORNE, R. T. "Racial Differences in Mental Growth and School Achievement: A Longitudinal Study." *Psychol Rep* 7:233–9 O '60. * (*PA* 35:2782)
83. RAMSEY, WALLACE. "An Analysis of Variables Predictive of Reading Growth." *J Develop Read* 3:158–64 sp '60. *
84. STAKE, ROBERT E., AND MEHRENS, WILLIAM A. "Reading Retardation and Group Intelligence Test Performance." *Excep Child* 26:497–501 My '60. * (*PA* 35:539)
85. WELNA, CECILIA THERESA. *A Study of Reasons for Success or Failure in College Mathematics Courses.* Doctor's thesis, University of Connecticut (Storrs, Conn.), 1960. (*DA* 21:1811)
86. ANDERSON, HARRY E., JR. "The Prediction of Reading and Language From the California Tests." *Ed & Psychol Meas* 21:1035–6 w '61. *
87. ANDERSON, HARRY E., JR. "A Study of Language and Nonlanguage Achievement." *Ed & Psychol Meas* 21:1037–8 w '61. *
88. CASSEL, RUSSELL N., AND STANCIK, EDWARD J. "California Test of Mental Maturity by Weights for Predicting a Composite Score on the Iowa Tests of Educational Development." *J Genetic Psychol* 98:119–26 Mr '61. * (*PA* 35:7074)
89. CENTI, PAUL. "Intellective and Language Factors Related to College Success." *Cath Ed R* 59:319–22 My '61. *
90. CLYMER, THEODORE. "A Study of the Validity of the California Test of Mental Maturity Elementary, Language Section." *Yearb Nat Council Meas Ed* 18:125–35 '61. *
91. FRENCH, JOSEPH L. "A Predictive Test Battery." *Nursing Res* 10:104–5 sp '61. *
92. LUCIER, OMER, AND BURNETTE, RICHARD. "The Lowry Reasoning Test Combination With Younger Adolescents." *J Social Psychol* 55:113–24 O '61. * (*PA* 36:4HD13L)
93. MCGUIRE, CARSON. "The Prediction of Talented Behavior in the Junior High School." *Proc Inv Conf Testing Probl* 1960:46–67 '61. *
94. BALDWIN, JOSEPH W. "The Relationship Between Teacher-Judged Giftedness, a Group Intelligence Test and an Individual Intelligence Test With Possible Gifted Kindergarten Pupils." *Gifted Child Q* 6:153–6 w '62. * (*PA* 37:8255)
95. CARNEY, RICHARD E., AND TROWBRIDGE, NORMA. "Intelligence Test Performance of Indian Children as a Function of Type of Test and Age." *Percept & Motor Skills* 14:511–4 Je '62. * (*PA* 37:2830)
96. CLARK, WILLIS W. "Item Selection Techniques for a Long-Range Continuous Mental Age Scale." *Yearb Nat Council Meas Ed* 19:72–7 '62. *
97. COBB, BART B. "Problems in Air Traffic Management: 2, Prediction of Success in Air Traffic Controller School." *Aerospace Med* 33:702–13 Je '62. *
98. NORMAN, RALPH D.; CLARK, BETTY P.; AND BESSEMER, DAVID W. "Age, Sex, IQ, and Achievement Patterns in Achieving and Nonachieving Gifted Children." *Excep Child* 29:116–23 N '62. * (*PA* 37:7159)
99. BALDAUF, ROBERT J. "Predicting Success in Eighth Grade Algebra." *Psychol Rep* 12:810 Je '63. * (*PA* 38:6580)
100. BOBBE, CAROL; CAMPBELL, WILLIAM; LAMBERTI, ELAINE; AND SHEPPARD, CHARLES. "A Correlation Analysis in Testing." *Ed* 83:375–8 F '63. *
101. CLINE, VICTOR B.; RICHARDS, JAMES M., JR.; AND NEEDHAM, WALTER E. "Creativity Tests and Achievement in High School Science." *J Appl Psychol* 47:184–9 Je '63. * (*PA* 37:8223)
102. CLYMER, THEODORE. "A Study of the Influence of Reading Ability on the Validity of Group Intelligence Tests." *Slow Learnng Child* 10:76–84 N '63. *
103. MACARTHUR, R. S., AND ELLEY, W. B. "The Reduction of Socioeconomic Bias in Intelligence Testing." *Brit J Ed Psychol* 33:107–19 Je '63. * (*PA* 38:4271)

For reviews by Frank S. Freeman and John E. Milholland of the 1957 edition, see 5:314; see also 4:282 (1 excerpt); for a review by Henry E. Garrett of an earlier edition, see 3:233 (2 excerpts); for reviews by Raymond B. Cattell and F. Kuhlmann, see 40:1384 (1 excerpt); for reviews by W. D. Commins,

Rudolf Pintner, and Arthur E. Traxler, see 38:1042 (1 excerpt). For reviews of the short form, see 443, 5:313, and 4:282.

[445]

★**Canadian Academic Aptitude Test (CAAT).** Grades 8.5–9.0; 1959–63; this test and tests 253 and 567 make up the *Canadian Test Battery*, grades 8–9; 3 scores: verbal, mathematical, non-verbal; 1 form; separate parts 1 ('62, verbal reasoning), 2 ('62, mathematical reasoning), 3 ('59, non-verbal reasoning), (4 pages); 2 editions of battery manual: hand scoring ('63, 11 pages), machine scoring ('63, 13 pages); supplementary data ('63, 6 pages) for the battery; battery profile ('63, 2 pages); separate answer sheets or cards must be used; $1.25 per 25 tests; $1 per set of 50 answer sheets and hand scoring manual; 20¢ per hand scoring stencil; 20¢ per 15 battery profiles; 50¢ per 25 IBM answer cards (machine scoring through the Department of Educational Research only); 10¢ per machine scoring manual; 50¢ per specimen set; $2.75 per battery specimen set; postage extra; 30 (40–45) minutes per part; Department of Educational Research, Ontario College of Education, University of Toronto; distributed by Guidance Centre (machine scoring manual and answer cards must be purchased from the Department of Educational Research). *

REFERENCES

1. D'OYLEY, VINCENT R. *Technical Manual for the Canadian Tests: Statistical Data on the Carnegie Study Tests of Academic Aptitude and Achievement in Grades 8, 9, and 10 in Ontario Schools and Grades 7 and 8 in Toronto Schools.* Carnegie Study of Identification and Utilization of Talent in High School and College, Bulletin No. 4. Toronto, Canada: Department of Educational Research, Ontario College of Education, University of Toronto, 1964. Pp. viii, 50. *
2. D'OYLEY, VINCENT R. *Testing: The First Two Years of the Carnegie Study 1959 to 1961: Analysis of Scores by Course, Sex, and Size of Municipality.* Carnegie Study of Identification and Utilization of Talent in High School and College, Bulletin No. 6. Toronto, Canada: Department of Educational Research, Ontario College of Education, University of Toronto, 1964. Pp. ix, 53. *

DONALD B. BLACK, *Professor of Education, University of Alberta, Edmonton, Alberta, Canada.*

This test consisting of three subtests, each of 30 minutes' length, can best be viewed as an experimental instrument. No alternate forms are available and by admission in the manual, no item analyses have been completed. This is not to suggest that the items are entirely new. Many items in the verbal reasoning subtest may be found in the intermediate and advanced levels of the *Group Test of Learning Capacity: Dominion Tests.* Unlike the Dominion Tests, however, the test format and item form is much improved. However, a serious defect that occurs in the test directions and which is common to all tests in the Canadian Test Battery for grades 8–9, is that no indication is given as to whether the student is to guess or that there will be a correction for guessing. This is considered important, particularly so since part of one of the tests (*Canadian English Achievement Test*) in the battery corrects for guessing at the grade 9 level.

The test, as part of the Carnegie Study of Identification and Utilization of Talent in High School and College, was administered to every grade 9 student in the province of Ontario in October and November 1959. The grade 9 percentile norms are based on this population which is in excess of 85,000 cases. No subnorms by type of school or community are given. The grade 8 norms are based on a "representative" sample of about 6,500 Ontario grade 8 students tested in May 1962. These latter norms are reported as percentiles correct to one place of decimal. No evidence is given as to the basis upon which these norms can be considered representative. It is interesting to note that for the verbal and nonverbal reasoning subtests, the mean and median scores for the grade 8 norms are higher in each case than those reported for grade 9. No mean and median are reported for the mathematical reasoning subtest for grade 9, but examination of the appropriate percentile norms would strongly suggest that the same pattern holds true for the median, at least. Just how reliable these differences are is not known since variability data are not provided, but the consistent trend shown would suggest that possibly the grade 8 norms are not as representative as they claim to be.

The publishers provide profile charts for each grade for interpreting the scores on the total battery. The grade 9 chart has minor inaccuracies. These could serve to magnify, in certain instances, misinterpretation of the battery results. The most serious defect is that nowhere in the manual nor on the charts is mention made of the standard error of measurement or its implications for interpreting scores. The absence of any variability and reliability data in the manual makes calculation of the standard errors of measurement impossible. A further disconcerting suggestion for interpreting scores is the suggestion in the manual that the percentile scores on the tests may be averaged to give class and student average performance.

A statistical supplement (October 31, 1963) containing reliability and validity data on the CAAT has been recently forwarded to the reviewer. Split-half reliabilities between .85 and .90 are reported for a sample of 200 grade 8 students and between .81 and .91 for a sample of 200 cases at the grade 9 level. Because of the nature of the item content in each subtest, the reviewer would much prefer K-R 20 reliability coefficients but, in the absence of item analysis and variability data noted above, the publisher obviously had little recourse than to use the split-half method.

The supplementary technical data sheets also include battery intercorrelation data and validity data for grade 9 average marks and year-end marks in English and mathematics based on a random sample of 1,000 cases. These data plus other data from the Carnegie Study and available in other reports, represent the most desirable aspect of this battery to the test user in Ontario schools. Intercorrelations of the subtests reveal coefficients of between .68 (Verbal Reasoning and Mathematical Reasoning) and .56 (Verbal Reasoning and Non-Verbal Reasoning). Considering the type of items, this is about what would be expected in light of similar correlations of other batteries of this type, and it suggests a high general intelligence factor. The validity data show correlations of .53 and .51 between Verbal Reasoning and grade 9 English grades and average grades, respectively. This, too, could be anticipated due to the heavy weighting of vocabulary-type items in the verbal reasoning test. Mathematical Reasoning correlates .40 with grade 9 English marks, .49 with mathematics marks, and .47 with average marks, and again this would be expected from the intercorrelation matrix. The nonverbal reasoning test, which contains conventional figure analogy items and a heavy weighting of "domino" items (15 of 40), correlates between .34 and .39 with the criterion scores. It is hoped that in subsequent editions the publisher, with the classroom teacher in mind, will devote some serious attention to the proper interpretation of these data and data from other studies for academic guidance purposes.

In summary, this is an excellent example of an experimental instrument being pushed into publication, presumably by demands from the schools for continued use of the test, before it was properly prepared. Why item analysis based even on pretesting data was not done, or why alternate forms were not prepared, or why complete statistical data were not reported before publication, is difficult to understand. It is difficult to accept the lack of sophistication of the manual and particularly the suggestions for the interpretation of test scores, for it has long been established that the test publisher owes the test consumer some concern for leadership in this regard. When these matters are attended to, and only when these are done, will the tests fully realize their potential for school use. Certainly, the provision of validity data, if only for Ontario schools, marks an excellent beginning in a most desirable direction.

GEORGE A. FERGUSON, *Professor of Psychology, McGill University, Montreal, Canada.*

The *Canadian Academic Aptitude Test* is part of a test battery developed for use in a Carnegie sponsored longitudinal study on the identification and utilization of talent in the high schools and colleges of Ontario. The test is restricted in use to the end of grade 8 and the beginning of grade 9. It consists of three subtests, Verbal Reasoning, Mathematical Reasoning, and Non-Verbal Reasoning. The verbal reasoning subtest contains items of the usual type, analogies, opposites, vocabulary, and classification. The mathematical reasoning subtest is composed of simple arithmetic and number series problems. The nonverbal reasoning subtest is constructed of figure analogy items, and a matrix-type item using dominoes.

Percentile rank norms are available for each subtest for grade 8 and grade 9. The grade 8 norms are based on a sample of 6,500 students in Ontario schools tested in 1962 near the end of the eighth grade year. The grade 9 norms are based on a complete, or almost complete, population of 85,000 grade 9 students tested in 1959 early in their ninth grade year. The standardization of tests on precisely defined complete populations is uncommon in North America, although in Britain the Moray House Tests, originally developed by Godfrey Thomson, have for many years been standardized on complete populations. A surprising feature of the standardization is that scores for grade 8 appear in general to be higher than for grade 9. For example, on the verbal reasoning subtest a score of 28 has a percentile rank of 49 for grade 8, whereas for grade 9 the same score has a percentile rank of 56. The test authors provide no explanation for this, although a variety of possible explanations come readily to mind, e.g., bias in the 1962 sample, dropout of superior students between grades 8 and 9, or some overall improvement in aptitude between the years 1959 and 1962.

No reliability or validity information are provided by the authors.[1] Much is known, however, about the reliability of this type of test material, and, assuming that conventional test construction methods have been used, we may assume that reliability coefficients of .90 or greater can be obtained for the subtests.[2] With regard to validity, detailed information on the relation between test scores and grade averages should shortly be available. Much is known, of course, about the validity of tests of this type in other contexts.

On the negative side the reviewer notes that this test contains no new or novel features either in content or construction. Tests of this kind have existed for many years. No arguments of a technical or scientific nature are advanced to justify their replication. It may well be that the authors wished to achieve a high degree of discrimination for a specific group, namely ending grade 8 and beginning grade 9 students, although this point is not discussed. A further negative point is that the three subtests are comprised of types of test material which are known to correlate highly. The minimum total time for administration is two hours. It seems probable that a shorter test might effectively accomplish about the same results.

Because the present test was developed for use in a comprehensive longitudinal study, the reviewer anticipates that the authors will in due course provide a body of substantive validity data which will enhance the test's usefulness.

[446]

★Cardall-Miles Test of Mental Alertness. Adults in business and industry; 1960–61; 1 form ('60, 3 pages); directions for administering ['61, 2 pages]; no data on reliability and validity; typewritten norms ('61, 1 page); norms also included in manual for *Cardall Test of Practical Judgment;* $8.50 per 100 tests; $1 per specimen set; postage extra; 15(20) minutes; Alfred J. Cardall and Gerald E. Miles; Cardall Associates. *

[447]

★The Carlton Picture Intelligence Test. Ages 6-3 to 7-9; 1962; Forms A, B, (16 pages); manual (16 pages); 22s. 6d. per 25 tests; 1s. per single copy; 2s. 6d. per manual; postage and purchase tax extra; 32(70) minutes in 2 sessions; W. K. Carlton; University of London Press Ltd. *

[1] This review was completed before the supplementary data referred to in the test entry preceding the review became available.—Editor.
[2] Obtained corrected odd-even coefficients were later reported as .88 and .91 for verbal, .81 and .85 for mathematical, and .88 and .90 for nonverbal.—Editor.

ELIZABETH D. FRASER, *Professor of Psychology, University of Aberdeen, Aberdeen, Scotland.*

This test is designed for children passing from the infant to the primary school, a transfer which normally takes place between the ages of 6 years 6 months and 7 years 6 months. The test in fact provides norms for the ages 6 years 3 months to 7 years 9 months.

There are two forms of the test, each consisting of eight sections with eight items in each section. The test is entirely pictorial; no writing is required of the child who simply marks the chosen answer with a cross; and detailed instructions are read out by the teacher or other person administering the test.

The tasks required of the child include picking out from a group of five pictures the one which has something silly in it; picking the one object in a group which is different from the rest; finding the missing part in a picture; completing pictorial analogies; choosing two things which a given object always has; ordering sets of four pictures into a time sequence; selecting from five objects the one which has something in common with a given set of three objects; and completing a series of symbols such as XOXOX_____. Each section of eight items is preceded by three sample items illustrating the type of problem. Many of the items are ingenious and most, though perhaps not all, should be within the range of experience of an average seven year old.

The test appears to have had a thorough tryout. The 128 items now used in Forms A and B are those which survived item analysis from the original test which consisted of 11 sections and of 330 items. The item analysis was carried out section by section on samples of 200 children of the appropriate age group.

Norms were based on a complete age group of Glasgow children, Forms A and B being given in two successive years to 29,863 and 29,950 children, respectively. The norms are presented in easily read tables with one-month age intervals on one axis, raw score on the other, and IQ appearing in the body of the table.

A great deal of care has obviously gone into the test, and the cooperation of the teaching profession has clearly been extremely valuable, especially in the standardisation process. The major criticism to be leveled against the test is that the drawings are occasionally difficult to identify, and this is true not only for adults. Part of the trouble is that since the drawings for each item appear in a strip across the page, scale has had to be sacrificed; thus, for example, an eye is the same size as a house, a nib is as large as an ink bottle, and so on. This is particularly noticeable in the sections where the child has to find the missing part and where he has to pick out two things an object always has. In both of these, identification without any clues to scale may be a matter of chance.

In other items, identification is difficult because of bad drawings: to the reviewer, at least, the car engine in section 4, item 4, Form A, looked like the remains of a car after a particularly bad smash, and the item had to be solved by guesswork.

In spite of these criticisms, the test can claim high reliability; by the Kuder-Richardson formula 20 it is .97 for Form A and .96 for Form B. The intercorrelation between the two forms is also high, .94 on a sample of 8,846 children, and the correlations with Terman-Merrill on a sample of 120 children were .86 for Form A and .85 for Form B.

Designed for a very specific age range, this test has something to offer. It is intrinsically interesting to the child, and it is pleasant to report on a test which, in spite of some drawbacks, has at least gone through the necessary trial stages before being placed on the market.

S. RACHMAN, *Lecturer in Psychology, Institute of Psychiatry, University of London, London, England.*

This new group intelligence test for children has been prepared for use in a limited age range—75 to 93 months. The two parallel forms, A and B, which are administered, scored, and interpreted in the same manner, each consist of eight sections. Apart from the tester's instructions and the examples which precede each section, the test takes 32 minutes to administer. The author states that it is essential to separate the first and second four sections with a 15 minute interval. The duration and timing of the rest interval appear to have been arbitrarily chosen and there is no information about the possible effects of varying this procedure. In the absence of such information, users are advised to adhere to Carlton's procedure.

The instructions for testers are concise and explicit and are unlikely to give rise to difficulties even if the test is administered by people without specialised training. The scoring of the tests is also explained in a lucid manner. The instructions which must be read to the children, however, are very detailed and sometimes rather involved. The test material is entirely pictorial and is all contained in a single booklet. While the great majority of the drawings are admirably simple and clear, three of those contained in section 7 of Form A appeared to the reviewer to be ambiguous (the eighth drawing in sample item A, the third drawing in item 7, and the sixth drawing in item 8).

The test was standardised on an impressively large sample—Form A was given to 29,863 children and Form B to 29,950 children. Unfortunately, the author provides no details of the methods used in the standardisation procedure beyond referring to an unpublished paper by Talman. It would be a valuable addition to the working manual if he included this information, perhaps as a technical appendix. The data which Carlton provides on the reliability and validity of the test are encouraging but not sufficiently comprehensive; these gaps will undoubtedly be filled in the future. The reliability coefficients of the two forms as calculated by the Kuder-Richardson formula 20 were .97 for Form A and .96 for Form B. These coefficients are extremely satisfactory but unfortunately the sample size was omitted. The two forms of the test were found to be highly correlated (.94) and there appears to be a negligible practice effect if Form A is administered first. Although this information is not entirely clear, it appears that the 8,846 children who participated in this study were given Form A followed by Form B five months later. In order to rule out the possibility of practice effect, a replication of this study should be conducted with Form B preceding Form A. Both forms of the test were found to correlate positively with Terman-Merrill IQ's (Form A, .86 and Form B, .85). Even allowing for the relative smallness of this sample ($n = 120$), these results are satisfactory.

Although the samples used by Carlton in ascertaining the reliability and stability of the test are of a salutary size, he unfortunately omitted details of the composition of the groups of children concerned. In the initial standardisation of the test he used "complete year groups of children" in two successive years. No further information about the social and geographical background of the children is given; one must assume, however, that they were all British schoolchildren. Neither the 8,846 children who participated in the test-retest study nor the 120 children in the validity study are described. For this reason, the possibility of sample bias cannot be effectively rejected.

The advantages of the Carlton test are those of any satisfactory group test. It is short and comparatively easy to administer and score. In addition, the available data on reliability and validity are encouraging as far as they go. The test promises to be of value as a screening instrument and should arouse reasonably wide interest, particularly if the age range is extended.

[448]

*Classification Test 40-A. Job applicants; 1957–59; 1 form ('57, 14 pages plus fold-out answer sheet); preliminary mimeographed manual ('57, 11 pages); general PPA mimeographed directions ['57, 7 pages]; norms ('59, 2 pages); no data on reliability; 10–49 tests, 68¢ each; $2 per specimen set; postpaid; 50(60) minutes; Public Personnel Association. *

N. M. DOWNIE, *Professor of Psychology, Purdue University, Lafayette, Indiana.*

As stated by the authors, the chief purpose of this test is "to assist in the selection of applicants for a wide variety of jobs where information about the applicant's general capacity to learn to do the job will be useful." They also note that the test will be of assistance in the placement, training, and promotion of employees.

The test is made up of 60 multiple choice items, equally divided among vocabulary, arithmetic reasoning, and picture classification varieties, the latter being reasoning items. The arithmetic reasoning items consist of the usual type of problems. The picture classification items are composed of sets of four pictures, three of which are in some way related. The vocabulary items are made up of short definitions of words. The examinee is to think of a word that fits the definition and begins with one of the four pairs of letters presented. The items are arranged in groups of five of a kind and these groups are in an ascending order of difficulty throughout the test.

Each copy of the test contains a fold-in answer sheet on which the responses are to be marked as on the usual IBM answer sheet, which may also be used. The answers are so arranged that verbal, numerical, and reasoning subscores may be obtained. An individual's score is the number correct.

Although part scores may be obtained, the authors recommend that they not be used in prediction because of their probable low reliability. It is suggested that these part scores may be used as an aid in placement or in understanding the strengths and weaknesses of a job applicant.

Page 1 consists of practice problems for which five minutes are allotted. Fifty minutes are allowed for the completion of the test. The authors state that the test is a power test. This is undoubtedly true as 50 minutes seems adequate for any examinee to answer about as many items as he ever would be able to.

According to the manual the test was developed on about 1,000 applicants or present employees of 12 public personnel agencies located "throughout the United States and Canada" and representing "a wide variety of occupational fields....including one sample of high school seniors." Apparently a 90-item form was first developed and this was subsequently shortened to the current 60-item form which is said to yield an almost perfect correlation with the longer form and to represent "the minimum number of items consistent with the required degree of reliability." It is interesting to note that this is the only mention of the reliability of the test in the 11-page manual.

Correlations between part and total scores are reported to range from .61 to .85. Intercorrelations among scores on the three parts of the test are said to fall between −.10 and .37. No details are given for the specific relationships.

In the manual itself no norms are presented. There is a general discussion of "absolute" and "flexible" passing points or percentages. Passing points, the authors note, must be determined locally, but they recommend that a score of 30 per cent correct be regarded as representing "minimum competence" and that passing points not be set below this point.

In a separate Test Service Memo, frequency distributions of scores are presented for a collection of 17 occupations based upon present employees and job applicants, the *n*'s varying from a low of 8 to a high of 280 with a median of 19.

It is interesting to note that not a single mention of validity is made in any of the materials accompanying this test.

In the Test Service Memo it is stated that

more than 100 agencies have purchased over 6,000 copies of the test. Since it is possible to use homemade answer sheets, probably many more individuals have been given this test by personnel managers of varying degrees of skill, competence, and training using a totally inadequate manual. The test seems well made and to have at least face validity. But there its goodness seems to stop. The test was published in 1957 with no reliability coefficients reported, no indication of the validity of the instrument for use in any specific type of personnel work, and no adequate or usable norms. An evaluation of the materials which the buyer gets with the test shows that practically nothing has been added in these three areas since the original publication.

The test seems to have some potential in that it differs from the typical test used in industry by being a power test rather than a heavily speeded one. For many types of positions, it seems to this reviewer that a power test would be a much more appropriate instrument than the 12 or 15 minute speed test. The authors could make this test acceptable. However, until they remedy the points discussed above, the test should be considered as unsatisfactory for the uses stated. Despite the claims made and the uses suggested by the authors, personnel managers should continue to use our more established tests such as the *Wonderlic Personnel Test* or the *Adaptability Test* in employee selection.

DAVID G. RYANS, *Director, Bureau of Educational Research, University of Hawaii, Honolulu, Hawaii.*

This test is intended to reflect "general capacity to learn" in job situations "which do not demand any special abilities." It is intended to be a power test and consists of 20 vocabulary, 20 arithmetic reasoning, and 20 picture classification items alternately presented in groups of 5 items of each type and arranged in order of difficulty. Working time (50 minutes) is for the test as a whole. A single score is obtained, the total number of correct responses to the 60 items. (Part scores may be obtained, but the potential user is warned that reliabilities of part scores are low.) No reliability data, either for part or for total scores, are provided.

Development of the test proceeded through several revisions, leading to production of a 90-item tryout form from which the present 60 items were selected after administration to 1,000 applicants and employees by 12 public personnel agencies. Part scores on the vocabulary, arithmetic reasoning, and picture classification items are reported to correlate .61 to .85 with total score, whereas intercorrelations between the part scores are given as from −.10 to .37.

A Test Service Memo dated April 1959 provides distributions (n's ranging from 8 to 280 per distribution; total $n = 776$) of raw scores of public service employees and candidates for public service jobs. Suggestions are offered by the manual for determining "absolute" and "flexible" passing points (adapted to agency policies) with regard to the raw score earned on the test.

No validity data are reported for the test. The items appear to be of standard quality, but little information is available about the test other than general statements relating to development procedures. Due to lack of technical information, use of the test cannot be recommended. Its usefulness as a predictor of a "general capacity to learn" in various job situations has not been demonstrated.

[449]

*College Entrance Examination Board Scholastic Aptitude Test.** Candidates for college entrance; 1926–63; for more complete information, see 760; 2 scores: verbal, mathematical; 180(210) minutes; program administered for the College Entrance Examination Board by Educational Testing Service. *

REFERENCES

1–22. See 4:285.
23–42. See 5:318.
43. DYER, HENRY S. *College Board Scores.* New York: College Entrance Examination Board, [1953]. Pp. xxiii, 70. * (*PA* 28:4936)
44. DYER, HENRY S., AND KING, RICHARD G. *College Board Scores: Their Use and Interpretation, No. 2.* New York: College Entrance Examination Board, 1955. Pp. viii, 192. * (*PA* 30:1616)
45. FISHMAN, JOSHUA A. *1957 Supplement to College Board Scores No. 2.* New York: College Entrance Examination Board, 1957. Pp. vi, 206. *
46. FLEMING, W. G. *Aptitude and Achievement Scores Related to Immediate Educational and Occupational Choices of Ontario Grade 13 Students.* Atkinson Study of Utilization of Student Resources, Report No. 3. Toronto, Canada: Department of Educational Research, Ontario College of Education, University of Toronto, 1958. Pp. xix, 380. *
47. FLEMING, W. G. *Ontario Grade 13 Students: Their Aptitude, Achievement, and Immediate Destination.* Atkinson Study of Utilization of Student Resources, Report No. 4. Toronto, Canada: Department of Educational Research, Ontario College of Education, University of Toronto, 1958. Pp. ix, 55. *
48. FRANZ, GRETCHEN; DAVIS, JUNIUS A.; AND GARCIA, DOLORES. "Prediction of Grades From Pre-Admissions Indices in Georgia Tax-Supported Colleges." *Ed & Psychol Meas* 18:841–4 w '58. * (*PA* 34:2097)
49. GARDNER, FRANK E. *A Study to Determine the Relationship Between High School Preparation, the College Entrance Examination Board Scholastic Aptitude Tests, and the First Semester College Grades.* Master's thesis, Whittier College (Whittier, Calif.), 1958.
50. HOLLAND, JOHN L. "Prediction of Scholastic Success for a High Aptitude Sample." *Sch & Soc* 86:290–3 Je 21 '58. *
51. ALTUS, WILLIAM D. "Personality Correlates of Verbal-

Classification Test 40-A

Quantitative Discrepancy Scores on the Scholastic Aptitude Test." *J Psychol* 48:219–25 O '59. * (*PA* 35:4868)
52. BLACK, D. B. "A Comparison of the Performance on Selected Standardized Tests to That on the Alberta Grade XII Departmental Examination of a Select Group of University of Alberta Freshmen." *Alberta J Ed Res* 5:180–90 S '59. * (*PA* 34:6559)
53. DUGGAN, JOHN M. "Puzzles and Powers in Junior SAT Scores." *Col Board R* 37:37–40 W '59. *
54. FLEMING, W. G. *Personal and Academic Factors as Predictors of First Year Success in Ontario Universities.* Atkinson Study of Utilization of Student Resources, Report No. 5. Toronto, Canada: Department of Educational Research, Ontario College of Education, University of Toronto, 1959. Pp. xi, 137. *
55. FRENCH, JOHN W., AND DEAR, ROBERT E. "Effect of Coaching on an Aptitude Test." *Ed & Psychol Meas* 19:319–30 au '59. * (*PA* 34:6568)
56. GILBERT, ARTHUR C. F. "The Efficiency of Certain Variables in Predicting Survival in an Engineering School." *Psychol Newsl* 10:311–3 My–Je '59. * (*PA* 34:1992)
57. GILBERT, ARTHUR C. F. "Prediction of Achievement in Chemistry." *Psychol Newsl* 10:135–7 Ja–F '59. * (*PA* 34:2099)
58. HILLS, JOHN R.; FRANZ, GRETCHEN; AND EMORY, LINDA B. *Counselor's Guide to Georgia Colleges.* Atlanta, Ga.: Office of Testing and Guidance, Regents of the University System of Georgia, December 1959. Pp. 32. *
59. HOLLAND, JOHN L. "The Prediction of College Grades From the California Psychological Inventory and the Scholastic Aptitude Test." *J Ed Psychol* 50:135–42 Ag '59. * (*PA* 35:2796)
60. SPAULDING, HELEN. "The Prediction of First-Year Grade Averages in a Private Junior College." *Ed & Psychol Meas* 19:627–8 w '59. * (*PA* 34:6574)
61. BLACK, DONALD B. "The Prediction of Freshman Success in the University of Alberta From Grade XII Departmental Results." *Alberta J Ed Res* 6:38–53 Mr '60. *
62. FRANKEL, EDWARD. "Effects of Growth, Practice and Coaching on Scholastic Aptitude Test Scores." *High Points* 42:34–45 Ja '60. *
63. FRANKEL, EDWARD. "Effects of Growth, Practice, and Coaching on Scholastic Aptitude Test Scores." *Personnel & Guid J* 38:713–9 My '60. * (*PA* 35:2790)
64. GILBERT, ARTHUR C. F. "Predicting Graduation From an Engineering School." *J Psychol Studies* 11:229–31 Jl–Ag '60. * (*PA* 35:7045)
65. HILLS, JOHN R.; EMORY, LINDA B.; AND FRANZ, GRETCHEN. *Freshman Norms for the University System of Georgia, 1958–59.* Atlanta, Ga.: Office of Testing and Guidance, Regents of the University System of Georgia, March 1960. Pp. ix, 91. *
66. HOLLAND, JOHN L. "The Prediction of College Grades From Personality and Aptitude Variables." *J Ed Psychol* 51:245–54 O '60. * (*PA* 36:1KL45H)
67. HURWITZ, HOWARD L. "Reflections on SAT Coaching and College Board Scores." *High Points* 42:48–9 O '60. *
68. JUOLA, ARVO E. "Predictive Validity of Five College-Level Academic Aptitude Tests at One Institution." *Personnel & Guid J* 38:637–41 Ap '60. * (*PA* 35:2791)
69. KETCHAM, HERBERT E., (MRS.) "Reading Tests and College Performance," pp. 63–6. In *Research and Evaluation in College Reading.* Ninth Yearbook of the National Reading Conference for College and Adults. Fort Worth, Tex.: Texas Christian University Press, 1960. Pp. 137. *
70. LORET, PETER G. *A History of the Content of the Scholastic Aptitude Test.* College Entrance Examination Board, Research and Development Reports, Test Development Memorandum TDM-60-1. [New York: the Board], October 1960. Pp. ii, 132. *
71. PIPHER, J. A. "An Appraisal of the Use of the Dominion Group Test of Learning Capacity (Advanced) in the Atkinson Study of Utilization of Student Resources." *Ont J Ed Res* 3:17–23 O '60. *
72. ROSEN, NED A. *A Validation Study of the College Entrance Examination Board Examinations and Other Predictors at Purdue University.* Purdue University, Division of Educational Reference, Studies in Higher Education, No. 90. Lafayette, Ind.: the Division, August 1960. Pp. 26. * (*PA* 35:2788)
73. WEXLER, AMELIA H. "Coaching and the SAT Tests." *High Points* 42:46–50 Ja '60. *
74. ALLEN, ROSCOE JACKSON. *An Analysis of the Relationship Between Selected Prognostic Measures and Achievement in the Freshman Program for Secretarial Majors at the Woman's College of the University of North Carolina.* Doctor's thesis, Pennsylvania State University (University Park, Pa.), 1961. (*DA* 23:122)
75. ALTUS, WILLIAM D. "Correlative Data for First-Semester Grade Averages at the University of California, Santa Barbara." *J Genetic Psychol* 98:303–5 Je '61. * (*PA* 36:2KJ03A)
76. ANGERS, WILLIAM P. "Pre-Engineering Characteristics of Entering Freshmen." *Voc Guid Q* 9:189–91 sp '61. * (*PA* 36:1KI89A)
77. HILLS, JOHN R.; EMORY, LINDA B.; AND MASTERS, PAULINE B. *Freshman Norms for the University System of Georgia, 1959–60.* Atlanta, Ga.: Office of Testing and Guidance, Regents of the University System of Georgia, September 1961. Pp. vii, 65. *
78. HILLS, JOHN R.; EMORY, LINDA B.; FRANZ, GRETCHEN; AND CROWDER, DOLORES GARCIA. "Admissions and Guidance Research in the University System of Georgia." *Personnel & Guid J* 39:452–7 F '61. * (*PA* 35:7102)
79. HILLS, JOHN R.; MASTERS, PAULINE B.; AND EMORY, LINDA B. *Supplement Counselor's Guide to Georgia Colleges.* Atlanta, Ga.: Office of Testing and Guidance, Regents of the University System of Georgia, 1961. Pp. ix, 35. *
80. HOLLAND, JOHN L. "Creative and Academic Performance Among Talented Adolescents." *J Ed Psychol* 52:136–47 Je '61. * (*PA* 38:3201)
81. MANN, M. JACINTA. "The Prediction of Achievement in a Liberal Arts College." *Ed & Psychol Meas* 21:481–3 su '61. * (*PA* 36:2KL81M)
82. MOCK, WILLIAM LINDSEY. *Selected Personality, Intellective, and Community Characteristics as Related to Academic Success of University of Georgia Students.* Doctor's thesis, University of Georgia (Athens, Ga.), 1961. (*DA* 22:1087)
83. PALLONE, NATHANIEL J. "Effects of Short- and Long-Term Developmental Reading Courses Upon S.A.T. Verbal Scores." *Personnel & Guid J* 39:654–7 Ap '61. * (*PA* 36:1KK54P)
84. SWANSON, EDWARD O., AND BERDIE, RALPH F. "Predictive Validities in an Institute of Technology." *Ed & Psychol Meas* 21:1001–8 w '61. Errata: 22:258 su '62. *
85. WATLEY, DONIVAN JASON. *Prediction of Academic Success in a College of Business Administration.* Doctor's thesis, University of Denver (Denver, Colo.), 1961. (*DA* 22:3527)
86. ANDERSON, SCARVIA B. *Letters to the Editor: SCAT and SAT.* Princeton, N.J.: Cooperative Test Division, 1962. Pp. 29. *
87. CHAUNCEY, HENRY. *Educational Testing Service Annual Report, 1961–62,* pp. 9–46. Princeton, N.J.: Educational Testing Service, 1962. Pp. 132. *
88. DARLEY, JOHN G. "The Basis for Equivalent Scores on the Annual Editions of the American Council on Education Psychological Examination (ACE), 1941 to 1954," pp. 170–83. In his *Promise and Performance: A Study of Ability and Achievement in Higher Education.* Berkeley, Calif.: Center for Study of Higher Education, University of California, 1962. Pp. vii, 191. *
89. ESSER, BARBARA F. "A Preliminary Factor Analysis of the Scholastic Aptitude Test Mathematics Section." *Yearb Nat Council Meas Ed* 19:83–93 '62. *
90. FLEMING, W. G. *The Use of Predictive Factors for the Improvement of University Admission Requirements.* Atkinson Study of Utilization of Student Resources, Report No. 9. Toronto, Canada: Department of Educational Research, Ontario College of Education, University of Toronto, 1962. Pp xi, 76. *
91. FOULKES, DAVID, AND HEAXT, SUSAN. "Concept Attainment and Self Concept." *Psychol Rep* 11:399–402 O '62. * (*PA* 37:7625)
92. FRENCH, JOHN W. "Effect of Anxiety on Verbal and Mathematical Examination Scores." *Ed & Psychol Meas* 22:553–64 au '62. * (*PA* 37:5082)
93. HILLS, JOHN R.; EMORY, LINDA B.; AND MASTERS, PAULINE B. *Freshman Norms for the University System of Georgia, 1960–61.* Atlanta, Ga.: Office of Testing and Guidance, Regents of the University System of Georgia, January 1962. Pp. xi, 65. *
94. JEFFREYS, LEONARD CHARLES, JR. *The Relationship of Selected Background Factors to the Academic Performance of Students of the Newark College of Arts and Sciences.* Doctor's thesis, Rutgers University (New Brunswick, N.J.), 1962. (*DA* 23:4224)
95. MASTEN, SHERMAN HASBROUCK. *The Value of Entrance Tests and Nine High School Variables in the Selection of Freshmen at Hofstra College: A Study in Differential Prediction.* Doctor's thesis, New York University (New York, N.Y.), 1962. (*DA* 23:886)
96. MICHAEL, WILLIAM B.; JONES, ROBERT A.; COX, ANNA; GERSHON, ARTHUR; HOOVER, MARVIN; KATZ, KENNETH; AND SMITH, DENNIS. "High School Record and College Board Scores as Predictors of Success in a Liberal Arts Program During the Freshman Year of College." *Ed & Psychol Meas* 22:399–400 su '62. * (*PA* 37:3872)
97. OLIVER, R. A. C. "The Selection of University Students: A 'Scholastic Aptitude Test'?" *Univ Q* 16:264–73 Je '62. *
98. REID, JOHN W.; JOHNSON, A. PEMBERTON; ENTWISLE, FRANK N.; AND ANGERS, WILLIAM P. "A Four-Year Study of the Characteristics of Engineering Students." *Personnel & Guid J* 41:38–43 S '62. * (*PA* 37:5655)
99. SHAW, HUBERT S. "Let's Simplify the Aptitude Test Schedule." *Col Board R* 47:20–2 sp '62. *
100. VICK, MARY CATHARINE, AND HORNADAY, JOHN A. "Predicting Grade Point Average at a Small Southern College." *Ed & Psychol Meas* 22:795–9 w '62. * (*PA* 37:7205)
101. WATLEY, DONIVAN J., AND MARTIN, H. T. "Prediction of Academic Success in a College of Business Administration." *Personnel & Guid J* 41:147–54 O '62. * (*PA* 37:5656)
102. WHITLA, DEAN K. "Effect of Tutoring on Scholastic

Aptitude Test Scores." *Personnel & Guid J* 41:32–7 S '62. * (*PA* 37:5660)

103. WILLINGHAM, WARREN W., AND STRICKLAND, JAMES A. "Conversion Tables for Otis Gamma and Scholastic Aptitude Test." *Personnel & Guid J* 41:356–8 D '62. * (*PA* 37:7183)

104. *Manual of Freshman Class Profiles, 1963 Edition.* Princeton, N.J.: College Entrance Examination Board, 1963. Pp. 642. *

105. AIKEN, LEWIS R., JR. "College Dropouts and Difference Scores." *Psychol Rep* 13:905–6 D '63. * (*PA* 38:9255)

106. AIKEN, LEWIS R., JR. "The Grading Behavior of a College Faculty." *Ed & Psychol Meas* 23:319–22 su '63. * (*PA* 38:1425)

107. ANGOFF, WILLIAM H. "Can Useful General-Purpose Equivalency Tables Be Prepared for Different College Admission Tests?" *Personnel & Guid J* 41:792–7 My '63. *

108. ANGOFF, WILLIAM H. "Can Useful General-Purpose Equivalency Tables Be Prepared for Different College Admissions Tests." *Proc Inv Conf Testing Probl* 1962:57–73 '63. * (*PA* 38:3187)

109. BURNS, RICHARD LEO. *An Investigation of the Value of the American College Testing Program, the Scholastic Aptitude Test and the Purdue Placement Tests as Predictors of Academic Success of Purdue University Freshmen.* Doctor's thesis, Purdue University (Lafayette, Ind.), 1963. (*DA* 24:1477)

110. COFFMAN, WILLIAM E. *The Scholastic Aptitude Test—1926–1962.* College Entrance Examination Board, Research and Development Reports, Test Development Report TDR-63-2. [New York: the Board], June 1963. Pp. i, 26. *

111. College Entrance Examination Board. *A Description of the College Board Scholastic Aptitude Test.* Princeton, N.J.: the Board, 1963. Pp. 53. * (Earlier editions published in 1960 and 1962.)

112. FUNKENSTEIN, DANIEL H. "Mathematics, Quantitative Aptitudes and the Masculine Role." *Dis Nerv System* 24(Sect 2):140–6 Ap '63. *

113. GRUBER, EDWARD C. *Practice for Scholastic Aptitude Tests: Complete Preparation.* New York: ARC Books, Inc., 1963. Pp. vi, 277. *

114. HILLS, JOHN R.; KLOCK, JOSEPH A.; AND LEWIS, SANDRA C. *Freshman Norms for the University System of Georgia, 1961–62.* Atlanta, Ga.: Office of Testing and Guidance, Regents of the University System of Georgia, June 1963. Pp. xi, 65. *

115. JACOBS, PAUL I. *A Study of Large Score Changes on the Scholastic Aptitude Test.* College Entrance Examination Board, Research and Development Reports, Research Bulletin RB-63-20. [New York: the Board], June 1963. Pp. iii, 47. *

116. JUOLA, ARVO E. "SAT Validities as Two-Variable Expectancy Tables." *Personnel & Guid J* 42:269–73 N '63. *

117. LEVINE, HAROLD G., AND LYONS, WILLIAM A. "Comparability of Scores on Three Examinations Sponsored by External Agencies in Secondary Schools in New York State." *Personnel & Guid J* 41:596–601 Mr '63. *

118. MICHAEL, WILLIAM B., AND JONES, ROBERT A. "Stability of Predictive Validities of High School Grades and of Scores on the Scholastic Aptitude Test of the College Entrance Examination Board for Liberal Arts Students." *Ed & Psychol Meas* 23:375–8 su '63. * (*PA* 38:1424)

119. MUELLER, KLAUS A., AND WIERSMA, WILLIAM, JR. "Correlation of Foreign Language Speaking Competency and Grades in Ten Midwestern Liberal Arts Colleges." *Mod Lang J* 47:353–5 D '63. *

120. SPAULDING, GERALDINE. "Relations Between the NAIS Junior Scholastic Aptitude Test and the CEEB Scholastic Aptitude Tests." *Ed Rec B* 84:55–62 Jl '63. *

121. WILLINGHAM, WARREN W. "Erroneous Assumptions in Predicting College Grades." Comment by Donald P. Hoyt. *J Counsel Psychol* 10:389–94 w '63. * (*PA* 38:9168)

JOHN E. BOWERS, *Director of Testing, Office of Admissions and Records, University of Illinois, Urbana, Illinois.* [Review of Form KSA45.]

The *College Entrance Examination Board Scholastic Aptitude Test* (SAT), introduced in 1926, has become one of the more familiar test instruments used by college and university personnel for predicting the scholastic achievement of college freshmen. Since an appraisal of the SAT should not ignore the reporting services associated with the admissions program of the College Entrance Examination Board, this reviewer will first describe the characteristics of the SAT and, secondly, comment upon aspects of the referral services.

Form KSA45 consists of five sections, beginning with a 30-minute section and followed by alternating 45-minute and 30-minute sections for a total of 180 minutes of testing time. Respondents are cautioned to guess prudently.

Two scores, verbal (based upon antonyms, sentence completion, analogies, and reading comprehension items) and mathematical (based upon word problems and data sufficiency items), are reported, each as a number on a scale between 200 and 800. Prior to 1941, both scores were scaled each year with a mean of 500 and a standard deviation of 100. The April 1941 national test administration results became the basis for equating all subsequent scales (*44*). At the present time, scaled scores for new forms introduced in each year are independently equated through a "double part-score equating" procedure [1] to two earlier reference forms.

Test-retest reliability coefficients of .89 for the verbal scale and .85 for the mathematical scale were found for time intervals up to 10 months. Reliability coefficients (K-R 20's modified by Dressel's procedure for use when there is a correction for guessing) for both scales for 14 1959–1962 SAT forms consistently approximate .90; standard errors of measurement for both scaled scores for these 14 forms vary, in general, between 30 and 35 points. Internal consistency reliability estimates appear not to contain a speed component.

The mean correlation between verbal and mathematical scores for the 14 forms introduced during the period 1959–1962 is .64. This is compared to the mean intercorrelation of .54 for six forms introduced during the period 1950–1953, .56 for six 1953–1956 forms, and .62 for nine 1956–1959 forms.

Percentile ranks of scaled scores are tabled separately by sex for secondary school seniors and for seniors who later entered college in *College Board Score Reports: A Guide for Counselors* and *College Board Score Reports: A Guide for Admissions Officers*. Norms for seniors were developed from scores on the *Preliminary Scholastic Aptitude Test* administered nation-wide in the fall of 1960, which were then converted to the SAT scale (multiplying

---

[1] ANGOFF, WILLIAM H., AND WAITE, ANNETTE C. *A Study of Double Part-Score Equating for the Scholastic Aptitude Test.* Unpublished statistical report, Educational Testing Service, Princeton, N.J., August 1959. Pp. 12. *

by 10) and adjusted for ability growth between the fall and winter of 1960. College-attending senior norms are based upon a fall 1961 follow-up study of the senior norm group. The publishers correctly point out that local norms, specific to the individual college, are perhaps of greater value to the high school and college counselor.

On each scale, coaching results in average gains of less than the associated standard errors of measurement (55). Practice resulting from the first administration of the SAT effects an increase of approximately 10 scaled score points on both sections for both sexes. Two administrations effect a gain of approximately 20 points on both sections for both boys and girls. Ability growth from May of the junior year in high school to January of the senior year in high school is reflected in an average gain of about 20 points on the verbal scale for both sexes; a 15-point average gain for boys and a 5-point average gain for girls is observed for the mathematical scale. Score changes resulting from practice on the mathematical sections also reflect the amount of mathematics taken in the senior year.[2]

Much validity data for a variety of colleges is summarized in *College Board Scores No. 2* (*44*). In general, the verbal scale has been found to predict freshman grades better than the mathematical scale in liberal arts colleges, while the mathematical scale has been more valid for engineering colleges.

A review of the SAT naturally invites comparison with its major competitor, the *American College Testing Program Examination*. The ACT and the SAT are administered throughout the nation at several Saturday test dates during the year. Each program also schedules Sunday test dates for respondents who, because of religious reasons, prefer not to be tested on Saturday. At the present time, the ACT and the SAT respondent may refer his score results to three institutions. Individual score results will be forwarded to additional institutions or agencies for a small fee. Both the ACT and the SAT reporting services are prompt, reliable, and provide punched-card information which may be immediately entered into local mechanized research systems.

In the reviewer's opinion, the advantages, at the present time, of the SAT program are: (*a*) SAT test forms are available for the handicapped; (*b*) there are overseas SAT administration centers; and (*c*) a list of the SAT respondents who select an institution as first, second, or third choice at each national test administration date is sent immediately to the institution.

The advantage of the ACT program is that the institutional "consumer" may assemble data which the ACT Research Service will summarize, tabulate, and analyze. For many institutions, these kinds of validity analyses might otherwise not be accomplished.

The choice of either instrument for use in situations involving subjects with fairly wide ranges of ability is probably a function of scale familiarity rather than discriminable utility. It would be a matter of empirical test to determine, for homogeneous ability level groupings, which instrument functions more validly. The unfortunate aspect for the prospective college student, undecided about his choice of college, is that he is often required to take both tests as "insurance" in order to meet different institutional entrance test requirements. This reviewer hopes that the evidence which might be accumulated from present duplicate testings will be collected in order to determine whether equivalencies between the ACT and the SAT are justified for some admissions purposes.

WAYNE S. ZIMMERMAN, *Test Officer, Los Angeles State College, Los Angeles, California.* [Review of Form KSA45.]

The SAT is a college entrance examination designed to measure general verbal and mathematical comprehension, the two abilities which the accumulation of statistical evidence argues are the most important cognitive traits contributing to success in academic work. The test was developed as an instrument to be administered to students who aspire to attend college. Its primary purpose is to provide information to college officials who are interested in selecting the most promising students from among those who apply for admission. The scores can be utilized also by high school counselors or other authorized officials to help guide a student either to an appropriate college or to consider an alternative pursuit, although the *Preliminary Scholastic Aptitude Test* has recently been designed specifically to serve this purpose.

---

[2] LEVINE, RICHARD S., AND ANGOFF, WILLIAM H. *The Effects of Practice and Growth on Scores on the Scholastic Aptitude Test.* Unpublished research report, Educational Testing Service, Princeton, N.J., February 1958. Pp. 22. *

The publishers expect that SAT scores will be used as a supplement to such information as previous school performance, biographical data, and scores from noncognitive inventories and questionnaires, plus scores on tests of other cognitive abilities.

Form KSA45 is similar in format to previous forms. The test is divided into five separately timed sections. Scores on two sections are combined to produce the total verbal score, scores on two sections are combined to produce the total mathematics score, and the fifth section is included for the purpose of obtaining data on new items which can be used later in the construction of additional alternative forms.

Items in the verbal sections are presented in four formats. In all instances the examinee is instructed to select the one correct answer from among five alternatives and to mark his choice on a separate machine scorable answer sheet. One verbal format requires a word to be selected which will correctly fill in a blank in a sentence. Another format requires an antonym to be selected for a given stimulus word. A third requires the examinee to select from the alternatives the second half of a verbal analogy, the first half being presented as a stimulus. The fourth presents questions based upon comprehension of content of written passages. Classically the first format would be recognized as a vocabulary test, the second as an antonym test, the third as a verbal analogies test, and the fourth a test of reading comprehension. In the theoretical framework of Guilford's structure of intellect, a vocabulary test might measure "cognition of semantic units," an antonym test, "cognition of semantic classes," a verbal analogies test, "cognition of semantic relations," and a reading comprehension test, "cognition of semantic systems" and cognition of semantic implications. Thus, there would appear to be a potentially good coverage of the Guilford factors of semantic cognition. In the analysis of similar tests, however, Guilford and his associates have found that where the vocabulary level is as high as it is throughout SAT "cognition of semantic units" predominates. This finding would appear to account for the very high correlations usually obtained among these potentially different measures and the fact that a well designed vocabulary test will substitute so well for the more comprehensive set of measures.

The mathematical sections begin with common arithmetical operations and, with difficulty increasing as the test progresses, move on to higher level reasoning type problems involving algebraic and elementary geometric concepts. Although some items are quite difficult, this difficulty is achieved through the level of reasoning required rather than through use of material which would be covered in more advanced mathematics courses. Theoretically, a student who has a grasp of first year high school algebra should be equipped to work all of the kinds of problems that are presented. The symbolic factors in Guilford's structure of intellect are not yet well determined. Consequently, only some very tentative conclusions can be drawn. SAT mathematical problems would be expected to cut across the realms of both symbolic-cognitive and symbolic-convergent production. Possibly one memory factor, "memory for symbolic implications," and one divergent production factor, "divergent production of symbolic relations" are present in some degree. The difficult word problems undoubtedly add some semantic variance, which would help to account for the moderate correlations between the SAT verbal and mathematical sections. Possibly the major portion of the SAT mathematics variance is in "cognition of symbolic systems."

Fourteen recent SAT forms are discussed in an ETS bulletin, covering the period from August 1959 to May 1961. Kuder-Richardson formula 20 reliability coefficients are listed for all forms. The reported verbal test reliabilities range from .88 to .91, while mathematics test reliabilities range from .87 to .91. The reliabilities of Form KSA45 are .92 for verbal and .93 for mathematical scores.

The selected validity coefficients reported for predicting success of male liberal arts students as measured by freshman average grades are modest. They range from .16 to .61 with a median of .35 for the verbal scores, and from .15 to .53 with a median of .33 for mathematics scores. Corresponding selected validity coefficients for female subjects cover approximately the same range with median values of .36 and .26 for verbal and mathematics scores, respectively. Validity coefficients are corrected for restriction in range, while multiple correlations are adjusted for shrinkage. One of the studies

College Entrance Examination Board Scholastic Aptitude Test

from which these data were selected[1] reports multiple correlations of the verbal and mathematics scores with first term grade averages ranging from .22 to .63 before correction and from .18 to .62 after correction for shrinkage. These corrected figures, however, cannot be relied upon as an indication of how well the reported multiple correlations would hold up in cross validation.

SAT has a number of major strengths which should be noted. In the first place, the test is very carefully constructed and it is thoroughly analyzed by appropriate methodology before being presented for use in the selection of students. Its range is sufficiently wide to differentiate among both the lowest and highest levels in the college bound or freshman samples. No other competing test publisher prepares so many alternate forms in which items are so carefully matched for content and difficulty and scores are so painstakingly equated. It is safe also to conclude that no other competing test publisher maintains as high a level of security. Trained security officers are available to be called to the scene immediately should a booklet be reported missing. In the few instances where booklets have been taken, the officers have a remarkably fine record of tracing and recovering them. No other test presents a greater abundance of normative data nor such a vast amount of detailed information concerning the test. Users who have time to read all of the reports are kept up to date by frequent bulletins and reports of new developments. It is not surprising, therefore, that the SAT continues to be the leading test for selection of college students throughout the nation, despite the fact that some inroads have been made. In the eastern states SAT is used almost exclusively. It is also the most frequently used test in the West. It is only in the Midwest and South where competing tests may be used more frequently.

If any adverse criticism were to be made of the SAT in this review, it would have to be aimed at the question of how much time is actually needed to measure two academic abilities. There is little question but what the SAT predicts academic achievement at the college level as well as or better than any competitive test, or at least that it adds more unique variance if it is used in conjunction with an evaluation of high school marks. The question is simply whether it is necessary and appropriate for a student to invest a half day of his time in order for school officials to obtain adequate measures of these two abilities. It seems reasonable to expect, in the light of more recent developments, that shorter factor analytically refined measures of the several verbal and numerical dimensions could be administered in considerably less time without a significant loss in predictive validity. The time saved in administering a shorter test could be utilized either in sampling other abilities and attributes, or for administering placement tests in at least the two areas that are particularly critical—college freshman English and mathematics. In this reviewer's opinion a one half day test composed of four sections designed to yield separate scores for verbal aptitude, quantitative aptitude, English proficiency, and mathematics proficiency would yield more useful information per unit of testing time.

In conclusion, where high school and college officials are satisfied to devote one half a day to the measurement of two abilities, there is probably no better test available to estimate the entering student's college level verbal and mathematical comprehension.

For a review by John T. Dailey of an earlier form, see 5:318; for a review by Frederick B. Davis of earlier forms, see 4:285.

[450]

*College Qualification Tests. Candidates for college entrance; 1955–61; 6 scores: verbal, numerical, science information, social studies information, total information, total; IBM; Forms A ('56), B ('56), C ('59); 2 editions; revised manual ('61, 61 pages); distribution of Forms B and C restricted to colleges and universities; separate answer sheets must be used; postpaid; George K. Bennett, Marjorie G. Bennett, Wimburn L. Wallace, and Alexander G. Wesman; Psychological Corporation. *

a) COMBINED BOOKLET EDITION. (14 pages); $5 per 25 tests; $3.50 per 50 IBM answer sheets; 75¢ per specimen set; 80(105) minutes.
b) SEPARATE BOOKLET EDITION. $2.50 per 25 tests; $2 per 50 IBM answer sheets; 90¢ per specimen set.
 1) *Test V [Verbal].* (5 pages); 15(25) minutes.
 2) *Test N [Numerical].* (6 pages); 35(45) minutes.
 3) *Test I [Information].* (6 pages); 3 scores: science information, social science information, total; 30(40) minutes.

REFERENCES

1. KIRK, BARBARA A. "Comparison of Transfer Students by Source of Origin With Entering Students on the College Qualification Test." *Jun Col J* 29:218–21 D '58. *
2. SEASHORE, HAROLD. "Academic Abilities of Junior College Students." *Jun Col J* 29:74–80 O '58. *

---

[1] OLSEN, MARJORIE. *Summary of Main Findings on the Validity of the CEEB Tests of Developed Ability as Predictors of College Grades.* Unpublished statistical report, Educational Testing Service, Princeton, N.J., October 1957. Pp. 59. *

3. SPAULDING, HELEN. "The Prediction of First-Year Grade Averages in a Private Junior College." *Ed & Psychol Meas* 19:627–8 w '59. * (PA 34:6574)
4. WESMAN, ALEXANDER G., AND BENNETT, GEORGE K. "Multiple Regression vs. Simple Addition of Scores in Prediction of College Grades." *Ed & Psychol Meas* 19:243–6 su '59. * (PA 34:4820)
5. JUOLA, ARVO E. "Predictive Validity of Five College-Level Academic Aptitude Tests at One Institution." *Personnel & Guid J* 38:637–41 Ap '60. * (PA 35:2791)
6. JUOLA, ARVO E. "The Differential Validity of the College Qualification Tests for Diverse Curricular Groups." *Personnel & Guid J* 39:721–4 My '61. * (PA 36:1KJ21J)
7. JUOLA, ARVO E. "Multi-Variable Grade Expectancy Tables: An Aid to Test Interpretation." *Yearb Nat Council Meas Ed* 18:91–9 '61. *
8. DARLEY, JOHN G. "The Basis for Equivalent Scores on the Annual Editions of the American Council on Education Psychological Examination (ACE), 1941 to 1954," pp. 170–83. In his *Promise and Performance: A Study of Ability and Achievement in Higher Education*. Berkeley, Calif.: Center for Study of Higher Education, University of California, 1962. Pp. vii, 191. *
9. RAO, S. NARAYANA. "Predicting Academic Achievement of Students in Science and Arts Colleges." *Psychol Studies* 7:16–9 Jl '62. * (PA 37:5669)
10. KIRK, BARBARA A.; CUMMINGS, ROGER W.; AND GOODSTEIN, LEONARD D. "The College Qualification Tests and Differential Guidance With University Freshmen." *Personnel & Guid J* 42:47–51 S '63. *
11. RAO, S. NARAYANA. "Prediction of Academic Achievement of Students in an Engineering College." *J Psychol Res* 7:114–7 S '63. *

RALPH F. BERDIE, *Professor of Psychology, and Director, Student Counseling Bureau, University of Minnesota, Minneapolis, Minnesota.*

When Educational Testing Service discontinued publishing new forms of the *American Council on Education Psychological Examinations* the authors of the *College Qualification Tests* assumed, and apparently correctly in light of the wide use of the CQT, that a brief, convenient, and relatively valid college aptitude test providing somewhat the same information as the old ACE was still worthwhile. Whereas some other college predicting tests have tended to include items more typical of the traditional academic achievement test, this test continues in the tradition of the old Army Alpha, the early Otis test, and the ACE.

The items in the vocabulary section of the tests require the student to select from four words the one that means the same as or the opposite of a fifth word. Since the early 1920's such vocabulary tests have proved to be among the best predictors of college success.

The numerical items consist of simple problems in mathematics covering fractions, decimals, square root, elementary algebra, and simple geometry.

The information test consists of items dealing with (*a*) physics, chemistry, and biology, and (*b*) history, government, economics, and geography. The items call for knowledge of facts and terminology and, as the title of the subtest implies, are designed to measure how much information the student has at his command rather than how he can use or interpret this information to solve problems. The information items can be scored to provide a science score and a social studies score as well as a total information score. The manual states that the test can be used for placement of students, but the items included in the information subtests do not resemble the items constructed by college teachers for inclusion in tests they use for classifying students in mathematics or social studies and no evidence is presented in the manual concerning the validity of the test for classification or placement purposes.

The manual has unusually complete information on reliability and standard errors of measurement. Reliability of the tests appears satisfactory. The coefficients for the verbal test vary between .84 and .95 with most of them being above .90. Those for the numerical test range between .77 and .93, with most being in or above the high .80's. The reliability coefficients for the total score on the information test range between .79 and .89, somewhat lower than those for either the verbal or numerical tests. The individual science and social studies scores have reliabilities in the .70's and low .80's. The manual does not present information concerning the reliability of the combined verbal and numerical scores, omitting the information section, but the inference appears justified that the reliability of this combined score would usually be in the low to mid .90's; these test scores would provide reliable information concerning college aptitude.

Validity data are presented in three tables, one containing data from publicly controlled four-year institutions, one data from privately controlled institutions, and one data from junior colleges. The institutions are identified only by geographical regions, within institutions data being classified by sex. Correlations are presented between the criterion (always college grades) and each of the six CQT scores.

In general, the size of the validity coefficient depends on the college being studied. Among the four-year publicly controlled institutions the correlation coefficients between verbal scores and grades range from .19 to .63; and the correlations between grades and total score range from .34 to .73. For the 47 correlations reported between total score and grades for the four-year institutions, the median correlation is .57. This is somewhat higher than the figure of .50 that for years people have used to describe the typical correlation between college aptitude test scores and freshman college grades. Somewhat discouraging, however, is the fact that good college aptitude tests available today still do not provide correlation coefficients consistently above the mid-fifties.

One considering using these tests for prediction purposes would wish to know the relative effectiveness of the verbal and numerical scores combined compared to the total CQT score. The manual does not provide this information, but some data from the Arts College of the University of Minnesota suggest the two scores combined provide as effective prediction as does the total score. In predicting first quarter grade-point average in 1962 the verbal test had a correlation with grades for men of .37, for women of .45. The numerical test had correlations of .39 and .45. The combined verbal and numerical scores provided correlations for the men of .49 and for the women of .57. Correlations between grades and total CQT scores were, for the men, .51 and for the women, .59, in each case only .02 higher than the correlations obtained from the combined verbal and numerical scores.

At Minnesota the multiple correlation coefficient between grades and scores predicted from the verbal and numerical scores was identical with the zero order correlations between grades and the totals of the verbal and numerical scores. The same thing was found when the verbal, numerical, science information, and social science information scores were combined in a multiple correlation coefficient and compared to the zero order correlation for the total test score. These results agree with the study by Wesman and Bennett (4) who found that the simple addition of three CQT scores predicted first-term college grades about as well as multiple regression equations. The use of the total test score provides the optimal weighting and adding the two information scores does not significantly increase the predictive efficiency of the test, particularly at the University of Minnesota.

Little information concerning the validity of the tests has been published other than that contained in the manual. One study (5) compared the predictive validities of five college aptitude tests and found that they differed only slightly in validity.

The normative information presented in the manual is superior to similar information presented in manuals for most aptitude tests. Norms are presented separately for men and women, and in light of known sex differences, it is surprising that so many test manuals fail to make this distinction. Not only are general norms for college freshmen presented, but norms also are presented for freshmen in state universities, in privately controlled universities, and for groups of college freshmen who are candidates for A.B. degrees, for B.S. degrees, and degrees in business, education, engineering, technical courses, and nursing. Geographical norms are also provided with separate norms for college freshmen in southern institutions, for freshmen in junior colleges, and for junior college freshmen registered in transfer and in terminal curricula. Finally norms are provided for high school students in grades 11 and 12.

Scores are reported as equivalent on Forms A and B and the same norm tables are presented for these forms. Separate norm tables are presented for Form C.

The three available forms of the test provide a significant advantage. Form A is available to high schools and colleges. Forms B and C are available only to colleges and colleges making use of these forms can be assured that candidates have not had experience with the forms being employed.

In summary, the *College Qualification Tests* are as good as but no better than the best of the other college aptitude tests. The tests have many advantages and no disadvantages that are not inherent in tests of this type. They are well constructed, edited, and printed. They have satisfactory reliability and are as valid as other tests available for these purposes; they are easy to administer and to score. The CQT is as adequate for identifying, admitting, classifying, and counseling college students as any other college aptitude test.

WARREN G. FINDLEY, *Professor of Education, and Coordinator of Educational Research, University of Georgia, Athens, Georgia.*

Two elements have been added since these tests were reviewed by three specialists as a new offering in the preceding issue of this yearbook. Form C, issued in 1960, constitutes a second restricted form for use in colleges and universities, but not in high schools. Also, the manual was revised in 1961 to incorporate the results of further validity and reliability studies.

Since the tests are offered as instruments for use in selective admissions, placement, and counseling, and since there were differing degrees of consensus among the previous reviewers regarding suitability of the tests for these various purposes, it will be well to organize this review along the line of suitability for the three purposes, respectively. The new data and argument will fall into place under these headings.

SUITABILITY FOR SELECTIVE ADMISSIONS. There was unanimous agreement among the previous reviewers on suitability of the tests for selective admissions purposes. The availability of a second restricted form and the promise of successive biennial forms for restricted use strengthen this use operationally. The fact that a Form D was not issued on schedule in 1962, or in 1963, suggests only that the need has not been as pressing as originally anticipated.

In addition to reporting an increased number of validity and reliability coefficients accumulated since the 1957 manual was published, the present manual includes illustrative expectancy tables for two institutions. These present graphically in parallel 100 per cent bars the proportions of freshmen attaining grade-point averages below 2.0, between 2.0 and 2.9, and between 3.0 and 4.0, for successive intervals of 10 percentile points on the CQT total score. These serve not only to underline the importance of local institutional norms, but also to provide a model form for their presentation and use.

Of course, the predictive power diminishes as one moves from the total score to the part scores and finally to the subpart scores. The medians of 65 correlations with college grade-point average for each of the scores are .51 for total score, .45 for Information, .44 for Numerical, .43 for Verbal, .39 for Science Information, and .38 for Social Studies Information. This is largely a function of the reliability of these part scores. It is interesting to note, however, that the medians of 12 reliability coefficients for each of the scores are .96 for total score, .93 for V, .89 for N, .86 for I, .79 for social studies, and .77 for science. It may be worth pondering that information scores prove quite as predictive of college GPA as either verbal or numerical scores despite their appreciably lower reliability. It is also noticeable that the reliability coefficients for boys run higher than those for girls for five of the six scores, while the reverse is true of the validity coefficients.

Failure of the verbal test to show higher predictive validity may be due partially to the item types used. This reviewer found it quite awkward to shift from seeking synonyms to seeking opposites and back again. In the opposites section he became frustrated at times at inability to find a synonym, only to realize suddenly that opposites were to be sought. It may also be questioned whether the verbal score should reflect only what a vocabulary test can measure. Most competing test offerings use reading comprehension in some form in arriving at the verbal measure.

The numerical test is a power test of problem solving ability based on fundamental concepts and operations of arithmetic, algebra, and geometry. Its somewhat lower reliability is shared by mathematics scores in other batteries. The fact that its median predictive validity is comparable to that of other parts involves a sex difference in college courses chosen. For boys the numerical score tends to be relatively more predictive, while for girls it tends to be relatively less predictive, than the verbal and information scores.

Inclusion of an information test gives this battery an advantage over most competing measures of scholastic aptitude. Some may wish to quarrel with the highly factual nature of the content on grounds not only of its face validity, but also of its influence on instruction in preparatory institutions. The first criticism is met directly by the validity coefficients, showing this test, if anything, slightly more predictive of GPA than the verbal and numerical tests are.

The criticism of unfavorable impact on instruction is more serious. For years this has deterred the College Entrance Examination Board from considering the introduction of such a section in its Scholastic Aptitude Test despite the probability that the predictive power of that measure would be enhanced thereby. Such criticism on a policy level is not to be met by statistical evidence. It is met in the American College Testing Program and related offerings by inclusion of reading comprehension tests in the subject fields; these tests contain small segments of items based on general knowledge of each area not involved in the content of the reading passages. The policy choice made for the *College Qualifica-*

tion Tests is to supplement the factorially based verbal and numerical sections found in so many academic aptitude batteries with this distinct element.

It should be noted in regard to this issue that scholastic aptitude measures which lack an information section are also subject to criticism on two counts, predictive and instructional. The predictive criticism, *supported by validity coefficients,* is that structured knowledge of useful factual information is quite as basic a characteristic of a vigorous mind as are the "basic skills" of verbal comprehension and quantitative reasoning. A proper sample of as many as 75 items of *significant* information from science and social studies can represent this area of substantive knowledge in the scholastic aptitude battery in much the same relative proportion to verbal comprehension and quantitative reasoning as prevails in the high school curriculum. It may be that some students will have had better instruction than others in these substantive areas, but that is equally true of mathematics and reading. To the degree that this reviewer is correct in the supposition that the predictiveness of reading comprehension and quantitative reasoning tests is attributable to the fact that rudimentary instruction in both areas has been generally available to those who have completed high school and that excellence on these tests reflects one's motivation and ability to learn these "basic" skills, a well constructed test of information may likewise be said to achieve its predictiveness by reflecting students' motivation and ability to learn equally "basic" substantive knowledge. Moreover, such a test need be no more coachable than tests of verbal and numerical skill. A good general education would be the best preparation. And those who sought to add to their knowledge and to structure it for effective recall would be strengthening their intellectual competence quite as intrinsically as those who now review their basic arithmetic and put it into more usable form.

The scholastic aptitude battery that lacks an information test may be criticized for favoring those with basic skills who have not put their skills to use in mastering substantive knowledge, over students with somewhat lesser basic skills who have put their skills to good use in acquiring structured knowledge. Many have viewed with concern the apparent emphasis put on scores from the *College Entrance Examination Board Scholastic Aptitude Test* in determination of scholarship awards, for example. It is an excellent test for prediction of college achievement and has the added virtue of being a common measure, taken by all competitors, which is relatively uninfluenced by special preparation or superior teaching. As of the date of writing this review, that test has not incorporated in it any measure of substantive knowledge. Some would argue that achievement tests, specifically those of the College Board, should be used for this purpose. It must be remembered, however, that such achievement tests measure advanced work much influenced by availability and by quality of advanced instruction. What is called for is a test of substantive knowledge with the characteristics already cited as characterizing the verbal and mathematics sections of the SAT.

The resolution of the issue would thus appear to depend on development of a *general* test of *significant* structured knowledge in a form least likely to be considered by students and their parents and teachers as a test requiring or favoring rote memorization of encyclopedic information.

Regarding the usefulness of this battery in admissions programs, one further question arises. The College Entrance Examination Board and the American College Testing Program offer their tests under secure administrative procedures that do not require the individual college to handle this considerable chore, fraught as it is with possibilities of loss of security when operated under ordinary circumstances. These programs also make provision, through multiple test administration (four or five times a year) and special arrangements, to achieve the local flexibility that is achievable through use of the *College Qualification Tests.* These two secure programs are rapidly gaining acceptance nationwide over such offerings as the *College Qualification Tests.* It would appear, then, that the future of the CQT as an instrument of college admissions must lie in extending to it the secure administration and scoring service the publishers now offer for testing of prospective graduate students, executives, and research and management personnel.

SUITABILITY FOR ACADEMIC PLACEMENT. To the extent that placement in curriculums, courses, and sections within courses is viewed simply as an extension of selective admission to college to selective admission *within* college, the same validity coefficients that establish the suitability of these tests for college admission also establish their suitability for placement purposes. There are several points to be borne in mind, however. First, since assignment within college generally deals with a narrower range of competence on each test than does selection for admission, a heavier strain is placed on validity and reliability. Second, assignment to curriculums and courses requires evidence of differential prediction. Norms for national groups specializing in different college curriculums are only suggestive and are not directly interpretable. The offer of the publishers to cooperate in local norms studies becomes important here. Also, the user will want to pay greater attention to high school grades and/or placement tests of prerequisite study for both course assignment and sectioning. The CQT would help in general sectioning and, in cases of extremely high or low scores in the verbal and numerical tests, in curriculum assignment. The total information score would play its part primarily as a contributor to total CQT score. The part scores for science and social studies information are not sufficiently reliable for differential use. Differences between them and differences from other scores would be useful only as they confirm or are confirmed by other evidence, such as differences in reported high school grades. Class sectioning needs to be done subject by subject, as is widely recommended for high school and college and has been done in a number of colleges for many years. And it is at least as important that provision be made for reassignment to the most appropriate section at an early evaluation point in each course as for proper initial assignment. Viewed in this light, initial sectioning must be considered tentative. Initial assignment should be made as valid as possible by taking into account as much relevant information about students as possible, but always with the expectation that some individuals will prove to have been incorrectly assigned and to require reassignment.

SUITABILITY FOR HIGH SCHOOL AND COLLEGE COUNSELING. College counseling may be considered a still further extension of selective admissions, beyond selective placement. Counseling implies less directive action by the institution, however, and more joint planning with the student or simply advisement of the student. Once in the college, the student can be properly advised only in terms of expectancy tables or charts showing him probabilities of attaining given averages in each of several curriculums in that college in the light of his tested aptitude and previous academic achievement. Counseling regarding advanced professional training during upperclass years would require similar expectancy tables for success in graduate work in particular fields within particular institutions.

High school counseling regarding college choice can be considerably helped by results of the *College Qualification Tests.* Again, this reviewer would strongly recommend use of expectancy tables of the sort provided in the *Counselor's Guide to Georgia Colleges,* prepared and distributed by the Office of Testing and Guidance of the Regents of the University System of Georgia. This publication and its supplements present in separate tables for each institution, and for each curriculum within each institution, separately by sex, the probability of attaining a grade average of C or better, B or better, or A, for high school students with particular values of predictive composites based on high school grades and, in this publication, College Board SAT scores. The CQT would do better to take advantage of high school grade averages as a supplement in such prediction rather than offer to supplant such grade averages. The practical value of a test for high school counseling is to be judged not in terms of its own unaided predictive power, but in terms of the extent to which it improves the predictive power of automatically available data like high school grade averages. The long and creditable history of predictive power which these averages have, makes it especially appropriate to evaluate tests as supplementary measures.

For counseling to be most effective, individual profiles of scores should be provided as accessories. It would be particularly helpful if such profiles incorporated the percentile band device of the Cooperative Test Division's STEP and SCAT series, or the difference device used in the CQT publisher's own *Differential Aptitude Tests,* to indicate when differences between an individual's scores on the separate tests warrant notice and differential prediction.

The value of the tables of special norms provided so generously in the CQT manual is real, but limited. State universities differ among themselves, as do privately controlled institutions (and their subdivisions that lead to different degrees and specializations), southern universities, and junior colleges and their subgroups of students in terminal and transfer programs. The norms of the samples just mentioned, calculated separately for the two sexes, reveal a number of significant general relations that provide a useful background for counseling. However, consider the norms for education majors and arts and sciences majors. These favor arts and sciences generally, more for boys than for girls. But research has shown that for many years students in teachers colleges in certain states have compared favorably with the national norms for arts and sciences majors, and even more favorably with arts and sciences majors from certain individual institutions or groups of institutions. The sample of privately controlled institutions is notably unrepresentative, while the sample of southern institutions is so varied as to make the norms not truly representative of any of them. The high school norms are more extensive, but not certainly representative. In fairness to the tests' authors, it should be noted that they argue for local norms and provide the model already cited for their calculation and presentation in the form of expectancy charts. However, these recommendations and strictures on interpretation, so carefully stated, are often overlooked or forgotten in preoccupation with seemingly appropriate special norms. This discussion should be viewed as an attempt to reinforce the authors' thoroughly professional presentation, rather than to criticize it.

SUMMARY. The *College Qualification Tests* are well conceived, show excellence in item construction, are supported by varied and substantial data on reliability, validity, and norms, which are in turn reported with professional rigor and contain a significant emphasis on substantive knowledge which is unique for a scholastic aptitude battery. They are appropriate for selective admissions but must compete with complete admissions testing services. They can serve academic placement and counseling uses as presently constituted but might be strengthened in ways indicated in this review. Users may rely on this instrument as sound and in some ways unique. Competing offerings abound and present a variety of important decisions to make.

For reviews by Gustav J. Froehlich, A. E. G. Pilliner, and David V. Tiedeman, see 5:320.

[451]

Concept Mastery Test. Grades 15–16 and graduate students and applicants for executive and research positions; 1956, c1950; IBM; Form T ('56, 4 pages); manual ('56, 9 pages); separate answer sheets must be used; $3.50 per 25 tests; $2 per 50 IBM answer sheets; 40¢ per set of manual and scoring key; 50¢ per specimen set; postpaid; (35–45) minutes; Lewis M. Terman; Psychological Corporation. *

REFERENCES

1–4. See 5:321.
5. MCNEMAR, QUINN. Chap. 12, "Intellectual Status of the Gifted Subjects as Adults," pp. 140–6. In *The Gifted Child Grows Up: Twenty-Five Years' Follow-Up of a Superior Group.* By Lewis M. Terman and others. Genetic Studies of Genius, Vol. 4. Stanford, Calif.: Stanford University Press, 1947. Pp. xiv, 448. * (PA 22:2080)
6. TERMAN, LEWIS M., AND ODEN, MELITA H.; IN ASSOCIATION WITH NANCY BAYLEY, HELEN MARSHALL, QUINN MCNEMAR, AND ELLEN B. SULLIVAN. Chap. 11, "Intelligence Tests of 1940," pp. 125–39. In their *The Gifted Child Grows Up: Twenty-Five Years' Follow-Up of a Superior Group.* Genetic Studies of Genius, Vol. 4. Stanford, Calif.: Stanford University Press, 1947. Pp. xiv, 448. * (PA 22:2080)
7. TERMAN, LEWIS M., AND ODEN, MELITA H. Chap. 5, "Intellectual Status at Mid-Life," pp. 52–63. In their *The Gifted Group at Midlife: Thirty-Five Years' Follow-Up of the Superior Child.* Genetic Studies of Genius, Vol. 5. Stanford, Calif.: Stanford University Press, 1959. Pp. xv, 187. * (PA 33:7905)
8. MACKINNON, DONALD W. "Fostering Creativity in Students of Engineering." *J Eng Ed* 52:129–42 D '61. * (PA 36:4HD29M)
9. CAMP, WILLIAM L., AND ROTHNEY, JOHN W. M. "Use of the Concept Mastery Test in Study of Superior High School Seniors." *Voc Guid Q* 10:223–5 su '62. * (PA 37:7181)
10. CURTIS, H. A., AND KROPP, R. P. "Standard and Visual Administrations of the Concept Mastery Test." *Audiovis Commun R* 10:38–42 Ja-F '62. * (PA 37:1193)
11. KENNEDY, WALLACE A., AND SMITH, ALVIN H. "Norms for Mathematically Gifted Adolescents on the Concept Mastery Test." *Percept & Motor Skills* 17:698 D '63. * (PA 38:6059)
12. TAYLOR, DONALD W. Chap. 19, "Variables Related to Creativity and Productivity Among Men in Two Research Laboratories," pp. 228–50. In *Scientific Creativity: Its Recognition and Development.* Edited by Calvin W. Taylor and Frank Barron. New York: John Wiley & Sons, Inc., 1963. Pp. xxiv, 419. * (PA 38:2689)

For reviews by J. A. Keats and Calvin W. Taylor, see 5:321.

[452]

***Cooperative School and College Ability Tests.** Grades 4–6, 6–8, 8–10, 10–12, 12–14, 15–16; 1955–63; also called SCAT; 3 scores: verbal, quantitative, total; IBM, NCS, and Grade-O-Mat; 6 levels; STEP-SCAT student report ('58, 4 pages); STEP-SCAT profile ('57, 2 pages); accessories for levels 1–5: directions for administering ('57, 11 pages), manual for interpreting ['57, 49 pages], technical report ['57, 43 pages], 1958 SCAT-STEP supplement ('58, 32 pages), 1962 SCAT-STEP supplement ('62, 48 pages), 1963 SCAT-STEP supplement of urban norms ('63, 16 pages), letters to the editor—SCAT and SAT ('62, 29 pages); manual for upper level ('63, 24 pages); separate answer sheets must be used; $4 per 20 tests; $1 per 20 IBM scorable answer sheets; $1 per 10 scoring stencils (answer pattern must be punched out locally); $1 per 20 Scribe answer sheets (see 763 for scoring service); see 666 for prices of Grade-O-Mat cards; see 671 for prices of NCS answer sheets; $1 per 20 student reports; $1 per 20 profiles; $1 per manual for interpreting; $1 per technical report; $1 per supplement; $1 per manual for upper level; postage extra; $1.25 per combined specimen set of levels 1–5; $1 per specimen set of upper level; cash orders postpaid; 70(95) minutes; Cooperative Test Division. *

a) SCHOOL ABILITY TEST. Grades 4–6, 6–8, 8–10, 10–12; 1955–63; 2 forms (12–14 pages); 4 levels.
  1) [*Level 5.*] Grades 4–6; Forms 5A, 5B, ('56).
  2) [*Level 4.*] Grades 6–8; Forms 4A, 4B, ('56).
  3) [*Level 3.*] Grades 8–10; Forms 3A, 3B, ('56).
  4) [*Level 2.*] Grades 10–12; Forms 2A, 2B, ('55).

b) COLLEGE ABILITY TEST. Grades 12–14, 15–16; 1955–63; 2 levels.
  1) [*Level 1.*] Grades 12–14; Forms 1A, 1B, 1C, 1D, ('55, 12 pages); Forms 1C and 1D available only by special arrangement for use with students in college.
  2) *Level U.* Grades 15–16; Forms UA, UB, ('61, 16 pages); Form UB available only by special arrangement.

REFERENCES

1–7. See 5:322.
8. WILLIAMS, CECIL L. *A Study of the Relative Effectiveness of the ACE Psychological Examination and the School and College Ability Test in Predicting First Semester Grade Point Averages.* Master's thesis, University of Kansas (Lawrence, Kan.), 1957.
9. BLACK, D. B. "A Study of the Relationship of the Grade IX Principal's Rating to Performance on the Alberta Grade IX Departmental Examinations." *Alberta J Ed Res* 4:227–36 D '58. * (*PA* 34:2089)
10. FLEMING, W. G. *Aptitude and Achievement Scores Related to Immediate Educational and Occupational Choices of Ontario Grade 13 Students.* Atkinson Study of Utilization of Student Resources, Report No. 3. Toronto, Canada: Department of Educational Research, Ontario College of Education, University of Toronto, 1958. Pp. xix, 380. *
11. FLEMING, W. G. *Ontario Grade 13 Students: Their Aptitude, Achievement, and Immediate Destination.* Atkinson Study of Utilization of Student Resources, Report No. 4. Toronto, Canada: Department of Educational Research, Ontario College of Education, University of Toronto, 1958. Pp. ix, 55. *
12. KENNEDY, PHYLLIS E. "The Validity of the School and College Ability Test for Prediction of College Achievement." *Calif J Ed Res* 9:67–71 Mr '58. * (*PA* 33:9044)
13. MAYER, ROBERT W. "A Study of the STEP Reading, SCAT and WISC Tests, and School Grades." *Reading Teach* 12:11 + D '58. * (*PA* 34:3441)
14. BLACK, D. B. "A Comparison of the Performance on Selected Standardized Tests to That on the Alberta Grade XII Departmental Examination of a Select Group of University of Alberta Freshmen." *Alberta J Ed Res* 5:180–90 S '59. * (*PA* 34:6559)
15. BROAD, ELMER J. *An Investigation of the Relative Effectiveness of the American Council on Education Psychological Examination and the School and College Ability Test in Predicting College Grade Point Averages.* Master's thesis, San Francisco State College (San Francisco, Calif.), 1959.
16. ENGELHART, MAX D. "Obtaining Comparable Scores on Two or More Tests." *Ed & Psychol Meas* 19:55–64 sp '59. * (*PA* 34:114)
17. FLEMING, W. G. *Personal and Academic Factors as Predictors of First Year Success in Ontario Universities.* Atkinson Study of Utilization of Student Resources, Report No. 5. Toronto, Canada: Department of Educational Research, Ontario College of Education, University of Toronto, 1959. Pp. xi, 137. *
18. KLUGH, HENRY E., AND BIERLEY, ROBERT. "The School and College Ability Test and High School Grades as Predictors of College Achievement." *Ed & Psychol Meas* 19:625–6 w '59. * (*PA* 34:6569)
19. LEASE, GUS C. *A Study of the Musicality, Intelligence, and Music Achievement of Vocalists and Instrumentalists in Selected High Schools.* Doctor's thesis, State University of South Dakota (Vermillion, S.D.), 1959. (*DA* 19:3631)
20. MOTT, DONALD B. *An Actuarial Study of Scores Received by High School Seniors on the Cooperative School and College Ability Test and These Students' Grades Received During the First Year of Attendance in South Dakota Colleges.* Master's thesis, South Dakota State College (Brookings, S.D.), 1959.
21. WEEKS, JAMES S. "The Predictive Validity of A.C.E. and S.C.A.T." *Personnel & Guid J* 38:52–4 S '59. *
22. WHITE, ARDEN JUNIOR. *A Comparison of the Flanagan Aptitude Classification Tests With the Wechsler Adult Intelligence Scale, the School and College Ability Test, and Three Other Measures of Mental Variables at the High School Level.* Doctor's research study No. 1, Colorado State College (Greeley, Colo.), 1959.
23. BARTLETT, CLAUDE J., AND BAUMEISTER, ALFRED A. "Prediction of Classroom Discipline Problems." *Excep Child* 27:216–8+ D '60. * (*PA* 36:4JO16B)
24. BERRY, CHARLES A., AND JONES, ARLYNNE L. "A Further Note on the Predictive Value of the National Freshman Testing Program." *Negro Ed R* 11:120–5 Jl '60. *
25. BLACK, DONALD B. "The Prediction of Freshman Success in the University of Alberta From Grade XII Departmental Results." *Alberta J Ed Res* 6:38–53 Mr '60. *
26. BUEGEL, HERMANN F. "Comparison of SCAT Scores of High School Juniors in Parochial and Public Schools." *Psychol Rep* 7:497–8 D '60. * (*PA* 35:2789)
27. CASSEL, RUSSELL N. "Expected Achievement Beta Weights on SCAT (Form 1A) for College Freshmen." *Psychol Rep* 6:401–2 Je '60. * (*PA* 35:7100)
28. DEWEES, JOSEPH P. *Predicting College Success for Freshmen at the College of the Pacific From Scores Made on the SCAT Test.* Master's thesis, College of the Pacific (Stockton, Calif.), 1960.
29. JONES, ARLYNNE LAKE. *An Investigation of the Response Patterns Which Differentiate the Performance of Selected Negro and White Freshmen on SCAT.* Doctor's thesis, University of Colorado (Boulder, Colo.), 1960. (*DA* 21:2986)
30. JUOLA, ARVO E. "Predictive Validity of Five College-Level Academic Aptitude Tests at One Institution." *Personnel & Guid J* 38:637–41 Ap '60. * (*PA* 35:2791)
31. KIMBELL, FONTELLA THOMPSON. *The Use of Selected Standardized Tests as Predictors of Academic Success at Oklahoma College for Women.* Doctor's thesis, University of Oklahoma (Norman, Okla.), 1960. (*DA* 20:4335)
32. LONG, JOHN MARSHALL. *The Prediction of College Success From a Battery of Tests and From High School Achievement.* Doctor's thesis, University of Virginia (Charlottesville, Va.), 1960. (*DA* 21:1100)
33. MILAM, OTIS H., JR., AND WARD, GEORGE, II. "The 1961–62 State College Selective Admissions Policy: Some Data." *Proc W V a Acad Sci* 32:209–13 D '60. * (*PA* 36: 3KA09M, title only)
34. O'SHAUGHNESSY, MARY MICHAEL. *Some Effects of Praise and Reproof on Test Performances on School Ability and Reading Achievement Tests.* Catholic University of America, Educational Research Monograph, Vol. 24, No. 2. Washington, D.C.: Catholic University of America Press, December 2, 1960. Pp. x, 114. *
35. PIPHER, J. A. "An Appraisal of the Use of the Dominion Group Test of Learning Capacity (Advanced) in the Atkinson Study of Utilization of Student Resources." *Ont J Ed Res* 3:17–23 O '60. *
36. TEMPERO, HOWARD E., AND IVANOFF, JOHN M. "The Cooperative School and College Ability Test as a Predictor of Achievement in Selected High School Subjects." *Ed & Psychol Meas* 20:835–8 w '60. * (*PA* 35:3976)
37. TRAXLER, ARTHUR E. "Some Independent School Results on the Cooperative School and College Ability Tests, Levels 2–5." *Ed Rec B* 76:57–64 F '60. *
38. ZABEL, RONALD L. *The Determination of the Ability of the Total Score of the Cooperative School and College Ability Test, the Total Reading Comprehension Score of the Cooperative English Test, and High School Rank to Predict Scholastic Success of Freshmen at Western Illinois University.* Master's thesis, Western Illinois University (Macomb, Ill.), 1960.
39. CLYDE, ROBERT BURDETTE. *An Empirical Comparison of the School and College Ability Test and the American Council on Education Psychological Examination.* Doctor's thesis, University of Southern California (Los Angeles, Calif.), 1961. (*DA* 22:151)
40. CURTIS, H. A., AND KROPP, R. P. "A Comparison of Scores Obtained by Administering a Test Normally and Visually." *J Exp Ed* 29:249–60 Mr '61. *
41. EELLS, KENNETH. "How Effective Is Differential Prediction in Three Types of College Curricula?" *Ed & Psychol Meas* 21:459–71 su '61. * (*PA* 36:2KJ59E)
42. GUSTAFSON, MONTY C. "Relationships Between Scholastic Aptitude Scores and Achievement of Junior College Freshmen." *Jun Col J* 32:147–50 N '61. *
43. KENNEDY, PHYLLIS E. "The Predictive Value of the College Ability Test for a Group of College Freshmen." *Calif J Ed Res* 12:174–7 S '61. *
44. LUCIER, OMER, AND FARLEY, JOHN. "The Lowry Reasoning Test Combination as a Status Free Technique." *J Social Psychol* 55:125–31 O '61. * (*PA* 36:4HB25L)
45. MANN, M. JACINTA. "The Prediction of Achievement in a Liberal Arts College." *Ed & Psychol Meas* 21:481–3 su '61. * (*PA* 36:2KL81M)
46. WAICHES, VINCENT CASIMIR. *Intellectual and Personality Changes in College Students as Measured by the Cooperative College Ability Test and the Personal Judgment Scale.* Doctor's thesis, University of Texas (Austin, Tex.), 1961. (*DA* 21:3706)
47. ZUCKOWSKY, LEO MARK. *The Efficiency of SCAT and Other Selected Variables in Predicting Success in the Various Lower Division College Curricula.* Doctor's thesis, University of Notre Dame (Notre Dame, Ind.), 1961. (*DA* 22:2297)
48. ANDERSON, SCARVIA B. *Letters to the Editor: SCAT and SAT.* Princeton, N.J.: Cooperative Test Division, 1962. Pp. 29. *
49. DARLEY, JOHN G. "The Basis for Equivalent Scores on the Annual Editions of the American Council on Education Psychological Examination (ACE), 1941 to 1954," pp. 170–83. In his *Promise and Performance: A Study of Ability and Achievement in Higher Education.* Berkeley, Calif.: Center

for Study of Higher Education, University of California, 1962. Pp. vii, 191. *
50. JOHNSON, ELMIRA LAYAGUE. *The Performance of Filipino College Freshmen on the School and College Ability Test.* Doctor's thesis, University of Wisconsin (Madison, Wis.), 1962. *(DA 22:3922)*
51. KIRK, BARBARA A.; CUMMINGS, ROGER W.; AND GOODSTEIN, LEONARD D. "The Differential Validity of the College Ability Test for Transfer Students in Six Curricular Fields." *Jun Col J* 33:131–40 O '62. *
52. LEWIS, JOHN W. "Comparing Zero-Order Correlation From SCAT Total and Multiple Correlation From SCAT Q and V at Southern Illinois University." *Ed & Psychol Meas* 22:397–8 su '62. * *(PA 37:3870)*
53. LEWIS, JOHN W. "Utilizing the Stepwise Multiple Regression Procedure in Selecting Predictor Variables by Sex Group." *Ed & Psychol Meas* 22:401–4 su '62. * *(PA 37:3871)*
54. PEARSON, MARGARET ADELLE. *The Establishment of School and College Ability Test Norms for Blind Children in Grades 4, 5, and 6.* Doctor's thesis, University of Oklahoma (Norman, Okla.), 1962. *(DA 23:890)*
55. REID, JOHN W.; JOHNSON, A. PEMBERTON; ENTWISLE, FRANK N.; AND ANGERS, WILLIAM P. "A Four-Year Study of the Characteristics of Engineering Students." *Personnel & Guid J* 41:38–43 S '62. * *(PA 37:5655)*
56. RUDD, JOHN PAUL. *A Study of the Validity of Selected Predictors for Placement in Three-Rail Curricula.* Doctor's research study No. 1, Colorado State College (Greeley, Colo.), 1962. *(DA 24:184)*
57. VICK, MARY CATHARINE, AND HORNADAY, JOHN A. "Predicting Grade Point Average at a Small Southern College." *Ed & Psychol Meas* 22:795–9 w '62. * *(PA 37:7205)*
58. CHEERS, ARLYNNE LAKE, AND SHERMAN, DOROTHY M. "Response Pattern Differences of Selected Negro and White Subjects on S.C.A.T." *Personnel & Guid J* 41:582–9 Mr '63. * *(PA 39:1482)*
59. DOLEYS, ERNEST J., AND RENZAGLIA, GUY A. "Accuracy of Student Prediction of College Grades." *Personnel & Guid J* 41:528–30 F '63. *
60. ENDLER, NORMAN S., AND STEINBERG, DANNY. "Prediction of Academic Achievement at the University Level." *Personnel & Guid J* 41:694–9 Ap '63. * *(PA 39:2888)*
61. FORTNA, RICHARD O. "A Factor-Analytic Study of the Cooperative School and College Ability Tests and Sequential Tests of Educational Progress." *J Exp Ed* 32:187–90 w '63. *
62. GOLDMAN, BERT A. "SCAT Versus WAIS: An Enigma." *J Ed Res* 57:51–3 S '63. *
63. LIGGITT, WILLIAM A. "An Evaluation of General Education in Elementary Teacher Preparation." *J Ed Res* 57:156–9 N '63. *
64. OSBORN, LYNN R. "An Analysis of the Relationship Between Speech Performance and Performance on Written Examinations of Course Content in a Beginning College Speech Course as Reflected in Assigned Grades." *Univ Kans B Ed* 17:68–71 F '63. *
65. PEARSON, MARGARET ADELLE. "The Establishment of School and College Ability Test Norms for Blind Children in Grades 4, 5, and 6." *Int J Ed Blind* 12:110–2 My '63. * *(PA 38:1213)*
66. PEMBERTON, W. A. *Ability, Values, and College Achievement.* University of Delaware Studies in Higher Education, No. 1. Newark, Del.: the University, 1963. Pp. xii, 77. * *(PA 38:6573)*
67. SARASON, IRWIN G. "Test Anxiety and Intellectual Performance." *J Abn & Social Psychol* 66:73–5 Ja '63. * *(PA 37:5672)*
68. SMITH, W. N. "Differential Prediction of Two Test Batteries." *J Ed Res* 57:39–42 S '63. *
69. SOMMERFELD, ROY E., AND TRACY, NEAL H. "A Study of Selected Predictors of Success in Second-Year Algebra in High School." *H Sch J* 46:234–40 Ap '63. *
70. TERWILLIGER, JAMES S. "Dimensions of Occupational Preference." *Ed & Psychol Meas* 23:525–42 au '63. * *(PA 38:6698)*
71. WELLCK, A. A. "Statewide Tests and Academic Success at the University of New Mexico." *Personnel & Guid J* 42:403–5 D '63. *

RUSSEL F. GREEN, *Associate Professor of Psychology, The University of Rochester, Rochester, New York.*

The SCAT series of six tests, covering grades 4 through 16, can best and most directly be described as academic aptitude tests. They were constructed specifically to "aid in estimating the capacity of a student to undertake the academic work of the next higher level of schooling." Their standardization is probably equal to that of any of their competitors and may be about as good as one can expect in a very large and relatively free society.

ETS has published some 260 pages of text and tables in nine manuals that describe SCAT's development, interpretation, uses, and statistical characteristics. Probably because ETS is attempting to write for both specialists and non-specialists, their literature is, in its entirety, somewhat confusing and in places even somewhat misleading. This confusion centers in statements of purposes, descriptions of what is measured, and, to some extent, the interpretation of test results.

In various descriptions of the purpose or function of the tests such phrases as measuring academic aptitude, estimating the capacity for academic work, predicting end-of-year grades, and "serving a function in guidance at four transitional periods" are used. Whatever phrase one chooses, he *can* use the tests to *help* make predictions about a student's probable academic performance, at least for the following two years. The validity of the tests as aids for such predictions, at least from grade 5 up, has been well demonstrated by a considerable number of research projects. Correlations between SCAT scores and either grade-point averages (GPA) or specific courses appear to be highest at about grade 7, ranging in the .70's and up for prediction of seventh grade math and English grades, and GPA. Prediction of college freshman GPA appears to range from about .4 to .6. These validities compare quite favorably with those obtained with other tests. However, two trends should be noted. The first is that the SCAT scores appear to predict academic achievement somewhat better among women than they do among men. The second is that the SCAT total score usually predicts English grades better than they are predicted by the verbal score. The quantitative score tends to predict math grades better than the SCAT total but the difference is often small and even reversed. This means that the best use of all three scores for prediction and guidance probably involves more complexity than is presented in the manuals. If it were not for trying to make more refined inferences from the "profile" than one can make from the total score, one would have no reason to get the verbal score at all. How much predictive efficiency is gained from including the verbal score in a "profile" has not been formally investigated; hence, one includes it primarily as an act of faith.

The publisher has, in various manuals, described SCAT as measuring: two kinds of school-related abilities (Q and V); four kinds of abilities (verbal comprehension, manipulating numbers and applying number concepts, comprehending the sense of a sentence read, and quantitative problems); and, finally, "'school learned abilities' directly, rather than psychological characteristics....which afford indirect measurement of *capacity* for school learning" [italics added]. Confusion over what is measured and for what purpose stems from trying to avoid talking about specific abilities or dimensions of intellect.

ETS obtained samples of behavior on four kinds of tasks and reduced these to two subscores, Q and V. Clearly, each must be regarded as arising from a complex set of abilities. These two subscores are combined into a single score which can confidently be interpreted as a measure of "general intelligence." (General intelligence scores can probably be most clearly described as one of the important elements in the measurement of scholastic aptitude.) This point is supported by the following observations. SCAT total correlates with the *Wechsler Adult Intelligence Scale* total at about .84 and with WAIS verbal at about .88. Both of these correlations were obtained on 84 eleventh and twelfth grade boys, and, therefore, from a somewhat restricted range of ability. In large samples tested in a junior college, the correlations of SCAT with the *Otis Quick-Scoring Mental Ability Tests* were .77 and .81. Clearly there is good evidence for concurrent validity with general intelligence.

The "school learned" abilities which are measured by the various levels of the tests are not clearly and directly related to content of specific course work beyond grammar school. This is especially true of the arithmetic sections. Very little algebra appears at any level and no mathematics higher than algebra is used; in fact at level U (for grades 15 and 16) well over half the problems do not require calculations on paper. (One can presume that this last point was intentional and it clearly is desirable.) The implied proposition that advanced math courses contribute to scoring ability has to be taken on faith, since no direct evidence is presented.

The principal device used by ETS for interpreting test scores is to transform raw scores into percentile bands. The use of percentile bands is an excellent device for avoiding the tendency to regard a number as representing something exactly or precisely determined. There are difficulties, however, which the publisher has not solved as satisfactorily as one might wish. These difficulties start with one of the two statistics on which the width of the band depends, the reliability coefficient. They also involve the difficulty level of the tests and the proper use of percentile bands.

The reliability of SCAT, while probably substantial, is not known. The authors report internal consistency reliability for the total test of about .95 for each level. Since, however, the tests are speeded to an unknown extent, this estimate is high to an unknown extent. The test authors hold that the speeding that occurs is probably relatively unimportant because "all but the slowest students can complete [the tests] in the time limits allowed." However, these "slowest students" turn out to include up to 35 per cent on sentence completion, up to 20 per cent on vocabulary, up to 52 per cent on computation, and up to 40 per cent on arithmetic reasoning. How much of the failure to finish is due to time and how much due to difficulty is undetermined. Most observers would conclude that speeding could be important and should have been allowed for in the method of estimating reliability used. The estimate of the reliability affects the size of the band widths. Due to the fact that the tests are to some extent speeded, the band widths probably should be somewhat wider.

For the careful reader, the interpretations by ETS of the band widths will cause some confusion and perhaps some error, even though the kind of error involved may not be of practical importance. The difficulty comes from inconsistency in the use of bands. For a person whose band width is 82–89, it is stated in the manual that he scored lower than 11 per cent of the cases. It is also stated that students are not to be considered different unless their percentile bands do not overlap. *Less* than 11 per cent of the *bands* of other students will fail to include the 89th percentile. The 11 per cent figure comes from reverting to the counting of other students' scores as percentile *points*. Perhaps a three class interpretation would be suitable: (*a*) percentage of higher non-overlapping bands; (*b*) percentage of overlapping bands;

Cooperative School and College Ability Tests

and (c) percentage of lower nonoverlapping bands. Lacking such interpretation one might better just use the simple percentile scores.

A final word about difficulty seems needed. In spite of the confusion between speed and difficulty, most of the tests may be reasonable in difficulty. However, 24 per cent of the quantitative scores of fourth graders fall in the chance range. Hence, if one wants discrimination at the low level, the test should not be used for this grade.

SUMMARY. The SCAT series, then, can be confidently regarded as a set of very good scholastic aptitude tests which probably is in most ways the equal of any of its competitors. In most ways, also, it is a good model of how such a series should be planned, developed, standardized, and validated. The most disturbing lack is that throughout all its voluminous and sometimes contradictory literature one is never given any real insight into the philosophy of measurement which guided the developers—if there really was one. We are never satisfactorily told why four "kinds" of tasks were used (even though it is apparent that three would have produced somewhat better results) to produce two scores which are associated with two "abilities"—verbal and numerical—which are, in turn, combined into a single total score which the authors seem reluctant to defend as representative of anything definite even though it is clearly defensible as an important component in "scholastic aptitude."

The nature and extent of use to which SCAT can be put will depend on the objectives that are sought through a testing program. If one is concerned with diagnosis of scholastic difficulties, the "profile" obtained from the three SCAT scores is certainly of limited, if not dubious, value. Other tests, such as SAT, will be preferred.

If, however, one is primarily concerned with prediction of general overall levels of future performance, SCAT can clearly be recommended for use from grades 5 through 16. Or if one wishes to install a system which will focus on academic aptitude while at the same time avoiding the use of IQ labels with all the potential for mischief that such labels carry, then SCAT appears to be ready made for him. It is a good general IQ test from which one cannot legitimately calculate IQ's. This may be a real virtue. We probably would be wise to deemphasize the IQ concept and, through the use of a test series such as SCAT, to emphasize instead statements of relative likelihood of success in specific situations.

For reviews by Frederick B. Davis, Hanford M. Fowler, and Julian C. Stanley of the tests for grades 4–14, see 5:322.

[453]

*Culture Fair Intelligence Test.** Ages 4-8 and mentally defective adults, 8-13 and average adults, grades 10-16 and superior adults; 1933-63; formerly called *Culture Free Intelligence Test;* 2 editions; Raymond B. Cattell and A. K. S. Cattell (Scales 2 and 3).

a) IPAT CULTURE FAIR INTELLIGENCE TEST. 1933-63; title on test is *Test of g: Culture Fair;* 3 levels; cash orders postpaid; Institute for Personality and Ability Testing. *

1) *Scale 1.* Ages 4-8 and mentally defective adults; 1933-62; identical with *Cattell Intelligence Tests, Scale 0: Dartington Scale;* individual in part; 1 form ('50, 12 pages); manual ('62, 14 pages, identical with manual copyrighted in 1960 except for format and one word change in text); no data on reliability; $3.50 per 25 tests; $3 per set of cards for classification test; 50¢ per scoring key; 75¢ per manual; $1.35 per specimen set; materials for following directions test must be assembled locally; (22-60) minutes.

2) *Scale 2.* Ages 8-13 and average adults; 1949-63; Forms A ('57, c1949-57), B ('61 edition, c1949-60, essentially the same as test copyrighted in 1956 except for some item and option order changes and revision in 8 items), (8 pages); Form A also available, either separately or in combination with the *Sixteen Personality Factor Questionnaire,* in a special edition ('63, 8 pages) for use with tape recorded directions; manual ('58, 35 pages); supplementary directions sheet ('60); manual ('63, 8 pages) for tape administration of Form A; $3.30 per 25 tests; separate answer sheets may be used; $2.25 per 50 answer sheets; 50¢ per either booklet or answer sheet hand scoring key; $1.60 per manual; $2.20 per specimen set; $30-$58 per examiner's kit of tape edition of Form A (includes 2 tests, 50 answer sheets, 3¾ ips tape, and manuals); 12.5(30) minutes.

3) *Scale 3.* Grades 10-16 and superior adults; 1950-63; Forms A ('63, c1950-63, identical with 1959 second edition except for printing and redrawing of some figures), B ('61, c1950-61), (8 pages); manual, 1961 edition (c1959, 51 pages); $3.30 per 25 tests; separate answer sheets may be used; $2.25 per 50 answer sheets; 50¢ per either booklet or answer sheet hand scoring key; $1.90 per manual; $2.45 per specimen set; 12.5(30) minutes.

b) CATTELL CULTURE FAIR INTELLIGENCE TEST. 1960-61; IBM; 1 form (16 pages, a single-booklet printing—labeled parts 1 and 2—of the current IPAT Forms A and B of each level); parts 1 or 2 may be administered alone although use of both parts is recommended; 2 levels; $5.75 per 35 tests; separate answer sheets may be used; 7¢ per IBM scorable answer sheet; 40¢ per scoring stencil; 75¢ per specimen set of either level; postage extra; Bobbs-Merrill Co., Inc. *

1) *Scale 2.* Ages 8-14 and average adults; 1 form ('60, c1949-60, 16 pages); manual ('60, c1949-60, 23 pages, a modification—with additional norms—for school use of the 1958 IPAT manual); 25(50) minutes for the full test.

2) *Scale 3.* Grades 9-16 and superior adults; 1 form ('61, c1950-61, 16 pages); manual ('60, c1959-60,

23 pages, a modification for school use of the 1961 IPAT manual); 25(30–60) minutes for the full test.

REFERENCES

1–2. See 4:300.
3–13. See 5:343.
14. XYDIAS, NELLY. "R. B. Cattell's Intelligence Test," pp. 333-44. In *Social Implications of Industrialization and Urbanization in Africa South of the Sahara.* Prepared under the auspices of Unesco by the International African Institute. Paris: Unesco, 1956. Pp. 743. *
15. BUSS, F. HOWARD. *The Effect of Socio-Economic Factors Upon a Culture-Bound Test and the Cattell Culture Free Test.* Master's thesis, Kent State University (Kent, Ohio), 1959.
16. CHAMBERS, JACK A. "Preliminary Screening Methods in the Identification of Intellectually Superior Children." *Excep Child* 26:145–50 N '59. * (PA 35:3249)
17. RODD, WILLIAM G. "A Cross-Cultural Study of Taiwan's Schools." *J Social Psychol* 50:3–36 Ag '59. * (PA 35:3960)
18. KIDD, ALINE HALSTEAD. *A Factor and Item Analysis of the Test of G; Culture-Free and the Stanford-Binet, Form L.* Doctor's thesis, University of Arizona (Tucson, Ariz.), 1960. (DA 21:366)
19. KNAPP, ROBERT R. "The Effects of Time Limits on the Intelligence Test Performance of Mexican and American Subjects." *J Ed Psychol* 51:14–20 F '60. * (PA 34:7395; 35:2197)
20. FARRANT, ROLAND HARVARD. *A Factor Analytic Study of the Intellective Abilities of Deaf and Hard of Hearing Children Compared With Normal Hearing Children.* Doctor's thesis, Northwestern University (Evanston, Ill.), 1961. (DA 22:2870)
21. BARRATT, ERNEST S.; CLARK, MARJORIE; AND LIPTON, JAMES. "Critical Flicker Frequency in Relation to Cattell's Culture Fair Intelligence Score." *Am J Psychol* 75:324–5 Je '62. * (PA 37:4952)
22. COOPER, JAMES G. "The Culture-Free Intelligence Test in a College of the Western Pacific." *Personnel & Guid J* 41:123–5 O '62. * (PA 37:5659)
23. KIDD, ALINE H. "The Culture-Fair Aspects of Cattell's Test of g: Culture-Free." *J Genetic Psychol* 101:343–62 D '62. * (PA 37:6702)
24. MEYERS, E.; ORPET, R. E.; ATTWELL, A. A.; AND DINGMAN, H. F. *Primary Abilities at Mental Age Six.* Monographs of the Society for Research in Child Development, Vol. 27, No. 1, Serial No. 82. Lafayette, Ind.: Child Development Publications, 1962. Pp. 40. * (PA 38:8462)
25. ALVI, SABIR ALI. *Traditional and "Culture Fair" Aptitude Test Performance of College Students From Different Academic and Cultural Backgrounds.* Doctor's thesis, Indiana University (Bloomington, Ind.), 1963. (DA 24:2775)
26. CATTELL, RAYMOND B. "Theory of Fluid and Crystallized Intelligence: A Critical Experiment." *J Ed Psychol* 54:1–22 F '63. * (PA 37:7991)
27. JORDHEIM, G. D., AND OLSEN, INGER A. "The Use of a Non-Verbal Intelligence Test of Intelligence in the Trust Territory of the Pacific." *Am Anthrop* 65:1122–5 O '63. *
28. MACARTHUR, R. S., AND ELLEY, W. B. "The Reduction of Socioeconomic Bias in Intelligence Testing." *Brit J Ed Psychol* 33:107–19 Je '63. * (PA 38:4271)

JOHN E. MILHOLLAND, *Professor of Psychology, The University of Michigan, Ann Arbor, Michigan.*

The two major claims made for these scales are that they have high saturation on general ability, *g,* and that they are relatively independent of school achievement, social advantages, and various other environmental influences. In Scale 1, however, only four of the eight subtests are represented as being fully culture free. All tests are paper and pencil tests, except Test 5 of Scale 1 which requires that the examiner have various specific objects.

The four subtests of Scale 1 which Cattell considers to be culture fair are symbol copying, classification of pictures, mazes, and identification of similar drawings. The other four tests involve selecting familiar objects when named, following directions, identifying what is wrong with pictures of familiar objects, and riddles.

The room in which Scale 1 is administered should have at least one oblong table low enough for a child easily to survey the top, two additional chairs, and a door which a child can open and shut.

Scale 1 is identical with Scale 0 (Dartington Scale) of the *Cattell Intelligence Tests* and thus shares Scale 0's research basis which, according to the manual, is reported in a paper by Cattell and Bristol.[1] Scores on 18 tests, each composed of only one item type, were intercorrelated in a sample of 100 six-year-olds. Thirteen of the tests were drawn from tests in common use; the other five were devised especially for this study. The eight tests with highest mean correlations with the others were used to form the Dartington Scale. The distribution of tetrad differences for the correlation matrix had a mean of approximately zero and a quartile deviation of .04, and these data were taken as sufficient to indicate that the tests were measuring just one factor, presumably *g.* The tests now constitute Scale 1 of the culture fair tests.

The standardization for this scale was based on "more than 400 cases combining American and British samples." A table of mental age equivalents of raw scores and one for converting raw scores to IQ's are provided. A table for converting IQ's to percentile ranks is based on an IQ standard deviation of 20 points. Cattell thinks the correct standard deviation for ratio IQ's is about 25, arguing that the reduced scatter in traditional intelligence tests is due to contamination of intelligence with achievement.

Scales 2 and 3 have four subtests: Series, which requires that the examinee complete a sequence of four drawings by choosing one from among five options; Classifications, which requires that he pick out one of a set of five drawings that is different from the rest; Matrices, requiring the selection of a drawing to complete a matrix; and Conditions, which requires that the examinee select from among five drawings of overlapping geometric figures the one in which one or two dots could be placed to fit the specifications of a model. These two scales each have a Form A and a Form B (called Parts 1 and 2 in the Bobbs-Merrill single booklet edition) which are par-

[1] CATTELL, RAYMOND B., AND BRISTOL, HILDA. "Intelligence Tests for Mental Ages of Four to Eight Years." *Brit J Ed Psychol* 3:142–69 Je '33.

allel in form, and if time presses only one part may be given. The authors advise against this.

The manual for Scale 2 of the Bobbs-Merrill edition recommends that users of the test construct their own norms, but nonetheless provides six tables of normative data. The only information about the standardization group is that it consisted of 4,328 boys and girls, "sampled from varied regions" of the United States and Britain. Percentile and normalized standard score IQ equivalents of raw scores for the two parts of the scale, separately and combined, are given, as well as a table of special norms (based on 14- and 15-year-olds only) for administration under unspeeded conditions and a table for converting IQ's to percentile ranks.

The norms tables for Scale 3 that appear in the Bobbs-Merrill manual are not entirely the same as those given in the 1961 IPAT Handbook. The "Usual, Routine Norm Table" in the IPAT Handbook is the same as the Bobbs-Merrill table for converting raw scores directly into IQ's, except that the former is reported to be based on 3,140 "American High School students....and young adults in a stratified job sample," while the latter is based on 3,140 high school students with no mention of the employed young adults. Both manuals contain a table for converting IQ's to standard scores and percentiles for the general adult population ($n = 1,788$), but the row of the IPAT table geared to an IQ standard deviation of 24 is omitted from the Bobbs-Merrill table. In both these tables there are different norms for Part 1 scores, depending on whether the examinee has had experience with the test before. A third table in each manual provides a conversion of raw scores to standard scores and percentile ranks for college students, and is based on a sample of 1,097 undergraduates, mainly sophomores, from two north central state universities, one southern university, and a medium sized private college. Finally, there is in each manual a table of age corrections after early adulthood, to be applied only to speeded administrations. The IPAT Handbook gives one additional table which does not appear in the Bobbs-Merrill manual: a "Research Norm Table" based on a sample of 3,140 high school students and young adults (presumably the same sample as the sample for the "Usual, Routine Norm Table"). The research table, however, is geared to an IQ standard deviation of 24 points, the other to one of 16 points.

The underlying rationale that it would be good to have a test as independent of circumstantial factors and as near to measuring innate ability as possible, is certainly a sound one. There are two facets to the problem: the measurement of what we think of as general intelligence, and the avoidance of cultural influences. The attainment of one objective without the other may be considerably easier than accomplishing both together. As one of the manuals states, "pictorial tests still involve cultural influence, while performance tests often avoid intelligence in avoiding culture!"

A sound rationale, however, is no guarantee of successful execution. No one yet has produced a satisfactory culture fair test, and we need to see the evidence bearing on the extent to which the Cattell test meets its goals of providing a test of g that is minimally susceptible to cultural influences. The manuals are woefully inadequate in meeting this requirement. The most convincing exhibit would be some factor matrices which would enable the reader to see for himself the basis for claims made. Instead, there appear only some isolated factor loadings, purporting to come from the list of references (numbering 62 in the 1961 edition of the IPAT Handbook for Scale 3). One who tries to check these data, however, is in for a frustrating experience. I was unable to locate a number of the references, and the ones I did find did not provide the information cited. For example, one paragraph which appears in the section titled "Proof of Validity, and the Correct Technical Definition of Intelligence" in both the IPAT and Bobbs-Merrill manuals for Scales 2 and 3 cites seven references as containing data in support of the correlation with g of the four subtests. I was able to examine five of these references and in none of them did I find any evidence of the g saturation of the tests. (One of the cited references, in fact, is I. Macfarlane Smith's review in the Fifth Yearbook and the only data cited in it are from the test manual. This kind of research referencing seems a bit circular.)

The foregoing indicates that one must not be overwhelmed by the array of references cited in the text of the manuals. The necessity (and sometimes, the impossibility) of tracking down each citation also makes it hard on the conscientious reviewer. This reviewer strongly

Culture Fair Intelligence Test

urges that diligent editing be applied to these manuals.

The picture is not completely dark, however. Cattell (*26*) has recently published a factor analytic study to test his hypothesis that *g* may be separated into "fluid" and "crystallized" intelligence. He believes that fluid intelligence is closer to unadulterated *g* and that the culture fair test should load on it. Included in the test battery in this study were two forms of the *SRA Primary Mental Abilities* (verbal, spatial, number, reasoning, fluency) and two forms of the *IPAT High School Personality Questionnaire* with 14 scores on each form. Subjects were 277 seventh and eighth graders. Two second-order factors were interpreted as fluid and crystallized intelligence. The loadings for the culture fair subtests on the fluid factor were: Series, .35; Classification, .63; Matrices, .50; and Conditions, .51. The only other substantial loading on this factor was .32 for the PMA spatial subtest. The PMA V, R, and N and the culture fair Series subtest also loaded on crystallized intelligence. These results are consonant with Cattell's hypothesis, but hardly enough to convince a skeptic that the factor underlying the culture fair test is *g*.

It must be acknowledged that the demonstration of freedom from culture bias is very tricky. The manuals have cited a few cross cultural studies, but most of them are not readily available in the literature. Again, one must be prepared to be unimpressed by the citations of references. For example, the following statement appears in the IPAT manual for Scale 3: "In the originally reported research....the CF test was administered to foreign language immigrants to the USA at the time of entry and again after some degree of acclimation." In the study cited, the immigrants were tested after living approximately 14 months in this country and then retested after 77 more days. After the estimated gain attributable to practice effects with the test was taken out, the following standard score gains were recorded: Binet, .45; Culture Fair, .17; Arthur, .09; ACE, .13; and Ferguson formboards, —.14. These results hardly seem to furnish definitive evidence of the outstanding freedom from culture effects of the culture fair test.

The manuals are deficient in other respects, being long on theoretical discussion and short on precise and definite information about the tests themselves. It seems a shame that a test that has been in published form for so long should still be criticized for lack of satisfactory manuals, but the necessary research to support the claims made for the Cattell tests either has not been done or has not been thoroughly and clearly presented in the manuals.

Culture fair tests would seem to have possibilities for great usefulness on the current scene, now that we are getting more and more concerned about culturally deprived segments of our population. Not only would it be eminently desirable to locate persons of high intelligence who did not show up well on our conventional tests, but it would be a good thing to have a fair assessment of everyone's potential regardless of the level at which he could eventually function. I would need to see some real longitudinal validity data before I could become convinced that the Cattell culture fair tests are suitable for this job. On the other hand, it seems to me they show promise, and I would like to see the research undertaken that would evaluate them.

ABRAHAM J. TANNENBAUM, *Associate Dean, Graduate School of Education, Yeshiva University, New York, New York.*

The IPAT is offered as a culture fair test of intelligence, a tool that enables psychometrists to depart from allegedly antiquated practices in mental measurement. Its design is based on Cattell's (*26*) theory of fluid general ability in contrast to the traditional concepts of crystallized intelligence. The two characterizations of mental activity differ in a variety of ways:

a) Crystallized intelligence (g_c) is reflected in cognitive performance that has become patterned through earlier learning experiences. Fluid ability (g_f), on the other hand, manifests itself through adaptive mental behavior in situations so unfamiliar that previously learned skills can be of no help in guiding such behavior.

b) Diversity in cultural interests and opportunities produces more individual differences in g_c than in g_f, even before biological maturity (age 15–25) has been reached.

c) Both types of ability reach their growth peaks at different ages, g_f leveling off sometime in early adolescence, while g_c may continue to grow in late adolescence and early adulthood, depending on the length of participation in cultural pursuits.

d) Standardized tests measuring g_c show a much smaller sigma than does a test like IPAT, measuring g_f. The reason is that in a given subculture the previous learning experiences which strongly influence g_c scores are so circumscribed that they tend to reduce the variance at a given age level. One example of the restrictive nature of learning activity may be found in the typical classroom where a wide range of potential is funneled into narrow-range performance as bright pupils are restrained from moving ahead and dull pupils are pushed to achieve more than they can.

e) With g_f rooted relatively more in heredity and physiology and g_c based relatively more on environment and experience, the latter type of measure will show greater fluctuation in test norms over the years.

In order to achieve cultural fairness, the IPAT tests were constructed to include mostly nonsense material, universally unfamiliar, and some commonplace material, universally familiar. The effects of special previous training could, therefore, not be transferred to the problems posed in these instruments, and the supposedly contaminating effects of social class, ethnicity, and even nationality on test results are said to be filtered out.

Scale 1 was restandardized after 1960 on a sample of under 500 cases drawn from America and Great Britain. Although larger than previous standardizing samples, the current group is still quite small, and there is no information provided on the size of the various age subgroups. It is interesting to note, however, that no difference was found between the American and British subsamples at any age level. Also, the age plots from 3½ to 12 years reportedly "show internal consistency and smooth progression," although no statistical evidence is presented to support these observations. Nor does the 1962 Handbook include data relating to the vital matters of reliability and validity. It is therefore difficult to assess the value of Scale 1 until the Handbook's assurance that "a more extensive standardization is in progress" results in a detailed report.

Scale 2 was standardized on 4,328 subjects from various parts of Great Britain and the U.S.A. No breakdown by age is noted. Scale 3 was standardized on 3,140 American youth divided equally among high school freshmen, sophomores, juniors, and seniors, and "young adults in a stratified job sample."

Evidence of validity is impressive, as far as it goes. Subtest correlations with Spearman's *g* (general mental capacity) range from .53 to .99 on American samples and from .78 to .83 on French samples. Full test correlations are reported on the order of .59 with the ACE, .84 with the Wechsler-Bellevue, anywhere from .56 to .85 with the Stanford-Binet, and an average of .73 with the Otis group test.

Evidence on the validity of the test in predicting scholastic achievement is not impressive. One study reports a correlation of .36 with the *Stanford Achievement Test* as against a Stanford-Binet correlation of .25 with the same measure. However, the sample was not only small in size ($n = 28$) but restricted in ability range, the group consisting of pupils in summer school, half of whom were making up academic deficiencies. Additional evidence taken from small samples shows that the IPAT tends to predict achievement test scores better than does the Otis. Other than these scant bits of information the only comment in the manuals on predictive validity is a speculative one to the effect that a culture fair test might have done a better job than conventional IQ measures in forecasting future accomplishment for such "late bloomers" as Darwin, Winston Churchill, and the Wright brothers.

Both Scales 2 and 3 show moderate internal consistency. Split-half and test-retest coefficients exceeded .80 in most samples tested. The author, however, urges the use of both forms in order to obtain more valid and reliable results.

Since the IPAT is designed to be culture fair, one basic question is whether it succeeds in eliminating the so-called contaminating effects of culture. At best, one can only answer that the success is partial. On the credit side, the manuals refer to studies showing that test norms for Taiwan and France did not differ from our own. On the other hand, mention is made of findings that detect norm differences between Indian and British-American populations; between Belgian Congo and American groups; and between Puerto Rican immigrants to America and native born Americans. Moreover, there is reference to data revealing a positive correlation between IPAT scores and socioeconomic status in this country.

In essence, then, it must be admitted that the long-pursued goal of demonstrating equality among national and international subpopulations on some measure of general ability has not been reached by this test. Is it, indeed, a goal worth pursuing? Even if it were possible to devise a test so antiseptic as to clean out inequality not only among subcultures but also among other groups showing differences in test intelligence, such as those classified by sex, age, education, geographic origin, body type, physical health, personality structure, and family unity—what kind of instrument would we then have? Since such a test must perforce be so thoroughly doctored as to omit tasks that reveal these group differences, or substitute others that show "no difference," what could it possibly measure? What could it predict? Covering up group differences in this way does not erase test bias. Rather, it delimits drastically the kinds of information one can gather about problem solving strengths and weaknesses associated with groups as well as individuals.[1]

It might be argued that the effort to eliminate cultural bias in the IPAT is only derivative of an attempt to assess latent potential rather than learned skills. This is, after all, a test designed to measure fluid, not crystallized, intelligence, and the assumption is that although there may be *individual* differences in fluid intelligence, *group* differences are unthinkable except to a racist. It should be borne in mind, however, that the concept of fluid intelligence is predicated on the belief that ability is fixed and its growth predetermined. It assumes that nature and nurture are *additive* components contributing to human behavior. Recent commentary on the subject, however, marshals considerable evidence to suggest that the two elements may be *interactive* instead.[2] A valuable encounter with environment enriches mental functioning just as proper nutrients contribute to physical development. It is quite possible that heredity and environment *affect each other* in setting the growth limits in both instances. There is even reason to believe that experiential impoverishment early in life inhibits intellectual growth regardless of how much compensatory experience may be supplemented in later years. It is therefore by no means certain that any test of latent potential can obtain a score that is free of cultural "contamination" if the very essence it purports to measure may itself be so "contaminated."

In the last analysis, a test of intelligence must provide practical insights. The emphasis in the IPAT is on the location of "hidden potential" or "real capacity." If such exists in the fixed, pure sense as assumed by the test authors, it should be possible to forecast accomplishment by combining test data with an analysis of the learning environment. Or, it could have predictive validity in circumstances where it is possible to control human experi-

[1] LORGE, IRVING. "Difference or Bias in Tests of Intelligence." *Proc Inv Conf Testing Probl* 1952:76–83 '53. *
[2] HUNT, J. McV. *Intelligence and Experience*. New York: Ronald Press Co., 1961. Pp. ix, 416. * (PA 36:4AD16H)

Culture Fair Intelligence Test

ence and opportunity. This has yet to be tested. Until such an evaluation is made, one is forced to suspend endorsement of the IPAT and of its underlying theory of fluid ability.

For a review by I. Macfarlane Smith of the IPAT edition, see 5:343; for reviews by Raleigh M. Drake and Gladys C. Schwesinger, see 4:300.

[454]

★**The D48 Test.** Grades 5 and over; 1963, c1961–63; translation of the French edition published in 1948; for research use only; 1 form ('61, 10 pages); preliminary manual ['63, 12 pages]; American norms for grades 5–6 only; separate answer sheets must be used; $5.25 per 25 tests; $2.20 per 50 answer sheets; $1.50 per set of hand scoring stencils and manual; postage extra; specimen set not available; 25(35) minutes; translation and American manual by John D. Black; Consulting Psychologists Press, Inc. *

REFERENCES
1. KEEHN, J. D., AND PROTHRO, E. TERRY. "Non-Verbal Tests as Predictors of Academic Success in Lebanon." *Ed & Psychol Meas* 15:495–8 w '55. * (PA 30:7765)
2. CRONHOLM, BORJE, AND SCHALLING, DAISY. "Intellectual Deterioration After Focal Brain Injury." *Arch Surgery* 86:670–87 Ap '63. *
3. GOUGH, HARRISON G., AND DOMINO, GEORGE. "The D 48 Test as a Measure of General Ability Among Grade School Children." *J Consult Psychol* 27:344–9 Ag '63. * (PA 38:266?)

PAUL C. DAVIS, *Dean and Professor of Psychology, Los Angeles Pacific College, Los Angeles, California.*

The *D48 Test* consists of pictured arrangements containing from 4 to 14 dominoes. The examinee's task is to determine the numbers of dots that should be in the blank domino in each arrangement in order for it to fit correctly into the set or series shown. The examinee is provided with an answer sheet showing the arrangement of dominoes for each item but without dots. He writes the correct numbers in the two halves of the domino shown in dotted outline. Time for the test, after instructions and sample items, is 25 minutes.

The test is simple in format, easy to administer and score, and is apparently homogeneous in content, although one who is multiple-factor oriented may suspect the presence of much more complexity than Vernon found in his bifactor analysis (loading of .87 in g).

Gough and Domino (*3*) emphasize the familiarity of many cultures with dominoes and identify the D48 as an approach to culture free testing involving general *familiarity* rather than *unfamiliarity* with the medium. In this same connection the test is recommended as "almost entirely non-verbal." In view of the extensive verbal directions and the importance of the testee's *understanding* the samples and requirements of the test, it is the reviewer's attitude that more than opinion is needed before the nonverbal characterization can be accepted.

The test's validity as an instrument for estimating intellectual level or predicting achievement has been explored. Gough and Domino summarized the results of French, Belgian, Italian, and American studies involving testing of a total of some 3,000 persons from about age 10 to adulthood. This summary indicates that (a) for the same age and educational level, mean scores tend to be similar in different countries; (b) there tends to be a steady upward progression in mean scores with age and educational level; (c) overall results show no consistent sex difference in mean score; and (d) studies of fifth and sixth grade American students ($n = 86$) showed that the test predicted total GPA well; in fact, approximately as well as does previous year GPA.

According to the test manual two studies of reliability have been reported. Odd-even reliability of .89 was obtained while a test-retest reliability study yielded a correlation of .69. Item difficulty has also been studied by Gough and Domino. They found the items generally to be in ascending order of difficulty, but report some apparent misplacements of items; e.g., item 22 is one of the most difficult while item 33 is passed by more than half of the group. They also found that difficulties are similar among the different populations reported.

SUMMARY. The *D48 Test* is a simple instrument that offers encouraging possibilities. Foreign administration plus administration to limited groups of American children suggests that the test may be a good predictor of academic achievement. It appears to be adequately reliable and mean scores appear to increase methodically with age and educational level. While percentile norms for various age groups based on data from French studies are given in the manual, the D48 is, for American users, essentially an experimental instrument. It is hoped that norms for American populations may soon be forthcoming.

S. S. DUNN, *Assistant Director, Australian Council for Educational Research, Hawthorn, Victoria, Australia.*

The manual for the *D48 Test* contains the following notice: "This test is for experimental use only: adequate normative and validity data on United States populations are *not* available."

The test was developed by the staff of the Centre de Psychologie Appliquée in France, based on the British Army Dominoes Test prepared by Anstey. The manual contains some information of French origin as well as "one study based on fifth and sixth graders in a California school and one report of means and sigmas on a group of American college students." The comments which follow are based on the material given in the American manual which has been adapted from the French.

The directions for administration allow great freedom to the examiner. He is told that it is his responsibility to see that the testee understands all four examples. For those who prefer to use them, verbatim instructions are included. In the opinion of the reviewer, understanding by testees is more likely to come from a carefully prepared standard set of directions than from allowing too great freedom to examiners.

The answer sheet repeats the pattern of the domino boxes with a domino space for the answer outlined in broken lines. This may help people of limited ability, but no reason is given for using this layout, which requires two pages and a more complicated scoring key, rather than a one-page answer sheet giving the answer space only.

The section on development gives some background history. It also contains a paragraph beginning "Research has demonstrated that:" followed by three statements. For the first statement no research evidence is given, the second finishes with a sentence beginning "Experience has shown that," and the third has nothing to do with research, but is merely a statement that the D48, being an open-ended test, is not subject to guessing answers by chance.

The evidence of difficulty in Table 1, based on California children, suggests that before the test is distributed in the United States, further testing is warranted to check the order of difficulty of questions. Several items (17, 18, 22, 24, and 25) seem badly misplaced.

The data on reliability show a satisfactory split-half reliability ($r = .89$), but a relatively low test-retest figure ($r = .69$) after a time interval of two months. The standard deviations of this group do not appear unduly restricted.

The validity data given are mostly of French

origin and not of a kind likely to be useful to an American user. A reference is made to the use of the test in the measurement of mental deterioration. Two references in French are given to deterioration studies.

Until the publishers produce evidence that this test is equal or superior to the many non-verbal tests published in the United States, it has little to commend it for use in guidance situations. The fact that it is a test of a single item type may make it useful for certain factor analytic studies.

[455]

★Deeside Non-Verbal Reasoning Test: English-Welsh Bilingual Version. Ages 10–12; 1961–63; 2 forms: test 1 ('61), test 2 ('63), (16 pages); separate mimeographed manuals for test 1 ['61, 17 pages], test 2 ['63, 19 pages]; distribution restricted to directors of education; 25s. per 25 tests; 7s. 6d. per manual; postage and purchase tax extra; 37–38(60) minutes; W. G. Emmett; George G. Harrap & Co. Ltd. *

[456]

*Doppelt Mathematical Reasoning Test. Grades 16–17 and employees; 1954–63; IBM; Form A ('54, 4 pages); manual ('58, 10 pages); bulletin of information ('63, 36 pages); revised procedures for testing center operation ('63, 8 pages); distribution restricted and test administered at specified licensed university centers; scoring and reporting handled by the local center; examination fee to centers: $1 per examinee; fees to examinees are determined locally and include reporting of scores to the examinee and to 3 institutions or companies designated at the time of testing; additional score reports may be secured from the publisher at a fee of $1 each; 50(60) minutes; Jerome E. Doppelt; Psychological Corporation. *

REFERENCES

1. SCHWARTZ, MILTON M., AND CLARK, F. EUGENE. "Prediction of Success in Graduate School at Rutgers University." *J Ed Res* 53:109–11 N '59. * (PA 35:1223)
2. ROEMMICH, HERMAN. "The Doppelt Mathematical Reasoning Test as a Selection Device for Graduate Engineering Students." *Ed & Psychol Meas* 21:1009–10 w '61. *

W. V. CLEMANS, *Director, Test Department, Science Research Associates, Inc., Chicago, Illinois.*

The *Doppelt Mathematical Reasoning Test* contains 50 problems that differ from the usual pattern for multiple choice questions in that there are no stems. The task facing the examinee is defined once for the entire set in the directions which state:

> Each problem in this test consists of five mathematical figures or expressions. Four of these have something in common which is not shared by the remaining one. You are to choose the *one* figure or expression which does *not* belong with the other four and mark the letter corresponding to your choice in the proper place on the answer sheet.

None of the problems involves mathematics beyond the usual secondary school level. The test can be easily administered to large groups or to individuals.

The manual states that the test "was designed primarily as an aid in the selection of students for graduate work" and that it "may also be useful in the classification and assignment of college graduates applying for positions in industry which require mathematical reasoning."

Correlations of the DMRT with faculty ratings or grades for three groups of 41, 57, and 109 graduate students taking mathematics suggest that the test may have some value for selecting graduate students. The coefficients obtained were .52, .71, and .43, respectively. Similar coefficients are reported for 28 graduate students in chemistry and 26 undergraduates in a psychometrics course, but a coefficient of only .32 was found for 29 medical students. This latter finding is hardly significant, but is the only coefficient reported for a criterion group whose course work is not primarily quantitative. The Psychological Corporation supplies summaries of five studies reported by independent investigators that tend to corroborate the claim that the test relates to measures of success in graduate study in mathematics or statistics. Apparently no systematic approach has been made to determining how valuable the test is for graduate students in other areas. Validity data for industrial criteria have not yet been supplied.

In the norms section of the manual percentile equivalents are given for five small student samples ranging in size from 102 to 145 students selected from 15 colleges and universities. The groups consisted of senior psychology students, medical students, psychology majors, education majors, and graduate students taking courses in statistics. Percentile equivalents are also given for a group of 388 engineers from one industrial organization.

Reliability coefficients were computed for each of the six groups using the odd-even approach and the Spearman-Brown formula. The coefficients range from .78 to .85. The author points out that the lowest values were found for the most homogeneous groups. He fails to point out, however, that the three groups yielding the highest reliability coefficients (all .85) not only had the largest standard deviations but also the lowest means. This phenomenon suggests to this reviewer that the higher values may have been due to speededness. The author claims that the time limit is adequate for most examinees to finish, but no data are supplied to indicate what is meant by "most" or how the different "norm" groups fared in this regard.

Several correlation coefficients obtained between the DMRT and other tests are given. Nine coefficients are given for the DMRT and the *Miller Analogies Test*. The median value is .34. Only one study is reported correlating the DMRT with the *Minnesota Engineering Analogies Test*. The coefficient is .71 and was obtained on 132 employed engineers. This value is exceptionally high considering the fact that the reliability for the DMRT obtained on a similar group of employed engineers is only .78.

In summary, five points should be stressed. First, claims are made for the test which could produce misleading impressions. Second, considering its reliability, the test is very highly related to the *Minnesota Engineering Analogies Test*. Third, norms are limited. Fourth, quantitative information on speededness for reliability samples is not given. Finally, no validity data are given for one suggested use of the test (classification in industry). It must be concluded that if this test is a gem, it is an unpolished one.

[457]

*Figure Reasoning Test: A Non-Verbal Intelligence Test, Second Edition. Ages 10 and over; 1949–62; 1 form ('62, 55 pages, identical with 1949 edition except for format); manual ('62, 15 pages, 1949 norms remain unchanged); separate answer sheets must be used; 4s. 6d. per test; 1s. 6d. per manual (free with 20 tests); postage extra; answer sheets must be duplicated and scoring stencils constructed locally; 30(40) minutes; John C. Daniels; Crosby Lockwood & Son, Ltd. *

A. W. Heim, *Medical Research Council, The Psychological Laboratory, University of Cambridge, Cambridge, England.*

This test is described, on its cover and in its manual, as "a non-verbal intelligence test." As with other tests so designated, this signifies a test with a strong visual (diagrammatic) bias. It consists of 45 test items and 6 preliminary examples, every one of which is of the same form. In the top half of the page is a large square containing two rows of three diagrams and one row of two diagrams; in the lower half of the page are two rows of three diagrams, one and only one of which correctly completes the third row in the top half of the page. The subject's task is to select the appropriate one of these six diagrams.

The test is distinguishable from the *Progressive Matrices* in three respects: (a) the test booklet is much smaller; (b) the subject is required to make his selection always from six alternatives (Sets C to E in *Progressive Matrices* offer eight alternative solutions); and (c) preliminary examples are given. Apart from these differences the two tests are remarkably similar both in the drawing of the diagrams and the principles employed. These principles include addition, subtraction, deletion, superimposition, and progressions of various kinds.

For the reviewer, these intelligence tests whose questions all have the same bias and whose questions, moreover, all take identical form, have "face-monotony." The manual suggests, however, that the *Figure Reasoning Test* has good validity (reaching .93, not surprisingly, when correlated with *Progressive Matrices,* and only slightly lower coefficients when compared with other well known tests such as the WISC) and high consistency—whether the criterion chosen be split-half (.96) or test-retest with an interval of one year (.89). The test author writes also of the "information that has been gathered on the *Figure Reasoning Test's* predictive efficiency when used for specific educational purposes." But having thus whetted our curiosity he does nothing further in the manual to allay it.

It seems to the reviewer that Daniels makes a bid, on two occasions in the manual, to have things both ways. First, he describes the test as "a measure of 'non-verbal' intelligence" (p. 12)—and, indeed, there is not one word in the test itself. Yet, later (p. 14) he writes that subjects "have to solve these problems by the use of fairly complex language skills" and that they "will be required to undertake fairly complex, theoretical, and therefore to a degree, verbal tasks." It is, of course, perfectly possible to engage in "complex, theoretical" problem solving without the use of words: examples of this may be found in mathematics, for instance. Secondly, he gives a table for converting test scores into standard scores with mean 100 and standard deviation 15, which "to all intents and purposes, we can treat....as if they were IQ's." It is as though Daniels wishes to claim the benefit of the IQ umbrella whilst disclaiming responsibility for the holes in the fabric which he and others have observed.

The manual gives the impression of having

been got out rather on the cheap: no frequency distribution curves are shown and no headings are given for the second page of the conversion table—which renders it slow to read. The text has not been carefully checked: for example, the second "C" on page 10 should read "E"; the answer to the fifth preliminary example is not given; and the fact that the phrase "Modern views" on page 14 is followed by a singular rather than a plural verb adds to the considerable confusion of the long sentence in question. The actual printing in the test occasionally leaves something to be desired, notably for items 11, 30, 32, and 43.

It is not possible for a 17-year-old (or older) to gain an IQ on this test of more than 128, even if he gets right all 45 items; nor is it possible for a 10-year-old to gain an IQ of less than 66, even if his score be zero. A score of 8, i.e., around chance, gained by a 10-year-old who tackles every question gives him an IQ of 81. The time limit is described by Daniels as generous.

Despite these objections, the test may well be useful in certain circumstances. The booklet is exceptionally small, lightweight, and neat; the actual testing time is only 30 minutes; the question of item order has been carefully considered, and the cogency of most of the items is beyond reproach. As stated above, the test fulfils the necessary conditions of consistency and of validity based on other standard tests and also on factorial analysis criteria. This is more than can be said for many of the current paper and pencil tests of intelligence.

For reviews by E. J. G. Bradford and James Maxwell, see 4:291 (1 excerpt).

[458]
*General Verbal Practice Tests. Ages 10 to 11-11; 1954–61; to be given at least 3 weeks before administering a verbal intelligence test in order to equalize coaching effects; keys are not provided since scoring of the test is not recommended; 3 forms; distribution restricted to directors of education; 8d. per manual for any one test; prices include purchase tax; postage extra; published for the National Foundation for Educational Research in England and Wales; Newnes Educational Publishing Co. Ltd. *
a) GENERAL VERBAL PRACTICE TEST G1. 1954; test (8 pages); manual (4 pages); 8s. per 12 tests; 9d. per single copy; 45(50) minutes.
b) GENERAL VERBAL PRACTICE TEST G2. 1959; test (4 pages); manual (4 pages); 5s. per 12 tests; 6d. per single copy; 25(30) minutes.
c) GENERAL VERBAL PRACTICE TEST G3. 1961; test (6 pages); manual (4 pages); 8s. per 12 tests; 9d. per single copy; 30(35) minutes.

Figure Reasoning Test

[459]
★Gestalt Continuation Test. Illiterate and semi-literate Bantu industrial workers; 1960–63; experimental form; administered orally or in pantomime; Forms A ('62), B ('63), C ('63), (1 page); manual ('63, 11 pages); no norms; R5.00 per 100 tests; R.40 per specimen set of all 3 forms; postage extra; a demonstration sheet for group administration is also available; [5–10] minutes; H. Hector; National Institute for Personnel Research. *

REFERENCES
1. HECTOR, H. "Results From a Simple Gestalt Continuation Test Applied to Illiterate Black Mineworkers." *J Nat Inst Personnel Res* 8:145-7 D '60. * (PA 35:4858)
2. TEKANE, I. "A New and Objective Scoring Method for the Gestalt Continuation Test." *J Nat Inst Personnel Res* 8:148-50 D '60. * (PA 35:4864)
3. MUNDY-CASTLE, A. C., AND NELSON, G. K. "A Neuropsychological Study of the Knysna Forest Workers." *Psychologia Africana* 9:240-72 '62. * (PA 37:4822)

[460]
*Goodenough-Harris Drawing Test. Ages 3–15; 1926–63; revision and extension of the *Goodenough Intelligence Test*; 1 form ('63, 4 pages); manual ('63, 80 pages, reprinted from *135* below); quality scale cards ('63, 24 cards); $3 per 35 tests; $2.50 per set of quality scale cards; $1 per manual; postage extra; (15–20) minutes; Florence L. Goodenough and Dale B. Harris; Harcourt, Brace & World, Inc. *

REFERENCES
1–60. See 4:292.
61–94. See 5:335.
95. SILVER, ARCHIE A. "Diagnostic Value of Three Drawing Tests for Children." *J Pediatrics* 37:129-43 Jl '50. * (PA 25:3191)
96. UTSUGI, ETSUKO, AND OHTSUKI, KATSUKO. "A Study on the Human Figure Drawing of Children." *Tohoku Psychologica Folia* 14:131-45 '54-55. * (PA 30:1067)
97. EISEN, VIRGINIA W. *Comparison of Human Figure Drawings by Behavior Problem and Normal Control Boys.* Doctor's thesis, Fordham University (New York, N.Y.), 1956.
98. PHATAK, PRAMILA. "Draw-A-Man Test: Survey of Investigations." *Indian J Psychol* 31:31-40 Ja-Je '56. * (PA 32:5522)
99. GROSS, DEAN G. *An Experiment With the Columbia Mental Maturity Scale and the Goodenough Draw-A-Man Test to Determine Their Utility as Testing Devices for the Severely Mentally Retarded as Compared to the Stanford-Binet.* Master's thesis, San Francisco State College (San Francisco, Calif.), 1958.
100. COLEMAN, J. M.; ISCOE, IRA; AND BRODSKY, MARVIN. "The 'Draw-A-Man' Test as a Predictor of School Readiness and as an Index of Emotional and Physical Maturity." *Pediatrics* 24:275-81 Ag '59. *
101. HARRIS, DALE B. "A Note on Some Ability Correlates of the Raven Progressive Matrices (1947) in the Kindergarten." *J Ed Psychol* 50:228-9 O '59. * (PA 36:1FE28H)
102. HENDERSON, KENT. "Objective Evaluation of a Remotivation Project on a Deteriorated Ward of Mental Hospital Patients." *Ont Hosp Psychol B* 5:4-9 D '59. *
103. LEVINSON, BORIS M. "A Comparison of the Performance of Bilingual and Monolingual Native Born Jewish Preschool Children of Traditional Parentage on Four Intelligence Tests." *J Clin Psychol* 15:74-6 Ja '59. * (PA 34:2729)
104. MITCHELL, ANNA CARR. "A New Maximum CA for the Draw-A-Man Test." *J Consult Psychol* 23:555-7 D '59. * (PA 34:5586)
105. PHATAK, PRAMILA. "Application of Phatak's Draw-A-Man Scale for Indian Children of Gujarat." *Psychol Studies* 4:45-54 Jl '59. *
106. POPPLESTONE, JOHN A. "Clinical Status and the Draw-A-Man Test: Congruence and Divergence." *Percept & Motor Skills* 9:131-3 Je '59. * (PA 38:4281)
107. RICHEY, MARJORIE H., AND SPOTTS, JAMES V. "The Relationship of Popularity to Performance on the Goodenough Draw-A-Man Test." *J Consult Psychol* 23:147-50 Ap '59. * (PA 34:1414)
108. ARMON, VIRGINIA. "Some Personality Variables in Overt Female Homosexuality." *J Proj Tech* 24:292-309 S '60. * (PA 35:818)
109. DENNIS, WAYNE. "The Human Figure Drawings of Bedouins." *J Social Psychol* 52:209-19 N '60. * (PA 35:4758)
110. KOPPITZ, ELIZABETH MUNSTERBERG. "Teacher's Attitude and Children's Performance on the Bender Gestalt Test and Human Figure Drawings." *J Clin Psychol* 16:204-8 Ap '60. * (PA 36:2HE04K)
111. MAGNUSSON, DAVID. "Some Personality Tests Applied

on Identical Twins." *Scandinavian J Psychol* 1(2):55–61 '60. * (*PA* 35:6424)

112. STEER, M. D., AND DREXLER, HAZEL G. "Predicting Later Articulation Ability From Kindergarten Tests." *J Speech & Hearing Disorders* 25:391–7 N '60. * (*PA* 35:3911)

113. TOBIAS, JACK, AND GORELICK, JACK. "The Utility of the Goodenough Scale in the Appraisal of Retarded Adults." *Am J Mental Def* 65:64–8 Jl '60. * (*PA* 35:3792)

114. WARREN, SUE ALLEN, AND COLLIER, HERBERT L. "Suitability of the Columbia Mental Maturity Scale for Mentally Retarded Institutionalized Females." *Am J Mental Def* 64: 916–20 Mr '60. * (*PA* 35:6846)

115. WEST, JOHN HAMILTON. "Correlates of the Draw-A-Scene Test." *J Clin Psychol* 16:44–5 Ja '60. * (*PA* 36:1HB44W)

116. ESTES, BETSY WORTH; CURTIN, MARY ELLEN; DEBURGER, ROBERT A.; AND DENNY, CHARLOTTE. "Relationships Between 1960 Stanford-Binet, 1937 Stanford-Binet, WISC, Raven, and Draw-A-Man." *J Consult Psychol* 25:388–91 O '61. *

117. HANNA, RALPH; COLEMAN, JAMES M.; ISCOE, IRA; KELTON, W. W.; PRICE, P. CLIFT; SEDBERRY, MILES E.; AND WEIR, MORTON W. "'Draw-A-Man' Test." *Tex State J Med* 57:707–11 Ag '61. *

118. HIRSCHENFANG, SAMUEL. "A Comparison of the Revised Columbia Mental Maturity Scale (CMMS) and Goodenough Draw-A-Man Test in Children With Speech Disorders." *J Clin Psychol* 17:381–2 O '61. * (*PA* 38:8918)

119. ISARD, ELEANORE S., AND LASKY, DAVID I. "A Discrepancy Score Method in Predicting Scholastic Achievement of College Freshmen Counseled During Probation." *Personnel & Guid J* 39:725–8 My '61. * (*PA* 36:1KL25I)

120. LESSING, ELISE ELKINS. "A Note on the Significance of Discrepancies Between Goodenough and Binet IQ Scores." *J Consult Psychol* 25:456–7 O '61. * (*PA* 37:3130)

121. NIELSEN, HELLE H. "Human Figure Drawings by Normal and Physically Handicapped Children: Draw-A-Person Test." *Scandinavian J Psychol* 2(3):129–38 '61. *

122. PHATAK, P. "Comparative Study of Revised Draw-A-Man Scale (Harris) and Phatak Draw-A-Man Scale for Indian Children." *Psychol Studies* 6:12–7 Jl '61. * (*PA* 38:2674)

123. SINGH, BALWANT. "Development of Visuo-Motor Capacities in Children from 6–11 Years." Abstract of master's thesis. *Brit J Ed Psychol* 31:299–302 N '61. *

124. THOMAS, R. MURRAY, AND SJAH, ANWAR. "The Draw-A-Man Test in Indonesia." *J Ed Psychol* 52:232–5 O '61. * (*PA* 38:2678)

125. CARKHUFF, ROBERT R. "The Goodenough Draw-A-Man Test as a Measure of Intelligence in Noninstitutionalized Subnormal Adults." Abstract. *J Consult Psychol* 26:476 O '62. *

126. CARNEY, RICHARD E., AND TROWBRIDGE, NORMA. "Intelligence Test Performance of Indian Children as a Function of Type of Test and Age." *Percept & Motor Skills* 14:511–4 Je '62. * (*PA* 37:2830)

127. CLAWSON, AILEEN. "Relationship of Psychological Tests to Cerebral Disorders in Children: A Pilot Study." *Psychol Rep* 10:187–90 F '62. * (*PA* 37:1655)

128. GILBERT, JEANNE G., AND HALL, MARION R. "Changes With Age in Human Figure Drawing." *J Gerontol* 17:397–404 O '62. * (*PA* 37:4775)

129. LINDNER, RONALD S. *The Goodenough Draw-A-Man Test: Its Relationship to Intelligence, Achievement, and Cultural Variables of Negro Elementary School Children in the Southeast United States.* Doctor's thesis, Florida State University (Tallahassee, Fla.), 1962. (*DA* 23:703)

130. ROHRS, FREDERICK W., AND HAWORTH, MARY R. "The 1960 Stanford-Binet, WISC, and Goodenough Tests With Mentally Retarded Children." *Am J Mental Def* 66:853–9 My '62. * (*PA* 37:1704)

131. VANE, JULIA R., AND EISEN, VIRGINIA W. "The Goodenough Draw-A-Man Test and Signs of Maladjustment in Kindergarten Children." *J Clin Psychol* 18:276–9 Jl '62. * (*PA* 39:1874)

132. ALEXANDER, THERON. "The Effect of Psychopathology in Children's Drawing of the Human Figure." *J Psychol* 56: 273–82 O '63. *

133. CHODORKOFF, JOAN, AND WHITTEN, CHARLES F. "Intellectual Status of Children With Sickle Cell Anemia." *J Pediatrics* 63:29–35 Jl '63. *

134. GRANICK, SAMUEL. "Comparative Performance of Normal and Psychoneurotic Children on the Draw-A-Person Test." *J Germantown Hosp* 4:17–22 F '63. * (*PA* 38:2623)

135. HARRIS, DALE B. *Children's Drawing as Measures of Intellectual Maturity: A Revision and Extension of the Goodenough Draw-A-Man Test.* New York: Harcourt, Brace & World, Inc., 1963. Pp. xv, 367. * (*PA* 39:1697)

136. PRINGLE, M. L. KELLMER, AND PICKUP, K. T. "The Reliability and Validity of the Goodenough Draw-A-Man Test: A Pilot Longitudinal Study." *Brit J Ed Psychol* 33:297–306 N '63. * (*PA* 38:8424)

137. THOMPSON, JACK M., AND FINLEY, CARMEN J. "The Relationship Between the Goodenough Draw-A-Man Test and the Stanford-Binet Form L-M in Children Referred for School Guidance Services." *Calif J Ed Res* 14:19–22 Ja '63. * (*PA* 37:7875)

For a review by Naomi Stewart of the original edition, see 4:292.

[461]

***The Graduate Record Examinations Aptitude Test.** Grades 16–17; 1949–63; for more complete information, see 762; 2 scores: verbal, quantitative; 150(170) minutes; Educational Testing Service. *

REFERENCES

1–2. See 4:293.
3–9. See 5:336.

10. CONWAY, MADONNA THERESE. *The Relationship of the Graduate Record Examination Results to Achievement in the Graduate School at the University of Detroit.* Master's thesis, University of Detroit (Detroit, Mich.), 1955.

11. RUPIPER, OMER JOHN. "An Analysis of the Graduate Record Examinations for Doctoral Majors in Education." *Peabody J Ed* 36:279–85 Mr '59. *

12. WILLIAMS, OLIVER HOYT. *Criteria for Admission to the Graduate School of the University of Texas in Relation to the Aptitude Test of the Graduate Record Examinations.* Doctor's thesis, University of Texas (Austin, Tex.), 1959. (*DA* 20:2685)

13. BESCO, ROBERT ORIN. *The Measurement and Prediction of Success in Graduate School.* Doctor's thesis, Purdue University (Lafayette, Ind.), 1960. (*DA* 21:1994)

14. KING, DONALD C., AND BESCO, ROBERT O. "The Graduate Record Examination as a Selection Device for Graduate Research Fellows." *Ed & Psychol Meas* 20:853–8 w '60. * (*PA* 35:3972)

15. LAW, ALEXANDER. "The Prediction of Ratings of Students in a Doctoral Training Program." *Ed & Psychol Meas* 20:847–51 w '60. * (*PA* 35:3973)

16. MICHAEL, WILLIAM B.; JONES, ROBERT A.; AND GIBBONS, BILLIE D. "The Prediction of Success in Graduate Work in Chemistry From Scores on the Graduate Record Examination." *Ed & Psychol Meas* 20:859–61 w '60. * (*PA* 35:3957)

17. ROBERTSON, MALCOLM, AND NIELSEN, WINNIFRED. "The Graduate Record Examination and Selection of Graduate Students." *Am Psychologist* 16:648–50 O '61. * (*PA* 36:4KJ48R)

18. SLEEPER, MILDRED L. "Relationship of Scores on the Graduate Record Examination to Grade Point Averages of Graduate Students in Occupational Therapy." *Ed & Psychol Meas* 21:1039–40 w '61. *

19. THOMSEN, STEPHEN J. "Academic Achievement and Institutional Testing Program Scores: A Longitudinal Study of One Class at a Liberal Arts College." *Proc W Va Acad Sci* 33:120–3 N '61. * (*PA* 36:5KL20T)

20. HOWARD, JANICE S. *A Study of the Graduate Record Examination Aptitude Tests and Other Selected Factors in Predicting Graduate School Success at Rhode Island College.* Master's thesis, Rhode Island College (Providence, R.I.), 1962.

21. JOHNSON, JANET WILDMAN. *An Investigation of Relationships Between College and Senior Student Characteristics and Performance on the Aptitude and Area Tests of the Graduate Record Examination at the George Washington University.* Doctor's thesis, George Washington University (Washington, D.C.), 1962.

22. MABERLY, NORMAN CHARLES. *The Validity of the Graduate Record Examinations as Used With English-Speaking Foreign Students.* Doctor's thesis, University of Southern California (Los Angeles, Calif.), 1962. (*DA* 23:2424)

23. TULLY, G. EMERSON. "Screening Applicants for Graduate Study With the Aptitude Test of the Graduate Record Examinations." *Col & Univ* 38:51–60 f '62. *

24. BORG, WALTER R. "GRE Aptitude Scores as Predictors of GPA for Graduate Students in Education." *Ed & Psychol Meas* 23:379–82 su '63. * (*PA* 38:1419)

25. MABERLY, NORMAN C. "The Validity of the Graduate Record Examinations as Used With English-Speaking Foreign Students." *Ed & Psychol Meas* 23:785–8 w '63. *

26. RUDMAN, JACK. *Graduate Record Examination: How to Pass Aptitude Test: Questions and Answers.* Brooklyn, N.Y.: College Publishing Corporation, 1963. Pp. v, 294. *

ROBERT L. FRENCH, *Vice President for Research and Testing, Science Research Associates, Inc., Chicago, Illinois.* [Review of Forms GGR and LGR1.]

The first forms of this test of scholastic aptitude, XGR and YGR, were published in the period 1949–51 and reviewed in *The Fourth Mental Measurements Yearbook.* Since that time several new forms have been produced.

Form EGR was reviewed in *The Fifth Mental Measurements Yearbook*. The most recent form available for review, LGR1, appears to differ in no substantial way from Form EGR. The test continues in its successive forms to be a well constructed, suitably difficult, and otherwise conventional test of general scholastic potential. Reliability remains satisfactory, normative data extensive, validity data sparse. Administrative literature pertinent to the test is quite complete, but the score interpretation booklet does not adequately bring together all of the information required for technical evaluation (e.g., item data), nor identify the specific forms with which particular sets of data were obtained.

The paucity of validity information is especially unfortunate. In the present atmosphere, critics of testing are bound to ask whether an aptitude test is appropriate or necessary for applicants who have recorded 16 or so years of school achievement and taken a number of similar tests in the process. Other and more sympathetic critics may well wonder at the lack of continuing exploration and appraisal of a variety of factors in graduate performance, some of which they might suspect of being both more accessible and more important than scholastic aptitude for differentiating applicants. Intelligent responses cannot be made to either set of critics without data from studies of criteria and the relative predictive value of various measures. It may be hoped that the publisher of the GRE will attack this problem more vigorously in the future than in the past, despite the obvious difficulties involved.

WARREN W. WILLINGHAM, *Director of Evaluation Studies, Georgia Institute of Technology, Atlanta, Georgia.* [Review of Forms GGR and LGR1.]

The Graduate Record Examinations include the Aptitude Test (verbal and quantitative), 3 Area Tests (social science, natural science, and humanities), and 20 Advanced Tests in specialized curriculum areas. This review is concerned only with the Aptitude Test, but since all of the GRE tests are designed to complement one another, the prospective user might well examine the reviews of the achievement tests also.

The Aptitude Test is similar in format to the familiar *College Entrance Examination Board Scholastic Aptitude Test* but pitched at a higher level of difficulty. The verbal score is based upon verbal reasoning and reading comprehension items. The quantitative section includes computation, reasoning, and data interpretation. These items presuppose no more than high school mathematics but a college senior's quantitative score would undoubtedly suffer had he taken no mathematics in college.

The verbal and quantitative scores have satisfactory K-R 20 reliabilities (.91 for Form GGR verbal, .90 for GGR quantitative, and .92 for each score on LGR1). No alternate form reliability estimates, long term retest reliability estimates, or reliability estimates based upon subgroups with a restricted range are reported. The score interpretation booklet, Scores for Basic Reference Groups, does provide a useful table showing the probability that selected score differences do not represent real differences.

This booklet does not contain any information pertaining to the predictive validity of the Aptitude Test. In the reviewer's opinion, this is an unfortunate omission. Available research (*11, 14–8, 23–4*) indicates that correlations between the Aptitude Test and graduate grade-point average range from moderately high to zero. The validity coefficients tend to become smaller when any criterion less prosaic than the point average is used. Since the criterion of graduate success varies widely among institutions and among disciplines, it would seem all the more necessary to document the predictive validity as extensively as possible.

The score interpretation booklet and other reports available from the publisher contain a very large amount of normative material for the Aptitude Test and its associated GRE tests. These include Aptitude Test norms for students in different curricula. There are signs here and there of the extreme difficulty of obtaining representative norms for different graduate populations, but this problem is mitigated to some extent by accurate descriptions of the norm groups included. The publisher has recently introduced a novel and promising solution to the norms problem. For a modest fee an institution can obtain norms based upon any 10 or more institutions selected from a longer list. At present this service is offered through the Institutional Testing Program and is somewhat limited in terms of the norm groups available. If the service expands it could prove quite useful, particularly in conjunction with institutional evaluation.

Graduate Record Examinations Aptitude Test

Typical for the publisher, the Aptitude Test has well designed supplementary materials. Directions for administering are complete; instructions to candidates are informative; brochures are attractive and professional. The score interpretation booklet should be very helpful to the non-specialist. As noted above, however, it does not contain several types of technical information normally considered essential.

The chief competitor of the Aptitude Test is the *Miller Analogies Test*. Both are well constructed tests which have their individual appeals.

In summary, the Aptitude Test is recommended as a good measure of high level verbal and quantitative ability. With its related tests and extensive system of norms, it should be useful in institutional evaluation. Many schools will find the test useful in selecting graduate students, but local validity studies are strongly recommended.

For a review by John T. Dailey of an earlier form, see 5:336; for reviews by J. P. Guilford and Carl I. Hovland of earlier forms, see 4:293. For a review of the testing program, see 5:601.

[462]
*The Henmon-Nelson Tests of Mental Ability, Revised Edition. Grades 3–6, 6–9, 9–12, 13–17; 1931–61; previous edition (see 4:299) still available; IBM and MRC; 4 levels; $2.55 per 100 MRC answer cards (machine scoring service, by Measurement Research Center, Inc., may be arranged through the publisher); postage extra; Tom A. Lamke, M. J. Nelson, and Paul C. Kelso (*d*); Houghton Mifflin Co. *

a) GRADES 3–6. 1931–60; 2 editions: consumable, reusable; Forms A (consumable edition, '57, 4 pages; reusable edition, '60, 7 pages), B (consumable edition, '58, 4 pages; reusable edition, '60, 7 pages); manual ('57, 24 pages) for both editions; separate answer sheets must be used with reusable edition; $3.60 per 35 tests; $1.38 per 35 IBM answer sheets; 21¢ per scoring stencil; $2.25 per specimen set including *b* and *c* below; 30(35) minutes.

b) GRADES 6–9. 1931–60; forms, prices, and time same as for grades 3–6.

c) GRADES 9–12. 1931–60; forms, prices, and time same as for grades 3–6.

d) GRADES 13–17. 1931–61; 3 scores: quantitative, verbal, total; Forms A, B, ('61, 7 pages); manual ('61, 19 pages); norms for college freshmen only; separate answer sheets must be used; $3.60 per 35 tests; $2.52 per 35 self-marking answer sheets; $2.91 per 100 IBM answer sheets; 64¢ per set of scoring stencils; $1 per specimen set; 40(45) minutes.

REFERENCES

1–25. See 4:299.
26–39. See 5:342.
40. KACZKOWSKI, HENRY R. "Using Expectancy Tables to Validate Test Procedures in High School." *Ed & Psychol Meas* 19:675–7 w '59. * (PA 34:6536)
41. KNIGHT, R., AND STENNETT, R. G. "Intelligence and Academic Success: Preliminary Report." *Ont Hosp Psychol B* 5:2–3 D '59. *
42. LAVER, A. B. "Testing in Canada: Report No. 1." *Can Psychologist* 8:102–3 O '59. *
43. BARRETT, HARRY O. "The Predictive Efficiency of Grade 8 Objective Tests in Terms of Grade 9 Achievement." *Ont J Ed Res* 2:101–7 Ap '60. *
44. CONDELL, JAMES F. "Comparison of Henmon-Nelson and Jastak Scores of Seventh Graders." *Psychol Rep* 9:622 D '61. *
45. KIRK, BARBARA A.; CUMMINGS, ROGER W.; AND GOODSTEIN, LEONARD D. "Predicting Student Success in Graduate Business Courses." *Calif Mgmt R* 5:63–6 f '62. *
46. SAX, GILBERT, AND CARR, ALBERT. "An Investigation of Response Sets on Altered Parallel Forms." *Ed & Psychol Meas* 22:371–6 su '62. * (PA 37:3267)
47. BLOSSER, GEORGE H. "Group Intelligence Tests as Screening Devices in Locating Gifted and Superior Students in the Ninth Grade." *Except Child* 29:282–6 F '63. * (PA 38:2434)
48. JURJEVICH, RATIBOR. "An Evaluation of the Henmon-Nelson Group *IQ* Test With Delinquent Girls." *J General Psychol* 69:227–33 O '63. * (PA 39:1778)
49. SCHROEDER, WAYNE LEE. *Factors Related to the Academic Success of Male College Students From Five Selected Wisconsin Counties.* Doctor's thesis, University of Wisconsin (Madison, Wis.), 1963. (*DA* 23:4207)
50. WEINER, MAX, AND TOBIAS, SIGMUND. "Chance Factors in the Interpretation of Group Administered Multiple-Choice Tests." *Personnel & Guid J* 41:435–7 Ja '63. * (PA 39:1771)

NORMAN E. WALLEN, *Associate Professor of Educational Psychology, University of Utah, Salt Lake City, Utah.* [Review of the college level.]

This review is restricted to the college level of this test which appeared on the market in 1961. The format is much the same as for the lower levels of the test although the number of items is increased from 90 to 100. With respect to item content, format, and general adequacy of the manual, this level conforms to the high standard demonstrated in the lower levels. One interesting departure, however, is the provision of separate verbal and quantitative scores in addition to the overall score. The manual is still pessimistic about the value of these separate scores and gives the impression that they have been included primarily as a result of social pressure. Although the test is intended for use from the freshman through the first year of graduate school the norms provided are based only on beginning college freshmen. The authors report that their attempts "to obtain cluster sampling stratified by size, location, and type of institution" were unsuccessful and hence they resorted to a random sample "stratified by location, size, and type of institution." For these variables the distribution of cases conforms quite closely to national data. Approximately one hundred colleges and universities are represented in the normative group which totals 1,002.

Only percentile norms are provided. It is difficult to understand why some form of standard score is not provided for the measures, particularly since one may certainly expect that differences between Q and V will be examined and the difficulties inherent in comparing differences in raw scores or in percentile ranks are well known.

The odd-even reliabilities, based on 100 cases, are .92 and .89 for Q, .92 and .93 for V, and .95 and .94 for total score on Forms A and B, respectively. Alternate forms testing with an interval of approximately 35 days provided reliabilities of .84 for the quantitative, .88 for the verbal, and .89 for the total score. A slight practice effect amounting to four raw score points, due almost entirely to the quantitative items, was noted. The standard error of measurement is reported for all three scores. Considerable effort has, it is stated, resulted in the two forms being very closely parallel but data to this effect should be reported.

With respect to validity, the first argument offered is in terms of the internal consistency of the scores resulting from a considerable amount of statistical tryout to assure homogeneity of items. Regarding congruent and predictive validity a few correlations with other tests and grades are presented. Correlations with freshman first semester grade point, based on a sample of 95 college freshmen, are of the expected magnitude, ranging from .46 to .54 across the three scores. Correlations between 120 preliminary items and ACE scores show correlations of .55 between the corresponding quantitative and total scores and .75 with the verbal scores.

One of the interesting features of this test has to do with the item types to be found. Of the total of 100 items, 47 were classified by this reviewer as straight vocabulary definition, 22 as number series, 17 as arithmetic reasoning, 12 as verbal analogies. Of the remaining two, one is a sentence arrangement item and the other is a combination of verbal reasoning and arithmetic skills. This is in contrast, at least, to the next lower level of the test, intended for grades 9 to 12, which comes much closer to approximating an omnibus type test containing a greater number of different type items, although the largest number of items is still vocabulary. This difference in item content may to some extent be responsible for the relatively low stability data reported by comparing the college level scores with scores obtained on the level 9 to 12 test with time interval ranging from 4 to 18 months. Based on 88 cases, this correlation for the total college level test is .79. It may also be, of course, that the correlations simply reflect changes in the individuals made possible by a longer time interval.

Of the competing tests, SCAT, CQT, and OSUPE seem to be more heavily dependent on prior school learning and hence are likely to be better predictors of academic success. If, however, one wants an index of intellectual skills which is less a function of schooling and individual testing is not feasible, this test has considerable appeal, especially in view of the short time required.

J Counsel Psychol 10:201–3 su '63. John O. Crites. [Review of college level.] * The authors....have made a commendable attempt to take into consideration some of the criticisms which were made of earlier editions and have been successful in large part in overcoming the more serious defects of the older forms. * Unlike its predecessors, the present edition.... yields Verbal and Quantitative part scores as well as a Total score. The V scale consists of 60 items, whereas the Q scale is comprised of only 40 items, which may be undesirable for several reasons. Not only is the reliability of the Q score adversely affected....but the test is more heavily weighted with the V factor. Also, a count of the items keyed to the two scales in each succeeding fifth of the test reveals that there is a disproportionate number of Q items in the last section of the test. Thus, for the slower examinee who fails to complete the test, the total score is based upon a higher ratio of V to Q items than for the examinee who finishes within the time limit. * One obvious omission in the description of the normative sample is the percentages of males and females included in it. The Manual states only that the Ss were college freshmen, which in itself is a somewhat disappointing if not misleading fact, since the test is advertised as applicable to students at all levels from the first year of college to the first year of graduate school. The test's authors suggest that local norms are more useful than national norms for graduate students, which is not only a debatable observation but one which tells nothing about the value of the test for the selection and guidance of advanced students. It is unfortunate that the nature of the national normative data restricts the applicability of the test to college freshmen. * It would appear that the test is very difficult for even the brightest college freshmen. Perhaps this is a desirable characteristic for a test which is supposed to be as wide-ranging as the Henmon-Nelson, but it may reduce the test's predictive validity at the lower levels by restricting its effective range, which would be the effect of a steep difficulty gradient. * Forms A and B were constituted from....200 items, which were matched on each of the item indices. The actual data on the latter, however, are not reported in the Manual, so that it is not possible to gain an explicit impression of the comparability of the "equivalent forms" or of the nature of the item difficulty gradients. Since the two forms were combined to develop norms for the test, it is important to know how similar they are. * It would be interesting and informative, however....to determine the correlations of the test with a factorial battery, such as the PMA or DAT. * the 1961 revision....rather closely approximates the ideal for measures of its kind. It is relatively short, easily administered, quickly scored, acceptably reliable, and reasonably valid. It would be extremely valuable to have norms for students at the higher college and beginning graduate school levels which are national in scope but hopefully these will be made available through the efforts of the test's authors and their cooperating colleges and universities. Also, it would be very useful to have data on the relationships of Henmon-Nelson test scores to eventual occupational membership and attainment for purposes of vocational counseling. At present, the test is primarily useful for educational rather than vocational guidance. As a final observation on the rationale for the revision, it would seem that the Henmon-Nelson Test has retained its usefulness as a predictor of academic success despite the recent emphasis upon multi-factor aptitude batteries and the test authors' acquiescence to this *Zeitgeist* as manifested in their development of the Q and V scales. It still remains to be demonstrated that the factorial batteries are supplements, and not merely complements, for a good measure of general scholastic aptitude.

For reviews by D. Welty Lefever and Leona E. Tyler of a-c, see 5:342 (1 excerpt); for a review by H. M. Fowler of the previous edition, see 4:299; for reviews by Anne Anastasi, August Dvorak, Howard Easley, and J. P. Guilford, see 40:1398 (1 excerpt).

[463]
★**Inventory No. 2.** Ages 16 and over; 1956; "a mental ability test"; 1 form ['56, 4 pages]; manual (3 pages); $3 per 25 tests; $1 per set of manual and key; postage extra; specimen set not available; 15(20) minutes; Stevens, Thurow & Associates Inc. *

[464]
*****Junior Scholastic Aptitude Test, Revised Edition.** Grades 7-9; 1935-60; tests copyrighted 1959-60 identical with those copyrighted 1957 except for cover page directions; for independent schools; 2 scores: verbal, numerical; IBM; Forms A ('59), B ('59), C ('60), (14 pages); directions ['59, 4 pages]; technical data and independent school norms presented in various issues of *Ed Rec B;* separate answer sheets must be used; tests rented only; examination fee: $1 per student, postage extra; fee includes scoring service; 60(80) minutes in 1 or 2 sessions; Secondary Education Board (original edition); [Geraldine Spaulding] (revised edition); distributed for the National Association of Independent Schools by Educational Records Bureau. *

REFERENCES

1-3. See 3:233.
4-10. See 5:345.
11. SPAULDING, GERALDINE. "Some Observations on the Results of the Revised Junior Scholastic Aptitude Test." *Ed Rec B* 76:53-6 F '60. *
12. SPAULDING, GERALDINE. "Some Data on the Relation Between the Junior Scholastic Aptitude Test and the General School Ability Test Used in the Secondary School Admission Test Program." *Ed Rec B* 79:62-4 Jl '61. *
13. VECCHIONE, NICHOLAS. "Summary of Results of the Revised Forms of the Junior Scholastic Aptitude Test in the Fall and Spring Testing Programs for Independent School Pupils in Grades 7, 8, and 9." *Ed Rec B* 80:66-9 F '62. *
14. JUNGEBLUT, ANN. "Stability of Results on the Junior Scholastic Aptitude Test." *Ed Rec B* 83:61-6 F '63. *
15. SPAULDING, GERALDINE. "Relations Between the NAIS Junior Scholastic Aptitude Test and the CEEB Scholastic Aptitude Tests." *Ed Rec B* 84:55-62 Jl '63. *

JEROME E. DOPPELT, *Assistant Director,* **Test Division,** *The Psychological Corporation,* **New York, New York.**

The earliest edition of the *Junior Scholastic Aptitude Test* (JSAT) was developed in the latter 1930's by the Bureau of Research of the Secondary Education Board to measure the verbal and numerical aptitudes of pupils in grades 7, 8, and 9. Three forms of the JSAT were prepared and after slight revision these became known as Forms DR, ER, and FR. The tests were turned over to the Educational Records Bureau for distribution, with the understanding that the test would be handled on a controlled basis with required scoring at the Bureau. Since 1939, the JSAT has been included in testing programs conducted by the Educational Records Bureau in independent (private) schools. Each of Forms DR, ER, and FR consisted of eight subtests from which a verbal score and a numerical score were obtained. A considerable amount of time was needed to administer one of these forms. In addition to 76 minutes of actual working time, a rather lengthy practice booklet was administered before the regular testing session.

In 1957 and 1958, the staff of the Educational Records Bureau undertook a revision of the JSAT intended primarily to shorten working time for the test and to incorporate the practice material into the administration of the test. Some items in the old forms were replaced or rewritten but items considered to be functioning well were retained. After experimental tryout in 1958, the revised forms were produced and designated as Forms A, B, and C.

Each revised form contains five parts and the entire test can be administered in about 80 minutes. A verbal score is obtained from 90 items in three parts which include paired opposites (selection of the two words that have opposite meanings), double definitions (selection of two missing words to complete a definition), and verbal analogies. The numerical score is based on 50 items in two parts which include number series and arithmetic reasoning. The verbal and numerical raw scores are translated into converted scores for which 500 represents the average performance of independent school pupils in the spring of grade 8 and 100 is the standard deviation of this group. Percentile norms corresponding to converted scores are available for each form and grade. The norms are based on the performance of independent school pupils and the tables are revised as additional data for a particular form become available.

The test items reflect good craftsmanship and are clearly presented with adequate directions. The test booklets are sealed and numbered in keeping with the concept of control of materials. Instructions to the examiner are also presented clearly in a four-page leaflet. The lack of a single manual containing technical data is an inconvenience. These data are given in different Bulletins of the Educational Records Bureau. Although it may be assumed that schools using the JSAT receive the Bulletins of the Bureau, it would be desirable to have the relevant information in one document.

The reliability coefficients reported for the verbal and numerical scores range from .93 to .95 for verbal, and from .91 to .95 for numerical. These are odd-even reliability coefficients which are not appropriate for speeded tests. Since the directions on the cover page of the test booklet acknowledge the effects of speed by the statement, "It is expected that many pupils will not have time to answer all the items," one must assume that the coefficients overestimate reliability. Correlations are reported between scores on Forms A and B administered, with an average time interval of about six months, to two groups: 344 students tested first in grade 7 and then in grade 8; 100 students tested first in grade 8 and then in grade 9. These correlations, which may be regarded as stability coefficients, were .88 and .84 for verbal; for numerical, the coefficients were .80 and .88, in the two groups respectively. Reliability coefficients based on immediate retesting with an alternate form would probably be somewhat higher than the stability coefficients. It would be helpful to have means and standard deviations for the reliability samples as well as for the norms groups but these are not presented. There is, indeed, a conspicuous absence of means and standard deviations in the statistical reports. This prevents the user from determining whether or not the groups for which reliability and other data are reported are similar to his own groups.

Correlations were computed between scores on the JSAT and scores on various achievement tests, when all tests were given in the same testing program. These correlations tend to be high where one would expect them to be high; however, exception may be taken to the conclusion that "correlations with various achievement measures indicate that the Verbal Score may be considered a good predictor of achievement in school subjects that are chiefly verbal in nature, and that the Numerical Score should provide a good prediction of achievement in mathematical subjects." The conclusion may well be true but it is not supported by evidence based on tests administered in the same program since there is no true prediction involved. A time interval between the predictors and the criteria is necessary.

Data were obtained on the relationship between the JSAT and the *Secondary School Admissions Tests: General School Ability and Reading Test.* The latter battery is taken by students who plan to enter an independent secondary school. On the basis of these data a table of equivalent percentiles on the two tests was prepared. The July 1963 Educational Records Bureau Bulletin includes tables of equivalence between grade 9 JSAT scores and scores on the PSAT in grade 11 and on the SAT in grade 12. These should provide useful information to counselors in the independent schools but it is to be hoped that they will evaluate the accuracy of the predictions for their own students.

In a study of the correlations between fall 1957 scores on one of the older forms and spring 1958 scores on the revised forms, the coefficients between verbal scores on the old and the new editions varied between .81 and .90; the coefficients for the numerical scores were between .75 and .82. There is obviously considerable similarity between the old and new tests but it would be desirable to collect and report validity data for the revised edition. It is reasonable to suppose such studies will be undertaken by the Educational Records Bureau.

The revised forms of the JSAT, like the earlier editions of that test, were developed for independent schools. Other published tests are probably equally suitable for measuring verbal and numerical aptitudes but independent schools may prefer a controlled test intended primarily for their use. The new forms are well constructed measures but additional supporting data would be desirable. More detailed reporting of results and evidence on the prediction of success in school would permit better evaluation of the revised JSAT as a functioning instrument.

[465]

*The Kingston Test of Intelligence. Ages 10-0 to 12-11; 1953–63; Forms A ('53), B ('62), (8 pages); practice sheet ['53, 2 pages]; manual ('63, 20 pages, identical with 1954 manual except for wording changes and addition of Form B norms); no data on reliability of Form B; no data on validity; 12s. 6d. per 25 tests of Form A; 15s. per 25 tests of Form B; 8d. per single copy; 3s. per manual; postage and purchase tax extra; 33(78) minutes; M. E. Hebron; George G. Harrap & Co. Ltd. *

H. J. SANTS, *Lecturer in Education, University College of North Wales, Bangor, Wales.*

Upon opening these compact test booklets and manual both teacher and pupil are likely to get the impression that they have an intelligence test which they can manage: the manual is concerned with administration rather than construction; the test booklets have instructions which are brief, with words to be underlined or small spaces to be filled as the test response required. But this apparent concern to put both manual and booklet into the language of the classroom has created some unsatisfactory features.

The children work for 33 minutes on the test proper, having first worked 15 minutes on a practice test and spent 10 to 15 minutes in discussion. The inclusion of standardised coaching is to be commended but testers will surely have difficulties in "following verbatim the standardized method." What the tester has to say, although admirably phrased for putting children at their ease, is so lengthy that a teacher would need either a better than average memory, or a special skill at reading as though talking spontaneously. With these long passages administration is unlikely to remain standard in the strictest sense, especially as the words to be used by the tester are not clearly separated from the remainder of the instructions. In the 1963 manual, the same instructions are used for both forms.

From the child's point of view the content of these tests is a good deal more inviting than that of many objective tests. The items are simple but not dull, e.g., "Linoleum is to Carpet as Mackintosh is to (Coat, Hat, Gloves, Rug)." Besides the verbal analogies section there are four other sections in each test: number series, diagrammatic analogies (occupying three and a half pages of the total eight), classification, and arranging words in order of size and intensity. Heim criticised the logic of the classification test in *The Fifth Mental Measurements Yearbook* and this section in Form B is again curiously constructed. Having been asked to "underline the word which may be *sometimes* true but *not always* so," the child is given such sentences, "All Clocks are essential, reliable, purchasable, mechanical." The correct answer listed for this example is "reliable." In choosing *reliable* rather than *essential* the child is having to choose the answer he thinks the teacher would prefer. This calls for conformity as well as intelligence. A child may be intellectually capable of deciding which answer the tester would favour but be emotionally incapable of giving it to him.

In addition, the Note on the Construction and Standardization of the Tests is no more satisfactory in the 1963 manual than in the earlier one. Its brevity can only irritate the expert and mislead the layman. The note should either be expanded technically with more data or replaced by a general cautionary note.

These criticisms have been made from inspection, and in the same way the attraction of using the test in the classroom can also be seen. A teacher meeting a new class might find results from these tests a useful addition to scholastic results obtained from school records, thus getting closer to an assessment of the intellectual potential of his pupils.

For a review by A. W. Heim, see 5:347.

[466]
*Kuhlmann-Anderson Intelligence Tests, Seventh Edition. Grades kgn, 1, 2, 3–4, 4–5, 5–7, 7–9, 9–12; 1927–63; sixth edition (see 5:348) still available; 3 scores for grades 7–12: verbal, quantitative, total; IBM for grades 4–12; 8 levels (labeled Booklets K, A, B, CD, D, EF, G, and H); *Booklets K, A, B, and CD* (grades kgn, 1, 2, 3–4) : 1 form ('63, 9–10 pages), administration and norms manual ('63, 36–51 pages) for each level, technical manual ('63, 31 pages) for all levels; *Booklets D and EF* (grades 4–5, 5–7) : 1 form ('60, c1927–60, 10 pages), manual for administering ('61, 23 pages) for each level, norms manual ('61, 20 pages) for both levels, technical manual ('62, 26 pages) for both levels; *Booklets G and H* (grades 7–9, 9–12) : 1 form ('60, c1927–60, 9 pages), manual for administering ('60, c1927–60, 22 pages) for each level, revised norms manual ('63, c1960–62, 34 pages) for both levels, revised technical manual ('63, c1960–62, 49 pages) for both levels, student's interpretive report form ('63, 1 page) ; supplementary norms manual ('63, 23 pages) for Booklets D–H; separate answer sheets must be used with Booklets D–H; $3 per 25 tests; $2.40 per 50 IBM answer sheets; 25¢ per set of scoring stencils; $1.10 per 50 student's interpretive report forms; 25¢ per norms manual; 50¢ per technical report; 50¢ per supplementary norms manual; $1 per specimen set of Booklets A and CD, D and EF, or G and H; postpaid; 22(45) minutes for Booklets K and A, 20(40–45) minutes for Booklet B, 26(45) minutes for Booklet CD, 30(60) minutes for Booklets D and EF, 23(50) minutes for Booklets G and H; F. Kuhlmann (fourth and earlier editions) and Rose G. Anderson; Personnel Press, Inc. *

REFERENCES

1–15. See 40:1404.
16–40. See 3:236.
41–50. See 4:302.
51–65. See 5:348.
66. HOLSOPPLE, ILA G. *Factorial Analysis of the Kuhlmann-Anderson Intelligence Tests and the Stanford Achievement Tests at Fourth and Eighth Grade Levels.* Doctor's thesis, Pennsylvania State College (State College, Pa.), 1948.
67. LLOYD, CLAUDE J. *The Relationship Between the Scores Made by Pupils on the Primary Mental Abilities Test, the Metropolitan Achievement Reading Test, and the Kuhlmann-Anderson Intelligence Test.* Master's thesis, University of Southern California (Los Angeles, Calif.), 1958.
68. CABANSKI, CAROLYN L. *The Predictive Value of the Kuhlmann-Anderson Subtests Regarding Reading Improvement.* Master's thesis, Loyola University (Chicago, Ill.), 1959.
69. CHAMBERS, JACK A. "Preliminary Screening Methods in the Identification of Intellectually Superior Children." *Excep Child* 26:145–50 N '59. * (PA 35:3249)
70. KNIGHT, ROBERT. "Intelligence Test Data From One Public and Two High Schools." *Ont Hosp Psychol B* 5:6–8 Ag '59. *
71. RACKY, DONALD J. "Predictions of Ninth Grade Woodshop Performance From Aptitude and Interest Measures." *Ed & Psychol Meas* 19:629–36 w '59. * (PA 34:6572)
72. VECCHIONE, NICHOLAS. "Stability of Kuhlmann-Anderson IQ's of Independent School Pupils in Elementary Grades Covering Six Testings Over a Five-Year Period." *Ed Rec B* 79:65–72 Jl '61. *
73. NORTH, ROBERT D. "Results of the Seventh Edition Kuhlmann-Anderson Test for Independent School Pupils in Grades 7–12." *Ed Rec B* 80:56–65 F '62. *
74. NORTH, ROBERT D. "A Further Analysis of the Kuhlmann-Anderson Seventh Edition Test." *Ed Rec B* 83:53–60 F '63. * (PA 38:962)
75. SCHENA, RICHARD A. "A Search for Talented Pupils." *J Exp Ed* 32:27–41 f '63. *
76. SNIFFEN, ALLAN MEAD. *A Correlation Study of Group Intelligence Tests With Achievement in Reading and Arithmetic in Grade Four: An Investigation of the Effectiveness of Using Group Intelligence Test Scores for Evaluating Academic Achievement in the Tool Subject Areas of Reading and Arithmetic in Public Elementary Schools.* Doctor's thesis, New York University (New York, N.Y.), 1963. (DA 24:826)

WILLIAM B. MICHAEL, *Professor of Education and Psychology, University of California, Santa Barbara, California.*

That the same excellent standards of workmanship as those associated with previous editions of the Kuhlmann-Anderson tests have been perpetuated in the series of eight coordinated tests of the new seventh edition is unmistakably evident from an examination of the carefully constructed items in the various forms, from exploration of the lucid norms manuals in which explicit directions are given concerning problems of scoring and interpretation, from inspection of the readily applied manuals for administration, and from detailed study of the three comprehensive and competently prepared technical manuals. Although the sixth edition is still available, the seventh edition introduces several new features that are in agreement with a great deal of modern thinking about the assessment of intelligence. Moreover nearly 40 per cent of the content of the seventh edition is new.

For Booklets K, A, B, and CD, which are intended for use in kindergarten, grade 1, grade 2, and grades 3 and 4, respectively, 8 tests instead of the former 10 are used, although the number of items in each test has been augmented. Another change is the introduction of grade percentile ranks for total scores on the A, B, and CD booklets. In place of the IQ's based on the ratio of mental age to chronological age, deviation IQ's for total scores are presented corresponding to intervals of three months in chronological age.

Similarly for Booklets D and EF, which are planned to be administered in grades 4 and 5 and in grades 5, 6, and 7, respectively, the same types of modifications have been effected. In addition both a verbal (V) score and a quantitative (Q) score may be derived for use in research studies, although the admonition has been set forth that the scores are not sufficiently independent for purposes of analysis of differential aptitudes. In contrast to the previous edition, the test booklets may be reused, and IBM answer sheets may be scored mechanically.

For the third sequence of booklets, G and H, which are appropriate for grades 7, 8, and 9 and for grades 9, 10, 11, and 12, respectively, the same kinds of revisions were undertaken. However, grade percentile ranks are provided for both V and Q scores (as well as for T scores) in view of the existence of a sufficient degree of independence and reliability of each of these part scores for differential use.

Several other praiseworthy improvements in the seventh edition should be briefly cited. In the current forms for the earlier grade levels, as compared with the corresponding forms of the sixth edition, the ceiling limitation has been obviated. Moreover, through use of the deviation IQ the standard deviations of scores from one grade level to the next have been shown in empirical studies to be not only wider, but also more nearly constant than in the instance of the forms of the sixth edition in which ratio IQ's were derived. Hence improved discrimination among pupils has been realized, particularly among those within either the higher or lower segments of the range of ability. In addition—apparently in view of the widespread use of standard scores by several school systems—the author has furnished stanine equivalents for the deviation IQ scores.

Another commendable effort in the presentation of normative data has been the introduction of percentile bands for a realistic interpretation of V, Q, and T scores for Booklets G and H. To enable the examinee in junior or senior high school to understand the meaning of percentile bands for each of his three scores, a Student's Interpretive Report Form has been developed. Although a conscientious attempt has been made to explain the significance of test bands upon the MAP (Measure of Academic Potential) profile, the reviewer has serious reservations regarding whether most high school students will be able to grasp the import of the discussion. A graphically portrayed example would be helpful.

Great care has been exercised in the development of representative norms, in the acquisition of data furnishing indices of both predictive and concurrent validity, and in the presentation of standard errors of measurement and of various types of reliability estimates.

On both a relative and absolute basis the seventh edition of the Kuhlmann-Anderson tests compares favorably with any other competitive instrument measuring general intelligence. The various manuals are noteworthy not only for their comprehensive and discerning exposition about the test forms but also for their cautious and modest statements. Finding little to criticize either concerning the construction and standardization of the test or regarding the adequacy of the interpretative data furnished, the reviewer can only hope that the teachers, counselors, principals, and other responsible persons will take pains to study and to apply the wealth of information to be found in the general and technical manuals. Both the author (Rose G. Anderson) and the publisher have attained a standard of excellence of which both the psychometric specialist and practitioner in the schools can be most appreciative.

DOUGLAS A. PIDGEON, *Deputy Director, National Foundation for Educational Research in England and Wales, Slough, Bucks, England.*

The changes made in the seventh edition of these well known tests, while probably more drastic than any made hitherto, are such as to retain most of the character of the original tests, and yet at the same time to bring them more in line with modern practices. As with previous editions, the tests appear in separate booklets, but the overlapping between adjacent booklets has been somewhat reduced. Also the correspondence of grade to booklet has been changed slightly from the sixth edition, and now a choice of booklet is available for pupils in grades 4, 5, 7, and 9. The number of tests in each booklet has been reduced from 10 to 8, but the number of items in each test has been increased, resulting in larger standard deviations and thus affording better discrimination among high and low scorers.

About 40 per cent of the content of this edition is new. The new items were tried out with the sixth edition and item analyses performed using the median mental age on the sixth edition as a criterion. This procedure was presumably adopted in order to ensure continuity of item content, and, as the technical manuals state, "The validity of the Sixth Edition was built into the Seventh Edition tests." It is to be noted, however, that the correlations quoted between the sixth and seventh edition booklets are no higher, and indeed tend to be lower, than those quoted between adjacent booklets of the seventh edition despite a somewhat smaller proportion of common items in the latter. Booklets D and EF, for example, correlate together about .86, but only .80 and .77 with the corresponding sixth edition Booklets D and E.

In general no a priori justification is made for the inclusion of any particular item type. From Booklet D onwards certain subtests have been added, however, so that separate verbal and quantitative scores could be obtained, although the user is warned against employing those derived from Booklets D and EF except for research purposes since, in the few empirical studies quoted, no sizable differences occur at these levels among the correlations of V and Q scores and grades in verbal and quantitative subjects. The inclusion of a perceptual test among the other quantitative tests at these levels is questionable.

It can be argued that, unlike achievement tests, nationally representative norms are of paramount importance for intelligence tests. This certainly appears to be the view held by the test authors, yet, while the difficulties involved in carrying out this task appear to have been fully appreciated, the steps taken to obtain a representative sample fall far short of ideal. Despite uneasiness, however, about the methods employed to select schools, a remarkably close agreement was found in one study with a group of fourth graders, between the means and standard deviations for IQ's derived from these tests (123.0 and 19.2) and from Stanford-Binet Form L-M (123.6 and 18.5). A comparison with WAIS IQ's for a group of twelfth graders did not produce such agreement.

Perhaps the greatest change in this edition is in the reporting of scores, and the author is to be congratulated on the clarity with which different methods of doing this are presented. Grade percentile ranks are provided for each booklet for the beginning, middle, and end of the school year, and users are gently encouraged to employ them. Tables of deviation IQ's, with a mean of 100 and a standard deviation of 16, are also provided, and for those who find difficulty in weaning themselves from the concept, instructions are given for estimating mental ages. Finally, apparently again to encourage broader grouping of scores, there are tables for converting IQ's into stanine equivalents.

Data on reliability are extensively and well reported in the manuals, and the coefficients quoted are generally satisfactory if not high. Test-retest coefficients, with as much as two grades between testings, range from .83 to .92; while testing with adjacent forms produces correlations from .77 to .89. For Booklets K to CD split-half coefficients range from .93 to .95, and in Booklets D, EF, G, and H, factor analyses of subtests were carried out, from which estimates of the reliability for the total score were made ranging from .85 to .95. The reliabilities of the V and Q scores from Booklets G and H estimated from the same data were much lower, and the reliability of the V-Q difference, lower still. Users, however, are clearly warned against any rash interpretations of such differences.

As was stated above, it is claimed that the validity of the sixth edition was "built into the Seventh" by the method of item analysis employed. However, despite a proportion of common content, the range of correlations reported between similar level booklets in the two editions is little different from what might be obtained between separate measures of, say, arithmetic and English, and hence constitutes no valid argument for supposing that the tests of the two editions are in fact measuring the same thing. Nor is this reviewer really impressed with the numerous (more than 150) correlations reported between these tests and other tests of intelligence and measures of achievement. These range, over all booklets, from the high .40's to the high .80's; but a good vocabulary test would also yield correlations of this order. The fact is that no evidence of concurrent validity will ever *prove* that these tests are measuring "intelligence" or "academic potential."

That these tests are measuring academic potential is certainly more assumed than proved. The manuals give no evidence, for example, to show that, given appropriate remedial treatment, pupils of low achievement but apparently high potential according to the tests are more likely to show improvement in school subjects than pupils of similar achievement levels who are apparently already working up to their potential.

An obvious point that is worth stressing yet again is that intelligence tests should only be used if satisfactory empirical evidence is available to show that the tests are valid for the purposes intended, be it grouping, predicting academic success, diagnosing underachievement, or whatever. Furthermore, such evidence should be based on groups as similar as possible to those to whom the tests are to be given. Unfortunately, while some quite satisfactory evidence is given in the manuals concerning the predictive validity of these tests, insufficient descriptive data (means, SD's, etc.) are given to enable a user to judge its relevance for his own group.

In summary it can be said that the reputation of these Kuhlmann-Anderson tests should be distinctly enhanced by the seventh edition, which now incorporates most of the desirable features that the user of modern tests requires. It is to be hoped that further validatory evidence, relevant to the actual use to which these tests will be put, will be published shortly.

Personnel & Guid J 40:481–4 Ja '62. Frederick B. Davis. [Review of Booklets G and H.] * attractively printed * An excellent *Manual of Directions for Administering and Scoring the Test* and a comprehensive *Technical Manual* are ....provided. * The seventh edition yields verbal, quantitative, and total raw scores, percentile ranks for each of these scores in each of grades seven through twelve (based on beginning-of-the-year testing), and deviation IQ scores corresponding to the total raw scores. IQ scores are not provided for the verbal and quantitative scores separately. * the verbal and quantitative scores are highly correlated * No convenient way of evaluating the difference between an individual's verbal and quantitative score is provided. The V and Q scores are not directly comparable so the method for evaluating their statistical significance given on page 27 of the *Technical Manual* cannot properly be used in the manner illustrated. * The reliability coefficients of the V, Q, and Total scores and of the IQ's derived from the Total scores are very satisfactory for tests of this type that take only 45 minutes to administer. * Some counselors and psychologists have been worried by the fact that most pupils do not have a chance to try all of the items in the parts of the Kuhlmann-Anderson tests. Scores, therefore, are greatly influenced by the rate at which pupils try the items. Data provided in the *Technical Manual* show this to be a fact. Pupils at the same level in capacity to understand concepts, to remember and use word meanings correctly, and to make arithmetic computations accurately work at different rates of speed. Habit, predisposition, and motivation greatly affect speed of mental operation. Counselors and psychologists who prefer to measure level of performance separately from speed of performance will not find the seventh edition of these tests any more to their liking than previous editions. In the *Technical Manual*, Dr. Anderson indicates a belief that intelligence tests should measure speed of mental functioning. Data are presented that show that doubling the time limits for the parts of the Kuhlmann-Anderson tests increases only slightly the correlations of V and Q scores with various achievement-test scores and with academic grades. It seems reasonable to conclude that these tests measure ability to succeed in school as well as any tests of their type. A commendable effort was made to obtain norm groups representative of all American school children in the grades for which the tests are appropriate for use. * Inspection of the items reveals them to be in generally good shape. The brightest pupils may be a bit troubled by some of the items in Test 2 of Booklet G. The procedure for getting the keyed response to items in this test consists sometimes of dropping out one number to leave a rule-following set of four numbers (as in Sample X) and sometimes of changing a number to create a rule-following set of five numbers (as in Sample Y). If the examinee creates a rule-following set of five numbers by changing, say 4, 6, 8, 9, 10 to 4, 6, 8, 10, 12, he will get no credit for the item if he marks both changes (9 to 10 and 10 to 12) or if he marks only the change of 10 to 12. In item 19 of this test, a rule-following series of five numbers can be created by changing choice E (17) to 15. But the response keyed as correct assumes the creation of a rule-following series of four numbers by dropping out choice B (10). * Since correction for chance is not employed, the answer sheets must be carefully inspected prior to scoring for excess marks per item. More than one mark is proper for some items so this inspection is more of a chore than usual. Then the excess marks must be erased (for machine scoring) or crossed out (for hand scoring). Since the tests were constructed to be administered with time limits so short that very few examinees would reach items near the end of any part, correction for chance success would be of maximum usefulness in scoring them. As they are scored, examinees who disregard the directions to "avoid careless guessing" and proceed to mark a response to every item (guessing when necessary) will tend to have an advantage over conscientious examinees who try to follow instructions to the letter. Finally, it should be pointed out that a large amount of very interesting and useful information about the development and uses of the test is given in the *Norms Manual* and the *Technical Manual*. The author and publisher are to be congratulated.

For reviews by Henry E. Garrett and David Segel of the sixth edition, see 4:302; for reviews by W. G. Emmett and Stanley S. Marzolf of an earlier edition, see 3:236; for a review by Henry E. Garrett, see 40:1404; for reviews by Psyche Cattell, S. A. Courtis, and Austin H. Turney, see 38:1049.

[467]

*The Lorge-Thorndike Intelligence Tests. Grades kgn–1, 2–3, 4–6, 7–9, 10–12; 1954–62; IBM and MRC for grades 4–12; Forms A, B, ('54, 6–11 pages); 5 levels; 2 tests (nonverbal, verbal) and 2 editions (consumable, reusable) of each test for levels 3–5; manual ('57, 20–32 pages) for each level (1–5); MRC manual ('59, 32 pages) for each level (3–5); revised technical manual ('62, 24 pages); *Levels 1–2*: $3.45 per 35 tests; *Levels 3–5*: $2.70 per 35 copies of either test of consumable edition, separate answer sheets must be used with reusable edition, $3 per 35 copies of either test of reusable edition, $1.44 per 35 IBM answer sheets for either test, 24¢ per scoring stencil, $7.50 per 100 MRC answer sheets for both tests, 45¢ per MRC stencil for hand scoring (machine scoring service, by Measurement Research Center, Inc., may be arranged through the publisher), 45¢ per MRC manual; 45¢ per technical manual; 45¢ per combined specimen set of levels 1–2; 45¢ per specimen set of any one of levels 3–5; $2.25 per complete specimen set; postage extra; Spanish directions available for nonverbal batteries; Irving Lorge and Robert L. Thorndike; Houghton Mifflin Co. *

a) LEVEL 1, NONVERBAL BATTERY. Grades kgn–1; (35) minutes in 2 or 3 sessions.
b) LEVEL 2, NONVERBAL BATTERY. Grades 2–3; (35) minutes.
c) LEVEL 3. Grades 4–6; IBM and MRC.
 1) *Verbal Battery.* 34(44–49) minutes.
 2) *Nonverbal Battery.* 27(37–39) minutes.
d) LEVEL 4. Grades 7–9; IBM and MRC.
 1) *Verbal Battery.* 34(44–49) minutes.
 2) *Nonverbal Battery.* 27(37–39) minutes.
e) LEVEL 5. Grades 10–12; IBM and MRC.
 1) *Verbal Battery.* 34(44–49) minutes.
 2) *Nonverbal Battery.* 27(37–39) minutes.

REFERENCES

1–6. See 5:350.
7. HAGE, DEAN SILVERS. *The Effect of Reading Proficiency on Intelligence Scores.* Doctor's thesis, State University of Iowa (Iowa City, Iowa), 1957. (DA 18:930)
8. HAGE, DEAN S., AND STROUD, JAMES B. "Reading Proficiency and Intelligence Scores, Verbal and Nonverbal." *J Ed Res* 52:258–62 Mr '59. * (PA 34:4813)
9. KNIEF, LOTUS M., AND STROUD, JAMES B. "Intercorrelations Among Various Intelligence, Achievement, and Social Class Scores." *J Ed Psychol* 50:117–20 Je '59. * (PA 35:779)
10. GNAUCK, JOHANNA, AND KACZKOWSKI, HENRY. "Prediction of Junior High School Performance." *Ed & Psychol Meas* 21:485–8 su '61. * (PA 36:2KL85G)
11. ANDERSON, WILLIAM F. "Relation of Lorge-Thorndike Intelligence Test Scores of Public School Pupils to the Socio-Economic Status of Their Parents." *J Exp Ed* 31:73–6 S '62. * (PA 37:7990)
12. BROMER, JOHN A.; JOHNSON, J. MYRON; AND SEVRANSKY, PAUL. "Validity Information Exchange, No. 15-02: D.O.T. Code 4-97.010, 4-75.120, 4-85.040, Craft Foremen Correspond to Foremen I; 5-91.275, 5-91.088, 5-91.091, 5-91.831, 5-91.812, Process, Production, and Warehouse Foremen Correspond to Foremen II." *Personnel Psychol* 15:107–9 sp '62. *
13. DOHERTY, VICTOR W., AND INGEBO, GEORGE S. "The Development of a School Ability Measure Based on the Lorge-Thorndike Intelligence Test." *Yearb Nat Council Meas Ed* 19:67–71 '62. *
14. KILGORE, LEONARD LOUIS, JR. *Relationships Between Socioeconomic Levels and Changes in Measured Intelligence.* Doctor's thesis, George Peabody College for Teachers (Nashville, Tenn.), 1962. (DA 23:2009)
15. WOMER, FRANK B. "BJMP Test Project Establishes Local Norms." *Mich Ed J* 39:522–3+ Ap '62. *
16. CAPLAN, STANLEY W.; RUBLE, RONALD A.; AND SEGEL, DAVID. "A Theory of Educational and Vocational Choice in Junior High School." *Personnel & Guid J* 42:129–35 O '63. *
17. MACARTHUR, R. S., AND ELLEY, W. B. "The Reduction of Socioeconomic Bias in Intelligence Testing." *Brit J Ed Psychol* 33:107–19 Je '63. * (PA 38:4271)

For reviews by Frank S. Freeman, John E. Milholland, and D. A. Pidgeon, see 5:350.

[468]

★Lowry-Lucier Reasoning Test Combination. Grades 5–16 and adults; 1956–59; 3 scores: total and 2 scores listed below; 2 tests; manual ('59, 15 pages); no data on reliability; tentative norms; $3.50 per 25 copies of either test; $6.50 per 25 sets of both tests; $1 per key; 50¢ per manual; postage extra; specimen set not available; Ellsworth Lowry (test) and Omer Lucier; distributed by Rowland & Co. *

a) TEST A. Sequential relations; 1 form ('56, 3 pages); 15(20) minutes.
b) TEST B. Spatial relations; 1 form ('56, 3 pages); 20(25) minutes.

REFERENCES

1. LUCIER, OMER, AND BURNETTE, RICHARD. "The Lowry Reasoning Test Combination With Younger Adolescents." Abstract. *Am Psychologist* 12:373 Jl '57. *
2. BURNETT, ELIZABETH LEE. *A Study of the Validity and Reliability of the Lowry Reasoning Test Combination in Grades Five, Six, and Seven.* Master's thesis, University of Richmond (Richmond, Va.), 1958.
3. LEBO, DELL; ANDREWS, ROBERT S.; AND LUCIER, OMER. "The Lowry Test: A Simple Status-Free Measure of Intellectual Ability." *J Appl Psychol* 43:411–2 D '59. * (PA 34:7352)
4. ANDREWS, ROBERT S.; LEBO, DELL; AND LUCIER, OMER. "A Pragmatic Validation of a Simple, Status Free Measure of Intellectual Ability." *J Social Psychol* 54:273–82 Ag '61. * (PA 36:3LD73A)
5. LUCIER, OMER, AND BURNETTE, RICHARD. "The Lowry Reasoning Test Combination With Younger Adolescents." *J Social Psychol* 55:113–24 O '61. * (PA 36:4HD13L)
6. LUCIER, OMER, AND FARLEY, JOHN. "The Lowry Reasoning Test Combination as a Status Free Technique." *J Social Psychol* 55:125–31 O '61. * (PA 36:4HB25L)

ANDREW R. BAGGALEY, *Professor of Psychology, Temple University, Philadelphia, Pennsylvania.*

These two tests represent an attempt to develop a short measure of reasoning ability that is relatively uninfluenced by cultural experiences. Test A contains questions concerning serial relationships among days of the week, and Test B contains problems involving the elimination of match sticks from rectangular designs to obtain specified results. Both tests are quite steeply graded in difficulty. The homogeneous nature of the items probably justifies the temporary absence of measures of internal consistency, but it would be highly desirable for the test manual to report retest reliabilities. The instructions for administration are appropriately detailed, especially for examinees under 15 years of age.

Recently published research indicates that the *Lowry-Lucier Reasoning Test Combination* is less correlated with measures of social status than each of three commonly used intelligence tests. In one of these studies, the correlation was lower within the groups of middle and low status examinees than within the high status examinees. Yet the Lowry-Lucier test gave somewhat higher validities for predicting criterion performance of soldiers and school children. The test manual reports the means and standard deviations of test scores for pupils in the fifth, sixth, and seventh grades, college freshmen, and soldiers.

The authors suggest that their test may be particularly valuable in "the selection of college freshmen from rural areas and lower class homes." In view of the data that have been reported so far, such research seems to be well worth undertaking.

Russel F. Green, *Associate Professor of Psychology, The University of Rochester, Rochester, New York.*

Information concerning the properties of this test is as yet too sketchy to permit its recommendation for any specific situation except one: it can be used as a research instrument if it appears appropriate to one's needs. However, it might also prove useful as a measure of scholastic aptitude which is freer than usual of bias from formal education and social class, *providing* the user is willing to develop his own norms, to carry out his own validation and reliability studies, and probably also even to perform his own item analyses.

The authors stress the idea that the test is essentially free of class bias. It probably is not entirely free of such bias but one can agree that it is more so than the usual IQ test. This is achieved by using more familiar materials to construct problems than is normally done.

The test is divided into two parts and involves the use of two rather novel kinds of materials. Subtest A uses manipulations of time relationships defined in terms of the days of the week. Subtest B uses a series of match stick problems. Contrary to the expectations of the authors, experience on both subtests is not really constant since similar ideas have occurred as parlor games and puzzles.

The authors state that the test "estimates" reasoning abilities: part A, verbal reasoning interacting with immediate memory; part B, spatial visualization. No validation for these claims is offered. Apparently the test correlates with measures of "general intelligence" somewhere in the range of .5 to .7, so that while it overlaps up to half of the variance of IQ tests, it is no substitute for them. It has, however, predicted proficiency ratings of a small group of servicemen at least as well as one general intelligence measure (.45 versus .34), and it has predicted grade-point averages of a seventh grade class as well as another such measure (.59 versus .57). If on further analysis validities such as these continue to be found, then it might be that greater utility could be achieved with this test than with most intelligence tests since it is briefer than most of them.

Anyone interested in trying to use the test should look closely at the possibility that the later items in subtest B might not correlate well with the earlier items of the subtest. For some of these items the solutions can be found only by correctly inferring that additional instructions are contained in the solutions to immediately preceding items. The subject is not warned of this. This procedure is rather unusual and may well have undesirable effects. If it does, then improvements in the instructions might yield improved results.

In summary, the test contains an interesting idea which may prove quite useful if and when it is adequately standardized and validated.

[469]

★**Maddox Verbal Reasoning Test.** Ages 9.5–10.5; 1960; 1 form (12 pages); manual (14 pages); 5d. per test; 1s. 9d. per manual; postage and purchase tax extra; 45(60) minutes; H. Maddox; Oliver & Boyd Ltd. *

T. R. Miles, *Professor of Psychology, University College of North Wales, Bangor, Wales.*

"Assuming that a child has had an ordinary schooling and the usual educational opportunities," says Maddox, "verbal tests of this type are the best available predictors of school performance." This claim may well be true, but it is unfortunate that no references are given in support. Despite this criticism, however, the test can certainly be commended; it is clearly the work of a skilled educationalist who has taken considerable trouble over standardisation and related matters.

There is little to criticise on the practical side. However, in question 50 ("We painted the chair....not the table") the only correct word for filling the blank is given as "but," whereas there are surely contexts where "and" is as good (e.g., if we did not have time to paint both or misunderstood which of the two we were supposed to paint). Also (question 60) it is false that a game always has player*s* (in the plural); patience has only one player. As regards unfair items, however, this test seems to the reviewer to compare very favourably with others of the same kind.

On the theoretical side one is far less happy. The test is said to provide "a measure of verbal intelligence for children between the ages of 9½ and 10½"; but in the very next paragraph the author states, "It should be regarded as measuring scholastic aptitude rather than pure intelligence," while two paragraphs later one reads, "It should not be assumed, however, that a low score on the test necessarily indicates lack of intelligence." Finally, the manual tells how to convert the scores into IQ's; but unless "IQ" is being redefined out of all recognition this surely means that the test *is* measuring intelligence after all. Thus in four sentences one is apparently told twice that the test does measure intelligence and twice that it does not! If Maddox had limited himself to saying "This is a test that will be useful in helping to 'stream' children in the junior school" and had added the proviso that one should be cautious in interpreting a low score, he could have omitted the controversial references to "intelligence" and "IQ" altogether. In the reviewer's opinion the concept of "IQ" is one of the biggest disasters in the history of psychology; because of its connexion with the word "intelligence" it is ambiguous, and in addition it implies a false view as to what can be done to *improve* children's intelligence.

Of its kind this is undoubtedly a good test; but it cannot be too much emphasised that the justification for using such tests is pragmatic and is not based on universally agreed theoretical premises.

A. E. G. PILLINER, *Senior Lecturer in Education, University of Edinburgh, Edinburgh, Scotland.*

In his description of this "omnibus" test the author points out that it is intended to measure scholastic aptitude rather than pure intelligence. Unfortunately it is probably necessary still to issue such a warning with tests of this sort.

The test proper, occupying 45 minutes without pauses, is preceded by a practice test lasting 15 minutes. In the latter most (but not all) of the item types included in the test proper are exemplified and worked by the children under the guidance of the teacher who (though this is insufficiently stressed) is expected to adhere exactly to the text presented.

The items employed in the test are conventional in type: alphabet items, similarities (several forms), opposites, "doesn't belong," missing words, "always has," order, series, and problems. The author is perhaps wise to limit himself to these well tried types which, however, have now been employed so extensively that other constructors will find many old friends amongst the items in this test. This is not a serious defect, provided the items are well constructed, which, in the main, they are. However, few tests are perfect in this respect, and the Maddox test is not one of them. Thus item 4 ("Which is the last letter of the alphabet that appears in DESERT but not in DANGER?") might be more intelligible to the testees if it read "Which is the letter latest in the alphabet that appears...." Also the notorious difficulty of avoiding ambiguity in classification items is exemplified here. Are a crab and a lobster "more alike," because they are crustaceans, than a herring and an eel, which are fish? Are fish and meat, both fleshy foods, "more alike" than peas and apples, both spherical? Again, items in which missing words are to be inserted sometimes present difficulties. The gap in "We painted the chair _____ not the table" is filled better by "but" than by "and"; but the latter (which is not credited) conforms to the requirement of being "sensible and right." So, too, in circumstances not too difficult to conceive, is "told" (not credited) used to fill the gap in "He _____ me what I was doing," though certainly it would be less usual than the required response "asked." Finally, the familiar "cyclic" difficulty again crops up. Which are the extremes in May,

Maddox Verbal Reasoning Test

July, January, September, March? It all depends on where one starts. Is the child who starts at May and finishes at March to be penalised for his unconventionality?

There are a few further points which can be easily dealt with in later editions. One item refers to ten men and 5 days. In another, the answer £1 is given credit, but not, apparently, 20 shillings, which seems hard. Yet another, in which different breeds of dog are to be assigned to their owners—a good item, this—is overdetermined.

The test norms presented in the manual are of the type now conventional. They relate testees' total raw scores and ages to standardised scores normally distributed with a standard deviation of 15 about a mean of 100. Standardisation is based on a representative sample of 4,518 children in Birmingham and Staffordshire, but the method of selecting the sample is not reported. The only reliability coefficient presented in the manual is K-R 20 = .95, a somewhat low result which, however, cannot be properly evaluated since no information is given about the nature of the sample from which it was obtained. Information is lacking also about the sample of 108 children, all from one school, for whom the correlation between scores on this test and scores on Schonell's *Essential Intelligence Test* was .86. The reviewer suggests that subsequent editions of the manual should report the Maddox test mean and standard deviation for the group so that interpretation of this validity coefficient is made possible. It would be useful also if the author were to report the procedure used in particularly designing the test "to give reliable scores in the I.Q. (standardised score) range 100 to 120," and to present evidence of the success achieved.

Finally, this reviewer cannot agree with the statement made in the manual that "at this age (9½–10½) it first becomes possible to obtain reliable test scores by the group test method." Evidence of group test-retest correlations at 7+ of nearly .9, and at 9+ of .95, is available.

To sum up: the criticisms made of the test are generally of a minor character. On the whole it is sound, though it displays few original features. The manual would benefit by a fuller reporting of the nature of the standardisation sample and of reliability and validity data. It remains to add that the publishers are to be congratulated on the excellent appearance of the test.

This reviewer agrees with the author that the test "should prove useful as an internal school examination and assist in allocating children to classes within the junior school."

Brit J Ed Psychol 30:289–90 N '60. Almost all group intelligence tests for children below 10½ use the Mental Age method of scoring, thus this new one will be a welcome addition for testing third-year juniors. It closely resembles a Moray House Verbal Reasoning test with deviation-quotient norms, though in fact, it does not register below I.Q. 78 at 9½ years. It was standardised on some 4,500 children in the Midlands. The one-hundred items are of conventional type, and 45 minutes are allowed. It is preceded by a practice sheet taking about 15 minutes, but thereafter, the children have to read the instructions and items for themselves. The author admits its dependence on reading, and prefers to regard it as a measure of "scholastic aptitude" rather than "intelligence."

[470]

Manchester General Ability Test (Senior). Ages 12-10 to 14-6, 13-6 to 15-2; 1952-59; 2 levels; no data on validity; postage and purchase tax extra; Stephen Wiseman; University of London Press Ltd. *
a) MANCHESTER GENERAL ABILITY TEST (SEN.) I. Ages 12-10 to 14-6; 1 form ['52, 8 pages]; manual ['52, 11 pages]; practice test ['52, 1 page]; 5s. 6d. per 12 tests; 7d. per single copy; 1s. per 12 practice tests; 1d. per single copy; 9d. per manual; 10(15) minutes for practice test, 45(50) minutes for test.
b) MANCHESTER GENERAL ABILITY TEST (SEN.) 2. Ages 13-6 to 15-2; 1 form ('59, 8 pages); manual ('59, 8 pages); 5s. 6d. per 12 tests; 7d. per single copy; 1s. 6d. per manual; 60(65) minutes.

REFERENCES

1. WRIGLEY, JACK. "The Factorial Nature of Ability in Elementary Mathematics." *Brit J Ed Psychol* 28:61–78 F '58. * (PA 33:6845)

A. W. HEIM, *Medical Research Council, The Psychological Laboratory, University of Cambridge, Cambridge, England.*

These two group tests are fun to do. They comprise a wide variety of verbal and numerical problems, some of which have original and entertaining features. The verbal items include analogies, series, sames-opposites, "scrambled" words, and classification questions; the numerical items include the supplying of omitted digits in multiplication and division calculations and the completion of ingenious tables such as a table of school cricket scores with "some of the scores....omitted owing to the carelessness of our scorer, Blenkinsop." There are no diagrammatic or pictorial items. Wiseman states that these tests "are designed to measure 'general ability' or what is usually known as 'verbal intelligence.'" The reviewer considers the equating of these two concepts to be controversial and, in view of the substantial minority of numerically biased items, questions the exclusively verbal nature of what is tested here.

There is, however, little doubt that the 13- to 15-year-olds for whom the tests are intended will enjoy doing them and this important condition for successful testing seems often to be forgotten. The original features include among other things: the instruction in the sames-opposites sections to "choose the numbered word which means nearly the same *or* nearly the opposite of the first word"; the requirement in analogy items of choice from three words in each of two parts of the analogy; and, in the classification questions, the precautionary measure, "In these questions you have to find the word in the second line [six words] which is most like the three words in capitals [first line] and is different from the rest."

Despite this precaution, some of the classifications—as seems almost inevitable with such items—appear to the reviewer to lack cogency. For example, in the question, "BUT IF OR 1. go 2. and 3. man 4. yes 5. perhaps 6. when," the correct answer, according to the manual, is 2. Surely an equally good case could be made for 6.

Similar objections apply to some of the sames-opposites—which do, of course, require particular care in view of their instruction to choose a word which means nearly the same *or* nearly the opposite. For instance, in the question, "*PERMIT:* 1. JUDGE 2. FORGIVE 3. BLAME 4. ALLOW 5. ADMIT 6. DENY," 4 and 6 are equally defensible. It seems especially unfortunate that this should be the first item in one of the tests. And in view of current butcher terminology, in the following question, 4 seems as apt as 5! "*PIG* is to PORK as 1. *BEEF* 2. *VEAL* 3. *SHEEP* is to 4. LAMB 5. MUTTON 6. CALF."

These doubtful questions are rare, however; they occur more frequently in classifications than in any other type of item; and, not unnaturally, they are more frequent in the harder than in the easier questions. A more serious criticism is the lack of a preliminary test for Sen. 2 for the subjects to work through on their own, and the inadequacy of the preliminary examples which are provided in the practice test for Sen. 1. These latter examples (*a*) offer only four alternatives from which to choose, as opposed to the six offered in the test itself, and (*b*) are, apart from this, intrinsically easier problems than occur on the whole in the test proper. In addition, the tester is specifically told, in the manual, that whether the subjects "are getting the right answers or not does not matter—what is important is that they are not *writing* an answer if a *number* is required." Thus some of the most vital reasons for having preliminary examples for the subject to work through are explicitly ignored.

There are some minor objections to the layout. For instance, in the supply-digits calculations where alignment is important there is occasional misalignment, and the presentation of question numbers which are printed on a level with the answer numbers and are identical with these in shape and size, is apt to be confusing, especially as this occurs at the very beginning of the test.

The manuals are satisfactory apart from the points already made about preliminary practice and what the tests are designed to measure. On the latter point, it is worth mentioning that absolutely no reference to validation is made in either manual. The reliability is over .90 both on split-half (Spearman-Brown formula correction) and on an unspecified Kuder-Richardson formula. Test-retest reliability is not mentioned. The test instructions are simple and clear; the directions to scorers are exceptionally careful and detailed; and the notes on the interpretation of scores might with benefit be added to every test manual.

For Sen. 1 the standardisation is based on the scores of 4,175 children, aged 13-1 to 14-0 years but conversion tables are given covering the ages 12-10 to 14-6. Instructions are given for converting the test scores of children aged 14-7 to 15-0, inclusive, by means of extrapolation. For Sen. 2 the standardisation is based on the scores of 13,442 children, aged 14-1 to 15-0 years and conversion tables are given covering the ages 13-6 to 15-2. For this test, neither extrapolation nor IQ is mentioned under the conversion tables but for both tests the standard scores are said to be "comparable

Manchester General Ability Test (Senior)

with 'I.Q.s' from other group tests of intelligence, *provided that* the constructors of such other tests have used a standard deviation of 15 in compiling their conversion tables."

The reviewer is disquieted by the following combination of facts: (*a*) Sen. 1 is ostensibly for subjects aged 12-10 to 14-6 whilst Sen. 2 is ostensibly for ages 13-6 to 15-2, but (*b*) the two tests, each comprising 100 items, are described as "parallel" although one has a time limit of 45 minutes and the other has a time limit of an hour, yet (*c*) a score of, for example, 10 points gained by a 14½-year-old yields an IQ of 80 on Sen. 1 and of 84 on Sen. 2—the latter test having *the longer time limit*. Such anomalies occur also at the top end of the scale (though not around IQ's of 100). They are due to the fact that Sen. 2, having the same number of items as Sen. 1 but a longer time limit, produces a considerably wider range of scores.

The variety of questions and their subject matter, however, is likely to achieve good motivation and to render the tests more "general" than are the exclusively diagrammatic type of intelligence test. They might well prove a useful pair of tests for the somewhat neglected age groups for which they cater, if satisfactory validation data were adduced.

ARTHUR B. ROYSE, *Lecturer in Psychology, The University of Hull, Hull, England.*

These tests are parallel group verbal tests of conventional type, designed to extend the existing range of tests used for academic selection in English schools to include the neglected ages of 13 to 14 (Sen. 1) and 14 to 15 (Sen. 2). According to the manual, they are thus "more appropriately to be used in the secondary grammar school and the upper ability levels of the secondary modern school." But no indication is given of specific purposes for which they can validly be used. Indeed, no validation data of any kind are given. The author contents himself with the statement that the test provides "a measure of general ability in the verbal and academic field."

This claim appears to be based on nothing stronger than the assumption that because most of the items are of conventional type—sames and opposites, series, analogies, classifications, insertion of missing numbers in sums, etc.—the test must be highly correlated with any similar test for which validation is available.

The same preference for face validity over statistical decision is apparent in the choice of test items. No statistical evidence was collected to justify the inclusion of individual items nor to determine their order of presentation in the tests. Despite this, however, internal consistency is moderately good, "boosted" split-half reliability coefficients of .95 (Sen. 1) and .96 (Sen. 2) and Kuder-Richardson coefficients of .93 (Sen. 1) and .95 (Sen. 2) being obtained. Unfortunately, however, no test-retest reliability coefficients are reported.

The layout and typography of the tests is excellent and the instructions for administration and scoring are lucid and comprehensive. Scoring is simple, each item being scored 0 or 1, and, in the interests of accuracy, the marking instructions are rigid. No credit is allowed for a "correct" answer unless it is indicated in the authorised manner. The provision of a practice test provides an opportunity for the child to learn these rigid requirements while supervisors "make sure all the children are doing the questions in the correct *way*."

Standardisation was thorough, 4,175 children aged 13-1 to 14 being used for Sen. 1 and 13,442 children aged 14-1 to 15 being used for Sen. 2. In both cases, the group was a virtually complete age group in the area selected. Raw scores are converted to give standardised "quotients" with a mean of 100 and a standard deviation of 15. The conversion tables include extrapolations to cover ages 12-1 to 14-6 for Sen. 1 and 13-6 to 15-2 for Sen. 2, but the basis and justification for these extrapolations is not given. No information is given concerning possible sex differences and no sex differentiation is given in the tables.

The tables indicate that the conventional aim of such tests—that of providing a skewed distribution of raw scores to ensure a wide range of scores in the critical area of decision—was achieved. For the median age group of Sen. 1 the raw scores at the 15th, 50th, 84th, and 95th percentiles are approximately 10, 23, 40, and 53, respectively; for the median age group for Sen. 2 the comparable raw scores are 11, 28, 56, and 74. These data suggest that both tests, but particularly Sen. 1, are rather difficult.

The manual claims that the standardised quotients, although not comparable with IQ's derived from mental age, are comparable with quotients from other group verbal tests having the same standard deviation. The warning

Manchester General Ability Test (Senior)

against confusion with Binet-type quotients is to be applauded but the claim to comparability with other tests is misleading. If it is meant only to indicate that the MGAT shares with other tests a common method of conversion of raw scores, then the statement is trivial. If, however, it is meant to imply that MGAT quotients are interchangeable with others for purposes of selection, prediction, etc., then it is inaccurate. The claim would be justified only if the two quotients were obtained from tests which (a) have been standardised on the same age group, (b) are highly correlated, and (c) have been converted to the same standard deviation by identical conversion formulae.

Quotients from the two MGAT forms are comparable, however, with each other. Although not standardised on the same age group, both tests were given to the second standardisation group. A correlation of .934 is quoted but despite its computation to three places of decimals, its value is limited because (a) it is based only on scores for the 14-1 to 15-0 group and no evidence is given to justify extrapolation to the other groups, (b) no evidence is given to justify the assumption of linearity of regression, and (c) no indication is given of whether the figure includes corrections for attenuation or for restriction of sample.

On the whole, the MGAT is a good example of the type of verbal test used for academic selection in English schools. Its limitations are shared with many such tests and there is nothing to suggest that it is better than the best of them or worse than the worst of them. The lack of competing tests in the age range covered should ensure its use among those testers who share the compiler's faith in its face validity. But for those testers who believe that intuitive judgment is a poor substitute for statistical decision in selection, and who demand indices of forecasting efficiency for use with specified external criteria in clearly defined situations, the test has little to offer.

For a review by A. E. G. Pilliner of a, see 5:351.

[471]

*Mill Hill Vocabulary Scale. Ages 4 and over; 11–14, 14 and over; 1943–58; 2 editions; manual ('58, 66 pages); 15s. per 50 tests; 20s. per key; 5s. 6d. per manual; 25s. per specimen set including 5 copies of each form and a specimen set of the complementary *Standard Progressive Matrices;* postage and purchase tax extra; (15–20) minutes; John C. Raven; H. K. Lewis & Co. Ltd. *
a) ORAL DEFINITIONS FORM. Ages 4 and over; consists of all words from both forms of the junior and senior levels below; individual; 1 form ('48, 4 pages).
b) WRITTEN TEST. Ages 11–14, 14 and over; Forms 1, 2, ('48, 4 pages); 2 levels: junior, senior. (Australian edition of senior level: Australian Council for Educational Research.)

REFERENCES

1–3. See 3:239.
4–10. See 4:303.
11. PINKERTON, PHILIP, AND KELLEY, JOSEPH. "An Attemped Correlation Between Clinical and Psychometric Findings in Senile-Arteriosclerotic Dementia." *J Mental Sci* 98: 244–55 Ap '52. * (*PA* 27:585)
12. DUNSDON, M. I. "The Application of Vocabulary Tests to a Large Sample of Children." Abstract. *B Brit Psychol Soc* 26:22 inset My '55. *
13. DUNSDON, M. I., AND ROBERTS, J. A. FRASER. "A Study of the Performance of 2,000 Children on Four Vocabulary Tests: 1, Growth Curves and Sex Differences." *Brit J Stat Psychol* 8:3–15 My '55. * (*PA* 30:3363)
14. DUNSDON, M. I., AND ROBERTS, J. A. FRASER. "A Study of the Performance of 2,000 Children on Four Vocabulary Tests: 2, Norms, With Some Observations on the Relative Variability of Boys and Girls." *Brit J Stat Psychol* 10:1–16 My '57. * (*PA* 33:2155)
15. ORME, J. E. "Non-Verbal and Verbal Performance in Normal Old Age, Senile Dementia, and Elderly Depression." *J Gerontol* 12:408–13 O '57. *
16. FOULDS, G. A. "The Relative Stability of Personality Measures Compared With Diagnostic Measures." *J Mental Sci* 105:783–7 Jl '59. * (*PA* 34:6016)
17. DESAI, MAHESH M. "Intelligence and Verbal Knowledge in Relation to Epstein's Overinclusion Test." *J Clin Psychol* 16:417–9 O '60. * (*PA* 37:3226)
18. DUNSDON, M. I., AND ROBERTS, J. A. FRASER. Chap. 3, "A Study of the Performance of 2000 Children on Four Vocabulary Tests," pp. 41–76. In *Stoke Park Studies: Mental Subnormality (Second Series): World Mental Health Year Memorial Volume.* Edited by J. Jancar. Bristol, England: John Wright & Sons Ltd., 1961. Pp. x, 135. *
19. LYNN, R., AND GORDON, I. E. "The Relation of Neuroticism and Extraversion to Intelligence and Educational Attainment." *Brit J Ed Psychol* 31:194–203 Je '61. * (*PA* 36:3HD94L)
20. VENABLES, ETHEL C. "Placement Problems Among Engineering Apprentices in Part-Time Technical College Courses: Part 2, Level of Ability Needed for Success in National Certificate Courses." *Brit J Ed Psychol* 31:56–8 F '61. * (*PA* 36:1KJ56V)
21. COSTA, LOUIS D., AND VAUGHAN, HERBERT G., JR. "Performance of Patients With Lateralized Cerebral Lesions: 1, Verbal and Perceptual Tests." *J Nerv & Mental Dis* 134: 162–8 F '62. *
22. FOULDS, G. A., AND DIXON, PENELOPE. "The Nature of Intellectual Deficit in Schizophrenia: Part 1, A Comparison of Schizophrenics and Neurotics." *Brit J Social & Clin Psychol* 1:7–19 F '62. * (*PA* 37:1788)
23. FOULDS, G. A., AND DIXON, PENELOPE. "The Nature of Intellectual Deficit in Schizophrenia: Part 3, A Longitudinal Study of the Sub-Groups." *Brit J Social & Clin Psychol* 1:199–207 O '62. * (*PA* 37:5488)
24. FOULDS, G. A.; DIXON, PENELOPE; McCLELLAND, MARILYN; AND McCLELLAND, W. J. "The Nature of Intellectual Deficit in Schizophrenia: Part 2, A Cross-Sectional Study of Paranoid, Catatonic, Hebephrenic and Simple Schizophrenics." *Brit J Social & Clin Psychol* 1:141–9 Je '62. * (*PA* 37:3685)
25. GRAHAM, CONRAD. "Differential Marking of Two Vocabulary Tests." *Psychol Rep* 12:421 Ap '63. * (*PA* 38:4275)
26. HAMILTON, VERNON. "I.Q. Changes in Chronic Schizophrenia." *Brit J Psychiatry* 109:642–8 S '63. * (*PA* 38:6506)

MORTON BORTNER, *Chief Psychologist, Department of Physical Medicine and Rehabilitation, New York Medical College, New York, New York.*

The author recommends that this test be used in conjunction with his *Progressive Matrices.* This vocabulary test consists of two sets (A and B) of 44 words of graduated difficulty.

There are three variations of this basic set of words. The first version is individually administered and consists of the examiner reading the words from both Sets A and B to the testee and writing down the responses. In the manual this is called the Standard Scale and is also referred to as the Oral Definitions Test. On the test form it is called the Definitions Form, and the normative data for this test are under the heading Oral Test. This kind of presentation of information is likely to lead to some confusion.

The second version, called the Written Test, consists of the first 33 words of each set; it is administered as follows: the testee writes his definitions to Set A and chooses from multiple choice items on Set B. This method makes the test feasible for group testing and also provides one with two comparison scores which the author believes to be clinically useful. A more difficult third version, the senior level of the Written Test, consists of the last 33 words of the original 44 and is administered in the same way as described for the second version.

Retest reliability figures for the Written Test range from .87 to .98. No reliability data are offered for the Oral Test. No validity coefficients are offered for either test.

It may be difficult to interpret poor performance on that portion of the test which requires the testee to write his answers, for poor spelling ability may lead him to use inappropriate substitute words, or his general expressive ability may be systematically inferior to his actual comprehension as indicated by an oral test. These considerations suggest that this test is measuring more than merely the "acquired information" the author seeks in order to supplement his *Progressive Matrices*.

The suggestion that this test be used together with the *Standard Progressive Matrices* helps to counterbalance the latter's excessively perceptual approach to the measurement of intelligence. It does not go far enough, since it still leaves unmeasured the variety of measureable abilities commonly subsumed under the matrix of intelligence.

All good clinicians are aware of a hierarchy of cognitive levels implied in different vocabulary responses. They also interpret many vocabulary responses in the light of personality psychodynamics. The suggestions by the author dealing with qualitative analyses of these factors are valuable and point the way to a use of the test that goes beyond its resultant scores.

For a review by David Wechsler, see 3:239.

[472]

*Miller Analogies Test. Candidates for graduate school; 1926-63; IBM; Forms G ('47), H ('50), J ('52), K ('59), (4 pages); use of Form G restricted to special projects approved by the publisher; Form H also published under the title *Advanced Personnel Test* for use in business; revised manual ('60, 23 pages); bulletin of information ('63, 36 pages); revised procedures for testing center operation ('63, 8 pages); distribution restricted and test administered at specified licensed university centers; scoring and reporting handled by the local center; examination fee to centers: $1 per examinee; fees to examinees are determined locally and include reporting of scores to the examinee and to 3 institutions or companies designated at the time of testing; additional score reports may be secured from the publisher at a fee of $1 each; 50(55) minutes: W. S. Miller; Psychological Corporation. *

REFERENCES

1-16. See 4:304.
17-44. See 5:352.
45. MOFFETT, CHARLES R. *Operational Characteristics of Beginning Master's Students in Educational Administration and Supervision.* Doctor's thesis, University of Tennessee (Knoxville, Tenn.), 1954.
46. LUTON, JAMES N. *A Study of the Use of Standardized Tests in the Selection of Potential Educational Administrators.* Doctor's thesis, University of Tennessee (Knoxville, Tenn.), 1955.
47. NUNNERY, MICHAEL Y. *A Study in the Use of Psychological Tests in Determining Effectiveness and Ineffectiveness Among Practicing School Administrators.* Doctor's thesis, University of Tennessee (Knoxville, Tenn.), 1958. (DA 19:1276)
48. BADAL, ALDEN WESLEY. *The Relationship of Selected Test Measures to Administrator Success in the Elementary School.* Doctor's thesis, Stanford University (Stanford, Calif.), 1959. (DA 20:1263)
49. KELLY, E. LOWELL, AND GOLDBERG, LEWIS R. "Correlates of Later Performance and Specialization in Psychology: A Follow-Up Study of the Trainees Assessed in the VA Selection Research Project." *Psychol Monogr* 73(12):1-32 '59. * (PA 34:7952)
50. NUNNERY, MICHAEL Y. "How Useful Are Standardized Psychological Tests in the Selection of School Administrators." *Ed Adm & Sup* 45:349-56 N '59. * (PA 35:7092)
51. PLATZ, ARTHUR; MCCLINTOCK, CHARLES; AND KATZ, DANIEL. "Undergraduates Grades and the Miller Analogies Test as Predictors of Graduate Success." *Am Psychologist* 14:285-9 Je '59. * (PA 34:4817)
52. SCHWARTZ, MILTON M., AND CLARK, F. EUGENE. "Prediction of Success in Graduate School at Rutgers University." *J Ed Res* 53:109-11 N '59. * (PA 35:1223)
53. SPIELBERGER, CHARLES D. "Evidence of a Practice Effect on the Miller Analogies Test." *J Appl Psychol* 43:259-63 Ag '59. * (PA 34:6408)
54. WAGGONER, GLEN HASTINGS. *Administrator's Scores on Selected Standardized Tests and His Administrative Performance as Reported by Classroom Teachers.* Doctor's thesis, Stanford University (Stanford, Calif.), 1959. (DA 20:3169)
55. BOYCE, RICHARD DUDLEY. *An Empirical Evaluation of Five Tests for Administrator Selection: The Composite Study.* Doctor's thesis, Stanford University (Stanford, Calif.), 1960. (DA 21:2546)
56. BURDOCK, E. I.; CHEEK, FRANCES; AND ZUBIN, JOSEPH. "Predicting Success in Psychoanalytic Training," pp. 176-91. In *Current Approaches to Psychoanalysis.* Proceedings of the 48th Annual Meeting of the American Psychopathological Association Held in New York City, February 1958. Edited by Paul H. Hoch and Joseph Zubin. New York: Grune & Stratton, Inc., 1960. Pp. 207. * (PA 36:4IE07H)
57. COLADARCI, ARTHUR P. "An Analysis of Miller Analogies Test Score Changes." *Ed & Psychol Meas* 20:817-23 w '60. * (PA 35:3405)
58. EBERT, FRANCIS JOHN. *An Empirical Evaluation of Five Tests for the Selection of Elementary School Principals.* Doctor's thesis, Stanford University (Stanford, Calif.), 1960. (DA 21:2548)
59. JAMES, KENNETH RAYMOND. *An Empirical Evaluation of Five Tests for Administrator Selection in a Metropolitan School District.* Doctor's thesis, Stanford University (Stanford, Calif.), 1960. (DA 21:2556)

60. NELSON, ROBERTA J., AND ENGLAND, GEORGE W. "Graduate Training in Industrial Relations: An Early Look." *Personnel & Guid J* 39:53–7 S '60. * (*PA* 35:4021)
61. BESSENT, EDGAR WAILAND. *The Predictability of Selected Elementary School Principals' Administrative Behavior.* Doctor's thesis, University of Texas (Austin, Tex.), 1961. (*DA* 22:3479)
62. COLVER, ROBERT M., AND SPIELBERGER, CHARLES D. "Further Evidence of a Practice Effect on the Miller Analogies Test." *J Appl Psychol* 45:126–7 Ap '61. * (*PA* 36: 3HD26C)
63. GREENBERG, BRADLEY S. "Predicting Journalism Student Ability." *Journalism Ed* 16:60–5 su '61. *
64. MOORE, ROBERT BURKLAND. *A Comparison of Test Performance and Current Status of Administrative Candidates in Twenty-Four School Districts.* Doctor's thesis, Stanford University (Stanford, Calif.), 1961. (*DA* 22:476)
65. LOCKE, LAWRENCE F. "Performance of Administration Oriented Male Physical Educators on Selected Psychological Tests." *Res Q* 33:418–29 O '62. *
66. SCOTT, C. WINFIELD, AND WEXLER, NORMAN. "Concurrent Validity of the Miller Analogies Test in a Graduate School of Education." *Yearb Nat Council Meas Ed* 19:134–9 '62. *
67. STEFFLRE, BUFORD; KING, PAUL; AND LEAFGREN, FRED. "Characteristics of Counselors Judged Effective by Their Peers." *J Counsel Psychol* 9:335–40 w '62. * (*PA* 39:2312)
68. TULLY, G. EMERSON. "Screening Applicants for Graduate Study With the Aptitude Test of the Graduate Record Examinations." *Col & Univ* 38:51–60 f '62. *
69. *Normative Information: Manager and Executive Testing.* New York: Richardson, Bellows, Henry & Co., Inc., May 1963. Pp. 45. *
70. MEDNICK, MARTHA T. "Research Creativity in Psychology Graduate Students." *J Consult Psychol* 27:265–6 Je '63. * (*PA* 38:958)

LLOYD G. HUMPHREYS, *Professor of Psychology and Head of the Department, University of Illinois, Urbana, Illinois.*

The *Miller Analogies Test* is well known, it has been reviewed earlier by Dailey and others, and there has been little change in recent years other than the publication of a revised manual in 1960. It is a good test, has high reliability in the homogeneous graduate student population, has plenty of top, and has fairly substantial predictive validity for the criterion of graduate school grades. It exists in four alternate forms of which only the earliest (Form G) shows any significant discrepancy from the others in terms of its raw score equivalents. The remaining three forms appear to be about as close to the classical definition of parallel forms as one can find in the psychological literature.

This reviewer's criticisms are directed not so much at the present test as at practices used in its norming and validation, practices that are common to many tests and to many test publishers. The norms, for example, are virtually meaningless. Samples represent in no case any well defined population having general meaning to the test user. For selection purposes this is not critical since norms developed from one's own applicants are most meaningful. The chief competitor of the Miller test, the *Graduate Record Examinations Aptitude Test,* probably has no better norms. The one thing that is certain is that the two sets of norms are based upon quite different groups.

The procedures used in validating the Miller test are deplorable though commonplace. People who have used the test in a particular institution have reported their data in the literature or contributed their data to the author and publisher on a voluntary basis. One wonders, however, how much voluntary suppression of data in which correlations were low has taken place at the local level. The reviewer happens to know of one case in which a negative correlation between the test and graduate grades was not submitted. Research workers, both pure and applied, tend to bury negative findings. The author and publisher have no control over this tendency. It would clearly be better, though more difficult, to obtain in some one year the cooperation of 20 or more large graduate schools, give the test, obtain similar criteria, and report a single coefficient for each criterion (though probably on a within-groups basis).

The present manual reports many validity studies of various kinds, with various criteria, and with many samples. The bewildering array of coefficients presented is difficult to comprehend, though the manual provides some ready-made rationalizations for the range of values provided. Thus, the reader is told that the reliability of course grades varies, the homogeneity of groups varies, some courses are more difficult than others, and some courses require little other than rote memory. The conclusion is: "Each of these conditions would affect the validity coefficients in a specific situation." This reviewer was just a little annoyed with the attitude underlying this section. Each of the propositions is testable, yet none was tested. Furthermore, an even more likely contributor to variance among correlation coefficients, sampling errors associated with small n's, was not mentioned.

It is still probably safe to conclude that this test will make a contribution toward the prediction of academic success in graduate school in most situations. It most nearly parallels the verbal scale of the GRE Aptitude Test, but is not by any means a parallel form of that scale. For reasons of heterogeneity of sources of words used, the reasoning content, or both, it is probably more valid than the GRE verbal scale for appropriate criteria. There is less similarity between the Miller test and the GRE quantitative scale. For criteria for which the latter scale has substantial validity, one would probably not be able to substitute the Miller test. There are no good comparative data, to this reviewer's knowledge, however. This seems surprising considering the very common use of selection tests by departments of psychology, particularly.

WILLIAM B. SCHRADER, *Director of Statistical Analysis, Educational Testing Service, Princeton, New Jersey.*

This well known test has followed faithfully the pattern established by the late W. S. Miller 38 years ago. Initially designed to measure scholastic aptitude at the graduate school level, it has also been found useful in selection for high level positions in business. The difficulty level is well adapted to these uses. Administration is conducted on a decentralized basis with effective procedures for maintaining test security. The test manual, revised in 1960, is attractive and comprehensive.

Empirical validation necessarily plays a prominent role in the interpretation of scores on this test. In all, 95 validity coefficients for the test and tables showing performance of 9 contrasted groups are reported in the manual. These data are accompanied by succinct summaries of the studies in which they were obtained. Users should find this extensive summary helpful.

The manual also includes a general discussion of factors which cause the test to be more effective in one situation than another. The discussion does not mention the fact that correlation coefficients based on small samples have a large sampling error. All but 16 of the 95 validity coefficients are based on samples of less than 100 and 25 are based on samples of less than 50. There is no methodological discussion of the vexing problems of validating tests at the graduate level, so that the reader is not cautioned about the special difficulties that arise when data are pooled across departments in the same university or across universities. Finally, the manual does not state any conclusions about the test on the basis of the data presented. Perhaps no conclusions should be drawn, since the groups and the criteria are exceedingly diverse. However, 11 coefficients from 10 studies related test scores to average grades for graduate students in education, psychology, or both. The median coefficient is .38. This figure should be regarded as reasonably satisfactory when account is taken of the heterogeneity of programs followed by different students, the less than perfect reliability of graduate school grades, and the likelihood that test scores were used in selecting at least some of the groups. The validity evidence as a whole indicates that the test measures abilities which are related to performance in academic and other intellectual fields.

A persistent question about the test is whether or not it measures important abilities over and above verbal ability. That it is predominantly a measure of verbal ability is reasonably clear from the high correlations with verbal tests reported in the manual. (For some reason, the dates for the studies of correlations with other tests have been omitted.) The correlations with verbal tests are undoubtedly lower than the corresponding reliabilities. It appears that a factor study would be needed to clarify the nature of what the test measures.

Norms distributions are given for 18 academic groups and for 5 industrial groups. Means and standard deviations are given for 13 additional industrial groups. Like the validity results, these data suffer from the fact that they are essentially compilations rather than reports of studies conducted by the publisher to answer specific questions. The manual makes no claim that any of the norms groups is representative of anything but itself, but the user is not cautioned that the norms groups may not be representative. For most of the academic groups, the number of students drawn from each academic institution included is specified. Even if it is recognized that local norms should play the chief role in score interpretation, it would seem that efforts to secure data on more nearly representative samples would result in more useful norms.

Beginning in February 1963, scores have been released to the examinees. In spite of the extensive controversy about revealing scores on psychological tests to examinees, the decision to reveal scores to MAT examinees was undoubtedly a wise one. Interestingly enough, this decision raises the norms question discussed in the preceding paragraph in a more acute form. In reporting scores to examinees, condensed normative data for first year graduate students in each of nine major fields are shown. Although the reader of the test manual knows that the norms are not necessarily comparable from field to field, the examinee has no way of knowing this. As a result, the norms data given are of doubtful value and may be misleading. This situation could be remedied by adding to the otherwise excellent statement to the examinee a frank admission that the data presented are probably not representative of all first year graduate students in the various fields.

The reliability coefficients for current forms are satisfactory. Both odd-even and test-retest coefficients are reported. An interesting technical question arises in evaluating the test-retest figures. In computing these coefficients, all cases were used even though half had taken one form first and the other half had taken the other form first. As shown in the manual, the correlation between Form J and Form K was .91 regardless of which form was taken first. When the data for both orders were combined, the coefficient was .87, and this figure is taken as the test-retest reliability of Form J versus Form K. It would seem that this procedure gives undue weight to practice effect, which is small but not negligible, in determining the error variance, and thus underestimates the reliability. One final comment with respect to reliability is that the usefulness of the standard error of measurement in score interpretation is not pointed out. Standard errors of measurement are not reported for the various forms.

The *Miller Analogies Test* is a well constructed, secure, convenient, single-score test of high difficulty level. Excellent aids to score interpretation have been provided for its users.

WARREN W. WILLINGHAM, *Director of Evaluation Studies, Georgia Institute of Technology, Atlanta, Georgia.*

The *Miller Analogies Test* (MAT) consists of 100 verbal analogy items which cover a broad range of knowledge. The test is quite difficult and was designed to aid in the selection of graduate students and high level personnel. Despite (or perhaps because of) very tight security regulations, the MAT has been used extensively for many years.

Data reported in the manual indicate that the test is quite reliable (.85 to .94) for heterogeneous groups of seniors and graduate students. The manual does not contain reliability estimates based upon more restricted groups which would be encountered commonly in operational use of the test. However, extensive summary statistics are included which indicate how much restriction in ability may be expected in special groups. In one study (57) the retest reliability of the MAT was found to be .82 after a median time lapse of 16 months. Higher retest reliability (.87 to .89) was found in a recent unpublished study conducted by the publisher.

The validity section of the manual is unusually complete in several respects. A large number of prediction studies are reported objectively and in sufficient detail. Mean MAT score is also reported for various groups of employees and successful and unsuccessful students. While the MAT is frequently a good predictor of performance in graduate school, it is evident that wide variations occur from one institution to another. Another important consideration in evaluating the validity of the MAT is the extent to which it adds useful information to the undergraduate grade-point average. The manual contains relatively little information on this question, but it is crucial since virtually all graduate schools refer to the undergraduate record in selecting students. This fact plus the variability among institutions and curricula underscore the necessity for systematic local studies.

The construct validity of the MAT is more difficult to evaluate. On the one hand it is clear that the test measures largely verbal comprehension in the context of general information. On the other hand it has been called a hodgepodge of subject matter which reflects no clear philosophy of graduate education. This criticism may be true; it may also put the cart before the horse. Systematic analyses of what constitutes successful graduate work are largely nonexistent. A hodgepodge predictor may provide the best available answer to an inadequate question. Unless the goals of a graduate department are articulated with considerably more precision than is typical, there does not appear to be any compelling reason to prefer or reject, a priori, the particular content of the MAT.

The usefulness of a test like the MAT is greatly improved by diverse normative data. The manual includes a great deal of normative information from both business and educational institutions, but the shortcomings of incidentally available norms are illustrated in several instances. For example, the norms for psychology graduate students appear to be fairly representative, while those for several other groups are based only upon students at two large midwestern universities. The normative groups are carefully described, however, and this should allow the reader to judge their comparability. It is worth noting at this point that the publisher has recently changed the security regulations which have governed the dissemination of MAT scores. Scores are now available to the candidate plus any three persons he designates, many of whom will not have a manual. In this regard the MAT is now in line with other similar tests.

The MAT manual is a joy. It starts with modest claims and proceeds inexorably to describe, explain, and document. It is brief yet remarkably complete. Few manuals follow more closely the letter and spirit of the technical recommendations of the American Psychological Association.

The chief competitor of the MAT is the *Graduate Record Examinations Aptitude Test*. Even if there were extensive comparative validity studies on the two tests, it is quite doubtful that either could be judged superior for all purposes. Both are well constructed tests which have their individual appeals.

In summary, the *Miller Analogies Test* is a very difficult, well constructed test. It has been subjected to a considerable amount of research and is supported by an excellent manual. The test is recommended as a measure which is likely to be useful in screening high level personnel and graduate students.

For a review by John T. Dailey, see 5:352; for reviews by J. P. Guilford and Carl I. Hovland, see 4:304.

[473]
★**Mitchell Vocabulary Test.** Adults; 1958; 1 form (2 pages); instructions and norms contained in manual for *Diagnostic Performance Tests* (see 1 below); reliability and validity data and norms based on an earlier version (same as present version except for item order and instructions); 14s. per pad of 50 tests; 35s. per DPT manual; prices include purchase tax; postpaid within U.K.; 15(20) minutes; [A. Mitchell]; distributed by the National Foundation for Educational Research in England and Wales. *

REFERENCES
1. SEMEONOFF, BORIS, AND TRIST, ERIC. Appendix 3, "The Mitchell Vocabulary Test," pp. 135-47. In their *Diagnostic Performance Tests: A Manual for Use With Adults.* London: Tavistock Publications Ltd., 1958. Pp. xvi, 176. *

[474]
*[Moray House Intelligence Tests.] Ages 8.5-10.5, 10-12, 10-12 of above average ability, 12-14, 13.5 and over; 1930-63; 5 levels; distribution restricted to education authorities; 37s. 6d. per 100 tests (except a, 56s.); 7d. per single copy (except a, 9d.); 11s. per 100 practice tests for b or d; 1s. 6d. per manual for any one form of any one test (except c, 2s.); postpaid; purchase tax extra; Department of Education, University of Edinburgh; University of London Press Ltd. *

a) MORAY HOUSE JUNIOR REASONING TEST FOR NINE YEAR OLDS. Ages 8.5-10.5; 1947-58; 2 forms: *Junior Intelligence Test 1a* ['56, 12 pages], *Junior Reasoning Test 2* ['58, 12 pages]; manual [dates same as for tests, 18 pages] for each form; 41.5(91.5) minutes for form 1a, 45(104) minutes for form 2.

b) MORAY HOUSE VERBAL REASONING TEST. Ages 10-12; 1930-63; earlier forms called *Moray House Intelligence Tests;* 2–3 new forms issued annually; 14 forms (8 pages) currently available: forms 60 ['58], 61 ['58], 62 ['59], 63 ['59], 64 ['60], 65 ['60], 66 ['61], 67 ['61], 68 ['61], 69 ['62], 70 ['62], 71 ['63], 72 ['63], 73 ['63]; manual [dates same as for tests, 12 pages] for each form; practice test [dates generally same as for test, 2 pages] for each form; 10(15) minutes for practice test, 45(50) minutes for test.

c) [MORAY HOUSE VERBAL REASONING TEST: VERNIER TEST 2.] Ages 10-12 of above average ability; 1954-57; a "slightly more difficult" test than the tests in b above; 1 form ['57, 8 pages]; manual ['57, 12 pages]; 45(50) minutes.

d) MORAY HOUSE VERBAL REASONING TEST (ADV.). Ages 12-14; 1940-56; forms 6 ['49], 8 ['53], 9 ['55], 10 ['56], (8 pages); manual [dates same as for test, 12 pages] for each form; practice tests (2 pages) 5 ['52, for form 6], 6 ['53, for forms 8–9], 7 ['54, for form 10]; 10(15) minutes for practice test, 45(50) minutes for test.

e) MORAY HOUSE ADULT INTELLIGENCE TEST 1. Ages 13.5 and over; 1952; 1 form ['52, 8 pages]; manual ['52, 15 pages]; 45(50) minutes.

REFERENCES
1-2. See 3:241.
3-4. See 5:353.
5. THOMSON, GODFREY H. "The Standardization of Group Tests and the Scatter of Intelligence Quotients: A Contribution to the Theory of Examining." *Brit J Ed Psychol* 2:92-112, 125-38 F, Je '32. * (PA 6:3031)
6. THOMSON, GODFREY H. "Following Up Individual Items in a Group Intelligence Test." *Brit J Psychol* 32:310-7 Ap '42. * (PA 16:2908)
7. LAMBERT, CONSTANCE M. "Symposium on Selection of Pupils for Different Types of Secondary Schools: 7, A Survey of Ability and Interest at the Stage of Transfer." *Brit J Ed Psychol* 19:67-81 Je '49. *
8. PEEL, E. A. "Symposium on Selection of Pupils for Different Types of Secondary Schools: 6, Evidence of a Practical Factor at the Age of Eleven." *Brit J Ed Psychol* 19:1-15 F '49. *
9. PEEL, E. A. "A Note on Practice Effects in Intelligence Tests." *Brit J Ed Psychol* 21:122-5 Je '51. * (PA 26:929)
10. EMMETT, W. G., AND WILMUT, F. S. "The Prediction of School Certificate Performance in Specific Subjects." *Brit J Ed Psychol* 22:52-62 F '52. * (PA 27:667)
11. JONES, W. R. "The Language Handicap of Welsh-Speaking Children: A Study of Their Performance in an English Verbal Intelligence Test in Relation to Their Non-Verbal Mental Ability and Their Reading Ability in English." *Brit J Ed Psychol* 22:114-23 Je '52. * (PA 27:2197)
12. PEEL, E. A. "Practice Effects Between Three Consecutive Tests of Intelligence." *Brit J Ed Psychol* 22:196-9 N '52. * (PA 27:5156)
13. WISEMAN, STEPHEN, AND WRIGLEY, JACK. "The Comparative Effects of Coaching and Practice on the Results of Verbal Intelligence Tests." *Brit J Psychol* 44:83-94 My '53. * (PA 28:2261)
14. EMMETT, W. G. "Secondary Modern and Grammar School Performance Predicted by Tests Given in Primary Schools." *Brit J Ed Psychol* 24:91-8 Je '54. * (PA 29:3036)
15. PEEL, E. A., AND ARMSTRONG, H. G. "Symposium: The Use of Essays in Selection at 11+; 2, The Predictive Power of the English Composition in the 11+ Examination." *Brit J Ed Psychol* 26:163-71 N '56. * (PA 31:8840)
16. NISBET, JOHN, AND BUCHAN, JIM. "The Long-Term Follow-Up of Assessments at Age Eleven." *Brit J Ed Psychol* 29:1-8 F '59. * (PA 34:3444)
17. HERBERT, N., AND TURNBULL, G. H. "Personality Factors and Effective Progress in Teaching." *Ed R* 16:24-31 N '63. *

For a review by Patrick Slater of earlier forms, see 3:241.

[475]

*Moray House Picture Test 2. Ages 6.5–8.0; 1944–61; earlier test called *Moray House Picture Intelligence Test 1*; 1 form ('61, 15 pages); manual ('61, 16 pages); no data on validity; distribution restricted to education authorities; 65s. per 100 tests; 2s. per manual; postpaid; purchase tax extra; 32(75) minutes; Department of Education, University of Edinburgh; University of London Press Ltd. *

REFERENCES

1–5. See 4:306.

For reviews by Gertrude Keir and M. L. Kellmer Pringle of the earlier test, see 4:306.

[476]

★Multi-Racial Picture Intelligence Tests Suitable for Use in African and Asian Schools. Ages 10–11.5; 1955; 1 form ['55, 16 pages]; instructions ['55, 4 pages]; no data on validity; no norms; 6d. per test; 1s. per key; postage and purchase tax extra; 60(90) minutes; Y. K. Lule; A. Wheaton & Co., Ltd. *

[477]

★[N. B. Group Tests.] Ages 5–6, 7–8; 1958; 1 form ['58, 8 pages]; 2 levels; mimeographed manual ['58, 35 pages]; no data on validity; R 1.40 per 100 tests, postage extra; manual free; specimen set not available; (65–75) minutes; National Bureau of Educational and Social Research. *
a) N. B. GROUP TEST FOR FIVE AND SIX YEAR OLDS.
b) N. B. GROUP TEST FOR SEVEN AND EIGHT YEAR OLDS.

[478]

★Non-Verbal Reasoning Test. Job applicants and industrial employees; 1961; 1 form (7 pages); manual (17 pages); norms for men only; $3 per 20 tests, postage extra; $1 per specimen set, postpaid; (15–30) minutes; Raymond J. Corsini and Measurement Research Division, Industrial Relations Center, University of Chicago (manual); Education-Industry Service. *

JAMES E. KENNEDY, *Associate Professor of Psychology, University of Wisconsin, Madison, Wisconsin.*

The *Non-Verbal Reasoning Test* is described in its manual as a measure of "a person's capacity to think logically through the medium of pictorial problems." A paper and pencil test, it may be administered to groups and requires no writing. The test consists of sets of five pictures. The subject is instructed to look at the first picture and then from the remaining four to pick out the one which "goes best with" the first picture. There are 44 items ordered for difficulty; total score is the number answered correctly. A key for hand scoring is provided.

This test has been revised several times; an earlier and longer form was item analyzed against total score and the poorest items were deleted. The final form was found, for various groups, to have reliabilities, ranging from .61 to .85 as estimated by the K-R 20 and K-R 21 formulae. Split-half reliability (corrected) was reported as .79; test-retest reliability was not judged to be appropriate. In an effort to minimize the effects of cultural factors, the items were shown to a sample of at least 30 individuals of widely different backgrounds and the only items retained were those having elements recognizable to at least 90 per cent of the group. The manual claims that since test performance is "not influenced by facility in language, it is fair to people who have not had much formal education, who are not accustomed to taking tests, or who are not familiar with paper-and-pencil activity." Some, or all, of these claims may be true to some degree, but no evidence is presented to support them.

In the manual "two approaches to validity" are discussed. The first consists in showing that this test correlated in the low .30's with *Verbal Reasoning,* developed by the same author. On the basis of this result, the author concludes only that "the test measures in the general area of mental abilities." The second approach involved reporting that the mean score for a group of "unskilled and semi-skilled employees" was *not* significantly different from the mean score for a group of "foremen, foremen trainees, and leadmen" and that the mean score for this latter group *was* significantly different from that of a group of "salesmen, office staff employees, engineers, middle and top management personnel." No further statement is made to suggest in what way this result might be interpreted as support, or lack of support, of the validity of the test, however validity might be defined. The unwary test user might misinterpret the discussion of these results under the heading of "validity," especially with the emphasis on the occupational characteristics of the groups, and infer that in some way this shows the test to be useful for selection and placement purposes. No correlations are reported between this test and any other psychologically relevant variable, such as other measures of nonverbal reasoning, general intelligence tests, age at time of testing, number of years of schooling, etc.

In summary, this test must be considered as an experimental instrument which measures with moderate reliability a capacity which might quite reasonably be called nonverbal reasoning. Sometime in the future it might conceivably make a contribution to theory or practice. At its present stage of development, its value is extremely limited by the total lack of information about its validity as that term is defined in any conventional manner. There is certainly no evidence to recommend its use for selection and placement in business and industry.

DAVID G. RYANS, *Director, Bureau of Educational Research, University of Hawaii, Honolulu, Hawaii.*

This is a 44-item test, each item consisting of five horizontally displayed pictures of objects, geometric forms, symbols, or configurations of objects, forms, or symbols. The first picture in each row is intended to establish a frame of reference and the testee is directed to draw a diagonal line through one of the remaining four pictures which "goes best with" the first picture. The current test represents a fourth version of an instrument originally called the Picture Test, and the 44 items in the current instrument were selected from a preceding 56-item version in light of analyses of the scores of 371 male industrial employees (same sample for which standard scores and percentiles and reliability and validity data are reported for the current instrument).

The score on the test is the number of the testee's responses corresponding to the scoring key. Normalized standard scores and percentile score equivalents are provided for the sample of 371 males, consisting of three subsamples: group 1, 125 unskilled and semiskilled industrial employees; group 2, 122 foremen, foremen trainees, and leadmen; and group 3, 124 salesmen, office workers, engineers, and management personnel. For this group of 371 males, the score mean was 33.90 and the standard deviation 5.85.

Reliabilities estimated by Kuder-Richardson indices vary among the three subsamples. For K-R 21 and K-R 20, respectively, coefficients are reported as .61 and .72 for group 1, .80 and .85 for group 2, and .67 and .72 for group 3. (Group 3 showed the smallest variance and the highest mean; groups 1 and 2 are similar with respect to mean score, but the standard deviation is higher for group 2.) Differences significant at the .001 level between the mean scores of groups 1 and 3 and groups 2 and 3 are presented as evidence of validity. Correlations of .31, .33, and .61 between the *Non-Verbal Reasoning Test* and another test, *Verbal Reasoning,* based, respectively, on 66 laborers, 71 management personnel, and the combined group "show that the test measures in the general area of mental abilities."

The *Non-Verbal Reasoning Test* may be of limited use for providing gross estimates of general ability when administered to groups. The reliability is too low to make the test useful for individual prediction except possibly for individuals whose scores deviate substantially from the mean.

The manual provides very little useful information. Normative, reliability, and validity data are inadequate, being restricted to the three loosely defined subsamples of male industrial workers. From the data presented it cannot be presumed that the *Non-Verbal Reasoning Test* and *Verbal Reasoning* are equivalent in any sense. No information is provided about the differential predictive effectiveness of the test scores for different purposes. In addition to more extensive data relating to the test use, it also would have been well to have determined the extent to which the *Non-Verbal Reasoning Test* scores correspond to those yielded by well known and widely used instruments purporting to measure general ability; and also how these scores relate to tests of special abilities such as those measured by the *Differential Aptitude Tests.* The test should not be made available and recommended for general use in the absence of a systematic effort to obtain and make available more extensive data. No one possessing even moderate sophistication in behavioral measurement would use this instrument in its present form.

[479]

*Non-Verbal Tests. Ages 8 to 11-0, 10 to 12-11, 10 to 15, 12 to 13-11; 1947-60; 4 levels; prices include purchase tax; postage extra; published for the National Foundation for Educational Research in England and Wales; Newnes Educational Publishing Co. Ltd. *

a) NON-VERBAL TESTS 1-2. Ages 10 to 12-11; 1947-59; title on test is *A Scale of Non-Verbal Mental Ability;* 2 forms (12 pages); optional practice test ['50, 3 pages]; no data on validity; distribution restricted to directors of education; 10s. per 12 tests; 1s. per single copy; 5s. per 12 practice tests; 6d. per single copy; 2s. 6d. per manual for either form; 10(15) minutes for practice test, 30(35) minutes for test.

1) *Non-Verbal Test 1.* 1947-59; 1 form ['49]; revised manual ('59, 20 pages); no norms for ages 12 to 12-11 for administration with practice test; Welsh edition ['54] available; J. W. Jenkins.

2) *Non-Verbal Test 2.* 1948–51; 1 form ['49]; manual ['51]; supplementary provisional norms ['51, for ages 10-3 to 11-2 only] for administration with practice test; D. M. Lee and J. W. Jenkins.

b) NON-VERBAL TEST 3. Ages 10 to 15; 1953–58; 1 form ['53, 28 pages]; may be administered as a short form for ages 10-6 to 12-0; revised manual ('58, 8 pages); no data on reliability; separate answer sheets must be used; 20s. per 12 tests; 2s. per single copy; 2s. 6d. per 12 answer sheets; 1s. 6d. per manual and stencil; 50(60) minutes for full test, 35(45) minutes for short version; B. Calvert (test) and I. Macfarlane Smith (original manual).

c) NON-VERBAL TEST 4. Ages 12 to 13-11; 1951–60; 1 form ['51, 11 pages]; manual ('60, 8 pages, with 1951 norms]; no data on validity; 10s. per 12 tests; 1s. per single copy; 1s. 3d. per manual; 40(50) minutes.

d) NON-VERBAL TEST 5. Ages 8 to 11-0; 1953–58; 1 form ['53, 17 pages]; revised manual ('58, 15 pages); no data on validity; 15s. per 12 tests; 1s. 6d. per single copy; 1s. 6d. per manual; 20(40) minutes; D. A. Pidgeon.

REFERENCES

1–3. See 4:307.
4. See 5:356.
5. LEWIS, D. G. "Bilingualism and Non-Verbal Intelligence: A Further Study of Test Results." *Brit J Ed Psychol* 29:17–22 F '59. * (*PA* 34:2730)

T. R. MILES, *Professor of Psychology, University College of North Wales, Bangor, Wales.*

Alas! these tests are for the most part merely "the mixture as before." There are a few refinements which were absent from some of the earlier group tests: the "standard error" of each test is calculated (apparently as a function of reliability, though details are not given); the number of children used for standardisation purposes is somewhat larger than previously; and in the manual for Test 5 test users are reminded, sensibly enough, to check their stopwatches beforehand. It is all very painstaking—and utterly unsatisfactory.

The time is ripe, in the reviewer's opinion, for a rethinking of fundamentals. In particular, one would welcome a clear statement of why it is considered desirable to take up the time of young people by making them do tests of this kind. In what ways are these so-called "non-verbal" tests an improvement on tests of English or mathematics? Do they point the way to any new and exciting psychological theory? Is there any good evidence as to their validity (as distinct from reliability) in terms of independent criteria? Are there any new facts emerging which would enable us to pass beyond the old and barren controversies about the existence of "*g*" and such matters? A manual of test instructions is admittedly no place for detailed discussion of theory; but if the above doubts can indeed be answered at all the reader should surely have been told where to look for the answers. The information given is in fact minimal. Thus Test 4 is said to have been designed "to obtain a measure of....non-verbal ability"; but surely no one can claim that "non-verbal ability" is a concept calling for no further justification or elucidation. Even Pidgeon, whose Test 5 impresses perhaps more than the others by its general competence, is constrained to talk of the child's "'true' score"; but his inverted commas round the word "true" merely underline the basic problem and do not solve it.

From suitably constructed tests of this kind there could well be material for useful research. Thus it would be interesting to do further studies on the growth of the ability to distinguish, e.g., vertical lines with a semicircle on the top left from vertical lines with a semicircle on the top right, on the ability to recognise conventional symbols (e.g., letters of the alphabet or Arabic numerals) as compared with ability to recognise meaningless shapes, on the difference between ability to recognise and ability to reproduce, on the difference between ability to organise in terms of visual space and ability to organise in terms of kinaesthetic space, and on the ability to describe complex patterns verbally; also one would welcome theoretical discussion on the question whether in any important sense these tests are "non-verbal" at all. If only research workers in this field would spend more time considering fundamentals and less time on the proliferation of actual tests—administered, incidentally, in conditions where the child's approach and performance cannot easily be watched in detail—we would all be the gainers. It should be remembered, too, that one inspired idea can often be worth many pages of norms, and that a few original observations on a single child can sometimes be of more value to psychology than the most elaborate and painstaking survey.

JOHN NISBET, *Professor of Education, University of Aberdeen, Aberdeen, Scotland.*

The *Non-Verbal Tests* vary so greatly in content, form, and age range that a separate review could be written for each test. They do not constitute a series of parallel tests but are rather a succession of experiments in group testing by differing methods.

Test 1 suffers from premature publication. Designed for the "11-plus" age group, it was originally used with printed instructions which were read by the children before they attempted the nonverbal problems. A subsequent revised procedure removed this verbal element by substituting a preliminary practice test and oral instructions. Two sets of norms are given, one for each procedure; but the norms for the revised procedure do not cover the whole age range.

Test 3 seems to have had a chequered career. Originally standardised for ages 10-6 to 12-0, it was subsequently used experimentally with those "aged between 14 and 15 years." Norms are now given for ages 10-0 through 15-0. There is also a shortened form for the younger children.

Tests 4 and 5 limit the variety of types of problem and give systematic practice before testing. The age range for Test 5 is 8-0 to 11-0; but the test is too difficult at age 8-0 (median raw score only 20 out of 100) and it is not until age 10 that the full range of scores is used. The cypher subtest in Test 5, with 100 items to be coded in 3½ minutes, is a speed test. Test 4 for ages 12-0 to 13-11 appears to be the best of the series.

Standardisation has been done on substantial numbers, but the manuals give inadequate information on the composition of the standardisation groups. For Test 1 it is merely stated: "The scores of 2700 children were collected." Reliability coefficients are .92 or above, although for Test 3 this information is given in the catalogue and not in the manual.

No attempt is made to control guessing, though there are some multiple choice items with only four possibilities. Norms are given for scores below chance; but we cannot assume that dull children do not realise that they might guess.

It is possible to make many criticisms and to regret that the National Foundation has not set a higher standard in publishing these tests. Nevertheless, we must recognise that these are the best nonverbal group tests in England for restricted age ranges. *Progressive Matrices* is much easier to administer, but its range of difficulty is so extensive that within one age group of children individual differences depend on as few as 12 items, some of the test being much too easy and some much too hard. The *Non-Verbal Tests* give a much wider scatter of raw scores.

These tests should be regarded as experimental tests, exploring the problem of how to present nonverbal material in a form suitable for group testing and yet still relevant to the school situation. Tests 4 and 5 are as good as any other English test of this particular type. They cannot be recommended for general use in educational guidance since there are still many sources of error in the scores they produce and the manuals fail to give adequate data on construction, validity, and relation to other tests.

For a review by Cyril A. Rogers of tests 1–3, see 5:356; for a review by E. A. Peel of the original edition, see 4:307.

[480]

Otis Group Intelligence Scale. Grades kgn–4, 5–16 and adults; 1918–40; 2 levels; no data on reliability; no data on validity presented in manuals; specimen set not available; postage extra; Arthur S. Otis; [Harcourt, Brace & World, Inc.]. * (British edition: George G. Harrap & Co. Ltd.)

a) PRIMARY EXAMINATION. Grades kgn–4; 1920–40; Forms A, B, ('20, 8 pages); revised manual ('40, 10 pages); $3.60 per 35 tests; (40) minutes.

b) ADVANCED EXAMINATION. Grades 5–16 and adults; 1918–29; Forms A, B, ('19, 11 pages); manual ('29, 12 pages); $4.50 per 35 tests; (60) minutes.

REFERENCES

1. OTIS, A. S. "An Absolute Point Scale for the Group Measure of Intelligence." J Ed Psychol 9:239–61, 333–48 My, Je '18. *
2. ARMENTROUT, W. D. "Classification of Junior High School Pupils by the Otis Scale." J Ed Psychol 11:165–8 Mr '20. *
3. DICKSON, VIRGIL E. "Use of Group Mental Tests in the Guidance of Eighth-Grade and High-School Pupils." J Ed Res 2:601–10 O '20. *
4. LOOMIS, A. K. "Some Correlations With the Otis Scale." J Ed Res 2:594 S '20. *
5. MONROE, WALTER S. "Some Correlations Between Otis Scale and Rogers Mathematical Tests." J Ed Res 2:774–6 N '20. *
6. SMITH, WILLIAM H. "The Otis Group Intelligence Tests and High-School Grades." Sch & Soc 12:71–2 Jl 17 '20. *
7. COLVIN, STEPHEN S. "Some Recent Results Obtained From the Otis Group Intelligence Scale." J Ed Res 3:1–12 Ja '21. *
8. COXE, WARREN W. "Norms for the Otis Group Intelligence Scale." J Ed Res 3:313–4 Ap '21. *
9. COXE, WARREN W. "School Variation in General Intelligence." J Ed Res 4:187–94 O '21. *
10. DICKSON, VIRGIL E., AND NORTON, J. K. "The Otis Group Intelligence Scale Applied to the Elementary School Graduating Classes of Oakland, California." J Ed Res 3:106–15 F '21. *
11. STENQUIST, JOHN L. "Unreliability of Individual Scores in Mental Measurements." J Ed Res 4:347–54 D '21. *
12. WEST, ROSCOE L. "An Experiment With the Otis Group Intelligence Scale in the Needham, Massachusetts, High School." J Ed Res 3:261–8 Ap '21. *
13. GARRISON, S. C., AND TIPPETT, JAMES S. "Comparison of the Binet-Simon and Otis Tests." J Ed Res 6:42–8 Je '22. *
14. GEYER, DENTON L. "The Reliability of Rankings by Group Intelligence Tests." J Ed Psychol 13:43–9 Ja '22. *
15. HOKE, ELMER. "Intelligence Tests and College Success." J Ed Res 6:177 S '22. *
16. JOHNSON, O. J. "Group Intelligence Examinations for Primary Pupils." J Appl Psychol 6:403–16 D '22. *
17. JORDAN, A. M. "Correlations of Four Intelligence Tests With Grades." J Ed Psychol 13:419–29 O '22. *
18. ROOT, W. T. "Correlations Between Binet Tests and Group Tests." J Ed Psychol 13:286–92 My '22. *
19. VITELES, MORRIS S. "A Comparison of Three Tests of 'General Intelligence.'" J Appl Psychol 6:391–402 D '22. *
20. GATES, ARTHUR I. "The Unreliability of M.A. and I.Q. Based on Group Tests of General Mental Ability." J Appl Psychol 7:93–100 Mr '23. *

21. JORDAN, A. M. "The Validation of Intelligence Tests." *J Ed Psychol* 14:348-66, 414-28, S, O '23. *
22. McGEOCH, JOHN A. "Some Results From Three Group Intelligence Tests." *Sch & Soc* 17:196 F 17 '23. *
23. MORRISON, J. CAYCE; CORNELL, W. B.; AND CORNELL, ETHEL. "A Study of Intelligence Scales for Grades Two and Three." *J Ed Res* 9:46-56 Ja '24. *
24. WILSON, J. H. "Comparison of Certain Intelligence Scales." *Brit J Psychol* 15:44-63 Jl '24. *
25. ACKERSON, LUTON, AND ESTABROOKS, GEORGE H. "On the Correlation of Intelligence Test Scores With Imputed Intelligence." *Brit J Psychol* 18:455-9 Ap '28. *
26. KUHLMANN, F. "The Kuhlmann-Anderson Intelligence Tests Compared With Seven Others." *J Appl Psychol* 12:545-94 D '28. * (*PA* 3:1751)
27. COLE, ROBERT D. "A Conversion Scale for Comparing Scores on Three Secondary School Intelligence Tests." *J Ed Res* 20:190-8 O '29. * (*PA* 4:439)
28. STECKEL, MINNIE L. "The Restandardization of IQ's of Different Tests." *J Ed Psychol* 21:278-83 Ap '30. *
29. CHARLES, C. M. "A Comparison of the Intelligence Quotients of Three Different Mental Tests Applied to a Group of Incarcerated Delinquent Boys." *J Appl Psychol* 17:581-4 O '33. * (*PA* 8:2662)
30. EDDS, JESS H., AND McCALL, W. MORRISON. "Predicting the Scholastic Success of College Freshmen." *J Ed Res* 27:127-30 O '33. * (*PA* 8:595)
31. MILLER, W. S. "Variation of IQ's Obtained From Group Tests." *J Ed Psychol* 24:468-74 S '33. * (*PA* 8:662)
32. TERRY, PAUL W. "The Prognostic Value of Different Types of Tests in Courses in Educational Psychology." *J Appl Psychol* 18:231-40 Ap '34. * (*PA* 8:5251)
33. ROBERTS, J. A. FRASER; NORMAN, R. M.; AND GRIFFITHS, RUTH. "Studies on a Child Population: 1, Definition of the Sample, Method of Ascertainment, and Analysis of the Results of a Group Intelligence Test." *Ann Eug* 6:319-38 D '35. * (*PA* 10:3766)
34. WILSON, J. H. "The Exactness of 'g' as Determined by Certain Intelligence Tests." *Brit J Psychol* 26:93-8 Jl '35. *
35. ADKINS, DOROTHY C. "The Effects of Practice on Intelligence Test Scores." *J Ed Psychol* 28:222-31 Mr '37. * (*PA* 11:3629)
36. ROBERTS, J. A. FRASER, AND GRIFFITHS, RUTH. "Studies on a Child Population: 2, Retests on the Advanced Otis and Stanford-Binet Scales, With Notes on the Use of a Shortened Binet Scale." *Ann Eug* 8:15-45 O '37. * (*PA* 12:2179)
37. ROBERTS, J. A. FRASER; NORMAN, R. M.; AND GRIFFITHS, RUTH. "Studies on a Child Population: 3, Intelligence and Family Size." *Ann Eug* 8:178-215 Ja '38. * (*PA* 12:4260)
38. ROBERTS, J. A. FRASER; NORMAN, R. M.; AND GRIFFITHS, RUTH. "Studies on a Child Population: 4, The Form of the Lower End of the Frequency Distribution of Standard-Binet Intelligence Quotients and the Fall of Low Intelligence Quotients With Advancing Age." *Ann Eug* 8:319-36 Ag '38. * (*PA* 13:798)
39. CURETON, EDWARD E. "Note on the IQ Obtained From the Otis Group Intelligence Scale, Advanced Examination." *J Appl Psychol* 23:416-7 Je '39. * (*PA* 13:5938)
40. TIFFIN, JOSEPH, AND GREENLY, R. J. "Employee Selection Tests for Electrical Fixture Assemblers and Radio Assemblers." *J Appl Psychol* 23:240-63 Ap '39. * (*PA* 13:4840)
41. KIRK, HARRY A. *The Relation Between Intelligence Rating and Achievement in Shorthand and Typing.* Master's thesis, Kent State University (Kent, Ohio), 1942.
42. McRAE, HUGH. "The Inconstancy of Group Test I.Q.'s." *Brit J Psychol* 12:59-70 F '42. * (*PA* 16:2905)
43. MORGAN, C. L., AND STEINMAN, C. C. "An Evaluation of a Testing Program in Educational Psychology." *J Ed Psychol* 34:495-502 N '43. * (*PA* 18:1891)
44. COFER, CHARLES N., AND BIEGEL, MARK M. "A Study of the Kent and Buck Screen Tests of Mental Ability in Relation to Otis and Stanford Achievement Test Scores." *J Consult Psychol* 12:187-9 My-Je '48. * (*PA* 22:4943)

D. WELTY LEFEVER, *Professor of Education, University of Southern California, Los Angeles, California.*

The *Otis Group Intelligence Scale* is one of the oldest standardized tests still listed in the catalogue of a major publishing house in 1963. Although several widely used intelligence tests may be regarded as lineal descendants of the *Otis Group Intelligence Scale,* the test in its present form has remained essentially unchanged since 1920. The Advanced Examination is perhaps the most important pioneer group intelligence test. It was almost completed when the United States entered World War I. Otis' research and experience made an indispensable contribution to the development of the Army Alpha and the subsequent success of group mental tests.

Otis' test received an enthusiastic reception when it was published in 1918. An early brochure about the test stated:

The success of the Otis Scale has been entirely unprecedented in the history of American schoolbook publishing. After the first edition issued in March it was necessary to put through a second printing in June of a hundred thousand; and in September it was found necessary to print a third of a million more. Plans were then laid for a still larger printing in December in order to supply schools examining pupils at the mid-year.

Lewis M. Terman wrote:

The *Otis Group Intelligence Scale* was the first scientifically grounded and satisfactory scale for testing subjects in groups, and it probably comes as near testing raw "brain power" as any system of tests yet devised. It is a necessity in schools, industries, armies, or any other institution or situation in which the mental ability of human beings is a factor for consideration.

The publishers of the new test promised enthusiastically:

The 1929 edition of the *Otis Group Intelligence Scale* is a valid measure of general mental ability. It will enable a teacher or school administrator to measure the native mental ability of pupils in groups rapidly and accurately for the purpose of (1) *classification* in regard to the native capacities to learn; (2) *elimination of the feeble minded* who should be placed in special institutions; (3) *selection of the vocation* in which the degree of mentality indicates the highest possible attainment; and (4) *determination of cases of probable delinquency* or potential delinquency and the proper punishment or remedial action for many criminal acts.

In the introduction to the test manual of the Otis scale dated 1921 Terman prophesied with great clairvoyance:

Thanks to the use of such [intelligence] tests in the United States Army, their experimental period is a thing of the past. * It would be surprising to find teachers and school principals lacking that openmindedness toward psychological methods which was so conspicuously present in army officers, and we may confidently look forward to seeing millions of school children classified annually on the basis of intelligence tests.

It is interesting to note the amount of optimism expressed by the psychologists and publishers of 40 years ago regarding the purchase and use of a new and largely untried device. No doubt such a confident outlook was both prompted and basically justified by the tremendous flood of publicity which the administration of the Army Alpha test to nearly two million men in World War I produced.

The test manual makes no direct mention of reliability. For a discussion of reliability and validity of the test the manual refers the test purchaser to two articles (*1*) published in 1918. The reliability coefficient reported is a correlation of .97 between two experimental forms of the scale. The sample studied in this pioneer development was 121 pupils in grades 4, 6, and 8. Such a large interform correlation would be regarded as spuriously high today because of the heterogeneity of a sample which included fourth, sixth, and eighth grade pupils. This reliability coefficient has been quoted in the textbook references to the *Otis Group Intelligence Scale* ever since. As far as this reviewer knows no other reliability data have been provided.

Incidentally, those of us who can recall having administered objective tests in schools that had never seen such an instrument before can appreciate Otis' experiences administering the test to the experimental groups. "Pupils were adjured at the beginning of the testing not to give or receive aid during the taking of any test. On the whole the pupils were orderly and attentive."

The evidence of concurrent validity presented in the journal article includes three correlations between Otis scores and teachers' marks of .80 (43 fourth grade pupils); .41 (40 sixth grade pupils); and .50 (38 eighth grade pupils). Two additional kinds of evidence for test validity are available in the test manual but not so designated. The point scores on the scale were tabulated in relation to the chronological age of the sample. The norm table for the Advanced Examination in the 1921 Manual of Directions is based on some 25,000 cases from grades 4 through 12, and shows a systematic increase of average scores with each advancing age group. A second source of information on validity presented in the 1921 manual, but not labeled as such, is the table of Binet mental age equivalents which indicates a definite relationship between Otis scores and Binet mental age values.

Research involving the scores of 800 pupils on both the Primary Examination and the *Otis Quick-Scoring Mental Ability Tests* reported in 1938, showed that the original norms were too low by more than 50 per cent at the 6 year and 7 year age levels. The differences between 1920 and 1938 norms diminish to less than 2 per cent at the 12 year level. However, since the 1938 norms are the latest reported one wonders whether any additional shifts in norm values would be shown if more recent surveys were conducted.

As we look back to those pioneering times when aptitude tests were new and appeared to possess psychological and statistical magic we may well ask ourselves how much real progress we have made in the past 50 years in the measurement of human intelligence. Have we accomplished any major breakthroughs like those made by Binet, Terman, Otis, et al.?

Certainly in 1963 we honor the *Otis Group Intelligence Scale* as a milestone in the history of aptitude measurement but we wish that it were either thoroughly updated or accorded an honorable retirement from the catalogues of a highly respected publishing house. By today's standards the information furnished the consumer of the *Otis Group Intelligence Scale* is both antiquated and inadequate.

[481]

*Otis Quick-Scoring Mental Ability Tests. Grades 1.5–4, 4–9, 9–16; 1936–62; IBM and MRC; 3 levels; Forms As of Alpha Test, EM and FM of Beta Test, and EM and FM of Gamma Test are labeled New Edition; pre-1954 forms of Beta and Gamma Tests are revisions of *Otis Self-Administering Tests of Mental Ability* (still available, see 5:363); 40¢ per specimen set of any one level; postage extra; Arthur S. Otis; Harcourt, Brace & World, Inc. *

a) ALPHA TEST. Grades 1.5–4; 1936–54; 2 editions.

1) Alpha Test [Long Form]. 3 scores: nonverbal, verbal, total (either subtest may be administered alone); Forms A ('36), B ('38), (11 pages); manual ('39, c1936–39, 22 pages); $3.75 per 35 tests; 20(25) minutes for nonverbal subtest, (30) minutes for verbal subtest.

2) Alpha Short Form. Form As ('53, c1936–52, 7 pages); the Form Bs listed in the publisher's 1963–64 catalog was withdrawn before publication; manual ('54, c1936–54, 15 pages); $3 per 35 tests; (35) minutes.

b) BETA TEST. Grades 4–9; 1937–62; IBM (Forms CM, DM, EM, FM) and MRC (Forms EM, FM); hand scored Forms A, B, ('37, 6 pages); machine scorable Forms CM ('37), DM ('39), EM ('54), FM ('54), (6 pages); manual ('37, 12 pages) for hand scored forms; manual ('54, c1939–54, 8 pages) for machine scorable forms; IQ tables ['62, 4 pages] for Forms CM and DM; $2.65 per 35 tests of hand scorable forms; $3.10 per 35 tests of machine scorable forms; separate answer sheets or cards may be used with machine scorable forms; $1.40 per 35 IBM answer sheets; 20¢ per scoring stencil; $2 per 100 Harbor answer cards (machine scoring service, by Measurement Research Center, Inc., may be arranged through the publisher); 30(35) minutes.

c) GAMMA TEST. Grades 9–16; 1937–62; IBM (Forms AM, BM, EM, FM) and MRC (Forms EM, FM);

hand scored Forms C, D, ('39, 6 pages); machine scorable Forms AM ('37), BM ('37), EM ('54), FM ('54), (6 pages); manual ('39, 8 pages) for hand scored forms; manual ('54, c1939-54, 6 pages) for machine scorable forms; IQ tables ['62, 4 pages] for all forms; prices same as for Beta Test; 30(35) minutes.

REFERENCES

1-9. See 3:249.
10-42. See 5:362.
43. HOLMES, JACK A. "Factors Underlying Major Reading Disabilities at the College Level." *Genetic Psychol Monogr* 49:3-95 F '54. * (*PA* 28:8982)
44. SHAW, GERALDINE SAX. "Prediction of Success in Elementary Algebra." *Math Teach* 49:173-8 Mr '56. *
45. DUFFICY, EDWARD C. *The Relationship Between Scores on the Otis Gamma Quick Scoring Mental Ability Test, the Gordon Personal Profile, and Success in Latin in a Minor Seminary.* Master's thesis, De Paul University (Chicago, Ill.), 1957.
46. CAMPBELL, ROBERT J. *An Analysis to Determine the Value of Otis I.Q. Test and the Iowa Silent Reading Test in Predicting Final Academic Success of Adams State College Students.* Master's thesis, Adams State College (Alamosa, Colo.), 1958.
47. MCQUEEN, ROBERT, AND WILLIAMS, KENNETH C. "Predicting Success in Beginning High School Algebra." *Psychol Rep* 4:603-6 D '58. * (*PA* 34:2009)
48. CROFT, ELLA JOYCE. "Prediction of Clothing Construction Achievement of High School Girls." *Ed & Psychol Meas* 19:653-5 w '59. * (*PA* 34:6562)
49. ENGELHART, MAX D. "Obtaining Comparable Scores on Two or More Tests." *Ed & Psychol Meas* 19:55-64 sp '59. * (*PA* 34:114)
50. LAVER, A. B. "Testing in Canada: Report No. 1." *Can Psychologist* 8:102-3 O '59. *
51. NORTON, DANIEL P. "The Relationship of Study Habits and Other Measures to Achievement in Ninth-Grade General Science." *J Exp Ed* 27:211-7 Mr '59. * (*PA* 35:1283)
52. CASS, JOHN C., AND TIEDEMAN, DAVID V. "Vocational Development and the Election of a High School Curriculum." *Personnel & Guid J* 38:538-45 Mr '60. *
53. DARBES, ALEX. "Relationships Among College Students Scores on ACE, Otis, and WAIS Tests." *Proc W Va Acad Sci* 32:214-6 D '60. * (*PA* 36:3KK14D)
54. DI BONA, LUCILLE J. "Predicting Success in Shorthand." *J Bus Ed* 35:213-4 F '60. *
55. ROSINSKI, EDWIN F. "Must All Tests Be Multi-Factor Batteries?" *J Exp Ed* 28:235-40 Mr '60. *
56. MARINACCIO, LAWRENCE V. *Relationships Between Work Experience and Intelligence Quotients of Secondary School Pupils.* Doctor's thesis, University of Connecticut (Storrs, Conn.), 1961. (*DA* 22:2693)
57. ROBERTS, HELEN ERSKINE. "Comparison of Otis and Stanford-Binet IQ's." *Calif J Ed Res* 12:8-15 Ja '61. * (*PA* 36:1HD08R)
58. SIEBERT, LAWRENCE A. "Otis IQ Scores of Delinquents." *J Clin Psychol* 18:517 O '62. * (*PA* 39:5720)
59. VON WITTICH, BARBARA. "Prediction of Success in Foreign Language Study." *Mod Lang J* 46:208-12 My '62. *
60. WILLINGHAM, WARREN W., AND STRICKLAND, JAMES A. "Conversion Tables for Otis Gamma and Scholastic Aptitude Test." *Personnel & Guid J* 41:356-8 D '62. * (*PA* 37:7183)
61. ALVI, SABIR ALI. *Traditional and "Culture Fair" Aptitude Test Performance of College Students From Different Academic and Cultural Backgounds.* Doctor's thesis, Indiana University (Bloomington, Ind.), 1963. (*DA* 24:2775)
62. BLOSSER, GEORGE H. "Group Intelligence Tests as Screening Devices in Locating Gifted and Superior Students in the Ninth Grade." *Excep Child* 29:282-6 F '63. * (*PA* 38:2434)
63. CLYMER, THEODORE. "A Study of the Influence of Reading Ability on the Validity of Group Intelligence Tests." *Slow Learning Child* 10:76-84 N '63. *
64. HIGGINS, CONWELL. "Multiple Predictor Score Cut-Offs Versus Multiple-Regression Cut-Offs in Selection of Academically Talented Children in Grade 3." *Yearb Nat Council Meas Ed* 20:153-64 '63. * (*PA* 38:9247)
65. SIEBERT, LAWRENCE A. "Matched Otis and Wechsler IQ Scores of Delinquents." *J Clin Psychol* 19:215-6 Ap '63. *
66. WEINER, MAX, AND TOBIAS, SIGMUND. "Chance Factors in the Interpretation of Group Administered Multiple-Choice Tests." *Personnel & Guid J* 41:435-7 Ja '63. * (*PA* 39:1771)

For reviews by D. Welty Lefever and Alfred Yates of the New Edition forms, see 5:362; for a review by Frederic Kuder of the earlier forms, see 3:249; for reviews by F. Kuhlmann and C. Spearman, see 40:1413; for reviews by Psyche Cattell and R. Pintner, see 38:1053 (2 excerpts).

[482]

★**Performance Alertness "PA" (With Pictures): Individual Placement Series (Area I).** Adults; 1961; Form C (4 pages); no manual; no data on reliability and validity; no description of normative population; separate answer sheets must be used; $12.50 per 25 tests; $1 per 25 answer sheets; $1 per key; $2.50 per specimen set; postpaid; 12(17) minutes; J. H. Norman; the Author. *

[483]

★**Personal Classification Test.** Business and industry; 1953-59; Forms H, R, ('53, 3 pages); mimeographed manual ['53, 2 pages] for Form R; no manual for Form H; Form H norms ('59, 1 page); no data on reliability and validity of Form H; $4 per 25 tests, postpaid; 10(15) minutes; W. E. Brown, W. H. E. Geiger, R. W. Henderson, and L. C. Steckle; William, Lynde & Williams. *

[484]

Personnel Research Institute Classification Test. Adults; 1943-54; formerly called *Classification Test for Industrial and Office Personnel;* Forms A ('47, revision of 1943 form), B ('47), (4 pages); revised manual ('54, 4 pages); $3 per 25 tests; 50¢ per specimen set; postage extra; 15(20) minutes; Jay L. Otis, Evelyn Katz (A), Robert W. Henderson (A), Mary Aiken (A), David J. Chesler (B), and Gardner E. Lindzey (B); Personnel Research Institute. *

REFERENCES

1. OTIS, JAY L., AND CHESLER, DAVID J. "A Short Test of Mental Ability." *J Appl Psychol* 33:146-50 Ap '49. * (*PA* 24:16)
2. CAMPBELL, JOEL T. "Validity Information Exchange, No. 16-04: D.O.T. Code 7-36.250, Gas Deliveryman." *Personnel Psychol* 16:181-3 su '63. *

JAMES R. GLENNON, *Director, Employee Relations Research, Standard Oil Company (Indiana), Chicago, Illinois.*

An industrial psychologist concerned with problems of selection from among applicants for almost any job within business or industry will surely include a test or tests of mental ability in his selection battery. Assuming that the hierarchy of jobs applies in his selection situation, he will first be concerned with the more numerous selections to be made for entry level jobs in plant or office. Confronted with the comparatively modest educational achievements and mental ability of the majority of applicants for lower level jobs, he will most likely choose from one or more of the short, easily administered mental ability tests.

The *Personnel Research Institute Classification Test* would appear to fit the foregoing prescription in that it is short (15 minutes) and presents 100 multiple choice items in a simple, easily administered form. The manual describes the purpose in the development of the test as one of meeting "the need for a short, easily administered test for use with office, shop, and sales personnel." The test differs from most mental ability tests in that the items are at the same level of difficulty and that level is by design a relatively low level. This constitutes an advantage, in the authors' eyes, over tests which present items of increasing difficulty, since these more difficult instruments discourage individuals of lesser ability. On the other hand, the test is a speed test with only 4 per cent of a college population able to complete the 100 items in less than the 15-minute time limit. This would be discouraging to many individuals from all levels of ability.

In an article by two of the authors (*I*) the argument is made that the *Classification Test for Industrial and Office Personnel* (the former title of this instrument) would be useful as a screening or pretest instrument for application in industry or in vocational counseling. Performance on this low-powered test would suggest the kind of further testing which might then be indicated. This reviewer would accept that as a feasible use for the Classification Test, but would prefer other short mental ability tests with a broader range of difficulty for use in general selection practices meant to include all or several levels of jobs.

Wider general application is suggested by the change in the name of the test, and the absence in the manual of any suggestion that the test could not serve for general selection. Norm groups shown in the four-page manual include college students, college applicants, and even high level administrative and research personnel. The higher ability groups, as might be expected, appear to knock the practical ceiling out of the instrument, averaging almost 75 per cent correct answers. In view of the avowed low horizon of the test, the classical criticism of the adequacy of the norms can be reversed and the comment made that the instrument is inadequate for some of its norms.

Norm groups reported in the manual total almost 24,000 and include in addition to those noted in the preceding paragraph, more appropriate norm populations, such as service station personnel, transit operators, factory workers, clerical applicants, and the like. Lower groups on the average answer about 50 of the 100 items correctly.

The manual covers construct validity by presenting a table of correlations between the test and several other tests of mental maturity with correlations ranging from .62 to .83. The authors' explanation of these modest correlations is the limited difficulty range of the Classification Test. Of more pertinence to the industrial user is evidence of concurrent validity given in a table of correlations of test results with "Measures of Job Success." Four of these criteria are based on ratings and show correlations in the .30's and .40's. One "hard" criterion, total sales for two years for a group of 45 maintenance salesmen, shows a relationship of .21, which is the lowest relationship reported. The manual does not define "maintenance" salesmen nor explain how ratings were made or by whom.

Reliability between Forms A and B is reported as .86 when the tests were given to groups of high school and college students. Reversing the order to B-A resulted in slightly lower reliability for similar groups.

The Classification Test used in accordance with what presumably was the authors' original intention—as a low-level screening device—could have certain applications in counseling and doubtless some limited use in industry. Weighed against the advantages of other short pencil and paper mental ability tests which do have items of increasing difficulty, this reviewer would prefer the *Adaptability Test* or *Wonderlic Personnel Test* for industrial selection.

MELVIN R. MARKS, *Professor of Business Administration, The University of Rochester, Rochester, New York.*

Each form of this 15-minute test consists of 100 multiple choice items, spiraled in series of five as follows: vocabulary, general information, arithmetic, general information, analogy. A special feature of the test is that all items are claimed to be of relatively constant difficulty.

Item content is typical for a general intelligence test with the following exceptions: there are no spatial items; verbal ability is measured both by vocabulary and analogy items; there are no mechanical items. For some of the items, the "rightness" of the designated correct alternatives lacks rigor. For example, "picture is to frame as stamp is to *envelope*"; "to revise means to overhaul"; "an improbable event is *unlikely*" (in the context where "uncertain" is also an alternative). However, this reviewer's overall evaluation of item content is favorable, especially since no anachronisms appear even though the test was last revised in 1954.

Two kinds of validity data are supplied. First, seven correlations with other intelligence tests are presented, but without information about the means and standard deviations of the groups tested. These coefficients range from .62 for 254 nursing applicants to .83 for 44 junior clerks. Second, correlations between scores and job success are presented for maintenance salesmen, heater salesmen, junior clerks, and semiskilled laborers. The job performance criteria include ratings of sales performance, total sales, "sales ability," "job rating," "progress rating," and "performance rating." The validity coefficients range from .21 to .49. These coefficients offer reasonable prediction of criteria which are certainly not limited to cognitive elements. On the other hand, the included jobs do not involve technical and spatial abilities; this suggests that validity coefficients might be lower for such jobs, since the test has no corresponding predictor.

Reliability data are furnished in terms of alternate form coefficients (appropriate for a speeded test) which range from .80 to .86 on groups varying from 72 to 159 examinees. The data indicate that the forms are almost completely equivalent in difficulty.

Normative data by tenths are furnished for 15 special samples of various classes of students, clerks, salesmen, factory personnel, etc. Sample sizes range from 113 college students to 6,679 undifferentiated factory personnel. Minimum raw score (out of a possible 100) necessary for the 90th percentile ranges from 67 for telephone operators to 90 for college applicants.

There is no explanation as to why the test is called a classification test. This term is usually reserved for batteries from which the scores of parts are combined in different ways to yield differential prediction of various jobs.

In summary, the test is well constructed, with adequate reliability and validity for use in a variety of job situations. Because of the short time required for administration, the test would appear to be very suitable for screening purposes and for vocational counseling, with resulting economy for both employer and applicant. In the absence of validity data for jobs involving mechanical or spatial skills, the test should not be used to make employment decisions on applicants for such jobs.

[485]
Personnel Research Institute Factory Series Test. Applicants for routine industrial positions; 1950–56; Form B ('50, 3 pages); manual ['56, 7 pages]; no data on validity; $3 per 25 tests; 35¢ per specimen set; postage extra; 10(15) or 15(20) minutes; Jay L. Otis and Alfred H. Exton; Personnel Research Institute. *

N. M. DOWNIE, *Professor of Psychology, Purdue University, Lafayette, Indiana.*

This test is another of those short, easily administered tests of mental ability widely used in industry for general employment practices. The test consists of 50 items—measuring general knowledge, ability in arithmetic, and block counting skill—similar to those found on the Otis tests. The items are arranged in a spiral order of difficulty and are mostly of an academic nature.

The test can be administered using either a 10-minute or 15-minute time limit. The examinee puts his answers on the test booklet, where they can be scored by using strip keys. The score is the number correct.

Split-half reliability coefficients of .931 for the 10-minute and .934 for the 15-minute administration lead the authors to state that the test may be employed with confidence using either time limit. Just what one has confidence in is unknown, for the authors have neither determined exactly what the test measures or shown that it selects the most intelligent or most satisfactory workers. A test with a 1950 copyright date and no demonstrated validity is still being distributed 13 years later.

Percentile norms are given for both the 10- and 15-minute time limit. Nothing whatever is said about the number or type of individuals on whom these norms were based.

While this test appears similar to such established industrial tests as the *Wonderlic Personnel Test* and the *Adaptability Test,* there is no reason why the use of these should be abandoned in favor of the test under review. The authors have yet to demonstrate the validity of their test or to establish norms for groups upon whom the test is to be used. The present inadequate manual offers little to help the personnel man, especially the inexperienced one, in using the test.

[486]
*** Picture Test 1.** Ages 7 to 8-1; 1955–62; formerly called *Picture Intelligence Test 1;* 1 form ['62, 16

pages, identical with test published in 1955 except for title]; manual ('58, 8 pages, identical with 1955 manual); no data on validity; 12s. 6d. per 12 tests; 1s. 3d. per single copy; 1s. per manual; prices include purchase tax; postage extra; 22(45) minutes; Joan E. Stuart; published for the National Foundation for Educational Research in England and Wales; Newnes Educational Publishing Co. Ltd. *

For reviews by Charlotte E. K. Banks and M. L. Kellmer Pringle, see 5:367.

[487]
★The Preliminary Scholastic Aptitude Test. Grades 11-12; 1959-63; abbreviated adaptation of the *College Entrance Examination Board Scholastic Aptitude Test* for guidance and scholarship testing; administered annually in October at participating secondary schools; 2 scores: verbal, mathematical; supervisor's manual ('63, 18 pages); score report booklet for students ('63, 18 pages); score report booklet for counselors ('63, 40 pages, also covers the Admissions Testing Program, see 760); bulletin of information ('63, 17 pages); examination fee: $1 per student; fee includes reporting of scores to the secondary school (schools may release scores to students at their discretion); 120(140) minutes; program administered for the College Entrance Examination Board by Educational Testing Service. *

REFERENCES
1. COFFMAN, WILLIAM E. "Evidence of Cultural Factors in Responses of African Students to Items in an American Test of Scholastic Aptitude." *Yearb Nat Council Meas Ed* 20:27-37 '63. * (PA 38:9272)
2. SEIBEL, DEAN W. "Prediction of College Attendance." *Voc Guid Q* 11:265-72 su '63. * (PA 38:4657)

WAYNE S. ZIMMERMAN, *Test Officer, Los Angeles State College, Los Angeles, California.* [Review of Forms HPT2 and KPT.]

The *Preliminary Scholastic Aptitude Test* (PSAT) is a shortened version of the *College Entrance Examination Board Scholastic Aptitude Test* (SAT). It is designed for use in secondary school guidance programs. The scores can be interpreted by high school counselors and other authorized officials in guiding a student either to select an appropriate college or to consider alternative goals.

The PSAT is parallel to the SAT both in form and in content. Items for the PSAT are drawn from the same pool as those for the SAT, or from obsolete forms of the SAT. The PSAT is designed so that it will discriminate best at the eleventh and twelfth year levels. Comparatively easier items are selected, therefore, than those selected for the college level SAT.

Like SAT, the PSAT measures verbal and mathematical comprehension. The test is composed of two sections, each one hour long. The design of the test is dictated by the College Board philosophy that only two cognitive traits contribute significantly to success in academic work. As its name implies the PSAT is intended for use in conjunction with the SAT. In other words, it is a preliminary test to be administered one or two years before the student is eligible to take the SAT. Because of the similarity between the two tests the PSAT is expected to predict how well the student should perform when later he becomes eligible to take the SAT.

Since the PSAT is designed to predict performance on the SAT its effectiveness depends not only on how well it does this but also on how well the SAT predicts college performance. A summary of data gathered between 1959 and 1962 shows correlations between PSAT and SAT verbal scores ranging from .83 to .88, and correlations between PSAT and SAT mathematical scores ranging from .82 to .85. The sizes of these samples range from 337 to 984. The correlations approach the reported reliabilities. The Kuder-Richardson formula 20 reliability estimates available to the reviewer range from .86 to .91 for PSAT verbal scores, and from .88 to .91 for PSAT mathematical scores. These reliabilities compare with reliabilities of .90 to .93 and .88 to .92 reported for the same two scores on SAT. It would appear that the scores on the PSAT are excellent predictors of SAT scores. The interested reader is referred to the review of the SAT (see 449) for a discussion of its effectiveness in predicting college success.

Like all tests produced and administered on a large scale by Educational Testing Service, norming procedures are thorough and as satisfactory as can reasonably be expected. Percentile norms based on a regional stratified national sampling of high schools are given for both eleventh and twelfth grade students.

Because the PSAT is a preliminary and parallel version of the SAT, most of the same criticisms that apply to the SAT apply to it. The major criticism of the SAT raised by this reviewer concerns the amount of time devoted to the measurement of two academic abilities. The PSAT administration time is two hours, compared to the SAT time of four hours. For a discussion of this issue the reader again is referred to the SAT review.

The PSAT has no competing test. It does the job that it was designed to do and does it well.

[488]

★[Pressey Classification and Verifying Tests.] Grades 1–2, 3–6, 7–12 and adults; 1922–58; IBM for grades 7–12 and adults; 3 levels; no data on reliability; no description of normative population; 50¢ per specimen set of any one test; postage extra; S. L. Pressey (except *a*) and L. C. Pressey; Bobbs-Merrill Co., Inc. *

a) PRIMARY CLASSIFICATION TEST. Grades 1–2; 1922; Form A (4 pages); manual (4 pages); mimeographed norms (1 page); $2.80 per 35 tests; (30–40) minutes.

b) PRESSEY INTERMEDIATE CLASSIFICATION-VERIFYING TESTS. Grades 3–6; 1922–58; 1 form ('58, 4 pages, same as tests copyrighted in 1922 and 1923 except for format, directions, and minor changes in a few items); 2 tests; publisher recommends administration of *b* a day or so after *a* and use of the higher of the two scores; manual ('58, 4 pages); $3.50 per 35 self-marking tests; 14(25) minutes per test.
 1) *Pressey Intermediate Classification Test.*
 2) *Pressey Intermediate Verifying Test.*

c) PRESSEY SENIOR CLASSIFICATION-VERIFYING TESTS. Grades 7–12 and adults; 1922–58; 2 tests; publisher recommends administration of *b* a day or so after *a* and use of the higher of the two scores; manual ('58, 4 pages); 16(25) minutes per test.
 1) *Pressey Senior Classification Test.* IBM; 1 form; 2 editions (differing in item order and 4 items): self-marking edition ('58, 4 pages, same as test copyrighted in 1922 except for format, directions, and minor changes in a few items), machine scoring edition (1940 edition, c1922, 2 pages); $3.50 per 35 self-marking tests; 15¢ per IBM test-answer sheet; 40¢ per set of machine scoring stencils.
 2) *Pressey Senior Verifying Test.* 1 form ('58, 4 pages, same as test copyrighted in 1922 except for format, directions, and minor changes in a few items); $3.50 per 35 self-marking tests.

REFERENCES

1. HENMON, V. A. C., AND STREITZ, RUTH. "A Comparative Study of Four Group Scales for the Primary Grades." *J Ed Res* 5:185–94 Mr '22. *
2. PRESSEY, S. L., AND PRESSEY, L. C. "A Revision of the Pressey Primer and Cross-Out Scales." *J Ed Res* 6:178–9 S '22. *
3. MILLER, W. S. "The Variation and Significance of Intelligence Quotients Obtained From Group Tests." *J Ed Psychol* 15:359–66 S '24. *
4. SANGREN, PAUL V. "Comparative Validity of Primary Intelligence Tests." *J Appl Psychol* 13:394–412 Ag '29. * (PA 3:4324)
5. MILLER, W. S. "Variation of IQ's Obtained From Group Tests." *J Ed Psychol* 24:468–74 S '33. * (PA 8:662)
6. FINCH, F. H. "Equating Intelligence Quotients From Group Tests." *J Ed Res* 28:589–92 Ap '35. * (PA 9:3929)
7. GREEN, HELEN J., AND BERMAN, ISABEL R.; UNDER THE DIRECTION OF DONALD G. PATERSON AND M. R. TRABUE. *A Manual of Selected Occupational Tests for Use in Public Employment Offices*, pp. 8, 23–31. University of Minnesota, Bulletins of the Employment Stabilization Research Institute, Vol. 2, No. 3. Minneapolis, Minn.: University of Minnesota Press, July 1936. Pp. 31. *
8. LORGE, IRVING. "A Table of Percentile Equivalents for Eight Intelligence Tests Frequently Used With Adults." *J Appl Psychol* 20:392–5 Je '36. * (PA 10:5552)
9. HACKMAN, RAY CARTER. *The Differential Prediction of Success in Two Contrasting Vocational Areas.* Doctor's thesis, University of Minnesota (Minneapolis, Minn.), 1940.
10. GHISELLI, EDWIN E. "The Use of the Strong Vocational Interest Blank and the Pressey Senior Classification Test in the Selection of Casualty Insurance Agents." *J Appl Psychol* 26:793–9 D '42. * (PA 17:2452)
11. BENDER, W. R. G., AND LOVELESS, H. E. "Validation Studies Involving Successive Classes of Trainee Stenographers." *Personnel Psychol* 11:491–508 w '58. * (PA 34:2143)

WALTER N. DUROST, *Associate Professor of Education, University of New Hampshire, Durham, New Hampshire.*

The justification for including a review of the *Pressey Classification and Verifying Tests* in this edition of the MMY must come from the opportunity it affords to pay tribute to one of the truly great men in educational psychology and testing. The original tests were copyrighted in the early 20's and although they never obtained the wide currency won by certain other tests such as the *Otis Group Intelligence Test* or the *National Intelligence Test*, the Pressey tests nevertheless represented a pioneer effort in the measurement of intelligence.

The current editions of the intermediate and advanced level tests have a copyright date of 1958 but this copyright date most obviously must have been based upon the inclusion of a very minute amount of new material since by no stretch of the imagination are the present tests representative of the 1958 period of test development. The continued publication of these instruments in their present form is, in fact, inexcusable in this day and age; they should be either withdrawn or revised.

There is a complete lack of any information on reliability and validity, and almost no data whatsoever concerning the nature and extent of the populations upon which the norms for these tests are based. "B scores" are provided, but an examination of a single sheet insert reveals that these "B scores" are nothing but the traditional grade equivalents which have been largely discredited in achievement testing, at least at the professional and technical level, and which certainly have little place in mental ability measurement. They do *not* serve to make the Pressey test results comparable with achievement test grade equivalents.

One has to examine the tests themselves to see the spark of quality that is consistent with the man who devised them. When one recalls that these test items were written in the 1920's, when knowledge of test item writing techniques was almost nonexistent, it is nothing short of astonishing that so many of them stand up under critical scrutiny as still being good items. This is not to deny that the quality of the item writing varies; it does—from poor to excellent —but by far the larger proportion of the items are on the plus side of good.

The self-scoring device invented by Pressey, making use of a carbon deposit underlying the answer spaces, is very useful and its close connection to his interest in teaching machines is obvious.

The idea of a second test to "verify" the results of the first administration, just as worthy now as it was when it was initiated, deserves emulation by others. It is much better than just giving advice to the user to verify by using a second form, advice he rarely takes.

To be more detailed would be to labor the shortcomings of the test as it presently appears and this would be to deny the very purpose of this review. It pleased the writer to be asked to review this test, not for the opportunity it afforded to provide a constructively critical appraisal of a colleague's work, but for the opportunity to pay personal tribute to one of the very few living pioneers in the field of testing.

[489]

*Primary Verbal Tests. Ages 8.0–10.5, 9.0–11.5, 10.0–12.0; 1953–62; 3 levels; 7s. 6d. per 12 tests; 9d. per single copy; 1s. per manual for any one level; postage extra; published for the National Foundation for Educational Research in England and Wales; Newnes Educational Publishing Co. Ltd. *
a) PRIMARY VERBAL TEST 1. Ages 8.0–10.5; 1953–58; formerly called *Primary School Verbal Intelligence Test 1*; adaptation of *A.C.E.R. Junior A Test* and *A.C.E.R. Junior B Test;* 1 form ['53, 8 pages]; manual ('58, 7 pages, essentially the same as 1953 manual except for additional validity data); 30(40) minutes; D. A. Pidgeon.
b) PRIMARY VERBAL TEST 2. Ages 9.0–11.5; 1959; 1 form ['59, 8 pages]; manual ['59, 7 pages]; 35(50) minutes; Valerie Land.
c) PRIMARY VERBAL TEST 3. Ages 10.0–12.0; 1962; 1 form ['62, 8 pages]; manual ['62, 12 pages]; (45–50) minutes; Neville Postlethwaite.

REFERENCES

1. MADDOX, H. "Mental Age Scales." *Brit J Ed Psychol* 29:72-3 F '59. * (*PA* 34:2731)

For reviews by John Nisbet and F. W. Warburton of a, see 5:369.

[490]

*Progressive Matrices. Ages 5 and over; 1938–63; 3 levels; postage and purchase tax extra (postpaid); J. C. Raven; H. K. Lewis & Co. Ltd. (U.S. distributor: Psychological Corporation.) * (Australian edition of a and c: Australian Council for Educational Research.)
a) STANDARD PROGRESSIVE MATRICES. Ages 6 and over; 1938–60; manual also uses the title *Progressive Matrices (1938), 1956 Revision;* 1 form ('56, 62 pages, identical with test copyrighted in 1938 except for change in one item and order of items); revised manual ('60, 25 pages, identical with 1956 manual except for bibliography); no norms for individual administration for ages 14 and over; separate record forms or answer sheets must be used; 210s. ($14) per 25 (10) tests; 12s. 6d. ($1.50) per 50 record forms (answer sheets); 30s. (75¢) per scoring key (set of scoring key and manual); 3s. 6d. per manual; 25s. per specimen set including 5 copies of the complementary *Mill Hill Vocabulary Scale* ($2.85 per specimen set); (60) minutes.
b) COLOURED PROGRESSIVE MATRICES. Ages 5–11 and mental patients and senescents; 1947–63; individual for ages 5–6; 1 form ('56, 38 pages, subtest Sets A and B same as subtest Sets A and B of the *Standard Progressive Matrices* except for color); revised manual ('63, 43 pages, identical with 1958 and 1960 manuals except for bibliography and revision in norms tables); record booklet (no date); separate record forms or answer sheets must be used for group administration; 210s. ($14.50) per 25 (10) tests; 17s. 6d. ($1.50) per 50 record forms (answer sheets); 5s. 6d. (80¢) per manual (set of scoring key and manual); 22s. 6d. per specimen set including 12 copies of the complementary *Crichton Vocabulary Scale* ($3 per specimen set); [30] minutes.
c) ADVANCED PROGRESSIVE MATRICES. Ages 11 and over; 1943–62; 2 editions; manual ('48, 20 pages); 12s. 6d. per 50 record forms for both editions; 30s. per scoring key for both editions.
1) *Progressive Matrices (1947)*: Set 1. For use either as a practice test for Set 2 or as a rough screening test; 1 form ('47, 14 pages); 50s. per 25 tests; 5s. per single copy ($3.30 per specimen set including *Mill Hill Vocabulary Scale* and *Crichton Vocabulary Scale*); (10) minutes.
2) *Advanced Progressive Matrices, Set 2: 1962 Revision.* For use either as "a test of intellectual capacity" when used without a time limit or as "a test of intellectual efficiency" when used with a time limit ("usually of 40 minutes"); 1 form ('62, 38 pages, a revision and abbreviation of the 1947 Set 2); no data on reliability and validity and no norms for revised form; distribution restricted to registered users who after signing an agreement and paying an annual service fee may either borrow the materials for indefinite periods at 150s. per set of 25 tests or for 4 weeks at 20s. per set of 25 tests, or purchase the materials at 340s. per 25 tests or 25s. per single copy; specimen set not available; [40] minutes.

REFERENCES

1-8. See 40:1417.
9-21. See 3:258.
22-53. See 4:314.
54-115. See 5:370.
116. BIESHEUVEL, S.; JACOBS, G. F.; AND COWLEY, J. J. "Maladjustments of Military Personnel." *J Nat Inst Personnel Res* 5:138-68 D '53. * (*PA* 29:3119)
117. RATH, R. "Correlation of Progressive Matrices With Verbal Intelligence Tests and Written Tests on Some Other Subjects." *Ed & Psychol* 1(4-5):20-5 '54. * (*PA* 31:3804)
118. ALLEN, ROBERT M., AND COLLINS, MARJORIE G. "Suggestions for the Adaptive Administration of Intelligence Tests for Those With Cerebral Palsy: Part 1, Administration of the Ammons Full-Range Picture Test, Columbia Mental Maturity Test, Raven's Progressive Matrices and Leiter International Performance Scale." *Cerebral Palsy R* 16:11-4+ My-Je '55. * (*PA* 30:3284)
119. WYSOCKI, BOLESLAW A., AND CANKARDAS, AYDIN. "A New Estimate of Polish Intelligence." *J Ed Psychol* 48:525-33 D '57. * (*PA* 33:3298)
120. CATTELL, RAYMOND B., AND SCHEIER, IVAN H. "The Objective Test Measurement of Neuroticism, U.I. 23 (—)." *Indian J Psychol* 33:217-36 pt 4 '58. *
121. FOULDS, G. A., AND CAINE, T. M. "Personality Factors and Performance on Timed Tests of Ability." *Occup Psychol* 32:102-5 Ap '58. *
122. HIGGINS, CONWELL, AND SIVERS, CATHRYNE H. "A Comparison of Stanford-Binet and Colored Raven Progressive Matrices IQs for Children With Low Socioeconomic Status." *J Consult Psychol* 22:465-8 D '58. * (*PA* 33:9919)
123. MUNDY, LYDIA, AND MAXWELL, A. E. "Assessment of the Feeble-minded." *Brit J Med Psychol* 31:201-10 pt 3 & 4 '58. * (*PA* 34:1673)
124. TRACHT, VERNON SLOAN. *A Comparative Study of Cerebral Palsied and Normal Adults on Two Forms of Raven's "Progressive Matrices."* Doctor's thesis, Loyola University (Chicago, Ill.), 1958.
125. VOGGENTHALER, ANN LOUISE. *A Comparison of the Progressive Matrices (1947), Set II, With Certain Group*

Tests Used With High School Students and School Grades. Master's thesis, University of Texas (Austin, Tex.), 1958.

126. COSTELLO, C. G. "Aphasic Cerebral Palsied Children's Wrong Answers on Raven's 'Progressive Matrices.'" *J Clin Psychol* 15:76-7 Ja '59. * (*PA* 34:3342)

127. DASH, S. C., AND KANUNGO, R. "Progressive Matrices and School Success: A Factor Analytical Study." *Psychologia* 2:246-50 D '59. * (*PA* 35:3952)

128. FOULDS, G. A. "The Relative Stability of Personality Measures Compared With Diagnostic Measures." *J Mental Sci* 105:783-7 Jl '59. * (*PA* 34:6016)

129. HARRIS, DALE B. "A Note on Some Ability Correlates of the Raven Progressive Matrices (1947) in the Kindergarten." *J Ed Psychol* 50:228-9 O '59. * (*PA* 36:1FH28H)

130. JENSEN, ARTHUR R. "A Statistical Note on Racial Differences in the Progressive Matrices." *J Consult Psychol* 23:272 Je '59. *

131. JORDAN, THOMAS E. "Formboard Comparability in the Colored Progressive Matrices." *J Clin Psychol* 15:422-3 O '59. * (*PA* 36:1HC22J)

132. JORDAN, THOMAS E., AND DECHARMS, RICHARD. "The Achievement Motive in Normal and Mentally Retarded Children." *Am J Mental Def* 64:457-66 N '59. * (*PA* 34:8011)

133. KNIEF, LOTUS M., AND STROUD, JAMES B. "Intercorrelations Among Various Intelligence, Achievement, and Social Class Scores." *J Ed Psychol* 50:117-20 Je '59. * (*PA* 35:779)

134. KURODA, JITSUO. "Application of the Colored Progressive Matrices Test for the Japanese Kindergarten Children." *Psychologia* 2:173-7 S '59. * (*PA* 35:3253)

135. LEVINSON, BORIS M. "A Comparison of the Coloured Progressive Matrices (CPM) With the Wechsler Adult Intelligence Scale (WAIS) in a Normal Aged White Male Population." *J Clin Psychol* 15:288-91 Jl '59. * (*PA* 35:3299)

136. LEVINSON, BORIS M. "A Comparison of the Performance of Bilingual and Monolingual Native Born Jewish Preschool Children of Traditional Parentage on Four Intelligence Tests." *J Clin Psychol* 15:74-6 Ja '59. * (*PA* 34:2729)

137. LORANGER, ARMAND W., AND MISIAK, HENRYK. "Critical Flicker Frequency and Some Intellectual Functions in Old Age." *J Gerontol* 14:323-7 Jl '59. * (*PA* 34:4153)

138. MEHROTRA, S. N. "An Educational-Vocational Guidance Project for Intermediate Students: A Follow-Up Study." *Indian J Psychol* 34:148-62 pt 3 '59. * (*PA* 36:4KJ48M)

139. MOSHIN, S. M. "Plea for a Scientific Aptitude Test and a Preliminary Report of the Development of Such Test." *Indian J Psychol* 34:36-42 pt 1 '59. *

140. SPERRAZZO, GERALD, AND WILKINS, WALTER L. "Racial Differences on Progressive Matrices." *J Consult Psychol* 23:273-4 Je '59. * (*PA* 34:4266)

141. VALENTINE, MAX. "Psychometric Testing in Iran." *J Mental Sci* 105:93-107 Ja '59. * (*PA* 34:1065)

142. DESAI, MAHESH M. "Intelligence and Verbal Knowledge in Relation to Epstein's Overinclusion Test." *J Clin Psychol* 16:417-9 O '60. * (*PA* 37:3226)

143. DILS, CHARLES W. "The Colored Progressive Matrices as an Indicator of Brain Damage." *J Clin Psychol* 16:414-6 O '60. * (*PA* 37:3530)

144. HAZARI, ANANDI. "The Stability of Raven's Coloured Progressive Matrices Scores for Selected Children." *J Psychol Res* 4:102-4 S '60. * (*PA* 35:5371)

145. LORANGER, ARMAND W., AND MISIAK, HENRYK. "The Performance of Aged Females on Five Non-Language Tests of Intellectual Functions." *J Clin Psychol* 16:189-91 Ap '60. * (*PA* 36:2FI89L)

146. LUNZER, E. A. "Aggressive and Withdrawing Children in the Normal School: 2, Disparity in Attainment." *Brit J Ed Psychol* 30:119-23 Je '60. *

147. MACARTHUR, R. S. "The Coloured Progressive Matrices as a Measure of General Intellectual Ability for Edmonton Grade III Boys." *Alberta J Ed Res* 6:67-75 Je '60. * (*PA* 36:2HD67M)

148. MAHER, BRENDAN A. "Position Errors and Primitive Thinking in the Progressive Matrices Test." *Am J Mental Def* 64:1016-20 My '60. * (*PA* 35:6407)

149. MALPASS, LESLIE F.; BROWN, RONALD; AND HAKE, DONALD. "The Utility of the Progressive Matrices (1956 Edition) With Normal and Retarded Children." *J Clin Psychol* 16:350 Jl '60. * (*PA* 36:2JI50M)

150. MASON, P. L., AND CASEY, D. L. "The Use of Psychological Tests for Selecting Tabulating Machine Operators." *Personnel Prac B* 16:39-41 S '60. * (*PA* 35:4063)

151. NYMAN, G. EBERHARD, AND SMITH, GUDMUND J. W. "Serial Performance Patterns in Raven's Progressive Matrices." *Scandinavian J Psychol* 1(3):103-11 '60. * (*PA* 35:4862)

152. URMER, ALBERT H.; MORRIS, ANN B.; AND WENDLAND, LEONARD V. "The Effect of Brain Damage on Raven's Progressive Matrices." *J Clin Psychol* 16:182-5 Ap '60. * (*PA* 36:2JF82U)

153. WOLF, WILLAVENE SHEETS. *The Contribution of Speed of Response in Mental Measurement.* Doctor's thesis, State University of Iowa (Iowa City, Iowa), 1960. (*DA* 21:1467)

154. CLARK, PHILIP J.; VANDENBERG, STEVEN G.; AND PROCTOR, CHARLES H. "On the Relationship of Scores on Certain Psychological Tests With a Number of Anthropometric Characters and Birth Order in Twins." *Hum Biol* 33:163-80 My '61. * (*PA* 36:3DP63C)

155. CROOKES, T. G., AND FRENCH, J. G. "Intelligence and Wastage of Student Mental Nurses." *Occup Psychol* 35:149-54 Jl '61. * (*PA* 37:2046)

156. ESTES, BETSY WORTH; CURTIN, MARY ELLEN; DEBURGER, ROBERT A.; AND DENNY, CHARLOTTE. "Relationships Between 1960 Stanford-Binet, 1937 Stanford-Binet, WISC, Raven, and Draw-A-Man." *J Consult Psychol* 25:388-91 O '61. * (*PA* 37:3127)

157. FEINBERG, IRWIN, AND GARMAN, EUGENIE M. "Studies of Thought Disorder in Schizophrenia: 2, Plausible and Implausible Errors on a Modification of the Progressive Matrices Test." *Arch Gen Psychiatry* 4:191-201 F '61. * (*PA* 35:6924)

158. HIGDON, BETTINA P. *Raven's Progressive Matrices, Set I, Administered to Even-Aged Students From 6 to 16.* Master's thesis, Alabama College (Montevallo, Ala.), 1961.

159. JAMUAR, K. K. "Personality and Achievement." *Psychol Studies* 6:59-65 Jl '61. * (*PA* 38:3203)

160. LYNN, R., AND GORDON, I. E. "The Relation of Neuroticism and Extraversion to Intelligence and Educational Attainment." *Brit J Ed Psychol* 31:194-203 Je '61. * (*PA* 36:3HD94L)

161. MCLEOD, H. N., AND RUBIN, J. "Correction Between the Raven Matrices (Rev. 1956) and the Wechsler Adult Intelligence Scale (1955)." *Ont Hosp Psychol B* 6:47-9 Mr '61. *

162. ORME, J. E. "The Coloured Progressive Matrices as a Measure of Intellectual Subnormality." *Brit J Med Psychol* 34:291-2 pt 3 & 4 '61. * (*PA* 37:1698)

163. VENABLES, ETHEL C. "Changes in Intelligence Test Scores of Engineering Apprentices Between the First and Third Years of Attendance at College." *Brit J Ed Psychol* 31:257-64 N '61. * (*PA* 36:5KK57V)

164. Venables, Ethel C. "Placement Problems Among Engineering Apprentices in Part-Time Technical College Courses: Part 2, Level of Ability Needed for Success in National Certificate Courses." *Brit J Ed Psychol* 31:56-8 F '61. * (*PA* 36:1KJ56V)

165. WOLF, WILLAVENE, AND STROUD, JAMES B. "The Contribution of Response in Mental Measurement." *J Ed Psychol* 52:249-53 O '61. * (*PA* 38:3192)

166. YATES, AUBREY J. "Item Analysis of Progressive Matrices (1947)." *Brit J Ed Psychol* 31:152-7 Je '61. * (*PA* 36:3HD52Y)

167. BLAZSANYIK, J. "Clinical Diagnostic Use of P.M. 38 and Verbal Tests." *Austral J Psychol Res* 3:5-8 au '62. *

168. ELLEY, W. B., AND MACARTHUR, R. S. "The Standard Progressive Matrices as a Culture-Reduced Measure of General Intellectual Ability." *Alberta J Ed Res* 8:54-65 Mr '62. * (*PA* 37:3126)

169. FOULDS, G. A., AND DIXON, PENELOPE. "The Nature of Intellectual Deficit in Schizophrenia: Part 1, A Comparison of Schizophrenics and Neurotics." *Brit J Social & Clin Psychol* 1:7-19 F '62. * (*PA* 37:1788)

170. FOULDS, G. A., AND DIXON, PENELOPE. "The Nature of Intellectual Deficit in Schizophrenia: Part 3, A Longitudinal Study of the Sub-Groups." *Brit J Social & Clin Psychol* 1:199-207 O '62. * (*PA* 37:5488)

171. FOULDS, G. A.; DIXON, PENELOPE; MCCLELLAND, MARILYN; AND MCCLELLAND, W. J. "The Nature of Intellectual Deficit in Schizophrenia: Part 2, A Cross-Sectional Study of Paranoid, Catatonic, Hebephrenic and Simple Schizophrenics." *Brit J Social & Clin Psychol* 1:141-9 Je '62. * (*PA* 37:3685)

172. JORDAN, THOMAS E. "Normative Data on the Progressive Matrices (1938)." *Psychol Rep* 10:122 F '62. * (*PA* 37:1204)

173. KNEHR, CHARLES A. "Factor Analyses of Schizophrenic and Organic Test Data." *J Psychol* 54:467-71 O '62. * (*PA* 37:6759)

174. LEVINSON, BORIS M. "Positional and Figural Errors Made by the Aged on Raven Coloured Progressive Matrices." *J Genetic Psychol* 100:183-92 Je '62. * (*PA* 37:2955)

175. MCDONNELL, M. W. "The Prediction of Academic Achievement of Superior Grade Three Pupils." *Alberta J Ed Res* 8:111-8 Je '62. * (*PA* 37:3886)

176. MCLEOD, HUGH N., AND RUBIN, JOSEPH. "Correlation Between Raven Progressive Matrices and the WAIS." *J Consult Psychol* 26:190-1 Ap '62. * (*PA* 37:4960)

177. MEYERS, E.; ORPET, R. E.; ATTWELL, A. A.; AND DINGMAN, H. F. *Primary Abilities at Mental Age Six.* Monographs of the Society for Research in Child Development, Vol. 27, No. 1, Serial No. 82. Lafayette, Ind.: Child Development Publications, 1962. Pp. 40. * (*PA* 38:8462)

178. NICKOLS, JOHN E., JR. "Insight, Superior Intelligence, and the Raven Progressive Matrices, Set E." *J Clin Psychol* 18:351 Jl '62. * (*PA* 39:1752)

179. RAO, S. NARAYANA. "Predicting Academic Achievement of Students in Science and Arts Colleges." *Psychol Studies* 7:16-9 Jl '62. * (*PA* 37:5669)

180. SCHEPERS, J. M. "A Components Analysis of a Complex Psychomotor Learning Task." *Psychologia Africana* 9:294-329 '62. * (*PA* 37:4314)

181. YOUNG, HARBEN BOUTOURLINE; TAGIURI, RENATO; TESI, GINO; AND MONTEMAGNI, GABRIELLA. "Influence of Town and

Country Upon Children's Intelligence." *Brit J Ed Psychol* 32:151–8 Je '62. * (*PA* 37:2883)

182. BURNETT, A.; BEACH, H. D.; AND SULLIVAN, A. M. "Intelligence in a Restricted Environment." *Can Psychologist* 4:126–36 O '63. * (*PA* 38:6050)

183. EDWARDS, ALLAN E., AND WINE, DAVID B. "Personality Changes With Age: Their Dependency on Concomitant Intellectual Decline." *J Gerontol* 18:182–4 Ap '63. * (*PA* 38:4099)

184. EVANS, RAY B., AND MARMORSTON, JESSIE. "Psychological Test Signs of Brain Damage in Cerebral Thrombosis." *Psychol Rep* 12:915–30 Je '63. * (*PA* 38:6413)

185. HAMILTON, VERNON. "I.Q. Changes in Chronic Schizophrenia." *Brit J Psychiatry* 109:642–8 S '63. * (*PA* 38:6506)

186. HIGASHIMACHI, WILFRED H. "The Construct Validity of the Progressive Matrices as a Measure of Superego Strength in Juvenile Delinquents." *J Consult Psychol* 27:415–9 O '63. * (*PA* 38:4302)

187. KING, W. H. "The Development of Scientific Concepts in Children." *Brit J Ed Psychol* 33:240–52 N '63. * (*PA* 38:8062)

188. MACARTHUR, R. S., AND ELLEY, W. B. "The Reduction of Socioeconomic Bias in Intelligence Testing." *Brit J Ed Psychol* 33:107–19 Je '63. * (*PA* 38:4271)

189. NELSON, MARVEN O., AND EDELSTEIN, GERALD. "Raven Progressive Matrices, Non-Language Multi-Mental Test, and California Test of Mental Maturity: Intercorrelations." *Psychol Rep* 13:46 Ag '63. * (*PA* 38:6061)

190. RAO, S. NARAYANA. "Prediction of Academic Achievement of Students in an Engineering College." *J Psychol Res* 7:114–7 S '63. *

191. RICH, CHARLES CLIFTON. *The Validity of an Adaptation of Raven's Progressive Matrices Test for Use With Blind Children.* Doctor's thesis, Texas Technological College (Lubbock, Tex.), 1963. (*DA* 24:1714)

192. SIGEL, IRVING E. "How Intelligence Tests Limit Understanding of Intelligence." *Merrill-Palmer Q* 9:39–56 Ja '63. * (*PA* 39:1791)

193. VENABLES, ETHEL C. "Social Differences Among Day-Release Students in Relation to Their Recruitment and Examination Success." *Brit J Social & Clin Psychol* 2:138–52 Je '63. * (*PA* 38:4659)

MORTON BORTNER, *Chief Psychologist, Department of Physical Medicine and Rehabilitation, New York Medical College, New York, New York.*

These tests represent an attempt to measure intellectual functioning within the context of Spearman's concept of *"g."* The tasks or matrices consist of designs which require completion. The testee chooses from multiple choice options the design or design part which best fits. An answer which fits may: (*a*) complete a pattern, (*b*) complete an analogy, (*c*) systematically alter a pattern, (*d*) introduce systematic permutations, or (*e*) systematically resolve figures into parts. The number of items correctly solved is the score which is then translated into a percentile rank. The author recommends that the *Standard Progressive Matrices* be used in conjunction with the *Mill Hill Vocabulary Scale* and that the *Coloured Progressive Matrices* be used in conjunction with the *Crichton Vocabulary Scale* in order to supplement the Matrices' measure of "capacity" with a measure of acquired information.

The accumulating literature dealing with the validity and reliability of these scales is equivocal. Continuing revisions of the tests have dealt with the adequacy of the designs, but have not departed from the original strategy of the test which is to measure *"g"* via various forms of "perceptual reasoning." Although the author breaks the perceptual task down into subcategories of perceptual functioning (enumerated above) their relevance to intellectual functioning in general remains to be documented.

These tests should be quite helpful as screening devices for groups where estimates of levels of intelligence need to be determined. They have already been found helpful in comparing various psychiatric, socioeconomic, and ethnic groups. (See *112* for an extensive review of the literature.) *Progressive Matrices* should also be helpful in estimating general level of intellectual functioning of individuals who have communication disorders as no verbal responses are required. The tests are easy to administer, require little verbal instruction, and are relatively brief. For the above reasons, these tests will probably continue to be justifiably used.

The value of the tests as clinical instruments is limited. The use of perceptual items, however finely the author breaks them down into subcategories, seems to provide a measure of perceptual adequacy rather than of intellectual capacity. The fact that perceptual adequacy and intellectual capacity are highly related in the normal hardly provides a basis for using one as the measure of the other, especially in the abnormal. Unless we are merely interested in a score, the diagnostic value of most tests of intellectual capacity comes from an analysis of the errors made and from observations made of the subject's attempts to deal with the task. Such analyses and observations are not forthcoming from the Matrices, hence nothing is known about what the subject is thinking when he is thinking wrong. For that matter, very little is known about what he is thinking when he is thinking right. That is, what does it signify to be able to break up designs into constituent parts, to find perceptual analogies, to complete a design, etc.? In the absence of developmental data concerning these aspects of perceptual adequacy, and their relation to other factors in intelligence, they remain theoretical constructs which might better serve the cause of perceptual research than psychometric testing.

Special groups such as the deaf, cerebral palsied, and individuals with communication disorders often are not easily tested with the standard procedures, and the Matrices will be helpful in establishing a mental level for them. However, the clinical usefulness of the Matrices as indicators of "process" in thinking is less than that of such tests as the *Leiter International Performance Scale* or the *Arthur Point Scale of Performance Tests,* where the clinician in addition to getting his score has opportunity to observe and make inferences about responses to a wide variety of tasks, many if not all of which have practical significance for life experiences even if they are not factorially pure.

The *Progressive Matrices (1947),* titled *Advanced Progressive Matrices* on the test booklet, was constructed with a view to evaluating "people of more than average intellectual capacity." Estimated percentile norms are available for the age range 11–40 for the 1947 Set 2. Reliability coefficients range from .76 to .91. Norms and technical data for the 1962 revision of Set 2 are not yet available. The validity of the 1947 test receives some favorable support from a study incorporated in the manual dealing with a comparison of advantaged and disadvantaged children with the expected differences occurring. The value of this test as a large scale screening device for identifying various levels of superior functioning remains unknown despite its use since 1943 when the original form was drafted for use by the War Officer Selection Boards in Great Britain.

A word about the manuals. The author seems to have combined in his manuals both something more and something less than what a manual should be. Much of the information offered might better be submitted as journal articles. Some of the information might better be offered not at all. Some prospective users might be confused to learn that a "board form" of the *Coloured Progressive Matrices* discussed in much detail is not commercially available, or that the working time for Set 2 of the *Advanced Progressive Matrices* "can be adjusted [from 15 minutes to an hour] to secure the type of score distribution one requires." In addition, as noted above, the manual for Advanced Set 2 does not yet cover the 1962 revision. Revision of the manuals is in order.

For reviews by Charlotte Banks, W. D. Wall, and George Westby, see 4:314; for reviews by Walter C. Shipley and David Wechsler of the 1938 edition, see 3:258; for a review by T. J. Keating, see 40:1417.

[491]
Purdue Non-Language Test. Grades 9–12 and adults; 1957–58; Forms A, B, ('57, 3 pages); preliminary manual ('58, 4 pages); $1.75 per 20 tests; 30¢ per specimen set of both forms; postage extra; 25(30) minutes; Joseph Tiffin, Alan Gruber, and Kay Inaba; Science Research Associates, Inc. *

JOHN D. HUNDLEBY, *Research Assistant Professor of Psychology, University of Illinois, Urbana, Illinois.*

Each item in the *Purdue Non-Language Test* consists of five designs or geometric shapes. The subject's task is to indicate which design is different from the other four. There are two parallel forms, A and B, both consisting of 48 items.

As presented by the publisher's 1963-1964 catalog, the specimen set contains a copy of both Forms A and B and a manual. On inspection, however, the manual is that published in March 1958, and designated at that time as a "preliminary manual." Further, the term "Experimental Form" appears on the specimen set package, but not on the test itself. This ambiguity is likely to be misleading to the user and needs to be corrected. For present purposes the test and manual will be evaluated as judged satisfactory by the authors and publishers for general distribution.

The manual is brief and overly concise. Thus norms for United States and Venezuelan high school students are given separately, while industrial supervisory personnel and civil service laborers are presented without national identification or further detail of group compositions. Another example is in the description of groups upon which reliability estimates were based. Here, two Cuban groups are described as "San Jose, Cuba (applicants), Rural" and "Havana, Cuba (applicants), Urban." "Applicants for what?" one may ask.

The section on norms occupies about one third of one page and is inadequate. To present test users with norms based on 77 cases (as for "U.S. High School"), 89 cases (for "Venezuelan High School"), 184 (for "Industrial Supervisory Personnel"), or 99 cases (for "Civil Service Laborers"), is clearly an overoptimistic use of normative procedures. Particularly is this true when *no information at all* is given on age, sex, grade level, socioeconomic class, or on any of the generally accepted ways in which normative populations are described. No information is presented suggesting the extent to which the normative groups may be regarded as representative of some larger population. Indeed if the U.S. and Venezuelan students came from single high schools without any attempt at sampling, it is impossible to judge the extent to which the reported differences may reflect discrepancies between high schools rather than between U.S. and Venezuelan children.

The *Purdue Non-Language Test* is described as "a 'culture fair' test designed to measure mental ability." It is stated that "since it consists entirely of geometric forms, there is evidence to show that it can be used effectively with persons having markedly different cultural or educational backgrounds." To describe a test as culture fair simply because geometric forms are used is somewhat hazardous, and indeed what little empirical evidence there is—the U.S. versus Venezuela comparison referred to above—is not supportive. Why such national differences should occur in a "culture fair" test is not even commented upon. Correlations with the *Adaptability Test* are reported of .65 for 184 industrial salaried employees and .55 for 99 laborers, and this appears to be the sole evidence that the test is a measure of general ability rather than of any particular specific ability (such as spatial relations) or combination of such abilities. No attempt was made to correlate the test with standard measures of roughly similar intent and no factor-analytic evidence is presented. The latter would appear to be mandatory in validating a general ability test of this type.

Equivalent forms reliabilities of this test range from .78 to .88, and internal consistency (usually odd-even) reliabilities from .90 to .93. These figures would be acceptable if it were not for the apparent assumption that this is a power test. With 48 items to be completed in 25 minutes (a rate of 32 seconds per item) this is questionable. If total score does include speed elements, then the reliability coefficients are likely to be too large, and certain rather undesirable implications appear for the test's validity. Unfortunately, no data are reported that would clear up this matter, and information on item difficulty level appears to be based upon the original pool of items from which both forms of the test were constructed. Presumably this original administration was untimed.

No mention of guessing is made in the manual and it would appear advisable to make appropriate additions to the administrator's instructions, and possibly to utilize appropriate correction formulas. Certainly if, as the reviewer suspects, this test may be speeded at least for groups of low educational background or ability, this problem becomes more acute.

This review, in summary, has been very critical of the *Purdue Non-Language Test*. In many ways the test falls short of generally accepted standards and at present there is not enough supportive evidence for the test user to prefer this over most other nonlanguage or culture fair tests that are available. If this test is to play any part in the future measurement of ability, then more research is necessary and a satisfactory pattern of correlation with other measures must be presented. Finally, a considerably revised and expanded manual with statistical information based upon a substantial normative sample is needed before this test can be recommended for general use.

BENJAMIN ROSNER, *Director, Test Development Division, Educational Testing Service, Princeton, New Jersey.*

Reviewing an experimental test presents major difficulties. Does one evaluate need, promise, or current status? And by what criteria? Present need? Conventional standards of test utility? The promise of further research? Or are experimental forms exempted from rigorous psychometric evaluation and, if so, for how long? When, specifically, are experimental editions no longer experimental? At the publisher's discretion? After some reasonable but arbitrarily imposed time limit? When experimentation ceases?

The case in point, the *Purdue Non-Language Test,* was published in 1958 as an experimental "culture fair" test of mental ability. In 1963, five years later, the review set contained the same preliminary manual and test materials. Is the test still experimental? The publisher apparently thinks so. But if so, where is the evidence of continued experimentation? Surely "experimental" denotes experimentation. Are we not, consequently, to anticipate periodic revision of the test manual? Or are we to regard the presence of unaltered experimental materials five years after initial publication as evidence of publisher disinterest? Or lack of faith? Or is the test to stand on its own?

Had I reviewed the test in 1958 I would have called attention to its gross inadequacies but I would probably have encouraged further research. Initially I would have questioned the need for another "culture fair" test if only because reliance on geometric forms duplicated more fully developed nonverbal instruments of similar constructs. The issue, however, is moot.

Secondly, I would have questioned the reliability data, particularly the odd-even versions, because of the speed factor that seems to permeate the task. Although each test form contains only 48 items, 25 minutes of testing time places a premium on speed for the intended examinee population. Moreover, although the more appropriate alternate form reliabilities of approximately .84 suggest minimally acceptable levels—certainly encouraging for experimental editions—these, too, are somewhat spurious for the data seem to have been derived from the sample providing the initial item statistics. At least this is not clear, for descriptions of the samples are rather fragmentary.

Next I would have underscored the need for predictive validity studies against appropriate academic and vocational criteria. There is some evidence of congruent validity in terms of correlations with the *Adaptability Test*. Since these data are encouraging, why weren't the "situational validity" tests carried out or reported? The manual almost suggests they were forthcoming.

Finally, I would have pointed to the woefully inadequate normative material. Not only are descriptions of the norming samples virtually absent, but the number of cases, ranging from 77 "U.S. High School" students to 184 "Industrial Supervisory Personnel," are obviously substandard.

In every regard, then, the experimental edition cannot stand on its own. It is, obviously, unacceptable for practical usage. If it is still experimental, the publishers must assume their experimental obligations to restore our faith.

[492]
★**Quantitative Evaluative Device.** Entering graduate students; 1959–62; also called QED; tests administered at college centers established by the author; "potential for quantitative sophistication"; Form D ('59, 8 pages); manual ('62, 4 pages); no data on reliability of present form; separate answer sheets must be used; tests rented only; rental fee: $1 per student, postpaid; IBM answer sheets must be purchased elsewhere; 50(60) minutes; R. E. Stake; [Lincoln Test Service]. *

REFERENCES
1. STAKE, ROBERT E. "A Non-Mathematical Quantitative Aptitude Test for the Graduate Level: The QED." *J Exp Ed* 31:81–3 S '62. * (PA 37:8280)

[493]
*__Quick-Scoring Group Test of Learning Capacity: Dominion Tests.__ Grades 7–9, 10–13 and adults; 1934–63; quick scoring edition of *Group Test of Learning Capacity: Dominion Tests* (see 5:341); Forms A, B; 2 levels; 2 editions; no data on reliability and validity; postage extra; 30(40) minutes; Department of Educational Research, Ontario College of Education, University of Toronto; distributed by Guidance Centre (manual and answer cards for *b* must be purchased from the Department of Educational Research). *

a) [HAND SCORING EDITION.] 1934–58; Forms A, B, ('58, 4 pages); 2 levels; separate answer sheets must be used; $1.75 per 25 tests; 20¢ per scoring key; 75¢ per complete specimen set.
 1) *Intermediate.* Grades 7–9; 1958; manual ('58, 4 pages).
 2) *Advanced.* Grades 10–13 and adults; 1955–58; manual ('58, 8 pages).
b) MACHINE-SCORING EDITION. 1962–63; Forms A, B, ('62, 6 pages); 2 levels: intermediate, advanced; manual ('63) in 2 parts: Parts 1 (6 pages), 2 (4 pages); separate answer cards must be used; $1.25 per 25 tests; 50¢ per 25 IBM answer cards (machine scoring through the Department of Educational Research only); 10¢ per manual; 20¢ per specimen set.

DONALD B. BLACK, *Professor of Education, University of Alberta, Edmonton, Alberta, Canada.*

The tests under review can best be appreciated by a study of their genealogy. The original test or rather the earliest form available to the reviewer was the 1934 *Group Test of Learning Capacity*. These were revised in 1939 (advanced) and 1950 (intermediate) to give omnibus editions of 75 items each. The 1939 manual was not available to the reviewer but the 1950 manual for the intermediate level gives Hoyt and parallel form reliabilities for this level of .93 based on a sample of urban students. The 1940 manual for the advanced level reports reliabilities of .81–.90. Revised norms for the two levels were produced in 1952 and 1954 for the intermediate and advanced levels, respectively. The 1950 (intermediate) and 1940 (advanced) reliability data are reproduced in the manuals containing these norms. The 1958 Quick-Scoring Edition represents a change from a consumable test booklet form to conventional multiple choice form with a separate answer sheet. This has meant, basically, only the provision of alternates for the mathematical items and a revising of the order of the stem for the number series items for the new edition. The 1963 Machine-Scoring Edition is a shortened version (70 items) of the 1958 editions. All items but three on the one form at one level examined by the reviewer are taken directly from the same form and level of the 1958 edition. In other words, the two tests under review are very similar in content to each other and to the earlier 1939 and 1950 Omnibus Editions.

No reliability data are reported for the current tests. Instead the reader is referred to the earlier manuals for the *Group Test of Learning Capacity* and the 1939 and 1950 data for the omnibus tests. No form to form or edition to edition data are available for the 1958 and 1963 editions. There is no evidence of item analyses. The alternates in the 1958 edition often violate good practice, presumably to ensure a proper distribution of correct responses. The 1963 edition has fewer instances of this and on the whole has a better general format.

The manuals for the 1958 edition note that Ontario pupils in 17 and 30 rural and urban schools were tested using the intermediate and advanced forms, respectively, in February 1957. "It was found that the 1952 [1954 for the advanced level] mental age equivalents were valid also for the Quick-Scoring [1958] Edition," and thus the earlier norms were used. The intermediate manual indicates these earlier (1952) norms were adjusted to give a mean IQ slightly higher than 100 for reasons of selection, a standard deviation of approximately 16, and a reasonably normal distribution. For the 2,500 cases of the 1952 norming sample, the mean IQ was 102.3; the standard deviation, 16.1; and the distribution of IQ's was normal. The advanced level 1954 norms are based on 13,468 students in grades 9 to 13 tested in the fall of 1953. No adult norming groups are defined nor is there any description of the adjustments of IQ's as in the intermediate level. However, a table of CA (months) adjustments is provided presumably to achieve the same end. The February 1957 testing with the 1958 edition contained no adults nor grade 13 students.

The procedure to obtain IQ's is the ratio method. The test scores are converted first to mental ages even though it has been adequately established that the use of this concept for the age ranges covered by these tests is highly suspect.

The 1963 edition norms, on the other hand, are based on a new norming population of a "representative" sample of Ontario students in grades 7–12. No evidence is given as to the basis on which the norming sample could be called representative nor are reliability and comparability of form data given. The norms for this test are reported in percentiles for each grade. It is interesting to note that the cover of the advanced level test booklet suggests the advanced form covers a grades 10 to 13 range. As noted, grade 12 is the highest level of norms provided. (The reader may be confused by the Ontario grade system in which all tests were normed and by grade 13 in particular. The latter could be best considered as college bound high school seniors.)

Several other comments should be directed to the manuals on points of administration. There is nothing to suggest to the student whether to guess or not, or that a correction for guessing will or will not be made, or that the best answer is to be selected. The Machine-Scoring Edition is so called because the manual directs use of a special IBM mark-sensing answer card. The Quick-Scoring Edition uses a special answer sheet which appears to be a conventional IBM mark-sensing answer sheet. However, a hand scoring key is provided. No mention is made of possible use of a scoring machine for these answer sheets. If the answer sheets provided with the specimen sets supplied for review are typical answer sheets, difficulty would be experienced in machine scoring because of poor cutting. It would seem that the publisher should provide answer sheets capable of machine scoring and that these should also be provided as an alternative to the IBM cards for the 1963 edition for those who have local machine scoring facilities and need not rely on the special facilities which are needed for the IBM cards and which are available only in Toronto.

Further, while the test items are generally typical of the type associated with single score or omnibus type IQ tests, there is nothing to suggest that these particular items have virtue for Canadian schools or disadvantage for American schools; there is no evidence that item analysis reflected any national differences from similar items in American tests. With 70 or 75 items to be attempted in 30 minutes, there obviously is a high speed factor in any score reported. No factorial weightings are reported in the manuals.

In summary, it would appear that the publishers could greatly assist the discriminating test consumer by even a cursory adherence to the suggestions of the Technical Recommendations.

GEORGE A. FERGUSON, *Professor of Psychology, McGill University, Montreal, Canada.*

Both tests are adaptations of the *Group Test of Learning Capacity: Dominion Tests.* They are composed of vocabulary, analogies, arithmetic reasoning, number sequence, classification, and related types of items commonly used in group tests of intelligence. The items have been carefully selected from earlier Dominion Tests. The user is assured that from a test construction viewpoint much technical skill has been exercised by the test authors.

The hand-scored Quick-Scoring Edition has essentially the same content as the Machine-Scoring Edition. The only difference of any consequence is that the former contains 75 and the latter 70 items. The Quick-Scoring Edition uses a separate answer sheet with a plastic stencil for hand scoring. The Machine-Scoring Edition uses an answer card with electrographic pencils. The Department of Educational Research, University of Toronto, through its Test Scoring and Item Analysis Section, will score the Machine-Scoring Edition and provide statistical data to the test user. The tests may also be scored locally by hand scoring answer keys provided in the manuals.

Norms for the Quick-Scoring Edition, advanced level, are based on over 13,000 secondary school students tested in Ontario in 1954. The norms provide mental age equivalents which, with chronological ages, may be used in the calculation of IQ's. A two-page nomograph is provided in the manual for converting raw score and chronological age to IQ. This appears to be a clumsy substitute for a very simple arithmetical calculation. Norms for the Quick-Scoring Edition, intermediate level, are the same as the 1952 norms for the Omnibus Edition of the intermediate level *Group Test of Learning Capacity: Dominion Tests.* The Machine-Scoring Edition was separately standardized in 1961–62 and percentile rank norms are based on about 1,000–3,000 Ontario pupils per grade.

No useful purpose is served by a discussion of either the validity or reliability of these tests. Although no data are provided in the manuals for the present tests, relevant data are available in the manuals of earlier editions of the *Group Tests of Learning Capacity.* Tests of this type have been widely used for many years, and their validity and reliability checked in many contexts.

On the whole these are well constructed tests of a conventional kind. No reasons exist to suppose that their usefulness for educational progress has diminished, or that their content has been superceded by some new and superior variety of test material.

[494]

Revised Beta Examination. Ages 16–59; 1931–57; revision of *Army Group Examination Beta* ('20); nonlanguage; 1 form ('35, 14 pages); revised manual ('57, 11 pages); norms for men only; $4.50 per 25 tests; 50¢ per specimen set; postpaid; French edition available; 15(30) minutes; 1946 revision by Robert M. Lindner and Milton Gurvitz; basic revision by C. E. Kellogg and N. W. Morton; Psychological Corporation. *

REFERENCES

1–4. See 40:1419.
5–9. See 3:259.
10–23. See 5:375.
24. ALPER, THELMA G., AND BORING, EDWIN G. "Intelligence-Test Scores of Northern and Southern White and Negro Recruits in 1918." *J Abn & Social Psychol* 39:471–4 O '44. * (*PA* 19:455)
25. GARRETT, HENRY E. "Comparison of Negro and White Recruits on the Army Tests Given in 1917–1918." *Am J Psychol* 58:480–95 O '45. * (*PA* 20:855)
26. MONTAGU, M. F. ASHLEY. "Intelligence of Northern Negroes and Southern Whites in the First World War." *Am J Psychol* 58:161–88 Ap '45. * (*PA* 19:2299)
27. MARCUSE, F. L., AND BITTERMAN, M. E. "Notes on the Results of Army Intelligence Testing in World War I." *Sci* 104:231–2 S 6 '46. * (*PA* 21:204)
28. PASTORE, NICHOLAS. "A Fallacy Underlying Garrett's Use of the Data of the Army Alpha and Beta Tests—A Comment." Letter. *Sci Mo* 69:279–80 O '49. * (*PA* 24:1145)
29. CUOMO, SYLVIA, AND MEYER, HERBERT H. "Validity Information Exchange, No. 8-19: D.O.T. Code 6-78.632, Floor Assembler." *Personnel Psychol* 8:270 su '55. *
30. NI, LIAN, AND HSIAO, SHIH-LANG. "A Study of Mental Declination With Aging Among the Retired Servicemen Tested in Nuan-Nuan Center." *Acta Psychologica Taiwanica* (1):9–47 N '58. * (*PA* 34:2849)
31. COHEN, LEONARD MARLIN. *The Relationship Between Certain Personality Variables and Prior Occupational Stability of Prison Inmates.* Doctor's thesis, Temple University (Philadelphia, Pa.), 1959. (*DA* 20:3375)
32. DOPPELT, JEROME E., AND SEASHORE, HAROLD G. "Psychological Testing in Correctional Institutions." *J Counsel Psychol* 6:81–92 sp '59. * (*PA* 34:6012)
33. PANTON, JAMES H. "Beta-WAIS Comparisons and WAIS Subtest Configurations Within a State Prison Population." *J Clin Psychol* 16:312–7 Jl '60. * (*PA* 36:2HD12P)
34. DURRETT, HAROLD L. "Validity Information Exchange, No. 14-03: D.O.T. Code 5-21.010, Continuous Miner Operator (Bituminous Coal Industry)." *Personnel Psychol* 14:453–5 w '61. *
35. COPPINGER, NEIL W.; BORTNER, RAYMAN W.; AND SAUCER, RAYFORD T. "A Factor Analysis of Psychological Deficit." *J Genetic Psychol* 103:23–43 S '63. * (*PA* 39:174)
36. TWAIN, DAVID C., AND BROOKS, EDWARD M. "A Comparison of Wechsler, Revised Beta and Otis Scores of Delinquents." *Brit J Criminol* 3:288–90 Ja '63. *

BERT A. GOLDMAN, *Associate Professor of Education, and Associate, Counseling Service, State University of New York at Albany, Albany, New York.*

In 1934, Kellogg and Morton published the *Revised Beta Examination* which was a revision of the *Army Group Examination Beta* developed during World War I. Following, in 1943, the authors prepared a revised manual. Three years later, 1946, Lindner and Gurvitz published a manual which described a procedure for converting Beta raw scores into IQ's resembling the scheme in the *Wechsler-Bellevue Intelligence Scale*. The present manual, revised in 1957 by Lindner and Gurvitz, is essentially the same as their 1946 edition and accompanies the original Kellogg and Morton *Revised Beta Examination* now some 30 years old. Apparently, the only major difference between the 1946 manual and the 1957 edition is the omission of the Kellogg-Morton standardization data from the latter. In place of this information a few reliability coefficients and correlations with other instruments have been added.

A paucity of statistical data is presented to support the authors' claim that the test is intended "to serve as a measure of general intellectual ability of persons who are relatively illiterate or who are non-English speaking." With the exception of two correlation coefficients, apparently all data are based upon the performance of white, male, adult prisoners at the U.S. Federal Penitentiary, Lewisburg, Pennsylvania.

The Lindner-Gurvitz standardization sample comprises 1,225 inmates of the Lewisburg penitentiary. Although the authors point out that these men were selected so that their education and socioeconomic status were in proportion to the 1940 census the fact is the sample is devoid of non-whites, females, and non-convicts. How closely does this sample represent the relatively illiterate or non-English speaking populations for whom the test is intended? Further, why was so *selected* a sample used? In lieu of an explanation, this reviewer assumes that such a captive group was used to effect a relatively easy task of standardization; but if this be the case, why should one run the risk of using unrepresentative norms merely for the convenience of the authors?

In an attempt to establish validity, two correlations are provided. One coefficient of .92 based upon 168 prisoners is reported between the *Revised Beta Examination* and the *Wechsler-Bellevue Intelligence Scale*. The second, a coefficient of .71 between the Beta and the *Otis Self-Administering Tests of Mental Ability*, utilized 198 prisoners. While the correlations are quite significant, especially the .92, additional studies involving a less restricted sample of subjects would add greatly to the notion that the test is a measure of general intelligence.

Reliability coefficients of .81 and .75 based, respectively, upon 199 and 104 prisoners are cited. They were obtained by correlating weighted scores on the three odd-numbered subtests with scores on the three even-numbered subtests. No rationale is provided for splitting the test in this fashion; nor is the reader told whether these coefficients embrace the split-half correction. The standard error of measurement was also determined for each of the two groups and found to be 4.8 and 4.3, respectively. The manual contains a third reliability coefficient of .90 which may be of dubious quality in that it was "estimated from intercorrelations of subtests." The authors provide no explanation for determining reliability in this fashion.

Intercorrelations among the six subtests ranging from .51 to .76 suggest that each subtest is far from measuring an independent factor. Correlations of subtests with the total weighted score range from .68 to .86.

Additional correlations reported by Bennett and Wesman in 1947 between the *Revised Beta Examination* and the *Hand-Tool Dexterity Test* (.36) and the *Tests of Mechanical Comprehension* (.56) are included in the manual, but owing to the content of the latter two instruments these correlations afford little if any support for validity of the *Revised Beta Examination* as a measure of intelligence. Likewise, little is added to the test's validity by including a few additional corelations ranging from .51 to .75 between Beta and the *PTI Oral Directions Test* and the verbal score on the *Wesman Personnel Classification Test*. Such correlations appear to do nothing more than pad the manual's dearth of statistical data.

It seems that ample time has passed during which a representative sample could have been secured for the purpose of building satisfactory norms; it is high time an item analysis of the test itself be conducted. Additional validity and reliability studies are equally in order. The statistical section of the present manual appears to contain nothing more than data helpful perhaps to those who would screen white, male adults at the U.S. Federal Penitentiary, Lewisburg, Pennsylvania; and at that, one must consider such data are more than 17 years old.

For reviews by Raleigh M. Drake and Walter C. Shipley, see 3:259; for reviews by S. D. Porteus and David Wechsler, see 40: 1419.

[495]
*SRA Tests of Educational Ability, 1962 Edition.** Grades 4–6, 6–9, 9–12; 1957–63; tests identical with those published in 1957 and 1958 except for minor changes in format and directions; 4–5 scores: language, reasoning, quantitative, total, (grades 4–6 only) nonreading total; IBM; 1 form; 3 levels; revised profile ('62, 1 page); technical supplement, third edition ('63, c1957–63, 41 pages); separate answer sheets must be used; $7 per 20 tests; $7 per 100 IBM answer sheets; 50¢ per scoring stencil; $1 per technical supplement; 75¢ per specimen set of any one level; scoring service available; fee: 25¢ per student; test materials may also be rented with either IBM or DocuTran answer sheets and scored by the publisher; fee: 45¢ per student; postage extra; L. L. Thurstone and Thelma Gwinn Thurstone; Science Research Associates, Inc. *
a) GRADES 4–6. 1958–63; 1 form ('62, c1958, 14 pages); revised manual ('62, c1958–62, 33 pages); 26(52) minutes.
b) GRADES 6–9. 1958–63; 1 form ('62, c1958, 13 pages); revised manual ('62, c1958–62, 32 pages); 42(67) minutes.
c) GRADES 9–12. 1957–63; 1 form ('62, c1957, 11 pages); revised manual ('62, c1958–62, 26 pages); 27(45) minutes.

REFERENCES
1. NORTH, ROBERT D. "An Appraisal of the SRA Tests of General Ability Based on Independent School Results." *Ed Rec B* 78:68–76 F '61. *

J. STANLEY AHMANN, *Professor of Psychology and Head of the Department, Colorado State University, Fort Collins, Colorado.*

As in the case of the 1958 edition, the 1962 edition of the *SRA Tests of Educational Ability* (TEA) provides "three aptitude measures for use by the teacher and counselor in judging a student's potentiality for success in school." Language, reasoning, and quantitative scores are available, and are usually combined to obtain a total score which can then be converted to an IQ score or a percentile rank. The scores are available for all three levels of the TEA. In addition, the first level (for grades 4–6) provides a total nonreading score. This score is based entirely on test items containing a picture or a drawing as the item stem.

Accompanying the three levels of the TEA is a technical supplement. This is the third edition of such a supplement and contains highly useful information. In addition, the technical supplement is well written. Teachers and counselors should find it an easy task to obtain the information about validity, reliability, and norms which they wish to have from this supplement.

FORMAT. The format of the tests is extremely well designed. The printing is attractive. In all cases the directions to the test administrator for the process of administration, scoring, and interpretation of scores seem to be as complete as needed.

The most striking feature of the format is the manner in which color is used. Each of the three levels is given a distinctive color, namely, blue for the first level (grades 4–6), green for the second level (grades 6–9), and red for the third level (grades 9–12). The use of the assigned color is completely consistent throughout the manual of directions for the tests of that level, the test itself, the answer sheets, whether IBM or DocuTran, and the keys for hand scoring. In the case of the manual of directions, the edges of important pages which give specific directions for the administration of the test are marked with the appropriate color. In addition, throughout the manual key sentences and headings are printed in the color appropriate for the level. Certainly the consistent use of a single color for a single level should simplify the task of the teacher as he uses that level and should minimize the likelihood of confusing the various materials provided for each level. Multi-level test batteries of all kinds might well profit from the same careful use of color as applied by the publishers of TEA.

VALIDITY AND RELIABILITY. Considerable attention has been given the questions related to the degree of validity and reliability of the TEA. The emphasis of the presentation is changed somewhat since the 1958 edition included normative profiles in its technical supplement. The use of such profiles automatically raised considerations with regard to the intercorrelations between the language, reasoning, and quantitative scores. In addition, the reliability of these scores had to be interpreted in view of this proposed use of the scores. Reviewers of the 1958 edition often felt that the intercorrelations were somewhat high and the reliabilities of the three test scores somewhat low to justify such normative profiles. All mention of normative profiles has been eliminated from the 1962 technical supplement, thereby simplifying the presentation of validity and reliability data since the total score is rec-

Revised Beta Examination

ommended as the score which is generally most useful.

Correlations between the total score of the TEA and the total scores of other common tests of mental ability are found to be quite high. For example, these correlations with various levels of the Kuhlmann-Anderson range from .69 to .82. In the case of the *California Test of Mental Maturity*, the correlations range from .66 to .79. In the case of the publisher's *Tests of General Ability* they range between .51 and .78.

Predictive validity data were determined on the basis of samples of students from the western, midwestern, and northeastern sections of the United States. Correlation coefficients between the three subtest scores and the total score were found for high school grade-point averages and scores on the *SRA Achievement Series*. The length of time which elapsed between the administration of the TEA and the determination of the criterion value was relatively short. Evidently it did not exceed two months. The correlations are very high. They range from .57 to .72 for the lowest level, from .68 to .84 for the middle level, and from .68 to .80 for the highest level.

Only one study is mentioned in the technical supplement with regard to the use of multiple regression techniques to predict some meaningful criterion on the basis of a number of part scores from the TEA. Multiple correlation coefficients were computed between the three TEA subscores and grade-point averages and composite scores on three achievement batteries. The authors conclude that "a comparison of the multiple coefficients of correlation and the product-moment coefficients of correlation for the unweighted sum of the raw scores indicates that, in general, little would be gained by weighting the subtest scores in accordance with the regression coefficients."

The coefficients of reliability for the total score are quite acceptable. Typically these values exceeded .90. The standard error of measurement for the IQ scores derived from the total score did not exceed four IQ units in any of the determinations. The authors quite properly point out that "this precision compares favorably with that attained in individually administered tests of intelligence." The foregoing findings were derived from samples of students drawn from grades 6 through 12 only. In the case of grades 4 through 6, the reliability is slightly less.

THE STANDARDIZATION SAMPLE. The authors made a serious attempt to draw a suitable standardization sample. Although recognizing that norms for intelligence measures are characteristically age oriented rather than grade oriented, the authors decided to base their sample on those individuals still in public school at the time of the standardization testing. A nationwide sampling for standardization took place in April 1962, and was based on a directory of public secondary schools compiled by the United States Office of Education. Three preliminary sample lists of secondary schools were drawn. These schools were stratified on the basis of regional location and school size. Secondary schools in the initial sample were contacted first. If the school could not participate, its counterpart in the second sample was contacted. If the second secondary school could not participate, then its counterpart in the third sample was contacted. Elementary schools were identified by asking the cooperation of the feeder school closest to the participating secondary school. A total of 20,338 pupils in 64 schools representing 25 school systems participated in the standardization.

For the purpose of drawing the sample, the United States was divided into eight regions. Due to the fact that some secondary schools were unable to cooperate, some regions were under-represented, and others therefore are over-represented. The two regions under-represented to the greatest degree were the mideast (Delaware, District of Columbia, Maryland, New Jersey, New York, and Pennsylvania) and the southwest (Arizona, New Mexico, Oklahoma, and Texas). The three areas over-represented to the greatest degree are the plains (Iowa, Kansas, Minnesota, Missouri, Nebraska, South Dakota, and North Dakota), the Rocky Mountains (Colorado, Idaho, Montana, Utah, and Wyoming), and New England (Connecticut, Maine, Massachusetts, New Hampshire, Rhode Island, and Vermont).

It is not surprising that the standardization sample reveals considerable age variation within each grade level. Also, there is a sharp drop in the number of students tested in the eleventh grade as compared with the tenth grade. The fact that, in most states, school attendance is no longer mandatory in the eleventh grade and thereafter is no doubt the reason for this phenomenon.

Table 12 of the technical supplement shows a careful comparison of the proportions of pupils in the standardization sample within three months of a given birthday for the TEA and within one month of a given birthday for the Stanford-Binet (1937) as distributed by grade. Except for grades 11 and 12 the proportion of older students in each grade is almost identical for both samples. The 1937 Binet sample had a higher proportion of younger children within each grade.

Since it is impossible to obtain an unbiased age sampling through the use of school systems, the authors took steps to adjust for the bias in determining the IQ norms. Based on the reports of four earlier investigations, estimates were made of the expected mean IQ for each of grades 4–12.

SUMMARY. The *SRA Tests of Educational Ability* are carefully designed and described tests of educational ability. The administration of the tests is not difficult, and the time required is relatively short. Considerably more data are available about the reliability, validity, and norms of these tests than was true in the case of the 1958 edition, and one can safely assume that additional data in large quantity will be made available in the future.

Although the normative profiles of TEA are not useful, there is much to recommend these tests provided the need of the individual selecting the tests is for a single score representing scholastic aptitude. This score is then to be used primarily in a predictive validity sense. In other words, anticipations are to be made of future academic success. The tests have a high educational loading and hence correlate very highly with common criterion measures such as grade-point averages and achievement test scores. In summary, these tests should be of value to public school teachers and guidance counselors within the framework of formal education.

JOHN E. HORROCKS, *Professor of Psychology, The Ohio State University, Columbus, Ohio.*

The 1962 standardization of the TEA is based on an April testing of 20,338 students enrolled in 64 schools representing 25 school systems scattered broadly over the United States. Representativeness of the normative sample was achieved by a stratified (regional location and school size) random drawing of schools from the United States Office of Education *Directory of Public Secondary Schools, 1958–59*. The random sample was supplemented by elementary and junior high schools feeding into the selected schools. Standardization subjects for each of the grades 4 through 12 contained in the total normative sample ranged from a low of 1,661 for grade 12 to a high of 3,282 for grade 9. Eight regions of the United States were represented, although unavailability of selected schools in some regions has loaded the sample with some regional inequalities. Regional weighting was not attempted to compensate for such bias since it was felt that weighting would only serve to magnify rather than to reduce the bias. It would appear, however, that the regional bias is not serious and that the TEA 1962 norms, as compared to those of other similar measures, are both reasonably representative and numerically adequate. Obviously no normative sample is perfect and a question could be raised as to the comprehensiveness of norms representing 25 school districts and 20,388 cases even when the selection was made on a stratified random basis. Latest data on the TEA are provided by the third edition of a technical supplement carrying the date 1963. Each of the three levels of the TEA is provided with a well written manual giving explicit administration and scoring directions.

The purpose of the TEA is cited as that of providing measures of "aptitude for schoolwork," which places it directly in the tradition of those tests which approach intelligence through an analysis of an individual's ability to learn as evidenced by his acquisition of the skills and knowledges learned in school. While the TEA is defined by its authors as an academic aptitude test, the possibility of converting the total scores into an IQ makes it necessary to evaluate it as a general line measure of intelligence. The concept of IQ dies hard, but it would appear that elimination of the possibility of deriving IQ ratios would have emphasized the status of the TEA as an academic aptitude measure and would have avoided the possible abuses of interpretation so often accorded the IQ in the public schools and in parents' aspirations. The three subscores, language, reasoning, and quantitative, fall short of the more diagnostically useful factors of the earlier Thurstone tests, but do represent an expansion of the L and Q scores of the old ACE. Actually, TEA, which is an outgrowth of the *SRA Primary Mental Abilities,* really represents nothing new in intelligence testing. Its items taken out of context are typical of the kinds of items perennially appearing on measures of intelligence since the days of the Army Alpha and Beta and the earlier work of the Thurstones. Perhaps the TEA can be thought of as striking a middle ground between a multi-factor or differential analysis and the single score global approach of some of the earlier measures of intelligence following World War I. It is unfortunate that there have been so few innovations in intelligence testing since 1917. Newer tests such as the TEA can only justify their presence and selection over similar existing measures if they offer something new and better—something that the TEA has really failed to do. It is a good test as such tests go and has been well worked up, but it is a fair question to ask why it appeared in the first place. The 1963 manual points to the possibly "unique contribution" of its part scores "when multiple-regression techniques are applied in order to predict some meaningful criterion," but cites only one preliminary study in support of such application.

Validity of the TEA is cited in terms of grade-point average and scores on the *SRA Achievement Series.* Grade-point average correlations with TEA total scores range from .69 to .73 depending on the level, with language scores showing a higher relationship (.67 to .69) than do either reasoning or quantitative scores (.45 to .66). SRA achievement composite scores correlate .72 with TEA 4–6 total scores, .84 with TEA 6–9 total scores and .80 with TEA 9–12 total scores. The part score intercorrelations do not exceed .66 at any level, but do not go lower than .36 in any case. TEA correlations with other intelligence tests range from .51 to .82 for the TEA total score, .59 to .75 for the L score, .42 to .67 for the R score, and .24 to .81 for the Q score.

In general, while TEA represents nothing new in intelligence testing it is a good example of its type and should prove as satisfactory as any other available group measure of general intelligence. More validity information would be helpful, and the technical manual could present its validity, reliability, and background information in a somewhat more coherent style, particularly aimed at teachers who will be the primary consumers of the test.

J Counsel Psychol 6:249 f '59. Laurence Siegel. * Each battery includes only those tests which correlate substantially with school success. Thus TEA is not particularly suitable when the aim of testing is to secure an estimate of ability apart from the influence of formal educational experiences. The series emphasizes power rather than speed, and the difficulty gradient is rather steep. It follows then, that although TEA will identify pupils of unusually low ability, it will not discriminate as well between such pupils as it will at the middle and upper ability levels. Finally, the series does not strive for score stability over a period of time in the sense that IQ measures strive for stability. The referrent in establishing TEA norms was grade level rather than age level. Consequently, this battery is not suitable as a measure of "brightness" relative to the population at large of a given age. The foregoing statements are neither criticism nor deficiencies of TEA. *

For reviews by Joshua A. Fishman, William B. Michael, and E. A. Peel of the 1957–58 edition of c, *see 5:377.*

[496]
★[SRA] Tests of General Ability. Grades kgn–2, 2–4, 4–6, 6–9, 9–12; 1959–60, c1957–60; 3 scores: information, noncultural reasoning, total; IBM for grades 4–12; Form A ('59, except for tests for grades 4–12 which are copyrighted 1957); 5 levels; $1 per technical report ('60, 39 pages); $2.50 per complete specimen set; postage extra; tests for grades 4–12 may be rented; fee (45¢ per student) includes scoring service; Spanish edition available; (35–45) minutes; John C. Flanagan; Science Research Associates, Inc. *
a) GRADES KGN–2. 12 pages; manual ('59, 19 pages); $3.20 per 20 tests; 50¢ per specimen set.
b) GRADES 2–4. Details same as for grades kgn–2.
c) GRADES 4–6. 15 pages; manual ('59, 21 pages); separate answer sheets must be used; $4.25 per 20 tests; $5 per 100 IBM scorable answer sheets; 50¢ per scoring stencil; 75¢ per specimen set.
d) GRADES 6–9. Details same as for grades 4–6 except: manual ('59, 25 pages).
e) GRADES 9–12. Details same as for grades 4–6 except: manual ('59, 19 pages).

JOHN E. HORROCKS, *Professor of Psychology, The Ohio State University, Columbus, Ohio.*

Equating general ability, general intelligence, and "basic ability to learn" as the same thing, the TOGA series provides a scale of equal units for five consecutive grade levels. That intelligence and ability to learn, if not exactly interchangeable concepts, are at least so closely related that an individual's ability to learn offers a good approach to the measurement of his intelligence is nothing new to ability testing. Numerous measures of intelligence have been described by their authors as well as by others as measures of learning ability—their difference consists in the kinds of learning experiences stressed and the kinds of items selected as most likely to offer adequate measures of that learning. TOGA represents a relatively new departure by attempting to eliminate, or at least place less stress upon, school learned skills such as reading, writing, and arithmetic. For that reason TOGA should offer a fairer testing context for those who, for one reason or another, have had limited or atypical opportunities to learn.

All TOGA test items at all levels are multiple choice and are pictorial in form. Two classes of items are represented: those which require reasoning on the part of the examinee and those which require information, vocabulary, and concepts. Information required, particularly at the younger levels, is of the kind ordinarily gained outside of the classroom, and stress is placed upon application rather than upon knowledge accumulation. Eight kinds of information items are included: (a) recognition of a pictured object when it is named, (b) recognition of an object from its classification, (c) recognition of an object on the basis of its similarity to another object, (d) recognition of an object's symbolic status, (e) selection of a picture as representative of an abstract concept, (f) selection of an object which involves a concept determining its use, (g) selection of an object as representative of the application of a principle, and (h) selection of an object depicting an element basic to an idea or a social institution. Content settings for information items include home, community, nature and recreation, science, and social science. Reasoning items present five line drawings, four of which are constructed on the basis of a specific rule, the fifth being different in that the rule does not apply. Speed has been eliminated in determining information performance and has been minimized for the reasoning section as a way, according to the author, of providing "'purer' measures of information depth and reasoning power." The question here is the advisability of de-emphasizing speed as an aspect of intellectual functioning. In life, behavior takes place under time conditions and an individual's effectiveness is often judged in terms of his "alertness" or ability to respond quickly. Insofar as speed is actually an aspect of real life effective functioning it would appear to beg the issue to eliminate it under the excuse of "power" in a measure designed to assess an individual's capacity to function in the cognitive domain.

Preliminary tryouts of TOGA items took place in 22 public and parochial schools in the Pittsburgh area and items included at the various levels in the final forms had to meet three criteria: (a) internal consistency as demonstrated by a correlation of "about" .40 or better with other items of the same type at all levels, (b) item difficulty figures which showed a trend of increase with respondents' age, and (c) a difficulty range between 30 and 70 per cent for the middle grade of the level at which the item was placed. Norms are based on 8,041 students enrolled in 40 schools in 20 school systems located in 12 different states. With the exception of Texas (Austin and Bryan) southern and southwestern states are not included in the normative sample, nor are the states in New England and the northwest. A more complete normative picture is needed if TOGA is to find defensible use as a nationally applicable test, although its normative background is already superior to some measures of intelligence which have been on the market considerably longer.

Since TOGA is a relatively new test (1957) potential users will have to depend upon reliability and validity information supplied by the very adequate technical report provided for users of the test. The report cites 20 reliability studies of TOGA total scores, with coefficients ranging for the various levels from .77 to .90. Correlations cited (19 studies) between TOGA total scores and those of other intelligence tests vary with the level being tested but range from a low of .41 (TOGA 6–9 level and Kuhlmann-Anderson) to a high of .80 (TOGA 6–9 and Kuhlmann-Anderson). Correlations with various measures of achievement tend to cluster between .50 and .60 and range from .38 to .81. Correlations between TOGA part scores (10 studies) ranged from .25 to .67, and part score split-half reliabilities (20 studies) ranged from .69 to .83. Part score correlations with other intelligence and achievement measures present about the same picture as that provided by the total score. In general TOGA Part 1 (information) scores appear to relate most closely to Thurstone's verbal comprehension factor, and Part 2 (reasoning) scores to his reasoning factor.

TOGA is a promising, carefully constructed general measure of verbal intelligence whose author has provided excellent quantitative background information for prospective users. Further and more representative normative data are needed as well as independent data on reliability and validity. The attempt to eliminate school centered information in writing test items is a particularly strong feature, but this reviewer would question the de-emphasis of the speed factor in a general line intelligence test. Such de-emphasis, insofar as it is tenable at all, would appear more appropriate in a school learning centered academic aptitude measure.

RICHARD E. SCHUTZ, *Professor of Education, and Director, Testing Service, Arizona State University, Tempe, Arizona.*

This test is graphic proof that the technology involved in the production of general ability tests has achieved an unprecedented level of sophistication. Major test publishers have facilities at their disposal to produce a complete intelligence test series with minimal effort and expense. These technical procedures can be counted on to produce a new test that will do almost, if not everything, that currently available tests do and will have gimmick appeal for a specified audience. Find a name that has acrostic characteristics with positive evaluative connotations, produce it in an artistic package, and you have an attractive seller. Although these reproductive efforts increase the population of test instruments, the desirability of such a population explosion is questionable.

The *Tests of General Ability* (TOGA) were "designed to provide measures of basic learning ability (general intelligence) without the use of test materials that are explicitly dependent upon school-learned skills such as reading, writing, and arithmetic." This is an accurate descriptive statement. Each form of the five levels of the tests contains two parts. Part 1 is composed of information items. Each item presents five pictured choices. The examinee is required to mark the drawing that best meets the specifications read orally by the examiner. The items sample a wide range of content. They are intended to test "the individual's ability to grasp meanings, recognize relationships, and understand the basic concepts and underlying principles of our natural and social environment." The K–2 and 2–4 levels include 35 items. The upper levels include 45 items.

Part 2 is composed of figure relationship items designed to test the examinee's abstract reasoning skill. Each item presents five line drawings of geometric forms. "Four of the drawings are constructed on the basis of a specific rule. The remaining figure is different; the rule does not apply." The examinee is required to select the figure representing the exception to the rule. The K–2 and 2–4 levels include 28 items; the upper levels, 40 items. The test as a whole requires 35 to 45 minutes.

The claim is made that Part 2 of the test is culture fair: "Part 2 avoids any cultural content * This part of the test presents an equal challenge to all children regardless of their cultural backgrounds." Herein lies the special appeal of the tests. "These tests are designed to provide a relatively fair measure of intelligence for all individuals, even those who have had atypical opportunities to learn."

No data are presented to support this culture fair validity claim. Rather, the validity of the tests is defended on a definition basis: "The validity of the TOGA series rests primarily on its definition of intelligence as basically involving information (including verbal concepts) and reasoning abilities, and its emphasis on test materials that do not require school-learned skills."

It would have been a straightforward task to check the claim that "the following types of students possessing *good general intelligence,* but *poor educational achievement* can be expected to obtain high scores on one or both parts of the *Tests of General Ability*" (italics in original). These groups include "children who may not have had the usual amount of schooling....who come from home environments where there are bilingual or other language problems....who attend schools in which the quality of instruction is clearly deficient....who come from homes where learning opportunities are limited because of parental neglect, parental illness, or other factors." By administering TOGA and some other commonly used test of general intelligence, it could easily have been determined whether any or all of the groups specified actually receive higher scores on TOGA. No such data are presented, however. A suggestive set of descriptive statistics are hidden away in a table of TOGA normative equivalence to other IQ tests. The mean IQ's for "a low-income area public school in New York City" at grade 6 are 80.5 on TOGA and 84.2 on the Otis Beta.

The accessory materials make no reference whatsoever to predictive validity. But the concurrent validity coefficients and other external correlations that are presented in the technical report suggest that TOGA scores function in much the same way as other general intelligence test scores. For example, the correlations of the TOGA total score with 19 other intelligence test scores range from .41 to .80 with a median of .62. The correlations of the TOGA total score with various achievement test scores are of the same order, ranging from .39 to .81 with a median of .58. The correlations with teacher grade averages range from .38 to .65 with a median of .49. These correlations are all in line with what one would anticipate for a conventional group intelligence test.

Neither does the pattern of part score correlations support the overall TOGA rationale. The median correlation of each of the parts with 10 other intelligence test scores is .59 for Part 1 and .55 for Part 2. The correlations with achievement test scores are of the same magnitude, with Part 1 correlating consistently higher than Part 2. The widest discrepancy in the part score correlations is found with the *SRA Reading Record,* where Part 1 has a median correlation of .70 versus .50 for Part 2.

Among the lowest correlations presented for the part scores are those between the part scores themselves at various grade levels. The coefficients range from .25 to .67, with a median of .43. These coefficients indicate that the two parts of the test sample nonoverlapping response classes. In fact, the low magnitude of the correlations calls to question the rationale for deriving a single IQ based on the total number of correct responses to the test as a whole.

By and large, the raw score standard deviations of Part 1 are higher than those of Part 2, indicating that the information items in Part 1 contribute more heavily to the IQ than the figural reasoning items in Part 2. This is particularly true for the high school level of the tests where the standard deviations run 7.5 versus 4.9 at grade 9 and 8.0 versus 5.5 at grade 12.

The steps in the production of TOGA are clearly outlined in the technical report. A blueprint is presented for each part of the test classifying the items in Part 1 by function and content area and those in Part 2 by function. Only summaries are shown for each level, however, so that it is impossible to cross check the classification item by item. On the three independent classifications I made, there were a number of discrepancies between my totals and those shown in the report. Lacking more detailed information from the TOGA report, it is impossible to clarify the reasons for the discrepancies.

A similar superficiality is evident with respect to the description of the item analysis procedures. While the statistical procedures involved in making the analysis are described in good detail, no information is given concerning the size or the characteristics of the examinees involved in the analysis other than that they were "at all levels from kindergarten through the twelfth grade." It is difficult to evaluate the adequacy of the item analysis without further information concerning the representativeness of the population and sample involved.

The IQ norms for the tests were derived by first equating TOGA raw scores to grade equivalents on the *SRA Achievement Series* in grades 1–9 and to the *Iowa Tests of Educational Development* in grades 9–12 using equipercentile procedures. The grade equivalents were then converted to mental age equivalents by adding a constant of 5.2, the average age at entrance to kindergarten. "At the higher levels, extrapolated equivalent mental ages were obtained in accordance with the usual practice." (I assume that this is a euphemistic way of saying someone arbitrarily extended the penciled curve with a deft twist of the wrist.) Ratio IQ's were then computed and are presented in the manual for each level along with the grade equivalents.

The manuals create the erroneous impression that the IQ's and grade expectancies are two independent scores: "The tests provide two scores for each child: an IQ and a grade expectancy score. The grade expectancy score shows the school level of the child's ability." Actually the grade expectancy scores represent nothing more than the IQ numerators. Moreover, the examples given in the manual in connection with the instructions for reading the norms table contain highly misleading statements. For example, a fourth grade pupil, "Linda" is shown to have an IQ of 114 and a "grade expectancy" of 5.2. The manual states: "Although Linda is in the fourth grade the test also shows that she is capable of doing school work as advanced as the first half of the fifth grade." "Joe" is in the sixth grade and has an IQ of 133 with a "grade expectancy" of 9.8. "The *Tests of General Ability* show that Joe has a very superior IQ. Although Joe is in the sixth grade, the test also shows that he is capable of doing school work as advanced as the last half of the ninth grade." An unsophisticated user could do serious damage to a child if he attempted to generalize this interpretation to his own situation.

The entire standardization of the tests involved a very modest total of 8,041 students from 40 schools in 20 school systems. Each of the schools completed a descriptive questionnaire, but no data concerning their responses are presented beyond the statement that "the procedure was found to be effective in providing a group of schools and school systems which yielded a reasonably representative sample of the nation's students." How the completion of a questionnaire could accomplish this highly desirable objective is not specified. No information is given concerning the number of grades or students tested in each school nor the criteria for their selection. Norms interlock studies were conducted in two individual schools. A norms continuity study was conducted in a single school. The equating of adjacent levels was based on samples ranging from 475 to 594 students.

Despite these small and inadequately described samples, TOGA norms appear to be fairly comparable to those of other IQ tests with respect to mean scores. TOGA IQ standard deviations, however, run consistently higher than those of other tests. This greater variability is an important consideration, particularly in testing at the extremes of the IQ scale.

Split-half and Kuder-Richardson 21 reliability coefficients are presented for the total and part scores. Total score split-half reliability ranges from .80 to .90 with a median of .87. K-R reliabilities run .01 to .05 points lower with a median coefficient of .83. The part score reliabilities hold up reasonably well, with median split-half coefficients of .84 for Part 1 and .80 for Part 2 and K-R 21 coefficients of .80 and .77. While not spectacularly high in comparison with other tests, the coefficients are at least minimally respectable.

Turning to practical considerations, the tests are attractively printed. Although some of the pictured objects are rather small, the detail is not emphasized and should be well within the range of the normally sighted child. The directions for administering the tests are clear. However, a good deal is left to the examiner's discretion, particularly in Part 1. "In general, specific instructions are to be read only once, but the examiner must use judgment in following such a rule. It is permissible to repeat instructions if it appears that the pupils have not understood them." Standardizing the timing of the items in Part 1 constitutes a problem. The routine is: read the item, pause 2 seconds, repeat the item, pause 5 seconds. The examiner is instructed to do the timing by counting "slowly to yourself." Even in Part 2, where there is a 15-minute time limit, the instructions to the examiner leave room for variability in interpretation: "Remind the pupils once or twice during the test to work as quickly as they can * It is essential that they do not stop concentrating on the test or become restless." Thus, the examiner load in monitoring the tests is reasonably heavy compared to other group intelligence tests. With the wide availability of tape recorders in the modern school, the publishers might give thought to tape recording the directions. This would not only relieve the teacher of a burdensome chore but would standardize the test conditions.

Separate IBM 805 machine or hand scoring answer sheets are used for the upper levels beginning at 4–6. For K–2 and 2–4 the keyed responses are printed in the manual with the suggestion that "the teacher make a key in a test booklet to help in scoring the tests more quickly." This is not very adequate service. Strip keys could easily be provided which would reduce the probability of error both in the preparation of the keys and their use in scoring and would also save the teacher's time.

Altogether, TOGA appears to be new wine in old bottles. Although the application of modern psychometric brewing processes has yielded a series which has most of the same characteristics as its related ancestors, one should not expect the results of the test to be

SRA Tests of General Ability

any more beneficially intoxicating than those of predecessor group intelligence tests.

J Counsel Psychol 8:91–2 sp '61. Laurence Siegel. * Flanagan's TOGA is particularly well-tailored (oops!) to intellectual assessment when opportunities for formal schooling have been deficient. Beyond this, brevity, technical quality, and soundness of rationale appear to commend it for wide use as an all-purpose measure of general intelligence. The utility of TOGA will be further enhanced when two of its current deficiencies are rectified. First, the absence of reported predictive validities, and of any mention of the necessity for such studies, is disappointing in an instrument of otherwise good quality. Second, since alternate forms of the series are not yet available, group administration in cramped quarters and readministration for the purpose of score verification in suspect cases is impeded.

[497]

★Safran Culture Reduced Intelligence Test. Grades 1–6; 1960–62; 1 form ('60, 42 pages); mimeographed manual ('62, 9 pages); mimeographed instructions for group administration ['61, 6 pages]; mimeographed instructions for individual administration ['61, 1 page]; mimeographed tentative norms ['62, 1 page]; separate answer sheets must be used; 43¢ per test; $1.50 per 100 mimeographed answer sheets; postage extra; (30–45) minutes; C. Safran; the Author. *

REFERENCES
1. SAFRAN, C. "An Introduction to the Safran Culture Reduced Intelligence Test and Some Reports on Its Validity From Current Studies." *Alberta J Ed Res* 9:36–44 Mr '63. * (PA 37:8274)

[498]

*Schrammel General Ability Test. Grades 9–17; 1953–59; based in part upon *Army Group Examination Alpha* and revisions; IBM; Forms A ('53), B ('55), C ('56), D ('57), (6 pages); manual ('59, 9 pages); $1.50 per 25 tests; separate answer sheets may be used; 85¢ per 25 IBM answer sheets; 30¢ per set of either hand or machine scoring stencils; postage extra; 35¢ per specimen set, postpaid; 50(60) minutes; H. E. Schrammel; Bureau of Educational Measurements. *

For a review by Henry E. Garrett, see 5:381.

[499]

★Secondary Verbal Tests. Ages 11-0 to 13-6, 13-0 to 15-6; 1960–62; 2 levels; 8s. per 12 tests; 9d. per single copy; 1s. per manual for *a*; prices include purchase tax; postage extra; Valerie Land and Olive Wood (*a*); published for the National Foundation for Educational Research in England and Wales; Newnes Educational Publishing Co. Ltd. *

a) SECONDARY VERBAL TEST 1. Ages 11-0 to 13-6; 1960; 1 form ('60, 8 pages]; manual ['60, 7 pages]; 40(45) minutes.
b) SECONDARY VERBAL TEST 2. Ages 13-0 to 15-6; 1962; 1 form ['62, 8 pages]; no manual; no data on reliability and validity; no norms; 45(50) minutes.

STANLEY NISBET, *Professor of Education, University of Glasgow, Glasgow, Scotland.* [Review of Test 1.]

This is a well composed, clearly printed group intelligence test, designed for use in the first two years of secondary schools in England. The manual claims that the test measures "general scholastic ability" for purposes of classification, but, rather strangely perhaps, insists that it "should not be regarded as providing in any way a measure of capacity for learning." The items seem to be sound, although it is surprising, especially in a test with this title, to find so many which involve juggling with the positions of letters and figures and so few which involve the understanding of straightforward sentences or passages. As for minor flaws or ambiguities, the reviewer thinks items 1, 4, 35, 53, 54, and 76 might possibly be improved.

Although no limitation of use to the upper ranges of ability (e.g., to use in English grammar schools) is suggested in the manual, the table of norms shows clearly that the test discriminates much better at the upper end. The median child in the 11-0 age group scores only 12 points out of 90, and even at the top end of the table the median child in the 13-6 age group scores less than half the total. For use within the prescribed ages, therefore, one would hesitate to recommend the test to English secondary modern or comprehensive schools if good differentiation in the lower reaches was desired.

In short, this is a useful and soundly constructed test, easy to administer and well standardized, but it differentiates better among the abler children than it does among the less able.

[500]

Ship Destination Test. Grades 9 and over; 1955–56; general reasoning; IBM; Form A ('55, 3 pages); manual ('56, 3 pages); separate answer sheets must be used; $2.50 per 25 tests; 15¢ per single copy; 5¢ per IBM answer sheet; $1 per scoring stencil; 35¢ per manual; postage extra; 15(20) minutes; Paul R. Christensen and J. P. Guilford; Sheridan Supply Co. *

REFERENCES
1. BERGER, R. M.; GUILFORD, J. P.; AND CHRISTENSEN, P. R. "A Factor-Analytic Study of Planning Abilities." *Psychol Monogr* 71(6):1–31 '57. * (PA 33:6967)
2. HILLS, JOHN R. "Factor-Analyzed Abilities and Success in College Mathematics." *Ed & Psychol Meas* 17:615–22 w '57. * (PA 33:4696)
3. HANEY, RUSSELL; MICHAEL, WILLIAM B.; AND JONES, ROBERT A. "Identification of Aptitude and Achievement Factors in the Prediction of the Success of Nursing Trainees." *Ed & Psychol Meas* 19:645–7 w '59. * (PA 34:6164)

4. KETTNER, NORMAN W.; GUILFORD, J. P.; AND CHRISTENSEN, PAUL R. "A Factor Analytic Study Across the Domains of Reasoning, Creativity, and Evaluation." *Psychol Monogr* 73(9):1–31 '59. * (*PA* 34:7333)
5. MICHAEL, WILLIAM B.; JONES, ROBERT A.; AND HANEY, RUSSELL. "The Development and Validation of a Test Battery for Selection of Student Nurses." *Ed & Psychol Meas* 19:641–3 w '59. * (*PA* 34:6171)
6. MARKS, ALVIN; MICHAEL, WILLIAM B.; AND KAISER, HENRY F. "Dimensions of Creativity and Temperament in Officer Evaluation." *Psychol Rep* 9:635–8 D '61. *
7. MARKS, ALVIN; MICHAEL, WILLIAM B.; AND KAISER, HENRY F. "Sources of Noncognitive Variance in 21 Measures of Creativity." *Psychol Rep* 9:287–90 O '61. *
8. MERRIFIELD, P. R.; GUILFORD, J. P.; CHRISTENSEN, P. R.; AND FRICK, J. W. "The Role of Intellectual Factors in Problem Solving." *Psychol Monogr* 76(10):1–21 '62. *

WILLIAM B. SCHRADER, *Director of Statistical Analysis, Educational Testing Service, Princeton, New Jersey.*

This interesting test requires the subject to perform a series of easy additions and subtractions for each item. The numbers to be added or subtracted are determined by a set of rules. The specific rules governing the work are different for each set of 3 items, and the complexity of the rules increases with each successive set of 12 items. The task is described to the subject in terms of conditions affecting the progress of a ship from one point to another. No doubt the formulation of the task in those more concrete terms makes the instructions easier to understand and keep in mind. Essentially, however, the problems seem to be artificial and formal.

A series of factor studies conducted in Guilford's laboratory have shown consistently that this test is a good measure of the factor designated as general reasoning and that it is a relatively pure measure of that factor. Thus, it should be useful in further factor research as a reference or "marker" test. Probably of more general interest is the fact that arithmetical reasoning, which is widely used in tests of intelligence and scholastic aptitude, has relatively high loadings on general reasoning and on numerical facility (*1*). This finding raises the interesting question of the relative importance of numerical facility and of general reasoning in making the arithmetical reasoning test effective in prediction. The test manual reports some fairly substantial correlation coefficients for the *Ship Destination Test* with course grades at the Coast Guard Academy and with performance rankings of 20 operations analysts, but notes that another study yielded essentially zero validities for an earlier form of the test with mathematics grades. Further validation work should be decidedly useful, particularly if both the *Ship Destination Test* and a measure of arithmetical reasoning were studied for the same groups.

As a practical instrument, the test has certain limitations which should be pointed out. First, only a single form is available. Second, since the test is somewhat speeded, the lack of a parallel form results in reliability estimates that are not entirely rigorous, as the authors point out. They used Tucker's modification of Kuder-Richardson formula 21, but do not indicate what account was taken of the fact that the test is formula scored in computing the various reliability coefficients reported. Third, no item analysis was done, on the grounds that the content of the items is homogeneous and that the relative difficulty of the items is apparent. Although these considerations are relevant, certain possible weaknesses of the test might have been avoided if an item analysis had been made. Thus, inspection of the norms table for men and women students enrolled in San Diego State College suggests that the test is somewhat too easy for the men, but about right for the women. (The norms tables must be interpreted in the light of the fact that the score is defined as rights plus one fifth omits. However, only about one fourth of the men and about one half of the women are below a score of 30, which is halfway between a chance score and a perfect score.) It is possible that the jump in difficulty from the third to the fourth set of 12 items is greater than it should be. Item analysis might also have shown that some of the more difficult items are ambiguous. Fourth, if this test were to be used widely in selection programs, the possible effect of special practice, using similar materials, on test performance should be investigated.

This test is imaginatively conceived, excellently printed, and psychologically meaningful. The brief, four-page manual provides a substantial amount of relevant data to aid in test use. For research purposes, it should be a very valuable instrument. For purposes of counseling or selection, however, its limitations, particularly with regard to empirical validation, definitely restrict its present usefulness.

For a review by C. J. Adcock, see 5:383.

[501]
The Simplex GNV Intelligence Tests. Ages 11–13.0; 1952–57; titles on tests are, for example for form 1, *The Simplex Intelligence Test GNV 1*; forms 1 ('52), 2 ('54), 3 ('54), 4 ('55), 5 ('56), 6 ('57),

(8 pages); manual for each form (dates as for tests, 7 pages); no data on reliability and validity; 10s. 6d. per 25 tests; 6d. per single copy; 1s. per manual; postage and purchase tax extra; 60(70) minutes; C. A. Richardson; George G. Harrap & Co. Ltd. *

REFERENCES

1. SHUTTLEWORTH, CLIFFORD W. "Tests of Technical Aptitude." *Occupational Psychol* 16:175-82 O '42. *
2. NISBET, JOHN D. "Contributions to Intelligence Testing and the Theory of Intelligence: IV, Intelligence and Age: Retesting With Twenty-Four Years' Interval." *Brit J Ed Psychol* 27:190-8 N '57. *

PHILIP M. LEVY, *Lecturer in Psychology, Institute of Education, University of Birmingham, Birmingham, England.*

Aimed primarily at the English "eleven-plus" testing market, these tests neither display nor indeed claim any originality. They appear to be competent productions in the usual "eleven-plus" mould. The items, numbering between 75 and 89 in each test, display the usual range of functions and include verbal analogies, number series, classification tasks, coding, opposites and similarities, syllogisms, and verbal and numerical reasoning tasks. The tests are easy to administer: the children read through the instructions for each item type for themselves.

The manuals tell the user only how to administer and score the tests. No other information is given. Indeed, this is clearly the author's intention, for he titles the manuals "Directions for Setting and Scoring." While no reliability or validity data are available, the publishers report (private communication) that the tests were standardised on "two or three thousand children from urban and rural areas in Great Britain." It appears that the potential user must accept the face validity of the tests or assume that data available from earlier Simplex tests are transferable.

The scoring keys, a list of right answers given in small print within the manuals, must be inconvenient to use and the scorer will be driven to devise his own. The two tables giving conversions to standard scores (mean 100, standard deviation 15) and mental ages provide values only for steps of 5 raw score units. Contrary to the author's statement in the manual, interpolation is not easy: 5 raw score units variously correspond to between 2 and 7 standard points and between 5 and 14 months of mental age. The routine user is again inconvenienced unnecessarily.

The author does not suggest why it might be "sometimes desired to obtain IQ's from mental ages" when he quotes the unnecessary, and surely discredited, age ratio formula. His warning that "Such IQ's will differ from the standard IQ's owing to differences in standard deviation" is only part of the story for there are also likely to be differences in the means. Those who make this outdated calculation may also be puzzled by the small discrepancies between the two tables: the chronological age at which a raw score has the standard score equivalent of 100 sometimes differs by a month or two from the mental age equivalent of the same raw score. No doubt there is a good answer to this admittedly minor point, but why encourage this practice at all?

In summary, these tests are easy to administer and have high face validity; but they are totally unsupported by their manuals, which even fail to give convenient scoring keys and conversion tables. It is doubtful whether these six tests can offer the same overall service as the 70 or so produced by the Moray House organisation or the growing numbers produced by the National Foundation for Educational Research.

[502]

*Sleight Non-Verbal Intelligence Test.** Ages 8-9, 6-10; 1931-63; 2 levels; no data on reliability and validity; tentative norms; postage and purchase tax extra; George F. Sleight and Preston Education Committee (revision of *a*); George G. Harrap & Co. Ltd. *

a) SLEIGHT NON-VERBAL INTELLIGENCE TEST: PRESTON REVISION. Ages 8-9; 1 form ('63, 16 pages); mimeographed manual ['63, 13 pages]; distribution restricted to directors of education; 25s. per 25 tests; 1s. 3d. per single copy; 7s. 6d. per manual; 27(75) minutes.

b) SLEIGHT NON-VERBAL INTELLIGENCE TEST. Ages 6-10; 1 form ['31, 20 pages]; manual ('31, 31 pages); 17s. 6d. per 25 tests; 9d. per single copy; 1s. per manual; 20(75) minutes.

REFERENCES

1. LYTTON, H. "Symposium: Contributions to the Diagnosis and Remedial Treatment of Reading Difficulties: 6, An Experiment in Selection for Remedial Education." *Brit J Ed Psychol* 31:79-95 F '61. * (*PA* 36:1KE79L)

For reviews by John C. Daniels and M. L. Kellmer Pringle of b, *see 5:387.*

[503]

★Survey of Mental Maturity: California Survey Series. Grades 7-9, 10-12 and adults; 1959; all items from *California Test of Mental Maturity, 1957 Edition;* 3 scores: language, nonlanguage, total; IBM; Forms 1, 2, (11 pages); 2 levels: junior high, advanced; manual (20 pages) for each level; $2.80 per 35 tests; separate answer sheets may be used; 5¢ per IBM answer sheet; 20¢ per scoring stencil; 10¢ per series class record sheet; 2¢ per series individual record sheet; postage extra; 50¢ per specimen set of either level, postpaid; 30(35) minutes; Willis W. Clark, Elizabeth T. Sullivan, and Ernest W. Tiegs; California Test Bureau. *

NAOMI STEWART, *Formerly Staff Associate, Educational Testing Service, Princeton, New Jersey.*

The *Survey of Mental Maturity,* the newest instrument in the *California Test of Mental Maturity* series, is intended for use by teachers and counselors "as a screening device to obtain mental ages and intelligence quotients." The Survey yields language and nonlanguage scores. The nonlanguage section consists of spatial relationship items, pictorial analogies, opposites, similarities, and number series items. The language section includes vocabulary, quantitative reasoning problems, and items requiring syllogistic reasoning. Each section contains 40 items, and the two sections are separately timed, each being allotted 15 minutes.

The manual for each level provides percentile values and standard scores for the language and the nonlanguage scores, separately for each of a large number of age groups. The total score may be converted into a mental age, and thence to an intelligence quotient, or it may be converted into a percentile rank or a standard score for a variety of age groups. Through an elaborate equating procedure which is briefly described in the manual, all of these values for the scores on the *Survey of Mental Maturity* have been articulated into the standardization data for the 1957 edition of the *California Test of Mental Maturity* and the *California Achievement Tests,* so that scores on the *Survey of Mental Maturity* can presumably be interpreted in the context of this large mass of already-available data.

It is apparent that a great deal of effort has gone into the preparation of this test, and it is regrettable that the result is of only fair quality. The major failing seems to lie in the test items themselves, particularly the nonlanguage items, and this is especially ironic inasmuch as the *Survey of Mental Maturity,* according to the manuals, "contains a selection of the most discriminating portions of the *California Test of Mental Maturity.*" For the advanced level, items were taken from the junior high and advanced levels of the CTMM; for the junior high school level, items were taken from the secondary and elementary levels of the parent instrument. In each case, 100 language items and 90 nonlanguage items were tentatively selected, made up into two experimental forms, and administered without time limits to obtain difficulty and discrimination indices. The best 80 language and the best 80 nonlanguage items were retained to form two parallel forms of 80 items each.

The procedure for item selection is not described in sufficient detail to make it possible to judge why it proved inadequate, but it certainly did allow some items of very dubious quality to slip through the screening process. Perhaps the initial pool of items was not large enough. In any event, the nonlanguage items are not very good. Some are absurdly easy and some are very difficult indeed, but for the wrong reasons. Most of the nonlanguage items —all, in fact, but the number series items— involve drawings of various kinds. Unfortunately, the drawings are not always clear enough to convey the meaning that is intended. Many of the items, too, require a very high degree of visual acuity almost as a minimum prerequisite. Time and again, for example, particularly in the spatial visualization items, the choice will narrow down to two alternative figures so nearly identical that differences between them are almost microscopic. (A magnifying glass, come to think of it, would make an ideal "crib" for this test!) Forcing the examinee to detect these minute differences is presumably intentional, though almost certainly ill advised, but many of the drawings, or the reproductions of the drawings, are of such poor quality as to be almost indecipherable.

Nonlanguage items generally, and indecipherable nonlanguage items in particular, are time consuming, yet the examinee is given no more time for the 40 nonlanguage items than for the 40 language items—15 minutes in each case. Although no data on speededness are presented, it would seem that the nonlanguage section is much more highly speeded than the language section. Unfortunately, this element of speededness, coupled with the item deficiencies already noted, operates to exert a systematic downward pull on the nonlanguage scores of the most intelligent examinees. (While increasing error variance generally, an indecipherable illustration does nothing to hurt the score of an examinee who would not be able to answer the item correctly in any event, and an item not reached does nothing to hurt the score of an examinee who would not be able to answer it correctly if he reached it.) Since the total score on the test—the basic measure from which mental ages and intelligence quotients are obtained—is the sum of the raw scores on the language and nonlanguage sections, there is also an artificial lowering of total raw scores for the most intelligent examinees.

The poor quality of the nonlanguage items, then, results in introducing both unreliability and systematic bias into the total score, particularly blunting the precision of discriminations made in the upper part of the intelligence range. For examinees of high intelligence of a scholastic nature, the addition of the nonlanguage score to the language score will result in an under-assessment of ability; this under-assessment is likely to be quite drastic in the case of very bright examinees whose vision is slightly defective. It is necessary therefore to be very cautious in interpreting total scores on the test, and probably unwise to use the test for such purposes as identifying highly superior students.

According to the manual, "these two types of response patterns [language and nonlanguage] are tested and scored separately....so that individual differences in the pattern of language and nonlanguage ability can be studied." Despite this encouragement from the manual, it seems quite inadvisable to make judgments about a student's language ability relative to his nonlanguage ability on the basis of the subscores. To give only one of a number of technical reasons, the errors of measurement associated with the two sets of raw scores are such that a difference of seven or eight raw score points can easily arise through chance alone. Now, to pick an example quite at random, a 13-year-old who got scores of 31 on the language section and 24 on the nonlanguage section of the junior high level test would have percentile ranks of 84 and 34, respectively. For a 14-year-old the same raw scores would yield percentiles of 66 and 18, respectively. The norms for other ages give different figures, but the tenor is the same: except for extreme scores, a 7-point difference in raw scores gives rise to roughly a 50-point difference in percentile scores below the age of 15 and about a 35- to 40-point difference in percentiles above the age of 15.

The suggestion that either the nonlanguage score or the language score may be used by itself to obtain a rough estimate of the examinee's IQ also seems inadvisable. Although the manual does not give mental age or IQ equivalents for the raw scores on the two sections directly, it sketches a procedure whereby IQ equivalents for these scores may be obtained by first converting the raw scores into standard scores and then looking up the IQ equivalent for the particular standard score or percentile. This is a shaky procedure because of the large amount of error introduced by the use of successive conversions or equivalences, each of which is in itself merely an approximation.

The general saturation of the norms tables with conversions and equivalences, and the multiplicity of breakdowns (including, for example, such generally useless and confusing information as that given in the column headed "Intelligence (M.A.) Grade Placement") gives a misleading impression of rigorous exactitude. In point of fact, most of the actual figures in the tables were obtained by equating new data to earlier data, and interpolating and extrapolating as necessary. Even with sizable numbers of cases in the equating population, there are so many breakdowns that the number of experimental observations nailing down any given figure is quite small.

The least objectionable procedure would probably be to use the language score by itself, but to do so twice, i.e., to administer both Form 1 and Form 2 to each student, calculate mental age separately each time, and then average the two. This is not to be taken as a suggested procedure for general use—merely as a reasonably acceptable way of "making do" with this test if one is forced to use it. Overall, the test is not recommended.

[504]

★**Test of Learning Ability.** Business and industry; 1947-63; Forms S, T, ('47, 5 pages), ST ('57, 8 pages); Form ST is a long form combination of Forms S and T; manual for Forms S and T ['63, 24 unnumbered pages]; manual for Form ST ['63, 8 unnumbered pages]; Form ST norms for males only; $3.50 per 25 tests of Form S or T; 10¢ per key; $2 per manual; $5.50 per 25 tests of Form ST; 15¢ per key; $1 per manual; postage extra; $1 per specimen set of Form S or T; $1.25 per specimen set of Form ST; postpaid; 15(20) minutes for Forms S and T, 25(30) minutes for Form ST; Richardson, Bellows, Henry & Co., Inc. *

REFERENCES
1. PERRINE, MERVYN WILLIAM. "The Selection of Drafting Trainees." *J Appl Psychol* 39:57–61 F '55. * (*PA* 30:1725)
2. SPARKS, CHARLES P., AND WAITE, W. DUDLEY. "Normative Data Information Exchange, No. 10-18." *Personnel Psychol* 10:238–40 su '57. *

[505]

★**Test of Non-Verbal Reasoning.** Business and industry; 1948-63; 1 form; 2 editions: long form ('48, 5 pages), short form ('50, 3 pages); manual ['63, 9–10 unnumbered pages] for each edition; $3.50 per 25 tests of long form; $3 per 25 tests of short form; 10¢ per key; $1 per manual for either edition; postage extra; $1 per specimen set, postpaid; Spanish edition of long form and Spanish, French, and Arabic editions of short form available; 10(15) minutes for short form, 15(20) minutes for long form; Richardson, Bellows, Henry & Co., Inc. *

REFERENCES

1. CUOMO, SYLVIA. "Validity Information Exchange, No. 8-17: D.O.T. Code 5-92.601, Foreman II." *Personnel Psychol* 8:268 su '55. *
2. CUOMO, SYLVIA, AND MEYER, HERBERT H. "Validity Information Exchange, No. 8-16: D.O.T. Code 5-92.601, Foreman II." *Personnel Psychol* 8:267 su '55. *
3. KIRCHNER, WAYNE; HANSON, RICHARD; AND BENSON, DALE. "Selecting Foremen With Psychological Tests." *Personnel Adm* 23:27–30 N-D '60. *

[506]

Tests AH4 and AH5. Ages 10 and over, 13 and over; 1955–56; 1 form; 2 levels; separate answer sheets must be used; 5s. per 25 answer sheets; postpaid within U.K.; A. W. Heim; distributed by the National Foundation for Educational Research in England and Wales. *

a) TEST AH4: GROUP TEST OF INTELLIGENCE. Ages 10 and over; 1955; 1 form ['55, 8 pages]; manual ['55, 16 pages]; no norms for age 10; 18s. per 25 tests; 6s. per set of scoring key and manual; 7s. per specimen set; 20(30–45) minutes.

b) TEST AH5: GROUP TEST OF HIGH-GRADE INTELLIGENCE. Ages 13 and over; 1956; 1 form ['56, 8 pages]; manual ['56, 20 pages]; 19s. per 25 tests; 5s. per set of scoring key and manual; 8s. per specimen set; 40(60–70) minutes.

REFERENCES

1–11. See 5:390.

JOHN LIGGETT, *Senior Lecturer in Psychology, University College of South Wales and Monmouthshire, University of Wales, Cardiff, Wales.*

Tests AH4 and AH5 are group tests of general intelligence employing similar question and answer materials and similar methods of administration and scoring. They are, however, of very different levels of difficulty. AH4 is intended for "a cross section of the adult population," whereas AH5 is designed for use with selected highly intelligent adult subjects ("students and research workers, and potential entrants to the university and the professions"). AH4 allows 20 minutes for questions and the more difficult AH5 allows 40 minutes. Further time is required in each case for initial practice with examples—an aspect of the administration of the test which the author considers particularly important.

The items in both tests are similar in character. In Part 1 of each test there are verbal directions, opposites, analogies, synonyms, numerical series, and numerical computations. Part 2 of each is composed of diagrammatic problems—analogies, sames, subtractions, series, directions, and superimpositions. A novel type of item, "similar relationships," is introduced in Part 1 of AH5. The subject is asked to choose from several given words the one which bears a similar relation to each of another two words. He has, in fact, to find out for himself whether the required relationship is one of sameness or opposition. A further variant of this idea is introduced in Part 2 of AH5 in the diagrammatic items which the author calls "features in common." The subject is shown five diagrams from which he has to select the "odd man out." As a guide he is given two further diagrams, each of which is declared to possess the odd feature. In this way the author has sought to avoid the ambiguity often found in classification test items.

The test booklets, separate answer sheets, and keys are quite conventional. The test score (the number of items correct) is readily convertible to a grade from A to E by reference to the norms representing the percentage distribution 10-20-40-20-10.

Test-retest consistency and validity are carefully considered in the manual. For AH4 the test-retest correlation is .92 ($n = 100$). For AH5 a test-retest correlation of .84 was obtained with 94 Cambridge undergraduates. Three sorts of validity data are presented for each test: correlations with other tests, comparisons with "real life" criteria such as examination results, and demonstration of the regular rise of test scores with chronological age. On this latter point the author makes the interesting report that the AH5 score may continue to increase even beyond the age of 18.

The manuals are well written in a modest, clear, and honest style, though their almost identical appearance invites confusion between the two tests. The test sheets themselves are poorly printed in a quaint mixture of old type faces and the diagrams are poorly reproduced. This is much less than the tests deserve.

In constructing AH4, Heim was attempting to provide a brief group test of general intelligence with items drawn from a wide field. In AH5 her major concern was to provide an instrument which would effect discrimination between highly intelligent subjects. Both of these aims she has achieved with a good deal to spare and there is little doubt that both AH4 and AH5 will do much valuable work. They are imaginatively based, soundly constructed, and well documented.

For reviews by George A. Ferguson of Test AH4 and J. A. Keats of Test AH5, see 5:390.

[507]
*Tests of General Ability: Cooperative Inter-American Tests.** Grades kgn and first grade entrants, 1–3.5, 4–7, 8–13, 10–13; 1950–63; levels 1 and 5 (*a* and *e* below) called *Test of General Ability: Inter-American Series*; a series of parallel tests and manuals in English and Spanish; IBM for grades 4–13; 5 levels; tentative norms (publisher recommends use of local norms); separate answer sheets must be used for grades 4–13; postage extra; 30¢ per specimen set of any one level, postpaid; prepared under the direction of Herschel T. Manuel; Guidance Testing Associates. *

a) LEVEL 1—PRIMARY. Grade kgn and first grade entrants; 1962–63; 3 scores: verbal and numerical, nonverbal, total; English language Form CE ('62, 9 pages); Spanish language Form CEs ('62, 11 pages); pretest ('62, 4 pages) for use in teaching testing procedures to immature children; directions ['62, 11 pages]; tentative norms ('63, 1 page); $3.50 per 25 tests; 5¢ per pretest (3¢ when purchased with test booklet); 30¢ per specimen set of either English or Spanish edition; 50¢ per combined specimen set; [40–50] minutes in 2 sessions.

b) PRIMARY LEVEL. Grades 1–3.5; 1950; 4 scores: oral vocabulary, classification, association, total; English language Forms AE, BE, ('50, 9 pages); Spanish language Forms AS, BS, ('50, 9 pages); directions ('50, 10 pages); series manual ('50, 18 pages); no data on reliability; no norms for subscores; $3 per 25 tests; 30¢ per set of keys; (30–40) minutes.

c) INTERMEDIATE LEVEL. Grades 4–7; 1950; 3 scores: nonverbal, verbal, total; IBM; English language Forms AE, BE, ('50, 12 pages); Spanish language Forms AS, BS, ('50, 12 pages); combined directions ('50, 7 pages) for this and *d* below; series manual ('50, 18 pages); no data on reliability; no norms for subscores; $3 per 25 tests; 5¢ per IBM answer sheet; 30¢ per set of scoring stencils; 34(50) minutes.

d) ADVANCED LEVEL. Grades 8–13; 1950; 3 scores: nonverbal, verbal, total; IBM; English language Forms AE, BE, ('50, 12 pages); Spanish language Forms AS, BS, ('50, 12 pages); combined directions ('50, 7 pages) for this and *c* above; series manual ('50, 18 pages); no data on reliability; no norms for subscores; prices same as for intermediate level; 34(50) minutes.

e) LEVEL 5—ADVANCED. Grades 10–13; 1962–63; 4 scores: verbal, nonverbal, numerical, total; IBM; English language Form CE ('62, 15 pages); Spanish language Form CEs ('62, 15 pages); directions ['62, 7 pages]; tentative norms and technical data ['63, 7 pages] for this and the level 5 reading test of the series; $4 per 25 tests; 5¢ per IBM answer sheet; 30¢ per set of scoring stencils; 30¢ per specimen set of either English or Spanish edition; 50¢ per combined specimen set; 52(65) minutes.

REFERENCES

1–8. See 4:325.

For reviews by Raleigh M. Drake and Walter N. Durost of b–d, see 4:325.

[508]
★**The Verbal Power Test of Concept Equivalence.** Ages 14 and over; 1959–63; Forms A, B, ('59, 2 pages) on a single sheet; manual ('63, 12 pages); $6 per set of 25 tests, key, and manual; $2 per manual; postpaid; (10–15) minutes; E. Francesco; Western Psychological Services. *

REFERENCES

1. FRANCESCO, E. "The Verbal Power Test of Concept Equivalents (VPT)." *J Psychol* 49:213–6 Ap '60. * (*PA* 34:7349)

2. FRANCESCO, E. "Below Chance Performance on a Verbal Test Using Paired Concepts." *J Clin Psychol* 17:312–5 Jl '61. * (*PA* 38:8412)
3. FRANCESCO, E. "Below Chance Performance on a Verbal Test: A Replication." *Psychol Rep* 10:601–2 Ap '62. * (*PA* 37:3868)

[509]
★**Verbal Reasoning.** Job applicants and industrial employees; 1958–61; 1 form ('58, 3 pages); manual ('61, c1959–61, 20 pages); norms for males only; $3 per 20 tests, postage extra; $1 per specimen set, postpaid; 15(20) minutes; Raymond J. Corsini, Richard Renck, and Measurement Research Division, Industrial Relations Center, University of Chicago (manual); Education-Industry Service. *

JAMES E. KENNEDY, *Associate Professor of Psychology, University of Wisconsin, Madison, Wisconsin.*

Verbal Reasoning is described in the manual as a measure of "a person's capacity to reason logically from written material." The test consists of 12 problems stated in words; each problem gives a verbal description of the activities of four brothers, followed by a three-part question. The answers may be deduced from the information given in the descriptions and the three-part questions. A paper and pencil test, *Verbal Reasoning* is suitable for administration to groups and has a strict time limit of 15 minutes. The items are said to be ordered for difficulty, although the description of the procedure followed is obscure. In its present format the test must be hand scored; the total score, ranging from 0 to 36, is the number of right answers. Only one form of the test is available. The sole estimate of the test's reliability is a test-retest correlation of .69 based on 68 cases.

While the organization and format of the manual are good, information about important features of the test is either missing or vague. Taking the positive features first, the instructions for administering and scoring the test are intelligible and should present no difficulties for the inexperienced. Rationales for percentile scores and normalized standard scores are well presented and procedures for converting raw scores are clear. Norm groups are reasonably large and are described in more detail than in most manuals for tests of this kind, although more information about age and education distributions would have been helpful.

On the negative side, the principal limitation of the manual is the incomplete and ambiguous discussion of validity and related issues. The manual provides no explanation of why, on theoretical grounds, the authors believe this test might be a useful measure of a capacity they call "verbal reasoning," in what ways the test is similar to or different from existing tests of either verbal reasoning in particular or intelligence in general, or why measurement of this capacity has been limited to a single type of item with only minor variations. Nowhere in the manual is there a statement, or an explicit suggestion, as to the purposes for which the test might be used. While these omissions are serious, the reviewer's objections would not be as strong if the manual reported the empirical relationships between performance on this test and performance on a variety of standard, relevant psychological measures. If this had been done the reader might have been able to infer for himself what the test does or does not measure and for what purposes it might be useful.

The validity of the test is said to be approached in two ways. The first consists in showing that low positive correlations (.10 to .55) exist between this test and three other tests: Thelma Thurstone's *Understanding Communication (Verbal Comprehension)*, Corsini's *Non-Verbal Reasoning Test,* and his *Word Fluency*. (These are newly published, equally untried tests by the same group that developed *Verbal Reasoning*.) On the basis of these results, and with no further elaboration, the authors conclude "the test measures in the area of mental abilities." The second approach consists in showing that mean scores on the test differ, sometimes significantly and sometimes not, for various skill levels of industrial personnel. No interpretation of these results is made. Since this analysis was discussed under the heading "validity," the authors presumably believed the results have some bearing on the test's validity, but they do not say what it might be. While this situation is considerably better than making unfounded claims for validity, it is undesirable in that it might be misinterpreted by the unwary or inexperienced test user as evidence that this test has demonstrated validity for selection or placement purposes. Incidentally, the skill groups among which the test discriminated were widely different in educational levels and possibly differed significantly in age. The authors take no interpretative note of this.

In summary, we can say only that this test may prove in the future to be a useful contribution to theory or practice, but at its present stage of development it must be considered as an experimental test of good face validity, moderate reliability, but of no demonstrated validity of any kind. There is certainly no evidence to indicate it has predictive validity for use in business and industry.

DAVID G. RYANS, *Director, Bureau of Educational Research, University of Hawaii, Honolulu, Hawaii.*

This test is intended to estimate an individual's "capacity to reason logically from written material." It is made up of 12 problems selected by an approximation method of item analysis from "preliminary research forms" administered to small groups of job applicants, and presented in order of difficulty. Directions printed on the cover page of the test read: "This booklet contains problems about four brothers: Art(A), Bill(B), Carl(C), and Dan(D). Each question refers to *one of the four brothers*. For each answer cross out either A-B-C-or-D." A sample problem which follows the directions reads: "On their jobs, Art wears a white coat, Bill a uniform, Carl overalls and Dan a business suit." The examinee must judge from this information which brother is the plumber, which the butcher, and which the policeman. Three responses are required to each problem situation, resulting in a total possible score of 36. (Within a given problem the three responses obviously are not independent.) An individual's score on the test is the number of correct responses. Raw scores may be converted to normalized standard scores and percentile ranks.

Test-retest results, based upon administration of the problems to 68 employed men over intervals of from six to eight weeks, yielded a correlation coefficient of .69, which is presumed to reflect test reliability. Validity is judged by two approaches: (*a*) comparisons of test results with other test data, and (*b*) t-tests between paired means of different groups. Correlation with Corsini's *Non-Verbal Reasoning Test* scores yielded coefficients of .31 for 66 laborers and .33 for 71 management personnel; with Thelma Thurstone's *Understanding Communication* scores coefficients of .52 for 193 unskilled employees and .48 for 45 professional executive employees were found; and with Corsini's *Word Fluency* scores correlations ranged from .10 to .55 with a median of .27. The t-tests between paired means of six different groups showed statistically significant differences between the means of groups of "unskilled and semi-skilled employees" and "foremen," and between means of each of these groups and those of groups of "engineers and chemists," "executives and middle management," "white collar and junior executives," and "salesmen." (The n for the unskilled and semiskilled employee group was 244 and for the engineers and chemists, 146; the other group n's ranged from 35 to 59.)

The test-retest reliability coefficient reported is based on too small a sample to provide generalization and the interval between testing leaves doubt about whether the data yield an acceptable test reliability index. If, however, the obtained coefficient is accepted as a reliability index, it would argue against use of the test; it is far too low to be acceptable. Evidence of concurrent validity is not convincing due to the low correlations with other tests. Use should have been made of analysis of variance in comparing differences between mean scores of different groups of employees.

Normalized standard score equivalents are given for raw scores of a group of 1,486 industrial personnel which showed a raw score mean of 16.58 and standard deviation of 7.04. Means and standard deviations are provided for six subgroups: professionals, executives, junior executives, salesmen, foremen, and hourly workers. (Interestingly, the mean for 35 salesmen in the "validity" study was reported to be 22.37; for 150 salesmen in the norms group the mean is 16.36.)

The Test Administration Manual is nontechnical and, indeed, unsophisticated (e.g., "The results shown in Tables 1 and 2 show that the Verbal Reasoning test measures in the general area of mental abilities"). The manual also is confusing and nonspecific in its statements about the test and its interpretation. It would have been desirable to have indicated the extent to which this short test of 12 problems and 36 responses correlates with various "abilities" measured by widely used tests of differential abilities and with factorially pure tests of such factors as deductive reasoning and inductive inference.

The test cannot be recommended for use due to lack of supporting information. If used, it definitely should be considered a trial test that has not been fully developed.

[510]
*Verbal Test (Adv.).** Ages 12 to 13-11; 1954-60; 4 forms; practice test [dates same as for tests, 2 pages] for each test; no data on validity; distribution restricted to directors of education; 10s. per 12 tests; 1s. per single copy; 2s. 6d. per 12 practice tests; 4d. per single copy; 1s. 3d. per manual for any one test; prices include purchase tax; postage extra; 10(15) minutes for practice test, 45(55) minutes for test (except for a); D. A. Pidgeon (a); published for National Foundation for Educational Research in England and Wales; Newnes Educational Publishing Co. Ltd. *
a) VERBAL TEST (ADV.) 1. 1954-55; 1 form ['54, 10 pages]; manual ('55, 10 pages); 50(60) minutes.
b) VERBAL TEST (ADV.) 2. 1957; 1 form ['57, 11 pages]; manual ('57, 11 pages).
c) VERBAL TEST (ADV.) 3. 1958; 1 form ['58, 11 pages]; manual ('58, 9 pages).
d) VERBAL TEST (ADV.) 4. 1960; 1 form ['60, 11 pages]; manual ('60, 9 pages).

J. S. LAWES, *Senior Lecturer in Education, Westminster College, North Hinksey, Oxford, England.*

These four tests are included in the series published by the National Foundation for Educational Research for use by Local Education Authorities particularly in selection and guidance procedures. Basically the tests contain similar material, the majority of the items being of types common to all four tests although the balance between different types of items varies from test to test. For example, Test 2 and Test 3 contain approximately 25 per cent analogy type questions, Test 1 about 15 per cent, and Test 4 only 5 per cent. Tests 2 and 3 show the greatest degree of similarity containing exactly the same types with only slight variations in the proportions. These examples show that although the tests are similar and designed for similar purposes they are not in fact exact parallel forms. It would be useful to collect information regarding intertest correlation.

The manuals of these tests are evidence of the continued adequacy of the standards of construction demanded by the National Foundation. In addition to complete administration and scoring instructions and conversion tables, full description of the standardisation and reliability procedures is given. The reliability coefficients, obtained by Kuder-Richardson formula 20 on samples of 200 to 300 pupils, are all .97 or a little higher. The manuals for Tests 2, 3, and 4 contain a warning to the effect that, although the reliability is very high, errors attached to a child's score are not inconsiderable and the reliability should be taken into account in any allocation procedure. This warning could well be included in any new edition of the manual for Test 1.

The standardisation of Tests 1, 2, and 3 is good in that it was carried out in each case on a complete population of the appropriate age range, with populations numbering between 1,500 and 2,000, but it is to be noted that each standardisation population was from one area only. Test 4 was not standardised on a complete population but calibrated against Test 3 on "a small but representative group of children"—in fact, 532 children. A direct standardisation on a larger population would be a useful check. The conversion tables provide standardised scores with a mean of 100 and a standard deviation of 15. For Test 2 only, separate conversion tables are provided for boys and girls since the rates of increase in score with age for the two sexes show a highly significant difference. The only other significant sex difference quoted is for raw scores on Test 3, but it is good to find in each manual a recommendation that for any allocation procedure the two sexes should be considered independently.

The one piece of information which is missing from the manuals is that important one, "Validation Data." Unfortunately the Foundation is unable to provide such data, having itself been unable to follow up pupils who have worked the tests. This reviewer can offer the meagre information that when correlating Test 1 scores with school examination marks for small groups of secondary school boys he has obtained significant correlations of the order .50 to .60 with performance in English. If those who have used the tests, especially on a large scale, were able to provide follow-up data the value of the tests would be greatly enhanced.

In conclusion, these tests are soundly constructed and well presented. Some format problems, such as the effort to place all responses on the right hand side of each page in Test 1, an arrangement which can be confusing to some children, have been avoided in the later tests. The manuals are fully informative. Standardisation is in the main adequate but could well be repeated in other geographical areas. The only reservation against full recommendation is the lack of validation data.

John Nisbet, *Professor of Education, University of Aberdeen, Aberdeen, Scotland.*

This series of tests is designed for selection in English secondary schools, particularly among pupils at the end of their second year of secondary education. Consequently, the tests discriminate well among the middle two thirds of a fairly restricted age range but are less accurate at the extremes of high and low ability. They have been soundly constructed, using representative samples of over 1,500 cases (except Test 4 which was merely calibrated against Test 3). Reliability coefficients are all at least .97.

But recommendation of the use of these tests depends on the reputation of the National Foundation for Educational Research and personal knowledge of the high standards of their test construction, rather than on any evidence presented in the manuals. Since it is assumed that the tests will be used in a routine official testing programme (sale is restricted to education authorities, though the tests may be made available for research projects) the manuals are little more than marking keys with instructions for teachers administering the tests. Scanty data are given for assessing the adequacy of the standardisation: a single page is devoted to details of construction and much of the information is not precise. The standardisation groups are referred to in terms such as "all children in a chosen area aged between 12-0 and 14-0," without specifying such details as whether the area was urban or mixed rural-urban. No comparison with other tests is reported, and norms are given in one form only, the deviation quotient used in English selection procedures. This makes for economy in cost, but one would have hoped that the National Foundation might set an example to commercial publishers in the information given.

Performance in these tests is heavily dependent on reading skill and speed, since most items have separate instructions and there are 100 items to answer in 45–50 minutes. Below IQ 80 scores cannot be valid, though norms down to 70 are given.

Test 2 is different from the others, being at an easier level and therefore lacking discrimination in the upper range of ability. (Boys aged 13-11 must have over 97 items right out of 100 to score over 120.) Test 2 differs also in that it presents separate norms for boys and for girls. The sex differences are disconcertingly large and cast doubt on the standardisation: at age 12-0, the median raw score is 41 for boys and 65 for girls.

Verbal Test (Adv.)

With the exception of Test 2, these are sound tests which can be recommended for use in assessing scholastic aptitude of 12- and 13-year-olds in the middle range of ability. They are very similar to the *Moray House Verbal Reasoning Test (Advanced)*, but the Moray House series is preferable in that it has fewer defects and presents slightly more information in its manuals.

[511]

*Verbal Tests 1–2, 4–13. Ages 10–12; 1951–63; 12 tests (8–10 pages); new test published annually; practice test (2 pages, dates same as for test except for Test 7) for each test; no data on validity; distribution restricted to directors of education; 8s. per 12 tests; 9d. per single copy; 2s. 6d. per 12 practice tests; 4d. per single copy; manual for any one test: 1s. for Tests 1, 4, 5, 1s. 3d. for Tests 2, 6–13; prices include purchase tax; postage extra; 10(15) minutes for practice test, 45(50) minutes for test (except for Test 1); I. Macfarlane Smith (a–d), M. A. Brimer (e), and others; published for the National Foundation for Educational Research in England and Wales; Newnes Educational Publishing Co. Ltd. *

a) VERBAL TEST 1. 1951–53; 1 form ['51]; manual ('53, 8 pages); 50(55) minutes.
b) VERBAL TEST 2. 1952–53; 1 form ['52]; manual ['53, 11 pages]; no norms for ages 11-7 to 11-11.
c) VERBAL TEST 4. 1953–58; 1 form ['53]; manual ('58, 8 pages).
d) VERBAL TEST 5. 1954–55; 1 form ['54]; manual ('55, 8 pages); no norms for ages 11-7 to 11-11.
e) VERBAL TEST 6. 1955–57; 1 form ['55]; manual ('57, 9 pages).
f) VERBAL TEST 7. 1957–59; forms 7A, 7B, ['57]; practice tests: 7A ['59], 7B ['58]; manuals: 7A ('59, 9 pages, identical with 1957 manual), 7B ('57, 9 pages).
g) VERBAL TEST 8. 1957–58; forms 8A ['57], 8B ['58]; manual ('58, 12 pages) for each form.
h) VERBAL TEST 9. 1959; forms 9A, 9B, ['59]; manual ('59, 9 pages) for each form.
i) VERBAL TEST 10. 1959–60; forms 10A, 10B, ['59]; manual ('60, 10 pages) for each form.
j) VERBAL TEST 11. 1960–61; forms 11A, 11B, 11C, ['60]; manual ('61, 11 pages) for each form.
k) VERBAL TEST 12. 1961–62; forms 12A, 12B, ['61]; manual ('62, 11 pages) for each form.
l) VERBAL TEST 13. 1962–63; forms 13A, 13B, ['62]; manual ('63, 11 pages) for each form.

REFERENCES

1. MORETON, C. ANNE, AND BUTCHER, H. J. "Are Rural Children Handicapped by the Use of Speeded Tests in Selection Procedures?" *Brit J Ed Psychol* 33:22–30 F '63. * (PA 38:684)

ARTHUR B. ROYSE, *Lecturer in Psychology, The University of Hull, Hull, England.*

These group tests are designed for use in the annual allocation of children to selected English secondary schools. To ensure that no child has had previous experience with the test, a new test (or a new parallel form) is produced for each year and circulation is restricted to directors of education. The several authors deserve congratulation for consistently producing tests of high reliability in the limited time available.

The layout of the tests is good and the instructions for administration and marking are detailed and lucid. A praiseworthy feature is the use of a scoring system which allows the child credit for his intentions, however expressed, but which is sufficiently detailed to ensure consistency of marking by different examiners. Information regarding standardisation groups, sex differences, reliability coefficients, and methods of interpretation of scores is given clearly and concisely.

Unfortunately, no validation data are given. Serious in any test, this omission is especially so for these tests. Because of their eminence, the method of construction has been copied in detail by many other compilers of tests used for the same—and even for different—purposes. The obvious criterion of validity would be the test's ability to predict success in grammar school or, alternatively, a high correlation with an existing test whose predictive ability has been established. Clearly the first could not be obtained, since each new test has to be in use before such evidence can be collected. But failure to collect the second type of evidence appears to be due solely to the authors' belief that such correlation could be assumed without test.

The resultant loss of scientific rigour might be regarded as negligible if each new test involved only minor deviations from the old and, indeed, this is true for the earlier one-author tests. But the earlier procedure was clearly regarded as an unnecessary handicap, for, in a review of previous tests, the manual to Test 7 (1957) states that "there is a danger when one person writes all the items that in successive years he will repeat and restrict the content." From this test on, items were collected from several contributors and a number of new types of item and variations in the format of conventional items appear.

The implicit assumption that the infinite population of possible verbal items, of whatever form or content, is homogeneous with respect to abilities measured and variables predicted becomes explicit in the manual to Test 10 (1960) which claims, "The validity of verbal tests as predictors of success in the Grammar School has been firmly established in the light of empirical evidence obtained from various follow-up studies." Published evidence that *some* verbal tests have been successful in such predictions appears to have been taken as a license to include in subsequent NFER tests any item which could be classified as a verbal item, irrespective of its form or content. From this test on, the differences between earlier and later tests become even more marked, the most significant trend being the decline in the proportion of items requiring the child to educe relations from given data in favour of items requiring him to search his memory store for exemplars of a given rule.

In contrast, standardisation is good, each test being administered to all the children forming the top year group in primary schools in a number of selected areas. The number of children, varying from 4,167 (Test 4) to 19,256 (Test 2) and comprising approximately equal numbers of boys and girls, is given but the basis of selection of areas is not. Raw scores are converted to standardised scores having a mean of 100 and a standard deviation of 15. The difference between mean scores for boys and girls is given and, where the difference is statistically significant, it is wisely recommended that the sexes be considered independently in allocation procedures. But separate conversion tables are not given unless the regression coefficients of score on age also show significant differences. No indication is given of how these regression coefficients are derived and no justification is offered to support the assumption of linearity of regression or the extrapolations to age groups included in the tables but not in the standardisation groups.

Internal consistency coefficients (Kuder-Richardson formula 20) are computed from small random subsamples of around 200 scripts. They are generally high, the majority being around .98 with none lower than .95. Unfortunately, except for a few of the earlier tests, no test-retest reliability coefficients are given; for these earlier tests, values around .94 were obtained from small samples of less than 100 scripts.

Despite their weakness in scientific rigour and statistical refinement, these tests provide an invaluable service to education authorities. They succeed in providing a reliable scale which has a wide range of raw scores in the area critical for selection and can be recommended strongly to those who are prepared to accept as reasonable the compilers' assumptions of validity. Even for those who would prefer a firmer basis for statistical decision these tests can be recommended as being as good as the best in this special field.

[512]

★The Western Personnel Tests. College and adults; 1962; Forms A, B, C, D, (3 pages); manual (4 pages); $5.50 per 25 tests, postpaid; specimen set not available; Spanish edition available; 5(10) minutes; Robert L. Gunn and Morse P. Manson; Western Psychological Services. *

LEWIS E. ALBRIGHT, *Assistant Director, Employee Relations Research, Standard Oil Company (Indiana), Chicago, Illinois.*

The *Western Personnel Tests* (W-P-T) are four parallel forms designed as alternate short measures of mental ability. Testing time required is five minutes for any one form, each form containing 24 items arranged in order of difficulty. The content of the items is typical of that of most short mental ability tests, including number series, word meaning, disarranged sentences, and arithmetic reasoning. Three sample items precede the test problems. The format is attractive, with large, readable type throughout.

The manual states that the W-P-T was designed for use in business and industry, and suggests that the tests may also be useful in clinics, schools, hospitals, institutional settings, and government agencies. Unfortunately, the norms provided would be of little help in these other situations. The norms, in fact, are quite inadequate even for industrial settings. There are five "occupational" norm groups and a "general population" group which is the total of the five occupational groups. The five groups are professional workers, college students, clerical workers, skilled workers, and unskilled workers. The number of cases in each group for any one form is very small, ranging from 25 to 72.

No detailed description of the groups' composition is given. The college student group, for example, consists of "first year students through graduate students working for Ph.D.s," with no indication of how many students at each level. Nothing is said regarding the amount of education of the other groups; also unspecified are the age and sex composition of all groups. This latter omission is certainly contrary to accepted practice and runs counter to much evidence of important sex differences on mental ability as well as other types of tests.

When a test is as short as the W-P-T, we

may properly be concerned about its reliability. Here again, the manual is disappointing. Split-half coefficients in the high .80's and low .90's are given for the four forms, but these must be spuriously high precisely because of the speeded nature of the test. Verifying this suspicion is a subsequent table of interform correlations ranging from the low to middle .80's. What one would like to see, of course, are retest reliabilities, but they are not to be found.

The evidence for validity is even less satisfying, consisting merely of correlations of each W-P-T form with Form B of the *Wonderlic Personnel Test*. Although these coefficients are of the same magnitude as the interform correlations cited above, some evidence of the *predictive* or, at least, *concurrent* validity of the W-P-T is needed. One can argue that, because this test is easy to administer and score (as it appears to be) and because it requires only five minutes of testing time, we have a right to expect the authors to conduct validation studies of their instrument against relevant criteria of job success. Until the findings of such research can be presented, it would have been better to delay publication.

Besides its other omissions, the manual contains no reference to the American Psychological Association technical recommendations on test validity and reliability. Similarly, there is no description of the item analysis procedures used in constructing the test. On the subject of administration and scoring of the W-P-T, the novice test administrator would hardly be enriched by this instruction from the manual: "If questions are raised [by those taking the test], they should be answered simply and clearly." How should the administrator deal with a question about guessing, for example? Is he to encourage guessing or discourage it?

In sum, brevity is unquestionably a virtue of tests designed for industrial use and because the W-P-T yields a mental ability score in only five minutes, it may achieve some measure of popularity on this account. Brevity of test manuals is quite another matter, however, and here the W-P-T suffers to the point of incompleteness compared with such tests as the *Wonderlic Personnel Test*, the *Otis Quick-Scoring Mental Ability Tests*, or the *Adaptability Test*. The personnel officer who has accumulated experience with any of these or similar instruments would be well advised to conduct careful studies to determine the effectiveness of the W-P-T before discarding the old standbys just to gain a few minutes of testing time.

ERWIN K. TAYLOR, *President, Personnel Research and Development Corporation, Cleveland, Ohio.*

The three-page manual for this device claims to provide "the essential information about the W-P-T, its construction, normative data, administration, scoring, and interpretation." Primarily designed for use in industry, the W-P-T comes in four forms. The intercorrelations among these (apparently administered on a timed basis) vary from .81 to .87. Each of the four forms consists of a hodgepodge of 24 items of World War I vintage, apparently patterned after the highly speeded Wonderlic and its predecessor the Otis. The conglomerate includes items in vocabulary, arithmetic reasoning, number series, paper formboards, name and number checking, and verbal reasoning.

The four forms are reasonably parallel since in the case of each form the rank order correlation between the item number and its difficulty is to all intents and purposes minus one as is the rank order correlation of the item difficulties among the several forms. That these item difficulties were determined from highly speeded administrations is evidenced by the magnitude of this correlation and by the fact that the same undescribed populations were apparently used in correlating the scores from this instrument with the Wonderlic. These correlations, incidentally, ranging from .81 to .85, are the manual's sole claim to "validity." Under such highly speeded conditions it is safe to assume that the item difficulty values given are more a measure of the proportion of the population that reached the item than a measure of how difficult the item would have been had the test been administered on a power basis. Aside from this table of item difficulties on this undescribed population the manual makes no mention of the source of items, the nature of the test construction and item analysis, or of any other basis—rational or statistical—for including the particular set of questions which constitute the device.

The manual further claims that the W-P-T provides:

1. *Rapid* tests to measure mental ability....
2. *Practical* and *inexpensive* measures of intelligence and *learning ability*.

Western Personnel Tests

3. Means for *selecting* and *evaluating* new employees, trainees, and present employees relative to hiring, placement, training, promotion, transfer, reassignment and other personnel purposes.

8. *Rapid measures of intellectual functions* such as the use of language, size of vocabulary, reasoning ability, numerical skills, perceptiveness, general alertness, and scope of background.

9. Tests to *reinforce measurements of non-intellectual* abilities and traits: interests, aptitudes, skills, personality characteristics.

10. Tests which are *reliable* and *valid* measurements of intelligence.

The six examples of the 12 claims made for the test in the manual seem to this reviewer to go far beyond anything supported by the data. As a matter of fact, he wonders if these claims do not border on the unethical.

The "reliability" of this highly speeded form (based on the same populations apparently as the item difficulties) is determined by applying the Spearman-Brown formula to the odd-even item correlations administered under highly speeded conditions. Similarly, the intercorrelations among the four versions of the device, although ranging from .81 to .87, cannot, assuming that they were not administered under power conditions, be considered any more than a measure of the reliability of speed, if that.

There are norms for professional ($n = 27$ to 35), college ($n = 25$ to 47), clerical ($n = 37$ to 45), skilled ($n = 34$ to 72), and unskilled ($n = 39$ to 53) populations.

Perhaps the greatest affront to the intelligence of the reader of the manual is the section entitled "Interpretation of the W-P-T Scores." Here the authors present three hypothetical applicants for a clerical job. Their general population percentile scores (based on an n of 200) are 99, 70, and 35, respectively, while their clerical group percentile scores ($n = 45$) are 95, 65, and 20, respectively. Without reference to the nature or complexity of the job, the manual states with respect to the top scoring candidate, "On the basis of intellectual capacity only, he appears to be an exceptionally strong candidate." The other two applicants are discussed as follows: "Harry H. places at the 70th percentile of the General Population, and at the 65th percentile in the Clerical group; this suggests he is above the average for the General Population and for the Clerical group. He would be a good risk, but not as strong as John W. Robert S. with a raw score of 7 places at the 35th percentile in the General Population, and at the 20th percentile in the Clerical group. He appears to be a poor risk for a clerical job."

The manual pays the usual lip service to the desirability of individual organizations building their own norms and suggests that such data can be useful for many purposes, such as validation, besides selecting and training employees.

Such instruments are grist for the mills of the Grosses, the Hoffmans, and the Whites. Such instruments, available to anyone with access to a business letterhead and sufficient money to make the purchase, unfortunately afford considerable veracity to the contentions of these critics of testing. It is devoutly to be desired that no personnel manager considering the use of tests is so gullible as to install this instrument.

[513]

*Wonderlic Personnel Test. Adults; 1939–61; Forms D and F are adaptations, for business and industrial use, of *Otis Self-Administering Tests of Mental Ability,* Higher Form; Forms A ('42), B ('42), D ['39], F ['39], 1 ('59), 2 ('59), 4 ('59), 5 ('59), EM ('59), (3 pages); revised manual ('61, 11 pages); norms supplement ('61, 14 pages); distribution of Form EM restricted to employment agencies; $8 per 100 tests and manual; 50¢ per manual; postage extra; norms supplement and 3 other reports free on request; $4 per introductory package of manual, norms supplement, 3 other reports, and 20 copies each of Forms A and B or 1 and 2; postpaid; 12(20) minutes; E. F. Wonderlic; E. F. Wonderlic & Associates. *

REFERENCES

1–2. See 40:1415.
3–9. See 3:269.
10–68. See 5:400.
69. BARTON, GLADYS. *The Personnel Test (Wonderlic) and Its Effectiveness in the Selection of Clerical Workers (Ticket Sorters).* Master's thesis, Temple University (Philadelphia, Pa.), 1958.
70. HUTTNER, LUDWIG, AND STENE, D. MIRIAM. "Foremen Selection in Light of a Theory of Supervision." *Personnel Psychol* 11:403–9 au '58. * (*PA* 33:11090)
71. SKOLNICKI, JOHN. "Normative Data Information Exchange, Nos. 11-17, 11-18." *Personnel Psychol* 11:447–8 au '58. *
72. ALBRIGHT, LEWIS E.; SMITH, WALLACE J.; AND GLENNON, J. R. "A Follow-Up on Some 'Invalid' Tests for Selecting Salesmen." *Personnel Psychol* 12:105–12 sp '59. * (*PA* 34:3463)
73. BUSCH, ALLEN C., AND WOODWARD, RICHARD H. "Normative Data Information Exchange, No. 12-27." *Personnel Psychol* 12:646 w '59. *
74. BUSCH, ALLEN C., AND WOODWARD, RICHARD H. "Validity Information Exchange, No. 12-18: D.O.T. Code 0-18.01, Industrial Engineer." *Personnel Psychol* 12:481 au '59. *
75. KAZMIER, LEONARD J. "Normative Data Information Exchange, No. 12-21." *Personnel Psychol* 12:503 au '59. *
76. KAZMIER, LEONARD J., AND BROWNE, C. G. "Comparability of Wonderlic Test Forms in Industrial Testing." *J Appl Psychol* 43:129–32 Ap '59. * (*PA* 34:3474)
77. MACKINNEY, ARTHUR C., AND WOLINS, LEROY. "Validity Information Exchange, No. 12-19: D.O.T. Code 1-36.05, Coding Clerk; 1-17.02, File Clerk II, Circulation Clerk." *Personnel Psychol* 12:482–3 au '59. *
78. CAMPBELL, JOEL T.; PRIEN, ERICH P.; AND BRAILEY, LESTER B. "Predicting Performance Evaluations." *Personnel Psychol* 13:435–40 w '60. * (*PA* 36:1LD35C)
79. HAWKINS, WILLIAM ANDREW. *Deviant Responses, Response Variability, and Paired-Associate Learning.* Doctor's thesis, Louisiana State University (Baton Rouge, La.), 1960. (*DA* 21:2365)
80. KIRCHNER, WAYNE; HANSON, RICHARD; AND BENSON, DALE. "Selecting Foremen With Psychological Tests." *Personnel Adm* 23:27–30 N-D '60. *
81. NEEL, ROBERT G., AND DUNN, ROBERT E. "Predicting Success in Supervisory Training Programs by the Use of

Psychological Tests." *J Appl Psychol* 44:358–60 O '60. * (*PA* 35:4081)
82. COATS, J. E.; WITH THE ASSISTANCE OF R. G. GARNER. *A Study of the Nature of the Chemical Operator's Occupation and the Personal Qualities That Contribute to Successful Operator Performance.* Midland, Mich.: Dow Chemical Co., March 1961. Pp. iv, 112. *
83. ROBBINS, JAMES E., AND KING, DONALD C. "Validity Information Exchange, No. 14-02: D.O.T. Code 0-97.61, Manager, Sales." *Personnel Psychol* 14:217–9 su '61. *
84. MCNAMARA, WALTER J. "Retraining of Industrial Personnel." *Personnel Psychol* 16:233–47 au '63. * (*PA* 38:6728)
85. SHOTT, GERALD L.; ALBRIGHT, LEWIS E.; AND GLENNON, J. R. "Predicting Turnover in an Automated Office Situation." *Personnel Psychol* 16:213–9 au '63. * (*PA* 38:6714)

N. M. DOWNIE, *Professor of Psychology, Purdue University, Lafayette, Indiana.*

Since the appearance of the last *Mental Measurements Yearbook,* five new forms of this test have appeared, 1, 2, 4, 5, and EM. Each of these, like the earlier forms, is a spiral-omnibus type of intelligence test of 50 items of an academic nature with a 12-minute time limit. The two original forms, D and F, were developed from the Higher Form of the *Otis Self-Administering Tests of Mental Ability.* Wonderlic's purpose was to develop a test for measuring mental ability of adults for hiring and placement in business and industry.

The author suggests that each company employ two forms and rotate their use. He also suggests that when this is done the following combinations be used: A and B, A and 5, 1 and 2, 1 and 4, or 2 and 4. Although the manual covers the 12-minute administration only, Wonderlic suggests that the test may be used as a power test with unlimited time. However, no suggestions are given concerning the interpretation of such scores. He also suggests that, if time is available, each applicant be given two forms to increase reliability.

Scoring with strip keys is rapid and simple; the score is the number right. Normative data are presented on some 50,000 adults in the age range 20–65 for the five newer forms and on about 35,000 adults for the earlier forms. Wonderlic recommends the use of raw scores rather than the IQ's for all practical uses of the instrument.

The new forms, like the earlier ones, have the items arranged from very easy to very difficult. Difficulty values are normally distributed with a mean of about 60 per cent. Correlation between position in the test and item difficulty is said to be above .90.

The reliability of the tests with a 12-minute time limit, one test being immediately followed by another, was found to vary between .82 and .94. Odd-even internal consistency coefficients ranging between .88 and .94 are also reported.

The author states that validity is demonstrated because the number of correct answers "distinguishes between good and poor groups of employees differentiated on work records accumulated over a period of five years."

Tables are presented to aid in interpreting results. Among these is a listing of minimum scores for various occupations. Another table shows the effect of age with suggestions that points be added to the score to compensate for score decrements related to age. For ages 60–69 this is 11 points. Although scores are shown to be related to educational level, as might be expected, there is considerable variance among scores in any one educational level. Finally, tables are provided for sex and last grade in school attended, for age, for applicants for clerical work in a bank, and for male applicants with types of work not specified. Conversion tables are presented for comparing forms and for transforming scores to Otis scores. In the 1961 supplement to the norms, distributions of scores by educational levels, stabilized for age groups, for males and females on each form are also given.

In summary this is an economical, generally adequate, and convenient instrument for measuring mental ability in an industrial situation. However, certain things leave much to be desired. The discussion of validity is inadequate. The validity of the test should be demonstrated for particular jobs, and for showing relationship to success in training for specific jobs. Expectancy charts for various occupations would be useful. Normative data should be presented for workers in different types of work and for variations in any job category. For example, it is not enough to give norms for clerical work; information should be available on bank clerks, time clerks, supply clerks, file clerks, etc. Percentile ranks or some type of standard score would be useful in giving more meaning to the raw scores used by Wonderlic.

MARVIN D. DUNNETTE, *Professor of Psychology, University of Minnesota, Minneapolis, Minnesota.*

The *Wonderlic Personnel Test* is a 50-item, timed (12 minutes), omnibus measure of intelligence. Forms D and F were formed from items contained in the Otis S-A tests and were standardized for industrial use and published in 1938. Forms A and B, consisting of new and more diverse item content, were published in

1942, and Forms 1, 2, 4, 5, and EM were published in 1959. The manual suggests, on the basis of "extremely high" correlations, that Forms 1, 2, 4, and 5 may be substituted, respectively, for Forms A, B, D, and F without requiring a restandardization. Form EM was developed for the exclusive use of fee employment agencies in order to avoid the possible conflict of interest between industrial employment departments and the private agencies. However, there is no evidence that these good intentions are backed up with any administrative device to insure that employment agencies do not also purchase the other forms. The manual, the norms booklet, and most of the reports on the Wonderlic test carry an order blank urging "any personnel executive" to purchase the tests. The easy availability of the *Wonderlic Personnel Tests* must, therefore, be regarded as one of the major disadvantages to their use. It is probably a rare applicant who is not exposed to the Wonderlic test several times during any given job search; the promotional literature on the test claims that over 6,500 organizations are using it for selection and placement procedures.

For such a widely used test, it is surprising and very disappointing to find such a paucity of information about the test in the manual. The manual carries a copyright date of 1961; yet, it contains only 16 references about the test, and many of these are from trade journals such as the *Mellon Bank News* or the *Wall Street Journal*. Furthermore, the references are old—10 dated in the late 30's and 40's and only 6 in the 50's, the most recent being 1958. Citations also are given to some of the classic texts such as Tiffin's *Industrial Psychology* and Yoder's *Personnel Management and Industrial Relations*. Here again, the citations are to the hopelessly out-of-date 1942 editions of these books. The Tiffin volume is now in its fourth edition and the Yoder in its fifth. One wonders what the more recent editions have to say about the *Wonderlic Personnel Test*. Thus, the manual seems *not* to include results of any recent studies by other investigators even though it does present information on a 1960–61 so-called restudy in which over 50,000 adults were tested. Unfortunately, however, the impressive n of 50,000 cannot make up for the lack of technical information on reliability and validity.

Reliability has been estimated in two ways. Equivalent form coefficients (one form given *immediately* after another) ranging from .82 to .94 are cited, but no n's are given, and the nature of the samples used is not described. Also, odd-even coefficients ranging from .88 to .94 are cited. Again no information is given about n's, the kinds of samples employed, or the forms to which the coefficients apply. Even more serious is the fact that an odd-even reliability estimate is clearly inappropriate for this highly speeded test.

No evidence of validity is given in the manual, although the flat claim is made that "This test has been shown to be a valid instrument in determining success on a number of different jobs." It is probably true that many studies have shown the Wonderlic test to be a valid indicator of job success; however, the potential user of the test should not have to make his own literature search to find evidence of validity nor should he be required to accept on faith the author's claim that "the test is valid." It is too bad that this up-dated manual was prepared without heeding the 1955 APA Technical Recommendations for the preparation of test manuals. Had they been heeded, a comprehensive and useful summary of the many studies using the test would have been included as well as carefully documented evidence for the content, predictive, concurrent, and construct validities of the Wonderlic tests. As it is, 25 years of research is very nearly ignored in favor of presenting a simplified and innocuous manual seemingly designed for businessmen rather than for psychologists. The only other evidence of validity is given in a supplemental publication titled "Summary of Experiences with the Wonderlic Personnel Test" which consists of a potpourri of anecdotal accounts, average scores obtained by different employees, frequencies with which the test is used, etc., etc.

A complete and careful job of norming (based on 27,366 males and 25,988 females) for the many forms of the test has been done; the norms are presented in a supplemental publication titled "Performance Norms," and separate norms are available by sex and educational level for each of the forms of the test. In addition, a table is provided enabling the user to convert raw scores from one form to equivalent scores on any of the other forms. The manual still suggests that corrections should be made for the effect of age on test scores; however, the correction tables are obviously based on cross-sectional comparisons, and the rationale for making the correction seems questionable.

In summary, the *Wonderlic Personnel Test* is a widely used, convenient, and easily available measure of general intelligence. It is also likely that the tests are adequately reliable and that they are also valid for a variety of jobs and for a variety of situations. It is extremely unfortunate, however, that these tests, in use now for 25 years, are not more rigorously described in the test manual. Instead, the manual and other supplementary materials seem primarily designed to sell tests rather than to inform the user in the appropriate use of the tests. I personally believe that these tests have a good deal of merit for use in industry, but I would hate to try to support such a claim solely on the basis of the *non-evidence* presented by the author and publisher.

For reviews by H. E. Brogden, Charles D. Flory, and Irving Lorge, see 3:269.

[Other Tests]

For tests not listed above, see the following entries in *Tests in Print*: 706–7, 710, 713, 715, 717–21, 726–7, 730, 734–5, 737, 741, 744–6, 748–54, 757–8, 760, 765–8, 770–1, 774–6, 778–81, 783, 785, 796, 801–3, 805–13, 818–9, 824, 826–7, 832, 835, 837–8, 840, 843, 845, 847–9, 854–5, 857, 860, 862, 865–8, and 871–4; out of print: 723, 739, 747, 756, 769, 814, 839, 844, 851, 859, and 861; status unknown: 728 and 786.

INDIVIDUAL

[514]

*Alexander Performance Scale: A Performance Scale for the Measurement of Practical Ability. Ages 7–19; 1935–58; individual; 1 form; 3 tests; manual ('46, 66 pages); record sheet ('58, 1 page); 162s. per set of testing materials, 50 record sheets, and manual; 12s. per 50 record sheets; 8s. per manual; prices include purchase tax; postpaid within U.K.; (40–50) minutes; W. P. Alexander; distributed by National Foundation for Educational Research in England and Wales. *

a) THE PASSALONG TEST. 1932–37; may be administered alone as a quick measure of practical ability; (15) minutes.
b) KOHS' BLOCK DESIGN TEST. 1919–36; a modification of the original Kohs' *Block-Design Test*.
c) CUBE CONSTRUCTION TEST. 1918–25.

REFERENCES

1–3. See 40:1376.
4. See 3:270.
5–8. See 4:334.
9. SLATER, PATRICK. "Evidence on Selection for Technical Schools." *Occup Psychol* 21:135–40 Jl '47. * (PA 22:460)
10. LEFF, BARBARA. *Some Aspects of the Measurement of Technical Aptitude in Boys Aged 12 Years, With Special Reference to Alexander's Performance Scale.* Master's thesis, University of London (London, England), 1949.
11. NELSON, CALVIN CLAYTON. *A Comparison of Retarded and Normal Children With Respect to Alexander's "F" Factor.*

Doctor's thesis, University of Oregon (Eugene, Ore.), 1958. (DA 19:1015)

H. GWYNNE JONES, *Senior Lecturer in Psychology, St. George's Hospital Medical School, London, England.*

This performance scale was developed in Britain to aid in the allocation of children to different types of secondary education at about the age of 11 years. In particular, it was designed to assess "practical ability," operationally defined as "that ability necessary for success in a technical school." Paper and pencil group tests had proved unsuitable for this purpose.

Each of the three subtests which make up the scale consists of graded series of items involving the solution of spatial problems and the manipulation of coloured wooden blocks. The adaptation of Kohs' well known *Block-Design Test* requires the reproduction of two-dimensional patterns; the *Cube Construction Test* extends this principle into the third dimension, and the *Passalong Test* requires the execution of a planned series of moves from an initial to a final pattern. The test materials are convenient, robust, and attractive, and, although the examiner needs to study the manual carefully and familiarise himself thoroughly with the material to achieve smoothness of administration, the instructions are clear and precise. Scoring is based jointly on level achieved and speed of performance.

Separate norms for boys and girls are provided for the total scale and for the *Passalong Test* alone. These are in the form of mental ages from 7 to 19 years to be converted into *practical ability ratios* equivalent to IQ's. No precise information is given concerning the distribution of these scores, but it is claimed that the norms were arranged so as to approximate to a mean of 100 and a standard deviation of 15. Certainly its standardisation is the weakest aspect of this scale, as indicated by the inclusion in the manual of a request for additional data from users. Evidence from the references quoted suggests that this weakness is least serious within the age range of 10 to 13, for which the norms are based on several hundred scores.

The reliability of the scale is not outstandingly high but is as high as can be expected for a performance scale of this kind and length: the test-retest correlation is of the order of .8.

Allowing for this, the *Kohs' Block Design Test* and the *Passalong Test* are very closely related (corrected correlation .96) but have lower correlations with the *Cube Construction Test* (corrected correlations .63 and .73, respectively). Factor analyses indicate that the scale is a good measure of general intellectual ability, and also of "practical ability," which most contemporary psychologists would identify with spatial ability.

The validity of the scale has been mainly assessed in terms of its predictive power in relation to success in technical school subjects. Whereas a verbal scale is a more efficient predictor of performance in the more academic verbal and science subjects, the performance scale is greatly superior for the more technical subjects, such as machine drawing and lathe work.

At one time the Alexander scale was very frequently used in Britain, in conjunction with the Binet scale, for the all round intellectual assessment of children for various purposes. During the last decade, the WISC has tended to become the popular tool for use with school age children. Whereas the WISC has many advantages over the earlier combination, it is by no means certain that the WISC performance scale is superior to the Alexander. The Block Design and Object Assembly subtest of the WISC are probably measures of the same spatial ability as that assessed by the Alexander scale, but this is not necessarily true of the overall performance IQ, which is also partially determined by various other abilities reflected in the other subtest scores. One definite advantage of the Alexander is the provision of separate sex norms: there is ample clear evidence of appreciable sex differences in spatial ability. In an experimental or other situation for which the adequacy of the initial standardisation data is not of the first importance, the Alexander might well still be the performance scale of choice for the appropriate age group.

[515]

*Cattell Infant Intelligence Scale. Ages 3–30 months; 1940–60; downward extension of the *Revised Stanford-Binet Intelligence Scale, Second Revision* (see 5:413); individual; 1 form; revised manual ('60, c1940, see *18* below, essentially the same as previous edition); record form ('40, 4 pages); $60 per set of testing materials, carrying case, and 25 record blanks; $1.70 per 25 record blanks; $6 per manual; postpaid; (20–30) minutes; Psyche Cattell; Psychological Corporation. *

REFERENCES

1. CATTELL, PSYCHE. *The Measurement of Intelligence of Infants and Young Children.* New York: Psychological Corporation, 1940. Pp. 274. * (PA 15:2397)
2. CATTELL, PSYCHE. "Intelligence of Infants and Its Measurement." *Trans N Y Acad Sci,* Series II 3:162–71 Ap '41. * (PA 15:4041)
3. GERSTEIN, REVA APPLEBY. "An Analysis of Infant Behavioural Development." Abstract. *B Can Psychol Assn* 5:73–5 O '45. * (PA 20:938, title only)
4. ESCALONA, SIBYLLE. "The Predictive Value of Psychological Tests in Infancy: A Report on Clinical Findings." Abstract. *Am Psychologist* 3:281 Jl '48. * (PA 22:5366, title only)
5. ESCALONA, SIBYLLE. "The Use of Infant Tests for Predictive Purposes." *B Menninger Clinic* 14:117–28 Jl '50. * (PA 25:5387)
6. HARMS, IRENE E. *A Study of Some Variables Affecting the Reliability of Intelligence Test Scores During Late Infancy.* Doctor's thesis, State University of Iowa (Iowa City, Iowa), 1951.
7. WATSON, ROBERT I. *The Clinical Method in Psychology,* pp. 333–40. New York: Harper & Bros., 1951. Pp. xii, 779. * (PA 26:5577)
8. KLATSKIN, ETHELYN HENRY. "Intelligence Test Performance at One Year Among Infants Raised With Flexible Methodology." *J Clin Psychol* 8:230–7 Jl '52. * (PA 27:5764)
9. MILLER, ELSA, AND ROSENFELD, GEORGE B. "The Psychologic Evaluation of Children With Cerebral Palsy and Its Implications in Treatment: Preliminary Report." *J Pediatrics* 41:613–21 N '52. * (PA 27:6706)
10. CATTELL, PSYCHE. "Infant Intelligence Scale," pp. 507–9. (PA 27:7759) In *Contributions Toward Medical Psychology: Theory and Psychodiagnostic Methods, Vol. II.* Edited by Arthur Weider. New York: Ronald Press Co., 1953. Pp. xi, 459–885. *
11. GALLAGHER, JAMES J. "Clinical Judgment and the Cattell Infant Intelligence Scale." *J Consult Psychol* 17:303–5 Ag '53. * (PA 28:4353)
12. CAVANAUGH, MAXINE C.; COHEN, IRA; DUNPHY, DONAL; RINGWALL, EGAN A.; AND GOLDBERG, IRVING D. "Prediction From the Cattell Infant Intelligence Scale." *J Consult Psychol* 21:33–7 F '57. * (PA 32:266)
13. FROMM, ERIKA; HARTMAN, LENORE DUMAS; AND MARSCHAK, MARIAN. "Children's Intelligence Tests as a Measure of Dynamic Personality Functioning." *Am J Orthopsychiatry* 27:134–44 Ja '57. * (PA 32:1621)
14. NORRIS, MIRIAM; SPAULDING, PATRICIA J.; AND BRODIE, FERN H. *Blindness in Children.* Chicago, Ill.: University of Chicago Press, 1957. Pp. xv, 217. * (PA 32:824)
15. ALLEN, ROBERT M. "Suggestions for the Adaptive Administration of Intelligence Tests for Those With Cerebral Palsy: Part 2, Administration of the Vineland Social Maturity Scale, the Gesell Preliminary Behavior Inventory, and the Cattell Infant Intelligence Scale." *Cerebral Palsy R* 19:6–7 Mr–Ap '58. * (PA 33:8853)
16. HARMS, IRENE E., AND SPIKER, CHARLES C. "Factors Associated With the Performance of Young Children on Intelligence Scales and Tests of Speech Development." *J Genetic Psychol* 94:3–22 Mr '59. * (PA 36:4FE03H)
17. KRALOVICH, ANNE MARIE. "A Study of Performance Differences on the Cattell Infant Intelligence Scale Between Matched Groups of Organic and Mongoloid Subjects." *J Clin Psychol* 15:198–9 Ap '59. * (PA 35:5178)
18. CATTELL, PSYCHE. *The Measurement of Intelligence of Infants and Young Children,* Revised 1960. New York: Psychological Corporation, 1940 [published 1960]. Pp. 274. * [Although "Revised 1960" appears on the title page, the publisher has informed the MMY that the book is only a reprinting of the original edition (*1*) with corrections of a few typographical errors.]
19. WIGGIN, MARTHA K. *The Use of Certain Items From the Cattell Intelligence Scale for Infants and Young Children With Deaf-Blind Children.* Master's thesis, Boston University (Boston, Mass.), 1960.
20. ESCALONA, SIBYLLE K., AND MORIARTY, ALICE. "Prediction of Schoolage Intelligence From Infant Tests." *Child Develop* 32:597–605 S '61. * (PA 36:4FE97E)
21. PEASE, DAMARIS; ROSAUER, JOSEPHINE KEEFE; AND WOLINS, LEROY. "Reliability of Three Infant Developmental Scales Administered During the First Year of Life." *J Genetic Psychol* 98:295–8 Je '61. * (PA 36:2FB95P)
22. LONDON, SUSAN KATHERINE. *The Stability of the IQ of Mentally Retarded Pre-School Children.* Doctor's thesis, University of Michigan (Ann Arbor, Mich.), 1962. (DA 23:310)

For reviews by Florence M. Teagarden and Beth L. Wellman, see 3:281 (1 excerpt).

[516]

★Children's Picture Information Test. Ages 2–6 with motor handicaps; 1959; individual; 1 form (41 pages); instructions for administering (1 page); norms-technical data (7 pages, reprint of *2* below); $10 per set of testing materials, postpaid; [10–25] minutes; Kate L. Kogan and Richard L. Crager; Spastic Aid Council, Inc. *

REFERENCES

1. KOGAN, KATE L. "A Method of Assessing Capacity in Preschool Cerebral Palsied Children." *J Clin Psychol* 13:54–6 Ja '57. *
2. KOGAN, KATE L., AND CRAGER, RICHARD L. "Standardization of the Children's Picture Information Test." *J Clin Psychol* 15:405–11 O '59. * (*PA* 36:1HCo5K)

DOROTHY EICHORN, *Associate Research Psychologist, and Administrator, Harold E. Jones Child Study Center, Institute of Human Development, University of California, Berkeley, California.*

This test consists of 40 sets of colored pictures, and the child indicates, by pointing or responding in some other discriminable way, which of four alternatives "goes with" the picture. Instructions for administration are clear and a specimen record form is provided, but examiners must number the pages of the test booklet and supply record forms. The authors emphasize that the test was devised for the "relatively rapid" assessment of young children lacking oral and manipulative skills, and "Under no circumstances would....be preferred if more extensive and varied examination" were possible. They are equally specific in describing the procedures used in establishing norms and estimating reliability and validity.

From a total of 568 normal children aged 2 through 6 years, tested in Seattle, 400 were chosen for the standardization population. Limitations of size and geographic sampling are mitigated by the attention given to selecting for each age interval a sample of 50 balanced for sex, age in months across the six-month range, and conformity of parental occupation to the distribution of the 1950 census. Norms are in the form of normalized *T*-scores and centiles because the raw score distributions were skewed—positively at the younger ages and negatively at the older ages—and of unequal variance. Increases in median score between successive age groups were significant at the one per cent level only from 2½ through 5½ years.

Two subgroups of 50 subjects each, balanced for age distribution from 2 to 6 years and with parental occupations approximating the census groupings, were also selected. The "reliability group" was retested after one to three weeks; the "validity group" received the Stanford-Binet, Form L. Binet and CPIT scores were also available for 59 handicapped children. The product-moment correlations between CPIT score and Binet mental age for the normal and handicapped groups were .89 and .80, respectively. Lower coefficients might be expected with a more restricted age range. The test-retest correlation was .93. Split-half reliability correlations, computed for 4 one-year age intervals of 100 subjects each and corrected by the Spearman-Brown formula, ranged from .85 to .90.

Test construction is only briefly discussed, but apparently was done less carefully than standardization. The pictures are cut from children's books, rather than designed to standard specifications. The authors claim that mounting the pictures of one set on paper of the same color eliminates any possible influence of color preference. However, the pictures differ in hue, brightness, scale relationships, fineness of detail, clarity, figure-ground contrast, and contrast with the mounting paper. Among the cerebral palsied, for whom the test is intended, are individuals whose performance may be particularly affected by such uncontrolled variables. "An effort was made to restrict the content largely to everyday household situations" with which an "immobilized child of confined environment" would be familiar. Some of the pictures do not meet this criterion, e.g., an igloo and a factory, but in the main this objective has been achieved.

Kogan and Crager recognize that factors in addition to "amount of information assimilated" influence performance, but overlook the cognitive processes involved in classifying the correct alternative as "belonging with" the key. A variety of principles of abstraction are required. One of the more frequent is a part-whole strategy, in which the key is a part of the correct alternative, or vice versa. Several sets require functional matching, e.g., a child's overalls and a flatiron. A third basis for matching is conventional proximity, such as ocean water (very indistinct) and a fish. Some sets admit of more than one method of classification, e.g., color matching and another strategy. The two strategies do not always lead to the same response. A frying pan is the correct match for the stove, but a chair is the only other piece of furniture. Such ambiguities may produce nondiscriminating items, either because equal proportions of different ability groups pass, using different conceptual bases of choice, or because incorrect choices are based on higher order abstractions. There is no indication that sets were pretested either to eliminate nondiscriminating items or to insure that the decoys in a set were of equal appeal and difficulty. Structuring the test to include several strategies should, however, strengthen it as a source of information about intellectual function by sampling more widely of cognitive processes—a real advantage when the clinician is asked to assess a child on the basis of relatively little material. Further, if some strategies are more difficult than others, tabulation of passes in terms of classification systems is a potentially powerful tool for item construction and selection.

The skewed distributions and poor discrimination at both ends of the age range indicate that the CPIT lacks "floor" and "ceiling." Items could be added without lengthening testing time if sets were arranged in order of difficulty and testing restricted to a critical range, from basal to ceiling. At present all sets must be given, although the medians at the lower ages are only 25 to 50 per cent of the total, and at the upper ages approximate the ceiling.

Despite the deficiencies in test construction, the standardization data indicate that Kogan and Crager have had considerable success in developing a test to meet a real need. It is easily administered, discriminates between adjacent six-month intervals from 2½ to 5½ years, produces satisfactory reliability coefficients, and correlates reasonably well with a conventional test of intelligence. For immediate use with young handicapped children, many may prefer the *Peabody Picture Vocabulary Test*. It is at least as easy and quick to administer and has the advantages of more "bottom" and "top," demonstration items, an alternate form, MA and IQ norms as well as percentiles, and more carefully constructed pictures. However, the potential which the CPIT offers for assessing aspects of intellectual function beyond sheer accumulation of information is a strong argument for its further use and refinement.

T. ERNEST NEWLAND, *Professor of Educational Psychology, University of Illinois, Urbana, Illinois.*

The test materials consist of a booklet of forty 10 by 11 inch pages on each of which appears a stimulus picture and four possible response pictures, generally 1½ by 2½ inches in size. The subject's attention is called to the stimulus picture and he then is asked to identify which of the possible response pictures "belongs with," or "goes with" the stimulus picture. The subject may be trained to whatever extent the examiner deems desirable, but he receives no score in any items used in training. In all but 5 of the 200 test item elements the figure-ground contrast is sharply delineated. The positional placements of the correct responses are well randomized. All of the 200 figures depicted are in color, 68 per cent of them being on a white background. Colored mats offset the elements from the black pages of the booklet. In terms of the kinds of behavior sampled, 9 items involve the categorization of stimulus and response elements (Hallowe'en pumpkin-witch); 10 items involve the recognition of whole-part or part-whole relationships (desk-telephone; chimney-house); and the remaining items call for the identification of use relationships (object-user; user-object; object-use; and joint use).

On a disabled population of 59 subjects, presumably of varying degrees and kinds of cerebral palsied involvement, and of unspecified age and sex distribution, CPIT scores correlated with "mental age ratings" .80. Test-retest reliability obtained on scores of 50 nondisabled subjects (26 males and 24 females), who presumably were equally distributed over the eight six-month age groups, is reflected in a product-moment coefficient of .93. On the basis of the results obtained on 400 nondisabled subjects, T-score equivalents are presented for each possible CPIT raw score for half-year age groups and for full-year age groups. A further table is provided for converting the T-score equivalents into centiles.

Children and clinicians being what they are, it is highly likely that the CPIT will make possible a helpful discrimination among children in this age range—certainly in the case of nondisabled youngsters, probably among disabled youngsters, and possibly among the highly heterogenous group of cerebral palsied youngsters. The light which scores on the CPIT will throw on the psychological functioning of cerebral palsied children in the preferred age ranges must be regarded as limited. The authors rightly point out that the CPIT "appears to measure the amount of information the child has assimilated," and, as in the case of so much "intelligence" testing, this is taken as the basis for inferring subsequent capacity to assimilate. Very properly, the authors perceive their device as capable of reflecting only certain "facets of intelligence," and recognize that psychological evaluation beyond the use of the CPIT will be needed. The CPIT is presented as a device developed for the purpose of better obtaining a kind of measurement of the learning aptitude of cerebral palsied children. Yet the only evidence presented to support this intent is a reasonably high correlation between the scores on the CPIT and the mental ages obtained by means of the Stanford-Binet Form L. Since it was because of the limitations of the Binet that a new device was conceived, this type of correlational validation has a highly involutional aspect to it, and actually could be self-defeating.

The authors, like others who have tried to produce devices presumably clinically more appropriate for measuring the "intelligence" (or facets of it) of physically deviant groups, such as the cerebral palsied, the deaf, and the blind, have been caught in a near-unresolvable dilemma. On the one hand, a device is developed, is standardized on a nondeviant population, and is concurrently validated—still on the nondeviant population—against the device which has been criticized. The two devices then are applied to a deviant population and if the resulting correlation is high enough, the appropriateness of the new device for use with the deviant population is taken as established. On the other hand, a newly developed device is standardized entirely on a deviant population and if the content validity appears satisfactory, it is assumed to yield results connoting the same kind of psychological functioning which extant (but criticized) devices yield on nondeviant populations. The authors, who have much company, have pursued the former course. But those who compare results obtained on cerebral palsied populations will need to be quite cautious when they try to rationalize correlations between results obtained by means of the CPIT and those obtained by means of other devices. The fact that so much of the precise statistical work was done on CPIT results obtained on a nondeviant population and so little on a cerebral palsied population will have to be kept clearly in mind.

More specifically, it is most unfortunate that the physical conditions (kinds of cerebral palsy, degrees of involvement, sensory conditions), age distribution, and sex distribution of the cerebral palsied population are not specified. From a test administration standpoint, it is quite possible that if at least the response elements were arranged and presented parallel to the bottom of the page, rather than vertical to it, the pointing responses of young involved subjects might be facilitated. As is so often true in newly developed devices, subjects may give perfectly justifiable responses which are not provided for in the key. Such would appear to be possible on items such as these: electric iron–overalls, as contrasted with iron–bus (both metal); little girl–tricycle (girl–moving van); tree–bird (tree–door, both wood); sleeping girl–bed (girl–toy); and Hallowe'en pumpkin–witch (pumpkin–turkey). Only a systematic analysis of response "errors" can establish the validity or invalidity of such concern.

[517]

*Columbia Mental Maturity Scale, Revised Edition.** Mental ages 3–12; 1954–59; 1 form ('59, 100 cards, same as 1954 edition except for 17 new items and reordering of items); manual ('54, 15 pages); hectographed supplementary data ('59, 3 pages); revised norms ['59, 1 page]; individual record, revised ('59, c1954–59, 1 page); no data on reliability of revised edition; $35 per examiner's kit of cards and manual (owners of earlier edition may purchase revised cards only for $5.50); $1.40 per 35 individual records; $5.75 per carrying case; postage extra; (15–30) minutes; Bessie B. Burgemeister, Lucille Hollander Blum, and Irving Lorge; [Harcourt, Brace & World, Inc.]. *

REFERENCES

1–13. See 5:402.
14. BLUM, LUCILLE H.; BURGEMEISTER, BESSIE B.; AND LORGE, IRVING D. "The Mental-Maturity Scale for the Motor Handicapped." *Sch & Soc* 73:232–3 Ap 14 '51. *
15. BLUM, LUCILLE H.; BURGEMEISTER, BESSIE B.; AND LORGE, IRVING. "Trends in Estimating the Mental Maturity of the Cerebral-Palsied Child." *J Excep Child* 17:174–7 Mr '51. *
16. ALLEN, ROBERT M., AND COLLINS, MARJORIE G. "Suggestions for the Adaptive Administration of Intelligence Tests for Those With Cerebral Palsy: Part 1, Administration of the Ammons Full-Range Picture Test, Columbia Mental Maturity Test, Raven's Progressive Matrices and Leiter International Performance Scale." *Cerebral Palsy R* 16:11–4+ My–Je '55. * (PA 30:3284)
17. BERKO, MARTIN J. "The Measurement in Intelligence of Children With Cerebral Palsy: The Columbia Mental Maturity Scale." *J Pediatrics* 47:253–60 Ag '55. * (PA 30:5078)
18. GUSLOFF, RICHARD F. *Comparability of Columbia Mental Maturity Scale Quotients.* Master's thesis, Illinois Normal University (Normal, Ill.), 1955.
19. ALLEN, ROBERT M., AND SANDLER, JACK. "Concerning the Variation of Responses on the Columbia Mental Maturity Scale." *Cerebral Palsy R* 17:38+ Mr–Ap '56. * (PA 31:4668)
20. FRENCH, JOSEPH, AND WORCESTER, D. A. "A Critical Study of the Columbia Mental Maturity Scale." *Excep Child* 23:111–3+ D '56. * (PA 31:7912)
21. GALLAGHER, JAMES J.; BENOIT, E. PAUL; AND BOYD, HERBERT F. "Measures of Intelligence in Brain Damaged Children." *J Clin Psychol* 12:69–72 Ja '56. * (PA 30:5093)
22. GALLAGHER, JAMES J. *A Comparison of Brain-Injured and Non-Brain-Injured Mentally Retarded Children on Several Psychological Variables.* Monograph of the Society for Research in Child Development, Vol. 22, No. 2. Lafayette, Ind.: Child Development Publications, 1957. Pp. 79. * (PA 33:1632)
23. GROSS, DEAN G. *An Experiment With the Columbia*

Mental Maturity Scale and the Goodenough Draw-A-Man Test to Determine Their Utility as Testing Devices for the Severely Mentally Retarded as Compared to the Stanford-Binet. Master's thesis, San Francisco State College (San Francisco, Calif.), 1958.

24. BLIGH, HAROLD F. "Concurrent Validity Evidence on Two Intelligence Measures for Young Children." *Yearb Nat Council Meas Used Ed* 16:56–66 '59. * (PA 34:7345)

25. DUNN, LLOYD M., AND HARLEY, RANDALL K. "Comparability of Peabody, Ammons, Van Alstyne, and Columbia Test Scores With Cerebral Palsied Children." *Excep Child* 26:70–4 O '59. * (PA 35:3733)

26. ESTES, BETSY WORTH; KODMAN, FRANK; AND AKEL, MACY. "The Validity of the Columbia Mental Maturity Scale." Abstract. *J Consult Psychol* 23:561 D '59. * (PA 34:5578)

27. WITSAMAN, L. R., AND JONES, REGINALD L. "Reliability of the Columbia Mental Maturity Scale With Kindergarten Pupils." *J Clin Psychol* 15:66–8 Ja '59. * (PA 34:2740)

28. LEVINSON, BORIS M., AND BLOCK, ZELICK. "Research Note on Columbia Mental Maturity Scale (CMMS) and Revised Stanford Binet (L) in a Preschool Population." *J Clin Psychol* 16:158–9 Ap '60. * (PA 36:2HC58L)

29. WARREN, SUE ALLEN, AND COLLIER, HERBERT L. "Suitability of the Columbia Mental Maturity Scale for Mentally Retarded Institutionalized Females." *Am J Mental Def* 64:916–20 Mr '60. * (PA 35:6846)

30. HIRSCHENFANG, SAMUEL. "A Comparison of the Revised Columbia Mental Maturity Scale (CMMS) and Goodenough Draw-A-Man Test in Children With Speech Disorders." *J Clin Psychol* 17:381–2 O '61. * (PA 38:8918)

31. HIRSCHENFANG, SAMUEL. "Further Studies on the Columbia Mental Maturity Scale (CMMS) and Revised Stanford Binet (L) in Children With Speech Disorders." *J Clin Psychol* 17:171 Ap '61. * (PA 38:956)

32. SMITH, BESSIE S. "The Relative Merits of Certain Verbal and Non-Verbal Tests at the Second-Grade Level." *J Clin Psychol* 17:53–4 Ja '61. * (PA 37:3595)

33. FLEMING, KATHRYN. *A Comparison of Mental Age Scores on the Revised Columbia Mental Maturity Scale and the Stanford-Binet Intelligence Test, Form L, at the Five Through Eight Year Mental Age Levels.* Master's thesis, Bowling Green State University (Bowling Green, Ohio), 1962.

34. KODMAN, FRANK, JR.; WATERS, JERRY E.; AND WHIPPLE, CLIFFORD I. "Psychometric Appraisal of Deaf Children Using the Columbia Mental Maturity Scale." *J Speech & Hearing Disorders* 27:275–9 Ag '62. * (PA 37:3488)

35. MASCIA, GEORGE V. *An Investigation Into the Use of the Revised Columbia Mental Maturity Scale as a Psychometric Instrument Sensitive to Brain Injury.* Master's thesis, University of Kansas (Lawrence, Kan.), 1962.

MARSHALL S. HISKEY, *Professor of Educational Psychology, and Director, Educational Psychological Clinic, University of Nebraska, Lincoln, Nebraska.*

Designed to measure intelligence of handicapped children, this pictorial type classification test "calls for no verbal response and a minimum of motor response." Each of the 100 items has a series of three to five drawings presented on a card which is 6 by 19 inches. The test, an untimed individual type scale, utilizes perceptive discriminations involving color, shape, size, use, number, kind, missing parts, and symbolic material. The subject responds by selecting the picture in each series which is different from, or unrelated to, the others.

In general, children enjoy this test. The pictures are large and clear and the test can be administered in 15 to 20 minutes. The record blank makes recording an easy procedure, and the conversion of the raw score to a mental age is a simple matter.

The present revision (1959) of the original scale (1954) took place after reports of research gave highly conflicting evidence in regard to validity and reliability coefficients, adequacy of norms, item difficulty, and the rationale for responses. The original scale had some items that contained printed words, thus making it necessary for the child to have considerable word recognition ability in order to complete the item successfully. Furthermore, some pictures in the original scale were not clearly discernible.

The replacement of 17 cards with new items and the rearrangement of items in terms of difficulty should alleviate some of the shortcomings of the original scale. Unfortunately, the reporting on the revision is such that one is unable to determine the extent to which it is an improvement over the original issue.

Items have been arranged in a new sequence on the basis of analysis of successive age groups, but no pertinent figures or tables are presented. The revised table of norms provokes some questions regarding item difficulty and the retention of certain items. For example, at the lower end of the scale there are several instances where three successive scores or two successive scores yield the same mental age. By contrast, differences of one point at the upper end of the scores listed result in mental age differences of two to five months each. Putting it another way, scores from 1 to 30 show a mental age difference of only 12 months while scores of 61 to 90 give a range of 90 months. It would seem feasible, on the basis of item analysis, to eliminate a number of items at the lower level and perhaps to add a few additional items at the upper level. Since there is no magic in having 100 items, there is little reason to retain items which add little or nothing to the effectiveness of the scale.

A new manual was not developed for the revised scale. A few pages of hectographed material are provided for insertion in the original manual. It would appear that a test that merits revision also merits a revised manual. The manual (1954) shows that the original scale was standardized on 957 normal children ranging from 3 to 12 years of age whereas the insertion (1959) states that "the revised edition....was administered to selected samples of boys and girls at each age level from 4 to 12."

On the original standardization, all children in the sample were given the Stanford-Binet. The revision makes comparison with the Stanford-Binet at the four- and five-year levels only. Children in grades 1 through 4 were given group tests of intelligence. These results were utilized in the norming process. It is not clear as to what procedure was used with children above the fourth grade. The reader is quite properly advised that the procedure utilized "will tend to perpetuate, in the Columbia norms, any systematic errors present in the norms for the other tests." The new norms for the revised Columbia should result in somewhat lower IQ's for high scoring subjects than did the original norms. No reference is made to the reliability of the revised edition.

Experience with the scale, as well as reports of research, reveal that younger children, retarded children, and deaf children have difficulty comprehending what the examiner wants when he asks them to indicate the one that does *not* belong. The concept of different or not belonging is much more elusive and subtle than is the concept of "same," "alike," or "go together." Perhaps this is why numerous young and/or handicapped children tend to perseverate in their responses. At the lower levels perseveration may be encouraged by the fact that the correct answer tends to appear on the same number consecutively, especially at the lower end of the scale. The tendency to perseverate could give an advantage or penalize the subject. For example, if the subject should by chance make the correct response (the first) on item 1 and should perseverate to the extent of the first 21 items, he would have 11 correct responses. Should he continue such perseveration through the next 13 items he would not have a single correct response.

In summary, the *Columbia Mental Maturity Scale* is a nonverbal test which is enjoyed by most children and one which can be administered in a relatively short time. The test has promise but needs not only further study and statistical analysis, but also an up-to-date manual. In spite of certain limitations, this test can be a useful part of a battery of tests, especially where nonverbal instruments are mandatory. Through observation of the child during the testing, the trained examiner can get quality judgments of the child and his method of attacking problems. The norms to interpret the performance of the child should be utilized with caution, especially at the extremes. The revised CMMS appears to be more satisfactory than the original version.

T. ERNEST NEWLAND, *Professor of Educational Psychology, University of Illinois, Urbana, Illinois.*

The 1959 revision differs from the 1954 edition in three ways: 17 cards have been replaced; the items have been rearranged in order of difficulty; and new norms have been established. The new cards reduce the sampling of acculturation (less reading, less demand on geographic and historical information). Order of difficulty has been determined for successive chronological year levels. The new norms reflect relationships between performances on the revised CMMS and (*a*) 1937 Stanford-Binet mental ages (196 kindergarten children), and (*b*) group test raw scores on children in grades 1–4 inclusive. The numbers of cases in the several group tests range for each grade level from 117 to 201. No criterion test was administered more than a month after the CMMS was given. Order of test administration was not randomized. On the school age children, the results on the different group tests were statistically synthesized by a method of "equipercentiles," the publishers forthrightly recognizing the assumption of the comparability of the group tests and the possibility of the resulting CMMS norms reflecting, or perpetuating, any systematic errors present in the norms of these group tests. No information on sex distribution is given on either the group or individual test populations. The preschool subjects were from the New Haven area and from Florida; the school age children were from New York City.

The new norms yield mental ages from 41 months to 167 months in contrast to the 29 to 195 range for the earlier standardization. From the four-year level upward, the scores yield mental age equivalents discernibly lower than on the 1954 form: 7 months lower at the five-year level; 12 months lower at the six-year level, and up to 34 months lower at the ten-year level. Below the four-year level, mental age equivalents are higher on the 1959 revision than on the 1954 norms. Regardless of the question of the general validity of the particular mental ages, the revision should yield smaller standard deviations than did its precursor. Whether the mental age equivalents will have the generality which is so often presumed will have to be determined by subsequent research. The 1959 CMMS mental ages

Columbia Mental Maturity Scale

show no discrimination between grade 3 and grade 4, although those for the group tests did. Just why the publishers present certain of their background normative data in terms of grade levels rather than in terms of the chronological ages of the children in those grades is not clear.

Four published studies have been made on nondisabled populations, in the four- to nine-year age range. The studies on disabled populations are quite diverse, both as to kind of disability and age range: institutionalized mentally retarded women (9 to 30 years of age); residential school deaf pupils (6–22); a mixed speech impaired group (3–15); and a public school, special class group of cerebral palsied children (7–16). Such heterogeneity, further complicated by a multiplicity of tests checked against (10) and by differing methodologies, provides little basis for generalizing about how the revised CMMS is performing. Sigmas on the revision appear to be relatively smaller than those of the 1954 form; they tend either to approximate or somewhat to exceed those for other tests (25, 28–9, 31–2). Revised CMMS IQ's correlated .88 with 1937 Binet IQ's on a speech impaired population (31); .39 with 1960 Binet IQ's on a nondisabled group of four- and five-year-olds (28), whereas correlations of .78 and .62 with 1937 Binet IQ's were found on these year levels, respectively—the latter apparently on the publisher's revision groups (24); .61 and .73 with Otis Alpha nonverbal IQ's on a deaf population (34); .68 to .70 with IQ's on the Wechsler's on female institutionalized defectives (29); .45 and .52, respectively, with WISC verbal and WISC performance IQ's on a nondisabled second grade population (32). Revised CMMS MA's correlated in the low .80's with MA's on the *Peabody Picture Vocabulary Test* and on the *Full Range Picture Vocabulary Test* on a cerebral palsied group, as compared with a .87 correlation with the *Van Alstyne Picture Vocabulary Test* (25). More significant for the educator is the fact that, in this latter study, the revised CMMS MA's tended to be one half to two years lower than those on the PPVT and on the FRPVT. Observations regarding the 1959 CMMS ranged from "improved" (25), to not yielding as good a single IQ measure as the (Norwegian) Binet and the Raven Matrices,[1] to "only partially successful" with six- to eight-year-old deaf children (34), to need for further scoring revision (31), to skepticism regarding its value below the four-year level (25), and to error in level placement of two cards (28).

As was true of the 1954 CMMS, the 1959 revision has been standardized only on a nonhandicapped population. Stemming from a desire to develop a psychometric device which could be used with the cerebral palsied (14), and later more generally "with subjects having serious verbal and motor impairment," the present revision, whatever its strengths and weaknesses, must be regarded as capable of throwing more light upon the learning aptitude of nondisabled children than on that of disabled children, particularly the cerebral palsied and the acoustically impaired. Any inference drawn regarding the psychologically sound usability of this device with either of these disabled groups has in its favor the fact that psychological processes essential to learning are being tapped. But the extent to which such an inference is valid in the case of the cerebral palsied, or even of the deaf, is yet to be determined. For children of the age for which this device is intended, the problem is not one of ascertaining whether it orders the members of a given age or grade group pretty much in the same manner as does some extant and validated device. Such a correlational approach can throw no light upon whether a CMMS mental age of, say, six should suggest educational expectations for the child earning it—as does, say, a 1960 Binet mental age of six. And this type of need is what is experienced by the teacher or occupational therapist of the cerebral palsied. It would seem that studies purporting to show high correlations between any pair of tests or to show that a level score (MA) on one is similar to a level score on another must be based upon the demonstrated psychological comparability of behavior samplings in the two tests, or upon the fact that the different behaviors sampled by the two devices have a sufficiently large underlying common factor (say, "*g*") to warrant a belief in reasonable interchangeability of the two level scores. The statistical treatment in the revision process and in connection with studies involving the use of

[1] LANDMARK, MARGRETE, AND GRINDE, TURID. "Undersøkelse av en gruppe normale barn med forskjellige intelligensprøver." *Nordisk Psykologi* 14(4):171–85 '62. *

the 1959 CMMS has little, if any, bearing upon the concepts presented.

Actually, the studies on this test, as well as the publisher's revision data, throw only limited light upon possible educational or clinical values of the 1959 CMMS. Concurrent validity correlational approaches are highly involutional in nature; they yield one kind of information to the psychometrist but may actually mislead educators. Any inspection of the revision data would make one most cautious to use 1959 CMMS results below the 4-year or above the 10-year levels. The critical user of this test will be aware of the possibility that East Coast norms may not be generally applicable. The complete absence of any direct evidence on the reliability of the revision seems inexcusable. Those who are interested in the psychological processes by which subjects arrive at their responses to tests will have difficulty accepting certain of the publisher's unique correct responses, especially to four of the new ones: items 69, 76, 83, and 97. Those working clinically, rather than psychometrically, with subjects will be tempted to depart from the directions for the use of this test and let the subject give either volunteered verbal or required pointing responses, as mentioned by one user (*28*). The directions in the manual, prepared with speech impaired subjects in mind, could be adapted so that the subject could be helped to employ whatever manner of response would be effective in his communication process, whether it be speaking, pointing, looking, or some clear combination of these. More systematic study and preparation of this device is needed before it can have the clinical and educational (and even psychometric) value which lies largely dormant within it.

[518]

Crichton Vocabulary Scale. Ages 4–11; 1950; individual; 1 form; combined record form (4 pages) for this test and the complementary *Coloured Progressive Matrices;* manual (15 pages); 17s. 6d. per 50 record forms; 3s. 6d. per manual; 22s. 6d. per specimen set including 12 record forms and a specimen set of the *Coloured Progressive Matrices;* postage and purchase tax extra; (15–20) minutes; John C. Raven; H. K. Lewis & Co. Ltd. *

REFERENCES

1. RAVENETTE, A. T. "An Empirical Approach to the Assessment of Reading Retardation: 7, Vocabulary Level and Reading Attainment." *Brit J Ed Psychol* 31:96–103 F '61. * (PA 36:1KF96R)

MORTON BORTNER, *Chief Psychologist, Department of Physical Medicine and Rehabilitation, New York Medical College, New York, New York.*

This test is recommended by its author for use in conjunction with the *Coloured Progressive Matrices*. Its use is intended to supplement the Matrices with a measure of acquired information. The test consists of two sets of 40 words each, both of which are orally administered. Set one consists of the first 40 words of the *Mill Hill Vocabulary Scale*. Both sets combine to give a raw score which is translated into a percentile rank. The test is addressed to children of defective intelligence or for all children from 4 to 11 years of age.

Retest reliability coefficients are .87, .95, and .98 for three separate age groups. Concurrent validity is suggested by reported correlations of .84 and .79 with the Terman-Merrill scale, for six- and nine-year-olds, respectively.

The directions contain a flexibility of administration which raises some question as to the significance of any particular score. As usual, the child is encouraged to explain in his own words the meaning of each word. As is *not* usual in similar tests, "The person giving the test can say: 'You know what a cap is? What is it? Tell me what a cap is? What is a cap like? What do you do with a cap?'" Such leading questions clearly set up different tasks of varying difficulty and suggest that not merely "acquired information," but various aspects of comprehension, are being measured.

This test was constructed to fill a gap the author felt was left by the *Coloured Progressive Matrices*. The two together now constitute a battery for the measurement of two important aspects of intelligence. It is desirable that they be further supplemented by additional measures of different modes of intellectual functioning. As presently constituted these two tests offer no advantages over the more well known and clinically more useful WISC or Stanford-Binet.

For reviews by Charlotte Banks and W. D. Wall, see 4:337.

[519]

★**Diagnostic Performance Tests.** Adults; 1958; "behavior related to disturbances in cognitive function"; individual; 5 tests; manual (185 pages, see *1*) also presents instructions and norms for *Mitchell Vocabulary Test;* instructions listed below are largely excerpted from the manual; no data on reliability except for *c;* tentative norms; 35s. per manual; prices include purchase tax; postpaid within U.K.; Boris

Semeonoff and Eric Trist; distributed by National Foundation for Educational Research in England and Wales. *

a) SEMEONOFF-VIGOTSKY TEST. Adults of average and above average intelligence; adaptation of *Concept Formation Test* (see 4:35); conceptual thinking; 1 form (22 blocks); instructions (6 pages); 59s. per set of testing materials and instructions; (40–60) minutes.

b) TRIST-HARGREAVES TEST. Adults of average and below average intelligence; conceptual thinking; 1 form (12 pieces); instructions (4 pages); scoring sheet (1 page); 67s. per set of testing materials, instructions, and pad of 50 scoring sheets; [20–30] minutes.

c) TRIST-MISSELBROOK-KOHS TEST. Primarily adults (although age norms down to age 8 are also presented); modification of Kohs' *Block-Design Test*; 1 form (24 blocks); instructions (3 pages); scoring sheet (1 page); norms for immediate retesting of adults also presented; 116s. per set of testing materials, instructions, and pad of 50 scoring sheets; (15–20) minutes for test, (30) minutes including retest.

d) CARL HOLLOW SQUARE TEST. Primarily adults (although age norms down to age 8 are also presented); essentially the same as *Carl Hollow Square Scale* except for norms and some modifications in instructions; 1 form (29 blocks, identical with original Carl blocks); instructions (8 pages); scoring sheet (1 page); 182s. per set of testing materials, instructions, and pad of 50 scoring sheets; administration time not reported.

e) THE REVISED PASSALONG TEST. Adults; modification, especially in scoring system, of *The Passalong Test*; 1 form (set of blocks and 8 cards); instructions (8 pages); scoring sheet (1 page); 77s. per set of testing materials, instructions, and pad of 50 scoring sheets; administration time not reported.

REFERENCES

1. SEMEONOFF, BORIS, AND TRIST, ERIC. *Diagnostic Performance Tests: A Manual for Use With Adults.* London: Tavistock Publications Ltd., 1958. Pp. xvi, 176. *

H. GWYNNE JONES, *Senior Lecturer in Psychology, St. George's Hospital Medical School, London, England.*

This battery of tests is not intended only as an orthodox performance scale for the objective and quantitative assessment of nonverbal intellectual abilities. This function is made subordinate to the qualitative, diagnostic, clinical assessment of abnormalities and other personality traits. Thus each test is regarded as a miniature stress situation, and emphasis is laid on the interpersonal aspects of individual testing, on flexibility of administration procedures, and on the intuitive interpretation of the testee's style and methods of dealing with the material and problems. Deliberate and systematic use is made of prompting techniques akin to those employed by Goldstein and in Rorschach limits testing. The battery was used originally in a clinical situation but was developed and extended in a wartime military selection setting.

Five tests are included in the battery, but it is not intended that all five be administered to all subjects. Two are tests of conceptual thinking of the sorting variety: the Semeonoff-Vigotsky is similar to Haufmann and Kasanin's *Concept Formation Test*, while the *Trist-Hargreaves Test* is an original sorting test intended as an "easier alternative" to the former. Kohs' *Block-Design Test* appears in a greatly modified form designed to facilitate its use as a learning situation. The *Carl Hollow Square* "formboard" test is included in its original form, and Alexander's *Passalong Test* is modified only in terms of the scoring system in order to make it more suitable for adults. The difficulty range of the latter may also be extended by use of an additional item. The test materials are well made and packed in convenient boxes. Brief instructions for the administration of each test are provided as separate leaflets, but an examiner needs to have studied the book-length manual.

Critical evaluation is difficult owing to the multi-purpose nature of the battery. As a straightforward intelligence test it has serious shortcomings. No formal data concerning reliability and validity are given, except for the intercorrelations between the tests in the battery and between these and certain conventional intelligence tests. These correlations are generally low, but they are based on very restricted populations. Factor analyses provide evidence for "general intellectual," "spatial," and "conceptual" factors. Because of the intended flexibility of administration it must be assumed that tester reliability would be relatively low. The standardisation is tentative and, although a table of estimated general population percentile norms is provided, it is based on highly selected military populations.

However, the authors stress that the psychometric aspects of the battery are secondary to its diagnostic value. It is in terms of the latter that these techniques must be assessed, but the reviewer is given little upon which to base his judgment. Isolated examples of tentative interpretations of idiosyncratic behaviour are given; two illustrative cases are described in some detail, and four more in outline. The authors had hoped to carry out a full validation study on the military data, but security considerations prevented this and the only surviving evidence of validity is the general impression of all concerned that a rating based on these techniques

Diagnostic Performance Tests

had roughly similar status to any other single portion of an elaborate selection procedure.

Clearly, the *Diagnostic Performance Tests* do not provide a ready-made solution for any of the problems of psychological assessment, but this limitation does not imply that they should be dismissed. The work described in the manual is best regarded as a large scale pilot study, the results of which point to various directions in which further work might be fruitful. The basic notion that important aspects of personality are revealed in a person's approach to problems of an intellectual nature is a sound one. Semeonoff and Trist have made a serious and valuable attempt to combine qualitative and quantitative methods of assessment, and flexibility and rigour of approach. Their diagnostic battery could be employed with advantage for further research in this field.

For excerpts from reviews of the manual, see B449.

[520]

★**English Picture Vocabulary Test.** Ages 5-0 to 8-11, 7-0 to 11-11; 1962–63; derived from *Peabody Picture Vocabulary Test;* individual for Test 1; 1 form ('62); 2 levels: Test 1 (44 pages), Test 2 (47 pages); manual ('63, 39 pages); separate answer sheets (for group administration, Test 2 only) or record sheets (for individual administration) must be used; 8s. per test; 5s. per 25 record sheets; 5s. per 50 answer sheets; 6d. per scoring stencil for answer sheets; 5s. per manual; 13s. per specimen set of either level; prices include purchase tax; postpaid within U.K.; [15–45] minutes; M. A. Brimer and Lloyd M. Dunn; distributed by National Foundation for Educational Research in England and Wales. *

L. B. BIRCH, *Senior Lecturer in Educational Psychology, Institute of Education, University of Sheffield, Sheffield, England.*

These tests are derived from Dunn's *Peabody Picture Vocabulary Test* and make use of the same pictures. They are, however, completely reconstructed and standardised for English children. Their purpose is to assess levels of listening vocabulary independent of the ability to read. Although essentially for use with normal children, they can be used with children with gross motor impairment.

Each test is of 40 items, the task in each being to identify from among four pictures the one which corresponds to a spoken stimulus word. Test 1, for children under 9 years, is an individual test; Test 2 can be administered either individually or to a group and covers ages 7 to 11 years. In either case, administration, scoring, and scaling of results are all very simple and well able to be carried out by class teachers.

The manual is an exemplar which other testmakers could well follow. Instructions for the use of the tests are simple, complete, and unambiguous, the methods of construction and standardisation are clearly given, and conversion tables and norms are easy to read. The norms are expressed as normalised scores with a mean of 100 and standard deviation of 15; these can be converted by a table into percentile ranks. The standardisation sample consisted of some 3,200 children for Test 1 and more than 5,000 for Test 2, taken from some 90 schools selected to represent closely the total population of England and Wales. There was a small sex difference in favour of boys comparable with that found by other investigators, but separate norms are not provided.

The tests seem satisfactorily reliable. Kuder-Richardson estimates range from .87 to .92 for different age groups on Test 1 and from .88 to .96 on Test 2. Estimates of the standard error of measurement are given together with a note explaining its meaning in nonstatistical terms. Evidence for the validity of the tests is, of course, somewhat more limited. A convincing case is made out for the adequacy of their content validity. The construct they claim to represent is that of "listening vocabulary" but, as is fairly pointed out in the manual, performance may depend to some extent upon other cues than the spoken word, e.g., visual perceptual cues. The testmakers were aware of this possible contamination and took appropriate steps to avoid it. Correlation coefficients between scores on Test 2 and three other tests were high; that with Schonell's *Graded Word Reading Test* was .80 and with the WISC vocabulary was .76.

At this stage it is difficult to predict how valuable a knowledge of children's listening vocabulary may be to clinical practice and teaching, but these two new tests may provide very good tools for finding out.

PHILIP M. LEVY, *Lecturer in Psychology, Institute of Education, University of Birmingham, Birmingham, England.*

This test, based on the *Peabody Picture Vocabulary Test,* is "designed to assess levels of listening vocabulary" in a manner which is "functionally independent of reading skill." The tester calls out a word and the child responds by identifying that one of four line drawings to which the word refers. Increase in difficulty, it is claimed, is brought about through the essential word difficulty and not by perceptual difficulty.

The two reusable test booklets are clearly printed and are strongly constructed as is appropriate for materials which are to be handled by young children. The separate answer sheets both for individual administration (Tests 1 and 2) and group administration (Test 2) are neatly designed. By contrast, the manual which serves both test booklets is an uneven product: the print is rather small (being photographically reduced typescript), and the early sequence of headings and subheadings is not as logically arranged as it could be. It does, however, contain adequate instructions for administration by teachers (the "experienced teacher"). The directions for scoring and the tables for score conversion to standardised scores and percentiles are clear and convenient.

The analyses appear to be particularly thorough in several respects: a large initial pool of items was used; distractors were checked for their distraction validity; reliabilities were calculated from samples other than those used for item analysis; most of the standardisation data were obtained by teachers, the potential users, and not by professional testers; and the essential equivalence of individual and group administration was established for Test 2 by a special experiment which took account of the order of testing.

Reliability data are presented in what perhaps is confusing variety: corrected split-half, Kuder-Richardson formula 20, and test-retest coefficients are variously reported for a number of age ranges and different samples. The coefficients do, however, show a high agreement among themselves, a typical value for a single year group being .88 for Test 1 and .92 for Test 2. The "eleven-plus" type of verbal ability and English tests gave correlations of .79 and .82, respectively, with Test 2 for the 11-year-old children. Correlations between the EPVT and other vocabulary tests range from .61 to .80, but these are for the full four-year age range of Test 2.

The test is said to be "diagnostically relevant to the understanding of reading difficulties and other verbal learning handicaps" and to provide "reading-free predictors of future language attainment." It may be too soon to demand experimental evidence to support these claims. Meanwhile, the test users, particularly the teachers, deserve some guidance in the manual about the interpretation and use of the scores so that the EPVT does not become just another test which claims but does not prove "diagnostic relevance" and "predictive value" with reference to reading skills. The test obviously deserves further research to support its use.

In summary then, the EPVT is a well produced and well documented instrument and deserves further research. The manual, however, needs an improved quality of production, a better layout, and some instructions on the use and interpretation of scores.

[521]

Full-Range Picture Vocabulary Test. Ages 2 and over; 1948; individual; Forms A, B, (16 cards, used with both forms); instructions (1 card); mimeographed norms (6 pages); record sheet (1 page) for each form; $7.50 per set of cards, instructions, norms, and sample record sheets; $1.10 per 25 record sheets; postage extra; specimen set not available; (10–15) minutes; Robert B. Ammons and Helen S. Ammons; Psychological Test Specialists. *

REFERENCES

1–10. See 4:340.
11. KATZ, IRVING STANLEY. *A Validation Study of the Full-Range Picture Vocabulary Test at the Lower Grade Levels.* Master's thesis, Pennsylvania State College (State College, Pa.), 1951.
12. TUCKER, D. A. *A Study of Adult Male Negroes With the Full-Range Picture Vocabulary Test.* Master's thesis, University of Louisville (Louisville, Ky.), 1951.
13. COPPINGER, NEIL W., AND AMMONS, R. B. "The Full-Range Picture Vocabulary Test: 8, A Normative Study of Negro Children." *J Clin Psychol* 8:136–40 Ap '52. * (PA 27:1952)
14. ALLEN, ROBERT M.; THORNTON, THOMAS E.; AND STENGER, CHARLES A. "Ammons and Wechsler Test Performances of College and Psychiatric Subjects." *J Clin Psychol* 10:378–81 O '54. * (PA 29:4022)
15. RICHARDSON, ELIZABETH J., AND KOBLER, FRANK J. "Testing the Cerebral Palsied." *Excep Child* 21:101–3+ D '54. * (PA 29:6108)
16. SLOAN, WILLIAM, AND BENSBERG, GERARD J. "An Exploratory Study of the Full-Range Picture Vocabulary Test With Mental Defectives." *Am J Mental Def* 58:481–5 Ja '54. * (PA 28:7700)
17. SMITH, LOUIS M., AND FILLMORE, ARLINE R. "The Ammons FRPV Test and the WISC for Remedial Reading Cases." Abstract. *J Consult Psychol* 18:332 O '54. * (PA 29:5799, title only)
18. ALLEN, ROBERT M., AND COLLINS, MARJORIE G. "Suggestions for the Adaptive Administration of Intelligence Tests for Those With Cerebral Palsy: Part 1, Administration of the Ammons Full-Range Picture Test, Columbia Mental Maturity Test, Raven's Progressive Matrices and Leiter International Performance Scale." *Cerebral Palsy R* 16:11–4+ My-Je '55. * (PA 30:3284)
19. ALLEN, ROBERT M.; THORNTON, THOMAS E.; AND STENGER, CHARLES A. "A Note on the Ammons Full-Range Picture Vocabulary Test as a Screening Device for College Students." *Psychol Rep* 1:459–60 D '55. * (PA 30:6329)
20. RABIN, A. I.; KING, G. F.; AND EHRMANN, J. C. "Vocabulary Performance of Short-Term and Long-Term Schizophrenics." *J Abn & Social Psychol* 50:255–8 Mr '55. * (PA 30:1361)
21. SANDERS, CHRISTOPHER C., JR. *The Reliability and "Validity" of the Ammons Full-Range Picture Vocabulary Test.* Master's thesis, University of Tennessee (Knoxville, Tenn.), 1955.
22. ALLEN, ROBERT M.; THORNTON, THOMAS E.; AND STENGER, CHARLES A. "The Full-Range Picture Vocabulary

Test Compared With Two Short Forms of the Wechsler Scale." *J Ed Res* 50:133–7 O '56. * (*PA* 32:933)

23. TEMPLIN, MILDRED C. Chap. 6, "Vocabulary," pp. 105–20. In her *Certain Language Skills in Children*. University of Minnesota, Institute of Child Welfare Monograph Series, No. 26. Minneapolis, Minn.: University of Minnesota Press, 1957. Pp. xviii, 183. * (*PA* 31:7556)

24. BLACK, A. D., AND GRINDER, R. E. "Reliability of the Ammons FRPV Test and the Relationship Between Two Measures of Verbal Comprehension for a Japanese-American Sample." *Psychol Rep* 5:261–3 Je '59. * (*PA* 34:2938)

25. BLATT, SIDNEY J. "Recall and Recognition Vocabulary: Implications for Intellectual Deterioration." *A.M.A. Arch Gen Psychiatry* 1:473–6 N '59. * (*PA* 34:6005)

26. CONDELL, JAMES F. "Note on the Use of the Ammons Full-Range Picture Vocabulary Test With Retarded Children." *Psychol Rep* 5:150 Mr '59. * (*PA* 34:1408)

27. DUNN, LLOYD M.; AND HARLEY, RANDALL K. "Comparability of Peabody, Ammons, Van Alstyne, and Columbia Test Scores With Cerebral Palsied Children." *Excep Child* 26:70–4 O '59. * (*PA* 35:3733)

28. WINITZ, HARRIS. "Relationships Between Language and Nonlanguage Measures of Kindergarten Children." *J Speech & Hearing Res* 2:387–91 D '59. * (*PA* 34:5896)

29. CARSON, ARNOLD S., AND RABIN, A. I. "Verbal Comprehension and Communication in Negro and White Children." *J Ed Psychol* 51:47–51 Ap '60. * (*PA* 35:2049)

30. FISHER, GARY M.; SHOTWELL, ANNA M.; AND YORK, DOROTHY H. "Comparability of the Ammons Full-Range Picture Vocabulary Test With the WAIS in the Assessment of Intelligence of Mental Retardates." *Am J Mental Def* 64:995–9 My '60. * (*PA* 35:6830)

31. MORGAN, ELMER F., JR. "Efficacy of Two Tests in Differentiating Potentially Low From Average and High First Grade Achievers." *J Ed Res* 53:300–4 Ap '60. *

32. NORMAN, RALPH D., AND MEAD, DONALD F. "Spanish-American Bilingualism and the Ammons Full-Range Picture-Vocabulary Test." *J Social Psychol* 51:319–30 My '60. * (*PA* 34:7650)

33. SCOGGINS, BETTY JOANNE. *A Comparative Study of the Full-Range Picture Vocabulary Test and the Peabody Picture Vocabulary Test*. Master's thesis, Vanderbilt University (Nashville, Tenn.), 1960.

34. STERNE, DAVID M. "Use of the Ammons FRPV With the Long-Term Chronically Ill." *J Clin Psychol* 16:192–3 Ap '60. * (*PA* 36:2HD92S)

35. SMITH, BESSIE S. "The Relative Merits of Certain Verbal and Non-Verbal Tests at the Second-Grade Level." *J Clin Psychol* 17:53–4 Ja '61. * (*PA* 37:3595)

36. MEYERS, E.; ORPET, R. E.; ATTWELL, A. A.; AND DINGMAN, H. F. *Primary Abilities at Mental Age Six*. Monographs of the Society for Research in Child Development, Vol. 27, No. 1, Serial No. 82. Lafayette, Ind.: Child Development Publications, 1962. Pp. 40. * (*PA* 38:8462)

37. SCHUELL, HILDRED; JENKINS, JAMES J.; AND CARROLL, JOHN B. "A Factor Analysis of the Minnesota Test for Differential Diagnosis of Aphasia." *J Speech & Hearing Res* 5:349–69 D '62. * (*PA* 37:5358)

38. HO, DAVID, AND WHITE, DELILAH T. "Use of the Full-Range Picture Vocabulary Test With the Mentally Retarded." *Am J Mental Def* 67:761–4 Mr '63. * (*PA* 38:1275)

39. MOED, GEORGE; WIGHT, BYRON W.; AND JAMES, PATRICIA. "Intertest Correlations of the Wechsler Intelligence Scale for Children and Two Picture Vocabulary Tests." *Ed & Psychol Meas* 23:359–63 su '63. * (*PA* 38:960)

40. SIMKINS, LAWRENCE, AND BURGIN, JUDITH. "A Comparison of Individual and Group Administrations of the Full-Range Picture Vocabulary Test." *J Ed Res* 57:189–92 D '63. *

For reviews by William D. Altus and William M. Cruickshank, see 4:340.

[522]

Gesell Developmental Schedules, 1940 Series. Ages 4 weeks to 6 years; 1925-49; individual; 1 form ('49); manuals: *The First Five Years of Life* ('40, see *20*), *Developmental Diagnosis, Second Edition* ('47, see *31*), and *Infant and Child in the Culture of Today* ('43, see *34*, which is for use with behavior day charts and which contains supplementary normative data); general instructions booklet ('49, 15 pages); 10 record forms: Forms 1A (for ages 4–8 weeks), 1B (for ages 12–20 weeks), 1C (for ages 24–32 weeks), 1D (for ages 36–44 weeks), 1E (for ages 48–56 weeks), 1F (for ages 15–21 months), 1G (for ages 21–30 months), 1H (for ages 30–42 months), 1I (for ages 42–54 months), 1J (for ages 54–72 months), ['40, 1 page]; analytic forms: Forms 2A (postural behavior), 2B (prehensory behavior), 2C (perceptual behavior), 2D (adaptive behavior), 2E (language-social behavior), 2F (analytic scoring sheet), ['40, 1 page]; observation record, Form 3 ['40, 1 page]; interview sheet, Form 4 ['40, 2 pages]; summary sheet, Form 5 ['40, 1 page]; behavior day chart, form 6 ['43, 2 pages]; preliminary behavior inventory, Form 7 ['43, 1 page]; $85 per set of testing materials, carrying case, and record forms; 90¢ per 25 record forms except form 6; $1.50 per 25 behavior day charts (form 6); 90¢ per specimen set of record forms; postpaid; (20–40) minutes; Arnold Gesell and others; Psychological Corporation. *

REFERENCES

1–28. See 3:276.
29–33. See 4:341.

34. GESELL, ARNOLD, AND ILG, FRANCES L.; IN COLLABORATION WITH JANET LEARNED AND LOUISE B. AMES. *Infant and Child in the Culture of Today: The Guidance of Development in Home and Nursery School*. New York: Harper & Brothers, 1943. Pp. xiii, 399. *

35. SILVER, ARCHIE A. "Diagnostic Value of Three Drawing Tests for Children." *J Pediatrics* 37:129–43 Jl '50. * (*PA* 25:3191)

36. GESELL, ARNOLD. "Gesell Developmental Schedules," pp. 485–94. (*PA* 27:7767) In *Contributions Toward Medical Psychology: Theory and Psychodiagnostic Methods*, Vol. 2. Edited by Arthur Weider. New York: Ronald Press Co., 1953. Pp. xi, 459–885. *

37. SIEVERS, DOROTHY J., AND NORMAN, RALPH D. "Some Suggestive Results in Psychometric Testing of the Cerebral Palsied With Gesell, Binet, and Wechsler Scales." *J Genetic Psychol* 82:69–90 Mr '53. * (*PA* 27:7974)

38. MACRAE, JOHN M. "Retests of Children Given Mental Tests as Infants." *J Genetic Psychol* 87:111–9 S '55. * (*PA* 30:6976)

39. SIMON, ABRAHAM J., AND BASS, LIBBY G. "Toward a Validation of Infant Testing." *Am J Orthopsychiatry* 26:340–50 Ap '56. * (*PA* 31:4713)

40. WITTENBORN, J. R.; WITH THE COLLABORATION OF MYRTLE A. ASTRACHAN, MARJORIE W. DEGOOYER, W. WALLACE GRANT, IRMA Z. JANOFF, ROBERT B. KUGEL, BARBARA J. MYERS, ANNALIESE RIESS, AND ELLERY C. RUSSELL. "A Study of Adoptive Children: 2, The Predictive Validity of the Yale Developmental Examination of Infant Behavior." *Psychol Monogr* 70(2):59–92 '56. * (*PA* 31:5860)

41. WOLK, SHIRLEY MAE. *The Gesell Technique as Applied to Twenty-Five Children in a Study Clinic for Mental Retardation*. Master's thesis, Immaculate Heart College (Los Angeles, Calif.), 1957.

42. ALLEN, ROBERT M. "Suggestions for the Adaptive Administration of Intelligence Tests for Those With Cerebral Palsy: Part 2, Administration of the Vineland Social Maturity Scale, the Gesell Preliminary Behavior Inventory, and the Cattell Infant Intelligence Scale." *Cerebral Palsy R* 19:6–7 Mr-Ap '58. * (*PA* 38:8853)

43. GARDENER, D. BRUCE, AND SWIGER, MARYBELLE K. "Developmental Status of Two Groups of Infants Released for Adoption." *Child Develop* 29:521–30 D '58. * (*PA* 34:4120)

44. KNOBLOCH, HILDA; SAYERS, MARTIN P.; AND HOWARD, WILLIAM H. R. "The Relationships Between Findings in Pneumoencephalograms and Clinical Behavior." *Pediatrics* 22:13–9 Jl '58. * See also 46.

45. DRILLIEN, CECIL MARY. "A Longitudinal Study of the Growth and Development of Prematurely and Maturely Born Children: Part 3, Mental Development." *Arch Dis Childh* 34:37–45 F '59. *

46. KUGEL, ROBERT B. "Pneumoencephalograms and Clinical Behavior." Letter. *Pediatrics* 23:174–5 Ja '59. * Criticism of 44 above. Reply by Hilda Knobloch. *Pediatrics* 23:175–8 Ja '59. *

47. RUESS, A. L.; DOLLY, ANNE; AND LIS, EDWARD F. "The Gesell Developmental Schedules and the Physically Handicapped Child." *Am J Occup Ther* 13:117–24+ My-Je '59. * (*PA* 34:4769)

48. ILLINGWORTH, R. S. *The Development of the Infant and the Young Child: Normal and Abnormal*. Edinburgh, Scotland: E. & S. Livingston Ltd., 1960. Pp. viii, 318. *

49. KNOBLOCH, HILDA, AND PASAMANICK, BENJAMIN. "An Evaluation of the Consistency and Predictive Value of the 40 Week Gesell Developmental Schedule," pp. 10–31; discussion, pp. 32–41. (*PA* 36:1FB10K) In *Child Development and Child Psychiatry*. Edited by Charles Shagass and Benjamin Pasamanick. Psychiatric Research Reports 13. Washington, D.C.: American Psychiatric Association, 1960. Pp. ix, 225. *

50. DRILLIEN, CECIL MARY. "A Longitudinal Study of the Growth and Development of Prematurely and Maturely Born Children: Part 7, Mental Development 2–5 Years." *Arch Dis Childh* 36:233–40 Je '61. *

51. ESCALONA, SIBYLLE K., AND MORIARTY, ALICE. "Prediction of Schoolage Intelligence From Infant Tests." *Child Develop* 32:597–605 S '61. * (*PA* 36:4FE97E)

52. ILLINGWORTH, R. S. "The Predictive Value of Developmental Tests in the First Year, With Special Reference

to the Diagnosis of Mental Subnormality." *J Child Psychol & Psychiatry* 2:210–5 N '61. * (*PA* 36:5JI10I)
53. PEASE, DAMARIS; ROSAUER, JOSEPHINE KEEFE; AND WOLINS, LEROY. "Reliability of Three Infant Developmental Scales Administered During the First Year of Life." *J Genetic Psychol* 98:295–8 Je '61. * (*PA* 36:2FB95P)
54. PELZ, KURT S.; AMES, LOUISE B.; AND PIKE, FRANCES. "Measurement of Psychologic Function in Geriatric Patients." *J Am Geriatrics Soc* 9:740–54 S '61. *
55. SHARE, JACK; WEBB, ALLEN; AND KOCH, RICHARD. "A Preliminary Investigation of the Early Developmental Status of Mongoloid Infants." *Am J Mental Def* 66:238–41 S '61. * (*PA* 36:3JI38S)
56. KNOBLOCH, HILDA, AND PASAMANICK, BENJAMIN. "The Developmental Behavioral Approach to the Neurologic Examination in Infancy." *Child Develop* 33:181–98 Mr '62. * (*PA* 37:823)
57. AMES, LOUISE BATES, AND ILG, FRANCES L. "The Gesell Incomplete Man Test as a Measure of Developmental Status." *Genetic Psychol Monogr* 68:247–307 N '63. *
58. KOCH, RICHARD; SHARE, JACK; WEBB, ALLEN; AND GRALIKER, BETTY V. "The Predictability of Gesell Developmental Scales in Mongolism." *J Pediatrics* 62:93–7 Ja '63. *
59. LIDDICOAT, RENÉE, AND KOZA, CONSTANCE. "Language Development in African Infants." *Psychologia Africana* 10:108–16 D '63. * (*PA* 38:8009)
60. WILSON, MIRIAM G. "Gesell Developmental Testing." Editorial. *J Pediatrics* 62:162–4 Ja '63. *

EMMY E. WERNER, *Assistant Professor of Child Development, University of California, Davis, California.*

Since the last review in *The Third Mental Measurements Yearbook*, the *Gesell Developmental Schedules* have been used fairly extensively as a criterion measure in the follow-up of infants with complications at birth or as predictors of intellectual development in the preschool and early school years.

Information on standardization procedures, norms, and instructions for administration and scoring of the Gesell Schedules is scattered in three volumes: standardization data in *The Psychology of Early Growth* (*13*), which is out of print, instructions for the administration and scoring of the Schedules from 1 to 6 years in *The First Five Years of Life* (*20*), and instructions for the Schedules from 4 through 56 weeks in *Developmental Diagnosis* (*31*). It would be extremely helpful if the information considered essential for a test manual according to the APA recommendations could be assembled in one concise volume. This would also help lower the combined cost of test and manuals which now approaches $100.

This reviewer has noticed that the enthusiasm for the merits of the *Gesell Developmental Schedules* has continued to run high in the medical profession, especially among pediatricians and neurologists. Most psychologists, while not discounting the merits of the careful and detailed descriptions of a young child's behavior, have their enthusiasm dampened by the awareness that the Schedules lack many of the qualifications which would be considered *essential* for a psychological test or diagnostic technique.

THE STANDARDIZATION SAMPLE. There is a real need for a restandardization of the Gesell Schedules on a large sample of children representative of United States infants of the 1960's. There is reason to suspect: (*a*) that individual variation within the small groups of children on whom the Schedules were originally standardized may have unduly influenced item placement; (*b*) that over a period of almost two generations there have been changes in the "typical" pattern of infant behavior, probably due to better nutritional status, better pediatric care, and changed child rearing practices (Knobloch and Pasamanick, *49,* find a shift toward earlier "achievement" in both gross motor and personal-social behavior of 39-, 40-, and 41-week-old infants on samples 10 times as large as Gesell's original sample); and (*c*) that there are significant differences in the development of infants drawn from different socioeconomic strata and ethnic stock.

RELIABILITY. Knobloch and Pasamanick report the only reliability data this reviewer has found—correlations between the Developmental Quotients obtained by the examiner and several observers (all trained by the same examiner). Two sets of correlations were computed: one for clinical cases (one third abnormal), the other for normal infants participating in a longitudinal follow-up study. The r's reported vary from .90 to .99 on samples of 40-week-old infants with n's ranging from 12 to 44. These tester-observer reliability coefficients are surprisingly high, considering the vagueness of the scoring method. There is a pressing need for additional reliability studies, both tester-observer and test-retest, at different age levels.

CONCURRENT VALIDITY. Knobloch and Pasamanick report a high correlation between the *Gesell Developmental Schedules* for older children (three years old) and the Stanford-Binet ($r = .87, n = 195$). This is not surprising since a number of items in the Gesell Schedules at the three-year level are taken directly from the Binet.

Less encouraging is a finding by Gardner (*43*) in a study of 128 infants, age 4–92 days (mean 32 days). He obtains a moderately high *negative* correlation ($-.64$) between the DQ and CA, demonstrating the inadequate discriminative power of the Gesell Schedules during the early weeks of infancy.

PREDICTIVE VALIDITY. Follow-up studies of infants tested below eight months have shown little predictive value. Escalona and Moriarty (*51*) find no relationship between Gesell scores of normal infants tested between 3 weeks and 33 weeks and retested between 6 years and 9 years. Share, Webb, and Koch (*55*) find that the DQ's for mongoloids tested at median age of 7.5 months are not good predictors of later DQ's. In contrast, DQ's of the same 16 mongoloids tested at median age 17.0 months and median age 29.5 months yield a correlation of .86.

Knobloch and Pasamanick report an r of .51 between the Gesell scores of 40-week-old infants and their 3-year Gesell scores (.74 for 48 abnormal infants in this group, .43 for the 147 normal cases). Correlations between 40-week Gesell scores and 3-year Binet are in the same range ($r = .48$, $n = 195$). The same authors report a correlation of .50 between 40-week Gesell scores and 7-year intelligence test scores. Simon and Bass (*39*) obtained what seem essentially similar results by classifying infants' Gesell scores into three categories (dull normal and defective; average; above average and superior). Contingency coefficient correlations vary between .45 and .52 for children tested in infancy on the Gesell and retested after age 5 with the S-B or WISC.

SUMMARY EVALUATION AND RECOMMENDATION. The *Gesell Developmental Schedules* should not be considered as an infant and preschool intelligence test, but as detailed observational schedules for a young child's developmental status. They are in need of an extensive revision on a large and representative sample of present-day infants. In the hands of a carefully trained examiner who is aware of their limitations (including questionable reliability of scoring method) the Gesell Schedules can tell us a certain amount about the *present* position of the child in relation to developmental expectancies. Predictions about *future* development, especially intellectual development, cannot be made with the certainty which Gesell has us believe (see p. 116 in *Developmental Diagnosis*). Contrary to his assumption, evidence accumulated suggests that predictions regarding future developmental status are extremely hazardous in the first half, and not much better in the second half, of the first year. After that a gross classification of the infant's development into categories of below average, average, and above average bears a moderate relationship to preschool and school age intelligence test scores (.40–.60), too low for certainty about an individual case.

Nancy Bayley is presently undertaking a restandardization of her California Scales on a large sample of children of different ethnic stocks, items selected after careful test-retest and tester-observer reliability studies. Until the revised Bayley scale is on the market, this reviewer would prefer to use the *Cattell Infant Intelligence Scale* in the range from birth through two years and the *Stanford-Binet Intelligence Scale*, 1960 edition, thereafter.

For reviews by Nancy Bayley and Florence M. Teagarden, see 3:276. For excerpts from related book reviews, see 3:277–80 and 40: B912–6.

[523]

The Griffiths Mental Development Scale for Testing Babies From Birth to Two Years. 1951–55; 6 scores: locomotor, personal-social, hearing and speech, eye and hand, performance, total; individual; 1 form ('54); manual ('54, see *2*); revised record booklet ('55, 8 pages); test materials sold only to persons taking author's lecture course or a guidance course by correspondence; fee for lecture course, 315s.; fee for guidance course, 210s.; postpaid; 252s. per set of testing materials; 12s. per 25 record booklets; 30s. per manual; postage extra; [20–40] minutes; Ruth Griffiths; the Author. *

REFERENCES

1–3. See 5:404.
4. WOOLF, L. I.; GRIFFITHS, RUTH; MONCRIEFF, ALAN; COATES, STEPHEN; AND DILLISTONE, F. "Dietary Treatment of Phenylketonuria." *Arch Dis Childh* 33:31–45 F '58. *
5. GRIFFITHS, RUTH. "The Extension of the Griffiths Mental Development Scale to Cover the Years From Two to Seven." Abstract. *B Brit Psychol Soc* 41:44 My '60. *
6. HINDLEY, C. B. "The Griffiths Scale of Infant Development: Scores and Predictions From 3 to 18 Months." *J Child Psychol & Psychiatry* 1:99–112 Je '60. *
7. HINDLEY, C. B. "Social Class Influences on the Development of Ability in the First Five Years," pp. 29–41. (*PA* 37:4717) In *Child and Education.* Proceedings of the XIV International Congress of Applied Psychology, Vol. 3. Copenhagen, Denmark: Munksgaard, Ltd., 1962. Pp. 197. *

C. B. HINDLEY, *Research Psychologist, Centre for the Study of Human Development, Institutes of Education and Child Health, University of London, London, England.*

The author clearly set herself the task of "measuring intelligence" in babies and is hopeful of the possibility of doing so, but she also acknowledges doubts as to whether in fact her test procedure "can claim to measure this innate ability as efficiently as tests for older subjects." Hers is the only infant test standardized on British children.

The Griffiths scale consists of a total of 260

items covering the first two years. Like the Stanford-Binet it is an age scale, with three items for each week of credit in the first year, and two items per week in the second year. As the ceiling of the test is two years of developmental age, brighter children will reach this level from about the age of 18 months. The author suggests in such cases that the Stanford-Binet should be used and mental age credits of both tests combined to obtain an MA. A drawback here is that the standard deviations of the two tests differ. Quotients are obtained from the developmental ages.

The author attaches a great deal of importance to the five subscales: Locomotor, Personal-Social, Hearing and Speech, Eye and Hand, and Performance. The test contains an equal number of items in each subscale for each age period, and therefore it is possible to calculate separate DA's and quotients for the subscales. Although the author is hopeful about the value of profiles and presents some very convincing ones of children with marked deafness, blindness, or other defects, she also recognizes the possibility, suggested by Gesell, that development of normal children may follow a spiral course, with a child centring his interests in one direction at one period, only to be followed by progress in another direction a little later.

The test instructions are full, and the tester is sensibly enjoined to capitalize on the child's interests, rather than following any definite order of presenting the items. While the majority of items are tested for, in quite a number of instances reliance has to be placed on mothers' testimony, e.g., items regarding the number of different sounds the infant makes, whether he enjoys a bath, and whether he listens to music. A good deal of use is made of particular sorts of apparatus, such as formboards in the Performance Scale in the second year, so that a child who is not interested in them is likely to be penalized.

The main criticisms that can be made of the scale apply in greater or lesser degree to other baby tests. The standardization sample, consisting of children from a London borough and largely from infant welfare clinics and day nurseries, can be regarded neither as a random sample nor as a representative sample of any defined population. Samples ranged from 16 to 31 children at each month of age, amounting to a total of 571 children, some of whom were tested twice.

The scale was constructed from a wider number of items, some derived from other infant tests and some resulting from the author's own observations of infants. By a "cut and fit" procedure, items were allocated to appropriate ages in each subscale. A table is presented showing that mean numbers of items passed, both on the global scale and the subscales at each age, conform fairly clearly to the required numbers. After correction of MA's and CA's of eight months or less for "floor effect" (lack of credit for earlier items when testing is begun at the one-month level), the mean GQ ("general quotient") is 99.7 and the standard deviations of GQ's are similar at different ages, being about 12 points.

Unfortunately, no evidence is presented concerning how the various items correlate with the test as a whole, nor is there any evidence, such as a factor analysis might provide, to support the breakdown of the items into the five subscales. It is difficult to see much difference between the Performance and Eye and Hand Scales. Again, certain speech items are to be found in the Hearing and Speech Scale and others in the Personal-Social Scale; the latter seems a mixture of developmental items and others which depend on special training, such as "Bowel control complete" at 19 months. There is no table of standard deviations of the subscales, which makes the significance of any particular partial quotient the more doubtful.

The big question concerning baby tests is, of course, how far they are predictive of later intelligence. Griffiths does not make any great claims here, but she reports the rather astonishing value of $r = .87$ between first and second testing over an interval of an average of 30 weeks (range 7 to 70 weeks) on 60 cases in the standardization sample. This is far higher than other workers have reported with other infant tests, or than figures reported by the reviewer (6) for the Griffiths scale, and would be considered eminently satisfactory on such a standard instrument as the Stanford-Binet. As all the tests were given by the author alone, one wonders whether independent testers would have reached such a high level of agreement. Longer term predictions reported by the reviewer (correlations between Griffiths GQ's at ages 6 months or 18 months and Stanford-Binet IQ's at age 5 years) were not sufficiently high for practical purposes (.32 and .40, respectively), though they were somewhat higher than those reported for other tests (7).

It is quite possible that higher levels of prediction could be obtained among subjects with definite defects, such as blindness or spasticity, but this remains to be demonstrated.

The test has an obvious value for British users, despite the rather inadequate information on many points, because it is the only infant test standardized on a British population. For other users it has the advantage of having an unusually large number of items, equal numbers of items for each subscale at each age, and reasonable stability of mean quotients and standard deviations from age to age. As with other tests of infant development it is wise to consider the Griffiths scale as assessing the current level of development, and it would be unwise to rely on it for prediction among normal children. It can also be regarded as a suitable device for picking out cases of gross handicap. Insufficient evidence is given regarding the internal consistency and standard deviations of subscales, so that one must advise that profiles be used only with caution and be regarded as providing pointers to be confirmed by other means.

For a review by Nancy Bayley, see 5:404.

[524]

★**Kahn Intelligence Tests: Experimental Form.** Ages 1 month and over, particularly the verbally or culturally handicapped; 1960; uses same test objects as *Kahn Test of Symbol Arrangement;* main scale plus 6 optional scales: brief scale, concept formation, recall, motor coordination, scale for use with the deaf, scale for use with the blind; individual; 1 form (16 plastic objects); record form (4 pages); manual (34 pages, reprint of 2 below); $26 per set of testing materials including 50 record forms and manual; $2.50 per manual; cash orders postpaid; administration time not reported; Theodore C. Kahn; Psychological Test Specialists. *

REFERENCES
1. KAHN, T. C. "A New 'Culture-Free' Intelligence Test." *Psychol Rep* 6:239-42 Ap '60. * (PA 35:6402)
2. KAHN, THEODORE C. "Kahn Intelligence Tests: Experimental Form (KIT:EXP)." *Percept & Motor Skills* 10:123-53 Ap '60. * (PA 35:6383)

[525]

*****The Leiter Adult Intelligence Scale.** Adults; 1949-59; revision of the *Leiter-Partington Adult Performance Scale;* includes *The FR-CR Test, Pathways Test, The Leiter Adaptation of Arthur's Stencil Design Test,* and *The Leiter Adaptation of the Painted Cube Test;* individual; 3 scores: language, nonlanguage, total; 1 form ['56]; mimeographed manual ['56, 55 pages]; revised record booklet ('59, 4 pages); $30.50 per set of testing materials, 100 record booklets, and manual; $5 per 100 record booklets; $2 per manual; postage extra; (40-60) minutes; Russell Graydon Leiter; C. H. Stoelting Co. *

REFERENCES
1-4. See 4:350.
5. International Psychological Service Center. "The FR-CR Test With Quantitative Scores and a Qualitative Check List for Clinical Use in the Evaluation of Brain Injury." *Psychol Service Center J* 1:52-61 S '49. * (PA 24:2918)
6. LEITER, RUSSELL GRAYDON. "The Leiter Adaptation of Arthur's Stencil Design Test." *Psychol Service Center J* 1:62-8+ S '49. * (PA 24:2920)
7. LEITER, RUSSELL GRAYDON. "The Leiter Adaptation of the Painted Cube Test." *Psychol Service Center J* 1:29-45 S '49. * (PA 24:2921)
8. PARTINGTON, JOHN E. "Detailed Instructions for Administering Partington's Pathways Test." *Psychol Service Center J* 1:46-8 S '49. * (PA 24:3215)
9. PARTINGTON, JOHN E., AND LEITER, RUSSELL GRAYDON. "Partington's Pathways Test." *Psychol Service Center J* 1:9-20 Mr '49. * (PA 23:5528)
10. WATSON, NEAL. "A Qualitative Check List for the Clinical Use of Partington's Pathways Test in the Evaluation of Brain Injury." *Psychol Service Center J* 1:49-51 S '49. * (PA 24:3351)
11. WATSON, NEAL. "A Qualitative Check List for the Clinical Use of the Leiter Adaptation of Arthur's Stencil Design Test in the Evaluation of Brain Injury." *Psychol Service Center J* 1:69-70 S '49. * (PA 24:3350)
12. COZAN, LEE W. "Industrial Use of the Partington Pathways Test." *J Appl Psychol* 35:112-3 Ap '51. * (PA 25:8077)
13. LEITER, RUSSELL GRAYDON. "The Leiter Adult Intelligence Scale." *Psychol Service Center J* 3:1-52 D '51. *
14. SYDOW, DONALD WAYNE. *A Psychometric Differentiation Between Functional Psychotics and Non-Psychotics With Organic Brain Damage.* Doctor's thesis, University of Minnesota (Minneapolis, Minn.), 1953. (DA 13:1267)
15. COZAN, LEE W. "Short Mental Ability Test for Industrial Use." *J Personnel Adm & Ind Rel* 1:191-4 '54. * (PA 29:8054)
16. PAYNE, R. W.; MATTUSSEK, P.; AND GEORGE, E. I. "An Experimental Study of Schizophrenic Thought Disorder." *J Mental Sci* 105:627-52 Jl '59. * (PA 34:6384)
17. PAYNE, R. W., AND HEWLETT, J. H. G. Chap. 1, "Thought Disorder in Psychotic Patients," pp. 3-104. In *Experiments in Personality: Vol. 2, Psychodiagnostics and Psychodynamics.* Edited by H. J. Eysenck. London: Routledge & Kegan Paul Ltd., 1960. Pp. viii, 333. *
18. VINSON, DAVID B. "Objectivity in the Assessment of Psychobiologic Decline." *Vita Hum* 4(3):134-42 '62. *
19. VINSON, DAVID B., AND GAITZ, CHARLES M. "The Objective Measurement of Psychobiologic Decline: A Preliminary Report," pp. 578-82. In *Social and Psychological Aspects of Aging.* Proceedings of the Fifth Congress of the International Association of Gerontology. Edited by Clark Tibbitts and Wilma Donahue. New York: Columbia University Press, 1962. Pp. xviii, 952. *

PAUL C. DAVIS, *Dean and Professor of Psychology, Los Angeles Pacific College, Los Angeles, California.*

The author states frankly that he revised the original (1949) scale to its present form (1959) because it was criticized for lack of language content. To the Free Recall-Controlled Recall test he has added two more tests, Similarities-Differences and Digits Forward and Backward, to round out a language battery of three tests. The nonlanguage battery consists of the same three tests used in the original scale: Pathways, Stencil Design, and Painted Cubes. As was the original scale, the revised scale is designed only as an individual instrument primarily for clinical use.

Several advantages are likely to recommend the scale to potential users: (*a*) it is relatively easy to administer and simple to score, (*b*) it is economical of time, requiring an average of 40 minutes for administration, and (*c*) the material is varied and arouses considerable inherent interest in adults. The author also lists as a recommending characteristic the fact that one subscale can be administered, if necessary, entirely without verbal directions.

Certain minor technical errors may confuse the first-time user of the scale. In the Painted Cube test, the table for scoring Part 1 appears in the midst of instructions for Part 2. Also, tables for all three parts show minimum credits for up to 119, 239, and 239 seconds while maximum times are 120, 240, and 240. How are the exact maximum times to be scored? The reviewer would suggest revising the terminal limit of the last interval up to the maximum time.

Reliability data (unidentified K-R) are given, based on an n of 256. Respectable reliability is indicated for all tests except Digits (.65) and Stencil Design (.67). These latter low reliabilities call into special question the author's providing equivalent IQ's for raw scores on individual tests. Although the author says this is done so the examiner "can have some idea of how the subject is progressing.... and whether....performance on any given test is above average, average, or below average," this purpose could as well be served by converting raw scores to scaled scores with an arbitrary mean and standard deviation, a device employed by many test authors. The sophisticated user will of course be wary of the unreliability of individual test IQ's, but the author does a disservice by including conversion tables without warning to the user.

Using an n of 256, the author computed intercorrelations among the subtests, language and nonlanguage subscales, total scale, and the Stanford-Binet. Subtest correlations with the S-B ranged from .57 (Painted Cubes) to .75 (Similarities-Differences), while total language correlated .82, nonlanguage, .78, and total scale, .88, with the same criterion. Although of course the Stanford-Binet is not the ultimate criterion measure of intelligence it has been widely employed as *a* criterion so that the reported correlations give the user considerable confidence that the Leiter scale is a reasonably good measure of intelligence as commonly conceived.

SUMMARY. The new scale is undoubtedly superior to its predecessor in that it contains balanced language and nonlanguage subscales. The scale is easy and economical to administer and score, and is interesting to adults. Reliabilities of subtests are adequate if scores are used only in arriving at language, nonlanguage, and total scores. Providing individual test score IQ equivalents tends to encourage false confidence in the reliability of individual tests. Intercorrelations of tests, scales, and the Stanford-Binet indicate that the *Leiter Adult Intelligence Scale* and the Stanford-Binet measure similar intellectual functions. For those seeking a new or alternative individual measure of intelligence, the Leiter scale offers interesting possibilities. However, much more research and evidence will be required to put the scale in the class, say, of the *Wechsler Adult Intelligence Scale*.

FRANK B. JEX, *Professor of Educational Psychology, University of Utah, Salt Lake City, Utah.*

The *Leiter Adult Intelligence Scale* derives from the Army Individual Test of General Mental Ability (1944) which was standardized on a group of 256 unselected male war veterans between the ages of 19 and 36, about whom the manual provides no further background information.

The three tests comprising the language scale are: (*a*) Similarities-Differences (telling how pairs of words are alike, and how they are different); (*b*) Digits Forwards and Backwards (repeating number series presented orally, as in the Wechsler scales); (*c*) FR-CR (after listening to a lengthy paragraph, first repeating it as a measure of free recall, then responding to a series of related questions as a measure of controlled recall).

The three tests comprising the nonlanguage scale (previously published as the *Leiter-Partington Adult Performance Scale*) are: (*a*) Pathways (first drawing lines from number to number in sequence, and then from numbers to letters alternately); (*b*) Stencil Designs (reproducing designs which resemble military shoulder patches by superimposing circular stencils of colored paper); (*c*) Painted Cube Test (duplicating various designs by arranging one-inch cubes to conform to the stimulus cards).

The scale purports to measure "a sufficient variety of mental functions to indicate the learning capacity of the adult being tested." The author's criterion of learning capacity is score on the 1937 Stanford-Binet, developed for use with children and inappropriate as a criterion of adult intelligence. For the standardization group, Stanford-Binet scores correlate .82 with scores on the language scale, .78 with nonlanguage scores, and .88 with total scores. Kuder-Richardson estimates of the scale's reliability are: language scores, .90, nonlanguage scores, .88, total scale scores, .94.

In 1951, without the benefit of standardization on a more representative adult population, the Army scale was rechristened the *Leiter Adult Intelligence Scale* and made available for civilian use. In the meantime a few relationship and validational studies have begun to appear, but most of them have been confined to the *Psychological Service Center Journal,* founded, edited, and published by Leiter himself.

Since the appearance of the mimeographed manual in 1956, the *Leiter Profile* has been published, employing the individual patterning on the WAIS, the LAIS, and the *Porteus Maze Test* to arrive at a measure of social sufficiency among patients in mental hospitals. This research is not without promise, but the completely inadequate standardization of the LAIS remains to plague the user and to discourage serious research with the scale. Perhaps this inadequacy also explains the relatively limited clinical use of the LAIS, as contrasted to the WAIS, even though the much shorter LAIS is now reported by the publishers to correlate .93 with a Wechsler-Bellevue scale.

The six tests of the LAIS do have an interesting history (although little of this is reflected in the manual), and that they are administered and scored much after the fashion of the WAIS suggests that the two scales might be used as alternate forms for assessing adult intelligence. For purposes of this review both the LAIS and the WAIS were administered to 50 University of Utah students (26 males and 24 females) enrolled in the College of Education. For this sample LAIS language correlated .67 with WAIS verbal, LAIS nonlanguage correlated .52 with WAIS performance, and LAIS total correlated .68 with WAIS total. The LAIS IQ's ranged from 96 through 136 with a mean of 122 and a standard deviation of 9 (published standard deviation of 20). The WAIS IQ's ranged from 103 through 133 with a mean IQ of 119 and a standard deviation of 7 (published standard deviation of 15). Considering the differences in published standard deviations, these average performances are fairly comparable for the two scales. For this restricted range of ability, correlations with cumulative college GPA were: WAIS verbal IQ, .41; LAIS language IQ, .27; WAIS performance IQ, .19; LAIS nonlanguage IQ, .16; WAIS total IQ, .38; LAIS total IQ, .27. While most of these correlations are statistically significant, they are not large enough to be of much help for purposes of selection or prediction, and all appear to be less valid in our situation than scores on the *Henmon-Nelson Tests of Mental Ability,* which correlate .47 with college grades for this same group of students. These data also suggest that academic success is predicted as well by verbal IQ alone as by total IQ on either the WAIS or LAIS. (Indeed, scores on the WAIS vocabulary test alone correlate .38 with college grades for this sample.) The WAIS IQ's for our students are fairly normally distributed. The LAIS IQ's are truncated at the top end, which is largely attributable to the fact that 72 per cent of the group went off the top end of the norms on one or more of the tests in the scale. Clearly the LAIS lacks adequate ceiling for use with college students, while the WAIS is much more adequate in this respect, none of our sample having gone off the norms for any of the WAIS tests.

Administration time for the LAIS ranged from 37 to 63 minutes, with an average time of 49 minutes, which closely approximates the published time limits. On the WAIS, administration time ranged from 60 to 100 minutes, with an average time of 76 minutes, suggesting that the published time for the WAIS may be a considerable underestimate.

Scoring of the 6-test LAIS is obviously less time consuming than the 11-test WAIS, but the LAIS directions are more ambiguous and the criteria for scoring much less adequate. Small scoring discrepancies between the manual and the record booklet for the Pathways and the Painted Cubes constitute a further annoyance in the LAIS. Of greater concern is the weighting for arriving at the full scale IQ, raw scores for all six subtests being simply summed. This practice results in giving some tests two (and in one case nearly three) times as much weight as others, for which the author offers no defensible rationale.

Another serious limitation is evident in both the Painted Cubes and the Pathways, where a single mistake makes the difference between a high and a low score. The Pathways are scored in "all or none" fashion and contain only two scorable tasks. If one of the two is failed and the other passed with the highest possible credit, the Pathways IQ is 91. If both items are passed with the highest possible credit (a feat achieved by 10 per cent of our sample) the Pathways IQ is 149. These examples are merely indicative of the numerous and basic shortcomings of the LAIS as revealed in its use with 50 college students. In short, although more quickly administered and scored than the WAIS, in its present poorly standardized form the LAIS is not a suitable instrument for measuring adult intelligence, and cannot be recommended as an alternate to the WAIS.

J Consult Psychol 21:93 F '57. L(aurance) F. S(haffer). The *Leiter Adult Intelligence Scale* is a brief individual test for adults which requires about 40 minutes of administration time. It seems close kin to the Army Individual Test of World War II, to which the author made considerable contributions. The three language subtests are similarities-differences, digits forward and backward, and a story memory test; the three nonverbal are a pathways test, stencil designs, and painted cubes. * The manual contains sufficient directions for administering and scoring, and tables of adult IQ norms for each subtest, the two subtotals, and the total score. Reliabilities, intercorrelations, sex differences, and correlations with other tests are satisfactorily reported for several groups. There is no statement about the sample used for the derivation of the norms. Implications from previously published studies suggest that the IQ norms were obtained entirely from 256 young male veterans who had also been given the Stanford Binet. Since the reported studies of sex differences concern college women and men only, the extension of the norms to women, and indeed to men in general, seems a bit risky.

For reviews by Harold A. Delp and Herschel Manuel of the original edition, see 4:350 (*1 excerpt*); for a review by George K. Bennett of the Pathways Test, see 4:355 (*1 excerpt*); for additional information regarding the other subtests, see 4:347 (*1 excerpt*), 4:348 (*1 excerpt*), and 4:339.

[526]
Leiter International Performance Scale. Ages 2–18, 3–8; 1936–55; individual; 2 editions; postage extra; Russell Graydon Leiter and Grace Arthur (*b*); C. H. Stoelting Co. *

a) 1948 REVISION. Ages 2–18; 1936–52; 1 form ('48); manual in 2 parts: Parts 1 ['52, 75 pages, also published in 1959 as 45 below], 2 ('50, 85 pages, reprint of 27); record card ['48, 2 pages]; $187.50 per set of testing materials, 100 record cards, carrying case, and manual; $5 per 100 record cards; specimen set not available; [30–60] minutes.
b) ARTHUR ADAPTATION. Ages 3–8; 1952–55; author recommends use with *Arthur Point Scale of Performance Tests*; administered by pantomime; individual; 1 form ['52]; test materials consist of Trays 1 and 2 of the 1948 revision (*a* above); manual ('52, 78 pages); record card ['55, 2 pages]; $136.50 per set of testing materials, 100 record cards, carrying case, and manual; $5 per 100 record cards; $4 per manual; (30–60) minutes.

REFERENCES

1–25. See 4:349.
26–42. See 5:408.
43. ALLEN, ROBERT M., AND COLLINS, MARJORIE G. "Suggestions for the Adaptive Administration of Intelligence Tests for Those With Cerebral Palsy: Part 1, Administration of the Ammons Full-Range Picture Test, Columbia Mental Maturity Test, Raven's Progressive Matrices and Leiter International Performance Scale." *Cerebral Palsy R* 16:11–4+ My–Je '55. * (*PA* 30:3284)
44. WILSON, BARBARA A. *A Comparison of Intelligence Quotients for Readers and Non-Readers Using the Leiter International Performance Scale and the 1937 Revision of the Stanford-Binet.* Master's thesis, Sacramento State College (Sacramento, Calif.), 1958.
45. LEITER, RUSSELL GRAYDON. "Part I of the Manual for the 1948 Revision of the Leiter International Performance Scale." *Psychol Service Center J* 11:1–72 '59. * [Same as manual, part 1, issued in 1952.]
46. WOLF, WILLAVENE SHEETS. *The Contribution of Speed of Response in Mental Measurement.* Doctor's thesis, State University of Iowa (Iowa City, Iowa), 1960. (*DA* 21:1467)
47. BRENGELMANN, JOHANNES C., AND KENNY, JOSEPH T. "Comparison of Leiter, WAIS and Stanford-Binet IQ's in Retardates." *J Clin Psychol* 17:235–8 Jl '61. * (*PA* 38:8953)
48. HUNT, BETTY M. "Differential Responses of Mentally Retarded Children on the Leiter Scale." *Excep Child* 28:99–102 O '61. * (*PA* 37:1693)
49. WOLF, WILLAVENE, AND STROUD, JAMES B. "The Contribution of Response in Mental Measurement." *J Ed Psychol* 52:249–53 O '61. * (*PA* 38:3192)
50. MAISEL, RICHARD N.; ALLEN, ROBERT M.; AND TALLARICO, ROBERT B. "A Comparison of the Adaptive and Standard Administration of the Leiter International Performance Scale With Normal Children." *Cerebral Palsy R* 23:3–4+ S–O '62. * (*PA* 37:3549)
51. MIRA, MARY P. "The Use of the Arthur Adaptation of the Leiter International Performance Scale and the Nebraska Test of Learning Aptitude With Preschool Deaf Children." *Am Ann Deaf* 107:224–8 Mr '62. * (*PA* 37:1617)
52. BIRCH, JANE R.; STUCKLESS, E. ROSS; AND BIRCH, JACK W. "An Eleven Year Study of Predicting School Achievement in Young Deaf Children." *Am Ann Deaf* 108:236–40 Mr '63. * (*PA* 37:8132)

EMMY E. WERNER, *Assistant Professor of Child Development, University of California, Davis, California.* [Review of the Arthur adaptation.]

The Arthur adaptation of the *Leiter International Performance Scale,* a nonverbal scale for young children, is a point-scale which yields both an MA and an IQ. Arthur stresses the following assets of the adaptation: (*a*) It requires no verbalization on the part of the examiner or the child. This makes it especially useful for the testing of children with speech and hearing difficulties, mental retardates, foreign-born or bilingual children, and shy or withdrawn children. (*b*) It has no time limits. (*c*) It reaches down to lower chronological age levels than other performance scales. (*d*) The tests lowest in the scale are tests of ability to learn rather than tests of acquired skills or materials already learned. (*e*) The materials for the test are interesting to children.

The test contains 60 items, ranging in difficulty level from ages 2 to 12. It is considered most suitable for the testing of children from 3 to 8 years and others whose mental age falls within this range.

The materials consist of a response frame with an adjustable card holder. All tests are administered by attaching the appropriate picture card to the frame. Directions are pantomimed. The child chooses the matching blocks and inserts them into the frame. The types of tasks range from matching of colors and forms to completion of patterns, analogous designs, classification of objects. Most of the items require a good deal of perceptual organization and discrimination.

Some questions may be raised about: (*a*) The seeming unevenness in difficulty level (nowhere could this reviewer find a reference to percentage of passes by item and age level). (*b*) The outdatedness of certain pictures (e.g., items V-1, V-3, VII-4). (*c*) The extent of culture fairness of the scale. Tate (*32*), studying children from extremely heterogenous socioeconomic backgrounds, found as much variability among them on the Leiter as on the Stanford-Binet. Although intended for cross cultural study, there has been no extensive use of the scale with children in cross cultural research. (*d*) The question of content or construct validity. What abilities does the scale measure? There seems to be an abrupt shift in the content of items when one compares those below age eight with those above. Factor-analytical studies of the scale at different age levels might provide an answer. (*e*) The relatively small number of items which represent each year level; on the upper level accidental failure can severely penalize a child. Arthur has worked out a somewhat complicated bonus system to compute the basal age. In spite of it, mean scores on the scale run generally lower than those on the S-B or the WISC. Orgel and Dreger (*35*) find that this tendency is extreme where Binet scores are high.

The 1952 manual contains very little of the information considered essential in the APA Technical Recommendations. In 1952 (the full scale manual) and 1959 (*45*) Leiter published an extensive account of the standardization, reliability, and validity data which had accumulated on the different revisions of the *Leiter International Performance Scale,* including the Arthur adaptation. This material ought also to be incorporated in the manual for the adaptation.

The 289 children who comprise the standardization group for the scale came from a very homogenous (middle class, midwestern, metropolitan background). There were few cases at either extreme of the socioeconomic distribution and apparently few or none of the children for whom the scale was originally designed: i.e., children who would be handicapped on a verbal scale. It might be helpful to expand the norms to cover a more representative sample of children, and to test more adequately the claims of culture fairness which have been made for the scale.

Arthur gives no reliability data in her manual; split-half reliabilities quoted by Anastasi and Freeman in their texts are in the .90's. There is a real need to determine both tester-observer and test-retest reliability, in view of the few items which represent each age range.

A number of studies have been undertaken which establish the concurrent validity of the scale. Correlations between the scale and the S-B, on samples of 4-, 5-, 7-, and 8-year-old public school children, range between .69 and .93 (*28, 30*); correlations based on mentally retarded or brain damaged children run generally a little lower, between .56 and .86 (*29, 39*). The performance scale of the WISC correlates higher with the Arthur (.79–.80) than the verbal scale (.40–.78) and about as high as the total score (.77–.83). This reviewer knows of no study reporting on the predictive validity of the scale.

SUMMARY. It is evident that a lot of work still needs to be done to establish more comprehensive norms, a better scoring system and the predictive value of the Arthur adaptation. Given the fairly high correlations with the two most widely used individual intelligence tests for children which have been demonstrated, there is encouragement to pursue this "clean-up work." Within the limits of what we presently know about the construction of culture fair tests, the Arthur scale is a very promising instrument, and has made possible the testing of many children who could not be properly evaluated by the Stanford-Binet or WISC. Its use in cross cultural research with young children should be more encouraged; for the time being this reviewer recommends the Arthur adaptation for research purposes and as a special diagnostic instrument for the experienced clinician.

For a review by Gwen F. Arnold of a, see 4:349 (1 excerpt); for excerpts from a related book review, see 40:B989.

[527]

Merrill-Palmer Scale of Mental Tests. Ages 24-63 months; 1926-31; individual; 1 form; 15 tests: *Stutsman Color-Matching Test, Wallin Peg Boards, Stutsman Buttoning Test, Stick-and-String Test, Stutsman Language Test, Stutsman Picture Formboard, Mare and Foal Formboard,* modification of *Seguin-Goddard Formboard, Manikin Test, Decroly Matching Game, Stutsman Nested Cubes, Action Agent Test* (modification of *Action-Agent Association Test* ['11] by R. S. Woodworth and F. L. Wells), *Copying Test, Pyramid Test,* and *Little Pink Tower Test;* manual ('31, see 5); record blank [no data, 4 pages]; no data on reliability; $75 per set of testing materials, 50 record blanks, and manual (manual may also be purchased separately from the publisher, Harcourt, Brace & World, Inc.); $2.50 per 50 record blanks; postage extra; administration time not reported; Rachel Stutsman; C. H. Stoelting Co. *

REFERENCES

1-13. See 40:1406.
14. BARRETT, HELEN ELIZABETH, AND KOCH, HELEN LOIS. "The Effect of Nursery-School Training Upon the Mental-Test Performance of a Group of Orphanage Children." *J Genetic Psychol* 37:102-22 Mr '30. * (PA 4:2163)
15. ALDRICH, CECELIA G., AND DOLL, EDGAR A. "Comparative Intelligence of Idiots and Normal Infants." *J Genetic Psychol* 39:227-57 Je '31. * (PA 6:520)
16. SMITTER, FAITH WINTERS. *The Serviceability of the Merrill-Palmer and Stanford-Binet Scales for Ages Three to Six.* Master's thesis, University of Southern California (Los Angeles, Calif.), 1936.
17. COFFEY, HUBERT STANLEY. *A Study of Certain Mental Functions and Their Relation to Changes in the Intelligence of Preschool Children.* Doctor's thesis, University of Iowa (Iowa City, Iowa), 1938.
18. ANDERSON, L. DEWEY. "The Predictive Value of Infancy Tests in Relation to Intelligence at Five Years." *Child Develop* 10:203-12 S '39. * (PA 13:6507)
19. DE FOREST, RUTH. "A Study of the Prognostic Value of the Merrill-Palmer Scale of Mental Tests and the Minnesota Preschool Scale." *J Genetic Psychol* 59:219-23 S '41. * (PA 16:1231)
20. ALLAN, MARY ELIZABETH, AND YOUNG, FLORENE M. "The Constancy of the Intelligence Quotient as Indicated by Retests of 130 Children." *J Appl Psychol* 27:41-60 F '43. * (PA 17:2631)
21. EBERT, ELIZABETH, AND SIMMONS, KATHERINE. *The Brush Foundation Study of Child Growth and Development: I, Psychometric Tests.* Monographs of the Society for Research in Child Development, Vol. 8, No. 2, Serial No. 35. Washington, D.C.: the Society, National Research Council, 1943. Pp. xiv, 113. * (PA 18:3322)
22. HARRIS, DALE B. "An Item Analysis and Evaluation of the Merrill-Palmer Scale of Mental Tests for Preschool Children." Abstract. *Am Psychologist* 2:302 Ag '47. *
23. STUTSMAN, RACHEL. *Guide for Administering the Merrill-Palmer Scale of Mental Tests.* A reprint of Part 3 of the author's *Mental Measurement of Preschool Children* published in 1931. Yonkers, N.Y.: World Book Co., 1948. Pp. 139-262. *
24. HAINES, MIRIAM STEARNS. *Test Performance of Pre-School Children With and Without Organic Brain Pathology.* Doctor's thesis, Columbia University (New York, N.Y.), 1953. (DA 14:1099)
25. HAINES, MIRIAM STEARNS. "Test Performance of Preschool Children With and Without Organic Brain Pathology." *J Consult Psychol* 18:371-4 O '54. * (PA 29:5707)
26. WALSH, ROSALINE. *The Prognostic Value of the Merrill-Palmer Mental Tests and the Nebraska Test of Learning Aptitude for Pre-School Deaf Children.* Master's thesis, University of Buffalo (Buffalo, N.Y.), 1954.
27. HURST, JOHN G. "A Factor Analysis of the Merrill-Palmer With Reference to Theory and Test Construction." *Ed & Psychol Meas* 20:519-32 au '60. * (PA 35:3251)
28. HORTON, CARRELL P., AND CRUMP, E. PERRY. "Growth and Development 11: Descriptive Analysis of the Backgrounds of 76 Negro Children Whose Scores Are Above or Below Average on the Merrill-Palmer Scale of Mental Tests at Three Years of Age." *J Genetic Psychol* 100:255-65 Je '62. * (PA 37:2871)
29. HURST, JOHN G. "Factor Analysis of the Merrill-Palmer at Two Age Levels: Structure and Comparison." *J Genetic Psychol* 102:231-44 Je '63. * (PA 38:4074)

MARJORIE P. HONZIK, *Lecturer in Psychology, and Associate Research Psychologist, Institute of Human Development, University of California, Berkeley, California.*

The *Merrill-Palmer Scale of Mental Tests* was constructed to serve as a substitute for, or supplement to, revisions of the Binet scale. It differs in this respect from a number of other preschool mental tests (e.g., the *California Preschool Mental Scale,* and the *Minnesota Preschool Scale,* as well as the Stanford revisions) which include items from the Binet. The Merrill-Palmer's independence from the Stanford-Binet has made it a highly useful adjunct to the testing program in nursery schools and clinics, as well as in developmental research.

The Merrill-Palmer scale is composed of 3 to 14 test items per six-month age period beginning at 18 months and extending to 6 years. There are 10 or more items at each level except ages 60 to 65 months and 66 to 71 months. The majority of items depend in part on fine motor skill: pegboards, block building, tower building with blocks of varying sizes, drawing, formboards (Seguin), buttoning, and picture puzzles. There are a few verbal items: repetition of or memory for words and groups of words; questions such as "What does a doggie say?" and the Action Agent Test which asks "What sleeps?", "What roars?", etc.

This scale is a delightful one for both the young child and the examiner. It includes few verbal items but those which are included are interesting to young children. Another advantage of this test is the provision it makes for refusals. Rachel Stutsman Ball has given more thoughtful consideration to the problem of resistance in the test situation than have the authors of any other preschool tests. Her listing of the many factors in the test situation which influence the child's cooperation has remained the best available for over 30 years. Refused and omitted items are considered in arriving at a total score which may then be converted into mental age, sigma value, or percentile rank.

The provision for refusals suggests a marked

sensitivity to the characteristics of the preschool child; but an insensitive aspect and major fault of the Merrill-Palmer scale, which causes difficulty when examining the very young child, is the large proportion of timed tests. Not only the pegboards but also the block building, buttoning, and even the puzzle tasks are timed. The slow moving but thoughful child is severely penalized on this test.

Another difficulty of the scale is the scores which it yields. The standard deviations of the mental ages do not increase in proportion to advancing chronological ages so that IQ's cannot be computed. The author recommends that percentile ranks or standard deviation units be used. Since percentile ranks are not suitable measures to use for computation, and thus research, one is left with the standard scores which, for this scale, are presented in such a way as to cover a wide range of ability. Standard scores are computed to the nearest half standard deviation. This means that almost half of a normal sample would receive a standardized deviation score of −.5, 0, or .5.

The reliability of the scale was not reported by Stutsman in her manual but she states that the test is valid on the basis that it (*a*) is composed of items which differentiated between children judged bright or dull by other criteria; (*b*) yields high correlations with chronological age; (*c*) differentiates between feebleminded and normal children; and (*d*) yields high correlations with Stanford-Binet mental ages for a far too wide spread of chronological ages.

The Merrill-Palmer scale has been widely used at child research centers (e.g., those at the Universities of Minnesota, Iowa, and California), and its predictive value was reported by Ebert and Simmons (*21*) for the Brush Foundation's longitudinal study at Western Reserve. In this study the correlations between the Merrill-Palmer and Stanford-Binet for two-, three-, and four-year-old children were in the .60's. Prediction of later Stanford-Binet IQ's from the Merrill-Palmer given between the ages of 2 and 4 years "fluctuates within the rather narrow range from .39 to .54." In this same study the abilities measured by the Merrill-Palmer were less closely related to the Stanford-Binet IQ's than the performance test scores (*Kent-Shakow Formboard, Kohs' Block-Design Test,* and the *Minnesota Paper Form Board Test*), at least in boys.

In summary, the Merrill-Palmer scale is one which is enjoyed by children, partly because of the large proportion of performance items, has good provisions for handling refused tests, and has played an important role in assessing abilities not tested by Binet-type tests. The disadvantages lie in its restricted age range of usefulness, large proportion of timed test items, and method of presenting scores, and in the fact that it was standardized on a nonrepresentative and relatively small sample at each age level. It is to be hoped that this scale will be revised since its value has been proved in the clinic and as a research tool.

For reviews by Nancy Bayley, B. M. Castner, Florence L. Goodenough, and Florence M. Teagarden, see 40:1406; for excerpts from related book reviews, see 40:B1123.

[528]
Minnesota Preschool Scale. Ages 1.5-6; 1932-40; 3 scores: verbal, nonverbal (ages 3.0-6.0 only), total; individual; Form A ('32); manual ('40, 127 pages); record booklet ('40, 4 pages, same as record booklet copyrighted in 1932); $38 per set of testing materials, 25 record blanks, and manual; $1.60 per 25 record blanks; postage extra; $2.15 per specimen set, postpaid; [10–30] minutes; Florence L. Goodenough, Katherine M. Maurer, and M. J. Van Wagenen; Educational Test Bureau. *

REFERENCES
1-3. See 40:1407.
4-5. See 3:286.
6-7. See 4:351.
8. LYLE, J. G. "The Effect of an Institution Environment Upon the Verbal Development of Imbecile Children: 1, Verbal Intelligence." *J Mental Def Res* 3:122-8 D '59. *
9. LYLE, J. G. "The Effect of an Institution Environment Upon the Verbal Development of Imbecile Children: 2, Speech and Language; 3, The Brooklands Residential Family Unit." *J Mental Def Res* 4:1-23 Je '60. * (*PA* 35:2565-6)
10. LYLE, J. G. "A Comparison of the Verbal Intelligence of Normal and Imbecile Children." *J Genetic Psychol* 99:227-34 D '61. * (*PA* 36:3JI27L)

MARJORIE P. HONZIK, *Lecturer in Psychology, and Associate Research Psychologist, Institute of Human Development, University of California, Berkeley, California.*

In the manual for the *Minnesota Preschool Scale,* the authors wrote that they felt that there was "a real demand for a series of tests which....accurately reveal the development of mental ability in early childhood." Since the publication of these scales 30 years ago, several longitudinal studies have shown that whereas mental test scores after six years of age are fairly stable, marked changes in relative standing on mental tests are likely to occur during the first five years. Thus there is still need for good preschool mental scales to delineate the changes which take place during these years and the factors which are related to these changes. An important question, then, is why the well standardized *Minnesota Preschool Scale* has been so little used either in developmental research or for diagnostic purposes.

Forms A and B of the scale (Form B is out of print) each contain 26 tests equally divided into verbal and nonverbal items. Verbal tests include language comprehension (points to parts of body and to objects in pictures, follows directions, comprehends problem situations); language facility (names objects, describes pictures, knows colors, vocabulary, opposites, and verbal absurdities); memory for objects, incomplete pictures, and digits. The nonverbal tests involve drawing (both copying and imitating); block building; discrimination, recognition, and tracing of forms; picture puzzles; paper folding; recognition of omitted parts in pictures; and imitating position of clock hands.

These scales were rigorously standardized. The norms are based on the tests of 50 boys and 50 girls examined at half-year levels. Within each age level, the children were selected so as to represent a cross section of the population. The statistical analysis is impeccable and the resulting C scores can be converted into IQ equivalents.

The authors report, for half-year age ranges, reliabilities ranging from .68 to .94 for the verbal scale, and from .67 to .92 for the nonverbal scale, when the scores on alternate forms were correlated. For the combined verbal and nonverbal scores, reliabilities range from .80 to .94.

The test materials are conveniently boxed and the manual of instructions is clearly written. The test materials have not become dated since toys are few and the pictures to be described are reproductions of paintings which would be equally difficult for all children. Although the test materials include a doll, blocks, and puzzles, these scales have less appeal to children than other preschool tests. Form L-M of the Stanford-Binet, for example, has an attractive formboard, small cars, an engine, and other toys which help maintain rapport. In fact, formboards, pegboards, and small toys are found in greater numbers in all other preschool tests: *Gesell Developmental Schedules, California Preschool Mental Scale,* and the *Merrill-Palmer Scale of Mental Tests.* A further difficulty of the Minnesota scale is the requirement that with few exceptions all tests be given to each child and in the prescribed order. This makes for a long test which taxes the patience of the child and the ingenuity of the examiner. Additionally, there is no provision for refusals. Form L-M of the Stanford-Binet has alternate test items which can be given if one is refused or is inappropriate. The Merrill-Palmer and California scales have specific adjustments in scoring when tests are refused or when there is an error in the administration of a test item. If a child does not "cooperate actively" on the Minnesota scale, the examiner is instructed to discontinue the test and allow the child to play with other toys. The authors add that in the case of an unusually shy child, two or three preliminary visits may be advisable. In practice, it is not always possible to have preliminary sessions before the actual test is given.

A further reason why these scales are used so infrequently is the limited age range of usefulness. The Merrill-Palmer is the only other test with such a limited age range. Other scales articulate with either an infant scale or with tests for older children.

In summary, the *Minnesota Preschool Scale* is among the most carefully standardized preschool tests and, although published 30 years ago, the test materials are not unduly dated. The disadvantages of this scale lie in the limited age range of usefulness, and in the lack of appeal to the young child because the test materials are not interesting and the procedures are too inflexible. At the present time, Form L-M of the Stanford-Binet is the test of choice for research and clinic, since it covers the age range 2 to adulthood, is more flexible, includes test materials with more intrinsic appeal to the young child, and has been more widely used. However, it is fortunate that the *Minnesota Preschool Scale* is still available since alternate tests are often needed on research projects and in confirming a diagnosis in the clinic.

For a review by Beth L. Wellman, see 3:286; for reviews by Rachel Stutsman Ball, Nancy Bayley, and Florence M. Teagarden of the original edition, see 40:1407; for excerpts from related book reviews, see 4:352, 3:287, and 3:288.

[529]
*Non-Verbal Intelligence Tests for Deaf and Hearing Subjects. Ages 3–16; 1939–59; title on record booklet is *S.O.N. Snijders-Oomen Non-Verbal*

Intelligence Scale; administered orally or in pantomime; 9 scores: mosaic, picture memory, arrangement, analogies, completion, Knox cubes, drawing, sorting, I.Q.; individual; 2 forms ('58): Scales P (consisting of mosaic, picture memory, arrangement, and analogies subtests), Q (consisting of completion, Knox cubes, drawing, and sorting subtests); Scale Q can be used as parallel form or combined with Scale P for longer test; manual ('59, 140 pages); record booklet ['58, 4 pages]; $85 (600s.) per set of testing materials, 100 scoring forms, and manual; $1.50 (11s.) per 100 scoring forms; $3.75 (27s.) per manual; postage extra; Dutch, German, and French editions available; [45] minutes per scale; J. Th. Snijders and N. Snijders-Oomen; J. B. Wolters. *

REFERENCES

1. SNIJDERS, J. TH., AND SNIJDERS-OOMEN, N. *Non-Verbal Intelligence Tests for Deaf and Hearing Subjects: Snijders-Oomen Non-Verbal Scale, S.O.N.* Groningen, Netherlands: J. B. Wolters, 1959. Pp. 141. *
2. NEUHAUS, MAURY. "Measuring the Nonverbal Intelligence of Gifted Elementary-School Children." *Excep Child* 28:271-3 Ja '62. *

J. S. LAWES, *Senior Lecturer in Education, Westminster College, North Hinksey, Oxford, England.*

This scale, first constructed in 1939–42 for use with deaf children, has now been revised, enlarged, and restandardised on both deaf and hearing subjects. The first form aimed to sample four aspects of intelligence: form, combination, abstraction, and memory. This grouping has been retained. The new version has eight subtests, two for each aspect and thus consists of two parallel subscales P and Q which can be used separately or together.

Within each subtest the principle of construction has been to maintain the same type of material and the same manner of presentation over the whole age range from 3 to 16 years. The Knox cubes test used to assess the "Memory" aspect in Scale Q is an example. Where such continuity has not been possible a change to material of similar but not identical type takes place. For example the "Form" subtest of Scale P consists of simple mosaics with four or five red squares up to age 5-3, more complex mosaics with up to 16 red and white squares from 5-3 up to 8-6, then a modified version of Kohs' *Block-Design Test*. Of such changes the manual says, "the correlation of the adjoining parts has been examined and, when necessary, raised by revision of items," but no details are given. In structure the scale has the advantage over the various Binet revisions that its pattern is the same at all age levels and, like the Wechsler scales, it is a point scale rather than an age scale.

Each subtest forms a separate point scale and tables are provided to convert raw scores to standard scores with a mean of 25 and standard deviation 5. Further tables convert the sum of the standard scores into a deviation IQ of mean 100 and standard deviation 15. For those who desire scores expressed as mental ages, tables are given for converting raw score in each subtest into a mental age, called a subtest age. Mental age is defined as the median of the subtest ages. This scoring system is explained clearly in the manual and there is a good section on interpretation of scores.

The tables are based on a standardisation sample which included Dutch children only. For the "hearing" group 50 children were selected for each half year of age from 3 to 5½ years and 100 children for each year from 6 up to 16. This gives a praiseworthy sample size of 1,400 cases. We are told that "Each age-sample was selected in exactly the same manner. The criteria were: birthday, sex, residence, type of school, social level of parents," but it is not clear whether this means that within each age sample the whole range of "type of school," "social level of parents," etc. was included or simply that the same, restricted, range of types was included at each level. The "deaf" sample included "all pupils of the Dutch schools for the deaf up to age 16." Although this means variation in age group size and some extrapolation, it also means that the conversion tables for deaf children are based on a whole population.

Reliability is reported as split-half coefficients and standard errors of measurement. The split-half coefficients for the whole scale at ages 5 to 5½ years, 10 to 11 years, and 15 years are .94, .91, and .91 for hearing children, .95, .93, and .94 for deaf children. These compare well with WISC performance scale reliabilities. Of the two subscales P shows a reliability similar to that of the whole scale but Q has a slightly lower reliability and, particularly with hearing children, shows a tendency to be less reliable with older subjects, viz. .89, .80, and .76 at the three ages quoted above. Reliability figures for the separate subtests vary from .36 up to .93. The lowest figures are found in the two "memory" subtests and in these also the reliability drops considerably within the middle age range. This raises the question of the desirability of using the individual subtests in isolation or in "profile" analysis; but one notes that the authors do, in the manual, sound a note of caution here.

Linked with this question is that of the validity of the theoretical construct of four aspects of intelligence. No evidence is offered to support this apart from the comment "it has only partly been confirmed by the factorial analysis of the standardisation data." No details are given, nor are we given any data from this factorial analysis to demonstrate the validity of the scale as a whole.

Validity of the scale as a measure of intelligence rests, at present, on correlations with teachers' judgments. For two groups of pupils numbering 300–400 and for two smaller groups of 25 pupils, all groups being hearing children, correlation coefficients range from .38 to .57. A group of 78 deaf pupils was tested in 1952 and again in 1956. Correlations of the two sets of scores with teachers' judgments made in 1956 are .42 and .49, respectively. This hint of test stability is confirmed by the correlation between the IQ's obtained in 1952 and 1956. These are .80 for the whole scale, .81 for P scale, and .63 for Q scale.

This all adds up to a well constructed scale, composed of pleasant and easy to handle material—some familiar, some modified from familiar tests, and some original. The price however seems unduly high, especially when tax and duty for British purchasers are added. The authors' advice that Scale Q should be reserved for retesting or added to Scale P for an extended scale is to be commended. The manual is well translated into English and gives full information for administration and scoring. Given large-scale standardisation in the United States and Britain, this English translation could be a welcome addition to the available range of nonverbal and performance scales.

[530]

★Peabody Picture Vocabulary Test. Ages 2.5–18; 1959; individual; Forms A, B, (154-page picture booklet used with both forms); pictures also available in a plastic booklet; manual (29 pages); individual record (2 pages) for each form; $10 per examiner's kit of picture booklet, 25 individual records for each form, and manual ($15 with plastic booklet instead of regular picture booklet); $3 per 50 individual records; postage extra; (10–15) minutes; Lloyd M. Dunn; American Guidance Service, Inc. *

REFERENCES

1. Dunn, Lloyd M., and Harley, Randall K. "Comparability of Peabody, Ammons, Van Alstyne, and Columbia Test Scores With Cerebral Palsied Children." *Excep Child* 26:70–4 O '59. * (*PA* 35:3733)
2. Garrett, Jane. *Comparison of the Peabody Picture Vocabulary Test and Wechsler Intelligence Scale for Children.* Master's thesis, George Peabody College for Teachers (Nashville, Tenn.), 1959.
3. Dunn, Lloyd M., and Brooks, Sadye T. "Peabody Picture Vocabulary Test Performance of Educable Mentally Retarded Children." *Training Sch B* 57:35–40 Ag '60. * (*PA* 35:1043)
4. Kimbrell, Don L. "Comparison of Peabody, WISC, and Academic Achievement Scores Among Educable Mental Defectives." *Psychol Rep* 7:502 D '60. * (*PA* 35:2554)
5. Moss, James W., and Edmonds, Phyllis. "The Peabody Vocabulary Test With English Children." *Brit J Ed Psychol* 30:82 F '60. *
6. Norris, Raymond C.; Hottel, John V.; and Brooks, Sadye. "Comparability of Peabody Picture Vocabulary Test Scores Under Group and Individual Administration." *J Ed Psychol* 51:87–91 Ap '60. * (*PA* 35:2780)
7. Scoggins, Betty Joanne. *A Comparative Study of the Full-Range Picture Vocabulary Test and the Peabody Picture Vocabulary Test.* Master's thesis, Vanderbilt University (Nashville, Tenn.), 1960.
8. Dunn, Lloyd M., and Hottel, John V. "Peabody Picture Vocabulary Test Performance of Trainable Mentally Retarded Children." *Am J Mental Def* 65:448–52 Ja '61. * (*PA* 35:6829)
9. Tobias, Jack, and Gorelick, Jack. "The Validity of the Peabody Picture Vocabulary Test as a Measure of Intelligence of Retarded Adults." *Training Sch B* 58:92–8 N '61. * (*PA* 36:4J192T)
10. Hartman, Bernard-Thomas. *Comparative Investigation of the Peabody Picture Vocabulary Test With Three Etiologic Groups of Institutionalized Mentally Retarded Students.* Doctor's thesis, Indiana University (Bloomington, Ind.), 1962. (*DA* 23:2008)
11. Himelstein, Philip, and Herndon, James D. "Comparison of the WISC and Peabody Picture Vocabulary Test With Emotionally Disturbed Children." *J Clin Psychol* 18:82 Ja '62. * (*PA* 38:8420)
12. Mein, R. "Use of the Peabody Picture Vocabulary With Severely Subnormal Patients." *Am J Mental Def* 67:269–73 S '62. * (*PA* 37:3582)
13. Mueller, Max W. "Effects of Illustration Size on Test Performance of Visually Limited Children." *Excep Child* 29:124–8 N '62. *
14. Reger, Roger. "Brief Tests of Intelligence and Academic Achievement." *Psychol Rep* 11:82 Ag '62. * (*PA* 37:5654)
15. Shipe, Dorothy M. *Discrepancies Between the Peabody Picture Vocabulary Test and the WISC as Related to Emotional Disturbance in Children of Retarded and Normal Intelligence.* Doctor's thesis, George Peabody College for Teachers (Nashville, Tenn.), 1962. (*DA* 23:3984)
16. Wolfensberger, Wolf. "The Correlation Between PPVT and Achievement Scores Among Retardates: A Further Study." *Am J Mental Def* 67:450–1 N '62. * (*PA* 37:5425)
17. Budoff, Milton, and Purseglove, Eleanor Mathias. "Peabody Picture Vocabulary Test: Performance of Institutionalized Mentally Retarded Adolescents." *Am J Mental Def* 67:756–60 Mr '63. * (*PA* 38:1259)
18. Matthews, Charles G., and Reitan, Ralph M. "Relationship of Differential Abstraction Ability Levels to Psychological Test Performances in Mentally Retarded Subjects." *Am J Mental Def* 68:235–44 S '63. * (*PA* 38:6430)
19. Moed, George; Wight, Byron W.; and James, Patricia. "Intertest Correlations of the Wechsler Intelligence Scale for Children and Two Picture Vocabulary Tests." *Ed & Psychol Meas* 23:359–63 su '63. * (*PA* 38:960)
20. Taylor, John R. "Screening Intelligence." *J Speech & Hearing Disorders* 28:90–1 F '63. *
21. Weeks, Richard William. "Effectiveness of the Peabody Picture Vocabulary Test With College Students." *J Ed Res* 57:109–10 O '63. *

Howard B. Lyman, *Associate Professor of Psychology, University of Cincinnati, Cincinnati, Ohio.*

The PPVT is an untimed individual test, administered in 15 minutes or less, consisting of a booklet with 3 practice and 150 test plates, each with 4 numbered pictures. The same booklet is used for both Form A and Form B, the forms differing only in the stimulus word (and, therefore, the picture which is the correct response) for each of the 150 items. Answer sheets, different for each form, give the stimulus word for each item, the correct response number, and space for recording the subject's response; the reverse side contains space for identifying information and for recording behavioral observations.

The examiner reads the stimulus word, and the subject responds by pointing to, giving the number of, or otherwise indicating the picture best illustrating the word. The manual states that the examiner must not spell, define, or even show the word to the subject.

Items are arranged in ascending order of difficulty, and the subject responds only to the items between his "basal" (eight consecutive correct responses) and his "ceiling" (six failures out of eight consecutive responses). The manual suggests appropriate starting points for different ages. Scoring is rapid and objective. The examiner places a mark over the item number of incorrect responses; these are counted and subtracted from the ceiling score.

This total score can be converted to any of three types of derived score: percentile rank, mental age, or standard score deviation IQ with a mean of 100 and a standard deviation of 15. Present tables include values for raw scores of 5 to 150 for IQ's, 6 to 140 only for percentile ranks, and 5 to 111 only for mental ages. These tables should be expanded to include derived score equivalents for all possible raw scores.

In developing the PPVT, the author had line drawings made for 2,055 illustratable words (from a population of 3,885) found in *Webster's New Collegiate Dictionary, Second Edition* (1956). Level of difficulty and item placement were determined on a sample of 360 subjects ranging in ages from 2 through 18 years. In a second pretest study, 750 subjects were used in selecting the final 300 stimulus words and 150 plates. (Some pictures appear in more than one of the plates.)

Standardization was based entirely on 4,012 white children and youth in and around Nashville, Tennessee. Numbers ranging from a minimum of 92 to a maximum of 354, at 19 different age levels from 2.5 years to 18 years, were tested on both forms. Only younger children (under 9 years of age) were given the test individually. At and above this age, the PPVT was administered as a group test by using photographic slides; justification for this procedure is based on a study of four 15-pupil fifth grade classes, which showed "no significant or appreciable differences" for type of administration.

Apparently norms for both Forms A and B are based on the entire samples of cases rather than on only the approximately one half who took a given form first. It seems likely that all of the norms tables are biased to an indeterminate extent because of this procedure.

The publisher effects an economy in printing the manual by using 6-month (through 5 years) and 12-month chronological age classifications; however, the use of such gross intervals is reflected in big "jumps" in the IQ table. For example, for a raw score of 50, a child of 5-5 would receive an IQ of 101 while a child of 5-6 would receive an IQ of only 89. "Jumps" of as much as 20 IQ points can be found at the extremes for younger children. The Stanford-Binet, tabling CA's in one-month units, has much smaller "jumps" (rarely above 2 IQ points).

Alternate form reliabilities ranging from .67 at the 6-year level to .84 at the 17- and 18-year levels are cited in the manual. Also cited are alternate form reliabilities of .83, .87, and .97 with handicapped and retarded groups; however, these cover such a range in ages as to seem spurious. The .97 reliability coefficient was based on 20 cerebral palsied children ranging in age from 7-1 through 16-2 years.

Although several validity studies are mentioned in the manual, the author states that "all of the statistical validity on the test are limited and preliminary." In one study with 150 seventh grade children, researchers reported correlations of .58 between Form B and the *California Test of Mental Maturity*, and .61 between Form B and the *Henmon-Nelson Tests of Mental Ability*. All other validity coefficients reported appear to be spurious because of the great range in ages.

The test is attractive and should be interesting to most subjects. It is simple to administer and score. No specialized preparation is required of the examiner beyond assuring himself of the proper pronunciation of all stimulus words. No special equipment is needed; the examiner needs only the book of plates (about 7 by 8½ inches), an answer sheet, and a pencil.

In summary, the PPVT is a highly usable test, of moderate reliability, and largely unestablished validity. Considerable caution needs to be used in interpreting the norms, especially in communities other than Nashville.

Peabody Picture Vocabulary Test

ELLEN V. PIERS, *Associate Professor of Psychology, The Pennsylvania State University, University Park, Pennsylvania.*

The PPVT is designed "to provide a well-standardized estimate of a subject's *verbal intelligence* through measuring his hearing vocabulary." As in other picture vocabulary tests, the subject indicates in some fashion which one of four pictures best fits the stimulus word read aloud to him. Besides serving as a quick estimate of intelligence for normal subjects, it was developed for use with special groups for whom the standard intelligence tests are not always appropriate, e.g., persons with reading problems, speech problems, brain damage, cerebral palsy, mental retardation, or emotional withdrawal. The author states that administration of the test requires no special training.

Its purpose, then, is similar to the Ammons *Full-Range Picture Vocabulary Test.* It may have been developed in order to improve on the FRPV, and in many ways it appears to have succeeded. Operating on the principle that different pictures for each stimulus word would provide more interest, the PPVT has 150 plates in the form of a booklet, only a portion of which are used for any one subject. (A plastic version designed to last longer has also been published.) The added interest would appear to outweigh the economy of using 16 or, as in the new Ammons *Quick Test,* only one plate per form, and the simplicity of the first few pages makes it more useful at the lower levels. The format also permits gradually increasing difficulty in the form and nature of the decoys. The pictures are sharply and clearly drawn with little ambiguity even in the more detailed plates. They were selected according to carefully defined criteria from a large pool taken from all illustratable words in *Webster's New Collegiate Dictionary.* Content validity and "item" validity thus seem well established.

The manual is for the most part a model of clarity, and illustrates admirably many of the 1954 APA Technical Recommendations. Part 1 contains directions for administering and scoring and includes tables for deriving mental ages, deviation IQ's, and percentiles. The user may find it inconvenient that scores were carried out to only three standard deviations so that IQ's are limited to the range of 55 to 145. The author states in the manual that age norms are the most useful scores beyond this range, but has reported in a personal communication to the reviewer that work is under way on methods of extrapolating IQ's downward.

Part 2 describes the test construction and standardization. Alternate form reliability is courageously presented for each age level and ranges from .67 to .84 with standard errors of measurement from 6.00 to 8.61 IQ points. Studies with wider age ranges report correspondingly higher reliabilities, ranging from .83 to .97. No test-retest reliability is reported in the manual, but a recent study (*19*) reports a test-retest coefficient of .88 after one year, with 29 physically disabled children. Both coefficients of equivalence and temporal stability appear, therefore, to be adequate for such a short test.

Although the standardization sample consisted of 4,012 white subjects restricted as to geographical area, the author employed an ingenious method of attempting to counteract these limitations. Rather than the frequently used stratified occupational sample, he chose schools where pupils' previous IQ scores provided a composite normal probability curve, or drew a random sample in some schools until the available IQ scores approximated a normal distribution. Group administration was used with upper levels, after it was established that scores would not be affected significantly. This not only provided a larger standardization sample, but appears to permit a wider application of the test.

One might question the author's assumption that recognition vocabulary measures verbal intelligence *in the same way* that verbal definition vocabulary tests are said to measure it, and that the demonstrated predictive value for school success of the latter is thus automatically transferred to a picture vocabulary test.

The section on congruent validity also raises some questions. The author, although he quotes the results of several comparison studies, states that "correlating the PPVT with other intelligence tests probably has limited utility." This reviewer would agree that such correlations may be misleading when done with small samples and restricted IQ ranges and when it is not entirely clear, as in the manual, whether mental ages were correlated in all cases or whether some studies used IQ's. On the other hand, it is essential—certainly until more evidence for predictive validity is in—that users know what a PPVT score means. Most particularly it is important since no special training is required to administer the test and many nonpsychologists will be using it. So far, from studies reported in the manual and others published since, correlations with Stanford-Binet mental ages seem to be on the order of .70's and low .80's, with IQ correlations running lower. With WISC IQ's they seem to be in the high .70's and low .80's. Correlations with three group intelligence tests are reported to be in the .60's, but the PPVT does not seem to correlate as highly with achievement test scores as do some of the group tests, although, as would be expected, coefficients are higher with reading or language than with other areas.

Perhaps the greatest potential danger in the use of this test resides in the same qualities which make it convenient—its shortness, its simplicity, its adaptability to group administration. Picture vocabulary tests can be good substitutes for the standard individual intelligence tests whenever verbal and performance responses cannot be obtained. But the encouraging of judgments of intelligence from such short and restricted samples of behavior by untrained individuals is unwise, unless the user is aware that what Guilford might call the "cognition of figural units" is only one aspect of the very complex domain called intelligence.

In any case, in this reviewer's opinion the PPVT is probably now the best of its kind. It seems to do at least as well as the Ammons FRPV, and has considerably more range than the Van Alstyne. It is too early to make comparisons with the Ammons *Quick Test* but it is almost certainly more discriminating at the lower levels. The plates and format are attractive and the test has a good manual, something still anticipated for the FRPV. A substantial list of references is already available and the test is stimulating current research. The author, according to personal communication, plans soon to revise the reliability and validity sections of the manual to pull together results of research that have accumulated since its publication.

[531]

★**Pictorial Test of Intelligence.** Ages 3–8; 1964; prepublication titles were *North Central Individual Test of Mental Ability* and *Pictorial Intelligence Test;* 7 scores: picture vocabulary, form discrimination, information and comprehension, similarities, size and number, immediate recall, total; individual; 1 **form** (54 stimulus cards and 137 response cards); may also be administered to 3- and 4-year-olds as a short form; manual (64 pages); record form (4 pages); no data on reliability of subscores; $24 per examiner's kit of test cards, 35 record forms, manual, and metal carrying case; $1.68 per 35 record forms; $3 per manual; postage extra; (45) minutes for full test; Joseph L. French; Houghton Mifflin Co. *

REFERENCES

1. FRENCH, JOSEPH L. *Development of the North Central Individual Test of Mental Ability.* Doctor's thesis, University of Nebraska (Lincoln, Neb.), 1957. (DA 17:2498)
2. FRENCH, JOSEPH L. "Intellectual Appraisal of Physically Handicapped Children." *J Genetic Psychol* 94:131–41 Mr '59. * (PA 36:4FE31F)

[532]

*****The Porteus Maze Test.** Ages 3 and over; 1914–59; individual; 2 scores: quantitative, qualitative; 1 form; 3 editions and 2 supplements; no adult norms; Stanley D. Porteus. *

a) VINELAND REVISION. Ages 3 and over; 1914–24; 1 form ('21); 13 mazes: years 3–12, 14, adult 1, 2; manual ['24, 21 pages]; $11.50 per set of manual and 100 mazes of any one level; $1 per 100 copies of any one maze; postage extra; (15–60) minutes; C. H. Stoelting Co.

b) VINELAND REVISION: NEW SERIES. Ages 3 and over; 1914–59; 1 form ('33); 12 mazes: years 3–12, 14, adult 1; combined manual ('59, 208 pages, see 95 below) for New Series and Extension (*c* below); $13.50 per set of 100 copies of each maze and pad of 100 scoring sheets; $1.50 per 100 mazes of any one level; $5.60 per manual; postpaid; (15–60) minutes; Psychological Corporation.

c) PORTEUS MAZE EXTENSION. Ages 14 and over; 1953–59; for use only as a supplement to the *Vineland Revision: New Series;* 1 form ('53); 8 mazes: years 7–12, 14, adult; combined manual ('59, 208 pages, see 95 below) for Extension and New Series (*b* above); $9.75 per set of 100 copies of each maze and pad of 100 scoring sheets; $1.50 per 100 mazes of any one level; $5.60 per manual; postpaid; (25) minutes; Psychological Corporation.

d) PORTEUS MAZE SUPPLEMENT. Ages 7 and over; 1959; a retesting series; 1 form ('59); 8 mazes: years 7–12, 14, adult; supplementary manual ('59, 12 pages, including copies of all mazes); manual for *b* and *c* above must also be purchased; $8.75 per set of 100 copies of each maze; $1.50 per 100 mazes of any one level; 75¢ per supplementary manual; postpaid; (25) minutes; Psychological Corporation.

e) BRITISH EDITION. Ages 3 and over; 1914–52; 1 form ('52, same as *Vineland Revision: New Series* copyrighted in 1933 except for format); 12 mazes: years 3–12, 14, adult 1; manual ('52, 61 pages); 5s. per 100 mazes of any one level; 5s. per 100 scoring sheets; 6s. per manual; postage and purchase tax extra; [15–60] minutes; George G. Harrap & Co. Ltd.

REFERENCES

1–56. See 4:356.
57–84. See 5:412.
85. PIDDINGTON, MARJORIE, AND PIDDINGTON, RALPH. "Report of Field Work in Northwestern Australia." *Oceania* 2:342–58 Mr '32. *
86. JOSEPH, ALICE, AND MURRAY, VERONICA F. *Chamorros and Carolinians of Saipan: Personality Studies,* pp. 119–35, 329–36, passim. Cambridge, Mass.: Harvard University Press, 1951. Pp. xviii, 381. * (PA 26:3359)
87. SHIMOTA, HELEN EMMA. *The Relation of Psychomotor Performance to Clinical Status and Improvement in Schizophrenic Patients.* Doctor's thesis, University of Minnesota (Minneapolis, Minn.), 1956. (DA 16:2530)
88. FOULDS, G. A., AND CAINE, T. M. "Personality Factors and Performance on Timed Tests of Ability." *Occup Psychol* 32:102–5 Ap '58. *
89. PORTEUS, S. D. "What Do the Maze Tests Measure?" *Austral J Psychol* 10:245–56 D '58. * (PA 34:2780)
90. VERRILL, BERNARD VICTOR. *An Investigation of the*

Concept of Impulsivity. Doctor's thesis, University of Houston (Houston, Tex.), 1958. (*DA* 19:183)
91. FOULDS, G. A. "The Relative Stability of Personality Measures Compared With Diagnostic Measures." *J Mental Sci* 105:783-7 Jl '59. * (*PA* 34:6016)
92. FOULDS, G. A., AND CAINE, T. M. "Symptom Clusters and Personality Types Among Psychoneurotic Men Compared With Women." *J Mental Sci* 105:469-75 Ap '59. * (*PA* 34:4715)
93. LORANGER, ARMAND W., AND MISIAK, HENRYK. "Critical Flicker Frequency and Some Intellectual Functions in Old Age." *J Gerontol* 14:323-7 Jl '59. * (*PA* 34:4153)
94. PORTEUS, S. D. "Recent Maze Test Studies." *Brit J Med Psychol* 32:38-43 pt 1 '59. * (*PA* 34:2690)
95. PORTEUS, STANLEY D. *The Maze Test and Clinical Psychology.* Palo Alto, Calif.: Pacific Books, 1959. Pp. vii, 203. * (*PA* 34:3571)
96. ARONSON, H., AND KLEE, G. D. "Effect of Lysergic Acid Diethylamide (LSD-25) on Impulse Control." *J Nerv & Mental Dis* 131:536-9 D '60. *
97. DOCTER, RICHARD F. "Interrelationships Among Porteus Maze Test Qualitative Errors." *J Clin Psychol* 16:336-8 Jl '60. * (*PA* 36:2HE36D)
98. DOCTER, RICHARD F. "Test-Retest Performance of Schizophrenics on Two Forms of the Porteus Mazes." *J Clin Psychol* 16:185-7 Ap '60. * (*PA* 36:2JQ85D)
99. HENKER, BARBARA A. *The Porteus Maze Test and Female Delinquency: A Controlled Comparison of the Qualitative Score Performance of Delinquent and Non-Delinquent Girls.* Master's thesis, Sacramento State College (Sacramento, Calif.), 1960.
100. JUDSON, ABE J. "The Effects of Chlorpromazine on Psychological Test Scores." Abstract. *J Consult Psychol* 24:192 Ap '60. * (*PA* 34:7888)
101. LORANGER, ARMAND W., AND MISIAK, HENRYK. "The Performance of Aged Females on Five Non-Language Tests of Intellectual Functions." *J Clin Psychol* 16:189-91 Ap '60. * (*PA* 36:2FI89L)
102. PORTEUS, S. D., AND KLEMAN, J. P. "A New Anthropometric Approach." *Mankind Q* 1:23-30 Jl '60. *
103. PORTEUS, S. D.; BARCLAY, J. E.; CULVER, H. S.; AND KLEMAN, J. P. "Measurement of Subconscious Memory." *Percept & Motor Skills* 10:215-29 Je '60. * (*PA* 35:6448)
104. SARASON, SEYMOUR B.; DAVIDSON, KENNETH S.; LIGHTHALL, FREDERICK K.; WAITE, RICHARD R.; AND RUEBUSH, BRITTON K. *Anxiety in Elementary School Children: A Report of Research,* pp. 171-88. New York: John Wiley & Sons, Inc., 1960. Pp. viii, 351. * (*PA* 34:7494)
105. SMITH, AARON. "Changes in Porteus Maze Scores of Brain-Operated Schizophrenics After an Eight-Year Interval." *J Mental Sci* 106:967-78 Jl '60. * (*PA* 35:5044)
106. BAREY, JOHN R.; EVERSTINE, LOUIS; AND KLEMAN, JOHN P. "An Abbreviated Qualitative Score for the Porteus Mazes." *J Clin Psychol* 17:291 Jl '61. * (*PA* 38:8398)
107. JENSEN, MILTON B. "The 'Low Level' Airman in Retesting and Basic Training: A Sociopsychological Study." *J Social Psychol* 55:177-90 D '61. * (*PA* 36:3LD77J)
108. PORTEUS, S. D. "Ethnic Group Differences." *Mankind Q* 1:187-200 Ja '61. *
109. ZUBIN, JOSEPH; SUTTON, SAMUEL; SALZINGER, KURT; SALZINGER, SUZANNE; BURDOCK, E. I.; AND PERETZ, DAVID. Chap. 10, "A Biometric Approach to Prognosis in Schizophrenia," pp. 143-203. In *Comparative Epidemiology of the Mental Disorders.* The Proceedings of the Forty-Ninth Annual Meeting of the American Psychopathological Association, Held in New York City, February 1959. Edited by Paul H. Hoch and Joseph Zubin. New York: Grune & Stratton, Inc., 1961. Pp. xvi, 290. * (*PA* 36:2JV90H)
110. CRAFT, MICHAEL; FABISCH, WALTER; STEPHENSON, GEOFFRY; BURNAND, GORDON; AND KERRIDGE, DAVID. "100 Admissions to a Psychopathic Unit." *J Mental Sci* 108:564-83 S '62. * (*PA* 38:2138)
111. DENTLER, ROBERT A., AND MACKLER, BERNARD. "The Porteus Maze Test as a Predictor of Functioning Abilities of Retarded Children." *J Consult Psychol* 26:50-5 F '62. * (*PA* 37:5400)
112. PORTEUS, S. D. "Maze Test Reports." *Percept & Motor Skills* 14:58 F '62. * (*PA* 37:3230)
113. PORTEUS, S. D., AND DIAMOND, A. L. "Porteus Maze Changes After Psychosurgery." *J Mental Sci* 108:53-8 Ja '62. * (*PA* 37:1382)
114. PURCELL, KENNETH; TURNBULL, JOHN W.; AND BERNSTEIN, LEWIS. "Distinctions Between Subgroups of Asthmatic Children: Psychological Test and Behavior Rating Comparisons." *J Psychosom Res* 6:283-91 O-D '62. * (*PA* 37:8210)
115. TOBIAS, JACK, AND GORELICK, JACK. "The Porteus Maze Test and the Appraisal of Retarded Adults." *Am J Mental Def* 66:600-6 Ja '62. * (*PA* 36:4JI00T)
116. ARONSON, BERNARD S. "The Comparative Sensitivity of the Qualitative and Quantitative Porteus Maze Scores to Drug Effects." *J Clin Psychol* 19:184-5 Ap '63. * (*PA* 39:4180)
117. ANTHONY, ARISTOTLE A. "The Relationship Between Neuroticism, Stress, and Qualitative Porteus Maze Performance." *J Consult Psychol* 27:513-9 D '63. * (*PA* 38:9090)
118. ANTHONY, ARISTOTLE ARISTIDES. *The Relationship Between Anxiety and Qualitative Porteus Maze Performance.* Doctor's thesis, Columbia University (New York, N.Y.), 1963. (*DA* 24:2119)
119. BRIGGS, PETER F. "The Validity of the Porteus Maze Test Completed With the Non-Dominant Hand." *J Clin Psychol* 19:427-9 O '63. *
120. GREGOR, A. JAMES, AND MCPHERSON, D. ANGUS. "The Correlation of the Porteus Maze and the Gestalt Continuation as Personnel Selection Tests of Peripheral Peoples." *J Psychol* 56:137-42 Jl '63. * (*PA* 38:4276)
121. PORTEUS, S. D., AND GREGOR, A. JAMES. "Studies in Intercultural Testing." *Percept & Motor Skills* 16:705-24 Je '63. * (*PA* 38:6026)
122. RUEBUSH, BRITTON K.; BYRUM, MILDRED; AND FARNHAM, LOUISE J. "Problem Solving as a Function of Defensiveness and Parental Behavior." *J Abn & Social Psychol* 67:355-62 O '63. * (*PA* 38:4084)

For reviews by C. M. Louttit and Gladys C. Schwesinger, see 4:356; for excerpts from related book reviews, see B400, 4:357, 38:B453, and 36:B210.

[533]
★**Quick Screening Scale of Mental Development.** Ages 6 months to 10 years; 1963; individual; 6 mental age ratings: body coordination, manual performance, speech and language, listening attention and number, play interests, general mental level (mean of preceding 5 ratings); 1 form (4 pages); manual (6 pages); no data on reliability of subscores; tentative norms; no description of normative population; $10 per examiner's kit of 25 tests and manual (must be purchased to obtain manual); $5 per additional 25 tests; cash orders postpaid; specimen set not available; (30) minutes; Katharine M. Banham; Psychometric Affiliates. *

BOYD R. MCCANDLESS, *Professor of Education and Psychology; Director, University School Clinic Complex; and Chairman, Department of Special Education; Indiana University, Bloomington, Indiana.*

THE TEST. This scale consists of five sections, each of which contains 16 statements "of readily observable behavior." Each statement is keyed "to an age between six months and ten" years. Items are arranged in order of age, one item for each six months' level up to 6 years, and one item for each 12 months' level from 6 to 10 years. According to the author (and from inspection of the items), most items have been taken from already standardized tests of motor ability or general aptitude. Thus, despite the author's failure to indicate reliability either for individual items or for the five categories of the test, notions of the reliability of most individual items can be gained by patient research, and an estimate for the different categories can be formed. The "basal" for each category is passes on two successive items, the "ceiling" failures on two successive items.

Most of the items in Part 1, Bodily Coordination, from age 6 on are postural, and some of the items for the very young seem prematurely placed. In category 2, Manual Performance, all items from age 1-6 are drawing items, and six of them (and all from age 8 on) are draw-a-man items of one form or another. Category 3, Speech and Language, is conventional, although the reviewer believes that too much reliance is placed on parental report for verbalization items at 1-0 and 1-6 years. For category 4, Listening, Attention, and Number, items test attention and imitation through 2-0 years and thereafter are made up entirely of digit span (forward and backward), counting, and simple arithmetic tasks. Factorially, this is probably a rather complex category. Category 5, Play Interests, depends almost entirely on parental report for its scoring, or upon an inordinate amount of time spent in observing. Its first three items overlap with Manual Performance and Listening, Attention, and Number.

A "Mental Level" can be calculated for each of the five categories, although the term "Mental" appears ill suited for category 1, Bodily Coordination. Total mental level is estimated from a composite of scores for all five categories. Again, the inclusion of category 1 seems dubious in view of the essential lack of correlation, described in the literature, between motor-postural behavior and behavior more conventionally described as "mental" or "intellectual."

THE MANUAL. The author's goal—to help busy clinicians—is unexceptionable, although print in the manual is so fine that the busy clinician is likely to have to hunt out his reading glasses unless his eyes are young and strong. The presence of errors and careless reporting is disturbing to this reviewer: In one place, category 4 is referred to as category 3; in another spot, mention is made of "the four categories of behavior" and later of the "five mental levels." "Validity coefficients" (r's) with the Binet L-M and the Cattell—58 and 13 children, respectively, aged 6 months to 12 years—are reported as .89 and .95, respectively. These (chronologically heterogeneous) samples are not described, nor is the sample or its size for the reported test-retest correlation of .93, based on a one-month interval.

The reviewer was not happy with the rationale for the heavy infusion of digit span items: "because of their indicative value as an aid in discovering emotional disturbances."

Banham recommends a fluid testing procedure, gives adequate cautions about testing conditions, provides illustrative indirect questions for eliciting information from adult informants about Play Interests, and provides directions for administering and scoring each item. These strike the reviewer as particularly inadequate for many of the drawing items.

In sum, this is a rough screening instrument, only tentatively standardized, not well supported by its manual, and—the reviewer believes—of only modest usefulness to "busy clinicians" in its present form.

[534]

★The Quick Test. Ages 2 and over; 1958–62; picture vocabulary; individual; Forms 1, 2, 3, ('58, 1 card); provisional manual ('62, 54 pages, reprint of 2 below); instruction cardboard ('62, 1 page); item cardboard ('62, 1 page, includes words for all 3 forms); record-norms sheet ('62, 2 pages); norms for combinations of 2 or 3 forms also presented; $8 per set of testing materials including all 3 forms, 100 record sheets, and manual; $2.50 per manual; cash orders postpaid; specimen set not available (manual illustrates all materials); (3–10) minutes; R. B. Ammons and C. H. Ammons; Psychological Test Specialists. *

REFERENCES

1. BURGESS, THOMAS C. "Form Equivalence of the Ammons Quick Picture Vocabulary Test." *Psychol Rep* 5:276 Je '59. * (PA 34:3433)
2. AMMONS, R. B., AND AMMONS, C. H. "The Quick Test (QT): Provisional Manual." *Psychol Rep* 11:111–61 Ag '62. * (PA 37:4941)
3. BURGESS, THOMAS C., AND WRIGHT, DOLORES D. "Seventh-Grade Evaluation of the Ammons Quick Test (QT)." *Psychol Rep* 10:791–4 Je '62. * (PA 37:5644)

BOYD R. MCCANDLESS, *Professor of Education and Psychology; Director, University School Clinic Complex; and Chairman, Department of Special Education; Indiana University, Bloomington, Indiana.*

For discussion purposes, this test seems to the reviewer to be best approached in much the same way the examiner of any new test approaches it: first, he is curious about the smaller items of the kit, then moves on to its manual and standardization and finally, often with a peek ahead, to the test itself.

INSTRUCTION CARDBOARDS. These are two easily handled sheets, clearly printed, one of which gives suggestions for administration, scoring, and interpretation, while the other lists, in approximate order of difficulty, the 50 items (words) for each of the three forms of the test.

The former gives in admirably brief and simple form two easy sets of instructions for introducing the test to the testee, informs the examiner that, for each of the three forms, the base of the test is six consecutive passes, while its ceiling is six successive failures; gives a rationale about guessing and suggestions for minimizing it; indicates that probing for unusual responses should be carried out and gives suggestions for how to do this; makes a brief introduction to the norms and final scores; and suggests flexible administrative procedures.

PROVISIONAL MANUAL. The Manual is respectably complete, is simply written (even chattily at times), and is frank about the aspirations the authors hold for the test but also realistic about its weaknesses (although they perhaps pass rather lightly over the facts that the sample, first, is not particularly large for a test so ambitiously designed, second, does not extend beyond the age limit of 45 years, and third, is geographically circumscribed).

The test is modeled closely after the authors' *Full-Range Picture Vocabulary Test*. Preliminary work on the present offspring seems sound enough; the sample is rather well balanced from nursery school through grade 12, plus an occupationally stratified adult sample, evenly divided between men and women, of from 24 to 45 years (distribution by age within the sample is not reported). The sample for the school aged subjects is selected by grade rather than by age, and the increasing age heterogeneity as we move into the upper grades is duly noted.

Clear information about percentiles and quotients (mean quotient is about 100, SD about 15) is provided. A number of reliability statistics (conservatively given by restricted age ranges) are reported. The most meaningful reliabilities, perhaps, are the interform reliabilities. These range from .60 to .96, the latter being based on an exception to the narrow age ranges usually employed (it is based on subjects ranging from age 2 through twelfth grade).

Most of the reported validities concern correlations of the QT with the parent instrument. As might be expected, these are high, from the high .60's into the .90's.

There is a chatty and interesting section in the manual on who should use the test, how novices should be trained, and how guessing should be handled, as well as other potentially useful testing tips.

The limits of the upper score ranges (above IQ 135) are discussed frankly and accurately enough, in the reviewer's judgment; the reported gain from age 17 to maturity (at least to age 30) seems sensible enough, and adequate appendices are also provided.

THE TEST. There are three 50-word forms, each form having as its basis a single plate of four complex line drawings. These seem adequate to the reviewer, and could, in his judgment, be used easily in most western or industrial cultures. Terminal scores can be computed for the forms, separately or together.

The record sheets impressed the reviewer favorably. They are clear, handy, and self-contained in providing for recording, scoring, and final establishment of percentile, MA and —for adults—IQ scores, for each form singly, and for the combined forms.

In summary, the QT appears to be worth looking into further as a clinical instrument and as a possibly useful tool around which a nomothetic network may be built.

ELLEN V. PIERS, *Associate Professor of Psychology, The Pennsylvania State University, University Park, Pennsylvania.*

The *Quick Test* is described in the manual as the "little brother" of the *Full-Range Picture Vocabulary Test* (FRPV). It was developed to provide new stimulus materials, additional forms which could be used with the FRPV, and a *very brief* intelligence test. Its purpose is the same as the FRPV—that is, to provide rapid intelligence screening, or to estimate the intelligence of special groups such as the mentally or physically handicapped for whom standard measures cannot be used. For the screening of large groups, the saving of an additional five or so minutes may indeed be valuable. For clinical purposes, however, considering the length of time typically spent on a Rorschach or TAT, 5 or 10 minutes hardly seems worth saving, particularly when reliability suffers. This point is apparently recognized by the authors in that they frequently recommend giving all three forms of the test, or combining the QT with the FRPV.

Plates have been reduced from 16 for the two forms of the FRPV to one plate for each of three forms of the QT. No rationale is given for the choice of the original drawings, the process apparently having been completely empirical. The drawings are designed to elicit responses at all difficulty levels. Though an ingenious idea, it does not seem entirely successful. Not only is there a great deal of detail in many of the pictures, but the drawings themselves are made with such heavy lines as to render many details ambiguous. That this is unnecessary is evident when one looks either at the *Peabody Picture Vocabulary Test* or the *Van Alstyne Picture Vocabulary Test* whose drawings are sharp and clear.

The effect of this ambiguity will probably be most evident at the lower levels. Recently this reviewer observed the testing of a 12-year-old severe retardate without speech. On the Peabody he obtained a mental age of 2 years 2 months but he could not complete a single item on the *Quick Test*. The extrapolated scores presented for ages 2-0 and 1-5 should therefore (as the authors suggest) be used very cautiously until more evidence is available.

Reliability estimates are all alternate form. Mean interform coefficients for one age level or for restricted ranges are seldom above the .60's, although the two- and three-form coefficients predicted from these by the Spearman-Brown formula range from .75 to .92. Wider age ranges show correspondingly higher reliabilities. Standard errors are given only for raw scores and not for IQ's. But by using the standard deviation which was adjusted to 15 IQ points, one could predict standard errors of measurement of over 9 IQ points in some cases for a single form.

Validity data so far consist chiefly of comparisons with the FRPV, some school grades, and some achievement tests. The former comparisons are unfortunately limited to preschoolers or college age and above. Ignoring the corrections for attenuation, they range from .62 to .93. The authors feel that they are high enough so that the QT and FRPV can be used interchangeably, and that since FRPV correlates well with other measures of intelligence one can assume that the QT will also, and therefore has high validity. Although perhaps a reasonable assumption, the reviewer would prefer a little more evidence before accepting it as fact. Certainly the logic for their further deduction that the QT therefore comprises a better measure of intelligence than the Wechsler or Binet is extremely questionable.

Some materials of the QT are a considerable improvement over the FRPV. Answer sheets are printed, and usable for any form. Mental age norms for "458 white children and adults," and IQ's and percentiles for an unspecified number of white adults are on the back. However, IQ's are not reported for children, although it is suggested that one can divide MA's by CA's, particularly when all three forms are given. One wonders, why not deviation IQ's? For adults, IQ values are extrapolated beyond 65 and 135.

At first glance, the standardization sample of 458 cases ranging from 2 years to adulthood (plus 40 supplementary cases) seems woefully inadequate. The authors contend, however, that this was carefully controlled for age, grade placement, own (or husband's) or father's occupation, and sex. On the basis of previous work they felt that geographical control was not important.

In general, any weaknesses of the norms, both for preschoolers and adults, are clearly pointed out, and limitations of use suggested. Another good feature is the spelling out of restrictions concerning use of the test in general. The one-page test description says, "Critical decisions of considerable importance demand supporting data from other tests. Interpretations by non-psychologists should be cautious." Tests which are otherwise good, such as the Peabody, might incorporate some of these cautions.

Finally, the provisional manual is a great improvement after the years of inadequate information concerning the FRPV. But the authors have failed to make a distinction between a manual and a research monograph. A manual should be shorter and more concise. Important material seems buried in their present long narrative. This reviewer spent considerable time trying to find the answers to the usual questions which could be contained in a dozen pages. The rest is valuable but could be published separately.

In spite of the weaknesses of the *Quick Test*, it will probably, like the FRPV, be very useful as a large-scale screening test, particularly when time is at a premium. But it is doubtful, in view of the somewhat questionable standardization, the lack of established, first-hand validity, and the complexity and poor quality of the drawings, whether a clinician would choose it over other available instruments at this point. Final evaluation must await further research.

[535]

★**Slosson Intelligence Test (SIT).** Ages 1 month and over; 1961–64; based in part upon *Stanford-Binet Intelligence Scale, Third Revision* and *Gesell Developmental Schedules;* individual; 1 form ('63, c1961–63); manual ('63, c1961–63, 43 pages, including test questions, sample score sheet, IQ finder, and other materials); score sheet ('63, 2 pages); IQ classification chart ('64, 2 pages); $3.75 per examiner's kit of manual, pad of 20 score sheets, and pad of 20 copies of the *Slosson Oral Reading Test*; 75¢ per additional pad of 20 score sheets; 75¢ per pad of 20 IQ classification charts; postpaid; (10–30) minutes; Richard L. Slosson; Slosson Educational Publications. *

[536]
*Stanford-Binet Intelligence Scale, Third Revision. Ages 2 and over; 1916–60; a single-form combination of items selected from Forms L and M ('37) of the Second Revision, which is still available (see 5:413); individual; Form L-M ('60); manual ('60, 374 pages, see 657a below); record booklet ('60, 15 pages); record form ('60, 5 pages); no data on reliability; $33.20 (16os.) per set of test materials including manual; $4.40 (28s.) per 35 record booklets; $2.20 (14s.) per 35 abbreviated record forms; $4.48 (21s.) per manual; postage extra; (30–90) minutes; revised IQ tables by Samuel R. Pinneau; Lewis M. Terman and Maud A. Merrill; Houghton Mifflin Co. * (British edition: George G. Harrap & Co. Ltd.)

REFERENCES

1–134. See 40:1420.
135–351. See 3:292.
352–493. See 4:358.
494–620. See 5:413.
621. MATEER, FLORENCE. "The Future of Clinical Psychology." *J Deling* 6:283–93 Ja '21. *
622. GARRISON, S. C., AND TIPPETT, JAMES S. "Comparison of the Binet-Simon and Otis Tests." *J Ed Res* 6:42–8 Je '22. *
623. ROOT, W. T. "Correlations Between Binet Tests and Group Tests." *J Ed Psychol* 13:286–92 My '22. *
624. ROSANOFF, AARON J. Chap. 4, "Stanford Revision and Extension of the Binet-Simon Intelligence Scale," pp. 500–38. In his *Manual of Psychiatry, Sixth Edition*. New York: John Wiley & Sons, 1927. Pp. xvii, 697. *
625. ROBERTS, J. A. FRASER; NORMAN, R. M.; AND GRIFFITHS, RUTH. "Studies in a Child Population: 3, Intelligence and Family Size." *Ann Eug* 8:178–215 Ja '38. * (*PA* 12:4260)
626. LIDZ, THEODORE; GAY, JAMES R.; AND TIETZE, CHRISTOPHER. "Intelligence in Cerebral Deficit States and Schizophrenia Measured by Kohs Block Test." *Arch Neurol & Psychiatry* 48:568–82 O '42. * (*PA* 17:862)
627. McNEMAR, QUINN. Chap. 12, "Intellectual Status of the Gifted Subjects as Adults," pp. 140–6. In *The Gifted Child Grows Up: Twenty-Five Years' Follow-Up of a Superior Group*. By Lewis M. Terman and others. Genetic Studies of Genius, Vol. 4. Stanford, Calif.: Stanford University Press, 1947. Pp. xiv, 448. * (*PA* 22:2080)
628. TERMAN, LEWIS M., AND ODEN, MELITA H.; IN ASSOCIATION WITH NANCY BAYLEY, HELEN MARSHALL, QUINN McNEMAR, AND ELLEN B. SULLIVAN. Chap. 11, "Intelligence Tests of 1940," pp. 125–39. In their *The Gifted Child Grows Up: Twenty-Five Years' Follow-Up of a Superior Group*. Genetic Studies of Genius, Vol. 4. Stanford, Calif.: Stanford University Press, 1947. Pp. xiv, 448. * (*PA* 22:2080)
629. McFIE, J., AND PIERCY, M. F. "Intellectual Impairment With Localized Cerebral Lesions." *Brain* 75:292–311 S '52. * (*PA* 27:7649)
630. MILLER, ELSA, AND ROSENFELD, GEORGE B. "The Psychologic Evaluation of Children With Cerebral Palsy and Its Implications in Treatment: Preliminary Report." *J Pediatrics* 41:613–21 N '52. * (*PA* 27:6706)
631. BERKO, MARTIN J. "A Note on 'Psychometric Scatter' as a Factor in the Differentiation of Exogenous and Endogenous Mental Deficiency." *Cerebral Palsy R* 16:20 Ja–F '55. * (*PA* 29:8715)
632. BERKO, MARTIN J. "Psychometric Scatter: Its Application in the Clinical Prediction of Future Mental Development in Cases of Childhood Brain Injury." *Cerebral Palsy R* 16:16–8 Mr–Ap '55. * (*PA* 30:1011)
633. KATZ, ELIAS. "Intelligence Test Performance of 'Athetoid' and 'Spastic' Children With Cerebral Palsy." *Cerebral Palsy R* 16:17–8 My–Je '55. * (*PA* 30:3303)
634. KATZ, ELIAS. "Success on Stanford-Binet Intelligence Scale Test Items of Children With Cerebral Palsy as Compared With Non-Handicapped Children." *Cerebral Palsy R* 16:18–9 Ja–F '55. * (*PA* 29:8855)
635. KATZ, ELIAS. "A Method of Selecting Stanford-Binet Intelligence Scale Test Items for Evaluating the Mental Abilities of Children Severely Handicapped by Cerebral Palsy." *Cerebral Palsy R* 17:13–5 Ja–F '56. * (*PA* 31:1566)
636. FIRNHABER, EDGAR P. *Variations in Performance on the Stanford Binet Figure Completion Test Among Children of Different Mental Ages*. Master's thesis, University of Nebraska (Lincoln, Neb.), 1957.
637. GALLAGHER, JAMES J. *A Comparison of Brain-Injured and Non-Brain-Injured Mentally Retarded Children on Several Psychological Variables*. Monograph of the Society for Research in Child Development, Vol. 22, No. 2. Lafayette, Ind.: Child Development Publications, 1957. Pp. 79. * (*PA* 33:1632)
638. BRADWAY, KATHERINE P.; THOMPSON, CLARE W.; AND CRAVENS, RICHARD B. "Preschool IQs After Twenty-Five Years." *J Ed Psychol* 49:278–81 O '58. * (*PA* 36:2HD78B)
639. HIGGINS, CONWELL, AND SIVERS, CATHRYNE H. "A Comparison of Stanford-Binet and Colored Raven Progressive Matrices IQs for Children With Low Socioeconomic Status." *J Consult Psychol* 22:465–8 D '58. * (*PA* 33:9919)
640. MUNDY, LYDIA, AND MAXWELL, A. E. "Assessment of the Feebleminded." *Brit J Med Psychol* 31:201–10 pt 3 & 4 '58. * (*PA* 34:1673)
641. SCHACHTER, FRANCES FUCHS, AND APGAR, VIRGINIA. "Comparison of Preschool Stanford-Binet and School-Age WISC IQs." *J Ed Psychol* 49:320–3 D '58. * (*PA* 36:2HD20S)
642. WILSON, BARBARA A. *A Comparison of Intelligence Quotients for Readers and Non-Readers Using the Leiter International Performance Scale and the 1937 Revision of the Stanford-Binet*. Master's thesis, Sacramento State College (Sacramento, Calif.), 1958.
643. LEHMANN, IRVIN J. "Rural-Urban Differences in Intelligence." *J Ed Res* 53:62–8 O '59. * (*PA* 35:780)
644. LEVINSON, BORIS M. "A Comparison of the Performance of Bilingual and Monolingual Native Born Jewish Preschool Children of Traditional Parentage on Four Intelligence Tests." *J Clin Psychol* 15:74–6 Ja '59. * (*PA* 34:2729)
645. NALE, STANLEY LEO. *A Factor Analysis of the Stanford-Binet Scores of Mentally Defective Children*. Doctor's thesis, Pennsylvania State University (University Park, Pa.), 1959. (*DA* 20:760)
646. POST, MILDRED. *Differences in Performance on Stanford-Binet Items of Children Who Function Above and Below Grade Level in Word Recognition*. Doctor's thesis, Syracuse University (Syracuse, N.Y.), 1959. (*DA* 20:590)
647. BYRD, ENOLA. *The Equivalence of the Two Forms of the 1937 Revision of the Stanford-Binet Intelligence Scale*. Master's thesis, Atlanta University (Atlanta, Ga.), 1960.
648. DUNSDON, M. I.; CARTER, C. O.; AND HUNTLEY, R. M. C. "Upper End of Range of Intelligence in Mongolism." *Lancet* 7124:565–8 Mr 12 '60. *
649. FRANCEY, RUTH E. "Psychological Test Changes in Mentally Retarded Children During Training." *Can J Pub Health* 51:69–74 F '60. *
650. KaDELL, MARY BELLE. *A Factor Analysis of the Vineland Social Maturity Scale and the Stanford-Binet Intelligence Scale*. Master's thesis, University of Minnesota (Minneapolis, Minn.), 1960.
651. KIDD, ALINE HALSTEAD. *A Factor and Item Analysis of the Test of G; Culture-Free and the Stanford-Binet, Form L*. Doctor's thesis, University of Arizona (Tucson, Ariz.), 1960. (*DA* 21:366)
652. KONSTANS, D. JANICE. *Stanford-Binet Responses of Elementary School Children: A Relational Analysis of Range, Intellectual Performance, Race, and Sex*. Master's thesis, University of Chicago (Chicago, Ill.), 1960.
653. LEVINSON, BORIS M. "The Binet Non-Verbal Preschool Scale." *J Clin Psychol* 16:12–3 Ja '60. * (*PA* 36:1HC12L)
654. LEVINSON, BORIS M., AND BLOCK, ZELICK. "Research Note on Columbia Mental Maturity Scale (CMMS) and Revised Stanford Binet (L) in a Preschool Population." *J Clin Psychol* 16:158–9 Ap '60. * (*PA* 36:2HC58L)
655. MAXWELL, JAMES, AND PILLINER, A. E. G. "The Intellectual Resemblance Between Sibs." *Ann Hum Genetics* 24:23–32 Ap '60. * (*PA* 35:2199)
656. STEIN, ZENA, AND SUSSER, MERVYN. "Families of Dull Children: Part 4, Increments in Intelligence." *J Mental Sci* 106:1311–9 O '60. * (*PA* 35:5182)
657. STOTT, D. H. "Observations on Retest Discrepancy in Mentally Sub-Normal Children." *Brit J Ed Psychol* 30:211–9 N '60. *
657a. TERMAN, LEWIS M., AND MERRILL, MAUD A. *Stanford-Binet Intelligence Scale: Manual for the Third Revision, Form L-M*. With revised IQ tables by Samuel R. Pinneau. Boston, Mass.: Houghton-Mifflin Co., 1960. Pp. xi, 363. *
658. WEISE, PHILLIP. "Current Uses of Binet and Wechsler Tests by School Psychologists in California." *Calif J Ed Res* 11:73–8 Mr '60. * (*PA* 35:7098)
659. ZUK, G. H. "Size: Its Significance in the Copied Drawings of Children." *J Clin Psychol* 16:38–42 Ja '60. * (*PA* 36:1HE38Z)
660. ACK, MARVIN; MILLER, IRVING; AND WEIL, WILLIAM B., JR. "Intelligence of Children With Diabetes Mellitus." *Pediatrics* 28:764–70 N '61. *
661. ANASTASI, ANNE. *Psychological Testing, Second Edition*, pp. 189–212. New York: Macmillan Co., 1961. Pp. xiii, 657. * (*PA* 36:1HA57A)
662. BRADWAY, KATHERINE P., AND ROBINSON, NANCY M. "Significant IQ Changes in Twenty-Five Years: A Follow-Up." *J Ed Psychol* 52:74–9 Ap '61. * (*PA* 38:2484)
663. BRENGELMANN, JOHANNES C., AND KENNY, JOSEPH T.

"Comparison of Leiter, WAIS and Stanford-Binet IQ's in Retardates." *J Clin Psychol* 17:235–8 Jl '61. * (*PA* 38:8953)
664. Darbes, Alex. "A Comparison of Scores Achieved by 55 Subjects Administered the Wechsler and Binet Scales of Intelligence." *Proc W Va Acad Sci* 33:115–9 N '61. * (*PA* 36:5HD15D)
665. Drillien, Cecil Mary. "A Longitudinal Study of the Growth and Development of Prematurely and Maturely Born Children: Part 7, Mental Development 2–5 Years." *Arch Dis Childh* 36:233–40 Je '61. *
666. Dunsdon, M. I., and Roberts, J. A. Fraser. Chap. 3, "A Study of the Performance of 2000 Children on Four Vocabulary Tests," pp. 41–76. In *Stoke Park Studies: Mental Subnormality (Second Series): World Mental Health Year Memorial Volume*. Edited by J. Jancar. Bristol, England: John Wright & Sons Ltd., 1961. Pp. x, 135. *
667. Estes, Betsy Worth; Curtin, Mary Ellen; DeBurger, Robert A.; and Denny, Charlotte. "Relationships Between 1960 Stanford-Binet, 1937 Stanford-Binet, WISC, Raven, and Draw-A-Man." *J Consult Psychol* 25:388–91 O '61. * (*PA* 37:3127)
668. Fisher, Gary M.; Kilman, Beverly A.; and Shotwell, Anna M. "Comparability of Intelligence Quotients of Mental Defectives on the Wechsler Adult Intelligence Scale and the 1960 Revision of the Stanford-Binet." *J Consult Psychol* 25:192–5 Je '61. *
669. Gaskins, John R. *A Comparison of the Stanford-Binet Form L and Form L-M Results of Educable Mentally Retarded Children*. Master's thesis, Kent State University (Kent, Ohio), 1961.
670. Graham, Doris D. *Some Relationships Between Early Stanford-Binet Scores and Later Measures of Achievement*. Master's thesis, Claremont College (Claremont, Calif.), 1961.
671. Heaton-Ward, W. A. Chap. 4, "An Interim Report on a Controlled Trial of the Effect of Niamid on the Mental Age and Behaviour of Mongols," pp. 77–80. In *Stoke Park Studies: Mental Subnormality (Second Series): World Mental Health Year Memorial Volume*. Edited by J. Jancar. Bristol, England: John Wright & Sons Ltd., 1961. Pp. x, 135. *
672. Hirschenfang, Samuel. "Further Studies on the Columbia Mental Maturity Scale (CMMS) and Revised Stanford Binet (L) in Children With Speech Disorders." *J Clin Psychol* 17:171 Ap '61. * (*PA* 38:956)
673. Hunt, Dennis. *The Comparative Performance of a Ten-Year-Old Group of Children on the Wechsler Intelligence Scale for Children and the Revised Stanford-Binet Scale of Intelligence, Form L-M*. Master's thesis, University of Saskatchewan (Saskatoon, Sask., Canada), 1961.
674. Kennedy, Wallace A.; Moon, Harold; Nelson, Willard; Lindner, Ronald; and Turner, Jack. "The Ceiling of the New Stanford-Binet." *J Clin Psychol* 17:284–6 Jl '61. * (*PA* 38:8457)
675. Lessing, Elise Elkins. "A Note on the Significance of Discrepancies Between Goodenough and Binet IQ Scores." *J Consult Psychol* 25:456–7 O '61. * (*PA* 37:3130)
676. Lytton, H. "Symposium: Contributions to the Diagnosis and Remedial Treatment of Reading Difficulties: 6, An Experiment in Selection for Remedial Education." *Brit J Ed Psychol* 31:79–95 F '61. * (*PA* 36:1KE79L)
677. McFie, John. "The Effect of Education on African Performance on a Group of Intellectual Tests." *Brit J Ed Psychol* 31:232–40 N '61. * (*PA* 36:5HD32M)
678. Parsley, K. M., Jr., and Powell, Marvin. "Relationships Between the Lee-Clark Reading Readiness Test and the 1937 Revision of the Stanford-Binet Intelligence Test, Form L." *J Ed Res* 54:304–7 Ap '61. *
679. Payne, R. W. Chap. 6, "Cognitive Abnormalities," pp. 193–261. In *Handbook of Abnormal Psychology: An Experimental Approach*. Edited by H. J. Eysenck. New York: Basic Books, Inc., 1961. Pp. xvi, 816. * (*PA* 35:6719)
680. Pinneau, Samuel R. *Changes in Intelligence Quotient: Infancy to Maturity: New Insights From the Berkeley Growth Study With Implications for the Stanford-Binet Scales and Applications to Professional Practice*. Boston, Mass.: Houghton Mifflin Co., 1961. Pp. xi, 233. * (*PA* 37:6706)
681. Qureshi, Mohammed Y. "Effects of Various Scoring Cutoffs on Reliability Estimates." *Am J Mental Def* 65:753–60 My '61. * (*PA* 36:1HD53Q)
682. Roberts, Helen Erskine. "Comparison of Otis and Stanford-Binet IQ's." *Calif J Ed Res* 12:8–15 Ja '61. * (*PA* 36:1HD08R)
683. Scherer, Isidor W. "The Prediction of Academic Achievement in Brain Injured Children." *Excep Child* 28:103–6 O '61. *
684. Shine, Aileen. "Relationship Between Arithmetic Achievement and Item Performance on the Revised Stanford-Binet Scale." *Arith Teach* 9:57–9 F '61. *
685. Shine, Aileen Elizabeth. *Relationship Between Arithmetic Achievement and Item Performance on the Revised Stanford-Binet Scale*. Doctor's thesis, University of Colorado (Boulder, Colo.), 1961. (*DA* 22:3047)
686. Silverstein, A. B., and Fisher, Gary M. "An Evaluation of Two Short Forms of the Stanford-Binet, Form L-M, for Use With Mentally Retarded Adults." *Am J Mental Def* 65:486–8 Ja '61. * (*PA* 35:6818)
687. Stott, D. H. "I.Q. Changes Among Educationally Sub-Normal Children." *Special Ed* 50:11–4 Je '61. *

688. Baldwin, Joseph W. "The Relationship Between Teacher-Judged Giftedness, a Group Intelligence Test and an Individual Intelligence Test With Possible Gifted Kindergarten Pupils." *Gifted Child Q* 6:153–6 w '62. * (*PA* 37:8255)
689. Bradway, Katherine P., and Thompson, Clare W. "Intelligence at Adulthood: A Twenty-Five Year Follow-Up." *J Ed Psychol* 53:1–14 F '62. * (*PA* 37:1210)
690. Cleland, Donald L., and Toussaint, Isabella H. "The Interrelationships of Reading, Listening, Arithmetic Computation and Intelligence." *Reading Teach* 15:228–31 Ja '62. *
691. Fleming, Kathryn. *A Comparison of Mental Age Scores on the Revised Columbia Mental Maturity Scale and the Stanford-Binet Intelligence Test, Form L, at the Five Through Eight Year Mental Age Levels*. Master's thesis, Bowling Green State University (Bowling Green, Ohio), 1962.
692. Freeman, Frank S. *Theory and Practice of Psychological Testing, Third Edition*, pp. 197–240, 323–30. New York: Holt, Rinehart & Winston, Inc., 1962. Pp. xix, 697. *
693. Hartman, Bernard-Thomas. *Comparative Investigation of the Peabody Picture Vocabulary Test With Three Etiologic Groups of Institutionalized Mentally Retarded Students*. Doctor's thesis, Indiana University (Bloomington, Ind.), 1962. (*DA* 23:2008)
694. Hindley, C. B. "Social Class Influences on the Development of Ability in the First Five Years," pp. 29–41. (*PA* 37:4717) In *Child and Education*. Proceedings of the XIV International Congress of Applied Psychology, Vol. 3. Copenhagen, Denmark: Munksgaard, Ltd., 1962. Pp. 197. *
695. Holowinsky, Ivan. "IQ Constancy in a Group of Institutionalized Mental Defectives Over a Period of 3 Decades." *Training Sch B* 59:15–7 My '62. * (*PA* 37:3578)
696. Hurst, John G. "The Meaning and Use of Difference Scores Obtained Between the Performance on the Stanford-Binet Intelligence Scale and Vineland Social Maturity Scale." *J Clin Psychol* 18:153–60 Ap '62. * (*PA* 38:8422)
697. Jarvik, Lissy Feingold. "Biological Differences in Intellectual Functioning." *Vita Hum* 5(4):195–203 '62. * (*PA* 38:970)
698. Jarvik, Lissy Feingold; Kallmann, Franz J.; and Falek, Arthur. "Intellectual Changes in Aged Twins." *J Gerontol* 17:289–94 Jl '62. * (*PA* 37:2952)
699. Kidd, Aline H. "The Culture-Fair Aspects of Cattell's Test of g: Culture-Free." *J Genetic Psychol* 101:343–62 D '62. * (*PA* 37:6702)
700. Mein, R. "Use of the Peabody Picture Vocabulary With Severely Subnormal Patients." *Am J Mental Def* 67:269–73 S '62. * (*PA* 37:3582)
701. Nelson, Thomas M., and Bartley, S. Howard. "Various Factors Playing a Role in Children's Responses to Flat Copy." *J Genetic Psychol* 100:289–308 Je '62. * (*PA* 37:2874)
702. Rohrs, Frederick W., and Haworth, Mary R. "The 1960 Stanford-Binet, WISC, and Goodenough Tests With Mentally Retarded Children." *Am J Mental Def* 66:853–9 My '62. * (*PA* 37:1704)
703. Thweatt, Roger C. "A Rapid Technique for Stanford-Binet Test Object Placement." *J Clin Psychol* 18:355 Jl '62. * (*PA* 39:1795)
704. Van de Riet, Vernon. *The Standardization of the Third Revision of the Stanford-Binet Intelligence Scale on Negro Elementary-School Children in Grades One, Two, and Three in the Southeastern United States*. Doctor's thesis, Florida State University (Tallahassee, Fla.), 1962. (*DA* 23:3985)
705. White, James C., Jr. *The Standardization of the Third Revision of the Stanford-Binet Intelligence Scale on Negro Elementary-School Children in Grades Four, Five, and Six in the Southeastern United States*. Doctor's thesis, Florida State University (Tallahassee, Fla.), 1962. (*DA* 23:3969)
706. Wilk, Walter S. *A Comparative Study of the Wechsler Intelligence Scale for Children and the Revised Form of the Stanford-Binet Intelligence Scale*. Master's thesis, Southern Connecticut State College (New Haven, Conn.), 1962.
707. Zeaman, David, and House, Betty J. "Mongoloid MA Is Proportional to Log CA." *Child Develop* 33:481–8 S '62. *
708. Benson, Robert R. "The Binet Vocabulary Score as an Estimate of Intellectual Functioning." *J Clin Psychol* 19:134–5 Ja '63. * (*PA* 39:1715)
709. British Psychological Society, English Division of Professional Psychologists (Educational and Clinical). "Report of the Working Party on Subnormality." Prepared by J. H. F. Castell, A. D. B. Clarke, P. Mittler, and W. M. Woodward. *B Brit Psychol Soc* 16:37–50 O '63. *
710. Budoff, Milton, and Purseglove, Eleanor Mathias. "Forms L and LM of the Stanford Binet Compared for an Institutionalized Adolescent Mentally Retarded Population." *J Clin Psychol* 19:214 Ap '63. * (*PA* 39:5041)
711. Edwards, Allen Jack. "Using Vocabulary as a Measure of General Ability." *Personnel & Guid J* 42:153–4 O '63. *
712. Garfunkel, Frank, and Blatt, Burton. "The Standardization of Intelligence Tests on Southern Negro School Children." *Training Sch B* 60:94–9 Ag '63. * (*PA* 38:4274)
713. Higgins, Conwell. "Multiple Predictor Score Cut-Offs Versus Multiple-Regression Cut-Offs in Selection of Academically Talented Children in Grade 3." *Yearb Nat Council Meas Ed* 20:153–64 '63. * (*PA* 38:9247)
714. Ho, David, and White, Delilah T. "Use of the Full-

Range Picture Vocabulary Test With the Mentally Retarded." *Am J Mental Def* 67:761-4 Mr '63. * (*PA* 38:1275)

715. JARVIK, LISSY F., AND FALEK, ARTHUR. "Intellectual Stability and Survival in the Aged." *J Gerontol* 18:173-6 Ap '63. * (*PA* 38:4103)

715a. KENNEDY, WALLACE; VAN DE RIET, VERNON; AND WHITE, JAMES C., JR. *A Normative Sample of Intelligence and Achievement of Negro Elementary School Children in Southeastern United States.* Monographs of the Society for Research in Child Development, Vol. 28, No. 6. Lafayette, Ind.: Child Development Publications, 1963. Pp. 112. *

716. KENNEDY, WALLACE A.; VAN DE RIET, VERNON; AND WHITE, JAMES C., JR. "Use of the Terman-Merrill Abbreviated Scale on the 1960 Stanford-Binet Form L-M on Negro Elementary School Children of the Southeastern United States." *J Consult Psychol* 27:456-7 O '63. * (*PA* 38:4277)

717. NASH, PAT NEFF. *The Effectiveness of Composite Predictors of Reading Success in the First Grade.* Doctor's thesis, North Texas State University (Denton, Tex.), 1963. (*DA* 24:1482)

718. NEWLAND, T. ERNEST, AND MEEKER, MARY M. "Binet Behavior Samplings and Guilford's Structure of the Intellect." *J Sch Psychol* 2:55-9 w '63-64. *

719. PRINGLE, M. L. KELLMER, AND PICKUP, K. T. "The Reliability and Validity of the Goodenough Draw-A-Man Test: A Pilot Longitudinal Study." *Brit J Ed Psychol* 33:297-306 N '63. * (*PA* 38:8424)

720. RUSHTON, C. S., AND STOCKWIN, A. E. "Changes in Terman-Merrill I.Qs. of Educationally Sub-Normal Boys." *Brit J Ed Psychol* 33:132-42 Je '63. * (*PA* 38:4293)

721. SCHENA, RICHARD A. "A Search for Talented Pupils." *J Exp Ed* 32:27-41 f '63. *

722. SILVERSTEIN, A. B. "An Evaluation of Two Short Forms of the Stanford-Binet, Form L-M, for Use With Mentally Retarded Children." *Am J Mental Def* 67:922-3 My '63. * (*PA* 38:964)

723. SPEARMAN, LEONARD H. O. "A Profile Analysis Technique for Diagnosing Reading Disability." *Yearb Nat Council Meas Ed* 20:75-86 '63. * (*PA* 38:9235)

724. TATHAM, CLIFFORD B., AND DOLE, ARTHUR A. "A Note on the Relationship of CTMM-SF to the Revised Binet, Form L-M." *J Clin Psychol* 19:302 Jl '63. *

725. THOMPSON, JACK M., AND FINLEY, CARMEN J. "The Relationship Between the Goodenough Draw-A-Man Test and the Stanford-Binet Form L-M in Children Referred for School Guidance Services." *Calif J Ed Res* 14:19-22 Ja '63. * (*PA* 37:7875)

726. VALETT, ROBERT E. "A Clinical Profile for the Stanford-Binet." *J Sch Psychol* 2:49-54 w '63-64. *

727. WIENER, GERALD; RIDER, ROWLAND V.; AND OPPEL, WALLACE. "Some Correlates of IQ Changes in Children." *Child Develop* 34:61-7 Mr '63. * (*PA* 38:5777)

728. ZINGLE, HARVEY W., AND LAMBERT, ROLAND A. "Experimental Tests of Two Hypotheses Concerning Normalization of Form Perception." *Alberta J Ed Res* 9:147-56 S '63. *

ELIZABETH D. FRASER, *Professor of Psychology, University of Aberdeen, Aberdeen, Scotland.*

The most obvious feature of the 1960 revision of the *Stanford-Binet Intelligence Scale* is the condensation of the two earlier Forms L and M into one, the new L-M scale. The offspring of these 23-year-old parents inherits much more from the L parent than from M: the ratio of L to M items in the new scale is about 9 to 7.

Apart from this one major change, the test has been brought up to date by eliminating items that are no longer appropriate to the present day, and by reordering items which for some reason have altered in difficulty since 1937. The condensation into one form has allowed the selection of items which best satisfy the criteria of a good item, viz., that with increase in age there should be an increase in the percentage passing the item, and that the item should correlate well with the test as a whole.

In addition, a number of ambiguities in administration and scoring have been cleared up, the layout of the test material and of the test manual, especially the section on scoring standards, has been vastly improved, and the problem of fluctuating standard deviations of IQ's at different ages has at last been tackled.

Many of these changes are welcome, and even the loss of a parallel form is not likely to disturb the great majority of users. Form L was always much more widely used than Form M, and with the WISC now available as a second sound individual test, the need for a parallel form for the Stanford-Binet is less acute than it was in 1937.

The improvement in layout is particularly welcome. The clear differentiation between plus, Q, and minus answers for each item is a great improvement on the old manual. Scoring standards are still tucked away at the back of the book, and inexpert testers who have to check standards frequently will continue to be irritated. An arrangement by which each test item was followed by its scoring standards would inevitably lead to much duplication, but there might be something to be said for having scoring standards in a separate booklet altogether, so that one could have access to both test item and scoring criteria simultaneously.

The provision of conversion tables which automatically correct for differences in standard deviation at different ages, takes care of the old criticism that an IQ of 130 at age 6 did not mean the same as an IQ of 130 at age 8. But there is strong insistence on the fact that the Stanford-Binet is still an age scale making use of age standards of performance, although this begins to lose some of its point when one encounters at the adult levels mental ages of 22 years 11 months.

In all its fundamentals, however, the Stanford-Binet remains very much its old self. Minimal changes have been introduced into the items themselves, and at some ages it is almost exactly the old Form L. Testers experienced in the old version are not likely to find any difficulty in adjusting to the new.

The main criticism likely to be leveled at this revision is that these changes in subtest composition have been introduced without any restandardisation process. The putting together of the items with the greatest internal validity is well worthwhile, but there is no guarantee that the final test, taken as a whole, will give the same result as either the old Form L or Form M. Thus, even if items a + b + c + d + e + f from Form L were equivalent to items m + n + o + p + q + r from Form M, it is not necessarily true that a + b + m + d + q + r will be equivalent to either of the former groupings. This has yet to be shown to be the case.

Comparisons between the Stanford-Binet and the WISC will no doubt continue to be drawn, and the devotees of each test will continue to argue for the test of their choice. Some of the disadvantages of the Stanford-Binet have been eliminated, but it is still rather less convenient to administer than the WISC, and it does not attempt a breakdown analysis of the total score as WISC does. The advantages of the Stanford-Binet remain: better coverage at the lower end of the scale, and more reliable assessment of the extreme ranges of intelligence.

Austral J Ed 6:233–4 O '62. Marie D. Neale. This revision of the Stanford-Binet Intelligence Scale will be widely welcomed. Since its second revision in 1937, the scale has won outstanding recognition by psychologists working in diverse fields. It is not too much to claim that the scale has become a basic tool in psychological equipment for research and clinical diagnostic work. However, since the practical implications of an I.Q. obtained on the scale are extremely important, often affecting an individual's opportunities for schooling or placement within an educational setting, sensitive test users will be relieved to know that this revision addresses itself mainly to the provision of up-to-date content and more reliable norms. * In format, the 1960 revision has some pleasing features. Spiral binding has been used for the printed card material, making it easier for the examiner to locate and present particular test items in the correct sequence. From a limited use of the new scale, the reviewer would suggest that the presentation of the picture vocabulary in this form contributes greatly to the co-operation and interest of young subjects. The manual is well designed with clear, comprehensive directions for administering and scoring the test. The I.Q. tables, in particular, are well set out, attributing to both speed and efficiency in evaluating the results. * In summary, this revision is timely. Its material, manual and equipment are presented in an attractive format, while the changes in content and the revised I.Q. tables will assure it the respect and popularity which the 1937 revision has hitherto enjoyed.

Brit J Ed Psychol 32:214 Je '62. L. B. Birch. [Review of the British edition.] An anglicised version of the 1960 Terman and Merrill Test is now available in this country. * There is no doubt that the material in the new form is more appropriate to present-day conditions. This writer found it pleasant to use and easy to pick up from an intimate knowledge of the 1937 version. As yet, of course, we know nothing of the relevance of the norms for British children or whether corrections like that of Roberts and Mellone will be needed. A report by the Division of Professional Psychologists on field trials of the test will be welcomed.

Brit J Psychol 53:472 N '62. James Maxwell. [Review of the British Edition.] * The administration of the new scales will present no difficulty to users of the 1937 revision, and there seems justification for the claim that the more rigorous selection of items has improved the test. Another welcome improvement is the establishment of a uniform standard deviation of I.Q. for each age, so that an I.Q. of, say, 70 at age 6 means, relatively, the same as I.Q. 70 at age 12. Also, the book itself is well thought out in its presentation, with easy reference to test items and an adequate set of tables for conversions to I.Q. The new revision, however, is not wholly without debit items. The cost of an improved selection of items is the loss of the alternate version, which had its value in testing the Binet-sophisticated child. The cards and material accompanying the tests are well planned but are rather shoddy and somewhat expensive, and there seems also to be an unnecessarily profuse supply of different kinds of record forms. At the present stage, only the administration of the test can be assessed; the validity of the new item selection and the norms for British children is as yet unknown.

Personnel & Guid J 39:155–6 O '60. Benjamin Balinsky. * No basic changes were made in the revision. It is still an age scale and measures the same kind of mental activities as the original scale, mainly falling under the category of general intelligence. The changes are essentially in the subtests and their placement, and in certain improvements in the IQ Tables that eliminate atypical variability and make the IQ's for all ages comparable. The 1960 revision incorporates in a single scale the best of the subtests from the L and M Forms of the 1937 scale. * Much careful work seems to have been done in keeping the best test items and eliminating the worst. This revision is not a complete restandardization. The norms are essentially based on the 1937 standardization with adjustments resulting from the data obtained in the more recent samplings. The removal of obsolete items and the revised placement of certain of the subtests should make for a general improvement of the Scale. There are no validity data specific to the revision. Its validity is based upon the fact that the same type of tests are used as in the 1937 Scale. Because of the great amount of overlap and the careful selection of subtests to be used in the revision, the probability is high that the validity of the revision will be at least equal to if not greater than the 1937 version. * The book should serve its purposes very well. For any user of the revision it is a must. For students of intelligence testing it brings together succinctly the major outlines in the development of age scales and, if studied together with previous works on the subject, provides much important additional material.

Personnel & Guid J 39:226–7 N '60. *Julian C. Stanley.* * Constructing a well standardized age scale of intelligence is truly a formidable undertaking, and "retreading" an old one (published in 1937) is no chore for the fainthearted. We are indebted to the late Professor Terman and to his collaborators on the 1937 and 1960 versions—especially Professors Maud Merrill and Quinn McNemar for their great zeal, energy, patience, and skill in combining laboratory standards of exactitude with extensive statistical verification. Along with Pinneau, who constructed the new standard-score IQ tables, they have elevated the "cut and trying" of age scaling to a high art and infused into it considerable science. We must ponder seriously, however, whether it is any longer worthwhile to work this hard preserving the cumulated-months mental age, only to fly to standard-score IQ tables (desired mean at each age level 100, standard deviation 16). Devising point scales seems much more straightforward, and it is possible to supplement standard scores and percentile ranks with grade equivalents and "point mental ages." Practically everyone, including Terman and Merrill, seems to have given up the MA/CA ratio-type IQ, thereby removing one of the chief reasons for having intelligence scales scored on the basis of months of mental age. A large number of psychologists —school and otherwise—will be grateful for this improved version of their favorite standardized interviewing technique, as it might be called. Gone are obsolescent items that puzzled today's children. (But the American flag still has only 48 stars!) Put together in one neat package are the best items from Forms L and M, even more heavily weighted with a general intellectual factor ("manipulation of symbols"?) than before * This reviewer concurs with their "reasonable assurance to test users that the third Revision of the Stanford-Binet Scales can be relied upon to perform even more dependably the functions that have come to be expected of them" (p. v). The revision is by no means a complete restandardization, but it does seem to be a distinct improvement in several respects.

For reviews by Mary R. Haworth and Norman D. Sundberg of the Second Edition, see 5:413; for a review by Boyd R. McCandless, see 4:358; see also 40:1420 (3 excerpts); for reviews by Francis N. Maxfield, J. W. M. Rothney, and F. L. Wells, see 38:1062; for excerpts from related book reviews, see B396, 3:293, 3:294, 40:B1093, and 38:B497.

[537]

***Van Alstyne Picture Vocabulary Test.** Mental ages 2–7; 1929–61; revision of *Van Alstyne Picture Vocabulary Test for Pre-school Children* ('29); individual; 1 form ('60, 61-page picture booklet); manual ('61, 15 pages); record blank ('61, 1 page); $4.80 per examiner's kit of picture booklet, manual, and record blank; $1.50 per 35 record blanks; postage extra; (15) minutes; Dorothy Van Alstyne; Harcourt, Brace & World, Inc. *

REFERENCES

1. VAN ALSTYNE, DOROTHY. *The Environment of Three-Year-Old Children: Factors Related to Intelligence and Vocabulary Tests.* Columbia University, Teachers College, Contributions to Education, No. 366. New York: Bureau of Publications, the College, 1929. Pp. vii, 108. * (PA 4:386)
2. MOORE, JOSEPH E. "A Comparison of Negro and White Preschool Children on a Vocabulary Test and Eye-Hand Coordination Test." *Child Develop* 13:247–52 D '42. * (PA 17:2079)
3. SCHNEIDERMAN, NORMA. "A Study of the Relationship Between Articulatory Ability and Language Ability." *J Speech & Hearing Disorders* 20:359–64 D '55. * (PA 30:7690)
4. BLIGH, HAROLD F. "Concurrent Validity Evidence on Two Intelligence Measures for Young Children." *Yearb Nat Council Meas Used Ed* 16:56–66 '59. * (PA 34:7345)
5. DUNN, LLOYD M., AND HARLEY, RANDALL K. "Comparability of Peabody, Ammons, Van Alstyne, and Columbia Test Scores With Cerebral Palsied Children." *Excep Child* 26:70–4 O '59. * (PA 35:3733)
6. VECCHIONE, NICHOLAS. "An Appraisal of the Van Alstyne Picture Vocabulary Test for Use in Determining Readiness of Pre-School Children for First Grade." *Ed Rec B* 83:79–84 F '63. *

MARY R. HAWORTH, *Associate Professor of Medical Psychology, University of Nebraska*

College of Medicine, Omaha, Nebraska.

The current test is a revision of the 1929 *Van Alstyne Picture Vocabulary Test for Preschool Children,* which must have been one of the first tests of this type. Its chief competitors at the present time are the Ammons' *Full-Range Picture Vocabulary Test* (1948) and the *Peabody Picture Vocabulary Test* (1959). The manual describes the test as a "quick, individually administered screening test for mental ability" designed for children in the mental age range from two to seven years.

The test consists of a spiral booklet containing 60 plates, all of which are administered to the subject. No verbal response is required; the child is asked to point to the one of four pictures on the page which corresponds to the stimulus word given by the examiner. Administration takes approximately 15 minutes and scoring consists simply of summing correct responses and determining the appropriate mental age from a table listing all possible scores.

The nonverbal aspects of the test make it especially suited to children with delayed speech or speech handicaps and for those with motor impairments.

A commendable feature of the test is the rationale used in selecting the three "incorrect" pictures for each plate. In addition to being of equal order of frequency, the words chosen for representation are either commonly associated with the test word (e.g., thimble—thread, nail—hammer, sleeve—cuff) or have similar initial sounds (e.g., parrot—penguin, picking—peeking, crawl—cry). If errors of either type are made repeatedly, valuable qualitative clues are provided for further exploration of possible aphasic-like tendencies or difficulties in making fine auditory discriminations. The subject must also frequently make rather fine distinctions with respect to functions, activities, or species (e.g., smoke—flame, geese—swan). Perseverative trends can also be observed, especially in brain damaged youngsters, since the same picture may appear on several plates (but only be a correct response on one of them) and will continue to be picked out for its familiarity even though its selection is no longer appropriate for the stimulus word. Unfortunately, the author suggests scoring simply as pass or fail, thus discouraging collection of additional information needed for qualitative evaluations.

The standardization data presented in the manual are sketchy at best. Apparently the scores of fewer than 500 subjects between the ages of four and seven (second grade) served as the basis for the table of mental age equivalents which range from 2 years 1 month through 10 years 5 months. These mental ages were established by comparisons with scores achieved on the Stanford-Binet for the preschool subjects, but from a variety of group intelligence tests for first and second graders.

The only evidence offered for validity consists of correlations between the Van Alstyne and other intelligence tests (in terms of test scores and of IQ's). Since the outside criterion tests were also those used as the basis for arriving at the Van Alstyne mental age equivalents in the first place, one might expect this dubious procedure to yield spuriously high correlations. Instead they range from .49 to .71.

Split-half reliabilities for the four age groups range from .71 to .85 and the standard error of measurement is 2 raw score points at age seven, but close to 3 points for each of the younger age levels. Inspection of the table of mental ages shows that 1 score point generally represents 1 month of mental age up to four years of age; from four to six years of age, 1 score point is equivalent to 1 or 2 months of MA; beyond age six, 1 point represents 3 to 4 months of MA. Consequently, mental ages can be in error by as much as 6 to 8 months.

The manual suggests converting MA's to IQ's in the usual way (MA/CA) and presents a table of percentile ranks based on these IQ's. The author also states that the test provides an "estimate of mental ability....based on the child's vocabulary comprehension," and proceeds to point out that vocabulary items have generally correlated highly with total scores on standard intelligence tests. The assumption is made that the two methods of testing verbal comprehension, namely by pointing to a word named and by defining it in verbal terms, are tapping equivalent cognitive functions. This has yet to be demonstrated experimentally.

Nevertheless, a good case can be made for the test, and picture vocabulary tests in general, if their purpose is specifically stated as the measurement of comprehension of the spoken word without inferring the equivalence to mental ability in general. Consequently scoring might well be kept in terms of age equivalents rather than converting to mental ages and IQ's.

The Van Alstyne test seems superior to the Ammons for the under 10 age range since there are more items per year at the younger levels on the Van Alstyne. The Peabody test is quite similar to the Van Alstyne in format and a correlation of .94 has been reported between the two tests (5). The Van Alstyne appears to have some advantages over the Peabody in terms of the selection of pictures as mentioned above. On the other hand, the Peabody has more test plates at the youngest age levels, extends upwards to 18 years, and was standardized on a much larger sample. Also, two forms of the Peabody can be administered using the same plates.

The Van Alstyne test could be improved with the addition of more items at the younger levels; and also at the upper levels to allow for more ceiling for bright seven-year-olds. Other suggestions of a more mechanical nature include: a larger spiral binding so that the test plates can more readily be turned over and under; and the printing of the stimulus words on the recording blank so that the examiner does not need to refer back and forth to the manual and the blank. Some provision should also be made for easy recording of wrong responses (by numbering the pictures or descriptive words on the test blank) to aid in later qualitative evaluation of patterns of errors. The overall value of the test might also be increased if some number concepts were added, or more adjectival stimuli for discriminations at higher levels, and more items likely to elicit aphasic trends or associations (such as comb—brush, table—chair).

In summary, this test basically has merit if its stated purpose is kept in mind, i.e., as a screening test with minimal emphasis on deriving an IQ from the test scores. Its stature could be improved with additional standardization data. The test has promise of clinical usefulness in testing young normal and older retarded children and those subjects with verbal or motor impairments who cannot be adequately evaluated by the more usual testing procedures.

ELLEN V. PIERS, *Associate Professor of Psychology, The Pennsylvania State University, University Park, Pennsylvania.*

This is a revision of the 1929 *Van Alstyne Picture Vocabulary Test for Pre-school Children.* While an improvement over the original, it still has its weaknesses. Its stated purpose is to provide an estimate of the mental ability of children in the mental age range from two to seven years, based on vocabulary comprehension. There are now 60 stimulus words presented in two groups of odd-numbered cards and even-numbered cards, each with four pictures. The drawings are good, and the record blank simple. The manual is short and easy to read. Twenty-eight new words were selected from a basic vocabulary list. Decoys were selected which had an equal level of frequency, were associated in life situations, or had a similar initial sound to the test word.

The manual does not make clear the total number of standardization cases but says they were "selected groups of preschool children in New Haven, Connecticut and in several localities in Florida, and in-school groups in New York City." No basis for selection is given. No children were below four years of age or above second grade, so that norms below and above that level are based on deviant children, the number of whom is unknown. Preschool children were given the 1937 Stanford-Binet as well as the Van Alstyne, and school aged children apparently were given one (or more?) of the following: Columbia, Otis Quick-Scoring, Pintner-Cunningham or Pintner-Durost, and Lorge-Thorndike. The mental age of each child was established from these tests, and the percentage of subjects answering each Van Alstyne item correctly at successive mental ages was determined. Increase in percentage passing with increasing mental age was used largely in the choice of 60 items out of an original 70, and equivalent mental age scores for the Van Alstyne were then derived from the other tests. IQ tables are not presented but may be determined in the now out-of-date manner of dividing MA by CA. Percentile ranks are given for a normal distribution of IQ's with a standard deviation of 16, but where the latter was plucked from is not stated.

Having used the same sample for both item selection and standardization, the author proceeds to use it again to establish concurrent validity! In spite of being the source for the establishment of Van Alstyne's mental age norms, correlations of the other tests with the Van Alstyne, both for mental age, raw scores or IQ's, ranged only from .49 to .71.

Split-half reliability of raw scores for ages 4–8 ranged from .71 to .85. No other reliabilities are reported.

In spite of some glaring weaknesses in standardization, this little test may still be useful in its middle range—that is, from 3 or 4 to 6 or 7 years. One study (5) in which it was compared with the Peabody and Ammons picture vocabulary tests with 20 cerebral palsied children reported high intercorrelations, partially one expects because of the wide age range. Mean mental age scores, however, showed the Ammons significantly different from (higher than) the Van Alstyne, and it was felt that the latter had insufficient ceiling.

If the test were worth revising, it seems a pity that a more sophisticated job of revision could not be undertaken. In this reviewer's opinion the better choice of test for preschool children would probably be the *Peabody Picture Vocabulary Test*. More conclusive evaluation of the Van Alstyne will have to await further research.

For a review by Ruth W. Washburn of the original edition, see 3:296.

[538]
Wechsler Adult Intelligence Scale. Ages 16 and over; 1939–55; revision of Form 1 of *Wechsler-Bellevue Intelligence Scale;* also called WAIS; individual; 14 scores: verbal (information, comprehension, arithmetic, similarities, digit span, vocabulary, total), performance (digit symbol, picture completion, block design, picture arrangement, object assembly, total), total; 1 form ['55]; manual ('55, 116 pages); record booklet ('55, 4 pages); supplementary record sheet ('55, 1 page); $24 per set of testing materials, 25 record booklets, and manual; $2.10 per 25 record booklets; 90¢ per 25 supplementary record sheets; $3 per manual; postpaid; (40–60) minutes; David Wechsler; Psychological Corporation. (Australian edition of record form and manual amendment slips: Australian Council for Educational Research; British modification of test questions: National Foundation for Educational Research in England and Wales.) *

REFERENCES

1–42. See 5:414.
43. NEURINGER, CHARLES. *A Statistical Comparison of the Wechsler-Bellevue Intelligence Scale, Form I and the Wechsler Adult Intelligence Scale for a College Population.* Master's thesis, University of Kansas (Lawrence, Kan.), 1956.
44. BENNETT, GEORGE K. Chap. 11, "Relationship of Age and Mental Test Scores Among Older Persons," pp. 152–7. In *The New Frontiers of Aging.* Edited by Wilma Donahue and Clark Tibbitts. Ann Arbor, Mich.: University of Michigan Press, 1957. Pp. x, 209. * (PA 33:927)
45. EVANS, LaVON. *A Comparison of Test Scores for the 16–17 Year Age Group of Navaho Indians With Standardized Norms for the Wechsler Adult Intelligence Scale.* Master's thesis, Brigham Young University (Provo, Utah), 1957.
46. LEWIS, LENA L. "The Relation of Measured Mental Ability to School Marks and Academic Survival in the Texas School for the Blind." *Int J Ed Blind* 6:56–60 Mr '57. *
47. RICKS, JAMES H., JR. *Age and Vocabulary Test Performance: A Qualitative Analysis of the Responses of Adults.* Doctor's thesis, Columbia University (New York, N.Y.), 1957. (DA 19:182)
48. HEILBRUN, ALFRED B., JR. "The Digit Span Test and the Prediction of Cerebral Pathology." *A.M.A. Arch Neurol & Psychiatry* 80:228–31 Ag '58. * (PA 33:10334)
49. HOWARD, WILLIAM. "A Note on McNemar's 'On Abbreviated Wechsler-Bellevue Scales.' " *J Consult Psychol* 22:414 D '58. * (PA 33:9920, title only)
50. KLETT, WILLIAM G. *An Analysis of Item Order in Seven Subtests of the Wechsler Adult Intelligence Scale (WAIS).* Master's thesis, Loyola University (Chicago, Ill.), 1958.

51. MIELE, JOHN ANTHONY. *Sex Differences in Intelligence: The Relationship of Sex to Intelligence as Measured by the Wechsler Adult Intelligence Scale and the Wechsler Intelligence Scale for Children.* Doctor's thesis, New York University (New York, N.Y.), 1958. (DA 18:2213)
52. PLANT, WALTER T. "Mental Ability Scores for Freshmen in a California State College." *Calif J Ed Res* 9:72–3+ Mr '58. * (PA 33:9051)
53. PURDOM, GLEN A., JR. *Comparison of Performance of Competent and Incompetent Readers in a State Training School for Delinquent Boys on the WAIS and the Rosenzweig P-F Study.* Doctor's thesis, University of Oregon (Eugene, Ore.), 1958. (DA 19:1016)
54. BLOOM, BERNARD L. "Ecologic Factors in the WAIS Picture Completion Test." Abstract. *J Consult Psychol* 23:375 Ag '59. * (PA 34:4237)
55. CLAYTON, HUGH, AND PAYNE, DAN. "Validation of Doppelt's WAIS Short Form With a Clinical Population." Abstract. *J Consult Psychol* 23:467 O '59. * (PA 34:5603)
56. COONS, W. H., AND PEACOCK, E. P. "Inter-Examiner Reliability of the Wechsler Adult Intelligence Scale With Mental Hospital Patients." *O.P.A. Q* 12:33–7 Jl '59. *
57. DOPPELT, JEROME E., AND SEASHORE, HAROLD G. "Psychological Testing in Correctional Institutions." *J Counsel Psychol* 6:81–92 sp '59. * (PA 34:6012)
58. EISDORFER, CARL; BUSSE, EWALD W.; AND COHEN, LOUIS D. "The WAIS Performance of an Aged Sample: The Relationship Between Verbal and Performance IQ's." *J Gerontol* 14:197–201 Ap '59. * (PA 34:11136)
59. FISHER, GARY M., AND SHOTWELL, ANNA M. "An Evaluation of Doppelt's Abbreviated Form of the WAIS for the Mentally Retarded." *Am J Mental Def* 64:476–81 N '59. * (PA 34:8003)
60. GARFIELD, SOL L. "Problems in the Psychological Evaluation of the Subnormal Individual." *Am J Mental Def* 64:467–71 N '59. * (PA 34:8005)
61. HOWARD, WILLIAM. "Validities of WAIS Short Forms in a Psychiatric Population." Abstract. *J Consult Psychol* 23:282 Je '59. * (PA 34:4384)
62. JONES, NELSON FREDRICK, JR. *Validity of Clinical Judgments of Schizophrenic Pathology Based on Verbal Responses to Intelligence Test Items.* Doctor's thesis, Northwestern University (Evanston, Ill.), 1959. (DA 20:2383)
63. LADD, CLAYTON E. *An Analysis of the WAIS Performance of Brain Damaged and Neurotic Patients.* Master's thesis, State University of Iowa (Iowa City, Iowa), 1959.
64. LEVINSON, BORIS M. "A Comparison of the Coloured Progressive Matrices (CPM) With the Wechsler Adult Intelligence Scale (WAIS) in a Normal Aged White Male Population." *J Clin Psychol* 15:288–91 Jl '59. * (PA 35:3299)
65. LEVINSON, BORIS M. "Traditional Jewish Cultural Values and Performance on the Wechsler Tests." *J Ed Psychol* 50:177–81 Ag '59. * (PA 35:2059)
66. LORANGER, ARMAND W., AND MISIAK, HENRYK. "Critical Flicker Frequency and Some Intellectual Functions in Old Age." *J Gerontol* 14:323–7 Jl '59. * (PA 34:4153)
67. PLANT, WALTER T., AND LYND, CELIA. "A Validity Study and a College Freshman Norm Group for the Wechsler Adult Intelligence Scale." *Personnel & Guid J* 37:578–80 Ap '59. *
68. POLAND, RONAL G. *A Factor Analysis of the WAIS and the EPSAT.* Doctor's thesis, Universty of Denver (Denver, Colo.), 1959.
69. SAUNDERS, DAVID R. "On the Dimensionality of the WAIS Battery for Two Groups of Normal Males." *Psychol Rep* 5:529–41 S '59. * (PA 38:4283)
70. SINES, LLOYD K., AND SIMMONS, HELEN. "The Shipley-Hartford Scale and the Doppelt Short Form as Estimators of WAIS IQ in a State Hospital Population." *J Clin Psychol* 15:452–3 O '59. * (PA 36:1HD52S)
71. STINSON, PAIRLEE J., AND MORRISON, MILDRED M. "Sex Differences Among High School Seniors." *J Ed Res* 53:103–8 N '59. *
72. WAGNER, EDWIN ERIC. *Predicting Success for Young Executives From Objective Test Scores and Personal Data.* Doctor's thesis, Temple University (Philadelphia, Pa.), 1959. (DA 20:3371)
73. WIENS, ARTHUR N.; MATARAZZO, JOSEPH D.; AND GAVER, KENNETH D. "Performance and Verbal IQ in a Group of Sociopaths." *J Clin Psychol* 15:191–3 Ap '59. * (PA 35:5102)
74. BORGATTA, EDGAR F., AND CORSINI, RAYMOND J. "The Quick Word Test (QWT) and the WAIS." *Psychol Rep* 6:201 Ap '60. * (PA 35:6397)
75. BRIGGS, PETER F. "The Validity of WAIS Performance Subtests Completed With One Hand." *J Clin Psychol* 16:318–20 Jl '60. * (PA 36:2HC18B)
76. DARBES, ALEX. "Relationships Among College Students Scores on ACE, Otis, and WAIS Tests." *Proc W Va Acad Sci* 32:214–6 D '60. * (PA 36:3KK14D)
77. FIELD, J. G. "Two Types of Tables for Use With Wechsler's Intelligence Scales." *J Clin Psychol* 16:3–7 Ja '60. * (PA 36:1HCo3F)
78. FISHER, GARY M. "The Altitude Quotient as an Index of Intellectual Potential: I, WAIS Data for Familial and Undifferentiated Mental Retardates." *Am J Mental Def* 65:252–5 '60. * (PA 35:3779)
79. FISHER, GARY M. "A Corrected Table for Determining the Significance of the Difference Between Verbal and Per-

formance IQ's on the WAIS and the Wechsler-Bellevue." *J Clin Psychol* 16:7–8 Ja '60. * (*PA* 36:1HC07F)
80. FISHER, GARY M. "Differences in WAIS Verbal and Performance IQ's in Various Diagnostic Groups of Mental Retardates." *Am J Mental Def* 65:256–60 S '60. * (*PA* 35:3780)
81. FISHER, GARY M.; DOOLEY, MILTON D.; AND SILVERSTEIN, ARTHUR B. "Wechsler Adult Intelligence Scale Performance of Familial and Undifferentiated Mental Subnormals." *Psychol Rep* 7:268 O '60. * (*PA* 35:2552)
82. FISHER, GARY M.; SHOTWELL, ANNA M.; AND YORK, DOROTHY H. "Comparability of the Ammons Full-Range Picture Vocabulary Test With the WAIS in the Assessment of Intelligence of Mental Retardates." *Am J Mental Def* 64:995–9 My '60. * (*PA* 35:6830)
83. GARDNER, MARGARET SEYMOUR. *Factors Associated With Success in First Grade Teaching.* Doctor's thesis, Northwestern University (Evanston, Ill.), 1960. (*DA* 21:2609)
84. GOLDMAN, BERT ARTHUR. *Relationships Between Intelligence and Immediate Memory-Reasoning.* Doctor's thesis, University of Virginia (Charlottesville, Va.), 1960. (*DA* 21:2192)
85. HIRSCHENFANG, SAMUEL. "A Comparison of WAIS Scores of Hemiplegic Patients With and Without Aphasia." *J Clin Psychol* 16:351 Jl '60. * (*PA* 36:2JF51H)
86. HUNT, WILLIAM A.; WALKER, RONALD E.; AND JONES, NELSON F. "The Validity of Clinical Ratings for Estimating Severity of Schizophrenia." *J Clin Psychol* 16:391–3 O '60. * (*PA* 37:3220)
87. KALDEGG, A. "A Note on the Application of Doppelt's Short Form of the Wechsler Adult Intelligence Scale to a Clinical Population." *Brit J Med Psychol* 33:221–3 pt 3 '60. *
88. KENNEDY, WALLACE A.; NELSON, WILLARD; LINDNER, RON; TURNER, JACK; AND MOON, HAROLD. "Psychological Measurements of Future Scientists." *Psychol Rep* 7:515–7 D '60. * (*PA* 35:1522)
89. LEVINSON, BORIS M. "A Research Note on Subcultural Differences in WAIS Between Aged Italians and Jews." *J Gerontol* 15:197–8 Ap '60. * (*PA* 35:6403)
90. LEVINSON, BORIS M. "A Research Note on the Knox Cubes as an Intelligence Test for Aged Males." *J Gerontol* 15:85–6 Ja '60. * (*PA* 35:6234)
91. LORANGER, ARMAND W., AND MISIAK, HENRYK. "The Performance of Aged Females on Five Non-Language Tests of Intellectual Functions." *J Clin Psychol* 16:189–91 Ap '60. * (*PA* 36:2FI89L)
92. MAXWELL, A. E. "Obtaining Factor Scores on the Wechsler Adult Intelligence Scale." *J Mental Sci* 106:1060–2 Jl '60. * (*PA* 35:4861)
93. PANTON, JAMES H. "Beta-WAIS Comparisons and WAIS Subtest Configurations Within a State Prison Population." *J Clin Psychol* 16:312–7 Jl '60. * (*PA* 36:2HD12P)
94. PARSONS, OSCAR A., AND KEMP, DAVID E. "Intellectual Functioning in Temporal Lobe Epilepsy." *J Consult Psychol* 24:408–14 O '60. * (*PA* 35:5156)
95. REITAN, RALPH M. "The Significance of Dysphasia for Intelligence and Adaptive Abilities." *J Psychol* 50:355–76 O '60. * (*PA* 35:6767)
96. SAUNDERS, DAVID R. "A Factor Analysis of the Information and Arithmetic Items of the WAIS." *Psychol Rep* 6:367–83 Je '60. * (*PA* 35:6411)
97. SAUNDERS, DAVID R. "A Factor Analysis of the Picture Completion Items of the WAIS." *J Clin Psychol* 16:146–9 Ap '60. * (*PA* 36:2HD46S)
98. SCHAFER, ROY. "Representations of Perceiving and Acting in Psychological Test Responses," pp. 291–312. (*PA* 35:850) In *Festschrift for Gardner Murphy.* Edited by John G. Peatman and Eugene L. Hartley. New York: Harper & Brothers, 1960. Pp. xi, 411. *
99. SILVERSTEIN, A. B., AND FISHER, GARY M. "Reanalysis of Sex Differences in the Standardization Data of the Wechsler Adult Intelligence Scale." *Psychol Rep* 7:405–6 D '60. * (*PA* 35:2201)
100. SINNETT, KATHLEEN, AND MAYMAN, MARTIN. "The Wechsler Adult Intelligence Scale as a Clinical Diagnostic Tool: A Review." *B Menninger Clinic* 24:80–4 Mr '60. * (*PA* 35:3416)
101. STEIN, ZENA, AND SUSSER, MERVYN. "Families of Dull Children: Part 4, Increments in Intelligence." *J Mental Sci* 106:1311–9 O '60. * (*PA* 35:5182)
102. WAGNER, EDWIN E. "Differences Between Old and Young Executives on Objective Psychological Test Variables." *J Gerontol* 15:296–9 Jl '60. * (*PA* 35:1328)
103. WIENS, ARTHUR N., AND BANAKA, WILLIAM H. "Estimating WAIS IQ From Shipley-Hartford Scores: A Cross-Validation." *J Clin Psychol* 16:452 O '60. * (*PA* 37:3119)
104. WOLFF, B. BERTHOLD. "The Application of the Hewson Ratios to the WAIS as an Aid in the Differential Diagnosis of Cerebral Pathology." *J Nerv & Mental Dis* 131:98–109 Ag '60. *
105. WOLFSON, WILLIAM, AND BACHELIS, LEONARD. "An Abbreviated Form of the WAIS Verbal Scale." *J Clin Psychol* 16:421 O '60. * (*PA* 37:3102)
106. WOLFSON, WILLIAM, AND WELTMAN, ROBERT E. "Implications of Specific WAIS Picture Completion Errors." *J Clin Psychol* 16:9–11 Ja '60. * (*PA* 36:1H109W)
107. ALIMENA, BENJAMIN. "A Note on Norms for Scatter Analysis on the Wechsler Intelligence Scales." *J Clin Psychol* 17:61 Ja '61. * (*PA* 37:3103)
108. ANASTASI, ANNE. *Psychological Testing, Second Edition,* pp. 303–15, 320–5. New York: Macmillan Co., 1961. Pp. xiii, 657. * (*PA* 36:1HA57A)
109. BEARDSLEY, KATHARINE. "Analysis of Psychological Tests of Persons Diagnosed Sociopathic Personality Disturbance." *Arch Crim Psychodynam* 4:389–411 su '61. *
110. BIRREN, JAMES E. Chap. 12, "Research on the Psychology of Aging: Concepts and Findings," pp. 203–22; discussion by Joseph Zubin, pp. 223–6. In *Psychopathology of Aging.* The Proceedings of the Fiftieth Annual Meeting of the American Psychopathological Association, Held in New York City, February 1960. Edited by Paul H. Hoch and Joseph Zubin. New York: Grune & Stratton, Inc., 1961. Pp. xiv, 321. * (*PA* 36:3FI21H)
111. BIRREN, JAMES E., AND MORRISON, DONALD F. "Analysis of the WAIS Subtests in Relation to Age and Education." *J Gerontol* 16:363–9 O '61. * (*PA* 36:5FI63B)
112. BRADWAY, KATHERINE P., AND ROBINSON, NANCY M. "Significant IQ Changes in Twenty-Five Years: A Follow-Up." *J Ed Psychol* 52:74–9 Ap '61. * (*PA* 38:2484)
113. BRENGELMANN, JOHANNES C., AND KENNY, JOSEPH T. "Comparison of Leiter, WAIS and Stanford-Binet IQ's in Retardates." *J Clin Psychol* 17:235–8 Jl '61. * (*PA* 38:8953)
114. COOK, RICHARD A., AND HIRT, MICHAEL L. "Verbal and Performance IQ Discrepancies on the Wechsler Adult Intelligence Scale and Wechsler-Bellevue, Form 1." *J Clin Psychol* 17:382–3 O '61. * (*PA* 38:8446)
115. DUNCAN, DONN R., AND BARRETT, ALBERT M. "A Longitudinal Comparison of Intelligence Involving the Wechsler-Bellevue 1 and WAIS." *J Clin Psychol* 17:318–9 Jl '61. * (*PA* 38:8453)
116. EISDORFER, CARL, AND COHEN, LOUIS D. "The Generality of the WAIS Standardization for the Aged: A Regional Comparison." *J Abn & Social Psychol* 62:520–7 My '61. * (*PA* 36:4FI20E)
117. FISHER, G. M. "A Comparison of the Performance of Endogenous and Exogenous Mental Retardates on the Wechsler Adult Intelligence Scale." *J Mental Def Res* 5:111–4 D '61. * (*PA* 36:4JI11F)
118. FISHER, GARY M.; KILMAN, BEVERLY A.; AND SHOTWELL, ANNA M. "Comparability of Intelligence Quotients of Mental Defectives on the Wechsler Adult Intelligence Scale and the 1960 Revision of the Stanford-Binet." *J Consult Psychol* 25:192–5 Je '61. *
119. FISHER, GARY M.; RISLEY, TODD R.; AND SILVERSTEIN, ARTHUR B. "Sex Differences in the Performance of Mental Retardates on the Wechsler Adult Intelligence Scale." *J Clin Psychol* 17:170 Ap '61. * (*PA* 38:952)
120. GEISER, ROBERT LEE. *The Psychodiagnostic Efficiency of WAIS and Rorschach Scores: A Discriminant Function Study.* Doctor's thesis, Boston University (Boston, Mass.), 1961. (*DA* 22:915)
121. KEEFE, MARY KAREN. *An Abbreviated WAIS With Bilingual Women.* Master's thesis, Saint Louis University (Saint Louis, Mo.), 1961.
122. LANFELD, EILEEN S., AND SAUNDERS, D. R. "Anxiety as 'Effect of Uncertainty': An Experiment Illuminating the OA Subtest of the WAIS." *J Clin Psychol* 17:238–41 Jl '61. * (*PA* 38:8498)
123. MCCARTHY, DOROTHEA. "Administration of Digit Symbol and Coding Subtests of the WAIS and WISC to Left-Handed Subjects." *Psychol Rep* 8:407–8 Je '61. * (*PA* 36:2HD07M)
124. MCKEEVER, WALTER F. "The Validity of the Hewson Ratios: A Critique of Wolff's Study." *J Nerv & Mental Dis* 132:417–9 My '61. *
125. MCLEOD, H. N. "My Two-Hour Psychological Test Battery." *O.P.A. Q* 14:85–7 D '61. *
126. MCLEOD, H. N. "The Use of the Information and Block-Design Sub-Tests of the WAIS as a Measure of Intelligence in Psychiatric Hospital Patients." *Ont Hosp Psychol B* 7:5–7 Ag '61. * Supplement, 7:12 Ap '62. *
127. MCLEOD, H. N., AND RUBIN, J. "Correction Between the Raven Matrices (Rev. 1956) and the Wechsler Adult Intelligence Scale (1955)." *Ont Hosp Psychol B* 6:47–9 Mr '61. *
128. MAXFIELD, KATHRYN E., AND PERRY, JAMES D. "The Intelligence Status of Some Vocational Rehabilitation Clients." *New Outlook Blind* 55:19–20 Ja '61. *
129. MAXWELL, A. E. "Trends in Cognitive Ability in the Older Age Ranges." *J Abn & Social Psychol* 63:449–52 S '61. * (*PA* 37:973)
130. MILLER, D. R.; FISHER, G. M.; AND DINGMAN, H. F. "A Note on Differential Utility of WAIS Verbal and Performance IQ's." *Am J Mental Def* 65:482–5 Ja '61. * (*PA* 35:6855)
131. NORMAN, RUSSELL P., AND WILENSKY, HAROLD. "Item Difficulty of the WAIS Information Subtest for a Chronic Schizophrenic Sample." *J Clin Psychol* 17:56–7 Ja '61. * (*PA* 37:3227)
132. SAUNDERS, DAVID R. "Digit Span and Alpha Frequency: A Cross-Validation." *J Clin Psychol* 17:165–7 Ap '61. * (*PA* 38:394)
133. SCHWARTZMAN, A. E.; HUNTER, R. C. A.; AND PRINCE,

R. H. "Intellectual Factors and Academic Performance in Medical Undergraduates." *J Med Ed* 36:353–8 Ap '61. *

134. STOTSKY, BERNARD A. "A Study of Factors in Recovery of Aged Patients From Chronic Physical Illness." *J Psychol Studies* 12:28–34 Ja '61. *

135. WAITE, RICHARD R. "The Intelligence Test as a Psychodiagnostic Instrument." *J Proj Tech* 25:90–102 Mr '61. * (PA 36:1HD90W)

136. WARREN, SUE ALLEN, AND KRAUS, MATTHEW J., JR. "WAIS Verbal Minus Performance IQ Comparisons in Mental Retardates." *J Clin Psychol* 17:57–9 Ja '61. * (PA 37:3599)

137. WOLFF, B. BERTHOLD. "The Validity of the Hewson Ratios: A Reply to McKeever's Critique." *J Nerv & Mental Dis* 132:420–4 My '61. *

138. WOLFSON, WILLIAM, AND LOCASCIO, RALPH. "Digit Symbol Performance of Nursing School Applicants." *J Clin Psychol* 17:59 Ja '61. * (PA 37:3876)

139. ALLEN, ROBERT M. "The Real Question in Digit Span Performance." *Psychol Rep* 11:218 Ag '62. * (PA 37:4951)

140. AYLAIAN, ARSEN, AND MELTZER, MALCOLM L. "The Bender Gestalt Test and Intelligence." Abstract. *J Consult Psychol* 26:483 O '62. *

141. BECK, AARON T.; FESHBACH, SEYMOUR; AND LEGG, DONALD. "The Clinical Utility of the Digit Symbol Test." *J Consult Psychol* 26:263–8 Je '62. * (PA 38:1177)

142. BIRREN, JAMES E., AND SPIETH, WALTER. "Age, Response Speed, and Cardiovascular Functions." *J Gerontol* 17:390–1 O '62. * (PA 37:4772)

143. BLOOM, BERNARD L., AND GOLDMAN, RUTH K. "Sensitivity of the WAIS to Language Handicap in a Psychotic Population." *J Clin Psychol* 18:161–3 Ap '62. * (PA 38:8233)

144. BRADWAY, KATHERINE P., AND THOMPSON, CLARE W. "Intelligence at Adulthood: A Twenty-Five Year Follow-Up." *J Ed Psychol* 53:1–14 F '62. * (PA 37:1210)

145. BRILL, RICHARD G. "The Relationship of Wechsler IQ's to Academic Achievement Among Deaf Students." *Excep Child* 28:315–21 F '62. * (PA 37:1609)

146. COSTA, LOUIS D., AND VAUGHAN, HERBERT G., JR. "Performance of Patients With Lateralized Cerebral Lesions: 1, Verbal and Perceptual Tests." *J Nerv & Mental Dis* 134: 162–8 F '62. *

147. CRADDICK, RAY A., AND GROSSMANN, KLAUS. "Effects of Visual Distraction Upon Performance on the WAIS Digit Span." *Psychol Rep* 10:642 Je '62. * (PA 37:4954)

148. FISHER, GARY M. "The Efficiency of the Hewson Ratios in Diagnosing Cerebral Pathology." *J Nerv & Mental Dis* 134:80–3 Ja '62. *

149. FISHER, GARY M. "Further Evidence of the Invalidity of the Wechsler Adult Intelligence Scale for the Assessment of Intelligence of Mental Retardates." *J Mental Def Res* 6:41–3 Je '62. (PA 37:3571)

150. FISHER, GARY M. "A Note on the Validity of the Wechsler Adult Intelligence Scale for Mental Retardates." *J Consult Psychol* 26:391 Ag '62. * (PA 38:4273)

151. FOGEL, MAX L. "The Intelligence Quotient as an Index of Brain Damage." Abstract. *Am J Orthopsychiatry* 32:338–9 Mr '62. *

152. FREEMAN, FRANK S. *Theory and Practice of Psychological Testing, Third Edition*, pp. 241–79, 330–8. New York: Holt, Rinehart & Winston, Inc., 1962. Pp. xix, 697. *

153. GRIFFITH, RICHARD M.; ESTES, BETSY WORTH; AND ZEROF, SELWYN A. "Intellectual Impairment in Schizophrenia." *J Consult Psychol* 26:336–9 Ag '62. * (PA 38:4604)

154. GUERTIN, WILSON H.; RABIN, ALBERT I.; FRANK, GEORGE H.; AND LADD, CLAYTON E. "Research With the Wechsler Intelligence Scales for Adults: 1955–60." *Psychol B* 59:1–26 Ja '62. * (PA 37:1203)

155. HIRT, MICHAEL L., AND COOK, RICHARD A. "Use of a Multiple Regression Equation to Estimate Organic Impairment From Wechsler Scale Scores." *J Clin Psychol* 18:80–1 Ja '62. * (PA 38:8421)

156. HULICKA, IRENE MACKINTOSH. "Verbal WAIS Scores of Elderly Patients." *Psychol Rep* 10:250 F '62. * (PA 37:966)

157. HUNT, WILLIAM A., AND WALKER, RONALD E. "A Comparison of Global and Specific Clinical Judgments Across Several Diagnostic Categories." *J Clin Psychol* 18:188–94 Ap '62. * (PA 38:8574)

158. JONES, REGINALD L. "Analytically Developed Short Forms of the WAIS." *J Consult Psychol* 26:289 Je '62. * (PA 38:943)

159. KO, YUNG-HO. "The Discrepancy Between the B-G Score and the Sum of the Object-Assembly and the Block-Design Test Scores as an Indicator of Organicity." *Acta Psychologica Taiwanica* (4):72–7 Mr '62. * (PA 38:6367)

160. L'ABATE, LUCIANO. "The Relationship Between WAIS-Derived Indices of Maladjustment and MMPI in Deviant Groups." *J Consult Psychol* 26:441–5 O '62. * (PA 39:1742)

161. LABRECQUE, JEAN M. *The Rationale of the WAIS Block Design Subtest.* Master's thesis, University of Ottawa (Ottawa, Ont., Canada), 1962.

162. LEVINSON, BORIS M. "Jewish Subculture and WAIS Performance Among Jewish Aged." *J Genetic Psychol* 100: 55–68 Mr '62. * (PA 37:969)

163. MCLEOD, HUGH N., AND RUBIN, JOSEPH. "Correlation Between Raven Progressive Matrices and the WAIS." *J Consult Psychol* 26:190–1 Ap '62. * (PA 37:4960)

164. MINER, JOHN B. "Personality and Ability Factors in Sales Performance." *J Appl Psychol* 46:6–13 F '62. * (PA 36:5LD06M)

165. NICKOLS, JOHN E., JR. "Brief Forms of the Wechsler Intelligence Scales for Research." *J Clin Psychol* 18:167 Ap '62. * (PA 38:8500)

166. O'NEIL, W. M. "The Stability of the Main Pattern of Abilities With Changing Age." *Austral J Psychol* 14:1–8 Ap '62. * (PA 38:6025)

167. RAPAPORT, GERALD M., AND MARSHALL, ROBERT J. "The Prediction of Rehabilitative Potential of Stockade Prisoners Using Clinical Psychological Tests." *J Clin Psychol* 18:444–6 O '62. * (PA 39:5087)

168. RIEGEL, RUTH M., AND RIEGEL, KLAUS F. "A Comparison and Reinterpretation of Factor Structures of the W-B, the WAIS, and the HAWIE on Aged Persons." *J Consult Psychol* 26:31–7 F '62. * (PA 37:4965)

169. SARASON, IRWIN G., AND MINARD, JAMES. "Test Anxiety, Experimental Instructions, and the Wechsler Adult Intelligence Scale." *J Ed Psychol* 53:299–302 D '62. * (PA 37:4968)

170. SATZ, PAUL, AND MOGEL, STEVE. "An Abbreviation of the WAIS for Clinical Use." *J Clin Psychol* 18:77–9 Ja '62. * (PA 38:8436)

171. SHAFFER, JOHN W. "A Specific Cognitive Deficit Observed in Gonadal Aplasia (Turner's Syndrome)." *J Clin Psychol* 18:403–6 O '62. * (PA 39:5565)

172. SILVERSTEIN, A. B. "Length of Hospitalization and Intelligence Test Performance in Mentally Retarded Adults." *Am J Mental Def* 66:618–20 Ja '62. * (PA 36:4JI18S)

173. SILVERSTEIN, A B.; SHOTWELL, ANNA M.; AND FISHER, GARY M. "Cultural Factors in the Intellectual Functioning of the Mentally Retarded." *Am J Mental Def* 67: 396–401 N '62. * (PA 37:5420)

174. SMALL, JOYCE G.; MILSTEIN, VICTOR; AND STEVENS, JANICE R. "Are Psychomotor Epileptics Different? A Controlled Study." *Arch Neurol* 7:187–94 S '62. * (PA 37:3521)

175. WAHLER, H. J., AND WATSON, LUKE S. "A Comparison of the Shipley-Hartford as a Power Test With the WAIS Verbal Scale." Abstract. *J Consult Psychol* 26:105 F '62. * (PA 37:5001)

176. WALL, HARVEY W.; MARKS, EDMOND; FORD, DONALD H.; AND ZEIGLER, MARTIN L. "Estimates of the Concurrent Validity of the W.A.I.S. and Normative Distributions for College Freshmen." *Personnel & Guid J* 40:717–22 Ap '62. * (PA 37:1998)

177. *Normative Information: Manager and Executive Testing.* New York: Richardson, Bellows, Henry & Co., Inc., May 1963. Pp. 45. *

178. BENSON, ROBERT R. "The Binet Vocabulary Score as an Estimate of Intellectual Functioning." *J Clin Psychol* 19: 134–5 Ja '63. * (PA 39:1715)

179. BIRREN, JAMES E. "Research on the Psychological Aspects of Aging." *Geriatrics* 18:393–403 My '63. * (PA 38: 8121)

180. British Psychological Society, English Division of Professional Psychologists (Educational and Clinical). "Report of the Working Party on Subnormality." Prepared by J. H. F. Castell, A. D. B. Clarke, P. Mittler, and W. M. Woodward. *B Brit Psychol Soc* 16:37–50 O '63. *

181. CLORE, GERALD L., JR. "Kent E-G-Y: Differential Scoring and Correlation With the WAIS." Abstract. *J Consult Psychol* 27:372 Ag '63. * (PA 38:2665)

182. CRADDICK, RAY A., AND STERN, MICHAEL R. "Relation Between the WAIS and the Kahn Test of Symbol Arrangement." *Percept & Motor Skills* 17:583–5 O '63. * (PA 38: 6052)

183. EISDORFER, CARL. "Rorschach Performance and Intellectual Functioning in the Aged." *J Gerontol* 18:358–63 O '63. * (PA 38:5822)

184. EISDORFER, CARL. "The WAIS Performance of the Aged: A Retest Evaluation." *J Gerontol* 18:169–72 Ap '63. * (PA 38:4100)

185. ESTES, BETSY WORTH. "A Note on the Satz-Mogel Abbreviation of the WAIS." *J Clin Psychol* 19:103 Ja '63. * (PA 39:1727)

186. EVANS, RAY B., AND MARMORSTON, JESSIE. "Psychological Test Signs of Brain Damage in Cerebral Thrombosis." *Psychol Rep* 12:915–30 Je '63. * (PA 38:6413)

187. FRIEDMAN, ELLEN C., AND BARCLAY, ALLAN. "The Discriminative Validity of Certain Psychological Tests as Indices of Brain Damage in the Mentally Retarded." *Mental Retardation* 1:291–3 O '63. * (PA 38:8935)

188. GIANNELL, A. STEVEN, AND FREEBURNE, CECIL M. "The Comparative Validity of the WAIS and the Stanford-Binet With College Freshmen." *Ed & Psychol Meas* 23:557–67 au '63. * (PA 38:6057)

189. GOLDMAN, BERT A. "Relationships Between Intelligence and Reasoning With Immediately Remembered Discrete Materials." *J Exp Ed* 31:279–84 Mr '63. *

190. GOLDMAN, BERT A. "SCAT Versus WAIS: An Enigma." *J Ed Res* 57:51–3 S '63. *

191. GRANICK, SAMUEL. "Comparative Analysis of Psychotic Depressives With Matched Normals on Some Untimed Verbal

Intelligence Tests." *J Consult Psychol* 27:439-43 O '63. * (PA 38:4628)
192. HAMLIN, ROY W., AND JONES, ROBERT E. "Vocabulary Deficit in Improved and Unimproved Schizophrenic Subjects." *J Nerv & Mental Dis* 136:360-4 Ap '63. * (PA 38:4605)
193. HARDYCK, CURTIS, AND PETRINOVICH, LEWIS F. "The Patterns of Intellectual Functioning in Parkinson Patients." Abstract. *J Consult Psychol* 27:548 D '63. *
194. IMRE, PAUL D. "A Correlation Study of Verbal IQ and Grade Achievement." *J Clin Psychol* 19:218-9 Ap '63. *
195. JARVIK, LISSY F., AND FALEK, ARTHUR. "Intellectual Stability and Survival in the Aged." *J Gerontol* 18:173-6 Ap '63. * (PA 38:4103)
196. JURJEVICH, R. M. "Interrelationships of Anxiety Indices of Wechsler Intelligence Scales and MMPI Scales." *J General Psychol* 69:135-42 Jl '63. * (PA 38:4305)
197. JURJEVICH, RATIBOR. "An Analysis of the Altitude IQs of Delinquent Girls." *J General Psychol* 69:221-6 O '63. * (PA 39:1779)
198. JURJEVICH, RATIBOR. "An Evaluation of the Henmon-Nelson Group *IQ* Test With Delinquent Girls." *J General Psychol* 69:227-33 O '63. * (PA 39:1778)
199. KARP, STEPHEN A. "Field Dependence and Overcoming Embeddedness." *J Consult Psychol* 27:294-302 Ag '63. * (PA 38:2629)
200. KARRAS, ATHAN. "Predicting Full Scale WAIS IQs From WAIS Subtests for a Psychiatric Population." *J Clin Psychol* 19:100 Ja '63. * (PA 39:1737)
201. KENNEDY, WALLACE A.; WILLCUTT, HERMAN; AND SMITH, ALVIN. "Wechsler Profiles of Mathematically Gifted Adolescents." *Psychol Rep* 12:259-62 F '63. * (PA 38:3174)
202. LAVER, A. B. "Testing in Canada." *Can Psychologist* 4:22-3 Ja '63. *
203. LEVINSON, BORIS M. "The WAIS Quotient of Subcultural Deviation." *J Genetic Psychol* 103:123-31 S '63. * (PA 39:1810)
204. LEVINSON, BORIS M. "Wechsler M-F Index." *J General Psychol* 69:217-20 O '63. * (PA 39:1748)
205. MOGEL, STEVE, AND SATZ, PAUL. "Abbreviation of the WAIS for Clinical Use: An Attempt at Validation." *J Clin Psychol* 19:298-300 Jl '63. *
206. NEURINGER, CHARLES. "The Form Equivalence Between the Wechsler-Bellevue Intelligence Scale, Form 1 and the Wechsler Adult Intelligence Scale." *Ed & Psychol Meas* 23:755-63 w '63. * (PA 38:8427)
207. NICKOLS, JOHN. "Structural Efficiency of WAIS Subtests." *J Clin Psychol* 19:420-3 O '63. *
208. PAUKER, JEROME D. "Relationship of Rorschach Content Categories to Intelligence." *J Proj Tech & Pers Assess* 27:220-1 Je '63. * (PA 38:2725)
209. PAUKER, JEROME D. "A Split-Half Abbreviation of the WAIS." *J Clin Psychol* 19:98-100 Ja '63. * (PA 39:1755)
210. PIERCE, ROBERT C. "Note on Testing Conditions." *J Consult Psychol* 27:536-7 D '63. *
211. PRENTICE, NORMAN M., AND KELLY, FRANCIS J. "Intelligence and Delinquency: A Reconsideration." *J Social Psychol* 60:327-37 Ag '63. * (PA 38:4585)
212. RAFI, A. AH. "A Note on the Cultural Aspects of the WAIS Vocabulary Subtest in Relation to British Mental Patients." *Brit J Social & Clin Psychol* 2:44-5 F '63. * (PA 38:963)
213. REED, HOMER B. C., JR., AND REITAN, RALPH M. "A Comparison of the Effects of the Normal Aging Process With the Effects of Organic Brain-Damage on Adaptive Abilities." *J Gerontol* 18:177-9 Ap '63. * (PA 38:4108)
214. ROBERTSON, MALCOLM H., AND WOLTER, DOUGLAS J. "The Effect of Sensory Deprivation Upon Scores on the Wechsler Adult Intelligenec Scale." *J Psychol* 56:213-8 Jl '63. * (PA 38:3610)
215. ROSS, D. "A Short-Form of the WAIS for Use in Mental Subnormality." *J Mental Subnorm* 9:91-4 D '63. *
216. ROTH, ROBERT M. "The Comprehension Subtest of the Wechsler Adult Intelligence Scale as an Indicator of Social Awareness." *J Ed Res* 56:387-8 Mr '63. *
217. SIEBERT, LAWRENCE A. "Matched Otis and Wechsler IQ Scores of Delinquents." *J Clin Psychol* 19:215-6 Ap '63. *
218. SILVERSTEIN, A. B. "WISC and WAIS IQs for the Mentally Retarded." *Am J Mental Def* 67:617-8 Ja '63. *
219. SPENCE, JANET TAYLOR. "Patterns of Performance on WAIS Similarities in Schizophrenic, Brain-Damaged and Normal Subjects." *Psychol Rep* 13:431-6 O '63. * (PA 38:8381)
220. TWAIN, DAVID C., AND BROOKS, EDWARD M. "A Comparison of Wechsler, Revised Beta and Otis Scores of Delinquent Boys." *Brit J Criminol* 3:288-90 Ja '63. *
221. WEBB, ALLEN P. "A Longitudinal Comparison of the WISC and WAIS With Educable Mentally Retarded Negroes." *J Clin Psychol* 19:101-2 Ja '63. * (PA 39:1769)
222. WITTENBORN, J. R., AND PLANTE, MARC. "Patterns of Response to Placebo, Iproniazid and Electroconvulsive Therapy Among Young Depressed Females." *J Nerv & Mental Dis* 137:155-61 Ag '63. *

For reviews by Nancy Bayley and Wilson H. Guertin, see 5:414. For reviews of the Wechsler-Bellevue Scale, see 5:415, 4:361, 3:298, and 40:1429. For excerpts from related book reviews, see B503, 3:299, 3:300, 3:301, and 40:B1121.

[539]
Wechsler-Bellevue Intelligence Scale. Ages 10 and over; 1939-47; individual; 2 forms; record form ('47, 4 pages) for each form; $2.10 per 25 record forms; postpaid; (40-60) minutes; David Wechsler; Psychological Corporation. (South African adaptation: National Institute for Personnel Research; Australian edition of record form and manual supplementary sheet: Australian Council for Educational Research.) *
a) FORM 1. 1939-47; out of print except for record form; see 538 for a revision.
b) FORM 2. 1946-47; catalog states that "Form 2 is the retest instrument for the WAIS as well as for Form 1"; 14 scores: verbal (general information, general comprehension, digit span, arithmetic, similarities, vocabulary, total), performance (picture arrangement, picture completion, block design, object assembly, digit symbol, total), total; manual ('46, 97 pages); $21 per set of testing materials, 25 record forms, and manual; $2.25 per manual.

REFERENCES

1-2. See 40:1429.
3-121. See 3:298.
122-371. See 4:361.
372-625. See 5:415.
626. MCFIE, J., AND PIERCY, M. F. "Intellectual Impairment With Localized Cerebral Lesions." *Brain* 75:292-311 S '52. * (PA 27:7649)
627. DENTON, L. R. "Intelligence Test Performance and Personality Differences in a Group of Visually Handicapped Children." *B Maritime Psychol Assn* 3:47-50 D '54. * (PA 29:7786)
628. YATES, AUBREY J. "The Validity of Some Psychological Tests of Brain Damage." *Psychol B* 51:359-79 Jl '54. *
629. HARRIS, RILDA. *A Comparative Study of Two Groups of Boys, Delinquent and Non-Delinquent, on the Basis of Their Wechsler and Rorschach Test Performances.* Master's thesis, Dalhousie University (Halifax, N.S., Canada), 1956.
630. MARSHAK, M. D. *A Study of the Wechsler-Bellevue Intelligence Scale Applied to British School Children.* Doctor's thesis, University of London (London, England), 1956.
631. BROWN, MORONI H., AND BRYAN, G. ELIZABETH. "Sex as a Variable in Intelligence Test Performance." *J Ed Psychol* 48:273-8 My '57. * (PA 33:778)
632. MAHRER, ALVIN R. "Potential Intelligence Testing: A Case Study." *U S Armed Forces Med J* 8:684-92 My '57. * (PA 33:3286)
633. PARSONS, OSCAR A.; STEWART, KENNETH D.; AND ARENBERG, DAVID. "Impairment of Abstracting Ability in Multiple Sclerosis." *J Nerv & Mental Dis* 125:221-5 Ap-Je '57. * (PA 33:4478)
634. SIDDIQUE, HABIBA. *A Translation of the Wechsler-Bellevue Intelligence Scale for Children With Adaptations, Suitable to West Pakistan.* Master's thesis, Claremont College (Claremont, Calif.), 1957.
635. STERNBERG, ULRICH; SPITZ, HERMAN; AND GOYNE, JAMES B. "Evaluation of Chlorpromazine and Reserpine Therapy With Follow-Up Study." *J Clin & Exp Psychopathol* 18:258-68 S '57. * (PA 33:1504)
636. KLØVE, HALLGRIM, AND REITAN, RALPH M. "Effect of Dysphasia and Spatial Distortion on Wechsler-Bellevue Results." *A.M.A. Arch Neurol & Psychiatry* 80:708-13 D '58. *
637. GASTON, CHARLES OWEN. *The Predictive Power of Attitudinal and Behavioral Indices Versus Formal Test Scores on the Wechsler-Bellevue Test.* Doctor's thesis, University of Houston (Houston, Tex.), 1958. (DA 19:1816)
638. HAWARD, L. R. C. "Wechsler Bellevue Form 1." *Psychometric Res B* (2):[34-6] Ag '58. *
639. HEILBRUN, A. B., JR. "The Digit Span Test and the Prediction of Cerebral Pathology." *A.M.A. Arch Neurol & Psychiatry* 80:228-31 Ag '58. * (PA 33:10334)
640. HOLT, ROBERT R., AND LUBORSKY, LESTER; WITH THE COLLABORATION OF WILLIAM R. MORROW, DAVID RAPAPORT, AND SIBYLLE K. ESCALONA. *Personality Patterns of Psychiatrists: A Study of Methods for Selecting Residents, Vol. 1.* New York: Basic Books, Inc., 1958. Pp. xiv, 386. * (PA 33:5751)
641. HOWARD, WILLIAM. "A Note on McNemar's 'On Abbreviated Wechsler-Bellevue Scales.'" *J Consult Psychol* 22:414 D '58. * (PA 33:9920, title only)

642. LEIDING, WALDEMAR C. *A Comparison of the Content and Sign Approaches in Evaluating a Projective Test Battery and Its Component Tests.* Doctor's thesis, University of Houston (Houston, Tex.), 1958. (*DA* 19:1822)

643. LEVINE, MURRAY. "'Not Alike' Responses in Wechsler's Similarities Subtest." Abstract. *J Consult Psychol* 22: 480 D '58. * (*PA* 33:10742)

644. MUNDY, LYDIA, AND MAXWELL, A. E. "Assessment of the Feebleminded." *Brit J Med Psychol* 31:201–10 pt 3 & 4 '58. * (*PA* 34:1673)

645. PLANT, WALTER T. "Mental Ability Scores for Freshmen in a California State College." *Calif J Ed Res* 9:72–3+ Mr '58. * (*PA* 33:9051)

646. ARMSTRONG, DOLORES MARIE. *The Differential Predictive Value of the Wechsler-Bellevue Scale.* Doctor's thesis, Stanford University (Stanford, Calif.), 1959. (*DA* 20:1262)

647. BIESHEUVEL, S., AND LIDDICOAT, R. "The Effects of Cultural Factors on Intelligence-Test Performance." *J Nat Inst Personnel Res* 8:3–14 S '59. * (*PA* 34:5785)

648. BLATT, SIDNEY J. "Recall and Recognition Vocabulary: Implications for Intellectual Deterioration." *A.M.A. Arch Gen Psychiatry* 1:473–6 N '59. * (*PA* 34:6005)

649. BRIDGES, CECIL. "Nomographs for Computing the 'Validity' of WISC or Wechsler-Bellevue Short Forms." *J Consult Psychol* 23:453–4 O '59. * (*PA* 34:5576)

650. CAMPBELL, J. CHANDLER. *The Relationship Between the Wechsler-Bellevue Scale and High School Achievement.* Doctor's thesis, Indiana University (Bloomington, Ind.), 1959. (*DA* 20:4031)

651. GUERTIN, WILSON H. "Auditory Interference With Digit Span Performance." *J Clin Psychol* 15:349 Jl '59. * (*PA* 35:3407)

652. KAHN, MARVIN W. "A Comparison of Personality, Intelligence, and Social History of Two Criminal Groups." *J Social Psychol* 49:33–40 F '59. * (*PA* 35:5214)

653. KARLE, H. "Wechsler Bellevue." *Psychometric Res B* (4):[26–9] Ag '59. *

654. KLØVE, HALLGRIM. "Relationship of Differential Electroencephalographic Patterns to Distribution of Wechsler-Bellevue Scores." *Neurology* 9:871–6 D '59. * (*PA* 35:1014)

655. KNOWLES, J. B. "Wechsler Bellevue." *Psychometric Res B* (4):[5–7] Ag '59. *

656. LONG, JAMES ALAN. *A Longitudinal Study of Some Factors Influencing the Performance of Adolescents on the Wechsler Bellevue Intelligence Scale I.* Doctor's thesis, Louisiana State University (Baton Rouge, La.), 1959. (*DA* 19:3368)

657. MARTIN, HARRY JEROME, JR. *A Comparison of Sign and Clinical Approaches in Predicting Psychiatric Diagnosis.* Doctor's thesis, University of Houston (Houston, Tex.), 1959. (*DA* 20:3837)

658. MASLING, JOSEPH. "The Effects of Warm and Cold Interaction on the Administration and Scoring of an Intelligence Test." *J Consult Psychol* 23:336–41 Ag '59. * (*PA* 34:4395)

659. NORMAN, RALPH D., AND DALEY, MARVIN F. "Senescent Changes in Intellectual Ability Among Superior Older Women." *J Gerontol* 14:457–64 O '59. * (*PA* 34:4157)

660. REITAN, RALPH M. "The Comparative Effects of Brain Damage on the Halstead Impairment Index and the Wechsler-Bellevue Scale." *J Clin Psychol* 15:281–5 Jl '59. * (*PA* 35:3739)

661. REITAN, RALPH M. "Correlations Between the Trail Making Test and the Wechsler-Bellevue Scale." *Percept & Motor Skills* 9:127–30 Je '59. * (*PA* 38:4282)

662. RIOCH, MARGARET J., AND LUBIN, ARDIE. "Prognosis of Social Adjustment for Mental Hospital Patients Under Psychotherapy." *J Consult Psychol* 23:313–8 Ag '59. * (*PA* 34:4404)

663. SMITH, JEANNE BAKER. *Abbreviated Wechsler-Bellevue Intelligence Scales With a Select High School Population.* Doctor's thesis, Bradley University (Peoria, Ill.), 1959. (*DA* 20:3637)

664. STRONG, PASCHAL N., JR. "Correlation Between the Ohio Literacy Test, Grade Achieved in School, and Wechsler Bellevue IQ." *J Clin Psychol* 15:71–2 Ja '59. * (*PA* 34:3452)

665. THORP, THOMAS R., AND MAHRER, ALVIN R. "Predicting Potential Intelligence." *J Clin Psychol* 15:286–8 Jl '59. * (*PA* 35:3418)

666. VICTOR, MAURICE; HERMAN, KENNETH; AND WHITE, ELISABETH E. "A Psychological Study of the Wernicke-Korsakoff Syndrome: Results of Wechsler-Bellevue Intelligence Scale and Wechsler Memory Scale Testing at Different Stages in the Disease." *Q J Studies Alcohol* 20:467–79 S '59. * (*PA* 34:6401)

667. AZIMA, FERN CRAMER, AND KRAL, V. A. "Effects of Blindfolding on Persons During Psychological Testing: A Psychometric Study of Various Age Groups." *Geriatrics* 15:780–92 N '60. *

668. BELL, ANNE, AND ZUBEK, JOHN P. "The Effect of Age on the Intellectual Performance of Mental Defectives." *J Gerontol* 15:285–95 Jl '60. * (*PA* 35:1039)

669. BROWN, FRED. "Intelligence Test Patterns of Puerto Rican Psychiatric Patients." *J Social Psychol* 52:225–30 N '60. * (*PA* 35:4855)

670. FIELD, J. G. "The Performance-Verbal IQ Discrepancy in a Group of Sociopaths." *J Clin Psychol* 16:321–2 Jl '60. * (*PA* 36:2HI21F)

671. FISHER, GARY M. "A Corrected Table for Determining the Significance of the Difference Between Verbal and Performance IQ's on the WAIS and the Wechsler-Bellevue." *J Clin Psychol* 16:7–8 Ja '60. * (*PA* 36:1HC07F)

672. GARFIELD, SOL L. "An Appraisal of Object Assembly on the Wechsler-Bellevue and WAIS." *J Clin Psychol* 16:8–9 Ja '60. * (*PA* 36:1HC08G)

673. HEILBRUN, ALFRED B., JR. "Specificity of Immediate Memory Function Associated With Cerebral Cortex Damage." *J Mental Sci* 106:241–5 Ja '60. * (*PA* 35:6745)

674. JUDSON, ABE J. "The Effects of Chlorpromazine on Psychological Test Scores." Abstract. *J Consult Psychol* 24:192 Ap '60. * (*PA* 34:7888)

675. KINGSLEY, LEONARD. "Wechsler-Bellevue Patterns of Psychopaths." Abstract. *J Consult Psychol* 24:373 Ag '60. * (*PA* 35:2244)

676. LANSING, KENNETH M. "Intelligence and Art Ability." *Studies Art Ed* 1:73–84 sp '60. *

677. MCFIE, JOHN. "Psychological Testing in Clinical Neurology." *J Nerv & Mental Dis* 131:383–93 N '60. * (*PA* 35:3736)

678. MORAN, LOUIS J.; GORHAM, DONALD R.; AND HOLTZMAN, WAYNE H. "Vocabulary Knowledge and Usage of Schizophrenic Subjects: A Six-Year Follow-Up." *J Abn & Social Psychol* 61:246–54 S '60. * (*PA* 35:5253)

679. MUNDY-CASTLE, A. C. "Comments on Saunders' 'Further Implications of Mundy-Castle's Correlations Between EEG and Wechsler-Bellevue Variables.'" *J Nat Inst Personnel Res* 8:102–5 D '60. * (*PA* 35:5895)

680. MUNDY-CASTLE, A. C., AND NELSON, G. K. "Intelligence, Personality and Brain Rhythms in a Socially Isolated Community." *Nature* 185:484–5 F 13 '60. *

681. O'REILLY, P. O., AND HARRISON, K. "Experimentation With an Objective Test Battery." *Can Psychiatric Assn J* 5:108–23 Ap '60. *

682. PETERS, JAMES S., III. "A Study of the Wechsler-Bellevue Verbal Scores of Negro and White Males." *J Negro Ed* 29:7–16 w '60. *

683. PLUMEAU, F.; MACHOVER, S.; AND PUZZO, F. "Wechsler-Bellevue Performances of Remitted and Unremitted Alcoholics, and Their Normal Controls." *J Consult Psychol* 24: 240 2 Jc '60. * (*PA* 35:6871)

684. RIKLAN, MANUEL; DILLER, LEONARD; WEINER, HERMAN; AND COOPER, IRVING S. "Psychological Studies on Effects of Chemosurgery of the Basal Ganglia in Parkinsonism: 1, Intellectual Functioning." *A.M.A. Arch Gen Psychiatry* 2:22–32 Ja '60. * (*PA* 34:8265)

685. SAUNDERS, D. R. "Further Implications of Mundy-Castle's Correlations Between EEG and Wechsler-Bellevue Variables." *J Nat Inst Personnel Res* 8:91–101 D '60. * (*PA* 35:5896)

686. WIGGINS, NEWTON WAYNE. *A Comparative Evaluation of the Wechsler-Bellevue Scale Performance of Selected Brain-Injured and Non-Injured Subjects.* Doctor's thesis, Indiana University (Bloomington, Ind.), 1960. (*DA* 21:2602)

687. BALTHAZAR, EARL E., AND MORRISON, DON H. "The Use of Wechsler Intelligence Scales as Diagnostic Indicators of Predominant Left-Right and Indeterminate Unilateral Brain Damage." *J Clin Psychol* 17:161–5 Ap '61. * (*PA* 38:1236)

688. BALTHAZAR, EARL E.; TODD, RONALD E.; MORRISON, DON H.; AND ZIEBELL, PETER W. "Visuoconstructive and Verbal Responses in Chronic Brain-Damaged Patients and Familial Retardates." *J Clin Psychol* 17:293–6 Jl '61. * (*PA* 38:8932)

689. BONIER, RICHARD J., AND HANLEY, CHARLES. "Handedness and Digit Symbol Performance." *J Clin Psychol* 17:286–9 Jl '61. * (*PA* 38:8444)

690. COOK, RICHARD A., AND HIRT, MICHAEL L. "Verbal and Performance IQ Discrepancies on the Wechsler Adult Intelligence Scale and Wechsler-Bellevue, Form I." *J Clin Psychol* 17:382–3 O '61. * (*PA* 38:8446)

691. COROTTO, LOREN V. "The Relation of Performance to Verbal IQ in Acting Out Juveniles." *J Psychol Studies* 12:162–6 Jl '61 [issued Mr '63]. *

692. CRADDICK, RAY A. "Wechsler-Bellevue IQ Scores of Psychopathic and Non-Psychopathic Prisoners." *J Psychol Studies* 12:167–72 Jl '61 [issued Mr '63]. *

693. CROOKES, T. G. "Wechsler's Deterioration Ratio in Clinical Practice." *J Consult Psychol* 25:234–8 Je '61. *

694. DARBES, ALEX. "A Comparison of Scores Achieved by 55 Subjects Administered the Wechsler and Binet Scales of Intelligence." *Proc W Va Acad Sci* 33:115–9 N '61. * (*PA* 36:5HD15D)

695. DIBNER, ANDREW S., AND CUMMINS, JAMES F. "Intellectual Functioning in a Group of Normal Octogenarians." *J Consult Psychol* 25:137–41 Ap '61. * (*PA* 36:4FI3–D)

696. DOEHRING, DONALD G.; REITAN, RALPH M.; AND KLØVE, HALLGRIM. "Changes in Patterns of Intelligence Test Performance Associated With Homonymous Visual Field Defects." *J Nerv & Mental Dis* 132:227–33 Mr '61. * (*PA* 36:1JF27D)

697. DUNCAN, DONN R., AND BARRETT, ALBERT M. "A Longitudinal Comparison of Intelligence Involving the Wechsler-Bellevue 1 and WAIS." *J Clin Psychol* 17:318–9 Jl '61. * (*PA* 38:8453)

698. FISHER, GARY M. "Discrepancy in Verbal and Per-

Wechsler-Bellevue Intelligence Scale

formance IQ in Adolescent Sociopaths." *J Clin Psychol* 17:60 Ja '61. * (PA 37:3214)

699. FITZHUGH, KATHLEEN B.; FITZHUGH, LOREN C.; AND REITAN, RALPH M. "Psychological Deficits in Relation to Acuteness of Brain Dysfunction." *J Consult Psychol* 25:61–6 F '61. * (PA 36:3JF61F)

700. GASTON, CHARLES O., AND DELANGE, WALTER H. "The Relationship Between Wechsler-Bellevue Digit Symbol Performance and Psychosis." *Tex Rep Biol & Med* 19:76–9 sp '61. *

701. GILGASH, CURTIS A. "Thorazine Therapy With Catatonic Schizophrenics in Relation to Wechsler Verbal and Performance Subtest Comparison." *J Clin Psychol* 17:95 Ja '61. * (PA 37:3687)

702. HILER, E. WESLEY, AND NESVIG, DAVID. "Changes in Intellectual Functions of Children in a Psychiatric Hospital." *J Consult Psychol* 25:288–92 Ag '61. * (PA 37:1495)

703. LIDDICOAT, RENEE. "A Study of Non-Institutionalized Homosexuals." *J Nat Inst Personnel Res* 8:217–49 S '61. * (PA 36:4JL17L)

704. MCFIE, JOHN. "The Effect of Education on African Performance on a Group of Intellectual Tests." *Brit J Ed Psychol* 31:232–40 N '61. * (PA 36:5HD32M)

705. MURSTEIN, BERNARD I., AND LEIPOLD, WILLIAM D. "The Role of Learning and Motor Abilities in the Wechsler-Bellevue Digit Symbol Subtest." *Ed & Psychol Meas* 21:103–12 sp '61. * (PA 36:1HE03M)

706. PAYNE, R. W. Chap. 6, "Cognitive Abnormalities," pp. 193–261. In *Handbook of Abnormal Psychology: An Experimental Approach*. Edited by H. J. Eysenck. New York: Basic Books, Inc., 1961. Pp. xvi, 816. * (PA 35:6719)

707. SUGARMAN, LOLA. "Alpha Rhythm, Perception and Intelligence." *J Nat Inst Personnel Res* 8:170–9 S '61. * (PA 36:4DG70S)

708. CASSEL, ROBERT H.; JOHNSON, ANNA P.; AND BURNS, WILLIAM H. "The Order of Tests in the Battery." *J Clin Psychol* 18:464–5 O '62. * (PA 39:5042)

709. COYNE, WILLIAM J. *The Effect of Reading Instruction and Further Education Upon the Intelligence Quotient as Measured by the Wechsler-Bellevue Scale*. Master's thesis, Cardinal Stritch College (Milwaukee, Wis.), 1962.

710. FISHER, GARY M., AND PARSONS, PATRICIA A. "The Effect of Intellectual Level on the Rate of False Positive Organic Diagnoses From the Hewson and Adolescent Ratios." *J Clin Psychol* 18:125–6 Ap '62. * (PA 38:8924)

711. FITZHUGH, KATHLEEN B.; FITZHUGH, LOREN C.; AND REITAN, RALPH M. "Relation of Acuteness of Organic Brain Dysfunction to Trail Making Test Performances." *Percept & Motor Skills* 15:399–403 O '62. * (PA 37:8142)

712. FITZHUGH, KATHLEEN B.; FITZHUGH, LOREN C.; AND REITAN, RALPH M. "Wechsler-Bellevue Comparisons in Groups With 'Chronic' and 'Current' Lateralized and Diffuse Brain Lesions." *J Consult Psychol* 26:306–10 Ag '62. * (PA 38:4544)

713. GUERTIN, WILSON H.; RABIN, ALBERT I.; FRANK, GEORGE H.; AND LADD, CLAYTON E. "Research With the Wechsler Intelligence Scales for Adults: 1955–60." *Psychol B* 59:1–26 Ja '62. * (PA 37:1203)

714. HAUSER, RUSSELL JEROME. *The Validity of the Formal and Linguistic Aspects of the Rorschach in Predicting Intelligence*. Doctor's thesis, New York University (New York, N.Y.), 1962. (DA 24:833)

715. JARVIK, LISSY F.; KALLMANN, FRANZ J.; LORGE, IRVING; AND FALEK, ARTHUR. "Longitudinal Study of Intellectual Changes in Senescent Twins," pp. 839–59. In *Social and Psychological Aspects of Aging*. Proceedings of the Fifth Congress of the International Association of Gerontology. Edited by Clark Tibbitts and Wilma Donahue. New York: Columbia University Press, 1962. Pp. xviii, 952. *

716. JARVIK, LISSY FEINGOLD. "Biological Differences in Intellectual Functioning." *Vita Hum* 5(4):195–203 '62. * (PA 38:970)

717. JARVIK, LISSY FEINGOLD; KALLMANN, FRANZ J.; AND FALEK, ARTHUR. "Intellectual Changes in Aged Twins." *J Gerontol* 17:289–94 Jl '62. * (PA 37:2952)

718. KLØVE, HALLGRIM. "The Differential Relationships of Psychological Test Results to Electroencephalographic Criteria in Older and Younger Age Groups," pp. 873–9. In *Social and Psychological Aspects of Aging*. Proceedings of the Fifth Congress of the International Association of Gerontology. Edited by Clark Tibbitts and Wilma Donahue. New York: Columbia University Press, 1962. Pp. xviii, 952. *

719. KLØVE, HALLGRIM, AND FITZHUGH, KATHLEEN B. "The Relationship of Differential EEG Patterns to the Distribution of Wechsler-Bellevue Scores in a Chronic Epileptic Population." *J Clin Psychol* 18:334–7 Jl '62. * (PA 39:2475)

720. LASKOWITZ, DAVID. "Wechsler-Bellevue Performance of Adolescent Heroin Addicts." *J Psychol Studies* 13:49–59 Mr '62 [issued N '63]. *

721. LIDDICOAT, RENEE, AND ROBERTS, A. O. H. "Interim Standardization of the South African Version of the Wechsler-Bellevue Adult Intelligence Test." *Psychologia Africana* 9:273–85 '62. * (PA 37:4957)

722. MCFARLAND, ROBERT L.; NELSON, CHARLES L.; AND ROSSI, ASCANIO M. "Prediction of Participation in Group Psychotherapy From Measures of Intelligence and Verbal Behavior." *Psychol Rep* 11:291–8 Ag '62. * (PA 37:5190)

723. MANNE, SIGMUND H.; KANDEL, ARTHUR; AND ROSENTHAL, DAVID. "Differences Between Performance IQ and Verbal IQ in a Severely Sociopathic Population." *J Clin Psychol* 18:73–7 Ja '62. * (PA 38:9008)

724. MATTHEWS, CHARLES G.; GUERTIN, WILSON H.; AND REITAN, RALPH M. "Wechsler-Bellevue Subtest Mean Rank Orders in Diverse Diagnostic Groups." *Psychol Rep* 11:3–9 Ag '62. * (PA 37:4944)

725. MUNDY-CASTLE, A. C., AND NELSON, G. K. "A Neuropsychological Study of the Knysna Forest Workers." *Psychologia Africana* 9:240–72 '62. * (PA 37:4822)

726. NICKOLS, JOHN E., JR. "Brief Forms of the Wechsler Intelligence Scales for Research." *J Clin Psychol* 18:167 Ap '62. * (PA 38:8500)

727. REITAN, RALPH M., AND REED, HOMER B. C., JR. "Consistencies in Wechsler-Bellevue Mean Values in Brain-Damaged Groups." *Percept & Motor Skills* 15:119–21 Ag '62. * (PA 37:5046)

728. RIEGEL, KLAUS F., AND RIEGEL, RUTH M. "Analysis of Differences in Test and Item Difficulty Between Young and Old Adults." *J Gerontol* 17:97–105 Ja '62. * (PA 36:5FI97R)

729. RIEGEL, RUTH M., AND RIEGEL, KLAUS F. "A Comparison and Reinterpretation of Factor Structures of the W-B, the WAIS, and the HAWIE on Aged Persons." *J Consult Psychol* 26:31–7 F '62. * (PA 37:4965)

730. SHAPIRO, M. B.; BRIERLEY, J.; SLATER, P.; AND BEECH, H. R. "Experimental Studies of a Perceptual Anomoly: 7, A New Explanation." *J Mental Sci* 108:655–68 S '62. * (PA 38:2989)

731. ANGERS, WILLIAM P. "Patterns of Abilities and Capacities in the Epileptic." *J Genetic Psychol* 103:59–66 S '63. *

732. BALTHAZAR, EARL E. "The Alleged Refractory Nature of Verbal Subtest Scores in Brain-Damaged Cases." *Am J Mental Def* 67:871–8 My '63. * (PA 38:1235)

733. BALTHAZAR, EARL E. "Cerebral Unilateralization in Chronic Epileptic Cases: The Wechsler Object Assembly Subtest." *J Clin Psychol* 19:169–71 Ap '63. * (PA 39:5627)

734. BERKOWITZ, BERNARD, AND GREEN, RUSSEL F. "Changes in Intellect With Age: 1, Longitudinal Study of Wechsler-Bellevue Scores." *J Genetic Psychol* 103:3–21 S '63. *

735. BURNETT, A.; BEACH, H. D.; AND SULLIVAN, A. M. "Intelligence in a Restricted Environment." *Can Psychologist* 4:126–36 O '63. * (PA 38:6050)

736. CAPUTO, DANIEL V.; EDMONSTON, WILLIAM E., JR.; L'ABATE, LUCIANO; AND RONDBERG, SAMUEL R. "Type of Brain Damage and Intellectual Functioning in Children." Abstract. *J Consult Psychol* 27:184 Ap '63. *

737. COPPINGER, NEIL W.; BORTNER, RAYMAN W.; AND SAUCER, RAYFORD T. "A Factor Analysis of Psychological Deficit." *J Genetic Psychol* 103:23–43 S '63. *

738. CRONHOLM, BORJE, AND SCHALLING, DAISY. "Intellectual Deterioration After Focal Brain Injury." *Arch Surgery* 86:670–87 Ap '63. *

739. FITZHUGH, KATHLEEN B.; FITZHUGH, LOREN C.; AND REITAN, RALPH M. "Effects of 'Chronic' and 'Current' Lateralized and Non-Lateralized Cerebral Lesions Upon Trail Making Test Performances." *J Nerv & Mental Dis* 137:82–7 Jl '63. * (PA 38:3755)

740. GIANNELL, A. STEVEN, AND FREEBURNE, CECIL M. "The Comparative Validity of the WAIS and the Stanford-Binet With College Freshmen." *Ed & Psychol Meas* 23:557–67 au '63. * (PA 38:6057)

741. KLØVE, HALLGRIM, AND WHITE, PHILIP T. "The Relationship of Degree of Electroencephalographic Abnormality to the Distribution of Wechsler-Bellevue Scores." *Neurology* 13:423–30 My '63. *

742. MATTHEWS, CHARLES G., AND REITAN, RALPH M. "Relationship of Differential Abstraction Ability Levels to Psychological Test Performances in Mentally Retarded Subjects." *Am J Mental Def* 68:235–44 S '63. * (PA 38:6430)

743. NEURINGER, CHARLES. "The Form Equivalence Between the Wechsler-Bellevue Intelligence Scale, Form 1 and the Wechsler Adult Intelligence Scale." *Ed & Psychol Meas* 23:755–63 w '63. * (PA 38:8427)

744. PARSONS, OSCAR A.; MORRIS, FREDA; AND DENNY, J. PETER. "Agitation, Anxiety, Brain-Damage and Perceptual-Motor Deficit." *J Clin Psychol* 19:267–71 Jl '63. *

745. PRENTICE, NORMAN M., AND KELLY, FRANCIS J. "Intelligence and Delinquency: A Reconsideration." *J Social Psychol* 60:327–37 Ag '63. * (PA 38:4585)

746. REED, HOMER B. C., JR., AND REITAN, R. M. "Intelligence Test Performances of Brain Damaged Subjects With Lateralized Motor Deficits." *J Consult Psychol* 27:102–6 Ap '63. * (PA 37:8145)

747. REED, HOMER B. C., JR., AND REITAN, RALPH M. "Changes in Psychological Test Performance Associated With the Normal Aging Process." *J Gerontol* 18:271–4 Jl '63. *(PA 38:4109)

748. SILVERSTEIN, A. B.; FISHER, GARY M.; AND OWENS, EARL P. "The Altitude Quotient as an Index of Intellectual Potential: 3, Three Studies of Predictive Validity." *Am J Mental Def* 67:611–6 Ja '63. * (PA 37:7026)

For reviews by Murray Aborn and William D. Altus, see 4:361; for a review by Robert I.

Watson, see 3:298; for a review by F. L. Wells, see 40:1429 (2 excerpts); for excerpts from related book reviews, see 5:B332, 4:362, 3:299–301, and 40:B1121.

[540]

Wechsler Intelligence Scale for Children. Ages 5–15; 1949; downward extension of Form 2 of *Wechsler-Bellevue Intelligence Scale;* also called WISC; 15 scores: verbal (information, comprehension, arithmetic, similarities, vocabulary, digit span-optional, total), performance (picture completion, picture arrangement, block design, object assembly, mazes-optional, coding, total), total; individual; 1 form; record booklet (6 pages, revised slightly in 1958 but dated 1949); manual (117 pages); $25 per set of testing materials, 25 record booklets, and manual; $2.50 per 25 record booklets; $1.35 per 25 WISC Maze Tests, an alternate subtest which may be used in place of Coding; $3 per manual; postpaid; Spanish edition available; (40–60) minutes; David Wechsler; Psychological Corporation. * (Australian edition: Australian Council for Educational Research.)

REFERENCES

1–22. See 4:363.
23–133. See 5:416.
134. CHALMERS, JAMES MCNISH. *An Investigation Into the Nature of the Results Obtained on the WISC by Mentally Superior Children.* Master's thesis, University of Alberta (Edmonton, Alta., Canada), 1953.
135. DENTON, L. R. "Intelligence Test Performance and Personality Differences in a Group of Visually Handicapped Children." *B Maritime Psychol Ass'n* 3:47–50 D '54. * (*PA* 29:7786)
136. HUNTRESS, DAN W. *Wechsler Intelligence Scale for Children and Associative Learning Disability.* Master's thesis, Illinois Normal University (Normal, Ill.), 1955.
137. HARRIS, RILDA. "A Comparative Study of Two Groups of Boys, Delinquent and Non-Delinquent, on the Basis of Their Wechsler and Rorschach Test Performances." *B Maritime Psychol Assn* 6:21–8 sp '57. * (*PA* 33:4295)
138. LEWIS, LENA L. "The Relation of Measured Mental Ability to School Marks and Academic Survival in the Texas School for the Blind." *Int J Ed Blind* 6:56–60 Mr '57. *
139. INDOW, TAROW. "The Mental Growth Curve Defined on the Absolute Scale: Comparison of Japanese and Foreign Data." *Jap Psychol Res* 1:35–48 Jl '58. * (*PA* 34:2725)
140. MAYER, ROBERT W. "A Study of the STEP Reading, SCAT and WISC Tests, and School Grades." *Reading Teach* 12:117+ D '58. * (*PA* 34:3441)
141. MIELE, JOHN ANTHONY. *Sex Differences in Intelligence: The Relationship of Sex to Intelligence as Measured by the Wechsler Adult Intelligence Scale and the Wechsler Intelligence Scale for Children.* Doctor's thesis, New York University (New York, N.Y.), 1958. (*DA* 18:2213)
142. NELSON, CALVIN CLAYTON. *A Comparison of Retarded and Normal Children With Respect to Alexander's "F" Factor.* Doctor's thesis, University of Oregon (Eugene, Ore.), 1958. (*DA* 19:1015)
143. SCHACHTER, FRANCES FUCHS, AND APGAR, VIRGINIA. "Comparison of Preschool Stanford-Binet and School-Age WISC IQs." *J Ed Psychol* 49:320–3 D '58. * (*PA* 36:2HD20S)
144. BAROFF, GEORGE S. "WISC Patterning in Endogenous Mental Deficiency." *Am J Mental Def* 64:482–5 N '59. * (*PA* 34:7995)
145. BENISKOS, JEAN-MARIE. *WISC Patterns and Reading Achievement.* Doctor's thesis, University of Ottawa (Ottawa, Ont., Canada), 1959. (Abstract: *Can Psychologist* 1:112)
146. BRIDGES, CECIL. "Nomographs for Computing the 'Validity' of WISC or Wechsler-Bellevue Short Forms." *J Consult Psychol* 23:453–4 O '59. * (*PA* 34:5576)
147. CHAMBERS, JACK A. "Preliminary Screening Methods in the Identification of Intellectually Superior Children." *Excep Child* 26:145–50 N '59. * (*PA* 35:3249)
148. COHEN, JACOB. "The Factorial Structure of the WISC at Ages 7-6, 10-6, and 13-6." *J Consult Psychol* 23:285–99 Ag '59. *
149. FINLEY, CARMEN, AND THOMPSON, JACK. "Sex Differences in Intelligence of Educable Mentally Retarded Children." *Calif J Ed Res* 10:167–70 S '59. * (*PA* 34:8002)
150. JILLSON, RICHMOND P. *An Investigation of the Clinical Possibilities of Certain Abbreviated Forms of the Wechsler Intelligence Scale for Children.* Master's thesis, Boston University (Boston, Mass.), 1959.
151. JONES, S. *A Statistical Study of the Wechsler Intelligence Scale for Children.* Doctor's thesis, University of London (London, England), 1959.
152. LARR, ALFRED L., AND CAIN, EARL R. "Measurement of Native Learning Abilities of Deaf Children." *Volta R* 61: 160–2 Ap '59. *
153. LEVINSON, BORIS M. "A Comparison of the Performance of Bilingual and Monolingual Native Born Jewish Preschool Children of Traditional Parentage on Four Intelligence Tests." *J Clin Psychol* 15:74–6 Ja '59. * (*PA* 34:2729)
154. LEVINSON, BORIS M. "Traditional Jewish Cultural Values and Performance on the Wechsler Tests." *J Ed Psychol* 50:177–81 Ag '59. * (*PA* 35:2059)
155. MAXWELL, A. E. "A Factor Analysis of the Wechsler Intelligence Scale for Children." *Brit J Ed Psychol* 29:237–41 N '59. *
156. MAXWELL, A. E. "Tables to Facilitate the Comparison of Sub-Test Scores on the WISC." *J Clin Psychol* 15:293–5 Jl '59. *
157. ROGGE, HAROLD JOHN. *A Study of the Relationships of Reading Achievement to Certain Other Factors in a Population of Delinquent Boys.* Doctor's thesis, University of Minnesota (Minneapolis, Minn.), 1959. (*DA* 20:4037)
158. SHELDON, M. STEPHEN, AND GARTON, JEANETTE. "A Note on 'A WISC Profile for Retarded Readers.'" *Alberta J Ed Res* 5:264–7 D '59. * (*PA* 35:771)
159. SIMPSON, WILLIAM H., AND BRIDGES, CECIL C., JR. "A Short Form of the Wechsler Intelligence Scale for Children." *J Clin Psychol* 15:424 O '59. * (*PA* 36:1HC25S)
160. STOFFEL, CLARENCE M., JR. *A Study of the Wechsler Intelligence Scale for Children Subtest Scores of Homeless and Wayward Boys.* Master's thesis, Creighton University (Omaha, Neb.), 1959.
161. WHITE, ARDEN JUNIOR. *A Comparison of the Flanagan Aptitude Classification Tests With the Wechsler Adult Intelligence Scale, the School and College Ability Test, and Three Other Measures of Mental Variables at the High School Level.* Doctor's research study No. 1, Colorado State College (Greeley, Colo.), 1959.
162. WINITZ, HARRIS. "Relationships Between Language and Nonlanguage Measures of Kindergarten Children." *J Speech & Hearing Res* 2:387–91 D '59. * (*PA* 34:5896)
163. ALPER, ARTHUR EUGENE. *An Analysis of the Wechsler Intelligence Scale for Children With Institutionalized Mental Defectives.* Doctor's thesis, University of Florida (Tallahassee, Fla.), 1960. (*DA* 20:4711)
164. BURNS, ROBERT C. "Behavioral Differences Between Brain-Injured and Brain-Deficit Children Grouped According to Neuropathological Types." *Am J Mental Def* 65:326–34 N '60. * (*PA* 35:3732)
165. BURT, CYRIL. "The Factor Analysis of the Wechsler Scale." *Brit J Stat Psychol* 13:82–7 My '60. *
166. CARSON, ARNOLD S., AND RABIN, A. I. "Verbal Comprehension and Communication in Negro and White Children." *J Ed Psychol* 51:47–51 Ap '60. * (*PA* 35:2049)
167. DOCKRELL, W. B. "The Use of Wechsler Intelligence Scale for Children in the Diagnosis of Retarded Readers." *Alberta J Ed Res* 6:86–91 Je '60. * (*PA* 36:2KF86D)
168. FIELD, J. G. "Two Types of Tables for Use With Wechsler's Intelligence Scales." *J Clin Psychol* 16:3–7 Ja '60. * (*PA* 36:1HC03F)
169. FISHER, GARY M. "A Cross-Validation of Baroff's WISC Patterning in Endogenous Mental Deficiency." *Am J Mental Def* 65:349–50 N '60. * (*PA* 35:3406)
170. FROST, BARRY P. "An Application of the Method of Extreme Deviations to the Wechsler Intelligence Scale for Children." *J Clin Psychol* 16:420 O '60. * (*PA* 37:3216)
171. HAFNER, A. JACK; POLLIE, DONALD M.; AND WAPNER, IRWIN. "The Relationship Between the CMAS and WISC Functioning." *J Clin Psychol* 16:322–3 Jl '60. * (*PA* 36:2FC22H)
172. HIRST, LYNNE SCHELLBERG. "The Usefulness of a Two-Way Analysis of WISC Subtests in the Diagnosis of Remedial Reading Problems." *J Exp Ed* 29:153–60 D '60. *
173. HOLLAND, WILLIAM R. "Language Barrier as an Educational Problem of Spanish-Speaking Children." *Excep Child* 27:42–50 S '60. *
174. JACKSON, M. A. "The Factor Analysis of the Wechsler Scale." *Brit J Stat Psychol* 13:79–82 My '60. *
175. KILMAN, BEVERLY A., AND FISHER, GARY M. "An Evaluation of the Finley-Thompson Abbreviated Form of the WISC for Undifferentiated, Brain-Damaged and Functional Retardates." *Am J Mental Def* 64:742–6 Ja '60. * (*PA* 35:1030)
176. KIMBRELL, DON L. "Comparison of Peabody, WISC, and Academic Achievement Scores Among Educable Mental Defectives." *Psychol Rep* 7:502 D '60. * (*PA* 35:2554)
177. LEVINSON, BORIS M. "Subcultural Variations in Verbal and Performance Ability at the Elementary School Level." *J Genetic Psychol* 97:149–60 S '60. * (*PA* 35:6404)
178. LITTELL, WILLIAM M. "The Wechsler Intelligence Scale for Children: Review of a Decade of Research." *Psychol B* 57:132–56 Mr '60. * (*PA* 34:7353)
179. LUCITO, LEONARD, AND GALLAGHER, JAMES. "Intellectual Patterns of Highly Gifted Children on the WISC." *Peabody J Ed* 38:131–6 N '60. * (*PA* 35:4860)
180. MAXWELL, A. E. "Discrepancies in the Variances of Test Results for Normal and Neurotic Children." *Brit J Stat Psychol* 13:165–72 N '60. * (*PA* 36:3HD65M)

181. MOLLER, HELLA. *Stuttering, Predelinquent, and Adjusted Boys: A Comparative Analysis of Personality Characteristics as Measured by the WISC and the Rorschach Test.* Doctor's thesis, Boston University (Boston, Mass.), 1960. (DA 21:1461)
182. MUKHERJEE, BISHWA NATH. "A Report on the Preliminary Item-Analysis of a Tryout Form of WISC for Gujerati Children." *Psychol Studies* 5:118–26 Jl '60. * (PA 38:2672)
183. OGDON, DONALD P. "WISC IQs for the Mentally Retarded." *J Consult Psychol* 24:187–8 Ap '60. * (PA 34:8014)
184. ROBECK, MILDRED C. "Subtest Patterning of Problem Readers on WISC." *Calif J Ed Res* 11:110–5 My '60. * (PA 35:7034)
185. SALVATI, SAVERIO R. *A Comparison of WISC I.Q.'s and Altitude Scores as Predictors of Learning Ability of Mentally Retarded Subjects.* Doctor's thesis, New York University (New York, N.Y.), 1960. (DA 21:2370)
186. SCHWARTZ, LEWIS, AND LEVITT. EUGENE E. "Short-Forms of the Wechsler Intelligence Scale for Children in the Educable, Non-Institutionalized, Mentally Retarded." *J Ed Psychol* 51:187–90 Ag '60. * (PA 35:3786)
187. SCOTT, EDWARD M. "Psychological Examination of Quadruplets." *Psychol Rep* 6:281–2 Ap '60. * (PA 35:5980)
188. STUMPF, JOHN C. *The Correlation Between the Wechsler Intelligence Scale for Children and Reading Scores From the Stanford Achievement Test.* Master's thesis, University of Utah (Salt Lake City, Utah), 1960.
189. TALBOT, SHELAGH C. *A Cross Validation Study With the Wechsler Intelligence Scale for Children of the Diagnostic Signs for the Syndrome Sociopathy.* Master's thesis, Drake University (Des Moines, Iowa), 1960.
190. WEISE, PHILLIP. "Current Uses of Binet and Wechsler Tests by School Psychologists in California." *Calif J Ed Res* 11:73–8 Mr '60. * (PA 35:7098)
191. ALIMENA, BENJAMIN. "A Note on Norms for Scatter Analysis on the Wechsler Intelligence Scales." *J Clin Psychol* 17:61 Ja '61. * (PA 37:3103)
192. ANASTASI, ANNE. *Psychological Testing, Second Edition,* p. 315. New York: Macmillan Co., 1961. Pp. xiii, 657. * (PA 36:1HA57A)
193. BALTHAZAR, EARL E., AND MORRISON, DON H. "The Use of Wechsler Intelligence Scales as Diagnostic Indicators of Predominant Left-Right and Indeterminate Unilateral Brain Damage." *J Clin Psychol* 17:161–5 Ap '61. * (PA 38:1236)
194. BAUMEISTER, ALFRED A. *The Dimensions of Ability for Retardates on the Wechsler Intelligence Scale for Children.* Doctor's thesis, George Peabody College for Teachers (Nashville, Tenn.), 1961.
195. COROTTO, LOREN V. "The Relation of Performance to Verbal IQ in Acting Out Juveniles." *J Psychol Studies* 12: 162–6 Jl '61 [issued Mr '63]. *
196. DARLEY, FREDERIC L., AND WINITZ, HARRIS. "Comparison of Male and Female Kindergarten Children on the WISC." *J Genetic Psychol* 99:41–9 S '61. * (PA 36:FE41D)
197. DUNSDON, M. I., AND ROBERTS, J. A. FRASER. Chap. 3, "A Study of the Performance of 2000 Children on Four Vocabulary Tests," pp. 41–76. In *Stoke Park Studies: Mental Subnormality (Second Series): World Mental Health Year Memorial Volume.* Edited by J. Jancar. Bristol, England: John Wright & Sons Ltd., 1961. Pp. x, 135. *
198. ENBURG, RICHARD; ROWLEY, VINTON N.; AND STONE, BETH. "Short Forms of the WISC for Use With Emotionally Disturbed Children." *J Clin Psychol* 17:280–4 Jl '61. * (PA 38:8454)
199. ESTES, BETSY WORTH; CURTIN, MARY ELLEN; DEBURGER, ROBERT A.; AND DENNY, CHARLOTTE. "Relationships Between 1960 Stanford-Binet, 1937 Stanford-Binet, WISC, Raven, and Draw-A-Man." *J Consult Psychol* 25:388–91 O '61. * (PA 37:3127)
200. FISHER, GARY M. "The Altitude Quotient as an Index of Intellectual Potential: 2, WISC Data for Familial and Undifferentiated Mental Retardates." *J Psychol Studies* 12:126–7 My '61. *
201. GALLAGHER, JAMES J., AND LUCITO, LEONARD J. "Intellectual Patterns of Gifted Compared With Average and Retarded." *Excep Child* 27:479–82 My '61. * (PA 36:4KE79G)
202. GOODENOUGH, DONALD R., AND KARP, STEPHEN A. "Field Dependence and Intellectual Functioning." *J Abn & Social Psychol* 63:241–6 S '61. * (PA 37:1214)
203. HOPKINS, KENNETH D., AND MICHAEL, WILLIAM B. "The Diagnostic Use of WISC Subtest Patterns." *Calif J Ed Res* 12:116–7+ My '61. * (PA 36:3HD16H)
204. HUNT, DENNIS. *The Comparative Performance of a Ten-Year-Old Group of Children on the Wechsler Intelligence Scale for Children and the Revised Stanford-Binet Scale of Intelligence, Form L-M.* Master's thesis, University of Saskatchewan (Saskatoon, Sask., Canada), 1961.
205. KALLOS, GEORGE L.; GRABOW, JOHN M.; AND GUARINO, EUGENE A. "The WISC Profile of Disabled Readers." *Personnel & Guid J* 39:476–8 F '61. * (PA 35:7084)
206. LEVINSON, BORIS M. "Subcultural Values and IQ Stability." *J Genetic Psychol* 98:69–82 Mr '61. * (PA 35:6405)
207. MCCARTHY, DOROTHEA. "Administration of Digit Symbol and Coding Subtests of the WAIS and WISC to Left-Handed Subjects." *Psychol Rep* 8:407–8 Je '61. * (PA 36: 2HD07M)
208. MARKS, JOHN B., AND KLAHN, JAMES E. "Verbal and Perceptual Components in WISC Performance and Their Relation to Social Class." Abstract. *J Consult Psychol* 25:273 Je '61. *
209. MAXWELL, A. E. "Discrepancies Between the Pattern of Abilities for Normal and Neurotic Children." *J Mental Sci* 107:300–7 Mr '61. * (PA 36:2FF00M)
210. MAXWELL, A. E. "Inadequate Reporting of Normative Test Data." *J Clin Psychol* 17:99–101 Ja '61. * (PA 37:3116)
211. NEVILLE, DONALD. "A Comparison of the WISC Patterns of Male Retarded and Non-Retarded Readers." *J Ed Res* 54:195–7 Ja '61. * (PA 35:6842)
212. PAVLOS, ANDREW JOHN. "Sex Differences Among Rural Negro Children on the Wechsler Intelligence Scale for Children." *Proc W Va Acad Sci* 33:109–14 N '61. * (PA 36: 5FE09P)
213. PELZ, KURT S.; AMES, LOUISE B.; AND PIKE, FRANCES. "Measurement of Psychologic Function in Geriatric Patients." *J Am Geriatrics Soc* 9:740–54 S '61. *
214. PINNEAU, SAMUEL R. Chap. 12, "Wechsler Intelligence Scale for Children," pp. 106–11. In his *Changes in Intelligence Quotient: Infancy to Maturity: New Insights From the Berkeley Growth Study With Implications for the Stanford-Binet Scales and Applications to Professional Practice.* Boston, Mass.: Houghton Mifflin Co., 1961. Pp. xi, 233. * (PA 37:6706)
215. REGER, ROGER, AND DAWSON, ANTOINETTE. "The Use of Psychological Tests to Predict Manual Abilities in Mentally Retarded Boys." *Am J Occup Ther* 15:204+ S–O '61. * (PA 36:5JI04R)
216. ROWLEY, VINTON N. "Analysis of the WISC Performance of Brain Damaged and Emotionally Disturbed Children." Abstract. *J Consult Psychol* 25:553 D '61. * (PA 37:5382)
217. SAWA, HIDEHISA. "Interference of Intelligence With Temperament." *Psychologia* 4:235–41 D '61. * (PA 38:974)
218. SMITH, BESSIE S. "The Relative Merits of Certain Verbal and Non-Verbal Tests at the Second-Grade Level." *J Clin Psychol* 17:53–4 Ja '61. * (PA 37:3595)
219. STOUT, DONALD H. *The Wechsler Intelligence Scale for Children and the Wechsler Adult Intelligence Scale: A Comparison Study.* Master's thesis, Fresno State College (Fresno, Calif.), 1961.
220. WILLIAMS, JESSIE M. "Children Who Break Down in Foster Homes: A Psychological Study of Patterns of Personality Growth in Grossly Deprived Children." *J Child Psychol & Psychiatry* 2:5–20 Je '61. * (PA 36:2FF05W)
221. BAUMEISTER, ALFRED, AND BARTLETT, CLAUDE J. "Further Factorial Investigations of WISC Performance of Mental Defectives." *Am J Mental Def* 67:257–61 S '62. * (PA 37: 3557)
222. BAUMEISTER, ALFRED A., AND BARTLETT, CLAUDE J. "A Comparison of the Factor Structure of Normals and Retardates on the WISC." *Am J Mental Def* 66:641–6 Ja '62. * (PA 36:4JI41B)
223. BELLUOMINI, HENRY M. *Wechsler Intelligence Scale for Children: Predicting Success in Corrective Reading.* Master's thesis, Sacramento State College (Sacramento, Calif.), 1962.
224. BORTNER, MORTON, AND BIRCH, HERBERT G. "Perceptual and Perceptual-Motor Dissociation in Cerebral Palsied Children." *J Nerv & Mental Dis* 134:103–8 F '62. * (PA 37:1667)
225. BRILL, RICHARD G. "The Relationship of Wechsler IQ's to Academic Achievement Among Deaf Students." *Excep Child* 28:315–21 F '62. * (PA 37:1609)
226. CLAWSON, AILEEN. "Relationship of Psychological Tests to Cerebral Disorders in Children: A Pilot Study." *Psychol Rep* 10:187–90 F '62. * (PA 37:1655)
227. FREEMAN, FRANK S. *Theory and Practice of Psychological Testing, Third Edition,* pp. 269–79, 330–8. New York: Holt, Rinehart & Winston, Inc., 1962. Pp. xix, 697. *
228. FROST, BARRY P., AND FROST, RUTH. "The Pattern of WISC Scores in a Group of Juvenile Sociopaths." *J Clin Psychol* 18:354–5 Jl '62. * (PA 39:2603)
229. GAINER, W. L. "The Ability of the WISC Subtests to Discriminate Between Boys and Girls of Average Intelligence." *Calif J Ed Res* 13:9–16 Ja '62. * (PA 36:5HD09G)
230. GAINER, WILLIAM LEE. *An Abbreviated Form of the Wechsler Intelligence Scale for Children.* Doctor's thesis, University of the Pacific (Stockton, Calif.), 1962. (DA 23:690)
231. HIMELSTEIN, PHILIP, AND HERNDON, JAMES D. "Comparison of the WISC and Peabody Picture Vocabulary Test With Emotionally Disturbed Children." *J Clin Psychol* 18:82 Ja '62. * (PA 38:8420)
232. JOHNSON, OLIVE L. *A Study of Scaled Scores on the Wechsler Intelligence Scale for Children in Relation to Organic Impairment Affecting Language Acquisition.* Master's thesis, Northwestern University (Evanston, Ill.), 1962.
233. JONES, SHEILA. "The Wechsler Intelligence Scale for Children Applied to a Sample of London Primary School Children." *Brit J Ed Psychol* 32:119–32 Je '62. * (PA 37: 2872)
234. LAVOS, GEORGE. "W.I.S.C. Psychometric Patterns Among Deaf Children." *Volta R* 64:547–52 N '62. *
235. O'NEIL, W. M. "The Stability of the Main Pattern of Abilities With Changing Age." *Austral J Psychol* 14:1–8 Ap '62. * (PA 38:6025)
236. OSBORNE, R. TRAVIS, AND ALLEN, JERRY. "Validity of Short Forms of the WISC for Mental Retardates." *Psychol Rep* 11:167–70 Ag '62. * (PA 37:4945)

Wechsler Intelligence Scale for Children

237. PELZ, KURT; PIKE, FRANCES; AND AMES, LOUISE B. "A Proposed Battery of Childhood Tests for Discriminating Between Different Levels of Intactness of Function in Elderly Subjects." *J Genetic Psychol* 100:23-40 Mr '62. * (*PA* 37:975)
238. RAVENETTE, A. T., AND KAHN, J. H. "Intellectual Ability of Disturbed Children in a Working-Class Area." *Brit J Social & Clin Psychol* 1:208-12 O '62. * (*PA* 37:5456)
239. REGER, ROGER. "Repeated Measurements With the WISC." *Psychol Rep* 11:418 O '62. * (*PA* 37:7987)
240. ROBECK, MILDRED C. "Children Who Show Undue Tension When Reading: A Group Diagnosis." *Int Rdg Assn Conf Proc* 7:133-8 '62. *
241. ROHRS, FREDERICK W., AND HAWORTH, MARY R. "The 1960 Stanford-Binet, WISC, and Goodenough Tests With Mentally Retarded Children." *Am J Mental Def* 66:853-9 My '62. * (*PA* 37:1704)
242. SHAFFER, JOHN W. "A Specific Cognitive Deficit Observed in Gonadal Aplasia (Turner's Syndrome)." *J Clin Psychol* 18:403-6 O '62. * (*PA* 39:5565)
243. SHIPE, DOROTHY M. *Discrepancies Between the Peabody Picture Vocabulary Test and the WISC as Related to Emotional Disturbance in Children of Retarded and Normal Intelligence.* Doctor's thesis, George Peabody College for Teachers (Nashville, Tenn.), 1962. (*DA* 23:3984)
244. SHORE, MILTON F. "The Utilization of the Patient-Examiner Relationship in Intelligence Testing of Children." *J Proj Tech* 26:239-43 Je '62. *
245. SIEGMAN, ARON WOLFE. "A Cross-Cultural Investigation of the Relationship Between Religiosity, Ethnic Prejudice and Authoritarianism." *Psychol Rep* 11:419-24 O '62. * (*PA* 37:7936)
246. TEAHAN, JOHN E., AND DREWS, ELIZABETH M. "A Comparison of Northern and Southern Negro Children on the WISC." *J Consult Psychol* 26:292 Je '62. * (*PA* 38:966)
247. THOMPSON, JACK M., AND FINLEY, CARMEN J. "A Further Comparison of the Intellectual Patterns of Gifted and Mentally Retarded Children." *Excep Child* 28:379-81 Mr '62. *
248. THOMPSON, JACK M., AND FINLEY, CARMEN J. "The Validation of an Abbreviated Wechsler Intelligence Scale for Children for Use With the Educable Mentally Retarded." *Ed & Psychol Meas* 22:539-42 au '62. * (*PA* 37:4970)
249. THRONE, FRANCES M.; SCHULMAN, JEROME L.; AND KASPAR, JOSEPH C. "Reliability and Stability of the Wechsler Intelligence Scale for Children for a Group of Mentally Retarded Boys." *Am J Mental Def* 67:455-7 N '62. * (*PA* 37:5421)
250. VIITAMÄKI, R. OLAVI. *Psychoses in Children: A Psychological Follow-Up Study.* Annals of the Finnish Academy of Science and Letters, Series B, Vol. 125, Part 2. Helsinki, Finland: Suomalainen Tiedeakatemia, Academia Scientiarum Fennica, 1962. Pp. 52. * (*PA* 39:2650)
251. WEMPEN, EDITH H. *A Comparative Study of WISC Subtests for Achievers and Underachievers.* Master's thesis, Chico State College (Chico, Calif.), 1962.
252. WIGHT, BYRON W., AND SANDRY, MARTIN. "A Short Form of the Wechsler Intelligence Scale for Children." *J Clin Psychol* 18:166 Ap '62. * (*PA* 38:8511)
253. WILK, WALTER S. *A Comparative Study of the Wechsler Intelligence Scale for Children and the Revised Form of the Stanford-Binet Intelligence Scale.* Master's thesis, Southern Connecticut State College (New Haven, Conn.), 1962.
254. WUNDERLIN, ROBERT J., AND MCPHERSON, MARION WHITE. "Sensitivity to Imbalance in Normal and Anoxic Damaged Children." *J Clin Psychol* 18:410-3 O '62. *
255. BAUMEISTER, ALFRED A.; BARTLETT, CLAUDE J.; AND HAWKINS, WILLIAM F. "Stimulus Trace as a Predictor of Performance." *Am J Mental Def* 67:726-9 Mr '63. * (*PA* 38:1255)
256. BELDOCH, MICHAEL. "Applicability of the Norms of the Wechsler Intelligence Scale for Children to Five-Year-Olds." *J Consult Psychol* 27:263-4 Je '63. * (*PA* 38:950)
257. CAPUTO, DANIEL V.; EDMONSTON, WILLIAM E., JR.; L'ABATE, LUCIANO; AND RONDBERG, SAMUEL R. "Type of Brain Damage and Intellectual Functioning in Children." Abstract. *J Consult Psychol* 27:184 Ap '63. *
258. CHODORKOFF, JOAN, AND WHITTEN, CHARLES F. "Intellectual Status of Children With Sickle Cell Anemia." *J Pediatrics* 63:29-35 Jl '63. *
259. COHEN, THEODORE B. "Prediction of Underachievement in Kindergarten Children." *Arch Gen Psychiatry* 9:444-50 N '63. * (*PA* 38:8040)
260. COLEMAN, JAMES C. "Stability of Intelligence Test Scores in Learning Disorders." *J Clin Psychol* 19:295-8 Jl '63. *
261. COLEMAN, JAMES C., AND RASOF, BEATRICE. "Intellectual Factors in Learning Disorders." *Percept & Motor Skills* 16:139-52 F '63. * (*PA* 38:1377)
262. GRAHAM, CONRAD. "Differential Marking of Two Vocabulary Tests." *Psychol Rep* 12:421-2 Ap '63. * (*PA* 38:4275)
263. JURJEVICH, RATIBOR. "An Analysis of the Altitude IQs of Delinquent Girls." *J General Psychol* 69:221-6 O '63. * (*PA* 39:1779)
264. JURJEVICH, RATIBOR. "An Evaluation of the Henmon-Nelson Group IQ Test With Delinquent Girls." *J General Psychol* 69:227-33 O '63. * (*PA* 39:1778)
265. LANDRUM, JACK PORTER. *A Study of the WISC Performance of Under-Achievers in Comparison to Average-Achievers and Over-Achievers.* Doctor's thesis, University of Colorado (Boulder, Colo.), 1963. (*DA* 23:4606)
266. LESSING, ELISE ELKINS, AND LESSING, JOHN CURTIS. "WISC Subtest Variability and Validity of WISC IQ." *J Clin Psychol* 19:92-5 Ja '63. * (*PA* 39:1746)
267. MCHUGH, ANN F. "WISC Performance in Neurotic and Conduct Disturbances." *J Clin Psychol* 19:423-4 O '63. *
268. MAHAN, THOMAS W., JR. "Diagnostic Consistency and Prediction: A Note on Graduate Student Skills." *Personnel & Guid J* 42:364-7 D '63. * (*PA* 39:2880)
269. MOED, GEORGE; WIGHT, BYRON W.; AND JAMES, PATRICIA. "Interest Correlations of the Wechsler Intelligence Scale for Children and Two Picture Vocabulary Tests." *Ed & Psychol Meas* 23:359-63 su '63. * (*PA* 38:960)
270. NICKOLS, JOHN, AND NICKOLS, MARCIA. "Brief Forms of the WISC for Research." *J Clin Psychol* 19:425 O '63. *
271. OSBORNE, R. T. "Factorial Composition of the Wechsler Intelligence Scale for Children at the Pre-school Level." *Psychol Rep* 13:443-8 O '63. * (*PA* 38:6915)
272. PATERRA, MARY ELIZABETH. "A Study of Thirty-Three WISC Scattergrams of Retarded Readers." *El Engl* 40:394-405 Ap '63. *
273. PRENTICE, NORMAN M., AND KELLY, FRANCIS J. "Intelligence and Delinquency: A Reconsideration." *J Social Psychol* 60:327-37 Ag '63. * (*PA* 38:4585)
274. PRINGLE, M. L. KELLMER, AND PICKUP, K. T. "The Reliability and Validity of the Goodenough Draw-A-Man Test: A Pilot Longitudinal Study." *Brit J Ed Psychol* 33:297-306 N '63. * (*PA* 38:8424)
275. REID, WILLIAM RESA. *Psychological Subtest Patterns and Reading Achievement.* Doctor's thesis, State University of Iowa (Iowa City, Iowa), 1963. (*DA* 24:2366)
276. ROWLEY, VINTON N., AND STONE, F. BETH. "A Further Note on the Relationship Between WISC Functioning and the CMAS." *J Clin Psychol* 19:426 O '63. *
277. SHINAGAWA, FUJIRO. "Studies on the Relationship Between Intelligence Structure and Personality Traits: An Analysis of WISC Discrepancy." *Jap Psychol Res* 5:55-62 Jl '63. * (*PA* 38:6033)
278. SIEBERT, LAWRENCE A. "Matched Otis and Wechsler IQ Scores of Delinquents." *J Clin Psychol* 19:215-6 Ap '63. *
279. SILVERSTEIN, A. B. "Effects of Proration on the WISC IQs of Mentally Retarded Children." *Psychol Rep* 12:646 Je '63. * (*PA* 38:6068)
280. SILVERSTEIN, A. B. "WISC and WAIS IQs for the Mentally Retarded." *Am J Mental Def* 67:617-8 Ja '63. *
281. SILVERSTEIN, A. B., AND MOHAN, PHILIP J. "Conceptual Area Analysis of the Test Performance of Mentally Retarded Adults." *J Abn & Social Psychol* 66:255-60 Mr '63. * (*PA* 37:8165)
282. SOLKOFF, NORMAN, AND CHRISIEN, GIL. "Frustration and Perceptual-Motor Performance." *Percept & Motor Skills* 17:282 Ag '63. *
283. SPEARMAN, LEONARD H. O. "A Profile Analysis Technique for Diagnosing Reading Disability." *Yearb Nat Council Meas Ed* 20:75-86 '63. * (*PA* 38:9235)
284. TALERICO, MARGUERITE, AND BROWN, FRED. "Intelligence Test Patterns of Puerto Rican Children Seen in Child Psychiatry." *J Social Psychol* 61:57-66 O '63. * (*PA* 38:8066)
285. THOMPSON, BERTHA BOYA. "A Longitudinal Study of Auditory Discrimination." *J Ed Res* 56:376-8 Mr '63. *
286. THOMPSON, JACK M., AND FINLEY, CARMEN J. "An Abbreviated WISC for Use With Gifted Elementary School Children." *Calif J Ed Res* 14:167-77 S '63. * (*PA* 38:6072)
287. TWAIN, DAVID C., AND BROOKS, EDWARD M. "A Comparison of Wechsler, Revised Beta and Otis Scores of Delinquents." *Brit J Criminol* 3:288-90 Ja '63. *
288. WEBB, ALLEN P. "A Longitudinal Comparison of the WISC and WAIS With Educable Mentally Retarded Negroes." *J Clin Psychol* 19:101-2 Ja '63. * (*PA* 39:1769)

ALVIN G. BURSTEIN, *Associate Professor of Psychology, Neuropsychiatric Institute, University of Illinois College of Medicine, Chicago, Illinois.*

In an era when fads in test construction and test consumption combine to produce rapid obsolescence and turnover, the WISC can be regarded as a highly successful test, if only on the grounds of durability. In the nearly 15 years since its introduction, it has not displaced the older Stanford-Binet, but has certainly come to rival its predecessor as an instrument of choice in the testing of school age children. In fact, the one time infant offspring of the

Wechsler-Bellevue now boasts offspring of its own in the shape of short forms and foreign language versions.

Proliferation of derivative forms might be taken as an index of success, indicating successful negotiation of the gantlet and elevation from the status of experimental test to criterion variable. A second reflection of the WISC's success is its popularity as the subject of journal notes and articles. Interest on this front continues, with more than 150 new articles having appeared in print since WISC was reviewed in *The Fifth Mental Measurements Yearbook*.

The interested reader may wish to refer to the six reviews of WISC in the last two *Mental Measurements Yearbooks* and to Littell's (*178*) more recent review for accounts of the literature prior to 1958; the literature since that time will be the focus of this review.

Overall, any judgment of the WISC on the basis of the current literature must be tempered by the unhappy realization that far too many studies are inadequately conducted or reported. The siren call of the subtest scores appears to lure many a researcher into a helter-skelter atheoretical attempt to dredge up a "significant" correlation with some dependent variable or other and then to rush into print without careful cross validation. Generally, too, little precision is involved in the choice of dependent variables or in the constituency of the sample representing that variable.

The literature which has accumulated on the WISC may be regarded as falling into four major categories. The first of these consists essentially of studies of the instrument in which effort is directed at determining how consistently WISC scores approximate those of earlier administrations of the WISC, or of other tests of intelligence. These reliability and concurrent validity studies, accounting for perhaps a fifth of the recent literature, are quite consistent with earlier work of this sort, characterizing the WISC as a well standardized, stable instrument, correlating well with other tests of intelligence.

The second major category contains those studies which deal with derivatives of the instrument. In this group, one would include accounts dealing with foreign language equivalents of the WISC (French, German, Japanese, and Puerto Rican) and with the development of short forms. Prescriptions for short forms vary somewhat, in part because some are developed for general use, some for use with retarded or brain damaged children. However, the consensus is that correlations in the .80's with full scale scores are possible with abbreviated administrations consisting of five or six subtests from both Verbal and Performance scales. In order of popularity, scales chosen have been Block Design, Information, Picture Completion, Picture Arrangement, and Coding; Arithmetic, Similarities, Vocabulary, and Object Assembly have also been used, though less frequently. The chief reason for abbreviating the test would appear to be time savings; these would appear to be on the order of 30 minutes. In cases where there is a good deal of between-test scatter such a time saving would appear both excessively hazardous and expensive in terms of lost information.

The third basic category of current research on the WISC deals with what might be termed psychopathological applications. Here the WISC or some part of the test is given to some special group in the hope of learning more about the group, in terms of either theory or diagnostic characteristics, or of learning more about the capacities tapped by the various parts of the WISC. Hence, reports are available dealing with special intellectual states (mentally retarded, gifted, brain damaged, school achievement, or inhibition), with socio-cultural effects (sex differences, cross cultural studies, socio-economic status differences), with psychiatric symptomatology (enuresis, interpersonal difficulty, psychopathic personality), and with basic psychic processes (anxiety, perceptual organization). This area of psychopathological investigation is unfortunately most prone to the experimental and theoretical liabilities already mentioned. Therefore, though results are sometimes intriguing, they are never definitive.

The final, and to my mind most important, category consists of those reports in which the nature and purpose of intelligence testing is directly examined. Psychological testing has a highly heterogeneous past; many very different traditions (psycho-physical, psychiatric, educational) make themselves felt in current practice. In general, though, there seems to be a trend for psychological tests, originally developed for special purposes, to become utilized in more and more general ways, generating conclusions about general personality function. Outstanding examples of this tendency are to be seen in the amplified usages of the Bender's *Visual Motor Gestalt Test* and the *Machover Draw-A-Person Test.* There is some evidence that similar changes are occurring in the use of both the WAIS and the WISC in recent articles by Sinnett and Mayman [1] and by Fromm and others [2] and foreshadowed by Rapaport.[3] The general approach is to analyze test protocols not only from the point of view of subscale or subtest scores, but from a much more microscopic analysis of responses to individual items, making inferences not only in terms of intelligence, but also in terms of total personality variables involved. Hence, Fromm outlines some 40 variables, including derivatives of the psychoanalytic model of ego functions of motility, memory, and perception, and including id, superego, and cultural variables as well. Less formally and less structurally, Sinnett and Mayman seem to view the test as a means of eliciting associations to widely varied stimuli, describing the vocabulary subtest of the WAIS as "a tool with which to assess the clarity, conciseness, and subtlety of a subject's thought processes and his facility in communicating thoughts" and suggesting that clues with respect to "capacity for impulse modulation....for empathy; and his capacity to grasp subtle subjective processes in himself and others" may be available.

Clearly such a broadening and diffusion of the test's use will send shudders coursing down the spine of many a psychometrical purist who depends upon criterion clarity. Nevertheless, the effort to integrate intelligence and concepts of general personality with their differing backgrounds is an important effort for general psychology, and the ultimate test of any construction placed upon data is its pragmatic utility. Broad-gauge clinical use of the test should not be prohibited or avoided, only made explicit and pragmatically assessed. Hopefully this will be the direction of future research with the WISC and similar devices.

For reviews by Elizabeth D. Fraser, Gerald R. Patterson, and Albert I. Rabin, see 5:416; for reviews by James M. Anderson, Harold A.

1 SINNETT, KATHLEEN, AND MAYMAN, MARTIN. "The Wechsler Adult Intelligence Scale as a Clinical Diagnostic Tool: A Review." *B Menninger Clinic* 24:80–4 Mr '60. * (PA 35:3416)
2 FROMM, ERIKA; HARTMAN, LENORE DUMAS; AND MARSCHAK, MARIAN. "Children's Intelligence Tests as a Measure of Dynamic Personality Functioning." *Am J Orthopsychiatry* 27:134–44 Ja '57. * (PA 32:1621)
3 RAPAPORT, DAVID. "Projective Techniques and the Theory of Thinking." *J Proj Tech* 16:269–75 S '52. *

Delp, and Boyd R. McCandless, see 4:363 (1 excerpt).

[541]
★**Williams Intelligence Test for Children With Defective Vision.** Ages 5–15 (blind and partially sighted); 1956; individual; 1 form ['56, a series of objects, orally presented tasks, and Braille cards]; handbook ('56, 54 pages plus fold-out IQ conversion tables); record form ['56, 4 pages]; no data on reliability and validity; 60s. per set of testing material; 2s. per 12 record forms; postage extra; 1s. per set of card material; 10s. per handbook; postpaid; prices include purchase tax; [60] minutes; M. Williams; University of Birmingham Institute of Education. *

REFERENCES
1. WILLIAMS, MYFANWY. "An Intelligence Test for Blind and Partially Sighted Children." Abstract. *B Brit Psychol Soc* (30):32 S '56. *
2. WILLIAMS, MYFANWY. "Research Into Intelligence Tests for Children With Defective Vision." *Teach Blind* 45:121–5 Jl '57. *

T. ERNEST NEWLAND, *Professor of Educational Psychology, University of Illinois, Urbana, Illinois.*

This 100-item test is patterned forthrightly on the *Revised Stanford-Binet Intelligence Scale.* At least 64 of the items have obvious Binet parentage, 45 coming from Form M, 7 from Form L, and 12 common to both forms. Twelve of the items have been adapted to make them usable with visually impaired subjects; three have been modified to provide for greater range in usage; and three have been culturally adapted to British subjects. Other items were taken from Valentine's *Intelligence Tests for Children,* from Burt's Reasoning Tests, and some from group tests. Four items have been included for optional use to arouse or sustain the interest of younger subjects, but they are not scored. The 40-word vocabulary test, the score on which is used only for determining the point of entry into the scale, is adapted from the *Wechsler Intelligence Scale for Children;* four new words have been substituted and a new order of difficulty has been established. No items necessitate the use of Braille.

After a preliminary tryout on 120 subjects, the items were administered to 939 children from age 4 up to 16. Subjects included both the blind and partially sighted. Since separate standardizations indicated no significant differences between performances of the two impaired groups, a single set of norms was established. No reliability or validity data are reported, and *Psychological Abstracts* records no formal publications on the test (through October 1963). Used as a point scale, deviation intelligence quotients are read directly from tables, at the intersections of raw scores and chronological ages (to the nearest month). Score distributions have been normalized so as to yield mean IQ's of 100 and sigmas of 15 for each age group, by month from 3 years 6 months to 16 years 0 months.

In terms of what is known about the value of the Binet in predicting academic learning in sighted children and in view of the nature of the psychological processes and the learning products sampled in this test (referred to by the author as the "Birmingham Scale"), one could assume that results obtained by means of this device should theoretically provide a fair basis for predicting the learning behavior of visually impaired children. However, it is highly likely that predictive validity coefficients obtained on sight impaired populations will tend to run lower than in a parallel case of Binet data on sighted children. Probably contaminating such correlations on visually impaired populations would be factors such as the unique nature of certain of the educational stimuli and responses in the form of Braille, the frequency of intervening emotional conditions, and the institutional practices and expectancies in many schools for the visually impaired—especially in the case of most residential schools. Any assumption that a Birmingham IQ of 100 on, say, a 10-year-old blind child has the same connotation regarding general learning aptitude as does a Binet IQ of 100 on a sighted child will have to be the responsibility of the one making such an assumption. Any assumption beyond that connoting averageness for a specified group (impaired or nonimpaired) will need to be most critically examined.

From an editorial standpoint, the title for item 61 is in error. Some may be curious about time specifications for at least items 80 and 91 (coding), and maybe items 95 and 99 (problem solving). However, the nature of the total testing situation is such that, in practically all instances, the setting of such time limits need not be crucial. From the standpoint of content validity, one could be justly concerned about items 79 and 92 (directions) and wonder how meaningful the terms "north," "south," "east," and "west" are, especially to the born blind. There is also an inconsistency in the ways in which the user is provided with the correct responses to certain items; this condition could be particularly important in the cases of those administering the test who are not well grounded in Binet testing.

In an overall sense the development of this device must be regarded as a potentially worthwhile contribution. Those who are Binet-oriented in their work with school children may miss the direct yielding of mental ages. Such persons can, however, make a reverse use of the tables and ascribe a mental age score to a child by finding the chronological age for which his obtained point score is the median and use that as the child's "mental age." Whether such mental age (or, better, "test age") will have the same implication for educational expectancies for visually impaired children as for nonimpaired children can be shown only by considerable research.

[Other Tests]

For tests not listed above, see the following entries in *Tests in Print*: 877–9, 884–5, 891–2, 894, 900, 903–4, 906, and 908–9; out of print: 889, 902, and 911.

SPECIFIC

[542]

★**Alternate Uses.** Grades 6–16 and adults; 1960; revision of *Unusual Uses;* experimental form; spontaneous flexibility; Form A (4 pages); mimeographed manual, second preliminary edition (7 pages); reliability data based on preliminary form; norms for grades 6, 9, and 13 only; $2 per 25 tests; 15¢ per single copy; 35¢ per manual; postage extra; 12(20) minutes; Paul R. Christensen, J. P. Guilford, Philip R. Merrifield, and Robert C. Wilson; Sheridan Supply Co. *

REFERENCES

1. BARRON, FRANK. "The Disposition Toward Originality." *J Abn & Social Psychol* 51:478–85 N '55. * (*PA* 31:2533)
2. GUILFORD, J. P. *Personality.* New York: McGraw-Hill Book Co., Inc., 1959. Pp. xiii, 562. *
3. BRITTAIN, W. LAMBERT, AND BEITTEL, KENNETH R. "A Study of Some Tests of Creativity to Performances in the Visual Arts." *Studies Art Ed* 2:54–65 sp '61. *
4. MARKS, ALVIN; MICHAEL, WILLIAM B.; AND KAISER, HENRY F. "Dimensions of Creativity and Temperament in Officer Evaluation." *Psychol Rep* 9:635–8 D '61. *
5. MARKS, ALVIN; MICHAEL, WILLIAM B.; AND KAISER, HENRY F. "Sources of Noncognitive Variance in 21 Measures of Creativity." *Psychol Rep* 9:287–90 O '61. *
6. ABDEL-RAZIK, TAHER MOHAMED. *An Investigation of Creative Thinking Among College Students.* Doctor's thesis, Ohio State University (Columbus, Ohio), 1963. (*DA* 24:2775)
7. BARRON, FRANK. Chap. 11, "The Disposition Toward Originality," pp. 139–52. In *Scientific Creativity: Its Recognition and Development.* Edited by Calvin W. Taylor and Frank Barron. New York: John Wiley & Sons, Inc., 1963. Pp. xxiv, 419. * (*PA* 38:2689)

[543]

Benton Visual Retention Test, Revised Edition. Ages 8 and over; 1946–55; title on manual is *Revised Visual Retention Test;* individual; Forms C, D, E, ('55, 10 cards) in a single booklet; manual ('55, 72 pages); record blank ('55, 1 page); $5 per set of cards, 50 record blanks, and manual; $2.30 per manual; postpaid; 5(10) minutes; Arthur L. Benton; distributed by Psychological Corporation. *

REFERENCES

1–3. See 4:360.
4–8. See 5:401.
9. CASTLETON, B. "Benton Visual Recognition." *Psychometric Res B* (4):[13–5] Ag '59. *

10. CROOKES, T. G. "Benton V.R." *Psychometric Res B* (5):[16–9] N '59. *
11. HEILBRUN, ALFRED B., JR. "Specificity of Immediate Memory Function Associated With Cerebral Cortex Damage." *J Mental Sci* 106:241–5 Ja '60. * (*PA* 35:6745)
12. MATUNAS, MARIAN ISABEL. *Test Performance of Psychotic Children With Organic Brain Pathology: A Study to Determine Whether the Bender-Gestalt Test, the Benton Visual Retention Test, and the Marble Board Test Can Detect the Presence of Organic Brain Pathology in Psychotic Children.* Doctor's thesis, New York University (New York, N.Y.), 1960. (*DA* 21:1257)
13. BENTON, ARTHUR L., AND SPREEN, OTFRIED. "Visual Memory Test: The Simulation of Mental Incompetence." *Arch Gen Psychiatry* 4:79–83 Ja '61. * (*PA* 35:6824)
14. ROWLEY, VINTON N., AND BAER, PAUL E. "Visual Retention Test Performance in Emotionally Disturbed and Brain-Damaged Children." *Am J Orthopsychiatry* 31:579–83 Jl '61. * (*PA* 36:4JG79R)
15. SCHNORE, MORRIS M. "Memory-for-Designs Tests in the Diagnosis of Brain Damage." *Ont Hosp Psychol B* 7:2–4 Ag '61. *
16. BENTON, ARTHUR L., AND FOGEL, MAX L. "Three-Dimensional Constructional Praxis: A Clinical Test." *Arch Neurol* 7:347–54 O '62. * (*PA* 37:5373)
17. BENTON, ARTHUR L., AND MCGAVREN, MUSETTA. "Qualitative Aspects of Visual Memory Test Performance in Mental Defectives." *Am J Mental Def* 66:878–83 My '62. * (*PA* 37:1680)
18. L'ABATE, LUCIANO; BOELLING, GARY M.; HUTTON, ROBERT D.; AND MATHEWS, DEWEY L., JR. "The Diagnostic Usefulness of Four Potential Tests of Brain Damage." Abstract. *J Consult Psychol* 26:479 O '62. *
19. LETON, DONALD A. "Visual-Motor Capacities and Ocular Efficiency in Reading." *Percept & Motor Skills* 15:407–32 O '62. * (*PA* 37:8253)
20. RIDDELL, S. A. "The Performance of Elderly Psychiatric Patients on Equivalent Forms of Tests of Memory and Learning." *Brit J Social & Clin Psychol* 1:70–1 F '62. * (*PA* 37:1208)
21. SHAFFER, JOHN W. "A Specific Cognitive Deficit Observed in Gonadal Aplasia (Turner's Syndrome)." *J Clin Psychol* 18:403–6 O '62. * (*PA* 39:5565)
22. SILVERSTEIN, A. B. "Perceptual, Motor, and Memory Functions in the Visual Retention Test." *Am J Mental Def* 66:613–7 Ja '62. * (*PA* 36:4JI13S)
23. BRILLIANT, PATRICIA J., AND GYNTHER, MALCOLM D. "Relationships Between Performance on Three Tests for Organicity and Selected Patient Variables." *J Consult Psychol* 27:474–9 D '63. * (*PA* 38:8404)
24. CANTER, ARTHUR. "A Background Interference Procedure for Graphomotor Tests in the Study of Deficit." *Percept & Motor Skills* 16:914 Je '63. * (*PA* 38:6348)
25. CRONHOLM, BORJE, AND SCHALLING, DAISY. "Intellectual Deterioration After Focal Brain Injury." *Arch Surgery* 86:670–87 Ap '63. *
26. FRIEDMAN, ELLEN C., AND BARCLAY, ALLAN. "The Discriminative Validity of Certain Psychological Tests as Indices of Brain Damage in the Mentally Retarded." *Mental Retardation* 1:291–3 O '63. * (*PA* 38:8935)
27. L'ABATE, LUCIANO; FRIEDMAN, WILLIAM H.; VOGLER, ROGER E.; AND CHUSED, THOMAS M. "The Diagnostic Usefulness of Two Tests of Brain-Damage." *J Clin Psychol* 19:87–91 Ja '63. * (*PA* 39:2477)
28. SILVERSTEIN, A. B. "Qualitative Analysis of Performance on the Visual Retention Test." *Am J Mental Def* 68:109–13 Jl '63. * (*PA* 38:4569)
29. SPREEN, OTFRIED, AND BENTON, ARTHUR L. "Simulation of Mental Deficiency on a Visual Memory Test." *Am J Mental Def* 67:909–13 My '63. * (*PA* 38:1281)
30. STRICKER, GEORGE, AND COOPER, ALLAN. "The Efficacy of the Benton Visual Retention Test at the 'Very Superior' Intelligence Level." *J General Psychol* 68:165–7 Ja '63. * (*PA* 38:2676)

For a review by Nelson G. Hanawalt, see 5:401; for reviews by Ivan Norman Mensh, Joseph Newman, and William Schofield of the original edition, see 4:360; see also 3:297 (1 excerpt).

[544]

★**Christensen-Guilford Fluency Tests.** Grades 7–16 and adults; 1957–63; 1 form; 4 tests; mimeographed manual, second edition ('59, 8 pages); mimeographed supplementary norms ['63, 2 pages]; $1.55 per complete specimen set; postage extra; Paul R. Christensen and J. P. Guilford; Sheridan Supply Co. *

a) WORD FLUENCY. Form A ('58, 3 pages); $2 per 25 tests; 15¢ per single copy; 4(10) minutes.
b) IDEATIONAL FLUENCY I. Form A ('57, 5 pages); $3.75 per 25 tests; 25¢ per single copy; 12(20) minutes.
c) ASSOCIATIONAL FLUENCY I. Form A ('57, 3 pages); $2 per 25 tests; 15¢ per single copy; 4(10) minutes.
d) EXPRESSIONAL FLUENCY. Form A ('58, 5 pages); $3.75 per 25 tests; 25¢ per single copy; 8(15) minutes.

REFERENCES
1. GUILFORD, J. P. *Personality.* New York: McGraw-Hill Book Co., Inc., 1959. Pp. xiii, 562. *
2. MERRIFIELD, P. R.; GUILFORD, J. P.; CHRISTENSEN, P. R.; AND FRICK, J. W. "The Role of Intellectual Factors in Problem Solving." *Psychol Monogr* 76(10):1–21 '62. *
3. ABDEL-RAZIK, TAHER MOHAMED. *An Investigation of Creative Thinking Among College Students.* Doctor's thesis, Ohio State University (Columbus, Ohio), 1963. (*DA* 24:2775)
4. CHRISTENSEN, PAUL R., AND GUILFORD, J. P. "An Experimental Study of Verbal Fluency Factors." *Brit J Stat Psychol* 16:1–26 My '63. * (*PA* 38:4879)

J. A. KEATS, *Reader in Psychology, University of Queensland, Brisbane, Australia.*

With these tests there is a danger that the intending user will reject them as trivial, particularly if he is not familiar with the extensive research programme conducted by Guilford and his co-workers. To call the number of words containing a specified letter which can be written in two minutes, a measure of "word fluency" seems arbitrary at best. The reasons for specifying one letter rather than two or three or none at all are not obvious. Similar comments might be made on the tests of expressional fluency, associational fluency, and ideational fluency. However these tests have arisen from factor analytic studies of the original verbal fluency factor of Thurstone and the justification for this particular form of the tests is given in Christensen and Guilford (*4*) and earlier studies. These references should be studied by intending users before final decisions are made.

There appears, however, to be one point that is not covered in either the research or the manual of instructions. The subject is not told that he is to respond only in English. Admittedly the instructions are in English as are the examples of acceptable responses, but it seems surprising that the problem has not arisen sufficiently often for this point to be covered either in the instructions to subjects or in the scoring procedures. Apart from the practical problem which may be trivial, this question raises the interesting experimental possibility of administering the tests to bilingual subjects—once in English and once in their other language. Using the careful experimental designs of Guilford and Christensen such a study might indicate clearly which, if any, of these fluency factors transcend the language medium.

From the point of view of practical use for selection or guidance these tests are still at the developmental stage. The reliabilities are of the order of .7 and no validity data are available apart from factorial validity. The tests are stated to cover grades 7-16 and adults, but the only norms based on identified groups are for naval and air force trainees, and then only for three of the four tests.[1] The reliability would have to be improved by adding more parts to the existing tests and, in view of the research findings, the only way to be certain that the extended tests had the desired factor structure would be to carry out a fresh factor study. This study could also include criterion measures so that validity data for the particular situation could be obtained. The four published tests could serve as reference measures in such a study. It is in this area of applied research that the current tests are likely to prove most valuable.

The scoring instructions for the four tests contain the following sentence: "The scorer should note carefully the exact specifications given in each item and should see that they are followed, but he may be *literal* in applying each specification" (reviewer's italics). This is either an awkward use of English or "literal" should be "liberal" and so change the meaning completely. The existing manual needs thorough revision to provide more information and clearer instructions for scoring and administration.

This battery of tests would need considerable developmental work before it could have much practical application. The intending user might well decide to construct his own tests from the published descriptions of test batteries and the factor analytic results. However, in checking his final tests by factor analysis or other methods, he might well find some use for the present battery as reference tests.

ALBERT S. THOMPSON, *Professor of Psychology and Education, Teachers College, Columbia University, New York, New York.*

This battery of tests of four types of fluency with verbal materials is designed to measure certain aspects of creative ability, or divergent thinking, to use the more technical term. All require the testee to produce words as rapidly as possible, in response to the following types of instructions: (*a*) Word Fluency—words containing a specified letter, (*b*) Ideational Fluency—names of things in a certain class such as "objects that move," (*c*) Association Fluency—words similar in meaning to a specified word, and (*d*) Expressional Fluency—four-word sentences beginning with specified letters for each word.

The total working time for the battery is 28 minutes. It can be administered to individuals or groups. Scoring requires judgment as to the acceptability of the response words. The manual presents the rationale and gives extensive examples of acceptable response.

The current manual (Second Edition, 1959) is an 8-page description of the administration and scoring procedures with one page devoted to interpretation of scores. The only norms presented are based on several hundred naval air cadets and naval officer candidates, described merely as typically high school graduates with some college education and with a general intellectual level substantially above average. No norms are presented for Expressional Fluency.[1]

Split-half reliabilities (corrected) range from .63 to .76 for the three tests, based on the Navy sample. No data on scorer agreement are presented.

It is clear that the tests are not yet in the operational stage—in the sense of being useful for individual or group appraisal in a service situation. However, they can be recommended for continued experimental use and for further research on the nature and correlates of creative behavior. Validity to date is of the construct, not predictive type, and is based on a number of factor analysis studies which have identified the existence of verbal fluency as a basic dimension of human ability and which have shed light on the nature of creative thinking.

Since tests of this type by their very nature must be open ended, they are subject to scorer unreliability and to testee variability in the ability to "create" at a specified moment of time. Data on these sources of variation should be made available.

Research referred to in the 12-item bibliography in the manual has certainly demonstrated the existence of verbal fluency and its impor-

---

[1] The supplementary norms referred to in the entry preceding the review present means for 229 boys, 228 girls, and 206 unidentified subjects in a "high-IQ group," and norms for all four tests. The norms group is not identified and the boys, girls, and high-IQ group are not described except for number.—Editor.

[1] See footnote 1 to the preceding review.—Editor.

tance in divergent thinking. Most of the studies, however, are directed toward the analytic study of human intellect rather than predictive validity of the instrument. What few prediction studies are found in the literature (but not reported in the manual) suggest relationship with creative performance of students, leadership behavior, and writing skill. Guilford's book *Personality* (*1*) is the basic source of information rather than the manual.

[545]

★**Closure Flexibility (Concealed Figures).** Industrial employees; 1956–63; revision of *Gottschaldt Figures;* formerly called *Concealed Figures: A Test of Flexibility of Closure;* Form A ('56, 8 pages); manual ('63, 20 pages); norms for males only; $5 per 20 tests, postage extra; $1 per specimen set, postpaid; 10(15) minutes; L. L. Thurstone (test), T. E. Jeffrey (test), and Measurement Research Division, Industrial Relations Center, University of Chicago (manual); Education-Industry Service. *

REFERENCES

1. CORTER, HAROLD M. "Factor Analysis of Some Reasoning Tests." *Psychol Monogr* 66(8):1–31 '52. * (*PA* 27:4995)
2. WECKOWICZ, T. E., AND BLEWETT, D. B. "Size Constancy and Abstract Thinking in Schizophrenic Patients." *J Mental Sci* 105:909–34 O '59. * (*PA* 34:6402)
3. GORDON, OAKLEY J., AND TIKOFSKY, RONALD S. "Performance of Brain-Damaged Subjects on Gottschaldt's Embedded Figures." *Percept & Motor Skills* 12:179–85 Ap '61. * (*PA* 36:1JG79G)
4. GORDON, OAKLEY; BRAYER, RICHARD; AND TIKOFSKY, RONALD. "Personality Variables and the Perception of Embedded Figures." *Percept & Motor Skills* 12:195–202 Ap '61. * (*PA* 36:1HJ95G)

LEONA E. TYLER, *Professor of Psychology, University of Oregon, Eugene, Oregon.*

One is likely to be a little puzzled by the name of this test, *Closure Flexibility,* unless he is familiar with Thurstone's classic monograph *A Factorial Study of Perception.*[1] One of the perceptual tests included in Thurstone's battery was the set of concealed figures Gottschaldt had used in studying the effects of experience on perception.[2] The present form of the test is a revision based on several research investigations carried out by Thurstone and his associates. The name is the label given the "second closure factor" which showed up repeatedly in these studies. The trait is defined as "the ability to hold a configuration in mind despite distraction."

It is a brief test, requiring only 10 minutes. On each line is a simple geometrical figure followed by four complex ones. The subject places a check mark under the complex figure if it contains the simple one, a zero if it does not. Thus the test is very easily scored. The only reliability data included in the manual are from the research studies mentioned above, a split-half coefficient of .78 reported by Thurstone on an earlier form and a corrected split-half coefficient of .94 reported by Pemberton[3] on the present form. It would obviously be advantageous to have more information about reliability. A split-half coefficient is not appropriate for a time-limited test like this.

The standard score norms provided by the present publishers are based on the test performance of 1,105 industrial employees. This norm group is made up of various numbers of professionals, executives, salesmen, foremen, and hourly workers. It does not constitute a representative sample of any definable population. Thus it is difficult to see just what use one would make of these standard scores.

Though both reliability and norms are inadequate, what the test needs more than anything else is more evidence as to what it measures, that is, what it is valid *for*. The authors of the manual summarize the results of the factor analytic studies by Thurstone and others.[4] These indicate that closure flexibility is related to mechanical aptitude and certain kinds of reasoning. They also summarize the evidence obtained by Pemberton that subjects who score high on this trait are more likely than those who score low to describe themselves on paper and pencil tests as socially retiring, not dependent on social conventions, having theoretical interests, and having a drive for achievement. Thurstone's findings that the test differentiated campus leaders from other students, and more successful public administrators from less successful, are also cited. In addition, the manual presents data on the industrial population used as a norm group. These data show a clear differentiation between most of the subgroups represented. Professional men are highest, hourly workers lowest. But since almost any intelligence test would differentiate these groups at least this well, it is not clear what the results are supposed to

[1] THURSTONE, L. L. *A Factorial Study of Perception.* Chicago, Ill.: University of Chicago Press, 1944. Pp. vi, 158.
[2] GOTTSCHALDT, KURT. "Über den Einfluss der Erfahrung auf die Wahrnehmung von Figuren: 2, Vergleichende Untersuchungen über die Wirkung figuraler Einprägung und den Einfluss spezifischer Geschehensverläufe auf die Auffassung optischer Komplexe." *Psychologische Forschung* 12:1–87 F '29. *

[3] PEMBERTON, CAROL L. *A Study of the Speed and Flexibility of Closure Factors.* Doctor's thesis, University of Chicago (Chicago, Ill.), 1951.
[4] BECHTOLDT, HAROLD P. *Factorial Study of Perceptual Speed.* Doctor's thesis, University of Chicago (Chicago, Ill.), 1947.
BOTZUM, WILLIAM A. *A Factorial Study of the Reasoning and Closure Factors.* Doctor's thesis, University of Chicago (Chicago, Ill.), 1950.
YELA, MARIANO. "Application of the Concept of Simple Structure to Alexander's Data." *Psychometrika* 14:121–35 Je '49. *

show about the particular trait of closure flexibility.

The conclusion follows that *Closure Flexibility* has not reached a stage of development where it is useful for any practical clinical, counseling, or selection purpose. It is to the credit of the publishers that they clearly specify that the test is to be used only under carefully prescribed conditions. What is a little puzzling about the presentation in the manual, however, is the detailed explanation about the meaning of standard scores. If the test is to be released only for research purposes, are such explanations necessary?

Since a much more extensive body of research knowledge has collected around another modification of the Gottschaldt test, the *Embedded Figures Test,* it might well be considered preferable to this one even for research. However, the fact that the Thurstone version is a short group test, easily scored, may constitute an advantage in many situations. Research on flexibility of closure has been suggestive and interesting. If the publication of this test in its present form facilitates more of it, it will have served a worthwhile purpose.

[546]

★**Closure Speed (Gestalt Completion).** Industrial employees; 1956-63; formerly called *Gestalt Completion: A Test of Speed of Closure;* Form A ('56, 3 pages); manual ('63, 16 pages); reliability data for present form based on college students only; norms for males only; $3 per 20 tests, postage extra; $1 per specimen set, postpaid; 3(8) minutes; L. L. Thurstone (test), T. E. Jeffrey (test), and Measurement Research Division, Industrial Relations Center, University of Chicago (manual); Education-Industry Service. *

REFERENCES

1. BASS, BERNARD M., AND COATES, CHARLES H. "Validity Information Exchange, No. 7-082: R.O.T.C. Cadets." *Personnel Psychol* 7:553-4 w '54. *
2. BASS, BERNARD M.; KARSTENDIEK, BARBARA; McCULLOUGH, GERALD; AND PRUITT, RAY C. "Validity Information Exchange, No. 7-024: D.O.T. Code 2-66.01, 2-66.11, 2-66.12, 2-66.23, Policemen and Detectives, Public Service." *Personnel Psychol* 7:159-60 sp '54. *
3. McCARTY, JOHN J. "Normative Data Information Exchange, No. 10-94." *Personnel Psychol* 10:537 w '57. *

LEONA E. TYLER, *Professor of Psychology, University of Oregon, Eugene, Oregon.*

The research L. L. Thurstone reported in 1944 in the monograph *A Factorial Study of Perception*[1] identified two "closure" factors. The first of these, labeled Closure Speed, showed up most clearly on a kind of test adapted from Street's *Gestalt Completion Test,*[2] in which the subject is required to identify a picture from incomplete material. Later studies by Thurstone and his students and associates contributed some information about the way in which this ability to "perceive an apparently disorganized or unrelated group of parts as a meaningful whole" is related to various other indicators of special ability and temperament.

The test is very short (24 items, 3-minute time limit) and its reliability for individual assessment is not really adequate (.68, .70, .67 in three studies), although the authors of the manual say that the reliabilities "are at an acceptable level for test scores." The fact that the first two of the figures cited were obtained by the split-half method, not legitimately used for timed tests, casts further doubt on the conclusion. The standard score norms are not of much value because the norm group of 1,252 male industrial employees does not constitute a representative sample of any intelligible population.

None of the evidence summarized under validity really tells the user very much about what the test is measuring. Most of it comes from Pemberton's dissertation[3] in which she showed that persons scoring above the mean on *Closure Speed* characterized themselves as socially outgoing, confident and optimistic, energetic and impulsive, not logical or theoretical, and possessing strong artistic interests. Pemberton[4] also produced some indications that spatial ability and inductive reasoning were related to Closure Speed, and Thurstone found that it differentiated between subjects high and low in mechanical interest and experience. The Industrial Relations Center, under whose auspices the test is now being published, adds to this factorial type of data some evidence that occupational groups are differentiated by their average scores. There seems to be a large amount of overlapping between groups at the successive levels, however, and it is a well known fact that many measures of ability and interest produce similar differentiations. Thus the contribution these results make to our understanding of the specific validity of the Gestalt completion test is slight.

It is apparent that the technical characteristics of this test are unsatisfactory if one is

[1] THURSTONE, L. L. *A Factorial Study of Perception.* Chicago, Ill.: University of Chicago Press, 1944. Pp. vi, 158.
[2] STREET, ROY F. *A Gestalt Completion Test: A Study of a Cross Section of Intellect.* Columbia University, Teachers College, Contributions to Education, No. 481. New York: Bureau of Publications, the College, 1931. Pp. vii, 65. *

[3] PEMBERTON, CAROL L. *A Study of the Speed and Flexibility of Closure Factors.* Doctor's thesis, University of Chicago (Chicago, Ill.), 1951.
[4] PEMBERTON, CAROL. "The Closure Factor Related to Other Cognitive Processes." *Psychometrika* 17:267-88 S '52. *

considering it for any practical purpose. In research studies where no conclusions will be drawn about the meaning of individual scores except on the basis of results actually obtained in the study, the test may have something to contribute. If such research findings accumulate and steps are taken to increase the reliability and improve the norms, the test may someday merit more extensive use.

[547]

★**Consequences.** Grades 9–16 and adults; 1958–62; 2 scores: originality, ideational fluency; 1 form ('58, 11 pages); mimeographed manual, second edition ['62, 24 pages]; $5 per 25 tests; 25¢ per single copy; $1 per manual; postage extra; 20(30) minutes; P. R. Christensen, P. R. Merrifield, and J. P. Guilford; Sheridan Supply Co. *

REFERENCES

1. BARRON, FRANK. "The Disposition Toward Originality." *J Abn & Social Psychol* 51:478–85 N '55. * (*PA* 31:2533)
2. BERGER, R. M.; GUILFORD, J. P.; AND CHRISTENSEN, P. R. "A Factor-Analytic Study of Planning Abilities." *Psychol Monogr* 71(6):1–31 '57. * (*PA* 33:6967)
3. GUILFORD, J. P. *Personality.* New York: McGraw-Hill Book Co., Inc., 1959. Pp. xiii, 562. *
4. KETTNER, NORMAN W.; GUILFORD, J. P.; AND CHRISTENSEN, PAUL R. "A Factor Analytic Study Across the Domains of Reasoning, Creativity, and Evaluation." *Psychol Monogr* 73(9):1–31 '59. * (*PA* 34:7333)
5. BRITTAIN, W. LAMBERT, AND BEITTEL, KENNETH R. "A Study of Some Tests of Creativity to Performances in the Visual Arts." *Studies Art Ed* 2:54–65 sp '61. *
6. MCGUIRE, CARSON. "The Prediction of Talented Behavior in the Junior High School." *Proc Inv Conf Testing Probl* 1960:46–67 '61. *
7. MARKS, ALVIN; MICHAEL, WILLIAM B.; AND KAISER, HENRY F. "Dimensions of Creativity and Temperament in Officer Evaluation." *Psychol Rep* 9:635–8 D '61. *
8. MARKS, ALVIN; MICHAEL, WILLIAM B.; AND KAISER, HENRY F. "Sources of Noncognitive Variance in 21 Measures of Creativity." *Psychol Rep* 9:287–90 O '61. *
9. CLINE, VICTOR B.; RICHARDS, JAMES M., JR.; AND ABE, CLIFFORD. "The Validity of a Battery of Creativity Tests in a High School Sample." *Ed & Psychol Meas* 22:781–4 w '62. * (*PA* 37:7184)
10. ABDEL-RAZIK, TAHER MOHAMED. *An Investigation of Creative Thinking Among College Students.* Doctor's thesis, Ohio State University (Columbus, Ohio), 1963. (*DA* 24:2775)
11. BARRON, FRANK. Chap. 11, "The Disposition Toward Originality," pp. 139–52. In *Scientific Creativity: Its Recognition and Development.* Edited by Calvin W. Taylor and Frank Barron. New York: John Wiley & Sons, Inc., 1963. Pp. xxiv, 419. * (*PA* 38:2689)
12. CLINE, VICTOR B.; RICHARDS, JAMES M., JR.; AND NEEDHAM, WALTER E. "Creativity Tests and Achievement in High School Science." *J Appl Psychol* 47:184–9 Je '63. * (*PA* 37:8223)
13. JACOBSEN, T. L., AND ASHER, J. J. "Validity of the Concept Constancy Measure of Creative Problem Solving." *J General Psychol* 68:9–19 Ja '63. * (*PA* 38:2684)

GOLDINE C. GLESER, *Professor of Psychology, University of Cincinnati Medical School, Cincinnati, Ohio.*

Consequences is one of a large battery of group administered tests which were developed in order to explore systematically the "structure of the intellect" and isolate the factors of creative thinking. The test consists of 10 items each requiring the subject to list what the results might be if some unusual situation came to pass, as for example, "What would be the results if none of us needed food any more in order to live?" Relevant, nonduplicated responses are classified as "obvious" or "remote," the frequency of the former yielding a score of ideational fluency and the latter a score on originality.

This is an interesting and ingenious test in a field where relatively few good tests are available. However, one receives the impression that the authors have reluctantly taken time out from their own factor analytic studies to publish it for use in other research and that they are totally uninterested in developing it as a clinical tool. The samples on which statistics are based are inadequately described. Minimal attention has been given to insuring comparability of results by different scorers. While guidelines and examples are given for differentiating remote and obvious responses, many of the distinctions made are tenuous at best. For example, in response to the item mentioned above, "more neurosis" is scored as remote whereas "more suicides" is scored as obvious. Likewise, the criterion of what constitutes a relevant nonduplicated response is extremely vague. The authors recognize the latter as a source of difficulty in developing norms or comparing scores obtained by different scorers. However, they report no studies investigating scorer reliability or the magnitude of this "leniency bias." Such studies could give an indication of the extent to which effort should be expended in tightening the scoring system.

Estimates of internal consistency reliability are given for the two scores for ninth grade students and young adult males separately. The reliability of the obvious score is estimated at .86 for the 10-item test over all samples. The remote score is less reliable, particularly with ninth graders (.67). This may not reflect any difference between the groups in variability of scores over items but rather may reflect the greater homogeneity (smaller variance) of the ninth graders in the ability tapped by this score. The authors indicate that with adults four or five items may be sufficiently accurate for some research purposes.

The many studies undertaken by Guilford and his associates to verify, modify, and reconfirm the hypotheses on the structure of the intellect also yield much information on the construct validity of this test. The obvious score has an average validity of .62 for the factor DMU (ideational fluency) on the basis of five samples of young adult males each consisting of over 200 cases. In most of these samples only four items of the test were used. A slightly lower average loading (.54) was found for this factor in four samples of ninth graders. Thus, from 29 to 38 per cent of the score variance is attributable to this one factor. Loadings on other intellectual factors, including originality, are negligible with the exception that for the ninth graders an average loading of .33 was found for DMI (elaboration).

The remote score has its largest average loading (.42) on the factor DMT (originality) for young adults. For ninth graders, however, the highest loading (.40) is for DMC (spontaneous flexibility). It is difficult to evaluate the importance of this difference, particularly since the authors indicate that these factors are difficult to separate experimentally. From a practical standpoint factorial purity is not necessarily desirable. A test measuring several aspects of creativity or originality may have more predictive validity than a pure test. Some indication of this fact is given in the one study of practical validity reported in the manual in which it was found that for 80 engineering students the obvious score correlated .17 while the remote score correlated .44 with grade-point average. That the latter correlation is not simply attributable to verbal intelligence is indicated by the fact that the remote score in other studies correlated only .23 with vocabulary and .18 with reading comprehension.

In summary, *Consequences* shows considerable promise as a test of intellectual factors not usually covered in the objectively scored aptitude tests. It is recommended as a research instrument, particularly to explore its usefulness in various decisions where flexibility and originality might be important. However, scorer reliability should be investigated, and efforts should be made to tighten the scoring system and provide ways of reducing scorer bias regarding what constitutes an "acceptable" response. One helpful method might be to provide a set of protocols which a potential user might score and then compare his results with that of the authors to determine and correct bias.

[548]

★**Decorations.** Grades 9–16 and adults; 1963; "divergent production of figural implications" or "ability to add meaningful details"; Form A (5 pages); mimeographed manual (4 pages); norms for ninth graders only; $3.75 per 25 tests; 20¢ per single copy; 25¢ per manual; postage extra; 12(16) minutes; Arthur Gershon, Sheldon Gardner, Philip R. Merrifield, and J. P. Guilford; Sheridan Supply Co. *

REFERENCES
1. GUILFORD, J. P. *Personality.* New York: McGraw-Hill Book Co., Inc., 1959. Pp. xiii, 562. *

[549]

★**Illinois Test of Psycholinguistic Abilities, Experimental Edition.** Ages 2.5–9; 1961–63; based in part upon the unpublished *Differential Language Facilities Test* by Dorothy J. Sievers; 10 scores: auditory-vocal automatic, visual decoding, motor encoding, auditory-vocal association, visual-motor sequencing, vocal encoding, auditory-vocal sequencing, visual-motor association, auditory decoding, total; individual; 1 form ('61, 113-page picture booklet, 21 cards, and a series of objects); manual ('61, 137 pages); selected studies monograph ('63, 101 pages, see 22 below); record form ('61, 4 pages); $32 per examiner's kit of testing materials, 25 record forms, selected studies monograph, and manual; $3.75 per 25 record forms; $2.50 per selected studies monograph; $3.50 per manual; postage extra; (45–60) minutes; James J. McCarthy and Samuel A. Kirk; distributed by University of Illinois Press. *

REFERENCES
1. SIEVERS, DOROTHY JEAN. *Development and Standardization of a Test of Psycholinguistic Growth in Preschool Children.* Doctor's thesis, University of Illinois (Urbana, Ill.), 1955. (DA 16:286)
2. GALLAGHER, JAMES J. *A Comparison of Brain-Injured and Non-Brain-Injured Mentally Retarded Children on Several Psychological Variables.* Monograph of the Society for Research in Child Development, Vol. 22, No. 2. Lafayette, Ind.: Child Development Publications, 1957. Pp. 79. * (PA 33:1632)
3. MCCARTHY, JAMES J. *Qualitative and Quantitative Differences in the Language Abilities of Young Cerebral Palsied Children.* Doctor's thesis, University of Illinois (Urbana, Ill.), 1957. (DA 18:499)
4. SIEVERS, DOROTHY J. "A Study to Compare the Performance of Brain-Injured and Non-Brain-Injured Mentally Retarded Children on the Differential Language Facility Test." *Am J Mental Def* 63:839–47 Mr '59. * (PA 34:4583)
5. MCCARTHY, JAMES J. "A Test for the Identification of Defects in Language Usage Among Young Cerebral Palsied Children." *Cerebral Palsy R* 21:3–5 Ja–F '60. * (PA 35:6444)
6. OLSON, JAMES LADD. *A Comparison of Sensory Aphasic, Expressive Aphasic, and Deaf Children on the Illinois Test of Language Ability.* Doctor's thesis, University of Illinois (Urbana, Ill.), 1960. (DA 21:2950)
7. SIEVERS, DOROTHY J., AND ROSENBERG, CARL M. "The Differential Language Facility Test and Electroencephalograms of Brain-Injured Mentally Retarded Children." *Am J Mental Def* 65:46–50 Jl '60. * (PA 35:3787)
8. KIRK, SAMUEL A., AND MCCARTHY, JAMES J. "The Illinois Test of Psycholinguistic Abilities: An Approach to Differential Diagnosis." *Am J Mental Def* 66:399–412 N '61. * (PA 36:4HI99K)
9. QURESHI, MOHAMMED Y. "Effects of Various Scoring Cutoffs on Reliability Estimates." *Am J Mental Def* 65:753–60 My '61. * (PA 36:1HD53Q)
10. SIEVERS, DOROTHY J., AND ESSA, SHIRLEY H. "Language Development in Institutionalized and Community Mentally Retarded Children." *Am J Mental Def* 66:413–20 N '61. * (PA 36:4JI13S)
11. HERMANN, ANITA LOUISE. *An Experimental Approach to the Educability of Psycholinguistic Functions in Children.* Master's thesis, University of Illinois (Urbana, Ill.), 1962.
12. KIRK, SAMUEL A., AND BATEMAN, BARBARA. "Diagnosis and Remediation of Learning Disabilities." *J Excep Child* 29:73–8 O '62. * (PA 37:6758)
13. SIEVERS, DOROTHY J., AND ROSENBERG, CARL M. "The Differential Language Facility Test and Electroencephalograms of Brain-Injured Mentally Retarded Children," pp. 567–72. In *Proceedings of the London Conference on the Scientific Study of Mental Deficiency, 1960, Vol. 2.* Edited by B. W. Richards. Dagenham, England: May & Baker Ltd., 1962. Pp. 353–690. *
14. BATEMAN, BARBARA D. "Reading and Psycholinguistic Process of Partially Seeing Children," pp. 70–86. In *Selected Studies on the Illinois Test of Psycholinguistic Abilities.* By Dorothy J. Sievers and others. [Urbana, Ill.: University of Illinois Press], 1963. Pp. vi, 96. *
15. CENTER, WILLIAM RUSSELL. *A Factor Analysis of Three Language and Communication Batteries.* Doctor's thesis, University of Georgia (Athens, Ga.), 1963. (DA 24:1918)
16. JAECKEL, LINDA RUTH. *A Study in the Comparison of Teachers' Ratings and the Illinois Test of Psycholinguistic Abilities in Determining the Language Ability of Deaf and Hard of Hearing Children.* Master's thesis, University of Kansas (Lawrence, Kan.), 1963.
17. KASS, CORRINE E. "Some Psychological Correlates of

Severe Reading Disability (Dyslexia)," pp. 87–96. In *Selected Studies on the Illinois Test of Psycholinguistic Abilities.* By Dorothy J. Sievers and others. [Urbana, Ill.: University of Illinois Press], 1963. Pp. vi, 196. *

18. McCarthy, James J. "Qualitative and Quantitative Differences in the Language Abilities of Young Cerebral Palsied Children," pp. 27–45. In *Selected Studies on the Illinois Test of Psycholinguistic Abilities.* By Dorothy J. Sievers and others. [Urbana, Ill.: University of Illinois Press], 1963. Pp. vi, 96. *

19. Myers, Patricia Irene. *A Comparison of Language Disabilities in Young Spastic and Athetoid Children.* Doctor's thesis, University of Texas (Austin, Tex.), 1963. (*DA* 24: 2788)

20. Olson, James L. "A Comparison of Receptive Aphasic, Expressive Aphasic, and Deaf Children on the Illinois Test of Psycholinguistic Abilities," pp. 46–69. In *Selected Studies on the Illinois Test of Psycholinguistic Abilities.* By Dorothy J. Sievers and others. [Urbana, Ill.: University of Illinois Press], 1963. Pp. vi, 96. *

21. Sievers, Dorothy J. "Development and Standardization of a Test of Psycholinguistic Growth in Preschool Children," pp. 1–26. In *Selected Studies on the Illinois Test of Psycholinguistic Abilities.* By Dorothy J. Sievers and others. [Urbana, Ill.: University of Illinois Press], 1963. Pp. vi, 96. *

22. Sievers, Dorothy J., and others. *Selected Studies on the Illinois Test of Psycholinguistic Abilities.* [Urbana, Ill.: University of Illinois Press], 1963. Pp. vi, 96. *

[550]

★**Jensen Alternation Board.** Ages 5 and over; 1959–60; learning age; individual; 2 forms on 1 board ['59]; mimeographed manual ['59, 5 pages]; supplementary data ('60, 15 pages, reprint of 2 below); $59 per board, postage extra; (5–70) minutes; Milton B. Jensen; Lafayette Instrument Co. *

REFERENCES

1. Jensen, Milton B. "A Light-Switch Alternation Apparatus." *Am J Psychol* 71:441–2 Je '58. * (*PA* 33:7238)
2. Jensen, Milton B. "Alternation Learning and Mental Pathology: Test Procedures and Findings." *J Psychol* 50:211–25 O '60. *

[551]

★**Kit of Reference Tests for Cognitive Factors, 1963 Revision.** Various grades 6–16; 1954–63; previously called *Kit of Selected Tests for Reference Aptitude and Achievement Factors;* for factorial research; groups of 3–5 tests which separately define 24 factors (listed below); manual ('63, 126 pages); no data on reliability and validity; no norms; $7.50 per set of manual and 1 copy of each test; cash orders postpaid on ETS orders; postage extra on Sheridan Supply Co. orders; additional copies of Sheridan Supply Co. tests (excluding m_1, p_1, s_2, w_2, and x_1 below) must be ordered directly from that publisher; all other tests may be reproduced without permission; kit of tests compiled and manual written by John W. French, Ruth B. Ekstrom, and Leighton A. Price; Educational Testing Service. *

a) FACTOR CF: FLEXIBILITY OF CLOSURE. Grades 6–16; 1962; 1 form (3–5 pages); 3 tests.
  1) *Hidden Figures Test, Cf-1.* $2.75 per 25 tests; 20(25) minutes.
  2) *Hidden Patterns Test, Cf-2.* $2.75 per 25 tests; 4(8) minutes.
  3) *Copying Test, Cf-3.* $2 per 25 tests; 6(10) minutes.

b) FACTOR CS: SPEED OF CLOSURE. Grades 6–16; 1962; 1 form (5 pages); 2 tests; $2.75 per 25 tests; 6(10) minutes.
  1) *Gestalt Completion Test, Cs-1.*
  2) *Concealed Words Test, Cs-2.*

c) FACTOR FA: ASSOCIATIONAL FLUENCY. Grades 6–16; 1957–62; 3 tests.
  1) *Controlled Associations Test, Fa-1.* 1962; 1 form (3 pages); $2 per 25 tests; 12(15) minutes.
  2) *Associational Fluency I,* [*Fa-2*]. See 544c; 1957; Form A (3 pages); $2 per 25 tests; 4(10) minutes; Paul R. Christensen and J. P. Guilford; Sheridan Supply Co.
  3) *Associations 4, Fa-3.* 1962; 1 form (3 pages); $2 per 25 tests; 14(18) minutes; J. P. Guilford.

d) FACTOR FE: EXPRESSIONAL FLUENCY. Grades 8–16; 1958–62; 3 tests.
  1) *Expressional Fluency,* [*Fe-1*]. See 544d; 1958; Form A (5 pages); $3.75 per 25 tests; 8(12) minutes; Paul R. Christensen and J. P. Guilford; Sheridan Supply Co.
  2) *Simile Interpretations, Fe-2.* 1962; 1 form (3 pages); $2 per 25 tests; 4(10) minutes; J. P. Guilford.
  3) *Word Arrangement, Fe-3.* 1962; 1 form (3 pages); $2 per 25 tests; 8(12) minutes; J. P. Guilford.

e) FACTOR FI: IDEATIONAL FLUENCY. Grades 8–16; 1962; 1 form (3 pages); 3 tests; $2 per 25 tests.
  1) *Topics Test, Fi-1.* 8(12) minutes.
  2) *Theme Test, Fi-2.* 8(12) minutes.
  3) *Thing Categories Test, Fi-3.* 6(10) minutes.

f) FACTOR FW: WORD FLUENCY. Grades 6–16; 1962; 1 form (3 pages); 3 tests; $2 per 25 tests; 6(10) minutes.
  1) *Word Endings Test, Fw-1.*
  2) *Word Beginnings Test, Fw-2.*
  3) *Word Beginnings and Endings Test, Fw-3.*

g) FACTOR I: INDUCTION. Grades 8–16; 1962; 3 tests.
  1) *Letter Sets Test, I-1.* 1 form (3 pages); $2 per 25 tests; 14(20) minutes.
  2) *Locations Test, I-2.* 1 form (3 pages); $2 per 25 tests; 12(17) minutes.
  3) *Figure Classification, I-3.* 1 form (9 pages); $3.75 per 25 tests; 16(20) minutes.

h) FACTOR LE: LENGTH ESTIMATION. Grades 6–16; 1962; 1 form (3 pages); 3 tests; $2 per 25 tests.
  1) *Estimation of Length Test, Le-1.* 6(10) minutes.
  2) *Shortest Road Test, Le-2.* 4(8) minutes.
  3) *Nearer Point Test, Le-3.* 4(8) minutes.

i) FACTOR MA: ASSOCIATIVE (ROTE) MEMORY. Grades 6–16; 1962; 1 form (6 pages); 3 tests; $3.75 per 25 tests.
  1) *Picture-Number Test, Ma-1.* 14(20) minutes.
  2) *Object-Number Test, Ma-2.* 10(15) minutes.
  3) *First and Last Names Test, Ma-3.* 10(15) minutes.

j) FACTOR MK: MECHANICAL KNOWLEDGE. 1962; 1 form (5–7 pages); 3 tests.
  1) *Tool Knowledge Test, Mk-1.* Grades 6–16; $2.75 per 25 tests; 10(15) minutes.
  2) *Mechanical Information Test, Mk-2.* Grades 8–16; $3.75 per 25 tests; 10(15) minutes.
  3) *Electrical Information Test, Mk-3.* Grades 8–16; $3.75 per 25 tests; 12(17) minutes.

k) FACTOR MS: MEMORY SPAN. Grades 6–16; 1962; 1 form (2 pages); 3 tests; $2 per 25 tests; (10) minutes.
  1) *Auditory Number Span Test, Ms-1.*
  2) *Visual Number Span Test, Ms-2.*
  3) *Auditory Letter Span Test, Ms-3.*

l) FACTOR N: NUMBER FACILITY. Grades 6–16; 1962; 1 form (3 pages); 3 tests; $2 per 25 tests; 4(10) minutes.
  1) *Addition Test, N-1.*
  2) *Division Test, N-2.*
  3) *Subtraction and Multiplication Test, N-3.*

m) FACTOR O: ORIGINALITY. Grades 10–16; 1958–62; 3 tests.
  1) *Plot Titles, O-1.* 1962; 1 form (3 pages); $2 per 25 tests; 6(10) minutes; Sheridan Supply Co.
  2) *Symbol Production, O-2.* 1962; 1 form (5 pages); $2.75 per 25 tests; 10(15) minutes; J. P. Guilford.
  3) *Consequences.* See 547; 1958; 1 form (11 pages); $5 per 25 tests; 20(30) minutes; P. R. Christensen, P. R. Merrifield, and J. P. Guilford; Sheridan Supply Co.

n) FACTOR P: PERCEPTUAL SPEED. Grades 6–16; 1962; 3 tests.
  1) *Finding A's Test, P-1.* 1 form (11 pages); $5 per 25 tests; 4(10) minutes.
  2) *Number Comparison Test, P-2.* 1 form (3 pages); $2 per 25 tests; 3(8) minutes.
  3) *Identical Pictures Test, P-3.* 1 form (5 pages); $2.75 per 25 tests; 3(8) minutes.
o) FACTOR R: GENERAL REASONING. 1955–62; 4 tests.
  1) *Mathematics Aptitude Test, R-1.* Grades 6–12; 1962; 1 form (7 pages); $3.75 per 25 tests; 20(25) minutes.
  2) *Mathematics Aptitude Test, R-2.* Grades 11–16; 1962; 1 form (7 pages); $3.75 per 25 tests; 20(25) minutes.
  3) *Ship Destination Test, [R-3].* See 500; 1955; Form A (3 pages); $2.50 per 25 tests; 15(20) minutes; Paul R. Christensen and J. P. Guilford; Sheridan Supply Co.
  4) *Necessary Arithmetic Operations Test, R-4.* Grades 6–16; 1962; 1 form (7 pages); $3.75 per 25 tests; 10(15) minutes.
p) FACTOR RE: SEMANTIC REDEFINITION. Grades 10–16; 1962; 1 form (3–4 pages); 3 tests.
  1) *Gestalt Transformation, Re-1.* $2 per 25 tests; 10(15) minutes; Sheridan Supply Co.
  2) *Object Synthesis, Re-2.* $2 per 25 tests; 10(15) minutes; J. P. Guilford.
  3) *Picture Gestalt, Re-3.* $2.75 per 25 tests; 9(15) minutes; J. P. Guilford.
q) FACTOR RS: SYLLOGISTIC REASONING. Grades 11–16; 1955–62; 3 tests.
  1) *Nonsense Syllogisms Test, Rs-1.* 1962; 1 form 3 pages); $2 per 25 tests; 8(12) minutes.
  2) *Logical Reasoning [Rs-2].* See 5:694; 1955; Form A (7 pages); $4 per 25 tests; 20(25) minutes; Alfred F. Hertza and J. P. Guilford; Sheridan Supply Co.
  3) *Inference Test, Rs-3.* 1962; 1 form (7 pages); $3.75 per 25 tests; 12(17) minutes.
r) FACTOR S: SPATIAL ORIENTATION. 1947–62; 3 tests.
  1) *Card Rotations Test, S-1.* Grades 8–16; 1962; 1 form (3 pages); $2 per 25 tests; 8(12) minutes.
  2) *Cube Comparisons Test, S-2.* Grades 8–16; 1962; 1 form (3 pages); $2 per 25 tests; 6(10) minutes.
  3) *Guilford-Zimmerman Aptitude Survey: Part 5, Spatial Orientation, [S-3].* See 772e; 1947; Form A (8 pages); $4 per 25 tests; 10(20) minutes; J. P. Guilford and Wayne S. Zimmerman; Sheridan Supply Co.
s) FACTOR SEP: SENSITIVITY TO PROBLEMS. Grades 8–16; 1962; 1 form (5–7 pages); 3 tests.
  1) *Apparatus Test, Sep-1.* $2.75 per 25 tests; 14(20) minutes; J. P. Guilford.
  2) *Seeing Problems, Sep-2.* $2.75 per 25 tests; 12(15) minutes; Sheridan Supply Co.
  3) *Seeing Deficiencies, Sep-3.* $3.75 per 25 tests; 20(25) minutes; J. P. Guilford.
t) FACTOR SS: SPATIAL SCANNING. Grades 6–16; 1962; 1 form (3–6 pages); 3 tests.
  1) *Maze Tracing Speed Test, Ss-1.* $2 per 25 tests; 6(10) minutes.
  2) *Choosing a Path, Ss-2.* $3.75 per 25 tests; 14(20) minutes.
  3) *Map Planning Test, Ss-3.* $2 per 25 tests; 6(10) minutes.
u) FACTOR V: VERBAL COMPREHENSION. 1962; 1 form (3 pages); 5 tests; $2 per 25 tests.
  1) *Vocabulary Test, V-1.* Grades 7–12; 8(12) minutes.
  2) *Vocabulary Test, V-2.* Grades 7–12; 8(12) minutes.
  3) *Wide Range Vocabulary Test, V-3.* Grades 7–16; 12(17) minutes.
  4) *Advanced Vocabulary Test, V-4.* Grades 11–16; 8(12) minutes.
  5) *Vocabulary Test, V-5.* Grades 11–16; 8(12) minutes.
v) FACTOR VZ: VISUALIZATION. Grades 9–16; 1962; 1 form (3–5 pages); 3 tests.
  1) *Form Board Test, Vz-1.* $2.75 per 25 tests; 16(20) minutes.
  2) *Paper Folding Test, Vz-2.* $2 per 25 tests; 6(10) minutes.
  3) *Surface Development Test, Vz-3.* $2.75 per 25 tests; 12(15) minutes.
w) FACTOR XA: FIGURAL ADAPTIVE FLEXIBILITY. Grades 11–16; 1962; 3 tests.
  1) *Match Problems 2, Xa-1.* 1 form (4 pages); $3.75 per 25 tests; 14(20) minutes; Sheridan Supply Co.
  2) *Match Problems 5, Xa-2.* 1 form (3 pages); $2 per 25 tests; 10(15) minutes; Sheridan Supply Co.
  3) *Planning Air Maneuvers, Xa-3.* 1 form (7 pages); $3.75 per 25 tests; 16(25) minutes.
x) FACTOR XS: SEMANTIC SPONTANEOUS FLEXIBILITY. Grades 6–16; 1960–62; 3 tests.
  1) *Utility Test, Xs-1.* 1962; 1 form (3 pages); $2 per 25 tests; 10(15) minutes; Sheridan Supply Co.
  2) *Alternate Uses, [Xs-2].* See 542; 1960; 1 form (4 pages); $2 per 25 tests; 12(17) minutes; J. P. Guilford, Philip R. Merrifield, and Robert C. Wilson; Sheridan Supply Co.
  3) *Object Naming, Xs-3.* 1962; 1 form (3 pages); $2 per 25 tests; 4(8) minutes; J. P. Guilford.

[552]
★**Making Objects.** Grades 9–16 and adults; 1963; "divergent production of figural systems" or "figural expressional fluency"; Form A (3 pages); mimeographed manual (4 pages); no data on reliability; norms for ninth graders and adult males only; $2 per 25 tests; 10¢ per single copy; 25¢ per manual; postage extra; [3(10)] minutes; Sheldon Gardner, Arthur Gershon, Philip R. Merrifield, and J. P. Guilford; Sheridan Supply Co. *

REFERENCES
1. GUILFORD, J. P. *Personality.* New York: McGraw-Hill Book Co., Inc., 1959. Pp. xiii, 562. *

[553]
★**Marianne Frostig Developmental Test of Visual Perception, Third Edition.** Ages 3–8; 1961–64; 6 scores: eye-motor coordination, figure-ground discrimination, form constancy, position in space, spatial relations, total, perceptual quotient; 1 form ('63, c1961, 19 pages); demonstration cards ['63, 11 cards]; administration and scoring manual ('64, c1961–64, 37 pages); monograph on 1963 standardization ('64, 38 pages, *Percept & Motor Skills* 19:463-99 O '64); $10.50 per examiner's kit of 10 tests, scoring keys, demonstration cards, monograph, and manual; $5 per specimen set (without demonstration cards); postage extra; (30–45) minutes for individual administration, (40–60) minutes for group administration; Marianne Frostig in collaboration with D. Welty Lefever, John R. B. Whittlesey, and Phyllis Maslow (monograph); Consulting Psychologists Press, Inc. * [The reviews which follow are of the third edition materials which were previously published by the Marianne Frostig School of Educational Therapy and which, except for format, were essentially the same as the materials described in this entry.]

REFERENCES
1. FROSTIG, MARIANNE; LEFEVER, D. WELTY; AND WHITTLESEY, JOHN R. B. "A Developmental Test of Visual Perception for Evaluating Normal and Neurologically Handicapped Children." *Percept & Motor Skills* 12:383-94 Je '61. * (*PA* 36:2JF83F)

2. FROSTIG, MARIANNE. "Visual Perception in the Brain-Damaged Child." Abstract. *Am J Orthopsychiatry* 32:279-80 Mr '62. *

3. FROSTIG, MARIANNE, AND HORNE, DAVID. "Assessment of Visual Perception and Its Importance in Education." *A.A.M.D. Ed Reporter* 2:11-2 Ap '62. *

4. SCHELLENBERG, ERNEST DAVID. *A Study of the Relationship Between Visual-Motor Perception and Reading Disabilities of Third Grade Pupils.* Doctor's thesis, University of Southern California (Los Angeles, Calif.), 1962. (*DA* 23:3785)

5. CORAH, NORMAN L., AND POWELL, BARBARA J. "A Factor Analytic Study of the Frostig Developmental Test of Visual Perception." *Percept & Motor Skills* 16:59-63 F '63. * (*PA* 38:677)

6. FROSTIG, MARIANNE. "Visual Perception in the Brain-Injured Child." *Am J Orthopsychiatry* 33:665-71 Jl '63. * (*PA* 38:7979)

7. FROSTIG, MARIANNE; LEFEVER, WELTY; AND WHITTLESEY, JOHN. "Disturbances in Visual Perception." *J Ed Res* 57:160-2 N '63. *

JAMES M. ANDERSON, *Research Consultant, Institute of Therapeutic Psychology, Santa Ana, California.*

According to the authors, "The test is designed to measure certain operationally defined perceptual functions, and to pinpoint the age at which they normally develop." There are five subtests: Test 1, Eye-Motor Coordination (16 items); Test 2, Figure-Ground (8 items); Test 3, Form Constancy (17 items); Test 4, Position in Space (8 items); and Test 5, Spatial Relations (8 items). Results are reported in terms of age equivalents, scale scores, and perceptual quotients (analogous in appearance, though not in method of derivation, to Wechsler type intelligence quotients).

All of the materials supplied with the specimen set range in aesthetic quality from mediocre to poor. This statement holds for both the quality of the art work and the printing. This seems hardly excusable for a "third" edition.

The directions on the whole are clear and concise. However, lack of time limits or instructions for what to do with the laggards should prove a handicap for some teachers. (I may be presumptuous here since there is no indication of the level of training needed for scoring or interpretation.) The directions for Test 2 could be improved if they were made more consistent. The examiner is told: "It is important to explain 'outline' and to use this word consistently throughout the remainder of the test. The expression 'draw around' is often interpreted literally by the child, and he may draw a circle around the figure." Yet for item 2 of this test the child is instructed to "Find the long box and trace around it." The same directions are employed for items 3 and 4 of this test. (The reviewer is here quoting from a typed second revision of the third edition of the Administration Manual supplied by the senior author and apparently intended to obviate the difficulty encountered in the manual supplied with the specimen set, which contains the instruction to "draw around.") Similarly, on Test 3 the inclusion of the word "mark" in the instructions introduces a confusing element since the scoring standards require outlining within fairly strict limits. Then, for two items in Test 3 the instructions are, "You are to draw around all of the balls (circles)" when outlining is required. Although the test is untimed, in Test 3 the examiner is advised, "If one child takes longer than the rest of the group, stop him and continue the test." From this it would follow that the last child finishing would be interrupted on each item of this test.

Instructions for scoring are straightforward and clear. Good examples illustrate the criteria for scoring each item. The Scoring and Evaluation Booklet should prove most helpful to users of the test. A paradoxical situation, however, prevails in the scoring of Test 1 wherein items 5 and 9, the most difficult items, receive decreased weight. No rationale is presented for this paradox.

Information for evaluating this test is at best incomplete if not haphazardly presented. The latest edition of the Scoring and Evaluation Booklet refers to the "Fourth preliminary standardization....on 2116 unselected school children at the nursery school, kindergarten, first, second and third grade levels." Nowhere in this booklet is there presented a breakdown of the composition of this standardization population. One cannot help but wonder if this increased *n,* increased over any previously published figure, represents a cumulation of cases accumulated under questionable conditions of variation in both test materials and directions.

The authors of this test have such a real contribution to offer to educators and psychologists alike that it is regrettable that they have apparently prematurely offered their test as a finished product. In a prepublication report on the 1962 standardization, this reviewer finds evidence of much thought and careful work as well as an excellent start at standardization. The concepts of perceptual age and perceptual quotient appear most useful and intriguing. Both reliability and validity studies reported in this paper are promising and even exciting though they are done on inadequate samples and on varying age groups.

The primary use of this instrument at this

time would seem to be that of predicting learning success in the primary grades. It contains types of items commonly found in reading readiness tests. The authors have apparently chosen to build a test of low band width (complexity of information) and high fidelity (exactness of information). In this they seem to have succeeded. It is hoped that when a complete manual on the test is presented it will present the authors' theoretical position in the field of perception as well as some attempt at construct validity.

MARY C. AUSTIN, *Professor of Education, Western Reserve University, Cleveland, Ohio.*

Frostig and her co-workers consider vision a developmental process which is directly related to early school success. They have evolved a series of tests for young children to measure their perceptual abilities and "to pinpoint the age at which they normally develop." To the extent that school success depends on these abilities it can, they believe, be predicted from the test. The severity of the perceptual disturbances can be evaluated, regardless of their etiology, and training procedures designed to correct the specific disabilities can be provided.

During the testing period the child attempts carefully graded tasks in five areas of visual perception. In eye-hand coordination, he must draw straight and curved lines between increasingly narrow boundaries or a straight line to a target. In figure-ground perception, he must discriminate between intersecting shapes and find hidden figures. In the form constancy subtest, he must discriminate circles and squares, in different shadings, sizes, and positions, from other shapes on the page. Subtest four, a measure of the perception of position in space, requires the child to differentiate between figures in an identical position and those in a reversed or rotated position. In the final test, one of spatial relationships, the task is to copy patterns by linking dots. Obviously, the tasks are varied, and the use of colored pencils on some of the items should further capture the child's interest. Even so, the time element involved appears lengthy for the attention span of young children.

Directions for administering the test are relatively clear from the examiner's standpoint. The initial directions to children, however, may be somewhat confusing for them, particularly the concept of not lifting the pencil from the paper in the eye-hand coordination test. There is some evidence also of inappropriate vocabulary for young children, i.e., the word "tunnel" which is necessary to the successful completion of the first test item. The test booklet itself may be too bulky for nursery and first grade youngsters to handle. Folding pages back is difficult for children at these ages. The stated optimum number for group testing at the kindergarten level is 6 to 8 (8 to 10 in a typewritten copy of the second revision of the manual for administration), and this size group would make the testing of an entire group too time consuming in most school situations.

Scoring of the Frostig test is for the most part objective and easy to learn. A perceptual quotient as well as a perceptual age can be derived from the score. The perceptual quotient (PQ) shows the developmental level of the child in relation to his chronological age. There may be a tendency, especially for the untrained and inexperienced, to interpret the perceptual quotient as something akin to the intelligence quotient. A thorough explanation of the PQ would have to be undertaken before the results of the test could be used effectively. Some examiners have questioned the practice of giving no credit in the eye-hand coordination subtest for an exercise with lines drawn too short or too long, underdrawing and overdrawing being measured to an eighth of an inch and a half inch, respectively. The scoring standards on subtests 3a and 3b (Form Constancy) are somewhat difficult to interpret and understand.

The test has been standardized on over 1,800 apparently "normal" children, with no tests given by untrained examiners. Sampling appears adequate within the five- to nine-year age range. This is not true at the lower levels, and more subjects at the preschool level should be tested. The authors' proposals for future research include the possibility of gathering additional samples for the purpose of comparing the norms of nursery school children with those in day care centers and those children not attending any nursery school. Hopefully, such comparisons may shed light on the question of differential performance at this age level. In any event, children of lower socioeconomic classes should be included since there are almost none of them in the present standardization group.

Test-retest reliability of the perceptual quo-

Marianne Frostig Developmental Test of Visual Perception

tient ($n = 35$ first and 37 second graders tested two weeks apart) is reported as .80 for the total sample. Subtest scale score test-retest correlations are reported to range from .42 (Figure-Ground) to .80 (Form Constancy). Validity has been investigated through correlations between scaled scores and teacher ratings of classroom adjustment (.44), motor coordination (.50), and intellectual functioning (.50). Correlations between Frostig and Goodenough scores range from .32 to .46. In a study of 25 children the Frostig test "proved to be highly accurate" in identifying children who would not attempt to learn to read when "exposed to reading material but not forced to use it." Low test scores are also reported to be related to the presence of severe learning difficulties.

The Frostig test appears to be a significant one. It has proved useful as a screening tool with groups of nursery school, kindergarten, and first grade children, primarily because it permits identification of those children who need special perceptual training in five important areas of visual perception. It should also be valuable as a clinical tool with children beyond first grade.

[554]
★**Match Problems.** Grades 9–16 and adults; 1963; formerly called *Match Problems 2;* "divergent production of figural transformations" or "originality in dealing with concrete visual material"; Form A (4 pages); mimeographed manual, preliminary edition (3 pages); scoring guide (5 pages); norms for ninth graders on the current form and adults on an earlier form only; $3.75 per 25 tests; 20¢ per single copy; 50¢ per set of manual and scoring guide; postage extra; 14(22) minutes; Raymond M. Berger and J. P. Guilford; Sheridan Supply Co. *

REFERENCES

1. BERGER, R. M.; GUILFORD, J. P.; AND CHRISTENSEN, P. R. "A Factor-Analytic Study of Planning Abilities." *Psychol Monogr* 71(6):1–31 '57. * (*PA* 33:6967)
2. GUILFORD, J. P. *Personality.* New York: McGraw-Hill Book Co., Inc., 1959. Pp. xiii, 562. *
3. BRITTAIN, W. LAMBERT, AND BEITTEL, KENNETH R. "A Study of Some Tests of Creativity to Performances in the Visual Arts." *Studies Art Ed* 2:54–65 sp '61. *
4. MARKS, ALVIN; MICHAEL, WILLIAM B.; AND KAISER, HENRY F. "Dimensions of Creativity and Temperament in Officer Evaluation." *Psychol Rep* 9:635–8 D '61. *
5. MARKS, ALVIN; MICHAEL, WILLIAM B.; AND KAISER, HENRY F. "Sources of Noncognitive Variance in 21 Measures of Creativity." *Psychol Rep* 9:287–90 O '61. *
6. CLINE, VICTOR B.; RICHARDS, JAMES M., JR.; AND ABE, CLIFFORD. "The Validity of a Battery of Creativity Tests in a High School Sample." *Ed & Psychol Meas* 22:781–4 w '62. * (*PA* 37:7184)
7. CLINE, VICTOR B.; RICHARDS, JAMES M., JR.; AND NEEDHAM, WALTER E. "Creativity Tests and Achievement in High School Science." *J Appl Psychol* 47:184–9 Je '63. * (*PA* 37:8223)

[555]
*****Nufferno Tests of Speed and Level.** Mental Ages 11 and over; 1956–62; 5 tests; 6s. per 25 tests; postage extra; W. D. Furneaux; distributed by University of London Press Ltd. *

a) NUFFERNO SPEED TESTS. 1956–62; 5 scores: speed (stressed or unstressed), speed-range, speed slope, stress speed-gain, accuracy; 2 tests; manual ['56, 34 pages] plus 18 mimeographed pages ['62] of corrections and revisions; 9s. 6d. per manual and supplementary pages; 10s. per specimen set.
  1) *Nufferno Sheet 1: Test GIS/14E.36.* Mental ages 11–15; Forms A(1), A(2), ['56, both forms on 1 sheet]; (15) minutes.
  2) *Nufferno Sheet 2: Test GIS/14E.36.* Mental ages 13 and over; Forms A(2), B(1), ['56, both forms on 1 sheet]; (20) minutes.
b) NUFFERNO LEVEL TESTS. 1956; 3 tests; manual ['56, 22 pages]; 6s. 6d. per manual; 7s. 6d. per specimen set.
  1) *Nufferno Level Test Cards: Test IL/2(AB)36.* Mental ages 11 and over; individual; 2 scores: personal level, situation level; 1 form ['56, 54 cards]; 17s. 6d. per set of cards; (40) minutes.
  2) *Nufferno Sheet 3: Test GL/2C.46.* Adults with IQ's 100 and over; 1 form ['56, 2 pages]; (40) minutes.
  3) *Nufferno Sheet 4: Test GL/3A.35.* Mental ages 11 and over; 1 form ['56, 2 pages]; (40) minutes.

REFERENCES

1–3. See 5:357.
4. PAYNE, R. W.; MATTUSSEK, P.; AND GEORGE, E. I. "An Experimental Study of Schizophrenic Thought Disorder." *J Mental Sci* 105:627–52 Jl '59. * (*PA* 34:6384)
5. PAYNE, R. W., AND HEWLETT, J. H. G. Chap. 1, "Thought Disorder in Psychotic Patients," pp. 3–104. In *Experiments in Personality: Vol. 2, Psychodiagnostics and Psychodynamics.* Edited by H. J. Eysenck. London: Routledge & Kegan Paul Ltd., 1960. Pp. viii, 333. *
6. BRIERLEY, HARRY. "The Speed and Accuracy Characteristics of Neurotics." *Brit J Psychol* 52:273–80 Ag '61. * (*PA* 36:3HI73B)
7. PAYNE, R. W. Chap. 6, "Cognitive Abnormalities," pp. 193–261. In *Handbook of Abnormal Psychology: An Experimental Approach.* Edited by H. J. Eysenck. New York: Basic Books, Inc., 1961. Pp. xvi, 816. * (*PA* 35:6719)

For reviews by John Liggett and E. A. Peel, see 5:357.

[556]
★**Perceptual Speed (Identical Forms).** Grades 9–16 and industrial employees; 1959, c1956–59; 1 form ('56, 8 pages); manual ('59, 13 pages); norms for males only; $4 per 20 tests, postage extra; $1 per specimen set, postpaid; 5(10) minutes; L. L. Thurstone (test), T. E. Jeffrey (test), and Measurement Research Division, Industrial Relations Center, University of Chicago (manual); Education-Industry Service. *

LEROY WOLINS, *Associate Professor of Psychology and Statistics, Iowa State University, Ames, Iowa.*

This test is very likely a good measure of the perceptual speed factor, which, in turn, is known to be predictive of performance in certain types of jobs. However, the manual presents only a few validity studies involving small samples and it is not clear whether the reliability data reported are specific to this instrument.

The normative data presented are not useful since the manual does not describe the sample adequately. It merely states that the sample consists of 182 male industrial employees.

More useful normative data are available from the publisher.

In summary, the only acceptable portion of the manual is the instructions for administration and scoring. This reviewer is pleased that this test has been made available and would not discourage its use for those who wish to find out if it is valid in their particular situation.

[557]

★**Pertinent Questions.** Grades 9–16 and adults; 1960; experimental form; conceptual foresight; Form A (3 pages); duplicated manual, preliminary edition (13 pages); no norms for high school; $2 per 25 tests; 15¢ per single copy; 50¢ per manual; postage extra; 12(20) minutes; Raymond M. Berger, J. P. Guilford, and P. R. Merrifield (manual); Sheridan Supply Co. *

REFERENCES

1. MARKS, ALVIN; MICHAEL, WILLIAM B.; AND KAISER, HENRY F. "Dimensions of Creativity and Temperament in Officer Evaluation." *Psychol Rep* 9:635–8 D '61. *
2. MARKS, ALVIN; MICHAEL, WILLIAM B.; AND KAISER, HENRY F. "Sources of Noncognitive Variance in 21 Measures of Creativity." *Psychol Rep* 9:287–90 O '61. *
3. MERRIFIELD, P. R.; GUILFORD, J. P.; CHRISTENSEN, P. R.; AND FRICK, J. W. "The Role of Intellectual Factors in Problem Solving." *Psychol Monogr* 76(10):1–21 '62. *

[558]

★**Possible Jobs.** Grades 6–16 and adults; 1963; "divergent production of semantic implications" or "ability to suggest alternative deductions"; Form A (3 pages); mimeographed manual (6 pages); norms based on sixth, ninth, and tenth graders only; $2 per 25 tests; 10¢ per single copy; 35¢ per manual; postage extra; 10(15) minutes; Arthur Gershon and J. P. Guilford; Sheridan Supply Co. *

REFERENCES

1. GUILFORD, J. P. *Personality*. New York: McGraw-Hill Book Co., Inc., 1959. Pp. xiii, 562. *

[559]

★**The Rutgers Drawing Test.** Ages 4–6, 6–9; 1952–61; 2 levels labeled forms; no data on reliability; $2 per 25 tests; $1 per specimen set of both levels; postpaid; (5–10) minutes; Anna Spiesman Starr; the Author. *

a) [FORM A.] Ages 4–6; 1952; test ['52, 1 page]; manual ('52, 21 pages, reprint of *1* below).
b) FORM B. Ages 6–9; 1959–61; test ('59, 1 page); manual ('61, 31 pages).

REFERENCES

1. STARR, ANNA SPIESMAN. "The Rutgers Drawing Test." *Training Sch B* 49:45–64 My '52. * (PA 27:444)
2. LETON, DONALD A. "A Factor Analysis of Readiness Tests." *Percept & Motor Skills* 16:915–9 Je '63. * (PA 38:6584)

[560]

★**Subsumed Abilities Test.** Ages 9 and over; 1957–63; subtitle on manual is *A Measure of Learning Efficiency*; 5 scores: recognition, abstraction, conceptualization, total (demonstrated abilities), potential abilities; 1 form ('57, 8 pages); manual ('63, 12 pages); no data on reliability of subscores or potential abilities score; no norms for potential abilities score; $6.25 per 25 tests; $2.75 per 25 scoring key-tabulation sheets; $1.75 per manual; $2.50 per specimen set; cash orders postpaid; 30(40) minutes; Joseph R. Sanders; Martin M. Bruce. *

NAOMI STEWART, *Formerly Staff Associate, Educational Testing Service, Princeton, New Jersey.*

This test is made up of 30 items, to each of which the examinee must give not one but two responses. Each item consists of four line drawings; the examinee must identify three that are alike in some way (shape, size, content, position, or whatever) and then, again, three (which may or may not be the same three) that are alike in a different way.

In theory, at least, success on the *Subsumed Abilities Test* depends on three "subsumed" or "hierarchical" perceptual skills: the first, Recognition, is, according to the manual, a prerequisite of the second, Abstraction, which, in turn, is a prerequisite of the third, Conceptualization. Of the 30 items, 10 are supposed on a purely a priori basis to be recognition items, another 10, abstraction items, and the remaining 10, conceptualization items. The three sets of items are loosely matched with respect to general character of the line drawings they comprise—e.g., items 1, 11, and 21, supposedly measuring Recognition, Abstraction, and Conceptualization, respectively, all contain vaguely canoe-shaped figures; items 4, 14, and 24, supposedly measuring Abstraction, Conceptualization, and Recognition, in that order, all contain rectangular figures. One point is given for each correct response. The maximum possible score on each subtest is 20 and the maximum possible total score, called the "Demonstrated Abilities Score," is 60.

Provision is also made for calculating still another score, namely, the "Potential Abilities Score." In this calculation, a correct response to a conceptualization item earns 3 points regardless of whether the companion recognition and abstraction items are correct or incorrect. An incorrect answer to a conceptualization item earns 1 point if the corresponding recognition item is right but the abstraction item is wrong, and 2 points if the abstraction item is right regardless of the response to the recognition item.

This is an exceedingly elaborate structure of scores, subscores, and superscores to base on a total of 30 items, especially when the available reliability figures are thin and fragmentary. No reliability data are given for Recognition, Abstraction, or Conceptualization, or for Potential Abilities. With respect to Demonstrated Abilities (which is simply the total number of correct responses), odd-even reliability figures of .97, .81, and .35, respectively, are reported for 30 hospitalized psychotic veterans, 21 fifth and sixth grade students, and 26 tenth grade students; a split-half reliability of .96 is given for a group of 26 open ward psychotics; and a test-retest reliability of .64 is reported for a group of college students (number of cases not given).

So far as validity data are concerned, the figures are even more fragmentary. Moreover, it is almost impossible to ascertain what the test is intended to measure or what it is actually measuring. There are at least three different, and to some extent mutually incompatible, foci of emphasis or "motifs" running through the various statements in the Examiner's Manual: first, the "subsumed abilities" motif (stressing the idea that the test is supposedly measuring a hierarchy of perceptual skills) for which no empirical support is ever given; secondly, what might be called the "fluidity" motif; and third, the "learning efficiency" motif.

Because an examinee must make more than one response to each item, the test presumably involves an element of fluidity, or ability to make appropriate shifts in perceptual responses. This "fluidity" aspect of the test is given major emphasis in the historical background section of both the original (1958) and the revised (1963) Examiner's Manual. Both manuals trace the relationship and similarity of the test to certain earlier (individually administered) tests requiring flexibility of perceptual response, which successfully differentiated psychotic from normal subjects. But whereas the original manual extends and enlarges upon this general train of thought—stating, e.g., "The purpose of the Subsumed Abilities Test is to measure intellectual abilities in relation to emotional state. It is a measure of a person's ability to perform complex intellectual tasks under varying degrees of stress"—the revised manual soft-pedals this motif outside of the historical background section. It makes no mention of stress or of measuring intellectual abilities in relation to emotional state. Without any qualification it terms the test "a measure of learning efficiency," and talks of its applicability to the junior and senior high school counseling situation, to the personnel hiring situation, to employee placement, and to rehabilitation counseling.

The publisher's catalog, too, omits any reference to stress, the differentiation of psychotics from nonpsychotics, and similar matters, and describes the test as a "non-verbal test measuring ability to handle abstractions and concepts," characterizing it as "a valuable aid in diagnosing the ability to learn." This shift toward an emphasis on the *general* applicability of the *Subsumed Abilities Test* seems most unfortunate, inasmuch as the validity of the test as a general measure of learning ability, or learning efficiency, has in no way been established.[1] Moreover, such data as appear in the manual tend to refute, rather than confirm, the likelihood that the test possesses any useful discriminating power except perhaps in the very special type of circumstances found in a mental hospital.

Of all the various figures given in the manual, only the data for psychotics versus nonpsychotics reveal a difference in demonstrated ability score (DAS) means that is large enough to possess any practical significance: (*a*) 26 open ward psychotics—mean DAS 45.35, SD 7.60; (*b*) 15 closed ward psychotics—mean DAS 36.46, SD 12.98; (*c*) 30 hospitalized psychotic veterans—mean DAS 41.40, SD 9.95; (*d*) "normal" group of college students (very roughly equal in age and education to groups *a* and *b*)—mean DAS 51.88, SD 5.59. Unfortunately, the data are not only based on very small numbers of cases but also are not readily accessible in the original; the figures for group *c* are reported as coming from a personal communication to the test author, and the remaining ones from an unpublished master's thesis.

The lack of general applicability of the test may be seen by examining the demonstrated ability score distributions given in the manual for various "normative" groups. For example, the 193 college psychology students (mean DAS 52.50, SD 8.71) and the 291 salesmanship students (mean DAS 51.68, SD 5.31) perform about on a par with the 45 sixth grade school children (mean DAS 51.63, SD 7.96) and the 21 fifth and sixth grade school children (mean DAS 52.57, SD 4.11), but not

---

[1] The 1958 Examiner's Manual at least was frank in that respect, stating (page 12): "*To what extent does performance on the S.A.T. correspond to one's ability to learn a novel skill or subject?* Copies of the group version of the S.A.T. and this manual are being distributed in order to gather answers to this and related questions." If any answers were gathered they are not given in the 1963 Examiner's Manual, and the question itself has been deleted from the text, which now fails to make explicit what is still perfectly true.

Subsumed Abilities Test

quite so well as the 26 tenth grade children (mean DAS 55.27, SD 2.44). The 74 supervisors—middle management and executive personnel, including such job titles as factory superintendent, chief chemist, personnel director, and vice president for sales—do about as well (mean DAS 49.65, SD 6.41) as the 23 factory workers who were applying for jobs as lappers, grinders, and inspectors in a ball bearing factory (mean DAS 49.70, SD 6.21)!

Presumably to forestall this very type of criticism, the 1963 Examiner's Manual furnishes a disclaimer under Conclusions (page 7):

> These studies suggest that the SAT is a relatively valid and reliable instrument when used as a screening device for separating those who are willing and able to learn or to utilize visual symbol systems from those for whom either an interview or further testing is needed to determine if such willingness and ability are present. It does not appear to be a highly reliable instrument for differentiating among individuals currently demonstrating relatively good ability to learn and to utilize visual symbol systems (e.g., accelerated tenth graders and college students). These findings are consistent with the purpose and rationale of the test, and are reflected in the limits recommended for interpreting scores.

Regrettably, of the three sentences that make up this quotation, the first and last are not substantiated by any data given in the manual, while the disclaimer itself is too well buried in a mass of verbiage to be of much use as a deterrent to anyone contemplating the purchase of the test.

The failure of the demonstrated abilities score to differentiate among the various groups is not really surprising. Even a superficial examination of the items making up the test reveals that in a great many instances it is possible to arrive at a "wrong" answer that is just as good by many standards as the answer keyed as correct. Some of the correct responses, moreover, are so obvious as to be almost insulting, and consequently in many instances the more intelligent examinee is more likely than the less intelligent one to produce a "wrong" answer. This is particularly true of the recognition items, as evidenced by the fact that (a) the mean recognition score is above 19 for nine of the ten "normative" groups (18.92 for the tenth), 20 being the maximum possible score, and (b) the only individuals who gave as many as 7 incorrect responses to the 10 recognition items were college students, professional, white collar, and secretarial applicants, and supervisors. None of the grade school children or factory workers made this many errors! Some of the abstraction items also appear to be operating in reverse, and this is borne out by examination of the abstraction score distributions. The conceptualization score seems to be least affected by this kind of attenuation. (Parenthetically, one might note in this connection that if the potential abilities score has any useful discriminating power—and there are no data on this point in the manual—it is undoubtedly because the largest contributor to the variance of the potential abilities score is the number of correct conceptualization responses.)

There are a number of additional criticisms that might be made, particularly of the misleading and certainly over-optimistic use in the manual of such terms as "cross-validation group," "content validity studies," and "concurrent validity studies," but there seems no point in belaboring this matter further. If the *Subsumed Abilities Test* is a valid measure of anything at all, this has yet to be demonstrated, and so far as this reviewer is concerned, it is highly questionable whether it should be offered for sale as a testing device.

[561]

*Wechsler Memory Scale. Adults; 1945-63; individual; Forms 1, 2; record forms for Forms 1 ('62, c1945), 2 ('63, c1948), (2 pages, slight revisions of the forms copyrighted in 1945 and 1948); manual ('62, 21 pages, a combined reprinting of 1 and 2 published in 1945 and 1946); $3.75 per set of 50 record forms and set of cards for visual reproduction subtest; 75¢ per manual; $1 per specimen set of both forms; postpaid; (15) minutes; David Wechsler and Calvin P. Stone (Form 2); Psychological Corporation. *

REFERENCES

1-3. See 3:302.
4-9. See 4:364.
10. WEIDER, ARTHUR. "Wechsler Memory Scale," pp. 757-9. (PA 27:7806) In *Contributions Toward Medical Psychology: Theory and Psychodiagnostic Methods*, Vol. II. Edited by Arthur Weider. New York: Ronald Press Co., 1953. Pp. xi, 459-885. *
11. HOWARD, ALVIN R. "Further Validation Studies of the Wechsler Memory Scale." *J Clin Psychol* 10:164-7 Ap '54. * (PA 29:926)
12. PARKER, JAMES W. "The Validity of Some Current Tests for Organicity." *J Consult Psychol* 21:425-8 O '57. * (PA 33:1297)
13. SHONTZ, FRANKLIN C. "Evaluation of Intellectual Potential in Hemiplegic Individuals." *J Clin Psychol* 13:267-9 Jl '57. * (PA 32:5816)
14. STROTHER, CHARLES R.; SCHAIE, K. WARNER; AND HORST, PAUL. "The Relationship Between Advanced Age and Mental Abilities." *J Abn & Social Psychol* 55:166-70 S '57. * (PA 33:3294)
15. WALTON, D. "The Diagnostic and Predictive Accuracy of the Wechsler Memory Scale in Psychiatric Patients Over 65." *J Mental Sci* 104:1111-8 O '58. * (PA 33:10793)
16. BLOOM, BERNARD L. "Comparison of the Alternate Wechsler Memory Scale Forms." *J Clin Psychol* 15:72-4 Ja '59. * (PA 34:3261)
17. VICTOR, MAURICE; HERMAN, KENNETH; AND WHITE, ELISABETH E. "A Psychological Study of the Wernicke-Korsakoff Syndrome: Results of Wechsler-Bellevue Intelligence Scale and Wechsler Memory Scale Testing at Different Stages in the Disease." *Q J Studies Alcohol* 20:467-79 S '59. * (PA 34:6401)

18. SHAW, JAMES HOWARD. *Memory Processes in Schizophrenics and Normals.* Doctor's thesis, Washington State University (Pullman, Wash.), 1960. (*DA* 21:2371)

For reviews by Ivan Norman Mensh and Joseph Newman, see 4:364; for a review by Kate Levine Kogan, see 3:302.

[562]

★**Word Fluency.** Industrial employees; 1959–61; 1 form ('61, 2 pages); manual ('59, 30 pages); norms for males only; $2 per 20 tests, postage extra; $1 per specimen set, postpaid; 10(15) minutes; Raymond J. Corsini and Measurement Research Division, Industrial Relations Center, University of Chicago; Education-Industry Service. *

JAMES E. KENNEDY, *Associate Professor of Psychology, University of Wisconsin, Madison, Wisconsin.*

Word Fluency attempts to measure "the speed (or quickness) of verbal associations" in such a way that "verbal comprehension and limited vocabulary do not have a significant bearing on the score." The subject is presented with 16 letters of the alphabet and 5 categories: automobiles, flowers, countries, colors, and tools. For each category he must write an example which starts with each of the letters. The test may be administered on a group basis; the time limit is set at 10 minutes; the total score is the number of acceptable responses (spelling is not important). It is reported that the test has been used "principally with male industrial subjects" but the purpose for which it has been used is not stated.

The manual gives adequate instructions for administering and scoring the test, for converting raw scores to standard scores, and for interpreting converted scores. A scoring key provides examples of acceptable responses for each category. The norms provided are based on 1,045 industrial personnel of varied occupation.

In a section headed "Background Research" the manual notes that L. L. Thurstone in his early studies of primary mental abilities identified two relatively distinct verbal factors: word fluency and verbal comprehension. Thurstone's test to measure word fluency, which required the subject to produce three synonyms for each of a list of stimulus words, was found to have "a high correlation with the word fluency factor and a negligible correlation with the verbal-comprehension factor." The manual does not explain why the new Corsini test of word fluency was developed, or in what ways the author believes it to be similar to or different from the Thurstone test. No evidence is provided to indicate how well the new test measures the word fluency factor or how it correlates with the verbal comprehension factor.

Test-retest reliability, based on a sample of 48 subjects, was found to be .78; Kuder-Richardson formula 21 estimates range from .67 to .84 for various occupational groups.

According to the manual, "two approaches to the validity of the test were taken." The first concerned the fact that *Word Fluency* correlated, for various occupational groups, between .10 and .55 with *Verbal Reasoning* and between −.02 and .56 with *Understanding Communication.* The author concludes that these results "indicate [the test] measures in the area of mental abilities"; no further interpretation is made. Correlations between *Word Fluency* and each of six subscale scores of the *Paired Comparison Temperament Schedule,* an earlier edition of the *Temperament Comparator,* were found to range, for six different occupational groups, from −.30 to .52. Two of these 42 correlations are identified as being "of interest" but the reason given for this belief is vague and unconvincing.

The second "approach to validity" consisted of comparing the mean scores of groups of industrial personnel at different skill levels. Some of the comparisons indicated significant differences; others did not. Since these results are presented under the heading of "validity," the author presumably believes they have some relevance for that topic but does not say what it might be.

In summary, this test presumably was designed to measure Thurstone's word fluency factor. No evidence is presented to demonstrate that it does. No evidence is provided to indicate that it is, as the author intended, independent of verbal comprehension and vocabulary factors. Although the test has been used principally with male industrial personnel, nowhere does the manual state for what purpose it has been used or for what purpose it might be used. There is certainly no evidence to indicate it has predictive validity for use in the selection and placement of industrial personnel.

[Other Tests]

For tests not listed above, see the following entries in *Tests in Print:* 918, 922–4, 925, 927–30, 934–5, and 937–8; out of print: 921.

Wechsler Memory Scale

REPRINTED FROM *The Seventh Mental Measurements Yearbook*

INTELLIGENCE—SEVENTH MMY

REVIEWS BY J. *Stanley Ahmann, Anne Anastasi, J. Douglas Ayres, Leonard L. Baird, Robert H. Bauernfeind, George K. Bennett, Alvin G. Burstein, H. J. Butcher, Joel T. Campbell, John B. Carroll, Clinton I. Chase, Roberta R. Collard, Lee J. Cronbach, Richard F. Docter, Robert C. Droege, Philip H. DuBois, James A. Dunn, Dorothy H. Eichorn, John P. Foley, Jr., David Freides, Joseph L. French, Eric F. Gardner, Bert A. Goldman, Marcel L. Goldschmid, Russel F. Green, Albert J. Harris, Philip Himelstein, Marshall S. Hiskey, Raymond H. Holden, Marjorie P. Honzik, Kenneth D. Hopkins, John L. Horn, Jane V. Hunt, Arthur R. Jensen, Raymond A. Katzell, James E. Kennedy, Kenneth Lovell, Howard B. Lyman, Boyd R. McCandless, Arthur C. MacKinney, William B. Michael, John E. Milholland, Alice E. Moriarty, T. Ernest Newland, John Nisbet, Stanley Nisbet, Robert D. North, Jum C. Nunnally, R. T. Osborne, David A. Payne, John H. Rosenbach, Richard E. Schutz, Melvyn I. Semmel, A. B. Silverstein, Charles D. Smock, Erwin K. Taylor, Hugh Taylor, Robert L. Thorndike, Carol K. Tittle, Philip E. Vernon, David A. Walker, Wimburn L. Wallace, Henry Weitz, and Emmy E. Werner.*

GROUP

[328]

*A.C.E.R. Advanced Test B40. Ages 13 and over; 1940–66; formerly called *Adult Test (B40)*; 1 form ['65, 4 pages, identical with test copyrighted in 1940 except for 2 revised items]; mimeographed manual ('66, 9 pages, identical—including norms—with manual published in 1964 except for key to 2 items); Aus 50¢ per 10 tests; 40¢ per manual; 45¢ per specimen set; postpaid within Australia; 55(65) minutes; Australian Council for Educational Research. *

REFERENCES

1–3. See 5:296.
4. ANDERSON, A. W. "Reading Ability and Intelligence of Students: A Study of New Admissions to the University of Western Australia in 1957." *Educand* 3:108–12 Mr '57. *
5. HOGBEN, D. "School of Entry and First Year Performance of Medical Students in the University of Western Australia." *Austral J Higher Ed* 2:79–83 N '64. *
6. ANDERSON, A. W. "Intelligence and Reading Scores of Entrants to the University of Western Australia 1954–65." *Austral J Higher Ed* 2:177–82 N '65. *

7. HOGBEN, D. "The Prediction of Academic Success in Relation to Student Selection in Medicine at the University of Western Australia." *Austral J Higher Ed* 2:152-60 N '65. *

For a review by C. Sanders, see 5:296.

[329]

★**A.C.E.R. Lower Grades General Ability Scale, Second Edition.** Ages 6-6 to 9-1; 1962–66; 5 scores: picture vocabulary, picture arrangement, picture analogies, picture series, total; 1 form ['64, 16 pages in 2 booklets labeled Part A and Part B]; test identical with first edition copyrighted in 1962 except for minor revisions in format; manual ('66, 45 pages); no norms for part scores; Aus $1.50 per 10 tests; $1 per set of keys; $1.25 per manual; $2.45 per specimen set; postpaid within Australia; (110–120) minutes in 2 sessions; M. L. Clark (manual) and the Australian Council for Educational Research; the Council. *

[330]

*****ACT Test Battery of the American College Testing Program.** Candidates for college entrance; 1959–70; ACT; tests administered 5 times a year (October, December, February, April, July) at centers established by the publisher; 5 scores: English usage, mathematics usage, social studies reading, natural sciences reading, composite; test booklet also includes a biographical inventory (Student Profile Section) of nonacademic achievements, aspirations, special campus needs, and perceptions of college; 3 new forms published annually; supervisor's manual, 1970–71 edition ('70, c1968, 20 pages); counselor's handbook ('70, 39 pages); technical report ('65, 43 pages); student information booklet ['70, 24 pages]; interpretive booklet for students ('70, 32 pages); guide for use of ACT services on campus ('70, 35 pages); reprint of student profile section ('70, 8 pages); announcement of ACT research services ('70, 44 pages); separate answer sheets (MRC) must be used; examination fee, $6 per student; fee includes reporting of scores to the student, his high school, and 3 colleges designated at time of application; 195(240) minutes; American College Testing Program. *

REFERENCES

1–14. See 6:1.
15. RAY, PHILIP BOND. *A Descriptive Study of Certain Characteristics of "High Creative" Freshman Arts College Students as Compared With "High Academic Potential" Students.* Doctor's thesis, University of Minnesota (Minneapolis, Minn.), 1962. (*DA* 24:1924)
16. ADKINS, ARLIE ANDREW. *Prediction of College Success at Middle Tennessee State College.* Doctor's thesis, University of Florida (Gainesville, Fla.), 1963. (*DA* 25:211)
17. CHASE, CLINTON I.; LUDLOW, H. GLENN; POMEROY, MARTHA C.; AND BARRITT, L. SPENCER. *Predicting Individual Course Success for Entering Freshmen.* Indiana Studies in Prediction No. 2. Bloomington, Ind.: Bureau of Educational Studies and Testing, Indiana University, 1963. Pp. i, 41. *
18. CHASE, CLINTON I.; LUDLOW, H. GLENN; POMEROY, MARTHA C.; AND BARRITT, L. SPENCER. *Predicting Success for University Freshmen.* Indiana Studies in Prediction No. 1. Bloomington, Ind.: Bureau of Educational Studies and Testing, Indiana University, 1963. Pp. vi, 47. *
19. FRIESEN, WALTER S. *A Descriptive Study of Freshman Performance in English Composition I at Kansas State University, 1961, in Relation to Fifty-Two Variables.* Doctor's research study No. 1, Colorado State College (Greeley, Colo.), 1963. (*DA* 25:290)
20. HIGGINS, WILLIAM. *A Comparison of the ACT Program With Other Available Criteria for Predicting Success of Students at Bismarck Junior College.* Master's thesis, Northern State College (Aberdeen, S.D.), 1963.
21. LIBBY, DOUGLAS F., JR. *The American College Testing Program and High School Achievement as Contributing Predictors of Success for Technical Institute Students.* Doctor's thesis, Boston University (Boston, Mass.), 1963. (*DA* 25:1657)
22. MAY, LOMAX LOUIS. *A Study of the Relationships Between Achievement on a Complex Visual-Auditory Learning Task and Certain Selected Variables.* Doctor's thesis, University of Alabama (University, Ala.), 1963. (*DA* 25:1750)
23. VAUGHAN, GEORGE ELLIS, JR. *Some Characteristics of College Freshmen According to Sex and Ethnic Group and the Relationship of These Characteristics to Academic Achievement.* Doctor's thesis, North Texas State University (Denton, Tex.), 1963. (*DA* 25:1017)
24. BLEDSOE, LUTHER, AND WARD, GEORGE. "An Analysis of the West Virginia State College Admissions Policy and Academic Performance at Marshall University." *Proc W Va Acad Sci* 36:184-7 S '64. *
25. BOYCE, RICHARD W. "The Prediction of Achievement in College Algebra." *Ed & Psychol Meas* 24:419–20 su '64. * (*PA* 39:5976)
26. BROWN, MARY MARGARET. *A Study of the Relationships of Selected Tests and Grade Point Averages for a Land Grant Institution.* Doctor's thesis, University of South Dakota (Vermillion, S.D.), 1964. (*DA* 27:664A)
27. DIZNEY, HENRY F., AND ROSKENS, RONALD W. "Comparing Aptitude and Achievement of American and Foreign Students in an American University." *J Col Stud Personnel* 5:146-51 Mr '64. *
28. FIRNBERG, JAMES W. *The Use of the American College Testing Program Test in the Prediction of Academic Achievement.* Master's thesis, Louisiana State University (Baton Rouge, La.), 1964.
29. FISHER, JAMES LEE. *Factors Affecting Academic Success.* Doctor's thesis, Northwestern University (Evanston, Ill.), 1964. (*DA* 25:3970)
30. KELLOGG, T. E.; TRUMP, PAUL L.; PEARSON, RICHARD; FOOSE, ROBERT L.; BENSON, LOREN; AND GROESBECK, BYRON L. "National Admissions Testing Programs—Their Value to Colleges—Their Impact on Secondary Schools." *Col & Univ* 39:488–514 su '64. *
31. LINDQUIST, E. F. "Equating Scores on Non-Parallel Tests." *J Ed Meas* 1:5–9 Je '64. * (*PA* 39:7777)
32. NORRED, ROBERT GAINES. *The Effect of Certain Selected Variables on Performance in Football.* Doctor's thesis, University of Alabama (University, Ala.), 1964. (*DA* 25:7066)
33. PETERSEN, LORENZ J. *The Significance of Score Discrepancies on a Test Battery.* Master's thesis, Illinois State University (Normal, Ill.), 1964.
34. QUINLAN, CLAIRE A. *The Prediction of Freshman Academic Success at Colorado State College by Means of Selected Standardized Tests and Admission Data.* Doctor's research study No. 1, Colorado State College (Greeley, Colo.), 1964. (*DA* 25:5124)
35. RYAN, ROBERT DALE. *A Study of Student Performance in First Year Technical Drawing at St. Cloud State College as Related to Certain High School Courses and ACT Scores.* Doctor's research study No. 1, Colorado State College (Greeley, Colo.), 1964. (*DA* 25:5031)
36. WALKER, PETER. *Is Either the SAT or the ACT a Superior Instrument for Predicting Academic Success at National College of Education.* Master's thesis, National College of Education (Evanston, Ill.), 1964.
37. WEBER, LOUISE A. *The Predictive Validity of the SCAT and the ACT at a Liberal Arts College for Women.* Master's thesis, John Carroll University (Cleveland, Ohio), 1964.
38. BOSSEN, DORIS STEPHENS. *The Relation of Four Nonintellective Factors to the Matriculation of High School Senior Girls.* Master's thesis, Ohio State University (Columbus, Ohio), 1965.
39. BOYCE, RICHARD W., AND PAXSON, R. C. "The Predictive Validity of Eleven Tests at One State College." *Ed & Psychol Meas* 25:1143–7 w '65. * (*PA* 40:3563)
40. BOYD, JOSEPH D. "Vocational Interest Measurement in High School: What Do the Findings Mean?" *J Assn Col Adm Officers* 10:9–14 w '65. *
41. BROWN, FREDERICK G., AND WOLINS, LEROY. "An Empirical Evaluation of the American College Testing Program." *Personnel & Guid J* 43:451–6 Ja '65. * (*PA* 39:10813)
42. CHASE, CLINTON I. *The University Freshman Dropout.* Indiana University, Monograph of the Bureau of Educational Studies and Testing, Indiana Studies in Prediction, No. 6. Bloomington, Ind.: the Bureau, 1965. Pp. 36. *
43. CRAIG, MARY J. *A Study of the Effectiveness of the Interpretation of the ACT Program Scores Through Group Guidance With Freshman Women.* Master's thesis, Texas Woman's University (Denton, Tex.), 1965.
44. CRIBB, GEORGE ROBERT. *The Comparative Effectiveness of Conventional and Programed Instructional Procedures in Teaching Fundamentals of Music.* Doctor's thesis, North Texas State University (Denton, Tex.), 1965. (*DA* 25:7098)
45. DESENA, PAUL A., AND WEBER, LOUISE ANN. "The Predictive Validity of the School College Ability Test (*SCAT*) and the American College Test (*ACT*) at a Liberal Arts College for Women." *Ed & Psychol Meas* 25:1149–51 w '65. * (*PA* 40:4603)
46. DIZNEY, HENRY F.; ELFNER, ELINOR A.; AND PAGE, HORACE A. "American College Test (ACT) Performance as a Function of Examinee Acceptance of Test." *Ed & Psychol Meas* 25:547–53 su '65. * (*PA* 39:15223)
47. DUBOIS, LLOYD VERRELL. *A Study of Factors Related to Persistence and Withdrawal Among Sophomore Students in the College of Education at Oklahoma State University.*

Doctor's thesis, Oklahoma State University (Stillwater, Okla.), 1965. (*DA* 27:50A)
48. ELLIOTT, EUGENE W. "An Evaluation of Some Tests for Placement in College Chemistry." *Mont Acad Sci* 25: 106–9 '65. *
49. FOSTER, JAMES M., AND DANSKIN, DAVID G. "The American College Test (ACT) Tested Three Ways." *Personnel & Guid J* 43:904–9 My '65. * (*PA* 39:16438)
50. FUNCHES, DELARS. "A Correlation Between the ACT Scores and the Grade Point Averages of Freshmen at Jackson State College." *Col & Univ* 40:324–6 sp '65. *
51. GALLANT, THOMAS FRANCIS. *Academic Achievement of College Freshmen and Its Relationship to Selected Aspects of the Student's Background.* Doctor's thesis, Western Reserve University (Cleveland, Ohio), 1965. (*DA* 26:6468)
52. GARLAND, CALVIN BOOTH. *A Comparative Study of High School Grades, Class Rank, and ACT Test Scores as Predictors of College Success at East Tennessee State University, 1964–65.* Master's thesis, East Tennessee State University (Johnson City, Tenn.), 1965.
53. HOLLAND, JOHN L., AND RICHARDS, JAMES M., JR. "Academic and Non-Academic Accomplishment: Correlated or Uncorrelated?" *ACT Res Rep* 2:1–26 Ap '65. *
54. HOLLAND, JOHN L., AND RICHARDS, JAMES M., JR. "Academic and Nonacademic Accomplishment: Correlated or Uncorrelated?" *J Ed Psychol* 56:165–74 Ag '65. * (*PA* 39:15293)
55. JOHNSON, RICHARD W. "Are SVIB Interests Correlated With Differential Academic Achievement?" *J Appl Psychol* 49:302–9 Ag '65. * (*PA* 39:15357)
56. KEEFER, KARL ELTON. *Self-Prediction of Academic Achievement by College Students.* Doctor's thesis, University of Tennessee (Knoxville, Tenn.), 1965. (*DA* 26:4337)
57. McIFF, LYLE HATCH. *The Relationship of Certain Selected Factors to the Success or Failure of Second-Quarter Accounting Students at Utah State University.* Doctor's thesis, University of Southern California (Los Angeles, Calif.), 1965. (*DA* 26:5767)
58. MUNDAY, LEO. "Comparative Predictive Validities of the American College Tests and Two Other Scholastic Aptitude Tests." *ACT Res Rep* 6:2–14 Ag '65. *
59. MUNDAY, LEO. *An Investigation of the Relationships of Selected Factors to the Predictability of College Grades.* Doctor's thesis, State University of Iowa (Iowa City, Iowa), 1965. (*DA* 26:2591)
60. MUNDAY, LEO. "Predicting College Grades in Predominantly Negro Colleges." *J Ed Meas* 2:157–60 D '65. *
61. MUNDAY, LEO, AND HOYT, DONALD P. "Predicting Academic Success for Nursing Students." *Nursing Res* 14:341–4 f '65. *
62. PHAY, JOHN E., AND McDONALD, DOUGLAS. *Four Years of Academic Achievement and Disposition of the 1961–62 Entering Freshmen at the University of Mississippi Compared With American College Test Scores.* University, Miss.: Bureau of Institutional Research, University of Mississippi, 1965. Pp. xvi, 161. *
63. RICHARDS, JAMES M., JR., AND HOLLAND, JOHN L. "Academic and Nonacademic Accomplishment: Correlated or Uncorrelated?" Abstract. *Proc Ann Conv Am Psychol Assn* 73:309–10 '65. * (*PA* 39:15293)
64. ROA, CLAYTON DURWARD. *An Investigation of Factors Leading to the Withdrawal of Waldorf Junior College Freshmen.* Doctor's thesis, Michigan State University (East Lansing, Mich.), 1965. (*DA* 27:681A)
65. ROBINSON, FRANCES K. *An Investigation of the Value of the ACT Battery, the College Board Scholastic Aptitude Test, the Differential Aptitude Test Battery, and the University of Kansas Placement Battery as Predictors of University of Kansas Freshmen Grades.* Master's thesis, University of Kansas (Lawrence, Kan.), 1965.
66. SASSENRATH, JULIUS M., AND PUGH, RICHARD. "Relationships Among CEEB Scholastic Aptitude Test and American College Test Scores and Grade Point Average." *J Ed Meas* 2:199–205 D '65. *
67. STANSBERRY, CHARLES WAYNE. *A Comparative Study of First Year Academic Achievement as Related to Predicted Achievement of Freshmen Enrolled in Elementary Education at Frostburg State College.* Doctor's thesis, Pennsylvania State University (University Park, Pa.), 1965. (*DA* 26:2028)
68. STEINBRECHER, ANDREW W. *Characteristic Personality Factors of Students With Marked Interest Variability on the A.C.T.* Master's thesis, Illinois State University (Normal, Ill.), 1965.
69. ABE, CLIFFORD. "A Factor Analytic Study of Some Non-Intellectual Indices of Academic Achievement." *J Ed Meas* 3:39–44 sp '66. *
70. ANDERSON, ROGER CLARE. *A Study of Academic and Biographical Variables for Predicting Achievement in Technical Programs at the North Dakota State School of Science.* Doctor's thesis, University of North Dakota (Grand Forks, N.D.), 1966. (*DA* 27:2046A)
71. BAILEY, CLARENCE W. *Description of Patterns of the American College Testing Program Scores of Academically Dismissed Students at Plymouth State College, Plymouth, New Hampshire.* Master's thesis, Plymouth State College (Plymouth, N.H.), 1966.

72. BRADLEY, NOLEN EUGENE, JR. *The Negro Undergraduate Student: Factors Relative to Performance in Predominantly White State Colleges and Universities in Tennessee.* Doctor's thesis, University of Tennessee (Knoxville, Tenn.), 1966. (*DA* 27:1534A)
73. BRISTOW, RONALD MILTON. *English and Native Language Test Score Relationships to College Grade Point Average for Japanese Students.* Doctor's thesis, University of Southern California (Los Angeles, Calif.), 1966. (*DA* 27:2062A)
74. BROWN, FREDERICK G., AND SCOTT, DAVID A. "The Unpredictability of Predictability." *J Ed Meas* 3:297–301 w '66. *
75. CHANDLER, JOSEPH DOUGLAS. *An Analysis of Competence in the Social Sciences by Elementary Education Majors at the University of Tennessee.* Doctor's thesis, University of Tennessee (Knoxville, Tenn.), 1966. (*DA* 27:3246A)
76. CHASE, CLINTON I., AND BARRITT, L. SPENCER. "A Table of Concordance Between ACT and SAT." *J Col Stud Personnel* 7:105–8 Mr '66. * Comment by William H. Angoff and reply by the authors, 7:194–6 Jl '66. *
77. COLLINS, MILTON EUGENE. *A Predictive and Item Study of the Cognitive Structure of a College Aptitude Test.* Doctor's thesis, University of Michigan (Ann Arbor, Mich.), 1966. (*DA* 27:3287A)
78. COPPEDGE, FLOYD LEVON. *The Relationship of Selected Factors to Occupational and College Success.* Doctor's thesis, University of Oklahoma (Norman, Okla.), 1966. (*DA* 26:6441)
79. DEMOS, GEORGE D., AND WEIJOLA, MERRILL J. "Achievement-Personality Criteria as Selectors of Participants and Predictors of Success in Special Programs in Higher Education." *Calif J Ed Res* 17:186–92 S '66. * (*PA* 41:1923)
80. DOHNER, CHARLES WESLEY. *The Relation of Non-Intellective Factors to the Academic Achievement of College Freshmen at the Ohio State University.* Doctor's thesis, Ohio State University (Columbus, Ohio), 1966. (*DA* 27:2826A)
81. HALL, WESTON ADRIAN. *The Construction of Scales From Selected Variables for Predicting Academic Success in a Junior College.* Doctor's thesis, University of Houston (Houston, Tex.), 1966. (*DA* 27:3325B)
82. HANSON, ROBERT NELTON. *Visual Stimulus Versus Combined Audio-Visual Stimuli for Out-of-Class Practice in First-Semester College Gregg Shorthand.* Doctor's thesis, University of North Dakota (Grand Forks, N.D.), 1966. (*DA* 27:3224A)
83. HOLLAND, JOHN L. "The Research and Development Division in the American College Testing Program." *J Counsel Psychol* 13:117–9 sp '66. *
84. HOLLAND, JOHN L., AND RICHARDS, JAMES M., JR. "Academic and Non-Academic Accomplishment in a Representative Sample Taken From a Population of 612,000." *ACT Res Rep* 12:1–28 My '66. * (*PA* 40:10451)
85. HOOVER, HELENE MAE PERRY. *Concept Development of College Students Exposed to Systematic, Organized Learning Experiences in Family Relationships.* Doctor's thesis, Oklahoma State University (Stillwater, Okla.), 1966. (*DA* 27:4465B)
86. HOYT, DONALD P. "Predicting Grades in Two-Year Terminal Programs: An Experiment in Predicting the College Ability of 'Non-Academically Oriented' Students." *Jun Col J* 36:20–3 F '66. *
87. HOYT, DONALD P., AND MUNDAY, LEO. "Academic Description and Prediction in Junior Colleges." *ACT Res Rep* 10:1–22 F '66. * (*PA* 40:8035)
88. JEX, FRANK B. *Predicting Academic Success Beyond High School.* Salt Lake City, Utah: University of Utah Bookstore, 1966. Pp. vi, 41. *
89. JOHNSON, RICHARD W. "Interpretation of ACT Difference Scores." *J Col Stud Personnel* 7:109–12 Mr '66. *
90. KAHNK, DONALD LEE. *Differential Value of Selected Pre-Matriculation Data for Predicting Collegiate Persistence.* Doctor's thesis, University of Nebraska (Lincoln, Neb.), 1966. (*DA* 27:1263A)
91. LEWIS, LESLIE. *A Multivariate Analysis of Variables Associated With Academic Success Within a College Environment.* Doctor's thesis, Oklahoma State University (Stillwater, Okla.), 1966. (*DA* 27:4134A)
92. LINS, L. JOSEPH; ABELL, ALLAN P.; AND HUTCHINS, H. CLIFTON. "Relative Usefulness in Predicting Academic Success of the ACT, the SAT, and Some Other Variables." *J Exp Ed* 35:1–29 w '66. *
93. MILLER, AARON JULIUS. *A Study of Engineering and Technical Institute Freshman Enrollees and Dropouts in Terms of Selected Intellective and Non-Intellective Factors.* Doctor's thesis, Oklahoma State University (Stillwater, Okla.), 1966. (*DA* 27:4050A)
94. MOSLEMI, MARLENE H. *ACT English Scores and General Studies English First Grade Point Average as Predictors of Academic Achievement on the Undergraduate Level at Southern Illinois University.* Master's thesis, Southern Illinois University (Carbondale, Ill.), 1966.
95. MUNDAY, LEO A.; HOYT, DONALD P.; AND LUTZ, SANDRA W. *College Student Profiles: Norms for the ACT Assessment, 1966–67 Edition.* Iowa City, Iowa: American College Testing Program, Inc., 1966. Pp. xii, 292. * (*PA* 41:10950)
96. PAPPAS, JOHN G. *The Effects of Three Approaches to College Orientation on Two Groups of Entering Freshmen*

Students at Kent State University. Doctor's thesis, Kent State University (Kent, Ohio), 1966. *(DA 28:401A)*

97. RAND, LEONARD PETER. *A Study of the Relationship Between the Matching of Student and Institutional Characteristics and College Choice Satisfaction.* Doctor's thesis, University of Iowa (Iowa City, Iowa), 1966. *(DA 27:2832A)*

98. RICHARDS, JAMES M., JR.; HOLLAND, JOHN L.; AND LUTZ, SANDRA W. "The Prediction of Student Accomplishment in College." *ACT Res Rep* 13:1–38 Je '66. * *(PA 40: 11491)*

99. RIVIERE, ANN L. *A Study of the Relationship Between American College Test Scores and College Grade Point Averages of Selected Tennessee Technological University Education Majors.* Master's thesis, Tennessee Technological University (Cookeville, Tenn.), 1966.

100. RUNDE, ROBERT M. "Freshman Placement Uses of a Nationwide Test." *Col & Univ* 41:190–8 w '66. *

101. SASSENRATH, JULIUS M., AND PUGH, RICHARD. "Note: Relationships Among CEEB Scholastic Aptitude Test and American College Test Scores and Grade Point Average: A Replication." *J Ed Meas* 3:37–8 sp '66. *

102. SEGRIST, ALLEN EDWARD. *Admission of Transfer Students.* Doctor's thesis, Ohio State University (Columbus, Ohio), 1966. *(DA 27:2053A)*

103. SHANA'A, JOYCE ADRIAN. *A Statistical Analysis of the Placement Program in Mathematics for Freshmen at the University of Oklahoma.* Doctor's thesis, University of Oklahoma (Norman, Okla.), 1966. *(DA 27:1629A)*

104. SHRADER, EDWARD FRANKLYN. *A Descriptive Study of Students in the Precollege Summer Session Program, the University of Maryland, 1964–1965.* Doctor's thesis, George Washington University (Washington, D.C.), 1966. *(DA 27:4104A)*

105. SIMONIAN, CHARLES. *A Descriptive Analysis of Selected Male Freshmen Majoring in Physical Education at the Ohio State University.* Doctor's thesis, Ohio State University (Columbus, Ohio), 1966. *(DA 27:2858A)*

106. SPARKS, THOMASINE P. *A Study of the Relationships Between ACT Scores and Grades of Female Elementary Education Students.* Master's thesis, Texas College of Arts and Industries (Kingsville, Tex.), 1966.

107. WALKUP, MARY JO COLEMAN. *The Predictability of Success in Bowling and Badminton.* Doctor's thesis, University of Iowa (Iowa City, Iowa), 1966. *(DA 27:4119A)*

108. WILLIAMS, JACK. *An Investigation of the Relationships Between Selected Factors Concerning Student Teachers and Their Success in Student Teaching.* Doctor's thesis, University of Houston (Houston, Tex.), 1966. *(DA 27:2820A)*

109. ANDERSON, JAMES, AND WHITTEMORE, ROBERT G. "Predictive Utility of Certain Criteria for Advanced Freshman Mathematics Courses." *Math Teach* 60:619–20 O '67. *

110. BAIRD, LEONARD L. "The Educational Goals of College-Bound Youth." *ACT Res Rep* 19:1–28 Ap '67. *

111. BAIRD, LEONARD L. "Family Income and the Characteristics of College-Bound Students." *ACT Res Rep* 17:1–26 F '67. *

112. BARNETT, THOMAS MARVIN. *The Predictive Validities, as Measured by Multiple Correlation, of Two Batteries Using Academic Achievement as Criterion.* Doctor's thesis, North Texas State University (Denton, Tex.), 1967. *(DA 28:2006A)*

113. BOWERS, JOHN E. "Prediction of Freshman Achievement With a Moderator Model." *Ed & Psychol Meas* 27: 427–8 su '67. * *(PA 41:14213)*

114. BOWERS, JOHN E. "A Test of Variation in Grading Standards." *Ed & Psychol Meas* 27:429–30 su '67. * *(PA 41:12822)*

115. BROWN, F. G., AND SCOTT, D. A. "Differential Predictability in College Admissions Testing." *J Ed Meas* 4:163–6 f '67. *

116. DAVIS, KENNETH MARTIN. *Predicting College Success for Five Area Schools.* Master's thesis, Eastern Illinois University (Charleston, Ill.), 1967.

117. ELTON, CHARLES F. "Male Career Role and Vocational Choice: Their Prediction With Personality and Aptitude Variables." *J Counsel Psychol* 14:99–105 Mr '67. * *(PA 41:7879)*

118. ELTON, CHARLES F., AND ROSE, HARRIETT A. "Traditional Sex Attitudes and Discrepant Ability Measures in College Women." *J Counsel Psychol* 14:538–43 N '67. * *(PA 42:4471)*

119. FUNCHES, DELARS. "Correlation Between Secondary School Transcript Averages and Grade Point Averages and Between ACT Scores and Grade Point Averages of Freshmen at Jackson State College." *Col & Univ* 43:52–4 f '67. *

120. HENDERSON, HARVEY CRIMMINS. *The Relationship Between Scholastic Aptitude and Confirmed vs. Non-Confirmed Responses to a Linear Program in the Physics of Sound as It Relates to Phonation.* Doctor's thesis, Ohio University (Athens, Ohio), 1967. *(DA 28:3797A)*

121. HIMMEL, KEITH LAVERN. *The Number of Years of High School Science as a Predictor of First Year College Success Compared With Other Predictors.* Doctor's thesis, Montana State University (Missoula, Mont.), 1967. *(DA 28:3364A)*

122. HOLLAND, JOHN L., AND RICHARDS, JAMES M., JR. "Academic and Nonacademic Accomplishment in a Representative Sample of Students Taking the American College Tests." *Col & Univ* 43:60–71 f '67. *

123. HOLT, JUDITH MARKHAM. *A Study of the Relationship Between American College Test Scores and Achievement of Indian Students at Brigham Young University.* Master's thesis, Brigham Young University (Provo, Utah), 1967.

124. HUSTON, BEATRICE MOORE. *A Normative Survey of the Personal and Academic Characteristics of the Freshmen Women Students Enrolled in Mary Hardin-Baylor College, 1966–1967.* Doctor's thesis, Baylor University (Waco, Tex.), 1967. *(DA 28:1209A)*

125. JOHNSON, RICHARD, AND WARD, GEORGE, II. "A Comparison of the Wherry-Doolittle and Multiple Cutting Score Methods in Predicting Academic Performance." *Proc W Va Acad Sci* 39:75–7 '67. *

126. LANE, JAMES ALBERT. *Assessment of Physically Handicapped Adult Students in College.* Doctor's thesis, Ohio State University (Columbus, Ohio), 1967. *(DA 28:3511A)*

127. McCARY, ARTHUR DALE. *Personality Variables Associated With Five Levels of Academic Achievement Within Five Levels of Ability.* Doctor's thesis, University of Mississippi (University, Miss.), 1967. *(DA 28:56A)*

128. MARZOLF, STANLEY S. "Individual Variability on the ACT Tests." *J Ed Res* 61:184–5 D '67. *

129. MORRISON, W. LEE, AND ROMOSER, R. C. "'Traditional' Classroom Attitudes, the A.C.T. and the 16 P.F." *J Ed Res* 60:326–9 Mr '67. *

130. MUNDAY, LEO. "Predicting College Grades Using ACT Data." *Ed & Psychol Meas* 27:401–6 su '67. * *(PA 41:14221)*

131. PASSONS, WILLIAM R. "Predictive Validities of the ACT, SAT and High School Grades for First Semester GPA and Freshman Courses." *Ed & Psychol Meas* 27:1143–4 w '67. * *(PA 42:9427)*

132. POWELL, HOBART L. *A Comparative Study of the Relationship Between ACT Composite Scores and G.P.A. of Washington County Students at ETSU, 1965–66.* Master's thesis, East Tennessee State University (Johnson City, Tenn.), 1967.

133. RANGE, LEO HARRY. *A Comparison of ACT and SAT Standard Scores.* Master's thesis, St. Louis University (St. Louis, Mo.), 1967.

134. RICHARDS, JAMES M., JR., AND LUTZ, SANDRA W. "Predicting Student Accomplishment in College From the ACT Assessment." *ACT Res Rep* 21:1–38 Ag '67. * *(PA 41:15295)*

135. RICHARDS, JAMES M., JR.; HOLLAND, JOHN L.; AND LUTZ, SANDRA W. "Prediction of Student Accomplishment in College." *J Ed Psychol* 58:343–55 D '67. * *(PA 42:4582)*

136. SASSENRATH, J. M. "Anxiety, Aptitude, Attitude, and Achievement." *Psychol Sch* 4:341–6 O '67. * *(PA 42:2949)*

137. SMITH, HAROLD T. *An Analysis of Intellectual Factors Bearing on Success in the College of Business, Brigham Young University, Provo, Utah.* Doctor's thesis, Brigham Young University (Provo, Utah), 1967. *(DA 28:2048A)*

138. STEINBERG, MARVIN; SEGEL, RUEBEN H.; AND LEVINE, HARRY D. "Psychological Determinants of Academic Success: A Pilot Study." *Ed & Psychol Meas* 27:413–22 su '67. * *(PA 41:14226)*

139. VAN ERDEWYK, ZENO MARTIN. *Academic and Non-Academic Variables Related to Persistence, Transfer, and Attrition of Engineering Students.* Doctor's thesis, University of North Dakota (Grand Forks, N.D.), 1967. *(DA 28:4453A)*

140. WALKER, JIMMY REEVES. *A Study of Selected Psychosocial Correlates of College Student Subcultures.* Doctor's thesis, Oklahoma State University (Stillwater, Okla.), 1967. *(DA 28:4883A)*

141. WALTERS, ALTON W. *An Analysis of Freshman Year Grade Point Average and Expected Grade Point Average Compared to ACT Research Predictions.* Master's thesis, East Tennessee State University (Johnson City, Tenn.), 1967.

142. WILLIAMS, JACK, AND FOX, A. M. "Prediction of Performance in Student Teaching." *Ed & Psychol Meas* 27: 1169–70 w '67. * *(PA 42:9491)*

143. WORK, GERALD GEORGE. *Correlates of Academic Achievement for Female Sophomore Elementary Education Majors.* Doctor's thesis, Ohio University (Athens, Ohio), 1967. *(DA 28:2926A)*

144. ZIMMERMAN, WAYNE S., AND MICHAEL, WILLIAM B. "A Comparison of the Criterion-Related Validities of Three College Entrance Examinations With Different Content Emphases." *Ed & Psychol Meas* 27:407–12 su '67. * *(PA 41: 12845)*

145. ABRAMS, AMANDA ULM. *Magic Thinking and Anxiety in Junior College Freshmen.* Doctor's thesis, University of Maryland (College Park, Md.), 1968. *(DA 29:3450A)*

146. BAIRD, LEONARD L. "The Achievements of Bright and Average Students." *Ed & Psychol Meas* 28:891–9 au '68. * *(PA 43:4514)*

147. BAIRD, LEONARD L., AND RICHARDS, JAMES M., JR. "The Effects of Selecting College Students by Various Kinds of High School Achievement." *ACT Res Rep* 23:1–30 F '68. *

148. BAKKEN, ORLIN D. *Does the American College Test Serve as a Valid Predictor for the Electronics Technology Curriculum at the North Dakota State School of Science.* Master's thesis, North Dakota State University (Fargo, N.D.), 1968.

149. BENNETT, JAMES WELDON. *The Interrelationship of College Press, Student Needs, and Academic Aptitudes as Measured by Grade Point Average in a Southern Denominational College.* Doctor's thesis, North Texas State University (Denton, Tex.), 1968. (*DA* 29:474A)

150. BRADSHAW, OTTIE LEON. *The Relationship of Selected Measures of Aptitude, Interest, and Personality to Academic Achievement in Engineering and Engineering Technology.* Doctor's thesis, Oklahoma State University (Stillwater, Okla.), 1968. (*DAI* 30:979A)

151. BROOKS, WINONA NOLAND. *Relationships of Variables Identified With Success in College Clothing Construction Courses: A View Toward Advanced Placement and Improved Learning.* Doctor's thesis, University of Southern California (Los Angeles, Calif.), 1968. (*DA* 29:1701A)

152. BROWN, THOMAS O. *The Urban University Student: Selected Factors Related to Continuation and Withdrawal.* Doctor's thesis, Kent State University (Kent, Ohio), 1968. (*DA* 29:4318A)

153. BROWN, WILLIAM THOMAS. *Consideration of the Interrelationship of Five Aptitude and Achievement Factors in Successful Male Undergraduate Students at the University of Montana.* Doctor's thesis, University of Montana (Missoula, Mont.), 1968. (*DA* 29:3411A)

154. CLEVENGER, WALTER SCHOBAL. *A Study to Determine the Relationship Between Certain Academic Factors and the Grade Earned in Business Education 347 at Northern Illinois University.* Master's thesis, Northern Illinois University (DeKalb, Ill.), 1968. (Abstract: *Nat Bus Ed Q* 38:9)

155. CORSINI, RAYMOND J., AND BORGATTA, EDGAR F. "The Quick Number Test (QNT)." *J Exp Ed* 36:7–10 su '68. *

156. DOBBINS, HOWARD JACK. *The Relationship of the Variability of the Subtest Scores on the American College Test and Prediction of Academic Achievement of College Freshmen.* Doctor's thesis, University of Tulsa (Tulsa, Okla.), 1968. (*DAI* 30:128A)

157. FISHER, RHEUA DALE SPICKELMIER. *A Study of Grades and Test Scores in a Selective Admissions Program for Teacher Education.* Doctor's thesis, Oklahoma State University (Stillwater, Okla.), 1968. (*DAI* 30:986A)

158. GRAY, STUART C. "A Study of the Relationships of Prospective Teachers' Choice of Subject Matter Field to Their Academic Aptitudes." Abstract. *J Teach Ed* 19:116–7 sp '68. *

159. GREEN, JOHNNIE HENDERSON. *An Analysis of Academic Proficiency of the 1965–66 Beginning Freshman Class, School of Business, Texas Southern University, Houston, Texas.* Doctor's thesis, University of Houston (Houston, Tex.), 1968. (*DA* 29:3323A)

160. HANSEN, EDA A. *The Relationship Between Grade Point Averages of the Henmon-Nelson Test of Mental Ability and the American College Test.* Master's thesis, Utah State University (Logan, Utah), 1968.

161. HOYT, DONALD P. "Description and Prediction of Diversity Among Four-Year Colleges." *Meas & Eval Guid* 1:16–26 sp '68. *

162. HOYT, DONALD P. "Description and Prediction of Diversity Among Junior Colleges." *Personnel & Guid J* 46:997–1004 Je '68. *

163. HOYT, DONALD P. "Forecasting Academic Success in Specific Colleges." *ACT Res Rep* 27:1–52 Ag '68. *

164. HOYT, DONALD P. "Generalized Academic Prediction in Four-Year Colleges." *Personnel & Guid J* 47:130–6 O '68. * (*PA* 43:11926)

165. HOYT, DONALD P., AND MUNDAY, LEO A. *Your College Freshmen: Interpretative Guide to ACT Research Services for Higher Education, 1968–69 Edition.* Iowa City, Iowa: American College Testing Program, Inc., 1968. Pp. vii, 249. *

166. HUMPHREYS, LLOYD G. "The Fleeting Nature of the Prediction of College Academic Success." *J Ed Psychol* 59:375–80 O '68. * (*PA* 42:19409)

167. JENNINGS, JO ANN. *Preadmission Information and First Quarter Persistence of Freshman Students Admitted on Probation at a Large Midwestern University.* Doctor's thesis, St. Louis University (St. Louis, Mo.), 1968. (*DA* 29:2481A)

168. KISH, GEORGE B., AND DONNENWERTH, GREGORY. "Sex Differences in the Relationship Between Sensation-Seeking and Scholastic Aptitude." *Newsl Res Psychol* 10:10–2 My '68. *

169. LEDBETTER, PEGGY JEAN. *An Analysis of the Performance of Graduates of a Selected Baccalaureate Program in Nursing With Regard to Selected Standardized Examinations.* Doctor's thesis, University of Alabama (University, Ala.), 1968. (*DA* 29:3381A)

170. LUTZ, SANDRA W. "Do They Do What They Say They Will Do?" *ACT Res Rep* 24:1–31 Mr '68. *

171. MARSHALL, JOSEPH JEMERSON. *Non-Cognitive Variables as a Predictor of Academic Achievement Among Freshmen, Sophomores, and Juniors at Abilene Christian College.* Doctor's thesis, Baylor University (Waco, Tex.), 1968. (*DA* 29:3833A)

172. MERCADO, AUREA ADRIAS. *American College Test Assessment of Educational Hierarchies and Scholastic Survival at the University of the Philippines.* Doctor's thesis, University of Maryland (College Park, Md.), 1968. (*DA* 29:3422A)

173. MILLER, RICHARD HADDEN. *A Descriptive Study of the Relationship Between Potential and Performance of Freshman Students at the University of South Dakota.* Doctor's thesis, University of South Dakota (Vermillion, S.D.), 1968. (*DA* 29:2612A)

174. MONTERO, PAUL. *The Predictive Validity of the National Merit Scholarship Qualifying Test, the American College Test, and Three Year High School Grade Point Average for Academic Success at Louisiana State University in New Orleans.* Master's thesis, University of Alabama (University, Ala.), 1968.

175. MUNDAY, LEO. "Correlations Between ACT and Other Predictors of Academic Success in College." *Col & Univ* 44:67–76 f '68. *

176. MUNDAY, LEO A. "A Comparison of Junior College Students in Transfer and Terminal Curricula." *J Col Stud Personnel* 9:325–9 S '68. *

177. PAVEK, FRANCIS LESLIE. *The Relationship of Non-Academic High School Variables to College Achievement and Participation in Selected Extra-Curricular Activities.* Doctor's thesis, University of North Dakota (Grand Forks, N.D.), 1968. (*DA* 29:2968A)

178. PETERS, BILL EUGENE. *Comparison of 1966 and 1967 Freshman Students at the Colorado State College Admitted Under Two Sets of Admission Standards.* Doctor's thesis, Colorado State College (Greeley, Colo.), 1968. (*DA* 29:2492A)

179. PLANISEK, R. J., AND MERRIFIELD, P. R. "Ability, Study Habits, and Academic Performance Correlates of the Theoretical-Practical Value Characteristics Inventory (TPCI)." Abstract. *Proc 76th Ann Conv Am Psychol Assn* 3:159–60 '68. *

180. PRATT, MICHAEL, AND ALEAMONI, LAWRENCE M. *Predicting the Academic Performance of the Fall, 1967 Freshmen Engineering Students.* Research Report No. 277. Champaign, Ill.: Measurement and Research Division, Office of Instructional Resources, University of Illinois, 1968. Pp. 6. *

181. PUGH, RICHARD C., AND SASSENRATH, JULIUS M. "Comparable Scores for the CEEB Scholastic Aptitude Test and the American College Test Program." *Meas & Eval Guid* 1:103–9 su '68. * (*PA* 44:9266)

182. READ, JOHN WILLIAM. *An Investigation of the Relationship of Selected Variables to Sight-Singing Ability.* Doctor's thesis, North Texas State University (Denton, Tex.), 1968. (*DAI* 30:358A)

183. REDFORD, JEANETTE. *A Comparison of Selected Factors in the Prediction of Academic Success at Southwest Mississippi Junior College.* Doctor's thesis, University of Southern Mississippi (Hattiesburg, Miss.), 1968. (*DA* 29:1109A)

184. RICHARDS, JAMES M., JR., AND LUTZ, SANDRA W. "Predicting Student Accomplishment in College From the ACT Assessment." *J Ed Meas* 5:17–29 sp '68. * (*PA* 42:14503)

185. SEVERINSEN, K. NORMAN. "A.C.T., W.A.I.S. Test Scores and College Grades." *J Ed Meas* 5:161–2 su '68. *

186. SPENCER, RICHARD E., AND STALLINGS, WILLIAM M. "The Student Profile Section of ACT Related to Academic Success." *J Col Stud Personnel* 9:177–9 My '68. *

187. SPURLIN, MELVIN DAVID. *A Study of the Relationship of Sex, Ability Level and Biology Preparation to Achievement in Freshman Biology at Metropolitan State College.* Doctor's thesis, University of Colorado (Boulder, Colo.), 1968. (*DA* 29:1173A)

188. TURNER, VERAS DEAN. *Prediction of Success as a Mathematics Major at the Minnesota State Colleges.* Doctor's thesis, University of Oklahoma (Norman, Okla.), 1968. (*DA* 29:2099A)

189. TURNIPSEED, JORJA POUND. *Academic Success of Junior College Transfer Students as Compared to Native Students at the University of Southern Mississippi.* Doctor's thesis, University of Southern Mississippi (Hattiesburg, Miss.), 1968. (*DA* 29:2908A)

190. YARINGTON, DAVID JON. *A Study of the Relationships Between the Reading Done by College Freshmen and Aptitude and Scholastic Achievement.* Doctor's thesis, University of Pennsylvania (Philadelphia, Pa.), 1968. (*DA* 29:1694A)

191. *The Two-Year College and Its Students: An Empirical Report.* Monograph Two. Iowa City, Iowa: American College Testing Program, 1969. Pp. vii, 157. *

192. BAIRD, LEONARD L. "Prediction of Academic and Nonacademic Achievement in Two-Year Colleges From the ACT Assessment." *Ed & Psychol Meas* 29(2):421–30 su '69. * (*PA* 44:17500)

193. BAIRD, LEONARD L. "The Prediction of Grades in Occupational and Academic Curricula in 2-Year Colleges." *J Ed Meas* 6(4):247–54 w '69. * (*PA* 44:17501)

194. BALDWIN, JEAN MARGARET. *An Analysis of the Relationship Between Self-Esteem, Academic Achievement, and Academic Level of Aspiration for a Group of College Students.* Doctor's thesis, University of Maryland (College Park, Md.), 1969. (*DAI* 31:209A)

195. BECHTOLD, DONALD WILLIAM. *Dynamic Structures of Occupational Choice of High School Seniors.* Doctor's thesis, Catholic University of America (Washington, D.C.), 1969. (*DAI* 30:2322A)

196. BOGUE, E. G., AND FOX, RAY P. "Feedback of College Grades to High Schools." *Personnel & Guid J* 48(3):210–7 N '69. *

197. CASSEL, RUSSELL N., AND EICHSTEADT, ARDEN C. "Factorial Structure of CQT, ACT, and SAT Test Scores for 50

Available College Freshmen." *J Psychol* 71(2):199–204 Mr '69. * (*PA* 43:8675)

198. CHRISTENSON, JEFFRY MILTON. *A Study of the Differences Between Seekers and Non-Seekers at a College Counseling Center.* Doctor's thesis, University of South Dakota (Vermillion, S.D.), 1969. (*DAI* 30:2326A)

199. COLE, NANCY S. "Differential Validity in Tests of Academic Ability." Abstract. *Proc 77th Ann Conv Am Psychol Assn* 4(1):175–6 '69. * (*PA* 43:17904)

200. COLE, NANCY S. "Differential Validity in the ACT Tests." *ACT Res Rep* 30:1–8 Ag '69. * (*PA* 45:2943)

201. DENISON, WALTER MARSHALL. *A Study of Three Interest Inventories Currently in Use at Central Virginia Community College.* Doctor's thesis, University of Virginia (Charlottesville, Va.), 1969. (*DAI* 31:996A)

202. DUBLIN, JAMES E.; ELTON, CHARLES F.; AND BERZINS, JURIS I. "Some Personality and Aptitudinal Correlates of the 'A-B' Therapist Scale." *J Consult & Clin Psychol* 33(6):739–45 D '69. * (*PA* 44:3595)

203. DYRHAUG, DONALD ROBERT. *Expectations Concerning the College Experience as They Relate to the Academic Achievement and Persistence of Freshmen.* Doctor's thesis, University of Minnesota (Minneapolis, Minn.), 1969. (*DAI* 30:2373A)

204. ELTON, CHARLES F. "Prediction of Educational Outcomes Among Junior College Students." *J Col Stud Personnel* 10(1):44–6 Ja '69. *

205. ELTON, CHARLES F., AND SHEVEL, LINDA R. "Who Is Talented? An Analysis of Achievement." *ACT Res Rep* 31:1–13 S '69. * (*PA* 45:3058)

206. FAIRCHILD, PATRICIA CARLETTE. *Grade Point Average and Variance as Criteria of College Academic Performance.* Doctor's thesis, University of Oklahoma (Norman, Okla.), 1969. (*DAI* 30:3318A)

207. FLAMINI, DOMINIC WILLIAM. *Competitive Strategies in Obtaining Grades.* Doctor's thesis, University of Oklahoma (Norman, Okla.), 1969. (*DAI* 30:580A)

208. GOLDBERG, LEONARD SEYMOUR. *Negroid-Caucasoid Differences Among College Freshmen.* Doctor's thesis, Ohio State University (Columbus, Ohio), 1969. (*DAI* 30:2724A)

209. GORDON, JAMES HALE. *A Comparison of Selected Characteristics of Students Entering Five Campuses of Ohio University.* Doctor's thesis, Ohio University (Athens, Ohio), 1969. (*DAI* 30:2332A)

210. GRADY, WILLIAM ELLIS. *Selected Variables Related to Academic Achievement of American and Canadian Male Freshmen at the University of North Dakota.* Doctor's thesis, University of North Dakota (Grand Forks, N.D.), 1969. (*DAI* 30:3725A)

211. GROENKE, GLENN RUSSELL. *The Relationship of the Entrance Examination Score to Grade Point Average of Junior College Freshmen When Classified by Age, Sex, and Curriculum.* Doctor's thesis, Arizona State University (Tempe, Ariz.), 1969. (*DAI* 30:3709A)

212. HARMAN, ROBERT LEE. *Predicting Persistence in College From Information in High School Cumulative Records.* Doctor's thesis, University of Nebraska (Lincoln, Neb.), 1969. (*DAI* 30:1397A)

213. HARRINGTON, CHARLES. "Forecasting College Performance From Biographical Data." *J Col Stud Personnel* 10(3):156–60 My '69. *

214. HAYES, VIRGINIA. *A Study of Personality and Achievement Variables of Successful and Unsuccessful Shorthand Students at the University of Alabama.* Doctor's thesis, University of Alabama (University, Ala.), 1969. (*DAI* 31:66A)

215. HOWLETT, JOHN L. "A Study of Placement Methods for Entering College Freshmen in the Proper Mathematics Sequence at Michigan Technological University." *Math Teach* 62(8):651–9 D '69. *

216. HUCKABEE, MALCOM W. "Personality and Academic Aptitude Correlates of Cognitive Control Principles." *South J Ed Res* 3(1):1–9 Ja '69. *

217. IRVIN, FLOYD S. "The Relationship Between Manifest Anxiety and Measures of Aptitude, Achievement, and Interest." *Ed & Psychol Meas* 29(4):957–61 w '69. * (*PA* 44:20950)

218. JONES, ANN O. *The Prediction of Physical Education Skill Grade Point Average Based Upon Motor Ability and ACT Scores.* Master's thesis, San Diego State College (San Diego, Calif.), 1969.

219. KEEFER, KARL E. "Self-Prediction of Academic Achievement by College Students." *J Ed Res* 63(2):53–6 O '69. *

220. LENNING, OSCAR THOMAS. *Student Factors Related to Educational Growth at a Church Related Liberal Arts College.* Doctor's thesis, University of Iowa (Iowa City, Iowa), 1969. (*DAI* 30:4225A)

221. LENNING, OSCAR T.; MUNDAY, LEO A.; AND MAXEY, E. JAMES. "Student Educational Growth During the First Two Years of College." *Col & Univ* 44(2):145–53 w '69. *

222. LONNING, PHILIP EUGENE. *Characteristics of Full-Time Students Enrolled in Area II and Area V Community Colleges.* Doctor's thesis, Iowa State University (Ames, Iowa), 1969. (*DAI* 30:4779A)

223. MCCLENNEY, BYRON NELSON. *A Comparison of Personality Characteristics, Self-Concepts, and Academic Aptitude of Selected College Men Classified According to Performance on a Test of Physical Fitness.* Doctor's thesis, University of Texas (Austin, Tex.), 1969. (*DAI* 30:1423A)

224. MAIN, NOBLE JAMES. *A Study of the Dropouts Among Music Majors in Four Church Related Liberal Arts Colleges.* Doctor's thesis, University of Oklahoma (Norman, Okla.), 1969. (*DAI* 30:3281A)

225. MOEGENBURG, LOUIS ARTHUR. *An Experimental Comparison of Programed Instruction Versus Video-Tape Television in Teaching Selected Orthographic Projection Concepts.* Doctor's thesis, Texas A & M University (College Station, Tex.), 1969. (*DAI* 30:4802A)

226. MOORE, JAMES C. "Using 'ACT' Battery to Recruit Honors Students." *Improving Col & Univ Teach* 17(3):215–6 su '69. *

227. MRIZEK, DAVID EMIL. *The Effects of Interest and Scholastic Ability Upon Listening Retention.* Master's thesis, Eastern Illinois University (Charleston, Ill.), 1969.

228. NIELSON, CHARLES L. *A Study of the Relation Between Selected Academic Factors and Performance on the I-E Scale.* Doctor's thesis, University of North Dakota (Grand Forks, N.D.), 1969. (*DAI* 30:1402A)

229. PARASKEVOPOULOS, JOHN, AND ROBINSON, L. F. "Comparison of College Performance of Cold War Veterans and Non-Veterans." *Col & Univ* 44(2):189–91 w '69. *

230. PARSONS, TERRY WAYNE. *A Descriptive Analysis of the Achievement Level Realized by Grant-in-Aid Athletes as Compared to Matched Non-Athletes at the Ohio State University.* Doctor's thesis, Ohio State University (Columbus, Ohio), 1969. (*DAI* 30:4263A)

231. PEERSON, RICHARD HAWES. *Analysis of Variables Predictive of Student Success in Community Colleges.* Doctor's thesis, United States International University (San Diego, Calif.), 1969. (*DAI* 30:2808A)

232. PROUSE, HOWARD, AND TURNER, V. DEAN. "Factors Contributing to Success in Calculus II." *J Ed Res* 62(10):439–40 Jl-Ag '69. *

233. RAMOS, ROBERT ANTHONY. *An Investigation of the Effect of Moderator Variables on the Regression and Factor Structure of Predictors and Criteria.* Doctor's thesis, University of Tennessee (Knoxville, Tenn.), 1969. (*DAI* 30:5275B)

234. REID, BARBARA ANN. *A Comparison Between Undergraduate Special Education Students Who Changed and Those Who Did Not Change Their Major.* Doctor's thesis, Colorado State College (Greeley, Colo.), 1969. (*DAI* 30:1757A)

235. RUSSO, JOSEPH FRANK. *Predicting Academic Achievement of Students in Arizona Junior Colleges.* Doctor's thesis, Arizona State University (Tempe, Ariz.), 1969. (*DAI* 30:2309A)

236. SCHLICK, EARL FRANK. *Academic Success of Junior College Students Admitted on Basis of High School Equivalency Certificates.* Doctor's thesis, Arizona State University (Tempe, Ariz.), 1969. (*DA* 29:2077A)

237. SIEVEKING, NICHOLAS A., AND SAVITSKY, JEFFREY C. "Evaluation of an Achievement Test, Prediction of Grades, and Composition of Discussion Groups in College Chemistry." *J Res Sci Teach* 6(4):374–6 '69. *

238. STALLINGS, WILLIAM M., AND ANDERSON, FRANCES E. "Some Characteristics and Correlates of the Meier Art Test of Aesthetic Perception Under Two Systems of Scoring." *J Ed Meas* 6(3):179–85 f '69. * (*PA* 44:14571)

239. STONE, THOMAS CARL. *A Case Study: Predictors of Success in Post-High School Vocational Trade, Industrial, and Technical Programs.* Doctor's thesis, Colorado State University (Ft. Collins, Colo.), 1969. (*DAI* 30:4348A)

240. TAYLOR, RONALD G., AND HANSON, GARY R. "Pre-College Math-Workshop and Freshman Achievement." *J Ed Res* 63(4):157–60 D '69. *

241. TOWNER, JOHN C. *The Relationship Between Area of Study and American College Testing Scores of Recent Degree Graduates at Wisconsin State University—River Falls.* Master's thesis, Wisconsin State University (River Falls, Wis.), 1969.

242. VRAA, CALVIN WOODROW. *The Relation of Selected Academic, Biographical and Personality Factors to the Achievement of Canadian College Freshmen.* Doctor's thesis, University of North Dakota (Grand Forks, N.D.), 1969. (*DAI* 31:168A)

243. WELKER, JAMES DOYT. *Selected Factors and Achievement in an Audio-Tutorial Introductory College Biology Course.* Doctor's thesis, Indiana University (Bloomington, Ind.), 1969. (*DAI* 31:249A)

244. WHEELER, JUDITH E. *Usefulness of the ACT Scores and High School Rank in Predicting Academic Success of Freshmen at Wisconsin State University—Platteville.* Master's thesis, Wisconsin State University (Platteville, Wis.), 1969.

245. WHIPKEY, KENNETH LEE. *A Study of the Interrelationship Between Mathematical Attitude and Mathematical Achievement.* Doctor's thesis, Case Western Reserve University (Cleveland, Ohio), 1969. (*DAI* 30:3808A)

246. WHORTON, JAMES EDWARD. *A Study of Academic Predictors for College Students Majoring in Special Education.* Doctor's thesis, Colorado State College (Greeley, Colo.), 1969. (*DAI* 30:1904A)

247. WORSLEY, ROGER LEWIS. *An Analysis of Selected Variables and the Prediction of the Educational Achievement of Junior College Freshmen.* Doctor's thesis, Arizona State University (Tempe, Ariz.), 1969. (*DAI* 30:3705A)

248. WORTHINGTON, LOIS ELAINE HUCKO. *A Study of Factors Related to First Quarter Academic Success at the University of Utah.* Doctor's thesis, University of Utah (Salt Lake City, Utah), 1969. (*DAI* 30:1884A)
249. ABE, CLIFFORD. *The Prediction of Academic Achievement of Mexican-American Students.* Doctor's thesis, University of Arizona (Tucson, Ariz.), 1970. (*DAI* 31:4535A)
250. ABELL, WILLIAM RUSSELL. *A Comparison of Selected Characteristics of Successful and Unsuccessful Students in a Junior College Remedial Program.* Doctor's thesis, Wayne State University (Detroit, Mich.), 1970. (*DAI* 31:3284A)
251. BERDIE, RALPH F.; PILAPIL, BONIFACIO; AND IM, IN JAE. "Entrance Correlates of University Satisfaction." *Am Ed Res J* 7(2):251–66 Mr '70. *
252. BIGGS, DONALD A., AND TINSLEY, DIANE J. "Student-Made Academic Predictions." *J Ed Res* 63(5):195–7 Ja '70. *
253. CARLSON, STANLEY LLOYD. *Differences in Aptitude, Previous Achievement, and Nonintellectual Traits (Personality, Values, Interest, and Attitude Toward Mathematics) of Freshmen Mathematics Majors and Transfers From the Mathematics Major at the University of Northern Colorado.* Doctor's thesis, University of Northern Colorado (Greeley, Colo.), 1970. (*DAI* 31:3768A)
254. CHAMBLISS, CHARLES ALVAH. *The Use of Personality Variables and Personal Data in Predicting Student Preference for a Proposed Set of Degree Requirements.* Doctor's thesis, University of Arkansas (Fayetteville, Ark.), 1970. (*DAI* 31:1031A)
255. DAVIS, SAMUEL C.; LOEB, JANE W.; AND ROBINSON, LEHYMANN F. "A Comparison of Characteristics of Negro and White College Freshman Classmates." *J Negro Ed* 39(4):359–66 f '70. *
256. ELTON, CHARLES F., AND ROSE, HARRIETT A. "Male Occupational Constancy and Change: Its Prediction According to Holland's Theory." *J Counsel Psychol Monogr* 17(6):1–19 N '70. * (*PA* 45:5123)
257. ERNEST, DAVID J. "The Predication of Academic Success of College Music Majors." *J Res Music Ed* 18(3):273–6 f '70. * (*PA* 45:8994)
258. GANSER, CARL J. "Understanding of Economic Concepts by Business Education and Social Studies Undergraduate Teaching Majors." *Delta Pi Epsilon J* 12(4):10–21 Ag '70. *
259. HANSON, GARY R., AND TAYLOR, RONALD G. "Interaction of Ability and Personality: Another Look at the Drop-Out Problem in an Institute of Technology." *J Counsel Psychol* 17(6):540–5 N '70. * (*PA* 45:3036)
260. HARRIS, GEORGE. *A Study Predicting Probable Success in College Among Freshmen at Tougaloo College Utilizing ACT Scores.* Master's thesis, Jackson State College (Jackson, Miss.), 1970.
261. HOFLAND, DEAN MYRON. *A Study of Selected Characteristics of Freshman Male Students Who Choose a Major and Those Who Do Not Choose a Major Upon Matriculation.* Doctor's thesis, University of South Dakota (Vermillion, S.D.), 1970. (*DAI* 31:3269A)
262. HOUNTRAS, PETER T., AND BRANDT, KENNETH R. "Relation of Student Residence to Academic Performance in College." *J Ed Res* 63(8):351–4 Ap '70. *
263. HOUNTRAS, PETER T.; GRADY, WILLIAM E.; AND VRAA, CALVIN W. "Manifest Anxiety and Academic Achievement of American and Canadian College Freshmen." *J Psychol* 76(1):3–8 S '70. * (*PA* 45:3037)
264. KIMBALL, JACK E., AND TOLMAN, HUBERT. "College ACT Data Information Storage and Retrieval." *J Ed Data Processing* 7(4):229–38 '70. *
265. LAUTZ, ROBERT; MACLEAN, G. DONALD; VAUGHAN, ANDREW T.; AND OLIVER, THOMAS C. "Characteristics of Successful Students Following Academic Suspension." *Col & Univ* 45(2):192–202 w '70. *
266. LOEB, JANE W., AND MUELLER, DANIEL J. "The Use of a Scale of High Schools in Predicting College Grades." *Ed & Psychol Meas* 30(2):381–6 su '70. * (*PA* 45:3063)
267. MILLSAPS, TEDDY W. *A Study Using the ACT and Four Year GPA to Establish the Predictive Validity for Academic Success at Middle Tennessee University for Graduates of Red Bank High School.* Master's thesis, University of Alabama (University, Ala.), 1970.
268. MORGAN, MARGARET KNOX. *The OPI, the ACT and University Attrition: A Discriminant Analysis.* Doctor's thesis, University of Kentucky (Lexington, Ky.), 1970. (*DAI* 31:3906A)
269. MUNDAY, LEO A. "Factors Influencing the Predictability of College Grades." *Am Ed Res J* 7(1):99–107 Ja '70. *
270. NASH, JOHN MORTON. *Prediction of Academic Achievement of Women at a Private Junior College Through Use of Certain Intellective and Family Relationships Measures.* Doctor's thesis, Boston University (Boston, Mass.), 1970. (*DAI* 31:2113A)
271. PARASKEVOPOULOS, JOHN, AND ROBINSON, L. F. "Comparison of Regression Equations Predicting College Performance From High School Record and Admissions Test Scores for Males and Females." *Col & Univ* 45(2):211–6 w '70. *
272. PARKS, KATHRYN J. *A Study to Determine the Relationship of Motor Educability and American College Test Scores to Skill Achievement.* Master's thesis, San Diego State College (San Diego, Calif.), 1970.
273. PEHRSON, PATRICIA J. *A Comparison of Student Achievement in Shorthand and Performance on the Turse Test and the ACT Test at Mankato State College.* Master's thesis, Mankato State College (Mankato, Minn.), 1970.
274. PITTMAN, FRANK MALLORY, JR. *An Investigation of the Predictive Value of Selected Factors on Achievement in Beginning Woodworking, Metalworking, and Electricity-Electronics Courses at the College Level.* Doctor's thesis, Texas A & M University (College Station, Tex.), 1970. (*DAI* 31:2149A)
275. SANDERS, ROBERT GENE. *The Relationship of Achievement and Personality Variables for Graduating Seniors Between Test Performances on the American College Test and the Edwards Personality Preference Schedule.* Doctor's thesis, University of Oklahoma (Norman, Okla.), 1970. (*DAI* 31:648A)
276. SMART, JOHN C.; ELTON, CHARLES F.; AND BURNETT, COLLINS W. "Underachievers and Overachievers in Intermediate French." *Mod Lang J* 54(6):415–20 O '70. *
277. SOLES, JAMES HENRY. *A Comparative Study of the Academic Performance of Three Selected Groups of Students Entering Troy State University.* Doctor's thesis, University of Alabama (University, Ala.), 1970. (*DAI* 31:1554A)
278. WILLIAMS, OSCAR C. *A Study of the Relationship Between High School Averages and College Success and Between ACT Composite Score and College Success.* Master's thesis, Jackson State College (Jackson, Miss.), 1970.
279. WYNNE, JOHN T., AND MURPHY, PATRICK S. "Using the Strong Vocational Interest Blank Diversity Scale Score as a Predictor of Freshman Academic Success." *Col Ed Rec* 55(9):203–6 Je '70. *

WIMBURN L. WALLACE, *Director, Professional Examinations Division, The Psychological Corporation, New York, New York.*

The American College Testing Program was initiated in 1959. Its adoption as a college admission examination has grown very rapidly since that time to the point where nearly a million students now take it annually throughout the country.

ACT's student assessment program comprises four tests of educational development and scholastic ability plus a questionnaire about high school grades, vocational and educational plans, family background, extracurricular activities, etc. The four tests are in English usage, mathematics usage, social studies reading, and natural sciences reading. They are direct descendants of the *Iowa Tests of Educational Development.*

Recent forms of the English usage test contain 75 items with a 40-minute time limit. Earlier forms contained 80 items with a time of 50 minutes. The test consists of four fairly lengthy, contiguous reading passages in which words or phrases are underlined and alternates of "no change" or different expressions are offered for the underlined sections. The task is to select the alternative "that best expresses the idea, makes the statement grammatically correct or [sic] more precise, or is worded most consistently with the style and tone of the passage as a whole." With these somewhat vague instructions, unequivocal right answers might occasionally be difficult to defend. Several ACT publications state that this test "measures the student's understanding and use of the basic elements in correct and effective writing—punctuation, capitalization, usage, phraseology, style, and organization." Although such may be the intent or goal, no evidence is presented that the test actually does measure these skills, especially the student's use of the basic elements listed.

The mathematics usage test consists of 40 items in arithmetic, algebra, and plane geometry with a 50-minute time limit. The emphasis on geometry varies among different forms of the test. The problems are of the traditional variety, reflecting little or no "modern mathematics." In an apparent attempt to give the test some flavor of practicality, there are many wordy problems; the stem for one item contains 69 words. This format would seem to vitiate the independence of this test from the three other parts of the ACT which are all essentially reading tests.

The social studies reading test contains 52 items. Although earlier forms with the same number of items had a time limit of 40 minutes, current forms allow only 35 minutes. Thirty-seven of the items are based on four reading passages, and the remaining 15 are miscellaneous information from the social studies area. Descriptions about the test state that it measures "the evaluative reasoning and problem-solving skills needed in the social studies." Evidence for this claim is lacking; indeed, it would be most difficult to substantiate any such statement.

Similarly, the natural sciences reading test is a 52-item, 35-minute (formerly 40-minute) section with 37 of the items based on four reading passages of scientific content and 15 items of general science knowledge. Content is not limited to "natural" science as differentiated from "physical science"; the section could more simply and accurately be labeled just "science." It is claimed that the test "measures the critical reasoning and problem-solving skills required in the natural sciences." This assertion generates an appreciable degree of skepticism.

All the items in the ACT are of the multiple choice type. Those in the mathematics section have five options, while the rest have four options. The reason for this discrepancy is not evident. The arrangement of the items in the test booklets is excellent with adequate spacing and easy readability. However, the quality of the construction of many of the items is poor. Stems often fail to define the question or problem at all, and nonparallel options are not uncommon. Following are some examples of inadequate stems:

> The weight of an object
> The deadlock between Hindu and Moslem
> Speaker 4's argument is
> Joule's experiments were
> Which of the following is most likely true of the author?
> Why is $(7 - 5) - 3 \neq 7 - (5 - 3)$?
> Which of the following is a name for 1?

For this last item, one option is "$2[(\frac{1}{3})(\frac{3}{2})]$," and another is "none of these."

Among the social studies and natural science items there are a great many stems which begin, "Which of the following" usually requiring the student to read through all the options to find the accurate one. This type devolves into a series of four true-false statements rather than a central question or problem to be recognized and answered.

Although most ACT publications are revised and updated annually, the latest ACT Technical Report available for this review was the 1965 edition. The report describes the development and equating of new test forms, scales and norms, reliability estimates, and summaries of some validity studies.

Draft items for new forms of the ACT are tried out on Iowa high school students, and item analysis is performed with the ITED as the criterion measure. Final forms are equated by the equipercentile method to old forms, using principally students at regular ACT centers in Iowa. Since each of the ACT subtests is equated to the corresponding ITED subtest, the national norms for the latter can be used for interpreting ACT scores of high school students. Beyond that, ACT has developed many sets of norms for individual colleges, regions, type of school, etc. There is a great abundance of normative data on the ACT fully accompanied by helpful descriptive information.

The scale score system used for the ACT is the same as that for the ITED. Scale scores range from 1 to 36 with the standard deviation intentionally set at approximately 5 so that the probable error of measurement would conveniently be about one scale score unit if the reliability coefficient were .91. Unfortunately, reliabilities for the ACT tend to be lower than for ITED, so the rule of thumb about the probable error of measurement does not so readily apply. The mean scale score for unselected first semester high school seniors is approximately 16,

ACT Test Battery of the American College Testing Program

while the mean for college bound seniors is about 20.

Although summaries or distributions of item analysis data are not published for the ACT, printouts of item difficulties and validities and of distributions of responses on the forms used in 1968–1969 were provided to this reviewer. In general these data are satisfactory despite the fact that the discrimination index for several items fell below .20 with one reaching into the negative area at −.09. Item difficulties have a wide range. The difficulty of the mathematics items is such that an average of about 45 percent of the students get each item correct, while an average of about 60 percent answer each item correctly in the English usage test. The mean difficulty of items in the other two tests falls between these extremes. Why such a discrepancy was created among the tests is not evident.

Reliabilities of successive forms of the ACT are estimated by the odd-even procedure. The Technical Report asserts that this method is recommended by Gulliksen in his *Theory of Mental Tests,* whereas actually Gulliksen (pp. 236–237) specifically warns against the use of this procedure with speeded tests. Since many students do not finish the parts of the ACT within the time limits, it may be concluded that the reliability coefficients reported are spuriously high. One inadequate study of parallel form reliability is reported in the Technical Report. It is based on 433 high school students who had been nominated for a competitive scholarship program in 1964. Interform correlations ranged from .69 in natural sciences to .86 on the Composite. Further studies of alternate form reliability are needed. Current evidence indicates that ACT reliabilities may be somewhat low for individual decisions.

Validation of the ACT has been very extensive with consistently good results. There is a vigorous and ongoing program of checking the validity of the ACT for predicting college grades. For every participating college that cooperates by providing the necessary criterion data, separate validity studies are performed. Furthermore, the predictive effectiveness of the ACT scores is analyzed by course or subject-matter groupings within schools as well as by programs such as business administration, engineering, education, and art. This wide variety of situations, of course, yields a broad range of validity coefficients, but it is estimated that the central tendency of the distribution of correlations between ACT Composite scores and overall grade point averages is about .50. In spite of the numerous criticisms of the ACT in this review, it must be emphasized that the most crucial characteristic of the examination, its predictive validity, proves to be as satisfactory as the state of the measurement art currently permits.

To enhance the accuracy of the prediction of college grades, ACT regularly incorporates self-reported high school grades with the test scores. The combined index provides a moderate gain in validity coefficients over either predictor alone, as might be expected.

In the Technical Report and other ACT literature there is an appeal to reviewers to consider the content validity of the ACT. It asks the reader "to try to determine the intellectual processes required to respond correctly to each item. In this way the reviewer can determine for himself to what degree the skills and understandings required by [sic] the examinee are similar to those required for the student in reading and study situations in college." This suggestion is patently inappropriate. In the case of the ACT, the topic of validity should be left well enough alone with the ample evidence of good predictive validity.

The few available reports of intercorrelations among the four ACT tests yield sets of data somewhat different from each other presumably because of sampling variations. In general these interrelationships are high, tending to confirm the observation that the ACT contains a redundancy of similar intellectual exercises all dependent to some degree on reading comprehension. A more telling indication of this condition is the fact that there is extremely little incremental validity gained by the addition of more of the parts of the ACT after the first test in a multiple correlation pattern. Indeed, all four parts optimally weighted appear to have practically no advantage over the one best predictor of the four.

There have been essentially no efforts made toward the development of new test types for the ACT. There is need for such work. A reasonable portion of the resources of ACT should be devoted to the exploration of improved testing techniques. Some varieties of assessments of intellectual skills are particularly called for in this battery which currently comprises such a concentration of reading comprehension. Although the ITED prototype has proved useful in the prediction of academic success, some improvements on that 30-year-old model should be attempted.

The ancillary services offered by ACT are extensive and splendid. The Student Profile Report contains a good deal more information beyond the ACT scores themselves. All the information gathered in the personal questionnaire section of the ACT is reflected in potentially useful categorized form on the report. High school grade averages in the areas corresponding to the parts of the ACT appear next to the test scores, and both local (for the college to which the scores are sent) and national percentile equivalents are provided for the ACT standard scores. Furthermore, for colleges participating in ACT's basic research service by providing grades, Student Profile Reports contain tables of grade predictions and probabilities of students' attaining C or higher in separate curricular areas and overall. Detailed, attractive, clear, helpful manuals accompany the reports containing useful guides to interpretation and suggestions for uses of the host of data provided.

Research services offered to participating colleges at no cost include distributions of ACT scores, high school grades, and college freshman grades; multiple regression analyses of ACT scores and high school grades as predictors of college grades; intercorrelations of all these variables; and comparative local and national norms. Subgrouping and local predictors are also included in analyses under certain conditions. A 250-page book entitled *Your College Freshmen* is provided with reports as an interpretive guide to the results of the research services. When unusual findings occur in the results of the research services for any college, individual communications are directed to that college concerning them.

ACT offers additional services associated directly in some instances and peripherally in others with the testing program itself. These include special punched card reports, magnetic tape reports, high school and college address files, financial aid information and reports, and a high school profile service. Most of these extra services are at additional cost.

Generally distributed periodic publications of ACT include *ACTivity,* a newsletter of the organization, and ACT Research Reports, which describe discrete studies in measurement or student personnel fields and are usually of general interest and high quality.

In summary, ACT is one of the two most widely used admission testing programs in the country. The other is the *College Board Scholastic Aptitude Test.* ACT contains four tests in English usage, mathematics usage, social studies reading, and natural sciences reading. A student profile questionnaire of background, high school grades, educational plans, and occupational goals is also an integral part of the program. Results are reported to the students and colleges in a very complete fashion with ample explanation accompanying them.

There is an overdependence on reading comprehension in the ACT. The four tests have high intercorrelations and the incremental validities of the addition of the second, third, and fourth tests in predicting collegiate success are minuscule. Reliabilities of the four tests are low for individual student assessment. Construction of the items in the ACT is of uneven quality; many of the items could benefit from more careful editing. There are extensive norms for the ACT, well developed and described and appropriately selected for the intended uses and interpretations of the test results. Despite some of the psychometric weaknesses of the ACT cited, the tests display highly satisfactory predictive validities against criteria of college grades, and this is in essence the most important property of all.

There has been a reprehensible neglect of new test development or experimentation associated with the ACT. Intensive attempts toward the evolvement of more varied yet pertinent measures of intellectual skills are long overdue.

The ancillary services of ACT in the forms of explanatory publications, extensive individual reports, local analyses of test and associated data, and research services for participating colleges are well executed, attractively presented, and potentially highly useful to those who will peruse them.

ACT suffers by comparison with the SAT in psychometric care and sophistication, is about equal in validity for predicting collegiate success, and excels somewhat in the variety and extent of ancillary services offered.

For reviews by Max D. Engelhart and Warren G. Findley of an earlier program, see 6:1 (1 excerpt).

ACT Test Battery of the American College Testing Program

[331]

*AH4, AH5, and AH6 Tests. Ages 10 and over, 13 and over, 16 and over; 1955–70; 2 levels: general intelligence, high-level intelligence; 4 tests; separate answer sheets must be used; 50p per 25 answer sheets; postage extra; A. W. Heim, K. P. Watts (AH6), and V. Simmonds (AH6); NFER Publishing Co. Ltd. *

a) AH4: GROUP TEST OF GENERAL INTELLIGENCE (1968 REVISION). Ages 10 and over; 1955–70; 1 form ('68, 14 pages); revised manual ('70, 18 pages); £2 per 25 tests; 10p per key; 50p per manual; £1 per specimen set; 20(30–45) minutes.

b) AH5: GROUP TEST OF HIGH-GRADE INTELLIGENCE. Ages 13 and over; 1956–68; 1 form ['56, 8 pages]; revised manual ('68, 25 pages); £1.15 per 25 tests; 15p per key; 50p per manual; £1 per specimen set; 40(60–70) minutes.

c) AH6: GROUP TESTS OF HIGH-LEVEL INTELLIGENCE. Ages 16 and over; 1970; 2 tests (12 pages): SEM for Scientists, Engineers and Mathematicians (potential or qualified), AG for Arts and General; manual (30 pages); £2.25 per 25 tests; 30p per set of keys; 70p per manual; £1.37 per specimen set; 40(60–75) minutes for SEM, 35(60–75) minutes for AG.

REFERENCES

1–11. See 5:390.
12. BEARD, R. M. "The Structure of Perception: A Factorial Study." *Brit J Ed Psychol* 35:210–22 Je '65. *
13. KELVIN, R. P.; LUCAS, C. J.; AND OJHA, A. B. "The Relation Between Personality, Mental Health and Academic Performance in University Students." *Brit J Social & Clin Psychol* 4:244–53 D '65. * (PA 40:4573)
14. TARPEY, M. SIMEON. "Personality Factors in Teacher Trainee Selection." *Brit J Ed Psychol* 35:140–9 Je '65. * (PA 39:16480)
15. LUCAS, C. J.; KELVIN, R. P.; AND OJHA, A. B. "Mental Health and Student Wastage." *Brit J Psychiatry* 112:277–84 Mr '66. * (PA 40:7958)
16. PILKINGTON, G. W., AND HARRISON, G. J. "The Relative Value of Two High Level Intelligence Tests, Advanced Level, and First Year University Examination Marks for Predicting Degree Classification." *Brit J Ed Psychol* 37:382–9 N '67. * (PA 42:6148)
17. CORTIS, G. A. "Predicting Student Performance in Colleges of Education." *Brit J Ed Psychol* 38:115–22 Je '68. * (PA 42:17717)
18. DACEY, J.; MADAUS, G.; AND ALLEN, A. "The Relationship of Creativity and Intelligence in Irish Adolescents." *Brit J Ed Psychol* 39(3):261–6 N '69. * (PA 44:8234)
19. BANKS, C.; KARDAK, V. S.; JONES, E. M.; AND LUCAS, C. J. "The Relation Between Mental Health, Academic Performance and Cognitive Test Scores Among Chemistry Students." *Brit J Ed Psychol* 40(1):74–9 F '70. * (PA 44:11366)
20. GALLOP, R. "A Study of the B.Ed. Student." Thesis abstract. *Brit J Ed Psychol* 40(2):220 Je '70. *
21. HAMILTON, VERNON. "Non-Cognitive Factors in University Students' Examination Performance." *Brit J Psychol* 61(2):229–41 My '70. * (PA 44:15302)
22. MEHRYAR, A. H., AND SHAPURIAN, R. "The Application of a High-Grade Intelligence Scale (AH5) in Iran." *Brit J Ed Psychol* 40(3):307–13 N '70. * (PA 45:6335)
23. POVEY, ROBERT M. "Arts/Science Differences: Their Relationship to Curriculum Specialization." *Brit J Psychol* 61(1):55–64 F '70. * (PA 44:9215)

JOHN NISBET, *Professor of Education, University of Aberdeen, Aberdeen, Scotland.*

AH4 and AH5 have proved popular as measures of general ability for research studies in Britain over the past 15 years. One reason is that they have an attractive face validity, for they include both verbal and nonverbal items in equal numbers, with at least four different types of problems in each part, all within a reasonable time limit. The researcher in a hurry, with a limited budget and an already crowded test battery, might find these all-purpose tests convenient.

A recent revision has improved the older tests in this series. The original versions were criticised for poor printing and amateurish drawings and lettering (6:506). These defects have been removed in the 1968 reprinting of AH4. (The marked improvement in layout may invalidate the old norms.) New manuals have been issued for AH4 and AH5, with more extensive norms and fuller details on validity and reliability. Norms, however, are still presented in the crude form of score distributions from a variety of samples, and provide only a broad five-point categorization from A (top 10 percent) to E (bottom 10 percent), varying for each reference group. The process of revision has been taken a step further by the publication in 1970 of AH6, designed to improve on AH5 by a more appropriate mixture of verbal (V), numerical (N) and diagrammatic (D) items, and by the provision of separate norms for the V, N and D categories. Two forms of AH6 have been issued: SEM for those specializing in science, engineering and mathematics, and AG for the somewhat vague group described as "Arts and General Subjects." SEM has equal numbers of V, N and D items, while AG has more V and fewer N and D, but the two forms have a substantial overlap of common items. SEM has norms for V, N and D separately, based on 1,189 university science students; AG has norms for V and (N + D) based on 1,710 school and college students.

The manuals give a clear statement of testing procedure and precise information on validity and reliability. Emphasis is laid on the proper presentation of the practice items which precede the tests. No less than 18 practice items are given for AH6, and, unlike some tests, these examples are of the same level of difficulty as the first items in the test proper. The claim is made (in the manuals for AH4 and AH5, but not for AH6) that these tests are less dependent on speed than most others of their kind, but this is open to question. For AH4 the time limit allows only nine seconds per item on average; but all the manuals prescribe that "nothing should be said....about speed of work." For AH4, test-retest reliability is .92; for AH5 and AH6 it is lower as the tests are designed for selected groups (AH6, AG total score, .83 on test-retest). For all tests a range of reliability coefficients is given, derived from different samples and by different methods. Validity is reported in the form of correlations with other comparable tests and with other criteria, mostly academic performance.

The tests are good examples of their kind, relying on the conventional types of problem, such as analogies, relations and series in verbal, numerical and diagrammatic forms. For AH6 the items have been devised imaginatively, especially the verbal problems which make use of words with more than one meaning. The timed group test, relying on a variety of items to secure wide coverage and sustain interest, will continue to be useful as a research instrument, but will not be used, one hopes, for individual assessment or as a basis for counseling. AH6, with its alternative bias, is likely to arouse most interest. The rationale of the design of the two forms of this test is argued in the manual. Giving weight to verbal items with the AG group is surely correct; for science-based courses also, verbal items give a fair prediction of achievement. The argument is less convincing for retaining diagrammatic items if the test is regarded as a measure of scholastic aptitude. The manual argues that "visuality" is important for the scientist, but it does not report any factor analysis of the test, and the correlations reported between D scores and scores on other similar tests are all below .50. (The manual is at least to be commended for reporting the correlations fully—even one on the wrong side of zero.) It is to be hoped that those who use the separate score categories will bear in mind the small number of items from which these subtest scores are derived. Comparison across SEM and AG will be based on the still smaller number of common items. Nevertheless, AH6 represents an interesting development of this series and provides a welcome addition to the measures available for assessing high-ability subjects. However, the established pattern of scholastic aptitude test, with its two categories, verbal and numerical, is not yet seriously challenged by this development.

For a review by John Liggett of AH5 and the original edition of AH4, see 6:506; for reviews by George A. Ferguson of AH4 and J. A. Keats of AH5, see 5:390.

[332]

*Academic Alertness "AA": Individual Placement Series. Adults; 1957–66; 7 scores: general knowledge, arithmetic, vocabulary, reasoning ability, logical sequence, accuracy, total; Forms A, B, ('57, 6 pages); no specific manual; series manual ('66, 107 pages); no data on reliability of part scores; separate answer sheets must be used; $25 per 20 tests; $4 per 100 answer sheets; 50¢ per key; $2.50 per series manual; $4.45 per specimen set; cash orders postpaid; 20(25) minutes; J. H. Norman; Personnel Research Associates, Inc. *

JOEL T. CAMPBELL, *Senior Research Psychologist, Educational Testing Service, Princeton, New Jersey.*

This 100-item measure of general intelligence is arranged in spiral form, each spiral having groupings of five items for each subarea. An additional score, called accuracy, is calculated from the ratio of items correct to items completed.

The items are in a free response format; the scoring key lists several variations of acceptable responses (or a range of responses) but this still leaves the scorer with judgmental decisions.

The question wording has been kept short and simple, but at a cost of ambiguity in a number of instances. For example, in one question, "What is the largest city in the United States?" the term "largest" is used to mean population rather than area. However, in a similar question "smallest" is used to mean area. For a few questions, the keyed response will not be acceptable to specialists in the area, although no doubt most of the general population would consider the response correct.

Possibly the most serious challenge to question wording will come from the standpoint of minority groups who will have considerable justification in claiming that the test has irrelevant cultural detail. This test was developed about 1956, before employers' attention had been forcibly directed to the problem of minority employment and differences in cultural background. Some of the questions ask for fairly common knowledge or for common sense interpretations or for fairly simple arithmetic computation. Other questions call for more esoteric information and it would be difficult to justify the need for such information on most jobs.

No item analyses are given. Correlations of the area scores with the total score range from .72 to .78, while area score intercorrelations range from .36 to .53. These correlations are low enough to indicate that the areas measure somewhat different abilities.

Table 1 in the manual is supposed to show the equivalence of the two forms, but the reviewer is unable to understand it. Columns 2 and 3 of this table, for example, give "number of misses" for each area and the total, but "number of misses" is nowhere defined. Test-retest reliability is given as .92 for an undescribed group of 100.

Evidence of validity is presented in three ways. Correlations of the two forms of the test with the Wonderlic, Army Beta, and Army General Classification Tests range from .69 to .88. Median scores by job classifications (total scores and area scores) for 20 different jobs show reasonable progression by job level from laborer to engineer. A third way in which validity information is presented is by expectancy charts for four occupations, comparing test performance with rated job performance.

Here, however, there is confusion in the figures for at least one of the charts. The text says "The length of each bar on the charts reflects the percent of employees who were rated as above average employees who scored in a given interval. Chart 6, for example, indicates that 88 percent of the guards who scored between 54 and 100 had been rated as superior performers; whereas only 12 percent of those who scored between 0 and 43 were rated as superior performers." The middle category had 57 percent. Since chart 6 was based on an N of 12, it is not possible to come up with any grouping of numbers which will permit these percentages!

In fairness, it should be stated that the other three expectancy charts are based on more respectable N's. They report, however, lower validity coefficients: .32 for 45 assembly engineers, .45 for 72 machine parts inspectors, and .18 for 116 junior engineers.

Normative data are based on unusually large numbers of cases. The total industry norm is based on 31,143 cases. Norms are also reported for clerical workers, shop workers, engineers, and supervisors.

The reviewer does not feel that this test can be recommended over such alternate possibilities as the verbal and numerical tests of the *Fundamental Achievement Series,* for lower level jobs, and the *Personnel Tests for Industry* for somewhat higher level factory or office jobs, even though these alternatives do require more testing time than does the AA.

[333]

*Adaptability Test. Job applicants; 1942–67; Forms A, B, ('42, 3 pages); manual ('67, 12 pages); $5.30 per 25 tests; 40¢ per manual; $1.25 per specimen set; postage extra; 15(20) minutes; Joseph Tiffin and C. H. Lawshe; Science Research Associates, Inc. *

REFERENCES

1–3. See 3:216.
4–16. See 5:305.
17. PAGE, HOWARD E. "A Note on Norms for the Purdue Industrial Mathematics Test and the Adaptability Test." *J Appl Psychol* 34:306–8 O '50. * (PA 26:559)
18. CHANDLER, ROBERT E. *Validation of Apprentice Screening Tests in an Oil Refinery.* Doctor's thesis, Purdue University (Lafayette, Ind.), 1956. (DA 27:325B)
19. KAZMIER, LEONARD J. "Normative Data Information Exchange, No. 12–22." *Personnel Psychol* 12:504 au '59. *
20. GRUENFELD, LEOPOLD WILHELM. *Selection of Executives for a Training Program.* Doctor's thesis, Purdue University (Lafayette, Ind.), 1960. (DA 21:1247)
21. BUEL, WILLIAM D., AND BAEHNER, VIRGINIA M. "The Assessment of Creativity in a Research Setting." *J Appl Psychol* 45:353–8 D '61. * (PA 37:1211)
22. GUION, ROBERT M. "Synthetic Validity in a Small Company: A Demonstration." *Personnel Psychol* 18:49–63 sp '65. * (PA 39:16490)

For a review by John M. Willits, see 5:305; for reviews by Anne Anastasi and Marion A. Bills, see 3:216.

[334]

★Analysis of Learning Potential. Grades 1, 2–3, 4–6, 7–9, 10–12; 1970; ALP; *complete test option:* 2 scores derived from the same total raw score: learning potential ("estimate of the pupil's general learning ability" compared to his age group), general composite ("estimate of the pupil's general learning ability" compared to his grade group); in grades 4–12 a reading-mathematics difference score (called "reading-mathematics composite prognostic differential") is also reported; *reading prognostic subtests option:* reading composite prognostic score ("an estimate of the pupil's capacity for school learning" in reading compared to his grade group); *mathematics prognostic subtests option:* mathematics composite prognostic score ("an estimate of the pupil's capacity for school learning" in mathematics compared to his grade group); the same test booklets but different answer sheets are used for the 3 options; 1 form; 5 levels; preliminary technical report (59 pages); no data on predictive validity; no norms for difference scores; use of local norms recommended; separate answer sheets (Digitek, IBM 805, IBM 1230, MRC) must be used for grades 4–12; $5.50 per 35 Digitek or IBM 1230 answer folders; $4.20 per 35 IBM 805 answer folders; $10 per 100 MRC answer sheets; $1.20 per set of MRC hand scoring keys; $2 per technical report; MRC scoring service: complete test (56¢ and over for grades 1–3, 43¢ and over for grades 4–12), either the reading prognostic subtests or the mathematics prognostic subtests (51¢ and over for grades 1–3, 38¢ and over for grades 4–12); postage extra; Walter N. Durost, Eric F. Gardner, Richard Madden, and George A. Prescott; Harcourt Brace Jovanovich, Inc. *
a) PRIMARY 1 BATTERY. Grade 1; Form A (12 pages); 2 editions: hand scored, MRC scored; manual (35 pages); norms (8 pages); $10.80 per 35 hand scored tests; $1 per key; $2 per specimen set; $13.80 per 35 MRC scored tests; (84) minutes in 3 sessions for complete test, (32) for reading, (27) for mathematics.
b) PRIMARY 2 BATTERY. Grades 2–3; Form A (12 pages); 2 editions: hand scored, MRC scored; manual (34 pages); norms (10 pages); $11 per 35 hand scored tests; $1 per key; $2 per specimen set; $14 per 35 MRC scored tests; (85) minutes in 3 sessions for complete test, (32) for reading, (31) for mathematics.
c) ELEMENTARY BATTERY. Grades 4–6; Form A (9 pages); manual (38 pages); norms (10 pages);

$11.50 per 35 tests; $2.10 per set of Digitek or IBM keys; $2.25 per specimen set; 50(75) minutes in 2 sittings for complete test, 19(28) for reading, 22(30) for mathematics.

d) ADVANCED 1 BATTERY. Grades 7–9; Form A (12 pages); manual (40 pages); norms (11 pages); $11.50 per 35 tests; $2.80 per set of Digitek or IBM 1230 keys; $2.10 per set of IBM 805 keys; $2.25 per specimen set; 68(93) minutes in 2 sittings for complete test, 23(31) for reading, 21(29) for mathematics.

e) ADVANCED 2 BATTERY. Grades 10–12; Form A (12 pages); manual (40 pages); norms (10 pages); prices same as for d; 68(93) minutes in 2 sittings for complete test, 31(40) for reading, 21(29) for mathematics.

LEE J. CRONBACH, *Vida Jacks Professor of Education, Stanford University, Stanford, California.*

ALP is made up of newly designed subtests which allegedly "have demonstrated their ability to predict specific criteria of scholastic success while....relatively free from....[content] specifically taught in school." The Index of Learning Potential is an indicator of "general capacity for school learning." A more accurate claim would be that the test measures the pupil's present level of general educational development; it requires reasoning, vocabulary, and computational skill.

Let us deal thoroughly with the Elementary battery, and examine its statistics at grade 5. Regarding batteries for earlier and later grades, it will then be necessary to note only a few variations from this basic pattern. The seven subtests at the Elementary level are for the most part variations on old themes. The variations are ingenious and avoid the "guess what I have in mind" character of items in many group mental tests. Verbal classification here takes the form

    door   kitchen   painted   garage   basement   porch

Number series is turned into a sort of analogy item:

    (4,2)   (5,3)   (7,—)   3 4 5 6 7

A numerical-reasoning task requires one to fill the blanks in

$$\frac{\Box\ 8}{5\ 6}\ \Box$$

with the same digit, so as to make a sound calculation. To do this, one must decide whether addition, subtraction, or multiplication fits the problem. These numerical items require school-learned content, but it is content all pupils taking this battery will have covered. Facility in using and adapting very basic skills is tested, and performance hence will not reflect local variations in curricula. The items in all subtests are abstract and formal. There is no attempt to interest pupils by referring to real situations.

The total score is converted to ILP, a standard-score-within-age-group; 50 is the scale mean and 15 the standard deviation. The *Test Standards* urge publishers to employ a 50-10 scale unless there is a compelling reason for some alternative, since proliferation of scales confuses users. There is no warrant for this 50-15 scale. The authors recommend *stanines* (in an obscure paragraph certain to be overlooked by users) as "the most desirable method of interpreting scores on ALP." The manuals, however, at all points discuss the 50-15 standard scores, and the norm booklet makes an extra stage of conversion necessary to get stanines (or percentiles). Surely most users will mistakenly employ the over-refined standard-score scale.

Such labels as "learning potential" and "capacity" are even more objectionable than the term "intelligence," which the authors studiously avoid. The only sensible meaning that can be given to "learning potential" is "what the pupil could achieve if he were hereafter to be given the instruction optimal for him." There is of course no evidence to support such an interpretation here. ILP is a measure of what the pupil's past education, in school and out, has taught him. It indicates the rank in achievement to be anticipated for him if the school does nothing more effective in the future than it did in the past. To label the mediocre achiever as having mediocre "potential" is simply to reassure the school that it has done the best it could for him. The authors recommend that ILP be used together with other data in making educational plans for the pupil. Clearly, if ILP is less favorable than the other evidence, it has to be ignored, for how can a pupil achieve beyond his potential? If ILP is significantly higher than other indicators, the school should heed its signal. But in what fraction of cases will there be such a disparity? The manual gives no direct evidence, but it appears that ALP will agree so closely with concurrent achievement tests that disparity is likely to be noise, not signal.

The total score is also converted to GCSS (General Composite Standard Score), a number on a 50-15 scale that compares the pupil with the norm for his half-grade. ILP and GCSS will agree except for the child whose age is atypical for his grade. For raw score 70 in the first half of grade 5, the GCSS stanine is 5; and the ILP stanine is also 5 for pupils of normal age (10-3 to 11-5). For a 9-year-old the stanine is 7. The authors propose that GCSS, not ILP, be the basis for ability grouping, where ability grouping is practiced.

The statistics for the total score are what one would expect for a test requiring 75 minutes. Reliability (taking into account short-term pupil variability and form-to-form variability) is .90; the standard error is about six-tenths of the stanine unit. ILP correlates .83 with Lorge-Thorndike Verbal and Total IQ's, .70 with Non-Verbal. The concurrent correlation of GCSS with single subtests of the Metropolitan and Stanford Achievement batteries is generally in the .70's, and the (unreported) correlation with an achievement total is probably close to .90. The statistics support the view, then, that this is a transfer test of academic achievement over the verbal and numerical areas.

The composite score on an achievement battery is a good predictor of next year's success, and it is a reasonable guess that this measure will have predictive validity in the same range. There are, however, no predictive data of any sort on this test, a fact that is obscured by the authors' liberal use of the words "predictive" and "prognostic" in discussing data from concurrent testing. It is hard to believe that ALP will be a better predictor of achievement than the *Iowa Tests of Basic Skills* or some other fundamental-skills battery. Such a battery has immediate diagnostic relevance, and is not subject to intrusive misinterpretations invoked by words like "capacity." Hence it is hard to understand why ALP should be used in preference to an achievement battery, for start-of-year planning.

THE PROGNOSTIC COMPOSITES. The idea of predicting specific achievements, quoted in the first sentence of this review, is an echo of early plans that collapsed under the weight of evidence. An attempt was made to develop separate composites relevant to reading, mathematics, science, language arts, and social studies, using the subtests in different combinations. As the data came in the authors faced up to the fact that GCSS is at least as good a (concurrent) predictor of achievement in science as any set of subtests. Likewise for other categories of achievement. Hence GCSS is clearly the predictor to use and the manual says so.

It is possible for a school interested solely in reading to administer just the three subtests in the reading composite (RCPS). This short scale works reasonably well. Other three- or four-subtest combinations can be separately administered where information relevant specifically to mathematics (MCPS) or any other single subject is desired.

Hope dies hard. The authors have retreated step by painful step from their intent to offer a differential battery, and in the manuals, score reports, etc., the composites are not yet properly subordinated to GCSS. While the authors recommend that subscales not be interpreted, they suggest that the RCPS-MCPS difference be examined; a confidence-band technique is used to suppress small differences. Even though conclusions about the true difference reach the level of differential reliability customary in profile interpretation, its differential validity is in serious doubt. More significant is the fact that in any event teachers can make no practical decision on the basis of norm-referenced differences in these two variables. It appears to me that the score should not be calculated, and if reported should not be used.

Although the authors prize their "measurement technology," they are not up to date. They preserve the interpretation of confidence bands symmetric around the observed score, which Lord and Novick [1] have exposed as fallacious. The authors ignore recent work [2] on theory of difference scores; further limitations of classical work in this field are still emerging.[3]

OTHER LEVELS. The Advanced batteries require 93 minutes, and include a fairly difficult spatial subtest. The Syntactic Clues subtest is intriguing, with items like this: "Priffles and wurfles were umping piskly in the opple popple. Whangles are usually wurfy but not while _____." The correct answer choice is "umping" rather than "piskly" or another non-verb.

The GCSS reliability coefficient rises to about .93 in grade 6 and above. Concurrent correlations of GCSS with achievement battery sub-

---

[1] LORD, FREDERIC M., AND NOVICK, MELVIN R. *Statistical Theories of Mental Test Scores.* Reading, Mass.: Addison-Wesley Publishing Co., Inc., 1968. Pp. xvii, 568. *
[2] LORD, FREDERIC M. Chap. 2, "Elementary Models for Measuring Change," pp. 21–38. In *Problems in Measuring Change.* Edited by Chester W. Harris. Madison, Wis.: University of Wisconsin Press, 1963. Pp. x, 259. *
STANLEY, JULIAN C. "General and Special Formulas for Reliability of Differences." *J Ed Meas* 4:249–52 w '67. *
[3] CRONBACH, LEE J., AND FURBY, LITA. "How We Should Measure 'Change'—Or Should We?" *Psychol B* 74(1):68–80 Jl '70. *

Analysis of Learning Potential

tests spread over the range .70 to .85. The story on predictive composites is essentially the same as for the Elementary battery.

Primary 2, for grades 2 and 3, requires no reading. A dictated test asks the pupil to judge whether a word such as "suspect" does or does not apply to a picture (man behind bars). Other tasks have to do with computation, everyday information, figure series and vocabulary. A picture-story task displays two silhouette pictures that start a story, plus four additional pictures. The pupil is to mark 3 beneath the picture that fits as third in the sequence, and 4 beneath the correct fourth panel. This subtest falls below the usual excellence of execution: the task is complex, the drawings are tiny, and responses other than the keyed ones can be defended.

For Primary 2 the reliability of GCSS holds up, but concurrent correlations with achievement subtests drop to the .50's and .60's. At this level the attempt to interpret the RCPS-MCPS difference is abandoned, though the option of administering half the test to get either composite remains.

Primary 1 is similar. There are more pictorial tests, and numerical tasks are replaced with one on quantitative concepts. Primary 1 is more nearly a pictorial test of verbal and general abilities than are the achievement-related tests at later levels. It includes a maddening perceptual task calling for selection of similar *kanji*. In general, the demands upon visual acuity and attentiveness seem large for school beginners. A considerable concession to children's interests is made at this level, however. Reliability over a short interval falls off to .80. At this level in particular one wants the missing information on stability over several months, and on predictive validity.

EVALUATION. The manual and technical report are disappointing. The developers obviously made an effort to give honest advice, to qualify statements, and to present extensive evidence. Outright conflict with the *Test Standards* is rare. Yet the manual and technical report seem unlikely to give users a sound understanding of the test. The facts I have found salient in assessing the test are located in widely scattered places, sometimes deeply buried. Some of the needed statistics are not reported even though the data were in hand. There was massive data collection, yet no resources were allocated to one-year follow-up studies. Tabular data are amassed to the point of throwing dust in the reader's eyes. It is agreed, for example, that alternate-forms reliabilities are pertinent, and internal-consistency coefficients less suitable. Why precede the two tables of relevant alternate-forms coefficients with *three* tables of K-R 20 coefficients? (Worse, the K-R 20 values are computed by a lazy-man's formula that probably inflates the coefficients.)

In the discussion of norms the information overload is even greater. The three-stage sampling plan appears to have been very well designed. The technical report offers three tables by way of evidence on the adequacy of the norms. The first table defends the representativeness of the first-stage selection of 2,000 school districts, but leaves us with no direct report on the 69 systems actually used in the norms. The second table, presented without comment, is a regional breakdown of the actual sample. The careful reader discovers that pupils in the Southeast region are overrepresented by 50 percent, with corresponding deficits in Midwest and West. Since the Southeast usually has conspicuously different score distributions, this suggests that the norms are more in error than the developers intended. How much difference does this make? What went wrong in the sampling? Why is the unrepresentativeness not discussed? The third table displays, for each grade, the percentage of standardization cases from various sizes of school system, and shows that each of these distributions matches the distribution for the U.S. population for all grades pooled. But is the U.S. distribution uniform in all grades? One suspects not. In sum, despite a flood of technical information, our confidence in the norms has to rest on our confidence in the authors.

ALP is a carefully made test. Preparation of items is good on the whole. The technical characteristics are entirely adequate, despite the faults noted. Probably ALP will forecast end-of-year grades as well as other tests do, at least in grades beyond the second. Yet it is hard to see what niche it will fit into. It cannot supplant the achievement test a good testing program uses early in the school year. It will do less than a good test of nonverbal reasoning to shake up the school by detecting the many pupils who can reason well but who have not mastered basic educational skills. ALP is conservative in conception, identifying the child's achievement to date with his "potential" and emphasizing pre-

Analysis of Learning Potential

ARTHUR R. JENSEN, *Professor of Educational Psychology; and Research Psychologist, Institute of Human Learning; University of California, Berkeley, California.*

The ALP is the result of a major effort to produce a series of group mental tests for school use which can fully compete with the best and most widely used group intelligence tests now available. To this reviewer, the effort appears to have been successful.

The various subtests can be classified by inspection of their item contents as Word Relational Concepts, Number Concepts, and Figure Concepts, although, as we shall see, the factorial complexity of the tests is not as great as all the diverse subtest labels might suggest.

The time required for administration is reasonable and comparable to other good tests. The tests are given in two or three sittings.

The manual for administration is excellent and contains all the information one could wish to find in a test manual.

PUBLISHER'S CLAIMS VS. REALITY. In the present climate of popular criticism of intelligence tests, which has culminated in their being banned in some school systems, the publishers of ALP seem to have gone all-out to make their product appear to be something other than what it actually is, namely, a good intelligence test. The publisher's blurb, for example, claims the "ALP is more than just a new measure of scholastic aptitude—it is a totally new concept for assessing school ability." The title of the test itself is misleading. There is nothing "analytic" about the scores it yields; there are no profiles or special diagnostic ratios. And the concept of "potential" is quite meaningless with respect to scores on any psychological tests. Some readers are apt to construe the test's title as suggesting a measure of innate ability—a claim not made by the publishers and for which no appropriate evidence is available. Moreover, the test is not best regarded as a measure of "learning" ability. If "learning ability" means rate of acquisition of skills or knowledge, independent of initial status, then the ALP, to the extent that it is like other intelligence tests, is not a measure of "learning ability." The ALP is very much like most other intelligence tests, and ample research has shown that intelligence test scores have relatively low correlations with learning measures or "gain scores" which are independent of initial status.

WHAT ALP MEASURES. Actually, the ALP measures nothing new, nothing different from what is measured by, say, the *Lorge-Thorndike Intelligence Tests*. It is old wine in a new bottle. But the old wine is excellent and the new bottle is indeed attractive. As anyone who has had much experience in factor analyzing a large variety of mental ability tests can readily see from casual inspection of the various ALP subtests, the old wine is nothing other than Spearman's g, the general intelligence factor. The various subtests would be somewhat differentially loaded on what Cattell calls "fluid" and "crystallized" g, and they can also be grouped in a way that would correspond quite closely to the verbal and nonverbal parts of the Lorge-Thorndike. Through factor analytic experience with many kinds of tests one comes readily to recognize the types of items most heavily loaded with g. It would be extremely difficult to make up more different kinds of g-loaded items than the authors have succeeded in composing—g-loaded items appropriate in difficulty and interest for every grade level from 1 to 12. This heavy g characteristic of the ALP tests is most interesting in view of its authors' emphasizing in the manual for administration that the ALP "was *not* developed within a specific theoretical framework concerning the nature of mental ability or intelligence. Thus, the tests were designed to measure neither a single, general ability factor nor to provide factorially 'pure' measures of somewhat discrete mental functions. Tests appearing in each battery were selected solely from the standpoint of their contribution to the prediction of academic success."

FACTORIAL COMPOSITION. To determine the factorial complexity of the ALP, this reviewer performed a factor analysis separately on Forms A and B of each of the five batteries, using the matrix of subtest intercorrelations for each battery provided by the publisher. (Specifically, a principal components analysis was done, followed by a varimax rotation of the components having Eigenvalues greater than 1.) Factorially, Forms A and B are very equivalent. A general factor accounts for between 42 and 59 percent of the total variance in each battery. With few exceptions the various subtests are highly similar in the g loadings, which are almost uniformly high (i.e., .70 to .80). In two of the batteries (Primary 1 and Elemen-

Analysis of Learning Potential

tary) no second factor emerged. And in no battery did more than two factors emerge. Rotation of these factors simply divides the variance between verbal and nonverbal factors. In brief, the reviewer's analysis indicates that the variance in these tests is mainly attributable to a large general factor (g), accounting on the average for about 52 percent of the variance, and to two small group factors, verbal and nonverbal (or numerical-spatial), together accounting for about 10 to 13 percent of the variance. The remaining 30 to 35 percent of the variance is attributable to measurement error (less than 10 percent) and to factors specific to the various subtests (about 20 to 25 percent). We can estimate that the total score on the ALP correlates with g between .65 and .77 for the various batteries, with an average correlation of about .72. In this respect, then, the ALP closely resembles most other good tests of general intelligence, which means that it measures, more than anything else, the subject's ability to see complex or abstract relationships, or in Spearman's words, "the eduction of relations and correlates." Whether we like it or not, this is the ability which, more than any other, enters into scholastic achievement under the instructional conditions of present-day schools and as assessed by the traditional criteria of school grades and achievement test scores.

"CULTURE-FAIRNESS." In their manual the authors warn that "Pupils who are poorly motivated or who have not had the opportunity to learn the broad, general types of behaviors sampled by the tests should have these limiting factors taken into consideration by teachers and counselors in interpreting the test results. This is particularly true for pupils who have experienced severe cultural deprivation." Does this mean that the ALP has lower validity in predicting the scholastic performance of "culturally deprived" children? We do not know. But we can guess from experience with similar tests that it will predict scholastic achievement (under normal school conditions and assessed by standard tests) as well for the disadvantaged as the majority of children. If it is realized that the *causes* of any particular child's score are unknown (unless specifically investigated) and that the score is simply a statistical predictive device, there need be no concern about the test's "fairness" to all subpopulations of pupils. However, if one should imagine that he is getting at something more "profound" than this, he should be made aware that the test is no more "culture-fair" than most other group tests now on the market. So far as we know, all tests with a high g saturation, whether or not they are called "culture-fair" or look "culture-fair," show very substantial social class differences in performance. The ALP will be no exception. We can expect lower socio-economic status children, on the average, to score about one standard deviation below middle-class children on the ALP.

This reviewer would regard tests like the ALP (and all other standard intelligence tests) as "unfair" only in the sense that they assess such a limited and homogeneous set of abilities. These abilities can be called "intelligence" or g, which is indeed highly correlated with scholastic performance. But g is not the whole spectrum of human ability, nor is it the only ability that can be marshaled for scholastic achievement. One would like to see a broader assessment of children's abilities, especially among groups who are relatively low in g, in hopes of finding other abilities and talents which can serve in the educational process of making schooling rewarding even for children with below average academic aptitude. Although tests like the ALP may give the impression, with all their diverse subtests, that they are getting at a broad assessment of many abilities, they are actually very unidimensional. Unless supplemented by other forms of assessment they tend to rank-order pupils along a single dimension of aptitude. Does the form of school instruction in turn attempt to maximize the correlation between "scholastic aptitude" (as represented by non-scholastic tests of g) and scholastic achievement? Highly homogeneous tests of ability, yielding a single score, may not be the most useful instruments in schools tending toward a diversity of curricula and instructional programs intended to make school beneficial to a wide range of individual differences. Only by inventing additional tests with low loadings on g will we be able to discover possible areas of educationally relevant strengths in those children who are below the average in g-type abilities. Unfortunately, there is no standard test battery one can recommend at present to fill this need.

NORMS. The ALP norms are based on a sample of 165,000 pupils in 75 school systems selected so as to be highly representative of the U.S. school population according to the latest census. Norms for different regions of the U.S.

Analysis of Learning Potential

or for different types of communities (e.g., rural-urban, lower–class—middle–class, etc.) are not provided. The authors suggest that school systems should develop their own local norms, presumably by accumulating large numbers of test results and converting the raw ALP scores to normalized standard scores. A further step would be to determine the regression equation for the school's particular achievement measures as "predicted" from the ALP. Local norms, if properly established and maintained up-to-date, make a good deal of sense, considering the fact that the average level of scholastic achievement in a school or a community is highly related to a host of community characteristics over which the schools themselves have little or no control, such as the educational level of the adult population, home ownership, cost of housing, proportion of native-born whites, rate of unemployment, proportion of professional workers, etc. Comparison of a particular school's or community's scores with overall national norms, though it may serve the purpose of describing one aspect of the school population, is of little or no value in dealing with an individual pupil. On the other hand, there may be some value in comparing an individual's score on an intelligence test with an assessment of his scholastic achievement. This is best done by putting the intelligence and achievement scores on the same scale (e.g., normalized standard scores with the same mean and standard deviation) normed on the same reference population. The authors of the ALP emphasize, correctly, I believe, that the subtests are designed, for the most part, to be "relatively free from specific school-learned skills. The tests ....do assess learned abilities gained from a number of somewhat diffuse sources whose exact nature cannot be clearly specified." The detection of large and reliable discrepancies between a measure of extra-scholastically acquired skills and measures of scholastic achievement can be of diagnostic value, both for individual children and for the means of classrooms and of whole schools. Detection of "underachievers" for special attention is a useful function of ability tests. The ALP can serve this purpose as well as any other intelligence tests on the market. The "cutoff" discrepancy between ALP and achievement scores that would pick out "underachievers" is not specified, but it is a largely arbitrary matter anyway. (It should probably be at least twice the test's standard error of estimate.) The fact that there will be about as many "overachievers" as "underachievers" belies the test's label, "Analysis of Learning *Potential,*" since theoretically no one should be able to exceed his "potential."

SCALES AND SCORES. The ALP provides five types of derived scores, all of which can be found in tables in the Norms-Conversion Booklet. The Index of Learning Potential (ILP) is a normalized standard score with a mean of 50 and a standard deviation of 15. The reference group is based on chronological age, within 2 or 3 month intervals. Although the term IQ is assiduously avoided by the authors, the ILP is essentially a deviation IQ, comparing the individual's standing among others of his age, and thus it has the same meaning that IQ has on the Lorge-Thorndike or any other up-to-date tests of intelligence which provide deviation IQ's. To put the ILP on the same scale as the IQ, one must simply add 50 to the ILP.

The General Composite Standard Score (GCSS) is normed on pupils making normal progress within grade levels limited to an 18-month age range within each grade level, a range that comprises the middle 80 to 90 percent of pupils in any one grade. The GCSS also has a mean of 50 and a SD of 15.

So, if you want to know where a pupil stands with respect to those of similar chronological age, regardless of their grade level, you use the ILP. If you want to see where a pupil stands in relation to others in his grade who are making normal progress (presumably the middle 80 to 90 percent of the age range of children in regular classes), you use the GCSS.

The Composite Prognostic Score (CPS), also with a mean of 50 and a SD of 15, is a score based on a weighted combination of several subtests that correlates maximally with either reading or mathematics achievement. The CPS provides hardly any appreciable gain over the total ILP or GCSS in terms of correlation specifically with achievement in verbal or quantitative curricula.

Finally, the ALP raw scores can be converted to percentile ranks and to stanines.

The most useful score, one might think, would be one which is on the same scale as the scholastic achievement test, so that direct comparison of "intelligence" (i.e., extra-scholastic achievement) and scholastic achievement would be possible. But most standard achievement tests provide normalized T scores with a mean of 50 and a standard deviation of 10. The ILP unfortunately combines the mean of achievement tests (i.e., 50) with the standard deviation of IQ tests (i.e., 15).

Scoring of the ALP by hand (made easy by simple templates) or by machine is possible. IBM, MRC, and Digitek answer sheets are available, and scoring can be done locally or by the publisher's scoring service.

RELIABILITY. The internal consistency reliability (Kuder-Richardson) is very high, ranging from .92 to .97 in different grades. The alternate-forms reliability is also quite satisfactory (.80 to .94).

VALIDITY. The ALP is expressly intended to predict scholastic achievement. Its validity was established by correlating the GCSS scores at each grade level. In the high school grades the validities are nearly as high as reliability will permit. If the authors' chief aim was to "predict" concurrent scholastic achievement with the ALP, it is hard to see how they could have been any more successful. The ILP score was not used in the validation evidence but would probably yield validity coefficients very similar to those for the GCSS.

The ALP correlates .83 with Lorge-Thorndike total IQ (at grade 5) and has correlations between .29 (Mechanical) and .86 (Verbal Reasoning + Numerical Ability) with various parts of the *Differential Aptitude Tests*.

TECHNICAL INFORMATION. In addition to the very complete printed manual that accompanies the test, the publishers have prepared a mimeographed Preliminary Technical Report which contains much more detailed information about the construction and validation of the ALP. It contains information which will be of primary interest to educational researchers and could also serve as a model in courses on the theory and practice of test construction. One of its most useful features is an appendix which gives normalized standard scores, with a mean of 500 and SD of 50, for the entire five batteries. This puts all the five tests, spanning grades 1 to 12, on the same scale, a feature which enhances the test's usefulness for longitudinal studies. The method of scaling the various tests is fully described in this report.

USEFULNESS. If one wants to use a test of "general intelligence," or "IQ," or "scholastic aptitude," the ALP is about as good as any of the current top competitors in the field. Since it correlates almost as highly with tests of scholastic achievement as reliability permits, one might ask, Why use the ALP at all? Why not just measure achievement? Indeed, why not? Unless the school authorities have some special purpose intended which calls for a measure of ability which is not directly based on the subject matter of the curriculum, there would seem to be little justification for the time, bother, and expense involved in getting group-administered intelligence test scores on all pupils in a school. Achievement scores should suffice for most purposes. Other diagnostic measures (including nonscholastic measures of general intelligence) would be called for in those cases where a pupil's scholastic performance is markedly deviant. As previously suggested, an intelligence test used along with achievement tests can spot the underachievers who may then receive further diagnosis to determine the causes of the underachievement. Since the correlation is so high between ALP and achievement, those pupils who show a marked discrepancy between the two scores would warrant special attention, especially if achievement scores are markedly *below* the ALP scores. The ALP scores, reflecting more extra-school influences, could also be used in the same way for comparing the average achievement of whole classes, schools, or communities. The ALP can also serve as a control variable in educational experiments.

SUMMARY. From both technical and practical standpoints, the *Analysis of Learning Potential* (despite its title being a misnomer for "intelligence test") is an excellent battery of five group tests, covering grades 1 to 12, for measuring general intelligence or scholastic aptitude by means of test materials for the most part not specifically taught in school. Its correlations with tests of scholastic achievement are exceptionally high. The ALP appears to be fully competitive with the best group intelligence tests currently available.

[335]

★**Boehm Test of Basic Concepts.** Grades kgn–2; 1969–70, c1967–69; BTBC; Form A ('69, 16 pages in 2 booklets); manual ('70, 22 pages); $5.90 per 30 tests; 50¢ per manual; $1 per specimen set; postage extra; Spanish edition available; (30–40) minutes in 2 sessions; Ann E. Boehm; Psychological Corporation. *

REFERENCE

1. BOEHM, ANN ELIZABETH. *The Development of Comparative Concepts in Primary School Children.* Doctor's thesis, Columbia University (New York, N.Y.), 1966. (*DA* 27: 4109B)

Boyd R. McCandless, *Professor of Education and Psychology and Director, Educational Psychology, Emory University, Atlanta, Georgia.*

The purpose of the test, as stated by the author, is "to assess beginning school children's knowledge of frequently used basic concepts widely but sometimes mistakenly assumed to be familiar to children at their time of entry into kindergarten or first grade." The reviewer considers this statement accurate, modest, and realistic.

The test was inspired by the author's awareness that many children beginning school do not comprehend many of the printed or spoken instructions taken as "givens" by most teachers, and by her assumption (well supported by survey data) that deficits at the beginning of school are cumulative over time. She hopes to provide an instrument to pinpoint these deficits, lead the way to remedying them, and thus prevent irrelevant interference with school progress.

The initial item content was empirically and apparently somewhat subjectively determined by inspection of curriculum materials, together with checks to see what concepts were difficult or unfamiliar to substantial numbers of children.

The test was finally narrowed to 50 items placed in two test booklets to facilitate administration in two sessions to children in grades K, 1, 2, and 3. Items proved so easy for third graders that the final form of the test includes norms for only grades K through 2, but the test is too easy to be of great value for first graders from middle or higher socioeconomic levels or for second graders of any social class.

Two waves of preliminary testing were conducted before the final form of the test was set up. Item selection was made according to conservative and acceptable principles—e.g., sampling of a range of concepts, point biserial correlations exceeding .30, "even rises of percent-passing values across age levels," and "normal distribution of percent-passing values, centered around .50 for the kindergarten pupils."

Testing with two booklets, each including 25 questions to be answered by making X's on pictures, requires 15 to 20 minutes per booklet. Instructions to teachers state that groups of 8 to 12 may be tested. Although the reviewer has not tried the test with kindergartners, he is skeptical that it can be feasibly administered to groups of this size unless there is a generous supply of proctors.

The booklets are made up of black line drawings on white (Booklet 1) or buff (Booklet 2). For the most part, the drawings are clear, though a few seem ambiguous. The people in the illustrations are appropriately integrated racially. Scoring instructions are clear and the mechanics are about as simple as is possible when working with test protocols for children in kindergarten and grades 1 and 2.

The standardization sample came from five cities, one western, one south-midwestern, one southeastern, and two northeastern. School personnel in each city were asked to administer the test within one high, one middle, and one low socioeconomic school. A disproportionate number of the low socioeconomic class children come from the southeastern city school system. The test author makes no pretense to having a representative U.S. normative sample, but has sampled widely in reasonably representative school systems.

No validity evidence other than face validity is presented, although the face validity is convincing enough. As anyone familiar with kindergarten and first grade instruction will realize, the items tap concepts that children need to know. The author represents the BTBC modestly as a screening device and a guide for instruction. Used thoughtfully, it can be quite useful to teachers. A section in the manual devoted to interpretation and use of the results in instruction is very practical.

Charles D. Smock, *Professor of Psychology, The University of Georgia, Athens, Georgia.*

Children enter school with a variety of experiential backgrounds and variation in knowledge of the physical and social environments. Current interest in cognitive developmental theory and enrichment of the environments of "disadvantaged" children has increased concern for adequate assessment of their intellectual level upon entering school. Also, curriculum development specialists have found it necessary to modify the typical first grade curriculum in order to create effective learning conditions for these children. Of particular importance is the fact that both the available curriculum materials and "readiness" tests assume a set of fundamental concepts which many disadvantaged children do not yet understand; for example, the understanding necessary to follow directions in the procedures designed to determine "readiness" is often questionable. The primary reason for development of the *Boehm Test of Basic Concepts* was the recognition of this fact: the assumption that all children have mastered these fundamental concepts is fallacious.

The Boehm assessment procedure consists of 50 items concerning the child's understanding of space (location, direction, orientation, dimensions); time and quantity (number); plus a few miscellaneous concepts selected on the basis of their contribution to the internal consistency and validity of the test.

The criteria governing the initial item selection included both empirical and educational considerations. That is, the concepts selected were important for the understanding and following of directions and occurred frequently in curriculum materials but were not generally part of the usual instructional process. The final 50 items selected met the following criteria: correlation of each item with the total score on the 25-item booklet in which the item appeared; a fairly even increase in percent passing across the age levels; and a final set of items which would yield a normal distribution of percent passing with the kindergarten children achieving a 50 percent level. Tables of percent passing, based on subsequent data collections, for each item by grade and socioeconomic level at the beginning and middle of each year are presented. Reliability coefficients ranging from .68 to .90 are reported. "Content validity," the only validity reported, seems adequate since the items were selected on the basis of the relevance to currently used curriculum materials in kindergarten, first, and second grades.

The Boehm procedures should be valuable to teachers in the detection and remediation of deficiencies in verbal understanding. Appropriate qualifications and cautions are presented in the manual regarding interpretation of obtained scores; e.g., the scores do not reflect general intellectual level. The directions and test items (pictorial form) are clear and concise; the test could be administered by aides or paraprofessional personnel. The manual gives explicit instructions on procedures for administration and offers suggestions to the teacher on how to use the results to plan remedial instructional work for children who have not acquired specific concepts.

J Ed Meas 7(2):139–40 su '70. Victor H. Noll. * The manual presents various reasons for concept difficulty and suggests procedures for remedial instruction. It is emphasized that ideally instruction should result in mastery, though training on the test items is to be avoided "if post-training test results are to reflect more than rote memorization." This would seem to pose some difficulties if, as appears likely, synonyms for such concepts as top, bottom, whole, every, etc. are to be found and used without equating them directly with their counterparts in the test. * The norms tables reveal that the test is still too easy for second graders with mean scores of 43.5, 46.7, and 47.8 out of a possible 50 for the three socioeconomic levels. It appears that it also may be too easy for the upper levels of Grade 1. The mean score for the middle socioeconomic level of Grade 1 is 43.8 while that for the highest level of second graders is 47.8. It might therefore be concluded that the test is adequate in difficulty only for kindergarten and the lowest socioeconomic levels of first graders. For a test of 50 items at these grade levels, reliabilities are surprisingly good. * It is in this matter of validity that the Boehm Test is most seriously open to question. This weakness has two aspects. In the first place no information is given as to what materials the author examined and only vague statements descriptive of methods used to determine what concepts were to be retained as a basis for the test. The statement is made that they "occurred with considerable frequency." Further, we are told that they "were seldom if ever explicitly defined or were defined in their simple forms but subsequently used in complex forms without adequate transitions." Finally, that "they represented relatively abstract basic concepts or ideas." Such statements as "considerable frequency," "seldom if ever," "adequate transitions," and "relatively abstract" are too general and imprecise to convey any adequate understanding of the criteria. In the second place, the author supplies no information on the question of how necessary these concepts really are to "achievement in the first years of school." Is there any relation between mastery of them and quality of school achievement? If there is none or even very little, the whole *raison d'etre* for the test as a test would seem to disappear unless some evidence on this point can be determined. A teacher who gave the test, tabulated the results, and

Boehm Test of Basic Concepts

proceeded with careful remedial instruction would seem to be wasting time. In summary, the author of this test has gone through most of the accepted and established procedures for constructing and standardizing a test but has not provided adequate and essential information on how the concepts on which the test is based were determined and the evidence, if any is available, to show that these concepts are indeed "necessary for achievement in the first years of school." Perhaps someone might claim that it is self-evident that no child could do well in the first years of school without mastery of them. But the author presents no evidence in support of such a claim. Directions for administering are clear and complete. The publishers have done a fine job of production. The test may have considerable usefulness as a teaching device to help identify group and individual lack of understanding of the 50 concepts tested. However, for this purpose most of the statistical data provided are superfluous.

J Spec Ed 4 (2):249–51 *sp–su* '70. **Barton B. Proger.** * Interpretation of test results is clearly and carefully delineated in the manual. * This reviewer was pleased to see that the author provides guidelines for using the *BTBC* in pretest-posttest gain analyses to evaluate the effectiveness of remediation efforts. Teachers should be encouraged to engage in, at least, informal program evaluation; far too many shy away from it. * by and large, that the test items possess a high degree of internal consistency. The consistency of scores over time cannot be gauged from the manual, since test-retest coefficients are not provided; such data are most desirable. It should also be noted that no internal consistency reliability measures are given for start-of-the-year scores, although such information would have been easy to provide. Boehm is to be commended for her discussion of confidence intervals and standard errors of measurement. * In the areas of conceptualization, standardization, interpretation, reliability, etc., the Boehm test is better than most new test instruments appearing on the market. However, this is not saying much! The *BTBC* must be severely criticized on the grounds of insufficient validity studies. The author begs the issue: "For the *Boehm Test of Basic Concepts,* like any other test of educational achievement or mastery, validity is primarily a matter of the relevance of the test content to the school curriculum. This type of validity is usually called *content validity*" (p. 17). Content validity is important, but predictive, construct, and concurrent validity are also important and have been neglected here. Indeed, only one research reference is provided in the whole manual: Boehm's dissertation (1966). Also, a test's technical manual should provide a representative (and perhaps comprehensive) review of the literature relevant to the issues underlying the test's development. The *Boehm* fails us here as well. Unfortunately, a dearth of documentation is by no means peculiar to the *BTBC*. In summary, the manual and test materials for the *Boehm Test of Basic Concepts* appear to be of high quality; its rationale has considerable appeal. It is an instrument that the teacher can administer, interpret, and utilize in remedial work. It has implications for both the disadvantaged and the handicapped. Limitations in standardization efforts, and lack of validation studies and of test-retest reliability should make the user cautious in its deployment.

Nat Cath Guid Conf J 14(3):200–1 *sp* '70. **George Lawlor.** * The items appear to be well selected from a survey of curriculum material in the areas of reading, arithmetic and science. * The standardization sample was adequate, however, no nursery school subjects were used. * it is strongly felt that a sample of pre-kindergarten subjects should have been included. Furthermore, the test Booklet 1 appears too easy for grade 2 since only two items reported less than 90% passing. Booklet 2 presents a slightly better use for grade 2. * More meaningful validity information should have accompanied the test rather than the generalized and well known cliché concerning this important aspect of the test. The classification of concepts with four content categories is well developed in the test form. However, there is a preponderance of items dealing with space, e.g., 56%, 36% pertains to quantity; 26% to time, and 10% to miscellaneous. There is overlapping in that 7% of the items test two concepts and 6% tap a triad in one item. The question arises when the teacher sets up remediation: which concept was known or unknown? Is further testing needed to determine whether one, two, or three basic concepts were unknown? Maybe the test would serve its purpose better if each item dealt with only *one* basic concept. The statistics are adequately presented. The Tables are easy to interpret. The table to determine per cents passing each item is very useful and can be used in any situation with forty or less subjects. However, this reviewer found no statement for the teacher regarding the cut-off level determining the difficulty of a given item for a grade level. Should this be 50, 75, or 90%? The directions are well stated. The booklets are easily handled by young children and the pictures are large enough to be readily identified. Non-white subjects are used in the test illustrations. In the local situation the teacher may find the Boehm Test useful in the identification of individual children with deficiencies in the area of certain basic concepts. The test may have further use in pointing out the individual concepts which may be unfamiliar to many students in a class.

Prof Psychol 1(5):490 f '70. Frank S. Freeman. * The usual standardization procedures were followed, but the areas from which the population was drawn, as the author of the test recognizes, are not representative of the nation as a whole. Still, the test items can be useful in any class if the teacher believes the concepts included should be empirically tested. Validation was by content, the items having been selected from "relevant curriculum materials." The data provided in the manual, unfortunately, are inadequate to permit judgment regarding comprehensiveness and representativeness of the selected items as to the curriculum materials. Justification of selected items is given entirely in general terms. Split-half reliability correlations are fairly good (.60–.90) * This type of instrument can be useful only in providing teachers with symptoms, or clues, as to children's concept mastery or ignorance. Granted that the selected concepts are valid as to curriculum content, they cannot represent the entire range of concepts that a child should know, ideally, or needs to know. * I am often surprised by statements that reveal deficient information in the subject under discussion. Dr. Boehm states, "It is only in the last few years that attention has been focused on these developmental differences (in cognitive development) with respect to their nature, their origins, modifiability, and implications for future achievement" [Test Manual, p. 3]. This astonishing statement ignores the very considerable research and the many publications on nature-nurture and individual differences, as well as on the differences in instructional materials and methods demanded by individual differences. Dr. Boehm's statement also ignores the fact that children's differences in concept mastery have for many years been tested, in one way or another, by means of individual and group tests of intelligence, although these were not devised exclusively for that purpose, for example, Stanford-Binet, Wechsler scales, California Test of Mental Maturity, Lorge-Thorndike, Terman-McNemar, and among the very early scales, Dearborn Group Tests, Pintner-Cunningham Primary Test, the Non-Language Multi-Mental Test, and others. Dr. Boehm's unwarranted claim, however, does not reduce the value the test has for the purpose intended.

[336]
★**CGA Mental Ability Tests.** Grades 6–9, 9–12; 1957–68; items identical with *The Henmon-Nelson Tests of Mental Ability*; for use in Canada only; Forms A, B, ['62, 4 pages]; 2 levels; manuals: grades 6–9 ['68, 8 pages], grades 9–12 ['68, 10 pages]; Can $2.47 per 25 tests; 97¢ per scoring stencil; 30¢ per manual; $2.44 per specimen set of either level; 15% extra for postage and handling; 30(35) minutes; Canadian Guidance Associates; distributed by Guidance Centre. *

[337]
*****California Short-Form Test of Mental Maturity, 1963 Revision.** Grades kgn–1.0, 1.5–3, 3–4, 4–6, 6–7, 7–8, 9–12, 12–16 and adults; 1938–65; CTMM-SF; all items drawn from the long form, *California Test of Mental Maturity*; 7 scores: logical reasoning, numerical reasoning, verbal concepts, memory, language total, nonlanguage total, total; 1 form; 8 levels; interpretation guide ('64, 38 pages) for long and short forms; technical report ('65, 25 pages) for long and short forms; supplementary norms ('65, 5–8 pages) for levels 1, 1H, 2, and 3; $3 per 100 profiles; $1 per interpretation guide; $1.50 per technical report; postage extra; $1.25 per specimen set of any one level, postpaid; Elizabeth T. Sullivan, Willis W. Clark, and Ernest W. Tiegs; CTB/McGraw-Hill. *

a) [HAND SCORED LEVELS.] Grades kgn–1.0, 1.5–3, 3–4; profile ('62, 1 page, also on back of test booklet); $5.75 per 35 tests; scoring service, 45¢ and over per test.
1) *Level 0.* Grades kgn–1.0; 1963 S-Form ('62, 11 pages); manual ('63, 49 pages); 34(39) minutes.
2) *Level 1.* Grades 1.5–3; 1963 S-Form ('62, 12 pages); manual ('63, 53 pages) with 1964 norms; 41(46) minutes.
3) *Level 1H.* Grades 3–4; 1963 S-Form ('62, 10 pages); manual ('64, 56 pages) with 1965 norms; 42(47) minutes.

b) [MACHINE SCORABLE LEVELS.] Grades 1.5–3, 3–4, 4–6, 6–7, 7–8, 9–12, 12–16 and adults; profile ('61, 1 page, also on back of test booklet and back of answer sheet); Digitek directions ('68, 4 pages) for levels 2–5; IBM 1230 directions ('65, 4 pages) for levels 2–5; separate answer sheets (CompuScan [NCS], Digitek, IBM 1230, Scoreze) may be used for levels 2–5; tape recorded directions (3¾ ips) for administration of levels 2–5 available at $5.95 each.
1) *Level 1.* Grades 1.5–3; 1963 S-Form ('62, 12 pages); manual ('63, 53 pages) with 1964 norms; $8 per 35 tests; $1 per scoring key; CompuScan scoring service, 27¢ and over per test; 41(46) minutes.
2) *Level 1H.* Grades 3–4; 1963 S-Form ('62, 10 pages); manual ('64, 56 pages) with 1965 norms;

prices same as for machine scorable level 1; 42(47) minutes.

3) *Level 2.* Grades 4–6; 1963 S-Form ('61, 11 pages); manual ('63, 59 pages); $6 per 35 tests; $2.50 per 50 CompuScan, Digitek, or IBM answer sheets; $2.50 per 25 Scoreze answer sheets; 5¢ per NCS answer sheet; 75¢ per Digitek or IBM hand scoring stencil; CompuScan scoring service, 22¢ and over per test; IBM scoring service, 25¢ and over per test; NCS scoring service, 14¢ and over per test; 43(48) minutes.

4) *Level 2H.* Grades 6–7; 1963 S-Form ('61, 11 pages); manual ('63, 60 pages); prices same as for level 2; 41(46) minutes.

5) *Level 3.* Grades 7–8; 1963 S-Form ('61, 11 pages); manual ('63, 57 pages); prices same as for level 2; 41(46) minutes.

6) *Level 4.* Grades 9–12; 1963 S-Form ('61, 11 pages); manual ('63, 53 pages); prices same as for level 2; 39(45) minutes.

7) *Level 5.* Grades 12–16 and adults; 1963 S-Form ('61, 11 pages); manual ('63, 47 pages); prices same as for level 2; 39(45) minutes.

REFERENCES

1–15. See 5:313.
16–26. See 6:443.
27. McHugh, Ann F. *An Investigation of the Reliability and Concurrent Validity of Two Levels of the California Test of Mental Maturity, Short Form.* Master's thesis, Fordham University (New York, N.Y.), 1957.
28. Rooks, Ila. *Teaching Satisfaction in Relation to Intelligence, Interests, and Grade-Point Average of Selected University of Georgia Graduates.* Doctor's thesis, University of Georgia (Athens, Ga.), 1957. (DA 17:1953)
29. Bashaw, Joan Ann. *The Effects of Three Methods of Group Test Interpretation on Self-Esteem.* Doctor's thesis, Florida State University (Tallahassee, Fla.), 1962. (DA 23:527)
30. Denum, Donald C. "The Use of the Stanford-Binet Intelligence Scale, Form L-M, 1960 Revision as a Criterion Instrument for Norming All Levels of the 1963 Revision of the California Test of Mental Maturity Series." *Yearb Nat Council Meas Ed* 20:50–3 '63. * (PA 38:8409)
31. Mattick, William E. "Predicting Success in the First Grade." *El Sch J* 63:273–6 F '63. *
32. Mickler, Jacob Ernest, Jr. *A Predictive Index of Academic Success for Alabama High School Graduates Entering the State Colleges and Universities.* Doctor's thesis, University of Alabama (University, Ala.), 1963. (DA 24:4086)
33. Altenhaus, Corrinne Batlin. *An Exploration of the Relationship of Intelligence to Creativity in School Children.* Doctor's thesis, Rutgers—The State University (New Brunswick, N.J.), 1964. (DA 25:2842)
34. Cauble, Ben Leroy. *Anxiety in Intermediate Grade Children and Its Relationship With Their Scores on Measures of Intelligence, Academic Achievement, and Several Personality Factors.* Doctor's thesis, Southern Illinois University (Carbondale, Ill.), 1964. (DA 25:5150)
35. Drew, Alfred S. "The Relationship of General Reading Ability and Other Factors to School and Job Performance of Machine Apprentices." *J Indus Teach Ed* 2:47–60 f '64. *
36. Shaffer, Raymond George. *A Study of Four Group Intelligence Tests to Identify Ambiguous Pictures as a Factor Which Causes Some Children to Select Incorrect Answers.* Doctor's research study No. 1, Colorado State College (Greeley, Colo.), 1964. (DA 25:1014)
37. West, L. W., and MacArthur, R. S. "An Evaluation of Selected Intelligence Tests for Two Samples of Metis and Indian Children." *Alberta J Ed Res* 10:17–27 Mr '64. * (PA 39:12328)
38. Frost, Barry P. "Intelligence, Manifest Anxiety and Scholastic Achievement." *Alberta J Ed Res* 11:167–75 S '65. * (PA 40:1948)
39. Johnson, Halvin Sherwood. *The Relationship of Scores on Aptitude and Achievement Tests Taken at Late Elementary and Junior High School Levels to Scholarship in Ninth Grade.* Doctor's thesis, University of South Dakota (Vermillion, S.D.), 1965. (DA 26:4449)
40. Rainey, Robert G. "A Study of Four School-Ability Tests." *J Exp Ed* 33:305–19 su '65. * (PA 39:12306)
41. Slayton, Wilfred George. *A Comparison of Successful and Unsuccessful Bible College Students With Respect to Selected Personality Factors.* Doctor's thesis, University of Arizona (Tucson, Ariz.), 1965. (DA 26:1487)
42. Swan, Robert J., and Hopkins, Kenneth D. "An Investigation of Theoretical and Empirical Chance Scores on Selected Standardized Group Tests." *Calif J Ed Res* 16:34–41 Ja '65. * (PA 39:10156)
43. Allen, Joyce Carmen Yandell. *A Study of the Relationships Between Achievement and Intelligence Test Scores for Charleston High School Juniors and Seniors.* Master's thesis, Eastern Illinois University (Charleston, Ill.), 1966.
44. Bristol, John L. "Validity of the California Achievement and Mental Maturity Tests in Predicting Success in Five Different First Year High School Foreign Languages." *J Exp Ed* 34:57–61 sp '66. *
45. Finley, Carmen J.; Thompson, Jack M.; and Cognata, Albert. "Stability of the California Short Form Test of Mental Ability: Grades 3, 5, and 7." *Calif J Ed Res* 17:157–68 S '66. * (PA 41:996)
46. Jenkins, Alice Crawford. *The Relationship of Certain Measurable Factors to Academic Success in Freshman Biology.* Doctor's thesis, New York University (New York, N.Y.), 1966. (DA 27:2279A)
47. Kopff, Richard Garms. *Manager Performance as Related to Goal Setting, Intelligence, and Selected Personality Characteristics.* Doctor's thesis, Columbia University (New York, N.Y.), 1966. (DA 27:677A)
48. Mayhon, Woodrow G. *The Relationship of Creativity to Achievement and Other Student Variables.* Doctor's thesis, University of New Mexico (Albuquerque, N.M.), 1966. (DA 27:1713A)
49. Olson, Arthur V. "Relation of Achievement Test Scores and Specific Reading Abilities to the Frostig Developmental Test of Visual Perception." *Percept & Motor Skills* 22:179–84 F '66. * (PA 40:4750)
50. Olson, Arthur V. "Relation of Achievement Test Scores and Specific Reading Abilities to the Frostig Test of Visual Perception." *Optom Weekly* 57:31–4 Jl 14 '66. *
51. Barnett, Thomas Marvin. *The Predictive Validities, as Measured by Multiple Correlation, of Two Batteries Using Academic Achievement as Criterion.* Doctor's thesis, North Texas State University (Denton, Tex.), 1967. (DA 28:2006A)
52. Hanna, Gerald S. "The Use of Students' Predictions of Success in Geometry and Year of High School to Augment Predictions Made From Test Scores and Past Grades." *J Ed Meas* 4:137–41 f '67. *
53. MacNeil, Ronald Lauchlin. *A Study of the Effectiveness of the SCAT and CTMM-SF to Predict First Semester Averages.* Master's thesis, St. Francis Xavier University (Antigonish, N.S., Canada), 1967.
54. Olson, Norinne Hilchey. *An Analysis of the Relationship Between Conventional Reading Readiness Measures and Intellectual Functioning.* Doctor's thesis, University of Georgia (Athens, Ga.), 1967. (DA 28:4490A)
55. Burke, Barbara Patricia. *An Exploratory Study of the Relationships Among Third Grade Negro Chidren's Self-Concept Creativity and Intelligence and Teachers' Perceptions of Those Relationships.* Doctor's thesis, Wayne State University (Detroit, Mich.), 1968. (DAI 30:1327A)
56. Carbonari, Joseph Phillip, Jr. *An Investigation of Residual Gain and Its Correlates.* Doctor's thesis, Northern Illinois University (DeKalb, Ill.), 1968. (DA 29:2559A)
57. MacArthur, R. S. "Assessing Intellectual Potential of Native Canadian Pupils: A Summary." *Alberta J Ed Res* 14:115–22 Je '68. * (PA 44:4170)
58. Ramirez, Walter Gene. *Measures of Three Types of Information Processing Related to Language and Non-Language Intelligence.* Doctor's thesis, University of Oregon (Eugene, Ore.), 1968. (DA 29:3470A)
59. Bushey, James Thomas. *The Relationships Between a Preschool Measure of Readiness and Subsequent Test Performances Among a Group of Private Elementary School Children.* Doctor's thesis, Wayne State University (Detroit, Mich.), 1969. (DAI 30:3816A)
60. Carron, Theodore J. "Validity of Tests for Chemical Plant Personnel." *Personnel Psychol* 22(3):307–12 au '69. * (PA 44:9414)
61. Cashen, Valjean M., and Ramseyer, Gary C. "The Use of Separate Answer Sheets by Primary Age Children." *J Ed Meas* 6(3):155–8 f '69. * (PA 44:15297)
62. Furr, Karl D., and Wilson, F. Robert. "The California Short-Form Test of Mental Ability 1963 Edition as a Screening Device for Educable Mentally Retarded Programs." *J Sch Psychol* 7(4):47–9 '68–69 ['69]. * (PA 44:2793)
63. Hall, Lucien Talmage, Jr. *The Prediction of Success in Each of Six Four-Year Selections of Secondary Mathematics Courses.* Doctor's thesis, University of Virginia (Charlottesville, Va.), 1969. (DAI 30:4141A)
64. McCullough, James Leonard, Sr. *A Study of the Predictive Efficiency of the California Short-Form Test of Mental Maturity, Level 2, for Negro and White Subjects.* Doctor's thesis, Mississippi State University (State College, Miss.), 1969. (DAI 30:2260A)
65. Oas, Robert T. *A Study of the Relationships of Students' Aptitude, Academic Achievement and Attitude Toward School for Selected School Populations.* Doctor's thesis, University of South Dakota (Vermillion, S.D.), 1969. (DAI 30:3644A)
66. Mars, Paul Arne. *High School Geometry Achievement as Related to Reading Achievement, Arithmetic Achievement, and General Intelligence in the Public Schools of Lincoln Ne-*

braska. Doctor's thesis, University of Nebraska (Lincoln, Neb.), 1970. (*DAI* 31:1691A)
67. MILLER, BERNEICE BEADLES. *The Effects of Continuing or Changing Foreign Languages on Listening Comprehension and Selected Tests as Predictors of Success in Spanish or French at the Seventh-Grade Level.* Doctor's thesis, University of Oklahoma (Norman, Okla.), 1970. (*DAI* 31:2618A)

For a review by Julian C. Stanley, see 6:443; for a review by Cyril Burt of an earlier edition, see 5:313; see also 4:282 (1 excerpt). For reviews of the regular edition, see 338 (2 reviews), 5:314 (2 reviews), 4:282 (1 excerpt), 3:223 (1 review, 2 excerpts), 2:1384 (2 reviews, 1 excerpt), and 1:1042 (3 reviews, 1 excerpt).

[338]
*California Test of Mental Maturity, 1963 Revision. Grades kgn–1.0, 1.5–3, 4–6, 7–9, 9–12, 12–16 and adults; 1936–65; CTMM; for short form, see preceding entry; 8 scores: logical reasoning, spatial relationships, numerical reasoning, verbal concepts, memory, language total, non-language total, total; 1 form; 6 levels; interpretation guide ('64, 38 pages) for long and short forms; technical report ('65, 25 pages) for long and short forms; $2 per 100 profiles; $1 per interpretation guide; $1.50 per technical report; postage extra; $1.25 per specimen set of any one level, postpaid; Elizabeth T. Sullivan, Willis W. Clark, and Ernest W. Tiegs; CTB/McGraw-Hill. *

a) HAND SCORED LEVELS. Grades kgn–1.0, 1.5–3; profile ('62, 1 page, also on back of test booklet); $7.30 per 35 tests; scoring service, 70¢ and over per test.

1) *Level 0.* Grades kgn–1.0; 1 form ('62, 15 pages); manual ('64, 60 pages); 48(58) minutes.
2) *Level 1.* Grades 1.5–3; 1 form ('62, 16 pages); manual ('64, 68 pages); 63(73) minutes.

b) MACHINE SCORABLE LEVELS. Grades 4–6, 7–9, 9–12, 12–16 and adults; 1 form ('61, 19 pages); profile ('61, 1 page, also on back of test booklet and back of answer sheet); practice exercises ('64, 2 pages) for IBM answer sheets; IBM directions ('65, 4 pages); separate answer sheets (IBM 1230, Scoreze) may be used; $5 per 50 sets of IBM answer sheets; $5 per 25 sets of Scoreze answer sheets; $1.50 per set of IBM hand scoring stencils; $3 per 100 practice exercises; 15¢ per IBM directions; IBM scoring service, 25¢ and over per test.

1) *Level 2.* Grades 4–6; manual ('64, 66 pages); $8 per 35 tests; 83(93) minutes.
2) *Level 3.* Grades 7–9; manual ('64, 63 pages); $8 per 35 tests; 83(93) minutes.
3) *Level 4.* Grades 9–12; manual ('64, 61 pages); $8.80 per 35 tests; 81(91) minutes.
4) *Level 5.* Grades 12–16 and adults; manual ('64, 53 pages); $8.80 per 35 tests; 81(91) minutes.

REFERENCES

1–5. See 2:1384.
6–15. See 3:223.
16–39. See 4:282.
40–73. See 5:314.
74–103. See 6:444.
104. CLARK, JERRY H. "Interest Variability on the California Test of Mental Maturity in Relation to the Minnesota Multiphasic Personality Inventory." *J Consult Psychol* 14:32–4 F '50. * (*PA* 24:4112)
105. RAWLINGS, TRAVIS DEAN. *Mental Organization as a Function of Brightness.* Doctor's thesis, University of Kentucky (Lexington, Ky.), 1956. (*DA* 21:2778)
106. MOE, IVER L. *Auding as a Predictive Measure of Reading Performance in Primary Grades.* Doctor's thesis, University of Florida (Gainesville, Fla.), 1957. (*DA* 18:121)
107. GUNDERSEN, RICHARD OSCAR. *The Significance of Divergencies Between Verbal and Nonverbal Intelligence Scores.* Doctor's thesis, State University of Iowa (Iowa City, Iowa), 1959. (*DA* 20:2142)
108. HAROOTUNIAN, BERJ AVEDIS. *The Relationships Among Tests of Intelligence, Learning, and Reasoning.* Doctor's thesis, University of Pennsylvania (Philadelphia, Pa.), 1959. (*DA* 20:203)
109. CURRY, ROBERT LEE. *The Effect of Intelligence on the Scholastic Achievement of Sixth-Grade Children of Comparable Socio-Economic Status.* Doctor's thesis, University of Oklahoma (Norman, Okla.), 1960. (*DA* 20:3995)
110. HOFFMAN, CARL BENTLEY. *The Relationship of Immediate Recall, Delayed Recall, and Incidental Memory to Problem-Solving Ability.* Doctor's thesis, University of Pennsylvania (Philadelphia, Pa.), 1960. (*DA* 21:813)
111. JOHNSON, WYNNE ELTON. *Prediction of High School Achievement by the Use of an Attitude Scale and a Group Intelligence Test.* Doctor's thesis, Washington State University (Pullman, Wash.), 1960. (*DA* 21:2215)
112. VERTEIN, LESTER DALE. *A Study of the Personal-Social and Intellectual Characteristics of a Group of State College Students Preparing to Teach.* Doctor's thesis, University of Wisconsin (Madison, Wis.), 1960. (*DA* 21:1473)
113. MCGUIRE, CARSON; HINDSMAN, EDWIN; KING, F. J.; AND JENNINGS, EARL. "Dimensions of Talented Behavior." *Ed & Psychol Meas* 21:3–38 sp '61. * (*PA* 36:1KH03M)
114. WELTER, M. BORROMEO. *A Comparison of the California Test of Mental Maturity and the Pikunas Graphoscopic Scale as Measures of Intelligence and Academic Achievement.* Master's thesis, University of Detroit (Detroit, Mich.), 1961.
115. OLSON, D. R., AND MACARTHUR, R. S. "The Effect of Foreign Language Background on Intelligence Test Performance." *Alberta J Ed Res* 8:157–66 S '62. * (*PA* 37:8270)
116. RUBIN, SAMUEL SOLOMON. *The Relation of Fantasy Productions to Test Intelligence.* Doctor's thesis, Columbia University (New York, N.Y.), 1962. (*DA* 23:1080)
117. *Basic Data for Factor Analytic Studies With the California Test of Mental Maturity, 1963 Revision.* Monterey, Calif.: California Test Bureau, 1963. Pp. 34. *
118. GARDNER, SHELDON FRANK. *Creativity in Children: A Study of the Relationship Between Temperament Factors and Aptitude Factors Involved in the Creative Ability of Seventh Grade Children With Suggestions for a Theory of Creativity.* Doctor's thesis, University of Southern California (Los Angeles, Calif.), 1963. (*DA* 24:822)
119. HOPKINS, KENNETH D., AND BIBELHEIMER, MILO H. "Two and Four Year Constancy of CTMM Language and Non-Language IQs," pp. 93–7. (*PA* 38:6058) In *Towards a Professional Identity in School Psychology.* California Association of School Psychologists and Psychometrists, Fourteenth Annual Conference, March 28–30, 1963. [Los Angeles, Calif.: the Association, 1963.] Pp. v, 97. * (*PA* 38:4904)
120. MUMAW, MYRON JAY. *Test Predictability for Culturally Deprived Students.* Master's thesis, Ohio State University (Columbus, Ohio), 1963.
121. PLESSAS, GUS P. "Auding and Intelligence." *Calif J Ed Res* 14:90–4 Mr '63. * (*PA* 38:1415)
122. WALSH, NANCY E. *The Relationship Between Performance on Certain Long Problems and Intelligence Factors.* Doctor's thesis, Rutgers—The State University (New Brunswick, N.J.), 1963. (*DA* 24:2–93)
123. ANDERSON, HARRY E., JR., AND LETON, DONALD A. "Factor Analyses of the California Test of Mental Maturity." *Ed & Psychol Meas* 24:513–23 f '64. * (*PA* 39:3176)
124. BISH, GERTRUDE GANTZ. *A Study of the Relationships of Intelligence, Achievement, Creativity, Anxiety, and Confidence Among Intermediate Grade Pupils in a Suburban Area Elementary School.* Doctor's thesis, George Washington University (Washington, D.C.), 1964.
125. BONEY, JEW DON. *A Study of the Use of Intelligence, Aptitude, and Mental Ability Measures in Predicting the Academic Achievement of Negro Students in Secondary School.* Doctor's thesis, University of Texas (Austin, Tex.), 1964. (*DA* 25:5726)
126. BRADSHAW, DONALD H. "Stability of California Test of Mental Maturity IQ's From the Second to the Fourth Grade." *Ed & Psychol Meas* 24:935–9 w '64. * (*PA* 39:7741)
127. BUCK, JAMES R., JR. *Some Identifiable Characteristics of Students Entering Negro Senior Colleges in Mississippi.* Doctor's thesis, George Peabody College for Teachers (Nashville, Tenn.), 1964. (*DA* 25:5039)
128. COBB, BART B. "Problems in Air Traffic Management: 5, Identification and Potential of Aptitude Test Measures for Selection of Tower Air Traffic Controller Trainees." *Aerospace Med* 35:1019–27 N '64. * (*PA* 39:16518)
129. DE BOER, DOROTHY LOUISE. *A Study of the Relationship of Creativity to Intelligence and Achievement.* Doctor's thesis, Northwestern University (Evanston, Ill.), 1964. (*DA* 25:3968)
130. DIZNEY, HENRY. "The Performance in Specific Skill Areas of Gifted, Elementary Underachievers." *Psychol Sch* 1:178–81 Ap '64. *
131. DIZNEY, HENRY, AND FLEMING, ELYSE. "Sex and I.Q. Differences in Discrepancies Between Predicted and Obtained Achievement." *J Sch Psychol* 3:26–31 au '64. * (*PA* 39:13032)

132. JONGEWARD, PAUL A. *The Relationship of Reading Ability to Performance on the California Test of Mental Maturity.* Master's thesis, Sacramento State College (Sacramento, Calif.), 1964.
133. SMITH, ROBERT HOUSTON. *A Study of Pre-Adolescent Boys Demonstrating Varying Levels of Creativity With Regard to Their Social Adjustment, Peer Acceptance and Academically Related Behavior.* Doctor's thesis, North Texas State University (Denton, Tex.), 1964. (*DA* 25:4553)
134. TRITES, DAVID K. "Problems in Air Traffic Management: 6, Interaction of Training-Entry Age With Intellectual and Personality Characteristics of Air Traffic Control Specialists." *Aerospace Med* 35:1184-94 D '64. * (*PA* 39:16533)
135. WALDRON, CORMAC. *Differential Prediction of Achievement in Broad Curricular Areas in an Academic High School.* Doctor's thesis, Fordham University (New York, N.Y.), 1964. (*DA* 25:1764)
136. BOYCE, RICHARD W., AND PAXSON, R. C. "The Predictive Validity of Eleven Tests at One State College." *Ed & Psychol Meas* 25:1143-7 w '65. * (*PA* 40:3563)
137. BRADY, WILLIAM JOSEPH. *Twenty Quantitative Predictors of Academic Success in College as Measured by Grade Point Averages.* Doctor's thesis, University of Connecticut (Storrs, Conn.), 1965. (*DA* 26:5121)
138. BREEN, JOSEPH MICHAEL. *Differential Prediction of Intermediate Grade Skills Achievement From Primary Grade Aptitude and Achievement Measures.* Doctor's thesis, University of Connecticut (Storrs, Conn.), 1965. (*DA* 26:5260)
139. GUILFORD, J. P.; HOEFFNER, RALPH; AND PETERSEN, HUGH. "Predicting Achievement in Ninth-Grade Mathematics From Measures of Intellectual-Aptitude Factors." *Ed & Psychol Meas* 25:659-82 au '65. * (*PA* 40:3376)
140. MCCALL, ROZANNE A., AND MCCALL, ROBERT B. "A Comparison of First Grade Reading Tests." *Ill Sch Res* 2:32-7 O '65. *
141. MCCAULEY, JOHN HOWARD, JR. *Rorschach, WISC, and ITBS Patterns of Nine-Year-Old School Boys With Labile and Stabile IQ Scores.* Doctor's thesis, University of Maryland (College Park, Md.), 1965. (*DA* 27:1663A)
142. SPIERS, DUANE EDWIN. *A Study of the Predictive Validity of a Test Battery Administered to Theological Students.* Doctor's thesis, Purdue University (Lafayette, Ind.), 1965. (*DA* 26:1488)
143. BONEY, J. DON. "Predicting the Academic Achievement of Secondary School Negro Students." *Personnel & Guid J* 44:700-3 Mr '66. * (*PA* 40:8064)
144. COPPEDGE, FLOYD LEVON. *The Relationship of Selected Factors to Occupational and College Success.* Doctor's thesis, University of Oklahoma (Norman, Okla.), 1966. (*DA* 26:6441)
145. COPPEDGE, LLOYD LEON. *A Study of the Causes for Pupil Failure in High School.* Doctor's thesis, University of Oklahoma (Norman, Okla.), 1966. (*DA* 27:1579A)
146. CUNNINGHAM, WILLIAM. *A Thirteen-Year Retrospective Study of Standardized Test Data.* Doctor's thesis, Western Reserve University (Cleveland, Ohio), 1966. (*DA* 27:3305A)
147. DIRR, PIERRE MARIE. *Intellectual Variables in Achievement in Modern Algebra.* Doctor's thesis, Catholic University of America (Washington, D.C.), 1966. (*DA* 27:2873A)
148. FUQUA, NORMAN VINCE. *An Analysis of the Relationships and Differences Among Measures of Creative Thinking and Selected Other Factors in Educable and Less Educable Groups of Negro Children.* Doctor's thesis, Wayne State University (Detroit, Mich.), 1966. (*DA* 27:2314A)
149. GRIESS, JERALD ALFRED. *Selection of Trainees for a Twelve-Week Pre-Occupational Basic Education Program.* Doctor's thesis, Pennsylvania State University (University Park, Pa.), 1966. (*DA* 27:3704A)
150. GUILFORD, J. P., AND HOEFFNER, RALPH. "Creative Potential as Related to Measure of IQ and Verbal Comprehension." *Indian J Psychol* 41:7-16 Mr '66. * (*PA* 41:2877)
151. HAROOTUNIAN, BERJ. "Intellectual Abilities and Reading Achievement." *El Sch J* 66:386-95 Ap '66. *
152. HAROOTUNIAN, BERJ. "Intelligence and the Ability to Learn." *J Ed Res* 59:211-4 Ja '66. * (*PA* 40:6627)
153. KANDEL, ARTHUR. *Discrepancies Between the Stanford-Binet and Three Group Tests of Intelligence in the Identification of Low I.Q. Children.* Doctor's thesis, Catholic University of America (Washington, D.C.), 1966. (*DA* 27:1659A)
154. KEACH, CHARLES CAMPBELL. *Discrepancies Between the Stanford-Binet and Three Group Tests of Intelligence in the Identification of High I.Q. Children.* Doctor's thesis, Catholic University of America (Washington, D.C.), 1966. (*DA* 27:1660A)
155. PARISH, ROBERT L. *A Comparison of Scores Made on the Primary and Elementary Forms of the California Test of Mental Maturity and Their Relationship to Report Card Grades.* Master's thesis, San Jose State College (San Jose, Calif.), 1966.
156. PARKER, ADAH DONOHUE. *Projections for the Selection, Training and Retention of Sub-Professional Recreation Leaders Based on an Analysis of Personality, Interest, Aptitude, and Preference Data.* Doctor's thesis, University of Illinois (Urbana, Ill.), 1966. (*DA* 27:2059A)
157. BRENDEMUEHL, FRANK LOUIS. *The Influence of Reading Ability on the Validity of Group Non-Verbal Intelligence Tests.* Doctor's thesis, University of Minnesota (Minneapolis, Minn.), 1967. (*DA* 28:2088A)
158. CLEVELAND, GERALD ARTHUR, AND BOSWORTH, DOROTHY L. "A Study of Certain Psychological and Sociological Characteristics as Related to Arithmetic Achievement." *Arith Teach* 14:383-7 My '67. *
159. FULLER, GERALD B., AND ENDE, RUSSELL. "The Effectiveness of Visual Perception, Intelligence and Reading Understanding in Predicting Reading Achievement in Junior High School Children." *J Ed Res* 60:280-2 F '67. *
160. GILMAN, ROBERT H. *A Study of Intellectual Change of Deaf Students as Measured by Standard Tests of Intelligence.* Master's thesis, Springfield College (Springfield, Mass.), 1967.
161. LLOYD, BRUCE A., AND LLOYD, ROSALIE. "A Comparison of the Reading Readiness and Mental Maturity Scores of Selected First Grade Pupils in an American School and in a Belgian School: A Pilot Study." *J Read Specialist* 7:14-7 O '67. *
162. MANDEL, ROBERT. *A Study of the Performance of Disadvantaged Seventh Grade Males on the Colored Raven Progressive Matrices and the California Test of Mental Maturity.* Master's thesis, University of Tennessee (Knoxville, Tenn.), 1967.
163. TILKER, HARVEY A., AND SCHELL, ROBERT E. "Concurrent Validity of the Porteus Maze Test: A Comparative Study of Regular and Educationally Handicapped High School Students." *Ed & Psychol Meas* 27:447-55 su '67. * (*PA* 41:12840)
164. TRITES, DAVID K.; KUREK, ADOLPH; AND COBB, BART B. "Personality and Achievement of Air Traffic Controllers." *Aerospace Med* 38:1145-50 N '67. *
165. TULLY, G. EMERSON. "Test-Retest Reliability of the Raven Progressive Matrices Test (Form 1938) and the California Test of Mental Maturity, Level 4 (S-F 1963)." *Fla J Ed Res* 9:67-74 Ja '67. *
166. WAGNER, HILMAR ERNEST. *A Study of Physical, Mental and Musical Characteristics of Selected Band Members.* Doctor's thesis, North Texas State University (Denton, Tex.), 1967. (*DA* 28:2285A)
167. ARTH, ALFRED ARTHUR. *A Study of the Relationship Between Non-Completion and Intelligence Exhibited by Sixth Grade Elementary School Students.* Doctor's thesis, University of Oklahoma (Norman, Okla.), 1968. (*DA* 29:1666A)
168. COLGAN, RICHARD THOMAS. *A Longitudinal Study of the Relationship of Teacher Judgment Versus Objective Test Data With Respect to College Success.* Doctor's thesis, Southern Illinois University (Carbondale, Ill.), 1968. (*DA* 29:3413B)
169. COOKE, BRYAN EDWARD MARSHALL. *The Relationship Between Balance and Cognitive Abilities of Children Aged Eight to Thirteen Years.* Doctor's thesis, University of Illinois (Urbana, Ill.), 1968. (*DAI* 30:154A)
170. DEICH, RUTH F. "Correlations Between the PPVT and the CTMM." *Psychol Rep* 22:856 Je '68. * (*PA* 42:12982)
171. HATFIELD, ROBERT C. *A Study of the Relationships of Selected Components of Creativity, Cognitive Style, and Self-Concept Identified in a Random Sample of Twelfth Grade Students in One High School With Their Learning of Selected Information in the Social Studies.* Doctor's thesis, Wayne State University (Detroit, Mich.), 1968. (*DAI* 30:1334A)
172. LAUTEN, DORIS ANNE HIGGINS. *The Relationship Between Intelligence and Motor Proficiency in the Intellectually Gifted Child.* Doctor's thesis, University of North Carolina (Greensboro, N.C.), 1968. (*DAI* 31:1521B)
173. MCLEOD, JACK DONALD. *Prediction of Independent Study Performance in Secondary School.* Doctor's thesis, Stanford University (Stanford, Calif.), 1968. (*DA* 29:3044A)
174. MARSHALL, JOSEPH JEMERSON. *Non-Cognitive Variables as a Predictor of Academic Achievement Among Freshmen, Sophomores, and Juniors at Abilene Christian College.* Doctor's thesis, Baylor University (Waco, Tex.), 1968. (*DA* 29:3833A)
175. RATTAN, M. S., AND MACARTHUR, R. S. "Longitudinal Prediction of School Achievement for Metis and Eskimo Pupils." *Alberta J Ed Res* 14:37-41 Mr '68. * (*PA* 44:4249)
176. RAY, MARTHA ROBERTS. *A Study of the Relationship Between Children's Test Scores on the Sensory Perception Block and the California Test of Mental Maturity.* Master's thesis, University of Tennessee (Knoxville, Tenn.), 1968.
177. THOMAS, HOWARD. *An Analysis of the California Test of Mental Maturity and the California Achievement Test for Discriminative Use at High Levels of Intelligence.* Master's thesis, Sacramento State College (Sacramento, Calif.), 1968.
178. ANDERSON, HARRY E., JR.; WHITE, WILLIAM F.; AND STEVENS, JOHN C. "Student Creativity, Intelligence, Achievement, and Teacher Classroom Behavior." *J Social Psychol* 78(1):99-107 Je '69. * (*PA* 43:16427)
179. BARZ, ANITA I. *Prediction of Secondary School Achievement From Primary Grade Aptitude and Achievement Measures.* Doctor's thesis, St. John's University (Jamaica, N.Y.), 1969. (*DAI* 30:3271A)
180. CALLAWAY, WEBSTER R. "A Holistic Conception of Creativity and Its Relationship to Intelligence." *Gifted Child Q* 13(4):237-41 w '69. * (*PA* 44:15338)
181. COPPEDGE, FLOYD L. "Relation of Selected Variables

From High School Records to Occupational and College Success." *J Ed Res* 63(2):71–3 O '69. *
182. Cox, Otis. *Creative Thinking in a High School Experimental Humanities Program.* Doctor's thesis, University of Alabama (University, Ala.), 1969. *(DAI* 31:214A)
183. Hieronymus, A. N., and Stroud, James B. "Comparability of IQ Scores on Five Widely Used Intelligence Tests." *Meas & Eval Guid* 2(3):135–40 f '69. * (*PA* 44:13285)
184. Hopkins, Kenneth D., and Sitkei, E. George. "Predicting Grade One Reading Performance: Intelligence vs. Reading Readiness Tests." *J Exp Ed* 37(3):31–3 sp '69. *
185. Krop, Harry. "Effects of Extrinsic Motivation, Intrinsic Motivation, and Intelligence on Creativity: A Factorial Approach." *J General Psychol* 80(2):259–66 Ap '69. * (*PA* 43:11332)
186. Lovett, Carl James. *An Analysis of the Relationship of Several Variables to Achievement in First Year Algebra.* Doctor's thesis, University of Texas (Austin, Tex.), 1969. *(DAI* 30:1470A)
187. Maples, Virginia S. *The Use of the California Mental Maturity Test in Predicting Differential Aptitude Scores.* Master's thesis, Texas Technological College (Lubbock, Tex.), 1969.
188. Shields, Ruth V., and Gordon, Mary Alice. "Schematic Concept Formation in Relationship to Mental Ability in Adolescents." *Psychon Sci* 17(6):361–2 D 25 '69. * (*PA* 44:6539)
189. Smith, Philip D., Jr. "The Pennsylvania Foreign Language Research Project: Teacher Proficiency and Class Achievement in Two Modern Languages." *Foreign Lang Ann* 3(2):194–207 D '69. *
190. Sutherland, Kelley. *The Predictive Value of School and College Ability Test, Sequential Test of Educational Progress, Differential Aptitude Test, Iowa Silent Reading Test, and California Test of Mental Maturity Scores at Clintwood High School, Clintwood, Virginia.* Master's thesis, East Tennessee State University (Johnson City, Tenn.), 1969.
191. Willmarth, John Gary. *Factors Affecting the Vocational Choice of Women of Different Ages Selecting Clerical and Secretarial Occupations.* Doctor's thesis, Washington State University (Pullman, Wash.), 1969. *(DAI* 30:991A)
192. Arena, Thomas. "Social Maturity in the Prediction of Academic Achievement." *J Ed Res* 64(1):21–2 S '70. *
193. Caldwell, James R.; Michael, William B.; Schrader, Donald R.; and Meyers, C. E. "Comparative Validities and Working Times for Composites of Structure-of-Intellect Tests and Algebra Grades and Composites of Traditional Test Measures and Algebra Grades in the Prediction of Success in Tenth-Grade Geometry." *Ed & Psychol Meas* 30(4):955–9 w '70. *
194. Canabal, Juana Villanueva. *Comparison of Deaf and Normally Hearing Children on Analogy Items Under Different Methods of Instruction at Different Age Levels.* Doctor's thesis, St. John's University (Jamaica, N.Y.), 1970. *(DAI* 31:3700B)
195. Carroll, Imogene Vass. *A Comparison of the Intelligence Quotients of Sixth-Grade Children of Negro and Caucasian Educators and Non-Educators.* Doctor's thesis, University of Alabama (University, Ala.), 1970. *(DAI* 31:3161A)
196. Corrigan, Francis Vincent, Jr. *A Comparison of Self Concepts of American Indian Students From Public or Federal School Backgrounds.* Doctor's thesis, George Washington University (Washington, D.C.), 1970.
197. Damm, Vernon J. "Creativity and Intelligence: Research Implications for Equal Emphasis in High School." *Excep Children* 36(8):565–9 Ap '70. * (*PA* 46:1754)
198. Gates, John Anthony. *Selective Factors in Predicting Success in Learning Basic Sight Words and First Grade Reading Achievement.* Doctor's thesis, West Virginia University (Morgantown, W.Va.), 1970. *(DAI* 31:3775A)
199. Johnson, Janice K. "Effects of the Process Approach Upon I.Q. Measures of Disadvantaged Children." *Sci Ed* 54(1):45–8 Ja–Mr '70. *
200. Jones, Kenneth J., and Jones, Priscilla P. "Contribution of the Rorschach to Description of Personality Structure Defined by Several Objective Tests." *Psychol Rep* 26(1):35–45 F '70. * (*PA* 45:4281)
201. McCracken, Robert A., and Mullen, Neill D. "The Validity of Certain Measures in an I.R.I.," pp. 104–10. In *Reading Difficulties: Diagnosis, Correction, and Remediation.* Edited by William K. Durr. Newark, Del.: International Reading Association, 1970. Pp. vii, 276. *
202. Moulin, Eugene K. "The Effects of Client-Centered Group Counseling Using Play Media on the Intelligence, Achievement, and Psycholinguistic Abilities of Underachieving Primary School Children." *El Sch Guid & Counsel* 5(2):85–98 D '70. *
203. Ringness, Thomas A. "Identifying Figures, Their Achievement Values, and Children's Values as Related to Actual and Predicted Achievement." *J Ed Psychol* 61(3):174–85 Je '70. * (*PA* 44:13397)
204. Skubic, Vera, and Anderson, Marian. "The Interrelationship of Perceptual-Motor Achievement, Academic Achievement and Intelligence of Fourth Grade Children." *J Learn Dis* 3(8):413–20 Ag '70. *
205. Younge, James W. "A Study of High School Preparation and Freshman Failures at North Carolina College at Durham." *J Negro Ed* 39(1):96–9 w '70. *

Bert A. Goldman, *Dean of Academic Advising, The University of North Carolina at Greensboro, Greensboro, North Carolina.*

The CTMM purports to measure functional capacities deemed basic to learning, problem-solving, and responding to new situations, by means of five factors for each of six school levels and for adults. Although the 1963 series retains the rationale and basic structure of earlier editions, the authors maintain that it has undergone extensive modification in test content and composition and that it has been rescaled at all levels. Some of the changes include: replacement of the ratio IQ with the deviation IQ to conform to the 1960 revision of the Stanford-Binet; introduction of new items; rearrangement of tests and factors; modification of time limits; revision of the directions for administration; redrawing of all artwork; adoption of a new format and color scheme for the test booklets, manuals, and accessories; and simplification of the process of calculating derived scores.

An earlier review criticized the test authors "for using the term 'factors' for scores derived from tests whose development was not based on factor analysis" (Milholland, 5:314). This complaint may no longer be registered because the authors say they have factor analyzed the test employing the Thurstone centroid method which produced five discrete factors. They say that as a result of this factor analysis the only major revision involved transferring the Inferences test from the Logical Reasoning factor to the Verbal Concepts factor. Surprisingly, no statistical information concerning the factor analysis is provided in the Technical Report. The reader is simply referred to "a more complete report" (*117*) prepared by the California Test Bureau in 1963 but not listed in their catalog. This information should have been included in the Technical Report.

The standardization population seems to be representative. However, no explanation is given for using 49 instead of all 50 states. The excluded state is not identified.

Overall, the reliability coefficients indicate adequate reliability. Levels 0 and 1 present the weakest coefficients and when coefficients for the five factors are compared across all levels, it is noted that Spatial Relationships has the poorest reliability. The K-R 21 reliabilities reported for each type of score follow: the five factor scores, .48 to .94, median .77; language total, .71 to .95, median .90; nonlanguage total, .79 to .93, median .86; and total, .86 to .96, median .93.

Considerable validity data for the Short Form of the CTMM are presented, but no data are provided for the Long Form. As an earlier reviewer pointed out, there is need for evidence of the Long Form's use for "educational selection, prediction, and guidance at each of the several age and grade levels" (Freeman, 5:314). Also lacking are validity and reliability data indicating use with the intellectual extremes (i.e., mentally deficient and superior).

No rationale is given for using eight school levels with the Short Form and only six school levels with the Long Form. Further, five factors are included in the Long Form and only four in the Short Form. No reason is given for eliminating the Spatial Relationships factor from the Short Form. However, earlier in this review it was pointed out that among the five factors this one provided the poorest reliability coefficients.

In sum, as far as group tests of intelligence are concerned, the CTMM appears to rate among the best. Its format is clear and easy to follow, its material appears durable, the norms appear representative, and its reliability while being weaker at the lower levels generally seems satisfactory. Data on validity are lacking, but if its shorter version is comparable, then considerable evidence suggests that the Long Form is valid. This leads to a question that has long stood in this reviewer's mind. Why both tests? Why not just the CTMM-SF? The Short Form takes less time to administer than the Long Form, research is available concerning its validity, and in terms of reliability it does not contain the Long Form's weakest factor (Spatial Relationships).

JOHN H. ROSENBACH, *Professor of Educational Psychology and Head of the Department, State University of New York at Albany, Albany, New York.*

In reading the publisher's literature on the CTMM series, one gets the definite impression of a test package designed to provide something for everyone: an omnibus IQ test to estimate Stanford-Binet (S-B) scores; language nonlanguage, and total IQ's in the spirit of the Wechsler scales; factor scores for those who lean toward differential aptitudes; mental ages for those who were brought up in the old S-B tradition; short forms and long forms; tests for kindergarteners to adults; color-coded booklets; and student profile charts on which the data-oriented teacher can record a multitude of numbers—IQ's, MA's, standard scores, stanines, and even I.S.I.'s and A.A.G.P.'s, which translate to Intellectual Status Index and Anticipated Achievement Grade Placements.

Certainly the CTMM is presented to us in an attractive fashion. But what does it all add up to? At worst, probably, an invitation to the less sophisticated users to over-interpret, to be misled into believing they have much more useful information than they actually possess, and to misclassify and to err in making educational decisions, especially about individual students. At best, another run-of-the-mill scholastic aptitude test series whose total score and language subscore correlate quite highly with standardized achievement tests and other tests of mental ability.

The CTMM was first published in 1936 and the current revisions (both Long Form and Short Form) bear close resemblance to their predecessors. Not only has the test format remained basically unchanged but the reported reliability and validity coefficients are of the same magnitude. Thus, past MMY reviews, especially those of the 1957 revisions, are still relevant.

Changes in the content and format of the 1963 revision do include one completely new subtest (Delayed Recall), and new names for some subtests (e.g., Number Concepts is now Numerical Values, Numerical Quantity has become Number Problems, and Verbal Concepts is called Verbal Comprehension). Further, nine subtests have been revised by replacing from 11 to 55 percent of their items with new items. Test 10, Immediate Recall, is essentially unchanged and the time limits for the total battery are the same as for the 1957 revision.

Since the 1963 Short Form consists of items drawn from the Long Form (only subtests "Rights and Lefts," "Manipulation of Areas," "Immediate Recall," and "Inferences" do not appear on the Short Form), Stanley's review of the Short Form in the Sixth MMY can be considered, in toto, appropriate to the Long Form. One additional comment appears in order: Given the social turmoil of the fifties and sixties it is surprising to observe the continuing content bias reflecting white, middle class values. For example, all the pictures of dwellings are of single family houses; not an apartment building is included. Moreover, the only apparent reference to a minority group depicts an Indian, attired in "traditional" costume and holding a spear! Even if such content selection does not differentially affect subjects' scores, it is perhaps time that major test publishers view their instruments as educational and social forces as well as psychometric devices.

The major technical changes in this revision, according to the Technical Report, include, "(1) scaling to the Stanford-Binet, Form L-M, 1960 Revision; (2) independent scaling of the Total, Language, and Non-Language I.Q.'s; (3) replacement of the Ratio I.Q. with the deviation I.Q.; and (4) extension of the I.Q. and M.A. tables to allow for direct look-up."

Moving to a deviation IQ places the CTMM, somewhat belatedly, in step with other major mental ability tests, while the IQ-MA arrangement is a convenience to the individual who desires both scores. The scaling issue is, however, a somewhat different matter. Given certain assumptions, the scaling procedure appears to be legitimate, but there is some question as to whether it is of any particular value to the test user. The authors apparently wanted their instrument to be viewed as a group-test equivalent of the Stanford-Binet. Thus, they first scaled the Short Form total score to the S-B, such that the Short Form IQ could be considered an estimate of an S-B IQ, and then scaled the Long Form to the Short Form. Finally, the various subscores were scaled to the total Long Form IQ. Just what is accomplished by all this is problematical. Moreover, it is doubtful that the average person who administers and interprets the test will be able to wade through the rather muddled description given of the scaling procedures with any degree of comprehension. Worst of all, the authors do not present any clear statement of their rationale for following these procedures nor how what they have done is to the benefit of the test interpreter.

NORMING. The standardization of the 1963 revision, if accomplished as described in the various California publications, appears to have been done with care. Classes from 253 schools, representing seven geographic regions and 49 states, comprised the sample. In addition, the cooperating schools were "urged" to take certain measures in order to insure comparable testing conditions, e.g., classes were to be excluded if they had recently taken similar tests, and testing was to be done during midweek. Unfortunately, no mention is made of the extent to which schools actually followed these directions or even if efforts were made to gather such information. Thus, the reader is left to make his own inferences as to what may have happened in various schools and, worse, to speculate about how different contingencies may have affected the standardization results. It would seem that a major test publisher could be expected to be quite specific about something as basic as standardization procedures.

RELIABILITY. With the exception of the K-R 21 reliability coefficients, *all* reliability and validity information presented in the Technical Report are based on the Short Form. One could reason that whatever is detected about the short form of a test will surely be as good or better for a longer version of the test. Nonetheless, some research data on the Long Form would be welcomed, especially since the L-F includes several components which are completely absent on the S-F. Furthermore, most of the studies with the S-F dealing with test-retest reliability or reporting correlations with other tests, except for the *California Achievement Tests* which was normed simultaneously with the CTMM, are based on relatively small samples (most of the N's range from 100–200). Thus, once again, the reader is left to his own devices to guess what the results might have been if the L-F were to be substituted for the S-F.

In any event, the K-R 21 coefficients are typical for tests of this type and similar to those reported for past revisions. Except for the very young ages, up to about 8, the total score reliabilities range from .93 to .96, those for the language section in the low .90's, and for the nonlanguage section in the high .80's. The factor scores, as expected, yield lower reliabilities, which are quite variable from level to level. These reliabilities are conspicuously low at the younger ages (several in the .40's and .50's), while the Spatial Relationship factor is low at just about every level (for example, with adults it is only .56). It should also be noted that, despite claims to the contrary, there is an element of speed present throughout the battery, i.e., each subtest has a time limit and the sub-

California Test of Mental Maturity

jects are instructed to "work as fast as you can." Unfortunately, the effects of this speed factor are unknown, but, if anything, there would be a tendency to enhance these reliability coefficients.

A somewhat more encouraging picture, with notable exceptions, is presented in test-retest and adjacent test studies done with the Short Form over one year intervals. At about grade four and above (Levels 2 through 5) the total score and language section reliabilities tend to run in the mid to high .80's, with the nonlanguage section in the mid to high .70's. Below these ages, however, the reliabilities are shockingly low: of 9 coefficients, one is .39, three are in the .40's, two in the .50's, two in the .60's, and one at .70. Unfortunately, no data are presented for the factor scores.

One can only conclude, as have other reviewers, that little significance, if any, be attributed to the several subscores, with the exception of the language section, especially when dealing with individuals. Moreover, even the total scores and language scores are of questionable value for children under eight, and based on the data presented in the Technical Report, one would be tempted to recommend that Levels 0 and 1 *not* be given unless score interpretations are to be made by someone highly trained in measurement.

VALIDITY. Judged against the claims made for the CTMM in the publisher's manuals, the validity data presented are woefully inadequate. To cite but a few examples from the Guide to Interpretation: "The factor scores are useful in educational diagnosis and remedial instruction"; "When this procedure [profile analysis] is followed, the individual's unique pattern of mental functioning can be studied and the most appropriate actions can be taken in the instructional program"; "The CTMM provides information about the student's functional capacities that are basic to learning."

However, the only "validity" data included in any of the manuals are the now too familiar correlations with other tests: against the Stanford-Binet, the *California Achievement Tests* (CAT), and several group tests of mental ability. Interestingly enough, although the CTMM was originally designed to parallel the Stanford-Binet and, as indicated earlier, was even scaled to it, the correlations with this test tend to be the lowest of all reported (from .66 and .74). The highest correlations are with other group tests (mostly in the high .70's and .80's) and with the CAT (r's of .79, .81, .81, .84). With these correlations running so close to the reliabilities of the tests, one can only ask for the nth time what, if any, information is being added to our knowledge of human behavior or ability.

As far as the factor scores are concerned, the only validity correlations reported are with the various subsections of the CAT. However, in almost every possible instance (114 of 120 r's) the Language IQ correlates more highly with the subsections of the CAT than do the factor scores with the CAT. In addition, the Language IQ consistently correlates more highly with the CAT than does the Nonlanguage IQ (37 of 40 comparisons). In other words, it is difficult to see any particular advantage of using CTMM scores other than the Total and Language IQ's.

SUMMARY. As a simple, omnibus test of mental ability the CTMM is fairly comparable and probably on a par with so many other similar instruments. However, it is oversold in its various manuals and little if any use should be made of its various subscores or of the test as a whole with younger children. Adequate reliability data are lacking for the Long Form and there is simply a paucity of research evidence to support the claims made, explicitly and implicitly, in the manuals. Other than the fact that the Long Form should theoretically be somewhat more reliable than the Short Form, no persuasive case is made for using it in preference to more compact versions. The additional factor score provided by the L-F, Spatial Relationships, is not only of questionable value insofar as validity is concerned, but is singularly low in reliability.

Perhaps the most cogent comment about the CTMM was made by McNemar:[1] "the [CTMM]....serves as an illustration of factor icing a *g* cake * The advertising claims the measurement of not only factors but also *g*; not only *g* but also factors. This measurement absurdity is all too apt to go unrecognized by test users, and hence a sales advantage for the aptitude battery that produces both factor scores and an IQ."

For reviews by Frank S. Freeman and John E. Milholland of an earlier edition, see 5:314;

[1] McNemar, Quinn. "Lost: Our Intelligence? Why?" *Am Psychol* 19:871–82 D '64. *

for a review by Henry E. Garrett, see 3:223 (2 excerpts); for reviews by Raymond B. Cattell and F. Kuhlmann, see 2:1384 (1 excerpt); for reviews by W. D. Commins, Rudolf Pintner, and Arthur E. Traxler, see 1:1042 (1 excerpt). For reviews of the short form, see 6:443 (1 review), 5:313 (1 review), and 4:282 (1 excerpt).

[339]
*Canadian Academic Aptitude Test. Grades 8.5–9.0; 1959–68; CAAT; this test and tests 6:253 and 6:567 make up the *Canadian Test Battery*, grades 8–9; 3 scores: verbal, mathematical, non-verbal; 1 form; separate parts 1 ('62, 4 pages, verbal reasoning), 2 ('62, 4 pages, mathematical reasoning), 3 ('62, 6 pages, non-verbal reasoning, identical with test copyrighted in 1959); battery manual ('68, 5 pages); battery technical manual ('64, 59 pages); supplementary data ('68, 6 pages, identical with data copyrighted in 1963) for the battery; battery profile ('63, 1 page); separate answer sheets (Digitek) must be used; $1.75 per 25 tests; $3.50 per 50 answer sheets; 20¢ per hand scoring stencil; 20¢ per 15 battery profiles; 10¢ per battery manual; $1 per technical manual; 70¢ per specimen set; $3.25 per battery specimen set; postage extra; machine scoring service available from The Ontario Institute for Studies in Education; 30(40–45) minutes per part; Ontario Institute for Studies in Education; distributed by Guidance Centre. *

REFERENCES
1–2. See 6:445.
3. KHAN, S. B., AND ROBERTS, DENNIS M. "Relationships Among Study Habits and Attitudes, Aptitude and Grade 8 Achievement." *Ed & Psychol Meas* 29(4):951–5 w '69. * (PA 44:21525)

For reviews by Donald B. Black and George A. Ferguson, see 6:445.

[340]
★Canadian Cognitive Abilities Test. Grades kgn–1, 2–3; 1954–70; CCAT; adaptation of *Cognitive Abilities Test*; 2 levels; Form 1 ('70, 16 pages) for each level; manual ('70, 34 pages) for each level; Can $6.25 per 35 tests; $1.50 per specimen set; postage extra; original test by Robert L. Thorndike, Elizabeth Hagen, and Irving Lorge; adaptation by Edgar N. Wright; Thomas Nelson & Sons (Canada) Ltd. *
a) PRIMARY 1. Grades kgn–1; (45–55) minutes in 2 sessions.
b) PRIMARY 2. Grades 2–3; (55–60) minutes in 2 sessions.

[341]
★Canadian Lorge-Thorndike Intelligence Tests, Multi-Level Edition. Grades 3–9; 1954–67; CLTIT; adaptation of *Lorge-Thorndike Intelligence Tests, Multi-Level Edition*; 3 scores: verbal, non-verbal, composite; Form 1 ('67, 46 pages); Levels A (grade 3), B (4), C (5), D (6), E (7), F (8–9) in a single booklet; manual ('67, 84 pages); no norms or reliability data for composite score; separate answer sheets (MRC) must be used; Can 90¢ per test; $4 per 35 answer sheets for any one level; 60¢ per scoring stencil for any one level; $1.65 per manual; $3.25 per specimen set; postage extra; scoring service, 25¢ and over per test; 62(120) minutes in 2 sessions; original test by Irving Lorge, Robert L. Thorndike, and Elizabeth Hagen; adaptation by Edgar N. Wright; Thomas Nelson & Sons (Canada) Ltd. *

[342]
★The Carlton Intelligence Tests. Ages 10–12; 1962–65; CIT; 2 tests; 20p per specimen set of either test; postage extra; 10(15) minutes for practice test, 45(55) minutes for test; [W. K. Carlton]; University of London Press Ltd. *
a) TEST NO. 1. 1962; 1 form (16 pages); manual (11 pages); practice sheet (2 pages); 92½p per 20 tests; 30p per 20 practice sheets; 12½p per manual.
b) TEST NO. 2. 1965; 1 form (15 pages); manual (10 pages); practice sheet (2 pages); £1.05 per 20 tests; 25p per 20 practice sheets; 15p per manual.

STANLEY NISBET, *Professor of Education, University of Glasgow, Glasgow, Scotland.*

These two tests, originally designed to assist in the allocation of pupils to appropriate courses in the transition from primary to secondary education, contain most of the familiar types of intelligence test items (e.g., "odd man out," opposites, "is to....as," codes, anagrams, absurdities, missing elements, series) as well as a number of less common ones (e.g., "word ladders," interpreting simple tables of statistics). Each test includes a wide variety of verbal, numerical, spatial, alphabetical, and pictorial questions. Since the tests rest on such a broad base, the face validity is high.

In construction and standardisation procedures the tests are all that one could desire. Identical means (36) and standard deviations (20) were obtained for the two tests in the standardisation populations. These figures suggest a well constructed test with good discriminating power at all levels except the very lowest.

Each test is divided into two parts, A and B, the latter being "considerably more difficult" than A. No indication is given, however, as to whether the test user is to take any special account of this division; it is not suggested anywhere, for instance, that A and B could be used separately.

The only criticisms concern a few matters of detail: in one item, the opposite of "guess" is given as "prove." This seems dubious. At least three items are "dated": children can no longer be expected to know about half-crowns and furlongs, and some modern clocks do not have hands. Eight of the "always has" items are debatable. The instructions for subtest A-5 seem less clear than the fairly similar instructions for B-5. Similar criticisms may be made of a few other items.

A few items involve general knowledge as well as intelligence. The reviewer sees nothing wrong with this, but wonders if knowledge of the meaning of "mosque" and of the fact that hedgehogs hibernate or that most four legged animals can swim should be included in an intelligence test for 10–12 year olds.

To sum up, these are good tests and can be recommended as instruments of proven worth for measuring the general mental capacity of children between the ages of 10 and 12. They should be particularly efficient in the identification of academic potential among average and above-average children.

[343]

*Cognitive Abilities Test. Grades kgn–1, 2–3; 1954–68; CAT; revision of Levels 1 and 2 of still-in-print *Lorge-Thorndike Intelligence Tests;* 2 levels; $1.20 per specimen set, postage extra; Robert L. Thorndike, Elizabeth Hagen, and Irving Lorge; Houghton Mifflin Co. *

a) PRIMARY 1. Grades kgn–1; 2 editions; manual ('68, 34 pages) for each form; (45–55) minutes in 2 sessions.
   1) *Hand Scorable Edition.* Forms 1, 2, ('68, 15 pages); $5.25 per 35 tests.
   2) *Machine Scorable Edition.* Forms 1, 2, ('68, 16 pages); $9 per 35 tests; MRC scoring service, 45¢ and over per test.

b) PRIMARY 2. Grades 2–3; 2 editions; manual ('68, 34 pages) for each form; (55–60) minutes in 2 sessions.
   1) *Hand Scorable Edition.* Forms 1, 2, ('68, 15 pages); $5.25 per 35 tests.
   2) *Machine Scorable Edition.* Forms 1, 2, ('68, 16 pages); $9 per 35 tests; MRC scoring service, 45¢ and over per test.

MARCEL L. GOLDSCHMID, *Associate Professor of Psychology and Director, Centre for Learning and Development, McGill University, Montreal, Quebec, Canada.*

The CAT is part of an integrated series of intelligence tests. It can be used beginning in the second half of kindergarten through grade 3 and can be followed by the *Lorge-Thorndike Intelligence Tests, Multi-Level Edition,* which covers grades 3 through 13. The normative linking of the two tests makes it possible to obtain comparable test scores across the 14 grades.

The CAT can be given by teachers and scored by hand or machine and offers the further advantage of being designed for small group administration. The influence of reading competence is eliminated by the use of paced, oral, item-by-item directions. Unscored sample items, moreover, permit the child to get oriented to each of the four subtests. A shorter version of Primary 1 can be administered to children who are known to be slower than average in cognitive development. The deliberate overlap between the CAT and the Multi-Level Edition provides flexibility in selecting the most suitable type of test for each group of children. For repeated testing of the same group of children, two equivalent forms are available.

Besides explicit test administration instructions, the manual offers useful suggestions and directions for selecting the proper test form, scheduling of the tests, general testing considerations, and use of the test results. The hand scoring is simple and objective.

The normative samples for the CAT (approximately 5,000 subjects in each of grades 1, 2, 3, and 4 and over 2,600 subjects in kindergarten) were drawn from a cross section of schools which were used in the Multi-Level Edition (180,000 pupils in 40 states). The means and standard deviations of the two tests were then equalized and the distribution of IQ's normalized. By using the tables in the manual, raw scores can easily be converted into deviation IQ's, which, in turn, can be converted into percentile ranks, stanines, or grade percentiles.

The reliability coefficients (K-R 20) are all around .90 at each grade level (based on samples of 300 for each). The reliability of the shortened version is only slightly lower.

Very sparse information about the validity of the CAT is reported. The CAT and Level A of the Multi-Level Edition were both given to 300 pupils in third grade. A factor analysis of these scores demonstrated that both the CAT and the L-T load heavily on a general reasoning factor (83 percent of the variance). Unfortunately, other than this bit of construct validity, no other validity data are contained in the manual. Neither are there data on the statistical relationship between the two "equivalent" forms.

In summary, the CAT is a well constructed and standardized test with excellent reliability and is based on representative and very substantial normative samples. It lends itself particularly well to the testing of large numbers of children, since it can be administered by teachers to groups and machine scored. Most regrettably, however, no concurrent or predictive validity data are presented in the manual. Since the CAT is normatively linked with the Multi-Level Edition of the *Lorge-Thorndike Intelligence Tests,* the potential CAT user is forced to search for indirect validity data in the manual of the Multi-Level Edition.

CAROL K. TITTLE, *Assistant Professor of Teacher Education, City University of New York, New York, New York.*

The *Cognitive Abilities Test* has four subtests: Oral Vocabulary; Relational Concepts (over, under, most, least, and so on); "Multimental" (identifying one picture in a set that does not belong); and Quantitative Concepts (find the square with three sticks). All instructions and questions are given orally, and responses are represented pictorially.

The *Cognitive Abilities Test* was standardized in January and February of 1968, using 45 of the 72 communities in the 1963 standardization of the *Lorge-Thorndike Intelligence Tests*. The manuals for the CAT give very limited descriptions of the norming sample and procedures. The manuals do promise a special study to check interpolated values in the norm tables from fall to winter and from winter to spring. For the early ages being tested here, there would seem to be a clear need to establish values for fall and spring on empirical data for the norms.

Scores provided are deviation IQ scores, with a mean of 100 and standard deviation of 16, and grade percentiles; in addition there are tables for converting DIQ's to percentile ranks and stanines. The use of intelligence test scores for pupils with varying social class and language backgrounds has been the subject of considerable debate. An up-to-date manual should provide norms, or discussion of the validity of scores, for special groups of pupils.

The reliability data presented were based on samples of 300 per grade from the standardization group. K-R 20, rather than an alternate forms method, was used to estimate the reliability. The reliability figures are satisfactory—.89 to .90. The section on cautions in interpreting and using the test results implies that the standard error of measurement is about 5 DIQ points. This section could discuss the standard error of measurement more explicitly and present the standard error of measurement for various score levels.

No data on validity are given, with the exception of a factor analysis of the CAT and Level A (grade 3) of the verbal and nonverbal tests of the L-T Multi-Level Edition. The factor analysis shows one main factor for the subtest scores of all three tests, labelled as a "general reasoning factor" by the authors.

The uses suggested for the test, for which validity should be demonstrated, are determining the "rate of introduction of new material for group activities"; "identifying individuals who need special attention"; "grouping within classrooms"; "selecting curriculum materials and learning tasks"; "conferring with parents on status and progress"; and "deciding about grade placement." Validity remains to be established for these uses.

Some evidence of the relationship of the earlier versions of the *Cognitive Abilities Test* to school achievement and reading achievement is available. These studies indicate at least moderate correlations with school achievement. The possible validity of the earlier L-T primary test in predicting reading achievement specifically also appears to be moderate. Users should assess the validity of the *Cognitive Abilities Test* for these purposes on an empirical basis in their own situation. Validity cannot be considered to be well demonstrated.

The authors are to be commended for the discussion which introduces the section on uses of the test. The first paragraphs point out the influence of informal experiences in development of the skills being measured. It is also noted that the skills measured by the test are in part *learned* skills and that low scores do *not* constitute "an excuse for passing the child by." This viewpoint is reiterated in the section providing cautions in interpreting and using the results of the test. The cautions note that the test measures the present status of a child, that test results for young children are relatively unstable, and that the test does not relate perfectly to school success.

For the test booklet available for review—Primary 1, Form 2—one comment can be made about the artwork: it does not represent minority groups satisfactorily where the pictures include people.

In summary, the *Cognitive Abilities Test*, Primary 1 and 2, is the downward extension of a widely used and well-constructed set of group intelligence tests. The reliability of the Primary tests is satisfactory; validity data are very limited. Some evidence from studies of the earlier Lorge-Thorndike indicates at least moderate correlations with school achievement and reading. Users will need to determine the validity of the CAT for their particular use of the scores.

Cognitive Abilities Test

J Ed Meas 6(2):123–4 su '69. Richard C. Cox. * there are two general problems which must be taken into account when using the CAT. The first is that this test demands, as do most tests intended for this age group, a certain amount of listening ability on the part of the test taker since the test is administered orally. Secondly, the test requires rather acute visual discrimination between multiple-choice answers which appear in the form of small pictures. These problems are not mentioned by the authors nor is the basis for item selection cited. For the most part, the directions are stated clearly and succinctly. One exception is that, if the directions are followed verbatim, grammatical errors such as "put your fingers on a.... apple" occur several times. * In general, the directions and scoring procedures are adequate. One minor criticism is that, when the CAT is scored by hand, there is no convenient place to record either total or subtest scores. * Standard errors, which may be useful for test interpretation, are not reported. In the Technical Considerations section of the examiners manual, the words "factor analysis" appear as a major heading in place of the more common "validity." This is the case since the only validity evidence presented is that from a factor analysis of data from the joint administration of the CAT and the Lorge-Thorndike Intelligence Tests, Multi-Level Edition, Level A in grade 3. This construct validation procedure seems to be rather narrow in scope and does not provide enough information for the reviewer to say much about validity. It does indicate, though, that the CAT does have some validity as a downward extension of the Lorge-Thorndike Intelligence Test. The norming procedure for the CAT seems well done in terms of both the numbers involved and the appropriateness of norm groups. I.Q. equivalents, percentile ranks and stanines of deviation I.Q.'s, and grade percentiles are clearly described and are easy to interpret using the tables provided in the manual. Also provided in the manual is a section entitled, "Using the Test Results." This may be a blessing or a Pandora's box for the potential user. The suggested uses are appropriate but are not to be blindly adopted by the naive test user. It is this reviewer's hope that persons desirous of using the results of the CAT in one of the ways suggested will also carefully read the following page in the manual which deals with cautions to be used in the interpretation of the test results. To summarize, the CAT is impressive with respect to the adequacy of directions, general test design, norm data, and other practical features. It is designed as a group test to measure cognitive ability at an early age, an area practically void of available standardized tests. Further data pertinent to the reliability and the validity of the test for certain purposes would be helpful for further evaluation.

[344]

*College Board Scholastic Aptitude Test. Candidates for college entrance; 1926–71; SAT; tests administered each January, March, April, July, November, and December at centers established by the publisher; 2 scores: verbal, mathematical; descriptive booklet ('70, 55 pages); for additional information, see 663; examination fee, $5.75 per student; special editions available for the visually handicapped; 180 (240) minutes; program administered for the College Entrance Examination Board by Educational Testing Service. *

REFERENCES

1–22. See 4:285.
23–42. See 5:318.
43–121. See 6:449.
122. GIESSOW, FRED JUNIOR. *The Prediction of Success in First Year Natural Science Courses at Washington University.* Doctor's thesis, Washington University (St. Louis, Mo.), 1953. (*DA* 14:1046)
123. MARSH, FRANK EUGENE, JR. *An Analysis of Failure Among University Freshmen.* Doctor's thesis, Boston University (Boston, Mass.), 1959. (*DA* 20:2101)
124. BALLANTYNE, ROBERT HUBBARD. *An Analysis of Criteria for Selecting Freshmen Students for an Honors Program at Washington State University.* Doctor's thesis, Washington State University (Pullman, Wash.), 1962. (*DA* 23:2439)
125. QUILLER, GORDON FREDERICK. *A Study of College Predictors for First Year Students at Colorado State University.* Doctor's research study No. 1, Colorado State College (Greeley, Colo.), 1962. (*DA* 23:1253)
126. STEIGE, ROBERT. *A Differential Study of the Prognostic Value of Admission and Placement Criteria at the University of Colorado.* Doctor's thesis, University of Colorado (Boulder, Colo.), 1962. (*DA* 23:537)
127. TURRENTINE, EDGAR MAYER. *Predicting Success in Practice Teaching in Music.* Doctor's thesis, State University of Iowa (Iowa City, Iowa), 1962. (*DA* 23:2814)
128. CHASE, CLINTON I.; LUDLOW, H. GLENN; POMEROY, MARTHA C.; AND BARRITT, L. SPENCER. *Predicting Individual Course Success for Entering Freshmen.* Indiana Studies in Prediction No. 2. Bloomington, Ind.: Bureau of Educational Studies and Testing, Indiana University, 1963. Pp. i, 41. *
129. CHASE, CLINTON I.; LUDLOW, H. GLENN; POMEROY, MARTHA C.; AND BARRITT, L. SPENCER. *Predicting Success for University Freshmen.* Indiana Studies in Prediction No. 1. Bloomington, Ind.: Bureau of Educational Studies and Testing, Indiana University, 1963. Pp. vi, 47. *
130. CLARK, EUGENE WARREN. *An Evaluation of Predictive Criteria for a Group of High Ability College Freshmen.* Doctor's thesis, University of Denver (Denver, Colo.), 1963. (*DA* 25:957)
131. FINGER, JOHN A., AND SCHLESSER, GEORGE E. "Academic Performance of Public and Private School Students." *J Ed Psychol* 54:118–22 Ap '63. * (*PA* 37:8282)
132. LARE, JOAN HINCHMAN. *The Relationship of Ordinal Position and Sex of Sibling to Scholastic Aptitude Test Scores and the Academic Achievement of College Students From Two Child Families.* Doctor's thesis, Cornell University (Ithaca, N.Y.), 1963. (*DA* 24:275)
133. LEACH, ALICE REA. *Prediction of Academic Success in College Freshmen at the University of Denver.* Doctor's thesis, University of Denver (Denver, Colo.), 1963. (*DA* 24:5199)
134. NICHOLS, ROBERT C., AND HOLLAND, JOHN L. "Prediction of the First Year College Performance of High Aptitude Students." *Psychol Monogr* 77(7):1–29 '63. * (*PA* 38:4693)
135. RICHMAN, ELI. *College Admissions Based on S.A.T. Scores, 1962–1963.* [Chelsea, Mass.: the Author, School Department, 1963.] Pp. i, 63. *
136. RUSSELL, JAMES WILLIAM. *An Analysis of the Academic Performance of Transfer and Native Students and Their Major Fields in the College of Arts and Sciences at the University of*

Georgia. Doctor's thesis, University of Georgia (Athens, Ga.), 1963. (DA 25:1668)
137. THREATT, ROBERT. *A Study of Selected Characteristics and College Success of High- and Low-Achieving Negro Students on CEEB Scholastic Aptitude Test in Georgia.* Doctor's thesis, University of Oklahoma (Norman, Okla.), 1963. (DA 24:577)
138. AIKEN, LEWIS R., JR. "The Prediction of Academic Success and Early Attrition by Means of a Multiple-Choice Biographical Inventory." *Am Ed Res J* 1:127-35 Mr '64. * (PA 39:1692)
139. BACHMAN, JERALD G. "Prediction of Academic Achievement Using the Edwards Need Achievement Scale." *J Appl Psychol* 48:16-9 F '64. * (PA 38:9276)
140. BERKEY, ROSEMARY. *A Survey of Twelve High School Seniors Who Achieved Low Verbal Scores on the Scholastic Aptitude Test of the College Entrance Examination Boards.* Master's thesis, Glassboro State College (Glassboro, N.J.), 1964.
141. BOYDEN, BARTLETT W., AND HINDLE, PETER G. *How to Boost Your Marks in the S.A.T.* New York: Macfadden-Bartell Corporation, 1964. Pp. 143. *
142. CARLSMITH, LYN. "Effect of Early Father Absence on Scholastic Aptitude." *Harvard Ed R* 34:3-21 w '64. *
143. CHAUNCEY, HENRY. "What's Right With Testing." *Fla J Ed Res* 6:87-102 Ja '64. *
144. COLLEGE ENTRANCE EXAMINATION BOARD. *A Description of the College Board Scholastic Aptitude Test.* Princeton, N.J.: the Board, 1964. Pp. 55. *
145. COLLEGE ENTRANCE EXAMINATION BOARD. *Manual of Freshman Class Profiles, 1964 Edition.* Princeton, N.J.: the Board, 1964. Pp. xiv, 584. *
146. COOPER, CARL J. "Some Relationships Between Paired-Associates Learning and Foreign-Language Aptitude." *J Ed Psychol* 55:132-8 Je '64. * (PA 39:5823)
147. DIEPPA, JORGE J. "Developing the Spanish Version of the SAT." *Col Board R* 53:12-7 sp '64. *
148. FRENCH, JOHN W. "New Tests for Predicting the Performance of College Students With High-Level Aptitude." *J Ed Psychol* 55:185-94 Ag '64. * (PA 39:5979)
149. HART, MARCIA E., AND SHAY, CLAYTON T. "Relationship Between Physical Fitness and Academic Success." *Res Q* 35:443-5 O '64. * (PA 39:5971)
150. HILLS, JOHN R. "College Expectancy Tables for High School Counselors." *Personnel & Guid J* 42:479-83 Ja '64. *
151. HILLS, JOHN R. "Prediction of College Grades for All Public Colleges of a State." *J Ed Meas* 1:155-9 D '64. *
152. HILLS, JOHN R.; BUSH, MARILYN L.; AND KLOCK, JOSEPH A. "Predicting Grades Beyond the Freshman Year." *Col Board R* 54:23-5 f '64. *
153. HILLS, JOHN R.; KLOCK, JOSEPH A.; AND BUSH, MARILYN L. *Freshman Norms for the University System of Georgia, 1962-63.* Atlanta, Ga.: Office of Testing and Guidance, Regents of the University System of Georgia, March 1964. Pp. xi, 65. *
154. HILLS, JOHN R.; KLOCK, JOSEPH A.; AND BUSH, MARILYN L. "Scholastic Aptitude of an Entire State's Public College Students." *Col & Univ* 40:60-7 f '64. *
155. IVANOFF, JOHN M.; MALLOY, JOHN P.; AND ROSE, JANET R. "Achievement, Aptitude, and Biographical Measures as Predictors of Success in Nursing Training." *Ed & Psychol Meas* 24:389-91 su '64. * (PA 39:5972)
156. KAUFMANN, JAMES D., AND DEMPSTER, DENNIS. "Prediction of SAT Scores." *Personnel & Guid J* 42:1026-7 Je '64. * (PA 39:5069)
157. LINDQUIST, E. F. "Equating Scores on Non-Parallel Tests." *J Ed Meas* 1:5-9 Je '64. * (PA 39:7777)
158. MCCORMICK, JAMES H., AND ASHER, WILLIAM. "Aspects of the High School Record Related to the First Semester College Grade Point Average." *Personnel & Guid J* 42:699-703 Mr '64. *
159. MARKS, EDMOND. *Nonadditive Effects in the Prediction of Academic Achievement.* Doctor's thesis, Pennsylvania State University (University Park, Pa.), 1964. (DA 25:6752)
160. MICHAEL, WILLIAM B.; BAKER, DAVID; AND JONES, ROBERT A. "A Note Concerning the Predictive Validities of Selected Cognitive and Non-Cognitive Measures for Freshman Students in a Liberal Arts College." *Ed & Psychol Meas* 24: 373-5 su '64. * (PA 39:5984)
161. PAUL, GORDON L., AND ERIKSEN, CHARLES W. "Effects of Test Anxiety on 'Real-Life' Examinations." *J Personality* 32:480-94 S '64. * (PA 39:7961)
162. QUINLAN, CLAIRE A. *The Prediction of Freshman Academic Success at Colorado State College by Means of Selected Standardized Tests and Admission Data.* Doctor's research study No. 1, Colorado State College (Greeley, Colo.), 1964. (DA 25:5124)
163. SCHERER, GEORGE A. C., AND WERTHEIMER, MICHAEL. *A Psycholinguistic Experiment in Foreign-Language Teaching.* New York: McGraw-Hill Book Co., 1964. Pp. xiii, 256. *
164. SGAN, MATTHEW R. "An Alternative Approach to Scholastic Aptitude Tests as Predictors of Graduation Rank at Selective Colleges." *Ed & Psychol Meas* 24:347-52 su '64. * (PA 39:5986)
165. SMITH, PAUL M. "Some Implications for Freshman Orientation Activities With Negro College Students." *J Col Stud Personnel* 5:176-9+ Mr '64. *

166. VEAL, LELAND RAMON. *A Comparison of the Professional Growth of Student Teachers Under Two Different Time-Arrangements for Student Teaching at the Secondary Level.* Doctor's thesis, University of South Carolina (Columbia, S.C.), 1964. (DA 25:7104)
167. WALKER, PETER. *Is Either the SAT or the ACT a Superior Instrument for Predicting Academic Success at National College of Education.* Master's thesis, National College of Education (Evanston, Ill.), 1964.
168. WATLEY, DONIVAN J. "The Effectiveness of Intellectual and Non-Intellectual Factors in Predicting Achievement for Business Students." *J Ed Res* 57:402-7 Ap '64. *
169. WATLEY, DONIVAN J., AND MERWIN, JACK C. "The Effectiveness of Variables for Predicting Academic Achievement for Business Students." *J Exp Ed* 33:189-92 w '64. * (PA 39:8713)
170. WEBB, SAM C. "The Psychological Components of Scores for Two Tests of Report Writing Ability." *Ed & Psychol Meas* 24:31-46 sp '64. * (PA 39:1770)
171. ALTUS, WILLIAM D. "Birth Order and Scholastic Aptitude." *J Consult Psychol* 29:202-5 Je '65. * (PA 39:13030)
172. ANGOFF, WILLIAM H. "College Board SAT and the Superior Student." *Sup Stud* 7:10-5 Mr-Ap '65. *
173. BACHRACH, PAUL B., AND WEITZNER, MARTIN. "Factors Related to Academic Success in a College of Business Administration." *Psychol Sch* 2:156-61 Ap '65. *
174. BEHRING, DANIEL W. "Predicting College Achievement With an Activities-Preference Inventory." Abstract. *Proc Ann Conv Am Psychol Assn* 73:345-6 '65. * (PA 39:15182)
175. BIAGGIO, ANGELA M. B. *Relative Predictability of Freshman Grade-Point Averages From SAT Scores in Negro and White Southern Colleges.* Master's thesis, University of Wisconsin (Madison, Wis.), 1965.
176. BRADY, WILLIAM JOSEPH. *Twenty Quantitative Predictors of Academic Success in College as Measured by Grade Point Averages.* Doctor's thesis, University of Connecticut (Storrs, Conn.), 1965. (DA 26:5121)
177. CHANSKY, NORMAN M. "Aptitude, Personality, and Achievement in Six College Curricula." *Ed & Psychol Meas* 25:1117-24 w '65. * (PA 40:3564)
178. CHASE, CLINTON I. *The University Freshman Dropout.* Indiana University, Monograph of the Bureau of Educational Studies and Testing, Indiana Studies in Prediction, No. 6. Bloomington, Ind.: the Bureau, 1965. Pp. 36. *
179. COLLEGE ENTRANCE EXAMINATION BOARD. *Effects of Coaching on Scholastic Aptitude Test Scores.* Princeton, N.J.: the Board, 1965. Pp. 27. *
180. COSTELLO, JOHN JOSEPH. *A Study of the Relationship of College Board Scores and Physical Fitness to the Prediction of Academic Success in College.* Doctor's thesis, University of Connecticut (Storrs, Conn.), 1965. (DA 26:5150)
181. DYE, JAMES MCKINLEY. *An Experimental Study in Selected Sectioning of Freshman English Composition Students.* Doctor's thesis, University of Georgia (Athens, Ga.), 1965. (DA 26:6466)
182. FINGER, JOHN A., AND SCHLESSER, GEORGE E. "Non-Intellective Predictors of Academic Success in School and College." *Sch R* 73:14-29 sp '65. * (PA 39:10832)
183. FLEMING, W. G. Chap. 5, "The Predictive Value of Scholastic Aptitude Scores," pp. 32-5. In his *Characteristics and Achievements of Students in Ontario Universities.* Atkinson Study of Utilization of Student Resources, Report No. 11. Toronto, Ont., Canada: Ontario Institute for Studies in Education, 1965. Pp. xiii, 197. *
184. GALLANT, THOMAS FRANCIS. *Academic Achievement of College Freshmen and Its Relationship to Selected Aspects of the Student's Background.* Doctor's thesis, Western Reserve University (Cleveland, Ohio), 1965. (DA 26:6468)
185. HAUN, KENNETH W. "Note on Prediction of Academic Performance From Personality Test Scores." *Psychol Rep* 16: 294 F '65. * (PA 39:7687)
186. HEIL, LOUIS M. "Scholastic and Personality Variables Associated With Acceptance to and Success in the Brooklyn College Scholars' Program." *Sup Stud* 7:34-40 Mr-Ap '65. *
187. HERBSTRITT, RICHARD LLOYD. *The Identification of Potentially Successful Rejected College Applicants.* Doctor's thesis, Western Reserve University (Cleveland, Ohio), 1965. (DA 27:675A)
188. HILLS, JOHN R., AND KLOCK, JOSEPH A. "Predicting Grades for All Schools in a Large University." *Am Ed Res J* 2:145-50 My '65. *
189. HILLS, JOHN R.; KLOCK, JOSEPH A.; AND BUSH, MARILYN L. *Freshman Norms for the University System, 1963-64.* Atlanta, Ga.: Office of Testing and Guidance, Regents of the University System of Georgia, February 1965. Pp. xi, 65. *
190. HILLS, JOHN R.; KLOCK, JOSEPH A.; AND BUSH, MARILYN L. *Freshman Norms for the University System, 1964-65.* Atlanta, Ga.: Office of Testing and Guidance, Regents of the University System of Georgia, October 1965. Pp. xi, 68. *
191. HILLS, JOHN R.; KLOCK, JOSEPH A.; AND BUSH, MARILYN L. "The Use of Academic Prediction Equations With Subsequent Classes." *Am Ed Res J* 2:203-6 N '65. *
192. IRVINE, DONALD W. "Estimated Grades and Freshman Achievement." *Voc Guid Q* 13:193-5 sp '65. * (PA 40:1949)
193. LEAVER, THOMAS EUGENE. *The Prediction of Academic*

Achievement of Freshman Business Students at Saint Joseph's College. Doctor's thesis, Temple University (Philadelphia, Pa.), 1965. (DA 26:1429)

194. LEMONS, CLIFTON DALE. An Investigation of Relationships Between Mechanical Drawing Experience, Certain Measures of Academic Ability and Knowledge of Drawing Fundamentals to Determine Criteria for Assigning Students to Accelerated Sections of Engineering Drawing. Doctor's thesis, Texas A & M University (College Station, Tex.), 1965. (DA 26:6533)

195. McKELPIN, J. P. "Some Implications of the Intellectual Characteristics of Freshmen Entering a Liberal Arts College." J Ed Meas 2:161–6 D '65. *

196. MUNDAY, LEO. "Comparative Predictive Validities of the American College Tests and Two Other Scholastic Aptitude Tests." ACT Res Rep 6:2–14 Ag '65. *

197. PLAPP, JON M.; PSATHAS, GEORGE; AND CAPUTO, DANIEL V. "Intellective Predictors of Success in Nursing School." Ed & Psychol Meas 25:565–77 su '65. * (PA 39:15259)

198. ROBINSON, BEVERLY VICKERSTAFF. Predicting College Grades on the Basis of College Entrance Examination Scores and Participation in Student Activities. Doctor's thesis, University of Toledo (Toledo, Ohio), 1965. (DA 26:2550)

199. ROBINSON, FRANCES K. An Investigation of the Value of the ACT Battery, the College Board Scholastic Aptitude Test, the Differential Aptitude Test Battery, and the University of Kansas Placement Battery as Predictors of University of Kansas Freshman Grades. Master's thesis, University of Kansas (Lawrence, Kan.), 1965.

200. SASSENRATH, JULIUS M., AND PUGH, RICHARD. "Relationships Among CEEB Scholastic Aptitude Test and American College Test Scores and Grade Point Average." J Ed Meas 2:199–205 D '65. *

201. SKAGER, RODNEY W.; SCHULTZ, CHARLES B.; AND KLEIN, STEPHEN P. "Quality and Quantity of Accomplishments as Measures of Creativity." J Ed Psychol 56:31–9 F '65. * (PA 39:10180)

202. STAPLES, JOHN DIXON. An Experimental Study to Identify the Basic Abilities Needed to Detect Typescript Errors With Implications for the Improvement of Instruction in Typewriting. Doctor's thesis, University of North Dakota (Grand Forks, N.D.), 1965. (DA 27:1693A)

203. STARKMAN, STANLEY S. "The Effect of Training in Reading on Performance on a Scholastic Ability Test." Psychol Sch 2:137–40 Ap '65. *

204. STRICKER, GEORGE. "Intellective and Nonintellective Correlates of Grade-Point Average." Abstract. Proc Ann Conv Am Psychol Assn 73:305–6 '65. * (PA 39:16460)

205. WATLEY, DONIVAN J. "Personal Adjustment and Prediction of Academic Achievement." J Appl Psychol 49:20–3 F '65. * (PA 39:8598)

206. WHETSTONE, ROBERT DEAN. A Tri-Group Prediction Paradigm for College Performance Based on Deviate High School Achievement. Doctor's thesis, University of Denver (Denver, Colo.), 1965. (DA 26:884)

207. AIKEN, LEWIS R. "A Composite Normograph for Predicting Achievement in College." J Ed Res 60:127–9 N '66. *

208. BAER, DANIEL J. "Scholastic Aptitude and Smoking Attitude and Behavior of College Males." J Psychol 64:63–8 S '66. * (PA 40:12589)

209. BEHRING, DANIEL W. "Activities and Academic Achievement." Personnel & Guid J 44:734–7 Mr '66. * (PA 40:7199)

210. BELL, EVERETTE LYLE. Factors Relating to Employment of Graduates of Des Moines Technical High School. Doctor's thesis, Iowa State University (Ames, Iowa), 1966. (DA 27:892A)

211. CAMPBELL, JAMES PATRICK. A Multivariate Analysis of the Relationship of Selected Academic Interest and Aptitude Variables in Choice of Major Field. Doctor's thesis, Temple University (Philadelphia, Pa.), 1966. (DA 27:3663B)

212. CHASE, CLINTON I., AND BARRITT, L. SPENCER. "A Table of Concordance Between ACT and SAT." J Col Stud Personnel 7:105–8 Mr '66. * Comment by William H. Angoff and reply by the authors, 7:194–6 Jl '66. *

213. CRADDICK, RAY A. "Effect of Season of Birth on Achievement of College Students." Psychol Rep 18:329–30 F '66. * (PA 40:6625)

214. DICKEY, OUIDA WORD. A Study of the Effects of Three Schedules of Reinforcement Upon Achievement and Retention in a Linear Program in College Business Mathematics. Doctor's thesis, University of Georgia (Athens, Ga.), 1966. (DA 27:3363A)

215. FITZPATRICK, MARY REPARATRICE. A Study of Cognitive Factors as Evidenced in the College Board SAT Scores of Seniors in a Suburban Catholic High School. Doctor's thesis, Fordham University (New York, N.Y.), 1966. (DA 27:389A)

216. FLORA, LARRY DALE. Predicting Academic Success at Lynchburg College From Multiple Correlational Analysis of Four Selected Predictor Variables. Doctor's thesis, University of Virginia (Charlottesville, Va.), 1966. (DA 27:2276A) (Abstract: Ed R 4:53–5)

217. HALLADAY, ROY ELDON. The Effect of Certain Subcultural Background Factors on the Prediction of Grades at the University of Michigan. Doctor's thesis, Michigan State University (East Lansing, Mich.), 1966. (DA 27:2780A)

218. IRVINE, DONALD W. "Multiple Prediction of College Graduation From Pre-Admission Data." J Exp Ed 35:84–9 f '66. *

219. IVEY, ALLEN E.; PETERSON, FLOYD E.; AND TREBBE, E. STEWART. "The Personality Record as a Predictor of College Attrition: A Discriminant Analysis." Col & Univ 41:199–205 w '66. *

220. JACOBS, PAUL I. "Large Score Changes on the Scholastic Aptitude Test." Personnel & Guid J 45:150–6 O '66. * (PA 41:1004)

221. JEX, FRANK B. Predicting Academic Success Beyond High School. Salt Lake City, Utah: University of Utah Bookstore, 1966. Pp. vi, 41. *

222. JUDGE, ELLEN M. A Comparison of One Non-Accelerated and Two Accelerated Mathematics Programs on Achievement Scores of the Scholastic Aptitude Tests. Master's thesis, Marywood College (Scranton, Pa.), 1966.

223. KANTROWITZ, JUDY LEOPOLD. The Effects of Crisis on Academic Achievement. Doctor's thesis, Boston University (Boston, Mass.), 1966. (DA 27:1623B)

224. LINS, L. JOSEPH; ABELL, ALLAN P.; AND HUTCHINS, H. CLIFTON. "Relative Usefulness in Predicting Academic Success of the ACT, the SAT, and Some Other Variables." J Exp Ed 35:1–29 w '66. *

225. MALCOLM, RICHARD WARD. An Analysis of Selected Conditional Admissions at the University of Southern California. Doctor's thesis, University of Southern California (Los Angeles, Calif.), 1966. (DA 27:115A)

226. MEADOWS, MARK EUGENE. A Comparative Study of Selected Characteristics of Counseled and Non-Counseled Students in a College Counseling Center. Doctor's thesis, University of Georgia (Athens, Ga.), 1966. (DA 27:2404A)

227. NELSEN, EDWARD A., AND MACCOBY, ELEANOR E. "The Relationship Between Social Development and Differential Abilities on the Scholastic Aptitude Test." Merrill-Palmer Q 12:269–84 O '66. * (PA 41:5953)

228. O'ZEE, WILLIAM FREDERICK. A Study of College Predictors for Opportunity Program Participants at Colorado State University. Doctor's thesis, Colorado State College (Greeley, Colo.), 1966. (DA 27:3729A)

229. PRIEN, ERICH P., AND BOTWIN, DAVID E. "The Reliability and Correlates of an Achievement Index." Ed & Psychol Meas 26:1047–52 w '66. * (PA 41:4998)

230. ROWE, LAURA M. The Predictive Value of the College Entrance Examination Board's Scholastic Aptitude Verbal Test Score and High School Index in Determining the Academic Performance of College Arts and Sciences Freshmen. Master's thesis, American University (Washington, D.C.), 1966.

231. SASSENRATH, JULIUS M., AND PUGH, RICHARD. "Note: Relationships Among CEEB Scholastic Aptitude Test and American College Test Scores and Grade Point Average: A Replication." J Ed Meas 3:37–8 sp '66. *

232. SAUNDERS, H. REED. A Comparison of Multiple Regression, Predictive Pattern and Bayes Techniques for the Prediction of College Grades. Doctor's thesis, University of Wisconsin (Madison, Wis.), 1966. (DA 28:507A)

233. STOVALL, EULA MAE. Sex Differences in Learning a Complex Motor Task. Doctor's thesis, University of Southern California (Los Angeles, Calif.), 1966. (DA 26:7149)

234. SULLIVAN, GERTRUDE VERONICA. A Study of Predictive Factors and the College Success of Above and Below 110 IQ Large-City Public School Graduates Attending Local Colleges and Universities. Doctor's thesis, Temple University (Philadelphia, Pa.), 1966. (DA 27:889A)

235. TATHAM, CLIFFORD B., AND DOLE, ARTHUR A. "Academic Success of Foreign Undergraduates." J Col Stud Personnel 7:167–71 My '66. *

236. WEBB, SAM C. "Estimating Gains in Scholastic Aptitude Test Scores Attributable to Three Sources." Ed & Psychol Meas 26:633–41 au '66. *

237. Manual of Freshman Class Profiles, 1967–69. Princeton, N.J.: College Entrance Examination Board, 1967. Pp. xvi, 1242. *

238. Normative Data for the 1965–66 Freshman Class, University System of Georgia. Atlanta, Ga.: Regents of the University System of Georgia, December 1967. Pp. xi, 72. *

239. BENSON, PURNELL H. "Multiple-Regression Analysis of a Paired-Choice Division-of-Time Inventory in Relation to Grade-Point Average." J Appl Psychol 51:82–8 F '67. * (PA 41:4965)

240. BUTZOW, JOHN W., AND WILLIAMS, CLARENCE M. "College Freshman Achievement of Parochial and Public Secondary School Graduates." J Ed Res 60:215–7 Ja '67. *

241. CANNING, HELEN, AND MAYER, JEAN. "Obesity: An Influence on High School Performance?" Am J Clin Nutr 20:352–4 Ap '67. *

242. COFFMAN, WILLIAM E., AND PARRY, MARY ELLEN. "Effects of an Accelerated Reading Course on SAT-V Scores." Personnel & Guid J 46:292–6 N '67. * (PA 42:4481)

243. COLE, CHARLES W., AND MILLER, C. DEAN. "Relevance of Expressed Values to Academic Performance." J Counsel Psychol 14:272–6 My '67. * (PA 41:9363)

244. DOWD, ROBERT JOHN. Divergent Thinking as a Factor

Related to Achievement in College. Doctor's thesis, University of Connecticut (Storrs, Conn.), 1967. (*DA* 28:3993A)

245. FLOYD, WILLIAM A. "Longitudinal Study of the Scholastic Aptitude Test as a Predictor of College Success." *Sch Counselor* 14:138–42 Ja '67. *

246. FRIELDS, SUSAN IRENE. *A Comparison of the Relationships of the PSAT and SAT Test Scores for the Students of North Haven High School: 1965 and 1966.* Master's thesis, Southern Connecticut State College (New Haven, Conn.), 1967.

247. GALLESSICH, JUNE MARIE. *Factors Associated With Academic Success of Freshmen Engineering Students of the University of Texas.* Doctor's thesis, University of Texas (Austin, Tex.), 1967. (*DA* 28:1677A)

248. GARMS, JOE DEWAYNE. *Predicting Scholastic Achievement With Nonintellectual Variables.* Doctor's thesis, Texas Technological College (Lubbock, Tex.), 1967. (*DA* 28:3460B)

249. GERRY, ROBERT. *Computer-Learner Interaction in Problem Solving Tasks.* Doctor's thesis, University of Texas (Austin, Tex.), 1967. (*DA* 28:3997A)

250. HARRIS, JOHN, AND REITZEL, JOHN. "Negro Freshman Performance in a Predominantly Non-Negro University." *J Col Stud Personnel* 8:366–7 N 67. *

251. HILTON, THOMAS L., AND MYERS, ALBERT E. "Personal Background, Experience and School Achievement: An Investigation of the Contribution of Questionnaire Data to Academic Prediction." *J Ed Meas* 4:69–80 su '67. * (*PA* 42:4570)

252. JANSEN, DAVID G. "Verbal and Reading Skills of Students Participating in a University Reading and Study Skills Program." *J Col Stud Personnel* 8:181–4 My '67. *

253. KEENEN, CHARLES BENJAMIN. *Predicting Completion in a College of Liberal Arts by Content Analysis of the Candidate's Personal Application Statement.* Doctor's thesis, Boston University (Boston, Mass.), 1967. (*DA* 29:4285A)

254. KEESEE, CURTIS GORDON, JR. *The Relationship of Performance on the Scholastic Aptitude Test, the Meier Art Judgment Test, and the Graves Design Judgment Test to Successful Completion of Freshmen Commercial Art Courses.* Doctor's thesis, University of Virginia (Charlottesville, Va.), 1967. (*DA* 28:2516A) (Abstract: *Ed R* 5:58–60)

255. KENDRICK, S. A. "The Coming Segregation of Our Selective Colleges." *Col Board R* 66:6–13 w '67–68. *

256. KENDRICK, S. A. "When SAT Scores Go Down." *Col Board R* 64:5–11 su '67. *

257. LEATHERS, ROGER K. *A Study of the Relationships Between Physical Performance and Academic Achievement of Springfield College Students.* Doctor's thesis, Springfield College (Springfield, Mass.), 1967.

258. MAGOON, ROBERT ARNOLD. *The Prediction of Freshman Academic Performance in an Urban Southern College.* Doctor's thesis, University of Virginia (Charlottesville, Va.), 1967. (*DA* 28:3371A)

259. MEDNICK, MARTHA T., AND ANDREWS, FRANK M. "Creative Thinking and Level of Intelligence." *J Creative Behav* 1:428–31 f '67. *

260. PASSONS, WILLIAM R. "Predictive Validities of the ACT, SAT and High School Grades for First Semester GPA and Freshman Courses." *Ed & Psychol Meas* 27:1143–4 w '67. * (*PA* 42:9427)

261. PAYNE, DAVID A., AND VAUGHN, HAROLD A. "Forecasting Italian Language Proficiency of Culturally Immersed Students." *Mod Lang J* 51:3–6 Ja '67. *

262. RANGE, LEO HARRY. *A Comparison of ACT and SAT Standard Scores.* Master's thesis, St. Louis University (St. Louis, Mo.), 1967.

263. SACHTLEBEN, CLYDE CLINTON. *An Analysis of Selected Background Variables Which Affect Success in Physics in Liberal Arts Colleges.* Doctor's thesis, University of Iowa (Iowa City, Iowa), 1967. (*DA* 28:470A)

264. SASSENRATH, J. M. "Anxiety, Aptitude, Attitude, and Achievement." *Psychol Sch* 4:341–6 O '67. * (*PA* 42:2949)

265. STANLEY, J. C. "Further Evidence via the Analysis of Variance That Women Are More Predictable Academically Than Men." *Ont J Ed Res* 10:49–56 au '67. * (*PA* 42:6157)

266. STANLEY, JULIAN C., AND PORTER, ANDREW C. "Correlation of Scholastic Aptitude Test Score With College Grades for Negroes Versus Whites." *J Ed Meas* 4:199–218 w '67. * (*PA* 42:11210)

267. STEWART, CAROL J. *The Reliability and Validity of High School Grades and Scholastic Aptitude Test Scores for Predicting Freshman Success at Westminster College.* Master's thesis, University of Utah (Salt Lake City, Utah), 1967.

268. STIX, DANIEL L. "Discrepant Achievement in College as a Function of Anxiety and Repression." *Personnel & Guid J* 45:804–7 Ap '67. * (*PA* 41:12494)

269. SUTTER, EMILY MAY GEESEMAN. *Individual Differences and Social Conditions as They Affect Learning by Computer-Assisted Instruction.* Doctor's thesis, University of Texas (Austin, Tex.), 1967. (*DA* 28:4012A)

270. WALBERG, HERBERT J. "Scholastic Aptitude, the National Teacher Examinations, and Teaching Success." *J Ed Res* 61:129–31 N '67. *

271. WALTERS, NANCY ROCKHILL. *Predictive Characteristics of Depauw University Freshman Dropouts Over a Three Year Period.* Doctor's thesis, Indiana University (Bloomington, Ind.), 1967. (*DA* 28:3471A)

272. WEBB, SAM C. *The Relations of College Grades and Personal Qualities Considered Within Two Frames of Reference.* Multivariate Behavioral Research Monographs, No. 67-2. Ft. Worth, Tex.: Texas Christian University Press, 1967. Pp. 53. * (*PA* 42:9511)

273. WILLIAMS, RODNEY HOWE. *The Relationship Between the Vocational Development and Scholastic Achievement of Male College Students: A Correlational Analysis and Evaluation of the Relationship Between Scores of Vocational Maturity, Vocational Maladjustment, Intellectual Capacity, and Scholastic Index.* Doctor's thesis, New York University (New York, N.Y.), 1967. (*DA* 28:1318A)

274. WINDHOLZ, GEORGE, AND MCINTOSH, WILLIAM A. "Concurrent Validation of Guilford's Six Convergent Tests." *Ed & Psychol Meas* 27:393–400 su '67. * (*PA* 41:12843)

275. YEREMIAN, THAIS SHERMAN. *A Comparative Study of Divergent Thinking Ability and Academic Achievement of Students in the Honors Program at the University of Southern California.* Doctor's thesis, University of Southern California (Los Angeles, Calif.), 1967. (*DA* 28:109A)

276. ZIMMERMAN, WAYNE S., AND MICHAEL, WILLIAM B. "A Comparison of the Criterion-Related Validities of Three College Entrance Examinations With Different Content Emphases." *Ed & Psychol Meas* 27:407–12 su '67. * (*PA* 41:12845)

277. *Normative Data for the 1966–67 Freshman Class, University System of Georgia.* Atlanta, Ga.: Regents of the University System of Georgia, November 1968. Pp. xi, 84. *

278. AIKEN, LEWIS R., JR. "Three Alignment Charts for Use in Selective Admissions." *J Ed Res* 62:14–7 S '68. *

279. ANGOFF, WILLIAM H. "How We Calibrate College Board Scores." *Col Board R* 68:11–4 su '68. *

280. BEALS, ERNEST WESLEY. *Academic Characteristics and Academic Success Patterns of Community College Transfer Students at the University of Massachusetts.* Doctor's thesis, University of Massachusetts (Amherst, Mass.), 1968. (*DA* 29:2954A)

281. BROOKS, WINONA NOLAND. *Relationships of Variables Identified With Success in College Clothing Construction Courses: A View Toward Advanced Placement and Improved Learning.* Doctor's thesis, University of Southern California (Los Angeles, Calif.), 1968. (*DA* 29:1701A)

282. BUCKEYE, DONALD ANDREW. *The Effects of a Creative Classroom Environment on the Creative Ability of Prospective Elementary Mathematics Teachers.* Doctor's thesis, Indiana University (Bloomington, Ind.), 1968. (*DA* 29:1801A)

283. BUSZEK, BEATRICE R. "Differential Treatment of Test Scores." *Col & Univ* 43:294–307 sp '68. *

284. BUTLER, JOHN HARRISON. *Personality Factors as Correlates of Receptivity to Electronic Music.* Doctor's thesis, University of Georgia (Athens, Ga.), 1968. (*DA* 29:4514A)

285. CHASE, C. I.; PUGH, R. C.; AND LUDLOW, H. G. *Modern Language Placement: An Alternative to Testing.* Indiana University, Monograph of the Bureau of Educational Studies and Testing, Indiana Studies in Prediction, No. 10. Bloomington, Ind.: the Bureau, 1968. Pp. vii, 11. *

286. CLAWAR, HARRY J. "A Short Highly-Efficient Prediction of College Entrance Examination Board Scholastic Aptitude Test Performance." *Ed Rec B* 94:42–4 Jl '68. * (*PA* 44:21523)

287. CLEARY, T. ANNE. "Test Bias: Prediction of Grades of Negro and White Students in Integrated Colleges." *J Ed Meas* 5:115–24 su '68. *

288. CLEARY, T. ANNE, AND HILTON, THOMAS L. "An Investigation of Item Bias." *Ed & Psychol Meas* 28:61–75 sp '68. * (*PA* 42:11356)

289. COLGAN, RICHARD THOMAS. *A Longitudinal Study of the Relationship of Teacher Judgment Versus Objective Test Data With Respect to College Success.* Doctor's thesis, Southern Illinois University (Carbondale, Ill.), 1968. (*DA* 29:3413B)

290. COOK, RAYMOND L. *A Comparative Study of Scores on the CEEB Scholastic Aptitude Test Made by Graduates of Graded and Non-Graded High Schools.* Master's thesis, Stetson University (DeLand, Fla.), 1968.

291. CORSINI, RAYMOND J., AND BORGATTA, EDGAR F. "The Quick Number Test (QNT)." *J Exp Ed* 36:7–10 su '68. *

292. CROUCH, JOYCE G. *The Role of Sex, Anxiety and Independence as Moderator Variables in Achievement of College Freshmen.* Doctor's thesis, University of Tennessee (Knoxville, Tenn.), 1968. (*DA* 29:3827A)

293. DOERMANN, HUMPHREY. "Market for College Education." *Ed Rec* 49:49–57 w '68. *

294. DONNAN, HUGH. "Personality Factors Related to College Achievement and Attrition." *J Col Stud Personnel* 9:116–9 Mr '68. *

295. EVEN, ALEXANDER. *Patterns of Academic Achievement in Grade 12 Chemistry and Their Relationship to Personal Attitudinal and Environmental Factors.* Doctor's thesis, University of Toronto (Toronto, Ont., Canada), 1968. (*DAI* 31:1136A)

296. FLAUGHER, RONALD L., AND ROCK, DONALD A. "A Fixed Length Optimal Test Battery for Colleges Characterized by Diverse Aptitude Levels." *Am Ed Res J* 5:659–74 N '68. *

297. FLAUGHER, RONALD L.; MELTON, RICHARD S.; AND MYERS, CHARLES T. "Item Rearrangement Under Typical Test

Conditions." *Ed & Psychol Meas* 28:813-24 au '68. * (*PA* 43:4430)

298. FREMER, JOHN; COFFMAN, WILLIAM E.; AND TAYLOR, PHILIP H. "The College Board Scholastic Aptitude Test as a Predictor of Academic Achievement in Secondary Schools in England." *J Ed Meas* 5:235-41 f '68. * (*PA* 44:11411)

299. GAMBLE, KENNETH R., AND KELLNER, HAROLD. "Creative Functioning and Cognitive Regression." *J Pers & Social Psychol* 9:266-71 Jl '68. * (*PA* 42:13761)

300. GRAFF, ROBERT WALTER. *The Relationship of the Opinion, Attitude, and Interest Survey to College Achievement and Academic Adjustment Factors.* Doctor's thesis, State University of New York (Buffalo, N.Y.), 1968. (*DA* 29:2959A)

301. HAMM, BETTY HUGHIE. *A Study of Enrollee Characteristics in Schools of Nursing in Georgia.* Doctor's thesis, University of Georgia (Athens, Ga.), 1968. (*DA* 29:4324A)

302. HILLS, JOHN R., AND GLADNEY, MARILYN B. "Predicting Grades From Below Chance Test Scores." *J Ed Meas* 5:45-53 sp '68. *

303. HILLS, JOHN R., AND STANLEY, JULIAN C. "Prediction of Freshman Grades From SAT and From Level 4 of SCAT in Three Predominantly Negro State Colleges." Abstract. *Proc 76th Ann Conv Am Psychol Assn* 3:241-2 '68. *

304. HOWELL, JOHN J. "On the Meaning of SAT Scores Obtained by Foreign Students of Non-English Language Background." *Col & Univ* 43:225-32 w '68. *

305. HOYT, DONALD P. "Forecasting Academic Success in Specific Colleges." *ACT Res Rep* 27:1-52 Ag '68. *

306. JOHNSON, RICHARD W.; KFOCHAKIAN, SIMON V.; MORNINGSTAR, MONA; AND SOUTHWORTH, J. ALFRED. "Validation of Freshman Orientation Test Battery." *Ed & Psychol Meas* 28:437-40 su '68. * (*PA* 42:19274)

307. KIRK, CHARLES RICHARD. *The Suppression of Non-Valid Variance in Measures of Scholastic Aptitude as Predictors of Scholastic Achievement.* Doctor's thesis, Temple University (Philadelphia, Pa.), 1968. (*DA* 29:1835B)

308. KOVACS, ALBERTA ROSE. *Predicting Success in Three Selected Collegiate Schools of Nursing.* Doctor's thesis, Columbia University (New York, N.Y.), 1968. (*DAI* 31:266B)

309. LORD, FREDERIC M. "An Analysis of the Verbal Scholastic Aptitude Test Using Birnbaum's Three-Parameter Logistic Model." *Ed & Psychol Meas* 28:989-1020 w '68. * (*PA* 44:7266)

310. MCENTIRE, EVALYN M. *The Relationship Between the Scores Made on the Florida State-Wide Twelfth Grade and the Scholastic Aptitude Test by Applicants to Stetson University in 1966 and 1967.* Master's thesis, Stetson University (DeLand, Fla.), 1968.

311. MANNING, WINTON H. "The Measurement of Intellectual Capacity and Performance." *J Negro Ed* 37:258-67 su '68. *

312. MARQUETTE, ALLAN J. *A Study of the Correlation Between the Scholastic Aptitude Test and the Grade Achievement of Majors in Mathematics at Central Connecticut State College.* Master's thesis, Central Connecticut State College (New Britain, Conn.), 1968.

313. MILLER, CAROL L.; FELDHUSEN, JOHN F.; AND ASHER, J. WILLIAM. "The Prediction of State Board Examination Scores of Graduates of an Associate Degree Program." *Nursing Res* 17:555+ N-D '68. *

314. MORGAN, LEWIS B. "The 'Calculated Risks': A Study of Success." *Col & Univ* 43:203-6 w '68. *

315. MUNDAY, LEO. "Correlations Between ACT and Other Predictors of Academic Success in College." *Col & Univ* 44:67-76 f '68. *

316. PERTUSIO, CAROLYN BOYER. *A Study of the Effects of a Seminar of Test-Taking Techniques on the College Board Scores of Palmyra Area High School Students.* Master's thesis, Millersville State College (Millersville, Pa.), 1968.

317. PUGH, RICHARD C., AND SASSENRATH, JULIUS M. "Comparable Scores for the CEEB Scholastic Aptitude Test and the American College Test Program." *Meas & Eval Guid* 1:103-9 su '68. * (*PA* 44:9266)

318. RECK, MARTIN. "The Prediction of Achievement in a College Science Curriculum." *Ed & Psychol Meas* 28:943-4 au '68. * (*PA* 43:4517)

319. ROBERTS, BRUCE BEN. *The Leader, Group, and Task Variables of Leader Selection in College.* Doctor's thesis, Claremont Graduate School (Claremont, Calif.), 1968. (*DA* 29:2360A)

320. SCHOEMER, JAMES R. "The College Pushout." *Personnel & Guid J* 46:677-80 Mr '68. * (*PA* 42:16005)

321. STIMSON, ROGER C., JR. "Factor Analytic Approach to the Structural Differentiation of Description." *J Counsel Psychol* 15:301-7 Jl '68. *

322. VAUGHAN, RICHARD P. "College Dropouts: Dismissed vs. Withdrew." *Personnel & Guid J* 46:685-9 Mr '68. * (*PA* 42:16144)

323. VELDMAN, DONALD J. "Effects of Sex, Aptitudes, and Attitudes on the Academic Achievement of College Freshmen." *J Ed Meas* 5:245-9 f '68. * (*PA* 44:11403)

324. WHITLA, DEAN K. Chap. 14, "Evaluation of Decision Making: A Study of College Admissions," pp. 456-90. In his *Handbook of Measurement and Assessment in Behavioral Sciences.* Reading, Mass.: Addison-Wesley Publishing Co., Inc., 1968. Pp. xx, 508. *

325. WILLINGHAM, WARREN W. "Validity of Several Methods of Expressing High School Achievement Level." *Col & Univ* 40:49-54 f '68. *

326. WOOD, DONALD A., AND LEBOLD, WILLIAM K. "Differential and Overall Prediction of Academic Success in Engineering: The Complementary Role of DAT, SAT and HSR." *Ed & Psychol Meas* 28:1223-8 w '68. * (*PA* 44:7339)

327. ZARFOSS, NORMA J. *The Effects of the Study of Latin on SAT Verbal Scores.* Master's thesis, Millersville State College (Millersville, Pa.), 1968.

328. *Normative Data for the 1967-68 Freshman Class, University System of Georgia.* Atlanta, Ga.: Regents of the University System of Georgia, May 1969. Pp. xi, 87. *

329. *Normative Data for the 1968-69 Freshman Class, University System of Georgia.* Atlanta, Ga.: Regents of the University System of Georgia, October 1969. Pp. xi, 87. *

330. ALKER, HENRY A. "Rationality and Achievement: A Comparison of the Atkinson-McClelland and Kogan-Wallach Formulations." *J Personality* 37(2):207-24 Je '69. *

331. ALKER, HENRY A.; CARLSON, JULIA A.; AND HERMANN, MARGARET G. "Multiple-Choice Questions and Student Characteristics." *J Ed Psychol* 60(3):231-43 Je '69. * (*PA* 43:13299)

332. ANDERSON, CARL EDWIN. *A Study of Selected Psycho-Social Correlates of College Student Protesters and Non-Protesters.* Doctor's thesis, University of Maryland (College Park, Md.), 1969. (*DAI* 31:606A)

333. BECHTOLD, DONALD WILLIAM. *Dynamic Structures of Occupational Choice of High School Seniors.* Doctor's thesis, Catholic University of America (Washington, D.C.), 1969. (*DAI* 30:2322A)

334. BEHLING, MARY ALICE. *The Development of a Screening Program for the Selection and Retention of Women Physical Education Major Students.* Doctor's thesis, Florida State University (Tallahassee, Fla.), 1969. (*DAI* 30:4258A)

335. BEHRING, DANIEL WILLIAM. *Adaptive Functioning: A Rationale for the Prediction of Achievement in Nursing Education.* Doctor's thesis, Ohio University (Athens, Ohio), 1969. (*DAI* 31:1065A)

336. BRAUN, JOHN ROBERT. *The BWWM Chemistry Placement Test as a Predictor of Achievement of General Chemistry Students.* Doctor's thesis, University of Georgia (Athens, Ga.), 1969. (*DAI* 30:5394B)

337. BRODY, ERNESS B. "Intellectual Ability, Social Desirability, and Differential Teacher Effectiveness." *J Exp Ed* 38(1):13-5 f '69. *

338. BUESCHER, RUTH MARIE. *The Relationship Between Selected Noncognitive Variables and Academic Achievement of College Women in Various Fields of Study.* Doctor's thesis, Fordham University (New York, N.Y.), 1969. (*DAI* 30:1858A)

339. BURGESS, THOMAS C. "Estimating Average Freshman Class Ability From Preliminary Information." *J Col Stud Personnel* 10(3):161-3 My '69. *

340. CASSEL, RUSSELL N., AND FORSTEADT, ARDEN C. "Factorial Structure of CQT, ACT, and SAT Test Scores for 50 Available College Freshmen." *J Psychol* 71(2):199-204 Mr '69. * (*PA* 43:8675)

341. CHASTAIN, KENNETH. "Prediction of Success in Audio-Lingual and Cognitive Classes." *Lang Learning* 19(1-2):27-39 Je '69. *

342. CHERRY, ADA LOU. *A Comparison of Selected Characteristics of Graduated Students and Academically Disqualified Students Who Were Admitted With Warning to Ball State University Autumns, 1963 and 1964.* Doctor's thesis, Ball State University (Muncie, Ind.), 1969. (*DAI* 30:4217A)

343. CONLEY, HAROLD W. *The Analyses of the Academic Performance of "High Risk" and "Regular Admit" Negro Students Within a College Freshman Class.* Doctor's thesis, University of Connecticut (Storrs, Conn.), 1969. (*DAI* 30:577A)

344. DICKASON, DONALD G. "Predicting the Success of Freshman Engineers." *Personnel & Guid J* 47(10):1008-14 Je '69. * (*PA* 44:1369)

345. ESSER, BARBARA FELLER. *The Changing Relationship Between Verbal and Quantitative Aptitudes as Measured by the Scholastic Aptitude Test.* Doctor's thesis, Rutgers—The State University (New Brunswick, N.J.), 1969. (*DAI* 30:3780A)

346. EVANS, JAMES D. "The Relationships of Three Personality Scales to Grade Point Average and Verbal Ability in College Freshmen." *J Ed Res* 63(3):121-5 N '69. *

347. FLAUGHER, RONALD L., AND ROCK, DONALD A. "A Multiple Moderator Approach to the Identification of Over- and Underachievers." *J Ed Meas* 6(4):223-8 w '69. * (*PA* 44:17516)

348. HARVILLE, DENNIS L. "Early Identification of Potential Leaders." *J Col Stud Personnel* 10(4):333-5 S '69. *

349. HOWLETT, JOHN L. "A Study of Placement Methods for Entering College Freshmen in the Proper Mathematics Sequence at Michigan Technological University." *Math Teach* 62(8):651-9 D '69. *

350. JUDD, LARRY R., AND SMITH, CAROLYN. "Predicting

Success in the Basic College Speech Course." *Speech Teach* 18(1):13–7 Ja '69. *

351. KARAS, SHAWKY F. "Development of a Reduced Set of Composite Equations for Three Predictors." *Psychol Rep* 25(2):623–30 O '69. * (*PA* 44:5710)

352. KARLINS, MARVIN; SCHUERHOFF, CHARLES; AND KAPLAN, MARTIN. "Some Factors Related to Architectural Creativity in Graduating Architecture Students." *J General Psychol* 81(2):203–15 O '69. * (*PA* 44:6775)

353. LEE, ESSIE ELIZABETH. *The Examination and Evaluation of the Educational Experiences of "Risk Students" at an Urban Community College.* Doctor's thesis, Columbia University (New York, N.Y.), 1969. (*DAI* 30:3730A)

354. MAGRAB, PHYLLIS R. *Expectation-Press Congruence as a Psychological Variable in the Prediction of College Adaptation.* Doctor's thesis, University of Maryland (College Park, Md.), 1969. (*DAI* 30:5290A)

355. MILLER, DORIS METZGER, AND O'CONNOR, PATRICIA. "Achiever Personality and Academic Success Among Disadvantaged College Students." *J Social Issues* 25(3):103–16 su '69. *

356. NELSON, BRUCE EDWARD. *The Relationship of Mathematics in Oregon High Schools to Placement and Success in First-Year Mathematics at Oregon State University.* Doctor's thesis, Oregon State University (Corvallis, Ore.), 1969. (*DAI* 30:1401A)

357. NOTESTINE, EARL BRANDON. *A Comparative Study of Student Retention and Withdrawal in the School of Humanities, Social Science, and Education at Purdue University.* Doctor's thesis, Purdue University (Lafayette, Ind.), 1969. (*DAI* 30:1402A)

358. PREAS, NANCY BUSH. *A Study of the Relationship Between Selected Variables and Academic Achievement in a Community College.* Doctor's thesis, North Carolina State University (Raleigh, N.C.), 1969. (*DAI* 30:5245A)

359. PRICE, RICHARD LIONEL. *Scholastic Aptitude Test in Mathematics as a Predictor of Student Selection of Algebraic Versus Geometric Approaches to Problem Solving.* Doctor's thesis, Ohio State University (Columbus, Ohio), 1969. (*DAI* 30:4340A)

360. PUGH, RICHARD C.; HUTCHCRAFT, GILBERT; AND LUDLOW, H. GLENN. *An Analysis of Achievement Behavior in Selected Mathematics Courses.* Indiana Studies in Prediction No. 12. Bloomington, Ind.: Bureau of Educational Studies and Testing, Indiana University, August 1969. Pp. xiii, 42. *

361. REELING, PATRICIA ANN. *Undergraduate Female Students as Potential Recruits to the Library Profession.* Doctor's thesis, Columbia University (New York, N.Y.), 1969. (*DAI* 30:4470A)

362. ROBERTS, S. OLIVER; HORTON, CARRELL P.; AND ROBERTS, BARBARA T. "SAT Versus GRE Performance of Negro American College Students." Abstract. *Proc 77th Ann Conv Am Psychol Assn* 4(1):177–8 '69. * (*PA* 43:17912)

363. SHERRON, RONALD HOMER. *A Study of Academic and Nonacademic Predictors and Criteria of Success Among the Morehead Scholars at the University of North Carolina at Chapel Hill.* Doctor's thesis, University of North Carolina (Chapel Hill, N.C.), 1969. (*DAI* 30:3287A)

364. SIEGEL, ARTHUR I., AND PFEIFFER, MARK G. "Predicting Academic Success Through Application of Theory of Signal Detectability Variables." Abstract. *Proc 77th Ann Conv Am Psychol Assn* 4(1):145–6 '69. * (*PA* 43:17990)

365. SIEVEKING, NICHOLAS A., AND SAVITSKY, JEFFREY C. "Evaluation of an Achievement Test, Prediction of Grades, and Composition of Discussion Groups in College Chemistry." *J Res Sci Teach* 6(4):374–6 '69. *

366. SOCKLOFF, ALAN LEONARD. *The Analysis of Student Characteristics Associated With Grades for Varying Levels of College Freshman Grade Complexity.* Doctor's thesis, Emory University (Atlanta, Ga.), 1969. (*DAI* 31:903B)

367. SPIEGEL, JOSEPH A. *Test Score Performance on Irish and Italian College Freshmen.* Doctor's thesis, Rutgers—The State University (New Brunswick, N.J.), 1969. (*DAI* 30:3802A)

368. STONE, MICHAEL HORACE. *A Study of the Relationships Between Selected Variables and the Differential Academic Achievement of Freshmen in the University of Michigan School of Music.* Doctor's thesis, University of Michigan (Ann Arbor, Mich.), 1969. (*DAI* 30:1881A)

369. SZABO, MICHAEL. *The Relationship of Intellective, Personality, and Biographical Variables to Success and Its Prediction in an Independent Study Science Course at the College Level.* Doctor's thesis, Purdue University (Lafayette, Ind.), 1969. (*DAI* 30:4845A)

370. THOMAS, CHARLES LEO, AND STANLEY, JULIAN C. "Effectiveness of High School Grades for Predicting College Grades of Black Students: A Review and Discussion." *J Ed Meas* 6(4):203–15 w '69. * (*PA* 44:17514)

371. TOBIAS, SIGMUND. "Effect of Creativity, Response Mode, and Subject Matter Familiarity on Achievement From Programmed Instruction." *J Ed Psychol* 60(6):453–60 D '69. *

372. UTGARD, RUSSELL O. *Verbal Behavior of Recitation Teachers and Achievement of College Geology Students.* Doctor's thesis, Indiana University (Bloomington, Ind.), 1969. (*DAI* 30:4294A)

373. WATLEY, DONIVAN J. "Career Progress: A Longitudinal Study of Gifted Students." *J Counsel Psychol* 16(2):100–8 Mr '69. * (*PA* 43:10379)

374. WATSON, LARRY WAYNE. *The Relationship of the Mathematical Course Work of Teachers and the SAT-M Scores of Their Students.* Doctor's thesis, Duke University (Durham, N.C.), 1969. (*DAI* 30:2892A)

375. ZIMMERMAN, JOHN JAMES. *Relationships Among Scholastic Aptitude, Attitudes Toward Various Facets of College Life, and Academic Performance of Students at Lycoming College.* Doctor's thesis, Pennsylvania State University (University Park, Pa.), 1969. (*DAI* 30:4792A)

376. ADINOLFI, ALLEN A. "Characteristics of Highly Accepted, Highly Rejected, and Relatively Unknown University Freshmen." *J Counsel Psychol* 17(5):456–64 S '70. * (*PA* 45:2994)

377. BRODY, E. B. "The Effects of Creativity and Intelligence on Teacher Ratings." *Brit J Ed Psychol* 40(3):342–4 N '70. * (*PA* 45:7036)

378. BROTHERS, CASSANDRA THESAURUS. *The Construction, Validation, Analysis, Evaluation and Comparison of Scales for Predicting Academic Success in College.* Doctor's thesis, University of Houston (Houston, Tex.), 1970. (*DAI* 31:2953B)

379. BROWN, JANE LIGHTCAP, AND LIGHTSEY, RALPH. "Differential Predictive Validity of SAT Scores for Freshman College English." *Ed & Psychol Meas* 30(4):961–5 w '70. *

380. CAMPANILE, SALVATORE C. *Prediction of Academic Success and Description of Students in a Comprehensive Community College.* Doctor's thesis, Rutgers—The State University (New Brunswick, N.J.), 1970. (*DAI* 31:3331A)

381. CAMPBELL, DAVID P. "Report on Twenty Year Study of Dartmouth Freshmen Completing the Strong Vocational Interest Blank and Scholastic Aptitude Test." *Col & Univ* 45(4):585–605 su '70. *

382. CENTRA, JOHN A., AND LINN, ROBERT L. "On Interpreting Students' Perceptions of Their College Environments." *Meas & Eval Guid* 3(2):102–9 su '70. * (*PA* 45:12~5)

383. CENTRA, JOHN A.; LINN, ROBERT L.; AND PARRY, MARY ELLEN. "Academic Growth in Predominantly Negro and Predominantly White Colleges." *Am Ed Res J* 7(1):83–98 Ja '70. *

384. CHASE, CLINTON I., AND HEMMETER, JOHN T. *A Characterization of Honors Students.* Indiana Studies in Prediction No. 14. Bloomington, Ind.: Bureau of Educational Studies and Testing, 1970. Pp. vii, 26. *

385. COLLEGE ENTRANCE EXAMINATION BOARD. *College Board Score Reports: A Guide for Counselors and Admissions Officers: Preliminary Scholastic Aptitude Test, Scholastic Aptitude Test, and Achievement Tests.* Princeton, N.J.: the Board, 1970. Pp. 37. *

386. COLLEGE ENTRANCE EXAMINATION BOARD, COMMISSION ON TESTS, DAVID V. TIEDEMAN, CHAIRMAN. *Report of the Commission on Tests: Vol. 1, Righting the Balance; Vol. 2, Briefs.* Princeton, N.J.: College Entrance Examination Board, 1970. Pp. xvi, 118; x, 194. *

387. COMBS, HARRISON TYLER, JR. *An Investigation of the Relationship Between the Academic Achievement Scale of the Strong Vocational Interest Blank and First Year Academic Achievement in College.* Doctor's thesis, University of South Carolina (Columbia, S.C.), 1970. (*DAI* 31:3262A)

388. DELAURETIS, ROBERT J.; LEBOLD, WILLIAM K.; AND MOLNAR, GEORGE E. "A Multiple-Regressional Analysis of the Complementary Roles of Cognitive and Noncognitive Measures of Engineering Behavior." Abstract. *Proc 78th Ann Conv Am Psychol Assn* 5(2):607–8 '70. * (*PA* 44:19532)

389. DOMINO, GEORGE. "Interactive Effects of Achievement Orientation and Teaching Style on Academic Achievement." *ACT Res Rep* 39:1–9 D '70. *

390. DUNN, DAVID CAMERON. *Scholastic Aptitude and Vocational Interest as Factors in the Selection of Entering Students in the School of Hotel Administration at Cornell University.* Doctor's thesis, Cornell University (Ithaca, N.Y.), 1970. (*DAI* 31:953A)

391. FRICKE, BENNO G. "Creative Writing Course Grades, OAIS Creative Personality Test Scores, and Other Assessment Measures." Abstract. *Proc 78th Ann Conv Am Psychol Assn* 5(2):617–8 '70. * (*PA* 44:19533)

392. FUJITA, GEORGE Y., AND O'REILLY, JOSEPH P. "A Two-Stage Sequential Strategy in the Placement of Students in an Undergraduate Curriculum." *J Res Math Ed* 1(4):241–50 N '70. *

393. HARTNETT, RODNEY T. "Differences in Selected Attitudes and College Orientations Between Black Students Attending Traditionally Negro and Traditionally White Institutions." Abstract. *Proc 78th Ann Conv Am Psychol Assn* 5(2):609–10 '70. * (*PA* 44:19340)

394. HIGHLEY, FRANK S. "Verbal Ability, Quantitative Ability, and the Rod-and-Frame Test." *Percept & Motor Skills* 30(3):95–8 Je '70. * (*PA* 44:15715)

395. HILLS, JOHN R., AND STANLEY, JULIAN C. "Easier Test Improves Prediction of Black Students' College Grades." *J Negro Ed* 39(4):320–4 f '70. * (*PA* 45:10957)

396. IHLANFELDT, WILLIAM IVAN. *Personal Characteristics of Satisfied and Non-Satisfied Northwestern University Students.* Doctor's thesis, Northwestern University (Evanston, Ill.), 1970. (*DAI* 31:3293A)

397. JONES, JOHN G., AND GRIENEEKS, LAURABETH. "Meas-

ures of Self-Perception as Predictors of Scholastic Achievement." *J Ed Res* 63(5):201-3 Ja '70. * (*PA* 46:5702)
398. JORDAN, MARY LOU, AND MICHAEL, WILLIAM B. "An Evaluation of the Resident Honors Program for High School Seniors at the University of Southern California 1961-1967." *Ed & Psychol Meas* 30(4):977-82 w '70. *
399. LEMAY, MORRIS. "Birth Order and Scholastic Aptitude and Achievement." Abstract. *J Consult & Clin Psychol* 34(2):287 Ap '70. * (*PA* 44:11388)
400. LIN, YI-GUANG, AND MCKEACHIE, WILBERT J. "Aptitude, Anxiety, Study Habits, and Academic Achievement." *J Counsel Psychol* 1-(4):306-9 Jl '70. * (*PA* 44:21601)
401. LYDEN, BARBARA A. *A Study of the Validity of SAT Scores in Mathematics Placement and the Effectiveness of Remedial Instruction for Students With Low SAT Scores.* Master's thesis, Virginia State College (Petersburg, Va.), 1970.
402. MAIER, NORMAN R. F., AND CASSELMAN, GERTRUDE G. "The SAT as a Measure of Problem-Solving Ability in Males and Females." *Psychol Rep* 26(3):927-39 Je '70. * (*PA* 45:1287)
403. NICHOLSON, EVERARD. *Final Report of the Study of Success and Admission Criteria for Potentially Successful Risks.* Providence, R.I.: Brown University, 1970. Pp. iv, 264. *
404. PUGH, RICHARD C., AND MORGAN, JAMES M. *Predicting Success for University Freshmen.* Indiana Studies in Prediction, No. 1, Supplement 3. Bloomington, Ind.: Bureau of Educational Studies and Testing, Indiana University, February 1970. Pp. 8. *
405. REINER, JOHN R. "Students' Academic Ability and Perceptions of College Environment." *J Exp Ed* 38(3):69-71 sp '70. *
406. ROCK, DONALD A.; CENTRA, JOHN A.; AND LINN, ROBERT L. "Relationships Between College Characteristics and Student Achievement." *Am Ed Res J* 7(1):109-21 Ja '70. *
407. SHERRON, RONALD H. "A Study of Academic and Nonacademic Predictors and Criteria of Success Among Scholarship Recipients." *J Exp Ed* 38(3):72-82 sp '70. *
408. SKINNER, SAMUEL BALLOU. *A Study of the Effect of the St. Andrews Presbyterian College Natural Science Course Upon Critical Thinking Ability.* Doctor's thesis, University of North Carolina (Chapel Hill, N.C.), 1970. (*DAI* 31:3984A)
409. STEININGER, MARION. "Aptitude, Dogmatism, and College Press as Codeterminants of Academic Achievement." *J Social Psychol* 80(2):229-30 Ap '70. * (*PA* 44:15462)
410. STRAHAN, ROBERT. "More on Correlates of Success in Undergraduate Statistics." Letter. *Am Psychologist* 25(12):1175-6 D '70. *
411. STROUP, ATLEE L. "The Prediction of Academic Performance From Personality and Aptitude Variables." *J Exp Ed* 38(3):83-6 sp '70. *
412. VROMAN, CLYDE, AND WILCOX, LEE. "Research on A.I.D. Sponsored Foreign Students." *Col & Univ* 45(4):717-23 su '70. *
413. WEISS, KENNETH P. "A Multi-Factor Admissions Predictive System." *Col & Univ* 45(2):203-10 w '70. *
414. WILLIS, CARL G., AND NICHOLSON, JAMES. "Series II SCAT as a College Aptitude Measure." *Ed & Psychol Meas* 30(4):971-5 w '70. *
415. ANGOFF, WILLIAM H., EDITOR. *The College Board Admissions Testing Program: A Technical Report on Research and Development Activities Relating to the Scholastic Aptitude Test and Achievement Tests.* New York: College Entrance Examination Board, 1971. Pp. xv, 181. *
416. DONLON, THOMAS F., AND ANGOFF, WILLIAM H. Chap. 2, "The Scholastic Aptitude Test," pp. 15-47. In *The College Board Admissions Testing Program*, see 415. *
417. FREMER, JOHN, AND CHANDLER, MARJORIE O. Chap. 6, "Special Studies," pp. 147-81. In *The College Board Admissions Testing Program*, see 415. *
418. SCHRADER, W. B. Chap. 5, "The Predictive Validity of College Board Admissions Tests," pp. 117-45. In *The College Board Admissions Testing Program*, see 415. *
419. SCHRADER, W. B., AND STEWART, E. ELIZABETH. Chap. 4, "Descriptive Statistics on College Board Candidates and Other Reference Groups," pp. 79-115. In *The College Board Admissions Testing Program*, see 415. *

PHILIP H. DUBOIS, *Professor of Psychology, Washington University, St. Louis, Missouri.*

The *College Board Scholastic Aptitude Test* probably is not the test that has been taken by the largest number of individuals in the history of testing. In respect to use, it is outstripped by the *Army General Classification Test,* the *Armed Forces Qualification Test,* and, perhaps, by one or more of the commercially available intelligence tests which date back 40 years or more. In one respect, however, it is unquestionably outstanding. On no other test have there been expended so many man-years of planning, item writing, statistical analyses, and evaluation of its various forms.

Technically the SAT may be regarded as highly perfected—possibly reaching the pinnacle of the current state of the art of psychometrics. Actually it would be surprising if this were not so. Ever since the SAT was first administered in 1926, highly competent professional staffs have been available at all times to prepare new forms, being guided by objective findings on past administrations and on item analyses of experimental material.

Like many developments in measurement, the SAT is a direct descendant of the Army Alpha. The original plan was formulated by Robert M. Yerkes, Henry T. Moore, and Carl C. Brigham. Later Brigham became responsible for its development. A conscious effort was made to develop an instrument that would measure neither school achievement nor general mental alertness. With the passage of time, resemblance to its prototype lessened: subtests became fewer; speededness was reduced; and emphasis was placed upon two relatively homogeneous item types—verbal and mathematical. Currently the two subscores are referred to as SAT-V and SAT-M.

Even today, nearly three decades after Brigham's untimely death, the SAT continues a number of features which he initiated: (*a*) an attempt to measure "aptitude for college studies" rather than intelligence; (*b*) equating of numerous forms so that the predictive scores are stable irrespective of the time and place the student takes the test; (*c*) extensive and systematic use of item analysis; and (*d*) tryout of all new material before items are used operationally.

While the College Entrance Examination Board is responsible for the SAT, operations including test development, administration, score reports, and statistical analyses are carried out by the Educational Testing Service. The SAT is buttressed, of course, with not only an impressive array of managerial and psychometric talent but also the hardware (electronic scoring and computers) to make a magnificent program feasible. If only the hand methods used in the initial decade of the SAT were available now, the instrument either would be almost prohibitively expensive or supportive effort would have to be drastically reduced.

Items with known statistical characteristics are organized in sections requiring 30 or 45 minutes each for a total testing time of three hours. Within each block of items, arrangement is in terms of increasing difficulty, with "the mean difficulty of each block....equal to that of the test as a whole."

Test content is selected to avoid as far as possible inequities to any subclass of the intended population. The SAT-M requires as background only the mathematics taught in grades 1–9, while the SAT-V is related to social, political, scientific, artistic, philosophical, and literary areas. The earlier literary focus of the verbal items has been abandoned for a broader orientation, while the mathematical material now depends less on formal knowledge and more on "logical reasoning and....the perception of mathematical relationships."

As is well known, SAT scores are reported with mean 500 and standard deviation 100. It is not so well known that the standardization group consists of 10,654 students who took the test in April, 1941. Through somewhat involved methods, the various forms are equated accurately to one another and to the form yielding the initial norms.

Ask for any conventional statistic about the SAT and one can be practically certain that it will be available: reliabilities, validity coefficients, and item data. Not only are they available but they also reflect highly competent workmanship and are amazingly consistent from year to year, even though the program as a whole has undergone changes in conception and execution.

The internal consistency reliability estimates for 12 recent forms cluster closely around .91 and .90 for the verbal and mathematical scores, respectively; the parallel-form reliabilities average two points lower. In the 1950's the average correlation between the two parts was in the middle .50's; more recently, it has been in the high .60's, possibly reflecting a decreasing emphasis on specific knowledge in the two areas.

From the beginning, the SAT has been found to have reasonably good validities for predicting college achievement. Also it has been found consistently that the SAT increases the validity of the high school average or rank. Studies made in 1927 showed a median validity of the school record of .52, a median validity of the SAT of .34, and of the combination of both, .55.

For 38 years, most validity studies were made by participating colleges, but in 1964 the College Board Validity Study Service relieved the colleges of this chore.

Currently, typical validities are .39 for SAT-V, .33 for SAT-M, .55 for the high school record, with a multiple correlation of the order of .62. The picture today is not greatly changed from that in 1927 except that both SAT validities and school grade validities have increased, and the increment of the SAT over the high school record is a little greater than it was.

For schools of engineering, science, business, education, and liberal arts, the high school record is more valid than the SAT, but the SAT supplements the high school record with additional valid variance. Except in engineering, the SAT-V is generally more predictive than the SAT-M.

A somewhat surprising heritage from the past is the reliance on formulas for the correction of guessing. Although ETS has done some pertinent empirical studies, the studies seem to have been oriented more toward logical considerations and the effects of instructions on guessing behavior than toward validity. If wrong and right answers on the SAT measure different characteristics, this fact should be determinable in prediction studies. Few, if any, investigators have ever reported useful variance in the wrong answers on psychometric devices except in speeded perceptual tests. The trend in measurement generally, as in the SAT, has been away from speed, but the SAT has not followed the general trend toward exclusive reliance on the rights score.

The strategy of including in each SAT test booklet a number of "variant" items has been a long-standing practice. As far as the candidate is concerned, these variant items are indistinguishable from the operational items, which are exactly the same for all who take the SAT on a given day. On the other hand, in a given examination room the booklets may have 25 different sets of variant items, which are used later for equating forms and, after appropriate analyses, as operational material. This practice apparently has made possible great stability in test characteristics from form to form, as well as permitting incorporation of innovations after their probable effect has been ascertained.

College Board Scholastic Aptitude Test

The SAT is more of a system than a test. It is a system by which information of a defined type can be made available to college admissions officers. Security precautions in test development, printing, distribution, administration, and processing of results are such that the possibility of compromise is close to zero.

The SAT is not without its detractors, some of whom regard it as a "tool of the academic establishment." Of course it is! But it is a good tool, perhaps the best that can be devised with present psychometric technology. No attempt is made to adjust SAT scores for sex, socioeconomic status, race, or educational background. In this reviewer's opinion, such attempts would be difficult to justify. Adding substantially to the prediction of academic achievement as contrasted with the use of high school grades alone, the SAT has repeatedly proved its usefulness to colleges. It helps to pick those who fit in best in the program of a particular institution, and, of course, it can be supplemented with any other information that admissions officials may wish to use.

The question has arisen of whether or not it fits the needs of the students as well as those of the colleges and universities. No good end would be served by blunting this instrument. Certainly there are many aptitudes other than verbal and mathematical that some colleges might like to know about, such as musical, spatial, mechanical, and clerical abilities. College entrance examining could be broadened so that a profile of testable characteristics adequate for educational and vocational counseling would become available. The question is one of appropriate strategy, including how much testing should be required of all students; how much optional. The College Board already has an extensive program of achievement measurement which dates back to 1900, with frequent updating both in content and in measurement methods. Obviously the CEEB program could be broadened further. But even in a broadened program the present SAT measures would be important.

WIMBURN L. WALLACE, *Director, Professional Examinations Division, The Psychological Corporation, New York, New York.*

The SAT contains verbal ability and mathematical ability sections and yields separate scores in these two areas. Its purpose is to aid in assessing students' competence for satisfactory achievement in college, and it is designed to be effective over the full range of abilities of students applying for admission to colleges which run the gamut of academic standards. It is the most widely used collegiate entrance test; over one and one-half million candidates take it each year.

A long-overdue technical report has finally been prepared for the College Board Admissions Testing Program. A manuscript of that report plus a copy of Form RSA35 of the SAT provide the principal basis for this review. The report (*415*) is an excellent document, describing in detail and with candor most or all of the relevant information about the examinations.

Although there is a continuous program of development, standardization, and application of new parallel forms of the SAT, the content and format of the test have been essentially the same for a very long time. The verbal section (SAT-V) comprises 90 items in two separately timed parts for a total of 75 minutes, and the mathematics section (SAT-M) contains 60 items, also in two parts with a total time of 75 minutes. The reason for separately timed parts within the V and M sections is not evident. Both verbal parts contain some of each item type used, namely, sentence completions, antonyms, analogies, and reading comprehension. One of the mathematics parts is entirely general mathematics problems, while the other is about half general problems and half data sufficiency type items. Reference to the M section as "Arithmetic Reasoning" is somewhat misleading, since it contains a great deal of geometry and algebra. The mathematics problems are all of the conventional variety and show little or no influence of the terminology of the "new math"; this reviewer has no quarrel with that characteristic of the test. However, the items in the M section tend to be wordy, hence potentially introducing too great a verbal influence in a section intended to provide a reasonably independent dimension of assessment from that derived from the SAT-V.

All the items appearing in the SAT appear to be carefully constructed and edited. Items are always of the 5-option, multiple choice variety and are formula scored. The system of pretesting of items, analysis, and standardization of new forms exemplifies the most sophisticated procedures in modern psychometrics. Every step in the production of successive forms is no less than meticulous, and the methods of equating forms virtually guarantee parallelism of the highest order obtainable. Every form of the SAT includes about 30 minutes of experimental work devoted to items that are either being pretested or standardized.

The layout of the SAT test booklets is satisfactory but could be simplified in the interest of clarity. For instance, mathematics items might well be more precisely separated from each other and the options could be listed in a more consistent manner for easy reference and recognition. In the SAT-V there is a frequent shift of item type which does not seem entirely justifiable. The student would not have to change set so often if all the analogies were grouped together, all the antonyms, etc. In the same vein, a study should be made to ascertain whether fewer verbal item types would be as effective as the four now used.

The investigation of, or experimentation with, various and new test types for the SAT has been sporadic. There should be a sustained, regular effort toward new test development. The traditional test and item types are described historically and in great detail in the technical report, but the rationale for their persistence is somewhat thin. Internal validation is the main or only criterion for the survival of new items, whereas the use of an external criterion, e.g., college grades, would be a desirable supplementary or substitute means of identifying potentially powerful new items. When novel test types have been tried in the SAT program, careful statistical work has accompanied the effort, and appropriate validation studies carried out. However, the new types are usually discarded on the basis that they do not add sufficiently to the predictive effectiveness of the standard measures in the SAT to justify their permanent inclusion. Rarely does the question seem to be answered as to whether some combination of different tests would do a better job of predicting collegiate academic success than the traditional V and M measures. It is possible that the ultimate was reached decades ago in the practical, efficient, effective measurement of college potential by tests with the ingredients of the SAT; but it is discouraging to contemplate a permanent plateau in the state of the art.

Most of the psychometric characteristics of the SAT are above reproach. Internal consistency reliability coefficients are regularly about .91 for SAT-V and .90 for the SAT-M for recent forms. For those who prefer another method of estimating reliability, alternate-form coefficients of correlation are provided and closely substantiate the other data at levels of about .89 for SAT-V and .88 for SAT-M.

Many thousands of validity coefficients have been calculated between SAT scores and college grades. There is no meaningful way to summarize them briefly, since they are affected by the tremendous variety of the full spectrum of characteristics of American colleges and universities. Suffice it to say that the validities are as high as have been attained with any general testing instrument in comparable settings. The technical manual reports many illustrations of results of validity studies including those based on highly selective and least selective schools, specialized curricula, specific courses, classes with wide and with narrow dispersion of abilities, and other important categories. Extensive research has also been focused on the relative validities of the SAT for male versus female students and Negro versus white students. In neither of those sets of comparisons have any important differences been found. A common feature of many of the validity studies is the separate inclusion of high school record and College Board Achievement Tests as predictors of college grades. The increment in predictive effectiveness over the SAT alone is shown in these instances. Typically the high school record adds most, as might be expected, and the well-known importance of considering both types of predictors is given full support. A major shortcoming in otherwise commendably complete validation is the paucity of information on the relative weighting due the SAT-V and the SAT-M in predicting college success. Where multiple correlations are reported they usually include high school average, or achievement test scores, or both, but do not indicate the weights for V and M. The intercorrelation between V and M has been steadily and sharply increasing during the last 25 years to an average of .67 in 1969. The value of the separate scores needs concerted scrutiny in the light of this phenomenon.

Considerable attention has been given to such problems as concern about the effects of coaching, of practice and growth, and of fatigue and anxiety. Well-documented summaries of studies of these issues indicate insignificant improvement of scores by coaching and no deleterious effects from anxiety, but do show score changes

College Board Scholastic Aptitude Test

over periods of time between testings. Although the changes over time are not surprising, extensive description of their magnitude and possible causes is provided.

Supplementary services and explanatory information for students, counselors, and admissions officers in connection with the SAT are quite appropriate to the purposes of the program. Among the special services offered at no cost to colleges, the Validity Study Service is a most valuable one in which test scores, high school grades, and other data are analyzed for their effectiveness in predicting success at the individual college. Every college participating in the SAT program should take advantage of this service, as it should indicate the appropriateness of the SAT for that school regardless of nationwide data.

The descriptive booklets are clear, straightforward explanations of the nature, purposes, content, limitations, and interpretation of the SAT. They constitute a happy balance between extremes of insufficient information and a plethora of printed matter. The typical user, be he the student, counselor, or administrator, can readily find in them answers to pertinent questions about the tests without the frustrations of verbosity in too many overlapping publications.

The supervisor's manual for administering the SAT is explicit and detailed to a fault. Although it is essential that testing conditions be as uniform as possible for all candidates, some brevity in the directions for the sake of clarity and emphasis might contribute toward that goal. However, it is evident that the huge task of organizing, administering, scoring, and reporting results for the SAT is consistently carried out with rigorous care and accuracy.

Comparison between the SAT and the American College Testing Program, the major alternative available, favors the SAT overall. Although validities against college achievement criteria are not strikingly different, the content mix, psychometric quality, and pertinent research efforts appear to be superior in the SAT. Ancillary services available with the two programs are comparable, but those with the SAT are the more succinct.

For reviews by John E. Bowers and Wayne S. Zimmerman of an earlier form, see 6:449; for a review by John T. Dailey, see 5:318; for a review by Frederick B. Davis, see 4:285.

[345]
*College Qualification Tests. Candidates for college entrance; 1955–61; CQT; 6 scores: verbal, numerical, information (science, social studies, total), total; Forms A ('56), B ('56), C ('59); 2 editions; revised manual ('61, 61 pages); distribution of Forms B and C restricted to colleges and universities; separate answer sheets (IBM 805, IBM 1230) must be used; 50¢ per manual, postage extra; George K. Bennett, Marjorie G. Bennett, Wimburn L. Wallace, and Alexander G. Wesman; Psychological Corporation. *
a) COMBINED BOOKLET EDITION. 14 pages; $5.50 per 25 tests; $3.90 per 50 IBM 805 answer sheets; $4.10 per 50 IBM 1230 answer sheets; 70¢ per set of IBM 805 hand scoring stencils; $1 per set of IBM 805 machine scoring stencils; 75¢ per set of IBM 1230 hand scoring stencils; 90¢ per specimen set; 80(105) minutes.
b) SEPARATE BOOKLET EDITION. $2.50 per 25 tests; $2 per 50 IBM 805 answer sheets; $1.20 per specimen set.
  1) *Test V [Verbal]*. 5 pages; 15(25) minutes.
  2) *Test N [Numerical]*. 6 pages; 35(45) minutes.
  3) *Test I [Information]*. 6 pages; 3 scores: science, social studies, total; 30(40) minutes.

REFERENCES

1–11. See 6:450.
12. HARTFORD, DONALD LEROY. *An Investigation of a Profile Method for Predicting College Grades From Scores of the College Qualification Tests.* Doctor's thesis, University of Kentucky (Lexington, Ky.), 1959. (DA 26:4373)
13. BUNGER, FRED ANTON. *Cultural Forces and Academic Success in College Freshmen.* Bulletin of the Bureau of School Service, College of Education, University of Kentucky, Vol. 33, No. 1. Lexington, Ky.: the Service, September 1960. Pp. 91. *
14. IKENBERRY, STANLEY O. "Factors in College Persistence." *J Counsel Psychol* 8:322–9 w '61. * (PA 37:3834)
15. COOPER, CARL J. "Some Relationships Between Paired-Associates Learning and Foreign-Language Aptitude." *J Ed Psychol* 55:132–8 Je '64. * (PA 39:5823)
16. JUOLA, ARVO E. "The Prediction of College Dropout From Freshman Level Ability Test Scores." *J Ed Meas* 1:35–7 Je '64. *
17. BOYCE, RICHARD W., AND PAXSON, R. C. "The Predictive Validity of Eleven Tests at One State College." *Ed & Psychol Meas* 25:1143–7 w '65. * (PA 40:3563)
18. ELTON, CHARLES F. "A Comparative Study of Teacher Ratings, High School Average and Measures of Personality and Aptitude in Predicting College Success." *Psychol Sch* 2:47–52 Ja '65. *
19. LEHMANN, IRVIN J. "Curricular Differences in Selected Cognitive and Affective Characteristics." *J Ed Meas* 2:103–10 Je '65. * (PA 39:15160)
20. MCKAY, WILLIAM R. "Interpersonal Relationships, a Factor in Academic Success." *Calif J Ed Res* 16:189–96 S '65. * (PA 40:1943)
21. MILLS, DAVID H. "The Relationship of Abstraction to Selected Personality and Intellectual Variables." *Psychol* 2:10–5 N '65. * (PA 40:3091)
22. JUOLA, ARVO E. "Prediction of Successive Terms Performance in College From Tests and Grades." *Am Ed Res J* 3:191–7 My '66. *
23. KAFER, LOWELL GENE. *An Analysis of Selected Characteristics and Experiences of Freshman Students in the Michigan State University Justin Morrill College.* Doctor's thesis, Michigan State University (East Lansing, Mich.), 1966. (DA 27:4043A)
24. LINS, L. JOSEPH; ABELL, ALLAN P.; AND HUTCHINS, H. CLIFTON. "Relative Usefulness in Predicting Academic Success of the ACT, the SAT, and Some Other Variables." *J Exp Ed* 35:1–29 w '66. *
25. BAUER, ROGER; MEHRENS, WILLIAM A.; AND VINSONHALER, JOHN F. "Predicting Performance in a Computer Programming Course." *Ed & Psychol Meas* 28:1159–64 w '68. * (PA 44:7333)
26. BUSZEK, BEATRICE R. "Differential Treatment of Test Scores." *Col & Univ* 43:294–307 sp '68. *
27. CORSINI, RAYMOND J., AND BORGATTA, EDGAR F. "The Quick Number Test (QNT)." *J Exp Ed* 36:7–10 su '68. *
28. GREENLAND, THOMAS CHARLES. *Some Differential Relationships of Academic Ability and Personality Factors to Academic Status as Suggested by Inter-Institutional and Intra-Institutional Analyses of the Freshman Class at Four Campuses.* Doctor's thesis, University of Kentucky (Lexington, Ky.), 1968. (DAI 30:1921B)
29. LUEPTOW, LLOYD B. "Need for Achievement and Occupational Preferences: Some Operations With Value-Orientations as Intervening Variables in Need-Goal Relationships." *Sociometry* 31:304–12 S '68. *
30. CASSEL, RUSSELL N., AND EICHSTEADT, ARDEN C. "Fac-

torial Structure of CQT, ACT, and SAT Test Scores for 50 Available College Freshmen." *J Psychol* 71(2):199–204 Mr '69. * (*PA* 43:8675)

31. DREYER, DOROTHY E. *Listening Performance Related to Selected Academic and Psychological Measures.* Doctor's thesis, Michigan State University (East Lansing, Mich.), 1969. (*DAI* 30:5735B)

32. ELTON, CHARLES F. "Patterns of Change in Personality Test Scores." *J Counsel Psychol* 16(2):95–9 Mr '69. * (*PA* 43:10296)

33. JENKINS, NORMAN LEE. *An Analysis of the Relationship Between Academic Achievement and Selected Criteria for Junior College Freshmen in Terminal and Transfer Curricula.* Doctor's thesis, Purdue University (Lafayette, Ind.), 1969. (*DAI* 30:3728A)

34. JOHNSON, RICHARD J., AND LEONARD, LOUISE C. "Psychological Test Characteristics and Performance of Nursing Students." *Nursing Res* 19(2):147–50 Mr–Ap '70. *

35. VOHS, A. P. *A Study of First-Year Academic Performance as Related to Predicted Achievement of Freshmen Enrolled in Teacher Education at John Brown University, 1968–69.* Doctor's thesis, University of Arkansas (Fayetteville, Ark.), 1970. (*DAI* 31:2713A)

For reviews by Ralph F. Berdie and Warren G. Findley, see 6:450; for reviews by Gustav J. Froehlich, A. E. G. Pilliner, and David V. Tiedeman, see 5:320.

[346]

★**Cooperative Academic Ability Test.** Superior grade 12 students; 1963–64; AAT; also published in 1966 as Level 1 of *Cooperative School and College Ability Tests: Series 2*, Forms A and B; 3 scores: verbal, mathematical, total; Forms A, B, ('63, 7 pages); manual ('64, 16 pages); administration directions ('64, 1 page); separate answer sheets (Digitek, IBM 1230) must be used; no instructions on the use of specific answer sheets; $7 per 20 tests; $4 per 100 answer sheets; $1.25 per 10 IBM 1230 scoring stencils (answer pattern must be punched out locally); Digitek scoring stencils not available; $1 per manual; $2 per specimen set; cash orders postpaid; 40(50) minutes; Cooperative Tests and Services. *

REFERENCES

1. TRAXLER, ARTHUR E. "The New Cooperative Academic Aptitude Test Compared With the American Council Psychological Examination." *Ed Rec B* 85:55–64 F '64. *
2. CLAWAR, HARRY J. "A Short Highly-Efficient Prediction of College Entrance Examination Board Scholastic Aptitude Test Performance." *Ed Rec B* 94:42–4 Jl '68. * (*PA* 44:21523)
3. CONKLIN, R. C., AND OGSTON, D. G. "Prediction of Academic Success for Freshman at the University of Calgary." *Alberta J Ed Res* 14:185–92 S '68. * (*PA* 44:4244)

ERIC F. GARDNER, *Margaret O. Slocum Professor of Education and Psychology and Chairman, Department of Psychology; and Director, Psychological Services and Research Center; Syracuse University, Syracuse, New York.*

The *Cooperative Academic Ability Test* for superior grade 12 students was published in 1963–64 following a substantial amount of experimental work on the original SCAT series published in 1955–57. The AAT was designed to perform somewhat the same function as the SCAT but to require a much shorter total time for administration. Comments by previous MMY reviewers about the effectiveness of SCAT in achieving the purposes and objectives specified are appropriate for the AAT. The AAT in contrast to SCAT includes two item types and administrative parts as compared with four in SCAT, although three scores (verbal, mathematical, and total) are presented for each test. The AAT verbal items are of the analogy type which has been used in a number of other tests. The mathematical item type is a relatively unusual format and is intended to "place a minimum emphasis on reading, to require more resourcefulness and insight than straight computation problems, and to allow presentation of more items per unit of testing time....than most of the usual mathematical item types." No data are presented to support these claims. The format involves the presentation of pairs of quantitative expressions in parallel columns. The student is asked to select one of the following four options: (*a*) whether the quantity in column A is the greater, (*b*) whether the quantity in column B is the greater, (*c*) whether the two quantities are equal, or (*d*) whether the size relationship can not be determined from the information given.

The successful experience of ETS with the *Cooperative Academic Ability Test* caused them to completely revise SCAT in 1966. In this new revision the AAT was used as the highest level test in the battery and levels for lower grades with the same type of item format were constructed.

K-R 20 reliabilities range from .78 to .88 for the verbal portion, .86 to .92 for the mathematics portion, and .89 to .94 for the total test. Although these values are reasonably adequate, they (as the manual points out) were obtained for samples selected from several schools and as such are overestimates of what the reliability would be if they were obtained from a single class within a single school. To make matters worse these values are spuriously large also because they are based on *speeded* tests. In spite of the statement in the handbook that "Table 4 reveals that the Verbal sections of forms A and B are essentially unspeeded, while the Mathematical sections of both forms are characterized by a substantial amount of drop-out," it shows that only a little over half the students in each group completed the mathematical section and less than 75 percent of one group completed the verbal section. Although the manual suggests that test users should compute reliability coefficients for their own groups, it would have been more appropriate for the manual to present reliability coefficients more comparable to those needed by schools using the test.

The use of percentile bands rather than percentile points and the deficiencies in applying them to SCAT have been discussed in previous MMY reviews. In spite of the fact that the same difficulties are present in their application to the AAT, this reviewer is highly in favor of any device which will emphasize the need for the test user to consider errors of measurement and hence commends ETS for their presentation.

In addition to equating the two forms of the AAT with each other, the same procedure was used to equate the ACE (1948 College Edition) with the AAT. Comparable scores of this type have been requested by a number of test users. However, although the manual is careful to point out that the equating was done on a fairly large sample, the question of the extent to which the variables measured by the ACE and the AAT subtests are identical is not mentioned at all. Hence, the user, not receiving this kind of warning, may be under the impression that the corresponding scores given in the table actually represent identical performance. Caution should have been given that comparable scores on different instruments may not be entirely comparable with respect to content.

In general, the AAT is a test consisting of good items selected by appropriate experimental procedures and interpreted by a handbook which is well written.

WILLIAM B. MICHAEL, *Professor of Educational Psychology and Psychology, University of Southern California, Los Angeles, California.*

Published in 1963 to furnish measures of verbal and mathematical ability of those secondary school students of superior potential who are planning to attend college, the AAT requires only about 45 minutes of total administration time, yields in addition to a verbal score and mathematical score a total general ability score, possibly shows a relatively greater emphasis on power than on speed as compared with other well-known ability tests that have been prepared and distributed by ETS, utilizes a "number right" scoring procedure, and contains only two item types and two administrative sections (verbal and mathematics)—one item type per administrative section. The professional staff at ETS had apparently been so pleased with the initial outcomes of the AAT that in 1966 they incorporated the two AAT forms into the SCAT Series 2 for grade levels 12 through 14 and constructed a third parallel form as well. Thus to gain the maximum benefit from use of the AAT one needs to consult the 1967 handbook for SCAT Series 2, as this manual contains substantial new normative information as well as additional data on validity and reliability not reported in the 1964 handbook for the AAT.

The AAT and its incorporation within the SCAT Series 2 affords an attractive alternative to other commercially available instruments employed for college admissions and selection. With little or no loss in validity and reliability, the AAT requires only 40 minutes of working time and therefore only one class period for its administration.

This favorable state of affairs has been effected through the use of only two item types. Fifty 4-choice verbal analogy items have been employed to measure an examinee's understanding of words. It is apparent that each of these insightfully constructed and carefully pretested items demands a fine degree of discrimination on the part of the examinee. The other item type represented by 4-choice alternatives in the mathematics section constitutes an important innovation in test construction and probably a major breakthrough both in maximizing the reliability of a relatively short test in quantitative reasoning and in minimizing the amount of reading required. Given two columns, in which mathematical quantities—figural, symbolic, or semantic—are placed, the examinee must decide whether the quantity in column A is larger than that in column B, the quantity in column B is larger than the one in column A, the two quantities are equivalent, or that their relative magnitudes are indeterminate in light of the information presented. It goes almost without saying that the implications of this item format for tests of mathematical aptitude and achievement are great indeed.

The handbook for the AAT and especially the one for SCAT Series 2 are superior to most manuals. Based on large, carefully chosen representative samples of college-bound students, extensive normative data for each form are presented tabularly in raw scores and converted scores that are related to percentile bands—a concept which incidentally is quite clearly explained in the handbook. Scores can be readily equated from one test form to another in view of the application of quite precise equating procedures developed at ETS by Angoff, Lord, Tucker, and others. Substantial amounts of reliability data are also furnished, although the K-R 20 estimates may be slightly inflated in light of the somewhat speeded nature of the two tests—especially the mathematics forms.

In addition to showing what would be judged as satisfactory reliability characteristics, the test forms also compare favorably with other scales in criterion-related validity, although admittedly more data would be welcome. In a sample of 244 students the AAT and the SAT verbal sections showed validity coefficients of .49 and .57 respectively with normalized rank in class achievement. For the same criterion, the AAT and SAT mathematics parts yielded, respectively, validity coefficients of .50 and .48. Correlations between corresponding verbal and mathematics sections of the AAT and SAT were .83 and .86, respectively.

The reviewer has two major reservations regarding the AAT. First it would seem that the two subtests—especially the one in mathematics—are too highly speeded. The handbook for the SCAT Series 2 reports that only 54 percent of the examinees who took Form 1 reached the last test item, although 92 percent of them attained the three-quarters point. In the instance of the verbal part, the corresponding percentages were 77 and 98, respectively. An additional two minutes on the verbal subtest and another five minutes on the mathematics section would probably constitute an improvement that might well be reflected in a more positive attitude on the part of the examinees and perhaps in a higher degree of validity for the AAT—especially for students from culturally different backgrounds in which competitive activities involving clock watching are not strongly reinforced or rewarded. Even with an additional seven minutes for test taking, the total time of administration would not exceed 55 minutes.

The second concern relates to the need for a greater number of practice items at the beginning of each of the two test sections. Instead of the one practice item presented, four or five items would appear to be highly desirable. In taking one form of the AAT, the reviewer noted subjectively a practice effect after about the first six or seven questions in that he was able to work more and more rapidly, even though the items were becoming somewhat more difficult. Although it is true that an excellent study guide in the form of a one-sheet student bulletin for SCAT Series 2 consisting of five verbal and 10 mathematics items is available, there is a substantial risk that not all potential examinees may gain access to the form in view of the frailties or even disinterest of certain counselors or test officers.

In summary, the AAT and its counterpart in SCAT Series 2 yield a highly economical yet comparatively reliable and valid estimate of academic potential in college for the superior high school junior or senior. The accompanying manuals rich in normative and other statistical data are competently prepared and highly readable, even for the counselor or admissions officer with somewhat limited training in measurement and evaluation. It is to be anticipated that the innovative format of the mathematics items as well as the general simplicity of the entire instrument will exert a substantial impact upon future test construction. In short, the AAT and SCAT Series 2 forms furnish a viable alternative to other commercially available ability tests of much greater length in the prediction of academic success for students entering institutions of higher learning.

J Ed Meas 3:81–3 sp '66. Kenneth D. Hopkins and Darrell L. Sander. * The test wisely does not presume to measure native intelligence, yet it does not offer tasks which generally duplicate those encountered in a school setting. * One of the most important features of the AAT is the relatively small amount of testing time required; the two twenty-minute segments of actual testing time are very attractive when compared to other competitive tests. It is unfortunate, however, that no provision is made for informing the examinees of the time allowance. Response style variance of the speed vs. accuracy might have been reduced by providing some basis for self-pacing. This factor takes on additional significance when one considers that on the average two and one-half items per minute must be answered in order to complete each test in the time allowed. About 81% of the normative sample attempted the last item on the verbal test, but only 52% on the mathematics test (even though the tests are described as "essentially unspeeded"). No correction for chance is employed, even though it seems to be a situation in which such an exploration is warranted. The logic favoring its use was apparently strong enough for Traxler....to recommend its use in independent schools even

Cooperative Academic Ability Test

without empirical validation. The directions for administering and scoring are generally clear; however, some possible confusion could have been prevented by giving more orientation into the use of the new IBM 1230 answer sheets. Another minor point of confusion may result from the directions for both tests appearing prior to the initial (verbal) test. A suggestion that the test users develop their own local norms is quite appropriate in light of the limited information available. "The norms in this *AAT Handbook* are based on midyear performance of a representative group of high school seniors with two characteristics: they all intended to go to college and they are enrolled in high schools which send 75% or more of their graduates to college." No mention is made of what percent of the students in the schools would have "intended to go to college" if they had been asked near the middle of their senior year, a fact which introduced some ambiguity into the normative data. The term "representative" may be less appropriate than "restrictive," as only 52% (381 of 753) of the public secondary schools contacted in a related survey "produced usable response data," and of these only 9% (35 schools) had 75% or more of their graduating seniors attending college; and of these 9 (20%) did not participate in the norms testing program. The publishers are to be commended for the completeness with which they describe and report information about the tests even when it indicates certain limitations. A converted score scale is used with a mean of 150 and a standard deviation of 10 based on the senior norms sample. The rationale for this particular numerical base was not discussed. Percentile bands as well as mid-percentile ranks are given for the two tests as well as for the composite score. Negative skewing is present for all three distributions in the normative data. * This negative skewing suggests inadequate test ceiling for the select normative sample; the fact that the median scores were 65–70% of the total items on the two tests is also suggestive in this respect. The method of equating scores on Forms A and B appears satisfactory (using the ACE as a common equating test) although insufficiently described for the general test user. * All things considered, reliability seems quite satisfactory, especially in light of the limited testing time required. * Evidence for AAT's validity takes several forms. When correlating test scores from the normative sample with subsequent rank in graduating class correlations of .52, .51, and .55 were obtained for the AAT verbal, math, and total scores respectively. These values compared favorably with the SAT and rank-in-class correlations. Also reported are correlation coefficients of .83 and .86 between corresponding AAT-SAT tests. The reason for the considerably higher values than those reported by Traxler (1964 .65 and .77) are not discussed. The variabilities of the samples on which these correlations were obtained were not reported, making interpretation very difficult. Traxler (1964) also found the AAT-ACE interrelationships to be approximately equal to the AAT-SAT correlations. He also noted the ACE and AAT correlations with the SAT did not differ substantially. SUMMARY. The AAT is a quickly administered and yet satisfactory reliable test of academic ability. It seems to compare favorably with its competitors in reliability and in validity, even though the amount of data on the latter for the AAT is as yet quite limited. It correlates substantially with the SAT, although its predictive validity for college success has as yet to be determined. The major deficiency seems to be in the rather unusually defined and select normative data which make individual interpretation difficult. For schools relying heavily on local norms, this, of course, is no problem.

[347]

*Cooperative School and College Ability Tests: Series 2.** Grades 4–6, 7–9, 10–12, 12–14; 1955–70; SCAT; 3 scores: verbal, mathematical, total; 4 levels; handbook ('67, 54 pages); preliminary teacher's handbook for SCAT-STEP ('69, 48 pages); preliminary SCAT-STEP norms ('70, 64 pages); student bulletins for levels 1–3, 4, ('67, 2 pages); separate answer sheets (Digitek, Digitek-IBM 805, IBM 1230, SCRIBE) must be used; $7 per 20 tests; $4 per 100 answer sheets; $1.25 per 10 IBM scoring stencils (answer pattern must be punched out locally); Digitek and SCRIBE scoring stencils not available; $2 per handbook; $3 per 100 student bulletins; $3 per specimen set; SCRIBE scoring and statistical analysis service, 35¢ and over per test; 40(50) minutes; cash orders postpaid; Cooperative Tests and Services. *

a) LEVEL 4. Grades 4–6; Forms A ('66, 7 pages), B ('66, 8 pages).
b) LEVEL 3. Grades 7–9; Forms A, B, ('66, 7 pages).
c) LEVEL 2. Grades 10–12; Forms A, B, ('66, 8 pages).
d) LEVEL 1. Grades 12–14; Forms A, B, ('66, 7 pages, tests are identical to the tests copyrighted in 1963 under the title *Cooperative Academic Ability Tests*), C ('66, 8 pages); Form C available only by special arrangement for use with students in college. [The references which follow are for both editions of SCAT.]

REFERENCES

1–7. See 5:322.
8–71. See 6:452.

72. AMES, ROBERT. "Relationships Between Two Types of Verbal Ability." *Calif J Ed Res* 10:177–9 + S '59. * (*PA* 34:7344)
73. MALNIG, LAWRENCE R. *Differential Predictability of Academic Achievement From Aptitude Tests Administered Under Psychological Stress to Subjects With Varying Amounts of Anxiety.* Doctor's thesis, New York University (New York, N.Y.), 1959. (*DA* 20:3197)
74. STOKER, HOWARD W., AND KROPP, RUSSELL P. "The Predictive Validating and Factorial Content of the Florida State-Wide Ninth-Grade Testing Program Battery." *Fla J Ed Res* 2:105–14 Ja '60. *
75. LUNN, MERVEL SAMUEL, JR. *The Prediction of Success of Students Enrolled in Professional Education Courses at the University of Oklahoma.* Doctor's thesis, University of Oklahoma (Norman, Okla.), 1961. (*DA* 22:1490)
76. POLAND, HAROLD VINCENT. *The Relationship Between Self Concept and Supervisory and Peer Ratings of Success in Nurses' Training.* Doctor's thesis, Fordham University (New York, N.Y.), 1961. (*DA* 22:1260)
77. BROE, JOHN RICHARD. *Prediction of Success in Training Among Electronics Technicians.* Doctor's thesis, University of Southern California (Los Angeles, Calif.), 1962. (*DA* 23:2417)
78. DEHART, ARLA LANDO, JR. *Possible Selective Admissions Criteria for the California Public Junior College.* Doctor's thesis, Stanford University (Stanford, Calif.), 1962. (*DA* 22:4233)
79. OWEN, CRAMER. "An Investigation of Creative Potential at the Junior High Level." *Studies Art Ed* 3:16–33 sp '62. *
80. PERRY, JAMES OLDEN. *A Study of a Selective Set of Criteria for Determining Success in Secondary Student Teaching at Texas Southern University.* Doctor's thesis, University of Texas (Austin, Tex.), 1962. (*DA* 23:1617)
81. ANDERSON, RODNEY EARL. *A Comparison of the Performance of College Freshmen Participants and Non-Participants in an Honors Program on Four Psychological Measures.* Doctor's research study No. 1, Colorado State College (Greeley, Colo.), 1963. (*DA* 25:279)
82. BATES, CHARLES O. *A Study of Creative Potential as Found in Elementary Student Teachers.* Doctor's thesis, Ball State Teachers College (Muncie, Ind.), 1963. (*DA* 24:4561)
83. CRAWFORD, W. R., AND MOYEL, I. S. "Predicting Academic Achievement From Intelligence and Personality Data." *Fla J Ed Res* 5:19–28 Ja '63. *
84. DANIEL, KATHRYN LAVERNE BARCHARD. *A Study of Dropouts at the University of Alabama With Respect to Certain Academic and Personality Variables.* Doctor's thesis, University of Alabama (University, Ala.), 1963. (*DA* 25:1736)
85. DICK, WALTER. "Retention as a Function of Paired and Individual Use of Programed Instruction." *J Programed Instr* 2:17–23 f '63. * (*PA* 38:10409)
86. FORDHAM, SHELDON LEROY. *A Study of the Relationship of Selected Factors to Academic Success in Professional Physical Education at the University of Illinois (Chicago).* Doctor's thesis, Michigan State University (East Lansing, Mich.), 1963. (*DA* 25:1270)
87. HILLIARD, ASA GRANT, III. *An Exploratory Study of Relationships Between Student Teacher Personality, Ability, Lower Division Grades, and the Student Teacher's Evaluation of Pupils.* Doctor's thesis, University of Denver (Denver, Colo.), 1963. (*DA* 24:5193)
88. HOOD, ALBERT B. "Predicting Achievement in Dental School." *J Dental Ed* 27:148–55 Je '63. *
89. REAMS, JAKE W. *The Relationship of Selected Factors to the Scholarship of Industrial Arts Teacher Education Students at Ball State Teachers College.* Doctor's thesis, Indiana University (Bloomington, Ind.), 1963. (*DA* 24:3222)
90. WILLIAMS, ROBERT A. *An Assessment of the Success of C Average High School Graduates in Grand Rapids Junior College.* Doctor's thesis, Michigan State University (East Lansing, Mich.), 1963. (*DA* 25:317)
91. ALLGOOD, EARL VANN. *Prediction of Academic Success of Freshman Students in Three Divisions at Virginia State College.* Doctor's thesis, Pennsylvania State University (University Park, Pa.), 1964. (*DA* 25:2303)
92. ATKINSON, BEA HENRIETTA. *The Relationship Between Problem-Solving Strategies and Measures of Convergent and Divergent Thinking in a Selected Group of Secondary School Pupils.* Doctor's thesis, University of Florida (Gainesville, Fla.), 1964. (*DA* 25:7070)
93. BONEY, JEW DON. *A Study of the Use of Intelligence, Aptitude, and Mental Ability Measures in Predicting the Academic Achievement of Negro Students in Secondary School.* Doctor's thesis, University of Texas (Austin, Tex.), 1964. (*DA* 25:5726)
94. BOYCE, RICHARD W. "The Prediction of Achievement in College Algebra." *Ed & Psychol Meas* 24:419–20 su '64. * (*PA* 39:5976)
95. BRODSKY, STANLEY LEON. *Language Patterns of Repressors and Sensitizers in Personal and Impersonal Descriptions.* Doctor's thesis, University of Florida (Gainesville, Fla.), 1964. (*DA* 25:4256)
96. BRODSKY, STANLEY MARTIN. *Predicting the Academic Competence of Students in Certain Technical Curricula at the New York City Community College of Applied Arts and Sciences After an Experimental, Preliminary, Remedial Semester.* Doctor's thesis, New York University (New York, N.Y.), 1964. (*DA* 25:928)
97. COOPER, LELAND ROSS. *The Relationship of Selected Factors to the Continuance of Junior College Graduates at Senior Institutions.* Doctor's thesis, University of Florida (Gainesville, Fla.), 1964. (*DA* 25:3924)
98. ENDLER, NORMAN S. "Factors Related to the Prediction of Academic Success." *Ont J Ed Res* 7:147–54 w '64–65. *
99. ENGEN, HAROLD BERNARD, JR. *Differential Prediction of Academic Success and Attrition-Survival of Entering Freshmen at the University of South Dakota.* Doctor's thesis, State University of South Dakota (Vermillion, S.D.), 1964. (*DA* 25:2847)
100. EVANS, RICHARD WILLIAM. *The School Counselor and Objective Measures as Predictors of High School Achievement and Relationship of Load to Achievement.* Doctor's thesis, Rutgers—The State University (New Brunswick, N.J.), 1964. (*DA* 25:2848)
101. GRIFFIN, WILLIAM MAXWELL. *A Study of the Relationship of Certain Characteristics of High School Seniors to Effectiveness in Independent Study.* Doctor's thesis, Syracuse University (Syracuse, N.Y.), 1964. (*DA* 25:5787)
102. GROSS, ARTHUR THOMAS. *A Study to Determine Relationships of Physical Fitness to Motor Educability, Scholastic Aptitude, and Scholastic Achievement of College Men.* Doctor's thesis, Louisiana State University (Baton Rouge, La.), 1964. (*DA* 25:5713)
103. HARE, ROBERT D. "Relationship of Level of Abstraction to Intelligence and Academic Performance." *Psychol Rep* 14:601–2 Ap '64. * (*PA* 39:1666)
104. HAUGEN, EARL STUART. *A Study of the Validity of the WAIS, SCAT, and STEP as Predictors of Success in College Mathematics.* Doctor's research study No. 1, Colorado State College (Greeley, Colo.), 1964. (*DA* 28:124A)
105. LONG, JOHN M. "Sex Differences in Academic Prediction Based on Scholastic, Personality and Interest Factors." *J Exp Ed* 32:239–48 sp '64. * (*PA* 39:6058)
106. MCCORMICK, JAMES H., AND ASHER, WILLIAM. "Aspects of the High School Record Related to the First Semester College Grade Point Average." *Personnel & Guid J* 42:699–703 Mr '64. *
107. RITCHIE, RALPH WESTLEY, JR. *An Investigation of Factors Related to the Successful Completion of the Engineering Curriculum at California State Polytechnic College, Kellogg Campus.* Doctor's thesis, University of California (Los Angeles, Calif.), 1964. (*DA* 25:3446)
108. SHERMAN, VIVIAN MABEL STANLEY RUSHWORTH. *Personality Correlates of Differential Performance on Intelligence and Creativity Tests.* Doctor's thesis, Stanford University (Stanford, Calif.), 1964. (*DA* 25:4004)
109. STEWART, LAWRENCE H. "Factor Analysis of Nonoccupational Scales of the Strong Blank, Selected Personality Scales and the School and College Ability Test." *Calif J Ed Res* 15:136–41 My '64. * (*PA* 39:3201)
110. WAGNER, EDWIN E., AND SOBER, KATHRYN A. "Effectiveness of the Guilford-Zimmerman Temperament Survey as a Predictor of Scholastic Success in College." *J Counsel Psychol* 11:94–5 sp '64. *
111. WEBER, LOUISE A. *The Predictive Validity of the SCAT and the ACT at a Liberal Arts College for Women.* Master's thesis, John Carroll University (Cleveland, Ohio), 1964.
112. ACKERMAN, THOMAS J. *Language Laboratory Instruction and the Achievement of First-Year Students of Spanish in Florida.* Doctor's thesis, Florida State University (Tallahassee, Fla.), 1965. (*DA* 27:134A)
113. ANDERSON, HARRY E., JR., AND BARRY, JOHN R. "Occupational Choices in Selected Health Professions." *Personnel & Guid J* 44:177–84 O '65. * (*PA* 40:3419)
114. BARGER, BEN, AND HALL, EVERETTE. "Relation of Expected College Activities to Ability and Achievement." *J Col Stud Personnel* 6:300–4 S '65. *
115. BLACK, HUBERT PERRY. *The Predictive Value of Selected Factors for Achievement of Lee College Freshmen.* Doctor's thesis, University of Tennessee (Knoxville, Tenn.), 1965. (*DA* 27:618A)
116. BOYCE, RICHARD W., AND PAXSON, R. C. "The Predictive Validity of Eleven Tests at One State College." *Ed & Psychol Meas* 25:1143–7 w '65. * (*PA* 40:3563)
117. CHAMBERS, JAY L.; BARGER, BEN; AND LIEBERMAN, LEWIS R. "Need Patterns and Abilities of College Dropouts." *Ed & Psychol Meas* 25:509–16 su '65. * (*PA* 39:16372)
118. DAVIS, LUTHER EDWARD, JR. *A Study of Selected Traits of St. Petersburg Junior College Students and Their Value in Predicting Academic Success in Certain Courses of Study at the Senior College Level.* Doctor's thesis, Auburn University (Auburn, Ala.), 1965. (*DA* 26:791)
119. DESENA, PAUL A., AND WEBER, LOUISE ANN. "The Predictive Validity of the School College Ability Test (SCAT) and the American College Test (ACT) at a Liberal Arts College for Women." *Ed & Psychol Meas* 25:1149–51 w '65. * (*PA* 40:4603)
120. EDWARDS, MEREDITH PAYNE, AND TYLER, LEONA E. "Intelligence, Creativity, and Achievement in a Nonselective Public Junior High School." *J Ed Psychol* 56:96–9 Ap '65. * (*PA* 39:10171)

121. FELDHUSEN, JOHN F.; DENNY, TERRY; AND CONDON, CHARLES F. "Anxiety, Divergent Thinking, and Achievement." *J Ed Psychol* 56:40–5 F '65. * (*PA* 39:10771)
122. FOLDS, JONELL HEMPHILL. *A Comparison of the Recall of Test Scores and Change in Self-Concept of College Students Following Three Methods of Test Interpretation.* Doctor's thesis, University of Georgia (Athens, Ga.), 1965. (*DA* 26:2073)
123. FRANCIS, RICHARD LEE. *A Study of the Value of Selected Test Scores for Predicting Success in Analytic Geometry and Calculus.* Doctor's thesis, University of Missouri (Columbia, Mo.), 1965. (*DA* 26:7166)
124. GRIMSLEY, GLEN, AND SUMMERS, GEORGE W. "Selection Techniques for Pakistani Postgraduate Students of Business." *Ed & Psychol Meas* 25:1133–42 w '65. * (*PA* 40:4607)
125. HOLTBY, VANITA J. *A Set of Expectancy Tables for Use With SCAT-STEP Tests at Lewis and Clark Junior High School, Omaha, Nebraska.* Master's thesis, University of Kansas (Lawrence, Kan.), 1965.
126. KILPATRICK, ARNOLD ROY. *The Effectiveness of the School and College Ability Tests as a Predictor of Undergraduate Academic Achievement at Northeast Louisiana State College.* Doctor's thesis, Louisiana State University (Baton Rouge, La.), 1965. (*DA* 25:4380)
127. LEEP, ALBERT GENE. *Selected Pre-Service Measures as Predictors of First Year Teaching Performance of Elementary Teachers.* Doctor's thesis, Ball State Teachers College (Muncie, Ind.), 1965. (*DA* 26:3163)
128. LEUTENEGGER, RALPH R.; MUELLER, THEODORE H.; AND WERSHOW, IRVING R. "Auditory Factors in Foreign Language Acquisition." *Mod Lang J* 49:22–31 Ja '65. *
129. MORRIS, ROBERT O. *A Study of the Effects of Test Sequence on the Results of the SCAT-STEP Test Battery.* Master's thesis, University of Washington (Seattle, Wash.), 1965.
130. MUNDAY, LEO. "Comparative Predictive Validities of the American College Tests and Two Other Scholastic Aptitude Tests." *ACT Res Rep* 6:2–14 Ag '65. *
131. OTTE, HAROLD WILLIAM. *Comparisons of Abilities, Motivations, and Personality Traits of Continuing and Non-Continuing Freshmen in Colleges of the Lutheran Church-Missouri Synod.* Doctor's thesis, University of Colorado (Boulder, Colo.), 1965. (*DA* 26:6480)
132. POHLMANN, VERNON C. "The Inadequacy of Rank in High School Class as a Predictor of College Success." *Ill Sch Res* 2:16–9 O '65. *
133. PREDIGER, DALE J. "Prediction of Persistence in College." *J Counsel Psychol* 12:62–7 sp '65. * (*PA* 39:10725)
134. REILLY, HOWARD E. *A Comparative Analysis of Selected Characteristics of Admitted and Non-Admitted Students to the College of Education, Wayne State University.* Doctor's thesis, Wayne State University (Detroit, Mich.), 1965. (*DA* 27:988A)
135. SLAYTON, WILFRED GEORGE. *A Comparison of Successful and Unsuccessful Bible College Students With Respect to Selected Personality Factors.* Doctor's thesis, University of Arizona (Tucson, Ariz.), 1965. (*DA* 26:1487)
136. SMITH, ROBERT GOUGH. *An Evaluation of Selected Aspects of a Teacher Education Admissions Program.* Doctor's thesis, North Texas State University (Denton, Tex.), 1965. (*DA* 26:3771)
137. STONE, DONALD BRADFORD. *Predicting Student Retention and Withdrawal in a Selected State University College of New York.* Doctor's thesis, Cornell University (Ithaca, N.Y.), 1965. (*DA* 26:5184)
138. SWAN, ROBERT J., AND HOPKINS, KENNETH D. "An Investigation of Theoretical and Empirical Chance Scores on Selected Standardized Group Tests." *Calif J Ed Res* 16:34–41 Ja '65. * (*PA* 39:10156)
139. TULLY, G. EMERSON, AND HALL, BRUCE W. "Test-Retest Reliability of the School and College Ability Test." *J Ed Meas* 2:129 Je '65. *
140. WALLACH, MICHAEL A., AND KOGAN, NATHAN. *Modes of Thinking in Young Children: A Study of the Creativity-Intelligence Distinction,* pp. 25–65. New York: Henry Holt & Winston, Inc., 1965. Pp. ix, 357. *
141. BELK, FLOYD EDMOND. *The Construction of a Simple Instrument to Predict Junior College Freshmen Attrition.* Doctor's thesis, Oklahoma State University (Stillwater, Okla.), 1966. (*DA* 27:4061A)
142. BONEY, J. DON. "Predicting the Academic Achievement of Secondary School Negro Students." *Personnel & Guid J* 44:700–3 Mr '66. * (*PA* 40:8064)
143. BRAY, DOUGLAS W., AND GRANT, DONALD L. "The Assessment Center in the Measurement of Potential for Business Management." *Psychol Monogr* 80(17):1–27 '66. * (*PA* 41:850)
144. BYLER, JESSE THOMAS. *The Relative Influence of Selected Variables in Determining Level of Vocational Preference.* Doctor's thesis, University of Virginia (Charlottesville, Va.), 1966. (*DA* 27:2385A) (Abstract: *Ed R* 4:56–8)
145. DENHAM, EDWARD CHAPLINE. *The Prediction of College Success With Biographical Data and Self-Ratings.* Doctor's thesis, University of Arkansas (Fayetteville, Ark.), 1966. (*DA* 27:599A)

146. DISTEFANO, M. K., JR., AND RICE, MARY L. "Predicting Academic Performance in a Small Southern College." *Ed & Psychol Meas* 26:487–9 su '66. * (*PA* 40:12758)
147. FOLDS, JONELL H., AND GAZDA, GEORGE M. "A Comparison of the Effectiveness and Efficiency of Three Methods of Test Interpretation." *J Counsel Psychol* 13:318–24 f '66. * (*PA* 40:12332)
148. FORD, ZANE BREWER. *Factors Related to Background of Senior Teacher Education Students Enrolled in Arkansas Institutions of Higher Education During the Academic Year 1964-65.* Doctor's thesis, University of Arkansas (Fayetteville, Ark.), 1966. (*DA* 27:627A)
149. FORREST, DONALD VINCENT. *A Comparative Study of Male Secondary School Underachievers Matriculating at the University of South Dakota.* Doctor's thesis, University of South Dakota (Vermillion, S.D.), 1966. (*DA* 27:671A)
150. FRIEDMAN, STUART M. *Predicting Students' Success in a Comprehensive Junior College.* Doctor's thesis, University of Southern California (Los Angeles, Calif.), 1966. (*DA* 26:7112)
151. GROSS, NATHAN. *English Grades as a Function of Intellectual Ability, Performance, and the Congruency of Teacher-Pupil Perceptions of Interpersonal Values.* Doctor's thesis, Harvard University (Cambridge, Mass.), 1966. (*DA* 28:123A)
152. GUILLIAMS, CLARK IRVIN. *Predicting Creative Productivity in College Classes Where Creative Thinking Is Emphasized.* Doctor's thesis, University of Arkansas (Fayetteville, Ark.), 1966. (*DA* 27:675A)
153. LEARD, JERRY LYNN. *A Statistical Study in the Building of Theoretically-Derived Equivalency Tables for Two Forms of the School and College Ability Test.* Master's thesis, University of Texas (Austin, Tex.), 1966.
154. LUNDSTEEN, SARA W., AND MICHAEL, WILLIAM B. "Validation of Three Tests of Cognitive Style in Verbalization for the Third and Sixth Grades." *Ed & Psychol Meas* 26:449–61 su '66. * (*PA* 40:12763)
155. LYON, JOHN THOMAS, JR. *An Experimental Investigation of the Relation Between Personality and Vocal Characteristics of Selected Beginning Adult Singers.* Doctor's thesis, Indiana University (Bloomington, Ind.), 1966. (*DA* 27:4285A)
156. MEANS, HESTER RICE. *An Analysis of the First Freshman Class of the DeKalb Junior College.* Doctor's thesis, University of Georgia (Athens, Ga.), 1966. (*DA* 27:1552A)
157. MILLER, WILLIAM EDGAR. *Factor Analytic Study of Perception of Self, Others, and the Environment.* Doctor's thesis, University of Kansas (Lawrence, Kan.), 1966. (*DA* 28:969A)
158. MORPER, JACK. *An Investigation of the Relationship of Certain Predictive Variables and Academic Achievement of Spanish-American and Anglo Pupils in Junior High School.* Doctor's thesis, Oklahoma State University (Stillwater, Okla.), 1966. (*DA* 27:4051A)
159. SCHUSLER, MARIAN M. "Prediction of Grades by Computer for High School Students: A Cross-Validation and Experimental Placement Study." *J Ed Data Processing* 3:97–110 su '66. *
160. STIVERS, EARL R. "A Study of Probationary Students at Manatee Junior College." *Fla J Ed Res* 8:81–91 Ja '66. *
161. SWANSON, JAMES R., AND TULLY, G. EMERSON. "Answer Sheet Format as a Variable in the Test Performance." *J Col Stud Personnel* 7:33–6 Ja '66. *
162. BRADLEY, R. C., AND MARTIN, BILLIE EDWARD. "A Study and Assessment of the Value of Selected Placement Tests for Predicting Achievement in Spanish, French, and German for First Semester Freshmen." *J Exp Ed* 36:50–4 w '67. *
163. CHABASSOL, DAVID J., AND THOMAS, DAVID C. "Anxiety, Aptitude, Achievement and Performance in Female Teachers." *Alberta J Ed Res* 13:291–4 D '67. * (*PA* 44:4218)
164. CLARKE, ROBERT B., AND GELATT, H. B. "Predicting Units Needed for College Entrance." *Personnel & Guid J* 46:275–82 N '67. * (*PA* 42:4512)
165. DANIEL, KATHRYN BARCHARD. "A Study of College Dropouts With Respect to Academic and Personality Variables." *J Ed Res* 60:230–5 Ja '67. *
166. FERRIS, MANFORD J. "Validity as a Function of Empirical Scaling of Test Items by a Logistic Model." *Ed & Psychol Meas* 27:829–35 w '67. * (*PA* 42:8091)
167. FOX, LOGAN JORDAN. *A Study of Relationships Between Grades and Measures of Scholastic Aptitude, Creativity, and Attitudes in Junior College Students.* Doctor's thesis, University of Southern California (Los Angeles, Calif.), 1967. (*DA* 28:4477A)
168. GOOLSBY, THOMAS M., JR. "Comparability and Validity of Three Forms of SCAT." *Ed & Psychol Meas* 27:1041–5 w '67. * (*PA* 42:9419)
169. GRECO, GERALDINE F. *A Study of STEP and SCAT as Predictors of School Achievement.* Master's thesis, Central Connecticut State College (New Britain, Conn.), 1967.
170. HILTON, THOMAS L., AND MYERS, ALBERT E. "Personal Background, Experience and School Achievement: An Investigation of the Contribution of Questionnaire Data to Academic Prediction." *J Ed Meas* 4:69–80 su '67. * (*PA* 42:4570)
171. INGRAM, JOHN ALLEN. *Factors Affecting the Success*

of Transfer Students at Drake University. Doctor's thesis, Iowa State University (Ames, Iowa), 1967. (DA 28:1341A)
172. LOHNES, PAUL R., AND McINTIRE, PAUL H. "Classification Validities of a Statewide 10th Grade Test Program." Personnel & Guid J 45:561-7 F '67. *
173. McGUIRE, DOUGLAS. Multiple Discriminant Analysis of Test Scores and Biographical Data for the Description and Prediction of 12th Grade Educational Outcomes. Doctor's thesis, University of Illinois (Urbana, Ill.), 1967. (DA 28:2987A)
174. MACNEIL, RONALD LAUCHLIN. A Study of the Effectiveness of the SCAT and CTMM-SF to Predict First Semester Averages. Master's thesis, St. Francis Xavier University (Antigonish, N.S., Canada), 1967.
175. MADAUS, GEORGE F. "Divergent Thinking and Intelligence: Another Look at a Controversial Question." J Ed Meas 4:227-35 w '67. * (PA 42:10584)
176. MASSAD, CAROLYN EMRICK. A Comparative Study of Creativity, Language Aptitude, and Intelligence in Sixth-Grade Children From Low-Socioeconomic and Middle-Socioeconomic Levels. Doctor's thesis, Kent State University (Kent, Ohio), 1967. (DA 29:4331A)
177. PATTERSON, BARBARA. Comparison of Students From High and Low Socio-Economic Backgrounds Using Kuhlmann-Anderson and SCAT Total Test Scores. Master's thesis, California State College (Hayward, Calif.), 1967.
178. TENOPYR, MARY L. "Social Intelligence and Academic Success." Ed & Psychol Meas 27:961-6 w '67. * (PA 42:9509)
179. TENOPYR, MARY L. "Symbolic Tests as Predictors of High-School Grades." Ed & Psychol Meas 27:385-391 su '67. * (PA 41:14227)
180. THACKER, JAMES HOSEA. Pre-College Experience as Preparation for Success in a College of Agriculture. Doctor's thesis, University of Missouri (Columbia, Mo.), 1967. (DA 28:3941B)
181. WARD, JAMES. "An Oblique Factorization of Wallach and Kogan's 'Creativity' Correlations." Brit J Ed Psychol 37:380-2 N '67. * (PA 42:4784)
182. BROWN, WILLIAM THOMAS. Consideration of the Interrelationship of Five Aptitude and Achievement Factors in Successful Male Undergraduate Students at the University of Montana. Doctor's thesis, University of Montana (Missoula, Mont.), 1968. (DA 29:3411A)
183. CAMERON, HOWARD K. "Nonintellectual Correlates of Academic Achievement." J Negro Ed 37:252-7 su '68. * (PA 45:7074)
184. CHABASSOL, DAVID J., AND THOMAS, DAVID C. "Anxiety, Aptitude, Achievement and Performance in Male Elementary Teachers." Alberta J Ed Res 14:233-7 D '68. * (PA 44:4219)
185. DAVIS, SAMUEL EUGENE. Predicting Probable Failure in College-Level Music Theory Courses. Doctor's thesis, University of Montana (Missoula, Mont.), 1968. (DAI 30:354A)
186. DIXON, PAUL W.; FUKUDA, NOBUKO K.; AND BERENS, ANNE E. "The Influence of Ethnic Grouping on SCAT, Teachers' Ratings, and Rank in High School Class." Abstract. J Social Psychol 75:285-6 Ag '68. * (PA 42:17056)
187. FARRAR, RONALD DOUGLAS. The Non-Visa Foreign Student at Los Angeles City College: A Study of the Relation of Various Administrative and Academic Factors to the Immigrant Student. Doctor's thesis, University of California (Los Angeles, Calif.), 1968. (DAI 30:487A)
188. FEE, FRANCIS. "An Alternative to Ward's Factor Analysis of Wallach and Kogan's 'Creativity' Correlations." Comment by James Ward. Brit J Ed Psychol 38:319-21 N '68. * (PA 43:6128)
189. FONTES, PATRICIA JOYCE. The Effect of a Procedure for Simulating Norms for Newly Constructed Tests. Doctor's thesis, Boston College (Chestnut Hill, Mass.), 1968. (DAI 30:57A)
190. GAGNI, ARSENIO OREVILLO. The Differential Prediction of Selected Measurements in Ornamental Horticulture. Doctor's thesis, Cornell University (Ithaca, N.Y.), 1968. (DA 29:4181A)
191. GINTHER, MARY LOU. Relationships of Characteristics of Previous Education Obtained in Arkansas High Schools to Cumulative Grade-Point Averages of Seniors in the Various Undergraduate Colleges of the University of Arkansas in 1964-65. Doctor's thesis, University of Arkansas (Fayetteville, Ark.), 1968. (DA 29:59A)
192. HARDESTY, D. L., AND JONES, W. S. "Characteristics of Judged High Potential Management Personnel—The Operations of an Industrial Assessment Center." Personnel Psychol 21:85-98 sp '68. * (PA 42:16197)
193. HEDLEY, CAROLYN NEAL. "Learning Relationship Differences and Curriculum Choice." Improv Col & Univ Teach 16:268-72 au '68. *
194. HEDLEY, CAROLYN NEAL. "The Relationship of Personality Factors to Scientific and Mathematical Ability Factors." Sch Sci & Math 68:265-71 Ap '68. *
195. HILLS, JOHN R., AND STANLEY, JULIAN C. "Prediction of Freshman Grades From SAT and From Level 4 of SCAT in Three Predominantly Negro State Colleges." Abstract. Proc 76th Ann Conv Am Psychol Assn 3:241-2 '68. *
196. HUTCHINS, BOB E. The Relationship of Selected Factors to Performance of Teenage Teacher Aides in Eleven Appalachian School Districts. Doctor's thesis, Ohio University (Athens, Ohio), 1968. (DA 29:1041A)
197. KHAN, S. B. "The Relative Magnitude of Speed and Power in SCAT." J Ed Meas 5:327-9 w '68. * (PA 44:11222)
198. McGEE, JIM ED. Selected Factors Associated With Success or Failure on the Junior English Examination at the University of Arkansas. Doctor's thesis, University of Arkansas (Fayetteville, Ark.), 1968. (DA 29:99A)
199. MILLER, RICHARD HADDEN. A Descriptive Study of the Relationship Between Potential and Performance of Freshman Students at the University of South Dakota. Doctor's thesis, University of South Dakota (Vermillion, S.D.), 1968. (DA 29:2612A)
200. MUNDAY, LEO. "Correlations Between ACT and Other Predictors of Academic Success in College." Col & Univ 44:67-76 f '68. *
201. ORR, DAVID B., AND GRAHAM, WARREN R. "Development of a Listening Comprehension Test to Identify Educational Potential Among Disadvantaged Junior High School Students." Am Ed Res J 5:167-80 Mr '68. *
202. PRATT, MICHAEL, AND ALEAMONI, LAWRENCE M. Predicting the Academic Performance of the Fall, 1967 Freshmen Engineering Students. Research Report No. 277. Champaign, Ill.: Measurement and Research Division, Office of Instructional Resources, University of Illinois, 1968. Pp. 6. *
203. TSENG, MICHAEL. "Multiple Prediction of Programed Learning in Descriptive Statistics." Proc W Va Acad Sci 40:215-20 '68. *
204. VAN DERSLICE, JOHN FREDERICK. The Educational, Social, and Economic Background of Engineering and Technical Students Analyzed for the Purpose of Establishing Profiles for Use in Counseling. Doctor's thesis, Utah State University (Logan, Utah), 1968. (DA 29:1431A)
205. WILSON, ANAISE VICTORIANNE. A Study of the Relationship of Selected Factors to the Academic Achievement of College Freshmen in the School of Education of Tuskegee Institute. Doctor's thesis, New York University (New York, N.Y.), 1968. (DAI 30:144A)
206. AICHELE, DOUGLAS BRUCE. Predicting Success in Basic Concepts of Modern Mathematics From Selected Test Scores and High School Measures. Doctor's thesis, University of Missouri (Columbia, Mo.), 1969. (DAI 30:3623A)
207. CARVER, RONALD P. "Use of a Recently Developed Listening Comprehension Test to Investigate the Effect of Disadvantagement Upon Verbal Proficiency." Am Ed Res J 6(2):263-70 Mr '69. *
208. CUNNINGHAM, ROOSEVELT. A Study to Determine Whether There Were Any Relationships Between High School Grade Point Averages and SCAT and STEP Tests. Master's thesis, Virginia State College (Petersburg, Va.), 1969.
209. DE BERUFF, ELLEN. The Prediction of Success in Master's and Doctoral Programs. Doctor's thesis, University of Maryland (College Park, Md.), 1969. (DAI 31:1033A)
210. DIXON, PAUL W.; FUKUDA, NOBUKO K.; AND BERENS, ANNE E. "Teachers' Ratings, Sex, and SCAT as Predictors of Rank in High School Class." J Exp Ed 37(3):21-6 sp '69. *
211. DRUM, DAVID JOHN. A Study of the Relationships Between Level of Development of Educational Interests and Academic Performance in First-Year College Students. Doctor's thesis, American University (Washington, D.C.), 1969. (DAI 30:3317A)
212. FOLLMAN, JOHN; HERNANDEZ, DAVID; AND MILLER, WILLIAM. "Canonical Correlation of Scholastic Aptitude and Critical Thinking." Psychol 6(3):3-6 Ag '69. * (PA 44:2853)
213. FOLLMAN, JOHN; MILLER, WILLIAM; AND HERNANDEZ, DAVID. "Factor Analysis of Achievement, Scholastic Aptitude, and Critical Thinking Subtests." J Exp Ed 38(1):48-53 f '69. * (PA 45:10901)
214. FORD, ROBERT N.; BORGATTA, EDGAR F.; AND BOHRNSTEDT, GEORGE W. "Use of the Work Components Study With New College-Level Employees." J Appl Psychol 53(5):367-76 O '69. * (PA 44:1407)
215. FOSTER, GARRETT R. "An Analysis of Teacher Assigned Grades at Nova and Three Control Schools." Fla J Ed Res 11(1):1-24 Ja '69. *
216. GEORGE, WARREN EDWIN. Significant Predictors for College Achievement in Specified Areas of Music Education and Identification of Potential Graduates. Doctor's thesis, University of Kansas (Lawrence, Kan.), 1969. (DAI 30:3040A)
217. GOOLSBY, THOMAS M., JR.; FRARY, ROBERT B.; AND LASCO, RICHARD A. "Selecting and Supplementing an Appropriate Achievement Battery for an Experimental School—A Factor Analytic Approach." Ed & Psychol Meas 29(2):403-8 su '69. * (PA 44:17319)
218. HAAKONSEN, HARRY OLAV. An Investigation of the Relationships Between Selected Psychological Characteristics of Students and Performance in an Audio-Tutorial Genetics Program. Doctor's thesis, Syracuse University (Syracuse, N.Y.), 1969. (DAI 31:63A)
219. HALL, LUCIEN TALMAGE, JR. The Prediction of Success in Each of Six Four-Year Selections of Secondary Mathematics Courses. Doctor's thesis, University of Virginia (Charlottesville, Va.), 1969. (DAI 30:4141A)
220. HARVEY, EVA DAVIS. Relationships Between the National

Teacher Examinations, Certain Variables, and Secondary Teacher Education Curricula. Doctor's thesis, North Texas State University (Denton, Tex.), 1969. (*DAI* 30:4852A)

221. HAYES, EDWARD MAJELLA. *The Relationship of Race and Sex to Academic Achievement in Selected Rural Elementary and High Schools Before and After Desegregation.* Doctor's thesis, University of Virginia (Charlottesville, Va.), 1969. (*DAI* 31:149A)

222. HINRICHS, J. R. "Comparison of 'Real Life' Assessments of Management Potential With Situational Exercises, Paper-and-Pencil Ability Tests, and Personality Inventories." *J Appl Psychol* 53(5):425-32 O '69. * (*PA* 44:1442)

223. HUSEMOLLER, KENNETH E. *The Prediction of Freshmen Academic Success at Eastern New Mexico University, Roswell, by Means of Selected Demographic and Standardized Tests Data.* Doctor's thesis, Colorado State College (Greeley, Colo.), 1969. (*DAI* 30:1467A)

224. IRVINE, S. H. "Factor Analysis of African Abilities and Attainments: Constructs Across Cultures." *Psychol B* 71(1):20-32 Ja '69. * (*PA* 43:7553)

225. KOOKER, EARL W., AND BELLAMY, ROY Q. "Some Psychometric Differences Between Graduates and Dropouts." *Psychol* 6(2):65-70 My '69. * (*PA* 43:14868)

226. LYONS, RICHARD ALAN, SR. *A Comparison of the Effect of Conceptually and Non-Conceptually-Oriented Tests Upon Student Achievement and Attitude in Basic Electronics at the College Level.* Doctor's thesis, University of Missouri (Columbia, Mo.), 1969. (*DAI* 30:4254A)

227. MOTLEY, HESTER CHATTIN. *A Study of the Predictive Value of Certain Factors Related to Test Performance, Academic Achievement, and Educational Aspirations.* Doctor's thesis, American University (Washington, D.C.), 1969. (*DAI* 30:2807A)

228. PHILLIPS, RICHARD MARTIN. *A Multiple Regression Study of Academic Prediction at Gallaudet College.* Doctor's thesis, University of Maryland (College Park, Md.), 1969. (*DAI* 30:5257A)

229. RONAN, RICHARD JAMES. *A Study of the Relationships Between the Performance of College Freshmen in Mathematics and Selected Factors in Their Academic Background.* Doctor's thesis, University of New Mexico (Albuquerque, N.M.), 1969. (*DAI* 31:1694A)

230. SOURS, CHARLES F. RAY. *The Probability of Enrollment and Success of High School Seniors in an Industrial and Technical Teacher Education Program in the State of Arkansas.* Doctor's thesis, University of Arkansas (Fayetteville, Ark.), 1969. (*DAI* 30:1058A)

231. WEISGERBER, CHARLES A. *Psychological Assessment of Candidates for a Religious Order,* pp. 126-32. Chicago, Ill.: Loyola University Press, 1969. Pp. viii, 191. *

232. ALSPAUGH, CAROL ANN. *A Study of the Relationships Between Student Characteristics and Proficiency in Symbolic and Algebraic Computer Programming.* Doctor's thesis, University of Missouri (Columbia, Mo.), 1970. (*DAI* 31:4627B)

233. BOWERS, JOHN. "The Comparison of GPA Regression Equations for Regularly Admitted and Disadvantaged Freshmen at the University of Illinois." *J Ed Meas* 7(4):219-25 w '70. *

234. CARLETON, FREDERICK O. "Relationships Between Follow-Up Evaluations and Information Developed in a Management Assessment Center." Abstract. *Proc 78th Ann Conv Am Psychol Assn* 5(2):565-6 '70. * (*PA* 44:19655)

235. CROWELL, ORVILLE. *An Analysis of the Relationship of Measured Interests of Entering College Freshmen to Choice of Occupation Approximately Forty-Four Months Later.* Doctor's thesis, University of Arkansas (Fayetteville, Ark.), 1970. (*DAI* 31:2680A)

236. DIXON, PAUL W.; FUKUDA, NOBUKO K.; AND BERENS, ANNE E. "Cognitive and Personalogical Factor Patterns for Japanese-American High School Students in Hawaii." *Psychologia* 13(1):35-41 Mr '70. * (*PA* 45:8036)

237. DIXON, PAUL W.; FUKUDA, NOBUKO K.; AND BERENS, ANNE E. "Two-Factor Explanation of Post-High School Destinations in Hawaii." *J Exp Ed* 39(1):24-9 f '70. *

238. FARAGHER, JOHN P. *An Investigation of the Usefulness of the School and College Ability Tests as Utilized in the Tracking Process at Cleveland Heights High School.* Master's thesis, John Carroll University (Cleveland, Ohio), 1970.

239. FELDHUSEN, JOHN F.; TREFFINGER, DONALD J.; AND ELIAS, ROBERT M. "Prediction of Academic Achievement With Divergent and Convergent Thinking and Personality Variables." *Psychol Sch* 7(1):46-52 Ja '70. * (*PA* 44:11410)

240. FRANK, AUSTIN C., AND KIRK, BARBARA A. "Forestry Students Today." *Voc Guid Q* 19(1):119-22 D '70. *

241. GRANT, DONALD L., AND BRAY, DOUGLAS W. "Validation of Employment Tests for Telephone Company Installation and Repair Occupations." *J Appl Psychol* 54(1):7-14 F '70. *

242. GREEN, JOE L. *An Analysis of Factors Related to Academic Achievement in Introductory Geography at the University of Arkansas.* Doctor's thesis, University of Arkansas (Fayetteville, Ark.), 1970. (*DAI* 31:1510A)

243. HICKS, JACK M., AND WRIGHT, JOHN H. "Convergent-Discriminant Validation and Factor Analysis of Five Scales of Liberalism-Conservatism." *J Pers & Social Psychol* 14(2):114-20 F '70. * (*PA* 44:6741)

244. HILLS, JOHN R., AND STANLEY, JULIAN C. "Easier Test Improves Prediction of Black Students' College Grades." *J Negro Ed* 39(4):320-4 f '70. * (*PA* 45:10957)

245. KHAN, S. B. "Affective Correlates of Academic Achievement: A Longitudinal Study." *Meas & Eval Guid* 3(2):76-80 su '70. * (*PA* 45:1360)

246. KRANZLER, GERALD D. "Some Effects of Reporting Scholastic Aptitude Test Scores to High School Students." *Sch Counselor* 17(3):219-27 Ja '70. * (*PA* 44:21519)

247. LIBBY, WILLIAM L., JR. "Reaction Time and Remote Association in Talented Male Adolescents." *Develop Psychol* 3(3):285-97 N '70. * (*PA* 45:4001)

248. MILLER, BERNEICE BEADLES. *The Effects of Continuing or Changing Foreign Languages on Listening Comprehension and Selected Tests as Predictors of Success in Spanish or French at the Seventh-Grade Level.* Doctor's thesis, University of Oklahoma (Norman, Okla.), 1970. (*DAI* 31:2618A)

249. NASH, JOHN MORTON. *Prediction of Academic Achievement of Women at a Private Junior College Through Use of Certain Intellective and Family Relationships Measures.* Doctor's thesis, Boston University (Boston, Mass.), 1970. (*DAI* 31:2113A)

250. PACE, JESSE LEONARD, JR. *Relationships of the Dominant Value Constructs to Achieved Grade Point Averages of High and Low Ability Transfer Students in Two Age Groups at Phillips County Community College.* Doctor's thesis, University of Mississippi (University, Miss.), 1970. (*DAI* 31:1039A)

251. RARDIN, DONALD R., AND MOAN, CHARLES E. "Frustration Tolerance and College Grade Point Average." *Percept & Motor Skills* 31(3):1003-6 D '70. * (*PA* 46:1867)

252. RIECHARD, DONALD EDWARD. *The Acquisition of Selected Life-Science Concepts by Beginning Kindergarten Children From Three Different Community Settings.* Doctor's thesis, Ohio State University (Columbus, Ohio), 1970. (*DAI* 31:3366A)

253. ROSSMANN, JACK E., AND KIRK, BARBARA A. "Comparison of Counseling Seekers and Nonseekers." *J Counsel Psychol* 17(2):184-8 Mr '70. * (*PA* 44:9247)

254. ROSSMANN, JACK E., AND KIRK, BARBARA A. "Factors Related to Persistence and Withdrawal Among University Students." *J Counsel Psychol* 17(1):56-62 Ja '70. * (*PA* 44:5658)

255. SARUK, ALEC, AND GULUTSAN, METRO. "Academic Performance of Students and the Cultural Orientation of Their Parents." *Alberta J Ed Res* 16(3):189-95 S '70. * (*PA* 45:8988)

256. WEBB, JAMES BOYD. *A Comparative Study of the Relation of Broken Homes to the School Success of High School Students.* Doctor's thesis, George Washington University (Washington, D.C.), 1970. (*DAI* 31:3187A)

257. WILLIS, CARL G., AND NICHOLSON, JAMES. "Series II SCAT as a College Aptitude Measure." *Ed & Psychol Meas* 30(4):971-5 w '70. *

H. J. BUTCHER, *Professor of Educational Psychology, University of Sussex, Brighton, Sussex, England.*

This new and extended series of SCAT tests is designed to provide measures of basic verbal and mathematical ability for grades 4 to 14. The verbal and mathematical tests at each level consist, respectively, of verbal analogies and "quantitative comparisons." Item form in the verbal tests is uniform throughout, but varies quite widely in the quantitative tests. From inspection, both sections could be expected to have wide cross-cultural validity in all English-speaking countries in the sense that instructions and material contain little that is specific to American usage, although, of course, all the tables of norms are applicable only to the USA.

The tests are evidently the result of careful, scientific, and professionally expert construction. Items are generally ingenious, fair, and unambiguous, although an occasional diagram is misleadingly drawn. The handbook is in many ways a model of its kind and considerable pains have been taken to make it foolproof for the untrained administrator and to provide sufficient information for the expert psychometrist.

Details of how the tests should be given are clearly and briefly stated, and the main space is rightly given to score interpretation. Sufficient warning is provided about legitimate and illegitimate comparisons between different forms and levels and about the limitations of raw scores. For all forms and levels, tables are provided to enable the user easily to obtain first a converted score and then a percentile rank in terms of national norms. A welcome innovation is the provision of percentile bands extending one standard error of score above and below the percentile rank, this standard error being apparently derived, although this is not made quite explicit, from Kuder-Richardson coefficients. The percentile bands, besides giving the user a ready means of estimating the significance of differences between the scores of individuals and the differences between scores of one individual on different parts, also clearly indicate the varying precision of the tests for different levels of ability.

Selection of the national sample on which norms are based was thorough and professionally sophisticated. A probability sample was obtained of "all public school systems and church-related schools with an enrollment of at least 300 pupils," using the "probability proportional to size" method combined with systematic sampling through a list (with random start). Although this reviewer is not familiar enough with statistics of school size in the USA to estimate the proportion of schools thus excluded, it might be thought that the systematic exclusion of, e.g., small rural schools, would result in an upward bias of the resulting norms. Another possible source of bias is that, of 1,460 school superintendents selected in the sampling, only 835 agreed to participate. Again, the most plausible guess about the direction of such bias is that willingness to participate might be positively correlated with level of attainment in the system and thus raise the obtained norms to an unknown extent.

These speculative criticisms apart, the establishment of norms for SCAT was admirably done; also the handbook discussion of the separate components in the total error of measurement and of the factors determining their relative importance is thorough and instructive. Leaving aside possible error due to nonrandom sampling as discussed in the last paragraph, sampling error has a negligible effect on the precision of the percentile norms relative to test unreliability, except at the extremes of the score distribution.

There are at least two parallel forms at each level. How parallel is parallel? The handbook goes into this quite deeply. It provides no between-forms correlations, but interpreting a rather complex series of inferences from the mean scores on the two forms of randomly divided classes leads to the conclusion that unwanted variance from between-forms differences is not large. The interpretation of the scores of individual students should not be affected, though care may be needed in interpreting small differences in the means of groups that have taken different forms of the test.

The handbook has little to say about speededness and nothing about its effect upon the size of the internal consistency coefficients and hence, presumably, upon the confidence intervals of the percentile ranks. The degree of speededness is not negligible, especially in the mathematical sections, since at three out of four levels 40 percent or more of the normative group failed to complete the test.

Predictive and concurrent validity, assessed by comparison with school and college grades and with other standard measures such as the SAT, appear adequate and fall within the expected range.

In sum, although further cumulative evidence about their properties is still desirable, these tests have all the appearance of being well engineered and quite well proven instruments.

Am Ed Res J 6 (2):306–9 Mr '69. Esin Kaya. In reviewing tests published by the Educational Testing Service one need not be concerned with whether or not the tests are reliable, the norms are based on representative samples, or the forms are adequately equated. Indeed, ETS can hardly be surpassed in efficiency and thoroughness in obtaining and reporting test data. The ....[test] under review....[reflects] this typical efficiency and thoroughness. * It is ironical, in a sense, that the thoroughness with which test development procedures and data are reported reveals certain test properties some of which may be construed as shortcomings. For example, both the normative data and a quick glance at the test content indicate that levels 1A and 2A of *SCAT Series II* overlap to a large extent. One is unable to determine the practical usefulness of having both levels. This problem of comparability of adjacent levels is augmented when one wants to measure gains of student groups who have scores near the top of any given level since the gains may not be validly measured because of difficulties in scaling the extreme scores on adjacent levels. Examination of the possible use of test results in the schools raises several more practical questions. Since the school practitioner is rarely aware of statistical subtleties, many of the technical cautions given by ETS are likely to go unnoticed by users of these tests *before* the decision is made to use them. Second, children in the extremes of the normative distributions frequently do not have their verbal and quantitative abilities differentiated. Rather, the data reported in the *Handbook* for *SCAT Series II* indicate that those groups who do well on quantitative tests also do well on verbal tests. The implication of this for the usefulness of administering both tests to all groups in the schools needs examination. Third, the predictive validity indices reported for *SCAT Series II* show a very large range so that the average *r*'s, plus and minus one standard deviation, range from .18 to .84. When one notes, too, that midterm grades and cumulative grade point averages of the students were used as the validating criterion, the eternal question of the chicken or the egg applies. *

J Counsel Psychol 15:583–6 N '68. S. David Farr. * a set of tests covering the same range of grades and producing the same type of scores as the SCAT, but having shorter testing time, one less level, and different and more restricted item domains * The purpose of this series....is to produce scores useful in "comparing a student or class with other students or classes, comparing performance on the verbal and mathematical subtests, estimating growth of these basic skills over a period of time, and predicting success in related activities." The publisher has done a convincing job in terms of some of these objectives but has failed to produce useful information on others. * Each subtest consists of a single type of item—verbal analogies for the score labeled "verbal" and items demanding the judgment of relative magnitude of two stimuli for the "mathematical" score. * No rationale is presented for choosing these two item domains. As would be expected, the use of a single task leads to tests with high internal consistency coefficients in spite of relatively short testing times. Whether this narrow bandwidth high-fidelity approach produces a test which is also restricted in its range of applications cannot be determined from the data presented. * Although the handbook does not state the vocabulary level for the words used in the verbal analogies, it appears that at least for average and above average children the majority of the items pose a task of finding the relationships rather than of understanding the words used. The items which form Part II of each form and produce the mathematical score are of a less familiar sort. Each item presents two stimuli labeled A and B and the student is asked to judge whether the stimulus in Column A is greater, the stimulus in Column B is greater, the two parts are equal, or not enough information is given to decide. * Perhaps the primary question to be raised is whether all students in the range for which these tests are intended have an adequate concept of greater than and less than, in order that a lack in this concept should not interfere with the ability to make the keyed response when the rest of the task can be performed correctly. Evidence could undoubtedly be presented on this point, but CTD has not done so in the handbook. The format of the test booklets is good. Since the Part I directions are on the page facing the first 24 items of Part I, the perceptive student may use the time taken in giving directions to attempt the first few items of Part I, thereby giving him an advantage over the less test-wise student. The typeface used is small but clear. It is interesting to note that the text of the handbook is set in slightly larger type than the items of the test booklet, perhaps in regard for the older eyes which will be reading the handbook. The instructions are clearly and nicely stated. * The handbook accompanying the SCAT Series II is generally comprehensive (at least for a new test) and well written. * CTD probably should be complimented for inviting the criticism of reviewers by including discussion of certain topics for which they cannot yet provide adequate data, for example speededness * Three of the four objectives....deal at least in part with the description of individual differences, namely, the comparison of a student with other students, the comparison of performance on the verbal and mathematical subtests, and the estimation of growth in the basic skills represented by the items. SCAT Series II has achieved good accuracy for the first of these objectives, discrimination among students * As is typical, reliability information is provided for only one of the parallel forms, Form A. While one may question why CTD used shortcut procedures such as choosing small samples for the item statistics, and failing to study the reliability of Form B, there is no particular reason to expect that more elaborate or precise procedures would lead to different conclusions about the test. The publishers should be complimented for pointing out that since single school groups tend to be more homogeneous than the norm group, the within-school reliability will be somewhat less than that presented in the manual. * The second objective deals with the difference between verbal and mathematical scores for single students. The handbook provides an excellent discussion of the accuracy of such differences, at least to the extent of deciding whether differences are real. There is absolutely no data or even discussion, however, bearing on the meaning of such differences. Therefore, the discovery that a student is truly better in the verbal skills than in mathematical skills may be of little use. The third of the individual differences objectives has to do with estimating the growth of individuals. The handbook gives a minimum of information relevant to this objective. Short-term stability and practice-effect information are not presented. Concurrent interform correlations have been estimated from the correlation between part-class means on the two forms. This is inadequate, however, to deal with the problems of measuring growth. Interpretation of individual differences through relative position in a norm group has been well handled by the constructors of this series. A commendable job of national sampling has been done * Distinct advantages to placing the SCAT Series II on a scale that would enable the schools to "utilize data obtained on SCAT" (in some unspecified way) are implied on page 40 of the handbook, in spite of the fact that the importance of "lack of equivalence" is also noted on the same page. Granting the usefulness of such scaling, it appears that ETS has done a competent technical job. The reviewer feels, however, that the effort spent on scaling was misplaced, considering the minimal amount of data relevant to use of the test which had been assembled. * The question of speededness is discussed and the proportion of students in certain groups reaching the ¾ point and the last item of the test is reported. This is not the most relevant information, however, for determining whether a speed factor seriously affects relative position in the distribution of individual differences. * Evidence is presented which suggests that while students in modern math curricula score higher than those in traditional curricula, this phenomenon is approximately equal on the verbal and mathematical subtest. Some type of overall school differences seems a more reasonable hypothesis for explaining these data than does exposure to the modern math curriculum per se. The final technical topic is the formation of the total score. The definition of this score as the number right in the two subtests combined reflects a philosophy of defining a common domain of items rather than maintaining separate domains and combining scores in a way optimal to any given purpose. The fact that the correlations between the verbal and mathematical scores are substantially lower than the reliability of either part would support the reviewer's bias toward the latter philosophy rather than that adopted by CTD. USEFULNESS OF THE SERIES. Considering that the SCAT Series II "is intended primarily as a measure of a student's ability to succeed in future academic work," (*Handbook*, p. 41) only a trivial amount of relevant information is provided. * What is presented....tends to be concurrent correlations with marks and in some cases is based on the use of Level 1 outside of its recommended grade range. * The size of the coefficients suggests that the relationships between SCAT Series II and school marks are similar in strength to those found using other ability tests. However, the information is too skimpy to provide any real guidance in the use of this test. What, then, might the test user hope that ETS would make a serious attempt to provide in the future? While the benefits of local validity studies are not to be denied, it would seem that a responsible test publisher should provide some fairly specific predictive procedures for their tests. These are usually of two types. Regression data (not just correlation coefficients) are needed to predict relative position on some future measure, such as academic performance. On the other hand, to tell which of two or more clearly defined groups a student is more like, group distribution data, including covariance information, allows the description of similarity of a student to the various reference groups by multivariate classification procedures or some less formal process. The groups of interest may be academic groups, for example, college attenders versus non-college attenders or those attending various types of colleges, but the potential usefulness of abilities tests in career counseling should not be underestimated, as the ability tests are among the better discriminators among career groups. A third type of data helpful in both cases is the extent to which the information provided by the SCAT Series II duplicates that supplied by other typically available (or procurable) measures. Such information will allow a counselor to evaluate the wisdom of bringing additional data to bear on a particular question. Some of the data just described are impossible to develop during the few years taken to refine and produce this series. Those interested in mere description of individual differences can make use of the tests with the present data. Those interested in conducting research using the two domains represented will also find the present instrument useful. However, a user interested in prediction will have to either begin his own empirical investigation of the tests or wait until the publisher provides him with better information. It can be hoped that CTD will accept the responsibility to produce regression and group distribution data which will make the tests more useful. Scattered efforts of this type are represented in the supplements to the original SCAT Series. It is hoped by this reviewer that a more focused and well-planned program for developing the type of data described will be followed for Series II. SUMMARY. The present state of the SCAT Series II appears to reflect a philosophy by the publisher of providing a test which is technically excellent in terms of individual differences and letting the user generate his own data for the use of the test. The test is interesting in that of the two item domains represented, one is a well-established standard domain and the other appears to be a promising newer domain. The fidelity of the two part scores and total is acceptable and the norming processes commendable. It is hoped that the publisher will not take the short-sighted view that having done this much his job is finished. Only a well-considered program of studies, including substantial follow-up studies of students tested with appropriate levels of the series will turn SCAT Series II from an interesting, technically good test into a really useful instrument.

J Ed Meas 6(1):51–3 sp '69. *Douglas McKie and Peggy Rae Koopman.* Form IA and IB of SCAT II originally appeared in 1964 as forms of the Cooperative Academic Ability Test, reviewed in the *Journal of Educational Measurement* by Hopkins and Sander (1966). These were renormed on a more representative sample in 1966, when the remaining forms were normed. SCAT Handbook II contains little indication of why SCAT II was developed, and what differences in philosophy guided the authors in changing the types of test tasks used. The most obvious reason is to provide a much shorter predictive instrument than SCAT I. * The SCAT II items appear slightly less school-specific and slightly more abstract than those of SCAT I. No explanation of a change from one item type in SCAT I to another in SCAT II appears in the Handbook II. In discussing the purpose of the test, Handbook II provides correlational evidence suggesting that the V and M scores of SCAT II may have more in common than have the V and Q scores of SCAT I. They are certainly not *purer* measures of these abilities. These correlations range from .68 (Grade 5) to .77 (Grade 11) in SCAT II, and .71 (Grade 5) through .61 (Grade 11) to .53 (Grade 13) in SCAT I. Somewhat disturbing is the fact that though, in the case of SCAT I, these measures become more independent with increased amounts of schooling, the dependence seems to *increase* for SCAT II. RELIABILITY. Reliability data on SCAT II, as for SCAT I, are obtained using KR 20. Coefficients range from .87 (Verbal, Form 2A) to .94 (Total Score, all forms) within grades. For the most part, they run higher than would be predicted by the Spearman-Brown formula for tests four-sevenths as long as the originals, so that in this respect, at least, the change in item type may have been beneficial. Within grades for a given school, however, the coefficients are reported to run .02 to .08 less than the above, presumably because of greater homogeneity. These reliabilities will tend to overestimate coefficients that take account of "occasions-variance," no measures for which are reported. Consequently, the standard error of measurement will be underestimated, and percentile bands used in norm tables will, as in SCAT I, be smaller than would otherwise be obtained. Not only that, but they will be smaller to a degree that is unknown but which varies with different forms and subtests-within-forms because of variable speeding. In this connection, the element of speed that was quite marked in SCAT I has been somewhat reduced, though the Handbook gives data showing that the mathematical subtests are still too long for a sizeable percentage of the students to complete in the time allotted. VALIDITY. Validity data on SCAT II are meager. At the grade 12 level, scores obtained in the Fall on the Cooperative Academic Ability Test (Forms 1A and 1B of SCAT II) were correlated against rank-in-graduating class. Coefficients obtained were .52, .51, and .56 for V, M, and T, respectively. * Also at the Grade 12 level, average r's are quoted between scores on SCAT II, administered in the Fall, and midterm grades. They are .41 for V with English Composition, .46 for V with English (Literature plus Composition), .43 for M with Mathematics, and .59 for Total Score with G.P.A. These figures seem small for such a short period. * The most that can be said to date about SCAT II validities is that they are promising. For such a short instrument, they suggest that it is likely to be about as predictive as its longer predecessor (SCAT I). But the evidence for this conclusion is slender. More validity data are needed, particularly over longer time periods. No doubt they will soon begin to appear in the journals. SCAT II correlations with SAT scores are .83 (for V) and .86 (for M), compared with .86 (for SCAT I—V) and .78–.81 (for SCAT I—Q). Evidently, SCAT II should be useful to counselors who are asked questions like, "What are my chances on SAT?" However, the Handbook does not present either charts or expectancy tables from which probabilistic statements might be obtained. STANDARDIZATION AND NORMS. The norming....was conducted with the care typically associated with E.T.S. projects. Sampling was by grade, and an attempt was made to reflect percentages of students from each grade within regional areas. The attempt was not wholly successful because of unavoidable complications at the local level, but evidently the norm sample is fairly representative. No separate tables of norms are yet available for special groups like urban schools. However, considerable stress is placed upon the value of compiling local norms. Inspection of the tables of norms reveals that there is an element of negative skew in the score distributions for grades 8 to 12, with an accompanying lack of ceiling in some cases. The lack of ceiling is also apparent for one or two of the forms at lower levels. As in SCAT I, scores may be interpreted via "converted scores," percentile ranks, or percentile bands (covering plus and minus 1 S.E.). The converted scores permit comparisons of performance across levels and forms, but not across subtests. For comparing individual scores or school averages with the appropriate norm group performance, percentile ranks or bands need to be used. An added convenience of the SCAT II norm tables that the SCAT I tables do not have is that one can enter the tables with the raw score instead of having first to obtain the converted score from another table. With regard to the precision of the norms, the authors carefully note that the accuracy of a P.R. for an individual depends primarily upon two sources of error: (a) the standard error of measurement of the test, and (b) the standard error of the mean of the norm group. They then note that the standard error of measurement indicates the extent to which the sample of items actually used in the test represents the universe of items that might have been included. This statement is true if KR 20 is used as a reliability measure in obtaining the standard error of measurement, as in fact it was. But the statement does not properly conform to the description on page nine of the Handbook as to what constitutes "error"—namely, "such extraneous factors as fatigue and practice" (commonly subsumed under some such label as "occasions-variance") as well as different samples of items. If this is what "error" is (and it surely should be), then an alternate forms reliability coefficient that takes account of occasions-variance as well as differences in item sampling is called for. It has already been noted that a consequence of failure to use such a reliability measure is that percentile bands are overly narrow. However, the practical difficulties of double testing on a large scale are well known. SUMMARY. In summary, the authors of SCAT II have produced a set of tests, each of which can be administered within a single class period. These relatively short tests have impressively high reliabilities. The validity data need considerable supplementing. College-level prediction is at present an unknown quantity, and little information is available about lower levels. What data are available, however, suggest that SCAT II can serve its predictive purposes well. Tables of norms have been carefully prepared, using scores that are comparable over different levels of schooling as well as conventional percentile ranks and bands. The tables

Cooperative School and College Ability Tests

are easily read and should prove serviceable to counselors, but norms for specially defined groups are not yet available.

For a review by Russel F. Green of the original 70 minute edition, see 6:452; for reviews by Frederick B. Davis, Hanford M. Fowler, and Julian C. Stanley, see 5:322.

[348]

★**Dennis Test of Scholastic Aptitude.** Grades 4–8, 5–8; DTSA; 1961–63; 2 levels labeled Forms 2, 3; no data on reliability; $2.50 per 35 tests; postpaid; specimen set not available; William H. Dennis; the Author. *
a) FORM 2. Grades 4–8; 1961–63; 1 form ('61, 2 pages); manual ('61, 6 pages); revised norms ('63, 2 pages); (40) minutes.
b) FORM 3. Grades 5–8; 1962; 1 form (2 pages); mimeographed temporary manual (11 pages); (35) minutes.

[349]

*****Doppelt Mathematical Reasoning Test.** Grades 16–17 and employees; 1954–68; DMRT; Form A ('54, 4 pages); revised manual ('68, 12 pages); bulletin of information ('70, 61 pages); guide for testing center operation ['64, 8 pages]; distribution restricted and test administered at specified licensed university centers; separate answer sheets (IBM 805-1230) must be used; scoring and reporting handled by the local center; examination fee to centers: $3 per examinee; fees to examinees are determined locally and include reporting of scores to the examinee and to 3 institutions or companies designated at the time of testing; additional score reports may be secured from the publisher at a fee of $1 each; 50(60) minutes; Jerome E. Doppelt; Psychological Corporation. *

REFERENCES

1–2. See 6:456.
3. HARDESTY, D. L., AND JONES, W. S. "Characteristics of Judged High Potential Management Personnel—The Operations of an Industrial Assessment Center." *Personnel Psychol* 21: 85-98 sp '68. * (*PA* 42:16197)
4. CARLETON, FREDERICK O. "Relationships Between Follow-Up Evaluations and Information Developed in a Management Assessment Center." Abstract. *Proc 78th Ann Conv Am Psychol Assn* 5(2):565-6 '70. * (*PA* 44:19655)

For a review by W. V. Clemans, see 6:456.

[350]

★**Draw-A-Man Test for Indian Children.** Ages 6–10; 1956–66; adaptation of *Goodenough Intelligence Test;* 1 form (no date, 1 page); manual ('66, 105 pages); Rs. 20 per manual and 20 tests, postage extra; (30) minutes; Pramila Phatak; distributed by Anand Agencies. *

REFERENCES

1. PHATAK, PRAMILA. "Application of Phatak's Draw-A-Man Scale for Indian Children of Gujarat." *Psychol Studies* 4:45-54 Jl '59. *
2. PHATAK, P. "Comparative Study of Revised Draw-A-Man Scale (Harris) and Phatak Draw-A-Man Scale for Indian Children." *Psychol Studies* 6:12-7 Jl '61. * (*PA* 38:2674)
3. PHATAK, P. "Sex Differences on Phatak's Draw-A-Man Scale." *Ed & Psychol R* 2:24-9 Ja '62. * (*PA* 37:7995)
4. MISRA, AJODHYA NATH. *To Work Out General Mental Ability Norms for Primary School Children Through Human Figure Drawings.* Doctor's thesis, University of Gorakhpur (Gorakhpur, India), 1966. (Abstract: *Indian Psychol R* 4:161-2)

J Psychol Res 12:51 Ja '68. M. A. Faroqi. [Review of the manual.] Those familiar with the work of Dr. Phatak on development and standardization of the Draw-a-Man Test will welcome the present publication. It brings together all the information available on the test, some of it previously unpublished and some published in different journals. It gives detailed procedure for administering and scoring the test, provides carefully presented scoring exercises. * A book review perhaps is not the right place to evaluate the test as such. This is one of the small number of attempts to carry through a full programme of test development in this country. This is not just Goodenough test standardized for Indian children. A new conception of scoring has been evolved. The scale has a very satisfactory relationship with other tests and also good inter-observer agreement, which is the test of objectivity applied in such scoring situations. The assumptions and implications in developing separate norms for the five 'environmental levels' and the particular conception of 'environmental levels' employed here need careful examination. The present publication will serve as a useful starting point for research workers who need a simple, convenient intelligence test and are prepared to learn the scoring scheme.

[351]

★**Gilliland Learning Potential Examination.** Ages 6 and over; 1966; GLPE; an intelligence test "for use with remedial readers and the culturally disadvantaged"; 1 to 4 scores: total score for all subjects, non-reading-noncultural, predicted comprehension, and visual memory for subjects with reading problems; some subtests may be omitted in grades 3 and over to obtain a quick score and in grades 3 and under to obtain a primary score; 1 form (12 pages); manual (31 pages); norms booklet (12 pages); no data on reliability; 25¢ per test; 75¢ per set of keys, norms booklet, and manual (free with 50 or more tests); $1 per set of scoring templates; 75¢ per specimen set; postpaid; (40–50) minutes; Hap Gilliland; Montana Reading Clinic Publications. *

ALBERT J. HARRIS, *Emeritus Professor of Education, The City University of New York, New York, New York.*

This test is described by the author as an intelligence or scholastic aptitude test intended specifically for use with poor readers and "culturally handicapped" children. The test has not been fully standardized and is not recommended for use in its present state of development. Reasons for this statement are given below.

The test contains eight subtests. Test 1, Visual Memory, involves drawing from memory a series of designs held up by the examiner; it is not included in the total score, but used only to disclose an area of potential weakness. Test 2 is a symbol-substitution test called Symbolic Representation in which the symbols have some visual resemblance to the pictured objects they represent. In Test 3a the same symbols are employed and the task is to name them, in writing in group administration or orally in individual administration. In Test 3b, Symbol Interpretation, the task is to combine the sequence of symbols presented in Test 3a into a meaningful message. Tests 2 and 3 obviously were inspired by Indian picture writing. Test 4, called Relationships, is a pictorial analogies test. In Test 5, Listening Comprehension, a story about an Indian boy is read aloud by the examiner and 10 three-choice pictorial items test recall of details and comprehension. Test 6, Picture Completion, has an unusual format reminiscent of the old *Healy Pictorial Completion Test*, adapted to group testing; in each of 8 pictures, three or four white rectangles blot out parts of the picture, and the task is to select the correct choices from among 10 pictures and write their numbers in the correct spaces. Test 7, Information and Interests, uses a pictorial format in which 10 interest areas are sampled by five items each, using a picture matching form of response.

The test is intended to cover a wide range, ages 6 through 15. IQ norms are provided at six-month intervals, for a variety of scores: Total Score, NR (low reading or culturally different, omitting Tests 3b and 7), QS (quick scoring, based on the four subtests that are easiest to score), Pri (primary, omitting the two most difficult subtests), and PC (Predicted Comprehension, based on Tests 2 and 5 only). Norms are based on "2100 students in six western states." No information is given about sampling procedures used. There are also separate norms for Indian children based on 1250 cases. Time limits are quite short on some subtests, flexible on others.

Statistical information provided in the manual is far below expected standards. Absolutely no information of any kind is given concerning reliability. No information is given about item validity, correlations with achievement, or validation of the special scores provided. The manual provides one short paragraph on validity, which contains the following statement: "Statistical studies completed at the time of publication indicate a very high (above .80) correlation with the non-language portions of other highly regarded intelligence tests." If any further statistical work has been done on the test since its publication in 1966, the author did not supply information about it.

This test should be either further developed with the assistance of a competent statistician and testing specialist, or withdrawn from the market. At present it must be considered an experimental test not ready for general use, even with the populations for which the author intended it.

HOWARD B. LYMAN, *Associate Professor of Psychology, University of Cincinnati, Cincinnati, Ohio.*

The GLPE is a test of intelligence emphasizing nonreading content, designed for individual or group administration, especially to Indians and other rural Americans age 6 and over.

Eight subtests combine in various ways to yield 1 to 4 intelligence scores, a visual memory score, and 10 interest scores. Visual Memory involves reproducing a design, exposed for five seconds, after a five-second delay. Symbolic Representation is a picture-symbol substitution task; Symbolic Identification involves symbol-picture substitution from memory of the previous test; Symbolic Interpretation demands translating the Identification task into a story. Relationship (only 10 items, but of 3 different types!) demands recognition of an association among drawings. In Listening Comprehension, the examinee selects drawings most closely related to a 200-word story that has been read to him. Picture Completion, similar to the classic *Healy Pictorial Completion Test,* has the examinee select drawings which fit appropriately into cutouts in a larger picture. In General Information and Interests, the examinee has 20 seconds to decide which sets of pictorial items seem easiest to him and then 10 minutes to select the answers in whatever order desired.

All subtests except Visual Memory contribute to Total. Dropping Symbolic Interpretation and General Information yields the "Non Reading and Non Cultural" score (sometimes NR, sometimes NR-NC, and probably the NC—explained nowhere—used in norms "for reservation Indians and other isolated rural groups"). Dropping (additionally) Symbol Identification and replacing General Information and Picture Completion yields the Quick Scoring score. Dropping Picture Completion and General Information while replacing Symbol Identification yields the Primary score "for children in grade 2 or below" (although norms are shown through age 15-11). The Predicted Comprehension score is the sum of Symbolic Representation and Picture Completion and "should be figured for all children whose noncultural IQ scores are 5 or more points higher than their total IQ scores and for all children who are suspected of having reading problems."

Visual Memory is treated separately. The test must be difficult to score reliably, but no evidence of scorer reliability is cited. The logic of some scoring is questionable: e.g., simple reversal of a figure sometimes gives less credit than does no drawing at all. Without explanation, the lowest-scoring 4% on single-year age norms are rated Critical; 4-12%, Problem Area; 12-25%, Low; and Upper 75%, Normal.

In addition, the rows of the General Information test are scored separately and used as guides to 10 "reading interest" areas. Here as elsewhere, the author places great faith in *face* validity.

Validity is dismissed with a single sentence: "Statistical studies completed at the time of publication indicate a very high (above .80) correlation with the nonlanguage portions of other [sic!] highly accepted intelligence tests." A letter from the author reveals that this was a single study with the nonverbal part of the *California Short-Form Test of Mental Maturity*, where a correlation of "+.8506" was found between mental ages on the CTMM and the GLPE; based on a combination of 18 third grade and 22 sixth grade pupils, even this one correlation coefficient is spurious because of the heterogeneity of the group. Other statistical data are completely missing as is any statement of how the IQ's were derived. There is no mention of mental ages (used in the one study). There is no discussion of preliminary research or the rationale of item content.

The norms were based on "2100 students in six western states." "'Indian' scores were derived from 1250 rural and reservation Indians" in four northwestern states. It is uncertain whether the "2100 students" include the 1,250 Indians. No further information is given about the norms groups. Representativeness is doubtful, however, for there is at least one reversal in levels: slightly lower raw scores are needed for a given IQ at ages 12-6 through 12-11 than at ages 12-0 through 12-5.

The test booklet itself looks homemade. The drawings are rough and sometimes unclear. The booklet looks jumbled and crowded. The paper is not sufficiently opaque, for printing shows through on the opposite side of the sheet. This poor printing must be confusing on some tests (e.g., Visual Memory) and helpful on at least one other (Symbol Identification).

Gilliland's purpose of providing an intelligence test for rural and Indian youth is commendable. The test has some novel features, should be interesting to children, and does possess some face validity; but there is still much work that must be done on it. I suspect that, given some assistance (perhaps from a foundation or major test publisher), the author might be able to develop this instrument into a respectable test—especially if he could narrow his interest and concentrate on fewer scores. But in its present form, there is little to recommend it for use with Indians or anyone else.

[352]

Goodenough-Harris Drawing Test. Ages 3–15; 1926–63; GHDT; revision and extension of the *Goodenough Intelligence Test;* 1 form ('63, 4 pages); manual ('63, 80 pages, reprinted from *135* below); quality scale cards ('63, 24 cards); $3.90 per 35 tests; $2.90 per set of quality scale cards; $1.50 per manual; $5 per specimen set; postage extra; (10–15) minutes; Florence L. Goodenough and Dale B. Harris; Harcourt Brace Jovanovich, Inc. *

REFERENCES

1–60. See 4:292.
61–94. See 5:335.
95–137. See 6:460.
138. EARL, C. J. C. "The Human Figure Drawings of Adult Defectives." *J Mental Sci* 79:305-27 Ap '33. * (*PA* 8:5518)
139. HUNKIN, V. "Validation of the Goodenough Draw-A-Man Test for African Children." *J Social Res (Pretoria)* 1:52-63 Jl '50. * (*PA* 27:1181)
140. DÖRKEN, HERBERT, JR. "Personality Factors Associated With Paraplegia and Prolonged Hospitalization: A Clinical Note." *Can J Psychol* 5:134-7 S '51. * (*PA* 26:2922)
141. ANASTASI, ANNE, AND D'ANGELO, RITA Y. "A Comparison of Negro and White Preschool Children in Language Development and Goodenough Draw-A-Man IQ." *J Genetic Psychol* 81:147-65 D '52. * (*PA* 27:6492)
142. GOLDENBERG, SAMUEL. *Some Aspects of Diagnosis of Cerebral Damage in Children.* Doctor's thesis, University of Washington (Seattle, Wash.), 1953. (*DA* 13:1259)
143. DUNN, MICHAEL BUTLER. *Global Evaluation of Children's Drawings of "Person" and "Self."* Doctor's thesis, Columbia University (New York, N.Y.), 1955. (*DA* 15:1254)
144. DOWLEN, CAROLINE LAWTHER. *Parental Attitudes in Relation to Their Children's Social Acceptance, Intellectual Functioning Level and Emotional Adjustment.* Doctor's thesis, University of Houston (Houston, Tex.), 1956. (*DA* 16:2203)
145. VARVA, FRANK IRVIN. *An Investigation of the Effect of Auditory Deficiency Upon Performance With Special Reference to Concrete and Abstract Tasks.* Doctor's thesis, University of Pittsburgh (Pittsburgh, Pa.), 1956. (*DA* 16:2532)
146. WILSON, JOHN LEOD. *Changes in Brightness of Children, Age Three to Eleven, Living in a Low Socioeconomic Environment.* Doctor's thesis, Indiana University (Bloomington, Ind.), 1957. (*DA* 17:2211)
147. DENNIS, WAYNE. "Handwriting Conventions as Determinants of Human Figure Drawings." *J Consult Psychol* 22:293-5 Ag '58. * (*PA* 34:710)
148. ROBINAULT, ISABEL PICK. *Preschool Children's Accomplishments in Tactual and Visual Form Perception.* Doctor's thesis, Columbia University (New York, N.Y.), 1958. (*DA* 19:3219)
149. FULLER, CARL WELLINGTON. *A Study of the Growth and Organization of Certain Mental Abilities in Young Deaf Children.* Doctor's thesis, Northwestern University (Evanston, Ill.), 1959. (*DA* 20:2382)

150. Hozier, Ann. "On the Breakdown of the Sense of Reality: A Study of Spatial Perception in Schizophrenia." *J Consult Psychol* 23:185-94 Je '59. * (*PA* 34:4680)
151. Ogilvie, Douglas S. *A Pilot Study of an Extension of the Goodenough Draw-A-Man Test.* Master's thesis, Fordham University (New York, N.Y.), 1959.
152. Santos, Bertha. *A Comparison of Memory and Learning Ability With Social Competence and Social Participation in Aged Senile Dements in a Mental Institution.* Doctor's thesis, New York University (New York, N.Y.), 1959. (*DA* 20:1441)
153. Holden, Raymond Henry. *Changes in Body Imagery of Physically Handicapped Children Due to Summer Camp Experience.* Doctor's thesis, Boston University (Boston, Mass.), 1960. (*DA* 21:3165)
154. Levinson, Boris M. "A Comparative Study of the Verbal and Performance Ability of Monolingual and Bilingual Native Born Jewish Preschool Children of Traditional Parentage." *J Genetic Psychol* 97:93-112 S '60. * (*PA* 35:6190)
155. Phatak, P. "A Study of the Revised Goodenough Scale With Reference to Artistic and Non-Artistic Drawings." *J Voc & Ed Guid* 7:35-40 Ag '60. * (*PA* 36:1HD35P)
156. Cohen, Haskel. "Psychological Test Findings in Adolescents Having Ovarian Dysgenesis." *Psychosom Med* 24:249-56 Mr-Ap '62. * (*PA* 37:5107)
157. Corah, Norman L., and Corah, Patricia Laney. "A Study of Body Image in Children With Cleft Palate and Cleft Lip." *J Genetic Psychol* 103:133-7 S '63. * (*PA* 39:2414)
158. Redbird, Helen Marie. *A Study of the Intelligence of Children of Domestic Agricultural Migrant Workers in Colorado.* Doctor's thesis, University of Colorado (Boulder, Colo.), 1963. (*DA* 24:4486)
159. Singer, Margaret Thaler. Chap. 12, "Personality Measurements in the Aged," pp. 217-49. In *Human Aging: A Biological and Behavioral Study.* Edited by James E. Birren, Robert N. Butler, Samuel W. Greenhouse, Louis Sokoloff, and Marian R. Yarrow. National Institute of Mental Health, Public Health Service Publication No. 986. Washington, D.C.: United States Government Printing Office, 1963. Pp. xiii, 328. * (*PA* 38:5821)
160. Balinky, Jean Lahn. *A Configurational Approach to the Prediction of Academic Achievement in First Grade.* Doctor's thesis, Rutgers—The State University (New Brunswick, N.J.), 1964. (*DA* 25:2844)
161. Briggs, Peter F., and Nelson, Susan. "The Effect of Non-Dominant Hand Execution on the Goodenough Draw-A-Man Test." *J Clin Psychol* 20:496 O '64. * (*PA* 39:12277)
162. Broverman, Donald M. "Generality and Behavioral Correlates of Cognitive Styles." *J Consult Psychol* 28:487-500 D '64. * (*PA* 39:7680)
163. Danford, Bart Harland. *Some Correlates of Two Brief Intelligence Tests Used by Pediatricians.* Doctor's thesis, University of Houston (Houston, Tex.), 1964. (*DA* 26:1772)
164. Easley, Glenn Truett. *The Draw-A-Man Test as an Index of Reading Readiness.* Doctor's thesis, Washington State University (Pullman, Wash.), 1964. (*DA* 25:2881)
165. Fahmy, Mostafa. "Initial Exploring of the Intelligence of Shilluk Children: Studies in the Southern Sudan." *Vita Hum* 7(3-4):164-77 '64. * (*PA* 39:7815)
166. Farrant, Roland H. "The Intellective Abilities of Deaf and Hearing Children Compared by Factor Analyses." *Am Ann Deaf* 109:306-25 My '64. * (*PA* 39:2442)
167. Grinder, Robert E.; Spotts, Wendy S.; and Curti, Margaret Wooster. "Relationships Between Goodenough Draw-A-Man Test Performance and Skin Color Among Preadolescent Jamaican Children." *J Social Psychol* 62:181-8 Ap '64. * (*PA* 39:5121)
168. Kennedy, Wallace A., and Lindner, Ronald S. "A Normative Study of the Goodenough Draw-A-Man Test on Southeastern Negro Elementary School Children." *Child Develop* 35:33-62 Mr '64. * (*PA* 38:8425)
169. Ouellette, Florian E. *The Administration of the Goodenough Draw-A-Man Test to Canadian Eskimos.* Master's thesis, University of Ottawa (Ottawa, Ont., Canada), 1964.
170. Shipp, Donald E., and Loudon, Mary Lou. "The Draw-A-Man Test and Achievement in the First Grade." *J Ed Res* 57:518-21 Jl-Ag '64. *
171. Silver, Archie A., and Hagin, Rosa A. "Specific Reading Ability: Follow-Up Studies." *Am J Orthopsychiatry* 34:95-102 Ja '64. * (*PA* 39:2863)
172. Sweeney, Neil R. "Reliability of Experienced and Inexperienced Scorers on Goodenough Draw-A-Man Test." *J Psychol* 57:281-7 Ap '64. * (*PA* 39:1763)
173. Vane, Julia R., and Kessler, Rosalyn T. "The Goodenough Draw-A-Man Test: Long Term Reliability and Validity." *J Clin Psychol* 20:487-8 O '64. * (*PA* 39:12313)
174. West, Peggy C. *An Experimental Study of Growth of Visual Perception in Educable Mentally Retarded Children Through Art Instruction as Indicated by Test-Retest of the Goodenough Draw-A-Man Test.* Master's thesis, East Tennessee State University (Johnson City, Tenn.), 1964.
175. Alzobaie, Abdul Jalil. "The Validity of the Goodenough Draw-A-Man Test in Iraq." *J Exp Ed* 33:331-5 su '65. * (*PA* 39:12273)
176. Badri, Malik B. "Influence of Modernization on Goodenough Quotients of Sudanese Children." *Percept & Motor Skills* 20:931-2 Je '65. * (*PA* 39:15209)

177. Badri, Malik B. "The Use of Finger Drawing in Measuring the Goodenough Quotient of Culturally Deprived Sudanese Children." *J Psychol* 59:333-4 Mr '65. *
178. Eklund, Susan, and Scott, Myrtle. "Effects of Bilingual Instruction on Test Response of Latin American Children." *Psychol Sch* 2:280 Jl '65. *
179. Fukada, Nahiko; Vahar, Mall; and Holowinsky, Ivan Z. "Qualitative Interpretation of Draw-A-Person Reproductions by Japanese Children." *Training Sch B* 62:119-25 N '65. * (*PA* 40:2132)
180. Khatena, Joe. *A Study of Comparative Performance on the Raven's Coloured Progressive Matrices and the Goodenough Draw-A-Man Test in Two Singapore Primary Schools.* Master's thesis, University of Singapore (Singapore, Malaysia), 1965.
181. Koppitz, Elizabeth Munsterberg. "A Comparison of Pencil and Crayon Drawings of Young Children." *J Clin Psychol* 21:191-4 Ap '65. * (*PA* 39:12393)
182. Meier, John Henry. *An Exploratory Factor Analysis of Psychodiagnostic and Case Study Information From Children in Special Education Classes for the Educable Mentally Handicapped.* Doctor's thesis, University of Denver (Denver, Colo.), 1965. (*DA* 26:3153)
183. Rajalakshmi, R., and Jeeves, M. A. "Discrimination Learning and Reversal Learning in Children as Related to Performance on Certain WISC Items and on the Goodenough Draw-A-Man Test." *J Genetic Psychol* 106:149-56 Mr '65. * (*PA* 39:11993)
184. Richey, Marjorie H. "Qualitative Superiority of the 'Self' Figure in Children's Drawings." *J Clin Psychol* 21:59-61 Ja '65. * (*PA* 39:12402)
185. Schulman, Jerome L.; Kaspar, Joseph C.; and Throne, Frances M. *Brain Damage and Behavior: A Clinical-Experimental Study.* Springfield, Ill.: Charles C Thomas, Publisher, 1965. Pp. ix, 164. *
186. Stone, Patricia A., and Ansbacher, Heinz L. "Social Interest and Performance on the Goodenough-Harris Draw-A-Man Test." *J Indiv Psychol* 21:178-86 N '65. * (*PA* 40:2963)
187. Thorpe, Joseph S. "A Cross-Cultural Study of Personality Development: Selection of Test Measures." *Congr Inter-Am Soc Psychol* 9(1964):242-9 ['65]. *
188. Throne, Frances M.; Kaspar, Joseph C.; and Schulman, Jerome L. "The Peabody Picture Vocabulary Test in Comparison With Other Intelligence Tests and an Achievement Test in a Group of Mentally Retarded Boys." *Ed & Psychol Meas* 25:589-95 su '65. * (*PA* 39:16072)
189. Abercrombie, M. L. J., and Tyson, M. C. "Body Image and Draw-A-Man Test in Cerebral Palsy." *Develop Med & Child Neurol* 8:9-15 F '66. * (*PA* 40:6965)
190. Alexander, Duane; Ehrhardt, Anke A.; and Money, John. "Defective Figure Drawing, Geometric and Human, in Turner's Syndrome." *J Nerv & Mental Dis* 142:161-7 F '66. * (*PA* 40:11185)
191. Auricchio, Elizabeth Williams. "Comparison of Several Methods of Scoring Draw-A-Person Tests." *Percept & Motor Skills* 23:1124 D '66. * (*PA* 41:5981)
192. Brenner, May Woolf, and Gillman, Selma. "Visuomotor Ability in Schoolchildren: A Survey." *Develop Med & Child Neurol* 8:686-703 D '66. * (*PA* 41:4397)
193. Carkhuff, Robert R. "Variations in Performance of Non-Institutionalized Retardates." *J Clin Psychol* 22:168-70 Ap '66. * (*PA* 40:8015)
194. Dennis, Wayne. "Goodenough Scores, Art Experience, and Modernization." *J Social Psychol* 68:211-28 Ap '66. * (*PA* 40:7590)
195. Dodd, John M., and Randall, Robert R. "A Comparison of Negro Children's Drawings of a Man and a Woman." *J Negro Ed* 35:287-8 su '66. *
196. Hiler, E. Wesley. "Prognostic Indicators for Children in a Psychiatric Hospital." *J Consult Psychol* 30:169-71 Ap '66. * (*PA* 40:6773)
197. Hirschenfang, Samuel; Jaramillo, Selene; and Benton, Joseph G. "Comparison of Scores on the Revised Stanford-Binet (L), Columbia Mental Maturity Scale (CMMS) and Goodenough Draw-A-Man Test of Children With Neurological Disorders." *Psychol Rep* 19:15-6 Ag '66. * (*PA* 40:12564)
198. Kernan, John S. "Test Age Equivalents for the Goodenough-Harris Drawing Scales." *Psychol Sch* 3:271-2 Jl '66. * (*PA* 41:1946)
199. McAninch, Myrene. "Body Image as Related to Perceptual-Cognitive-Motor Disabilities," pp. 137-70. In *Learning Disorders, Vol. 2.* Edited by Jerome Hellmuth. Seattle, Wash.: Special Child Publications, 1966. Pp. 422. *
200. Medinnus, Gene R.; Bobitt, Diane; and Hullett, Jack. "Effects of Training on the Draw-A-Man Test." *J Exp Ed* 35:62-3 w '66. *
201. Painter, Genevieve. "The Effect of a Rhythmic and Sensory Motor Activity Program on Perceptual Motor Spatial Abilities of Kindergarten Children." *Excep Children* 33:113-6 O '66. * (*PA* 41:800)
202. Quast, Wentworth, and Ireton, Harold. "Utility of the Goodenough Draw-A-Man Test as a Screening Device." *Percept & Motor Skills* 23:778 D '66. * (*PA* 41:7328)
203. Robinson, H. Alan. "Reliability of Measures Related to Reading Success of Average, Disadvantaged, and Advan-

taged Kindergarten Children." Comments by Samuel Weintraub. *Read Teach* 20:203–9 D '66. * *(PA* 41:3344)
204. SELLS, S. B. *Evaluation of Psychological Measures Used in the Health Examination Survey of Children Ages 6–11,* pp. 34–53. Public Health Service Publication No. 1000, Series 2, No. 15. Washington, D.C.: United States Government Printing Office, March 1966. Pp. viii, 67. * *(PA* 40:7217)
205. SILVERSTEIN, A. B. "Anxiety and the Quality of Human Figure Drawings." *Am J Mental Def* 70:607–8 Ja '66. * *(PA* 40:5889)
206. TAUBER, ROSALYN. "Identification of Potential Learning Disabilities." *Acad Ther Q* 2:116–9+ w '66–67. * *(PA* 41:5004)
207. TAYLOR, JAMES B. "The Use of Human Figure Drawings With the Upper Level Mentally Retarded." *Am J Mental Def* 71:423–6 N '66. * *(PA* 41:1851)
208. WATKINS, DWIGHT G. *A Validity Study of the Goodenough-Harris Drawing Test (GHDT) in a School Setting.* Doctor's thesis, University of Cincinnati (Cincinnati, Ohio), 1966. *(DA* 27:2080A)
209. BRENNER, MAY WOOLF; GILLMAN, SELMA; ZANGWILL, O. L.; AND FARRELL, MARGARET. "Visuo-Motor Disability in School Children." *Brit Med J* 4:259–62 N 4 '67. *
210. BROMWICH, ROSE MEYER. *Some Correlates of Stimulus-Bound Versus Stimulus-Free Verbal Responses to Pictures by Young Negro Boys.* Doctor's thesis, University of California (Los Angeles, Calif.), 1967. *(DA* 28:1290A)
211. DATTA, LOIS-ELLIN. "Draw-A-Person Test as a Measure of Intelligence in Preschool Children From Very Low Income Families." *J Consult Psychol* 31:626–30 D '67. * *(PA* 42:2561)
212. DUNN, JAMES A. "Inter- and Intra-Rater Reliability of the New Harris-Goodenough Draw-A-Man Test." *Percept & Motor Skills* 24:269–70 F '67. * *(PA* 41:8148)
213. DUNN, JAMES A. "Note on the Relation of Harris' Draw-A-Woman to WISC IQs." *Percept & Motor Skills* 24:316 F '67. * *(PA* 41:8880)
214. DUNN, JAMES A. "Validity Coefficients for the New Harris-Goodenough Draw-A-Man Test." *Percept & Motor Skills* 24:299–301 F '67. * *(PA* 41:8149)
215. ETUK, ELIZABETH EME SAMSON. *The Development of Number Concepts: An Examination of Piaget's Theory With Yoruba-Speaking Nigerian Children.* Doctor's thesis, Columbia University (New York, N.Y.), 1967. *(DA* 28:1295A)
216. JOHNSON, DALE L.; JOHNSON, CARMEN A.; AND PRICE-WILLIAMS, DOUGLASS. "The Draw-A-Man Test and Raven Progressive Matrices Performance of Guatemalan Maya and Ladino Children." *Revista Interamericana de Psicología* 1:143–57 Je '67. * *(PA* 41:11919)
217. KHATENA, JOE, AND GOWAN, J. C. "Crosscultural Measurement of Intelligence With the DAM and CPM." *Gifted Child Q* 11:227–30 w '67. * *(PA* 42:7111)
218. LEPPKE, RONALD DEAN. *Perceptual Approaches for Disadvantaged Anglo- and Mexican-American Students.* Doctor's thesis, University of the Pacific (Stockton, Calif.), 1967. *(DA* 28:1302A)
219. MARSHALL, ANNE. *The Abilities and Attainments of Children Leaving Junior Training Centres.* London: National Association for Mental Health, 1967. Pp. i, 62. *
220. MASON, ANNE W. "Specific (Developmental) Dyslexia." *Develop Med & Child Neurol* 9:183–90 Ap '67. * *(PA* 41:14066)
221. MONEY, JOHN, AND WANG, CHRISTINE. "Human Figure Drawing: 2, Quality Comparisons in Gender-Identity Anomalies, Klinefelter's Syndrome and Precocious Puberty." *J Nerv & Mental Dis* 144:55–8 Ja '67. * *(PA* 41:12170)
222. MUZEKARI, LOUIS H. "Relationships Between the Goodenough DAM and Stanford-Binet in Negro and White Public School Children." *J Clin Psychol* 23:86–7 Ja '67. * *(PA* 41:6253)
223. OLIVIER, K., AND BARCLAY, A. "Stanford-Binet and Goodenough-Harris Test Performances of Head Start Children." *Psychol Rep* 20:1175–9 Je '67. * *(PA* 41:15275)
224. PANTHER, EDWARD E. "Prediction of First-Grade Reading Achievement." *El Sch J* 68:44–8 O '67. *
225. SAK, HELEN G.; SMITH, ALFRED A.; AND DAVIES, JOSEPH. "Psychometric Evaluation of Children With Familial Dysautonomia." *Am J Psychiatry* 124:682–7 N '67. * *(PA* 42:5959)
226. STEINMAN, WARREN M. "The Use of Ambiguous Stimuli to Predict General Competence." *J Sci Lab Denison Univ* 48:7–14 Je '67. * *(PA* 42:2599)
227. VANE, JULIA R. "An Evaluation of the Harris Revision of the Goodenough Draw-A-Man Test." *J Clin Psychol* 23:375–7 Jl '67. * *(PA* 41:14461)
228. VOGEL, FRANCIS XAVIER. *The Relationship of the Form of School Organization to Selected Classroom Behaviors of Pupils.* Doctor's thesis, Northwestern University (Evanston, Ill.), 1967. *(DA* 28:3957A)
229. WELLS, DONALD G., AND PEDRINI, DUILIO T. "Relationship Between the Stanford-Binet L-M and the Goodenough D-A-M." *Psychol Sch* 4:371–5 O '67. * *(PA* 42:2592)
230. WELLS, DONALD G., AND PEDRINI, DUILIO T. "Relationships Between the S-B L-M, G-H, and PPVT With Institutionalized Retardates." *Am J Mental Def* 72:412–5 N '67. * *(PA* 42:7680)
231. YULE, WILLIAM; LOCKYER, LINDA; AND NOONE, AHILYA. "The Reliability and Validity of the Goodenough-Harris Drawing Test." *Brit J Ed Psychol* 37:110–1 F '67. *
232. ARMSTRONG, JUDITH GLANTZ. *Intellectual Competence and Coping Behavior in Preschool Children.* Doctor's thesis, University of California (Berkeley, Calif.), 1968. *(DA* 29:4837B)
233. ARTH, ALFRED ARTHUR. *A Study of the Relationship Between Non-Completion and Intelligence Exhibited by Sixth Grade Elementary School Students.* Doctor's thesis, University of Oklahoma (Norman, Okla.), 1968. *(DA* 29:1666A)
234. BACH, LLOYD CARL. *A Comparison of Selected Psychological Tests Used With Trainable Mentally Retarded Children.* Doctor's thesis, University of South Dakota (Vermillion, S.D.), 1968. *(DA* 29:2990A)
235. BATLIN, R., AND KRAFT, IRVIN A. "Psycholinguistic Evaluation of Children Referred for Private Consultation to a Child Psychiatrist." *J Learn Dis* 1:600–5 O '68. * *(PA* 45:2995)
236. BUCHANAN, BARBARA A. *Adolescent Human Figure Drawings Evaluated by the Goodenough-Harris Scoring Procedure Under Timed and Untimed Conditions.* Master's thesis, Pennsylvania State University (University Park, Pa.), 1968.
237. DE MOREAU, MARGARET, AND KOPPITZ, ELIZABETH M. "Relationship Between Goodenough Draw-A-Man Test IQ Scores and Koppitz Human Figure Drawing Scores." *Revista Interamericana de Psicología* 2:35–40 Mr '68. * *(PA* 42:13753)
238. FINE, MARVIN J., AND TRACY, D. B. "Performance of Normal and EMR Boys on the FRPV and GHDT." *Am J Mental Def* 72:648–52 Mr '68. * *(PA* 42:11049)
239. GADDES, W. H.; MCKENZIE, AUDREY; AND BARNSLEY, ROGER. "Psychometric Intelligence and Spatial Imagery in Two Northwest Indian and Two White Groups of Children." *J Social Psychol* 75:35–42 Je '68. * *(PA* 42:13575)
240. GELLERT, ELIZABETH. "Comparison of Children's Self-Drawings With Their Drawings of Other Persons." *Percept & Motor Skills* 26:123–38 F '68. * *(PA* 42:10614)
241. GEORGAS, JAMES G., AND PAPADOPOULOU, ELLIE. "The Harris-Goodenough and the Developmental Form Sequence With Five-Year-Old Greek Children." *Percept & Motor Skills* 26:352–4 Ap '68. * *(PA* 42:11927)
242. HEPBURN, ANDREW W., AND DONNELLY, FRANK. "Psychometric Identification of Kindergarten Children With Visual Perceptual Impairment." *Excep Children* 34:708–9 My '68. *
243. KEOGH, BARBARA K. "The Copying Ability of Young Children." *Ed Res* 11:43–7 N '68. * *(PA* 45:6667)
244. KEOGH, BARBARA K., AND KEOGH, JACK F. "Pattern Walking: A Dimension of Visuomotor Performance." *Excep Children* 34:617–8 Ap '68. * *(PA* 42:17546)
245. KIRSCHNER, FREDERICK ERNST. *A Quasi-Experimental Study Using Human Figure Drawings for Predicting Intellectual Maturity in Kindergarten Children.* Doctor's thesis, University of Toledo (Toledo, Ohio), 1968. *(DA* 29:2566A)
246. KRAFT, MARCIA B. "The Face-Hand Test." *Develop Med & Child Neurol* 10:214–9 Ap '68. * *(PA* 42:13487)
247. KROP, HARRY D. "Education and the Self-Concept of the Mentally Retarded." *Training Sch B* 65:57–64 Ag '68. * *(PA* 44:4045)
248. LEVINE, HAROLD A., AND GROSS, MARILYN. "Suitability of the Harris Revision of the Goodenough Draw-A-Man Test for a Psychiatric Population." *J Clin Psychol* 24:350 Jl '68. * *(PA* 42:16415)
249. LEVY, IRWIN SAUL. *The Effect of Age as a Variable on the Scores of the Harris-Goodenough Drawing Test of Educable Retardates.* Doctor's thesis, University of North Carolina (Chapel Hill, N.C.), 1968. *(DA* 29:2123A)
250. LUONG, CORINA K. MONGCAL. *An Analysis of Factors Related to Difficulties in Learning and Adjustment Among Minority Group Children.* Doctor's thesis, Bryn Mawr College (Bryn Mawr, Pa.), 1968. *(DAI* 30:4795B)
251. MCCLELLAN, DORINDA ANN. *Factors Which Are Predictive of Reading Success of Low-Socio-Economic Children in Selected First Grades.* Doctor's thesis, Oklahoma State University (Stillwater, Okla.), 1968. *(DAI* 30:933A)
252. MIEZITIS, SOLVEIGA AUSMA. *An Exploratory Study of Divergent Production in Preschoolers.* Doctor's thesis, University of Toronto (Toronto, Ont., Canada), 1968. *(DAI* 30:589A)
253. MILLICHAP, J. GORDON; AYMAT, FERNANDO; STURGIS, LORETTA H.; LARSEN, KATHERINE W.; AND EGAN, ROSEMARY A. "Hyperkinetic Behavior and Learning Disorders: 3, Battery of Neuropsychological Tests in Controlled Trial of Methylphenidate." *Am J Dis Children* 116:235–44 S '68. * *(PA* 43:4123)
254. RAWL, MIRIAM FREEMAN. *A Study of the Relationship of Verbal Ability and Vocalization to Conceptual-Motor Tasks in Disadvantaged First-Grade Children.* Doctor's thesis, University of South Carolina (Columbia, S.C.), 1968. *(DAI* 30:1028A)
255. ROBERTON, MARY ANN. *The Ability of Children Three, Five, and Seven Years of Age to Imitate Body Positions.* Master's thesis, University of California (Berkeley, Calif.), 1968.
256. ROBINSON, H. ALAN, AND HANSON, EARL. "Reliability

of Measures of Reading Achievement." *Read Teach* 21:307–13+ Ja '68. * (*PA* 42:17652)

257. STERNLOF, R. E.; PARKER, H. J.; AND MCCOY, J. F. "Relationships Between the Goodenough DAM Test and the Columbia Mental Maturity Test for Negro and White Headstart Children." *Percept & Motor Skills* 27:424–6 O '68. *

258. STRÜMPFER, D. J. W., AND HUYSAMEN, G. K. "Correlates of the Communication Organ Score on the Harris-Goodenough Drawing Test." *J Indiv Psychol* 24:60–2 My '68. * (*PA* 42:12133)

259. STRÜMPFER, D. J. W., AND MIENIE, C. J. P. "A Validation of the Harris-Goodenough Test." *Brit J Ed Psychol* 38:96–100 F '68. * (*PA* 42:12134)

260. SUNDBERG, NORMAN, AND BALLINGER, THOMAS. "Nepalese Children's Cognitive Development as Revealed by Drawings of Man, Woman, and Self." *Child Develop* 39:969–85 S '68. * (*PA* 43:3765)

261. THOMPSON, CHARLES WILMER. *The Harris-Goodenough Draw-A-Man Test as a Predictor of Intelligence With Suspected Educable Retardates.* Doctor's thesis, University of North Carolina (Chapel Hill, N.C.), 1968. (*DA* 29:4339A)

262. BERKOWITZ, MICHAEL C. *A Revised Goodenough Draw-A-Man Test as a Measure of School Readiness.* Master's thesis, Kansas State Teachers College (Emporia, Kan.), 1969.

263. BEVAN, WILTSHIRE E., AND GRAY, JOHN E. "Draw-A-Man and Raven's Progressive Matrices (1938) Intelligence Test Performance of Reserve Indian Children." *Can J Behav Sci* 1(2):119–22 Ap '69. * (*PA* 44:12604)

264. BYRD, COLEEN, AND SPRINGFIELD, LYNN. "A Note on the Draw-A-Person Test With Adolescent Retardates." *Am J Mental Def* 73(4):578–9 Ja '69. * (*PA* 43:8571)

265. CAMPBELL, HENRY E. *The Influence of Motivation on Goodenough-Harris Intelligence Test Scores.* Master's thesis, Jersey City State College (Jersey City, N.J.), 1969.

266. DOKECKI, PAUL R.; FREDE, MARTHA C.; AND GAUTNEY, DONALD B. "Criterion, Construct, and Predictive Validities of the Wechsler Preschool and Primary Scale of Intelligence." Abstract. *Proc 77th Ann Conv Am Psychol Assn* 4(2):505–6 '69. * (*PA* 44:1253)

267. DUDEK, S. Z.; GOLDBERG, J. S.; LESTER, E. P.; AND HARRIS, B. R. "The Validity of Cognitive, Perceptual-Motor and Personality Variables for Prediction of Achievement in Grade 1 and Grade 2." *J Clin Psychol* 25(2):165–70 Ap '69. * (*PA* 43:14874)

268. HALL, JOSEPH CLARENCE. *A Comparative Study of Selected Measures of Intelligence as Predictors of First-Grade Reading Achievement in a Culturally Disadvantaged Population.* Doctor's thesis, Temple University (Philadelphia, Pa.), 1969. (*DAI* 31:1074A)

269. HENDERSON, NORMAN B.; GOFFENEY, BARBARA; AND BUTLER, BRUCE V. "Do Negro Children Project a Self-Image of Helplessness and Inadequacy in Drawing a Person?" Abstract. *Proc 77th Ann Conv Am Psychol Assn* 4(1):437–8 '69. * (*PA* 43:17226)

270. MALONEY, MICHAEL P., AND PAYNE, LAWRENCE E. "Validity of the Draw-A-Person Test as a Measure of Body Image." *Percept & Motor Skills* 29(1):119–22 Ag '69. * (*PA* 44:2366)

271. MINSKY, RAPHAEL. *An Investigation Into Children's Conceptualization of Proportionality as Expressed in Their Drawings of the Male Human Figure.* Doctor's thesis, University of Maryland (College Park, Md.), 1969. (*DAI* 31:1082A)

272. NASE, ROBERT R. *A Correlation Study of the Harris-Goodenough Draw-A-Man and the Wechsler Preschool and Primary Scale of Intelligence With Children Referred for Psychological Testing.* Master's thesis, Mankato State College (Mankato, Minn.), 1969.

273. NIELSEN, HELLE H., AND RINGE, KIRSTEN. "Visuo-Perceptive and Visuo-Motor Performance of Children With Reading Disabilities." *Scandinavian J Psychol* 10(4):225–31 '69. * (*PA* 44:9351)

274. ROCHE, DERMOT, AND ROCHE, P. J. D. "A Validity Study of the Goodenough-Harris Draw-A-Man Test." Abstract. *B Brit Psychol Soc* 22(76):215–6 Jl '69. *

275. VROEGH, KAREN, AND HANDRICH, MILLICENT. "The Validity of the Howard Maze Test as a Measure of Stimulus-Seeking in Preschool Children." *Ed & Psychol Meas* 29(2):495–502 su '69. * (*PA* 44:16395)

276. WATSON, BILLY LESLIE. *Field Dependence and Early Reading Achievement.* Doctor's thesis, University of California (Los Angeles, Calif.), 1969. (*DAI* 31:656A)

277. YATER, ALLAN C.; BARCLAY, ALLAN G.; AND MCGILLIGAN, ROBERT. "Inter-Rater Reliability of Scoring Goodenough-Harris Drawings by Disadvantaged Preschool Children." *Percept & Motor Skills* 28(1):281–2 F '69. * (*PA* 43:11364)

278. YEN, SHERMAN M. Y. *A Comparative Study of Test Variability With Peabody Picture Vocabulary Test, Goodenough's Draw-A-Man Test, and Stanford-Binet Intelligence Scale as Intellectual Measurement With a Group of Urban Low Socio-Economic Status Pre-School Pupils.* Doctor's thesis, Catholic University of America (Washington, D.C.), 1969. (*DAI* 30:2625A)

279. CARLSON, JERRY S. "A Note on the Relationships Between the Draw-A-Man Test, the Progressive Matrices Test, and Conservation." *J Psychol* 74(2):231–5 Mr '70. * (*PA* 44:12310)

280. CUNDICK, BERT P. "Measures of Intelligence on Southwest Indian Students." *J Social Psychol* 81(2):151–6 Ag '70. * (*PA* 44:20655)

281. EYSENCK, SYBIL B. G.; RUSSELL, T.; AND EYSENCK, H. J. "Extraversion, Intelligence, and Ability to Draw a Person." *Percept & Motor Skills* 30(3):925–6 Je '70. * (*PA* 44:16371)

282. GAYTON, WILLIAM F. "Validity of the Harris Quality Scale With a Child Guidance Population." *Percept & Motor Skills* 31(1):17–8 Ag '70. * (*PA* 45:4532)

283. GAYTON, WILLIAM F.; BASSETT, JOHN E.; AND BISHOP, JOHN S. "The Harris Revision of the Goodenough Draw-A-Man Test: Suitability for a Retarded Population." *J Clin Psychol* 26(4):522–3 O '70. * (*PA* 45:4790)

284. HARCKHAM, LAURA D. *Prediction of Reading Achievement in Grades One, Two, Three, and Four Using Kindergarten Measures.* Doctor's thesis, Fordham University (New York, N.Y.), 1970. (*DAI* 31:3266A)

285. HARMAN, CHARLES E., AND RAYMOND, CHRISTOPHER S. "Computer Prediction of Chronic Psychiatric Patients." *J Nerv & Mental Dis* 150(6):490–503 Je '70. * (*PA* 45:8497)

286. INGRAM, T. T. S.; MASON, A. W.; AND BLACKBURN, I. "A Retrospective Study of 82 Children With Reading Disability." *Develop Med & Child Neurol* 12(3):271–81 Je '70. *

287. MERZ, WILLIAM ROBERT, SR. *A Factor Analysis of the Goodenough-Harris Drawing Test Across Four Ethnic Groups.* Doctor's thesis, University of New Mexico (Albuquerque, N.M.), 1970. (*DAI* 31:1627A)

288. NASH, HARVEY, AND HARRIS, DALE B. "Body Proportions in Children's Drawings of a Man." *J Genetic Psychol* 117(1):85–90 S '70. * (*PA* 45:2181)

289. PETRIE, RONALD GENE. *A Comparison of Verbal Responses of Anglo-Migrant and Anglo-Resident Children.* Doctor's thesis, Oregon State University (Corvallis, Ore.), 1970. (*DAI* 31:3181A)

290. ROCHE, DERMOT. "On the Concurrent Validity of the Goodenough-Harris Draw-A-Person Test." *Papers Psychol* 4(1–2):5–7 Ap-O '70. *

291. SAUNDERS, MAUDERIE HANCOCK, AND TESKA, PERCY T. "An Analysis of Cultural Differences on Certain Projective Techniques." *J Negro Ed* 39(2):109–15 sp '70. *

292. SINHA, M. "A Study of the Harris Revision of the Goodenough Draw-A-Man Test." Thesis abstract. *Brit J Ed Psychol* 40(2):221–2 Je '70. *

293. SPADAFORE, GERALD JOSEPH. *Differences in Learning Between Retardates and Nonretardates on the Draw-A-Man Test.* Doctor's thesis, University of Nebraska (Lincoln, Neb.), 1970. (*DAI* 31:1633A)

294. WERNER, EMMY E., AND MURALIDHARAN, RAJALAKSHMI. "Nutrition, Cognitive Status and Achievement Motivation of New Delhi Nursery School Children." *J Cross-Cultural Psychol* 1(3):271–81 S '70. * (*PA* 45:3803)

295. WILLIAMS, BARBARA KATHLEEN. *The Goodenough-Harris Draw-A-Man Test and Reflection-Impulsivity.* Master's thesis, University of Alberta (Edmonton, Alta., Canada), 1970.

ANNE ANASTASI, *Professor of Psychology and Chairman of the Department, Fordham University, New York, New York.*

Development of this revision and extension of the Goodenough Draw-A-Man test is described in detail in Harris' *Children's Drawings as Measures of Intellectual Maturity (135)*. Part 2 of this book is reproduced in toto as a separately published manual for the convenience of test users. This manual, however, is concerned exclusively with instructions for administration, scoring, and use of norms. For any information on the construction and technical properties of the test, one must consult the original book, which also provides a comprehensive literature survey of the psychology of children's drawings, covering both empirical and theoretical publications and including the use of drawings not only as cognitive indicators but also as projective personality devices. Research on the Draw-A-Man, beginning with its first appearance in 1926, is reviewed in detail.

Like the original test, the present revision focuses on the child's accuracy of observation and on the development of conceptual thinking, rather than on artistic skill. The number of scorable items or points has been increased from 51 to 73. These items were selected from a pool of about 100 on the basis of age differentiation, relation to total scores on the provisional form, and relation to group intelligence test scores. Data for this purpose were obtained from 50 boys and 50 girls at each year of age from 6 to 15 years, drawn from a larger sample tested in rural and urban areas of Minnesota and Wisconsin and representative of the national distribution with regard to paternal occupation. The manual gives detailed instructions, with illustrations, for scoring the 73 points on an all-or-none basis. Raw scores are converted to standard scores with a mean of 100 and a standard deviation of 15. Norms were established on a new standardization sample of 2,975 children between the ages of 5 and 15 years, representative of the occupational distribution of the U.S. in 1950, and distributed among four major geographical areas. A table is provided for converting the standard scores to percentiles, although the limitations of percentile scores are noted and the use of standard scores is recommended.

In the present version of the test, the subject is also asked to draw a picture of a woman and of himself, in that order. The Woman scale is scored in terms of 71 items selected by the same procedures followed in developing the Man scale. Because the correlation of the Woman scale with the Man scale is about as high as the odd-even reliability of either scale alone, Harris recommends that their standard scores be averaged for higher reliability. The Self scale was included as a possible projective test of personality, but available findings from this application are not promising. Currently, the manual provides a qualitative checklist for assessing performance on this scale and comparing the Self drawing with the other two drawings. This checklist is presented as a subjective and thus far untested guide. It is also suggested that the Self scale be scored on the points of the Man or Woman scale (depending upon the subject's sex) and a standard score found from the corresponding normative table. The Self scale is offered principally as a device for further research.

In the new scale, as in the earlier version, scorer reliabilities are usually over .90. In part, such interscorer agreement reflects the fullness of the scoring instructions and the care exercised in selecting items that can be scored with a minimum of uncertainty. Split-half reliabilities, found on the earlier form, are in the .70's and .80's. Retest reliabilities obtained with the earlier form over intervals as long as three months fall mostly in the .60's and .70's. Short-term fluctuations in performance are negligible as indicated by a study of the scores obtained on the revised form by kindergarten children given the test on each of ten consecutive school days. Examiner variance has proved insignificant, as has the effect of art training in school upon test scores. Judged artistic merit of the drawings, moreover, bears little or no relation to the point scores assigned to the drawings. Scores in the revised Man scale correspond closely to those obtained with the original version, the correlations ranging from .91 to .98 in homogeneous age groups.

An alternative way of evaluating performance on both Man and Woman scales utilizes the Quality scales. These scales substitute a simplified, global, qualitative assessment of the entire drawing for the detailed point scoring. The scorer simply chooses one of twelve sample drawings that most closely matches the performance level of the subject's product and assigns the scale value of that sample to the drawing. A separate quality scale is provided for the Man and Woman drawings. The scale drawings were selected by having judges assign specimen drawings to categories by the method of equal-appearing intervals, the specific procedures being quite similar to those followed by Thurstone in developing attitude scales. Interscorer reliabilities of the Quality scales are mostly in the .80's. Correlations of standard scores derived from Quality scale ratings and from point scores cluster closely in the .80's but tend to be lower at the upper ages. The Quality scales also show less age differentiation than the point scales at the upper ages.

Harris summarizes correlations obtained between the earlier Draw-A-Man test and the Stanford-Binet, WISC, WAIS, PMA, and a few other intelligence and special aptitude tests. Nearly all these correlations are significant and most are substantial. It should be noted, however, that several correlations between MA's of children ranging widely in age are cited with the sole comment that "As would be expected,

MA scores correlate more highly than IQ scores" (p. 99). The reader is not cautioned that these correlations are spuriously high and had better be ignored. The principal evidence for the validity of the test, of course, derives from the item analysis procedures followed in developing the scales. The effectiveness of the age differentiation criterion employed in item selection is reflected in the consistent and sharp rises in mean raw point scores between ages 5 and 14. From age 14 to 15 there is a decided leveling off in the scores of both sexes on both Man and Woman scales.

In summary, the original Draw-A-Man test has been updated, extended, and restandardized; the crude ratio IQ has been replaced with standard scores; and a parallel form has been developed in the Woman scale. Efforts to extend the scale chronologically into the adolescent years have failed. On theoretical grounds, Harris proposes that the child's drawings reveal his conceptual maturity but cease to show increments when the child moves from concrete concepts to higher-order abstractions and turns increasingly to more practiced and more suitable verbal modes of expression. Attempts to utilize children's drawings as a projective technique for the assessment of personality characteristics likewise proved fruitless. Both the specific research with the present drawing test and an analysis of the published literature on children's drawings led Harris to conclude that "consistent and reliable patterns having diagnostic significance for personality probably cannot be found in children's drawings" and that such drawings "primarily express cognitive processes."

JAMES A. DUNN, *Director, Developmental Systems Division, American Institutes for Research, Palo Alto, California.*

The Draw-A-Man test was originally published in 1926 by Florence Goodenough. Since that time it has enjoyed widespread popularity. Twenty years after its introduction, Louttit and Browne found it was the third most frequently used test in clinical psychology. Fifteen years later, in 1961, Sundberg found it still in the "top ten." This record is especially impressive considering that the instrument is appropriate for use only with children.

The test calls for the child to "make a picture of a man." This is a simple task which seldom takes more than five or ten minutes to administer. It may be administered either individually or to groups. If it is administered individually, it is often given as the first test in a battery because it is nonthreatening, quick, and often elicits interesting comments on the part of the subject. Scoring time is also on the order of ten minutes.

In 1963 Harris (*135*) published the results of an extensive revision of the Draw-A-Man test. First, Harris extensively redeveloped the Goodenough scoring criteria on a highly objective, empirical basis. (Anyone who has used the old version of the Goodenough readily appreciates the increased specificity that Harris brings to the scoring of the test.) Second, Harris devoted extensive effort to a new standardization of the test (the quality of the standardization far exceeds that of the original). Third, Harris converted the IQ computation from the old mental age/chronological age ratio concept to the deviation IQ concept. Fourth, Harris introduced a companion Draw-A-Woman test. Finally, Harris introduced a drawing quality score.

In addition to material improvement in the Draw-A-Man test (it should add another 20 years of life to the Goodenough procedure, even at today's obsolescence rate), Harris has given us an excellent review of the use of children's drawings as measures of intelligence and an example of scientific caution in making generalizations as to the effectiveness of the use of children's drawings in personality assessment.

It is at this point that the first criticism of the *Goodenough-Harris Drawing Test* can be made. Anyone contemplating using the test should not buy the examiner's kit alone. The manual provided is for administration and scoring only. It is not a manual in the sense of the *Standards for Educational and Psychological Tests and Manuals*. Thus, from a technical professional point of view, the manual is inadequate. Considerations of scale development, standardization, reliability, and validity are treated in part one of Harris's book, *Children's Drawings as a Measure of Intellectual Maturity,* rather than in the administration manual. To be sure, the manual cites the book and refers to it as the "basic reference for the use of the test," but it is this reviewer's opinion that the case for purchasing the book and considering *it* as the actual manual is not made forcefully enough.

There is one major problem that bothers this

reviewer: the manner in which reliability and validity for the new scales were handled. The case for the reliability and validity of the Drawing Test scales rests with their obvious similarity to the 1926 test. Harris' 1963 book refers almost exclusively to 1926 Draw-A-Man reliabilities and validities. The manual cites only one study, involving four small samples of 75 subjects each, in which the interscorer reliabilities for the new scales are reported; and only one study, on Canadian-Indian children, which reports correlations between the 1926 scale and the 1963 scale. These latter correlations are on the order of .91 to .98, the same range as for correlations between scorings of the same protocols by independent scorers.

While there is a lack of information about test-retest reliability and correlations with other IQ tests for the new scales, there is no lack of comparable information reported for the Goodenough Draw-A-Man. Harris very systematically, and conscientiously, reports these. Test-retest reliabilities are on the order of .60 to .70. Interscorer reliabilities are on the order of .80 to .96 and correlations with the Stanford-Binet are on the order of .36 to .65 (Goodenough reported correlations with the Binet on the order of .74).

No correlations with academic achievement were offered in *Children's Drawings* for either the 1926 or 1963 scales.

In short, in view of the excellent standardization of the new scales on 2,975 children "representative of the occupational distribution of the U.S. in 1950," one cannot help but wish that, at the same time, data offering comprehensive validation had been collected. Similarly, in view of the scholarship reflected in *Children's Drawings,* this reviewer also wishes that Harris had found time to include a capstone chapter in which to summarize his views on the theoretical relevance of the Draw-A-Man test, to discuss its implications for future conceptualizations of intelligence, and to comment on its relationship to such other instruments as the Binet, the Bender-Gestalt, and perhaps the Raven Matrices.

All things considered, this reviewer has used the Goodenough-Harris scale in the past, he will use it in the future, and he commends it to others for their use. It is hoped, however, that users of the scale will reflect seriously upon the sober, cautious, scientifically oriented interpretations offered by Harris in his book and consider them as models for their own behavior.

Brit J Ed Psychol 34:338 N '64. M. L. Kellmer Pringle. [Review of *Children's Drawings as Measures of Intellectual Maturity (135)*.] * avowedly the work of a disciple rather than of a critic. The author has most ably met one of his aims, namely "to present a comprehensive survey of the literature on children's drawings in this country and abroad." * Since the presentation of past studies is, moreover, detailed enough to enable the researcher to make his own critical assessment, it is perhaps unreasonable to wish that the author had been more stringent in his evaluation of research designs, statistical methods and conclusions reached. It is probably more justified to regret that there are no suggestions for further research; for example, one would have thought there is a need for longitudinal studies of these revised and extended scales, all the more so in view of the lack of such studies with regard to Goodenough's original test. These criticisms, however, do not seriously detract from the great value of the book to the student of children's drawings, for whom it is likely to become a major source book. * Since the book provides both a comprehensive review of children's drawings and a fully illustrated and well-produced handbook for the revised and extended Draw-a-Man Test, its rather high cost seems justified.

Cont Psychol 11:28+ Ja '66. Marjorie P. Honzik. [Review of *Children's Drawings as Measures of Intellectual Maturity (135)*.] This is a good book. Developmental and clinical psychologists may assign it to students without qualm or qualification. Its merits lie in the value of children's drawings in understanding cognitive development, in the comprehensive coverage of the literature and in the fact that it is theoretically eclectic and written with extraordinary care and thoughtfulness. * Goodenough wrote the first book on the *Measurement of Intelligence by Drawings* in 1926. For almost forty years Goodenough's volume has been in continuous use. Harris's book brings the technique up-to-date with alternate forms, a more exact method of scoring, and new norms based on a well selected sampling of children. Harris clearly and repeatedly points out that the "Draw-a-Man-Test" is primarily a test of conceptual and intellectual maturity. * This test yields many valuable and fascinating findings. *

The only criticism of this book is that it does not always convey the excitement inherent in a medium that can be used to assess individuality from the first to the last year of life. Here is a test that is pleasurable to the testee at most ages, takes relatively little time, yet yields estimates of cognitive development, can indicate brain impairment, and has been employed extensively as a personality and projective test. The fact that correlations have been low between drawings' scores and personality characteristics is not surprising. A drawing is a small sample of the child's creativity and there are no easily available truly comprehensive and valid measures of a child's personality. * Harris's book is basic and we are grateful to him for its excellence, but there is more gold in this mine of drawings, and it should stimulate further active research. We now need even more ideas, new perspectives and methods of analysis and, most of all, increasing sensitivity to this method of communication.

Ed & Psychol Meas 25:636–7 su '65. Carol Hunter. [Review of *Children's Drawings as Measures of Intellectual Maturity (135)*.] * For the purposes of the school psychologist the "Quality" scale shows promise. One of the prime roles of schools today is prevention of school maladjustment. The Goodenough-Harris Drawing Test should be easily integrated with other screening tests into a battery which can be used to select children who should receive more detailed attention. Children can be quickly arranged in order of intellectual maturity in kindergarten and first grades when no group mental maturity test data are available. * School psychologists should find the Goodenough-Harris Drawing Test useful in screening primary children. Clinical psychologists should find the information provocative. One may hope that the ingenuity of psychologists is taxed in formulating experiments based on theories in order to clarify some of the issues which the author discussed.

J Proj Tech & Pers Assess 28:499–500 D '64. Adolph G. Woltmann. [Review of *Children's Drawings as Measures of Intellectual Maturity (135)*.] Psychologists in the 1930's and 1940's used the Goodenough "Draw A Man" test as a very important addition to their test batteries for children. This simple, non-verbal test yielded an I.Q. which correlated closely with the Stanford Binet Measurement of Intelligence. Post War psychology saw the emergence of "projective tests." The intelligence quotient yielding "Draw A Man" test....published in 1926....became less prominent * Harris has rescued this test from falling into oblivion. This alone should earn him the gratitude of the psychological profession. Yet, he has done more than merely revising and bringing up to date the pioneer research of Florence Goodenough. He extended the original number of scorable items from 51 points to 73 points. He also worked out an analogous point scale for the drawing of a woman which contains 71 scorable items. He further added a "drawing of the self," reasoning that this would make possible a more valid projective device for the study of the emerging self concept. Goodenough's scoring instructions were purely descriptive. Harris supplemented this with numerous illustrations which show graphically what to score and what not. * Aside from the fact that Dr. Harris used more representative samples than were available to Goodenough in the early 1920's, he subjected his data to a painstaking statistical analysis which included, among other means of verification and validity, extensive retesting, agreements among independent judges and correlating his collected material statistically with other well known tests of intelligence. This book contains other features which make it a "must reading" for psychologists, regardless of whether they approach childhood academically or are engaged in the human interaction of clinical practice. * Post War psychologists, trained in the "projective hypothesis," may take issue with Harris' chapter on "Clinical and Projective Use of Children's Drawings." They may feel that the author is not sympathetic towards the large body of research papers that have accumulated in this area. Hammer's book on *The Clinical Application of Projective Drawings,* which contains a very comprehensive bibliography on the projective use of children's drawings up to 1957, is not mentioned although it was published 5 years prior to the volume under review. * Harris approaches his topic with the true spirit of the researcher. The original "Draw A Man" test contained 192 references. He retained 40 of these and added 426 references about studies published since 1926. The total bibliography of 466 entries comprises all that has been written about children's art in regard to theory, practice, application and statistical treatment. The book is highly recommended to all who, in one way or another,

Goodenough-Harris Drawing Test

have contact with children, whether they be psychiatrists, psychologists, teachers or social workers. Researchers should find this well-printed and easily read book a gold mine for clues towards formulating new hypotheses. Dr. Harris is to be congratulated for having combined, in one volume, the revision of a test which has proven its worth and whose soundness in design and thinking will prevail. The profession is indebted to him for having tackled courageously, clarified and delineated this important aspect of child development.

Personnel & Guid J 43:830–1 Ap '65. Marvin S. Kaplan. [Review of *Children's Drawings as Measures of Intellectual Maturity* (135).] * this book....has much to recommend it beyond the presentation of a revised version of a useful test instrument. The book should be of great interest to anybody wishing to learn more about the literature, investigations and theories regarding children's thinking processes particularly as expressed through drawings. Harris comprehensively reviews the investigations regarding the projective uses of children's drawings and concludes that they have limited value in this regard. * Despite this quite skeptical conclusion regarding the use of children's drawings as measures of personality, Harris, as is the case with many of us, seems unable quite to accept the situation, i.e., that the drawing test evaluates primarily the ability to form concepts. He goes on to present us with a Guide for the Analysis of Self-Drawings. The Guide suggests the analysis of apparently idiosyncratic features and comparison with the like-sex and opposite-sex adult figures. He believes, however, that meaningful interpretations will be fairly obvious, "close to the surface" and interpretation does not require an elaborate theory of symbolism. * This is not only a much needed revision of the 1926 Goodenough Draw-A-Man Test but it is also a scholarly, comprehensive, carefully done survey of the literature on children's drawings. The test itself will be most useful to those working with elementary age children and will have only a limited applicability beyond the grade school level. The review of the literature and the theory should be fascinating to all who work with children and are interested in their thought processes.

Studies Art Ed 6:49–51 au '64. Mary J. Rouse. [Review of *Children's Drawings as Measures of Intellectual Maturity* (135).] * Harris' modest claim for his book is that it is only an attempt to restandardize Florence Goodenough's earlier version of the "Draw-a-Man" test. Harris....has accomplished his task with efficiency. This, however, is not the whole story. Happily for art educators, his efforts have gone far beyond the minimum required for a test revision. For, along with the restandardization materials, he has included chapters which form the most interesting and complete compilation of research on children's drawings that this reviewer has yet seen. This collection is of such importance that every serious student of graphic expression must inevitably place Harris' book on his "required reading" list. These informative chapters cover several different, but related, topics: a historical survey of research studies concerning drawing which begins with information first published in 1885; a discussion of the non-intellective and cultural influences on graphic expression; a chapter that includes an exceedingly rich store of empirical studies; another that discusses every reputable drawing theory extant; and finally, a chapter that goes beyond the narrow confines of "drawing" and delves into the broader aspects of child art in general. Of interest, also, is the section containing the conclusions which Mr. Harris draws from the empirical evidence he has assembled. From the point of view of an art educator, one of the most important of these is his discussion of the three major stages which he believes occur in most children's drawings. * Harris' continued emphasis of the fundamental importance of the cognitive in shaping the child's drawing behavior may seem confusing to the teacher who has been trained to believe that only "self-expression" was of value to the younger child and that harmful effects would undoubtedly result from the imposition of any kind of cognitive training in art activities. His reasoning, however, based as it is on existing evidence, seems logical to this reviewer, who has long wondered why children could be (and indeed, must be) "trained" in every other area of the school curriculum but never, never, in ours. It seems clearly consistent with current psychological knowledge to suppose that the child can be helped to build up a "vocabulary" of visually-oriented concepts which he can utilize later, just as he can be helped to build a repertory of words which he will use later for more advanced purposes. Similarly, it seems logical to suppose that if the child does *not* build these kinds of concepts, he will not draw later, just as he will not read or write adequately (and creatively) if he has not had sufficient prior experience in reading and writing words. Mr. Harris' discussion of these three stages and their consequents could be regarded as a mandate for considerable restructuring of art education curricula. His conclusions suggest that the emphasis in the elementary grades ought to be on the development of enriched visually-oriented concepts in the child, with attention given to helping him to organize and communicate them more efficiently. Provided with such a rich foundation, the program in the secondary grades might then emphasize the aesthetic and expressive. * Harris discusses and compares the perceptual theories which have application to our understanding of graphic behavior, describing the Gestalt, the Organismic, and the Empiricist schools in a concise manner. * In summary, this book offers a wealth of invaluable information to the art educator who believes that educational objectives and philosophies must be formulated on the basis of empirical evidence. And, whether one agrees with them or not, Mr. Harris' own conclusions which he draws from this information are fresh and provocative. We must compliment him on his efforts, and hope that others in our field will act upon the stimulating and challenging leads which he has provided for us.

For a review by Naomi Stewart of the original edition, see 4:292.

[353]
*The Graduate Record Examinations Aptitude Test. Graduate school candidates; 1949–70; GREAT; 2 scores: verbal, quantitative; 8 current forms ('65–70, 32–40 pages); for more complete information, see 667; 180(200) minutes; Educational Testing Service. *

REFERENCES

1–2. See 4:293.
3–9. See 5:336.
10–26. See 6:461.
27. BAILLIE, GORDON STUART. *An Investigation of Objective Admission Variables as They Relate to Academic and Job Success in One Graduate Library Education Program.* Doctor's thesis, Washington University (St. Louis, Mo.), 1961. (DA 22:2804)
28. JOHNSON, BOBBY GENE. *The Prediction of Success in the Doctoral Program in the College of Education at the University of Houston on the Basis of Objective Test Scores and Quality-Point Averages.* Doctor's thesis, University of Houston (Houston, Tex.), 1963. (DA 24:4066)
29. TULLY, G. EMERSON, AND KING, F. J. "Comparative Performance of Florida Teachers on the Common Examinations of the National Teacher Examinations and the Aptitude Test of the Graduate Record Examinations." *Fla J Ed Res* 5:41–6 Ja '63. *
30. ZIMMERMAN, WILLIAM GEORGE, JR. *An Analysis of Selected Aspects of the Master of Education Program at the University of Miami.* Doctor's thesis, University of Miami (Coral Gables, Fla.), 1963. (DA 28:95A)
31. BURDICK, LOIS A. *Academic Performance of Graduate Students at Indiana State University as Related to the Graduate Record Examination Results.* Master's thesis, Indiana State College (Terre Haute, Ind.), 1964. (Abstract: *Teach Col J* 36:217–8)
32. NICHOLS, ROBERT C. "Effects of Various College Characteristics on Student Aptitude Test Scores." *J Ed Psychol* 55:45–54 F '64. * (PA 38:9269)
33. PONIATOWSKI, ROBERT A. *A Study of the Predictive Value of the Graduate Record Examination Aptitude Tests and Success in the Graduate Division of Rhode Island College.* Master's thesis, Rhode Island College (Providence, R.I.), 1964.
34. ROBERTSON, MALCOLM, AND HALL, EVERETT. "Predicting Success in Graduate Study." *J General Psychol* 71:359–65 O '64. * (PA 39:5997)
35. CREAGER, JOHN A. *Predicting Doctorate Attainment With GRE and Other Variables.* Technical Report No. 25. Washington, D.C.: National Academy of Sciences—National Research Council, November 1965. Pp. iv, 48. *
36. ELTON, CHARLES F. "The Use and Abuse of the Graduate Record Examination Area Tests." *Psychol Sch* 2:245–9 Jl '65. *
37. MADAUS, GEORGE F., AND WALSH, JOHN J. "Departmental Differentials in the Predictive Validity of the Graduate Record Examination Aptitude Tests." *Ed & Psychol Meas* 25:1105–10 w '65. * (PA 40:3580)
38. MOGHRABI, KAMEL M. *An Analysis of Factors That Influence the Degree of Success or Failure of Foreign Students at Texas A & M University.* Doctor's thesis, Texas A & M University (College Station, Tex.), 1966. (DA 27:3232A)
39. PALMER, ROBERT H. *A Statistical Analysis of the Graduate Record Examination and the Miller Analogies Test for Predicting Success in Graduate School at East Tennessee State University.* Master's thesis, East Tennessee State University (Johnson City, Tenn.), 1966.
40. RINDONE, RONALD. *Relationship of Graduate Aptitude Test Scores to Achievement in Industrial Arts.* Master's thesis, California State College (Long Beach, Calif.), 1966.
41. TUCKER, HARMON. *A Statistical Study to Determine the Relationship Between Scores of the Cooperative English Test and the Aptitude Sections of the Graduate Record Examinations.* Master's thesis, Stetson University (DeLand, Fla.), 1966.
42. BREIMEIER, KENNETH H. *Relationship Between Various Psychological Measures in Use at Theological Seminaries.* Comments by James E. Dittes. Occasional Papers No. 1. Washington, D.C.: Ministry Studies Board, 1967. Pp. iii, 59. *
43. CURETON, EDWARD E., AND SCOTT, THOMAS B. "Equivalent Scores for the Graduate Record Verbal and Miller Analogies Tests." *Ed & Psychol Meas* 27:611–5 au '67. * (PA 42:122)
44. STRICKER, GEORGE, AND HUBER, J. T. "The Graduate Record Examination and Undergraduate Grades as Predictors of Success in Graduate School." *J Ed Res* 60:466–8 Jl–Ag '67. *
45. WHITE, GORDON W. *A Predictive Validity Study of the Graduate Records Examinations Aptitude Test at the University of Iowa.* Master's thesis, University of Iowa (Iowa City, Iowa), 1967.
46. WHITELEY, JOHN M.; SPRINTHALL, NORMAN A.; MOSHER, RALPH L.; AND DONAGHY, ROLLA T. "Selection and Evaluation of Counselor Effectiveness." *J Counsel Psychol* 14:226–34 My '67. * (PA 41:9423)
47. ALEXAKOS, CONSTANTINE E. "The Graduate Record Examination: Aptitude Tests as Screening Devices for Students in the College of Human Resources and Education, West Virginia University." *Col & Univ* 43:342–7 sp '68. *
48. CARBONARI, JOSEPH PHILLIP, JR. *An Investigation of Residual Gain and Its Correlates.* Doctor's thesis, Northern Illinois University (DeKalb, Ill.), 1968. (DA 29:2559A)
49. COLVIN, GERALD FRANKLIN. *The Value of Selected Variables in Predicting Academic Success in Graduate Education at the University of Arkansas.* Doctor's thesis, University of Arkansas (Fayetteville, Ark.), 1968. (DA 29:55A)
50. NEWMAN, RICHARD I. "GRE Scores as Predictors of GPA for Psychology Graduate Students." *Ed & Psychol Meas* 28:433–6 su '68. * (PA 42:102–7)
51. RICHTER, WALTER R. *The Graduate Record Examinations Aptitude Test and Success in Graduate Study in Business at San Diego State College.* Master's thesis, San Diego State College (San Diego, Calif.), 1968.
52. TOOKEY, MARY D. "Fathers' Occupations as Related to GRE Aptitude Test Scores of Eureka College Students." *Ill Sch Res* 4:22–6 My '68. *
53. WIGGINS, NANCY; BLACKBURN, MARGARET; AND HACKMAN, J. RICHARD. "Prediction of First-Year Graduate Success in Psychology." Abstract. *Proc 76th Ann Conv Am Psychol Assn* 3:237–8 '68. *
54. CHIMONIDES, STELIOS GEORGIOU. *Some Relationships Associated With Academic Success in Graduate Work at a Midwestern University.* Master's thesis, Western Michigan University (Kalamazoo, Mich.), 1969. (*Masters Abstracts* 7:200)
55. CIEBOTER, FRANK J. "Factors Related to the Performance of Foreign Graduate Students." *J Ed Res* 62(8):360–5 Ap '69. *
56. EWEN, ROBERT B. "The GRE Psychology Test as an Unobtrusive Measure of Motivation." *J Appl Psychol* 53(5):383–7 O '69. * (PA 44:1370)
57. FRANK, AUSTIN C., AND KIRK, BARBARA A. "Character-

istics and Attributes of Prospective City and Regional Planners." *J Col Stud Personnel* 10(4):317–23 S '69. *
58. GAB, DEL D. *Prediction of Success for Doctoral Students in Education at the University of North Dakota.* Doctor's thesis, University of North Dakota (Grand Forks, N.D.), 1969. (*DAI* 31:61A)
59. MEHRABIAN, ALBERT. "Undergraduate Ability Factors in Relationship to Graduate Performance." *Ed & Psychol Meas* 29(2):409–19 su '69. * (*PA* 44:17508)
60. RAWLS, JAMES R.; RAWLS, DONNA J.; AND HARRISON, C. WADE. "An Investigation of Success Predictors in Graduate School in Psychology." *J Psychol* 72(1):125–9 My '69. * (*PA* 43:16455)
61. ROBERTS, S. OLIVER; HORTON, CARRELL P.; AND ROBERTS, BARBARA T. "SAT Versus GRE Performance of Negro American College Students." Abstract. *Proc 77th Ann Conv Am Psychol Assn* 4(1):177–8 '69. * (*PA* 43:17912)
62. ROSCOE, JOHN T., AND HOUSTON, SAMUEL R. "The Predictive Validity of GRE Scores for a Doctoral Program in Education." *Ed & Psychol Meas* 29(2):507–9 su '69. * (*PA* 44:17512)
63. WIGGINS, NANCY; BLACKBURN, MARGARET; AND HACKMAN, J. RICHARD. "Prediction of First-Year Graduate Success in Psychology: Peer Ratings." *J Ed Res* 63(2):81–5 O '69. *
64. WILLIAMS, JOHN D., AND GAB, DEL. "Assessing the Doctoral Admission Policy." *Col Ed Rec* 55(1):14–20 O '69. *
65. WOODARD, DUDLEY BLAKESLEE, JR. *Predicting Success in Graduate School From Biographical Data.* Doctor's thesis, Ohio University (Athens, Ohio), 1969. (*DAI* 31:170A)
66. HACKMAN, J. RICHARD; WIGGINS, NANCY; AND BASS, ALAN R. "Prediction of Long-Term Success in Doctoral Work in Psychology." *Ed & Psychol Meas* 30(2):365–74 su '70. * (*PA* 45:3060)
67. MEHRABIAN, ALBERT. "Ability Factors of Candidates for Graduate School." *Am Psychologist* 25(6):560–3 Je '70. *
68. STEIN, RITA F., AND GREEN, EDITH J. "The Graduate Record Examination as a Predictive Potential in the Nursing Major." *Nursing Res* 19(1):42–6 Ja-F '70. *
69. WILLIAMS, JOHN D.; HARLOW, STEVEN D.; AND GAB, DEL. "A Longitudinal Study Examining Prediction of Doctoral Success: Grade Point Average as Criterion, or Graduation vs. Non-Graduation as Criterion." *J Ed Res* 64(4):161–4 D '70. *

For reviews by Robert L. French and Warren W. Willingham of earlier forms, see 6:461; for a review by John T. Dailey, see 5:336; for reviews by J. P. Guilford and Carl I. Hovland, see 4:293. For reviews of the testing program, see 667 (1 review) and 5:601 (1 review).

[354]
★**Group Test 91.** Industrial applicants; 1949–68; verbal intelligence; 1 form ['49, 4 pages]; mimeographed manual ('68, 8 pages); instructions ('68, 1 page); 40p per 10 tests; 8p per single copy; 8p per key; 7p per instructions; 15p per manual; postpaid within U.K.; 15(25) minutes; National Institute of Industrial Psychology. *

[355]
*****Group Tests 70 and 70B.** Ages 15 and over; 1939–70; subtest of *N.I.I.P. Engineering Apprentice Selection Test Battery;* nonverbal intelligence; forms 70, 70B; booklet 70/1 ['50, 6 pages] is common to both forms; booklet 70/23 ['43, 15 pages] completes form 70; booklet 70/23B ['68, 15 pages] completes form 70B; mimeographed manual ('68, 10 pages); instructions ('68, 2 pages); mimeographed battery manual ['69, 19 pages, with 1970 revision]; 40p per 10 70/1 booklets; 8p per single copy; £1.50 per 10 70/23 or 70/23B booklets; 30p per single copy; 18p per scoring stencil; 7p per instructions; 15p per manual; 20p per battery manual; postpaid within U.K.; 18(35) minutes; National Institute of Industrial Psychology. *

REFERENCES
1–5. See 4:297.
6. MEHROTRA, S. N. "Predicting Intermediate Examination Success by Means of Psychological Tests: A Follow-Up Study." *J Voc & Ed Guid* 4:157–65 My '58. *
7. DHAR, CHANDRAKALA, AND MARR, EVELYN. "A Study of the Practice Effect of Taking Ravens Matrices on Performance on the N.I.I.P. Group Test 70/23 and of the N.I.I.P. on the Ravens Matrices." *J Voc & Ed Guid* 5:187–9 My '59. * (*PA* 38:3188)
8. FRISBY, C. B.; VINCENT, D. F.; AND LANCASHIRE, RUTH. *Tests for Engineering Apprentices: A Validation Study.* National Institute of Industrial Psychology, Report 14. London: the Institute, 1959. Pp. iii, 24. *
9. JOG, R. N. "An Attempt to Predict Success at the 'First Year Engineering Examination.'" *J Voc & Ed Guid* 9:142–8 Ag '63. * (*PA* 38:6643)
10. JOG, R. N., AND AGA, H. "A Comparative Study of the Prediction of Academic Achievement of Engineering." *J Voc & Ed Guid* 12:45–50 My '66. *

For a review by George Westby of form 70, see 4:297.

[356]
★**Group Tests 72 and 73.** Industrial applicants; 1949–68; nonverbal intelligence; Group Tests 72 ['49, 12 pages], 73 ['50, 12 pages]; mimeographed manual ('68, 8 pages); instructions ('68, 2 pages); separate answer sheets must be used; £1.30 per 10 tests; 26p per single copy; 15p per 10 answer sheets; 15p per scoring stencil; 7p per instructions; 15p per manual; postpaid within U.K.; 15(30) minutes; National Institute of Industrial Psychology. *

REFERENCE
1. CASTLE, P. F. C., AND GARFORTH, F. I. DE LA P. "Selection, Training and Status of Supervisors: 1, Selection." *Occup Psychol* 25:109–23 Ap '51. * (*PA* 26:5858)

[357]
*****Group Tests 90A and 90B.** Ages 15 and over; 1950–70; subtest of *N.I.I.P. Engineering Apprentice Selection Test Battery;* verbal intelligence; forms 90A ['50, 12 pages], 90B ['57, 12 pages]; mimeographed manual ('68, 10 pages); instructions ('68, 2 pages); mimeographed battery manual ['69, 19 pages, with 1970 revision]; 60p per 10 tests; 12p per single copy; 12p per key; 7p per instructions; 15p per manual; 20p per battery manual; postpaid with U.K.; 20(30) minutes; National Institute of Industrial Psychology. *

REFERENCE
1. WILLIAMS, A. P. "The Selection of Maintenance Engineers for Data Processing Equipment." *Occup Psychol* 40:53–65 Ja-Ap '66. * (*PA* 41:851)

For a review by John Liggett of form 90A, see 5:340.

[358]
★**Illinois Index of Scholastic Aptitude.** Grades 9–12; 1966; IISA; 1 form (5 pages); manual (17 pages plus test); $8.50 per examiner's kit of 25 tests, key, and manual; $6.50 per 25 tests; $1 per key; $3 per manual; postpaid; 25(30) minutes; B. Everard Blanchard; Western Psychological Services. *

J. STANLEY AHMANN, *Professor of Psychology, Colorado State University, Fort Collins, Colorado.*

The *Illinois Index of Scholastic Aptitude* is a comparatively short group test designed for students in grades 9–12. It is intended to predict the probable success of high school students in four basic academic areas: English, social studies, science, and mathematics. In addition, the author believes that the IISA may be used for such purposes as (*a*) deciding if students are ready to begin the "regular" high school program, (*b*) deciding if preparatory work need be provided to students, and (c) scheduling classes by "ability grouping" techniques.

The content of the IISA is entirely verbal and is oriented toward formal education. Beyond a doubt, this test should be classified with the *CEEB Scholastic Aptitude Test* and with similar tests near the "crystallized achievement" end of the Cronbach spectrum for comparing tests of scholastic aptitude. Of the 108 items, 90 deal directly with vocabulary. They are four-option, multiple-choice items which require the selection of a synonym (55 items) or an antonym (35 items). The balance of the test (18 items) measures paragraph understanding. For each of six unrelated short paragraphs, three three-option, multiple choice items must be answered. The three parts are not separately timed; exactly 25 minutes is allowed for the entire test.

The development of the test is inadequately described. Evidently, many of the words for the vocabulary items were selected from the Declaration of Independence, the Gettysburg Address, and the Monroe Doctrine. No mention is made of any pretesting of these or of the paragraph understanding items. Item analysis data are not reported.

The sample of students used for standardizing the test is of questionable representativeness. Although the author's goal was to select a representative sample of high school students, examination of the list of participating high schools leads to the conclusion that he probably failed. For instance, of the 41 participating high schools, none is located in New York and only one in California. In contrast, five are Colorado schools. Furthermore, at least one-fourth of the 41 schools are private. Most significant of all, no description is given of the method by means of which the sample of schools was selected.

The number of students tested is comparatively small—only 1,850. Of these, 59 percent were students in the ninth and tenth grades. The proportions of male and female students are not given.

In view of the purposes of the IISA, the evidence concerning its validity is extremely limited. Amazingly, no evidence regarding predictive validity is reported. The degree of construct validity is represented by correlations with other common group mental ability tests. The largest correlation (.85) was found with the *California Test of Mental Maturity,* the lowest (.64) with the *Kuhlmann-Anderson Intelligence Test.* Only split-half reliability coefficients are cited, varying from a low of .85 to a high of .90.

The author's suggestions for interpreting the IISA scores are unusual. Rather than convert the raw scores to standard scores or percentile ranks, he classifies them in terms of seven categories ranging from "exceptional" (93 through 108) to "poor" (0 through 30). No explanation is offered as to why the size of the categories varies so greatly, with two as small as 5 units and two as large as 31.

On balance, the IISA must be judged as anything but a strong competitor to the many verbal group mental ability tests now widely used in high schools. On the basis of the information provided in the manual, one must conclude that the IISA was developed in a somewhat casual manner and that it produces raw scores of largely uncertain value. This is not to say that the test is without promise. It is possible that further validation efforts may establish it as worthwhile for use in the high school. Much, much work needs to be done.

DAVID A. PAYNE, *Professor of Educational Psychology and Curriculum and Supervision, The University of Georgia, Athens, Georgia.*

The evaluation of a test needs to be made against an authoritative and comprehensive set of criteria. Such a set of criteria can be found in the 1966 *Standards for Educational and Psychological Tests and Manuals.* Unfortunately, the IISA publication date is caught between the above Standards and the 1954 *Technical Recommendations for Psychological Tests and Diagnostic Techniques.* If the author and publisher cannot be held accountable for the letter of these standards, the spirit nevertheless applies.

ADMINISTRATION AND SCORING. Directions for administration, if one assumes appropriate motivational preparation for taking the test, are clear and concise. Examinees are allowed 25 minutes for the 90 four-choice, 18 three-choice, and 7 unscored sample items. There is no indication of how speed influences the scores.

VALIDITY. Beginning with the not unreasonable premise that vocabulary is the best single index of mental ability, at least as far as this concept is operationalized and employed in our tests and schools, the author describes the development of a verbal power test made up of word meaning (synonyms and antonyms)

Illinois Index of Scholastic Aptitude

and paragraph understanding items. Content was drawn from English, social studies, mathematics and science. All vocabulary items were derived from the Declaration of Independence, the Gettysburg Address, and the Monroe Doctrine. It was assumed that such a procedure would help to insure common vocabulary background. No other specification of the domain being sampled is mentioned.

The manual claims that the test may be used (a) to determine readiness for high school, (b) to identify academic deficiencies, (c) to predict success in four academic areas, (d) for ability grouping, and (e) in research. Unfortunately no validity data directly related to these uses are reported. Indirect evidence in the form of correlations with six reputable group general intelligence tests is provided. These correlations ranged from .64 to .85, with a mean correlation of .74. It was apparently assumed that any validity evidenced by these instruments would by association be possessed by the IISA. Such an assumption is open to serious question. No responsive data in the form of IISA-achievement correlations, expectancy tables, group differences, or criterion-related or construct validating procedures are reported. There is also the implication that differential prediction is possible, but no data are presented to support this implication.

RELIABILITY. The assumption of content homogeneity is verified by corrected split-half correlations ranging from .85 to .90 for each of grades 9-12, with a mean of .87. The size of these coefficients is probably positively influenced by the large samples used, ranging from 350 to 600. Inasmuch as the uses suggested for the IISA include prediction, one would expect some indication of stability over time. No such data are reported. A commendable effort is made in reporting standard errors of measurement, as well as tabled confidence intervals. As commendable as this effort is, the probability interpretation for individual scores is open to question. Another interpretation not accepted by authorities is that the square root of a reliability coefficient (index of reliability) may be taken as evidence of validity.

INTERPRETATION OF SCORES. Scores are initially reported as raw scores. These can then be further classified into one of three "Ability Levels" (High, Medium, and Low) and then into two or three "Scholastic Aptitude Levels" within each of the ability levels.

No discussion of the derivation of these classifications is presented, nor is validity evidence included to support the verbal case-study-like descriptions of individuals classified into one of the seven aptitude levels. Some of these descriptions—when one considers we are talking here only of a total score on a single instrument—defy understanding. For example, an *exceptional* student "generally is an overachiever, strongly self-motivated, able and more than ready to follow directions, prompt in making decisions, punctual with assignments, and inclined to do more than is required of him/her."

The standardization details are fairly well explicated, but one wonders (a) how many schools, when invited to participate, declined, and (b) exactly how the data resulting from the administration of an experimental edition of the IISA to "varied ethnic groups" were used to reduce bias.

SUMMARY. The IISA, although beginning with some interesting assumptions and ideas, has probably been marketed too early. It is not yet ready for general consumption. At the very minimum, the IISA in its present form should be considered and labeled an "experimental edition." The chief shortcoming must be considered lack of relevant validity information, which is at least available for most of the potential competitors of the IISA.

[359]
*Lorge-Thorndike Intelligence Tests, College Edition. Grades 12-13; 1954-66; LTIT-H; Level H of the Multi-Level Edition (see 360); revision of still-in-print Level 5 (Grades 10-12), Separate Level Edition (see 6:467); 2 scores: verbal, nonverbal; Forms 1, 2, ('64, 23 pages); manual ('64, 32 pages); battery technical manual ('66, 33 pages); norms for grade 13 based upon 1954 testing with Level 5 of the separate level edition; separate answer sheets (IBM 1230, MRC) must be used; $6 per 35 tests; $8.55 per 100 MRC answer sheets and 3 group record sheets; $5.70 per 100 IBM answer sheets; 60¢ per MRC scoring stencil; $1.20 per set of IBM scoring stencils; 60¢ per manual; $1.20 per battery technical manual; $2.25 per specimen set; postage extra; MRC scoring service, 48¢ and over per test; 62(120) minutes; Irving Lorge, Robert L. Thorndike, and Elizabeth Hagen; Houghton Mifflin Co. *

ERIC F. GARDNER, *Margaret O. Slocum Professor of Education and Psychology and Chairman, Department of Psychology; and Director, Psychological Services and Research Center; Syracuse University, Syracuse, New York.*

This test is Level H of the *Lorge-Thorndike*

Intelligence Tests: Multi-Level Edition, which is an outgrowth and revision of the separate level edition of the LTIT published in 1954. These earlier tests were reviewed thoroughly and favorably in *The Fifth Mental Measurements Yearbook.*

The present tests contain the same rubrics, same item format, and in fact many of the same items as the earlier tests. The major change involves the adoption of the multi-level design and rescaling. The term "multi-level" signifies that for each subtest in the battery there is a graded series of items divided into eight different but overlapping scales in the grade range 3 through 13. Each higher level of a subtest is formed by dropping off one modular unit from the beginning of the next lower subtest and adding one at the upper end. Items are selected to show a progression in difficulty within a module and an overlapping in difficulty in successive modules. By combining modular structure with this type of graded item difficulty, the authors have produced a test in which at each level most of the items are in the immediate difficulty range and consequently are contributing most effectively to test discrimination. The relatively high average internal-consistency coefficients reported in the technical manual indicate the success of the authors, although the coefficients reported for the College Edition are the lowest of all eight levels.

Two types of norms are presented: intelligence quotient equivalents (deviation IQ's) and grade 12 percentile norms. No college norms are given.

The authors maintain that American colleges differ so widely in the intellectual selectivity of their input that no general "college norms" have much meaning. The reviewer concurs. The authors recommend that colleges devise local norms. The merit of the stress on local norms needs no comment, but advocating the construction of local norms does not satisfy the desire of the user for more adequate frames of reference. In view of the care with which the normative data for the lower levels have been collected and presented, it is unfortunate that the same concern was not shown for the College Edition. Data from a variety of colleges should be presented along with that of the basic group of 18-year-olds.

The manual reports odd-even reliability coefficients, based on a sample of 949 high school seniors drawn from a high school senior standardization group, of .93 for verbal and .90 for nonverbal. No reliability coefficients are reported for college groups, although such information is needed for a test advocated for college students.

The previous reviewers spoke well of the technical manual but indicated that additional validity studies would have been desirable. The authors have been greatly concerned about the validity of the revised tests and have presented worthwhile discussions and data about content, predictive, concurrent, and construct validity. These include correlations with achievement test batteries, and correlations with other aptitude tests such as the DAT, CEEB, and ACT. Correlations with academic grades are given for the lower levels but not for Level H. Such information from specific colleges would be useful. However, in general the sections in the technical manual on reliability and validity, which are well written and well illustrated, should be of real value to the user. This manual, overall, is far superior to its predecessor but gives the least information for the College Edition.

In an effort to furnish the much sought-after comparable scores on different aptitude tests, a table described as "Score Equivalents of Lorge-Thorndike Multi-Level IQ's in Terms of College Board and American College Testing Program Tests" is provided. This information is useful. However, the only warning given to the users about these scores is that the number of cases used in the equating procedure was small. Of greater concern is the implication that the three tests are measuring identical functions and hence, for example, a score on the quantitative portion of the SAT, which contains many data-sufficiency items, has the same meaning as a specific score on the Lorge-Thorndike. The fault is essentially the old one of assuming that all IQ's of a particular size are equivalent regardless of the specific intelligence test used.

In general, the favorable comments made by reviewers of the earlier Lorge-Thorndike are warranted. In fact, these are superior test batteries with superior ancillary materials and should have great value for the purposes defined by their authors. The major weakness is that the College Edition, which obviously is being recommended for college students, has minimum data on college students compared with the kinds supplied at the lower levels.

Lorge-Thorndike Intelligence Tests, College Edition

WILLIAM B. MICHAEL, *Professor of Educational Psychology and Psychology, University of Southern California, Los Angeles, California.*

The College Edition (Level H) is the most advanced of eight overlapping levels of the *Lorge-Thorndike Intelligence Tests* and is designed for superior students in grade 12 and students beginning college. It consists of a verbal battery (V) and a nonverbal battery (NV). The V battery requires 35 minutes of actual working time and is made up of five subtests: Vocabulary, Sentence Completion, Arithmetic Reasoning, Verbal Classification, and Verbal Analogies. The NV battery requires 27 minutes of working time and is made up of three subtests: Figure Classification, Number Series, and Figure Analogies.

The administration manual furnishes tables for converting the total raw scores on each battery (V and NV) into percentile ranks and deviation IQ's. In view of the correlation of .66 between the V and NV total scores on Level H (the correlations reported for the other levels were higher), one could argue against the value of providing separate V and NV IQ's. Whether the Arithmetic Reasoning subtest should have been included in the V battery is debatable, as the V scores could thereby be somewhat contaminated with nonverbal sources of factorial variance. It may well be, however, that a single general factor accounts for most of the reliable test-score variance—a hypothesis that is supported by one reported factor analysis of the intercorrelations of all eight subtests for a group of 250 sixth-grade pupils from the national standardization sample (see table 10 of the technical manual). Only one rotated factor could be clearly identified, and its loadings varied from .49 on the Arithmetic Reasoning subtest to .84 on the Figure Analogies subtest, the median loading being .69.

It is evident from an inspection of the items in the subtests and a study of the technical manual that great care was taken in the preparation and standardization of the 1964 Multi-Level Edition of the LTIT. For Level H, the average internal-consistency coefficient (biserial correlation) on the eight subtests varied from .41 to .56 for Form 1 and from .40 to .61 for Form 2. This is reflected in odd-even reliability estimates for Form 1 of .93 and .90 for the V and NV batteries (N = 949), respectively, and in corresponding alternate-form estimates (based on combined 1–2 and 2–1 sequences) of .90 and .92 for samples of 69 and 57 cases and of .83 and .83 for a sample of about 500 students. Reported at selected raw-score points, the standard errors of measurement for deviation IQ's varied from 3.9 to 4.6 on the V battery and from 4.0 to 5.1 on the NV battery. Thus it appears that the precision of the V and NV scores on Level H is relatively high and essentially comparable to that found in most major competitive instruments.

In the technical manual the authors argue for the validity of the LTIT in terms of (*a*) how well the items when logically viewed represent activities related to behavior that would be described as intelligent according to six enumerated criteria, (*b*) how accurately the LTIT battery scores predict performance on well-known standardized achievement tests as well as school grades, and (*c*) how clearly the LTIT signifies a construct largely in terms of its relationship with other measures designed to tap intelligence. Although the argument regarding construct validity seems somewhat weak, it is supported by correlations of the V battery scores with part scores on standardized achievement tests ranging roughly from .65 to .85 and with composite scores ranging from .79 to .90. The NV correlations were lower. Somewhat comparable ranges in correlation were found between the V and NV battery scores and scores on well-known measures of intelligence. Unfortunately, the findings cited for Level H are considerably less plentiful than those for the other levels. However, the general patterns of correlation are similar. It may be that the familiar "jangle fallacy" has shown itself again, as evidenced by high interrelationships between achievement and aptitude measures, which differ in name but not in function or process required.

Although, for the most part, the statistical data reported for Level H appear to indicate the adequacy of its reliability, validity, and norms (although deviation IQ's are based on 1954 normative data from only two educational institutions), the reviewer is concerned about the practicality of administering so many relatively short tests as well as with the seeming inconvenience of a working-time requirement of 35 and 27 minutes, respectively, for the V and NV batteries. Competing instruments, such as the *Academic Ability Test* in SCAT Series 2 for grades 12 through 14, that require only 45 minutes—or one class period—for administration may offer as useful information as does the LTIT.

Another concern relates to the appropriateness of several of the alternative answers in the Sentence Completion and Verbal Classification subtests. In many instances, a bright or an unusually creative person—especially one whose background differed from that found in the white middle-class culture—could defend his selection of an unkeyed answer. A careful review of these tests suggests that changes in societal expectations that have occurred in the past five years may have made some of the items inappropriate and possibly obsolete.

Despite the limitations that have been mentioned, the LTIT is a well-constructed, carefully normed instrument that is sufficiently reliable and valid to meet the needs of many school communities. One hopes that a shorter form will be built that could be administered in one class period, that an early revision will remove or revise certain items that may be ambiguous or at least suspect in an examinee's value expectations, and that forms for culturally different groups can be devised and separately normed—not an easy undertaking. Nevertheless, the LTIT compares favorably with other tests of general intelligence that are available from commercial publishers. The College Edition (Level H) should continue to make an important contribution to the counseling and placement of superior high school students who are seeking admission to college.

JOHN H. ROSENBACH, *Professor of Educational Psychology and Head of the Department, State University of New York at Albany, Albany, New York.*

The *Lorge-Thorndike Intelligence Tests* have gained the reputation of being among the better group tests of mental ability. Various reviewers have commented favorably on the development of the underlying constructs, the general design and construction of the tests, the ease of administration and scoring, the adequate standardization and norms, the satisfactory reliability, and, perhaps most significantly, the sophistication of the manuals. Unlike so many others, the authors present their case in a modest and reasonable way. Moreover, the sections on reliability and, especially, validity are not only informative but also a delight to read. Although brief, they could serve as helpful supplements for students enrolled in a basic tests and measurements course.

Unfortunately, despite the many positive features of the tests, there are some serious shortcomings associated with the edition under consideration here, Level H, for grade 12 and college. There are neither adequate validity data nor norms for this level, in contrast to the information presented for Levels A through G (grades 3 through 11 or 12). The most recent standardization of the tests—referred to as a Multi-Level Edition because of the overlapping nature of the items—was done in 1963. The sample consisted of *pupils* in grades 3 through 12; neither dropouts nor college students were included. Thus, the only published norms available to the user of Form H are those based on the performance of twelfth grade students. The authors suggest that these norms be used "only as rather general bench marks" and "that most colleges using the tests will want to develop their own tables of local norms."

Data bearing on the empirical validity of Form H are similarly limited. Correlations with the *Iowa Tests of Educational Development* and with the *Tests of Academic Progress* at grade 12 are high. In fact, the correlations between the verbal section of the L-T and the composite scores of these achievement tests are so high (r's of .86, .90, and .895 based on N's of 138, 141, and 1,684, respectively) that one is led to suspect that the tests are measuring the same constructs. But this is certainly not a new or novel observation about mental ability and achievement tests.

Other "validity" data reported at grade 12 include correlations, within the typical range, with three other group intelligence tests (California, Kuhlmann-Anderson, and Otis), and with College Board and American College Testing Program scores. The CEEB and ACT data are based on extremely small N's (35 to 69) and narrowly selected samples; so much so, in fact, that Tables 24 (correlations) and 25 (score equivalents) of the Technical Manual, based on this material, appear virtually worthless. Their inclusion tends to mar the otherwise high quality of the manual.

No empirical information is presented for college-level students. The authors do state, however, that "experience with the items developed for Level H and tried out in several colleges and universities has indicated that the items discriminate well among individuals in college freshman groups."

An overall assessment of Level H leads one to mixed conclusions. The lack of appropriate norms and validity data is offset, in part, by the acknowledged overall quality of the items (content validity), satisfactory levels of reliability, and good performance characteristics of the lower level forms. Nonetheless, based on the information made available by the publisher, it would seem that this form has only limited applicability at the college level. The test user should be wary of making any other than the most general interpretations unless local norms and, hopefully, locally derived validity data are at his disposal.

[360]

*Lorge-Thorndike Intelligence Tests, Multi-Level Edition.** Grades 3-13; 1954-66; LTIT; revision of Levels 3-5 of the still-in-print *Lorge-Thorndike Intelligence Tests* (see 6:467); 3 scores: verbal, nonverbal, composite; Forms 1, 2, ('64, 52 pages); overlapping Levels A (grade 3), B (4), C (5), D (6), E (7), F (8-9), G (10-11), H (12-13) in a single booklet; Level H available as a separate (see 359); manual ('64, 95 pages); technical manual ('66, 33 pages); no norms or reliability data for composite score; most data on validity based upon the earlier edition; separate answer sheets (Digitek, IBM 805, IBM 1230, MRC) must be used; 78¢ per test; $36 per 500 Digitek answer sheets; $4.80 per 100 IBM 805 answer sheets; $5.70 per 100 IBM 1230 answer sheets; $8.55 per 100 MRC answer sheets; Digitek scoring stencils not available; $1.20 per set of IBM scoring stencils; 60¢ per MRC scoring stencil; $1.20 per technical manual; $1.20 per manual; $3 per specimen set; postage extra; MRC scoring service, 24¢ and over per test; MRC scorable test booklet is available for Level A, Form 1 ($15 per 35 tests, 45¢ per directions, 45¢ and over per test for scoring service); 62(120) minutes; Irving Lorge, Robert L. Thorndike, and Elizabeth Hagen; Houghton Mifflin Co. *

REFERENCES

1-6. See 5:350.
7-17. See 6:467.
18. ROBERTS, DODD EDWARD. *Some Effects of an Oral-Visual Presentation of a Group Intelligence Test to Selected Seventh Grade Pupils Reading at Varying Levels.* Doctor's thesis, University of Missouri (Columbia, Mo.), 1958. (*DA* 19:1621)
19. BALOW, IRVING H. *The Relationship of Lateral Dominance Characteristics to Reading Achievement in the First Grade.* Doctor's thesis, University of Minnesota (Minneapolis, Minn.), 1959. (*DA* 20:2138)
20. GUNDERSEN, RICHARD OSCAR. *The Significance of Divergencies Between Verbal and Nonverbal Intelligence Scores.* Doctor's thesis, State University of Iowa (Iowa City, Iowa), 1959. (*DA* 20:2142)
21. FITZGERALD, LOUIS ALLEN. *Some Effects of Reading Ability on Group Intelligence Test Scores in the Intermediate Grades.* Doctor's thesis, State University of Iowa (Iowa City, Iowa), 1960. (*DA* 21:1844)
22. FISCHER, ROBERT FREDERICK. *Relationships Between School Achievement and the Verbal and Nonverbal Abilities of Children.* Doctor's thesis, University of Wisconsin (Madison, Wis.), 1961. (*DA* 21:3357)
23. HARMS, CALLIS R. *The Relationship Between Intelligence, Physical Growth, Socio-Economic Status, Social Acceptance and Academic Achievement in the Elementary School.* Doctor's thesis, Arizona State University (Tempe, Ariz.), 1961. (*DA* 22:2631)
24. BARRETT, THOMAS CLIFFORD. *The Relationship Between Selected Reading Readiness Measures of Visual Discrimination and First Grade Reading Achievement.* Doctor's thesis, University of Minnesota (Minneapolis, Minn.), 1962. (*DA* 24:193)
25. KATZENMEYER, WILLIAM GILBERT. *Social Interaction and Differences in Intelligence Test Performance of Negro and White Elementary School Pupils.* Doctor's thesis, Duke University (Durham, N.C.), 1962. (*DA* 24:1904)
26. MORTENSEN, JAMES BENSON. *A Study of Variables Related to First Grade Success in Selected Colorado School Districts.* Doctor's research study No. 1, Colorado State College (Greeley, Colo.), 1962. (*DA* 23:1236)
27. OLSON, D. R., AND MACARTHUR, R. S. "The Effect of Foreign Language Background on Intelligence Test Performance." *Alberta J Ed Res* 8:157-66 S '62. * (*PA* 37:8270)
28. ABDEL-GHAFFAR, ABDEL-SALAM ABDEL-KADER. *Relationships Between Selected Creativity Factors and Certain Non-Intellectual Factors Among High School Students.* Doctor's thesis, University of Denver (Denver, Colo.), 1963. (*DA* 25:1728)
29. MATTICK, WILLIAM E. "Predicting Success in the First Grade." *El Sch J* 63:273-6 F '63. *
30. SCHLUETER, MARY PETER. *The Role of Intelligence, Personality, and Selected Psychological Factors in Remedial Reading Progress.* Doctor's thesis, University of Rochester (Rochester, N.Y.), 1963. (*DA* 24:4088)
31. SONNEMAN, LAWRENCE J. *A Study of the Relationships Between Four Tests of Intelligence and One Test of Scholastic Achievement.* Doctor's thesis, State University of South Dakota (Vermillion, S.D.), 1963. (*DA* 24:4555)
32. DEMOPOULOS, CONSTANTINE GEORGE. *A Comparison of Verbal and Nonverbal IQ Scores of Negro School Children Using the Lorge-Thorndike Intelligence Test.* Master's thesis, Marshall University (Huntington, W.Va.), 1964.
33. DEUTSCH, MARTIN, AND BROWN, BERT. "Social Influences in Negro-White Intelligence Differences." *J Social Issues* 20:24-35 Ap '64. * (*PA* 39:4734)
34. EDWARDS, ALLEN JACK, AND KIRBY, M. ELSIE. "Predictive Efficiency of Intelligence Test Scores: Intelligence Quotients Obtained in Grade One and Achievement Test Scores Obtained in Grade Three." *Ed & Psychol Meas* 24:941-6 w '64. * (*PA* 39:8699)
35. JUNGEBLUT, ANN. "Some Further Data on the Lorge-Thorndike Intelligence Tests." *Ed Rec B* 85:69-71 F '64. *
36. KERFOOT, JAMES FLETCHER. *The Relationship of Selected Auditory and Visual Reading Readiness Measures to First Grade Reading Achievement and Second Grade Reading and Spelling Achievement.* Doctor's thesis, University of Minnesota (Minneapolis, Minn.), 1964. (*DA* 25:1747)
37. KLEIN, ROBERT A. *An Investigation of the Lorge-Thorndike Intelligence Test as an Instrument in the Prediction of Creativity in Elementary School Children.* Master's thesis, University of Tennessee (Knoxville, Tenn.), 1964.
38. SARASON, SEYMOUR B.; HILL, KENNEDY T.; AND ZIMBARDO, PHILIP G. "A Longitudinal Study of the Relation of Test Anxiety to Performance on Intelligence and Achievement Tests." *Monogr Soc Res Child Develop* 29(7):1-51 '64. * (*PA* 39:15263)
39. SHAFFER, RAYMOND GEORGE. *A Study of Four Group Intelligence Tests to Identify Ambiguous Pictures as a Factor Which Causes Some Children to Select Incorrect Answers.* Doctor's research study No. 1, Colorado State College (Greeley, Colo.), 1964. (*DA* 25:1014)
40. SHEA, CAROL ANN. *Visual Discrimination of Words as a Predictor of Reading Readiness.* Doctor's thesis, University of Connecticut (Storrs, Conn.), 1964. (*DA* 25:6321)
41. TAYLOR, ALTON L. "The Prediction of Success Using Programed Science Materials." *J Res Sci Ed* 2(1):58-59 '64. *
42. WEST, L. W., AND MACARTHUR, R. S. "An Evaluation of Selected Intelligence Tests for Two Samples of Metis and Indian Children." *Alberta J Ed Res* 10:17-27 Mr '64. * (*PA* 39:12328)
43. WILLIAMS, BENNIE LEE. *The Concurrent Validity of the Lorge-Thorndike Verbal and Nonverbal Intelligence Tests Among Negro Children.* Master's thesis, Marshall University (Huntington, W.Va.), 1964.
44. YAMAMOTO, KAORU. "Role of Creative Thinking and Intelligence in High School Achievement." *Psychol Rep* 14:783-9 Je '64. * (*PA* 39:5140)
45. BAILEY, RUBELLIA JOHNSON. *The Relationship of Educational Background, Socio-Economic Status, Level of Aspiration, and Intelligence to Success in Business Education.* Doctor's thesis, Temple University (Philadelphia, Pa.), 1965. (*DA* 26:1396)
46. CONSTANTINIDES, PANAYIOTES DEMOSTHENOUS. *The Relationship of Critical Thinking Ability to Intelligence, to Personality, and to Teacher Evaluation of Pupil Personality.* Doctor's thesis, University of Virginia (Charlottesville, Va.), 1965. (*DA* 26:5861) (Abstract: *Ed R* 3:43-5)
47. GLAD, JOAN ROGERS BOURNE. *Evaluation of the Remedial Reading Program in Utah Public Schools.* Doctor's thesis, University of Utah (Salt Lake City, Utah), 1965. (*DA* 26:5864)
48. KANGAS, RONALD D. "Factors Related to Success in 7th Grade Foreign Language Study." *Mod Lang J* 49:97-8 F '65. *
49. KARZEN, JUDITH MILLER; SUVETOR, HELENE; AND THOMPSON, GLEN. "Predicting First Grade Reading Achievement." *Ill Sch Res* 2:20-2 O '65. *

50. RAINEY, ROBERT G. "A Study of Four School-Ability Tests." *J Exp Ed* 33:305–19 su '65. * (*PA* 39:12306)
51. RAY, JOHN RICHARD. *The Predictive Value of Selected Factors for Achievement of Seventh Grade Pupils.* Doctor's thesis, University of Tennessee (Knoxville, Tenn.), 1965. (*DA* 26:4396)
52. SWAN, ROBERT J., AND HOPKINS, KENNETH D. "An Investigation of Theoretical and Empirical Chance Scores on Selected Standardized Group Tests." *Calif J Ed Res* 16:34–41 Ja '65. * (*PA* 39:10156)
53. YOLOYE, EMMANUEL AYOTUNDE. *The Performance of Bilingual Nigerian Students on Verbal and Nonverbal Tests of Intelligence.* Doctor's thesis, Columbia University (New York, N.Y.), 1965. (*DA* 26:4466)
54. DYKSTRA, ROBERT. "Auditory Discrimination Abilities and Beginning Reading Achievement." *Read Res Q* 1:5–34 sp '66. * (*PA* 40:11011)
55. EAGLE, NORMAN. "The Stability of Lorge-Thorndike IQ Scores Between Grades Three and Four and Grade Eight." *J Ed Res* 60:164–5 D '66. *
56. KANDEL, ARTHUR. *Discrepancies Between the Stanford-Binet and Three Group Tests of Intelligence in the Identification of Low I.Q. Children.* Doctor's thesis, Catholic University of America (Washington, D.C.), 1966. (*DA* 27:1659A)
57. KEACH, CHARLES CAMPBELL. *Discrepancies Between the Stanford-Binet and Three Group Tests of Intelligence in the Identification of High I.Q. Children.* Doctor's thesis, Catholic University of America (Washington, D.C.), 1966. (*DA* 27:1660A)
58. MORPER, JACK. *An Investigation of the Relationship of Certain Predictive Variables and Academic Achievement of Spanish-American and Anglo Pupils in Junior High School.* Doctor's thesis, Oklahoma State University (Stillwater, Okla.), 1966. (*DA* 27:4051A)
59. OHNMACHT, FRED W. "Achievement, Anxiety and Creative Thinking." *Am Ed Res J* 3:131–8 Mr '66. *
60. WARD, GEORGE, II. "Lorge-Thorndike Nonverbal IQ's and Verbal Achievement Tests Among a Group of Negro Pupils." *Proc W Va Acad Sci* 37:282–5 F '66. * (*PA* 40:8827)
61. BRENDEMUEHL, FRANK LOUIS. *The Influence of Reading Ability on the Validity of Group Non-Verbal Intelligence Tests.* Doctor's thesis, University of Minnesota (Minneapolis, Minn.), 1967. (*DA* 28:2088A)
62. CAVE, RICHARD LESTER. *A Factorial Comparison of Creativity and Intelligence.* Doctor's thesis, University of Tennessee (Knoxville, Tenn.), 1967. (*DA* 28:4293B)
63. CROPLEY, A. J. "Creativity, Intelligence, and Achievement." *Alberta J Ed Res* 13:51–8 Mr '67. * (*PA* 41:15253)
64. LANIER, PERRY EUGENE. *A Study of Creativity, Intelligence and Discovery Teaching as Related to Performance in Elementary School Mathematics.* Doctor's thesis, University of Oklahoma (Norman, Okla.), 1967. (*DA* 28:1004A)
65. MCCOMAS, WILLIAM, AND WARD, GEORGE, II. "An Internal Factor Analysis of Lorge-Thorndike Scores of Negro Children." *Proc W Va Acad Sci* 39:59–61 '67. *
66. MCCOMAS, WILLIAM C. *Structure and Function of the Lorge-Thorndike Intelligence Test When Used With Negro School Children.* Master's thesis, Marshall University (Huntington, W.Va.), 1967.
67. PANTHER, EDWARD E. "Prediction of First-Grade Reading Achievement." *El Sch J* 68:44–8 O '67. *
68. RICE, VICTOR. *An Appraisal of the Predictive Value of Patterns of Subtest Scores in Achievement Test Batteries.* Doctor's thesis, American University (Washington, D.C.), 1967. (*DA* 28:1267A)
69. ROBERTSON, JOHN W. *The Lorge-Thorndike Intelligence Tests as Predictors of Achievement in Remedial Reading Classes.* Master's thesis, University of Utah (Salt Lake City, Utah), 1967.
70. WARTENBERG, HERBERT. *The Relationship Between Success in Beginning Reading and Various Predictive Measures.* Doctor's thesis, Temple University (Philadelphia, Pa.), 1967. (*DA* 28:979A)
71. ALZOBAIE, ABDUL JALIL; METFESSEL, NEWTON S.; AND MICHAEL, WILLIAM B. "Alternative Approaches to Assessing the Intellectual Abilities of Youth From a Culture of Poverty." *Ed & Psychol Meas* 28:449–55 su '68. * (*PA* 42:19264)
72. BOERSMA, FREDERIC J., AND O'BRYAN, KENNETH. "An Investigation of the Relationship Between Creativity and Intelligence Under Two Conditions of Testing." *J Personality* 36:341–8 S '68. * (*PA* 43:3993)
73. CICCHETTI, DOMENIC V., AND LERNER, EMANUEL. "Measures of Reliability and Validity of Verbal Intelligence Among Neuropsychiatric Patients." *J Abn Psychol* 73:420 O '68. * (*PA* 42:18084)
74. KAKKAR, S. B. "The Consistency of IQ Scores." *J Psychol Res* 12:111–3 S '68. *
75. KARNES, LUCIA ROONEY. *The Comparison of Scores of Eighth-Grade Reading and Nonreading Boys on the Lorge-Thorndike Tests, Wechsler Intelligence Scale for Children, the D 48 Test, and the Welsh Figure Preference Test, GW Scale.* Doctor's thesis, University of North Carolina (Chapel Hill, N.C.), 1968. (*DAI* 30:585A)
76. LEHRER, BARRY EUGENE. *An Investigation of the Role of Intellectual, Motivational, and Other Non-Intellectual Factors in the Prediction of Educational Achievement and Efficiency.* Doctor's thesis, University of Iowa (Iowa City, Iowa), 1968. (*DA* 29:3876A)
77. MACARTHUR, R. S. "Assessing Intellectual Potential of Native Canadian Pupils: A Summary." *Alberta J Ed Res* 14:115–22 Je '68. * (*PA* 44:4170)
78. MACARTHUR, RUSSELL. "Some Differential Abilities of Northern Canadian Native Youth." *Int J Psychol* 3(1):43–50 '68. *
79. MANCOTT, ANATOL. "Prediction of Academic Achievement in a First Semester College Chemistry Course for Medical Laboratory Technologists." *Ed & Psychol Meas* 28:945–6 au '68. * (*PA* 43:4516)
80. RATTAN, M. S., AND MACARTHUR, R. S. "Longitudinal Prediction of School Achievement for Metis and Eskimo Pupils." *Alberta J Ed Res* 14:37–41 Mr '68. * (*PA* 44:4249)
81. ROSEN, CARL L., AND OHNMACHT, FRED. "Perception, Readiness, and Reading Achievement in First Grade." *Proc Ann Conv Int Read Assn* 12(4):33–9 '68. *
82. SATTABANASUK, THIRAPAN. *Junior High Student Performance and Related Student and Parent Characteristics.* Doctor's thesis, Colorado State College (Greeley, Colo.), 1968. (*DA* 29:1052A)
83. SHEA, CAROL ANN. "Visual Discrimination of Words and Reading Readiness." *Read Teach* 21:361–7 Ja '68. *
84. WESTON, LESLIE DONALD. *An Exploration of the Interrelationships Among Children's Arithmetic Achievement, Their Styles of Learning, Their Responsibility for Intellectual Academic Achievement, and Their Parents' Attitudes.* Doctor's thesis, Wayne State University (Detroit, Mich.), 1968. (*DAI* 30:1087A)
85. WOLF, WILLAVENE; KING, MARTHA L.; AND HUCK, CHARLOTTE S. "Teaching Critical Reading to Elementary School Children." *Reading Res Q* 3:435–98 su '68. *
86. BLAND, ROSA BEATRICE. *Relation of Auditory Discrimination to Reading Achievement.* Doctor's thesis, University of Virginia (Charlottesville, Va.), 1969. (*DAI* 31:1655A)
87. DUDEK, S. Z.; GOLDBERG, J. S.; LESTER, E. P.; AND HARRIS, B. R. "The Validity of Cognitive, Perceptual-Motor and Personality Variables for Prediction of Achievement in Grade 1 and Grade 2." *J Clin Psychol* 25(2):165–70 Ap '69. * (*PA* 43:14874)
88. DUDEK, S. Z.; LESTER, E. P.; GOLDBERG, J. S.; AND DYER, G. B. "Relationship of Piaget Measures to Standard Intelligence and Motor Scales." *Percept & Motor Skills* 28(2):351–62 Ap '69. * (*PA* 43:15587)
89. FELTON, THOMAS A., JR. *Correlation Between Creativity as Measured by Torrance Tests of Creative Thinking Figural Forms A and B and Intelligence as Measured by the Lorge-Thorndike Intelligence Test of Fifty Sixth Grade Students.* Master's thesis, Old Dominion University (Norfolk, Va.), 1969.
90. HAYES, EDWARD MAJELLA. *The Relationship of Race and Sex to Academic Achievement in Selected Rural Elementary and High Schools Before and After Desegregation.* Doctor's thesis, University of Virginia (Charlottesville, Va.), 1969. (*DAI* 31:149A)
91. HIERONYMUS, A. N., AND STROUD, JAMES B. "Comparability of IQ Scores on Five Widely Used Intelligence Tests." *Meas & Eval Guid* 2(3):135–40 f '69. * (*PA* 44:13285)
92. LESSING, ELISE E., AND ZAGORIN, SUSAN W. "Correlation Between Lorge-Thorndike IQ and Factor B of the IPAT Children's Personality Questionnaire." *Psychol Rep* 24(2):569–70 Ap '69. * (*PA* 43:15590)
93. MACARTHUR, RUSSELL S. "Some Cognitive Abilities of Eskimo, White, and Indian-Métis Pupils Aged 9 to 12 Years." *Can J Behav Sci* 1(1):50–9 Ja '69. * (*PA* 44:12319)
94. MCCUTCHEON, NANCY SUSAN. *A Study of Relationships Among Creativity, Intelligence, and Test Anxiety of Middle-Class Fourth Grade Boys and Girls.* Doctor's thesis, University of South Carolina (Columbia, S.C.), 1969. (*DAI* 30:4833A)
95. MANCOTT, ANATOL. "Prediction of Performance in Chemistry." *Nursing Outl* 17(11):55 N '69. *
96. MEHRENS, WILLIAM A., AND LEHMANN, IRVIN J. *Standardized Tests in Education,* pp. 91–101. New York: Holt, Rinehart & Winston, Inc., 1969. Pp. xi, 323. *
97. MOTLEY, HESTER CHATTIN. *A Study of the Predictive Value of Certain Factors Related to Test Performance, Academic Achievement, and Educational Aspirations.* Doctor's thesis, American University (Washington, D.C.), 1969. (*DAI* 30:2807A)
98. NIKAS, GEORGE BILL. *Anxiety Levels of Upper-Middle and Upper-Lower Class First Grade Children Prior to and During Formal Reading Instruction.* Doctor's thesis, State University of New York (Buffalo, N.Y.), 1969. (*DAI* 30:2382A)
99. OAS, ROBERT T. *A Study of the Relationships of Students' Aptitude, Academic Achievement and Attitude Toward School for Selected School Populations.* Doctor's thesis, University of South Dakota (Vermillion, S.D.), 1969. (*DAI* 30:3644A)
100. RODGERS, DENIS CYRIL. *An Investigation of the Auditory Memory Abilities of Grade 2 Retarded-Underachieving Readers and Competent-Achieving Readers Under Conditions of Reinforcement and Non-Reinforcement.* Doctor's thesis,

University of Toronto (Toronto, Ont., Canada), 1969. (*DAI* 31:2196A)

101. SHIGAKI, IRENE SHIKIBU. *The Effects of Teacher Strength and Sensitivity and Pupil Intelligence and Creativity on the Production of Divergent Responses.* Doctor's thesis, Columbia University (New York, N.Y.), 1969. (*DAI* 30:3864A)

102. TORRANCE, E. PAUL. "Prediction of Adult Creative Achievement Among High School Seniors." *Gifted Child Q* 13(4):223–9 w '69. * (*PA* 44:14620)

103. WESTPHAL, M. ELIZABETH; LEUTENEGGER, RALPH R.; AND WAGNER, DOROTHEA L. "Some Psycho-Acoustic and Intellectual Correlates of Achievement in German Language Learning of Junior High School Students." *Mod Lang J* 53(4):258–66 Ap '69. * (*PA* 44:21623)

104. YOUNG, WILLIAM THOMAS. *An Investigation of the Relative and Combined Power of Musical Aptitude, General Intelligence, and Academic Achievement Tests to Predict Musical Attainment.* Doctor's thesis, University of Iowa (Iowa City, Iowa), 1969. (*DAI* 30:758A)

105. ALLISON, DONALD E. "Test Anxiety, Stress, and Intelligence-Test Performance." *Can J Behav Sci* 2(1):26–37 Ja '70. * (*PA* 44:13275)

106. CALDWELL, JAMES R.; MICHAEL, WILLIAM B.; SCHRADER, DONALD R.; AND MEYERS, C. E. "Comparative Validities and Working Times for Composites of Structure-of-Intellect Tests and Algebra Grades and Composites of Traditional Test Measures and Algebra Grades in the Prediction of Success in Tenth-Grade Geometry." *Ed & Psychol Meas* 30(4):955–9 w '70. *

107. CANABAL, JUANA VILLANUEVA. *Comparison of Deaf and Normally Hearing Children on Analogy Items Under Different Methods of Instruction at Different Age Levels.* Doctor's thesis, St. John's University (Jamaica, N.Y.), 1970. (*DAI* 31:3700B)

108. CAVE, RICHARD L. "A Combined Factor Analysis of Creativity and Intelligence." *Multiv Behav Res* 5(2):177–91 Ap '70. * (*PA* 44:16697)

109. LESTER, EVA P.; MUIR, R.; AND DUDEK, STEPHANIE Z. "Cognitive Structure and Achievement in the Young Child." *Can Psychiatric Assn J* 15(3):279–87 Je '70. * (*PA* 45:5058)

110. NYE, MAE REDDISH. *Changes in Lorge-Thorndike Scores and in Grade Point Averages Over Three Years.* Master's thesis, College of Idaho (Caldwell, Idaho), 1970.

111. SMITH, I. LEON. "IQ, Creativity, and the Taxonomy of Educational Objectives: Cognitive Domain." *J Exp Ed* 38(4):58–60 su '70. * (*PA* 46:5688)

112. WILLIS, JERRY. "Group Versus Individual Intelligence Tests in One Sample of Emotionally Disturbed Children." *Psychol Rep* 27(3):819–22 D '70. * (*PA* 45:10227)

CAROL K. TITTLE, *Assistant Professor of Teacher Education, City University of New York, New York, New York.*

The *Lorge-Thorndike Intelligence Tests* have been well received in previous reviews, and meet generally accepted standards for test construction and standardization procedures. Restandardization in 1963, administration of achievement tests to the same standardization sample, and the multi-level format are the main features to be noted in this revision. The revision for the multi-level edition includes about one-third new items; the major change is in the format and sequencing for the multi-level edition.

The standardization in 1963 was carried out with the *Iowa Tests of Basic Skills* (grades 3–8) and the *Tests of Academic Progress* (grades 9–12). The common standardization sample for both the intelligence and achievement tests will assist users in interpreting scores and making comparisons between the scores on the batteries. The standardization procedures appear in the main to have been carefully carried out; the problems encountered in participation (just over 50 percent of the first choice units agreed to participate) and resulting statistical adjustments to the data are probably not uncommon to major test standardizations.

A major feature of the new edition is the multi-level arrangement. On first look at the test booklet, one is easily put off by the interruptions of the various start and stop statements for the different levels. However, it is likely that students adjust readily and probably do not experience difficulty because of the extraneous material.

The technical manual does not present adequate data, such as the item difficulty data, to support the arrangement of the modules of items for the multi-level arrangement. The items within a module are to show a progression in difficulty, but each new module is also to include items of lower difficulty to overlap with the preceding module. While the data is not given on distributions of item difficulties, the results of this type of scaling procedure seem to be satisfactory as nearly as can be inferred from the norm tables. Where some levels were administered a grade lower than that recommended, the norms tend to show small percentages of students down in the chance score area, when the actual score range used is considered (see data on Level C, for example). The tests appear to have considerable ceiling, since the number of items in the grade percentile norm tables is well under the total number of items in the verbal and nonverbal tests.

The tests are said to be primarily power tests. One study (66) found the tests to be too highly speeded to calculate internal consistency reliability coefficients for a sample of black students in grades 7–12. The manual should present data to show what effect time has on score distributions earned by subjects in the lower half of the distribution and for groups of special interest.

Reliability of the test is appropriately assessed with the alternate forms methods, and most data reported in the technical manual are developed by this method. The reliability coefficients are satisfactory, although the set of coefficients presented in Table 4 are on the low side (verbal battery .83 to .91, nonverbal battery .80 to .88, for different grades). The data for the standard error of measurement was based on the odd-even reliabilities and consequently may be slightly underestimated.

The inclusion of discussion on the standard error of measurement and the provision of the standard error of measurement in deviation IQ scores by raw score level (10 point intervals in raw scores) for both verbal and nonverbal tests is highly commended. The data allow the user to gain some understanding of the possible variability of scores, particularly at the extremes of the score distribution. The discussion and table should also be included in the administration manual, however, since many users of the test scores probably never see the technical manual, in contrast with the greater availability of the administration manual.

The data on practice effects are difficult to understand, particularly those for the nonverbal battery. Quite small effects were noted for the verbal battery, on a sample described as fairly sophisticated test takers. It is not clear exactly what is meant by the statement: "Some downward adjustment would need to be made in interpreting a retest" (i.e., since published norms are based upon an initial testing). A question can be raised concerning the amount of experience likely to have occurred within the standardization population, and how the user is to judge the amount of experience his pupils have had "with this type of test." Perhaps larger practice effects would have been noted on a random sample from the standardization group.

Content, predictive, and construct validity are discussed in the technical manual (labeled as representing, predicting, and signifying, respectively). Two of these areas will be considered here, predictive and construct, since the uses suggested for the test are: selecting curriculum materials and learning tasks (for students on the basis of the Lorge-Thorndike); comparing level of achievement and aptitude; formation of classroom groups by ability level; grouping within classroom; identifying students who may need special attention; reporting progress; counseling students; and vocational guidance.

Some correlations and related data are cited for the Lorge-Thorndike with achievement tests and school grades, but no specific data on the use of scores in grouping, identifying students who may need special attention, counseling and vocational guidance. The latter is particularly important, since the distinction between the verbal and nonverbal batteries implies that differences may have significance in relation to reading level, school achievement, or educational and vocational planning. There is indirect evidence on the latter in the correlations with the *Differential Aptitude Tests*. These show higher correlations for the nonverbal IQ's with Space Relations, Abstract Reasoning, and Mechanical Reasoning.

Generally, the Lorge-Thorndike verbal and nonverbal tests provide relatively high correlations with tests of achievement (.60's to .70's, with some up to the .80's). The nonverbal typically provides the lower correlations within any set.

Two series of studies provide some data relevant to the use of the nonverbal score. In a group of studies of Eskimos and Indians, MacArthur and colleagues have found the nonverbal battery to compare favorably with the *Progressive Matrices* and other "culture reduced" tests in predicting school achievement (*27, 42, 77, 78, 80*). However, the MacArthur studies apparently did not include the L-T verbal, so direct comparisons cannot be made.

A series of studies by Ward and his students did use both the verbal and nonverbal tests with samples of black students. The nonverbal was found less effective in predicting school achievement, and Ward raised the question of the independence of the verbal and nonverbal in use with special populations, at least. Higher nonverbal IQ's were noted with increasing age, but were not more effective than the verbal IQ in predicting school achievement. Factor analytic studies also indicated one general factor. Ward's suggestion that the factor structure of the nonverbal be investigated seems reasonable (*32, 43, 60, 65, 66*). A study of the stability of verbal and nonverbal scores (grades 3 to 8) found the estimated true change for the nonverbal three times that for the verbal—indicating a greater instability in the nonverbal scores (*55*).

A study of Nigerian students also found the verbal and nonverbal correlated similarly with school marks. There was "no indication of the superiority of the verbal or nonverbal for educational guidance" (*53*). Lorge-Thorndike scores were not predictors of reading gains for elementary pupils in grades 2–6 in remedial reading classes (*69*).

Studies of construct validity cited included relationships with school achievement (as above) and with other tests that have acceptance as measures of intelligence. The most extensive study was conducted by Hieronymus and Stroud (*91*). In their study of the comparability of IQ's obtained from the Lorge-Thorndike and four other intelligence tests administered to pupils in Iowa in grades 4, 7, and 10, they note that the correlations were quite variable, and in most cases below the reliabilities of the test, indicating that the tests were measuring somewhat different traits. The nonverbal IQ scores of the L-T had lower correlations with the other intelligence test scores than the verbal. The Hieronymus and Stroud study also provides comparability data on the IQ's derived from the 1954 and 1963 editions of the Lorge-Thorndike. In their study the newer edition yielded slightly lower IQ's for the verbal score in grades 4, 7, and 10, and for the nonverbal in grades 7 and 10.

Other studies of the relationships of the L-T with IQ measures have been conducted by Rainey (50), Kandel (56), and Keach (57). In a study of 813 fourth grade pupils, 100 with Stanford-Binet IQ's below 75 were located; the *California Test of Mental Maturity* selected a higher percentage of those identified by the Stanford-Binet than did the L-T or Otis (56). A similar study with the 100 highest IQ children on the S-B found the L-T and the CTMM about equally satisfactory (57).

The Lorge-Thorndike IQ's correlate moderately to fairly highly with school achievement and with other IQ's derived from intelligence tests. The multi-level edition is a refinement and improvement over the earlier separate level edition. The issues raised in the review are intended to encourage further studies of this widely-used, well-constructed and presented series of tests.

For reviews by Frank S. Freeman, John E. Milholland, and D. A. Pidgeon of the Separate Level Edition, see 5:350.

[361]
*Lowry-Lucier Reasoning Test Combination. Grades 5–16 and adults; 1956–65; LLRC; 3 scores: sequential relations, spatial relations, total; 2 tests; revised manual ('65, 15 pages); no data on reliability of subscores; tentative norms; $3.50 per 25 copies of either test; $6.50 per 25 sets of both tests; $1 per key; $1 per manual; postage extra; $5 per specimen set, postpaid; Ellsworth Lowry (test) and Omer Lucier; B. M. Farley. *
a) LOWRY-LUCIER REASONING TEST A. Sequential relations; LLRA; 1 form ('56, 3 pages); 15(20) minutes.
b) LOWRY-LUCIER REASONING TEST B. Spatial relations; LLRB; 1 form ('56, 3 pages); 20(25) minutes.

REFERENCES
1–6. See 6:468.
7. WALLACE, EDWIN C., JR. "The Selection and Training of Men and Women Programmers in a Bank." *Comput & Autom* 14:23–5 Ap '65. *

For reviews by Andrew R. Baggaley and Russel F. Green, see 6:468.

[362]
★Mental Alertness. Job applicants with 9–11, 12 or more years of education; 1945–62; 2 levels; no manual; no data on reliability and validity; R3.75 per 25 tests; 70c per key; sample copy available for inspection; postpaid within South Africa; Afrikaans edition available; National Institute for Personnel Research. *
a) TEST A/2. Job applicants with 9–11 years of education; Forms A/2/1 ('62, 8 pages), A/2/2 ['62, 8 pages]; norms ('57, 1 page); 30(35) minutes.
b) TEST A/1. Job applicants with 12 or more years of education; Forms A/1/1 ('62, 8 pages), A/1/2 ('61, 8 pages); norms ('57, 1 page); 35(40) minutes.

[363]
*Miller Analogies Test. Candidates for graduate school; 1926–70; MAT; Forms J ('52, 4 pages), K ('59, 4 pages), M ('69, 4 pages), R ('50, 4 pages, formerly Form H); Forms J and R also published under the title *Advanced Personnel Test* for use in business; use of Form R restricted to retesting; revised manual ('70, 32 pages); bulletin of information ('70, 61 pages); guide for testing center operation ['64, 8 pages]; distribution restricted and test administered at specified licensed university centers; scoring and reporting handled by the local center; separate answer sheets (IBM 805-Digitek, IBM 1230) must be used; examination fee to centers: $3 per examinee; fees to examinees are determined locally and include reporting of scores to the examinee and to 3 institutions or companies designated at the time of testing; additional score reports may be secured from the publisher at a fee of $1 each; Braille and large type editions available; 50(55) minutes; W. S. Miller (test); Psychological Corporation. *

REFERENCES
1–16. See 4:304.
17–44. See 5:352.
45–70. See 6:472.
71. GLADING, JOHN CAMPBELL. *The Miller Analogies Test and Its Relationship to Other Tests and Scholastic Achievement at Springfield College.* Master's thesis, Springfield College (Springfield, Mass.), 1951.
72. HYMAN, SIDNEY ROBERT. *The Development of Criteria of Research Competence in Psychology and Their Prediction From Certain Intellectual and Achievement Measures.* Doctor's thesis, University of Pittsburgh (Pittsburgh, Pa.), 1954. (*DA* 14:2395)
73. BINFORD, MARJORIE LYNETTE. *A Study of the Relationship of Test Scores and Experience to Grades in a Graduate Engineering Program.* Master's thesis, George Washington University (Washington, D.C.), 1959.
74. BLATT, SIDNEY J., AND STEIN, MORRIS I. "Efficiency in Problem Solving." *J Psychol* 48:193–213 O '59. * (*PA* 35:4971)
75. ASHBROOK, JAMES BARBOUR. *Evaluating Seminary Students as Potential Ministers.* Master's thesis, Ohio State University (Columbus, Ohio), 1962.
76. ROSS, JOEL A. *Major Factors Related to Success in an M.A. Program in Psychology.* Master's thesis, Hofstra University (Hempstead, N.Y.), 1962.
77. BOONE, SAM W. *The Scholastic Achievement of Stetson University Freshmen Required to Take Remedial English.* Master's thesis, Stetson University (DeLand, Fla.), 1963.
78. LEHMKUHL, CARLTON BURDELL. *Test Performance Relationships Among Occupational Patterns of Educational Administration Program Graduates.* Doctor's thesis, University of Minnesota (Minneapolis, Minn.), 1963. (*DA* 24:4510)
79. CALLIS, ROBERT, AND PREDIGER, DALE J. "Predictors of Achievement in Counseling and Guidance Graduate Study." *Counselor Ed & Sup* 3:63–9 w '64. *
80. CAMPBELL, MARY LOU. *Verbal Analogies Tests: A Comparison of Vocabulary and Reasoning Components Using the Miller Analogies Test and the Concept Mastery Test.* Master's thesis, University of Utah (Salt Lake City, Utah), 1964.
81. DUNNETTE, MARVIN D.; WERNIMONT, PAUL; AND ABRAHAMS, NORMAN. "Further Research on Vocational Interest Differences Among Several Types of Engineers." *Personnel & Guid J* 42:484–93 Ja '64. * (*PA* 39:6040)
82. FEINBERG, ABRAHAM. *The Relative Efficiency of Several Variables Used in the Selection Process for Candidates in a*

Graduate Certification Program. Doctor's thesis, Rutgers—The State University (New Brunswick, N.J.), 1964. (*DA* 25:2871)

83. KOLTVEIT, THOMAS H. "A Critique of: A Comparison of Miller Analogies Test Scores, Undergraduate Grade Point Averages, and Faculty Ratings of Guidance Counselor Students." *Univ N Dak Col Ed Rec* 49:87–8 Mr '64. *

84. ROBERTSON, MALCOLM, AND HALL, EVERETT. "Predicting Success in Graduate Study." *J General Psychol* 71:359–65 O '64. * (*PA* 39:5997)

85. STERNAL, WILLIAM; CASH, W. LEVI, JR.; AND GADE, ELDON M. "A Comparison of Miller Analogies Test Scores, Undergraduate Grade Point Averages, and Faculty Ratings of Guidance Counselor Students." *Univ N Dak Col Ed Rec* 49: 75–6 F '64. *

86. BUTLER, MARJORIE JOHNSON. *Criteria for Creativity in Counseling.* Doctor's thesis, University of Pittsburgh (Pittsburgh, Pa.), 1965. (*DA* 27:977B)

87. LIEF, VICTOR F.; LIEF, HAROLD I.; AND YOUNG, KATHLEEN M. "Academic Success: Intelligence and Personality." *J Med Ed* 40:114–24 F '65. *

88. MONAHAN, RUSSELL D. *The Relationship Between the Miller Analogies Test and the Technical Vocabulary Test.* Master's thesis, University of Oregon (Eugene, Ore.), 1965.

89. AINSWORTH, L. L., AND FOX, A. M. "Prediction of Grades in Graduate Education Courses." *Ed & Psychol Meas* 26:499–500 su '66. *

90. BENTLEY, JOSEPH C. "Creativity and Academic Achievement." *J Ed Res* 59:269–72 F '66. * (*PA* 40:6631)

91. ECKHOFF, CONSTANCE M. "Predicting Graduate Success at Winona State College." *Ed & Psychol Meas* 26:483–5 su '66. * (*PA* 40:12759)

92. LANE, ROBERT G.; PENN, NOLAN E.; AND FISCHER, ROBERT F. "Miller Analogies Test: A Note on Permissive Retesting." *J Appl Psychol* 50:409–11 O '66. * (*PA* 40:13189)

93. MOORE, JAMES C. "The Relationship Between Time Taken to Complete the Example Questions and Raw Score on the Miller Analogies Test." *J Ed Meas* 3:175–7 su '66. *

94. PAYNE, DAVID A., AND TUTTLE, CYNTHIA E. "The Predictive Relationship of the Miller Analogies Test to Objective and Subjective Criteria of Success in a Graduate School of Education." *Ed & Psychol Meas* 26:427–30 su '66. * (*PA* 40:13534)

95. SCHOFIELD, WILLIAM, AND MERWIN, JACK C. "The Use of Scholastic Aptitude, Personality, and Interest Test Data in the Selection of Medical Students." *J Med Ed* 41:502–9 Je '66. *

96. THUMIN, FRED J., AND BOERNKE, CAROL. "Miller Analogies Test Performance as Related to Age, Sex, and Academic Field." *Psychol Rep* 19:751–4 D '66. * (*PA* 41:5005)

97. WARD, DOROTHY V. *The Prediction of Success in Graduate Education Based on Undergraduate Grade Point Averages and Miller Analogies Test Scores.* Master's thesis, Kent State University (Kent, Ohio), 1966.

98. WATLEY, DONIVAN J. "Counselor Variability in Making Accurate Predictions." *J Counsel Psychol* 13:53–62 sp '66. * (*PA* 40:5817)

99. CURETON, EDWARD E., AND SCOTT, THOMAS B. "Equivalent Scores for the Graduate Record Verbal and Miller Analogies Tests." *Ed & Psychol Meas* 27:611–5 au '67. * (*PA* 42:122)

100. JANSEN, DAVID G., AND JOHNSTON, FRED N. "Prediction of Graduate School Achievement." *J Col Stud Personnel* 8:296–9 S '67. *

101. MCGREEVY, C. PATRICK. "Factor Analysis of Measures Used in the Selection and Evaluation of Counselor Education Candidates." *J Counsel Psychol* 14:51–6 Ja '67. * (*PA* 41:3644)

102. MARASCUILO, LEONARD A., AND GILL, GARY. "Measurable Differences Between Successful and Unsuccessful Doctoral Students in Education." *Calif J Ed Res* 18:65–70 Mr '67. * (*PA* 41:9389)

103. SCHMITT, JOHN A. "A Note on the Miller Analogies Test and Selection of Graduate Students in Education." *J Teach Ed* 18:59–61 sp '67. *

104. SEIBEL, DEAN W. "Predicting the Classroom Behavior of Teachers." *J Exp Ed* 36:26–32 f '67. *

105. STORDAHL, KALMER E. "Predicting Grades in a Master's-Degree Program." *J Ed Meas* 4:119–22 su '67. *

106. WALLEN, NORMAN E., AND CAMPBELL, MARY LOU A. "Vocabulary and Non-verbal Reasoning Components of Verbal Analogies Tests (Miller Analogies Tests and Concept Mastery Test)." *J Ed Res* 61:87–9 O '67. *

107. WHITELEY, JOHN M.; SPRINTHALL, NORMAN A.; MOSHER, RALPH L.; AND DONAGHY, ROLLA T. "Selection and Evaluation of Counselor Effectiveness." *J Counsel Psychol* 14:226–34 My '67. * (*PA* 41:9423)

108. GRIMSRUD, RICHARD ARLO. *A Method for Predicting Success in a Counselor Education Training Program.* Doctor's thesis, University of Minnesota (Minneapolis, Minn.), 1968. (*DA* 29:2115A)

109. HARDESTY, D. L., AND JONES, W. S. "Characteristics of Judged High Potential Management Personnel—The Operations of an Industrial Assessment Center." *Personnel Psychol* 21:85–98 sp '68. * (*PA* 42:16197)

110. LAURENT, HARRY. Chap. 1, "Research on the Identification of Management Potential," pp. 1–34. In *Predicting Managerial Success.* Edited by John A. Myers, Jr. Ann Arbor, Mich.: Foundation for Research on Human Behavior, April 1968. Pp. v, 173. *

111. MERLE, SHERMAN. *The Selection of Students at a Graduate School of Social Work: A Study of the Incremental Value of a Pre-Admission Interview, and the Use of the Undergraduate Grade Point Average and Miller Analogy Test in Identifying the Successful and Unsuccessful Student.* Doctor's thesis, Brandeis University (Waltham, Mass.), 1968. (*DA* 29:101A)

112. CARLSON, RAE. "Rorschach Prediction of Success in Clinical Training: A Second Look." *J Consult & Clin Psychol* 33(6):699–704 D '69. * (*PA* 44:3697)

113. DE BERUFF, ELLEN. *The Prediction of Success in Master's and Doctoral Programs.* Doctor's thesis, University of Maryland (College Park, Md.), 1969. (*DAI* 31:1033A)

114. DIGIORGIO, ANTHONY JOSEPH. *Discriminant Function Analysis of Measured Characteristics Among Committed Career Groups With Requisite Graduate Training.* Doctor's thesis, Purdue University (Lafayette, Ind.), 1969. (*DAI* 30:4769A)

115. EWEN, ROBERT B. "The GRE Psychology Test as an Unobtrusive Measure of Motivation." *J Appl Psychol* 53(5): 383–7 O '69. * (*PA* 44:1370)

116. GAB, DEL D. *Prediction of Success for Doctoral Students in Education at the University of North Dakota.* Doctor's thesis, University of North Dakota (Grand Forks, N.D.), 1969. (*DAI* 31:61A)

117. MEHRABIAN, ALBERT. "Undergraduate Ability Factors in Relationship to Graduate Performance." *Ed & Psychol Meas* 29(2):409–19 su '69. * (*PA* 44:17508)

118. POSTON, WILLIAM KENNETH, JR. *Educational Administrator Job Performance and Training Program Admission Criteria.* Doctor's thesis, Arizona State University (Tempe, Ariz.), 1969. (*DAI* 30:532A)

119. RAWLS, JAMES R.; RAWLS, DONNA J.; AND HARRISON, C. WADE. "An Investigation of Success Predictors in Graduate School in Psychology." *J Psychol* 72(1):125–9 My '69. * (*PA* 43:16455)

120. SMOLINSKY, MERVIN PHILIP. *An Empirical Study of a Method of Measuring a Criterion for Graduate Student Success.* Doctor's thesis, University of Pittsburgh (Pittsburgh, Pa.), 1969. (*DAI* 30:1879A)

121. WILLIAMS, JOHN D., AND GAB, DEL. "Assessing the Doctoral Admission Policy." *Col Ed Rec* 55(1):14–20 O '69. *

122. CARLETON, FREDERICK O. "Relationships Between Follow-Up Evaluations and Information Developed in a Management Assessment Center." Abstract. *Proc 78th Ann Conv Am Psychol Assn* 5(2):565–6 '70. * (*PA* 44:19655)

123. FERNANDES, LUCIA M. *The Miller Analogies Test as a Predictor of Success in the Graduate School of Education, University of Pittsburgh.* Master's thesis, University of Pittsburgh (Pittsburgh, Pa.), 1970.

124. MEHRABIAN, ALBERT. "Ability Factors of Candidates for Graduate School." *Am Psychologist* 25(6):560–3 Je '70. *

125. PRIEN, ERICH P. "Measuring Performance Criteria of Bank Tellers." *J Indus Psychol* 5(1):29–36 Mr '70. *

126. SMITH, I. LEON. "Associational Achievement, Aptitude, and Creativity." *Ed & Psychol Meas* 30(4):999–1000 w '70. *

127. WILLIAMS, JOHN D.; HARLOW, STEVEN D.; AND GAB, DEL. "A Longitudinal Study Examining Prediction of Doctoral Success: Grade Point Average as Criterion, or Graduation vs. Non-Graduation as Criterion." *J Ed Res* 64(4):161–4 D '70. *

For reviews by Lloyd G. Humphreys, William B. Schrader, and Warren W. Willingham of Forms H, J, K, and an earlier form, see 6:472; for a review by John T. Dailey, see 5:352; for reviews by J. P. Guilford and Carl I. Hovland, see 4:304.

[364]

*Moray House Intelligence Tests. Ages 8.5–10.5, 10–12, 10–12 of above average ability, 12–14.5, 13.5 and over; 1930–70; MHIT; 5 levels; distribution restricted to education authorities; 75p per 20 tests (except *a*, £1); 5p per single copy; 12½p per manual for any one form of any one test; postage extra; Department of Education, University of Edinburgh; University of London Press Ltd. *

a) MORAY HOUSE JUNIOR REASONING TEST FOR NINE YEAR OLDS. Ages 8.5–10.5; 1947–70; 4 forms: *Junior Reasoning Test 2* ['58], *3* ('69), *6, 7,* ('70), (12 pages); manual (dates same as for test, 12–19 pages) for each form; 45(104) minutes for form *2*, 40(75) minutes for forms *3, 6, 7.*

b) MORAY HOUSE VERBAL REASONING TEST. Ages 10–12; 1930–70; earlier forms called *Moray House Intelligence Tests*; 2–3 new forms issued annually; 19 forms currently available: forms 65 ['60], 66 ('69), 67 ('68), 68 ('68), 69 ['62], 70 ['62], 71 ['63], 72 ['63], 74 ('68), 75 ('68), 76 ('65), 77 ('68), 78 ('68), 79 ('68), 80 ('68), 82 ('69), 85 ('68), 86 ('69), 87 ('70), (8 pages); manual (dates same as for test, 12 pages) for each form; practice test (dates generally same as for test, 2 pages) for each form; 10(15) minutes for practice test, 45(50) minutes for test.

c) [MORAY HOUSE VERBAL REASONING TEST: VERNIER TEST 2.] Ages 10–12 of above average ability; 1954–57; a "slightly more difficult" test than the tests in *b* above; 1 form ['57, 8 pages]; manual ['57, 12 pages]; 45(50) minutes.

d) MORAY HOUSE VERBAL REASONING TEST (ADV.). Ages 12–14.5; 1940–68; forms 7 ('61, 8 pages), 9, 10, (68, 8 pages); manual (dates same as for test, 12 pages) for each form; practice tests 6 ['53, 2 pages, for form 7], 7 ['54, 2 pages, for forms 9–10]; 10(15) minutes for practice test, 45(50) minutes for test.

e) MORAY HOUSE ADULT INTELLIGENCE TEST 1. Ages 13.5 and over; 1952; 1 form ['52, 8 pages]; manual ['52, 15 pages]; 45(50) minutes.

REFERENCES

1–2. See 3:241.
3–4. See 5:353.
5–17. See 6:474.
18. BOYNE, A. W., AND CLARK, J. R. "Secular Change in the Intelligence of 11-Year-Old Aberdeen Schoolchildren." *Hum Biol* 31:325–33 D '59. * (PA 35:690)
19. ENTWISTLE, N. J., AND WELSH, JENNIFER. "Correlates of School Attainment at Different Ability Levels." *Brit J Ed Psychol* 39(1):57–63 F '69. * (PA 43:17988)
20. MCINTOSH, D. M., AND WALKER, D. A. "The O Grade of the Scottish Certificate of Education." *Brit J Ed Psychol* 40(2):179–99 Je '70. * (PA 44:21528)

For a review by Patrick Slater of earlier forms, see 3:241; for a review by C. Ebblewhite Smith, see 2:1409.

[365]

*New South African Group Test. Ages 8–11, 10–14, 13–17; 1931–65; NSAGT; 3 scores: verbal, nonverbal, total; 3 levels; preliminary manual ('65, 44 pages) for junior and senior levels; separate answer sheets (hand scorable, IBM 1230) must be used; R2 per 10 tests; R2.40 per 100 hand scorable answer sheets; R4 per 100 IBM 1230 answer sheets; 30c per hand scoring stencil; 60c per manual; postpaid within South Africa; specimen set free; Afrikaans edition available; 55(100) minutes; Human Sciences Research Council. *

a) JUNIOR. Ages 8–11; 1931–65; Forms J, K, ['65, 32 pages].
b) INTERMEDIATE. Ages 10–14; 1931–63; Form G ['63, 32 pages]; manual ['63, 19 pages].
c) SENIOR. Ages 13–17; 1931–65; Forms S, T, ['65, 32 pages].

REFERENCES

1. ELDER, C. M. "The Statistical Procedure Adopted in the Construction and Standardization of the New South African Group Test." *J Social Res* (Pretoria) 8:1–12 '57. * (PA 34:3630)
2. SUGARMAN, LOLA. "Alpha Rhythm, Perception and Intelligence." *J Nat Inst Personnel Res* 8:170–9 S '61. * (PA 36:4DG70S)
3. STRÜMPFER, D. J. W., AND MIENIE, C. J. P. "A Validation of the Harris-Goodenough Test." *Brit J Ed Psychol* 38:96–100 F '68. * (PA 42:12134)

[366]

★Non-Readers Intelligence Test. Ages 6–9 to 8–11; 1964; no reading by examinees; 1 form; manual (31 pages); 32½p per 20 answer sheets; 12½p per scoring stencil; 25p per manual; postage extra; (60) minutes in 2 sessions; D. Young; University of London Press Ltd. *

[367]

*Non-Verbal Tests. Ages 8 to 11–0, 10 to 12–11, 10 to 15; 1947–65; 3 levels; postpaid within U.K.; published for the National Foundation for Educational Research in England and Wales; Ginn & Co. Ltd. *

a) NON-VERBAL TESTS 1–2. Ages 10 to 12–11; 1947–59; title on test is *A Scale of Non-Verbal Mental Ability*; 2 forms (12 pages); optional practice test ['50, 3 pages]; no data on validity; distribution restricted to directors of education; 7p per test; 4p per practice test; 15p per manual for either form; 10(15) minutes for practice test, 30(35) minutes for test.

1) *Non-Verbal Test 1*. 1947–59; 1 form ['49]; revised manual ('59, 20 pages); no norms for ages 12–0 to 12–11 for administration with practice test; Welsh edition ['54] available; J. W. Jenkins.
2) *Non-Verbal Test 2*. 1948–51; 1 form ['49]; manual ['51]; supplementary provisional norms ['51, for ages 10–3 to 11–2 only] for administration with practice test; D. M. Lee and J. W. Jenkins.

b) NON-VERBAL TEST DH. Ages 10 to 15; 1953–58; formerly called *Non-Verbal Test 3*; 1 form ['53, 28 pages]; may be administered as a short form for ages 10–6 to 12–0; revised manual ('58, 8 pages); no data on reliability; separate answer sheets must be used; 13p per test; 2p per answer sheet; 10p per manual and stencil; 50(60) minutes for full test, 35(45) minutes for short version; B. Calvert (test) and I. Macfarlane Smith (original manual).

c) NON-VERBAL TEST BD. Ages 8 to 11–0; 1953–65; formerly called *Non-Verbal Test 5*; 1 form ['53, 17 pages]; revised manual ('65, 15 pages); no data on validity; 10p per test; 10p per manual; 20(40) minutes; D. A. Pidgeon.

REFERENCES

1–3. See 4:307.
4. See 5:356.
5. See 6:479.
6. ENTWISTLE, N. J., AND WELSH, JENNIFER. "Correlates of School Attainment at Different Ability Levels." *Brit J Ed Psychol* 39(1):57–63 F '69. * (PA 43:17988)

For reviews by T. R. Miles and John Nisbet, see 6:479; for a review by Cyril A. Rogers, see 5:356; for a review by E. A. Peel of the original edition, see 4:307.

[368]

★OISE Picture Reasoning Test: Primary. Grades 1–2; 1969–70; PRT; replaces the *Group Test of Learning Capacity: Dominion Tests: Primary*; Forms A, B, ('69, 12 pages); manual ('70, 10 pages plus scoring keys); no data on reliability and validity; Can $4 per 20 tests and manual; $1 per specimen set; postage extra; 51(80) minutes; Ontario Institute for Studies in Education; distributed by Guidance Centre. *

[369]

★The Oregon Academic Ranking Test. Bright children grades 3–7; 1965; OART; for rapid identification of the top 3 percent; 9 scores: making sentences, making comparisons, numbers, secret words, working problems, reasoning, completing sentences, sayings, total; 1 form (4 pages); manual (16 pages plus test); no norms or reliability data for subscores; $7.50 per 25 tests and manual; $6.50 per 25 tests; $2 per manual; postpaid; (30–40) minutes; Charles H. Derthick; Western Psychological Services. *

ROBERT H. BAUERNFEIND, *Professor of Educational Psychology, Northern Illinois University, DeKalb, Illinois.*

The *Oregon Academic Ranking Test* was designed to identify the "exceptionally bright child"—the child who is talented in convergent skills (arithmetic and reading vocabulary) and who is also talented in divergent skills (using objects, completing sentences, and interpreting popular adages). This test, printed in a four-page folder, is divided into eight sections, each employing a different item type. Some sections are objectively scored and some subjectively scored. A perfect paper yields a score of 100 points.

I have mixed feelings about this test. The test questions are really very good—very clever, and they seem consistently relevant to the author's stated purposes. But after one praises the test questions, he finds that everything else is downhill.

The first fault involves format. The test materials have clearly been squeezed into a four-page format; the readability is quite poor, with small type and some line lengths exceeding seven inches; and, in the divergent sections, there is not nearly enough room for the handwriting of pupils in the elementary grades. In the very first test, the children are given only 3/16 of an inch of vertical space between lines on which they are to write. This test is for third and fourth graders? Maybe children in Salem, Oregon, are taught differently. But children in my area stumbled badly in reading the test problems, and they could not print or write their answers within the confines imposed by the test publisher. (I doubt that the publisher's own art director can write or print the word "Thursday" in that little box in item 5-E!) Those who designed this format were terribly insensitive to their audience—i.e., children aged 8 to 13. On the criterion of format alone, I cannot recommend this test for use below the seventh grade.

The second fault is that the manual is misleading in several places. First, it implies that the exceptionally bright children are in the top three percent of some undefined group. Why the top three percent instead of any other percent? There is no discussion of this point anywhere in the manual. Three percent of what group? There is no discussion of this matter either. But raw scores corresponding to a 97th percentile are prominently printed on the front cover of each test booklet. Where did these data come from? Well, they came from studies of children in Salem, Oregon, with an average N around 180 per grade. Since Salem is a large city, these children must have been selected in some manner. But the manual does not bother to mention the matter of selection.

If the manual had said, "Here's the story of how this test worked in one school system," that would be fine—interesting and professional. But when normative data from a single undefined group are printed on the front cover of every test booklet, the test reviewer simply must blow the whistle.

All technical data apparently are based on these same small undefined groups of children in Salem, Oregon. And these technical studies are largely meaningless. The reliability coefficients are irrelevant, since the stated purpose of the test is to select the top three percent of a school population. Thus, relevant data would show percentages of youngsters selected *both times* in test-retest studies. Under "validity," the manual shows three tables correlating OART with the Stanford-Binet. But on page 1 of the manual the author implies that OART is to measure something somewhat different from the Stanford-Binet. Do low correlations between the two tests then demonstrate the "validity" of OART? Well, maybe. But the author would have done much better by staying with his strong suit—content validity.

If asked to select the three percent most academically-talented pupils in a school district, I would give a general educational development test (such as the *Iowa Tests of Basic Skills*) districtwide for use with all pupils. Then I would list the top five or six percent on the total score and ask the teachers to select the final three percent by applying criteria of "divergent thinking" and "abstract reasoning."

In short, this is quite a good test except for its insensitive format, but it seems inefficient and unnecessary. It could be used with junior high pupils who like to write small, if the school personnel especially like the mix of item types. But they should make such a choice solely on the basis of the item mix. There are no statistical studies reported in the manual that are relevant or useful to anyone outside of Salem, Oregon.

[370]

*Otis-Lennon Mental Ability Test. Grades kgn, 1.0–1.5, 1.6–3.9, 4–6, 7–9, 10–12; 1936–70; OLMAT; revision of the still-in-print *Otis Quick-Scoring Men-*

tal Ability Tests; 2 forms; 6 levels; manual ('67, 23 pages) for grades 4 and over; technical handbook ('69, 52 pages); supplementary technical data report ('70, 2 pages); $2 per handbook; $2.25 per specimen set of any one level; postage extra; Arthur S. Otis and Roger T. Lennon; Harcourt Brace Jovanovich, Inc. *

a) PRIMARY I. Kgn; 1967–69; Forms J ('67, 8 pages), K ('68, 8 pages); manual for Forms J ('67, 21 pages), K ('68, 21 pages); norms booklet for Forms J ('67, 4 pages), K ('68, 4 pages); $6.50 per 35 tests; scoring service, 90¢ per test; (30–35) minutes.

b) PRIMARY 2. Grades 1.0–1.5; 1967–69; 2 editions; Forms J ('67, 8 pages), K ('68, 8 pages); manual for Forms J ('67, 22 pages), K ('68, 22 pages); norms booklet for Forms J ('67, 4 pages), K ('68, 4 pages); (30–35) minutes.
  1) *Hand Scorable Edition*. $6.50 per 35 tests; scoring service, 90¢ per test.
  2) *Machine Scorable Edition*. $9 per 35 tests; MRC scoring service, 36¢ and over per test.

c) ELEMENTARY I. Grades 1.6–3.9; 1936–69; 2 editions; Forms J ('67, 12 pages), K ('68, 12 pages); manual for Forms J ('67, 23 pages), K ('68, 23 pages); norms booklet for Forms J ('67, 6 pages), K ('68, 6 pages); (55–60) minutes.
  1) *Hand Scorable Edition*. $6.80 per 35 tests; scoring service, $1 per test.
  2) *Machine Scorable Edition*. $9.30 per 35 tests; MRC scoring service, 42¢ and over per test.

d) ELEMENTARY 2. Grades 4–6; 1936–69; Forms J ('67, 8 pages), K ('68, 8 pages); norms booklet for Forms J ('67, 6 pages), K ('68, 6 pages); $6.80 per 35 tests; separate answer sheets (Digitek, Harbor, IBM 805, IBM 1230) may be used; $2.80 per 35 Digitek or IBM 1230 answer sheets; $2.30 per 35 IBM 805 answer sheets; $3 per 100 Harbor answer cards; 70¢ per Digitek or IBM scoring stencil; Harbor or IBM scoring service, 21¢ and over per test; (45–50) minutes.

e) INTERMEDIATE. Grades 7–9; 1936–69; Forms J ('67, 8 pages), K ('68, 8 pages); norms booklet for Forms J ('67, 6 pages), K ('68, 6 pages); answer sheets, prices, and time same as for Elementary 2 level.

f) ADVANCED. Grades 10–12; 1936–69; Forms J ('67, 8 pages), K ('68, 8 pages); norms booklet for Forms J ('67, 6 pages), K ('68, 6 pages); answer sheets, prices, and time same as for Elementary 2 level.

REFERENCES

1. BURKHALTER, W. D., JR. *A Validation Study of the Otis-Lennon Mental Ability Test, Elementary 1 Level, Grade Three.* Doctor's thesis, University of Tulsa (Tulsa, Okla.), 1969. (*DAI* 30:1812A)
2. COX, OTIS. *Creative Thinking in a High School Experimental Humanities Program.* Doctor's thesis, University of Alabama (University, Ala.), 1969. (*DAI* 31:214A)
3. HANNA, GERALD S.; BLIGH, HAROLD F.; LENKE, JOANNE M.; AND ORLEANS, JOSEPH B. "Predicting Algebra Achievement With an Algebra Prognosis Test, IQs, Teacher Predictions, and Mathematics Grades." *Ed & Psychol Meas* 29(4): 903–7 w '69. * (*PA* 44:21615)
4. BREUER, CHARLES EDWARD, JR. *The Effect of Prejudice Upon Test Performance.* Doctor's thesis, University of South Carolina (Columbia, S.C.), 1970. (*DAI* 31:3259A)
5. COTLER, SHELDON, AND PALMER, RICHARD J. "The Relationships Among Sex, Sociometric, Self, and Test Anxiety Factors and the Academic Achievement of Elementary School Children." *Psychol Sch* 7(3):211–6 Jl '70. * (*PA* 45:5019)
6. SKRIPOL, JAMES N. *Correlation of the Otis-Lennon Intermediate and the Wechsler Intelligence Scale for Children.* Master's thesis, Springfield College (Springfield, Mass.), 1970.

JOHN E. MILHOLLAND, *Professor of Psychology, The University of Michigan, Ann Arbor, Michigan.*

The construction and norming of this test bespeaks adherence to the highest level of current standards. Sophisticated authorship apparently backed by the publisher's determination to spare no effort or expense has resulted in a product of exceptional merit.

The rationale comes from Vernon's description of the structure of mental abilities, embodying two major divisions, verbal-educational and practical-mechanical, integrated into Spearman's g. The Otis-Lennon test aims to cover only the verbal-educational half of the structure.

The standardization sample was chosen to represent the country's educational system, not the population at large. Controls were applied for size of school, family income, educational level of adults, types of school (public, private, church-related), geographic location (all 50 states were represented) and quality of school in terms of educational achievement within its own system. At the kindergarten level, 5,379 pupils were tested; for grades 1–12 the samples per grade varied in size from 11,866 to 14,746. The technical handbook gives a thorough account of the norming operations and the results.

The question arises, however, to what purpose is all this effort expended? Just what is the value of national norms? Has one learned anything by discovering that a school pupil, a grade, or a system is this or that far above or below a nationwide norm figure? Does it help to guide instructional policy? One can, of course, make many kinds of predictions, with reasonable accuracy, from norm-referenced scores. But couldn't just as good a job be done with scaled scores? The College Board has been doing fairly well with this kind of mechanism for some years.

It would seem that local school problems can be best attacked through the use of local norms, and that the only really significant function served by norms is furnishing a scale. This function can certainly be carried out effectively without the elaborate structure of "representative" national norms.

Scores on the Otis-Lennon tests may be expressed as deviation IQ's and as age and grade percentile ranks and stanines. Users are gently urged to interpret scores in terms of stanines rather than IQ's, and this may be a sign of a healthy trend. Deviation IQ's are only transformed standard scores anyway, and the IQ unit implies a precision that is not justified. The standard errors of measurement, based on alternate-forms reliability estimates, for IQ's from the Otis-Lennon vary from 3.9 to 7.0 points.

In addition to reliability and validity data, information on reading proficiency level required, speededness, and practice effect is provided in the handbook. The three lower levels of the test require no reading, and median reading grade-level ratings for the other three are below the lowest grade for which the test is intended. A few items, however, were rated at reading difficulty levels higher than the highest grade for which the test is recommended.

A speededness study showed a gain of 2.9 IQ points under untimed conditions for the Advanced Level tests; gains at all other levels were less than 2 points. Mean practice effect gains for a 2-week interval ranged from 1 to 3.6 points of IQ, giving an average gain of 2.5 points for practice effect.

An alternate forms reliability estimate is given for each grade and for each age. Those for grades 4 and below range from .83 to .89; beyond grade 4 they are all above .90. Below age 10 the estimates go from .81 to .90; above that age they are all .90 or better. Standard errors of measurement average about 4.5 IQ points at ages 10 or above, around 6 points at the lower ages. An unusual feature is the provision of IQ standard errors by stanine level.

The discussion of validity is organized in accordance with the content, criterion-related, and construct categories of the 1966 *Standards for Educational and Psychological Tests and Manuals*. The validity research was wide-ranging, and abundant data are provided. The test correlates adequately with educational criteria and with other measures of general scholastic aptitude. The Otis-Lennon test should perform well the functions it is intended to serve. These explicitly do not include measuring innate learning potential, and in the manuals special caution is advised in interpreting results for children who do not have normal backgrounds and motivation.

J Counsel Psychol 17(1):91–2 Ja '70. Arthur E. Smith. * A number of changes from the previous Otis series reflect attention to recent research and currently recommended practices in test development. While the fundamental theory about intelligence remains the same (reliable measure of "g"), nearly all the items are new or revised. * Primary I and II, however, are identical except for method of scoring and recommended use. The former is suggested for students in the last half of kindergarten and the latter in the first half of Grade 1 or the last half for "slower, less mature first graders." This distinction is misleading and serves no good purpose. It is impossible, moreover, to follow the authors' recommendation to administer Primary I in two sittings on the same day separated by a lunch period since kindergartens are typically half-day sessions. * The format of the items is similar to that used in the previous tests with a smaller proportion of verbal items at the upper levels. * Time limits appear to be ample and the authors' claim of a power measure are substantiated except that the study on speededness was conducted with students who were "somewhat" superior to typical students. Speed is a greater factor among lower levels of ability and hence studies at these levels should be conducted by the publishers as soon as possible. The procedures used in the selection of items are appropriate. The care taken to reduce the effects of reading handicaps on the student's performance is commendable. The scoring directions are excellent, particularly for the early series. Methods of scoring are flexible and probably meet the needs of any user. Extensive care and planning are evident in choosing the sample for standardization. Intelligence or scholastic ability is highly correlated with socioeconomic level. In the new Otis-Lennon series, a comparison of median family income and education completed for sampled school systems and for adults in the general population were virtually identical. * Obviously, stability over time cannot be determined immediately for a new test such as this. The comparisons of scores obtained over a 1-year lapse look promising with correlation coefficients ranging from .80 to .94 (highest at upper levels). The comparisons appear to be based on above-average students and hence these should be replicated on a more typical population. Nevertheless, estimates of reliability using alternate forms and split-half techniques give the user assurance that the results can be used with reasonable confidence. Standard errors of measurement indicate that the results may be used in an appropriate manner. As the authors point out, however, some of the levels have insufficient "top" and "bottom." Judging the validity of the Otis-Lennon is preliminary. The authors discuss content, criterion related, and construct validity and present data which supports the use of the instrument.

Correlation coefficients with other measures are in the expected magnitudes and some indicate substantial relationships with composite or total scores. * The Otis-Lennon Tests can be a useful tool for teachers, administrators, and counselors. The same careful work which marked the previous tests of this nature are evident in the new series. Future research is needed to determine the adequacy of their sampling techniques and general usefulness of the test in predicting academic performance.

J Ed Meas 6(2):111–3 su '69. *Arden Grotelueschen.* * The test booklets are well organized and designed, and the ease with which the test may be administered and scored is a continued positive feature. Raw scores are easily convertible to various types of normative scores * The authors state that the Primary I level is a downward extension of the Alpha Test. More specifically, they claim that "The downward extension of the Otis-Lennon series to include a level especially designed for use with kindergarten pupils (Primary I) is a noteworthy addition." This reviewer has some serious reservations about this latter statement. First, it could be argued that the Primary I level is not in and of itself a distinct level, because every item of this level is identical to that contained in the Primary II level. Apparently, the authors felt justified in differentiating between the Primary I and Primary II levels on the basis of response mode alone. For example, at the Primary I level the pupil is required to circle the item option representing his choice; with the Primary II level the pupil shades in a small oval beneath his choice. A sampling of several 4-year-olds, by the reviewer, indicates no difference in their ability to complete either the response mode of the Primary I level or the response mode of the Primary II level. Second, the technical data provided for the Primary I level are neither as complete nor as acceptable as those provided for the other test levels. For example, no validity information is given other than that with the Quick-Scoring Alpha Test administered to kindergarten pupils, for which the Alpha is not recommended. Presumably, part of the incompleteness results from the assumption that evidence for Primary II is directly applicable to Primary I, an assumption which contradicts the fact that the two tests are defined as two distinct levels. In summary, it would appear that the Otis-Lennon should have been published as five levels with one Primary level for kindergarten and first grade pupils. Also, validity data based on the performance of kindergarten pupils are lacking. The manual contains an excellent discussion of the use of the age and grade norms and the interpretation of test scores. In contrast, some sections of the Technical Data and Developmental Research parts of the manual lack specific information essential to test consumers. The most serious lack of data is that of validity. The authors intend well by stating that validity studies are being conducted and that the results will appear in a forthcoming Technical Handbook. * Information on the procedures for standardization, scaling and norming is presented in detail. Moreover, the procedures for each appear to have been carefully conceptualized and conducted. * Substantial evidence is provided to indicate that the Otis-Lennon is highly reliable. * The higher internal-consistency coefficients were assumed to have not been influenced by speed. This assumption was based on findings obtained from an experimental study designed to ascertain the effect of speed on test performance. The findings were interpreted to provide conclusive evidence that speed of responding had a negligible effect on test performance when administered within the specified time limits. Had the design of the study incorporated a group receiving the test under strictly power conditions, a more conclusive test of the effect of speed on test performance would have been ascertained. The authors should be applauded for facing up to an embarrassing situation—that of making explicit a rationale for a test which has been in existence for around 50 years. In the development of the rationale, it was reasoned that the Otis-Lennon series should continue to be a broadly based measure of general mental ability, defined more specifically as "verbal-educational *g*." * It would have been desirable if the authors had presented factor-analytic evidence to complement the logical claims for the test. The omission of a factor study, of available data, is of concern to this reviewer, especially since correlational evidence interpreted by the authors to support the construct validity of the test is inconclusive. For instance, the authors interpret the high correlations reported between the Otis-Lennon and various mental ability batteries as evidence for construct validity. No explanation is given, however, to account for similar high correlations reported between the Otis-Lennon and various achievement test scores. (The Otis-Lennon is not unique in this respect.) The high correlations, for example, between the Otis-Lennon and the *Iowa Tests of Basic Skills* composite score leaves only 5% of the nonerror variance unexplainable at the fifth and eighth grade levels, when both predictor and criterion are corrected for attenuation. This finding is not appreciably different than that observed between Forms J and K of the Otis-Lennon itself. Thus, the Otis-Lennon gives ample evidence for predicting scholastic success. However, without stronger evidence of construct validity, it may be concluded that the predictability of scholastic success is due to the fact that the Otis-Lennon is a direct measure of scholastic success. Stated more practically, present evidence indicates that schools with an achievement testing program may not be adding anything unique to the total testing program by using the Otis-Lennon as a measure of general mental ability. In summary, the Otis-Lennon is a marked improvement, both technically and substantively, over its immediate predecessor, the Otis Quick-Scoring series. Aside from the criticisms directed toward the test's purported construct validity and its downward extension, the Otis-Lennon is an outstanding test of its kind.

For reviews by D. Welty Lefever and Alfred Yates of the Otis Quick-Scoring Mental Ability Tests, *see 5:362; for a review by Frederic Kuder, see 3:249; for reviews by F. Kuhlmann and C. Spearman, see 2:1413; for reviews by Psyche Cattell and R. Pintner, see 1:1053 (2 excerpts).*

[371]
★**Pacific Reasoning Series Tests: Pacific Test Series.** Job applicants in Papua and New Guinea; 1962–68; PRST; Forms A, B, C, ('68, 4 pages); manual ('68, 29 pages); Aus 80¢ per 10 tests; $2.50 per manual; $2.80 per specimen set; postpaid within Australia; 45(50) minutes; I. G. Ord; Australian Council for Educational Research. *

REFERENCE
1. BENNETT, M. J. "Reasoning Test Response in Urban and Rural Fijian and Indian Groups in Fiji." *Austral Psychologist* 5(3):260–6 N '70. * (PA 46:5459)

[372]
*****Performance Alertness "PA" (With Pictures): Individual Placement Series.** Adults; 1961–66; Form C ('61, 4 pages); no specific manual; series manual ('66, 107 pages); separate answer sheets must be used; $12 per 20 tests; $4 per 100 answer sheets; 50¢ per scoring stencil; $2.50 per series manual; $3.75 per specimen set; cash orders postpaid; 12(17) minutes; J. H. Norman; Personnel Research Associates, Inc. *

JOEL T. CAMPBELL, *Senior Research Psychologist, Educational Testing Service, Princeton, New Jersey.*

This test is a 45-item measure of the ability to select rapidly the correct response to a set of incomplete drawings or diagrams. Of the 45 items, 23 are pictorial representations (scarecrow, man in a hospital bed, weight lifter, etc.), 17 are mosaic-type geometric patterns, and 5 are bar-chart type figures. The examinee is required to select the correct response to each item from a set of 120 possible choices. The correct response may be turned at a different angle. Since the 45 correct answers are scattered randomly through the 120 possible responses, the person taking the test must work very quickly to complete all items within the 12-minute time limit.

The fact that the 99th percentile for engineers includes scores from 36 to 45 is an indication that even persons of high ability are not likely to complete the test. No information is given on rationale for item development, nor are any item analysis data presented. Some of the pictorial items have a degree of cultural content which is probably not desirable—e.g., the shape of the devil's pitchfork.

Test-retest reliability with a six-month time interval is reported as .92 for a sample of 31 engineers. This level of reliability appears satisfactory, but the sample it is based on is quite small, particularly considering the number of cases in the norms tables. Validity coefficients are reported for five industrial jobs. The criterion was job performance, although there is no indication of how job performance was measured. The coefficient for production engineers is .02, but for the other four jobs, shop foremen, machinists, machine parts inspectors, and assemblers, the coefficients range from .34 to .45.

The manual also reports correlations with 5 other tests. The highest, .72, is with the "Army Beta Exam." The correlations with the *Army General Classification Test* and the *Tests of Mechanical Comprehension* are .51 and .45, respectively. *Performance Alertness* also correlates .60 with the Filing subtest of the Individual Placement Series, and −.43 with age. These latter correlations indicate that the test score is probably significantly influenced by perceptual speed.

Median scores are reported for 14 different

occupations, with N's ranging from 11 for tooling inspections to 41 for foremen. The median scores range from 14 for laborer to 26 for engineer, with a reasonable progression of scores corresponding to apparent job difficulty level in between.

Percentile score tables are based on over 7,000 industrial cases, with subgroupings reported for clerical workers, shop workers, engineers, and supervisors.

The manual states that "The [test] serves as an effective double check on the results of the Academic Alertness test, and is often a more accurate and suitable instrument for the individual who has been deprived of cultural and educational opportunities." This advice runs counter to the research findings that the largest minority group, Negroes, do relatively better on verbal tests than on tests in nonlanguage areas.[1] The fact that this test is highly speeded is probably additional reason not to use it with a disadvantaged group, unless the job for which selection is being done involves very highly speeded operations.

The test probably measures something useful to performance in some jobs which is not fully measured by a verbal or arithmetic test. If testing time were not a constraining factor, the reviewer would prefer to use the *Progressive Matrices* or the *Revised Minnesota Paper Form Board Test*.

[373]
*Personnel Tests for Industry. Trade school and adults; 1945–69; PTI; 3 tests; manual ('69, 23 pages) for *a* and *b*; 90¢ per specimen set including manual for *Oral Directions Test*; postage extra; Psychological Corporation. *
a) PTI-VERBAL TEST. 1952–69; PTI-V; Forms A, B, ('52, 3 pages), C, D, ('67, 3 pages); $3 per 25 tests; 5(15) minutes; Alexander G. Wesman.
b) PTI-NUMERICAL TEST. 1952–69; PTI-N; Forms A, B, ('52, 4 pages), C, D, ('67, 4 pages); $3 per 25 tests; 20(25) minutes; Jerome E. Doppelt.
c) PTI-ORAL DIRECTIONS TEST. 1945–54; ODT; 1 form; 2 formats: 33⅓ rpm record, 3¾ ips tape recording (or cassette); separate answer sheets must be used; preliminary manual ['54, 8 pages]; $12 per set of record, scoring key, 100 answer sheets, and manual; $12.50 ($13) per set of tape recording (cassette), scoring key, 100 answer sheets, and manual; $5 per 100 answer sheets; Spanish edition available on tape; (15) minutes; Charles R. Langmuir.

[1] LESSER, GERALD S.; FIFER, GORDON; AND CLARK, DONALD H. "Mental Abilities of Children From Different Social-Class and Cultural Groups." *Monogr Soc Res Child Develop* 30(4): 1–115 '65. *
STODOLSKY, SUSAN S., AND LESSER, GERALD. "Learning Patterns in the Disadvantaged." *Harvard Ed Rev* 37:546–93 f '67. *
VERNON, PHILIP E. "Ability Factors and Environmental Influences." *Am Psychologist* 20:723–33 S '65. *

REFERENCES
1. See 4:309.
2. CAMPBELL, SAMUEL C. *An Evaluation of the Oral Directions Tests of General Intelligence as an Effective Predictor of On-the-Job Performance of "Blue Collar" Workers*. Master's thesis, Fordham University (New York, N.Y.), 1958.
3. HABER, WILFRED. *The Contribution of Selected Variables to Success or Failure in a Vocational Rehabilitation Evaluation*. Doctor's thesis, New York University (New York, N.Y.), 1959. (*DA* 20:4171)
4. WOLFE, RAYMOND N., AND DAVIS, JOHN A. "Use of the Oral Directions Test in a Domiciliary Setting." *J Gerontol* 19:349–51 Jl '64. *

For a review by Erwin K. Taylor, see 5:366; for reviews by Charles D. Flory, Irving Lorge, and William W. Turnbull of the Oral Directions Test, *see 3:245.*

[374]
*Picture Test A. Ages 7-0 to 8-1; 1955–70; PTA; formerly called *Picture Test 1* and, earlier, *Picture Intelligence Test 1*; 1 form ['70, 16 pages, identical with test published in 1955 except for title]; manual ('61, 8 pages, identical with 1955 manual); no data on validity; 8p per test; 7p per manual; postpaid within U.K.; 22(45) minutes; Joan E. Stuart; published for the National Foundation for Educational Research in England and Wales; Ginn & Co. Ltd. *

For reviews by Charlotte E. K. Banks and M. L. Kellmer Pringle, see 5:367.

[375]
*The Preliminary Scholastic Aptitude Test. Grades 11–12; 1959–70; PSAT; abbreviated adaptation of the *College Board Scholastic Aptitude Test* for guidance and scholarship testing; test last administered in 1970, this test and the *National Merit Scholarship Qualifying Test* will be replaced by a new test, PSAT/NMSQT, in fall 1971; 2 scores: verbal, mathematical; Forms SPT1 ('70, 18 pages), SPT2 ('70, 21 pages); supervisor's manual ('70, 24 pages); score report booklet for students ('70, 15 pages); score report booklet for counselors and admissions officers ('70, 38 pages); bulletin of information ('70, 31 pages); 120(140) minutes; program administered for the College Entrance Examination Board by Educational Testing Service. *

REFERENCES
1–2. See 6:487.
3. KAUFMANN, JAMES D., AND DEMPSTER, DENNIS. "Prediction of SAT Scores." *Personnel & Guid J* 42:1026–7 Je '64. * (*PA* 39:5069)
4. BRADY, WILLIAM JOSEPH. *Twenty Quantitative Predictors of Academic Success in College as Measured by Grade Point Averages*. Doctor's thesis, University of Connecticut (Storrs, Conn.), 1965. (*DA* 26:5121)
5. SEIBEL, DEAN W. "The Relationships of Some Academic Ability Characteristics of High School Seniors to College Attendance and Performance." *Col & Univ* 42:41–52 f '66. *
6. FRIELDS, SUSAN IRENE. *A Comparison of the Relationships of the PSAT and SAT Test Scores for the Students of North Haven High School: 1965 and 1966*. Master's thesis, Southern Connecticut State College (New Haven, Conn.), 1967.
7. HILTON, THOMAS L., AND MYERS, ALBERT E. "Personal Background, Experience and School Achievement: An Investigation of the Contribution of Questionnaire Data to Academic Prediction." *J Ed Meas* 4:69–80 su '67. * (*PA* 42:4570)
8. CLAWAR, HARRY J. "A Short Highly-Efficient Prediction of College Entrance Examination Board Scholastic Aptitude Test Performance." *Ed Rec B* 94:42–4 Jl '68. * (*PA* 44:21523)
9. CLEARY, T. ANNE, AND HILTON, THOMAS L. "An Investigation of Item Bias." *Ed & Psychol Meas* 28:61–75 sp '68. * (*PA* 42:11356)
10. HELM, CARL E., AND HARASYMIW, STEFAN J. "Computer-Based Verbal Score Reports for the Preliminary Scholastic Aptitude Test." *Meas & Eval Guid* 1:27–35 sp '68. * (*PA* 44:7264)

11. MANNING, WINTON H. "The Measurement of Intellectual Capacity and Performance." *J Negro Ed* 37:258–67 su '68. *
12. COLLEGE ENTRANCE EXAMINATION BOARD. *College Board Score Reports: A Guide for Counselors and Admissions Officers: Preliminary Scholastic Aptitude Test, Scholastic Aptitude Test, and Achievement Tests.* Princeton, N.J.: the Board, 1970. Pp. 37. *

For a review by Wayne S. Zimmerman of earlier forms, see 6:487.

[376]

*Progressive Matrices. Ages 5 and over; 1938–65; PM; 3 levels; postage extra; J. C. Raven; H. K. Lewis & Co. Ltd. (U.S. distributor: Psychological Corporation.) *

a) STANDARD PROGRESSIVE MATRICES. Ages 6 and over; 1938–60; manual also uses the title *Progressive Matrices (1938), 1956 Revision*; 1 form ('56, 62 pages, identical with test copyrighted in 1938 except for change in one item and order of items); revised manual ('60, 25 pages, identical with 1956 manual except for bibliography); no norms for individual administration for ages 14 and over; separate record forms or answer sheets must be used; 210s. ($14) per 25 (10) tests; 12s. 6d. ($2.40) per 50 record forms (answer sheets); 30s. (75¢) per scoring key (set of scoring key and manual); 3s. 6d. per manual; 25s. per specimen set including 5 copies of the complementary *Mill Hill Vocabulary Scale* ($2.85 per specimen set); (60) minutes.

b) COLOURED PROGRESSIVE MATRICES. Ages 5–11 and mental patients and senescents; 1947–63; individual for ages 5–6; 1 form ('56, 38 pages, subtest Sets A and B same as subtest Sets A and B of the *Standard Progressive Matrices* except for color); revised manual ('63, 43 pages, identical with 1958 and 1960 manuals except for bibliography and revision in norms tables); record booklet (no date); separate record forms or answer sheets must be used for group administration; 210s. ($14.50) per 25 (10) tests; 17s. 6d. ($2.40) per 50 record forms (answer sheets); 7s. 6d. ($1.10) per manual (set of scoring key and manual); 25s. per specimen set including 12 copies of the complementary *Crichton Vocabulary Scale* ($3 per specimen set); [30] minutes.

c) ADVANCED PROGRESSIVE MATRICES. Ages 11 and over; 1943–65; 2 editions; manual ('65, 28 pages); 12s. 6d. ($2.40) per 50 record forms (answer sheets) for both editions; 30s. per scoring key ($1 per set of scoring key and manual) for both editions; 7s. 6d. per manual; 42s. ($5) per specimen set for both editions.

1) *Progressive Matrices (1947): Set 1.* For use either as a practice test for Set 2 or as a rough screening test; 1 form ('47, 14 pages); 50s. ($4) per 25 (10) tests; (60¢ per single copy); (10) minutes.

2) *Advanced Progressive Matrices, Set 2: 1962 Revision.* For use either as "a test of intellectual capacity" when used without a time limit, or as "a test of intellectual efficiency" when used with a time limit ("usually of 40 minutes"); 1 form ('62, 38 pages, a revision and abbreviation of the 1947 Set 2); no data on reliability and validity for revised form; estimated norms based on 1947 data; 340s. ($24) per 25 (10) tests; ($3 per single copy); [40] minutes.

REFERENCES

1–8. See 2:1417.
9–21. See 3:258.
22–53. See 4:314.
54–115. See 5:370.
116–193. See 6:490.
194. VARADACHAR, DORAISWAMY. *A Study of the Distribution of Intelligence Employing the Progressive Matrices.* Master's thesis, University of Mysore (Mysore, India), 1954.
195. VARVA, FRANK IRVIN. *An Investigation of the Effect of Auditory Deficiency Upon Performance With Special Reference to Concrete and Abstract Tasks.* Doctor's thesis, University of Pittsburgh (Pittsburgh, Pa.), 1956. (DA 16:2532)
196. STEPHENSON, GEORGE ROTHWELL. *Form Perception, Abstract Thinking and Intelligence Test Validity in Cerebral Palsy.* Doctor's thesis, Columbia University (New York, N.Y.), 1957. (DA 17:1600)
197. MEHROTRA, S. N. "Predicting Intermediate Examination Success by Means of Psychological Tests: A Follow-Up Study." *J Voc & Ed Guid* 4:157–65 My '58. *
198. DHAR, CHANDRAKALA, AND MARR, EVELYN. "A Study of the Practice Effect of Taking Ravens Matrices on Performance on the N.I.I.P. Group Test 70/23 and of the N.I.I.P. on the Ravens Matrices." *J Voc & Ed Guid* 5:187–9 My '59. * (PA 38:3188)
199. FULLER, CARL WELLINGTON. *A Study of the Growth and Organization of Certain Mental Abilities in Young Deaf Children.* Doctor's thesis, Northwestern University (Evanston, Ill.), 1959. (DA 20:2382)
200. RAAHEIM, KJELL. "The Ability to Name Functions for Common Objects." *Nordisk Psykologi* 11(5):215–24 '59. * (PA 34:5589)
201. RATH, R. "Standardization of Progressive Matrices Among College Students." *J Voc & Ed Guid* 5:167–71 My '59. * (PA 38:2675)
202. ROYO, D., AND MARTIN, F. "Standardized Psychometrical Tests Applied to the Analysis of the Effects of Anti-Convulsive Medication on the Intellectual Proficiency of Young Epileptics." *Epilepsia* 1:189–207 D '59. *
203. ESBENSHADE, ANN AUGUSTA. *Rigidity as a Function of Age and Intelligence.* Doctor's thesis, University of Pennsylvania (Philadelphia, Pa.), 1960. (DA 21:956)
204. GOETZINGER, C. P.; DIRKS, D. D.; AND BAER, C. J. "Auditory Discrimination and Visual Perception in Good and Poor Readers." *Ann Otol Rhinol & Laryngol* 69:121–36 Mr '60. *
205. LEVINSON, BORIS M. "A Comparative Study of the Verbal and Performance Ability of Monolingual and Bilingual Native Born Jewish Preschool Children of Traditional Parentage." *J Genetic Psychol* 97:93–112 S '60. * (PA 35:6190)
206. PHELPS, HENRY BEVERIDGE. *Conceptual Ability and the Perception of Interaction in Movement by Elderly Persons.* Doctor's thesis, Columbia University (New York, N.Y.), 1960. (DA 21:2007)
207. BANNISTER, D.; SLATER, PATRICK; AND RADZAN, M. "The Use of Cognitive Tests in Nursing Candidate Selection." *Occup Psychol* 36:75–8 Ja–Ap '62. *
208. FRISBY, C. B. "The Use of Cognitive Tests in Nursing Candidate Selection: A Comment." *Occup Psychol* 36:79–81 Ja–Ap '62. *
209. MONTGOMERY, G. W. G. "Predicting Success in Engineering." *Occup Psychol* 36:59–68 Ja–Ap '62. *
210. OLSON, D. R., AND MACARTHUR, R. S. "The Effect of Foreign Language Background on Intelligence Test Performance." *Alberta J Ed Res* 8:157–66 S '62. * (PA 37:8270)
211. ROSS, JEAN. "Predicting Practical Skill in Engineering Apprentices." *Occup Psychol* 36:69–74 Ja–Ap '62. *
212. TESI, GINO, AND YOUNG, H. BOUTOURLINE. "A Standardization of Raven's Progressive Matrices 1938 (Revised Order, 1956)." *Archivio di Psicologia, Neurologia e Psichiatria* 23:456–64 S–O '62. * (PA 37:4950)
213. BOTWINICK, JACK, AND BIRREN, JAMES E. Chap. 8, "Mental Abilities and Psychomotor Responses in Healthy Aged Men," pp. 97–108. In *Human Aging: A Biological and Behavioral Study.* Edited by James E. Birren, Robert N. Butler, Samuel W. Greenhouse, Louis Sokoloff, and Marian R. Yarrow. National Institute of Mental Health, Public Health Service Publication No. 986. Washington, D.C.: United States Government Printing Office, 1963. Pp. xiii, 328. * (PA 38:5821)
214. GIBBENS, T. C. N.; WITH THE ASSISTANCE OF A. MARRIAGE AND A. WALKER. *Psychiatric Studies of Borstal Lads,* pp. 143–84. London: Oxford University Press, 1963. Pp. vi, 230. *
215. MORRISON, MARY. "A Gaelic Translation of the Wechsler Intelligence Scale for Children." Undergraduate thesis abstract. *Brit J Ed Psychol* 33:89–90 F '63. *
216. YATES, AUBREY J. "A Further Study of Progressive Matrices (1947)." *Brit J Ed Psychol* 33:307–11 N '63. * (PA 38:8441)
217. ANDERSON, ROBERT ARNOLD. *Mathematical Student Achievement of Third Form (Ninth Grade) Students in London and St. Paul-Minneapolis Metropolitan Areas.* Doctor's thesis, University of Minnesota (Minneapolis, Minn.), 1964. (DA 25:5008)
218. BECK, ELIZABETH JOAN. *Relation Between Social Impact and Selected Intellectual Traits in Preadolescent Negro Boys.* Doctor's thesis, Fordham University (New York, N.Y.), 1964. (DA 25:1328)
219. BIRKEMEYER, FLORENCE. "The Relationship Between the Coloured Progressive Matrices and Individual Intelligence Tests." *Psychol Sch* 1:309–12 Jl '64. *
220. BRADLEY, BETTY HUNT. "Differential Responses in Perceptual Ability Among Mentally Retarded Brain-Injured Children." *J Ed Res* 57:421–4 Ap '64. *

221. EVANS, RAY B., AND MARMORSTON, JESSIE. "Scoring Raven's Coloured Progressive Matrices to Differentiate Brain Damage." *J Clin Psychol* 20:360-4 Jl '64. * *(PA* 39:10102)
222. FORBES, A. R. "An Item Analysis of the Advanced Matrices." *Brit J Ed Psychol* 34:223-36 N '64. * *(PA* 39:7756)
223. FOULDS, G. A. "Organization and Hostility in the Thematic Apperception Test Stories of Schizophrenics." *Brit J Psychiatry* 110:64-6 Ja '64. * *(PA* 38:8870)
224. GILES, GEORGE C., JR. "Predictive Validity of Progressive Matrices and Two Other Nonlanguage Tests of Mental Ability." *J Ed Meas* 1:65-7 Je '64. * *(PA* 39:7757)
225. JAIN, K. S. PRABHACHANDRA. "An Organismic Study of Cognitive Errors." *Manas* 11(2):105-13 '64. * *(PA* 39:7392)
226. KHATENA, JOE; KIANG, CHEW GUAN; AND GOWAN, J. C. "Reliability of Raven Progressive Matrices Test With Asian Children." *Ed Malaysia* 1(1):22 '64. *
227. KUNDU, RAMANATH, AND SEN (CHAKRABORTY), ANIMA. "Matrices Score With Time Limit and Without Time Limit and Its Relationship With Multiplication Score." *J Psychol Res* 8:120-3 S '64. * *(PA* 39:5073)
228. LARSON, KEITH HAROLD. *The Characteristics of Vocationally Successful Mentally Retarded Youth as Described by Two Types of Intelligence Tests.* Doctor's thesis, University of Oregon (Eugene, Ore.), 1964. *(DA* 25:2815)
229. LI, ANITA KING-FUN. "The Use of Ability Tests in Hong Kong." *Int J Exp Res Ed* 1(2):187-95 '64. *
230. MACARTHUR, R. S.; IRVINE, S. H.; AND BRIMBLE, A. R. *The Northern Rhodesia Mental Ability Survey 1963.* Rhodes-Livingstone Communication No. 27. Lusaka, Zambia: Rhodes-Livingstone Institute, 1964. Pp. ix, 100. *
231. MOGENSEN, ALAN. "Raven's Progressive Matrices in Twelve Pairs of Uniovular Twins Brought Up Apart." *Scandinavian J Psychol* 5(1):50-2 '64. * *(PA* 39:1787)
232. PHILLIPS, G. R. "A Study of Psychological Tests for the Selection of Trainee Nurses: 1, General Approach." *Personnel Prac B* 20:28-32 D '64. * *(PA* 39:10886)
233. TONN, MARTIN HELMUTH. *The Effect of Time in Mental Measurement.* Doctor's thesis, State University of Iowa (Iowa City, Iowa), 1964. *(DA* 25:5130)
234. WEST, L. W., AND MACARTHUR, R. S. "An Evaluation of Selected Intelligence Tests for Two Samples of Metis and Indian Children." *Alberta J Ed Res* 10:17-27 Mr '64. * *(PA* 39:12328)
235. WOLK, ROBERT L., AND RUSTIN, STANLEY L. "Psychologic Evaluation of Gerontologic Population: Comparison of Results With the Raven Progressive Matrices (1947) Versus the Wechsler Adult Intelligence Scale." *J Am Geriatrics Soc* 12:807-9 Ag '64. *
236. BIRKEMEYER, FLORENCE. "The Relationship Between Coloured Progressive Matrices and the Wechsler Intelligence Scale for Children." *Psychol Sch* 2:278-80 Jl '65. *
237. CASHDAN, ASHER. "Conditions Affecting Problem-Solving in the Mentally Subnormal." *Int Copenhagen Congr Sci Study Mental Retard* 1964:623-6 ['65]. *
238. DE RENZI, ENNIO, AND FAGLIONI, PIETRO. "The Comparative Efficiency of Intelligence and Vigilance Tests in Detecting Hemispheric Cerebral Damage." *Cortex* 1:410-33 Je-S '65. * *(PA* 40:1897)
239. GUPTA, KUNWAR PAL. *A Study of Two Non-Language Intelligence Tests With Deaf Subjects in the Intermediate and Advanced Departments of the Kansas School for the Deaf.* Master's thesis, University of Kansas (Lawrence, Kan.), 1965.
240. KAKKAR, ARUNA. "The Role of Intelligence in Adolescents' Adjustment." *Indian J Psychol* 40:179-84 D '65. * *(PA* 40:12179)
241. KEBBON, LARS. *The Structure of Abilities at Lower Levels of Intelligence: A Factor-Analytical Study.* Stockholm, Sweden: Skandinaviska Testförlaget AB, 1965. Pp. 112. *
242. KHATENA, J. "A Study on the Reliability of the Raven's Coloured Progressive Matrices 1947." *Ed J (Singapore)* 3:51-3 '65-66. *
243. KHATENA, JOE. *A Study of Comparative Performance on the Raven's Coloured Progressive Matrices and the Goodenough Draw-A-Man Test in Two Singapore Primary Schools.* Master's thesis, University of Singapore (Singapore, Malaysia), 1965.
244. KLEIN, JOSEPHINE. "Levels of Perceptual Organization and of Performance After Time for Reflection." *Brit J Ed Psychol* 35:60-2 F '65. * *(PA* 39:10820)
245. MCDONALD, RODERICK P. "Difficulty Factors and Non-Linear Factor Analysis." *Brit J Math & Stat Psychol* 18:11-23 My '65. * *(PA* 39:13277)
246. MAITRA, AMAL K. "An Examination of the Difficulty Index and Item Validity of Standard Progressive Matrices (1956) With Indian Data." *Indian J Psychol* 40:127-31 S '65. *
247. MEIER, JOHN HENRY. *An Exploratory Factor Analysis of Psychodiagnostic and Case Study Information From Children in Special Education Classes for the Educable Mentally Handicapped.* Doctor's thesis, University of Denver (Denver, Colo.), 1965. *(DA* 26:3153)
248. MUELLER, MAX W. *A Comparison of the Empirical Validity of Six Tests of Ability With Young Educable Retardates.* Institute of Mental Retardation and Intellectual Development, IMRID Behavioral Science Monograph No. 1. Nashville, Tenn.: Peabody College Bookstore, 1965. Pp. vii, 130. *
249. MUELLER, MAX WILLIAM. *A Comparison of the Empirical Validity of Six Tests of Ability With Educable Mental Retardates.* Doctor's thesis, George Peabody College for Teachers (Nashville, Tenn.), 1965. *(DA* 26:6853)
250. RICH, CHARLES C., AND ANDERSON, ROBERT P. "A Tactual Form of the Progressive Matrices for Use With Blind Children." *Personnel & Guid J* 43:912-9 My '65. * *(PA* 39:15197)
251. SHANAN, JOEL, AND SHARON, MIRIAM. "Personality and Cognitive Functioning of Israeli Males During the Middle Years." *Hum Develop* 8(1):2-15 '65. * *(PA* 39:14799)
252. SHAW, C. NEIL. "An Investigation of Scores Earned by Adults on the Raven Progressive Matrices Test." *Fla J Ed Res* 7:40-4 Ja '65. *
253. WIRT, ROBERT. *Raven-Coloured Progressive Matrices, Metropolitan Readiness, and Detroit First Grade Intelligence Tests as Predictors of Achievement in Primary Grades.* Master's thesis, Central Washington College of Education (Ellensburg, Wash.), 1965.
254. BINGHAM, WILLIAM C.; BURKE, HENRY R.; AND MURRAY, STEWART. "Raven's Progressive Matrices: Construct Validity." *J Psychol* 62:205-9 Mr '66. * *(PA* 40:7203)
255. CANTWELL, ZITA M. "Relationships Between Scores on the Standard Progressive Matrices (1938) and on the D.48 Test of Non-Verbal Intelligence and 3 Measures of Academic Achievement." *J Exp Ed* 34:28-31 su '66. * *(PA* 40:11152)
256. COLONNA, A., AND FAGLIONI, P. "The Performance of Hemisphere-Damaged Patients on Spatial Intelligence Tests." *Cortex* 2:293-307 Ap '66. * *(PA* 41:4895)
257. FITCH, MICHAEL JOHN. *Verbal and Performance Test Scores in Bilingual Children.* Doctor's research study No. 1, Colorado State College (Greeley, Colo.), 1966. *(DA* 27:1654A)
258. FREYBERG, P. S. "The Efficacy of the Coloured Progressive Matrices as a Group Test With Young Children." *Brit J Ed Psychol* 36:171-7 Je '66. * *(PA* 40:9922)
259. GUPTA, G. C., AND GUPTA, SARLA. "Norms for Raven's Coloured Matrices." *Manas* 13(2):87-9 '66. *
260. IRVINE, S. H. "Towards a Rationale for Testing Attainments and Abilities in Africa." *Brit J Ed Psychol* 36:24-32 F '66. * *(PA* 40:6103)
261. JACOBS, PAUL I. "Programed Progressive Matrices." Abstract. *Proc 74th Ann Conv Am Psychol Assn* 1:263-4 '66. * *(PA* 41:6291)
262. JOHNSON, SONIA ANN HARRIS. *Some Selected Classroom Variables and Their Relationship to Mathematics Achievement in Central Minnesota and the Greater London Area.* Doctor's thesis, Rutgers—The State University (New Brunswick, N.J.), 1966. *(DA* 27:139A)
263. KILBURN, KENT L., AND SANDERSON, ROBERT E. "Predicting Success in a Vocational Rehabilitation Program With the Raven Coloured Progressive Matrices." *Ed & Psychol Meas* 26:1031-4 w '66. * *(PA* 41:4843)
264. KILBURN, KENT L.; SANDERSON, ROBERT E.; AND MELTON, KYLE. "Relation of the Raven Coloured Progressive Matrices to Two Measures of Verbal Ability in a Sample of Mildly Retarded Hospital Patients." *Psychol Rep* 19:731-4 D '66. * *(PA* 41:4915)
265. LEY, P.; SPELMAN, M. S.; DAVIES, ANN D. M.; AND RILEY, S. "The Relationships Between Intelligence, Anxiety, Neuroticism and Extraversion." *Brit J Ed Psychol* 36:185-91 Je '66. * *(PA* 40:10100)
266. MONTGOMERY, G. W. G. "The Relationship of Oral Skills to Manual Communication in Profoundly Deaf Students." *Am Ann Deaf* 111:557-65 S '66. * *(PA* 41:1800)
267. ORME, J. E. "Hypothetically True Norms for the Progressive Matrices Tests." *Hum Develop* 9(4):223-9 '66. * *(PA* 41:2872)
268. RADFORD, J. "Verbalisation Effects in a 'Non-Verbal' Intelligence Test." *Brit J Ed Psychol* 36:33-8 F '66. * *(PA* 40:6643)
269. SEMLER, IRA J., AND ISCOE, IRA. "Structure of Intelligence in Negro and White Children." *J Ed Psychol* 57:326-36 D '66. * *(PA* 41:1418)
270. SHANTZ, CAROLYN UHLINGER. *A Developmental Study of Piaget's Theory of Logical Multiplication.* Doctor's thesis, Purdue University (Lafayette, Ind.), 1966. *(DA* 27:603B)
271. SITKEI, E. GEORGE, AND MICHAEL, WILLIAM B. "Predictive Relationships Between Items on the Revised Stanford-Binet Intelligence Scale (SBIS), Form L-M, and Total Scores on Raven's Progressive Matrices (PM), Between Items on the PM and Total Scores on the SBIS, and Between Selected Items on the Two Scales." *Ed & Psychol Meas* 26:501-6 su '66. * *(PA* 40:12784)
272. WANG, FUNG YEE. "A Study in General Ability Testing in Hong Kong: The Application of Ravens Progressive Matrices (1938) as a Group Timed Test and Its Relations to Attainments in Four Academic Areas." *J Ed (Hong Kong)* 23:56-9 '66. *
273. WETHERICK, N. E. "The Responses of Normal Adult Subjects to the Matrices Test." *Brit J Psychol* 57:297-300 N '66. *
274. WILLIAMS, JANETTE R., AND WILCOCK, JOAN C. "An Alternative to the Binet Mental Age Score as a Criterion in

Discrimination Learning." *J Mental Def Res* 10:27–32 Mr '66. * (*PA* 40:9420)
275. YATES, AUBREY J. "Level, Speed and Personality Factors in the Intellectual Performance of Young Children." *Brit J Ed Psychol* 36:312–6 N '66. * (*PA* 41:463)
276. YATES, AUBREY J. "A Note on Progressive Matrices (1962)." *Austral J Psychol* 18:281–3 D '66. * (*PA* 41:4571)
277. YATES, AUBREY J. "The Relationship Between Level and Speed on Two Intelligence Tests." *Brit J Ed Psychol* 36:166–70 Je '66. * (*PA* 40:9421)
278. ANDERSON, HARRY E., JR.; KERN, FRANK E.; AND COOK, CHARLOTTE. "Correlational and Normative Data for the Progressive Matrices With Retarded Populations." *J Psychol* 67:221–5 N '67. * (*PA* 42:1396)
279. ARCHIBALD, Y. M.; WEPMAN, J. M.; AND JONES, L. V. "Nonverbal Cognitive Performance in Aphasic and Nonaphasic Brain-Damaged Patients." *Cortex* 3:275–94 S '67. * (*PA* 42:9335)
280. ARCHIBALD, Y. M.; WEPMAN, J. M.; AND JONES, L. V. "Performance on Nonverbal Cognitive Tests Following Unilateral Cortical Injury to the Right and Left Hemisphere." *J Nerv & Mental Dis* 145:25–36 Jl '67. * (*PA* 42:4382)
281. BANNISTER, D., AND PRESLY, A. S. "Test Selection of Overseas Nursing Candidates: A Cross Validation Study." *B Brit Psychol Soc* 20:21–4 Jl '67. *
282. BUDOFF, MILTON. "Learning Potential Among Institutionalized Young Adult Retardates." *Am J Mental Def* 72:404–11 N '67. * (*PA* 42:7631)
283. CANTWELL, ZITA M. "The Performance of American Pupils on the Coloured Progressive Matrices." *Brit J Ed Psychol* 37:389–90 N '67. * (*PA* 42:5577)
284. CATE, CLARENCE C. "Test Behavior of ESL Students." *Calif J Ed Res* 18:184–7 S '67. * (*PA* 42:4480)
285. FLEMING, JEAN MCKEY. *Body Image and Learning of Deaf and Hearing Boys.* Doctor's thesis, University of Florida (Gainesville, Fla.), 1967. (*DA* 29:144A)
286. GANGULY, ARUN K. "An Experimental Study of the Variation in Concept Formation Ability of Young Adults Due to Socio-Economic Status." *Manas* 14:69–75 D '67. * (*PA* 43:11098)
287. GOETZINGER, CORNELIUS P.; WILLS, ROBERT C.; AND DEKKER, LYNN CROUTER. "Non-Language IQ Tests Used With Deaf Pupils." *Volta R* 69:500–6 O '67. *
288. HARFORD, THOMAS. "An Item Analysis of the Progressive Matrices Test for Samples of Male Schizophrenic Patients." *J Clin Psychol* 23:377–80 Jl '67. * (*PA* 41:15268)
289. HERON, ALASTAIR, AND CHOWN, SHEILA. *Age and Function.* London: J. & A. Churchill Ltd., 1967. Pp. x, 182. *
290. JOHNSON, DALE L.; JOHNSON, CARMEN A.; AND PRICE-WILLIAMS, DOUGLASS. "The Draw-A-Man Test and Raven Progressive Matrices Performance of Guatemalan Maya and Ladino Children." *Revista Interamericana de Psicología* 1:143–57 Je '67. * (*PA* 41:11919)
291. JURJEVICH, R. M. "Avoidable Errors on Raven Progressive Matrices and Psychopathological Indices." Abstract. *Psychol Rep* 21:364 O '67. *
292. JURJEVICH, R. M. "Intellectual Assessment With Gorham's Proverbs Test, Raven's Progressive Matrices, and WAIS." *Psychol Rep* 20:1285–6 Je '67. * (*PA* 41:15271)
293. KHATENA, J. "An Item Analysis of the Coloured Progressive Matrices With Asian Singapore Children." *Malaysian J Ed* 4:82–5 Je '67. *
294. KHATENA, JOE, AND GOWAN, J. C. "Crosscultural Measurement of Intelligence With the DAM and CPM." *Gifted Child Q* 11:227–30 w '67. * (*PA* 42:7111)
295. KLINGELHOFER, E. L. "Performance of Tanzanian Secondary School Pupils on the Raven Standard Progressive Matrices Test." *J Social Psychol* 72:205–15 Ag '67. * (*PA* 41:15272)
296. KUMAR, PRAMOD. "Intelligence and Student Leadership." *J Psychol Res* 11:45–8 My '67. * (*PA* 42:7332)
297. MAJUMDAR, P. K.; DASGUPTA, J.; BASU, K.; AND DUTTA, D. "On the Working of a Battery of Psychological Tests: Raven's Standard Progressive Matrices Test." *B Council Social & Psychol Res* 9:1–6 Jl '67. * (*PA* 45:699)
298. MANDEL, ROBERT. *A Study of the Performance of Disadvantaged Seventh Grade Males on the Colored Raven Progressive Matrices and the California Test of Mental Maturity.* Master's thesis, University of Tennessee (Knoxville, Tenn.), 1967.
299. MEARS, FREDERICK GARY. *Effects of Reward on the Raven Progressive Matrices With Normal and Retarded Children.* Master's thesis, Texas Christian University (Ft. Worth, Tex.), 1967.
300. NEWCOMB, WALDO BURKETT, JR. *Normal Achieving and Underachieving Hearing-Impaired Students' Performance on Raven's Progressive Matrices (1938) and the Hooper Visual Organization Test.* Master's thesis, University of Texas (Austin, Tex.), 1967.
301. NICKOLS, JOHN. "Structural Efficiency of the Raven Coloured Matrices." Abstract. *J Clin Psychol* 23:489 O '67. * (*PA* 42:1414)
302. RAFI, A. ABI. "The Progressive Matrices (1938) and the Dominoes (D48) Tests: A Cross-Cultural Study." *Brit J Ed Psychol* 37:117–9 F '67. *

303. SCHNELL, RICHARD R., AND DWARSHUIS, LOUIS. "Progressive Matrices—Scores and Time." *Ed & Psychol Meas* 27:485–7 su '67. * (*PA* 41:13599)
304. SEIDEL, H. E., JR.; BARKLEY, MARY JO; AND STITH, DORIS. "Evaluation of a Program for Project Head Start." *J Genetic Psychol* 110:185–97 Je '67. * (*PA* 41:11718)
305. SYDIAHA, DANIEL. "Prediction of WAIS IQ for Psychiatric Patients Using the Ammons' FRPV and Raven's Progressive Matrices." *Psychol Rep* 20:823–6 Je '67. * (*PA* 41:13602)
306. TAYLOR, A. J. W. "Prediction for Parole: A Pilot Study With Delinquent Girls." *Brit J Criminol* 7:418–24 O '67. *
307. TULLY, G. EMERSON. "Test-Retest Reliability of the Raven Progressive Matrices Test (Form 1938) and the California Test of Mental Maturity, Level 4 (S-F 1963)." *Fla J Ed Res* 9:67–74 Ja '67. *
308. ANDERSON, HARRY E., JR.; KERN, FRANK E.; AND COOK, CHARLOTTE. "Sex, Brain Damage, and Race Effects in the Progressive Matrices With Retarded Populations." *J Social Psychol* 76:207–11 D '68. * (*PA* 43:4329)
309. ARCHIBALD, Y. M., AND WEPMAN, J. M. "Language Disturbance and Nonverbal Cognitive Performance in Eight Patients Following Injury to the Right Hemisphere." *Brain* 91:117–30 Mr '68. * (*PA* 42:19160)
310. BLUMENKRANTZ, JACK; WILKIN, WENDELL R.; AND TUDDENHAM, READ D. "Relationships Between the Progressive Matrices and AGCT-3a Among Older Military Personnel." *Ed & Psychol Meas* 28:931–5 au '68. * (*PA* 43:3317)
311. CRICKMORE, LEON. "An Approach to the Measurement of Music Appreciation (II)." *J Res Music Ed* 16:291–301 w '68. * (*PA* 43:8756)
312. DAS, J. P., AND DUTTA, TAPATI. "Standardization of Coloured Progressive Matrices: Norms for 10, 11 and 12 Year Old School Children." *J Psychol Res* 12:143–8 S '68. *
313. DOMINO, GEORGE. "Culture-Free Tests and the Academic Achievement of Foreign Students." Abstract. *J Consult & Clin Psychol* 32:102 F '68. * (*PA* 42:7843)
314. ELKIN, LORNE. "Predicting Performance of the Mentally Retarded on Sheltered Workshop and Non-Institutional Jobs." *Am J Mental Def* 72:533–9 Ja '68. * (*PA* 42:7638)
315. FINNEY, BETTY JANE. *The Modification of Conceptual Tempo in Disadvantaged Boys.* Doctor's thesis, Case Western Reserve University (Cleveland, Ohio), 1968. (*DAI* 30:3782A)
316. FINNIE, FRANCES RUTH. *The Relationship Between Perceptual Field Articulation and Intellectual Functioning in Paranoid Male Schizophrenics.* Doctor's thesis, George Washington University (Washington, D.C.), 1968.
317. HARFORD, THOMAS. "An Item Analysis of the Progressive Matrices Test for Samples of Male Schizophrenic Patients." *J Clin Psychol* 24:204–7 Ap '68. * (*PA* 42:12472)
318. HUTCHINS, BOB E. *The Relationship of Selected Factors to Performance of Teenage Teacher Aides in Eleven Appalachian School Districts.* Doctor's thesis, Ohio University (Athens, Ohio), 1968. (*DA* 29:1041A)
319. JACOBS, PAUL I., AND VANDEVENTER, MARY. "Progressive Matrices: An Experimental, Developmental, Nonfactorial Analysis." *Percept & Motor Skills* 27:759–66 D '68. * (*PA* 43:8354)
320. KENCHAVEERAIAH, B., AND MENON, A. SREEKUMAR. "Relationship of Intelligence and Fluency Among Students." *Indian Psychol R* 4:123–5 Ja '68. * (*PA* 43:11322)
321. MACARTHUR, R. S. "Assessing Intellectual Potential of Native Canadian Pupils: A Summary." *Alberta J Ed Res* 14:115–22 Je '68. * (*PA* 44:4170)
322. MACARTHUR, RUSSELL. "Some Differential Abilities of Northern Canadian Native Youth." *Int J Psychol* 3(1):43–50 '68. *
323. MATTHEWS, CHARLES G.; CHUN, RAYMOND W. M.; GRABOW, JACK D.; AND THOMPSON, WAYNE H. "Psychological Sequelae in Children Following California Arboviros Encephalitis." *Neurol* 18:1023–30 O '68. * (*PA* 43:5771)
324. MEHROTRA, K. K. "The Relationship of the WISC to the Progressive Matrices." *J Psychol Res* 12:114–8 S '68. *
325. MEHROTRA, KRISHNA KANT. "A Comparative Study of WISC and Raven's Progressive Matrices." *Psychol Studies* 13:47–50 Ja '68. *
326. MUELLER, MAX W. "Validity of Six Tests of Ability With Educable Mental Retardates." *J Sch Psychol* 6:136–46 w '68. * (*PA* 42:11152)
327. MUNRO, HELLE. "Verbal Fluency in Test and Group Situations." *Brit J Proj Psychol & Pers Study* 13:25–9 Je '68. * (*PA* 45:946)
328. ORME, J. E. "A Comment on Estimating W.A.I.S. IQ From Progressive Matrices Scores." *J Clin Psychol* 24:94–5 Ja '68. *
329. PERIASWAMY, THIRU M. *Development of Norms for J. C. Raven's Intelligence Test on a Rural Sample.* Master's thesis, Meston Training College, University of Madras (Madras, India), 1968.
330. PHILLIPS, C. J., AND BANNON, W. J. "The Stanford-Binet, Form L-M, Third Revision: A Local English Study of Norms, Concurrent Validity and Social Differences." *Brit J Ed Psychol* 38:148–61 Je '68. * (*PA* 42:17600)
331. POTTASH, MYRA E. *An Evaluation of Raven's Progressive Matrices for the Measurement of Certain Ability,*

Achievement, and Personality Factors in Junior High School. Master's thesis, Bryn Mawr College (Bryn Mawr, Pa.), 1968.

332. RAO, S. NARAYANA, AND REDDY, I. K. S. "Development of Norms for the Raven's Coloured Progressive Matrices Test (Booklet Form) on Elementary School Children." *Psychol Studies* 13:105-7 Jl '68. *

333. RATTAN, M. S., AND MACARTHUR, R. S. "Longitudinal Prediction of School Achievement for Metis and Eskimo Pupils." *Alberta J Ed Res* 14:37-41 Mr '68. * (*PA* 44:4249)

334. SHEPPARD, CHARLES; FIORENTINO, DIANE; COLLINS, LOIS; AND MERLIS, SIDNEY. "Performance Errors on Ravens Progressive Matrices (1938) by Sociopathic and Schizotypic Personality Types." *Psychol Rep* 23:1043-6 D '68. * (*PA* 43:8462)

335. SHEPPARD, CHARLES; FIORENTINO, DIANE; COLLINS, LOIS; AND MERLIS, SIDNEY. "Ravens Progressive Matrices (1938): Normative Data on Male Narcotic Addicts." *Psychol Rep* 23:343-8 O '68. * (*PA* 43:10036)

336. SINHA, UMA. "The Use of Raven's Progressive Matrices Test in India." *Indian Ed R* 3:75-88 Ja '68. * (*PA* 42:13757)

337. TAMHANKAR, V. S. "Norms for the X Grade on Advanced Progressive Matrices (1962) and Some Correlates of Intelligence." *J Psychol Res* 12:85-9 My '68. * (*PA* 43:5894)

338. TULKIN, STEVEN R., AND NEWBROUGH, J. R. "Social Class, Race, and Sex Differences on the Raven (1956) Standard Progressive Matrices." *J Consult & Clin Psychol* 32:400-6 Ag '68. * (*PA* 42:17225)

339. VEJLESKOV, HANS. "An Analysis of Raven Matrix Responses in Fifth Grade Children, 1." *Scandinavian J Psychol* 9(3):177-86 '68. * (*PA* 43:4018)

340. WATTIMENA, DANIEL MARCUS. *The Impact of Motivation on Intelligence.* Doctor's thesis, University of California (Berkeley, Calif.), 1968. (*DA* 29:3011A)

341. AFTANAS, M. S., AND ROYCE, J. R. "A Factor Analysis of Brain Damage Tests Administered to Normal Subjects With Factor Score Comparisons Across Ages." *Multiv Behav Res* 4(4):459-81 O '69. * (*PA* 44:11030)

342. ALMGREN, PER-ERIK; ANDERSSON, ALF L.; AND KULLBERG, GUNVOR. "Differences in Verbally Expressed Cognition Following Left and Right Ventrolateral Thalamotomy." *Scandinavian J Psychol* 10(4):243-9 '69. * (*PA* 44:9042)

343. BEVAN, WILTSHIRE E., AND GRAY, JOHN E. "Draw-A-Man and Raven's Progressive Matrices (1938) Intelligence Test Performance of Reserve Indian Children." *Can J Behav Sci* 1(2):119-22 Ap '69. * (*PA* 44:12604)

344. BLUE, ARTHUR WILLIAM. *Prediction of Learning Ability Across Cultures.* Doctor's thesis, Iowa State University (Ames, Iowa), 1969. (*DAI* 30:5220B)

345. BURKE, HENRY R., AND BINGHAM, WILLIAM C. "Raven's Progressive Matrices: More on Construct Validity." *J Psychol* 72(2):247-51 Jl '69. * (*PA* 44:71)

346. COSTA, LOUIS D.; VAUGHAN, HERBERT G., JR.; HORWITZ, MORTON; AND RITTER, WALTER. "Patterns of Behavioral Deficit Associated With Visual Spatial Neglect." *Cortex* 5(3):242-63 S '69. * (*PA* 44:13142)

347. EISENTHAL, SHERMAN, AND HARFORD, THOMAS. "Variation in the Form and Administration of Raven's Progressive Matrices Scale in a Neuropsychiatric Population." *Psychol Rep* 24(1):262 F '69. * (*PA* 43:13533)

348. FRACCHIA, JOHN F.; FIORENTINO, DIANE; SHEPPARD, CHARLES; AND MERLIS, SIDNEY. "A Comparison of Techniques for the Scoring of Avoidable Errors on the Raven Progressive Matrices." *J Psychol* 72(1):93-8 My '69. * (*PA* 43:15804)

349. FRANK, HARRY, AND FIEDLER, EDNA R. "A Multifactor Behavioral Approach to the Genetic-Etiological Diagnosis of Mental Retardation." *Multiv Behav Res* 4(2):131-45 Ap '69. * (*PA* 43:16258)

350. GOETZINGER, MADELON R., AND HOUCHINS, ROLLIE R. "The 1947 Colored Raven's Progressive Matrices With Deaf and Hearing Subjects." *Am Ann Deaf* 114(2):95-101 Mr '69. * (*PA* 43:11730)

351. HARFORD, THOMAS, AND EISENTHAL, SHERMAN. "An Item Analysis of the Progressive Matrices Test for a Sample of Hospitalized Schizophrenics." *J Clin Psychol* 25(2):185 Ap '69. * (*PA* 43:14468)

352. HWANG, CHIEN-HOU. "Parent-Child Resemblance in Psychological Characteristics." *Psychol & Ed* 3:29-36 D '69. *

353. IRVINE, S. H. "Factor Analysis of African Abilities and Attainments: Constructs Across Cultures." *Psychol B* 71(1):20-32 Ja '69. * (*PA* 43:7553)

354. IRVINE, SIDNEY H. "Figural Tests of Reasoning in Africa: Studies in the Use of Raven's Progressive Matrices Across Cultures." *Int J Psychol* 4(3):217-28 '69. * (*PA* 45:6334)

355. KINGSLEY, LEONARD. "Functioning of Acute and Chronic Schizophrenics on Measures of Abstract Reasoning." *J Clin Psychol* 25(2):144-7 Ap '69. * (*PA* 43:14470)

356. LANGE, UNA ANN. *Differential Performances of Minimally Brain-Damaged Boys and of Non-Brain-Damaged Boys on Selected Tests.* Doctor's thesis, University of Nebraska (Lincoln, Neb.), 1969. (*DAI* 30:2852A)

357. MACARTHUR, RUSSELL S. "Some Cognitive Abilities of Eskimo, White, and Indian-Métis Pupils Aged 9 to 12 years." *Can J Behav Sci* 1(1):50-9 Ja '69. * (*PA* 44:12319)

358. MACDONALD, H. A., AND NETHERTON, A. H. "Contribution of a Non-Verbal General Ability Test to the Educational Assessment of Pupils in the Cross-Cultural Setting of the Canadian North." *J Ed Res* 62(7):315-9 Mr '69. *

359. MCNAMARA, J. REGIS; PORTERFIELD, CHARLES L.; AND MILLER, LAWRENCE E. "The Relationship of the Wechsler Preschool and Primary Scale of Intelligence With the Coloured Progressive Matrices (1956) and the Bender Gestalt Test." *J Clin Psychol* 25(1):65-8 Ja '69. * (*PA* 43:9766)

360. NICHOLSON, CHARLES L. "The Use of Four Screening Instruments." *Ann Inter Conf Assn Children Learn Dis* 6:101-7 '69. *

361. OWENS, RICHARD THOMAS. *A Study of the Performance of Minimally Brain-Damaged and Emotionally Disturbed Boys on Six Selected Psychological Tests.* Doctor's thesis, University of Nebraska (Lincoln, Neb.), 1969. (*DAI* 31:383B)

362. PANDE, C. G., AND KOTHARI, S. "Field Dependence and the Raven's Progressive Matrices." *Psychologia* 12(1):49-51 Mr '69. *

363. PAYNE, J. F. "A Comparative Study of the Mental Ability of Seven- and Eight-Year-Old British and West Indian Children in a West Midland Town." *Brit J Ed Psychol* 39(3):326-7 N '69. *

364. ROMNEY, DAVID. "The Validity of Certain Tests of Overinclusion." *Brit J Psychiatry* 115(522):591-2 My '69. * (*PA* 44:3689)

365. ROSENBERG, C. M. "Determinants of Psychiatric Illness in Young People." *Brit J Psychiatry* 115(525):907-15 Ag '69. * (*PA* 44:10505)

366. SHEPPARD, CHARLES; FIORENTINO, DIANE; COLLINS, LOIS; AND MERLIS, SIDNEY. "Further Study of Performance Errors on Ravens Progressive Matrices (1938)." *J Psychol* 71(1):127-32 Ja '69. * (*PA* 43:5430)

367. WOBER, MALLERY. "The Meaning and Stability of Raven's Matrices Test Among Africans." *Int J Psychol* 4(3):229-35 '69. * (*PA* 45:6337)

368. CANABAL, JUANA VILLANUEVA. *Comparison of Deaf and Normally Hearing Children on Analogy Items Under Different Methods of Instruction at Different Age Levels.* Doctor's thesis, St. John's University (Jamaica, N.Y.), 1970. (*DAI* 31:3700B)

369. CARLSON, JERRY S. "A Note on the Relationships Between the Draw-A-Man Test, the Progressive Matrices Test, and Conservation." *J Psychol* 74(2):231-5 Mr '70. * (*PA* 44:12310)

370. DAVIS, WILLIAM E.; DEWOLFE, ALAN S.; DIZZONNE, MICHAEL F.; AND AIR, DOROTHY HABERKAMP. "Relationship Between Schizophrenics' Premorbid History and Intelligence Test Performance." *Newsl Res Psychol* 12(4):5-6 N '70. *

371. FOULDS, G. A. "Progressive Matrices and the Mill Hill Vocabulary Scale as a Diagnostic Aid Among Psychiatric Patients." *Brit J Social & Clin Psychol* 9(1):80-2 F '70. *

372. FRACCHIA, JOHN; FIORENTINO, DIANE; SHEPPARD, CHARLES; AND MERLIS, SIDNEY. "Raven Progressive Matrices Avoidable Errors as a Measure of Psychopathological Ideational Influences Upon Reasoning Ability." *Psychol Rep* 26(2):359-62 Ap '70. * (*PA* 44:21168)

373. FRACCHIA, JOHN; SHEPPARD, CHARLES; MERLIS, MICHAEL; AND MERLIS, SIDNEY. "Atypical Reasoning Errors in Sociopathic, Paranoid, and Schizophrenic Personality Types." *J Psychol* 76(1):91-5 S '70. * (*PA* 45:4560)

374. GIBSON, H. B., AND WEST, D. J. "Social and Intellectual Handicaps as Precursors of Early Delinquency." *Brit J Criminol* 10(1):21-32 Ja '70. * (*PA* 44:16949)

375. GROSVENOR, THEODORE. "Refractive State, Intelligence Test Scores, and Academic Ability." *Am J Optom* 47(5):355-61 My '70. * (*PA* 46:4624)

376. HAZARI, ANANDI, AND THAKUR, GIRIDHAR P. "The Relation Between Manifest Anxiety and Intelligence." *J Ed & Psychol* 27(4):375-7 Ja '70. *

377. IRVING, G.; ROBINSON, R. A.; AND MCADAM, W. "The Validity of Some Cognitive Tests in the Diagnosis of Dementia." *Brit J Psychiatry* 117(537):149-56 Ag '70. *

378. JACOBS, PAUL I., AND VANDEVENTER, MARY. "Information in Wrong Responses." *Psychol Rep* 26(1):311-5 F '70. * (*PA* 45:4253)

379. JOHNSON, JAMES E., AND OZIEL, LEON J. "An Item Analysis of the Raven Colored Progressive Matrices Test for Paranoid and Non-Paranoid Schizophrenic Patients." *J Clin Psychol* 26(3):357-9 Jl '70. * (*PA* 45:1054)

380. KEAR-COLWELL, J. J. "The B Factor Scale of the 16 PF as a Measure of Intelligence in Psychiatric Patients." *J Clin Psychol* 26(4):477-9 O '70. * (*PA* 45:4540)

381. KOTHARI, S. "Relationship Between the Progressive Matrices Tests and the Cancellation Task." *Psychol Studies* 15(1):59-61 Ja '70. *

382. NICHOLSON, CHARLES L. "Correlations Among CMMS, PPVT, and RCPM for Cerebral Palsied Children." *Percept & Motor Skills* 30(3):715-8 Je '70. * (*PA* 44:17151)

383. ORME, J. E. "A Practical Guide to Estimating Intelligence, Attainments and Intellectual Profit." *Acta Psychologica* 32(2):145-61 Ap '70. * (*PA* 44:16684)

384. SCHUT, DIEN; BESIJN, J. W.; BOEKE, P. E.; AND ULEMAN, A. L. "Psychological Examination Before and After Stereotactic Operations in Parkinson Patients." *Psychiatria, Neurologia, Neurochirurgia* 73(5):375-86 S-O '70. *

385. SEIM, SOL. "The Teenagers Grow Up." *Int Congr Rorsch & Other Proj Tech* 7:387–98 '70. *
386. WARDER, JOHN; PRESLY, ALLAN S.; AND KIRK, JOAN. "Intelligence and Literacy in Prison and Hospital Populations." *Brit J Criminol* 10(3):286–7 Jl '70. * (*PA* 46:1469)
387. WEINGARTEN, GILAD, AND ALEXANDER, JOHN F. "Effects of Physical Exertion on Mental Performance of College Males of Different Physical Fitness Level." *Percept & Motor Skills* 31(2):371–8 O '70. * (*PA* 45:5441)

For a review by Morton Bortner, see 6:490; for reviews by Charlotte Banks, W. D. Wall, and George Westby, see 4:314; for reviews by Walter C. Shipley and David Wechsler of the 1938 edition, see 3:258; for a review by T. J. Keating, see 2:1417.

[377]
*Purdue Non-Language Personnel Test. Business and industry; 1957–69; PNPT; abbreviated revision of *Purdue Non-Language Test*; Forms A-S, B-S, ['69, 2 pages, all items taken from 1957 tests] ; preliminary manual ('69, 4 pages) ; $4 per 25 tests, postage extra; 75¢ per specimen set, postpaid; 10(15) minutes; Joseph Tiffin; University Book Store. *

For reviews by John D. Hundleby and Benjamin Rosner of the earlier test, see 6:491.

[378]
★Quick Word Test. Grades 4–6, 7–12 and average adults, college and professional adults; 1957–67; QWT; 3 levels; manuals: elementary level ('67, 14 pages), levels 1 and 2 ('64, 14 pages), supplementary report ('67, 6 pages) ; 70¢ per scoring stencil; $1.50 per specimen set; postage extra; scoring service, 19¢ and over per test; (15–20) minutes; Edgar F. Borgatta and Raymond J. Corsini; Harcourt Brace Jovanovich, Inc. *
a) ELEMENTARY LEVEL. Grades 4–6; 1967; Form Am (1 page) ; $3 per 35 IBM 805/Digitek test-answer sheets ; $3.30 per 35 IBM 1230 test-answer sheets.
b) LEVEL 1. Grades 7–12 and average adults; 1957–65; IBM 805 Forms Am, Bm, Cm, Dm, ('64, 1 page, identical with tests copyrighted 1957) ; IBM 1230 Forms Am ('64), Bm ('65), Cm ('65), Dm ('65), (1 page, identical with tests copyrighted 1957) ; Form Dm sales restricted; $3 per 35 IBM 805 test-answer sheets ; $3.30 per 35 IBM 1230 test-answer sheets.
c) LEVEL 2. College and professional adults; 1957–65; IBM 805 Forms Am, Bm, ('64, 1 page, identical with tests copyrighted 1957) ; IBM 1230 Forms Am ('64), Bm ('65), (1 page, identical with tests copyrighted 1957) ; Form Bm sales restricted; prices same as for Level 1.

REFERENCES
1. BORGATTA, EDGAR F., AND CORSINI, RAYMOND J. "The Quick Word Test." *J Ed Res* 54:15–9 S '60. *
2. BORGATTA, EDGAR F., AND CORSINI, RAYMOND J. "The Quick Word Test (QWT) and the WAIS." *Psychol Rep* 6:201 Ap '60. * (*PA* 35:6397)
3. BORGATTA, EDGAR F., AND BOHRNSTEDT, GEORGE W. "Elementary Forms of the Quick Word Test." *J Exp Ed* 35:57–61 w '66. *
4. GROTELUESCHEN, ARDEN, AND KNOX, ALAN B. "Analysis of Quick Word Test as an Estimate of Adult Mental Ability." *J Ed Meas* 4:169–77 f '67. * (*PA* 42:3197)
5. GROTELUESCHEN, ARDEN, AND LYONS, THOMAS J. "Quick Word Test Validity With Adults." *Psychol Rep* 20:488–90 Ap '67. * (*PA* 41:8151)
6. REUBUSH, FAY JAYNES. *A Concurrent Validity Study of the Quick Word Test.* Doctor's thesis, University of Virginia (Charlottesville, Va.), 1967. (*DA* 28:2604A)
7. WESTBROOK, BERT W., AND SELLERS, JAMES R. "Critical Thinking, Intelligence, and Vocabulary." *Ed & Psychol Meas* 27:443–6 su '67. * (*PA* 41:13634)

8. GROTELUESCHEN, ARDEN, AND MCQUARRIE, DUNCAN. "Cross-Validation of the Quick Word Test as an Estimator of Adult Mental Ability." *Adult Ed* 21(1):14–9 f '70. *

JUM C. NUNNALLY, *Professor of Psychology, Vanderbilt University, Nashville, Tennessee.*

The purpose of the QWT is to provide a quick, inexpensive, easily applied measure of general ability. It is based entirely on vocabulary items. The elementary form has 50 vocabulary items, and the other forms have 100 vocabulary items. The stem words for items were obtained by sampling the pages of dictionaries. Alternative response words were obtained from dictionary definitions. All stem words contain four letters, and all alternative choice words contain five letters. Numerous item analyses were undertaken to obtain words of moderate difficulty which correlated well with total test scores. Norms were obtained on large, representative groups of subjects at each age level.

Test manuals are clear and contain much useful information. Tables are presented for easily translating raw scores on the tests into percentiles and stanines. Impressive amounts of data are presented on various types of reliability and correlations with other measures of intelligence. Reliabilities in the neighborhood of .90 are reported for split-half and alternative form measures.

Because the original purpose for constructing the test was to obtain a quick estimate of general ability, it is important to inspect correlations between the test and established measures of intelligence. Numerous such correlations are reported in the test manuals, and many of them are surprisingly high. As an example, at the elementary level, the test correlates .86 with scores on the *Cooperative School and College Ability Test* and .84 with the *Lorge-Thorndike Intelligence Tests*.

The test is very simple to administer and score. All of the items are on a one-sided answer sheet. The test format is so simple to comprehend that directions to persons who are taking the test are adequately presented in a few short sentences on the answer sheet. Time for completing the test tends to vary between 10 minutes and less than 20, depending on the age level and differences among subjects in speed of work. Although the instructions urge the subject to work quickly, no time limit is put on the test. One would imagine that a very generous time limit for even the slowest of subjects would be 30 minutes. Thus, in that short amount of time, one can obtain much the same information that is obtained from some measures of general ability that are more time consuming, more expensive, and less simple to administer.

There are four important questions to ask about the QWT. First, why should one ever employ any other type of measure of general ability? If one is considering employing an instrument that is highly dependent on vocabulary scores, then in most cases (exceptions to be discussed later) one would be better off employing a simple vocabulary test like the *Quick Word Test*. For example, a correlation of .84 was found between scores on the QWT and scores on the *Wechsler Adult Intelligence Scale*. This is not much below the reliabilities of the two tests. The Wechsler test requires a highly expert professional examiner, and the test is much more expensive and time consuming to administer and score.

Before the answer to the first question lulls the reader into thinking that the millennium has been reached in the testing of general ability with very simple methods, however, we should ask a second question, one that is related to the first one: Can one measure general intelligence with simple vocabulary items? Such items are featured very prominently on the Wechsler scales and the Binet scales, and most group tests of intelligence also rely heavily on vocabulary items. However, on intuitive grounds and on the basis of a half century of factor analytic research, one could claim that a better measure of general ability could be obtained by mixing content from at least some other factors, in addition to verbal comprehension, particularly material from the general reasoning factor and the numerical facility factor. The latter would require a separate test with items like, "Which one of the following numbers is closest to 8.01?" The general reasoning factor, however, can be brought directly into the format of the vocabulary-type item by phrasing the items in terms of verbal analogies, which is done in some existing tests. This would make it more difficult to construct items, and such items might not be quite as simple for 4th grade children to understand; but bringing in the reasoning component logically would make a somewhat better measure of general ability than relying entirely on simple word knowledge, as is done in the QWT. However, to broaden the content in such a way as to bring in more of the central factors in intellectual functioning would tend to destroy the original purpose of the test. The purpose was to provide a simple, economical, quick approximation of scores obtained on existing tests of general intelligence. The *Quick Word Test* does those things well.

The third question regarding the QWT is: In what ways would the test be most validly employed? The test probably would serve very well to (*a*) screen out individuals who needed more detailed interviewing and testing, e.g., transfer students from one school system to another, (*b*) help in the industrial selection of personnel, e.g., bank tellers and secretaries, (*c*) obtain a quick measure of general ability as part of experiments in psychology, sociology, and education, and (*d*) add to personnel folders in the many instances in which an approximate measure of general ability is useful, e.g., in prisons.

The fourth and final question is: When it is feasible to do so, when would it probably be better to employ some other types of instruments than a simple vocabulary test like the *Quick Word Test?* First, because no test forms are available below the 4th grade level, it is obvious that one would have to employ some other type of measure below that level. For most purposes in elementary education, it would be better to employ other types of instruments. For preschool children, it is better to rely on individual intelligence tests or "readiness tests" that emphasize the understanding of simple concepts. In the elementary grades, most important educational decisions (e.g., sectioning and promotion) are based on teacher-made tests and commercially distributed achievement tests. It is difficult to see how these and other decisions about students in the elementary grades would be materially enhanced by a simple vocabulary test. Second, instruments other than simple vocabulary tests are more useful in the testing of various atypical groups—the deaf, the blind, the mentally ill, recent immigrants, and various culturally disadvantaged groups in our society. With some of these groups it is best to employ individually administered intelligence tests; with others it is best to employ so-called "culture fair tests" that contain nonverbal reasoning items. Third, the test would not be highly useful in career guidance, such as in the advisement of senior high school students about choices of careers and higher education. In career guidance, one needs as much differential information as can be obtained about the individual's abilities, interests, personality characteristics, and other attributes. When it is done well, such career guidance should be based on multifactor batteries of ability tests and tests of other kinds.

To mention these and other limitations of the potential effectiveness of the *Quick Word Test* is not meant to be a general condemnation. The test was not designed to do those things. Rather, it was designed to provide an inexpensive, quick, easily applied approximation of what is measured by traditional measures of general intelligence, and it does these things surprisingly well.

J Counsel Psychol 12:436–7 w '65. *Jack C. Merwin.* * In general, the *Quick Word Test* appears to be about as economical an approach to measuring general ability as could be attempted. Reliability and normative information are satisfactory for such a new and short test. While the correlation with other general aptitude tests would indicate a need for greater caution in the use of equivalent raw scores with Level 2 than that probably needed with Level 1, the test seems capable of providing a relatively efficient estimate of performance on other general ability tests. The individual user will have to study the extent to which it can be used as a substitute for the other tests in predicting his unique criteria. He may also find norms developed on his unique groups of more value than those presented in the manual, as suggested by the authors.

J Ed Meas 2:257–8 D '65. *Gilbert Sax and Ethel A. Oda.* * Each word to be defined contains five letters. Four synonym alternatives are given for each word. Most of the options are well selected and clear. However, with a 15 minute time limit, defining words out of context may produce some confusion. * Directions for administering and scoring the QWT are simple and clear. * An examination of the mean Otis Gamma IQ scores obtained from the same students provides a useful estimate of the amount of bias present in the norming procedure. According to the QWT manual, the mean Otis IQ for ninth graders was 107.3. It is likely that the systematic elimination of all small schools was at least partially responsible for the over-selection of relatively bright examinees. * Percentile and stanine norms are also provided. The norms tables are extremely clear and easy to use. * Alternate-form reliabilities have a median of .88, but are spuriously high inasmuch as data from two grades were combined. As a substitute for longer, more time consuming examinations, the QWT would seem to be able to provide reliable and useful information. Costs can also be reduced over other comparable types of tests because test items are printed directly on the answer sheet.

RBH Test of Learning Ability. Business and industry; 1947–63; TLA; 3 editions; directions (no date, 1 page) for each edition; 50¢ per key; $1.50 per manual; $1.50 per specimen set of any one edition; postage extra; Richardson, Bellows, Henry & Co., Inc. *
a) FORMS S AND T. Test ('47, 5 pages); manual ['63, 24 pages]; $4.50 per 25 tests; 15(20) minutes.
b) FORMS DS-12 AND DT-12. Identical with Forms S and T except for removal of directions from testing time; formerly titled *Test for Office Personnel;* test ('61, 5 pages, identical with 1947 tests); manual ['63, 27 pages, identical with manual for Forms S and T except for cover and 2 pages]; $4.50 per 25 tests; 12(20) minutes.
c) FORM ST. Consists of Forms S and T combined; test ('57, 8 pages); manual ['63, 8 pages]; $5.50 per 25 tests; 25(30) minutes.

REFERENCES

1–2. See 6:504.
3. ROSS, PAUL F., AND DUNFIELD, NEIL M. "Selecting Salesmen for an Oil Company." *Personnel Psychol* 17:75–84 sp '64. *
4. MOORE, CLAY L., JR.; MACNAUGHTON, JOHN F.; AND OSBURN, HOBART G. "Ethnic Differences Within an Industrial Selection Battery." *Personnel Psychol* 22(4):473–82 w '69. * (PA 44:13473)

ERWIN K. TAYLOR, *President, Personnel Research and Development Corporation, Cleveland, Ohio.*

Industrial test users constantly bring pressure on test publishers for tests with shorter and shorter time limits. RBH has responded to this pressure with this 12-minute spiral omnibus test (54 items) modeled after the 40-minute *Army General Classification Test* (150 items).

Manuals for Forms S and T are the same as for DS and DT except for the administration directions. The same norms are used for both tests since the difference in time limits, according to the publisher, has not changed the means or standard deviations to a substantial degree.

The manuals provide a wealth of normative, validity, and reliability data. A total of 16,993 male cases are reported. This population is broken into seven groups, varying in size from 48 technical and professional people to 10,576 industrial employees and applicants. Each of these seven groups is then further broken down into its component populations; means and standard deviations are provided for more than one hundred samples ranging in size from 5 to 1,500. A similarly bountiful list of relationships between Forms S and T and a large number of other tests, including personal background surveys, supervisory judgment tests, and personality tests are provided.

Female norms are based on a total of 6,386 cases, again divided into seven groups ranging in size from 67 statistical accounting and supply clerks to 3,550 miscellaneous or unspecified clerical applicants and employees. These are again broken down into the various specific populations of which the groups are constructed, with the N, mean, and standard deviation provided, and again a large number of correlations with a wide variety of other tests.

The reliability of the test is approximately .90 and is adequate for almost any purpose for which it is to be used. The manual also briefly describes about 20 validity studies conducted in 1963 or earlier and about 15 studies between 1967 and 1970. In those dated 1968 or later, both the N and the mean of minority group members are given in almost all cases. In one instance, a study of 64 office support personnel consisted of 27 minority and 37 nonminority group members. The test, validated against supervisory ratings, was in this small sample slightly more valid for the minority than for the nonminority group members.

The manuals mention that "The three types of items can be scored separately if desired." But they provide no rationale for doing so, nor do they provide normative, reliability, or validity data for the several item types separately.

Despite the test's reliability, we remain skeptical concerning the measurement of three intellectual variables (with 17 items for each) in 12 to 15 minutes. Considering the EEOC requirements for specific validity, we also question the value of an omnibus intelligence test. In the light of the Supreme Court decision in the Duke Power case, it seems that multiple factor tests are less likely to be acceptable to EEOC or OFCC than single factor tests validated against specific criteria. Sufficient short tests of verbal, numerical, and spatial ability exist to make these tests of questionable value.

[380]

RBH Test of Non-Verbal Reasoning. Business and industry; 1948-63; TNR; 1 form; 2 editions: long form ('48, 5 pages), short form ('50, 3 pages); catalog uses title *The RBH Non-Verbal Reasoning Test;* manual ['63, 10-11 pages] for each edition; directions (no date, 2 pages) for each edition; $4.50 per 25 tests of long form; $4 per 25 tests of short form; 50¢ per key; $1.50 per manual for either edition; $1.50 per specimen set of each edition; postage extra; 10(15) minutes for short form, 15(20) minutes for long form; Richardson, Bellows, Henry & Co., Inc. *

REFERENCES

1-3. See 6:505.
4. MOORE, CLAY L., JR.; MACNAUGHTON, JOHN F.; AND OSBURN, HOBART G. "Ethnic Differences Within an Industrial Selection Battery." *Personnel Psychol* 22(4):473-82 w '69. * (PA 44:13473)

ERWIN K. TAYLOR, *President, Personnel Research and Development Corporation, Cleveland, Ohio.*

Like many tests from this publisher, these instruments were modeled, constructed and developed by the Personnel Research Section of the Adjutant General's Office during and shortly after World War II. The long form, composed of 50 items, has a 15-minute time limit, while the short form, with 24 items, has a 10-minute time limit.

The figures used in the items are all abstract and probably as "culture-free" as any that might be devised. Aside from the directions (which could be easily translated into any language), the test is essentially independent of the language of the subject. The understanding of certain concepts, such as symmetry, rectilinearity, and angular bifurcation is all that is essential to the solution of the problem.

The tests do not employ separate answer sheets, and thus can become rather costly in an extensive program. Separate answer sheets could, of course, be readily devised, but in a test as speeded as this, they would require renormalization. The typography of the test leaves something to be desired, and the test would be improved by better printing on more opaque stock.

While the test (except for the directions) is independent of language, this reviewer seriously questions whether this or any other paper-and-pencil test of this type, such as the *Minnesota Paper Form Board Test* or the *SRA Pictorial Reasoning Test,* is not really responded to by at least a large portion of a tested population in a verbal (but probably subvocal) fashion. Both forms correlate substantially (according to data provided in the manuals) with standard verbal intelligence tests. It might perhaps be more correct to name the test "Abstract Reasoning," as is done in the *Differential Aptitude Tests,* than to imply that, because the items are themselves nonverbal in construction, they are solved on a nonverbal basis.

The manuals give extensive normative data. For the long form, the total N is 3,118. This population includes 2,113 managers and executives in the largest single group. In the short form norms table, there are 5,499 cases. Here, however, the populations are primarily lower level: almost 3,000 are industrial applicants; another 1,000 clerical applicants and employees; and there are 1,345 mechanical and operating employees. Thus, the longer form appears to have been used with higher level employees and applicants than the shorter form. Each manual presents the N, mean, and standard deviation of each of the samples from which the norms categories were developed. The manuals also present numerous correlations with other tests. Separate norms are presented for female personnel.

Split-half reliability coefficients are .86 and .84 for the long and short forms, respectively. Five validity studies are reported for the long form. These are primarily at the managerial and executive levels and range in sample size from 28 to 443. In the former study, tests correlated .14 with a complex composite criterion. The highest correlation reported is .36. Eleven validity studies are reported for the shorter form, and these, generally speaking, deal with hourly workers and first-level supervisors. Validities range from lows of −.02, .03, .07, and .08 to a high of .38.

While no data with respect to the proportion of subjects who complete the test are provided, both forms seem to be too highly speeded (the longer form, ironically, being more so than the shorter). To complete the long form in 15 minutes, the subject must respond to three items per minute, while to complete the short form in ten minutes, 2.4 responses per minute are required. It is our feeling that a moderate extension of the time limit might render the test considerably more valid, particularly with lower socioeconomic level personnel.

These tests, along with the DAT abstract reasoning test and the *Minnesota Paper Form Board Test,* are probably as culture free as a pencil-and-paper test can be made. All of these are too highly speeded and would be more valid with more generous time limits, particularly for nonexempt positions. The RBH tests have the disadvantage of having the most complicated verbal directions and, simultaneously, the advantage of lower than usual opportunity for getting the correct answer by chance. Their industrial standardization is better than average, but they have not demonstrated consistent validity, particularly for nonexempt positions and for lower levels of supervision.

[381]

★SRA Pictorial Reasoning Test. Ages 14 and over; 1966–67; PRT; for use "with all major American subcultural groups"; 1 form ('66, 7 pages); preliminary manual ('67, 21 pages); $5.95 per 25 tests; 75¢ per manual; $1.25 per specimen set; postage extra; untimed (30–45) minutes or timed 15(20) minutes; Robert N. McMurry and Phyllis D. Arnold; Science Research Associates, Inc. *

RAYMOND A. KATZELL, *Professor of Psychology and Head of the Department, New York University, New York, New York.*

A consequence of recent heightened concern with social justice for disadvantaged minorities has been renewed attention to the equitability of tests for such populations. A long established approach to this kind of problem has been the attempt to develop culture free or culture fair tests. That strategy has not been pursued much in recent years, partly because cultural effects were not eliminated by the earlier attempts and partly because of the growing suspicion that culture free tests are likely also to be validity free.

The test under consideration represents a latter-day revival of the culture fair strategy in developing a test of general mental ability intended to be applicable to all major American subcultural groups. Like other attempts along these lines, it utilizes a type of subject matter believed to be relatively immune to cultural influences. In this instance, items entail reasoning with nonverbal, pictorial materials of the sort employed in the earlier *SRA Non-Verbal Form.* However, in addition to trying to control for cultural influences through the choice of test content, the authors also used the interesting idea of empirically identifying those 80 items which, from an edited pool of 270 experimental items, exhibited minimal differences in difficulty among seven subcultures while at the same time correlating with total score on the experimental test. The items constituting the test are reported as having lower inter-group variability in mean difficulty than did the experimental items. Emphasis on selecting items which minimize inter-group differences may have cost some internal consistency, since the K-R 20 reliability is .75 for a heterogeneous sample of 1,250 cases, and falls to the .60's in several culturally homogeneous groups. Reliability coefficients in this range call for the conventional note of tentativeness, especially in interpreting and acting upon scores of individuals.

The seven subcultures represented in the experimental and normative samples were described simply as urban whites from deprived areas of large cities, Appalachian whites, urban Negroes from deprived areas of large cities, rural Negroes from areas of the South, Spanish-speaking bilinguals, French-speaking bilinguals, and nonurban whites from rural, suburban, and smaller city areas, this last group bearing the anomalous label of "control group." The normative sample, consisting of 3,598 who took the test with a time limit and 1,250 who took it untimed, was composed of both male and female students whose ages ranged from 13 to 19 and whose completed schooling ranged from grades 8 through 12. Norms are provided in the manual for several breakdowns of the sample but there are none, inexplicably, by sex. Unfortunately, insufficient information is given about the seven subcultural groups to determine how comparable they were in other respects, such as age, education, whether the urban whites and blacks were from the same cities, or whether the Spanish-speaking group consisted of, say, rural Mexican-Americans or urban Puerto Ricans.

The remaining big question is, of course, to what extent the test is fair and valid among the several subcultures studied. As to fairness, the major evidence advanced in the manual is that the means and distributions of all seven cultural subgroups are "nearly the same." It would have been helpful had there been further statistical analysis of these data such as testing the hypothesis that the several group means and distributions are equivalent, or calculating what portion of score variance is accounted for by subculture. It might also have been instructive had the intergroup differences found with this test been compared with results obtained by using other mental ability tests with the same or similar groups. From the results presented it would appear that in a timed administration of the test, the disadvantaged groups typically obtained mean scores about half a standard deviation below the "control group," which is not a particularly unusual result for such comparisons. Under untimed administration, however, the means of most of the disadvantaged groups exceeded the "control group" by about one-third of a standard deviation.

The picture of the test's cultural fairness is further clouded by the aforementioned lack of information about the composition of the several subcultures which are compared. That 198 urban whites and 63 urban blacks obtained essentially the same mean scores on the untimed version of the test is of interest, but a conclusion regarding culture-fairness can hardly be drawn unless we can be sure of the comparability of the two samples in age, education, sex, and other relevant respects; no assurances of such comparability are provided in the manual.

But the most critical variable on which different cultural groups must be compared in order to assess a test's fairness is a relevant criterion of performance, such as success in school or work. A test on which two cultural groups attain the same mean score cannot be said to be fair if one group were to score significantly higher on such a criterion. Conversely, a test may be regarded as unfair only when there is a significantly different discrepancy in the test performance as compared to the criterion performance of two or more groups.[1] The manual is devoid of such comparisons involving criteria together with test performance.

Mention of criteria immediately raises the remaining big question, that of validity. The only test-criterion correlations presented are 49 which involve grades of one or another cultural subgroup in one or another school subject. Interestingly, the higher correlations are usually found with the control group, judged as closest to the mainstream of American culture. None of the correlations based on disadvantaged or minority groups appears to be significantly greater than zero, although here again the persistent failure of the manual to provide information on statistical significance requires the consumer to be his own statistician.

In brief, the method of construction gives reason to hope that the test *may* turn out to be useful in measuring "the learning potential of individuals from diverse backgrounds with reading difficulties, whose potential for training and employment cannot be reliably and validly measured by verbal instruments." The results reported in the manual do not dampen this hope, but they are too limited and imperfect to nurture it either. The test should therefore not be used for the stated purpose unless one is prepared

---

[1] KIRKPATRICK, JAMES J.; EWEN, ROBERT B.; BARRETT, RICHARD S.; AND KATZELL, RAYMOND A. *Testing and Fair Employment: Fairness and Validity of Personnel Tests for Different Ethnic Groups*, p. 7. New York: New York University Press, 1968. Pp. x, 145. *

SRA Pictorial Reasoning Test

to do further research on its fairness and validity in various subcultures.

JOHN E. MILHOLLAND, *Professor of Psychology, The University of Michigan, Ann Arbor, Michigan.*

Only a preliminary manual is available for this test, and it claims that the test

can be used to measure the learning potential of individuals from diverse backgrounds with reading difficulties, whose potential for training and employment cannot be reliably and validly measured by verbal instruments * The PRT is designed to be used as a general index of ability, measuring a person's potential to learn jobs independent of his background or culture * The PRT was expressly designed to yield comparable measurement across subcultures. * The PRT can be used as a placement instrument to measure the learning potential of dropouts, adults in basic education programs, or persons in remedial reading programs.

The support for the claims comes from the fact that one criterion of item selection was equal difficulty across samples from the following subpopulations: rural white, urban white, Appalachian, urban Negro, rural Negro, Spanish-speaking bilinguals, and French-speaking bilingual Canadians.

In order for the claim to be substantiated it would appear that one of two situations must be true: (*a*) The samples have been equated on some criterion of learning potential; or (*b*) The subculture populations have the same distribution of learning potential *and* the samples are representative of the populations. No evidence is given that either situation obtains and therefore this test should not be recommended for operational use.

The test consists of 80 sets of 5 pictures or designs; the task is to select the one that differs from the rest in some way in which the other four are alike. It can be given with a 15-minute time limit, or untimed. The untimed administration is recommended, since norms for the various subsamples are more alike in this mode. Hand scoring is convenient, consisting of counting the marks registered by carbon paper in squares corresponding to the keyed options.

Reliabilities (K-R 20) in the norm samples range from .59 to .83. Fourteen correlations with other tests are given, 11 of them based on "control group" samples consisting of nonurban whites. Six of them are with the *SRA Non-Verbal Form,* but the items in this instrument were a part of the pool from which the PRT items were chosen! These six correlations range from .37 to .75 and perhaps should be regarded as reliability estimates. Their utility for this purpose, however, is diminished by the fact that every sample included individuals from grades 9 through 12. The other correlations are for single grade control group samples, with N's of 50 to 74. A number of correlations with school grades are also presented, but the authors quite rightly point out that conventional grades are unsuitable as criteria for this kind of a test.

The test was copyrighted in 1966, the preliminary manual in 1967, and here it is 1970. One suspects that no serious effort is going to be made to establish validity for the instrument.

J Ed Meas 6(1):41–3 sp '69. *John L. Horn.* * intended to provide a measure of a general ability for which the averages across various ethnic and social groups in the U.S.A. and Canada are not notably different. As the authors state: "The PRT is designed to be used as a general index of ability, measuring a person's potential to learn jobs independent of his background or culture." This purpose makes the test vulnerable to criticisms that would not be directed at tests based upon less ambitious designs. * Because the test is based upon only one kind of task, a substantial proportion of the variation in test scores is likely to represent a test-specific factor—a factor which need not be integral to the concept of intelligence. Probably it is desirable to regard the test as a measure of a primary-level factor, cognition of classes, rather than as a measure of a general intellective ability. Some of the drawings are difficult to identify with certainty (e.g., two peppers (?), a watermelon, a pile of bricks, a tape measure) and in several such cases it is necessary to make proper identification of the depicted object in order to reason properly to obtain the correct answer. Also, to the reviewer it seems that some of the depicted objects would be unfamiliar to those for whom the test is intended (e.g., a microphone, snowshoes, comets (?), molded jello (?), different kinds of ships). To some extent, however, the method for selection of items obviates this criticism. Not obviated by the item-selection method, however, is the fact that several of the items have more than one answer-choice satisfying the conditions for a correct answer—e.g., in item 15, choice D represents the only animal that is clearly winged (one can't be sure about the insect of choice A), yet E, presumably the only legless animal (though one can't be sure about this), is the one choice that is scored correct. This kind of problem arises with any ability test, of course; it may not be any more prevalent in this test than in others (the reviewer counted some 7 items for which this problem seemed to exist). In any case it no doubt produces some lowering of reliability and validity. * the test can be said to be self-administering only if subjects can read and understand such sentences as: "All four pictures except the phonograph are alike because they are musical instruments, and ONLY the phonograph repeats the sounds made by other instruments." * it is clear that one can find better tests than the PRT to predict academic performance. The test authors interpret the significant correlations between the PRT and the Nonverbal, Otis and DAT tests as supporting, or at least not overthrowing, an hypothesis that the PRT does, indeed, measure "learning potential." They imply that the low correlations between the PRT and measures of academic achievement indicate culture fairness. It is worth paying heed to the fact, however, that tests can show moderate correlation with so-called general ability tests and low correlation with academic performance and yet not be particularly culture fair, much less be measures of "learning potential." Fluency tests, for example, have these characteristics and yet are not regarded as culture fair. Low correlation with academic performance is by no means a necessary or sufficient indicator of culture fair measurement of "learning potential." SUMMARY. In the reviewer's opinion this test should be considered to be in an experimental stage of development. Institutional decisions should be based upon the use of this test only if additional research is done to establish the basis for the decision. Individual decisions based upon the use of this test should be made only with considerable caution and then only with the aid of a psychologist or educator who has a very good understanding of the measurement of human abilities.

[382]

★SRA Short Test of Educational Ability. Grades kgn-1, 2-3, 4-6, 7-8, 9-12; 1966-70; STEA; 2 editions; interpretive manual ('69, 9 pages); conversion tables ('70, 9 pages); approximately 80 per cent of the items in the series were taken from *SRA Primary Mental Abilities* and *SRA Tests of Educational Ability;* norms derived by equating with parent tests; 35¢ per interpretive manual; postage extra; Spanish edition available; Science Research Associates, Inc. *
a) HAND SCORED EDITION. Grades kgn-1, 2-3, 4-6, 7-8, 9-12; 5 levels in 3 booklets.

1) *Levels 1-2.* Grades kgn-1, 2-3; 2 overlapping levels in 1 booklet; 1 form ('66, 11 pages); manual ('66, 18 pages); $5.55 per 25 tests; $1.05 per specimen set; (30-40) minutes.
2) *Levels 3-4.* Grades 4-6, 7-8; 2 overlapping levels in 1 booklet; 1 form ('66, 7 pages, self-marking); manual ('66, 10 pages); $5.55 per 25 tests; $1.05 per specimen set; 20(30) minutes.
3) *Level 5.* Grades 9-12; 1 form ('66, 8 pages, self-marking); manual ('66, 8 pages); $4.80 per 25 tests; $1.05 per specimen set; 20(30) minutes.
b) MACHINE SCORABLE EDITION. Grades kgn-1, 2-3; 1 form ('66, 8 pages, NCS scorable); 2 levels; marking practice sheet ('66, 1 page); test materials and scoring service, 55¢ and over per test; specimen set not available; 30(40) minutes.
1) *Level 1.* Grades kgn-1; manual ('66, 14 pages).
2) *Level 2.* Grades 2-3; manual ('66, 13 pages).

REFERENCES

1. JONES, WILLIAM PAUL. *Predicting Academic Performance With the Short Test of Educational Ability Considering Social Class and Sex Differences.* Doctor's thesis, New Mexico State University (University Park, N.M.), 1968. (DA 29:3832A)
2. JONES, W. PAUL. "Sex Differences in Academic Prediction." *Meas & Eval Guid* 3(2):88-91 su '70. *

RUSSEL F. GREEN, *Research Consultant in Psychology and Education, Henrietta, New York.*

This test consists of five levels of increasing difficulty which are represented as spanning grades K through 12. The instructions are clearly written and seem to cover all details that might be needed. The format is easy to follow. The norms and conversion tables are well laid out and easy to follow.

Except for portions of Levels 1 and 5, the items used were taken from current editions of the *SRA Primary Mental Abilities* (PMA) or from the *SRA Tests of Educational Ability* (TEA). No standardization sample, as such, was used. Rather, these short forms were administered to students in six Chicago area schools, along with the PMA for grades K through 3 and the TEA for grades 4 through 11. IQ equivalents were then obtained by equating the STEA scores with the PMA and TEA scores using the equi-percentile method. The implication is that the norming of the STEA is equivalent to that of the PMA and the TEA.

Correlations between the STEA and PMA ranged from .53 to .78, averaging about .70. Correlations between the STEA and the TEA ranged from .54 to .82, averaging about .75. The implication here seems to be that the STEA is supposed to be valid for making the same kinds of predictions that the long forms (PMA and TEA) make. No other data relevant to validity are presented in the manual.

The STEA would appear to have quite limited usefulness and little reason for being published. There is a continuing desire on the part of educators to have tests which will provide valid predictors of academic achievement but which will not take much time away from instruction. This test represents another effort at developing a test which, presumably, is supposed to be better in some way than other tests on the market. No evidence that it is, is available. In fact, there are several shortcomings that the potential user should keep in mind.

First, the developers give no evidence that their choice of subtests or of items is the optimum set for the purpose. Developing such evidence would not have been difficult, and perhaps it was done; not mentioning it would represent a serious oversight.

Second, no evidence is presented to support the developers' claim that Levels 1 and 2 avoid "dependence on concurrent school achievement." Avoiding any items that depend on reading ability may accomplish this to some degree. There is substantial evidence, however, that avoiding verbal material is by no means a sufficient strategy for avoiding such dependence.

Third, the use of multiple choice items in a short-form test precludes the possibility of satisfactorily discriminating among students who are in the lower portion of the scale. *The mean for five-year olds on Level 1 is actually set at the theoretical chance score!* Hence for this test there probably is no discrimination at all in the entire lower two-thirds of the distribution. This situation improves somewhat at higher levels and ages but its discrimination is never satisfactory.

Fourth, added to the problem of poor discrimination among lower scores is the fact that the standard errors of measurement appear to be large (about 6.5) relative to the assumed standard deviations (16) for both Levels 1 and 2.

Fifth, the reliabilities of Levels 1 and 2 (.82 to .84) are too low for comfort if one wishes to make inferences about individuals. This probably is due to the chance element being so important in the lower half of the distributions.

Sixth, the IQ's obtained are too often poor estimates of the IQ's one would obtain from the longer, more reliable, more comprehensive versions from which these were constructed. The standard errors of estimate of predicting IQ's on the longer versions from the short forms are often more than one-half of the standard deviation.

CONCLUSION. It seems clear that the STEA fails in attempting to be a satisfactory short-form estimate of educational ability (aptitude). Its principal downfall can be traced to shortcomings inherent in the use of multiple choice items in short tests. If one is concerned only with differentiating among high aptitude students, the test might be suitable, but as age increases, the STEA becomes progressively more unsatisfactory for differentiating among the lower two-thirds to one-third of the students, depending on the level.

Educators, it seems, would be best advised to use long forms if their need is to make decisions about individual students in the lower one-third to two-thirds of the ability range.

As a short-form estimate to be used for some kinds of research on groups, Levels 2 through 5 probably would be quite satisfactory. One hesitates to recommend their use even for this purpose if the research is to depend on correlation estimates or covariance controls.

HENRY WEITZ, *Professor of Education and Director, Counseling Center, Duke University, Durham, North Carolina.*

The principal advantage claimed for the STEA is the limited time required for its administration. The 30 or so minutes required to administer most levels of the STEA represents an average of about half the time required for the *SRA Tests of Educational Ability* or the *SRA Primary Mental Abilities,* from which over 80 percent of the STEA items were drawn. This advantage was achieved at the cost of reduced reliability at some levels.

The test is said to be "designed to avoid reliance on achievement concepts and skills acquired in school" and, in the case of the first two levels, "or at home: the tests for Levels 1 and 2 do not, for example, require the pupil to read," while "the Level 3 and 4 tests....require only the simplest reading skills." The subtests of the first two levels, for example, purport to measure ability to identify cause and effect relationships, skill in simple problem solving, space visualization, pictorial vocabulary, and recognition of missing numbers in a series. Although these skills are rarely taught in the precise form in which they appear in the items, they do represent behavioral objectives of education at this level. Similar correspondence between skills measured by the test and educational objectives is found throughout the

STEA. And this is as it should be for a test designed to measure educational ability.

In the case of the Levels 1 and 2 tests, covering grades K-3, the split-half reliability coefficients reported, ranging from .82 to .84, represent a lower limit of usefulness for individual measurement. Split-half reliabilities for all other grades equal or exceed .90, which some will find acceptable for individual assessment. Slightly lower K-R 20's are also reported. Test-retest reliabilities would have been more meaningful.

Predictive validity data are not presently available, although the STEA is reported to correlate with the PMA and TEA. (The median correlation reported was .72, with correlations ranging from .53 to .82.) Thus it is difficult to say at this time how much, if any, this test can contribute to the management of the learning experiences of a student. The Interpretive Manual appropriately warns the prospective user that the test "should not be regarded as measuring all factors or processes usually associated with intelligence testing."

Conversions of raw scores to MA's and quotients for Levels 1 and 2 and to quotient scores, percentiles, and stanines for all levels are provided in the manuals. These norms were developed by an equi-percentile method relating the STEA raw scores to the raw scores of the parent test, the PMA or TEA. Hopefully, norms based on the STEA will be developed.

The STEA appears to be a moderately useful instrument for estimating educational ability if testing time is a crucial factor. Limited reliability and the lack of predictive validity information reduce its usefulness. Use of this instrument should be restricted to experimental administrations until local validity and reliability studies can be made or until the publishers provide adequate supporting information.

J Ed Meas 8(1):49–51 sp '71. Raynard J. Dooley. * Validity is mentioned only once: "Predictive validity is not available at this time." However, a concurrent type of validity is alluded to by establishing correlations between the STEA and the Primary Mental Abilities (PMA) or the STEA and the Tests of Educational Ability (TEA). The PMA and the TEA are parent tests of the STEA. The test publisher emphasizes these correlations by declaring: "The major value of the STEA lies in its....high correlation with existing tests that take somewhat longer to administer." But both the PMA and the TEA have had a weak validity history themselves, and the reported correlations are unimpressive when one considers the loss of content from the longer to the shorter form—from the PMA or the TEA to the STEA. * the entire process of relating the STEA to the PMA or the TEA can be called into question. First, the sample used to calibrate scores for the STEA were not equated with the anchor test norms (nor was matching intended by the test publisher). Second, the content of the tests was not similar even though the STEA was extracted from the PMA and TEA. Validity was sacrificed for reliability in the shorter form, as the test publisher apparently extracted only those items from the test that contributed the most to subtest score or total test score on the parent test. Content or factors of the parent test were not maintained in the shorter test * Third, the correlations, although high in the equating study, do not support the use of the equipercentile method. The correlations are spuriously high; identical items appear in both forms. The STEA illustrates the misuse of the split-half and the KR-20 formula in computing reliability. While reporting the upper level of the STEA to be somewhat speeded, the test publisher, nonetheless, employs these formulae in calculating the reliability coefficient. The STEA illustrates the inadequacies in measuring bright youngsters at grades 3, 6, and 8. Obviously, the bright youngsters tested with the STEA at their appropriate grade level would hit a ceiling at that level. But how does one identify a bright youngster: by school achievement, by previous test performance, or by intuition? Furthermore, should a 3-, 6-, or 8-grade student who reaches a ceiling at the appropriate grade level (assuming he is a student who has not been identified as bright before the test administration) be retested with the next level? The STEA manual answers neither question. Finally, are teachers who use this test willing to separate the bright youngsters from the group and test them separately, as is required in the STEA directions. The STEA illustrates an attempt to construct a test that avoids dependence on concurrent school achievement. However, the STEA was derived for most levels from the TEA. And the TEA was validated on common criterion measures such as grade point averages and achievement tests. The TEA score and, consequently, the STEA score are therefore estimates on ability derived from and predictive of formal educational encounters. Irrespective of STEA's claim that reading at the various levels is kept to a minimum, and omitted at the earlier levels, the parent test was originally related to school achievement criteria. Moreover, without further support for STEA, the claim of the test publisher appears unfounded. Summary. The test's strongest feaure is, of course, its brevity—administration time is only 30–35 minutes. The reliability coefficients are acceptable, ranging from .82 to .93. The test is easily scored, and converted scores are easily obtained in terms of quotients, mental ages, stanines, and percentiles. But validity information is nonexistent, except for what can be inferred from the equating study. However, the equating study in which the STEA scores were calibrated from the parent, reference test (either the PMA or the TEA) is a questionable approach. In conclusion, unless the person who uses the STEA is willing to do research on his own, the test has little to recommend its adoption.

J Ed Meas 8(1):51–2 sp '71. W. Paul Jones. [A rejoinder to the above review from the publisher.] * Dooley notes that "the PMA and TEA have had weak validity history themselves...." That point seems questionable to this writer. A review of TEA by Ahmann (1965) summarized that "the tests (TEA)....correlate very highly with common criterion measures such as grade point averages and achievement test scores." * The STEA is related to academic performance, because obviously an educational ability test without such relationship would be of little value. * Dooley's....key question seemed to be the lack of available data relating STEA scores to outside criteria. * Dooley....was correct in pointing out that the only validity information was that to be inferred from the parent instruments. * however, it should be noted that published data regarding the validity of STEA are now available * In summary, the STEA series seems to this writer to have attained the stated objective: to provide a reliable estimate of educational ability within a short administration time. Reliability coefficients are acceptable, and while there can probably never be "enough" validity data, the available data certainly suggest a significant relationship between STEA scores and academic performance criteria. Although a national standardization of STEA would certainly be preferable to the equated norms, the generally accepted procedures used to calibrate STEA to the anchor tests should have resulted in useful norms conversions. The debt owed by STEA to the parent instruments in terms of content is obvious, but the publisher's statement that STEA does not measure all processes associated with intelligence testing is prudent. The objective of a short time limit for administration certainly precludes any objective of total factorial coverage. To suggest that the STEA has no faults is not the purpose of this reply. However, the data now available do suggest that for those test users desiring a useful estimate of educational ability with a minimal investment in testing time, the STEA series has much to offer.

[383]

*****SRA Verbal Form.** Grades 7–16 and adults; 1946–67; formerly called *SRA Verbal Classification Form*; abbreviated adaptation of *Thurstone Test of Mental Alertness* which is an abbreviated adaptation of *American Council on Education Psychological Examination for High School Students*, 1940 Edition; 3 scores: quantitative, linguistic, total; self-marking; Forms A ('47, 4 pages), B ('55, 4 pages); manual, third edition ('67, 10 pages); $5.95 per 25 tests; 40¢ per manual; $1.25 per specimen set; postage extra; 15(25) minutes; Thelma Gwinn Thurstone (test) and L. L. Thurstone (test); Science Research Associates, Inc. *

REFERENCES

1. GRIGG, AUSTIN E., AND FILER, ROBERT J. "Norms for Scientists and Engineers on SRA Verbal Test." *J Indus Psychol* 3:52–3 Je '65. *
2. PHILLIPS, RICHARD MARTIN. *A Multiple Regression Study of Academic Prediction at Gallaudet College.* Doctor's thesis, University of Maryland (College Park, Md.), 1969. (*DAI* 30:5257A)

For reviews by W. D. Commins and Willis C. Schaefer, see 4:319.

[384]

*****Safran Culture Reduced Intelligence Test.** Grades 1–6, 4 and over; 1960–69; SCRIT; separate answer sheets must be used; Can 2¢ per mimeographed answer sheet, postage extra; C. Safran; the Author. *
a) [SCALE 1.] Grades 1–6; 1960–66; 1 form ('60, 42 pages); mimeographed manual ('62, reprint of *1* below); mimeographed instructions for group administration in grades 1–3 ['65, 4 pages]; mimeographed instructions for individual administration ['61, 1 page]; mimeographed norms ['65, 2 pages] for grades 1 and 3 only; 40¢ per test; 10¢ per norms; 10¢ per manual; (30–45) minutes.
b) [REVISED SCALE 2.] Grades 4 and over; 1960–69; 1 form ['69, c1960, 26 pages, consisting of 21 of the 60 items from the 1960 edition]; mimeographed instructions for administration ['69, 1 page]; mimeographed introduction ['69, 3 pages]; no norms; 30¢ per test; 15(20) minutes.

REFERENCES

1. See 6:497.
2. WEST, L. W., AND MACARTHUR, R. S. "An Evaluation of Selected Intelligence Tests for Two Samples of Metis and Indian Children." *Alberta J Ed Res* 10:17–27 Mr '64. * (*PA* 39:12328)

3. Frost, Barry P. "Intelligence, Manifest Anxiety and Scholastic Achievement." *Alberta J Ed Res* 11:167–75 S '65. * (*PA* 40:1948)
4. MacArthur, R. S. "Assessing Intellectual Potential of Native Canadian Pupils: A Summary." *Alberta J Ed Res* 14:115–22 Je '68. * (*PA* 44:4170)
5. MacArthur, Russell. "Some Differential Abilities of Northern Canadian Native Youth." *Int J Psychol* 3(1):43–50 '68. *
6. Rattan, M. S., and MacArthur, R. S. "Longitudinal Prediction of School Achievement for Metis and Eskimo Pupils." *Alberta J Ed Res* 14:37–41 Mr '68. * (*PA* 44:4249)
7. Solis, Miguela M. "A Pilot Study of the SCRIT in the Philippines." *Alberta Psychologist* 8(4):8–31 Ja '68. *

Lee J. Cronbach, *Vida Jacks Professor of Education, Stanford University, Stanford, California.*

SCRIT is in the figure analogies or figure series tradition. The 1969 revision consists of 21 items, each a brightly colored display of colored squares, circles, triangles, and other symbols. The examinee must induce a rule or pattern and select the figure, from 4 to 6 alternatives, that completes the pattern. Directions are somewhat complex, but the author expects the child to learn the rules of the game from the relatively easy items that begin the test. This revision is derived from a 60-item scale for grades 4–6, produced in 1960. A 36-item scale for the primary grades is still current.

SCRIT is in preliminary form and cannot be judged by the standards for a published test. Only bits and pieces of technical information are provided. The test should be regarded only as a set of items for possible use in research until norms and systematic information on validity are provided. A K-R 20 reliability of .76 (for sixth graders) indicates that SCRIT will function as a unit in a battery of tests but cannot be the sole basis for decisions.

SCRIT has been used in a number of studies in Alberta. These, in addition to the author's studies, provide scattered correlations of the 1960 forms with other measures. MacArthur finds SCRIT the near equal of *Progressive Matrices,* Lorge-Thorndike nonverbal sections, and a Cattell test, with respect to loading on a *g* factor. Safran reports correlations with teachers' marks of .43 to .78 for samples of unknown size and character. Apart from this the evidence is what one would expect for a short, internally consistent test with nonverbal displays that make strong demands on verbal mediation.

It is pointless to talk about "culture reduced" tests. Attending, encoding, and information-processing abilities, as well as the attitudes that go into successful test performance, are constructed through the child's interaction with his culture. The school psychologist should welcome tests that require little facility in any particular language. Such a test should not be rendered misleading by suggesting that it measures an inherited quality. Nor should psychologists abandon realism by arguing that on a truly valid test children from every subculture or Indian tribe will do equally well. Some cultures develop the skills and habits that make one capable at verbal reasoning about visual patterns, and some handicap the child in this regard. On the other hand, if there is any clearly intellectual task on which a disadvantaged minority has scores like those for the cultural majority, the school should strive to get equal educational results for those minority children.

Safran and MacArthur wisely emphasize that learning on a task like this takes place even in the few moments of the test itself. This thought should be pursued to its logical conclusion. The child who quickly gains insight into the task is exhibiting an easily-tapped readiness that is of undoubted significance. Perhaps many others could, by spending two weeks on practice exercises, greatly improve their scores and so earn a higher ranking in the group. The burden of proof is on those who contend that status at the beginning of the training period is a better index of educability than is performance at the end.

To defend a mental test simply on the ground that it manifestly requires reasoning and self-criticism is to evade the issue of relevance. A high score indicates a well-tuned mind, and if high-scoring children do poorly in school the school program is at fault. But what school program would be well suited to the child who scores high on SCRIT, Matrices, and similar tasks, while scoring at or below average on direct verbal tests? Until an investigator discovers the answer to this, and describes the successful instructional method so clearly that it can be used as a model, his test is of little use in education. Pointed questions are to be asked also about the child whose verbal reasoning is superior but whose SCRIT score is not. For some reason this child's intellectual skills are unbalanced, and a method of repairing the deficiency needs to be discovered. Predicting success in an established program is not a significant use for tests in education. When a society intends to educate everyone and can afford it, the educator has to plan alternative programs or instructional strategies, and tests have to have demonstrated relevance to the choice among the alternatives. This sort of relevance has never been demonstrated for group nonverbal tests. After half a century, such tests are still in the category of "promising."

[385]

*Scholastic Mental Ability Test. Grades kgn–1, 2–3, 4–5, 6–8; 1953–67; SMAT; various titles used by publisher; 1 form; 4 levels; statistical data ['62, 1 page] for grades 2–8; $5.95 per 35 tests, postage extra; 50¢ per specimen set of any one level, cash orders only; Oliver F. Anderhalter; Scholastic Testing Service, Inc. *
a) PRE-PRIMARY. Grades kgn–1; 1954–55; Form A ('55, 14 pages, identical to test copyrighted in 1954 except for format); revised manual ('55, 5 pages); no data on reliability and validity; (25–35) minutes.
b) PRIMARY. Grades 2–3; 1953–62; Form O ('61, 12 pages); manual ('62, 11 pages) with 1963 norms; (40–50) minutes.
c) ELEMENTARY. Grades 4–5; 1954–62; Form O ('61, 14 pages); manual ('62, 10 pages) with 1963 norms; separate answer sheets (Digitek) may be used; $5 per 50 answer sheets; $1.50 per school scoring kit; scoring service, 20¢ and over per test; (40–50) minutes.
d) ADVANCED. Grades 6–8; 1955–67; Form O ('61, 12 pages); 2 editions; prices same as for c; (40–50) minutes.
  1) *Digitek Edition.* 1955–67; manual ('67, 17 pages); separate answer sheets (Digitek) must be used.
  2) *IBM 1230 Edition.* 1955–66; manual ('66, 13 pages); separate answer sheets (IBM 1230) must be used.

For reviews by Walter N. Durost and Alexander G. Wesman of earlier editions, see 5:380.

[386]

*Schubert General Ability Battery. Grades 12–16 and adults; 1946–65; SGAB; 5 scores: vocabulary, analogies, arithmetic problems, syllogisms, total; 1 form ('65, 13 pages, identical with test copyrighted in 1946 except for revision of 4 items and omission of 3 items); manual ('65, 24 pages, identical with manual published in 1953 except for revised analogies norms for high school senior boys); 30¢ per test; $2 per manual; $3 per specimen set; postage extra; 16(25) or 32(40) minutes; Herman J. P. Schubert and Daniel S. P. Schubert (test); Herman J. P. Schubert. *

REFERENCE
1. NEIDT, CHARLES O., AND DREBUS, RICHARD W. "Characteristics Associated With the Creativity of Research Scientists in an Industrial Setting." *J Indus Psychol* 2:102–12 D '64. * (PA 40:11550)

For a review by William B. Schrader, see 5:382.

[387]

*Short Form Test of Academic Aptitude. Grades 1.5–2, 3–4, 5–6, 7–9, 9–12; 1936–70; SFTAA; revision of still-in-print *California Test of Mental Maturity;* 3 scores: language, nonlanguage, total; 1 form; 5 levels; preliminary interpretation guide ('70, 48 pages); technical bulletin ('70, 39 pages); individual record sheet ['70, 1 page]; optional tape recorded directions (3¾ ips) available for levels 2–5; no data on validity; separate answer sheets (CompuScan [NCS], Digitek, IBM 1230, Scoreze) must be used for b1, c, d, and e; $3 per 100 individual record sheets; $1.50 per guide; $2.50 per technical bulletin; $6.50 per tape recording of any one level; postage extra; $1.30 per specimen set of any one level, postpaid; Elizabeth T. Sullivan, Willis W. Clark, and Ernest W. Tiegs; CTB/McGraw-Hill. *
a) LEVEL 1. Grades 1.5–2; 2 editions; manual ('70, 47 pages); 31(40) minutes.
  1) *Hand Scorable Booklet.* 1 form ['70, 13 pages]; $6.50 per 35 tests.
  2) *CompuScan Machine Scorable Booklet.* 1 form ('70, 12 pages); $8.50 per 35 tests; scoring service, 27¢ and over per test.
b) LEVEL 2. Grades 3–4; 2 editions; 38(45) minutes.
  1) *Hand Scorable Booklet.* 1 form ('70, 13 pages); manual ('70, 45 pages); $6.50 per 35 tests; $2.50 per 50 CompuScan, Digitek, or IBM answer sheets; $2.50 per 25 Scoreze answer sheets; $1 per set of IBM hand scoring stencils; CompuScan scoring service, 22¢ and over per test.
  2) *CompuScan Machine Scorable Booklet.* 1 form ('70, 12 pages); manual ('70, 51 pages); prices same as for a2.
c) LEVEL 3. Grades 5–6; 1 form ('70, 12 pages); manual ('70, 45 pages); $7.50 per 35 tests; remaining prices same as for b1; 38(45) minutes.
d) LEVEL 4. Grades 7–9; 1 form ('70, 16 pages); manual ('70, 47 pages); $7.50 per 35 tests; remaining prices same as for b1; 38(45) minutes.
e) LEVEL 5. Grades 9–12; 1 form ('70, 15 pages); manual ('70, 47 pages); $7.50 per 35 tests; remaining prices same as for b1; 38(45) minutes.

[388]

★Spiral Nines, Sixth Edition. Job applicants with 7–8 years of education; 1960–65; SN; also called *Nines;* Forms A, B, ('65, 15 pages); no manual; preliminary norms for Form A ('66), Form B norms ('65); no data on reliability and validity; separate answer sheets must be used; R17.85 per 25 tests; 75c per single copy; 40c per 25 answer sheets; 40c per scoring stencil; postpaid within South Africa; 60(70) minutes; National Institute for Personnel Research. *

REFERENCES
1. MACARTHUR, R. S.; IRVINE, S. H.; AND BRIMBLE, A. R. *The Northern Rhodesia Mental Ability Survey 1963.* Rhodes-Livingstone Communication No. 27. Lusaka, Zambia: Rhodes-Livingstone Institute, 1964. Pp. ix, 100. *
2. IRVINE, S. H. "Factor Analysis of African Abilities and Attainments: Constructs Across Cultures." *Psychol B* 71(1): 20–32 Ja '69. * (PA 43:7553)

[389]

★Test of Adult College Aptitude. Evening college entrants; 1966; TACA; 1 form (2 pages); mimeographed manual (14 pages); preliminary norms; 10¢ per IBM 1230 test-answer sheet, postpaid; specimen set free; (45) minutes; King M. Wientge and Philip H. DuBois; TACA Development Fund. *

KENNETH D. HOPKINS, *Professor of Education and Director, Laboratory of Educational Research, University of Colorado, Boulder, Colorado.*

PURPOSE. TACA has been designed to be a "brief measure of the learning potential of the adult who is considering entering a program of continuing education." It is to be used to obtain "an objective index of learning capacity," needed to advise prospective adult students.

TEST DEVELOPMENT AND DESIGN. TACA grew out of the authors' previous research pertaining to predicting the achievement (GPA) of adult students at Washington University. Part 1 consists of 22 biographical questions selected from a pool of "55 items of non-threatening nature ....on the basis of their contribution to the prediction of course grade." Part 2 contains 54 items (42 verbal and 12 numerical) that were selected from a pool of 100 items on the basis of a "difficulty analysis." All require the selection of the dissimilar option. The rationale for selecting the items on a difficulty rather than a discrimination criterion is unexplained.

The test is contained on both sides of a specially printed IBM 1230 form which serves as both booklet and answer sheet. The directions for administering and taking the test are both simple and straightforward but no directions are given regarding guessing. The simplicity of the test and the ease with which it can be administered and scored are appealing features. The 45 minutes for completion of the test is said to be adequate although no supporting data are provided on this point.

NORMS. "Preliminary norms" (percentile ranks) are based on a group described only as "329 students enrolled in....the evening division of Washington University." No information regarding age, sex, previous education or occupation are given, hence this reference group is so amorphous that it is little, if any, better than none at all. A "representative" norm group cannot be reasonably expected for such a new test, but the failure to describe the available sample on which the norms are based can be criticized —particularly when this information is a portion of the biographical items contained in Part 1 of the TACA!

RELIABILITY. The K-R 20 reliability estimates given for Part 2 of TACA for three samples are very high (.95–.96). No information is given on the mean number of items attempted, hence the influence of speed and guessing probably contributes to some unknown extent to these high values. It is this reviewer's opinion that although the time limits appear ample, the tendency of several examinees not to attempt several items (no directions are given regarding guessing) probably resulted in considerably inflated K-R 20 estimates.

No reliability information is given for Part 1: "since the material is heterogeneous, an internal measure of reliability is not appropriate."

Part 1 reliability is no doubt very high, yet Parts 1 and 2 correlate only meagerly (.29, .25, .17). The correlation between true scores on the two parts using the authors' data is estimated to be only .32, hardly a satisfactory relationship for justifying the combining of scores in Parts 1 and 2 into a single score. (Norms are given only for the total TACA score.)

The reliability data presented do not directly address the consistency of TACA *total* scores, the type of reliability information most important for the user. In addition, it is not clear from the manual whether or not the 249 students used for the item selection were a part of the 386 on whom the reliability estimates are based; if so, the estimates would be considerably and spuriously inflated. Standard errors of measurement are not given and cannot be estimated readily since a reliability estimate for total score is not provided.

VALIDITY. It is axiomatic that the validity of a test must always be viewed in relation to its function. The authors would be much less vulnerable to criticism if they purported solely a prognostic function for the test. But as a measure of "learning capacity," the TACA must be evaluated in terms of construct validity considerations (which of course subsumes predictive relationships). From a predictive standpoint, the TACA functioned reasonably satisfactorily (at least in a relative sense) for three samples of 100–150 students (r's of .28–.36 for single courses; r's of .38–.54 with cumulative GPA). It would appear, however, that since both parts are probably quite reliable and yet the entire correlation between them is low, a multiple regression approach could have meaningfully increased the validity coefficients.

As a measure of "learning potential," however, the TACA is grossly inadequate. A logical study of the items (vocabulary and arithmetic) suggests that they measure academic achievement far more than aptitude. But the most serious defect is the absence of any underlying rationale for "scoring" of biographical information (as "number right") and combining this "score" in an undifferentiated fashion with the score on Part 2. How can one justify (in terms of construct validity) the fact that an examinee's "learning potential," or "college aptitude" is 20 points (2σ!) less because he happens to be: a 24-year-old (not older), unmarried clerk with no dependents, who graduated below the top quarter in his high school class, who has

Test of Adult College Aptitude

less than 30 college hours, is taking the course at his employer's request, who says grades reflect his ability only most of the time (but not always), is not a member of any career organization or community group, who does not attend church weekly, is not a home owner, has attended only one art exhibit in the past year, rates himself as only an average reader, has not read more than 5 nonfiction books in the past year, and owns less than 50 books.

Since the test interpretation as normed is made from the sum of the two part scores, it is misleading to call TACA an aptitude test. Its prognostic function is, of course, another matter.

SUMMARY. The TACA is a test in an embryonic stage. Fragmentary norms are based on a group of unknown characteristics. The TACA appears to have satisfactory reliability although an undisclosed portion of this is probably the result of reliability response styles on which there are wide and reliable individual differences. The TACA may have promised a quick convenient *predictive* measure of GPA in adult education, but, in its present form, it appears to have little promise of attaining its purported objective as a measure of learning potential. The problems cited above lead to the conclusion that, while the test has merit from an administrative viewpoint, whether or not it is a usable tool for the counselor has not been demonstrated. With the present version, users of the test must be able and willing to develop their own norms, reliability and validity data.

[390]

★**Test of Perceptual Organization.** Ages 12 and over; 1967–69; TPO; formerly called *Test of Abstract Reasoning;* 1 form ('69, 3 pages) ; manual ('69, 12 pages) ; $6.50 per 25 tests; 50¢ per scoring stencil; $3 per manual; $3.75 per specimen set; cash orders postpaid; 10(15) minutes; William T. Martin; Psychologists and Educators Press. *

REFERENCE

1. MARTIN, WILLIAM T. "Analysis of the Abstracting Function in Reasoning Using an Experimental Test." *Psychol Rep* 21:593–8 O '67. * (PA 42:4815)

[391]

*****Tests of General Ability: Inter-American Series.** Preschool, grades kgn–1.5, 2–3, 4–6, 7–9, 10–13.5; 1961–67; TGA; revision of still-in-print *Tests of General Ability: Cooperative Inter-American Tests;* a series of parallel tests and manuals in English and Spanish; 6 levels; series manual ('67, 99 pages) ; series technical report ('67, 70 pages) ; tentative norms, publisher recommends use of local norms; $1 per manual; $1 per technical report; postage extra; 50¢ per specimen set of any one level except preschool, postpaid; Herschel T. Manuel; Guidance Testing Associates. *

a) PRESCHOOL LEVEL, EXPERIMENTAL EDITION. Ages 4–5;

1966–67; 3 scores: verbal-numerical, nonverbal, total; individual; 1 form ('66, 100 cards) ; English, Spanish, directions ('66, 12 pages) ; $5 per set of cards, English, Spanish directions, and record sheet; $4 per 100 record sheets; (40–50) minutes in 2 sessions.

b) LEVEL 1—PRIMARY. Grades kgn–1.5; 1962–67; 3 scores same as in *a;* 2 editions; 2 forms; pretest ['64, 4 pages] for use in teaching testing procedures to immature children; 3¢ per pretest.

1) *Regular Edition.* English Forms CE, DE, ('62, 11 pages) ; Spanish Forms CEs, DEs, ('62, 11 pages) ; English, Spanish, directions ['66, 11 pages] ; $1.40 per 10 tests; (50–60) minutes in 2 sessions.

2) *Short Form.* English Forms CE-A, DE-A, ('63, 7 pages) ; Spanish Forms CEs-A, DEs-A, ('65, 7 pages) ; English, Spanish, directions ['66, 8 pages] ; $1.20 per 10 tests; (40–50) minutes in 2 sessions.

c) LEVEL 2—PRIMARY. Grades 2–3; 1964–67; 3 scores same as in *a;* English Forms CE, DE, ('64, 12 pages) ; Spanish Forms CEs, DEs, ('65, 12 pages) ; English, Spanish, directions ['66, 11 pages] ; $1.40 per 10 tests; (45–50) minutes.

d) LEVEL 3—ELEMENTARY. Grades 4–6; 1961–67; 4 scores: verbal, nonverbal, numerical, total; English Forms CE ('61, 15 pages), DE ('62, 15 pages) ; Spanish Forms CEs, DEs, ('62, 15 pages) ; English, Spanish, combined directions ['66, 7–8 pages] for Levels 3–5; separate answer sheets (IBM 805, IBM 1230) must be used for Levels 3–5; $1.60 per 10 tests; $5 per 100 answer sheets; 30¢ per IBM 805 scoring stencil; 15¢ per IBM 1230 scoring stencil; 52(65) minutes.

e) LEVEL 4—INTERMEDIATE. Grades 7–9; 1962–67; 4 scores same as in *d;* English Forms CE, DE, ('62, 15 pages) ; Spanish Forms CEs, DEs, ('62, 15 pages) ; remaining details same as for Level 3.

f) LEVEL 5—ADVANCED. Grades 10–13.5; 1962–67; 4 scores same as in *d;* English Forms CE, DE, ('62, 15 pages) ; Spanish Forms CEs, DEs, ('62, 15 pages) ; remaining details same as for Level 3.

REFERENCES

1–8. See 4:325.
9. MANUEL, HERSCHEL T. *The Preparation and Evaluation of Inter-Language Testing Materials.* Unpublished report to the U.S. Office of Education, Cooperative Research Project No. 681, University of Texas, 1963. Pp. vii, 112. * (ERIC ED 001 702)
10. MANUEL, HERSCHEL T. *Development of Inter-American Test Materials.* Unpublished report to the U.S. Office of Education, Cooperative Research Project No. 2621, University of Texas, December 1966. Pp. vii, 99. * (ERIC ED 010 670)

RUSSEL F. GREEN, *Research Consultant in Psychology and Education, Henrietta, New York.*

The objective of the author in preparing this test is a worthy one: to produce a new series of tests that will be parallel English and Spanish editions and which will yield "comparable" results when the Spanish edition is administered to Spanish-speaking people and the English edition is administered to English-speaking people. More narrowly, the objective was to select test items "common to the two cultures" and "of similar difficulty." The importance of the series lies primarily in the effort to produce parallel English and Spanish forms. This review is limited to an evaluation of this effort.

The tone of the author's writing is sincere, reasonable, and insightful. He is careful to write in language that persons with little background in testing should be able to understand. The author includes cautions concerning the interpretability of the test scores and especially the comparability of the scores obtained from the parallel English and Spanish versions.

Every item presented in one language is also presented in the parallel form of the other language. The tests consist of materials that are commonly found in tests of general ability. The language seems appropriate.

It is, of course, a difficult task to make a Spanish form acceptable to all Spanish-speaking subcultures. The solution adopted was to use rather formal Spanish that would be recognized as correct everywhere and to avoid local idioms or area usages. The result is that in almost every locality some items in the tests will sound a little strange to the examinee. This is unavoidable.

Many estimates of reliability are reported. The alternate-form reliabilities for the English total score range from .72 to .90 (median .80) and for the Spanish total score from .59 to .91 (median .88). Subtest reliabilities are, of course, somewhat lower. The verbal scores are a little more reliable than the nonverbal scores. This is a typical outcome for test materials of these kinds.

Quite a number of concurrent validity estimates are reported. These range from quite low to an occasional quite high correlation. Correlations with academic achievement, especially in reading, appear to average over .60 which seems quite good, especially in view of the apparently modest reliability of the tests.

No evidence is presented in the manuals that the parallel items are of equal difficulty in the two cultural settings. Many of them almost surely are not; nor is evidence presented that the distribution of difficulties of items is the same. The author states, "The Spanish items were administered to Spanish speaking children and the English items to English speaking children." The results were then compared for relative difficulty. Unfortunately, the groups to which the items were administered are not specified; the reader is expected to assume that the groups were equivalent in natural endowment and environmental advantages and that they would, therefore, have equivalent mastery of their native language and equivalent developmental histories such that the comparison of "relative difficulty" was valid. These are troublesome assumptions; to make them about undescribed samples of children seems too much of an act of faith to ask of potential users. It seems highly likely that the items of the parallel forms are not parallel in difficulty; appropriate populations probably were not used. Defining such a Spanish-speaking population would be virtually impossible. Even if this could be done, inherent differences in the two languages would make it all but impossible to achieve equal difficulties of all items. There are many concepts that are more easily expressed in one language than in the other. The number of words needed to express many concepts differs. To some degree the conceptual worlds of the two language groups are different. To evolve truly parallel forms in the two languages would involve a whole series of progressive approximations from appropriate samples to be successful.

There are three tables presented (one being relevant to the *Tests of General Ability*) from which one could easily get the impression that *scores* on parallel English and Spanish forms were equivalent. The technical manual shows that the alternate forms in English and in Spanish have closely equivalent scores. By presenting both the English forms and the Spanish forms comparisons in the same table one can easily get the impression that the English and Spanish scores presented are also equivalent to each other. The fact that this is not so (except for carefully selected subsets of undefined students) can be verified by comparing the appropriate sections of this table with four other such tables. The comparison makes it clear that numerically similar scores derived from parallel forms from the two language groups are not equivalent.

In an effort to provide useful norms, the test developers have "equated" the *Tests of General Ability* with a large number of other tests. All this results in a rather confusing variety of "norms" from which it is hoped that a potential user can find a set which will suit his purpose. Much of this "equating" was done on small undefined samples and hence is of doubtful value. However, a few sets of the equivalents are probably quite useful, such as those involving Project Talent Tests and the *College Board Scholastic Aptitude Test*.

Tentative within-grade norms for an "island-wide administration of tests in Puerto Rico" are presented for "a limited sampling of pupils

Tests of General Ability

in the public schools." Even if these norms are adequate for Puerto Rico, they still would be of limited usefulness to other Spanish-speaking groups because of varying cultural emphasis in such areas as language development and usage. Good norms are not available for any Spanish-speaking area.

So this reviewer must close on a note of regret. The unique objectives have not been met. The tests are not adequate for cross-cultural research or comparisons. For that we must wait for a much more definitive test development and normative effort.

RICHARD E. SCHUTZ, *Director, Southwest Regional Laboratory for Educational Research and Development, Los Alamitos, California.*

The history of these tests is unique in the annals of American testing. From an individual perspective, the history reflects the personal pioneer efforts of a persevering author. From a societal perspective, the history reflects the attitude of American society toward ethnic minorities which, in retrospect, appears clearly tokenistic, but which was unrecognized as such at the time of the test's development.

The test development began in Puerto Rico in the early 1940's, sponsored by the Committee on Modern Languages of the American Council on Education, as a subordinate objective of an effort designed to teach English as a second language. The purpose was to develop measuring instruments "which will yield comparable results in....English and Spanish," to provide "comparable measures of ability....in the bilingual situation." While current linguistic knowledge makes it clear that this objective is both simplistic and chauvinistic, it remains the purpose of the tests in their present form.

The tests were published by the Educational Testing Service from 1950–1959 as the Cooperative Inter-American Tests. In 1959, three interrelated events stimulated further development activity. ETS discontinued distribution of the tests. A new nonprofit corporation was established in Texas by Herschel Manuel "specifically to assume responsibility for the tests." The U.S. Office of Education awarded a research contract to be directed by Manuel to the University of Texas to "provide means now lacking or imperfectly developed for comparing the abilities and educational achievements of different languages and cultures."

The spirit of both the times and the test series is reflected in the objectives of the research project:

(1) the improvement of international cooperation and communication in educational research and in the educative process; (2) provision of comparable measures of ability and achievement in the bilingual situation—for example, when a school is educating children of different home languages or when the ability of the same person in two languages needs to be estimated; (3) an increase of the supply of useful measuring instruments in each of the languages. * The use of the tests for communication across linguistic barriers and for comparison of ability in different languages will be greatly limited unless the Spanish tests are generally useful and widely used with Spanish-speaking children and the English tests with English-speaking children.

One result of the research effort was a revision and refinement of the 1950 series tests into Levels 1–5. USOE research support from 1964–1966 produced the Preschool Level tests and a large number of correlational analyses based on administration of various forms of the series with other commonly used test series. Although the examinee samples for these analyses are not well defined, the concurrently administered tests are all in English and the samples all appear to be from the United States. The objective of "international cooperation and communication" clearly lost a good deal in the translation from research proposal to project results.

While the history of the series is pertinent to the present prospective user, he is necessarily concerned with its current characteristics. These as well as the history are documented accurately and fairly in the manual and technical report, which are also relevant to the companion reading test in the Inter-American Series. A prime characteristic of each series, fully emphasized in the documentation, is that the tests are essentially unnormed. "The Inter-American Tests are recommended for use primarily with regional or local norms to be prepared by those who use the tests." A few norm tables are presented, and equivalent scores are given for several well known and well normed tests. However, the size and nature of the samples involved are such that the user would be foolhardy to disregard the publisher's advice on this matter. A user should be prepared to construct his own norms if he plans to use this series.

The obvious distinctive characteristic of the series is that forms are available in Spanish. This is true of both test booklets and directions for administration. At the Preschool Level through Level 2, this characteristic is a moot distinction for the test booklets, since all items are nonverbal. At the upper levels, the verbal items are Spanish-English translations. At all levels, the items and subtests have familiar analogs with other available tests; the series is neither more or less unique nor more or less culturally influenced than competing series.

Were any competing test publisher interested in converting an available English general ability test to Spanish, it would be possible to quickly generate a Spanish translation that would create a series with all of the distinguishing features of the Inter-American Series. This is not to suggest that any publisher should do such a translation. Quite the contrary, since the limitations of such a series would be patently obvious. Although the Inter-American Series test development has quite different historical antecedents, it incorporates the same patent limitations, even though the series was generated "the hard way."

The Spanish-speaking child in an English-speaking country unquestionably poses difficult and complex policy, pedagogic, and psychometric problems which include but are not restricted to those relevant to the English-speaking child. These problems, however, are likely to be obscured rather than ameliorated by use of the Spanish forms of the Inter-American Series. That is, test interpretations which treat the resulting scores in the same manner that one would treat the scores from an English mental ability test will almost certainly detract from rather than contribute to the enhancement of the potential of the examinee. Ethnic minority leaders who have in general opposed mental ability tests for ideologic rather than psychometric reasons should not be duped by the ostensible linguistic relevance of the series. Basically, the Spanish tests share the ideologic deficiencies reputed in English mental ability tests and add some severe psychometric limitations.

Regretfully, no stronger endorsement can be given either for the use of the Spanish forms of the tests in Spanish-speaking contexts or for the use of the English forms in either English-speaking or Spanish-speaking contexts. The goal of solving inter-American communication problems through the alchemy of comparable ability tests is a fanciful and outmoded ideal. The Inter-American Series tests are of and for a bygone era.

For reviews by Raleigh M. Drake and Walter N. Durost of the earlier edition, see 4:325.

[392]

*****Thurstone Test of Mental Alertness.** Grades 9-12 and adults; 1943–68; TTMA; abbreviated adaptation of *American Council on Education Psychological Examination for High School Students,* 1940 Edition; for a shorter adaptation of this test, see *SRA Verbal Form;* 3 scores: quantitative, linguistic, total; Forms A ('52), B ('53), (9 pages, consumable booklet replacing original separate answer sheet edition); manual ('68, 16 pages); $5.95 per 25 tests; 40¢ per manual; $1.25 per specimen set; postage extra; 20(25) minutes; Thelma Gwinn Thurstone and L. L. Thurstone; Science Research Associates, Inc. *

REFERENCES

1-3. See 4:326.
4. PETERSON, FLOYD E. "Identification of Sub-Groups for Test Validation Research." *J Indus Psychol* 2:98–101 D '64. * (*PA* 40:10636)
5. VIVERS, BILLY B. *A Study of the Relationship Between Applicants Scores on the Thurstone Tests of Mental Alertness and the Allport, Vernon, Lindzey Study of Values and Subsequent Job Success as Psychiatric Aids.* Master's thesis, Kansas State College (Pittsburg, Kan.), 1965.
6. BENTZ, V. JON. Chap. 3, "The Sears Experience in the Investigation, Description and Prediction of Executive Behavior," pp. 59–152. In *Predicting Managerial Success.* Edited by John A. Myers, Jr. Ann Arbor, Mich.: Foundation for Research on Human Behavior, April 1968. Pp. v, 173. *
7. WHEELER, RICHARD WADE. *A Study of the Relationship Between Selected Interviewer Variables and the Interpretation of Interview Information.* Doctor's thesis, University of Houston (Houston, Tex.), 1969. (*DAI* 30:425B)

ROBERT D. NORTH, *Associate Director, Professional Examinations Division, The Psychological Corporation, New York, New York.*

Except for the addition of some new research and normative data to the manual, this test remains essentially unchanged from the 1952–53 edition. Each form of the test consists of 126 items of four types, arranged spirally and in order of difficulty. The seven items in each spiral segment occur in the following sequence: two same-opposites, one arithmetic reasoning (word-arithmetic problem), two definitions, and two number series. Although labelled a "test of mental alertness," it is actually a test of verbal and mathematical abilities.

Like its parent instrument, the time-honored *American Council on Education Psychological Examination,* this test yields separate linguistic (L) and quantitative (Q) scores, but unlike the ACE, the spiral arrangement of the items prevents separate timing of the sets of items that yield these scores. As a result, the interdependence of the two types of scores tends to be increased, since a student's hang-up on items of one type might keep him from progressing to some of the items of the other types that he could answer readily. Persistent students do not always heed the part of the directions stating: "Do not spend too much time on a single question."

The items are concise and are printed in easily readable type. In the case of the number series items—as well as the definition items, which call for identification of the correct response solely by its initial letter—traditional arguments about ambiguity or the justification of the keyed responses may be advanced.

Evidently the test is now going through a metamorphosis from the former reusable booklet style with "self-scoring" answer pads to a consumable booklet with an answer sheet, according to information given in the 1970 SRA catalog. The test booklets submitted for this review have a hybrid format, with the progressively narrowing columns of the step-down design being printed on full pages, flush right.

The percentile norms for high school students are based on the scores of 977 ninth grade students and 545 twelfth grade students "drawn in 1959 from four coeducational high schools representing diverse geographical areas of the country." Interpolated norms for the tenth and eleventh grades are also given. For a contemporary test of a major publisher, these school norms are scant.

Percentile norms are also presented for 15 categories of employees and job applicants, with the sizes of the norm groups ranging from 128 for secretaries to 4,447 for "Male Applicants with H.S. Education." The only information given about these norm groups is that they "are thought to be a cross section of most TMA takers." The publisher's advice that local norms should be developed for interpreting the test results might well be heeded.

Data given in the manual, based on a counterbalanced administration of the two forms to 202 twelfth graders in a 1962 study, indicate that Form A is somewhat easier than Form B, with the difference amounting to 3.8 total raw score points at the mean. This evidence should be taken into consideration in retesting situations, since a difference of about that magnitude corresponds to more than 10 percentile points in the 20–80 range of the twelfth grade norms. Correlations of equivalence between the two forms for the same 202 cases are reported as .79 for the L score, .81 for the Q score, and .85 for the total score.

Test-retest reliability coefficients over a 30-day interval for four groups of 55 to 89 twelfth grade students in two schools range from .84 to .96 for the part scores, and from .92 to .95 for the total score. As pointed out in the manual, the memory effect involved in retesting with the same form after 30 days probably inflates these coefficients. Making some allowance for this effect, and also for the small sizes of the groups tested, the reviewer judges that the reliabilities nevertheless approach those of other current mental ability tests of similar length.

For student groups in the ninth and twelfth grades in one to four schools, the total scores have correlations of .40 to .77 (median, .64) with grade-point averages, .83 to .85 with *Iowa Tests of Educational Development* composite scores, and .71 to .73 with *SRA High School Placement Test* composite scores. These correlations are fairly typical of those yielded by creditable tests of verbal and mathematical abilities. No evidence is given of any differential validity for the L and Q scores for student groups.

At the adult level in the industrial area, correlations with the "verbal subtest of the *Wechsler Adult Intelligence Scale*" are given as .60 for the L score, .18 for the Q score, and .62 for the total score. Since means and standard deviations for this sample of 200 cases, with an age range of 22 to 70, are not reported, these correlations cannot be interpreted without ambiguity.

Some evidence of the validity of the test for certain business and industrial personnel uses is given in the form of correlations with supervisors' ratings and mean score differences between groups of employees rated "good" and "poor." The samples consist of 27 to 404 individuals in managerial, supervisory, sales, clerical, and bank-teller positions. Some of the correlations are impressive—ranging up to .63. Nevertheless, since job-success criteria are likely to vary greatly from one place of employment to another, the test user would be well advised to follow the manual's admonition to base his interpretation of the scores on his cumulative experience with the instrument.

On the whole, the *Thurstone Test of Mental Alertness* warrants consideration for use with high school students, employment applicants, or employees when a relatively quick measure of verbal and numerical abilities in combination is desired. Careful consideration should be given to the limitations of the normative and validity data, however, in choosing this test over such others as the *Cooperative School and College Ability Tests,* the *SRA Tests of Educational*

Ability, or the Verbal and Numerical subtests of the *Differential Aptitude Tests.*

For a review by Joshua A. Fishman, see 5:391; for reviews by Anne Anastasi and Emily T. Burr of an earlier edition, see 3:265.

[393]
★**The Undergraduate Record Examinations: Aptitude Test.** Grades 15–16; 1969–70; 2 scores: verbal, quantitative; Forms K-RUR1 ('69, 23 pages), RUR2 ('69, 22 pages); descriptive booklet ('70, 20 pages); for more complete information, see 671; 90(110) minutes; Educational Testing Service. *

For reviews of the testing program, see 671 (2 reviews).

[394]
The Verbal Power Test of Concept Equivalence. Ages 14 and over; 1959–63; VPTCE; Forms A, B, ('59, 2 pages) on a single sheet; manual ('63, 12 pages); $6 per set of 25 tests, key, and manual; $1.50 per manual; postpaid; (10–15) minutes; E. Francesco; Western Psychological Services. *

REFERENCES
1–3. See 6:508.

ERWIN K. TAYLOR, *President, Personnel Research and Development Corporation, Cleveland, Ohio.*

The title *Verbal Power Test of Concept Equivalence* is a rather grandiose name for what turns out to be a test of synonyms. The manual, published in 1963, provides little information with respect to the nature or philosophy of item construction; also, there are no data provided with respect to the kind of item analysis performed or the basis of item selection.

The manual stipulates that the test "requires fourth grade reading ability." While it is true that only four-letter words are used, many of them are so archaic and arcane as to make this statement patently ridiculous. Form A, for example, contains such terms as "ovum," "elan," "limn," "dyad," "cote," and "rive." To these Form B adds additionally such terms as "abet," "opus," "kris," "lode," "quay," "gaol," and others. It would strain fourth grade level readers to recognize that a "dirk" is equivalent to a "kris." One might even quarrel with some of the keying, such as giving "shed" and "emit" the same meaning. Similarly, "soar" and "rise" are keyed as synonyms, as are "norm" and "mode." Even "dear" and "high" are considered synonyms, as are "clay" and "mire." The correlation between the two forms of the test (printed on opposite sides of the same page) is quoted as .86 for a "slightly longer test form than the present forms." Unidentified "between-test product-moment coefficients of correlation for Forms A and B" range from .61 to .94.

All of the "validity" data presented in the manual consist of correlations between the VPTCE and other intelligence tests, mostly from the 200 adult prisoners in a mid-Atlantic state prison. Unidentified additional studies from a variety of sources quote correlations between the test and the WAIS as ranging from .34 to .68. In the opinion of this reviewer, the VPTCE incorporates a high degree of cultural bias and offers little to the potential user that is not already available in comparable tests that are more highly standardized and better constructed; for example, the *Quick Word Test,* the verbal portions of the *Personnel Tests for Industry,* or the verbal comprehension test from the *Employee Aptitude Survey.* All three are equally short and can be administered as power tests (with the requisite restandardization) if so desired.

The VPTCE manual makes the usual suggestion (which few users are in a position to follow) that they construct their own norms. The norms in the manual are based on 1,096 subjects in five different groups. Four of these are academic, consisting of two populations (sophomores and seniors, respectively) from an unidentified Ivy League university, a population of freshmen from a Southwestern school of education, and a group of Eastern high school seniors. The only nonacademic population is an unselected group of prisoners in an "East Central" prison. Thus, with all of the types of populations for which normative data are presented, it is likely that more comprehensive and more adequately standardized measures of intelligence would be already available—making the administration of this device even less valuable than it would otherwise be.

It is indeed difficult for this reviewer to imagine a situation in which he would find it desirable to use the VPTCE in preference to any of the above-mentioned tests or short verbal tests available.

[395]
★**Verbal Test (Adv.).** Ages 12 to 13–11; 1954–67; 4 tests; practice test [dates same as for tests, 2 pages] for each test; no data on validity; distribution restricted to directors of education; 7p per test; 2p per practice test; 8p per manual for any one test except *d*; postpaid within U.K.; 10(15) minutes for practice test; D. A. Pidgeon (*a*); published for National Foundation for Educational Research in England and Wales; Ginn & Co. Ltd. *

a) VERBAL TEST (ADV.) 1. 1954–55; 1 form ['54, 10 pages]; manual ('55, 10 pages); 50(60) minutes.
b) VERBAL TEST (ADV.) 3. 1958; 1 form ['58, 11 pages]; manual ('58, 9 pages); 45(55) minutes.
c) VERBAL TEST (ADV.) 4. 1960; 1 form ['60, 11 pages]; manual ('60, 9 pages); 45(55) minutes.
d) VERBAL TEST (ADV.) 5. 1962–67; 1 form ['62, 11 pages]; mimeographed directions for administration ['62, 8 pages]; provisional norms ['67]; directions and norms free on request from NFER; 50(60) minutes.

For reviews by J. S. Lawes and John Nisbet of Tests 1–4, see 6:510.

[396]

*Verbal Tests BC, CD, C, and D. Ages 8-0 to 10-6, 9-0 to 11-6, 9-6 to 12-0; 1953–66; 3 levels; 5p per test; 7p per manual for Test BC or CD, 8p per manual for Test C or D; postpaid within U.K.; published for the National Foundation for Educational Research in England and Wales; Ginn & Co. Ltd. *
a) VERBAL TEST BC. Ages 8-0 to 10-6; 1953–62; formerly called *Primary Verbal Test 1*; adaptation of *A.C.E.R. Junior A Test* and *A.C.E.R. Junior B Test*; 1 form ['53, 8 pages]; revised manual ('62, 8 pages); 30(40) minutes; D. A. Pidgeon.
b) VERBAL TESTS CD AND C. Ages 9-0 to 11-6; 1959–66; 2 forms; 35(45) minutes.
  1) *Verbal Test CD.* Ages 9-0 to 11-6; formerly called *Primary Verbal Test 2;* 1 form ['59, 8 pages]; manual ['59, 7 pages]; Valerie Land.
  2) *Verbal Test C.* Ages 9-4 to 11-0; formerly called *Primary Verbal Test 2G;* 1 form ['65, 8 pages]; manual ['66, 9 pages].
c) VERBAL TEST D. Ages 9-6 to 12-0; 1962; formerly called *Primary Verbal Test 3;* 1 form ['62, 8 pages]; manual ['62, 11 pages]; 40(50) minutes; T. Neville Postlethwaite.

For reviews by John Nisbet and F. W. Warburton of a, see 5:369.

[397]

*Verbal Tests EF and GH. Ages 11.0–13.5, 13.5–15.0; 1960–66; 2 levels; 5p per test; 7p per manual for either level; postpaid within U.K.; Valerie Land and Olive Wood (a); published for the National Foundation for Educational Research in England and Wales; Ginn & Co. Ltd. *
a) VERBAL TEST EF. Ages 11.0–13.5; 1960; formerly called *Secondary Verbal Test 1;* 1 form ['60, 8 pages]; manual ['60, 7 pages]; 40(45) minutes.
b) VERBAL TEST GH. Ages 13.5–15.0; 1962–66; formerly called *Secondary Verbal Test 2;* 1 form ['62, 8 pages]; manual ['66, 7 pages]; 45(50) minutes.

For a review by Stanley Nisbet of a, see 6:499.

[398]

*Verbal Tests 14–21 and 69. Ages 10–12; 1951–70; 9 tests (8 pages); new test published annually; practice test (2 pages, dates same as for test) for each test; no data on validity; distribution restricted to directors of education; 5p per test; 2p per practice test; 8p per manual for any one test except g2 and h; postpaid within U.K.; 10(15) minutes for practice test, 45(50) minutes for Tests 18–21, 50(55) minutes for Tests 14–17 and 69; published for the National Foundation for Educational Research in England and Wales; Ginn & Co. Ltd. *

Verbal Test (Adv.)

a) VERBAL TEST 14. 1963–64; forms 14A, 14B, ['63]; manual ('64, 10 pages) for each form.
b) VERBAL TEST 15. 1964–65; forms 15A, 15B, ['64]; manual ('65, 10 pages) for each form.
c) VERBAL TEST 16. 1965–66; forms 16A, 16B, ['65]; manual ('66, 10 pages) for each form.
d) VERBAL TEST 17. 1966–67; forms 17A, 17B, ['66]; manual ('67, 10 pages) for each form.
e) VERBAL TEST 18. 1967–68; forms 18A, 18B, ['67]; manual ('68, 11 pages) for each form.
f) VERBAL TEST 19. 1968–69; forms 19A, 19B, ['68]; manual ('69, 11 pages) for each form.
g) VERBAL TESTS 20 AND 69. 1969–70; 2 editions.
  1) *Verbal Test 20.* 1969–70; forms 20A, 20B, ['69]; manual ('70, 11 pages) for each form.
  2) *Verbal Test 69.* 1969; multiple choice version of form 20A; 1 form ['69]; mimeographed instructions '69, 7 pages); provisional norms ['69, 2 pages]; no data on reliability; separate answer sheets (Parnall) must be used; 4p per answer sheet; 10p per scoring stencil; instructions and norms free on request from NFER.
h) VERBAL TEST 21. 1970; 1 form ['70]; mimeographed instructions (7 pages); no data on reliability; no norms; instructions free on request from NFER.

REFERENCE

1. See 6:511.

DAVID A. WALKER, *Formerly Director, The Scottish Council for Research in Education, Edinburgh, Scotland.* [Review of Tests 13–20.]

This series of tests is designed mainly to aid education authorities in England and Wales in allocating pupils to appropriate courses of secondary education. Each of the tests follows the same general pattern, there being 100 items in sections of six to eight items, each section preceded by instructions and an example.

All items are of the objective type and the answer keys provided in the manuals give the acceptable responses. The sections are separated only by the new instructions and an example; they bear no heading but cover the usual field of vocabulary, classification, analogies, coding, mixed sentences, and reasoning.

The manual which accompanies each test gives full instructions on administration, marking, and transformation of raw scores to standardised scores. It also contains a brief description of the method by which each test was constructed and the basis of standardisation. It is noticeable that the wording of the manuals is almost identical throughout the series, apart from the necessary changes in answer keys, in standardisation data and in conversion tables. This permanence of construction is possibly a reflection of the satisfaction expressed by the authorities using the tests over the years and their unwillingness to contemplate any radical changes.

There are several points which should be

noted about the standardisation of these tests. The numbers used are substantial, usually exceeding 10,000 for each test, but they are drawn from selected areas and usually from ages 10-2 to 11-5. No indication is given of the method of selecting the areas, but it seems almost certain that these were the areas using the test for allocating pupils to secondary schools. Many of the pupils taking the tests were probably highly motivated to obtain high scores and gain admission to grammar schools. If the norms obtained from these pupils are used for pupils who are not so highly motivated, the resulting scores may well be depressed by several points.

A factor operating in the opposite direction is the steady improvement of scores in tests of this type that has been shown over the years,[1] so that the norms especially for the earlier tests require adjustment. The norms for those aged 11-6 to 12-0 are obtained by extrapolation. Finally, the norms are given for boys and girls taken together, although the manual points out that girls, on average, score about three points higher than boys. The recommendation in the manual is that in an allocation procedure the two sexes be considered independently of each other.

No validity coefficients are given, the reader being referred to Yates and Pidgeon's *Admission to Grammar Schools* for evidence to support the claim that the validity of verbal tests as predictors of success in the grammar school has been firmly established from empirical evidence in follow-up studies. This was without doubt a justifiable claim in the days when the grammar school was the chosen method of educating the abler children of England and Wales. The position is constantly changing, however, as the number of schools described as comprehensive increases. What function would be served by tests of this type if the system became fully comprehensive? There is evidence that in that situation tests of this kind are still satisfactory predictors of success in the examinations that must be passed before entry is gained to academic courses in universities and similar institutions. It may well be that these tests will continue to be used by administrators and teachers to enable them to advise pupils and their parents on the selection of courses of study in the secondary school.

[1] PILLINER, A. E. G.; SUTHERLAND, J.; AND TAYLOR, E. G. "Zero Error in Moray House Verbal Reasoning Tests." *Brit J Ed Psychol* 30:53–62 F '60. *

For a review by Arthur B. Royse of earlier tests, see 6:511.

[399]
★**WLW Culture Fair Inventory.** Job applicants; 1969; CFI; intelligence; 1 form (8 pages); preliminary manual (8 pages); reliability and validity data based upon earlier experimental forms; preliminary norms; $15 per set of 100 tests and manual, postpaid; specimen set not available; [30–45] minutes; Barbara O. Murray (test), Lynde C. Steckle (test), and Robert W. Henderson; William, Lynde & Williams. *

ARTHUR R. JENSEN, *Professor of Educational Psychology; and Research Psychologist, Institute of Human Learning; University of California, Berkeley, California.*

The *WLW Culture Fair Inventory* (CFI) is a nontimed, nonverbal test intended to eliminate verbal and other cultural effects. The 30 items comprising the test consist of figural materials involving logical-spatial relationships. There are five parts: (a) selection of the one figure in a set of five that is most different, (b) block counting, (c) selection of the fifth figure in a series, (d) paper form board-type items, (e) selection of a figure which completes a pattern (matrices). Each of these parts is preceded by printed instructions and two examples with the correct answers given.

Judging from inspection of the items and this reviewer's experience with a wide variety of psychometric tests, it is inferred that the CFI measures reasoning and spatial abilities, much the same abilities as are assessed by Cattell's *Culture Fair Intelligence Tests,* Raven's *Progressive Matrices,* and Domino's *D48 Test,* although the CFI appears to be more loaded on a spatial factor.

The test manual claims that the test should "be suitable for minority groups or 'hard-core' individuals in hiring situations." The test, however, appears to be too difficult for this population. The 50th percentile for college students is only 18 items correct (out of 30), and the median for Negro clerical workers is only 10 items correct; the 99th percentile for this group is only 20 items correct. It is this reviewer's prediction that culturally disadvantaged minority persons will average lower on this test, in relation to middle class whites, than on most other standard tests, especially verbal tests.

The test has at least three advantages: (a) it is "nonverbal" and eliminates or minimizes the influence of reading ability and formal education; (b) it presents a variety of figural subtests, so that its total score should not contain a factor specific to a particular form of figural test material such as Matrices; (c) it is untimed and is thus a power test, but this also may introduce personality factors into the score variance. (The reviewer found a correlation of −.45 between time taken on the *Progressive Matrices* and the extraversion scale of the *Eysenck Personality Inventory* when subjects had no time limit. The more extraverted subjects tend to get through faster or to give up sooner when the items increase in difficulty.) Raven's PM shares advantages *a* and *c*; Cattell's CFT shares advantages *a* and *b*.

Several criticisms can be made of the CFI: (*a*) Some of the items depend as much upon perceptual or visual acuity as much as upon reasoning ability. (*b*) The figural materials are not as clearly printed as those in the Cattell and Raven tests. (*c*) The test is too difficult for the general population, being more suited to college level persons. (*d*) There are no really easy items at the beginning of each subtest to permit the subject to catch on readily to what is required and to gain practice before he is confronted with the more difficult problems. The Cattell and Raven tests are superior in this respect.

Finally, the test manual is totally inadequate and makes it obvious that the test has been published and marketed much too prematurely. The manual contains virtually no helpful information. The "norms" of the CFI are based on 50 male and 50 female college students, and 24 Negro and 46 women applicants for clerical jobs in an insurance company! The intercorrelations among the five subtests are remarkably low, ranging from .29 to .55. No data are given concerning the test's reliability. Correlations with other intelligence tests are so low as to make one wonder what the CFI actually measures. Aside from these correlations suggesting very low concurrent validity, the manual gives no other evidence of the test's validity or usefulness.

In conclusion, there is no good reason to recommend this test in its present inadequate stage of development. Testers who are seeking a good nonverbal "culture fair" test of general intelligence are urged to consider Cattell's *Culture Fair Intelligence Tests* or Raven's *Progressive Matrices* (these tests come in different forms for various ages and populations). The construction of these alternative tests, the adequacy of their manuals, their normative data, and the research behind them are totally unmatched by the *WLW Culture Fair Inventory*.

JAMES E. KENNEDY, *Professor of Psychology, The University of Wisconsin, Madison, Wisconsin.*

This 30-item test, consisting of five varieties of pictorial problems, requires no writing and was designed for group administration with no time limit. The test manual does not say what the test purports to measure. Since most of the items were adapted from or modeled after items from standard intelligence tests, one can infer that it was probably intended to measure one or more aspects of nonverbal reasoning or intelligence.

The test was developed to meet the expressed need of industrial clients for "a culture fair test that would largely discount the influence of environment and education." Toward this end, the test is untimed and limited to nonverbal items which "most people have not encountered in their daily lives." It is said to be suitable for use with "minority groups or 'hard-core' individuals in hiring situations."

The test manual offers only a vague and clumsy description of how the test was developed. Using a sample of students in a small women's liberal arts college, some type of item analysis was performed on the nonverbal section of the WLW Mental Alertness Inventory, the *Culture Fair Intelligence Test,* and the *Chicago Non-Verbal Examination* as a basis for the selection of 70 items. In some fashion or other these 70 items were reduced to the 30 items comprising the current form of the test. Reference is made to adopting items from other tests as well, but there is no explanation. (The manual does not explain why the authors thought it advisable to use an item-analysis sample of college students to develop a test for "minority groups or 'hard-core' individuals.")

Norms are available on 50 male and 50 female college students and on 24 black and 46 white female applicants for entry clerical jobs at an insurance company. No further description of these groups, such as educational level, age, or socioeconomic status, is provided.

The manual also presents a hodgepodge of correlations between part scores on the *WLW Culture Fair Inventory* and part or whole scores on several other tests. Since the WLW scores used were based on the preliminary 70-item form of the test, these correlations have little

WLW Culture Fair Inventory

relevance for the test being reviewed. No reliability estimates of the test are reported.

The manual reports a median score of 10 for the black applicants and 13 for the white applicants on this test and a median score of 20 for the blacks and 24 for the whites on the *Wonderlic Personnel Test*. While information of this kind is meaningless without a discussion of the comparability of these groups on other dimensions, it would not appear that this purportedly culture fair test operates differently from the Wonderlic, which makes no claims about culture fairness.

In summary, this test is not based on any stated theoretical grounds, the operations followed in its development are obscure, its reliability has not been estimated, and its validity has not been demonstrated nor even considered in the manual. The assumption that elimination of the time and verbal factor would "largely discount the influence of the environment and education" was at least naive, and, in my opinion, absurd. I know of no test that would serve the purpose for which this test was designed.

[400]

*Wesman Personnel Classification Test. Grades 8–16 and adults; 1946–65; WPCT; title on Forms A and B is *Personnel Classification Test*; 3 scores: verbal, numerical, total; Forms A ('46, 4 pages), B ('47, 4 pages), C ('64, 4 pages); revised manual ('65, 27 pages); $3 per 25 tests; 50¢ per specimen set; postage extra; 28(35) minutes; Alexander G. Wesman; Psychological Corporation. *

REFERENCES

1–3. See 4:331.
4–11. See 5:399.
12. Ash, Philip. "Validity Information Exchange, No. 13-05:D.O.T. Code 1-86.12, Salesmen, Typewriters." *Personnel Psychol* 13:454 w '60. *
13. Ash, Philip. "Validity Information Exchange, No. 13-06:D.O.T. Code 5-83.127, Typewriter Serviceman." *Personnel Psychol* 13:455 w '60. *
14. Dunnette, Marvin D., and Kirchner, Wayne K. "Psychological Test Differences Between Industrial Salesmen and Retail Salesmen." *J Appl Psychol* 44:121–5 Ap '60. * (PA 35:4029)
15. Vincent, Norman L., and Dugan, Robert D. "Validity Information Exchange, No. 15-03:D.O.T. Code 1-57.10, Salesman, Insurance." *Personnel Psychol* 15:223–5 su '62. *
16. Dunnette, Marvin D.; Wernimont, Paul; and Abrahams, Norman. "Further Research on Vocational Interest Differences Among Several Types of Engineers." *Personnel & Guid J* 42:484–93 Ja '64. * (PA 39:6040)
17. Welsch, Lawrence A. *The Supervisor's Employee Appraisal Heuristic: The Contribution of Selected Measures of Employee Aptitude, Intelligence and Personality.* Doctor's thesis, University of Pittsburgh (Pittsburgh, Pa.), 1967. (DA 28:4321A)
18. Parry, Mary Ellen. "Ability of Psychologists to Estimate Validities of Personnel Tests." *Personnel Psychol* 21:139–47 su '68. * (PA 42:14727)

Arthur C. MacKinney, *Dean of Graduate Studies, Wright State University, Dayton, Ohio.*

Everyone has come to expect high quality from both Wesman and the Psychological Corporation, and this test maintains the tradition. Overall, it appears to this reviewer to be an excellent example of a short, general-population-level, general intelligence test, composed of verbal and numerical subtests.

The verbal subtest is composed of 40 two-part analogy items arranged in increasing difficulty. The numerical subtest is composed of 20 items, mainly arithmetic, progressing from simple addition through more complex manipulations of fractions, square roots, and the like. Scores from both subtests are summed for a total score.

The manual is clear and well written, simple without being insulting. It is cautious and scholarly to an appropriate degree without compromising the obvious need for utility. Administration instructions are lucidly stated. Twenty-nine sets of norms are presented, encompassing many different occupational groups (ranging from "production workers" to "executive trainee" and "high level positions"), as well as several student groups (ranging from tenth grade students to college sophomores). Reliabilities (including the sub-score reliabilities), equivalence of forms, correlation between subtests and the influence of speed (negligible) are all within the acceptable range. Validity data of three general types are presented. First, correlations of this test with other tests give some good indication of the conceptual content being tapped. Second, the progression of mean scores across the occupational hierarchy is clearly demonstrated. Third, data from 12 concurrent validity studies show correlations primarily under .50. In general, these seem to follow the typical pattern of higher correlation for higher level jobs and for the more intellectual kinds of criteria. The user can be confident that the validity of this instrument will be no worse than that of similar tests, and probably better. In general, the use of this instrument seems indicated in those instances for which it was designed.

J Counsel Psychol 12:435–6 w '65. Jack C. Merwin. * Using two groups, one a high scoring group and one a lower scoring group, the proportion completing nine-tenths the items of each subtest in the stated time limits was calculated. * The proportion of the low scoring group completing nine-tenths of the numerical test, however, was only 43 per cent. The author interprets this as, "presumably a matter of running out of ability rather than out of time."

It is unfortunate that the low scoring group was not given additional time to finish so that this hypothesis could have been tested. It is encouraging to see a continuing updating of existing tests. Often the experience of various groups with a test over the years leads to identification of the real value of a test. The provision of a third form of this test is a significant addition. Inclusion of previous norms which have been in use along with the newer sets of norms should be helpful to the user. The new manual, with a relatively complete description of validity and reliability considerations, as well as data bearing on these considerations, is most readable. Study of the material presented in the revised manual by persons currently using the test should increase its value to them. This new material may also provide people who have previously considered the use of this test with new insights into its possibilities for their needs.

For reviews by John C. Flanagan and Erwin K. Taylor, see 4:331; see also 3:253 (1 excerpt).

[401]

*Wonderlic Personnel Test. Adults; 1938-71; WPT; Forms D and F are adaptations of *Otis Self-Administering Tests of Mental Ability*, Higher Form; 14 forms (3 pages): Forms A, B, ('42), D ['38], F ('59, identical with undated form published in 1938), 1, 2, 4, 5, EM, ('59), APT, BPT, CPT, T-11, T-21, ('67); manual ('70, 19 pages); norms research report ('70, 264 looseleaf pages); norms summary ('70, 38 pages); minimum occupational scores monograph ('66, 64 pages, see 96 below); position analysis reports ('71) for 34 positions: accountant (59 pages), accounting clerk (55 pages), administrator-executive (64 pages), bookkeeper (53 pages), cashier (51 pages), clerk-clerical (84 pages), computer operator (56 pages), custodian (57 pages), draftsman (57 pages), engineer (57 pages), file clerk (51 pages), foreman (58 pages), key punch operator (54 pages), lineman-utility (53 pages), maintenance (64 pages), manager-supervisor (83 pages), nurse's aide (56 pages), office-general (60 pages), police-patrolman (54 pages), programmer (53 pages), receptionist (52 pages), sales and service-customer service (62 pages), salesman-field representative (74 pages), secretary (61 pages), skilled labor and trades (85 pages), stenographer (58 pages), student-part time employee (54 pages), technician (67 pages), telephone operator (52 pages), teller (54 pages), typist (62 pages), unskilled labor (81 pages), warehouseman (59 pages), writer-news etc. (58 pages); no reliability data or norms for Forms D, F, BPT, CPT, T-11, and T-21; distribution of Forms EM, APT, BPT, and CPT restricted to employment agencies; distribution of Forms D, F, T-11, and T-21 restricted to users ordering 1,000 or more copies; $14.75 per 100 tests and manual, postage extra; $150 per norms report; $15 per norms summary; $7.50 per introductory package of 20 copies each of Forms 1 and 2, manual, and special reports; $5 per minimum occupational scores monograph; $15 to $12 per position analysis report; postpaid; 12(20) minutes; E. F. Wonderlic; E. F. Wonderlic & Associates, Inc. *

REFERENCES

1–2. See 2:1415.
3–9. See 3:269.
10–68. See 5:400.
69–85. See 6:513.
86. Rowe, Frederick B. *The Selection of Psychiatric Aides: Criterion Development and Prediction.* Doctor's thesis, University of Maryland (College Park, Md.), 1957. (*DA* 17:2674)
87. Mahoney, T. A.; Jerdee, T. H.; and Nash, A. N. "Predicting Managerial Effectiveness." *Personnel Psychol* 13: 147–63 su '60. * (*PA* 36:2LI47M)
88. Morrison, William E. *The Effectiveness of the Minnesota Clerical Test and the Wonderlic Personnel Test in the Selection of Clerk Typists and File Clerks.* Master's thesis, Springfield College (Springfield, Mass.), 1963.
89. Hodgson, Richard W. "Personality Appraisal of Technical and Professional Applicants." *Personnel Psychol* 17: 167–87 su '64. * (*PA* 39:6067)
90. Hoskins, John Emmett. *A Study of Certain Characteristics Which Have Predictive Value for Vocational Adjustment in a Rehabilitation Workshop.* Doctor's thesis, Wayne State University (Detroit, Mich.), 1964. (*DA* 26:4797)
91. Thumin, Fred J., and Wittenberg, Angela. "Personality as Related to Age and Mental Ability in Female Job Applicants." *J Gerontol* 20:105–7 Ja '65. *
92. Jex, Frank B. *Predicting Academic Success Beyond High School.* Salt Lake City, Utah: University of Utah Bookstore, 1966. Pp. vi, 41. *
93. Keim, Lawrence. *A Study of Psychometric Profile Patterns of Selected Associate Degree Technology Majors.* Doctor's thesis, Purdue University (Lafayette, Ind.), 1966. (*DA* 27: 2049A)
94. Kopff, Richard Garms. *Manager Performance as Related to Goal Setting, Intelligence, and Selected Personality Characteristics.* Doctor's thesis, Columbia University (New York, N.Y.), 1966. (*DA* 27:677A)
95. Penfield, Robert Verdon. *The Psychological Characteristics of Effective First-Line Managers.* Doctor's thesis, Cornell University (Ithaca, N.Y.), 1966. (*DA* 27:1610B)
96. Wonderlic, E. F. *A Cooperative Research Study of Minimum Occupational Scores for the Wonderlic Personnel Test.* Northfield, Ill.: E. F. Wonderlic & Associates, Inc., 1966. Pp. 64. *
97. Wonderlic, E. F. *A Selected, Annotated Bibliography for the Wonderlic Personnel Test.* Northfield, Ill.: E. F. Wonderlic & Associates, Inc., 1966. Pp. 104. *
98. Schuh, Allen J. "Application Blank Items and Intelligence as Predictors of Turnover." *Personnel Psychol* 20:59–63 sp '67. * (*PA* 41:11002)
99. Irish, Thomas E. *An Evaluation of the Effectiveness of the Wonderlic Personnel Test, the Cleaver Self-Description, Previous Job Tenure, and Previous Insurance Selling Experience in the Successful Selection of Insurance Salesmen.* Master's thesis, Springfield College (Springfield, Mass.), 1968.
100. Mitchell, M. D.; Albright, L. E.; and McMurry, F. D. "Biracial Validation of Selection Procedures in a Large Southern Plant." Abstract. *Proc 76th Ann Conv Am Psychol Assn* 3:575–6 '68. *
101. Parry, Mary Ellen. "Ability of Psychologists to Estimate Validities of Personnel Tests." *Personnel Psychol* 21: 139–47 su '68. * (*PA* 42:14727)
102. Ruda, Edward, and Albright, Lewis E. "Racial Differences on Selection Instruments Related to Subsequent Job Performance." *Personnel Psychol* 21:31–41 sp '68. * (*PA* 42: 16233)
103. Thumin, F., and Goldman, Sue. "Comparative Test Performance of Negro and White Job Applicants." *J Clin Psychol* 24:455–7 O '68. * (*PA* 43:4565)
104. Butler, Patrick C., and Rusmore, Jay T. "Illumination Intensities and Test Performance." *Percept & Motor Skills* 29(2):653–4 O '69. * (*PA* 44:4167)
105. Karlins, Marvin; Schuerhoff, Charles; and Kaplan, Martin. "Some Factors Related to Architectural Creativity in Graduating Architecture Students." *J General Psychol* 81(2):203–15 O '69. * (*PA* 44:6775)
106. Lord, Raymond Morrieson. *Profile Patterns of Selected Business Majors as a Basis for Intra-Occupational Differentiation.* Doctor's thesis, Indiana University (Bloomington, Ind.), 1969. (*DAI* 30:551A)
107. Richardson, Billy K. *Prediction of Rehabilitation Counselor Effectiveness: The Relationship of Counselor Characteristics to Supervisors' Ratings.* Doctor's thesis, University of Iowa (Iowa City, Iowa), 1969. (*DAI* 30:3738A)
108. Wille, Glenn R. *An Investigation of the Relationship Between the Wonderlic Personnel Test, Form I, and the General Clerical Test; the Relationship Between the Wonderlic Personnel Test, Form I, and Employee Job Performance.* Master's thesis, Wisconsin State University (Oshkosh, Wis.), 1969.
109. Keillor, James Sherwood. *The Effects of Experimentally Induced Consciousness Expansion and Consciousness Control Upon Creativity and Intellectual Functioning.* Doctor's

thesis, Wayne State University (Detroit, Mich.), 1970. *(DAI* 31:4339B)
110. PRIEN, ERICH P. "Measuring Performance Criteria of Bank Tellers." *J Indus Psychol* 5(1):29–36 Mr '70. * *(PA* 45:7135)
111. RONAN, W. W. "Evaluation of Three Criteria of Management Performance." *J Indus Psychol* 5(1):18–28 Mr '70. * *(PA* 45:7148)
112. THUMIN, FRED J. "Comparative Study of Three Mental Ability Tests." *J Indus Psychol* 5(1):1–7 Mr '70. * *(PA* 45:7117)
113. WEVRICK, L. "Evaluation of the Personnel Test Battery," pp. 1–5. In *Applied Research in Public Personnel Administration.* By L. Wevrick and others. Personnel Report No. 702. Chicago, Ill.: Public Personnel Association, 1970. Pp. 29. *

ROBERT C. DROEGE, *Research Psychologist, Manpower Administration, U.S. Department of Labor, Washington, D.C.*

The WPT is a 12-minute test of general learning ability. Each form of the test has 50 verbal, numerical, and spatial test items arranged in spiral omnibus format. First published in 1938, the Wonderlic has been widely used in industry for screening applicants for jobs at various levels of complexity. The basic character of the test is unchanged since it was reviewed in *The Sixth Mental Measurements Yearbook*. But additional material has been published, including new test forms, an annotated bibliography, a publication of occupational cutoff scores in use, a performance norms report, and a revised manual.

The new forms are for employment agencies only (Forms APT, BPT, and CPT) or for users of 1,000 or more copies (Forms T-11 and T-21). The items were taken from forms previously published but still operational. Form APT consists of 25 items from Form A and 25 items from Form B. The other new forms each include items selected from all seven of the older forms.

A bibliography (*97*) of 361 entries relevant to the WPT is now available. Not all are references to occupational norming, occupational validation, and other research studies, but enough are to make this publication a useful one to those interested in the Wonderlic data base. Even more useful would be an organized presentation of the pertinent research findings. Development of this material would be a big undertaking, but a worthwhile one.

The Minimum Occupational Scores Monograph reports the practice of 703 firms in the use of minimum (and sometimes maximum) cutting scores for over 700 specific jobs. Most of the major and many minor occupations are represented, illustrating the widely held assumption in industry that the Wonderlic is applicable to the entire range of jobs, with their varying requirements of literacy skills, training time, etc. Minimum scores range from 8 for janitors and other unskilled jobs to over 30 for some professional and managerial jobs. Convenient alphabetical listings of job titles with associated cutting scores invite potential users of the Wonderlic to make an immediate application to jobs in their own firms. It seems inevitable that this publication will be used for what it so obviously is—a means of selection of cutting scores to screen applicants for specific jobs. The fact is that no evidence is reported of validity underlying the use of any of these cutting scores by companies reporting them. The publication amounts to a guide to the use of a priori norms and cannot be justified.

Put together at considerable expense in both data collection and analysis (total cost estimated by the author at more than $500,000), the Norms Research Report is an example of the major accomplishments that can be achieved in developing a comprehensive data base for widely used tests such as the Wonderlic. Based on an analysis of data on 251,253 job applicants from 1,071 Wonderlic users, the report contains "performance norms" by age, sex, education, industry, geographic region, and position applied for. There are literally hundreds of tables and graphs in the ten sections of the report. For example, in section C "Test Scores by Education" there are 84 graphs showing the relationship between test scores and years of education for various age groups separately by sex and combined. And there is a table of means, standard deviations, and modes accompanying each graph. It is in this section of the report that the author tries to make a case for the validity of the test as a measure of "trainability" required both in school and on the job. Under this concept, proof of validity lies in the relationship between years of education and the Wonderlic test scores. (The correlations reported, however, are between years of education and *average* test scores for each of several age groups. These correlations are all .95 or above, considerably higher than would have been obtained if individual rather than average test scores had been used.) What the author is attempting to do is to make a virtue of what must be regarded as a severe limitation of general learning ability tests as screening instruments for jobs—their high relationships with educational achievement. For many jobs educational achievement is not a valid consideration and use of a test highly related to education leads to unfair discrimination against disadvantaged individuals. Twenty-eight alternate-form reliability coefficients, half of them .95 or higher, are presented. Detailed data on sample size and characteristics are shown for the various samples in the norms sections of the report, but none for the reliability samples. This is a curious omission in an otherwise detailed report.

The 1968 edition [1] of the manual is not much different from the previous editions, and this is too bad because it has the same serious defects. There still has been no attempt to meet the minimum requirements of the *Standards for Educational and Psychological Tests and Manuals.*

The reader of the manual is left with the impression that the validity of the test has been established for the entire range of occupations. The fact is that there are many studies which show that tests like the Wonderlic have no relevance for successful performance in many occupations. An example from occupational research with the *General Aptitude Test Battery* illustrates the point. Aptitude G (General Learning Ability) of the GATB has item content similar to that in the Wonderlic and studies have shown that the two measures correlate highly, indicating that they measure essentially the same abilities. Of the 413 occupational validation studies conducted with the GATB, as reported in the 1968 edition of the GATB manual, only 180 resulted in final selection test batteries that included Aptitude G. Thus, in less than half of the studies did Aptitude G contribute enough validity to enter into the final selection test battery established for the occupation.

There is evidence from the extensive bibliography on the Wonderlic that considerable occupational validation research has been conducted on this test, but the manual does not document it. It is time that a systematic effort was made to develop a comprehensive manual that will report the evidence of the extent to which the test does what the author states it does on page 4 of the 1968 (and 1961) edition of the manual: "This test has been shown to be a valid instrument in determining success on a number of different jobs. The number of questions right clearly distinguished between good and poor groups of employees differentiated on work records accumulated over a period of five years."

In summary, there is not nearly enough documented validation data to justify the current wide use of the *Wonderlic Personnel Test* in screening applicants for employment or candidates for promotion. Aptitude and intelligence tests are coming under increasing attack because of the possibility of unfair discrimination against minority groups in the application of the test results in selection. The Wonderlic is particularly vulnerable because of its known high relationship to formal education, the use of a priori norms, and the lack of documented evidence that it is a useful instrument in predicting success in many jobs. Unless the user first validates the test, preferably in combination with tests measuring other abilities, on a sample of his applicants or workers, he may find that he is in violation of Title VII of the Civil Rights Act of 1964. Companies considering the use of this test should first become familiar with the 1970 *Guidelines on Employee Selection Procedures,* published by the Equal Employment Opportunity Commission, Washington, D.C., and with the March 8, 1971 Supreme Court ruling in the case of Griggs, et al., vs. Duke Power Company.

JOHN P. FOLEY, JR., *President, J. P. Foley and Co., Inc., New York, New York.*

This well-known test continues to be widely used as a measure of adult intelligence in business and industry. As in the case of earlier forms, the more recent forms follow the same spiral omnibus pattern, with the 50 multiple choice items arranged in ascending order of difficulty. They are printed on the two inside pages of a four-page fold, the instructions, as well as sample and practice items, appearing on the first page. Although the test may be given with the work-limit method, i.e., unlimited time, most of the norms relate to a 12-minute time limit, which is satisfactory for most testing purposes. Scoring is done manually with strip keys and is simple and rapid. The test score is the number of items correct.

It is claimed that the first nine forms listed in the entry above "are equal and similar to a very high degree." Even so, it is admitted that "minor differences were observed in this study" and that "some of the test forms are more closely equated than others." A conversion table for the nine forms is provided on the same page

---

[1] At the time this review was being prepared, the 1970 manual was not available.—The Editor.

of the manual, with the individual correction values ranging from $+3$ to -3. However, a request by this reviewer for reference to the raw data from which the suggested conversion values were obtained failed to elicit the desired information.

Norms for male and female high school and college graduates are presented in the 1968 manual,[1] as are other educational, age and sex norms. The "central tendency" (evidently the median) and the quartile range of scores obtained by professional and executive, managerial, clerical, sales, plant staff and line, and other groups are also reported. Minimum critical scores for a number of different occupations are suggested, although no supporting data are provided. Test users are advised to establish their own critical scores "since job titles are not completely descriptive," since they "vary from plant to plant even with the same organization," and since "the critical score....must be moved up or down, depending upon the available supply of applicants."

Claims for "good reliability" are made in the 1968 manual, as are claims for proven validity. Although high correlation coefficients are cited, the paucity of supporting information makes it difficult, if not impossible, to evaluate the studies underlying these claims. Moreover, a separate booklet titled "Summary of Experiences with the Wonderlic Personnel Test" is little more than a disorganized series of quoted passages from journal articles, textbooks, and other publications.

A 36-page norms booklet summarizes data from a more comprehensive study of 251,253 cases, a study designed "to up-date and re-verify the central tendency and the dispersion statistics affecting Personnel Placement and Selection" and "to provide the users of the Personnel Test with additional supportive statistics essential to the improved conduct of their testing programs." Original data were supplied by 1,071 participating business, industrial, and governmental organizations. The data presented relate to all forms of the test combined, and to a testing time of 12 minutes, no correction being made for age, form administered, or other factors. Among the data presented are tables showing distribution of scores by educational level and position applied for, as well as statistics relating to region, age, sex, and racial grouping. Reliability coefficients are also presented, as are validity coefficients based on "the degree of covariance between years of education obtained and average test score achieved by level of education."

The *Wonderlic Personnel Test* is an appropriate screening device for use with clerical and other white-collar personnel. When combined with a clerical aptitude test, it constitutes an effective test battery for such an application. The availability of multiple forms is highly advantageous. Testing time and ease of administration represent favorable considerations. Moreover, the publisher is to be commended for recent efforts to accumulate normative information, as well as data relating to reliability and validity. And in the light of other materials available from the same publisher, it is implied that the test should form only one part of an overall selection or evaluation program, although this point is not always made explicit.

However, there is insufficient emphasis on the restricted applicability of the test, i.e., on the fact that it is most appropriate for a limited population, viz., white-collar employees. The widespread use and availability of the test tend to impair its effectiveness, although this limitation is to some extent mitigated by the multiple forms. More detailed percentile norms relating to occupational and other groups would be helpful, as would carefully designed and controlled validation studies. Much of the material in the manual and other supporting publications is loosely organized and presented. Just which test forms are available is not unequivocally stated. The term "central tendency" is not sufficiently explicit. A few passages in the manual are naive, such as the admonition: "In interpreting results, avoid trying to establish an I.Q. or any other psychological refinement. As a practical personnel man, you are interested *only* in finding the relationship of questions answered correctly." Some of the material in the supporting booklets is anecdotal in nature, consisting of little more than testimonials. And much of this material smacks too much of promotionalism, designed more to stimulate sale of the test than to provide relevant information. Lastly, there are signs of defensiveness, such as the reproduction of a letter from the president of the tabulating company which prepared the norms reports and the following statement contained in a letter from the publisher to this reviewer:

---

[1] At the time this review was being prepared, the 1970 manual was not available.—The Editor.

"Our construction methods have not and will not be published."

For reviews by N. M. Downie and Marvin D. Dunnette, see 6:513; for reviews by H. E. Brogden, Charles D. Flory, and Irving Lorge, see 3:269.

INDIVIDUAL

[402]

★**Bayley Scales of Infant Development.** Ages 2–30 months; 1969; BSID; 2 scores: mental, motor, plus 30 behavior ratings; the mental and motor scales "draw heavily upon" the *California First-Year Mental Scale,* the *California Preschool Mental Scale,* and the *California Infant Scale of Motor Development;* individual; 1 form; manual (185 pages); record booklets: mental scale (8 pages), motor scale (4 pages), infant behavior (6 pages); no data on validity of motor scale; no data on predictive validity of mental scale; $88 per set of testing materials including manual and 25 sets of record booklets; $3 per 25 mental scale record booklets; $2.25 per 25 motor scale or infant behavior record booklets; $5 per manual; (45–90) minutes for mental and motor scales; Nancy Bayley; Psychological Corporation. *

REFERENCES

1. BAYLEY, NANCY, AND SCHAEFFR, EARL S. "Correlations of Maternal and Child Behaviors With the Development of Mental Abilities: Data From the Berkeley Growth Study." *Monogr Soc Res Child Develop* 29(6):1–8 '64. * (PA 39:11895)
2. PHATAK, PRAMILA; POFFENBERGER, THOMAS; PATEL, ANJALI; AND BAROT, JYOTI. "Motor and Mental Development of Indian Infants of Ages 1 Month to 25 Months." *J Gujarat Res Soc* 27:106–13 Ap '65. *
3. COHEN, ABRAHAM I. "Hand Preference and Developmental Status of Infants." *J Genetic Psychol* 108:337–45 Je '66. * (PA 40:10986)
4. ESTES, BETSY, AND COMBS, ANN. "Perception of Quantity." *J Genetic Psychol* 108:333–6 Je '66. * (PA 40:11012)
5. KLATSKIN, ETHELYN H.; MCGARRY, MARY E.; AND STEWARD, MARGARET S. "Variability in Developmental Test Patterns as a Sequel of Neonatal Stress." *Child Develop* 37:819–26 D '66. * (PA 41:2668)
6. KOHEN-RAZ, REUVEN. "The Ring-Cube Test: A Brief Time Sampling Method for Assessing Primary Development of Coordinated Bilateral Grasp Responses in Infancy." *Percept & Motor Skills* 23:675–88 D '66. * (PA 41:7088)
7. WERNER, EMMY E., AND BAYLEY, NANCY. "The Reliability of Bayley's Revised Scale of Mental and Motor Development During the First Year of Life." *Child Develop* 37:39–50 Mr '66. * (PA 40:4770)
8. FRANCIS-WILLIAMS, JESSIE, AND YULE, WILLIAM. "The Bayley Infant Scales of Mental and Motor Development: An Exploratory Study With an English Sample." *Develop Med & Child Neurol* 9:391–401 Ag '67. * (PA 42:646)
9. KOHEN-RAZ, REUVEN. "Scalogram Analysis of Some Developmental Sequences of Infant Behavior as Measured by the Bayley Infant Scale of Mental Development." *Genetic Psychol Monogr* 76:3–21 Ag '67. * (PA 41:16466)
10. MENDELSON, MARTIN A. "Interdisciplinary Approach to the Study of the Exceptional Infant: A Large Scale Research Project," pp. 15–77. In *Exceptional Infant: The Normal Infant,* Vol. 1. Edited by Jerome Hellmuth. Seattle, Wash.: Special Child Publications, 1967. Pp. 568. *
11. ROBINSON, JOHN S., AND BAYLEY, NANCY. "Behavioral Criteria for Diagnosing Mental Retardation in the First Two Years of Life." Progress report. *Calif Mental Health Res Dig* 5:180–1 su '67. * (PA 42:2884)
12. GANNON, D. R. "Relationships Between 8-Mo. Performance on the Bayley Scales of Infant Development and 48-Mo. Intelligence and Concept Formation Scores." *Psychol Rep* 23:1199–205 D '68. * (PA 43:8104)
13. GERSON, ELAINE FREED. *Dimensions of Behavior in the First Half Year of Life and the Effect of Prenatal Parent Counseling.* Doctor's thesis, Pennsylvania State University (University Park, Pa.), 1968. (DA 29:4830B)
14. KOHEN-RAZ, REUVEN. "Mental and Motor Development of Kibbutz, Institutionalized, and Home-Reared Infants in Israel." *Child Develop* 39:489–504 Je '68. * (PA 42:13460)
15. GERSON, ELAINE F. "Dimensions of Infant Behavior in the First Six Months of Life." Abstract. *Proc 77th Ann Conv Am Psychol Assn* 4(1):269–70 '69. * (PA 43:17137)
16. CARR, JANET. "Mental and Motor Development in Young Mongol Children." *J Mental Def Res* 14(3):205–20 S '70. *
17. ERICKSON, MARILYN T.; JOHNSON, NANCY M.; AND CAMPBELL, FRANCES A. "Relationships Among Scores on Infant Tests for Children With Developmental Problems." *Am J Mental Def* 75(1):102–4 Jl '70. * (PA 45:926)
18. IRETON, HAROLD; THWING, EDWARD; AND GRAVEM, HOWARD. "Infant Mental Development and Neurological Status, Family Socioeconomic Status, and Intelligence at Age Four." *Child Develop* 41(4):937–45 D '70. * (PA 46:831)
19. MAN, EVELYN B.; ADELMAN, MAURICE; JONES, WALTER S.; AND LORD, ROBERT M., JR. "Development and BEI of Full-Term and Low-Birth-Weight Infants Through 18 Months." *Am J Dis Children* 119(4):298–307 Ap '70. * (PA 44:17246)
20. WILLERMAN, LEE; BROMAN, SARAH H.; AND FIEDLER, MIRIAM. "Infant Development, Preschool IQ, and Social Class." *Child Develop* 41(1):69–77 Mr '70. * (PA 44:8168)

ROBERTA R. COLLARD, *Assistant Professor of Human Development, University of Massachusetts, Amherst, Massachusetts.*

The *Bayley Scales of Infant Development* is a carefully standardized, well planned, and comprehensive measure of infant development from 2 months to 2½ years of age.

The BSID consists of three parts: a Mental Scale, a Motor Scale, and the Infant Behavior Record. The Mental Scale is made up of 163 items which measure responses to visual and auditory stimuli, manipulation and play with objects, and responses involving social interaction such as socialization and imitation. It also has items which measure discrimination of shapes, memory or object constancy, simple problem solving, and more abstract abilities such as naming objects, understanding prepositions, and the concept of the number one. The Motor Scale consists of 81 items which measure progressions of gross motor abilities such as sitting, standing, walking, and stair climbing as well as abilities involving finer motor coordination, such as those involved in grasping objects of various sizes. The Infant Behavior Record is a rating scale which measures various aspects of personality such as emotional and social behaviors, activity level, responses to objects, sensory areas of interest, and such ego functions as attention span, persistence, and endurance.

The BSID was designed to be used for both clinical and research purposes. The author states that the value of these scales in clinical practice does not lie in predicting a child's later abilities but in establishing his current developmental status in relation to others his age. These scales should prove useful in the recognition and diagnosis of sensory and neurological defects and emotional disturbances, and in indicating the possibility of environmental deficits. The value of the BSID as a research instrument lies in its careful standardization, high reliability, and broad coverage of many aspects of the behavior repertoire of infants, parts of which could be used as subscales in longitudinal studies.

The test materials are colorful, attractive, durable, washable, and have sufficient novelty to be intrinsically interesting to infants and young children and yet are similar to objects with which most subjects would be familiar. The use in the Motor Scale of heavy or bulky specially constructed stairs and a walking board may limit its use in some situations because of the difficulty of transporting these items.

The record forms include spaces for recording information about the child's health, prenatal or perinatal difficulties, educational and occupational level of parents, and family constellation.

The greatest advantage of the BSID over other tests of infant development lies in its excellent standardization. These scales were standardized on a sample of 1,262 infants and children, ranging from 2 to 30 months of age. The sample was selected to be representative of the U.S. population in terms of major geographic areas and residence (urban-rural) and was controlled for sex, race, and education of head of household. Only "normal" children living at home were included in the sample; prematures, institutional infants, and those from bilingual homes were excluded.

The split-half reliability coefficients reported for the 14 age groups range from .81 to .93 (median .88) on the Mental Scale and from .68 to .92 (median .84) on the Motor Scale.

To evaluate the neurological or mental developmental status of infants and young children, it is important to know the reliabilities of individual test items. The BSID items found to have high tester-observer and test-retest reliabilities are those having to do with eye-hand coordination directed toward a test object, those having to do with sustained attention toward a test object, those involving object constancy, and vocabulary items.

The validity of the Mental Scale was determined by correlating the scores of the two-year-olds in the standardization sample on this scale with their scores on the Stanford-Binet. The correlation was .57 over the 6-month age overlap of the two tests.

The directions in the manual are specific, clear, and logical. The items do not have to be given in a strict order but may be flexibly adapted to the infant's interest and state. Behaviors may be scored if they are observed before or after the administration of the test. Mother's reports of the occurrence of the behaviors tested are recorded and used in the evaluation of the adequacy of the test.

On the Mental Scale the 163 items are arranged in chronological order by tenths of months, and items are arranged in the same order in the manual. It is helpful that the items are also listed in categories or "situation codes" in which the same materials are used in different ways for different age levels. These categories are given letter names which appear near the items both in the manual and on the record forms. It would have been helpful if the age placement of the items had been listed after each item in the situation codes and if these categories were printed on the front and back of a cardboard card which could be consulted by the tester as the test is given. It is helpful that the pages in the manual for a particular scale are color coded to the record forms.

For one who is not familiar with infant tests (or even for one who is) the BSID is difficult to learn how to administer because of the overwhelming amount of information one must keep in mind while giving it. Not only does the large number of items in the scales make this difficult, but the variety of factors to remember in the instructions may make these scales seem formidable to an inexperienced tester. It is assumed that this difficulty would decrease for most testers with increasing practice and familiarity. Writing up detailed protocols of items and procedures before the first subjects in each age group are tested should prove helpful in learning how to administer these scales.

Scoring the BSID is straightforward and simple. The items are arranged by age level on the scoring forms, and each item passed is given a credit of one. Raw scores consist of each item passed plus the items below the basal level. Raw scores are easily changed to index scores by locating the former in the infant's age column in a table in the testing manual and finding the index score corresponding to the raw score on the same line.

An index score is a "normalized standard score" in which each infant is compared to others his age in the standardization sample. A Mental Development Index is derived from the Mental Scale, and a Psychomotor Development Index is based on the Motor Scale.

CONCLUSIONS. The *Bayley Scales of Infant Development* is the culmination of the development of mental and motor tests in the tradition of Binet and Gesell. The BSID is intermediate between the empirically constructed tests which sample the observed abilities of children in various situations and those tests which may be designed to measure specific mental processes such as memory, object constancy, generalization, learning to solve problems, or learning abstract language concepts. The BSID includes items involving these processes, but does not have sections which measure these processes specifically. Neither the Mental nor Motor Scale is designed to indicate specific neurological or sensory deficits nor is the Infant Behavior Record designed to indicate or measure kind or degree of emotional disturbance. However, because of the range of the items, the reliability of the scales, and their careful construction and standardization, the BSID is by far the best measure of infant development available today.

RAYMOND H. HOLDEN, *Professor of Psychology and Coordinator, Learning Center, Rhode Island College, Providence, Rhode Island.*

The *Bayley Scales of Infant Development* fills a long felt need for a well standardized and reliable instrument to assess the developmental progress of infants. Previous scales, based on test items formulated 20 to 40 years ago, utilized small samples of children of limited geographic and socioeconomic backgrounds. The present version of the BSID contains three parts: the Mental Scale, the Motor Scale, and the Infant Behavior Record.

The author states that "the indexes derived from the Mental and Motor Scales have limited value as predictors of later abilities, since rates of development for any given child in the first year or two of life may be highly variable over the course of a few months." According to the author, "the *primary* value of the development indexes is that they provide the basis for establishing a child's current status, and thus the extent of any deviation from normal expectancy."

Standardization was exceptionally well controlled. A stratified sample design was used, controlling "for sex and color within each age group, with further controls related to residence (urban-rural) and to education of the head of the household." The sample consisted of 1,262 children evenly distributed in age between 2 and 30 months.

The test materials are contained in a large black suitcase. The items have no particular standard place in the case; each repacking places them in a different location.

The manual presents detailed instructions to examiners on general testing considerations. One of the interesting rules stated is "Hurry yourself but do not hurry the child." Testing proceeds, like the Binet, from a basal level to the ceiling. The directions for administering are very clearly presented.

In summary, the *Bayley Scales of Infant Development* are well standardized developmental scales for infants and meet satisfactory standards of test reliability. The test is useful for the clinician and researcher alike.

Congratulations to Nancy Bayley and to the Psychological Corporation for the standards of scientific rigor provided in the standardization of this scale. It is a most useful and satisfactory addition to our test armamentarium in infancy and early childhood.

[403]
*Canadian Intelligence Test, 1966 Revision.** Ages 3–16; 1940–66; formerly called *Canadian Intelligence Examination;* a modification of the 1916 *Stanford Revision of the Binet-Simon Intelligence Scale;* individual; manual ('66, 86 pages); card book ('66, 31 pages); record booklet ('66, 8 pages); no data on reliability and validity; Can $2.50 per card book; $2 per 25 record booklets; $3.75 per manual; postage extra; specimen set available on 60 day approval; [60–75] minutes; Carman E. Stothers, Beverly R. Collier, James W. Covert, and James C. Williams; Ryerson Press. *

REFERENCE
1. See 3:272.

HUGH TAYLOR, *Assistant Professor of Education, University of Victoria, Victoria, British Columbia, Canada.*

The *Canadian Intelligence Test,* previously entitled the *Canadian Intelligence Examination,* is the second revision of a test originally published in 1940. It has a content and design similar to that of the Stanford-Binet. The test as a whole may be considered as measuring a highly verbal component of intelligence. Only a few items deal with the manipulation of materials. Beginning at Year 3, the test includes six or fewer items at each age level up to Year 14. Above Year 14 there are two levels entitled Young Adult 1 and Young Adult 2, each containing six items. This reviewer suspects that the average item is more difficult than that of the Stanford-Binet. Varying amounts of credit are assigned to each item passed and the resultant mental age score is used to calculate the traditional ratio intelligence quotient.

The 1966 revision of the test is a minor one. The content is basically the same as in previous editions. Three new words have replaced "copper," "outward," and "loiter" on the 55-word vocabulary test and two words have traded places at the 20th and 21st positions on the list. It would appear that these changes would have a very minor effect on scores, particularly at age 11 or over. The words in the vocabulary list seem to be free of any national bias when judged across the major English-speaking nations.

The testing materials—including the directions for administering, the card booklet, and the 8-page record form—are clearly written on high quality paper and well designed for effective use. Printing on each card page the year level for which it may be used would increase the efficient handling of the card booklet. Provision of a table for determining IQ scores or a mechanical IQ calculator would help the examiner avoid arithmetical errors as well as speed up and standardize the determination of the IQ score. A 2-page section in the manual entitled "Item Analysis of the Canadian Intelligence Test" does not contain any item analysis data. In fact, item difficulties and discrimination indices are not included in the test kit. A more appropriate title for the section would be "Content Outline of the Canadian Intelligence Test."

The *Canadian Intelligence Test* has only one form. The cost involved in developing an alternate form may not be desirable from the publisher's point of view. If this is the case, then a minimum substitute would be to provide the user with tables of score equivalents with other intelligence tests of parallel design.

Specific validity, reliability, and normative data for the 1966 revision are not included in the manual. There are general comments made relative to these concepts but the evidence cited is now over 30 years old! It is suggested that the publisher immediately proceed to re-norm this test, provide information on sex differences, produce current validity and reliability data as well as adopt the more prevalent deviation IQ score.

In summary, the *Canadian Intelligence Test* is simple in design, relatively easy to administer, but lacking in empirical data for use in the meaningful interpretation of scores. The authors' suggested use of the test, namely in the training of teachers in individual test administration, might well be considered its only legitimate use at this stage in its development. No evidence is presented to suggest that this test may be used in making important clinical decisions related to intelligence.

For a review by Gwen F. Arnold of the 1947 edition, see 4:336; see also 3:272 (2 excerpts).

[404]

★Cooperative Preschool Inventory, Revised Edition. Disadvantaged children ages 3–6; 1965–70; CPI; achievement in areas necessary for success in school; individual; 1 form ('70, 4 pages); manual ('70, 13 pages); technical report ('70, 35 pages); the "national norms" are based on children enrolled in 11 Head Start Centers; $2.50 per 20 tests; $1 per technical report; $1 per manual; $2 per specimen set; cash orders postpaid; (15) minutes; Bettye M. Caldwell; Cooperative Tests and Services. *

REFERENCES

1. ALLERHAND, MELVIN E. "Effectiveness of Parents of Head Start Children as Administrators of Psychological Tests." J Consult Psychol 31:286–90 Je '67. * (PA 41:10474)
2. CALDWELL, BETTYE M. "Descriptive Evaluations of Child Development and of Developmental Settings." Pediatrics 40: 46–54 Jl '67. *
3. DATTA, LOIS-ELLIN. "Draw-A-Person Test as a Measure of Intelligence in Preschool Children From Very Low Income Families." J Consult Psychol 31:626–30 D '67. * (PA 42:2561)
4. ASBURY, CHARLES ALEXANDER. Factors Associated With Discrepant Achievement in Rural Economically Deprived White and Negro First Graders. Doctor's thesis, University of North Carolina (Chapel Hill, N.C.), 1969. (DAI 31:208A)
5. HOWARD, MARSHALL J., JR.; HOOPS, H. RAY; AND MCKINNON, ARCHIE J. "Language Abilities of Children With Differing Socioeconomic Backgrounds." J Learn Dis 3(6): 328–35 Je '70. *

JOSEPH L. FRENCH, *Professor of Special Education and Educational Psychology and Head of the Department of Special Education, The Pennsylvania State University, University Park, Pennsylvania.*

"The *Cooperative Preschool Inventory* is a brief assessment and screening procedure designed for individual use with children in the age range of three-to-six years." While not an attempt to create a culture-fair instrument, the test was "developed to give a measure of achievement in areas regarded as necessary for success in school." The inventory comprises items of the "information" type and, to a lesser extent, items requiring ability to label quantities, identify serial positions, perceive shapes, and execute certain visual-motor basic drawing skills. It was anticipated that it would measure basic information children have about themselves, including their self-concept. A few easily obtained materials such as blank paper and crayons must be assembled locally prior to administration.

The revised 1970 edition contains 64 items scored as correct or incorrect and administered in 15 minutes. Responses are recorded in a four-page booklet in which the subjects may draw when necessary. Answers are found directly beneath the questions in the administrative manual. Internal design allows for administration by the child's own teacher, who is assumed to possess a minimal sophistication in measurement technique. Question and probe technique is similar to that of the Stanford-Binet. Periodically, however, the examiner is instructed to reinforce correct behavior. This revision includes minor changes in administrative procedure from the 1968 version which was known as the Standardization Edition. The final product is reduced considerably in length from the original 7-test inventory developed in 1965 by Bettye Caldwell during the original excitement surrounding the development of Project Head Start. Caldwell's inventory was designed for measuring a child's basic information vocabulary and number and space concepts prior to his enrolling in a Head Start program and at its conclusion. Subsequently, Donald Soule refined the scoring system and processed the data collected from the national field testing.

Standardization of the Revised Edition took place in 11 Head Start centers and the data are reported for those tested in English. Most of the technical data are available for the following age groups: 3-0 to 3-11, 4-0 to 4-5, 4-6 to 4-11, 5-0 to 5-5, 5-6 to 6-5. A larger number of subjects were tested at each level between ages 4-0 and 5-5 than at either extreme. Some regional normative data, based on 107 to 248 subjects per region at each age level, are available. Percentile ranks are available for each age group and for some regions.

K-R 20 reliability coefficients for the age groups range from .86 to .92. For the total standardization sample, the mean increases about four raw score points from one age group to another. The standard error of measurement for the age groups varies from 3.1 to 3.9.

The Stanford-Binet was used with 1,476 subjects during the standardization. Concurrent validity coefficients vary from .39 at age 3-0 to 3-11 to .65 at age 5-0 to 5-5. Additional data are expected to be reported in the professional press when the instrument becomes generally available.

Results from measurement of achievement before and after nursery school experiences were not available in the prepublication manual. Data indicating the power of the scores from this instrument to predict success in school were also unavailable. Analysis of the responses by the teacher may indicate some educational needs. Since its object is the identification of those individuals unprepared for traditional programs, studies which indicate the degree to which the items in the test are predictive of "success in school" will be of interest to many professionals concerned with child development.

J Ed Meas 6(1):33–5 sp '69. *Dale Carlson.* Referred to as the Cooperative Pre-school Inventory (CPSI) in the catalog, this little instrument sometimes carries the parenthetical subtitle, "Standardization Edition" or "Preliminary Version" to denote its embryonic if not germinal state of development. The publisher hopes to have a more complete edition out sometime in 1969. The catalog states that its purpose is to "provide an indication of a child's level of development prior to formal instruction in a variety of basic skills and concepts regarded as necessary for success in school." The author prefers to regard the CPSI as an achievement test which is sensitive to changes associated with educational intervention. Whether it is an achievement test or a readiness test as the catalog implies, the items are exceedingly similar to those of other preschool batteries. The test has a strong verbal emphasis, but is relatively light on tasks such as short-term memory, motor development, and visual perception. Only 4 of the 89 items tap the latter two functions. The four scales originated from a factor analysis of the initial test consisting of 161 items. Four factors emerged including one general factor which loaded on items requiring information from parents. Items from this factor were not included in the published edition. Instead, one factor was logically divided to yield scores for two of the four scales. On the Personal-Social Responsiveness variable, the items relating to the child's knowledge of his body actually loaded heavier on the discarded self-help factor. The items requiring the capacity to execute simple and complex directions are probably more deserving of the "activation" title than the scales which bear it. The second scale, Associative Vocabulary, is neither associative in any standard psychological sense, nor is it a vocabulary test. It has a few items of a motor-encoding variety, but is largely a test of information and comprehension in the Wechsler tradition. The Concept Activation-Numerical scale is clearly a measure of quantitative understanding and has several excellent items. The second part of that original factor, Concept Activation-Sensory, might better be called sensory-motor or perceptual motor. The manual is appropriately entitled, Directions for Administration and Scoring, for that is all it contains except for tables of norms and a three-page description of the test and its origin. No help is offered in the interpretation of scores in terms of meaning, applicability, or stability. Additional information in the technical report regarding reliability, relationships among sub-tests, and items statistics could easily have been included in the manual. This would have made a technical report unnecessary since the remainder of the technical report is devoted to what some would consider an irrelevant narrative of the details relating to the birth of the instrument and the convictions of the author. The instructions for administration are very explicit and complete. The general criteria for scoring are equally clear. The need for immediate feedback during administration is recognized and provided for by the placing of sample responses immediately following the question. The criteria for scoring appear to ensure objectivity, but no evidence on this dimension is provided. The claim is made for a total administration time of only fifteen minutes. This is probably an underestimate. * reports percentile conversion charts for ages 2-1 to 6-6 for both middle and lower class groups. These norms are based on a sample of 669. Although the schools from which the sample was drawn are listed, there is no mention of any scheme to ensure adequate sampling. The manual does faithfully point out, however, that 80% of the sample is from one city. The concept of presenting norms as a function of social class is appealing. No information is offered, however, regarding the criteria for placing children in either norm group; nor are such basic descriptive statistics as mean and standard deviation reported on either sample for any part of the test. * For the full-length experimental version the split half (odd-even) coefficient was .97. A coefficient of .95 is reported for the published edition. These were both computed on the initial standardization sample only. Is it possible that these coefficients are spuriously high? Inspection of the tests reveals clusters of items which are very similar in format. Although success on one item is not completely dependent upon success on other items, the items are probably so highly correlated that an odd-even coefficient could be seriously affected. These clusters are distributed throughout the test to contribute to the factor-based scores which are probably correlated, thereby compounding the problem. If not spuriously high, the reported coefficients probably approach upper-bound estimates. Coefficients which consider other sources of variance, such as time, are not reported. Separate reliability estimates of part scores are absent, as well as any discussion on the stability of part or whole scores in terms of standard error of measurement. No validity data are reported unless the factor analysis performed during the construction of the inventory would qualify as such. While this information helps to indicate what the test is measuring, the inclusion of some reference tests in the factor analysis would have buttressed the unstated construct validation claims. The only other evidence for construct validity, through a consideration of age differentiation, was also gathered during the process of building the instrument. A table showing the proportion of children passing each item at three age levels is not very reassuring. Many items show almost no differentiation and a few are actually negatively correlated with age. Unfortunately, there are no indications of the relationships between CPSI scores and other criteria, either concurrently with another preschool test, or predictively with such crucial variables as success in beginning reading. Focusing on the author's preference that it be considered an achievement test, the content validity picture is just as bleak. No attention is given to the definition of the universe of test behaviors which this test might represent, nor any assurance that items were systematically selected to assure representation. The qualities sought and probably captured in this instrument: speed and ease of administration, objectivity in scoring, and low cost, indicate the potential value of this instrument. However, a healthy skepticism is justified if not demanded in the use of this test which was hastily marketed with inadequate norms and meager reliability and validity data.

[405]

★**Denver Developmental Screening Test.** Ages 2 weeks to 6 years; 1968–70; DDST; 4 scores: gross motor, fine motor-adaptive, language, personal-social; individual; 1 form ('68, 2 pages and kit of small objects); manual, 1970 edition ('70, 65 pages); $1 per 100 tests; $6.25 per kit of objects; $1 per manual; cash orders (plus 5% for postage) only; [15–20] minutes; William K. Frankenburg and Josiah B. Dodds; Ladoca Project and Publishing Foundation, Inc. *

REFERENCES

1. FRANKENBURG, WILLIAM K., AND DODDS, JOSIAH B. "The Denver Developmental Screening Test." *J Pediatrics* 71:181–91 Ag '67. *
2. KOUPERNIK, CYRILLE. "The Denver Developmental Screening Test." *Develop Med & Child Neurol* 10:796–7 D '68. *
3. FRANKENBURG, WILLIAM K. "The Denver Developmental Screening Test." Reply by Cyrille Koupernik. *Develop Med & Child Neurol* 11(2):260–2 Ap '69. *
4. ROBISCHON, PAULETTE. *A Study of the Relationship Between Children's Developmental Level, Pica Practice, and Other Hand-Mouth Behavior.* Doctor's thesis, New York University (New York, N.Y.), 1970. (*DAI* 31:2786B)
5. SANDLER, LOUISE; VANCAMPEN, JACK; RATNER, GERALD; STAFFORD, CALVIN; AND WEISMAR, RICHARD. "Response of Urban Preschool Children to a Developmental Screening Test." *J Pediatrics* 77(7):775–81 N '70. *
6. SMITH, JOANN HORN. *A Study of the Relationship Between Dogmatic and Rigid Attitudes in the Mother and Early Developmental Progress in the Infant.* Doctor's thesis, New York University (New York, N.Y.), 1970. (*DAI* 31:4160B)

ALICE E. MORIARTY, *Senior Psychologist, The Menninger Foundation, Topeka, Kansas.*

Efforts to predict later intellectual functioning from measurement or observation of infant behavior have on the whole been disappointing. On the other hand, clinicians knowledgeable about infant behavior have documented qualitative differences in the range of behavior which discriminate between children who will later show neurological and intellectual deficits from those who will not. At the same time, increasing recognition of the importance of early development on later cognitive and affective functioning, along with needs for early diagnosis of delayed development or retardation in order to plan for effective care and treatment of deviant children, have pushed clinicians to formalize observations in normative sequences. One such effort with apparent promise is the *Denver Developmental Screening Test.*

Selecting 240 potentially discriminating items from 12 existing developmental and preschool tests, the authors, in a preliminary survey of 200 infants and preschool children, experimentally eliminated items felt to be ambiguous or insufficiently discriminating. From this survey, the authors culled 105 items which were administered to a standardization population of 1,036 children (543 males and 493 females) between the ages of 2 weeks and 6.4 years. Children who were adopted, premature, or known to be handicapped in any way were excluded from the sample, which quite closely approximated the ethnic and occupational groups of the population in the city of Denver according to the 1960 census. Computer calculations were then made of the age at which 25, 50, 75, and 90 percent of the sample passed each item. Though a relatively small number of children were retested by four separate examiners for reliability purposes, agreement between 90 and 100 percent on each of the items, arbitrarily assigned to the four measured areas of functioning (gross motor, fine motor-adaptive, language, and personal-social) appeared to justify the authors' claims for a high level of reliability in administration and scoring. Not made clear is why adaptive aspects of functioning were considered only in relation to motor functioning.

A parallel study of the correlation of the DDST scores with the Yale Developmental Examination yielded a correlation of .97, suggesting high validity, especially since there were few cases of discrepancy between the two tests in identifying normal and deviant children.

In our clinical use of the DDST, we have had some reason to question the circumscribed geographical selection of the sample and the applicability of norms in screening children from the lower socioeconomic groups, especially in the language area. Furthermore, even if the standardization sample is truly representative of the Denver population, we cannot automatically assume that the established norms are appropriate for assessment of individual minority group children outside of the population in the Denver area. Possible unfairness to minority group children could, of course, be stated as an objection leveled at almost all measurements of cognitive development and functioning in minority groups. To the extent that quantitative findings are assessed in the light of known deterrents to functioning and weighed against the observable assets in the child's style of functioning, these objections are reduced but not entirely eliminated. The authors' cautions against using the DDST as a diagnostic tool and their recommendations of close observation of qualitative aspects of test behavior in relation to motivation, dependency or hostility between mother and child, examiner-child interaction, and of the maintenance of optimal and standard testing conditions are therefore especially commendable.

With these reservations in mind and in the context of the purposes for which it was designed, the DDST is a practical, efficient, and dependable device. It is inexpensive, quick and easy to administer and evaluate with relatively little training or experience in testing. The manual is direct and clear, and scoring guides are explicit. The test seems to meet standards of reliability and validity for the purposes for which it was designed. The materials themselves are colorful and of inherent interest to young children. Furthermore, it has the advantage of providing graphic representation of passes and failures, allowing the examiner to look at the range of behavior in each infant, and to interpret meaningfully to parents the strengths and weaknesses in relative developmental pace in each of the areas assessed. This reviewer is impressed by the authors' continuing refinement of scoring techniques in a 1970 revision of the manual and by their awareness of the limits of the test's applicability and purposefulness.

In presenting the findings only in terms of developmental adequacy or inadequacy, the authors bypassed the question of relationship to later intelligence. It is likely, however, that the DDST is most useful in the intermediate range since there are relatively few items in the age range below three months, and there are many readily available and more clearly definitive diagnostic procedures, that is standard intelligence tests, for ages beyond four years. Within these limits, the DDST is a useful and acceptable screening device, particularly for those not specifically trained in test administration and evaluation. It is comparable to similar inventories, such as the *Developmental Screening Inventory,* based on the more extensive Gesell tests. In marginal or doubtful cases, it would seem important to remember the clinical need to look at the whole child in his specific environment. Specifically, one needs to keep in mind the effects of environmental experiences, such as the provision of opportunities for and freedom from deterrents to developmental progress, along with parental adequacy in reporting child behavior, and objective physical findings. For this purpose, the Hoopes Infant Rating Scale could serve as a useful extension of observed or reported functioning on the DDST items. With these reservations, this reviewer feels that the DDST, in the context of its stated aims to provide screening of developmental delay in young children, is an excellent addition to existing testing techniques.

EMMY E. WERNER, *Professor of Child Development and Research Child Psychologist, University of California, Davis, California.*

The DDST aims to be a simple, clinically useful tool for the detection of children with serious developmental delays for use by persons who have not had training in psychological testing. It evaluates four aspects of a child's functioning: gross motor, fine motor-adaptive, language, and personal-social development. More than 12 existing infant and preschool tests were surveyed to select 240 potential items which required no elaborate equipment and were easy to administer and score. After a pretest of 200 infants and preschool children, 105 items that best satisfied the above criteria were kept. The standardization group contained 1,036 normal children (543 M, 493 F) between the ages of 2 weeks and 6.4 years in Denver.

Test materials consist of a skein of red wool, a box of raisins, a rattle, a bottle, a bell, a tennis ball, and eight cubes. On the record form each test item in the four sectors is designated by a bar which indicates the ages at which 25, 50, 75, and 90 percent of the standardization population can perform the particular test item.

The results in each sector are categorized as normal, abnormal, and questionable. A child's performance in any sector is considered normal if he passes at least one item which is intersected by his age line and if he has no delays on any items in that sector (i.e., failure to perform any item passed by more than 90 percent of children his age). A child's performance in a sector is considered abnormal if he has two or more delays in that sector. It is considered questionable if he is delayed in just one item in each sector through which his age line passes.

The DDST is in use in Head Start programs, well-baby clinics and community health programs, and has gained popularity among pediatricians, medical students, and nonprofessional health workers. Although the authors, a pediatrician and a psychologist, state in the manual that the DDST was not designed to yield a developmental or mental age, or a developmental or intelligence quotient, this warning has not been heeded.

The test user should be aware of the following weaknesses of the DDST with regard to standardization, reliability, and validity. The norm group contains a significantly higher proportion of white children and of children whose fathers are in the professional, managerial, or sales occupation than the census distribution would warrant (*1*). The 105 items retained for the standardization were chosen on the basis of a pretest by four medical students. It is doubtful whether these students possessed the psychological training necessary to make such an examination meaningful.

Test-retest reliabilities and interexaminer reliabilities reported in the manual are based on extremely small samples of children (20 and 12, respectively), representing a wide age range, from 2 months to 5½ years. A more extensive tester-observer reliability study of 76 children, ranging in age from 4 to 77 months, and a test-retest reliability study (7 days apart) of 186 children between the ages of 1.5 and 76 months have been reported recently.[1] Mental ages were calculated for 13 age groups between 1.5 and 49 months, using the 50 percent pass method for each of the four sectors. Coefficients ranged between .66 and .93. Reliabilities were generally poor in the first and second years, but reached a more acceptable level in the third and fourth year. Of some concern is the fact that of the 28 items with the highest tester-observer and test-retest reliabilities, 17 could be passed by report of the mother, in contrast to only 5 of the 23 items with low tester-observer and test-retest reliabilities. The majority of the items on the DDST based on actual observations of the child's behavior had only low to moderate reliability. Thus the DDST seems to yield little more in the nature of reliable information than an interview with the mother, with the inherent distortion of developmental facts by recall.

The only preliminary validity study given in the 1968 manual is restricted to 18 children, ranging in age from 4 to 68 months who were given both the DDST and the Revised Yale Developmental Schedule (RYDS). Fifteen of the 18 children scored below 90 IQ on the RYDS. A correlation of .97 appears spuriously inflated, because the sample is small, skewed in the direction of abnormality, and encompasses a wide age range.

In a more extensive validity study,[2] 236 children were evaluated with the DDST and the following criterion tests: Stanford-Binet (N, 91; mean age, 52.5 months), RYDS (N, 64; mean age, 33 months), *Cattell Infant Intelligence Scale* (N, 50; mean age, 12.8 months) and *Bayley Scales of Infant Development* (N, 31; mean age, 6.2 months). Mental ages, mean DQ's/IQ's, and SD's on the criterion tests indicate that the majority of the children fell within the slow learner and mentally retarded range. Mental ages were obtained on the DDST by averaging scores for the four sectors and correlated with the scores on the criterion tests. Correlations ranged from .74 to .97. The agreement between the DDST and the criterion tests were compared in terms of co-positivity and co-negativity. The results of this analysis show a marked underselection by the DDST of children who received abnormal scores on the Bayley and Cattell tests. Seventy-one percent of the children called abnormal on the Bayley in the first year, and 43 percent of the children called abnormal on the Cattell in the second year were called normal on the DDST. Children over 30 months who were classified as abnormal on the RYDS and the Stanford-Binet were generally correctly identified on the DDST. There was a considerable overselection of normal children in the third year of life: 42 percent of normal children on the RYDS were called abnormal on the DDST. One wonders whether this may reflect on the insensitivity of untrained examiners to the period of negativism, shyness and distractibility that makes rapport with this age group a challenge to the most experienced tester.

In a report on the use of nonprofessional personnel for health screening of 298 Head Start children, comparisons were made between the referrals of health aides (mothers with less than high school education) and referrals made by psychologists and pediatricians.[3] Children whose scores the aides found to be below the 20th percentile on the DDST were compared with children scoring below IQ 80 on the Stanford-Binet. The aides referred only about half of the children below 80 IQ, and only one-fifth of the children identified by the pediatricians as having intellectual and developmental problems. The correlation between the aides' DDST scores and the psychologists' S-B scores for the same children was only .30.

---

[1] Frankenburg, W. K.; Camp, B. W.; Van Natta, P. A.; De Mersseman, J. A.; and Vorhess, S. F. "Reliability of the Denver Developmental Screening Test." Unpublished paper.
[2] Frankenburg, W. K.; Camp, B. W.; and Van Natta, P. A. "Validity of the Denver Developmental Screening Test." *Child Develop* 42(2):475-85 Je '71.

[3] Furuno, S., and Connor, A. "Use of Non-Professional Personnel for Health Screening of Head Start Children." Unpublished paper presented at *Annual Meeting of the American Orthopsychiatric Association*. San Francisco, California, March, 1970.

SUMMARY. At a time of great interest in developmental screening for the sake of early intervention, the search for a foolproof, quick and easy screening instrument is bound to become popular. Already there are available variations of the DDST. The user of these screening tools needs to keep in mind that available evidence indicates that the DDST is not as reliable, valid, sensitive, and specific as its authors had hoped. Its use under the age of 30 months should be discouraged since it is of questionable reliability in the first two years of life and misses a high proportion of children identified by technically more superior tests, such as the Bayley and Cattell. In the third year of life, it tends to overselect normal children, possibly because of the difficulty of an inexperienced tester in establishing rapport with this age group. The DDST appears to be a fairly satisfactory screening tool at 4–4½ years of age, but even here its concurrent validity is lower than that of other screening tests, such as the *Peabody Picture Vocabulary Test*.

Most important, it needs to be kept in mind that a screening tool, even the simplest, is only as good as the sensitivity of its user to the behavior of young children. It is doubtful whether the authors' claim is justified that "in a few hours training almost any adult can administer this test competently."

[406]

*Detroit Tests of Learning Aptitude. Ages 3 and over; 1935–68; DTLA; 20 scores: pictorial absurdities, verbal absurdities, pictorial opposites, verbal opposites, motor speed and precision, auditory attention span (for unrelated words, for related syllables), oral commissions, social adjustment A, visual attention span (for objects, for letters), orientation, free association, memory for designs, number ability, social adjustment B, broken pictures, oral directions, likenesses and differences, total; individual; 1 form; revised examiner's handbook ('67, 143 pages, with 1955 norms); supplement ('68, 15 pages); pictorial material ('58, 97 pages); revised record booklet ('59, 16 pages); no data on reliability for part scores; $3 per pictorial material; $5.90 per 35 record booklets; 30¢ per single copy; $4.45 per handbook; $1.20 per supplement; postage extra; (60–95) minutes; Harry J. Baker and Bernice Leland; Bobbs-Merrill Co., Inc. *

REFERENCES

1. See 3:275.
2. ASHLOCK, PATRICK ROBERT. *Visual Perception of Children in the Primary Grades and Its Relation to Reading Performance.* Doctor's thesis, University of Texas (Austin, Tex.), 1963. (DA 24:5186)
3. SANDSTEDT, BARBARA. "Relationship Between Memory Span and Intelligence of Severely Retarded Readers." *Read Teach* 17:246–50 Ja '64. *
4. ASHLOCK, PATRICK. "The Visual Perception of Children in the Primary Grades and Its Relation to Reading Performance." *Proc Ann Conv Int Read Assn* 10:331–3 '65. *
5. CHARRY, LAWRENCE BERNARD. *The Relationship Between Prereading and First Grade Reading Performances and Subsequent Achievement in Reading and Other Specified Areas.* Doctor's thesis, Temple University (Philadelphia, Pa.), 1967. (DA 28:960A)
6. WARTENBERG, HERBERT. *The Relationship Between Success in Beginning Reading and Various Predictive Measures.* Doctor's thesis, Temple University (Philadelphia, Pa.), 1967. (DA 28:979A)
7. CHIAPPONE, ANTHONY D. "Use of the Detroit Tests of Learning Aptitude With EMR." *Excep Children* 35:240–1 N '68. * (PA 43:13075)
8. BANAS, NORMA, AND WILLS, I. H. "The Vulnerable Child and Prescriptive Teaching." *Acad Ther* 4(3):215–9 sp '69. * (PA 43:17927)
9. BRUININKS, ROBERT H. "Auditory and Visual Perceptual Skills Related to the Reading Performance of Disadvantaged Boys." *Percept & Motor Skills* 29(1):179–86 Ag '69. * (PA 44:2835)
10. NELSON, C. MICHAEL, AND HUDSON, FLOYD G. "Predicting the Reading Achievement of Junior High School EMR Children." *Am J Mental Def* 74(3):415–20 N '69. *
11. ENGELHARDT, GEORGE M. "Predicting Rehabilitation of Socially Maladjusted Boys." *J Counsel Psychol* 17(6):546–9 N '70. * (PA 45:2619)

For a review by F. L. Wells, see 3:275; for reviews by Anne Anastasi and Henry Feinberg of an earlier edition, see 1:1058 (1 excerpt).

[407]

★A Developmental Screening Inventory. Ages 1–18 months; 1966; DSI; consists of selected items from the *Gesell Developmental Schedules;* abnormal development; history and observation ratings in 5 areas: adaptive, gross motor, fine motor, language, personal-social; individual; 1 form ['66, 6 pages]; manual (15 pages, reprint of *1* below); no data on reliability; $4.50 per 25 tests, postpaid; sample test free; test materials must be assembled locally; (5–30) minutes; Hilda Knobloch, Benjamin Pasamanick, and Earl S. Sherard, Jr.; Hilda Knobloch. *

REFERENCE

1. KNOBLOCH, HILDA; PASAMANICK, BENJAMIN; AND SHERARD, EARL S., JR. "A Developmental Screening Inventory for Infants." *Pediatrics* 38(sup):1095–108 D '66. *

[408]

*English Picture Vocabulary Test. Ages 5-0 to 8-11, 7-0 to 11-11; 1962–66; EPVT; derived from *Peabody Picture Vocabulary Test;* individual for Test 1; 1 form; 2 levels: Test 1 ('62, 44 pages), Test 2 ('62, 47 pages); manual, second edition ('66, 44 pages, 39 of which are identical, including norms, with 1963 manual); separate answer sheets (for group administration, Test 2 only) or record sheets (for individual administration) must be used; £1.40 per set of 25 tests, 25 record sheets, 25 answer sheets, scoring stencil, and manual; 35p per 25 record sheets; 35p per 25 answer sheets; 5p per scoring stencil for answer sheets; 50p per manual; postage extra; specimen set not available; [15–45] minutes; M. A. Brimer and Lloyd M. Dunn; distributed by Educational Evaluation Enterprises. *

REFERENCES

1. MARSHALL, ANNE. *The Abilities and Attainments of Children Leaving Junior Training Centres.* London: National Association for Mental Health, 1967. Pp. i, 62. *
2. PHILLIPS, C. J., AND BANNON, W. J. "The Stanford-Binet, Form L-M, Third Revision: A Local English Study of Norms, Concurrent Validity and Social Differences." *Brit J Ed Psychol* 38:148–61 Je '68. * (PA 42:17000)
3. BRIMER, M. A. "Sex Differences in Listening Comprehension." Discussion by John B. Carroll. *J Res & Develop Ed* 3(1):72–81 f '69. *
4. WEDELL, K., AND HORNE, I. EDNA. "Some Aspects of Perceptuo-Motor Disability in 5½-Year-Old Children." *Brit J Ed Psychol* 39(2):174–82 Je '69. * (PA 44:6514)
5. O'KELLY, E. "A Method for Detecting Slow Learning Juniors." *Ed Res* 12(2):135–9 F '70. *

KENNETH LOVELL, *Professor of Educational Psychology, The Institute of Education, The University, Leeds, England.*

The purpose of this test is to assess the levels of listening vocabulary among children in the age range 5-0 to 11-11. The EPVT was derived from the *Peabody Picture Vocabulary Test* and depends upon it for some of the preparatory constructional data. In essence a page of four pictures together with a spoken word makes a test item and the child's task is to identify the picture to which the word refers. The booklets which contain the pictures are stoutly constructed and, of course, reusable. Moreover, the accompanying manual sets out clearly and fully the directions for administering and scoring the tests; although the manual itself could be improved from the point of view of format, size of print, and durability.

The standardisation was carried out in Wiltshire—a predominantly rural county. Care was taken to stratify the maintained schools within the county by type, locality, and size. However, whether it is possible to build a sample representative of the U.K. from within Wiltshire is a point which might be argued. Conversion tables give standardised scores at monthly intervals and the percentile equivalents for standardised scores are also given. The manual recommends the values of .88 and .92 be accepted as the reliabilities of Tests 1 and 2, respectively. There is a consistent difference in raw scores in favour of boys—a characteristic feature of many orally administered vocabulary tests—but no separate conversion tables for the sexes.

Test 2 is also now available in a group form which employs expendable booklets. The pictures are set out horizontally in fours, instead of in a 2 × 2 array as in the individual arrangements. The accompanying manual sets out fully and precisely the directions for administering and scoring the tests in the new format.

Here are tests which can be used to assess listening vocabulary regardless of reading ability, while handicapped pupils can take the test providing they can evoke some movement to indicate the correct picture. However, it should be noted that when testing pupils who are very backward in number work, group administration demands that a child recognise the number of the page when its number name is called, and in the group form he must recognise the row number when its name is announced.

The most difficult question concerns the validity of the EPVT. At present no evidence exists that it will give an understanding of reading difficulties and other verbal handicaps, as is claimed in the manual. In a study involving children between the ages 8-0 and 11-0, Test 2 is reported to correlate .61 with one of Schonell's reading comprehension tests, .76 with WISC Vocabulary, and .80 with Schonell's *Graded Word Reading Test*. In another study, a correlation of .82 was found with Stanford-Binet Vocabulary. These suggest that Test 2 does measure some function which is common to other tests of vocabulary, although little more than this can be said at present.

In summary, the EPVT is recommended as an orally administered vocabulary test suitable for normal and for many kinds of handicapped pupils. It compares favourably with any other test designed to measure difficulty of listening vocabulary.

For reviews by L. B. Birch and Philip M. Levy, see 6:520.

[409]
★**Haptic Intelligence Scale for Adult Blind.** Blind and partially sighted adults; 1964; HIS; 7 scores: digit symbol, block design, object assembly, object completion, pattern board, bead arithmetic, total; individual; 1 form; manual (45 pages); record form (4 pages); $175 per set of testing materials, manual, and 100 record forms; $7 per 100 record forms; $2.50 per manual; postage extra; (90–120) minutes; Harriett C. Shurrager and Phil S. Shurrager; Psychology Research. *

REFERENCES
1. WATSON, SHIRLEY B. *Development and Standardization of a Performance Scale for Adult Blind.* Doctor's thesis, Illinois Institute of Technology (Chicago, Ill.), 1956.
2. KAMIN, HERBERT SPENCER, JR. *Onset and Duration of Blindness: Affecters of Haptic Intelligence Scale Performance.* Doctor's thesis, Illinois Institute of Technology (Chicago, Ill.), 1964.
3. DAUTERMAN, WILLIAM L.; SHAPIRO, BERNICE; AND SUINN, RICHARD M. "Performance Tests of Intelligence for Blind Reviewed." *Int J Ed Blind* 17:8–16 O '67. *
4. EBER, HERBERT W. "The Factor Structure of the WAIS-Verbal and HIS-Test Combination." *J Ed Res* 61:27–8 S '67. *
5. GALLAGHER, PATRICIA. "A Correlation Study of Haptic Subtest Scores and Travel Rating Skills of Blind Adolescents." *New Outl Blind* 62:240–6 O '68. *
6. NADDEO, CANDICE L., AND CURTIS, W. SCOTT. "Some Effects of the Disorientation of Tactile-Kinesthesia." *Int J Ed Blind* 18:69–72 O '68. *
7. STREITFELD, JULIAN W., AND AVERY, CONSTANCE D. "The WAIS and HIS Tests as Predictors of Academic Achievement in a Residential School for the Blind." *Int J Ed Blind* 18:73–7 O '68. * (PA 43:10178)
8. AVERY, CONSTANCE D., AND STREITFELD, JULIAN W. "An Abbreviation of the Haptic Intelligence Scale for Clinical Use." *Ed Visually Handicapped* 1(2):37–40 My '69. * (PA 43:14459)
9. SAXON, JOHN P.; ALSTON, PAUL P.; AND PORTER, THOMAS L. "Comparison of Haptic Intelligence Scale and WAIS Scores in a Population of Blind Psychotics." *Rehabil Counsel B* 13(1):49–51 S '69. *

MARSHALL S. HISKEY, *Professor of Educational Psychology and Measurements and Director, Educational-Psychological Clinic, University of Nebraska, Lincoln, Nebraska.*

Based on the assumption that existing tests were neither designed for nor adapted to the blind and that certain facets of their intelligence were not assessed adequately by verbal tests, the *Haptic Intelligence Scale* was developed as a nonverbal test to measure the intelligence of blind adults. The authors stress that the scale should be used in conjunction with verbal tests of intelligence in order to provide a more comprehensive evaluation of blind persons.

Four of the five subtests of the original or experimental scale were modified adaptations of the performance scale of the WAIS. Since the intercorrelations of the subtests of the experimental scale suggested that a common factor was involved to a large degree, two additional tests which required somewhat less fine tactile discrimination and skillful manipulation of parts were devised and included in the final scale.

Since the scale was designed to be used in conjunction with the verbal scale of the WAIS, Wechsler's procedures were followed with respect to establishing age categories and with the statistical treatment of the data.

The subjects in the standardization sample were from four designated geographic regions within the United States. Visual acuity did not exceed 5/200 in the better eye with correction. Both whites and nonwhites were included in proportion to their population (1950 census reports) but for stated and justifiable reasons the sample was not stratified on the basis of occupation and education.

Since the standardization procedure and the analyses of data replicate the methods utilized by Wechsler, little will be stated on this subject. The 20–34 age group was used as the reference group since they obtained the highest scores. The distribution of scores was converted to a scale with a mean scaled score of 10 and a standard deviation of 3. Since scaled score values do not vary with age, it is possible to compare a subject's performance with the reference group but not with the group to which he belongs. Relative ratings within a group can be obtained by comparing the IQ's listed with the conversion tables for the particular age group.

A retest of 136 subjects after six months or more gave reliability coefficients varying from .70 to .81. Test-retest reliability for the sum of five subtests (Bead Arithmetic was omitted) was .91 (N, 124). Odd-even reliabilities varied from a low of .79 on Object Assembly to a high of .94 on Bead Arithmetic. The total HIS IQ's showed a split-half reliability of .95. When utilized with the adult blind (ages 20–34) the HIS correlation with WAIS Verbal was .65.

Psychological examiners who are well versed in the administration and interpretation of the WAIS will have relatively little difficulty making the transition to the HIS. Due to the nature of the scale, the test materials are bulky. The materials are attractive and, in general, reveal fine craftsmanship. The manual is durable and contains a good review of the development and standardization of the scale as well as certain shortcomings, of which the authors are aware.

The test has some limitations when used with the partially sighted. Since it is based on a tactile approach even the slightest view of the materials would invalidate the subject's performance. Thus the partially-sighted person must wear a blindfold which often becomes irritating before the lengthy session is over. Likewise, there is the real question as to whether partially-sighted persons develop the tactile skills that were so much a part of the blind who were used in establishing the norms as the test was standardized.

In summary the *Haptic Intelligence Scale* is a nonverbal test patterned after the performance tests of the WAIS. The subtests are interesting and the blind enjoy them, but the administration time is rather long and perhaps should be divided in two sessions. The authors state that it is not a perfected test in its present form and should be administered and interpreted with caution. Its current value perhaps rests in the clinical clues it provides the trained psychologist. Users are cautioned that the HIS cannot be used with some blind persons of low ability or those who have psychological blockings. The obtained results correlate well with the WAIS but the authors stress that they in no way intend to imply that the HIS measures in the blind the same factors that the WAIS performance tests measure in the sighted. Nevertheless, it is a clinically useful instrument that should be valuable to those who work closely with the adult blind. A still greater service would have been rendered had the authors employed the same sample of blind adults to establish norms for the verbal scale of the WAIS.

[410]
*Hiskey-Nebraska Test of Learning Aptitude. Ages 3-16 (deaf and hearing); 1941–66; HNTLA; revision of *Nebraska Test of Learning Aptitude;* individual; 1 form ('66); revised manual ('66, 70 pages); record booklet ['66, 4 pages]; completion of drawings sheet ['66, 2 pages]; $56 per set of testing materials,

25 record booklets, and 25 drawing sheets; $3 per 50 record booklets; $1.75 per 50 drawing sheets; postage extra; (45-60) minutes; Marshall S. Hiskey; the Author. *

REFERENCES

1-3. See 3:289.
4. See 4:353.
5-12. See 5:409.
13. KIRK, SAMUEL A., AND PERRY, JUNE. "A Comparative Study of the Ontario and Nebraska Tests for the Deaf." *Am Ann Deaf* 93:315-23 S '48. * (*PA* 23:1902)
14. MACPHERSON, JANE G., AND LANE, HELEN S. "A Comparison of Deaf and Hearing on the Hiskey Test and on Performance Scales." *Am Ann Deaf* 93:178-84 Mr '48. * (*PA* 22:5103)
15. VARVA, FRANK IRVIN. *An Investigation of the Effect of Auditory Deficiency Upon Performance With Special Reference to Concrete and Abstract Tasks.* Doctor's thesis, University of Pittsburgh (Pittsburgh, Pa.), 1956. (*DA* 16:2532)
16. MIRA, MARY P. "The Use of the Arthur Adaptation of the Leiter International Performance Scale and the Nebraska Test of Learning Aptitude with Preschool Deaf Children." *Am Ann Deaf* 107:224-8 Mr '62. * (*PA* 37:1617)
17. CASJENS, CLIFFORD CURTIS. *Performance of Brain-Injured and Non-Brain Injured Mentally Retarded Children on the Hiskey-Nebraska Test of Learning Aptitude.* Doctor's thesis, University of Nebraska (Lincoln, Neb.), 1965. (*DA* 26:2048)
18. GIANGRECO, C. JOSEPH. *The Hiskey-Nebraska Test of Learning Aptitude as a Predictor of Academic Achievement of Deaf Children.* Doctor's thesis, University of Nebraska (Lincoln, Neb.), 1965. (*DA* 26:155)
19. GENTILE, J. RONALD. "In Search of Research: Four Children's Tests." *J Sch Psychol* 5:1-13 au '66. * (*PA* 41:3335)
20. GIANGRECO, C. JOSEPH. "The Hiskey-Nebraska Test of Learning Aptitude (Revised) Compared to Several Achievement Tests." *Am Ann Deaf* 111:566-77 S '66. * (*PA* 41:999)
21. BACH, LLOYD CARL. *A Comparison of Selected Psychological Tests Used With Trainable Mentally Retarded Children.* Doctor's thesis, University of South Dakota (Vermillion, S.D.), 1968. (*DA* 29:2990A)
22. MORRIS, BERNIECE EVELYN JEPSEN VANCAMP. *Responses by Adult Retardates to Visual Stimuli of Variable Fidelity.* Doctor's thesis, University of Nebraska (Lincoln, Neb.), 1968. (*DA* 29:1788A)
23. MORRIS, GEORGE LEE, JR. *Effects of Variation in Fidelity Level of Visual Stimuli.* Doctor's thesis, University of Nebraska (Lincoln, Neb.), 1968. (*DA* 29:1788A)
24. PAUL, GERALD THOMAS. *The Relationship Between Prenatal and Perinatal Experiences and Intellectual, Perceptual-Motor, and Conceptual Functioning in Preschool Adopted Children.* Doctor's thesis, Temple University (Philadelphia, Pa.), 1968. (*DAI* 30:1364B)
25. HOWARD, JANE OSBURN. *A Comparison of the Revised Stanford-Binet Intelligence Scale, Form L-M, and the Nebraska Test of Learning Aptitude, 1966 Revision, With Groups of Mentally Retarded, Deaf, and Normal Children.* Doctor's thesis, University of New Mexico (Albuquerque, N.M.), 1969. (*DAI* 30:3322A)
26. LEWIS, JAMES F. *Differential Evaluation of Selected Tests When Utilized With Institutionalized and Non-Institutionalized Trainable Mentally Retarded.* Doctor's thesis, University of Nebraska (Lincoln, Neb.), 1969. (*DAI* 30:3793A)

T. ERNEST NEWLAND, *Professor of Educational Psychology, University of Illinois, Urbana, Illinois.*

This test is a revision of the 1941 *Nebraska Test of Learning Aptitude,* which came to be regarded by the author as useful with hearing children. With an added test, Spatial Reasoning, the test was administered to 1,107 deaf children and 1,101 hearing children from 2-6 years to 17-5 years in 10 states.

Understandably, the number of children in the standardization populations at each year level varies more for the deaf (25 to 106, median 71) than for the hearing (47 to 85, median 76). Parental occupational level sampling for the hearing population (no such data on the deaf) corresponds closely to the U.S. census data. No breakdowns by race or sex are provided.

The total test age score is called "learning age" (LA) for deaf subjects and "mental age" for hearing subjects. Although the author recommends the use of age ratings, the deviation IQ may be computed for hearing children and "learning quotient" (LQ) for deaf children. The learning age is the median of the age scores on the subtests.

The split-half reliabilities reported (scores unspecified) are for wide-range populations: .95 for the deaf and .93 for the hearing in groups having an age range of 3 to 10; .92 and .90, respectively, in the range of 11 to 17. No other information is reported for these four groups.

The author presents four kinds of validity data: subtest intercorrelations, correlations between age ratings on the subtests and the median LA, correlations with the 1960 Stanford-Binet and the WISC for hearing children, and correlations with performance on achievement tests and teacher ratings for the deaf. For the deaf, subtest intercorrelations range from .33 to .74 (median .48) for the age range 3-10 and from .31 to .43 (median .37) for ages 11-17. For the hearing, the intercorrelations range from .32 to .78 (median .55) for ages 3-10 and .25 to .46 (median .34) for ages 11-17. The author reports a correlation of .86 (IQ's) with the S-B for 99 subjects ranging in age from 3 through 10 and a correlation of .78 for ages 11-17. For WISC, the correlation between IQ's is .82 on 52 subjects (age range 5-11) for the three groups.

It is this reviewer's opinion that, in spite of the absence of any discernable theory underlying the construction of the HNTLA, it does provide, at least in certain kinds of behavior samplings, a closer approximation to tapping the major psychological components necessary in the school learning of deaf children, especially the younger ones, than does, say, the WISC Performance test which is so widely used with deaf and seriously acoustically impaired children. The use of "learning ages" and "learning quotients" and the determination of the total test performance by taking the median subtest score are commendable. Test-retest information is needed, as is that on standard errors of measurement, at least for the year-age levels. The revised test is physically a distinct improvement over its predecessor in packaging and printing.

In spite of the impreciseness of much of the research cited in support of the HNTLA, this test is the most promising one available for assessing the "book learning" capability of deaf children. The behavior samplings in the areas of memory, picture identification, and picture association in particular have demonstrated relevance to the kinds of learning aptitude important in school work. The demands for testing time and highly technical test administration techniques are not great. Its nearest competitor is the *Leiter International Performance Scale*. More definitive research is needed, however, to demonstrate that the use of the HNTLA with hearing children can be as fruitful psycho-educationally over the age range claimed for it as is the Stanford-Binet or even the verbal portion of the WISC. For the lower portions of the HNTLA age range, the *Pictorial Test of Intelligence* appears to be a more promising test for use with hearing children.

For a review by William Sloan of an earlier edition, see 5:409; for a review by Mildred C. Templin, see 4:353.

[411]

Kahn Intelligence Tests: Experimental Form. Ages 1 month and over, particularly the verbally or culturally handicapped; 1960; KIT; uses same test objects as *Kahn Test of Symbol Arrangement*; main scale plus 6 optional scales: brief scale, concept formation, recall, motor coordination, scale for use with the deaf, scale for use with the blind; individual; 1 form (16 plastic objects); record form (4 pages); manual (34 pages, reprint of *2* below); $26 per set of testing materials including 50 record forms and manual; $2.50 per manual; cash orders postpaid; administration time not reported; Theodore C. Kahn; Psychological Test Specialists. *

REFERENCES

1-2. See 6:524.
3. KROSKE, WILLIAM H.; FRETWELL, LORETTA N.; AND CUPP, MARION E. "Comparison of the Kahn Intelligence Tests: Experimental Form, the Stanford-Binet and the WAIS for Familial Retardates." *Percept & Motor Skills* 21:428 O '65. * (PA 40:3310)
4. MCDANIEL, ERNEST D., AND CARSE, WILLIAM T. "Validation of the Kahn Intelligence Tests." *Ed & Psychol Meas* 25:1153-6 w '65. * (PA 40:3581)
5. CARSE, WILLIAM T. "Further Validation of the Kahn Intelligence Tests." *Ed & Psychol Meas* 27:1055-60 w '67. * (PA 42:8935)
6. EPPLEY, EDWIN B. *A Validity Study Comparing the Main Scale of the Kahn Intelligence Test With the Wechsler Intelligence Scale for Children.* Master's thesis, Millersville State College (Millersville, Pa.), 1968.
7. ROFFMAN, PAMELA OLCOTT. *Validation of the Kahn Intelligence Tests: Experimental Form With Southeastern Second-Graders.* Master's thesis, University of Georgia (Athens, Ga.), 1968.
8. CHOVAN, WILLIAM L., AND HATHAWAY, MILDRED L. "The Performance of Two Culturally Divergent Groups of Children on a Culture-Free Test." Abstract. *J Sch Psychol* 8(1):66 '70. * (PA 44:10126)

MARJORIE P. HONZIK, *Lecturer in Psychology, and Research Psychologist, Institute of Human Development, University of California, Berkeley, California.*

The KIT is an age scale extending from 1 month to adulthood. The test materials consist of a felt strip (numbered from 1 to 15), and 16 small, flat, plastic objects (3 dogs, 3 hearts, 3 stars, 2 butterflies, an anchor, a cross, a parrot, a circle, and a segment of a circle). These materials vary in color and size as well as shape, and are intrinsically interesting to persons of all ages.

The test items for this age scale are patterned after those of the *Gesell Developmental Schedules* and the *Stanford-Binet Intelligence Scale*. Kahn's use of the plastic objects to test different age levels is ingenious. This test is weakest at the youngest age levels, where development is most rapid. There are only 6 test items covering the first 12 months of life, in contrast to 103 in the *Bayley Scales of Infant Development* and 55 in the *Cattell Infant Intelligence Scale*. The 6 items available for each of the second and third years are also too few for adequate testing. Six tests per year for the age period 4 to 14 should prove sufficient, especially after year 6.

The inadequacy of the test series for the first year is further indicated by the age placements. For example, item 1 of the scale is definitely much more difficult than item 2. The relative age placements of these items on the Bayley Scale are 3.3 months and .5 months, respectively. Also, first-year items 5 and 6 require manipulation of very small plastic objects which babies find difficult to manage. Most infants less than a year old would be frustrated by the problem of making a small flat plastic dog stand up and would probably brush the materials aside. The first-year scale should be either improved by adding more test items or deleted entirely. In its present form, it is worse than nothing, since it might suggest retardation where none exists.

Many of the concepts which are basic to the Stanford-Binet are used in the Kahn tests. Binet considered "following directions" an important aspect of intelligence. Success on many of the Kahn tests is highly dependent on attending to instructions. For example, at year 3-4, all six test items require that the child understand and comply with instructions: "Find me one just like it," "Put them together the way I had them," "Find something else that can run....fly," "Put one red thing in the box," and "Show me a bigger." This test depends heavily not only on verbal comprehension but also on verbal facility. Beginning at year 4–5, the child is asked to respond verbally to one or two items at most levels. The test instructions become rather complex and contrived at the older age levels and at times have a negative tone. For example, at year 13–14, the subject is asked not only which object is different from the others but is told *not* to judge "by what the object could stand for," nor by "thickness, thinness, or transparency."

Kahn's claim of freedom from cultural bias is not supported by McDaniel and Carse's study (*4*) of 50 children between the ages of 4 and 6. These children were tested on both the KIT and the Stanford-Binet. The KIT IQ's were more closely related to socioeconomic status than the S-B IQ's, suggesting that the KIT may be at least as culturally biased as the S-B, if not more so.

STANDARDIZATION. The age placement of test items is based on testing 40 adults and 297 children ranging in age from 1 month to 17 years. Item difficulty was determined by the responses of at least 10 children at each age level whose MA fell within that year level on the WISC, S-B, or Gesell. Clearly, KIT is not adequately standardized. Kahn considers these scales "frankly experimental."

RELIABILITY. Kahn reports a test-retest reliability of .94 based on the MA's of 23 children ranging in age from 1 to 14 years. It is difficult to understand why there is no correction for age, either by using IQ's or by partialling out chronological age.

VALIDITY. Kahn reports a validity coefficient of .75 based on a correlation of the MA's on the KIT and S-B for the same 23 children used in the reliability study. Fortunately, more adequate evaluations of the validity of this test are available. McDaniel and Carse (*4*) report a correlation of .83 between IQ's on the KIT and S-B for 50 children whose parents held predominantly managerial or professional positions. This coefficient suggests a high degree of comparability between the two scales. At the other end of the ability scale, Kroske and others (*3*) report the KIT IQ's for 34 cultural-familial retarded children living in an institution. The mean IQ of this group on the KIT was 43; on the S-B, 47; and on the WAIS, 56. The Kahn IQ correlated .62 with the S-B IQ and .51, .73, and .66 with the WAIS Verbal, Performance, and the Full Scale, respectively, in spite of the restricted range of ability.

SUMMARY. The KIT consists of interesting test materials which yield information about the intellectual functioning of a child or adult. It should be used with extreme caution until adequately standardized. This test requires understanding of language but few verbal responses, and it is less culture free than the Binet tests. It is of little or no value as an infant test because of inadequate sampling of abilities. The test is worthy of consideration because it is intrinsically interesting, covers a wide age range, and correlates highly with the Binet and Wechsler scales in populations of both low and high ability. Also derived from this scale are shorter scales to estimate ability in areas of concept formation, recall, and motor coordination and special scales that can be administered by sign language and for testing the visually handicapped. The usefulness, reliability, and validity of these derived scales have not been determined.

[412]

★**New Guinea Performance Scales.** Pre-literates ages 17 and over; 1961–71; NGPS; based (except *f*) on the unpublished *PIR Test* used for screening for the Pacific Island Regiment; test (except *e*) is essentially the same as the *Queensland Test* except for minor differences in some of the testing materials and differences in administration, scoring, and norms population; 6 tests; 7 scores: cube imitation, bead threading, passalong, form assembly, observation, design construction, total; individual; 1 form; manual ('71, c1970, 274 pages, see *4* below); record form ('67, 2 pages); norms based on male Papuans and New Guineans; Aus $70 per set of testing materials; $9.50 (£2.75) per manual available from Jacaranda Press Pty Ltd. in Australia (Ginn & Co. Ltd. in Britain); postage extra; record form must be reproduced locally; (45–60) minutes; I. G. Ord; New Guinea Fund for Psychological Test Development. *

a) CUBE IMITATION TEST. An adaptation of Pintner's revision of the Knox test; (5) minutes.
b) BEAD THREADING TEST. (10) minutes.
c) PASSALONG TEST. Modification of a subtest of *Alexander Performance Scale*; test booklet title is *Passalong Test (New Guinea Version)*; 1 form ('61, 8 cards); (10–15) minutes.
d) FORM ASSEMBLY TEST. Single form, multiple form; (8–10) minutes.
e) OBSERVATION TEST (5–10) minutes.
f) DESIGN CONSTRUCTION TEST. Published separately as *Pacific Design Construction Test;* Form A ('65, 13 cards); (10–15) minutes.

REFERENCES

1. ORD, I. G. *Development of a Test of Cognitive Capacity for Indigenes of Papua-New Guinea.* Master's thesis, University of Queensland (Brisbane, Australia), 1959.
2. ORD, I. G. "The New Guinea Performance Scale and Its Educational Use." *Papua & New Guinea J Ed* 5:7–16 S '67. *
3. ORD, I. G. "The P.I.R. Test and Derivatives." *Austral Psychologist* 2:137–46 Mr '68. * (PA 42:18798)
4. ORD, I. G. *Mental Tests for Pre-Literates: Results Mainly*

From New Guinea Studies. London: Ginn & Co. Ltd., 1971 (c1970). Pp. xiii, 270. *

[413]

★**New South African Individual Scale.** Ages 6–17; 1964; NSAIS; 12 scores: verbal (vocabulary, comprehension, reasoning, problems, memory, total), nonverbal (pattern completion, blocks, absurdities, form board, total), total; both power and power-time scores are obtained for 4 subtests, the verbal and nonverbal test totals, and the overall total; individual; 1 form; preliminary manual in 3 booklets: background and standardisation (33 pages), instructions (27 pages), norms (50 pages); record booklet ['64, 4 pages]; R39 per set of testing materials and manual; R4 per 100 record booklets; R4 per 100 pattern completion practice sheets; R5 per set of manual booklets; postpaid within South Africa; Afrikaans edition available; (45–60) minutes; Human Sciences Research Council. *

REFERENCE

1. STRÜMPFER, D. J. W., AND MIENIE, C. J. P. "A Validation of the Harris-Goodenough Test." *Brit J Ed Psychol* 38: 96–100 F '68. * (PA 42:12134)

[414]

★**The Ohwaki-Kohs Tactile Block Design Intelligence Test for the Blind.** Blind ages 6 and over; 1965; OKTBD; record booklet title is *The Ohwaki-Kohs Tactile Block Design Intelligence Test;* adaptation of *Kohs' Block Design Test;* for American revision, see 427; individual; 1 form (blocks and design cards); record booklet (4 pages); manual (11 pages plus record booklet); norms based upon testing of Japanese subjects with Japanese edition first published in 1960; $47.50 per examiner's kit of testing materials, 25 record booklets, and manual; $42.50 per set of testing materials; $6.50 per 25 record booklets; $2.50 per manual; postpaid; administration time not reported; Yoshikazu Ohwaki; Western Psychological Services. *

REFERENCES

1. OHWAKI, YOSHIKAZU; TANNO, YUJI; OHWAKI, MIEKO; HARIU, TOHRU; HAYASAKA, KAZUKO; AND MIYAKE, KEIKO. "Construction of an Intelligence Test for the Blind (Ohwaki-Kohs Tactile-Block Intelligence Test)." *Tohuko Psychologica Folia* 18(2–4):45–65 '60. * (PA 34:8294)
2. BOZZO, MARIA TERESA, AND ZECCA, GRAZIELLA. "First Results of Applications on Italian Subjects of the Ohwaki-Kohs Intelligence Test for the Blind." *Psychologia* 7:121–3 Je '64. *
3. SUINN, RICHARD M. "The Ohwaki-Kohs Intelligence Test for the Blind: Standardization on American Adults." *Psychologia* 9:217–8 S '66. *
4. SUINN, RICHARD M.; DAUTERMAN, WILLIAM; AND SHAPIRO, BERNICE. "The Stanford Ohwaki-Kohs Tactile Block Design Intelligence Test for the Blind." *New Outl Blind* 60: 77–9 Mr '66. *

J Ed Meas 4:261–2 w '67. *Richard J. Rankin.* This test was developed in Japan with the current form basically an English translation. * The eleven page manual contains a relatively complete description of the test administration. Unfortunately there is little information about the normative sample, and the theoretical justification for use of a performance scale based on the single intellectual dimension tapped by block design is sketchy. The IQ is determined by summing the raw points obtained, converting to mental age, dividing by chronological age, and multiplying the result by 100. At age 13 and above, the mental age is divided by a correct chronological age. Interestingly, the corrected chronological ages parallel exactly those presented in the 1937 Stanford Binet Manual. Since the S. B. adjustment was specific to that scale, it cannot be generalized as a constant chronological age correction table for performance scales. The disadvantages of the ratio IQ have been stressed many times in literature and the lack of a constant variation with age is well known. Indicative of the general quality of the manual, example C for computing the IQ is incorrect. Further confusion occurs on the test protocol where the steps for determining IQ read "Step 3 IQ equals C.A. in months over M.A. in months times 100." No statistical information concerning the mean score or the S.D. of scores is presented in the manual, however, an IQ distribution for 278 totally blind Japanese children is presented. The distribution is bimodal with peaks in the IQ range 65–74 and 125–134. The manual claims that the maximum obtainable raw score is 131 points, but in actuality the maximum obtainable score is 134 points. (Summation Column 6 of Protocol.) This error occurs in Table 2 of the manual and on the test protocol booklet. The norming group is not described. The assumption can be made that the norm data are based upon the scores of 278 totally blind persons ranging in age from 8 to 20 years. However, mental age equivalents are given down to year 5.3. If, indeed, the norms presented are a translation for use with American blind from a Japanese population, the cultural differences are so great as to cast severe doubt upon their usefulness. The validity data given for the O-KTBD is sketchy. Figure 2 of the manual describes a linear relationship between increasing O-KTBD score and increasing CA. This figure is based upon 243 cases with a CA range of 8 through 20 years. The fallacy of using increasing score with increasing age as a validity coefficient is obvious. The curve has the same general shape as a curve for increase in height over the same span of years. The relationship does not justify the statement "This finding does demonstrate a fairly high validity for the O-KTBD." * The reliability data presented on the O-KTBD are scanty. A test, re-test study, based upon 33 totally blind individuals ranging from age 8 to 20 made with a 3½ month interval, reported a reliability coefficient of .846. This is interpreted as an indication "that the O-KTBD as an intelligence test for the blind has a high reliability." The direct statement is made in the manual that the O-KTBD is applicable for use as an intelligence scale with children of normal intelligence and vision between 2 and 6 years. No norms are provided for youngsters in this age group, nor are the instructions clear as to how a child with normal vision is to be tested. The reviewer attempted to test several sighted children blindfolded and found that they were incapable of performing. It was thus determined that normal vision children should be tested in a non-blindfolded condition. Following the instructions of the manual, 26 children obtained from public schools and private kindergarten in Oklahoma ranging in age from 3.5 years to 8.0 years were given both the 1960 Form L-M Stanford Binet and the O-KTBD Intelligence Test. The tests were presented one week apart and were given in counterbalanced order. * The correlation between the IQ's yielded by the scale was .56. Discrepancies in the scores were spectacular. The mean IQ difference was 41.42 points, with a S.D. of the differences of 38.49 points. In 23 of the 26 cases the O-KTBD score was higher than the S.B. score. One 5-year, 10-months male achieved an S.B. IQ of 154 and an O-KTBD IQ of 34! The mean S.B. IQ of the validation group is 112.23 with a S.D. of 18.40. The mean O-KTBD IQ is 153.65 with a standard deviation of 45.78. It is emphatically recommended that the O-KTBD be used with neither blind nor sighted individuals until the severe defects in the test are eliminated.

[415]

★Pacific Design Construction Test. Illiterates and semiliterates in Papua and New Guinea; 1962–68; PDCT; based upon *Kohs' Block-Design Test* and block design subtest of *Wechsler Adult Intelligence Scale*; subtest of *New Guinea Performance Scales*; subtest (with minor modifications) of *Queensland Test* in which it is called *Pattern Matching Test*; individual; 1 form ('68, 13 design cards, 32 titles, and 5 tile trays); manual ('68, 29 pages); record form ('68, 1 page); norms based on natives of Papua and New Guinea; Aus $30 per set of testing materials and 10 record forms; 40¢ per 10 record forms; $1.50 per manual; postpaid within Australia; I. G. Ord; Australian Council for Educational Research. *

REFERENCES

1. ORD, I. G. *Development of a Test of Cognitive Capacity for Indigenes of Papua-New Guinea.* Master's thesis, University of Queensland (Brisbane, Australia), 1959.
2. KEARNEY, GEORGE E. "Cognitive Capacity Among the Orokaiva." *New Guinea Res B* 13:1–25 '66. *
3. ORD, I. G. *Mental Tests for Pre-Literates: Results Mainly From New Guinea Studies.* London: Ginn & Co. Ltd., 1971 (c1970). Pp. xiii, 270. *

[416]

★Pacific Infants Performance Scale. Ages 5.5–8; 1970; PIPS; preschool screening; revision of *Elementary Performance Scale* which was an adaptation of 3 subtests of the *New Guinea Performance Scales*; 4 scores: block tapping, bead threading, design making, total; individual; 1 form; manual (21 pages); reliability data for earlier edition only; no norms, authors recommend use of local norms; Aus $9.45 per set of testing materials; $1.20 per 100 record sheets; postage extra; specimen set not available; [20] minutes; I. G. Ord and J. Schofield; Jacaranda Press Pty Ltd. *

REFERENCE

1. ORD, I. G. *Mental Tests for Pre-Literates: Results Mainly From New Guinea Studies.* London: Ginn & Co. Ltd., 1971 (c1970). Pp. xiii, 270. *

[417]

*Peabody Picture Vocabulary Test. Ages 2.5–18; 1959–70; PPVT; individual; no reading by examinees; Forms A, B, ('59, 154 page picture booklet used with both forms); plastic edition of pictures also available; expanded manual ('65, 51 pages); individual record ('70, 4 pages) for each form; $10 per set of testing materials including 25 individual records for each form ($15 with set of plastic plates); $3 per 50 individual records; postage extra; (10–15) minutes; Lloyd M. Dunn; American Guidance Service, Inc. *

REFERENCES

1–21. See 6:530.
22. PATTERSON, HENRY J. *A Concurrent Validation of the Peabody Picture Vocabulary Test.* Doctor's thesis, Kansas State Teachers College (Emporia, Kan.), 1961.
23. TENHOFF, MARVIN LE ROY. *Conditions Associated With Readiness for School Entrance at Selected Ages.* Doctor's thesis, University of Minnesota (Minneapolis, Minn.), 1962. (*DA* 24:150)
24. GRAVES, GORDON R. *A Study of the Use of the Peabody Picture Vocabulary Test for Identifying Mentally Retarded Children, Using the Wechsler Intelligence Scale for Children as a Criterion.* Master's thesis, Fresno State College (Fresno, Calif.), 1963.
25. KRIPPNER, STANLEY. "Correlates of Reading Improvement." *J Develop Read* 7:29–39 au '63. *
26. ROOD, THOMAS M. *The Effectiveness of the Peabody Vocabulary Pictures Tests: A Study of Reliability and Validity.* Master's thesis, Western State College (Gunnison, Colo.), 1963.
27. WINSCHEL, JAMES FRANCIS. *Performance of Normal and Mentally Retarded Children on Selected Motor and Intellectual Tasks as a Function of Incentive Conditions.* Doctor's thesis, University of Pittsburgh (Pittsburgh, Pa.), 1963. (*DA* 25: 6443)
28. ALLEN, ROBERT M.; HAUPT, THOMAS D.; AND JONES, R. WAYNE. "A Suggested Use and Non-Use for the Peabody Picture Vocabulary Test With the Retarded Child." *Psychol Rep* 15:421–2 O '64. * (*PA* 39:5034)
29. DANFORD, BART HARLAND. *Some Correlates of Two Brief Intelligence Tests Used by Pediatricians.* Doctor's thesis, University of Houston (Houston, Tex.), 1964. (*DA* 26:1772)
30. FLOYD, WILLIAM A. "Aptitude Testing With Mental Patients." *Voc Guid Q* 12:203–6 sp '64. *
31. JACKSON, CECIL LEE. *Factor Structure of the Wechsler Intelligence Scale for Children and Selected Reference Tests at Pre-School Level and After First Grade: A Longitudinal Study.* Doctor's thesis, University of Georgia (Athens, Ga.), 1964. (*DA* 25:6052)
32. MARLEY, ALBERT D. *A Validity Study of the Columbia Mental Maturity Scale and the Peabody Picture Vocabulary Test, Using the Wechsler Intelligence Scale for Children as the Validating Criterion, With a Selected Sample of Educable Mentally Retarded Children.* Doctor's research study No. 1, Colorado State College (Greeley, Colo.), 1964. (*DA* 25:5386)
33. MATTHEWS, CHARLES G., AND MANNING, GEORGE C., JR. "Psychological Test Performances in Three Electroencephalographic Classifications of Mentally Retarded Subjects." *Am J Mental Def* 68:485–92 Ja '64. * (*PA* 39:2526)
34. NATION, JAMES EDWARD. *A Comparative Study of Comprehension and Usage Vocabularies of Normal and Cleft Palate Preschool Children.* Doctor's thesis, University of Wisconsin (Madison, Wis.), 1964. (*DA* 25:3747)
35. RUGG, ROGER H. *A Comparison of the Relative Effectiveness of the Peabody Picture Vocabulary Test and the Ammons Full Range Picture Vocabulary Test With Educable Mentally Retarded Children.* Master's thesis, Sacramento State College (Sacramento, Calif.), 1964.
36. SCHARF, MURRAY PATRICK. *The Performance of Twelve-Year-Old and Thirteen-Year-Old Children on the Peabody Picture Vocabulary Test.* Master's thesis, University of Saskatchewan (Saskatoon, Sask., Canada), 1964.

37. TUTTLE, LESTER EUGENE, JR. *The Comparative Effect on Intelligence Test Scores of Negro and White Children When Certain Verbal and Time Factors Are Varied.* Doctor's thesis, University of Florida (Gainesville, Fla.), 1964. (DA 25:7093)
38. BURNETT, ALASTAIR. "Comparison of the PPVT, Wechsler-Bellevue, and Stanford-Binet on Educable Retardates." *Am J Mental Def* 69:712–5 Mr '65. * (PA 39:12715)
39. CORWIN, BETTY JANE. "The Influence of Culture and Language on Performance of Individual Ability Tests." *J Sch Psychol* 3:41–7 sp '65. * (PA 39:15217)
40. EKLUND, SUSAN, AND SCOTT, MYRTLE. "Effects of Bilingual Instruction on Test Response of Latin American Children." *Psychol Sch* 2:280 Jl '65. *
41. GAGE, GERALD E., AND NAUMANN, THEODOR F. "Correlation of the Peabody Picture Vocabulary Test and the Wechsler Intelligence Scale for Children." *J Ed Res* 58:466–8 Jl–Ag '65. * (PA 40:422)
42. HAMMILL, DONALD, AND IRWIN, ORVIS C. "Peabody Picture Vocabulary Test as a Measure of Intelligence for Mentally Subnormal Children." *Training Sch B* 62:126–31 N '65. * (PA 40:2135)
43. HEDGER, MABLE F. Chap. 3, "An Analysis of Three Picture Vocabulary Tests for Use With the Deaf," pp. 12–9. In *Research Studies on the Psycholinguistic Behavior of Deaf Children.* Edited by Joseph Rosenstein and Walter H. MacGinitie. CEC Research Monograph, Series B, No. B-2. Washington, D.C.: Council for Exceptional Children, 1965. Pp. v, 40. *
44. HUGHES, ROBERT B., AND LESSLER, KEN. "A Comparison of WISC and Peabody Scores of Negro and White Rural School Children." *Am J Mental Def* 69:877–80 My '65. * (PA 39:12289)
45. IRWIN, ORVIS C., AND HAMMILL, DONALD D. "Effect of Type, Extent and Degree of Cerebral Palsy on Three Measures of Language." *Cereb Palsy J* 26:7–9 N–D '65. *
46. IRWIN, ORVIS C., AND HAMMILL, DONALD D. "Regional and Sex Differences in the Language of Cerebral Palsied Children." *Cereb Palsy J* 26:11–2 S–O '65. * (PA 40:1899)
47. IVANOFF, JOHN M., AND TEMPERO, HOWARD E. "Effectiveness of the Peabody Picture Vocabulary Test With Seventh-Grade Pupils." *J Ed Res* 58:412–5 My–Je '65. * (PA 39:15242)
48. KORST, JOSEPH W. *A Comparison of the Results Obtained for the Peabody Picture Vocabulary Test and the Leiter International Performance Scale With Children Having Functional Articulatory Disorders.* Master's thesis, Wichita State University (Wichita, Kan.), 1965.
49. MEIER, JOHN HENRY. *An Exploratory Factor Analysis of Psychodiagnostic and Case Study Information From Children in Special Education Classes for the Educable Mentally Handicapped.* Doctor's thesis, University of Denver (Denver, Colo.), 1965. (DA 26:3153)
50. MUELLER, MAX W. *A Comparison of the Empirical Validity of Six Tests of Ability With Young Educable Retardates.* Institute of Mental Retardation and Intellectual Development, IMRID Behavioral Science Monograph No. 1. Nashville, Tenn.: Peabody College Bookstore, 1965. Pp. vii, 130. *
51. MUELLER, MAX WILLIAM. *A Comparison of the Empirical Validity of Six Tests of Ability With Educable Mental Retardates.* Doctor's thesis, George Peabody College for Teachers (Nashville, Tenn.), 1965. (DA 26:6853)
52. SHANE, JAMES F. *Effectiveness of the Peabody Picture Vocabulary Test in Comparison to Wechsler Intelligence Scale for Children and Stanford-Binet Test Scores in Identification of Mentally Retarded and Gifted School Children.* Master's thesis, California State College (Long Beach, Calif.), 1965.
53. STRONG, ROBERT THOMAS, JR. *The Identification of Primary School Age Children With Learning Handicaps Associated With Minimal Brain Disorder.* Doctor's thesis, University of Utah (Salt Lake City, Utah), 1965. (DA 26:1489)
54. THRONE, FRANCES M.; KASPAR, JOSEPH C.; AND SCHULMAN, JEROME L. "The Peabody Picture Vocabulary Test in Comparison With Other Intelligence Tests and an Achievement Test in a Group of Mentally Retarded Boys." *Ed & Psychol Meas* 25:589–95 su '65. * (PA 39:16072)
55. CHILDERS, PERRY R. "Concurrent Validity of a Group Administered Peabody Picture Vocabulary Test." *J Ed Res* 60:92–3 O '66. *
56. EMERICK, LONNIE L. *An Evaluation of Three Psychological Variables in Tonic and Clonic Stutterers and in Nonstutterers.* Doctor's thesis, Michigan State University (East Lansing, Mich.), 1966. (DA 28:317A)
57. FARGO, GEORGE; CROWELL, DORIS; AND NOYES, MARY. "Screening for Learning Problems: A New Use for Educational Television." *Audio Vis Instr* 11:762+ N '66. *
58. HAMMILL, DONALD D., AND IRWIN, ORVIS C. "Relations Among Measures of Language of Cerebral Palsied and of Mentally Retarded Children." *Cereb Palsy J* 27:8–9 Ja–F '66. * (PA 40:5860)
59. IRWIN, ORVIS C. "A Comparison of the Vocabulary of Use and of Understanding by Mentally Retarded Children." *Cereb Palsy J* 27:8–10 N–D '66. * (PA 41:3239)
60. IRWIN, ORVIS C. "A Comparison of the Vocabulary of Use and of Understanding of Cerebral Palsied Children." *Cereb Palsy J* 27:7–11 My–Je '66. * (PA 40:10390)
61. IRWIN, ORVIS C. "A Language Test for Use With Cerebral Palsied Children." *Cereb Palsy J* 27:6–8 S–O '66. * (PA 41:1816)
62. IRWIN, ORVIS C. "The Relation of Vocabularies of Use and Understanding by Cerebral Palsied Children to Several Variables." *Cereb Palsy J* 27:3–4 Jl–Ag '66. * (PA 41:1818)
63. IRWIN, ORVIS C. "Vocabulary Ability of Two Samples of Cerebral Palsied Children." *Cereb Palsy J* 27:14–5 My–Je '66. *
64. IRWIN, ORVIS C., AND HAMMILL, DONALD D. "Effect of Type of Mental Retardation on Three Language Measures." *Cereb Palsy J* 27:9–10 Ja–F '66. * (PA 40:5881)
65. KAHN, HARRIS. "Evidence for Long-Term Reliability of the PPVT With Adolescent and Young Adult Retardates." *Am J Mental Def* 70:895–8 My '66. * (PA 40:9160)
66. KICKLIGHTER, RICHARD M. "Correlation of Peabody Picture Vocabulary Test Scores and Stanford-Binet Intelligence Scale, Form L-M Scores in an Educable Mentally Retarded Population." Abstract. *J Sch Psychol* 5:75–6 au '66. *
67. KILBURN, KENT L.; SANDERSON, ROBERT E.; AND MELTON, KYLE. "Relation of the Raven Coloured Progressive Matrices to Two Measures of Verbal Ability in a Sample of Mildly Retarded Hospital Patients." *Psychol Rep* 19:731–4 D '66. * (PA 41:4915)
68. KORST, JOSEPH W. "A Comparison of Results From the Peabody Vocabulary Test and Leiter International Performance Scale With Children Having Functional Articulatory Disorders." *Cereb Palsy J* 27:3–5 Ja–F '66. * (PA 40:5851)
69. LINDSEY, JAMES MORRISON. *The Factorial Organization of Intelligence in Children as Related to the Variables of Age, Sex and Subculture.* Doctor's thesis, University of Georgia (Athens, Ga.), 1966. (DA 27:3664B)
70. MAYANS, ANNA E. *Early Differential Prediction of First Grade Reading Achievement Among Three Culturally Different Kindergarten Groups.* Doctor's thesis, University of Cincinnati (Cincinnati, Ohio), 1966. (DA 27:2891A)
71. RICE, DON MARTIN, SR. *The Effects of Visual Perception Techniques With Cerebral Palsied Individuals Functioning at a Mentally Retarded Level.* Doctor's thesis, Colorado State College (Greeley, Colo.), 1966. (DA 27:3732A)
72. ROSENBERG, LEON A., AND STROUD, MICHAEL. "Limitations of Brief Intelligence Testing with Young Children." *Psychol Rep* 19:721–2 D '66. * (PA 41:4999)
73. SHAW, DALE J.; MATTHEWS, CHARLES G.; AND KLØVE, HALLGRIM. "The Equivalence of WISC and PPVT IQs." *Am J Mental Def* 70:601–4 Ja '66. * (PA 40:5454)
74. SHIPE, DOROTHY; CROMWELL, RUE L.; AND DUNN, LLOYD M. "Responses of Emotionally Disturbed and Nondisturbed Retardates to PPVT Items of Human Versus Nonhuman Content." *J Consult Psychol* 30:439–43 O '66. * (PA 40:13457)
75. SILBERBERG, NORMAN E., AND FELDT, LEONARD S. "The Peabody Picture Vocabulary Test as an IQ Screening Technique for Primary Grade Referral Cases." *J Sch Psychol* 5:21–30 au '66. * (PA 41:3345)
76. TAUBER, ROSALYN. "Identification of Potential Learning Disabilities." *Acad Ther Q* 2:116–9+ w '66–67. * (PA 41:5004)
77. TILLINGHAST, B. S., JR., AND RENZULLI, JOSEPH S. "Reliability of the Peabody Picture Vocabulary Test: A Preliminary Report." *Ed R* 4:1–6 '66. *
78. TUTTLE, LESTER EUGENE, JR. "The Comparative Effect on Intelligence Test Scores of Negro and Caucasian Children When Certain Verbal and Time Factors Are Varied by Use of the WISC, PPVT and CMMS." *Fla J Ed Res* 8:49–61 Ja '66. *
79. WARD, WILLIAM CORNELIUS, JR. *Creativity and Impulsivity in Kindergarten Children.* Doctor's thesis, Duke University (Durham, N.C.), 1966. (DA 27:2127B)
80. WHIPPLE, CLIFFORD I., AND MAIER, LOUISE JO. "Perceptual-Motor Maturation and Language Development in Young Children." *Percept & Motor Skills* 23:1208 D '66. * (PA 41:5794)
81. ALLERHAND, MELVIN E. "Effectiveness of Parents of Head Start Children as Administrators of Psychological Tests." *J Consult Psychol* 31:286–90 Je '67. * (PA 41:10474)
82. BASHAW, W. L., AND AYERS, JERRY B. "An Evaluation of the Norms and Reliability of the PPVT for Pre-School Subjects." *Ed & Psychol Meas* 27:1069–75 w '67. * (PA 42:9416)
83. BIGELOW, GORDON SHOEMAKER. *Global Versus Analytical Cognitive Style in Children as a Function of Age, Sex, and Intelligence.* Doctor's thesis, Brigham Young University (Provo, Utah), 1967. (DA 28:958A)
84. BROMWICH, ROSE MEYER. *Some Correlates of Stimulus-Bound Versus Stimulus-Free Verbal Responses to Pictures by Young Negro Boys.* Doctor's thesis, University of California (Los Angeles, Calif.), 1967. (DA 28:1290A)
85. BROWN, LOUIS F., AND RICE, JAMES A. "The Peabody Picture Vocabulary Test: Validity for EMRs." *Am J Mental Def* 71:901–3 My '67. * (PA 41:12378)
86. CARR, DONALD L.; BROWN, LOUIS F.; AND RICE, JAMES A. "The PPVT in the Assessment of Language Deficits." *Am J Mental Def* 71:937–40 My '67. * (PA 41:11915)
87. CORWIN, BETTY JANE. "The Relationship Between Read-

88. Datta, Lois-Ellin. "Draw-A-Person Test as a Measure of Intelligence in Preschool Children From Very Low Income Families." *J Consult Psychol* 31:626–30 D '67. * (PA 42:2561)
89. Dockrell, W. B., and Brosseau, J. F. "The Correlates of Second Language Learning by Young Children." *Alberta J Ed Res* 13:295–8 D '67. * (PA 44:3452)
90. Fargo, George A.; Crowell, Doris C.; Noyes, Mary H.; Fuchigami, Robert Y.; Gordon, John M.; and Dunn-Rankin, Peter. "Comparability of Group Television and Individual Administration of the Peabody Picture Vocabulary Test: Implications for Screening." *J Ed Psychol* 58:137–40 Je '67. * (PA 41:10445)
91. Fulton, Robert T. "Task Adaptation and Word Familiarity of W-22 Discrimination Lists With Retarded Children." *J Auditory Res* 7:353–8 O '67. *
92. Gilmore, Stuart I., and Familant, Rosalee P. "Race, Residence, Socioeconomic Status, and Responses to Articulation Test Stimuli." *Southern Speech J* 33:44–9 f '67. *
93. Graubard, Paul S. "The Use of the Peabody Picture Vocabulary Test in the Prediction and Assessment of Reading Disability in Disturbed Children." *J Ed Res* 61:3–5 S '67. *
94. Greemore, Ruth. *A Comparative Study on the Abstract and the Concrete Method of Teaching New Words to Mentally Retarded Children, Using the Peabody Picture Vocabulary Tests as an Instructional Tool.* Master's thesis, University of Kansas (Lawrence, Kan.), 1967.
95. Hale, James Roy. *Peabody Picture Vocabulary Test: A Validity Study With Educable Mentally Retarded Children.* Master's thesis, University of Texas (Austin, Tex.), 1967.
96. Hammill, Donald D., and Irwin, Orvis C. "Factors Affecting Equivalency of PPVT and RSB When Used With Mentally Subnormal Children." *Am J Mental Def* 71:793–6 Mr '67. * (PA 41:8881)
97. Howard, Joyce L., and Plant, Walter T. "Psychometric Evaluation of an Operation Headstart Program." *J Genetic Psychol* 111:281–8 D '67. * (PA 42:6013)
98. Irwin, Orvis C. "Replications and Reliabilities of Four Speech Tests." *Cereb Palsy J* 28:5–6 My–Je '67. *
99. Irwin, Orvis C., and Korst, Joseph W. "Comparison of Scores of Cerebral Palsied, Subnormal and Normal Children on Five Speech Tests." *Cereb Palsy J* 28:10–1 My–Je '67. *
100. Irwin, Orvis C., and Korst, Joseph W. "Correlations Among Five Speech Tests and the WISC Verbal Scale." *Cereb Palsy J* 28:9–11 S–O '67. * (PA 42:3201)
101. Irwin, Orvis C., and Korst, Joseph W. "Summary of Reliability Coefficients of Six Speech Tests for Use With Handicapped Children." *Cereb Palsy J* 28:6–7 Jl–Ag '67. *
102. Koh, Tong-He, and Madow, Arnold A. "Relationship Between PPVT and Stanford-Binet Performance in Institutionalized Retardates." *Am J Mental Def* 72:108–13 Jl '67. * (PA 41:15728)
103. Lavitt, Jerry A. *A Comparative Evaluation of the Peabody Picture Vocabulary Test as a Measure of Ability for Children of Differing Reading Proficiency Levels.* Doctor's thesis, Oklahoma State University (Stillwater, Okla.), 1967. (DA 28:4877A)
104. Leppke, Ronald Dean. *Perceptual Approaches for Disadvantaged Anglo- and Mexican-American Students.* Doctor's thesis, University of the Pacific (Stockton, Calif.), 1967. (DA 28:1302A)
105. Lloyd, Lyle L.; Rolland, John C.; and McManis, Donald L. "Performance of Hearing Impaired and Normal Hearing Retardates on Selected Language Measures." *Am J Mental Def* 71:904–8 My '67. * (PA 41:12408)
106. Milgram, Norman A. "A Note on the PPVT in Mental Retardates." *Am J Mental Def* 72:496–7 N '67. * (PA 42:7658) See 147 for discussion of article.
107. Milgram, Norman A., and Ozer, Mark N. "Peabody Picture Vocabulary Test Scores of Preschool Children." *Psychol Rep* 20:779–84 Je '67. * (PA 41:13597)
108. Nelson, Pike Cornelius. *A Statistical Analysis of San Diego Summer Head Start Children on Seven Variables.* Doctor's thesis, Colorado State College (Greeley, Colo.), 1967. (DA 28:3463B)
109. Osborne, R. T.; Anderson, Harry E., Jr.; and Bashaw, W. L. "The Stability of the WISC Factor Structure at Three Age Levels." *Multiv Behav Res* 2:443–51 O '67. * (PA 42:6388)
110. Panther, Edward E. "Prediction of First-Grade Reading Achievement." *El Sch J* 68:44–8 O '67. *
111. Rice, James A., and Brown, Louis F. "Validity of the Peabody Picture Vocabulary Test in a Sample of Low IQ Children." *Am J Mental Def* 71:602–3 Ja '67. * (PA 41:5960)
112. Silverstein, A. B., and Hill, Thomas Vernon. "Comparability of Three Picture Vocabulary Tests With Retarded School Children." *Training Sch B* 64:58–61 Ag '67. * (PA 42:1057)
113. Smith, Peter Barker, Jr. *A Description of the Language Abilities of Institutionalized Phenylketonuric Individuals in the States of Washington, Oregon, Idaho, and Montana.* Doctor's thesis, University of Washington (Seattle, Wash.), 1967. (DA 28:3917B)
114. Sydiaha, Daniel. "Prediction of WAIS IQ for Psychiatric Patients Using the Ammons' FRPV and Raven's Progressive Matrices." *Psychol Rep* 20:823–6 Je '67. * (PA 41:13602)
115. Weaver, Ann Sullivan. *The Prediction of First Grade Reading Achievement in Culturally Disadvantaged Children.* Doctor's thesis, George Peabody College for Teachers (Nashville, Tenn.), 1967. (DA 28:3789A)
116. Wells, Donald G., and Pedrini, Duilio T. "Relationships Between the S-B L-M, G-H, and PPVT With Institutionalized Retardates." *Am J Mental Def* 72:412–5 N '67. * (PA 42:7680)
117. Anderson, Beatrice Betty. *Evaluation of a Checklist to Measure Specific Reading Readiness Factors in Beginning First Grade Pupils.* Doctor's thesis, University of Maryland (College Park, Md.), 1968. (DAI 30:480A)
118. Anderson, Darrell E., and Flax, Morton L. "A Comparison of the Peabody Picture Vocabulary Test With the Wechsler Intelligence Scale for Children." *J Ed Res* 62:114–6 N '68. *
119. Ando, Kyoko. "A Comparative Study of Peabody Picture Vocabulary Test and Wechsler Intelligence Scale for Children With a Group of Cerebral Palsied Children." *Cereb Palsy J* 29:7–9 My–Je '68. * (PA 42:15909)
120. Bach, Lloyd Carl. *A Comparison of Selected Psychological Tests Used With Trainable Mentally Retarded Children.* Doctor's thesis, University of South Dakota (Vermillion, S.D.), 1968. (DA 29:2990A)
121. Benger, Kathlyn. "The Relationships of Perception, Personality, Intelligence, and Grade One Reading Achievement." *Proc Ann Conv Int Read Assn* 12(4):112–23 '68. *
122. Bonner, Mary Winstead. *A Comparative Study of the Performance of Negro Seniors of Oklahoma City High Schools on the Wechsler Adult Intelligence Scale and the Peabody Picture Vocabulary Test.* Doctor's thesis, Oklahoma State University (Stillwater, Okla.), 1968. (DAI 30:921A)
123. Borosage, Vera. *A Study of the Effect of Nursery School Experience on Intellectual Performance at Two Socio-Economic Levels.* Doctor's thesis, Michigan State University (East Lansing, Mich.), 1968. (DA 29:2993A)
124. Cartwright, G. Phillip. "A Note on the Use of the Peabody Picture Vocabulary Test With Disadvantaged Children." *J Ed Res* 61:285 F '68. *
125. Coyle, F. A., Jr.; Dans, Clarice; and Cork, Elizabeth. "Form Equivalence of the PPVT on Children in Speech Therapy." *Psychol Rep* 23:1002 D '68. * (PA 43:9–37)
126. Deich, Ruth F. "Correlations Between the PPVT and the CTMM." *Psychol Rep* 22:856 Je '68. * (PA 42:12982)
127. DiLorenzo, Louis T. "Effects of Year-Long Prekindergarten Programs on Intelligence and Language of Educationally Disadvantaged Children." *J Exp Ed* 36:36–42 sp '68. *
128. DiLorenzo, Louis T., and Brady, James J. "Use of the Peabody Picture Vocabulary Test With Preschool Children." *Psychol Rep* 22:247–51 F '68. * (PA 42:10612)
129. Elkin, Lorne. "Predicting Performance of the Mentally Retarded on Sheltered Workshop and Non-Institutional Jobs." *Am J Mental Def* 72:533–9 Ja '68. * (PA 42:7638)
130. Ernhart, Claire B. "The Peabody Picture Vocabulary Test: Automated Application in a Statewide Psychiatric System." *Psychiatric Q Sup* 42(2):317–20 '68. * (PA 46:3313)
131. Gardner, Ann M., and Birnbrauer, J. S. "A Note on Possible Form Differences in the Peabody Picture Vocabulary Test." *Am J Mental Def* 73:86–7 Jl '68. * (PA 42:19184)
132. Hammill, Donald D.; Myers, Patricia I.; and Irwin, Orvis C. "Certain Speech and Linguistic Abilities in Subclasses of Cerebral Palsy." *Percept & Motor Skills* 26:511–4 Ap '68. * (PA 42:12630)
133. Haywood, H. Carl, and Heal, Laird W. "Retention of Learned Visual Associations as a Function of IQ and Learning Levels." *Am J Mental Def* 72:828–38 My '68. * (PA 42:14404)
134. Johnson, Carolyne Margaret. *The Creative Thinking, Verbal Intelligence, and Creative Writing Ability of Young Gifted Children.* Doctor's thesis, Case Western Reserve University (Cleveland, Ohio), 1968. (DA 29:4187A)
135. Kaplan, Burt Edward. *Psychophysiological and Cognitive Development in Children.* Doctor's thesis, Pennsylvania State University (University Park, Pa.), 1968. (DA 29:1859B)
136. Kaufman, Harvey I., and Ivanoff, John M. "Evaluating the Mentally Retarded With the Peabody Picture Vocabulary Test." *Am J Mental Def* 73:396–8 N '68. * (PA 43:8590)
137. McArthur, Charles R., and Wakefield, Homer E. "Validation of the PPVT With the Stanford-Binet-LM and the WISC on Educable Mental Retardates." *Am J Mental Def* 73:465–7 N '68. * (PA 43:8596)
138. McClellan, Dorinda Ann. *Factors Which Are Predictive of Reading Success of Low-Socio-Economic Children in Selected First Grades.* Doctor's thesis, Oklahoma State University (Stillwater, Okla.), 1968. (DAI 30:933A)
139. Malerstein, A. J., and Belden, E. "WAIS, SILS,

and PPVT in Korsakoff's Syndrome." *Arch Gen Psychiatry* 19:743-50 D '68. * (*PA* 43:8472)

140. MAUSER, AUGUST JOHN. *First Grade Children's Comprehension of Oral Language in Sentences and Success in Beginning Reading Instruction.* Doctor's thesis, Indiana University (Bloomington, Ind.), 1968. (*DAI* 30:70A)

141. MIEZITIS, SOLVEIGA AUSMA. *An Exploratory Study of Divergent Production in Preschoolers.* Doctor's thesis, University of Toronto (Toronto, Ont., Canada), 1968. (*DAI* 30:589A)

142. MUELLER, MAX W. "Validity of Six Tests of Ability With Educable Mental Retardates." *J Sch Psychol* 6:136-46 w '68. * (*PA* 42:11152)

143. NESBITT, MARY CATHERINE. *Auding Achievement of First Grade Pupils Related to Selected Pupil Characteristics.* Doctor's thesis, University of Georgia (Athens, Ga.), 1968. (*DA* 29:2445A)

144. PLANT, WALTER T., AND SOUTHERN, MARA L. "First Grade Reading Achievement Predicted From WPPSI and Other Scores Obtained 18 Months Earlier." Abstract. *Proc 76th Ann Conv Am Psychol Assn* 3:593-4 '68. *

145. RAWL, MIRIAM FREEMAN. *A Study of the Relationship of Verbal Ability and Vocalization to Conceptual-Motor Tasks in Disadvantaged First-Grade Children.* Doctor's thesis, University of South Carolina (Columbia, S.C.), 1968. (*DAI* 30:1028A)

146. RENZULLI, JOSEPH S., AND PAULUS, DIETER H. "An Investigation of the Validity of the Order of Items on the Peabody Picture Vocabulary Test." Abstract. *AERA Paper Abstr* 1968:256-7 '68. *

147. RICE, JAMES A. "A Note on the Milgram Article." [see *106*] Reply by Norman A. Milgram. Letters. *Am J Mental Def* 73:520-1 N '68. *

148. RIEBER, MORTON, AND WOMACK, MARCELEETE. "The Intelligence of Preschool Children as Related to Ethnic and Demographic Variables." *Excep Children* 34:609-14 Ap '68. * (*PA* 42:17001)

149. STARK, JOEL; COHEN, SYLVIA; AND EISENSON, JON. "Performances of Aphasic Children on the PPVT and Auditory Decoding Tests." *J Spec Ed* 2:435-7 su-f '68. * (*PA* 43:10213)

150. STERNE, DAVID M. "Validity of the PPVT, Knox Cubes and ITPA With Aphasic Adults." Abstract. *Psychol Rep* 22:1014 Je '68. * (*PA* 42:12997)

151. TILLINGHAST, B. S., JR., AND RENZULLI, JOSEPH S. "Reliability of a Group Form of the Peabody Picture Vocabulary Test." *J Ed Res* 61:311-4 Mr '68. *

152. ZUNICH, M., AND TOLLEY, J. "Performance on the Peabody Picture Vocabulary Test and Stanford-Binet by Institutionalized Mentally Retarded Children." *Psychol Rep* 22:1212 Je '68. * (*PA* 42:19210)

153. ABRAMSON, THEODORE. "The Influence of Examiner Race on First-Grade and Kindergarten Subjects' Peabody Picture Vocabulary Test Scores." *J Ed Meas* 6(4):241-6 w '69. * (*PA* 44:17313)

154. ALLEN, ROBERT M. "The Developmental Test of Visual Perception and the Bender Gestalt Test Achievement of Educable Mental Retardate." *Training Sch B* 66(2):80-5 Ag '69. * (*PA* 44:4029)

155. ALLEN, ROBERT M. "The Mental Age—Visual Perception Issue Assessed." *Excep Children* 35(9):748-9 My '69. * (*PA* 44:19186)

156. ALLEN, ROBERT M., AND WALLACH, EDWARD S. "Word Recognition and Definition by Educable Retardates." *Am J Mental Def* 73(6):883-5 My '69. * (*PA* 43:13233)

157. ASBURY, CHARLES ALEXANDER. *Factors Associated With Discrepant Achievement in Rural Economically Deprived White and Negro First Graders.* Doctor's thesis, University of North Carolina (Chapel Hill, N.C.), 1969. (*DAI* 31:208A)

158. BAUMANN, KAREN SUZANN. *The Effects of an Educational Program on the Test Performance of Children With Psychoneurological Learning Disabilities.* Doctor's thesis, Oklahoma State University (Stillwater, Okla.), 1969. (*DAI* 31:3865A)

159. BECKER, JOHN T. *The Effect of Group Administration of Selected Individual Tests of Language, Visual Perception, and Auditory Perception to Kindergarten, First-, Second-, and Third-Grade Children.* Doctor's thesis, Catholic University of America (Washington, D.C.), 1969. (*DAI* 30:2367A)

160. BLUE, C. MILTON. "PPVT Temporal Stability and Alternate Form Reliability With the Trainable Mentally Retarded." *Am J Mental Def* 73(5):745-8 Mr '69. * (*PA* 43:10218)

161. COCHRAN, MALCOLM L., AND PEDRINI, DUILIO T. "The Concurrent Validity of the 1965 WRAT With Adult Retardates." *Am J Mental Def* 73(4):654-6 Ja '69. * (*PA* 43:8574)

162. CRAWFORD, VEDA B. *Relationships of Scores on the Wechsler Preschool and Primary Scale of Intelligence, the Stanford-Binet Intelligence Scale, Form LM, and the Peabody Picture Vocabulary Test, Form A.* Master's thesis, Bowling Green State University (Bowling Green, Ohio), 1969.

163. CURRY, DAL ROY. *The Effect of Two Types of Auditory Discrimination Training on Language Performance and Acquisition in a Culturally Deprived Preschool Population.* Doctor's thesis, University of Kansas (Lawrence, Kan.), 1969. (*DAI* 30:5281A)

164. DILORENZO, LOUIS T., AND BRADY, JAMES J. "Use of the Peabody Picture Vocabulary Test." *Training Sch B* 65(4):117-21 F '69. * (*PA* 44:4169)

165. DUNDORE, JAMES M., JR. *A Study of the Relationship Between Scores Earned on the Columbia Mental Maturity Scale and Peabody Picture Vocabulary Test and School Achievement of Culturally Disadvantaged Negro Children.* Master's thesis, Mississippi State University (State College, Miss.), 1969.

166. ELLIOTT, RAYMOND N., JR. "Comparative Study of the Pictorial Test of Intelligence and the Peabody Picture Vocabulary Test." *Psychol Rep* 25(2):528-30 O '69. * (*PA* 44:5541)

167. ENGLISH, RICHARD A., AND KIDDER, JACK W. "Note on Relationships Among Mental Ability Scores, Teacher's Rankings, and Rate of Acquisition for Four-Year-Old Kindergarteners." *Psychol Rep* 24(2):554 Ap '69. * (*PA* 43:15568)

168. GROPPER, ROBERT L. *Comprehension of Narrative Passages by Fourth-Grade Children as a Function of Listening Rate and Eleven Predictor Variables.* Doctor's thesis, George Peabody College for Teachers (Nashville, Tenn.), 1969. (*DAI* 30:4827A)

169. HALL, JOSEPH CLARENCE. *A Comparative Study of Selected Measures of Intelligence as Predictors of First-Grade Reading Achievement in a Culturally Disadvantaged Population.* Doctor's thesis, Temple University (Philadelphia, Pa.), 1969. (*DAI* 31:1074A)

170. KEIM, RICHARD PAUL. *Visual-Motor Training, Readiness, and Intelligence of Kindergarten Children.* Doctor's thesis, Temple University (Philadelphia, Pa.), 1969. (*DAI* 31:1076A)

171. KIRK, GIRVIN EATON. *The Performance of Advantaged and Disadvantaged Preschool Children on Tests of Picture-Phonemic Discrimination and Picture-Word Recognition Skills.* Doctor's thesis, University of Illinois (Urbana, Ill.), 1969. (*DAI* 30:930A)

172. KLAPPER, ZELDA S., AND BIRCH, HERBERT G. "Perceptual and Action Equivalence to Objects and Photographs in Children." *Percept & Motor Skills* 29(3):763-71 D '69. *

173. MCCLARY, GEORGE OSCAR. *Cognitive and Affective Responses by Negro and White Children to Pictorial Stimuli.* Doctor's thesis, George Washington University (Washington, D.C.), 1969. (*DAI* 30:1901B)

174. MAZER, MARJORIE. *The Pre-School Inventory and the Peabody Picture Vocabulary Test With Preschool Children.* Master's thesis, Pennsylvania State University (University Park, Pa.), 1969.

175. MESSER, MICHAEL E., AND ALLEN, ROBERT M. "Verbal Recognition and Non-Verbal Reasoning of Retardates." *Percept & Motor Skills* 28(1):334 F '69. * (*PA* 43:11764)

176. MINSKY, RAPHAEL. *An Investigation Into Children's Conceptualization of Proportionality as Expressed in Their Drawings of the Male Human Figure.* Doctor's thesis, University of Maryland (College Park, Md.), 1969. (*DAI* 31:1082A)

177. MUELLER, MAX W. "Prediction of Achievement of Educable Mentally Retarded Children." *Am J Mental Def* 73(4):590-6 Ja '69. * (*PA* 43:8703)

178. NELSON, C. MICHAEL, AND HUDSON, FLOYD G. "Predicting the Reading Achievement of Junior High School EMR Children." *Am J Mental Def* 74(3):415-20 N '69. *

179. NICHOLSON, CHARLES L. "The Use of Four Screening Instruments." *Ann Inter Conf Assn Children Learn Dis* 6:101-7 '69. *

180. OMER, JANE L. "Investigation of Speech Discrimination Ability of Children Selected for Learning Disability." *Kan Studies Ed* 19(3):25-8 Ag '69. *

181. RENZULLI, JOSEPH S., AND PAULUS, DIETER H. "A Cross-Validation Study of the Item Ordering of the Peabody Picture Vocabulary Test." *J Ed Meas* 6(1):15-20 sp '69. * (*PA* 44:15308)

182. SABATINO, DAVID A., AND BECKER, JOHN T. "Relations Among Five Basic Tests of Behavior." *Percept & Motor Skills* 29(2):487-90 O '69. * (*PA* 44:3428)

183. SHIPE, DOROTHY, AND MIEZITIS, SOLVEIGA. "A Pilot Study in the Diagnosis and Remediation of Special Learning Disabilities in Preschool Children." *J Learn Dis* 2(11):579-92 N '69. * (*PA* 46:7521)

184. SHOTWELL, ANNA M.; O'CONNOR, GAIL; GABET, YVONNE; AND DINGMAN, HARVEY F. "Relation of the Peabody Picture Vocabulary Test IQ to the Stanford-Binet IQ." *Am J Mental Def* 74(1):39-42 Jl '69. * (*PA* 43:17485)

185. STRANDBERG, T. E.; GRIFFITH, J.; AND MINER, L. "Child Language and Screening Intelligence." *J Commun Disorders* 2(3):268-72 Ag '69. * (*PA* 44:3464)

186. TEASDALE, G. R. "Validity of the PPVT as a Test of Language Ability With Lower SES Children." *Psychol Rep* 25(3):746 D '69. * (*PA* 44:17787)

187. WALKER, AUDREY JEAN MASSEY. *A Descriptive Study of the Oral Language Progress of Selected Disadvantaged and Advantaged Kindergarten Children.* Doctor's thesis, University of Georgia (Athens, Ga.), 1969. (*DAI* 30:5354A)

188. WILLIAMS, TANNIS M., AND FLEMING, JACK W. "Methodological Study of the Relationship Between Associative Fluency and Intelligence." *Develop Psychol* 1(2):155-62 Mr '69. * (*PA* 43:8146)

189. YEN, SHERMAN M. Y. *A Comparative Study of Test Variability With Peabody Picture Vocabulary Test, Goodenough's Draw-A-Man Test, and Stanford-Binet Intelligence Scale as Intellectual Measurement With a Group of Urban Low Socio-Economic Status Pre-School Pupils.* Doctor's thesis, Catholic University of America (Washington, D.C.), 1969. (*DAI* 30:2625A)
190. ALLEN, ROBERT M. "The PPVT Is Not a Test of Visual Perceptual Maturation." *Percept & Motor Skills* 31(1): 262 Ag '70. * (*PA* 45:3969)
191. ANASTASIOW, NICHOLAS J.; SIBLEY, SALLY A.; LEONHARDT, TERESA M.; AND BORICH, GARY D. "A Comparison of Guided Discovery, Discovery and Didactic Teaching of Math to Kindergarten Poverty Children." *Am Ed Res J* 7(4):493-510 N '70. *
192. ANDERSON, B. BETTY. "Classroom Diagnosis of Reading Readiness Factors." *J Learn Dis* 3(5):260-3 My '70. *
193. ARCHER, LORENE STURDIVANT. *The Effect of an Eight Weeks Summer Program on Preschool Readiness in Longview Public Schools.* Doctor's thesis, East Texas State University (Commerce, Tex.), 1970. (*DAI* 31:1987A)
194. BECK, RAY, AND TALKINGTON, LARRY W. "Frostig Training With Headstart Children." *Percept & Motor Skills* 30(2):521-2 Ap '70. * (*PA* 46:7765)
195. BONNER, MARY W., AND BELDEN, BERNARD R. "A Comparative Study of the Performance of Negro Seniors of Oklahoma City High Schools on the Wechsler Adult Intelligence Scale and the Peabody Picture Vocabulary Test." *J Negro Ed* 39(4):354-8 f '70. * (*PA* 45:10662)
196. BRUININKS, ROBERT H., AND FELDMAN, DAVID H. "Creativity, Intelligence, and Achievement Among Disadvantaged Children." *Psychol Sch* 7(3):260-4 Jl '70. * (*PA* 45:5015)
197. BRUININKS, ROBERT H., AND LUCKER, WILLIAM G. "Change and Stability in Correlations Between Intelligence and Reading Test Scores Among Disadvantaged Children." *J Read Behav* 2(4):295-305 f '70. * (*PA* 46:5700)
198. CALLAWAY, BYRON. "Factors Related to Reading of Children Referred to a University Reading Clinic," pp. 61-6. In *Reading Difficulties: Diagnosis, Correction, and Remediation.* Edited by William K. Durr. Newark, Del.: International Reading Association, 1970. Pp. vii, 276. *
199. COCHRAN, MALCOLM L. "A Profile of Psychological Test Scores for Retarded Adults." *Am J Mental Def* 74(4): 582-4 Ja '70. * (*PA* 44:11052)
200. COSTELLO, JOAN. "Effects of Pretesting and Examiner Characteristics on Test Performance of Young Disadvantaged Children." Abstract. *Proc 78th Ann Conv Am Psychol Assn* 5(1):309-10 '70. * (*PA* 44:18295)
201. CUNDICK, BERT P. "Measures of Intelligence on Southwest Indian Students." *J Social Psychol* 81(2):151-6 Ag '70. * (*PA* 44:20655)
202. ERNHART, CLAIRE B. "The Correlation of Peabody Picture Vocabulary and Wechsler Adult Intelligence Scale Scores for Adult Psychiatric Patients." *J Clin Psychol* 26(4):470-1 O '70. * (*PA* 45:4528)
203. FITZGERALD, BERNARD J.; PASEWARK, RICHARD A.; AND GLOECKLER, TED. "Use of the Peabody Picture Vocabulary Test With the Educationally Handicapped." *J Sch Psychol* 8(4): 296-300 '70. * (*PA* 46:1800)
204. GALLI, ANTHONY P. *Reliability of Measures From the Peabody Picture Vocabulary Test and Their Relation to Articulation.* Master's thesis, Sacramento State College (Sacramento, Calif.), 1970.
205. GARBER, MALCOLM, AND WARE, W. B. "Relationship Between Measures of Home Environment and Intelligence Scores." Abstract. *Proc 78th Ann Conv Am Psychol Assn* 5(2):64-8 '70. * (*PA* 44:18353)
206. GOLDSTEIN, LEO S.; COLLER, ALAN R.; DILL, JOHN; AND TILIS, HOWARD S. "The Effect of a Special Curriculum for Disadvantaged Children on Test-Retest Reliabilities of Three Standardized Instruments." *J Ed Meas* 7(3):171-4 f '70. * (*PA* 45:4917)
207. GOODGLASS, HAROLD; GLEASON, JEAN BERKO; AND HYDE, MARY R. "Some Dimensions of Auditory Language Comprehension in Aphasia." *J Speech & Hearing Res* 13(3):595-606 S '70. *
208. GROSSMAN, MARVIN. "Perceptual Style, Creativity, and Various Drawing Abilities." *Studies Art Ed* 11(2):51-4 w '70. *
209. HUBSCHMAN, EVA; POLIZZOTTO, EMILIA ANN; AND KALISKI, MYRA S. "Performance of Institutionalized Retardates on the PPVT and Two Editions of the ITPA." *Am J Mental Def* 74(4):579-80 Ja '70. * (*PA* 44:11063)
210. JOSELSON, MAURICE L. *The Role of Language Skills Within the Perspective of Other Psychosocial Factors in a Select Prison Population.* Doctor's thesis, University of Florida (Gainesville, Fla.), 1970. (*DAI* 31:4385B)
211. KAPLAN, BURT E. "Psychophysiological and Cognitive Development in Children: The Relationship of Skin Conductance and Heart Rate to Word Associations and Task Requirements." *Psychophysiol* 7(1):18-26 Jl '70. * (*PA* 45:6014)
212. LESSLER, KEN; SCHOENINGER, D. W.; AND BRIDGES, JUDITH S. "Prediction of First Grade Performance." *Percept & Motor Skills* 31(3):751-6 D '70. * (*PA* 45:10959)
213. LOCKYER, LINDA, AND RUTTER, MICHAEL. "A Five- to Fifteen-Year Follow-Up Study of Infantile Psychosis: 4, Patterns of Cognitive Ability." *Brit J Social & Clin Psychol* 9(2): 152-63 Je '70. * (*PA* 44:16983)
214. MANDEL, ROBERT, AND MCLEOD, PHILIP. "A Longitudinal Investigation of the Stability of IQ's on the Peabody Picture Vocabulary Test With High and Low Socioeconomic Subjects." *Excep Children* 37(4):300-1 D '70. *
215. NICHOLSON, CHARLES L. "Correlations Among CMMS, PPVT, and RCPM for Cerebral Palsied Children." *Percept & Motor Skills* 30(3):715-8 Je '70. * (*PA* 44:17151)
216. NURCOMBE, B., AND MOFFITT, P. "'Cultural Deprivation and Language Defect: Project Enrichment of Childhood." *Austral Psychologist* 5(3):249-59 N '70. * (*PA* 46:5744)
217. PALMER, FRANCIS H. "Socioeconomic Status and Intellective Performance Among Negro Preschool Boys." *Develop Psychol* 3(1):1-9 Jl '70. * (*PA* 44:16374)
218. POOL, DONALD A., AND BROWN, ROBERT. "The Peabody Picture Vocabulary Test as a Measure of General Adult Intelligence." *J Consult & Clin Psychol* 34(1):8-11 F '70. * (*PA* 44:6772)
219. RASKIN, LARRY M., AND FONG, LOUELLA J. "Temporal Stability of the PPVT in Normal and Educable-Retarded Children." *Psychol Rep* 26(2):547-9 Ap '70. * (*PA* 44:21438)
220. ROBERTS, ARTHUR JAMES. *The Relationship Between Kindergarten Experience and Fine-Muscle Eye-Hand Coordination Abilities of First Grade Children.* Doctor's thesis, Oregon State University (Corvallis, Ore.), 1970. (*DAI* 31:2019A)
221. UHL, NORMAN P., AND NURSS, JOANNE R. "Socio-Economic Level Styles in Solving Reading-Related Tasks." *Read Res Q* 5(3):452-85 sp '70. *
222. WOODY, ROBERT H., AND BILLY, HEIDI T. "Influencing the Intelligence Scores of Retarded and Nonretarded Boys With Clinical Suggestion." *Am J Clin Hyp* 12(4):268-71 Ap '70. * (*PA* 44:18849)
223. ZAESKE, ARNOLD. "The Validity of Predictive Index Tests in Predicting Reading Failure at the End of Grade One," pp. 28-33. In *Reading Difficulties: Diagnosis, Correction, and Remediation.* Edited by William K. Durr. Newark, Del.: International Reading Association, 1970. Pp. vii, 276. *

For reviews by Howard B. Lyman and Ellen V. Piers, see 6:530.

[418]

Pictorial Test of Intelligence. Ages 3-8; 1964; PTI; prepublication titles were *North Central Individual Test of Mental Ability* and *Pictorial Intelligence Test;* 7 scores: picture vocabulary, form discrimination, information and comprehension, similarities, size and number, immediate recall, total; individual; 1 form (54 stimulus cards and 137 response cards); may also be administered to 3- and 4-year-olds as a short form; manual (64 pages); record form (4 pages); no data on reliability of subscores; $33 per examiner's kit of test cards, 35 record forms, manual, and metal carrying case; $1.95 per 35 record forms; $3.60 per manual; postage extra; (45) minutes for full test; Joseph L. French; Houghton Mifflin Co. *

REFERENCES

1-2. See 6:531.
3. FRENCH, JOSEPH L., AND GREER, DONALD. "Effect of Test-Item Arrangement on Physiological and Psychological Behavior in Primary-School Children." *J Ed Meas* 1:151-3 D '64. * (*PA* 39:10105)
4. JENSON, G., III. *A Statistical Analysis of the Reliability and Validity of the Pictorial Test of Intelligence and the Stanford-Binet Intelligence Scale.* Master's thesis, University of Missouri (Columbia, Mo.), 1964.
5. MUELLER, MAX W. *A Comparison of the Empirical Validity of Six Tests of Ability With Young Educable Retardates.* Institute of Mental Retardation and Intellectual Development, IMRID Behavioral Science Monograph No. 1. Nashville, Tenn.: Peabody College Bookstore, 1965. Pp. vii, 130. *
6. MUELLER, MAX WILLIAM. *A Comparison of the Empirical Validity of Six Tests of Ability With Educable Mental Retardates.* Doctor's thesis, George Peabody College for Teachers (Nashville, Tenn.), 1965. (*DA* 26:6853)
7. GENTILE, J. RONALD. "In Search of Research: Four Children's Tests." *J Sch Psychol* 5:1-13 au '66. * (*PA* 41:3335)
8. HONSTEAD, CAROLE ANN. *Relationships Between Socioeconomic Level, Intelligence, and Piagetian Concept Attainment in Kindergarten Children.* Master's thesis, Iowa State University (Ames, Iowa), 1966.
9. HOWARD, JOYCE L., AND PLANT, WALTER T. "Psychometric Evaluation of an Operation Headstart Program." *J Genetic Psychol* 111:281-8 D '67. * (*PA* 42:6013)
10. PASEWARK, R. A.; SAWYER, R. N.; SMITH, E.; WASSERBERGER, M.; DELL, D.; BRITO, H.; AND LEE, R. "Concur-

rent Validity of the French Pictorial Test of Intelligence." *J Ed Res* 61:179–83 D '67. *
11. BONFIELD, JOHN RONALD. *Predictors of Achievement for Educable Mentally Retarded Children.* Doctor's thesis, Pennsylvania State University (University Park, Pa.), 1968. (*DAI* 30:1009A)
12. MUELLER, MAX W. "Validity of Six Tests of Ability With Educable Mental Retardates." *J Sch Psychol* 6:136–46 w '68. * (*PA* 42:11152)
13. ORTIZ, KENNETH K. *A Concurrent Validation Study of a Spanish Version of the Pictorial Test of Intelligence and a Critical Analysis of the Use of the Wechsler Intelligence Scale for Children With Bilingual Mexican-American Children.* Master's thesis, California State College (Long Beach, Calif.), 1968.
14. PATTERSON, HENRY JAMES. *A Validation and Comparison of the Pictorial Test of Intelligence With the Stanford-Binet (L-M).* Doctor's thesis, University of Arizona (Tucson, Ariz.), 1968. (*DA* 29:485A)
15. PLANT, WALTER T., AND SOUTHERN, MARA L. "First Grade Reading Achievement Predicted From WPPSI and Other Scores Obtained 18 Months Earlier." Abstract. *Proc 76th Ann Conv Am Psychol Assn* 3:593–4 '68. *
16. SAWYER, R. N. "An Investigation of the Reliability of the French Pictorial Test of Intelligence." *J Ed Res* 61:211–4 Ja '68. *
17. VOGLER, JAMES DONALD. *The Influence of Ethnicity and Socioeconomic Status on the Pictorial Test of Intelligence.* Doctor's thesis, University of Arizona (Tucson, Ariz.), 1968. (*DA* 29:490A)
18. ELLIOTT, RAYMOND N., JR. "Comparative Study of the Pictorial Test of Intelligence and the Peabody Picture Vocabulary Test." *Psychol Rep* 25(2):528–30 O '69. * (*PA* 44:5541)
19. MUELLER, MAX W. "Prediction of Achievement of Educable Mentally Retarded Children." *Am J Mental Def* 73(4): 590–6 Ja '69. * (*PA* 43:8703)

PHILIP HIMELSTEIN, *Professor of Psychology and Head of the Department, The University of Texas at El Paso, El Paso, Texas.*

The PTI is a Binet type instrument which allows the subject to respond in a multiple choice fashion. The test requires only sufficient command of English to understand the simple instructions. Responses to the questions (e.g., "Find the one from which we tell the temperature") would usually take the form of pointing to one of four pictures on a test card. The drawings are spatially so arranged on the card that there could be little doubt of the subject's choices. The examiner merely records the position of the choice on an answer sheet by making a slash mark through the letter corresponding to the position on the card of the subject's choice. The total number of correct items (the raw score) is converted by table to MA units and to deviation IQ's.

While the PTI is presented as "a further development of Binet type scales," there are some dissimilarities to the Stanford-Binet. Items are not ordered according to mental age, but according to subtests, as in Wechsler scales. There are six subtests arranged in the order of difficulty. There is no base or ceiling to be obtained; instead, all items are administered (with a minor exception) regardless of the successes or failures of the subject. None of the subtests are timed. Finally, and most important for the test user, the PTI covers only the age range of 3 to 8, while the Stanford-Binet tests children between the ages of 2 and 18.

Standardization, completed in 1962, was based on 1,830 children randomly selected to compare—by regional area, community size, and occupational level of father—with the 1960 census. The manual reports test-retest reliability coefficients ranging from .90 to .96 for time intervals of two to six weeks. K-R 20 reliability estimates from the standardization sample range from .87 to .93, with the lowest estimates at the upper and lower age limits of the test. Validity studies reported in the manual range in sample size from 9 to 32, rather inadequate for a test author's claim of validity.

While the test has not had adequate tryout by other investigators in the six years since it was published, a few studies are available. Sawyer (*16*) reports a test-retest reliability of .77 for kindergarten children with a 45-day interval and .88 for second graders with a 53-day interval. While the split-half reliabilities range from .95 to .98, the test-retest reliabilities seem woefully inadequate. Pasewark et al. (*10*) obtained a correlation of .75 between PTI and WISC IQ with a kindergarten sample and .71 with second grade children. With the S-B, Patterson (*14*) reported a correlation of .78 for randomly selected children (.38 and .65 for superior and retarded children, respectively). Mueller (*6*) obtained a correlation of .72 between PTI and S-B. Elliott (*18*) compared the PTI to another picture intelligence test, the PPVT, and, after relating the two tests to WRAT scores, concluded that "overall, the PTI appeared to be a more effective measure of intelligence in predicting class placement of institutionalized, educable mentally retarded students."

Some nine criticisms of the test are leveled by Pasewark et al. (*10*), including the restricted ages covered by the test and the increased testing time necessitated by the demand that all subjects, regardless of age, begin each subtest with the first item. There are suggestions in the published research that the test is least reliable at age 8, the highest age at which the test is used. The validity correlation reported would suggest that the PTI correlates about as well (in the .70's) with the S-B as the WISC does, and better than another picture test, the PPVT.

In sum, I can say that, like many other instruments, the PTI needs additional research. It does appear to have adequate validity so that it can be used with some confidence. Its application to the study of children with motor or speech handicaps would seem to be a special advantage.

T. ERNEST NEWLAND, *Professor of Educational Psychology, University of Illinois, Urbana, Illinois.*

The PTI differs from its preliminary edition, the NCITMA, by being standardized on a two-year wider age range, with two to three times more subjects at each level, and on subjects in 37 states (vs. two); by the exclusion of some of the old items and the addition of more difficult items; and by providing, within it, for a short form for use with three- and four-year-olds.

Test-retest reliabilities ranging from .90 to .94 are reported for groups of 25 to 31 children at year levels 5, 6, and 7. K-R 20 reliabilities range from .87 to .93.

The author presumes that content validity is apparent in the similarity between his test items and those of other "recognized tests of intelligence." No firm predictive validity data are presented, although the author does present rank correlations from .74 to .82, on from 9 to 11 cases, between scores (IQ's or MA's?) on the NCITMA and mean scores on three achievement tests (after 4 years). The author also reports rank correlations, for groups of 18 and 28, of .68 and .77 between his test (IQ's?) and two group intelligence tests administered three to five years later. Concurrent validity data are based on correlational studies of performances of three populations of no more than 32 subjects each: PTI with the 1960 Stanford-Binet, .72; with WISC (Full Scale IQ's?), .65; and with the *Columbia Mental Maturity Scale* (IQ's?), .53.

While terminological ambiguity hampers precise communication and rigorous evaluation, the PTI appears to be in the same "ball park" as the other tests cited, but who is on what base is not clear. Further skepticism regarding some of the statistics reported in the manual must be entertained, since the author points out that these analyses were made "before the standardization was complete." This reviewer has difficulty accepting the author's claim that the increase in PTI scores from lower to higher occupational levels is evidence of construct validity.

Sawyer (*16*) found split-half reliabilities quite in accord with those in the manual, but, on 52 kindergarten children, found a retest reliability of .77 and, on 38 second graders, one of .88. He observed that the subtest intercorrelations were "much higher than those reported in the manual." He regarded the effectiveness of PTI at the 8-year level as "subject to some doubt."

It is dangerous to generalize to the "normal" population the implications of the published research on the use of the PTI with retarded subjects. Correlations have been computed more in terms of psychometric curiosity than in terms of psychological inquiry. To correlate the PTI total results with the Stanford-Binet or with the WISC Verbal reflects good presumptive thinking, whereas to correlate PTI total results with the PPVT involves the tacit assumption that the two tests sample comparable forms of behavior.

If one desires to measure the learning aptitude of young children in a molar manner, particularly for ages 3–6, the PTI deserves serious consideration. To use it as though it could yield the same kind of psychological information as the PPVT, the Leiter, the Raven, or the CMMS would be a near-waste of examination time.

Because the response card is placed in a rack before the child, the test has considerable potential value in the cases of verbally constricted (or expressively impaired) children: the child merely needs to point to the desired response. With children with motor involvement of the arms or hands, the examiner can observe easily the eye movements of the child who has been instructed just to look at his "answer," since the spacing and location of the response elements on the cards make this quite feasible. When the short form is used, care should be taken to guard against positional perseveration in response. The response cards should be revised so that there is a more equitable distribution of the placement of the correct responses: 17 are at the bottom of the card, 23 are at the subject's right, 31 are at his left, and 26 are at the top. The answer sheet is easily used and scored, and is facilitative to a behavioral description of the subject in the test situation.

Even though the PTI is not truly based on a discernible psychological theory, as is true of the Stanford-Binet and many other individual tests of learning aptitude, and although rigorous research on it is yet to appear, the kinds of behavior samplings made constitute a composite that is plausibly relatable to the general cognitive demands in the school learning of children. Certainly, by virtue of the potential psycho-educational relevance of the variety of behaviors sampled and its broad standardization base, the PTI holds more promise as an individual learning aptitude test for young children than most other such tests recently released, including the *Wechsler Preschool and Primary Scale of Intelligence.*

[419]

*The Porteus Maze Test. Ages 3 and over; 1914–65; PMT; individual; 2 scores: quantitative, qualitative; 1 form; 3 editions and 2 supplements; no data on reliability; no adult norms; postage extra; Stanley D. Porteus. *

a) VINELAND REVISION. Ages 3 and over; 1914–24; 1 form ('21); 13 mazes: years 3–12, 14, adult 1, 2; manual ['24, 21 pages]; $19 per set of manual and 100 mazes of any one level; $1.35 per 100 copies of any one maze; (15–60) minutes; Stoelting Co.

b) VINELAND REVISION: NEW SERIES. Ages 3 and over; 1914–65; 1 form ('33); 12 mazes: years 3–12, 14, adult 1; combined manual ('65, 324 pages, see *143* below); $14.50 per set of 100 copies of each maze and pad of 100 scoring sheets; $1.60 per 100 mazes of any one level; $7.60 per manual; (15–60) minutes; Psychological Corporation.

c) PORTEUS MAZE EXTENSION. Ages 14 and over; 1953–65; for use only as a supplement to the *Vineland Revision: New Series*; 1 form ('53); 8 mazes: years 7–12, 14, adult; combined manual as in *b*; $10 per set of 100 copies of each maze and pad of 100 scoring sheets; $1.50 per 100 mazes of any one level; $7.60 per manual; (25) minutes; Psychological Corporation.

d) PORTEUS MAZE SUPPLEMENT. Ages 7 and over; 1959–65; a retesting series; 1 form ('59); 8 mazes: years 7–12, 14, adult; combined manual as in *b*; $9.50 per set of 100 copies of each maze; $1.70 per 100 mazes of any one level; $7.60 per manual; (25) minutes; Psychological Corporation.

e) BRITISH EDITION. Ages 3 and over; 1914–65; 1 form ('52, same as *Vineland Revision: New Series* copyrighted in 1933 except for format); 12 mazes: years 3–12, 14, adult 1; manual ('65, 324 pages, see *143* below); 35p per 100 mazes of any one level; 35p per 100 scoring sheets; 52½p per manual; [15–60) minutes; George G. Harrap & Co. Ltd.

REFERENCES

1–56. See 4:356.
57–84. See 5:412.
85–122. See 6:532.
123. EBERT, ELIZABETH, AND SIMMONS, KATHERINE. *The Brush Foundation Study of Child Growth and Development: 1, Psychometric Tests.* Monographs of the Society for Research in Child Development, Vol. 8, No. 2, Serial No. 35. Washington, D.C.: the Society, National Research Council, 1943. Pp. xiv, 113. * (PA 18:3322)
124. CROWN, SIDNEY. "An Experimental Study of Psychological Changes Following Prefrontal Lobotomy." *J General Psychol* 47:3–41 Jl '52. * (PA 27:6024)
125. GOLDENBERG, SAMUEL. *Some Aspects of Diagnosis of Cerebral Damage in Children.* Doctor's thesis, University of Washington (Seattle, Wash.), 1953. (DA 13:1259)
126. JUSTISS, WILL ALAN. *The Electroencephalogram of the Frontal Lobes and Abstract Behavior in Old Age.* Doctor's thesis, University of Florida (Gainesville, Fla.), 1957. (DA 18:308)
127. CRAWFORD, PAUL L. "The Relative Sensitivity of the LAIS, WAIS, and PM in Differentiating Between Psychopathic and Psychotic Patients in a Mental Hospital." *Psychol Service Center J* 11(2):93–7 '59. * (PA 34:4374)
128. CRAWFORD, PAUL L. "The Statistical Significance of Difference in Performance on the Leiter Adult Intelligence Scale, the Wechsler Adult Intelligence Scale, and the Porteus Maze by a Heterogeneous Mental Hospital Population." *Psychol Service Center J* 11(2):89–92 '59. * (PA 34:4510)
129. FULLER, CARL WELLINGTON. *A Study of the Growth and Organization of Certain Mental Abilities in Young Deaf Children.* Doctor's thesis, Northwestern University (Evanston, Ill.), 1959. (DA 20:2382)
130. FOULDS, G. A. "Personality Traits and Neurotic Symptoms and Signs." *Brit J Med Psychol* 34:263–70 pt 4 '61. * (PA 37:1229)
131. GIBBENS, T. C. N.; WITH THE ASSISTANCE OF A. MARRIAGE AND A. WALKER. *Psychiatric Studies of Borstal Lads*, pp. 143–84. London: Oxford University Press, 1963. Pp. vi, 230. *
132. BROVERMAN, DONALD M. "Generality and Behavioral Correlates of Cognitive Styles." *J Consult Psychol* 28:487–500 D '64. * (PA 39:7680)
133. FAHMY, MOSTAFA. "Initial Exploring of the Intelligence of Shilluk Children: Studies in the Southern Sudan." *Vita Hum* 7(3–4):164–77 '64. * (PA 39:7815)
134. FOULDS, G. A., AND OWEN, ANNA. "Speed and Accuracy on Mazes in Relation to Diagnosis and Personality." *Brit J Social & Clin Psychol* 3:34–5 F '64. * (PA 38:8870)
135. WASSENAAR, G. M. C. "The Effect of General Anxiety as an Index of Lability on the Performance of Various Psychomotor Tasks." *J General Psychol* 71:351–7 O '64. * (PA 39:3667)
136. BLUMENKRANTZ, JACK; DAHLGREN, HELEN; AND BORUM, ELIZABETH. "An Abbreviated Scoring Method for Porteus Mazes." *Newsl Res Psychol* 7:19 F '65. *
137. CRAFT, MICHAEL. Chap. 3, "Diagnosis and Aetiology Illustrated by an Analysis of Admissions to a Psychopathic Unit," pp. 32–54. In *Ten Studies Into Psychopathic Personality: A Report to the Home Office and the Mental Health Research Fund.* Bristol, England: John Wright & Sons Ltd., 1965. Pp. 133. *
138. FELDMAN, RUTH CAMM. *A Study of Cognitive Style and Some Personality Variables in Relation to the Conceptual Performance of Emotionally Disturbed Adolescents.* Doctor's thesis, Temple University (Philadelphia, Pa.), 1965. (DA 26:1773)
139. FROST, BARRY P. "The Porteus Maze Test and Manual Proficiency." *Alberta J Ed Res* 11:17–20 Mr '65. * (PA 39:16418)
140. KAINER, ROCHELLE KRUGMAN. *The Porteus Maze Test and the Delay of Gratification.* Doctor's thesis, Columbia University (New York, N.Y.), 1965. (DA 26:4808)
141. LABARBA, RICHARD C. "Relation of Color Responses on the Rorschach to Qualitative Scores on the Porteus Maze Test." *Percept & Motor Skills* 21:61–2 Ag '65. * (PA 40:40)
142. PIERCE, ROBERT ALLYN. *Response Sets as Personality Variables: An Attempt at Validation.* Doctor's thesis, University of Rochester (Rochester, N.Y.), 1965. (DA 26:3490)
143. PORTEUS, STANLEY D. *Porteus Maze Test: Fifty Years' Application.* Palo Alto, Calif.: Pacific Books, Publishers, 1965. Pp. vii, 320. *
144. RILEY, J. E., AND ARMLIN, N. J. "The Dogmatism Scale and Flexibility in Maze Performance." *Percept & Motor Skills* 21:914 D '65. * (PA 40:4237)
145. ANDREWS, ROBERT SEWALL. *The Relationship Between Appropriateness of Emotional Response and Delay of Motor Behavior.* Doctor's thesis, Boston University (Boston, Mass.), 1966. (DA 27:1613B)
146. BARRY, JOHN R., AND FULKERSON, SAMUEL C. "Chronicity and the Prediction of Duration and Outcome of Hospitalization From Capacity Measures." *Psychiatric Q* 40:104–21 Ja '66. * (PA 40:6764)
147. ERIKSON, ROBERT V., AND ROBERTS, ALAN H. "A Comparison of Two Groups of Institutionalized Delinquents on Porteus Maze Test Performance." Abstract. *J Consult Psychol* 30:567 D '66. *
148. GAMBARO, SALVATORE, AND SCHELL, ROBERT E. "Prediction of the Employability of Students in a Special Education Work-Training Program Using the Porteus Maze Test and a Rating Scale of Personal Effectiveness." *Ed & Psychol Meas* 26:1021–9 w '66. * (PA 41:5012)
149. LEIBOWITZ, MARVIN. *Effects of Psychological Support on Test Performance of Four Types of Narcotic Addicts.* Doctor's thesis, New York University (New York, N.Y.), 1966. (DA 27:2873B)
150. MEIER, MANFRED J., AND RESCH, JOSEPH A. "Behavioral Correlates of Short-Term Change in Neurological Status Following Acute Onset of Cerebrovascular Symptomatology." *J Clin Psychol* 22:156–9 Ap '66. * (PA 40:8003)
151. RANKIN, R. J., AND THOMPSON, KENNETH. "A Factor Analytic Approach to Impulse as Measured by Arrow Dot I, Q, and SORT." *Percept & Motor Skills* 23:1239–45 D '66. * (PA 41:5262)
152. RANKIN, RICHARD, AND THOMPSON, KENNETH. "A Factorial Investigation of Scores on the Porteus Maze." *Percept & Motor Skills* 23:1255–60 D '66. * (PA 41:5263)

153. STERNE, DAVID M. "Use of the Porteus Mazes With Non-Retarded Adults." *Newsl Res Psychol* 8:51–3 My '66. *
154. BURNAND, G.; HUNTER, H.; AND HOGGART, K. "Some Psychological Test Characteristics of Klinefelter's Syndrome." *Brit J Psychiatry* 113:1091–6 O '67. * (PA 42:7632)
155. COOPER, G. DAVID; YORK, MICHAEL W.; DASTON, PAUL G.; AND ADAMS, HENRY B. "The Porteus Test and Various Measures of Intelligence With Southern Negro Adolescents." *Am J Mental Def* 71:787–92 Mr '67. * (PA 41:8879)
156. DAVID, KENNETH H. "Effect of Verbal Reinforcement on Porteus Maze Scores Among Australian Aborigine Children." *Percept & Motor Skills* 24:986 Je '67. *
157. DAVID, KENNETH H., AND BOCHNER, STEPHEN. "Teacher Ratings of IQ and Porteus Maze Scores of Pitjantjara Children." *Percept & Motor Skills* 25:639–40 O '67. * (PA 42:5578)
158. FISH, CAROLINE CHANDLER. *Impulsivity in Culturally Deprived Children.* Doctor's thesis, Boston University (Boston, Mass.), 1967. (DA 29:4322A)
159. MALMQUIST, CARL P.; KIRESUK, THOMAS J.; AND SPANO, ROBERT M. "Mothers With Multiple Illegitimacies." *Psychiatric Q* 41:339–54 Ap '67. * (PA 42:4189)
160. MEIER, M. J., AND STORY, J. L. "Selective Impairment of Porteus Maze Test Performance After Right Subthalamotomy." *Neuropsychologia* 5:181–9 My '67. * (PA 42:10045)
161. MEIER, MANFRED J., AND RESCH, JOSEPH A. "Behavioral Prediction of Short-Term Neurologic Change Following Acute Onset of Cerebrovascular Symptoms." *Mayo Clin Proc* 42:641–7 O '67. *
162. PORTEUS, S. D.; BOCHNER, S.; RUSSELL, J.; AND DAVID, KENNETH. "Age as a Factor in Australid Mentality." *Percept & Motor Skills* 25:3–16 Ag '67. * (PA 42:2563)
163. TILKER, HARVEY A., AND SCHELL, ROBERT E. "Concurrent Validity of the Porteus Maze Test: A Comparative Study of Regular and Educationally Handicapped High School Students." *Ed & Psychol Meas* 27:447–55 su '67. * (PA 41:12840)
164. BOURESTOM, NORMAN C., AND HOWARD, MARY T. "Behavioral Correlates of Recovery of Self-Care in Hemiplegic Patients." *Arch Phys Med & Rehabil* 49:449–54 Ag '68. *
165. GADDES, W. H.; MCKENZIE, AUDREY; AND BARNSLEY, ROGER. "Psychometric Intelligence and Spatial Imagery in Two Northwest Indian and Two White Groups of Children." *J Social Psychol* 75:35–42 Je '68. * (PA 42:13575)
166. GILBERSTADT, HAROLD. "Relationships Among Scores of Tests Suitable for the Assessment of Adjustment and Intellectual Functioning." *J Gerontol* 23:483–7 O '68. *
167. LEFKOWITZ, MONROE M. "Nonintellective Components in the School Performance of Juvenile Delinquents." *Percept & Motor Skills* 26:1185–6 Je '68. * (PA 42:19246)
168. MCALOON, FRANCIS WILLIAM. *The Inhibition Process, Stress, and Qualitative Performance on the Porteus Maze.* Doctor's thesis, Fordham University (New York, N.Y.), 1968. (DA 29:3089B)
169. MATTHEWS, CHARLES G.; CHUN, RAYMOND W. M.; GRABOW, JACK D.; AND THOMPSON, WAYNE H. "Psychological Sequelae in Children Following California Arboviros Encephalitis." *Neurology* 18:1023–30 O '68. * (PA 43:5771)
170. PALKES, HELEN; STEWART, MARK; AND KAHANA, BOAZ. "Porteus Maze Performance of Hyperactive Boys After Training in Self-Directed Verbal Commands." *Child Develop* 39:817–26 S '68. * (PA 43:3758)
171. PORTEUS, S. D. "New Applications of the Porteus Maze Tests." *Percept & Motor Skills* 26:787–98 Je '68. * (PA 42:14729)
172. ROBERTS, ALAN H., AND ERIKSON, ROBERT V. "Delay of Gratification, Porteus Maze Test Performance, and Behavioral Adjustment in a Delinquent Group." *J Abn Psychol* 73:449–53 O '68. * (PA 42:19056)
173. SCHALLING, DAISY, AND ROSÉN, ANNE-SOFIE. "Porteus Maze Differences Between Psychopathic and Non-Psychopathic Criminals." *Brit J Social & Clin Psychol* 7:224–8 S '68. * (PA 43:1115)
174. AFTANAS, M. S., AND ROYCE, J. R. "A Factor Analysis of Brain Damage Tests Administered to Normal Subjects With Factor Score Comparisons Across Ages." *Multiv Behav Res* 4(4):459–81 O '69. * (PA 44:11030)
175. COHEN, SHIRLEY. *Impulsivity in Low-Achieving and High-Achieving Lower Class Boys.* Doctor's thesis, Columbia University (New York, N.Y.), 1969. (DAI 30:4269A)
176. JARRAHI-ZADEH, ALI; KANE, F. J., JR.; VAN DE CASTLE, R. L.; LACHENBRUCH, P. A.; AND EWING, J. A. "Emotional and Cognitive Changes in Pregnancy and Early Puerperium." *Brit J Psychiatry* 115(524):797–805 Jl '69. * (PA 44:6605)
177. MEIER, MANFRED J., AND OKAYAMA, MASAHIRO. "Behavior Assessment." *Geriatrics* 24(11):95–110 N '69. *
178. PORTEUS, S. D. "The Porteus Maze and Clinical Psychology." *Prof Psychol* 1(1):52–4 N '69. * (PA 44:6833)
179. STERNE, DAVID M. "The Benton, Porteus and WAIS Digit Span Tests With Normal and Brain-Injured Subjects." *J Clin Psychol* 25(2):173–5 Ap '69. * (PA 43:14481)
180. TRAIL, BILLIE M. *Criminal Psychopathic vs Criminal Non-Psychopathic Scores on the Porteus Maze Test Series.* Master's thesis, Texas Woman's University (Denton, Tex.), 1969.
181. WHYBROW, P. C.; PRANGE, A. J., JR.; AND TREADWAY, C. R. "Mental Changes Accompanying Thyroid Gland Dysfunction: A Reappraisal Using Objective Psychological Measurement." *Arch Gen Psychiatry* 20(1):48–63 Ja '69. * (PA 43:11631)
182. COTLER, SHELDON, AND PALMER, RICHARD J. "The Effects of Test Anxiety, Sex of Subject, and Type of Verbal Reinforcement on Maze Performance of Elementary School Children." *J Personality* 38(2):216–34 Je '70. * (PA 44:17896)
183. LOOKER, ANDREW, AND CONNERS, C. KEITH. "Diphenylhydantoin in Children With Severe Temper Tantrums." *Arch Gen Psychiatry* 23(1):80–9 Jl '70. * (PA 44:18868)
184. MEIER, MANFRED J., AND MARTIN, WILLIAM E. "Intellectual Changes Associated With Levodopa Therapy." Letter. *J Am Med Assn* 213(3):465–6 Jl 20 '70. *
185. O'KEEFE, EDWARD JOHN. *Impulsivity and Its Relationship to Risk Taking.* Doctor's thesis, Fordham University (New York, N.Y.), 1970. (DAI 31:3000B)
186. QUERY, WILLIAM T. "A Comparative Study of the Relationship Between Need Affiliation and Need Achievement, and Success and Failure Among Indian and White Children." *Newsl Res Psychol* 12(2):95–6 My '70. *
187. ROSEN, MARVIN; KIVITZ, MARVIN S.; CLARK, GERALD R.; AND FLOOR, LUCRETIA. "Prediction of Postinstitutional Adjustment of Mentally Retarded Adults." *Am J Mental Def* 74(6):726–34 My '70. * (PA 44:17195)
188. SHARP, ELIZABETH YERXA. *The Relationship of Visual Closure to Speechreading Among Deaf Children.* Doctor's thesis, University of Arizona (Tucson, Ariz.), 1970. (DAI 31:2198A)
189. WERNER, EMMY E., AND MURALIDHARAN, RAJALAKSHMI. "Nutrition, Cognitive Status and Achievement Motivation of New Delhi Nursery School Children." *J Cross-Cultural Psychol* 1(3):271–81 S '70. * (PA 45:3803)

RICHARD F. DOCTER, *Professor of Psychology, San Fernando Valley State College, Northridge, California.*

The *Porteus Maze Test* is a performance test of intelligence yielding test age scores which may be converted into IQ estimates. In addition, by assigning various penalty scores to the subject's test-taking behavior regardless of his success in dealing with the mazes, a qualitative score (Q-score) is derived which has been shown to correlate with various indices of social adjustment and, especially, to differentiate delinquent youth from nondelinquents.

The materials consist of three different maze series: the Original or Vineland Series which is supposed to be given first, the Extension Series, and the Supplement Series. The latter two are intended as retest measures only. One of the nice things about this test is that almost everyone enjoys taking it. The mazes are seen by youngsters as puzzles similar to those they may have tried to do in comic books.

Porteus began the development of his test in 1914 and, like many other early test developers, his first concern was with the classification of mentally retarded youngsters and their assignment to a special school. There is considerable evidence from a variety of clinical settings spanning over half a century that the maze test can be a useful, sensitive, and powerful tool to assist in the differential assessment of both children and adults in the borderline range of intellectual endowment. This test, particularly when teamed with other measures of intelligence, often enhances the prediction of performance in training programs for mentally retarded children and for adults who might otherwise be considered untrainable. The test is entirely nonverbal, except for presentation of the instructions and even here it is possible to circumvent the use of spoken language.

TEST AGE SCORE. Porteus has long emphasized that maze solving requires planning capacity, foresight, and the ability to learn from experience. This may be true, but hard evidence to support the claim that this is what the mazes measure is difficult to come by. In general, the test author has been willing to accept as evidence of construct validity the results of many studies which show that maze scores correlate with ratings of social adjustment or trainability, often based on populations with borderline or low intelligence but these correlational studies do not prove what the maze test measures. At this point, the best we can say is that this test appears to have considerable face validity as a task requiring short term planning toward the solution of printed mazes; how this may generalize to other kinds of planning and learning essential to the solving of different kinds of problems remains to be seen. But there is no doubt that the mazes are indeed measuring intelligence. Numerous reports have been made showing the maze test age and various general intelligence tests as having correlations of from about .40 to .70. Thus, less than one-half of the variance of the maze test age score is accounted for by whatever it is that general intelligence tests are measuring. Since the maze test has been shown to detect performance changes following psychosurgery, while other tests including the Wechsler-Bellevue have failed to do so, it seems clear that maze solving calls for problem solving competencies not required by many other tests.

The test is disarming in its simplicity. To thread one's way through any but the most elementary of mazes it is necessary to perform some very complex behaviors. These include recognition of the goal (escape from the maze), identification of subgoals (landmarks along a successful track), short term memory for a preferred course of action, and, finally, carrying out one's plan without slipping into a blind alley. To better unravel maze-solving behavior, we shall have to learn more about individual differences in problem sets and in cognitive style, for it is the problem-attack strategy and the behavioral control essential to vicarious trial and error which are critical in maze solving. These are obviously very complex mental processes, and when combined with recognition that much learning goes on within the context of a single administration of a set of mazes, it is little wonder that no one has yet extracted the essence of what the maze test measures, at least not with the specificity and exactness that would be essential to consider the mazes a refined test.

The extension and supplement series were created to compensate for practice effects based on the original series, but their use in test-retest designs leaves many questions unanswered. A central difficulty is that while the group test age averages for the original and extension series are very similar, the correlation between scores on the two forms is only about .50. This similarity in group means is due mainly to the more difficult designs at the upper end of the extension series. This increase in difficulty has more of an effect on test age scores for subjects who have excelled on the original series than for those who did less well. In the absence of adequate evidence of high correlations among these three series, their application in test-retest designs does not appear justified.

THE Q-SCORE. The qualitative score is comprised of nine test performance characteristics (such as cutting corners, crossing lines, and lifting the pencil), none of which plays a direct part in the calculation of the test age score. The rationale for the Q-score is based on Porteus' observation that the test taking "style of response" was markedly different among various youngsters even when the test age score was held constant. He noted differences in "impulsiveness," carelessness in performance, and failure to follow the directions. While Porteus has termed this a "rough and ready" measure, it has consistently been shown to reflect differences between groups of delinquents and non-delinquents, and between other groups differing in social adjustment. The correlation between Q-score and various indices of intelligence has been shown to be in the range of about −.20 to −.40. While the reliability of scoring the qualitative errors tends to be very high (above .95), the test-retest correlation of the Q-score after a three-day interval was only .51 in a sample of psychiatric patients. A factor analysis of the Q-score revealed that about 70 percent of the variance of this measure is attributable to two errors: lift pencil and wavy lines. The subject who frequently lifts his pencil has either failed to learn the instructions or has failed to comply with them, while wavy lines reflect imprecision in motor performance. These two errors do not correlate with each other. Factor analytic evidence reveals that the Q-score should not be interpreted as indicative of a single trait such as "impulsivity" or impulse control. As with the test age score, the Q-score is deceptively simple, for it depends on the quality of attention and learning when the instructions are given, and on a multitude of personality and cognitive differences that can influence one's total style of response in maze solving behavior.

STANDARDIZATION. The trouble with the maze test is not that it lacks promise; the difficulty is that the standardization of the test was quite limited to begin with and is now long overdue for revision. Porteus' most recent book serves as the test manual, but it falls short of being satisfactory for this purpose. Its greatest fault is that standardization and validation data from previous studies have not been adequately pulled together and it is not possible for a maze test user to determine what subject samples were used in the establishment of norms. Other basic psychometric essentials, such as the standard deviation for test age scores by age level, are also missing. Far more would be accomplished by a thorough restandardization than would be lost by any possible test modification which would complicate the interpretation of existing maze test research.

After a lifetime of study with the maze test, Porteus, combining both the judgment of a sensitive clinician and extensive empirical data, is frank to admit that "the validation of the Maze Test is far less satisfactory than is desired." With this we must agree, for while there is much about the predictive validity of the test which is known, the full development of the test's potential has suffered from a lack of clearly focused validation research. If the mazes are to achieve the utilization that they may well deserve, the next step in their development would seem to be in pinning down more precisely those traits or abilities which appear to be uniquely measured by this test.

JOHN L. HORN, *Professor of Psychology, University of Denver, Denver, Colorado.*

In its basic form the Maze test of today differs little from the test first published in 1914. The test has a core set of 12 mazes and 2 extension forms, each consisting of 8 mazes. The extensions are graded in difficulty and standardized in a way designed to provide scores equivalent to the core series if they are given in a designated order. The purpose of this construction is to eliminate practice effects. This purpose is realized only to the extent that one can justify several rather strong assumptions about equality of units and change.

There is no manual for the test—at least, no manual of the kind recommended in *Standards for Educational and Psychological Tests and Manuals* (SEPTM). Instead, there is a book (*143*) which contains some of the information recommended in SEPTM. There is, however, no information on reliability, virtually no description of norms, and little indication of the qualifications required to administer and interpret the test, but there is an extended and lively discussion of the limitations of other tests and of the hazards of sampling and testing in Central Australia and South Africa. In conformance with SEPTM, the book deals rather fully (in a rambling and repetitious though entertaining way) with questions of validity, and there is a description of how the test is administered and scored.

The test is scored in three quite different ways to produce measurement of three distinct attributes. One scoring, recorded in mental age or test quotient units and here referred to as ability scores, indicates degree of success in solving the problems. A second scoring, producing a Q-score, indicates stylistic qualities and, loosely, the degree of sloppiness in pathway drawings. A third scoring provides what is called a Conformity-Variability score. It is important in evaluating results obtained with the Maze test to distinguish clearly between ability and qualitative scoring, for they are sometimes confused in writings about the test and yet the two appear to have quite different construct validities. The correlation between the two is about $-.40$.

The Maze ability scores have been found to correlate at well above the chance level with a variety of ability tests, both those comprised of one type of item (Block designs, Matrices) and omnibus measures of intelligence, such as the Binet and the Wechsler, in which several different kinds of items or subtests representing different primary abilities enter into the score. The test can be said to measure a process, or processes, involved in expressions of intelligence. Porteus has argued that this process is a capacity of foresight and planning which is measured also, but along with other things, in the tests with which the Maze is correlated.

The correlational evidence provides an indirect indication of the lower bound for the reliability of the Maze test. Since the test correlates about .75 with Knox Cubes, it can be reasoned that the reliability of the Maze is probably not less than .75.

The ability score has been found to correlate most highly with spatial tests such as Knox Cubes and Kohs Blocks. Such tests have been found to define a broad visual ability that can be distinguished from two equally broad intellectual factors referred to as fluid intelligence and crystallized intelligence.[1] Guilford[2] has classified Maze tests in the CFI (Cognition of Figural Implications) cell of the structure of intellect model.

Porteus finds that in a wide range of comparisons, males on the average obtain higher Maze scores than do females. This finding is consistent with several others showing differences in favor of males in tests involving figural content and calling for spatial-visualization ability. Nevertheless, these results should be tempered with an awareness that the sampling for males and females in most of the studies upon which the conclusion is based cannot be assumed to be equally representative and that, taken overall, the differences are not large.

Porteus bases a major part of his case for the usefulness of the Maze test on evidence relating test performance to effects produced by brain injuries. He suggests that the capacity measured by the Maze test is localized to a considerable extent in frontal lobe function. In keeping with the times, however, he also suggests that the midbrain reticular formation may govern Maze performance. Most of the relevant studies have been on the frontal lobes, in general, and leucotomy, in particular. The numbers of subjects in these studies were small and the experimental controls which might compensate for small N's were in all instances inadequate. The conclusions that can be drawn must therefore be regarded as tentative. Nevertheless, the results from most of the studies[3] suggest that the ability measured by the Maze test is reduced by removal of frontal lobe tissue. There are a few results[4] indicating gains (not losses) in Maze performance following leucotomy, but these findings appear to be due in part to practice effect and in part to relief of a psychotic condition which severely hampered performance in the pretest.

The evidence thus supports the claim that the Maze test is sensitive to effects produced by the brain damage of prefrontal leucotomy. That this sensitivity is not associated exclusively with damage to the frontal lobes is indicated by the careful reviews of Hebb,[5] Meyer,[6] and Willett[7] and, more specifically and recently, by the findings of Brown and others,[8] Meier and Story (*160*), and Sterne (*179*). In the Brown and others study, for example, decrement in maze performance was found to be associated with temporal lobe surgery. Also, to acknowledge that the Maze test is "sensitive" to the effects produced by brain damage is not to imply that one can predict with high accuracy the loss to be incurred by any given individual. Averaging over the data provided by Crown,[9] King,[10] and Petrie,[11] the point biserial correlation, indicating the loss to be predicted from knowledge that the surgery has been performed, is only .29.

It is a bit misleading for Porteus to suggest that the Maze test alone among existing tests is sensitive to the effects produced by brain damage—that "losses after operation have been

---

[1] Horn, John L. "The Organization of Abilities and the Development of Intelligence." *Psychol R* 75:242-59 My '68. *
Horn, John L., and Cattell, Raymond B. "Refinement and Test of the Theory of Fluid and Crystallized General Intelligences." *J Ed Psychol* 57:253-70 O '66. *
[2] Guilford, J. P. *The Nature of Human Intelligence.* New York: McGraw-Hill Book Co., Inc., 1967. Pp. xii, 538. *

[3] Crown, Sidney. "Psychological Changes Following Prefrontal Leucotomy: A Review." *J Mental Sci* 97:49-83 Ja '51. *
Meyer, V. Chap. 14, "Psychological Effects of Brain Change," pp. 529-65. In *Handbook of Abnormal Psychology: An Experimental Approach.* Edited by H. J. Eysenck. New York: Basic Books, Inc., Publishers, 1961. Pp. xvi, 816. *
Willett, R. A. Chap. 15, "The Effects of Psychosurgical Procedures on Behavior," pp. 566-610. In *Handbook of Abnormal Psychology: An Experimental Approach.* Edited by H. J. Eysenck. New York: Basic Books, Inc., Publishers, 1961. Pp. xvi, 816. *
[4] Jones, Robert E. "Personality Changes in Psychotics Following Prefrontal Lobotomy." *J Abn & Social Psychol* 44:315-28 Jl '49. *
Ström-Olsen, R.; Last, S. L.; and Brody, M. B. "Results of Prefrontal Leucotomy in Thirty Cases of Mental Disorder." *J Mental Sci* 89:165-74 Ap '43. *
[5] Hebb, D. O. "Man's Frontal Lobes: A Critical Review." *Arch Neurol & Psychiatry* 54:10-24 Jl '45. *
Hebb, D. O. *The Organization of Behavior: A Neuropsychological Theory.* New York: John Wiley & Sons, Inc., 1949. Pp. xix, 335. *
[6] Meyer, op. cit.
[7] Willett, op. cit.
[8] Brown, Ian A.; French, Lyle A.; Ogle, William S.; and Jahnson, Shirley. "Temporal Lobe Epilepsy: Its Clinical Manifestations and Surgical Treatment: A Preliminary Report, Part 1." *Medicine* 35:425-59 '56. *
[9] Crown, op. cit.
[10] King, Henry Eugene. Chap. 14, "Intellectual Function," pp. 178-207. In *Selective Partial Ablation of the Frontal Cortex.* Edited by Fred A. Mettler. New York: Paul B. Hoeber, Inc., 1949. Pp. xiv, 517. *
[11] Petrie, Asenath. "Preliminary Report of Changes After Prefrontal Leucotomy." *J Mental Sci* 95:449-55 Ap '49. *

inconsistent or slight except in the Maze." Porteus is correct in pointing out that omnibus tests of intelligence, such as the Binet and Wechsler, sometimes indicate little or no decrement when other tests, such as the Maze, show that there has been loss. This fact was emphasized by Hebb years ago. But a number of tests (such as Blocks, Matrices, Homographs, Associational Fluency, and Absurdities) are sensitive to this decrement—tests which require the subject to sustain attention in order to deduce complex and novel relations (and this may be at the core of capacity for planning). The Maze is apparently this kind of test, although the level of complexity of the most difficult items is relatively low. Indeed, it may be, as Robinson [12] suggested, that the Maze is mainly indicative of an ability, or inclination, to sustain attention, not a good measure of capacity for resolving complex relationships.

Related to these findings is a suggestion that relative to other tests which are sensitive to the effects of brain damage, there is, according to Porteus, a "greater resistance of Maze test performance to the inroads of old age." This is a particularly interesting conjecture in light of the evidence suggesting that "the inroads of old age" are, to a considerable extent, accumulations of brain injuries.[13] Unfortunately, there are few studies of aging in which the Maze test was used. In evaluating this evidence, one must wonder if the Maze test has sufficient ceiling to detect decline in persons who function at a relatively high level—say, above what is represented roughly by an IQ of 115. That this supposition has merit is suggested by unpublished results obtained by M. B. Jensen in 1961. These indicate decline in Maze performance between age 46 to 66 in adults who had had less than eight years of schooling, but not in adults whose formal education extended beyond the eighth grade. The results of a study by Porteus and others (*162*) are also consistent with this hypothesis.

A number of studies of relationships between Maze performance and the effects produced by drugs suggest that agents which induce ataraxia, namely the phenothiazines (such as chlorpromazine, i.e., Thorazine) produce a decrement in Maze performance, whereas analeptic stimulants (such as phenidylate, i.e., ritalin) produce an increase in scores. Porteus interprets these findings as indicating that midbrain activating functions support a capacity to maintain attention, which in turn supports the planning that is required for successful performance on the Maze test.

Porteus originally developed the Maze test for the purpose of providing more accurate diagnosis of mental retardation than was provided by other tests. The results from no fewer than 10 studies have suggested that in samples of persons who score in the lower fourth of the distribution of scores obtained with omnibus tests of intelligence, the Maze test provides a useful guide for discriminating between persons who are able to manage their affairs and support themselves in the community and persons who are not thus capable. The studies suffer from a number of detracting limitations in design and analysis, and Porteus consistently fails either to acknowledge the limitations or to neutralize criticisms which follow from them. For example, Porteus gives no indication that he is aware of the arguments put against a posteriori matched-group designs. Nevertheless, the consistency of the findings in this area is impressive.

A few studies have directly attacked hypotheses stipulating that the Maze measures capacity or inclination to plan, exercise forethought, sustain attention, and delay gratification. For example, Kainer (*140*) found that children who delayed gratification scored higher on the Maze than children who did not, and that this relationship could not be entirely accounted for by differences in verbal comprehension. Palkes and others (*170*) showed that when a random set of hyperactive boys were trained to verbalize self-directed commands designed to alter a heedless, slapdash approach to tasks, they improved in their performance on the Maze Extension Series relative to another random set of hyperactive boys who were not given the training.

These kinds of results thus suggest that an interesting ability is measured, with a reliability of about .75 or better, using the Maze diagrams and the ability-scoring procedures which Porteus has recommended. The ability is probably

---

12 ROBINSON, MARY FRANCES. "What Price Lobotomy?" *J Abn & Social Psychol* 41:421–36 O '46. *
13 HORN, JOHN L. Chap. 16, "The Organization of Data on Life-Span Development of Human Abilities," pp. 423–66. In *Life-Span Developmental Psychology: Research and Theory.* Edited by L. R. Goulet and Paul B. Baltes. New York: Academic Press, Inc., 1970. Pp. 580.
HORN, JOHN L., AND CATTELL, RAYMOND B. "Age Differences in Fluid and Crystallized Intelligence." *Acta Psychologica* 26:107–29 Mr '67. *
HORN, JOHN L., AND CATTELL, RAYMOND B. "Age Differences in Primary Mental Abilities." *J Gerontol* 21:210–20 Ap '66. *

best described as a capacity or inclination to sustain attention in the face of the difficulty involved in resolving moderately complex spatial relations. It is depressed by brain damage and treatments that induce ataraxia; it may be raised somewhat by treatment with central nervous system stimulants and training that teaches one to take a more considered, deliberate approach to intellectual tasks. The ability is important in distinguishing between persons of generally low intellectual ability who can and cannot take care of themselves in societies such as our own. The test appears to provide fairly accurate measurements among persons of generally low ability but may not have enough ceiling to discriminate finely among persons well above the average in general competence.

The qualitative score has been studied most fully for its relationship to delinquent, sociopathic, antisocial behavior and, in general, has been found to correlate with this kind of behavior, as well as with a variety of variables indicating extraversion, carelessness, impulsivity, a tendency to make errors, and a tendency to strive for speed rather than accuracy in ability tests (see Payne [14] for review). Thus, it would appear that the Q-score is mainly indicative of impulsivity or impetuousness— an inability or unwillingness to refrain from behaving in a hasty, slapdash manner.

The fact that the qualitative Maze score correlates about −.40 with the ability score indicates that some of the variance in what is interpreted as an ability to sustain attention may be due to the lack of impulse control which the qualitative score is assumed to measure. This suggests that for purposes of defining more clearly what the two scores measure, and in indicating the practical validities of the two scores, it will be useful to remove the variance in each score that can be accounted for by variance in the other. It is desirable, also, to obtain more precise information about the equivalency, reliability, and long-term stability of the qualitative and ability variables. More information on the factorial validity of the test would also be very useful.

The Maze test thus presents a paradox. On the one hand there is an accumulation of evidence indicating that it provides measurements of attributes which applied and clinical psychologists are often called upon to measure. On the other hand, there is the sad fact that the norms and the information on reliability are not of a quality sufficient to justify using the test in individual diagnosis. The test and the test manual fall far short of meeting the standards recommended by the APA-AERA-NCME Committee on Test Standards. To make the test truly appropriate for use in situations where it has the greatest promise of being useful—in diagnosis of brain damage and identification of the adaptability of poorly acculturated persons—the applied and clinical psychologist must yet determine by his own research such items as: (*a*) the norms which apply in the population with which he is concerned, (*b*) whether or not the test reliability is sufficient for his purposes, and (*c*) the long-term practical predictions which the test can support.

Thus, sadly, after over 50 years of research on the Maze test, it must be concluded that the test can be recommended only for research purposes and applied work that is based upon additional research appropriate to a particular setting. Yet, paradoxical though it may seem, the evidence supports the hypothesis that the test measures an important attribute not measured by other popular devices and thus is one of the more interesting and promising tests now known to psychology. It is to be hoped that these qualities may yet provoke psychologists, as Louttit (4:356) suggested almost 20 years ago, "to establish it on a firm technical base."

Brit J Criminol 7:236–7 Ap '67. H. B. Gibson. [Review of the manual (*143*).] The Porteus Maze test has a special interest for criminologists because results obtained with it have a feature which has been shown to be discriminative of delinquent populations. This is the well-known qualitative score, which reflects the degree to which the task has been executed in an apparently slovenly manner. What components of behaviour this score really represents have never yet been fully determined. Indeed, neither have the implications of the Test Quotient (a cognitive measure like an I.Q.) ever been adequately determined scientifically, in spite of a number of attempts by distinguished research workers. The test is a triumph of empiricism. Professor Porteus, the innovator of half a century ago, has been

---

[14] PAYNE, R. W. Chap. 6, "Cognitive Abnormalities," pp. 193–261. In *Handbook of Abnormal Psychology: An Experimental Approach.* Edited by H. J. Eysenck. New York: Basic Books, Inc., Publishers, 1961. Pp. xvi, 816. *

content to reiterate his opinions about what is supposedly measured, without showing great interest in research into the *mechanisms* involved, as distinct from what can be done with the test. Much of what appears in this book has been published before, but it is useful to have such an historical compendium. It was to Porteus' credit that in the early days of psychology he recognised the need for a test that was not heavily biased by verbal knowledge. For many years he waged a spirited campaign to show that his creation was a "better" test of intelligence than the Binet, and the whole story is now retold. Later on, he discovered the value of the qualitative score; still later, the use of the test in evaluating the effects of psychosurgery. The latest development is that Porteus has sought to invade the field of "projective" techniques with his Maze—there is nothing which cannot be attempted with it! This book contains a chapter wherein a most inappropriate comparison is made between the Rorschach and the Maze test. Many modern psychologists have come to the conclusion that the Rorschach test is a lot of nonsense anyway, and should be discreetly abandoned. It is a pity that the author of the Maze test, which has so much of scientific interest in it yet to be explored, should in his enthusiasm advocate it in a vague way as a competitor among the "projective devices." This book contains many curious data, anthropological and otherwise, gathered in the course of Porteus' indefatigable penetration of remote lands with his Maze. The Appendices contain normative data concerning the Test Quotient which recent studies have shown to be utterly inappropriate to two populations of modern British schoolchildren.

Brit J Psychol 57:470 N '66. *D. C. Kendrick.* [Review of the manual (*143*).] * traces the development of the Maze Test from its first uses with feeble-minded children in 1915 up to the production of a second parallel form of the test in 1959 * In his final chapter Porteus gives the latest instructions and scoring systems for the test, and the appendices contain all three forms of the test plus tables of test quotients and examples of scoring. Porteus considers his test to be one not only of intelligence but also one of foresight and planning. The main criticism of this book is that he fails to delineate in any clear fashion just what the test really is supposed to be measuring. There appears to be no extensive study reported in the literature which answers this question. A wealth of studies is cited in the book purporting to show what the test measures, but they become a little confusing after a while. The book itself is written in a rather peculiar style. It is a mixture of the historical novel, test manual and social anthropological report, peppered with the most extraordinary passages of preaching and scolding. Many readers may find this quite irritating and distracting.

Cont Psychol 11:517–8 N '66. *Laurance F. Shaffer.* [Review of the manual (*143*).] For any psychological test to evoke wide use and new research after half a century is rare enough. Even more remarkable is the appearance of a new book about such a test written by its originator. The present volume shows that the Porteus Maze Test is still a vigorous youngster. The book digs into the past, as one would expect, but it also deals with some very present concerns and takes not a few glances into the future. * Two chapters are devoted to the author's remarkable expeditions to observe and test the primitive natives of Australia, with new data obtained in 1962. Another chapter summarizes many studies with the Mazes of members of other preliterate societies. This material makes splendidly interesting reading, but much of it is good travelogue with only incidental relevance to the psychology of individual differences. The primitive subjects tested with the Mazes have in most instances constituted samples of expediency (one cannot say of convenience!) whose degree of representativeness is unknown. That these persons tested below white standards on the Mazes was inevitable; it is remarkable that they were able to perform so alien a task at all. Although the norms obtained in the Caucasian culture are inapplicable, the raw scores of the preliterates are pure prime data of some interest. Differences between the performances of groups are generally interpreted in cultural terms with no evidence of "racial" bias. While the book contains much good and relevant evidence about the Maze Test, the reviewer cannot suppress the wish that the data and their presentation might have been better and more complete. In all too many instances the reader needs to know more in order to interpret findings intelligently. An example is the typical absence of data on the dispersion of scores in samples. One cannot compare correlation coefficients without knowing the variances of the groups on which they were determined. Another technical fault is the absence of any evidence about the reliability of the Maze Test. This lack must be forgiven for the original single form which was unsuited for repeated administration or for breaking into equivalent parts, but the development of the two new forms for retesting—the "Extension" and "Supplement"—surely could have provided useful evidence on test stability. Equally vexing is the absence of sufficient data on the standardization of the test and of the derivation of the Test Quotients. There is, for example, no way to learn what the standard deviation of a TQ is at various ages, an essential bit of information if one is to compare the Maze Test with other instruments which use quotients. The last section of the book is a satisfactory guide for the administration and scoring, both quantitative and qualitative, of the three forms of the Maze Test. It is the handbook that a user needs, and supersedes earlier versions. But, lacking the detailed technical and normative data about the test, it is not a Manual as that term is now understood. What kind of a judgment can one make of the Maze Test as a whole? In spite of the lack of some technical information usually deemed essential, and in spite of some faults in the reporting of earlier studies relevant to validity, the test holds up well. The reviewer expresses his bias that empirical evidence about the concurrent and predictive powers of a test stands higher in the hierarchy of values than evidence about internal characteristics and standardization. But it would be gratifying to have both varieties of knowledge about the test, and the reviewer hopes that Dr. Porteus will some day furnish the missing pieces.

Ed & Psychol Meas 26:511–4 su '66. William D. Altus. [Review of the manual (*143*).] Stanley Porteus' life by almost any standard has been a highly successful one. He was vouchsafed fairly early an original insight in psychometrics and has carefully nursed his brain child along for over fifty years of application, research, and controversy. * Porteus....has never been accorded adequate professional recognition among American psychologists, possibly because he was something of an Ausländer among the natives. It seems more probable, though, that his espousal of tests as a touchstone for evaluating racial differences in intelligence in the long dead controversies of a generation back had more to do with the lack of acceptance of his mazes and the claims he has made for them. * For 20 years after its publication in 1916 the Stanford-Binet Intelligence Scale was accepted as the true measure of intelligence, against which any newcomer must be validated. Thus it can be seen that Porteus and his mazes gave many hostages to fortune while making a bid for professional recognition in the United States: Porteus was "foreign," he chose unpopular causes, and Terman's Stanford-Binet Intelligence Scale was already entrenched. Only through long life, energy, and persistence have these hostages been neutralized. This book tells the story—a successful one—of the tangled Odyssey of the mazes. * Porteus believed that the performance measure he invented in the maze test cut through the pitfalls of the purely verbal measure and got at some native aptitudes of a practical nature, especially of "planfullness." It has taken him a lifetime to document his original hunch, but he has done it in a number of specific ways. Aside from Porteus' own publications, one of the good early confirmations of the special extra quality to be found in the mazes but not in the Binet type test was a study of Poull and Montgomery in 1929. They gave the Stanford-Binet Intelligence Scale and the mazes to inmates of a youth facility on Randall's Island, New York, about one half of whom consisted of juvenile delinquents while the other half was relatively free of psychopathic tainting. Stanford-Binet Intelligence Scale showed no mean differences between the two groups; the mazes did—the juvenile delinquent group scoring nine points lower. Slowly here, more readily in England, the mazes began to be accepted as an adjunct test in the clinical armamentarium and increasingly often as the test of choice if the child or adult were non-English or nearly so. * The mazes would appear to measure something both quantitatively and qualitatively which discriminates against the impulsive individuals so frequently found among the delinquent and criminal. The Porteus Maze Test was found by Porteus and Peters, later by Landis and Zubin to be a sensitive measure of the cerebral insult of psychosurgery. Whereas the Wechsler-Bellevue Intelligence Scale showed no impairment subsequent to the operation, the mazes did. * Porteus also demonstrated from the beginning that the maze test is a measure much to be preferred to the traditional intelligence test when institutional groups—the feeble of mind, the criminal, or the delinquent—are to be sorted for training or treatment. * What has been reported makes it seem likely that the test is a valuable adjunct for the anthropologist to know about and to employ for research purposes in his investigations. * In 99 out of 105 studies Porteus has found the male to have a maze test mean superior to that of the female. Porteus does not exactly claim that this shows general male superiority of intelligence; he suggests that it probably represents inherent temperamental differences. Since he has so often equated temperamental differences with manifest intelligence, one wonders whether he does not feel about women's mental inferiority somewhat the way he did about the various non-Caucasian groups in Hawaii and their numerous crosses which he tested and found wanting a generation ago. One hastens to add that this claim is not made in this latest book of Porteus. It may be that he has succumbed to the Zeitgeist. It may also be that he feels it is better not to tilt at windmills without allies. We should be thankful to Porteus for his mazes and for his research. He is still a vigorous, undaunted sample of what originality, persistence, hard work, and long life can bring about. Let us hope that he brings us up-to-date once more when he reaches the century mark.

For reviews by C. M. Louttit and Gladys C. Schwesinger, see 4:356.

[420]
★**Preschool Attainment Record, Research Edition.** Ages 6 months to 7 years; 1966-67; PAR; 9 scores: ambulation, manipulation, rapport, communication, responsibility, information, ideation, creativity, total; individual; 1 form ('66, 5 pages plus profile); manual ['67, 24 pages plus test]; no data on reliability; no norms; $2.50 per 25 record blanks; $1.35 per manual; postage extra; $1.50 per specimen set, postpaid; [15–20] minutes; Edgar A. Doll; American Guidance Service, Inc. *

REFERENCES
1. DOLL, EDGAR A., AND MCKNIGHT, EDWARD L. "A Preschool Educational Attainment Scale." *Cereb Palsy J* 26:3–5 Jl–Ag '65. * (PA 40:744)
2. DOLL, EDGAR A. "An Attainment Scale for Appraising Young Children With Expressive Handicaps." *Cereb Palsy J* 27:3–5 S–O '66. * (PA 41:1815)
3. STEDMAN, DONALD J.; CLIFFORD, MIRIAM; AND SPITZNAGEL, ANNE. "A Comparison of Ratings of Mothers and Teachers on the Preschool Attainment Record of 17 Five Year Old Children." *Excep Children* 35(6):488–9 F '69. *
4. BLAIR, JOHN R. "A Comparison of Mother and Teacher Ratings on the Preschool Attainment Record of Four Year Old Children." *Excep Children* 37(4):299–300 D '70. *
5. OWENS, EARL P., AND BOWLING, DONALD H. "Internal Consistency and Factor Structure of the Preschool Attainment Record." *Am J Mental Def* 75(2):170–1 S '70. * (PA 45:8814)

ROBERTA R. COLLARD, *Assistant Professor of Human Development, University of Massachusetts, Amherst, Massachusetts.*

The *Preschool Attainment Record* is an expansion of the early age levels of the *Vineland Social Maturity Scale* and is designed to measure the physical, social, mental, and language attainments of children from 6 months to 7 years. The purpose of the PAR is to determine the child's usual behavior in the areas tested rather than what he is able to do. Like the VSMS, the PAR is administered as a structured interview with an adult closely associated with the child to be evaluated, or on the basis of direct observation of the child's behavior by the examiner.

The test is divided into eight areas with 14 age items in each category: one item for each half-year interval up to 7 years. The eight areas are: Ambulation, Manipulation, Rapport, Communication, Responsibility, Information, Ideation, and Creativity. Items are arranged in order of increasing difficulty; for example, the category Ambulation includes a range of behavior items from "Sits unsupported" to "Rides play vehicles."

The scale is intended to be used to determine the developmental level of children for whom verbal intelligence tests are not appropriate; for example, children with sensory or neuromuscular impairments, speech or language disabilities, emotional disturbances, resistance to testing, and cultural differences. More specifically, it is well adapted for testing deaf, blind, or aphasic children; children with cerebral palsy, mental retardation, autism, or schizophrenia; and children whose development has been impaired by sensory or cultural deprivation or who do not speak English. It has the advantage over tests such as the Stanford-Binet of including motor skills, social competencies, and creativity, as well as intellectual abilities. The record blank includes spaces for a description of the child's socioeconomic and cultural-linguistic background and family constellation and for medical referral notes on disabilities or illnesses.

Items are scored +, –, or ± for pass, fail, and doubtful, respectively. To determine the raw score, each item passed is counted as one, and ± scores are given half credit. As there are 16 items per year, the Attainment Age is calculated by dividing the total score by 16, or the raw score could be multiplied by .75 to derive the month value.

The procedure of using precise numerical scoring may be open to criticism because of the possibility of subjectivity of the adult's report on the child and the impreciseness of the behavioral measures. However, if the test score is interpreted with these limitations in mind and the test results are used to note areas of difficulty and strengths in the child's development, the use of a precise score should not necessarily be misleading. Because of the unreliability of some of the items, such a criticism could be leveled at most developmental tests based on observation.

As Doll mentions in the manual, there is considerable overlap in the classification of the areas of behavior sampled by the PAR, particularly in the areas of Communication, Ideation, and Information. Although this problem cannot be completely surmounted, the logic of some of the classifications could be improved. For example, an item which involves adding amounts up to 10 and counting by 5's to 30 is included under Communication, while several levels of counting are included under Ideation. The area of Communication could best be called Language, because some of the items such as "Babbling" and "Imitation" are not, strictly speaking, Communication.

The instructions on the administration of the test are generally clear, but this reviewer would have appreciated a larger number of specific examples of good questions to be asked to elicit the information to be scored. Most of the definitions of the behaviors are clear, but some need examples for clarity. Also, some of the categories contain several behaviors, and it is not clearly stated whether the child must show *all* of these behaviors to pass the item completely.

I find the age placement of some of the items questionable as the behaviors are now defined. For example, play is arranged into six levels: from parallel play (age 3.0) to playing simple group table games (age 7.0). Although most of the age placements appear reasonable in terms of systematic observations reported in the literature, item 91, "Plays pretend" (which includes imaginative play and role play with leading or following in evidence) is given a mean of 6.0 years, which seems high to me, as I have observed such play to be almost universal after age 4½ in both upper middle class and Head Start children if they have had an opportunity to play with other children before. On the other hand, in the area of Creativity, item 48, "Dramatizes stories," which includes dressing up or acting out roles is placed at age 3.0 which seems low. Item 50, "Throws objects" (flings object nonrandomly with arm, hand, and wrist), is given an age mean of 3.5 years, whereas in the *Gesell Developmental Schedules* the age at which most children are expected to throw a ball in a particular direction is 21 months. To answer or score this item accurately would require careful observation of the child's method of throwing an object.

Some of the items under Rapport and Responsibility indicate a high value placed on conformity and obedience, such as "Minds" (age 2.0), "Complies" (age 2.5), "Cleans up" (age 5.0), "Helps" (age 5.5), "Conforms" (age 6.0), and "Observes routines" (age 7.0). A qualifying phrase such as "reasonably often" would give these items less of an authoritarian ring. I miss items under Rapport which would indicate whether or not the child has friends or shows empathy. Affectionate responses are placed in the category Information. I also miss items on moral development which would indicate degree of internalization of control versus impulsivity. There are few items indicating qualities of ego strength, such as confidence, self-esteem, frustration tolerance, persistence at tasks, foresight, and ability to find or accept substitute gratification or to delay gratification. The test includes few items on emotions, none on fears or on aggression toward persons.

Despite these omissions and within the limits of the areas covered, the PAR appears to be a good basic inventory of the behaviors of infants and young children, based on maturation and social expectations in American culture. As a scale which does not require language and includes motor and social as well as intellectual competencies, it should prove useful in evaluating the developmental strengths and weaknesses of young children with physical, emotional, or culturally-based developmental difficulties.

Psychol Rep 21:1029 D '67. C. H. Ammons. * assessment is much like that required on the Vineland Social Maturity Scale. Some item definitions are lacking in specificity. No normative data are presented. No reliability or validity information is reported.

★Queensland Test. Ages 7 and over; 1968–70; QT; based (except for pattern matching subtest) on the unpublished *PIR Test* used for screening for the Pacific Island Regiment; essentially the same as 5 of the 6 subtests in the *New Guinea Performance Scales* except for minor differences in some of the testing materials and differences in administration, scoring, and norms population; for the selection of subjects "likely to be able to learn rapidly the complex skills of westernized urbanized cultures from among groups who had had little contact with that culture"; administered by pantomime; 6 scores: *Knox Cube Test,* beads, modified *Passalong Test,* form assembly, pattern matching, total; individual; 1 form; manual ('70, 179 pages); record form ['68, 4 pages]; 3 sets of norms: Australian school children, aboriginal children with a medium amount of European contact, aboriginal children with low contact; Aus $95 per set of testing materials, 50 record forms, and manual; $3 per 50 record forms; $7 per manual; postpaid within Australia; (45-65) minutes; D. W. McElwain, G. E. Kearney, and I. G. Ord (test and record form); Australian Council for Educational Research. *

REFERENCES

1. ORD, I. G. *Development of a Test of Cognitive Capacity for Indigenes of Papua-New Guinea.* Master's thesis, University of Queensland (Brisbane, Australia), 1959.
2. KEARNEY, GEORGE E. "Cognitive Capacity Among the Orokaiva." *New Guinea Res B* 13:1-25 '66. *
3. KEARNEY, JACQUELINE E. *A New Performance Scale of Cognitive Capacity for Use With Deaf Subjects.* Master's thesis, University of Queensland (Brisbane, Australia), 1967.
4. KEARNEY, GEORGE ENGLAND. *Some Aspects of the General Cognitive Ability of Various Groups of Aboriginal Australians as Assessed by the Queensland Test.* Doctor's thesis, University of Queensland (Brisbane, Australia), 1968.
5. ORD, I. G. "The P.I.R. Test and Derivatives." *Austral Psychologist* 2:137-46 Mr '68. * (PA 42:18-98)
6. KEARNEY, JACQUELINE E. "A New Performance Scale of Cognitive Capacity for Use With Deaf Subjects." *Am Ann Deaf* 114(1):2-14 Ja '69. * (PA 43:7197)
7. KEARNEY, JACQUELINE E. "Verbalization Tests." *Austral Psychologist* 5(2):164-76 Jl '70. * (PA 45:8719)

[422]

The Quick Test. Ages 2 and over; 1958-62; QT; picture vocabulary; individual; Forms 1, 2, 3, ('58, 1 card); provisional manual ('62, 54 pages, reprint of 2 below); instruction cardboard ('62, 1 page); item cardboard ('62, 1 page, includes words for all 3 forms); record-norms sheet ('62, 2 pages); norms for combinations of 2 or 3 forms also presented; $8 per set of testing materials including all 3 forms, 100 record sheets, and manual; $2.50 per manual; cash orders postpaid; specimen set not available (manual illustrates all materials); (3-10) minutes; R. B. Ammons and C. H. Ammons; Psychological Test Specialists. *

REFERENCES

1-3. See 6:534.
4. BIBB, JOHN JAMES, JR. *A Study of the Quick Test as a Screening Instrument for Educable Mentally Retarded Children.* Doctor's thesis, University of Virginia (Charlottesville, Va.), 1964. (DA 25:3386) (Abstract: Ed R 2:69-71)
5. METHVIN, MARILYN. "Quick Test Performances of Mentally Retarded Individuals." *Am J Mental Def* 68:540-2 Ja '64. *
6. CARLISLE, A. L. "Quick Test Performance by Institutional Retardates." *Psychol Rep* 17:489-90 O '65. * (PA 40:886)
7. DOYLE, EDWARD D. *A Comparison of IQ's on the WAIS and Q.T. With a Group of Spinal Cord Injury Patients.* Master's thesis, Loyola University (Chicago, Ill.), 1965.
8. OGILVIE, ROBERT D. "Correlations Between the Quick Test (QT) and the Wechsler Adult Intelligence Scale (WAIS) as Used in a Clinical Setting." *Psychol Rep* 16:497-8 Ap '65. * (PA 39:10081)
9. OTTO, WAYNE, AND McMENEMY, RICHARD A. "An Appraisal of the Ammons Quick Test in a Remedial Reading Program." *J Ed Meas* 2:193-8 D '65. * (PA 40:4769)
10. PLESS, I. BARRY; SNIDER, MARVIN; EATON, ANN E.; AND KEARSLEY, RICHARD B. "A Rapid Screening Test for Intelligence in Children: A Preliminary Report." *Am J Dis Children* 109:533-7 Je '65. * (PA 40:425)
11. WHITNEY, VIRGIL, AND METZGER, ROLLAND. "The Quick Test as an Intelligence Screening Device in a Large Scale Program of Employee Applicant Testing." *J Clin Psychol* 21:71-2 Ja '65. * (PA 39:12315)
12. ANDREWS, R. J., AND ANDERSON, J. "The Use of the Quick Test in a Number of Clinical and Routine Settings." *Austral Psychologist* 1:116-20 N '66. * (PA 42:3191)
13. ABIDIN, RICHARD R., JR., AND BYRNE, ALFRED V. "Quick Test Validation Study and Examination of Form Equivalency." *Psychol Rep* 20:735-9 Je '67. * (PA 41:13591)
14. COLE, SPURGEON, AND WILLIAMS, ROBERT. "The Quick Test as an Index of Intellectual Ability on a Negro Admission Ward." *Psychol Rep* 20:581-2 Ap '67. * (PA 41:8146)
15. KING, FRANCIS W. "Quick Test Inter-Form Reliability in Diverse Clinical Groups and the Effect of Age Correction Factor." *Psychol Rep* 20:193-4 F '67. * (PA 41:7502)
16. LAMP, ROBERT E., AND BARCLAY, A. "The Quick Test as a Screening Device for Intellectually Subnormal Children." *Psychol Rep* 20:763-6 Je '67. * (PA 41:13596)
17. MEDNICK, MARTHA T. "Relationship of the Ammons Quick Test of Intelligence to Other Ability Measures." *Psychol Rep* 20:523-6 Ap '67. * (PA 41:9390)
18. STEWART, HORACE; COLE, SPURGEON; AND WILLIAMS, ROBERT. "Relationship Between the QT and WAIS in a Restricted Clinical Sample." *Psychol Rep* 20:383-6 Ap '67. * (PA 41:9087)
19. WIRLS, CHARLES J., AND PLOTKIN, ROSALIE R. "Calculation of Quick Test IQs for Children With Mental Ages Seventeen and Above." *Psychol Rep* 20:603-5 Ap '67. * (PA 41:8172)
20. BONFIELD, JOHN RONALD. *Predictors of Achievement for Educable Mentally Retarded Children.* Doctor's thesis, Pennsylvania State University (University Park, Pa.), 1968. (DAI 30:1009A)
21. CONNOLLY, JOSEPH KENNETH. *The Discriminatory Functions of Brief Tests With the Educable Mentally Retarded.* Doctor's thesis, Fordham University (New York, N.Y.), 1968. (DA 29:2997A)
22. COYLE, F. A., JR., AND ERDBERG, PHILIP. "Quick Test Administration With Mental Retardates." *Psychol Rep* 22:1091-2 Je '68. * (PA 42:18997)
23. FELDMAN, SOLOMON E. "Utility of Some Rapid Estimations of Intelligence in a College Population." *Psychol Rep* 22:23-6 F '68. * (PA 42:10572)
24. HOUSTON, CAMILLE, AND OTTO, WAYNE. "Poor Readers' Functioning on the WISC, Slosson Intelligence Test and Quick Test." Abstract. *AERA Paper Abstr* 1968:120-1 '68. *
25. HOUSTON, CAMILLE, AND OTTO, WAYNE. "Poor Readers' Functioning on the WISC, Slosson Intelligence Test and Quick Test." *J Ed Res* 62:15-9 D '68. *
26. LAMP, ROBERT E., AND BARCLAY, A. "Comparisons of Scores on Quick Test and Stanford-Binet, Form L-M, for Retarded Children." *Psychol Rep* 23:401-2 O '68. * (PA 43:10229)
27. LEVINE, NIRA R. *Validation of the Quick Test for an Elderly Population.* Doctor's thesis, University of Virginia (Charlottesville, Va.), 1969. (DAI 31:646A)
28. MEDNICK, MARTHA T. "The Validity of the Ammons' Quick Test of Intelligence." *Psychol Rep* 24(2):388-90 Ap '69. * (PA 43:15012)
29. QUATTLEBAUM, LAWRENCE F., AND WHITE, WILLIAM F. "Relationship Between Two Quick Screening Measures of Intelligence for Neuropsychiatric Patients." *Psychol Rep* 24(3):691-3 Je '69. * (PA 44:868)
30. QUATTLEBAUM, LAWRENCE F., AND WHITE, WILLIAM F. "Relationships Among the Quick Test, Two Measures of Psychomotor Functioning, and Age." *Percept & Motor Skills* 29(3):824-6 D '69. * (PA 46:5150)
31. STRANDBERG, T. E.; GRIFFITH, J.; AND MINER, L. "Child Language and Screening Intelligence." *J Commun Disorders* 2(3):268-72 Ag '69. * (PA 44:3464)
32. CULL, JOHN G., AND COLVIN, CRAIG R. "Correlation Between the Quick Test (QT) and the WAIS Verbal Scale in the Rehabilitation Setting." *Psychol Rep* 27(1):105-6 Ag '70. * (PA 45:6807)
33. DAVIS, WILLIAM E., AND DIZZONNE, MICHAEL F. "Relationship Between the QT and the WAIS." *Psychol Rep* 26(2):457-8 Ap '70. * (PA 44:21167)

Brit J Psychol 55:117 F '64. B. Semeonoff. * essentially a shortened version of the....*Full Range Picture Vocabulary Test* * Each of its three "forms" is represented by a card bearing four line drawings. The subject is required to say, for each of 50 words associated with a given card, which of the four pictures "best fits it." The purpose of the test is to provide a means of "quick screening of verbal intelligence in practical situations." Separate norms (in the form of "I.Q." conversions) are provided for each form separately, any pair, or all three together. The idea is an attractive one, but the material published is open to criticism. Three points, in order of increasing seriousness, are as follows: First, the drawings are crude—though seldom really ambiguous. Secondly, some of the attributions of meaning, and the cues on which they rest, are highly dubious. Thus, *celerity* is regarded as appropriate to a picture of a restaurant because the waitress is "bending over in her hurry." Again, in the same picture the diner very definitely looks *bovine*—another of the key words, for which the correct choice is a drawing showing a cow by a stream, because, the manual says, this "is the only drawing with a cow on it." Thirdly, and finally, the method seems positively to encourage acceptance of loose use of language. Whether this is inherent in the method would seem to rest on further experiment with better pictures. Here everything seems to have been sacrificed to convenience, and one cannot help feeling that the validities claimed for the test and its parent FRPV (which are considerable) must have been achieved in spite of rather than because of their characteristic features. *

Ed & Psychol Meas 25:268–71 sp '65. Peter F. Merenda. [Review of the Provisional Manual.] This excellent monograph....is....a provisional manual....[and]....a combination of (*a*) an exposition on the merits of brief screening devices for estimating a wide range of human intellectual abilities; (*b*) a plea to critics of short psychological tests to consider factors other than brevity in their evaluation of such instruments; and (*c*) a review and summary of the professional literature reporting a great scope of research findings with the *QT* and its parent test—*The Full-Range Picture Vocabulary Test (FRPV)*. * the authors....maintain that they have found that reasonably intelligent adults with no formal training in testing can learn to administer the *QT* efficiently and that with some additional training such persons can be taught to interpret it adequately. They go on to say that it is better to train non-psychologists to administer and interpret these tests adequately rather than unrealistically to expect untrained persons to do absolutely no testing! In line with this reasoning, they have simplified the presentation of directions and materials in this manual. Such statements will undoubtedly elicit some strong negative reactions on the part of the authors' professional colleagues, but this reviewer for one, on the basis of his own personal experiences, is willing to agree with Ammons and Ammons. * the controversial nature of the contents of much of this provisional manual for the *QT* is deemed inevitable. There will be those who will undoubtedly be greatly concerned about the brevity of the tests, the relatively small samples utilized in the normative, reliability, and validity research, and the rather high correlation coefficients reported which suggest spuriousness. To these critics, and to all users or potential users of the *QT*, this reviewer can only advise others to consult the basic research literature on the *QT* to which the authors make repeated reference in the monograph. Of course, this reviewer is not necessarily willing to accept all the findings reported in the monograph at face value. Nevertheless, the data and arguments presented by Ammons and Ammons are both impressive and seemingly convincing. Therefore, they cannot be blindly ignored! If the *QT* is only partly as good as the data and findings reported in this provisional manual seem to imply, then the authors will have made an outstanding and lasting contribution to the field of psychological testing. It is necessary, however, for the discriminating user and researcher to go beyond the data reported herein and, as the authors themselves suggest, conduct his own research with the *QT*.

For reviews by Boyd R. McCandless and Ellen V. Piers, see 6:534.

[423]
★**Ring and Peg Tests of Behavior Development.** Birth to age 6; 1958–64; RPTBD; experimental; 6 scores: ambulative, manipulative, communicative, social adaptive, emotive, total; individual; 1 form ('58); mimeographed revised manual ('64, 164 pages, identical with 1958 manual except for 9 pages of inserts); administration booklet ('64, 10 pages); $15 per kit including 10 scoring sheets, 10 administration booklets, manual, and set of manipulation objects; $6 per manual; cash orders postpaid; (20–50) minutes; Katharine M. Banham; Psychometric Affiliates. *

JANE V. HUNT, *Assistant Research Psychologist, Institute of Human Development, University of California, Berkeley, California.*

This infant and preschool scale contains items derived from a number of existing mental tests. Ten items and ten alternates are included at each age level. Age levels are divided into monthly intervals during the first year, bimonthly intervals during the second year, and six-month intervals from 2½ through 6 years.

An alternate item is included for each item of the scale, to be given and scored when the basic item is omitted or failed. Many of the alternates provide for the administration of the item by a familiar adult when the examiner cannot elicit the desired response; other alternates allow for varying the position of the stimulus, accepting alternative behaviors with test materials, providing different materials for the same task, or assessing completely different tasks. The test is scored either as a cumulative total score, yielding a behavior age and a ratio developmental quotient, or as a developmental profile of the five behavioral categories of the test. These categories (ambulative, manipulative, communicative, social adaptive, and emotive) are systematically represented by two items at each age level.

Reliability and validity studies with normal infants and children are essentially lacking. Scores on the Ring and Peg tests have been compared with scores on the *Cattell Infant Intelligence Scale* or on the *Stanford-Binet Intelligence Scale* for small groups of children at ages of approximately 7 months, 8 months, 4 years, and 5 years. These groups varied in size from 10 to 39 children; mean IQ for the groups ranged from 50 to 86. Split-half reliability (odd and even numbers) yielded rank difference coefficients of correlation of .95 or higher. Rank difference correlations between this test and the Cattell scale for the infant groups were .86 and .75. The correlation between the Ring and Peg tests and the Cattell scale for the four-year-olds was .73; the correlation between this test and the Stanford-Binet for the five-year-olds was .89.

Because of the lack of standardization on a representative sample of normal children, the RPTBD should be used as an experimental scale only and should not be used in lieu of a more reliable instrument. The behavioral subscales of the test are particularly experimental, as there are few items in each category at each level and because no evidence is presented to substantiate content validity. Item selection appears to have been made on an ad hoc basis, a method often debatable, particularly in the domains of social adaptive behavior and emotive behavior.

The author stresses the compact size of the test as an asset, but the advantage of compactness is offset by the extremely limited amount of material available to capture the interest of the child. Repeated presentation of the rings and pegs in different situations can lead either to diminished interest in the materials or to perseverative attempts to use the materials in a manner other than that desired at a given moment. For example, at the nine-month level the infant is expected to drop the peg and wait for the adult response, but at the ten-month level he is expected to hold two pegs and reach for a third. An infant tested on both items might elect to continue the first behavior when handed the same material again. Infants and young children sometimes display idiosyncratic preferences for, or rejection of, particular test materials. If the infant rejected either the pegs or rings of this test, test reliability would be considerably diminished. An additional drawback of the compact size of the test is the very fine, almost unreadable print used in the small administration booklet.

SUMMARY. This test is an unstandardized developmental scale which may be elected for research purposes but should not be used as a replacement for existing tests having known reliability. The systematic effort to include items from each of five behavioral categories at each age level is laudable, but the small number of such items at each age level and the ad hoc decisions of item selection make individual profile analyses extremely dubious. Research is needed to test the validity of the functional divisions of the test. The inclusion of an alternate for each item is novel but, again, research is needed to measure the effects of this innovative approach on test reliability.

EMMY E. WERNER, *Professor of Child Development and Research Child Psychologist, University of California, Davis, California.*

The *Ring and Peg Tests of Behavior Development* was published in experimental form in 1958 to serve the needs of clinical psychologists, psychiatrists, and pediatricians attached to child guidance clinics, hospitals, institutions for the mentally retarded, and traveling mental health clinics.

Test materials are inexpensive, simple, attractive to children, and less dependent on cultural opportunities than materials used in other preschool scales. They consist of pencil and paper, shoelaces, a handkerchief, a box, and a yellow (or blue) plastic pegbase with three blue (or yellow) pegs and eight graded rings to fit over them, four blue and four yellow.

Ring and Peg Tests of Behavior Development

Behavior subtests were selected on the basis of similarity to items of existing scales, including the Stanford-Binet, the Gesell, the California, Minnesota, Merrill-Palmer, Cattell, Northwestern, Buehler, Griffiths, and Vineland scales, with age placements taken from these scales. A thorough standardization on representative samples of children and a careful item analysis remain to be done.

A cursory examination of the age placement of the items in the five behavior categories suggests that some of the items in the section on ambulative development are now passed at an earlier age, as the 1969 revision of the *Bayley Scales of Infant Development* indicates. The same appears to hold for some of the items on social-adaptive development that were taken from the Vineland Scale. The section on manipulative development is excellent in its imaginative use of simple materials to test form-perception and eye-hand coordination. The section on communicative development has more detailed observations on early vocalizations than other infant and preschool scales. The predictive value of these items in forecasting later cognitive development ought to be explored. The section on emotive development (motivation, interest, drive) besides being probably the weakest, is difficult to differentiate from the other subscales.

Assets of the tests are: (*a*) the selection of test items that involve learning and problem solving with little dependence on cultural opportunities; (*b*) the imaginative use of simple materials; (*c*) clearly stated instructions that make allowance for alternate items; and (*d*) test items that can be administered as either an age scale or a point scale.

Data on the validity and reliability continue to be only preliminary in the 1964 manual. Preliminary studies of concurrent validity are based on correlations (ranging from .73 to .89) between behavior age scores on some small samples and scores on the *Cattell Infant Intelligence Scale* and the Stanford-Binet. Mean scores on the RPTBD are generally somewhat lower than mean scores on the Cattell and Stanford-Binet for the same children, but the variability of the scores is somewhat higher. Unfortunately, no additional validation studies have been undertaken since the publication of the revised manual in 1964.

SUMMARY. The Ring and Peg tests are still in experimental form, 12 years after their publication. It is hoped that, after a long period of neglect, the present surge of interest in the early diagnosis of developmental defects, especially among the culturally deprived, and in cross-cultural research with young children may lead to a rediscovery of this simple, imaginative, inexpensive, and reliable instrument that covers a wider range of behavior than most infant and preschool tests on the market. The real job of standardization and validation, however, remains to be done.

[424]

Slosson Intelligence Test. Ages 2 weeks and over; 1961–63; SIT; based in part upon *Stanford-Binet Intelligence Scale, Third Revision* and *Gesell Developmental Schedules;* individual; 1 form ('63); manual ('63, 43 pages, including test questions, sample score sheets, IQ finder, and other materials); score sheet ('63, 2 pages); IQ classification chart ('62, 2 pages); $3.75 per examiner's kit of manual, pad of 20 score sheets, and pad of 20 copies of the *Slosson Oral Reading Test;* $1 per additional pad of 20 score sheets; 75¢ per pad of 20 IQ classification charts; postpaid; (10–30) minutes; Richard L. Slosson; Slosson Educational Publications. *

REFERENCES

1. DELAPA, GIACINTO. *Correlates of Slosson Intelligence Test, Stanford Binet, Form L-M, and Achievement Indices.* Doctor's thesis, West Virginia University (Morgantown, W.Va.), 1967. (*DA* 28:3498A)
2. O'KEEFE, STEPHEN LOUIS. *An Inquiry Into the Use of the Slosson Intelligence Test With Fast Learning.* Master's thesis, Ohio State University (Columbus, Ohio), 1967.
3. AMES, LOUISE BATES. "Academic Progress in Negro Schools." *J Learn Dis* 1:570–7 O '68. * (*PA* 45:3029)
4. BONFIELD, JOHN RONALD. *Predictors of Achievement for Educable Mentally Retarded Children.* Doctor's thesis, Pennsylvania State University (University Park, Pa.), 1968. (*DAI* 30:1009A)
5. BURNS, LORNA M. *The Slosson Intelligence Test as a Pre-Screening Instrument With Potentially Gifted Children.* Master's thesis, Sacramento State College (Sacramento, Calif.), 1968.
6. DELAPA, GIACINTO. "The Slosson Intelligence Test: A Screening and Retesting Technique for Slow Learners." Abstract. *J Sch Psychol* 6:224–5 sp '68. *
7. DUGGAN, MARY DIONYSIA. *A Study of the Relation Between the Slosson Reading and Intelligence Tests and Other Standardized Tests at the Second Grade Level.* Master's thesis, Cardinal Stritch College (Milwaukee, Wis.), 1968.
8. FAGERT, CHARLES M. *The Relationship Between the Slosson Intelligence Test and the Wechsler Intelligence Scale for Children.* Master's thesis, Kent State University (Kent, Ohio), 1968.
9. HOUSTON, CAMILLE, AND OTTO, WAYNE. "Poor Readers' Functioning on the WISC, Slosson Intelligence Test and Quick Test." Abstract. *AERA Paper Abstr* 1968:120–1 '68. *
10. HOUSTON, CAMILLE, AND OTTO, WAYNE. "Poor Readers' Functioning on the WISC, Slosson Intelligence Test and Quick Test." *J Ed Res* 62:157–9 D '68. *
11. KEANY, MARY. *A Study of the Relation Between the Slosson Reading and Intelligence Tests and Other Standardized Tests at the Sixth Grade Level.* Master's thesis, Cardinal Stritch College (Milwaukee, Wis.), 1968.
12. MCRAE, J. *A Comparison of the Wechsler Preschool and Primary Scale of Intelligence With the Slosson Intelligence Test.* Master's thesis, Eastern Washington State College (Cheney, Wash.), 1968.
13. WHITACRE, ROGER L. *Use of the Slosson Intelligence Test With the Stanford-Binet, L-M, as a Screening Device for Slow Learner Placement.* Master's thesis, Bowling Green State University (Bowling Green, Ohio), 1968.
14. HAMMILL, DONALD. "The Slosson Intelligence Test as a Quick Estimate of Mental Ability." *J Sch Psychol* 7(4):33–7 '68–69 ['69]. * (*PA* 44:2794)
15. HUTTON, JERRY B. "Practice Effects on Intelligence and School Readiness Tests for Preschool Children." *Training Sch B* 65(4):130–4 F '69. * (*PA* 44:4229)
16. JONGEWARD, PAUL A. "A Validity Study of the Slosson Intelligence Test for Use With Educable Mentally Retarded

Students." *J Sch Psychol* 7(4):59–63 '68–69 ['69]. * (*PA* 44:2702)
17. JONGEWARD, PAUL ALBERT. *A Validity Study of the Slosson Intelligence Test for Use With Educable Mentally Retarded Students.* Doctor's thesis, University of Oregon (Eugene, Ore.), 1969. (*DAI* 30:3323A)
18. KAUFMAN, HARVEY, AND IVANOFF, JOHN. "The Slosson Intelligence Test as a Screening Instrument With a Rehabilitation Population." *Excep Children* 35(9):745 My '69. * (*PA* 44:18977)
19. KILDUFF, CAROL T. *A Study of the Relation Between the Slosson Reading and Intelligence Tests and Other Standardized Tests at the Fourth Grade Level.* Master's thesis, Cardinal Stritch College (Milwaukee, Wis.), 1969.
20. NASH, MARY SAUNDERS. *The Development of Depth Perception in Intermediate Age Children.* Doctor's thesis, University of Kentucky (Lexington, Ky.), 1969. (*DAI* 30:3894B)
21. NICHOLSON, CHARLES L. "The Use of Four Screening Instruments." *Ann Inter Conf Assn Children Learn Dis* 6:101–7 '69. *
22. O'NEILL, HUGH DANIEL, JR. *Partial Validation of the Slosson Intelligence Test.* Doctor's thesis, University of Oklahoma (Norman, Okla.), 1969. (*DAI* 30:3797A)
23. SHEPHERD, CLYDE W., JR. "Childhood Chronic Illness and Visual Motor Perceptual Development." *Excep Children* 36(1):39–42 S '69. * (*PA* 44:21470)
24. CARLISLE, A. LINDSAY; SHINEDLING, MARTIN M.; AND WEAVER, RICHARD. "Note on the Use of the Slosson Intelligence Test With Mentally Retarded Residents." *Psychol Rep* 26(3):865–6 Je '70. * (*PA* 45:1191)
25. GILLESPIE, PATRICIA HALL. *A Study of the Performance of Dyslexic and Normal Readers on the Slosson Intelligence Test for Children and Adults.* Doctor's thesis, West Virginia University (Morgantown, W.Va.), 1970. (*DAI* 31:2003A)
26. HAMMILL, DONALD D.; CRANDELL, JOHN M., JR.; AND COLARUSSO, RONALD. "The Slosson Intelligence Test Adapted for Visually Limited Children." *Excep Children* 36(7):535–6 Mr '70. *
27. HUTTON, JERRY BOB. *Relationships Between Preschool Screening Test Data and First Grade Academic Performance for Head Start Children.* Doctor's thesis, University of Houston (Houston, Tex.), 1970. (*DAI* 31:395B)
28. MEISSLER, GEORGE R. *A Correlation of the Slosson Intelligence Test and the Wechsler Intelligence Scale When Administered to Atypical Children.* Doctor's thesis, Catholic University of America (Washington, D.C.), 1970. (*DAI* 31:2191A)
29. NICHOLSON, CHARLES L. "Analysis of Functions of the Slosson Intelligence Test." *Percept & Motor Skills* 31(2):627–31 O '70. * (*PA* 45:6336)
30. STUHLER, AGNES M. *An Experimental Study of the Relation Between the Slosson Reading and Intelligence Tests and Other Standardized Tests at the First Grade Level.* Master's thesis, Cardinal Stritch College (Milwaukee, Wis.), 1970.
31. SWANSON, MERLYN S., AND JACOBSON, ANITA. "Evaluation of the S.I.T. for Screening Children With Learning Disabilities." *J Learn Dis* 3(6):318–20 Je '70. * Reply by Richard L. Slosson. 3(9):466 S '70. *

PHILIP HIMELSTEIN, *Professor of Psychology and Head of the Department, The University of Texas at El Paso, El Paso, Texas.*

The *Slosson Intelligence Test* is a brief individual test of intelligence designed to be used by relatively untrained examiners as well as qualified professionals in working with both children and adults. Testing and scoring take from 10–30 minutes depending on how quickly the basal level (10 consecutive passes before the first error occurs) and the termination point (10 consecutive failures) are reached. Scoring is fairly objective and can be accomplished during testing without loss of rapport with the subject since each item is accompanied by the correct response.

The SIT is an adaptation of items from the Stanford-Binet, but with a lower base (2 weeks) and a higher ceiling (27 years) than the Binet. Many of the items in the lower age group are adapted from the *Gesell Developmental Schedules.* In spite of the higher ceiling, the chronological age for purposes of calculating the IQ never exceeds 16 years, thus limiting the test for use with adults. Although the test is essentially adapted from and validated against the Stanford-Binet (Form L-M) the SIT continues to employ the ratio IQ. The test, therefore, has all of the problems of the ratio IQ, although this is apparently not recognized by the test author. Witness the following quotation from the test manual: "For validation purposes ....the Stanford-Binet, Form L-M has been used. Thus, while the SIT IQ's have a ratio basis—they have all of the advantages of the 'deviation IQ.'" Since one of the advantages of the deviation IQ is that the mean and standard deviation are the same for all age groups, Slosson can hardly claim to share in that advantage.

The manual has many serious deficiencies. One of these is the use of testimonials, often representing the worst of the advertising world. The back cover of the manual has tributes from unspecified authorities, such as "director of research in an institute of child development," "associate principal of a girl's senior high school," and "casework supervisor of a home for boys." Letters from school people endorsing the product are enclosed with the test material.

The manual describes the construction of the test itself in about 25 lines. The manual states that "only those items which produced favorable results were included." The criteria for retention or rejection of an item are not specified. Since Slosson has modeled his test after the Stanford-Binet, one might wonder if he has used the percent-pass at specific ages as the basis for including an item on the test. The standardization sample, children and adults from both rural and urban populations in New York State, is not well described. Departures from census data are not described, so that the age, sex, ethnic membership, educational, and socioeconomic characteristics of the standardization group are not indicated.

Validity studies in the manual leave much to be desired. Five studies, with N's ranging from 10 to 24, are devoted only to average differences between IQ's obtained on the SIT and the Stanford-Binet or Wechsler. One table, the only true validity study reported, shows correlations between SIT IQ and Stanford-Binet IQ for ages 4 to 17, and 18 years and older. N's for the age groups range from 23 to 71 and correlations range from .90 (age 4) to .98 (ages 6 and 7). Since items from the SIT at the ages reported are essentially adaptations from the Stanford-Binet, the correlations are spuriously high. A test-retest reliability coefficient ("within a period of two months") of .97 is reported in the manual.

Published validity studies provide a rather confusing picture of the worth of the SIT. Reported correlations between SIT and Wechsler Full Scale IQ's range from .54 to .93; between SIT and Stanford-Binet, from .76 to .90. As might be anticipated, those studies that do not unduly restrict the range of scores obtain correlations of respectable proportions. Kaufman and Ivanoff (*18*), employing a sample of 45 rehabilitation clients, obtained a product-moment correlation of .93 between SIT and WAIS Full Scale IQ, and .96 and .70 between SIT and Verbal and Performance IQ, respectively. Much lower correlations were obtained by Houston and Otto (*10*) and Jongeward (*16*) with the WISC. In the first study, a correlation of .60 was obtained between SIT and Full Scale IQ with a sample of 56 pupils with reading problems, with correlations of .64 and .42 for Verbal and Performance IQ's, respectively. Jongeward compared the SIT with both the WISC and Stanford-Binet with retarded children. Obtained product-moment correlations between SIT and WISC Full, Verbal, and Performance IQ's are as follows: .54, .85, and .20, in that order.

With the Stanford-Binet, Jongeward reported correlations of SIT and Stanford-Binet IQ of .76 and .81 with MA. De Lapa (*1*) reported correlations between SIT and Stanford-Binet for both educable retardates and regular class students. For the retardates, the obtained correlation was .60, raised to .79 when corrected for restriction of range. For the regular classroom students, the correlation was .90. These results would indicate that an examiner could substitute the SIT for the Binet with more confidence than when substituting for the WISC.

The SIT appears to be valuable as a quick screening device. Since inexperienced testers can administer this instrument quickly and accurately (*14*), it has much to recommend it as a preliminary screening procedure. However, the uncritical use of the SIT as a substitute for Wechsler or Binet instruments is ill advised.

Additional research with larger samples of more typical subjects is needed for this test.

JANE V. HUNT, *Assistant Research Psychologist, Institute of Human Development, University of California, Berkeley, California.*

This test is designed as "an individual screening instrument....for the use of school teachers, principals, guidance counselors, social workers, and other responsible persons." Considerable emphasis has been given to a format which is easily administered and scored. The manual is readable and explicit, standards for correct responses are unambiguous and instantly available during testing, and the method of scoring used is a multi-step procedure designed to augment scoring accuracy.

The author reports test-retest reliability of .97 within a two-month interval for a heterogeneous sample of 139 individuals from ages 4 to 50.

Comparability of IQ scores between SIT and Stanford-Binet was a goal of test construction. The author reports product moment correlations yielding correlations ranging from .90 to .98 at each age from 4 to 18 and above, derived from a heterogeneous population of 701 individuals. The sample includes both gifted and retarded children, which would inflate the magnitude of the correlation. Some unpublished studies report correlations of .91 for a group of 30 children with low-normal to superior intelligence, .89 for a group of slow learners with IQ's ranging from 50 to 80, and .91 for 72 boys with IQ range of 69 to 134. The goal of general comparability with Binet IQ seems to be met, despite the fact that the SIT yields a ratio IQ, and the Binet score is a deviation IQ.

TESTING ABOVE 4 YEARS. All questions are presented verbally and require spoken responses. Item content stresses mathematical reasoning, vocabulary, auditory memory, and information. An advantage of the test is that no time limits are imposed. The high ceiling makes the test sufficiently challenging for bright adolescents and adults.

PRESCHOOL TESTING. Between 2 to 4 years, the verbal format places heavy emphasis on language skills. With one exception, items measure or rely on achievements in language comprehension and speech. Test validity is dubious for children with delayed language development and for those whose environments do not include middle class language patterns. For this age group, the author makes no claim for predictive validity, and the only pretesting reported is the finding of a correlation of .93 with the Binet for a group of 16 "bright children" between 2 and 3 years of age.

INFANT TESTING. The infant portion of the test (0.5 to 24 months) is derived from items in the *Gesell Developmental Schedules* and uses the original Gesell age placements for these items. The author disavows the validity of the infant IQ, presumably as a predictive measure, but this test fails to meet essential requirements for evaluating current status of mental development in the infant. There are few items at each month's level and a large proportion of these assess postural control and locomotion. Age placements of items are often not in close agreement with contemporary standardization of the same items in the *Bayley Scales of Infant Development*, sometimes differing by as much as 3 or 4 months. The author reports a correlation of .70 with the *Cattell Infant Intelligence Scale* for 20 children under two years, age not otherwise specified.

SUMMARY. The SIT is designed to provide screening information and when used for this purpose can be a useful tool in selecting individuals for more comprehensive evaluation of mental ability. It is preferable to a group test, as the author indicates. The test is designed to be administered by persons who are not accustomed to interpreting test results. Extreme caution should be taken in relying on SIT test scores in situations where important diagnostic decisions are required, such as special class placements. As is the case with all short tests, the amount of information derived from the test is limited and the time spent with the child is brief. The ratio IQ is likely to be unstable in a given individual across age, and is more unstable for certain ages than for others. The heavy emphasis on language skills makes it a difficult test for children who, for cultural or individual reasons, have language problems. This disadvantage is accentuated at the preschool level. The infant portion of the test is less useful for screening purposes than is a test, such as the *Denver Developmental Screening Test*, which separates mental from motor development and which is standardized on contemporary infants.

[425]

*Stanford-Binet Intelligence Scale, Third Revision.** Ages 2 and over; 1916–64; S-B; a single-form combination of items selected from Forms L and M ('37) of still-in-print Second Revision; individual; Form L-M ('60); manual ('60, 374 pages, see 657a below); directions for administering ('64, 60 pages); record booklet ('60, 15 pages); record form ('60, 5 pages); $45 per set of test materials including manual (£9 without manual); $4.65 (£1) per 35 (25) record booklets; $2.55 (60p) per 35 (25) abbreviated record forms; $2.40 per directions for administering; $5.80 (£1.05) per manual; postage extra; (30–90) minutes; revised IQ tables by Samuel R. Pinneau; Lewis M. Terman and Maud A. Merrill; Houghton Mifflin Co. * (British edition: George G. Harrap & Co. Ltd.)

REFERENCES

1–134. See 2:1420.
135–351. See 3:292.
352–493. See 4:358.
494–620. See 5:413.
621–728. See 6:536.
729. EBERT, ELIZABETH, AND SIMMONS, KATHERINE. *The Brush Foundation Study of Child Growth and Development: I, Psychometric Tests.* Monographs of the Society for Research in Child Development, Vol. 8, No. 2, Serial No. 35. Washington, D.C.: the Society, National Research Council, 1943. Pp. xiv, 113. * (PA 18:3322)
730. COLLINS, A. LOUISE, AND LENNOX, WILLIAM G. "The Intelligence of 300 Private Epileptic Patients." *Res Publ Assn Res Nerv & Mental Dis* 26:586–603 '47. *
731. KOLSTOE, OLIVER PAUL. *A Comparison of Mental Abilities of Bright and Dull Children Having the Same Mental Ages.* Doctor's thesis, State University of Iowa (Iowa City, Iowa), 1952. (DA 12:707)
732. ARMSTRONG, HUBERT COSLET. *The Relationship of the Auditory and Visual Vocabularies of Children.* Doctor's thesis, Stanford University (Stanford, Calif.), 1953. (DA 13:716)
733. GOLDENBERG, SAMUEL. *Some Aspects of Diagnosis of Cerebral Damage in Children.* Doctor's thesis, University of Washington (Seattle, Wash.), 1953. (DA 13:1259)
734. LEBERFELD, DORIS TREPEL. *An Investigation to Determine the Effect of Language and Speech Training on the Measurable Mental Abilities of Mentally Retarded Children.* Doctor's thesis, New York University (New York, N.Y.), 1953. (DA 14:735)
735. WELSH, GEORGE BYRON. *An Investigation of Some Predictive Factors in Auding Ability.* Doctor's thesis, University of Pittsburgh (Pittsburgh, Pa.), 1954. (DA 14:2407)
736. APGAR, VIRGINIA; GIRDANY, B. R.; MCINTOSH, R.; AND TAYLOR, H. C., JR. "Neonatal Anoxia: 1, A Study of the Relation of Oxygenation at Birth to Intellectual Development." *Pediatrics* 15:6653–62 Je '55. *
737. WEINLANDER, MAX MARTIN. *Differential Rates of Mental Development in Children.* Doctor's thesis, University of Michigan (Ann Arbor, Mich.), 1955. (DA 15:1558)
738. LEHMANN, IRVIN JACK. *Rural-Urban Differences in Intelligence.* Doctor's thesis, University of Wisconsin (Madison, Wis.), 1957. (DA 17:1937)
739. TOMS, DOLORES CATHERINE. *Progress in Reading With Reference to the Quantitative Measurements of the Binet: A Study of Longitudinal Records.* Doctor's thesis, University of Michigan (Ann Arbor, Mich.), 1957. (DA 18:1725)
740. TRACHTMAN, GILBERT M. *Personality and Developmental Characteristics of Children Rated Most and Least Ready for First Grade by Their Kindergarten Teachers.* Doctor's thesis, New York University (New York, N.Y.), 1958. (DA 19:3028)
741. ALPER, ARTHUR E., AND HORNE, BETTY M. "Changes in IQ of a Group of Institutionalized Mental Defectives Over a Period of Two Decades." *Am J Mental Def* 64:472–5 N '59. * (PA 34:7994)
742. HOFFMAN, CARL BENTLEY. *The Relationship of Immediate Recall, Delayed Recall, and Incidental Memory to Problem-Solving Ability.* Doctor's thesis, University of Pennsylvania (Philadelphia, Pa.), 1960. (DA 21:813)
743. LEVINSON, BORIS M. "A Comparative Study of the Verbal and Performance Ability of Monolingual and Bilingual Native Born Jewish Preschool Children of Traditional Parentage." *J Genetic Psychol* 97:93–112 S '60. * (PA 35:6190)
744. BERNSTEIN, LEWIS. "Psychological Testing: 1, Intelligence Tests." *J Child Asth Res Inst & Hosp* 1:205–17 Je '61. *
745. HAAG, CARL HERBERT. *An Exploratory Study to Determine the Significance of Early Longitudinal Records of Ability and Achievement as Predictors of Academic Achievement in College.* Doctor's thesis, University of Michigan (Ann Arbor, Mich.), 1961. (DA 21:3702)
746. MORIARTY, ALICE. "Coping Patterns of Preschool Children in Response to Intelligence Test Demands." *Genetic Psychol Monogr* 64:3–127 Ag '61. * (PA 36:2FF03M)
747. NAKAMURA, HIROMU. "Nature of Institutionalized Adult Mongoloid Intelligence." *Am J Mental Def* 66:456–8 N '61. * (PA 36:4JI56N)
748. RICHARDS, BERNA FLANDERS. *A Predictive Longitudinal*

748. *Study of Intellective and Non-Intellective Factors Affecting School Achievement of Gifted Children.* Doctor's thesis, Ohio State University (Columbus, Ohio), 1961. (DA 22:3526)
749. SANDLER, ANNE-MARIE, AND SANDLER, JOSEPH. "Piaget's Approach to Problems of Intellectual Development." *Cereb Palsy B* 3(1):25-8 '61. * (PA 36:1FE25S)
750. SHECHTMAN, AUBREY M. *The Relationship of Variability in Children's Verbal and Non-Language Test Performance to Current and Later Behavioral Functions.* Doctor's thesis, University of Minnesota (Minneapolis, Minn.), 1961. (DA 22:2065)
751. TOUSSAINT, ISABELLA HASTIE. *Interrelationships of Reading, Listening, Arithmetic, and Intelligence and Their Implications.* Doctor's thesis, University of Pittsburgh (Pittsburgh, Pa.), 1961. (DA 22:819)
752. WITKIN, H. A.; DYKE, R. G.; FATERSON, H. F.; GOODENOUGH, D. R.; AND KARP, S. A. *Psychological Differentiation: Studies of Development.* New York: John Wiley & Sons, Inc., 1962. Pp. xii, 418. * (PA 37:819)
753. ABBOTT, ROBERT FRANKLIN. *The Prediction of First Grade Reading and Numbers Achievement by Means of Psychological Tests.* Doctor's thesis, University of Tennessee (Knoxville, Tenn.), 1963. (DA 25:1020)
754. DENUM, DONALD C. "The Use of the Stanford-Binet Intelligence Scale, Form L-M, 1960 Revision as a Criterion Instrument for Norming All Levels of the 1963 Revision of the California Test of Mental Maturity Series." *Yearb Nat Council Meas Ed* 20:50-3 '63. * (PA 38:8409)
755. GOULET, L. R., AND BARCLAY, A. "The Vineland Social Maturity Scale: Utility in Assessment of Binet MA." *Am J Mental Def* 67:916-21 My '63. * (PA 38:1273)
756. LEVINSON, ELIZABETH JOHNSON. *The Effects of Training in the Verbalization of Photoconcepts on Intelligence.* Doctor's thesis, University of Maine (Orono, Me.), 1963. (DA 26:1186)
757. REDBIRD, HELEN MARIE. *A Study of the Intelligence of Children of Domestic Agricultural Migrant Workers in Colorado.* Doctor's thesis, University of Colorado (Boulder, Colo.), 1963. (DA 24:4486)
758. ROTMAN, CHARLES B. *A Study of the Effect of Practice Upon Motor Skills of the Mentally Retarded.* Doctor's thesis, Boston University (Boston, Mass.), 1963. (DA 25:1755)
759. SONNEMAN, LAWRENCE J. *A Study of the Relationships Between Four Tests of Intelligence and One Test of Scholastic Achievement.* Doctor's thesis, State University of South Dakota (Vermillion, S.D.), 1963. (DA 24:4555)
760. SPIETH, PHILLIP EARL. *Intelligence as It Relates to Three Creativity Categories: Science, Art, and Literature.* Doctor's thesis, University of Michigan (Ann Arbor, Mich.), 1963. (DA 25:1759)
761. THOMPSON, MARY MARTHA. "Psychological Characteristics Relevant to the Education of the Pre-School Mongoloid Child." *Mental Retard* 1:148-51+ Je '63. * (PA 38:9243)
762. BIRKEMEYER, FLORENCE. "The Relationship Between the Coloured Progressive Matrices and Individual Intelligence Tests." *Psychol Sch* 1:309-12 Jl '64. *
763. CAPOBIANCO, R. J., AND KNOX, STANLEY. "IQ Estimates and the Index of Marital Integration." *Am J Mental Def* 68:718-21 My '64. * (PA 39:2322)
764. EARHART, RICHARD H., AND WARREN, SUE ALLEN. "Long Term Constancy of Binet IQ in Retardation." *Training Sch B* 61:109-15 N '64. * (PA 39:7753)
765. HAAN, NORMA. "The Relationship of Ego Functioning and Intelligence to Social Status and Social Mobility." *J Abn & Social Psychol* 69:594-605 D '64. * (PA 39:7560)
766. HUTTON, JERRY B. "A Comparison of Digit Repetition Scores on the WISC and Revised Binet, Form L-M." *J Clin Psychol* 20:364-6 Jl '64. * (PA 39:10124)
767. JENSON, G., III. *A Statistical Analysis of the Reliability and Validity of the Pictorial Test of Intelligence and the Stanford-Binet Intelligence Scale.* Master's thesis, University of Missouri (Columbia, Mo.), 1964.
768. LEVINE, DAVID, AND DYSINGER, DON W. "Patterns of Intellectual Performance and the Outcome of Institutionalization in the Mentally Retarded." *Am J Mental Def* 68:784-8 My '64. * (PA 39:2523)
769. LINDHOLM, BYRON W. "Changes in Conventional and Deviation IQ's." *J Ed Psychol* 55:110-3 Ap '64. * (PA 39:1749)
770. NUNNALLY, JUM C. *Educational Measurement and Evaluation,* pp. 251-7. New York: McGraw-Hill Book Co., Inc., 1964. Pp. xv, 440. *
771. PALMER, ALBERT B., JR. *Stanford-Binet Responses as a Function of Motivational Cue Properties of Items and of Children's Motivation.* Doctor's thesis, Southern Illinois University (Carbondale, Ill.), 1964. (DA 25:2615)
772. PHILLIPS, C. J., AND WHITE, R. R. "The Prediction of Educational Progress Among Cerebral Palsied Children." *Develop Med & Child Neurol* 6:167-74 Ap '64. * (PA 39:5648)
773. ROBECK, MILDRED C., AND WILSON, JOHN A. R. "Comparison of Binet and the Kindergarten Evaluation of Learning Potential." *Ed & Psychol Meas* 24:393-7 su '64. * (PA 39:5088)
774. SILVERSTEIN, A. B. "A Further Evaluation of Two Short Forms of the Stanford-Binet." *Calif Mental Health Res Dig* 2:15-6 au '64. *
775. TAVRIS, EDWARD. "An Attempt to Distinguish Between 'Successful' and 'Unsuccessful' Separation Groups in a Hospital for Mentally Retarded Patients." *Training Sch B* 60:184-91 F '64. * (PA 39:5488)
776. TIBER, NORMAN, AND KENNEDY, WALLACE A. "The Effects of Incentives on the Intelligence Test Performance of Different Social Groups." Abstract. *J Consult Psychol* 28:187 Ap '64. *
777. BEARD, R. M. "The Structure of Perception: A Factorial Study." *Brit J Ed Psychol* 35:210-22 Je '65. *
778. BURNETT, ALASTAIR. "Comparison of the PPVT, Wechsler-Bellevue, and Stanford-Binet on Educable Retardates." *Am J Mental Def* 69:712-5 Mr '65. * (PA 39:12715)
779. CASTELL, J. H. F., AND MITTLER, P. J. "Intelligence of Patients in Subnormality Hospitals: A Survey of Admissions in 1961." *Brit J Psychiatry* 111:219-25 Mr '65. * (PA 39:10453)
780. CHURCH, JANE CAROLYN. *A Short-Term Longitudinal Study of Factors Related to IQ Change in White Southern Rural Adolescents.* Doctor's thesis, University of North Carolina (Chapel Hill, N.C.), 1965. (DA 27:299B)
781. CIEUTAT, VICTOR J. "Examiner Differences With the Stanford-Binet IQ." *Percept & Motor Skills* 20:317-8 F '65. * (PA 39:10187)
782. CORDINER, MARIAN ESPACH. *A Comparative Study of the 1960 Stanford-Binet and the Wechsler Intelligence Scale for Children and Other Selected Variables.* Master's thesis, University of Utah (Salt Lake City, Utah), 1965.
783. DIBBLE, MARY F. *An Analysis of the Performance of Thirty-Three Retarded Readers on the Subtests of the Revised Stanford-Binet Intelligence Test, Form LM.* Master's thesis, University of Kansas (Lawrence, Kan.), 1965.
784. ESTES, BETSY WORTH. "Relationships Between the Otis, 1960 Stanford-Binet and WISC." *J Clin Psychol* 21:296-7 Jl '65. * (PA 39:15230)
785. GOLDSCHMID, MARCEL L., AND DOMINO, GEORGE. "Some Para-Diagnostic Implications of the IQ Among Mentally Retarded Patients." *Training Sch B* 61:178-83 F '65. * (PA 39:10586)
786. JENKINS, C. DAVID. "The Weight Discrimination Test as an Indicator of Brain Pathology." *J Clin Psychol* 21:76-7 Ja '65. * (PA 39:12699)
787. KABACK, GOLDIE RUTH. "A Comparison of WAIS, Binet, and WISC Test Results of Mentally Retarded Young Adults Born in New York City and Puerto Rico." *Training Sch B* 62:108-12 N '65. * (PA 40:2138)
788. KEBBON, LARS. *The Structure of Abilities at Lower Levels of Intelligence: A Factor-Analytical Study.* Stockholm, Sweden: Skandinaviska Testförlaget AB, 1965. Pp. 112. *
789. KROSKE, WILLIAM H.; FRETWELL, LORETTA N.; AND CUPP, MARION E. "Comparison of the Kahn Intelligence Tests: Experimental Form, the Stanford-Binet and the WAIS for Familial Retardates." *Percept & Motor Skills* 21:428 O '65. * (PA 40:3310)
790. LINDHOLM, BYRON W. "A Longitudinal Study of Deviation IQs and Grades in School." *J Ed Meas* 2:123-8 Je '65. * (PA 39:14710)
791. MEEKER, MARY. "A Procedure for Relating Stanford Binet Behavior Samplings to Guilford's Structure of the Intellect." *J Sch Psychol* 3:26-36 sp '65. * (PA 39:15303)
792. MEIER, JOHN HENRY. *An Exploratory Factor Analysis of Psychodiagnostic and Case Study Information From Children in Special Education Classes for the Educable Mentally Handicapped.* Doctor's thesis, University of Denver (Denver, Colo.), 1965. (DA 26:3153)
793. MITCHELL, ROBERT JEFFERY, SR. *An Experimental Study to Determine the Effects of Inhaling Pure Oxygen on I.Q.* Doctor's thesis, University of Oklahoma (Norman, Okla.), 1965. (DA 26:1188)
794. MUELLER, MAX W. *A Comparison of the Empirical Validity of Six Tests of Ability With Young Educable Retardates.* Institute of Mental Retardation and Intellectual Development, IMRID Behavioral Science Monograph No. 1. Nashville, Tenn.: Peabody College Bookstore, 1965. Pp. vii, 130. *
795. MUELLER, MAX WILLIAM. *A Comparison of the Empirical Validity of Six Tests of Ability With Educable Mental Retardates.* Doctor's thesis, George Peabody College for Teachers (Nashville, Tenn.), 1965. (DA 26:6853)
796. NAKAMURA, HIROMU. "An Inquiry Into Systematic Differences in the Abilities of Institutionalized Adult Mongoloids." *Am J Mental Def* 69:661-6 Mr '65. * (PA 39:12743)
797. SATTLER, JEROME M. "Analysis of Functions of the 1960 Stanford-Binet Intelligence Scale, Form L-M." *J Clin Psychol* 21:173-9 Ap '65. * (PA 39:12308)
798. SCHULMAN, JEROME L.; KASPAR, JOSEPH C.; AND THRONE, FRANCES M. *Brain Damage and Behavior: A Clinical-Experimental Study.* Springfield, Ill.: Charles C Thomas, Publisher, 1965. Pp. ix, 164. *
799. SHANE, JAMES F. *Effectiveness of the Peabody Picture Vocabulary Test in Comparison to Wechsler Intelligence Scale for Children and Stanford-Binet Test Scores in Identification of Mentally Retarded and Gifted School Children.* Master's thesis, California State College (Long Beach, Calif.), 1965.
800. SILVERSTEIN, A. B. "Comparison of Two Item-Classifi-

cation Schemes for the Stanford-Binet." *Psychol Rep* 17:964 D '65. * (*PA* 40:4219)

801. SMART, RUSSELL C. "The Changing Composition of 'Intelligence': A Replication of a Factor Analysis." *J Genetic Psychol* 107:111–6 S '65. * (*PA* 39:15308)

802. STERNLICHT, MANNY. "A Downward Application of the 1960 Revised Stanford-Binet With Retardates." *J Clin Psychol* 21:79 Ja '65. * (*PA* 39:12326)

803. WEISE, PHILLIP; MEYERS, C. E.; AND TUEL, JOHN K. "PMA Factors, Sex, and Teacher Nomination in Screening Kindergarten Gifted." *Ed & Psychol Meas* 25:597–603 su '65. * (*PA* 39:14718)

804. BARCLAY, A., AND CAROLAN, PATRICIA. "A Comparative Study of the Wechsler Intelligence Scale for Children and the Stanford-Binet Intelligence Scale, Form L-M." Abstract. *J Consult Psychol* 30:563 D '66. *

805. BLACK, D. B.; KATO, J. G.; AND WALKER, G. W. R. "A Study of Improvement in Mentally Retarded Children Accruing From Siccacell Therapy." *Am J Mental Def* 70:499–508 Ja '66. * (*PA* 40:5869)

806. BURSON, GERALD EDWARD. *A Comparative Study of the Effects of Programed Presentations of Selected Portions of the Stanford-Binet Intelligence Test on Student Examiners.* Doctor's thesis, Oklahoma State University (Stillwater, Okla.), 1966. (*DA* 27:4124A)

807. CHURCHILL, WILLIAM D., AND SMITH, STUART E. "The Relationship of the 1960 Revised Stanford-Binet Intelligence Scale to Intelligence and Achievement Test Scores Over a Three-Year Period." *Ed & Psychol Meas* 26:1015–20 w '66. * (*PA* 41:4567)

808. COLMAN, P. G. "A Comparative Study of the Test Performances of Brain-Injured Children." *S Afric Med J* 40:945–50 O 22 '66. *

809. HIMELSTEIN, PHILIP. "Research With the Stanford-Binet, Form L-M: The First Five Years." *Psychol B* 65:156–64 Mr '66. * (*PA* 40:4764)

810. HIRSCHENFANG, SAMUEL; JARAMILLO, SELENE; AND BENTON, JOSEPH G. "Comparison of Scores on the Revised Stanford-Binet (L), Columbia Mental Maturity Scale (CMMS) and Goodenough Draw A Man Test of Children With Neurological Disorders." *Psychol Rep* 19:15–6 Ag '66. * (*PA* 40:12564)

811. KANDEL, ARTHUR. *Discrepancies Between the Stanford-Binet and Three Group Tests of Intelligence in the Identification of Low I.Q. Children.* Doctor's thesis, Catholic University of America (Washington, D.C.), 1966. (*DA* 27:1659A)

812. KEACH, CHARLES CAMPBELL. *Discrepancies Between the Stanford-Binet and Three Group Tests of Intelligence in the Identification of High I.Q. Children.* Doctor's thesis, Catholic University of America (Washington, D.C.), 1966. (*DA* 27:1660A)

813. KICKLIGHTER, RICHARD M. "Correlation of Peabody Picture Vocabulary Test Scores and Stanford-Binet Intelligence Scale, Form L-M Scores in an Educable Mentally Retarded Population," Abstract. *J Sch Psychol* 5:75–6 au '66. *

814. KILBURN, KENT L.; SANDERSON, ROBERT E.; AND MELTON, KYLE. "Relation of the Raven Coloured Progressive Matrices to Two Measures of Verbal Ability in a Sample of Mildly Retarded Hospital Patients." *Psychol Rep* 19:731–4 D '66. * (*PA* 41:4915)

815. KIMBRELL, DON L. "Comparison of PPVT, FRPVT, RS-B, and Academic Achievement Scores Among Institutionalized Educable Mental Retardates." *Percept & Motor Skills* 23:1178 D '66. * (*PA* 41:6185)

816. LUSZKI, WALTER A. "Intellectual Functioning of Spastic Cerebral Palsied." *Cereb Palsy J* 27:7–9 Mr-Ap '66. * (*PA* 40:8010)

817. MCKERRACHER, D. W., AND SCOTT, J. "I.Q. Scores and the Problem of Classification: A Comparison of the W.A.I.S. and S-B, Form L-M in a Group of Subnormal and Psychopathic Patients." *Brit J Psychiatry* 112:537–41 Je '66. * (*PA* 40:10101)

818. MATHENY, ADAM P., JR. "Improving Diagnostic Forecasts Made on a Developmental Scale." *Am J Mental Def* 71:371–5 N '66. * (*PA* 41:1706)

819. ROBERTS, DENNIS M. "Serial Position Effects in Two Stanford-Binet Subtests." *Psychol* 3:2–4 Ag '66. * (*PA* 40:12319)

820. ROSENBERG, LEON A., AND STROUD, MICHAEL. "Limitations of Brief Intelligence Testing with Young Children." *Psychol Rep* 19:721–2 D '66. * (*PA* 41:4999)

821. SATTLER, JEROME M. "Comments on Cieutat's 'Examiner Differences With the Stanford-Binet IQ.'" *Percept & Motor Skills* 22:612–4 Ap '66. * (*PA* 40:8270)

822. SATTLER, JEROME M. "Statistical Reanalysis of Canady's 'The Effect of "Rapport" on the I.Q.: A New Approach to the Problem of Racial Psychology.'" *Psychol Rep* 19:1203–6 D '66. * (*PA* 41:4444)

823. SIDERITS, MARY ANNE TERESA. *Indices of Change in the Cattell-Binet Ratings of Intellectually Sub-Average Children.* Doctor's thesis, University of Michigan (Ann Arbor, Mich.), 1966. (*DA* 27:2519B)

824. SILVERSTEIN, A. B. "A Further Evaluation of Two Short Forms of the Stanford-Binet." *Am J Mental Def* 70:928–9 My '66. * (*PA* 40:9174)

825. SILVERSTEIN, A. B. "Mental Growth in Mongolism." *Child Develop* 37:725–9 S '66. * (*PA* 40:12586)

826. SITKEI, E. GEORGE, AND MICHAEL, WILLIAM B. "Predictive Relationships Between Items on the Revised Stanford-Binet Intelligence Scale (SBIS), Form L-M, and Total Scores on Raven's Progressive Matrices (PM), Between Items on the PM and Total Scores on the SBIS, and Between Selected Items on the Two Scales." *Ed & Psychol Meas* 26:501–6 su '66. * (*PA* 40:12784)

827. SMITH, C. SIMPSON. "Changes in I.Q.'s of Educationally Subnormal Pupils: A Survey of West Riding Children." *Pub Health* 80:201–8 My '66. *

828. SMITH, HERBERT W.; MAY, W. THEODORE; AND LEBOVITZ, LEON. "Testing Experience and Stanford-Binet Scores." *J Ed Meas* 3:229–33 f '66. * (*PA* 41:11921)

829. STORMER, GEORGE EDWARD. *Dimensions of the Intellect Unmeasured by the Stanford-Binet.* Doctor's thesis, University of Illinois (Urbana, Ill.), 1966. (*DA* 27:2078A)

830. STOTT, LELAND H., AND BALL, RACHEL STUTSMAN. *Infant and Preschool Mental Tests: Review and Evaluation.* Monographs of the Society for Research in Child Development, Vol. 30, No. 3, Serial No. 101. Chicago, Ill.: University of Chicago Press, 1966. Pp. iv, 151. * (*PA* 40:7220)

831. VANE, JULIA R.; WEITZMAN, JONATHAN; AND APPLEBAUM, ADRIAN P. "Performance of Negro and White Children and Problem and Nonproblem Children on the Stanford Binet Scale." *J Clin Psychol* 22:431–5 O '66. * (*PA* 41:2875)

832. WALL, W. D., AND PRINGLE, M. L. KELLMER. "The Clinical Significance of Standard Score Discrepancies Between Intelligence and Social Competence." *Hum Develop* 9(3): 121–51 '66. *

833. WILLIAMS, JANETTE R., AND WILCOCK, JOAN C. "An Alternative to the Binet Mental Age Score as a Criterion in Discrimination Learning." *J Mental Def Res* 10:27–32 Mr '66. * (*PA* 40:9420)

834. BUDOFF, MILTON. "Learning Potential Among Institutionalized Young Adult Retardates." *Am J Mental Def* 72:404–11 N '67. * (*PA* 42:7631)

835. CIEUTAT, VICTOR J., AND FLICK, GRAD L. "Examiner Differences Among Stanford-Binet Items." *Psychol Rep* 21; 613–22 O '67. * (*PA* 42:4794)

836. DELAPA, GIACINTO. *Correlates of Slosson Intelligence Test, Stanford Binet, Form L-M, and Achievement Indices.* Doctor's thesis, West Virginia University (Morgantown, W.Va.), 1967. (*DA* 28:3498A)

837. DOBSON, JAMES CLAYTON, JR. *Intellectual and Linguistic Development in Treated and Untreated Phenylketonuric Children.* Doctor's thesis, University of Southern California (Los Angeles, Calif.), 1967. (*DA* 28:1294A)

838. DUNN, JAMES A. "Validity Coefficients for the New Harris-Goodenough Draw-A-Man Test." *Percept & Motor Skills* 24:299–301 F '67. * (*PA* 41:8149)

839. EISENMAN, RUSSELL, AND ROBINSON, NANCY. "Complexity-Simplicity, Creativity, Intelligence and Other Correlates." *J Psychol* 67:331–4 N '67. * (*PA* 42:2567)

840. HAMMILL, DONALD D., AND IRWIN, ORVIS C. "Factors Affecting Equivalency of PPVT and RSB When Used With Mentally Subnormal Children." *Am J Mental Def* 71:793–6 Mr '67. * (*PA* 41:8881)

841. HOWARD, JOYCE L., AND PLANT, WALTER T. "Psychometric Evaluation of an Operation Headstart Program." *J Genetic Psychol* 111:281–8 D '67. * (*PA* 42:6013)

842. KLAPPER, ZELDA S., AND BIRCH, HERBERT G. "A Fourteen Year Follow-Up Study of Cerebral Palsy: Intellectual Changes and Stability." *Am J Orthopsychiatry* 37:540–7 Ap '67. *

843. KOH, TONG-HE, AND MADOW, ARNOLD A. "Relationship Between PPVT and Stanford-Binet Performances in Institutionalized Retardates." *Am J Mental Def* 72:108–13 Jl '67. * (*PA* 41:15728)

844. KOPPITZ, ELIZABETH MUNSTERBERG. "Expected and Exceptional Items on Human Figure Drawings and IQ Scores of Children Age 5 to 12." *J Clin Psychol* 23:81–3 Ja '67. * (*PA* 41:5985)

845. KUNDU, RAMANATH. "A Comparison of Stanford-Binet and Wechsler-Bellevue Scales." *Indian Psychol R* 3:114–8 Ja '67. * (*PA* 41:8901)

846. MARSHALL, ANNE. *The Abilities and Attainments of Children Leaving Junior Training Centres.* London: National Association for Mental Health, 1967. Pp. i, 62. *

847. MASON, ANNE W. "Specific (Developmental) Dyslexia." *Develop Med & Child Neurol* 9:183–90 Ap '67. * (*PA* 41:14066)

848. MILLER, BILLY. *A Comparison of the Columbia Mental Maturity Scale, the Leiter International Performance Scale, and the Wright Short Form of the Stanford-Binet, Form L-M, With the Full Scale Stanford Binet, Form L-M, on a Group of Trainable Retardates.* Master's thesis, Central Missouri State College (Warrensburg, Mo.), 1967.

849. MISCEVICH, MADELEINE BECK. *Correlation of a Pre-School Test With the Stanford-Binet Intelligence Scale.* Master's thesis, Millersville State College (Millersville, Pa), 1967.

850. MOORE, TERENCE. "Language and Intelligence: A Longitudinal Study of the First Eight Years: Part 1, Patterns of Development in Boys and Girls." *Hum Develop* 10(2):88–106 '67. * (*PA* 41:7080)

Stanford-Binet Intelligence Scale

851. MUZEKARI, LOUIS H. "Relationships Between the Goodenough DAM and Stanford-Binet in Negro and White Public School Children." *J Clin Psychol* 23:86–7 Ja '67. * (*PA* 41:6253)

852. OLIVIER, K., AND BARCLAY, A. "Stanford-Binet and Goodenough-Harris Test Performances of Head Start Children." *Psychol Rep* 20:1175–9 Je '67. * (*PA* 41:15275)

853. PICKLES, D. G. "Intelligence Tests and the Ascertainment of the Educationally Subnormal: A Comparative Study of the Stanford-Binet and Wechsler Intelligence Scales." *Pub Health* 81:133–44 Mr '67. *

854. RASOF, BEATRICE; LINDE, LEONARD M.; AND DUNN, OLIVE JEAN. "Intellectual Development in Children With Congenital Heart Disease." *Child Develop* 38:1043–53 D '67. * (*PA* 42:7687)

855. RUSSELL, CAROL A. *A Comparison of Performance on the Stanford-Binet Intelligence Scale, Form L-M, and the Wechsler Intelligence Scale for Children With Mentally Retarded Subjects.* Master's thesis, University of Utah (Salt Lake City, Utah), 1967.

856. SATTLER, JEROME M., AND THEYE, FRED. "Procedural, Situational, and Interpersonal Variables in Individual Intelligence Testing." *Psychol B* 68:347–60 N '67. * (*PA* 42:2564)

857. SEELYE, BARBARA JANE. *An Investigation of Language Development in Non-Institutionalized Mentally Retarded Children.* Doctor's thesis, University of Denver (Denver, Colo.), 1967. (*DA* 28:821A)

858. SHEVERBUSH, ROBERT L., JR. *An Analysis of Subtest Performance by Gifted Students on the Stanford-Binet Intelligence Scale (1960 Form L-M).* Doctor's thesis, Colorado State College (Greeley, Colo.), 1967. (*DA* 28:2568A)

859. SIGEL, IRVING; JARMAN, P.; AND HANESIAN, HELEN. "Styles of Categorization and Their Intellectual and Personality Correlation in Young Children." *Hum Develop* 10(1):1–7 '67. * (*PA* 41:7146)

860. SILBERBERG, NORMAN; IVERSEN, IVER; AND SILBERBERG, MARGARET. "Predicting End of First Grade Developmental Reading Test Scores From Gates Reading Readiness Test Scores Administered in Kindergarten." Abstract. *Proc 75th Ann Conv Am Psychol Assn* 2:291–2 '67. * (*PA* 41:14224)

861. SILVERSTEIN, A. B.; MOHAN, PHILIP J.; AND FRANKEN, ROBERT E. "A Problem-Solving Approach to the Assessment of Intellectual Functioning." *Training Sch B* 63:159–62 F '67. * (*PA* 41:9299)

862. SMITH, HERBERT W., AND MAY, W. THEODORE. "Individual Differences Among Inexperienced Psychological Examiners." *Psychol Rep* 20:759–62 Je '67. * (*PA* 41:13601)

863. WEAVER, ANN SULLIVAN. *The Prediction of First Grade Reading Achievement in Culturally Disadvantaged Children.* Doctor's thesis, George Peabody College for Teachers (Nashville, Tenn.), 1967. (*DA* 28:3789A)

864. WELLS, DONALD G., AND PEDRINI, DUILIO T. "Relationship Between the Stanford-Binet L-M and the Goodenough D-A-M." *Psychol Sch* 4:371–5 O '67. * (*PA* 42:2592)

865. WELLS, DONALD G., AND PEDRINI, DUILIO T. "Relationships Between the S-B L-M, G-H, and PPVT With Institutionalized Retardates." *Am J Mental Def* 72:412–5 N '67. * (*PA* 42:7680)

866. WELLS, DONALD G., AND PEDRINI, DUILIO T. "Where to Begin Testing on the 1960 Stanford-Binet L-M." *J Clin Psychol* 23:182–4 Ap '67. * (*PA* 41:8888)

867. WILLIAMS, JEROLD R. *A Correctional Study of Adult Comprehension Performance on the Stanford-Binet (1937) Form L Test and the Wechsler Adult Intelligence Scale.* Master's thesis, Illinois State University (Normal, Ill.), 1967.

868. YATES, LOUISE GRAHAM. *Comparative Intelligence of Negro and White Children From a Rural-Southern Culture.* Doctor's thesis, University of North Carolina (Chapel Hill, N.C.), 1967. (*DA* 28:4768B)

869. ANASTASI, ANNE. *Psychological Testing, Third Edition,* pp. 188–206. New York: Macmillan Co., 1968. Pp. xiii, 665. *

870. ANDERSON, CATHERINE J.; PORRATA, ELENA; LORE, JAMES; ALEXANDER, SHIRLEY; AND MERCER, MARGARET. "A Multidisciplinary Study of Psychogeriatric Patients." *Geriatrics* 23:105–13 F '68. * (*PA* 42:14051)

871. ARMSTRONG, JUDITH GLANTZ. *Intellectual Competence and Coping Behavior in Preschool Children.* Doctor's thesis, University of California (Berkeley, Calif.), 1968. (*DA* 29:4837B)

872. BACH, LLOYD CARL. *A Comparison of Selected Psychological Tests Used With Trainable Mentally Retarded Children.* Doctor's thesis, University of South Dakota (Vermillion, S.D.), 1968. (*DA* 29:2990A)

873. BATEMAN, BARBARA. "Clinically' Obtained IQs Versus 'Production Line' IQs in a Mentally Retarded Sample." *J Sch Psychol* 7(1):29–33 '68–69. * (*PA* 43:10217)

874. BAUGHMAN, E. EARL, AND DAHLSTROM, W. GRANT. *Negro and White Children: A Psychological Study in the Rural South,* pp. 38–48, passim. New York: Academic Press Inc., 1968. Pp. xx, 572. *

875. BENGER, KATHLYN. "The Relationships of Perception, Personality, Intelligence, and Grade One Reading Achievement." *Proc Ann Conv Int Read Assn* 12(4):112–23 '68. *

876. BONFIELD, JOHN RONALD. *Predictors of Achievement for Educable Mentally Retarded Children.* Doctor's thesis, Pennsylvania State University (University Park, Pa.), 1968. (*DAI* 30:1009A)

877. BOROSAGE, VERA. *A Study of the Effect of Nursery School Experience on Intellectual Performance at Two Socio-Economic Levels.* Doctor's thesis, Michigan State University (East Lansing, Mich.), 1968. (*DA* 29:2993A)

878. BRITTAIN, MICHAEL. "A Comparative Study of the Use of the Wechsler Intelligence Scale for Children and the Stanford-Binet Intelligence Scale (Form L-M) With Eight-Year-Old Children." *Brit J Ed Psychol* 38:103–4 F '68. *

879. DILORENZO, LOUIS T. "Effects of Year-Long Prekindergarten Programs on Intelligence and Language of Educationally Disadvantaged Children." *J Exp Ed* 36:36–42 sp '68. *

880. DILORENZO, LOUIS T., AND BRADY, JAMES J. "Use of the Peabody Picture Vocabulary Test With Preschool Children." *Psychol Rep* 22:247–51 F '68. * (*PA* 42:10612)

881. DILORENZO, LOUIS T., AND NAGLER, ERIC. "Examiner Differences on the Stanford-Binet." *Psychol Rep* 22:443–7 Ap '68. * (*PA* 42:11402)

882. EISENMAN, RUSSELL; PLATT, JEROME J.; AND DARBES, ALEX. "Creativity, Intelligence and Achievement." *Psychol Rep* 22:749–54 Je '68. * (*PA* 42:13739)

883. ERICKSON, MARILYN T. "The Predictive Validity of the Cattell Infant Intelligence Scale for Young Mentally Retarded Children." *Am J Mental Def* 72:728–33 Mr '68. * (*PA* 42:11047)

884. GANNON, D. R. "Relationships Between 8-Mo. Performance on the Bayley Scales of Infant Development and 48-Mo. Intelligence and Concept Formation Scores." *Psychol Rep* 23:1199–205 D '68. * (*PA* 43:8104)

885. HIMELSTEIN, PHILIP. "Use of the Stanford-Binet, Form LM, With Retardates: A Review of Recent Research." *Am J Mental Def* 72:691–9 Mr '68. * (*PA* 42:11054)

886. LAMP, ROBERT E., AND BARCLAY, A. "Comparisons of Scores on Quick Test and Stanford-Binet, Form L-M, for Retarded Children." *Psychol Rep* 23:401–2 O '68. * (*PA* 43:10229)

887. LARSEN, MARY RUTH JUHAN. *Item Performance of Five-Year-Old Georgia Subjects on the Stanford-Binet Form L-M Compared With the Standardization Sample.* Doctor's thesis, University of Georgia (Athens, Ga.), 1968. (*DA* 29:2529A)

888. LEVY, PHILIP. "Short-Form Tests: A Methodological Review." *Psychol B* 69:410–6 Je '68. * (*PA* 42:11410)

889. LUONG, CORINA K. MONGCAL. *An Analysis of Factors Related to Difficulties in Learning and Adjustment Among Minority Group Children.* Doctor's thesis, Bryn Mawr College (Bryn Mawr, Pa.), 1968. (*DAI* 30:4795B)

890. MCARTHUR, CHARLES R., AND WAKEFIELD, HOMER E. "Validation of the PPVT With the Stanford-Binet-LM and the WISC on Educable Mental Retardates." *Am J Mental Def* 73:465–7 N '68. * (*PA* 43:8596)

891. MATTHEWS, CHARLES G.; CHUN, RAYMOND W. M.; GRABOW, JACK D.; AND THOMPSON, WAYNE H. "Psychological Sequelae in Children Following California Arboviros Encephalitis." *Neurol* 18:1023–9 O '68. * (*PA* 43:5771)

892. MIEZITIS, SOLVEIGA AUSMA. *An Exploratory Study of Divergent Production in Preschoolers.* Doctor's thesis, University of Toronto (Toronto, Ont., Canada), 1968. (*DAI* 30:589A)

893. MUELLER, MAX W. "Validity of Six Tests of Ability With Educable Mental Retardates." *J Sch Psychol* 6:136–46 w '68. * (*PA* 42:11152)

894. PATTERSON, HENRY JAMES. *A Validation and Comparison of the Pictorial Test of Intelligence With the Stanford-Binet (L-M).* Doctor's thesis, University of Arizona (Tucson, Ariz.), 1968. (*DA* 29:485A)

895. PHILLIPS, C. J., AND BANNON, W. J. "The Stanford-Binet, Form L-M, Third Revision: A Local English Study of Norms, Concurrent Validity and Social Differences." *Brit J Ed Psychol* 38:148–61 Je '68. * (*PA* 42:17000)

896. PLANT, WALTER T., AND SOUTHERN, MARA L. "First Grade Reading Achievement Predicted From WPPSI and Other Scores Obtained 18 Months Earlier." Abstract. *Proc 76th Ann Conv Am Psychol Assn* 3:593–4 '68. *

897. SCHREFFLER, ROY HOOVER. *Six Year Study of Three Groups of Students Screened for Sixth Grade Major Work Classes: Special and Regular Class Students of High Binet IQ, and Pseudogifted Students.* Doctor's thesis, Pennsylvania State University (University Park, Pa.), 1968. (*DA* 29:3473A)

898. SEKYRA, FRANCIS, III, AND ARNOULT, JOSEPH FRANCIS, III. "Negro Intellectual Assessment With Three Instruments Contrasting Caucasian and Negro Norms." *J Learn Dis* 1:564–9 O '68. * (*PA* 45:2174)

899. SHEVERBUSH, ROBERT L., JR. "An Analysis of Subtest Performance by Gifted Students on the Stanford-Binet Intelligence Scale (1960 Form L-M)." Abstract. *AERA Paper Abstr* 1968:324–5 '68. *

900. SHIPE, DOROTHY; VANDENBERG, STEVEN; AND WILLIAMS, R. D. BROOKE. "Neonatal Apgar Ratings as Related to Intelligence and Behavior in Preschool Children." *Child Develop* 39:861–6 S '68. * (*PA* 43:3762)

901. SULLIVAN, ROBYN A. *Adaptive Administration of the Stanford-Binet Intelligence Scale to Indian Children.* Master's thesis, Arizona State University (Tempe, Ariz.), 1968.

902. TUCHMAN, STEPHANIE B. *A Correlation Study of the*

Stanford-Binet and Academic Ability of Trainable Retarded Children. Master's thesis, Adelphi University (Garden City, N.Y.), 1968.

903. WHITACRE, ROGER L. *Use of the Slosson Intelligence Test With the Stanford-Binet, L-M, as a Screening Device for Slow Learner Placement.* Master's thesis, Bowling Green State University (Bowling Green, Ohio), 1968.

904. WHITE, LINDA ANN. *A Comparative Study of the Performance of Negro Head Start Students on the Wechsler Preschool and Primary Scale of Intelligence, the Wechsler Intelligence Scale for Children, and the Stanford-Binet, Form L-M.* Master's thesis, University of Texas (Austin, Tex.), 1968.

905. WISE, JAMES H. "Stick Copying of Designs by Preschool and Young School-Age Children." *Percept & Motor Skills* 27:1159–68 D '68. * (PA 43:9547)

906. ZIGLER, EDWARD, AND BUTTERFIELD, CARL C. "Motivational Aspects of Changes in IQ Test Performance of Culturally Deprived Nursery School Children." *Child Develop* 39:1–14 Mr '68. * (PA 42:10578)

907. ZUNICH, M., AND TOLLEY, J. "Performance on the Peabody Picture Vocabulary Test and Stanford-Binet by Institutionalized Mentally Retarded Children." *Psychol Rep* 22:1212 Je '68. * (PA 42:19210)

908. BABSON, S. GORHAM, AND KANGAS, JOHN. "Preschool Intelligence of Undersized Term Infants." *Am J Dis Children* 117(5):553–7 My '69. * (PA 44:440)

909. BARABASZ, ARREED F. "Test-Retest Reliability of the Torrance Tests of Creative Thinking, and the Relationship Between Intelligence and Figural Creativity." *Child Study Center B* 5(4–5):73–4 S–N '69. * (PA 44:16369)

910. BARCLAY, ALLAN, AND YATER, ALLAN C. "Comparative Study of the Wechsler Preschool and Primary Scale of Intelligence and the Stanford-Binet Intelligence Scale, Form L-M, Among Culturally Deprived Children." Abstract. *J Consult & Clin Psychol* 33(2):257 Ap '69. * (PA 43:9734)

911. BRUININKS, ROBERT H. "Auditory and Visual Perceptual Skills Related to the Reading Performance of Disadvantaged Boys." *Percept & Motor Skills* 29(1):179–86 Ag '69. * (PA 44:2835)

912. BUNUAN, JOSEFINA S. *Translation and Adaptation of the Stanford-Binet Intelligence Scale, Form L-M, for Filipino Children.* Doctor's thesis, Boston University (Boston, Mass.), 1969. (*DAI* 31:377B)

913. COCHRAN, MALCOLM L., AND PEDRINI, DUILIO T. "The Concurrent Validity of the 1965 WRAT With Adult Retardates." *Am J Mental Def* 73(4):654–6 Ja '69. * (PA 43:8574)

914. CORNWELL, ANNE C., AND BIRCH, HERBERT C. "Psychological and Social Development in Home-Reared Children With Down's Syndrome (Monogolism)." *Am J Mental Def* 74(3):341–50 N '69. * (PA 44:5539)

915. CRAWFORD, VEDA B. *Relationships of Scores on the Wechsler Preschool and Primary Scale of Intelligence, the Stanford-Binet Intelligence Scale, Form LM, and the Peabody Picture Vocabulary Test, Form A.* Master's thesis, Bowling Green State University (Bowling Green, Ohio), 1969.

916. DILORENZO, LOUIS T., AND BRADY, JAMES J. "Use of the Peabody Picture Vocabulary Test." *Training Sch B* 65(4):117–21 F '69. * (PA 44:4169)

917. DOKECKI, PAUL R.; FREDE, MARTHA C.; AND GAUTNEY, DONALD B. "Criterion, Construct, and Predictive Validities of the Wechsler Preschool and Primary Scale of Intelligence." Abstract. *Proc 77th Ann Conv Am Psychol Assn* 4(2):505–6 '69. * (PA 44:1253)

918. DUFFETT, JOHN WARREN. *The Influence of Stanford-Binet Items on Traditional Measures in Estimating First Grade Reading Success in a Selected Population.* Doctor's thesis, University of Pittsburgh (Pittsburgh, Pa.), 1969. (*DAI* 31:1683A)

919. ENGLISH, RICHARD A., AND KIDDER, JACK W. "Note on Relationships Among Mental Ability Scores, Teacher's Rankings, and Rate of Acquisition for Four-Year-Old Kindergartners." *Psychol Rep* 24(2):554 Ap '69. * (PA 43:15568)

920. FAGAN, JOEN; BROUGHTON, ELIZABETH; ALLEN, MILDRED; CLARK, BETTY; AND EMERSON, PATRICIA. "Comparison of the Binet and WPPSI With Lower-Class Five-Year-Olds." *J Consult & Clin Psychol* 33(5):607–9 O '69. * (PA 44:2135)

921. GIOIOSO, JOSEPH V., AND ADERMAN, MORRIS. "The Combination Test as a Quick Screening Device to Differentiate Levels of Retardation." *Psychol Rep* 25(3):843–8 D '69. * (PA 44:18906)

922. HIRSHOREN, ALFRED. "A Comparison of the Predictive Validity of the Revised Stanford-Binet Intelligence Scale and the Illinois Test of Psycholinguistic Abilities." *Excep Children* 35(7):517–21 Mr '69. * (PA 44:17505)

923. HOWARD, JANE OSBURN. *A Comparison of the Revised Stanford-Binet Intelligence Scale, Form L-M, and the Nebraska Test of Learning Aptitude, 1966 Revision, With Groups of Mentally Retarded, Deaf, and Normal Children.* Doctor's thesis, University of New Mexico (Albuquerque, N. M.), 1969. (*DAI* 30:3322A)

924. JONGEWARD, PAUL A. "A Validity Study of the Slosson Intelligence Test for Use With Educable Mentally Retarded Students." *J Sch Psychol* 7(4):59–63 '68–69 ['69]. * (PA 44:2702)

925. JONGEWARD, PAUL ALBERT. *A Validity Study of the Slosson Intelligence Test for Use With Educable Mentally Retarded Students.* Doctor's thesis, University of Oregon (Eugene, Ore.), 1969. (*DAI* 30:3323A)

926. KAMII, CONSTANCE K., AND RADIN, NORMA L. "The Retardation of Disadvantaged Negro Preschoolers: Some Characteristics Found From an Item Analysis of the Stanford-Binet Test." *Psychol Sch* 6(3):283–8 Jl '69. * (PA 44:4040)

927. KEIM, RICHARD PAUL. *Visual-Motor Training, Readiness, and Intelligence of Kindergarten Children.* Doctor's thesis, Temple University (Philadelphia, Pa.), 1969. (*DAI* 31:1076A)

928. KENNEDY, WALLACE A. "A Follow-Up Normative Study of Negro Intelligence and Achievement." *Monogr Soc Res Child Develop* 34(2):1–40 '69. * (PA 45:1350)

929. LEWIS, JAMES F. *Differential Evaluation of Selected Tests When Utilized With Institutionalized and Non-Institutionalized Trainable Mentally Retarded.* Doctor's thesis, University of Nebraska (Lincoln, Neb.), 1969. (*DAI* 30:3793A)

930. MASSARI, DAVID; HAYWEISER, LOIS; AND MEYER, WILLIAM J. "Activity Level and Intellectual Functioning in Deprived Preschool Children." *Develop Psychol* 1(3):286–90 My '69. * (PA 43:11105)

931. MAXWELL, JAMES. "Intelligence, Education and Fertility: A Comparison Between the 1932 and 1947 Scottish Surveys." *J Biosocial Sci* 1(3):247–71 Jl '69. * (PA 46:1184)

932. MEEKER, MARY NACOL. *The Structure of Intellect: Its Interpretation and Uses,* pp. 123–31. Columbus, Ohio: Charles E. Merrill Publishing Co., 1969. Pp. xix, 203. *

933. MUELLER, MAX W. "Prediction of Achievement of Educable Mentally Retarded Children." *Am J Mental Def* 73(4):590–6 Ja '69. * (PA 43:8703)

934. NEEDHAM, WALTER E.; BRAY, PATRICK F.; WISER, WILMER C.; AND BECK, EDWARD C. "Intelligence and EEG Studies in Families With Idiopathic Epilepsy." *J Am Med Assn* 207(8):1497–501 F 24 '69. * (PA 44:21418)

935. RELLAS, ARCHIE J. "The Use of the Wechsler Preschool and Primary Scale (WPPSI) in the Early Identification of Gifted Students." *Calif J Ed Res* 20(3):117–9 My '69. * (PA 45:8921)

936. ROWLAND, MARY SARA. *A Study of Cognitive Content in the Play Themes of Pre-School Children.* Doctor's thesis, St. Louis University (St. Louis, Mo.), 1969. (*DAI* 30:3335A)

937. SHOTWELL, ANNA M.; O'CONNOR, GAIL; GABET, YVONNE; AND DINGMAN, HARVEY F. "Relation of the Peabody Picture Vocabulary Test IQ to the Stanford-Binet IQ." *Am J Mental Def* 74(1):39–42 Jl '69. * (PA 43:17485)

938. SILVERSTEIN, A. B. "Analysis of Two Item-Classification Schemes for the Stanford-Binet." *Psychol Rep* 24(2):503–5 Ap '69. * (PA 43:16263)

939. SILVERSTEIN, A. B. "The Internal Consistency of the Stanford-Binet." *Am J Mental Def* 73(5):753–4 Mr '69. * (PA 43:10236)

940. TURNER, A. JACK, AND LAIR, CHARLES V. "The Use of Video Tape in Teaching and Evaluating Training of Individual Testing." *J Clin Psychol* 25(2):218–21 Ap '69. * (PA 43:13511)

941. YEN, SHERMAN M. Y. *A Comparative Study of Test Variability With Peabody Picture Vocabulary Test, Goodenough's Draw-A-Man Test, and Stanford-Binet Intelligence Scale as Intellectual Measurement With a Group of Urban Low Socio-Economic Status Pre-School Pupils.* Doctor's thesis, Catholic University of America (Washington, D.C.), 1969. (*DAI* 30:2625A)

942. ACHENBACH, THOMAS M. "Comparison of Stanford-Binet Performance of Nonretarded and Retarded Persons Matched for MA and Sex." *Am J Mental Def* 74(4):488–94 Ja '70. * (PA 44:11048)

943. ALPERN, GERALD D., AND KIMBERLIN, CAROLYN C. "Short Intelligence Test Ranging From Infancy Levels Through Childhood Levels for Use With the Retarded." *Am J Mental Def* 75(1):65–71 Jl '70. * (PA 45:1185)

944. BAYLEY, NANCY. Chap. 16, "Development of Mental Abilities," pp. 1163–209. In *Carmichael's Manual of Child Psychology, Third Edition, Vol. 1.* Edited by Paul H. Mussen. New York: John Wiley & Sons, Inc., 1970. Pp. xiii, 1519. *

945. BENNETT, DOROTHY KEMLER. *The Tester and Intelligence Testing: An Examination of Protocol Interpretation.* Doctor's thesis, Harvard University (Cambridge, Mass.), 1970. (*DAI* 31:2095A)

946. BERGER, M. "The Third Revision of the Stanford-Binet (Form L-M): Some Methodological Limitations and Their Practical Implications." *B Brit Psychol Soc* 23(78):17–26 Ja '70. * (PA 44:13629)

947. BLUM, JUNE E.; JARVIK, LISSY F.; AND CLARK, EDWARD T. "Rate of Change on Selective Tests of Intelligence: A Twenty-Year Longitudinal Study." *J Gerontol* 25(3):171–6 Jl '70. *

948. BRUININKS, ROBERT H., AND FELDMAN, DAVID H. "Creativity, Intelligence, and Achievement Among Disadvantaged Children." *Psychol Sch* 7(3):260–4 Jl '70. * (PA 45:5015)

949. BRUININKS, ROBERT H., AND LUCKER, WILLIAM G. "Change and Stability in Correlations Between Intelligence and Reading Test Scores Among Disadvantaged Children." *J Read Behav* 2(4):295–305 f '70. * (PA 46:5700)

950. BUTTERFIELD, EARL C., AND ZIGLER, EDWARD. "Preinstitutional Social Deprivation and IQ Changes Among Institutionalized Retarded Children." *J Abn Psychol* 75(1):83–9 F '70. * (*PA* 44:7155)
951. CALDWELL, MARK B., AND KNIGHT, DAVID. "The Effect of Negro and White Examiners on Negro Intelligence Test Performance." *J Negro Ed* 39(2):177–9 sp '70. * (*PA* 46:7443)
952. CALLAWAY, BYRON. "Factors Related to Reading of Children Referred to a University Reading Clinic," pp. 61–6. In *Reading Difficulties: Diagnosis, Correction, and Remediation*. Edited by William K. Durr. Newark, Del.: International Reading Association, 1970. Pp. vii, 276. *
953. COCHRAN, MALCOLM L. "A Profile of Psychological Test Scores for Retarded Adults." *Am J Mental Def* 74(4):582–4 Ja '70. * (*PA* 44:11052)
954. COSTELLO, JOAN, AND DICKIE, JOYCE. "Leiter and Stanford-Binet IQ's of Preschool Disadvantaged Children." Abstract. *Develop Psychol* 2(2):314 Mr '70. * (*PA* 44:6523)
955. CRANDALL, VIRGINIA C., AND BATTLE, ESTHER S. "The Antecedents and Adult Correlates of Academic and Intellectual Achievement." *Minn Symposia Child Psychol* 4:36–93 '70. *
956. DAVE, PRAFUL N. "Achievement Motivation and Risk-Taking in Kindergarten Children." *J Psychol Res* 14(1):7–13 Ja '70. *
957. DURKIN, DOLORES. "A Language Arts Program for Pre-First-Grade Children: Two-Year Achievement Report." *Read Res Q* 5(4):534–65 su '70. *
958. ENGELMANN, SIEGFRIED. "The Effectiveness of Direct Instruction on IQ Performance and Achievement in Reading and Arithmetic." *Disadvantaged Child* 3:339–61 '70. *
959. ESTES, ROBERT E., AND MORRIS, HUGHLETT L. "Relationship Among Intelligence, Speech Proficiency, and Hearing Sensitivity in Children With Cleft Palates." *Cleft Palate J* 7(9):763–73 Jl '70. *
960. FERINDEN, WILLIAM E., JR.; JACOBSON, SHERMAN; AND KOVALINSKY, THOMAS. *Educational Interpretation of the Stanford-Binet Intelligence Scale Form L-M and the Illinois Test of Psycholinguistic Abilities*. Linden, N.J.: Remediation Associates, Inc., 1970. Pp. 71. *
961. FISHER, MARY ANN, AND ZEAMAN, DAVID. "Growth and Decline of Retardate Intelligence." *Int R Res Mental Retard* 4:151–91 '70. *
962. FUTTERER, JAMES W. *An Investigation of the Relationship of the Wechsler Preschool and Primary Scale of Intelligence to the 1960 Revision of the Stanford-Binet Scale, Form L-M*. Master's thesis, Loyola University (Chicago, Ill.), 1970.
963. GAYTON, WILLIAM F. "Validity of the Harris Quality Scale With a Child Guidance Population." *Percept & Motor Skills* 31(1):17–8 Ag '70. * (*PA* 45:4532)
964. GOLDSTEIN, LEO S.; COLLER, ALAN R.; DILL, JOHN; AND TILIS, HOWARD S. "The Effect of a Special Curriculum for Disadvantaged Children on Test-Retest Reliabilities of Three Standardized Instruments." *J Ed Meas* 7(3):171–4 f '70. * (*PA* 45:4917)
965. HOFMEISTER, ALAN, AND ESPESETH, V. KNUTE. "Predicting Academic Achievement With TMR Adults and Teenagers." *Am J Mental Def* 75(1):105–7 Jl '70. *
966. HUMPHREYS, L. G. "Footnote to the Scottish Survey of Intelligence." *Brit J Ed Psychol* 40(1):72–4 F '70. * (*PA* 44:10411)
967. INGRAM, T. T. S.; MASON, A. W.; AND BLACKBURN, I. "A Retrospective Study of 82 Children With Reading Disability." *Develop Med & Child Neurol* 12(3):271–81 Je '70. *
968. IRETON, HAROLD; THWING, EDWARD; AND GRAVEM, HOWARD. "Infant Mental Development and Neurological Status, Family Socioeconomic Status, and Intelligence at Age Four." *Child Develop* 41(4):937–45 D '-o. * (*PA* 46:831)
969. KANGAS, JON ALAN. *Intelligence at Middle Age*. Doctor's thesis, Washington State University (Pullman, Wash.), 1970. (*DAI* 31:1520B)
970. KODMAN, FRANK, JR. "Effects of Preschool Enrichment on Intellectual Performance of Appalachian Children." *Excep Children* 36(7):503–7 Mr '71. * (*PA* 44:21495)
971. LARSEN, MARY JUHAN, AND ALLEN, JERRY C. "Effects of Certain Subject Variables on Stanford-Binet Item Performance of Five-Year-Old Children." *Psychol Rep* 26(3):975–84 Je '70. * (*PA* 45:517)
972. MEISSLER, GEORGE R. *A Correlation of the Slosson Intelligence Test and the Wechsler Intelligence Scale When Administered to Atypical Children*. Doctor's thesis, Catholic University of America (Washington, D.C.), 1970. (*DAI* 31:2191A)
973. MUMBAUER, CORINNE C., AND MILLER, J. O. "Socioeconomic Background and Cognitive Functioning in Preschool Children." *Child Develop* 41(2):471–80 Je '70. * (*PA* 44:14291)
974. NELSON, K. B., AND DEUTSCHBERGER, J. "Head Size at One Year as a Predictor of Four-Year IQ." *Develop Med & Child Neurol* 12(3):487–95 Je '70. * (*PA* 45:10490)
975. NICHOLSON, CHARLES L. "Analysis of Functions of the Slosson Intelligence Test." *Percept & Motor Skills* 31(2):627–31 O '70. * (*PA* 45:6336)
976. NURSS, JOANNE R. "A Diagnostic Comparison of Two Third Grade Reading Classes," pp. 42–54. In *Reading Difficulties: Diagnosis, Correction, and Remediation*. Edited by William K. Durr. Newark, Del.: International Reading Association, 1970. Pp. vii, 276. *
977. PALMER, FRANCIS H. "Socioeconomic Status and Intellective Performance Among Negro Preschool Boys." *Develop Psychol* 3(1):1–9 Jl '70. * (*PA* 44:16374)
978. PEDRINI, DUILIO T. AND PEDRINI, LURA N. *The Pedrini Supplementary Aid to the Administration of the Stanford-Binet Intelligence Scale (Form L-M): A Handbook*. Los Angeles, Calif.: Western Psychological Services, 1970. Pp. iii, 50. *
979. RAMSEY, PHILLIP H., AND VANE, JULIA R. "A Factor Analytic Study of the Stanford Binet With Young Children." *J Sch Psychol* 8(4):278–84 '70. * (*PA* 46:1778)
980. REES, ANN H., AND PALMER, FRANCIS H. "Factors Related to Change in Mental Test Performance." *Develop Psychol Monogr* 3(2):1–57 S '70. * (*PA* 45:464)
981. SILVERSTEIN, A. B. "The Measurement of Intelligence." *Int R Res Mental Retard* 4:193–227 '70. *
982. TAYLOR, JOHN F.; WINSLOW, CHARLES N.; AND PAGE, HORACE A. "An MA Growth Curve for Institutionalized Mild and Moderate Retardates." *Am J Mental Def* 75(1):47–50 Jl '70. * (*PA* 45:1213)
983. WALKER, KENNETH P., AND GROSS, FREDERICK L. "I.Q. Stability Among Educable Mentally Retarded Children." *Training Sch B* 66(4):181–7 F '70. * (*PA* 44:13185)
984. WASHINGTON, ERNEST D., AND TESKA, JAMES A. "Relations Between the Wide Range Achievement Test, the California Achievement Tests, the Stanford-Binet, and the Illinois Test of Psycholinguistic Abilities." *Psychol Rep* 26(1):291–4 F '70. * (*PA* 45:4931)
985. WILLERMAN, LEE; BROMAN, SARAH H.; AND FIEDLER, MIRIAM. "Infant Development, Preschool IQ, and Social Class." *Child Develop* 41(1):69–77 Mr '70. * (*PA* 44:8168)
986. ZIMMERMAN, IRLA LEE, AND WOO-SAM, JAMES. "The Utility of the Wechsler Preschool and Primary Scale of Intelligence in the Public School." *J Clin Psychol* 26(4):472 O '70. * (*PA* 45:6976)

DAVID FREIDES, *Associate Professor of Psychology, Emory University, Atlanta, Georgia.*

My comments in 1970 are not very different from those made by F. L. Wells 32 years ago in *The 1938 Mental Measurements Yearbook*. The Binet scales have been around a long time and their faults are well known.

In a simpler age, variations in accomplishment, especially in school performance, were explained by resort to the unitary concept of intelligence. This was measured by an instrument that yielded an index of underlying capability. The Stanford-Binet was the embodiment par excellence of this concept, the standard against which other instruments were evaluated. Unfortunately, if the score was low, the outlook was pessimistic: the explanation, hereditary. What could one do in the face of a fault in the biological past? Controversies raged (and still do) about the hereditary component of intelligence, while naive racial and hereditary concepts became part of the intellectual baggage in the field. Only recently has a sophisticated behavior genetics torn away the old naiveté and begun to show the inappropriateness of studying genic variations by examining so complexly determined a measure as IQ.

Meanwhile, many workers apparently disregarded unitary concepts and disdained pessimistic attitudes, with the result that a technology of (re)habilitation, (re)education, and (re)-motivation developed. A diversified evaluation, tapping different aspects of mental functioning and yielding indices of strength and weakness, had much greater utility than a singular index. Today, we remain a long way from systematic knowledge of the nature of intelligence and hence we still do not know exactly what to measure. But it is clear that this is the direction to go, which may explain why the Wechsler scales have largely superseded the Binet. Even when a Binet is used, patterns of successes and failures are analyzed and other tests are used to place the Binet result in perspective.

At present, no major, well standardized general intelligence test of the point scale type is available for children between 30 months, the ceiling of the *Bayley Scales of Infant Development,* and 48 months, the lowest age of the *Wechsler Preschool and Primary Scale of Intelligence.* Since tests are somewhat less reliable near the limits of the ages for which they were designed, the gap between these figures should be stretched some. But it is in filling this gap (especially along with the *Merrill-Palmer Scale of Mental Tests*) that the remaining utility of the Binet is found. Specifically to be avoided is its classic use in older cases of severe retardation in order to pinpoint levels of IQ below 50 or so. It is statistically meaningless to know that a subject is more than four or five standard deviations below the mean; however, the determination of a precise but meaningless number frequently precludes the search for behavioral potentials.

The *Stanford-Binet Intelligence Scale* is an old, old vehicle. It has led a distinguished life as a pioneer in the bootstrap operation that is the assessment enterprise. Its time is just about over. *Requiescat in pace.*

For a review by Elizabeth D. Fraser, see 6:536 (5 excerpts); for reviews by Mary R. Haworth and Norman D. Sundberg of the second edition, see 5:413; for a review by Boyd R. McCandless, see 4:358; see also 2:1420 (3 excerpts); for reviews by Francis N. Maxfield, J. W. M. Rothney, and F. L. Wells, see 1:1062.

[426]
★[Re Stanford-Binet Intelligence Scale] A Clinical Profile for the Stanford Binet Intelligence Scale (L-M). Ages 5 and over; 1965; title on profile is *A Profile for the Stanford Binet (L-M)*; an item classification system for use by school psychologists in analyzing and reporting performance in 6 categories: general comprehension, visual-motor ability, arithmetic reasoning, memory and concentration, vocabulary and verbal fluency, judgment and reasoning; profile (2 pages); manual (4 pages); no data on reliability and validity of item classifications; $2.50 per 50 profiles; 50¢ per specimen set; postage extra; Robert E. Valett; Consulting Psychologists Press, Inc. *

[427]
★Stanford-Ohwaki-Kohs Block Design Intelligence Test for the Blind: American Revision of the Ohwaki-Kohs Test. Blind and partially sighted ages 16 and over; 1965–66; uses same testing materials as *The Ohwaki-Kohs Tactile Block Design Intelligence Test for the Blind;* individual; 1 form (blocks and design cards); record sheet (1 page); manual (18 pages plus record sheet); $47.50 per set of testing materials, 25 record sheets, and manual; $42.50 per set of testing materials; $12.50 per 100 record sheets; $3.50 per manual; postpaid; [60–120] minutes; Richard M. Suinn and William L. Dauterman; Western Psychological Services. *

[428]
★Vane Kindergarten Test. Ages 4-0 to 6-11; 1968; VKT; 4 scores: perceptual motor, vocabulary, drawing a man, total; individually administered in part; 1 form (1 page); manual (35 pages, reprint of *1* below); $3.50 per 50 tests; $4 per manual; postpaid; [30] minutes; Julia R. Vane; Clinical Psychology Publishing Co., Inc. *

REFERENCES
1. VANE, JULIA R. "The Vane Kindergarten Test." *J Clin Psychol* 24:121–54 Ap '68. * (*PA* 42:12096)
2. ELLERMAN, RICHARD A., AND WADLEY, JOYCE A. "A Readiness Experiment." *Read Teach* 23(6):556–8 Mr '70. *
3. WILLIS, DIANE JANICE. *Perceptual and Cognitive Performance of Children as Functions of Socio-Economic Class.* Doctor's thesis, University of Oklahoma (Norman, Okla.), 1970. (*DAI* 31:3045A)

DOROTHY H. EICHORN, *Research Psychologist and Administrator, Child Study Center, Institute of Human Development, University of California, Berkeley, California.*

The *Vane Kindergarten Test* utilizes three subtests and behavioral observations made during testing to assess "the intellectual and academic potential and behavior adjustment of young children." A rather unusual feature is the combination of group and individual testing. The Perceptual Motor subtest, in which the child makes three copies each of a box, a cross, and a hexagon, and the Man subtest (similar to the *Goodenough Intelligence Test* and the *Goodenough-Harris Drawing Test*), in which the child draws a man, are administered to a group. Then each child is tested individually for the 11-item Vocabulary subtest. Following the latter, the examiner notes on the test blank "behavior with respect to attention, ability to follow directions, self-control, cooperation, hand dominance and speech."

Tables for converting point scores to IQ are provided for each subtest for each month of age from 4-0 to 6-11. Full IQ is the average of the three subtest IQ's. For each subtest, mental age equivalents of point scores are also tabled so that ratio IQ's (mental age divided by chronological age) can be derived for children younger than 4-0 or older than 6-11.

All three subtests draw on classes of items widely used in tests for young children, and the empirical rationale for their selection is straightforward. Cited references indicate that form-copying skills are developmental in nature and related to success in reading and writing in the primary grades. The high correlation of vocabulary scores with total score on general tests of intelligence and with academic success is well known. In this particular test, the author considers the easier words to sample general information and the more difficult ones to require language facility as well as knowledge. A lengthy list of studies on the use of human figure drawing as an index of intelligence, adjustment, and future achievement of young children is provided.

Considerable effort was expended in the development and assessment of the VKT before its publication. A large variety of words (drawn from published lists and primary readers) and forms (recommended by teachers and psychologists working with young children) were first administered to "992 children, aged 5 to 10 years, in a lower middle class school district." Next a reduced number—15 words and 5 forms—were "given to 1809 children, aged 4 to 10 years, in a number of different school districts. Final selection of the items was then made." The methods used in item evaluation are not mentioned, except for the Man subtest. For this, rapidity and consistency of scoring by a number of examiners of varying experience, and comparability of correlation with the Stanford-Binet (.49) to that obtained with scoring by the Goodenough method (.52) were the criteria. The final standardization sample consisted of 400 children ages 4½ to 6 (the manual states that there were 100 of each sex at each half-year level, a seeming misprint) from the states of New York and New Jersey. The number of classrooms sampled, a factor which the literature suggests is as important as sample size, is not stated. Socioeconomic class was defined by father's occupational category. The VKT percentages of urban and of rural whites and the total of nonwhites are almost identical to those of the 1960 census. However, the sample contained very few nonwhite rural children and overly represented nonwhite urban children in occupational categories IV through VIII. Norms for children younger or older than those in the standardization sample must be based on rescoring of tests from the pretest groups, a questionable procedure.

Intercorrelations among subtests range between .47 and .61. As would be expected from the averaging method for full IQ, the correlations of all subtests with full IQ are approximately the same, ranging from .78 to .86. Data on reliability come only from retests on very small groups—there is no alternate form of the VKT, and the brevity of the test contraindicates an odd-even assessment of reliability. Retesting of 14 kindergarten children after one week yielded high reliability coefficients: .97 for full IQ, .92 for the Man subtest, .82 for Perceptual Motor, and .81 for Vocabulary. Corresponding coefficients for 36 children tested in kindergarten in April and retested in the first grade the following October (at age levels in which the test is less discriminating) were .88, .79, .83, and .71. To assess the validity of full IQ's, correlations of the VKT with the Stanford-Binet were obtained in two samples. In one school district 212 children tested with the VKT in May of their kindergarten year were given the Binet sometime during the following two years. In another district the VKT was administered to 78 kindergarten children in October and the Binet was given in the same school year. Despite the temporal separations in testing, the correlation coefficient was about as high as would be expected under any circumstances (.76 for both samples), and the means on the two tests did not differ significantly.

The VKT is intended for use by school psychologists, not by teachers or other school personnel. This fact, of course, precludes its use in schools without psychological services. Among the advantages claimed for the VKT are "short administration time, simple directions, and rapid scoring," no disruption of school routine, and individual evaluation of "the influence of motivation, attention, perceptual motor skills or nonconforming behavior upon the test results." Although group tests require less time to administer, they do not offer the interpretative advantages of some individual contact.

For the most part, the directions for administration, both in terms of testing conditions and instructions to the children, and for scoring are clear and sufficiently detailed. Whether

Vane Kindergarten Test

chronological age is to be calculated to the last month's birthdate or to nearest month is not specified. Minor perils in scoring are variations in point allotments. Some disruption of class routine must occur. Only 10 to 12 kindergarten children should be tested at one time; the others must be taken out of the room. An assistant is also recommended to supervise the remainder of the group while the examiner is administering vocabulary tests. The fact that the latter are likely to be given in a corner of the classroom introduces two possible problems: the child being tested may be disturbed by the other activities in the room, and children yet to take the Vocabulary may overhear responses. A further source of bias in Vocabulary scores, particularly with older or bright children, is the listing of the words on the same sheet on which the children copy forms. The compact record sheet is an advantage in many respects, but children who can already read may benefit from this exposure. Behavioral adjustment is evaluated from "signs" on the figure drawing and from observations during testing. Vane is careful to urge appropriate cautions in interpreting these data.

Although the VKT needs more extensive evaluation with broader and larger samples, it appears promising for its intended use. To date, reliability and validity coefficients are as good as those for any group test for young children, and relatively few are available. Among other group tests for this age range, only the *IPAT Culture Fair Intelligence Test* includes partial individual evaluation. If factor analyses justify the use of differential subtest scoring, such scores offer additional evaluative and predictive possibilities now paralleled probably only in the *California Short-Form Test of Mental Maturity*. Against these advantages must be weighed those of a series of graded tests by which to extend the age range covered, a characteristic of competing tests.

MARCEL L. GOLDSCHMID, *Associate Professor of Psychology and Director, Centre for Learning and Development, McGill University, Montreal, Quebec, Canada.*

The VKT may offer a considerable saving of time over conventional intelligence tests, since two of its three subtests, the Perceptual Motor and Draw A Man, can be administered to groups of children (8 to 12 at a time, depending on their age). The scoring also takes relatively little time, but it requires some judgment as to the quality of the response. Unfortunately, no interscorer reliability figures are presented for any of the three subtests. Given a random sample of examiners scoring the same set of VKT protocols, a considerable range of total scores might conceivably emerge.

A conversion table, broken down month by month from 4-0 to 6-11, shows the IQ equivalents of the total raw scores for each subtest. The total IQ is calculated by taking the average of the three subtest IQ's. The child's adjustment is evaluated on the basis of his total test behaviour and his draw-a-man performance. No quantitative measure is obtained, and no reliability or validity data (except for a handful of "successful" case studies) are provided for this assessment or for that of the child's perceptual motor development.

The norms are based on 400 subjects, a small and geographically unrepresentative sample (all subjects were from New York and New Jersey). The sample is, however, representative (for the U.S. as a whole) of different rural-urban, white-nonwhite, and occupational groups. Boys and girls did equally well, but white collar and white urban subjects obtained higher IQ's than blue collar and nonwhite subjects, respectively. (Unfortunately, no cross-tabulations were made in any of these comparisons.) Intercorrelations among the three subtests (.47 to .55) and for each subtest with the full test (.81 to .84) are satisfactory.

Test-retest reliability coefficients for the full test were .97 after one week and .88 after five months, but the samples were small and undefined in both cases.

Two separate samples (N's 212 and 78) were given both the VKT and the Stanford-Binet. In the first sample, the VKT was administered in kindergarten and the S-B in the following two years. In the second, the VKT was followed by the S-B later in the same year (kindergarten). Again the two samples are undefined with respect to sex, socioeconomic status, etc. No significant differences between the two means emerged for either sample and the correlation between the VKT and S-B was .76 in both cases. This correlation could conceivably be somewhat higher if both tests were given at the same time. It would have been very instructive to know the correlations between each VKT subtest and the S-B, since the correlation between S-B and full VKT approaches that between the VKT subtests and the full VKT. VKT IQ's obtained in kindergarten were also correlated with achievement deviations from grade expectations (as measured by the Stanford or California achievement tests) in first, second, and third grade. The coefficients were .59, .60, and .60, respectively. Thus it would appear possible to make reasonably good predictions about children's achievement in third grade based on their kindergarten VKT score.

The manual concludes with brief summaries of four illustrated case studies intended to "show that by utilizing the full IQ score and all other data derived from testing, a good picture of the child's functioning may be obtained." Such a small and highly selected sample can hardly be convincing. If such a claim is made, it would be desirable to support it with the results from other correlative studies or a predictive study of a larger and representative sample, particularly if the predictor variables are to include not only the VKT IQ scores but also quantified test behaviour and adjustment scores. The case studies do serve, however, the purpose of further illustrating the author's proposed scoring of entire VKT protocols. They also demonstrate the relatively curtailed range of possible scores, particularly at the lower end. The lowest Vocabulary IQ possible for a 4-year-old, for example, is 100 (if he can identify at least one word) or 0 (if he does not know any of the very short list of 11 words). (Note that the Vocabulary subtest does in fact have the lowest test-retest reliability, .71 after a 5-month interval.)

In summary, the VKT offers the advantages that part of the test can be administered to groups; the total IQ is a fair approximation of the Stanford-Binet IQ; it is reasonably well correlated with later achievement test scores; and it appears to have satisfactory reliability. On the other hand, the normative sample was small and geographically unrepresentative. The VKT, furthermore, requires a fair amount of judgment and experience (both with respect to administration and scoring). It is, in fact, meant to be administered by psychologists, rather than teachers.

[429]
Wechsler Adult Intelligence Scale. Ages 16 and over; 1939-55; WAIS; revision of Form 1 of *Wechsler-Bellevue Intelligence Scale;* individual; 14 scores: verbal (information, comprehension, arithmetic, similarities, digit span, vocabulary, total), performance (digit symbol, picture completion, block design, picture arrangement, object assembly, total), total; 1 form ['55]; manual ('55, 116 pages); record booklet ('55, 4 pages); supplementary record sheet ('55, 1 page); $26 per set of testing materials, 25 record booklets, and manual; $2.70 per 25 record booklets; $1 per 25 supplementary record sheets; $3.25 per manual; postage extra; Spanish edition ('68) available; (40-60) minutes; David Wechsler; Psychological Corporation. *

REFERENCES
1-42. See 5:414.
43-222. See 6:538.
223. STAKER, JAMES EDWARD. *A Study of Academically Successful Students in a Large Secondary School.* Doctor's thesis, Northwestern University (Evanston, Ill.), 1954. (*DA* 14:2280)
224. WAHLER, HARRY JOE. *Analysis of the Performance of Brain-Damaged Patients on a Memory-For-Designs Test.* Doctor's thesis, State University of Iowa (Iowa City, Iowa), 1954. (*DA* 14:2406)
225. WECHSLER, D. "The Measurement and Evaluation of Intelligence of Older Persons," pp. 275-9. In *Old Age in the Modern World: Report of the Third Congress of the International Association of Gerontology, London, 1954.* Edinburgh, Scotland: E. & S. Livingstone Ltd., 1955. Pp. vii, 647. *
226. KIRSCHNER, DAVID. *An Analysis of Certain Relationships Between "Abstract" and "Concrete" Attitude, Avoidance Behavior, and Stimulus Generalization.* Doctor's thesis, University of Pittsburgh (Pittsburgh, Pa.), 1957. (*DA* 17:2314)
227. DREWES, HENRY WALTER. *An Experimental Study of the Relationship Between Electroencephalographic Imagery Variables and Perceptual-Cognitive Processes.* Doctor's thesis, Cornell University (Ithaca, N.Y.), 1958. (*DA* 19:87)
228. ALPER, ARTHUR E., AND HORNE, BETTY M. "Changes in IQ of a Group of Institutionalized Mental Defectives Over a Period of Two Decades." *Am J Mental Def* 64:472-5 N '59. * (*PA* 34:7994)
229. CRAWFORD, PAUL L. "The Relative Sensitivity of the LAIS, WAIS, and PM in Differentiating Between Psychopathic and Psychotic Patients in a Mental Hospital." *Psychol Service Center J* 11(2):93-7 '59. * (*PA* 34:4374)
230. CRAWFORD, PAUL L. "The Statistical Significance of Differences in Performance on the Leiter Adult Intelligence Scale, the Wechsler Adult Intelligence Scale, and the Porteus Maze by a Heterogeneous Mental Hospital Population." *Psychol Service Center J* 11(2):89-92 '59. * (*PA* 34:4510)
231. FLEMING, JACK WAYNE. *The Relationships Among Psychometric, Experimental, and Observational Measures of Learning Ability in Institutional, Endogenous Mentally Retarded Persons.* Doctor's thesis, University of Colorado (Boulder, Colo.), 1959. (*DA* 20:4183)
232. KARLIN, ISAAC W.; EISENSON, JON; HIRSCHENFANG, SAMUEL; AND MILLER, MAURICE H. "A Multi-Evaluational Study of Aphasic and Non-Aphasic Right Hemiplegic Patients." *J Speech & Hearing Disorders* 24:369-79 N '59. * (*PA* 34:8078)
233. SANTOS, BERTHA. *A Comparison of Memory and Learning Ability With Social Competence and Social Participation in Aged Senile Dements in a Mental Institution.* Doctor's thesis, New York University (New York, N.Y.), 1959. (*DA* 20:1441)
234. KOROTKIN, ARTHUR LEWIS. *Perception and Intelligence: The Relationship of Certain Visual-Perceptual Skills With Intelligence, Age, and Sex.* Doctor's thesis, Temple University (Philadelphia, Pa.), 1960. (*DA* 21:1637)
235. NELSON, LOIS AUDREY. *A Study of Certain Cognitive Aspects of the Speech of Multiple Sclerotic Patients.* Doctor's thesis, University of Wisconsin (Madison, Wis.), 1960. (*DA* 21:1666)
236. WERTS, CHARLES EARL, JR. *Multidimensional Analysis of Psychological Constructs.* Doctor's thesis, University of Minnesota (Minneapolis, Minn.), 1960. (*DA* 21:2008)
237. BELL, ANNE, AND ZUBEK, JOHN P. "Effects of Deanol on the Intellectual Performance of Mental Defectives." *Can J Psychol* 15:172-5 S '61. * (*PA* 36:4JI72B)
238. BERNSTEIN, LEWIS. "Psychological Testing: 1, Intelligence Tests." *J Child Asth Res Inst & Hosp* 1:205-17 Je '61. *
239. ILANIT, NATHAN. *Some Psychological Correlates of the Process-Reactive Concept of Schizophrenia.* Doctor's thesis, University of Southern California (Los Angeles, Calif.), 1961. (*DA* 21:3852)
240. GOUREVITCH, VIVIAN, AND FEFFER, MELVIN H. "A Study of Motivational Development." *J Genetic Psychol* 100:361-75 Je '62. * (*PA* 37:2891)
241. KOLE, DELBERT MERRILL. *A Study of Intellectual and Personality Characteristics of Medical Students.* Master's thesis, University of Oregon Medical School (Portland, Ore.), 1962.
242. MURDY, WILLIAM GEORGE, JR. *The Effect of Positive and Negative Administrations on Intelligence Test Performance.* Doctor's thesis, University of Florida (Gainesville, Fla.), 1962. (*DA* 23:1076)

243. NATHAN, PETER. *A Comparative Investigation of Conceptual Ability in Relation to Frustration Tolerance.* Doctor's thesis, Washington University (St. Louis, Mo.), 1962. (*DA* 24:394)

244. OBRIST, WALTER D.; BUSSE, EWALD W.; EISDORFER, CARL; AND KLEEMEIER, ROBERT W. "Relation of the Electroencephalogram to Intellectual Function in Senescence." *J Gerontol* 17:197–206 Ap '62. * (*PA* 37:2958)

245. WINER, DAVID. "The Relationship Among Intelligence, Emotional Stability, and Use of Auditory Cues by the Blind." *Am Found Blind Res B* 2:88–93 D '62. *

246. BERGER, LESLIE; BERNSTEIN, ALVIN; KLEIN, EDWARD; COHEN, JACOB; AND LUCAS, GERALD. "Effects of Aging and Pathology on the Factorial Structure of Intelligence." *Newsl Res Psychol* 5:35–6 Ag '63. * (*PA* 38:8442)

247. BERNSTEIN, ALVIN; KLEIN, EDWARD; BERGER, LESLIE; AND COHEN, JACOB. "The Influence of Institutionalization and Several Pre-Morbid and Demographic Variables on the Structure of Intelligence in Chronic Schizophrenics." *Newsl Res Psychol* 5:34–5 Ag '63. *

248. BIRREN, JAMES E.; BOTWINICK, JACK; WEISS, ALFRED D.; AND MORRISON, DONALD F. Chap. 10, "Interrelations of Mental and Perceptual Tests Given to Healthy Elderly Men," pp. 143–56. In *Human Aging: A Biological and Behavioral Study.* Edited by James E. Birren, Robert N. Butler, Samuel W. Greenhouse, Louise Sokoloff, and Marian R. Yarrow. National Institute of Mental Health, Public Health Service Publication No. 986. Washington, D.C.: United States Government Printing Office, 1963. Pp. xiii, 328. * (*PA* 38:5821)

249. BIRREN, JAMES E.; RIEGEL, KLAUS F.; AND MORRISON, DONALD F. Chap. 1, "Intellectual Capacities, Aging, and Man's Environment," pp. 9–44. In *Process of Aging: Social and Psychological Perspectives.* Edited by Richard H. Williams and others. New York: Atherton Press, 1963. Pp. xix, 587. *

250. BOTWINICK, JACK, AND BIRREN, JAMES E. Chap. 8, "Mental Abilities and Psychomotor Responses in Healthy Aged Men," pp. 97–108. In *Human Aging: A Biological and Behavioral Study.* Edited by James E. Birren, Robert N. Butler, Samuel W. Greenhouse, Louis Sokoloff, and Marian R. Yarrow. National Institute of Mental Health, Public Health Service Publication No. 986. Washington, D.C.: United States Government Printing Office, 1963. Pp. xiii, 328. * (*PA* 38:5821)

251. CAMPO, ROBERT ETTORE. *Clinical Versus Automated Administration of a Mental Test: A Study of Examiner Influence.* Doctor's thesis, University of Arizona (Tucson, Ariz.), 1963. (*DA* 25:285)

252. CANCRO, RALPH. *The Relation of Laterality of Brain Lesion to Intellectual Dysfunction.* Doctor's thesis, Columbia University (New York, N.Y.), 1963. (*DA* 24:2120)

253. DESROCHES, HARRY F.; BALLARD, H. TED; AND KIMBREALL, GORDON M. "Note on the Reliability of the WAIS Vocabulary Test in the Aged." *Newsl Res Psychol* 5:10 N '63. *

254. FLINN, DON E.; HARTMAN, BRYCE O.; POWELL, DOUGLAS H.; AND MCKENZIE, RICHARD E. "Psychiatric and Psychological Evaluation," pp. 199–230. In *Aeromedical Evaluation for Space Pilots.* Edited by Lawrence E. Lamb. Brooks Air Force Base, Tex.: USAF School of Aerospace Medicine, July 1963. Pp. viii, 276. * (*PA* 38:4728)

255. GALLAHER, PHILLIP JAMES. *Effects of Increased Verbal Scale Difficulty and Failure on WAIS Digit Symbol Performance.* Doctor's thesis, University of Denver (Denver, Colo.), 1963. (*DA* 24:5544)

256. JENNINGS, CHARLES L. "Psychologic Test Profiles of Special Groups." *Proc Ann Conf Air Force Clin Psychologists* 4:105–16 '63. *

257. KLETT, WILLIAM G. "An Analysis of Item Order in Seven Subtests of the Wechsler Adult Intelligence Scale." *Newsl Res Psychol* 5:30–2 N '63. *

258. MACKIE, JAMES BENJAMIN. *A Comparative Study of Brain Damaged and Normal Individuals on Tests of Intelligence, Perception and Rigidity.* Doctor's thesis, University of Utah (Salt Lake City, Utah), 1963. (*DA* 24:1700)

259. NICKOLS, JOHN. "Mental Deficit, Schizophrenia and the Benton Test." *J Nerv & Mental Dis* 136:279–82 Mr '63. * (*PA* 38:4615)

260. PARKER, ROLLAND S., AND DAVIDSON, NORMAN L. "A Comparison of Students of Nursing and Hospitalized Patients on Scores Derived From an Intelligence Test (WAIS)." *Psychiatric Q Sup* 37:298–306 pt 2 '63. * (*PA* 38:8431, 39:1789)

261. PASRICHA, PREM, AND PAGEDAR, RAJAMI M. "Adaptation of 'WAIS' to the Gujarati Population: Try-out With the School and College Population." *J Voc & Ed Guid* 9:174–84 N '63. * (*PA* 38:8432)

262. RUBIN, EDMUND JOSEPH. *Performance of Totally-Blind and Sighted Subjects on Tests of Abstraction.* Doctor's thesis, Fordham University (New York, N.Y.), 1963. (*DA* 24:2989)

263. SPIETH, PHILLIP EARL. *Intelligence as It Relates to Three Creativity Categories: Science, Art, and Literature.* Doctor's thesis, University of Michigan (Ann Arbor, Mich.), 1963. (*DA* 25:1759)

264. STEINER, FELIX. *Pictorial and Conceptual Thinking as Related to Personality.* Doctor's thesis, Yeshiva University (New York, N.Y.), 1963. (*DA* 25:2056)

265. WEBB, ALLEN P. "Some Issues Relating to the Validity of the WAIS in Assessing Mental Retardation," pp. 87–92. (*PA* 38:6075) In *Towards a Professional Identity in School Psychology.* California Association of School Psychologists and Psychometrists, Fourteenth Annual Conference, March 28–30, 1963. [Los Angeles, Calif.: the Association, 1963.] Pp. v, 97. * (*PA* 38:4904)

266. BERGER, LESLIE; BERNSTEIN, ALVIN; KLEIN, EDWARD; COHEN, JACOB; AND LUCAS, GERALD. "Effects of Aging and Pathology on the Factorial Structure of Intelligence." *J Consult Psychol* 28:199–207 Je '64. † (*PA* 39:4631)

267. BERMAN, ISAAC. *Wechsler Scores vs. Piaget Levels: A Study of the Cognitive Efficiency of Institutionalized Retardates.* Doctor's thesis, University of Southern California (Los Angeles, Calif.), 1964. (*DA* 25:2040)

268. BERMAN, ISAAC, AND RHONE, DORIS ELLEN. "Wechsler Scores VS. Piaget Levels: Cognitive Efficiency of Institutionalized Retardates." *Calif Mental Health Res Dig* 2:18 au '64. *

269. BEVERFELT, EVA; NYAARD, MARIT; AND NORDVIK, HILMAR. "Factor Analysis of Wechsler Adult Intelligence Scale Performance of Elderly Norwegians." *J Gerontol* 19:49–53 Ja '64. *

270. BUTLER, ALFRED J., AND CONRAD, W. GLENN. "Psychological Correlates of Abnormal Electroencephalographic Patterns in Familial Retardates." *J Clin Psychol* 20:338–43 Jl '64. * (*PA* 39:10572)

271. DENNERLL, RAYMOND D. "Prediction of Unilateral Brain Dysfunction Using Wechsler Test Scores." *J Consult Psychol* 28:278–84 Je '64. * (*PA* 39:5618)

272. DENNERLL, RAYMOND D.; DEN BROEDER, JOAN; AND SOKOLV, SHERWIN L. "WISC and WAIS Factors in Children and Adults With Epilepsy." *J Clin Psychol* 20:236–40 Ap '64. * (*PA* 39:8347)

273. FEINBERG, M. R., AND PENZER, W. N. "Factor Analysis of a Sales Selection Battery." *Personnel Psychol* 17:319–24 au '64. * (*PA* 39:8794)

274. FISKE, DONALD W.; CARTWRIGHT, DESMOND S.; AND KIRTNER, WILLIAM L. "Are Psychotherapeutic Changes Predictable?" *J Abn & Social Psychol* 69:418–26 O '64. * (*PA* 39:8058)

275. FITZHUGH, KATHLEEN B., AND FITZHUGH, LOREN C. "WAIS Results for Ss With Longstanding, Chronic, Lateralized and Diffuse Cerebral Dysfunction." *Percept & Motor Skills* 19:735–9 D '64. * (*PA* 39:8353)

276. FITZHUGH, LOREN C., AND FITZHUGH, KATHLEEN B. "Relationships Between Wechsler-Bellevue Form I and WAIS Performances of Subjects With Longstanding Cerebral Dysfunction." *Percept & Motor Skills* 19:539–43 O '64. * (*PA* 39:8348)

277. FOGEL, MAX L. "The Intelligence Quotient as an Index of Brain Damage." *Am J Orthopsychiatry* 34:555–62 Ap '64. *

278. GENDEL, HOWARD, AND RICE, WARREN. "Correlation of the Kent EGY With WAIS IQ's and Scaled Scores." *Newsl Res Psychol* 6:43–4 Ag '64. *

279. GERDINE, PHILIP VAN HORN, JR. *Patterns of Ego Function in Psychophysiological Skin Disorders.* Doctor's thesis, Boston University (Boston, Mass.), 1964. (*DA* 25:3108)

280. GUYETTE, ANNA; WAPNER, SEYMOUR; WERNER, HEINZ; AND DAVIDSON, JOHN. "Some Aspects of Space Perception in Mental Retardates." *Am J Mental Def* 69:90–100 Jl '64. * (*PA* 39:2514)

281. HAUGEN, EARL STUART. *A Study of the Validity of the WAIS, SCAT, and STEP As Predictors of Success in College Mathematics.* Doctor's research study No. 1, Colorado State College (Greeley, Colo.), 1964. (*DA* 28:124A)

282. HUFF, FREDERICK WARE. *Reliability of Clinical, Psychological Judgment as a Function of Information Presentation and Response Classification.* Doctor's thesis, University of Georgia (Athens, Ga.), 1964. (*DA* 25:3110)

283. HUNT, WILLIAM A.; SCHWARTZ, MELVIN L.; AND WALKER, RONALD E. "The Correctness of Diagnostic Judgment as a Function of Diagnostic Bias and Population Base Rate." *J Clin Psychol* 20:143–5 Ja '64. * (*PA* 39:10278)

284. JASTAK, J. F., AND JASTAK, S. R. "Short Forms of the WAIS and WISC Vocabulary Subtests." *J Clin Psychol* 20:167–99 Ap '64. * (*PA* 39:7820)

285. JOHNSON, JAMES J. *The Significance of Verbal Sub-Test Discrepancies on the Wechsler Tests.* Master's thesis, Illinois State University (Normal, Ill.), 1964.

286. JURKO, M. F., AND ANDY, O. J. "Psychological Aspects of Diencephalotomy." *J Neurol Neurosurg & Psychiatry* 27:516–21 D '64. * (*PA* 39:9508)

287. KENDRICK, D. C. "Assessment of Pre-Morbid Intelligence of Elderly Patients With Diffuse Brain Pathology." *Psychol Rep* 15:188 Ag '64. * (*PA* 39:1389)

288. KETTELL, MARJORIE EDYTHE. *Integrity of Ego Processes in Aged Females.* Doctor's thesis, Boston University (Boston, Mass.), 1964. (*DA* 25:3111)

289. KRIPPNER, STANLEY. "The Relationship Between MMPI and WAIS Masculinity-Femininity Scores." *Personnel & Guid J* 42:695–8 Mr '64. * (*PA* 39:5072)

290. LADD, CLAYTON E. "WAIS Performances of Brain Damaged and Neurotic Patients." *J Clin Psychol* 20:114–7 Ja '64. * (*PA* 39:10132)

291. LASKY, JULIAN J. "Relationships Between Measures of Ego Strength, Intelligence and Anxiety." *Newsl Res Psychol* 6:52–3 My '64. *

292. LEVINSON, BORIS M. "The 'Beat' Phenomenon in Wechsler Tests." *J Clin Psychol* 20:118–20 Ja '64. * (PA 39:10133)

293. LEVINSON, BORIS M. "A Comparative Study of the WAIS Performance of Native-Born Negro and White Homeless." *J Genetic Psychol* 105:211–8 D '64. * (PA 39:7562)

294. LUSZKI, WALTER ALOISE. *Degree of Hearing Loss Related to Intelligence as Measured by the WAIS and WISC.* Doctor's thesis, University of Georgia (Athens, Ga.), 1964. (DA 25:3113)

295. MAJUMDAR, P. K. "Wechsler-Bellevue Adult Intelligence Scale in a Foreign Language." *B Council Social & Psychol Res* 3:11–6 Jl '64. * (PA 40:2872)

296. MATARAZZO, JOSEPH D.; ALLEN, BERNADENE V.; SASLOW, GEORGE; AND WIENS, ARTHUR N. "Characteristics of Successful Policemen and Firemen Applicants." *J Appl Psychol* 48:123–33 Ap '64. * (PA 39:6047)

297. MONEY, JOHN. "Two Cytogenetic Syndromes: Psychologic Comparisons: 1, Intelligence and Specific-Factor Quotients." *J Psychiatric Res* 2:223–31 O '64. * (PA 39:15981)

298. NUNNALLY, JUM C. *Educational Measurement and Evaluation*, pp. 257–62. New York: McGraw-Hill Book Co., 1964. Pp. xv, 440. *

299. OLSEN, INGER A., AND JORDHEIM, GERALD D. "Use of W.A.I.S. in a Student Counseling Center." *Personnel & Guid J* 42:500–3 Ja '64. * (PA 39:5512)

300. QUERESHI, MOHAMMED Y. "Maximum Versus Minimum Testing: A Problem in Individual Appraisal." *Univ N Dak Col Ed Rec* 49:89–92 Mr '64. *

301. SHAW, DALE JEAN. *An Analysis of Wechsler Adult Intelligence Scale Protocols of Students in a Midwestern University.* Doctor's thesis, Purdue University (Lafayette, Ind.), 1964. (DA 26:1175)

302. SWENSON, EDWIN WAYNE. *A Comparison of the Wechsler-Bellevue, Form I, and the Wechsler Adult Intelligence Scale for a Population of Average Intelligence.* Master's thesis, University of Utah (Salt Lake City, Utah), 1964.

303. TOLOR, ALEXANDER. "Abstract Ability in Organics and Schizophrenics." *J Proj Tech & Pers Assess* 28:357–62 S '64. * (PA 39:8520)

304. WALKER, RONALD E., AND SPENCE, JANET TAYLOR. "Relationship Between Digit Span and Anxiety." *J Consult Psychol* 28:220–3 Je '64. * (PA 39:5245)

305. WATSON, CHARLES GORDON. *Differences Between Brain-Damaged and Schizophrenic Patients in Three Aspects of Wechsler Adult Intelligence Scale Performance.* Doctor's thesis, University of Iowa (Iowa City, Iowa), 1964. (DA 25:1348)

306. WEBB, ALLEN P. "Some Issues Relating to the Validity of the WAIS in Assessing Mental Retardation." *Calif J Ed Res* 15:130–5 My '64. * (PA 39:5672)

307. WHEELER, LAWRENCE. "Complex Behavioral Indicies Weighted by Linear Discriminant Functions for the Prediction of Cerebral Damage." *Percept & Motor Skills* 19:907–23 D '64. * (PA 39:8357)

308. WOLK, ROBERT L., AND RUSTIN, STANLEY L. "Psychologic Evaluation of Gerontologic Population: Comparison of Results With the Raven Progressive Matrices (1947) Versus the Wechsler Adult Intelligence Scale." *J Am Geriatrics Soc* 12:807–9 Ag '64. *

309. BERKOWITZ, BERNARD, AND GREEN, RUSSEL F. "Changes in Intellect With Age: 5, Differential Changes as Functions of Time Interval and Original Score." *J Genetic Psychol* 107:179–92 D '65. * (PA 40:5284)

310. BERNSTEIN, ALVIN S.; KLEIN, EDWARD B.; BERGER, LESLIE; AND COHEN, JACOB. "Relationship Between Institutionalization, Other Demographic Variables, and the Structure of Intelligence in Chronic Schizophrenics." *J Consult Psychol* 29:320–4 Ag '65. * (PA 39:16181)

311. BLATT, SIDNEY J.; ALLISON, JOEL; AND BAKER, BRUCE L. "The Wechsler Object Assembly Subtest and Bodily Concerns." *J Consult Psychol* 29:223–30 Je '65. * (PA 39:12225)

312. CARLISLE, A. L. "Quick Test Performance by Institutional Retardates." *Psychol Rep* 17:489–90 O '65. * (PA 40:886)

313. CASTELL, J. H. F., AND MITTLER, P. J. "Intelligence of Patients in Subnormality Hospitals: A Survey of Admissions in 1961." *Brit J Psychiatry* 111:219–25 Mr '65. * (PA 39:10453)

314. CONRY, ROBERT, AND PLANT, WALTER T. "WAIS and Group Test Predictions of an Academic Success •Criterion: High School and College." *Ed & Psychol Meas* 25:493–500 su '65. * (PA 39:15216)

315. COSLETT, STEPHEN B. "The WAIS Masculinity-Femininity Index in a Paranoid Schizophrenic Population." *J Clin Psychol* 21:62 Ja '65. * (PA 39:12840)

316. CRAFT, MICHAEL. Chap. 3, "Diagnosis and Aetiology Illustrated by an Analysis of Admissions to a Psychopathic Unit," pp. 32–54. In *Ten Studies Into Psychopathic Personality: A Report to the Home Office and the Mental Health Research Fund.* Bristol, England: John Wright & Sons Ltd., 1965. Pp. 133. *

317. DE MILAN, JEAN. "Bilingualism and the Wechsler Vocabulary Scales." *J Clin Psychol* 21:298 Jl '65. * (PA 39:15346)

318. DOYLE, EDWARD D. *A Comparison of IQ's on the WAIS and Q.T. With a Group of Spinal Cord Injury Patients.* Master's thesis, Loyola University (Chicago, Ill.), 1965.

319. EDWARDS, HENRY P. *EEG and WAIS Intelligence in a Sample of Cultural-Familial Deficients.* Master's thesis, University of Ottawa (Ottawa, Ont., Canada), 1965.

320. FOGEL, MAX L. "The Proverbs Test in the Appraisal of Cerebral Disease." *J General Psychol* 72:269–75 Ap '65. * (PA 39:12281)

321. FOGEL, MAX L., AND BLUMKLOTZ, F. PETER. "Effects of Different Training Tasks on Digit Symbol Performance." *J Clin Psychol* 21:109–11 Ja '65. * (PA 39:12318)

322. GIBEAU, PHILIP JOSEPH. *Field Dependency and the Process-Reactive Dimension in Schizophrenia.* Doctor's thesis, Purdue University (Lafayette, Ind.), 1965. (DA 26:1775)

323. GREEN, HARRY BRUCE, JR. *A Statistical Comparison of the Wechsler Intelligence Scale for Children and the Wechsler Adult Intelligence Scale.* Doctor's thesis, University of Virginia (Charlottesville, Va.), 1965. (DA 26:5866) (Abstract: *Ed R* 3:61–3)

324. GREENWOOD, DENNIS I., AND TAYLOR, CHARLES. "Adaptive Testing in an Older Population." *J Psychol* 60:193–8 Jl '65. * (PA 40:32)

325. HALLENBECK, CHARLES E.; FINK, STEPHEN L.; AND GROSSMAN, JOEL S. "Measurement of Intellectual Inefficiency." *Psychol Rep* 17:339–49 O '65. * (PA 40:1590)

326. HAMLIN, ROY M., AND WARD, WILLIAM D. "Aging, Hospitalization, and Schizophrenic Intelligence." Abstract. *Proc Ann Conv Am Psychol Assn* 73:221–2 '65. * (PA 39:16202)

327. HASKELL, SIMON H. "The Use of the Shortened Form of the W.A.I.S. With Cerebral Palsied Adults." *Int Copenhagen Congr Sci Study Mental Retard* 1964:636–41 ['65]. *

328. HENNING, JOHN J. *Analysis of Examiner Variance on the Wechsler Adult Intelligence Scale.* Master's thesis, Loyola University (Chicago, Ill.), 1965.

329. HIMELSTEIN, PHILIP. "College Failure on the WAIS 'Population' Item." *Psychol Rep* 17:824 D '65. * (PA 40:4215)

330. HOLMES, DOUGLAS S.; ARMSTRONG, HUBERT E., JR.; JOHNSON, MONTY H.; AND RIES, HAROLD A. "Further Evaluation on an Abbreviated Form of the WAIS." *Psychol Rep* 16:1163–4 Je '65. * (PA 39:15238)

331. KABACK, GOLDIE RUTH. "A Comparison of WAIS, Binet, and WISC Test Results of Mentally Retarded Young Adults Born in New York City and Puerto Rico." *Training Sch B* 62:108–12 N '65. * (PA 40:2138)

332. KAHN, MARVIN W. "A Factor-Analytic Study of Personality, Intelligence, and History Characteristics of Murderers." Abstract. *Proc Ann Conv Am Psychol Assn* 73:227–8 '65. * (PA 39:16125)

333. KENNEDY, WALLACE A., AND WALSH, JOHN. "A Factor Analysis of Mathematical Giftedness." *Psychol Rep* 17:115–9 Ag '65. * (PA 40:1553)

334. KNOX, WILMA J. "The Effects of Alcoholic Overindulgence on Selected WAIS Sub-Test Scores in Domiciliary Members." *Newsl Res Psychol* 7:33–5 Ag '65. *

335. KOLE, DELBERT M., AND MATARAZZO, JOSEPH D. "Intellectual and Personality Characteristics of Two Classes of Medical Students." *J Med Ed* 40:1130–44 D '65. *

336. KRAMER, ERNEST, AND FRANCIS, PAUL S. "Errors in Intelligence Estimation With Short Forms of the WAIS." Abstract. *J Consult Psychol* 29:490 O '65. *

337. KRAUS, J. "Cattell Anxiety Scale Scores and WAIS Attainment in Three Groups of Psychiatric Patients." *Austral J Psychol* 17:229–32 D '65. * (PA 40:5451)

338. KRAUS, J. "Psychiatric Classification and Differential Value of WAIS Subtest Scores." *Austral J Psychol* 17:137–9 Ag '65. * (PA 40:894)

339. KRAUS, J., AND SELECKI, B. R. "Brain Atrophy and Assessment of Intellectual Deterioration on the Wechsler Adult Intelligence Scale." *J Nerv & Mental Dis* 141:119–22 Jl '65. * (PA 40:2468)

340. KROSKE, WILLIAM H.; FRETWELL, LORETTA N.; AND CUPP, MARION E. "Comparison of the Kahn Intelligence Tests: Experimental Form, the Stanford-Binet and the WAIS for Familial Retardates." *Percept & Motor Skills* 21:428 O '65. * (PA 40:3310)

341. LEVINSON, BORIS M. "Note on the Intelligence and WAIS Pattern of White First-Time Applicants for Shelter Care." *Psychol Rep* 16:524 Ap '65. * (PA 39:10602)

342. LUSZKI, WALTER A. "Hearing Loss and Intelligence Among Retardates." *Am J Mental Def* 70:93–101 Jl '65. * (PA 39:16056)

343. MCKEEVER, WALTER F.; MAY, PHILIP R. A.; AND TUMA, A. HUSSAIN. "Prognosis in Schizophrenia: Prediction of Length of Hospitalization From Psychological Test Variables." *J Clin Psychol* 21:214–21 Ap '65. * (PA 39:12856)

344. MEER, BERNARD, AND BAKER, JANET A. "Reliability of Measurements of Intellectual Functioning of Geriatric Patients." *J Gerontol* 20:410–4 Jl '65. *

345. NEWTON, G. MACKIE. "A Comparison of the Immediate Test and WAIS Verbal Scale in Vocational Rehabilitation Use." *J Clin Psychol* 21:300 Jl '65. * (PA 39:15368)

346. OGILVIE, ROBERT D. "Correlations Between the Quick Test (QT) and the Wechsler Adult Intelligence Scale (WAIS) as Used in a Clinical Setting." *Psychol Rep* 16:497–8 Ap '65. * (PA 39:10081)

347. PASRICHA, PREM, AND PAGEDAR, RAJANI M. "Item

347. Analysis of the Translation and Adaptation of WAIS for a Gujarati Speaking Population." *J Voc & Ed Guid* 11:12–7 F '65. * (PA 39:10243)

348. PETTIT, DONALD E. "A Note on the Satz-Mogel WAIS Abbreviation for Prison Populations." *Can J Correct* 7:111 Ja '65. *

349. PRADO, WILLIAM M., AND SCHNADT, FREDERICK. "Differences in WAIS—WB Functioning of Three Psychiatric Groups." *J Clin Psychol* 21:184–6 Ap '65. * (PA 39:12305)

350. RAMALINGASWAMI, PRABHA. "The Use of Block Design Test Among Illiterate Low Economic Group of People." *Indian J Psychol* 40:153–60 D '65. * (PA 40:11666)

351. SCHWARTZ, MARK S. "Relationships Between the Kent EGY and WAIS Scores, Functioning Levels and Subtests in a Veterans Neuropsychiatric Population." *Newsl Res Psychol* 7:8–9 My '65. *

352. SEGAL, STANLEY J.; NACHMANN, BARBARA; AND MOULTON, ROBERT. "The Wechsler Adult Intelligence Scale (WAIS) in the Counseling of Students With Learning Disorders." *Personnel & Guid J* 43:1018–23 Je '65. * (PA 39:16432)

353. SHAW, DALE J. "Sexual Bias in the WAIS." *J Consult Psychol* 29:590–1 D '65. * (PA 40:2874)

354. SMART, REGINALD G. "The Relationships Between Intellectual Deterioration, Extraversion and Neuroticism Among Chronic Alcoholics." *J Clin Psychol* 21:27–9 Ja '65. * (PA 39:12771)

355. SMITH, LAURENCE C., JR. "The Effects of Heat Stroke on Cognitive Functioning." *Proc Ann Conf Air Force Behav Sci* 11:130–42 Jl '65. *

356. STONE, LEROY A., AND RAMER, JOHN C. "Estimating WAIS IQ From Shipley Scale Scores: Another Cross-Validation." *J Clin Psychol* 21:297 Jl '65. * (PA 39:15276)

357. TEMMER, HELENA W. "Wechsler Intelligence Scores and Bender-Gestalt Performance in Adult Male Mental Defectives." *Am J Mental Def* 70:142–7 Jl '65. * (PA 39:16070)

358. WACHTEL, PAUL L., AND BLATT, SIDNEY J. "Energy Deployment and Achievement." *J Consult Psychol* 29:302–8 Ag '65. * (PA 39:16395)

359. WALKER, RONALD E.; HUNT, WILLIAM A.; AND SCHWARTZ, MELVIN L. "The Difficulty of WAIS Comprehension Scoring." *J Clin Psychol* 21:427–9 O '65. * (PA 40:1555)

360. WALKER, RONALD E.; NEILSEN, MARY KAY; AND NICOLAY, ROBERT C. "The Effects of Failure and Anxiety on Intelligence Test Performance." *J Clin Psychol* 21:400–2 O '65. * (PA 40:1556)

361. WATSON, CHARLES G. "Intratest Scatter in Hospitalized Brain-Damaged and Schizophrenic Patients." Abstract. *J Consult Psychol* 29:596 D '65. *

362. WATSON, CHARLES G. "WAIS Error Types in Schizophrenics and Organics." *Psychol Rep* 16:527–30 Ap '65. * (PA 39:10164)

363. WATSON, CHARLES G. "WAIS Profile Patterns of Hospitalized Brain-Damaged and Schizophrenic Patients." *J Clin Psychol* 21:294–5 Jl '65. * (PA 39:15377)

364. WHITE, J. GRAHAM, AND KNOX, S. J. "Some Psychological Correlates of Age and Dementia." *Brit J Social & Clin Psychol* 4:259–65 D '65. * (PA 40:4114)

365. WILLNER, ALLEN, AND REITZ, WILLARD. "Association as an Essential Variable in Tests of Abstract Reasoning." Abstract. *Proc Ann Conv Am Psychol Assn* 73:287–8 '65. * (PA 39:14009)

366. ZYTOWSKI, DONALD G., AND HUDSON, JACQUELINE. "The Validity of Split-Half Abbreviations of the WAIS." *J Clin Psychol* 21:292–4 Jl '65. * (PA 39:15284)

367. ABRAMS, STANLEY, AND NATHANSON, IRA A. "Intellectual Deficit in Schizophrenia: Stable or Progressive." *Dis Nerv System* 27:115–7 F '66. *

368. AFFLECK, D. CRAIG, AND FREDERICKSON, WILBUR K. "Testing Limits of WAIS Picture Arrangement Test." *Am J Mental Def* 70:605–6 Ja '66. * (PA 40:5863)

369. BERRY, ROSE AUERSPERG. *An Analysis of the Relationship Between Certain Variables of Students With Behavioral Disorders and Successful Completion of Vocational Training.* Doctor's thesis, University of Arkansas (Fayetteville, Ark.), 1966. (DA 27:1194A)

370. BINGHAM, WILLIAM C.; BURKE, HENRY R.; AND MURRAY, STEWART. "Raven's Progressive Matrices: Construct Validity." *J Psychol* 62:205–9 Mr '66. * (PA 40:7203)

371. BLATT, BENJAMIN, AND TSUSHIMA, WILLIAM. "A Psychological Study of Uremic Patients Being Considered for the Artificial Kidney Machine Programs (Hemodialysis)." *Newsl Res Psychol* 8:17–8 F '66. *

372. BLAZER, JOHN A. "Leg Position and Psychological Characteristics in Women." *Psychol* 3:5–12 Ag '66. * (PA 40:12361)

373. BOLTON, N.; BRITTON, P. G.; AND SAVAGE, R. D. "Some Normative Data on the WAIS and Its Indices in an Aged Population." *J Clin Psychol* 22:184–8 Ap '66. * (PA 40:7204)

374. BRITTON, P. G., AND SAVAGE, R. D. "A Short Form of the WAIS for Use With the Aged." *Brit J Psychiatry* 112:417–8 Ap '66. * (PA 40:9428)

375. CHANSKY, NORMAN M. "Measuring the Intelligence and Achievement of School Dropouts With the Benton Visual Retention Test." *Am J Mental Def* 71:191–5 S '66. * (PA 40:13186)

376. CRADDICK, RAY A. "WISC and WAIS IQs as a Function of Season of Birth." *Psychol Rep* 18:259–64 F '66. * (PA 40:6626)

377. DICKSTEIN, LOUIS S., AND BLATT, SIDNEY J. "Death Concern, Futurity, and Anticipation." *J Consult Psychol* 30:11–7 F '66. * (PA 40:4230)

378. DOHERTY, MARY AUSTIN, AND WALKER, RONALD E. "The Relationship of Personality Characteristics, Awareness, and Attitude in a Verbal Conditioning Situation." *J Personality* 34:504–16 D '66. *

379. EDWARDS, GENE A. "Anxiety Correlates of the Wechsler Adult Intelligence Scale." *Calif J Ed Res* 17:144–7 My '66. * (PA 40:10099)

380. FLYNN, WILLIAM F. "How Biased Was This Sample?" *Newsl Res Psychol* 8:45–7 N '66. *

381. FRIEDMAN, JOEL. *The Relationship Between Intelligence and Channel Capacity.* Doctor's thesis, Texas Technological College (Lubbock, Tex.), 1966. (DA 28:1191B)

382. GATHERCOLE, C. E. "I.Q. Scores and the Problem of Classification." Letter. *Brit J Psychiatry* 112:1181–2 N '66. *

383. GUERTIN, WILSON H.; LADD, CLAYTON E.; FRANK, GEORGE H.; RABIN, ALBERT I.; AND HIESTER, DOUGLAS S. "Research With the Wechsler Intelligence Scales for Adults: 1960–1965." *Psychol B* 66:385–409 N '66. * (PA 41:40)

384. HIGBEE, WALTER R. "Supervisors as Raters in the Assessment of Workshop Performance of Retarded Sheltered Employees." *Am J Mental Def* 71:447–50 N '66. * (PA 41:1838)

385. HIRSCHENFANG, SAMUEL, AND BENTON, JOSEPH G. "Note on Intellectual Changes in Multiple Sclerosis." *Percept & Motor Skills* 22:786 Je '66. * (PA 40:11405)

386. HOLDEN, RAYMOND H.; MENDELSON, MARTIN A.; AND DEVAULT, SPENCER. "Relationship of the WAIS to the SRA Non-Verbal Test Scores." *Psychol Rep* 19:987–90 D '66. * (PA 41:3721)

387. HOLMES, DOUGLAS S.; ARMSTRONG, HUBERT E., JR.; JOHNSON, MONTY H.; AND RIES, HAROLD A. "Validity and Clinical Utility of the Satz and Mogel Abbreviated Form of the WAIS." *Psychol Rep* 18:992–4 Je '66. * (PA 40:9435)

388. HOROWITZ, FRANCES DEGEN. "The Relationship Between Wechsler Intelligence Quotients and Parsons Language-Sample Scores of Mentally Retarded Children." *J Genetic Psychol* 108:59–63 Mr '66. * (PA 40:10400)

389. HUNT, WILLIAM A., AND WALKER, RONALD E. "Validity of Diagnostic Judgment as a Function of Amount of Test Information." *J Clin Psychol* 22:154–5 Ap '66. * (PA 40:7847)

390. HUNT, WILLIAM A.; QUAY, HERBERT C.; AND WALKER, RONALD E. "The Validity of Clinical Judgments of Asocial Tendency." *J Clin Psychol* 22:116–8 Ja '66. * (PA 40:4410)

391. JENNINGS, CHARLES L. "The Hewson Ratios Revisited via the WAIS." *Proc Ann Conf Air Force Behav Sci* 13:181–94 S '66. *

392. JOSLIN, HANNAH FAE. *Intelligence and Social Awareness: An Investigation of the Relationship Between Social Awareness, Planfulness and Performance on the Wechsler Picture Arrangement Subtests.* Doctor's thesis, New York University (New York, N.Y.), 1966. (DA 27:2871B)

393. KLØVE, H., AND MATTHEWS, C. G. "Psychometric and Adaptive Abilities in Epilepsy With Differential Etiology." *Epilepsia* 7:330–8 D '66. *

394. KRAUS, J. "On the Method of Indirect Assessment of Intellectual Impairment: A Modified WAIS Index." *J Clin Psychol* 22:66–9 Ja '66. * (PA 40:4216)

395. LEVINSON, BORIS M. "A Comparative Study of Northern and Southern Negro Homeless Men." *J Negro Ed* 35:144–50 sp '66. * (PA 44:10415)

396. LIBOWITZ, JUSTUS M. *The Effect of the Perceived Degree of Examiner Congruence Upon WAIS IQs.* Doctor's thesis, Yeshiva University (New York, N.Y.), 1966. (DA 28:1167B)

397. LUSZKI, MARGARET B.; DAWES, ROBYN M.; SCHULTZ, WILLIAM; AND LAYWELL, H. ROBERT. "A Study of an Abbreviated Form of the Wechsler Adult Intelligence Scale." *Newsl Res Psychol* 8:14–5 N '66. *

398. LUSZKI, WALTER A. "An Idiot Savant on the WAIS?" *Psychol Rep* 19:603–9 O '66. * (PA 41:719)

399. MCKERRACHER, D. W., AND SCOTT, J. "I.Q. Scores and the Problem of Classification: A Comparison of the W.A.I.S. and S-B, Form L-M in a Group of Subnormal and Psychopathic Patients." *Brit J Psychiatry* 112:537–41 Je '66. * (PA 40:10101)

400. MATTHEWS, C. G.; SHAW, D. J.; AND KLØVE, H. "Psychological Test Performances in Neurologic and 'Pseudo-Neurologic' Subjects." *Cortex* 2:244–53 Ap '66. * (PA 41:672)

401. MEIER, MANFRED J., AND RESCH, JOSEPH A. "Behavioral Correlates of Short-Term Change in Neurological Status Following Acute Onset of Cerebrovascular Symptomatology." *J Clin Psychol* 22:156–9 Ap '66. * (PA 40:8003)

402. MILLS, DAVID H., AND TUCKER, LEDYARD R. "A Three-Mode Factor Analysis of Clinical Judgment of Schizophrenicity." *J Clin Psychol* 22:136–9 Ap '66. * (PA 40:7913)

403. MONROE, KENTON L. "Note on the Estimation of the WAIS Full Scale IQ." *J Clin Psychol* 22:79–81 Ja '66. * (PA 40:4217)

404. MORGAN, DONALD W. "WAIS 'Analytic Index' and Rehospitalization of Schizophrenic Servicemen." *J Consult Psychol* 30:267–9 Je '66. * (PA 40:9052)

405. NORMAN, RALPH D. "A Revised Deterioration Formula

for the Wechsler Adult Intelligence Scale." *J Clin Psychol* 22:287–94 Jl '66. * (*PA* 40:11293)

406. PAYNE, DAVID A., AND LEHMAN, IRVIN J. "A Brief WAIS Item Analysis." *J Clin Psychol* 22:296–7 Jl '66. * (*PA* 40:10635)

407. RADCLIFFE, J. A. "WAIS Factorial Structure and Factor Scores for Ages 18 to 54." *Austral J Psychol* 18:228–38 D '66. * (*PA* 41:3699)

408. REITZ, WILLARD E. "Association, Abstraction, and Intelligence." Abstract. *Proc 74th Ann Conv Am Psychol Assn* 1:239–40 '66. * (*PA* 41:5959)

409. RUSALEM, HERBERT; LIPTON, ROBERT; AND GOLDSAMT, MILTON. "Changes in Psychologic Test (WAIS) Scores of Older Disabled Persons During a Vocational Rehabilitation Program." *J Am Geriatrics Soc* 14:875–8 Ag '66. *

410. SANNITO, THOMAS C., AND HANNUM, THOMAS E. "Relationship Between the WAIS and Indices of Sociopathy in an Incarcerated Female Population." *J Res Crime & Del* 3:63–70 Ja '66. *

411. SAXE, ETTA LOU GLUCKSTEIN. *Intra-Test Scatter on the WAIS as a Diagnostic Sign: A Comparison of Schizophrenic, Neurotic, and Normal Groups.* Doctor's thesis, University of Michigan (Ann Arbor, Mich.), 1966. (*DA* 27:2517B)

412. SCHALON, CHARLES LAWRENCE. *Performance Following Failure Stress as a Function of Level of Self-Esteem.* Doctor's thesis, University of Iowa (Iowa City, Iowa), 1966. (*DA* 27:3296B)

413. SCHILL, THOMAS. "The Effects of MMPI Social Introversion on WAIS PA Performance." *J Clin Psychol* 22:72–4 Ja '66. * (*PA* 40:4239)

414. SCHWARTZ, MELVIN L. "The Scoring of WAIS Comprehension Responses by Experienced and Inexperienced Judges." *J Clin Psychol* 22:425–7 O '66. * (*PA* 41:2267)

415. SIMS, NEIL B., AND CLOWER, ROBERT P. "Correlation Between WAIS IQ's and 16 PF B Factor Scores of General Hospital Patients." *Newsl Res Psychol* 8:10–1 My '66. *

416. SMITH, AARON. "Talkers and Doers, or Education, Intelligence, and WAIS Verbal-Performance Ratios in Psychiatric Patients." Abstract. *Proc 74th Ann Conv Am Psychol Assn* 1:233–4 '66. * (*PA* 41:5975)

417. SPRAGUE, ROBERT L., AND QUAY, HERBERT C. "A Factor Analytic Study of the Responses of Mental Retardates on the WAIS." *Am J Mental Def* 70:595–600 Ja '66. * (*PA* 40:5891)

418. SPREEN, OTFRIED, AND ANDERSON, CHARLES W. G. "Sibling Relationship and Mental Deficiency Diagnosis as Reflected in Wechsler Test Patterns." *Am J Mental Def* 71:406–10 N '66. * (*PA* 41:1850)

419. STERNBERG, DAVID, AND SCHIFF, STANLEY. "Reality Checking Ability and Cognitive Functioning in Functional Psychiatric Disorders." *Psychiatric Q Sup* 40:306–14 pt 2 '66. * (*PA* 41:16823)

420. STERNE, DAVID M. "The Knox Cubes as a Test of Memory and Intelligence With Male Adults." *J Clin Psychol* 22:191–3 Ap '66. * (*PA* 40:7219)

421. TAYLOR, JAMES B. "The Use of Human Figure Drawings With the Upper Level Mentally Retarded." *Am J Mental Def* 71:423–6 N '66. * (*PA* 41:1851)

422. THOMAS, CHARLES A., JR. "The 'Yell Fire' Response as an Indicator of Impaired Impulse Control." *J Clin Psychol* 22:221–3 Ap '66. * (*PA* 40:7720)

423. THUNE, JEANNE; TINE, SEBASTIAN; AND CHERRY, NANCY. "Personality Characteristics of Successful Older Leaders." *J Gerontol* 21:463–70 Jl '66. *

424. VEALE, SARA OSTEEN. *Evaluating Two Approaches to Remedial Reading and Analyzing WAIS Profiles of Participants in DeKalb College.* Doctor's thesis, University of Georgia (Athens, Ga.), 1966. (*DA* 27:3325A)

425. VELLUTINO, FRANK R., AND HOGAN, TERRENCE P. "The Relationship Between the Ammons and WAIS Test Performances of Unselected Psychiatric Subjects." *J Clin Psychol* 22:69–71 Ja '66. * (*PA* 40:4221)

426. WATSON, CHARLES G. "Evidence on the Utilities of Three WAIS Short Forms." Abstract. *J Consult Psychol* 30:181 Ap '66. *

427. WEINER, IRVING B. *Psychodiagnosis in Schizophrenia.* New York: John Wiley & Sons, Inc., 1966. Pp. xiv, 573. * (*PA* 41:4753)

428. WILLNER, A. E., AND REITZ, W. E. "Association, Abstraction, and the Conceptual Organization of Recall: Implications for Clinical Tests." *J Abn Psychol* 71:315–27 O '66. * (*PA* 40:13178)

429. WILLNER, ALLEN E. "Associative Meaning and Vocabulary Tests." Abstract. *Proc 74th Ann Conv Am Psychol Assn* 1:241–2 '66. * (*PA* 41:5979)

430. WITKIN, HERMAN A.; FATERSON, HANNA F.; GOODENOUGH, DONALD R.; AND BIRNBAUM, JUDITH. "Cognitive Patterning in Mildly Retarded Boys." *Child Develop* 37:301–16 Je '66. * (*PA* 40:9184)

431. ABIDIN, RICHARD R., JR., AND BYRNE, ALFRED V. "Quick Test Validation Study and Examination of Form Equivalency." *Psychol Rep* 20:735–9 Je '67. * (*PA* 41:13591)

432. ANDERSON, HARRY E., JR.; KERN, FRANK E.; AND COOK, CHARLOTTE. "Correlational and Normative Data for the Progressive Matrices With Retarded Populations." *J Psychol* 67:221–5 N '67. * (*PA* 42:1396)

433. BAER, P.; MERRYMAN, P.; AND GAITZ, C. "Performance Deficit Related to Chronic Brain Syndrome, Schizophrenia and Age." *Gerontologist* 7(3, pt 2):37 S '67. * (*PA* 41:16721)

434. BERKE, NORMAN DANIEL. *An Investigation of Adult Negro Illiteracy: Prediction of Reading Achievement and Description of Educational Characteristics of a Sample of City Core Adult Negro Illiterates.* Doctor's thesis, State University of New York (Buffalo, N.Y.), 1967. (*DA* 28:931A)

435. BLATT, SIDNEY J., AND QUINLAN, PAUL. "Punctual and Procrastinating Students: A Study of Temporal Parameters." *J Consult Psychol* 31:169–74 Ap '67. * (*PA* 41:7317)

436. BRIGHAM, BRUCE W. *A Study of the Reading Achievement and Certain Characteristics of Adult Males Convicted of Felonies.* Doctor's thesis, Temple University (Philadelphia, Pa.), 1967. (*DA* 28:4279B)

437. BRITTON, PETER G.; BERGMANN, KLAUS; KAY, DAVID W. K.; AND SAVAGE, R. DOUGLASS. "Mental State, Cognitive Functioning, Physical Health, and Social Class in the Community Aged." *J Gerontol* 22:517–21 O '67. *

438. BROWN, ORIL. "Relation of WAIS Verbal and Performance IQs for Four Psychiatric Conditions." *Psychol Rep* 20:1015–20 Je '67. * (*PA* 41:13951)

439. BUDOFF, MILTON. "Learning Potential Among Institutionalized Young Adult Retardates." *Am J Mental Def* 72:404–11 N '67. * (*PA* 42:7631)

440. BURNAND, G.; HUNTER, H.; AND HOGGART, K. "Some Psychological Test Characteristics of Klinefelter's Syndrome." *Brit J Psychiatry* 113:1091–6 O '67. * (*PA* 42:7632)

441. CATE, CLARENCE C. "Test Behavior of ESL Students." *Calif J Ed Res* 18:184–7 S '67. * (*PA* 42:4480)

442. DE LINT, JAN. "Note on Birth Order and Intelligence Test Performance." *J Psychol* 66:15–7 My '67. * (*PA* 41:10444)

443. DICKSTEIN, LOUIS S., AND BLATT, SIDNEY J. "The WAIS Picture Arrangement Subtest as a Measure of Anticipation." *J Proj Tech & Pers Assess* 31:32–8 Je '67. * (*PA* 41:13613)

444. DOORBAR, RUTH RAE. "Psychological Testing of Transsexuals: A Brief Report of Results from the Wechsler Adult Intelligence Scale, the Thematic Apperception Test, and the House-Tree-Person Test." *Trans N Y Acad Sci* 29:455–62 F '67. * (*PA* 41:16827)

445. DOTY, BARBARA A. "Some Academic Characteristics of the Mature Coed." *J Ed Res* 61:163–5 D '67. *

446. DUKE, ROBERT B. "Intellectual Evaluation of Brain-Damaged Patients With a WAIS Short Form." Abstract. *Psychol Rep* 20:858 Je '67. *

447. EBER, HERBERT W. "The Factor Structure of the WAIS-Verbal and HIS-Test Combination." *J Ed Res* 61:27–8 S '67. *

448. GAMEWELL, JOYCE. *An Investigation of the Use of Two Instruments for Assessing Intellective and Nonintellective Aspects of Intelligence as Predictors of Post Degree Success of Psychology Graduate Students.* Doctor's thesis, Colorado State College (Greeley, Colo.), 1967. (*DA* 28:3022A)

449. GIBSON, JOHN, AND LIGHT, PHYLLIS. "Intelligence Among University Scientists." *Nature* 213:441–3 F 4 '67. * (*PA* 41:11916)

450. GILBERSTADT, HAROLD, AND SAKO, YOSHIO. "Intellectual and Personality Changes Following Open-Heart Surgery." *Arch Gen Psychiatry* 16:210–4 F '67. * (*PA* 41:7763)

451. GILMAN, ROBERT H. *A Study of Intellectual Change of Deaf Students as Measured by Standard Tests of Intelligence.* Master's thesis, Springfield College (Springfield, Mass.), 1967.

452. GOLDSTEIN, STEVEN G., AND LUNDY, CHARLES T. "Utilization of the Wechsler Adult Intelligence Scale (WAIS) in Predicting Success With Low Average High School Students." *Ed & Psychol Meas* 27:457–61 su '67. * (*PA* 41:14216)

453. GRISSO, J. THOMAS, AND MEADOW, ARNOLD. "Test Interference in a Rorschach-WAIS Administration Sequence." *J Consult Psychol* 31:382–6 Ag '67. * (*PA* 41:13617)

454. GROTELUESCHEN, ARDEN, AND LYONS, THOMAS J. "Quick Word Test Validity With Adults." *Psychol Rep* 20:488–90 Ap '67. * (*PA* 41:8151)

455. HARONIAN, FRANK, AND SAUNDERS, DAVID R. "Some Intellectual Correlates of Physique: A Review and a Study." *J Psychol Studies* 15:57–105 Je '67. *

456. HARWOOD, B. THOMAS. "Some Intellectual Correlates of Schizoid Indicators: WAIS and MMPI." Abstract. *J Consult Psychol* 31:218 Ap '67. *

457. HENNING, JOHN J., AND LEVY, RUSSELL H. "Verbal-Performance IQ Differences of White and Negro Delinquents on the WISC and WAIS." *J Clin Psychol* 23:164–8 Ap '67. * (*PA* 41:9127)

458. JONES, REGINALD L. "Validities of Short WAIS Batteries." Abstract. *J Consult Psychol* 31:103 F '67. *

459. JURJEVICH, R. M. "Intellectual Assessment With Gorham's Proverbs Test, Raven's Progressive Matrices, and WAIS." *Psychol Rep* 20:1285–6 Je '67. * (*PA* 41:15271)

460. KAUFMAN, HARVEY ISIDORE. *Cognitive and Noncognitive Indices of Employability in a Sampling of 17 to 21 Year Old Mentally Retarded Individuals.* Doctor's thesis, Marquette University (Milwaukee, Wis.), 1967. (*DA* 28:3027A)

461. KLAPPER, ZELDA S., AND BIRCH, HERBERT G. "A Fourteen Year Follow-Up Study of Cerebral Palsy: Intellectual Changes and Stability." *Am J Orthopsychiatry* 37:540–7 Ap '67. *

462. KRAUS, J., AND SELECKI, B. R. "Assessment of Laterality in Diffuse Cerebral Atrophy Using the WAIS." *J Clin Psychol* 23:91–2 Ja '67. * (*PA* 41:5958)

463. LABAK, ALEX S. *A Comparative Study of Three Short Individual Intelligence Tests, Using the Wechsler Adult Intelligence Scale as a Validating Criterion, With a Selected Group of Slow Learners.* Master's thesis, Moorehead State College (Moorehead, Minn.), 1967.

464. LASSMAN, FRANK M., AND ENGELBART, ELAINE S. "Methodology in Digit Memory Testing of College Students." *J Speech & Hearing Res* 10:268–76 Je '67. * (*PA* 41:15819)

465. LOWE, C. MARSHALL. "Prediction of Posthospital Work Adjustment by the Use of Psychological Tests." *J Counsel Psychol* 14:248–52 My '67. * (*PA* 41:9197)

466. LUSZKI, MARGARET B.; SCHULTZ, WILLIAM; LAYWELL, H. ROBERT; AND DAWES, ROBYN M. "A Study of an Abbreviated Form of the Wechsler Adult Intelligence Scale." *Newsl Res Psychol* 9:39–41 My '67. *

467. MCCARTHY, DOROTHEA; SCHIRO, FREDERICK M.; AND SUDIMACK, JOHN P. "Comparison of WAIS *M-F* Index With Two Measures of Masculinity-Femininity." *J Consult Psychol* 31:639–40 D '67. * (*PA* 42:2587)

468. MCDONALD, K. G., AND CROOKES, T. G. "The WAIS Picture Arrangement Test in British Psychiatric Patients." *Brit J Social & Clin Psychol* 6:72 F '67. *

469. MATTHEWS, C. G., AND KLØVE, H. "Differential Psychological Performances in Major Motor, Psychomotor, and Mixed Seizure Classifications of Known and Unknown Etiology." *Epilepsia* 8:117–28 Je '67. *

470. MONEY, JOHN, AND EPSTEIN, RALPH. "Verbal Aptitude in Eonism and Prepubertal Effeminacy—A Feminine Trait." *Dis Nerv System* 29:448–54 F '67. *

471. MURRAY, JOHN B. "College Students' IQs." *Psychol Rep* 20:743–7 Je '67. * (*PA* 41:13598)

472. NEWLAND, T. ERNEST, AND SMITH, PATRICIA A. "Statistically Significant Difference Between Subtest Scaled Scores on the WISC and the WAIS." *J Sch Psychol* 5:122–7 w '67. * (*PA* 41:8884)

473. OBERLEDER, MURIEL. "Adapting Current Psychological Techniques for Use in Testing the Aging." *Gerontologist* 7(3, pt 1):188–91 S '67. * (*PA* 42:3801)

474. OGDON, DONALD P. Section 2, "The Wechsler Scales," pp. 3–10, 75–7. In his *Psychodiagnostics and Personality Assessment: A Handbook.* Beverly Hills, Calif.: Western Psychological Services, 1967. Pp. v, 96. *

475. PAUL, MARY E. *The Effect of Stress on WAIS Digit Span, Digit Symbol and Picture Completion Performances.* Master's thesis, Loyola University (Chicago, Ill.), 1967.

476. REED, JAMES C., AND FITZHUGH, KATHLEEN B. "Factor Analysis of WB-1 and WAIS Scores of Patients With Chronic Cerebral Dysfunction." *Percept & Motor Skills* 25:517–21 O '67. * (*PA* 42:5964)

477. RHUDICK, P. J., AND GORDON, C. "Test-Retest IQ Changes in Bright Aging Individuals." Abstract. *Gerontologist* 7(3, pt 2):34 S '67. * (*PA* 41:16550)

478. RICHMAN, JOSEPH. "Reporting Diagnostic Test Results to Patients and Their Families." *J Proj Tech & Pers Assess* 31:62–70 Je '67. * (*PA* 41:13733)

479. ROSS, DONALD RUFUS. *Test Performance of Deaf Adults Under Two Modes of Test Administration.* Doctor's thesis, University of Arizona (Tucson, Ariz.), 1967. (*DA* 28:2992A)

480. ROSS, ROBERT T., AND MORLEDGE, JUNE. "Comparison of the WISC and WAIS at Chronological Age Sixteen." *J Consult Psychol* 31:331–2 Je '67. * (*PA* 41:10449)

481. RUBY, THOMAS M. *Performance on the Wechsler Adult Intelligence Scale by High and Low Anxious College Students.* Master's thesis, Southern Methodist University (Dallas, Tex.), 1967.

482. SATTLER, JEROME M., AND THEYE, FRED. "Procedural, Situational, and Interpersonal Variables in Individual Intelligence Testing." *Psychol B* 68:347–60 N '67. * (*PA* 42:2564)

483. SATZ, PAUL; RICHARD, WAYNE; AND DANIELS, AUBREY. "The Alteration of Intellectual Performance After Lateralized Brain-Injury in Man." *Psychon Sci* 7:369–70 Ap 5 '67. * (*PA* 41:8428)

484. SHAW, DALE J. "Estimating WAIS IQ From Progressive Matrices Scores." *J Clin Psychol* 23:184–5 Ap '67. * (*PA* 41:8886)

485. SHAW, DALE J. "Factor Analysis of the Collegiate WAIS." Abstract. *J Consult Psychol* 31:217 Ap '67. *

486. SILVERSTEIN, A. B. "A Short Short Form of the WISC and WAIS for Screening Purposes." *Psychol Rep* 20:682 Ap '67. * (*PA* 41:8164)

487. SILVERSTEIN, A. B. "Validity of WAIS Short Forms." *Psychol Rep* 20:37–8 F '67. * (*PA* 41:6463)

488. SINGH, UDAI PRATAP. "Intelligence in Criminals." *Indian J Social Work* 27:269–74 O '67. * (*PA* 41:4569) Reprinted 27:393–8 Ja '67. * (*PA* 41:9124)

489. SJOGREN, DOUGLAS D. "Achievement as a Function of Study Time." *Am Ed Res J* 4:337–43 N '67. * (*PA* 42:17816)

490. STEINBERG, MARVIN; SEGEL, RUEBEN H.; AND LEVINE, HARRY D. "Psychological Determinants of Academic Success: A Pilot Study." *Ed & Psychol Meas* 27:413–22 su '67. * (*PA* 41:14226)

491. STEINMAN, WARREN M. "The Use of Ambiguous Stimuli to Predict General Competence." *J Sci Lab Denison Univ* 48:7–14 Je '67. * (*PA* 42:2590)

492. STEWART, HORACE; COLE, SPURGEON; AND WILLIAMS, ROBERT. "Relationship Between the QT and WAIS in a Restricted Clinical Sample." *Psychol Rep* 20:383–6 Ap '67. * (*PA* 41:9087)

493. STIER, SERENA AUSTER. *Developmental Attainment, Outcome and Symbolic Performance in Schizophrenia.* Doctor's thesis, University of California (Los Angeles, Calif.), 1967. (*DA* 28:4766B)

494. SUINN, RICHARD M.; DAUTERMAN, WILLIAM; AND SHAPIRO, BERNICE. "The WAIS as a Predictor of Educational and Occupational Achievement in the Adult Blind." *New Outl Blind* 61:41–3 F '67. *

495. SYDIAHA, DANIEL. "Prediction of WAIS IQ for Psychiatric Patients Using the Ammons' FRPV and Raven's Progressive Matrices." *Psychol Rep* 20:823–6 Je '67. * (*PA* 41:13602)

496. TELLEGEN, AUKE, AND BRIGGS, PETER F. "Old Wine in New Skins: Grouping Wechsler Subtests Into New Scales." *J Consult Psychol* 31:499–506 O '67. * (*PA* 41:16071)

497. TEMPLER, DONALD I. "Relation Between Immediate and Short-Term Memory and Clinical Implications." *Percept & Motor Skills* 24:1011–2 Je '67. * (*PA* 41:13086)

498. THALER, VICTOR HUGO. *Personality Dimensions Derived From Multiple Instruments.* Doctor's thesis, Columbia University (New York, N.Y.), 1967. (*DA* 28:509A)

499. TOOLSON, REX NOBLE. *An Investigation of the Relationship Between Measures of Intelligence and Season of Birth.* Doctor's thesis, Colorado State College (Greeley, Colo.), 1967. (*DA* 28:2572A)

500. WAGNER, RUDOLPH FRED. *An Explication of Gittinger's Internalizer-Externalizer Dimension by Factor Analysis Based Upon Related Personality Measures.* Doctor's thesis, George Washington University (Washington, D.C.), 1967.

501. WANG, H. A.; OBRIST, W. D.; AND BUSSE, E. W. "Electroencephalographic and Intellectual Changes in Healthy Elderly: A Longitudinal Study." Abstract. *Gerontologist* 7(3, pt 2):23 S '67. *

502. WILLIAMS, JEROLD R. *A Correctional Study of Adult Comprehension Performance on the Stanford-Binet (1937) Form L Test and the Wechsler Adult Intelligence Scale.* Master's thesis, Illinois State University (Normal, Ill.), 1967.

503. WILTBERGER, ARLENE CAMPBELL. *A Comparative Study of the Wechsler Intelligence Scale for Children and the Wechsler Adult Intelligence Scale With High IQ Level and Low IQ Level Subjects.* Master's thesis, Cornell University (Ithaca, N.Y.), 1967.

504. WINTER, GERALD DAVID. *Intelligence, Interest, and Personality Characteristics of a Selected Group of Students: A Description and Comparison of White and Negro Students in a Vocational Rehabilitation Administration Program in Bassick and Harding High Schools, Bridgeport, Connecticut.* Doctor's thesis, Columbia University (New York, N.Y.), 1967. (*DA* 28:4920A)

505. WIRLS, CHARLES J., AND PLOTKIN, ROSALIE R. "Calculation of Quick Test IQs for Children With Mental Ages Seventeen and Above." *Psychol Rep* 20:603–5 Ap '67. * (*PA* 41:8172)

506. WIRTH, GARY. *A Comparison of Wechsler Verbal, Performance and Full Scale IQ's for Schizophrenia, Anxiety Reaction, Psychoneurosis Brain Damage, and Mental Retardation.* Master's thesis, East Tennessee State University (Johnson City, Tenn.), 1967.

507. WOLFSON, WILLIAM, AND BACHELIS, LEONARD. "Time of Year as a Factor in Success on WAIS Items." *Psychol Rep* 21:268 Ag '67. *

508. ALLISON, JOEL; BLATT, SIDNEY J.; AND ZIMET, CARL N. Chap. 2, "The Wechsler Adult Intelligence Scale," pp. 20–88, passim. In their *Interpretation of Psychological Tests.* New York: Harper & Row, Publishers, Inc., 1968. Pp. x, 342. *

509. ANASTASI, ANNE. *Psychological Testing, Third Edition,* pp. 271–82. New York: Macmillan Co., 1968. Pp. xiii, 665. *

510. ANDERSON, CATHERINE J.; PORRATA, ELENA; LORE, JAMES; ALEXANDER, SHIRLEY; AND MERCER, MARGARET. "A Multidisciplinary Study of Psychogeriatric Patients." *Geriatrics* 23:105–13 F '68. * (*PA* 42:14051)

511. ANDERSON, HARRY E., JR.; KERN, FRANK E.; AND COOK, CHARLOTTE. "Sex, Brain Damage, and Race Effects in the Progressive Matrices With Retarded Populations." *J Social Psychol* 76:207–11 D '68. * (*PA* 43:4329)

512. AVERY, CONSTANCE. "A Psychological Study of Patients With Behavior Problems and 6 and 14 per Second Positive Spikes in Their Electroencephalograms." *J Clin Psychol* 24:171–3 Ap '68. * (*PA* 42:11777)

513. AX, ALBERT F., AND BAMFORD, JACQUELINE L. "Validation of a Psychophysiological Test of Aptitude for Learning Social Motives." *Psychophysiol* 5:316–32 S '68. * (*PA* 43:3943)

514. BARTZ, WAYNE R. "Relationship of WAIS, BETA and Shipley-Hartford Scores." *Psychol Rep* 22:676 Ap '68. * (*PA* 42:12089)

515. BAYLEY, NANCY. "Behavioral Correlates of Mental

Growth: Birth to Thirty-Six Years." *Am Psychologist* 23:1-17 Ja '68. * (*PA* 42:8705)

516. BAYLEY, NANCY. Chap. 9, "Cognition and Aging," pp. 97-119. In *Theory and Methods of Research on Aging.* Edited by K. Warner Schaie. Morgantown, W.Va.: West Virginia University, 1968. Pp. iv, 197. *

517. BIELEFELD, MARTIN OLIVER. *Prediction of Concept Attainment From the PAS.* Doctor's thesis, University of Missouri (Columbia, Mo.), 1968. (*DA* 29:3077B)

518. BLATT, SIDNEY J., AND ALLISON, JOEL. Chap. 14, "The Intelligence Test in Personality Assessment," pp. 421-60. In *Projective Techniques in Personality Assessment: A Modern Introduction.* Edited by A. I. Rabin. New York: Springer Publishing Co., Inc., 1968. Pp. x, 638. *

519. BONNER, MARY WINSTEAD. *A Comparative Study of the Performance of Negro Seniors of Oklahoma City High Schools on the Wechsler Adult Intelligence Scale and the Peabody Picture Vocabulary Test.* Doctor's thesis, Oklahoma State University (Stillwater, Okla.), 1968. (*DAI* 30:921A)

520. BOOR, MYRON, AND SCHILL, THOMAS. "Subtest Performance on the Wechsler Adult Intelligence Scale as a Function of Anxiety and Defensiveness." *Percept & Motor Skills* 27:33-4 Ag '68. * (*PA* 43:2609)

521. BOURESTOM, NORMAN C., AND HOWARD, MARY T. "Behavioral Correlates of Recovery of Self-Care in Hemiplegic Patients." *Arch Phys Med & Rehabil* 49:449-54 Ag '68. *

522. BROWN, FRED. "Applicability of the Jastak Short Form Revision of the WAIS Vocabulary Subtest to Psychiatric Patients." *J Clin Psychol* 24:454-5 O '68. * (*PA* 43:4145)

523. BURTON, D. A. "The Jastak Short Form WAIS Vocabulary Applied to a British Psychiatric Population." *J Clin Psychol* 24:345-7 Jl '68. * (*PA* 42:16404)

524. CARTWRIGHT, JERRY LEE. *A Comparison of a Generalized and a Differential Predictor of Risk Taking.* Doctor's thesis, University of Missouri (Columbia, Mo.), 1968. (*DA* 29:3077B)

525. CHABASSOL, DAVID J. "A Comparison of Measures of Masculinity-Femininity." *Meas & Eval Guid* 1:173-4 f '68. *

526. CLUM, GEORGE ARTHUR. *The Relationships Between Measures of Classical and Operant Conditioning, Psychiatric Diagnoses and Statistically Derived Classificatory Groups.* Doctor's thesis, St. John's University (Jamaica, N.Y.), 1968. (*DA* 29:3899B)

527. CONNOR, MARJORIE WELLS. *Learning Characteristics of Able Nonachievers in Audiolingual Foreign Language Classes.* Doctor's thesis, University of Cincinnati (Cincinnati, Ohio), 1968. (*DA* 29:1446A)

528. CRONHOLM, BÖRJE, AND SCHALLING, DAISY. "Cognitive Test Performances in Cerebrally Palsied Adults Without Mental Retardation." *Acta Psychiatrica Scandinavica* 44(1):37-50 '68. * (*PA* 43:2937)

529. DELUCA, JOSEPH. "Predicting the Full Scale WAIS IQ of Army Basic Trainees." *J Psychol* 68:83-6 Ja '68. * (*PA* 42:7326)

530. DESAI, ARVINDRAI N. "Behavioral Characteristics of Alcoholic Delinquents." *Indian J Appl Psychol* 5:54-61 Jl '68. *

531. DICKINSON, THOMAS C.; NEUBERT, JOAN; AND MCDERMOTT, DOROTHY. "Relationship of Scores on the Full-Range Picture Vocabulary Test and the Wechsler Adult Intelligence Scale in a Vocational Rehabilitation Setting." *Psychol Rep* 23:1263-6 D '68. * (*PA* 43:8448)

532. DOMINO, GEORGE. "A Non-Verbal Measure of Intelligence for Totally Blind Adults." *New Outl Blind* 62:247-52 O '68. *

533. DUKE, ROBERT B.; BLOOR, BYRON M.; NUGENT, G. ROBERT; AND MAJZOUB, HISHAM S. "Changes in Performance on WAIS, Trail Making Test and Finger Tapping Test Associated With Carotid Artery Surgery." *Percept & Motor Skills* 26:399-404 Ap '68. * (*PA* 42:12653)

534. DUNN, JAMES A. "Anxiety, Stress, and the Performance of Complex Intellectual Tasks: A New Look at an Old Question." *J Consult & Clin Psychol* 32:669-73 D '68. * (*PA* 43:4014)

535. ELKIN, LORNE. "Predicting Performance of the Mentally Retarded on Sheltered Workshop and Non-Institutional Jobs." *Am J Mental Def* 72:533-9 Ja '68. * (*PA* 42:7638)

536. ERNHART, CLAIRE B. "The Peabody Picture Vocabulary Test: Automated Application in a Statewide Psychiatric System." *Psychiatric Q Sup* 42(2):317-20 '68. * (*PA* 46:3313)

537. FELDMAN, SOLOMON E. "Utility of Some Rapid Estimations of Intelligence in a College Population." *Psychol Rep* 22:23-6 F '68. * (*PA* 42:10572)

538. FINNIE, FRANCES RUTH. *The Relationship Between Perceptual Field Articulation and Intellectual Functioning in Paranoid Male Schizophrenics.* Doctor's thesis, George Washington University (Washington, D.C.), 1968.

539. FISHER, GARY. "Intellectual Impairment in a Patient With Hepatolenticular Degeneration (Wilson's Disease)." *J Mental Subnorm* 14:91-5 D '68. * (*PA* 44:2624)

540. FREEDMAN, SAUL. *The Relationship Between Selected Variables and Success in Transcribing Typing for Trainees Who Are Blind.* Doctor's thesis, New York University (New York, N.Y.), 1968. (*DA* 29:3000A)

541. FUNKHOUSER, THOMAS R. "Correlational Study of the 'Revised Beta Examination' in a Female Retarded Population." *Am J Mental Def* 72:875-8 My '68. * (*PA* 42:13754)

542. GALLAGHER, HELEN C. "Intelligence and Learning Structured Tasks." *Am J Occup Ther* 22:264-8 Jl-Ag '68. * (*PA* 43:2864)

543. GILBERSTADT, HAROLD. "Relationships Among Scores of Tests Suitable for the Assessment of Adjustment and Intellectual Functioning." *J Gerontol* 23:483-7 O '68. *

544. GONEN, JAY Y., AND BROWN, LOUIS. "'Role of Vocabulary in Deterioration and Restitution of Mental Functioning.' Abstract. *Proc 76th Ann Conv Am Psychol Assn* 3:469-70 '68. *

545. GONEN, YECHIEL. "Does Vocabulary Resist Mental Deterioration?" *J Clin Psychol* 24:341-3 Jl '68. * (*PA* 42:17529)

546. HANNA, GERALD S.; HOUSE, BETTY; AND SALISBURY, LEE H. "WAIS Performance of Alaskan Native University Freshmen." *J Genetic Psychol* 112:57-61 Mr '68. * (*PA* 42:10574)

547. HOLMES, J. STEVEN. "Acute Psychiatric Patient Performance on the WAIS." *J Clin Psychol* 24:87-91 Ja '68. * (*PA* 42:8938)

548. HOLT, ROBERT R. "Concerning Scatter and the WAIS," pp. 161-71. In *Diagnostic Psychological Testing.* New York: International Universities Press, Inc., 1968. Pp. xi, 562. *

549. JACOBSON, LEONARD I.; ELENEWSKI, JEFFREY J.; LORDAHL, DANIEL S.; AND LIROFF, JEFFREY H. "Role of Creativity and Intelligence in Conceptualization." *J Pers & Social Psychol* 10:431-6 D '68. * (*PA* 43:6752)

550. KAHN, EDWIN, AND FISHER, CHARLES. "Individual Differences and Amount of Rapid Eye Movement Sleep in Aged Adulthood." Abstract. *Psychophysiology* 4:393-4 Ja '68. * (*PA* 42:15311)

551. KAHN, EDWIN, AND FISHER, CHARLES. "The Relationship of REM Sleep to Various Measures in the Aged." Abstract. *Psychophysiol* 5:228-9 S '68. * (*PA* 43:14153)

552. KAHN, MARVIN W. "Superior Performance IQ of Murderers as a Function of Overt Act or Diagnosis." *J Social Psychol* 76:113-6 O '68. * (*PA* 43:2823)

553. KASTL, ALBERT J.; DAROFF, ROBERT B.; AND BLOCKER, W. WEBSTER. "Psychological Testing of Cerebral Malaria Patients." *J Nerv & Mental Dis* 147:553-61 D '68. * (*PA* 43:14654)

554. KELLY, FRANCIS D. *An Investigation of the Performance of Schizophrenic Patients on the Picture Completion Subtest of the WAIS.* Master's thesis, Springfield College (Springfield, Mass.), 1968.

555. KNOX, ALAN B.; GROTELUESCHEN, ARDEN; AND SJORGREN, DOUGLAS D. "Adult Intelligence and Learning Ability." *Adult Ed* 18:188-96 sp '68. *

556. KRAUS, J., AND WALKER, WENDY. "A Pilot Study of Factors in WAIS 'Patterns' in Diffuse Brain Atrophy." *Am J Mental Def* 72:900-4 My '68. * (*PA* 42:14061)

557. LEVY, PHILIP. "Short-Form Tests: A Methodological Review." *Psychol B* 69:410-6 Je '68. * (*PA* 42:11410)

558. LEVY, RUSSELL H. "Group Administered Intelligence Tests Which Appropriately Reflect the Magnitude of Mental Retardation Among Wards of the Illinois Youth Commission." *J Correct Ed* 20:7-10 su '68. *

559. LEWIS, FARRELL W. *A Comparison of Wechsler Adult Intelligence Scale Scores of Dogmatic and Open-Minded Students.* Master's thesis, Brigham Young University (Provo, Utah), 1968.

560. LOGUE, VALENTINE; DURWARD, MARJORIE; PRATT, R. T. C.; PIERCY, MALCOLM; AND NIXON, W. L. B. "The Quality of Survival After Rupture of an Anterior Cerebral Aneurysm." *Brit J Psychiatry* 114:137-60 F '68. * (*PA* 42:8433)

561. LUND, RONALD DEAN. *Wechsler Subtest Patterns and Personality: An Application of Gittinger's Personality Assessment System to Verbal Activity, Self-Descriptions and Sociometric Choices.* Doctor's thesis, University of Colorado (Boulder, Colo.), 1968. (*DA* 29:3491B)

562. MCKERRACHER, D. W.; WATSON, R. A.; LITTLE, A. J.; AND WINTER, K. S. "Validation of a Short Form Estimation of W.A.I.S. in Subnormal and Psychopathic Patients." *J Mental Subnorm* 14:96-7 '68. * (*PA* 44:2530)

563. MCLELLAND, PAUL EUGENE. *A Comparative Study of the Reasoning Ability of Two Groups of Hearing Impaired Children in a Residential School.* Doctor's thesis, University of Virginia (Charlottesville, Va.), 1968. (*DA* 29:3005A)

564. MALERSTEIN, A. J., AND BELDEN, E. "WAIS, SILS, and PPVT in Korsakoff's Syndrome." *Arch Gen Psychiatry* 19:743-50 D '68. * (*PA* 43:8472)

565. MASSER, EDWARD V., AND ARNETTE, JOHNNY L. "The Use of the Satz-Mogel WAIS Short Form With Prison. Inmates." *J Correct Ed* 20:7+ sp '68. *

566. MEIKLE, STEWART. "The Effect on Subtest Differences of Abbreviating the WAIS." *J Clin Psychol* 24:196-7 Ap '68. * (*PA* 42:12092)

567. MOORE, ANTHONY BRYAN. *Reasoning Ability and Verbal Proficiency in Deaf and Hearing Children.* Doctor's thesis, University of Massachusetts (Amherst, Mass.), 1968. (*DA* 29:4381B)

568. MOORE, WILLIAM BATEMAN. *Drawings of Human Figures in Relation to Psychopathology and Intellectual Function-*

ing. Doctor's thesis, George Washington University (Washington, D.C.), 1968. *(DA* 29:2657B)

569. MUSKERA, DAVID J. *The Effects of Verbal Reinforcement and Instructional Set on the Similarities Subtests of the WAIS.* Master's thesis, Marshall University (Huntington, W.Va.), 1968.

570. ORME, J. E. "A Comment on Estimating W.A.I.S. IQ From Progressive Matrices Scores." *J Clin Psychol* 24:94-5 Ja '68. *

571. PATRICK, JERRY H., AND OVERALL, JOHN E. "Validity of Beta IQ's for White Female Patients in a State Psychiatric Hospital." *J Clin Psychol* 24:343-5 Jl '68. * *(PA* 42:16422)

572. PEAK, DANIEL T. "Changes in Short-Term Memory in a Group of Aging Adults." *J Gerontol* 23:9-16 Ja '68. *

573. PELOSI, JOHN WILLIAM. *A Study of the Effects of Examiner Race, Sex, and Style on Test Responses of Negro Examinees.* Doctor's thesis, Syracuse University (Syracuse, N.Y.), 1968. *(DA* 29:4105A)

574. PIERCE, RICHARD M. "Comment on the Prediction of Posthospital Work Adjustment With Psychological Tests." *J Counsel Psychol* 15:386-7 Jl '68. * *(PA* 42:15539)

575. PIHL, ROBERT O. "The Degree of the Verbal-Performance Discrepancy on the WISC and the WAIS and Severity of EEG Abnormality in Epileptics." *J Clin Psychol* 24:418-20 O '68. * *(PA* 43:4327)

576. POLLACK, MAX; WOERNER, MARGARET G.; AND KLEIN, DONALD F. "IQ Differences Between Hospitalized Schizophrenic and Personality-Disorder Patients and Their Normal Siblings." Abstract. *Proc 76th Ann Conv Am Psychol Assn* 3:491-2 '68. *

577. PRICE, A. COOPER, AND GENTRY, WILLIAM D. "Schizophrenic Thought Process: Analysis of the WAIS." Abstract. *Psychol Rep* 22:1099-100 Je '68. * *(PA* 42:19092)

578. QURESHI, M. Y. "The Optimum Limits of Testing on the Wechsler Intelligence Scales." *Genetic Psychol Monogr* 78:141-90 N '68. * *(PA* 43:4016)

579. QURESHI, MOHAMMED Y. "The Comparability of WAIS and WISC Subtest Scores and IQ Estimates." *J Psychol* 68:73-82 Ja '68. * *(PA* 42:7334)

580. ROSEN, MARVIN; STALLINGS, LINDA; FLOOR, LUCRETIA; AND NOWAKIWSKA, MYRA. "Reliability and Stability of Wechsler IQ Scores for Institutionalized Mental Subnormals." *Am J Mental Def* 73:218-25 S '68. * *(PA* 43:4352)

581. SAUNDERS, DAVID R., AND GITTINGER, JOHN W. "Patterns of Intellectual Functioning and Their Implications for the Dynamics of Behavior," pp. 377-90, discussion 403-18. In *The Role and Methodology of Classification in Psychiatry and Psychopathology.* Edited by Martin M. Katz and others. Public Health Service Publication No. 1584. Washington, D.C.: United States Government Printing Office, 1968. Pp. ix, 590. *

582. SAVAGE, R. D., AND BOLTON, N. "A Factor Analysis of Learning Impairment and Intellectual Deterioration in the Elderly." *J Genetic Psychol* 113:177-82 D '68. * *(PA* 43:4391)

583. SAVAGE, R. DOUGLASS, AND BRITTON, PETER G. "The Factorial Structure of the WAIS in an Aged Sample." *J Gerontol* 23:183-6 Ap '68. *

584. SCHILL, THOMAS; KAHN, MALCOLM; AND MUEHLEMAN, THOMAS. "Verbal Conditionability and Wechsler Picture Arrangement Scores." *J Consult & Clin Psychol* 32:718-21 D '68. * *(PA* 43:4037)

585. SCHILL, THOMAS; KAHN, MALCOLM; AND MUEHLEMAN, THOMAS. "WAIS PA Performance and Participation in Extracurricular Activities." *J Clin Psychol* 24:95-6 Ja '68. * *(PA* 42:8943)

586. SCHUCMAN, HELEN, AND THETFORD, WILLIAM N. "Expressed Symptoms and Personality Traits in Conversion Hysteria." *Psychol Rep* 23:231-43 Ag '68. * *(PA* 43:7148)

587. SCHWARTZ, MERVIN L.; DENNERLL, RAYMOND D.; AND LIN, YI-GUANG. "Neuropsychological and Psychosocial Predictors of Employability in Epilepsy." *J Clin Psychol* 24:174-7 Ap '68. * *(PA* 42:12633)

588. SEVERINSEN, K. NORMAN. "A.C.T., W.A.I.S. Test Scores and College Grades." *J Ed Meas* 5:161-2 su '68. *

589. SHERMAN, A. ROBERT, AND BLATT, SIDNEY J. "WAIS Digit Span, Digit Symbol, and Vocabulary Performance as a Function of Prior Experiences of Success and Failure." *J Consult & Clin Psychol* 32:407-12 Ag '68. * *(PA* 42:17224)

590. SILVERSTEIN, A. B. "Evaluation of a Split-Half Short Form of the WAIS." *Am J Mental Def* 72:839-40 My '68. * *(PA* 42:13756)

591. SILVERSTEIN, A. B. "Validity of a New Approach to the Design of WAIS, WISC, and WPPSI Short Forms." *J Consult & Clin Psychol* 32:478-9 Ag '68. * *(PA* 42:16432)

592. SILVERSTEIN, A. B. "Variance Components in Five Psychological Tests." *Psychol Rep* 23:141-2 Ag '68. * *(PA* 43:6920)

593. SIMPSON, ROBERT LEE. *A Study of the Comparability of the WISC and the WAIS and the Factors Contributing to Their Differenecs.* Doctor's thesis, University of Southern California (Los Angeles, Calif.), 1968. *(DA* 29:1794A)

594. SINOWITZ, MELVIN, AND BROWN, FRED. "Wechsler's MF Score as an Indicator of Masculinity and Femininity in a Psychiatric Population." *J Clin Psychol* 24:92-4 Ja '68. *

595. SORENSEN, MOURITS A., AND CLIFTON, SILAS W. "Client Opinions of WAIS Interpretations." *Meas & Eval Guid* 1:168-72 f '68. * *(PA* 44:11281)

596. STEIN, HENRY. *Intellectual Functioning in Hospitalized Nonchronic Schizophrenic Patients: The Relationship of Early Characteristics to Adult I.Q.* Doctor's thesis, New York University (New York, N.Y.), 1968. *(DA* 29:488A)

597. STERNLICHT, MANNY; SIEGEL, LOUIS; AND DEUTSCH, MARTIN R. "WAIS Subtest Characteristics of Institutionalized Retardates." *Ed & Psychol Meas* 28:465-8 su '68. * *(PA* 42:19207)

598. STRATTON, ALBERT J. "Validity of the SRA Non-Verbal Form for Adults." *Psychol Rep* 22:163-7 F '68. * *(PA* 42:10577)

599. STREITFELD, JULIAN W., AND AVERY, CONSTANCE D. "The WAIS and HIS Tests as Predictors of Academic Achievement in a Residential School for the Blind." *Int J Ed Blind* 18:73-7 O '68. * *(PA* 43:10178)

600. WAGNER, NATHANIEL N. "The 'Intelligence' of Malaysian Medical Students." *Brit J Med Ed* 2:24-7 Mr '68. *

601. WATSON, CHARLES G., AND KLETT, WILLIAM G. "Prediction of WAIS IQ's From the Shipley-Hartford, the Army General Classification Test and the Revised Beta Examination." *J Clin Psychol* 24:338-41 Jl '68. * *(PA* 42:16437)

602. WHITE, J. G., AND PATTEN, MARY P. "Intellectual Performance, Activity Level, and Physical Health in Old Age." Discussion by D. B. Bromley. *Gerontologia Clinica* 10(3):157-73 '68. *

603. WILSON, JOHN D. "Predicting Student Performance in First Year Arts and Science." *Scottish Ed Studies* 1:68-74 My '68. *

604. ZUNG, WILLIAM W. K., AND GIANTURCO, JUDITH. "Further Validation of the Ohio Literacy Test: Correlation With the Wechsler Adult Intelligence Scale and Grade Achieved in School." *J Clin Psychol* 24:197-8 Ap '68. * *(PA* 42:12829)

605. ABRAM, HARRY S.; ALLAN, J. HAMILTON; HUGHES, DEANNA; SMITH, BURKE M.; HALL, WILLIAM E.; AND LEWIS, DAVID W. "A Multidisciplinary Computerized Approach to the Study of Adjustment to Lower Limb Amputation." *South Med J* 62(9):1072-6 S '69. *

606. ASSO, DOREEN. "W.A.I.S. Scores in a Group of Parkinson Patients." *Brit J Psychiatry* 115(522):555-6 My '69. * *(PA* 44:3963)

607. ASSO, DOREEN; CROWN, SIDNEY; RUSSELL, JOHN A.; AND LOGUE, VALENTINE. "Psychological Aspects of the Stereotactic Treatment of Parkinsonism." *Brit J Psychiatry* 115(522):541-53 My '69. * *(PA* 44:3964)

608. BARCLAY, A.; FRIEDMAN, ELLEN C.; AND FIDEL, YILDIZ. "A Comparative Study of WISC and WAIS Performances and Score Patterns Among Institutionalized Retardates." *J Mental Def Res* 13(2):99-105 Je '69. * *(PA* 44:9089)

609. BASSETT, JOHN E., AND GAYTON, WILLIAM F. "The Use of Doppelt's Abbreviated Form of the WAIS With Mental Retardates." *J Clin Psychol* 25(3):276-7 Jl '69. * *(PA* 44:4030)

610. BURGESS, MICHAEL M., AND DUFFEY, MARGERY. "The Prediction of Success in a Collegiate Program of Nursing." *Nursing Res* 18(1):68-72 Ja-F '69. *

611. BURKE, HENRY R., AND BINGHAM, WILLIAM C. "Raven's Progressive Matrices: More on Construct Validity." *J Psychol* 72(2):247-51 Jl '69. * *(PA* 44:71)

612. CALLENS, CHARLOTTE J., AND MELTZER, MALCOLM L. "Effect of Intelligence, Anxiety, and Diagnosis on Arithmetic and Digit Span Performance on the WAIS." Abstract. *J Consult & Clin Psychol* 33(5):630 O '69. * *(PA* 44:2523)

613. CANTER, ARTHUR, AND STRAUMANIS, JOHN J. "Performance of Senile and Healthy Aged Persons on the BIP Bender Test." *Percept & Motor Skills* 28(3):695-8 Je '69. * *(PA* 43:17618)

614. COCHRAN, MALCOLM L., AND PEDRINI, DUILIO T. "The Concurrent Validity of the 1965 WRAT With Adult Retardates." *Am J Mental Def* 73(4):654-6 Ja '69. * *(PA* 43:8574)

615. COSTA, LOUIS D.; VAUGHAN, HERBERT G., JR.; HORWITZ, MORTON; AND RITTER, WALTER. "Patterns of Behavioral Deficit Associated With Visual Spatial Neglect." *Cortex* 5(3):242-63 S '69. * *(PA* 43:13142)

616. CRAIG, ROBERT J. "An Illustration of the Wechsler Picture Arrangement Subtest as a Thematic Technique." *J Proj Tech & Pers Assess* 33(3):286-9 Je '69. * *(PA* 43:14311)

617. CRANDALL, FAYE ELIZABETH. *A Cross-Cultural Study of Ahtena Indian and Non-Indian High School Students in Alaska on Selected Value Orientations and Measured Intellectual Ability.* Doctor's thesis, Clark University (Worcester, Mass.), 1969. *(DAI* 31:214A)

618. DANA, JEAN M., AND DANA, RICHARD H. "Experimenter-Bias and the WAIS." *Percept & Motor Skills* 28(3):694 Je '69. * *(PA* 43:16652)

619. DAVIS, WILLIAM E. "Effect of Prior Failure on Subjects' WAIS Arithmetic Subtest Scores." *J Clin Psychol* 25(1):72-3 Ja '69. * *(PA* 43:9760)

620. DAVIS, WILLIAM E.; PEACOCK, WILLIAM; FITZPATRICK, PHILIP; AND MULHERN, MICHAEL. "Examiner Differences, Prior Failure, and Subjects' WAIS Arithmetic Scores." *J Clin Psychol* 25(2):178-80 Ap '69. * *(PA* 43:14465)

621. DICKSTEIN, LOUIS S. "Prospective Span as a Cognitive Ability." *J Consult & Clin Psychol* 33(6):757-60 D '69. * *(PA* 44:3616)

622. ELWOOD, DAVID L. "Automation of Psychological Testing." *Am Psychologist* 24(3):287-9 Mr '69. * *(PA* 44:3011)

623. EME, ROBERT F., AND WALKER, RONALD E. "The WAIS as a Group Test of Intelligence." *J Clin Psychol* 25(3):277-8 Jl '69. * (*PA* 44:3618)
624. FIELDS, FRANCIS R. J., AND WHITMYRE, JOHN W. "Verbal and Performance Relationships With Respect to Laterality of Cerebral Involvement." *Dis Nerv System* 30(3):177-9 Mr '69. * (*PA* 44:1070)
625. FOSTER, ASHLEY. "The Use of Psychological Testing in Rehabilitation Planning for Alaskan Native People." *Austral Psychologist* 4(2-3):146-52 N '69. * (*PA* 46:5260)
626. FOX, ELIZABETH, AND BLATT, SIDNEY J. "An Attempt to Test Assumptions About Some Indications of Negativism on Psychological Tests." *J Consult & Clin Psychol* 33(3):365-6 Je '69. * (*PA* 43:12965)
627. GLICK, IRA D., AND STERNBERG, DAVID. "Performance I.Q. as Predictor of Hospital Treatment Outcome." *Comprehen Psychiatry* 10(5):365-8 S '69. * (*PA* 44:14863)
628. GOLDFARB, WILLIAM; GOLDFARB, NATHAN; AND POLLACK, RUTH C. "Changes in IQ of Schizophrenic Children During Residential Treatment." *Arch Gen Psychiatry* 21(6):673-90 D '69. * (*PA* 44:10887)
629. GREEN, RUSSEL F. "Age-Intelligence Relationship Between Ages Sixteen and Sixty-Four: A Rising Trend." *Develop Psychol* 1(5):618-27 S '69. * (*PA* 43:16634)
630. GRESSETT, JOHN D. "Prediction of Job Success Following Heart Attack." *Rehabil Counsel B* 13(1):10-4 S '69. *
631. GROSSMAN, JOEL LAWRENCE. *A Comparison of Cautious Behavior of Elderly and Young Persons on WAIS Subtest Performance.* Doctor's thesis, State University of New York (Buffalo, N.Y.), 1969. (*DAI* 30:2908B)
632. HERRANS, LAURA LETICIA. *Sex Differences in the Spanish WAIS Scores.* Doctor's thesis, Catholic University of America (Washington, D.C.), 1969. (*DAI* 30:1432A)
633. HODGES, WILLIAM F., AND SPIELBERGER, CHARLES D. "Digit Span: An Indicant of Trait or State Anxiety?" *J Consult & Clin Psychol* 33(4):430-4 Ag '69. * (*PA* 43:15857)
634. HOGAN, TERRENCE P. "Relationship Between the Ammons IQ Norms and WAIS Test Performances of Psychiatric Subjects." *J Clin Psychol* 25(3):275-6 Jl '69. * (*PA* 44:3679)
635. HOLLENDER, JOHN W., AND BROMAN, HARVEY J. "Intellectual Assessment in a Disadvantaged Population." *Meas & Eval Guid* 2(1):19-24 sp '69. *
636. HOLMES, DOUGLAS S. "Note on Levy's Methodological Review of Studies on Short-Forms of the WAIS." *Psychol Rep* 24(1):49-50 F '69. * (*PA* 43:14312)
637. JAMBOR, K. L. "Cognitive Functioning in Multiple Sclerosis." *Brit J Psychiatry* 115(524):765-75 Jl '69. * (*PA* 44:7136)
638. JOHNSON, DALE T. "Introversion, Extraversion, and Social Intelligence: A Replication." *J Clin Psychol* 25(2):181-3 Ap '69. * (*PA* 43:14469)
639. KAHN, EDWIN, AND FISHER, CHARLES. "Some Correlates of Rapid Eye Movement Sleep in the Normal Aged Male." *J Nerv & Mental Dis* 148(5):495-505 My '69. * (*PA* 44:507)
640. KANTER, HAROLD M. *The Identification of Elements Which Contribute to Occupational Success and Failure of Adults Classified as Educable Mentally Retarded.* Doctor's thesis, Arizona State University (Tempe, Ariz.), 1969. (*DAI* 30:3790A)
641. KAUFMAN, HARVEY, AND IVANOFF, JOHN. "The Slosson Intelligence Test as a Screening Instrument With a Rehabilitation Population." *Excep Children* 35(9):745 My '69. * (*PA* 44:18977)
642. KOESTLINE, W. CHARLES, AND DENT, ORAN B. "Verbal Mediation in the WAIS Digit Symbol Subtest." *Psychol Rep* 25(2):377-8 O '69. * (*PA* 44:5156)
643. L'ABATE, LUCIANO, AND GALE, ELLIOT N. "Neurological Status and Psychological Functioning." *Percept & Motor Skills* 29(3):999-1007 D '69. * (*PA* 46:5330)
644. LEVINE, NIRA R. *Validation of the Quick Test for an Elderly Population.* Doctor's thesis, University of Virginia (Charlottesville, Va.), 1969. (*DAI* 31:646A)
645. LEVINSON, BORIS M. "Factor Scales in Evaluation of Intellectual Deficit." *Psychol Rep* 25(3):898 D '69. * (*PA* 44:18916)
646. LEVY, PHILIP. "Short Forms of the WAIS: A Reply." *Psychol Rep* 24(2):654 Ap '69. * (*PA* 43:15807)
647. LOVE, HENRY G. I. "Validity of the Doppelt Short Form WAIS in a Psychiatric Population." *Brit J Social & Clin Psychol* 8(2):185-6 Je '69. * (*PA* 43:15011)
648. MCDONALD, CARRICK. "Clinical Heterogeneity in Senile Dementia." *Brit J Psychiatry* 115(520):267-71 Mr '69. * (*PA* 43:13272)
649. MANN, EDWARD T. "Male Drug Addiction and the Kahn Test of Symbol Arrangement." *Percept & Motor Skills* 29(3):875-80 D '69. * (*PA* 46:5154)
650. MEIER, MANFRED J., AND OKAYAMA, MASAHIRO. "Behavior Assessment." *Geriatrics* 24(11):95-110 N '69. *
651. MORRIS, LARRY W., AND LIEBERT, ROBERT M. "Effects of Anxiety on Timed and Untimed Intelligence Tests: Another Look." *J Consult & Clin Psychol* 33(2):240-4 Ap '69. * (*PA* 43:9-68)
652. MOSES, JOSEPH L. "Automation of Testing Procedures." Letter. *Am Psychologist* 24(12):1174 D '69. *
653. NADEL, ROBERT S. *Social Responsibility as a Criterion for the Prediction of Success of Volunteers: A Study of the Characteristics of People Who Volunteer to Serve.* Doctor's thesis, New York University (New York, N.Y.), 1969. (*DAI* 30:3549A)
654. NEEDHAM, WALTER E.; BRAY, PATRICK F.; WISER, WILMER C.; AND BECK, EDWARD C. "Intelligence and EEG Studies in Families With Idiopathic Epilepsy." *J Am Med Assn* 207(8):1497-501 F 24 '69. * (*PA* 44:21418)
655. NEURINGER, CHARLES; WHEELER, GAYLE R.; AND BEARDSLEY, JAMES V. "Rating Diversity and Measures of Convergent and Divergent Intelligence." *J General Psychol* 80(1):73-9 Ja '69. * (*PA* 43:6919)
656. ORGASS, B., AND POECK, K. "Assessment of Aphasia by Psychometric Methods." *Cortex* 5(4):317-30 D '69. * (*PA* 44:17125)
657. PALMORE, ERDMAN B. "Physical, Mental, and Social Factors in Predicting Longevity." *Gerontologist* 9(2):103-8 su '69. * (*PA* 46:2787)
658. PARSONS, OSCAR A.; VEGA, ARTHUR, JR.; AND BURN, JULIAN. "Different Psychological Effects of Lateralized Brain Damage." *J Consult & Clin Psychol* 33(5):551-7 O '69. * (*PA* 44:2695)
659. PHILLIPS, RICHARD MARTIN. *A Multiple Regression Study of Academic Prediction at Gallaudet College.* Doctor's thesis, University of Maryland (College Park, Md.), 1969. (*DAI* 30:5257A)
660. QUATTLEBAUM, LAWRENCE F., AND WHITE, WILLIAM F. "Relationship Between Two Quick Screening Measures of Intelligence for Neuropsychiatric Patients." *Psychol Rep* 24(3):691-3 Je '69. * (*PA* 44:868)
661. RENEAR, KATHERINE ROBERTS. *Field Dependence and Parole Success.* Doctor's thesis, Claremont Graduate School (Claremont, Calif.), 1969. (*DAI* 30:56;8B)
662. ROSENQUIST, CARL M., AND MEGARGEE, EDWIN I. *Delinquency in Three Cultures*, pp. 208-24. Austin, Tex.: University of Texas Press, 1969. Pp. xvi, 554. *
663-4. ROSICKI, MARIA. *A Comparison of the Critical Flicker Frequency and Other Perceptual Tasks in Mental Defectives and Normals.* Doctor's thesis, Fordham University (New York, N.Y.), 1969. (*DAI* 30:5697B)
665. SABER-MOTAMEDI, HOUSHANG. *A Comparison of Test Scores of Foreign College Students With American College Students on the Wechsler Adult Intelligence Scale at ETSU and Tusculum.* Master's thesis, East Tennessee State University (Johnson City, Tenn.), 1969.
666. SAN DIEGO, ELLINOR AQUIO. *A Comparison of M-F Scores of American and Philippine Ss on the WAIS and the MMPI.* Master's thesis, Loyola University (Chicago, Ill.), 1969.
667. SATTLER, JEROME M.; WINGET, BARBARA M.; AND ROTH, ROSEMARY J. "Scoring Difficulty of WAIS and WISC Comprehension, Similarities, and Vocabulary Responses." *J Clin Psychol* 25(2):175-7 Ap '69. * (*PA* 43:14478)
668. SAXON, JOHN P.; ALSTON, PAUL P.; AND PORTER, THOMAS L. "Comparison of Haptic Intelligence Scale and WAIS Scores in a Population of Blind Psychotics." *Rehabil Counsel B* 13(1):49-51 S '69. *
669. SCHOOLER, CARMI, AND SILVERMAN, JULIAN. "Perceptual Styles and Their Correlates Among Schizophrenic Patients." *J Abn Psychol* 74(4):459-70 Ag '69. * (*PA* 43:16089)
670. SILVERSTEIN, A. B. "An Alternative Factor Analytic Solution for Wechsler's Intelligence Scales." *Ed & Psychol Meas* 29(4):763-7 w '69. * (*PA* 44:20972)
671. SILVERSTEIN, A. B., AND FISHER, GARY. "WAIS Subtest Characteristics of Institutionalized Retardates." *Psychol Rep* 25(2):397-8 O '69. * (*PA* 44:5570)
672. SINGER, PAUL R. Chap. 9, "Psychological Testing: Thematic Apperception Test, Rorschach Test, and WAIS Vocabulary Scale," pp. 110-43. In *The Psychological World of the Teen-Ager: A Study of Normal Adolescent Boys.* By Daniel Offer and others. New York: Basic Books, Inc., Publishers, 1969. Pp. xiv, 286. *
673. SINGH, UDAI PRATAP. "Movement From One's Own Position Towards a Group Norm as a Function of Intellect." *Psychol Studies* 14(2):88-93 Jl '69. *
674. SONG, A. Y., AND SONG, R. H. "Prediction of Job Efficiency of Institutionalized Retardates in the Community." *Am J Mental Def* 73(4):567-71 Ja '69. * (*PA* 43:8603)
675. STERNE, DAVID M. "The Benton, Porteus and WAIS Digit Span Tests With Normal and Brain-Injured Subjects." *J Clin Psychol* 25(2):173-5 Ap '69. * (*PA* 43:14481)
676. STRICKER, GEORGE; MERBAUM, MICHAEL; AND TANGEMAN, PAUL. "WAIS Short Forms, Information Transmission and Approximations of Full Scale IQ." *J Clin Psychol* 25(2):170-2 Ap '69. * (*PA* 43:14482)
677. TEMPLER, DONALD I., AND HARTLAGE, LAWRENCE C. "Physicians' I.Q. Estimates and Kent I.Q. Compared With WAIS I.Q." *J Clin Psychol* 25(1):74-5 Ja '69. * (*PA* 43:10025)
678. VEGA, ARTHUR, JR., AND PARSONS, OSCAR A. "Relationship Between Sensory-Motor Deficits and WAIS Verbal and Performance Scores in Unilateral Brain Damage." *Cortex* 5(3):229-41 S '69. * (*PA* 44:13157)
679. VITALE, JOHN H.; STEINHELBER, JOHN C.; DRAKE, WILLIAM E., JR.; AND DAHLGREN, HELEN. "Psychological Dimensions of Cerebrovascular Insufficiency." *Percept & Motor Skills* 29(2):555-63 O '69. * (*PA* 44:3996)
680. WEINSTOCK, COMILDA SUNDEEN. *The Relations Be-*

tween Social Isolation, Social Cognition and Related Cognitive Skills in the Aged. Doctor's thesis, Columbia University (New York, N.Y.), 1969. (*DAI* 30:3376B)

681. WICKSTROM, MARGARET LEE. *The Relationship of Future Time Perspective to Rehabilitation Performance on a Leg Prosthesis.* Doctor's thesis, Columbia University (New York, N.Y.), 1969. (*DAI* 30:4802B)

682. WOLFF, RICHARD, AND WASDEN, RONALD. "Measured Intelligence and Estimates by Nursing Instructors and Nursing Students." *Psychol Rep* 25(1):77–8 Ag '69. * (*PA* 44:3622)

683. ADAR, LEA D. *An Investigation of the Relationship of Some Aspects of Frustration to Pulmonary Tuberculosis.* Doctor's thesis, New York University (New York, N.Y.), 1970. (*DAI* 31:4322B)

684. BEN-YISHAY, YEHUDA; DILLER, LEONARD; AND MANDLEBERG, IAN. "Ability to Profit From Cues as a Function of Initial Competence in Normal and Brain-Injured Adults: A Replication of Previous Findings." *J Abn Psychol* 76(3): 378–9 D '70. * (*PA* 45:8763)

685. BEN-YISHAY, YEHUDA; DILLER, LEONARD; GERSTMAN, LOUIS; AND GORDON, WAYNE. "Relationship Between Initial Competence and Ability to Profit From Cues in Brain-Damaged Individuals." *J Abn Psychol* 75(3):248–59 Je '70. * (*PA* 44:15125)

686. BEN-YISHAY, YEHUDA; GERSTMAN, LOUIS; DILLER, LEONARD; AND HAAS, ALBERT. "Prediction of Rehabilitation Outcomes From Psychometric Parameters in Left Hemiplegics." *J Consult & Clin Psychol* 34(3):436–41 Je '70. * (*PA* 44:15081)

687. BERSOFF, DONALD N. "The Revised Deterioration Formula for the Wechsler Adult Intelligence Scale: A Test of Validity." *J Clin Psychol* 26(1):71–3 Ja '70. * (*PA* 44:10460)

688. BLATT, SIDNEY J.; BAKER, BRUCE L.; AND WEISS, JAY. "Wechsler Object Assembly Subtest and Bodily Concern: A Review and Replication." *J Consult & Clin Psychol* 34(2): 269–74 Ap '70. * (*PA* 44:10408)

689. BONNER, MARY W., AND BELDEN, BERNARD R. "A Comparative Study of the Performance of Negro Seniors of Oklahoma City High Schools on the Wechsler Adult Intelligence Scale and the Peabody Picture Vocabulary Test." *J Negro Ed* 39(4):354–8 f '70. * (*PA* 45:10662)

690. BURGESS, MICHAEL M.; KODANAZ, ALTAN; AND ZIEGLER, DEWEY K. "Prediction of Brain Damage in a Neurological Population With Cerebrovascular Accidents." *Percept & Motor Skills* 31(2):595–601 O '70. * (*PA* 45:6841)

691. BURGESS, MICHAEL M.; KODANAZ, ALTAN; ZIEGLER, DEWEY; AND GREENBURG, HOWARD. "Prediction of Brain Damage in Two Clinical Populations." *Percept & Motor Skills* 30(2):523–32 Ap '70. * (*PA* 46:7299)

692. COCHRAN, MALCOLM L. "A Profile of Psychological Test Scores for Retarded Adults." *Am J Mental Def* 74(4):582–4 Ja '70. * (*PA* 44:11052)

693. COONS, W. H., AND PEACOCK, E. P. "Interpersonal Interaction and Personality Change in Group Psychotherapy." *Can Psychiatric Assn J* 15(4):347–55 Ag '70. * (*PA* 44:21108)

694. COOPER, GERTRUDE V. *Effects of Anxiety and Color Among Male and Female Subjects on the Block Design Subtest of the Wechsler Adult Intelligence Scale.* Doctor's thesis, American University (Washington, D.C.), 1970. (*DAI* 31:3701B)

695. CROOKES, T. G., AND PEARSON, P. R. "WAIS IQ, Sixteen PF B Score and Education." *J Clin Psychol* 26(3):348–9 Jl '70. * (*PA* 45:672)

696. CULL, JOHN G., AND COLVIN, CRAIG R. "Correlation Between the Quick Test (QT) and the WAIS Verbal Scale in the Rehabilitation Setting." *Psychol Rep* 27(1):105–6 Ag '70. * (*PA* 45:6807)

697. DAVIS, WILLIAM E., AND DIZZONNE, MICHAEL F. "Relationship Between the QT and the WAIS." *Psychol Rep* 26(2):457–8 Ap '70. * (*PA* 44:21167)

698. DAVIS, WILLIAM E.; DEWOLFE, ALAN S.; DIZZONNE, MICHAEL F.; AND AIR, DOROTHY HABERKAMP. "Relationship Between Schizophrenics' Premorbid History and Intelligence Test Performance." *Newsl Res Psychol* 12(4):5–6 N '70. *

699. DUNCAN, D. F. "LSD and Intelligence: An Exploratory Study." *Psychol* 7(2):6–7 My '70. * (*PA* 44:20905)

700. ELWOOD, DAVID L. "Automation of Testing Procedures: Elwood Replies to Moses." Letter. *Am Psychologist* 25(8): 764–5 Ag '70. *

701. ERNHART, CLAIRE B. "The Correlation of Peabody Picture Vocabulary and Wechsler Adult Intelligence Scale Scores for Adult Psychiatric Patients." *J Clin Psychol* 26(4):470–1 O '70. * (*PA* 45:4528)

702. FERNALD, PETER S. "Consensus Intelligence Testing in Compatible and Incompatible Groups." *J Proj Tech & Pers Assess* 34(3):238–40 Je '70. * (*PA* 44:18690)

703. FRANK, GEORGE H. "The Measurement of Personality From the Wechsler Tests." *Prog Exp Pers Res* 5:169–94 '70. *

704. GOLDSTEIN, GERALD; NEURINGER, CHARLES; AND KLAPPERSACK, BERNARD. "Cognitive, Perceptual, and Motor Aspects of Field Dependency in Alcoholics." *J Genetic Psychol* 117(2): 253–66 D '70. * (*PA* 45:6611)

705. GOLLAND, JEFFREY H.; HERRELL, JAMES M.; AND HAHN, MICHAEL. "Should WAIS Subjects Explain Picture Arrangement Stories?" *J Consult & Clin Psychol* 35(2):157–8 O '70. * (*PA* 45:4252)

706. GONEN, JAY Y. "The Use of Wechsler's Deterioration Quotient in Cases of Diffuse and Symmetrical Cerebral Atrophy." *J Clin Psychol* 26(2):174–7 Ap '70. * (*PA* 44:15117)

707. GREENBERG, IRWIN M. "Clinical Correlates of Fourteen- and Six-Cycles-Per-Second Positive EEG Spiking and Family Pathology." *J Abn Psychol* 76(3):403–12 D '70. * (*PA* 45:6649)

708. GROTELUESCHEN, ARDEN, AND MCQUARRIE, DUNCAN. "Cross-Validation of the Quick Word Test as an Estimator of Adult Mental Ability." *Adult Ed* 21(1):14–9 f '70. *

709. HANNON, JOHN E., AND KICKLIGHTER, RICHARD. "WAIS Versus WISC in Adolescents." *J Consult & Clin Psychol* 35(2):179–82 O '70. * (*PA* 45:2202)

710. HUSTMYER, FRANK E., JR. "Eye Movements, Intelligence and Field Dependency in Schizophrenics." *Percept & Motor Skills* 30(3):703–6 Je '70. * (*PA* 44:17000)

711. JORTNER, SIDNEY. "Overinclusion Responses to WAIS Similarities as Suggestive of Schizophrenia." *J Clin Psychol* 26(3):346–8 Jl '70. * (*PA* 45:1055)

712. KANGAS, JON ALAN. *Intelligence at Middle Age.* Doctor's thesis, Washington State University (Pullman, Wash.), 1970. (*DAI* 31:1520B)

713. KAPLAN, MARVIN L.; COLARELLI, NICK J.; GROSS, RUTH BRILL; LEVENTHAL, DONALD B.; AND SIEGAL, SAUL M. *The Structural Approach to Psychological Testing.* New York: Pergamon Press, Inc., 1970. Pp. xi, 195. *

714. KASSINOVE, HOWARD; ROSENBERG, EDWIN; AND TRUDEAU, PAUL. "Cross Validation of the Environmental Participation Index in a Group of Economically Deprived High School Students." *J Consult & Clin Psychol* 26(3):373–6 Jl '70. * (*PA* 45:575)

715. KAUFMAN, HARVEY I. "Diagnostic Indices of Employment With the Mentally Retarded." *Am J Mental Def* 74(6): 777–9 My '70. * (*PA* 44:17178)

716. KLONOFF, HARRY; FEBIGER, CHRISTOPHER H.; AND HUTTON, GORDON H. "Neuropsychological Patterns in Chronic Schizophrenia." *J Nerv & Mental Dis* 150(4):291–300 Ap '70. * (*PA* 45:8632)

717. KNOX, WILMA J., AND GRIPPALDI, RICARDO. "High Levels of State or Trait Anxiety and Performance on Selected Verbal WAIS Subtests." *Psychol Rep* 27(2):375–9 O '70. * (*PA* 45:6319)

718. KUNCE, JOSEPH T., AND WORLEY, BERT. "Simplified Prediction of Occupational Adjustment of Distressed Clients." *J Counsel Psychol* 17(4):326–30 Jl '70. * (*PA* 44:21338)

719. LACKS, PATRICIA BRILLIANT, AND KEEFE, KATHRYN. "Relationships Among Education, the MMPI, and WAIS Measures of Psychopathology." *J Clin Psychol* 26(4):468–70 O '70. * (*PA* 45:4542)

720. LEWIS, WAYNE M. *A Study of the Relationship Between Personality and Intelligence.* Master's thesis, Springfield College (Springfield, Mass.), 1970.

721. LOOFT, WILLIAM R. "Note on WAIS Vocabulary Performance by Young and Old Adults." *Psychol Rep* 26(3): 943–6 Je '70. * (*PA* 45:698)

722. LUSZKI, MARGARET BARRON; SCHULTZ, WILLIAM; LAYWELL, H. ROBERT; AND DAWES, ROBYN M. "Long Search for a Short WAIS: Stop Looking." *J Consult & Clin Psychol* 34(3):425–31 Je '70. * (*PA* 44:13631)

723. MCCARTHY, DOROTHEA; ANTHONY, ROBERT J.; AND DOMINO, GEORGE. "A Comparison of the CPI, Franck, MMPI, and WAIS Masculinity-Femininity Indexes." *J Consult & Clin Psychol* 35(3):414–6 D '70. * (*PA* 45:4284)

724. MACK, JAMES L. "A Comparative Study of Group Test Estimates of WAIS Verbal, Performance, and Full Scale IQs." *J Clin Psychol* 26(2):177–9 Ap '70. * (*PA* 44:14870)

725. MCKEE, JAMES LEE. *Intellectual and Behavioral Correlates of Chronic Exposure to Toxic Chemicals.* Doctor's thesis, University of Denver (Denver, Colo.), 1970. (*DAI* 31:4341B)

726. MALEY, ROBERT F. "The Relationship of Premorbid Social Activity Level of Psychiatric Patients to Test Performance on the WAIS and the MMPI." *J Clin Psychol* 26(1): 75–6 Ja '70. * (*PA* 44:10494)

727. MATTHEWS, CHARLES G.; CLEELAND, CHARLES S.; AND HOPPER, CORNELIUS L. "Neuropsychological Patterns in Multiple Sclerosis." *Dis Nerv System* 31(3):161–70 Mr '70. * (*PA* 44:13128)

728. MEIER, MANFRED J., AND MARTIN, WILLIAM E. "Intellectual Changes Associated With Levodopa Therapy." Letter. *J Am Med Assoc* 213(3):465–6 Jl 20 '70. *

729. PAULSON, MORRIS J., AND LIN, TIEN-TEH. "Age: The Neglected Variable in Constructing an Abbreviated WAIS." *J Clin Psychol* 26(3):336–43 Jl '70. * (*PA* 45:950)

730. PAULSON, MORRIS J., AND LIN, TIEN-TEH. "Predicting WAIS IQ From Shipley-Hartford Scores." *J Clin Psychol* 26(4):453–61 O '70. * (*PA* 45:4546)

731. PECK, DAVID F. "The Conversion of Progressive Matrices and Mill Hill Vocabulary Raw Scores Into Deviation IQ's." *J Clin Psychol* 26(1):67–70 Ja '70. * (*PA* 44:10420)

732. POOL, DONALD A., AND BROWN, ROBERT. "The Peabody Picture Vocabulary Test as a Measure of General Adult Intelligence." *J Consult & Clin Psychol* 34(1):8–11 F '70. * (*PA* 44:6772)

733. POWELL, BARBARA J. "Role of Verbal Intelligence in the Field Approach of Selected Groups of Psychotics." *J Abn Psychol* 76(1):47–9 Ag '70. * (PA 44:21246)

734. QUERESHI, M. Y., AND MILLER, JEFFREY M. "The Comparability of the WAIS, WISC, and WBII." *J Ed Meas* 7(2):105–11 su '70. * (PA 44:18711)

735. QUERESHI, M. Y., AND WIDLAK, FREDERIC W. "Perceptual Diversity as a Function of Intelligence." Abstract. *Proc 78th Ann Conv Am Psychol Assn* 5(1):379–80 '70. * (PA 44:18613)

736. ROCHESTER, DEAN E., AND BODWELL, AARON. "Beta-WAIS Comparisons for Illiterate and Indigent Male and Female Negroes." *Meas & Eval Guid* 3(3):164–8 f '70. * (PA 45:9974)

737. ROSEN, MARVIN; KIVITZ, MARVIN S.; CLARK, GERALD R.; AND FLOOR, LUCRETIA. "Prediction of Postinstitutional Adjustment of Mentally Retarded Adults." *Am J Mental Def* 74(6):726–34 My '70. * (PA 44:17195)

738. ROSENZWEIG, STANLEY P., AND HARFORD, THOMAS. "Correlates of the Psychotic Reaction Profile in an Outpatient Psychiatric Sample." *J Consult & Clin Psychol* 35(2):244–7 O '70. * (PA 45:4549)

739. RUBINO, CARL A. "Psychometric Procedures and the Detection and Exploration of Behavioral Deficits Due to Cerebral Dysfunction in Men." *Can Psychologist* 11(3):239–60 Jl '70. * (PA 44:21180)

740. RUSSELL, ELBERT W. "A WAIS Factor Analysis With Brain Damage Subjects Using Criterion Measures." *Newsl Res Psychol* 12(4):1–2 N '70. *

741. SAN DIEGO, ELLINOR A.; FOLEY, JEANNE M.; AND WALKER, RONALD E. "WAIS Scores for Highly Educated Young Adults From the Philippines and the United States." *Psychol Rep* 27(2):511–5 O '70. * (PA 45:6139)

742. SATTLER, JEROME M., AND WINGET, BARBARA M. "Intelligence Testing Procedures as Affected by Expectancy and IQ." *J Clin Psychol* 26(4):446–8 O '70. * (PA 45:4257)

743. SATTLER, JEROME M.; HILLIX, WILLIAM A.; AND NEHER, LINDA A. "Halo Effect in Examiner Scoring of Intelligence Test Responses." *J Consult & Clin Psychol* 34(2):172–6 Ap '70. * (PA 44:10422)

744. SCHUCMAN, HELEN, AND THETFORD, WILLIAM N. "A Comparison of Personality Traits in Ulcerative Colitis and Migraine Patients." *J Abn Psychol* 76(3):443–52 D '70. * (PA 45:6910)

745. SHIMKUNAS, ALGIMANTAS M. "Reciprocal Shifts in Schizophrenic Thought Processes." *J Abn Psychol* 76(3):423–6 D '70. * (PA 45:6724)

746. SHINN, STEVEN M. *A Comparative Investigation of Three Predictors of Academic Success at Springfield College.* Master's thesis, Springfield College (Springfield, Mass.), 1970.

747. SILVERSTEIN, A. B. "The Measurement of Intelligence." *Int R Res Mental Retard* 4:193–227 '70. *

748. SILVERSTEIN, A. B. "Reappraisal of the Validity of a Short Short Form of Wechsler's Scales." *Psychol Rep* 26(2):559–61 Ap '70. * (PA 44:20973)

749. SILVERSTEIN, A. B. "Reappraisal of the Validity of WAIS, WISC, and WPPSI Short Forms." *J Consult & Clin Psychol* 34(1):12–4 F '70. * (PA 44:5886)

750. SIMPSON, ROBERT L. "Study of the Comparability of the WISC and the WAIS." *J Consult & Clin Psychol* 34(2):156–8 Ap '70. * (PA 44:10423)

751. SINGH, S. B., AND VIRMANI, VIMLA. "Differential WAIS Pattern Study in the Cases of General, Focal and Psychomotor Seizures." *Psychol Studies* 15(2):95–100 Jl '70. *

752. SMITH, HARRY ELMER. *The Beta-WAIS Relationship and the Intercorrelations Among Beta Subtests for a Youthful Offender Population.* Master's thesis, Millersville State College (Millersville, Pa.), 1970.

753. SOLTZ, WILLIAM HOWARD. *Comparative Study of Negro-White Differences on the MMPI and PAS.* Doctor's thesis, University of Missouri (Columbia, Mo.), 1970. (DAI 31:3009B)

754. TAYLOR, JOHN F. "Brief Note on Simplified Administration of the Object Assembly Subtest." *J Clin Psychol* 26(2):182 Ap '70. * (PA 44:14607)

755. THETFORD, WILLIAM N., AND SCHUCMAN, HELEN. "Conversion Reactions and Personality Traits." *Psychol Rep* 27(3):1005–6 D '70. * (PA 45:10346)

756. WALKER, KENNETH P., AND GROSS, FREDERICK L. "I.Q. Stability Among Educable Mentally Retarded Children." *Training Sch B* 66(4):181–7 F '70. * (PA 44:13185)

757. WALKER, RONALD E.; SANNITO, THOMAS C.; AND FIRETTO, ANTHONY C. "The Effect of Subjectively Reported Anxiety on Intelligence Test Performance." *Psychol Sch* 7(3):241–3 Jl '70. * (PA 45:4259)

758. WANG, H. SHAN; OBRIST, WALTER D.; AND BUSSE, EWALD W. "Neurophysiological Correlates of the Intellectual Function of Elderly Persons Living in the Community." *Am J Psychiatry* 126(9):1205–12 Mr '70. * (PA 44:14399)

759. WATKINS, JOHN T., AND KINZIE, WAYNE B. "Exaggerated Scatter and Less Reliable Profiles Produced by the Satz-Mogel Abbreviation of the WAIS." *J Clin Psychol* 26(3):343–5 Jl '70. * (PA 45:703)

760. WESSLER, RICHARD L. "Estimating IQ: Expertise or Examiner Effect?" *Percept & Motor Skills* 30(1):268 F '70. *

761. YOUNG, JOEL R. *A Study of WAIS Performance Varying Pretest Examiner-Subject Relationships.* Master's thesis, Springfield College (Springfield, Mass.), 1970.

762. ZIMMERMAN, S. F.; WHITMYRE, J. W.; AND FIELDS, F. R. J. "Factor Analytic Structure of the Wechsler Adult Intelligence Scale in Patients With Diffuse and Lateralized Cerebral Dysfunction." *J Clin Psychol* 26(4):462–5 O '70. * (PA 45:4776)

ALVIN G. BURSTEIN, *Professor and Chief, Division of Psychology, The University of Texas Medical School at San Antonio, San Antonio, Texas.*

The *Wechsler Adult Intelligence Scale* can be regarded as the psychological test apotheosized. In the two decades since its introduction as an updating of its prototype, the *Wechsler-Bellevue Intelligence Scale,* it has enjoyed unparalleled success. It is virtually impossible to imagine a setting in which the psychological testing of adults occurs in which the WAIS is not well known, just as it is virtually impossible to imagine a course in psychological testing which does not make liberal reference to this test.

Accordingly, no attempt will be made in this review to duplicate the readily available excellent descriptions of the history, development, and nature of the WAIS. Nor will an attempt be made to summarize fully the voluminous research efforts involving this test. The reader seeking such information will find it represented in previous editions of the *Mental Measurements Yearbook,* and in the work of Guertin and others (*154, 383*), as well as in a new review of the research literature scheduled for publication in 1972 (Guertin, private communication). The focus of this reviewer's concern will be rather to define some crucial questions regarding the clinical use of the WAIS and to review the recent literature in those specific areas.

Any evaluation of the clinical utility of the WAIS depends upon a clear understanding of the clinical concept of intelligence. Initially a clearly irreal construct intended as a mediating variable between the factors of test performance and school performance, the concept "intelligence" has undergone two important developments. The first is its assessment as a personality variable held in a kind of logical distinction from "dynamic" factors, and the second is its reification.

The urgency with which intelligence test scores are sought as things valuable in themselves by students, parents, and clinicians is familiar to anyone who has worked in counseling and laboratory school settings as well as to most people in many other clinical settings. The consumer not infrequently feels deprived if he is offered in place of the "real" score on the intelligence test a projected grade point average or other performance projection. This unhappy state of affairs, probably the joint product of poor consumer relations on the part of professional psychologists and the development of highly restricted and specialized notions of what human characteristics may be thought of as valuable, has reached a crescendo in the controversy surrounding the recent works of Jensen,[1] described in more detail below.

The tendency to regard intelligence as a personality variable to be distinguished from "dynamic" or "emotional" factors is embodied in the production of psychological reports by many generations of psychological diagnosticians in which these two variables are separately treated; the tendency is fostered by an unwitting commitment to the notion that feelings and thinking are somehow incompatible. Many able theoreticians, such as Schachtel,[2] have pointed out the limitations of such views, but their writing has done little to deflect the tendency for this distinction to be made.

Review of these general notions helps to define several crucial areas of research on the WAIS. The first comprises studies relating WAIS performance to sociocultural factors; the second, studies using the WAIS to predict specific areas of performance outside the school setting; and the third, work articulating theoretically the concept of intelligence and relating it to general personality theory.

The social developments of recent years, including the explosion of concern with minority civil rights and the rioting in and around black and white urban centers and university campuses, are considered by many to constitute a mandate for increased attention by the behavioral sciences to sociocultural issues. It is in that sense unfortunate that work relating sociocultural factors and WAIS performance is so scanty and of such poor quality. The tendency to use over-crude independent variables (e.g.,

black versus white, without regard for cultural characteristics) or to sample inadequately is one common defect; another is the tendency to design the studies as though variation from group to group in the configuration of scores were the primary interest rather than variation in the predictive meaning of scores. It is only in this latter sense that the issue of "cultural bias" has meaning. From the point of view of rhetoric and semantics, substituting the term "culturally specific validities" for the term "cultural bias" might help to sharpen the scientific issues involved.

Easily the most notorious controversy surrounding the cultural bias issue—though not involving the WAIS in particular—is that which ensued from the publication of Jensen's opinions that intelligence is largely genetically determined, and that remedial programs for the culturally deprived have been ill conceived to the extent that they depend on the assumption that cultural deprivation rather than genetic differences account for the differences in test and school performance. The polemic level to which some of the participants have sunk has obscured the highly specialized variable that Jensen is discussing and contributed to the unfortunate tendency to further reify the concept of "g." The central issue of the cultural specificity of the predictive validities of WAIS scores has simply not been dealt with adequately in the literature.

Turning from the confusions generated by the surplus meanings of the term intelligence, our attention is attracted to two areas of inquiry relative to the WAIS. The first deals with the predictive value of the WAIS performance relative to other specific performance, and the second deals with theoretical refinement and elaboration of the variable intelligence.

With respect to the first area, the **classical** target performance is, of course, academic success, and there is little reason to question the value of IQ scores in the prediction of academic success defined in the most generalized terms. However, when the type of academic performance is highly specific, there is room for considerable question. Although the number of recent studies is unfortunately small, the variability of WAIS scores among Oxford scientists (*449*) and the relative lack of success in relating IQ to success in specific curricular areas (*281, 452, 471, 527, 599*) suggest that

---

[1] JENSEN, ARTHUR R. "How Much Can We Boost IQ and Scholastic Achievement?" *Harvard Ed R* 39(1):1–123 w '69. *
JENSEN, ARTHUR R. "Reducing the Heredity-Environment Uncertainty: A Reply." *Harvard Ed R* 39(3):449–83 su '69. *
KAGAN, JEROME S.; HUNT, J. McV.; CROW, JAMES F.; BERNREITER, CARL; ELKIND, DAVID; CRONBACH, LEE J.; AND BRAZZIEL, WILLIAM F. "Discussion: How Much Can We Boost IQ and Scholastic Achievement?" *Harvard Ed R* 39(2):273–356 sp '69. *
[2] SCHACHTEL, ERNEST G. *Metamorphosis: On the Development of Affect, Perception, Attention, and Memory.* New York: Basic Books, Inc., Publishers, 1959. Pp. 344.

multiple factors, including nonintellectual ones, should be evaluated in such predictions.

The only nonacademic target performance given systematic attention in the current literature is employability. Here, if appropriate methodological cautions are invoked, as indicated by Kaufman (*460*) and Pierce (*574*), there is reason to believe that meaningful relationships with WAIS performance can be established. Then, too, as the population studied becomes more restricted and the employment behavior more highly specified, factors in addition to "g," or full scale IQ, score became increasingly relevant.

Overall, it seems that the use of WAIS performance to predict other concrete behaviors is an underworked area. For it to be explored fruitfully will require moving away from simplistic research designs utilizing IQ as the single, bipolar independent variable. Intelligence test performance itself is complex, and many aspects of it are potentially quantifiable; condensing the performance into a single score is inadequate.

Beyond relating intelligence test performance to subsequent behaviors of high pragmatic interest (e.g., school or job performance) is the goal of articulating theoretically the variable of intelligence by systematic exploration of patterns of test performance. Guilford's recent book,[3] though it does not focus on the WAIS, reflects an important and comprehensive effort in this direction. Recent factor analytic studies of the WAIS itself, such as Shaw's (*485*), confirm earlier studies identifying "verbal comprehension" and "perceptual organization" as general factors in WAIS performance. In addition, Shaw suggests the importance of motivational variables.

Other recent investigators have attempted to estimate, as reflected in WAIS performance, such variables as intellectual efficiency (*325*), nonintellective aspects of intelligence—described by Wechsler as such traits as persistence, zest, and desire to succeed—and to explore the substructure of the problem solving effort (*429*). The absolute incidence of such studies is small and none of the studies are definitive, but they represent an enormously exciting area of research.

The above work focuses on internal elaboration of the concept of intelligence; a convergent scientific goal is pursued by researchers attempting to relate WAIS performance to motivational or other aspects of general personality. Perhaps the most ambitious such effort is the Gittinger Personality Assessment System, which is based upon WAIS performance. The details of Gittinger's system have not been widely available in literature, but three recent studies (*517, 561, 586*) indicate that the system, though highly complex, merits careful evaluation. In addition to the PAS anxiety, risk taking behavior (*524*), impulsivity (*422*), and future orientation (*435, 443*) have all been explored as relating to WAIS performance.

In general, the more carefully specified the personality variable, the more encouraging the research results. For example, relatively crude measures of anxiety yield less promising results than more sophisticated measures distinguishing between trait and state anxiety (*633*). Given that intellectual performance does not occur separately from motivational systems, and given the importance of such systems in determining human behavior, the importance of continued work in this area is clear.

In summary, I would hope that the utilization of the WAIS in basic personality research is considerably expanded, in part because of the clinical success of the test. Such utilization of the WAIS will be facilitated by abandoning the notion that the extended range of complex behaviors that constitute an individual's performance is best compressed into a single number. It will also require a commitment to the notion that intellectual activity is most productively viewed as one aspect of total psychological functioning, and should be assessed in the context of other relevant psychological factors.

HOWARD B. LYMAN, *Associate Professor of Psychology, University of Cincinnati, Cincinnati, Ohio.*

As Bayley and Guertin suggest in their earlier reviews (5:414), the WAIS is certainly the best of the adult individual tests of intelligence. It was carefully constructed and carefully standardized. The norms were intelligently conceived and meticulously developed. As Guertin suggested, this test has become *the* standard against which other adult tests can be compared.

But there is room for improvement. For example, Wechsler says nothing in the manual about his theory of intelligence—for anything about the meaning of intelligence one must

---

[3] GUILFORD, J. P. *The Nature of Human Intelligence.* New York: McGraw-Hill Book Co., Inc., 1967. Pp. xii, 538. *

consult Wechsler's *The Measurement and Appraisal of Adult Intelligence* (*41*).

I wonder, too, whether the norms, based on tests given prior to 1955, are an honest reflection of the 1970's. After more than 15 years of extensive use, how much of the WAIS content is still unknown to mental hospital patients and to others who may have had several contacts with the test (e.g., in courts, psychiatric clinics, and the like)? All test publishers, of course, have a constant dilemma: whether to change items and improve a test or to make no changes and thereby take advantage of experience with proven items. Nevertheless, I think that most of us would be happier with some new content.

Some of the present items are in need of immediate change. For example: The scoring limits "130–190 million" for the population of the United States (Information, item 20) are unrealistic when the true population is in excess of 200 million. (I wonder whether some examiners actually use those limits shown in the manual—and fail subjects who give a close approximation of the present population.)

Other items seem more culture bound than necessary. Particularly for the foreign born, many of whom *do* take the WAIS, some of the information items seem particularly unfair (for example: identification of Longfellow or of Washington's birthdate). More satisfactory results probably could be obtained if greater attention were paid to the advisability of including items which rely so completely on American schooling.

In addition to the need for improvement and updating of items is the need for improvement in directions and in the format of both the manual and the record form. Particularly on the Vocabulary subtest are occasional subjects penalized. Directions tell the examiner to query further if "it is difficult to determine whether a subject does or does not know the meaning of a word." Obviously such a query may result in a clarification worth full credit (i.e., 2 points); however, a subject may receive only partial credit (1 point) for a clear, but not specific, definition. For example, "one of the seasons" is clearly a 1-point definition for *Winter;* therefore, an examiner should not query—despite the fact that the subject, if asked for more information, might give a 2-point response. My graduate students invariably report greater difficulty in scoring the WAIS Vocabulary than they had (in an earlier course) in scoring the Stanford-Binet vocabulary items.

No set of scoring criteria and scoring samples can, of course, be sufficient to answer all questions; however, more attention should be given to the scoring samples to make them as helpful as possible—for Vocabulary and for the other subtests.

The manual is not conveniently arranged for the examiner. Scoring samples (for most subtests) are buried many pages away from the directions for administration. Certainly it would be easier for all examiners to have the samples immediately following the directions; conceivably, this latter arrangement could keep some examiners from making many mistakes in scoring.

The record form is economically arranged for saving paper, but not designed efficiently for the school or clinical psychologist who believes that he should make behavioral observations of the subject while testing. Available at extra cost is a supplementary sheet on which such observations may be made, but the standard record form contains barely enough space for the minimal recording of responses.

Several features of the record form for the *Wechsler Preschool and Primary Scale of Intelligence* should be used for the WAIS record form: (*a*) printing a statement of the number of successive failures needed for termination of a subtest; inasmuch as the directions for termination differ for the various subtests, even the skilled examiner can make mistakes; (*b*) printing a reminder about the need for (or acceptability of) further queries; and (*c*) allowing sufficient space for recording responses and for making behavioral observations.

Some examiners may memorize the standard layout of pieces for the Object Assembly subtest, but I usually have to check with the manual. Wouldn't it save many examiners a lot of fumbling if the directions told us to lay out the pieces *before testing* on separate sheets of cardboard? This procedure permits the examiner to review his layout without losing rapport with his subject or spoiling the pace of his testing.

It seems unfortunate that Wechsler and The Psychological Corporation neglect to give us any sort of bibliography, for there is an impressive list of works which might have been cited (see, for example, those listed above).

Nevertheless, the facts remain that the WAIS

is still the best we have, that clinical and school psychologists find the test very helpful, and that the standardization was very carefully done.

For reviews by Nancy Bayley and Wilson H. Guertin, see 5:414. For references to reviews of an earlier edition, see 6:539.

[430]
★[Re Wechsler Adult Intelligence Scale] Rhodes WAIS Scatter Profile. Ages 16 and over; 1971; a form for profiling WAIS scores; profile (2 pages); manual (4 pages); $4.50 per 50 profiles, postage extra; Fen Rhodes; Educational and Industrial Testing Service. *

[431]
Wechsler Intelligence Scale for Children. Ages 5–15; 1949; WISC; downward extension of Form 2 of *Wechsler-Bellevue Intelligence Scale;* 13–15 scores: verbal (information, comprehension, arithmetic, similarities, vocabulary, digit span [optional], total), performance (picture completion, picture arrangement, block design, object assembly, mazes [optional], coding, total), total; individual; 1 form; record booklet (6 pages, revised slightly in 1958 but dated 1949); manual (117 pages); $27.50 per set of testing materials, 25 record booklets, and manual; $2.75 per 25 record booklets; $1.35 per 25 WISC Maze Tests, an alternate subtest which may be used in place of Coding; $3.25 per manual; postage extra; Spanish edition available; (40–60) minutes; David Wechsler; Psychological Corporation. [Australian Edition. 1968; record booklet (8 pages); manual (93 pages); Aus $27.50 per set of testing materials, 90¢ per 10 record booklets; 45¢ per 10 WISC Maze Tests; $3.50 per manual; manual by J. A. Radcliffe and F. E. Trainer; Australian Council for Educational Research.] *

REFERENCES

1–22. See 4:363.
23–133. See 5:416.
134–288. See 6:540.
289. KOLSTOE, OLIVER PAUL. *A Comparison of Mental Abilities of Bright and Dull Children Having the Same Mental Ages.* Doctor's thesis, State University of Iowa (Iowa City, Iowa), 1952. (DA 12:707)
290. ELLIS, EARNEST. *A Comparison of the Weschler Intelligence Scale for Children and the I.P.A.T. Free Intelligence Test.* Master's thesis, San Francisco State College (San Francisco, Calif.), 1953.
291. GOLDENBERG, SAMUEL. *Some Aspects of Diagnosis of Cerebral Damage in Children.* Doctor's thesis, University of Washington (Seattle, Wash.), 1953. (DA 13:1259)
292. BANAGHAN, WILLIAM FRANCIS. *A Study of Variability of Performance on the Wechsler Intelligence Scale for Children and Its Relationship to Diagnostic Categories.* Master's thesis, San Diego State College (San Diego, Calif.), 1955.
293. COLEMAN, LEONARD. *An Investigation of the Relationship Between Categorizing Behavior and Intelligence in School Children.* Doctor's thesis, Michigan State University (East Lansing, Mich.), 1955. (DA 15:1648)
294. MORGAN, CARL E. *Criteria for Diagnosis and Prediction in a Remedial Reading Program.* Doctor's thesis, University of Houston (Houston, Tex.), 1956. (DA 16:1507)
295. MORRISON, ERNEST BRUCE. *A Comparison of Mental Abilities of Average-Bright and Dull Children With Comparable Mental Ages.* Doctor's thesis, State University of Iowa (Iowa City, Iowa), 1957. (DA 17:2922)
296. PATTESON, RICHARD F. *A Longitudinal Analysis of the Relationship Between Growth Rate and Mental Development in Children Between the Ages of Four and Ten Years.* Doctor's thesis, Florida State University (Tallahassee, Fla.), 1958. (DA 18:1869)
297. FLEMING, JACK WAYNE. *The Relationships Among Psychometric, Experimental, and Observational Measures of Learning Ability in Institutional, Endogenous Mentally Retarded Persons.* Doctor's thesis, University of Colorado (Boulder, Colo.), 1959. (DA 20:4183)
298. GEUTING, MARY P. *Validities of Abbreviated Scales of the Wechsler Intelligence Scale for Children.* Master's thesis, Fordham University (New York, N.Y.), 1959.
299. HUGHES, DOROTHY HALE. *A Study of Concept Formation in a Group of Superior, Average and Mentally Retarded Children of Similar Mental Age: A Comparison of the Concept Formation of Boys and Girls Whose Mental Ages Are Between 9-6 and 10-6, but Whose Intellectual Levels Vary From Superior to Mentally Retarded.* Doctor's thesis, New York University (New York, N.Y.), 1959. (DA 20:3378)
300. BASTENDORF, WILLIAM LEON. *Activation Level, as Measured by Palmer Conductance, and Intelligence in Children.* Doctor's thesis, Claremont Graduate School (Claremont, Calif.), 1960. (DA 21:3156)
301. LEVINSON, BORIS M. "A Comparative Study of the Verbal and Performance Ability of Monolingual and Bilingual Native Born Jewish Preschool Children of Traditional Parentage." *J Genetic Psychol* 97:93–112 S '60. * (PA 35:6190)
302. TRAPP, E. PHILIP, AND EVANS, JANET. "Functional Articulatory Defect and Performance on a Nonverbal Task." *J Speech & Hearing Disorders* 25:176–80 My '60. * (PA 35:6808)
303. AURIA, CARL. *Differences in Specific Intellectual Functioning Among Children of the Same General Intellectual Ability but of Different Chronological Ages.* Doctor's thesis, University of Buffalo (Buffalo, N.Y.), 1961. (DA 22:2679)
304. BERNSTEIN, LEWIS. "Psychological Testing: 1, Intelligence Tests." *J Child Asth Res Inst & Hosp* 1:205–17 Je '61. *
305. SOSULSKI, MICHAEL CARL. *A Validation of the Finley-Thompson Short Form of the WISC for the Educable Mentally Retarded.* Master's thesis, Assumption University of Windsor (Windsor, Ont., Canada), 1961.
306. THOMPSON, BERTHA BOYA. *The Relation of Auditory Discrimination and Intelligence Test Scores to Success in Primary Reading.* Doctor's thesis, Indiana University (Bloomington, Ind.), 1961. (DA 22:785)
307. CLEMENTS, SAM D., AND PETERS, JOHN E. "Minimal Brain Dysfunction in the School-Age Child: Diagnosis and Treatment." *Arch Gen Psychiatry* 6:185–97 Mr '62. * (PA 37:3512)
308. FELDHUSEN, JOHN F., AND KLAUSMEIER, HERBERT J. "Anxiety, Intelligence, and Achievement in Children of Low, Average, and High Intelligence." *Child Develop* 33:403–9 Je '62. * (PA 37:3867)
309. GOUREVITCH, VIVIAN, AND FEFFER, MELVIN H. "A Study of Motivational Development." *J Genetic Psychol* 100:361–75 Je '62. * (PA 37:2891)
310. REGER, ROGER. "Brief Tests of Intelligence and Academic Achievement." *Psychol Rep* 11:82 Ag '62. * (PA 37:5654)
311. SAFRIN, RENATE KERSTEN. *Differences in Visual Perception and in Visual-Motor Functioning Between Psychotic and Nonpsychotic Children.* Doctor's thesis, Columbia University (New York, N.Y.), 1962. (DA 23:1080)
312. TANYZER, HAROLD JOSEPH. *The Relationship of Change in Reading Achievement to Change in Intelligence Among Retarded Readers.* Doctor's thesis, University of Connecticut (Storrs, Conn.), 1962. (DA 23:1612)
313. WITKIN, H. A.; DYKE, R. G.; FATERSON, H. F.; GOODENOUGH, D. R.; AND KARP, S. A. *Psychological Differentiation: Studies of Development.* New York: John Wiley & Sons, Inc., 1962. Pp. xii, 418. * (PA 37:819)
314. ANDERSON, LINNEA MAE. *Factors Affecting High and Low Achievement Among Adolescents Enrolled in Special Classes for the Mentally Handicapped.* Doctor's thesis, Wayne State University (Detroit, Mich.), 1963. (DA 25:279)
315. ASHLOCK, PATRICK ROBERT. *Visual Perception of Children in the Primary Grades and Its Relation to Reading Performance.* Doctor's thesis, University of Texas (Austin, Tex.), 1963. (DA 24:5186)
316. CONVERSE, HAROLD DALE. *Screening for Non-Intellective Factors of Children With Emotional Handicaps.* Doctor's research study No. 1, Colorado State College (Greeley, Colo.), 1963. (DA 25:640)
317. GRAVES, GORDON R. *A Study of the Use of the Peabody Picture Vocabulary Test for Identifying Mentally Retarded Children, Using the Wechsler Intelligence Scale for Children as a Criterion.* Master's thesis, Fresno State College (Fresno, Calif.), 1963.
318. KOUTSTAAL, CORNELIS W. *A Relationship Between the Intelligence and the Speech of Deaf Children.* Master's thesis, Springfield College (Springfield, Mass.), 1963.
319. KRIPPNER, STANLEY. "Correlates of Reading Improvement." *J Develop Read* 7:29–39 au '63. *
320. MCLEAN, TERRY KEITH. *A Comparison of the Subtest Performance of Two Groups of Retarded Readers With Like Groups of Non-Retarded Readers on the Wechsler Intelligence Scale for Children.* Doctor's thesis, University of Oregon (Eugene, Ore.), 1963. (DA 24:4800)
321. MORRISON, MARY. "A Gaelic Translation of the Wechsler Intelligence Scale for Children." Undergraduate thesis abstract. *Brit J Ed Psychol* 33:89–90 F '63. *
322. O'CONNELL, APRIL WELSH. *Sensori-Perceptual Differences Between Academically and Non-Academically Retarded Children.* Doctor's thesis, Ohio State University (Columbus, Ohio), 1963. (DA 24:4782)
323. SHOHEN, SAMUEL SUTLAND. *The Relationship Between*

Verbal Intelligence and Critical Reading Ability of Superior Readers. Doctor's thesis, Temple University (Philadelphia, Pa.), 1963. (*DA* 24:2979)

324. SONNEMAN, LAWRENCE J. *A Study of the Relationships Between Four Tests of Intelligence and One Test of Scholastic Achievement.* Doctor's thesis, State University of South Dakota (Vermillion, S.D.), 1963. (*DA* 24:4555)

325. WALKER, CARL. *The Relationship of Certain Selected Variables to First Grade Achievement.* Doctor's thesis, University of New Mexico (Albuquerque, N.M.), 1963. (*DA* 24:3242)

326. WEBB, ALLEN P. "Some Issues Relating to the Validity of the WAIS in Assessing Mental Retardation," pp. 87–92. (*PA* 38:6075) In *Towards a Professional Identity in School Psychology.* California Association of School Psychologists and Psychometrists, Fourteenth Annual Conference, March 28–30, 1963. [Los Angeles, Calif.: the Association, 1963.] Pp. v, 97. * (*PA* 38:4904)

327. WINSCHEL, JAMES FRANCIS. *Performance of Normal and Mentally Retarded Children on Selected Motor and Intellectual Tasks as a Function of Incentive Conditions.* Doctor's thesis, University of Pittsburgh (Pittsburgh, Pa.), 1963. (*DA* 25:6443)

328. ABERCROMBIE, M. L. J., AND JONCKHEERE, J. "Visual, Perceptual and Visuomotor Impairment in Physically Handicapped Children: 5, Wechsler Intelligence Scale for Children." Discussion by M. L. J. Abercrombie. *Percept & Motor Skills* 18:574–82, 609–20 Ap '64. * (*PA* 39:5574)

329. AMES, LOUISE B., AND WALKER, RICHARD N. "Prediction of Later Reading Ability From Kindergarten Rorschach and IQ Scores." *J Ed Psychol* 55:309–13 D '64. * (*PA* 39:8662)

330. BAUMEISTER, ALFRED A. "Use of the WISC With Mental Retardates: A Review." *Am J Mental Def* 69:183–94 S '64. * (*PA* 39:5036)

331. BERMAN, ISAAC, AND RHONE, DORIS ELLEN. "Wechsler Scores vs. Piaget Levels: Cognitive Efficiency of Institutionalized Retardates." Abstract. *Calif Mental Health Res Dig* 2:18 au '64. * (*PA* 39:12712)

332. BIBB, JOHN JAMES, JR. *A Study of the Quick Test as a Screening Instrument for Educable Mentally Retarded Children.* Doctor's thesis, University of Virginia (Charlottesville, Va.), 1964. (*DA* 25:3386) (Abstract: *Ed R* 2:69–71)

333. BIRKEMEYER, FLORENCE. "The Relationship Between the Coloured Progressive Matrices and Individual Intelligence Tests." *Psychol Sch* 1:309–12 Jl '64. *

334. BUCHMAN, MARCIA D. *Speed of Response on the Wechsler Intelligence Scale for Children Under Varying Conditions of Test Administration.* Master's thesis, University of Chicago (Chicago, Ill.), 1964.

335. CROPLEY, A. J. "Differentiation of Abilities, Socioeconomic Status, and the WISC." *J Consult Psychol* 28:512–7 D '64. * (*PA* 39:7749)

336. DENNERLL, RAYMOND D.; DEN BROEDER, JOAN; AND SOKOLOV, SHERWIN L. "WISC and WAIS Factors in Children and Adults With Epilepsy." *J Clin Psychol* 20:236–40 Ap '64. * (*PA* 39:8347)

337. EISENMAN, RUSSELL, AND MCBRIDE, JOHN W., JR. "'Balls' on the WISC." *Psychol Rep* 14:266 F '64. * (*PA* 39:1725)

338. FROMMELT, LEO ALOIS. *An Analysis of the WISC Profiles of Successful and Unsuccessful Readers in the Elementary School.* Doctor's thesis, State University of South Dakota (Vermillion, S.D.), 1964. (*DA* 25:2849)

339. GARNER, EDITH H. *An Investigation of the Coding of the Wechsler Scales in Relation to Reading Achievement of the Mentally Retarded.* Master's thesis, Boston University (Boston, Mass.), 1964.

340. GROSSBERG, JOHN M. "A Comparison of the Full-Range Picture Vocabulary Test and WISC in Clinical Use." Abstract. *J Consult Psychol* 28:188 Ap '64. *

341. HOLROYD, JEAN COREY. *Neurological Implications of WISC Verbal-Performance Discrepancies in a Psychiatric Setting.* Doctor's thesis, University of Minnesota (Minneapolis, Minn.), 1964. (*DA* 25:2048)

342. HOPKINS, KENNETH D. "An Empirical Analysis of the Efficacy of the WISC in the Diagnosis of Organicity in Children of Normal Intelligence." *J Genetic Psychol* 105:163–72 S '64. * (*PA* 39:2466)

343. HUTTON, JERRY B. "A Comparison of Digit Repetition Scores on the WISC and Revised Binet, Form L-M." *J Clin Psychol* 20:364–6 Jl '64. * (*PA* 39:10124)

344. IRWIN, DALE ORVIS. *The Reliability and the Stability of the Wechsler Intelligence Scale for Children.* Doctor's thesis, State University of Iowa (Iowa City, Iowa), 1964. (*DA* 25:5018)

345. ISCOE, IRA, AND PIERCE-JONES, JOHN. "Divergent Thinking, Age, and Intelligence in White and Negro Children." *Child Develop* 35:785–97 S '64. * (*PA* 39:4589)

346. JACKSON, CECIL LEE. *Factor Structure of the Wechsler Intelligence Scale for Children and Selected Reference Tests at Pre-School Level and After First Grade: A Longitudinal Study.* Doctor's thesis, University of Georgia (Athens, Ga.), 1964. (*DA* 25:6052)

347. JASTAK, J. F., AND JASTAK, S. R. "Short Forms of the WAIS and WISC Vocabulary Subtests." *J Clin Psychol* 20:167–99 Ap '64. * (*PA* 39:7820)

348. JENKIN, NOEL; SPIVACK, GEORGE; LEVINE, MURRAY; AND SAVAGE, WILLIAM. "Wechsler Profiles and Academic Achievement in Emotionally Disturbed Boys." Abstract. *J Consult Psychol* 28:290 Je '64. *

349. KAISER, MERLE DALLAS. *The Wechsler Intelligence Scale for Children as an Instrument for Diagnosing Sociopathy.* Doctor's thesis, Florida State University (Tallahassee, Fla.), 1964. (*DA* 25:2612)

350. KOOS, EUGENIA M. "Manifestations of Cerebral Dominance and Reading Retardation in Primary-Grade Children." *J Genetic Psychol* 104:155–65 Mr '64. * (*PA* 39:5940)

351. KRIPPNER, STANLEY. "Relationship Between Reading Improvement and Ten Selected Variables." *Percept & Motor Skills* 19:15–20 Ag '64. * (*PA* 39:5941)

352. KRIPPNER, STANLEY. "WISC Comprehension and Picture Arrangement Subtests as Measures of Social Competence." *J Clin Psychol* 20:366–7 Jl '64. * (*PA* 39:10130)

353. LARSON, KEITH HAROLD. *The Characteristics of Vocationally Successful Mentally Retarded Youth as Described by Two Types of Intelligence Tests.* Doctor's thesis, University of Oregon (Eugene, Ore.), 1964. (*DA* 25:2815)

354. LOVELL, K.; GRAY, E. A.; AND OLIVER, D. E. "A Further Study of Some Cognitive and Other Disabilities in Backward Readers of Average Nonverbal Reasoning Scores." *Brit J Ed Psychol* 34:275–9 N '64. * (*PA* 39:8668)

355. LUSIENSKI, DEAN RICHARD. *An Analysis of the Scores of Urban Negro Boys on the Wechsler Intelligence Scale for Children.* Doctor's thesis, University of Nebraska (Lincoln, Neb.), 1964. (*DA* 25:2854)

356. LUSZKI, WALTER ALOISE. *Degree of Hearing Loss Related to Intelligence as Measured by the WAIS and WISC.* Doctor's thesis, University of Georgia (Athens, Ga.), 1964. (*DA* 25:3113)

357. MAC VICAR, DONALD B. *A Study of Relationships Between WISC Subtest Scores and Reading Ability.* Master's thesis, Sacramento State College (Sacramento, Calif.), 1964.

358. MARLEY, ALBERT D. *A Validity Study of the Columbia Mental Maturity Scale and the Peabody Picture Vocabulary Test, Using the Wechsler Intelligence Scale for Children as the Validating Criterion, With a Selected Sample of Educable Mentally Retarded Children.* Doctor's research study No. 1, Colorado State College (Greeley, Colo.), 1964. (*DA* 25:5386)

359. MONEY, JOHN. "Two Cytogenetic Syndromes: Psychologic Comparisons: 1, Intelligence and Specific-Factor Quotients." *J Psychiatric Res* 2:223–31 O '64. * (*PA* 39:15981)

360. MUMPOWER, DANIEL L. "The Fallacy of the Short Form." *J Clin Psychol* 20:111–3 Ja '64. * (*PA* 39:10144)

361. NUNNALLY, JUM C. *Educational Measurement and Evaluation,* pp. 257–62. New York: McGraw-Hill Book Co., Inc., 1964. Pp. xv, 440. *

362. OSBORNE, R. TRAVIS. "WISC Factor Structure for Normal Negro Pre-School Children." *Psychol Rep* 15:543–8 O '64. * (*PA* 39:5133)

363. QUERESHI, MOHAMMED Y. "Maximum Versus Minimum Testing: A Problem in Individual Appraisal." *Univ N Dak Col Ed Rec* 49:89–92 Mr '64. *

364. ROBECK, MILDRED C. "Effects of Prolonged Reading Disability: A Preliminary Study." *Percept & Motor Skills* 19:7–12 Ag '64. * (*PA* 39:5945)

365. ROBECK, MILDRED C. "Intellectual Strengths and Weakness Shown by Reading Clinic Subjects on the WISC." *J Develop Read* 7:120–9 w '64. *

366. SAFRIN, RENATE KERSTEN. "Differences in Visual Perception and in Visual-Motor Functioning Between Psychotic and Nonpsychotic Children." *J Consult Psychol* 28:41–5 F '64. * (*PA* 38:9025)

367. SANDSTEDT, BARBARA. "Relationship Between Memory Span and Intelligence of Severely Retarded Readers." *Read Teach* 17:246–50 Ja '64. *

368. SAWYER, RITA. *A Study of Discrimination by the Sub-Tests of the Wechsler Intelligence Scale for Children Between Mildly Disabled and Severely Disabled Readers Diagnosed at the Syracuse Reading Center, September, 1958 to June, 1963.* Doctor's thesis, Syracuse University (Syracuse, N.Y.), 1964. (*DA* 26:2594)

369. SOLKOFF, NORMAN. "Frustration and WISC Coding Performance Among Brain-Injured Children." *Percept & Motor Skills* 18:54 F '64. * (*PA* 39:2482)

370. TUTT, MARY L. *A Comparison of the Wechsler Intelligence Scale for Children and the SRA Primary Mental Abilities Test.* Master's thesis, Northern Illinois University (DeKalb, Ill.), 1964.

371. TUTTLE, LESTER EUGENE, JR. *The Comparative Effect on Intelligence Test Scores of Negro and White Children When Certain Verbal and Time Factors Are Varied.* Doctor's thesis, University of Florida (Gainesville, Fla.), 1964. (*DA* 25:7093)

372. VIITAMÄKI, R. OLAVI. "A Psychological Follow-up Study: Psychoses in Childhood, Part 2." *Acta Psychiatrica Scandinavica Supplement* 174:33–93 '64. * (*PA* 39:8464)

373. WEBB, ALLEN P. "Some Issues Relating to the Validity of the WAIS in Assessing Mental Retardation." *Calif J Ed Res* 15:130–5 My '64. * (*PA* 39:5672)

374. WENDT, R. A., AND BURWELL, ELINOR. "Test Performance of Jewish Day-School Students." *J Genetic Psychol* 105:99–103 S '64. * (*PA* 39:1492)

Wechsler Intelligence Scale for Children

375. WOODY, ROBERT HENLEY. *The Use of Electroencephalography and Mental Abilities Tests in the Diagnosis of Behavioral Problem Males.* Doctor's thesis, Michigan State University (East Lansing, Mich.), 1964. *(DA* 26:204)
376. ALLEN, ROBERT M.; HAUPT, THOMAS D.; AND JONES, R. WAYNE. "Visual Perceptual Abilities and Intelligence in Mental Retardates." *J Clin Psychol* 21:299–300 Jl '65. * *(PA* 39:16039)
377. ASHLOCK, PATRICK. "The Visual Perception of Children in the Primary Grades and Its Relation to Reading Performance." *Proc Ann Conv Int Read Assn* 10:331–3 '65. *
378. BIRKEMEYER, FLORENCE. "The Relationship Between Coloured Progressive Matrices and the Wechsler Intelligence Scale for Children." *Psychol Sch* 2:278–80 Jl '65. *
379. BLATT, SIDNEY J.; ALLISON, JOEL; AND BAKER, BRUCE L. "The Wechsler Object Assembly Subtest and Bodily Concerns." *J Consult Psychol* 29:223–30 Je '65. * *(PA* 39:12225)
380. CHURCHILL, JOHN A. "The Relationship Between Intelligence and Birth Weight in Twins." *Neurology* 15:341–7 Ap '65. * *(PA* 39:15288)
381. CLEMENTS, GLADYS R. "An Abbreviated Form of the Wechsler Intelligence Scale for Children." Abstract. *J Consult Psychol* 29:92 F '65. *
382. CORDINER, MARIAN ESPACH. *A Comparative Study of the 1960 Stanford-Binet and the Wechsler Intelligence Scale for Children and Other Selected Variables.* Master's thesis, University of Utah (Salt Lake City, Utah), 1965.
383. CORWIN, BETTY JANE. "The Influence of Culture and Language on Performance of Individual Ability Tests." *J Sch Psychol* 3:41–7 sp '65. * *(PA* 39:15217)
384. COYLE, F. A., JR. "Another Alternate Wording on the WISC." *Psychol Rep* 16:1276 Je '65. * *(PA* 39:15219)
385. DEAL, MARGARET. "A Summary of Research Concerning Patterns of WISC Sub-test Scores of Retarded Readers." *J Read Specialist* 4:101–11 My '65. *
386. DI NELLO, MARIO C. *WISC Subtest Patterns as Predictors of Reading Achievement of First Grade Boys.* Doctor's thesis, University of Iowa (Iowa City, Iowa), 1965. *(DA* 26:5862)
387. ESTES, BETSY WORTH. "Relationships Between the Otis, 1960 Stanford-Binet and WISC." *J Clin Psychol* 21:296–7 Jl '65. * *(PA* 39:15230)
388. FORD, JUNE BROOKS. *Identification of a Specific Language Disability (Dyslexia).* Doctor's thesis, University of Oklahoma (Norman, Okla.), 1965. *(DA* 26:1827)
389. FRANSELLA, FAY, AND GERVER, DAVID. "Multiple Regression Equations for Predicting Reading Age From Chronological Age and WISC Verbal I.Q." *Brit J Ed Psychol* 35:86–9 F '65. * *(PA* 39:10818)
390. FURTH, HANS G., AND MILGRAM, NORMAN A. "Verbal Factors in Performance on WISC Similarities." *J Clin Psychol* 21:424–7 O '65. * *(PA* 40:1414)
391. GAGE, GERALD E., AND NAUMANN, THEODOR F. "Correlation of the Peabody Picture Vocabulary Test and the Wechsler Intelligence Scale for Children." *J Ed Res* 58:466–8 Jl–Ag '65. * *(PA* 40:422)
392. GAINER, W. L. "The Ability of the WISC Subtests to Discriminate Between Boys and Girls Classified as Educable Mentally Retarded." *Calif J Ed Res* 16:85–92 Mr '65. * *(PA* 39:10106)
393. GARIBAY, CARMEN. *A Study of the Performance of Mexican-American Children on English and Spanish Versions of the Wechsler Intelligence Scale for Children.* Master's thesis, Fresno State College (Fresno, Calif.), 1965.
394. GILBERT, J. G., AND RUBIN, E. J. "Evaluating the Intellect of Blind Children: An Evaluation of the Relative Merits of the Hayes-Binet and the WISC in Examining the Intelligence of Blind Children." *New Outl Blind* 59:238–40 S '65. *
395. GOLEN, M. EVARISTA. *A Comparison of WISC and the PGS in Prediction of School Achievement.* Master's thesis, University of Detroit (Detroit, Mich.), 1965.
396. GREEN, HARRY BRUCE, JR. *A Statistical Comparison of the Wechsler Intelligence Scale for Children and the Wechsler Adult Intelligence Scale.* Doctor's thesis, University of Virginia (Charlottesville, Va.), 1965. *(DA* 26:5866) (Abstract: *Ed R* 3:61–3)
397. GREENMUN, RENNY. *Abbreviated Forms of the Wechsler Intelligence Scale for Children.* Master's thesis, Texas Christian University (Ft. Worth, Tex.), 1965.
398. HASKELL, SIMON H., AND HUGHES, V. A. "Some Observations on the Performance of Squinters and Non-Squinters on the Wechsler Intelligence Scale for Children." *Percept & Motor Skills* 21:107–12 Ag '65. * *(PA* 40:537)
399. HECHT, PATRICIA J., AND NEWLAND, T. ERNEST. "Learning Potential and Learning Achievement of Educationally Blind Third-Eighth Graders in a Residential School." *Int J Ed Blind* 15:33–8 My '65. * *(PA* 40:3386)
400. HOLROYD, JEAN, AND WRIGHT, FRANCIS. "Neurological Implications of WISC Verbal-Performance Discrepancies in a Psychiatric Setting." *J Consult Psychol* 29:206–12 Je '65. * *(PA* 39:12690)
401. HUGHES, ROBERT B., AND LESSLER, KEN. "A Comparison of WISC and Peabody Scores of Negro and White Rural School Children." *Am J Mental Def* 69:877–80 My '65. * *(PA* 39:12289)
402. KABACK, GOLDIE RUTH. "A Comparison of WAIS, Binet, and WISC Test Results of Mentally Retarded Young Adults Born in New York City and Puerto Rico." *Training Sch B* 62:108–12 N '65. * *(PA* 40:2138)
403. KRIEGMAN, LOIS S., AND KRIEGMAN, GEORGE. "The PaTE Report: A New Psychodynamic and Therapeutic Evaluative Procedure." *Psychiatric Q* 39:646–74 O '65. * *(PA* 40:3006)
404. LOPER, DORIS JEAN. *Auditory Discrimination, Intelligence, Achievement, and Background of Experience and Information in a Culturally Disadvantaged First-Grade Population.* Doctor's thesis, Temple University (Philadelphia, Pa.), 1965. *(DA* 26:5873)
405. LUSZKI, WALTER A. "Hearing Loss and Intelligence Among Retardates." *Am J Mental Def* 70:93–101 Jl '65. * *(PA* 39:16056)
406. MCCAULEY, JOHN HOWARD, JR. *Rorschach, WISC, and ITBS Patterns of Nine-Year-Old School Boys With Labile and Stabile IQ Scores.* Doctor's thesis, University of Maryland (College Park, Md.), 1965. *(DA* 27:1663A)
407. MCLEOD, J. "A Comparison of WISC Sub-Test Scores of Pre-Adolescent Successful and Unsuccessful Readers." *Austral J Psychol* 17:220–8 D '65. * *(PA* 40:5240)
408. MCMULLEN, CATHERINE P. *WISC Profiles in Relation to Specific Aspects of Reading Disability.* Master's thesis, National College of Education (Evanston, Ill.), 1965.
409. MALIN, A. J. "An Indian Adaptation of the WISC." *J Voc & Ed Psychol* 10:128–31 N '65. * *(PA* 39:10136)
410. MASSEY, JAMES O. *WISC Scoring Supplement for the Wechsler Intelligence Scale for Children, Third Edition.* Palo Alto, Calif.: Consulting Psychologists Press, Inc., 1965. Pp. 46. *
411. MEIER, JOHN HENRY. *An Exploratory Factor Analysis of Psychodiagnostic and Case Study Information From Children in Special Education Classes for the Educable Mentally Handicapped.* Doctor's thesis, University of Denver (Denver, Colo.), 1965. *(DA* 26:3153)
412. MUEHL, SIEGMAR; KNOTT, JOHN R.; AND BENTON, ARTHUR L. "EEG Abnormality and Psychological Test Performance in Reading Disability." *Cortex* 1:434–40 Je–S '65. * *(PA* 40:1419)
413. NAAR, RAY. "A Note on the Intelligence of Delinquents in Richmond, Virginia." *Brit J Criminol* 5:82–5 Ja '65. *
414. OSBORNE, R. TRAVIS. "Factor Structure of the Wechsler Intelligence Scale for Children at Pre-School Level and After First Grade: A Longitudinal Analysis." *Psychol Rep* 16:637–44 Ap '65. * *(PA* 39:9799)
415. OTTO, WAYNE, AND MCMENEMY, RICHARD A. "An Appraisal of the Ammons Quick Test in a Remedial Reading Program." *J Ed Meas* 2:193–8 D '65. * *(PA* 40:4769)
416. OWENS, KAYE DON. *A Comparison of the Behavioral Patterns of the Mentally Retarded and Average Children During the Administration of the Wechsler Intelligence Scale for Children.* Doctor's research study No. 1, Colorado State College (Greeley, Colo.), 1965. *(DA* 26:875)
417. PLESS, I. BARRY; SNIDER, MARVIN; EATON, ANN E.; AND KEARSLEY, RICHARD B. "A Rapid Screening Test for Intelligence in Children: A Preliminary Report." *Am J Dis Children* 109:533–7 Je '65. * *(PA* 40:425)
418. RAJALAKSHMI, R., AND JEEVES, M. A. "Discrimination Learning and Reversal Learning in Children as Related to Performance on Certain WISC Items and on the Goodenough Draw-A-Man Test." *J Genetic Psychol* 106:149–56 Mr '65. * *(PA* 39:11993)
419. RICH, CHARLES C., AND ANDERSON, ROBERT P. "A Tactual Form of the Progressive Matrices for Use With Blind Children." *Personnel & Guid J* 43:912–9 My '65. * *(PA* 39:15197)
420. SAWYER, RITA I. "Does the Wechsler Intelligence Scale for Children Discriminate Between Mildly and Severely Disabled Readers?" *El Sch J* 66:97–103 N '65. * *(PA* 40:2920)
421. SCHULMAN, JEROME L.; KASPAR, JOSEPH C.; AND THORNE, FRANCES M. *Brain Damage and Behavior: A Clinical-Experimental Study.* Springfield, Ill.: Charles C Thomas, Publisher, 1965. Pp. ix, 164. *
422. SHANE, JAMES F. *Effectiveness of the Peabody Picture Vocabulary Test in Comparison to Wechsler Intelligence Scale for Children and Stanford-Binet Test Scores in Identification of Mentally Retarded and Gifted School Children.* Master's thesis, California State College (Long Beach, Calif.), 1965.
423. SILBERBERG, NORMAN ESAU. *An Investigation to Identify Intellectual and Perceptual Correlates of Disability in Word Recognition.* Doctor's thesis, State University of Iowa (Iowa City, Iowa), 1965. *(DA* 26:878)
424. THORPE, JOSEPH S. "A Cross-Cultural Study of Personality Development: Selection of Test Measures." *Congr Inter-Am Soc Psychol* 9(1964):242–9 ['65].*
425. THRONE, FRANCES M.; KASPAR, JOSEPH C.; AND SCHULMAN, JEROME L. "The Peabody Picture Vocabulary Test in Comparison With Other Intelligence Tests and an Achievement Test in a Group of Mentally Retarded Boys." *Ed & Psychol Meas* 25:589–95 su '65. * *(PA* 39:16072)
426. UFFORD, MARY SOLANUS. *A Design and Application for the Evaluation of Effectiveness of Speech Therapy.* Doctor's thesis, Wayne State University (Detroit, Mich.), 1965. *(DAI* 30:3424B)
427. VANDERPOOL, JAMES. *An Investigation of the Potential*

Use of WISC Scores for Differential Diagnosis. Master's thesis, Loyola University (Chicago, Ill.), 1965.
428. WALLACH, MICHAEL A., AND KOGAN, NATHAN. *Modes of Thinking in Young Children: A Study of the Creativity-Intelligence Distinction*, pp. 25-65. New York: Henry Holt & Winston, Inc., 1965. Pp. ix, 357. *
429. WASSING, H. E. "Cognitive Functioning in Early Infantile Autism: An Examination of Four Cases by Means of the Wechsler Intelligence Scale for Children." *Acta Paedopsychiatrica* 32:122-35 Ap '65. * (*PA* 39:15376)
430. WECHSLER, DAVID, AND JAROS, EUGENIA. "Schizophrenic Patterns on the WISC." *J Clin Psychol* 21:288-91 Jl '65. * (*PA* 39:15378)
431. AHMAD, FARRUKH Z. "A Study of the Relationship Between Test Intelligence and Delinquency." *Psychologia* 9:24-6 Mr '66. * (*PA* 41:1729)
432. BARCLAY, A., AND CAROLAN, PATRICIA. "A Comparative Study of the Wechsler Intelligence Scale for Children and the Stanford-Binet Intelligence Scale, Form L-M." Abstract. *J Consult Psychol* 30:563 D '66. *
433. BAUMEISTER, ALFRED A., AND HAWKINS, WILLIAM F. "WISC Scores of Retardates in Relation to Learning Ability." *J Clin Psychol* 22:75-6 Ja '66. * (*PA* 40:4549)
434. BELMONT, LILLIAN, AND BIRCH, HERBERT G. "The Intellectual Profile of Retarded Readers." *Percept & Motor Skills* 22:787-816 Je '66. * (*PA* 40:11497)
435. BERG, VERNA. *The Effect of Timing on Performance on the Wechsler Intelligence Scale for Children*. Master's thesis, University of Utah (Salt Lake City, Utah), 1966.
436. BERLIN, MARTIN ALBERT. *The Use of a Modified Block Design Technique in the Assessment of Educability for Boys From Lower Socio-Economic Environments*. Doctor's thesis, Rutgers—The State University (New Brunswick, N.J.), 1966. (*DA* 27:4121A)
437. BRANSFORD, LOUIS ALEXANDER. *A Comparative Investigation of Verbal and Performance Intelligence Measures at Different Age Levels With Bilingual Spanish-Speaking Children in Special Classes for the Mentally Retarded*. Doctor's research study No. 1, Colorado State College (Greeley, Colo.), 1966. (*DA* 27:226-A)
438. BREESKIN, JOHN. *The Development of Time Estimation in Children*. Doctor's thesis, University of Texas (Austin, Tex.), 1966. (*DA* 27:3267B)
439. CAMP, BONNIE WEBB. "WISC Performance in Acting-Out and Delinquent Children With and Without EEG Abnormality." *J Consult Psychol* 30:350-3 Ag '66. * (*PA* 40:11181)
440. CRADDICK, RAY A. "WISC and WAIS IQs as a Function of Season of Birth." *Psychol Rep* 18:259-64 F '66. * (*PA* 40:6626)
441. DAVIS, LEO J., JR. "The Internal Consistency of the WISC With the Mentally Retarded." *Am J Mental Def* 70:714-6 Mr '66. * (*PA* 40:6972)
442. DWYER, ROBERT CORCORAN. *Development of Three Subtests of Verbal Intelligence for Use With Severely Response Handicapped Children*. Doctor's thesis, George Peabody College for Teachers (Nashville, Tenn.), 1966. (*DA* 27:3718A)
443. EGELAND, BYRON RICKER. *The Relationship of Intelligence, Visual-Motor Skills and Psycholinguistic Abilities With Achievement in the First Grade*. Doctor's thesis, University of Iowa (Iowa City, Iowa), 1966. (*DA* 27:388A)
444. EKWALL, ELDON EDWARD. *The Use of WISC Subtest Profiles in the Diagnosis of Reading Difficulties*. Doctor's thesis, University of Arizona (Tucson, Ariz.), 1966. (*DA* 27:950A)
445. EXNER, JOHN E., JR. "Variations in WISC Performances as Influenced by Differences in Pretest Rapport." *J General Psychol* 74:299-306 Ap '66. * (*PA* 40:7194)
446. FITCH, MICHAEL JOHN. *Verbal and Performance Test Scores in Bilingual Children* Doctor's research study No. 1, Colorado State College (Greeley, Colo.), 1966. (*DA* 27:1654A)
447. FOLEY, MARY VENARD. *A Study of the Differences Between Boys and Girls, and Between Boys and Girls of Different IQ Levels, on a Certain Selection of Subtests of the Wechsler Intelligence Scale for Children*. Master's thesis, Cardinal Stritch College (Milwaukee, Wis.), 1966.
448. FULLER, GERALD B. "A Comparison of Intelligence and Perception in Emotionally Disturbed Children." *J Clin Psychol* 22:193-5 Ap '66. * (*PA* 40:7890)
449. HARTE, MARY LABOURE. *Anxiety and Defensiveness as Related to Measurable Intelligence and Scholastic Achievement of Selected Institutionalized Children*. Doctor's thesis, Fordham University (New York, N.Y.), 1966. (*DA* 27:2884A)
450. HOLTZMAN, WAYNE H. "Intelligence, Cognitive Style, and Personality: A Developmental Approach," pp. 1-32. In *Intelligence: Perspectives 1965: The Terman-Otis Memorial Lectures*. By Orville G. Brim, Jr., Richard S. Crutchfield, and Wayne H. Holtzman. New York: Harcourt Brace & World, Inc., 1966. Pp. x, 101. *
451. HOPKINS, KENNETH D., AND MCGUIRE, LENORE. "Mental Measurement of the Blind: The Validity of the Wechsler Intelligence Scale for Children." *Int J Ed Blind* 15:65-73 My '66. * (*PA* 40:7985)
452. HOROWITZ, FRANCES DEGEN. "The Relationship Between Wechsler Intelligence Quotients and Parsons Language Sample Scores of Mentally Retarded Children." *J Genetic Psychol* 108:59-63 Mr '66. * (*PA* 40:10400)
453. IRWIN, DALE O. "Reliability of the Wechsler Intelligence Scale for Children." *J Ed Meas* 3:287-92 w '66. * (*PA* 41:11918)
454. KISSEL, STANLEY. "Juvenile Delinquency and Psychological Differentiation: Differences Between Social and Solitary Delinquents." *J Clin Psychol* 22:442 O '66. * (*PA* 41:3090)
455. KISSEL, STANLEY. "Schizophrenic Patterns on the WISC: A Missing Control." *J Clin Psychol* 22:201 Ap '66. * (*PA* 40:7910)
456. LAUER, BARBARA A. *The Relationship Between Creativity and Subtest Scores on the WISC*. Master's thesis, Kent State University (Kent, Ohio), 1966.
457. LERAND, LESLIE WAYNE. *Intelligence and Reading Level of Girls*. Doctor's research study No. 1, Colorado State College (Greeley, Colo.), 1966. (*DA* 27:2137B)
458. LINDSEY, JAMES MORRISON. *The Factorial Organization of Intelligence in Children as Related to the Variables of Age, Sex and Subculture*. Doctor's thesis, University of Georgia (Athens, Ga.), 1966. (*DA* 27:3664B)
459. MCELHANEY, MARK LUCAS. *A Comparison of Temporal Lobe With Non-Temporal Lobe Brain Damage as Shown by Various Psychological Tests*. Doctor's thesis, University of Houston (Houston, Tex.), 1966. (*DA* 27:1625B)
460. MCGRAW, JOSEPH J. *A Comparison of Mean Subtest Raw Scores on the Wechsler Intelligence Scale for Children of Regular and Over-Achieving Readers With Under-Achieving Readers*. Doctor's thesis, University of Oklahoma (Norman, Okla.), 1966. (*DA* 27:1552A)
461. MCLEOD, JOHN. *Some Psychological and Psycholinguistic Aspects of Severe Reading Disability in Children*. Doctor's thesis, University of Queensland (Brisbane, Australia), 1966.
462. MONEY, JOHN, AND EHRHARDT, ANKE A. "Preservation of IQ in Hypoparathyroidism of Childhood." *Am J Mental Def* 71:237-43 S '66. * (*PA* 40:13235)
463. MORPER, JACK. *An Investigation of the Relationship of Certain Predictive Variables and Academic Achievement of Spanish-American and Anglo Pupils in Junior High School*. Doctor's thesis, Oklahoma State University (Stillwater, Okla.), 1966. (*DA* 27:4051A)
464. NICKOLS, JOHN, AND NICKOLS, MARCIA. "A Brief Arthur's Stencils Test, Form I." *J Clin Psychol* 22:436-8 O '66. * (*PA* 41:2263)
465. OSBORNE, R. T. "Stability of Factor Structure of the WISC for Normal Negro Children From Pre-School Level to First Grade." *Psychol Rep* 18:655-64 Ap '66. * (*PA* 40:8862)
466. REGER, ROGER. "WISC, WRAT, and CMAS Scores in Retarded Children." *Am J Mental Def* 70:717-21 Mr '66. * (*PA* 40:6987)
467. REID, WILLIAM R., AND SCHOER, LOWELL A. "Reading Achievement, Social-Class and Subtest Pattern on the WISC." *J Ed Res* 59:469-72 Jl-Ag '66. * (*PA* 40:11490)
468. SELLS, S. B. *Evaluation of Psychological Measures Used in the Health Examination Survey of Children Ages 6-11*, pp. 2-23. Public Health Service Publication No. 1000, Series 2, No. 15. Washington, D.C.: United States Government Printing Office, March 1966. Pp. viii, 67. * (*PA* 40:7217)
469. SEMLER, IRA J., AND ISCOE, IRA. "Structure of Intelligence in Negro and White Children." *J Ed Psychol* 57:326-36 D '66. * (*PA* 41:1418)
470. SHAW, DALE J.; MATTHEWS, CHARLES G.; AND KLØVE, HALLGRIM. "The Equivalence of WISC and PPVT IQs." *Am J Mental Def* 70:601-4 Ja '66. * (*PA* 40:5454)
471. SHEARER, PAUL D. *A Study of the Relationship Between the WISC and School Success of Emotionally Disturbed Children*. Master's thesis, University of Richmond (Richmond, Va.), 1966.
472. SILBERBERG, NORMAN E., AND FELDT, LEONARD S. "The Peabody Picture Vocabulary Test as an IQ Screening Technique for Primary Grade Referral Cases." *J Sch Psychol* 5:21-30 au '66. * (*PA* 41:3345)
473. SPREEN, OTFRIED, AND ANDERSON, CHARLES W. G. "Sibling Relationship and Mental Deficiency Diagnosis as Reflected in Wechsler Test Patterns." *Am J Mental Def* 71:406-10 N '66. * (*PA* 41:1850)
474. TEIGLAND, JOHN J.; WINKLER, RONALD C.; MUNGER, PAUL F.; AND KRANZLER, GERALD D. "Some Concomitants of Underachievement at the Elementary School Level." *Personnel & Guid J* 44:950-5 My '66. * (*PA* 40:10429)
475. TILLMAN, MURRAY HOWELL. *A Comparison of the Factor Structure of Blind and Normals on the Verbal WISC*. Doctor's thesis, University of Georgia (Athens, Ga.), 1966. (*DA* 27:3665B)
476-7. TUTTLE, LESTER EUGENE, JR. "The Comparative Effect on Intelligence Test Scores of Negro and Caucasian Children When Certain Verbal and Time Factors Are Varied by Use of the WISC, PPVT and CMMS." *Fla J Ed Res* 8:49-61 Ja '66. *
478. WISSER, ROBERT E. *The Relationship Between WISC Verbal-Performance Discrepancy and Degree of Delinquency*. Master's thesis, Springfield College (Springfield, Mass.), 1966.
479. WITKIN, HERMAN A.; FATERSON, HANNA F.; GOODENOUGH, DONALD R.; AND BIRNBAUM, JUDITH. "Cognitive Patterning in Mildly Retarded Boys." *Child Develop* 37:301-16 Je '66. * (*PA* 40:9184)

480. YUDIN, LEE WILLIAM. "An Abbreviated Form of the WISC for Use With Emotionally Disturbed Children." *J Consult Psychol* 30:272-5 Je '66. * (*PA* 40:8274)
481. ZEDLER, EMPRESS Y. "A Screening Scale for Children With High Risk of Neurological Impairment." *Ann Inter Conf Assn Children Learn Dis* 3:20-8 '66. *
482. ZLODY, RUDOLPH L.; AND FITZGERALD, MARY CALLISTA. "WISC Scores Made by Children With Articulatory Speech Difficulties." *Cath Ed R* 64:551-4 N '66. *
483. ALPER, ARTHUR E. "An Analysis of the Wechsler Intelligence Scale for Children With Institutionalized Mental Retardates." *Am J Mental Def* 71:624-30 Ja '67. * (*PA* 41:6174)
484. BEAN, WILLIAM JAMES. *The Isolation of Some Psychometric Indices of Severe Reading Disability.* Doctor's thesis, Texas Technological College (Lubbock, Tex.), 1967. (*DA* 28:3012A)
485. BELMONT, IRA; BIRCH, HERBERT G.; AND BELMONT, LILLIAN. "The Organization of Intelligence Test Performance in Educable Mentally Subnormal Children." *Am J Mental Def* 71:969-76 My '67. * (*PA* 41:12371)
486. BIRCH, HERBERT G.; BELMONT, LILLIAN; BELMONT, IRA; AND TAFT, LAWRENCE T. "Brain Damage and Intelligence in Educable Mentally Subnormal Children." *J Nerv & Mental Dis* 144:247-57 Ap '67. * (*PA* 41:15702)
487. BORNSTEIN, ALAN VANDAM. *The Effects of Examiner Approval and Disapproval Upon the Performance of Subjects on the Performance Scale of the Wechsler Intelligence Scale for Children.* Doctor's thesis, Florida State University (Tallahassee, Fla.), 1967. (*DA* 28:3047B)
488. BRODT, AUDREY. *An Investigation of WISC Vocabulary Instructions.* Master's thesis, Loyola University (Chicago, Ill.), 1967.
489. BUTLER, KATHARINE GORRELL. *Psychogenic Articulation Disorders Related to Verbal Skills and Intelligence as Measured by the Wechsler Intelligence Scale for Children.* Doctor's thesis, Michigan State University (East Lansing, Mich.), 1967. (*DA* 28:4332B)
490. CATE, CLARENCE C. "Test Behavior of ESL Students." *Calif J Ed Res* 18:184-7 S '67. * (*PA* 42:4480)
491. CHANG, THOMAS M. C., AND CHANG, VIVIAN A. C. "Relation of Visual-Motor Skills and Reading Achievement in Primary-Grade Pupils of Superior Ability." *Percept & Motor Skills* 24:51-3 F '67. * (*PA* 41:8701)
492. CHARRY, LAWRENCE BERNARD. *The Relationship Between Prereading and First Grade Reading Performances and Subsequent Achievement in Reading and Other Specified Areas.* Doctor's thesis, Temple University (Philadelphia, Pa.), 1967. (*DA* 28:960A)
493. COLE, SPURGEON N.; WILLIAMS, ROBERT J.; NIX, ALICE P.; AND LITAKER, ROBERT G. "Validity of an Abbreviated WISC Scale for Retarded and Borderline Children." *Psychol Rep* 21:571-2 O '67. * (*PA* 42:4795)
494. CONKLIN, R. C., AND DOCKRELL, W. B. "The Predictive Validity and Stability of WISC Scores Over a Four Year Period." *Psychol Sch* 4:263-6 Jl '67. * (*PA* 41:15871)
495. CORWIN, BETTY JANE. "The Relationship Between Reading Achievement and Performance on Individual Ability Tests." Abstract. *J Sch Psychol* 5:156-7 w '67. * (*PA* 41:9386)
496. DAVIS, LEO J., JR., AND REITAN, RALPH M. "Dysphasia and Constructional Dyspraxia Items, and Wechsler Verbal and Performance IQs in Retardates." *Am J Mental Def* 71:604-8 Ja '67. * (*PA* 41:6179)
497. DEBRULER, RALPH MILES. *An Investigation of Relationships Between Subtest Scores on the Wechsler Intelligence Scale for Children and Reading Ability.* Doctor's thesis, University of Oregon (Eugene, Ore.), 1967. (*DA* 29:143A)
498. DUDEK, S. Z.; LESTER, L. P.; AND HARRIS, B. R. "Variability on Tests of Cognitive and Perceptual-Motor Development in Kindergarten Children." *J Clin Psychol* 23:461-4 O '67. * (*PA* 42:2400)
499. DUNN, JAMES A. "Note on the Relation of Harris' Draw-A-Woman to WISC IQs." *Percept & Motor Skills* 24:316 F '67. * (*PA* 41:8880)
500. DUNN, JAMES A. "Validity Coefficients for the New Harris-Goodenough Draw-A-Man Test." *Percept & Motor Skills* 24:299-301 F '67. * (*PA* 41:8149)
501. EGELAND, BYRON. "Influence of Examiner and Examinee Anxiety on WISC Performance." *Psychol Rep* 21:409-14 O '67. * (*PA* 42:6082)
502. ELITCHER, HELENE. *Children's Causal Thinking as a Function of Cognitive Style and Question Wording.* Doctor's thesis, New York University (New York, N.Y.), 1967. (*DA* 28:1294A)
503. ERIKSON, ROBERT V. "Abbreviated Form of the WISC: A Reevaluation." Abstract. *J Consult Psychol* 31:641 D '67. * (*PA* 42:2562)
504. FAST, ROBERT ERWIN. *The Effects of Verbal and Monetary Reward on the Individual Intelligence Test Performance of Children of Differing Socio-Economic Status.* Doctor's thesis, Rutgers—The State University (New Brunswick, N.J.), 1967. (*DA* 28:1703A)
505. FERNALD, PETER S., AND WISSER, ROBERT E. "Using WISC Verbal-Performance Discrepancy to Predict Degree of Acting Out." *J Clin Psychol* 23:92-3 Ja '67. * (*PA* 41:5957)
506. FLEMING, JEAN MCKEY. *Body Image and Learning of Deaf and Hearing Boys.* Doctor's thesis, University of Florida (Gainesville, Fla.), 1967. (*DA* 29:144A)
507. FROSTIG, MARIANNE. "Testing as a Basis for Educational Therapy." *J Spec Ed* 2:15-34 f '67. * (*PA* 42:7770)
508. GALVAN, ROBERT ROGERS. *Bilingualism as It Relates to Intelligence Test Scores and School Achievement Among Culturally Deprived Spanish-American Children.* Doctor's thesis, East Texas State University (Commerce, Tex.), 1967. (*DA* 28:3021A)
509. GLASSER, ALAN J., AND ZIMMERMAN, IRLA LEE. *Clinical Interpretation of the Wechsler Intelligence Scale for Children (WISC).* New York: Grune & Stratton, Inc., 1967. Pp. v, 152. *
510. GRAUBARD, PAUL S. "The Use of the Peabody Picture Vocabulary Test in the Prediction and Assessment of Reading Disability in Disturbed Children." *J Ed Res* 61:3-5 S '67. *
511. HENNING, JOHN J., AND LEVY, RUSSELL H. "Verbal-Performance IQ Differences of White and Negro Delinquents on the WISC and WAIS." *J Clin Psychol* 23:164-8 Ap '67. * (*PA* 41:9127)
512. HERSHENSON, DAVID B. "Body-Image (Hand) and Arithmetic Ability." *Percept & Motor Skills* 25:967-8 D '67. * (*PA* 42:8994)
513. HOPKINS, KENNETH D., AND MCGUIRE, LENORE. "IQ Constancy and the Blind Child." *Int J Ed Blind* 16:113-4 My '67. * (*PA* 41:10945)
514. HUEFTLE, M. KEENE. *A Factor Analytic Study of the Frostig Developmental Test of Visual Perception, the Illinois Test of Psycholinguistic Abilities, and the Wechsler Intelligence Scale for Children.* Doctor's thesis, Colorado State College (Greeley, Colo.), 1967. (*DA* 28:2139B)
515. IRWIN, ORVIS C., AND KORST, JOSEPH W. "Correlations Among Five Speech Tests and the WISC Verbal Scale." *Cereb Palsy J* 28:9-11 S-O '67. * (*PA* 42:3201)
516. JACOBSON, FRANK N. "Differences on the WISC Digit Span Between Outpatient Clinic and Delinquent Boys." *Percept & Motor Skills* 25:840 D '67. * (*PA* 42:9160)
517. JONES, GENTRY THOMAS, JR. *An Experimental Investigation of Family Relationships Among Mental Retardates.* Doctor's thesis, University of Oklahoma (Norman, Okla.), 1967. (*DA* 27:4125B)
518. KOPPITZ, ELIZABETH MUNSTERBERG. "Expected and Exceptional Items on Human Figure Drawings and IQ Scores of Children Age 5 to 12." *J Clin Psychol* 23:81-3 Ja '67. * (*PA* 41:5985)
519. LAMP, ROBERT E., AND BARCLAY, A. "The Quick Test as a Screening Device for Intellectually Subnormal Children." *Psychol Rep* 20:-63-6 Je '67. * (*PA* 41:13596)
520. LAVITT, JERRY A. *A Comparative Evaluation of the Peabody Picture Vocabulary Test as a Measure of Ability for Children of Differing Reading Proficiency Levels.* Doctor's thesis, Oklahoma State University (Stillwater, Okla.), 1967. (*DA* 28:4877A)
521. LOVELL, K., AND SHIELDS, J. B. "Some Aspects of a Study of the Gifted Child." *Brit J Ed Psychol* 37:201-8 Je '67. * (*PA* 41:15273)
522. MCLEOD, JOHN. "Some Psycholinguistic Correlates of Reading Disability in Young Children." *Read Res Q* 2:5-31 sp '67. * (*PA* 41:11883)
523. MILGRAM, NORMAN A. "A Note on the PPVT in Mental Retardates." *Am J Mental Def* 72:496-7 N '67. * (*PA* 42:7658)
524. MONEY, JOHN, AND EPSTEIN, RALPH. "Verbal Aptitude in Eonism and Prepubertal Effeminacy: A Feminine Trait." *Trans N Y Acad Sci* 29:448-54 F '67. * (*PA* 41:16833)
525. NALVEN, FREDRIC B. "Relationship Between Digit Span and Distractibility Ratings in Emotionally Disturbed Children." *J Clin Psychol* 23:466-7 O '67. * (*PA* 42:2731)
526. NAMY, ELMER. "Intellectual and Academic Characteristics of Fourth Grade Gifted and Pseudogifted Students." *Excep Children* 34:15-8 S '67. * (*PA* 41:17073)
527. NEUHAUS, MAURY. "Modifications in the Administration of the WISC Performance Subtests for Children With Profound Hearing Losses." *Excep Children* 33:573-4 Ap '67. * (*PA* 41:8883)
528. NEWLAND, T. ERNEST, AND SMITH, PATRICIA A. "Statistically Significant Difference Between Subtest Scaled Scores on the WISC and the WAIS." *J Sch Psychol* 5:122-7 w '67. * (*PA* 41:8884)
529. NICKOLS, JOHN. "Explorations on Productive Thinking Tasks for Group Testing." *Psychiatric Q Sup* 41:128-42 pt 1 '67. * (*PA* 44:8745)
530. OGDON, DONALD P. Section 2, "The Wechsler Scales," pp. 3-10, 75-7. In his *Psychodiagnostics and Personality Assessment: A Handbook.* Beverly Hills, Calif.: Western Psychological Services, 1967. Pp. v, 96. *
531. OKI, TADAHIKO. "A Psychological Study of Early Childhood Neuroses." *B Osaka Med Sch Sup* 12:344-59 '67. *
532. OSBORNE, R. T., AND TILLMAN, M. H. "Normal and Retardate WISC Performance: An Analysis of the Stimulus Trace Theory." *Am J Mental Def* 72:257-61 S '67. * (*PA* 42:2882)
533. OSBORNE, R. T.; ANDERSON, HARRY E., JR.; AND BASHAW, W. L. "The Stability of the WISC Factor Structure at Three Age Levels." *Multiv Behav Res* 2:443-51 O '67. * (*PA* 42:6388)

534. OSBORNE, R. TRAVIS, AND LINDSEY, JAMES M. "A Longitudinal Investigation of Change in the Factorial Composition of Intelligence With Age in Young School Children." *J Genetic Psychol* 110:49–58 Mr '67. * (*PA* 41:7141)
535. OSMAN, HASSAN HAFEZ. *An Investigative Study in the Creative Thinking of Emotionally Disturbed Children in Special Classes.* Doctor's thesis, University of Kansas (Lawrence, Kan.), 1967. (*DA* 28:5210B)
536. PASEWARK, R. A.; SAWYER, R. N.; SMITH, E.; WASSERBERGER, M.; DELL, D.; BRITO, H.; AND LEE, R. "Concurrent Validity of the French Pictorial Test of Intelligence." *J Ed Res* 61:179–83 D '67. *
537. PICKLES, D. G. "Intelligence Tests and the Ascertainment of the Educationally Subnormal: A Comparative Study of the Stanford-Binet and Wechsler Intelligence Scales." *Pub Health* 81:133–44 Mr '67. *
538. REED, JAMES C. "Reading Achievement as Related to Differences Between WISC Verbal and Performance IQ's." *Child Develop* 38:835–40 S '67. * (*PA* 41:16696)
539. ROCKWELL, G. JAMES, JR. "WISC Object Assembly and Bodily Concern." Abstract. *J Consult Psychol* 31:221 Ap '67. *
540. ROSS, ROBERT T., AND MORLEDGE, JUNE. "Comparison of the WISC and WAIS at Chronological Age Sixteen." *J Consult Psychol* 31:331–2 Je '67. * (*PA* 41:10449)
541. RUSSELL, CAROL A. *A Comparison of Performance on the Stanford-Binet Intelligence Scale, Form L-M, and the Wechsler Intelligence Scale for Children With Mentally Retarded Subjects.* Master's thesis, University of Utah (Salt Lake City, Utah), 1967.
542. SAK, HELEN G.; SMITH, ALFRED A.; AND DAVIES, JOSEPH. "Psychometric Evaluation of Children With Familial Dysautonomia." *Am J Psychiatry* 124:682–7 N '67. * (*PA* 42:5959).
543. SATTLER, JEROME M., AND THEYE, FRED. "Procedural, Situational, and Interpersonal Variables in Individual Intelligence Testing." *Psychol B* 68:347–60 N '67. * (*PA* 42:2564)
544. SATZ, PAUL; VAN DE RIET, HANI; AND MOGEL, STEVE. "An Abbreviation of the WISC for Clinical Use." Abstract. *J Consult Psychol* 31:108 F '67. *
545. SCHUBERT, JOSEF. "Effect of Training on the Performance of the W.I.S.C. 'Block Design' Subtest." *Brit J Social & Clin Psychol* 6:144–9 Je '67. * (*PA* 41:13600)
546. SCOTTISH COUNCIL FOR RESEARCH IN EDUCATION. *The Scottish Standardisation of WISC.* Publications of the Scottish Council for Research in Education 55. London: University of London Press Ltd., 1967. Pp. 71. * (*PA* 39:15281)
547. SILVERSTEIN, A. B. "Estimating Full Scale IQs From WISC Short Forms." *Psychol Rep* 20:1264 Je '67. *
548. SILVERSTEIN, A. B. "A Short Short Form of the WISC and WAIS for Screening Purposes." *Psychol Rep* 20:682 Ap '67. * (*PA* 41:8164)
549. SILVERSTEIN, A. B. "Validity of WISC Short Forms at Three Age Levels." *J Consult Psychol* 31:635–6 D '67. * (*PA* 42:1415)
550. SILVERSTEIN, ARTHUR B. "Validity of WISC Short Forms at Three Age Levels." *Calif Mental Health Res Dig* 5:253–4 au '67. * (*PA* 42:138)
551. STEVENS, DOUGLAS A.; BOYDSTUN, JAMES A.; DYKMAN, ROSCOE A.; PETERS, JOHN E.; AND SINTON, DAVID W. "Presumed Minimal Brain Dysfunction in Children: Relationship to Performance on Selected Behavioral Tests." *Arch Gen Psychiatry* 16:281–5 Mr '67. * (*PA* 41:0252)
552. STONE, LEROY A. "The Devaluated Shilling and the WISC." *Psychol Rep* 20:280 F '67. * (*PA* 41:6466)
553. TAVA, EDWARD GERALD. *A Review of the Short Forms of the Wechsler Intelligence Scale for Children.* Master's thesis, Western Michigan University (Kalamazoo, Mich.), 1967. (*Masters Abstracts* 6:157)
554. TELLEGEN, AUKE, AND BRIGGS, PETER F. "Old Wine in New Skins: Grouping Wechsler Subtests Into New Scales." *J Consult Psychol* 31:499–506 O '67. * (*PA* 41:16071)
555. THORNTON, CARL L., AND BARRETT, GERALD V. "Psychological Differentiation and WISC 'Analytical IQ,' Methodological Note." *Percept & Motor Skills* 25:704 D '67. * (*PA* 42:8971)
556. TILLMAN, M. H. "The Performance of Blind and Sighted Children on the Wechsler Intelligence Scale for Children: Study 1." *Int J Ed Blind* 16:65–74 Mr '67. * (*PA* 41:10948)
557. TILLMAN, M. H. "The Performances of Blind and Sighted Children on the Wechsler Intelligence Scale for Children: Study 2." *Int J Ed Blind* 16:106–12 My '67. * (*PA* 41:10949)
558. TRIEGLAFF, ANNETTE L. *The Relationship Between the Wechsler Intelligence Scale for Children and Reading Scores for the Stanford Achievement Test.* Master's thesis, Sacramento State College (Sacramento, Calif.), 1967.
559. TURNER, R. K.; MATHEWS, A.; AND RACHMAN, S. "The Stability of the WISC in a Psychiatric Group." *Brit J Ed Psychol* 37:194–200 Je '67. * (*PA* 41:14459)
560. WARD, JAMES. "An Oblique Factorization of Wallach and Kogan's 'Creativity' Correlations." *Brit J Ed Psychol* 37:380–2 N '67. * (*PA* 42:4784)
561. WARRINGTON, ELIZABETH K. "The Incidence of Verbal Disability Associated With Retardation Reading." *Neuropsychologia* 5:175–9 My '67. * (*PA* 42:11212)

562. WILLERMAN, LEE, AND CHURCHILL, JOHN A. "Intelligence and Birth Weight in Identical Twins." *Child Develop* 38:623–9 S '67. * (*PA* 41:16697)
563. WILTBERGER, ARLENE CAMPBELL. *A Comparative Study of the Wechsler Intelligence Scale for Children and the Wechsler Adult Intelligence Scale With High IQ Level and Low IQ Level Subjects.* Master's thesis, Cornell University (Ithaca, N.Y.), 1967.
564. WOODY, ROBERT H. "Diagnosis of Behavioral Problem Children: Electroencephalography and Mental Abilities." *J Sch Psychol* 5:116–21 w '67. * (*PA* 41:9383)
565. YULE, WILLIAM. "Predicting Reading Ages on Neale's Analysis of Reading Ability." *Brit J Ed Psychol* 37:252–5 Je '67. * (*PA* 41:15822)
566. ANASTASI, ANNE. *Psychological Testing, Third Edition,* pp. 282–8. New York: Macmillan Co., 1968. Pp. xiii, 665. *
567. ANDERSON, DARRELL E., AND FLAX, MORTON L. "A Comparison of the Peabody Picture Vocabulary Test With the Wechsler Intelligence Scale for Children." *J Ed Res* 62:114–6 N '68. *
568. ANDO, KYOKO. "A Comparative Study of Peabody Picture Vocabulary Test and Wechsler Intelligence Scale for Children With a Group of Cerebral Palsied Children." *Cereb Palsy J* 29:7–9 My–Je '68. * (*PA* 42:15909)
569. ARMSTRONG, JUDITH GLANTZ. *Intellectual Competence and Coping Behavior in Preschool Children.* Doctor's thesis, University of California (Berkeley, Calif.), 1968. (*DA* 29:4837B)
570. BAE, AGNES Y. "Factors Influencing Vocational Efficiency of Institutionalized Retardates in Different Training Programs." *Am J Mental Def* 72:871–4 My '68. * (*PA* 42:14397)
571. BATTIN, R., AND KRAFT, IRVIN A. "Psycholinguistic Evaluation of Children Referred for Private Consultation to a Child Psychiatrist." *J Learn Dis* 1:600–5 O '68. * (*PA* 45:2995)
572. BECK, FRANCES. "Performance of Retarded Readers on Parts of the Wechsler Intelligence Scale for Children." *Sup Ed Monogr* 97:91–103 Ag '68. *
573. BOWLES, FRANK LOUIS. *Sub-Test Score Changes Over Twenty Months on the Wechsler Intelligence Scale for Children for White and Negro Special Education Students.* Doctor's thesis, University of Florida (Gainesville, Fla.), 1968. (*DAI* 30:54A)
574. BRITTAIN, MICHAEL. "A Comparative Study of the Use of the Wechsler Intelligence Scale for Children and the Stanford-Binet Intelligence Scale (Form L-M) With Eight-Year-Old Children." *Brit J Ed Psychol* 38:103–4 F '68. *
575. BRUNSON, FORREST WARD. *Comparative Ratings of Intelligence and of Achievement of Children From Low- and Middle-Socioeconomic Areas.* Doctor's thesis, University of Nebraska (Lincoln, Neb.), 1968. (*DA* 29:4318A)
576. BURCH, CHARLES WILLIAM. *Assessment Variables Relevant to the Referral and Placement of Pupils in Educationally Handicapped Classes.* Doctor's thesis, University of Southern California (Los Angeles, Calif.), 1968. (*DA* 29:2995A)
577. BURNES, DONNA KAY STANDLEY. *A Study of Relationships Between Measured Intelligence and Non-Intellective Factors for Children of Two Socioeconomic Groups and Races.* Doctor's thesis, Washington University (St. Louis, Mo.), 1968. (*DA* 29:4839B)
578. BUTTERFIELD, EARL C. "Stimulus Trace in the Mentally Retarded, Defect or Developmental Lag?" *J Abn Psychol* 73:358–62 Ag '68. * (*PA* 42:17539)
579. CACCAVO, EMIL. *The Listening Comprehension Level of an Informal Reading Inventory as a Predictor of Intelligence of Elementary School Children.* Doctor's thesis, New York University (New York, N.Y.), 1968. (*DAI* 30:164A)
580. CALDWELL, MARCUS B., AND SMITH, TIMOTHY A. "Intellectual Structure of Southern Negro Children." *Psychol Rep* 23:63–71 Ag '68. * (*PA* 43:6915)
581. CHAIN, RHODA U. *A Comparative Study of the Performance of Obese and Non-Obese Children on the Wechsler Intelligence Scale for Children.* Master's thesis, Southern Connecticut State College (New Haven, Conn.), 1968.
582. CHIAPPONE, ANTHONY D. "Use of the Detroit Tests of Learning Aptitude With EMR." *Excep Children* 35:240–1 N '68. * (*PA* 43:13075)
583. CHURCHILL, JOHN A.; WILLERMAN, LEE; GRISELL, JAMES; AND AYERS, MELVERN A. "Effect of Head Position at Birth on WISC Verbal and Performance IQ." *Psychol Rep* 23:495–8 O '68. * (*PA* 43:9492)
584. CONNOLLY, JOSEPH KENNETH. *The Discriminatory Functions of Brief Tests With the Educable Mentally Retarded.* Doctor's thesis, Fordham University (New York, N.Y.), 1968. (*DA* 29:2997A)
585. DAHLKE, ANITA B. *The Use of WISC Scores to Predict Reading Improvement After Remedial Tutoring.* Doctor's thesis, University of Florida (Gainesville, Fla.), 1968. (*DAI* 30:165A)
586. DUDEK, S. Z., AND LESTER, E. P. "The Good Child Facade in Chronic Underachievers." *Am J Orthopsychiatry* 38:153–60 Ja '68. * (*PA* 42:17778)
587. DUFF, MARIGENE MULLIGAN. *Language Functions in Children With Learning Disabilities.* Doctor's thesis, Northwestern University (Evanston, Ill.), 1968. (*DA* 29:3958B)

Wechsler Intelligence Scale for Children

588. EPPLEY, EDWIN B. *A Validity Study Comparing the Main Scale of the Kahn Intelligence Test With the Wechsler Intelligence Scale for Children.* Master's thesis, Millersville State College (Millersville, Pa.), 1968.
589. FAGERT, CHARLES M. *The Relationship Between the Slosson Intelligence Test and the Wechsler Intelligence Scale for Children.* Master's thesis, Kent State University (Kent, Ohio), 1968.
590. FEE, FRANCIS. "An Alternative to Ward's Factor Analysis of Wallach and Kogan's 'Creativity' Correlations." Comment by James Ward. *Brit J Ed Psychol* 38:319-21 N '68. * *(PA* 43:6128)
591. FLEEMAN, GEORGE W. *The Significance of Differences Between Non-Prorated and Prorated Scores for Verbal Performance and Full Scale I.Q.'s on the Wechsler Intelligence Scale for Children.* Master's thesis, East Tennessee State University (Johnson City, Tenn.), 1968.
592. FROSTIG, MARIANNE. "Testing as a Basis for Educational Therapy," pp. 64-86. In *Assessment of the Cerebral Palsied Child for Education.* Edited by James Loring. London: William Heinemann Ltd., 1968. Pp. vii, 112. *
593. GADDES, W. H.; MCKENZIE, AUDREY; AND BARNSLEY, ROGER. "Psychometric Intelligence and Spatial Imagery in Two Northwest Indian and Two White Groups of Children." *J Social Psychol* 75:35-42 Je '68. * *(PA* 42:13575)
594. GARDNER, RILEY W., AND MORIARTY, ALICE. Chap. 8, "Individuality in Wechsler's Intelligence Scale for Children," pp. 129-33, passim. In their *Personality Development at Preadolescence: Explorations of Structure Formation*, see 595. *
595. GARDNER, RILEY W., AND MORIARTY, ALICE. *Personality Development at Preadolescence: Explorations of Structure Formation.* Seattle, Wash.: University of Washington Press, 1968. Pp. xi, 344. *
596. HARRIS, A. J., AND LOVINGER, R. J. "Longitudinal Measures of the Intelligence of Disadvantaged Negro Adolescents." *Sch R* 76:60-6 Mr '68. * *(PA* 43:3138)
597. HOLROYD, JEAN. "When WISC Verbal IQ Is Low." *J Clin Psychol* 24:457 O '68. * *(PA* 43:3754)
598. HOMMEL, RONALD WILLIAM. *An Index of Creativity as Derived From an Extended Form of Intelligence Testing.* Doctor's thesis, Rutgers—The State University (New Brunswick, N.J.), 1968. *(DA* 29:2618B)
599. HOUSTON, CAMILLE, AND OTTO, WAYNE. "Poor Readers' Functioning on the WISC, Slosson Intelligence Test and Quick Test." Abstract. *AERA Paper Abstr* 1968:120-1 '68. *
600. HOUSTON, CAMILLE, AND OTTO, WAYNE. "Poor Readers' Functioning on the WISC, Slosson Intelligence Test and Quick Test." *J Ed Res* 62:157-9 D '68. *
601. INGHAM, J. G. "Comment on Effect of Training on the Performance of the WISC 'Block Design' Subtest by Josef Schubert." Reply by Josef Schubert. *Brit J Social & Clin Psychol* 7:149-50 Je '68. * *(PA* 42:16413, 16429)
602. JACKSON, ELIZABETH M. *The WISC Sub-Scores and Achievement in Reading Clinic.* Master's thesis, California State College (Long Beach, Calif.), 1968.
603. KASPAR, JOSEPH C.; THRONE, FRANCES M.; AND SCHULMAN, JEROME L. "A Study of the Inter-Judge Reliability in Scoring the Responses of a Group of Mentally Retarded Boys to Three WISC Subscales." *Ed & Psychol Meas* 28:469-77 su '68. * *(PA* 42:18797)
604. LEVY, PHILIP. "Short-Form Tests: A Methodological Review." *Psychol B* 69:410-6 Je '68. * *(PA* 42:11410)
605. LEVY, RUSSELL H. "Group Administered Intelligence Tests Which Appropriately Reflect the Magnitude of Mental Retardation Among Wards of the Illinois Youth Commission." *J Correct Ed* 20:7-10 su '68. *
606. LUONG, CORINA K. MONGCAL. *An Analysis of Factors Related to Difficulties in Learning and Adjustment Among Minority Group Children.* Doctor's thesis, Bryn Mawr College (Bryn Mawr, Pa.), 1968. *(DAI* 30:4795B)
607. LYLE, J. G. "Errors of Retarded Readers on Block Designs." *Percept & Motor Skills* 26:1222 Je '68. * *(PA* 42:19419)
608. LYTTON, H. "Some Psychological and Sociological Characteristics of 'Good' and 'Poor Achievers' (Boys) in Remedial Reading Groups." *Hum Develop* 11(4):260-76 '68. *
609. MCARTHUR, CHARLES R., AND WAKEFIELD, HOMER E. "Validation of the PPVT With the Stanford-Binet-LM and the WISC on Educable Mental Retardates." *Am J Mental Def* 73:465-7 N '68. * *(PA* 43:8596)
610. MCKERRACHER, D. W., AND WATSON, R. A. "Validation of a Short Form WISC With Clinic Children." *Brit J Ed Psychol* 38:205-8 Je '68. * *(PA* 42:16418)
611. MATTHEWS, CHARLES G.; CHUN, RAYMOND W. M.; GRABOW, JACK D.; AND THOMPSON, WAYNE H. "Psychological Sequelae in Children Following California Arboviros Encephalitis." *Neurology* 18:1023-30 O '68. * *(PA* 43:5771)
612. MEHROTRA, K. K. "The Relationship of the WISC to the Progressive Matrices." *J Psychol Res* 12:114-8 S '68. *
613. MEHROTRA, KRISHNA KANT. "A Comparative Study of WISC and Raven's Progressive Matrices." *Psychol Studies* 13:47-50 Ja '68. *
614. MIEZITIS, SOLVEIGA AUSMA. *An Exploratory Study of Divergent Production in Preschoolers.* Doctor's thesis, University of Toronto (Toronto, Ont., Canada), 1968. *(DAI* 30:589A)

615. MORDOCK, JOHN B., AND BOGAN, STEVE. "Wechsler Patterns and Symptomatic Behaviors of Children Diagnosed as Having Minimal Cerebral Dysfunction." Abstract. *Proc 76th Ann Conv Am Psychol Assn* 3:663-4 '68. *
616. NALVEN, FREDERIC B., AND PULEO, VINCENT T. "Relationship Between Digit Span and Classroom Distractibility in Elementary School Children." *J Clin Psychol* 24:85-7 Ja '68. * *(PA* 42:9426)
617. ORTIZ, KENNETH K. *A Concurrent Validation Study of a Spanish Version of the Pictorial Test of Intelligence and a Critical Analysis of the Use of the Wechsler Intelligence Scale for Children With Bilingual Mexican-American Children.* Master's thesis, California State College (Long Beach, Calif.), 1968.
618. PEDERSEN, DARHL M.; SHINEDLING, MARTIN M.; AND JOHNSON, DEE L. "Effects of Sex of Examiner and Subject on Children's Quantitative Test Performance." *J Pers & Social Psychol* 10:251-4 N '68. * *(PA* 43:3760)
619. PIHL, ROBERT O. "The Degree of the Verbal-Performance Discrepancy on the WISC and the WAIS and Severity of EEG Abnormality in Epileptics." *J Clin Psychol* 24:418-20 O '68. * *(PA* 43:4327)
620. QUERESHI, M. Y. "Intelligence Test Scores as a Function of Sex of Experimenter and Sex of Subject." *J Psychol* 69:277-84 Jl '68. * *(PA* 42:15462)
621. QUERESHI, M. Y. "The Optimum Limits of Testing on the Wechsler Intelligence Scales." *Genetic Psychol Monogr* 78:141-90 N '68. * *(PA* 43:4016)
622. QUERESHI, MOHAMMED Y. "The Comparability of WAIS and WISC Subtest Scores and IQ Estimates." *J Psychol* 68:73-82 Ja '68. * *(PA* 42:7334)
623. QUERESHI, MOHAMMED Y. "The Internal Consistency of the WISC Scores for Ages 5 to 16." *J Clin Psychol* 24:192-5 Ap '68. * *(PA* 42:12093)
624. QUERESHI, MOHAMMED Y. "Practice Effects on the WISC Subtest Scores and IQ Estimates." *J Clin Psychol* 24:79-85 Ja '68. * *(PA* 42:8942)
625. RAINWATER, HAROLD G. "Reading Problem Indicators Among Children With Reading Problems." *Psychol* 5:81-3 N '68. *
626. REED, JAMES C. "Cognitive Factors Associated With Achievement in Reading at the Elementary Grades." Abstract. *AERA Paper Abstr* 1968:72 '68. *
627. REID, WALTER B.; MOORE, DANA; AND ALEXANDER, DWAYNE. "Abbreviated Form of the WISC for Use With Brain-Damaged and Mentally Retarded Children." Abstract. *J Consult & Clin Psychol* 32:236 Ap '68. * *(PA* 42:8103)
628. ROSEN, MARVIN; STALLINGS, LINDA; FLOOR, LUCRETIA; AND NOWAKIWSKA, MYRA. "Reliability and Stability of Wechsler IQ Scores for Institutionalized Mental Subnormals." *Am J Mental Def* 73:218-25 S '68. * *(PA* 43:4352)
629. RYMSZA, JANUSZKA SOFIA DE LILIO. *Factor Analysis of Measures of Divergent Thinking Obtained From the Children's Apperception Test and Measures of Intelligence Obtained From the Wechsler Intelligence Scale for Children.* Doctor's thesis, Florida State University (Tallahassee, Fla.), 1968. *(DAI* 30:831B)
630. SABATINO, DAVID A.; ASSISTED BY R. L. JONES, CURTISS BROWN, AND W. M. GIBSON. "The Relationship Between Twenty-Three Learning Disability Behavioral Variables," pp. 149-61. In *CEC Selected Convention Papers.* 46th Annual International Convention, 1968. Washington, D.C.: Council for Exceptional Children, [1968]. Pp. xii, 346. *
631. SABATINO, DAVID A.; WICKHAM, WILLIAM, JR.; AND BURNETT, CALVIN W. "The Psychoeducational Assessment of Learning Disabilities." *Cath Ed R* 66:327-41 My '68. *
632. SCALLON, RICHARD J. *Field Articulation: A Study of the Perceptual Style of Enuretic Boys.* Doctor's thesis, St. John's University (Jamaica, N.Y.), 1968. *(DA* 29:4369B)
633. SEKYRA, FRANCIS, III, AND ARNOULT, JOSEPH FRANCIS, III. "Negro Intellectual Assessment With Three Instruments Contrasting Caucasian and Negro Norms." *J Learn Dis* 1:564-9 O '68. * *(PA* 45:2174)
634. SILBERBERG, NORMAN, AND FELDT, LEONARD S. "Intellectual and Perceptual Correlates of Reading Disabilities." *J Sch Psychol* 6:237-45 su '68. * *(PA* 42:3033)
635. SILVERSTEIN, A. B. "Simple Summation vs Differential Weighting in the Construction of WISC Short Forms." *Psychol Rep* 23:960 D '68. * *(PA* 43:9743)
636. SILVERSTEIN, A. B. "Validity of a New Approach to the Design of WAIS, WISC, and WPPSI Short Forms." *J Consult & Clin Psychol* 32:478-9 Ag '68. * *(PA* 42:16432)
637. SILVERSTEIN, A. B. "Variance Components in Five Psychological Tests." *Psychol Rep* 23:141-2 Ag '68. * *(PA* 43:6920)
638. SILVERSTEIN, A. B. "WISC and WPPSI IQs for the Gifted." *Psychol Rep* 22:1168 Je '68. * *(PA* 42:18801)
639. SILVERSTEIN, A. B. "WISC Subtest Patterns of Retardates." *Psychol Rep* 23:1061-2 D '68. * *(PA* 43:8601)
640. SIMPSON, ROBERT LEE. *A Study of the Comparability of the WISC and the WAIS and the Factors Contributing to Their Differences.* Doctor's thesis, University of Southern California (Los Angeles, Calif.), 1968. *(DA* 29:1794A)
641. SLOBODZIAN, EVELYN BIRDSALL. *The Relationship Between Certain Readiness Measures and Reading Achievement*

at Level One. Doctor's thesis, Temple University (Philadelphia, Pa.), 1968. (DA 29:1053A)
642. TILLMAN, M. H., AND BASHAW, W. L. "Multivariate Analysis of the WISC Scales for Blind and Sighted Children." Psychol Rep 23:523–6 O '68. * (PA 43:9745)
643. TOWNES, BRENDA, AND CHRIST, ADOLPHE E. "Psychological Testing: Its Usefulness in Teaching Psychotherapy and Psychodynamics to Medical Students." Arch Gen Psychiatry 19:487–90 O '68. * (PA 43:4068)
644. TOZIER, LEONARD LESLIE. Modifications of the WISC Block Design Subtest. Master's thesis, San Diego State College (San Diego, Calif.), 1968.
645. TYSON, MARTHA HARALSON. The Effect of Prior Contact With the Examiner on the Wechsler Intelligence Scale for Children Scores of Third-Grade Children. Doctor's thesis, University of Houston (Houston, Tex.), 1968. (DA 29:4372B)
646. VANCINI, JOHN PAUL. The Stability and Utility of an Abbreviated Form of the WISC. Doctor's thesis, University of Colorado (Boulder, Colo.), 1968. (DA 29:3499B)
647. WHITE, LINDA ANN. A Comparative Study of the Performance of Negro Head Start Students on the Wechsler Preschool and Primary Scale of Intelligence, the Wechsler Intelligence Scale for Children, and the Stanford-Binet, Form L-M. Master's thesis, University of Texas (Austin, Tex.), 1968.
648. WIDMAN, JOANNE B. Wechsler Intelligence Scale for Children: A Study of Scores Obtained by Aleut Elementary School Students, St. Paul Island, Alaska. Master's thesis, Pacific Lutheran University (Tacoma, Wash.), 1968.
649. WIENER, G.; RIDER, R. V.; OPPEL, W. C.; AND HARPER, P. A. "Correlates of Low Birth Weight: Psychological Status at Eight to Ten Years of Age." Pediatric Res 2:110–8 Mr '68. * (PA 42:15299)
650. WILLARD, LOUISA A. "A Comparison of Culture Fair Test Scores With Group and Individual Intelligence Test Scores of Disadvantaged Negro Children." J Learn Dis 1:584–9 O '68. * (PA 45:3968)
651. WOLF, CLIFTON W. A Statistical Study of Specific Dyslexia-Characteristics and Syndrome Patterns. Doctor's thesis, University of Houston (Houston, Tex.), 1968. (DA 29:2643B)
652. WOODY, ROBERT H. "Diagnosis of Behavioral Problem Children: Mental Abilities and Achievement." J Sch Psychol 6:111–6 w '68. * (PA 42:11148)
653. ZEDLER, EMPRESS Y. "Screening Underachieving Pupils for Risk of Neurological Impairment." Learning Disorders 3:249–74 '68. *
654. ABRAMS, STANLEY. "The Upper Weight Level Premature Child." Dis Nerv System 30(6):414–7 Je '69. * (PA 44:6420)
655. BANAS, NORMA, AND WILLS, I. H. "The Vulnerable Child and Prescriptive Teaching." Acad Ther 4(3):215–9 sp '69. * (PA 43:17927)
656. BARCLAY, A.; FRIEDMAN, ELLEN C.; AND FIDEL, YILDIZ. "A Comparative Study of WISC and WAIS Performances and Score Patterns Among Institutionalized Retardates." J Mental Def Res 13(2):99–105 Je '69. * (PA 44:9089)
657. BAUMANN, KAREN SUZANN. The Effects of an Educational Program on the Test Performance of Children With Psychoneurological Learning Disabilities. Doctor's thesis, Oklahoma State University (Stillwater, Okla.), 1969. (DAI 31:3865A)
658. BORTNER, MORTON, AND BIRCH, HERBERT G. "Patterns of Intellectual Ability in Emotionally Disturbed and Brain-Damaged Children." J Spec Ed 3(4):351–69 w '69. * (PA 44:14652)
659. BRODT, AUDREY M., AND WALKER, RONALD E. "Techniques of WISC Vocabulary Administration." J Clin Psychol 25(2):180–1 Ap '69. * (PA 43:14324)
660. BYRD, COLEEN, AND SPRINGFIELD, LYNN. "A Note on the Draw-A-Person Test With Adolescent Retardates." Am J Mental Def 73(4):578–9 Ja '69. * (PA 43:8571)
661. CANNON, THOMAS MILTON, JR. The Wechsler Intelligence Scale for Children as a Prediction of Adjustment of First Grade Students. Doctor's thesis, Texas Technological University (Lubbock, Tex.), 1969. (DAI 31:143A)
662. CHAWLA, TILAK R. "An Evaluative Study of New Culture-Free Intelligence Test (Kit:Exp)." J Psychol Res 13(2):74–6 My '69. * (PA 45:4248)
663. CRAWFORD, VEDA B. Relationships of Scores on the Wechsler Preschool and Primary Scale of Intelligence, the Stanford-Binet Intelligence Scale, Form LM, and the Peabody Picture Vocabulary Test, Form A. Master's thesis, Bowling Green State University (Bowling Green, Ohio), 1969.
664. CROCKETT, DAVID; KLONOFF, HARRY; AND BJERRING, JAMES. "Factor Analysis of Neuropsychological Tests." Percept & Motor Skills 29(3):791–802 D '69. * (PA 46:4665)
665. DE MARCO, WILLIAM. The Scatter of Intellectual Abilities of the Hard of Hearing as Assessed by the Wechsler Intelligence Scale for Children. Doctor's thesis, University of Illinois (Urbana, Ill.), 1969. (DAI 30:3383B)
666. DOUBROS, STEVE G., AND MASCARENHAS, JULIET. "Relations Among Wechsler Full-Scale Scores, Organicity-Sensitive Subtest Scores and Bender-Gestalt Errors Scores." Percept & Motor Skills 29(3):719–22 D '69. * (PA 46:4666)
667. DUDEK, S. Z.; GOLDBERG, J. S.; LESTER, E. P.; AND HARRIS, B. R. "The Validity of Cognitive, Perceptual-Motor and Personality Variables for Prediction of Achievement in Grade 1 and Grade 2." J Clin Psychol 25(2):165–70 Ap '69. * (PA 43:14874)
668. DUDEK, S. Z.; LESTER, E. P.; GOLDBERG, J. S.; AND DYER, G. B. "Relationship of Piaget Measures to Standard Intelligence and Motor Scales." Percept & Motor Skills 28(2):351–62 Ap '69. * (PA 43:15587)
669. EGELAND, BYRON. "Examiner Expectancy: Effects on the Scoring of the WISC." Psychol Sch 6(3):313–5 Jl '69. * (PA 44:3617)
670. ERTL, JOHN P., AND SCHAFER, EDWARD W. P. "Brain Response Correlates of Psychometric Intelligence." Nature 223(5204):421–2 Jl 26 '69. *
671. FEDIO, PAUL, AND MIRSKY, ALLAN F. "Selective Intellectual Deficits in Children with Temporal Lobe or Centrencephalic Epilepsy." Neuropsychologia 7(4):287–300 S '69. *
672. FERINDEN, WILLIAM E., JR.; JACOBSON, SHERMAN; AND KOVALINSKY, THOMAS. Educational Interpretation of the Wechsler Intelligence Scale for Children (WISC). Linden, N.J.: Remediation Associates, 1969. Pp. ii, 36. *
673. FLEMING, JUANITA WILSON. The Interrelationship of Early Developmental Factors on the Academic Failure of Children. Doctor's thesis, Catholic University of America (Washington, D.C.), 1969. (DAI 30:1429A)
674. FRIEDRICH, DOUGLAS; FULLER, GERALD B.; AND HAWKINS, WILLIAM F. "Relationship Between Perception (Input) and Execution (Output)." Percept & Motor Skills 29(3):923–34 D '69. * (PA 46:5346)
675. GIOIOSO, JOSEPH V., AND ADERMAN, MORRIS. "The Combination Test as a Quick Screening Device to Differentiate Levels of Retardation." Psychol Rep 25(3):843–8 D '69. * (PA 44:18906)
676. GOENS, BERT DOUGLAS. Comparisons of the Wechsler Preschool and Primary Scale of Intelligence With the Wechsler Intelligence Scale for Children. Master's thesis, Western Michigan University (Kalamazoo, Mich.), 1969. (Masters Abstracts 7:119)
677. HALL, LEON P., AND LADRIERE, LAVERNE. "Patterns of Performance on WISC Similarities in Emotionally Disturbed and Brain-Damaged Children." J Consult & Clin Psychol 33(3):357–64 Je '69. * (PA 43:13078)
678. HEMBERGER, LANCE WARNER. A Longitudinal Study of the Factorial Organization of Intelligence as Related to Socioeconomic Variables. Doctor's thesis, University of Georgia (Athens, Ga.), 1969. (DAI 30:3321A)
679. HENDERSON, NORMAN B.; BUTLER, BRUCE V.; AND GOFFENEY, BARBARA. "Effectiveness of the WISC and Bender-Gestalt Test in Predicting Arithmetic and Reading Achievement for White and Nonwhite Children." J Clin Psychol 25(3):268–71 Jl '69. * (PA 44:4246)
680. HERRELL, JAMES M., AND GOLLAND, JEFFREY H. "Should WISC Subjects Explain Picture Arrangement Stories?" J Consult & Clin Psychol 33(6):761–2 D '69. * (PA 44:3678)
681. HEWITT, PATRICIA S., AND MASSEY, JAMES O. Clinical Clues From the WISC, Wechsler Intelligence Scale for Children: With Special Sections on Testing Black and Spanish-Speaking Children. Palo Alto, Calif.: Consulting Psychologists Press, Inc., 1969. Pp. 46. *
682. JOHNSON, CLIFFORD IVY. An Analysis of the Predictive Validity of Selective Reading Readiness Factors to Third Grade Reading Achievement. Doctor's thesis, University of Georgia (Athens, Ga.), 1969. (DAI 30:3363A)
683. JOHNSON, DONALD DAVID. A Comparative Analysis of Special Education and Regular Program Students' Scores on Selected Subtests of the Wechsler Intelligence Scale for Children. Doctor's thesis, New Mexico State University (University Park, N.M.), 1969. (DAI 30:3816A)
684. JONGEWARD, PAUL A. "A Validity Study of the Slosson Intelligence Test for Use With Educable Mentally Retarded Students." J Sch Psychol 7(4):59–63 '68–69 ['69]. * (PA 44:2702)
685. JONGEWARD, PAUL ALBERT. A Validity Study of the Slosson Intelligence Test for Use With Educable Mentally Retarded Students. Doctor's thesis, University of Oregon (Eugene, Ore.), 1969. (DAI 30:3323A)
686. KARP, STEPHEN A.; SILBERMAN, LESTER; AND WINTERS, STEPHEN. "Psychological Differentiation and Socioeconomic Status." Percept & Motor Skills 28(1):55–60 F '69. * (PA 43:11306)
687. KASS, CORRINE E. "Learning Disabilities." R Ed Res 39(1):71–82 F '69. * (PA 44:5671)
688. KEARNEY, JACQUELINE E. "A New Performance Scale of Cognitive Capacity for Use With Deaf Subjects." Am Ann Deaf 114(1):2–14 Ja '69. * (PA 43:7197)
689. LOCKYER, LINDA, AND RUTTER, MICHAEL. "A Five- to Fifteen-Year Follow-up Study of Infantile Psychosis: 3, Psychological Aspects." Brit J Psychiatry 115(525):865–82 Ag '69. * (PA 44:10847)
690. LYLE, J. G. "Reading Retardation and Reversal Tendency: A Factorial Study." Child Develop 40(3):833–43 S '69. * (PA 44:2706)
691. LYLE, J. G., AND GOYEN, JUDITH. "Performance of Retarded Readers on the WISC and Educational Tests." J Abn Psychol 74(1):105–12 F '69. * (PA 43:8790)
692. MARGACH, CHARLES, AND KERN, KATE CONDIT. "Visual

Impairment, Partial-Sight and the School Psychologist." *J Learn Dis* 2(8):407–14 Ag '69. * (*PA* 45:6995)
693. MARSDEN, GERALD, AND KALTER, NEIL. "Bodily Concerns and the WISC Object Assembly Subtest." *J Consult & Clin Psychol* 33(4):391–5 Ag '69. * (*PA* 43:15808)
694. MEEKER, MARY NACOL. *The Structure of Intellect: Its Interpretation and Uses*, pp. 132–46. Columbus, Ohio: Charles E. Merrill Publishing Co., 1969. Pp. xix, 203. *
695. MILLER, HAROLD R. "WISC Performance Under Incentive Conditions: Case Report." *Psychol Rep* 24(3):835–8 Je '69. * (*PA* 44:479)
696. NALVEN, FREDRIC B. "Classroom-Administered Digit Span and Distractibility Ratings for Elementary School Pupils." *Psychol Rep* 24(3):734 Je '69. * (*PA* 44:1222)
697. NALVEN, FREDRIC B., AND BIERBRYER, BRUCE. "Predicting Elementary School Children's Classroom Comprehension From Their WISC Results." *J Clin Psychol* 25(1):75–6 Ja '69. * (*PA* 43:10328)
698. NALVEN, FREDRIC B.; HOFMANN, LOUIS J.; AND BIERBRYER, BRUCE. "The Effects of Subjects' Age, Sex, Race, and Socioeconomic Status on Psychologists' Estimates of 'True IQ' From WISC Scores." *J Clin Psychol* 25(3):271–4 Jl '69. * (*PA* 44:3620)
699. NEEDHAM, WALTER E.; BRAY, PATRICK F.; WISER, WILMER C.; AND BECK, EDWARD C. "Intelligence and EEG Studies in Families With Idiopathic Epilepsy." *J Am Med Assn* 207(8):1497–501 F 24 '69. * (*PA* 44:21418)
700. NELSON, C. MICHAEL, AND HUDSON, FLOYD G. "Predicting the Reading Achievement of Junior High School EMR Children." *Am J Mental Def* 74(3):415–20 N '69. *
701. OAKLAND, JAMES A. "WISC Coding as a Measure of Motivation." *J Clin Psychol* 25(4):411–2 O '69. * (*PA* 44:10981)
702. O'NEILL, HUGH DANIEL, JR. *Partial Validation of the Slosson Intelligence Test*. Doctor's thesis, University of Oklahoma (Norman, Okla.), 1969. (*DAI* 30:3797A)
703. REED, JAMES C. "Children's Figure Drawing—A Clue to Reading Progress." *Read Teach* 23(2):132–6 N '69. * (*PA* 44:21620)
704. REED, JAMES C., AND REITAN, RALPH M. "Verbal and Performance Differences Among Brain-Injured Children With Lateralized Motor Deficits." *Percept & Motor Skills* 29(3):747–52 D '69. * (*PA* 46:5334)
705. REILLEY, ROBERT R. "Student Reactions to Use of Video Taped WISC Instruction." *Counselor Ed & Sup* 8(3):233–5 sp '69. *
706. RHODES, L. E.; DUSTMAN, R. E.; AND BECK, E. C. "The Visual Evoked Response: A Comparison of Bright and Dull Children." *Electroencephalography & Clin Neurophysiol* 27(4):364–72 O '69. * (*PA* 45:2142)
707. SABATINO, DAVID A., AND CRAMBLETT, HENRY. "A Longitudinal Study of Children With Learning Disabilities Subsequent to Hospitalization for Viral Encephalitis Part I." *J Learn Dis* 2(2):65–75 F '69. * (*PA* 45:6854)
708. SABATINO, DAVID A., AND CRAMBLETT, HENRY G. "A Longitudinal Study of Children With Learning Disabilities Subsequent to Hospitalization for Viral Encephalitis—Part II." *J Learn Dis* 2(3):124–35 Mr '69. * (*PA* 45:6855)
709. SATTLER, JEROME M. "Effects of Cues and Examiner Influence on Two Wechsler Subtests." *J Consult & Clin Psychol* 33(6):716–21 D '69. * (*PA* 44:4171)
710. SATTLER, JEROME M.; WINGET, BARBARA M.; AND ROTH, ROSEMARY J. "Scoring Difficulty of WAIS and WISC Comprehension, Similarities, and Vocabulary Responses." *J Clin Psychol* 25(2):175–7 Ap '69. * (*PA* 43:14478)
711. SCALLON, RICHARD J., AND HERRON, WILLIAM G. "Field Articulation of Enuretic Boys and Their Mothers." *Percept & Motor Skills* 28(2):407–13 Ap '69. * (*PA* 43:15604)
712. SILBERBERG, NORMAN E.; IVERSEN, IVER A.; AND SILBERBERG, MARGARET C. "A Model for Classifying Children According to Reading Level." *J Learn Dis* 2(12):634–43 D '69. *
713. SILVERSTEIN, A. B. "An Alternative Factor Analytic Solution for Wechsler's Intelligence Scales." *Ed & Psychol Meas* 29(4):763–7 w '69. * (*PA* 44:20972)
714. SIMON, WILLIAM E. "Expectancy Effects in the Scoring of Vocabulary Items: A Study of Scorer Bias." *J Ed Meas* 6(3):159–64 f '69. * (*PA* 44:13628)
715. SMITH, NATHANIEL CUTRIGHT, JR. *Factors Underlying WISC Performance in Juvenile Public Offenders*. Doctor's thesis, Ohio State University (Columbus, Ohio), 1969. (*DAI* 30:1888B)
716. SMITH, TIMOTHY A., AND CALDWELL, MARCUS B. "Intellectual Differences in Negro and White Mental Defectives." *Psychol Rep* 25(2):559–65 O '69. * (*PA* 44:5571)
717. SOLLEE, NATALIE DOSICK. *Verbal Competence and the Acquisition of Conservation*. Doctor's thesis, Boston University (Boston, Mass.), 1969. (*DAI* 30:2409B)
718. STRECKER, REBECCA V. *A Comparison of WISC Subtest Scores of Mentally Retarded Mexican-American and Caucasian Students*. Master's thesis, Chapman College (Orange, Calif.), 1969.
719. SWEET, ROGER CHARLES. *Variations in the Intelligence Test Performance of Lower-Class Children as a Function of Feedback or Monetary Reinforcement*. Doctor's thesis, University of Wisconsin (Madison, Wis.), 1969. (*DAI* 31:648A)

720. TALKINGTON, LARRY W., AND RIEKER, GRACE A. "A Short Form of the WISC for Use With the Mentally Retarded." *Psychol Rep* 25(2):461–2 O '69. * (*PA* 44:5574)
721. TALMADGE, MAX; HAYDEN, BENJAMIN S.; AND SCHIFF, DONALD. "Longitudinal Analysis of Intellectual and Educational Achievement Change in Culturally Deprived, Emotionally Disturbed Boys." *Percept & Motor Skills* 29(2):435–40 O '69. * (*PA* 44:3795)
722. TILLMAN, H. M., AND OSBORNE, R. T. "The Performance of Blind and Sighted Children on the Wechsler Intelligence Scale for Children: Interaction Effects." *Ed Visually Handicapped* 1(1):1–4 Mr '69. * (*PA* 43:13192)
723. TRAINER, F. E. *Australian Revision of the Wechsler Intelligence Scale for Children*. Master's thesis, University of Sydney (Sydney, N.S.W., Australia), 1969.
724. VANBRAMER, PETER J. *The Use of the Wechsler Intelligence Scale for Children in Selecting Students for Remedial Reading*. Master's thesis, Wisconsin State University (Platteville, Wis.), 1969.
725. WALLACE, GERALD. *A Study of the Relationship of Selected Visual Perceptual Capabilities and Intelligence to Achievement in Reading of Educable Mentally Retarded Children*. Doctor's thesis, University of Oregon (Eugene, Ore.), 1969. (*DAI* 30:3336A)
726. ALLOR, BARBARA A. *A Comparison of Good and Poor Readers on the Wechsler Intelligence Scale for Children at the Seventh Grade Level*. Master's thesis, Cardinal Stritch College (Milwaukee, Wis.), 1970.
727. BAIRD, ROBERT KAY. *A Comparison of the Performance of High and Low Sociometric Fourth Graders on Two Subtests of the Wechsler Intelligence Scale for Children*. Master's thesis, Brigham Young University (Provo, Utah), 1970.
728. BAR-OR, O.; SKINNER, J.; BERGSTEIN, V.; HAAS, J.; SHEARBURN, C.; AND BUSKIRK, E. Chap. 4, "Measures of Performance and Related Physiological Characteristics," pp. 47–73. In *Factors Related to the Speech-Hearing of Children of Below Normal Intelligence*, see 787. *
729. BARTON, BRENDA. *A Study of the Relationship Between School Anxiety and Performance on the Wechsler Intelligence Scale for Children*. Master's thesis, University of Texas (Austin, Tex.), 1970.
730. BLATT, SIDNEY J.; BAKER, BRUCE L.; AND WEISS, JAY. "Wechsler Object Assembly Subtest and Bodily Concern: A Review and Replication." *J Consult & Clin Psychol* 34(2):269–74 Ap '70. * (*PA* 44:10408)
731. BROCKWAY, ROBERT L. *Is There a Significant Difference Between the Verbal and Performance Scores of Juvenile Delinquents on the Wechsler Intelligence Scale for Children?* Master's thesis, Southern Connecticut State College (New Haven, Conn.), 1970.
732. BROWNE, DAUNA BELL, AND TIAHRT, HELEN GERTRUDE. *An Exploration of the Usefulness of Four Descriptive Clusters of Subtest Scores of the Wechsler Intelligence Scale for Children*. Doctor's thesis, University of Northern Colorado (Greeley, Colo.), 1970. (*DAI* 31:4983B)
733. BURNES, KAY. "Patterns of WISC Scores for Children of Two Socioeconomic Classes and Races." *Child Develop* 41(2):493–500 Je '70. * (*PA* 44:14344)
734. CHRISTIANSEN, TED, AND LIVERMORE, GARY. "A Comparison of Anglo-American and Spanish-American Children on the WISC." *J Social Psychol* 81(1):9–14 Je '70. * (*PA* 44:18706)
735. COYLE, F. A., JR., AND BELLAMY, EDWARD E. "Use of the California Abbreviated WISC With Institutionalized Retardates." *Am J Mental Def* 74(4):578 Ja '70. * (*PA* 44:11053)
736. CUNDICK, BERT P. "Measures of Intelligence on Southwest Indian Students." *J Social Psychol* 81(2):151–6 Ag '70. * (*PA* 44:20655)
737. EAVES, LINDA, AND KLONOFF, HARRY. "A Comparison of Blind and Sighted Children on a Tactual and Performance Test." *Excep Children* 37(4):269–73 D '70. *
738. EGELAND, BYRON; DI NELLO, MARIO; AND CARR, DONALD. "The Relationship of Intelligence, Visual-Motor, Psycholinguistic and Reading-Readiness Skills With Achievement." *Ed & Psychol Meas* 30(2):451–8 su '70. * (*PA* 43:3056)
739. ESTES, ROBERT E., AND MORRIS, HUGHLETT L. "Relationship Among Intelligence, Speech Proficiency, and Hearing Sensitivity in Children With Cleft Palates." *Cleft Palate J* 7(9):763–73 Jl '70. *
740. FITZGERALD, BERNARD J.; PASEWARK, RICHARD A.; AND GLOECKLER, TED. "Use of the Peabody Picture Vocabulary Test With the Educationally Handicapped." *J Sch Psychol* 8(4):296–300 '70. * (*PA* 46:1800)
741. FRETZ, BRUCE R. "Factor Structure of Intellectual, Visual Perception, and Visuomotor Performance of Poorly Coordinated Boys." *J Motor Behav* 2(2):69–78 Je '70. *
742. FRIEDMAN, RONALD. "The Reliability of the Wechsler Intelligence Scale for Children in a Group of Mentally Retarded Children." *J Clin Psychol* 26(2):181–2 Ap '70. * (*PA* 44:15147)
743. GARMS, JOE D. "A Validation Study of the Illinois Test of Psycholinguistic Abilities." *Psychol* 7(1):9–12 F '70. * (*PA* 44:13282)
744. GAYTON, WILLIAM F.; WILSON, WINSTON T.; AND BERNSTEIN, STEPHEN. "An Evaluation of an Abbreviated Form of

the WISC." *J Clin Psychol* 26(4):466–8 O '70. * (*PA* 45:4533)

745. GILLINGHAM, WILLIAM HARVEY. *An Investigation of Examiner Influence on Wechsler Intelligence Scale for Children Scores.* Doctor's thesis, Michigan State University (East Lansing, Mich.), 1970. (*DAI* 31:2178A)

746. GRIMALDI, JOSEPH, JR. *A Factor Analytic Study of WISC Patterns in Children With CNS Dysfunction.* Doctor's thesis, St. John's University (Jamaica, N.Y.), 1970. (*DAI* 31:3706B)

747. HAFNER, LAWRENCE E.; WEAVER, WENDELL W.; AND POWELL, KATHRYN. "Psychological and Perceptual Correlates of Reading Achievement Among Fourth Graders." *J Read Behav* 2(4):281–90 f '70. * (*PA* 46:5663)

748. HALL, LEON P., AND LA DRIERE, M. LAVERNE. "Evaluation of WISC Similarities Responses According to Cognitive Style and Error Analysis: A Comparative Study." *Psychol Rep* 26(1):175–80 F '70. * (*PA* 45:4537)

749. HANNON, JOHN E., AND KICKLIGHTER, RICHARD. "WAIS Versus WISC in Adolescents." *J Consult & Clin Psychol* 35(2):179–82 O '70. * (*PA* 45:2202)

750. HARRIS, HELENA. "Development of Moral Attitudes in White and Negro Boys." *Develop Psychol* 2(3):376–83 My '70. * (*PA* 44:12259)

751. HARTLAGE, LAWRENCE C. "Differential Diagnosis of Dyslexia, Minimal Brain Damage and Emotional Disturbances in Children." *Psychol Sch* 7(4):403–6 O '70. * (*PA* 46:1422)

752. HINE, W. D. "The Abilities of Partially Hearing Children." *Brit J Ed Psychol* 40(2):171–8 Je '70. * (*PA* 44:21362)

753. HINE, W. D. "Verbal Ability and Partial Hearing Loss." *Teach Deaf* 68(404):450–9 N '70. *

754. HIRSCH, ERNEST A. *The Troubled Adolescent: As He Emerges From Psychological Tests.* New York: International Universities Press, Inc., 1970. Pp. xv, 645. *

755. HUELSMAN, CHARLES B., JR. "The WISC Subtest Syndrome for Disabled Readers." *Percept & Motor Skills* 30(2):535–50 Ap '70. * (*PA* 46:7506)

756. KRIPPNER, STANLEY. "Reading Improvement and Its Correlates." *Percept & Motor Skills* 31(3):727–31 D '70. * (*PA* 45:10694)

757. LESSING, ELISE E.; ZAGORIN, SUSAN W.; AND NELSON, DOROTHY. "WISC Subtest and IQ Score Correlates of Father Absence." *J Genetic Psychol* 117(2):181–95 D '70. * (*PA* 45:6017)

758. LESTER, EVA P.; MUIR, R.; AND DUDEK, STEPHANIE Z. "Cognitive Structure and Achievement in the Young Child." *Can Psychiatric Assn J* 15(3):279–87 Je '70. * (*PA* 45:5058)

759. LEWIS, FRANKLIN D.; BELL, D. BRUCE; AND ANDERSON, ROBERT P. "Reading Retardation: A Bi-Racial Comparison." *J Read* 13(6):433–6, 474–8 Mr '70. *

760. LOCKYER, LINDA, AND RUTTER, MICHAEL. "A Five- to Fifteen-Year Follow-Up Study of Infantile Psychosis: 4, Patterns of Cognitive Ability." *Brit J Social & Clin Psychol* 9(2):152–63 Je '70. * (*PA* 44:16983)

761. LOVINGER, SOPHIE L. "Observation on the Arithmetic Subtest of the Wechsler Intelligence Scale for Children." Letter. *J Sch Psychol* 8(4):322 '70. *

762. MCFIE, J., AND THOMPSON, J. A. "Intellectual Abilities of Immigrant Children." *Brit J Ed Psychol* 40(3):348–51 N '70. * (*PA* 45:7025)

763. MARSDEN, GERALD. "Intelligence and the Rorschach Whole Response." *J Proj Tech & Pers Assess* 34(6):470–6 D '70. * (*PA* 45:7873)

764. MAYCOCK, GEORGE ALBERT. *Emotional, Social, and Academic Adjustment of the Mentally Retarded as Related to Socio-Economic Level.* Doctor's thesis, Texas Technological University (Lubbock, Tex.), 1970. (*DAI* 31:3375A)

765. MILLER, CHARLES K.; CHANSKY, NORMAN M.; AND GREDLER, GILBERT R. "Rater Agreement on WISC Protocols." *Psychol Sch* 7(2):190–3 Ap '70. * (*PA* 45:700)

766. MOON, W. HAROLD, AND LAIR, CHARLES V. "Manifest Anxiety, Induced Anxiety and Digit Symbol Performance." *Psychol Rep* 26(3):947–50 Je '70. * (*PA* 45:134)

767. MUNZ, ADAM. *The Relationship Between Central Nervous System Functions and Verbal Communication.* Doctor's thesis, New York University (New York, N.Y.), 1970. (*DAI* 31:2193A)

768. NURSS, JOANNE R. "A Diagnostic Comparison of Two Third Grade Reading Classes," pp. 42–54. In *Reading Difficulties: Diagnosis, Correction, and Remediation.* Edited by William K. Durr. Newark, Del.: International Reading Association, 1970. Pp. vii, 276. *

769. ORPET, R. E., AND MYERS, C. E. "Discriminant Function Analysis of Conservation Stages by Structure of Intellect and Conceptual Style Variables." Abstract. *Proc 78th Ann Conv Am Psychol Assn* 5(1):279–80 '70. * (*PA* 44:18342)

770. POST, JOSEPH MARTIN. *The Effects of Vocalization on the Ability of Third Grade Students to Complete Selected Performance Subtests From the Wechsler Intelligence Scale for Children.* Doctor's thesis, University of South Carolina (Columbia, S.C.), 1970. (*DAI* 31:1579A)

771. QUERESHI, M. Y., AND MILLER, JEFFREY M. "The Comparability of the WAIS, WISC, and WBII." *J Ed Meas* 7(2):105–11 su '70. * (*PA* 44:18711)

772. QUERESHI, M. Y., AND WIDLAK, FREDERIC W. "Perceptual Diversity as a Function of Intelligence." Abstract. *Proc 78th Ann Conv Am Psychol Assn* 5(1):379–80 '70. * (*PA* 44:18613)

773. QUERY, WILLIAM T. "A Comparative Study of the Relationship Between Need Affiliation and Need Achievement, and Success and Failure Among Indian and White Children." *Newsl Res Psychol* 12(2):95–6 My '70. *

774. REES, ANN H., AND PALMER, FRANCIS H. "Factors Related to Change in Mental Test Performance." *Develop Psychol Monogr* 3(2):1–57 S '70. * (*PA* 45:464)

775. RICE, DONALD B. "Learning Disabilities: An Investigation in Two Parts." *J Learn Dis* 3(3):149–55 Mr '70. *

776. ROSIER, F. N. G. "A Study of Juvenile Delinquents in a Remand Home." *Papers Psychol* 4(1–2):54–5 Ap-O '70. *

777. RUBINO, CARL A. "Psychometric Procedures and the Detection and Exploration of Behavioral Deficits Due to Cerebral Dysfunction in Man." *Can Psychologist* 11(3):239–60 Jl '70. * (*PA* 44:21180)

778. SABATINO, DAVID A., AND HAYDEN, DAVID L. "Information Processing Behaviors Related to Learning Disabilities and Educable Mental Retardation." *Excep Children* 37(1):21–9 S '70. * (*PA* 46:5527)

779. SABATINO, DAVID A., AND HAYDEN, DAVID L. "Psycho-Educational Study of Selected Behavioral Variables With Children Failing the Elementary Grades." *J Exp Ed* 38(4):40–57 su '70. * (*PA* 46:5680–1)

780. SABATINO, DAVID A., AND HAYDEN, DAVID L. "Variation in Information Processing Behaviors: As Related to Chronological Age Differences for Children Failing in the Elementary Grades." *J Learn Dis* 3(8):404–12 Ag '70. *

781. SATTLER, JEROME M.; HILLIX, WILLIAM A.; AND NEHER, LINDA A. "Halo Effect in Examiner Scoring of Intelligence Test Responses." *J Consult & Clin Psychol* 34(2):172–6 Ap '70. * (*PA* 44:10422)

782. SCHOONOVER, SARAH M., AND HERTEL, RICHARD K. "Diagnostic Implications of WISC Scores." *Psychol Rep* 26(3):967–73 Je '70. * (*PA* 45:956)

783. SCHWARTZ, MELVIN L., AND DENNERLL, RAYMOND D. "Neuropsychological Assessment of Children With, Without, and With Questionable Epileptogenic Dysfunction." *Percept & Motor Skills* 30(1):111–21 F '70. *

784. SCHWEBEL, ANDREW I., AND BERNSTEIN, ANDREW J. "The Effects of Impulsivity on the Performance of Lower-Class Children on Four WISC Tests." *Am J Orthopsychiatry* 40(4):629–36 Jl '70. * (*PA* 45:7943)

785. SCOTT, RALPH; KELL, E. R.; AND SALISBURY, DONALD L. "Cognitive Profiles of 'Retarded' Children: A Survey of Inter- and Intra-child Differences." *Psychol Sch* 7(3):288–91 Jl '70. * (*PA* 45:4957)

786. SHATSWELL, DAVID WAYNE. *A WISC Profile of the Disabled Reader.* Master's thesis, Chico State College (Chico, Calif.), 1970.

787. SIEGENTHALER, BRUCE M., AND OTHERS. *Factors Related to the Speech-Hearing of Children of Below Normal Intelligence.* An unpublished report to the U.S. Office of Education, Project No. 8-0426, Pennsylvania State University, 1970. Pp. vi, 134. *

788. SILVERSTEIN, A. B. "The Measurement of Intelligence." *Int R Res Mental Retard* 4:193–227 '70. *

789. SILVERSTEIN, A. B. "Reappraisal of the Validity of a Short Short Form of Wechsler's Scales." *Psychol Rep* 26(2):559–61 Ap '70. * (*PA* 44:20973)

790. SILVERSTEIN, A. B. "Reappraisal of the Validity of WAIS, WISC, and WPPSI Short Forms." *J Consult & Clin Psychol* 34(1):12–4 F '70. * (*PA* 44:5886)

791. SIMPSON, ROBERT L. "Reading Tests Versus Intelligence Tests as Predictors of High School Graduation." *Psychol Sch* 7(4):363–5 O '70. * (*PA* 46:18;0)

792. SIMPSON, ROBERT L. "Study of the Comparability of the WISC and the WAIS." *J Consult & Clin Psychol* 34(2):156–8 Ap '70. * (*PA* 44:10423)

793. SKRIPOL, JAMES N. *Correlation of the Otis-Lennon Intermediate and the Wechsler Intelligence Scale for Children.* Master's thesis, Springfield College (Springfield, Mass.), 1970.

794. SPREEN, OTFRIED, AND TRYK, H. EDWARD. "WISC Information Subtest in a Canadian Population." *Can J Behav Sci* 2(4):294–8 O '70. * (*PA* 45:4258)

795. STEWART, R. R.; WALKER, W.; AND SAVAGE, R. D. "A Developmental Study of Cognitive and Personality Characteristics Associated With Haemolytic Disease of the Newborn." *Develop Med & Child Neurol* 12(1):16–26 F '70. * (*PA* 44:17249)

796. SWANSON, MERLYN S., AND JACOBSON, ANITA. "Evaluation of the S.I.T. for Screening Children With Learning Disabilities." *J Learn Dis* 3(6):318–20 Je '70. *

797. TAYLOR, JOHN F. "Brief Note on Simplified Administration of the Object Assembly Subtest." *J Clin Psychol* 26(2):182 Ap '70. * (*PA* 44:14607)

798. THEYE, FRED W. "Violation of Standard Procedure on Wechsler Scales." *J Clin Psychol* 26(1):70–1 Ja '70. * (*PA* 44:10424)

799. THOMPSON, WILLIAM WARREN. "A Northern Iceland Standardization of the Vocabulary Subtest of the Wechsler Intelligence Scale for Children." *Papers Psychol* 4(1–2):28–30 Ap-O '70. *

800. VOGELSANG, MARCIA P. *The Performance of Culturally Deprived Negro Preschool Children on the Wechsler Preschool*

and Primary Scale of Intelligence. Master's thesis, Texas Woman's University (Denton, Tex.), 1970.

801. WAGNER, EDWIN E. "Results of Psychological Testing on a Child with Gilles De La Tourette's Disease." *J Clin Psychol* 26(1):52–7 Ja '70. * (PA 44:10955)

802. WAGONER, OMER LEON. *The Relation Between Reading Ability and Piaget's Developmental Stages as Determined by WISC Sub-Test Profiles.* Doctor's thesis, University of Michigan (Ann Arbor, Mich.), 1970. (*DAI* 31:3976A)

803. WALKER, KENNETH P., AND GROSS, FREDERICK L. "I.Q. Stability Among Educable Mentally Retarded Children." *Training Sch B* 66(4):181–7 F '70. (PA 44:13185)

804. WARD, BYRON J. "Two Measures of Reading Readiness and First Grade Reading Achievement." *Read Teach* 23(7): 637–9 Ap '70. * (PA 45:3070)

805. WEINBERG, SHEILA, AND RABINOWITZ, JOSHUA. "A Sex Difference in the Wechsler IQ Vocabulary Score as a Predictor of Strategy in a Probability-Learning Task Performed by Adolescents." *Develop Psychol* 3(2): 218–24 S '70. * (PA 44:20696)

806. WILLIS, JERRY. "Group Versus Individual Intelligence Tests in One Sample of Emotionally Disturbed Children." *Psychol Rep* 27(3):819–22 D '70. * (PA 45:10227)

807. WUSSLER, MARILYN, AND BARCLAY, A. "Cerebral Dominance, Psycholinguistic Skills and Reading Disability." *Percept & Motor Skills* 31(2):419–25 O '70. * (PA 45:4015)

DAVID FREIDES, *Associate Professor of Psychology, Emory University, Atlanta, Georgia.*

A twenty-second century museum devoted to intellectual history might include in a display of the beginnings of mental testing, three sets of Wechsler block design materials, from the set borrowed from Kohs (who borrowed from whom?) through the streamlined version found in the *Wechsler Preschool and Primary Scale of Intelligence.* The caption might explain that changes in the materials came about by trial and error and that although not much was known in the twentieth century about what was being measured, psychologists did the best they could and achieved a modicum of practical success.

This fantasy, and the knowledge that it took Wechsler and The Psychological Corporation 28 years and five test editions to simplify the blocks, militates against undue complacency when measuring intelligence. Our methods are quite primitive. We are working with an accumulated lore consisting of procedures that enable us to compare people but not to measure innate qualities or specified skills. The Wechsler tests represent the acme of such pragmatic accumulation.

The appeal of the Wechsler tests lies in their organized diversity. There are separate verbal and performance scales and individual subtests. Clinicians and learning disability specialists consider the pattern of strengths and deficits in formulating treatment plans. There is much art in this process and relatively little science. Research on score patterns has yielded no systematic confirmation and some work, especially on children, has even challenged the verbal-performance distinction. Nonetheless, the practice of distinguishing between the two persists, apparently because enough practical validation occurs to warrant its continuation in the absence of anything better. On the research side, the issue is certainly not yet settled. There is some evidence, for example, that the verbal and performance scales may be at least a preliminary way of approaching the knotty issue of lateral hemispheric differences in adults.

If we are to deal with present inadequacies in a fundamental way, new measurement concepts must be generated. There is promise of such development emerging from research in developmental psychology, neuropsychology, cognition, and information processing. But genuinely new instruments for general assessment are probably years away, while continuing widespread use of the Wechsler tests can be anticipated over the next two decades. This 21-year-old test is probably more directly instrumental in influencing life decisions on school age children than any other, yet the greatest part of its content was borrowed from a test for adults, Form 2 of the *Wechsler-Bellevue Intelligence Scale.* There is a need for revision and restandardization of the WISC now, and it can be accomplished without major theoretical innovation. Many obvious weaknesses can be corrected while retaining the same format. Since the publishers are planning a revision, due approximately in 1972, some suggestions follow:

a) A test covering age 30 months (the ceiling on the Bayley) to senility is both feasible and desirable. The *Wechsler Adult Intelligence Scale* (ages 16 and up) is now 15 years old and will soon need revising. Combining the accumulated lore from WAIS and WISC with that recently obtained in the standardization of the WPPSI would be most helpful to psychological assessment. There would be special advantages for longitudinal research, large gains in efficiency in educating psychologists and psychometricians, efficiencies in the economics of clinical practice, and technical advances contributing to the assessment of regressive and deficit conditions. Perhaps more importantly, such a test might help obliterate artificial distinctions between childhood and adulthood and would emphasize, instead, the continuity of development that is life but which eludes much clinical thinking.

b) Wechsler emphasizes that an IQ is no more than a score comparing a person with his peers. I wonder how much of his contribution is vitiated when the score attained is interpreted according to the table of intelligence classifications printed in all editions of his tests. The central group in the distribution is designated, appropriately, as average, a term whose meaning is essentially statistical, but adjacent groups are termed dull normal and bright normal. Granted that "normal" has a statistical meaning, it also has many other meanings, and these are frequently invidious and culture bound. Terms with less surplus meaning, possibly dull average and bright average, are much to be preferred.

c) Many of the Comprehension questions in the WISC are clearly inappropriate for children and should be replaced. Since appropriateness has been accomplished in excellent fashion on the WPPSI, it should present no difficulty here. However, care should be taken that revisions do not follow the example of the WAIS, where proverb interpretations were added to Comprehension, thereby mixing concept formation with practical judgment and muddling both.

d) WISC Comprehension also poses a methodological problem of some importance. Several items require the subject to give two correct answers spontaneously for full credit. This penalizes an individual who is content to provide a single answer to a single question while it rewards obsessive and talkative types. It confounds ability with response style. Although opportunity for the assessment of both skill and response style is needed, tests should be structured so that the two can be distinguished. It seems appropriate for intelligence tests to emphasize skill and ability and to de-emphasize response style. Once again, this has been accomplished in the WPPSI, where the examiner is instructed to request an additional response when it is not spontaneously given.

Criteria and procedure must vary from subtest to subtest, depending on what is being measured. For example, Vocabulary should be treated as a recognition task aimed at determining passive familiarity and/or understanding. To this end, the multiple choice synonym or antonym technique used in paper and pencil tests can be adapted to the individual testing situation. Or the method of requesting a definition can be retained with modification of follow-up questioning to get at the issue being assessed. For example, examiners can be allowed to ask for description of an object (How does it look? Describe it.) after the subject indicates that the word refers to the object. This method contrasts with the noncommittal and awkward "Please explain a little more." (Incidentally, the introductory instruction on Vocabulary, "I want to see how many words you know," should be eliminated. It is threatening, unnecessary, and untrue.)

On the other hand, Similarities or other tests of concept formation might well be judged on the basis of the subject's production of categorizations, rather than merely on the recognition that a category is appropriate. Here the test construction problem is to find a means to be explicit about the level of categorization required for maximum credit. The WISC is imprecise. The question, "In what way are a plum and a peach alike?" is not specific as to the level of response desired. The responses "You eat both" and "Both are fruit" are equally true. It is not known whether a child who gives the former response could or could not have given the latter. Hence, it is not known whether conceptual style or conceptual ability is being assessed.

e) Wechsler's tests are compendia of previously studied materials, and the recent publication of the WPPSI indicates that he is prepared to borrow anew. The Geometric Designs of the WPPSI, borrowed from Bender (who borrowed from Wertheimer who borrowed from whom?), is an excellent choice and should certainly be represented in the WISC and also in the proposed lifetime test. Using scoring considerations and techniques advanced by Graham and Kendall (*Memory-for-Designs Test*), Beery and Buktenica (*Developmental Test of Visual-Motor Integration*), Fuller, (*Minnesota Percepto-Diagnostic Test*), and Koppitz (*Bender-Gestalt Test for Young Children*), it would be possible to devise a test of considerable range, even for adults.

f) The Picture Completion test, though showing up as a significant component of Witkin's field independence factor, is a rather banal and diagnostically unimportant test. I would substitute a test of figure-ground relationships such as the combination of overlapping figures and embedded figures contained in Ayres' *Southern California Figure-Ground Visual Perception Test* (borrowed from Witkin, borrowed from Gottschaldt, borrowed from whom?).

g) The Block Design test always shows up as a valuable assessment tool in both research and clinical work and should be retained, but two different kinds of errors appear at the

Wechsler Intelligence Scale for Children

easier levels: difficulty with spatial orientation and figure-ground confusion. It would be helpful to have more items explicitly designed to challenge each area of functioning.

h) There is no test of memory, verbal or nonverbal, in the Wechsler battery except perhaps the Digit Span. Schafer[1] and those in the Rapaport tradition borrowed the old Babcock-Levy Story Recall for this purpose. All studies indicate that Digit Span is the least reliable of the verbal subtests and in the WISC it was actually excluded from the computation of the norms. Although the Coding, or digit symbol, subtest in the Performance group is at times purported to reflect a memory factor, it is hardly a test of memory. I would suggest that Digit Span be replaced by a meaningful verbal memory test, made up of memory for phrases, sentences, and stories (like the Babcock-Levy or the *Wechsler Memory Scale*); and that Coding be replaced by a nonverbal recognition task involving figural identifications ranging from simple designs to faces.

i) Next to Digit Span, Arithmetic generally shows the least correlation with Verbal IQ. Neurological evidence and factor analysis both indicate independence in verbal and mathematical factors. In practice, results of the Arithmetic test have a nebulous significance. If they are inconsistent with other findings, the data are generally disregarded, perhaps because the test is just a collection of increasingly difficult arithmetical problems with no attention paid to the cognitive operations underlying this function. Pending the development of instruments which get at the structure of mathematical thinking, Arithmetic should be relegated to the status of a supplementary test, used in those instances when there is some special need for data in this area.

j) Wechsler uses Mazes (borrowed from Porteus who borrowed from whom?) as a supplementary test in the WISC and as a main test in the WPPSI. Its administration is somewhat cumbersome, but I favor its retention as a supplementary test on the WISC or the proposed lifetime test. It has a more promising research background (as a measure of planning, attention, and mental control) than many other procedures commonly in use.

k) Order of administration is least boring

---

[1] SCHAFER, ROY. *The Clinical Application of Psychological Tests: Diagnostic Summaries and Case Studies.* The Menninger Foundation Monograph Series No. 6. New York: International Universities Press, Inc., 1948. Pp. 346. *

when Verbal and Performance tests are intermixed, as is done in the WPPSI.

l) Culture free tests and tests not favoring one social group over another may not be even theoretically attainable (the mind must grow on something and that, inevitably, is slanted culturally) and certainly will not be available in the near future. However, care can be exercised in the wording of items so as not to confound unduly the variables being measured with social class variables. "Why is it generally better to give money to an organized charity than to a street beggar?" is clearly inappropriate and "to pay bills by check [rather] than by cash" may be unsuitable for many adults, let alone children. Close scrutiny of the questions and careful consultation with experts in the various subcultures of the country is a sine qua non for the next revision.

To conclude, the WISC is currently the best available compendium of individually administered, subject comparison techniques purporting to measure intelligence. The test needs revision and restandardization, and the cumulation of available Wechsler lore should make possible a cradle-to-grave version that would be a real boon to clinical work and research.

R. T. OSBORNE, *Professor of Psychology and Director, Testing and Evaluation Center, The University of Georgia, Athens, Georgia.*

Despite the efforts of some well intentioned but misinformed school administrators, guidance counselors, and legislators to restrict the use of psychological tests in general and of intelligence tests in particular, the WISC has become of age and remains the individual intelligence test of choice for use with children in the 6 to 13 age range. For the WISC just to have survived the last six years in an atmosphere of test burnings, Congressional investigations, restrictive legislation, and claims that the IQ test is an instrument of subtle torture is no small accomplishment. For the WISC to have survived and grown in professional respect lends further support to Burstein's characterization of the WISC in *The Sixth Yearbook* as "a well standardized, stable instrument, correlating well with other tests of intelligence." There is nothing in the WISC literature of over 200 articles published since 1963 to suggest a substantial change in the earlier evaluation.

The four major WISC categories covered by Burstein, (*a*) reliability and validity, (*b*) derivatives of the WISC, including foreign translations, (c) psychopathological applications, and (d) nature and purpose of intelligence testing, will not be reviewed here. The interested reader should refer to *The Sixth Yearbook* and to the over 280 earlier references.

Burstein hopefully predicted that future research with the WISC would involve a broad-gauge application of the scale to total personality variables. In the opinion of this reviewer, Glasser and Zimmerman have made a significant effort to integrate intelligence and concepts of general personality in their manual, *Clinical Interpretations of the Wechsler Intelligence Scale for Children* (509). Using the broad base of 18 years of WISC research and their own clinical experiences, they have delineated certain examiner and child variables not ordinarily considered in the analysis of objective intelligence testing. The authors say "these qualitative factors permit valuable inferences to be drawn and can greatly enhance understanding of the individual child."

Space does not permit the discussion of the application of the WISC to special populations —retarded, blind, dyslexic, gifted, brain damaged, Negro, and other minority groups. Suffice it to say, little new knowledge has been added in these areas since 1963.

There are, however, some new and exciting WISC related investigations which may be of relevance to the growing body of knowledge linking genetics with behavior. Alexander and others,[1] Shaffer (242), and Money (359) have observed a specific cognitive deficit in gonadal aplasia (Turner's Syndrome) which may stem from an organic defect related to the chromosomal anomaly involved. It was noted that women with Turner's Syndrome and persons with lesions of the parietal lobes have similar impairments reflected in specific WISC factor patterns identified by Cohen (148) and confirmed by Osborne (414). There is evidence to suggest that the sex chromosome complement and related sex differences in biochemical processes may underlie sex differences in spatial and numerical abilities.

Both the WISC and WAIS have been used with encouraging results to evaluate electrophysiological correlates of intelligence. Correla-

tions as high as .70 between the Wechsler scales and the visually evoked response have been reported by Osborne,[2] Rhodes (806), and Vogel.[3]

The WISC design and standardization weaknesses recognized in earlier Yearbooks will hopefully be corrected in the revision of the scale tentatively scheduled for 1972. Misuses of the scale apparent to any first-day graduate student are another matter. Unfortunately, the weaknesses of misuse cannot be corrected in the next revision.

The WISC is a stable, general purpose, individual intelligence test and is a useful and valid measure of immediate or present mental functioning.

For a review by Alvin G. Burstein, see 6:540; for reviews by Elizabeth D. Fraser, Gerald R. Patterson, and Albert I. Rabin, see 5:416; for reviews by James M. Anderson, Harold A. Delp, and Boyd R. McCandless, see 4:363 (1 excerpt).

[432]
★[Re Wechsler Intelligence Scale for Children] California Abbreviated WISC. Educable mentally retarded ages 8–13.5, intellectually gifted elementary school children; 1966; CAW-MR, CAW-IG; consists of 5 subtests of *Wechsler Intelligence Scale for Children;* 6 scores: information, picture arrangement, picture completion, block design, coding (Form 1), similarities (Form 2), total; individual; 2 levels: Form 1 (4 pages) for the educable mentally retarded child, Form 2 (4 pages) for the intellectually gifted child; manual (12 pages plus tests); WISC testing materials must be used; $7 per examiner's kit of 10 sets of record booklets and manual; $6.50 per 25 record booklets; $3 per manual; postpaid; (20–30) minutes; Carmen J. Finley and Jack M. Thompson; Western Psychological Services. *

REFERENCE
1. COYLE, F. A., JR., AND BELLAMY, EDWARD E. "Use of the California Abbreviated WISC With Institutionalized Retardates." *Am J Mental Def* 74(4):578 Ja '70. * (PA 44: 11053)

A. B. SILVERSTEIN, *Research Specialist, Pacific State Hospital, Pomona, California.*

Developing short forms of Wechsler's tests has been a popular pastime of psychologists for years, but to the reviewer's knowledge, the CAW is the first of these to be published with a manual and protocol booklets of its own.

The CAW-MR was standardized on a sample of 309 educable mentally retarded children (IQ's 50–80) from California. The data for

---

1 ALEXANDER, DUANE, AND MONEY, JOHN. "Turner's Syndrome and Gerstmann's Syndrome: Neuropsychologic Comparisons." *Neuropsychologia* 4:265–73 Jl '66. *
ALEXANDER, DUANE; WALKER, H. T., JR.; AND MONEY, JOHN. "Studies in Direction Sense: I, Turner's Syndrome." *Arch Gen Psychiatry* 10:337–9 Ap '64. *

2 OSBORNE, R. T. "Heritability Estimates for the Visual Evoked Response." *Life Sci* 9(9, pt 2):481–90 My 8 '70. *
3 VOGEL, WILLIAM, AND BROVERMAN, DONALD M. "Relationship Between EEG and Test Intelligence: A Critical Review." *Psychol B* 62:132–44 Ag '64. *

10 WISC subtests (Digit Span and Mazes omitted) were analyzed by the Wherry-Doolittle method, and the combination of five subtests having the highest multiple correlation with the Full Scale (R = .89) was selected. For a second sample, of 173 children, IQ's estimated on the basis of the original regression equation had a correlation of .86 with the IQ's actually obtained.

A similar, but not identical, procedure was used in the case of the CAW-IG, which was standardized on a sample of 400 intellectually gifted children (IQ's 125+), also from California. The same method was used to select the "best" combination of five subtests, but then the subtest scores were simply summed, not differentially weighted. The correlation between estimated and actual IQ's was .75 for the standardization sample, and .84 for a second sample of 151 children.

Even if one accepts the premise that developing a short form of the WISC is a worthwhile endeavor (not everyone would agree), a number of questions can be raised about the proper way of going about it.

How should the test be shortened? The two basic approaches are by reducing the number of subtests and by reducing the number of items within subtests. There is evidence, based on the WISC standardization data, that short forms developed by the second approach have validities—i.e., correlations with the Full Scale—which are comparable to those of short forms comprised of the best combination of five subtests. Moreover, advocates of this second approach point out that it does not sacrifice the variety of functions tapped by the Full Scale. Finley and Thompson cannot be faulted for proceeding as they have, but research is needed to compare the *external* validities of short forms developed by the two approaches.

Should subtest scores be differentially weighted? Most short forms involve only simple summation. Short forms that entail differential weighting will naturally afford something of an advantage, but the gain may not be worth the additional effort required. A re-analysis of the CAW standardization data shows that simple summation would reduce the validity of the CAW-MR by only .01, whereas differential weighting would increase the validity of the CAW-IG by .04. In the light of these findings, it is puzzling that Finley and Thompson elected to employ differential weighting for the CAW-MR and simple summation for the CAW-IG.

What is the appropriate standardization sample for a shortened test? Twenty years ago, McNemar argued convincingly for using the sample on which the test was originally standardized, rather than samples of exceptional children, adult schizophrenics, prisoners, student nurses, etc. For certain purposes, to be sure, it may be desirable to gather local data on special groups, but then one must question the propriety of publishing these data for general use. More specifically, are Finley and Thompson's findings on retarded and gifted children from California generalizable to children in other parts of the country?

How should validity be determined? When scores on a short form and those on the Full Scale are obtained from the same administration of the test, the resulting validity is spuriously high. In effect, this procedure implies that the subtests are all perfectly reliable, since those items passed on the Full Scale must also be passed on the short form. For the WISC standardization sample, the validities of the CAW-MR and the CAW-IG (using simple summation) are .94 and .95, respectively, but when allowance is made for subtest unreliability, the corresponding values drop to .88 and .90. The validities reported by Finley and Thompson would presumably drop similarly if subtest reliability were taken into account.

As alternatives to the CAW, the reviewer would recommend short forms based on available analyses of the WISC standardization data, or possibly short forms based on the analysis of one's own data on subjects of special interest.

[433]
★[Re Wechsler Intelligence Scale for Children] Rhodes WISC Scatter Profile. Ages 5-15; 1969; a form for profiling WISC scores; profile (2 pages); manual (4 pages); $4.50 per 50 profiles, postage extra; Fen Rhodes; Educational and Industrial Testing Service. *

[434]
★Wechsler Preschool and Primary Scale of Intelligence. Ages 4-6.5; 1967, c1949-67; WPPSI; 8 of the 11 tests provide the same measures as the *Wechsler Intelligence Scale for Children* and approximately ⅓ of the total number of items are essentially the same; 14 scores: verbal (information, vocabulary, arithmetic, similarities, comprehension, sentences-optional, total), performance (animal house, picture completion, mazes, geometric design, block design, total), total; individual; 1 form; manual (139 pages); record form (6 pages); $26 per set of testing materials including 50 geometric design sheets, 25 maze tests, 25 record forms, and manual; $2.50 per 25 record

forms; $2.80 per 25 maze tests; $1.50 per 50 design sheets; $3.25 per manual; postage extra; (50-75) minutes; David Wechsler; Psychological Corporation.* (Australian edition: Australian Council for Educational Research.)

REFERENCES

1. SILVERSTEIN, A. B. "A Short Short Form of Wechsler's Scales for Screening Purposes." *Psychol Rep* 21:842 D '67. * (*PA* 42:7335)
2. BACH, LLOYD CARL. *A Comparison of Selected Psychological Tests Used With Trainable Mentally Retarded Children.* Doctor's thesis, University of South Dakota (Vermillion, S.D.), 1968. (*DA* 29:2990A)
3. BONFIELD, JOHN RONALD. *Predictors of Achievement for Educable Mentally Retarded Children.* Doctor's thesis, Pennsylvania State University (University Park, Pa.), 1968. (*DAI* 30:1009A)
4. CAMPANELLA, SAM. *The Validity and Use of the WPPSI in Predicting School Achievement.* Master's thesis, Utah State University (Logan, Utah), 1968.
5. FULLER, BARBARA L. *A Factor Analysis of the Wechsler Pre-School and Primary Scale of Intelligence.* Master's thesis, California State College (Long Beach, Calif.), 1968.
6. HERMAN, DAVID O. "A Study of Sex Differences on the Wechsler Preschool and Primary Scale of Intelligence." Abstract. *Proc 76th Ann Conv Am Psychol Assn* 3:455-6 '68. *
7. KNOLL, DONNA B. *A Comparison of the ABC Inventory and Wechsler Preschool and Primary Scale of Intelligence for Predicting Success in Kindergarten.* Master's thesis, Fort Hays Kansas State College (Hays, Kan.), 1968.
8. MCRAE, J. *A Comparison of the Wechsler Preschool and Primary Scale of Intelligence With the Slosson Intelligence Test.* Master's thesis, Eastern Washington State College (Cheney, Wash.), 1968.
9. PAUL, GERALD THOMAS. *The Relationship Between Prenatal and Perinatal Experiences and Intellectual, Perceptual-Motor, and Conceptual Functioning in Preschool Adopted Children.* Doctor's thesis, Temple University (Philadelphia, Pa.), 1968. (*DAI* 30:1364B)
10. PLANT, WALTER T., AND SOUTHERN, MARA L. "First Grade Reading Achievement Predicted From WPPSI and Other Scores Obtained 18 Months Earlier." Abstract. *Proc 76th Ann Conv Am Psychol Assn* 3:593-4 '68. *
11. RICHARDS, JOHN THOMAS. *The Effectiveness of the Wechsler Preschool and Primary Scale of Intelligence in the Identification of Mentally Retarded Children.* Doctor's thesis, University of Virginia (Charlottesville, Va.), 1968. (*DA* 29:3880A)
12. SILVERSTEIN, A. B. "Validity of a New Approach to the Design of WAIS, WISC, and WPPSI Short Forms." *J Consult & Clin Psychol* 32:478-9 Ag '68. * (*PA* 42:16432)
13. SILVERSTEIN, A. B. "Validity of WPPSI Short Forms." *J Consult & Clin Psychol* 32:229-30 Ap '68. * (*PA* 42:8108)
14. SILVERSTEIN, A. B. "Variance Components in Five Psychological Tests." *Psychol Rep* 23:141-2 Ag '68. * (*PA* 43:6920)
15. SILVERSTEIN, A. B. "WISC and WPPSI IQs for the Gifted." *Psychol Rep* 22:1168 Je '68. * (*PA* 42:1880)
16. SILVERSTEIN, A. B. "WPPSI IQs for the Mentally Retarded." *Am J Mental Def* 73:446 N '68. * (*PA* 43:8602)
17. SMITH, RALPH A. *Abbreviated Forms of the Wechsler Preschool and Primary Scale of Intelligence for a Kindergarten Population.* Master's thesis, Fort Hays Kansas State College (Hays, Kan.), 1968.
18. WHITE, LINDA ANN. *A Comparative Study of the Performance of Negro Head Start Students on the Wechsler Preschool and Primary Scale of Intelligence, the Wechsler Intelligence Scale for Children, and the Stanford-Binet, Form L-M.* Master's thesis, University of Texas (Austin, Tex.), 1968.
19. BARCLAY, ALLAN, AND YATER, ALLAN C. "Comparative Study of the Wechsler Preschool and Primary Scale of Intelligence and the Stanford-Binet Intelligence Scale, Form L-M, Among Culturally Deprived Children." Abstract. *J Consult & Clin Psychol* 33(2):257 Ap '69. * (*PA* 43:9734)
20. BRITTAIN, MICHAEL. "The WPPSI: A Midlands Study." *Brit J Ed Psychol* 39(1):14-7 F '69. * (*PA* 43:17903)
21. BRUDENELL, GERALD ALFRED. *Predicting Achievement of Head Start Children Using Personal, Testing, and Rating Data.* Doctor's thesis, Colorado State College (Greeley, Colo.), 1969. (*DAI* 30:4269A)
22. CURRY, DAL ROY. *The Effect of Two Types of Auditory Discrimination Training on Language Performance and Acquisition in a Culturally Deprived Preschool Population.* Doctor's thesis, University of Kansas (Lawrence, Kan.), 1969. (*DAI* 30:5281A)
23. DIENSTAG, ROBERT. *The Efficacy of the Wechsler Preschool and Primary Scale of Intelligence in Diagnosing Minimal Cerebral Dysfunction.* Master's thesis, California State College (Long Beach, Calif.), 1969.
24. DOKECKI, PAUL R.; FREDE, MARTHA C.; AND GAUTNEY, DONALD B. "Criterion, Construct, and Predictive Validities of the Wechsler Preschool and Primary Scale of Intelligence." Abstract. *Proc 77th Ann Conv Am Psychol Assn* 4(2):505-6 '69. * (*PA* 44:1253)
25. FAGAN, JOEN; BROUGHTON, ELIZABETH; ALLEN, MILDRED; CLARK, BETTY; AND EMERSON, PATRICIA. "Comparison of the Binet and WPPSI With Lower-Class Five-Year-Olds." *J Consult & Clin Psychol* 33(5):607-9 O '69. * (*PA* 44:2135)
26. GARVER, SHERRY A. *A Comparison of the Verbal IQ Scores of the Wechsler Preschool and Primary Scale of Intelligence and the Wechsler Intelligence Scale for Children at the Kindergarten Level.* Master's thesis, Wisconsin State University (River Falls, Wis.), 1969.
27. GOENS, BERT DOUGLAS. *Comparisons of the Wechsler Preschool and Primary Scale of Intelligence With the Wechsler Intelligence Scale for Children.* Master's thesis, Western Michigan University (Kalamazoo, Mich.), 1969. (*Masters Abstracts* 7:119)
28. GREEN, REGINA MIRIAM. *The Relationship of Nutritional States, Performance I.Q. and Self Concept in 4-6 Year Old Inner City Children.* Doctor's thesis, University of Maryland (College Park, Md.), 1969. (*DAI* 31:2085B)
29. KAVAJECZ, LEONARD GARY. *A Study of Results on the Wechsler Preschool and Primary Scale of Intelligence of Inadequate Readers.* Doctor's thesis, Colorado State College (Greeley, Colo.), 1969. (*DAI* 30:4143A)
30. KREBS, ELEONORE GOODLIN. *The Wechsler Preschool and Primary Scale of Intelligence and Prediction of Reading Achievement in First Grade.* Doctor's thesis, Rutgers—The State University (New Brunswick, N.J.), 1969. (*DAI* 30:4279A)
31. LICHTMAN, MARILYN VICKMAN. *Intelligence, Creativity, and Language: An Examination of the Interrelationships of Three Variables Among Preschool, Disadvantaged Negro Children.* Doctor's thesis, George Washington University (Washington, D.C.), 1969. (*DAI* 31:1625A)
32. LIVO, NORMA JOAN. *The Degree of Relationship Among a Number of Readiness Factors and Success in Beginning Reading.* Doctor's thesis, University of Pittsburgh (Pittsburgh, Pa.), 1969. (*DAI* 30:2379A)
33. MCNAMARA, J. REGIS; PORTERFIELD, CHARLES L.; AND MILLER, LAWRENCE E. "The Relationship of the Wechsler Preschool and Primary Scale of Intelligence With the Coloured Progressive Matrices (1956) and the Bender Gestalt Test." *J Clin Psychol* 25(1):65-8 Ja '69. * (*PA* 43:9766)
34. MEEKER, MARY NACOL. *The Structure of Intellect: Its Interpretation and Uses*, pp. 132-46. Columbus, Ohio: Charles E. Merrill Publishing Co., 1969. Pp. xix, 203. *
35. MILLIREN, ALAN P., AND NEWLAND, T. ERNEST. "Statistically Significant Differences Between Subtest Scaled Scores for the WPPSI." *J Sch Psychol* 7(3):16-9 '68-69 ['69]. * (*PA* 44:2188)
36. NASE, ROBERT R. *A Correlation Study of the Harris-Goodenough Draw-A-Man and the Wechsler Preschool and Primary Scale of Intelligence With Children Referred for Psychological Testing.* Master's thesis, Mankato State College (Mankato, Minn.), 1969.
37. RELLAS, ARCHIE J. "The Use of the Wechsler Preschool and Primary Scale (WPPSI) in the Early Identification of Gifted Students." *Calif J Ed Res* 20(3):117-9 My '69. * (*PA* 45:8921)
38. SHIPE, DOROTHY, AND MIEZITIS, SOLVEIGA. "A Pilot Study in the Diagnosis and Remediation of Special Learning Disabilities in Preschool Children." *J Learn Dis* 2(11):579-92 N '69. * (*PA* 46:7521)
39. SILVERSTEIN, A. B. "An Alternative Factor Analytic Solution for Wechsler's Intelligence Scales." *Ed & Psychol Meas* 29(4):763-7 w '69. * (*PA* 44:20972)
40. VINGOE, FRANK J.; BIRNEY, S. DARYL; AND KORDINAK, S. THOMAS. "Note on Psychological Screening of Preschool Children." *Percept & Motor Skills* 29(2):661-2 O '69. * (*PA* 44:4182)
41. YULE, W.; BERGER, M.; BUTLER, S.; NEWHAM, V.; AND TIZARD, J. "The WPPSI: An Empirical Evaluation With a British Sample." *Brit J Ed Psychol* 39(1):1-13 F '69. * (*PA* 43:17914)
42. CUNDICK, BERT P. "Measures of Intelligence on Southwest Indian Students." *J Social Psychol* 81(2):151-6 Ag '70. * (*PA* 44:20655)
43. DELANEY, RICHARD J. *Short Forms of the WPPSI for Screening and Research.* Master's thesis, Loyola University (Chicago, Ill.), 1970.
44. FUTTERER, JAMES W. *An Investigation of the Relationship of the Wechsler Preschool and Primary Scale of Intelligence to the 1960 Revision of the Stanford-Binet Scale, Form L-M.* Master's thesis, Loyola University (Chicago, Ill.), 1970.
45. GRAHAM, GERALDINE AGNES. *The Effects of Material and Social Incentives on the Performance on Intelligence Test Tasks by Lower Class and Middle Class Negro Preschool Children.* Doctor's thesis, George Washington University (Washington, D.C.), 19-0. (*DAI* 31:4311B)
46. HANDLEY, WILLIAM B. *A Validity and Reliability Study of the Wechsler Preschool and Primary Scale of Intelligence Using Six Year Old Children.* Master's thesis, University of Saskatchewan (Saskatoon, Sask., Canada), 1970.
47. JONES, ELOISE LORRAINE HARRISS. *The Effects of a Language Development Program on the Psycholinguistic Abili-*

ties and IQ of a Group of Preschool Disadvantaged Children. Doctor's thesis, University of Arkansas (Fayetteville, Ark.), 1970. (*DAI* 31:2761A)
48. NURCOMBE, B., AND MOFFITT, P. "Cultural Deprivation and Language Defect: Project Enrichment of Childhood." *Austral Psychologist* 5(3):249–59 N '70. * (*PA* 46:5744)
49. O'KEEFE, GERALD S. *The Factorial Structure of the Wechsler Preschool and Primary Scale of Intelligence.* Master's thesis, Loyola University (Chicago, Ill.), 1970.
50. RICHARDS, JOHN T. "Internal Consistency of the WPPSI With the Mentally Retarded." *Am J Mental Def* 74(4):581–2 Ja '70. * (*PA* 44:11072)
51. SILVERSTEIN, A. B. "Reappraisal of the Validity of a Short Short Form of Wechsler's Scales." *Psychol Rep* 26(2):559–61 Ap '70. * (*PA* 44:20973)
52. SILVERSTEIN, A. B. "Reappraisal of the Validity of WAIS, WISC, and WPPSI Short Forms." *J Consult & Clin Psychol* 34(1):12–4 F '70. *
53. TAYLOR, VERA COOK. *An Evaluation of Three Compensatory Education Kindergarten Programs.* Doctor's thesis, University of Southern California (Los Angeles, Calif.), 1970. (*DAI* 31:2749A)
54. WASIK, JOHN L., AND WASIK, BARBARA H. "A Note on Use of the WPPSI in Evaluating Intervention Programs." *Meas & Eval Guid* 3(1):54–6 sp '70. * (*PA* 45:2958)
55. WORKS, MARIAN NEWMAN. *Some Variables Involved in the Reading Process.* Doctor's thesis, University of Oklahoma (Norman, Okla.), 1970. (*DAI* 31:2765AAA)
56. ZIMMERMAN, IRLA LEE, AND WOO-SAM, JAMES. "The Utility of the Wechsler Preschool and Primary Scale of Intelligence in the Public School." *J Clin Psychol* 26(4):472 O '70. * (*PA* 45:6976)

DOROTHY H. EICHORN, *Research Psychologist and Administrator, Child Study Center, Institute of Human Development, University of California, Berkeley, California.*

In composition and in both positive and negative characteristics, the youngest member of the family of Wechsler scales strongly resembles its older siblings. All five of the regular verbal subtests and three of the five performance subtests are downward extensions of like-named subtests of the WISC. The new supplementary verbal test (Sentences) is in lieu of the Digit Span subtest of the WISC and WAIS, and Animal House (one of the two new performance subtests) is analogous to Coding in the older scales. Geometric Design, the other new performance subtest, involves copying forms (circle, square, etc.), an item long popular on tests for young children.

Among the desirable traits of the WPPSI are the usual advantages of point scales over age scales (comparison of an individual only with his age peers, equality of means and standard deviations across ages, less variation in administration time, and avoidance of terminating the test with a long succession of failures), compact and attractive test materials, standardization closely approximating the American Psychological Association standards, and reliabilities satisfactorily high for individual evaluation.

Less satisfactory traits require more extended comment. The only validity data reported in the manual were obtained by administering the WPPSI, *Stanford-Binet Intelligence Scale, Peabody Picture Vocabulary Test,* and the *Pictorial Test of Intelligence* to 98 children aged 5 to 6 years from a single school district. Although the means of the various tests were all within four points of one another (highest on the S-B), the correlations with the WPPSI Full Scale IQ ranged from .58 (PPVT) to .75 (S-B). Almost all studies appearing since the publication of the manual report higher mean scores on the Stanford-Binet than on the WPPSI (*19, 24, 25, 37*). This direction of the difference was found for culturally disadvantaged as well as advantaged and gifted groups. Correlations between the WPPSI and the S-B were about of the order reported in the WPPSI manual, supporting Wechsler's comment that the tests are not interchangeable. In general, the correlations with the Stanford-Binet are higher for the Verbal than for the Performance IQ of the WPPSI. Correlations of WPPSI IQ's and subtest scores with a number of other tests have also been reported. With the exception of the *SRA Primary Mental Abilities,* correlations were lower than those of the WPPSI with the S-B. Predictive validity, as assessed by later performance on achievement tests, appears to be better for the WPPSI than for the Stanford-Binet, Peabody, Bender-Gestalt, and Draw-a-Person (*10, 24*).

Most of the reliabilities reported in the manual are based on corrected split-half correlations. Odd-even correlations of a comparably high order have been reported for a random sample of 60 5½-year-olds from Nottingham, England (*20*) and 40 mentally retarded children from a clinic in the southern U.S. (*50*). Except for the Animal House subtest, for which reliability was calculated from an immediate retest, the only test-retest reliabilities presented in the manual are correlations of .86, .89, and .92 for the Verbal, Performance, and Full Scales IQ's, respectively, obtained from a sample of 50 children aged about 5½ years and retested after an average of 11 weeks. Substantiation of these estimates, as well as item-rater reliabilities for subtests requiring examiner discretion in scoring, are needed.

A format of subtest scores and separate verbal and performance IQ's offers temptations for overinterpretation. Although factor analyses and analyses of variance components (*14, 24, 39*) contraindicate pattern analysis of subtest scores, they do suggest the existence of two major factors in the WPPSI (as in the WISC and WAIS). Interpretation of Verbal-Performance differences must, however, be tempered by the finding of discrepancies much greater than those observed in the standardization sample by several investigators (*20, 24, 41*).

Queries of experienced examiners and a review of the literature to date on the WPPSI revealed several recurrent complaints. A minor annoyance, also characteristic of the WISC and WAIS, is the use in the vocabulary subtests of words which have homonyms (e.g., fur) or near-homonyms (e.g., gamble). Other irritants are the necessity for interrupting the child after error on the mazes, asking for additional reasons on some items, and the obviousness of failure—all of which were seen as making discomfort for the child. Disconcerting to examiners were the subjectivity of scoring of a number of subtests and changes in materials or directions for administration within subtests. More major complaints concerned the length of the test and limited degree to which it extended the age range downward from the WISC. Although administration time does vary less than that for the Stanford-Binet, many testers find the WPPSI unduly long for preschool children. This problem was not often reported to be serious with children of five years or over, but even for children of this age, needs for rapid screening have precipitated a rash of short forms. Reviewers of the WISC noted its limited sensitivity and discrimination at its lower age limit. This fact and the desirability of having a point scale of intelligence for children younger than five made for eager anticipation of the WPPSI. Unfortunately, it suffers from the same sorts of limitations with respect to age and ability. The youngest age for which norms are given is 3 years, 10 months, 16 days. A child can receive a scaled score greater than zero without passing a single item, and gifted children may earn a sum of scaled scores higher than those for which IQ equivalents are tabled.

In view of the fact that much of the pressure for a downward extension of the WISC arose from programs of early educational intervention, most of which enroll children by at least three years of age, the relatively high "bottom" of the WPPSI and the length of administration time are disappointing restrictions on its utility. On the other hand, some of a generally good thing is better than none. For the age and ability range covered the WPPSI is the best standardized and most up-to-date individual test available.

A. B. SILVERSTEIN, *Research Specialist, Pacific State Hospital, Pomona, California.*

Although it is a separate and distinct test, the WPPSI bears such a strong family resemblance to the WISC that it appears reasonable to appraise the new test by comparing and contrasting it with its older "sibling."

ORGANIZATION. The WPPSI contains 11 subtests, 6 verbal and 5 performance. Except for Sentences, which replaces Digit Span as the supplementary subtest, the names of the verbal subtests are the same as those on the WISC, and they incorporate many of the same items. Modifications in the performance scale are more extensive: Animal House and Geometric Design replace Picture Arrangement, Object Assembly, and Coding, and there is no supplementary subtest, Mazes having been promoted to regular status. These changes are intended to increase the suitability of the test for younger children, and Wechsler suggests that the WPPSI be used in place of the WISC at age levels where the two tests overlap.

STANDARDIZATION. "The WPPSI was standardized on a sample of 100 boys and 100 girls in each of six age groups, ranging by half-years from 4 through 6.5." As with the WISC, the sample was stratified with respect to geographic region, urban-rural residence, and father's occupation, but on the basis of the 1960 census, rather than that of 1940. A noteworthy innovation was the stratification of the WPPSI sample with respect to color (white versus nonwhite). In general, the data reported in the manual support the representativeness of the sample.

ADMINISTRATION AND SCORING. In contrast to the WISC, the WPPSI is administered with the verbal and performance subtests intermixed, a procedure which should facilitate the use of the test with younger children. The examiner is free, however, to change the prescribed order to meet the needs of the testing situation.

The procedures for translating raw scores to scaled scores and converting sums of scaled scores to IQ's are identical to those for the WISC, and the same methods are used to obtain "equivalent MAs" (or "test ages"). Although the scaled scores on both tests have the same means and standard deviations, their possible range on the WPPSI is from 1 to 19, whereas on the WISC it is from 0 to 20. Thus, a child of 4 with a raw score of zero on every subtest should receive a total of 32 scaled score points, and a Full Scale IQ of 51. However, Wechsler recommends that IQ's not be calculated unless a child obtains raw scores greater than zero on at least two verbal and two performance subtests.

As on the WISC, if only four subtests are given on either scale, proration must be used to calculate the IQ's. However, if Sentences is administered in addition to the other verbal subtests, it is *not* used in calculating the IQ's. This represents an improvement over the WISC procedure, where proration is used when six subtests are given on either scale.

PSYCHOMETRIC PROPERTIES. Split-half reliabilities are reported at each age level for every subtest except Animal House, for which test-retest reliabilities are given. (In the WISC manual, reliabilities are reported at only three "representative" age levels.) The average reliabilities of six of the eight subtests which are common to both tests are higher for the WPPSI than for the WISC. The average reliabilities of the Verbal, Performance, and Full Scale IQ's on the WPPSI are .94, .93, and .96, respectively; the corresponding values on the WISC are .94, .88, and .94.

In addition to the reliability data given for the standardization sample, data on stability are reported for an independent sample of 50 children. With a mean retest interval of approximately 11 weeks, the reliabilities of individual subtests ranged from .60 to .93. The reliabilities of the Verbal, Performance, and Full Scale IQ's were .86, .88, and .91, respectively. On almost every subtest, the mean scaled score was higher on the second testing than on the first; the Verbal, Performance, and Full Scale IQ's rose 3.0, 6.6, and 3.6 points, respectively. No comparable data are given in the WISC manual.

Data on the correlations with three other intelligence tests are reported from a special study of 98 children. The correlations between the Full Scale IQ and IQ's on the *Stanford-Binet Intelligence Scale*, the *Peabody Picture Vocabulary Test*, and the *Pictorial Test of Intelligence* were .75, .58, and .64, respectively. The correlation with the Stanford-Binet is in the range usually reported between the WISC and the Stanford-Binet (although again, no comparable data are given in the WISC manual), and, as is also found with the WISC, the Verbal IQ correlated more highly with the Stanford-Binet than did the Performance IQ. The *greatest* difference between the mean Full Scale IQ and the mean IQ on any of the other three tests was less than 2 points.

One feature of the WPPSI manual which does not appear in the WISC manual is a table showing the critical values of differences between scaled scores on all possible pairs of subtests. A similar table shows the critical values of differences between Verbal and Performance IQ's. Since the manual does not state what interpretations are intended for the scores on individual subtests, or even for the IQ's on the two scales, it is not clear what use the examiner is to make of these data.

SUMMARY. Test users who prefer the WISC to the Stanford-Binet will be pleased to have a highly similar test designed especially for use with younger children. Those who prefer the Stanford-Binet to the WISC will presumably see no reason to switch to the WPPSI.

J Ed Meas 5:347–8 w '68. O. A. Oldridge and E. E. Allison. * An improvement over the WISC in the norms and hence usefulness of the WPPSI results from the inclusion of non-whites (14%) in the standardization sample. This seems particularly important since extensive use will be made of this instrument in the assessment of the mental ability of non-whites in pre-school situations. * The WPPSI, like the WISC, appears to suffer from inadequate floor to differentiate abilities at the lower end of the scale. A four-year-old making no correct responses would obtain a Verbal I.Q. of 56, Performance I.Q. of 57, and Full-Scale I.Q. of 53. Although the manual's recommendation that no I.Q.'s be computed unless the child obtains a raw score greater than zero on two of the Verbal tests and two of the Performance tests, its usefulness for differentiating among the moderately to severely retarded is absent. The manual suggests the tests may be too difficult for four-year-olds with I.Q.'s below 75. This rules out 5% of the four-year-old population (as reported in Table 6) and would seem to cast considerable doubt upon the test's value for this group of children at a very critical point. This deficiency would have been avoided if a few more very easy items had been included in each subtest. Verbal-Performance and subtest differences necessary for significance at the 15% level of confidence are included to reduce the common tendency toward type-I errors in interpretation. Since the common minimum acceptable confidence levels are 5% and 1%, it would have been valuable to have included subtest difference values for those levels. The manual reports that obtained differences of approximately three points (one standard deviation) between scaled scores on any pair of tests are significant at the 15% level, but a difference of at least 4 is needed to be significant at the 5% level and slightly more than 5 to be significant at the 1% level. The manual gives extensive reliability figures. Odd-even reliability coefficients appear to be quite substantial for the Verbal (.89 to .90), Performance (.84 to .91), and Full-Scale I.Q.'s (.92 to .94) but somewhat less so for the subtest scores (.62 to .88). These values are inflated to the extent that certain pupils could correctly answer items after the cut-off criterion had been reached for each subtest. No data are given as to whether the cut-off criteria were determined empirically or intuitively. The inclusions of retest reliabilities is a helpful addition. Stability coefficients over a three month period for fifty five-year-olds were .86, .89, and .92 for Verbal, Performance, and Full-Scale I.Q. scores, respectively. The subtest reliabilities were considerably lower, with ten of the eleven yielding coefficients of less than .8, five of these below .7, suggesting that the cut-off scoring did not result in inflated odd-even reliability coefficients for the subtests. The reliability of the Verbal, Performance, and Full-Scale I.Q.'s are satisfactory, but the subtests are not sufficiently stable to be of much value for individual use. McNemar's (1956, p. 127) statement regarding the WAIS is also relevant to the WPPSI: "....the author of the WAIS has attempted an impossible task; the construction of a scale to measure general (global) intelligence which at the same time will provide differences among subtests which are of a diagnostic value." Only the global objective appears to be well-achieved. Valuable concurrent validity data are also included which show the expected substantial relationship (r = .76) between the WPPSI-Verbal and the Stanford-Binet (Form L-M) for approximately 100 five- to six-year-olds. The less-than-normal variability (S = 12.8) for this sample makes the estimate conservative. The long administration time necessary for some children is also a concern to the reviewers. In many cases, especially with the younger or with "handicapped" children, the test requires two sessions. The extent to which this break affects the normative data and thus affects the validity of the results is uncertain; the manual only states that some children will need two sessions for the test. In the standardization sample it was found that about 10% of those tested needed one and one-half hours or more to complete the test. Summary: The WPPSI is a carefully developed and well standardized instrument of general intelligence that warrants widespread acceptance, although the value of subtest scores for individual use remains yet to be established.

Psychol Rep 21:1029 D '67. C. H. Ammons. * items are interesting and materials are satisfactorily sturdy * The sample of 600 boys and 600 girls seems adequately controlled for obvious factors judging from the data presented in the manual. Reliability estimates range from .71 to .94 depending on the subtest and age group, but SE_m varies sufficiently to require caution in comparing profiles of groups or points within profiles. * *Much* research is called for as the variance of WPPSI scores is not currently adequately accounted for. Tabled summaries and score equivalents in the manual will be useful in that undertaking as well as in clinical assessments.

SPECIFIC

[435]

*Closure Flexibility (Concealed Figures).** Industrial employees; 1956–65; CF; revision of *Gottschaldt Figures;* formerly called *Concealed Figures: A Test of Flexibility of Closure;* Form A ('56, 8 pages); manual ('65, 20 pages, identical—including norms—with manual published in 1963); norms for males only; $4 per 20 tests, postage extra; $2 per specimen set, postpaid; 10(15) minutes; L. L. Thurstone (test), T. E. Jeffrey (test), and Manpower Research and Development Division, Industrial Relations Center, University of Chicago (manual); the Center. *

REFERENCES

1–4. See 6:545.
5. UHLMANN, FRANK WALTER. *Retention of Anxiety Material as a Function of Cognitive Style.* Doctor's thesis, Wayne State University (Detroit, Mich.), 1962. (*DA* 28:5196B)
6. DAUGHERTY, ROBERT ALTON. *Perceiving One's Own Performance Level as a Function of Cognitive Control and Motivation.* Doctor's thesis, Wayne State University (Detroit, Mich.), 1963. (*DA* 29:405B)
7. LEWIN, PAUL B. *Validity of Thurstone's Test of Closure Flexibility to Predict Student Teaching Effectiveness.* Master's thesis, East Tennessee State University (Johnson City, Tenn.), 1966.
8. MANGAN, GORDON L. "Studies of the Relationship Between Neo-Pavlovian Properties of Higher Nervous Activity and Western Personality Dimensions: 4, A Factor Analytic Study of Extraversion and Flexibility, and the Sensitivity and Mobility of the Nervous System." *J Exp Res Personality* 2:124–7 My '67. * (*PA* 41:11908)
9. OHNMACHT, FRED W. "Factorial Invariance of the Teacher Characteristics Schedule and Measures of Two Cognitive Styles." *J Psychol* 69:193–9 Jl '68. * (*PA* 42:15472)
10. STEINMETZ, ANDRÉS. *Perceptual Style and Response to*

Single Concept Science Films. Doctor's thesis, Indiana University (Bloomington, Ind.), 1968. (*DAI* 30:504A)
11. BAEHR, MELANY E.; FURCON, JOHN E.; AND FROEMEL, ERNEST C. *Psychological Assessment of Patrolman Qualifications in Relation to Field Performance.* Washington, D.C.: United States Government Printing Office, 1969. Pp. vii, 246. *
12. GARDNER, RILEY W., AND LOHRENZ, LEANDER J. "Some Old and New Group Tests for the Study of Cognitive Controls and Intellectual Abilities." *Percept & Motor Skills* 29(3):935-50 D '69. * (*PA* 46:4981)
13. SCHEIBNER, RUTH MARTIN. *Field Dependence-Independence as a Basic Variable in the Measurement of Interest and Personality.* Doctor's thesis, Temple University (Philadelphia, Pa.), 1969. (*DAI* 30:3375B)

For a review by Leona E. Tyler, see 6:545.

[436]

★Closure Speed (Gestalt Completion). Industrial employees; 1956-66; formerly called *Gestalt Completion: A Test of Speed of Closure;* Form A ('56, 3 pages); revised manual ('66, 18 pages); norms for males only; $3 per 20 tests, postage extra: $2 per specimen set, postpaid; 3(8) minutes; L. L. Thurstone (test), T. E. Jeffrey (test), and Norman J. Kantor (manual); Industrial Relations Center, University of Chicago. *

REFERENCES

1-3. See 6:546.
4. BAEHR, MELANY E.; FURCON, JOHN E.; AND FROEMEL, ERNEST C. *Psychological Assessment of Patrolman Qualifications in Relation to Field Performance.* Washington, D.C.: United States Government Printing Office, 1969. Pp. vii, 246. *
5. SANDERS, JAY W., AND COSCARELLI, JANET E. "The Relationship of Visual Synthesis Skill to Lipreading." *Am Ann Deaf* 115(1):23-6 Ja '70. * (*PA* 44:10988)

For a review by Leona E. Tyler, see 6:546.

[437]

★Concept Assessment Kit—Conservation. Ages 4-7; 1968; CAKC; individual; 2 tests; manual (16 pages plus record forms); $23.50 per kit of testing materials, 1 copy of each record form, and manual; $1.25 per manual; postage extra; Marcel L. Goldschmid and Peter M. Bentler; Educational and Industrial Testing Service. *
a) FORMS A AND B. 13 scores: 2 scores (behavior, explanation) in each of 6 areas (2-dimensional space, number, substance, continuous quantity, weight, discontinuous quantity), total; Forms A, B, (4 pages); $4 per 25 record forms; (15-20) minutes.
b) FORM C. 13 scores: 2 scores (behavior, explanation) in area (3 scores) and length (3 scores), total; Form C (2 pages); $3.50 per 25 record forms; (10-15) minutes.

REFERENCES

1. GOLDSCHMID, MARCEL L. "Different Types of Conservation and Nonconservation and Their Relation to Age, Sex, IQ, MA, and Vocabulary." *Child Develop* 38:1229-46 D '67. * (*PA* 42:7086)
2. GOLDSCHMID, MARCEL L. "The Relation of Conservation to Emotional and Environmental Aspects of Development." *Child Develop* 39:579-89 Je '68. *
3. GOLDSCHMID, MARCEL L., AND BENTLER, P. M. "The Dimensions and Measurement of Conservation." *Child Develop* 39:787-802 S '68. * (*PA* 43:3774)
4. BAKER, EUGENE AUSTIN. *Conservation and Two Related Cognitive Functions.* Doctor's thesis, University of Missouri (Columbia, Mo.), 1970. (*DAI* 31:4965B)
5. BENTLER, P. M. "Evidence Regarding Stages in the Development of Conservation." *Percept & Motor Skills* 31(3):855-9 D '70. * (*PA* 45:9648)

J. DOUGLAS AYERS, *Professor of Education, University of Victoria, Victoria, British Columbia, Canada.*

The *Concept Assessment Kit—Conservation* is designed to assess young children's attainment of the principles involved in comprehending conservation. As such, it is a type of intelligence test, limited to a narrow age range and to conservation tasks and excluding such other important Piagetian concepts as seriation, classification, and transitivity. As with all Piagetian scales, the focus is on measuring optimal performance of the process aspect of intelligence rather than maximum performance of the content component (e.g., number of synonyms recognized).

Forms A and B are parallel tests composed of a series of tasks that present the child with two objects or sets of objects that are the same with respect to amount of matter of a given type: particled material (discontinuous quantity), plastic material (substance), blocks of solid material (two-dimensional space), liquid (continuous quantity), pieces (number), and weight. In Form C the objects are the same with respect to length or area. One object or set of objects is then changed spatially or in shape and the child is asked, e.g., "Is there as much corn in *this* glass as in *that* one, or does one have more in it?" If the child answers "the same," he gets one point for behavior. He is then asked "Why?" to measure comprehension. An adequate explanation adds another point for that task.

The three forms were determined primarily by multidimensional homogeneity scaling of an initial battery consisting of three to seven tasks representing each of 10 types of conservation. The battery, containing 44 behavior items and 43 explanation items, was administered in two 45-minute sessions to 142 children in kindergarten, first, and second grades. Three dimensions, or factors, emerged for explanation. A general dimension, amount of matter, included the six types of conservation in the two parallel forms, A and B. Form C was composed of two minor dimensions, length and area.

That the six types of conservation in Forms A and B are unidimensional is not surprising. Five of the tasks obviously involve conservation of amount or quantity. The sixth task, weight conservation, as used in Forms A and B, involves balls of Playdoh of the same amount as well as same weight, making a quantity interpretation possible.

In addition to dimensionality, other criteria governing final selection of tasks for the scales are reported as high internal consistency, reliability, and between-forms reliability. Because all statistics are based on the complete range of grades, they are spuriously high, but it might be argued that no real harm is done except to give an unrealistic impression of the characteristics of the tryout battery. This would be true if the tryout were used only for item selection, but most of the reliability and validity data reported in the manual are based on the initial tryout and not on the final scales. Also, several of the tables fail to indicate that the data are based on the tryouts and the discussion implies that Forms A, B, and C are separate entities and not purely hypothetical tests that require cross-validation. The manual also fails to report that the content of several of the tasks was changed between the tryout and the final scales.

The manual states that norms are based on 560 children tested individually with either Forms A and C, or B and C, from 20 schools, day care centers, and Head Start centers in the Los Angeles area. The schools were selected to represent the entire spectrum of socioeconomic status and race, but the sample is said to be biased slightly toward lower-middle-class children. The only norms reported are percentile ranks, and these, together with means and standard deviations, are provided for a confusing variety of age ranges. But for the critical ages 5½ to 7½, the norms for Forms A and B are based on too few children, approximately 75 of each sex for each form. Also, there is no mention of the limitations of percentile ranks and the dangers of overinterpretation. Despite the higher reported reliability, the standard error is 1¼ points on a 12-item test.

The data also reveal that the test is difficult for children below age 6½. For example, in the 5½ to 6½ age range, the expected chance score on Form A is equivalent to a percentile rank of 69, and in the 4 to 5½ age range, in which the percentile norms are the same for each half-year age, the expected chance score on Form A is equivalent to a percentile rank of 94. To administer these scales routinely to children under the age of 5½, when only two or three percent will obtain a score of 4 in 12, is futile. The normative data, as well as general experience, indicate that the age range should be 5½ to 7½, rather than the recommended 4 to 7.

For a test of 12 items at these grade levels the K-R 20, parallel-form, and retest reliabilities are very high, typically .94 or .95, but they are based on a three-grade spread instead of single age groups.

Content validity was established by multidimensional homogeneity scaling of the tryout battery and was confirmed in the standardization. Adequate predictive and concurrent validity data are also provided.

The authors are to be commended for developing a record form that contains all of the essential directions in a very convenient format. The directions for each task are separated into five columns: pictorial illustration, specific procedures, verbal instructions and questions, recording of responses, and score. Such a format is very efficient because the examiner quickly learns the procedures but has the verbal instructions and questions column as a guide for uniform administration. He is further assisted by the italicizing and indenting of each instruction and question. Two other points warrant approval. Because the correct answer to all conservation questions is "the same," the authors have included two tasks that require a "more" answer, in order to ensure that there will be no response set. Also, in agreement with research findings, manipulation of materials by children is minimized.

The authors have diligently pursued procedures that would ensure uniform administration, yet the question remains, have they established psychometric standardization? For example, there has been little or no attempt to control the situational variables, particularly form and style of questioning and comprehension of instructions. In traditional testing, understanding of directions is controlled by sample and practice exercises, especially with unfamiliar tasks and in the primary grades. It would seem essential to provide the equivalent for Piagetian tasks. This criticism is aimed not only at this instrument, but at nearly all Piagetian measurement procedures. Administering Piagetian tasks in a uniform fashion does not necessarily ensure standardization in the psychometric sense.

The authors have apparently given considerable thought to the questioning techniques; the critical question for each task uses the phrase "as much _____," rather than the more usual, "Is there the same amount of _____, or ...." The new wording may be preferable, particularly for inexperienced administrators, as there is no chance of indicating the correct answer by inflection. On the other hand, it precludes the use of the more precise term "amount." The effect of these and other variations in wording may be minimal, especially with older children, but because each task is really measured with a single item, it is essential that conditions be such as to ensure optimal performance. As yet, very little research has been done on the effects of varying questioning techniques with Piagetian tasks.

There are also several specific criticisms of the questioning techniques. For two-dimensional space and for number tasks, the children are asked if the amounts in the two objects are the same to begin with, but in all other tasks they are told that the amounts are the same. The former would seem to be preferable because it eliminates extra verbiage and does not suggest the answer. There is also no apparent reason for including extraneous running commentary, such as, "See, I am making this ball into a hotdog." This can only tend to make conditions less standard.

In summary, the authors have assembled three scales that have clear directions; attractive, well-organized format; together with considerable data on homogeneity, reliability, and validity. However, they have failed to provide essential details of test development and to include cautionary statements regarding norms and their interpretation.

As this is a first-of-its-kind instrument, measuring a single Piagetian task in the 4 to 7 age range (this reviewer, however, recommends that its use be limited to ages 5½ to 7½), and as our knowledge of measurement techniques in this area is not fully developed, the *Concept Assessment Kit—Conservation* must be considered essentially experimental.

J Ed Meas 6(4):263–6 w '69. Rheta DeVries and Lawrence Kohlberg. * is directed toward providing a measure of conservation as an indicator of cognitive change from the prelogical mode of thought to the concrete operational mode which Piaget found to occur roughly at about age seven or eight years. * In summary, effort aimed toward providing test materials and procedures for assessment of qualitative aspects of intellectual functions which differ from the traditional psychometrically assessed functions is to be applauded. However, it must be cautioned that the Concept Assessment Kit—Conservation provides only a limited measure of conservation and cannot be used alone to establish the presence of concrete operational thought. While it may be a desirable goal to depart from Piaget's clinical method of assessing the presence of conservation and to develop a more standardized technique, the challenge lies in preserving the opportunity for expression of subtleties in thinking which frequently do not appear with more limited procedures. The inclusion of standard probes and ceiling-level items would help to make the instrument under review less equivocal on individual assessment. If the realization of the goal of a satisfactory standardized measure of Piagetian cognitive development is possible at all, continued research is necessary to establish just how much and what kind of test procedures constitute a minimal requirement. [See original review for critical comments not excerpted.]

J Ed Meas 6(4):266–9 w '69. Vernon C. Hall and Michael Mery. * The tasks involving types of conservation are taken from a specific theory (Piaget's), but the procedures, scoring, and even the purpose of the test (as understood by the present authors) seem unrelated to this theory. * In many ways, then, the test resembles the conventional intelligence test which was noted by Goldschmid and Bentler as inappropriate, *i.e.,* numerical scores which give no obvious indication as to how they came about. The general issue, as we see it, is how to specify the abilities required to conserve and the assessment techniques, including criteria, which follow from that specification. In any future revision of the test under review, we would suggest incorporating many diverse procedures in the attempt to provide sufficient *standardized* data of a diagnostic nature in order to attempt to specify the subject's (or subjects') developmental level in terms of Piagetian theory. Such procedures might include counter-suggestion, extinction, standardized probing, etc. We would also suggest changing the scoring procedure. As the test now stands, one point is given for a correct answer and one for a correct explanation regardless of the skill the item is testing. This leads to problems in interpreting a score based upon, for example, different combinations of correct answers across tasks and/or correct items and explanations combined within and across tasks. As is the case with most intelligence tests, it is difficult to determine how a subtest or a combined score was achieved. Another issue in current conservation research concerns the antecedents necessary for conservation to take place. It is probably not reasonable to expect a child to conserve successfully without first determining whether he knows the adult meaning of important terms, *e.g.*, same, different, longer, etc. It is also important that we learn more about the relationship between meaning of these terms for children and conservation behavior * Goldschmid and Bentler recognize this difficulty as seen by their suggestion that *S*s under four years of age not be given the test because "part of the difficulty appears to be related to the children's lack of understanding of relational terms such as 'more' or 'same.'" In their procedures, however, they simply have the Examiner state the relationship between the objects rather than assessing the *S*s' use of relevant terms. We would prefer to see such an assessment as an integral part of the instrument. Turning to item format we find problems which in themselves might serve to influence results. We would think that including items which begin with different amounts as well as the same amount (included in the test to guard against a response set of saying "same" every time) should be included in all types of conservation assessed. Part of being a conserver is to understand that if two objects originally have different amounts of "something," changing an irrelevant dimension does not change this relationship. Finally, the verbal instructions remain constant throughout the test. In all questions the ending phrase is "or does one have more?" By varying this wording across items, it would have been possible to determine if the subject was being led by the experimenter and in what way. Additional problems tend to follow from the general issues already discussed. For instance, why are item difficulties based on a total sample of different aged subjects relevant? Why did the authors include correlations between academic achievement and total test scores? Although the correlations are substantial, a Piagetian would neither be surprised nor view the information as particularly relevant. In summary, we view the attempt at standardizing procedures in conservation research as being laudable. We feel, however, that such an instrument must recognize that measurement procedures are influenced by the purpose for which they are going to be used. We have raised only a few of what we feel to be important issues in the validation of Piaget's theory in general and conservation specifically which should influence measurement procedures. Goldschmid and Bentler seemingly did not find these issues sufficiently important

Concept Assessment Kit—Conservation

and thus will probably find limited circulation for their test. [See original review for critical comments not excerpted.]

Prof Psychol 1(5):491–3 f '70. Charles D. Smock. * provides, at best, a limited measure of conservation. It is not recommended to establish either the presence of generalized concrete operational thought nor for conservation in a particular content area. The Kit can be very useful in providing the novice an opportunity to gain experience in the Piagetian approach and the demonstration of the subtleties involved in children's thinking. However, the realization of the goal for standardized measure of an important aspect of cognitive development à la Piaget will require a more thorough analytical and empirical inquiry into the theory and the invention of procedures that constitute minimal requirements for testing that theory.

[438]
★**Fret Continuation Test, I.B.P. Edition 1968.** Semiliterate adults; 1966–69; perceptual analysis; no reading by examinees; 1 form ('66, 14 pages); manual ('69, 17 pages, English and Venda); no data on validity; R3.60 per 25 tests; 16c per single copy; R2 per manual; postpaid within South Africa; (25–30) minutes; G. V. Grant (manual); National Institute for Personnel Research. *

[439]
★**Fret Repetition Test, I.B.P. Edition 1968.** Illiterate adults; 1966–69; perceptual analysis; 1 form ('66, 16 pages); manual ('69, 16 pages, English and Venda); no data on validity; R4 per 25 tests; 16c per single copy; R2 per manual; postpaid within South Africa; (20–25) minutes; G. V. Grant (manual); National Institute for Personnel Research. *

[440]
*****Hidden Figures Test.** Grades 6–16; 1962–63; HFT; for research use only; flexibility of closure; 2 tests; no data on reliability and validity; no norms; cash orders postpaid; Educational Testing Service. *
a) FORM CF-1. 1962–63; 1 form ('62, 5 pages); no specific manual; combined manual ('63, 126 pages) for this and other tests in 6:551; 20¢ per test; $2.40 per manual; 20(25) minutes; manual by John W. French, Ruth B. Ekstrom, and Leighton B. Price.
b) FORM 5. 1962; 1 form (33 pages); no manual; 75¢ per test; scoring key not available; 10(15) minutes.

REFERENCES
1. RICHARDS, JAMES M., JR.; CLINE, VICTOR B.; AND NEEDHAM, WALTER E. "Creativity Tests and Teacher and Self Judgments of Originality." *J Exp Ed* 32:281–5 sp '64. * (*PA* 39:5135)
2. ANDERSON, C. C., AND CROPLEY, A. J. "Some Correlates of Originality." *Austral J Psychol* 18:218–27 D '66. * (*PA* 41:4572)
3. BECKERLE, GERALD PAUL. *Behavioral Traits Related to Psychological Differentiation in Pre-Adolescent Boys.* Doctor's thesis, Michigan State University (East Lansing, Mich.), 1966. (*DA* 28:336B)
4. CROPLEY, A. J. "Creativity and Intelligence." *Brit J Ed Psychol* 36:259–66 N '66. * (*PA* 41:5-3)
5. ACKER, MARY BRYANT. *The Relation of Achievement Need, Time Perspective, and Field Articulation to Academic Performance.* Doctor's thesis, University of California (Berkeley, Calif.), 1967. (*DA* 29:1492B)
6. BRIGHAM, BRUCE W. *A Study of the Reading Achievement and Certain Characteristics of Adult Males Convicted of*

Felonies. Doctor's thesis, Temple University (Philadelphia, Pa.), 1967. (*DA* 28:4279B)
7. CROPLEY, A. J. "Creativity, Intelligence, and Achievement." *Alberta J Ed Res* 13:51–8 Mr '67. * (*PA* 41:15253)
8. DAVIS, JON KENT. *Concept Identification as a Function of Cognitive Style, Complexity, and Training Procedures.* Doctor's thesis, University of Wisconsin (Madison, Wis.), 1967. (*DA* 28:4476A)
9. FREDRICK, WAYNE CLARENCE. *Information Processing and Concept Learning at Grades Six, Eight, and Ten as a Function of Cognitive Styles.* Doctor's thesis, University of Wisconsin (Madison, Wis.), 1967. (*DA* 28:4478A)
10. BARRETT, GERALD V.; CABE, PATRICK A.; AND THORNTON, CARL L. "Relation Between Hidden Figures Test and Rod and Frame Test Measures of Perceptual Style." *Ed & Psychol Meas* 28:551–4 su '68. * (*PA* 42:18139)
11. BOERSMA, FREDERIC J. "Test-Retest Reliability of the Cf-1 Hidden Figures Test." *Ed & Psychol Meas* 28:555–9 su '68. * (*PA* 42:18083)
12. BRYAN, VINCENT. *The Experimental Induction of Stress in Relation to Field Articulation.* Doctor's thesis, Yeshiva University (New York, N.Y.), 1968. (*DAI* 30:1354B)
13. FARR, ROBERTA SIEGEL. *Personality Variables and Problem Solving Performance: An Investigation of the Relationships Between Field-Dependence-Independence, Sex-Role Identification, Problem Difficulty and Problem Solving Performance.* Doctor's thesis, New York University (New York, N.Y.), 1968. (*DA* 29:2561A)
14. WERBEL, STEPHEN A. *Response to Loss and Its Relation to Personality Measures.* Doctor's thesis, University of Kansas (Lawrence, Kan.), 1968. (*DA* 29:2213B)
15. BARRETT, GERALD V.; THORNTON, CARL L.; AND CABE, PATRICK A. "Relation Between Embedded Figures Test Performance and Simulator Behavior." *J Appl Psychol* 53(3): 253–4 Je '69. * (*PA* 43:11980)
16. BARTELT, CLAUDIA ANN. *The Relation Between Field Articulation, Locus of Control and Subjective Probability of Success.* Doctor's thesis, University of California (Berkeley, Calif.), 1969. (*DAI* 31:1571A)
17. BRINTON, GEORGE, AND ROULEAU, ROBERT A. "Automating the Hidden and Embedded Figures Tests." *Percept & Motor Skills* 29(2):401–2 O '69. * (*PA* 44:3652)
18. CONKLIN, R. C., AND ZINGLE, H. W. "Counsellor Sensitivity and Cognitive Style." *West Psychologist* 1(1):19–28 S '69. * (*PA* 45:8948)
19. DUVALL, NANCY SHERMAN. *Field Articulation and the Repression-Sensitization Dimension in Perception and Memory.* Doctor's thesis, University of North Carolina (Chapel Hill, N.C.), 1969. (*DAI* 30:3864B)
20. ERGINEL, ADNAN. *The Relation of Cognitive Style and Intelligence to Achievement and Errors in Thinking.* Doctor's thesis, Lehigh University (Bethlehem, Pa.), 1969. (*DAI* 31:216A)
21. HUCKABEE, MALCOM W. "Personality and Academic Aptitude Correlates of Cognitive Control Principles." *South J Ed Res* 3(1):1–9 Ja '69. *
22. TITUS, H. EDWIN. "Prediction of Supervisory Success by Use of Standard Psychological Tests." *J Psychol* 72(1): 35–40 My '69. * (*PA* 43:16503)
23. BARRETT, GERALD V.; THORNTON, CARL L.; AND CABE, PATRICK A. "Cue Conflict Related to Perceptual Style." *J Appl Psychol* 54(3):258–64 Je '70. * (*PA* 44:11696)
24. CREGO, CLYDE A. "A Pattern Analytic Approach to the Measure of Modes of Expression of Psychological Differentiation." *J Abn Psychol* 76(2):194–8 O '70. * (*PA* 45:4277)
25. DAVIS, J. KENT, AND KLAUSMEIER, HERBERT J. "Cognitive Style and Concept Identification as a Function of Complexity and Training Procedures." *J Ed Psychol* 61(6):423–30 D '70. * (*PA* 45:7431)
26. GRUENFELD, LEOPOLD W., AND WEISSENBERG, PETER. "Field Independence and Articulation of Sources of Job Satisfaction." *J Appl Psychol* 54(5):424–6 O '70. * (*PA* 45:3159)
27. KAZELSKIS, RICHARD. "Field Independence and the Free-Recall of Nonsense Syllables." *Percept & Motor Skills* 31(2): 351–4 O '70. * (*PA* 45:6317)
28. MCWHINNIE, HAROLD J. "A Third Study of Some Relationships Between Creativity and Perception in 6th Grade Children." *Calif J Ed Res* 21(1):35–42 Ja '70. *
29. MAUSNER, BERNARD, AND GRAHAM, JUDITH. "Field Dependence and Prior Reinforcement as Determinants of Social Interaction in Judgment." *J Pers & Social Psychol* 16(3): 486–93 N '70. * (*PA* 45:4127)
30. OHNMACHT, FRED W.; WEAVER, WENDELL W.; AND KOHLER, EMMETT T. "Cloze and Closure: A Factorial Study." *J Psychol* 74(2):205–17 Mr '70. * (*PA* 44:12542)
31. SHARP, ELIZABETH YERXA. *The Relationship of Visual Closure to Speechreading Among Deaf Children.* Doctor's thesis, University of Arizona (Tucson, Ariz.), 1970. (*DAI* 31:2198A)

[441]
★**Higgins-Wertman Test: Threshold of Visual Closure.** Ages 5–15; 1968; manual title is *Visual Closure Assessment*; 6 scores: initial closure, final closure, number of responses prior to final closure (whole and detail), perseveration, impotence; Forms 1, 2, (23 scales in separate 14–22 page booklets, 11 scales per form plus alternate scale); mimeographed manual (139 pages); $65 per set of both forms; $5.25 per 25 record blanks of each form; $7.50 per manual; postpaid; (30) minutes; Conwell Higgins and Howard Wertman; Higgins-Wertman Associates. *

REFERENCE
1. RUSCH, REUBEN R. "Reliability of the Higgins-Wertman Test of Visual Closure." *Percept & Motor Skills* 30(3):879–85 Je '70. * (*PA* 44:17513)

[442]
***Illinois Test of Psycholinguistic Abilities, Revised Edition.** Ages 2–10; 1961–68; ITPA; 11–13 scores: auditory reception, visual reception, visual sequential memory, auditory association, auditory sequential memory, visual association, visual closure, verbal expression, grammatic closure, manual expression, auditory closure (optional), sound blending (optional), total; individual; 1 form ('68); manual ('68, 134 pages); record form ['68, 16 pages]; visual closure picture strips ['68, 5 pages]; $43.50 per set of testing materials, carrying case, 25 record forms, and 25 sets of picture strips; $7.75 per 25 record forms and sets of picture strips; $5.75 per manual; cash orders from individuals; (45–60) minutes; Samuel A. Kirk, James J. McCarthy, and Winifred D. Kirk; University of Illinois Press. *

REFERENCES
1–22. See 6:549.
23. OLSON, JAMES L. "Deaf and Sensory Aphasic Children." *Excep Children* 27:422–4 Ap '61. * (*PA* 36:4JD220)
24. BATEMAN, BARBARA DEE. *Reading and Psycholinguistic Processes of Partially Sighted Children.* Doctor's thesis, University of Illinois (Urbana, Ill.), 1962. (*DA* 23:2416)
25. KASS, CORRINE EVELYN. *Some Psychological Correlates of Severe Reading Disability (Dyslexia).* Doctor's thesis, University of Illinois (Urbana, Ill.), 1962. (*DA* 23:2421)
26. SMITH, JAMES OTTO. *Effects of a Group Language Development Program Upon the Psycholinguistic Abilities of Educable Mental Retardates.* Doctor's thesis, George Peabody College for Teachers (Nashville, Tenn.), 1962. (*DA* 23:3821)
27. BATEMAN, BARBARA D. *Reading and Psycholinguistic Processes of Partially Seeing Children.* CEC Research Monograph, Series A, No. 5. Washington, D.C.: Council for Exceptional Children, National Education Association, 1963. Pp. v, 46. *
28. FERRIER, ELMER EARL. *An Investigation of Psycholinguistic Factors Associated With Functional Defects of Articulation.* Doctor's thesis, University of Illinois (Urbana, Ill.), 1963. (*DA* 25:290)
29. HAMLIN, CAROLYN S. *A Study Using the Illinois Test of Psycholinguistic Abilities in the Determination of the Language Abilities of Hearing Impaired Children.* Master's thesis, University of Kansas (Lawrence, Kan.), 1963.
30. MCCARTHY, JAMES J., AND KIRK, SAMUEL A. *The Construction, Standardization and Statistical Characteristics of the Illinois Test of Psycholinguistic Abilities.* [Urbana, Ill.: University of Illinois Press], 1963. Pp. vii, 90. *
31. MIRON, MURRAY S. Appendix B, "A Psycholinguistic Analysis of Some Frequently Used Tests for Aphasia," pp. 176–99. In *Approaches to the Study of Aphasia: A Report of an Interdisciplinary Conference on Aphasia.* Edited by Charles E. Osgood and Murray S. Miron. Urbana, Ill.: University of Illinois Press, 1963. Pp. vii, 210. * (*PA* 38:4504)
32. MUELLER, MAX W. "Peabody College Research on the Illinois Test of Psycholinguistic Abilities," pp. 183–7. In *Selected Convention Papers: 41st Annual CEC Convention, Philadelphia, Pennsylvania, 1963.* Washington, D.C.: Council for Exceptional Children, National Education Association, [1963]. Pp. iv, 235. *
33. BLESSING, KENNETH RICHARD. *An Investigation of a Psycholinguistic Deficit in Educable Mentally Retarded Children: Detection, Remediation and Related Variables.* Doctor's thesis, University of Wisconsin (Madison, Wis.), 1964. (*DA* 25:2372)
34. CARR, DONALD LEE. *The Concept Formation and Psycholinguistic Abilities of Normal and Mentally Retarded Children of Comparable Mental Age.* Doctor's thesis, State University of Iowa (Iowa City, Iowa), 1964. (*DA* 25:997)
35. GUNZBURG, H. C. "The Reliability of a Test of Psycholinguistic Abilities (I.T.P.A.) in a Population of Young Male Subnormals." *J Mental Subnorm* 10:101–12 D '64. * (*PA* 39:10116)
36. HASTEROK, GERALD S. "The Training of Mentally Re-

tarded Children With Sense Modality Disabilities," pp. 128–31. In *Inspection and Introspection of Special Education.* Selected Convention Papers, 42nd Annual CEC Convention, 1964. Washington, D.C.: Council for Exceptional Children, [1964]. Pp. v, 288. *

37. KENNEY, ELEANORE T. "The Small Classroom—A Developmental Idiosyncratic Approach to Learning and Behavioral Disorders in Children of Normal Intelligence," pp. 208–16. In *Inspection and Introspection of Special Education.* Selected Convention Papers, 42nd Annual CEC Convention, 1964. Washington, D.C.: Council for Exceptional Children, [1964]. Pp. v, 288. *

38. MCCARTHY, JAMES J. "The Importance of Linguistic Ability in the Mentally Retarded." *Mental Retard* 2:90–6 Ap '64. *

39. MCCARTHY, JAMES J. "The Use and Usefulness of the ITPA," pp. 195–202. In *Inspection and Introspection of Special Education.* Selected Convention Papers, 42nd Annual CEC Convention, 1964. Washington, D.C.: Council for Exceptional Children, [1964]. Pp. v, 288. *

40. MCCARTHY, JAMES J., AND OLSON, JAMES L. *Validity Studies on the Illinois Test of Psycholinguistic Abilities.* [Urbana, Ill.: University of Illinois Press], 1964. Pp. viii, 106. *

41. MCLEOD, J. "The Search for Measurable Intellectual Causes of Reading Disability." *Slow Learning Child* 11:80–94 Jl '64. * (*PA* 39:16413)

42. MUELLER, MAX W. "Comparison of Psycholinguistic Patterns of Gifted and Retarded Children," pp. 143–9. In *Inspection and Introspection of Special Education.* Selected Convention Papers, 42nd Annual CEC Convention, 1964. Washington, D.C.: Council for Exceptional Children, [1964]. Pp. v, 288. *

43. MUELLER, MAX W. "Language Profiles of Mentally Retarded Children," pp. 149–53. In *Inspection and Introspection of Special Education.* Selected Convention Papers, 42nd Annual CEC Convention, 1964. Washington, D.C.: Council for Exceptional Children, [1964]. Pp. v, 288. *

44. MUELLER, MAX W., AND WEAVER, S. JOSEPH. "Psycholinguistic Abilities of Institutionalized and Non-Institutionalized Trainable Mental Retardates." *Am J Mental Def* 68:775–83 My '64. * (*PA* 39:2529)

45. OUTRIDGE, MARGARET. "Psycholinguistic Abilities of Five Children Attending Baroona Opportunity School." *Spec Sch B* 6:8–21 My '64. *

46. RAGLAND, GILBERT GRAY. *The Performance of Educable Mentally Handicapped Students of Differing Reading Ability on the Illinois Test of Psycholinguistic Abilities.* Doctor's thesis, University of Virginia (Charlottesville, Va.), 1964. (*DA* 25:3407)

47. RAYNOR, JUDITH E. *Effect of an Immediate Visual Memory Factor in the Visual Decoding Subtest of the Illinois Test of Psycholinguistic Abilities.* Master's thesis, University of Washington (Seattle, Wash.), 1964.

48. STRUNK, DEFOREST LIVINGSTON, II. *An Analysis of the Psycholinguistic Abilities of a Selected Group of Mongoloids.* Doctor's thesis, University of Virginia (Charlottesville, Va.), 1964. (*DA* 26:203) (Abstract: *Ed R* 3:46–8)

49. WELSH, JOAN B. *Differences in Language Performance as Measured by the Illinois Test of Psycholinguistic Abilities Among Groups of Children With Severe Language Disorders: Deaf Children and Brain Injured Deaf Children.* Master's thesis, University of Pittsburgh (Pittsburgh, Pa.), 1964.

50. WISEMAN, DOUGLAS E. "Program Planning for Retarded Children With Psycholinguistic Abilities," pp. 241–52. In *Inspection and Introspection of Special Education.* Selected Convention Papers, 42nd Annual CEC Convention, 1964. Washington, D.C.: Council for Exceptional Children, [1964]. Pp. v, 288. *

51. BATEMAN, BARBARA. *The Illinois Test of Psycholinguistic Abilities in Current Research: Summary of Studies.* [Urbana, Ill.: University of Illinois Press], 1965. Pp. iii, 43. *

52. BATEMAN, BARBARA. "The Role of the ITPA in Differential Diagnosis and Program Planning for Mentally Retarded." *Am J Orthopsychiatry* 35:465–72 Ap '65. * (*PA* 39:10088)

53. BATEMAN, BARBARA, AND WETHERELL, JANIS. "Psycholinguistic Aspects of Mental Retardation." *Mental Retard* 3:8–13 Ap '65. * (*PA* 39:10569)

54. BILOVSKY, DAVID, AND SHORE, JACK. "The ITPA and Down's Syndrome: An Exploratory Study." *Am J Mental Def* 70:78–82 Jl '65. * (*PA* 39:16042)

55. ENSMINGER, E. EUGENE, AND SMITH, JAMES O. "Language Development and the ITPA." *Training Sch B* 62:97–107 N '65. * (*PA* 40:3301)

56. ESPESETH, VERNON KNUTE. *An Investigation of Visual Sequential Memory in the Deaf Child.* Doctor's thesis, University of Wisconsin (Madison, Wis.), 1965. (*DA* 26:5288)

57. FORD, JUNE BROOKS. *Identification of a Specific Language Disability (Dyslexia).* Doctor's thesis, University of Oklahoma (Norman, Okla.), 1965. (*DA* 26:1827)

58. GRAUBARD, PAUL STUART. *Psycholinguistic Correlates of Reading Disability in Disturbed Children.* Doctor's thesis, Yeshiva University (New York, N.Y.), 1965. (*DA* 26:3172)

59. HARRIES, W. T. *The Illinois Test of Psycholinguistic Abilities (ITPA): An Appraisal.* Australian Council for Educational Research, Memorandum No. 1. Victoria, Australia: the Council, January 1965. Pp. ii, 19. *

60. MCCARTHY, JAMES J. "Notes on the Validity of the ITPA." *Mental Retard* 3:25–6 Ap '65. * (*PA* 39:10139)

61. MCCARTHY, JEANNE MCRAE. *Patterns of Psycholinguistic Development of Mongoloid and Non-Mongoloid Severely Retarded Children.* Doctor's thesis, University of Illinois (Urbana, Ill.), 1965. (*DA* 26:872)

62. MCLEOD, JOHN. *Some Psychological and Physiological Aspects of Severe Reading Disability in Children.* Doctor's thesis, University of Queensland (Brisbane, Australia), 1965.

63. MILLS, ESTHER BROWNELL. *Relationships Between Psycholinguistic Abilities of Educable Mentally Retarded Pupils and the Effectiveness of Four Instructional Approaches in the Language Arts.* Doctor's thesis, University of Maryland (College Park, Md.), 1965. (*DA* 27:145A)

64. MUELLER, MAX W. "Comparison of Psycholinguistic Patterns of Gifted and Retarded Children." *J Sch Psychol* 3:18–25 sp '65. * (*PA* 39:15126)

65. MUELLER, MAX W. *A Comparison of the Empirical Validity of Six Tests of Ability With Young Educable Retardates.* Institute of Mental Retardation and Intellectual Development, IMRID Behavioral Science Monograph No. 1. Nashville, Tenn.: Peabody College Bookstore, 1965. Pp. vii, 130. *

66. MUELLER, MAX WILLIAM. *A Comparison of the Empirical Validity of Six Tests of Ability With Educable Mental Retardates.* Doctor's thesis, George Peabody College for Teachers (Nashville, Tenn.), 1965. (*DA* 26:6853)

67. MYERS, PATRICIA. "A Study of Language Disabilities in Cerebral Palsied Children." *J Speech & Hearing Res* 8:129–36 Je '65. * (*PA* 39:15127)

68. OLSON, JAMES L.; HAHN, HANS R.; AND HERMANN, ANITA L. "Psycholinguistic Curriculum." *Mental Retard* 3:14–9 Ap '65. *

69. OUTRIDGE, MARGARET. "Psycholinguistic Abilities of Five Children Attending a Brisbane Opportunity School." *Slow Learning Child* 11:165–74 Mr '65. * (*PA* 39:12997)

70. PURKHISER, CAROL ANNE. *A Comparative Investigation of the Verbal Behavior and Psycholinguistic Abilities of a Group of Hydrocephalic Children and Their Matched Controls.* Doctor's thesis, Northwestern University (Evanston, Ill.), 1965. (*DA* 26:3538)

71. RADUS, LIBBY. *Dysphasia: Musical Perception as a Stimulus in Communication.* Doctor's thesis, University of Florida (Gainesville, Fla.), 1965. (*DA* 26:6230)

72. RANTUCCI, DORIS A. *A Correlation Study of the Visual and Auditory Subtests of the Detroit Tests of Learning Aptitudes With the Illinois Tests of Psycholinguistic Abilities.* Master's thesis, University of Kansas (Lawrence, Kan.), 1965.

73. STRONG, ROBERT THOMAS, JR. *The Identification of Primary School Age Children With Learning Handicaps Associated With Minimal Brain Disorder.* Doctor's thesis, University of Utah (Salt Lake City, Utah), 1965. (*DA* 26:1489)

74. VEST, MARY LOU R. *The Determination of Some Variables Which Are Related to the Auditory Decoding Subtest of the Illinois Test of Psycholinguistic Abilities.* Master's thesis, University of Kansas (Lawrence, Kan.), 1965.

75. WISEMAN, DOUGLAS EDMUND. *The Effects of an Individualized Remedial Program on Mentally Retarded Children With Psycholinguistic Disabilities.* Doctor's thesis, University of Illinois (Urbana, Ill.), 1965. (*DA* 26:5143)

76. BATEMAN, BARBARA. "The Application of Language and Communication Models in Programs for the Trainable Retarded," pp. 45–9. In *Special Education: Strategies for Educational Progress.* Selected Convention Papers, 44th Annual CEC Convention, 1966. Washington, D.C.: Council for Exceptional Children, [1966]. Pp. viii, 259. *

77. BRADLEY, BETTY HUNT; MAURER, RUTH; AND HUNDZIAK, MARCEL. "A Study of the Effectiveness of Milieu Therapy and Language Training for the Mentally Retarded." *Excep Children* 33:143–50 N '66. * (*PA* 41:1824)

78. CRIPE, ANTJE G., AND WILSON, BETTY ANN. "Auditory and Visual Learning Related to ITPA Sensory Channels," pp. 153–6. In *Special Education: Strategies for Educational Progress.* Selected Convention Papers, 44th Annual CEC Convention, 1966. Washington, D.C.: Council for Exceptional Children, [1966]. Pp. viii, 259. *

79. CRIPE, ANTJE GREEN. *Auditory and Visual Learning Related to ITPA Sensory Channels.* Doctor's thesis, Purdue University (Lafayette, Ind.), 1966. (*DA* 27:635B)

80. DILLON, EDWARD JOSEPH. *An Investigation of Basic Psycholinguistic and Reading Abilities Among the Cerebral Palsied.* Doctor's thesis, Temple University (Philadelphia, Pa.), 1966. (*DA* 27:949A)

81. EGELAND, BYRON RICKER. *The Relationship of Intelligence, Visual-Motor Skills and Psycholinguistic Abilities With Achievement in the First Grade.* Doctor's thesis, University of Iowa (Iowa City, Iowa), 1966. (*DA* 27:388A)

82. FERRIER, E. E. "An Investigation of the ITPA Performance of Children With Functional Defects of Articulation." *Excep Children* 32:625–9 My '66. * (*PA* 40:7992)

83. GENTILE, J. RONALD. "In Search of Research: Four Children's Tests." *J Sch Psychol* 5:1–13 au '66. * (*PA* 41:3335)

84. HART, N. W. M.; SEARLE, E. B.; AND PHILLIPS, B. "The Use of I.T.P.A. and an Associated Language Program

With Partially Sighted Children." *Spec Sch B* 8:16–24 Ag '66. *

85. HORNER, RALPH D. *A Comparison of the Illinois Test of Psycholinguistic Abilities and the Parsons Language Sample in Assessing the Linguistic Abilities of Institutionalized Mentally Retarded Children.* Master's thesis, Kansas State College (Pittsburg, Kan.), 1966.

86. JOHNSON, GLEN BROOKS. *A Comparison of Scores Earned by Certain Groups of Residential School Deaf Children and the Standardization Sample of the Illinois Test of Psycholinguistic Abilities on Four Selected Subtests.* Doctor's thesis, University of Oregon (Eugene, Ore.), 1966. (DA 27:3723A)

87. KASS, CORRINE E. "Psycholinguistic Disabilities of Children With Reading Problems." *Excep Children* 32:533–9 Ap '66. * (PA 40:6515)

88. KIRK, SAMUEL A. *The Diagnosis and Remediation of Psycholinguistic Disabilities.* Urbana, Ill.: University of Illinois Press, 1966. Pp. x, 250. *

89. KIRK, SAMUEL A., AND McLEOD, JOHN. "Research Studies in Psycholinguistic Disabilities," pp. 173–84. In *Special Education: Strategies for Educational Progress.* Selected Convention Papers, 44th Annual CEC Convention, 1966. Washington, D.C.: Council for Exceptional Children, [1966]. Pp. viii, 259. *

90. McLEOD, JOHN. "Psychological and Psycholinguistic Aspects of Severe Reading Disability in Children: Some Experimental Studies." *Ann Inter Conf Assn Children Learn Dis* 3:186–205 '66. *

91. PAINTER, GENEVIEVE. "The Effect of a Rhythmic and Sensory Motor Activity Program on Perceptual Motor Spatial Abilities of Kindergarten Children." *Excep Children* 33:113–6 O '66. * (PA 41:800)

92. RAGLAND, GILBERT. "Performance of Educable Mentally Handicapped Students of Differing Reading Ability on the ITPA," pp. 69–72. In *Special Education: Strategies for Educational Progress.* Selected Convention Papers, 44th Annual CEC Convention, 1966. Washington, D.C.: Council for Exceptional Children, [1966]. Pp. viii, 259. *

93. ROBERTS, LAURENCE H. *A Study of the Value of the American Council on Education Psychological Examinations for Predicting Student Achievement in an Independent School.* Master's thesis, Trinity College (Hartford, Conn.), 1966.

94. SPICKER, HOWARD H. "The Remediation of Language Deficiencies of Educable Mentally Retarded Children." *Ed & Train Mental Retard* 1:137–40 O '66. *

95. STARK, JOEL. "Performance of Aphasic Children on the ITPA." *Excep Children* 33:153–8 N '66. * (PA 41:1203)

96. STEARNS, KEITH EUGENE. *Experimental Group Language Development for Psycho-Socially Deprived Preschool Children.* Doctor's thesis, Indiana University (Bloomington, Ind.), 1966. (DA 27:2078A)

97. SUMNER, JOSEPH WILLIAM. *A Comparison of Some Psycholinguistic Abilities of Educable Mentally Retarded Readers and Non-Readers.* Doctor's thesis, University of North Carolina (Chapel Hill, N.C.), 1966. (DA 27:2411A)

98. SWEARENGEN, MARY-B MOSLEY. *The Psycholinguistic Abilities of Beginning First-Grade Children and Their Relationship to Reading Achievement.* Doctor's thesis, University of New Mexico (Albuquerque, N.M.), 1966. (DA 27:1808A)

99. TUBBS, VIRGINIA K. "Types of Linguistic Disability in Psychotic Children." *J Mental Def Res* 10:230–40 S '66. * (PA 41:4792)

100. WEBER, MARYLOU ADAM. *The Motor Behavior Characteristics of Children With Operant Language Disorder.* Doctor's thesis, University of Arizona (Tucson, Ariz.), 1966. (DA 27:2381A)

101. ANDERSON, GLADYS L., AND MAGARY, JAMES F. "The Illinois Test of Psycholinguistic Abilities and the School Psychologist," pp. 342–54. In *School Psychological Services: In Theory and Practice: A Handbook.* Edited by James F. Magary. Englewood Cliffs, N.J.: Prentice Hall, Inc., 1967. Pp. xxi. 774. *

102. BATEMAN, BARBARA. "A Reference Line for Use With the ITPA." *J Sch Psychol* 5:128–35 w '67. * (PA 41:8715)

103. BROWN, LOUIS F., AND RICE, JAMES A. "Psycholinguistic Differentiation of Low IQ Children." *Mental Retard* 5:16–20 F '67. * (PA 41:7730)

104. CANNON, BONNIE G. *A Comparative Study of ITPA Verbal Scores With the Verbal Behavior of Children in a Child-Child Interaction.* Master's thesis, Utah State University (Logan, Utah), 1967.

105. CARR, DONALD L.; BROWN, LOUIS F.; AND RICE, JAMES A. "The PPVT in the Assessment of Language Deficits." *Am J Mental Def* 71:937–40 My '67. * (PA 41:11915)

106. CAWLEY, JOHN F. "Psycholinguistic Characteristics of Preschool Children." *Training Sch B* 64:95–101 N '67. * (PA 42:5385)

107. DICKSON, STANLEY. "Clinical Judgement of Language Delay and ITPA Measurements." *J Commun Disorders* 1:35–40 My '67. * (PA 41:17014)

108. DOBSON, JAMES CLAYTON, JR. *Intellectual and Linguistic Development in Treated and Untreated Phenylketonuric Children.* Doctor's thesis, University of Southern California (Los Angeles, Calif.), 1967. (DA 28:1294A)

109. FROSTIG, MARIANNE. "Testing as a Basis for Educational Therapy." *J Spec Ed* 2:15–34 f '67. * (PA 42:7770)

110. GRAUBARD, PAUL S. "Psycholinguistic Correlates of Reading Disability in Disturbed Delinquent Children." *J Spec Ed* 1:363–8 su '67. * (PA 42:4503)

111. GRAUBARD, PAUL S. "The Use of the Peabody Picture Vocabulary Test in the Prediction and Assessment of Reading Disability in Disturbed Children." *J Ed Res* 61:3–5 S '67. *

112. HAMALUK, OREST J. *The Effectiveness of the Illinois Test of Psycholinguistic Abilities in Predicting Reading Achievement.* Master's thesis, University of Alberta (Edmonton, Alta., Canada), 1967.

113. HIRSHOREN, ALFRED. *The Prognostic and Diagnostic Utility and the Stability of the Illinois Test of Psycholinguistic Abilities.* Doctor's thesis, University of Illinois (Urbana, Ill.), 1967. (DA 28:3026A)

114. HORNER, R. DON. "A Factor Analysis Comparison of the ITPA and PLS With Mentally Retarded Children." *Excep Children* 34:183–9 N '67. * (PA 42:9359)

115. HUEFTLE, M. KEENE. *A Factor Analytic Study of the Frostig Developmental Test of Visual Perception, the Illinois Test of Psycholinguistic Abilities, and the Wechsler Intelligence Scale for Children.* Doctor's thesis, Colorado State College (Greeley, Colo.), 1967. (DA 28:2139B)

116. KING, JOHN D., AND MASAT, LARRY J. "Implications of the Illinois Test of Psycholinguistic Abilities for Teachers of Educable Mentally Retarded Children." *Ed & Train Mental Retard* 2:107–11 O '67. *

117. McLEOD, JOHN. "Some Perceptual Factors Related to Childhood Dyslexia." *Slow Learning Child* 14:5–12 Jl '67. * (PA 42:569)

118. McLEOD, JOHN. "Some Psycholinguistic Correlates of Reading Disability in Young Children." *Read Res Q* 2:5–31 sp '67. * (PA 41:11883)

119. MATHEWS, PAULA R. *A Study of the Concurrent and Diagnostic Validity of the Illinois Test of Psycholinguistic Abilities.* Master's thesis, Utah State University (Logan, Utah), 1967.

120. MESSINEO, JOSEPH F. *The Environmental Utilization of Psycholinguistic Abilities of Disadvantaged Slow Learners in Relation to the Ecology of Test Intelligence.* Doctor's thesis, University of Rochester (Rochester, N.Y.), 1967. (DA 28:4006A)

121. MINSKOFF, JOSEPH GERALD. *A Psycholinguistic Approach to Remediation With the Retarded-Disturbed.* Doctor's thesis, Yeshiva University (New York, N.Y.), 1967. (DA 28:1625A)

122. MITCHELL, RUTH SMITH. *A Study of the Effects of Specific Language Training on Psycholinguistic Scores of Headstart Pupils.* Doctor's thesis, Florida State University (Tallahassee, Fla.), 1967. (DA 28:1709A)

123. NELSON, CHARLES DONALD. *Comparison of Sensory Modality Differences in Children With Communication Disorders.* Doctor's thesis, University of Washington (Seattle, Wash.), 1967. (DA 28:1921A)

124. QURESHI, MOHAMMED Y. "Patterns of Psycholinguistic Development During Early and Middle Childhood." *Ed & Psychol Meas* 27:353–65 su '67. * (PA 41:13420)

125. RECHNER, JOAN, AND WILSON, BETTY ANN. "Relation of Speech Sound Discrimination and Selected Language Skills." *J Commun Disorders* 1:26–30 My '67. * (41:16658)

126. RICE, JAMES A. "The ITPA: A Note on Critical Evaluations." Letter. *Excep Children* 34:71–2 S '67. *

127. ROBERTS, THOMAS GENE. *An Investigation of Language Abilities and Their Relation to School Achievement in Educable Mentally Retarded Children.* Doctor's thesis, University of North Carolina (Chapel Hill, N.C.), 1967. (DA 28:3037A)

128. SCHWARTZ, SOL; DEUTSCH, CYNTHIA P.; AND WEISSMANN, ANN. "Language Development in Two Groups of Socially Disadvantaged Young Children." *Psychol Rep* 21:169–78 Ag '67. * (PA 42:2381)

129. SEELYE, BARBARA JANE. *An Investigation of Language Development in Non-Institutionalized Mentally Retarded Children.* Doctor's thesis, University of Denver (Denver, Colo.), 1967. (DA 28:821A)

130. SILVERSTEIN, A. B. "Variance Components in the Illinois Test of Psycholinguistic Abilities." *Percept & Motor Skills* 24:1315–6 Je '67. * (PA 41:14455)

131. SMITH, HERBERT W., AND MAY, W. THEODORE. "Individual Differences Among Inexperienced Psychological Examiners." *Psychol Rep* 20:759–62 Je '67. * (PA 41:13601)

132. SMITH, HERBERT W., AND MAY, W. THEODORE. "Influence of the Examiner on the ITPA Scores of Negro Children." *Psychol Rep* 20:499–502 Ap '67. * (PA 41:8862)

133. SMITH, PETER BARKER, JR. *A Description of the Language Abilities of Institutionalized Phenylketonuric Individuals in the States of Washington, Oregon, Idaho, and Montana.* Doctor's thesis, University of Washington (Seattle, Wash.), 1967. (DA 28:3917B)

134. STARK, JOEL. "A Comparison of the Performance of Aphasic Children on Three Sequencing Tests." *J Commun Disorders* 1:31–4 My '67. * (PA 41:17016)

135. TOBACK, CHARLES. *Speech Intelligibility of Congenitally Deaf Children as Related to Intelligence and Language Ability.* Doctor's thesis, New York University (New York, N.Y.), 1967. (DA 28:4395A)

136. WARDEN, PAUL G. *The Validity of the Illinois Test of*

Psycholinguistic Abilities as a Predictor of Academic Achievement of First Grade Students. Master's thesis, Kent State University (Kent, Ohio), 1967.

137. WEAVER, ANN SULLIVAN. *The Prediction of First Grade Reading Achievement in Culturally Disadvantaged Children.* Doctor's thesis, George Peabody College for Teachers (Nashville, Tenn.), 1967. (*DA* 28:3789A)

138. WEAVER, S. JOSEPH, AND WEAVER, ANN. "Psycholinguistic Abilities of Culturally Deprived Negro Children." *Am J Mental Def* 72:190–7 S '67. * (*PA* 42:2536)

139. WEENER, PAUL; BARRITT, LOREN S.; AND SEMMEL, MELVYN I. "A Critical Evaluation of the Illinois Test of Psycholinguistic Abilities," pp. 373–80. Response by James J. McCarthy, pp. 380–2. Reply by authors, pp. 382–4. *Excep Children* 33:373–84 F '67. * (*PA* 41:5282, 41:5278, 41:5283)

140. WISLAND, MILTON V., AND MANY, WESLEY. "A Study of the Stability of the Illinois Test of Psycholinguistic Abilities." *Ed & Psychol Meas* 27:367–70 su '67. * (*PA* 41:12844)

141. BACH, LLOYD CARL. *A Comparison of Selected Psychological Tests Used With Trainable Mentally Retarded Children.* Doctor's thesis, University of South Dakota (Vermillion, S.D.), 1968. (*DA* 29:2990A)

142. BATEMAN, BARBARA. "The Efficacy of an Auditory and a Visual Method of First Grade Reading Instruction With Auditory and Visual Learners." *Proc Ann Conv Int Read Assn* 12(4):105–12 '68. *

143. BATEMAN, BARBARA. *Interpretation of the 1961 Illinois Test of Psycholinguistic Abilities: With Reproductions of Original Profiles.* Seattle, Wash.: Special Child Publications, 1968. Pp. 108. *

144. BATTIN, R., AND KRAFT, IRVIN A. "Psycholinguistic Evaluation of Children Referred for Private Consultation to a Child Psychiatrist." *J Learn Dis* 1:600–5 O '68. * (*PA* 45:2995)

145. BLOUNT, WILLIAM R. "Language and the More Severely Retarded: A Review." *Am J Mental Def* 73:21–9 Jl '68. * (*PA* 42:19171)

146. BONFIELD, JOHN RONALD. *Predictors of Achievement for Educable Mentally Retarded Children.* Doctor's thesis, Pennsylvania State University (University Park, Pa.), 1968. (*DAI* 30:1009A)

147. COHEN, LINDA. *Performance of Cleft Palate Children on the Illinois Test of Psycholinguistic Abilities.* Master's thesis, Queens College (Flushing, N.Y.), 1968.

148. ETIENNE, JERALD FRANCIS. *The Relationship Between Language and Employment of Caucasian, Negroid, and Spanish-American Male Educable Mentally Retarded Adults.* Doctor's thesis, Colorado State College (Greeley, Colo.), 1968. (*DA* 29:1037A)

149. Fox, FRANK HEWITT. *A Description of Language and Perceptual Function of Culturally Deprived Children.* Doctor's thesis, University of Wisconsin (Madison, Wis.), 1968. (*DA* 29:4323A)

150. FROSTIG, MARIANNE. "Testing as a Basis for Educational Therapy," pp. 64–86. In *Assessment of the Cerebral Palsied Child for Education.* Edited by James Loring. London: William Heinemann Ltd., 1968. Pp. vii, 112. *

151. FROSTIG, MARIANNE, AND MASLOW, PHYLLIS. "Language Training: A Form of Ability Training." *J Learn Dis* 1:105–15 F '68. * (*PA* 44:5680)

152. GATES, MAXINE FULLER. *A Comparison of the Learning Characteristics of Hyperactive and Hypoactive Children With Related Central Nervous System Dysfunctions.* Doctor's thesis, Ohio State University (Columbus, Ohio), 1968. (*DAI* 30:166A)

153. GELHART, ROBERT PRESTON. *Auditory Discrimination in the Educable Mentally Retarded.* Doctor's thesis, University of Southern California (Los Angeles, Calif.), 1968. (*DA* 29:833A)

154. GENTILE, LOUIS ANDREW. *An Investigation of the Relationship Between the Reflective-Impulsivity Cognitive Dimension and Psycholinguistic Abilities.* Doctor's thesis, University of Maryland (College Park, Md.), 1968. (*DA* 29:1449A)

155. HEPBURN, ANDREW WATSON. *The Performance of Normal Children of Differing Reading Ability on the Illinois Test of Psycholinguistic Abilities.* Doctor's thesis, University of Minnesota (Minneapolis, Minn.), 1968. (*DA* 29:2116A)

156. HURLEY, OLIVER L. "Perceptual Integration and Reading Problems." *Excep Children* 35:207–15 N '68. * (*PA* 43:13365)

157. JOYNT, DENIS, AND CAMBOURNE, BRIAN. "Psycholinguistic Development and the Control of Behaviour." *Brit J Ed Psychol* 38:249–60 N '68. * (*PA* 43:6747)

158. KASS, CORRINE E. "The Psycholinguistic Abilities of Retarded Readers." *Kan Studies Ed* 18:35–47 Ap '68. *

159. KIRK, SAMUEL A. "Illinois Test of Psycholinguistic Abilities: Its Origin and Implications." *Learning Disorders* 3:395–427 '68. *

160. LUONG, CORINA K. MONGCAL. *An Analysis of Factors Related to Difficulties in Learning and Adjustment Among Minority Group Children.* Doctor's thesis, Bryn Mawr College (Bryn Mawr, Pa.), 1968. (*DAI* 30:4795B)

161. MASSENGILL, JANET. *A Comparison of the Performance of Aphasic and Nonaphasic Male Adults of the Illinois Test of Psycholinguistic Abilities and the Minnesota Test for Differential Diagnosis of Aphasia.* Master's thesis, East Tennessee State University (Johnson City, Tenn.), 1968.

162. MOULIN, EUGENE KARL. *The Effects of Client-Centered Group Counseling Utilizing Play Media on the Intelligence, Achievements, and Psycholinguistic Abilities of Underachieving Primary School Children.* Doctor's thesis, University of Toledo (Toledo, Ohio), 1968. (*DA* 29:1425A)

163. MUELLER, MAX W. "Validity of Six Tests of Ability With Educable Mental Retardates." *J Sch Psychol* 6:136–46 w '68. * (*PA* 42:11152)

164. NORTH, GEORGE E. "The Illinois Test of Psycholinguistic Abilities (ITPA) Before and After a Poverty Area Program." *J Ed Res* 62:93 O '68. *

165. OGLAND, VANETTA SUYDAM. *Performance of Special Class Educable Mentally Retarded Children on the ITPA and Other Language Measures as a Function of Selected Variables.* Doctor's thesis, University of Minnesota (Minneapolis, Minn.), 1968. (*DAI* 30:174A)

166. O'GRADY, DONALD JOHN. *Psycholinguistic Abilities in Primary School Age Children With Learning Disabilities.* Doctor's thesis, University of Cincinnati (Cincinnati, Ohio), 1968. (*DA* 29:1848B)

167. PHILLIPS, C. J. "The Illinois Test of Psycholinguistic Abilities: A Report on Its Use With English Children and a Comment on the Psychological Sequelae of Low Birth-Weight." *Brit J Dis Commun* 3:143–9 O '68. * (*PA* 45:9681)

168. SIGEL, IRVING E., AND PERRY, CERETA. "Psycholinguistic Diversity Among 'Culturally Deprived' Children." *Am J Orthopsychiatry* 38:122–6 Ja '68. * (*PA* 42:17002)

169. SILVERSTEIN, A. B. "Variance Components in Five Psychological Tests." *Psychol Rep* 23:141–2 Ag '68. * (*PA* 43:6920)

170. SLOBODZIAN, EVELYN BIRDSALL. *The Relationship Between Certain Readiness Measures and Reading Achievement at Level One.* Doctor's thesis, Temple University (Philadelphia, Pa.), 1968. (*DA* 29:1053A)

171. SMITH, ROBERT M., AND MCWILLIAMS, BETTY JANE. "Psycholinguistic Abilities of Children With Clefts." *Cleft Palate J* 5:238–49 Jl '68. *

172. SMITH, ROBERT M., AND MCWILLIAMS, BETTY JANE. "Psycholinguistic Considerations in the Management of Children With Cleft Palate." *J Speech & Hearing Disorders* 33:26–33 F '68. * (*PA* 42:9321)

173. STARK, JOEL; COHEN, SYLVIA; AND EISENSON, JON. "Performances of Aphasic Children on the PPVT and Auditory Decoding Tests." *J Spec Ed* 2:435–7 su–f '68. * (*PA* 43:10213)

174. STEPHENSON, BOBBY LYNN. *A Study of Sex and Race Variables and Psycholinguistic Abilities of Lower Socioeconomic Status First Grade Children.* Doctor's thesis, University of Alabama (University, Ala.), 1968. (*DA* 29:3475A)

175. STERNE, DAVID M. "Validity of the PPVT, Knox Cubes and ITPA With Aphasic Adults." Abstract. *Psychol Rep* 22:1014 Je '68. * (*PA* 42:12997)

176. WEBB, PATRICIA KIMBERLEY. *A Comparison of the Psycholinguistic Abilities of Anglo-American, Negro, and Latin-American Lower-Class Preschool Children.* Doctor's thesis, North Texas State University (Denton, Tex.), 1968. (*DA* 29:3351A)

177. WISEMAN, DOUGLAS E. "The ITPA and Remediation." *Ann Inter Conf Assn Children Learn Dis* 5:81–7 '68. *

178. ASTILL, DOLORES ELLEN. *Visual Memory Deficits and Reading Disabilities.* Doctor's thesis, University of Utah (Salt Lake City, Utah), 1969. (*DAI* 30:3310A)

179. AYRES, A. JEAN. "Deficits in Sensory Integration in Educationally Handicapped Children." *J Learn Dis* 2(3):160–8 Mr '69. * (*PA* 45:6978)

180. BAKER, GEORGIA ANN PITCHER. *The Efficiency of Diagnostic, Readiness, and Achievement Instruments as Predictors of Language Arts Achievement: A Longitudinal Study From Kindergarten Through Second Grade.* Doctor's thesis, Purdue University (Lafayette, Ind.), 1969. (*DAI* 30:3624A)

181. BANAS, NORMA, AND WILLS, I. H. "The Vulnerable Child and Prescriptive Teaching." *Acad Ther* 4(3):215–9 sp '69. * (*PA* 43:17927)

182. BANNATYNE, ALEX D. "A Comparison of Visuo-Spatial and Visuo-Motor Memory for Designs and Their Relationship to Other Sensori-Motor and Psycholinguistic Variables." *J Learn Dis* 2(9):451–66 S '69. * (*PA* 45:6004)

183. BANNATYNE, ALEX D., AND WICHIARAJOTE, PENNY. "Hemispheric Dominance, Handedness, Mirror Imaging, and Auditory Sequencing." *Excep Children* 36(1):27–36 S '69. * (*PA* 44:20147)

184. BANNATYNE, ALEX D., AND WICHIARAJOTE, PENNY. "Relationships Between Written Spelling, Motor Functioning and Sequencing Skills." *J Learn Dis* 2(1):4–16 Ja '69. * (*PA* 45:7915)

185. BRUININKS, ROBERT H. "Auditory and Visual Perceptual Skills Related to the Reading Performance of Disadvantaged Boys." *Percept & Motor Skills* 29(1):179–86 Ag '69. * (*PA* 44:2835)

186. CRITTENDEN, JERRY BLICKMAN. *An Empirical Investigation of the Behavioral Dimensions of Four Tests of Learning Disabilities.* Doctor's thesis, Michigan State University (East Lansing, Mich.), 1969. (*DAI* 30:5310A)

187. DUGGER, JAMES G. "The ITPA as a Diagnostic Instru-

ment for Reading Disability Problems in Mental Deficiency." *Psychol* 6(4):47-51 N '69. * (*PA* 44:9122)
188. Efron, Marvin. *The Influence of Communication Ability on the Incidence of Over-Referral in the Use of the School Vision Tester.* Doctor's thesis, University of South Carolina (Columbia, S.C.), 1969. (*DAI* 30:4825A)
189. Espeseth, V. K. "An Investigation of Visual-Sequential Memory in Deaf Children." *Am Ann Deaf* 114(4):786-9 S '69. * (*PA* 44:7120)
190. Evans, David. "The Assessment of Language Abilities in Subnormal Children With Special Reference to the Illinois Test of Psycholinguistic Abilities." *Med Officer* 122(17):219-22 O 24 '69. *
191. Gerber, Sanford E., and Hertel, Christina G. "Language Deficiency of Disadvantaged Children." *J Speech & Hearing Res* 12(2):270-80 Je '69. *
192. Golden, Nancy E., and Steiner, Sharon R. "Auditory and Visual Functions in Good and Poor Readers." *J Learn Dis* 2(9):476-81 S '69. * (*PA* 45:6666)
193. Gordon, Susan B. *The Relationship Between the English Language Abilities and Home Language Experiences of First-Grade Children, From Three Ethnic Groups, of Varying Socioeconomic Status and Varying Degrees of Bilingualism.* Doctor's thesis, University of New Mexico (Albuquerque, N.M.), 1969. (*DAI* 31:2252A)
194. Hatch, Eric J. *A Stability and Validity Study of the Illinois Test of Psycholinguistic Abilities With Educable Mental Retardates.* Master's thesis, Pennsylvania State University (University Park, Pa.), 1969.
195. Hirshoren, Alfred. "A Comparison of the Predictive Validity of the Revised Stanford-Binet Intelligence Scale and the Illinois Test of Psycholinguistic Abilities." *Excep Children* 35(7):517-21 Mr '69. * (*PA* 44:17505)
196. Kastner, Sheldon B. "Reversal Shifts and Problem-Solving Abilities at Ages 4-7." *Genetic Psychol Monogr* 79(2): 211-49 My '69. * (*PA* 43:15589)
197. Kuske, Irwin I., Jr. *Psycholinguistic Abilities of Sioux Indian Children.* Doctor's thesis, University of South Dakota (Vermillion, S.D.), 1969. (*DAI* 30:4280A)
198. Lombardi, Thomas Philip. *Psycholinguistic Abilities of Papago Indian Children.* Doctor's thesis, University of Arizona (Tucson, Ariz.), 1969. (*DAI* 30:1891A)
199. Lucas, Marilyn Steude. *The ITPA and the Coding Process in Mental Retardates.* Doctor's thesis, Ohio State University (Columbus, Ohio), 1969. (*DAI* 30:3374B)
200. Macione, Joseph R. *Psychological Correlates of Reading Disability as Defined by the Illinois Test of Psycholinguistic Abilities.* Doctor's thesis, University of South Dakota (Vermillion, S.D.), 1969. (*DAI* 30:3817A)
201. Mann, Lester. "Are We Fractionating Too Much?" *Acad Ther* 5(2):85-91 w '69-70 [*69]. * (*PA* 44:15347)
202. Meyers, C. E. "What the ITPA Measures: A Synthesis of Factor Studies of the 1961 Edition." *Ed & Psychol Meas* 29(4):867-76 w '69. * (*PA* 44:20897)
203. Mittler, Peter. "Genetic Aspects of Psycholinguistic Abilities." *J Child Psychol & Psychiatry* 10(3):165-76 N '69. * (*PA* 44:8198)
204. Mueller, Max W. "Prediction of Achievement of Educable Mentally Retarded Children." *Am J Mental Def* 73(4): 590-6 Ja '69. * (*PA* 43:8703)
205. Okada, Doris Mamiya. *The Effects of Perceptual and Perceptual-Motor Training on the Visual Perception, Auditory Perception, and Language Performance of Institutionalized Educable Mental Retardates.* Doctor's thesis, New York University (New York, N.Y.), 1969. (*DAI* 30:2857A)
206. Paraskevopoulos, John N., and Kirk, Samuel A. *The Development and Psychometric Characteristics of the Revised Illinois Test of Psycholinguistics.* Urbana, Ill.: University of Illinois Press, 1969. Pp. x, 243. *
207. Perozzi, Joseph Anthony. *The Relationship Between Speech Sound Discrimination Skills and Language Abilities of Kindergarten Children.* Doctor's thesis, University of Washington (Seattle, Wash.), 1969. (*DAI* 30:5278B)
208. Rice, James A. "Confusion in Laterality: A Validity Study With Bright and Dull Children." *J Learn Dis* 2(7): 368-73 Jl '69. * (*PA* 45:6889)
209. Ryckman, David B., and Wiegerink, Ronald. "The Factors of the Illinois Test of Psycholinguistic Abilities: A Comparison of 18 Factor Analyses." *Excep Children* 36(2): 107-13 O '69. * (*PA* 44:19766)
210. Schiller, Jerome J., and Deignan, Margaret C. "An Approach to Diagnosis and Remediation of Learning Disabilities." *J Learn Dis* 2(10):508-19 O '69. * (*PA* 45:7011)
211. Sears, Charles Richards. *A Comparison of the Basic Language Concepts and Psycholinguistic Abilities of Second Grade Boys Who Demonstrate Average and Below Average Levels of Reading Achievement.* Doctor's thesis, Colorado State College (Greeley, Colo.), 1969. (*DAI* 30:1758A)
212. Shipe, Dorothy, and Miezitis, Solveiga. "A Pilot Study in the Diagnosis and Remediation of Special Learning Disabilities in Preschool Children." *J Learn Dis* 2(11):579-92 N '69. * (*PA* 46:7521)
213. Simmons, Helen. *Decision Strategy as a Function of Sensory Modality.* Doctor's thesis, University of Oregon (Eugene, Ore.), 1969. (*DAI* 31:1089A)
214. Smith, Carolyn Meredith. *The Relationship of Reading Method and Reading Achievement to ITPA Sensory Modalities.* Doctor's thesis, University of Georgia (Athens, Ga.), 1969. (*DAI* 30:2916A)
215. Teska, James Allen. *Success and Failure in Five Different Programs of Preschool Intervention With Culturally Disadvantaged Children.* Doctor's thesis, University of Illinois (Urbana, Ill.), 1969. (*DAI* 30:2917A)
216. Wisland, Milton, and Many, Wesley A. "A Factorial Study of the Illinois Test of Psycholinguistic Abilities With Children Having Above Average Intelligence." *Ed & Psychol Meas* 29(2):367-76 su '69. * (*PA* 44:17341)
217. Brickman, Lillian. *A Study of Anxiety and Performance on the IPTA by Children With Minimal Cerebral Dysfunction.* Master's thesis, California State College (Long Beach, Calif.), 1970.
218. Brochu, Edith Williamson. *A Study of Selected Communication Abilities of Boys in All-Male and Traditional Kindergarten and First Grade Classes.* Doctor's thesis, University of Northern Colorado (Greeley, Colo.), 1970. (*DAI* 31:4031A)
219. Bruininks, Robert H.; Lucker, William G.; and Gropper, Robert L. "Psycholinguistic Abilities of Good and Poor Reading Disadvantaged First-Graders." *El Sch J* 70(7): 378-86 Ap '70. *
220. Chovan, William L. "Vocal Mediating Responses in Short-Term Memory of Severely and Profoundly Deaf Children." *Percept & Motor Skills* 31(2):539-44 O '70. * (*PA* 45:6826)
221. Clark, Alice, and Foster, James. "Objective Measures and Occupational Success." *Mental Retard* 8(4):41-4 Ag '70. *
222. Durkin, Dolores. "A Language Arts Program for Pre-First-Grade Children: Two-Year Achievement Report." *Read Res Q* 5(4):534-65 su '70. *
223. Egeland, Byron; Di Nello, Mario; and Carr, Donald. "The Relationship of Intelligence, Visual-Motor, Psycholinguistic and Reading-Readiness Skills With Achievement." *Ed & Psychol Meas* 30(2):451-8 su '70. * (*PA* 45:3056)
224. Ferinden, William E., Jr.; Jacobson, Sherman; and Kovalinsky, Thomas. *Educational Interpretation of the Stanford-Binet Intelligence Scale Form L-M and the Illinois Test of Psycholinguistic Abilities.* Linden, N.J.: Remediation Associates, Inc., 1970. Pp. 71. *
225. Flynn, Pauline T., and Byrne, Margaret C. "Relationship Between Reading and Selected Auditory Abilities of Third-Grade Children." *J Speech & Hearing Res* 13(4): 731-40 D '70. *
226. Garms, Joe D. "A Validation Study of the Illinois Test of Psycholinguistic Abilities." *Psychol* 7(1):9-12 F '70. * (*PA* 44:13282)
227. Goodstein, H. A.; Whitney, G.; and Cawley, J. F. "Prediction of Perceptual Reading Disability Among Disadvantaged Children in the Second Grade." *Read Teach* 24(1): 23-8 O '70. * (*PA* 45:10955)
228. Hofmeister, Alan, and Espeseth, V. Knute. "Predicting Academic Achievement With TMR Adults and Teenagers." *Am J Mental Def* 75(1):105-7 Jl '70. *
229. Howard, Marshall J., Jr.; Hoops, H. Ray; and McKinnon, Archie J. "Language Abilities of Children With Differing Socioeconomic Backgrounds." *J Learn Dis* 3(6):328-35 Je '70. *
230. Hubschman, Eva; Polizzotto, Emilie Ann; and Kaliski, Myra S. "Performance of Institutionalized Retardates on the PPVT and Two Editions of the ITPA." *Am J Mental Def* 74(4):579-80 Ja '70. * (*PA* 44:11063)
231. Jones, Eloise Lorraine Harriss. *The Effects of a Language Development Program on the Psycholinguistic Abilities and IQ of a Group of Preschool Disadvantaged Children.* Doctor's thesis, University of Arkansas (Fayetteville, Ark.), 1970. (*DAI* 31:2761A)
232. Joselson, Maurice L. *The Role of Language Skills Within the Perspective of Other Psychosocial Factors in a Select Prison Population.* Doctor's thesis, University of Florida (Gainesville, Fla.), 1970. (*DAI* 31:4385B)
233. Karr, Sharon Kay Studer. *Differences in Psycholinguistic Abilities and Intellectual Maturity Among Sierra Leonean Children From Four Cultural Systems of Varying Degrees of Modernization.* Doctor's thesis, Southern Illinois University (Carbondale, Ill.), 1970. (*DAI* 31:3958A)
234. Leeds, Donald S. "Illinois Test of Psycholinguistic Abilities: Summary of Research and Commentary." *J Read Specialist* 9(4):169-83 My '70. *
235. Leventhal, Donald S., and Stedman, Donald J. "A Factor Analytic Study of the Illinois Test of Psycholinguistic Abilities." *J Clin Psychol* 26(4):473-7 O '70. * (*PA* 45:4923)
236. Lokerson, Jean Elizabeth. *An Investigation of Visual Perception and the Psycholinguistic Process: The Comparative Performance of First Grade Boys on the Illinois Test of Psycholinguistic Abilities Adapted for Visual-Perceptual Impairment.* Doctor's thesis, University of Maryland (College Park, Md.), 1970. (*DAI* 31:3992A)
237. Lombardi, Thomas P. "Psycholinguistic Abilities of Papago Indian School Children." *Excep Children* 36(7):485-93 Mr '70. * (*PA* 44:21498)
238. Mittler, P., and Ward, J. "The Use of the Illinois Test of Psycholinguistic Abilities on British Four-Year-Old

Children: A Normative and Factorial Study." *Brit J Ed Psychol* 40(1):43–53 F '70. * (*PA* 44:11226)
239. MITTLER, P.; WARD, J.; AND MARINOSSON, GRETAR. "Suggestions for Re-Wording of Items From the Revised Edition of the Illinois Test of Psycholinguistic Abilities for Use With British Children." *Brit J Ed Psychol* 40(1):53–4 F '70. *
240. MOULIN, EUGENE K. "The Effects of Client-Centered Group Counseling Using Play Media on the Intelligence, Achievement, and Psycholinguistic Abilities of Underachieving Primary School Children." *El Sch Guid & Counsel* 5(2):85–98 D '70. *
241. NURCOMBE, B., AND MOFFITT, P. "Cultural Deprivation and Language Defect: Project Enrichment of Childhood." *Austral Psychologist* 5(3):249–59 N '70. * (*PA* 46:5744)
242. NURSS, JOANNE R. "A Diagnostic Comparison of Two Third Grade Reading Classes," pp. 42–54. In *Reading Difficulties: Diagnosis, Correction, and Remediation.* Edited by William K. Durr. Newark, Del.: International Reading Association, 1970. Pp. vii, 276. *
243. ORPET, R. E., AND MYERS, C. E. "Discriminant Function Analysis of Conservation Stages by Structure of Intellect and Conceptual Style Variables." Abstract. *Proc 78th Ann Conv Am Psychol Assn* 5(1):279–80 '70. * (*PA* 44:18342)
244. RICE, JAMES A., AND DOUGHTIE, EUGENE B. "IQ and the ITPA Classification Versus Diagnosis." *J Learn Dis* 3(9):471–4 S '70. *
245. SABATINO, DAVID A., AND HAYDEN, DAVID L. "Information Processing Behaviors Related to Learning Disabilities and Educable Mental Retardation." *Excep Children* 37(1):21–9 S '70. * (*PA* 46:5527)
246. SABATINO, DAVID A., AND HAYDEN, DAVID L. "Psycho-Educational Study of Selected Behavioral Variables With Children Failing the Elementary Grades." *J Exp Ed* 38(4):40–57 su '70. * (*PA* 46:5680–1)
247. SABATINO, DAVID A., AND HAYDEN, DAVID L. "Variation in Information Processing Behaviors: As Related to Chronological Age Differences for Children Failing in the Elementary Grades." *J Learn Dis* 3(8):404–12 Ag '70. *
248. ST. GEORGE, ROSS. "The Psycholinguistic Abilities of Children From Different Ethnic Backgrounds." *Austral J Psychol* 22(1):85–9 Ap '70. * (*PA* 45:4053)
249. SEVERSON, ROGER A., AND GUEST, KRISTIN E. Chap. 15. "Toward the Standardized Assessment of the Language of Disadvantaged Children," pp. 309–34. In *Language and Poverty: Perspectives on a Theme.* Edited by Frederick Williams. Chicago, Ill.: Markham Publishing Co., 1970. Pp. xii, 459. *
250. SHARP, ELIZABETH YERXA. *The Relationship of Visual Closure to Speechreading Among Deaf Children.* Doctor's thesis, University of Arizona (Tucson, Ariz.), 1970. (*DAI* 31:2198A)
251. SLOBODZIAN, EVELYN B. "Use of the Illinois Test of Psycholinguistic Abilities as a Readiness Measure," pp. 43–8. In *Reading Diagnosis and Evaluation.* Edited by Dorothy L. De Boer. Newark, Del.: International Reading Association, 1970. Pp. vi, 138. *
252. SMITH, JOAN MELVIN. *Utilization of the Illinois Test of Psycholinguistic Abilities With Educationally Handicapped Children.* Doctor's thesis, University of the Pacific (Stockton, Calif.), 1970. (*DAI* 31:3973A)
253. TEN BRINK, TERRY D. "Critique of Hirshoren's ITPA Validity Study." Reply by Alfred Hirshoren. *Excep Children* 36(5):351–6 Ja '70. *
254. UHL, NORMAN P., AND NURSS, JOANNE R. "Socio-Economic Level Styles in Solving Reading-Related Tasks." *Read Res Q* 5(3):452–85 sp '70. *
255. WADDELL, KATHLEEN J., AND CAHOON, DELWIN D. "Comments on the Use of the Illinois Test of Psycholinguistic Abilities With Culturally Deprived Children in the Rural South." *Percept & Motor Skills* 31(1):56–8 Ag '70. * (*PA* 45:3967)
256. WASHINGTON, ERNEST D., AND TESKA, JAMES A. "Relations Between the Wide Range Achievement Test, the California Achievement Tests, the Stanford-Binet, and the Illinois Test of Psycholinguistic Abilities." *Psychol Rep* 26(1):291–4 F '70. * (*PA* 45:4931)
257. WEYCHERT, MARIE C. *The Utilization of Illinois Test of Psycholinguistic Abilities Profiles to Provide a Structured, Language Oriented Curriculum for Mentally Retarded Children.* Master's thesis, Cardinal Stritch College (Milwaukee, Wis.), 1970.
258. WISEMAN, DOUGLAS E. "Remedial Education: Global or Learning-Disability Approach?" *Acad Ther* 5(3):165–75 sp '70. * (*PA* 44:19423)
259. WORKS, MARIAN NEWMAN. *Some Variables Involved in the Reading Process.* Doctor's thesis, University of Oklahoma (Norman, Okla.), 1970. (*DAI* 31:2765AAA)
260. WUSSLER, MARILYN, AND BARCLAY, A. "Cerebral Dominance, Psycholinguistic Skills and Reading Disability." *Percept & Motor Skills* 31(2):419–25 O '70. * (*PA* 45:4015)
261. ZBINDEN, WILLIAM ROSS. *Psycholinguistic and Perceptual Correlates of Spelling in Educable Mentally Handicapped Children.* Doctor's thesis, University of Illinois (Urbana, Ill.), 1970. (*DAI* 31:2765AAA)

JOHN B. CARROLL, *Senior Research Psychologist, Educational Testing Service, Princeton, New Jersey.*

It requires some stretching of meaning to call the ITPA a measure of "psycholinguistic abilities." The interdisciplinary field of psycholinguistics studies the role of natural language systems in human communication and thinking—in particular, the way in which individuals acquire and use such systems. Only about half of the subtests in the ITPA **clearly** involve a natural language system, i.e., English; the remainder of the tests are essentially "non-language" tests that could be performed, conceivably, by individuals who had never acquired any language system at all, and with appropriate translation of instructions, they could be performed by non-English speakers. In the construction and development of this test, a "psycholinguistic ability" was apparently viewed as any ability that reflects or involves some kind of "communicative" transaction between the individual and his environment, whether or not this transaction requires the use of symbols in a particular language such as English. But by this definition, almost any testable cognitive ability could be regarded as "psycholinguistic." The title of the ITPA is a misnomer, and users should be cautioned to look carefully at the true nature of the test, which might less misleadingly have been named something like the "Illinois Diagnostic Test of Cognitive Functioning."

From the present title, a potential user might feel justified in expecting it to cover such language skills as reading, writing, and spelling. Actually, tests of these skills were deliberately excluded from the battery, since the authors' intention was to measure basic cognitive skills that are not usually attained through schooling.

The confusion that the test engenders about what kinds of abilities are "psycholinguistic" is aggravated when a user of the test claims that the difficulties it reveals are "psycholinguistic in nature," as Ferrier (*82*) did in a report on his use of the test with a group of children with "functional defects of articulation."

If the ITPA were truly a test of psycholinguistic abilities, it would limit its attention to language functions, but it would provide information on a much wider range of such functions, with considerably more detail and precision.

The authors' original purpose was to develop a diagnostic test of a variety of basic mental functions that might be relevant in the analysis

Illinois Test of Psycholinguistic Abilities

of intellectual deficits exhibited in cases of mental retardation, "learning disability," and the like. They were convinced that tests of global intelligence such as the Stanford-Binet or the WISC do not provide sufficient diagnostic information. To develop the experimental version of the test, they made use of a model of the communication process that had been proposed by C. E. Osgood, a psycholinguist on the University of Illinois faculty. The model purported to analyze the individual's communication with the environment and with other individuals in terms of *channels, levels of organization,* and *processes. Channels* referred to auditory, visual, tactual, and other sensory modalities (on the receptive side), and to vocal and motor classes of responses (on the output side). Three *levels of organization* were postulated: a "projection" level, dealing primarily with physiological processes; an integrative or "automatic" level, mediating the habitual processing of symbols and response chains; and a "representational" level, dealing with the meanings of stimuli. *Processes* included decoding and encoding of symbols and the finding of associations among stimuli. The ITPA's authors considered the possibility of constructing tests for 48 possible combinations of channels, levels, and processes suggested by the Osgood model, but found it impracticable to do so. The experimental version of the ITPA comprised nine tests designed to tap what were considered to be the more important of these combinations—primarily, combinations that would contrast the "representational" and the "automatic" levels, "auditory-vocal" and "visual-motor" channels, and (at the "representational" level) "decoding," "associational," and "encoding" processes. It was intended in this way to measure nine more or less independent abilities. The Revised Edition retains the basic plan of the experimental edition but adds a test of one "new" ability, Visual Closure (to measure "visual-motor automatic function"), and two further tests claimed to measure "auditory-vocal automatic functions."

The ITPA's model of cognitive function invites comparison with Guilford's "structure of intellect" model. The pitfalls of model-making are starkly illustrated by this comparison, for there is little coincidence between the models. Possibly Guilford's "operations" correspond in a limited way to Osgood's "processes," if we assume that "cognition" corresponds to "decoding" and that "convergent production" and "divergent production" are types of "encoding." There seems to be nothing in the ITPA model that would correspond to Guilford's "contents" and "products." But Guilford's model is largely an arbitrary construction, and if the abilities tested at different intersections of his model are truly independent, it cannot be firmly supported even by factor-analytic evidence. The logic by which the authors of the ITPA expected the tests at the intersections of *their* model to be independent is certainly not clear. One would think that they ought to expect, for example, that all tests measuring the "representational" level would have at least some covariance on this account. This possibility has now been recognized by those associated with the development of the revised edition (*206*).

Fortunately, factor-analytic studies (mainly for the experimental version) that enable one to appraise the validity of some aspects of the ITPA cognitive model are available. One must, however, largely discount the numerous studies that have factor-analyzed the ITPA with little or no use of external reference tests, for such studies would automatically fail to identify unique abilities in the separate tests. Silverstein (*130, 169*) has reported that the nine tests in the experimental edition have considerable variance in common; this is also apparent from inspection of correlation matrices presented by the test authors. Meyers (*202*) attempted to synthesize the factor analyses of the experimental edition of the ITPA and reported that it appears to measure "six separate and established abilities, and possibly a seventh." Meyers suggested how these factors might be labeled according to Guilford's system. He also discussed the extent to which the factor-analytic results seem to provide confirmation of the postulated model of communicative abilities. While separation by "channel" does occur, the "representational" level is identified mainly with the well-known verbal comprehension factor. The concept of an "automatic" level is not well supported, and the notion of different "processes" is "completely unsubstantiated," according to Meyers, who further states that the "sequential" tests are just tests of "short-term memory."

Probably the most useful factorial study of the ITPA is that by Uhl and Nurss (*254*), which used a large number of reference tests and which was able to identify only three or four interpretable factors in the 1961 version. These factors were: (*a*) a factor of "vocabulary," which for upper-middle-class children was significantly tapped by at least six of the nine tests, but which split into "expressive" and "receptive" verbal factors for lower-class children; (*b*) an "immediate memory span" factor, present for both upper-middle- and lower-class children; and (*c*) a factor of "auditory processing," which was found only in the data for lower-class children. Uhl and Nurss interpreted this last factor as representing the extent to which the children understood the dialect of the examiner.

A casual inspection of the subtests will reinforce the conclusion that many of them, even the "non-language" ones, measure a "vocabulary" factor, or rather, a factor having to do with the range of cultural experiences to which the child has been exposed—cultural experiences symbolized by *words* in some tests and by *pictures* and visual symbols in others. For example, in the Auditory Reception test of the Revised Edition, the child may be asked such questions (orally) as "Do bugles camouflage?" or "Do meteorites collide?" (meteorites *do* collide, according to the answer key, although I have never heard of their colliding with each other). In Visual Association, the child may be shown an item requiring him to make an association between a microscope and a telescope. In Visual Reception, he may have to associate a picture of a regular table-top pencil sharpener with the miniature variety one can put in one's purse, or an ordinary screwdriver with the automatic type one can insert in the chuck of an electric hand drill. It seems hardly necessary to point out that such items involve quite specific knowledges that can be expected only of children who have had wide cultural experiences.

It is somewhat ironic, however, that in a test of "psycholinguistic abilities" the test on Verbal Expression, scored as directed in the manual, affords little information on the expressive linguistic development of the child. Scoring of this test focuses on the number of ideas within certain restricted types that are present in the child's talk when he is asked to "tell about" a few simple objects. There is, for example, no scoring for mean length of utterance in morphemes, a measure that has been found to be highly indicative of level of linguistic development. Whether the score on the test of Grammatic Closure is an adequate substitute for such a measure is not indicated.

To a degree, then, the ITPA may be regarded as just another test of a limited number of intellectual abilities—verbal comprehension and general information, immediate memory span, and perhaps special capacities in the visual and auditory perceptual domains, as well as a special kind of expressive verbal fluency. The precise factorial composition of the Revised Edition is still to be explored, but it is likely to contain few surprises. Although the test was intended as a "diagnostic" instrument, the manual gives directions for computing and interpreting scaled scores based on an unweighted sum of the subtest scores. These scaled scores generally have correlations in the .80's with the Stanford-Binet MA or similar measures, according to several studies (e.g., *256*). The considerably lower correlations with Stanford-Binet MA's reported by the test authors are for highly restricted ranges in terms of ability and age.

It would seem that much care and effort were expended in construction and refining the test materials. Technical characteristics such as reliability seem to be highly satisfactory. However, the ITPA is a fairly complicated battery to administer. Despite the many improvements in the Revised Edition to facilitate administration, one finds it hard to believe that the battery can typically be given in 45, or even 60, minutes, as claimed by the authors. Several studies of the experimental edition (*55, 131, 132*) suggest that there can be fairly wide variation in scores due to examiner differences. Whether the ITPA is more sensitive to examiner differences than other individually administered clinical instruments is an open question.

It has already been noted in the literature (*139*) that the standardization procedures adopted by the test authors were somewhat unusual and possibly open to question. For both the Experimental Edition and the Revised Edition, the standardization samples consisted of groups of "normal," "average" children. The authors justified their procedure by saying that they desired a reference group against which deficits of learning disability and mental retardate cases could be evaluated. For the Revised Edition, the norm group comprised 962 children (about 120 children in each of eight age-groups) who were carefully screened to have "average" intelligence (IQ 84 to 116), to be from schools with achievements in a "middle

Illinois Test of Psycholinguistic Abilities

range" in middle-class communities, and to be free from physical handicaps, emotional disturbances, etc. Only 4 percent were Negro; all samples were from medium-sized cities or towns in the Midwest. There is a distinct possibility that the normative sample had average IQ's below the average for the populations from which the samples were drawn.

There may be some merit in the authors' standardization procedures, but those procedures can be criticized on the ground that the norms do not include data on groups of children representative of the "learning disability" and mental retardate populations for which the test was presumably designed. It has been left to other investigators to collect such norms, but the available literature contains few, if any, studies of respectably large groups of systematically selected "learning disability" cases. A user of the ITPA should not be surprised if he finds that on a given subtest a particular child scores at or below the lowest possible score in the norms given for "average" children. He would probably be justified in concluding that the child is in some way deviant from "average" children, but he would still not know how to relate the score to those typically obtained by "learning disability" cases, mental retardates, etc.

If the use of the ITPA were to be restricted to certain types of learning disability cases, the authors' standardization procedures might be regarded as acceptable. There is, however, a serious issue latent in the fact that nowhere in the materials accompanying the test do the authors make a clear and explicit statement concerning the types of populations for which the test is designed. They make vague references to "learning disabilities" and mental retardation, but one gathers that the kinds of cases they are referring to are those that are found with significant frequency in middle-class, white, English-speaking communities, not only in the Midwest, of course, but throughout the country. At least, their selection of norm groups from such communities suggests such an interpretation. It would appear, however, from studies reported in the literature, that by far the greatest use of the ITPA has been in the assessment of the "psycholinguistic" abilities of lower-class children, particularly from minority groups—Blacks, Chicanos, and even Papago Indians. The test has also been applied to adolescent and adult mental retardates. Little justification for such uses is to be found in the standardization of the test. If fault is to be found, at least some of it must be attributed to the authors for not making suitable cautionary statements regarding the use of the test with lower-class and minority groups. From an inspection of test content and in view of a number of research studies, one can raise serious questions concerning the validity of the test for such groups.

Consider, first, the fact that the test is replete with materials that are characteristic of middle-class culture—pictures of electric mixers, violins, tennis rackets, and motor-driven hand tools, and words like *cosmetics, meteorite, beverage,* and *architect.* Consider also the fact that several of the tests require the child to exhibit his familiarity with, or his ability to conform to, the lexical and grammatical norms of "standard" American English (as opposed to the many varieties of "nonstandard" or "substandard" English). Consider the fact that Uhr and Nurss's study suggested that the "auditory" factors in the test might be associated more with the child's ability to understand the dialect of the examiner than with any defect of auditory perception. Howard, Hoops, and McKinnon (*229*) have made pointed criticism of the test on the grounds that the scoring often unjustly penalizes the child who happens to have been reared in a community with nonstandard speech patterns. For such cases, low ITPA scores cannot be interpreted as necessarily reflecting any real intellectual deficit, unless one believes in the discredited notion that nonstandard speech patterns betoken faulty intellectual functioning. Consider also the fact that Verbal Expression (Vocal Encoding in the experimental edition) —a test requiring the child to "talk about" each of a series of such objects as a wooden block, an envelope, etc.—is very likely to "tongue-tie" a child from a lower-class environment when he is confronted with a strange and (possibly) ethnically-different examiner. The sociolinguist William Labov [1] has dramatically illustrated how such children can be highly verbal and fluent when they are observed in a situation which is less unnatural to them than a test. Severson and Guest (*249*) have written a particularly valuable discussion of the limitations of the ITPA when it is used with disadvantaged children.

[1] LABOV, WILLIAM. Chap. 9, "The Logic of Nonstandard English," pp. 153–89. In *Language and Poverty: Perspectives on a Theme.* Edited by Frederick Williams. Chicago, Ill.: Markham Publishing Co., 1970. Pp. xii, 459. *

Illinois Test of Psycholinguistic Abilities

Thus, the use of the ITPA in evaluating the effects of language programs for the disadvantaged is highly questionable, unless one views the purpose of such testing as that of finding out how much these programs advance the child towards certain middle-class language norms. And even if that is the purpose, the ITPA is hardly adequate for the task. One doubts that the test can be used to assess progress of these groups in "intellectual functioning" per se because the cultural element is too dominant. Much caution must be urged in interpreting the results of studies that have used the ITPA with lower-class minority groups.

If we must doubt the validity of the ITPA for children from lower socioeconomic classes or from nonstandard language backgrounds, we may nevertheless inquire into its validity and usefulness for the types of children for whom it was designed. The "average" middle-class children in the norms groups exhibited considerable variability in performance. The test authors display data based on the norms groups (*206*, Table 7-6) showing that differences among subtest scores are in general highly reliable, a finding that supports the notion that the test shows promise for diagnostic use. Kirk (*88*) has published a number of case studies showing how "psycholinguistic disabilities" can be diagnosed by the test in its experimental form; presumably the Revised Edition would be useful in similar ways. He also illustrates a variety of remedial techniques, including programmed instruction, whose use would be indicated by certain profiles of subtest scores. Nevertheless, there are few systematic studies in the literature concerning the effectiveness of remedial procedures selected in accordance with test results. Weener, Barritt, and Semmel (*139*) pointed to the need for "evidence....to show how subscale performance is related to educationally relevant behaviors." Ferrier (*82*), working with functional disorders of articulation, complained that the remedial procedures that would be suggested by test performances "would, in most cases, bear little resemblance to what is usually considered speech therapy." Ogland (*165*), studying educable mental retardates, found that the test showed no significant differences between subjects with and without language training, but Okada (*205*) found the ITPA was useful in measuring the effects of certain kinds of perceptual training.

Studies are divided on the usefulness of the test in prediction or diagnosis of reading disabilities. Some favorable evidence is presented by Bateman (*27*), Kass (*87*), and Macione (*200*). (Macione's study is one of the few that concerns the Revised Edition.) However, Sears (*211*) found no significant differences between average and disabled readers in any of the ITPA skill areas, and Smith (*214*) found no interaction between reading method and "auditory" vs. "visual" types as identified by the test.

Reviewing the material on the use of the test in diagnosis and remediation, one gets the impression that its main contribution might be to differentiate deficits in the "auditory" and "visual" areas, with secondary values in cases of poor verbal expression. The authors have an obligation to report further research supporting the usefulness of the ITPA for the major purpose for which it was designed—diagnosis and remediation. As matters stand, it is difficult to see wherein the ITPA represents a diagnostic instrument that is markedly superior to other tests of this genre, such as the Stanford-Binet and the WISC—tests that are more extensively standardized and in general, one would judge, more appealing to children.

CLINTON I. CHASE, *Professor of Educational Psychology and Chairman of the Department; and Director, Bureau of Educational Studies and Testing; Indiana University, Bloomington, Indiana.*

The ITPA departs from the standard kit of individual tests in the psychometrist's cabinet in that it is not intended to be an intelligence test and it emphasizes intraindividual, rather than interindividual, differences. It is a test of language, perception, and short-term memory abilities. Since so many school learning problems are tied to these skills, this test presents a unique tool for diagnosing school learning difficulties. The test also has the desirable quality of being based on a reasonably well developed psycholinguistic theory, Charles Osgood's model. This theory describes the receptive process for language; the organizing process—which deals with the internal manipulation of percepts, concepts, and symbols; and the expressive process. The ITPA attempts to assess quality of performance within each of these three processes. Visual and auditory channels of input, and vocal and motor channels of output provide the bases for assessment.

The 1968 ITPA departs from the 1961 edition primarily in that the revised edition attempts to tease out the assessment of processes into more specific operations. Therefore, 12 subscales are included in the test, whereas the 1961 edition had only 9. The new tests are designed primarily to extend the assessment of the child's ability to put bits of a communication together into an organized whole. These new tests include a test of Visual Closure, Auditory Closure, and Sound Blending. The last two subtests are for optional use.

Since the test is designed to identify departures from "normal," the standardization population included only children who demonstrated average intellectual functioning, average school achievement, average personal-social adjustment, who had sensory-motor integrity, and who came from predominantly English-speaking homes. Therefore, norms are available for average children alone and run from ages 2 to 10. The children tested for normative data came from five Midwestern towns of moderate size. A wider sample of children probably would have been desirable, including both large metropolitan and clearly rural areas.

The standardization sample was also from homes slightly above the national average in income and education, with middle occupational levels slightly overrepresented at the expense of lower levels. The sample clearly underrepresents Negroes, and the number of Spanish-American children is not reported. In addition, it is interesting to note that almost none of the preschool children screened were rejected from the normative group, whereas more than half of the school-age children screened were rejected. One wonders if the character of preschool norms, compared to norms on older children, is influenced by this factor.

In the collection of normative data, 17 examiners were employed. Only three of these were male. Noting differences in responses obtained by different examiners on individual tests, one may wonder if the disproportionately large number of female examiners influenced the normative data.

Since the profile of tests is designed to be diagnostic, subtest reliabilities and intercorrelations are especially important. Because the standardization sample for the ITPA is limited to "normal" children, an obvious restriction in range of scores must occur. Since this typically results in lower reliabilities, the authors have reported both the obtained reliabilities and estimates of the reliabilities for "the full range of intelligence." There are 12 subtests and a composite at each of eight age levels, resulting in 104 internal consistency coefficients. Of the 104 uncorrected reliabilities, 51 fall below .80, 23 below .70, and 15 above .90. The corresponding numbers for the corrected-for-range estimates are 15, 6, and 40, respectively. The tests appear to be reasonably reliable at each age level, with Visual Closure and Auditory Closure the least reliable subtests in the battery. Visual Closure reliabilities range from .49 to .71 (corrected estimates, .67 to .83). The Auditory Closure data are only slightly better.

As a measure of stability, a retest of the ITPA was conducted after a five- to six-month interval for three age groups (71 4-year-olds, 55 6-year-olds, and 72 8-year-olds). The retest reliabilities for the 12 subtests range from .12 to .86, with median .50; the corrected-for-range estimates range from .28 to .90, with median .71. The retest correlations for the Composite score are .83, .70, and .70, respectively, for the three age groups.

If a test such as the ITPA is going to be diagnostic, the differences between pairs of scores in a child's profile must be stable. The authors report median reliabilities of the differences among all subtest pairs, ranging from .57 to .88, with median .74; the corrected-for-range reliabilities range from .67 to .91, with median .81. Score profiles appear to be moderately stable.

Several types of validity data are available that fit the construct on which the ITPA was based. The tests correlate poorly with social class and poorly with Stanford-Binet scores. However, a substantial amount of validity information still must be collected before hard data can be presented to define the behaviors associated with performance on each of the subtests in the ITPA.

In summary, the revised ITPA allows the examiner to assess psycholinguistic behavior in more detail than the earlier edition, and does it with moderate reliability and with a fairly stable profile of scores. However, scores hold up only fairly well with time. Further, the standardization group has a "middle America" bias, with minority groups clearly underrepresented. Much research is still needed before confident statements can be made concerning validity. Nevertheless, the test has been carefully constructed and goes far toward extending

Illinois Test of Psycholinguistic Abilities

the psychometrist's ability to diagnose learning difficulties effectively.

[443]

★[Re Illinois Test of Psycholinguistic Abilities] A Filmed Demonstration of the ITPA. 1969; black and white 16 mm. instructional sound film demonstrating the administration of the ITPA; $360 per film, cash orders postpaid; rental fee, $12 (available from University of Illinois Visual Aids Service); running time, 43 minutes; University of Illinois Press.

Except Children 36(8):631 Ap '70. *Don Mahler.* Of all the new tests introduced during the Decade of the 60's (to borrow a current popular phrase) and used by special educators, the Illinois Test of Psycholinguistic Abilities certainly must be one of the most popular. Experienced administrators of individual tests probably can teach themselves the ITPA in a reasonably short time without this film, but its use should shorten the learning period as well as result in a more standardized administration. For the neophyte, the film should provide an invaluable introduction and supplement to the manual. The film itself is simple in format. Mrs. Kirk administers the test to a young boy while Dr. Samuel Kirk provides occasional narration. Some items of the ITPA have been eliminated in order to reduce the overall length, but all of the subtests are included. This reviewer is mindful of the problems inherent in making a testing film but would like to offer a few comments. Using other camera angles— perhaps one from the right to show more of John's expressions and another to illustrate the actual scoring more clearly—would provide more visual interest as well as more information to the student examiner. A brief guide addressed specifically to some of the questions apt to be generated by the contents would be helpful. This latter comment arises because about half way through the film the examinee shows signs of tiredness/anxiety and near the end he appears to be saying, "Let's stop. I've had enough." Several natural questions arise. For example, Do the authors of the ITPA feel this is significant in this instance? How might the examiner deal with it? Was the filming session a major contributing factor? In the reviewer's opinion, the film should be shown only after the viewer has read the manual and has developed some familiarity with the test materials. Maximum benefits will be obtained from two viewings, with the second broken into segments for discussion purposes if used in a training class.

[444]

*Perceptual Speed (Identical Forms). Grades 9–16 and industrial employees; 1956–66; 1 form ('56, 8 pages); revised manual ('66, 20 pages); norms for males only; $4 per 20 tests, postage extra; $2 per specimen set, postpaid; 5(10) minutes; L. L. Thurstone (test), T. E. Jeffrey (test), and Norman J. Kantor (manual); Industrial Relations Center, University of Chicago. *

REFERENCES
1. BOND, GUY L., AND DYKSTRA, ROBERT. "The Cooperative Research Program in First-Grade Reading Instruction." *Read Res Q* 2:5–142 su '67. * (*PA* 42:4557)
2. BAEHR, MELANY E.; FURCON, JOHN E.; AND FROEMEL, ERNEST C. *Psychological Assessment of Patrolman Qualifications in Relation to Field Performance.* Washington, D.C.: United States Government Printing Office, 1969. Pp. vii, 246. *

For a review by Leroy Wolins, see 6:556.

[445]

★Remote Associates Test. College and adults; 1967, c1959–67; RAT; "ability to think creatively"; Forms 1 ('67, 4 pages), 2 ('67, 4 pages, "in an experimental stage"); manual ('67, 17 pages); $3.60 per 35 tests; 60¢ per manual; $1.20 per specimen set; postage extra; 40(45) minutes; Sarnoff A. Mednick and Martha T. Mednick; Houghton Mifflin Co. *

REFERENCES
1. ANDREWS, FRANK MEREDITH. *Creativity and the Scientist.* Doctor's thesis, University of Michigan (Ann Arbor, Mich.), 1962. (*DA* 23:3524)
2. MEDNICK, SARNOFF A. "The Associative Basis of the Creative Process." *Psychol R* 69:220–32 My '62. * (*PA* 37:6161)
3. MEDNICK, SARNOFF A., AND MEDNICK, MARTHA T. "A Theory and Test of Creative Thought," pp. 40–7. (*PA* 37:4961) In *Industrial and Business Psychology.* Proceedings of the XIV International Congress of Applied Psychology, Vol. 5. Copenhagen, Denmark: Munksgaard Ltd., 1962. Pp. 229. *
4. JENKINS, ADELBERT HOWARD. *Tolerance for Unrealistic Experience as a Cognitive Control.* Doctor's thesis, University of Michigan (Ann Arbor, Mich.), 1963. (*DA* 24:834)
5. LAHN, MARION. *Some Effects of Conflict on Creative Thinking.* Doctor's thesis, University of Michigan (Ann Arbor, Mich.), 1963. (*DA* 24:835)
6. MEDNICK, MARTHA T. "Research Creativity in Psychology Graduate Students." *J Consult Psychol* 27:265–6 Je '63. * (*PA* 38:958)
7. WALKER, HOWARD EDGAR. *Relationships Between Predicted School Behavior and Measures of Creative Potential.* Doctor's thesis, University of Michigan (Ann Arbor, Mich.), 1963. (*DA* 24:636)
8. WHITTEMORE, ROBERT GEORGE, JR. *Modification of Originality Responses in Academically Talented, Male University Freshmen.* Doctor's thesis, Arizona State University (Tempe, Ariz.), 1963. (*DA* 25:6403)
9. DATTA, LOIS-ELLIN. "A Note on the Remote Associates Test, United States Culture, and Creativity." *J Appl Psychol* 48:184–5 Je '64. * (*PA* 39:6064)
10. DATTA, LOIS-ELLIN. "Remote Associates Test as a Predictor of Creativity in Engineers." *J Appl Psychol* 48:183 Je '64. * (*PA* 39:6063)
11. EASTERBROOK, CAROLYN M. *Pursuit of a Quest: Mortalities Along the Way. A Study of a Selected Group of Variables Relative to the Holding Power of the Art Teaching Profession.* Doctor's thesis, Wayne State University (Detroit, Mich.), 1964. (*DA* 26:4478)
12. FLEISCHER, GERALD. *The Effects of Anxiety Upon Tests of Creativity.* Doctor's thesis, State University of New York (Buffalo, N.Y.), 1964. (*DA* 25:5372)
13. GINSBURG, GERALD PHILLIP. *Creative Potential and Childhood Antecedents.* Doctor's thesis, University of Michigan (Ann Arbor, Mich.), 1964. (*DA* 25:3725)
14. MALTZMAN, IRVING; BELLONI, MARIGOLD; AND FISHBEIN, MARTIN. "Experimental Studies of Associative Variables in Originality." *Psychol Monogr* 78(3):1–21 '64. * (*PA* 39:1785)
15. MEDNICK, MARTHA T.; MEDNICK, SARNOFF A.; AND JUNG, CHARLES C. "Continual Association as a Function of Level of Creativity and Type of Verbal Stimulus." *J Abn & Social Psychol* 69:511–5 N '64. * (*PA* 39:7824)
16. MEDNICK, MARTHA T.; MEDNICK, SARNOFF A.; AND MEDNICK, EDWARD V. "Incubation of Creative Performance and Specific Associative Priming." *J Abn & Social Psychol* 69:84–8 Jl '64. * (*PA* 39:1786)
17. RAINWATER, JANETTE MUNKITTRICK. *Effects of Set on*

Relation to Nursing. Doctor's thesis, Indiana University (Bloomington, Ind.), 1962. *(DA* 23:4323)

4. PHATAK, PRAMILA. "Exploratory Study of Creativity and Intelligence and Scholastic Achievement." *Psychol Studies* 7:1–9 Ja '62. * *(PA* 37:2013)

5. RAY, PHILIP BOND. *A Descriptive Study of Certain Characteristics of "High Creative" Freshman Arts College Students as Compared With "High Academic Potential" Students.* Doctor's thesis, University of Minnesota (Minneapolis, Minn.), 1962. *(DA* 24:1924)

6. TORRANCE, E. PAUL. *Guiding Creative Talent,* pp. 44–64, 213–54. Englewood Cliffs, N.J.: Prentice-Hall, Inc., 1962. Pp. xi, 278. *

7. ANDERSON, RODNEY EARL. *A Comparison of the Performance of College Freshmen Participants and Non-Participants in an Honors Program on Four Psychological Measures.* Doctor's research study No. 1, Colorado State College (Greeley, Colo.), 1963. *(DA* 25:279)

8. BLOCKHUS, WANDA ALEXANDER. *Creativity and Money Management Understandings.* Doctor's thesis, University of Minnesota (Minneapolis, Minn.), 1963. *(DA* 25:2373)

9. EVEN, ROBERT LAWRENCE. *An Experimental Study of the Comparative Effect of Selected Art Experiences on the Creative Performance and Attitudes of Academically Superior Students.* Doctor's thesis, University of Minnesota (Minneapolis, Minn.), 1963. *(DA* 24:4470)

10. JOHNSON, RICHARD THEODORE. *The Growth of Creative Thinking Abilities in Western Samoa.* Doctor's thesis, University of Minnesota (Minneapolis, Minn.), 1963. *(DA* 24:1922)

11. KETCHERSIDE, WILLIAM JOSEPH. *Creative and Adjustive Factors Involved in Educational Development Beyond Expectancy.* Doctor's thesis, University of Missouri (Columbia, Mo.), 1963. *(DA* 24:4545)

12. LUCHT, WAYNE EDWARD. *Creativity: A Study of Relationships.* Doctor's thesis, State University of Iowa (Iowa City, Iowa), 1963. *(DA* 24:4085)

13. McELVAIN, JUDITH L.; FRETWELL, LORETTA N.; AND LEWIS, ROLAND B. "Relationships Between Creativity and Teacher Variability." *Psychol Rep* 13:186 Ag '63. * *(PA* 38:6665)

14. ROUGHTON, EDGAR LEROY. *Creativity as a Factor in Reading Achievement.* Doctor's thesis, University of South Carolina (Columbia, S.C.), 1963. *(DA* 25:1012)

15. ROUSE, SUE THOMPSON. *Effects of a Training Program on the Productive Thinking of Educable Mental Retardates.* Doctor's thesis, George Peabody College for Teachers (Nashville, Tenn.), 1963. *(DA* 25:1053)

16. WODTKE, KENNETH HENRY. *A Study of the Reliability and Validity of Creativity Tests at the Elementary School Level.* Doctor's thesis, University of Utah (Salt Lake City, Utah), 1963. *(DA* 24:4091)

17. BECK, ELIZABETH JOAN. *Relation Between Social Impact and Selected Intellectual Traits in Preadolescent Negro Boys.* Doctor's thesis, Fordham University (New York, N.Y.), 1964. *(DA* 25:1328)

18. BISH, GERTRUDE GANTZ. *A Study of the Relationships of Intelligence, Achievement, Creativity, Anxiety, and Confidence Among Intermediate Grade Pupils in a Suburban Area Elementary School.* Doctor's thesis, George Washington University (Washington, D.C.), 1964.

19. CICIRELLI, VICTOR GEORGE. *The Relationship Between Measures of Creativity, IQ, and Academic Achievement; Interaction and Threshold Effects.* Doctor's thesis, University of Michigan (Ann Arbor, Mich.), 1964. *(DA* 25:3388)

20. DEVER, WAYMAN TODD. *The Relationship Between the Creative Thinking Ability of Selected Fourth Graders and Parental Attitudes.* Doctor's thesis, North Texas State University (Denton, Tex.), 1964. *(DA* 25:3390)

21. DUKES, BEN MARSHALL. *Anxiety, Self Concept, Reading Achievement, and Creative Thinking in Four Socio-Economic Status Levels.* Doctor's thesis, University of Alabama (University, Ala.), 1964. *(DA* 25:7076)

22. ELLINGER, BERNICE DEES. *The Home Environment and the Creative Thinking Ability of Children.* Doctor's thesis, Ohio State University (Columbus, Ohio), 1964. *(DA* 25:6308)

23. GOLDMAN, R. J. "The Minnesota Tests of Creative Thinking." *Ed Res* 7:3–14 N '64. * *(PA* 39:10114)

24. HANSON, DORIS ELIZABETH. *Home Economists in Overseas Work.* Doctor's thesis, Columbia University (New York, N.Y.), 1964. *(DA* 26:346)

25. HAVEN, GEORGE A., JR. *Creative Thought, Productivity, and the Self-Concept.* Doctor's thesis, University of Minnesota (Minneapolis, Minn.), 1964. *(DA* 25:2030)

26. MEARIG, JUDITH SUZANNE. *Fluency and Dependency as Predictors of Sex Differences in Ability and Achievement.* Doctor's thesis, University of Michigan (Ann Arbor, Mich.), 1964. *(DA* 25:3401)

27. OWENS, RICHARD E. *The Relationship of Creative Thinking Ability to Extreme Over and Underachievement.* Doctor's thesis, Colorado State College (Greeley, Colo.), 1964. *(DA* 25:5122)

28. POGUE, BETTY CASKEY. *An Exploration of the Interrelationship Among Creativity, Self-Esteem and Race.* Doctor's thesis, Ball State Teachers College (Muncie, Ind.), 1964. *(DA* 26:3155)

29. RAGOUZIS, PERRY NICHOLAS. *An Experimental Study of the Effects of Non-Grading of Student Art Products on Selected Aspects of Creativity, Personality Adjustment and Art Quality in Art Education Courses for Elementary School Teachers.* Doctor's thesis, University of Minnesota (Minneapolis, Minn.), 1964. *(DA* 26:877)

30. RAMBO, FLORENCE LASSETER. *Pupil Characteristics Related to Creativity.* Doctor's thesis, University of Georgia (Athens, Ga.), 1964. *(DA* 25:2857)

31. SMITH, ROBERT HOUSTON. *A Study of Pre-Adolescent Boys Demonstrating Varying Levels of Creativity With Regard to Their Social Adjustment, Peer Acceptance and Academically Related Behavior.* Doctor's thesis, North Texas State University (Denton, Tex.), 1964. *(DA* 25:4553)

32. TRUE, SALLY RALSTON. *A Study of the Relation of General Semantics and Creativity.* Doctor's thesis, University of Wisconsin (Madison, Wis.), 1964. *(DA* 25:2390)

33. WALLACE, HAROLD RONALD. *Creative Thinking: A Factor in the Performance of Industrial Salesmen.* Doctor's thesis, University of Minnesota (Minneapolis, Minn.), 1964. *(DA* 26:4463)

34. WODTKE, KENNETH H. "Some Data on the Reliability and Validity of Creativity Tests at the Elementary School Level." *Ed & Psychol Meas* 24:399–408 su '64. * *(PA* 39:5110)

35. YAMAMOTO, KAORU. "Evaluation of Some Creativity Measures in a High School With Peer Nominations as Criteria." *J Psychol* 58:285–93 O '64. * *(PA* 39:5138)

36. YAMAMOTO, KAORU. *Experimental Scoring Manuals for Minnesota Tests of Creative Thinking and Writing.* Kent State University, Bureau of Educational Research, Research Monograph Series, No. 1. Kent, Ohio: the Bureau, May 1964. Pp. 160. *

37. YAMAMOTO, KAORU. "Role of Creative Thinking and Intelligence in High School Achievement." *Psychol Rep* 14:783–9 Je '64. * *(PA* 39:5140)

38. YEE, GEORGE FONG. *The Influences of Problem-Solving Instruction and Personal-Social Adjustment Upon Creativity Test Scores of Twelfth Grade Students.* Doctor's thesis, Pennsylvania State University (University Park, Pa.), 1964. *(DA* 26:916)

39. CICIRELLI, VICTOR G. "Form of the Relationship Between Creativity, IQ, and Academic Achievement." *J Ed Psychol* 56:303–8 D '65. * *(PA* 40:3373)

40. DAUW, DEAN CHARLES. *Life Experiences, Vocational Needs and Choices of Original Thinkers and Good Elaborators.* Doctor's thesis, University of Minnesota (Minneapolis, Minn.), 1965. *(DA* 26:5223)

41. DAVIS, O. L., JR., AND YAMAMOTO, KAORU. "Creative Thinking and Achievement Item Responses of Elementary School Pupils: A Preliminary Investigation." *J Peabody Ed* 42:349–55 My '65. *

42. EASTWOOD, GORDON R. "Divergent Thinking and Academic Success." *Ont J Ed Res* 7:241–54 sp '65. * *(PA* 39:16453)

43. GOWAN, J. C., AND TORRANCE, E. P. "An Intercultural Study of Non-Verbal Ideational Fluency." *Gifted Child Q* 9:13–5+ sp '65. * *(PA* 39:12005)

44. HADLEY, DONALD JAMES. *Experimental Relationships Between Creativity and Anxiety.* Doctor's thesis, University of Michigan (Ann Arbor, Mich.), 1965. *(DA* 26:2586)

45. KELLY, GEORGE RICHARD. *Creativity, School Attitude, and Intelligence Relationships in Grades: Four, Six, and Eight.* Doctor's thesis, University of New Mexico (Albuquerque, N.M.), 1965. *(DA* 25:6390)

46. KELSON, FLORENCE. *An Assessment of Creativity in the Retarded Child.* Doctor's thesis, Yeshiva University (New York, N.Y.), 1965. *(DA* 26:3478)

47. KIRSH, JACK LORIN. *Relationship Between Certain Teacher Personality Traits and Background Experiences and Teacher Preference for Working With Children Who Exhibit a High Degree of Originality.* Doctor's thesis, University of Florida (Gainesville, Fla.), 1965. *(DA* 27:704A)

48. PALERMO, RICHARD RANDOLPH. *A Study of the Relationship of Students' Descriptions of Teachers' Styles of Teaching and Teachers' Creativity.* Doctor's thesis, Western Reserve University (Cleveland, Ohio), 1965. *(DA* 27:130A)

49. PATON, CORA LOUISE. *Divergent Thinking and Language Enrichment of Nursery School Children.* Doctor's thesis, Florida State University (Tallahassee, Fla.), 1965. *(DA* 26:4456)

50. RODERICK, JAMES LEROY. *An Investigation of Selected Factors of the Creative Thinking Ability of Music Majors in a Teacher Training Program.* Doctor's thesis, University of Illinois (Urbana, Ill.), 1965. *(DA* 26:409)

51. ROUSE, SUE T. "Effects of a Training Program on the Productive Thinking of Educable Mental Retardates." *Am J Mental Def* 69:666–73 Mr '65. * *(PA* 39:13001)

52. SCOTT, LEON EDWARD. *Underachievers as Contrasted to Overachievers With Respect to Creative Ability, Achievement Motivation, Self-Control, and Parental Aspirations.* Doctor's thesis, University of Nebraska (Lincoln, Neb.), 1965. *(DA* 26:5881)

53. SHELDON, MARGARET JEAN REED. *A Statistical Study of the Reliability of a Single Paper and Pencil Test of Creativity.* Master's thesis, American University (Washington, D.C.), 1965. *(Masters Abstracts* 5:4)

54. TORRANCE, E. PAUL. "Scientific Views of Creativity and Factors Affecting Its Growth." *Daedalus* 94:663–81 su '65. *
55. TORRANCE, E. PAUL, AND DAUW, DEAN C. "Aspirations and Dreams of Three Groups of Creatively Gifted High School Seniors and a Comparable Unselected Group." *Gifted Child Q* 9:177–82 w '65. * (*PA* 40:5281)
56. TUCKER, CASEY ALLEN. *Creativity and Its Relationship to Success in College as Measured by the Grade Point Average.* Doctor's research study No. 1, Colorado State College (Greeley, Colo.), 1965. (*DA* 26:5275)
57. VAN PELT, BOBBY NEWELL. *A Study of Creativity and Other Selected Variables as Related to Academic Achievement in the Upper Elementary Grades.* Doctor's thesis, University of New Mexico (Albuquerque, N.M.), 1965. (*DA* 26:5884)
58. YAMAMOTO, KAORU. "Effects of Restriction of Range and Test Unreliability on Correlation Between Measures of Intelligence and Creative Thinking." *Brit J Ed Psychol* 35:300–5 N '65. * (*PA* 40:2876)
59. CAREY, JOSEPH EDWARD. *The Relationship Between Creative Thinking Ability, Intellectual Ability, Educational Achievement, and Writing Ability of Sixth Grade Children.* Doctor's thesis, Indiana University (Bloomington, Ind.), 1966. (*DA* 27:2095A)
60. CICIRELLI, VICTOR G. "Vocational Aspirations and Creativity." *J Ed Res* 60:68–70 O '66. *
61. COLLINS, DWANE R.; COLLINS, MYRTLE T.; AND LETON, DONALD A. "The Effects of the Flight Technique of Teaching on Creativity Scores." *J Exp Ed* 34:32–7 su '66. * (*PA* 40:11154)
62. DAUW, DEAN C. "Career Choices of High and Low Creative Thinkers." *Voc Guid Q* 15:135–40 D '66. * (*PA* 41:12658)
63. DAUW, DEAN C. "Life Experiences of Original Thinkers and Good Elaborators." *Excep Children* 32:433–40 F '66. * (*PA* 40:6632)
64. DAUW, DEAN C. "Personality Self-Descriptions of Original Thinkers and Good Elaborators." *Psychol Sch* 3:78–9 Ja '66. *
65. DAUW, DEAN C. "Scholastic Aptitudes and Vocational Needs of Original Thinkers and Good Elaborators." *Personnel & Guid J* 45:171–5 O '66. *
66. DAVIS, DONALD JACK. *The Effects of Two Methods of Teaching Art Upon Creative Thinking, Art Attitudes, and Aesthetic Quality of Art Products in Beginning College Art Students.* Doctor's thesis, University of Minnesota (Minneapolis, Minn.), 1966. (*DA* 27:2272A)
67. DUENK, LESTER G. "A Study of the Concurrent Validity of the Minnesota Tests of Creative Thinking for Eighth Grade Industrial Arts Students." *J Indus Teach Ed* 3:30–5 sp '66. *
68. DUENK, LESTER GERALD. *A Study of the Concurrent Validity of the Minnesota Tests of Creative Thinking, Abbr. Form VII, for Eighth Grade Industrial Arts Students.* Doctor's thesis, University of Minnesota (Minneapolis, Minn.), 1966. (*DA* 27:1653A)
69. FUQUA, NORMAN VINCE. *An Analysis of the Relationships and Differences Among Measures of Creative Thinking and Selected Other Factors in Educable and Less Educable Groups of Negro Children.* Doctor's thesis, Wayne State University (Detroit, Mich.), 1966. (*DA* 27:2314A)
70. GROVER, BURTON L. "Prediction of Achievement in Divergent and Convergent Learning Situations." *J Ed Res* 59: 402–5 My-Je '66. * (*PA* 40:11488)
71. GUTH, ROBERT OTTO. *Creativity, Competitive Drive, and Interest Patterns Associated With Success in a Program for Academically Talented High School Students.* Doctor's thesis, Temple University (Philadelphia, Pa.), 1966. (*DA* 27:3692A)
72. HAMBY, TRUDY M. *An Investigation of the Relationship Between Teacher Structuring and Change in Children's Creative Performance and Self-Ideal Self Reports.* Doctor's thesis, University of Maryland (College Park, Md.), 1966. (*DA* 27:993A)
73. HUGUELET, PATRICIA WILLIAMS. *A Perceptual Approach to the Creative Process.* Doctor's thesis, University of Michigan (Ann Arbor, Mich.), 1966. (*DA* 27:2069A)
74. LAYNOR, HAROLD ARTHUR. *Some Indicators of Levels of Creativity in Eighth Grade Pupils (A Comparison of Artwork Judgment and Teacher Choice With Selected Tests From the Minnesota Creativity Test Battery).* Doctor's thesis, State University of New York (Albany, N.Y.), 1966. (*DA* 27:4047A)
75. MACDOUGALL, MARY JULIA. *Relationship of Critical Reading and Creative Thinking Abilities in Children.* Doctor's thesis, Ohio State University (Columbus, Ohio), 1966. (*DA* 27:3779A)
76. MAYHON, WOODROW G. *The Relationship of Creativity to Achievement and Other Student Variables.* Doctor's thesis, University of New Mexico (Albuquerque, N.M.), 1966. (*DA* 27:1713A)
77. OLSON, DAVID R.; RUMLEY, EVELYN; REARDON, BARBARA; AND GILL, MARY JANE. "Creativity and Social Acceptability." *Can Ed & Res Dig* 6:205–8 S '66. *
78. PERRY, JOYCE MARLENE. *Correlates of Teacher Prediction for Student Success Six Years Beyond Sixth Grade.* Doctor's thesis, University of Illinois (Urbana, Ill.), 1966. (*DA* 27:2012A)
79. SMITH, DAVID LYLE. *An Exploratory Study of a Means for Assessing Both Creativity and Conformity of First Graders.* Doctor's thesis, Michigan State University (East Lansing, Mich.), 1966. (*DA* 28:158A)
80. STAFFORD, RICHARD LINDSAY. *The Effects of Creativity and Intelligence on Information Seeking Strategies Used in a Problem Solving Task by Sixth Grade Boys.* Doctor's thesis, University of Houston (Houston, Tex.), 1966. (*DA* 27:973B)
81. TORRANCE, E. PAUL, AND DAUW, DEAN C. "Attitude Patterns of Creatively Gifted High School Seniors." *Gifted Child Q* 10:53–7 su '66. * (*PA* 41:788)
82. TRUE, SALLY. "A Study of the Relation of General Semantics and Creativity." *J Exp Ed* 34:34–40 sp '66. * (*PA* 40:8079)
83. WIRTH, JANINA WIRPSA. *Relationships Between Teacher Opinions of Disadvantaged Children and Measures of Selected Characteristics of These Children.* Doctor's thesis, University of Florida (Gainesville, Fla.), 1966. (*DA* 27:1290A)
84. YAMAMOTO, KAORU, AND CHIMBIDIS, MARIA E. "Achievement, Intelligence, and Creative Thinking in Fifth Grade Children: A Correlational Study." *Merrill-Palmer Q* 12:233–41 Jl '66. * (*PA* 41:5818)
85. YAMAMOTO, KAORU, AND FRENGEL, BARBARA A. "An Exploratory Component Analysis of the Minnesota Tests of Creative Thinking." *Calif J Ed Res* 17:220–9 S '66. * (*PA* 41:28–8)
86. BELLIN, ADELAIDA PEINADO. *Creative Thinking Ability and Its Relationship to Reading Comprehension and Intelligence of Fourth Grade Pupils.* Doctor's thesis, University of Minnesota (Minneapolis, Minn.), 1967. (*DA* 28:2429A)
87. BENTON, JOHN ELDON. *A Study of the Relationship of Openness and Drive to Creativity.* Doctor's thesis, Arizona State University (Tempe, Ariz.), 1967. (*DA* 28:995A)
88. BILON, LOUISA RUSSELL. *Improving Children's Creative Thinking Through Group Discussion Treatment of Mothers: An Experimental Study of the Impact of Group Discussion on Maternal Attitudes and on Children's Creative Thinking.* Doctor's thesis, George Washington University (Washington, D.C.), 1967. (*DA* 28:2618B)
89. BROOME, LILLIAN WISLER. *The Effect of Teachers' Creativity on Children's Learning.* Doctor's thesis, Temple University (Philadelphia, Pa.), 1967. (*DA* 28:4040A)
90. CAWLEY, JOHN F., AND CHASE, DONNA V. "Productive Thinking in Retarded and Non-Retarded Children." *Brit J Ed Psychol* 37:356–60 N '67. * (*PA* 42:5977)
91. CUMMINGS, SUSAN PAULINE NOLL. *Curiosity as a Measure of Cortical Potential.* Doctor's thesis, Arizona State University (Tempe, Ariz.), 1967. (*DA* 28:1323A)
92. DAUW, DEAN C. "Vocational Interests of Highly Creative Computer Personnel." *Personnel J* 46:653–9 N '67. * (*PA* 42:4632)
93. FLETCHER, KENNETH RICHARD. *Congruence of Self and Ideal-Self in Original and Non-Original High School Seniors.* Doctor's thesis, University of Minnesota (Minneapolis, Minn.), 1967. (*DA* 28:4907A)
94. GENSEMER, IRA BENNETT. *A Study of Psychometric Measures of Creativity and Their Relationship to Field-Dependency, Teacher Proficiency and Attitudes.* Doctor's thesis, Temple University (Philadelphia, Pa.), 1967. (*DA* 29:1128A)
95. GOLDMAN, R. J., AND CLARKE, D. F. "The Minnesota Tests of Creative Thinking—A Note on Scorer Reliability in Follow-Up Studies With English Primary School Children." *Brit J Ed Psychol* 37:115–7 F '67. *
96. HAHN, MARSHALL STERLING. *The Influence of Creativity on the Effectiveness of Two Methods of Instruction.* Doctor's thesis, University of Minnesota (Minneapolis, Minn.), 1967. (*DA* 28:2895A)
97. HENSON, JAMES PINKNEY. *The Creative Thinking Abilities of Elementary Students in Public and Parochial Schools.* Doctor's thesis, Indiana University (Bloomington, Ind.), 1967. (*DA* 28:2094A)
98. HINE, WILLA WASSON. *An Evaluation of Creativity as a Factor in the Development of Problems for Some School Children.* Doctor's thesis, University of Denver (Denver, Colo.), 1967. (*DA* 28:4875A)
99. IRONS, JERRY LEE. *Creative Thinking Abilities of Rural and Urban Elementary School Students.* Doctor's thesis, East Texas State University (Commerce, Tex.), 1967. (*DA* 28:2897A)
100. JENNINGS, BETTY LEA. *A Comparison of Creative and Non-Creative Pre-Service Teachers on Scholastic Aptitude, Academic Achievement, Personality, and Item Sorts on Behavioral Classroom Situation Variables.* Doctor's thesis, University of Oklahoma (Norman, Okla.), 1967. (*DA* 28:987A)
101. JOHNSON, JENNINGS OLIVER. *The Relationship Between Science Achievement and Selected Student Characteristics.* Doctor's thesis, University of Minnesota (Minneapolis, Minn.), 1967. (*DA* 28:2029A)
102. KARIOTH, EMIL JOSEPH. *Creative Dramatics as an Aid in Developing Creative Thinking Abilities.* Doctor's thesis, University of Minnesota (Minneapolis, Minn.), 1967. (*DA* 28:5180A)
103. KUO, YOU-YUH. *A Comparative Study of Creative Thinking Between Delinquent Boys and Non-Delinquent Boys.* Doctor's thesis, University of Maryland (College Park, Md.), 1967. (*DA* 28:1166B)
104. KUO, YOU-YUH. "Creative Thinking: Delinquent vs. Nondelinquent Boys." *J Creative Behav* 1:411–8 f '67. *

105. LANIER, PERRY EUGENE. *A Study of Creativity, Intelligence and Discovery Teaching as Related to Performance in Elementary School Mathematics.* Doctor's thesis, University of Oklahoma (Norman, Okla.), 1967. (*DA* 28:1004A)
106. MCDANIEL, SARAH W. "Counselor Selection: An Evaluation of Instruments." *Counselor Ed & Sup* 6:142-4 w '67. *
107. MACKLER, BERNARD, AND SHONTZ, FRANKLIN C. "Characteristics of Responses to Tests of Creativity." *J Clin Psychol* 23:73-80 Ja '67. * (*PA* 41:5961)
108. MADAUS, GEORGE F. "A Cross-Cultural Comparison of the Factor Structure of Selected Tests of Divergent Thinking." *J Social Psychol* 73:13-21 O '67. * (*PA* 42:650)
109. MADAUS, GEORGE F. "Divergent Thinking and Intelligence: Another Look at a Controversial Question." *J Ed Meas* 4:227-35 w '67. * (*PA* 42:10584)
110. MERRYMAN, EDWARD PAUL. *An Analysis of Open-Closed-Mindedness and Selected Variables as Predictors of Creativity.* Doctor's thesis, Ball State University (Muncie, Ind.), 1967. (*DA* 28:1303A)
111. MIDDENTS, GERALD JOHN. *The Relationship of Creativity and Anxiety.* Doctor's thesis, University of Minnesota (Minneapolis, Minn.), 1967. (*DA* 28:2562A)
112. MITCHELL, BRUCE MARVIN. *An Assessment of Changes in Creativity Factors of Elementary School Children Involved in a Creativity Project.* Doctor's thesis, University of Denver (Denver, Colo.), 1967. (*DA* 28:3376A)
113. MOSS, JEROME, JR., AND DUENK, LESTER G. "Estimating the Concurrent Validity of the Minnesota Tests of Creative Thinking." *Am Ed Res J* 4:387-96 N '67. * (*PA* 42:16421)
114. NEAL, JOYCE A. *A Study of the Creative Ability of Mental Retardates Compared With That of Normal and Gifted Pupils Through Use of the Minnesota Tests of Creative Thinking and Writing.* Master's thesis, University of Louisville (Louisville, Ky.), 1967.
115. OSMAN, HASSAN HAFEZ. *An Investigative Study in the Creative Thinking of Emotionally Disturbed Children in Special Classes.* Doctor's thesis, University of Kansas (Lawrence, Kan.), 1967. (*DA* 28:5210B)
116. PHILIPP, JOAN ALICE. *The Comparison of Motor Creativity With Figural and Verbal Creativity, and Selected Motor Skills.* Doctor's thesis, University of Michigan (Ann Arbor, Mich.), 1967. (*DA* 28:4899A)
117. PLOGMAN, BERNARD EDWARD. *The Creative Relationship Between Art Teachers and Their Ninth Grade Art Students in Art Room Practices, Personality and Pencil Drawing in Catholic Schools.* Doctor's thesis, University of Cincinnati (Cincinnati, Ohio), 1967. (*DA* 28:3534A)
118. POPE, ALLEN LAWRENCE. *An Exploratory Study of Certain Aspects of the Personal-Social Relations of the Highly Creative Student as Compared to the Academically-Intelligent Student.* Doctor's thesis, University of Montana (Missoula, Mont.), 1967. (*DA* 28:1629A)
119. RODERICK, JESSIE ALICE. *Some Relationships Between Creativity and the Reading Preferences and Choices of a Group of Sixth Graders.* Doctor's thesis, Temple University (Philadelphia, Pa.), 1967. (*DA* 28:1012A)
120. ROGERS, DONALD WESLEY. *A Comparison of Selected Art Abilities of Elementary School Students From Varying Socio-economic Levels.* Doctor's thesis, University of Connecticut (Storrs, Conn.), 1967. (*DA* 28:3381A)
121. SOLIMAN, ABDALLA MAHMOUD. *A Study of the Relationships Between Creativity, Social Class, Social Mobility, and Vocational Goals of High School Seniors.* Doctor's thesis, University of Minnesota (Minneapolis, Minn.), 1967. (*DA* 28:3518A)
122. STUBBINGS, JOHN ROBERT, JR. *A Comparison of the Torrance Tests of Creative Thinking and Guilford's Measures of Creative Ability on Sex, Cognitive, and Personality Variables.* Doctor's thesis, University of Virginia (Charlottesville, Va.), 1967. (*DA* 28:4496A)
123. TORRANCE, E. PAUL. "The Minnesota Studies of Creative Behavior: National and International Extensions." *J Creative Behav* 1:137-54 sp '67. * (*PA* 41:15284)
124. WEBER, WILFORD ALEXANDER. *Teacher Behavior and Pupil Creativity.* Doctor's thesis, Temple University (Philadelphia, Pa.), 1967. (*DA* 29:159A)
125. AMRAM, FRED M., AND WILLIAMS, FRANK E. "Creative Thinking Skills and Personality Traits: A Study of Their Relationship Among Young Adults." *J Nat Assn Women Deans & Counselors* 31:176-81 su '68. *
126. ARASTEH, JOSEPHINE D. "Creativity and Related Processes in the Young Child: A Review of the Literature." *J Genetic Psychol* 112:77-108 Mr '68. * (*PA* 42:10353)
127. BELEFF, NICHOLAS. *An Experiment to Increase Ideational Fluency Gain Scores of Ninth Grade Students Through Brainstorming and Questioning Methods, Developmental Exercises, and Social Studies Content.* Doctor's thesis, Indiana University (Bloomington, Ind.), 1968. (*DA* 29:1668A)
128. BOERSMA, FREDERIC J., AND O'BRYAN, KENNETH. "An Investigation of the Relationship Between Creativity and Intelligence Under Two Conditions of Testing." *J Personality* 36:341-8 S '68. * (*PA* 43:3993)
129. BRADFIELD, ROBERT HARRISON. *Divergent and Convergent Thinking: Achievement Motivated Processes.* Doctor's thesis, University of California (Berkeley, Calif.), 1968. (*DA* 29:4272A)
130. BREWTON, BARNEY CAMBON. *Relationships of Sex-Role Identification and Conformity to Creative Thinking.* Doctor's thesis, University of Georgia (Athens, Ga.), 1968. (*DAI* 30:828B)
131. BURKE, BARBARA PATRICIA. *An Exploratory Study of the Relationships Among Third Grade Negro Children's Self-Concept Creativity and Intelligence and Teachers' Perceptions of Those Relationships.* Doctor's thesis, Wayne State University (Detroit, Mich.), 1968. (*DAI* 30:1327A)
132. CALVERT, JOHN F. *An Exploration of Some of the Relationships Between Sense of Humor and Creativity in Children.* Doctor's thesis, Syracuse University (Syracuse, N.Y.), 1968. (*DA* 29:1494B)
133. COONE, JIM GARON. *A Cross-Cultural Study of Sex Differences in the Development of Selected Creative Thinking Abilities.* Doctor's thesis, University of Georgia (Athens, Ga.), 1968. (*DA* 29:4828B)
134. COVINGTON, NEIL RONALD. *Creativity in Culturally Deprived Adolescent Boys.* Doctor's thesis, Florida State University (Tallahassee, Fla.), 1968. (*DA* 29:1608A)
135. DAUW, DEAN C. "Creativity Research on Actuaries." *J Creative Behav* 2:274-80 f '68. * (*PA* 43:14316)
136. FREYERMUTH, ROBERT ALLAN. *A Comparison of the Effects of Various Preschool Experiences Upon the Imaginative Visual Expression of Five-Year-Olds.* Doctor's thesis, University of Miami (Coral Gables, Fla.), 1968. (*DA* 29:2603A)
137. GALLAGHER, MARIE SPELLMAN. *A Comparative Study of the Most Creative and Least Creative Student in Grades 4-8 at the Boston School for the Deaf, Randolph, Massachusetts.* Doctor's thesis, Boston College (Chestnut Hill, Mass.), 1968. (*DAI* 30:130A)
138. GLASS, GENE V. "Correlations With Products of Variables: Statistical Formulation and Implications for Methodology." *Am Ed Res J* 5:721-8 N '68. *
139. HATFIELD, ROBERT C. *A Study of the Relationships of Selected Components of Creativity, Cognitive Style, and Self-Concept Identified in a Random Sample of Twelfth Grade Students in One High School With Their Learning of Selected Information in the Social Studies.* Doctor's thesis, Wayne State University (Detroit, Mich.), 1968. (*DAI* 30:1334A)
140. HOLMAN, EUGENE RILEY. *An Experimental Investigation Designed to Enhance the Creative Potential and Teaching Ability of Students Majoring in Elementary Education.* Doctor's thesis, Brigham Young University (Provo, Utah), 1968. (*DA* 29:1165A)
141. INGMIRE, BRUCE DOUGLAS. *Relationships Between Creativity Scores and Leadership Behavior in a Group of High School Seniors.* Doctor's thesis, Arizona State University (Tempe, Ariz.), 1968. (*DA* 29:1365A)
142. IRVINE, FLEET RAYMOND. *A Study of Creative Thinking Ability, and Its Relationship to Psychomotor Ability, Mechanical Reasoning Ability, and Vocational Aptitude of Selected High School Industrial Arts Students.* Doctor's thesis, Utah State University (Logan, Utah), 1968. (*DA* 29:1768A)
143. JOHNSON, CAROLYNE MARGARET. *The Creative Thinking, Verbal Intelligence, and Creative Writing Ability of Young Gifted Children.* Doctor's thesis, Case Western Reserve University (Cleveland, Ohio), 1968. (*DA* 29:4187A)
144. KERNALEGUEN, ANNE PAULE. *Creativity Level, Perceptual Style and Peer Perception of Attitudes Towards Clothing.* Doctor's thesis, Utah State University (Logan, Utah), 1968. (*DA* 29:2960B)
145. MANY, WESLEY A., AND ELLIS, JOSEPH R. "Relationships Between Creativity and Report of Self-Concept of Ability for Upper Elementary School Children." *Ill Sch Res* 5:11-5 N '68. *
146. O'ROURKE, RICHARD HUGH. *A Study of the Creative Thinking Abilities, Attitudes, and Achievement of Academically Talented Students in the Honors Program and Regular Classes at Cooley High School, 1962-65.* Doctor's thesis, Wayne State University (Detroit, Mich.), 1968. (*DAI* 30:962A)
147. PANG, HENRY, AND HORROCKS, CAROL. "An Exploratory Study of Creativity in Deaf Children." *Percept & Motor Skills* 27:844-6 D '68. * (*PA* 43:8551)
148. PAULUS, DIETER H., AND RENZULLI, JOSEPH S. "Scoring Creativity Tests by Computer." *Gifted Child Q* 12:79-83 su '68. *
149. RAINA, M. K. "A Study Into the Effect of Competition on Creativity." *Gifted Child Q* 12:217-20 w '68. * (*PA* 43:14318)
150. RITTMAYER, JANE FOEHL. *Relationships Among High Verbal, High Non-Verbal and High Total Creativity Scores and Intelligence, Academic Achievement, Socio-Economic Status and Teacher Judgements.* Doctor's thesis, Rutgers—The State University (New Brunswick, N.J.), 1968. (*DA* 28:4913A)
151. RODERICK, JESSIE A. "Some Relationships Between Creativity and the Reading Preferences and Choices of a Group of Sixth Graders." *Ed Leadership* 26:49-52 O '68. *
152. SCHMIDT, RUSSELL HARRIS. *A Comparative Study of Students; Teachers, and Scientists as Judges of Science Fair Projects.* Doctor's thesis, University of Florida (Gainesville, Fla.), 1968. (*DAI* 30:224A)
153. SHAPIRO, R. J. *Creative Research Scientists.* Psychologica Africana Monograph Supplement No. 4. Johannesburg, South Africa: National Institute for Personnel Research, 1968. Pp. 180. *

154. SHELDON, ERIC. *Parental Child-Rearing Attitudes and Their Relationship to Cognitive Functioning of Their Pre-Adolescent Sons.* Doctor's thesis, Syracuse University (Syracuse, N.Y.), 1968. (*DA* 29:4370B)
155. SOLOMON, ANITA OSTRIN. *A Comparative Analysis of Creative and Intelligent Behavior of Elementary School Children With Different Socio-Economic Backgrounds.* Doctor's thesis, American University (Washington, D.C.), 1968. (*DA* 29:1457A)
156. STEINMETZ, CLOYD S. "Creativity Training: A Testing Program That Became a Sales Training Program." *J Creative Behav* 2:179–86 su '68. * (*PA* 43:6028)
157. THOMPSON, RICHARD ARLEN. *An Evaluation of a Two-Week Workshop in Education (Exploring Creativity).* Doctor's thesis, Ball State University (Muncie, Ind.), 1968. (*DA* 29:1470A)
158. TIBBETTS, JOHN WESLEY. *Relationships of Creativity to Socioeconomic Status, Race, Sex, IQ, Age and Grade-Point Average in an Adolescent Population.* Doctor's thesis, University of Southern California (Los Angeles, Calif.), 1968. (*DA* 29:1174A)
159. TORRANCE, E. PAUL. Chap. 7, "The Measurement of Creative Behavior in Children," pp. 199–222; comments by William J. Tisdall and Charles E. Bish. In *Productive Thinking in Education.* Edited by Mary Jane Aschner and Charles E. Bish. Washington, D.C.: National Education Association, 1968. Pp. x, 349. *
160. TORRANCE, E. PAUL. "Examples and Rationales of Test Tasks for Assessing Creative Abilities." *J Creative Behav* 2:165–78 su '68. * (*PA* 43:5166)
161. TORRANCE, E. PAUL. "A Longitudinal Examination of the Fourth Grade Slump in Creativity." *Gifted Child Q* 12:195–9 w '68. * (*PA* 43:14129)
162. TORRANCE, E. PAUL. *Minnesota Studies of Creative Behavior, 1958–1966.* Greensboro, N.C.: Creativity Research Institute of The Richardson Foundation, Inc., February 1968. Pp. i, 63. *
163. TORRANCE, E. PAUL, AND FORTSON, LAURA R. "Creativity Among Young Children and the Creative-Aesthetic Approach." *Ed* 89:27–30 S-O '68. *
164. TRYK, H. EDWARD. "The Torrance Tests of Creative Thinking," pp. 44–9. In *Advances in Psychological Assessment, Vol. 1.* Edited by Paul McReynolds. Palo Alto, Calif.: Science & Behavior Books, Inc., 1968. Pp. xiii, 336. *
165. ALIOTTI, NICHOLAS CASPER. *The Effects of Warm-Up Activities on the Verbal Creative Thinking Abilities of Disadvantaged First Grade Children.* Doctor's thesis, University of Georgia (Athens, Ga.), 1969. (*DAI* 30:5275A)
166. BAHLKE, SUSAN JOYCE MOORE. *Componential Evaluation of Creativity Instructional Materials.* Doctor's thesis, Purdue University (Lafayette, Ind.), 1969. (*DAI* 30:1426A)
167. BARABASZ, ARREED F. "Test-Retest Reliability of the Torrance Tests of Creative Thinking, and the Relationship Between Intelligence and Figural Creativity." *Child Study Center B* 5(4–5):73–4 S-N '69. * (*PA* 44:16369)
168. BOLTON, SHIRLEY L. "An Introductory Study of Art as Creative Learning for the Rural Culturally Disadvantaged." *Studies Art Ed* 10:50–6 w '69. *
169. BOWERS, JOHN. "Interactive Effects of Creativity and IQ on Ninth-Grade Achievement." *J Ed Meas* 6(3):173–7 f '69. * (*PA* 44:15469)
170. CICIRELLI, VICTOR G. "University Supervisors' Creative Ability and Their Appraisal of Student Teachers' Classroom Performance: An Exploratory Study." *J Ed Res* 62(8):375–81 Ap '69. *
171. COX, OTIS. *Creative Thinking in a High School Experimental Humanities Program.* Doctor's thesis, University of Alabama (University, Ala.), 1969. (*DAI* 31:214A)
172. DACEY, J.; MADAUS, G.; AND ALLEN, A. "The Relationship of Creativity and Intelligence in Irish Adolescents." *Brit J Ed Psychol* 39(3):261–6 N '69. * (*PA* 44:8234)
173. DAVIS, DONALD JACK. "The Effects of Depth and Breadth Methods of Art Instruction Upon Creative Thinking, Art Attitudes, and Aesthetic Quality of Art Products in Beginning College Students." *Studies Art Ed* 10(2):27–40 w '69. *
174. DENT, PAULA ANN. *Creativity in Inner-City Children, in Relation to Aptitude, Achievement, and Background.* Doctor's thesis, Wayne State University (Detroit, Mich.), 1969. (*DAI* 31:1682A)
175. ELSOM, BILLY FRED. *Creative Ability and Perceived Parent-Child Relations.* Doctor's thesis, North Texas State University (Denton, Tex.), 1969. (*DAI* 31:59A)
176. FELTON, THOMAS A., JR. *Correlation Between Creativity as Measured by Torrance Tests of Creative Thinking Figural Forms A and B and Intelligence as Measured by the Lorge-Thorndike Intelligence Test of Fifty Sixth Grade Students.* Master's thesis, Old Dominion University (Norfolk, Va.), 1969.
177. FRICK, RALPH CARL. *An Inquiry Into Certain Aspects of Intuition.* Doctor's thesis, Northern Illinois University (DeKalb, Ill.), 1969. (*DAI* 30:2376A)
178. GROSSMAN, MARVIN JAY. *Developing Aesthetic and Creative Visual Abilities in Kindergarten Children Through a Structured Developmental Art Program.* Doctor's thesis, University of Georgia (Athens, Ga.), 1969. (*DAI* 30:3375A)

179. HILLERY, MILTON C. *The Effects of Lack of Formal School Experience on Performance on Tests of Creative Thinking.* Doctor's thesis, Michigan State University (East Lansing, Mich.), 1969. (*DAI* 30:2376A)
180. JOHNSON, JENNINGS O. "The Relationship Between Science Achievement and Selected Student Characteristics." *Sci Ed* 53(4):307–18 O '69. *
181. JUFFER, VIRGINIA MAHANNAH. *Socialization of Children With Varying Levels of Originality: An Analysis of Parent-Child Interaction.* Doctor's thesis, Iowa State University (Ames, Iowa), 1969. (*DAI* 30:1253A)
182. KALTSOUNIS, BILL. *Factors Related to Creative Thinking Among Deaf and Hearing Children.* Doctor's thesis, University of Georgia (Athens, Ga.), 1969. (*DAI* 30:3324A)
183. KALTSOUNIS, BILL. "Impact of Instruction on Development of Deaf Children's Originality of Thinking." *Percept & Motor Skills* 29(1):298 Ag '69. * (*PA* 44:2802)
184. KOBAYASHI, MICHAEL JUNICHI. *Relationships of Intelligence and Creativity to Anxiety and Extroversion-Introversion in Ninth Grade Japanese Boys.* Doctor's thesis, Boston College (Chestnut Hill, Mass.), 1969. (*DAI* 30:3730A)
185. LICHTMAN, MARILYN VICKMAN. *Intelligence, Creativity, and Language: An Examination of the Interrelationships of Three Variables Among Preschool, Disadvantaged Negro Children.* Doctor's thesis, George Washington University (Washington, D.C.), 1969. (*DAI* 31:1625A)
186. MCCORMACK, ALAN JOSEPH. *The Effect of Selected Teaching Methods on Creative Thinking, Self-Evaluation, and Achievement of Students Enrolled in an Elementary Science Education Methods Course.* Doctor's thesis, Colorado State College (Greeley, Colo.), 1969. (*DAI* 30:4311A)
187. MCCUTCHEON, NANCY SUSAN. *A Study of Relationships Among Creativity, Intelligence, and Test Anxiety of Middle-Class Fourth Grade Boys and Girls.* Doctor's thesis, University of South Carolina (Columbia, S.C.), 1969. (*DAI* 30:4833A)
188. MCWHINNIE, HAROLD J. "Some Relationships Between Creativity and Perception in Fourth Grade Children." *Acta Psychologica* 31(2):169–75 Ag '69. * (*PA* 44:14345)
189. MIDDLETON, FRANCES TALLULAH. *Creative Thinking Abilities of Selected Sixth-Grade Children.* Doctor's thesis, University of Georgia (Athens, Ga.), 1969. (*DAI* 30:5348A)
190. NUTTALL, ENA VAZQUEZ. *Creativity in Boys: A Study of the Influence of Social Background, Educational Achievement, and Parental Attitudes on the Creative Behavior of Ten Year Old Boys.* Doctor's thesis, Boston University (Boston, Mass.), 1969. (*DAI* 31:231A)
191. ORLANDI, LISANIO ROBERT. *Social Class and Subcultural Patterns of Performance in Divergent Thinking of Students in Urban Elementary Schools.* Doctor's thesis, Boston College (Chestnut Hill, Mass.), 1969. (*DAI* 30:4282A)
192. PHILIPP, JOAN A. "Comparison of Motor Creativity With Figural and Verbal Creativity, and Selected Motor Skills." *Res Q* 40(1):163–73 Mr '69. *
193. POLLERT, LESLIE H.; FELDHUSEN, JOHN F.; VAN MONDFRANS, ADRIAN P.; AND TREFFINGER, DONALD J. "Role of Memory in Divergent Thinking." *Psychol Rep* 25(1):151–6 Ag '69. * (*PA* 44:3471)
194. PORTER, CHARLES MACK. *Figures of Speech, Divergent Thinking, and Activation Theory.* Doctor's thesis, North Texas State University (Denton, Tex.), 1969. (*DAI* 30:2384A)
195. RAINA, M. K. "A Study of Sex Differences in Creativity in India." *J Creative Behav* 3(2):111–4 sp '69. *
196. SHERWOOD, DAVID WILLIAM. *The Differential Effects of Assessment Context and Scoring Method on Creativity Performance in Children.* Doctor's thesis, Duke University (Durham, N.C.), 1969. (*DAI* 30:1888B)
197. SHIGAKI, IRENE SHIKIBU. *The Effects of Teacher Strength and Sensitivity and Pupil Intelligence and Creativity on the Production of Divergent Responses.* Doctor's thesis, Columbia University (New York, N.Y.), 1969. (*DAI* 30:3864A)
198. SMITH, GEORGE PRITCHY. *The Relationships Among Selected Variables of Creative Thinking and Visual, Auditory, and Tactual Sensory Perception.* Doctor's thesis, North Texas State University (Denton, Tex.), 1969. (*DAI* 30:4839A)
199. SPRINGER, THOMAS A. *An Experimental Study of the Effects of Group Counseling Upon the Creative Thinking of Selected Senior High School Students.* Doctor's thesis, Ball State University (Muncie, Ind.), 1969. (*DAI* 31:165A)
200. STEVENS, JOHN CULVER. *A Study of the Relationships Between Field Independence, Dogmatism, and Creativity in Rural Seventh Grade Students.* Doctor's thesis, University of Georgia (Athens, Ga.), 1969. (*DAI* 30:2863A)
201. STIMELING, WILLIAM F. *An Investigation of the Relationship of Selected Attributes of Creativity and Success Evaluations of Indiana Public School Superintendents.* Doctor's thesis, Indiana University (Bloomington, Ind.), 1969. (*DAI* 30:4746A)
202. TORRANCE, E. PAUL. "Curiosity of Gifted Children and Performance on Timed and Untimed Tests of Creativity." *Gifted Child Q* 13(3):155–8 au '69. * (*PA* 44:12332)
203. TORRANCE, E. PAUL. "Prediction of Adult Creative Achievement Among High School Seniors." *Gifted Child Q* 13(4):223–9 w '69. * (*PA* 44:14620)
204. TORRANCE, E. PAUL, AND ALIOTTI, NICHOLAS C. "Sex

Differences in Levels of Performance and Test-Retest Reliability on the Torrance Tests of Creative Thinking Ability." *J Creative Behav* 3(1):52–7 w '69. *

205. WALKER, PERRY CRANE. *A Study of Creativity Among Mexican School Children.* Doctor's thesis, University of Georgia (Athens, Ga.), 1969. (*DAI* 31:650A)

206. WELTNER, WILLIAM HAROLD. *Evaluations by Teacher Educators of Observable Behavior Characteristics Used to Predict Creative Teaching Potential of Elementary Education Student Teachers.* Doctor's thesis, Ball State University (Muncie, Ind.), 1969. (*DAI* 31:1128A)

207. WOOD, REBECCA HOLCOMBE. *Three Environmental Press Variables and Their Relationship to Coping Behavior and Creativity in Children.* Doctor's thesis, University of Alabama (University, Ala.), 1969. (*DAI* 30:5306A)

208. BACHTOLD, LOUISE M., AND WERNER, EMMY E. "An Evaluation of Teaching Creative Skills to Gifted Children in Grades 5 and 6." *J Ed Res* 63(6):253–6 F '70. * (*PA* 46:5761)

209. BADER, LAWRENCE JOSEPH. *The Effects of Task-Taking Atmosphere, Level of Creativity and Field-Independence on Creative Production.* Doctor's thesis, Boston University (Boston, Mass.), 1970. (*DAI* 31:2974B)

210. BAILEY, JUNE T.; MCDONALD, FREDERICK J.; AND CLAUS, KAREN E. "Evaluation of the Development of Creative Behavior in an Experimental Nursing Program." *Nursing Res* 19(2):100–8 Mr–Ap '70. *

211. BARRISH, BERNARD. *Inductive Versus Deductive Teaching Strategies With High and Low Divergent Thinkers.* Doctor's thesis, Stanford University (Stanford, Calif.), 1970. (*DAI* 31:4029A)

212. BRUININKS, ROBERT H., AND FELDMAN, DAVID H. "Creativity, Intelligence, and Achievement Among Disadvantaged Children." *Psychol Sch* 7(3):260–4 Jl '70. * (*PA* 45:5015)

213. BURSTINER, IRVING. *Effects of a Workshop in Creative Thinking for Secondary School Department Chairmen—On Their Perceptions of Supervisory Activities, on Problem-Solving, and on Creativity Test Scores.* Doctor's thesis, St. John's University (Jamaica, N.Y.), 1970. (*DAI* 31:3197A)

214. CAVE, RICHARD L. "A Combined Factor Analysis of Creativity and Intelligence." *Multiv Behav Res* 5(2):177–91 Ap '70. * (*PA* 44:16697)

215. CICIRELLI, VICTOR G., AND CICIRELLI, JEAN S. "Counselors' Creative Ability and Attitude in Relation to Counseling Behavior With Disadvantaged Counselees." *J Counsel Psychol* 17(2):177–83 Mr '70. * (*PA* 44:8550)

216. CLARK, PHILIP M., AND MIRELS, HERBERT L. "Fluency as a Pervasive Element in the Measurement of Creativity." *J Ed Meas* 7(2):83–6 su '70. * (*PA* 44:19354)

217. DEWING, K. "Some Correlates of Creativity Test Performance in Seventh Grade Children." *Austral J Psychol* 22(3):269–76 D '70. * (*PA* 46:889)

218. DEWING, KATHLEEN. "The Reliability and Validity of Selected Tests of Creative Thinking in a Sample of Seventh-Grade West Australian Children." *Brit J Ed Psychol* 40(1):35–42 F '70. * (*PA* 44:10128)

219. GROSSMAN, MARVIN. "Perceptual Style, Creativity, and Various Drawing Abilities." *Studies Art Ed* 11(2):51–4 w '70. *

220. HARVEY, O. J.; HOFFMEISTER, JAMES K.; COATES, CAROLIE; AND WHITE, B. JACK. "A Partial Evaluation of Torrance's Tests of Creativity." *Am Ed Res J* 7(3):359–72 My '70. *

221. HURLEY, JOHN DONALD. *The Relationship of Dogmatism With Two Measures of Originality.* Doctor's thesis, Boston University (Boston, Mass.), 1970. (*DAI* 31:2183A)

222. JONES, JOAN C. *A Study of the Effect of a Teaching Strategy in Divergent Thinking Upon the Behavior of Student-Teachers and the Children They Teach.* Doctor's thesis, Boston University (Boston, Mass.), 1970. (*DAI* 31:2231A)

223. KALTSOUNIS, BILL. "Comparative Study of Creativity in Deaf and Hearing Children." *Child Study J* 1(1):11–9 f '70. *

224. KALTSOUNIS, BILL. "Differences in Verbal Creative Thinking Abilities Between Deaf and Hearing Children." *Psychol Rep* 26(3):727–33 Je '70. * (*PA* 45:1133)

225. KALTSOUNIS, BILL. "Intellectual Functioning of Deaf Children." *Percept & Motor Skills* 30(1):49–50 F '70. *

226. KARIOTH, JOSEPH. "Creative Dramatics as Aid in Developing Creative Thinking Abilities." *Speech Teach* 19(4):301–9 N '70. *

227. KEENAN, JUNE F. *The Relationship of Certain Socio-Cultural and Community Factors Among Sixth Grade Students to Creativity in Art.* Doctor's thesis, North Texas State University (Denton, Tex.), 1970. (*DAI* 31:3782A)

228. LANDRY, RICHARD GEORGE. *The Relationship of Second Language Learning to Divergent Thinking Abilities of Students in Urban Schools.* Doctor's thesis, Boston College (Chestnut Hill, Mass.), 1970. (*DAI* 31:2615A)

229. LINDSEY, JAMES F., AND HICKS, DAVID. "A Note on Teaching for Creativity." *Calif J Ed Res* 21(2):84–7 Mr '70. *

230. MCWHINNIE, HAROLD J. "A Third Study of Some Relationships Between Creativity and Perception in 6th Grade Children." *Calif J Ed Res* 21(1):35–42 Ja '70. *

231. MARTIN, FELIX. "Questioning Skills Among Advantaged and Disadvantaged Children in First Grade." *Psychol Rep* 27(2):617–8 O '70. * (*PA* 45:6068)

232. PAULUS, DIETER H. "Are Sub-Tests of the Torrance Test Independent?" Abstract. *Am Ed Res Assn 1970 Ann Meeting Abstr* 2:42–3 '70. *

233. PESCI, MICHAEL LINDEN. *Psychological Differences Between Research, Development and Product Engineers and Their Implications for Placement Decisions.* Doctor's thesis, University of Minnesota (Minneapolis, Minn.), 1970. (*DAI* 31:3048B)

234. RAIA, JAMES R., AND OSIPOW, SAMUEL H. "Creative Thinking Ability and Susceptibility to Persuasion." *J Social Psychol* 82(2):181–6 D '70. * (*PA* 45:6341)

235. RAINA, MAHARAJ K. "Creative, Critical and Power Motivations of High and Low Creative Students." *J Psychol Res* 14(3):107–12 S '70. *

236. RAINA, MAHARAJ K. "Creativity and Teaching Success." *Psychol Rep* 26(1):70 F '70. * (*PA* 45:5001)

237. RAINA, MAHARAJ K. "A Study of Creativity in Teachers." *Psychol Studies* 15(1):28–33 Ja '70. *

238. RAPPEL, DOROTHY. *Teacher-Pupil Interaction at the Elementary Grade Level and Pupil Creativity.* Doctor's thesis, Catholic University of America (Washington, D.C.), 1970. (*DAI* 31:2965B)

239. TORRANCE, E. PAUL. "Influence of Dyadic Interaction on Creative Functioning." *Psychol Rep* 26(2):391–4 Ap '70. * (*PA* 44:20849)

240. TORRANCE, E. PAUL; GOWAN, JOHN C.; WU, JING-JYI; AND ALIOTTI, NICHOLAS C. "Creative Functioning of Monolingual and Bilingual Children in Singapore." *J Ed Psychol* 61(1):72–5 F '70. * (*PA* 44:6532)

241. TREFFINGER, DONALD J., AND RIPPLE, RICHARD E. "Teachers' Ratings of Pupil Creativity." *Child Study J* 1(1):5–10 f '70. *

242. TREFFINGER, DONALD J.; FELDHUSEN, JOHN F.; AND THOMAS, SUSAN BAHLKE. "Relationship Between Teachers' Divergent Thinking Abilities and Their Ratings of Pupils' Creative Thinking Abilities." *Meas & Eval Guid* 3(3):169–76 f '70. * (*PA* 45:10616)

243. BATES, OPAL ELAINE. *The Correlation of Children's Perception of Locus of Control to Originality in Selected Groups of Sixth Grade Children.* Doctor's thesis, Oregon State University (Corvallis, Ore.), 1971. (*DAI* 31:3865A)

LEONARD L. BAIRD, *Research Psychologist, Educational Testing Service, Princeton, New Jersey.*

The *Torrance Tests of Creative Thinking* were designed to measure four aspects of "creative thinking"—fluency, flexibility, originality, and elaboration. Two scores for each aspect are provided—verbal and figural (although norms are not provided for the verbal elaboration scores). The author and publisher recommend that the TTCT be used in research studies of cognitive functioning, individualized instruction, remedial programs, and new educational programs, but also suggest its use for assessing individual students' potentials.

ADMINISTRATION AND SCORING. The manual and administration guide provide clear, detailed and comprehensive directions for administering and scoring the TTCT. The TTCT can be administered individually or in groups. Three figural tests can be given in 30 minutes of testing time, with additional time required for instructions. Seven verbal tasks require 45 minutes of testing time. Since the subjects give free responses to semistructured tasks, the test must be scored by hand. The guides for scoring are quite clear, and the manual discusses scoring errors to avoid. While a rationale is provided for each scale, no empirical evidence of the development of the scoring methods is discussed, with the exception of the originality scale. (The originality scale is based on the statistical rarity of the responses.) A scorer requires some training and experience with the instrument. The reported correlations between scores of inexperienced and experienced scorers are generally in the high 90's, ranging from .66 to .99. However, the inter-scorer agreement among inexperienced scorers (such as some school teachers) will probably be lower. The manual and scoring guide do not provide estimates of the time needed to score each test, but it appears that scoring a test would take a considerable time, even for an experienced scorer. (A scoring service is available through the publisher.)

CONTENT. While the manual includes a sentence that the tests attempt to assess "these test activities in terms of Guilford's divergent thinking factors," no evidence is provided for any relation with Guilford's model, and no effort is made to seek logical connections with Guilford's work. (No correlations of the TTCT with the Guilford battery are reported.) In general the tests seem to be derived from Torrance's long thinking about creativity and tend to be eclectic, rather than based on a systematic theory of creativity. They may be best interpreted as an attempt to measure certain particular aspects of creativity, and not as an attempt to measure all of the important dimensions of creative thinking. Some of the rationales given for the scales are rather vague and discursive. The relation between a scale score and the interpretation provided for the score in some cases seems to be based more on the rationale for the scale than on the evidence provided for it.

RELIABILITY. Creative thinking may be influenced by personality and situational variables, so, as the manual points out, "it is to be expected that motivational conditions affect test-retest reliability" and that motivational aspects are probably controlled more adequately in research studies than in normative studies. Thus, test-retest reliabilities range from .50 to .93 over one- to two-week periods, and from .35 to .73 over three-year periods. Although the reliability studies of the TTCT are well summarized in the manual, many of the studies used only one or a few scales. These studies are not fully reported, so it is difficult to assess them in some cases. However, the diversity of studies and samples suggests that the scales have adequate reliability.

VALIDITY. The manual summarizes more than 50 studies of the validity of the test. The majority of the studies concerned with construct validity are studies of the personalities of high and low scorers. Many of these studies utilize extreme groups without any information about students in the middle; others use designs that compare "creatives" with an "unselected" sample. In spite of these weak designs and many results that show only slight relations, the studies do suggest that the test does measure behaviors consistent with the literature on creative behavior.

In a section on concurrent validity, the TTCT seems to have only slight relations to peer nominations and low relations to teacher nominations. The TTCT seems to be related to both academic intelligence and educational achievement test scores, both in the studies reported in the manual and in subsequent work. This last fact leads to some question about the extent to which the TTCT scales are saturated with general academic aptitude.

The manual partially reports only one study of predictive validity. This same study is the only one involving criteria of *real-life* creative accomplishment. (There is a great difference between a measure of "Planfulness" and actually having "had scientific or scholarly paper published in a scientific or professional journal.") This leads to two criticisms of the TTCT. First, there needs to be much more work examining the predictive validity of the test. Second, the TTCT needs to be firmly linked to reality by showing that it predicts socially valuable creative behavior. It may be that a student could think of many unusual ways to improve a toy in the testing situation but make no original and useful contributions in real-life situations. While the studies in the manual suggest that there could be some predictive validity, the relation remains to be established. And, ultimately, without considerable work on the validity of the test for predicting real-life creativity, it is difficult to evaluate the utility of the test or to compare it with other tests.

NORMS AND INTERPRETATION. Means and standard deviations are provided for a number of samples, most somewhat restricted. The basic groups used for the two main score conversion tables are 118 fifth graders in St. Croix, Wisconsin, and 108 seventh graders. (These identifications are tentative, because the manual is not as clear as it might be about these groups.) No other conversion tables are provided, and

Torrance Tests of Creative Thinking

the scores are converted into T scores, but not to centile ranks or other scales. Of course, one could construct his own conversion tables from the means and standard deviations of other groups, as the manual suggests. The means and standard deviations for the groups used for the conversion tables sometimes vary considerably from the means and standard deviations reported in the manual for other fifth and seventh grade groups. For example, on one scale the mean of the fifth graders in one sample is at the 90th percentile of the one used for the tables. Thus, any interpretation of a score must be quite tentative, at best. Although this would seem to be a major limitation, the manual states, "The author and publisher will continue to accumulate comparison group norms on a variety of kinds of populations ranging from kindergarten through graduate school. There is no plan at the present time to compile what might be called 'children-in-general' type norms." Thus, the norms will apparently continue to be based on restricted, available samples. This tends to make any interpretation of the scores, even in research projects, very tentative. The interpretations provided for the scale scores are clear, but seem to go beyond the evidence presented in the manual.

The scales are supposed to measure independent traits, but the intercorrelations presented in the manual, as well as some factor-analytic evidence (e.g., *232*), suggest that there is a great deal of overlap in the scales.

The manual provides a good deal of information about the studies using the test, but in many places the writing seems to be straining to be persuasive. In a few places, reliance seems to be placed on the "author's belief." There are also occasional arguments with critics. The general format of the manual could be much improved.

SUMMARY EVALUATION. The TTCT seems to be useful as a basis for further research into the nature and nurture of creativity. The work already done with the TTCT has made a considerable contribution to the literature on creative behavior. However, without better norms, studies of predictive validity, and anchoring of the test to real-life creative behavior, the TTCT should probably be used for assessment of an individual's creative potential only with great caution. If the author and publisher could make these changes, as well as other improvements promised in the manual, the test could be a powerful and useful tool for research and practice, thus joining Torrance's other significant contributions to our understanding of creativity.

ROBERT L. THORNDIKE, *Professor of Psychology and Education, Teachers College, Columbia University, New York, New York.*

There seems little question that "creativity" is one of the "in" things in psychology of 1970. Thus, whereas the number of references under this heading in the *Psychological Abstracts* of 1949 was 7 out of 6,530, or 1.1 per 1,000, in 1969 the number was 218 out of 18,068, or 12.1 per 1,000. The curve during this period was positively accelerated and need be extrapolated only about another 20 years for the topic to take over the PA completely.

It is natural, therefore, that the period should have yielded creativity tests. Whereas Guilford's tests were embedded in his larger Structure of Intellect, being primarily measures of various cells in the slab labelled "divergent thinking," Torrance's tests stand as a single and separate publication.

Torrance's tests are of two main types, tests involving words (semantic material, in Guilford's terms) and tests involving pictorial material (figural content). The several verbal subtests appear in one booklet, and the several pictorial in another. Two forms of each are available. It is claimed that either the verbal or the pictorial test can be used from kindergarten through graduate school, though data on reliability and validity are typically limited to elementary and secondary school students. Rather full manuals are provided to guide both the administration and the scoring of the tests.

From each of his tests Torrance extracts scores for fluency, flexibility, originality, and elaboration. Fluency is simply the number of relevant responses given; flexibility is the number of different categories of response; originality is a sum of credits where some routine responses count zero, less common responses get a unit score, and, in some cases, responses too infrequent to be on the list in the manual get a credit of two; and the elaboration score is a count of the additional details used in each response totaled over responses. It is not surprising, under these circumstances, that the fluency, flexibility, and originality scores tend to be highly correlated, since all are accumulated over the same set of responses given by the examinee. Harvey and others (*220*), working with the seven subtests of the verbal test, found the average correlation of the different traits within a single subtest to be .54, while the average correlation for a single trait over the different subtests was .50 for fluency, .32 for flexibility, and .25 for originality. In another study (*19*), the following intercorrelations were obtained among the verbal tests: .79 between fluency and flexibility, .80 between fluency and originality, and .74 between flexibility and originality. The corresponding correlations reported for the figural tests are .77, .68, and .66. An average of the correlations of verbal with pictorial scores gave the following: same trait correlated across tests, .44; different traits correlated across tests, .40. Thus, the evidence of consistently different meaning for the fluency, flexibility, and originality scores is almost vanishingly small.

Results such as these raise serious question as to whether any attention should be paid to the separate scores on each form of the test, or whether a single score for the verbal and one for the pictorial would be more appropriate. The author gives no clear guidance on this point. Scoring and norms emphasize the separate scores, but much of the research on validity of the instrument seems to use a total score as a variable, or contrasting groups formed on the basis of a total score. Unless adequate evidence is provided that the separate scores are accomplishing measurement of really different attributes, and this seems unlikely, it would seem better to think of each test as yielding a **single** total score. It would be desirable that some uniform way of arriving at that score be specified in the scoring guide, so that comparable results might be obtained from one user to another.

Scores on flexibility and originality are so contaminated by the basic fluency component that it is difficult to interpret data on the reliability of either scoring or performance for the flexibility and originality components, after basic fluency of responding has been partialed out. A total score apparently would have fairly adequate alternate-forms reliability—perhaps .85 to .90 for the verbal test and .70 to .80 for the figural test.

The author reports a variety of interesting correlates of scores on one or another of the tests that have gone into the battery. Many of the studies relate to component subtests or to earlier versions of the material, so it is somewhat difficult to pull together a coherent picture of the validity of the instrument in its current published form. However, it should be recognized that the author presents the tests to potential users as a "research edition." Hopefully, their existence in a standard format will lead to a more coherent body of research that will provide systematic information both on their internal structure and their external correlates, so that the would-be user can better judge to what extent they merit their somewhat ambitious title.

Am Ed Res J 5:272–81 Mr '68. Michael A. Wallach. By publishing the *Torrance Tests of Creative Thinking* as a commercial undertaking, the author of these materials is recommending their use as a standard set of assessment procedures that are different from intelligence tests but that, like intelligence tests, will help teachers sift out more from less talented students. * Although called a "research edition," advertising matter presents the tests, together with a series of workbooks and phonograph records, as "a complete program in creative development." The intent, then, is to make available for general use instruments that are presumed to be not just tests of intelligence but tests of creative thinking. Torrance gives a definition of creativity that indicates concern for assessing problem-solving in a general sense. * Effective dealing with the environment, the hallmark of intelligence as generally defined, thus represents the core of Torrance's construal of creative thinking. * The crucial issue....in evaluating the Torrance tests is, of course, their psychological meaning. * the Torrance instruments themselves correlate substantially with intelligence * Rather than viewing peer judgments for fluency as validation for fluency scores from the creativity tests, or peer judgments for flexibility as validation for flexibility scores from the creativity tests, in the manner suggested by Torrance, we have to entertain seriously the more parsimonious hypothesis that general intelligence alone accounts for the degree to which the peer judgments correlate with Torrance scores. * One is led to suspect....that whatever small degree of enhanced predictability of academic achievement comes about from adding the Torrance tests as a predictor arises not because a new cognitive domain of "creativity" in thinking is being sampled but rather because these tests offer an alternate measure of general intelligence. * In sum, we have been able to find little evidence in support of an interpretation of the Torrance tests that would construe them as "creative thinking" rather than simply as "thinking." * that the Torrance tests seem to be functioning essentially as a battery of general intelligence assessors should come as no surprise in the light of the Torrance definition of creative thinking * this definition is quite close to the traditional conception of intelligence, including everything, say, that Wechsler's definition of general intelligence includes, with the addition of greater specific emphasis upon hypothesis-search activities in seeking problem solutions * We turn, finally, to the question of recommending the applied use of the Torrance tests. It is evident that we feel extreme caution is necessary. Most of the scoring practices commented upon in the Technical Manual seem to yield results that are hard to distinguish from assessment of general intelligence. At least no convincing empirical separability from intelligence has yet been demonstrated. If we view the Torrance materials as a possible supplement to intelligence testing, it is not evident that one will obtain results that differ clearly from what can be obtained by spending an equivalent amount of time with additional assessors of general intelligence. While the Torrance battery may function as a substitute for a general intelligence test, the user can be misled by the creativity label into believing that he is assessing something different from intelligence as usually defined. The consequence, ironically enough, is that the students of high intelligence will also be identified as creative. Such considerations are by no means intended to imply, of course, that one should be satisfied with general intelligence as a definition of talent. On the contrary, the importance of moving away from a unidimensional conception of talent centered upon general intelligence has in recent years become increasingly apparent. Furthermore, the Torrance materials for assessing fluency may represent an approach that has the potential for defining a considerably different kind of talent than is caught in the net of the general intelligence concept, but this would constitute a very different kind of emphasis than the Torrance battery provides. Efforts to determine the usefulness of fluency levels in selection are certainly needed. While publication of the *Torrance Tests of Creative Thinking* may encourage such efforts, we are left with the nagging suspicion that the major effect of the tests will be to give intelligence assessment a more fashionable name. [See original review for additional comments not excerpted.]

J Counsel Psychol 15:297–8 My '68. John L. Holland. * Because a subject gives free responses to several semistructured tasks, the scoring must be done by hand. A "Directions Manual and Scoring Guide" is provided for each form of the verbal and figural batteries (Forms A and B). These guides are unusually clear, complete, and explicit. Many test authors will find them helpful models. The specific origin of the interpretation of a person's responses is not always clear. Except for the originality scales, all keys or scoring guides were evolved rationally during the long period of the tests' development. Torrance provides an extensive rationale for each scale, but no empirical evidence about scale development except for the originality scales. These scales were developed by categorizing statistically rare responses as "original." More information about scoring is contained in the "Norms-Technical Manual." That publication suggests that interscorer reliability is usually above .90 for individual scales scored by elementary teachers. Other studies with similar reliabilities are alluded to but not reported. These interscorer reliabilities are impressive, but more explicit reporting and more evidence are desirable. The normative information is helpful, although much more information for larger, clearly defined populations is needed. On the other hand, there is enough information to distinguish high, middle, and low scores for a wide range of age groups. A related, interpretative section is less satisfactory. The relationship between the interpretation of a scale score and the evidence for the meaning of that score appears to rest more on its rationale than the evidence. Despite extensive work, much more is required to clarify and substantiate the scale interpretations. The evidence for the test-retest and equivalent-forms reliability of the Torrance batteries is more extensive and satisfactory. In 15 studies using equivalent forms or time intervals from 1 week to 3 years, the majority of reliability coefficients exceeded .70. Although these studies are not fully reported, the diversity of samples and time intervals strongly suggests that the TTCT scales have useful reliability. The validity of the TTCT rests on more than 50 investigations using samples of children, adolescents, and adults.

Of these, only one incompletely reported study is concerned with the predictive validity of the tests. Most investigations are concerned with construct and concurrent validities. An inordinate number of these validation studies capitalize on extreme group comparisons without any information about the excluded middle; many others use weak designs—"creative" versus "unselected" sample, simple matching of controls and "creatives." Despite these gross statistical deficiencies and weak designs, most of the evidence seems internally consistent and generally consistent with the literature of creative behavior. The failure to deal with external predictive validity remains a serious deficiency. It is quite possible that a subject can give many unusual uses for a brick or a cardboard box, but fail to perform originally in real-life situations. Unless tests like the TTCT are tied to reality by studies of their external validity, it will never be known whether high scores identify original people or crazy bricklayers and packers. The current evidence about the TTCT *implies* that it may have some predictive validity, but explicit evidence is needed about its ability to forecast socially relevant creative behavior. It would also be helpful to know more about the relationships between the TTCT scales and other common measures of originality or creative behavior. Normally, the writing, printing, and format of a test manual do not warrant comment. In this instance, Torrance's valuable substantive contributions are blurred by a dull, sometimes ugly and hard-to-read layout and typography. But, more important, the writing of the manual is poor, containing intrusive arguments with critics, promises of things to come, and excessive persuasion. And, although I enjoyed Torrance's encounters with critics (there should be a 1-month open season for this kind of activity), these, and other intrusions, make it difficult to quickly locate and interpret the guts of the evidence about the tests. At this time, the TTCT appear to have useful reliability and validity for research purposes. If they can be linked both to other common tests of originality and to criteria of greater social relevance, they will become powerful and valuable tools for research and practice. I wonder, however, if it might be more helpful, in education at least, to sensitize teachers to original behavior and its development rather than to have teachers use a somewhat laborious technique to find out who is "creative." In several publications for teachers, Torrance himself has already demonstrated how. Whatever the eventual uses of the TTCT, Torrance has made a large, substantive contribution to our knowledge of creative imagination.

J Ed Meas 4:191–2 f '67. *Ralph Hoepfner.* * an early attempt to measure an area of individual differences about which much more needs to be learned, and as such, is designed to be used for research purposes, and not for counseling or guiding the lives of people. With this in mind, it is surprising that the manual for this test so persistently underplays an objective scientific appraisal in favor of a sales pitch. *Interpretation.* Information supporting the values and interpretations of the tests is extensive and easily understood. Test-score interpretations are explained clearly in the manual and are simplified in scoring forms, but the names applied to the scores for tests may be open to misinterpretation. Different names imply different concepts, but different test scores don't necessarily imply different independent trait standings. As the intercorrelations among the test scores amply indicate, there is a great deal of overlap and nonindependence in each of the test scores. *Scoring.* The test manual is most comprehensive with regard to the administration of the tests (maintaining appropriate tone and intent) and in the necessarily complex scoring procedures, which are clearly detailed and based upon rational analysis of responses. The necessary training for scorers is described, and the reported inter-scorer reliabilities (.76 to .99; most in the high .90's) is evidence of the care taken in the training of scorers. But scorer training cannot be expected to be of so high a standard for all novices who will use these tests, and therefore inter-scorer agreement may be expected to be of a much lower level. Although there is no estimate of time required to score a test battery, one may assume that it will be a long affair. *Content.* The eight possible scores....purport to measure eight aspects of creative thinking, but the universe of behavior described as creative thinking is considerably larger. The manual readily admits to this inadequate coverage, which is, incidentally, not due entirely to the state of our knowledge. The logical basis of trait coverage stresses the complexity of creative thinking, but the scores are supposed to reflect unitary factor-like traits.

Further, the scores are supposed to be free from technical or subject-matter content (which they must surely be) and are also supposed to be appropriate to all age levels (regardless of the fact that one's educated psychological intuition, supported by the age-norm data, would strongly disagree). *Validity and Reliability.* The predictive ability of the tests is quite in line with other, unpublished, measures of creative potential—low. The relationships of the TTCT performance to other constructs which one might hypothesize to be related to creative potential, experimental measures of "preferred ways of learning," "long-range aspirations," or "attitude patterns," add a great deal of interest to these tests, but do fail to strongly anchor the test score meanings more firmly into the concept of creative potential. Because creative thinking, as measured, may take into account the influences of many personality and situational variables that fluctuate, we might expect the stability of test scores to suffer. They do. Test-retest reliabilities ranged from .71 to .93 over two-week intervals, and from .35 to .73 over three-year intervals. Although the studies on the reliability of the TTCT are well summarized, as are those concerned with test validity, the summaries do not contain the descriptive statistics, like means and standard deviations, necessary to make generalizations or to measure the comparability of forms or the absolute constancy of scores. *Norms.* Raw scores from the tests are to be converted to T-scores, but such a scale is not converted to centile ranks, or any other well-known scales. The scales and normative data were gathered on rather restricted samples, presumably on the basis of availability only, which may make generalizations, even for research purposes, somewhat ill-advised. * these tests do not measure up to the level of "format" quality one would expect as a product from a major publishing house and prominent psychologist and educator. Although the TTCT may have significance as a stimulant to further research, one certainly hopes that the author's and publisher's promise of major improvements will be actualized as soon as possible, so that the revision may offer theoretical, scientific, and practical values not yet incorporated into this bold venture into the mystery of creativity.

Torrance Tests of Creative Thinking

TIP II SCANNING INDEX

This classified index of all tests in *Tests in Print II* can be used to determine what tests are available in areas besides intelligence. Citations are to test entry numbers in TIP II. The population for which a test is intended is included. Stars indicate tests not previously listed in an MMY; asterisks indicate tests revised or supplemented since last listed. The intelligence portion of this index, the only part relevant to this monograph, is repeated at the end of this volume.

ACHIEVEMENT BATTERIES

Academic Proficiency Battery [South Africa], college entrants, see 1

Adult Basic Education Student Survey, poorly educated adults in basic education classes, see 2

Adult Basic Learning Examination, adults with achievement levels grades 1–12, see 3

American School Achievement Tests, grades 1–9, see 4

Bristol Achievement Tests [England], ages 8–13, see 5

*CLEP General Examinations: Humanities, 1–2 years of college or equivalent, see 6

*California Achievement Tests, grades 1–14, see 7

Canadian Tests of Basic Skills [Canada], grades 3–8, see 8

Classification and Placement Examination, grade 8 and high school entrants, see 9

*College-Level Examination Program General Examinations, 1–2 years of college or equivalent, see 10

*Comprehensive Tests of Basic Skills, grades kgn–12, see 11

Cooperative Primary Tests, grades 1.5–3, see 12

★*Educational Skills Tests: College Edition,* open-door college entrants, see 13

General Tests of Language and Arithmetic [South Africa], standards 5–7, see 14

Gray-Votaw-Rogers General Achievement Tests, grades 1–9, see 15

★*Guidance Test for Junior Secondary Bantu Pupils in Form 3* [South Africa], see 16

High School Fundamentals Evaluation Test, grades 9–12, see 17

Iowa High School Content Examination, grades 11–13, see 18

*Iowa Tests of Basic Skills, grades 1.7–9, see 19

*Iowa Tests of Educational Development, grades 9–12, see 20

Ligondé Equivalence Test [Canada], adults who left elementary or secondary school 15–20 years ago, see 21

*Metropolitan Achievement Tests, grades kgn–9, see 22

National Achievement Tests, grades 4–9, see 23

*National Educational Development Tests, grades 7–10, see 24

*National Teacher Examinations: Common Examinations, college seniors and teachers, see 25

Peabody Individual Achievement Test, grades kgn–12, see 26

★*Primary Survey Tests,* grades 2–3, see 27

Public School Achievement Tests, grades 3–8, see 28

*SRA Achievement Series, grades 1–9, see 29

*SRA Assessment Survey, grades 1–12, see 30

*SRA High School Placement Test, grade 9 entrants, see 31

*STS Closed High School Placement Test, grade 9 entrants, see 32

*STS Educational Development Series, grades 2–12, see 33

*Scholastic Proficiency Battery [South Africa], standards 8–10, see 34

*Sequential Tests of Educational Progress, grades 4–14, see 35

*Stanford Achievement Test, grades 1.5–9, see 36

Stanford Achievement Test: High School Basic Battery, grades 9–12, see 37

*Stanford Early School Achievement Test, grades kgn–1.5, see 38

★*Stanford Test of Academic Skills,* grades 8–12 and first year junior/community college, see 39

Survey of College Achievement, grades 13–14, see 40

*Teacher Education Examination Program: General Professional Examinations, college seniors preparing to teach, see 41

*Test for High School Entrants, high school entrants, see 42

Test of Reading and Number: Inter-American Series, grade 4 entrants, see 43

*Tests of Academic Progress, grades 9–12, see 44

Tests of Adult Basic Education, adults at reading levels of children in grades 2–9, see 45
★*Tests of Arithmetic and Language for Indian South Africans* [South Africa], standards 6–8, see 46
Tests of Basic Experiences, prekgn–grade 1, see 47
Tests of General Educational Development, candidates for high school equivalency certificates, see 48
Undergraduate Program Area Tests, college, see 49
Wide Range Achievement Test, ages 5 and over, see 50

ENGLISH

Advanced Placement Examination in English, high school students desiring credit for college level courses or admission to advanced courses, see 51
American School Achievement Tests: Language and Spelling, grades 4–9, see 52
Analytical Survey Test in English Fundamentals, grades 9–13, see 53
Barrett-Ryan English Test, grades 7–13, see 54
★*Berry-Talbott Language Test: Comprehension of Grammar,* ages 5–8, see 55
Bristol Achievement Tests: English Language [England], ages 8–13, see 56
Business English Test: Dailey Vocational Tests, grades 8–12 and adults, see 57
CLEP General Examinations: English Composition, 1–2 years of college or equivalent, see 58
CLEP Subject Examination in English Composition, 1 year or equivalent, see 59
★*CLEP Subject Examination in Freshman English,* 1 year or equivalent, see 60
California Achievement Tests: Language, grades 1–14, see 61
Canadian Achievement Test in English [Canada], grade 10, see 62
Canadian English Achievement Test [Canada], grades 8.5–9, see 63
★*Canadian English Language Achievement Test* [Canada], candidates for college entrance, see 63A
College Board Achievement Test in English Composition, candidates for college entrance, see 64
College English Placement Test, college entrants, see 65
College English Test: National Achievement Tests, grades 12–13, see 66
College Placement Tests in English Composition, entering college freshmen, see 67
Comprehensive Tests of Basic Skills: Language, grades 2.5–12, see 68
Cooperative English Tests, grades 9–14, see 69
Cooperative Primary Tests: Writing Skills, grades 2.5–3, see 70
Cotswold Junior English Ability Test [Scotland], ages 8.5–10.5, see 71
Cotswold Measurement of Ability: English [Scotland], ages 10–12, see 72
English Expression: Cooperative English Tests, grades 9–14, see 73
English IX–XII: Achievement Examinations for Secondary Schools, grades 9–12, see 74
English Progress Tests [England], ages 7-3 to 15-6, see 75
English Test FG [England], ages 12–13, see 76
English Test: Municipal Tests, grades 3–8, see 77
English Test: National Achievement Tests, grades 3–12, see 78
English Tests (Adv.) [England], ages 12–13, see 79
English Tests 14–20 and 22 [England], ages 10–11, see 80
Essentials of English Tests, grades 7–13, see 81
★*Functional Grammar Test,* high school and college, see 82
Grammar and Usage Test Series, grades 7–12, see 83
Grammar, Usage, and Structure Test and Vocabulary Test, college entrants, see 84
Hoyum-Sanders English Tests, 1–2 semesters in grades 2–8, see 85
Iowa Placement Examinations: English Aptitude, grades 12–13, see 86
Iowa Placement Examinations: English Training, grades 12–13, see 87
Iowa Tests of Educational Development: Correctness and Appropriateness of Expression, grades 9–12, see 88
★*Language Arts Diagnostic Probes,* grades 3–9, see 89
Language Arts: Minnesota High School Achievement Examinations, grades 7–12, see 90
Language Arts Tests: Content Evaluation Series, grades 7–9, see 91
Language Perception Test, business and industry, see 92
Language Usage: Differential Aptitude Tests, grades 8–12 and adults, see 93–4
Moray House English Tests [England], ages 8.5–14, see 95
National Teacher Examinations: English Language and Literature, college seniors and teachers, see 96
Nationwide English Composition Examination, grades 4–12, see 97
Nationwide English Grammar Examination, grades 4–12, see 98
New Purdue Placement Test in English, grades 11–16, see 99
Objective Tests in Constructive English, grades 7–12, see 100
Objective Tests in Punctuation, grades 7–12, see 101
Pacific Tests of English Attainment and Skills: Pacific Test Series [Australia], job applicants in Papua New Guinea, see 102
Picture Story Language Test, ages 7–17, see 103
Pressey Diagnostic Tests in English Composition, grades 7–12, see 104
Purdue High School English Test, grades 9–12, see 105
RBH Spelling Test and Word Meaning Test, business and industry, see 106
RBH Test of Language Skills, business and industry, see 107
SRA Achievement Series: Language Arts, grades 2–9, see 108–9
Schonell Diagnostic English Tests [Scotland], ages 9.5–16, see 110
Senior English Test [England], technical college entrants, see 111
★*Sequential Tests of Educational Progress, Series 2: English Expression,* grades 4–14, see 112
Sequential Tests of Educational Progress: Writing, grades 4–14, see 113
Stanford Achievement Test: High School English and Spelling Tests, grades 9–12, see 114
Stanford Achievement Test: Spelling and Language Tests, grades 4–9, see 115
Survey Tests of English Usage, grades 9–13, see 116
Teacher Education Examination Program: English Language and Literature, college seniors preparing to teach secondary school, see 117

Test of English Usage [India], English-speaking high school and college students and adults, see 118
Tests of Academic Progress: Composition, grades 9–12, see 119
**Tests of Basic Experiences: Language*, prekgn–grade 1, see 120
Tressler English Minimum Essentials Test, grades 8–12, see 121
Walton-Sanders English Test, 1–2 semesters in grades 9–13, see 122
Watson English Usage and Appreciation Test [Canada], grades 4–8, see 123
Writing Skills Test, grades 9–12, see 124
Writing Test: McGraw-Hill Basic Skills System, grades 11–14, see 125

LITERATURE

**American Literature Anthology Tests*, high school, see 126
★*CLEP Subject Examination in American Literature*, 1 year or equivalent, see 127
**CLEP Subject Examination in Analysis and Interpretation of Literature*, 1 year or equivalent, see 128
**CLEP Subject Examination in English Literature*, 1 year or equivalent, see 129
**College Board Achievement Test in Literature*, candidates for college entrance, see 130
**College Placement Test in Literature*, entering college freshmen, see 131
★*Cooperative Literature Tests*, grades 9–12, see 132
**English Literature Anthology Tests*, high school, see 133
English Tests for Outside Reading, grades 9–12, see 134
**Graduate Record Examinations Advanced Literature in English Test*, graduate school candidates, see 135
Hollingsworth-Sanders Junior High School Literature Test, grades 7–8, see 136
Hoskins-Sanders Literature Test, 1–2 semesters in grades 9–13, see 137
**Iowa Tests of Educational Development: Ability to Interpret Literary Materials*, grades 9–12, see 138
Literature Test: National Achievement Tests, grades 7–12, see 139
**Literature Tests/Objective*, high school, see 140
Look at Literature: NCTE Cooperative Test of Critical Reading and Appreciation, grades 4–6, see 141
★*Poetry Test/Objective*, grades 7–12, see 142
Tests of Academic Progress: Literature, grades 9–12, see 143
**Undergraduate Program Field Tests: Literature Tests*, college, see 144
★*World Literature Anthology Tests*, high school, see 145

SPELLING

Buckingham Extension of the Ayres Spelling Scale, grades 2–9, see 146
★*Correct Spelling*, grades 10–13, see 147
Group Diagnostic Spelling Test, grades 9–13, see 148
Iowa Spelling Scales, grades 2–8, see 149
Kansas Spelling Tests, grades 3–8, see 150
Kelvin Measurement of Spelling Ability [Scotland], ages 7–12, see 151
Lincoln Diagnostic Spelling Tests, grades 2–12, see 152
N.B. Spelling Tests [South Africa], standards 1–10 for English pupils and 3–10 for Afrikaans pupils, see 153
Nationwide Spelling Examination, grades 4–12, see 154
New Iowa Spelling Scale, grades 2–8, see 155
Sanders-Fletcher Spelling Test, 1–2 semesters in grades 9–13, see 156
**Spelling: Differential Aptitude Tests*, grades 8–12 and adults, see 157
Spelling Errors Test, grades 2–8, see 158
Spelling Test for Clerical Workers, stenographic applicants and high school, see 159
Spelling Test: McGraw-Hill Basic Skills System, grades 11–14, see 160
Spelling Test: National Achievement Tests, grades 3–12, see 161
Traxler High School Spelling Test, grades 9–12, see 162

VOCABULARY

A.C.E.R. Word Knowledge Test [Australia], ages 18 and over, see 163
American Literacy Test, adults, see 164
Bruce Vocabulary Inventory, business and industry, see 165
**Iowa Tests of Educational Development: General Vocabulary*, grades 9–12, see 166
Johnson O'Connor English Vocabulary Worksamples, ages 9 and over, see 167
Johnson O'Connor Vocabulary Tests, professionals, see 168
Nationwide English Vocabulary Examination, grades 4–12, see 169
Purdue Industrial Supervisors Word-Meaning Test, supervisors, see 170
RBH Vocabulary Test, applicants for clerical and stenographic positions, see 171
Sanders-Fletcher Vocabulary Test, 1–2 semesters in grades 9–13, see 172
Survey Test of Vocabulary, grades 3–12, see 173
Test of Active Vocabulary, grades 9–12, see 174
★*Vocabulary Survey Test*, grades kgn–1, see 175
Vocabulary Test for High School Students and College Freshmen, grades 9–13, see 176
Vocabulary Test: McGraw-Hill Basic Skills System, grades 11–14, see 177
Vocabulary Test: National Achievement Tests, grades 3–12, see 178
Wide Range Vocabulary Test, ages 8 and over, see 179
Word Clue Tests, grades 7–13 and adults, see 180
Word Dexterity Test, grades 7–16, see 181
Word Understanding, grades 6–12, see 182

FINE ARTS

ART

★*Advanced Placement Examination in Art*, high school students desiring credit for college level courses or admission to advanced courses, see 183
Art Vocabulary, grades 6–12, see 184
Graves Design Judgment Test, grades 7–16 and adults, see 185
Horn Art Aptitude Inventory, grades 12–16 and adults, see 186

Knauber Art Ability Test, grades 7–16, see 187
Knauber Art Vocabulary Test, grades 7–16, see 188
Meier Art Tests, grades 7–16 and adults, see 189
**National Teacher Examinations: Art Education,* college seniors and teachers, see 190
★*Teacher Education Examination Program: Art Education,* college seniors preparing to teach secondary school, see 191
**Undergraduate Program Field Tests: Art History Test,* college, see 192

MUSIC

★*Advanced Placement Examination in Music,* high school students desiring credit for college level courses or admission to advanced courses, see 193
Aliferis-Stecklein Music Achievement Tests, music students college level entrance and over, see 194
★*Belwin-Mills Singing Achievement Test,* grades 5–16, see 195
★*Elementary Rhythm and Pitch Test,* grades 4–8, see 196
**Graduate Record Examinations Advanced Music Test,* graduate school candidates, see 197
Gretsch-Tilson Musical Aptitude Test, grades 4–12, see 198
**Iowa Tests of Music Literacy,* grades 4–12, see 199
Jones Music Recognition Test, grades 4–16, see 200
Knuth Achievement Tests in Music, grades 3–12, see 201
Kwalwasser-Dykema Music Tests, grades 4–16 and adults, see 202
Kwalwasser Music Talent Test, grades 4–16 and adults, see 203
Kwalwasser-Ruch Test of Musical Accomplishment, grades 4–12, see 204
Kwalwasser Test of Music Information and Appreciation, high school and college, see 205
Measures of Musical Abilities [England], ages 7–14, see 206
Music Achievement Tests, grades 3–12, see 207
★*Music Aptitude Test,* grades 4–8, see 208
Musical Aptitude Profile, grades 4–12, see 209
**National Teacher Examinations: Music Education,* college seniors and teachers, see 210
Seashore Measures of Musical Talents, grades 4–16 and adults, see 211
Snyder Knuth Music Achievement Test, elementary education and music majors, see 212
**Teacher Education Examination Program: Music Education,* college seniors preparing to teach secondary school, see 213
Test of Musicality, grades 4–12, see 214
**Undergraduate Program Field Tests: Music Tests,* college, see 215
Watkins-Farnum Performance Scale, music students, see 216
Wing Standardised Tests of Musical Intelligence [England], ages 8 and over, see 217

FOREIGN LANGUAGES

Foreign Language Prognosis Test, grades 8–9, see 218
**Graduate School Foreign Language Testing Program,* graduate level degree candidates required to demonstrate foreign language reading proficiency, see 219
Iowa Placement Examinations: Foreign Language Aptitude, grades 12–13, see 220
Modern Language Aptitude Test, grades 9 and over, see 221
Modern Language Aptitude Test—Elementary, grades 3–6, see 222
Pimsleur Language Aptitude Battery, grades 6–12, see 223

ARABIC

**First Year Arabic Final Examination,* 1 year college, see 224

CHINESE

Harvard-MLA Tests of Chinese Language Proficiency, college and adults, see 225

ENGLISH

Comprehensive English Language Test for Speakers of English as a Second Language, non-native speakers of English, see 226
Diagnostic Test for Students of English as a Second Language, applicants from non-English language countries for admission to American colleges, see 227
English Knowledge and Comprehension Test [India], high school, see 228
★*English Placement Test,* college entrants from non-English language countries, see 229
**English Usage Test for Non-Native Speakers of English,* non-native speakers of English, see 230
Examination in Structure (English as a Foreign Language), college entrants from non-English language countries, see 231
★*Michigan Test of Aural Comprehension,* college applicants from non-English language countries, see 232
**Michigan Test of English Language Proficiency,* college applicants from non-English language countries, see 233
Oral Rating Form for Rating Language Proficiency in Speaking and Understanding English, non-native speakers of English, see 234
★*Test A/65: English Language Achievement Test* [South Africa], matriculants and higher, see 235
Test of Aural Perception in English for Japanese Students, Japanese students in American colleges, see 236
Test of Aural Perception in English for Latin-American Students, Latin-American students of English, see 237
**Test of English as a Foreign Language,* college applicants from non-English language countries, see 238
**Vocabulary and Reading Test for Students of English as a Second Language,* non-native speakers of English, see 239

FRENCH

**Advanced Placement Examination in French,* high school students desiring credit for college level courses or admission to advanced courses, see 240

Foreign Languages

Baltimore County French Test, 1 year high school, see 241
*Canadian Achievement Test in French [Canada], grade 10, see 242
★*College Board Achievement Test in French Listening-Reading,* candidates for college entrance with 2-4 years high school French, see 243
*College Board Achievement Test in French Reading, candidates for college entrance with 2-4 years high school French, see 244
*College Placement Test in French Listening Comprehension, entering college freshmen, see 245
★*College Placement Test in French Listening-Reading,* entering college freshmen, see 246
*College Placement Test in French Reading, entering college freshmen, see 247
Cooperative French Listening Comprehension Test, 2-5 semesters high school or college, see 248
First Year French Test, high school and college, see 249
Ford-Hicks French Grammar Completion Tests [Canada], high school, see 250
French I and II: Achievement Examinations for Secondary Schools, 1-2 years high school, see 251
*Graduate Record Examinations Advanced French Test, graduate school candidates, see 252
*Graduate School Foreign Language Test: French, graduate level degree candidates required to demonstrate reading proficiency in French, see 253
Iowa Placement Examinations: French Training, grades 12-13, see 254
MLA Cooperative Foreign Language Proficiency Tests: French, French majors and advanced students in college, see 255
MLA-Cooperative Foreign Language Tests: French, 1-4 years high school or 1-2 years college, see 256
*National Teacher Examinations: French, college seniors and teachers, see 257
Pimsleur French Proficiency Tests, grades 7-16, see 258
Second Year French Test, high school and college, see 259
*Teacher Education Examination Program: French, college seniors preparing to teach secondary school, see 260
*Undergraduate Program Field Tests: French Test, college, see 261

GERMAN

*Advanced Placement Examination in German, high school students desiring credit for college level courses or admission to advanced courses, see 262
★*College Board Achievement Test in German Listening-Reading,* candidates for college entrance with 2-4 years high school German, see 263
*College Board Achievement Test in German Reading, candidates for college entrance with 2-4 years high school German, see 264
*College Placement Test in German Listening Comprehension, entering college freshmen, see 265
★*College Placement Test in German Listening-Reading,* entering college freshmen, see 266
*College Placement Test in German Reading, entering college freshmen, see 267
German I and II: Achievement Examinations for Secondary Schools, 1-2 years high school, see 268
*Graduate Record Examinations Advanced German Test, graduate school candidates, see 269
*Graduate School Foreign Language Test: German, graduate level degree candidates required to demonstrate reading proficiency in German, see 270

MLA Cooperative Foreign Language Proficiency Tests: German, German majors and advanced students in college, see 271
MLA-Cooperative Foreign Language Tests: German, 1-4 years high school or 1-2 years college, see 272
*National German Examination for High School Students, 2-4 years high school, see 273
*National Teacher Examinations: German, college seniors and teachers, see 274
Pimsleur German Proficiency Tests, grades 7-16, see 275
*Undergraduate Program Field Tests: German Test, college, see 276

GREEK

*College Placement Test in Greek Reading, entering college freshmen, see 277

HEBREW

★*Achievement Test—Hebrew Language,* grades 5-7, see 278
*College Board Achievement Test in Hebrew, candidates for college entrance with 2-4 years high school Hebrew, see 279
*College Placement Test in Hebrew Reading, entering college freshmen, see 280
NCRI Achievement Tests in Hebrew, grades 5-9, see 281
Test on the Fundamentals of Hebrew, grades 2-7, see 282

ITALIAN

*College Placement Test in Italian Listening Comprehension, entering college freshmen, see 283
★*College Placement Test in Italian Listening-Reading,* entering college freshmen, see 284
*College Placement Test in Italian Reading, entering college freshmen, see 285
MLA Cooperative Foreign Language Proficiency Tests: Italian, Italian majors and advanced students in college, see 286
MLA-Cooperative Foreign Language Tests: Italian, 1-4 years high school or 1-2 years college, see 287

LATIN

*Advanced Placement Examination in Classics, high school students desiring credit for college level courses or admission to advanced courses, see 288
*College Board Achievement Test in Latin, candidates for college entrance with 2-4 years high school Latin, see 289
*College Placement Test in Latin Reading, entering college freshmen, see 290
Cooperative Latin Test: Elementary and Advanced Levels, grades 9-16, see 291
Emporia First Year Latin Test, 1 year high school, see 292
Emporia Second Year Latin Test, 2 years high school, see 293
Latin I and II: Achievement Examinations for Secondary Schools, 1-2 years high school, see 294

RUSSIAN

★*College Board Achievement Test in Russian Listening-Reading,* candidates for college entrance with 2-4 years high school Russian, see 295

College Placement Test in Russian Listening Comprehension, entering college freshmen, see 296
★*College Placement Test in Russian Listening-Reading,* entering college freshmen, see 297
College Placement Test in Russian Reading, entering college freshmen, see 298
Graduate School Foreign Language Test: Russian, graduate level degree candidates required to demonstrate reading proficiency in Russian, see 299
MLA Cooperative Foreign Language Proficiency Tests: Russian, Russian majors and advanced students in college, see 300
MLA-Cooperative Foreign Language Tests: Russian, 1–4 years high school or 1–2 years college, see 301

SPANISH

Advanced Placement Examination in Spanish, high school students desiring credit for college level courses or admission to advanced courses, see 302
Baltimore County Spanish Test, 1 year high school, see 303
★*College Board Achievement Test in Spanish Listening-Reading,* candidates for college entrance with 2–4 years high school Spanish, see 304
College Board Achievement Test in Spanish Reading, candidates for college entrance with 2–4 years high school Spanish, see 305
College Placement Test in Spanish Listening Comprehension, entering college freshmen, see 306
★*College Placement Test in Spanish Listening-Reading,* entering college freshmen, see 307
College Placement Test in Spanish Reading, entering college freshmen, see 308
First Year Spanish Test, high school and college, see 309
Furness Test of Aural Comprehension in Spanish, 1–3 years high school or 1–2 years college, see 310
Graduate Record Examinations Advanced Spanish Test, graduate school candidates, see 311
Graduate School Foreign Language Test: Spanish, graduate level degree candidates required to demonstrate reading proficiency in Spanish, see 312
Iowa Placement Examinations: Spanish Training, grades 12–13, see 313
MLA Cooperative Foreign Language Proficiency Tests: Spanish, Spanish majors and advanced students in college, see 314
MLA-Cooperative Foreign Language Tests: Spanish, 1–4 years high school or 1–2 years college, see 315
National Spanish Examination, 1–5 years junior high school and high school, see 316
National Teacher Examinations: Spanish, college seniors and teachers, see 317
Pimsleur Spanish Proficiency Tests, grades 7–16, see 318
Second Year Spanish Test, high school and college, see 319
Spanish I and II: Achievement Examinations for Secondary Schools, 1–2 years high school, see 320
Teacher Education Examination Program: Spanish, college seniors preparing to teach secondary school, see 321
Undergraduate Program Field Tests: Spanish Test, college, see 322

INTELLIGENCE

GROUP

A.C.E.R. Advanced Test B40 [Australia], ages 13 and over, see 323
A.C.E.R. Advanced Tests AL and AQ [Australia], college and superior adults, see 324
A.C.E.R. Higher Tests [Australia], ages 13 and over, see 325
A.C.E.R. Intermediate Test A [Australia], ages 10–13, see 326
A.C.E.R. Intermediate Tests C and D [Australia], ages 10–13, see 327
A.C.E.R. Junior Non-Verbal Test [Australia], ages 8.5–11, see 328
A.C.E.R. Junior Test A [Australia], ages 8.5–11, see 329
A.C.E.R. Lower Grades General Ability Scale [Australia], ages 6-6 to 9-1, see 330
AH4, AH5, and AH6 Tests [England], ages 10 and over, see 331
APT Performance Test, adults, see 332
Abstract Reasoning: Differential Aptitude Tests, grades 8–12 and adults, see 333
Academic Alertness "AA," adults, see 334
Academic Aptitude Test: Non-Verbal Intelligence: Acorn National Aptitude Tests, grades 7–16 and adults, see 335
Academic Aptitude Test: Verbal Intelligence: Acorn National Aptitude Tests, grades 7–16 and adults, see 336
Adaptability Test, job applicants, see 337
Advanced Test N [Australia], ages 15 and over, see 338
American School Intelligence Test, grades kgn–12, see 339
Analysis of Learning Potential, grades 1–12, see 340
Analysis of Relationships, grades 12–16 and industry, see 341
Army Alpha Examination: First Nebraska Revision, grades 6–16 and adults, see 341A
Army General Classification Test, First Civilian Edition, grades 9–16 and adults, see 342
★*BITCH Test (Black Intelligence Test of Cultural Homogeneity),* adolescents and adults, see 343
Boehm Test of Basic Concepts, grades kgn–2, see 344
Business Test, clerical workers, see 345
CGA Mental Ability Tests [Canada], grades 6–12, see 346
★*C.P. 66 Test* [England], ages 13 and over, see 347
California Short-Form Test of Mental Maturity, grades kgn–16 and adults, see 348
California Test of Mental Maturity, grades kgn–16 and adults, see 349
Canadian Academic Aptitude Test [Canada], grades 8.5–9.0, see 350
Canadian Cognitive Abilities Test [Canada], grades kgn–3, see 351
Canadian Lorge-Thorndike Intelligence Tests [Canada], grades 3–9, see 352
★*Canadian Scholastic Aptitude Test* [Canada], candidates for college entrance, see 353
Cattell Intelligence Tests [England], mental ages 4 and over, see 354
Chicago Non-Verbal Examination, ages 6 and over, see 355
Cognitive Abilities Test, grades kgn–12, see 356

College Board Scholastic Aptitude Test, candidates for college entrance, see 357
College Qualification Tests, candidates for college entrance, see 358
Concept Mastery Test, grades 15–16 and graduate students and applicants for executive and research positions, see 359
Cooperative Academic Ability Test, superior grade 12 students, see 360
Cooperative School and College Ability Tests, grades 4–16, see 361
Cotswold Junior Ability Tests [Scotland], ages 8.5–10.5, see 362
Cotswold Measurement of Ability [Scotland], ages 10–12, see 363
Culture Fair Intelligence Test, ages 4 and over, see 364
D48 Test, grades 5 and over, see 365–6
Deeside Non-Verbal Reasoning Test [England], ages 10–12, see 367
Deeside Picture Puzzles [England], ages 6.5–8.5, see 368
Dennis Test of Scholastic Aptitude, grades 4–8, see 369
Detroit General Intelligence Examination, grades 7–12, see 370
Doppelt Mathematical Reasoning Test, grades 16–17 and employees, see 371
Draw-A-Man Test for Indian Children [India], ages 6–10, see 372
Essential Intelligence Test [Scotland], ages 8–12, see 373
Executive Employment Review, applicants for executive level positions, see 374
Figure Reasoning Test [England], ages 10 and over, see 375
Fundamental Achievement Series, semiliterate job applicants and employees, see 376–7
General Mental Ability Test, job applicants, see 378
General Verbal Practice Test G1–G3 [England], ages 10–11, see 379
Gilliland Learning Potential Examination, ages 6 and over, see 380
Goodenough-Harris Drawing Test, ages 3–15, see 381
Graduate Record Examinations Aptitude Test, graduate school candidates, see 382
★Group Test for Indian South Africans [South Africa], standards 4–10, see 383
Group Test 36 [England], ages 10–14, see 384
Group Test 75 [England], ages 12–13, see 385
Group Test 91 [England], industrial applicants, see 386
★Group Test 95 [England], ages 14 and over, see 386A
Group Test of Learning Capacity: Dominion Tests [Canada], grades kgn–1, 4–12 and adults, see 387
Group Tests 70 and 70B [England], ages 15 and over, see 388
Group Tests 72 and 73 [England], industrial applicants, see 389
Group Tests 90A and 90B [England], ages 15 and over, see 390
Henmon-Nelson Tests of Mental Ability, grades kgn–17, see 391
Illinois Index of Scholastic Aptitude, grades 9–12, see 392
Inventory No. 2, ages 16 and over, see 393
Junior Scholastic Aptitude Test, grades 7–9, see 394
Kelvin Measurement of Ability in Infant Classes [Scotland], ages 5–8, see 395
Kelvin Measurement of Mental Ability [Scotland], ages 8–12, see 396
Kingston Test of Intelligence [England], ages 10–12, see 397

Kuhlmann-Anderson Test, grades kgn–12, see 398
Kuhlmann-Finch Tests, grades 1–12, see 399
Lorge-Thorndike Intelligence Tests, grades kgn–13, see 400
Lorge-Thorndike Intelligence Tests, College Edition, grades 12–13, see 401
Mental Alertness: Tests A/1 and A/2 [South Africa], job applicants with 9 or more years of education, see 402
Mill Hill Vocabulary Scale [England], ages 4 and over, see 403
Miller Analogies Test, candidates for graduate school, see 404
★Minnesota Scholastic Aptitude Test, high school and college, see 405
Mitchell Vocabulary Test [England], adults, see 406
Modified Alpha Examination Form 9, grades 7–12 and adults, see 407
Moray House Picture Tests [England], ages 6.5–8.5, see 408
Moray House Verbal Reasoning Tests [England], ages 8.5 and over, see 409
N.B. Group Tests [South Africa], ages 5–8, see 410
New South African Group Test [South Africa], ages 8–17, see 411
★Non-Language Test of Verbal Intelligence [India], class 8 (ages 11–13), see 412
Non-Readers Intelligence Test [England], ages 6–8, see 413
Non-Verbal Reasoning Test, job applicants and industrial employees, see 414
Non-Verbal Tests [England], ages 8–15, see 415
Northumberland Mental Tests [England], ages 10–12.5, see 416
OISE Picture Reasoning Test: Primary [Canada], grades 1–2, see 417
Ohio Penal Classification Test, penal institutions, see 418
Ohio State University Psychological Test, grades 9–16 and adults, see 419
★Oral Verbal Intelligence Test [England], ages 7.5–14, see 419A
Oregon Academic Ranking Test, gifted children grades 3–7, see 420
O'Rourke General Classification Test, grades 12–13 and adults, see 421
"Orton" Intelligence Test, No. 4 [Scotland], ages 10–14, see 422
Otis Employment Tests, applicants for employment, see 423
Otis-Lennon Mental Ability Test, grades kgn–12, see 424
Otis Quick-Scoring Mental Ability Tests, grades 1–16, see 425
Otis Self-Administering Tests of Mental Ability, grades 4–16, see 426
Pacific Reasoning Series Tests [Australia], job applicants in Papua New Guinea, see 427
Pattern Perception Test [England], ages 6 and over, see 428
Performance Alertness "PA" (With Pictures), adults, see 429
Personal Classification Test, business and industry, see 430
Personnel Research Institute Classification Test, adults, see 431
Personnel Research Institute Factory Series Test, applicants for routine industrial positions, see 432
Personnel Tests for Industry, trade school and adults, see 433
Picture Test A [England], ages 7-0 to 8-1, see 434
Pintner-Cunningham Primary Test, grades kgn–2, see 435

Preliminary Scholastic Aptitude Test/National Merit Scholarship Qualifying Test, grades 10-12, see 436
★*Preschool and Early Primary Skill Survey*, ages 3-3 to 7-2, see 437
Pressey Classification and Verifying Tests, grades 1-12 and adults, see 438
Progressive Matrices [England], ages 5 and over, see 439
Proverbs Test, grades 5-16 and adults, see 440
Public School Primary Intelligence Test, grades 2-4, see 441
Purdue Non-Language Personnel Test, business and industry, see 442
Quantitative Evaluative Device, entering graduate students, see 443
RBH Test of Learning Ability, business and industry, see 444
RBH Test of Non-Verbal Reasoning, business and industry, see 445
Reasoning Tests for Higher Levels of Intelligence [Scotland], college entrants, see 446
Revised Beta Examination, ages 16-59, see 447
Ryburn Group Intelligence Tests [Scotland], ages 6.5-15.5, see 448
*SRA Nonverbal Form, ages 12 and over, see 449
*SRA Pictorial Reasoning Test, ages 14 and over, see 450
*SRA Short Test of Educational Ability, grades kgn-12, see 451
*SRA Verbal Form, grades 7-16 and adults, see 452
Safran Culture Reduced Intelligence Test [Canada], grades 1 and over, see 453
Scholastic Mental Ability Tests, grades kgn-8, see 454
Schubert General Ability Battery, grades 12-16 and adults, see 455
Scott Company Mental Alertness Test, applicants for office positions, see 456
Ship Destination Test, grades 9 and over, see 457
Short Form Test of Academic Aptitude, grades 1.5-12, see 458
Simplex GNV Intelligence Tests [England], ages 11-12, see 459
Simplex Group Intelligence Scale [England], ages 10 and over, see 460
Simplex Junior Intelligence Tests [England], ages 7-14, see 461
Sleight Non-Verbal Intelligence Test [England], ages 6-10, see 462
Southend Test of Intelligence [England], ages 10-12, see 463
Spiral Nines [South Africa], job applicants with 7-8 years of education, see 464
Test of Adult College Aptitude, evening college entrants, see 465
*Test of Perceptual Organization, ages 12 and over, see 466
Tests of General Ability, grades kgn-12, see 467
*Tests of General Ability: Inter-American Series, preschool and grades kgn-13.5, see 468
Thurstone Test of Mental Alertness, grades 9-12 and adults, see 469
*Undergraduate Program Aptitude Test, grades 15-16, see 470
Verbal Power Test of Concept Equivalence, ages 14 and over, see 471
Verbal Reasoning, job applicants and industrial employees, see 472
*Verbal Reasoning: Differential Aptitude Tests, grades 8-12 and adults, see 473
Verbal Tests (Adv.) [England], ages 12-13, see 474
Verbal Tests BC, CD, C, and D [England], ages 8-11, see 475
Verbal Tests EF and GH [England], ages 11-14, see 476
Verbal Tests 15-23 and 69 [England], ages 10-12, see 477
★*WLW Employment Inventory III*, job applicants, see 478
★*WLW Mental Alertness Inventory*, job applicants, see 479
Wesman Personnel Classification Test, grades 8-16 and adults, see 480
Western Personnel Tests, college and adults, see 481
*Wonderlic Personnel Test, adults, see 482

INDIVIDUAL

Arthur Point Scale of Performance Tests, ages 4.5 to superior adults, see 483
Bayley Scales of Infant Development, ages 2-30 months, see 484
★*Bingham Button Test*, disadvantaged children ages 3-6, see 485
Canadian Intelligence Test [Canada], ages 3-16, see 486
Cattell Infant Intelligence Scale, ages 3-30 months, see 487
★*Classification Tasks* [Australia], ages 5-9, see 488
*Columbia Mental Maturity Scale, ages 3.5-9, see 489
Cooperative Preschool Inventory, ages 3-6, see 490
Crichton Vocabulary Scale [England], ages 4-11, see 491
Denver Developmental Screening Test, ages 2 weeks to 6 years, see 492
Detroit Tests of Learning Aptitude, ages 3 and over, see 493
Developmental Screening Inventory, ages 1-18 months, see 494
*English Picture Vocabulary Test [England], ages 5 and over, see 495
Full-Range Picture Vocabulary Test, ages 2 and over, see 496
Gesell Developmental Schedules, ages 4 weeks to 6 years, see 497
Haptic Intelligence Scale for Adult Blind, blind and partially sighted adults, see 498
Hiskey-Nebraska Test of Learning Aptitude, ages 3-17, see 499
Immediate Test: A Quick Verbal Intelligence Test, adults, see 500
★*Individual Scale for Indian South Africans* [South Africa], ages 8-17, see 501
Kahn Intelligence Tests, ages 1 month and over (particularly the verbally or culturally handicapped), see 502
Kent Series of Emergency Scales, ages 5-14, see 503
*Leiter Adult Intelligence Scale, adults, see 504
Leiter International Performance Scale, ages 2-18, see 505
★*McCarthy Scales of Children's Abilities*, ages 2.5-8.5, see 506
Merrill-Palmer Scale of Mental Tests, ages 24-63 months, see 507
★*Minnesota Child Development Inventory*, ages 1-6, see 508
Minnesota Preschool Scale, ages 1.5-6.0, see 509
New Guinea Performance Scales [Papua New Guinea], pre-literates ages 17 and over, see 510
New South African Individual Scale [South Africa], ages 6-17, see 511
Non-Verbal Intelligence Tests for Deaf and Hearing Subjects [The Netherlands], ages 3-16, see 512
Ohwaki-Kohs Tactile Block Design Intelligence Test for the Blind, blind ages 6 and over, see 513
Pacific Design Construction Test [Australia], illiterates and semiliterates in Papua New Guinea, see 514

Passalong Test: A Performance Test of Intelligence, ages 8 and over, see 515
Peabody Picture Vocabulary Test, ages 2.5–18, see 516
Pictorial Test of Intelligence, ages 3–8, see 517
Porteus Maze Test, ages 3 and over, see 518
Preschool Attainment Record, ages 6 months to 7 years, see 519
Queensland Test [Australia], ages 7 and over, see 520
Quick Screening Scale of Mental Development, ages 6 months to 10 years, see 521
Quick Test, ages 2 and over, see 522
Ring and Peg Tests of Behavior Development, birth to age 6, see 523
Slosson Intelligence Test, ages 2 weeks and over, see 524
**Stanford-Binet Intelligence Scale,* ages 2 and over, see 525; *Clinical Profile for the Stanford Binet Intelligence Scale (L–M),* ages 5 and over, see 526
Stanford-Ohwaki-Kohs Block Design Intelligence Test for the Blind, blind and partially sighted ages 16 and over, see 527
Vane Kindergarten Test, ages 4–6, see 528
Wechsler Adult Intelligence Scale, ages 16 and over, see 529; *Rhodes WAIS Scatter Profile,* see 530; ★*WAIS Test Profile,* see 531
Wechsler-Bellevue Intelligence Scale, ages 10 and over, see 532
Wechsler Intelligence Scale for Children, ages 5–15, see 533; *California Abbreviated WISC,* educable mentally retarded ages 8–13.5 and intellectually gifted elementary school children, see 534; *Rhodes WISC Scatter Profile,* see 535; ★*WISC Mental Description Sheet,* see 536; ★*WISC Test Profile,* see 537
Wechsler Preschool and Primary Scale of Intelligence, ages 4–6.5, see 538; ★*WPPSI Test Profile,* see 539
Williams Intelligence Test for Children With Defective Vision [England], blind and partially sighted ages 5–15, see 540

SPECIFIC

★*Abstract Spatial Relations Test* [South Africa], Bantu industrial workers with 0–12 years of education, see 541
Alternate Uses, grades 6–16 and adults, see 542
Benton Visual Retention Test, ages 8 and over, see 543
★*Biographical Inventory—Creativity,* "adolescents and young adults," see 544
Block-Design Test, mental ages 5–20, see 545
**Christensen-Guilford Fluency Tests,* grades 7–16 and adults, see 546
Closure Flexibility (Concealed Figures), industrial employees, see 547
Closure Speed (Gestalt Completion), industrial employees, see 548
Concept Assessment Kit—Conservation, ages 4–7, see 549
★*Concept Attainment Test* [South Africa], college and adults, see 550

Consequences, grades 9–16 and adults, see 551
★*Consequences* [South Africa], ages 15 and over, see 552
★*Creativity Attitude Survey,* grades 4–6, see 553
★*Creativity Tests for Children,* grades 4–6, see 554
Decorations, grades 9–16 and adults, see 555
Feature Profile Test: Pintner-Paterson Modification, ages 4 and over, see 556
★*Gottschaldt Figures* [South Africa], job applicants with at least 10 years of education, see 557
Healy Pictorial Completion Tests, ages 5 and over, see 558
Hidden Figures Test, grades 6–16, see 559
Higgins-Wertman Test: Threshold of Visual Closure, ages 5–15, see 560
Jensen Alternation Board, ages 5 and over, see 560A
Kit of Reference Tests for Cognitive Factors, grades 6–16, see 561
Making Objects, grades 9–16 and adults, see 562
Manikin Test, ages 2 and over, see 563
Match Problems, grades 9–16 and adults, see 564
**Match Problems 5,* grades 9–16, see 565
★*Memory for Events,* grades 9–13, see 566
★*Memory for Meanings,* grades 7–16, see 567
**New Uses,* grades 10–16, see 568
★*Pattern Relations Test* [South Africa], college graduates, see 569
Perceptual Speed (Identical Forms), grades 9–16 and industrial employees, see 570
Pertinent Questions, grades 9–16 and adults, see 571
**Plot Titles,* grades 9–16, see 572
Possible Jobs, grades 6–16 and adults, see 573
**Remote Associates Test,* grades 9–16 and adults, see 574
Rutgers Drawing Test, ages 4–9, see 575
★*Seeing Faults* [South Africa], ages 15 and over, see 576
**Seeing Problems,* grades 9–16, see 577
Seguin-Goddard Formboard, ages 5–14, see 578
**Simile Interpretations,* grades 10–16, see 579
★*Similes Test,* grades 4–16 and adults, see 580
★*Sketches,* grades 9 and over, see 581
Subsumed Abilities Test, ages 9 and over, see 582
★*Symbol Identities,* grades 10 and over, see 583
Symbol Series Test [South Africa], illiterate and semiliterate adults, see 584
★*Test of Concept Utilization,* ages 4.5–18.5, see 585
★*Test of Creative Potential,* grades 2–12 and adults, see 586
★*Thinking Creatively With Sounds and Words,* grades 3–12 and adults, see 587
Time Appreciation Test, ages 10 and over, see 588
Torrance Tests of Creative Thinking, kgn through graduate school, see 589
Two-Figure Formboard, ages 4 and over, see 590
**Utility Test,* grades 9–12, see 591
Wechsler Memory Scale, adults, see 592
★*Willner Instance Similarities Test,* adults, see 593
Word Fluency, industrial employees, see 594

MATHEMATICS

★*ACER Mathematics Tests* [Australia], grades 4–6, see 595
ACT Mathematics Placement Examination, college entrants, see 596
**Advanced Mathematics (Including Trigonometry): Minnesota High School Achievement Examinations,* high school, see 597
★*Annual High School Mathematics Examination,* high school students competing for individual and school awards, see 598
**Basic Mathematics Tests* [England], ages 7–14.5, see 599
Bristol Achievement Tests: Mathematics [England], ages 8–13, see 600

CLEP General Examinations: Mathematics, 1–2 years of college or equivalent, see 601
CLEP Subject Examination in College Algebra and Trigonometry, 1 semester or equivalent, see 602
California Achievement Tests: Mathematics, grades 1–14, see 603
Canadian Achievement Test in Mathematics [Canada], grade 10, see 604
Canadian Achievement Test in Technical and Commercial Mathematics [Canada], grade 10, see 605
Canadian Mathematics Achievement Test [Canada], grades 8.5–9.0, see 606
College Board Achievement Test in Mathematics, Level 1, candidates for college entrance, see 607
College Board Achievement Test in Mathematics, Level 2, candidates for college entrance, see 608
College Placement Test in Advanced Mathematics, entering college freshmen, see 609
College Placement Test in Intermediate Mathematics, entering college freshmen, see 610
College Placement Test in Mathematics, Level 1, entering college freshmen, see 611
College Placement Test in Mathematics, Level 2, entering college freshmen, see 612
Cooperative Mathematics Tests: Structure of the Number System, grades 7–8, see 613
Cooperative Primary Tests: Mathematics, grades 1.5–3, see 614
★Diagnostic Test in Mathematics—Level 1 [Canada], grades 8–9, see 615
ERB Modern Mathematics Test, grades 7–8, see 616
General Mathematics III: Achievement Examinations for Secondary Schools, grade 9, see 617
Graded Arithmetic-Mathematics Test: Decimal Currency Edition [England], ages 7–21, see 618
Graduate Record Examinations Advanced Mathematics Test, graduate school candidates, see 619
★Group Mathematics Test [England], ages 6.5–8.5, see 620
Iowa Placement Examinations: Mathematics Aptitude, grades 12–13, see 621
Iowa Placement Examinations: Mathematics Training, grades 12–13, see 622
Iowa Tests of Educational Development: Ability to Do Quantitative Thinking, grades 9–12, see 623
Junior High School Mathematics Test: Acorn Achievement Tests, grades 7–9, see 624
★Leicester Number Test [England], ages 7-1 to 8-1, see 625
★Mathematics Attainment Test EF [England], ages 11–12, see 626
Mathematics Attainment Tests C1 and C3 [England], ages 9-3 to 10-8, see 627
Mathematics Attainment Tests DE1 and DE2 [England], ages 10–11, see 628
Mathematics Attainment Tests (Oral) [England], ages 7 to 9-8, see 629
★Mathematics Inventory Tests, grades 4–12, see 630
Mathematics: Minnesota High School Achievement Examinations, grades 7–9, see 631
Mathematics Test (Adv.) 6 [England], ages 12–13, see 632
Mathematics Test: Content Evaluation Series, grades 7–9, see 633
Mathematics Test for Grades Four, Five and Six, grades 4–6, see 634
Mathematics Test: McGraw-Hill Basic Skills System, grades 11–14, see 635
Mathematics Tests 20–22 [England], ages 10–11, see 636
Metropolitan Achievement Tests: Mathematics Tests, grades 3–9, see 637
Minimum Essentials for Modern Mathematics, grades 6–8, see 638

Modern Mathematics Supplement to the Iowa Tests of Basic Skills, grades 3–9, see 639
Moray House Mathematics Tests [England], ages 8.5–12, see 640
★Moreton Mathematics Tests—Level 2 [Australia], grades 3–5, see 641
N.B. Mathematics Tests [South Africa], standards 7–8 (ages 14–15), see 642
National Teacher Examinations: Mathematics, college seniors and teachers, see 643
Numerical Ability: Differential Aptitude Tests, grades 8–12 and adults, see 644
★Objective Tests in Mathematics: Arithmetic and Trigonometry [England], ages 15 and over, see 645
Portland Prognostic Test for Mathematics, grades 6.9–8, see 646
★Prescriptive Mathematics Inventory, grades 4–8, see 647
★Prescriptive Mathematics Inventory Interim Evaluation Tests, grades 4–7, see 648
★Primary Mathematics Survey Tests, grades 2–3, see 649
Purdue Industrial Mathematics Test, adults, see 650
Senior Mathematics Test [England], technical college entrants, see 651
Sequential Tests of Educational Progress: Mathematics, grades 4–14, see 652
Stanford Achievement Test: High School Mathematics Test, grades 9–12, see 653
Stanford Achievement Test: High School Numerical Competence Test, grades 9–12, see 654
Stanford Achievement Test: Mathematics Tests, grades 1.5–9, see 655
Stanford Modern Mathematics Concepts Test, grades 5.5–9.5, see 656
Teacher Education Examination Program: Mathematics, college seniors preparing to teach secondary school, see 657
★Test A/16: Mathematical Achievement Test [South Africa], job applicants with at least 10 years of education, see 658
Tests of Academic Progress: Mathematics, grades 9–12, see 659
Tests of Achievement in Basic Skills: Mathematics, grades 4–12, see 660
Tests of Basic Experiences: Mathematics, prekgn–grade 1, see 661
Undergraduate Program Field Tests: Mathematics Tests, college, see 662
★Watson Diagnostic Mathematics Test: Computation [Canada], grades 1–10, see 663

ALGEBRA

Advanced Algebra: Achievement Examinations for Secondary Schools, high school, see 664
Algebra Readiness Test, grades 8–9, see 665
Algebra Test for Engineering and Science, college entrants, see 666–7
Blyth Second-Year Algebra Test, grades 9–12, see 668
Breslich Algebra Survey Test, 1–2 semesters high school, see 669
CLEP Subject Examination in College Algebra, 1 semester or equivalent, see 670
California Algebra Aptitude Test, high school, see 671
Cooperative Mathematics Tests: Algebra I and II, grades 8–12, see 672
Cooperative Mathematics Tests: Algebra III, high school and college, see 673
Diagnostic Test in Basic Algebra [Australia], 2–3 semesters high school, see 674

*ERB Modern Elementary Algebra Test, grades 8-9, see 675
ERB Modern Second Year Algebra Test, high school, see 676
Elementary Algebra: Achievement Examinations for Secondary Schools, high school, see 677
*Elementary Algebra: Minnesota High School Achievement Examinations, high school, see 678
First Year Algebra Test: National Achievement Tests, 1 year high school, see 679
Illinois Algebra Test, 1-2 semesters high school, see 680
Iowa Algebra Aptitude Test, grade 8, see 681
Kepner Mid-Year Algebra Achievement Tests, 1 semester high school, see 682
Lankton First-Year Algebra Test, grades 8-12, see 683
Lee Test of Algebraic Ability, grades 7-8, see 684
Mid-Year Algebra Test, high school, see 685
★Modern Algebra Test: Content Evaluation Series, 1 year high school, see 686
★Objective Tests in Mathematics: Algebra [England], ages 15 and over, see 687
Orleans-Hanna Algebra Prognosis Test, grades 7-11, see 688
Survey Test of Algebraic Aptitude, grade 8, see 689

ARITHMETIC

A.C.E.R. Arithmetic Tests: Standardized for Use in New Zealand [New Zealand], ages 9-12, see 690
A.C.E.R. Number Test [Australia], ages 13.5 and over, see 691
★Adston Diagnostic Instruments in Elementary School Mathematics: Whole Numbers, grades 4-8, see 692
American Numerical Test, adults in "that great middle and upper middle block of vocations which emphasize shop and white collar skills involving number competence," see 693
American School Achievement Tests: Arithmetic Readiness, grades kgn-1, see 694
American School Achievement Tests: Part 2, Arithmetic, grades 2-9, see 695
Analytical Survey Test in Computational Arithmetic, grades 7-12, see 696
Arithmetic Computation: Public School Achievement Tests, grades 3-8, see 697
Arithmetic Reasoning: Public School Achievement Tests, grades 3-8, see 698
Arithmetic Reasoning Test, clerical applicants and high school, see 699
Arithmetic Test (Fundamentals and Reasoning): Municipal Tests, grades 3-8, see 700
Arithmetic Test: National Achievement Tests, grades 3-8, see 701
*Arithmetic Tests EA2A and EA4 [England], ages 14.5 and over, see 702
*Arithmetical Problems: Test A/68 [South Africa], job applicants with at least 10 years of education, see 703
Basic Skills in Arithmetic Test, grades 6-12, see 704
Bobbs-Merrill Arithmetic Achievement Tests, grades 1-9, see 705
Brief Survey of Arithmetic Skills, grades 7-12, see 706
*Comprehensive Tests of Basic Skills: Arithmetic, grades 2.5-12, see 707
Computation Test A/67 [South Africa], job applicants with at least 6 years of education, see 708
Cooperative Mathematics Tests: Arithmetic, grades 7-9, see 709
*Cotswold Junior Arithmetic Ability Tests [Scotland], ages 8.5-10.5, see 710

*Cotswold Measurement of Ability: Arithmetic [Scotland], ages 10-12, see 711
*Diagnostic Arithmetic Tests [South Africa], standards 2-5 (ages 9-12), see 712
Diagnostic Chart for Fundamental Processes in Arithmetic, grades 2-8, see 713
★Diagnostic Decimal Tests 1-3 [Australia], ages 9-13, see 714
Diagnostic Fractions Test 3 [Australia], ages 7-11, see 715
Diagnostic Number Tests 1-2 [Australia], ages 8-12, see 716
Diagnostic Tests and Self-Helps in Arithmetic, grades 3-12, see 717
*ERB Modern Arithmetic Test, grades 5-6, see 718
Emporia Arithmetic Tests, grades 1-8, see 719
Kelvin Measurement of Ability in Arithmetic [Scotland], ages 7-12, see 720
★KeyMath Diagnostic Arithmetic Test, grades kgn-7, see 721
Moray House Arithmetic Test [England], ages 10-12, see 722
★Moreton Arithmetic Tests [Australia], grades 6-7, see 723
N.B. Arithmetic Tests [South Africa], standards 2-8 (ages 9-15), see 724
Number Test DE [England], ages 10.5-12.5, see 725
*Office Arithmetic Test, job applicants, see 726
RBH Arithmetic Fundamentals Test, business and industry, see 727
RBH Arithmetic Reasoning Test, business and industry, see 728
RBH Shop Arithmetic Test, industry, see 729
Revised Southend Attainment Test in Mechanical Arithmetic [England], ages 7-15, see 730
SRA Achievement Series: Arithmetic, grades 1-9, see 731
SRA Arithmetic Index, job applicants with poor educational backgrounds, see 732-3
Schonell Diagnostic Arithmetic Tests [Scotland], ages 7-13, see 734
*Seeing Through Arithmetic Tests, grades 1-6, see 735
Southend Attainment Test in Mechanical Arithmetic [England], ages 6-14, see 736
Staffordshire Arithmetic Test [England], ages 7-15, see 737
Stanford Diagnostic Arithmetic Test, grades 2.5-8.5, see 738
Survey Tests of Arithmetic Fundamentals [Canada], grades 3-8, see 739
Test A/8: Arithmetic [South Africa], technical college students and applicants for clerical and trade positions with 8-12 years of education, see 740
Watson Number-Readiness Test [Canada], grades kgn-1, see 741

CALCULUS

*Advanced Placement Examination in Mathematics: Calculus, high school students desiring credit for college level courses or admission to advanced courses, see 742
*CLEP Subject Examination in Introductory Calculus, 1 year or equivalent, see 743
Cooperative Mathematics Tests: Calculus, high school and college, see 744

GEOMETRY

Cooperative Mathematics Tests: Analytic Geometry, high school and college, see 745

Cooperative Mathematics Tests: Geometry, grades 10–12, see 746
Diagnostic Test in Basic Geometry [Australia], 1–2 years high school, see 747
Geometry (Including Plane and Solid Geometry): Minnesota High School Achievement Examinations, high school, see 748–9
Howell Geometry Test, grades 9–12, see 750
Iowa Geometry Aptitude Test, high school, see 751
Mid-Year Geometry Test, high school, see 752
★Modern Geometry Test: Content Evaluation Series, grades 10–12, see 753
★Objective Tests in Mathematics: Geometry [England], ages 15 and over, see 754
Orleans-Hanna Geometry Prognosis Test, grades 8–11, see 755
Plane Geometry: Achievement Examinations for Secondary Schools, high school, see 756
Plane Geometry: National Achievement Tests, high school, see 757
*Solid Geometry: Achievement Examinations for Secondary Schools, high school, see 758
Solid Geometry: National Achievement Tests, high school, see 759

SPECIAL FIELDS

★Decimal Currency Test [England], primary and secondary school, see 760
★NM Consumer Mathematics Test, grades 9–12, see 761

TRIGONOMETRY

*CLEP Subject Examination in Trigonometry, 1 semester or equivalent, see 762
Cooperative Mathematics Tests: Trigonometry, high school and college, see 763
Plane Trigonometry: National Achievement Tests, grades 10–16, see 764
*Trigonometry: Minnesota High School Achievement Examinations, high school, see 765

MISCELLANEOUS

Modern Photography Comprehension Test, photography students, see 766
★NM Consumer Rights and Responsibilities Test, grades 9–12, see 767

AGRICULTURE

★Agribusiness Achievement Test, grades 9–12, see 768

BLIND

Colorado Braille Battery: Literary Code Tests, grades 1 and over, see 769
Colorado Braille Battery: Nemeth Code Tests, grades 4 and over, see 770
Lorimer Braille Recognition Test [England], students (ages 7–13) in grade 2 Braille, see 771
Roughness Discrimination Test, blind children in grades kgn–1, see 772
★Stanford Multi-Modality Imagery Test, blind and partially sighted ages 16 and over, see 773
Tooze Braille Speed Test [England], students (ages 7–13) in grades 1 or 2 Braille, see 774

BUSINESS EDUCATION

Bookkeeping: Achievement Examinations for Secondary Schools, high school, see 775
*Bookkeeping: Minnesota High School Achievement Examinations, high school, see 776
*Bookkeeping Test: National Business Entrance Tests, grades 11–16 and adults, see 777
*Business Fundamentals and General Information Test: National Business Entrance Tests, grades 11–16 and adults, see 778
*Business Relations and Occupations: Achievement Examinations for Secondary Schools, high school, see 779
Clerical Aptitude Test: Acorn National Aptitude Tests, grades 7–16 and adults, see 780
*Clerical Speed and Accuracy: Differential Aptitude Tests, grades 8–12 and adults, see 781
Clerical Tests FG and 2 [England], ages 12–13, see 781A
Detroit Clerical Aptitudes Examination, grades 9–12, see 782
*General Office Clerical Test: National Business Entrance Tests, grades 11–16 and adults, see 783
Hiett Simplified Shorthand Test (Gregg), 1–2 semesters high school, see 784
*Machine Calculation Test: National Business Entrance Tests, grades 11–16 and adults, see 785
*National Business Entrance Tests, grades 11–16 and adults, see 786
*National Teacher Examinations: Business Education, college seniors and teachers, see 787
★Office Information and Skills Test: Content Evaluation Series, high school, see 788
Reicherter-Sanders Typewriting I and II, 1–2 semesters high school, see 789
Russell-Sanders Bookkeeping Test, 1–2 semesters high school, see 790
SRA Clerical Aptitudes, grades 9–12 and adults, see 791
SRA Typing Skills, grades 9–12 and adults, see 792
Shorthand Aptitude Test [Australia], high school, see 793
Stenographic Aptitude Test, grades 9–16, see 794
*Stenographic Test: National Business Entrance Tests, grades 11–16 and adults, see 795
*Tapping Test: A Predictor of Typing and Other Tapping Operations, high school, see 796
*Teacher Education Examination Program: Business Education, college seniors preparing to teach secondary school, see 797
Turse Shorthand Aptitude Test, grades 8 and over, see 798
*Typewriting Test: National Business Entrance Tests, grades 11–16 and adults, see 799
*Undergraduate Program Field Tests: Business Test, college, see 800
United Students Typewriting Tests, 1–4 semesters, see 801

COMPUTATIONAL & TESTING DEVICES

★Bowman Chronological Age Calculator, see 802
Bowman M.A. and I.Q. Kalkulator, see 803
*Chronological Age Computer, ages 3-7 to 19-5, see 804
Dominion Table for Converting Mental Age to I.Q. [Canada], see 805
Grade Averaging Charts, see 806
I.Q. Calculator, see 807
★Mental Age Calculator, see 808
*Multiple Purpose Self Trainer, high school and adults, see 809
Psychometric Research and Service Chart Showing the Davis Difficulty and Discrimination Indices for Item Analysis [India], see 810
Rapid-Rater, see 811
★Ratio I.Q. Computer, see 812

COURTSHIP & MARRIAGE

★Albert Mate Selection Check List, premarital counselees, see 813
California Marriage Readiness Evaluation, premarital counselees, see 814
Caring Relationship Inventory, marital counselees, see 815
Courtship Analysis, adults, see 816
Dating Problems Checklist, high school and college, see 817
El Senoussi Multiphasic Marital Inventory, premarital and marital counselees, see 818
★I-Am Sentence Completion Test, marital counselees, see 819
Individual and Family Developmental Review, counselees and therapy patients, see 820
★Love Attitudes Inventory, grades 12-16, see 821
Male Impotence Test, adult males, see 822
Marital Communication Inventory, adults, see 823
★Marital Diagnostic Inventory, marital counselees, see 824
Marital Roles Inventory, marital counselees, see 825
Marriage Adjustment Form, adults, see 826
Marriage Adjustment Inventory, marital counselees, see 827
Marriage Adjustment Sentence Completion Survey, marital counselees, see 828
Marriage Analysis, married couples in counseling, see 829
★Marriage Expectation Inventories, engaged and married couples, see 830
Marriage-Personality Inventory, individuals and couples, see 831
Marriage Prediction Schedule, adults, see 832
Marriage Role Expectation Inventory, adolescents and adults, see 833
*Marriage Scale (For Measuring Compatibility of Interests), premarital or married counselees, see 834
★Marriage Skills Analysis, marital counselees, see 835
Otto Pre-Marital Counseling Schedules, adult couples, see 836
★Pair Attraction Inventory, college and adults, see 837
Sex Knowledge Inventory, sex education classes in high school and college and adults, see 838
Sexual Development Scale for Females, adult females, see 839
*Taylor-Johnson Temperament Analysis, grades 7-16 and adults, see 840
Thorman Family Relations Conference Situation Questionnaire, families receiving therapy, see 841

DRIVING & SAFETY EDUCATION

*American Automobile Association Driver Testing Apparatus, drivers, see 842
*Bicycle Safety—Performance and Skill Tests, ages 10-16, see 843
Driver Attitude Survey, drivers, see 844
★Driving Skill Exercises, automobile drivers, see 845
General Test on Traffic and Driving Knowledge, drivers, see 846
Hannaford Industrial Safety Attitude Scales, industry, see 847
McGlade Road Test for Use in Driver Licensing, Education and Employment, prospective drivers, see 848
Road Test Check List for Passenger Car Drivers, passenger car drivers, see 849
Siebrecht Attitude Scale, grades 9-16 and adults, see 850
★Simplified Road Test, drivers, see 851

EDUCATION

Academic Freedom Survey, college students and faculty, see 852
*CLEP Subject Examination in History of American Education, 1 semester or equivalent, see 853
*CLEP Subject Examination in Tests and Measurements, 1 semester or equivalent, see 854
★Classroom Atmosphere Questionnaire, grades 4-9, see 855
★Comprehensive Teaching and Training Evaluation, college and training programs, see 856
★Counseling Services Assessment Blank, college and adult counseling clients, see 857
★Course Evaluation Questionnaire, high school and college, see 858
Diagnostic Teacher-Rating Scale, grades 4-12, see 859
★Educational Values Assessment Questionnaire, adults, see 860
Faculty Morale Scale for Institutional Improvement, college faculty, see 861
★General Tests of Language and Arithmetic for Students [South Africa], first and second year Bantu candidates for primary teacher's certificate, see 862
*Graduate Record Examinations Advanced Education Test, graduate school candidates, see 863
*Illinois Course Evaluation Questionnaire, college, see 864
Illinois Ratings of Teacher Effectiveness, grades 9-12, see 865
Illinois Teacher Evaluation Questionnaire, grades 7-12, see 866
*Junior Index of Motivation, grades 7-12, see 867
Minnesota Teacher Attitude Inventory, elementary and secondary school teachers and students in grades 12-17, see 868
*National Teacher Examinations, college seniors and teachers, see 869
*National Teacher Examinations: Early Childhood Education, college seniors and teachers, see 870
*National Teacher Examinations: Education in an Urban Setting, college seniors and teachers, see 871
*National Teacher Examinations: Education in the Elementary School, college seniors and teachers, see 872
*National Teacher Examinations: Education of Mentally Retarded, college seniors and teachers, see 873
★National Teacher Examinations: Educational Administration and Supervision, prospective principals, see 874
★National Teacher Examinations: Guidance Counselor, prospective guidance counselors, see 875

National Teacher Examinations: Media Specialist—Library and Audio-Visual Services, college seniors and teachers, see 876
Ohio Teaching Record: Anecdotal Observation Form, teachers, see 877
★*Oral School Attitude Test,* grades kgn–3, see 878
Pictographic Self Rating Scale, high school and college, see 879
Purdue Instructor Performance Indicator, college teachers, see 880
Purdue Rating Scale for Instruction, college teachers, see 881
Purdue Student-Teacher Opinionaire, student teachers, see 882
Purdue Teacher Evaluation Scale, grades 7-12, see 883
Purdue Teacher Opinionaire, teachers, see 884
Remmlein's School Law Test, teacher education classes in school law, see 885
★*School Administration and Supervision,* prospective elementary school administrators and supervisors, see 886
★*School Atmosphere Questionnaire,* grades 7-12, see 887
★*School Attitude Test,* grades 4–6, see 888
★*School Personnel Research and Evaluation Services,* teachers and prospective administrators and supervisors, see 889
★*School Survey of Interpersonal Relationships,* teachers, see 890
★*Secondary School Administration,* prospective secondary school administrators, see 891
★*Secondary School Supervision,* prospective secondary school supervisors, see 892
Self Appraisal Scale for Teachers, teachers, see 893
★*Student Instructional Report,* college teachers, see 894
★*Student Reactions to College,* two-year college, see 895.
Student's Rating Scale of an Instructor, high school and college, see 896
★*Survey of Educational Leadership Practices,* teachers and school administrators, see 897
Teacher Education Examination Program, college seniors preparing to teach, see 898
Teacher Education Examination Program: Early Childhood Education, college seniors preparing to teach kgn–grade 3, see 899
Teacher Education Examination Program: Elementary School Education, college seniors preparing to teach grades 1–8, see 900
Teacher Opinionaire on Democracy, teachers, see 901
Teacher Preference Schedule, elementary school teachers and prospective teachers, see 902
★*Teacher Self-Rating Inventory,* teachers, see 903
Teaching Aptitude Test, grades 12–16, see 904
Teaching Evaluation Record, teachers, see 905
Undergraduate Program Field Tests: Education Test, college, see 906
Wilson Teacher-Appraisal Scale, ratings by students in grades 7–16, see 907

HANDWRITING

Ayres Measuring Scale for Handwriting: Gettysburg Edition, grades 5–8, see 908
Expessional Growth Through Handwriting Evaluation Scale, grades 1–12, see 909

HEALTH & PHYSICAL EDUCATION

★*AAHPER Cooperative Health Education Test,* grades 5–9, see 910

AAHPER Cooperative Physical Education Tests, grades 4–12, see 911
AAHPER-Kennedy Foundation Special Fitness Test for the Mentally Retarded, ages 8–18, see 912
AAHPER Sport Skills Tests, ages 10–18, see 913
AAHPER Youth Fitness Test, ages 10–30 (grades 5–16), see 914
Action-Choice Tests for Competitive Sports Situations, high school and college, see 915
Attitude Inventory, college women, see 916
Basic Fitness Tests, ages 12–18, see 917
Belmont Measures of Athletic Performance, females grades 9–16, see 918
CAHPER Fitness-Performance Test [Canada], ages 7–44, see 919
CLEP Subject Examination in Human Growth and Development, 1 semester or equivalent, see 920
College Health Knowledge Test, college, see 921
★*Drug Abuse Knowledge Test,* grades 10–12, see 922
Drug Knowledge Inventory, grades 7–16 and adults, see 923
Emporia Elementary Health Test, grades 6–8, see 924
Emporia High School Health Test, high school and college, see 925
Health and Safety Education Test, grades 3–6, see 926
Health Behavior Inventory, grades 3–16, see 927
Health Education Test: Knowledge and Application, grades 7–13, see 928
Health Knowledge Test for College Freshmen, grade 13, see 929
Health Test: National Achievement Tests, grades 3–8, see 930
Illinois Ratings of Character in Physical Education, high school, see 931
Indiana Physical Fitness Test, grades 4–12, see 932
Information Test on Drugs and Drug Abuse, grades 9–16 and adults, see 933
Information Test on Human Reproduction, grades 9–16 and adults, see 934
Kilander-Leach Health Knowledge Test, grades 12–16, see 935
Modified Sjöstrand Physical Work Capacity Test [Canada], ages 7–44, see 936
National Teacher Examinations: Men's Physical Education, college seniors and teachers, see 937
National Teacher Examinations: Women's Physical Education, college seniors and teachers, see 938
Patient's Self-History Form, patients, see 939
★*Self Administered Health Questionnaire for Secondary School Students,* high school, see 940
Swimming Ability Scales for Boys in Secondary Schools: National Swimming Norms [England], boys ages 11–18, see 941
Teacher Education Examination Program: Physical Education, college seniors preparing to teach secondary school, see 942
★*Tests for Venereal Disease Education,* junior high school, high school and college, see 943
★*Thompson Smoking and Tobacco Knowledge Test,* grades 7–16, see 944
Undergraduate Program Field Tests: Physical Education Test, college, see 945
★*VD Knowledge Test,* grades 6 and over, see 946
Wetzel Grid Charts, ages birth–18, see 947

HOME ECONOMICS

Compton Fabric Preference Test, females in grades 7 and over, see 948
Emporia Clothing Test, high school, see 949
Emporia Foods Test, high school, see 950

Minnesota Check List for Food Preparation and Serving, grades 7–16 and adults, see 951
**National Teacher Examinations: Home Economics Education,* college seniors and teachers, see 952
**Nutrition Information Test,* grades 9–16 and adults, see 953
Scales for Appraising High School Homemaking Programs, pupils, teachers, community members, and administrators, see 954
★*Teacher Education Examination Program: Home Economics Education,* college seniors preparing to teach secondary school, see 955
★*Test of Family Life Knowledge and Attitudes,* grade 12 boys and girls seeking Betty Crocker college scholarships and awards, see 956–66

INDUSTRIAL ARTS

Drawing: Cooperative Industrial Arts Tests, 1 semester grades 7–9, see 967
Electricity/Electronics: Cooperative Industrial Arts Tests, 1 semester grades 7–9, see 968
Emporia Industrial Arts Test, high school, see 969
General Industrial Arts: Cooperative Industrial Arts Tests, 1 year grades 7–9, see 970
Metals: Cooperative Industrial Arts Tests, 1 semester grades 7–9, see 971
**National Teacher Examinations: Industrial Arts Education,* college seniors and teachers, see 972
**Teacher Education Examination Program: Industrial Arts,* college seniors preparing to teach secondary school, see 973
Technical and Scholastic Test: Dailey Vocational Tests, grades 8–12 and adults, see 974
Woods: Cooperative Industrial Arts Tests, 1 semester grades 7–9, see 975

LEARNING DISABILITIES

★*Automated Graphogestalt Technique,* grades 1–4, see 976
★*Basic Screening and Referral Form for Children With Suspected Learning and Behavioral Disabilities,* grades 1–12, see 977
★*Cutrona Child Study Profile of Psycho-Educational Abilities,* grades kgn–3, see 978
First Grade Screening Test, first grade entrants, see 979
★*Grassi Basic Cognitive Evaluation,* ages 3–9, see 980
Illinois Test of Psycholinguistic Abilities, ages 2–10, see 981; *Filmed Demonstration of the ITPA,* see 982
★*Individual Learning Disabilities Classroom Screening Instrument,* grades 1–3, see 983
Meeting Street School Screening Test, grades kgn–1, see 984
★*Psychoeducational Inventory of Basic Learning Abilities,* ages 5–12 with suspected learning disabilities, see 985
Psychoeducational Profile of Basic Learning Abilities, ages 2–14 with learning disabilities, see 986
★*Pupil Rating Scale: Screening for Learning Disabilities,* grades 3–4, see 987
Screening Test for the Assignment of Remedial Treatments, ages 4-6 to 6-5, see 988
Screening Tests for Identifying Children With Specific Language Disability, grades 1–4, see 989
Specific Language Disability Test, "average to high IQ" children in grades 6–8, see 990
Valett Developmental Survey of Basic Learning Abilities, ages 2–7, see 991

LISTENING COMPREHENSION

**Assessment of Children's Language Comprehension,* ages 2–6, see 992
Brown-Carlsen Listening Comprehension Test, grades 9–16 and adults, see 993
Cooperative Primary Tests: Listening, grades 1.5–3, see 994
Orr-Graham Listening Test, junior high school boys, see 995
★*Progressive Achievement Tests of Listening Comprehension* [New Zealand], standards 1–4 and Forms I–IV (ages 7–14), see 996
Sequential Tests of Educational Progress: Listening, grades 4–14, see 997
★*Tests for Auditory Comprehension of Language,* ages 3–7, see 997A

PHILOSOPHY

**Graduate Record Examinations Advanced Philosophy Test,* graduate school candidates, see 998
**Undergraduate Program Field Tests: Philosophy Test,* college, see 999
**Undergraduate Program Field Tests: Scholastic Philosophy Test,* college, see 1000

PSYCHOLOGY

Aden-Crosthwait Adolescent Psychology Achievement Test, college, see 1001
**CLEP Subject Examination in Educational Psychology,* 1 semester or equivalent, see 1002
**CLEP Subject Examination in General Psychology,* 1 semester or equivalent, see 1003
Cass-Sanders Psychology Test, high school and college, see 1004
**Graduate Record Examinations Advanced Psychology Test,* graduate school candidates, see 1005
**Undergraduate Program Field Tests: Psychology Test,* college, see 1006

RECORD & REPORT FORMS

**A/9 Cumulative Record Folder,* grades kgn–12, see 1007
American Council on Education Cumulative Record Folders, grades 1–16, see 1008
California Cumulative Record and Health Insert, grades 1–12, see 1009
**Cassel Developmental Record,* birth to death, see 1010
Florida Cumulative Guidance Record, grades 1–12, see 1011
G.C. Anecdotal Record Form [Canada], teachers' recordings of student actions, see 1012
**Guidance Cumulative Folder and Record Forms,* grades kgn–12, see 1013
**Height Weight Interpretation Folders,* ages 4–17, see 1014
Junior High School Record, grades 7–10, see 1015
**Ontario School Record System* [Canada], grades kgn–13, see 1016
★*Permanent Record Folder,* exceptional children, see 1017
★*Psychodiagnostic Test Report Blank,* psychologists' test data on clients, see 1018
**Secondary-School Record,* grades 9–12, see 1019

RELIGIOUS EDUCATION

Achievement Test in Jewish History, junior high school, see 1020
★*Achievement Test—Jewish Life and Observances,* grades 5–7, see 1021
★*Achievement Test—The State of Israel,* "pupils who have completed an organized course of study on the State of Israel," see 1022
★*Bible and You,* ages 13 and over, see 1023
★*Biblical Survey Test,* college, see 1024
Concordia Bible Information Inventory, grades 4–8, see 1025
Inventory of Religious Activities and Interests, high school and college students considering church-related occupations and theological school students, see 1025A
Religious Attitudes Inventory, religious counselees, see 1026
Standardized Bible Content Tests, Bible college, see 1027
Theological School Inventory, incoming seminary students, see 1028
Youth Research Survey, ages 13–19, see 1029

SCORING MACHINES & SERVICES

Automata EDT 1200 Educational Data Terminal, see 1030
Hankes Scoring Service, see 1031
IBM 1230 Optical Mark Scoring Reader, see 1032
★*IBM 3881 Optical Mark Reader,* see 1033
MRC Scoring and Reporting Services, see 1034
NCS Scoring and Reporting Services, see 1035
NCS Sentry 70, see 1036
OpScan Test Scoring and Document Scanning System, see 1037
Psychological Resources, see 1038

SOCIOECONOMIC STATUS

American Home Scale, grades 8–16, see 1039
Environmental Participation Index, culturally disadvantaged ages 12 and over, see 1040
Home Index, grades 4–12, see 1040A
Socio-Economic Status Scales [India], urban students, adults, and rural families, see 1041

STATISTICS

CLEP Subject Examination in Statistics, 1 semester or equivalent, see 1042
★*Objective Tests in Mathematics: Statistics* [England], ages 15 and over, see 1043

TEST PROGRAMS

ACT Assessment, candidates for college entrance, see 1044
Advanced Placement Examinations, high school students desiring credit for college level courses or admission to advanced courses, see 1045
Canadian Test Battery, Grade 10 [Canada], see 1046
Canadian Test Battery, Grades 8–9 [Canada], grades 8.5–9.0, see 1047
College Board Admissions Testing Program, candidates for college entrance, see 1048
★*College Guidance Program,* grade 11, see 1049
College-Level Examination Program, 1–2 years of college or equivalent, see 1050
College Placement Tests, entering college freshmen, see 1051
Comparative Guidance and Placement Program, entrants to two-year colleges and vocational-technical institutes, see 1052
Graduate Record Examinations: National Program for Graduate School Selection, graduate school candidates, see 1053
Junior College Placement Program, junior college entrants, see 1054
National Guidance Testing Program, grades 1.5–14, see 1055
National Science Foundation Graduate Fellowship Testing Program, applicants for N.S.F. fellowships for graduate study in the sciences, see 1056
★*Ohio Survey Tests,* grades 4, 6, 8, and 10, see 1057
Project Talent Test Battery, grades 9–12, see 1058
Secondary School Admission Test, grades 5–10, see 1059
★*Service for Admission to College and University Testing Program* [Canada], candidates for college entrance, see 1060
★*Testing Academic Achievement,* high school students desiring credit for college level courses or advanced placement, entering college freshmen, and 1–2 years of college or equivalent, see 1061
Undergraduate Program for Counseling and Evaluation, college, see 1062

MULTI-APTITUDE BATTERIES

Academic Promise Tests, grades 6–9, see 1063
★*Academic-Technical Aptitude Tests* [South Africa], "coloured pupils" in standards 6–8, see 1064
★*Aptitude Test for Junior Secondary Pupils* [South Africa], Bantus in Form I, see 1065
Aptitude Tests for Occupations, grades 9–13 and adults, see 1066
★*Armed Services Vocational Aptitude Battery,* high school, see 1067
Detroit General Aptitudes Examination, grades 6–12, see 1068
Differential Aptitude Tests, grades 8–12 and adults, see 1069
Differential Test Battery [England], ages 7 to "top university level," see 1070
Employee Aptitude Survey, ages 16 and over, see 1071
Flanagan Aptitude Classification Tests, grades 9–12 and adults, see 1072
General Aptitude Test Battery, grades 9–12 and adults, see 1073
Guilford-Zimmerman Aptitude Survey, grades 9–16 and adults, see 1074
High Level Battery: Test A/75 [South Africa], adults with at least 12 years of education, see 1075
★*International Primary Factors Test Battery,* grades 5 and over, see 1076
Jastak Test of Potential Ability and Behavior Stability, ages 11.5–14.5, see 1077
Job-Tests Program, adults, see 1078
★*Junior Aptitude Tests for Indian South Africans* [South Africa], standards 6–8, see 1079
Measurement of Skill, adults, see 1080

Multi-Aptitude Test, college courses in testing, see 1081
Multiple Aptitude Tests, grades 7-13, see 1082
N.B. Aptitude Tests (Junior) [South Africa], standards 4-8, see 1083
National Institute for Personnel Research Intermediate Battery [South Africa], standards 7-10 and job applicants with 9-12 years of education, see 1084
★National Institute for Personnel Research Normal Battery [South Africa], standards 6-10 and job applicants with 8-11 years of education, see 1085
★Nonreading Aptitude Test Battery, disadvantaged grades 9-12 and adults, see 1086
SRA Primary Mental Abilities, grades kgn-12 and adults, see 1087
★Senior Aptitude Tests [South Africa], standards 8-10 and college and adults, see 1088

PERSONALITY

NONPROJECTIVE

★*Ai3Q: A Measure of the Obsessional Personality or Anal Character* [England], sixth form and intelligent adults, see 1089
A-S Reaction Study, college and adults, see 1090
★Activity Vector Analysis, ages 16 and over, see 1091
★Adaptive Behavior Scales, mentally retarded and emotionally maladjusted ages 3 and over, see 1092
Addiction Research Center Inventory, drug addicts, see 1093
Adjective Check List, grades 9-16 and adults, see 1094
Adjustment Inventory, grades 9-16 and adults, see 1095
★*Adolescent Alienation Index,* ages 12-19, see 1096
★*Affect Scale,* college, see 1097
Alcadd Test, adults, see 1098
★*Animal Crackers: A Test of Motivation to Achieve,* grades kgn-1, see 1099
Anxiety Scale for the Blind, blind and partially sighted ages 13 and over, see 1100
Attitude-Interest Analysis Test, early adolescents and adults, see 1101
Attitudes Toward Industrialization, adults, see 1102
Attitudes Toward Parental Control of Children, adults, see 1103
Ayres Space Test, ages 3 and over, see 1104
Babcock Test of Mental Efficiency, ages 7 and over, see 1105
Baker-Schulberg Community Mental Health Ideology Scale, mental health professionals, see 1106
★*Balthazar Scales of Adaptive Behavior,* "profoundly and severely mentally retarded adults and the younger less retarded," see 1107
★*Barclay Classroom Climate Inventory,* grades 3-6, see 1108
Barron-Welsh Art Scale, ages 6 and over, see 1109
Behavior Cards, delinquents having a reading grade score 4.5 or higher, see 1110
Behavior Status Inventory, psychiatric inpatients, see 1111
Bristol Social Adjustment Guides [England], ages 5-15, see 1112
Brook Reaction Test [England], ages 13 and over, see 1113
Burks' Behavior Rating Scale for Organic Brain Dysfunction, grades kgn-6, see 1114
Burks' Behavior Rating Scales, preschool and grades kgn-8, see 1115
C-R Opinionaire, grades 11-16 and adults, see 1116
Cain-Levine Social Competency Scale, mentally retarded children ages 5-13, see 1117
California Life Goals Evaluation Schedules, ages 15 and over, see 1118
California Medical Survey, medical patients ages 10-18 and adults, see 1119
California Preschool Social Competency Scale, ages 2.5-5.5, see 1120
California Psychological Inventory, ages 13 and over, see 1121; *★Behaviordyne Psychodiagnostic Lab Service,* see 1122
California Test of Personality, grades kgn-14 and adults, see 1123
Cassel Group Level of Aspiration Test, grades 5-16 and adults, see 1124
Chapin Social Insight Test, ages 13 and over, see 1125
Child Behavior Rating Scale, grades kgn-3, see 1126
★Children's Embedded Figures Test, ages 5-12, see 1127
Children's Hypnotic Susceptibility Scale, ages 5-16, see 1128
★Children's Personality Questionnaire [South Africa], ages 8-12, see 1129
Client-Centered Counseling Progress Record, adults and children undergoing psychotherapeutic counseling, see 1130
Clinical Analysis Questionnaire, ages 18 and over, see 1131
Clinical Behavior Check List and Rating Scale, clinical clients, see 1132
College and University Environment Scales, college, see 1133
College Inventory of Academic Adjustment, college, see 1134
★College Student Questionnaires, college entrants and students, see 1135
★*College Student Satisfaction Questionnaire,* college, see 1136
Community Adaptation Schedule, normals and psychiatric patients, see 1137
Community Improvement Scale, adults, see 1138
Comrey Personality Scales, ages 16 and over, see 1139
Concept Formation Test, normal and schizophrenic adults, see 1140
★*Concept-Specific Anxiety Scale,* college and adults, see 1141
★*Conceptual Systems Test,* grades 7 and over, see 1142
Conservatism Scale [England], ages 12 and over, see 1143
Cornell Index, ages 18 and over, see 1144
Cornell Medical Index, ages 14 and over, see 1145
Cornell Word Form 2, adults, see 1146
Cotswold Personality Assessment P.A.1 [Scotland], ages 11-16, see 1147
★*Crawford Psychological Adjustment Scale,* psychiatric patients, see 1148
Cree Questionnaire, industrial employees, see 1149
Current and Past Psychopathology Scales, psychiatric patients and nonpatients, see 1150
DF Opinion Survey, grades 12-16 and adults, see 1151
Defense Mechanism Inventory, ages 16 and over, see 1152
Demos D Scale: An Attitude Scale for the Identification of Dropouts, grades 7-12, see 1153
Depression Adjective Check Lists, grades 9-16 and adults, see 1154
Detroit Adjustment Inventory, grades kgn-12, see 1155

Developmental Potential of Preschool Children, handicapped children ages 2–6, see 1156
Devereux Adolescent Behavior Rating Scale, normal and emotionally disturbed children ages 13–18, see 1157
Devereux Child Behavior Rating Scale, emotionally disturbed and mentally retarded children ages 8–12, see 1158
Devereux Elementary School Behavior Rating Scale, grades kgn–6, see 1159
Diplomacy Test of Empathy, business and industry, see 1160
★*Discharge Readiness Inventory,* psychiatric patients, see 1161
Dynamic Personality Inventory [England], ages 15 or 17 and over with IQ's of 80 and over, see 1162
**Early School Personality Questionnaire,* ages 6–8, see 1163
Edwards Personal Preference Schedule, college and adults, see 1164
Edwards Personality Inventory, grades 11–16 and adults, see 1165
Ego-Ideal and Conscience Development Test, ages 12–18, see 1166
Ego Strength Q-Sort Test, grades 9–16 and adults, see 1167
Elizur Test of Psycho-Organicity, ages 6 and over, see 1168
**Embedded Figures Test,* ages 10 and over, see 1169
Emo Questionnaire, adults, see 1170
Empathy Test, ages 13 and over, see 1171
Evaluation Modality Test, adults, see 1172
★*Experiential World Inventory,* disturbed adolescents and adults, see 1173
Eysenck Personality Inventory [England], grades 9–16 and adults, see 1174
Eysenck-Withers Personality Inventory [England], institutionalized subnormal adults, see 1175
**FIRO Scales,* grades 4–16 and adults, see 1176
★*Fairview Development Scale,* infirm mentally retarded, see 1177
★*Fairview Problem Behavior Record,* mentally retarded, see 1178
★*Fairview Self-Help Scale,* mentally retarded, see 1179
★*Fairview Social Skills Scale,* mentally retarded, see 1180
Family Adjustment Test, ages 12 and over, see 1181
Family Relations Test [England], ages 3 and over, see 1182
Famous Sayings, grades 9–16 and business and industry, see 1183
Fatigue Scales Kit, adults, see 1184
Fear Survey Schedule, college and adults, see 1185
Fels Parent Behavior Rating Scales, parents, see 1186
**Forty-Eight Item Counseling Evaluation Test,* adolescents and adults, see 1187
Freeman Anxiety Neurosis and Psychosomatic Test, mental patients, see 1188
★*Frost Self Description Questionnaire* [Canada], ages 8–14, see 1189
Getting Along, grades 7–9, see 1190
Gibson Spiral Maze [England], ages 8.5 and over, see 1191
Goldstein-Scheerer Tests of Abstract and Concrete Thinking, brain damaged adults, see 1192
Gordon Personal Inventory, grades 9–16 and adults, see 1193
Gordon Personal Profile, grades 9–16 and adults, see 1194
Gottschalk-Gleser Content Analysis Scales, ages 14 and over, see 1195
Grassi Block Substitution Test, mental patients, see 1196
Grayson Perceptualization Test, detection of cortical impairment, see 1197

Grid Test of Schizophrenic Thought Disorder [England], adults, see 1198
Group Cohesiveness: A Study of Group Morale, adults, see 1199
Group Dimensions Descriptions Questionnaire, college and adult groups, see 1200
★*Group Embedded Figures Test,* ages 10 and over, see 1201
Group Psychotherapy Suitability Evaluation Scale, patients in group therapy, see 1202
**Guidance Inventory,* high school, see 1203
Guilford-Holley L Inventory, college and adults, see 1204
Guilford-Martin Inventory of Factors GAMIN, grades 12–16 and adults, see 1205
Guilford-Martin Personnel Inventory, adults, see 1206
Guilford-Zimmerman Temperament Survey, grades 12–16 and adults, see 1207
★*Hahn Self Psychoevaluation Materials,* ages 40 and over, see 1208
★*Hahnemann High School Behavior Rating Scale,* grades 7–12, see 1209
Handicap Problems Inventory, ages 16 and over with physical disabilities, see 1210
**Hartman Value Profile,* ages 12 and over, see 1211
Harvard Group Scale of Hypnotic Susceptibility, college and adults, see 1212
Hellenic Affiliation Scale, college, see 1213
Hill Interaction Matrix, psychotherapy groups, see 1214
Hoffer-Osmond Diagnostic Test, mental patients, see 1215
Hooper Visual Organization Test, ages 14 and over, see 1216
Hospital Adjustment Scale, mental patients, see 1217
Hostility and Direction of Hostility Questionnaire [England], mental patients and normals, see 1218
★*How I See Myself Scale,* grades 3–12, see 1219
How Well Do You Know Yourself?, high school, college, office and factory workers, see 1220
Human Relations Inventory, grades 9–16 and adults, see 1221
Humm-Wadsworth Temperament Scale, adults, see 1222
**Hunt-Minnesota Test for Organic Brain Damage,* chronological ages 16–70 and mental ages 8 and over, see 1223
Hysteroid-Obsessoid Questionnaire [England], mental patients and normals, see 1224
**IPAT Anxiety Scale Questionnaire,* ages 14 and over, see 1225
IPAT Contact Personality Factor Test, high school and adults, see 1226
**IPAT 8-Parallel-Form Anxiety Battery,* ages 14 or 15 and over, see 1227
IPAT Humor Test of Personality, high school and adults, see 1228
IPAT Neurotic Personality Factor Test, grades 9–16 and adults, see 1229
Independent Activities Questionnaire, high school and college, see 1230
★*Inferred Self-Concept Scale,* grades 1–6, see 1231
Inpatient Multidimensional Psychiatric Scale, hospitalized mental patients, see 1232
Institute of Child Study Security Test [Canada], grades 1–8, see 1233
Institutional Functioning Inventory, college faculty and administrators, see 1234
★*Institutional Goals Inventory,* college faculty and students, see 1235
Institutional Self-Study Service Survey, college students, see 1236
Integration Level Test Series, adults, see 1237
Interest Inventory for Elementary Grades, grades 4–6, see 1238

Inter-Person Perception Test, ages 6 and over, see 1239
*Interpersonal Check List, adults, see 1240
★*Interpersonal Communication Inventory,* grades 9–16 and adults, see 1241
★*Interpersonal Orientation Scale,* college and adults, see 1242
Interpersonal Perception Method [England], married couples and other 2-person or 2-group situations, see 1243
**Inventory of College Activities,* college, see 1244
Inventory of Factors STDCR, grades 9–16 and adults, see 1245
★*"Is of Identity" Test,* grades 4–16, see 1246
It Scale for Children, ages 5–6, see 1247
★*Jesness Behavior Checklist,* ages 10 and over, see 1248
**Jesness Inventory,* disturbed children and adolescents ages 8–18 and adults, see 1249
**Job Analysis and Interest Measurement,* adults, see 1250
Jones Personality Rating Scale, grades 9–12 and adults, see 1251
Junior Eysenck Personality Inventory [England], ages 7–15, see 1252
**Jr.-Sr. High School Personality Questionnaire,* ages 12–18, see 1253
KD Proneness Scale and Check List, ages 7 and over, see 1254
Katz Adjustment Scales, normal and mentally disordered adults, see 1255
Kuder Preference Record—Personal, grades 9–16 and adults, see 1256
Kundu's Neurotic Personality Inventory [India], adults, see 1257
★*Kupfer-Detre System,* psychiatric patients, see 1258
Leadership Ability Evaluation, grades 9–16 and adults, see 1259
Leadership Q-Sort Test, adults, see 1260
Level of Aspiration Board, mental ages 12.5 and over, see 1261
Life Adjustment Inventory, high school, see 1262
Lüscher Color Test, adults, see 1263
**MACC Behavioral Adjustment Scale,* psychiatric patients, see 1264
**M-B History Record,* psychiatric patients and penal groups, see 1265
**M-Scale: An Inventory of Attitudes Toward Black/White Relations in the United States,* college and adults, see 1266
★*Maferr Inventory of Feminine Values,* older adolescents and adults, see 1267
★*Maferr Inventory of Masculine Values,* older adolescents and adults, see 1268
Manchester Scales of Social Adaptation [England], ages 6–15, see 1269
Mandel Social Adjustment Scale, psychiatric patients and others, see 1270
Manson Evaluation, adults, see 1271
**Martin S-D Inventory,* clients and patients, see 1272
Maryland Parent Attitude Survey, parents, see 1273
★*Mathematics Anxiety Rating Scale,* college and adults, see 1274
Maudsley Personality Inventory [England], college and adults, see 1275
Maxfield-Buchholz Scale of Social Maturity for Use With Preschool Blind Children, infancy–6 years, see 1276
Memory-For-Designs Test, ages 8.5 and over, see 1277
Mental Status Schedule, psychiatric patients and nonpatients, see 1278
Middlesex Hospital Questionnaire [England], ages 18 and over, see 1279
Minnesota Counseling Inventory, high school, see 1280
Minnesota Multiphasic Personality Inventory, ages 16 and over, see 1281; **Behaviordyne Psychodiagnostic Lab Service,* see 1282; **MMPI-ICA Computer Report,* see 1283; *The Psychological Corporation MMPI Reporting Service,* see 1284; **Roche MMPI Computerized Interpretation Service,* see 1285
Minnesota Rating Scale for Personal Qualities and Abilities, college and adults, see 1286
★*Missouri Children's Picture Series,* ages 5–16, see 1287
★*Mood Altering Substances,* high school and college, see 1288
Mooney Problem Check List, grades 7–16 and adults, see 1289
Mother-Child Relationship Evaluation, mothers, see 1290
Motivation Analysis Test, ages 17 and over, see 1291
Multidimensional Maturity Scale, grades kgn–12, see 1292
Multiple Affect Adjective Check List, grades 8–16 and adults, see 1293
Myers-Briggs Type Indicator, grades 9–16 and adults, see 1294
Neuroticism Scale Questionnaire, ages 13 and over, see 1295
New Junior Maudsley Inventory [England], ages 9–16, see 1296
Northampton Activity Rating Scale, mental patients, see 1297
Nurses' Observation Scale for Inpatient Evaluation, mental patients, see 1298
Object Sorting Scales [Australia], adults, see 1299
Objective-Analytic (O-A) Anxiety Battery, ages 14 and over, see 1300
Ohio College Association Rating Scale, high school, see 1301
Omnibus Personality Inventory, college, see 1302
Opinion, Attitude, and Interest Survey, high school seniors and college students, see 1303
★*Opinions Toward Adolescents,* college and adults, see 1304
Organic Integrity Test, ages 5 and over, see 1305
Orientation Inventory, college and industry, see 1306
★*Ottawa School Behavior Check List* [Canada], ages 6–12, see 1307
**PHSF Relations Questionnaire* [South Africa], standards 6–10 and college and adults, see 1308
PRADI Autobiographical Form, clinical clients, see 1309
Parent-Adolescent Communication Inventory, high school and adults, see 1310
**Perceptual Maze Test* [England], ages 6–16 and adults, see 1311
**Personal Adjustment Index,* job applicants, see 1312
Personal Adjustment Inventory, ages 9–13, see 1313
Personal Audit, grades 9–16 and adults, see 1314
Personal Orientation Inventory, grades 9–16 and adults, see 1315
Personal Preference Scale, ages 15 and over, see 1316
★*Personal Values Abstract,* ages 13 and over, see 1317
Personal Values Inventory, grades 12–13, see 1318
Personality Evaluation Form, ages 2 and over, see 1319
Personality Inventory, grades 9–16 and adults, see 1320
Personality Rating Scale, grades 4–12, see 1321
Personality Research Form, college, see 1322
**Personnel Reaction Blank,* adults, see 1323
Philo-Phobe, ages 10 and over, see 1324
Pictorial Study of Values, ages 14 and over, see 1325
Piers-Harris Children's Self Concept Scale, grades 3–12, see 1326
Polarity Scale, college and adults, see 1327
Polyfactorial Study of Personality, adults, see 1328
Power of Influence Test, grades 2–13, see 1329

Practical Policy Test, adults, see 1330
★*Preschool Embedded Figures Test*, ages 3–5, see 1331
Preschool Self-Concept Picture Test, ages 4–5, see 1332
Press Test, industrial employees, see 1333
★*Primary Self-Concept Inventory*, grades kgn–4, see 1334
Problem Check List: Form for Rural Young People, ages 16–30, see 1335
Process for In-School Screening of Children With Emotional Handicaps, grades kgn–12, see 1336
★*Profile of Mood States*, college and psychiatric outpatients, see 1337
**Progress Assessment Chart of Social Development* [England], mentally handicapped children and adults, see 1338
Psychiatric Evaluation Form, psychiatric patients and nonpatients, see 1339
Psychiatric Status Schedules, psychiatric patients and nonpatients, see 1340
Psychological Audit for Interpersonal Relations, marriage counselees and industrial personnel, see 1341
★*Psychological Screening Inventory*, ages 16 and over, see 1342
Psychometric Behavior Checklist, adults, see 1343
Psycho-Somatic Inventory, older adolescents and adults, see 1344
Psychotic Inpatient Profile, mental patients, see 1345
Psychotic Reaction Profile, mental patients, see 1346
Pupil Behavior Inventory, grades 7–12, see 1347
Purdue Master Attitude Scales, grades 7–16, see 1348
Purdue Rating Scale for Administrators and Executives, administrators and executives, see 1349
Purpose in Life Test, adults, see 1350
Q-Tags Test of Personality [Canada], ages 6 and over, see 1351
★*Reactions to Everyday Situations* [South Africa], ages 16 and over, see 1352
*Reid Report, job applicants, see 1353
Richardson Emergency Psychodiagnostic Summary, mental patients, see 1354
★*Risk-Taking-Attitude-Values Inventory*, ages 3 and over, see 1354A
★*Rokeach Value Survey*, grades 7–16 and adults, see 1355
★*Runner Studies of Attitude Patterns*, job applicants, see 1356
Rutgers Social Attribute Inventory, adults, see 1357
SAQS Chicago Q Sort, college and adults, see 1358
S-D Proneness Checklist, clients and patients, see 1359
**STS Junior Inventory*, grades 4–8, see 1360
**STS Youth Inventory*, grades 7–12, see 1361
Scale of Socio-Egocentrism, grades 7–16, see 1362
Scale to Measure Attitudes Toward Disabled Persons, disabled and nondisabled adults, see 1363
★*School Attitude Survey*, grades 3–6, see 1364
School Interest Inventory, grades 7–12, see 1365
School Inventory, high school, see 1366
School Motivation Analysis Test, ages 12–17, see 1367
Science Research Temperament Scale, grades 12–16 and adults, see 1368
★*Secondary School Research Program*, high school students, teachers, and administrators, see 1369
Security-Insecurity Inventory, grades 9–16 and adults, see 1370
Self-Analysis Inventory, adults, see 1371
★*Self-Concept Adjective Checklist*, grades kgn–8, see 1372
★*Self-Concept and Motivation Inventory*, age 4 and grades kgn–12, see 1373
★*Self-Esteem Questionnaire*, ages 9 and over, see 1374
Self-Interview Inventory, adult males, see 1375
Self Perception Inventory, ages 12 and over, see 1376
Self-Rating Depression Scale, adults, see 1377

★*Self-Report Inventory*, college, see 1378
Sherman Mental Impairment Test, adults, see 1379
Shipley-Institute of Living Scale for Measuring Intellectual Impairment, adults, see 1380
★*Situational Attitude Scale*, college, see 1381
★*Situational Preference Inventory*, grades 9–16 and adults, see 1382
**Sixteen Personality Factor Questionnaire*, ages 16 and over, see 1383
Slosson Drawing Coordination Test for Children and Adults, ages 1.5 and over, see 1384
Social Competence Inventories, adults, see 1385
Social Intelligence Test, grades 9–16 and adults, see 1386
Spiral Aftereffect Test, ages 5 and over, see 1387
**Stamp Behaviour Study Technique* [Australia], preschool–kgn, see 1388
Stanford Hypnotic Susceptibility Scale, college and adults, see 1389
Stanford Profile Scales of Hypnotic Susceptibility, college and adults, see 1390
State-Trait Anxiety Inventory, grades 9–16 and adults, see 1391
★*State-Trait Anxiety Inventory for Children*, grades 4–8, see 1392
Stereopathy-Acquiescence Schedule, college, see 1393
**Stern Activities Index*, grades 7–16 and adults, see 1394
**Stern Environment Indexes*, grades 7 through graduate school, see 1395
Stockton Geriatric Rating Scale, hospital or nursing home patients aged 65 and over, see 1396
★*Structured and Scaled Interview to Assess Maladjustment*, mental patients, see 1397
Structured Clinical Interview, mental patients, see 1398
Student Attitude Inventory [Australia], college, see 1399
Student Description Form, grades 9–12, see 1400
★*Student Evaluation Scale*, grades 1–12, see 1401
Study of Choices, ages 16 and over, see 1402
Study of Values, grades 10–16 and adults, see 1403; British Edition [England], college and adults, see 1404
Style of Mind Inventory, college and adults, see 1405
★*Suinn Test Anxiety Behavior Scale*, college and adults, see 1406
Survey of Interpersonal Values, grades 9–16 and adults, see 1407
Survey of Personal Attitude "SPA" (With Pictures), adults, see 1408
Survey of Personal Values, grades 11–16 and adults, see 1409
Symptom Sign Inventory [England], mental patients, see 1410
Systematic Interview Guides [England], mothers, see 1411
★*T.M.R. Performance Profile for the Severely and Moderately Retarded*, ages 4 and over, see 1412
Temperament Comparator, adults, see 1413
★*Temperament Questionnaire* [South Africa], standards 8 and over, see 1414
Tennessee Self Concept Scale, ages 12 and over, see 1415
Test for Developmental Age in Girls, girls ages 8–18, see 1416
Test of Basic Assumptions, adults, see 1417
Test of Behavioral Rigidity, ages 21 and over, see 1418
Test of Social Insight, grades 6–16 and adults, see 1419
Test of Work Competency and Stability [Canada], ages 21 and over, see 1420
Tests of Social Intelligence, high school and adults, see 1421

Personality INTELLIGENCE TESTS AND REVIEWS [1050

Thorndike Dimensions of Temperament, grades 11–16 and adults, see 1422
Thurstone Temperament Schedule, grades 9–16 and adults, see 1423
Trait Evaluation Index, college and adults, see 1424
Triadal Equated Personality Inventory, adult males, see 1425
★*Tri-Cultural Attitude Scale*, grades kgn–6, see 1426
Tulane Factors of Liberalism-Conservatism, social science students, see 1427
Vineland Social Maturity Scale, birth to maturity, see 1428
Visual-Verbal Test, schizophrenic patients, see 1429
Vocational Preference Inventory, grades 12–16 and adults, see 1430
WLW Personal Attitude Inventory, business and industry, see 1431
★*Wahler Physical Symptoms Inventory*, psychiatric patients and counselees, see 1432
★*Wahler Self-Description Inventory*, grades 7 and over and psychiatric patients, see 1433
Walker Problem Behavior Identification Checklist, grades 4–6, see 1434
Ward Behavior Inventory, mental patients, see 1435
Weighted-Score Likability Rating Scale, ages 6 and over, see 1436
Welsh Figure Preference Test, ages 6 and over, see 1437
Western Personality Inventory, adults, see 1438
What I Like to Do, grades 4–7, see 1439
★*Whitaker Index of Schizophrenic Thinking*, mental patients, see 1440
**William, Lynde & Williams Analysis of Personal Values*, business and industry, see 1441
★*Work Environment Preference Schedule*, grades 11–16 and adults, see 1442
★*Y.E.M.R. Performance Profile for the Young Moderately and Mildly Retarded*, ages 5–9, see 1443

PROJECTIVE

African T.A.T. [South Africa], urban African adults, see 1444
Association Adjustment Inventory, normal and institutionalized adults, see 1445
Auditory Apperception Test, grades 9 and over, see 1446
Bender-Gestalt Test, ages 4 and over, see 1447
Blacky Pictures, ages 5 and over, see 1448
Braverman-Chevigny Auditory Projective Test, ages 4 and over, see 1449
Buttons, grades 7–9, see 1450
Children's Apperception Test, ages 3–10, see 1451
Color Pyramid Test [Switzerland], ages 6 and over, see 1452
Columbus: Picture Analysis of Growth Towards Maturity [Switzerland], ages 5–20, see 1453
Curtis Completion Form, grades 11–16 and adults, see 1454
Draw-A-Person, ages 5 and over, see 1455
Draw-A-Person Quality Scale, ages 16–25, see 1456
Driscoll Play Kit, ages 2–10, see 1457
★*Education Apperception Test*, preschool and elementary school, see 1458
Family Relations Indicator, emotionally disturbed children and their parents, see 1459
Five Task Test, ages 8 and over, see 1460
**Forer Structured Sentence Completion Test*, ages 10–18 and adults, see 1461
Forer Vocational Survey, adolescents and adults, see 1462
Franck Drawing Completion Test [Australia], ages 6 and over, see 1463

★*Gerontological Apperception Test*, ages 66 and over, see 1464
Graphoscopic Scale, ages 5–16 and over, see 1465
Group Personality Projective Test, ages 11 and over, see 1466
Group Projection Sketches for the Study of Small Groups, ages 16 and over, see 1467
HFD Test, ages 5–12, see 1468
H-T-P: House-Tree-Person Projective Technique, ages 3 and over, see 1469
*Hand Test, ages 6 and over, see 1470
Holtzman Inkblot Technique, ages 5 and over, see 1471; *Computer Scoring Service for the Holtzman Inkblot Technique*, see 1472
Howard Ink Blot Test, adults, see 1473
Human Figure Drawing Techniques, see 1474
IES Test, ages 10 and over and latency period girls, see 1475
Incomplete Sentence Test, employees and college, see 1476
Industrial Sentence Completion Form, employee applicants, see 1477
Kahn Test of Symbol Arrangement, ages 6 and over, see 1478
Ka-Ro Inkblot Test [Japan], ages 3 and over, see 1479
Kent-Rosanoff Free Association Test, ages 4 and over, see 1480
Machover Draw-A-Person Test, ages 2 and over, see 1481
Make a Picture Story, ages 6 and over, see 1482
Measurement of Self Concept in Kindergarten Children, kgn, see 1483
Miner Sentence Completion Scale, managers and management trainees, see 1484
**Minnesota Percepto-Diagnostic Test*, ages 5–16, see 1485
**Object Relations Technique* [England], ages 11 and over, see 1486
PRADI Draw-A-Person Test, clinical clients, see 1487
**Pain Apperception Test*, adults, see 1488
Pickford Projective Pictures [England], ages 5–15, see 1489
**Picture Identification Test*, high school and college, see 1490
Picture Impressions Test, adolescents and adults, see 1491
★*Picture Situation Test* [South Africa], adult males, see 1492
Picture Story Test Blank, clinical clients, see 1493
Picture World Test, ages 6 and over, see 1494
★*Politte Sentence Completion Test*, grades 1–12, see 1495
Psychiatric Attitudes Battery, adults, see 1496
Rock-A-Bye, Baby, ages 5–10, see 1497
Rohde Sentence Completions Test, ages 12 and over, see 1498
Rorschach [Switzerland], ages 3 and over, see 1499
**Rosenzweig Picture-Frustration Study*, ages 4 and over, see 1500
Rotter Incomplete Sentences Blank, grades 9–16 and adults, see 1501
Ruth Fry Symbolic Profile, ages 14 and over, see 1502
School Apperception Method, grades kgn–9, see 1503
Self Explorations Inventory, college and adults, see 1504
Self Valuation Test [England], ages 7–15 and adults, see 1505
Sentence Completion Blank, college and adults, see 1506
★*Sentence Completion Test*, high school and college, see 1507
Seven Squares Technique [Sweden], ages 5 and over, see 1508

Social Relations Test [South Africa], adult males, see 1509
Sound-Apperception Test, ages 16 and over, see 1510
South African Picture Analysis Test [The Netherlands], ages 5-13, see 1511
Structured Doll Play Test, ages 2-6, see 1512
Structured-Objective Rorschach Test, adults, see 1513
Symbol Elaboration Test, ages 6 and over, see 1514
Symonds Picture-Story Test, grades 7-12, see 1515
Szondi Test [Switzerland], ages 5 and over, see 1516
★*Tasks of Emotional Development Test*, ages 6-11 and adolescents, see 1517
Test of Family Attitudes [Belgium], ages 6-12, see 1518
Thematic Apperception Test, ages 4 and over, see 1519
Thematic Apperception Test for African Subjects [South Africa], ages 10 and over, see 1520
★*This I Believe Test*, grades 9 and over, see 1521
Tomkins-Horn Picture Arrangement Test, ages 10 and over, see 1522
Toy World Test [France], ages 2 and over, see 1523
Tree Test [Switzerland], ages 9 and over, see 1524
Twitchell-Allen Three-Dimensional Personality Test, ages 3 and over (sighted and sightless), see 1525
Visual Apperception Test '60, ages 6 and over, see 1526
Washington University Sentence Completion Test, ages 12 and over, see 1527
Zulliger Individual and Group Test [Switzerland], ages 3 and over, see 1528

READING

A.C.E.R. Lower Grades Reading Test: Level 1 [Australia], grade 1, see 1529
★*ACER Primary Reading Survey Tests* [Australia], grades 3-6, see 1530
A.C.E.R. Silent Reading Tests: Standardized for Use in New Zealand [New Zealand], ages 9-12, see 1531
American School Achievement Tests: Reading, grades 2-9, see 1532
American School Reading Tests, grades 10-13, see 1533
Buffalo Reading Test for Speed and Comprehension, grades 9-16, see 1534
Burnett Reading Series: Survey Test, grades 1.5-12, see 1535
★*California Achievement Tests: Reading*, grades 1-14, see 1536
★*Carver-Darby Chunked Reading Test*, grades 9-16 and adults, see 1537
Commerce Reading Comprehension Test, grades 12-16 and adults, see 1538
Comprehension Test for Training College Students [England], training college students and applicants for admission, see 1539
Comprehensive Primary Reading Scales, grade 1, see 1540
Comprehensive Reading Scales, grades 4-12, see 1541
★*Comprehensive Tests of Basic Skills: Reading*, grades kgn-12, see 1542
Cooperative Primary Tests: Reading, grades 1.5-3, see 1543
Cooperative Reading Comprehension Test, Form Y [Australia], secondary forms 5-6 and university, see 1544
Cooperative Reading Comprehension Test, Forms L and M [Australia], secondary forms 2-4, see 1545
Davis Reading Test, grades 8-13, see 1546
Delaware County Silent Reading Test, grades 1.5-8, see 1547
★*Edinburgh Reading Tests* [England], ages 8.5-12.5, see 1548
Emporia Reading Tests, grades 1-8, see 1549
GAP Reading Comprehension Test [Australia], grades 2-7, see 1550
★*GAPADOL* [Australia], ages 10 and over, see 1551
★*Gates-MacGinitie Reading Tests*, grades 1-9, see 1552
Gates-MacGinitie Reading Tests: Survey F, grades 10-12, see 1553
Group Reading Assessment [England], end of first year junior school, see 1554
Group Reading Test [England], ages 6-10, see 1555
High School Reading Test: National Achievement Tests, grades 7-12, see 1556
Individual Reading Test [Australia], ages 6-0 to 9-9, see 1557
★*Informal Reading Assessment Tests* [Canada], grades 1-3, see 1558
★*Inventory-Survey Tests*, grades 4-8, see 1559
★*Iowa Silent Reading Tests*, grades 4-16, see 1560
Kelvin Measurement of Reading Ability [Scotland], ages 8-12, see 1561
Kingston Test of Silent Reading [England], ages 7-11, see 1562
Lee-Clark Reading Test, grades 1-2, see 1563
McGrath Test of Reading Skills, grades 1-13, see 1564
McMenemy Measure of Reading Ability, grades 3 and 5-8, see 1565
Maintaining Reading Efficiency Tests, grades 7-16 and adults, see 1566
★*Metropolitan Achievement Tests: Reading Tests*, grades 2-9, see 1567
Minnesota Reading Examination for College Students, grades 9-16, see 1568
Monroe's Standardized Silent Reading Test, grades 3-12, see 1569
N.B. Silent Reading Tests (Beginners): Reading Comprehension Test [South Africa], substandard B, see 1570
★*National Teacher Examinations: Reading Specialist*, college seniors and teachers, see 1571
Nelson-Denny Reading Test, grades 9-16 and adults, see 1572
Nelson Reading Test, grades 3-9, see 1573
New Developmental Reading Tests, grades 1-6, see 1574
OISE Achievement Tests in Silent Reading: Advanced Primary Battery [Canada], grade 2, see 1575
Pressey Diagnostic Reading Tests, grades 3-9, see 1576
★*Primary Reading Survey Tests*, grades 2-3, see 1577
Primary Reading Test: Acorn Achievement Tests, grades 2-3, see 1578
Progressive Achievement Tests of Reading [New Zealand], standards 2-4 and Forms I-IV (ages 8-14), see 1579
RBH Basic Reading and Word Test, disadvantaged adults, see 1580
RBH Test of Reading Comprehension, business and industry, see 1581
★*Reading Comprehension: Canadian English Achievement Test* [Canada], grades 8.5-9.0, see 1582
Reading Comprehension: Cooperative English Tests, grades 9-14, see 1583
Reading Comprehension Test, college entrants, see 1584
★*Reading Comprehension Test DE* [England], ages 10-12.5, see 1585
Reading Comprehension Test: National Achievement

Tests [Crow, Kuhlmann, and Crow], grades 4–9, see 1586
Reading Comprehension Test: National Achievement Tests [Speer and Smith], grades 3–8, see 1587
*Reading for Understanding Placement Test, grades 3–16, see 1588
★Reading Progress Scale, grades 3–12, see 1589
Reading: Public School Achievement Tests, grades 3–8, see 1590
Reading Test AD [England], ages 7-6 to 11-1, see 1591
Reading Test (Comprehension and Speed): Municipal Tests, grades 3–8, see 1592
Reading Test: McGraw-Hill Basic Skills System, grades 11–14, see 1593
*Reading Tests A and BD [England], 1–4 years primary school, see 1594
Reading Tests EH 1–3 [England], first 4 years of secondary school, see 1595
SRA Achievement Series: Reading, grades 1–9, see 1596
SRA Reading Record, grades 6–12, see 1597
Schrammel-Gray High School and College Reading Test, grades 7–16, see 1598
*Sequential Tests of Educational Progress: Reading, grades 4–14, see 1599
Silent Reading Tests [South Africa], standards 1–10 (ages 7–17), see 1600
Southgate Group Reading Tests [England], ages 6–8, see 1601
Stanford Achievement Test: High School Reading Test, grades 9–12, see 1602
*Stanford Achievement Test: Reading Tests, grades 1.5–9, see 1603
★Sucher-Allred Reading Placement Inventory, reading level grades 1–9, see 1604
Survey of Primary Reading Development, grades 1–4, see 1605
Survey of Reading Achievement, grades 7–12, see 1606
Survey Tests of Reading, grades 3–13, see 1607
Tests of Academic Progress: Reading, grades 9–12, see 1608
Tests of Reading: Inter-American Series, grades 1–13, see 1609
Traxler High School Reading Test, grades 10–12, see 1610
Traxler Silent Reading Test, grades 7–10, see 1611
Van Wagenen Analytical Reading Scales, grades 4–12, see 1612
W.A.L. English Comprehension Test [Australia], high school, see 1613
★Wide-span Reading Test [England], ages 7–15, see 1614
Williams Primary Reading Test, grades 1–3, see 1615
Williams Reading Test for Grades 4–9, see 1616

DIAGNOSTIC

California Phonics Survey, grades 7–12 and college, see 1617
*Classroom Reading Inventory, grades 2–10, see 1618
★Cooper-McGuire Diagnostic Word-Analysis Test, grades 1 and over, see 1619
Cooperative Primary Tests: Word Analysis, grades 1.5–3, see 1620
Denver Public Schools Reading Inventory, grades 1–8, see 1621
Diagnostic Examination of Silent Reading Abilities, grades 4–12, see 1622
Diagnostic Reading Examination for Diagnosis of Special Difficulty in Reading, grades 1–4, see 1623
*Diagnostic Reading Scales, grades 1–6 and retarded readers in grades 7–12, see 1624
Diagnostic Reading Test: Pupil Progress Series, grades 1.9–8, see 1625
*Diagnostic Reading Tests, grades kgn–13, see 1626
*Doren Diagnostic Reading Test of Word Recognition Skills, grades 1–4, see 1627
Durrell Analysis of Reading Difficulty, grades 1–6, see 1628
Gates-McKillop Reading Diagnostic Tests, grades 2–5, see 1629
★Gillingham-Childs Phonics Proficiency Scales, grades 1–12, see 1630
Group Diagnostic Reading Aptitude and Achievement Tests, grades 3–9, see 1631
★Group Phonics Analysis, reading level grades 1–3, see 1632
★LRA Standard Mastery Tasks in Language, grades 1–2, see 1633
McCullough Word-Analysis Tests, grades 4–6, see 1634
★McGuire-Bumpus Diagnostic Comprehension Test, reading levels grades 2.5–6, see 1635
★Phonics Criterion Test, reading level grades 1–3, see 1636
Phonics Knowledge Survey, grades 1–6, see 1637
Phonovisual Diagnostic Test, grades 3–12, see 1638
★Prescriptive Reading Inventory, grades 1.5–6.5, see 1639
★Prescriptive Reading Inventory Interim Tests, grades 1.5–6.5, see 1640
Primary Reading Profiles, grades 1–3, see 1641
★Reading Diagnostic Probes, grades 2–9, see 1642
Roswell-Chall Diagnostic Reading Test of Word Analysis Skills, grades 2–6, see 1643
Reading Skills Diagnostic Test, grades 2–8, see 1644
★SPIRE Individual Reading Evaluation, grades 1–10, see 1645
Schonell Reading Tests [Scotland], ages 5–15, see 1646
Silent Reading Diagnostic Tests, grades 2–6, see 1647
★Sipay Word Analysis Tests, grades 2–12, see 1648
Standard Reading Inventory, grades 1–7, see 1649
Standard Reading Tests [England], reading ages up to 9, see 1650
*Stanford Diagnostic Reading Test, grades 2.5–8.5, see 1651
★Swansea Test of Phonic Skills [England], reading ages below 7.5, see 1652
*Test of Individual Needs in Reading, grades 1–6, see 1653
★Test of Phonic Skills, reading level grades kgn–3, see 1654
★Wisconsin Tests of Reading Skill Development: Word Attack, grades kgn–6, see 1655
★Woodcock Reading Mastery Tests, grades kgn–12, see 1656

MISCELLANEOUS

Basic Sight Word Test, grades 1–2, see 1657
Botel Reading Inventory, grades 1–12, see 1658
Cumulative Reading Record, grades 9–12, see 1659
Durrell Listening-Reading Series, grades 1–9, see 1660
Durrell-Sullivan Reading Capacity and Achievement Tests, grades 2.5–6, see 1661
Dyslexia Schedule, children having reading difficulties and first grade entrants, see 1662
Individual Reading Placement Inventory, youth and adults with reading levels up to grade 7, see 1663
★Instant Word Recognition Test, reading level grades 1–4, see 1664
★Inventory of Teacher Knowledge of Reading, elementary school teachers and college students in methods courses, see 1665
Learning Methods Test, grades kgn–3, see 1666
★National Test of Basic Words, grades 1–5, see 1667

OC Diagnostic Syllabizing Test, grades 4–6, see 1668
Phonics Test for Teachers, reading methods courses, see 1669
Reader Rater With Self-Scoring Profile, ages 15 and over, see 1670
Reader's Inventory, entrants to a reading improvement course for secondary and college students and adults, see 1671
Reading Eye II, grades 1–16 and adults, see 1672
Reading Versatility Test, grades 5–16, see 1673
Roswell-Chall Auditory Blending Test, grades 1–4, see 1674
Word Discrimination Test, grades 1–8, see 1675
★Word Recognition Test [England], preschool to age 8.5, see 1676

ORAL

★Concise Word Reading Tests [Australia], ages 7–12, see 1677
Flash-X Sight Vocabulary Test, grades 1–2, see 1678
Gilmore Oral Reading Test, grades 1–8, see 1679
Graded Word Reading Test [England], ages 5 and over, see 1680
Gray Oral Reading Test, grades 1–16 and adults, see 1681
Holborn Reading Scale [England], ages 5.5–10, see 1682
*Neale Analysis of Reading Ability [England], ages 6–13, see 1683
★Oral Reading Criterion Test, reading level grades 1–7, see 1684
Oral Word Reading Test [New Zealand], ages 7–11, see 1685
★Reading Miscue Inventory, grades 1–7, see 1686
★St. Lucia Graded Word Reading Test [Australia], grades 2–7, see 1687
Slosson Oral Reading Test, grades 1–8 and high school, see 1688
Standardized Oral Reading Check Tests, grades 1–8, see 1689
Standardized Oral Reading Paragraphs, grades 1–8, see 1690

READINESS

ABC Inventory to Determine Kindergarten and School Readiness, entrants to kgn and grade 1, see 1691
APELL Test, Assessment Program of Early Learning Levels, ages 4.5–7, see 1692
Academic Readiness and End of First Grade Progress Scales, grade 1, see 1693
American School Reading Readiness Test, first grade entrants, see 1694
★Analysis of Readiness Skills: Reading and Mathematics, grades kgn–1, see 1695
Anton Brenner Developmental Gestalt Test of School Readiness, ages 5–6, see 1696
Basic Concept Inventory, preschool and kgn, see 1697
Binion-Beck Reading Readiness Test for Kindergarten and First Grade, grades kgn–1, see 1698
Clymer-Barrett Prereading Battery, first grade entrants, see 1699
Contemporary School Readiness Test, first grade entrants, see 1700
★Delco Readiness Test, first grade entrants, see 1701
Gates-MacGinitie Reading Tests: Readiness Skills, grades kgn–1, see 1702
*Gesell Developmental Tests, ages 5–10, see 1703
Group Test of Reading Readiness, grades kgn–1, see 1704
Harrison-Stroud Reading Readiness Profiles, grades kgn–1, see 1705

★Initial Survey Test, first grade entrants, see 1706
★Inventory of Primary Skills, grades kgn–1, see 1707
★Kindergarten Behavioural Index [Australia], grades kgn–1, see 1708
Kindergarten Evaluation of Learning Potential, kgn, see 1709
★LRS Seriation Test, ages 4–6, see 1710
Lee-Clark Reading Readiness Test, grades kgn–1, see 1711
*Lippincott Reading Readiness Test, grades kgn–1, see 1712
McHugh-McParland Reading Readiness Test, grades kgn–1, see 1713
Macmillan Reading Readiness Test, first grade entrants, see 1714
Maturity Level for School Entrance and Reading Readiness, grades kgn–1, see 1715
Metropolitan Readiness Tests, grades kgn–1, see 1716
Murphy-Durrell Reading Readiness Analysis, first grade entrants, see 1717
Parent Readiness Evaluation of Preschoolers, ages 3–9 to 5–8, see 1718
★Pre-Reading Assessment Kit [Canada], grades kgn–1, see 1719
★Prereading Expectancy Screening Scales, first grade entrants, see 1720
Pre-Reading Screening Procedures, first grade entrants of average or superior intelligence, see 1721
★Preschool and Kindergarten Performance Profile, preschool and kgn, see 1722
Primary Academic Sentiment Scale, ages 4-4 to 7-3, see 1723
Reading Aptitude Tests, grades kgn–1, see 1724
★Reading Inventory Probe 1, grades 1–2, see 1725
Reversal Test [Sweden], grade 1 entrants, see 1726
Riley Preschool Developmental Screening Inventory, ages 3–5, see 1727
School Readiness Checklist, ages 5–6, see 1728
School Readiness Survey, ages 4–6, see 1729
Screening Test of Academic Readiness, ages 4-0 to 6-5, see 1730
Sprigle School Readiness Screening Test, ages 4–6 to 6–9, see 1731
Steinbach Test of Reading Readiness, grades kgn–1, see 1732
Van Wagenen Reading Readiness Scales, first grade entrants, see 1733
Watson Reading-Readiness Test [Canada], grades kgn–1, see 1734

SPECIAL FIELDS

*ANPA Foundation Newspaper Test, grades 7–12, see 1735
Adult Basic Reading Inventory, functionally illiterate adolescents and adults, see 1736
*Iowa Tests of Educational Development: Ability to Interpret Reading Materials in the Social Studies, grades 9–12, see 1737
*Iowa Tests of Educational Development: Ability to Interpret Reading Materials in the Natural Sciences, grades 9–12, see 1738
Purdue Reading Test for Industrial Supervisors, supervisors, see 1739
RBH Scientific Reading Test, employees in technical companies, see 1740
Reading Adequacy "READ" Test: Individual Placement Series, adults in industry, see 1741
Reading: Adult Basic Education Student Survey, poorly educated adults, see 1742
Reading Comprehension Test for Personnel Selection [England], applicants for technical training programs with high verbal content, see 1743

★*Reading/Everyday Activities in Life*, high school and "adults at basic education levels," see 1744
Robinson-Hall Reading Tests, college, see 1745
SRA Reading Index, job applicants with poor educational backgrounds, see 1746
Understanding Communication (Verbal Comprehension), industrial employees at the skilled level or below, see 1747

SPEED

*Basic Reading Rate Scale, grades 3–12, see 1748
Minnesota Speed of Reading Test for College Students, grades 12–16, see 1749

STUDY SKILLS

Bristol Achievement Tests: Study Skills [England], ages 8–13, see 1750
College Adjustment and Study Skills Inventory, college, see 1751
*Comprehensive Tests of Basic Skills: Study Skills, grades 2.5–12, see 1752
★*Cornell Class-Reasoning Test*, grades 4–12, see 1753
★*Cornell Conditional-Reasoning Test*, grades 4–12, see 1754
Cornell Critical Thinking Test, grades 7–16, see 1755
★*Cornell Learning and Study Skills Inventory*, grades 7–16, see 1756
Evaluation Aptitude Test, candidates for college and graduate school entrance, see 1757

*Iowa Tests of Educational Development: Use of Sources of Information, grades 9–12, see 1758
Library Orientation Test for College Freshmen, grade 13, see 1759
★*Library Tests*, college, see 1760
Logical Reasoning, grades 9–16 and adults, see 1761
★*National Test of Library Skills*, grades 2–12, see 1762
Nationwide Library Skills Examination, grades 4–12, see 1763
OC Diagnostic Dictionary Test, grades 5–8, see 1764
SRA Achievement Series: Work-Study Skills, grades 4–9, see 1765
★*Study Attitudes and Methods Survey*, high school and college, see 1766
Study Habits Checklist, grades 9–14, see 1767
Study Habits Inventory, grades 12–16, see 1768
Study Performance Test, high school and college, see 1769
Study Skills Counseling Evaluation, high school and college, see 1770
Study Skills Test: McGraw-Hill Basic Skills System, grades 11–14, see 1771
Survey of Study Habits and Attitudes, grades 7–14, see 1772
Test on Use of the Dictionary, high school and college, see 1773
★*Uncritical Inference Test*, college, see 1774
Watson-Glaser Critical Thinking Appraisal, grades 9–16 and adults, see 1775
★*Wisconsin Tests of Reading Skill Development: Study Skills*, grades kgn–7, see 1776

SCIENCE

Adkins-McBride General Science Test, high school, see 1777
Borman-Sanders Elementary Science Test, grades 5–8, see 1778
*CLEP General Examinations: Natural Sciences, 1–2 years of college or equivalent, see 1779
Cooperative Science Tests: Advanced General Science, grades 8–9, see 1780
Cooperative Science Tests: General Science, grades 7–9, see 1781
Elementary Science Test: National Achievement Tests, grades 4–6, see 1782
Emporia General Science Test, 1–2 semesters high school, see 1783
★*General Science Test* [South Africa], matriculants and higher, see 1784
General Science Test: National Achievement Tests, grades 7–9, see 1785
General Science III: Achievement Examinations for Secondary Schools, high school, see 1786
*Iowa Tests of Educational Development: General Background in the Natural Sciences, grades 9–12, see 1787
*National Teacher Examinations: Biology and General Science, college seniors and teachers, see 1788
*National Teacher Examinations: Chemistry, Physics and General Science, college seniors and teachers, see 1789
SRA Achievement Series: Science, grades 4–9, see 1790
*Science: Minnesota High School Achievement Examinations, grades 7–9, see 1791
Science Tests: Content Evaluation Series, grades 8–9, see 1792

Scientific Knowledge and Aptitude Test [India], high school, see 1793
*Sequential Tests of Educational Progress: Science, grades 4–14, see 1794
Stanford Achievement Test: High School Science Test, grades 9–12, see 1795
Stanford Achievement Test: Science, grades 5.5–9.9, see 1796
*Teacher Education Examination Program: Biology and General Science, college seniors preparing to teach secondary school, see 1797
*Teacher Education Examination Program: Chemistry, Physics and General Science, college seniors preparing to teach secondary school, see 1798
Tests of Academic Progress: Science, grades 9–12, see 1799

BIOLOGY

*Advanced Placement Examination in Biology, high school students desiring credit for college level courses or admission to advanced courses, see 1800
*BSCS Achievement Tests, grade 10, see 1801
*Biological Science: Interaction of Experiments and Ideas, grades 10–12, see 1802
*Biology: Minnesota High School Achievement Examinations, high school, see 1803
*CLEP Subject Examination in Biology, 1 year or equivalent, see 1804
*College Board Achievement Test in Biology, candidates for college entrance, see 1805
*College Placement Test in Biology, entering college freshmen, see 1806

Cooperative Biology Test: Educational Records Bureau Edition, high school, see 1807
Cooperative Science Tests: Biology, grades 10–12, see 1808
Emporia Biology Test, 1–2 semesters high school, see 1809
General Biology Test: National Achievement Tests, high school, see 1810
Graduate Record Examinations Advanced Biology Test, graduate school candidates, see 1811
Nelson Biology Test, grades 9–13, see 1812
Undergraduate Program Field Tests: Biology Test, college, see 1813

CHEMISTRY

ACS Cooperative Examination Brief Course in Organic Chemistry, 1 semester college, see 1814
ACS Cooperative Examination in Analytical Chemistry, Graduate Level, entering graduate students, see 1815
ACS Cooperative Examination in Biochemistry, college, see 1816
ACS Cooperative Examination in Brief Physical Chemistry, 1 semester college, see 1817
ACS Cooperative Examination in Brief Qualitative Analysis, college, see 1818
ACS Cooperative Examination in General Chemistry, 1 year college, see 1819
ACS Cooperative Examination in Inorganic Chemistry, grades 15–16, see 1820
ACS Cooperative Examination in Inorganic Chemistry, Graduate Level, entering graduate students, see 1821
ACS Cooperative Examination in Inorganic-Organic-Biological Chemistry (for Paramedical Programs), 1–2 semesters of chemistry for nursing, home economics, and other paramedical students, see 1822
ACS Cooperative Examination in Instrumental Analysis, grades 15–16, see 1823
ACS Cooperative Examination in Organic Chemistry, 1 year college, see 1824
ACS Cooperative Examination in Organic Chemistry, Graduate Level, entering graduate students, see 1825
ACS Cooperative Examination in Physical Chemistry, 1 year college, see 1826
ACS Cooperative Examination in Physical Chemistry, Graduate Level, entering graduate students, see 1827
ACS Cooperative Examination in Qualitative Analysis, college, see 1828
ACS Cooperative Examination in Quantitative Analysis, college, see 1829
ACS-NSTA Cooperative Examination in High School Chemistry, 1 year high school, see 1830
ACS-NSTA Cooperative Examination in High School Chemistry: Advanced Level, advanced high school classes, see 1831
Advanced Placement Examination in Chemistry, high school students desiring credit for college level courses or admission to advanced courses, see 1832
CLEP Subject Examination in General Chemistry, 1 year or equivalent, see 1833
Chemistry: Achievement Examinations for Secondary Schools, high school, see 1834
Chemistry Achievement Test for CHEM Study or Equivalent, high school, see 1835
Chemistry: Minnesota High School Achievement Examinations, high school, see 1836
College Board Achievement Test in Chemistry, candidates for college entrance, see 1837
College Placement Test in Chemistry, entering college freshmen, see 1838
Cooperative Chemistry Test: Educational Records Bureau Edition, high school, see 1839

Cooperative Science Tests: Chemistry, grades 10–12, see 1840
Emporia Chemistry Test, 1–2 semesters high school, see 1841
General Chemistry Test: National Achievement Tests, grades 10–16, see 1842
Graduate Record Examinations Advanced Chemistry Test, graduate school candidates, see 1843
Iowa Placement Examinations: Chemistry Aptitude, grades 12–13, see 1844
Iowa Placement Examinations: Chemistry Training, grades 12–13, see 1845
RBH Test of Chemical Comprehension, employee applicants and applicants for nurses' training, see 1846
Toledo Chemistry Placement Examination, college entrants, see 1847
Undergraduate Program Field Tests: Chemistry Test, college, see 1848

GEOLOGY

CLEP Subject Examination in Geology, 1 year or equivalent, see 1849
Graduate Record Examinations Advanced Geology Test, graduate school candidates, see 1850
Undergraduate Program Field Tests: Geology Test, college, see 1851

MISCELLANEOUS

Butler Life Science Concept Test, grades 1–6, see 1852
Dubins Earth Science Test, grades 8–12, see 1853
★NM Concepts of Ecology Test, grades 6–8, see 1854
★Science Attitude Questionnaire [England], secondary school, see 1855
Test on Understanding Science, grades 9–12, see 1856
Tests of Basic Experiences: Science, prekgn–grade 1, see 1857

PHYSICS

Advanced Placement Examination in Physics, high school students desiring credit for college level courses or admission to advanced courses, see 1858
College Board Achievement Test in Physics, candidates for college entrance, see 1859
College Placement Test in Physics, entering college freshmen, see 1860
Cooperative Physics Test: Educational Records Bureau Edition, high school, see 1861
Cooperative Science Tests: Physics, grades 10–12, see 1862
Dunning-Abeles Physics Test, grades 10–13, see 1863
Emporia Physics Test, 1–2 semesters high school, see 1864
General Physics Test: National Achievement Tests, grades 10–16, see 1865
Graduate Record Examinations Advanced Physics Test, graduate school candidates, see 1866
Iowa Placement Examinations: Physics Aptitude, grades 12–13, see 1867
Iowa Placement Examinations: Physics Training, grades 12–13, see 1868
★Objective Tests in Physics, high school, see 1869
Physics: Achievement Examinations for Secondary Schools, high school, see 1870
Physics: Minnesota High School Achievement Examinations, high school, see 1871
Tests of the Physical Science Study Committee, high school, see 1872
Undergraduate Program Field Tests: Physics Test, college, see 1873

SENSORY-MOTOR

D-K Scale of Lateral Dominance, grades 2-6, see 1874
Developmental Test of Visual-Motor Integration, ages 2-15, see 1875
★Frostig Movement Skills Test Battery, ages 6-12, see 1876
Harris Tests of Lateral Dominance, ages 7 and over, see 1877
*Leavell Hand-Eye Coordinator Tests, ages 8-14, see 1878
MKM Picture Arrangement Test, grades kgn-6, see 1879
*Moore Eye-Hand Coordination and Color-Matching Test, ages 2 and over, see 1880
Perceptual Forms Test, ages 5-8, see 1881
Primary Visual Motor Test, ages 4-8, see 1882
Purdue Perceptual-Motor Survey, ages 6-10, see 1883
★Rosner Perceptual Survey, ages 5-12, see 1884
Southern California Kinesthesia and Tactile Perception Tests, ages 4-8, see 1885
Southern California Perceptual-Motor Tests, ages 4-8, see 1886
*Southern California Sensory Integration Tests, ages 4-10 with learning problems, see 1887
★Spatial Orientation Memory Test, ages 5-8, see 1888
★Symbol Digit Modalities Test, ages 8 and over, see 1889
Trankell's Laterality Tests [Sweden], left-handed children in grades 1-2, see 1890
★Wold Digit-Symbol Test, ages 6-16, see 1891
★Wold Sentence Copying Test, grades 2-8, see 1892
★Wold Visuo-Motor Test, ages 6-16, see 1893

MOTOR

★Devereux Test of Extremity Coordination, emotionally handicapped and neurologically impaired ages 4-10, see 1894
Lincoln-Oseretsky Motor Development Scale, ages 6-14, see 1895
★Manual Accuracy and Speed Test, ages 4 and over, see 1896
*Motor Problems Inventory, preschool-grade 5, see 1897
Oseretsky Tests of Motor Proficiency: A Translation From the Portuguese Adaptation, ages 4-16, see 1898
Perrin Motor Coordination Test, adults, see 1899
Rail-Walking Test, ages 5 and over, see 1900
Smedley Hand Dynamometer, ages 6-18, see 1901
Southern California Motor Accuracy Test, ages 4-7 with nervous system dysfunction, see 1902
★Teaching Research Motor-Development Scale, moderately and severely retarded (preschool-grade 12), see 1903
★Test of Motor Impairment [Canada], ages 5-14, see 1904

VISION

A-B-C Vision Test for Ocular Dominance, ages 5 and over, see 1905
AO Sight Screener, adults, see 1906
Atlantic City Eye Test, grades 1 and over, see 1907
Basic Screen Test—Vision: Measurement of Skill Test 12, job applicants, see 1908
Burnham-Clark-Munsell Color Memory Test, adults, see 1909
Dennis Visual Perception Scale, grades 1-6, see 1910
Dvorine Pseudo-Isochromatic Plates, ages 3 and over, see 1911
Farnsworth Dichotomous Test for Color Blindness: Panel D-15, ages 12 and over, see 1912
Farnsworth-Munsell 100-Hue Test for the Examination of Color Discrimination, mental ages 12 and over, see 1913
★Guy's Colour Vision Test for Young Children [England], ages 3-5 and handicapped, see 1914
*Inter-Society Color Council Color Aptitude Test, adults, see 1915
Keystone Ready-to-Read Tests, school entrants, see 1916
Keystone Tests of Binocular Skill, grades 1 and over, see 1917
*Keystone Visual Screening Tests, preschool and over, see 1918
MKM Binocular Preschool Test, preschool, see 1919
MKM Monocular and Binocular Reading Test, grades 1 and over, see 1920
Marianne Frostig Developmental Test of Visual Perception, ages 3-8, see 1921
★Motor-Free Visual Perception Test, ages 4-8, see 1922
Ortho-Rater, adults, see 1923
*Pseudo-Isochromatic Plates for Testing Color Perception, ages 7 and over, see 1924
School Vision Tester, grades kgn and over, see 1925
★Sheridan Gardiner Test of Visual Acuity [England], ages 5 and over, see 1926
★Sloan Achromatopsia Test, individuals suspected of total color blindness, see 1927
Southern California Figure-Ground Visual Perception Test, ages 4-10, see 1928
Spache Binocular Reading Test, nonreaders and grades 1 and over, see 1929
★Speed of Color Discrimination Test, college, see 1930
Stycar Vision Tests [England], ages 6 months to 7 years, see 1931
Test for Colour-Blindness [Japan], ages 4 and over, see 1932
★3-D Test of Visualization Skill, ages 3-8, see 1933
Titmus Vision Tester, ages 3 and over, see 1934
*Visualization Test of Three Dimensional Orthographic Shape, high school and college, see 1935

SOCIAL STUDIES

American History—Government—Problems of Democracy: Acorn Achievement Tests, grades 9-16, see 1936
American School Achievement Tests: Social Studies and Science, grades 4-9, see 1937
*CLEP General Examinations: Social Sciences and History, 1-2 years of college or equivalent, see 1938
*College Board Achievement Test in American History and Social Studies, candidates for college entrance, see 1939
*College Board Achievement Test in European History

and World Cultures, candidates for college entrance, see 1940
*College Placement Test in American History and Social Studies, entering college freshmen, see 1941
*College Placement Test in European History and World Cultures, entering college freshmen, see 1942
History and Civics Test: Municipal Tests, grades 3–8, see 1943
*Iowa Tests of Educational Development: Understanding of Basic Social Concepts, grades 9–12, see 1944
*National Teacher Examinations: Social Studies, college seniors and teachers, see 1945
Primary Social Studies Test, grades 1–3, see 1946
SRA Achievement Series: Social Studies, grades 4–9, see 1947
*Sequential Tests of Educational Progress: Social Studies, grades 4–14, see 1948
*Social Studies: Minnesota High School Achievement Examinations, grades 7–9, see 1949
Social Studies Test: Acorn National Achievement Tests, grades 7–9, see 1950
Social Studies Test: National Achievement Tests, grades 4–9, see 1951
Stanford Achievement Test: High School Social Studies Test, grades 9–12, see 1952
Stanford Achievement Test: Social Studies Tests, grades 5.5–9, see 1953
*Teacher Education Examination Program: Social Studies, college seniors preparing to teach secondary school, see 1954
Tests of Academic Progress: Social Studies, grades 9–12, see 1955
*Tests of Basic Experiences: Social Studies, prekgn–grade 1, see 1956
Zimmerman-Sanders Social Studies Test, grades 7–8, see 1957

CONTEMPORARY AFFAIRS

*Current News Test, grades 9–12, see 1958
*Newsweek NewsQuiz, grades 9–12, see 1959
*School Weekly News Quiz, high school, see 1960
*Time Current Affairs Test, grades 9–12 and adults, see 1961
★*Time Monthly News Quiz,* grades 9–12 and adults, see 1962

ECONOMICS

*CLEP Subject Examination in Introductory Economics, 1 year or equivalent, see 1963
★*Economics/Objective Tests,* 1 semester high school, see 1964
*Graduate Record Examinations Advanced Economics Test, graduate school candidates, see 1965
★*Modern Economics Test: Content Evaluation Series,* grades 10–12, see 1966
★*Primary Test of Economic Understanding,* grades 2–3, see 1967
Test of Economic Understanding, high school and college, see 1968
★*Test of Elementary Economics,* grades 4–6, see 1969
Test of Understanding in College Economics, 1–2 semesters college, see 1970
★*Test of Understanding in Personal Economics,* high school, see 1971
*Undergraduate Program Field Tests: Economics Test, college, see 1972

GEOGRAPHY

Brandywine Achievement Test in Geography for Secondary Schools, grades 7–12, see 1973
*Economic Geography: Achievement Examinations for Secondary Schools, high school, see 1974
Geography Test: Municipal Tests, grades 3–8, see 1975
Geography Test: National Achievement Tests, grades 6–8, see 1976
*Graduate Record Examinations Advanced Geography Test, graduate school candidates, see 1977
Hollingsworth-Sanders Geography Test, grades 5–7, see 1978
*Undergraduate Program Field Tests: Geography Test, college, see 1979

HISTORY

*Advanced Placement Examination in American History, high school students desiring credit for college level courses or admission to advanced courses, see 1980
*Advanced Placement Examination in European History, high school students desiring credit for college level courses or admission to advanced courses, see 1981
★*American History: Junior High—Objective,* grades 7–9, see 1982
*American History: Senior High—Objective, 1–2 semesters high school, see 1983
American History Test: National Achievement Tests, grades 7–8, see 1984
★*CLEP Subject Examination in Afro-American History,* 1 semester or equivalent, see 1985
*CLEP Subject Examination in American History, 1 year or equivalent, see 1986
*CLEP Subject Examination in Western Civilization, 1 year or equivalent, see 1987
Cooperative Social Studies Tests: American History, grades 7–8, 10–12, see 1988
Cooperative Social Studies Tests: Modern European History, grades 10–12, see 1989
Cooperative Social Studies Tests: World History, grades 10–12, see 1990
Cooperative Topical Tests in American History, high school, see 1991
Crary American History Test, grades 10–13, see 1992
Emporia American History Test, 1–2 semesters high school, see 1993
*Graduate Record Examinations Advanced History Test, graduate school candidates, see 1994
Hollingsworth-Sanders Intermediate History Test, grades 5–6, see 1995
Meares-Sanders Junior High School History Test, grades 7–8, see 1996
Modern World History: Achievement Examinations for Secondary Schools, high school, see 1997
Sanders-Buller World History Test, 1–2 semesters high school, see 1998
*Social Studies Grade 10 (American History): Minnesota High School Achievement Examinations, grade 10, see 1999
*Social Studies Grade 11 (World History): Minnesota High School Achievement Examinations, grade 11, see 2000
*Undergraduate Program Field Tests: History Test, college, see 2001
*World History/Objective Tests, 1–2 semesters high school, see 2002
World History Test: Acorn National Achievement Tests, high school and college, see 2003

POLITICAL SCIENCE

*CLEP Subject Examination in American Government, 1 semester or equivalent, see 2004
Cooperative Social Studies Tests: American Government, grades 10–12, see 2005
Cooperative Social Studies Tests: Civics, grades 8–9, see 2006
Cooperative Social Studies Tests: Problems of Democracy, grades 10–12, see 2007
★Government/Objective Tests, 1 semester grades 11–12, see 2008
*Graduate Record Examinations Advanced Political Science Test, graduate school candidates, see 2009
★National Teacher Examinations: Texas Government, college seniors and teachers, see 2010
Patterson Test or Study Exercises on the Constitution of the United States, grades 9–16 and adults, see 2011
Principles of Democracy Test, grades 9–12, see 2012
Sare-Sanders American Government Test, high school and college, see 2013
Sare-Sanders Constitution Test, high school and college, see 2014
*Social Studies Grade 12 (American Problems): Minnesota High School Achievement Examinations, grade 12, see 2015
*Undergraduate Program Field Tests: Political Science Test, college, see 2016

SOCIOLOGY

*CLEP Subject Examination in Introductory Sociology, 1 year or equivalent, see 2017
*Graduate Record Examinations Advanced Sociology Test, graduate school candidates, see 2018
Sare-Sanders Sociology Test, high school and college, see 2019
*Undergraduate Program Field Tests: Sociology Test, college, see 2020

SPEECH AND HEARING

★Diagnostic Test of Speechreading, deaf children ages 4–9, see 2021
★Multiple-Choice Intelligibility Test, college, see 2022
★Ohio Tests of Articulation and Perception of Sounds, ages 5–8, see 2023
Preschool Language Scale, ages 2–6, see 2024
Reynell Developmental Language Scales [England], children ages 1–5 with delayed or deviant language development, see 2025
*Undergraduate Program Field Tests: Speech Pathology and Audiology Test, college, see 2026

HEARING

*Ambco Audiometers, ages 10 and over, see 2027
Ambco Speech Test Record, ages 3 and over, see 2027A
*Auditory Discrimination Test, ages 5–8, see 2028
★Auditory Memory Span Test, ages 5–8, see 2029
★Auditory Sequential Memory Test, grades 5–8, see 2030
Auditory Tests, grades 2 and over, see 2031
*Beltone Audiometers, grades kgn and over, see 2032
Comprehension of Oral Language: Inter-American Series, grade 1, see 2033
*Eckstein Audiometers, grades kgn and over, see 2034
★Flowers-Costello Tests of Central Auditory Abilities, grades kgn–6, see 2035
★Four Tone Screening for Older Children and Adults, ages 8 and over, see 2036
Goldman-Fristoe-Woodcock Test of Auditory Discrimination, ages 4 and over, see 2037
*Grason-Stadler Audiometers, ages 6 and over, see 2038
Hearing of Speech Tests, ages 3–12, see 2039
Hollien-Thompson Group Hearing Test, grades 1 and over, see 2040
★Kindergarten Auditory Screening Test, grades kgn–1, see 2041
★Lindamood Auditory Conceptualization Test, grades kgn–12, see 2042
*Maico Audiometers, grades kgn and over, see 2043
*Maico Hearing Impairment Calculator, see 2044
Massachusetts Hearing Test, grades 1–16 and adults, see 2045
Modified Rhyme Hearing Test, grades 4 and over, see 2046
*National Teacher Examinations: Audiology, college seniors and teachers, see 2047
New Group Pure Tone Hearing Test, grades 1 and over, see 2048
★Oliphant Auditory Discrimination Memory Test, grades 2–6, see 2049
★Oliphant Auditory Synthesizing Test, grade 1, see 2050
Pritchard-Fox Phoneme Auditory Discrimination Tests: Test Four, kgn and over, see 2051
Robbins Speech Sound Discrimination and Verbal Imagery Type Tests, ages 4 and over, see 2052
Rush Hughes (PB 50): Phonetically Balanced Lists 5–12, grades 2 and over, see 2053
Screening Test for Auditory Perception, grades 2–6, see 2054
Stycar Hearing Tests [England], ages 6 months to 7 years, see 2055
Test of Listening Accuracy in Children, ages 5–9, see 2056
★Test of Non-Verbal Auditory Discrimination, ages 6–8, see 2057
★Tracor Audiometers, infants and older, see 2058
Verbal Auditory Screening for Children, ages 3–8, see 2059
★Washington Speech Sound Discrimination Test, ages 3–5, see 2060
★Word Intelligibility by Picture Identification, hearing impaired children ages 5–13, see 2061
★ZECO Pure Tone Screening for Children, ages 3–8, see 2062
*Zenith Audiometers, preschool and over, see 2063–4

SPEECH

Arizona Articulation Proficiency Scale, mental ages 2–14 and over, see 2065
★Boston Diagnostic Aphasia Examination, aphasic patients, see 2066
★Bzoch-League Receptive-Expressive Emergent Language Scale: For the Measurement of Language Skills in Infancy, birth to age 3, see 2067
Communicative Evaluation Chart From Infancy to Five Years, see 2068
Deep Test of Articulation, all reading levels, see 2069

★*Edinburgh Articulation Test* [Scotland], ages 3–5, see 2070
Examining for Aphasia, adolescents and adults, see 2071
★*Fairview Language Evaluation Scale*, mentally retarded, see 2072
★*Fisher-Logemann Test of Articulation Competence*, preschool and over, see 2073
Forms From Diagnostic Methods in Speech Pathology, children and adults with speech problems, see 2074
**Goldman-Fristoe Test of Articulation*, ages 2 and over, see 2075
Halstead Aphasia Test, adults, see 2076
Houston Test for Language Development, ages 6 months to 6 years, see 2077
Language Facility Test, ages 3 and over, see 2078
Language Modalities Test for Aphasia, adults, see 2079
**Minnesota Test for Differential Diagnosis of Aphasia*, adults, see 2080
**National Teacher Examinations: Speech-Communication and Theatre*, college seniors and teachers, see 2081
**National Teacher Examinations: Speech Pathology*, college seniors and teachers, see 2082
Nationwide Speech Examination, grades 4–12, see 2083
★*Northwestern Syntax Screening Test*, ages 3–7, see 2084

Orzeck Aphasia Evaluation, mental and brain damaged patients, see 2085
Photo Articulation Test, ages 3–12, see 2086
**Porch Index of Communicative Ability*, adults, see 2087
Predictive Screening Test of Articulation, grade 1, see 2088
**Riley Articulation and Language Test*, grades kgn–2, see 2089
Screening Deep Test of Articulation, grades kgn and over, see 2090
**Screening Speech Articulation Test*, ages 3.5–8.5, see 2091
**Sklar Aphasia Scale*, brain damaged adults, see 2092
Speech Defect Questionnaire, ages 6 and over, see 2093
Speech Diagnostic Chart, grades 1–8, see 2094
Templin-Darley Tests of Articulation, ages 3 and over, see 2095
★*Undergraduate Program Field Tests: Drama and Theatre Test*, college, see 2096
Utah Test of Language Development, ages 1.5 to 14.5, see 2097
**Verbal Language Development Scale*, birth to age 15, see 2098
Weidner-Fensch Speech Screening Test, grades 1–3, see 2099

VOCATIONS

★*ACT Assessment of Career Development*, grades 8–11, see 2100
★*ACT Career Planning Program*, entrants to postsecondary educational institutions, see 2101
**Aptitude Inventory*, employee applicants, see 2102
★*Career Maturity Inventory*, grades 6–12, see 2103
★*Classification Test Battery* [South Africa], illiterate and semiliterate applicants for unskilled and semiskilled mining jobs, see 2104
Dailey Vocational Tests, grades 8–12 and adults, see 2105
*ETSA Tests, job applicants, see 2106
**Flanagan Industrial Tests*, business and industry, see 2107
Individual Placement Series, high school and adults, see 2108
★*New Mexico Career Education Test Series*, grades 9–12, see 2109
Personal History Index, job applicants, see 2110
Steward Basic Factors Inventory, applicants for sales and office positions, see 2111
Steward Personnel Tests, applicants for sales and office positions, see 2112
TAV Selection System, adults, see 2113
Vocational Planning Inventory, vocational students in grades 8–12 and grade 13 entrants, see 2114
WLW Employment Inventory, adults, see 2115
★*Wide Range Employment Sample Test*, ages 16–35 (normal and handicapped), see 2116

CLERICAL

ACER Short Clerical Test—Form C [Australia], ages 13 and over, see 2117
A.C.E.R. Speed and Accuracy Tests [Australia], ages 13.5 and over, see 2118
APT Dictation Test, stenographers, see 2119
★*Appraisal of Occupational Aptitudes*, high school and adults, see 2120
Clerical Skills Series, clerical workers and applicants, see 2121

Clerical Tests, applicants for clerical positions, see 2122
Clerical Tests, Series N, applicants for clerical positions not involving frequent use of typewriter or verbal skill, see 2123
Clerical Tests, Series V, applicants for typing and stenographic positions, see 2124
Clerical Worker Examination, clerical workers, see 2125
Cross Reference Test, clerical job applicants, see 2126
Curtis Verbal-Clerical Skills Tests, applicants for clerical positions, see 2127
**General Clerical Ability Test*, job applicants, see 2128
**General Clerical Test*, grades 9–16 and clerical job applicants, see 2129
*Group Test 20 [England], ages 15 and over, see 2130
**Group Tests 61A, 64, and 66A* [England], clerical applicants, see 2131
**Hay Clerical Test Battery*, applicants for clerical positions, see 2132
L & L Clerical Tests, applicants for office positions, see 2133
McCann Typing Tests, applicants for typing positions, see 2134
Minnesota Clerical Test, grades 8–12 and adults, see 2135
Office Skills Achievement Test, employees, see 2136
**Office Worker Test*, office workers, see 2137
O'Rourke Clerical Aptitude Test, Junior Grade, applicants for clerical positions, see 2138
Personnel Institute Clerical Tests, clerical personnel and typists-stenographers-secretaries, see 2139
Personnel Research Institute Clerical Battery, applicants for clerical positions, see 2140
Personnel Research Institute Test of Shorthand Skills, stenographers, see 2141
Purdue Clerical Adaptability Test, applicants for clerical positions, see 2142
RBH Checking Test, applicants for clerical and stenographic positions, see 2143
RBH Classifying Test, business and industry, see 2144
RBH Number Checking Test, business and industry, see 2145

RBH Test of Dictation Speed, stenographers, see 2146
RBH Test of Typing Speed, applicants for clerical positions, see 2147
Seashore-Bennett Stenographic Proficiency Test, adults, see 2148
Secretarial Performance Analysis, employees, see 2149
Selection Tests for Office Personnel, insurance office workers and applicants, see 2150
*Short Employment Tests, applicants for clerical positions, see 2151
Short Occupational Knowledge Test for Bookkeepers, job applicants, see 2152
Short Occupational Knowledge Test for Office Machine Operators, job applicants, see 2153
Short Occupational Knowledge Test for Secretaries, job applicants, see 2154
Short Tests of Clerical Ability, applicants for office positions, see 2155
Shorthand Test: Individual Placement Series, adults, see 2156
Skill in Typing: Measurement of Skill Test 9, job applicants, see 2157
Stenographic Dictation Test, applicants for stenographic positions, see 2158
*Stenographic Skill-Dictation Test, applicants for stenographic positions, see 2159
*Stenographic Skills Test, job applicants, see 2160
Survey of Clerical Skills: Individual Placement Series, adults, see 2161
Thurstone Employment Tests, applicants for clerical and typing positions, see 2162
*Typing Skill, typists, see 2163
Typing Test for Business, applicants for typing positions, see 2164
Typing Test: Individual Placement Series, adults, see 2165
USES Clerical Skills Tests, applicants for clerical positions, see 2166

INTERESTS

ACT Guidance Profile, junior college, see 2167
A.P.U. Occupational Interests Guide [England], ages 14–18, see 2168
*Applied Biological and Agribusiness Interest Inventory, grade 8, see 2169
*California Occupational Preference Survey, grades 9–16 and adults, see 2170
California Pre-Counseling Self-Analysis Protocol Booklet, student counselees, see 2171
★*Career Guidance Inventory,* grades 7–13 students interested in trades, services and technologies, see 2172
Chatterji's Non-Language Preference Record [India], ages 11–16, see 2173
College Interest Inventory, grades 11–16, see 2174
Connolly Occupational Interests Questionnaire [England], ages 15 and over, see 2175
*Crowley Occupational Interests Blank [England], ages 13 and over of average ability or less, see 2176
Curtis Interest Scale, grades 9–16 and adults, see 2177
*Educational Interest Inventory, grades 11–13 and adults, see 2178
Factorial Interest Blank [England], ages 11–16, see 2179
*Geist Picture Interest Inventory, grades 8–16 and adults, see 2180
Geist Picture Interest Inventory: Deaf Form: Male, deaf and hard of hearing males (grades 7–16 and adults), see 2181
Gordon Occupational Check List, high school students not planning to enter college, see 2182
Gregory Academic Interest Inventory, grades 13–16, see 2183
Guilford-Shneidman-Zimmerman Interest Survey, grades 9–16 and adults, see 2184
Guilford-Zimmerman Interest Inventory, grades 10–16 and adults, see 2185
Hackman-Gaither Vocational Interest Inventory, grades 9–12 and adults, see 2186
*Hall Occupational Orientation Inventory, grades 7–16 and adults, see 2187
Henderson Analysis of Interest, grades 9–16 and adults, see 2188
How Well Do You Know Your Interests, high school, college, adults, see 2189
*Interest Check List, grades 9 and over, see 2190
★*Interest Questionnaire for Indian South Africans* [South Africa], standards 6–10, see 2191
Inventory of Vocational Interests: Acorn National Aptitude Tests, grades 7–16 and adults, see 2192
Kuder General Interest Survey, grades 6–12, see 2193
Kuder Occupational Interest Survey, grades 11–16 and adults, see 2194
*Kuder Preference Record—Vocational, grades 9–16 and adults, see 2195
★*Milwaukee Academic Interest Inventory,* grades 12–14, see 2196
Minnesota Vocational Interest Inventory, males ages 15 and over not planning to attend college, see 2197
19 Field Interest Inventory [South Africa], standards 8–10 and college and adults, see 2198
Occupational Interest Inventory, grades 7–16 and adults, see 2199
Occupational Interest Survey (With Pictures), industrial applicants and employees, see 2200
*Ohio Vocational Interest Survey, grades 8–12, see 2201
Phillips Occupational Preference Scale [Australia], ages 14 and over, see 2202
Pictorial Interest Inventory, adult males, particularly poor readers and nonreaders, see 2203
★*Pictorial Inventory of Careers,* grades 3–14 and disadvantaged adults, see 2204
Picture Interest Inventory, grades 7 and over, see 2205
Preference Analysis [South Africa], standards 8 and over, see 2206–7
Rothwell-Miller Interest Blank [Australia], ages 13 and over, see 2208
Rothwell-Miller Interest Blank, British Edition [England], ages 11 and over, see 2209
Safran Student's Interest Inventory [Canada], grades 8–12, see 2210
★*Self Directed Search: A Guide to Educational and Vocational Planning,* high school and college and adults, see 2211
Strong Vocational Interest Blank for Men, ages 16 and over, see 2212
Strong Vocational Interest Blank for Women, ages 16 and over, see 2213
Thurstone Interest Schedule, grades 9–16 and adults, see 2214
VALCAN Vocational Interest Profile [Canada], ages 15 and over, see 2215
Vocational Apperception Test, college, see 2216
Vocational Interest and Sophistication Assessment, retarded adolescents and young adults, see 2217
Vocational Interest Profile [Canada], ages 15 and over, see 2218
★*Wide Range Interest-Opinion Test,* grades 8–12 and adults, see 2219
*William, Lynde & Williams Analysis of Interest, male adults, see 2220
Work Values Inventory, grades 7–16 and adults, see 2221

MANUAL DEXTERITY

*APT Manual Dexterity Test, automobile and truck mechanics and mechanics' helpers, see 2222
Crawford Small Parts Dexterity Test, high school and adults, see 2223
Crissey Dexterity Test, job applicants, see 2224
Hand-Tool Dexterity Test, adolescents and adults, see 2225
Manipulative Aptitude Test, grades 9–16 and adults, see 2226
Minnesota Rate of Manipulation Test, grade 7 to adults, see 2227
O'Connor Finger Dexterity Test, ages 14 and over, see 2228
O'Connor Tweezer Dexterity Test, ages 14 and over, see 2229
★One Hole Test, job applicants, see 2230
Pennsylvania Bi-Manual Worksample, ages 16 and over, see 2231
Practical Dexterity Board, ages 8 and over, see 2232
*Purdue Hand Precision Test, ages 17 and over, see 2233
*Purdue Pegboard, grades 9–16 and adults, see 2234
Stromberg Dexterity Test, trade school and adults, see 2235
Yarn Dexterity Test, textile workers and applicants, see 2236

MECHANICAL ABILITY

A.C.E.R. Mechanical Comprehension Test [Australia], ages 13.5 and over, see 2237
A.C.E.R. Mechanical Reasoning Test [Australia], ages 13–9 and over, see 2238
Bennett Mechanical Comprehension Test, grades 9–12 and adults, see 2239
Chriswell Structural Dexterity Test, grades 7–9, see 2240
*College Placement Test in Spatial Relations, entering college freshmen, see 2241
Cox Mechanical and Manual Tests [England], boys ages 10 and over, see 2242
Curtis Object Completion and Space Form Tests, applicants for mechanical and technical jobs, see 2243
Detroit Mechanical Aptitudes Examination, grades 7–16, see 2244
Flags: A Test of Space Thinking, industrial employees, see 2245
Form Perception Test [South Africa], illiterate and semiliterate adults, see 2246
Form Relations Group Test [England], ages 14 and over, see 2247
Group Test 80A [England], ages 15 and over, see 2248
Group Test 81 [England], ages 14 and over, see 2249
Group Test 82 [England], ages 14.5 and over, see 2250
MacQuarrie Test for Mechanical Ability, grades 7 and over, see 2251
Mechanical Aptitude Test: Acorn National Aptitude Tests, grades 7–16 and adults, see 2252
Mechanical Comprehension Test [South Africa], male technical apprentices and trainee engineer applicants, see 2253
Mechanical Information Test [England], ages 15 and over, see 2254
Mechanical Movements: A Test of Mechanical Comprehension, industrial employees, see 2255
*Mechanical Reasoning: Differential Aptitude Tests, grades 8–12 and adults, see 2256
Mellenbruch Mechanical Motivation Test, grades 6–16 and adults, see 2257
Minnesota Spatial Relations Test, ages 11 and over, see 2258
O'Connor Wiggly Block, ages 16 and over, see 2259
O'Rourke Mechanical Aptitude Test, grades 7–12 and adults, see 2260
Perceptual Battery [South Africa], job applicants with at least 10 years of education, see 2261
Primary Mechanical Ability Tests, applicants for positions requiring mechanical ability, see 2262
Purdue Mechanical Adaptability Test, males ages 15 and over, see 2263
RBH Three-Dimensional Space Test, industrial workers in mechanical fields, see 2264
RBH Two-Dimensional Space Test, business and industry, see 2265
Revised Minnesota Paper Form Board Test, grades 9–16 and adults, see 2266
SRA Mechanical Aptitudes, grades 9–12 and adults, see 2267
*Space Relations: Differential Aptitude Tests, grades 8–12 and adults, see 2268
Spatial Tests EG, 2, and 3 [England], ages 10–13 and 15–17, see 2269
Spatial Visualization Test: Dailey Vocational Tests, grades 8–12 and adults, see 2270
Vincent Mechanical Diagrams Test [England], ages 15 and over, see 2271
Weights and Pulleys: A Test of Intuitive Mechanics, engineering students and industrial employees, see 2272

MISCELLANEOUS

Alpha Biographical Inventory, grades 9–12, see 2273
Biographical Index, college and industry, see 2274
Business Judgment Test, adults, see 2275
*Conference Evaluation, conference participants, see 2276
Conference Meeting Rating Scale, conference leaders and participants, see 2277
★Continuous Letter Checking and Continuous Symbol Checking [South Africa], ages 12 and over, see 2278–9
Gullo Workshop and Seminar Evaluation, workshop and seminar participants, see 2280
Job Attitude Analysis, production and clerical workers, see 2281
Mathematical and Technical Test [England], ages 11 and over, see 2282
*Minnesota Importance Questionnaire, vocational counselees, see 2283
★Minnesota Job Description Questionnaire, employees and supervisors, see 2284
Minnesota Satisfaction Questionnaire, business and industry, see 2285
Per-Flu-Dex Tests, college and industry, see 2286
RBH Breadth of Information, business and industry, see 2287
Self-Rating Scale for Leadership Qualifications, adults, see 2288
Tear Ballot for Industry, employees in industry, see 2289
Test Orientation Procedure, job applicants and trainees, see 2290
Tests A/9 and A/10 [South Africa], applicants for technical and apprentice jobs, see 2291
Whisler Strategy Test, business and industry, see 2292
Work Information Inventory, employee groups in industry, see 2293

SELECTION & RATING FORMS

APT Controlled Interview, applicants for employment, see 2294
Application Interview Screening Form, job applicants, see 2295
Career Counseling Personal Data Form, vocational counselees, see 2296
Employee Competency Scale, employees, see 2297
Employee Evaluation Form for Interviewers, adults, see 2298
Employee Performance Appraisal, business and industry, see 2299
★*Employee Progress Appraisal Form,* rating of office employees, see 2300
*Employee Rating and Development Forms, executive, industrial, office, and sales personnel, see 2301
*Executive, Industrial, and Sales Personnel Forms, applicants for executive, industrial, office, or sales positions, see 2302
*Job Application Forms, job applicants and employees, see 2303
Lawshe-Kephart Personnel Comparison System, for rating any aspect of employee performance by the paired comparison technique, see 2304
★*McCormick Job Performance Measurement "Rate-$-Scales,"* employees, see 2305
McQuaig Manpower Selection Series, applicants for office and sales positions, see 2306
*Martin Performance Appraisal, employees, see 2307
Merit Rating Series, industry, see 2308
Nagel Personnel Interviewing and Screening Forms, job applicants, see 2309
Performance Review Forms, employees and managers, see 2310
Personal Data Blank, counselees ages 15 and over, see 2311
Personnel Interviewing Forms, business and industry, see 2312
Personnel Rating Scale, employees, see 2313
RBH Individual Background Survey, business and industry, see 2314
San Francisco Vocational Competency Scale, mentally retarded adults, see 2315
Selection Interview Forms, business and industry, see 2316
Speech-Appearance Record, job applicants, see 2317
*Stevens-Thurow Personnel Forms, business and industry, see 2318
★*Tickmaster,* job applicants, see 2319
Wonderlic Personnel Selection Procedure, applicants for employment, see 2320
Work Reference Check, job applicants, see 2321

SPECIFIC VOCATIONS

ACCOUNTING

Account Clerk Test, job applicants, see 2322
*American Institute of Certified Public Accountants Testing Programs, grades 13-16 and accountants, see 2323
*CLEP Subject Examination in Introductory Accounting, 1 year or equivalent, see 2324

BUSINESS

*Admission Test for Graduate Study in Business, business graduate students, see 2325
*CLEP Subject Examination in Introduction to Business Management, 1 semester or equivalent, see 2326
*CLEP Subject Examination in Introductory Business Law, 1 semester or equivalent, see 2327
*CLEP Subject Examination in Introductory Marketing, 1 semester or equivalent, see 2328
*CLEP Subject Examination in Money and Banking, 1 semester or equivalent, see 2329
Organizational Value Dimensions Questionnaire, adults, see 2330

COMPUTER PROGRAMMING

Aptitude Assessment Battery: Programming, programmers and trainees, see 2331
*CLEP Subject Examination in Computers and Data Processing, 1-2 semesters or equivalent, see 2332
★*CLEP Subject Examination in Elementary Computer Programming—Fortran IV,* 1 semester or equivalent, see 2333
*Computer Programmer Aptitude Battery, applicants for computer training or employment, see 2334
Diebold Personnel Tests, programmers and systems analysts for automatic data processing and computing installations, see 2335
★*Programmer Aptitude/Competence Test System,* computer programmers and applicants for programmer training, see 2336

DENTISTRY

*Dental Admission Testing Program, dental school applicants, see 2337
Dental Hygiene Aptitude Testing Program, dental hygiene school applicants, see 2338
★*Ohio Dental Assisting Achievement Test,* grades 11-12, see 2339

ENGINEERING

AC Test of Creative Ability, engineers and supervisors, see 2340
Engineering Aide Test, engineering aides, see 2341
*Garnett College Test in Engineering Science [England], 1-2 years technical college, see 2342
*Graduate Record Examinations Advanced Engineering Test, graduate school candidates, see 2343
Minnesota Engineering Analogies Test, candidates for graduate school and industry, see 2344
*N.I.I.P. Engineering Apprentice Selection Test Battery [England], engineering apprentices, see 2345
*National Engineering Aptitude Search Test: The Junior Engineering Technical Society, grades 9-12, see 2346
Purdue Creativity Test, applicants for engineering positions, see 2347
*Undergraduate Program Field Tests: Engineering Test, college, see 2348

LAW

*Law School Admission Test, law school applicants, see 2349

MEDICINE

★*CLEP Subject Examination in Clinical Chemistry,* medical technologists, see 2350
★*CLEP Subject Examination in Hematology,* medical technologists, see 2351
★*CLEP Subject Examination in Immunohematology and Blood Banking,* medical technologists, see 2352
★*CLEP Subject Examination in Microbiology,* medical technologists, see 2353

Colleges of Podiatry Admission Test, grades 14 and over, see 2354
Medical College Admission Test, applicants for admission to member colleges of the Association of American Medical Colleges, see 2355
Medical School Instructor Attitude Inventory, medical school faculty members, see 2356
★*Optometry College Admission Test,* optometry college applicants, see 2357
Veterinary Aptitude Test, veterinary school applicants, see 2358

MISCELLANEOUS

Architectural School Aptitude Test, architectural school applicants, see 2359
Chemical Operators Selection Test, chemical operators and applicants, see 2360
Fire Promotion Tests, prospective firemen promotees, see 2361
Firefighter Test, prospective firemen, see 2362
Fireman Examination, prospective firemen, see 2363
General Municipal Employees Performance (Efficiency) Rating System, municipal employees, see 2364
Journalism Test, high school, see 2365
★*Law Enforcement Perception Questionnaire,* law enforcement personnel, see 2366
Memory and Observation Tests for Policeman, prospective policemen, see 2367
Police Performance Rating System, policemen, see 2368
Police Promotion Tests, prospective policemen promotees, see 2369
Policeman Examination, prospective policemen, see 2370
Policeman Test, policemen and prospective policemen, see 2371
Potter-Nash Aptitude Test for Lumber Inspectors and Other General Personnel Who Handle Lumber, employees in woodworking industries, see 2372
★*Test for Firefighter B-1,* firemen and prospective firemen, see 2373
★*Test for Police Officer A-1,* policemen and prospective policemen, see 2374
Visual Comprehension Test for Detective, prospective police detectives, see 2375

NURSING

Achievement Tests in Nursing, students in schools of registered nursing, see 2376
Achievement Tests in Practical Nursing, practical nursing students, see 2377
Empathy Inventory, nursing instructors, see 2378
Entrance Examination for Schools of Nursing, nursing school applicants, see 2379
Entrance Examination for Schools of Practical Nursing, practical nursing school applicants, see 2380
George Washington University Series Nursing Tests, prospective nurses, see 2381
Luther Hospital Sentence Completions, prospective nursing students, see 2382
NLN Achievement Tests for Schools Preparing Registered Nurses, students in state-approved schools preparing registered nurses, see 2383
NLN Aide Selection Test, applicants for aide positions in hospitals and home health agencies, see 2384
NLN Practical Nursing Achievement Tests, students in state-approved schools of practical nursing, see 2385
NLN Pre-Admission and Classification Examination, practical nursing school entrants, see 2386
NLN Pre-Nursing and Guidance Examination, applicants for admission to state-approved schools preparing registered nurses, see 2387
Netherne Study Difficulties Battery for Student Nurses [England], student nurses, see 2388
Nurse Attitudes Inventory, prospective nursing students, see 2389
PSB-Aptitude for Practical Nursing Examination, applicants for admission to practical nursing schools, see 2390

RESEARCH

Research Personnel Review Form, research and engineering and scientific firms, see 2391
Supervisor's Evaluation of Research Personnel, research personnel, see 2392
Surveys of Research Administration and Environment, research and engineering and scientific firms, see 2393
Technical Personnel Recruiting Inventory, research and engineering and scientific firms, see 2394

SELLING

Aptitudes Associates Test of Sales Aptitude, applicants for sales positions, see 2395
Combination Inventory, Form 2, prospective debit life insurance salesmen, see 2396
Detroit Retail Selling Inventory, candidates for training in retail selling, see 2397
Evaluation Record, prospective life insurance agency managers, see 2398
Hall Salespower Inventory, salesmen, see 2399
Hanes Sales Selection Inventory, insurance and printing salesmen, see 2400
Information Index, life and health insurance agents, see 2401
LIAMA Inventory of Job Attitudes, life insurance field personnel, see 2402
Personnel Institute Hiring Kit, applicants for sales positions, see 2403
SRA Sales Attitudes Check List, applicants for sales positions, see 2404
Sales Aptitude Test, job applicants, see 2405
Sales Comprehension Test, applicants for sales positions, see 2406
Sales Method Index, life insurance agents, see 2407
Sales Motivation Inventory, applicants for sales positions, see 2408
Sales Sentence Completion Blank, applicants for sales positions, see 2409
Steward Life Insurance Knowledge Test, applicants for life insurance agent or supervisory positions, see 2410
Steward Occupational Objectives Inventory, applicants for supervisory positions in life insurance companies or agencies, see 2411
Steward Personal Background Inventory, applicants for sales positions, see 2412
Test for Ability to Sell: George Washington University Series, grades 7–16 and adults, see 2413
★*Test of Retail Sales Insight,* retail clerks and students, see 2414

SKILLED TRADES

Electrical Sophistication Test, job applicants, see 2415
Fiesenheiser Test of Ability to Read Drawings, trade school and adults, see 2416
Mechanical Familiarity Test, job applicants, see 2417
Mechanical Handyman Test, maintenance workers, see 2418
Mechanical Knowledge Test, job applicants, see 2419

Ohio Auto Body Achievement Test, grades 11-12, see 2420
Ohio Automotive Mechanics Achievement Test, grades 11-12, see 2421
★*Ohio Carpentry Achievement Test,* grades 11-12, see 2422
★*Ohio Communication Products Electronics Achievement Test,* grades 11-12, see 2423
★*Ohio Construction Electricity Achievement Test,* grades 11-12, see 2424
Ohio Cosmetology Achievement Test, grades 11-12, see 2425
★*Ohio Industrial Electronics Achievement Test,* grades 11-12, see 2426
Ohio Machine Trades Achievement Test, grades 11-12, see 2427
Ohio Mechanical Drafting Achievement Test, grades 11-12, see 2428
Ohio Printing Achievement Test, grades 11-12, see 2429
Ohio Sheet Metal Achievement Test, grades 11-12, see 2430
Ohio Trade and Industrial Education Achievement Test Program, grades 11-12, see 2431
Ohio Welding Achievement Test, grades 11-12, see 2432
Purdue Industrial Training Classification Test, grades 9-12 and adults, see 2433
Purdue Interview Aids, applicants for industrial employment, see 2434
Purdue Trade Information Test for Sheetmetal Workers, sheetmetal workers, see 2435
Purdue Trade Information Test in Carpentry, vocational school and adults, see 2436
Purdue Trade Information Test in Engine Lathe Operation, vocational school and adults, see 2437
Purdue Trade Information Test in Welding, vocational school and adults, see 2438
Short Occupational Knowledge Test for Auto Mechanics, job applicants, see 2439
Short Occupational Knowledge Test for Carpenters, job applicants, see 2440
Short Occupational Knowledge Test for Draftsmen, job applicants, see 2441
Short Occupational Knowledge Test for Electricians, job applicants, see 2442
Short Occupational Knowledge Test for Machinists, job applicants, see 2443
Short Occupational Knowledge Test for Plumbers, job applicants, see 2444
Short Occupational Knowledge Test for Tool and Die Makers, job applicants, see 2445
Short Occupational Knowledge Test for Welders, job applicants, see 2446
Technical Tests [South Africa], standards 6-8 (ages 13-15), see 2447

SUPERVISION

How Supervise?, supervisors, see 2448
Ideal Leader Behavior Description Questionnaire, supervisors, see 2449
★*In-Basket Test* [South Africa], applicants for high level executive positions, see 2450
Leader Behavior Description Questionnaire, supervisors, see 2451
Leader Behavior Description Questionnaire, Form 12, supervisors, see 2452
Leadership Evaluation and Development Scale, prospective supervisors, see 2453
Leadership Opinion Questionnaire, supervisors and prospective supervisors, see 2454
★*Leadership Practices Inventory,* supervisors, see 2455
Managerial Scale for Enterprise Improvement, supervisors, see 2456
RAD Scales, supervisors, see 2457
RBH Test of Supervisory Judgment, business and industry, see 2458
Supervisory Index, supervisors, see 2459
Supervisory Inventory on Communication, supervisors and prospective supervisors, see 2460
★*Supervisory Inventory on Discipline,* supervisors, see 2461
★*Supervisory Inventory on Grievances,* supervisors, see 2462
Supervisory Inventory on Human Relations, supervisors and prospective supervisors, see 2463
★*Supervisory Inventory on Labor Relations,* supervisors in unionized firms, see 2464
Supervisory Inventory on Safety, supervisors and prospective supervisors, see 2465
Supervisory Practices Test, supervisors, see 2466
★*Survey of Management Perception,* supervisors, see 2467
WPS Supervisor-Executive Tri-Dimensional Evaluation Scales, supervisors, see 2468

TRANSPORTATION

American Transit Association Tests, transit operating personnel, see 2469
Driver Selection Forms and Tests, truck drivers, see 2470
McGuire Safe Driver Scale and Interview Guide, prospective motor vehicle operators, see 2471
Road Test Check List for Testing, Selecting, Rating, and Training Coach Operators, bus drivers, see 2472
Road Test in Traffic for Testing, Selecting, Rating and Training Truck Drivers, truck drivers, see 2473
Short Occupational Knowledge Test for Truck Drivers, job applicants, see 2474
Truck Driver Test, drivers of light and medium trucks, see 2475
Wilson Driver Selection Test, prospective motor vehicle operators, see 2476

PUBLISHERS DIRECTORY AND INDEX

This directory and index gives the addresses and tests of all publishers represented in this volume. References are to entry numbers, not to page numbers. Stars indicate test publishers with test catalogs listing 10 or more tests. Tests not originating in the country of publication are identified by listing in brackets the country in which the test was originally prepared and published. All foreign tests distributed by United States publishers are listed; however, United States tests distributed by foreign publishers are listed only if the tests have been revised or supplemented for foreign use.

★American Guidance Service, Inc., Publishers' Bldg., Circle Pines, Minn. 55014:
Kuhlmann-Finch Tests, 399
Minnesota Preschool Scale, 509
Peabody Picture Vocabulary Test, 516
Preschool Attainment Record, 519

American Printing House for the Blind, Inc., 1839 Frankfort Ave., Louisville, Ky. 40206:
Cooperative School and College Ability Tests, 361

Anand Agencies, 1433 A Shukrawar, Poona 2, India:
Draw-A-Man Test for Indian Children, 372

Aptitude Test Service, Inc., P.O. Box 16, Golf, Ill. 60029:
Business Test, 345

Associated Personnel Technicians, Inc., Box 1036, Wichita, Kan. 67201:
APT Performance Test, 332

★Australian Council for Educational Research, P.O. Box 210, Hawthorn, Vic. 3122, Australia:
A.C.E.R. Advanced Test B40, 323
A.C.E.R. Advanced Tests AL and AQ, 324
ACER Higher Tests, 325
A.C.E.R. Intermediate Test A, 326
A.C.E.R. Intermediate Tests C and D, 327
A.C.E.R. Junior Non-Verbal Test, 328
A.C.E.R. Junior Test A, 329
A.C.E.R. Lower Grades General Ability Scale, 330
Advanced Test N, 338
Classification Tasks, 488
Jenkins Non-Verbal Test [England], 415a1
Mill Hill Vocabulary Scale [England], 403
Otis Self-Administering Tests of Mental Ability [United States], 426
Pacific Design Construction Test, 514
Pacific Reasoning Series Tests: Pacific Test Series, 427
Queensland Test, 520
Wechsler Intelligence Scale for Children [United States], 533

Bingham Button Test, 46211 North 125th St. East, Lancaster, Calif. 93534:
Bingham Button Test, 485

★Bobbs-Merrill Co., Inc. (The), 4300 West 62nd St., Indianapolis, Ind. 46268:
American School Intelligence Test, 339
Cattell Culture Fair Intelligence Test, 364b
Detroit General Intelligence Examination, 370
Detroit Tests of Learning Aptitude, 493
Pressey Classification and Verifying Tests, 438
Public School Primary Intelligence Test, 441

★Bruce (Martin M.), Ph.D., Publishers, 340 Oxford Road, New Rochelle, N.Y. 10804:
Subsumed Abilities Test, 582

★CTB/McGraw-Hill, Del Monte Research Park, Monterey, Calif. 93940:
California Short-Form Test of Mental Maturity, 348
California Test of Mental Maturity, 349
Short Form Test of Academic Aptitude, 458

Case Western Reserve University. *See* Personnel Research Institute.

Clinical Psychology Publishing Co., Inc., 4 Conant Square, Brandon, Vt. 05733:
Vane Kindergarten Test, 528

Cognitive Test Center, East Neck Road, Huntington Bay, N.Y. 11743:
Willner Instance Similarities Test, 593

College Entrance Examination Board, 888 Seventh Ave., New York, N.Y. 10019:
College Board Scholastic Aptitude Test, 357
Preliminary Scholastic Aptitude Test/National Merit Scholarship Qualifying Test, 436

★Consulting Psychologists Press, Inc., 577 College Ave., Palo Alto, Calif. 94306:
Analysis of Relationships, 341
Clinical Profile for the Stanford Binet Intelligence Scale (L-M), 526
D48 Test, 365
WAIS Test Profile, 531
WISC Test Profile, 537
WPPSI Test Profile, 539

★Cooperative Tests and Services, Educational Testing Service, Princeton, N.J. 08540:
Cooperative Academic Ability Test, 360
Cooperative Preschool Inventory, 490
Cooperative School and College Ability Tests, 361

Crosby Lockwood Staples, Frogmore, St. Albans, Herts, AL2 2NF, England:
Figure Reasoning Test, 375

Dennis (William H.), Trumbull County Reading Clinic, 255 Bonnie Brae Ave. N.E., Warren, Ohio 44483:
Dennis Test of Scholastic Aptitude, 369

★Educational and Industrial Testing Service, P.O. Box 7234, San Diego, Calif. 92107:
Biographical Inventory—Creativity, 544
Concept Assessment Kit—Conservation, 549
Queensland Test [Australia], 520
Rhodes WAIS Scatter Profile, 530
Rhodes WISC Scatter Profile, 535

Educational Evaluation Enterprises, 5 Marsh St., Bristol 1, Glos., England:
English Picture Vocabulary Test, 495

Educational Records Bureau, Box 619, Princeton, N.J. 08540:
Junior Scholastic Aptitude Test, 394

★Educational Testing Service, Princeton, N.J. 08540 (*See also* College Entrance Examination Board, Cooperative Tests and Services, Educational Records Bureau, and Educational Testing Service [Atlanta Office]):
Graduate Record Examinations Aptitude Test, 382
Undergraduate Program Aptitude Test, 470

Educational Testing Service (Atlanta Office), Suite 100, 17 Executive Park Drive, Atlanta, Ga. 30329:
Hidden Figures Test, 559
Kit of Reference Tests for Cognitive Factors, 561

★Educators'-Employers' Tests & Services Associates, 120 Detzel Place, Cincinnati, Ohio 45219:
General Mental Ability Test, 378

Gibson (Robert) & Sons, Glasgow, Ltd., 17 Fitzroy Place, Glasgow G37SF, Scotland:
Cotswold Junior Ability Tests, 362
Cotswold Measurement of Ability, 363
Kelvin Measurement of Ability in Infant Classes, 395
Kelvin Measurement of Mental Ability, 396
"Orton" Intelligence Test, No. 4, 422
Ryburn Group Intelligence Tests, 448

★Ginn & Co. Ltd., Elsinore House, Buckingham St., Aylesbury, Bucks, England:
General Verbal Practice Tests G1-G3, 379
Non-Verbal Tests, 415
Picture Test A, 434
Verbal Tests (Adv.), 474
Verbal Tests BC, CD, C, and D, 475
Verbal Tests EF and GH, 476
Verbal Tests 15-23 and 69, 477

★Guidance Centre, University of Toronto, 1000 Yonge St., Toronto, Ont. M4W 2K8, Canada:
CGA Mental Ability Tests, 346
Canadian Academic Aptitude Test, 350
Group Test of Learning Capacity, 387
OISE Picture Reasoning Test, 417

Guidance Testing Associates, 6516 Shirley Ave., Austin, Tex. 78752:
Tests of General Ability: Inter-American Series, 468

★Harcourt Brace Jovanovich, Inc., 757 Third Ave., New York, N.Y. 10017:
Analysis of Learning Potential, 340
Columbia Mental Maturity Scale, 489
Goodenough-Harris Drawing Test, 381
Otis Employment Tests, 423
Otis-Lennon Mental Ability Test, 424
Otis Quick-Scoring Mental Ability Tests, 425
Otis Self-Administering Tests of Mental Ability, 426
Pintner-Cunningham Primary Test, 435

★Harrap (George G.) & Co. Ltd., P.O. Box 70, 182/4 High Holborn, London WC1V 7AX, England:
Cattell Intelligence Tests, 354
Deeside Non-Verbal Reasoning Test, 367
Deeside Picture Puzzles, 368
Kingston Test of Intelligence, 397
Northumberland Mental Tests, 416
Porteus Maze Test [United States]: British Edition, 518e
Simplex GNV Intelligence Tests, 459
Simplex Group Intelligence Scale, 460
Simplex Junior Intelligence Tests, 461
Sleight Non-Verbal Intelligence Test, 462
Southend Test of Intelligence, 463
Stanford-Binet Intelligence Scale [United States], 525

Higgins-Wertman Associates, P.O. Box 9012, Delaware Station, Albany, N.Y. 12209:
Higgins-Wertman Test: Threshold of Visual Closure, 560

Hiskey (Marshall S.), 5640 Baldwin, Lincoln, Neb. 68508:
Hiskey-Nebraska Test of Learning Aptitude, 499

★Houghton Mifflin Co., 110 Tremont St., Boston, Mass. 02107:
Cognitive Abilities Test, 356
Henmon-Nelson Tests of Mental Ability, 391
Lorge-Thorndike Intelligence Tests, 400
Lorge-Thorndike Intelligence Tests, College Edition, 401
Pictorial Test of Intelligence, 517
Remote Associates Test, 574
Stanford-Binet Intelligence Scale, 525

★Human Sciences Research Council, Private Bag 41, Pretoria, Republic of South Africa:
Group Test for Indian South Africans, 383
Individual Scale for Indian South Africans, 501
N.B. Group Tests, 410
New South African Group Test, 411
New South African Individual Scale, 511
Non-Verbal Intelligence Tests for Deaf and Hearing Subjects [The Netherlands], 512

★Industrial Relations Center, University of Chicago, 1225 East 60th St., Chicago, Ill. 60637 (This publisher has not replied to our four requests to check the accuracy of the entries for the tests listed below.):
Closure Flexibility (Concealed Figures), 547
Closure Speed (Gestalt Completion), 548
Non-Verbal Reasoning Test, 414
Perceptual Speed (Identical Forms), 570
Verbal Reasoning, 472
Word Fluency, 594

★Institute for Personality and Ability Testing, 1602 Coronado Drive, Champaign, Ill. 61820:
IPAT Culture Free Intelligence Test, 364a

Kennedy-Galton Centre, Harperbury Hospital, Harper Lane, Shenley, Radlett, Herts WD7 9HQ, England:
Pattern Perception Test, 428

Knobloch (Hilda), Albany Medical College, Albany, N.Y. 12208:
Developmental Screening Inventory, 494

L & L Associates, P.O. Box 20473, Charlotte, N.C. 28202:
Executive Employment Review, 374

Ladoca Project and Publishing Foundation, Inc., East 51st Ave. and Lincoln St., Denver, Colo. 80216:
Denver Developmental Screening Test, 492

Lafayette Instrument Co., P.O. Box 1279, North 9th St. Road and Sagamore Parkway, Lafayette, Ind. 47902:
Jensen Alternation Board, 560A

Layton (Wilbur L.), 3604 Ross Road, Ames, Iowa 50010:
Minnesota Scholastic Aptitude Test, 405
Ohio State University Psychological Test, 419

Lewis (H. K.) & Co. Ltd., P.O. Box 66, 136 Gower St., London WC1E 6BS, England:
Crichton Vocabulary Scale, 491
Mill Hill Vocabulary Scale, 403
Progressive Matrices, 439

Lincoln Test Service, 304 West Iowa St., Urbana, Ill. 61801:
Quantitative Evaluative Device, 443

McGraw-Hill Ryerson Ltd., 330 Progress Ave., Scarborough, Ont., Canada:
Canadian Intelligence Test, 486

Mafex Associates, Inc., 111 Barron Ave., Johnstown, Pa. 15906:
Preschool and Early Primary Skill Survey, 437

★Monitor, P.O. Box 2337, Hollywood, Calif. 90028:
Test of Creative Potential, 586

Montana Reading Publications, 419 Stapleton Bldg., Billings, Mont. 59101:
Gilliland Learning Potential Examination, 380

NCS Interpretive Scoring Systems, 4401 West 76th St., Minneapolis, Minn. 55435:
Minnesota Child Development Inventory, 508

★NFER Publishing Co. Ltd., 2 Jennings Bldgs., Thames Ave., Windsor, Berks SL4 1QS, England:
AH4, AH5, and AH6 Tests, 331
C.P. 66 Test, 347
Group Test 36, 384
Group Test 75, 385
Group Test 91, 386
Group Test 95, 386A
Group Tests 70 and 70B, 388
Group Tests 72 and 73, 389
Group Tests 90A and 90B, 390
Mitchell Vocabulary Test, 406
Wechsler Adult Intelligence Scale [United States], 529
Wechsler Intelligence Scale for Children [United States], 533
Wechsler Preschool and Primary Scale of Intelligence [United States], 538
Williams Intelligence Test for Children With Defective Vision, 540

★National Institute for Personnel Research, P.O. Box 10319, Johannesburg, Republic of South Africa:
Abstract Spatial Relations Test, 541
Concept Attainment Test, 550
Consequences, 552
Gottschaldt Figures, 557
Mental Alertness: Tests A/1 and A/2, 402
Pattern Relations Test, 569
Seeing Faults, 576
Spiral Nines, 464
Symbol Series Test, 584
Wechsler Adult Intelligence Scale [United States], 529
Wechsler-Bellevue Intelligence Scale [United States], 532

★Nelson (Thomas) & Sons (Canada) Ltd., 81 Curlew Drive, Don Mills 400, Ont., Canada:
Canadian Cognitive Abilities Test [United States], 351
Canadian Lorge-Thorndike Intelligence Tests [United States], 352

New Zealand Council for Educational Research, Education House, 178 Willis St., Wellington C.2, New Zealand:
Otis Self-Administering Tests of Mental Ability [United States], 426

Oliver & Boyd, Croythorn House, 23 Ravelston Terrace, Edinburgh EH4 3TJ, Scotland:
Essential Intelligence Test, 373
Reasoning Tests for Higher Levels of Intelligence, 446

O'Rourke Publications, P.O. Box 1118, Lake Alfred, Fla. 33850:
O'Rourke General Classification Test, 421

Personnel Press, Education Center, P.O. Box 2649, Columbus, Ohio 43216:
Kuhlmann-Anderson Test, 398
Thinking Creatively With Sounds and Words, 587
Torrance Tests of Creative Thinking, 589

Personnel Research Associates, Inc., 701 Metropolitan Bldg., 1407 Main St., Dallas, Tex. 75202:
Individual Placement Series
Academic Alertness "AA," 334
Performance Alertness "PA," 429

Personnel Research Institute, Case Western Reserve University, 1695 Magnolia Drive, Cleveland, Ohio 44106:
Personnel Research Institute Classification Test, 431
Personnel Research Institute Factory Series Test, 432

★Psychological Corporation (The), 304 East 45th St., New York, N.Y. 10017:
Arthur Point Scale of Performance Tests, 483
Bayley Scales of Infant Development, 484
Benton Visual Retention Test, 543
Boehm Test of Basic Concepts, 344
Cattell Infant Intelligence Scale, 487
Chicago Non-Verbal Examination, 355
College Qualification Tests, 358
Concept Mastery Test, 359
Differential Aptitude Tests
Abstract Reasoning, 333
Verbal Reasoning, 473
Doppelt Mathematical Reasoning Test, 371
Fundamental Achievement Series, 376
Gesell Developmental Schedules, 497
Kent Series of Emergency Scales, 503
McCarthy Scales of Children's Abilities, 506
Miller Analogies Test, 404
Modified Alpha Examination Form 9, 407
Personnel Tests for Industry, 433
Porteus Maze Test, 518
Progressive Matrices [England], 439
Revised Beta Examination, 447
Wechsler Adult Intelligence Scale, 529
Wechsler-Bellevue Intelligence Scale, 532
Wechsler Intelligence Scale for Children, 533
Wechsler Memory Scale, 592
Wechsler Preschool and Primary Scale of Intelligence, 538
Wesman Personnel Classification Test, 480

Psychological Test Specialists, Box 1441, Missoula, Mont. 59801:
Full-Range Picture Vocabulary Test, 496
Kahn Intelligence Tests, 502
Proverbs Test, 440
Quick Test, 522

★Psychologists and Educators, Inc., Suite 212, 211 West State St., Jacksonville, Ill. 62650:
Creativity Attitude Survey, 553
Test of Perceptual Organization, 466
WISC Mental Description Sheet, 536

★Psychometric Affiliates, Box 3167, Munster, Ind. 46321:
Acorn National Aptitude Tests
Academic Aptitude Test: Non-Verbal Intelligence, 335
Academic Aptitude Test: Verbal Intelligence, 336
Ohio Penal Classification Test, 418
Quick Screening Scale of Mental Development, 521
Ring and Peg Tests of Behavior Development, 523

Research Psychologists Press, Inc., 36 St. John St., Goshen, N.Y. 10924:
Similes Test, 580

★Richardson, Bellows, Henry & Co., Inc., 1140 Connecticut Ave. N.W., Washington, D.C. 20036:
RBH Test of Learning Ability, 444
RBH Test of Non-Verbal Reasoning, 445

Safran (C.), Calgary School Board, Calgary, Alta., Canada:
Safran Culture Reduced Intelligence Test, 453

★Scholastic Testing Service, Inc., 480 Meyer Road, Bensenville, Ill. 60106:
Scholastic Mental Ability Tests, 454

Schubert (Herman J. P.), 500 Klein Road, Buffalo, N.Y. 14221:
Schubert General Ability Battery, 455

★Science Research Associates, Inc., 259 East Erie St., Chicago, Ill. 60611:
Adaptability Test, 337
Army General Classification Test, 342
SRA Nonverbal Form, 449
SRA Pictorial Reasoning Test, 450
SRA Short Test of Educational Ability, 451
SRA Verbal Form, 452
Tests of General Ability, 467
Thurstone Test of Mental Alertness, 469

Service for Admission to College and University, 151 Slater St., Ottawa 4, Ont., Canada:
Canadian Scholastic Aptitude Test, 353

★Sheridan Psychological Services, Inc., P.O. Box 6101, Orange, Calif. 92667:
Alternate Uses, 542
Army Alpha Examination: First Nebraska Revision, 341A
Christensen-Guilford Fluency Tests, 546
Consequences, 551
Creativity Tests for Children, 554
Decorations, 555
Immediate Test, 500
Making Objects, 562
Match Problems, 564
Match Problems 5, 565
Memory for Events, 566
Memory for Meanings, 567
New Uses, 568
Pertinent Questions, 571
Plot Titles, 572
Possible Jobs, 573
Seeing Problems, 577
Ship Destination Test, 457
Simile Interpretations, 579
Sketches, 581
Symbol Identities, 583
Utility Test, 591

Shurrager (Harriett C.), Department of Psychology and Education, Illinois Institute of Technology, Chicago, Ill. 60616:
Haptic Intelligence Scale for Adult Blind, 498

Slosson Educational Publications, Inc., 140 Pine St., East Aurora, N.Y. 14052:
Slosson Intelligence Test, 524

Society for New Guinea Psychological Research and Publications, P.O. Box 5008, Boroto, Papua New Guinea:
New Guinea Performance Scales, 510

Starr (Anna Spiesman), 126 Montgomery St., Highland Park, N.J. 08904:
Rutgers Drawing Test, 575

Statistical Publishing Society, 204/1 Barrackpore Trunk Road, Calcutta-35, India:
Non-Language Test of Verbal Intelligence, 412

Stevens, Thurow & Associates, Inc., 105 West Adams St., Chicago, Ill. 60603:
Inventory No. 2, 393

★Stoelting Co., 1350 South Kostner Ave., Chicago, Ill. 60623:
Arthur Point Scale of Performance Tests, 483
Block-Design Test, 545
Feature Profile Test, 556
Healy Pictorial Completion Tests, 558
Leiter Adult Intelligence Scale, 504
Leiter International Performance Scale, 505
Manikin Test, 563

Merrill-Palmer Scale of Mental Tests, 507
Passalong Test, 515
Porteus Maze Test: Vineland Revision, 518a
Scott Company Mental Alertness Test, 456
Seguin-Goddard Formboard, 578
Two-Figure Formboard, 590

Swets & Zeitlinger B. V., Keizersgracht 487, Amsterdam-C, The Netherlands:
Non-Verbal Intelligence Tests for Deaf and Hearing Subjects, 512

TACA Development Fund, University of Missouri, 8001 Natural Bridge, St. Louis, Mo. 63121:
Test of Adult College Aptitude, 465

★University Book Store, 360 State St., West Lafayette, Ind. 47906:
Purdue Non-Language Personnel Test, 442

University of Chicago. *See* Industrial Relations Center.

★University of London Press Ltd., St. Paul's House, Warwick Lane, London EC4P 4AH, England:
Moray House Picture Tests, 408
Moray House Verbal Reasoning Tests, 409
Non-Readers Intelligence Test, 413
Oral Verbal Intelligence Test, 419A

University of Toronto. *See* Guidance Centre.

★Western Psychological Services, 12031 Wilshire Blvd., Los Angeles, Calif. 90025:
California Abbreviated WISC, 534
Illinois Index of Scholastic Aptitude, 392
Ohwaki-Kohs Tactile Block Design Intelligence Test for the Blind [Japan], 513
Oregon Academic Ranking Test, 420
Stanford-Ohwaki-Kohs Block Design Intelligence Test for the Blind [Japan], 527
Test of Concept Utilization, 585
Time Appreciation Test, 588
Verbal Power Test of Concept Equivalence, 471
Western Personnel Tests, 481

Williams and Associates, 7201 Creveling Drive, St. Louis, Mo. 63130:
BITCH Test, 343

William, Lynde & Williams, 153 East Erie St., Painesville, Ohio 44077:
Personal Classification Test, 430
WLW Employment Inventory III, 478
WLW Mental Alertness Inventory, 479

Wonderlic (E. F.) & Associates, Inc., Box 7, Northfield, Ill. 60093:
Wonderlic Personnel Test, 482

INDEX OF TITLES

This index lists (a) intelligence tests in print as of February 1, 1974, and (b) intelligence tests out of print, status unknown, or reclassified since last listed in the intelligence section of a *Mental Measurements Yearbook* (MMY). Citations are to test entries, not to pages. Numbers without colons refer to in print tests listed in this volume; numbers with colons refer to tests out of print, status unknown, or reclassified. Unless preceded by the word *"consult,"* all numbers containing colons refer to tests in this volume. The guide numbers next to the outside margins in the running heads of the reprint sections should be used to locate a particular test. The first reprint section, from *Tests in Print II* (TIP II), has guide numbers in the range 323 to 594; the second reprint section, from the 1st MMY, 1:1037 to 1:1062; the third reprint section, from the 2nd MMY, 2:1376 to 2:1430.1; etc. To obtain the latest information on a test no longer classified with intelligence tests, the reader must consult either TIP II (if the test is in print) or an MMY (if the test is out of print). For example, "Illinois Test of Psycholinguistic Abilities, 7:442; reclassified, *consult* T2:981" indicates that the ITPA, test 7:442 in the section of this volume reprinted from the 7th MMY, has since been reclassified and for the latest information, test 981 in TIP II must be consulted. Superseded titles are listed with cross references to the current title. Tests which are part of a series are listed under their individual titles and also their series titles. Acronyms for tests having 10 or more references are presented at the end of this title index.

A.C.E.R. Adult Test (B40), *see* A.C.E.R. Advanced Test B40, 323
A.C.E.R. Advanced Test B40, 323
A.C.E.R. Advanced Tests AL and AQ, 324
A.C.E.R. General Ability Test: Advanced M, *see* A.C.E.R. Higher Tests, 325
A.C.E.R. General Tests A and C, *see* A.C.E.R. Intermediate Tests A and C, 326-7
A.C.E.R. Higher Tests, 325
A.C.E.R. Intermediate Test A, 326
A.C.E.R. Intermediate Tests C and D, 327
A.C.E.R. Junior A Test, *see* A.C.E.R. Junior Test A, 329
A.C.E.R. Junior B Test, 6:435
A.C.E.R. Junior Non-Verbal Test, 328
A.C.E.R. Junior Test A, 329
A.C.E.R. Lower Grades General Ability Scale, 330
A.C.E.R. Non-Verbal Test, 4:272
A.C.E.R. Test L, 4:273
A.C.E.R. Test W.N.V., 6:436
ACT Test Battery of the American College Testing Program, 7:330; reclassified, *consult* ACT Test Assessment, T2:1044
AH4, AH5, and AH6 Tests, 331
APT Performance Test, 332
Abstract Reasoning: Differential Aptitude Tests, 333
Abstract Spatial Relations Test, 541
Academic Alertness "AA," 334

Academic Aptitude Test: Non-Verbal Intelligence, 335; Verbal Intelligence, 336
Acorn National Aptitude Tests: Academic Aptitude Test: Non-Verbal Intelligence, 335; Verbal Intelligence, 336
Adaptability Test, 337
Adding Decorations: Creativity Tests for Children, 554a
Addition Test, N-1, 561I1
Adult Test (B40), *see* A.C.E.R. Advanced Test B40, 323
Advanced Perception of Relations Scales, 3:251b
Advanced Personnel Test, *see* Miller Analogies Test, 404
Advanced Progressive Matrices, 439c
Advanced Test N, 338
Advanced Vocabulary Test, V-4, 561u4
Akron Classification Test, 4:276
Alexander Performance Scale, 6:514
Alternate Uses, 542; Xs-2, 561x2
American Council on Education Psychological Examination for College Freshmen, 6:438; for High School Students, 5:309
American School Intelligence Test, 339
Analysis of Learning Potential, 340
Analysis of Relationships, 341
Andover School-Entrance Test, *see* Kent Series of Emergency Scales, 503a

Animal Puzzles, 1:1057
Apparatus Test, Sep-1, 561s1
Aptitude Test C.P.66, see C.P.66 Test, 347
Aptitude Test: Undergraduate Record Examinations, see Undergraduate Program Aptitude Test, 470
Army Alpha Examination: First Nebraska Revision, 341A
Army General Classification Test, First Civilian Edition, 342
Army Group Examination Alpha, 4:281; for revisions, see Army Alpha Examination: First Nebraska Edition, 341A; Army Group Examination Alpha: Schrammel-Brannan Revision, 3:220h; Bureau Test VI, Mental Alertness, 3:220a; Modified Alpha Examination Form 9, 407; Revised Alpha Examination Forms 5 and 7, 4:315; Revised Alpha Examination Form 6, Short Form, 4:316; Revision of Army Alpha Examination, 4:317; Scovill Classification Test, 4:320
Army Group Examination Alpha: Schrammel-Brannan Revision, 3:220h
Army Group Examination Beta, see Revised Beta Examination, 447
Arthur Point Scale of Performance Tests, 483
Associational Fluency 1: Christensen-Guilford Fluency Tests, 546c
Associational Fluency 1, Form A, Fa-2, 561c2
Associations 4, Fa-3, 561c3
Auditory Letter Span Test, Ms-3, 561k3
Auditory Number Span Test, Ms-1, 561k1
Auditory Scale for Group Measurement of General Mental Ability, 1:1041
BITCH Test, 343
Basic Employment Test, 3:221b
Bayley Scales of Infant Development, 484
Benge Employment Tests (status unknown), 3:221
Benton Visual Retention Test, 543
Bingham Button Test, 485
Biographical Inventory—Creativity, 544
Bitch-100: A Culture-Specific Test, see BITCH Test, 343
Black Intelligence Test of Cultural Homogeneity, see BITCH Test, 343
Block-Design Test, 545
Boehm Test of Basic Concepts, 344
Bristol Group Reasoning Tests, 2:1381
Bureau Test VI: Mental Alertness, 3:220b
Business Test, 345
CGA Mental Ability Tests, 346
C.P.66 Test, 347
California Abbreviated WISC, 534
California Analogies and Reasoning Test, 6:442
California Capacity Questionnaire, 3:222
California First-Year Mental Scale, 2:1382
California Preschool Mental Scale, 2:1383
California Short-Form Test of Mental Maturity, 348
California Survey Series: Survey of Mental Maturity, 6:503
California Test of Mental Maturity, 349
Canadian Academic Aptitude Test, 350
Canadian Cognitive Abilities Test, 351
Canadian Intelligence Examination, see Canadian Intelligence Test, 486
Canadian Intelligence Test, 486
Canadian Lorge-Thorndike Intelligence Tests, 352
Canadian Scholastic Aptitude Test, 353
Card Rotations Test, S-1, 561r1
Cardall-Miles Test of Mental Alertness (status unknown), 6:446
Carl Hollow Square Scale, 3:273
Carl Hollow Square Test, 6:519d
Carlton Intelligence Tests, 7:342
Carlton Picture Intelligence Test, 6:447
Carnegie Mental Ability Tests, 3:224

Cattell Culture Fair Intelligence Test, 364b
Cattell Infant Intelligence Scale, 487
Cattell Intelligence Tests, 354
Chicago Non-Verbal Examination, 355
Chicago Tests of Primary Mental Abilities, 3:225; reclassified, consult SRA Primary Mental Abilities, T2:1087
Children's Picture Information Test, 6:516
Choosing a Path, Ss-2, 561t2
Christensen-Guilford Fluency Tests, 546
Classification Tasks, 488
Classification Test for Industrial and Office Personnel, see Personnel Research Institute Classification Test, 431
Classification Test 40-A, 6:448
Clinical Profile for the Stanford Binet Intelligence Scale (L-M), 526
Closure Flexibility (Concealed Figures), 547
Closure Speed (Gestalt Completion), 548
Cognitive Abilities Test, 356
Cole-Vincent Group Intelligence Test for School Entrants, 3:226
College Ability Test, see College Transfer Test, 4:286
College Board Scholastic Aptitude Test, 357
College Entrance Examination Board Scholastic Aptitude Test, see College Board Scholastic Aptitude Test, 357
College Placement Test [SRA], 5:319
College Qualification Tests, 358
College Transfer Test, 4:286
Coloured Progressive Matrices, 439b
Columbia Mental Maturity Scale, 489
Concealed Figures: A Test of Flexibility of Closure, see Closure Flexibility (Concealed Figures), 547
Concealed Words Test, Cs-2, 561b2
Concept Assessment Kit—Conservation, 549
Concept Attainment Test, 550
Concept Mastery Test, 359
Consequences, 551; [NIPR], 552; 0-1 [10-Item Edition], 561m3
Construction Puzzle, see Dearborn Formboard 3, 2:1391
Controlled Associations Test, Fa-1, 561c1
Cooperative Academic Ability Test, 360
Cooperative Inter-American Tests: Tests of General Ability, see Inter-American Series: Tests of General Ability, 468
Cooperative Preschool Inventory, 490
Cooperative School and College Ability Tests, 361
Copying Test, Cf-3, 561a3
Cornell-Coxe Performance Ability Scale, 2:1388
Cotswold Junior Ability Tests, 362
Cotswold Measurement of Ability, 363
Cotswold Measurement of Mental Ability, see Cotswold Measurement of Ability, 363
Cotswold Mental Ability Test, see Cotswold Measurement of Ability, 363
Creativity Attitude Survey, 553
Creativity Tests for Children, 554
Crichton Vocabulary Scale, 491
Cube Comparisons Test, S-2, 561r2
Culture Fair Intelligence Test, 364
Culture Free Intelligence Test, see Culture Fair Intelligence Test, 364
Culture-Free Test, 4:287
Curtis Classification Form, 4:338
D48 Test, 365
Daneshill Intelligence Test, 5:325
Davis-Eells Games, see Davis-Eells Test of General Intelligence, 5:326
Davis-Eells Test of General Intelligence or Problem-Solving Ability, 5:326
Dawson Mental Test, 2:1389
Dearborn-Anderson Formboards 2 and 2b, 2:1390

INDEX OF TITLES

Dearborn Formboard 3, 2:1391
Decorations, 555
Deeside Non-Verbal Reasoning Test, 367
Deeside Picture Puzzles, 368
Dennis Test of Scholastic Aptitude, 369
Denver Developmental Screening Test, 492
Detroit Advanced First-Grade Intelligence Test, 2:1392
Detroit Advanced Intelligence Test, 5:329c
Detroit Alpha Intelligence Test, 5:329b
Detroit Beginning First-Grade Intelligence Test, 1:1044
Detroit First Grade Intelligence Test, *see* Detroit Beginning First Grade Intelligence Test, 1:1044
Detroit General Intelligence Examination, 370
Detroit Kindergarten Test, 3:274
Detroit Primary Intelligence Test, *see* Public School Primary Intelligence Test, 441
Detroit Tests of Learning Aptitude, 493
Developmental Screening Inventory, 494
Diagnostic Performance Tests, 6:519
Different Letter Groups: Creativity Tests for Children, 554b
Differential Aptitude Tests: Abstract Reasoning, 333; Verbal Reasoning, 473
Distributed Attention, *see* Partington's Pathways Test, 4:355
Division Test, N-2, 561I2
Dominion Group Test of Intelligence, 5:330
Dominion Group Test of Learning Capacity, *see* Group Test of Learning Capacity, 387
Dominion Higher Test, *see* Dominion Group Test of Intelligence, 5:330
Dominion Tests: Group Test of Learning Capacity, 387; Machine-Scoring Group Test of Learning Capacity, 387c; Quick-Scoring Group Test of Learning Capacity, 6:493
Dominion Tests of Learning Capacity, *see* Group Test of Learning Capacity: Dominion Tests, 387
Doppelt Mathematical Reasoning Test, 371
Draw-A-Man Test for Indian Children, 372
Duplex Series of Ability Tests, 4:289
Easel Age Scale, 5:332
Electrical Information Test, Mk-3, 561j3
Emergency Test, *see* Kent Series of Emergency Scales, 503c
Employment Test, 3:221a
English Picture Vocabulary Test, 495
Essential Intelligence Test, 373
Essential Junior Intelligence Test, *see* Essential Intelligence Test, 373
Estimation of Length Test, Le-1, 561h1
Executive Employment Review, 374
Expressional Fluency: Christensen-Guilford Fluency Tests, 546d; [Fe-1], 561d1
FR-CR Test, 4:339; now available only as a subtest of Leiter Adult Intelligence Scale, 504
Feature Profile Test: Pintner-Paterson Modification, 556
Ferguson Formboards, 2:1394
Figure Classification, I-3, 561g3
Figure Reasoning Test, 375
Fiji Test of General Ability, 2:1395
Finding A's Test, P-1, 561n1
First and Last Names Test, Ma-3, 561i3
Form Board Test, Vz-1, 561v1
Fret Continuation Test, 7:438
Fret Repetition Test, 7:439
Full-Range Picture Vocabulary Test, 496
Fundamental Achievement Series, 376
General Employment Review, *see* Executive Employment Review, 374
General Intelligence Test for Africans, 2:1396
General Interest Review, *see* Executive Employment Review, 374

General Mental Ability Test: ETSA Test, 378
General Test T, *see* A.C.E.R. Junior Test A, 329
General Verbal Practice Tests G1-G3, 379
George Washington University Series: Mental Alertness Test, 3:238
Gesell Developmental Schedules, 497
Gestalt Completion: A Test of Speed of Closure, *see* Closure Speed (Gestalt Completion), 548
Gestalt Completion Test, Cs-1, 561b1
Gestalt Continuation Test (status unknown), 6:459
Gestalt Transformation, Re-1, 561p1
Gibson's Intelligence Tests, 1:1045
Gilliland Learning Potential Examination, 380
Gilliland-Shotwell Intelligence Scale, *see* Northwestern Intelligence Tests, 5:411
Goodenough-Harris Drawing Test, 381
Goodenough Intelligence Test, *see* Goodenough-Harris Drawing Test, 381
Gottschaldt Figures, *see* Closure Flexibility (Concealed Figures), 547, and Gottschaldt Figures [NIPR], 557
Gottschaldt Figures [NIPR], 557
Graduate Record Examinations Aptitude Test, 382
Griffiths Mental Development Scale for Testing Babies From Birth to Two Years, 6:523
Group Selective Test No. 1, 5:337
Group Test for Indian South Africans, 383
Group Test of General Intelligence: AH4, 331a
Group Test of High-Grade Intelligence: AH5, 331b
Group Test of Intelligence, *see* Group Test of Learning Capacity, 387
Group Test of Learning Capacity: Dominion Tests, 387
Group Test 33 and 33B, 5:339
Group Test 36, 384
Group Test 70 and 70B, 388
Group Test 72 and 73, 389
Group Test 75, 385
Group Test 90A and 90B, 390
Group Test 91, 386
Group Test 95, 386A
Group Tests of High-Level Intelligence: AH6, 331c
Guilford-Zimmerman Aptitude Survey, Part 5, Spatial Orientation, S-3, 561r3
Haptic Intelligence Scale for Adult Blind, 498
Healy Pictorial Completion Tests, 558
Henmon-Nelson Tests of Mental Ability, 391
Herring Revision of the Binet-Simon Tests, 2:1399
Hidden Figures Test, 559; Cf-1, 559a, 561a1; Form 5, 559b
Hidden Letters: Creativity Tests for Children, 554c
Hidden Patterns Test, Cf-2, 561a2
Higgins-Wertman Test: Threshold of Visual Closure, 560
Hiskey-Nebraska Test of Learning Aptitude, 499
IPAT Culture Fair Intelligence Test, 364a
IPAT Culture Free Intelligence Test, *see* IPAT Culture Fair Intelligence Test, 364a
Ideational Fluency 1: Christensen-Guilford Fluency Tests, 546b
Identical Pictures Test, P-3, 561n3
Illinois Index of Scholastic Aptitude, 392
Illinois Test of Psycholinguistic Abilities, 7:442; reclassified, *consult* T2:981
Immediate Test, 500
Individual Scale for Indian South Africans, 501
Inductive Reasoning Test, 3:232
Infant Intelligence Scale, *see* Cattell Infant Intelligence Scale, 487
Inference Test, Rs-3, 561q3
Intelligence Tests for Children, 5:405
Intelligence Tests for Young Children, *see* Intelligence Tests for Children, 5:405
Inter-American Series: Tests of General Ability, 468
Inventory No. 2, 393

JNB Time Test, *see* Time Appreciation Test, 588
Jenkins Non-Verbal Test, *see* Non-Verbal Test 1, 415a1
Jensen Alternation Board, 560A
Junior Mental Ability, *see* Cotswold Junior Ability Tests, 362
Junior Mental Ability A and B, *see* Cotswold Junior Ability Tests, 362
Junior Mental Ability D and F, *see* Cotswold Junior Ability Tests, 362
Junior Scholastic Aptitude Test, 394
Junior School Grading Test, 2:1400
Kahn Intelligence Tests, 502
Kelvin Measurement of Ability in Infant Classes, 395
Kelvin Measurement of Mental Ability, 396
Kent E-G-Y Test, *see* Kent Series of Emergency Scales, 503c
Kent Series of Emergency Scales, 503
Kentucky Classification Battery, 4:301
Kentucky Classification Test, *see* Kentucky General Ability Test, 3:234
Kentucky General Ability Test, 3:234
Kentucky General Scholastic Ability Test, *see* Kentucky General Ability Test, 3:234
Kinds of People: Creativity Tests for Children, 554d
Kingston Test of Intelligence, 397
Kingsway Intelligence Tests, 3:235
Kit of Reference Tests for Cognitive Factors, 561
Kit of Selected Tests for Reference Aptitude and Achievement Factors, *see* Kit of Reference Tests for Cognitive Factors, 561
Koh's Block-Design Test, *see* Block-Design Test, 545
Kuhlmann-Anderson Intelligence Tests, *see* Kuhlmann-Anderson Test, 398
Kuhlmann-Anderson Measure of Academic Potential, *see* Kuhlmann-Anderson Test, 398
Kuhlmann-Anderson Test, 398
Kuhlmann-Finch Scholastic Aptitude Tests, *see* Kuhlmann-Finch Tests, 399
Kuhlmann-Finch Tests, 399
Kuhlmann Tests of Mental Development, *see* Tests of Mental Development, 2:1426
Laycock Mental Ability Test, 3:237
Leiter Adaptation of Arthur's Stencil Design Test, 4:347; now available only as a subtest of Leiter Adult Intelligence Scale, 504
Leiter Adaptation of the Painted Cube Test, 4:348; now available only as a subtest of Leiter Adult Intelligence Scale, 504
Leiter Adult Intelligence Scale, 504
Leiter International Performance Scale, 505
Leiter-Partington Adult Performance Scale, *see* Leiter Adult Intelligence Scale, 504
Letter Sets Test, I-1, 561g1
Linfert-Hierholzer Scale for Measuring the Mental Development of Infants During the First Year of Life, 3:285
Locations Test, I-2, 561g2
Logical Reasoning, Rs-2, 561q2
Lorge-Thorndike Intelligence Tests, 400; College Edition, 401
Lowry-Lucier Reasoning Test Combination, 7:361
McCarthy Scales of Children's Abilities, 506
Machine-Scoring Group Test of Learning Capacity, 387c
Maddox Verbal Reasoning Test, 6:469
Make Something Out of It: Creativity Tests for Children, 554e
Making Objects, 562
Manchester General Ability Test (Senior), 6:470
Manikin Test, 563
Map Planning Test, Ss-3, 561t3
Marianne Frostig Developmental Test of Visual Perception, 6:553; reclassified, *consult* T2:1921
Match Problems, 564; 2, Xa-1, 561w1; 5, 565; 5, Xa-2, 561w2
Match Problems 2, *see* Match Problems, 564
Mathematics Aptitude Test, R-1, 561o1; R-2, 561o2
Maze Tracing Speed Test, Ss-1, 561t1
Mechanical Information Test, Mk-2, 561j2
Memory for Events, 566
Memory for Meanings, 567
Mental Alertness Test: George Washington University Series, 3:238
Mental Alertness: Tests A/1 and A/2, 402
Merrill-Palmer Scale of Mental Tests, 507
Mill Hill Vocabulary Scale, 403
Miller Analogies Test, 404
Minnesota Child Development Inventory, 508
Minnesota Preschool Scale, 509
Minnesota Scholastic Aptitude Test, 405
Minnesota Tests of Creative Thinking, *see* Torrance Tests of Creative Thinking, 589
Mitchell Vocabulary Test, 406
Modification of the Kent-Shakow Formboard, 2:1408
Modified Alpha Examination Form 9, 407
Moray House Adult Intelligence Test, *see* Moray House Verbal Reasoning Test (Adult) 1, 409e
Moray House Intelligence Tests, *see* Moray House Verbal Reasoning Test, 409b
Moray House Junior Intelligence Test, *see* Moray House Junior Reasoning Test for Nine Year Olds, 409a
Moray House Junior Reasoning Test for Nine Year Olds, 409a
Moray House Picture Intelligence Test 1, 408a
Moray House Picture Tests, 408
Moray House Test 10, *see* Moray House Verbal Intelligence Tests, 409b
Moray House Verbal Reasoning Tests, 409
Multi-Mental Scale, 3:242
Multi-Racial Picture Intelligence Tests Suitable for Use in African and Asian Schools, 6:476
N.B. Group Tests, 410
Names for Stories: Creativity Tests for Children, 554g
National Merit Scholarship Qualifying Test, *see* Preliminary Scholastic Aptitude Test/National Merit Scholarship Qualifying Test, 436
Nearer Point Test, Le-3, 561h3
Nebraska Test of Learning Aptitude, *see* Hiskey-Nebraska Test of Learning Aptitude, 499
Necessary Arithmetic Operations Test, R-4, 561o4
New Guinea Performance Scales, 510
New Rhode Island Intelligence Test, 5:354
New South African Group Test, 411
New South African Individual Scale, 511
New Uses, 568
Nines, *see* Spiral Nines, 464
Non-Language Multi-Mental Test, 3:243
Non-Language Test of Verbal Intelligence, 412
Non-Readers Intelligence Test, 413
Nonsense Syllogisms Test, Rs-1, 561q1
Non-Verbal Intelligence Tests for Deaf and Hearing Subjects, 512
Non-Verbal Reasoning Test, 414
Non-Verbal Test 3, *see* Non-Verbal Test DH, 415b
Non-Verbal Tests, 415
North Central Individual Test of Mental Ability, *see* Pictorial Test of Intelligence, 517
Northox Group Intelligence Test, 2:1410
Northumberland Mental Tests, 416
Northwestern Intelligence Tests, 5:411
Nufferno Tests of Speed and Level, 6:555
Number Comparison Test, P-2, 561n2
OISE Picture Reasoning Test: Primary, 417
Object Naming, Xs-3, 561x3
Object-Number Test, Ma-2, 561i2
Object Synthesis, Re-2, 561p2

Ohio Classification Test, *see* Ohio Penal Classification Test, 418
Ohio Penal Classification Test, 418
Ohio State University Psychological Test, 419
Ohwaki-Kohs Tactile Block Design Intelligence Test for the Blind, 513
Onomatopeia and Images, 587b
Ontario School Ability Examination, 2:1411
Oral Directions Test, *see* PTI-Oral Directions Test, 433c
Oral Verbal Intelligence Test, 419A
Orally Presented Group Test of Intelligence for Juniors, 5:360
Oregon Academic Ranking Test, 420
O'Rourke General Classification Test, 421
"Orton" Intelligence Test, 422
Otis Classification Test, 3:247
Otis Employment Tests, 423
Otis General Intelligence Examination, 3:248
Otis Group Intelligence Scale, 6:480
Otis-Lennon Mental Ability Test, 424
Otis Quick-Scoring Mental Ability Tests, 425
Otis Self-Administering Tests of Mental Ability, 426
P.C. Verbal Capacity Sampler, *see* Verbal Capacity Sampler, 5:394
PTI-Numerical Test, 433b
PTI-Oral Directions Test, 433c
PTI-Verbal Test, 433a
Pacific Design Construction Test, 514
Pacific Infants Performance Scale, 7:416
Pacific Reasoning Series Tests, 427
Paper Folding Test, Vz-2, 561v2
Partington's Pathways Test, 4:355; now available only as a subtest of Leiter Adult Intelligence Scale, 504
Passalong Test, 515
Pattern Perception Test, 428
Pattern Relations Test, 569
Peabody Picture Vocabulary Test, 516
Peel Group Tests of Practical Ability, 4:313
Perception of Relations Scales, 3:251
Perceptual Speed (Identical Forms), 570
Performance Alertness "PA" (With Pictures), 429
Performance Tests of Intelligence, 3:290
Personal Classification Test, 430
Personnel Classification Test [Henderson], 3:252
Personnel Classification Test [Wesman], *see* Wesman Personnel Classification Test, 480
Personnel Research Institute Classification Test, 431
Personnel Research Institute Factory Series Test, 432
Personnel Tests for Industry, 433
Pertinent Questions, 571
Pictorial Intelligence Test, *see* Pictorial Test of Intelligence, 517
Pictorial Test of Intelligence, 517
Picture Gestalt, Re-3, 561p3; for a revision, *see* New Uses, 568
Picture Intelligence Test 1, *see* Moray House Picture Intelligence Test 1, 408a, and Picture Test A, 434
Picture-Number Test, Ma-1, 561i1
Picture Test A, 434
Picture Test 1, *see* Picture Test A, 434
Pintner Advanced Test, 5:368d
Pintner-Cunningham Primary Mental Test, *see* Pintner-Cunningham Primary Test, 435
Pintner-Cunningham Primary Test, 435
Pintner-Durost Elementary Test, 5:368b
Pintner General Ability Tests: Non-Language Series, 3:254; Verbal Series, 5:368
Pintner Intelligence Test, *see* Pintner Intermediate Test, 5:368c
Pintner Intermediate Test, 5:368c
Pintner Non-Language Primary Mental Test, 3:256
Pintner-Paterson Scale of Performance Tests, 1:1061
Planning Air Maneuvers, Xa-3, 561w3

Plot Titles, 572; O-1, 561m1
Plumb IQ Slide Rule, 4:362
Point Scale of Performance Tests, *see* Arthur Point Scale of Performance Tests, 483
Porteus Maze Test, 518
Possible Jobs, 573
Preliminary Scholastic Aptitude Test, *see* Preliminary Scholastic Aptitude Test/National Merit Scholarship Qualifying Test, 436
Preliminary Scholastic Aptitude Test/National Merit Scholarship Qualifying Test, 436
Preliminary Test of Intelligence, 3:291
Preschool and Early Primary Skill Survey, 437
Preschool Attainment Record, 519
Preschool Inventory, *see* Cooperative Preschool Inventory, 490
Pressey Classification and Verifying Tests, 438
Pressey Intermediate Classification Test, 438b1; Verifying Test, 438b2
Pressey Senior Classification Test, 438c1; Verifying Test, 438c2
Primary Classification Test, 438a
Primary School Verbal Intelligence Test 1, *see* Verbal Test BC, 475a
Primary Verbal Tests 1, 2, 2G, and 3, *see* Verbal Tests BC, CD, C, and D, 475
Profile for the Stanford Binet (L-M), *see* Clinical Profile for the Stanford Binet Intelligence Scale (L-M), 526
Profion Dealltwriaeth Cyfaddasiad Cymbraeg, 3:257
Progressive Matrices, 439
Proverbs Test, 440
Psychological Examination, 2:1418
Public School Primary Intelligence Test, 441
Purdue Non-Language Personnel Test, 442
Purdue Non-Language Test, *see* Purdue Non-Language Personnel Test, 442
Quantitative Evaluative Device, 443
Queensland Test, 520
Quick-Scoring Test of Learning Capacity, *see* Group Test of Learning Capacity, 387
Quick Screening Scale of Mental Development, 521
Quick Test, 522
Quick Word Test, 7:378
RBH Non-Verbal Reasoning Test, *see* RBH Test of Non-Verbal Reasoning, 445
RBH Test of Learning Ability, 444
RBH Test of Non-Verbal Reasoning, 445
Reasoning Tests for Higher Levels of Intelligence, 446
Reconstruction Puzzle, *see* Dearborn-Anderson Formboards 2 and 2b, 2:1390
Remote Associates Test, 574
Revised Alpha Examination, Form 5, 4:315; Form 6, Short Form, 4:316
Revised Beta Examination, 447
Revised Passalong Test, 6:519e
Revised Stanford-Binet Scales, *see* Stanford-Binet Intelligence Scale, 525a
Revised Visual Retention Test, *see* Benton Visual Retention Test, 543
Revision of Army Alpha Examination, 4:317
Rhode Island Intelligence Test, *see* New Rhode Island Intelligence Test, 5:354
Rhodes WAIS Scatter Profile, 530
Rhodes WISC Scatter Profile, 535
Ring and Peg Tests of Behavior Development, 523
Rutgers Drawing Test, 575
Ryburn Group Intelligence Tests, 448
S.O.N. Snijders-Oomen Non-Verbal Intelligence Scale, *see* Non-Verbal Intelligence Tests for Deaf and Hearing Subjects, 512
SRA College Classification Tests, 5:376
SRA Non-Verbal Classification Form, *see* SRA Non-verbal Form, 449

SRA Nonverbal Form, 449
SRA Pictorial Reasoning Test, 450
SRA Short Test of Educational Ability, 451
SRA Tests of Educational Ability, 6:495
SRA Tests of General Ability, see Tests of General Ability, 467
SRA Verbal Classification Form, see SRA Verbal Form, 452
SRA Verbal Form, 452
Safran Culture Reduced Intelligence Test, 453
Scale of Non-Verbal Mental Ability, see Non-Verbal Tests 1–2, 415a
Scholarship Qualifying Test, 5:379
Scholastic Mental Ability Tests, 454
School Aptitude Test: Thanet Mental Tests, 2:1422
Schrammel General Ability Test, 6:498
Schubert General Ability Battery, 455
Scott Company Mental Alertness Test, 456
Scovill Classification Test, 4:320
Secondary Verbal Tests 1 and 2, see Verbal Tests EF and GH, 476
Seeing Deficiencies, Sep-3, 561s3
Seeing Faults, 576
Seeing Problems, 577; Sep-2, 561s2
Seguin-Goddard Formboard, 578
Semeonoff-Vigotsky Test, 6:519a
Ship Destination Test, 457; R-3, 561o3
Short Form Test of Academic Aptitude, 458
Shortest Road Test, Le-2, 561h2
Similar Meanings: Creativity Tests for Children, 554h
Simile Interpretations, Fe-2, 561d2; for revised edition, see 579
Similes Test, 580
Simplex GNV Intelligence Tests, 459
Simplex Group Intelligence Scale, 460
Simplex Intelligence Test GNV, see Simplex GNV Intelligence Tests, 459
Simplex Junior "A" Intelligence Test, 461b
Simplex Junior "A" Test, see Simplex Junior "A" Intelligence Test, 461b
Simplex Junior Intelligence Scale, 461
Sketches, 581
Sleight Non-Verbal Intelligence Test, 462
Slosson Intelligence Test, 524
Sounds and Images, 587a
Southend Group Test of Intelligence, see Southend Test of Intelligence, 463
Southend Test of Intelligence, 463
Spiral Nines, 464
Standard Progressive Matrices, 439a
Stanford-Binet Intelligence Scale, 525
Stanford-Binet Scale, see Stanford-Binet Intelligence Scale, 525
Stanford-Ohwaki-Kohs Block Design Intelligence Test for the Blind, 527
Stanford Revision of the Binet-Simon Intelligence Test, see Stanford-Binet Intelligence Scale, 525
Stencil Design Tests, 4:359
Subsumed Abilities Test, 582
Subtraction and Multiplication Test, N-3, 561l3
Surface Development Test, Vz-3, 561v3
Survey of Mental Maturity, 6:503
Symbol Identities, 583
Symbol Production, O-2, 561m2
Symbol Series Test, 584
Teachers College Psychological Examination, see Psychological Examination, 2:1418
Terman Group Test of Mental Ability, see Terman-McNemar Test of Mental Ability, 4:324
Terman-McNemar Test of Mental Ability, 4:324
Test for Office Personnel, see RBH Test of Learning Ability, 444b

Test of Abstract Reasoning, see Test of Perceptual Organization, 466
Test of Adult College Aptitude, 465
Test of Concept Utilization, 585
Test of Creative Potential, 586
Test of g: Culture Fair, see Culture Fair Intelligence Test, 364
Test of General Knowledge, 2:1425
Test of Learning Ability, see RBH Test of Learning Ability, 444
Test of Non-Verbal Reasoning, see RBH Test of Non-Verbal Reasoning, 445
Test of Perceptual Organization, 466
Test of Word-Number Ability, 5:389
Tests A/1 and A/2: Mental Alertness, 402
Tests AH4 and AH5, see AH4, AH5, and AH6 Tests, 331
Tests for Primary Mental Abilities, 2:1427; reclassified, consult SRA Primary Mental Abilities, T2:1087
Tests of General Ability, 467; Inter-American Series, 468
Tests of General Ability: Cooperative Inter-American Tests, see Tests of General Ability: Inter-American Series, 468
Tests of Mental Development, 2:1426
Tests of Primary Mental Abilities for Ages 5 and 6, 3:264; reclassified, consult SRA Primary Mental Abilities, T2:1087a
Thanet Mental Tests: School Aptitude Test, 2:1422
Theme Test, Fi-2, 561e2
Thing Categories Test, Fi-3, 561e3
Thinking Creatively With Pictures, see Torrance Tests of Creative Thinking, 589b
Thinking Creatively With Sounds and Words, 587
Thinking Creatively With Words, see Torrance Tests of Creative Thinking, 589a
Thurstone Test of Mental Alertness, 469
Time Appreciation Test, 588
Tomlinson Junior School Test, 5:392
Tool Knowledge Test, Mk-1, 561j1
Topics Test, Fi-1, 561e1
Torrance Tests of Creative Thinking, 589
Trist-Hargreaves Test, 6:519b
Trist-Misselbrook-Kohs Test, 6:519c
Two-Figure Formboard, 590
Undergraduate Program Aptitude Test, 470
Undergraduate Record Examinations: Aptitude Test, see Undergraduate Program Aptitude Test, 470
Unit Scales of Aptitude, 2:1428
Unusual Uses, see Alternate Uses, 542
Utility Test, 591; Xs-1, 561x1
V.G.C. Intelligence Indicator, 4:327
Van Alstyne Picture Vocabulary Test, 6:537
Vane Kindergarten Test, 528
Verbal and Non-Verbal Test 1, 5:393
Verbal Capacity Sampler, 5:394
Verbal Intelligence Test, 5:395
Verbal Intelligence Test for Business Executives, see Verbal Intelligence Test, 5:395
Verbal Power Test of Concept Equivalence, 471
Verbal Reasoning, 472
Verbal Reasoning: Differential Aptitude Tests, 473
Verbal Tests (Adv.), 474
Verbal Tests BC, CD, and D, 475; EF and GH, 476; 15–23 and 69, 477
Visual Closure Assessment, see Higgins-Wertman Test: Threshold of Visual Closure, 560
Visual Number Span Test, Ms-2, 561k2
Visual Retention Test for Clinical Use, see Benton Visual Retention Test, 543
Vocabulary Test, V-1, 561u1
Vocabulary Test, V-2, 561u2
Vocabulary Test, V-5, 561u5

Vocabulary Tests, 5:398
WAIS Test Profile, 531
WISC Mental Description Sheet, 536
WISC Test Profile, 537
WLW Culture Fair Inventory, 7:399
WLW Employment Inventory III, 478
WLW Mental Alertness Inventory, 479
WPPSI Test Profile, 539
Wechsler Adult Intelligence Scale, 529
Wechsler-Bellevue Intelligence Scale, 532
Wechsler Intelligence Scale for Children, 533
Wechsler Memory Scale, 592
Wechsler Preschool and Primary Scale of Intelligence, 538
Wesman Personnel Classification Test, 480
"West Riding" Tests of Mental Ability, 2:1430
"West Yorkshire" Group Test of Intelligence, 4:332
Western Personnel Tests, 481
What To Do With It: Creativity Tests for Children, 554i
Wide Range Vocabulary Test, V-3, 561u3
Williams Intelligence Test for Children With Defective Vision, 540
Willis-Smith Advanced Mental Test, 3:268
Willner Instance Similarities Test, 593
Wonderlic Personnel Test, 482
Word Arrangement, Fe-3, 561d3
Word Beginnings and Endings Test, Fw-3, 561f3
Word Beginnings Test, Fw-2, 561f2
Word Endings Test, Fw-1, 561f1
Word Fluency, 594
Word Fluency: Christensen-Guilford Fluency Tests, 546a
Word-Number Test of Scholastic Aptitude, see Test of Word-Number Ability, 5:389
Writing Sentences: Creativity Tests for Children, 554j

ACRONYMS

AGCT, Army General Classification Test, 342
BVRT, Benton Visual Retention Test, 543
CAKC, Concept Assessment Kit—Conservation, 549
CFIT, Culture Fair Intelligence Test, 364
CMMS, Columbia Mental Maturity Scale, 489
CMT, Concept Mastery Test, 359
CQT, College Qualification Tests, 358
CTMM, California Test of Mental Maturity, 349
CTMM-SF, California Short-Form Test of Mental Maturity, 348
DDST, Denver Developmental Screening Test, 492
DTLA, Detroit Tests of Learning Aptitude, 493
GDS, Gesell Developmental Schedules, 497
GREAT, Graduate Record Examinations Aptitude Test, 382
HFT, Hidden Figures Test, 559
HIS, Haptic Intelligence Scale for Adult Blind, 498
HNTLA, Hiskey-Nebraska Test of Learning Aptitude, 499
KAT, Kuhlmann-Anderson Test, 398
LAIS, Leiter Adult Intelligence Scale, 504
LTIT, Lorge-Thorndike Intelligence Tests, 400
MAT, Miller Analogies Test, 404
MPS, Minnesota Preschool Scale, 509
MSAT, Minnesota Scholastic Aptitude Test, 405
OSUPT, Ohio State University Psychological Test, 419
PM, Progressive Matrices, 439
PMT, Porteus Maze Test, 518
PPVT, Peabody Picture Vocabulary Test, 516
PSAT/NMSQT, Preliminary Scholastic Aptitude Test/National Merit Scholarship Qualifying Test, 436
PTI, Pictorial Test of Intelligence, 517
QT, Quick Test, 522
RAT, Remote Associates Test, 574
SAT, College Board Scholastic Aptitude Test, 357
S-B, Stanford-Binet Intelligence Scale, 525
SCAT, Cooperative School and College Ability Tests, 361
SIT, Slosson Intelligence Test, 524
TCSW, Thinking Creatively With Sounds and Words, 587
TGA, Tests of General Ability, 468
TTCT, Torrance Tests of Creative Thinking, 589
TTMA, Thurstone Test of Mental Alertness, 469
VKT, Vane Kindergarten Test, 528
WAIS, Wechsler Adult Intelligence Scale, 529
W-B, Wechsler-Bellevue Intelligence Scale, 532
WISC, Wechsler Intelligence Scale for Children, 533
WPCT, Wesman Personnel Classification Test, 480
WPPSI, Wechsler Preschool and Primary Scale of Intelligence, 538
WPT, Wonderlic Personnel Test, 482

INDEX OF NAMES

This analytical index indicates whether a citation refers to authorship of a test, test review, excerpted review, or a reference for a specific test. Citations are to test numbers, not to page numbers. In the reprint sections, the numbers of the first and last tests on facing pages are given in the running heads next to the outside margins. Numbers without colons refer to in print tests presented in the section reprinted from TIP II. Interpret abbreviations and numbers for in print tests as follows: "test, 517" indicates authorship of test 517; "rev, 358," authorship of a review of test 358; "exc, 532," authorship of an excerpted review of test 532; and "ref, 425," authorship of one or more references for test 425. (The Cumulative Name Index for that test must be consulted to locate the references.) Numbers with colons (e.g., 6:438, test 438 in the 6th MMY) refer to out of print tests included in the material reprinted from the MMY's, unless otherwise indicated. In the reprint sections, the yearbook digit preceding the colon is given in the running head only.

AAMODT, G. P.: ref, 426
Aaronson, B. S.: ref, 518
Abbott, R. F.: ref, 525
Abdel-Ghaffar, A. S. A. K.: ref, 400
Abdel-Razik, T. M.: ref, 542, 546, 551
Abe, C.: ref, 551, 564
Abel, T. M.: ref, 381, 483, 525, 558, 578
Abell, A. P.: ref, 357-8
Abelson, H. H.: ref, 525
Abercrombie, M. L.: ref, 381
Abercrombie, M. L. J.: ref, 533
Abernethy, E. M.: ref, 525
Abidin, R. R.: ref, 522, 529
Ables, B. S.: ref, 381, 525, 533
Abney, C. W.: ref, 574
Aborn, M.: rev, 532; ref, 525, 532
Abou-Ghorra, I. M.: ref, 542
Abraham, C.: ref, 542, 546, 551
Abrahams, N.: ref, 404, 480
Abram, H. S.: ref, 529
Abrams, J.: ref, 532
Abrams, J. C.: ref, 533
Abrams, S.: ref, 529, 533
Abramson, H. A.: ref, 532
Abramson, T.: ref, 516
Abt, I. A.: ref, 525
Abt, L. E.: ref, 426, 480, 529
Abudabbeh, N. N.: ref, 381
Achard, F. H.: ref, 426
Achenbach, T. M.: ref, 525
Achilles, P. S.: ref, 3:220(49)

Ack, M.: ref, 525
Acker, M. B.: ref, 559
Ackerman, P. T.: ref, 533
Ackerman, T. J.: ref, 361
Ackerson, L.: ref, 525, 6:480(25)
Acuff, N. H.: ref, 381
Adams, D. K.: exc, 497
Adams, F. J.: ref, 525, 3:217(75)
Adams, H. B.: ref, 496, 518
Adams, J.: ref, 543
Adams, J. C.: ref, 542, 551, 561
Adams, N. A.: ref, 532-3
Adams, P. A.: ref, 381, 533
Adams, R. D.: ref, 532, 592
Adams, R. H.: test, 373
Adar, L. D.: ref, 529
Adcock, C.: ref, 388, 439
Adcock, C. J.: rev, 457; ref, 323, 364, 532, 559, 561, 564
Addison, E. M.: ref, 3:217(80)
Adelman, M.: ref, 484
Aderman, M.: ref, 489, 496, 525, 533
Adinolfi, A. A.: ref, 357
Adjutant General's Office, Personnel Research Section: test, 342; ref, 342, 504, 4:347(1), 4:348(1), 4:355(1)
Adkins, A. A.: ref, 426
Adkins, D. C.: ref, 398, 2:1377(41), 2:1378(1), 3:217(134), 6:480(35)
Adkins, M. M.: ref, 525
Adkisson, J.: ref, 424

Adler, D. L.: ref, 525
Adler, E.: ref, 532, 543
Adler, H. M.: ref, 525
Adlerstein, A. M.: ref, 529
Affleck, D. C.: ref, 529
Aftanas, M. S.: ref, 439-40, 518
Aga, H.: ref, 388, 426
Agnew, M.: ref, 518
Agnew, N.: ref, 518
Aguero, A.: ref, 496
Ahlgren, A.: ref, 391
Ahmad, F. Z.: ref, 425, 533
Ahmann, J. S.: rev, 392, 6:495; ref, 5:308(370)
Aichele, D. B.: ref, 361
Aijaz, S. M.: ref, 473
Aiken, L. R.: exc, 376; ref, 357
Aiken, M.: test, 431
Ainsworth, L. L.: ref, 404, 425
Ainsworth, M. E.: ref, 364
Air, D. H.: ref, 439, 529
Aita, J. A.: ref, 532
Akamine, T.: ref, 6:438(457)
Akel, M.: ref, 489
Al-Amir, H.: ref, 382
Albee, G. W.: ref, 532
Albert, K.: ref, 525
Albrecht, R.: ref, 592
Albright, L. E.: rev, 481; ref, 337, 482
Albright, R. J.: ref, 592
Alcorn, J. D.: ref, 364, 516
Alderdice, E. T.: ref, 525, 532
Aldrich, C. G.: ref, 497, 507

1076

INDEX OF NAMES

Aleamoni, L. M.: *ref*, 361
Alegre, C. E.: *ref*, 551, 574
Alessi, S. L.: *ref*, 447, 532
Alexakos, C. E.: *ref*, 359, 382
Alexander, D.: *ref*, 381, 533, 543
Alexander, E. B.: *ref*, 5:326(19)
Alexander, F. S.: *ref*, 532
Alexander, J. F.: *ref*, 439
Alexander, S.: *ref*, 525, 529
Alexander, S. M.: *ref*, 529, 561
Alexander, T.: *ref*, 381
Alexander, W. P.: *test*, 515, 2:1400, 2:1422, 6:514; *ref*, 515, 2:1376(1-3)
Ali, F.: *ref*, 516
Alimena, B.: *ref*, 529, 532-3
Aliotti, N. C.: *ref*, 589
Alker, H. A.: *ref*, 357, 542
Allan, J. H.: *ref*, 529
Allan, M. E.: *ref*, 507, 525
Allebach, N. L.: *ref*, 439
Allen, A.: *ref*, 331, 589
Allen, B. V.: *ref*, 529
Allen, J.: *ref*, 533
Allen, J. C.: *ref*, 525
Allen, J. C. Y.: *ref*, 348
Allen, K.: *ref*, 529
Allen, L.: *ref*, 525, 532
Allen, M.: *ref*, 525, 538
Allen, M. K.: *ref*, 525
Allen, M. M.: *ref*, 398
Allen, R. D.: *ref*, 525
Allen, R. J.: *ref*, 357
Allen, R. M.: *ref*, 355, 375, 391, 407, 425, 439, 487, 489, 496-7, 505, 516, 529, 532-3
Allen, S.: *ref*, 529, 592
Allerhand, M. E.: *ref*, 490, 516
Alley, G. R.: *ref*, 543
Allgood, E. V.: *ref*, 361
Alling, R. L.: *ref*, 489, 525
Allison, D. E.: *ref*, 400
Allison, E. E.: *exc*, 538
Allison, G.: *ref*, 4:277(158)
Allison, J.: *ref*, 529, 533
Allison, R. B.: *ref*, 357
Allor, B. A.: *ref*, 533
Alluisi, E. A.: *ref*, 419
Almgren, P. E.: *ref*, 439
Alper, A. E.: *ref*, 505, 525, 529, 533
Alper, T. G.: *ref*, 447, 4:281(81)
Alpern, G. D.: *ref*, 487, 525
Alspaugh, C. A.: *ref*, 361
Alston, D. J.: *ref*, 589
Alston, P. P.: *ref*, 498, 529
Alteneder, L. E.: *ref*, 391
Altenhaus, C. B.: *ref*, 348
Altmaier, C. L.: *ref*, 525
Altman, C. H.: *ref*, 525
Altrocchi, J.: *ref*, 532
Altus, G. T.: *ref*, 349, 533, 5:326(20)
Altus, W. D.: *rev*, 496, 532; *exc*, 518, 529, 532; *ref*, 342, 357, 361, 525, 532, 4:277(231), 5:308(288, 430)
Altus, W. S.: *ref*, 525
Alvi, S. A.: *ref*, 364, 425
Alvis, H. J.: *ref*, 592
Alzobaie, A. J.: *ref*, 364, 381, 400, 561-2, 591
Amacher, P. L.: *ref*, 525
Amarel, M.: *ref*, 361
Amatruda, C. S.: *ref*, 497

Amdur, J. L. R.: *ref*, 516
American Gas Association: *ref*, 349, 482
Ames, L. B.: *ref*, 497, 524, 533
Ames, R.: *ref*, 361
Ames, V.: *ref*, 426
Ames, W. S.: *ref*, 400
Amin, D. L.: *ref*, 515, 3:270(4)
Ammon, M. S.: *ref*, 439, 516
Ammons, C. H.: *test*, 522; *exc*, 519, 538; *ref*, 522
Ammons, H. S.: *test*, 496; *ref*, 496
Ammons, R. B.: *test*, 496, 522; *ref*, 496, 522
Amoss, H.: *test*, 2:1411; *ref*, 2:1411(1)
Amram, F. M.: *ref*, 589
Amunrud, K. D.: *ref*, 349
Anastasi, A.: *rev*, 337, 381, 391, 469, 493, 1:1037, 2:1424, 3:222; *exc*, 532; *ref*, 364, 381, 525, 529, 533, 542, 544, 551
Anastasiow, N. J.: *ref*, 516
Anderhalter, O. F.: *test*, 454
Andersen, A. L.: *ref*, 532
Anderson, A. W.: *ref*, 323
Anderson, B. B.: *ref*, 516
Anderson, C. A.: *ref*, 435
Anderson, C. C.: *ref*, 559, 561, 574, 577
Anderson, C. E.: *ref*, 357
Anderson, C. J.: *ref*, 525, 529
Anderson, C. W. G.: *ref*, 529, 532-3
Anderson, D. E.: *ref*, 516, 533
Anderson, D. L.: *ref*, 364, 574
Anderson, E. E.: *ref*, 525, 532, 3:217(98)
Anderson, E. M.: *ref*, 426
Anderson, G. L.: *ref*, 525
Anderson, G. V.: *exc*, 6:442
Anderson, H. D.: *ref*, 381, 525
Anderson, H. E.: *ref*, 349, 361, 439, 496, 516, 529, 533, 561, 572, 591
Anderson, J.: *ref*, 522
Anderson, J. E.: *test*, 2:1390; *exc*, 497; *ref*, 2:1390(1), 2:1391(1), 3:220(8)
Anderson, J. M.: *rev*, 533, 3:295
Anderson, K. E.: *ref*, 6:438(474-5, 491)
Anderson, L.: *ref*, 5:308(371)
Anderson, L. D.: *ref*, 497, 507, 525, 3:285(6)
Anderson, L. M.: *ref*, 533
Anderson, M.: *ref*, 349
Anderson, M. L.: *ref*, 574
Anderson, M. R.: *ref*, 5:308(341)
Anderson, R.: *ref*, 545
Anderson, R. A.: *ref*, 439
Anderson, R. E.: *ref*, 361, 589, 5:308(399)
Anderson, R. G.: *test*, 398; *ref*, 398, 5:308(310)
Anderson, R. J.: *ref*, 342, 546, 551, 561, 591
Anderson, R. P.: *ref*, 439, 533
Anderson, S. B.: *ref*, 357, 361, 425, 5:308(311)
Anderson, S. F.: *ref*, 525, 532, 3:217(98)
Anderson, W. F.: *ref*, 400
Anderson, W. W.: *ref*, 503, 592
Andersson, A. L.: *ref*, 439

Ando, K.: *ref*, 516, 533
Andrew, D. C.: *ref*, 5:308(369)
Andrews, F. M.: *ref*, 357, 574
Andrews, R. G.: *ref*, 349
Andrews, R. J.: *ref*, 522
Andrews, R. S.: *ref*, 518, 6:468(3-4)
Andy, O. J.: *ref*, 529
Angelino, H.: *ref*, 391, 5:326(10)
Angers, W. P.: *ref*, 357, 361, 532
Angier, R. P.: *ref*, 357, 426
Angoff, W. H.: *ref*, 357, 382, 5:308(289, 416), 6:438(515-6)
Anneser, R.: *ref*, 419, 5:308(400)
Annesley, F.: *ref*, 398
Ansbacher, H. L.: *ref*, 381
Antell, M. J.: *ref*, 574
Anthony, A. A.: *ref*, 518
Anthony, E. J.: *ref*, 533
Anthony, R. J.: *ref*, 529
Apgar, V.: *ref*, 497, 525, 533
Appelbaum, S. A.: *ref*, 532
Applebaum, A. P.: *ref*, 525
Arasteh, J. D.: *ref*, 589
Arbuthnot, J. B.: *ref*, 564
Archambault, F. X.: *ref*, 589
Archer, L. S.: *ref*, 516
Archibald, Y. M.: *ref*, 439
Arena, T.: *ref*, 349
Arenberg, D.: *ref*, 532
Arieli, S.: *ref*, 529
Arlitt, A. H.: *ref*, 525
Armbrust, R.: *ref*, 425
Armentrout, J. A.: *ref*, 381
Armentrout, W. D.: *ref*, 6:480(2)
Armitage, S. G.: *ref*, 504, 532
Armlin, N. J.: *ref*, 518
Armon, V.: *ref*, 381
Armstrong, C. L. G.: *ref*, 542, 564
Armstrong, C. P.: *ref*, 525, 532
Armstrong, D. M.: *ref*, 532
Armstrong, E. M.: *ref*, 381, 507, 525
Armstrong, H. C.: *ref*, 404, 525
Armstrong, H. E.: *ref*, 529
Armstrong, H. G.: *ref*, 409
Armstrong, J. G.: *ref*, 381, 525, 533
Armstrong, R. G.: *ref*, 532-3
Armstrong, R. J.: *ref*, 524-5
Armstrong, W.: *ref*, 559, 561
Arn, E. H. R.: *ref*, 5:308(312)
Arndt, J. R.: *ref*, 358
Arnette, J. L.: *ref*, 529
Arnhoff, F. N.: *ref*, 532
Arnold, E. M.: *ref*, 439
Arnold, E. R.: *ref*, 349
Arnold, F. C.: *ref*, 525, 533
Arnold, G. F.: *rev*, 486, 505; *ref*, 505, 518, 532
Arnold, P. D.: *test*, 450
Arnold, P. R.: *ref*, 496
Arnold, R. D.: *ref*, 364
Arnoult, J. F.: *ref*, 489, 533
Arnsfield, P.: *ref*, 533
Aron, J. E.: *ref*, 423
Aronow, M.: *ref*, 5:326(13)
Aronson, H.: *ref*, 518
Arps, G. F.: *ref*, 3:220(10, 14)
Arth, A. A.: *ref*, 349, 381, 425
Arthur, G.: *test*, 483, 505, 4:359; *ref*, 483, 505, 525, 4:359(1-2)
Arvidson, R. M.: *ref*, 574
Asbury, C. A.: *ref*, 490, 516
Ash, P.: *ref*, 480

Ashbrook, J. B.: *ref*, 404
Asher, E. J.: *test*, 3:234; *ref*, 525, 2:1402(2)
Asher, J. J.: *ref*, 551
Asher, J. W.: *ref*, 357, 589
Asher, P.: *ref*, 525
Asher, W.: *ref*, 357, 361, 425
Ashlock, P.: *ref*, 493, 533
Ashlock, P. R.: *ref*, 493, 533
Askar, A. M.: *ref*, 532
Asso, D.: *ref*, 529
Astin, A. W.: *ref*, 357
Astrachan, M. A.: *ref*, 497
Ataullah, K.: *ref*, 5:326(2)
Atchison, C. O.: *ref*, 533
Atkey, R. R.: *ref*, 532
Atkins, R.: *ref*, 440
Atkinson, B. H.: *ref*, 361, 546, 561, 577
Atkinson, J. A.: *ref*, 6:438(501)
Atkinson, S. M.: *ref*, 439
Attwell, A. A.: *ref*, 364, 439, 496
Atwell, C. R.: *test*, 4:316; *exc*, 532; *ref*, 525, 3:220(44), 4:315(3), 4:316(1)
Augoustaki, O.: *ref*, 518, 529, 533
Auria, C.: *ref*, 533
Auricchio, E. W.: *ref*, 381
Aursand, I. M.: *ref*, 482, 5:308(366)
Austin, G. R.: *ref*, 361
Australian Council for Educational Research: *test*, 323, 326, 329, 338, 4:272–3, 5:298a, 5:330, 6:435–6
Avakian, S. A.: *ref*, 435
Avery, C.: *ref*, 529
Avery, C. D.: *ref*, 498, 529
Avery, G. T.: *ref*, 525, 2:1399(3), 2:1424(3)
Ax, A. F.: *ref*, 364, 529
Axelbaum, E. M.: *ref*, 525, 545
Ayers, J. B.: *ref*, 404, 516
Ayers, J. D.: *rev*, 549; *ref*, 559, 561
Ayers, M. A.: *ref*, 533
Aylaian, A.: *ref*, 529
Aylesworth, H. C.: *ref*, 342
Aymat, F.: *ref*, 381
Ayres, A. J.: *ref*, 497
Azima, F. C.: *ref*, 532

BABBOTT, E. F.: *ref*, 425
Babcock, H.: *ref*, 525
Babcock, M. E.: *ref*, 518
Babigian, H.: *ref*, 440
Babson, S. G.: *ref*, 525
Bach, L. C.: *ref*, 381, 499, 516, 525, 538
Bachelis, L.: *ref*, 529
Bachelis, L. A.: *ref*, 542, 546, 551
Bachman, A. M.: *ref*, 361
Bachman, J. G.: *ref*, 357
Bachrach, P. B.: *ref*, 357
Bachtold, L. M.: *ref*, 589
Backe, E. B.: *ref*, 348
Backer, W.: *test*, 512
Backhouse, J. K.: *ref*, 446
Backman, M. E.: *ref*, 357, 529
Backus, R.: *ref*, 516
Bacon, A. M.: *ref*, 525
Bacon, C. S.: *ref*, 532–3
Badal, A. W.: *ref*, 361, 404
Bader, L. J.: *ref*, 574, 589
Badgett, J. L.: *ref*, 357

Badri, M. B.: *ref*, 381
Bae, A. Y.: *ref*, 533
Baehner, V. M.: *ref*, 337
Baehr, M. E.: *ref*, 414, 547–8, 570
Baer, C. J.: *ref*, 439
Baer, D. J.: *ref*, 357
Baer, P.: *ref*, 529, 592
Baer, P. E.: *ref*, 543
Baggaley, A. R.: *rev*, 6:468; *ref*, 357
Baggett, M. P.: *ref*, 532
Bagley, M. L.: *test*, 5:389
Bagur, J. S.: *ref*, 516
Bagwell, F. I.: *ref*, 533
Bahlke, S. J. M.: *ref*, 589
Baier, D. E.: *ref*, 480
Bailey, A. E.: *ref*, 349, 391, 398, 425–6, 435, 3:255(13), 3:263(46), 5:329(6)
Bailey, D. W.: *ref*, 4:277(260)
Bailey, H. K.: *ref*, 349, 398, 525
Bailey, H. W.: *ref*, 342, 4:277(170)
Bailey, J. T.: *ref*, 589
Bailey, K. G.: *ref*, 425
Bailey, L. J.: *ref*, 425
Bailey, L. L.: *ref*, 364, 525
Bailey, M. A.: *ref*, 532
Bailey, R. B.: *ref*, 381, 6:438(488)
Bailey, R. J.: *ref*, 400
Baillie, G. S.: *ref*, 382
Bair, J. T.: *ref*, 426
Baird, L. L.: *rev*, 574, 589
Baird, R. K.: *ref*, 533
Baker, B. L.: *ref*, 529, 533
Baker, C. T.: *ref*, 525
Baker, C. W.: *ref*, 3:220(55)
Baker, D.: *ref*, 357
Baker, E. A.: *ref*, 549
Baker, H. J.: *test*, 370, 441, 493, 1:1044, 2:1392, 3:274, 5:329b-c; *ref*, 525
Baker, J. A.: *ref*, 503, 529, 592
Baker, P. C.: *ref*, 5:308(372)
Baldauf, R. J.: *ref*, 349
Baldwin, A. L.: *exc*, 532; *ref*, 525
Baldwin, B. T.: *ref*, 507, 525
Baldwin, G. B.: *test*, 3:232
Baldwin, J. W.: *ref*, 349, 525
Baldwin, T. S.: *ref*, 457, 561
Balinky, J. L.: *ref*, 381, 575
Balinsky, B.: *rev*, 4:359; *ref*, 426, 525, 529, 532
Balken, E. R.: *ref*, 483
Ball, R. S.: *rev*, 509; *exc*, 487; *ref*, 487, 497, 507, 525
Ball, T. S.: *ref*, 525
Ballantyne, R. H.: *ref*, 357
Ballard, H. T.: *ref*, 529
Ballard, P. B.: *ref*, 416
Ballinger, T.: *ref*, 381
Balow, I. H.: *ref*, 400
Balthazar, E. E.: *ref*, 532–3
Balyeat, R. M.: *ref*, 426
Bamford, J. L.: *ref*, 364, 529
Banaghan, W. F.: *ref*, 533
Banaka, W. H.: *ref*, 589
Banas, N.: *ref*, 493, 533
Band, R. I.: *ref*, 439
Banham, K. M.: *test*, 521, 523
Banker, H. J.: *ref*, 3:247(1)
Banks, C.: *rev*, 439, 491; *ref*, 331, 439, 446
Banks, C. E. K.: *rev*, 368, 434
Bannister, D.: *ref*, 439

Bannochie, M. N.: *ref*, 381, 493, 503, 505, 533, 558
Bannon, W. J.: *ref*, 439, 495, 525
Barabasz, A. F.: *ref*, 525, 589
Barbe, W.: *ref*, 391
Barbe, W. B.: *ref*, 426
Barbee, E. W.: *ref*, 349, 533
Barber, L. W.: *ref*, 497
Barclay, A.: *ref*, 381, 522, 525, 529, 533, 538, 543
Barclay, A. G.: *ref*, 381
Barclay, J. E.: *ref*, 518
Barger, B.: *ref*, 361
Barham, R.: *ref*, 559
Barik, H.: *ref*, 592
Barker, D.: *test*, 569
Barker, G. B.: *ref*, 532
Barker, L. L.: *ref*, 542, 561
Barker, R. G.: *ref*, 426
Barkley, M. J.: *ref*, 355, 439
Barlow, D. H.: *ref*, 357, 425
Barlow, F. P.: *ref*, 525
Barnabas, B.: *test*, 332; *ref*, 426, 482
Barnes, C. M.: *ref*, 543
Barnes, M. W.: *ref*, 3:217(114–5)
Barnes, P. J.: *ref*, 425
Barnett, A.: *ref*, 4:277(158)
Barnett, I.: *ref*, 532
Barnett, T. M.: *ref*, 348
Barnette, W. L.: *ref*, 342, 425, 2:1377(43), 4:277(200, 261)
Barnhart, E. L.: *ref*, 6:438(491)
Barnowe, T. J.: *ref*, 349, 398, 5:329(8)
Barnsley, R.: *ref*, 364, 381, 518, 533
Baroff, G. S.: *ref*, 533
Bar-Or, O.: *ref*, 533
Barot, J.: *ref*, 484
Baroya, G. M.: *ref*, 473
Barratt, E. S.: *ref*, 364, 439, 489, 525, 533
Barrell, R. P.: *ref*, 529
Barrett, A. M.: *ref*, 529, 532
Barrett, D. M.: *ref*, 5:308(290)
Barrett, G. V.: *ref*, 533, 559
Barrett, H. E.: *ref*, 507
Barrett, H. O.: *ref*, 391, 425
Barrett, R. S.: *ref*, 333, 342, 449, 482, 5:308(431)
Barrett, S. B.: *ref*, 357
Barrett, T. C.: *ref*, 400
Barrington, B. L.: *ref*, 529
Barrish, B.: *ref*, 589
Barritt, L. S.: *ref*, 357
Barron, B. A.: *ref*, 381
Barron, E. M.: *ref*, 425
Barron, F.: *ref*, 542, 546, 551, 561, 572
Barron, R. C.: *ref*, 533
Barrows, T. N.: *test*, 426
Barry, A. J.: *ref*, 439
Barry, C. A.: *ref*, 349
Barry, J. R.: *ref*, 361, 518, 532
Bart, L. E.: *ref*, 439, 489, 516
Bartelme, P.: *ref*, 497, 525
Bartelt, C. A.: *ref*, 559
Barthelmess, H. M.: *ref*, 3:242(2)
Barthol, R. P.: *ref*, 359
Bartin, N. G.: *ref*, 533
Bartlett, C. J.: *ref*, 361, 419, 425, 469, 533
Bartlett, E. M.: *exc*, 4:345
Bartley, S. H.: *ref*, 525

Barton, B.: *ref,* 533
Barton, G.: *ref,* 482
Barton, K.: *ref,* 364
Bartz, W. R.: *ref,* 447, 529
Barz, A. I.: *ref,* 349
Bashaw, J. A.: *ref,* 348
Bashaw, W. L.: *ref,* 496, 516, 533
Basiul, W. J.: *ref,* 4:277(232)
Bass, A. R.: *ref,* 382
Bass, B. M.: *ref,* 469, 482, 548, 5: 308(342)
Bass, H.: *ref,* 426
Bass, L. G.: *ref,* 487, 497
Bassett, D. M.: *ref,* 518
Bassett, J. E.: *ref,* 381, 529
Bastendorf, W. J.: *ref,* 533
Basu, K.: *ref,* 439
Batcheldor, K. J.: *ref,* 529
Bateman, B.: *ref,* 525
Bates, B. C.: *ref,* 589
Bates, C. O.: *ref,* 361
Bates, O. E.: *ref,* 589
Bath, J. A.: *ref,* 400
Batman, R. H.: *ref,* 532
Battin, R.: *ref,* 381, 533
Battle, E. S.: *ref,* 497, 525, 532
Batts, V.: *ref,* 331
Bauer, D. H.: *ref,* 361
Bauer, R.: *ref,* 358
Bauer, R. W.: *ref,* 439, 529
Bauernfeind, R. H.: *rev,* 420
Baugh, V. S.: *ref,* 447
Baughman, E. E.: *ref,* 525
Baumann, K. S.: *ref,* 516, 533
Baumeister, A.: *ref,* 533
Baumeister, A. A.: *ref,* 361, 533
Baumgarten, D. L.: *ref,* 525, 533
Baumgold, J.: *ref,* 529
Bavelas, A.: *ref,* 381
Baxter, B.: *rev,* 3:221, 3:252; *ref,* 426
Bay, M. S.: *ref,* 532
Bayley, N.: *rev,* 497, 507, 509, 529, 3:285, 5:404, 5:411; *test,* 484, 2: 1382; *exc,* 497, 509; *ref,* 359, 484, 487, 497, 525, 529, 532, 2:1382 (1), 4:324(60)
Baylor, C. C.: *ref,* 349
Bayuk, R. J.: *ref,* 400, 424
Beach, H. D.: *ref,* 439, 532
Beach, J. E.: *ref,* 439, 529
Beach, S.: *ref,* 398, 5:326(33)
Beals, E. W.: *ref,* 357
Beaman, G. C.: *ref,* 3:217(81)
Beamer, G. C.: *ref,* 425-6
Bean, A. G.: *ref,* 357
Bean, K. L.: *ref,* 426, 525
Bean, W. J.: *ref,* 533
Beans, D. T.: *ref,* 505
Bear, R. B.: *ref,* 426
Bear, R. M.: *ref,* 426
Beard, B. B.: *ref,* 529
Beard, J. G.: *ref,* 361
Beard, R. M.: *ref,* 331, 525
Beardsley, J. V.: *ref,* 529
Beardsley, K.: *ref,* 529
Beauchamp, J. M.: *ref,* 435
Beaver, A. P.: *ref,* 5:308(401)
Bechtold, D. W.: *ref,* 357
Becica, B.: *ref,* 364, 574
Beck, A. T.: *ref,* 529
Beck, E. C.: *ref,* 525, 529, 533
Beck, E. J.: *ref,* 439, 525, 589
Beck, F.: *ref,* 533

Beck, H. S.: *ref,* 533
Beck, R.: *ref,* 516
Beck, R. L.: *ref,* 419
Beck, S. J.: *exc,* 507
Becker, B. C.: *ref,* 529
Becker, G. J.: *ref,* 532
Becker, J. A.: *ref,* 426
Becker, J. T.: *ref,* 516, 533
Beckerle, G. P.: *ref,* 559
Beckham, A. S.: *ref,* 391, 525
Beckman, R. O.: *ref,* 438
Beckwith, L.: *ref,* 487, 497
Beech, H. R.: *ref,* 532
Beechley, R. M.: *ref,* 525
Beeson, M. F.: *ref,* 525
Begg, T. L.: *ref,* 525
Behling, M. A.: *ref,* 357
Behrens, B.: *ref,* 529
Behring, D. W.: *ref,* 357
Beinke, J. L.: *ref,* 425
Beittel, K. R.: *ref,* 542, 551, 564
Belai, L.: *ref,* 6:438(446)
Belcher, T. L.: *ref,* 391, 574, 589
Belden, B. R.: *ref,* 516, 529
Belden, E.: *ref,* 516, 529
Beldoch, M.: *ref,* 533
Beleff, N.: *ref,* 589
Belk, F. E.: *ref,* 361, 419
Bell, A.: *ref,* 529, 532
Bell, D. A.: *ref,* 533
Bell, D. B.: *ref,* 533
Bell, E. L.: *ref,* 357
Bell, G. B.: *ref,* 419
Bell, J. E.: *ref,* 532
Bellak, L.: *ref,* 525
Bellamy, E. E.: *ref,* 533-4, 589
Bellamy, R. Q.: *ref,* 361
Beller, E. K.: *ref,* 381, 516, 525
Bellico, R. P.: *ref,* 357
Bellin, A. P.: *ref,* 589
Belloni, M.: *ref,* 574
Bellows, R. M.: *exc,* 2:1416
Belluomini, H. M.: *ref,* 533
Belman, H. S.: *ref,* 4:277(262)
Belmont, I.: *ref,* 533
Belmont, L.: *ref,* 532-3
Belsky, T. B.: *ref,* 357
Belz, H. F.: *ref,* 357
Bender, L.: *ref,* 381
Bender, W. R. G.: *ref,* 438
Bendig, A. W.: *ref,* 5:308(382)
Benefiel, R. C.: *ref,* 505
Benezet, L. T.: *ref,* 4:277(152)
Benge, E. J. *test,* 2:1425, 3:221; *ref,* 2:1425(1)
Benger, K: *ref,* 516, 525
Beniskos, J. M.: *ref,* 533
Bennett, C. M.: *ref,* 439
Bennett, D. K.: *ref,* 525
Bennett, E.: *ref,* 388, 439
Bennett, E. M.: *ref,* 381
Bennett, G. K.: *rev,* 574, 4:355; *test,* 333, 358, 376, 473; *ref,* 358, 407, 447, 529
Bennett, H. J.: *ref,* 518
Bennett, M. G.: *test,* 358
Bennett, M. J.: *ref,* 427
Bennett, M. W.: *ref,* 3:263(44, 49)
Bennett, R.: *ref,* 529
Benninger, C. A.: *ref,* 516
Benoit, E. P.: *ref,* 349, 489, 505, 525
Bensberg, G. J.: *ref,* 364, 483, 496, 505, 525, 532-3

Benson, C. E.: *ref,* 3:220(19)
Benson, D.: *ref,* 445, 482
Benson, P. H.: *ref,* 357
Benson, R. R.: *ref,* 525, 529
Benson, S.: *ref,* 532
Bentler, P. M.: *test,* 549; *ref,* 516, 549
Bentley, J. C.: *ref,* 404
Bentley, M.: *exc,* 518
Benton, A. L.: *test,* 543; *ref,* 426, 503, 525, 529, 532-3, 543, 545
Benton, J. E.: *ref,* 589
Benton, J. G.: *ref,* 381, 489, 525, 529
Bentz, V. J.: *ref,* 469, 5:308(313)
Ben-Yishay, Y.: *ref,* 529
Beran, M.: *ref,* 447, 592
Berdie, R. F.: *rev,* 358; *ref,* 357, 381, 404-5, 3:217(109), 4:277 (233, 263), 5:308(291), 6:438 (502)
Bereiter, C. E.: *ref,* 545
Berens, A. E.: *ref,* 361
Beretta, S.: *ref,* 589
Berg, B. C.: *ref,* 435
Berg, I. A.: *ref,* 337, 348, 3:217 (139), 4:277(172)
Berg, N. L.: *ref,* 516
Berg, S. D.: *ref,* 516
Berg, T.: *ref,* 449, 452
Berg, V.: *ref,* 533
Bergan, A.: *ref,* 533
Berger, A.: *ref,* 381, 525
Berger, D.: *ref,* 349
Berger, D. G.: *ref,* 532
Berger, L.: *ref,* 529, 532
Berger, M.: *ref,* 525, 538
Berger, R. M.: *test,* 564, 571-2; *ref,* 457, 551, 564
Berger, S. E.: *ref,* 525, 529
Berger, V. F.: *ref,* 391
Berges, J.: *ref,* 483
Bergman, R. L.: *ref,* 525
Bergmann, K.: *ref,* 529
Bergstein, V.: *ref,* 533
Berk, R. L.: *ref,* 525, 532
Berke, N. D.: *ref,* 504, 529
Berkey, R.: *ref,* 357
Berkman, P. L.: *ref,* 503
Berko, M. J.: *ref,* 489, 497, 525, 578
Berkowitz, B.: *ref,* 529, 532
Berkowitz, M. C.: *ref,* 381
Berkowitz, P. H.: *ref,* 592
Berks, M. D.: *ref,* 532
Berks, M. D. D.: *ref,* 4:354(5)
Berkshire, R.: *ref,* 4:277(234)
Berlin, M. A.: *ref,* 533
Berman, A.: *ref,* 489
Berman, A. B.: *ref,* 525
Berman, G.: *ref,* 391
Berman, I.: *ref,* 529, 533
Berman, I. R.: *ref,* 438, 518, 525, 532
Berman, J. R.: *ref,* 574
Bernard, H. W.: *ref,* 419
Bernard, J.: *ref,* 342
Bernardoni, L. C.: *ref,* 467
Berner, W.: *ref,* 5:308(282)
Bernreuter, R. G.: *rev,* 355, 4:320; *ref,* 518, 525, 545, 578
Bernstein, A.: *ref,* 529, 532
Bernstein, A. J.: *ref,* 533
Bernstein, A. S.: *ref,* 529

Bernstein, L.: *ref,* 518, 525, 529, 532-3
Bernstein, R.: *ref,* 532
Bernstein, S.: *ref,* 533
Berrien, F. K.: *ref,* 381
Berringer, D. E.: *ref,* 529
Berry, C. A.: *ref,* 361, 5:308(432)
Berry, G. S.: *ref,* 391
Berry, H. K.: *ref,* 525
Berry, J. W.: *ref,* 439, 545
Berry, R. A.: *ref,* 529
Bersoff, D. N.: *ref,* 525, 529, 533, 538
Berson, P. M.: *ref,* 398
Bertrand, J. R.: *ref,* 5:308(373)
Besco, R. O.: *ref,* 382
Besijn, J. W.: *ref,* 439, 532
Bessell, H.: *ref,* 355, 391, 407, 425
Bessemer, D. W.: *ref,* 349
Bessent, E. W.: *ref,* 404
Bessent, T. E.: *ref,* 505
Betts, G. L.: *test,* 5:354
Betz, R. C.: *ref,* 529
Bevan, W. E.: *ref,* 381, 439
Bevans, H. G.: *ref,* 439
Beverfelt, E.: *ref,* 529
Beverly, L.: *ref,* 505, 525
Beyel, V.: *ref,* 439
Beyer, F. N.: *ref,* 381
Bhattacharyya, C. C.: *ref,* 515
Bhushan, V.: *ref,* 425
Biaggio, A. M. B.: *ref,* 357
Biamonte, A. J.: *ref,* 482
Bianchi, G. N.: *ref,* 520
Bibb, J. J.: *ref,* 489, 522, 533
Bibelheimer, M.: *ref,* 349
Bibelheimer, M. H.: *ref,* 349
Bickley, A. C.: *ref,* 425
Bickley, R.: *ref,* 425
Bickley, R. T.: *ref,* 357
Bidder, T. G.: *ref,* 543, 592
Biddle, A. E.: *ref,* 525
Bidinian, R. J.: *ref,* 361
Biegel, M. M.: *ref,* 503, 588, 6:480(44)
Bielefeld, M. O.: *ref,* 529
Bierbryer, B.: *ref,* 533
Bieri, J.: *ref,* 357, 381, 525
Bierley, R.: *ref,* 361
Bierman, J. M.: *ref,* 487
Biesheuvel, S.: *ref,* 439, 515, 518, 532, 545
Bigelow, G. S.: *ref,* 516
Biggs, D. A.: *ref,* 405
Biggs, J. B.: *ref,* 439
Bijou, S. W.: *ref,* 483, 525
Biles, D.: *ref,* 426
Bilger, R. C.: *ref,* 545, 558, 578
Bilka, L. P.: *ref,* 435, 570
Billeter, P. E.: *ref,* 342
Bills, M. A.: *rev,* 336-7, 421, 3:221; *ref,* 3:220(20, 48), 4:320(1)
Billy, H. T.: *ref,* 516
Bilodeau, I. M.: *ref,* 503, 532
Bilon, L. R.: *ref,* 589
Binford, M. L.: *ref,* 404
Bingham, W. C.: *ref,* 342, 439, 529
Bingham, W. J.: *test,* 485
Bingham, W. V.: *ref,* 342, 3:220(32)
Bininger, M. L.: *ref,* 425
Binks, V.: *ref,* 533
Binks, V. M.: *ref,* 532
Binnewies, W. G.: *ref,* 426

Birch, H. G.: *ref,* 516, 525, 529, 532-3
Birch, J. R.: *ref,* 505
Birch, J. W.: *ref,* 381, 505, 525
Birch, L. B.: *rev,* 495; *exc,* 525
Bird, G. E.: *test,* 5:354; *ref,* 5:354(2-3)
Birkemeyer, F.: *ref,* 439, 525, 533
Birnbaum, J.: *ref,* 529, 533
Birnbrauer, J. S.: *ref,* 516
Birney, R. C.: *ref,* 542, 561, 572
Birney, S. D.: *ref,* 489, 538
Birns, B.: *ref,* 487, 525
Birren, J. E.: *ref,* 439, 529, 532
Bischof, L. J.: *ref,* 4:277(235, 264)
Bish, G. G.: *ref,* 349, 589
Bishop, H.: *ref,* 2:1402(3), 2:1424(24)
Bishop, H. M.: *ref,* 483
Bishop, J. S.: *ref,* 381
Bishop, R.: *ref,* 404
Bitterman, M. E.: *ref,* 447, 4:281(84)
Bittner, R. H.: *ref,* 342, 4:317(2)
Bixler, H. H.: *rev,* 3:268
Bjerring, J.: *ref,* 533
Black, A. D.: *ref,* 496
Black, A. H.: *ref,* 532
Black, B. G.: *ref,* 533
Black, D. B.: *rev,* 350, 387; *ref,* 349, 357, 361, 525, 6:438(458, 477)
Black, F. W.: *ref,* 533
Black, H. P.: *ref,* 361
Black, I. S.: *ref,* 525
Black, J. D.: *test,* 365; *ref,* 425
Black, R. B.: *ref,* 492
Blackburn, A. R.: *ref,* 532
Blackburn, H. L.: *ref,* 529
Blackburn, I.: *ref,* 381, 525
Blackburn, J. M.: *rev,* 2:1376
Blackburn, M.: *ref,* 382
Blackhurst, A. E.: *ref,* 542, 546, 551, 561, 577, 594
Blacklock, C.: *exc,* 486
Blai, B.: *ref,* 361
Blaine, H. M.: *ref,* 484
Blair, G. M.: *ref,* 426
Blair, J. R.: *ref,* 519
Blake, M. E.: *ref,* 543
Blake, R. R.: *ref,* 404, 532
Blakemore, A.: *ref,* 482
Blakemore, A. M.: *ref,* 341A, 426
Blakemore, J. R.: *ref,* 533
Blakeney, A. L.: *ref,* 426
Blanchard, B. E.: *test,* 392
Blanchard, B. M.: *ref,* 529
Blanchard, H. L.: *ref,* 4:277(201)
Blanchard, M. B.: *ref,* 525
Blanchard, P.: *ref,* 525
Blanchfield, W. C.: *ref,* 357
Bland, R. B.: *ref,* 400
Blank, L.: *ref,* 532
Blank, S. S.: *ref,* 482
Blanton, W. E.: *ref,* 439
Blatt, B.: *ref,* 525, 529
Blatt, S. J.: *ref,* 404, 496, 529, 532-3
Blauvelt, J.: *ref,* 525, 532
Blazer, J. A.: *test,* 536; *ref,* 529
Blazsanyik, J.: *ref,* 426, 439
Blewett, D. B.: *ref,* 547, 5:357(1)
Bliesmer, E. P.: *ref,* 348-9, 398, 525
Bligh, H. F.: *ref,* 424, 489, 6:537(4)
Bliss, M.: *ref,* 381

Block, J. B.: *ref,* 529
Block, Z.: *ref,* 489, 525
Blocker, L. P.: *ref,* 589
Blocker, W. W.: *ref,* 529, 592
Blockhus, W. A.: *ref,* 589
Blommers, P.: *ref,* 533
Bloom, B. L.: *ref,* 529, 592
Bloor, B. M.: *ref,* 529
Blosser, G. H.: *ref,* 391, 425
Blue, A. W.: *ref,* 439
Blue, C. M.: *ref,* 516
Bluett, C. G.: *ref,* 447, 4:315(9)
Blum, J. E.: *ref,* 525, 532
Blum, L. H.: *test,* 489; *ref,* 489
Blum, M. L.: *ref,* 426
Blumberg, A.: *ref,* 532
Blumberg, E.: *ref,* 532
Blumenfeld, W.: *ref,* 4:324(58)
Blumenkrantz, J.: *ref,* 342, 439, 518
Blumkoltz, F. P.: *ref,* 529
Blundell, E.: *ref,* 504, 529, 532
Bobbe, C.: *ref,* 349
Bobbitt, J. M.: *ref,* 357, 5:308(296, 302)
Bobitt, D.: *ref,* 381
Bochner, S.: *ref,* 518
Bock, R. D.: *ref,* 529
Bodily, G. P.: *test,* 5:394
Bodley, P.: *ref,* 592
Bodwell, A.: *ref,* 447, 529
Boehm, A. E.: *test,* 344; *ref,* 344, 532
Boehncke, F. C.: *ref,* 381, 505
Boeke, P. E.: *ref,* 439, 532
Boeker, E.: *ref,* 525
Boelling, G. M.: *ref,* 543
Boernke, C.: *ref,* 404
Boersma, F. J.: *ref,* 400, 559, 589
Bogan, S.: *ref,* 533
Bogartz, W.: *ref,* 533
Boger, J. H.: *ref,* 349, 425
Boguslavsky, G. W.: *ref,* 342
Bohrnstedt, G. W.: *ref,* 357, 361, 522, 7:378(3)
Bolanovich, D. J.: *ref,* 482
Bolin, B. J.: *ref,* 425, 439, 5:308(374)
Bolin, S. F.: *ref,* 431
Boll, T. J.: *ref,* 532-3
Bollinger, R. L.: *ref,* 439
Bolt, R. A.: *exc,* 497
Bolton, B.: *ref,* 439, 447
Bolton, E. B.: *ref,* 3:217(70), 5:308(292, 343)
Bolton, F. B.: *ref,* 349, 425, 439, 3:263(50)
Bolton, I. A.: *ref,* 525
Bolton, N.: *ref,* 409, 529, 589
Bolton, S. L.: *ref,* 589
Bonaccorsi, M. T.: *ref,* 487
Bond, C. M.: *ref,* 425
Bond, E. A.: *ref,* 391, 525
Bond, G.: *ref,* 426, 525
Bond, G. L.: *ref,* 342, 391, 398, 419, 426, 435, 525, 570
Bone, R. N.: *ref,* 574
Boneau, C. A.: *ref,* 482
Boney, J. D.: *ref,* 349, 361
Bonfield, J. R.: *ref,* 517, 522, 524-5, 538
Bongiovanni, A. M.: *ref,* 503
Bonier, R. J.: *ref,* 532
Bonk, E. C.: *ref,* 419, 425-6
Bonner, M. W.: *ref,* 516, 529

Bonney, M. E.: *ref,* 349, 398
Boone, D. R.: *ref,* 489
Boone, S. W.: *ref,* 404
Boor, M.: *ref,* 529
Bordeaux, E. A.: *ref,* 570
Bordin, E. S.: *exc,* 6:442
Borg, W. R.: *ref,* 382, 469, 4:277 (202)
Borgatta, E. F.: *test,* 7:378; *ref,* 357–8, 361, 471, 522, 529, 7:378 (1–3)
Borgen, J. S.: *ref,* 551, 561, 591
Borich, G. D.: *ref,* 516
Boring, E. G.: *ref,* 426, 447, 4:281 (81)
Bornstein, A. V.: *ref,* 533
Borosage, V.: *ref,* 516, 525
Borreson, P. M.: *ref,* 533
Bortner, M.: *rev,* 403, 439, 491; *ref,* 532–3
Bortner, R. W.: *ref,* 447, 532
Borum, E.: *ref,* 518
Boruszak, R. J.: *ref,* 525, 533
Bosworth, D. L.: *ref,* 349
Botel, M.: *ref,* 357
Bottegal, J. D.: *ref,* 482
Botwin, D. E.: *ref,* 357, 419
Botwinick, J.: *ref,* 439, 529, 532
Boulger, C.: *ref,* 4:359(2)
Bourestom, N. C.: *ref,* 483, 518, 529, 578, 592
Bousfield, M. B.: *ref,* 426
Bovee, A. G.: *ref,* 525
Bovinette, R. L.: *ref,* 357
Bowers, J.: *ref,* 361, 425, 589
Bowers, J. E.: *rev,* 357
Bowers, K.: *ref,* 551
Bowers, K. S.: *ref,* 529, 551, 574
Bowie, C. C.: *ref,* 532
Bowie, S.: *ref,* 416
Bowles, F. L.: *ref,* 533
Bowling, D. H.: *ref,* 519
Bowman, A. E.: *ref,* 6:438(517)
Bowman, H. L.: *ref,* 426
Bowman, K. M.: *ref,* 532
Boyce, R. D.: *ref,* 404
Boyce, R. W.: *ref,* 349, 358, 361
Boyd, H. F.: *ref,* 349, 489, 505, 525
Boyd, J. D.: *ref,* 357, 419
Boyd, M. E.: *ref,* 365
Boyd, M. W.: *ref,* 538
Boyden, B. W.: *ref,* 357
Boydstun, J. A.: *ref,* 533
Boyer, L. E.: *ref,* 419, 5:308(402)
Boyer, R. A.: *ref,* 5:308(403)
Boyes, F. E.: *ref,* 532
Boyne, A. W.: *ref,* 409
Boynton, P. L.: *exc,* 483; *ref,* 398, 426
Bozarth, D. C.: *ref,* 525
Bozzo, M. T.: *ref,* 513
Braasch, W. F.: *ref,* 425
Braaten, L. J.: *ref,* 482, 5:308(366)
Brackbill, G. A.: *ref,* 532
Bradburn, W. M.: *ref,* 357
Bradfield, A. F.: *ref,* 404
Bradfield, R. H.: *ref,* 589
Bradford, E. J. G.: *rev,* 375, 588; *ref,* 439, 515, 545
Bradley, A. D.: *ref,* 342
Bradley, B. H.: *ref,* 439
Bradley, C.: *ref,* 525
Bradley, G. H.: *ref,* 342
Bradley, M.: *ref,* 426

Bradley, R. C.: *ref,* 361
Bradley, R. W.: *ref,* 361
Bradley, W. A.: *ref,* 3:217(116)
Bradshaw, D. H.: *ref,* 349
Bradt, K. H.: *ref,* 419
Bradway, K.: *ref,* 525, 529, 532
Bradway, K. P.: *ref,* 398, 525, 529
Brady, J. J.: *ref,* 516, 525
Brady, W. J.: *ref,* 349, 357, 425, 436
Braen, B. B.: *ref,* 525, 533
Braff, R. A.: *ref,* 543
Braff, R. G.: *ref,* 533
Bragg, E. W.: *ref,* 5:308(404)
Bragg, J. K.: *ref,* 467
Brailey, L. G.: *ref,* 482
Bramble, W.: *ref,* 529
Brammer, L. M.: *ref,* 4:277(260)
Brams, J. M.: *ref,* 404
Branca, A. A.: *ref,* 449
Branch, L. G.: *ref,* 359
Brandenburg, G. C.: *ref,* 3:220(6)
Brandenburg, J. B.: *ref,* 357
Brane, M.: *ref,* 381
Brannan, C. V.: *test,* 3:220h
Brannom, E.: *ref,* 438
Bransford, L. A.: *ref,* 533
Braucht, G. N.: *ref,* 516, 522, 529
Braun, J. R.: *ref,* 357
Braun, J. S.: *ref,* 381
Braund, R. A.: *ref,* 561, 591
Bray, D. W.: *ref,* 333, 361
Bray, P. F.: *ref,* 525, 529, 533
Bray, W. J.: *ref,* 426
Brayer, R.: *ref,* 547
Brecher, S.: *ref,* 532
Bredt, C. V.: *ref,* 4:277(183)
Breen, J. M.: *ref,* 349
Breen, L. J.: *ref,* 358
Breeskin, F.: *ref,* 533
Bregman, E. O.: *test,* 4:317; *ref,* 4:281(76)
Bregman, M.: *ref,* 5:308(418)
Bregoli, E. J.: *ref,* 348
Breiger, B.: *ref,* 532
Breimeier, K. H.: *ref,* 382, 419
Brendemuehl, F. L.: *ref,* 349, 400
Brengelmann, J. C.: *ref,* 439, 489, 505, 516, 525, 529, 543
Brennan, J. G.: *ref,* 529
Brennan, J. T.: *ref,* 425
Brennan, T. F.: *ref,* 482
Brenner, A.: *ref,* 381, 435
Brenner, M. W.: *ref,* 381, 543
Brentlinger, W. H.: *ref,* 438
Breskin, S.: *ref,* 398
Bressler, M. B.: *ref,* 532
Breuer, C. E.: *ref,* 424
Brewer, C.: *ref,* 529, 543
Brewer, E. J.: *ref,* 533
Brewton, B. C.: *ref,* 589
Brice, M. M.: *ref,* 425–6, 5:308(417)
Brickman, P.: *ref,* 357
Bridger, W.: *ref,* 487, 525
Bridges, C.: *ref,* 532–3
Bridges, C. C.: *ref,* 533
Bridges, C. I.: *ref,* 553
Bridges, J. S.: *ref,* 516
Bridges, J. W.: *ref,* 3:220(9)
Bridgman, C. S.: *ref,* 482
Brierley, H.: *ref,* 331, 532, 6:555 (6)
Brierley, J.: *ref,* 532
Brigger, G.: *ref,* 525

Briggs, P. F.: *ref,* 381, 518, 529, 533
Brigham, B. W.: *ref,* 529, 559
Brigham, C. C.: *ref,* 357, 426
Bright, H. A.: *ref,* 533
Bright, I. J.: *ref,* 2:1424(1)
Brilhart, B. L.: *ref,* 559, 561
Brilhart, J. K.: *ref,* 559, 561
Brill, M.: *ref,* 381, 525, 2:1388(2), 2:1401(6)
Brill, R. G.: *ref,* 529, 533
Brilliant, P. J.: *ref,* 543
Brimble, A. R.: *ref,* 439, 464
Brimer, M. A.: *test,* 495; *ref,* 495
Brinegar, V.: *ref,* 419
Brinton, G.: *ref,* 559
Brislin, R.: *ref,* 561
Bristol, H.: *ref,* 354, 507
Bristol, J. L.: *ref,* 348
British Psychological Society, English Division of Professional Psychologists (Educational and Clinical): *ref,* 525, 529
Brito, H.: *ref,* 517, 533
Brittain, M.: *ref,* 525, 533, 538
Brittain, W. L.: *ref,* 542, 551, 564
Britton, J. H.: *ref,* 381, 592
Britton, P. G.: *ref,* 529
Broad, E. J.: *ref,* 361, 6:438(459)
Broadhurst, A.: *ref,* 439
Brockway, R. L.: *ref,* 533
Brod, D.: *ref,* 357
Brodie, F. H.: *ref,* 487
Brodsky, M.: *ref,* 349, 381
Brodsky, S. L.: *ref,* 361
Brodsky, S. M.: *ref,* 361
Brodt, A.: *ref,* 533
Brodt, A. M.: *ref,* 533
Brody, A. B.: *ref,* 532
Brody, E. B.: *ref,* 357, 574
Brody, L.: *ref,* 525
Brody, M. B.: *ref,* 525
Broe, J. R.: *ref,* 361
Brogden, H. E.: *rev,* 482
Brolyer, C. R.: *ref,* 357
Broman, H. J.: *ref,* 342, 529
Broman, S. H.: *ref,* 484, 525
Bromer, J. A.: *ref,* 400
Bromley, A.: *ref,* 4:277(236)
Bromley, D. B.: *ref,* 439, 518, 532
Bromwich, R. M.: *ref,* 381, 516
Bronner, A. F.: *ref,* 2:1390(3), 2:1391(6), 2:1394(3), 2:1401(2)
Brookhouse, D. B.: *ref,* 533
Brooks, B. R.: *ref,* 525
Brooks, E.: *ref,* 3:217(56)
Brooks, E. M.: *ref,* 426, 447, 529, 533
Brooks, F. D.: *ref,* 426, 525, 2:1424(8)
Brooks, L. E.: *ref,* 532
Brooks, S.: *ref,* 516
Brooks, S. T.: *ref,* 516
Brooks, W. N.: *ref,* 357
Broom, E.: *ref,* 518, 525, 545
Broom, M. E.: *ref,* 426, 525
Broome, L. W.: *ref,* 589
Brosseau, J. F.: *ref,* 516
Brothers, C. T.: *ref,* 357
Brothers, W. L.: *ref,* 4:277(237)
Broughton, E.: *ref,* 525, 538
Brousseau, M. A.: *ref,* 357
Brousseau, P. J.: *ref,* 349

Broverman, D. M.: *ref,* 381, 518, 532
Brower, D.: *ref,* 426, 532
Brown, A. E.: *ref,* 484
Brown, A. J.: *ref,* 545, 2:1394(4)
Brown, A. M.: *ref,* 538
Brown, A. W.: *rev,* 348, 2:1399; *test,* 355; *ref,* 355, 426, 483, 525, 3:256(2)
Brown, B.: *ref,* 400
Brown, C.: *ref,* 533
Brown, C. C.: *ref,* 532
Brown, C. W.: *ref,* 497
Brown, D. A.: *ref,* 529
Brown, D. J.: *ref,* 419
Brown, D. L.: *ref,* 525
Brown, D. V.: *ref,* 532
Brown, E. A.: *ref,* 419
Brown, F.: *ref,* 525, 529, 532-3
Brown, F. G.: *ref,* 405, 419
Brown, G. L.: *ref,* 525
Brown, H. S.: *ref,* 4:277(238)
Brown, J.: *ref,* 525
Brown, J. F.: *ref,* 532
Brown, J. L.: *ref,* 357
Brown, L.: *ref,* 529
Brown, L. F.: *ref,* 516
Brown, M. H.: *ref,* 532
Brown, M. N.: *ref,* 532
Brown, O.: *ref,* 529
Brown, R.: *ref,* 439, 516, 529
Brown, R. C.: *ref,* 504
Brown, R. R.: *ref,* 525, 532
Brown, S. W.: *ref,* 457, 542, 546, 551, 561, 572, 591
Brown, T. E.: *ref,* 426
Brown, W. E.: *test,* 430, 478-9
Brown, W. M.: *ref,* 426
Brown, W. T.: *ref,* 361
Browne, C. G.: *ref,* 482
Browne, D. B.: *ref,* 533
Brownless, V. T.: *ref,* 327, 415
Bruce, M.: *ref,* 398, 483, 525
Bruce, M. M.: *ref,* 426, 582
Bruce, P.: *ref,* 533
Bruch, C.: *ref,* 525
Bruch, C. B.: *ref,* 525, 542
Brudenell, G. A.: *ref,* 538
Bruininks, R. H.: *ref,* 493, 516, 525, 589
Brunje, J.: *ref,* 489
Brunschwig, L.: *ref,* 543, 592
Brunson, F. W.: *ref,* 533
Bryan, A. I.: *ref,* 525, 3:217(60, 99)
Bryan, G. E.: *ref,* 532
Bryan, Q. R.: *ref,* 398
Bryan, V.: *ref,* 559, 561
Buchan, J.: *ref,* 409
Buchanan, B. A.: *ref,* 381
Buchanan, C. E.: *ref,* 439
Buchman, M. D.: *ref,* 533
Buck, C.: *ref,* 525
Buck, C. W.: *ref,* 532
Buck, J.: *ref,* 588
Buck, J. N.: *test,* 588
Buck, J. R.: *ref,* 349
Buckeye, D. A.: *ref,* 357
Buckingham, B. R.: *ref,* 525
Buckley, F.: *ref,* 529
Bucklow, M.: *ref,* 439
Buckton, L.: *ref,* 404
Budde, E. H.: *ref,* 424

Budoff, M.: *ref,* 439, 516, 525, 529, 545, 589
Buegel, H. F.: *ref,* 361
Buel, W. D.: *ref,* 337
Buescher, R. M.: *ref,* 357
Buffmire, J. A.: *ref,* 489
Bugden, C. W.: *ref,* 525
Buhler, C.: *ref,* 525
Bumgarner, F.: *ref,* 419
Bunger, F. A.: *ref,* 358
Bunuan, J. S.: *ref,* 525
Burack, M.: *ref,* 4:277(265)
Burch, C. W.: *ref,* 533
Burchard, E. M. L.: *ref,* 483, 503
Burchard, K. A.: *ref,* 525
Burchinal, L. G.: *ref,* 425
Burdick, A.: *ref,* 382
Burdock, E. I.: *ref,* 404, 518
Burgemeister, B. B.: *test,* 489; *ref,* 483, 489, 525, 532
Burger, B.: *ref,* 426
Burgess, M. M.: *ref,* 529, 543, 574
Burgess, T. C.: *ref,* 357, 522
Burgess, W. V.: *ref,* 589
Burgin, J.: *ref,* 496
Burik, T. E.: *ref,* 532
Burke, B. P.: *ref,* 348, 589
Burke, C. J.: *ref,* 529
Burke, H. R.: *ref,* 342, 439, 529
Burke, J. L.: *ref,* 532
Burke, R. J.: *ref,* 357, 574
Burkett, B.: *ref,* 6:438(460)
Burkhalter, W. D.: *ref,* 424
Burkheimer, G. J.: *ref,* 578
Burks, B. S.: *exc,* 507; *ref,* 525
Burks, H. F.: *ref,* 533
Burland, R.: *ref,* 516
Burley, W.: *ref,* 400
Burn, J.: *ref,* 529
Burnand, G.: *ref,* 518, 529
Burnes, D. K. S.: *ref,* 533
Burnes, K.: *ref,* 533
Burnett, A.: *ref,* 439, 516, 525, 532
Burnett, C. W.: *ref,* 533
Burnett, E. L.: *ref,* 6:468(2)
Burnette, R.: *ref,* 349, 6:468(1, 5)
Burnham, C. A.: *ref,* 532
Burnham, P. S.: *ref,* 357, 3:217(131)
Burnham, R. E.: *ref,* 589
Burns, G. W.: *ref,* 516, 533
Burns, H. M.: *ref,* 525
Burns, L.: *ref,* 533
Burns, L. M.: *ref,* 524
Burns, P. P.: *ref,* 505
Burns, R. C.: *ref,* 533
Burns, R. L.: *ref,* 357
Burns, W. H.: *ref,* 532
Burnside, L. H.: *ref,* 525
Burr, E. T.: *rev,* 469, 3:222
Burrell, L. F.: *ref,* 404
Burson, G. E.: *ref,* 525
Burstein, A. G.: *rev,* 529, 533
Burstiner, I.: *ref,* 589
Burt, C.: *rev,* 348, 5:326; *test,* 4:295; *exc,* 525, 3:283, 4:345; *ref,* 518, 525, 533
Burton, A.: *ref,* 525, 532
Burton, D. A.: *ref,* 529
Burtt, H. E.: *ref,* 3:220(10)
Burwell, E.: *ref,* 533
Busby, W. A.: *ref,* 473
Busch, A. C.: *ref,* 482
Busch, J. C.: *ref,* 400

Bush, M. L.: *ref,* 357
Bush, W. J.: *ref,* 533
Bushey, J. T.: *ref,* 348
Bushong, G. E.: *ref,* 391
Buskirk, E.: *ref,* 533
Buss, F. H.: *ref,* 364
Busse, E. W.: *ref,* 529
Busse, T. V.: *ref,* 542, 564, 574
Bussis, A. M.: *ref,* 436
Buswell, G. T.: *ref,* 449
Buszek, B. R.: *ref,* 357-8, 425
Butcher, H. J.: *rev,* 361; *ref,* 364, 477
Butler, A.: *ref,* 532
Butler, A. J.: *ref,* 525, 529, 532-3
Butler, B. V.: *ref,* 381, 484, 516, 533
Butler, G. D.: *ref,* 533
Butler, J. H.: *ref,* 357
Butler, K. G.: *ref,* 533
Butler, M. J.: *ref,* 404, 546, 551, 574
Butler, P. C.: *ref,* 482
Butler, R. B.: *ref,* 391
Butler, S.: *ref,* 538
Butsch, R. L. C.: *ref,* 2:1377(37)
Butterfield, C. C.: *ref,* 525
Butterfield, E. C.: *ref,* 525, 533
Buttle, D.: *ref,* 439, 529
Butzow, J. W.: *ref,* 357
Byerly, R. L.: *ref,* 405
Byers, J. L.: *ref,* 359
Byler, J. T.: *ref,* 361
Byrd, C.: *ref,* 381, 533
Byrd, E.: *ref,* 525
Byrne, A. V.: *ref,* 522, 529
Byrne, M. A.: *ref,* 542, 546, 561
Byrne, P. S.: *ref,* 331
Byrns, R.: *ref,* 391
Byrns, R. K.: *ref,* 419
Byrum, M.: *ref,* 518
Bytheway, B.: *ref,* 373, 408-9

CTB/McGRAW-HILL: *ref,* 349
Cabanski, C. L.: *ref,* 398
Cabe, P. A.: *ref,* 559
Caccavo, E.: *ref,* 533
Cacha, F. B.: *ref,* 589
Cadman, W. H.: *ref,* 532
Caffrey, J.: *ref,* 349, 5:326(11, 18)
Cahoon, D. D.: *ref,* 447, 529
Cahow, A. C.: *ref,* 419
Cain, E. R.: *ref,* 533
Cain, R. W.: *ref,* 473
Caine, T. A.: *ref,* 439
Caine, T. M.: *ref,* 518
Calden, G.: *ref,* 532
Caldwell, B. M.: *test,* 490; *ref,* 381, 490, 532, 592
Caldwell, H. H.: *ref,* 525
Caldwell, J. R.: *ref,* 349, 400
Caldwell, M. B.: *ref,* 525, 532-3
Calhoun, F. J.: *ref,* 525
California Test Bureau. *See* CTB/McGraw-Hill
Callahan, C. M.: *ref,* 589
Callaway, B.: *ref,* 516, 522, 525, 533
Callaway, E.: *ref,* 439
Callaway, W. R.: *ref,* 349
Callens, C. J.: *ref,* 529
Callis, R.: *ref,* 342, 404, 419, 5:308(345)
Calvert, B.: *test,* 415
Calvert, J. F.: *ref,* 589
Calvin, A. D.: *ref,* 5:308(394)

Cameron, D. E.: *ref*, 592
Cameron, H. K.: *ref*, 361
Camp, B. W.: *ref*, 492, 533
Camp, W. L.: *ref*, 359
Campanella, S.: *ref*, 538
Campanile, S. C.: *ref*, 357
Campbell, B. A.: *test*, 450, 452
Campbell, D. P.: *ref*, 357, 405
Campbell, E. F.: *ref*, 532
Campbell, F. A.: *ref*, 484, 487
Campbell, H. E.: *ref*, 381
Campbell, J. C.: *ref*, 532
Campbell, J. P.: *ref*, 357, 405
Campbell, J. T.: *rev*, 334, 429; *ref*, 431, 482, 6:438(503)
Campbell, M. L.: *ref*, 359, 404
Campbell, M. L. A.: *ref*, 359, 404
Campbell, R. J.: *ref*, 425
Campbell, S. C.: *ref*, 433
Campbell, W.: *ref*, 349
Campo, R. E.: *ref*, 529
Canabal, J. V.: *ref*, 349, 400, 439, 512
Canadian Guidance Associates: *test*, 346
Canady, H. G.: *ref*, 525
Cancro, R.: *ref*, 529
Candee, B.: *ref*, 426, 525
Cane, V. R.: *ref*, 331
Canfield, A. A.: *ref*, 482
Cankardas, A.: *ref*, 439
Cannell, C. F.: *ref*, 518, 525
Cannicott, R. G.: *ref*, 503, 532
Canning, H.: *ref*, 357
Cannon, R. C.: *ref*, 532
Cannon, T. M.: *ref*, 533
Canter, A.: *ref*, 489, 529, 543
Canter, A. H.: *ref*, 342, 532
Cantoni, L. J.: *ref*, 398
Cantwell, Z. M.: *ref*, 365, 439
Capellini, J.: *ref*, 5:308(405)
Caplan, S. W.: *ref*, 400
Capobianco, R. J.: *ref*, 525, 533
Capps, M. P.: *ref*, 382
Caputo, D. V.: *ref*, 357, 425, 532-3
Capwell, D. F.: *ref*, 482-3
Carbonari, J. P.: *ref*, 348, 382
Cardall, A. J.: *test*, 6:446
Cardone, S. S.: *ref*, 496
Carey, J. E.: *ref*, 589
Caring, L. C.: *ref*, 533
Carkhuff, R. R.: *ref*, 381, 529
Carl, G. P.: *test*, 3:273; *ref*, 3:273 (1-2)
Carl, P. M.: *ref*, 349
Carleton, F. O.: *ref*, 361, 371, 404, 439, 525, 533
Carlile, A. B.: *ref*, 391, 419, 5:329(9)
Carlin, L. C.: *ref*, 5:308(314)
Carlin, L. O.: *ref*, 4:277(266)
Carlisle, A. L.: *ref*, 522, 524, 529
Carlsmith, L.: *ref*, 357
Carlson, D.: *exc*, 490
Carlson, H. B.: *ref*, 349
Carlson, J. A.: *ref*, 357, 542
Carlson, J. J.: *ref*, 525
Carlson, J. S.: *ref*, 381, 439, 516
Carlson, R.: *ref*, 404
Carlson, W. A.: *ref*, 482
Carlton, T.: *ref*, 398, 525
Carlton, W. K.: *test*, 6:447, 7:342
Carment, D. W.: *ref*, 532
Carmichael, L.: *ref*, 525

Carney, R. E.: *ref*, 349, 381
Carolan, P.: *ref*, 525, 533
Carp, A.: *ref*, 532
Carpenter, C. C.: *ref*, 525
Carpenter, C. T.: *ref*, 361
Carpenter, R. S.: *ref*, 558
Carr, A.: *ref*, 391
Carr, A. C.: *ref*, 529
Carr, D.: *ref*, 533
Carr, D. L.: *ref*, 516, 543
Carr, E. J.: *ref*, 525
Carr, J.: *ref*, 484
Carrillo, L. W.: *ref*, 5:308(293)
Carroll, H. A.: *ref*, 525, 2:1399(10)
Carroll, I. V.: *ref*, 349
Carroll, J. B.: *ref*, 496
Carroll, L. T.: *ref*, 440
Carroll, V. M.: *ref*, 516
Carroll, W. R.: *ref*, 592
Carron, T. J.: *ref*, 348
Carr-Saunders, A. M.: *ref*, 460
Carruth, B. R.: *ref*, 357
Carruth, B. R. R.: *ref*, 357
Carscallen, H. B.: *ref*, 532
Carse, D.: *ref*, 532
Carse, W. T.: *ref*, 502
Carson, A. S.: *ref*, 496, 533
Carson, M. K.: *ref*, 518, 525
Cartee, J. K.: *ref*, 525, 533
Carter, C. O.: *ref*, 525
Carter, G. C.: *ref*, 4:277(236)
Carter, J. D.: *ref*, 545
Carter, J. P.: *ref*, 525
Carter, R. S.: *ref*, 425
Carter, W. R.: *ref*, 419
Cartwright, D. S.: *ref*, 529
Cartwright, G. P.: *ref*, 516
Cartwright, J. L.: *ref*, 529
Carver, R. P.: *ref*, 361
Cary, L. A.: *ref*, 355
Case, H. W.: *ref*, 426
Casey, D. L.: *ref*, 325, 439
Casey, J. E.: *ref*, 5:308(344)
Casey, M. L.: *ref*, 525
Cash, W. L.: *ref*, 404, 419, 6:438(504)
Cashdan, A.: *ref*, 439, 489, 516
Cashen, V. M.: *ref*, 348-9
Cashman, J. P.: *ref*, 425
Casjens, C. C.: *ref*, 499
Cass, J. C.: *ref*, 425
Cassel, R. H.: *ref*, 439, 532
Cassel, R. N.: *ref*, 349, 357-8, 361, 391
Casselman, G. G.: *ref*, 357
Cassingham, C. C.: *ref*, 525
Castell, J. H. F.: *ref*, 525, 529
Castelli, C. D.: *ref*, 542, 551
Castetter, J. S.: *ref*, 439
Castiglione, L. V.: *ref*, 425, 546, 574
Castle, P. F. C.: *ref*, 386, 389
Castleton, B.: *ref*, 543
Castner, B. M.: *rev*, 507, 2:1383; *ref*, 497
Cate, C. C.: *ref*, 364, 439, 467, 529, 533
Cattell, A. K. S.: *test*, 364
Cattell, P.: *rev*, 398, 425, 1:1044, 3:256, 3:274; *test*, 487; *ref*, 398, 426, 487, 525
Cattell, R. B.: *rev*, 349, 2:1389; *test*, 354, 364, 4:287; *exc*, 525; *ref*, 354, 364, 388, 439, 473, 525, 3:228(1, 4)
Catterall, C. D.: *ref*, 532
Cauble, B. L.: *ref*, 348
Cautela, J. R.: *ref*, 357, 425
Cavanaugh, M. C.: *ref*, 487
Cave, R. L.: *ref*, 400, 589
Cavell, A. C.: *ref*, 398
Cawley, J. F.: *ref*, 589
Cawte, J. E.: *ref*, 520
Center, C. C.: *ref*, 349
Centi, P.: *ref*, 349
Centra, J. A.: *ref*, 357
Cerbus, G.: *ref*, 533
Chabassol, D. J.: *ref*, 361, 529
Chahbazi, P.: *ref*, 419
Chaika, J. J.: *ref*, 419
Chain, R. U.: *ref*, 533
Challman, A.: *ref*, 525
Chalmers, J. M.: *ref*, 533
Chambers, E. G.: *ref*, 4:295(1)
Chambers, J. A.: *ref*, 349, 364, 398, 533
Chambers, J. F.: *ref*, 357, 529
Chambers, J. L.: *ref*, 361
Chambers, W. R.: *ref*, 529, 532
Champion, J. M.: *ref*, 419
Chance, J.: *ref*, 532
Chancellor, G. A.: *ref*, 349
Chandler, M. O.: *ref*, 357
Chandler, R. E.: *ref*, 337
Chang, T. M. C.: *ref*, 533
Chang, V. A. C.: *ref*, 533
Chansky, N.: *ref*, 398
Chansky, N. M.: *ref*, 357, 381, 516, 529, 533, 543, 5:308(418)
Chapa, D. G.: *ref*, 560A
Chapanis, A.: *ref*, 398, 426
Chapman, H. M.: *ref*, 5:308(375-6)
Chappell, T. L.: *test*, 478-9; *ref*, 342, 5:308(345)
Chappell, W. H. E.: *test*, 478
Charles, C. M.: *ref*, 398, 425, 525, 6:480(29)
Charles, D. C.: *ref*, 532, 6:438(461)
Charlton, N. W.: *ref*, 524
Charry, L. B.: *ref*, 493, 533
Chase, C. I.: *ref*, 357, 359, 425
Chase, D. V.: *ref*, 589
Chase, H. W.: *ref*, 525
Chase, J. M.: *ref*, 381
Chase, V. E.: *ref*, 354
Chassell, C. F.: *ref*, 525
Chassell, L. M.: *ref*, 525
Chassell, M. A.: *ref*, 525
Chastain, K.: *ref*, 357
Chatterjee, N.: *ref*, 515, 545
Chatterji, S.: *test*, 412; *ref*, 412
Chaudhry, G. M.: *ref*, 473
Chauncey, H.: *ref*, 357
Chawla, T. R.: *ref*, 502, 533
Cheek, F.: *ref*, 404
Cheek, F. E.: *ref*, 361
Cheers, A. L.: *ref*, 361
Chenault, V. M.: *ref*, 468
Cheong, G. S. C.: *ref*, 324
Cherdack, A. N.: *ref*, 357
Cherry, A. L.: *ref*, 357
Cherry, N.: *ref*, 529, 545
Chesire, L. E.: *ref*, 507, 525
Chesler, D. J.: *test*, 431; *ref*, 431, 482
Chesrow, E. J.: *ref*, 532
Cheyne, W. M.: *ref*, 439, 495

Chiappone, A. D.: *ref,* 493, 533
Child, D.: *ref,* 331, 516
Child, I. L.: *test,* 3:291; *ref,* 357
Childers, P. R.: *ref,* 516
Childs, H. G.: *ref,* 525
Chimbidis, M. E.: *ref,* 589
Chimonides, S. G.: *ref,* 382
Chipman, C. E.: *ref,* 525
Chissom, B. S.: *ref,* 365, 424–5
Choate, H. H.: *ref,* 349
Chodorkoff, J.: *ref,* 381, 525, 533
Chopra, S. L.: *ref,* 439
Chovan, W. L.: *ref,* 502
Chown, S.: *ref,* 403, 439
Chrisien, G.: *ref,* 533
Christ, A. E.: *ref,* 533
Christ, A. F.: *ref,* 391
Christakos, A. C.: *ref,* 503
Christensen, L.: *ref,* 425
Christensen, P. R.: *test,* 457, 542, 546, 551, 561c2, 561d1, 561m3, 561o3, 561x2, 579; *ref,* 457, 546, 551, 561, 564, 571
Christensen, T. E.: *ref,* 342
Christeson, B.: *test,* 325
Christiansen, A. O.: *ref,* 2:1390(1), 2:1391(1)
Christiansen, T.: *ref,* 533
Christoff, P. L.: *ref,* 357
Chun, R. W. M.: *ref,* 439, 518, 525, 533
Church, A. M.: *ref,* 349
Church, H. V.: *ref,* 3:220(2)
Church, J. C.: *ref,* 525
Churchill, J. A.: *ref,* 533
Churchill, W. D.: *ref,* 525
Chused, T. M.: *ref,* 543
Chyatte, C.: *ref,* 342
Cicchetti, D. V.: *ref,* 400
Cicero, J.: *ref,* 381
Cicirelli, J. S.: *ref,* 574, 589
Cicirelli, V. G.: *ref,* 348, 574, 589
Cieboter, F. J.: *ref,* 382
Cieutat, V. J.: *ref,* 525
Cisler, L. E.: *ref,* 525
Clapson, L.: *ref,* 551
Clark, B.: *ref,* 525, 538
Clark, B. P.: *ref,* 349
Clark, E. A.: *ref,* 525
Clark, E. T.: *ref,* 525, 532
Clark, E. W.: *ref,* 357
Clark, F. E.: *ref,* 371, 404
Clark, G. E.: *ref,* 425, 5:326(29)
Clark, G. R.: *ref,* 518, 529
Clark, G. Y.: *ref,* 419, 426, 438
Clark, H. V.: *test,* 448, 3:257
Clark, J. H.: *ref,* 349, 525, 532
Clark, J. M.: *ref,* 504, 529
Clark, J. R.: *ref,* 409
Clark, K.: *ref,* 357
Clark, K. C.: *ref,* 558
Clark, M.: *ref,* 364
Clark, M. L.: *test,* 325, 327, 330; *ref,* 529
Clark, N. C.: *ref,* 361
Clark, P. J.: *ref,* 439
Clark, P. M.: *ref,* 574, 589
Clark, S.: *ref,* 525
Clark, W. H.: *ref,* 426
Clark, W. M.: *ref,* 525, 533
Clark, W. W.: *test,* 348–9, 458, 3:222, 6:503; *ref,* 349, 525
Clarke, A. D. B.: *ref,* 525, 529, 532
Clarke, A. M.: *ref,* 532

Clarke, B. R.: *ref,* 533
Clarke, D. F.: *ref,* 589
Clarke, D. P.: *ref,* 525
Clarke, F. H.: *ref,* 426
Clarke, F. R.: *ref,* 525, 532–3
Clarke, H. J.: *ref,* 532
Clarke, R. B.: *ref,* 361
Clarke, R. R.: *ref,* 382, 404
Clarke, W. M.: *ref,* 533
Clarke, W. V.: *exc,* 532
Claus, K. E.: *ref,* 589
Clawar, H. J.: *ref,* 357, 360, 394, 436
Clawson, A.: *ref,* 381, 533
Clayton, H.: *ref,* 529
Cleary, T. A.: *ref,* 357, 436
Cleeland, C. S.: *ref,* 529
Cleeton, G. U.: *test,* 3:224
Clegg, H. D.: *ref,* 348
Clegg, S. J.: *ref,* 505
Cleland, D. L.: *ref,* 525
Clemans, W. V.: *rev,* 371
Clements, D.: *ref,* 3:217(55)
Clements, G. R.: *ref,* 533
Clements, S. D.: *ref,* 533
Cleveland, G. A.: *ref,* 349
Cleveland, S. E.: *ref,* 532–3
Cliff, R.: *ref,* 361
Clifford, M.: *ref,* 519
Clifton, S. W.: *ref,* 529
Cline, R.: *ref,* 529
Cline, V. B.: *ref,* 349, 551, 559, 564
Clore, G. L.: *ref,* 503, 529
Close, R. L.: *ref,* 525
Closson, M. B.: *ref,* 357
Clower, R. P.: *ref,* 529
Clum, G. A.: *ref,* 529
Clyde, R. B.: *ref,* 361, 6:438(492)
Clymer, T.: *ref,* 349, 399, 425
Coates, C.: *ref,* 589
Coates, C. H.: *ref,* 548, 5:308(342)
Coates, G. E.: *ref,* 545
Coates, S.: *ref,* 6:523(4)
Coats, J. E.: *ref,* 482
Cobb, B. B.: *ref,* 349
Cobb, K.: *ref,* 381
Cobb, M. V.: *ref,* 525
Coberly, R. L.: *ref,* 6:438(517)
Cochran, M. L.: *ref,* 516, 525, 529
Cochran, S. W.: *ref,* 4:277(239)
Cochrane, C. M.: *ref,* 449
Cochrane, R. G.: *ref,* 328
Cockrum, L. V.: *ref,* 404
Coell, A.: *ref,* 516
Coers, W. C.: *ref,* 398
Cofer, C. N.: *rev,* 588; *ref,* 503, 532, 588, 6:480(44)
Coffey, F. H.: *ref,* 349, 589
Coffey, H. S.: *ref,* 349, 507, 509, 525
Coffman, W. E.: *ref,* 357, 436
Coghill, G. E.: *exc,* 497
Cognata, A.: *ref,* 348
Cohen, A. I.: *ref,* 484
Cohen, B.: *ref,* 532
Cohen, B. D.: *ref,* 483, 525, 533
Cohen, D.: *ref,* 532
Cohen, D. N.: *ref,* 381
Cohen, E.: *ref,* 532
Cohen, E. R.: *ref,* 426, 3:263(40)
Cohen, H.: *ref,* 381
Cohen, I.: *ref,* 487
Cohen, I. S.: *ref,* 359, 542, 551, 574

Cohen, J.: *rev,* 3:270; *exc,* 4:344; *ref,* 529, 532–3, 592
Cohen, L.: *ref,* 533
Cohen, L. D.: *ref,* 529
Cohen, L. M.: *ref,* 447
Cohen, M.: *ref,* 532, 543
Cohen, R. D.: *ref,* 467
Cohen, S.: *ref,* 516, 518, 542, 546, 551, 574
Cohen, S. A.: *ref,* 533
Cohen, S. M.: *ref,* 381
Cohen, T. B.: *ref,* 533
Coladarci, A. P.: *ref,* 349, 404
Colarelli, N. J.: *ref,* 529
Colarusso, R.: *ref,* 524
Cole, C. W.: *ref,* 357
Cole, D.: *ref,* 529, 532–3
Cole, E. M.: *ref,* 532
Cole, J. O.: *ref,* 533
Cole, L. W.: *test,* 3:226; *ref,* 525
Cole, R.: *ref,* 525
Cole, R. D.: *ref,* 426, 2:1424(13), 6:480(27)
Cole, S.: *ref,* 522, 529, 533, 578
Cole, S. N.: *ref,* 533
Coleman, J. C.: *ref,* 349, 425, 533
Coleman, J. M.: *ref,* 349, 381, 447, 522, 529, 592
Coleman, L.: *ref,* 533
Coleman, W.: *ref,* 399, 5:308(315), 5:326(12)
Colgan, C. M.: *ref,* 532
Colgan, R. T.: *ref,* 349, 357
Colla, P.: *ref,* 532
Collard, R. R.: *rev,* 484, 519; *ref,* 497
Collart, D. S.: *ref,* 525, 533
College Entrance Examination Board: *test,* 357, 436, 4:286, 5:379; *ref,* 357, 436
Coller, A. R.: *ref,* 489, 516, 525
Collier, B. R.: *test,* 486
Collier, H. L.: *ref,* 381, 489
Collier, M. J.: *ref,* 483, 525, 533
Collins, A. L.: *ref,* 525, 532
Collins, C. C.: *ref,* 5:308(377)
Collins, D. R.: *ref,* 589
Collins, J.: *ref,* 525
Collins, J. J.: *ref,* 532
Collins, L.: *ref,* 439
Collins, M.: *test,* 3:290; *ref,* 3:290(2)
Collins, M. G.: *ref,* 439, 489, 496, 505
Collins, M. T.: *ref,* 589
Collins, N. T.: *ref,* 543
Collister, E. G.: *ref,* 425
Collmann, R. D.: *ref,* 525
Colloton, C.: *ref,* 525
Colman, P. G.: *ref,* 525
Colonna, A.: *ref,* 439
Colver, R. M.: *ref,* 404
Colvin, C. R.: *ref,* 522, 529
Colvin, G. F.: *ref,* 382
Colvin, S. S.: *ref,* 525, 6:480(7)
Combs, A.: *ref,* 484
Combs, H. T.: *ref,* 357
Commins, W. D.: *rev,* 341A, 349, 449, 452, 1:1040, 3:217, 3:224; *ref,* 426, 3:242(3)
Compton, M. F.: *ref,* 542, 551, 561
Comrey, A.: *ref,* 533
Comrey, A. L.: *ref,* 349
Comstock, J. A.: *ref,* 439, 516

Conaway, B. D.: *ref*, 425
Condell, J. F.: *ref*, 391, 496
Condit, P. M.: *ref*, 2:1377(8)
Condon, C. F.: *ref*, 361, 542, 551
Congdon, N. A.: *ref*, 3:217(101)
Conger, J. A.: *ref*, 3:285(3)
Conklin, B. B.: *ref*, 391
Conklin, R.: *ref*, 561
Conklin, R. C.: *ref*, 360, 533, 559
Conklyn, E. D.: *ref*, 574
Conley, H. W.: *ref*, 357
Conn, L. K.: *ref*, 467
Connaughton, I. M.: *test*, 347; *ref*, 347
Conner, H. T.: *ref*, 419
Connors, C. K.: *ref*, 381, 518
Connolly, J. K.: *ref*, 522, 533
Connor, A.: *ref*, 487
Connor, M. W.: *ref*, 529
Conover, D. M.: *ref*, 342
Conrad, H. S.: *ref*, 357, 525, 3:220(45)
Conrad, R.: *ref*, 495
Conrad, W. G.: *ref*, 529
Conry, R.: *ref*, 529
Constantinides, P. D.: *ref*, 400
Constantoulakis, M.: *ref*, 518, 529, 533
Consulting Psychologists Press: *test*, 531, 537, 539
Converse, H. D.: *ref*, 400, 533
Conway, M. T.: *ref*, 382
Cook, C.: *ref*, 439, 529
Cook, J. J.: *ref*, 525, 533
Cook, J. M.: *ref*, 423, 483, 525
Cook, M.: *ref*, 532
Cook, P. H.: *ref*, 323, 426
Cook, R. A.: *ref*, 529, 532
Cook, R. L.: *ref*, 357
Cook, W. W.: *ref*, 404
Cooke, B. E. M.: *ref*, 349
Cooley, J. C.: *ref*, 6:438(493)
Coon, G. P.: *ref*, 532
Coone, J. G.: *ref*, 589
Coons, W. H.: *ref*, 529
Coop, R. H.: *ref*, 533
Cooper, A.: *ref*, 543
Cooper, C. J.: *ref*, 357-8
Cooper, G. D.: *ref*, 496, 518
Cooper, G. V.: *ref*, 529
Cooper, I. S.: *ref*, 439, 529, 532, 592
Cooper, J. G.: *ref*, 349, 364, 489, 505, 533, 5:326(34)
Cooper, L. R.: *ref*, 361
Cooper, W.: *ref*, 559, 561
Cooperative Tests and Services: *test*, 360-1, 5:309, 6:438; *ref*, 4:277(198-9, 229-30, 259), 5:308(287)
Cooprider, H. A.: *ref*, 419, 4:277(184)
Copeland, H. A.: *ref*, 426
Coppedge, F. L.: *ref*, 349
Coppedge, L. L.: *ref*, 349
Coppinger, N. W.: *ref*, 447, 496, 532
Copple, G. E.: *ref*, 532
Corah, N. L.: *ref*, 381, 516, 533
Corah, P. L.: *ref*, 381
Corder, B. F.: *ref*, 542
Cordiner, M. E.: *ref*, 525, 533
Cordova, F. A.: *ref*, 364
Corey, S. M.: *exc*, 493; *ref*, 493

Cork, E.: *ref*, 516
Corlett, F.: *ref*, 574
Cornell, E.: *ref*, 6:480(23)
Cornell, E. L.: *test*, 2:1388; *exc*, 525; *ref*, 525, 2:1388(1)
Cornell, W. B.: *ref*, 6:480(23)
Cornwell, A. C.: *ref*, 525
Cornwell, J.: *test*, 5:360; *ref*, 5:360(1-2)
Corotto, L. V.: *ref*, 532-3, 6:438(518)
Correll, R. E.: *ref*, 529
Corrie, C. C.: *ref*, 532
Corrigan, F. V.: *ref*, 349
Corsini, R.: *ref*, 500
Corsini, R. J.: *test*, 414, 472, 500, 594, 7:378; *ref*, 357-8, 529, 532, 7:378(1-2)
Corter, H. M.: *ref*, 525, 532-3, 547
Cortes, C. F.: *ref*, 532
Cortis, G. A.: *ref*, 331
Corwin, B. J.: *ref*, 489, 516, 533
Corwin, C. G.: *ref*, 538
Coscarelli, J. E.: *ref*, 548
Coslett, S. B.: *ref*, 529
Costa, J.: *ref*, 487, 525
Costa, L. D.: *ref*, 403, 439, 529
Costello, C. G.: *ref*, 439
Costello, J.: *ref*, 505, 516, 525
Costello, J. J.: *ref*, 357
Costello, T. W.: *ref*, 525
Cotler, S.: *ref*, 424, 518
Cottle, W. C.: *ref*, 480, 5:308(303, 422)
Cotton, C. B.: *ref*, 355
Cotzin, M.: *ref*, 532
Counts, P. D.: *ref*, 400
Courtis, S. A.: *rev*, 398
Courtney, J. M.: *ref*, 400, 533
Covert, J. W.: *test*, 486
Covington, N. R.: *ref*, 589
Cowden, J. E.: *ref*, 364, 426, 529
Cowdery, K. M.: *ref*, 525
Cowles, K.: *ref*, 518
Cowley, J. J.: *ref*, 439, 532
Cowne, L.: *ref*, 348
Cox, A.: *ref*, 357
Cox, G. M.: *ref*, 497
Cox, J. F.: *ref*, 525
Cox, K. J.: *ref*, 4:315(8)
Cox, O.: *ref*, 349, 424, 589
Cox, R. C.: *exc*, 356
Cox, T.: *ref*, 525
Cox, W. K.: *ref*, 482
Coxe, W. W.: *test*, 2:1388; *ref*, 2:1388(1), 6:480(8-9)
Coy, M.: *ref*, 357
Coyle, F. A.: *ref*, 516, 522, 533-4
Coyne, L.: *ref*, 532
Coyne, W. J.: *ref*, 532
Cozan, L. W.: *ref*, 504
Craddick, R. A.: *ref*, 357, 529, 532-3
Craft, M.: *ref*, 518, 529
Crager, R. L.: *test*, 585, 6:516; *ref*, 585, 6:516(2)
Craig, A. L.: *ref*, 505
Craig, C. R.: *test*, 5:354
Craig, J.: *ref*, 532
Craig, R. J.: *ref*, 529
Cramblett, H.: *ref*, 533
Cramer-Azima, F.: *ref*, 529, 532, 592
Crandall, F. E.: *ref*, 529

Crandall, V. C.: *ref*, 497, 525, 532
Crandell, J. M.: *ref*, 524
Crane, W. J.: *ref*, 426
Crary, H. L.: *ref*, 543, 592
Cravens, R. B.: *ref*, 525
Craver, A. A.: *ref*, 542, 574
Crawford, A.: *ref*, 439
Crawford, A. B.: *ref*, 357, 3:217(131)
Crawford, F. W.: *ref*, 382
Crawford, J. E.: *ref*, 3:224(2)
Crawford, J. M.: *ref*, 354, 439, 518, 525, 545
Crawford, P. L.: *ref*, 504, 518, 529
Crawford, V. B.: *ref*, 516, 525, 533, 538
Crawford, W. R.: *ref*, 361
Crawshaw, J. E.: *ref*, 331
Creager, J. A.: *ref*, 382
Creed, C. D.: *ref*, 495, 533
Creekmore, F.: *ref*, 589
Creelman, A. G.: *ref*, 426
Crego, C. A.: *ref*, 559
Creighton, S. L.: *ref*, 357
Creutzer, W. A.: *ref*, 3:217(61)
Crickmore, L.: *ref*, 439
Crider, B.: *ref*, 426
Crissey, O. L.: *ref*, 398, 525
Cristantiello, P. D.: *ref*, 6:438(505)
Crites, J. O.: *exc*, 391; *ref*, 342, 419, 426, 6:438(513)
Crittenden, J. B.: *ref*, 533
Crockett, D.: *ref*, 533
Croft, E. J.: *ref*, 425
Croft, L. W.: *test*, 4:301
Crofts, I. E.: *ref*, 533
Croke, K.: *ref*, 525
Crokes, T. G.: *ref*, 532
Cromwell, R. L.: *ref*, 516
Cronbach, L. J.: *rev*, 340, 453, 5:379; *exc*, 509, 518; *ref*, 525, 532, 5:308(300)
Cronholm, B.: *ref*, 365, 529, 532, 543
Cronin, M.: *ref*, 438
Cronin, R.: *ref*, 533
Cronon, D.: *ref*, 592
Crook, H.: *ref*, 503
Crookes, T. G.: *ref*, 439, 529, 532-3, 543
Crooks, W. R.: *ref*, 426
Cropley, A. J.: *ref*, 400, 425, 533, 551, 559, 561, 574, 577
Crosby, D. W.: *ref*, 382
Crouch, H. H.: *ref*, 342
Crouch, J. G.: *ref*, 357
Crouch, M. S.: *ref*, 425
Crow, C. B.: *ref*, 4:277(160)
Crow, J. L.: *ref*, 357
Crowder, D. G.: *ref*, 357
Crowell, D.: *ref*, 516
Crowell, D. C.: *ref*, 516
Crowell, O.: *ref*, 361
Crowley, F.: *test*, 3:238
Crowley, M. E.: *ref*, 503
Crown, P. J.: *ref*, 533
Crown, S.: *ref*, 403, 518, 529
Crowne, D.: *ref*, 467
Cruickshank, W. M.: *rev*, 496; *ref*, 525
Crumley, F. S.: *ref*, 349
Crump, E. P.: *ref*, 507
Crutchlow, E.: *ref*, 532

Csikszentmihalyi, M.: ref, 482, 542, 546
Cull, J. G.: ref, 500, 522, 529
Cullina, J. J.: ref, 589
Culver, H. S.: ref, 518
Cummings, D. E.: ref, 421
Cummings, R. W.: ref, 358, 361, 391
Cummings, S. B.: ref, 503, 532
Cummings, S. P. N.: ref, 589
Cummins, E. J.: ref, 358
Cummins, J. F.: ref, 532
Cundick, B. P.: ref, 381, 516, 533, 538
Cuneo, I.: ref, 525
Cunningham, B. V.: test, 435; ref, 381, 435, 525, 3:255(1)
Cunningham, K. S.: ref, 518
Cunningham, R.: ref, 361
Cunningham, W.: ref, 349, 398
Cunnington, B. F.: test, 587
Cuomo, S.: ref, 445, 447, 482
Cupp, M. E.: ref, 502, 525, 529
Cureton, E. E.: rev, 4:317, 4:320; exc, 532; ref, 342, 382, 404, 525, 2:1377(38), 6:480(39)
Cureton, L. W.: ref, 404
Curr, W.: ref, 439, 461, 525
Currie, C.: ref, 425
Currie, J. S.: ref, 342
Curry, D. R.: ref, 516, 538
Curry, R. L.: ref, 349
Curti, M.: exc, 497
Curti, M. W.: ref, 381, 497, 509
Curtin, J. T.: ref, 349
Curtin, M. E.: ref, 381, 439, 525, 533
Curtis, H. A.: ref, 359, 361
Curtis, J. W.: test, 4:338
Curtis, W. S.: ref, 498
Cushman, C. L.: ref, 426, 525
Cutts, R. A.: ref, 525, 532
Czaczkes, J. W.: ref, 381, 439, 545

DACEY, J.: ref, 331, 589
Dacey, J. S.: ref, 331, 400, 574, 589
Daffron, M. R.: ref, 589
Dahlgren, H.: ref, 518, 529, 543, 592
Dahlke, A. B.: ref, 533
Dahlke, A. E.: ref, 361
Dahlstrom, W. G.: ref, 525
Dailey, J. T.: rev, 342, 357, 382, 404, 4:281
Dale, A. B.: test, 2:1381; ref, 460, 2:1381(1)
Dale, R. R.: rev, 446
Dales, R. J.: ref, 497
Daley, M. F.: ref, 532
Dallenbach, K. M.: ref, 342, 4:277(170)
Damm, V. J.: ref, 349, 574
Dampel, D. D.: ref, 361
Dana, J. M.: ref, 529
Dana, R. H.: ref, 361, 529, 532, 574
Daneel, D.: test, 569
Danford, B. H.: ref, 381, 516
Dangel, H. L.: ref, 533
D'Angelo, R.: ref, 528
D'Angelo, R. D.: ref, 357
D'Angelo, R. Y.: ref, 381
Daniel, K. B.: ref, 361
Daniel, K. laV. B.: ref, 361
Daniels, A.: ref, 529
Daniels, J. C.: rev, 462, 5:392; tests, 375; ref, 375
Daniere, A.: ref, 357
Danks, J. H.: ref, 574
Dans, C.: ref, 516
Danskin, D. G.: ref, 6:438(478)
Darbes, A.: ref, 425, 525, 529, 532, 6:438(479)
Darby, H. E.: ref, 505
Darcy, N. T.: ref, 525, 5:368(19)
Dargel, R.: ref, 559, 561
Darke, R. A.: ref, 381
Darley, F. L.: ref, 533
Darley, J. G.: ref, 342, 357-8, 361, 419, 426, 6:438(506)
Daroff, R. B.: ref, 529, 592
Darsie, M. L.: ref, 525
Das, J. P.: ref, 439
Das, R. S.: ref, 388, 439
Dasgupta, J.: ref, 439
Dash, S. C.: ref, 439
Dashiell, J. F.: ref, 525
Daston, P. G.: ref, 496, 518, 592
Datta, A.: ref, 381
Datta, L.: ref, 381, 490
Datta, L. E.: ref, 348, 516, 574
Daugherty, R. A.: ref, 547
Daughtrey, J. P.: ref, 4:277(177)
Dauterman, W.: ref, 513, 529
Dauterman, W. L.: test, 527; ref, 498
Dauw, D. C.: ref, 589
Davage, P. P. E.: ref, 439
Dave, P. N.: ref, 525
Davenport, C. B.: ref, 525
Davenport, E. L.: ref, 381
Davenport, K. S.: ref, 4:277(203)
Davey, H.: ref, 529
David, K.: ref, 518
David, K. H.: ref, 518, 542, 574
Davidson, C. M.: ref, 421, 3:220(56–7, 60)
Davidson, H. P.: ref, 525
Davidson, J.: ref, 529
Davidson, J. F.: ref, 525, 533
Davidson, J. L.: ref, 532
Davidson, K. S.: ref, 518, 532
Davidson, M.: ref, 439, 525
Davidson, M. A.: ref, 331
Davidson, N. L.: ref, 529
Davies, A. D. M.: ref, 403, 439
Davies, F. R. J.: ref, 426, 4:272(2)
Davies, J.: ref, 381, 533
Davies, J. E.: ref, 2:1377(25)
Davies-Eysenck, M.: ref, 403, 439
Davis, A.: test, 5:326; ref, 348, 391, 398, 425
Davis, A. J.: ref, 525
Davis, B. H.: ref, 398
Davis, D. J.: ref, 589
Davis, D. R.: ref, 525, 533
Davis, E. A.: ref, 525
Davis, F. B.: rev, 357, 361; exc, 398; ref, 525, 4:277(239)
Davis, G. A.: ref, 391, 542, 574, 589
Davis, H.: ref, 3:220(21)
Davis, H. L.: ref, 4:301(4)
Davis, J. A.: ref, 357, 433
Davis, J. C.: ref, 532
Davis, J. K.: ref, 559, 561
Davis, K. A.: ref, 499
Davis, L.: ref, 439
Davis, L. E.: ref, 361
Davis, L. J.: ref, 532–3, 592
Davis, O. L.: ref, 589
Davis, O. U.: test, 4:301
Davis, P. C.: rev, 365, 504; ref, 532
Davis, R.: ref, 525, 545
Davis, R. M.: ref, 525
Davis, S. E.: ref, 361
Davis, T. R.: ref, 426
Davis, W. A.: ref, 349, 391, 398, 425, 4:324(59)
Davis, W. E.: ref, 439, 522, 529
Davis, W. M.: ref, 528
Davis, W. T.: ref, 3:220(32)
Davison, D. G.: ref, 467
Davison, L.: ref, 439
Dawes, R. M.: ref, 529
Dawis, R. V.: ref, 561
Dawson, A.: ref, 533
Dawson, C. D.: ref, 525
Dawson, J. L. M.: ref, 545
Dawson, S.: test, 2:1389; ref, 525
Day, H. I.: ref, 574
Day, J. F.: ref, 4:277(204)
Day, R.: ref, 525
Dayal, P.: ref, 473
Deahl, K.: ref, 483, 525
Deal, M.: ref, 533
Dean, C. C.: ref, 505
Dean, D. A.: ref, 525
Dean, R. F. A.: ref, 497
Dean, S.: ref, 525, 533
Deane, M. A.: ref, 532
Dear, R. E.: ref, 357
Dearborn, W. F.: test, 2:1390–1; ref, 525, 2:1390(1–2), 2:1391(1–2)
Deb, S.: ref, 515
DeBerardinis, A.: ref, 349
De Beruff, E.: ref, 361, 404
DeBlassie, R.: ref, 533
DeBlassie, R. R.: ref, 451
De Boer, D. L.: ref, 349
de Bottari, L.: ref, 425
DeBruler, R. M.: ref, 533
DeBurger, R. A.: ref, 381, 439, 525, 533
DeBusk, B. W.: ref, 525
DeCamp, J. E.: ref, 525, 3:220(22)
de Castro, F. J.: ref, 503
DeCharms, R.: ref, 439
Decker, R. L.: ref, 348, 482
DeCosta, F. A.: ref, 382
Dee, H. L.: ref, 543
DeForrest, R.: ref, 507, 509
DeGooyer, M. H.: ref, 497
De Haan, H.: ref, 532
DeHart, A. L.: ref, 361
de Heus, J. H.: ref, 5:329(5)
Deich, R. F.: ref, 349, 516
Deignan, F. J.: ref, 6:438(462)
deJesús, C.: ref, 381
Dejmek, F. W.: ref, 349
Dekker, L. C.: ref, 355, 439
de Lacey, P. R.: ref, 516
Delancy, E. O.: ref, 425
Delaney, R. J.: ref, 538
DeLange, W. H.: ref, 532
DeLapa, G.: ref, 524–5
Delattre, L.: ref, 532–3
Delauretis, R. J.: ref, 357
Del Gaudio, A. C.: ref, 574
de L. Horne, D. J.: ref, 592
de Lint, J.: ref, 529
Dell, D.: ref, 517, 533
Della Piana, G. M.: ref, 532

INDEX OF NAMES

Dellas, M.: *ref*, 542, 551
Delli Colli, P.: *ref*, 532
DeLong, J. J.: *ref*, 358
Delp, H. A.: *rev*, 504, 533; *ref*, 503, 533
DeLuca, J.: *ref*, 529
De Luca, J. N.: *ref*, 349, 529
Demand, J. W.: *ref*, 391, 407
De Marco, W.: *ref*, 533
Demaree, R. G.: *rev*, 341A
Demarest, R.: *ref*, 503, 525, 532
DeMartino, H. A.: *ref*, 532
Demers, R. G.: *ref*, 529
De Milan, J.: *ref*, 529, 532
de Mille, R.: *ref*, 457, 532, 546, 561, 577
Demopoulos, C. G.: *ref*, 400
de Moreau, M.: *ref*, 381
Dempsey, M. P.: *ref*, 497
Dempster, D.: *ref*, 357, 436
Dempster, J. J. B.: *ref*, 409
Den Broeder, J.: *ref*, 529, 533
Denham, E. C.: *ref*, 361
Dennehy, R. F.: *ref*, 357
Dennerll, R. D.: *ref*, 529, 533
Denney, L. L.: *ref*, 419
Dennis, F. E.: *ref*, 391
Dennis, R. A.: *ref*, 482
Dennis, W.: *ref*, 381, 487, 518
Dennis, W. H.: *test*, 369
Denny, C.: *ref*, 381, 439, 525, 533
Denny, E. C.: *ref*, 525, 2:1377(2), 2:1424(10)
Denny, J. P.: *ref*, 357, 532
Denny, T.: *ref*, 361, 542, 551
De-Nour, A. K.: *ref*, 381, 439, 545
Dent, O. B.: *ref*, 529
Dent, P. A.: *ref*, 589
Dentler, R. A.: *ref*, 518
Denton, L. R.: *ref*, 532-3
Denum, D. C.: *ref*, 348, 525
Denworth, K. M.: *ref*, 525
Deputy, E. C.: *ref*, 435
De Renzi, E.: *ref*, 439
DeRidder, L. M.: *ref*, 400, 5:308 (316)
Derner, G. F.: *ref*, 525, 532
Derrick, S. M.: *ref*, 525
Dershowitz, Z.: *ref*, 533
Derthick, C. H.: *test*, 420
Desai, A. N.: *ref*, 529
Desai, M.: *ref*, 403, 439
Desai, M. M.: *ref*, 403, 439, 518, 532
De Sante, D. A.: *ref*, 419
DeSena, P. A.: *ref*, 361
Deshpande, M. V.: *ref*, 439
Desiderato, O.: *ref*, 574
Desing, M. F.: *ref*, 398
Deskins, A.: *ref*, 503, 592
Desmersseman, J. A.: *ref*, 492
Despert, J. L.: *ref*, 525
Desroches, H. F.: *ref*, 529
Dessotnekoff, N.: *ref*, 426
DeStephens, W. P.: *ref*, 532
Destrooper, J.: *ref*, 487
Deutsch, M.: *ref*, 400
Deutsch, M. R.: *ref*, 529
Deutschberger, J.: *ref*, 525
DeVault, S.: *ref*, 449, 529
Dever, W. T.: *ref*, 589
Devonshire, M. E.: *ref*, 532
DeVoss, J. C.: *ref*, 525
DeVries, R.: *exc*, 549
DeWees, J. P.: *ref*, 361

Dewey, D. M.: *ref*, 518, 545, 578
Dewing, K.: *ref*, 327, 589
DeWitt, W. R.: *ref*, 349
DeWolfe, A. S.: *ref*, 439, 529
Dexter, E. S.: *ref*, 391
Dhapola, T. S.: *ref*, 532
Dhar, C.: *ref*, 388, 439
Diamond, A. L.: *ref*, 518
Diamond, S.: *ref*, 532
Dibble, M. F.: *ref*, 525
Dibner, A. S.: *ref*, 532
Di Bona, L. J.: *ref*, 425
Dick, R. M.: *ref*, 516
Dick, W.: *ref*, 361
Dickason, D. G.: *ref*, 357
Dicken, C. F.: *ref*, 425
Dicker, L.: *ref*, 439
Dickey, O. W.: *ref*, 357
Dickie, J.: *ref*, 505, 525
Dickinson, T. C.: *ref*, 496, 529
Dicks-Mireaux, M. J.: *ref*, 497
Dickson, E. J.: *ref*, 358
Dickson, V.: *ref*, 525
Dickson, V. E.: *ref*, 525, 6:480 (3, 10)
Dickstein, L. S.: *ref*, 529, 547, 561
Dickter, M. R.: *ref*, 357
Dielman, T. E.: *ref*, 364, 419
Dienstag, R.: *ref*, 538
Dieppa, J. J.: *ref*, 357
Diers, W. C.: *ref*, 532
Dietsch, M. K.: *ref*, 525
DiGiorgio, A. J.: *ref*, 404, 419
Dignan, F.: *ref*, 482
Dilcher, R. C.: *ref*, 589
Dill, J.: *ref*, 489, 516, 525
Dill, J. R.: *ref*, 589
Diller, J. C.: *ref*, 532
Diller, L.: *ref*, 525, 529, 532
Dilling, H. J.: *ref*, 387, 425
Dillistone, F.: *ref*, 6:523(4)
Dillon, L. E.: *ref*, 525
DiLorenzo, L. T.: *ref*, 516, 525
Dils, C. W.: *ref*, 439
Dimalta, V. F.: *ref*, 357
Di Nello, M.: *ref*, 533
Di Nello, M. C.: *ref*, 533
Dingman, H. F.: *ref*, 364, 439, 496, 516, 525, 529
Dingman, R. L.: *ref*, 559, 561
Dinnan, J. A.: *ref*, 357, 425
Dirks, D. D.: *ref*, 439
Dirr, P. M.: *ref*, 349, 425
DiScipio, W. J.: *ref*, 357
Dispenzieri, A.: *ref*, 436, 529
Distefano, M. K.: *ref*, 361
DiTolla, E. E.: *ref*, 483
Dittes, J. E.: *ref*, 419
DiVesta, F. J.: *ref*, 419, 5:308(346)
Dixon, J. C.: *ref*, 439, 522, 529, 542, 592
Dixon, P.: *ref*, 403, 439
Dixon, P. W.: *ref*, 361
Dizney, H.: *ref*, 349
Dizney, H. F.: *ref*, 348, 398
Dizzone, M. F.: *ref*, 439, 522, 529
Dobson, J. C.: *ref*, 525
Dockrell, W. B.: *ref*, 409, 516, 533
Docter, R. F.: *rev*, 518; *ref*, 518
Dodd, J. M.: *ref*, 381
Dodd, W. E.: *ref*, 426
Dodds, J. B.: *test*, 492; *ref*, 492
Dodge, A. B.: *ref*, 3:242(2)
Dodge, A. F.: *ref*, 438

Dodson, M. H.: *ref*, 391, 5:308 (277)
Doehring, D. G.: *ref*, 496, 532
Doerman, L. H.: *ref*, 504
Doermann, H.: *ref*, 357
Doerring, P. L.: *ref*, 504
Doherty, M. A.: *ref*, 529, 574
Doherty, V. W.: *ref*, 400
Dokecki, P. R.: *ref*, 381, 525, 538
Dolby, L. L. L.: *ref*, 574
Dole, A. A.: *ref*, 357, 361, 364, 525
Doleys, E. J.: *ref*, 361
Doll, E. A.: *test*, 519; *exc*, 497; *ref*, 497, 507, 519, 525, 545
Doll, P. A.: *ref*, 516
Dolly, A.: *ref*, 497
Domino, G.: *ref*, 357, 364-5, 439, 447, 525, 529
Domrath, R. P.: *ref*, 381, 399, 533, 543
Donaghy, R. T.: *ref*, 382, 404
Donahue, D.: *ref*, 529
Donelson, K. L.: *ref*, 426
Donlon, T. F.: *ref*, 357
Donnan, H.: *ref*, 357
Donnell, G.: *ref*, 497
Donnelly, E. F.: *ref*, 532
Donnelly, F.: *ref*, 381
Donofrio, A. F.: *ref*, 497
Donohue, H. H.: *ref*, 425
Dooley, M. D.: *ref*, 529
Dooley, R. J.: *exc*, 451
Doorbar, R. R.: *ref*, 529
Doppelt, J.: *ref*, 532-3
Doppelt, J. E.: *rev*, 394, 500; *test*, 371, 376, 433; *ref*, 404, 433, 447, 529
Doran, S.: *test*, 3:238
Dorcus, M. D.: *ref*, 558
Dorcus, R. M.: *ref*, 532
Dore, J. J.: *ref*, 532
Doris, R. E.: *ref*, 381, 533
Dörken, H.: *ref*, 381, 532
Dorsey, T. E.: *ref*, 489
Doty, B. A.: *ref*, 529
Doub, B. A.: *ref*, 482
Doubros, S. G.: *ref*, 533
Dougherty, M. L.: *ref*, 525
Doughty, E.: *ref*, 348
Doughty, P.: *ref*, 439
Douglas, M. J.: *ref*, 426
Doust, J. W. L.: *ref*, 532
Dowd, R. J.: *ref*, 357
Dowis, J. L.: *ref*, 439
Dowlen, C. L.: *ref*, 381
Downey, J. E.: *ref*, 525
Downie, N. M.: *rev*, 432, 482, 6:448
Downing, L. N.: *ref*, 529
Doyle, E. D.: *ref*, 522, 529
D'Oyley, V. R.: *ref*, 350, 353
Dozier, J. P.: *ref*, 532
Dragositz, A.: *ref*, 525
Drake, L. E.: *ref*, 391, 2:1377(28), 5:308(317)
Drake, R. M.: *rev*, 355, 364, 447, 468, 4:287, 5:326
Drake, W. E.: *ref*, 529, 543, 592
Drash, P. W.: *ref*, 381, 525, 532-3
Drebus, R. W.: *ref*, 455
Dreger, R. M.: *ref*, 505, 525
Dressel, P. L.: *ref*, 4:277(263)
Drever, J.: *rev*, 515; *test*, 3:290; *ref*, 3:290(2)
Drew, A. L.: *ref*, 533

Drew, A. S.: *ref,* 348
Drew, L. J.: *ref,* 4:334(5)
Drewery, J.: *exc,* 518
Drewes, H. W.: *ref,* 529
Drews, E. M.: *ref,* 533
Drexler, H. G.: *ref,* 381
Dreyer, A. S.: *ref,* 533
Dreyer, C. A.: *ref,* 533
Dreyer, D. E.: *ref,* 358
Drillien, C. M.: *ref,* 497, 525
Driscoll, G. P.: *ref,* 507
Driscoll, J. A.: *ref,* 349, 5:368(20)
Droege, R. C.: *rev,* 482
Druger, M.: *ref,* 357
Drum, D. J.: *ref,* 361
Drummond, M. D.: *ref,* 4:354(3)
Drummond, W. A.: *ref,* 503
Dryman, I.: *ref,* 533
Dubin, S. S.: *ref,* 532
DuBois, P. H.: *rev,* 357; *test,* 465; *ref,* 342, 532
Dubois, T. E.: *ref,* 419
Dudek, S. Z.: *ref,* 381, 400, 533, 575
Dudley, H. K.: *ref,* 447
Duenk, L. G.: *ref,* 589
Duerfeldt, P. H.: *ref,* 489
Duff, M. M.: *ref,* 533
Duffett, J. W.: *ref,* 525
Duffey, M.: *ref,* 529, 574
Dufficy, E. C.: *ref,* 425
Duffy, R. J.: *ref,* 533
Dugan, R. D.: *ref,* 480
Dugan, W. E.: *ref,* 404
Duggan, J. M.: *ref,* 357
Duggan, M. D.: *ref,* 524
Dujovne, B. E.: *ref,* 529, 592
Duke, R. B.: *ref,* 529
Duke, R. L.: *ref,* 349
Dukes, B. M.: *ref,* 589
Dulsky, S. G.: *ref,* 482, 525
du Mas, F. M.: *ref,* 426
Dumler, M. J.: *ref,* 404
Duncan, A. J.: *ref,* 342
Duncan, C. P.: *ref,* 419
Duncan, D. F.: *ref,* 529
Duncan, D. R.: *ref,* 529, 532
Duncan, J. O.: *ref,* 525, 532
Dundore, J. M.: *ref,* 489, 516
Dunfield, N. M.: *ref,* 341, 444
Dungan, E. W.: *ref,* 5:308(378)
Dunham, C. V.: *ref,* 468
Dunham, R. E.: *ref,* 447, 532
Dunham, R. M.: *ref,* 533
Dunlap, J. W.: *rev,* 2:1377
Dunn, D. C.: *ref,* 357
Dunn, H. G.: *ref,* 381, 525, 533
Dunn, J. A.: *rev,* 381; *ref,* 381, 525, 529, 533
Dunn, L. M.: *test,* 495, 516; *ref,* 489, 496, 516, 6:537(5)
Dunn, M. B.: *ref,* 381
Dunn, O. J.: *ref,* 487, 497, 525
Dunn, R. E.: *ref,* 482
Dunn, R. F.: *ref,* 574
Dunn, S.: *ref,* 327-8, 415
Dunn, S. S.: *rev,* 365; *ref,* 327, 415, 6:435(1)
Dunnette, M. D.: *rev,* 482; *ref,* 404, 480, 529
Dunn-Rankin, P.: *ref,* 516
Dunphy, D.: *ref,* 487, 525
Dunsdon, M. I.: *ref,* 403, 525, 533
Du Pan, R. M.: *ref,* 497
Duperre, M. R.: *exc,* 382

Durea, M. A.: *ref,* 525, 532
Durflinger, G. W.: *ref,* 6:438(519-20)
Durham, J. A.: *ref,* 361
Durkin, D.: *ref,* 525
Durling, D.: *ref,* 518, 525
Durnall, E. J.: *ref,* 404, 5:308(318)
Durojaiye, M. O. A.: *ref,* 507, 525, 533
Durost, W. N.: *rev,* 399, 438, 454, 468; *test,* 340, 435, 5:368b-d
Durr, L.: *ref,* 439
Durrell, D. D.: *ref,* 425-6, 525
Durrett, H. L.: *ref,* 447
Durward, M.: *ref,* 529
Dusek, E. R.: *ref,* 559, 561
Dustman, R. E.: *ref,* 533
Duthler, B. T.: *ref,* 358
Dutta, D.: *ref,* 439
Dutta, T.: *ref,* 439
Duvall, N. S.: *ref,* 559
Dvorak, A.: *rev,* 391
Dwarshuis, L.: *ref,* 439
Dwyer, R. C.: *ref,* 533
Dye, J. M.: *ref,* 357
Dyer, G. B.: *ref,* 400, 533
Dyer, H. S.: *ref,* 357
Dyett, E. G.: *ref,* 381
Dyke, R. G.: *ref,* 525, 533
Dyken, M. L.: *ref,* 532
Dykman, R. A.: *ref,* 533
Dykstra, R.: *ref,* 400, 435, 570
Dysinger, D. W.: *ref,* 525, 532

EAGLE, N.: *rev,* 418; *ref,* 400
Earhart, R. H.: *ref,* 525
Earl, C. J. C.: *exc,* 525; *ref,* 381, 515, 518, 525, 545, 2:1401(7)
Earle, E. S.: *ref,* 505
Earle, F. M.: *test,* 4:289; *ref,* 4:289(1-2)
Early, G. H.: *ref,* 533
Easley, G. T.: *ref,* 381
Easley, H.: *rev,* 391, 2:1418, 2:1424
Easterbrook, C. M.: *ref,* 574
Eastwood, G. R.: *ref,* 589
Eaton, A. E.: *ref,* 522, 533
Eaton, H. T.: *ref,* 525
Eattell, E. A.: *ref,* 525
Eaves, L.: *ref,* 533
Eaves, L. C.: *ref,* 381, 525, 533
Eber, H. W.: *ref,* 449, 498, 529
Ebert, E.: *ref,* 426, 507, 518, 525, 545
Ebert, E. H.: *ref,* 525
Ebert, F. J.: *ref,* 404
Eccles, A. M.: *ref,* 558
Echeverria, B. P.: *ref,* 348, 425, 447
Eckermann, A. C.: *ref,* 3:217(64)
Eckhoff, C. M.: *ref,* 404
Eckman, R.: *ref,* 525, 533, 538
Economidou, J.: *ref,* 518, 529, 533
Edberg, G.: *ref,* 419
Edds, J. H.: *ref,* 6:480(30)
Eddy, B. B.: *ref,* 361
Edelstein, G.: *ref,* 348, 439
Edgar, M.: *ref,* 348, 399, 425
Edgerton, H. A.: *ref,* 419
Edholm, O. G.: *ref,* 439
Edmonds, P.: *ref,* 516
Edmonds, W. S.: *ref,* 361
Edmondson, M. B.: *ref,* 525
Edmonson, L. D.: *test,* 478-9; *ref,* 426

Edmonston, W. E.: *ref,* 532-3
Edrington, T. C.: *ref,* 532
Educational Records Bureau: *ref,* 2:1377(33)
Educational Testing Service: *test,* 382, 470, 559
Edwards, A. B.: *ref,* 542, 546, 561, 572
Edwards, A. E.: *ref,* 439
Edwards, A. J.: *ref,* 400, 525, 561
Edwards, A. S.: *exc,* 497
Edwards, C. N.: *ref,* 467
Edwards, G. A.: *ref,* 529
Edwards, H. P.: *ref,* 529
Edwards, K. R.: *ref,* 529, 592
Edwards, M. P.: *ref,* 361
Edwards, R. M.: *ref,* 398
Eells, K.: *test,* 5:326; *ref,* 348, 361, 391, 398, 425, 5:326(6)
Eells, W. C.: *ref,* 381, 525
Egan, R. A.: *ref,* 381
Egeland, B.: *ref,* 533, 543
Egeland, B. R.: *ref,* 533
Eggers, M. M.: *ref,* 381
Eglash, A.: *ref,* 532
Ehrhardt, A.: *ref,* 543
Ehrhardt, A. A.: *ref,* 381, 529, 533, 543
Ehrhart, P. M.: *ref,* 400, 424
Ehrmann, J. C.: *ref,* 496, 532
Eichelberger, R. T.: *ref,* 424
Eichorn, D.: *rev,* 6:516
Eichorn, D. H.: *rev,* 528, 538
Eichsteadt, A. C.: *ref,* 357-8
Eigler, P.: *ref,* 545
Eimicke, V. W.: *ref,* 407
Einspahr, M. H.: *ref,* 6:438(463)
Eisdorfer, C.: *ref,* 529
Eisen, V. W.: *ref,* 381, 532
Eisenberg, L.: *ref,* 518
Eisenberg, M.: *ref,* 391
Eisenman, R.: *ref,* 525, 533
Eisenson, J.: *ref,* 516, 529
Eisenstadt, J. M.: *ref,* 542, 551
Eisenthal, S.: *ref,* 439
Eklund, S.: *ref,* 381, 516
Ekstrom, R. B.: *test,* 559, 561; *ref,* 561
Ekwall, E. E.: *ref,* 533
El-Abd, H. A.: *ref,* 561
Elberfeld, S.: *ref,* 361
Elder, C. M.: *ref,* 411
Elder, H. E.: *ref,* 426
Elefano, I. P.: *ref,* 348, 439
Elenewski, J. J.: *ref,* 529, 574
El-Gundy, T.: *ref,* 532
Eliakim, M.: *ref,* 439
Elias, J. Z.: *ref,* 349, 447
Elias, R. M.: *ref,* 361, 542, 551
Elitcher, H.: *ref,* 533
Elkin, L.: *ref,* 439, 516, 529, 545
Elkind, D.: *ref,* 533
Elkins, J.: *ref,* 328, 330, 426
Ellerd, A. A.: *ref,* 381
Ellerman, R. A.: *ref,* 528
Elley, W. B.: *ref,* 348-9, 353, 364, 400, 426, 439
Ellinger, B. D.: *ref,* 589
Ellington, W.: *ref,* 525
Elliott, D. N.: *ref,* 4:277(214)
Elliott, H. A.: *ref,* 353
Elliott, M. H.: *ref,* 361
Elliott, R.: *ref,* 516, 525
Elliott, R. N.: *ref,* 516-7

Ellis, A.: *ref*, 532
Ellis, E.: *ref*, 364, 533
Ellis, J. R.: *ref*, 589
Ellis, N. R.: *ref*, 525
Ellison, R. L.: *ref*, 349, 357
Elmore, C. M.: *ref*, 440
Elonen, A. S.: *ref*, 439, 525
Elsom, B. F.: *ref*, 589
Elster, R. S.: *ref*, 382
Elton, C. F.: *ref*, 358, 382, 446
Elwood, D. L.: *ref*, 529
Elwood, M. I.: *ref*, 503, 525
Embree, R. B.: *ref*, 391, 3:217 (132), 4:277(240)
Emch, M. A.: *ref*, 525
Eme, R. F.: *ref*, 529
Emerick, L. L.: *ref*, 516
Emerick, L. M.: *ref*, 391
Emerson, M. R.: *exc*, 483
Emerson, P.: *ref*, 525, 538
Emmett, W. C.: *ref*, 408
Emmett, W. G.: *rev*, 387, 398, 4: 289; *test*, 367–8; *ref*, 409
Emory, L. B.: *ref*, 357
Emrick, C. S.: *ref*, 589
Enburg, R.: *ref*, 533
Ende, R.: *ref*, 349
Ende, R. S.: *ref*, 349
Endler, N. S.: *ref*, 361
Engel, A. M.: *test*, 1:1044
Engelbart, E. S.: *ref*, 529
Engelhardt, G. M.: *ref*, 493
Engelhart, M. D.: *ref*, 361, 425–6, 4:286(1)
Engelmann, S.: *ref*, 525
Engen, H. B.: *ref*, 361
Engen, T.: *ref*, 532
England, G. W.: *ref*, 404, 561
Engle, T. L.: *ref*, 588
English, H. B.: *ref*, 525
English, R. A.: *ref*, 516, 525
Enriquez, V. G.: *ref*, 574
Entin, A. D.: *ref*, 533
Entwisle, F. N.: *ref*, 357, 361
Entwistle, N. J.: *ref*, 373, 408–9, 415
Eppley, E. B.: *ref*, 502, 533
Eppley, M. V. (B.): *ref*, 532
Epstein, R.: *ref*, 529, 533
Equinozzi, A. M.: *ref*, 529
Erdberg, P.: *ref*, 522
Erffmeyer, C. E.: *ref*, 419
Erginel, A.: *ref*, 559
Erickson, E. L.: *ref*, 533
Erickson, M. T.: *ref*, 484, 487, 525
Eriksen, C. W.: *ref*, 357
Erikson, R. V.: *ref*, 518, 533
Erlandson, F. L.: *ref*, 349, 6:438 (467)
Erlick, D.: *ref*, 518
Ernest, D. J.: *ref*, 405
Ernhart, C. B.: *ref*, 516, 522, 529
Ertl, J. P.: *ref*, 425, 533
Erwin, E. F.: *ref*, 532
Esbenshade, A. A.: *ref*, 439
Escalona, S.: *ref*, 487, 497
Escalona, S. K.: *ref*, 532
Esen, F. M.: *ref*, 518
Esher, F. J. S.: *ref*, 439
Eshleman, E. R.: *ref*, 525
Espeseth, V. K.: *ref*, 525
Esser, B. F.: *ref*, 357
Estabrooks, G. H.: *ref*, 525, 6:480 (25)

Estes, B.: *ref*, 484
Estes, B. W.: *ref*, 342, 381, 425, 439, 489, 525, 529, 533
Estes, R. E.: *ref*, 525, 533
Estes, S. G.: *ref*, 532, 3:273(4)
Etuk, E. E. S.: *ref*, 381
Evans, E. G. S.: *ref*, 331, 446
Evans, F. J.: *ref*, 559
Evans, F. R.: *ref*, 357, 551, 561
Evans, G. T.: *ref*, 353
Evans, H. E.: *ref*, 381
Evans, J.: *ref*, 533
Evans, J. D.: *ref*, 357
Evans, K. A.: *ref*, 381
Evans, L.: *ref*, 439, 529, 533
Evans, M. C.: *ref*, 349, 4:277(185)
Evans, M. L.: *ref*, 505, 525
Evans, R. B.: *ref*, 439, 529
Evans, R. N.: *ref*, 4:277(262)
Evans, R. W.: *ref*, 361
Evans Brothers Ltd.: *test*, 3:235
Even, A.: *ref*, 357
Even, R. L.: *ref*, 589
Evenson, A. B.: *ref*, 357, 361, 5: 308(433)
Everett, E. G.: *ref*, 532
Everett, G. D.: *ref*, 533
Everson, R. R.: *ref*, 532
Everstine, L.: *ref*, 518
Ewen, R. B.: *ref*, 333, 382, 404, 449
Ewert, J. C.: *ref*, 439, 529, 592
Ewing, J. A.: *ref*, 518
Ewing, R. M.: *ref*, 355
Ewing, T. N.: *ref*, 5:308(300)
Exner, J. E.: *ref*, 533
Exton, A. H.: *test*, 432
Eyde, L. D.: *ref*, 6:438(521)
Eysenck, H. J.: *exc*, 509; *ref*, 381, 403, 425, 439
Eysenck, M. D.: *ref*, 439
Eysenck, S. B. G.: *ref*, 381

FABISCH, W.: *ref*, 518
Fagan, J.: *ref*, 525, 538
Fagert, C. M.: *ref*, 524, 533
Faglioni, P.: *ref*, 439
Fagot, H. J.: *ref*, 516
Fahey, G. L.: *ref*, 404
Fahmy, M.: *ref*, 381, 515, 518, 578
Failor, L. M.: *ref*, 349, 391, 426, 4:315(6)
Fairchild, P. C.: *ref*, 425
Falberg, R. M.: *ref*, 529
Falconer, A. D.: *ref*, 518, 543, 592
Falek, A.: *ref*, 525, 529, 532
Falk, L. J.: *ref*, 493, 516, 533
Falk, R.: *ref*, 525, 3:242(2)
Falstein, E. K.: *ref*, 483
Familant, R. P.: *ref*, 516
Fandal, A. W.: *test*, 492
Fanelli, G. C.: *ref*, 592
Fangman, M. W.: *ref*, 543
Faragher, J. P.: *ref*, 361
Farber, I. E.: *ref*, 532
Farber, R. H.: *ref*, 4:277(267)
Farbro, P. C.: *ref*, 423
Fargo, G.: *ref*, 516
Fargo, G. A.: *ref*, 516
Farley, F. H.: *ref*, 403
Farley, J.: *ref*, 361, 6:468(6)
Farmer, E.: *ref*, 4:295(1)
Farnham, L. J.: *ref*, 518
Farnsworth, P. R.: *ref*, 419
Farnum, H. B.: *ref*, 426

Faroqi, M. A.: *exc*, 372; *ref*, 439
Farr, J. L.: *ref*, 425, 469
Farr, R. S.: *ref*, 559
Farr, S. D.: *exc*, 361
Farrant, R. H.: *ref*, 355, 364, 381
Farrar, R. D.: *ref*, 361
Farrell, M.: *ref*, 381
Farson, M. R.: *ref*, 525
Farthing, M.: *ref*, 525
Fassett, K. K.: *ref*, 532
Fast, R. E.: *ref*, 533
Faterson, H. F.: *ref*, 525, 529, 533
Fattu, N. A.: *ref*, 6:438(532)
Fauls, J. T.: *ref*, 532
Fauth, D. L.: *ref*, 529
Fay, L. C.: *ref*, 525
Fay, W. H.: *ref*, 516
Fear, R. A.: *ref*, 447
Febiger, C. H.: *ref*, 529
Fedell, J. C.: *ref*, 357
Fedio, P.: *ref*, 516, 533
Fee, F.: *ref*, 361, 533
Fee, M.: *ref*, 426, 2:1424(16), 3: 242(7)
Feeney, M. M.: *ref*, 357
Feeney, S.: *ref*, 467
Feffer, M. H.: *ref*, 529, 533
Feifel, H.: *ref*, 525
Feil, M. H.: *ref*, 4:277(186)
Fein, S. R.: *ref*, 439
Feinberg, A.: *ref*, 404, 419
Feinberg, H.: *rev*, 493; *ref*, 525
Feinberg, I.: *ref*, 439
Feinberg, M. R.: *ref*, 529
Feingold, S. N.: *ref*, 3:228(2, 4)
Feinstein, A. R.: *ref*, 533
Feldhusen, J. F.: *ref*, 357, 361, 533, 542, 546, 551, 561, 589
Feldman, D. H.: *ref*, 516, 525, 589
Feldman, M. J.: *ref*, 404
Feldman, R. C.: *ref*, 518
Feldman, S. E.: *ref*, 522, 529, 533
Feldt, L. S.: *ref*, 348, 516, 533
Felix, R.: *ref*, 529
Felker, S. A.: *ref*, 404
Fellers, G. L.: *ref*, 532
Felton, T. A.: *ref*, 400, 589
Fendrick, P.: *ref*, 426, 525
Ference, C.: *ref*, 589
Ferguson, C.: *ref*, 525, 532, 3:217 (98)
Ferguson, G. A.: *rev*, 331, 350, 387, 419, 3:237, 4:327
Ferguson, G. O.: *test*, 2:1394; *ref*, 2:1394(1)
Ferguson, H. H.: *ref*, 426
Ferguson, L. W.: *ref*, 426
Ferinden, W. E.: *ref*, 525, 533
Fernald, M. R.: *ref*, 525
Fernald, P. S.: *ref*, 529, 533
Fernandes, L. M.: *ref*, 404
Fernandez, P.: *ref*, 533
Ferneau, L.: *ref*, 525
Fernow, D. L.: *ref*, 525
Ferris, D. R.: *ref*, 589
Ferris, M. J.: *ref*, 361
Ferson, R. F.: *ref*, 342
Feshbach, S.: *ref*, 529
Fey, W. F.: *ref*, 532
Fialkin, H. N.: *ref*, 438
Ficca, S. C.: *ref*, 532
Fidel, Y.: *ref*, 529, 533
Fiedler, E. R.: *ref*, 439, 496
Fiedler, F. E.: *ref*, 381

Fiedler, M.: *ref*, 484, 525
Field, J. G.: *ref*, 529, 532-3
Fielder, W. R.: *ref*, 467
Fields, D. L.: *ref*, 525
Fields, F. R. J.: *ref*, 529, 592
Fife, I. E.: *ref*, 469
Fife, R. H.: *ref*, 468
Filer, R. J.: *ref*, 452
Filler, M. G.: *ref*, 3:220(3)
Fillmore, A. R.: *ref*, 496, 533
Finch, F. H.: *test*, 399; *ref*, 426, 438, 2:1424(19, 22), 3:220(52, 58)
Findley, W. G.: *rev*, 358
Fine, B. J.: *ref*, 559, 561
Fine, M. J.: *ref*, 381, 496
Finger, J. A.: *ref*, 357
Fingert, H. H.: *ref*, 381
Fink, M.: *ref*, 532
Fink, S. L.: *ref*, 529
Finkelstein, M.: *ref*, 532
Finley, C.: *ref*, 533
Finley, C. J.: *test*, 534; *ref*, 348, 381, 525, 533
Finley, J. R.: *ref*, 357
Finley, K. H.: *ref*, 525, 533
Finnerty, R. J.: *ref*, 533
Finney, B. J.: *ref*, 439
Finnie, F. R.: *ref*, 439, 529
Fiorentino, D.: *ref*, 439
Firestone, M. H.: *exc*, 497
Firestone, R. W.: *ref*, 342
Firetto, A. C.: *ref*, 529
Firnhaber, E. P.: *ref*, 525
Fischer, A.: *ref*, 503, 592
Fischer, R. F.: *ref*, 400, 404
Fish, B.: *ref*, 497
Fish, C. C.: *ref*, 518
Fish, H. L.: *ref*, 407
Fishbein, M.: *ref*, 574
Fishbein, S.: *ref*, 532
Fisher, C.: *ref*, 529, 592
Fisher, G.: *ref*, 529
Fisher, G. C.: *ref*, 532
Fisher, G. M.: *ref*, 496, 525, 529, 532-3
Fisher, H. R.: *ref*, 3:224(1)
Fisher, J.: *ref*, 381, 529
Fisher, K. A.: *ref*, 532
Fisher, M. A.: *ref*, 525
Fisher, S.: *ref*, 381, 518, 532-3
Fishler, K.: *ref*, 497
Fishman, J. A.: *rev*, 469, 5:377; *ref*, 357
Fishman, S.: *ref*, 525
Fisichelli, V. R.: *ref*, 487, 525
Fiske, D. W.: *ref*, 404, 482, 529
Fitch, M. J.: *ref*, 439, 533
Fitt, A. B.: *ref*, 354, 525
Fitzgerald, B. J.: *ref*, 516, 533
Fitzgerald, D.: *ref*, 439
Fitzgerald, L. A.: *ref*, 400, 425
Fitzgerald, M. C.: *ref*, 533
Fitz-Gibbon, C. T.: *ref*, 439
Fitzgibbon, T. J.: *ref*, 5:308(347)
Fitzhugh, K. B.: *ref*, 529, 532
Fitzhugh, L. C.: *ref*, 529, 532
Fitzpatrick, C. H.: *ref*, 558
Fitzpatrick, E. D.: *ref*, 482
Fitzpatrick, M. R.: *ref*, 357
Fitzpatrick, P.: *ref*, 529
Fitzsimmons, E. K.: *ref*, 439
Fitzwater, M. E.: *ref*, 558
Fjeld, S. P.: *ref*, 543

Flanagan, J. C.: *rev*, 480, 1:1054, 3:252; *test*, 467; *exc*, 525
Flanagan, M. L.: *ref*, 574
Flanary, W.: *ref*, 532
Flanders, J. K.: *ref*, 525
Flanigan, P. J.: *ref*, 525, 533, 538
Flaugher, R. L.: *ref*, 357
Flax, M.: *ref*, 400
Flax, M. L.: *ref*, 516, 533, 542, 546, 551
Fleeman, G. W.: *ref*, 533
Fleet, D.: *ref*, 4:277(234)
Fleischer, G.: *ref*, 359, 542, 551, 574
Fleishman, J. J.: *ref*, 559, 561
Fleming, C. M.: *test*, 362-3, 395-6; *exc*, 509
Fleming, E.: *ref*, 349
Fleming, E. S.: *ref*, 589
Fleming, J. M.: *ref*, 439, 533
Fleming, J. W.: *ref*, 516, 529, 533
Fleming, K.: *ref*, 489, 525
Fleming, V. V. D.: *ref*, 525
Fleming, W. G.: *ref*, 357, 361
Fleminger, J. J.: *ref*, 592
Flemming, C. W.: *ref*, 426, 525, 558
Flemming, E. G.: *ref*, 426
Fletcher, K. R.: *ref*, 589
Flewelling, R. W.: *ref*, 516, 533
Flick, G. L.: *ref*, 525, 529, 560A, 592
Flinn, D. E.: *ref*, 529
Floor, L.: *ref*, 518, 529, 533
Flora, L. D.: *ref*, 357
Florence Louise, Sister M.: *ref*, 3:217(140)
Flory, C. D.: *rev*, 433, 482, 3:251; *ref*, 2:1377(44)
Flottman, E. A.: *ref*, 426
Flower, R. M.: *ref*, 522, 533
Floyd, J. A.: *test*, 5:389
Floyd, W. A.: *ref*, 357, 516
Flynn, E.: *ref*, 525
Flynn, J. J.: *ref*, 532
Flynn, W. F.: *ref*, 529
Fogel, J.: *ref*, 532
Fogel, M. L.: *ref*, 440, 529, 543
Folds, J. H.: *ref*, 361
Foley, J. M.: *ref*, 425, 529
Foley, J. P.: *rev*, 482, 5:395
Foley, M. V.: *ref*, 533
Folk, E. D.: *ref*, 532
Follman, J.: *ref*, 361, 400
Fong, L. J.: *ref*, 516
Font, M. M.: *ref*, 525
Fontes, P. J.: *ref*, 361
Fooks, G.: *ref*, 518
Foote, R. P.: *ref*, 449
Foran, T. G.: *ref*, 435, 438
Forbes, A. R.: *ref*, 439
Ford, C. A.: *ref*, 525
Ford, D. H.: *ref*, 529
Ford, E. D.: *ref*, 562, 564
Ford, J. B.: *ref*, 533
Ford, R. N.: *ref*, 361
Ford, Z. B.: *ref*, 361
Fordham, S. L.: *ref*, 361
Foree, S. S.: *ref*, 357
Forehand, G. A.: *ref*, 361
Forehand, R.: *ref*, 525
Forlano, G.: *ref*, 426, 525
Formanek, R.: *ref*, 490
Forrest, D. V.: *ref*, 361
Forrest, T.: *ref*, 381, 533
Forster, C. R.: *ref*, 532

Fortna, R. O.: *ref*, 361
Fortson, C. B.: *ref*, 532
Fortson, L. R.: *ref*, 589
Foster, A.: *ref*, 447, 529, 532
Foster, A. L.: *ref*, 532
Foster, C.: *ref*, 532
Foster, C. G.: *ref*, 532
Foster, D.: *ref*, 533
Foster, D. V.: *ref*, 532-3
Foster, G. R.: *ref*, 361
Foster, L. S.: *ref*, 3:217(86)
Foster, M. E.: *ref*, 348-9, 425
Foulds, G. A.: *ref*, 403, 439, 518
Foulkes, D.: *ref*, 357
Fowler, H. L.: *ref*, 515, 2:1394(12)
Fowler, H. M.: *rev*, 361, 391, 5:308
Fowler, O. F.: *ref*, 426
Fowler, R. S.: *ref*, 592
Fowler, W. L.: *ref*, 348, 364, 391, 5:326(21, 30), 5:329(10-1)
Fox, A. M.: *ref*, 404, 425
Fox, C.: *rev*, 2:1381; *ref*, 532
Fox, D. G.: *ref*, 349, 357
Fox, E.: *ref*, 529
Fox, E. J.: *ref*, 435
Fox, J. T.: *ref*, 518
Fox, L. J.: *ref*, 361
Fox, V.: *ref*, 342
Fox, W. C.: *ref*, 435
Fox, W. H.: *ref*, 3:217(122), 4:277(173)
Foxe, A. N.: *exc*, 497
Foxwell, N. H.: *ref*, 439, 529
Foxworth, C. L.: *ref*, 361
Fracchia, J.: *ref*, 439
Fracchia, J. F.: *ref*, 439
Francesco, E.: *test*, 471; *ref*, 471
Francey, R. E.: *ref*, 525
Francis, G. M.: *ref*, 525
Francis, P. S.: *ref*, 529
Francis, R. L.: *ref*, 361
Francis-Williams, J.: *ref*, 484
Frandsen, A.: *ref*, 525
Frandsen, A. N.: *ref*, 399, 525, 532-3, 5:326(31)
Frank, A. C.: *ref*, 361, 382
Frank, G.: *ref*, 419
Frank, G. H.: *ref*, 529, 532
Frank, H.: *ref*, 439, 496
Frankel, E.: *ref*, 357
Franken, R. E.: *ref*, 525
Frankenburg, W. K.: *test*, 492; *ref*, 492
Frankle, A. H.: *ref*, 480
Franklin, J. C.: *ref*, 532
Fransella, F.: *ref*, 331, 533
Franz, G.: *ref*, 357
Franzen, R.: *ref*, 2:1424(2)
Frary, R. B.: *ref*, 361
Fraser, D.: *ref*, 525
Fraser, E. D.: *rev*, 525, 533, 5:360, 5:405, 6:447
Fraser, W. D.: *ref*, 525
Frasier, G. W.: *ref*, 525
Frazeur, H. A.: *ref*, 483, 525
Frede, M. C.: *ref*, 381, 525, 538
Frederick, W. C.: *ref*, 559
Frederickson, W. K.: *ref*, 529
Frederiksen, N.: *rev*, 376; *ref*, 357, 551, 561, 5:308(294)
Freeburne, C. M.: *ref*, 529, 532, 6:438(522)

Freedheim, D. K.: *ref,* 487, 525, 533
Freedman, J. L.: *ref,* 574
Freedman, S.: *ref,* 529
Freehill, M. F.: *ref,* 5:308(295, 348)
Freeman, A. V.: *ref,* 532
Freeman, F. N.: *exc,* 525; *ref,* 525
Freeman, F. S.: *rev,* 349, 400; *exc,* 344; *ref,* 419, 525, 529, 532–3, 2: 1377(11)
Freeman, J.: *ref,* 331, 439, 529
Freeman, K. H.: *ref,* 426
Freeman, P.: *ref,* 331
Freer, F. J.: *ref,* 533, 538, 543
Freides, D.: *rev,* 525, 533
Freinek, W. R.: *ref,* 439, 529
Fremer, J.: *ref,* 357
French, E. G.: *ref,* 532
French, F. E.: *ref,* 487
French, J.: *ref,* 489
French, J. G.: *ref,* 439
French, J. L.: *rev,* 490; *test,* 391, 517; *ref,* 349, 517
French, J. W.: *test,* 559, 561; *ref,* 357, 5:308(296, 302)
French, L. A.: *ref,* 518, 525, 529, 532, 592
French, R. L.: *rev,* 382
Frengel, B. A.: *ref,* 589
Freston, C. W.: *ref,* 518
Fretwell, L. N.: *ref,* 502, 525, 529, 589
Fretz, B. R.: *ref,* 533
Freud, S. L.: *ref,* 529
Freudenberg, R. K.: *ref,* 545
Frey, J. H.: *ref,* 489
Freyberg, P. S.: *ref,* 439
Freyermuth, R. A.: *ref,* 589
Freymark, B. A.: *ref,* 529
Frick, J. W.: *ref,* 457, 546, 551, 561, 571, 5:308(406)
Frick, R. C.: *ref,* 589
Fricke, B. G.: *ref,* 357
Friedline, C. L.: *ref,* 525
Friedman, A. S.: *ref,* 529
Friedman, E. C.: *ref,* 529, 533, 543
Friedman, G. H. P.: *ref,* 533
Friedman, I.: *ref,* 532
Friedman, J.: *ref,* 529
Friedman, M.: *ref,* 545
Friedman, R.: *ref,* 533
Friedman, S. M.: *ref,* 361
Friedman, W. H.: *ref,* 543
Friedrich, D.: *ref,* 533
Friedrichs, T. D.: *ref,* 348
Frields, S. I.: *ref,* 357, 436
Frisby, C. B.: *ref,* 384, 388, 439
Fritz, M. F.: *ref,* 5:308(349)
Fritz, R. A.: *ref,* 3:217(52)
Froehlich, G. J.: *rev,* 341, 358, 5: 319; *exc,* 509; *ref,* 391, 525, 3: 217(82)
Froemel, E. C.: *ref,* 414, 547–8, 570
Fromm, E.: *ref,* 487, 525
Frommelt, L. A.: *ref,* 533
Frook, W. F.: *ref,* 391
Frost, B. P.: *ref,* 348, 453, 518, 533
Frost, R.: *ref,* 533
Frost, R. B.: *ref,* 425
Frostig, M.: *ref,* 533
Fruchter, B.: *ref,* 342, 425
Fruin, D. J.: *ref,* 551, 561, 572
Fry, H. R.: *ref,* 518
Fry, L. M.: *ref,* 532

Frye, U. C.: *ref,* 532
Fryer, D.: *ref,* 456, 4:281(78)
Fryett, H. L.: *ref,* 405
Fuchigami, R. Y.: *ref,* 516
Fuchs, E. F.: *ref,* 342
Fujita, G. Y.: *ref,* 357
Fukuda, N.: *ref,* 381
Fukuda, N. K.: *ref,* 361
Fukuda, T.: *ref,* 525
Fulk, B. E.: *ref,* 342
Fulkerson, S. C.: *ref,* 518, 532
Fuller, B. L.: *ref,* 538
Fuller, C. W.: *ref,* 381, 439, 518
Fuller, E. M.: *ref,* 404, 3:217(133)
Fuller, G. B. *ref,* 349, 533
Fuller, R.: *ref,* 497
Fulton, R. T.: *ref,* 516
Funkenstein, D. H.: *ref,* 357
Funkhouser, T. R.: *ref,* 447, 529
Fuqua, N. V.: *ref,* 349, 589
Furcon, J.: *ref,* 561, 574, 577
Furcon, J. E.: *ref,* 414, 547–8, 570
Furfey, P. H.: *ref,* 3:285(1, 5)
Furneaux, W. D.: *test,* 6:555; *ref,* 403, 439, 5:357(2)
Furr, K. D.: *ref,* 348, 439
Furst, E. J.: *ref,* 4:277(241)
Furth, H. G.: *ref,* 533
Fuschillo, J.: *ref,* 532
Fusfeld, I. S.: *ref,* 4:277(205)
Futterer, J. W.: *ref,* 525, 538

GAB, D.: *ref,* 382, 404
Gab, D. D.: *ref,* 404
Gabet, Y.: *ref,* 516, 525
Gabler, E. R.: *exc,* 525
Gabriel, K. R.: *ref,* 439
Gaddes, W. H.: *ref,* 364, 381, 518, 533
Gade, E. M.: *ref,* 404
Gage, G. E.: *ref,* 516, 533
Gage, N. L.: *ref,* 4:277(193, 214–5)
Gagni, A. O.: *ref,* 361
Gagnon, J.: *ref,* 487
Gaier, E. L.: *rev,* 440
Gainer, W. L.: *ref,* 532–3
Gaitz, C.: *ref,* 529, 592
Gaitz, C. M.: *ref,* 504
Galbreath, N.: *ref,* 525
Galdieri, A. A.: *ref,* 533
Gale, E. N.: *ref,* 440, 529, 543
Galinsky, M. D.: *ref,* 357, 524, 533
Gall, M.: *ref,* 574
Gall, M. D.: *ref,* 574
Gallagher, H. C.: *ref,* 529
Gallagher, J.: *ref,* 533
Gallagher, J. J.: *ref,* 349, 487, 489, 505, 525, 532–3
Gallagher, M. S.: *ref,* 589
Gallagher, P.: *ref,* 498
Gallaher, P. E.: *ref,* 529, 532
Gallant, T. F.: *ref,* 357
Gallessich, J. M.: *ref,* 357
Galli, A. P.: *ref,* 516
Gallop, R.: *ref,* 331
Gallup, H. F.: *ref,* 574
Galvan, R. R.: *ref,* 533
Gambaro, S.: *ref,* 518
Gamble, K. R.: *ref,* 357, 574
Gamewell, J.: *ref,* 359, 529
Ganguly, A. K.: *ref,* 439
Gannon, D. R.: *ref,* 484, 525
Gantcher, P.: *ref,* 381
Ganter, R. L.: *ref,* 533

Gantz, B. S.: *ref,* 574
Garber, M.: *ref,* 516
Garber, W. F.: *ref,* 480
Garcia, D.: *ref,* 357
Gardener, D. B.: *ref,* 497
Gardiner, C. S.: *ref,* 425
Gardner, A. M.: *ref,* 516
Gardner, E. F.: *rev,* 360, 401; *test,* 340
Gardner, F. E.: *ref,* 357
Gardner, M. J.: *ref,* 518, 532
Gardner, M. S.: *ref,* 529
Gardner, R. K.: *ref,* 592
Gardner, R. W.: *ref,* 533, 547, 561
Gardner, S.: *test,* 554–5, 562, 581
Gardner, S. F.: *ref,* 349
Gardner, W. H.: *exc,* 497
Garfield, S. L.: *ref,* 518, 529, 532, 6:438(490)
Garforth, F. I. de la P.: *ref,* 386, 389
Garfunkel, F.: *ref,* 525
Garibay, C.: *ref,* 533
Garman, E. M.: *ref,* 439
Garms, J. D.: *ref,* 357, 533
Garner, E. H.: *ref,* 533
Garner, J.: *ref,* 533
Garner, R. G.: *ref,* 482
Garrett, H. E.: *rev,* 349, 398–9, 5:381; *exc,* 525; *ref,* 447, 525, 2:1394(6), 2:1399(12), 4:281(82)
Garrett, J.: *ref,* 516
Garrett, J. F.: *ref,* 525
Garrett, W. S.: *ref,* 419, 3:224(3)
Garrison, K. C.: *ref,* 426
Garrison, M.: *ref,* 518, 524–5
Garrison, N. L.: *ref,* 3:242(2)
Garrison, S. C.: *ref,* 525, 6:480(13)
Garside, R. F.: *ref,* 390
Garth, T. R.: *ref,* 3:256(6)
Garton, J.: *ref,* 533
Garver, S. A.: *ref,* 538
Garwood, D. S.: *ref,* 542, 551, 561, 564
Gaskill, A. R.: *ref,* 435
Gaskill, H. V.: *ref,* 3:274(1)
Gaskill, P.: *ref,* 388, 439, 512, 532
Gaskins, J. R.: *ref,* 525
Gast, I. M.: *test,* 1:1041
Gaston, C. O.: *ref,* 532
Gates, A. I.: *ref,* 435, 525, 3:255(11), 6:480(20)
Gates, D. O.: *ref,* 560A
Gates, J. A.: *ref,* 349
Gathercole, C. E.: *ref,* 529
Gatien, R.: *ref,* 3:218(9)
Gaudet, F. J.: *ref,* 426
Gaudry, E.: *ref,* 324
Gault, R. H.: *ref,* 558
Gault, U.: *ref,* 533
Gautney, D. B.: *ref,* 381, 525, 538
Gaver, K. D.: *ref,* 529
Gaw, E. A.: *ref,* 525
Gaw, F.: *ref,* 518, 558, 578, 2:1391(5)
Gay, C. J.: *ref,* 425
Gay, J. R.: *ref,* 525, 545
Gayton, W. F.: *ref,* 381, 525, 529, 533
Gazda, G. M.: *ref,* 361
Gearan, J. S.: *ref,* 3:217(71)
Geber, M.: *ref,* 497
Geertsma, R.: *ref,* 404, 532

Gehman, I. H.: *ref,* 525, 533
Geiger, H. E.: *ref,* 3:217(77)
Geiger, W. H. E.: *test,* 430, 478-9
Geil, G. A.: *ref,* 381, 532
Geiser, R. L.: *ref,* 529
Geist, H.: *ref,* 5:326(8)
Gelatt, H. B.: *ref,* 361
Gellerman, S. W.: *ref,* 483
Gellert, E.: *ref,* 381
Gendel, H.: *ref,* 503, 529
Gensemer, I. B.: *ref,* 589
Gentile, J. R.: *ref,* 499, 505, 517
Gentry, D. E.: *ref,* 398, 419
Gentry, J.: *ref,* 357, 361
Gentry, W. D.: *ref,* 529
Georgas, J. G.: *ref,* 381, 529
George, E. I.: *ref,* 504, 6:555(4)
George, W. E.: *ref,* 361
Gerberich, J. R.: *ref,* 2:1377(16), 3:217(50)
Gerboth, R.: *ref,* 532
Gerdine, P. V. H.: *ref,* 529
Gerken, C. d'A.: *ref,* 480, 5:308(309)
Gerlach, H. M.: *ref,* 4:277(206)
Gerlach, M.: *ref,* 525
Germain, G. L.: *ref,* 532
Gerry, R.: *ref,* 357
Gershon, A.: *test,* 554-5, 562, 573, 581; *ref,* 357
Gerson, E. F.: *ref,* 484, 487, 497
Gerstein, A. I.: *ref,* 364, 532
Gerstein, R. A.: *ref,* 487, 497, 532
Gerstein, S.: *ref,* 525
Gerstman, L.: *ref,* 529
Gerstman, L. J.: *ref,* 529
Gerver, D.: *ref,* 533
Gerver, J. M.: *ref,* 525
Gesell, A.: *test,* 497; *ref,* 497
Gesell, A. L.: *ref,* 497
Gettys, R. H.: *ref,* 357
Getz, S. B.: *ref,* 532
Getzels, J. W.: *ref,* 482, 533, 542, 546
Geuting, M. P.: *ref,* 533
Gewirtz, J. L.: *ref,* 525
Geyer, D. L.: *ref,* 6:480(14)
Ghiselli, E. E.: *test,* 341; *ref,* 341, 438
Ghosh, S.: *ref,* 416
Ghosh, S. P.: *ref,* 525
Ghozeil, S.: *ref,* 525, 533
Giangreco, C. J.: *ref,* 499
Giannell, A. S.: *ref,* 529, 532, 6:438(522)
Giannitrapani, D.: *ref,* 529
Gianturco, J.: *ref,* 529
Gibbens, T. C. N.: *ref,* 439, 518
Gibbons, B. D.: *ref,* 382
Gibbons, C. C.: *ref,* 398
Gibbons, K. C.: *ref,* 331
Gibby, R. G.: *ref,* 425, 532
Gibeau, P. J.: *ref,* 529
Gibson, D.: *ref,* 525
Gibson, F. J.: *ref,* 525, 532
Gibson, H. B.: *exc,* 518; *ref,* 403, 439
Gibson, J.: *ref,* 529
Gibson, J. W.: *ref,* 542, 561
Gibson, Q. H.: *ref,* 364, 439
Gibson, R. M.: *ref,* 503
Gibson, W. M.: *ref,* 533
Gibson (Robert) & Sons, Glasgow, Ltd.: *test,* 422, 1:1045

Giebink, J. W.: *ref,* 516
Giedt, H. M.: *ref,* 532
Giese, W. J.: *ref,* 337
Giessow, F. J.: *ref,* 357
Gifford, D. W.: *ref,* 3:217(83)
Gifford, E.: *ref,* 525
Gifford, E. V.: *ref,* 525
Gilberstadt, H.: *ref,* 518, 529, 592
Gilbert, A. C. F.: *ref,* 357
Gilbert, H. B.: *ref,* 480
Gilbert, J.: *ref,* 426, 6:438(497)
Gilbert, J. G.: *ref,* 381, 533
Gilbert, W. M.: *ref,* 5:308(300)
Giles, G. C.: *ref,* 333, 439
Gilgash, C. A.: *ref,* 532
Gilhooly, F. M.: *ref,* 532
Gill, G.: *ref,* 404
Gill, L. N.: *ref,* 398
Gill, M.: *ref,* 532
Gill, M. J.: *ref,* 589
Gill, M. M.: *ref,* 532
Gill, M. P.: *test,* 387; *ref,* 398
Gill, M. R.: *ref,* 439, 525
Gillespie, H. F.: *ref,* 6:438(507)
Gillespie, P. H.: *ref,* 524
Gillette, A. L.: *ref,* 525
Gilliland, A. R.: *test,* 5:411; *ref,* 532, 4:354(1-4, 6-9)
Gilliland, H.: *test,* 380
Gillingham, W. H.: *ref,* 533
Gillman, S.: *ref,* 381, 543
Gilman, R. H.: *ref,* 349, 529
Gilmore, S. I.: *ref,* 516
Ginett, L. E.: *ref,* 532
Giniger, S.: *ref,* 436, 529
Ginsburg, G. P.: *ref,* 574
Ginther, M. L.: *ref,* 361
Gioioso, J. V.: *ref,* 489, 496, 525, 533
Girard, J. A. F.: *ref,* 340
Girdany, B. R.: *ref,* 497, 525
Girdner, J.: *ref,* 592
Githens, W. H.: *ref,* 382
Gitlitz, H. B.: *ref,* 381
Gittelman, M.: *ref,* 525, 533
Gittinger, J. W.: *ref,* 529
Givens, P. R.: *ref,* 542, 546, 551
Glad, J. R. B.: *ref,* 359, 400
Glading, J. C.: *ref,* 404
Gladney, M. B.: *ref,* 357
Gladstein, G. A.: *ref,* 5:326(4)
Glaister, B. R.: *ref,* 543
Glanville, A. D.: *ref,* 525
Glaser, R.: *ref,* 342, 404, 482
Glass, G. V: *ref,* 589
Glasser, A. J.: *ref,* 533
Gleason, J. B.: *ref,* 516
Glenn, I.: *ref,* 525
Glenn, R. T.: *ref,* 505, 525
Glenn, W. D.: *ref,* 525
Glennon, J. R.: *rev,* 431; *ref,* 482
Gleser, G. C.: *rev,* 551
Glick, H. N.: *ref,* 525
Glick, I. D.: *ref,* 529
Glidden, G. W.: *ref,* 391
Glik, E. E.: *ref,* 532
Gloeckler, T.: *ref,* 516, 533
Glowatsky, E.: *ref,* 381, 483, 533
Glucksberg, S.: *ref,* 574
Glucksman, M. L.: *ref,* 381
Glueck, E.: *ref,* 532
Glueck, S.: *ref,* 532
Gluskinos, U.: *ref,* 482
Gnauck, J.: *ref,* 400, 435

Goddard, H. H.: *test,* 578
Godfrey, L. L.: *ref,* 525
Goeckerman, R. W.: *ref,* 419
Goedicke, R.: *ref,* 361
Goens, B. D.: *ref,* 533, 538
Goertzen, S. M.: *ref,* 503
Goetzinger, C. P.: *ref,* 355, 439, 532, 543
Goetzinger, M. R.: *ref,* 439
Goff, C. E.: *ref,* 398
Goffeney, B.: *ref,* 381, 484, 533
Goldberg, B.: *ref,* 525
Goldberg, I. D.: *ref,* 487
Goldberg, J. S.: *ref,* 381, 400, 533, 575
Goldberg, L. R.: *ref,* 404, 532
Goldberg, W.: *ref,* 426
Golden, M.: *ref,* 487, 525
Goldenberg, S.: *ref,* 381, 518, 525, 533
Goldfarb, N.: *ref,* 529
Goldfarb, W.: *ref,* 426, 525, 529, 532, 545
Goldhor, H.: *ref,* 482
Goldman, B. A.: *rev,* 342, 349, 447; *ref,* 361, 529
Goldman, G. D.: *ref,* 532
Goldman, M.: *ref,* 532
Goldman, R.: *ref,* 525, 532
Goldman, R. J.: *ref,* 589
Goldman, R. K.: *ref,* 529
Goldman, S.: *ref,* 482
Goldsamt, M.: *ref,* 529
Goldsamt, M. R.: *ref,* 504
Goldschmid, M. L.: *rev,* 356, 528; *test,* 549; *ref,* 525, 549
Goldsmith, R. W.: *ref,* 543
Goldstein, A. D.: *ref,* 492
Goldstein, G.: *ref,* 529
Goldstein, H. S.: *ref,* 381, 533
Goldstein, K.: *ref,* 532
Goldstein, L. S.: *ref,* 489, 516, 525
Goldstein, M. J.: *ref,* 532
Goldstein, N. N.: *ref,* 532
Goldstein, N. P.: *ref,* 529, 592
Goldstein, R. H.: *ref,* 440
Goldstein, S. G.: *ref,* 529
Goldwasser, M. L.: *ref,* 532
Golen, M. E.: *ref,* 533
Golland, J. H.: *ref,* 529, 533
Gonen, J. Y.: *ref,* 529
Gonen, Y.: *ref,* 529
Goo, V.: *ref,* 382
Good, C. V.: *exc,* 497
Good, R. K.: *ref,* 349
Goodell, H.: *ref,* 529
Goodenough, D. R.: *ref,* 525, 529, 533
Goodenough, F. L.: *rev,* 507, 2:1382-3; *test,* 381, 509; *exc,* 497, 525; *ref,* 381, 507, 509, 525
Goodey, D. J.: *ref,* 525
Goodglass, H.: *ref,* 516
Goodling, R. A.: *ref,* 419
Goodman, J.: *ref,* 518, 533
Goodman, P.: *ref,* 561, 574, 577
Goodner, S.: *ref,* 426
Goodstein, L. D.: *ref,* 358, 361, 391, 532-3
Goodwin, N. L.: *ref,* 364
Goolishian, H. A.: *ref,* 532
Goolsby, T. M.: *ref,* 357, 361
Gordon, B. F.: *ref,* 482
Gordon, C.: *ref,* 529

INDEX OF NAMES

Gordon, D. A.: *ref,* 525
Gordon, E.: *ref,* 391
Gordon, G.: *ref,* 538, 574, 578
Gordon, H. C.: *ref,* 426
Gordon, I. E.: *ref,* 403, 439
Gordon, J. M.: *ref,* 516
Gordon, J. R.: *ref,* 387, 398
Gordon, K.: *ref,* 525
Gordon, K. K.: *ref,* 357
Gordon, L. V.: *ref,* 433, 525
Gordon, M. A.: *ref,* 349
Gordon, O.: *ref,* 547
Gordon, O. J.: *ref,* 547
Gordon, R. E.: *ref,* 357
Gordon, R. G.: *ref,* 507
Gordon, W.: *ref,* 529
Gorelick, J.: *ref,* 381, 516, 518
Gorham, D. R.: *test,* 440; *ref,* 440, 532
Goshal, A. H. S.: *ref,* 425
Gothberg, L. C.: *ref,* 525, 532
Gough, H. G.: *ref,* 365
Goulard, L. J.: *ref,* 505
Goulard, S. E.: *ref,* 505
Gould, G.: *ref,* 4:277(178)
Goulet, L. R.: *ref,* 525
Gourevitch, V.: *ref,* 529, 533
Gourlay, N.: *ref,* 439, 461, 525
Gowan, J. C.: *ref,* 381, 439, 589, 5:308(419, 434), 6:438(480–1)
Goyen, J.: *ref,* 533
Goyne, J. B.: *ref,* 532
Grabow, J. D.: *ref,* 439, 518, 525, 533
Grabow, J. M.: *ref,* 533
Grace, A. G.: *ref,* 426
Graczykowska-Koczorowska, A.: *ref,* 532
Grad, B.: *ref,* 529, 532, 592
Graff, R. W.: *ref,* 357
Gragg, D. B.: *ref,* 525, 3:217(75)
Graham, C.: *ref,* 403, 533
Graham, D.: *ref,* 354, 373, 408, 425, 462
Graham, D. D.: *ref,* 525
Graham, E. E.: *ref,* 529, 532–3
Graham, G. A.: *ref,* 538
Graham, J.: *ref,* 559
Graham, J. L.: *ref,* 426
Graham, L. F.: *ref,* 5:308(385)
Graham, V. T.: *ref,* 525, 545
Graham, W. R.: *ref,* 361, 5:308(350)
Grajales, M. C.: *ref,* 518, 532
Graliker, B.: *ref,* 497
Graliker, B. V.: *ref,* 497
Grandovic, M. C.: *ref,* 381, 533
Granick, S.: *ref,* 381, 439, 496, 525, 529
Grant, A.: *ref,* 435, 3:255(9–10)
Grant, D. L.: *ref,* 333, 361
Grant, G. V.: *test,* 584, 7:438–9; *ref,* 541
Grant, T. N.: *ref,* 543
Grant, W. V.: *ref,* 4:277(242)
Grant, W. W.: *ref,* 497
Grantham-McGregor, S. M.: *ref,* 497
Grassi, J. R.: *ref,* 532
Grater, H.: *ref,* 5:308(379)
Graubard, P. S.: *ref,* 516, 533
Gravem, H.: *ref,* 484, 525
Graves, G. R.: *ref,* 516, 533
Graves, K. B.: *ref,* 525

Gray, C. V.: *ref,* 532
Gray, E. A.: *ref,* 533
Gray, J.: *ref,* 525, 532, 3:217(98)
Gray, J. A.: *ref,* 348
Gray, J. E.: *ref,* 381, 439
Gray, J. J.: *ref,* 546, 561, 572–3, 591
Gray, M. G.: *ref,* 503
Gray, P. L.: *ref,* 525
Greco, G. F.: *ref,* 361
Gredler, G. R.: *ref,* 533
Greemore, R.: *ref,* 516
Green, C. W.: *ref,* 425
Green, E.: *ref,* 525
Green, E. J.: *ref,* 382
Green, H. B.: *ref,* 529, 533
Green, H. J.: *ref,* 438, 525
Green, J. H.: *ref,* 425
Green, J. L.: *ref,* 361
Green, M. W.: *ref,* 439
Green, R.: *ref,* 532
Green, R. B.: *ref,* 400, 439
Green, R. F.: *rev,* 361, 451, 468, 6:468; *ref,* 529, 532
Green, R. M.: *ref,* 538
Greenberg, B. L.: *ref,* 364
Greenberg, B. S.: *ref,* 404
Greenberg, G.: *ref,* 529
Greenberg, I. M.: *ref,* 529
Greenberg, N. E.: *ref,* 525, 532
Greenberg, S. H.: *ref,* 364
Greenblatt, M.: *ref,* 532
Greenbloom, G. C.: *ref,* 532
Greenburg, H.: *ref,* 529, 543
Greene, C. L.: *ref,* 381
Greene, E. B.: *ref,* 525, 545, 3:217(72)
Greene, J. E.: *ref,* 419, 4:277(211, 250)
Greene, J. F.: *ref,* 589
Greene, K. B.: *ref,* 525
Greene, M. C. L.: *ref,* 533
Greene, P. C.: *ref,* 3:217(84)
Greenfield, A.: *ref,* 559, 561
Greenland, T. C.: *ref,* 358
Greenly, R. J.: *ref,* 426, 6:480(40)
Greenmun, R.: *ref,* 533
Greenwood, D. I.: *ref,* 529
Greenwood, E. D.: *ref,* 503, 532
Greenwood, R. L.: *ref,* 6:438(508)
Greer, D.: *ref,* 517
Greeson, L. E.: *ref,* 525
Gregg, R.: *ref,* 525
Gregor, A. J.: *exc,* 518; *ref,* 518
Gregory, C. L.: *ref,* 419
Grehl, P. F.: *ref,* 6:438(447)
Gremillion, B. J.: *ref,* 361
Gressett, J. D.: *ref,* 529
Grice, J. E.: *ref,* 525, 538
Grief, E. G.: *ref,* 533
Grieneeks, L.: *ref,* 357
Griess, J. A.: *ref,* 349
Grieve, T. D.: *ref,* 559, 561
Griffin, D. C.: *ref,* 533
Griffin, J. V.: *ref,* 348, 425, 447
Griffin, W. M.: *ref,* 361, 542, 551
Griffith, J.: *ref,* 516, 522
Griffith, R. M.: *ref,* 342, 529, 532
Griffiths, A. W.: *ref,* 529
Griffiths, J. S.: *ref,* 532
Griffiths, R.: *test,* 6:523; *ref,* 525, 5:404(1–3), 6:480(33, 36–8), 6:523(4–5)
Grigg, A. E.: *ref,* 452

Grilk, W.: *ref,* 391
Grimaldi, J.: *ref,* 533
Grimes, J. W.: *ref,* 399, 5:326(31)
Grimsley, G.: *ref,* 361
Grimsley, W. G.: *ref,* 542, 546, 551, 561, 577
Grimsrud, R. A.: *ref,* 359, 404, 419
Grinder, R. E.: *ref,* 381, 496
Grippaldi, R.: *ref,* 529
Grisell, J.: *ref,* 533
Grisso, J. T.: *ref,* 529
Griswold, B. B.: *ref,* 529, 574
Grohmann, M.: *ref,* 529
Grohsmeyer, F. A.: *ref,* 482
Gropper, R. L.: *ref,* 425, 516
Gross, A. T.: *ref,* 361
Gross, D. G.: *ref,* 381, 489
Gross, F. L.: *ref,* 525, 529, 533
Gross, J. B.: *ref,* 529, 592
Gross, M.: *ref,* 381, 489, 516, 525
Gross, M. B.: *ref,* 525
Gross, N.: *ref,* 361
Gross, R. B.: *ref,* 529
Grossberg, J. M.: *ref,* 496, 533
Grossman, J. L.: *ref,* 529
Grossman, J. S.: *ref,* 529
Grossman, M.: *ref,* 516, 589
Grossman, M. J.: *ref,* 589
Grossmann, K.: *ref,* 529
Grosvenor, T.: *ref,* 426, 439
Grotelueschen, A.: *exc,* 424; *ref,* 529, 7:378(4–5, 8)
Grove, W. R.: *rev,* 483; *test,* 2:1408; *ref,* 533, 2:1401(5), 2:1408(1–3)
Grover, B. L.: *ref,* 589
Grover, V. M.: *ref,* 507
Groves, J. W.: *ref,* 426
Groves, M. H.: *ref,* 532
Growden, C. H.: *ref,* 525
Gruber, A.: *test,* 6:491
Gruber, E. C.: *ref,* 357
Gruber, J. J.: *ref,* 357
Gruen, A.: *ref,* 529
Gruen, R. S.: *ref,* 424
Gruenfeld, L. W.: *ref,* 337, 442, 559
Gruneberg, M. M.: *ref,* 357
Guarino, E. A.: *ref,* 533
Guazzo, J. J.: *ref,* 5:308(351)
Guerrant, J.: *ref,* 503, 592
Guertin, W. H.: *rev,* 529; *ref,* 529, 532
Guest, K. E.: *ref,* 538
Guest, L.: *ref,* 482
Guiler, W. S.: *ref,* 419, 426, 525, 2:1424(9)
Guilford, J. P.: *rev,* 382, 391, 404, 419, 3:217, 3:238, 5:326; *test,* 341A, 457, 542, 546, 551, 554–5, 561c2–3, 561d1–3, 561d3, 561m3, 561o3, 561p2–3, 561q2, 561r3, 561s1, 561s3, 561x2–3, 562, 564–8, 571–3, 577, 579, 581, 583, 591; *ref,* 341A, 349, 457, 542, 546, 551, 555, 561–2, 564, 571–3, 577, 579, 581, 591, 4:281(80)
Guilliams, C. I.: *ref,* 361, 574
Guinagh, B. J.: *ref,* 439
Guinn, M. P.: *ref,* 5:308(279)
Guion, R. M.: *ref,* 337
Gulutsan, M.: *ref,* 361
Gummere, J. F.: *ref,* 357
Gundersen, R. O.: *ref,* 348–9, 400
Gunn, R. L.: *test,* 481

Gunnell, D. C.: *ref,* 426
Gunning, I. C.: *ref,* 419
Gunther, M. K.: *ref,* 381
Gunzburg, H. C.: *ref,* 381
Gupta, G. C.: *ref,* 439
Gupta, K. P.: *ref,* 439
Gupta, S.: *ref,* 439
Gurevitz, S.: *ref,* 381, 525
Gurvitz, M.: *test,* 447; *ref,* 447
Gurvitz, M. S.: *ref,* 532, 4:315(11)
Gusloff, R. F.: *ref,* 489
Gustafson, E. A.: *ref,* 425
Gustafson, M. C.: *ref,* 361
Gustafson, R. G.: *ref,* 400
Gutekunst, J. G.: *ref,* 545, 6:438 (464)
Guth, R. O.: *ref,* 589
Guthrie, G. M.: *ref,* 525, 533, 561
Gutman, B.: *ref,* 532
Guy, W.: *ref,* 532
Guyette, A.: *ref,* 529
Gwaltney, W.: *ref,* 349, 516, 522, 533
Gwaltney, W. K.: *ref,* 398
Gwynne Jones, H.: *ref,* 439
Gynther, M. D.: *ref,* 440, 503, 529, 543

HAAG, C. H.: *ref,* 525
Haag, R. A.: *ref,* 542, 574
Haak, L. A.: *ref,* 405
Haakonsen, H. O.: *ref,* 361, 546
Haan, N.: *ref,* 525
Haanstad, M.: *ref,* 439, 529
Haas, A.: *ref,* 529
Haas, J.: *ref,* 533
Haas, L.: *ref,* 391
Haas, M. G.: *ref,* 425, 542
Haber, W.: *ref,* 433, 532
Hackett, J. R.: *ref,* 426
Hackman, J. R.: *ref,* 382
Hackman, R. B.: *ref,* 349, 532
Hackman, R. C.: *ref,* 438
Hackney, K. U.: *ref,* 469
Haddon, F. A.: *ref,* 409, 589
Hadley, D. J.: *ref,* 589
Hadley, J. M.: *ref,* 337
Hadley, S. T.: *test,* 378
Hafemeister, N.: *ref,* 447, 525
Hafner, A. J.: *ref,* 533
Hafner, L. E.: *ref,* 349, 533
Hage, D. S.: *ref,* 400
Hagen, E.: *test,* 351-2, 356, 400-1
Hagen, E. P.: *ref,* 533
Hagenah, T.: *ref,* 405, 6:438(502)
Haggerty, A. D.: *ref,* 532
Hagin, R. A.: *ref,* 381, 538
Hahn, M.: *ref,* 529
Hahn, M. E.: *ref,* 404
Hahn, M. S.: *ref,* 589
Haines, E. M.: *ref,* 3:217(143)
Haines, M. S.: *ref,* 507
Haines, R. B.: *ref,* 529
Hake, D.: *ref,* 439
Hakel, M. D.: *ref,* 405
Halcrow, J. H.: *ref,* 361
Hale, J. R.: *ref,* 516
Hale, P. P.: *ref,* 5:308(319)
Hales, N. M.: *ref,* 3:220(41)
Hales, W. M.: *ref,* 398
Hall, A. E.: *ref,* 574
Hall, B. W.: *ref,* 361
Hall, E.: *ref,* 361, 382, 404
Hall, H. E.: *ref,* 425

Hall, J. C.: *ref,* 381, 439, 516, 529, 532, 543
Hall, K. R. L.: *ref,* 532
Hall, L. P.: *ref,* 533
Hall, L. T.: *ref,* 348, 361
Hall, M. R.: *ref,* 381
Hall, V. C.: *exc,* 549
Hall, W. E.: *ref,* 529
Halladay, R. E.: *ref,* 357
Hallberg, M. C.: *ref,* 532
Hallenbeck, C. E.: *ref,* 529
Halliday, R. W.: *ref,* 426
Hallowell, D. K.: *ref,* 525
Hallworth, H. J.: *ref,* 409, 439, 446
Halperin, S. L.: *ref,* 532
Halpern, A. S.: *ref,* 529
Halpern, F.: *ref,* 525, 532
Halpern, S. K.: *ref,* 574
Halstead, H.: *ref,* 354, 403, 439, 532, 3:273(5)
Halverson, H. M.: *ref,* 497
Ham, D. G.: *ref,* 574
Hamby, T. M.: *ref,* 589
Hamilton, D. D. H.: *ref,* 391
Hamilton, J.: *ref,* 532
Hamilton, M. E.: *ref,* 483, 525
Hamilton, V.: *ref,* 331, 403, 439
Hamister, R. C.: *ref,* 532
Hamlett, I. C.: *ref,* 532, 588
Hamlin, R.: *ref,* 525, 558, 578
Hamlin, R. M.: *ref,* 529, 532
Hamlin, R. W.: *ref,* 529
Hamm, B. H.: *ref,* 357
Hammer, E. F.: *ref,* 349, 588
Hammill, D.: *ref,* 516, 524
Hammill, D. D.: *ref,* 516, 524-5
Hammond, L. L.: *ref,* 400
Hanawalt, N. G.: *rev,* 543
Hanchey, G. B.: *ref,* 4:277(151)
Hand, J.: *ref,* 533
Handel, A.: *ref,* 439
Handley, W. B.: *ref,* 538
Handrich, M.: *ref,* 381
Haner, C.: *ref,* 532
Haner, C. F.: *ref,* 480, 482, 532, 5:308(352)
Hanes, B.: *ref,* 426, 447
Hanesian, H.: *ref,* 525
Haney, R.: *ref,* 457
Hanfmann, E.: *ref,* 558
Hanley, C.: *ref,* 532
Hanna, G. S.: *ref,* 348, 424, 529
Hanna, J. V.: *ref,* 419, 5:308(297)
Hanna, R.: *ref,* 381
Hannaford, A. E.: *ref,* 533
Hänninen, H.: *ref,* 529, 543
Hannon, J. E.: *ref,* 529, 533
Hannum, T. E.: *ref,* 529
Hansen, C. F.: *ref,* 3:220(23)
Hansen, C. W.: *ref,* 349
Hansen, D. N.: *ref,* 524, 529
Hansen, E. A.: *ref,* 391
Hansen, F. W.: *ref,* 532
Hansen, L. H.: *ref,* 471, 522
Hansen, W. L.: *ref,* 382
Hanske, C. F.: *ref,* 3:263(37)
Hanson, A. J.: *ref,* 5:308(283)
Hanson, D. E.: *ref,* 589
Hanson, E.: *ref,* 381
Hanson, G. R.: *ref,* 405
Hanson, H. B.: *ref,* 518, 525, 532
Hanson, R.: *ref,* 445, 482
Hanvik, L. J.: *ref,* 381
Haralson, S.: *ref,* 529

Harasymiw, S. J.: *ref,* 436
Harckham, L. D.: *ref,* 381
Hardaway, C.: *ref,* 5:308(320)
Hardesty, D. L.: *ref,* 361, 371, 404
Hardin, R. A.: *ref,* 419
Harding, D. W.: *ref,* 439
Harding, F. D.: *ref,* 482
Harding, W. T.: *ref,* 361
Hardy, J. B.: *ref,* 381, 484, 525, 533
Hardy, M. C.: *ref,* 525
Hardy, M. P.: *ref,* 516, 533
Hardy, R. E.: *ref,* 500, 529
Hardyck, C.: *ref,* 529
Hardyck, C. D.: *ref,* 551
Hare, J.: *test,* 331
Hare, R. D.: *ref,* 361
Harford, T.: *ref,* 439, 529
Haritos-Fatouros, M.: *ref,* 518, 529, 533
Hariu, T.: *ref,* 513
Harkey, S. M.: *ref,* 440
Harless, B. B.: *test,* 5:394
Harley, R. K.: *ref,* 489, 496, 516, 6:537(5)
Harlow, J. E.: *ref,* 525, 533
Harlow, S. D.: *ref,* 382, 404, 551, 561, 591
Harman, C. E.: *ref,* 381
Harman, H. H.: *ref,* 525
Harmon, L. R.: *test,* 3:251
Harms, C. R.: *ref,* 400
Harms, I. E.: *ref,* 487
Haronian, F.: *ref,* 529
Harootunian, B.: *ref,* 349, 425
Harootunian, B. A.: *ref,* 349, 425
Harper, A. E.: *ref,* 532
Harper, M.: *ref,* 525
Harper, P.: *ref,* 494, 497
Harper, P. A.: *ref,* 533
Harrell, M. S.: *ref,* 342
Harrell, T. W.: *ref,* 342, 423
Harrell, W.: *ref,* 426
Harriman, P. L.: *ref,* 525
Harrington, M. J.: *ref,* 425
Harris, A. J.: *rev,* 380; *ref,* 364, 425-6, 525, 533
Harris, B. R.: *ref,* 381, 400, 533, 575
Harris, C. W.: *ref,* 457, 561
Harris, D. B.: *test,* 381; *exc,* 525; *ref,* 381, 439, 507
Harris, H.: *ref,* 533
Harris, H. I.: *ref,* 503
Harris, J.: *ref,* 357
Harris, J. A.: *ref,* 382
Harris, J. D.: *ref,* 503
Harris, R.: *ref,* 532-3, 574
Harris, R. E.: *ref,* 381, 532
Harris, Y. Y.: *ref,* 361
Harrison, A. W.: *ref,* 403
Harrison, B.: *ref,* 426
Harrison, C. W.: *ref,* 382, 404
Harrison, G. J.: *ref,* 331, 446
Harrison, K.: *ref,* 440, 532
Harrison, M. R.: *ref,* 3:217(100)
Harrison, R.: *ref,* 482
Harrison, R. H.: *ref,* 525
Harrower, M.: *ref,* 532
Harrower, M. R.: *ref,* 532
Harshman, R. C.: *ref,* 403
Hart, A. M.: *ref,* 589
Hart, H.: *ref,* 525
Hart, M. E.: *ref,* 357
Hart, N. W. M.: *ref,* 512

Harte, M. L.: *ref*, 533
Harter, D. I.: *ref*, 525
Harter, S.: *ref*, 525
Hartford, D. L.: *ref*, 358
Hartlage, L. C.: *ref*, 503, 529, 533
Hartley, J.: *ref*, 331
Hartman, A. A.: *ref*, 3:220(63), 4:317(3)
Hartman, B.: *ref*, 525
Hartman, B. O.: *ref*, 529
Hartman, B. T.: *ref*, 516
Hartman, L. D.: *ref*, 487, 525
Hartman, R. K.: *ref*, 381, 533, 538, 589
Hartnett, R. T.: *ref*, 357
Hartsock, W. W.: *ref*, 404
Hartson, L. D.: *ref*, 391, 398, 419, 426, 525, 3:263(45), 4:324(56)
Hartson, L. S.: *rev*, 419
Harvey, E. D.: *ref*, 361
Harvey, J.: *ref*, 529
Harvey, O. J.: *ref*, 589
Harville, D. L.: *ref*, 357
Harwood, B. T.: *ref*, 529
Harwood, E.: *ref*, 529
Hascall, E. O.: *ref*, 426
Häseth, K.: *ref*, 439, 547–8
Hashmi, S. A.: *ref*, 473
Haskell, S. H.: *ref*, 529, 533
Haslam, P.: *ref*, 483, 507
Hasson, D. J.: *ref*, 424
Hatfield, R. C.: *ref*, 349, 589
Hathaway, M. L.: *ref*, 502
Hatt, E.: *ref*, 507, 525
Haugen, E. S.: *ref*, 361, 529
Haughey, C.: *ref*, 391, 533
Haun, K. W.: *ref*, 357
Haupt, T. D.: *ref*, 516, 533
Haury, G.: *ref*, 525
Hause, E.: *ref*, 3:242(5)
Hauser, L. J. M.: *ref*, 4:277(207)
Hauser, R. J.: *ref*, 532
Haven, G. A.: *ref*, 589
Havens, R. I.: *ref*, 419
Havens, V.: *ref*, 4:277(187)
Havighurst, R. J.: *ref*, 348–9, 381, 391, 398, 425, 483, 518, 525, 532, 4:324(59)
Haw, A. B.: *ref*, 525
Haward, L. R. C.: *ref*, 381, 532
Hawke, W. A.: *ref*, 497
Hawkes, N. J.: *ref*, 426
Hawkins, H. M.: *ref*, 518, 532
Hawkins, W. A.: *ref*, 482
Hawkins, W. F.: *ref*, 533
Haworth, M. R.: *rev*, 525, 6:537; *ref*, 381, 525, 533
Hay, E. N.: *test*, 345; *exc*, 525; *ref*, 341A, 426, 482
Hayasaka, K.: *ref*, 513
Hayden, B. S.: *ref*, 533
Hayden, D. L.: *ref*, 425, 533
Hayden, M. P.: *ref*, 543
Hayden, S. J.: *ref*, 532
Hayes, E. M.: *ref*, 361, 400
Hayes, S. P.: *ref*, 525, 532
Haynes, C. R.: *ref*, 542, 546, 573
Haynes, E. F.: *ref*, 349
Haynes, J. O.: *ref*, 5:308(380)
Hays, W.: *ref*, 532
Hayweiser, L.: *ref*, 525
Haywood, H. C.: *ref*, 516
Haywood, N. R.: *ref*, 538
Hazari, A.: *ref*, 439

Heal, L. W.: *ref*, 516
Healy, W.: *test*, 558; *ref*, 558, 2:1390(3), 2:1391(6), 2:1394(3), 2:1401(2)
Heard, W. G.: *ref*, 357
Heathers, L. B.: *ref*, 532, 5:308(328)
Heaton, J. M.: *ref*, 361
Heaton-Ward, W. A.: *ref*, 525
Heaxt, S.: *ref*, 357
Heber, R. F.: *ref*, 398
Hebron, M. E.: *test*, 397, 463
Hecht, I.: *ref*, 532
Hecht, P. J.: *ref*, 533
Hecht, R.: *ref*, 426
Hecht, R. M.: *ref*, 423
Hecker, A. O.: *ref*, 532
Heckman, S. B.: *ref*, 381, 435, 438, 525
Hector, H.: *test*, 6:459; *ref*, 6:459(1)
Hedger, M. F.: *ref*, 496, 516
Hedl, J. J.: *ref*, 524, 529
Hedley, C. N.: *ref*, 361
Hedlund, D. E.: *ref*, 357, 359
Hegge, T. G.: *ref*, 439
Heil, L. M.: *ref*, 357
Heilbrun, A. B.: *rev*, 440; *ref*, 529, 532, 543
Heilman, J. D.: *ref*, 525, 3:217(101)
Heim, A. W.: *rev*, 363, 375, 397, 428, 5:325, 6:470; *test*, 331; *ref*, 331, 439
Heimann, R. A.: *ref*, 574, 587
Heinichen, F. W. O.: *test*, 383, 501
Heiss, W. E.: *ref*, 533
Heister, D. S.: *ref*, 532
Helin, W. C.: *ref*, 364, 574
Heller, A. D.: *ref*, 381
Helm, C. E.: *ref*, 436
Helme, W. H.: *ref*, 381, 525
Helmick, J. S.: *ref*, 532
Helper, M. M.: *ref*, 518
Helseth, B. J.: *ref*, 497
Helson, R.: *ref*, 542
Hemberger, L. W.: *ref*, 533
Hemenway, J.: *test*, 586
Hemmeter, J. T.: *ref*, 357
Henderson, E. H.: *ref*, 589
Henderson, E. M.: *ref*, 497
Henderson, H. L.: *ref*, 5:308(407, 420), 6:438(465)
Henderson, K.: *ref*, 381
Henderson, N.: *ref*, 349, 525
Henderson, N. B.: *ref*, 381, 484, 533, 6:438(466)
Henderson, R. W.: *test*, 430–1, 478–9, 3:252, 4:276, 7:399
Hendrick, I.: *exc*, 497
Hendrickson, G.: *ref*, 426, 3:220(40)
Hendrickson, G. F.: *ref*, 357
Hendrix, O. R.: *ref*, 419, 5:308(321, 353)
Hendrix, R.: *ref*, 533
Heninger, G. R.: *ref*, 529
Henker, B. A.: *ref*, 518
Henmon, V. A. C.: *rev*, 1:1038; *ref*, 391, 438, 525, 2:1377(28)
Henning, J. A.: *ref*, 426
Henning, J. J.: *ref*, 529, 533
Henning, R. L.: *ref*, 532
Henrickson, P. R.: *ref*, 589

Henry, E. R.: *rev*, 4:316–7
Henry, J. A.: *ref*, 525
Henry, M. B.: *ref*, 398
Henson, J. P.: *ref*, 589
Hepburn, A. W.: *ref*, 381
Herbert, N.: *ref*, 409
Herbstritt, R. L.: *ref*, 357
Herke, M. L.: *ref*, 5:308(322)
Herman, D. O.: *ref*, 538
Herman, K.: *ref*, 532, 592
Herman, S. J.: *ref*, 484
Hermann, M. G.: *ref*, 357, 542
Hermann, R. S.: *ref*, 496
Hernandez, D.: *ref*, 361
Herndon, C. N.: *ref*, 532
Herndon, J. D.: *ref*, 516, 533
Heron, A.: *ref*, 403, 439
Herr, S. E.: *ref*, 435
Herrans, L. L.: *ref*, 529
Herrell, J. M.: *ref*, 529, 533
Herrick, C. J.: *ref*, 505, 518, 525
Herrick, V. E.: *ref*, 348, 391, 398, 425
Herring, F. H.: *ref*, 532
Herring, J. P.: *test*, 2:1399; *ref*, 518, 525, 2:1399(1, 4–7)
Herrmann, M.: *ref*, 349, 532
Herron, W. G.: *ref*, 381, 440, 529, 533
Hersh, J. B.: *ref*, 525
Hershenson, D. B.: *ref*, 533
Hertel, J. P.: *ref*, 419
Hertel, R. K.: *ref*, 533
Hertzberg, O. E.: *ref*, 507, 525
Hertzig, M. E.: *ref*, 525, 533
Hertzka, A. F.: *test*, 561q2
Hess, R. D.: *ref*, 5:326(3)
Heston, J. C.: *ref*, 419, 518, 525, 4:277(179, 188)
Hetrick, S. H.: *ref*, 561
Heussenstamm, F. K.: *ref*, 542, 555, 564, 573, 594
Hewer, V. H.: *ref*, 405, 419, 5:308(421)
Hewes, A.: *ref*, 525
Hewitt, B. A.: *ref*, 357
Hewitt, P. S.: *ref*, 533
Hewlett, J. H. G.: *ref*, 504, 6:555(5)
Hewson, L. R.: *ref*, 532
Heydenberk, W. R.: *ref*, 340, 516
Heyer, A. W.: *ref*, 532
Hichens, J. H.: *ref*, 439
Hicks, D.: *ref*, 589
Hicks, J. A.: *ref*, 518
Hicks, J. M.: *ref*, 361
Hicks, V. C.: *ref*, 525
Hierholzer, H. M.: *test*, 3:285; *ref*, 3:285(2)
Hieronymus, A. N.: *ref*, 349, 391, 398, 400, 425
Hiester, D. S.: *ref*, 529
Higashimachi, W. H.: *ref*, 439
Higbee, W. R.: *ref*, 529
Higdon, B. P.: *ref*, 439
Higgins, C.: *test*, 560; *ref*, 425, 439, 525
Higgins, J.: *ref*, 574
Higginson, J. B.: *ref*, 525, 533
High, W. S.: *ref*, 349
Highfield, M. E.: *ref*, 525
Highley, F. S.: *ref*, 357
Higuchi, J. L.: *ref*, 484
Hilbun, S.: *ref*, 4:277(195)

Hildebrand, H. P.: *ref,* 439
Hilden, A. H.: *ref,* 398, 483, 525, 532
Hildman, L. K.: *ref,* 533
Hildreth, G.: *test,* 1:1057, 1:1061; *exc,* 497, 2:1426; *ref,* 381, 525
Hildreth, G. H.: *ref,* 525
Hiler, E. W.: *ref,* 381, 532
Hilkevitch, R. R.: *ref,* 483
Hill, A. H.: *ref,* 572, 577
Hill, B. E.: *ref,* 492
Hill, G. H.: *ref,* 423
Hill, H. S.: *ref,* 426, 525
Hill, K. T.: *ref,* 400
Hill, S. D.: *ref,* 419
Hill, T. V.: *ref,* 496, 516
Hillery, M. C.: *ref,* 589
Hilliard, A. G.: *ref,* 361
Hillix, W. A.: *ref,* 529, 533
Hillman, W. A.: *ref,* 489, 505, 516, 529
Hills, D. A.: *ref,* 439
Hills, J. R.: *rev,* 6:442; *ref,* 357, 361, 457
Hilton, A. C.: *ref,* 431
Hilton, T. L.: *ref,* 357, 361, 436
Hilty, D. P.: *ref,* 525
Himbert, J. D.: *ref,* 516
Himelstein, P.: *rev,* 517, 524; *ref,* 516, 525, 529, 533
Himmelweit, H. T.: *ref,* 388, 403, 439
Himwich, H. E.: *ref,* 529
Hindle, P. G.: *ref,* 357
Hindley, C. B.: *rev,* 6:523; *ref,* 525, 6:523(6-7)
Hindsman, E.: *ref,* 349, 542, 551
Hine, W. D.: *ref,* 533
Hine, W. W.: *ref,* 589
Hines, H. C.: *ref,* 2:1424(4)
Hinkelman, E. A.: *ref,* 398
Hinman, M. E. H.: *ref,* 525
Hinman, S. L.: *ref,* 426
Hinrichs, J. R.: *ref,* 359, 361
Hinrichs, W. E.: *ref,* 381
Hinton, B. L.: *ref,* 542, 551, 564
Hinton, G. G.: *ref,* 516, 533
Hinton, R. T.: *ref,* 483, 525
Hippe, D. L.: *ref,* 364, 574
Hirsch, E. A.: *ref,* 532-3
Hirsch, J.: *ref,* 381
Hirsch, M. J.: *ref,* 349, 525
Hirsch, N. D. M.: *ref,* 435, 3:255 (2)
Hirschenfang, S.: *ref,* 381, 489, 525, 529
Hirshoren, A.: *ref,* 525
Hirst, L. S.: *ref,* 533
Hirt, M. L.: *ref,* 529, 532
Hirt, Z. I.: *ref,* 525
Hiskey, M. S.: *rev,* 489, 498; *test,* 499; *ref,* 499, 525
Hite, L.: *ref,* 533
Hittinger, J.: *ref,* 525, 532, 3:217 (98)
Ho, D.: *ref,* 496, 525
Hoakley, Z. P.: *ref,* 483, 525
Hobbs, G. E.: *ref,* 532
Hoch, P.: *ref,* 525
Hoch, P. M.: *ref,* 532
Hochman, S. H.: *ref,* 559, 561
Hockey, S. W.: *ref,* 409
Hodges, W. F.: *ref,* 529
Hodgins, A. S.: *ref,* 516, 525

Hodgson, G. L.: *ref,* 532
Hodgson, R. W.: *ref,* 482
Hoefer, C.: *ref,* 507, 525
Hoepfner, R.: *test,* 567-8, 579, 583, 586; *exc,* 589; *ref,* 349, 457, 542, 546, 551, 561, 572, 577, 579, 581, 591
Hoerres, M. A.: *ref,* 5:308(354)
Hoffeditz, E. L.: *ref,* 398, 503
Hoffman, C. B.: *ref,* 349, 525
Hoffman, M.: *ref,* 532
Hoffman, P. J.: *ref,* 364
Hoffmeister, J. K.: *ref,* 589
Hofforth, R. A.: *ref,* 339
Hofmann, L. J.: *ref,* 533
Hofmeister, A.: *ref,* 525
Hofstaetter, P. R.: *ref,* 391
Hogan, H. P.: *ref,* 503, 525
Hogan, T. P.: *ref,* 496, 529
Hogben, D.: *ref,* 323
Hoggart, K.: *ref,* 518, 529
Hohenshil, T. H.: *ref,* 400
Hohman, L. B.: *ref,* 487, 525, 533
Hohne, H. H.: *ref,* 323
Hoke, E.: *ref,* 6:480(15)
Holcomb, G. W.: *ref,* 3:217(51)
Holden, R. H.: *rev,* 484; *ref,* 381, 439, 449, 496, 529
Holland, G. A.: *ref,* 525, 533
Holland, J. L.: *exc,* 589; *ref,* 357
Holland, P. E.: *ref,* 398, 525
Holland, W. R.: *ref,* 533
Hollender, J. W.: *ref,* 342, 529
Holliday, F.: *ref,* 384, 5:339(4, 6-8)
Hollingsworth, B. H.: *ref,* 532-3
Hollingsworth, J. D.: *ref,* 489
Hollingworth, L. S.: *ref,* 525, 2:1399(10), 4:281(79)
Hollock, N. J.: *ref,* 4:277(195)
Holloway, H. D.: *ref,* 533
Holly, K. A.: *ref,* 349
Holman, E. R.: *ref,* 589
Holmes, D. S.: *ref,* 529
Holmes, F. J.: *ref,* 426, 482
Holmes, J. A.: *ref,* 425
Holmes, J. C.: *ref,* 496
Holmes, J. L.: *ref,* 419, 5:308(363)
Holmes, J. S.: *ref,* 529
Holmes, M.: *ref,* 353
Holmes, W. R.: *ref,* 516
Holowinsky, I.: *ref,* 525
Holowinsky, I. Z.: *ref,* 381, 425
Holroyd, J.: *ref,* 533
Holroyd, J. C.: *ref,* 533
Holsopple, I. G.: *ref,* 398
Holt, J.: *ref,* 331
Holt, M.: *ref,* 525
Holt, R. R.: *ref,* 529, 532
Holt, W. G.: *ref,* 480, 5:308(355, 422)
Holtby, V. J.: *ref,* 361
Holtzman, W. H.: *ref,* 381, 440, 532-3
Holzberg, J. D.: *ref,* 447, 532
Holzinger, K. J.: *ref,* 525
Holzman, P. S.: *exc,* 529, 532
Hommel, R. W.: *ref,* 533
Honstead, C. A.: *ref,* 517
Honzik, M. P.: *rev,* 502, 507, 509; *exc,* 381; *ref,* 487, 525, 532-3
Hood, A. B.: *ref,* 361, 405
Hood, H. B.: *ref,* 4:334(6)
Hood, R. W.: *ref,* 574

Hooker, E.: *ref,* 529
Hooper, S.: *ref,* 533
Hoopes, J. L.: *ref,* 349
Hoops, H. R.: *ref,* 490
Hoover, M.: *ref,* 357
Hope, L. H.: *ref,* 357
Hopka, E.: *ref,* 349
Hopkins, B.: *ref,* 403, 439, 532
Hopkins, K. D.: *rev,* 465; *exc,* 360; *ref,* 348-9, 361, 391, 400, 533
Hopper, C. L.: *ref,* 529
Horlick, R. S.: *ref,* 532
Horn, J. L.: *rev,* 518; *exc,* 450; *ref,* 364
Hornaday, J. A.: *ref,* 357, 361
Horne, B. M.: *ref,* 525, 529
Horne, I. E.: *ref,* 495
Horobin, G.: *ref,* 373, 408-9
Horowitz, F. D.: *ref,* 529, 532-3
Horrall, B. M.: *ref,* 4:277(208)
Horrocks, C.: *ref,* 589
Horrocks, J. E.: *rev,* 467, 6:495
Horst, P.: *ref,* 592
Horton, C. P.: *ref,* 357, 382, 507
Horton, K. B.: *ref,* 525
Horton, S. P.: *ref,* 447
Horwitz, M.: *ref,* 439, 529, 532
Hoskins, J. E.: *ref,* 482
Hottel, J. V.: *ref,* 516
Houchins, R. R.: *ref,* 439
Houk, C. C.: *ref,* 419
Houlihan, R. A. M.: *ref,* 525
Hountras, P. T.: *ref,* 404
House, B.: *ref,* 529
House, B. J.: *ref,* 525
House, F. R.: *ref,* 525
Houser, J. D.: *ref,* 525
Houston, C.: *ref,* 522, 524, 533
Houston, J. P.: *ref,* 574
Houston, S. R.: *ref,* 382
Hover, G. L.: *ref,* 532
Hovey, H. B.: *ref,* 532
Hovland, C. I.: *rev,* 382, 404, 3:218, 3:263; *ref,* 426, 482
Howard, A. R.: *ref,* 592
Howard, J. L.: *ref,* 516-7, 525
Howard, J. O.: *ref,* 499, 525
Howard, J. S.: *ref,* 382
Howard, L.: *ref,* 525
Howard, M. J.: *ref,* 490
Howard, M. T.: *ref,* 518, 529, 578, 592
Howard, W.: *ref,* 529, 532
Howard, W. H. R.: *ref,* 497
Howell, A. A.: *ref,* 525
Howell, I. L.: *ref,* 532, 545
Howell, J. J.: *ref,* 357
Howell, R. J.: *ref,* 440, 529, 532
Howell, R. W.: *ref,* 533
Howell, W. J.: *ref,* 357
Howie, D.: *rev,* 324; *ref,* 328
Howlett, J. L.: *ref,* 357
Hoyt, C. J.: *rev,* 419
Hoyt, D. P.: *ref,* 357, 419, 5:308 (356), 6:438(478)
Hozier, A.: *ref,* 381
Hrdlicka, A.: *exc,* 497
Hsiao, H. H.: *ref,* 525, 3:220(45)
Hsiao, S. L.: *ref,* 447
Hubbard, O. S.: *ref,* 525
Huber, J. T.: *ref,* 382
Huber, T. G.: *ref,* 543
Hubschman, E.: *ref,* 516
Huck, C. S.: *ref,* 400

Huckabee, M. W.: *ref,* 559, 561
Hudson, F. G.: *ref,* 425, 493, 516, 533
Hudson, J.: *ref,* 529
Hudson, L.: *ref,* 331
Hueftle, M. K.: *ref,* 533
Huelsman, C. B.: *ref,* 533
Huesing, R.: *ref,* 381
Huff, B.: *ref,* 349, 361
Huff, F. W.: *ref,* 529
Huffman, W. J.: *ref,* 5:308(284)
Huggett, A. J.: *ref,* 5:354(6)
Hughes, B. E.: *ref,* 419
Hughes, D.: *ref,* 529
Hughes, D. H.: *ref,* 533
Hughes, D. L.: *ref,* 361
Hughes, H. O.: *ref,* 408
Hughes, J. M.: *ref,* 426
Hughes, L.: *ref,* 419
Hughes, L. S.: *ref,* 381
Hughes, R. B.: *ref,* 516, 533
Hughes, V. A.: *ref,* 533
Hughes, W. H.: *ref,* 398
Huguelet, P. W.: *ref,* 589
Huizinga, R. J.: *ref,* 525, 533
Hulicka, I. M.: *ref,* 529, 592
Hullett, J.: *ref,* 381
Hult, E.: *ref,* 391
Hultsch, C. L.: *ref,* 483, 525
Human Sciences Research Council: *test,* 383, 410-1, 511
Humm, K. A.: *ref,* 483
Humphreys, L. G.: *rev,* 404; *ref,* 364, 525
Humphries, C. C.: *ref,* 592
Hundal, P. S.: *ref,* 364, 439
Hundleby, J. D.: *rev,* 442, 6:491
Hunka, S.: *ref,* 561
Hunkin, V.: *ref,* 381
Hunsicker, L.: *ref,* 2:1377(14)
Hunt, B.: *ref,* 381
Hunt, B. M.: *ref,* 505, 525
Hunt, D.: *ref,* 525, 533
Hunt, E. P.: *rev,* 2:1400, 2:1410; *exc,* 483
Hunt, J. V.: *rev,* 523-4; *ref,* 484
Hunt, W.: *ref,* 482
Hunt, W. A.: *ref,* 503, 525, 529, 532
Hunt, W. L.: *ref,* 532
Hunter, C.: *exc,* 381
Hunter, D.: *ref,* 529
Hunter, E. C.: *ref,* 3:217(102)
Hunter, E. J.: *ref,* 533
Hunter, H.: *ref,* 518, 529
Hunter, H. T.: *ref,* 3:220(4)
Hunter, M.: *ref,* 505, 518, 525, 533
Hunter, R. C. A.: *ref,* 529
Hunter, T. A.: *ref,* 426
Huntley, R. M. C.: *ref,* 525
Huntress, D. W.: *ref,* 533
Hurd, A. W.: *ref,* 425-6
Hurley, J. D.: *ref,* 589
Hurley, J. R.: *ref,* 349
Hurst, J. G.: *ref,* 419, 507, 525
Hurt, R. W.: *ref,* 349
Hurwitz, H. L.: *ref,* 357
Husemoller, K. E.: *ref,* 361
Huskey, J. F.: *ref,* 426
Husted, J.: *ref,* 487
Hustmyer, F. E.: *ref,* 529
Huston, B. M.: *ref,* 425
Hutchcraft, G.: *ref,* 357
Hutchens, W. H.: *ref,* 503
Hutcheon, N. B.: *ref,* 4:277(154)

Hutchings, M.: *ref,* 3:242(2)
Hutchins, B. E.: *ref,* 361, 439
Hutchins, H. C.: *ref,* 357-8
Huth, R. W.: *ref,* 496
Hutson, B. T.: *ref,* 425
Hutt, M. L.: *ref,* 525, 545
Huttner, L.: *ref,* 482
Hutton, G. H.: *ref,* 529
Hutton, J. B.: *ref,* 524-5, 533
Hutton, R. D.: *ref,* 543
Huysamen, G. K.: *ref,* 381
Hvistendahl, J. K.: *ref,* 6:438(448)
Hwang, C. H.: *ref,* 439
Hyde, M. R.: *ref,* 516
Hylan, N. W.: *ref,* 426
Hylbert, K. W.: *ref,* 342
Hyman, I.: *ref,* 538, 578
Hyman, J. R.: *ref,* 489
Hyman, S. R.: *ref,* 404

IHLANFELDT, W. I.: *ref,* 357
Ikenberry, S. O.: *ref,* 358
Ilanit, N.: *ref,* 529
Ilg, F. L.: *ref,* 497
Illesley, R.: *ref,* 373, 408-9
Illingworth, R. S.: *ref,* 497
Im, I. J.: *ref,* 405
Imre, P. D.: *ref,* 529
Inaba, K.: *test,* 6:491
Indow, T.: *ref,* 533
Industrial Relations Center: *test,* 414, 472, 547, 594
Ingebo, G. S.: *ref,* 400
Ingham, J. G.: *ref,* 533
Inglis, J.: *ref,* 496, 529, 532
Ingmire, B. D.: *ref,* 589
Ingram, J. A.: *ref,* 361
Ingram, L. M.: *ref,* 419
Ingram, T. T. S.: *ref,* 381, 525
International Psychological Service Center: *ref,* 504, 4:339(1)
Ipson, W. M.: *ref,* 532
Ireton, H.: *ref,* 381, 484, 525
Ireton, H. R.: *test,* 508
Irish, T. E.: *ref,* 482
Irons, J. L.: *ref,* 589
Irvine, D. J.: *ref,* 542, 546, 551
Irvine, D. W.: *ref,* 357
Irvine, F. R.: *ref,* 589
Irvine, J.: *ref,* 516, 533
Irvine, S. H.: *ref,* 361, 439, 464
Irving, G.: *ref,* 403, 439
Irwin, D. O.: *ref,* 533
Irwin, O. C.: *exc,* 497; *ref,* 516, 525, 533
Isaac, D. M.: *ref,* 532
Isaacs, A.: *ref,* 426
Isaacson, L. E.: *ref,* 5:308(298)
Isard, E. S.: *ref,* 381, 419
Iscoe, I.: *ref,* 349, 355, 381, 439, 532-3, 542
Ismail, A. H.: *ref,* 364, 425
Ison, M. G.: *ref,* 529, 533
Israel, H.: *ref,* 525, 532
Israelite, J.: *ref,* 381
Ivanoff, J.: *ref,* 524, 529
Ivanoff, J. M.: *ref,* 357, 361, 516, 6:438(494)
Iversen, I.: *ref,* 525
Iverson, I. A.: *ref,* 533
Ivey, A. E.: *ref,* 357
Ivinskis, A.: *ref,* 529, 592

JACHUCK, K.: *ref,* 439
Jackson, B. J.: *ref,* 349
Jackson, C. L.: *ref,* 496, 516, 533
Jackson, C. V.: *ref,* 532
Jackson, D. N.: *ref,* 561
Jackson, E. M.: *ref,* 533
Jackson, M.: *ref,* 382
Jackson, M. A.: *ref,* 533
Jackson, M. M.: *ref,* 503
Jackson, P. W.: *ref,* 533
Jackson, R.: *ref,* 4:277(243)
Jackson, R. A.: *ref,* 5:308(381)
Jackson, R. L.: *ref,* 542, 546, 551
Jackson, T. A.: *ref,* 482
Jacobs, E. A.: *ref,* 592
Jacobs, G. F.: *ref,* 439, 532
Jacobs, O.: *ref,* 342, 404
Jacobs, P. I.: *ref,* 357, 439
Jacobs, R.: *ref,* 4:277(209, 244), 5:308(357)
Jacobs, R. E.: *ref,* 349
Jacobsen, T. L.: *ref,* 551
Jacobson, A.: *ref,* 524, 533
Jacobson, C. F.: *ref,* 482
Jacobson, F. N.: *ref,* 533
Jacobson, L. I.: *ref,* 525, 529, 574
Jacobson, S.: *ref,* 525, 533
Jacoby, J.: *ref,* 574
Jaffa, A. S.: *test,* 2:1383; *ref,* 2:1383(1)
Jaggers, C. H.: *ref,* 398, 426
Jahoda, G.: *ref,* 439, 491, 495
Jain, K. S. P.: *ref,* 439
Jamal, S.: *ref,* 425, 439
Jambor, K. L.: *ref,* 529
James, A.: *ref,* 525
James, E. B.: *ref,* 525
James, K. R.: *ref,* 404
James, L. R.: *ref,* 349, 357
James, P.: *ref,* 496, 516, 533
James, R. J.: *ref,* 357
James, R. W.: *ref,* 419
Jamieson, E.: *ref,* 435
Jamieson, G. H.: *ref,* 384-5, 403, 439
Jamuar, K. K.: *ref,* 439
Janke, L. L.: *ref,* 381, 518, 525, 532
Janoff, I. Z.: *ref,* 497
Jansen, D. G.: *ref,* 357, 404, 419
Janssen, C.: *ref,* 542, 546, 561, 572
Janssen, C. W.: *ref,* 542, 546, 561, 572
Janssen, R. H. C.: *ref,* 532
Janus, M.: *ref,* 426
Jaramillo, S.: *ref,* 381, 489, 525
Jardin, R. P.: *ref,* 382, 404
Jarman, P.: *ref,* 525
Jarmin, M. V.: *ref,* 419
Jaros, E.: *ref,* 533
Jaros, R. M.: *ref,* 503, 592
Jarrahi-Zadeh, A.: *ref,* 518
Jarrett, R. F.: *ref,* 518
Jarvie, H.: *ref,* 439
Jarvik, L. F.: *ref,* 525, 529, 532
Jaspen, N.: *ref,* 525
Jastak, J.: *ref,* 439, 525, 532
Jastak, J. F.: *ref,* 529, 533
Jastak, S. R.: *ref,* 529, 533
Jayagopal, R.: *ref,* 533
Jayalakshmi, G.: *ref,* 515, 545
Jeeves, M. A.: *ref,* 381, 533
Jeffree, D. M.: *ref,* 489, 516
Jeffress, S.: *ref,* 525, 3:217(75)
Jeffrey, T. E.: *test,* 547-8, 570
Jeffreys, L. C.: *ref,* 357

Jenkin, N.: *ref,* 532-3
Jenkins, A. C.: *ref,* 348
Jenkins, A. H.: *ref,* 574
Jenkins, C. D.: *ref,* 518, 525, 529, 543
Jenkins, J.: *ref,* 496
Jenkins, J. J.: *ref,* 419, 496
Jenkins, J. M.: *ref,* 542, 546, 561, 572
Jenkins, J. W.: *test,* 415; *exc,* 497
Jenkins, M. D.: *ref,* 525
Jenkins, N. L.: *ref,* 358
Jenkins, R. L.: *ref,* 525
Jennings, B. L.: *ref,* 589
Jennings, C. L.: *ref,* 529
Jennings, E.: *ref,* 349, 542, 551
Jennings, E. E.: *ref,* 482
Jensen, A. R.: *rev,* 340, 7:399; *ref,* 400, 439
Jensen, D. E.: *ref,* 381
Jensen, J. A.: *ref,* 524-5
Jensen, K.: *exc,* 497
Jensen, M. B.: *test,* 560A; *ref,* 342, 482, 496, 518, 560A
Jensen, O. M. J.: *ref,* 381
Jenson, G.: *ref,* 517, 525
Jenson, R. E.: *ref,* 404
Jerdee, T. H.: *ref,* 482
Jerrolds, B. W.: *ref,* 516, 522, 533
Jeruchimowicz, R.: *ref,* 516
Jewett, S. P.: *ref,* 525
Jex, F. B.: *rev,* 504; *ref,* 357, 425, 482, 6:438(442)
Jha, J.: *ref,* 543
Jillson, R. P.: *ref,* 533
Jimenez, C.: *ref,* 525
Jimmerson, S.: *ref,* 533
Joesting, J.: *ref,* 516, 522, 525, 533, 589
Joesting, R.: *ref,* 516, 522, 525, 533, 589
Jog, R. N.: *ref,* 388, 426
Johannsen, D. E.: *ref,* 381
John, E.: *ref,* 525
John, M. A. T.: *ref,* 546
Johns, D. J.: *ref,* 358
Johnson, A. P.: *ref,* 357, 361, 381, 426, 525, 532, 3:217(103-4), 5:308(323)
Johnson, B.: *ref,* 525, 558
Johnson, B. F.: *test,* 5:389
Johnson, B. G.: *ref,* 382
Johnson, B. J.: *ref,* 525, 558
Johnson, C. A.: *ref,* 381, 439, 516, 525
Johnson, C. I.: *ref,* 533
Johnson, C. M.: *ref,* 516, 589
Johnson, D. A.: *ref,* 574
Johnson, D. D.: *ref,* 533
Johnson, D. E.: *ref,* 439, 529
Johnson, D. L.: *ref,* 381, 439, 447, 482, 516, 525, 533
Johnson, D. M.: *ref,* 391
Johnson, D. R.: *ref,* 525, 532, 592
Johnson, D. T.: *ref,* 529
Johnson, E. E.: *ref,* 425, 588
Johnson, E. H.: *ref,* 355
Johnson, E. L.: *ref,* 361
Johnson, E. Z.: *ref,* 439, 483, 525
Johnson, G.: *ref,* 426, 5:308(299)
Johnson, G. B.: *ref,* 381, 426
Johnson, G. O.: *ref,* 489, 525
Johnson, H. H.: *ref,* 359
Johnson, H. S.: *ref,* 348

Johnson, J. A.: *ref,* 533
Johnson, J. E.: *ref,* 439
Johnson, J. J.: *ref,* 529
Johnson, J. K.: *ref,* 349
Johnson, J. M.: *ref,* 400
Johnson, J. O.: *ref,* 589
Johnson, J. T.: *ref,* 398
Johnson, J. W.: *ref,* 382
Johnson, L. C.: *ref,* 532-3
Johnson, M. C.: *ref,* 398
Johnson, M. H.: *ref,* 529
Johnson, M. L.: *ref,* 391, 561
Johnson, N. M.: *ref,* 484, 487
Johnson, O. J.: *ref,* 6:480(16)
Johnson, O. L.: *ref,* 533
Johnson, R.: *ref,* 400
Johnson, R. E. L.: *ref,* 528
Johnson, R. H.: *ref,* 342, 391, 398, 419, 426
Johnson, R. J.: *ref,* 358
Johnson, R. T.: *ref,* 589
Johnson, R. W.: *ref,* 357
Johnson, S. A. H.: *ref,* 439
Johnson, T. F.: *ref,* 532
Johnson, W. E.: *ref,* 349
Johnson, W. R.: *ref,* 533
Johnston, F. N.: *ref,* 404
Johnston, R. A.: *ref,* 6:438(534)
Joiner, L. M.: *ref,* 533
Jonckheere, J.: *ref,* 533
Jones, A. H.: *ref,* 3:220(37)
Jones, A. L.: *ref,* 349, 361, 5:308(432)
Jones, A. M.: *ref,* 525
Jones, A. W.: *ref,* 381
Jones, B. M.: *ref,* 439
Jones, C. H.: *ref,* 435
Jones, D. C.: *ref,* 460
Jones, E. L. H.: *ref,* 538
Jones, E. M.: *ref,* 331, 446
Jones, E. S.: *ref,* 3:220(11)
Jones, F. D.: *ref,* 518
Jones, G. A. A.: *ref,* 2:1377(22)
Jones, G. L.: *ref,* 558
Jones, G. T.: *ref,* 533
Jones, H. E.: *ref,* 525, 3:220(45)
Jones, H. G.: *rev,* 6:514, 6:519; *ref,* 525, 529
Jones, J. C.: *ref,* 589
Jones, J. G.: *ref,* 357
Jones, K. J.: *ref,* 349, 426, 6:438(523)
Jones, L. V.: *ref,* 439, 525
Jones, N. F.: *ref,* 529
Jones, P. P.: *ref,* 349
Jones, R. A.: *ref,* 357, 382, 457
Jones, R. D.: *ref,* 4:277(174)
Jones, R. E.: *ref,* 529
Jones, R. L.: *ref,* 489, 529, 533, 6:438(509)
Jones, R. W.: *ref,* 516, 533
Jones, S.: *ref,* 533
Jones, S. A.: *ref,* 516
Jones, V. A.: *ref,* 525
Jones, W. A.: *ref,* 6:438(441)
Jones, W. J.: *exc,* 3:247
Jones, W. P.: *exc,* 451; *ref,* 451
Jones, W. R.: *ref,* 363, 409, 415
Jones, W. S.: *test,* 478; *ref,* 361, 371, 404, 484
Jongeward, P. A.: *ref,* 349, 524-5, 533
Jordan, A. M.: *rev,* 2:1392; *ref,* 525, 2:1424(5), 3:220(26, 29), 3:263(26), 5:368(16), 6:480(17, 21)
Jordan, J. S.: *ref,* 525
Jordan, M. L.: *ref,* 357
Jordan, R. C.: *test,* 5:389
Jordan, T. E.: *ref,* 439, 519, 522, 525, 533
Jordheim, G. D.: *ref,* 364, 529
Jorgensen, C.: *ref,* 2:1377(19), 3:220(50)
Jortner, S.: *ref,* 529
Jose, T. A.: *ref,* 398, 589
Joselson, M. L.: *ref,* 516
Joseph, A.: *ref,* 483, 518
Joslin, H. F.: *ref,* 529
Judah, L. N.: *ref,* 518, 532
Judd, L. R.: *ref,* 357
Judge, C. H.: *ref,* 558
Judge, E. M.: *ref,* 357
Judson, A. J.: *ref,* 518, 532
Juel-Nielsen, N.: *ref,* 439, 532
Juffer, V. M.: *ref,* 589
Jui, A. H.: *ref,* 532
Jung, C. C.: *ref,* 574
Jungeblut, A.: *ref,* 394, 400
Juola, A. E.: *ref,* 357-8, 361, 419, 6:438(482)
Jurjevich, R.: *ref,* 391, 529, 533
Jurjevich, R. M.: *ref,* 439-40, 529
Jurko, M. F.: *ref,* 529
Justiss, W. A.: *ref,* 518
Justman, J.: *ref,* 391, 425, 525, 533, 5:326(13), 5:368(21)

KABACK, G. R.: *ref,* 525, 529, 533
Kaczkowski, H.: *ref,* 400, 435
Kaczkowski, H. R.: *ref,* 391
KaDell, M. B.: *ref,* 525
Kaelbling, R.: *ref,* 592
Kafer, L. G.: *ref,* 358
Kagan, J. R.: *ref,* 381
Kahana, B.: *ref,* 518
Kahn, D. F.: *ref,* 337
Kahn, E.: *ref,* 529, 592
Kahn, H.: *ref,* 516, 532, 4:277(210)
Kahn, J. H.: *ref,* 533
Kahn, M.: *ref,* 529
Kahn, M. W.: *ref,* 529, 532
Kahn, T. C.: *test,* 502; *ref,* 502
Kainer, R. K.: *ref,* 518
Kaiser, H. F.: *ref,* 457, 542, 551, 561, 564, 571-2
Kaiser, M. D.: *ref,* 533
Kaiser, R. L.: *test,* 479
Kakkar, A.: *ref,* 439
Kakkar, S. B.: *ref,* 364, 400
Kaldegg, A.: *ref,* 439, 529, 532
Kalehoff, D. W.: *ref,* 364
Kaliappan, K. V.: *ref,* 592
Kalinkowitz, B. N.: *ref,* 532
Kaliski, M. S.: *ref,* 516
Kallingal, A.: *ref,* 358
Kallingal, A. K.: *ref,* 358
Kallmann, F. J.: *ref,* 525, 532
Kallos, G. L.: *ref,* 533
Kaloger, J. H.: *ref,* 357, 361
Kalter, N.: *ref,* 533
Kaltsounis, B.: *ref,* 589
Kamano, D.: *ref,* 529
Kamat, V. V.: *ref,* 525
Kamii, C. K.: *ref,* 349, 525
Kamin, H. S.: *ref,* 498
Kamman, G. R.: *ref,* 532
Kamman, J. F.: *ref,* 426

Kammann, R. A.: *ref*, 6:438(524)
Kandel, A.: *ref*, 349, 400, 425, 525, 532
Kanderian, S. S.: *ref*, 364, 561-2, 591
Kane, F. J.: *ref*, 518
Kane, R. B.: *ref*, 542, 546, 561
Kanfer, F. H.: *ref*, 489
Kangas, J.: *ref*, 525, 529
Kangas, J. A.: *ref*, 525, 529
Kangas, R. D.: *ref*, 400
Kanitz, H. E.: *ref*, 589
Kanter, H. M.: *ref*, 529
Kantor, N. J.: *test*, 548, 570
Kantor, R. E.: *ref*, 532
Kantrowitz, J. L.: *ref*, 357
Kanungo, R.: *ref*, 439
Kao, K. S.: *ref*, 3:242(2)
Kapat, G.: *ref*, 515
Kapel, D. E.: *ref*, 524
Kapel, M. B.: *ref*, 524
Kaplan, B. E.: *ref*, 516
Kaplan, E.: *ref*, 525
Kaplan, H. K.: *ref*, 543
Kaplan, M.: *ref*, 357, 482, 561, 574
Kaplan, M. F.: *ref*, 574
Kaplan, M. L.: *ref*, 529
Kaplan, M. S.: *exc*, 381
Kaplan, O.: *ref*, 525
Kappelman, M. M.: *ref*, 533
Karadenes, M.: *ref*, 525
Karas, S. F.: *ref*, 357
Kardak, V. S.: *ref*, 331, 446
Kardos, M. S.: *ref*, 525, 533
Karelitz, R.: *ref*, 487, 525
Karelitz, S.: *ref*, 487, 525
Karioth, E. J.: *ref*, 589
Karioth, J.: *ref*, 589
Karle, H.: *ref*, 532
Karlin, I. W.: *ref*, 529
Karlins, M.: *ref*, 357, 482, 561, 574
Karlsen, B.: *ref*, 381, 533
Karnes, L. R.: *ref*, 365, 400
Karnes, M. B.: *ref*, 516, 525
Karp, S. A.: *ref*, 525, 529, 533, 547
Karpeles, L. M.: *ref*, 518
Karras, A.: *ref*, 529
Karson, S.: *ref*, 529, 532
Karsten, M. O.: *ref*, 561-2, 577, 591
Karstendiek, B.: *ref*, 482, 548
Karzen, J. M.: *ref*, 400
Kasambi, K.: *ref*, 497
Kaspar, J. C.: *ref*, 381, 516, 525, 533
Kasper, S.: *ref*, 439, 529
Kass, C. E.: *ref*, 533
Kass, W.: *ref*, 532
Kassinove, H.: *ref*, 529
Kastl, A. J.: *ref*, 529, 592
Kaswan, J.: *ref*, 529
Katakis, H.: *ref*, 529
Kato, J. G.: *ref*, 525
Katz, D.: *ref*, 404
Katz, E.: *test*, 431; *ref*, 525
Katz, F. M.: *ref*, 516
Katz, I. S.: *ref*, 496
Katz, J.: *ref*, 532
Katz, K.: *ref*, 357
Katz, L.: *ref*, 503
Katz, S. S.: *ref*, 361
Katzell, R. A.: *rev*, 450; *ref*, 333, 449
Katzenmeyer, W. G.: *ref*, 400
Kauffman, J. M.: *ref*, 400

Kaufman, A. S.: *ref*, 400
Kaufman, H.: *ref*, 524, 529
Kaufman, H. I.: *ref*, 516, 529
Kaufman, M. J.: *ref*, 533
Kaufman, M. R.: *ref*, 532
Kaufmann, H. J.: *test*, 3:274
Kaufmann, J. D.: *ref*, 357, 436
Kaulfers, W. V.: *ref*, 3:263(30)
Kaunitz, R. M.: *ref*, 525, 4:281 (79)
Kavajecz, L. G.: *ref*, 538
Kavruck, S.: *ref*, 525
Kawin, E.: *exc*, 525; *ref*, 507
Kay, D. W. K.: *ref*, 529
Kaya, E.: *exc*, 361
Kayani, M. R.: *ref*, 473
Kays, D.: *ref*, 574
Kazelskis, R.: *ref*, 559, 561
Kazmier, L. J.: *ref*, 337, 423, 482
Keach, C. C.: *ref*, 349, 400, 425, 525
Keany, M.: *ref*, 524
Kear-Colwell, J. J.: *ref*, 403, 439
Kearney, G. E.: *test*, 520; *ref*, 364, 514, 520
Kearney, J. E.: *ref*, 512, 520, 533
Kearsley, R. B.: *ref*, 522, 533
Keating, T. J.: *rev*, 439, 515, 2:1385
Keats, J. A.: *rev*, 331, 359, 546
Kebbon, L.: *ref*, 439, 525
Kedar, H.: *ref*, 439
Keefe, K.: *ref*, 529
Keefe, M. K.: *ref*, 529
Keehn, J. D.: *ref*, 364-5, 439, 532
Keeler, C. E.: *ref*, 364, 505, 529
Keeler, H. J.: *ref*, 5:308(408)
Keeling, K. R.: *ref*, 574
Keen, A. M.: *ref*, 525
Keen, C. F.: *ref*, 589
Keenan, J. F.: *ref*, 589
Keenen, C. B.: *ref*, 357
Keener, E. E.: *ref*, 426
Keener, H. E.: *ref*, 5:308(406)
Keesee, C. G.: *ref*, 357
Keevil-Rogers, P.: *ref*, 529
Kefauver, G. N.: *ref*, 426, 2:1424 (14), 3:263(31)
Keffer, C. E.: *ref*, 391, 533
Keillor, J. S.: *ref*, 482, 574
Keim, L.: *ref*, 482
Keim, R. P.: *ref*, 516, 525
Keir, G.: *rev*, 408, 463; *ref*, 439, 461, 507, 525
Keiser, T. W.: *ref*, 547
Kell, E. R.: *ref*, 533
Kelleher, E. J.: *ref*, 418
Kellenberger, L. R.: *ref*, 589
Keller, A. J.: *ref*, 532
Keller, J. E.: *ref*, 533, 5:326(15-6)
Keller, M.: *test*, 3:291
Kelley, E.: *ref*, 532
Kelley, F.: *ref*, 468
Kelley, J.: *ref*, 403, 439
Kelley, J. W.: *ref*, 529
Kellner, H.: *ref*, 357, 574
Kellogg, C. E.: *test*, 447; *ref*, 447, 2:1377(9), 3:220(38)
Kelly, E. L.: *ref*, 404
Kelly, F. D.: *ref*, 529
Kelly, F. J.: *ref*, 529, 532-3, 561
Kelly, G. R.: *ref*, 589
Kelly, J. P.: *ref*, 425

Kelly, P. O.: *ref*, 398, 3:242(6), 3:263(39), 5:329(4)
Kelmovitz, J.: *test*, 541
Kelsey, A. E.: *ref*, 348
Kelso, P.: *ref*, 4:277(263)
Kelso, P. C.: *test*, 391
Kelson, F.: *ref*, 589
Kelton, W. W.: *ref*, 381
Kelvin, R. P.: *ref*, 331
Kemler, D.: *ref*, 589
Kemp, D. E.: *ref*, 529
Kempler, H. L.: *ref*, 533
Kenchaveeraiah, B.: *ref*, 439
Kendall, W. E.: *ref*, 404
Kendig, I.: *exc*, 532; *ref*, 525
Kendrick, D. C.: *exc*, 518; *ref*, 403, 529
Kendrick, S. A.: *ref*, 357
Kennedy, J. E.: *rev*, 414, 472, 594, 7:399
Kennedy, M.: *ref*, 543, 592
Kennedy, P. E.: *ref*, 361
Kennedy, V.: *ref*, 525
Kennedy, W.: *ref*, 525
Kennedy, W. A.: *ref*, 359, 381, 525, 529, 533
Kennedy-Fraser, D.: *ref*, 525
Kennett, K. F.: *ref*, 425
Kenny, J. T.: *ref*, 505, 525, 529
Kent, E. G.: *ref*, 342
Kent, G. H.: *rev*, 515, 2:1390-1, 2:1394, 2:1426, 3:273; *test*, 503; *exc*, 525, 532; *ref*, 503, 525, 545, 2:1401(1, 3)
Kent, N.: *ref*, 525, 533
Kent, R. A.: *ref*, 2:1377(5)
Keochakian, S. V.: *ref*, 357
Keogh, B. K.: *ref*, 381
Keogh, J. F.: *ref*, 381
Keough, M. J.: *ref*, 419
Kepka, E. J.: *ref*, 357
Kepner, R. D.: *ref*, 518, 525
Kerfoot, J. F.: *ref*, 400
Kerley, S. A.: *ref*, 357
Kern, D. W.: *ref*, 5:308(324)
Kern, F. E.: *ref*, 439, 529
Kern, K. C.: *ref*, 533
Kernaleguen, A. P.: *ref*, 589
Kernan, J. S.: *ref*, 381
Kernoff, P.: *ref*, 357
Kerr, G.: *ref*, 425
Kerr, W. A.: *ref*, 418
Kerridge, D.: *ref*, 518
Kessell, R.: *ref*, 518, 529
Kessler, M. R.: *ref*, 545
Kessler, R. T.: *ref*, 381
Keston, M. J.: *ref*, 525
Ketcham, H. E. (Mrs.): *ref*, 357, 419
Ketcherside, W. J.: *ref*, 589
Kettell, M. E.: *ref*, 529
Kettner, N. W.: *ref*, 457, 551
Keys, N.: *ref*, 2:1424(25), 3:263(42)
Khan, S. B.: *ref*, 350, 361, 561
Khatena, J.: *test*, 587; *ref*, 381, 439, 587, 589
Khullar, B. M. P.: *ref*, 545
Kiang, C. G.: *ref*, 439
Kibler, R. J.: *ref*, 542, 561
Kicklighter, R.: *ref*, 529, 533
Kicklighter, R. M.: *ref*, 516, 525
Kidd, A. H.: *ref*, 364, 525
Kidder, J. W.: *ref*, 516, 525

Kienlen, J. S.: *ref,* 391
Kilbride, J. E.: *ref,* 484
Kilbride, P. L.: *ref,* 484
Kilburn, K. L.: *ref,* 439, 516, 525
Kilduff, C. T.: *ref,* 524
Kilgore, J. H.: *ref,* 467
Kilgore, L. L.: *ref,* 400
Killen, J. R.: *ref,* 381, 493, 503, 505, 533, 558
Killian, C. D.: *ref,* 525
Killian, L. R.: *ref,* 533
Kilman, B. A.: *ref,* 525, 529, 533
Kilpatrick, A. R.: *ref,* 361
Kim, K. S.: *ref,* 5:308(423)
Kimball, C. P.: *ref,* 529, 545
Kimball, W. H.: *ref,* 361
Kimbell, F. T.: *ref,* 361
Kimberlin, C. C.: *ref,* 487, 525
Kimble, G.: *ref,* 5:308(438)
Kimble, J. P.: *ref,* 561
Kimbles, S. L.: *ref,* 361
Kimbreall, G. M.: *ref,* 529
Kimbrell, D. L.: *ref,* 496, 516, 525, 533
Kincannon, S. G.: *ref,* 357
Kinder, E. F.: *ref,* 518, 525, 532
King, A. J.: *ref,* 381
King, A. R.: *ref,* 364
King, D. C.: *ref,* 382, 482
King, D. M.: *ref,* 532
King, D. T.: *ref,* 6:438(525)
King, F. J.: *ref,* 349, 382, 542, 551
King, F. W.: *ref,* 522
King, G. F.: *ref,* 496, 532
King, J. D.: *ref,* 525, 533, 538
King, J. E.: *test,* 449
King, M. L.: *ref,* 400
King, N. W.: *ref,* 409
King, P.: *ref,* 349, 404, 6:438(467)
King, R. G.: *ref,* 357
King, S. H.: *ref,* 505, 516
King, W. H.: *ref,* 439, 461
Kingsley, L.: *ref,* 342, 439–40, 532
Kingston, A. J.: *ref,* 419
Kinnie, E. J.: *ref,* 538
Kinsbourne, M.: *ref,* 439
Kinzer, J. R.: *ref,* 419
Kinzer, L. G.: *ref,* 419
Kinzie, W. B.: *ref,* 529
Kipnis, D.: *ref,* 357
Kirby, B. J.: *ref,* 361
Kirby, M. E.: *ref,* 400
Kirchner, E. P.: *ref,* 574
Kirchner, J. H.: *ref,* 425, 439
Kirchner, W.: *ref,* 445, 482
Kirchner, W. K.: *ref,* 404, 480, 529
Kiresuk, T. J.: *ref,* 518
Kirk, B. A.: *ref,* 358–9, 361, 382, 391
Kirk, C. R.: *ref,* 357
Kirk, G. E.: *ref,* 516
Kirk, H. A.: *ref,* 419, 6:480(41)
Kirk, J.: *ref,* 403, 439
Kirk, R. E.: *ref,* 559, 561
Kirk, S. A.: *ref,* 499
Kirkendall, D. R.: *ref,* 357, 364, 425
Kirkpatrick, F. H.: *exc,* 525; *ref,* 419, 426, 3:217(73), 3:255(12), 5:368(14)
Kirkpatrick, J. J.: *ref,* 333, 342, 449
Kirschner, D.: *ref,* 529, 532
Kirschner, F. E.: *ref,* 381
Kirsh, J. L.: *ref,* 589
Kirtner, W. L.: *ref,* 529

Kissel, S.: *ref,* 533
Kissin, B.: *ref,* 532
Kittell, J. E.: *ref,* 348
Kittredge, W. B.: *ref,* 525
Kitzinger, H.: *ref,* 532
Kivitz, M. S.: *ref,* 518, 529
Klahn, J. E.: *ref,* 533
Klappauf, J.: *ref,* 529
Klapper, Z. S.: *ref,* 516, 525, 529
Klappersack, B.: *ref,* 529
Klatskin, E. H.: *ref,* 484, 487, 507, 525, 578
Klausmeier, H. J.: *ref,* 457, 533, 559, 561
Klebanoff, S. G.: *ref,* 503, 525, 532
Klee, G. D.: *ref,* 518
Kleemeier, R. W.: *ref,* 529
Klein, A.: *ref,* 3:263(33)
Klein, D. F.: *ref,* 529, 532
Klein, E.: *ref,* 529, 532
Klein, G. S.: *ref,* 532
Klein, J.: *ref,* 439
Klein, P.: *ref,* 574
Klein, R. A.: *ref,* 400
Klein, S. P.: *ref,* 357, 542, 551, 561
Kleman, J. P.: *ref,* 518
Klett, W. G.: *ref,* 342, 447, 529
Kleyle, H. M.: *ref,* 425
Kline, M. V.: *ref,* 532
Klingelhofer, E. L.: *ref,* 439
Klock, J. A.: *ref,* 357
Klonoff, H.: *ref,* 381, 439, 525, 529, 432–3, 543, 592
Kløve, H.: *ref,* 516, 529, 532–3
Kluever, R.: *ref,* 533
Klugh, H. B.: *ref,* 5:308(382)
Klugh, H. E.: *ref,* 361
Klugman, S. F.: *ref,* 348, 447, 525, 532, 5:308(424)
Knapp, R. H.: *ref,* 359
Knapp, R. R.: *ref,* 364
Knapp, W.: *ref,* 447
Knauft, E. B.: *ref,* 482
Knecht, W. W.: *ref,* 349
Knehr, C. A.: *ref,* 426, 439
Knezevich, S. J.: *ref,* 349, 391
Knickerbocker, K. L.: *ref,* 4:277 (268)
Knief, L. M.: *ref,* 400, 439, 5:326 (32)
Knight, D.: *ref,* 364, 525
Knight, J.: *test,* 5:389
Knight, M. W.: *ref,* 483, 525
Knight, R.: *ref,* 391, 398
Knight, R. P.: *ref,* 532
Knights, R. M.: *ref,* 516, 533
Knittle, J. L.: *ref,* 381
Knobloch, H.: *test,* 494; *ref,* 494, 497
Knoll, D. B.: *ref,* 538
Knollin, H. E.: *ref,* 525
Knopf, I. J.: *ref,* 532–3
Knott, J. R.: *ref,* 503, 532–3
Knowles, J. B.: *ref,* 532
Knox, A. B.: *ref,* 529, 7:378(4)
Knox, P.: *ref,* 391
Knox, S.: *ref,* 525
Knox, S. J.: *ref,* 529
Knox, W. J.: *ref,* 529
Ko, Y. H.: *ref,* 529
Kobal, A.: *test,* 335–6
Kobayashi, M. J.: *ref,* 589
Kobler, F. J.: *ref,* 398, 439, 496, 525
Koch, H. L.: *exc,* 497; *ref,* 435, 507

Koch, R.: *ref,* 497
Kodanaz, A.: *ref,* 529, 543
Kodman, F.: *ref,* 489, 525
Koenig, F. J.: *ref,* 503
Koerth, W.: *ref,* 3:220(31)
Koestline, W. C.: *ref,* 529
Kogan, K. L.: *rev,* 592, 4:339; *test,* 6:516; *ref,* 381, 426, 483, 525, 532, 6:516(1–2)
Kogan, N.: *ref,* 361, 533
Kogan, W. S.: *rev,* 4:339; *ref,* 532
Koh, T. H.: *ref,* 516, 525
Kohen-Raz, R.: *ref,* 484
Kohlberg, L.: *exc,* 549
Kohler, E. T.: *ref,* 559, 561
Kohn, H. A.: *ref,* 419, 2:1377(34), 3:218(3)
Kohs, S. C.: *test,* 545; *ref,* 525
Kohut, S.: *ref,* 489
Koken, J. E.: *ref,* 419, 5:308(402)
Kolasa, B. J.: *ref,* 4:277(245)
Kolb, L.: *ref,* 525
Kole, D. M.: *ref,* 529
Koller, J. R.: *ref,* 525
Kolstoe, O. P.: *ref,* 525, 533, 543
Koltveit, T. H.: *ref,* 404
Konstans, D. J.: *ref,* 525
Koo, G. Y.: *ref,* 348
Kooker, E. W.: *ref,* 361, 404
Kool, K. A.: *ref,* 532
Kools, J. A.: *ref,* 516
Koons, N.: *ref,* 589
Koopman, P. R.: *exc,* 361
Koos, E. M.: *ref,* 533
Kopel, D.: *exc,* 349
Kopff, R. G.: *ref,* 348, 482
Koplyay, J. B.: *ref,* 425
Koppitz, E. M.: *ref,* 381, 525, 533
Koran, M. L.: *ref,* 561
Kordinak, S. T.: *ref,* 489, 538
Koriat, A.: *ref,* 574
Korner, A. F.: *ref,* 525, 532
Kornhauser, A. W.: *ref,* 426
Korotkin, A. L.: *ref,* 529
Korst, J. W.: *ref,* 505, 516, 533
Kortmeyer, H. A.: *ref,* 349
Kosc, L.: *ref,* 545
Koshuk, R. P.: *exc,* 497
Kostlan, A.: *ref,* 440
Kothari, S.: *ref,* 439
Koupernik, C.: *ref,* 492
Koutstaal, C. W.: *ref,* 533
Kovacs, A. R.: *ref,* 357
Kovalinsky, T.: *ref,* 525, 533
Kowitz, G. T.: *ref,* 483
Koza, C.: *ref,* 497
Kraft, I. A.: *ref,* 381, 529, 533, 592
Kraft, M. B.: *ref,* 381
Kral, V. A.: *ref,* 529, 532, 592
Kralovich, A. M.: *ref,* 487, 533
Kram, C.: *ref,* 532
Kramar, E. J. J.: *ref,* 532, 5:308 (383)
Kramer, E.: *ref,* 529
Kramish, A. A.: *ref,* 532
Krantz, L. L.: *ref,* 349
Kranzler, G. D.: *ref,* 361, 533
Krathwohl, D. R.: *ref,* 5:308(300)
Krato, J. C.: *ref,* 532
Krattiger, J. T.: *ref,* 426
Kraus, J.: *ref,* 529, 532
Kraus, M. J.: *ref,* 529
Kraut, A. I.: *ref,* 359, 457
Krebs, E. G.: *ref,* 538

Krebs, S. O.: *ref,* 349
Kreezer, G. L.: *ref,* 525
Kriegman, G.: *ref,* 532-3
Kriegman, L. S.: *ref,* 533
Krippner, S.: *ref,* 516, 529, 533
Krocco, D.: *ref,* 505, 533
Kronenberger, E. J.: *ref,* 545
Krop, H.: *ref,* 349, 551
Krop, H. D.: *ref,* 381, 551, 574
Kropp, R. P.: *ref,* 349, 359, 361, 561
Kroske, W. H.: *ref,* 502, 525, 529
Krout, M. H.: *ref,* 482
Krueger, A. F.: *ref,* 419
Krueger, R. L.: *ref,* 426
Krueger, W. C. F.: *ref,* 426
Krugman, J. I.: *ref,* 525, 533
Krugman, M.: *exc,* 525; *ref,* 525, 533
Krusen, M. M. M.: *ref,* 538
Kubala, A. L.: *ref,* 532
Kuder, F.: *rev,* 425-6, 3:248
Kuder, G. F.: *ref,* 357, 3:217(92)
Kuderna, J. G.: *ref,* 3:220(25)
Kugel, R. B.: *ref,* 497
Kuhlmann, F.: *rev,* 349, 425; *test,* 398, 2:1426; *ref,* 398, 426, 435, 441, 525, 2:1424(12), 3:255(4), 4:288(1), 6:480(26)
Kukkonen, S.: *ref,* 592
Kullberg, G.: *ref,* 439
Kumar, P.: *ref,* 439
Kumin, E.: *ref,* 2:1394(10)
Kunce, J. T.: *ref,* 529
Kundu, R.: *ref,* 439, 515, 525, 532
Kunze, K. R.: *test,* 335-6
Kuo, Y. Y.: *ref,* 589
Kurek, A.: *ref,* 349
Kureth, G.: *ref,* 525, 533
Kurko, V. K.: *ref,* 525
Kurland, A. A.: *ref,* 439, 529
Kuroda, J.: *ref,* 439
Kushmar, H. S.: *ref,* 482
Kushner, R.: *ref,* 525
Kushner, R. E.: *ref,* 426
Kutash, S. B.: *ref,* 525, 532
Kvaraceus, W. C.: *ref,* 525
Kyte, G. C.: *ref,* 525

L & L ASSOCIATES: *test,* 374
Labak, A. S.: *ref,* 529
LaBarba, R. C.: *ref,* 518
L'Abate, L.: *ref,* 381, 440, 489, 516, 529, 532-3, 543
Laberteaux, T. E.: *ref,* 529
Labrecque, J. M.: *ref,* 529
Lachenbruch, P. A.: *ref,* 518
Lachmann, F. M.: *ref,* 543, 545
Lacks, P. B.: *ref,* 529, 543
Lacy, L. D.: *ref,* 426, 525
Lacy, W. I.: *ref,* 525
Ladd, A. H.: *ref,* 532
Ladd, C. E.: *ref,* 529, 532
Ladieu, G. B.: *ref,* 419
Ladner, J. L.: *ref,* 589
LaDriere, L.: *ref,* 533
LaDriere, M. L.: *ref,* 533
Lafave, H. G.: *ref,* 532
Lahey, T. H.: *ref,* 381
Lahn, M.: *ref,* 574
Laing, D. M.: *ref,* 482
Lair, C. V.: *ref,* 525, 533
Laird, D. S.: *ref,* 533
Lake, A. E.: *ref,* 542
Lam, R. L.: *ref,* 533

Lamb, M. W.: *ref,* 357
Lambert, C. M.: *ref,* 409, 4:313(1), 4:334(7)
Lambert, P.: *ref,* 357, 471, 522
Lambert, R. A.: *ref,* 525
Lamberti, E.: *ref,* 349
Lamke, T. A.: *test,* 391; *ref,* 391
Lamm, S. S.: *exc,* 497
Lamontagne, C. W.: *ref,* 542, 551
Lamp, R. E.: *ref,* 522, 525, 533
Lampton, T. D.: *ref,* 433, 447, 529, 592
Lamson, E. E.: *ref,* 525
Lancashire, R.: *ref,* 384, 388
Land, M.: *ref,* 419
Land, V.: *test,* 475-6
Landis, C.: *ref,* 518
Landis, L.: *ref,* 496
Landisberg, S.: *ref,* 532, 545, 588
Landrum, J. P.: *ref,* 533
Landrus, G.: *ref,* 439
Landry, H. A.: *ref,* 357
Landry, R. G.: *ref,* 364, 589
Lane, B. R.: *ref,* 349
Lane, E. A.: *ref,* 532
Lane, G. G.: *ref,* 419, 426
Lane, H. A.: *ref,* 525
Lane, H. S.: *ref,* 499
Lane, J. A.: *ref,* 419
Lane, M. O'K.: *ref,* 532
Lane, R. G.: *ref,* 404
Laney, A. R.: *ref,* 482
Laney, B. J.: *ref,* 516, 533
Lanfeld, E. S.: *ref,* 529
Lang, M. J.: *ref,* 6:438(483)
Lange, I. D.: *ref,* 426
Lange, U. A.: *ref,* 439, 543
Langevin, R.: *ref,* 425, 439, 574
Langgulung, H.: *ref,* 589
Langland, L.: *ref,* 349
Langley, C. W.: *ref,* 547
Langlie, T. A.: *rev,* 419
Langmuir, C. R.: *rev,* 3:232; *test,* 433
Langsam, R. S.: *ref,* 3:217(85), 4:277(161)
Langston, R. D.: *ref,* 532
Lanier, L. H.: *ref,* 426
Lanier, P. E.: *ref,* 400, 589
Lanigan, M. A.: *ref,* 426, 4:277(180)
Lansdell, H.: *ref,* 532
Lansing, K. M.: *ref,* 532
Lantz, B.: *test,* 5:332; *ref,* 489, 525
Lantz, C. M. B.: *ref,* 525
Laosa, L. M.: *ref,* 381
Lapp, C. J.: *ref,* 357
Lare, J. H.: *ref,* 357
Larimore, D. L.: *ref,* 357
Larr, A. L.: *ref,* 533
Larsen, K. W.: *ref,* 381
Larsen, M. J.: *ref,* 525
Larsen, M. R. J.: *ref,* 525
Larsen, R. P.: *ref,* 425
Larsen, T. M.: *ref,* 5:308(425)
Larson, A. A.: *ref,* 399
Larson, K. H.: *ref,* 439, 533
Larson, R. E.: *ref,* 398
Larson, R. K.: *ref,* 545
Larson, S. S.: *ref,* 355, 364
Larson, W. L.: *ref,* 496
Larwood, H. J. C.: *ref,* 5:339(10-1)
LaSalle, J.: *ref,* 525

Lasco, R. A.: *ref,* 361
Laskowitz, D.: *ref,* 532
Lasky, D. I.: *ref,* 381, 419
Lasky, J. J.: *ref,* 529
Lasky, L.: *ref,* 440
Laslett, H. R.: *ref,* 419, 426, 2:1377(22), 3:217(51), 4:277(184)
Lassman, F. M.: *ref,* 529
LaTourelle, C. W.: *ref,* 532
Lauber, M.: *ref,* 533
Lauderbach, J. C.: *ref,* 435, 3:242(5), 3:255(6)
Lauer, B. A.: *ref,* 533
Laughlin, P. R.: *ref,* 359, 574
Laughlin, W. P.: *ref,* 419, 4:277(159)
Laurent, H.: *ref,* 404, 414
Lauten, D. A. H.: *ref,* 349
Laver, A. B.: *ref,* 391, 425-6, 529
Lavitt, J. A.: *ref,* 516, 533
Lavos, G.: *ref,* 355, 447, 533
Law, A.: *ref,* 382
Lawder, E.: *ref,* 349
Lawes, J. S.: *rev,* 474, 512
Lawlor, G.: *exc,* 344
Lawrence, E. M.: *ref,* 461, 525
Lawrence, P. J.: *ref,* 426, 589
Lawrence, R. M.: *ref,* 529, 532
Lawrence, W. A.: *ref,* 4:277(153)
Lawrence, W. C.: *ref,* 355
Laws, A. R.: *ref,* 416
Lawshe, C. H.: *test,* 337; *ref,* 337, 421
Lawson, J. R.: *ref,* 381, 538
Lawson, T.: *ref,* 533
Lawton, G.: *exc,* 532
Laycock, S. R.: *test,* 3:237; *ref,* 525, 4:277(154)
Layman, J. W.: *ref,* 342, 525
Laynor, H. A.: *ref,* 589
Layton, W. L.: *test,* 405; *ref,* 404-5, 419, 5:308(291), 5:309(12), 6:438(502)
Laywell, H. R.: *ref,* 529
Lazar, M.: *ref,* 3:242(2)
Leach, A. R.: *ref,* 357
Leach, K. W.: *ref,* 348
Leaf, C. T.: *ref,* 3:217(74)
Leafgren, F.: *ref,* 404
Leahy, A. M.: *ref,* 426, 525
Leahy, D. M.: *ref,* 6:438(455, 468)
Leard, J. L.: *ref,* 361
Learned, J.: *ref,* 497
Lease, G. C.: *ref,* 361
Leathers, R. K.: *ref,* 357
Leaver, T. E.: *ref,* 357
Leavitt, H. J.: *ref,* 342
Leberfeld, D. T.: *ref,* 525
Lebo, D.: *ref,* 6:468(3-4)
LeBold, W. K.: *ref,* 357
Lebovitz, L.: *ref,* 525
Lecrone, E. M.: *ref,* 381
Ledford, K. B.: *ref,* 382
Ledgerwood, R.: *rev,* 1:1048
Lee, D.: *ref,* 331
Lee, D. M.: *test,* 415
Lee, E. E.: *ref,* 357
Lee, F. J.: *ref,* 532
Lee, J.: *ref,* 529
Lee, J. M.: *ref,* 398
Lee, M. V.: *ref,* 525
Lee, P. J.: *ref,* 5:308(358)
Lee, R.: *ref,* 517, 533
Lee, T.: *ref,* 428

Leep, A. G.: *ref,* 361
Lefcourt, H. M.: *ref,* 574
Lefever, D. W.: *rev,* 391, 425, 6:480
Leff, B.: *ref,* 6:514(10)
Lefkowitz, M. M.: *ref,* 518
Legg, D.: *ref,* 529
Lehman, E. B.: *ref,* 381, 533
Lehmann, I. J.: *ref,* 358, 400, 525, 529
Lehmann, M. M.: *ref,* 525, 533
Lehmkuhl, C. B.: *ref,* 404
Lehrer, A. C.: *ref,* 542, 546, 564
Lehrer, B. E.: *ref,* 400
Leibowitz, M.: *ref,* 518
Leichman, N. S.: *ref,* 529
Leichtman, S. R.: *ref,* 533
Leiding, W. C.: *ref,* 532
Leipold, W. D.: *ref,* 532
Leitch, M.: *ref,* 525
Leiter, R. G.: *test,* 504–5, 4:339, 4:347–8, 4:355; *exc,* 497; *ref,* 504–5, 4:359(3)
Leithwood, K. A.: *ref,* 525
Leland, B.: *test,* 493
LeMay, M.: *ref,* 357
Lemke, E. A.: *ref,* 425, 439, 457, 561
Lemons, C. D.: *ref,* 357
Lenke, J. M.: *ref,* 424
Lennon, R. T.: *rev,* 5:379; *test,* 424; *ref,* 425, 4:324(62), 5:368(17–8, 23)
Lennox, W. G.: *ref,* 525, 532
Leon, J. F.: *ref,* 398
Leonard, L. C.: *ref,* 358
Leonhardt, T. M.: *ref,* 516
Lepley, W. M.: *ref,* 6:438(469)
Leppke, R. D.: *ref,* 381, 516
Lerand, L. W.: *ref,* 533
Lerche, M.: *ref,* 3:242(2)
Lerea, L.: *ref,* 489
Lerner, E.: *ref,* 400
Lescarbeau, W. J.: *ref,* 361
LeShan, L.: *ref,* 342
Leskosky, R.: *ref,* 381, 538
Leskosky, R. J.: *ref,* 381
Leslie, P. T.: *ref,* 533
Lessard, C. S.: *ref,* 561, 591
Lessing, E. E.: *ref,* 381, 400, 525, 533
Lessing, J. C.: *ref,* 533
Lessler, K.: *ref,* 516, 524, 533
Lester, D. W.: *ref,* 503
Lester, E. P.: *ref,* 381, 400, 533, 575
Lester, L. P.: *ref,* 533, 575
Lester, O. P.: *ref,* 518, 545
Lester, R. A.: *ref,* 405
Leton, D. A.: *ref,* 349, 543, 575, 589
Lett, W. R.: *ref,* 542, 546, 551
LeUnes, A.: *ref,* 425
Leutenegger, R. R.: *ref,* 361, 391, 400
Levenson, M.: *ref,* 529
Leventhal, D. B.: *ref,* 529
Levesque, C. E.: *ref,* 497
Levi, H. S.: *ref,* 381, 533
Levi, J.: *ref,* 525, 532
Levin, J.: *ref,* 525, 532–3
Levin, J. R.: *ref,* 439, 516
Levine, A.: *ref,* 532
Levine, B.: *ref,* 355, 439, 532
Levine, B. D.: *ref,* 439, 532
Levine, B. L.: *ref,* 447
Levine, D.: *ref,* 525

Levine, H. A.: *ref,* 381
Levine, H. D.: *ref,* 529
Levine, H. G.: *ref,* 357
Levine, J.: *ref,* 532
Levine, L. G.: *ref,* 419
Levine, L. S.: *ref,* 532
Levine, M.: *ref,* 532–3
Levine, N. R.: *ref,* 522, 529
Levine, R. L.: *ref,* 357
Levinson, B. M.: *ref,* 381, 439, 483, 489, 525, 529, 532–3, 5:326(22)
Levinson, E. J.: *ref,* 525, 533
Levit, H. I.: *ref,* 532
Levita, E.: *ref,* 439, 529, 532, 592
Levitt, E. A.: *ref,* 532
Levitt, E. E.: *ref,* 533
Levreault, L. P.: *ref,* 532
Levy, B. I.: *ref,* 381, 529, 533, 592
Levy, I. S.: *ref,* 381
Levy, L. E.: *ref,* 483
Levy, L. R.: *ref,* 381
Levy, M.: *ref,* 436, 529
Levy, P.: *ref,* 525, 529, 533
Levy, P. M.: *rev,* 459, 495
Levy, R.: *ref,* 592
Levy, R. H.: *ref,* 426, 447, 449, 529, 533
Lewin, P. B.: *ref,* 547
Lewinski, R. J.: *ref,* 503, 532
Lewinsohn, P. M.: *ref,* 440
Lewis, B. I.: *ref,* 545
Lewis, D. G.: *ref,* 415, 525
Lewis, D. W.: *ref,* 529
Lewis, F. D.: *ref,* 533
Lewis, F. W.: *ref,* 529
Lewis, J. F.: *ref,* 499, 525
Lewis, J. M.: *ref,* 426
Lewis, J. W.: *ref,* 361
Lewis, L. L.: *ref,* 529, 533
Lewis, L. W.: *ref,* 391
Lewis, M. M.: *test,* 5:337
Lewis, O. F.: *ref,* 561, 591
Lewis, R.: *ref,* 525
Lewis, R. B.: *ref,* 589
Lewis, S. C.: *ref,* 357
Lewis, V.: *ref,* 381, 525, 533
Lewis, V. G.: *ref,* 529, 533
Lewis, W. D.: *ref,* 398
Lewis, W. M.: *ref,* 529
Ley, P.: *ref,* 403, 439
Lezine, I.: *ref,* 483
Li, A. K.: *ref,* 439
Li, A. K. F.: *ref,* 331
Libb, J. W.: *ref,* 447, 522, 529, 592
Libby, W. L.: *ref,* 361, 574
Libowitz, J. M.: *ref,* 529
Licht, L.: *ref,* 542
Lichtman, M. V.: *ref,* 538, 589
Liddicoat, R.: *ref,* 497, 532
Lidz, T.: *ref,* 525, 545
Lieberman, J. N.: *ref,* 516
Lieberman, L. R.: *ref,* 361
Liebert, R. M.: *ref,* 529
Liedtke, W.: *ref,* 348
Lief, H. I.: *ref,* 404
Lief, V. F.: *ref,* 404
Lien, A. J.: *ref,* 391, 5:308(301)
Liggett, J.: *rev,* 331, 390, 5:340, 5:357
Liggitt, W. A.: *ref,* 361
Light, M. L.: *ref,* 529, 532
Light, P.: *ref,* 529
Lighthall, F.: *ref,* 425
Lighthall, F. K.: *ref,* 518

Lightsey, R.: *ref,* 357, 365, 425
Lilly, R. S.: *ref,* 561
Lin, T. T.: *ref,* 529
Lin, Y. G.: *ref,* 357, 529
Lincoln, E. A.: *ref,* 525, 2:1390(2), 2:1391(2), 3:273(3)
Lincoln, H.: *ref,* 2:1388(3)
Lindahl, L. E. H.: *ref,* 439
Linde, L. M.: *ref,* 487, 497, 525
Lindeman, R. H.: *ref,* 357
Linder, M. G.: *ref,* 507
Lindholm, B. W.: *ref,* 525
Lindner, R.: *ref,* 525, 529
Lindner, R. M.: *test,* 447; *ref,* 447
Lindner, R. S.: *ref,* 381
Lindquist, E. F.: *ref,* 357
Lindsey, J. F.: *ref,* 589
Lindsey, J. M.: *ref,* 496, 516, 533
Lindzey, G.: *ref,* 482
Lindzey, G. E.: *test,* 431; *ref,* 482, 532
Line, W.: *rev,* 2:1393, 2:1411; *exc,* 349, 483, 497, 507; *ref,* 525
Lines, J.: *ref,* 2:1394(8–9)
Linfert, H. E.: *test,* 3:285; *ref,* 3:285(2)
Lingwood, J.: *ref,* 439
Linker, J. M.: *ref,* 561
Linn, M. R.: *ref,* 357
Linn, R. L.: *ref,* 357
Lins, L. J.: *ref,* 357–8, 391, 4:277(175, 189, 246), 5:308(325)
Lipton, J.: *ref,* 364
Lipton, M. B.: *ref,* 532
Lipton, R.: *ref,* 529
Liroff, J. H.: *ref,* 529, 574
Lis, E. F.: *ref,* 497
Liske, R. E.: *ref,* 6:438(503)
Lister, J. L.: *ref,* 382
Listiak, R. L.: *ref,* 364, 574
Litaker, R. G.: *ref,* 533
Littell, W. M.: *ref,* 533
Little, A. J.: *ref,* 529
Little, J. K.: *ref,* 391
Little, K.: *ref,* 4:277(189)
Lively, M. L.: *ref,* 525
Livermore, G.: *ref,* 533
Livesay, T. M.: *ref,* 2:1377(26, 29, 39), 3:218(7), 4:277(164)
Livingston, J. S.: *ref,* 525
Livo, N. J.: *ref,* 538
Lloyd, B. A.: *ref,* 349
Lloyd, C. J.: *ref,* 398
Lloyd, D. O.: *ref,* 348
Lloyd, F.: *ref,* 415
Lloyd, L. L.: *ref,* 516
Lloyd, R.: *ref,* 349
Lobl, M.: *ref,* 525
LoCascio, R.: *ref,* 529
Locke, E. A.: *ref,* 457, 546, 551, 571
Locke, L. F.: *ref,* 404
Lockyer, L.: *ref,* 381, 516, 533
Lodge, T.: *ref,* 525
Loevinger, J.: *rev,* 4:333
Loewenson, R. B.: *ref,* 518, 529, 533
Loewer, H. D.: *ref,* 529, 543
Lofquist, L. H.: *ref,* 561
Logothetis, J.: *ref,* 518, 529, 533
Logue, P. E.: *ref,* 529
Logue, V.: *ref,* 529
Lohnes, P. R.: *ref,* 361, 435
Lohrenz, L. J.: *ref,* 547, 561
Loiselle, R. H.: *ref,* 543

Lomangino, L.: *ref,* 528
London, S. K.: *ref,* 487
Long, B. H.: *ref,* 589
Long, E.: *ref,* 3:242(2)
Long, G. S.: *ref,* 438
Long, H. H.: *ref,* 398, 525
Long, J. A.: *test,* 437; *exc,* 425; *ref,* 532, 3:242(2)
Long, J. M.: *ref,* 361
Long, J. R.: *ref,* 425
Long, L.: *ref,* 4:277(181)
Long, R. I.: *ref,* 547
Longenecker, E. D.: *ref,* 6:438(510)
Longworth, A.: *ref,* 512
Lonigan, M. A.: *ref,* 3:217(141)
Looft, W. R.: *ref,* 529
Looker, A.: *ref,* 518
Loomis, A. K.: *ref,* 6:480(4)
Loos, F. M.: *ref,* 533
Loper, D. J.: *ref,* 533
Loranger, A. W.: *ref,* 439, 518, 529
Lord, E. E.: *exc,* 497; *ref,* 497
Lord, F. M.: *ref,* 357
Lord, R. M.: *ref,* 482, 484
Lordahl, D. S.: *ref,* 529, 574
Lore, J.: *ref,* 525, 529
Lorenz, A. B.: *ref,* 419
Loret, P. G.: *ref,* 357
Lorge, I.: *rev,* 433, 482; *test,* 351–2, 356, 400–1, 489, 3:243; *exc,* 532; *ref,* 426, 438, 489, 525, 532, 4:315(2), 4:317(1), 5:326(7)
Lorge, I. D.: *ref,* 489
Lorr, M.: *ref,* 525
Lotesta, P.: *ref,* 532
Lotsof, E. J.: *ref,* 532–3
Lott, H. V.: *ref,* 3:217(65)
Lott, W. J.: *ref,* 532
Louden, M. V.: *ref,* 525
Loudon, M. L.: *ref,* 381
Lourie, D. K.: *ref,* 525
Louttit, C. M.: *rev,* 518; *exc,* 487; *ref,* 518, 525, 558
Love, B.: *ref,* 361
Love, D. B.: *ref,* 532
Love, H. G. I.: *ref,* 529
Love, J. O.: *ref,* 6:438(451)
Love, L. R.: *ref,* 532
Love, M. I.: *ref,* 398, 5:326(33)
Lovegren, L. A.: *ref,* 404
Loveless, H. E.: *ref,* 438
Lovell, K.: *rev,* 495; *ref,* 415, 533
Lovett, C. J.: *ref,* 349
Lovinger, R. J.: *ref,* 364, 425, 533
Lovinger, S. L.: *ref,* 533
Lovius, B. B. J.: *ref,* 403, 439
Low, H. E.: *ref,* 589
Lowden, G. L.: *ref,* 525
Lowe, A. J.: *ref,* 400
Lowe, C. M.: *ref,* 529
Lowe, G. M.: *ref,* 2:1390(3), 2:1391(6), 2:1394(3), 2:1401(2)
Lowe, J. D.: *ref,* 533
Lowe, P. E.: *ref,* 426
Lowe, W. E.: *ref,* 349
Lowell, F. E.: *ref,* 525
Lowell, R. E.: *ref,* 467
Lower, K. D.: *ref,* 349
Lowrey, J. B.: *ref,* 529
Lowrie, K. H.: *ref,* 419
Lowry, C. E.: *ref,* 5:308(426)
Lowry, E.: *test,* 7:361
Lozoff, M.: *ref,* 532

Luber, S. A.: *ref,* 504
Lubin, A.: *ref,* 532
Luborsky, L.: *ref,* 532
Lucas, C. J.: *ref,* 331, 446
Lucas, D.: *ref,* 6:438(517)
Lucas, F. H.: *ref,* 574
Lucas, G.: *ref,* 529, 532
Luchins, A. S.: *ref,* 532
Luchins, E. H.: *ref,* 532
Lucht, W. E.: *ref,* 589
Lucier, O.: *test,* 7:361; *ref,* 349, 361, 6:468(1, 3–6)
Lucito, L.: *ref,* 533
Lucito, L. J.: *ref,* 533
Luck, E.: *ref,* 533
Lucker, W. G.: *ref,* 516, 525
Luckey, B.: *ref,* 525
Ludlow, H. G.: *ref,* 357, 359, 5:326(23)
Ludlow, M. E.: *ref,* 499, 525
Lueptow, L. B.: *ref,* 358
Lufkin, H. M.: *ref,* 3:220(24)
Luh, C. W.: *ref,* 525
Luker, A. G.: *ref,* 4:277(269)
Lule, Y. K.: *test,* 6:476
Lumsden, J.: *rev,* 327; *ref,* 525
Lund, R. D.: *ref,* 529
Lundgren, E. J.: *ref,* 405
Lundquist, R. M.: *ref,* 361
Lundsteen, S. W.: *ref,* 361
Lundy, C. T.: *ref,* 529
Lunn, M. S.: *ref,* 361, 419
Lunzer, E. A.: *ref,* 439
Luong, C. K. M.: *ref,* 381, 525, 533
Lusienski, D. R.: *ref,* 533
Luszki, M. B.: *ref,* 529
Luszki, W. A.: *ref,* 487, 525, 529, 533
Luton, J. N.: *ref,* 404
Lyden, B. A.: *ref,* 357
Lyerly, O.: *ref,* 342
Lyle, J. G.: *ref,* 509, 533
Lyman, G.: *ref,* 525
Lyman, H. B.: *rev,* 342, 380, 516, 529; *test,* 4:301
Lynch, M. D.: *ref,* 574
Lynch, P. L.: *ref,* 419
Lynch, W. J.: *ref,* 529
Lynd, C.: *ref,* 529
Lynn, R.: *ref,* 403, 439
Lyon, J. T.: *ref,* 361
Lyon, V. E.: *ref,* 391, 419
Lyon, V. W.: *ref,* 426
Lyons, R. A.: *ref,* 361
Lyons, T. J.: *ref,* 529, 7:378(5)
Lyons, W. A.: *ref,* 357
Lysaught, J. P.: *ref,* 425
Lytton, H.: *ref,* 409, 462, 525, 533, 589

MABERLY, N. C.: *ref,* 382
McAdam, M.: *ref,* 403, 439
McAdams, H. E.: *ref,* 6:438(495)
Macaitis, L.: *test,* 452
McAloon, F. W.: *ref,* 518
McAlpin, A. S.: *ref,* 398
McAninch, M.: *ref,* 381
McAnulty, E. A.: *ref,* 525
McArthur, C. R.: *ref,* 516, 525, 533
MacArthur, R.: *ref,* 364, 400, 425, 439, 453
MacArthur, R. S.: *ref,* 348–9, 364, 400, 425, 439, 453, 464
McBeath, M.: *ref,* 533

McBee, G.: *ref,* 349
McBrearty, J. F.: *ref,* 483, 533
McBride, D. W.: *ref,* 505
McBride, J. W.: *ref,* 533
MacBride, K.: *ref,* 426
McBride, K.: *ref,* 525
McBride, K. E.: *ref,* 381, 518, 525
McCall, C. I.: *ref,* 516
McCall, J. N.: *ref,* 357, 5:308(340)
McCall, J. R.: *ref,* 349, 5:368(22)
McCall, R. A.: *ref,* 349
McCall, R. B.: *ref,* 349
McCall, W. A.: *test,* 3:242–3; *ref,* 3:242(1–2)
McCall, W. M.: *ref,* 6:480(30)
McCandless, B. R.: *rev,* 344, 521–2, 525, 533; *ref,* 483, 525
McCann, B.: *ref,* 542
McCarthy, D.: *test,* 506; *ref,* 381, 529, 533
McCarty, B. S.: *ref,* 532
McCarty, J. J.: *ref,* 482, 548
McCauley, J. H.: *ref,* 349, 533
McCaulley, S.: *ref,* 558
Macchia, W.: *ref,* 357, 361
McClary, G. O.: *ref,* 516
McClellan, D. A.: *ref,* 381, 516
McClelland, M.: *ref,* 403, 439
McClelland, W. J.: *ref,* 403, 439
McClintock, C.: *ref,* 404
McCloskey, E. P.: *ref,* 525
McCloud, T. E.: *ref,* 359
McClure, W. E.: *ref,* 419, 525
Maccoby, E. E.: *ref,* 357
McComas, W.: *ref,* 400
McComas, W. C.: *ref,* 400
M'Comisky, J. G.: *ref,* 439, 529
McConnell, D. S.: *ref,* 357
McConnell, F.: *ref,* 439, 496, 525
McConnell, T. R.: *ref,* 2:1377(20)
McConochie, W. A.: *ref,* 533
McCook, W.: *ref,* 516
McCord, C. P.: *exc,* 532
McCormack, A. J.: *ref,* 589
McCormick, A. G.: *ref,* 425
McCormick, C. C.: *ref,* 381, 516, 529
McCormick, J. H.: *ref,* 357, 361, 425
McCoy, J. F.: *ref,* 381, 489
McCracken, R. A.: *ref,* 349
McCranie, J.: *ref,* 468
McCreary, J. R.: *ref,* 426, 532
McCrory, M. A.: *ref,* 425
McCuen, T. L.: *ref,* 3:263(34)
McCulloch, T. L.: *exc,* 487; *ref,* 525, 533
McCullough, B. R.: *ref,* 525
McCullough, G.: *ref,* 482, 548
McCullough, J. L.: *ref,* 348
McCullough, M. W.: *ref,* 532
McCully, R. S.: *ref,* 381
McCurdy, H. G.: *ref,* 381
McCutcheon, N. S.: *ref,* 400, 589
McDaniel, E. D.: *ref,* 502
McDaniel, S. W.: *ref,* 589
McDermid, C. D.: *ref,* 359
McDermott, D.: *ref,* 496, 529
McDonagh, J. M.: *ref,* 559, 561
McDonald, C.: *ref,* 529
McDonald, D.: *ref,* 349
McDonald, D. C.: *ref,* 574
McDonald, F. J.: *ref,* 561, 589
MacDonald, G. L.: *ref,* 419

Macdonald, H. A.: *ref,* 439
McDonald, J. R.: *ref,* 518, 545
McDonald, K. G.: *ref,* 529
McDonald, M. A.: *ref,* 543
McDonald, N. L. H.: *ref,* 589
MacDonald, R.: *test,* 5:325
McDonald, R. L.: *ref,* 503
McDonald, R. P.: *ref,* 439
McDonnell, M. W.: *ref,* 348, 439
MacDougall, M. J.: *ref,* 589
McDowell, F.: *ref,* 529
McElhaney, M. L.: *ref,* 533
McElvain, J. L.: *ref,* 589
McElwain, D. W.: *test,* 520; *ref,* 520
McElwee, E. W.: *ref,* 381, 525
McEntire, E. M.: *ref,* 357
MacEvitt, M.: *ref,* 529
McFadden, J. H.: *exc,* 518; *ref,* 525
McFarland, J. A.: *ref,* 419
McFarland, R. L.: *ref,* 532
Macfarlane, J. W.: *ref,* 525, 532
McFarlane, M.: *ref,* 2:1394(2)
McFie, J.: *ref,* 525, 532–3, 545
McGarry, M. E.: *ref,* 484
McGaughey, M. V.: *ref,* 574
McGavren, M.: *ref,* 543
McGee, E.: *ref,* 439, 518, 525, 532
McGee, J. E.: *ref,* 361
McGehee, E. M.: *ref,* 418
McGehee, W.: *ref,* 426, 2:1377(35), 3:217(117)
McGeoch, J. A.: *ref,* 426, 3:220 (30), 6:480(22)
McGilligan, R.: *ref,* 381
McGilligan, R. P.: *ref,* 381
McGlothlin, M. S.: *ref,* 542, 546, 551, 574
McGlothlin, W. H.: *ref,* 542, 546, 551, 574
McGowan, J. R.: *ref,* 400, 424
Mc Gown, W. P.: *ref,* 559, 561
McGrath, R. F.: *ref,* 525
McGraw, J. J.: *ref,* 533
McGraw, M. L.: *ref,* 435, 438
McGreevy, C. P.: *ref,* 404
McGuire, C.: *ref,* 349, 542, 551
McGuire, D.: *ref,* 361
McGuire, L.: *ref,* 533
Machen, L. H.: *ref,* 4:277(247)
Machi, V. S.: *ref,* 533
Machover, S.: *ref,* 532
McHugh, A. F.: *ref,* 348–9, 381, 533
McHugh, G.: *ref,* 381, 525
McIntire, J. T.: *ref,* 503
McIntire, P. H.: *ref,* 361
McIntosh, D. M.: *ref,* 409
McIntosh, R.: *ref,* 497, 525
McIntosh, W. A.: *ref,* 357, 542, 546, 561, 572
McIntyre, G. A.: *ref,* 4:272(1)
McIntyre, W.: *ref,* 415
Mack, J. L.: *ref,* 529
Mack, L. L.: *ref,* 6:438(526)
MacKane, K.: *ref,* 483, 3:290(1)
McKay, B. E.: *ref,* 525
MacKay, D. N.: *ref,* 516, 525
Mackay, G. W. S.: *ref,* 381
McKay, W. R.: *ref,* 358
McKeachie, W. J.: *ref,* 357
McKee, J. L.: *ref,* 529
McKeever, W. F.: *ref,* 529, 532
McKelpin, J. P.: *ref,* 357

McKenna, B.: *ref,* 532
McKenzie, A.: *ref,* 364, 381, 518, 533
Mackenzie, D. M.: *ref,* 391
McKenzie, R. E.: *ref,* 529, 532
McKerracher, D. W.: *ref,* 403, 525, 529, 533
McKie, D.: *exc,* 361
Mackie, J. B.: *ref,* 529
McKinlay, M.: *ref,* 403, 439
MacKinney, A. C.: *rev,* 480; *ref,* 348, 423, 482
McKinney, J. D.: *ref,* 525, 533
McKinnon, A. J.: *ref,* 490
MacKinnon, D. W.: *ref,* 359
McKinstry, E.: *ref,* 525, 532, 3:217 (98)
Mackler, B.: *ref,* 518, 555, 589
McKnight, E. L.: *ref,* 519
McLauchlin, J. A.: *ref,* 4:277(149)
McLean, O. S.: *ref,* 532
McLean, T. K.: *ref,* 533
McLelland, P. E.: *ref,* 355, 529
McLeod, H. N.: *ref,* 439, 529
McLeod, J.: *ref,* 533
McLeod, J. D.: *ref,* 349
McLeod, P.: *ref,* 516
McManis, D. L.: *ref,* 516, 533
Macmeeken, A. M.: *ref,* 525
McMenemy, R. A.: *ref,* 522, 533
McMorris, R. F.: *ref,* 561, 574
McMullen, C. P.: *ref,* 533
MacMullen, M. R.: *ref,* 532
MacMurray, D.: *ref,* 525
McMurry, F. D.: *ref,* 482
McMurry, R. N.: *test,* 449–50; *ref,* 426, 447, 482
McNamara, J. R.: *ref,* 439, 538
McNamara, W. J.: *ref,* 426, 482
MacNaughton, J. F.: *ref,* 444–5
McNeal, B. F.: *ref,* 532
McNeil, E. B.: *ref,* 532
MacNeil, R. L.: *ref,* 348, 361
McNeilly, A.: *ref,* 538
McNemar, Q.: *test,* 4:324; *exc,* 509, 532; *ref,* 359, 525, 529, 532
McNinch, G. H. W.: *ref,* 533
Macomber, L.: *ref,* 525
MacPhail, A. H.: *ref,* 357, 426, 3:217(86, 105)
MacPhee, E. D.: *ref,* 2:1394(4)
MacPhee, H. M.: *ref,* 503, 532
McPherson, D. A.: *ref,* 518
MacPherson, J. G.: *ref,* 499
McPherson, M. W.: *ref,* 381, 533
McProuty, V. H.: *ref,* 533
McQuarrie, D.: *ref,* 529, 7:378(8)
McQuary, J. P.: *ref,* 391
McQueen, R.: *ref,* 425
McQuitty, J. V.: *ref,* 2:1402(1)
McQuitty, L. L.: *rev,* 341A; *ref,* 361
McRae, H.: *ref,* 409, 461, 525, 3: 263(47), 6:480(42)
McRae, J.: *ref,* 524, 538
MacRae, J. M.: *ref,* 497, 525, 5: 326(14)
Macvaugh, G. S.: *ref,* 4:315(4–5)
Mac Vicar, D. B.: *ref,* 533
McWhinnie, H. J.: *ref,* 559, 589
Madaus, G.: *ref,* 331, 589
Madaus, G. F.: *ref,* 331, 361, 382, 400, 574, 589
Madden, R.: *test,* 340; *ref,* 525

Maddox, H.: *test,* 6:469; *ref,* 373, 461
Madeley, C. B.: *ref,* 505
Madigan, M. E.: *ref,* 3:217(108)
Madoff, E.: *ref,* 398
Madonick, M. J.: *ref,* 532
Madow, A. A.: *ref,* 516, 525
Madsen, I. N.: *ref,* 525, 3:220(5, 12–3)
Magaret, A.: *exc,* 532; *ref,* 525, 532
Magaret, G. A.: *ref,* 532
Magnusson, D.: *ref,* 381
Magoon, R. A.: *ref,* 357
Magrab, P. R.: *ref,* 357
Mahal, B. K.: *ref,* 542
Mahan, H. C.: *ref,* 483, 525
Mahan, T. W.: *ref,* 533
Maher, B. A.: *ref,* 439
Maher, H.: *ref,* 469
Mahler, C. A.: *ref,* 532
Mahoney, T. A.: *ref,* 482
Mahrer, A. R.: *ref,* 532
Maier, L. J.: *ref,* 516
Maier, N. R. F.: *ref,* 357
Mailer, A. B.: *ref,* 532
Main, H. V.: *ref,* 426
Mainord, W. A.: *ref,* 532
Mainwaring, J.: *rev,* 460, 463
Maisel, R. N.: *ref,* 505
Maitra, A. K.: *ref,* 439
Maity, H.: *ref,* 525
Maizlish, I. L.: *ref,* 525, 532
Major, C. L.: *ref,* 419
Majumdar, P. K.: *ref,* 439, 529
Majumdar, S. K.: *ref,* 372, 381
Majzoub, H. S.: *ref,* 529
Maksimczyk, W. J.: *ref,* 532
Malamud, W.: *ref,* 525
Malcolm, R. W.: *ref,* 357
Malcove, L.: *exc,* 497
Malecki, G. S.: *ref,* 357, 5:308 (359)
Malerstein, A. J.: *ref,* 516, 529
Maley, R. F.: *ref,* 529
Malin, A. J.: *ref,* 533
Maller, J. B.: *ref,* 426
Mallinson, G. G.: *ref,* 419
Malloy, J. P.: *ref,* 357, 5:308(326, 384–5)
Malmquist, C. P.: *ref,* 518
Malnig, L. R.: *ref,* 361
Maloney, M. P.: *ref,* 381, 516, 522
Malos, H. B.: *ref,* 532
Malpass, L. F.: *ref,* 439
Maltzman, I.: *ref,* 542, 574
Malueg, E.: *ref,* 6:438(466)
Man, E. B.: *ref,* 484
Manahan, N.: *ref,* 496
Mancott, A.: *ref,* 400
Mandel, R.: *ref,* 349, 439, 516
Mandelbaum, D.: *ref,* 517
Mandell, M. M.: *ref,* 3:217(134)
Mandleberg, I.: *ref,* 529
Mandler, G.: *ref,* 532, 545
Mangan, G. L.: *ref,* 542, 546–7, 551, 561, 572, 591
Mangold, M. C.: *ref,* 435, 438
Manley, D. R.: *ref,* 409
Mann, A.: *ref,* 525
Mann, C. W.: *test,* 2:1395; *ref,* 525, 2:1395(1–2)
Mann, E. T.: *ref,* 529
Mann, H. P.: *ref,* 525

Mann, L.: *ref*, 391, 400, 424, 533
Mann, M. J.: *ref*, 357, 361
Manne, S. H.: *ref*, 532
Manning, F. L.: *ref*, 426
Manning, G. C.: *ref*, 516, 532
Manning, J.: *ref*, 426
Manning, W. H.: *ref*, 357, 436
Manolakes, G.: *ref*, 349, 483, 525
Manske, M. E.: *ref*, 542
Manson, G. E.: *ref*, 3:220(34)
Manson, G. G.: *ref*, 361
Manson, M. P.: *test*, 481; *ref*, 349
Manuel, H. T.: *rev*, 504, 2:1428; *test*, 468, 5:389; *ref*, 361, 381–2, 468, 525, 3:217(75), 5:308(327, 427), 5:389(1)
Manwiller, C. E.: *ref*, 426
Many, W. A.: *ref*, 589
Maples, V. S.: *ref*, 349
Marascuilo, L. A.: *ref*, 404
Marburg, G. S.: *ref*, 589
Marches, J. R.: *ref*, 6:438(484)
Marchi, J. U.: *ref*, 533
Marcus, B.: *ref*, 439
Marcuse, F. L.: *ref*, 447, 4:281(84)
Marden, M. L.: *ref*, 516
Margach, C.: *ref*, 533
Mar'i, S. K.: *ref*, 589
Mariani, R. R.: *ref*, 532
Marinaccio, L. V.: *ref*, 425
Marine, E. L.: *ref*, 525
Marino, C.: *ref*, 542
Mark, J. C.: *ref*, 532
Markham, S.: *ref*, 532
Markides, M.: *ref*, 496
Markin, K. E.: *ref*, 532
Marks, A.: *ref*, 457, 542, 551, 561, 564, 571–2
Marks, C. H.: *ref*, 542, 546, 551, 561, 577, 594
Marks, C. S.: *ref*, 592
Marks, E.: *ref*, 357, 529
Marks, E. S.: *ref*, 525
Marks, J. B.: *ref*, 533
Marks, M. R.: *rev*, 431; *ref*, 532
Markwardt, F. C.: *ref*, 6:438(485)
Markwell, E. D.: *ref*, 532
Marley, A. D.: *ref*, 489, 516, 533
Marlowe, D.: *ref*, 419
Marmorston, J.: *ref*, 439, 529
Marquart, D. I.: *ref*, 364, 525
Marquette, A. J.: *ref*, 357
Marquis, D. P.: *ref*, 381
Marr, E.: *ref*, 388, 439
Marriage, A.: *ref*, 439, 518
Mars, P. A.: *ref*, 348
Marsan, C. A.: *ref*, 529, 592
Marschak, M.: *ref*, 487, 525
Marsden, G.: *ref*, 533
Marsden, R. E.: *ref*, 525
Marsh, C. J.: *ref*, 518, 558
Marsh, F. E.: *ref*, 357
Marshak, M. D.: *ref*, 532
Marshall, A.: *ref*, 381, 495, 525, 578
Marshall, F. B.: *ref*, 497
Marshall, H.: *ref*, 359, 525
Marshall, J. J.: *ref*, 349
Marshall, M. S.: *ref*, 516
Marshall, M. V.: *ref*, 3:217(123)
Marshall, R. J.: *ref*, 529
Marshall, T. A.: *ref*, 349
Marshall, T. O.: *ref*, 435
Marston, A. R.: *ref*, 382
Martin, A. H.: *exc*, 525

Martin, A. W.: *ref*, 439, 533
Martin, B.: *ref*, 489
Martin, B. E.: *ref*, 361
Martin, D. R.: *ref*, 439, 5:339(9)
Martin, F.: *ref*, 439, 482, 525, 532, 589
Martin, F. M.: *ref*, 4:277(248)
Martin, H. J.: *ref*, 532, 4:277(249)
Martin, H. T.: *ref*, 357
Martin, J. D.: *ref*, 533
Martin, J. P.: *ref*, 419
Martin, J. R.: *ref*, 391
Martin, R. B.: *ref*, 574
Martin, R. P.: *ref*, 447
Martin, R. R.: *ref*, 5:308(360)
Martin, S.: *ref*, 533
Martin, S. B.: *ref*, 532
Martin, W. E.: *ref*, 518, 529
Martin, W. T.: *test*, 466; *ref*, 333, 440, 466
Martinson, B.: *ref*, 525
Martinson, M. P.: *ref*, 3:217(66)
Marum, O.: *ref*, 403, 439
Marvin, S.: *ref*, 342
Marx, B.: *ref*, 525
Marx, R. W.: *ref*, 533
Marzolf, S. S.: *rev*, 398, 3:255; *ref*, 439
Mascarenhas, J.: *ref*, 533
Mascia, G. V.: *ref*, 489
Masica, D. N.: *ref*, 529, 533
Masling, J.: *ref*, 532
Masling, J. M.: *ref*, 525, 533
Mason, A. W.: *ref*, 381, 525
Mason, C. F.: *ref*, 342
Mason, C. T.: *ref*, 3:217(87)
Mason, E. P.: *ref*, 503
Mason, P. L.: *ref*, 325, 439
Massa, E.: *ref*, 400, 424
Massad, C. E.: *ref*, 361
Massari, D.: *ref*, 525
Masser, E. V.: *ref*, 529
Massey, J. O.: *ref*, 533
Masten, S. H.: *ref*, 357, 6:438(465)
Masters, P. B.: *ref*, 357
Matarazzo, J. D.: *ref*, 529, 532, 592
Matarazzo, R. G.: *ref*, 532, 592
Mateer, F.: *ref*, 525
Mathae, D. E.: *ref*, 407
Matheny, A. P.: *ref*, 487, 516, 525, 533, 538
Mather, L. J.: *ref*, 439, 505, 533
Mather, M. D.: *ref*, 592
Mathews, A.: *ref*, 533
Mathews, D. L.: *ref*, 543
Mathews, J.: *ref*, 525
Mathis, C.: *ref*, 357
Mattar, J. C.: *ref*, 532
Matthew, J.: *ref*, 525
Matthews, C. G.: *ref*, 439, 516, 518, 525, 529, 532–3, 578
Matthews, J.: *ref*, 505
Mattick, W. E.: *ref*, 348, 400
Mattussek, P.: *ref*, 504, 6:555(4)
Matunas, M. I.: *ref*, 543
Matyas, R. P.: *ref*, 525, 533
Maul, T. L.: *ref*, 589
Maupin, E. W.: *ref*, 529
Maurer, K. M.: *test*, 509; *ref*, 381, 509, 525
Maurer, S.: *ref*, 483
Mauser, A. J.: *ref*, 516
Mausner, B.: *ref*, 559
Maxfield, F. N.: *rev*, 525, 1:1061,
2:1388, 2:1426; *exc*, 391, 483, 525; *ref*, 349, 525
Maxfield, K. E.: *ref*, 529
Maxwell, A. E.: *ref*, 439, 518, 525, 529, 532–3
Maxwell, E.: *ref*, 529
Maxwell, J.: *rev*, 375; *exc*, 525; *ref*, 525
Maxwell, M. J.: *ref*, 6:438(486)
Maxwell, M. T.: *ref*, 524–5, 533
May, A. E.: *ref*, 440
May, L. L.: *ref*, 546
May, P. R. A.: *ref*, 529
May, W. T.: *ref*, 489, 525
Mayans, A. E.: *ref*, 516
Maycock, G. A.: *ref*, 533
Mayer, A. D.: *ref*, 503
Mayer, B. A.: *ref*, 525
Mayer, J.: *ref*, 357
Mayer, R. W.: *ref*, 361, 533
Mayhon, W. G.: *ref*, 348, 589
Mayman, M.: *ref*, 525, 529, 532
Mazer, M.: *ref*, 516
Mazur, J. L.: *ref*, 398
Mead, A. R.: *ref*, 419
Mead, D. F.: *ref*, 496
Mead, M.: *ref*, 497
Meadow, A.: *ref*, 529, 542, 561, 572
Meadows, M. E.: *ref*, 357
Meals, D. W.: *ref*, 532
Means, H. R.: *ref*, 361
Mearig, J. S.: *ref*, 589
Mears, F. G.: *ref*, 439
Mech, E.: *ref*, 532
Mechling, J.: *ref*, 357
Medinnus, G. R.: *ref*, 381
Mednick, E. V.: *ref*, 574
Mednick, M. T.: *test*, 574; *ref*, 357, 404, 522, 574
Mednick, S. A.: *test*, 574; *ref*, 574
Mee, E. A.: *ref*, 532
Meehan, K. S.: *ref*, 425
Meeker, M.: *ref*, 525
Meeker, M. M.: *ref*, 525
Meeker, M. N.: *ref*, 525, 533, 538
Meenes, M.: *ref*, 398
Meer, B.: *ref*, 404, 503, 529, 532, 592
Meerbach, J. C.: *ref*, 589
Mefferd, R. B.: *ref*, 561
Megargee, E. I.: *ref*, 529, 533
Mehrabian, A.: *ref*, 382, 404
Mehrens, W. A.: *ref*, 349, 358, 400
Mehrotra, K. K.: *ref*, 439, 533
Mehrotra, S. N.: *ref*, 388, 439
Mehryar, A. H.: *ref*, 331
Meichenbaum, D. H.: *ref*, 518, 533
Meier, J. H.: *ref*, 381, 439, 516, 525, 533
Meier, L. D.: *ref*, 532
Meier, M. J.: *ref*, 518, 529, 578
Meier, N. C.: *ref*, 381, 398, 426
Meikle, S.: *ref*, 529
Mein, R.: *ref*, 516, 525
Meissler, G. R.: *ref*, 524–5
Meister, R. K.: *ref*, 525
Melchert, P. A.: *ref*, 533
Melikian, L.: *ref*, 381
Mellenbruch, P. L.: *test*, 3:234
Mellits, D.: *ref*, 516, 533
Mellits, E. D.: *ref*, 381, 484, 525, 533
Mellone, M. A.: *test*, 408; *ref*, 408, 525

Mellsop, G. W.: *ref,* 403
Melton, K.: *ref,* 439, 516, 525
Melton, R. S.: *ref,* 357, 5:308(386)
Meltzer, M. L.: *ref,* 529
Melville, N. T.: *ref,* 418
Mendelsohn, G. A.: *ref,* 574
Mendelson, M. A.: *ref,* 449, 484, 529
Mendenhall, D. R.: *ref,* 399
Mendola, V. S.: *ref,* 532
Menon, A. S.: *ref,* 439
Mensh, I. N.: *rev,* 500, 503, 543, 592; *ref,* 503, 525, 532, 592
Menzel, E. W.: *ref,* 381
Meranski, S.: *ref,* 525
Merbaum, M.: *ref,* 529
Mercer, M.: *ref,* 525, 529, 532
Merenda, P. F.: *exc,* 522; *ref,* 382, 522
Merle, S.: *ref,* 404
Merlis, M.: *ref,* 439
Merlis, S.: *ref,* 439
Merrifield, P. R.: *test,* 542, 551, 554–5, 561m3, 561x2, 562, 565, 571, 577, 581, 591; *ref,* 457, 546, 551, 561, 571
Merrill, M. A.: *test,* 525; *ref,* 525
Merrill, R. M.: *ref,* 419, 532, 5:308 (328)
Merriman, C.: *ref,* 525
Merryman, E. P.: *ref,* 589
Merryman, P.: *ref,* 529, 592
Merwin, J. C.: *exc,* 480, 7:378; *ref,* 357, 404–5
Mery, M.: *exc,* 549
Merz, W. R.: *ref,* 381
Mesinger, J. F.: *ref,* 524
Meskin, J.: *ref,* 525
Meskin, J. D.: *ref,* 589
Mesner, D. M.: *ref,* 5:308(413)
Messer, M. E.: *ref,* 375, 516
Messick, S. J.: *ref,* 561
Metfessel, N. S.: *ref,* 364, 400, 561–2, 591
Methvin, M.: *ref,* 522
Metzger, R.: *ref,* 522
Metzger, S. M.: *ref,* 6:438(449)
Meyer, B.: *ref,* 6:438(470)
Meyer, H. H.: *ref,* 445, 447, 482
Meyer, M. M.: *ref,* 532
Meyer, V.: *ref,* 403, 439, 532, 592
Meyer, W. J.: *ref,* 525
Meyers, C. E.: *ref,* 349, 400, 525, 533
Meyers, E.: *ref,* 364, 439, 496
Michael, J. J.: *ref,* 516
Michael, W. B.: *rev,* 360, 398, 401, 5:308–9, 5:377; *ref,* 349, 357, 361, 364, 382, 400, 439, 457, 525, 533, 542, 551, 561–2, 564, 571–2, 591
Michaels, J. J.: *ref,* 525
Michalski, S. F.: *ref,* 357
Michea, C. A.: *ref,* 505
Mickler, J. E.: *ref,* 348
Middents, G. J.: *ref,* 589
Middleton, F. T.: *ref,* 589
Midkiff, K. L.: *ref,* 381, 439
Miele, J. A.: *ref,* 529, 533
Mienie, C. J. P.: *ref,* 381, 411, 511
Miezitis, S.: *ref,* 516, 538
Miezitis, S. A.: *ref,* 381, 505, 516, 525, 533
Mignone, R. J.: *ref,* 532
Miklich, D. R.: *ref,* 533

Milam, O. H.: *ref,* 361, 5:308 (329)
Miles, C. C.: *ref,* 426
Miles, D. T.: *ref,* 561, 572
Miles, D. W.: *ref,* 503
Miles, G. E.: *test,* 6:446
Miles, G. H.: *ref,* 529
Miles, T. R.: *rev,* 415, 5:337, 5:393, 6:469
Miles, W. R.: *ref,* 426
Milgram, N. A.: *ref,* 516, 525, 533
Milholland, J. E.: *rev,* 349, 364, 400, 424, 450
Mill, C. R.: *ref,* 489
Millard, M. S.: *ref,* 518, 525
Miller, A. J.: *ref,* 426
Miller, B.: *ref,* 489, 525
Miller, B. B.: *ref,* 348, 361, 516
Miller, B. P.: *ref,* 447
Miller, C. D.: *ref,* 357
Miller, C. K.: *ref,* 524, 533
Miller, C. L.: *ref,* 357
Miller, D. M.: *ref,* 357
Miller, D. R.: *ref,* 529
Miller, E.: *ref,* 487, 489, 525
Miller, F. M.: *ref,* 439
Miller, G. L.: *ref,* 592
Miller, H.: *ref,* 525
Miller, H. R.: *ref,* 533
Miller, I.: *ref,* 525
Miller, J. M.: *ref,* 357, 529, 532–3
Miller, J. O.: *ref,* 525, 561
Miller, J. S.: *ref,* 532
Miller, L. E.: *ref,* 439, 538
Miller, L. L.: *ref,* 5:329(7)
Miller, L. R.: *ref,* 498, 525, 529
Miller, M. H.: *ref,* 529
Miller, R. B.: *ref,* 482
Miller, R. E.: *ref,* 6:438(487)
Miller, R. H.: *ref,* 361
Miller, V. J.: *ref,* 525
Miller, W.: *ref,* 361, 400
Miller, W. E.: *ref,* 361
Miller, W. S.: *test,* 404; *ref,* 426, 438, 2:1424(6, 15), 3:220(33, 46), 3:263(28), 6:480(31)
Millham, J.: *ref,* 525, 529
Millichap, J. G.: *ref,* 381, 516
Milligan, E. E.: *ref,* 4:277(189)
Milliren, A. P.: *ref,* 538
Mills, D. H.: *ref,* 358, 529
Mills, L. F.: *ref,* 388, 415, 439
Milne, G. G.: *ref,* 532
Milstein, V.: *ref,* 529, 532–3
Milton, C. R.: *ref,* 426
Milton, E. O.: *ref,* 532
Milton, O.: *ref,* 473
Minard, J.: *ref,* 529
Mindess, H.: *ref,* 532
Miner, J. B.: *ref,* 529
Miner, L.: *ref,* 516, 522
Minogue, B. M.: *ref,* 525
Minski, L.: *ref,* 518
Minsky, R.: *ref,* 381, 516
Mintz, J.: *ref,* 489
Mira, M. P.: *ref,* 499, 505
Mirels, H. L.: *ref,* 589
Miron, M.: *ref,* 400
Mirsky, A. F.: *ref,* 516, 529, 532–3, 592
Misbach, L.: *ref,* 532
Miscevich, M. B.: *ref,* 525
Mishra, S. P.: *ref,* 525, 529, 533
Misiak, H.: *ref,* 439, 518, 529

Misra, A. N.: *ref,* 372
Misra, M. N.: *ref,* 543
Misselbrook, B. D.: *exc,* 532
Mitchell, A.: *test,* 406
Mitchell, A. C.: *ref,* 381
Mitchell, B.: *ref,* 589
Mitchell, B. C.: *ref,* 525
Mitchell, B. M.: *ref,* 589
Mitchell, C.: *test,* 6:442; *ref,* 426, 2:1424(20)
Mitchell, D.: *ref,* 525
Mitchell, J. H.: *ref,* 5:339(3)
Mitchell, J. V.: *ref,* 348, 391, 425
Mitchell, K. E.: *ref,* 400
Mitchell, L.: *ref,* 439
Mitchell, M. B.: *ref,* 525, 532
Mitchell, M. D.: *ref,* 482
Mitchell, R. J.: *ref,* 525
Mitra, A. K.: *ref,* 439
Mitrano, A. J.: *ref,* 4:315(7)
Mittler, P.: *ref,* 525, 529
Mittler, P. J.: *ref,* 525, 529
Miyake, K.: *ref,* 513
Moan, C. E.: *ref,* 361, 549
Mock, W. L.: *ref,* 357
Moe, I. L.: *ref,* 349
Moed, G.: *ref,* 496, 516, 533
Moeny, W. C.: *ref,* 533
Moffat, G. W.: *ref,* 3:242(2)
Moffett, C. R.: *ref,* 404
Moffie, D. J.: *ref,* 426
Moffitt, P.: *ref,* 516, 538
Mogel, S.: *ref,* 529, 533
Mogensen, A.: *ref,* 439
Moghrabi, K. M.: *ref,* 382
Mogor, A. G.: *ref,* 364
Mohan, J.: *ref,* 439
Mohan, P. J.: *ref,* 525, 533
Mohan, V.: *ref,* 439
Mohr, E.: *ref,* 507
Moldawsky, P. C.: *ref,* 532
Moldawsky, S.: *ref,* 532
Molema, S. Y.: *ref,* 381, 439
Molino, H. S.: *ref,* 505
Molish, H. B.: *ref,* 529, 592
Mollenkopf, W. G.: *ref,* 357
Moller, H.: *ref,* 533
Molnar, G. E.: *ref,* 357
Molomo, R. R-S.: *ref,* 561
Monahan, J. E.: *ref,* 525
Monahan, R. D.: *ref,* 404
Moncrieff, A.: *ref,* 6:523(4)
Money, J.: *ref,* 381, 525, 529, 532–3, 543
Monroe, J.: *ref,* 532
Monroe, J. J.: *ref,* 532
Monroe, K. L.: *ref,* 481, 529
Monroe, W. S.: *ref,* 6:480(5)
Montagu, M. F. A.: *ref,* 447, 4:281 (83)
Montemagni, G.: *ref,* 439
Montgomery, G. W. G.: *ref,* 403, 439, 512, 533
Montgomery, R. P.: *ref,* 518
Moon, H.: *ref,* 525, 529
Moon, W. H.: *ref,* 533
Mooney, R. F.: *ref,* 524–5
Moore, A. B.: *ref,* 529
Moore, B. G. R.: *ref,* 354, 439
Moore, C. L.: *ref,* 444–5
Moore, C. W.: *ref,* 5:308(435)
Moore, D.: *ref,* 533
Moore, E. J.: *ref,* 398

Moore, H.: *ref,* 357, 426, 2:1424 (17), 3:220(51)
Moore, J. C.: *ref,* 404
Moore, J. E.: *ref,* 426, 447, 6:537 (2)
Moore, J. H.: *ref,* 532
Moore, L. B.: *ref,* 357
Moore, M.: *ref,* 381, 503, 533
Moore, M. C.: *ref,* 533
Moore, N. I.: *ref,* 496
Moore, R. B.: *ref,* 404
Moore, R. V.: *ref,* 364
Moore, T.: *ref,* 525
Moore, T. I.: *ref,* 533
Moore, W. B.: *ref,* 529
Moore, W. E.: *ref,* 426, 447, 449, 529, 533
Moran, F. A.: *ref,* 532
Moran, L. J.: *ref,* 440, 532, 561
Morán, R. E.: *ref,* 439, 525, 533
Mordock, J. B.: *ref,* 533
More, A.: *ref,* 349, 361, 425
Moreau, M.: *ref,* 435
Moreton, C. A.: *ref,* 477
Morgan, A. B.: *test,* 5:395
Morgan, C. E.: *ref,* 533
Morgan, C. L.: *ref,* 6:480(43)
Morgan, D. W.: *ref,* 529
Morgan, E. F.: *ref,* 435, 496
Morgan, F.: *ref,* 3:263(43)
Morgan, G. A. V.: *rev,* 5:405; *ref,* 415
Morgan, J. J. B.: *ref,* 4:354(1)
Morgan, J. M.: *ref,* 357
Morgan, L. B.: *ref,* 357
Morgan, R. E.: *ref,* 357
Morgan, W. J.: *test,* 5:395; *ref,* 3:220(71)
Morgart, H. S.: *ref,* 425
Morgenthau, D. R.: *ref,* 518, 525, 558
Moriarty, A.: *ref,* 487, 497, 507, 525, 533
Moriarty, A. E.: *rev,* 492
Morice, H. O.: *ref,* 6:438(527)
Morledge, J.: *ref,* 529, 533
Morley, C. A.: *ref,* 426
Morningstar, M.: *ref,* 357
Morper, J.: *ref,* 361, 400, 533
Morris, A. B.: *ref,* 439
Morris, B. E. J. VanC.: *ref,* 499
Morris, C. M.: *ref,* 391, 518
Morris, F.: *ref,* 532
Morris, G. L.: *ref,* 499
Morris, H. L.: *ref,* 525, 533
Morris, L. W.: *ref,* 529
Morris, M.: *test,* 437
Morris, R. O.: *ref,* 361
Morrison, D. F.: *ref,* 529
Morrison, D. H.: *ref,* 532-3
Morrison, E. B.: *ref,* 533
Morrison, H. E.: *ref,* 425
Morrison, I. E.: *ref,* 348
Morrison, J.: *ref,* 6:438(528)
Morrison, J. C.: *ref,* 6:480(23)
Morrison, J. W.: *ref,* 357
Morrison, M.: *ref,* 439, 533
Morrison, M. M.: *ref,* 529
Morrison, N. C.: *ref,* 3:242(2)
Morrison, W. E.: *ref,* 482
Morrison, W. J.: *ref,* 2:1411(2)
Morrow, R. S.: *ref,* 532, 3:217(88)
Morrow, W. R.: *ref,* 532
Morse, N. C.: *ref,* 381, 435

Mortensen, J. B.: *ref,* 400
Morton, N. W.: *test,* 447; *ref,* 447
Mortvedt, A. R.: *ref,* 5:308(330)
Moser, R. J.: *ref,* 364, 574
Moser, W. E.: *ref,* 391
Moses, J. L.: *ref,* 529
Mosher, L. R.: *ref,* 529
Mosher, R. L.: *ref,* 382, 404
Moshin, S. M.: *ref,* 388, 439, 473
Mosier, C. I.: *ref,* 2:1377(23)
Mosier, J. A.: *ref,* 589
Moss, A.: *ref,* 487, 525
Moss, J.: *ref,* 589
Moss, J. W.: *ref,* 516
Mosychuk, H.: *ref,* 364, 400, 439
Motley, H. C.: *ref,* 361, 400
Mott, D. D.: *ref,* 361
Mott, S. M.: *ref,* 381
Motter, M. E.: *ref,* 525, 532, 3:217(98)
Moulin, E. K.: *ref,* 348-9
Moulton, R.: *ref,* 529
Mouly, G. J.: *ref,* 348, 399, 425
Mowrer, W. M. C.: *ref,* 507, 509, 525
Moyel, I. S.: *ref,* 361
Moyles, E. W.: *ref,* 439
Muehl, S.: *ref,* 533
Muehleman, T.: *ref,* 529
Muehlenbein, J. M.: *ref,* 3:285 (4-5)
Mueller, K. A.: *ref,* 357
Mueller, M. W.: *ref,* 439, 516-7, 525
Mueller, T. H.: *ref,* 361
Muench, G. A.: *ref,* 518, 525
Muhlenkamp, A. F.: *ref,* 357
Muhr, J. P.: *ref,* 525, 533
Muir, R.: *ref,* 400, 533
Muir, W.: *ref,* 559
Mukerjee, M.: *test,* 412; *ref,* 412
Mukherjee, A.: *ref,* 525
Mukherjee, B. N.: *ref,* 533
Mulero, R.: *ref,* 529
Mulhern, M.: *ref,* 529
Mullen, F. A.: *ref,* 398, 503, 525
Mullen, N. D.: *ref,* 349
Mullineaux, J. E.: *ref,* 342
Mullins, C. J.: *ref,* 5:308(387)
Mumaw, M. J.: *ref,* 349, 391
Mumbauer, C. C.: *ref,* 525
Mumpower, D. L.: *ref,* 533
Munday, L.: *ref,* 357, 361, 391, 405, 419
Mundy, J. P.: *ref,* 532
Mundy, L.: *ref,* 439, 525, 532
Mundy-Castle, A. C.: *ref,* 532, 6:459(3)
Munger, P.: *ref,* 419
Munger, P. F.: *ref,* 419, 533
Munn, N. L.: *exc,* 497
Munro, H.: *ref,* 403, 439
Munroe, R. L.: *ref,* 4:277(190)
Munson, G.: *ref,* 525
Muntyan, M.: *ref,* 4:278(10)
Munz, A.: *ref,* 533
Munz, D. C.: *ref,* 391
Muralidharan, R.: *ref,* 381, 497, 518
Murdy, W. G.: *ref,* 529
Murfett, B. J.: *ref,* 532-3
Murphree, O. D.: *ref,* 518, 532
Murphy, D. B.: *ref,* 532
Murphy, K. P.: *ref,* 388, 532
Murphy, L. J.: *ref,* 533

Murphy, L. W.: *ref,* 398, 447, 4:324(55)
Murphy, M.: *ref,* 525
Murphy, M. M.: *ref,* 381, 532
Murray, B. O.: *test,* 7:399
Murray, J. B.: *ref,* 529
Murray, J. E.: *ref,* 407
Murray, S.: *ref,* 342, 439, 529
Murray, T.: *ref,* 5:308(361)
Murray, V. F.: *ref,* 483, 518
Murstein, B. I.: *ref,* 532-3
Musgrove, W. J.: *ref,* 381, 538
Muskera, D. J.: *ref,* 529
Mussen, P.: *ref,* 525, 533
Mussen, P. H.: *ref,* 518
Muth, M. J.: *ref,* 5:308(388)
Muzekari, L. H.: *ref,* 381, 525
Myatt, M. F.: *ref,* 518
Myers, A. E.: *ref,* 357, 361, 436
Myers, B. J.: *ref,* 497
Myers, C. E.: *ref,* 533
Myers, C. R.: *ref,* 525
Myers, C. T.: *ref,* 357
Myers, P. I.: *ref,* 516
Myers, R. A.: *ref,* 447, 529
Myers, R. C.: *ref,* 357
Myers, R. E.: *ref,* 391, 589
Myers, S. S.: *ref,* 529
Myklebust, H. R.: *ref,* 381, 483, 493, 503, 505, 533, 558

NAAR, R.: *ref,* 533
Nachmann, B.: *ref,* 529
Naddeo, C. L.: *ref,* 498
Nadeau, C.: *ref,* 349, 364, 400
Nadel, A. B.: *ref,* 545
Nadel, R. S.: *ref,* 529
Nadler, E. B.: *ref,* 529
Nagler, E.: *ref,* 525
Nair, R. K.: *ref,* 349
Najarian, P.: *ref,* 381, 487, 518
Nakamura, H.: *ref,* 525
Nale, S.: *ref,* 525, 533
Nale, S. L.: *ref,* 525
Nalven, F. B.: *ref,* 533
Namy, E.: *ref,* 533
Nanassy, L. C.: *rev,* 345
Napp, F. P.: *ref,* 5:308(389)
Narosny, E. H.: *ref,* 483, 525
Nase, R. R.: *ref,* 381, 538
Nash, A. N.: *ref,* 482
Nash, H.: *ref,* 381
Nash, J.: *ref,* 543
Nash, J. M.: *ref,* 361
Nash, M. S.: *ref,* 524
Nash, P. G.: *ref,* 398
Nash, P. N.: *ref,* 525
Nathan, P.: *ref,* 529
Nathan, S.: *ref,* 381
Nathanson, I. A.: *ref,* 529
Nation, J. E.: *ref,* 516
National Foundation for Educational Research in England and Wales: *test,* 379, 415, 474-7, 5:393
National Institute for Personnel Research: *test,* 402, 464, 529, 557, 5:339-40
National Institute of Industrial Psychology: *test,* 384-6, 386A, 388-90
National Merit Scholarship Corporation: *test,* 436

National Research Council: *test*, 4:281
Naumann, T. F.: *ref*, 516, 533
Naylor, G. F. K.: *ref*, 529
Neal, C. D.: *ref*, 439
Neal, J. A.: *ref*, 589
Neale, M. D.: *exc*, 525
Neaves, A. I.: *ref*, 533
Nebelkopf, E. B.: *ref*, 533
Nebergall, R. E.: *ref*, 419
Nedler, S.: *ref*, 505, 516
Needham, N. R.: *ref*, 381, 525
Needham, W. E.: *ref*, 349, 525, 529, 533, 551, 559, 561, 564, 577
Neel, M. O.: *ref*, 419
Neel, R. G.: *ref*, 482
Neely, J. H.: *ref*, 489, 525
Neher, L. A.: *ref*, 529, 533
Neidt, C. O.: *rev*, 399; *ref*, 357, 359, 455
Neilsen, M. K.: *ref*, 529
Neilson, J. R.: *ref*, 512
Neisworth, J. T.: *ref*, 542, 546, 551, 561-2, 577, 589
Nelsen, E. A.: *ref*, 357
Nelson, A. G.: *ref*, 349
Nelson, A. K.: *exc*, 497; *ref*, 419
Nelson, B. E.: *ref*, 357
Nelson, C. C.: *ref*, 533, 6:514(11)
Nelson, C. L.: *ref*, 532
Nelson, C. M.: *ref*, 425, 493, 516, 533
Nelson, C. W.: *ref*, 3:217(106)
Nelson, D.: *ref*, 533
Nelson, D. A.: *ref*, 503
Nelson, E. H.: *ref*, 5:357(3)
Nelson, G. K.: *ref*, 532, 6:459(3)
Nelson, K. B.: *ref*, 525
Nelson, L. A.: *ref*, 529, 592
Nelson, L. T.: *ref*, 473
Nelson, M. J.: *test*, 391; *ref*, 391, 2:1377(2), 2:1424(10)
Nelson, M. O.: *ref*, 348, 439
Nelson, P. C.: *ref*, 516
Nelson, R. J.: *ref*, 404
Nelson, S.: *ref*, 381
Nelson, T. M.: *ref*, 525
Nelson, V.: *ref*, 497, 525
Nelson, V. L.: *ref*, 497, 525
Nelson, W.: *ref*, 525, 529
Nemzek, C. L.: *ref*, 398, 426, 438, 525, 2:1399(11, 13), 3:220(47), 5:329(5)
Nesbitt, M. C.: *ref*, 516
Nesvig, D.: *ref*, 532
Netherton, A. H.: *ref*, 439
Netley, C. T.: *ref*, 403
Neubert, J.: *ref*, 496, 529
Neuhaus, M.: *ref*, 512, 533
Neuringer, C.: *ref*, 529, 532
Nevill, E. M.: *exc*, 525
Neville, D.: *ref*, 533
Neville, M. H.: *ref*, 453
Nevins, F. A.: *ref*, 525
New York Public Schools, Division of Tests and Measurements: *ref*, 525
New Zealand Council for Educational Research: *test*, 426
Newbrough, J. R.: *ref*, 439
Newcomb, W. B.: *ref*, 439
Newham, V.: *ref*, 538
Newland, T. E.: *rev*, 489, 499, 517, 540, 6:516; *ref*, 355, 525, 529, 533, 538
Newlyn, D.: *ref*, 525
Newman, A. P.: *ref*, 533
Newman, J.: *rev*, 543, 592
Newman, J. R.: *ref*, 532-3
Newman, R. I.: *ref*, 382
Newman, S. E.: *ref*, 419
Newman, S. H.: *ref*, 357, 5:308 (296, 302)
Newton, B. M.: *ref*, 400
Newton, B. W.: *ref*, 532
Newton, G. M.: *ref*, 500, 529
Newton, R. L.: *ref*, 532
Ni, L.: *ref*, 447
Nicholi, A. M.: *ref*, 357
Nichols, J. E.: *ref*, 532
Nichols, R. C.: *ref*, 357, 382, 440
Nicholson, A.: *ref*, 349, 425
Nicholson, C. L.: *ref*, 439, 489, 516, 524-5
Nicholson, E.: *ref*, 357
Nicholson, J.: *ref*, 357, 361
Nickols, J.: *ref*, 439, 529, 533, 543
Nickols, J. E.: *ref*, 439, 529
Nickols, M.: *ref*, 533
Nicolay, G. C.: *ref*, 542, 551
Nicolay, R. C.: *ref*, 529
Nielsen, H. H.: *ref*, 381
Nielsen, W.: *ref*, 382
Niemela, W. A.: *ref*, 3:217(67)
Niemi, G. M.: *ref*, 426
Nijhawan, H. K.: *ref*, 416
Nikas, G. B.: *ref*, 400
Nilson, K.: *ref*, 398
Nisbet, J.: *rev*, 331, 415, 474-5, 5:398; *ref*, 409
Nisbet, J. D.: *ref*, 373, 408-9, 415, 459
Nisbet, S.: *rev*, 476, 7:342
Nisbet, S. D.: *rev*, 4:289
Nix, A. P.: *ref*, 533
Nixon, M.: *test*, 488; *ref*, 488
Nixon, W. L. B.: *ref*, 529
Noble, E. L.: *ref*, 3:220(14)
Noble, H.: *ref*, 525
Nolan, E. G.: *ref*, 349
Noll, V. H.: *exc*, 344
Noller, P. A.: *ref*, 525, 533
Noone, A.: *ref*, 381
Nordén, K.: *ref*, 381, 439
Nordvik, H.: *ref*, 529
Norman, J. H.: *test*, 334, 429
Norman, R. D.: *ref*, 349, 381, 439, 496-7, 525, 529, 532
Norman, R. M.: *ref*, 525, 6:480(33, 37-8)
Norman, R. P.: *ref*, 529
Norman, W. T.: *ref*, 419, 5:308 (356)
Norrell, G.: *ref*, 349, 6:438(467)
Norris, B. N.: *ref*, 357
Norris, M.: *ref*, 487
Norris, R. C.: *rev*, 5:354; *ref*, 516
Norsworthy, N.: *test*, 578
North, G. E.: *ref*, 532
North, R. D.: *rev*, 469; *test*, 4:301; *ref*, 348, 361, 398, 400, 425, 5:308(409, 428), 6:438(529), 6:495(1)
Norton, D. P.: *ref*, 425
Norton, J. A.: *ref*, 533
Norton, J. K.: *ref*, 525, 6:480(10)
Notcutt, B.: *ref*, 381, 439
Notestine, E. B.: *ref*, 357
Nott, P. N.: *ref*, 592
Nottingham, R. D.: *ref*, 525, 558, 578
Nowakiwska, M.: *ref*, 529, 533
Nowka, H. E.: *ref*, 357
Noyes, M.: *ref*, 516
Noyes, M. H.: *ref*, 516
Nuckols, R.: *ref*, 482
Nugent, G. R.: *ref*, 529
Nuhn, D.: *ref*, 349
Nunnally, J. C.: *rev*, 7:378; *ref*, 525, 529, 533
Nunnery, M. Y.: *ref*, 404
Nurcombe, B.: *ref*, 516, 538
Nurss, J. R.: *ref*, 516, 525, 533
Nuttall, E. V.: *ref*, 589
Nuttall, J. C.: *ref*, 381, 525, 533
Nutting, R. E.: *ref*, 426
Nyaard, M.: *ref*, 529
Nye, M. R.: *ref*, 400
Nyman, G. E.: *ref*, 439

OAKLAND, J. A.: *ref*, 533
Oakland, T. D.: *ref*, 525, 533, 538
Oakley, C. A.: *ref*, 381
Oas, R. T.: *ref*, 348, 400
Oates, W. E.: *ref*, 357
Obelkevich, H.: *ref*, 525
Oberheim, G. M.: *ref*, 3:217(107)
Oberleder, M.: *ref*, 529
Oberlin, D. S.: *ref*, 507
Oberstein, R. M.: *ref*, 349
Oblinger, B.: *ref*, 525
O'Brien, C. C.: *ref*, 532
O'Brien, F. P.: *ref*, 3:263(29)
O'Brien, T. G.: *ref*, 381
Obrist, W. D.: *ref*, 529
O'Bryan, K.: *ref*, 400, 589
Obst, F.: *ref*, 358, 6:438(471)
Obuchowski, K.: *ref*, 532
Ochs, E.: *ref*, 381
O'Connell, A. W.: *ref*, 533
O'Connor, D. J.: *ref*, 425
O'Connor, G.: *ref*, 516, 525
O'Connor, J. P.: *ref*, 391, 532
O'Connor, N.: *ref*, 354, 439, 518, 525, 545
O'Connor, P.: *ref*, 357
O'Connor, P. A.: *ref*, 503
Oda, E. A.: *exc*, 7:378
O'Dea, J. D.: *ref*, 5:308(354)
Odell, C. W.: *ref*, 426, 525
Odell, L. M.: *ref*, 449, 516
O'Dell, P. L.: *ref*, 532
Oden, M. H.: *ref*, 359, 525
Odgers, J. G.: *ref*, 419
Odhner, F.: *ref*, 398
Odoroff, M. E.: *ref*, 398, 426, 525, 2:1424(22), 3:220(58)
Oeschler, H.: *ref*, 3:242(2)
Oexle, H. M.: *ref*, 525
Offenbach, S. I.: *ref*, 516
Offer, D.: *ref*, 529
Ogdon, D. P.: *ref*, 529, 533
Ogilvie, D. S.: *ref*, 381
Ogilvie, R. D.: *ref*, 522, 529
Ogletree, E.: *ref*, 589
Ogletree, E. J.: *ref*, 589
O'Grady, D. J.: *ref*, 525
Ogston, D. G.: *ref*, 360
Ohlsen, M. M.: *ref*, 391
Ohlsen, R. L.: *ref*, 496
Ohnmacht, F.: *ref*, 400

Ohnmacht, F. W.: *ref,* 400, 547, 559, 561, 574
Ohtsuki, K.: *ref,* 381
Ohwaki, M.: *ref,* 513
Ohwaki, Y.: *test,* 513; *ref,* 513
Ojha, A. B.: *ref,* 331
Okayama, M.: *ref,* 518, 529, 578
O'Keefe, E. J.: *ref,* 518
O'Keefe, G. S.: *ref,* 538
O'Keefe, R.: *ref,* 381
O'Keefe, S. L.: *ref,* 524
O'Kelly, E.: *ref,* 495, 525
Oki, T.: *ref,* 533
Olander, H. T.: *ref,* 391, 398, 425–6
Olch, D. R.: *ref,* 532
Olczak, P. V.: *ref,* 574
Older, H. J.: *ref,* 426, 503
Oldman, D.: *ref,* 373, 408–9
Oldridge, O. A.: *exc,* 538
O'Leary, B. S.: *ref,* 425, 469
Oléron, P.: *ref,* 439
Oleson, D. S.: *ref,* 542, 546, 551, 555, 562, 564, 573
Olin, T. D.: *ref,* 529
Olive, H.: *ref,* 542, 546, 551
Oliver, D. E.: *ref,* 533
Oliver, J. A.: *ref,* 404
Oliver, J. E.: *ref,* 543
Oliver, R. A. C.: *test,* 2:1396; *ref,* 357, 2:1396(1–4)
Olivier, K.: *ref,* 381, 525
Olsen, I. A.: *ref,* 364, 529
Olsen, M. A.: *ref,* 357
Olshin, D.: *ref,* 533, 538
Olson, A. V.: *ref,* 348
Olson, D. R.: *ref,* 349, 400, 439, 589
Olson, G. R.: *ref,* 425
Olson, N. H.: *ref,* 348
Olson, R. E.: *ref,* 496
Olson, R. W.: *ref,* 532
Olson, W. C.: *exc,* 509
Omer, J. L.: *ref,* 516
Ommen, D. F.: *ref,* 6:438(496)
Omwake, K. T.: *ref,* 391
Omwake, L.: *test,* 3:238
Onarheim, J.: *ref,* 349
O'Neal, C. E.: *ref,* 5:308(303)
O'Neil, H. F.: *ref,* 524, 529
O'Neil, W. J.: *ref,* 348
O'Neil, W. M.: *ref,* 529, 533
O'Neill, H. D.: *ref,* 524, 533
O'Neill, J. J.: *ref,* 532
Ontario Commercial Teachers' Association: *ref,* 387
Ontario Institute for Studies in Education: *test,* 350, 387, 417
Oosthuizen, S.: *test,* 383
O'Piela, J. M.: *ref,* 348, 516
Oppel, W.: *ref,* 525
Oppel, W. C.: *ref,* 533
Oppenheim, D. B.: *ref,* 357
Oppenheim, H.: *ref,* 532
Oppenheim, S.: *ref,* 532
Oppermann, A. F.: *ref,* 3:242(2)
Orchinik, C. W.: *ref,* 532, 592
Ord, I. G.: *test,* 427, 510, 514, 520, 7:416; *ref,* 510, 514, 520, 7:416(1)
Ordahl, G.: *ref,* 525
Ordahl, L. E.: *ref,* 525
Ordahl, V. E.: *ref,* 349, 426, 525
O'Reilly, J. P.: *ref,* 357
O'Reilly, P. O.: *ref,* 440, 532
Orgass, B.: *ref,* 529, 543

Orgel, A. R.: *ref,* 505, 525
Orlandi, L. R.: *ref,* 589
Orleans, J. B.: *ref,* 424
Orme, J. E.: *ref,* 403, 439, 529
Oros, J. A.: *ref,* 533
O'Rourke, L. J.: *test,* 421
O'Rourke, R. H.: *ref,* 589
Orpet, R. E.: *ref,* 364, 439, 496, 533
Orr, D. B.: *ref,* 361
Orr, D. H.: *ref,* 503
Orr, K. N.: *ref,* 533
Ortar, G.: *ref,* 533
Ortiz, K. K.: *ref,* 517, 533
Orton, R.: *ref,* 439, 5:339(9)
Osborn, L. R.: *ref,* 361, 6:438(530)
Osborn, R. C.: *ref,* 419
Osborne, A. E.: *ref,* 426
Osborne, R. T.: *rev,* 533; *ref,* 349, 447, 496, 516, 533, 4:277(211, 250)
Osburn, H. G.: *ref,* 444–5
O'Shaughnessy, M. M.: *ref,* 361
Osipow, S. H.: *ref,* 555, 589
Osman, H. H.: *ref,* 533, 589
Oster, Z. H.: *ref,* 439
Ostrander, J. M.: *ref,* 532
Ostrow, P.: *ref,* 532
Otis, A. S.: *test,* 423–6, 3:247–8, 6:480; *ref,* 525, 6:480(1)
Otis, J. L.: *test,* 431–2; *ref,* 426, 431, 6:438(503)
Otte, H. W.: *ref,* 361
Otterness, W. B.: *ref,* 342
Ottman, D. K.: *ref,* 480, 5:308(422)
Otto, W.: *ref,* 522, 524, 533
Ouellette, F. E.: *ref,* 381
Outhit, M. C.: *ref,* 525
Overall, J. E.: *ref,* 447, 529
Overstreet, G. C.: *ref,* 589
Owen, A.: *ref,* 403, 518
Owen, C.: *ref,* 361, 561, 564
Owen, D. R.: *ref,* 533
Owen, F. W.: *ref,* 381, 533
Owen, J. C.: *ref,* 349, 400
Owen, R.: *ref,* 3:242(2)
Owen, S. V.: *ref,* 542, 551
Owens, E. P.: *ref,* 519, 532
Owens, K. D.: *ref,* 523
Owens, R. E.: *ref,* 589
Owens, R. T.: *ref,* 439, 543
Owens, T. R.: *ref,* 419
Owens, W. A.: *ref,* 2:1377(3), 3:220(35), 4:277(212), 4:281(87)
Oxlade, M.: *ref,* 426, 439
Oxlade, M. N.: *ref,* 426
O'Zee, W. F.: *ref,* 357
Ozer, M. N.: *ref,* 516
Oziel, L. J.: *ref,* 439, 533

PACE, J. L.: *ref,* 361
Pacht, A. R.: *ref,* 364, 426, 529
Paeratakul, C.: *ref,* 419
Page, B. H.: *ref,* 348
Page, H. A.: *ref,* 525
Page, H. E.: *ref,* 337
Page, H. F.: *ref,* 439
Page, J. D.: *ref,* 525
Page, K.: *ref,* 532
Page, S.: *ref,* 529, 533
Pagedar, R. M.: *ref,* 529
Paine, R. W.: *ref,* 529, 533
Painter, G.: *ref,* 381

Painter, P.: *ref,* 533
Paitich, D.: *ref,* 439
Pal, S.: *ref,* 525
Palermo, R. R.: *ref,* 589
Palkes, H.: *ref,* 518
Pallone, N. J.: *ref,* 357
Palmer, A. B.: *ref,* 525
Palmer, E. M.: *ref,* 525
Palmer, F. H.: *ref,* 516, 525, 533
Palmer, J. O.: *ref,* 532
Palmer, R. H.: *ref,* 382
Palmer, R. J.: *ref,* 424, 518
Palmore, E. B.: *ref,* 529
Panda, T. P.: *ref,* 439
Pande, C. G.: *ref,* 439
Pandey, R. E.: *ref,* 361
Paney, H.: *ref,* 589
Pang, H.: *ref,* 589
Pankove, E. W.: *ref,* 542
Panther, E. E.: *ref,* 381, 400, 516, 575
Panton, J. H.: *ref,* 447, 529
Paolino, A. F.: *ref,* 532
Papadopoulou, E.: *ref,* 381
Papania, N.: *ref,* 525, 5:326(15–6)
Papavassiliou, I. T.: *ref,* 381
Papurt, M. J.: *ref,* 525
Paredes, A.: *ref,* 529
Parish, R. L.: *ref,* 349
Park, G. R.: *ref,* 349
Park, Y. H.: *ref,* 357
Parker, A. D.: *ref,* 349
Parker, A. L.: *ref,* 518
Parker, D. H. H.: *ref,* 415
Parker, H. J.: *ref,* 381, 489
Parker, H. T.: *ref,* 525
Parker, J.: *ref,* 533
Parker, J. W.: *ref,* 431, 532, 592
Parker, L. L.: *ref,* 425
Parker, M. M.: *exc,* 532
Parker, R. S.: *ref,* 529
Parks, E.: *ref,* 435
Parks, P.: *ref,* 561
Parkyn, G. W.: *ref,* 525
Parlett, T. A. A.: *ref,* 559, 561
Parmelee, A. H.: *ref,* 497
Parmenter, M. D.: *test,* 4:327
Parnell, R. W.: *ref,* 331
Parnes, S. J.: *ref,* 542, 546, 551, 561, 572
Parres, J. G.: *ref,* 357
Parry, J. B.: *ref,* 388, 439, 4:295(2)
Parry, M. E.: *ref,* 357, 480, 482
Parsley, J. F.: *ref,* 361
Parsley, K. M.: *ref,* 525
Parsons, O. A.: *ref,* 529, 532
Parsons, P. A.: *ref,* 532
Partin, R. L.: *ref,* 425, 436
Partington, J. E.: *test,* 4:350, 4:355; *ref,* 504, 532
Pasamanick, B.: *test,* 494; *ref,* 494, 497
Pascal, G. R.: *ref,* 532
Paschal, F. C.: *ref,* 558
Pasewark, R. A.: *ref,* 516–7, 525, 533, 538
Pasricha, P.: *ref,* 333, 529
Passmore, M.: *ref,* 538
Passons, W. R.: *ref,* 357
Pastore, N.: *ref,* 447, 4:281(86)
Pastovic, J. J.: *ref,* 525, 533
Patel, A.: *ref,* 484
Paterra, M. E.: *ref,* 533

Paterson, D. G.: *test*, 556; *ref*, 404, 438, 558, 1:1061(1), 2:1401(8), 2:1424(23)
Patinka, P. J.: *ref*, 337
Paton, C. L.: *ref*, 589
Paton, R.: *ref*, 522, 525
Patrick, J. H.: *ref*, 447, 529
Patrick, J. R.: *ref*, 419
Patten, M. P.: *ref*, 529
Patterson, B.: *ref*, 361, 398
Patterson, C. H.: *ref*, 342, 532
Patterson, G. R.: *rev*, 533
Patterson, H.: *ref*, 426
Patterson, H. J.: *ref*, 516–7, 525
Patterson, R. M.: *ref*, 381, 483, 532
Patteson, R. F.: *ref*, 533
Patton, W. M.: *ref*, 337
Pauk, W. J.: *ref*, 5:308(390)
Pauker, J. D.: *ref*, 529
Paul, G. L.: *ref*, 357
Paul, G. T.: *ref*, 499, 538
Paul, L. M.: *ref*, 533
Paul, M. E.: *ref*, 529
Paulsen, G. B.: *ref*, 419
Paulson, M. J.: *ref*, 529
Paulus, D. H.: *ref*, 516, 589
Pavlos, A. J.: *ref*, 533
Paxson, R. C.: *ref*, 349, 358, 361
Payne, D.: *ref*, 529
Payne, D. A.: *rev*, 339, 392; *ref*, 357, 382, 404, 529
Payne, J. F.: *ref*, 439, 491
Payne, L. E.: *ref*, 381
Payne, R. W.: *ref*, 403, 504, 525, 532, 6:555(4–5, 7)
Pazeian, B.: *ref*, 525, 2:1401(9)
Peacock, E. P.: *ref*, 529
Peacock, W.: *ref*, 529
Peak, D. T.: *ref*, 529, 532
Peak, H.: *ref*, 426
Pearl, D.: *ref*, 529, 532, 543, 592
Pearson, J. S.: *ref*, 525
Pearson, M. A.: *ref*, 361
Pearson, P. R.: *ref*, 529
Pearson, R.: *ref*, 357
Pearson, R. E.: *ref*, 391
Pearson, W.: *ref*, 529
Pease, D.: *ref*, 487, 497
Peatman, J. G.: *exc*, 497; *ref*, 525
Peatman, L. B.: *ref*, 525
Peck, D. F.: *ref*, 403, 529
Peck, R.: *ref*, 381, 533
Pedersen, D. M.: *ref*, 361, 533
Pedersen, F.: *ref*, 419
Pedrini, D. T.: *ref*, 381, 516, 525, 529, 532
Pedrini, L. N.: *ref*, 525
Peel, E. A.: *rev*, 415, 5:357, 5:377; *test*, 4:313; *ref*, 354, 373, 408–9, 415, 425, 439, 462–3, 4:313(2)
Pegnato, C. V.: *ref*, 425
Pegram, E. L.: *ref*, 525
Peiser, W. G.: *ref*, 3:217(57)
Peisner, E. F.: *ref*, 505
Peixotto, H. E.: *ref*, 357, 532
Pelc, R. E.: *ref*, 381
Pelosi, J. W.: *ref*, 364, 529
Pelton, R. B.: *ref*, 364
Pelz, D. C.: *ref*, 574
Pelz, K.: *ref*, 497, 533
Pelz, K. S.: *ref*, 497, 533
Pemberton, W. A.: *ref*, 361
Pendergast, M. C.: *ref*, 419

Penfield, R. V.: *ref*, 482
Penfold, D. J.: *ref*, 391, 439, 533
Penn, N. E.: *ref*, 404
Penny, R. K.: *ref*, 542
Penny, S.: *ref*, 543
Penrose, L. S.: *rev*, 3:228; *test*, 428; *ref*, 428, 439, 518, 525
Penzer, W. N.: *ref*, 529
Pepinsky, H. N.: *ref*, 404
Perce, F. C.: *ref*, 525
Percy, L. M.: *ref*, 533
Peretz, D.: *ref*, 518
Periaswamy, T. M.: *ref*, 439
Perkins, J. C.: *ref*, 447, 592
Perkins, R. E.: *ref*, 525
Perkins, S. A.: *ref*, 574
Perl, R. E.: *ref*, 3:217(60)
Perlman, L. G.: *ref*, 342
Perloff, R.: *ref*, 342
Perrett, L.: *ref*, 529, 543
Perrine, M. W.: *ref*, 444, 480
Perrone, J. V.: *ref*, 574
Perry, D. E.: *ref*, 558
Perry, H. W.: *ref*, 489, 525
Perry, I. F.: *ref*, 348
Perry, J.: *ref*, 499
Perry, J. A.: *ref*, 499
Perry, J. D.: *ref*, 529, 545, 4:277(181)
Perry, J. M.: *ref*, 589
Perry, J. O.: *ref*, 361
Pertusio, C. B.: *ref*, 357
Pesci, M. L.: *ref*, 589
Pescor, M. J.: *ref*, 2:1394(7)
Pessin, V.: *ref*, 487, 525
Peters, F. R.: *ref*, 419
Peters, H. D.: *ref*, 349, 381, 425
Peters, H. N.: *exc*, 518; *ref*, 518
Peters, J. E.: *ref*, 533
Peters, J. S.: *ref*, 532
Peters, M. F.: *ref*, 518
Petersen, H.: *ref*, 349
Petersen, P. W.: *ref*, 529
Peterson, B. H.: *ref*, 3:217(89)
Peterson, D. F.: *ref*, 349
Peterson, F. E.: *ref*, 357, 469
Peterson, H.: *test*, 3:238
Peterson, H. A.: *ref*, 3:220(25)
Peterson, J.: *ref*, 381, 426, 518
Peterson, L. H.: *ref*, 5:308(285)
Peterson, L. R.: *ref*, 342
Peterson, M. E.: *ref*, 6:438(472)
Peterson, P. G.: *ref*, 532
Peterson, R.: *ref*, 532
Peterson, R. E.: *ref*, 357
Peterson, T. T.: *ref*, 404
Peterson, W. M.: *ref*, 364, 426, 529
Petit, J. L.: *ref*, 425
Petrie, A.: *ref*, 403, 428, 439, 518, 532
Petrie, R. G.: *ref*, 381
Petrik, N. D.: *ref*, 405
Petrinovich, L. F.: *ref*, 529
Pettifor, R. E.: *ref*, 543
Pettinato, G. C.: *ref*, 439
Pettit, D. E.: *ref*, 529
Peyman, D. A. R.: *ref*, 532
Pfeifer, C. M.: *ref*, 357
Pfeiffer, M. G.: *ref*, 357
Phatak, P.: *test*, 372; *ref*, 372, 381, 484, 589
Phelps, A. M.: *ref*, 361
Phelps, H. B.: *ref*, 439, 532
Philipp, J. A.: *ref*, 589

Phillips, A.: *ref*, 525
Phillips, A. J.: *ref*, 387, 3:242(8)
Phillips, C. J.: *ref*, 439, 495, 525
Phillips, D. C.: *ref*, 519, 525
Phillips, E. L.: *ref*, 518, 525, 532
Phillips, G. R.: *ref*, 325, 439
Phillips, J. C.: *ref*, 482, 5:308(436)
Phillips, L. N.: *ref*, 357
Phillips, R.: *ref*, 449, 452
Phillips, R. M.: *ref*, 361, 447, 449, 452, 529
Phillips, V. K.: *ref*, 574, 589
Philpott, S. J. F.: *exc*, 4:345
Phipps, G. T.: *ref*, 425
Pichot, P.: *ref*, 439
Pickles, D. G.: *ref*, 525, 533
Pickup, K. T.: *ref*, 381, 525, 533
Piddington, M.: *ref*, 518
Piddington, R.: *ref*, 518
Pidgeon, D. A.: *rev*, 328, 398, 400; *test*, 415, 474–5; *ref*, 415
Pierce, H. O.: *ref*, 525
Pierce, R. A.: *ref*, 518
Pierce, R. C.: *ref*, 503, 529
Pierce, R. M.: *ref*, 529
Pierce-Jones, J.: *ref*, 364, 533, 542, 4:277(251)
Piercy, M.: *ref*, 529
Piercy, M. F.: *ref*, 525, 532, 545
Piercy, M. M.: *ref*, 439, 529, 532
Pierleoni, R. G.: *ref*, 425
Piers, E. V.: *rev*, 516, 522, 6:537; *ref*, 574
Pierson, L. R.: *ref*, 419
Pignatelli, M. L.: *rev*, 355, 2:1426; *ref*, 525
Pihl, R. O.: *ref*, 529, 533
Pihlblad, C. T.: *ref*, 419
Pike, F.: *ref*, 497, 533
Pilkington, G. W.: *ref*, 331, 446
Pilliner, A. E. G.: *rev*, 338, 358, 5:351, 6:469; *ref*, 409, 525
Pimsleur, P.: *ref*, 457
Pindner, G. D.: *ref*, 381
Pine, I.: *ref*, 532
Piness, G.: *ref*, 525
Pinkard, C. A.: *ref*, 542, 546, 551
Pinkerton, P.: *ref*, 403, 439
Pinneau, S. R.: *test*, 525; *ref*, 525, 533
Pintel, G.: *ref*, 357
Pintner, R.: *ref*, 349, 419, 425; *test*, 435, 556, 563, 590, 1:1061, 3:254, 3:256, 5:368b-d; *exc*, 518; *ref*, 435, 525, 558, 1:1061(1), 3:255(1, 3), 3:256(1, 3–4), 3:263(38)
Piotrowski, Z. A.: *ref*, 525
Pipher, J. A.: *ref*, 357, 361, 387
Pippert, R. R.: *ref*, 391
Pishkin, V.: *ref*, 529
Pisula, D.: *ref*, 381
Pitt, H.: *ref*, 5:308(325)
Pitts, R.: *ref*, 439
Pitts, V. A.: *ref*, 533
Pizam, A.: *ref*, 574
Pizzat, F. J.: *ref*, 532
Plant, W. T.: *ref*, 516–7, 525, 529, 532–3, 538
Plante, M.: *ref*, 529
Plapp, J. M.: *ref*, 357, 425
Platt, J. J.: *ref*, 525
Platz, A.: *ref*, 404
Pless, I. B.: *ref*, 522, 533

Plessas, G. P.: *ref,* 349
Plog, E. L.: *ref,* 419
Plogman, B. E.: *ref,* 561, 589, 591
Plotkin, L.: *ref,* 357
Plotkin, R. R.: *ref,* 522, 529
Plumb, G. R.: *test,* 4:362; *ref,* 349, 532
Plumeau, F.: *ref,* 532
Plumleigh, G. E.: *ref,* 349
Poe, C. A.: *ref,* 405
Poe, W. A.: *ref,* 337, 348
Poeck, K.: *ref,* 529, 543
Poffenberger, T.: *ref,* 484
Pogue, B. C.: *ref,* 589
Pohlmann, V. C.: *ref,* 361
Pohndorf, R. H.: *ref,* 364
Poindexter, C. C.: *ref,* 361
Poland, H. V.: *ref,* 361
Poland, R. G.: *ref,* 529
Polizzoto, E. A.: *ref,* 516
Pollack, M.: *ref,* 529, 532
Pollack, R. C.: *ref,* 529
Pollard, A. G.: *ref,* 348, 364, 400
Pollard, J. R.: *ref,* 5:308(410)
Pollens, B.: *ref,* 532
Pollert, L. H.: *ref,* 589
Polley, D.: *ref,* 533
Pollie, D. M.: *ref,* 533
Pollin, W.: *ref,* 529
Pollitt, E.: *ref,* 525, 533
Polnaya, M.: *ref,* 592
Pomerantz, N. E.: *ref,* 349
Pomeroy, M. C.: *ref,* 357, 359
Pond, F. L.: *ref,* 426
Pond, L.: *ref,* 323–4
Pond, M.: *ref,* 3:220(48), 4:320 (1)
Poniatowski, R. A.: *ref,* 382
Pool, D. A.: *ref,* 516, 529
Pool, K. B.: *ref,* 529, 532
Pope, A. L.: *ref,* 589
Popovics, A. J.: *ref,* 497
Popplestone, J. A.: *ref,* 381
Poppleton, P. K.: *ref,* 331
Porozny, G. H. J.: *ref,* 404
Porrata, E.: *ref,* 525, 529
Portenier, L. G.: *ref,* 419, 4:277 (191–2)
Porter, A.: *ref,* 419
Porter, A. C.: *ref,* 357
Porter, C. M.: *ref,* 589
Porter, E. H.: *ref,* 2:1426(1)
Porter, J. P.: *ref,* 419
Porter, M. P.: *ref,* 435, 3:255(6)
Porter, R. B.: *test,* 339
Porter, T. L.: *ref,* 498, 529
Porterfield, C. L.: *ref,* 439, 538
Porteus, S. D.: *rev,* 355, 447; *test,* 518; *ref,* 381, 505, 518, 525, 545, 578
Portnoy, B.: *ref,* 532–3
Portwood, P. F.: *ref,* 525, 533
Poruben, A.: *ref,* 426, 480
Post, F.: *ref,* 403, 439, 532
Post, J. M.: *ref,* 533
Post, M.: *ref,* 525
Postlethwaite, T. N.: *test,* 475
Poston, W. K.: *ref,* 404
Pottash, M. E.: *ref,* 439
Potter, E. H.: *ref,* 545
Potter, M. C.: *ref,* 425
Potts, E.: *ref,* 408
Potts, L.: *ref,* 592

Poull, L. E.: *ref,* 518, 525, 5:354 (4)
Pounders, C. J.: *ref,* 440
Pounds, R. L.: *ref,* 5:308(391)
Povey, R. M.: *ref,* 331
Powell, B. J.: *ref,* 529
Powell, D. B.: *ref,* 4:277(213)
Powell, D. H.: *ref,* 529
Powell, J. A.: *ref,* 525, 532
Powell, J. C.: *ref,* 440
Powell, K.: *ref,* 533
Powell, M.: *ref,* 348, 525
Powell, M. B.: *ref,* 403, 428
Powell, R. R.: *ref,* 364
Powers, G. F.: *ref,* 6:438(531)
Powers, R. J.: *ref,* 357
Powers, S. M.: *ref,* 528
Prado, W. M.: *ref,* 529, 532
Prager, D.: *ref,* 525, 532
Prandoni, J. R.: *ref,* 381
Prange, A. J.: *ref,* 518
Prasad, R.: *ref,* 525
Pratt, C. C.: *ref,* 525
Pratt, I. E.: *ref,* 381
Pratt, K. C.: *ref,* 3:217(62)
Pratt, M.: *ref,* 361
Pratt, R. T. C.: *ref,* 529
Pratt, W. E.: *test,* 339
Preas, N. B.: *ref,* 357
Pred, G. D.: *ref,* 337, 4:277(252)
Prediger, D. J.: *ref,* 361, 404, 419
Preische, W. A.: *ref,* 425
Prentice, N. M.: *ref,* 381, 525, 529, 532–3
Prescott, G. A.: *test,* 340
Presly, A. S.: *ref,* 403, 439
Pressey, L. C.: *test,* 438; *ref,* 435, 438
Pressey, L. W.: *ref,* 438
Pressey, S. L.: *test,* 438; *ref,* 438
Preston, C. E.: *ref,* 532
Preston, R. C.: *ref,* 357
Preston Education Committee: *test,* 462
Price, A. C.: *ref,* 342, 525, 529, 533
Price, E. J. J.: *ref,* 515, 545
Price, H. G.: *ref,* 532
Price, J. C.: *ref,* 532
Price, J. D.: *ref,* 439, 533
Price, J. R.: *ref,* 532–3
Price, J. St. C.: *ref,* 426
Price, L. A.: *test,* 561
Price, L. B.: *test,* 559
Price, O. K.: *ref,* 398
Price, P. C.: *ref,* 381
Price, R. L.: *ref,* 357
Price-Williams, D.: *ref,* 381, 439
Prien, E. P.: *ref,* 357, 404, 419, 482, 6:438(503)
Primac, D. W.: *ref,* 529, 592
Prince, R. H.: *ref,* 529
Pringle, M. L. K.: *rev,* 368, 408, 434, 462; *exc,* 381; *ref,* 381, 525, 533
Pringle, R. K.: *ref,* 439, 529
Prinsloo, R. J.: *test,* 383, 501
Pritchard, S. A.: *ref,* 6:438(461)
Proctor, C. H.: *ref,* 439
Proctor, W. M.: *ref,* 525
Proger, B. B.: *exc,* 344; *ref,* 400, 424
Prosser, N. S.: *ref,* 525, 533, 538
Prothro, E. T.: *ref,* 364–5, 391, 439
Pruitt, R. C.: *ref,* 482, 548

Pruyser, P. W.: *ref,* 532, 592
Prywes, M.: *ref,* 439
Psathas, G.: *ref,* 357, 425
Psychological Services Bureau: *test,* 378
Ptacek, J. E.: *ref,* 532
Public Personnel Association: *test,* 6:448
Pugh, G. S.: *ref,* 425
Pugh, L. A.: *ref,* 529
Pugh, R.: *ref,* 357
Pugh, R. C.: *ref,* 357, 359, 425, 589
Puleo, V. T.: *ref,* 533
Puletti, F.: *ref,* 529
Pulleine, R. H.: *ref,* 518
Pullias, C. M.: *ref,* 382
Pumfrey, P. D.: *ref,* 408
Purcell, C. K.: *ref,* 532
Purcell, K.: *ref,* 518, 532
Purdom, G. A.: *ref,* 529
Purdy, B. F.: *ref,* 425
Purdy, R. S.: *ref,* 532
Purseglove, E. M.: *ref,* 516, 525
Putnam, T. J.: *ref,* 483, 525, 532
Puzzo, F.: *ref,* 532
Puzzo, F. S.: *ref,* 532
Pyle, R. F.: *ref,* 533
Pyle, W. H.: *ref,* 525

QUADFASEL, A. F.: *ref,* 532, 592
Quaid, T. D. D.: *ref,* 419, 3:217 (58, 63)
Qualtere, T. J.: *ref,* 439, 525
Quandt, R. E.: *ref,* 357
Quast, W.: *ref,* 381
Quattlebaum, L. F.: *ref,* 522, 529
Quay, H. C.: *ref,* 529, 532
Quay, L. C.: *ref,* 525
Quayle, M. S.: *ref,* 426
Quereshi, M. Y.: *ref,* 525, 529, 532–3
Query, W. T.: *ref,* 518, 533
Quiller, G. F.: *ref,* 357
Quinlan, C. A.: *ref,* 357
Quinlan, P.: *ref,* 529

RAAHEIM, K.: *ref,* 439
Rabin, A. I.: *ref,* 341A, 496, 525, 529, 532–3
Rabinovitz, A.: *ref,* 532
Rabinowitz, D.: *ref,* 533
Rachiele, L. D.: *ref,* 496, 533
Rachman, S.: *rev,* 6:447; *ref,* 533
Racky, D. J.: *ref,* 398
Radcliffe, J. A.: *test,* 533; *ref,* 529
Radford, J.: *ref,* 439
Radin, N.: *ref,* 516, 525
Radin, N. L.: *ref,* 525
Radzan, M.: *ref,* 439
Raffel, S. C.: *ref,* 433, 447, 529, 592
Rafi, A. A.: *ref,* 365, 439, 529
Ragland, R.: *ref,* 529
Ragland, R. E.: *ref,* 529
Ragouzis, P. N.: *ref,* 589
Raia, J. R.: *ref,* 555, 589
Raina, M. K.: *ref,* 589
Raine, L. M.: *ref,* 532
Rainey, R. G.: *ref,* 348, 398, 400
Rainier, R. N.: *ref,* 3:217(108)
Rainwater, H. G.: *ref,* 533
Rainwater, J. M.: *ref,* 542, 551, 561, 564, 574

Rajalakshmi, R.: *ref,* 381, 533
Rajatasilpin, A.: *ref,* 533
Rakhawy, Y. T.: *ref,* 532
Rakusin, J.: *ref,* 532
Raleigh, W. H.: *ref,* 348, 525, 533
Ralph, D. W.: *ref,* 518
Ralston, N. C.: *ref,* 6:438(511)
Ramalingaswami, P.: *ref,* 529
Rambo, F. L.: *ref,* 589
Ramer, J. C.: *ref,* 529
Ramirez, J. V.: *ref,* 439, 589
Ramirez, W. G.: *ref,* 348
Ramsay, R.: *ref,* 532
Ramsey, P. H.: *ref,* 525
Ramsey, W.: *ref,* 349
Ramseyer, G. C.: *ref,* 348-9
Rand, G.: *ref,* 525
Randall, F. B.: *ref,* 525
Randall, R. E.: *ref,* 391
Randall, R. R.: *ref,* 381
Randall, R. V.: *ref,* 529, 592
Range, L. H.: *ref,* 357
Rankin, R.: *ref,* 518, 5:308(371)
Rankin, R. J.: *exc,* 513; *ref,* 518
Ranzau, M. L.: *ref,* 589
Ranzoni, J. H.: *ref,* 357
Rao, C. K. V.: *ref,* 439, 515, 518
Rao, S.: *ref,* 364
Rao, S. N.: *ref,* 358, 439
Rapaport, D.: *ref,* 532
Rapaport, G. M.: *ref,* 529
Rapaport, I.: *ref,* 525, 533
Raphael, S.: *ref,* 400
Rapp, D.: *ref,* 529, 533
Rappaport, M. E.: *ref,* 525
Rappaport, S. R.: *ref,* 525, 532
Rappel, D.: *ref,* 589
Rardin, D. R.: *ref,* 361, 549
Rardin, M. W.: *ref,* 525, 538
Rarick, H. J.: *ref,* 3:217(76)
Rashkis, H. A.: *ref,* 532
Raskin, L. M.: *ref,* 516
Rasmussen, E. M.: *ref,* 5:308(304)
Rasof, B.: *ref,* 487, 497, 525, 533
Rath, R.: *ref,* 439
Ratner, G.: *ref,* 492
Rattan, M. S.: *ref,* 349, 400, 439, 453
Raub, E. S.: *ref,* 532
Rautman, A. L.: *ref,* 503, 525
Raven, J. C.: *test,* 403, 439, 491; *ref,* 403, 439
Ravenette, A. T.: *ref,* 491, 533
Rawl, M. F.: *ref,* 381, 516
Rawlings, G.: *exc,* 1:1043
Rawlings, T. D.: *ref,* 349
Rawls, D. J.: *ref,* 382, 404
Rawls, J. R.: *ref,* 382, 404
Rawn, M. L.: *ref,* 532
Ray, J. B.: *ref,* 525
Ray, J. R.: *ref,* 400
Ray, M. R.: *ref,* 349
Ray, P. B.: *ref,* 405, 589
Ray, T.: *ref,* 515
Ray, T. S.: *ref,* 529
Ray, W.: *ref,* 357
Ray, W. S.: *ref,* 542
Raybold, E.: *ref,* 435, 525, 545
Ray-Chowdhury, K.: *ref,* 515, 545
Raymond, C. S.: *ref,* 381
Read, C. B.: *ref,* 419
Ream, M. J.: *ref,* 3:220(23)
Reams, J. W.: *ref,* 361
Reardon, B.: *ref,* 589

Rebhun, A. M.: *ref,* 525, 533
Rebish, D.: *ref,* 533
Reck, M.: *ref,* 357
Redbird, H. M.: *ref,* 381, 525
Reddy, I. K. S.: *ref,* 439
Reddy, M. J.: *ref,* 532
Redlich, F. C.: *test,* 3:291
Redmond, M.: *ref,* 426, 4:272(2)
Redmond, N. J.: *ref,* 533
Reed, H. B. C.: *ref,* 529, 532, 578
Reed, H. C.: *ref,* 532
Reed, H. R.: *ref,* 525, 532
Reed, J. C.: *ref,* 529, 532-3
Reed, J. L.: *ref,* 440
Reeling, P. A.: *ref,* 357
Rees, A. H.: *ref,* 525, 533
Rees, W. L.: *ref,* 403, 439
Reese, H. W.: *ref,* 542, 546, 551, 561
Reger, R.: *ref,* 516, 533
Rehfeld, F. W.: *ref,* 3:217(108)
Reich, H.: *ref,* 532
Reichard, J. D.: *ref,* 518, 525
Reichard, S.: *ref,* 532
Reichart, R. R.: *ref,* 5:308(293)
Reichenberg-Hackett, W.: *ref,* 381
Reichman, W.: *ref,* 436, 529
Reid, J. W.: *ref,* 357, 361
Reid, W. B.: *ref,* 533
Reid, W. R.: *ref,* 533
Reidy, M. E.: *ref,* 533
Reilley, R. R.: *ref,* 533
Reilly, H. E.: *ref,* 361
Reilly, R.: *ref,* 382
Reilly, W. J.: *ref,* 5:308(392)
Reimanis, G.: *ref,* 529, 532
Reiner, J. R.: *ref,* 357
Reinhart, R. A.: *ref,* 525
Reinitz, A. H.: *ref,* 532
Reitan, R. M.: *ref,* 516, 529, 532-3, 578
Reitman, E. E.: *ref,* 533
Reitz, W.: *exc,* 532; *ref,* 529
Reitz, W. E.: *ref,* 529
Reitzel, J.: *ref,* 357
Rellas, A. J.: *ref,* 525, 538
Remmers, H. H.: *ref,* 2:1399(9), 3:217(77), 4:277(193, 214-5)
Renck, R.: *test,* 472
Renear, K. R.: *ref,* 529
Renfer, M. E. F.: *ref,* 391
Renner, J. C.: *ref,* 542
Renner, V.: *ref,* 542, 551
Renzaglia, G. A.: *ref,* 342, 361, 5:308(345)
Renzulli, J. S.: *ref,* 516, 589
Requena, M.: *ref,* 439
Resch, J. A.: *ref,* 518, 529, 578
Resnick, H.: *ref,* 547
Resnick, J. H.: *ref,* 357
Resnick, R. J.: *ref,* 533
Restell, M.: *ref,* 543
Reswick, J.: *ref,* 525, 533
Reubush, F. J.: *ref,* 7:378(6)
Reusser, W. C.: *ref,* 419
Reuter, J.: *ref,* 489
Reymert, M. L.: *ref,* 525
Reynell, W. R.: *ref,* 532
Reynolds, F.: *ref,* 391
Reynolds, G. A.: *ref,* 532
Reynolds, M. C.: *ref,* 525
Reznikoff, M.: *ref,* 529
Rheingold, H. L.: *ref,* 525

Rhinehart, J. B.: *ref,* 525, 2:1377(15)
Rhoades, F. L.: *ref,* 3:263(41)
Rhode, J. F.: *ref,* 423
Rhoderick, W. A.: *ref,* 532
Rhodes, F.: *test,* 530, 535
Rhodes, L. E.: *ref,* 533
Rhone, D. E.: *ref,* 529, 533
Rhudick, P. J.: *ref,* 529
Ribble, M. A.: *exc,* 497
Rice, D. B.: *ref,* 533
Rice, D. M.: *ref,* 516
Rice, J.: *ref,* 543
Rice, J. A.: *ref,* 424, 516, 543
Rice, M. L.: *ref,* 361
Rice, V.: *ref,* 400
Rice, W.: *ref,* 503, 529
Rich, C. C.: *ref,* 439, 533
Rich, G. J.: *exc,* 497
Rich, K. D.: *ref,* 398
Rich, T. A.: *ref,* 381, 542, 546, 551
Richard, W.: *ref,* 529
Richards, B. F.: *ref,* 525
Richards, B. W.: *ref,* 525
Richards, H. E.: *ref,* 533
Richards, J. M.: *ref,* 349, 419, 551, 559, 561, 564
Richards, J. T.: *ref,* 538
Richards, P. N.: *ref,* 409, 589
Richards, T. D.: *ref,* 559, 561
Richards, T. W.: *ref,* 497, 525, 532-3
Richardson, B. K.: *ref,* 482
Richardson, Bellows, Henry & Co., Inc.: *test,* 444-5
Richardson, C. A.: *test,* 459-61; *ref,* 461, 525
Richardson, E. J.: *ref,* 439, 496, 525
Richardson, H.: *ref,* 532
Richardson, H. D.: *ref,* 4:324(54)
Richardson, H. M.: *ref,* 533
Richardson, J.: *ref,* 5:308(371)
Richardson, M. W.: *ref,* 525
Richey, M. H.: *ref,* 381
Richie, A.: *ref,* 398, 5:326(9)
Richman, E.: *ref,* 357
Richman, J.: *ref,* 529
Richmond, B. O.: *ref,* 400, 542, 551, 589
Richmond, D. M.: *ref,* 328
Richmond, W.: *exc,* 532
Richmond, W. V.: *ref,* 525
Richter, W. R.: *ref,* 382
Ricks, J. H.: *rev,* 345; *ref,* 529
Riddell, S. A.: *ref,* 543
Rider, R.: *ref,* 494, 497
Rider, R. V.: *ref,* 525, 533
Ridgway, R. W.: *ref,* 543, 592
Ridley, D. R.: *ref,* 542, 561, 572
Ridley, W. N.: *ref,* 425
Rieber, M.: *ref,* 516
Riechard, D. E.: *ref,* 361
Riegel, K. F.: *ref,* 529, 532
Riegel, R. M.: *ref,* 529, 532
Rieker, G. A.: *ref,* 533
Ries, A. J.: *ref,* 426
Ries, H. A.: *ref,* 529
Riess, A.: *ref,* 497
Riess, B.: *ref,* 426
Riffel, P. A.: *ref,* 358
Riggs, M. M.: *ref,* 525
Righthand, H.: *ref,* 391
Riker, B. L.: *ref,* 426

INDEX OF NAMES

Riklan, M.: *ref,* 439, 529, 532, 592
Riley, C. S.: *ref,* 373
Riley, G.: *ref,* 483, 525
Riley, J. E.: *ref,* 518
Riley, R. C.: *ref,* 6:438(450–1)
Riley, S.: *ref,* 403, 439
Rimoldi, H. J. A.: *ref,* 439
Rindone, R.: *ref,* 382
Ringe, K.: *ref,* 381
Ringness, T. A.: *ref,* 349, 533
Ringwall, E. A.: *ref,* 487
Rinsland, H. D.: *exc,* 505; *ref,* 349, 419, 4:277(216)
Rioch, M. J.: *ref,* 532
Ripple, R. E.: *ref,* 589
Risch, F.: *ref,* 525, 532
Rishel, D. F.: *ref,* 419
Risley, T. R.: *ref,* 529
Ritchie, J. E.: *ref,* 532
Ritchie, R. W.: *ref,* 361
Ritter, W.: *ref,* 439, 529
Rittmayer, J. F.: *ref,* 589
Ritzinger, R. C.: *ref,* 533
Rivoire, J. L.: *ref,* 364
Roach, C. B.: *ref,* 525
Roach, J. H. L.: *ref,* 419
Roaden, A. L.: *ref,* 419
Robb, G. P.: *ref,* 419
Robbins, J. E.: *ref,* 482
Robbins, M. C.: *ref,* 484
Robeck, M. C.: *ref,* 525, 533
Roberton, M. A.: *ref,* 381
Roberts, A. D.: *ref,* 483, 525, 532
Roberts, A. H.: *ref,* 518
Roberts, A. J.: *ref,* 516
Roberts, A. O. H.: *ref,* 532
Roberts, B. B.: *ref,* 357
Roberts, B. T.: *ref,* 357, 382
Roberts, C. S.: *ref,* 525
Roberts, D.: *ref,* 349
Roberts, D. E.: *ref,* 400
Roberts, D. M.: *ref,* 350, 525
Roberts, G. L.: *ref,* 3:220(6)
Roberts, H. C.: *ref,* 349
Roberts, H. E.: *ref,* 425, 525
Roberts, J.: *ref,* 381, 533
Roberts, J. A. F.: *ref,* 403, 525, 533, 6:480(33, 36–8)
Roberts, J. P.: *ref,* 357, 361
Roberts, P. T.: *ref,* 382
Roberts, R. C.: *ref,* 3:217(90)
Roberts, R. W.: *ref,* 529
Roberts, S. O.: *ref,* 357, 382, 4:277(194)
Roberts, W. H.: *ref,* 482
Robertson, J. P. S.: *ref,* 529, 545
Robertson, J. W.: *ref,* 400
Robertson, M.: *ref,* 382, 404
Robertson, M. H.: *ref,* 358, 529
Robinault, I. P.: *ref,* 381
Robinowitz, R.: *ref,* 503, 532–3
Robinson, B. V.: *ref,* 357
Robinson, C.: *ref,* 3:242(2)
Robinson, D. W.: *ref,* 382, 404
Robinson, E. L.: *ref,* 525
Robinson, F. K.: *ref,* 357
Robinson, H. A.: *ref,* 381, 489
Robinson, H. B.: *ref,* 484, 490, 505, 516, 538
Robinson, J. S.: *ref,* 484
Robinson, M. L.: *ref,* 398
Robinson, M. S.: *ref,* 525
Robinson, N.: *ref,* 525
Robinson, N. M.: *ref,* 484, 490, 505, 516, 525, 529, 538
Robinson, R.: *ref,* 349
Robinson, R. A.: *ref,* 403, 439
Robinson, S. J.: *ref,* 525, 533
Robinson, W. P.: *ref,* 495, 533
Robischon, P.: *ref,* 492
Robison, R. K.: *exc,* 532
Robitaille, H. J.: *ref,* 525
Roche, D.: *ref,* 381
Roche, P. J. D.: *ref,* 381
Rochester, D. E.: *ref,* 447, 529
Rock, D. A.: *ref,* 357
Rockwell, G. J.: *ref,* 533
Rodahl, K.: *ref,* 439
Rodd, W. G.: *ref,* 364
Roden, A. H.: *ref,* 359
Roderick, J. A.: *ref,* 589
Roderick, J. L.: *ref,* 589
Rodger, A. G.: *ref,* 409
Rodgers, D. C.: *ref,* 400
Roe, A.: *ref,* 381, 518, 525
Roe, K. V.: *ref,* 497
Roelke, P. L.: *ref,* 542
Roemmich, H.: *ref,* 371
Roesel, H. A.: *ref,* 5:308(305)
Roff, M.: *ref,* 400, 525
Roffman, P. O.: *ref,* 502
Rogal, R.: *ref,* 532
Rogers, A. L.: *ref,* 525
Rogers, B. E.: *ref,* 545
Rogers, C. A.: *rev,* 415; *ref,* 354
Rogers, D. C.: *ref,* 357, 426
Rogers, D. W.: *ref,* 589
Rogers, L. L.: *ref,* 364
Rogers, L. S.: *ref,* 532
Rogers, M. I.: *ref,* 551
Rogge, H. J.: *ref,* 533
Roggenkamp, R. R.: *ref,* 357, 425
Rogo, R. A.: *ref,* 5:308(362)
Rohan, J. C.: *ref,* 354, 525
Rohlf, R. J.: *ref,* 359
Rohrer, J. H.: *ref,* 381, 426
Rohrer, P. L.: *test,* 355
Rohrs, D. K.: *ref,* 6:438(512)
Rohrs, F. W.: *ref,* 381, 525, 533
Rohwer, W. D.: *ref,* 400, 439, 516
Rokicki, R. R.: *ref,* 503
Rokosz, S.: *ref,* 529
Roland, W. A.: *ref,* 381
Rolfe, J. F.: *ref,* 3:217(125)
Rolland, J. C.: *ref,* 516
Roller, R. D.: *ref,* 525
Romney, D.: *ref,* 403, 439
Ronan, R. J.: *ref,* 361
Ronan, W. W.: *ref,* 482
Rondberg, S. R.: *ref,* 532–3
Ronning, R. R.: *ref,* 419
Rood, T. M.: *ref,* 516
Rooks, I.: *ref,* 348
Roos, P.: *ref,* 426
Root, W. T.: *ref,* 525, 6:480(18)
Roper, G. E.: *ref,* 355
Rosanoff, A. J.: *ref,* 525
Rosauer, J. K.: *ref,* 487, 497
Roscoe, J. T.: *ref,* 382
Rose, D. M.: *ref,* 532
Rose, J.: *ref,* 561, 574, 577
Rose, J. R.: *ref,* 357
Rosén, A. S.: *ref,* 518
Rosen, C. L.: *ref,* 400
Rosen, E. K.: *ref,* 381
Rosen, M.: *ref,* 518, 529, 533
Rosen, N. A.: *ref,* 357, 574
Rosenau, C. B.: *ref,* 400
Rosenbach, J. H.: *rev,* 349, 401
Rosenberg, B. G.: *ref,* 532
Rosenberg, C. M.: *ref,* 439
Rosenberg, E.: *ref,* 529
Rosenberg, J. B.: *ref,* 516
Rosenberg, L. A.: *ref,* 489, 516, 525
Rosenberg, M.: *ref,* 525, 533
Rosenberger, P. B.: *ref,* 533
Rosenblatt, S. M.: *ref,* 532
Rosenblith, J. F.: *ref,* 484
Rosenblum, J.: *ref,* 489
Rosenblum, S.: *ref,* 5:326(15–6)
Rosenfeld, G. B.: *ref,* 487, 489, 525
Rosenfeld, M.: *ref,* 361
Rosenfield, L.: *ref,* 487, 525
Rosenow, C.: *ref,* 525
Rosenquist, C. M.: *ref,* 529, 533
Rosensteel, R. K.: *ref,* 337
Rosenstein, J.: *ref,* 496
Rosenstein, J. L.: *ref,* 4:277(146)
Rosenthal, D.: *ref,* 532
Rosenthal, R.: *ref,* 467
Rosenzweig, S.: *ref,* 381, 426, 483, 525, 532
Rosenzweig, S. P.: *ref,* 529
Rosevear, D.: *ref,* 353
Rosicki, M.: *ref,* 529
Rosier, F. N. G.: *ref,* 533
Rosilda, M.: *ref,* 349
Rosinski, E. F.: *ref,* 425
Roslow, S.: *ref,* 398
Rosner, B.: *rev,* 442, 6:491; *ref,* 400
Ross, A. O.: *ref,* 342
Ross, D.: *ref,* 529
Ross, D. R.: *ref,* 529
Ross, G.: *ref,* 499
Ross, J.: *ref,* 403, 439
Ross, J. A.: *ref,* 404
Ross, L. W.: *ref,* 447
Ross, P. F.: *ref,* 341, 444
Ross, R. T.: *ref,* 529, 533
Rossi, A. M.: *ref,* 532
Rossi, P. D.: *ref,* 532
Rossiter, J. R.: *ref,* 574
Rossmann, J. E.: *ref,* 361
Rostker, L. E.: *ref,* 3:217(126)
Rosvold, H. E.: *ref,* 529, 592
Roth, J. D.: *ref,* 405
Roth, M.: *ref,* 439, 532
Roth, R. J.: *ref,* 529, 533
Roth, R. M.: *ref,* 426, 529, 6:438(497)
Roth, S.: *ref,* 497
Rothbart, H. B.: *ref,* 525
Rothman, A. I.: *ref,* 391
Rothney, J. W. M.: *rev,* 525; *ref,* 359, 525
Rothstein, H. J.: *ref,* 532
Rotman, C. B.: *ref,* 525
Rotter, D. M.: *ref,* 349
Rotter, J. B.: *ref,* 342, 482
Rottersman, L.: *ref,* 381, 525, 533
Roughton, E. L.: *ref,* 589
Rouleau, R. A.: *ref,* 559
Rourke, B. P.: *ref,* 516, 533
Rouse, M. J.: *exc,* 381
Rouse, S. T.: *ref,* 589
Rousey, C. L.: *ref,* 532
Rousseau, C. A.: *ref,* 516
Rowe, F. B.: *ref,* 482
Rowe, L. M.: *ref,* 357
Rowland, M. S.: *ref,* 525

Rowles, E.: *ref,* 419
Rowley, V. N.: *ref,* 533, 543
Royce, J. R.: *ref,* 439–40, 518
Royer, F. L.: *ref,* 529
Royer, J. E.: *ref,* 5:308(393)
Royo, D.: *ref,* 439, 532
Royse, A. B.: *rev,* 461, 477, 6:470
Rozynko, V.: *ref,* 349
Rubin, E. J.: *ref,* 407, 440, 529, 533
Rubin, H.: *ref,* 532
Rubin, J.: *ref,* 439, 529
Rubin, S. S.: *ref,* 349
Rubino, C. A.: *ref,* 505, 529, 532–3
Rubin-Rabson, G.: *ref,* 532
Rubinstein, E. A.: *ref,* 532
Ruble, R. A.: *ref,* 400
Ruby, T. M.: *ref,* 529
Ruch, F. L.: *ref,* 525
Ruch, G. M.: *ref,* 525, 3:220(15, 31)
Ruda, E.: *ref,* 482
Rudd, J. P.: *ref,* 361
Rudel, R. G.: *ref,* 533
Rudman, J.: *ref,* 382
Rudnick, M.: *ref,* 400
Rudolf, G. de M.: *ref,* 439, 503, 525, 532
Rudolph, L.: *ref,* 524, 529
Ruebush, B.: *ref,* 425
Ruebush, B. K.: *ref,* 518
Ruedisili, C. H.: *ref,* 3:217(78), 4:277(162–3)
Ruess, A. L.: *ref,* 497, 533, 5:326(35)
Rugg, H.: *ref,* 525
Rugg, L. S.: *ref,* 525
Rugg, R. H.: *ref,* 496, 516
Rumley, E.: *ref,* 589
Rupiper, O. J.: *ref,* 382
Rupp, R. A.: *ref,* 3:255(12)
Rusalem, H.: *ref,* 529
Rusch, R. R.: *ref,* 560
Ruschival, M. L.: *ref,* 533, 538
Rush, A. C.: *ref,* 349
Rush, H.: *ref,* 438
Rushton, C. S.: *ref,* 525
Rushton, S. Y.: *ref,* 543
Rusmore, J.: *ref,* 482
Rusmore, J. T.: *ref,* 482
Russell, C. A.: *ref,* 525, 533
Russell, E. C.: *ref,* 497
Russell, E. W.: *ref,* 529
Russell, G. E.: *ref,* 532
Russell, H. H.: *ref,* 387, 425
Russell, I. L.: *ref,* 5:326(24)
Russell, J.: *ref,* 518
Russell, J. A.: *ref,* 529
Russell, J. B.: *ref,* 416
Russell, J. W.: *ref,* 357
Russell, L.: *ref,* 532, 592
Russell, R. W.: *ref,* 381
Russell, T.: *ref,* 381
Russell, W. P.: *ref,* 361
Rustin, S. L.: *ref,* 439, 529
Rutherford, B. M.: *ref,* 425
Rutland, E.: *ref,* 436
Rutter, D.: *ref,* 409
Rutter, M.: *ref,* 516, 533
Ruzicka, W. R.: *ref,* 522, 533
Ryan, B.: *ref,* 361
Ryan, M. S.: *exc,* 497
Ryan, S. E.: *ref,* 419
Ryans, D. G.: *rev,* 414, 472, 6:448; *exc,* 497; *ref,* 398

Ryback, R. S.: *ref,* 561, 591
Rychlak, J. F.: *ref,* 533
Rymsza, J. S. D.: *ref,* 533

SAAM, T.: *ref,* 525
Sabatino, D. A.: *ref,* 516, 533
Sabeh, R.: *ref,* 419, 532
Saber-Motamedi, H.: *ref,* 529
Sachs, D. A.: *ref,* 533
Sachtleben, C. C.: *ref,* 357
Sacks, E. L.: *ref,* 525
Sacks, J. M.: *ref,* 518
Sacks, L.: *ref,* 533
Saddler, L. E.: *test,* 479
Sadnavitch, J. M.: *ref,* 525
Sadowsky, D.: *ref,* 532
Saffir, M. A.: *ref,* 525
Safford, H. W.: *ref,* 529
Safran, C.: *test,* 453; *ref,* 453
Safrin, R. K.: *ref,* 533
Sak, H. G.: *ref,* 381, 533
Sako, Y.: *ref,* 529
Salisbury, D. L.: *ref,* 533
Salisbury, L. H.: *ref,* 529
Salley, R. E.: *ref,* 3:217(130), 4:277(217)
Salopek, T. F.: *ref,* 525, 533
Saltzgaver, L. D.: *ref,* 6:438(443)
Saltzman, S.: *ref,* 525
Salvati, S. R.: *ref,* 533
Salzinger, K.: *ref,* 518
Salzinger, S.: *ref,* 518
Salzman, L. F.: *ref,* 440
Samenfeld, H. W.: *ref,* 419, 5:308(331)
Sampson, O. C.: *ref,* 381, 403, 439, 525
Sams, C. C.: *ref,* 419
Sanborn, M. P.: *ref,* 361
Sánchez, G. I.: *ref,* 525
Sanchez, J. T.: *ref,* 332
Sand, P. L.: *ref,* 529
Sander, D. L.: *exc,* 360
Sandercock, M. G.: *ref,* 525, 533
Sanders, C.: *rev,* 323, 325, 338
Sanders, C. C.: *ref,* 496
Sanders, J. R.: *test,* 582; *ref,* 532
Sanders, J. W.: *ref,* 548
Sanders, M. W.: *ref,* 4:277(253)
Sanders, W. B.: *ref,* 4:277(211, 250)
Sanderson, M. H.: *ref,* 518, 532
Sanderson, R. E.: *ref,* 439, 516, 525
San Diego, E. A.: *ref,* 529
Sandiford, P.: *ref,* 435
Sandler, A. M.: *ref,* 525
Sandler, J.: *ref,* 489, 525
Sandler, L.: *ref,* 492
Sandry, M.: *ref,* 533
Sands, H.: *ref,* 532
Sandstead, H. H.: *ref,* 525
Sandstedt, B.: *ref,* 493, 533
Sandy, C. A.: *ref,* 435
Sangren, P. V.: *ref,* 435, 438, 3:255(5), 5:354(5)
Sannito, T. C.: *ref,* 529
Santoro, R. M.: *ref,* 425, 483, 578
Santos, B.: *ref,* 381, 529, 592
Sants, H. J.: *rev,* 397
Sanua, V. D.: *ref,* 433
Sapir, S. G.: *ref,* 381, 533
Sappenfield, B. R.: *ref,* 532
Sarason, E. K.: *ref,* 483, 525, 545
Sarason, I. G.: *ref,* 357, 361, 529

Sarason, S.: *ref,* 425
Sarason, S. B.: *ref,* 400, 483, 518, 525, 532, 545, 3:218(6), 3:228(3–4)
Sargent, R. F.: *ref,* 3:247(2)
Sartain, A. Q.: *ref,* 337, 426, 525, 532, 3:217(135), 3:220(74–5)
Sartorius, I. C.: *ref,* 3:242(2)
Saruk, A.: *ref,* 361
Saslow, G.: *ref,* 529
Sassenrath, J. M.: *ref,* 357, 5:308(371), 6:438(532)
Satlow, I. D.: *rev,* 5:389
Sattabanasuk, T.: *ref,* 400
Sattel, L.: *ref,* 533
Satter, G.: *ref,* 439, 518, 525, 532
Sattler, J. M.: *ref,* 525, 529, 532–3
Satz, M. A.: *ref,* 5:308(332)
Satz, P.: *ref,* 440, 529, 533
Saucer, R. T.: *ref,* 447, 532
Saum, A. L.: *ref,* 419
Saum, J. A.: *ref,* 382
Saunders, D. R.: *ref,* 529, 532
Saunders, H. R.: *ref,* 357
Saunders, M. H.: *ref,* 381
Saunders, W. J.: *ref,* 423, 426
Savage, B. M.: *ref,* 407
Savage, R. D.: *ref,* 331, 425, 529, 533
Savage, W.: *ref,* 532–3
Saville, P.: *test,* 331, 529, 533, 538
Savitsky, J. C.: *ref,* 357
Sawa, H.: *ref,* 533
Sawrey, J. M.: *ref,* 435, 532, 5:326(17)
Sawyer, C. R.: *ref,* 398, 5:329(3)
Sawyer, R.: *ref,* 533
Sawyer, R. I.: *ref,* 533
Sawyer, R. N.: *ref,* 517, 533
Sax, G.: *exc,* 7:378; *ref,* 391
Saxe, E. L. G.: *ref,* 529
Saxon, J. P.: *ref,* 498, 529
Sayers, M. P.: *ref,* 497
Scallon, R. J.: *ref,* 533
Scarborough, B. B.: *ref,* 532
Scarf, R. C.: *ref,* 6:438(444)
Scarr, E. H.: *ref,* 525
Schachter, F. F.: *ref,* 525, 533
Schaefer, C. E.: *test,* 544, 553, 580; *ref,* 381, 542, 544, 551, 553, 580, 587
Schaefer, E.: *ref,* 348
Schaefer, E. S.: *ref,* 484
Schaefer, W. C.: *rev,* 452, 4:281
Schafer, E. W. P.: *ref,* 425, 533
Schafer, R.: *ref,* 529, 532
Schafer, S.: *ref,* 525
Schaie, K. W.: *ref,* 592
Schalling, D.: *ref,* 365, 518, 529, 532, 543
Schalon, C. L.: *ref,* 529
Scharf, M. P.: *ref,* 516
Scheibner, R. M.: *ref,* 547
Scheidemann, N. V.: *exc,* 487
Scheier, I. H.: *ref,* 388, 439, 473
Schein, E. H.: *ref,* 532
Schell, M.: *ref,* 525
Schell, R. E.: *ref,* 349, 518
Schellenberg, E. D.: *ref,* 349
Schellhammer, J. R.: *ref,* 357
Schena, R. A.: *ref,* 398, 525
Schenck, H. U.: *ref,* 516, 522
Schepers, J. M.: *test,* 550; *ref,* 439
Scherer, G. A. C.: *ref,* 357

Scherer, I. W.: *ref,* 504, 525, 532
Schieffelin, B.: *ref,* 558, 2:1390(4), 2:1391(8), 2:1394(5), 2:1401(4)
Schiff, D.: *ref,* 533
Schiff, S.: *ref,* 529
Schilder, P.: *ref,* 381
Schill, T.: *ref,* 529
Schiller, B.: *ref,* 381
Schilling, M. E.: *ref,* 525
Schillo, R. J.: *ref,* 532
Schindler, R.: *ref,* 439
Schiro, F. M.: *ref,* 529
Schlesser, G. E.: *ref,* 357, 3:217 (90), 4:277(254)
Schlicht, W. J.: *ref,* 364, 574
Schlosser, J. R.: *ref,* 532
Schlueter, M. P.: *ref,* 400
Schmid, J.: *ref,* 496, 518
Schmidt, A. G.: *exc,* 497, 507, 518, 532, 2:1426
Schmidt, D. G.: *ref,* 532
Schmidt, H. E.: *test,* 552, 576
Schmidt, R. H.: *ref,* 589
Schmitt, J. A.: *ref,* 404
Schmitz, R. M.: *ref,* 419, 5:308 (363)
Schmitz, S. B.: *ref,* 426, 2:1377 (30), 3:220(59)
Schmuck, R. A.: *ref,* 399
Schmuck, R. W.: *ref,* 399
Schnack, G. F.: *ref,* 525
Schnadt, F.: *ref,* 529, 532
Schneck, M. R.: *ref,* 2:1394(6), 2:1399(12)
Schneideman, N. V.: *exc,* 487
Schneider, B.: *ref,* 532-3
Schneider, J. H.: *ref,* 533
Schneider, R. A.: *ref,* 532
Schneiderman, N.: *ref,* 6:537(3)
Schneidler, G. G.: *ref,* 438, 2:1401 (8), 2:1424(23), 3:217(109)
Schnell, R. R.: *ref,* 439
Schneyer, J. W.: *ref,* 357
Schneyer, S.: *ref,* 532
Schnitzer, L. P.: *ref,* 551, 561, 572
Schnobrich, J. N.: *ref,* 381, 516, 529
Schnore, M. M.: *ref,* 529, 543
Schoel, D. R.: *ref,* 542, 574
Schoemer, J. R.: *ref,* 357
Schoeninger, D. W.: *ref,* 516
Schoer, L. A.: *ref,* 533
Schofield, J.: *test,* 7:416
Schofield, L. F.: *ref,* 529
Schofield, M.: *test,* 450, 452
Schofield, W.: *rev,* 543; *ref,* 404, 532
Scholl, G.: *ref,* 533
Schon, M.: *ref,* 532
Schonell, F. E.: *ref,* 525
Schonell, F. J.: *rev,* 4:272; *test,* 373
Schonhorn, R.: *ref,* 533
Schooler, C.: *ref,* 529
Schoonover, S. M.: *ref,* 525, 533
Schorr, M.: *ref,* 348
Schott, E. L.: *ref,* 525
Schrader, D. R.: *ref,* 349, 400
Schrader, E. N.: *ref,* 3:217(91)
Schrader, W. B.: *rev,* 335-6, 404, 455, 457, 4:329; *ref,* 357, 5:308 (294)
Schramm, T. A.: *ref,* 525, 533
Schrammel, H. E.: *test,* 3:220h, 4:281, 6:498

Schreck, J. F.: *ref,* 361
Schreck, T. C.: *ref,* 333
Schreffler, R. H.: *ref,* 525
Schreiber, E. W.: *ref,* 426
Schreurs, E.: *ref,* 2:1377(5)
Schriefer, L.: *ref,* 525, 558
Schroeder, W. L.: *ref,* 391
Schubert, D. S. P.: *test,* 455
Schubert, H. J. P.: *test,* 455
Schubert, J.: *ref,* 533
Schucman, H.: *ref,* 529, 532
Schuell, H.: *ref,* 496
Schuerhoff, C.: *ref,* 357, 482, 561, 574
Schuh, A. J.: *ref,* 482
Schuh, B.: *ref,* 3:242(2)
Schulberg, H. C.: *ref,* 529
Schulman, J. L.: *ref,* 381, 516, 525, 533
Schulte, F. J.: *ref,* 497
Schultz, C. B.: *ref,* 357, 436, 542, 561
Schultz, D. G.: *ref,* 357
Schultz, M. K.: *ref,* 382
Schultz, R. S.: *ref,* 3:220(49), 4:277(147)
Schultz, W.: *ref,* 529
Schulz, R. E.: *ref,* 5:308(394)
Schurdak, J. J.: *ref,* 391
Schusler, M. M.: *ref,* 361, 425
Schut, D.: *ref,* 439, 532
Schutte, T. H.: *ref,* 426
Schutz, R. E.: *rev,* 467-8; *ref,* 425, 5:368(23)
Schwartz, A. A.: *ref,* 525
Schwartz, E. M.: *ref,* 503
Schwartz, H. G.: *ref,* 532, 592
Schwartz, I. H.: *ref,* 364
Schwartz, L.: *ref,* 533
Schwartz, M. L.: *ref,* 529, 532-3
Schwartz, M. M.: *ref,* 371, 404
Schwartz, M. S.: *ref,* 503, 529
Schwartzman, A. E.: *ref,* 529
Schwarz, R. H.: *ref,* 525, 533, 538
Schwebel, A. I.: *ref,* 533
Schwegler, R. A.: *ref,* 525
Schweiker, R.: *test,* 387
Schwellenbach, J. A.: *ref,* 349
Schwerin, E.: *ref,* 558
Schwesinger, G. C.: *rev,* 364, 518; *ref,* 558, 2:1390(4), 2:1391(8), 2:1394(5), 2:1401(4)
Schwinger, W. A.: *ref,* 5:308(333)
Schwitzgoebel, R. R.: *ref,* 533
Science Research Associates, Inc.: *test,* 451, 5:319, 5:376
Sciortino, R.: *ref,* 419
Scoggins, B. J.: *ref,* 496, 516
Scollay, R. W.: *test,* 418
Scollon, R. W.: *ref,* 447, 592
Scoonover, D. L.: *ref,* 516
Scott, C. W.: *ref,* 404
Scott, D. A.: *ref,* 405
Scott, E. M.: *ref,* 533
Scott, G. C.: *ref,* 415
Scott, G. R.: *ref,* 525, 533
Scott, J.: *ref,* 525, 529
Scott, L. E.: *ref,* 589
Scott, M.: *ref,* 381, 516
Scott, R.: *ref,* 533
Scott, R. B.: *ref,* 487, 497
Scott, R. H.: *ref,* 425
Scott, T. B.: *ref,* 382, 404
Scott Co.: *test,* 456

Scottish Council for Research in Education: *ref,* 525, 533
Scovill, M. S.: *ref,* 558
Scovill Manufacturing Co.: *test,* 4:320
Scripture, M. K.: *ref,* 525
Scudder, K. J.: *ref,* 3:263(32)
Seagoe, M. V.: *ref,* 398, 426, 435, 441, 2:1424(18), 3:255(7), 4:288(2)
Sealy, A. P.: *ref,* 364
Seaquist, M. R.: *ref,* 532
Searls, E. F.: *ref,* 533, 538
Sears, R.: *ref,* 381, 532
Seashore, H.: *ref,* 357-8, 426, 532-3, 5:308(364)
Seashore, H. G.: *rev,* 4:338; *test,* 333, 473; *ref,* 358, 381, 426, 433, 447, 482, 525, 529, 532-3
Seashore, R. H.: *ref,* 419, 426
Sebera, P.: *ref,* 505, 516
Secondary Education Board: *test,* 394
Seda, M. S. A.: *ref,* 516
Sedal, V. S.: *ref,* 525
Sedberry, M. E.: *ref,* 381
Seder, M.: *ref,* 2:1377(40, 45)
Sedlacek, W. E.: *ref,* 357
Seelye, B. J.: *ref,* 525
Seeman, W.: *ref,* 532
Segal, S. J.: *ref,* 529, 532
Segel, D.: *rev,* 398, 1:1037; *ref,* 400, 2:1377(16)
Segel, R. H.: *ref,* 529
Seguin, E.: *test,* 578
Seibel, D. W.: *ref,* 404, 436
Seidel, H. E.: *ref,* 355, 439
Seidenfeld, M. A.: *ref,* 426
Seidl, J. C.: *ref,* 483, 525
Seigle, W. F.: *ref,* 5:308(365)
Seim, S.: *ref,* 439
Seither, F. G.: *ref,* 349
Seitz, E. K.: *ref,* 538
Seitz, F. C.: *ref,* 522, 529
Seitz, T. L.: *ref,* 542, 546, 551
Sekyra, F.: *ref,* 489, 525, 533
Selecki, B. R.: *ref,* 529
Sell, D. E.: *test,* 418
Sella, A. P.: *ref,* 490, 525
Selland, C. T.: *ref,* 398
Sellers, J. R.: *ref,* 391, 7:378(7)
Sells, S. B.: *ref,* 381, 400, 533
Selman, R. L.: *ref,* 516
Selover, R. B.: *ref,* 419
Seltzer, C. C.: *ref,* 357, 407
Semeonoff, B.: *test,* 6:519; *exc,* 522; *ref,* 406, 6:519(1)
Semler, I. J.: *ref,* 439, 533
Semmel, M. I.: *rev,* 575
Sen, A.: *ref,* 439
Sen, R.: *ref,* 525
Senour, A. C.: *ref,* 3:256(5)
Senti, M. M.: *ref,* 503, 532
Serafetinides, E. A.: *ref,* 532
Serota, K. E.: *ref,* 525
Service for Admission to College and University: *test,* 353
Servis, M.: *ref,* 425
Severance, K. M.: *ref,* 5:308(334)
Severinsen, K. N.: *ref,* 529
Severson, R. A.: *ref,* 543
Sevier, F. A. C.: *ref,* 357
Sevransky, P.: *ref,* 400
Sewell, W. H.: *ref,* 391

Seybold, F. R.: *ref,* 532
Seymore, S.: *ref,* 542
Seymour, J. H.: *ref,* 532, 592
Seymour, O. J.: *ref,* 4:277(144)
Seymour, W. R.: *ref,* 361
Sgan, M. R.: *ref,* 357
Shaalan, M.: *ref,* 532
Shackel, D. S. J.: *ref,* 589
Shaffer, J. W.: *ref,* 439, 529, 533, 543
Shaffer, L. F.: *exc,* 348, 391, 504–5, 518, 532–3, 4:347–8, 4:354–5, 4:362
Shaffer, R. G.: *ref,* 348, 398, 400, 425
Shagass, C.: *ref,* 439, 547–8
Shah, S. A.: *ref,* 426
Shah, V. P.: *ref,* 391
Shaheen, O.: *ref,* 532
Shakow, D.: *ref,* 518, 525, 2:1401 (1, 3, 9)
Shaltiel, J.: *ref,* 381, 439, 545
Shanan, J.: *ref,* 439, 532, 543
Shane, J. F.: *ref,* 516, 525, 533
Shanley, L. A.: *ref,* 425
Shanner, W. M.: *ref,* 349, 357, 3:217(92)
Shannon, W.: *ref,* 532
Shantz, C. U.: *ref,* 439
Shapiro, B.: *ref,* 498, 513, 529
Shapiro, E.: *ref,* 533
Shapiro, M. B.: *ref,* 518, 529, 532, 545, 5:357(3)
Shapiro, R. J.: *ref,* 551, 589
Shapton, D.: *ref,* 415, 533
Shapurian, R.: *ref,* 331
Sharan (Singer), S.: *ref,* 532
Share, J.: *ref,* 497
Sharon, M.: *ref,* 439
Sharp, A. A.: *ref,* 503
Sharp, E. Y.: *ref,* 518, 559, 561
Sharp, H. C.: *ref,* 419, 505, 525, 533
Sharpe, T. M.: *ref,* 533
Shatswell, D. W.: *ref,* 533
Shatus, E. L.: *ref,* 525, 538
Shaver, J. P.: *ref,* 349
Shaw, C. N.: *ref,* 439
Shaw, D. J.: *ref,* 516, 529, 533
Shaw, E.: *ref,* 529, 592
Shaw, E. A.: *ref,* 2:1390(2), 2:1391(2)
Shaw, F.: *ref,* 542
Shaw, G. S.: *ref,* 425
Shaw, H. S.: *ref,* 357
Shaw, H. W.: *ref,* 529
Shaw, J. H.: *ref,* 592
Shay, C. T.: *ref,* 357
Shay, J. B.: *ref,* 425
Shea, C. A.: *ref,* 400
Shea, J. A.: *ref,* 5:308(395)
Shea, M.: *ref,* 505, 533
Shearburn, C.: *ref,* 533
Shearer, P. D.: *ref,* 533
Shearn, C. R.: *ref,* 496
Shechtman, A. M.: *ref,* 483, 525
Shedd, C. L.: *ref,* 5:326(10)
Sheddan, B. R.: *ref,* 419
Sheehan, P. W.: *ref,* 542
Sheffield, E. F.: *ref,* 4:277(165)
Sheldon, E.: *ref,* 589
Sheldon, H. J.: *ref,* 533
Sheldon, M. J. R.: *ref,* 589
Sheldon, M. S.: *ref,* 533
Sheldon, W. D.: *ref,* 349, 483, 525

Sheldon, W. H.: *ref,* 357, 525
Shelly, C. H.: *ref,* 529
Shepard, E. L.: *ref,* 425
Shepherd, C. W.: *ref,* 524
Sheppard, C.: *ref,* 349, 439
Sherard, E. S.: *test,* 494; *ref,* 494, 497
Sherman, A. R.: *ref,* 529
Sherman, D. M.: *ref,* 361
Sherman, E. A.: *ref,* 349
Sherman, O.: *ref,* 4:277(155)
Sherman, R. C.: *ref,* 405
Sherman, V. M. S. R.: *ref,* 361
Sherrill, D.: *ref,* 357
Sherron, R. H.: *ref,* 357
Sherwood, D. W.: *ref,* 589
Sherwood, E. J.: *ref,* 419
Sheverbush, R. L.: *ref,* 525
Shields, J. B.: *ref,* 533
Shields, R. V.: *ref,* 349
Shier, D. A.: *ref,* 532
Shigaki, I. S.: *ref,* 400, 589
Shimberg, M. E.: *ref,* 2:1390(3), 2:1391(6), 2:1394(3), 2:1401(2)
Shimkunas, A. M.: *ref,* 440, 529
Shimota, H. E.: *ref,* 518, 532
Shinagawa, F.: *ref,* 533
Shine, A.: *ref,* 525
Shine, A. E.: *ref,* 525
Shinedling, M. M.: *ref,* 524, 533
Shinn, S. M.: *ref,* 357, 529
Shipe, D.: *ref,* 516, 518, 525, 538
Shipe, D. M.: *ref,* 516, 533
Shipley, W. C.: *rev,* 439, 447, 3:228; *ref,* 525
Shipp, D. E.: *ref,* 381
Shirley, M.: *exc,* 497
Shively, J. E.: *ref,* 589
Shneidman, E. S.: *ref,* 529, 532
Shoben, E. J.: *ref,* 532
Shohen, S. S.: *ref,* 533
Shontz, F. C.: *ref,* 483, 489, 529, 555, 589, 592
Shor, J.: *ref,* 525
Shore, C.: *ref,* 529
Shore, H.: *ref,* 529
Shore, M. F.: *ref,* 533
Shore, R. P.: *ref,* 423
Shott, G. L.: *ref,* 482
Shotwell, A. M.: *test,* 5:411; *ref,* 483, 496, 516, 525, 529, 4:354(2)
Shrimali, P. L.: *ref,* 381
Shrivastava, R. P.: *ref,* 545
Shrubsall, F. C.: *exc,* 483
Shry, S. A.: *ref,* 574
Shuey, A. M.: *ref,* 3:217(110), 4:277(166, 195, 255)
Shukla, T. R.: *ref,* 543
Shultz, I. T.: *ref,* 426, 438
Shuman, J. T.: *ref,* 425
Shurrager, H. C.: *test,* 498
Shurrager, P. S.: *test,* 498
Shuttleworth, C. W.: *ref,* 384, 459
Shuttleworth, F. K.: *exc,* 483, 532
Sibley, S. A.: *ref,* 516
Siddique, H.: *ref,* 532
Siderits, M. A. T.: *ref,* 487, 525
Sidle, A. C.: *ref,* 542, 551, 561
Siebert, L. A.: *ref,* 425, 529, 533
Siegal, R. S.: *ref,* 532
Siegal, S. M.: *ref,* 529
Siegel, A. I.: *ref,* 357
Siegel, L.: *exc,* 467, 6:495; *ref,* 529, 6:438(509)

Siegel, S. M.: *ref,* 381
Siegelman, M.: *ref,* 357
Siegenthaler, B. M.: *ref,* 533
Siegman, A. W.: *ref,* 533
Sieveking, N. A.: *ref,* 357
Sievers, D. J.: *ref,* 497, 525, 532
Sigal, S.: *ref,* 574
Sigel, I.: *ref,* 525
Sigel, I. E.: *ref,* 439
Silber, D. E.: *ref,* 574
Silberberg, M.: *ref,* 525
Silberberg, M. C.: *ref,* 533
Silberberg, N.: *ref,* 525, 533
Silberberg, N. E.: *ref,* 483, 516, 533
Silberman, L.: *ref,* 533
Siloac, K. T.: *ref,* 516
Silva, J. J.: *ref,* 592
Silvaroli, N. J.: *ref,* 425
Silver, A. A.: *ref,* 381, 497, 538
Silver, C. E.: *ref,* 348, 532, 5:308(280)
Silver, M. R.: *ref,* 342
Silverberg, R. A.: *ref,* 589
Silverman, H.: *ref,* 532
Silverman, J.: *ref,* 529
Silverstein, A. B.: *rev,* 534, 538; *exc,* 525; *ref,* 381, 496, 516, 525, 529, 532–3, 538, 543
Silvey, H. M.: *ref,* 4:277(218, 270)
Sim, M.: *ref,* 529
Simkin, J. S.: *ref,* 532
Simkins, L.: *ref,* 496
Simmers, C. P.: *ref,* 525, 533
Simmonds, V.: *test,* 331
Simmons, A. A.: *ref,* 532
Simmons, H.: *ref,* 529
Simmons, K.: *ref,* 426, 507, 518, 525, 545
Simmons, P. W.: *ref,* 525
Simmons, R.: *ref,* 435
Simms, J. T.: *ref,* 542, 546
Simms, L. G.: *ref,* 543
Simon, A.: *ref,* 439, 532
Simon, A. J.: *ref,* 487, 497
Simon, L. M.: *ref,* 532
Simon, L. R.: *ref,* 574
Simon, W. E.: *ref,* 533
Simonian, K.: *ref,* 487
Simpson, C. D.: *ref,* 529
Simpson, D. J.: *ref,* 542, 546, 562, 573
Simpson, M. M.: *ref,* 532
Simpson, R. L.: *ref,* 529, 533
Simpson, S. A.: *ref,* 543
Simpson, W. H.: *ref,* 533
Sims, N. B.: *ref,* 529
Sims, V. M.: *ref,* 426
Sinaiko, H. W.: *ref,* 561
Sinclair, J. K.: *ref,* 489
Sines, J. O.: *ref,* 533
Sines, L. K.: *ref,* 529, 532
Singer, E.: *ref,* 532, 4:277(210)
Singer, M. T.: *ref,* 381, 532
Singer, P. R.: *ref,* 529
Singh, A.: *ref,* 331, 364
Singh, B.: *ref,* 381
Singh, M.: *ref,* 439
Singh, R. N.: *ref,* 364
Singh, S. B.: *ref,* 529
Singh, U. P.: *ref,* 529
Sinha, M.: *ref,* 381
Sinha, U.: *ref,* 439
Sinks, N. B.: *ref,* 348

INDEX OF NAMES

Sinnett, E. R.: *ref*, 381
Sinnett, K.: *ref*, 529
Sinowitz, M.: *ref*, 529
Sinton, D. W.: *ref*, 533
Sisk, H. L.: *ref*, 3:217(68), 4:277 (156)
Sisson, E. R.: *ref*, 361
Sitkei, E. G.: *ref*, 349, 439, 525
Sivers, C. H.: *ref*, 439, 525
Sjah, A.: *ref*, 381
Sjorgren, D. D.: *ref*, 529
Skager, R. W.: *ref*, 357, 436, 542, 561
Skaggs, E. B.: *ref*, 525, 558
Skalet, M.: *ref*, 525
Skard, O.: *ref*, 482, 5:308(366)
Skeels, H. M.: *ref*, 398, 483, 507, 525
Skene, D. M.: *ref*, 525
Skinner, J.: *ref*, 533
Skinner, S. B.: *ref*, 357
Sklar, M.: *ref*, 532
Skodak, M.: *ref*, 525
Skolnicki, J.: *ref*, 482
Skripol, J. N.: *ref*, 424, 533
Skubic, V.: *ref*, 349
Skurnik, L. S.: *ref*, 347
Slakter, M. J.: *ref*, 359
Slater, M. M.: *ref*, 5:308(306)
Slater, P.: *rev*, 409; *ref*, 354, 388, 403, 439, 532, 3:273(5), 5:339(5), 6:514(9)
Slater, R. D.: *ref*, 425
Slaughter, D. T.: *ref*, 490, 525
Slaymaker, R. R.: *ref*, 3:217(142)
Slayton, W. G.: *ref*, 348, 361
Sleeper, M. L.: *ref*, 382
Sleight, G. F.: *test*, 462
Sless, B.: *ref*, 525
Slivinske, A. J.: *ref*, 349
Sloan, W.: *rev*, 499; *ref*, 364, 483, 496, 503, 505, 525, 532-3
Sloane, R. B.: *ref*, 403
Slobodzian, E. B.: *ref*, 533
Slocombe, C. S.: *ref*, 525
Slosson, R. L.: *test*, 524
Slutzky, J. E.: *ref*, 425, 525
Small, I. F.: *ref*, 543, 592
Small, J. F.: *ref*, 348
Small, J. G.: *ref*, 529, 543, 592
Small, J. J.: *ref*, 323
Small, K.: *ref*, 518
Small, S. M.: *ref*, 592
Smart, R. C.: *ref*, 525
Smart, R. G.: *ref*, 529
Smith, A.: *ref*, 518, 529, 532
Smith, A. A.: *ref*, 381, 533
Smith, A. B.: *ref*, 419
Smith, A. E.: *exc*, 424; *ref*, 532
Smith, A. H.: *ref*, 359
Smith, B. M.: *ref*, 529
Smith, B. S.: *ref*, 489, 496, 533
Smith, C.: *ref*, 357
Smith, C. A.: *ref*, 354
Smith, C. E.: *rev*, 409, 2:1422
Smith, C. S.: *ref*, 525
Smith, D.: *ref*, 357
Smith, D. D.: *ref*, 4:277(256)
Smith, D. E.: *ref*, 357, 361, 5:308(433)
Smith, D. L.: *ref*, 589
Smith, D. M.: *ref*, 358
Smith, E.: *ref*, 517, 533
Smith, F. F.: *ref*, 4:277(171)
Smith, F. O.: *ref*, 381
Smith, F. W.: *ref*, 525
Smith, G. B.: *ref*, 5:308(411)
Smith, G. J. W.: *ref*, 439
Smith, G. P.: *ref*, 589
Smith, G. R.: *ref*, 398
Smith, H.: *ref*, 525, 529, 533
Smith, H. A.: *ref*, 349
Smith, H. E.: *test*, 3:268; *ref*, 447, 529
Smith, H. P.: *ref*, 419
Smith, H. W.: *ref*, 525
Smith, I. L.: *ref*, 400, 404, 551, 573-4
Smith, I. M.: *rev*, 354, 364; *test*, 415; *ref*, 409, 415, 425, 439
Smith, J.: *ref*, 503
Smith, J. B.: *ref*, 532
Smith, J. H.: *ref*, 492
Smith, J. M.: *ref*, 3:217(93)
Smith, J. S.: *ref*, 357
Smith, K.: *ref*, 440, 529
Smith, L.: *ref*, 358
Smith, L. C.: *ref*, 440, 529, 543
Smith, L. M.: *ref*, 404, 496, 533
Smith, M.: *ref*, 525, 529, 533
Smith, M. E.: *ref*, 4:277(167)
Smith, M. M.: *ref*, 533
Smith, M. P.: *ref*, 516, 525
Smith, N. C.: *ref*, 533
Smith, O. D.: *ref*, 3:256(6)
Smith, P.: *rev*, 2:1381, 2:1389
Smith, P. A.: *ref*, 529, 533
Smith, P. B.: *ref*, 516
Smith, P. D.: *ref*, 348-9
Smith, P. M.: *ref*, 357
Smith, R. A.: *ref*, 538
Smith, R. C.: *ref*, 440
Smith, R. E.: *exc*, 533
Smith, R. G.: *ref*, 361
Smith, R. H.: *ref*, 349, 589
Smith, R. L.: *ref*, 425
Smith, R. M.: *ref*, 542, 546, 551, 561-2, 577, 589
Smith, R. S.: *ref*, 487
Smith, S. E.: *ref*, 525
Smith, T. A.: *ref*, 533
Smith, T. W.: *ref*, 349, 5:326(11, 18, 25-6)
Smith, V. E.: *ref*, 391
Smith, W. H.: *ref*, 6:480(6)
Smith, W. J.: *ref*, 482
Smith, W. L.: *ref*, 525, 529
Smith, W. N.: *ref*, 361
Smith, W. T.: *ref*, 529
Smithers, A.: *ref*, 331
Smitter, F. W.: *ref*, 507, 525
Smock, C. D.: *rev*, 344; *exc*, 549
Smolinsky, M. P.: *ref*, 404
Smotherman, T. E.: *ref*, 4:277(271)
Smouse, A. D.: *ref*, 391
Smykal, A.: *ref*, 532
Smyth, V. O. G.: *ref*, 439, 529, 532
Snedden, D.: *exc*, 483
Snell, J.: *ref*, 525
Snider, H. L.: *ref*, 503, 532
Snider, J. G.: *ref*, 349
Snider, M.: *ref*, 522, 533
Snider, S.: *ref*, 525
Sniffen, A. M.: *ref*, 398-9
Snijders, J. T.: *test*, 512; *ref*, 512
Snijders-Oomen, N.: *test*, 512; *ref*, 512
Snow, R. E.: *ref*, 561
Snyder, C. R.: *ref*, 357
Snyder, W. U.: *ref*, 504
Sober, K. A.: *ref*, 361
Sobol, A.: *ref*, 426
Sockloff, A. L.: *ref*, 357
Sodhi, S.: *ref*, 361
Soika, G. R.: *ref*, 5:308(335)
Sokolov, S. L.: *ref*, 529, 533
Soliman, A. M.: *ref*, 589
Solis, M. M.: *ref*, 453
Solkoff, N.: *ref*, 425-6, 533
Sollee, N. D.: *ref*, 533
Solomon, A. O.: *ref*, 589
Solomon, L. E.: *ref*, 5:308(278)
Solomon, M.: *ref*, 532
Solomon, P.: *ref*, 503
Soltys, J. J.: *ref*, 533
Soltz, W. H.: *ref*, 529
Solyom, L.: *ref*, 592
Somasundaram, C. P.: *ref*, 592
Somerset, H. C. A.: *ref*, 532
Sommerfeld, R. E.: *ref*, 361
Song, A. Y.: *ref*, 529
Song, R. H.: *ref*, 529
Sonneman, L. J.: *ref*, 400, 489, 525, 533
Sontag, L. W.: *ref*, 525
Sontag, M.: *ref*, 490, 525
Sopchak, A. L.: *ref*, 5:308(437)
Soper, M. E.: *ref*, 5:308(336)
Sorensen, M. A.: *ref*, 529
Sorenson, H.: *ref*, 404
Sorsby, F. B.: *ref*, 532
Sosulski, M. C.: *ref*, 533
Sours, C. F. R.: *ref*, 361
South, E. B.: *ref*, 419, 426, 438
Southern, M. L.: *ref*, 516-7, 525, 533, 538
Southworth, J. A.: *ref*, 357
Space, M. N.: *ref*, 405
Spache, G.: *ref*, 398, 525, 532
Spache, G. D.: *ref*, 533
Spadafore, G. J.: *ref*, 381
Spaethe, M.: *ref*, 482
Spaner, F. E.: *ref*, 529, 532
Spaner, S. D.: *ref*, 522
Spaney, E.: *ref*, 6:438(440)
Spanier, S. W.: *ref*, 532
Spano, R. M.: *ref*, 518
Sparks, C. P.: *ref*, 444
Sparling, E. J.: *ref*, 456, 4:281(78)
Sparling, M. E.: *ref*, 518, 525
Spaulding, G.: *test*, 394; *ref*, 357, 394, 398
Spaulding, H.: *ref*, 357-8, 419
Spaulding, P. J.: *ref*, 487, 525
Spearman, C.: *rev*, 425; *exc*, 525; *ref*, 439
Spearman, C. E.: *ref*, 439
Spearman, L. H. O.: *ref*, 525, 533
Spearritt, D.: *test*, 324-5, 327-8, 426; *ref*, 327-8, 415, 6:435(1)
Speedie, S. M.: *ref*, 589
Speer, G. S.: *ref*, 425, 525
Speevack, M.: *ref*, 525
Spelman, M. S.: *ref*, 403, 439
Spence, A. G.: *ref*, 525, 533
Spence, J. T.: *ref*, 529
Spence, R. B.: *ref*, 426
Spencer, S. J. G.: *ref*, 331
Sperber, Z.: *ref*, 529
Sperrazzo, G.: *ref*, 439
Speyer, H.: *exc*, 487

Spiegel, H.: *ref,* 525
Spiegel, J. A.: *ref,* 357
Spielberger, C. D.: *ref,* 324, 357, 404, 529, 6:438(452)
Spiers, D. E.: *ref,* 349
Spieth, P. E.: *ref,* 525, 529
Spieth, W.: *ref,* 529
Spiker, C. C.: *ref,* 487
Spilka, B.: *ref,* 5:308(438), 6:438(453)
Spitz, H.: *ref,* 532
Spitzer, M. E.: *ref,* 426
Spitznagel, A.: *ref,* 519
Spivack, G.: *ref,* 532-3
Spock, A.: *ref,* 381, 516
Spoerl, D. T.: *ref,* 381, 391, 525
Spohrer, M. A.: *ref,* 342, 4:308(345)
Spotts, J. V.: *ref,* 381, 555
Spotts, W. S.: *ref,* 381
Sprague, A. L.: *ref,* 496
Sprague, R. L.: *ref,* 529
Spreen, O.: *ref,* 525, 529, 532-3, 543
Spriggs, A. J.: *test,* 585; *ref,* 585
Spring, L. E.: *ref,* 5:308(367)
Springer, N. N.: *ref,* 381, 503, 532
Springer, T. A.: *ref,* 589
Springfield, L.: *ref,* 381, 533
Sprinthall, N. A.: *ref,* 382, 404
Sprow, A. J.: *ref,* 391, 398, 419, 3:263(45)
Staats, A. W.: *ref,* 357
Stabenau, J. R.: *ref,* 529
Stacey, C. L.: *ref,* 439, 525, 532-3
Stack, S. E.: *ref,* 348, 6:438(473)
Stackhouse, H. A.: *ref,* 419
Stackman, H.: *ref,* 518, 525
Stackman, H. A.: *ref,* 525
Stacy, B. F.: *ref,* 348
Staffieri, J. R.: *ref,* 516, 522
Stafford, C.: *ref,* 492
Stafford, J. W.: *ref,* 382, 404
Stafford, R. E.: *ref,* 484
Stafford, R. L.: *ref,* 425, 589
Stagner, R.: *ref,* 469
Stainer, W. J.: *ref,* 416
Stake, R. E.: *test,* 443; *ref,* 349, 443
Staker, J. E.: *ref,* 529
Stallings, L.: *ref,* 529, 533
Stalnaker, E. M.: *ref,* 525, 3:217(111)
Stalnaker, J. M.: *ref,* 357, 2:1377(6), 3:217(49)
Stalnaker, R. C.: *ref,* 357
Stancik, E. J.: *ref,* 349
Standen, J. L.: *ref,* 489
Standlee, L. S.: *ref,* 592
Stanger, M.: *ref,* 525
Stanley, J. C.: *rev,* 348, 361; *exc,* 525; *ref,* 357, 361, 525, 532-3
Stanton, J. M.: *ref,* 532
Staples, J. D.: *ref,* 357, 425
Stapleton, M. R.: *ref,* 4:277(219)
Starer, E.: *ref,* 532
Stark, I.: *exc,* 532
Stark, J.: *ref,* 516
Stark, R.: *ref,* 533
Starkman, S. S.: *ref,* 357
Starr, A. S.: *test,* 575; *ref,* 575
Start, K. B.: *ref,* 323
Staton, T. F.: *ref,* 419
Staudt, V. M.: *ref,* 426
Stead, L. S. G.: *ref,* 532

Stecher, L. I.: *ref,* 525
Stechler, G.: *ref,* 497
Steckel, M. L.: *ref,* 398, 426, 497, 6:480(28)
Steckle, L. C.: *test,* 430, 478-9, 7:399
Stedman, D. J.: *ref,* 381, 516, 519
Stedman, M. B.: *ref,* 3:263(35)
Steer, M. D.: *ref,* 381, 426
Stefflre, B.: *ref,* 404
Stefic, E. C.: *ref,* 532
Steggerda, M.: *ref,* 497, 509
Stegman, E. J.: *ref,* 5:308(341)
Steige, R.: *ref,* 357
Stein, H.: *ref,* 529
Stein, H. L.: *ref,* 349
Stein, J.: *ref,* 405
Stein, M. I.: *ref,* 404, 532
Stein, M. L.: *ref,* 545, 3:220(36)
Stein, R. F.: *ref,* 382
Stein, S.: *ref,* 426
Stein, S. P.: *test,* 355
Stein, Z.: *ref,* 525, 529
Steinbach, A. A.: *ref,* 525
Steinberg, D.: *ref,* 361
Steinberg, J.: *ref,* 578
Steinberg, M.: *ref,* 529
Steindler, F. M.: *ref,* 357, 529
Steiner, F.: *ref,* 529
Steiner, M. A.: *ref,* 525
Steinhelber, J. C.: *ref,* 529, 543, 592
Steininger, M.: *ref,* 357
Steinman, C. C.: *ref,* 6:480(43)
Steinman, W. M.: *ref,* 381, 529
Steinmetz, A.: *ref,* 547
Steinmetz, C. S.: *ref,* 589
Steinmetz, J. R.: *ref,* 439
Steisel, I. M.: *ref,* 532
Stempel, E. F.: *ref,* 533
Stenbäck, A: *ref,* 592
Stene, D. M.: *ref,* 482
Stenger, C. A.: *ref,* 496, 532
Stennett, R. G.: *ref,* 391
Stenquist, J. L.: *ref,* 525, 5:326(7), 6:480(11)
Stephans, P.: *ref,* 348
Stephens, H. G.: *ref,* 589
Stephenson, G.: *ref,* 518
Stephenson, G. R.: *ref,* 439, 489, 496
Stephenson, R. S.: *ref,* 361
Stephenson, W.: *test,* 463
Stern, D. J.: *ref,* 497
Stern, F.: *ref,* 433
Stern, J. A.: *ref,* 533
Stern, M. R.: *ref,* 529
Sternal, W.: *ref,* 404
Sternberg, D.: *ref,* 529
Sternberg, T. H.: *ref,* 532
Sternberg, U.: *ref,* 532
Sterne, D. M.: *ref,* 496, 516, 518, 529, 543
Sternfield, M.: *ref,* 381
Sternlicht, M.: *ref,* 525, 529
Sternlof, R. E.: *ref,* 381, 489, 538
Sterritt, G. M.: *ref,* 400
Stevens, D. A.: *ref,* 533
Stevens, F. A. B.: *ref,* 349
Stevens, H.: *ref,* 589
Stevens, J. C.: *ref,* 349, 561, 572, 589, 591
Stevens, J. R.: *ref,* 529, 592
Stevens, M. C.: *ref,* 575
Stevens, S. N.: *ref,* 426

Stevens, W. C.: *ref,* 3:217(94)
Stevens, Thurow and Associates, Inc.: *test,* 393
Stevenson, V. M.: *ref,* 533
Stevenson, W. D.: *ref,* 532
Steward, M. S.: *ref,* 484
Stewart, C. J.: *ref,* 357
Stewart, E. E.: *ref,* 357
Stewart, H.: *ref,* 522, 529
Stewart, H. F.: *ref,* 364, 505, 529
Stewart, J. G.: *ref,* 533
Stewart, K. D.: *ref,* 532
Stewart, L. H.: *ref,* 361
Stewart, M.: *ref,* 518
Stewart, N.: *rev,* 381, 582, 5:332, 6:503; *ref,* 342
Stewart, R. A. C.: *ref,* 551, 561, 572
Stewart, R. R.: *ref,* 533
Stewart, W. A. C.: *ref,* 363, 415
Stickland, C. A.: *rev,* 4:334
Stier, S. A.: *ref,* 529
Stierhem, R. J.: *ref,* 361
Stillwell, L.: *ref,* 5:326(36)
Stimeling, W. F.: *ref,* 589
Stimson, R. C.: *ref,* 357, 542, 546
Stinson, P. J.: *ref,* 529, 6:438(454)
Stith, D.: *ref,* 355, 439
Stivers, E. R.: *ref,* 361
Stix, D. L.: *ref,* 357
Stock, W. H.: *ref,* 425, 574
Stockford, L. B. O.: *ref,* 426
Stockwin, A. E.: *ref,* 525
Stoddard, G. D.: *exc,* 497
Stoffel, C. M.: *ref,* 533
Stogdill, E. L.: *exc,* 532
Stoke, S. M.: *ref,* 525
Stoker, H. W.: *ref,* 361, 561
Stokes, C. W.: *ref,* 461
Stolz, L. M.: *ref,* 381, 533
Stone, B.: *ref,* 533
Stone, C. L.: *exc,* 518; *ref,* 357, 426, 3:220(27)
Stone, C. P.: *test,* 592; *ref,* 426, 532, 592, 4:281(85)
Stone, D. B.: *ref,* 361
Stone, D. R.: *ref,* 533
Stone, F. B.: *ref,* 533
Stone, I. R.: *ref,* 426
Stone, J. B.: *ref,* 5:308(368)
Stone, L. A.: *ref,* 529, 533
Stone, M. H.: *ref,* 357
Stone, P. A.: *ref,* 381
Stone, S.: *ref,* 5:308(429)
Stonesifer, F. A.: *ref,* 381, 592
Stopher, E. C.: *ref,* 419, 3:217(95)
Stordahl, K. E.: *ref,* 404
Stormer, G. E.: *ref,* 525
Storrs, S. V.: *ref,* 532
Story, J. L.: *ref,* 518
Stothers, C. E.: *test,* 486; *ref,* 486
Stotsky, B. A.: *ref,* 447, 518, 529, 532
Stott, D. H.: *ref,* 525
Stott, L. H.: *ref,* 487, 497, 507, 525
Stott, M. B.: *ref,* 525
Stouffer, G. A. W.: *test,* 339, 378, 437
Stough, K. F.: *ref,* 467
Stout, D. H.: *ref,* 533
Stoutenborough, A.: *ref,* 423
Stovall, E. M.: *ref,* 357
Stovall, F. L.: *ref,* 468
Strabel, E.: *ref,* 419, 3:217(54, 59)

Strachan, L.: *ref,* 525, 3:220(15)
Strahan, R.: *ref,* 357
Strain, J. J.: *ref,* 543, 592
Strandberg, T. E.: *ref,* 516, 522
Strang, R.: *ref,* 349
Strange, F. B.: *ref,* 532
Stratton, A. J.: *ref,* 449, 529
Straumanis, J. J.: *ref,* 439, 529, 547-8
Straus, M. A.: *ref,* 349
Strauss, A. A.: *ref,* 525
Strauss, M. E.: *ref,* 559, 561
Strecker, R. V.: *ref,* 533
Street, R. F.: *ref,* 525
Streit, L. R.: *ref,* 404
Streitfeld, J. W.: *ref,* 498, 529
Streitz, R.: *ref,* 438
Stribling, F.: *ref,* 3:242(2)
Stricker, G.: *ref,* 357, 382, 529, 543
Strickland, J. A.: *ref,* 357, 425
Stringer, P.: *ref,* 331
Stromberg, E. L.: *ref,* 337
Stromer, W. F.: *ref,* 525
Strong, P. N.: *ref,* 532
Strong, R. T.: *ref,* 516
Strong, S. R.: *ref,* 405
Strother, C. R.: *ref,* 489, 525, 532, 592
Strothers, C. E.: *test,* 486
Stroud, J. B.: *ref,* 349, 391, 398, 400, 425, 438-9, 505, 533
Stroud, M.: *ref,* 489, 516, 525
Stroup, A. L.: *ref,* 357
Strowig, R. W.: *ref,* 404
Struckett, P. B. A.: *ref,* 439, 532, 543, 592
Struempfer, D. J. W.: *ref,* 381
Struening, E. L.: *ref,* 342
Struhs, I.: *ref,* 439, 525
Strum, I. S.: *ref,* 589
Strümpfer, D. J. W.: *ref,* 381, 411, 511
Stuart, J. E.: *test,* 434
Stubbings, J. R.: *ref,* 589
Stuckless, E. R.: *ref,* 505
Stucky, M. O.: *ref,* 6:438(474-5)
Studer, M. R.: *ref,* 589
Stuhler, A. M.: *ref,* 524
Stuit, D. B.: *ref,* 419
Stumpf, J. C.: *ref,* 533
Sturgis, L. H.: *ref,* 381
Stutsman, R.: *test,* 507; *ref,* 507, 525
Such, M.: *ref,* 507, 525, 533
Sudimack, J. P.: *ref,* 529
Suehs, J. E.: *ref,* 440, 592
Suepsaman, B.: *ref,* 533
Sugarman, L.: *ref,* 411, 532
Suinn, R. M.: *test,* 527; *ref,* 498, 513, 529
Sullivan, A.: *ref,* 439, 532
Sullivan, A. M.: *ref,* 439, 532
Sullivan, B. A.: *ref,* 4:277(221)
Sullivan, D. S.: *ref,* 533
Sullivan, E. B.: *ref,* 359, 525, 532
Sullivan, E. G.: *ref,* 525
Sullivan, E. T.: *test,* 348-9, 458, 3:222, 6:503; *ref,* 525
Sullivan, G. V.: *ref,* 357
Sullivan, L. R.: *ref,* 558
Sullivan, R. A.: *ref,* 525
Summerfield, A.: *ref,* 388
Summers, G. W.: *ref,* 361
Summerskill, J.: *ref,* 532

Sundberg, N.: *ref,* 381
Sundberg, N. D.: *rev,* 525; *ref,* 589
Sundean, D. A.: *ref,* 525, 533
Sunne, D.: *ref,* 525
Sunukjian, H.: *ref,* 518, 532
Supeau, G. A.: *ref,* 5:308(396)
Super, D. E.: *ref,* 342, 425-6, 532, 2:1377(46), 4:277(220), 6:438(513)
Surko, E. F.: *ref,* 533
Surratt, C.: *ref,* 545, 5:326(1)
Surwillo, W. W.: *ref,* 439, 533
Susser, M.: *ref,* 525, 529
Suter, B. A.: *ref,* 574
Sutherland, B. S.: *ref,* 525
Sutherland, H. E. G.: *ref,* 409
Sutherland, J.: *ref,* 409
Sutherland, K.: *ref,* 349
Sutherland, T. E.: *test,* 478
Sutter, E. M. G.: *ref,* 357
Sutter, N. A.: *ref,* 4:277(233)
Sutton, R. V.: *ref,* 439
Sutton, S.: *ref,* 518
Suvetor, H.: *ref,* 400
Suziedelis, A.: *ref,* 391
Suzuki, N.: *ref,* 439, 516
Sved, S.: *ref,* 592
Swade, R. E.: *ref,* 533
Swan, R. J.: *ref,* 348, 361, 391, 400
Swanson, E.: *ref,* 533
Swanson, E. O.: *ref,* 357, 405, 6:438(502)
Swanson, J. R.: *ref,* 361
Swanson, M. S.: *ref,* 524, 533
Swart, D. J.: *test,* 501
Swartz, B. K.: *ref,* 426
Swartz, J. D.: *ref,* 381
Sweeney, F. J.: *ref,* 349
Sweeney, N. R.: *ref,* 381
Sweeny, M. E.: *ref,* 507, 525
Sweet, R. C.: *ref,* 533
Sweet, R. D.: *ref,* 529
Sweney, A. B.: *ref,* 364
Swenson, E. W.: *ref,* 529, 532
Swenson, L. G.: *ref,* 5:308(337)
Swenson, W. M.: *ref,* 592
Swiger, M. K.: *ref,* 497
Swink, E.: *ref,* 574
Swink, R.: *ref,* 433, 447, 529, 592
Swize, L. M.: *ref,* 489, 516, 533, 549
Swize, M. T.: *ref,* 489, 549
Sydiaha, D.: *ref,* 439, 496, 529
Sydow, D. W.: *ref,* 439, 504, 518
Sylvester, R. H.: *ref,* 3:220(5)
Symmes, E. F.: *ref,* 497
Symonds, P. M.: *ref,* 426, 525, 2:1424(11)
Szabo, M.: *ref,* 357

TABER, T.: *ref,* 364
Taft, L. T.: *ref,* 533
Taft, R.: *ref,* 542, 574
Tagg, H. R.: *ref,* 349
Tagiuri, R.: *ref,* 439, 525, 532
Tahmisian, J.: *ref,* 357
Taibl, R. M.: *ref,* 439
Takacs, C. P.: *ref,* 507, 538
Talbert, W.: *ref,* 525
Talbot, S. C.: *ref,* 533
Talerico, M.: *ref,* 533
Talkington, L. W.: *ref,* 516, 533
Talkoff, A.: *ref,* 532
Talland, G. A.: *ref,* 532, 592
Tallarico, R. B.: *ref,* 505

Tallent, N.: *ref,* 532
Talmadge, M.: *ref,* 533
Tamarin, S.: *ref,* 532
Tamhankar, V. S.: *ref,* 439
Tamminen, A. W.: *ref,* 342, 532
Tanck, R. H.: *ref,* 532
Tangeman, P.: *ref,* 529
Tannenbaum, A. J.: *rev,* 364
Tanno, Y.: *ref,* 513
Tanyzer, H. J.: *ref,* 533
Taranta, A.: *ref,* 533
Tarnopol, L.: *ref,* 529, 547
Tarpey, M. S.: *ref,* 331
Tate, M. E.: *ref,* 505
Tate, M. W.: *ref,* 349, 5:326(27)
Taterka, J. H.: *ref,* 532
Tatham, C. B.: *ref,* 357, 364, 525
Tatham, L. J.: *ref,* 525, 533
Tatom, M. H.: *ref,* 532
Tauber, R.: *ref,* 381, 516
Taulbee, G. C.: *ref,* 6:438(533)
Tava, E. G.: *ref,* 533
Tavernier, A.: *ref,* 532
Tavris, E.: *ref,* 525, 532
Taylor, A. J. W.: *ref,* 439, 545
Taylor, A. L.: *ref,* 349, 361, 400
Taylor, C.: *ref,* 529
Taylor, C. W.: *rev,* 359; *ref,* 349, 357
Taylor, D. H.: *ref,* 426
Taylor, D. W.: *ref,* 359
Taylor, E. A.: *ref,* 348, 489
Taylor, E. G.: *ref,* 409
Taylor, E. K.: *rev,* 433, 444-5, 471, 480-1, 4:276; *ref,* 431
Taylor, G. A.: *ref,* 525
Taylor, G. J.: *ref,* 532
Taylor, H.: *rev,* 486
Taylor, H. C.: *ref,* 497, 525
Taylor, H. R.: *ref,* 3:217(53)
Taylor, J. B.: *ref,* 381, 529
Taylor, J. F.: *ref,* 525, 529, 533, 3:242(4)
Taylor, J. R.: *ref,* 516
Taylor, J. W.: *ref,* 532
Taylor, M. W.: *ref,* 507
Taylor, P. H.: *ref,* 357
Taylor, R. G.: *ref,* 405
Taylor, V. C.: *ref,* 538
Taylor, W. C.: *ref,* 533
Teachers College Personnel Association: *test,* 2:1418
Teagarden, F. M.: *rev,* 487, 497, 507, 509, 5:332; *ref,* 503, 525
Teahan, J. E.: *ref,* 533
Teasdale, G. R.: *ref,* 516
Tedford, W. H.: *ref,* 542
Teegarden, L.: *rev,* 2:1401
Teepe, E. A.: *ref,* 426
Teicher, M. I.: *ref,* 532
Teigland, J. J.: *ref,* 533
Tekane, I.: *ref,* 6:459(2)
Teledgi, M. S.: *ref,* 574
Telegdy, G. A.: *ref,* 533
Telford, C. W.: *ref,* 381, 518
Tellegen, A.: *ref,* 529, 533
Temmer, H. W.: *ref,* 529
Temp, G.: *ref,* 357
Tempero, H. E.: *ref,* 361, 516
Templer, D. I.: *ref,* 503, 529, 543
Templin, M. C.: *rev,* 499, 4:354; *ref,* 496
Tenhoff, M. L.: *ref,* 516
Tennyson, W. W.: *rev,* 419

Tenopyr, M. L.: *ref,* 361
Terman, E. L.: *test,* 3:243; *ref,* 3:243(1)
Terman, L. M.: *test,* 359, 525, 4:324; *ref,* 359, 525, 3:220(1)
Terry, P. W.: *ref,* 6:480(32)
Terwilliger, J. S.: *ref,* 361
Terwilliger, R. F.: *ref,* 357
Tesi, G.: *ref,* 439
Teska, J. A.: *ref,* 516, 525
Teska, P. T.: *ref,* 381
Teuber, H. L.: *ref,* 342, 533, 578
Thacker, J. H.: *ref,* 361
Thackray, D. V.: *ref,* 395
Thakur, G. P.: *ref,* 439
Thaler, M.: *ref,* 532
Thaler, V. H.: *ref,* 529
Thalman, W. A.: *ref,* 5:308(379)
Theaman, M.: *ref,* 532
Thetford, W. N.: *ref,* 529, 532
Theye, F.: *ref,* 525, 529, 533
Theye, F. W.: *ref,* 533
Thiesen, J. W.: *ref,* 525
Thomann, D. F.: *ref,* 4:277(196), 4:278(11)
Thomas, A.: *ref,* 533
Thomas, C. A.: *ref,* 529
Thomas, C. D.: *ref,* 516
Thomas, C. L.: *ref,* 357
Thomas, D. C.: *ref,* 361
Thomas, H.: *ref,* 349
Thomas, J.: *ref,* 5:308(371)
Thomas, J. R.: *ref,* 424
Thomas, R. M.: *ref,* 381
Thomas, R. R.: *ref,* 518
Thomas, S. B.: *ref,* 589
Thomas, W. F.: *ref,* 5:308(317)
Thompson, A. S.: *rev,* 546
Thompson, B. B.: *ref,* 533
Thompson, C. E.: *ref,* 482
Thompson, C. W.: *ref,* 381, 525, 529, 532
Thompson, E. M.: *ref,* 525
Thompson, G.: *ref,* 400
Thompson, G. G.: *ref,* 425
Thompson, G. M.: *ref,* 533
Thompson, H.: *ref,* 497
Thompson, J.: *ref,* 533
Thompson, J. A.: *ref,* 533
Thompson, J. M.: *test,* 534; *ref,* 348, 381, 525, 533
Thompson, K.: *ref,* 518
Thompson, L. M.: *ref,* 3:217(143)
Thompson, M. D.: *ref,* 3:247(3)
Thompson, M. M.: *ref,* 525
Thompson, R. A.: *ref,* 589
Thompson, R. B.: *ref,* 342, 419, 4:277(168)
Thompson, W. H.: *ref,* 439, 518, 525, 533
Thompson, W. W.: *ref,* 533
Thomsen, S. J.: *ref,* 382, 6:438(498)
Thomson, G. H.: *rev,* 354; *test,* 416, 3:241; *ref,* 409, 416, 545
Thomson, W. A.: *ref,* 2:1377(47), 4:277(157)
Thomure, E.: *ref,* 499
Thorndike, R. L.: *rev,* 589, 2:1377, 3:224, 3:263; *test,* 351-2, 356, 400-1, 525; *ref,* 357, 359, 426, 490, 525, 4:277(182, 197)
Thorne, G. D.: *ref,* 532-3
Thornton, C. L.: *ref,* 533, 559

Thornton, G. R.: *ref,* 337, 421
Thornton, T. E.: *ref,* 496, 532
Thorp, T. R.: *ref,* 532
Thorpe, J. S.: *ref,* 381, 533
Thorsen, E. E.: *ref,* 439, 589
Threatt, R.: *ref,* 357
Throne, F. M.: *ref,* 381, 516, 525, 533
Throne, J. M.: *ref,* 533
Throp, J. L.: *ref,* 529
Thumin, F. J.: *ref,* 482
Thumin, F. J.: *ref,* 404, 426, 482
Thune, J.: *ref,* 529, 545
Thurston, D.: *ref,* 533
Thurston, J. R.: *ref,* 532, 542, 551
Thurstone, L. L.: *test,* 452, 469, 547-8, 570, 5:309, 6:438, 6:495; *ref,* 525, 2:1377(1, 4, 7, 10, 12-3, 17, 21, 24, 27, 31, 36, 41, 48), 2:1378(1-2), 3:217(96, 112, 118, 124, 127, 136), 3:218(8)
Thurstone, T. G.: *test,* 452, 469, 5:309, 6:438, 6:495; *ref,* 2:1377(10, 12-3, 17, 21, 24, 27, 31, 36, 41, 48), 2:1378(1-2), 3:217(96, 112, 118, 124, 127, 136), 3:218(8)
Thweatt, R. C.: *ref,* 525
Thwing, E.: *ref,* 484, 525
Thwing, E. J.: *test,* 508
Tiahrt, H. G.: *ref,* 533
Tibbetts, J. W.: *ref,* 589
Tiber, N.: *ref,* 525
Tiebout, C.: *ref,* 381, 398, 426
Tiedeman, D. V.: *rev,* 358, 4:301, 5:319; *ref,* 357, 425-6, 5:308(364)
Tiegs, E. W.: *test,* 348-9, 458, 3:222, 6:503; *ref,* 349
Tietze, C.: *ref,* 525, 545
Tiffin, J.: *test,* 337, 442, 6:491; *ref,* 337, 426, 6:480(40)
Tigay, B.: *ref,* 533
Tikofsky, R.: *ref,* 547
Tikofsky, R. S.: *ref,* 496, 547
Tilis, H. S.: *ref,* 489, 516, 525
Tilker, H. A.: *ref,* 349, 518
Tillinghast, B. S.: *ref,* 357, 516
Tillman, C. G.: *ref,* 532
Tillman, H. M.: *ref,* 533
Tillman, M. H.: *ref,* 533
Tillmans, S. J.: *ref,* 516
Tilton, J. W.: *exc,* 518; *ref,* 398, 441, 4:324(57), 5:368(15)
Tine, S.: *ref,* 529, 545
Tinker, M. A.: *ref,* 419
Tippett, J. S.: *ref,* 525, 6:480(13)
Tisdale, J. C.: *ref,* 361
Tisdall, W. J.: *ref,* 542, 546, 551, 561, 577, 594
Tittle, C. K.: *rev,* 356, 400
Titus, H. E.: *ref,* 559
Tizard, J.: *ref,* 354, 439, 518, 525, 538, 545
Toal, R.: *ref,* 447
Tobias, J.: *ref,* 381, 516, 518
Tobias, M.: *ref,* 349
Tobias, S.: *ref,* 357, 391, 425, 574
Tobin, J. C.: *ref,* 592
Todd, R. E.: *ref,* 532
Toliver, G. D.: *ref,* 516
Toll, C. H.: *ref,* 426, 4:277(145), 4:281(77), 4:324(52)
Tollefson, B. E.: *ref,* 419
Tolley, J.: *ref,* 516, 525

Tolor, A.: *ref,* 425, 529, 532
Tomlinson, H.: *ref,* 525, 3:217(75)
Tomlinson, J. P.: *test,* 4:332
Tomlinson, T. P.: *test,* 2:1430, 5:392
Toms, D. C.: *ref,* 525
Tonn, M. H.: *ref,* 439
Tookey, M. D.: *ref,* 382
Toolson, R. N.: *ref,* 529
Toomey, T. C.: *ref,* 529
Toops, H. A.: *test,* 405, 419; *ref,* 419
Tooth, G.: *ref,* 532, 545
Topetzes, N. J.: *ref,* 349, 532
Toppen, J. T.: *ref,* 529
Torgerson, T. L.: *ref,* 426
Torrance, E. P.: *test,* 587, 589; *ref,* 400, 574, 587, 589
Torrance, P.: *ref,* 532
Tortorella, W. M.: *ref,* 574
Tousignant, F.: *ref,* 487
Toussaint, I. H.: *ref,* 525
Tow, P. M.: *ref,* 518
Town, C. H.: *ref,* 5:354(1)
Townes, B.: *ref,* 533
Townsend, A.: *ref,* 394, 398, 5:308(338)
Townsend, R. R.: *ref,* 525
Tozer, A. H. D.: *ref,* 5:339(10-1)
Tozer, G. E.: *ref,* 3:263(36)
Tozier, L. L.: *ref,* 533
Trabue, M. R.: *test,* 339; *ref,* 438
Tracht, V. S.: *ref,* 439
Trachtman, G. M.: *ref,* 525
Tracy, D. B.: *ref,* 381, 496
Tracy, N. H.: *ref,* 361
Trad, M.: *ref,* 400
Trafton, H.: *ref,* 357, 426, 2:1424(17), 3:220(51)
Trail, B. M.: *ref,* 518
Trainer, F. E.: *test,* 533; *ref,* 533
Trapp, C. E.: *ref,* 525
Trapp, E. P.: *ref,* 533
Traster, S.: *ref,* 4:324(51)
Traub, R. E.: *test,* 387
Travers, R. M. W.: *ref,* 404, 4:277(257)
Travis, L. E.: *ref,* 426
Traxler, A. E.: *rev,* 349; *exc,* 525; *ref,* 349, 357, 360-1, 394, 398, 400, 426, 2:1377(42), 3:217(79, 97, 113, 119, 128), 5:308(307, 397-8, 412)
Treadway, C. R.: *ref,* 518
Treadwell, Y.: *ref,* 574
Treat, K.: *ref,* 518
Trebbe, E. S.: *ref,* 357
Treffinger, D. J.: *ref,* 361, 542, 551, 589
Trefsgar, T. F.: *ref,* 391, 533
Trehub, A.: *ref,* 532
Treumann, M. J.: *ref,* 4:277(221)
Trevorrow, R. L.: *ref,* 400, 424
Trider, M. S.: *ref,* 424
Trieglaff, A. L.: *ref,* 533
Trieschmann, R. B.: *ref,* 529
Trigg, C. W.: *ref,* 4:324(53)
Triggs, F.: *ref,* 532-3
Triggs, F. O.: *ref,* 525, 533, 4:277(256, 272)
Triplett, R. J.: *ref,* 426
Trist, E.: *test,* 6:519; *ref,* 406, 6:519(1)
Trist, E. L.: *ref,* 532

Trites, D. K.: *ref,* 349, 4:277(222)
Tronca, W. F.: *ref,* 404
Trost, H.: *ref,* 525
Trowbridge, L.: *ref,* 503
Trowbridge, N.: *ref,* 349, 381
Troy, E. M.: *ref,* 358
Trudeau, P.: *ref,* 529
True, S.: *ref,* 589
True, S. R.: *ref,* 589
Trussell, W. D.: *exc,* 533
Tryk, H. E.: *ref,* 533, 589
Tsai, L. S.: *ref,* 529
Tsao, D. F.: *ref,* 381
Tseng, M.: *ref,* 361
Tsushima, W.: *ref,* 529
Tuchman, S. B.: *ref,* 525
Tuck, J. A.: *ref,* 532
Tucker, C. A.: *ref,* 589
Tucker, D. A.: *ref,* 496
Tucker, H.: *ref,* 382
Tucker, L. R.: *ref,* 529, 5:308(296)
Tucker, W. F.: *ref,* 425
Tuddenham, R. D.: *exc,* 529, 532; *ref,* 342, 439, 4:315(10)
Tuel, J. K.: *ref,* 525
Tueller, R. L.: *ref,* 542
Tulchin, S. H.: *ref,* 525
Tulkin, S. R.: *ref,* 439
Tully, G. E.: *ref,* 349, 361, 382, 404, 439
Tuma, A. H.: *ref,* 529
Tunstall, O. A.: *ref,* 425, 439
Turknett, R. L.: *ref,* 589
Turnbull, G. H.: *ref,* 409
Turnbull, J. W.: *ref,* 518
Turnbull, W. W.: *rev,* 433
Turner, A. J.: *ref,* 525
Turner, C. J.: *ref,* 489
Turner, E.: *ref,* 529
Turner, G. H.: *ref,* 391, 439, 533
Turner, J.: *ref,* 525, 529
Turner, R. K.: *ref,* 533
Turner, T. N.: *ref,* 589
Turner, W. J.: *ref,* 440
Turney, A. H.: *rev,* 398, 2:1378; *ref,* 426, 2:1424(16), 3:242(7)
Turney, J. R.: *ref,* 574
Turrentine, E. M.: *ref,* 357, 419, 425
Tuska, S. A.: *ref,* 381
Tutt, M. L.: *ref,* 533
Tuttle, C. E.: *ref,* 404
Tuttle, L. E.: *ref,* 489, 516, 533
Twain, D. C.: *ref,* 426, 447, 529, 533
Tyler, F. T.: *rev,* 387, 3:237, 3:268; *ref,* 364, 3:263(48), 4:277(251)
Tyler, L. E.: *rev,* 391, 547-8; *ref,* 361, 589
Tyler, R. W.: *ref,* 348, 391, 398, 425
Tyson, M.: *ref,* 331
Tyson, M. C.: *ref,* 381
Tyson, M. H.: *ref,* 533

UECKER, A. E.: *ref,* 525, 532, 592
Ufford, M. S.: *ref,* 533
Uhl, N. P.: *ref,* 516
Uhlmann, F. W.: *ref,* 547
Uhrbrock, R. S.: *ref,* 354, 419
Uleman, A. L.: *ref,* 439, 532
Ulin, R. O.: *ref,* 357
Umberger, J. P.: *ref,* 503, 532

University of Edinburgh, Godfrey Thomson Unit: *test,* 409
University of Toronto, Ontario College of Education, Department of Educational Research: *ref,* 387
Updegraff, R.: *ref,* 507, 525
Upshall, C. C.: *ref,* 2:1377(32)
Uray, R. M.: *ref,* 425
Urbach, N.: *ref,* 532
Urlocker, W. T.: *ref,* 425
Urmer, A. H.: *ref,* 439, 529
Utgard, R. O.: *ref,* 357
Utsugi, E.: *ref,* 381

VAAGE, M.: *ref,* 487
Vaccaro, J. J.: *ref,* 426, 433
Vahar, M.: *ref,* 381
Valentine, C. W.: *test,* 446, 5:405; *exc,* 497, 509; *ref,* 446, 4:343(2-3), 5:405(4-5)
Valentine, M.: *ref,* 439
Valett, R. E.: *test,* 526; *ref,* 525
Van Alstyne, D.: *test,* 6:537; *ref,* 525, 6:537(1)
Vanbramer, P. J.: *ref,* 533
VanCampen, J.: *ref,* 492
Vance, S. B.: *ref,* 489, 533
Vance, T. F.: *ref,* 507, 578
Vancini, J. P.: *ref,* 533
Van de Castle, R. L.: *ref,* 518
Vandenberg, S.: *ref,* 525
Vandenberg, S. G.: *ref,* 439, 457, 529, 533, 561
Vanderberg, S. G.: *ref,* 484
Vanderhost, L.: *ref,* 532-3
Van De Riet, H.: *ref,* 529, 533
Van De Riet, V.: *ref,* 525, 529, 533
Van Der Jagt, E. R.: *ref,* 5:308(413)
Van der Kolk, J. J.: *ref,* 518
van der Meulen, S. J.: *ref,* 551
Vanderpool, J.: *ref,* 533
Van Derslice, J. F.: *ref,* 361
Vander Zwaag, R.: *ref,* 525
Vandeventer, M.: *ref,* 439
Vane, J. R.: *test,* 528; *ref,* 344, 381, 525, 528, 532
van Lennep, J. E.: *ref,* 532
Van Mondfrans, A. P.: *ref,* 589
Van Natta, P. A.: *ref,* 492
Van Pelt, B. N.: *ref,* 589
Van Vorst, R. B.: *ref,* 532
Van Wagenen, M. J.: *test,* 509, 2:1428, 3:251; *ref,* 3:220(16)
Varadachar, D.: *ref,* 439
Varma, S. K.: *ref,* 525
Varnado, G. R.: *ref,* 3:217(69)
Varner, D. G.: *ref,* 425
Varva, F. I.: *ref,* 381, 439, 483, 499, 505
Varvel, W. A.: *exc,* 532
Vasa, S. F.: *ref,* 499, 533
Vassiliou, V.: *ref,* 529
Vaughan, H. G.: *ref,* 403, 439, 529
Vaughan, M.: *ref,* 391, 589
Vaughan, R. P.: *ref,* 357
Vaughn, C. L.: *exc,* 532
Vaughn, H. A.: *ref,* 357
Vaughn, K. L.: *ref,* 503
Veal, L. R.: *ref,* 357
Veale, S. O.: *ref,* 529
Vecchione, N.: *ref,* 394, 398, 6:537(6)
Veeder, B. S.: *exc,* 497

Vega, A.: *ref,* 529
Vejleskov, H.: *ref,* 439
Veldman, D. J.: *ref,* 357
Vellutino, F. R.: *ref,* 496, 529
Venables, E. C.: *ref,* 403, 439
Venables, P. H.: *ref,* 525
Veon, D. H.: *ref,* 5:308(281)
Vernon, L. N.: *test,* 418
Vernon, P. E.: *rev,* 574; *exc,* 525, 4:289; *ref,* 381, 388, 439, 515, 518, 525, 558, 578, 4:295(2)
Verrill, B. V.: *ref,* 518
Vertein, L. D.: *ref,* 349
Very, P. S.: *ref,* 457, 561
Vick, G.: *ref,* 525, 532, 3:217(98)
Vick, M. C.: *ref,* 357, 361
Vickers, M. J.: *ref,* 516
Victor, M.: *ref,* 532, 592
Viehweg, R.: *ref,* 522, 533
Viel, B.: *ref,* 439
Viele, A. B.: *ref,* 435
Vignos, P. J.: *ref,* 525
Viitamäki, R. O.: *ref,* 533, 592
Vincent, D. F.: *ref,* 384, 388, 390
Vincent, L.: *ref,* 361, 5:308(439)
Vincent, L. E.: *test,* 3:226
Vincent, N. L.: *ref,* 480
Vincent, N. M.: *ref,* 425
Vineyard, E. E.: *ref,* 6:438(488)
Vingoe, F. J.: *ref,* 489, 538
Vinoda, K. S.: *ref,* 403
Vinson, D. B.: *ref,* 504
Vinson, L.: *test,* 5:389
Vinsonhaler, J. F.: *ref,* 358
Vint, V. H.: *ref,* 561, 572
Virene, E. P.: *ref,* 357
Virmani, V.: *ref,* 529
Vistica, N. J.: *ref,* 532
Vitale, H. J.: *ref,* 529, 543, 592
Viteles, M. S.: *ref,* 3:220(28), 6:480(19)
Vivers, B. B.: *ref,* 469
Voelker, P. H.: *test,* 370
Vogel, F. X.: *ref,* 381
Vogelsang, M. P.: *ref,* 533
Voggenthaler, A. L.: *ref,* 439
Vogler, J. D.: *ref,* 517
Vogler, R. E.: *ref,* 543
Vohs, A. P.: *ref,* 358
Volle, F. O.: *ref,* 533
Von Wittich, B.: *ref,* 425
Voorhees, S. F.: *ref,* 492
Vorhaus, P. G.: *ref,* 532
Vormeland, O.: *ref,* 381
Vorreyer, W. J.: *ref,* 419
Voss, C. E.: *ref,* 349, 5:326(27)
Votaw, D. F.: *ref,* 404, 3:217(137-8)
Vroegh, K.: *ref,* 381
Vroman, C.: *ref,* 357, 364

WACHTEL, P. L.: *ref,* 529
Waddle, C.: *ref,* 525
Wade, S. E.: *ref,* 542, 546, 551
Wadley, J. A.: *ref,* 528
Waelsch, H.: *ref,* 525
Waggoner, G. H.: *ref,* 404
Waggoner, R. W.: *ref,* 349, 525, 532
Wagman, M.: *ref,* 361
Wagner, D. L.: *ref,* 391, 400
Wagner, E. E.: *ref,* 361, 529, 533
Wagner, H. E.: *ref,* 349
Wagner, M. E.: *ref,* 3:217(54, 59)

Wagner, N. N.: *ref,* 529
Wagner, R. F.: *ref,* 529
Wagner, W. K.: *ref,* 525, 533
Wagoner, L. C.: *ref,* 381, 507, 525
Wagoner, O. L.: *ref,* 533
Wagonseller, B. R.: *ref,* 533
Wahler, H. J.: *ref,* 529, 543
Waiches, V. C.: *ref,* 361
Wainrib, B.: *ref,* 592
Waite, A.: *ref,* 439
Waite, R. R.: *ref,* 518, 529
Waite, W. D.: *ref,* 444
Waits, J. V.: *ref,* 2:1377(18), 4:277 (148)
Wake, F. R.: *ref,* 381
Wakefield, H. E.: *ref,* 516, 525, 533
Wakelam, B. B.: *ref,* 4:343(1)
Walberg, H. J.: *ref,* 357, 391
Walcott, G. D.: *ref,* 525, 3:220(7)
Waldfogel, S.: *ref,* 532
Waldron, C.: *ref,* 349
Waldrop, R. S.: *ref,* 6:438(521)
Walker, A.: *ref,* 439, 518
Walker, A. J. M.: *ref,* 516
Walker, B. S.: *ref,* 391, 398, 426
Walker, C.: *ref,* 533
Walker, C. E.: *ref,* 357
Walker, D. A.: *rev,* 477; *ref,* 409
Walker, E. W.: *ref,* 435, 3:255(8)
Walker, F. C.: *ref,* 482
Walker, G. W. R.: *ref,* 525
Walker, H. A.: *ref,* 533
Walker, H. E.: *ref,* 574
Walker, J. L.: *ref,* 364, 574
Walker, K. F.: *ref,* 426
Walker, K. P.: *ref,* 525, 529, 533
Walker, L. D.: *ref,* 391
Walker, M. A.: *ref,* 558
Walker, P.: *ref,* 357
Walker, P. C.: *ref,* 589
Walker, R. E.: *ref,* 425, 504, 529, 532-3
Walker, R. N.: *ref,* 533
Walker, W.: *ref,* 529, 533
Walker, W. B.: *ref,* 431
Wall, H. W.: *ref,* 529
Wall, K. W.: *ref,* 357
Wall, W. D.: *rev,* 439, 491; *ref,* 525
Wallace, E. C.: *ref,* 7:361(7)
Wallace, G.: *ref,* 533
Wallace, H. R.: *ref,* 589
Wallace, J. G.: *ref,* 331, 439
Wallace, S. R.: *ref,* 337
Wallace, W. L.: *rev,* 341, 357, 6:442; *test,* 358; *ref,* 404, 529, 4:277(223, 257, 273-4)
Wallach, E. S.: *ref,* 516
Wallach, M. A.: *exc,* 589; *ref,* 357, 361, 533
Wallbrown, F. H.: *ref,* 533
Wallen, N. E.: *rev,* 391; *ref,* 359, 404, 589
Wallihan, R. S.: *ref,* 398, 435
Wallin, J. E. W.: *ref,* 483, 525
Wallin, K.: *ref,* 487
Walsh, J.: *ref,* 528-9
Walsh, J. F.: *ref,* 528
Walsh, J. J.: *ref,* 382
Walsh, M. A.: *ref,* 532
Walsh, N. E.: *ref,* 349
Walsh, R.: *ref,* 499, 507
Walshaw, J. B.: *ref,* 403

Walters, C. E.: *ref,* 497
Walters, F. C.: *ref,* 525
Walters, N. R.: *ref,* 357
Walters, R. H.: *ref,* 532
Walton, D.: *ref,* 439, 525, 592
Walton, J. M.: *ref,* 589
Wamba, D. E.: *ref,* 439
Wampler, J. F.: *ref,* 561
Wang, C.: *ref,* 381
Wang, F. Y.: *ref,* 439
Wang, H. A.: *ref,* 529
Wang, H. S.: *ref,* 529
Wapner, I.: *ref,* 533
Wapner, S.: *ref,* 529
Warburton, F. W.: *rev,* 373, 475, 5:325; *ref,* 439, 525
Ward, A. W.: *ref,* 399, 5:326(12)
Ward, B. J.: *ref,* 533
Ward, D. V.: *ref,* 404
Ward, G.: *ref,* 361, 365, 400
Ward, J.: *ref,* 361, 533
Ward, J. H.: *ref,* 404, 532
Ward, M. P.: *ref,* 516, 522
Ward, W. C.: *ref,* 516
Ward, W. D.: *ref,* 529, 5:308(339)
Warder, J.: *ref,* 403, 439
Wardeska, B. C.: *ref,* 574
Ware, W. B.: *ref,* 516
Warhapdande, N. R.: *ref,* 545
Warinner, E. M.: *ref,* 525, 533
Warner, S. J.: *ref,* 532
Warren, E. C.: *ref,* 4:277(150)
Warren, N. S.: *ref,* 415, 533
Warren, P. A.: *ref,* 348
Warren, S. A.: *ref,* 381, 489, 525, 529
Warren, T. F.: *ref,* 574, 589
Warrington, E. K.: *ref,* 529, 533
Wartenberg, H.: *ref,* 400, 493
Wasden, R.: *ref,* 529
Washburn, A. A.: *exc,* 497
Washburn, M. F.: *ref,* 525, 558
Washburn, R. W.: *rev,* 3:226, 3:274, 3:296
Washburne, C. W.: *ref,* 525
Washburne, N. F.: *ref,* 5:308(369)
Washington, E. D.: *ref,* 525
Wasik, B. H.: *ref,* 538, 549
Wasik, J. L.: *ref,* 538, 549
Wassenaar, G. M. C.: *ref,* 504, 518
Wasserberger, M.: *ref,* 517, 533
Wassing, H. E.: *ref,* 533
Waters, J. E.: *ref,* 489
Waters, T. J.: *ref,* 525, 547
Waters, W. E.: *ref,* 331
Watkins, D. G.: *ref,* 381
Watkins, E. O.: *ref,* 560A
Watkins, J. T.: *ref,* 529
Watley, D. J.: *ref,* 357, 404-5
Watson, B. L.: *ref,* 381
Watson, C. G.: *ref,* 342, 447, 529, 543
Watson, L. S.: *ref,* 529
Watson, L. W.: *ref,* 357
Watson, N.: *ref,* 504, 4:359(4)
Watson, R. A.: *ref,* 529, 533
Watson, R. I.: *rev,* 532; *ref,* 342, 483, 487, 518, 525, 532, 592
Watson, S. B.: *ref,* 498
Watters, G. V.: *ref,* 404
Wattimena, D. M.: *ref,* 439
Watts, F.: *test,* 5:398
Watts, K. P.: *test,* 331; *ref,* 331
Way, J. G.: *ref,* 533, 538

Weaver, A.: *ref,* 400
Weaver, A. S.: *ref,* 516, 525
Weaver, H. B.: *ref,* 482, 504
Weaver, R.: *ref,* 524
Weaver, S. J.: *ref,* 400
Weaver, W. W.: *ref,* 419, 533, 559, 561
Webb, A.: *ref,* 497
Webb, A. P.: *ref,* 529, 533
Webb, B.: *ref,* 532
Webb, H. Q.: *ref,* 361
Webb, J. B.: *ref,* 361
Webb, L. W.: *ref,* 3:220(17)
Webb, S. C.: *ref,* 357, 419, 5:308 (340, 414)
Webb, W. B.: *ref,* 425, 532
Webber, V. L.: *ref,* 6:438(455)
Webberley, M.: *ref,* 323, 364, 559, 561, 564
Weber, C. O.: *ref,* 357, 4:277(169)
Weber, D. S.: *ref,* 425
Weber, E. G.: *ref,* 425, 3:217(129)
Weber, G. H.: *ref,* 532
Weber, L. A.: *ref,* 361
Weber, L. E.: *ref,* 425
Weber, W. A.: *ref,* 589
Webster, E. C.: *ref,* 404
Wechsler, D.: *rev,* 403, 439, 447, 3:228; *test,* 529, 532-3, 538, 592; *ref,* 525, 529, 532-3, 545, 556, 563, 592, 3:220(42)
Wechsler, I. R.: *ref,* 482
Weckowicz, T. E.: *ref,* 547
Wedell, K.: *ref,* 495
Weeks, A. L.: *ref,* 525
Weeks, J. S.: *ref,* 361, 6:438(476)
Weeks, R. W.: *ref,* 516
Wegman, M.: *ref,* 447, 525
Weider, A.: *ref,* 482, 525, 532-3, 592
Weikart, D. P.: *ref,* 349
Weil, W. B.: *ref,* 525
Weinberg, H.: *ref,* 529
Weinberg, R. S.: *ref,* 533
Weinberg, S.: *ref,* 533
Weiner, H.: *ref,* 532
Weiner, I. B.: *ref,* 529
Weiner, M.: *ref,* 391, 425
Weiner, P. S.: *ref,* 439, 505, 516, 533
Weingarten, G.: *ref,* 439
Weinik, H. M.: *ref,* 341A
Weinlander, M. M.: *ref,* 525
Weinstein, B.: *ref,* 525
Weinstein, M. R.: *ref,* 503, 592
Weinstein, S.: *ref,* 342, 578
Weinstock, C.: *ref,* 529
Weinstock, C. S.: *ref,* 529
Weintraub, R. G.: *ref,* 3:217(130), 4:277(217)
Weintraub, S.: *ref,* 489, 589
Weir, M. W.: *ref,* 381
Weise, P.: *ref,* 525, 533
Weisenburg, T.: *ref,* 381, 518, 525
Weiser, J. C.: *ref,* 589
Weisgerber, C. A.: *ref,* 361, 525, 532-3
Weisman, F.: *ref,* 525
Weisman, S. E.: *ref,* 525
Weismar, R.: *ref,* 492
Weiss, A. D.: *ref,* 529
Weiss, D. J.: *ref,* 561
Weiss, I.: *ref,* 5:308(308)
Weiss, J.: *ref,* 529, 533

Weiss, K. P.: *ref*, 357
Weiss, M.: *ref*, 5:326(5)
Weissenberg, P.: *ref*, 559
Weissman, H.: *ref*, 440
Weissman, S. L.: *ref*, 529
Weissmann, S.: *ref*, 525, 533
Weitz, H.: *rev*, 451; *ref*, 357
Weitzman, J.: *ref*, 525
Weitzner, M.: *ref*, 357
Welborn, E. L.: *ref*, 3:217(120), 4:277(176)
Welch, L.: *exc*, 497
Welch, W. B.: *ref*, 349
Welch, W. W.: *ref*, 391
Welcher, D. W.: *ref*, 381, 484, 525, 533
Weleba, L.: *ref*, 529
Wellck, A. A.: *ref*, 361
Weller, D. C.: *ref*, 419
Wellman, B. L.: *rev*, 487, 509; *ref*, 507, 509, 525
Wellman, F. E.: *ref*, 425
Wells, C. G.: *ref*, 533
Wells, D. G.: *ref*, 381, 516, 525, 529
Wells, F. L.: *rev*, 493, 525, 532, 2:1426; *test*, 407, 4:315–6; *ref*, 407, 426, 525, 532, 2:1391(7), 3:220(44), 4:315(1), 4:316(1)
Wells, R. A.: *ref*, 382, 404
Welman, A. J.: *ref*, 532
Welna, C. T.: *ref*, 349, 6:438(489)
Welsch, L. A.: *ref*, 426, 480
Welsh, G. B.: *ref*, 525
Welsh, G. S.: *ref*, 359, 365, 532
Welsh, J.: *ref*, 409, 415
Welsh, M. L.: *ref*, 419, 5:308(286)
Welter, M. B.: *ref*, 349
Weltman, R. E.: *ref*, 529
Weltner, W. H.: *ref*, 589
Wempen, E. H.: *ref*, 533
Wendland, L. V.: *ref*, 439, 529
Wendt, R. A.: *ref*, 533
Wenk, E.: *ref*, 349
Wentworth, M. M.: *ref*, 525, 3:220(18)
Wentworth-Rohr, I.: *ref*, 532
Wepman, J. M.: *ref*, 439
Werbel, S. A.: *ref*, 559
Werner, E.: *ref*, 487
Werner, E. E.: *rev*, 492, 497, 505, 523; *ref*, 381, 484, 487, 518, 589
Werner, F. J.: *test*, 4:276
Werner, H.: *ref*, 525, 529, 558, 2:1394(11)
Wernimont, P.: *ref*, 404, 480
Wershow, I. R.: *ref*, 361
Wertheimer, M.: *ref*, 357, 532
Wertman, H.: *test*, 560
Werts, C. E.: *ref*, 529, 532
Wesman, A.: *ref*, 532–3
Wesman, A. G.: *rev*, 454; *test*, 333, 358, 433, 473, 480; *ref*, 358, 447, 525, 529, 532
Wessler, R. L.: *ref*, 529
West, A. A.: *ref*, 529, 532
West, D. J.: *ref*, 403, 439
West, D. N.: *ref*, 503
West, J. H.: *ref*, 381
West, L. W.: *ref*, 348, 400, 439, 453
West, P. C.: *ref*, 381
West, R. L.: *ref*, 6:480(12)
Westberg, W. C.: *ref*, 482

Westbrook, B. W.: *ref*, 391, 7:378(7)
Westbrook, C. H.: *exc*, 532
Westby, G.: *rev*, 388, 439, 4:313
Westcott, M. R.: *ref*, 357
Westerhold, R.: *ref*, 532
Weston, L. D.: *ref*, 400
Westphal, M. E.: *ref*, 391, 400
Wetherell, R. H.: *ref*, 349
Wetherick, N. E.: *ref*, 439
Wevrick, L.: *ref*, 482
Wexberg, E.: *ref*, 525
Wexler, A. H.: *ref*, 357
Wexler, M.: *ref*, 532
Wexler, N.: *ref*, 404
Whaley, E. R.: *ref*, 6:438(517)
Wharton, L. H.: *ref*, 543
Whatley, R. G.: *ref*, 533
Wheatley, M. M.: *ref*, 532
Wheeler, E. T.: *ref*, 532
Wheeler, G. R.: *ref*, 529
Wheeler, J. A.: *ref*, 503
Wheeler, J. I.: *ref*, 381, 532
Wheeler, L.: *ref*, 529
Wheeler, L. R.: *ref*, 4:277(224–5, 275)
Wheeler, R. G.: *ref*, 357
Wheeler, R. W.: *ref*, 469
Wheeler, V. D.: *ref*, 4:277(225, 275)
Wheeler, W. M.: *ref*, 532
Whetstone, R. D.: *ref*, 357
Whinery, S. M.: *ref*, 419
Whipple, C. I.: *ref*, 489, 516
Whitacre, R. L.: *ref*, 524–5
Whitcomb, M. A.: *ref*, 525, 532
White, A. J.: *ref*, 361, 533
White, B. J.: *ref*, 589
White, D. T.: *ref*, 496, 525
White, E. E.: *ref*, 532, 592
White, G.: *ref*, 381, 525
White, G. W.: *ref*, 382
White, J. C.: *ref*, 525
White, J. G.: *ref*, 529
White, K.: *ref*, 542, 551
White, L. A.: *ref*, 525, 533, 538
White, L. E.: *ref*, 542, 574
White, M. F. R.: *ref*, 381
White, M. L.: *ref*, 525
White, P. T.: *ref*, 532
White, R. R.: *ref*, 525
White, W. F.: *ref*, 349, 505, 522, 529, 561, 572, 591
Whitehouse, D.: *ref*, 533
Whiteley, J. M.: *ref*, 382, 404
Whiteman, D. B.: *ref*, 532
Whiteman, M.: *ref*, 532
Whiteside, O. R.: *ref*, 6:438(514)
Whitla, D. K.: *ref*, 357
Whitman, J. R.: *ref*, 529
Whitman, M. A.: *ref*, 516
Whitmer, C. A.: *rev*, 483, 2:1388, 3:243, 3:254, 3:256
Whitmyre, J. W.: *ref*, 529
Whitney, V.: *ref*, 522
Whittemore, R. G.: *ref*, 348, 425, 447, 551, 574, 587
Whitten, C. F.: *ref*, 381, 525, 533
Whybrow, P. C.: *ref*, 518
Wickham, M.: *ref*, 439
Wickham, W.: *ref*, 533
Wickstrom, M. L.: *ref*, 529
Wickwire, P. J. N.: *ref*, 349, 381
Wideen, M. F.: *ref*, 435

Widener, S. E.: *ref*, 404
Widlak, F. W.: *ref*, 529, 532–3
Widman, J. B.: *ref*, 533
Wiechers, J. E.: *ref*, 439, 533
Wiemers, I. H.: *ref*, 487, 497
Wiener, G.: *ref*, 525, 529, 533
Wiens, A. N.: *ref*, 529
Wientge, K. M.: *test*, 465
Wiersma, W.: *ref*, 357
Wigdor, B. T.: *ref*, 592
Wiggin, M. K.: *ref*, 487
Wiggins, J. G.: *ref*, 532
Wiggins, N.: *ref*, 364, 382
Wiggins, N. W.: *ref*, 532, 6:438(456)
Wiggins, P. Y.: *ref*, 529, 592
Wight, B. W.: *ref*, 496, 516, 533
Wightwick, B.: *ref*, 426
Wikoff, R. L.: *ref*, 525
Wilcock, J. C.: *ref*, 439, 525
Wilcott, R. C.: *ref*, 518
Wilcox, L.: *ref*, 357, 364
Wilder, D. H.: *ref*, 426
Wile, I. S.: *exc*, 497, 545; *ref*, 525
Wilensky, H.: *ref*, 529
Wiley, L. N.: *ref*, 349, 532, 4:277(258)
Wiley, R.: *ref*, 400
Wilhelm, H. M.: *ref*, 357
Wilhelm, R.: *ref*, 533
Wilk, W. S.: *ref*, 525, 533
Wilkie, F.: *ref*, 529
Wilkin, W. R.: *ref*, 342, 439
Wilkins, T. B.: *ref*, 3:217(87)
Wilkins, W. L.: *ref*, 439, 503, 532
Wilkinson, V. J.: *ref*, 439
Willard, D. W.: *ref*, 3:263(27)
Willard, L. A.: *ref*, 364, 532–3
Willcutt, H.: *ref*, 529
Wille, G. R.: *ref*, 482
Willenson, D.: *ref*, 532
Willerman, L.: *ref*, 484, 525, 533
Willett, E. A.: *ref*, 358
Willett, G. W.: *ref*, 4:277(226)
Willhauk, R. C.: *ref*, 468
Williams, A. F.: *ref*, 516
Williams, A. P.: *ref*, 390
Williams, B. K.: *ref*, 381
Williams, B. L.: *ref*, 400
Williams, C. D.: *ref*, 551, 574
Williams, C. L.: *ref*, 361, 6:438(445)
Williams, C. M.: *ref*, 357
Williams, F. E.: *ref*, 589
Williams, G. P.: *test*, 2:1410
Williams, G. W.: *ref*, 2:1394(8–9)
Williams, H. B.: *ref*, 357
Williams, H. M.: *ref*, 447, 507, 525
Williams, H. V.: *ref*, 391
Williams, J.: *ref*, 425
Williams, J. C.: *test*, 486; *ref*, 357
Williams, J. D.: *ref*, 382, 400, 404, 447, 551, 561, 591
Williams, J. E.: *ref*, 480, 516, 5:308(309), 6:438(534)
Williams, J. H.: *ref*, 381, 525
Williams, J. M.: *ref*, 533
Williams, J. R.: *ref*, 349, 439, 525, 529
Williams, K. C.: *ref*, 425
Williams, M.: *test*, 540; *ref*, 439, 503, 525, 532, 540, 592
Williams, M. L.: *ref*, 381
Williams, N.: *ref*, 333, 473

Williams, O. H.: *ref*, 382
Williams, P. R.: *ref*, 349, 364
Williams, R.: *ref*, 522, 529
Williams, R. A.: *ref*, 361
Williams, R. D. B.: *ref*, 525
Williams, R. H.: *ref*, 357
Williams, R. J.: *ref*, 533
Williams, R. L.: *test*, 343; *ref*, 533, 589
Williams, R. M.: *ref*, 505
Williams, S. B.: *ref*, 342, 503
Williams, T. M.: *ref*, 516
Williams, W. C.: *ref*, 398
Williamson, D. A.: *ref*, 357
Williamson, E. G.: *ref*, 438, 2:1401(8), 2:1424(23)
Williamson, H. T.: *ref*, 400, 542
Williamson, M. L.: *ref*, 361
Willig, S. N.: *ref*, 516, 533
Willingham, W. W.: *rev*, 382, 404; *ref*, 357, 425
Willis, C. B.: *test*, 3:268
Willis, C. G.: *ref*, 357, 361
Willis, D. J.: *ref*, 528
Willis, J.: *ref*, 400, 533
Willits, J. M.: *rev*, 337, 5:389
Willmarth, J. G.: *ref*, 349
Willmott, J. N.: *ref*, 425
Willner, A.: *ref*, 529, 532
Willner, A. E.: *test*, 593; *ref*, 529, 593
Wills, I. H.: *ref*, 493, 533
Wills, R. C.: *ref*, 355, 439
Wilmot, W. G.: *ref*, 3:218(4)
Wilmut, F. S.: *ref*, 409
Wilner, C. F.: *ref*, 525, 2:1399(2, 8)
Wilson, A. V.: *ref*, 361
Wilson, B. A.: *ref*, 505, 525
Wilson, C. A.: *ref*, 507, 525
Wilson, F. R.: *ref*, 348
Wilson, F. T.: *ref*, 558
Wilson, G. D.: *ref*, 425, 439
Wilson, G. E.: *ref*, 349
Wilson, G. M.: *ref*, 525
Wilson, G. O.: *ref*, 533
Wilson, J. A. R.: *ref*, 525
Wilson, J. D.: *ref*, 409, 529
Wilson, J. H.: *ref*, 416, 460, 2:1424(7, 21), 6:480(24, 34)
Wilson, J. L.: *ref*, 381
Wilson, J. T.: *ref*, 461
Wilson, K. M.: *ref*, 357
Wilson, L.: *ref*, 439, 533
Wilson, M. G.: *ref*, 497
Wilson, M. O.: *ref*, 532
Wilson, M. T.: *exc*, 497; *ref*, 426, 503, 525
Wilson, R. C.: *test*, 542, 561x2, 591
Wilson, R. M.: *ref*, 435
Wilson, W. R.: *ref*, 419
Wilson, W. S.: *ref*, 381
Wilson, W. T.: *ref*, 533
Wilsoncroft, W. E.: *ref*, 525
Wiltberger, A. C.: *ref*, 529, 533
Wilton, K.: *ref*, 559
Wiltse, K. T.: *ref*, 529
Wimberly, S. E.: *ref*, 398
Wimby, E. B.: *ref*, 425
Wimby, E. G.: *ref*, 398
Winans, J. M.: *ref*, 349
Winder, C. L.: *ref*, 518
Windholz, G.: *ref*, 357, 542, 546, 561, 572-3

Wine, D. B.: *ref*, 439
Winer, D.: *ref*, 529
Wing, C. W.: *ref*, 357
Winget, B. M.: *ref*, 529, 533
Wining, M. H.: *ref*, 5:308(415)
Winitz, H.: *ref*, 496, 533
Winkler, R. C.: *ref*, 533
Winn, A.: *ref*, 404
Winn, E.: *ref*, 525
Winne, J. F.: *ref*, 504, 532
Winpenny, N.: *ref*, 533
Winschel, J. F.: *ref*, 516, 533
Winslow, C. N.: *ref*, 525
Winston, W. E.: *ref*, 425
Winter, G. D.: *ref*, 529
Winter, K. S.: *ref*, 529
Winter, P. M.: *ref*, 592
Winter, W. D.: *ref*, 381
Winter, W. N.: *ref*, 525
Winterbourn, R.: *rev*, 329, 373, 5:300
Winters, S.: *ref*, 533
Winthrop, H.: *ref*, 496
Wirls, C. J.: *ref*, 522, 529
Wirt, R.: *ref*, 439
Wirth, G.: *ref*, 529
Wirth, J. W.: *ref*, 589
Wirwick-Van Dusen, M.: *ref*, 574
Wise, J. H.: *ref*, 525
Wiseman, S.: *test*, 6:470; *ref*, 409
Wiser, W. C.: *ref*, 525, 529, 533
Wishner, J.: *ref*, 532
Wiskoff, M.: *ref*, 382
Wisler, M. L.: *ref*, 483, 525
Wisser, R. E.: *ref*, 533
Witherspoon, P.: *ref*, 6:438(531)
Witherspoon, R. P.: *ref*, 6:438(499)
Witherspoon, Y. T.: *ref*, 533
Witkin, H. A.: *ref*, 525, 529, 533
Witmer, J. M.: *ref*, 533
Witmer, L.: *ref*, 525
Witmer, L. R.: *ref*, 419
Witryol, S. L.: *ref*, 425
Witsaman, L. R.: *ref*, 489
Witt, E. L.: *ref*, 532
Witt, N. E.: *ref*, 426
Wittenberg, A.: *ref*, 482
Wittenborn, J. R.: *ref*, 425, 497, 529, 532
Wittman, P.: *ref*, 532
Wittmer, J.: *ref*, 382
Wittson, C. L.: *ref*, 503
Witty, P. A.: *ref*, 525, 3:242(4)
Wladkowsky, E.: *ref*, 525, 532
Wober, M.: *ref*, 439
Wodtke, K. H.: *ref*, 589
Woehlke, A. B.: *ref*, 426
Woerner, E. M.: *ref*, 3:217(121)
Woerner, M. G.: *ref*, 529
Wolf, C. W.: *ref*, 533
Wolf, G. P.: *ref*, 516
Wolf, R.: *ref*, 489, 525
Wolf, R. R.: *ref*, 357
Wolf, S.: *ref*, 439, 529
Wolf, S. J.: *ref*, 525
Wolf, W.: *ref*, 400, 439, 505
Wolf, W. C.: *ref*, 525
Wolf, W. S.: *ref*, 439, 505
Wolfe, R. N.: *ref*, 433
Wolfensberger, W.: *ref*, 516
Wolfensberger, W. P.: *ref*, 532
Wolff, B. B.: *ref*, 529
Wolff, R.: *ref*, 529

Wolff, S. J.: *ref*, 532
Wolfle, D.: *rev*, 407, 4:315-6
Wolfson, W.: *ref*, 529
Wolins, L.: *rev*, 570; *ref*, 342, 348, 423, 482, 487, 497
Wolins, M.: *ref*, 439
Wolk, R. L.: *ref*, 439, 529
Wolk, S. M.: *ref*, 497
Wollowick, H. B.: *ref*, 426
Wolpin, M.: *ref*, 6:438(490)
Wolter, D. J.: *ref*, 529
Woltmann, A. G.: *exc*, 381
Womack, M.: *ref*, 516
Womer, F. B.: *rev*, 339; *ref*, 400
Wonderlic, E. F.: *test*, 482; *ref*, 426, 482
Wonzer, A. C.: *ref*, 349, 589
Wood, D. A.: *ref*, 357
Wood, E. R.: *test*, 4:281
Wood, L.: *ref*, 558, 2:1394(10)
Wood, M. M.: *ref*, 426
Wood, O.: *test*, 476
Wood, R. H.: *ref*, 589
Woodall, C. S.: *ref*, 525, 3:220(39)
Woodard, D. B.: *ref*, 382
Wooden, H.: *ref*, 487
Woodrow, H.: *ref*, 483
Woodruff, A. D.: *ref*, 419
Woods, E. L.: *ref*, 525
Woods, J. E.: *ref*, 447, 529
Woods, R. C.: *ref*, 4:277(276)
Woods, W. A.: *ref*, 447
Woodward, J. C.: *ref*, 515
Woodward, M.: *ref*, 497
Woodward, R. H.: *ref*, 482
Woodward, W. M.: *ref*, 525, 529
Woodworth, R. S.: *ref*, 525
Woody, C.: *ref*, 348-9, 3:218(5, 9)
Woody, R. H.: *ref*, 516, 533
Woog, P.: *ref*, 490
Wooley, H. T.: *ref*, 507, 525
Woolf, H.: *exc*, 532
Woolf, L. I.: *ref*, 6:523(4)
Woo-Sam, J.: *ref*, 525, 529, 532, 538
Wooster, A. D.: *ref*, 439, 491, 495
Worbois, G. M.: *ref*, 525
Worcester, D. A.: *rev*, 2:1418, 3:242, 3:255; *exc*, 493, 518; *ref*, 489, 493, 525, 4:317(2)
Worden, D. K.: *ref*, 525
Worell, L.: *ref*, 357
Works, M. N.: *ref*, 538
Worley, B.: *ref*, 529
Worthen, B. R.: *ref*, 574
Worthington, M. R.: *ref*, 518, 525, 558, 578
Wosika, P. H.: *ref*, 532
Wozencraft, M.: *ref*, 398
Wrenn, C. G.: *ref*, 404, 419, 525, 4:277(227)
Wright, C.: *ref*, 518, 525, 532
Wright, D. D.: *ref*, 522
Wright, E. L.: *ref*, 525
Wright, E. N.: *test*, 351-2
Wright, F.: *ref*, 533
Wright, H. C.: *ref*, 533
Wright, H. F.: *ref*, 503, 532
Wright, J. H.: *ref*, 361, 482
Wright, L.: *ref*, 533
Wright, M. T.: *ref*, 382, 404
Wright, R. E.: *ref*, 525
Wright, S. C.: *ref*, 532
Wrightsman, L. S.: *ref*, 337

INDEX OF NAMES

Wrightstone, J. W.: *test*, 335–6; *exc*, 435, 532, 2:1416; *ref*, 391, 425, 525, 533, 5:368(21)
Wrigley, J.: *ref*, 409, 6:470(1)
Wu, J. J.: *ref*, 589
Wu, T. M.: *ref*, 525
Wunderlin, R. J.: *ref*, 533
Wussler, M.: *ref*, 533
Wyatt, F.: *ref*, 532
Wyeth, E. R.: *ref*, 382
Wyke, M.: *ref*, 529
Wyne, M. D.: *ref*, 533
Wynn Jones, L.: *rev*, 2:1430
Wysocki, A. C.: *ref*, 532
Wysocki, B. A.: *ref*, 439, 532, 5:308(385)

XYDIAS, N.: *ref*, 364
Xydis, G. A.: *ref*, 533

YACORZYNSKI, G. K.: *ref*, 532, 545
Yahav, A. L.: *ref*, 574
Yalowitz, J. M.: *ref*, 533
Yamahiro, R. S.: *ref*, 529, 532
Yamamoto, K.: *ref*, 348, 398, 400, 589
Yamarat, V.: *ref*, 533
Yap, P. M.: *ref*, 403, 439
Yater, A. C.: *ref*, 381, 525, 538
Yates, A.: *rev*, 425
Yates, A. J.: *ref*, 403, 439, 532, 545, 592
Yates, L. G.: *ref*, 525
Yeats, L. C.: *ref*, 532
Yee, G. F.: *ref*, 589
Yela, M.: *ref*, 426, 515, 545, 4:324(61), 4:334(8)
Yen, S. M. Y.: *ref*, 381, 516, 525
Yepsen, L. N.: *ref*, 381
Yerbury, E. C.: *ref*, 447
Yeremian, T. S.: *ref*, 357

Yerkes, R. M.: *ref*, 447, 525, 2:1391(3–4), 3:220(18a, 25a)
Yoakum, C. S.: *ref*, 447, 2:1391(3), 3:220(18a)
Yoloye, E. A.: *ref*, 400
York, D. H.: *ref*, 496, 529
York, M. W.: *ref*, 496, 518
Young, C.: *ref*, 439, 496
Young, D.: *test*, 413, 419A
Young, F. A.: *ref*, 349, 525
Young, F. L.: *ref*, 533
Young, F. M.: *ref*, 507, 525, 532–3
Young, G. C.: *ref*, 516, 533
Young, H. B.: *ref*, 439
Young, J. R.: *ref*, 529
Young, K. M.: *ref*, 404, 543
Young, M. B.: *ref*, 482
Young, R. O.: *ref*, 357
Young, W. T.: *ref*, 400
Younge, J. W.: *ref*, 349
Yudin, L. W.: *ref*, 533, 575
Yule, D. L. G.: *ref*, 387
Yule, W.: *ref*, 381, 484, 533, 538

ZABEL, R. L.: *ref*, 361
Zabin, D. H.: *ref*, 525
Zaccaria, M. A.: *ref*, 468
Zaeske, A.: *ref*, 516
Zagorin, S. W.: *ref*, 400, 533
Zagorski, H. J.: *ref*, 404
Zahn, J.: *ref*, 391
Zahn, J. C.: *ref*, 359
Zakolski, F. C.: *ref*, 426, 447
Zamora, E. L.: *ref*, 592
Zangwill, O. L.: *ref*, 381
Zarfoss, N. J.: *ref*, 357
Zeaman, D.: *ref*, 525
Zeaman, J. B.: *ref*, 532
Zecca, G.: *ref*, 513
Zeckel, A.: *ref*, 518
Zedeck, S.: *ref*, 364
Zedler, E. Y.: *ref*, 533

Zeidler, R.: *ref*, 525
Zeigler, M. L.: *ref*, 529
Zeigler, T. W.: *ref*, 349, 525, 532
Zemanek, D.: *ref*, 525
Zerfas, P. G.: *ref*, 532
Zerof, S. A.: *ref*, 342, 529
Ziebell, P. W.: *ref*, 532
Ziegler, D. K.: *ref*, 529, 543
Zienkiewicz, H.: *ref*, 532
Zigler, E.: *ref*, 525
Zimbardo, P. G.: *ref*, 400
Zimet, C. N.: *ref*, 529, 532
Zimmerer, A. M.: *ref*, 6:438(535)
Zimmerman, F. T.: *ref*, 483, 525, 532
Zimmerman, I. L.: *ref*, 525, 532–3, 538
Zimmerman, J. J.: *ref*, 357
Zimmerman, M. C.: *ref*, 532
Zimmerman, S. F.: *ref*, 529
Zimmerman, W. G.: *ref*, 382, 419
Zimmerman, W. S.: *rev*, 357, 436; *test*, 561r3; *ref*, 357
Zingle, H. W.: *ref*, 525, 559
Zlody, R. L.: *ref*, 533
Zoob, I.: *ref*, 574
Zook, H. A.: *ref*, 361
Zubek, J. P.: *ref*, 529, 532, 542, 546, 551, 555, 562, 564, 573
Zubin, J.: *ref*, 404, 518
Zuckerman, M.: *ref*, 592
Zuckowsky, L. M.: *ref*, 361, 6:438(500)
Zuk, G. H.: *ref*, 525
Zung, W. W. K.: *ref*, 529
Zunich, M.: *ref*, 516, 525
Zweibelson, I.: *ref*, 425, 5:326(28)
Zwibelman, B.: *ref*, 529
Zwier, M. D.: *ref*, 398
Zwilling, V. T.: *ref*, 4:277(228)
Zwirner, W.: *ref*, 403
Zytowski, D. G.: *ref*, 529

INTELLIGENCE SCANNING INDEX

This scanning index is an expanded table of contents listing all tests in this volume. Foreign tests are identified by listing the country of origin in brackets immediately after the title. The population for which a test is intended is presented to facilitate the search for tests for use with a particular group. Stars indicate tests not previously listed in a *Mental Measurements Yearbook*; asterisks indicate tests revised or supplemented since last listed. Numbers refer to test entries, not to pages.

INTELLIGENCE

GROUP

A.C.E.R. Advanced Test B40 [Australia], ages 13 and over, see 323
*A.C.E.R. Advanced Tests AL and AQ [Australia], college and superior adults, see 324
*A.C.E.R. Higher Tests [Australia], ages 13 and over, see 325
A.C.E.R. Intermediate Test A [Australia], ages 10–13, see 326
*A.C.E.R. Intermediate Tests C and D [Australia], ages 10–13, see 327
A.C.E.R. Junior Non-Verbal Test [Australia], ages 8.5–11, see 328
A.C.E.R. Junior Test A [Australia], ages 8.5–11, see 329
A.C.E.R. Lower Grades General Ability Scale [Australia], ages 6-6 to 9-1, see 330
*AH4, AH5, and AH6 Tests [England], ages 10 and over, see 331
APT Performance Test, adults, see 332
*Abstract Reasoning: Differential Aptitude Tests, grades 8–12 and adults, see 333
Academic Alertness "AA," adults, see 334
Academic Aptitude Test: Non-Verbal Intelligence: Acorn National Aptitude Tests, grades 7–16 and adults, see 335
Academic Aptitude Test: Verbal Intelligence: Acorn National Aptitude Tests, grades 7–16 and adults, see 336
Adaptability Test, job applicants, see 337
Advanced Test N [Australia], ages 15 and over, see 338
American School Intelligence Test, grades kgn–12, see 339

*Analysis of Learning Potential, grades 1–12, see 340
Analysis of Relationships, grades 12–16 and industry, see 341
Army Alpha Examination: First Nebraska Revision, grades 6–16 and adults, see 341A
Army General Classification Test, First Civilian Edition, grades 9–16 and adults, see 342
★BITCH Test (Black Intelligence Test of Cultural Homogeneity), adolescents and adults, see 343
*Boehm Test of Basic Concepts, grades kgn–2, see 344
*Business Test, clerical workers, see 345
CGA Mental Ability Tests [Canada], grades 6–12, see 346
★C.P. 66 Test [England], ages 13 and over, see 347
California Short-Form Test of Mental Maturity, grades kgn–16 and adults, see 348
California Test of Mental Maturity, grades kgn–16 and adults, see 349
Canadian Academic Aptitude Test [Canada], grades 8.5–9.0, see 350
Canadian Cognitive Abilities Test [Canada], grades kgn–3, see 351
Canadian Lorge-Thorndike Intelligence Tests [Canada], grades 3–9, see 352
★Canadian Scholastic Aptitude Test [Canada], candidates for college entrance, see 353
Cattell Intelligence Tests [England], mental ages 4 and over, see 354
Chicago Non-Verbal Examination, ages 6 and over, see 355
*Cognitive Abilities Test, grades kgn–12, see 356
*College Board Scholastic Aptitude Test, candidates for college entrance, see 357
College Qualification Tests, candidates for college entrance, see 358

Concept Mastery Test, grades 15–16 and graduate students and applicants for executive and research positions, see 359
Cooperative Academic Ability Test, superior grade 12 students, see 360
*Cooperative School and College Ability Tests, grades 4–16, see 361
*Cotswold Junior Ability Tests [Scotland], ages 8.5–10.5, see 362
*Cotswold Measurement of Ability [Scotland], ages 10–12, see 363
*Culture Fair Intelligence Test, ages 4 and over, see 364
D48 Test, grades 5 and over, see 365–6
Deeside Non-Verbal Reasoning Test [England], ages 10–12, see 367
Deeside Picture Puzzles [England], ages 6.5–8.5, see 368
Dennis Test of Scholastic Aptitude, grades 4–8, see 369
Detroit General Intelligence Examination, grades 7–12, see 370
Doppelt Mathematical Reasoning Test, grades 16–17 and employees, see 371
Draw-A-Man Test for Indian Children [India], ages 6–10, see 372
Essential Intelligence Test [Scotland], ages 8–12, see 373
Executive Employment Review, applicants for executive level positions, see 374
Figure Reasoning Test [England], ages 10 and over, see 375
*Fundamental Achievement Series, semiliterate job applicants and employees, see 376–7
*General Mental Ability Test, job applicants, see 378
General Verbal Practice Test G1–G3 [England], ages 10–11, see 379
*Gilliland Learning Potential Examination, ages 6 and over, see 380
Goodenough-Harris Drawing Test, ages 3–15, see 381
*Graduate Record Examinations Aptitude Test, graduate school candidates, see 382
★Group Test for Indian South Africans [South Africa], standards 4–10, see 383
Group Test 36 [England], ages 10–14, see 384
Group Test 75 [England], ages 12–13, see 385
Group Test 91 [England], industrial applicants, see 386
★Group Test 95 [England], ages 14 and over, see 386A
*Group Test of Learning Capacity: Dominion Tests [Canada], grades kgn–1, 4–12 and adults, see 387
Group Tests 70 and 70B [England], ages 15 and over, see 388
Group Tests 72 and 73 [England], industrial applicants, see 389
Group Tests 90A and 90B [England], ages 15 and over, see 390
*Henmon-Nelson Tests of Mental Ability, grades kgn–17, see 391
Illinois Index of Scholastic Aptitude, grades 9–12, see 392
Inventory No. 2, ages 16 and over, see 393
Junior Scholastic Aptitude Test, grades 7–9, see 394
Kelvin Measurement of Ability in Infant Classes [Scotland], ages 5–8, see 395
Kelvin Measurement of Mental Ability [Scotland], ages 8–12, see 396
Kingston Test of Intelligence [England], ages 10–12, see 397
*Kuhlmann-Anderson Test, grades kgn–12, see 398
Kuhlmann-Finch Tests, grades 1–12, see 399
Lorge-Thorndike Intelligence Tests, grades kgn–13, see 400

Lorge-Thorndike Intelligence Tests, College Edition, grades 12–13, see 401
*Mental Alertness: Tests A/1 and A/2 [South Africa], job applicants with 9 or more years of education, see 402
Mill Hill Vocabulary Scale [England], ages 4 and over, see 403
Miller Analogies Test, candidates for graduate school, see 404
★Minnesota Scholastic Aptitude Test, high school and college, see 405
Mitchell Vocabulary Test [England], adults, see 406
Modified Alpha Examination Form 9, grades 7–12 and adults, see 407
Moray House Picture Tests [England], ages 6.5–8.5, see 408
*Moray House Verbal Reasoning Tests [England], ages 8.5 and over, see 409
N.B. Group Tests [South Africa], ages 5–8, see 410
New South African Group Test [South Africa], ages 8–17, see 411
★Non-Language Test of Verbal Intelligence [India], class 8 (ages 11–13), see 412
Non-Readers Intelligence Test [England], ages 6–8, see 413
Non-Verbal Reasoning Test, job applicants and industrial employees, see 414
Non-Verbal Tests [England], ages 8–15, see 415
Northumberland Mental Tests [England], ages 10–12.5, see 416
OISE Picture Reasoning Test: Primary [Canada], grades 1–2, see 417
Ohio Penal Classification Test, penal institutions, see 418
*Ohio State University Psychological Test, grades 9–16 and adults, see 419
★Oral Verbal Intelligence Test [England], ages 7.5–14, see 419A
Oregon Academic Ranking Test, gifted children grades 3–7, see 420
O'Rourke General Classification Test, grades 12–13 and adults, see 421
"Orton" Intelligence Test, No. 4 [Scotland], ages 10–14, see 422
Otis Employment Tests, applicants for employment, see 423
Otis-Lennon Mental Ability Test, grades kgn–12, see 424
Otis Quick-Scoring Mental Ability Tests, grades 1–16, see 425
Otis Self-Administering Tests of Mental Ability, grades 4–16, see 426
Pacific Reasoning Series Tests [Australia], job applicants in Papua New Guinea, see 427
Pattern Perception Test [England], ages 6 and over, see 428
Performance Alertness "PA" (With Pictures), adults, see 429
Personal Classification Test, business and industry, see 430
Personnel Research Institute Classification Test, adults, see 431
Personnel Research Institute Factory Series Test, applicants for routine industrial positions, see 432
Personnel Tests for Industry, trade school and adults, see 433
Picture Test A [England], ages 7-0 to 8-1, see 434
*Pintner-Cunningham Primary Test, grades kgn–2, see 435
*Preliminary Scholastic Aptitude Test/National Merit Scholarship Qualifying Test, grades 10–12, see 436
★Preschool and Early Primary Skill Survey, ages 3-3 to 7-2, see 437

Pressey Classification and Verifying Tests, grades 1-12 and adults, see 438
Progressive Matrices [England], ages 5 and over, see 439
Proverbs Test, grades 5-16 and adults, see 440
Public School Primary Intelligence Test, grades 2-4, see 441
Purdue Non-Language Personnel Test, business and industry, see 442
Quantitative Evaluative Device, entering graduate students, see 443
RBH Test of Learning Ability, business and industry, see 444
RBH Test of Non-Verbal Reasoning, business and industry, see 445
Reasoning Tests for Higher Levels of Intelligence [Scotland], college entrants, see 446
Revised Beta Examination, ages 16-59, see 447
Ryburn Group Intelligence Tests [Scotland], ages 6.5-15.5, see 448
*SRA Nonverbal Form, ages 12 and over, see 449
*SRA Pictorial Reasoning Test, ages 14 and over, see 450
*SRA Short Test of Educational Ability, grades kgn-12, see 451
*SRA Verbal Form, grades 7-16 and adults, see 452
Safran Culture Reduced Intelligence Test [Canada], grades 1 and over, see 453
Scholastic Mental Ability Tests, grades kgn-8, see 454
Schubert General Ability Battery, grades 12-16 and adults, see 455
Scott Company Mental Alertness Test, applicants for office positions, see 456
Ship Destination Test, grades 9 and over, see 457
Short Form Test of Academic Aptitude, grades 1.5-12, see 458
Simplex GNV Intelligence Tests [England], ages 11-12, see 459
Simplex Group Intelligence Scale [England], ages 10 and over, see 460
Simplex Junior Intelligence Tests [England], ages 7-14, see 461
Sleight Non-Verbal Intelligence Test [England], ages 6-10, see 462
Southend Test of Intelligence [England], ages 10-12, see 463
Spiral Nines [South Africa], job applicants with 7-8 years of education, see 464
Test of Adult College Aptitude, evening college entrants, see 465
*Test of Perceptual Organization, ages 12 and over, see 466
Tests of General Ability, grades kgn-12, see 467
*Tests of General Ability: Inter-American Series, preschool and grades kgn-13.5, see 468
Thurstone Test of Mental Alertness, grades 9-12 and adults, see 469
*Undergraduate Program Aptitude Test, grades 15-16, see 470
Verbal Power Test of Concept Equivalence, ages 14 and over, see 471
Verbal Reasoning, job applicants and industrial employees, see 472
*Verbal Reasoning: Differential Aptitude Tests, grades 8-12 and adults, see 473
Verbal Tests (Adv.) [England], ages 12-13, see 474
Verbal Tests BC, CD, C, and D [England], ages 8-11, see 475
Verbal Tests EF and GH [England], ages 11-14, see 476
*Verbal Tests 15-23 and 69 [England], ages 10-12, see 477
★*WLW Employment Inventory III,* job applicants, see 478
★*WLW Mental Alertness Inventory,* job applicants, see 479
Wesman Personnel Classification Test, grades 8-16 and adults, see 480
Western Personnel Tests, college and adults, see 481
*Wonderlic Personnel Test, adults, see 482

INDIVIDUAL

Arthur Point Scale of Performance Tests, ages 4.5 to superior adults, see 483
Bayley Scales of Infant Development, ages 2-30 months, see 484
★*Bingham Button Test,* disadvantaged children ages 3-6, see 485
Canadian Intelligence Test [Canada], ages 3-16, see 486
Cattell Infant Intelligence Scale, ages 3-30 months, see 487
★*Classification Tasks* [Australia], ages 5-9, see 488
*Columbia Mental Maturity Scale, ages 3.5-9, see 489
Cooperative Preschool Inventory, ages 3-6, see 490
Crichton Vocabulary Scale [England], ages 4-11, see 491
Denver Developmental Screening Test, ages 2 weeks to 6 years, see 492
Detroit Tests of Learning Aptitude, ages 3 and over, see 493
Developmental Screening Inventory, ages 1-18 months, see 494
*English Picture Vocabulary Test [England], ages 5 and over, see 495
Full-Range Picture Vocabulary Test, ages 2 and over, see 496
Gesell Developmental Schedules, ages 4 weeks to 6 years, see 497
Haptic Intelligence Scale for Adult Blind, blind and partially sighted adults, see 498
Hiskey-Nebraska Test of Learning Aptitude, ages 3-17, see 499
Immediate Test: A Quick Verbal Intelligence Test, adults, see 500
★*Individual Scale for Indian South Africans* [South Africa], ages 8-17, see 501
Kahn Intelligence Tests, ages 1 month and over (particularly the verbally or culturally handicapped), see 502
Kent Series of Emergency Scales, ages 5-14, see 503
*Leiter Adult Intelligence Scale, adults, see 504
Leiter International Performance Scale, ages 2-18, see 505
★*McCarthy Scales of Children's Abilities,* ages 2.5-8.5, see 506
Merrill-Palmer Scale of Mental Tests, ages 24-63 months, see 507
★*Minnesota Child Development Inventory,* ages 1-6, see 508
Minnesota Preschool Scale, ages 1.5-6.0, see 509
New Guinea Performance Scales [Papua New Guinea], pre-literates ages 17 and over, see 510
New South African Individual Scale [South Africa], ages 6-17, see 511
Non-Verbal Intelligence Tests for Deaf and Hearing Subjects [The Netherlands], ages 3-16, see 512
Ohwaki-Kohs Tactile Block Design Intelligence Test for the Blind, blind ages 6 and over, see 513
Pacific Design Construction Test [Australia], illiterates and semiliterates in Papua New Guinea, see 514
Passalong Test: A Performance Test of Intelligence, ages 8 and over, see 515
Peabody Picture Vocabulary Test, ages 2.5-18, see 516

Pictorial Test of Intelligence, ages 3–8, see 517
Porteus Maze Test, ages 3 and over, see 518
Preschool Attainment Record, ages 6 months to 7 years, see 519
Queensland Test [Australia], ages 7 and over, see 520
Quick Screening Scale of Mental Development, ages 6 months to 10 years, see 521
Quick Test, ages 2 and over, see 522
Ring and Peg Tests of Behavior Development, birth to age 6, see 523
Slosson Intelligence Test, ages 2 weeks and over, see 524
**Stanford-Binet Intelligence Scale*, ages 2 and over, see 525; *Clinical Profile for the Stanford Binet Intelligence Scale (L–M)*, ages 5 and over, see 526
Stanford-Ohwaki-Kohs Block Design Intelligence Test for the Blind, blind and partially sighted ages 16 and over, see 527
Vane Kindergarten Test, ages 4–6, see 528
Wechsler Adult Intelligence Scale, ages 16 and over, see 529; *Rhodes WAIS Scatter Profile*, see 530; ★*WAIS Test Profile*, see 531
Wechsler-Bellevue Intelligence Scale, ages 10 and over, see 532
Wechsler Intelligence Scale for Children, ages 5–15, see 533; *California Abbreviated WISC*, educable mentally retarded ages 8–13.5 and intellectually gifted elementary school children, see 534; *Rhodes WISC Scatter Profile*, see 535; ★*WISC Mental Description Sheet*, see 536; ★*WISC Test Profile*, see 537
Wechsler Preschool and Primary Scale of Intelligence, ages 4–6.5, see 538; ★*WPPSI Test Profile*, see 539
Williams Intelligence Test for Children With Defective Vision [England], blind and partially sighted ages 5–15, see 540

SPECIFIC

★*Abstract Spatial Relations Test* [South Africa], Bantu industrial workers with 0–12 years of education, see 541
Alternate Uses, grades 6–16 and adults, see 542
Benton Visual Retention Test, ages 8 and over, see 543
★*Biographical Inventory—Creativity*, "adolescents and young adults," see 544
Block-Design Test, mental ages 5–20, see 545
**Christensen-Guilford Fluency Tests*, grades 7–16 and adults, see 546
Closure Flexibility (Concealed Figures), industrial employees, see 547
Closure Speed (Gestalt Completion), industrial employees, see 548
Concept Assessment Kit—Conservation, ages 4–7, see 549
★*Concept Attainment Test* [South Africa], college and adults, see 550
Consequences, grades 9–16 and adults, see 551
★*Consequences* [South Africa], ages 15 and over, see 552
★*Creativity Attitude Survey*, grades 4–6, see 553
★*Creativity Tests for Children*, grades 4–6, see 554
Decorations, grades 9–16 and adults, see 555
Feature Profile Test: Pintner-Paterson Modification, ages 4 and over, see 556
★*Gottschaldt Figures* [South Africa], job applicants with at least 10 years of education, see 557
Healy Pictorial Completion Tests, ages 5 and over, see 558
Hidden Figures Test, grades 6–16, see 559
Higgins-Wertman Test: Threshold of Visual Closure, ages 5–15, see 560
Jensen Alternation Board, ages 5 and over, see 560A
Kit of Reference Tests for Cognitive Factors, grades 6–16, see 561
Making Objects, grades 9–16 and adults, see 562
Manikin Test, ages 2 and over, see 563
Match Problems, grades 9–16 and adults, see 564
*Match Problems 5, grades 9–16, see 565
★*Memory for Events*, grades 9–13, see 566
★*Memory for Meanings*, grades 7–16, see 567
*New Uses, grades 10–16, see 568
★*Pattern Relations Test* [South Africa], college graduates, see 569
Perceptual Speed (Identical Forms), grades 9–16 and industrial employees, see 570
Pertinent Questions, grades 9–16 and adults, see 571
*Plot Titles, grades 9–16, see 572
Possible Jobs, grades 6–16 and adults, see 573
**Remote Associates Test*, grades 9–16 and adults, see 574
Rutgers Drawing Test, ages 4–9, see 575
★*Seeing Faults* [South Africa], ages 15 and over, see 576
*Seeing Problems, grades 9–16, see 577
Seguin-Goddard Formboard, ages 5–14, see 578
**Simile Interpretations*, grades 10–16, see 579
★*Similes Test*, grades 4–16 and adults, see 580
★*Sketches*, grades 9 and over, see 581
Subsumed Abilities Test, ages 9 and over, see 582
★*Symbol Identities*, grades 10 and over, see 583
Symbol Series Test [South Africa], illiterate and semiliterate adults, see 584
★*Test of Concept Utilization*, ages 4.5–18.5, see 585
★*Test of Creative Potential*, grades 2–12 and adults, see 586
★*Thinking Creatively With Sounds and Words*, grades 3–12 and adults, see 587
Time Appreciation Test, ages 10 and over, see 588
Torrance Tests of Creative Thinking, kgn through graduate school, see 589
Two-Figure Formboard, ages 4 and over, see 590
*Utility Test, grades 9–12, see 591
Wechsler Memory Scale, adults, see 592
★*Willner Instance Similarities Test*, adults, see 593
Word Fluency, industrial employees, see 594

Ref
Z
5814
P8
I 53

MAR 2 1 1980